THE WORLD ALMANAC®

AND BOOK OF FACTS

2025

WORLD ALMANAC BOOKS

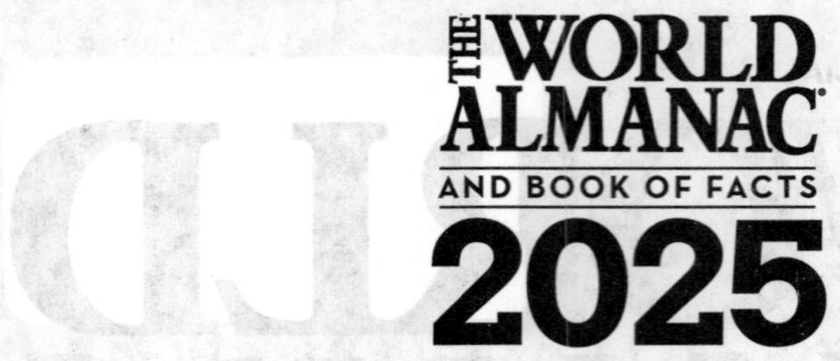

Executive Editor: Sarah Janssen

Contributors: Emily Dolbear, Robert Famighetti, Marshall Gerometta, Jacqueline Laks Gorman, Richard Hantula, M. L. Liu, Laurence A. Marschall, William A. McGeveran Jr., Jessica A. Newport, Janet M. Olson, John Rosenthal, Stevonnie Ross, Peter J. Schmidtke, Matthew Silverman, Edward A. Thomas, Lori P. Wiesenfeld

Production: Newgen North America
Design and Production, Year in Pictures: Chris Schultz, Skyhorse Publishing
Design, Cover: Takeshi Takahashi
Photo Research: Edward A. Thomas
Index Editor: Nan Badgett

Image credits: Cover: Getty Images, Shutterstock. **Interior pages:** Photos are Getty Images unless noted below. Photos on pages 458-677 in public domain unless noted. **Alamy Stock Photos:** PA Images: Alice Munro, 799. **California State Library:** Chinese Exclusion Act, 463. **Jimmy Carter Library and Museum:** Carter, 521. **William J. Clinton Presidential Library:** 671. **FEMA:** Andrea Booher: 473. **Gerald R. Ford Presidential Library and Museum:** Ford, 521. **Lyndon Baines Johnson Library and Museum:** Johnson, 520. **Library of Congress:** 462; 464; 466; 468; U.S. presidents, unless otherwise noted, 514-524; Grant, 517; 659; 663; Henry Kissinger, 798. **National Archives and Records Administration:** 481; 483; 666. **NASA:** 469; Butch Wilmore and Suni Williams, 797. **National Transportation Safety Board:** Francis Scott Key Bridge, 246. **New Jersey Dept. of Military and Veterans Affairs:** Mark C. Olsen, 478. **Shutterstock:** 649; 651; 653; 654; 658; 664; 675. **U.S. Coast Guard:** 474. **U.S. Dept. of Defense:** Staff Sgt. Victor Mancilla, 677. **U.S. Government:** hostage release, 246. **U.S. Navy:** Photographer's Mate 2nd Class Jim Watson, 672. **U.S. Senate:** Joe Lieberman, 799. **Univ. of Virginia:** 459. **White House:** Adam Schultz: Evan Gershkovich, 245; Biden, 524. Eric Draper: George W. Bush, 522. Pete Souza: Obama, 522. Shealah Craighead: Trump, 523. Rosalyn Carter, 798. **White House Historical Society:** Madison, 514.

The World Almanac®
An imprint of Skyhorse Publishing, Inc.
Visit our website at www.skyhorsepublishing.com.
Please follow our publisher Tony Lyons on Instagram @tonylyonsisuncertain.

Hardcover
ISBN-13: 978-1-5107-8087-3
ISBN-10: 1-5107-8087-4

Ebook
ISBN-13: 978-1-5107-8088-0
ISBN-10: 1-5107-8088-2

Paperback
ISBN-13: 978-1-5107-8086-6
ISBN-10: 1-5107-8086-6

International Standard Serial Number
0084-1382

The World Almanac® and Book of Facts 2025
Book printed and bound in the United States of America
Date printed: November 2024
10 9 8 7 6 5 4 3 2 1

CONTENTS

2024: SPECIAL FEATURES AND YEAR IN REVIEW

THE WORLD ALMANAC AND BOOK OF FACTS 2025

Top 10 News Topics of 2024

1. Trump Claims Second Term in Historic Comeback; GOP Wins Senate Control. Former Pres. Donald Trump (R) won the Nov. 5 presidential election, overcoming incumbent Vice Pres. Kamala Harris (D), the first Black and South Asian nominee of a major party. Only the second U.S. president elected to non-consecutive terms and the first elected with a criminal conviction, Trump campaigned heavily on the economy while also maintaining his rallying cry against undocumented immigration. By Nov. 7, Trump had flipped the key swing states of Georgia, Michigan, Pennsylvania, and Wisconsin and looked likely to also take the battleground states Arizona and Nevada. Republicans gained control of the Senate after a net gain of four seats with one race still uncalled by the AP; House control was not yet determined. The election followed an extraordinary campaign season during which Biden easily secured the party's nomination but withdrew July 21, after concerns over his age and fitness for office were amplified by a disastrous debate performance in late June. On July 13, a gunman attempted to assassinate Trump at a rally in Butler, PA, and the Secret Service's protective capacity was called into question.

2. Israel Continues War on Gaza, Expands Offensive Across Region. The Israel Defense Forces' (IDF) war against the militant Palestinian group Hamas in Gaza—sparked by its surprise attack against Israel on Oct. 7, 2023—passed the one-year mark. More than 43,000 Palestinians had been killed by the end of Oct. 2024, according to Gaza's health ministry, with frequent airstrikes, including on residential and humanitarian zones, causing the majority of fatalities. On Oct. 16, IDF forces killed Hamas's leader, Yahya Sinwar. Though the U.S. continued to supply arms to Israel, Pres. Biden publicly voiced concern over civilian deaths and the worsening humanitarian crisis (about 1.9 mil in Gaza were displaced according to the UN, which also reported extreme food insecurity). Israeli Prime Min. Benjamin Netanyahu faced major domestic protests over his slow pursuit of a cease-fire agreement to free approx. 100 known hostages—including 36 presumed dead—remaining in Gaza as of Nov. 1. In late Sept., the IDF sharply escalated airstrikes against the militant Hamas-allied group Hezbollah in neighboring Lebanon, killing hundreds including Hezbollah leader Hassan Nasrallah, before launching a "limited ground invasion." Since Oct. 2023, IDF military action killed more than 2,400 people in Lebanon, according to officials there.

3. Russian Invasion of Ukraine Persists. Russia's ongoing invasion of Ukraine passed the 32nd month in late Oct. Though it held on to most of the territory it regained in late 2022, Ukraine suffered major damage to its energy infrastructure over nearly seven months during which the U.S. Congress deadlocked over providing military aid, which it ultimately approved in late Apr. Ukraine's military attacked infrastructure inside Russia via drones and missiles, and in Aug. seized about 500 sq mi in Russia's Kursk region. Though Russia's military continued to make grinding gains along Ukraine's eastern front, it suffered heavy losses, prompting North Korea to reportedly deploy 10,000 troops to Russia by late Oct. The U.S. in early Oct. assessed Russia's combat casualties at 615,000 (115,000 killed). A Sept. *Wall Street Journal* report cited a confidential Ukrainian estimate of 80,000 Ukrainian soldiers killed and 400,000 wounded.

4. Trump Convicted in Hush Money Case; Three More Cases Effectively Stall. Former Pres. Trump was found guilty May 30 of all 34 felony counts against him of falsifying business records to conceal payments made to an adult-film star in order to influence the 2016 presidential election. The New York State Supreme Court jury's verdict made Trump the only U.S. president to be convicted of a felony (no president had been charged with one). His sentencing was delayed until late Nov., after the election. None of the three other criminal cases against Trump went to trial by Nov. In a historic 6-3 ruling July 1, the conservative-majority Supreme Court granted Trump substantial immunity from prosecution pertaining to a federal indictment over his alleged attempt to overturn the 2020 election.

5. Biden Issues Strict Border Rule as Immigration Debate Continues. Pres. Biden June 4 signed an order turning back, with some exceptions, migrants seeking asylum who come to the U.S. illegally when crossings reach emergency levels. Border patrol encounters with unauthorized migrants fell by 40% over the three weeks following the order, according to the Dept. of Homeland Security. The measure was criticized by human rights activists and drew legal challenges. The Senate's long-sought bipartisan immigration and border security package was blocked in early Feb. by Republican lawmakers after former Pres. Trump opposed it. A record 2.48 mil U.S. Customs and Border Protection encounters with migrants at the U.S.-Mexico border in FY2023 fell to fewer than 2.14 mil in FY2024.

6. Hurricanes Fueled by Record Temps Pummel Southeast U.S. NOAA designated June-Aug. 2024 the Northern Hemisphere's hottest summer on record, with Aug. capping a record 15-straight months of record-high monthly average global temperatures. In addition to setting record-high temperatures in numerous cities, incl. Las Vegas, NV (120 °F), and Palm Springs, CA (124°F), climate change was blamed for boosting the likelihood of extreme weather events, including three highly destructive storms: Beryl, the earliest-forming Category 5 hurricane on record in the Atlantic Ocean, before it diminished and impacted Texas July 8 (40+ fatalities); Helene, which made landfall in Florida's Big Bend region Sept. 26 (200+ people killed in at least six states, according to an AP tally, nearly half of which occurred in hardest-hit North Carolina); and Milton, which battered Florida's southern Gulf Coast Oct. 9 (25+ deaths). According to USAID, flooding in West and Central Africa killed more than 1,000 people by mid-Sept. and left up to 4 mil in need of humanitarian aid. Flash flooding killed more than 210 people in Valencia, Spain, Oct. 29.

7. Stubborn Inflation Ebbs as Most Economic Indicators Remain Steady. Annual U.S. inflation continued its sometimes bumpy decline, from a 40-year-high of 9.1% in June 2022 to 2.4% in Sept. 2024. The Federal Reserve on Sept. 18 lowered its 23-year-high benchmark interest rate by a half point. Average interest rates on 30-year fixed mortgages in Oct. (6.7%) stood a full point below their level a year prior but over double the average in late Oct. 2021. Though annual wage growth continued to exceed inflation, polls showed many Americans continued to view the economy negatively, citing food and housing costs. GDP grew at an annualized rate of 2.8% in third quarter 2024 as the unemployment rate held steady at 3.7%-4.3% Jan.-Oct.

8. Overdue Funding Bill Averts Government Shutdown. Ending a six-month impasse, Pres. Biden Mar. 23 signed a $1.2-trillion measure funding most of the government. Though it did not include deep cuts to nonmilitary spending far-right House Republicans demanded, the bill raised defense spending by roughly 3.5%, funded 2,000 more border patrol agents, and provided $300 mil in military assistance to Ukraine. On Apr. 23, Congress passed a long-awaited comprehensive security package directing roughly $61 bil in new aid to Ukraine, $14 bil to Israel, and $8 bil to Taiwan and other Indo-Pacific U.S. allies.

9. Legislation Seeks to Ban TikTok Amid Tumultuous Tech Year. Pres. Biden signed bipartisan legislation Apr. 24 requiring the Chinese parent company of short-form video app TikTok to either sell its U.S. operations by Jan. 19, 2025, or cease operating in the U.S. Though free-speech advocates criticized the measure, lawmakers cited the risk of China's authoritarian government using the app to spread misinformation and access user data. A federal judge Aug. 5 ruled that Google's online search business violated antitrust law through restrictive contracts making Google the default search engine on many devices. The EU Court of Justice in Sept. upheld a $2.7 bil fine against Google for boosting its shopping search results over those of rivals. On Sept. 5, the U.S., UK, EU, and seven other countries signed the first legally binding international treaty on artificial intelligence use.

10. SpaceX Steps in for Troubled Boeing to Transport Stranded Astronauts. Boeing's Starliner carried its first crew into space June 5 for an eight-day mission to the Intl. Space Station, but their return trip was postponed due to ship malfunctions; NASA in Aug. scheduled SpaceX to return the pair of astronauts in Feb. 2025. In Jan., Japan soft-landed an unmanned spacecraft on the moon, and in Feb., U.S. company Intuitive Machines' robotic Nova-C made the first commercial landing there. China's *Chang'e 6* unmanned lunar mission returned to Earth in late June with the first-ever samples from the moon's far side. NASA's uncrewed Europa Clipper launched Oct. 14 to investigate an underground reservoir on Jupiter's Europa moon. On Apr. 8, millions of people across North America viewed a total solar eclipse.

THE WORLD AT A GLANCE

Number Ones

World's biggest urban area by population .... Tokyo, Japan, 37.1 million population in 2024 *(p. 731)*
North America's biggest urban area by population........ Mexico City, Mexico, 22.5 million population in 2024 *(p. 731)*
World's wealthiest person........ Bernard Arnault and family, $233.0 billion net worth as of Apr. 2024 *(p. 77)*
Most-used U.S. search engine .... Google, 74.2% of all searches in July 2024 *(p. 327)*
Most popular U.S. smartphone app .... YouTube, accessed by 75% of adult users in May 2024 *(p. 328)*
U.S. airline that carried the most passengers........ Southwest Airlines, 171.8 million passengers in 2023 *(p. 117)*
Busiest world airport by passenger traffic .... Hartsfield-Jackson Atlanta Intl., 104.7 million passengers in 2023 *(p. 117)*
Nations with the most days off work per year........ Austria and Malta, 38 days off *(p. 736)*
Most popular musical artist by digital sales .... Drake, 244.0 million units sold as of Aug. 2024 *(p. 282)*
Most popular YouTuber........ MrBeast, 309.0 million subscribers as of Aug. 2024 *(p. 275)*
World's all-time top-grossing movie .... *Avengers: Endgame* (2019), $2.8 billion gross as of Sept. 2024 *(p. 272)*
World's top-grossing movie of 2024 .... *Inside Out 2*, $1.7 billion gross as of Sept. 2024 *(p. 272)*
Highest-rated prime-time TV show...... *Sunday Night Football*, watched in 10.4% of TV-owning households in 2023-24 *(p. 285)*
Highest-rated syndicated TV show........ *Jeopardy!* watched in 5.0% of TV-owning households in 2023-24 *(p. 284)*
Highest-rated basic cable TV series........ *The Five*, watched in 2.0% of TV-owning households in 2023-24 *(p. 285)*
Highest-rated premium cable TV series .... *House of the Dragon*, watched in 1.0% of TV-owning households in 2023-24 *(p. 286)*
Most watched original streaming series........ *Bridgerton*, viewed for 20.6 billion minutes in 2023-24 *(p. 284)*
Most watched acquired streaming series........ *Bluey*, viewed for 55.7 billion minutes in 2023-24 *(p. 284)*
Most watched streaming movie .... *The Super Mario Bros. Movie*, viewed for 16.3 billion minutes in 2023-24 *(p. 284)*

Surprising Facts

Average test scores for 13-year-olds in 2023 declined 4 points in reading and 9 points in math compared to 2020. Average test scores for 9-year-olds in 2022 declined 5 points in reading and 7 points in math compared to 2020. *(p. 409)*

More than 10% of female high school students and 6.6% of male high school students did not go to school at least once in 2021 due to safety concerns. *(p. 412)*

In 2023, 35.7% of 12th graders said they had ever tried vaping nicotine, marijuana, or just flavoring, compared to 15.0% who had ever tried smoking cigarettes. *(p. 175)*

The U.S. divorce rate has declined steadily since it peaked at 5.3 per 1,000 pop. in 1981; in 2022, it was 2.4. *(p. 191)*

In 2021, U.S. life expectancy fell for the second straight year, primarily due to deaths from COVID-19. Life expectancy in 2021 was 76.4 years, declining from 78.8 years in 2019, before ticking back up to 77.5 years in 2022. *(p. 200)*

Overdose deaths in the U.S. increased more than 540% between 1999, when 16,849 died of overdose, and 2022, when overdoses numbered 107,941. *(p. 198)*

The median amount of debt outstanding on home loans in 2023 was $160,000, up from $120,000 in 2011. *(p. 100)*

Americans paid an average of 24.2% of their gross earnings in income tax and Social Security contributions in 2023; Belgians, who had some of the highest personal income tax rates, paid an average of 39.9%. *(p. 735)*

U.S. workers saw their productivity and compensation grow at similar rates, 1948-79, with 117.5% and 107.3% growth, respectively. But in 1979-2022, those rates diverged, with 64.7% in productivity gains and just 14.8% in compensation growth. *(p. 126)*

The number of refugees in the world increased from 14.4 million in 2014 to 31.6 million in 2023. The number of internally displaced persons (IDPs) increased even more steeply, from 32.3 million in 2014 to a record-high 63.3 million in 2023. *(p. 737)*

In 1950, the U.S. produced 75.7% of the world's motor vehicles manufactured that year; by 2023, that number had dropped to 11.3% (up from a low of 9.5% in 2009). *(p. 108)*

In 2023, the Ford F-Series, the top-selling truck in the U.S., sold 694,237—more than twice as many vehicles as the top-selling car (Toyota Camry, 290,649 sold). Light trucks (including CUVs, SUVs, vans, and pickups) have outsold cars in the U.S. since at least 2013. *(p. 111)*

Milestone Birthdays

100
June Lockhart, June 25
Dick Van Dyke, Dec. 13

90
Dalai Lama, July 6
Julie Andrews, Oct. 1

80
Rod Stewart, Jan. 10
Tom Selleck, Jan. 29
Debbie Harry, July 1
Helen Mirren, July 26
Steve Martin, Aug. 14
Rod Carew, Oct. 1
John Lithgow, Oct. 19
Jaclyn Smith, Oct. 26
Henry Winkler, Oct. 30
Goldie Hawn, Nov. 21
Bette Midler, Dec. 1
Diane Sawyer, Dec. 22

70
J. K. Simmons, Jan. 9
Kevin Costner, Jan. 18
Jeff Daniels, Feb. 19
Kelsey Grammer, Feb. 21
Gary Sinise, Mar. 17
Bruce Willis, Mar. 19
Reba McEntire, Mar. 28
Laurie Metcalf, June 16
Jimmy Smits, July 9
Willem Dafoe, July 22
Iman, July 25
Billy Bob Thornton, Aug. 4
Yo-Yo Ma, Oct. 7
Bill Gates, Oct. 28
Kris Jenner, Nov. 5
Whoopi Goldberg, Nov. 13

60
Diane Lane, Jan. 22
Alan Cumming, Jan. 27
Chris Rock, Feb. 7
Sarah Jessica Parker, Mar. 25
Robert Downey Jr., Apr. 4
Martin Lawrence, Apr. 16
Kevin James, Apr. 26
Brooke Shields, May 31
J. K. Rowling, July 31
Viola Davis, Aug. 11
Shania Twain, Aug. 28
Charlie Sheen, Sept. 3
Steve Kerr, Sept. 27
Ben Stiller, Nov. 30

50
Dax Shepard, Jan. 2
Bradley Cooper, Jan. 5
Drew Barrymore, Feb. 22
Eva Longoria, Mar. 15
Pedro Pascal, Apr. 2
Zach Braff, Apr. 6
Johnny Galecki, Apr. 30
David Beckham, May 2
André 3000, May 27
Angelina Jolie, June 4
Tobey Maguire, June 27
Charlize Theron, Aug. 7
Jason Sudeikis, Sept. 18
Kate Winslet, Oct. 5
Tiger Woods, Dec. 30

40
Issa Rae, Jan. 12
Keira Knightley, Mar. 26
Carey Mulligan, May 28
Hasan Minhaj, Sept. 23
Bruno Mars, Oct. 8
Kaley Cuoco, Nov. 30
Chrissy Teigen, Nov. 30
Janelle Monáe, Dec. 1
Amanda Seyfried, Dec. 3

30
Megan Thee Stallion, Feb. 15
Gigi Hadid, Apr. 23
Post Malone, July 4
Dua Lipa, Aug. 22
Patrick Mahomes, Sept. 17
Kendall Jenner, Nov. 3
Timothée Chalamet, Dec. 27

21
Millie Bobby Brown, Feb. 19

ELECTION, 2024

Trump Returns to Power as Republicans Also Take the Senate

Former Pres. Donald Trump (R) decisively defeated Vice Pres. Kamala Harris (D) to reclaim the White House, capping an extraordinary 2024 campaign that saw a candidate convicted on criminal charges, two assassination attempts, and the sitting president, Joe Biden, coast through the primaries only to bow out less than four months before Election Day, Nov. 5, 2024. By early morning Nov. 6, the Associated Press (AP) and other news organizations projected Trump as the eventual winner of the electoral vote, with a number of closely fought states—notably Georgia, North Carolina, Pennsylvania, and Wisconsin—having completed enough of their ballot counting for an Electoral College winner to become clear. Republicans also appeared to win a narrow majority in the Senate; the House, as of Nov. 7, still had too many close outstanding race results to call. Trump's victory—with Sen. JD Vance (R, OH) replacing former Trump running mate Vice Pres. Mike Pence—marked only the second time in U.S. history a president was elected to nonconsecutive terms and the first time Americans elected a convicted felon to its highest office. Vice Pres. Harris, with Minnesota Gov. Tim Walz (D) as her running mate, was the first Black woman and first Indian American to lead a major party presidential ticket.

The First Campaign

National polls ahead of early 2024 caucuses and primary voting showed both 81-year-old Pres. Biden (D) and 78-year-old former Pres. Trump (R) would easily win their respective nominations to create a repeat matchup of the 2020 presidential race. (Trump since 2020 had maintained without evidence that fraud had cost him his rightful reelection.)

Trump secured the nomination over an initial field of 12 other candidates by Mar. 12, 2024; only his closest competitor, former UN Ambassador Nikki Haley, won any contests (Washington, DC, and Vermont). Biden faced no serious challengers and clinched his own nomination the same day.

Both Trump and Biden offered dire warnings for the future of the country if the other won the election. Trump pledged to implement anti-immigrant policies and expand the president's power over the federal government, and criticized Pres. Biden, especially his handling of the economy and immigration. Biden claimed credit for the country's economic recovery from COVID and for infrastructure funding and the 2022 Inflation Reduction Act. He also committed to passing a "billionaire minimum income tax" and argued that a second Trump administration would threaten American democracy.

The first scheduled Trump-Biden debate, June 27, 2024, seen by more than 51.3 mil viewers, amplified concerns over Biden's fitness for office as he misused words and delivered meandering arguments in a weak voice. Democratic party leaders and high-profile donors—some publicly, others privately—called for the president to withdraw. He announced July 21, 2024, that he was ending his campaign and endorsing 59-year-old Vice Pres. Kamala Harris.

Trump vs. Harris

Vice Pres. Harris drew immediate, widespread support from the Democratic base, raising over $81 mil in donations in the first 24 hours after Biden bowed out. She named two-term Minnesota Gov. Tim Walz (D) as her vice-presidential running mate Aug. 6, after her nomination was made official by a virtual delegate roll call (Aug. 1-5) ahead of the Democratic National Convention.

Much of the Biden campaign apparatus, including its war chest, transferred to Harris, whose policy stances were also similar to Biden's, though she argued more forcefully for national abortion protections. The Trump campaign, meanwhile, sought to tie Harris to Biden administration policies on immigration, inflation, and "Bidenomics."

Harris and Trump met in their only presidential debate Sept. 10, 2024, seen by 67.1 mil viewers. Harris delivered a pointed performance, with many remarks seemingly intended to needle the former president and move him off message. CNN fact-checkers found that Trump made more than 30 false claims during the debate and Harris only one. In the wake of the debate, singer-songwriter Taylor Swift endorsed Harris and encouraged her 283 mil Instagram followers to vote.

Harris drew endorsements from disaffected Republicans, such as former Vice Pres. Dick Cheney (R) and former Rep. Liz Cheney (R, WY), and an assortment of former Trump staffers. At the same time, the powerful Teamsters Union declined to endorse either candidate after six straight Democratic presidential candidate endorsements. A number of high-profile news outlets, such as the *L.A. Times*, *Washington Post*, and *USA Today*, did not endorse any candidate. Trump's endorsements included fellow 2024 presidential candidate Robert F. Kennedy Jr., who had been running as an independent since late 2023 but suspended his campaign to endorse Trump Aug. 23, 2024.

Both Harris and Trump found ways to reach out via nontraditional media, making appearances with TikTok influencers and on highly rated podcasts (e.g., Harris on *Call Her Daddy*, Oct. 6; Trump on *The Joe Rogan Experience*, Oct. 26). But each candidate also frequently campaigned via more conventional large-scale rallies.

Balance of Power, 2024

(as of Nov. 9, 2024)

Party	Senate Before	Senate After	House Before[1]	House After	Governors Before	Governors After
Dem.	47	44	212	202	23	23
Rep.	49	53	220	213	27	27
Ind.	4[2]	2[2]	—	—	—	—

Note: One Senate race and 20 House races were not yet called. (1) Includes three vacancies. (2) Independent senators caucus with Democrats.

Electoral Votes for President, 2024

Electoral votes based on the 2020 Census were in force beginning with the 2024 elections.

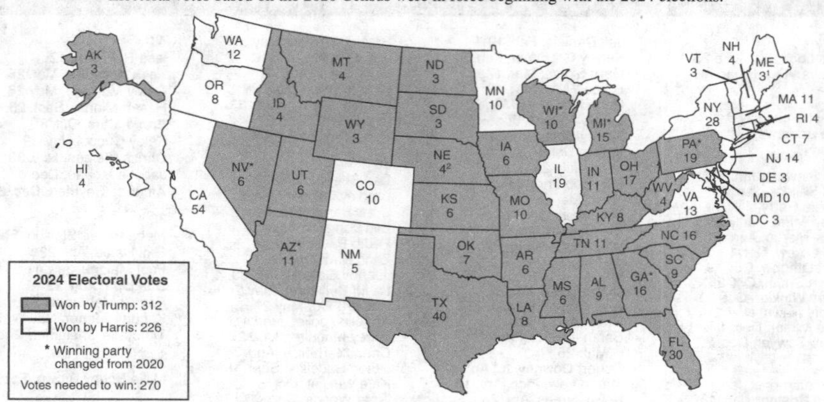

Note: Two states (Arizona and Nevada) had not yet been called for either candidate. Map reflects electoral forecast based on vote as of Nov. 7, 2024. (1) Trump was awarded one of Maine's four electoral votes. (2) Harris was awarded one of Nebraska's five electoral votes.

According to the RealClearPolitics polling average Nov. 4, 2024, Trump led narrowly in five of the seven major swing states; most were within the margin of error.

According to AP VoteCast, an Election Day survey of more than 115,000 voters nationwide, Harris voters said they were motivated by concern over the fate of democracy, Trump supporters by immigration and economic issues. As in 2020, more than 8 in 10 Trump voters were white, and about 1 in 10 were nonwhite. However, slightly larger numbers of voters under 30 supported Trump in 2024 (about 4 in 10) compared to 2020 (about one-third). Black and Latino voters also appeared slightly more likely to support Trump in 2024.

Congressional Contests

Republicans were optimistic about winning control of the Senate because Democrats were defending seats in a number of states that had previously voted for former Pres. Trump. Gov. Jim Justice (R) defeated Glenn Elliott (D) by a 40-point margin to take the West Virginia seat vacated by Sen. Joe Manchin (D/I). In Ohio, car dealer Bernie Moreno (R) flipped the seat held by three-term incumbent Sen. Sherrod Brown (D). Tim Sheehy (R) likewise was declared the victor in Montana, where three-term incumbent Sen. Jon Tester (D) unsuccessfully defended his seat.

Both parties still maintained hope of winning control of the House, with results in around two dozen races still outstanding as of Nov. 7. In notable races, Sarah McBride (D) was elected the first openly transgender member of Congress, representing Delaware. Trump impeachment whistleblower Eugene Vindman (D) won a highly competitive seat in Virginia.

Statehouses and Ballot Issues

There were 11 governorships on 2024 ballots; Republicans won eight and Democrats won three. North Carolina's Atty. Gen. Josh Stein (D) easily defeated scandal-plagued Lt. Gov. Mark Robinson (R). Atty. Gen. Bob Ferguson (D) won out over former U.S. Rep. Dave Reichert (R) to win the open governor's seat in Washington State.

Voters weighed in on dozens of statewide ballot measures. Right-to-abortion-related measures passed in Arizona, Colorado, Maryland, Missouri, Montana, and Nevada, but were rejected in Florida, Nebraska, and South Dakota. Florida also rejected a measure that would have legalized recreational marijuana. Eight states passed measures requiring proof of citizenship to vote: Idaho, Iowa, Kentucky, Missouri, North Carolina, Oklahoma, South Carolina, and Wisconsin.

Electoral and Popular Vote, 2020 and 2024

Source: 2024 results preliminary as of Nov. 7, 2024,

Two states (AZ, NV) had not yet been called by AP; 2024 electoral vote assignments reflect count forecast as of Nov. 7, 2024.

	2020				2024				
	Electoral vote		Popular vote		Electoral vote		Popular vote		
State	Biden	Trump	Biden	Trump	Harris	Trump	Harris	Trump	State
AL	0	9	849,624	1,441,170	0	9	768,974	1,456,985	AL
AK	0	3	153,778	189,951	0	3	102,969	141,470	AK
AZ	11	0	1,672,143	1,661,686	0	11	1,167,898	1,303,793	AZ
AR	0	6	423,932	760,647	0	6	395,716	758,523	AR
CA	55	0	11,110,639	6,006,518	54	0	5,750,004	4,023,693	CA
CO	9	0	1,804,352	1,364,607	10	0	1,466,125	1,157,765	CO
CT	7	0	1,080,831	714,717	7	0	920,758	709,153	CT
DE	3	0	296,268	200,603	3	0	289,585	214,184	DE
DC	3	0	317,323	18,586	3	0	255,899	18,669	DC
FL	0	29	5,297,045	5,668,731	0	30	4,676,871	6,103,182	FL
GA	16	0	2,473,633	2,461,854	0	16	2,540,272	2,656,906	GA
HI	4	0	366,130	196,864	4	0	312,384	193,169	HI
ID	0	4	287,021	554,119	0	4	265,876	594,935	ID
IL	20	0	3,471,915	2,446,891	19	0	2,837,428	2,393,355	IL
IN	0	11	1,242,498	1,729,857	0	11	1,135,903	1,689,218	IN
IA	0	6	759,061	897,672	0	6	705,310	924,143	IA
KS	0	6	570,323	771,406	0	6	523,249	735,586	KS
KY	0	8	772,474	1,326,646	0	8	700,606	1,335,516	KY
LA	0	8	856,034	1,255,776	0	8	766,405	1,208,233	LA
ME	3	1	435,072	360,737	3	1	402,750	348,412	ME
MD	10	0	1,985,023	976,414	10	0	1,485,253	920,393	MD
MA	11	0	2,382,202	1,167,202	11	0	2,071,333	1,233,687	MA
MI	16	0	2,804,040	2,649,852	0	15	2,714,167	2,795,917	MI
MN	10	0	1,717,077	1,484,065	10	0	1,653,745	1,516,341	MN
MS	0	6	539,398	756,764	0	6	411,051	674,737	MS
MO	0	10	1,253,014	1,718,736	0	10	1,190,806	1,739,020	MO
MT	0	3	244,786	343,602	0	4	216,876	336,208	MT
NE	1	4	374,583	556,846	1	4	353,106	551,343	NE
NV	6	0	703,486	669,890	0	6	647,247	698,169	NV
NH	4	0	424,937	365,660	4	0	410,966	388,074	NH
NJ	14	0	2,608,400	1,883,313	14	0	2,096,873	1,893,210	NJ
NM	5	0	501,614	401,894	5	0	471,294	419,702	NM
NY	29	0	5,244,886	3,251,997	28	0	4,336,052	3,434,451	NY
NC	0	15	2,684,292	2,758,775	0	16	2,684,549	2,876,398	NC
ND	0	3	115,042	235,751	0	3	112,028	246,019	ND
OH	0	18	2,679,165	3,154,834	0	17	2,476,003	3,116,579	OH
OK	0	7	503,890	1,020,280	0	7	499,043	1,035,217	OK
OR	7	0	1,340,383	958,448	8	0	1,008,708	777,459	OR
PA	20	0	3,458,229	3,377,674	0	19	3,341,223	3,474,923	PA
RI	4	0	307,486	199,922	4	0	281,922	212,934	RI
SC	0	9	1,091,541	1,385,103	0	9	1,024,728	1,479,046	SC
SD	0	3	150,471	261,043	0	3	146,806	271,895	SD
TN	0	11	1,143,711	1,852,475	0	11	1,055,039	1,964,499	TN
TX	0	38	5,259,126	5,890,347	0	40	4,806,487	6,375,442	TX
UT	0	6	560,282	865,140	0	6	375,889	577,551	UT
VT	3	0	242,820	112,704	3	0	235,705	119,366	VT
VA	13	0	2,413,568	1,962,430	13	0	2,227,756	2,003,384	VA
WA	12	0	2,369,612	1,584,651	12	0	1,694,782	1,130,757	WA
WV	0	5	235,984	545,382	0	4	210,223	527,704	WV
WI	10	0	1,630,866	1,610,184	0	10	1,668,045	1,697,679	WI
WY	0	3	73,491	193,559	0	3	69,508	192,576	WY
Total	**306**	**232**	**81,283,501**	**74,223,975**	**226**	**312**	**67,962,195**	**72,647,570**	**U.S.**

Note: Maine and Nebraska are the only two states with laws that allow electoral votes to be split between candidates.

Presidential Popular Vote, 2024

Source: 2024 results preliminary as of Nov. 7, 2024, © Associated Press, all rights reserved.

Candidate	Votes	Percent of vote
Donald Trump, Republican	72,647,570	50.9%
Kamala Harris, Democrat	67,962,195	47.6
Jill Stein, Green	641,091	0.5
Robert F. Kennedy Jr., Independent	616,095	0.4
Chase Oliver, Libertarian	575,895	0.4
Claudia De la Cruz, Socialism and Liberation	101,645	<0.1
Cornel West, Independent	63,417	<0.1
Randall Terry, Constitution	40,363	<0.1
Shiva Ayyadurai, No party affiliation	26,792	<0.1
Peter Sonski, American Solidarity	24,133	<0.1
None of These Candidates	17,179	<0.1
Richard Duncan, No party affiliation	12,532	<0.1
Joel Skousen, Independent American	9,105	<0.1
Jay Bowman, Independent	5,856	<0.1%
Chris Garrity, Independent	5,137	<0.1
Joseph Kishore, Socialist Equality	4,256	<0.1
Rachele Fruit, Socialist Workers	3,965	<0.1
Mattie Preston, Godliness, Truth, Justice	2,857	<0.1
Total write-ins	1,994	<0.1
Blake Huber, Approval Voting	1,761	<0.1
Lucifer Everylove, Unaffiliated	1,548	<0.1
Michael Wood, Prohibition	1,142	<0.1
Vermin Supreme, Independent/Conservative/Pirate Party	914	<0.1
Laura Ebke, Liberal	848	<0.1
William Stodden, Socialist	360	<0.1
Robert Wells, Independent	356	<0.1
Total votes	**142,769,006**	

Note: Party designations vary from one state to another; party label listed may not necessarily represent a political party organization.

Total Cost of U.S. Elections, 1998-2024

Source: OpenSecrets.org, Center for Responsive Politics

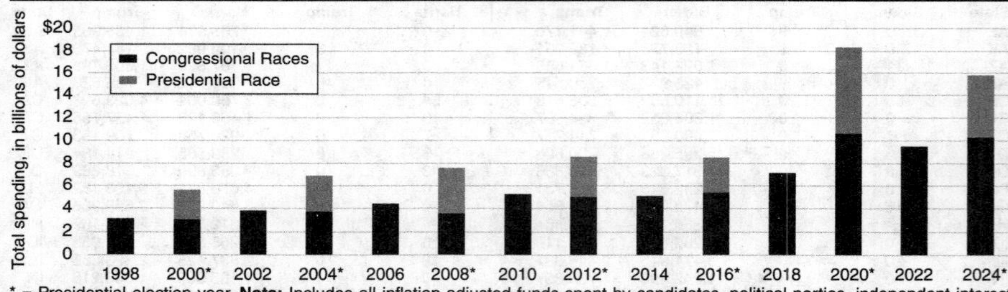

* = Presidential election year. **Note:** Includes all inflation-adjusted funds spent by candidates, political parties, independent interest groups, and political action committees (PACs) trying to influence federal elections; also includes PAC overhead expenses, 2014-24.

Top Congressional Campaign Fundraisers, 2024

Source: Federal Election Commission

House

Candidate (affiliation)	Total funds raised
1. Hakeem Jeffries (D, NY)	$21,831,973
2. Mike Johnson (R, LA)	17,385,170
3. Adam Frisch (D, CO)	16,502,296
4. Eugene Vindman (D, VA)	15,686,040
5. Kevin McCarthy (R, CA)	15,429,688
6. Elise M. Stefanik (R, NY)	14,082,734
7. Steve Scalise (R, LA)	13,425,804
8. Alexandria Ocasio-Cortez (D, NY)	13,266,704
9. Jim Jordan (R, OH)	12,460,333
10. Will Rollins (D, CA)	11,510,839
11. Mary Peltola (D, AK)	11,383,692
12. Marie Gluesenkamp Perez (D, WA)	10,699,161
13. Raja Krishnamoorthi (D, IL)	10,236,640
14. Ro Khanna (D, CA)	10,036,480
15. Josh Gottheimer (D, NJ)	9,547,636
16. Michelle Steel (R, CA)	9,441,899
17. Ryan Zinke (R, MT)	9,366,073
18. Tom Suozzi (D, NY)	9,275,135
19. George Whitesides (D, CA)	9,258,624
20. Mondaire Jones (D, NY)	9,057,157

Senate

Candidate (affiliation)	Total funds raised
1. Sherrod Brown (D, OH)	$91,399,138
2. Jon Tester (D, MT)	88,163,151
3. Ted Cruz (R, TX)	86,316,192
4. Colin Allred (D, TX)	80,059,292
5. David Trone (D, MD)	63,726,337
6. Ruben Gallego (D, AZ)	56,843,786
7. Bob Casey Jr. (D, PA)	52,879,738
8. Tammy Baldwin (D, WI)	52,311,613
9. Jacky Rosen (D, NV)	46,500,385
10. Adam Schiff (D, CA)	46,098,413
11. Elissa Slotkin (D, MI)	45,761,795
12. Rick Scott (R, FL)	40,410,331
13. Bernie Sanders (Ind., VT)	35,165,028
14. Katie Porter (D, CA)	32,402,044
15. Debbie Mucarsel-Powell (D, FL)	31,410,999
16. Eric Hovde (R, WI)	29,531,138
17. Angela Alsobrooks (D, MD)	28,461,432
18. Dave McCormick (R, PA)	27,698,653
19. Josh Hawley (R, MO)	26,290,023
20. Tim Sheehy (R, MT)	26,161,680

Note: Funds raised for the period Jan. 1, 2023, to Oct. 16, 2024, for House candidates and Jan. 1, 2019, to Oct. 16, 2024, for Senate candidates. Not all affiliations represent current offices held; some candidates had not yet been elected or had been eliminated in primary elections.

Campaign Trail Quotes

"I don't care what the hell happens in this world. If President Trump gets reelected, the border's going to be sealed, the military will be deployed, the National Guard will be activated, and the illegals are going home."

—**Trump adviser Stephen Miller** in a Nov. 2023 podcast interview with Charlie Kirk, reported on in Feb. 2024 by the *Washington Post*, on Republican post-election plans.

"He's so obsessed with his own demons from the past, he can't focus on delivering a future Americans deserve."

—**Nikki Haley**, former Trump UN Ambassador and Republican presidential primary candidate, on Pres. Donald Trump, Feb. 20, 2024.

"My predecessor and some of you here seek to bury the truth about Jan. 6th. I will not do that … You can't love your country only when you win."

—**Pres. Joe Biden** during his State of the Union address to Congress Mar. 7, 2024.

"I don't know if you call them people. In some cases they're not people, in my opinion."

—**Former Pres. Donald Trump**, referring to immigrants, at a rally near Dayton, OH, Mar. 16, 2024.

"Biden had a very low bar going into the debate and failed to clear even that bar. He seemed unprepared, lost, and not strong enough to parry effectively with Trump, who lies constantly."

—**Former HUD Sec. Julián Castro**, June 27, 2024, in a tweet about Pres. Biden's debate performance.

"I know nothing about Project 2025. I have no idea who is behind it. I disagree with some of the things they're saying and some of the things they're saying are absolutely ridiculous and abysmal. Anything they do, I wish them luck, but I have nothing to do with them."

—**Former Pres. Trump**, in an official statement released July 5, 2024, on social media website Truth Social.

"Look, the thing on immigration is that no one can avoid that it has made our societies poorer, less safe, less prosperous, and less advanced."

—**Sen. JD Vance** (R, OH) at NatCon 4, the National Conservatism Conference, July 10, 2024.

"Disagreement is inevitable in American democracy. It's part of human nature. But politics must never be a literal battlefield and, God forbid, a killing field."

—**Pres. Biden** in an address to the nation July 14, 2024, in response to an assassination attempt on former Pres. Trump at a Butler, PA, campaign rally.

"… a bunch of childless cat ladies who are miserable at their own lives and the choices that they've made and so they want to make the rest of the country miserable, too."

—**Sen. Vance**, referring to those in power, in a 2021 Tucker Carlson interview, which resurfaced on social media July 22, 2024.

"In those roles I took on perpetrators of all kinds. Predators who abused women. Fraudsters who ripped off consumers. Cheaters who broke the rules for their own gain. So hear me when I say I know Donald Trump's type."

—**Vice Pres. Kamala Harris**, reflecting on her years as a prosecutor after Pres. Biden withdrew his reelection bid, July 22, 2024.

"I'm telling you: these guys are weird."

—**Gov. Tim Walz** (D, MN) in July 23, 2024, tweet emphasizing his other public comments on Republicans.

"I didn't know she was Black until a number of years ago when she happened to turn Black, and now she wants to be known as Black. So I don't know, is she Indian, or is she Black?"

—**Former Pres. Trump** at the National Association of Black Journalists convention, July 31, 2024.

"Who's going to tell him that the job he's currently seeking might just be one of those Black jobs?"

—**Former first lady Michelle Obama**, Aug. 20, 2024, speaking about former Pres. Trump at the Democratic National Convention.

"Never underestimate a public school teacher."

—**Gov. Walz**, accepting the vice-presidential nomination at the Democratic National Convention, Aug. 21, 2024.

"Cheney and I agree on nothing. No issues. But what we do believe in is that the United States should retain its democratic foundations … I applaud the Cheneys for their courage in defending democracy."

—**Sen. Bernie Sanders** (I, VT) on *Meet the Press*, Sept. 8, 2024, on Kamala Harris's endorsements by former Vice Pres. Dick Cheney and former Rep. Liz Cheney (R, WY).

"These dictators and autocrats are rooting for you to be president again, because they're so clear, they can manipulate you with flattery and favors."

—**Vice Pres. Harris** commenting on Donald Trump's relationships with authoritarian leaders, in the presidential debate held Sept. 10, 2024, in Philadelphia.

"In Springfield, they're eating the dogs, the people that came in. They're eating the cats. They're eating—they're eating the pets of the people that live there."

—**Former Pres. Trump** repeating a debunked social media rumor about Haitian immigrants in Springfield, OH, in the presidential debate held Sept. 10, 2024, in Philadelphia.

"If I have to create stories so that the American media actually pays attention to the suffering of the American people, then that's what I'm going to do."

—**Sen. Vance** in a CNN interview with Dana Bash, Sept. 15, 2024, addressing the false claims he previously made about Haitian immigrants eating pets in Springfield, OH.

"I am your protector. I want to be your protector … you will no longer be abandoned, lonely, or scared. You will no longer be in danger … you will no longer be thinking about abortion."

—**Former Pres. Trump**, trying to reach reluctant voters in a campaign speech Sept. 23, 2024.

"The rules were that you guys weren't going to fact-check."

—**Sen. Vance** to debate moderator Margaret Brennan, during the vice-presidential debate Oct. 1, 2024, after she followed his debunked comments on Haitian migrants with, "And just to clarify for our viewers, Springfield, Ohio, does have a large number of Haitian migrants who have legal status. Temporary protected status."

"Nobody's even trying to kill Kamala because it's pointless. What do you achieve? Nothing, you just bought another puppet."

—**X, SpaceX, and Tesla magnate Elon Musk**, Oct. 8, 2024, in an interview with Tucker Carlson.

"Why should anyone other than the woman herself have the power to determine what she does with her own body? A woman's fundamental right of individual liberty, to her own life, grants her the authority to terminate her pregnancy if she wishes."

—**Former first lady Melania Trump** in her memoir *Melania*, released Oct. 8, 2024.

"Oh you guys are at the wrong rally—no, I think you meant to go to the smaller one down the street."

—**Vice Pres. Harris**, responding Oct. 17, 2024, to hecklers at a La Crosse, WI, campaign event.

"Certainly the former president is in the far-right area, he's certainly an authoritarian, admires people who are dictators—he has said that. So he certainly falls into the general definition of fascist, for sure."

—**John Kelly**, former Trump chief of staff, when questioned if Donald Trump met the definition of a fascist, in a *NY Times* interview, Oct. 22, 2024.

"We're a dumping ground. We're like a garbage can for the world. That's what's happened."

—**Former Pres. Trump**, Oct. 24, 2024, in Tempe, AZ, regarding immigration to the U.S.

"I don't know if you guys know this, but there's literally a floating island of garbage in the middle of the ocean right now. I think it's called Puerto Rico."

—**Tony Hinchcliffe**, a stand-up comic, at former Pres. Trump's highly anticipated rally at Madison Square Garden in New York City, Oct. 27, 2024.

"I shouldn't have left."

—**Former Pres. Trump**, at a Lititz, PA, rally Nov. 3, 2024.

Members of the 119th Congress: U.S. Senate

Boldface denotes the 2024 election winner. * = Incumbent. Third-party, independent, or write-in candidates receiving fewer than 70,000 votes are not necessarily listed.

Terms are for six years and end Jan. 3 of the year preceding the senator's name in the following table. Annual salary: $174,000; President Pro Tempore, Majority Leader, and Minority Leader: $193,400. To be eligible to serve in the Senate, a person must be at least 30 years old, a U.S. citizen for at least nine years, and a resident of the state from which elected.

D = Democrat; R = Republican; DFL = Dem.-Farmer-Labor; Ind. = Independent; LB = Libertarian; D-NPL = Dem.-Nonpartisan League.

Term ends	Senator/candidate (party); service from	2024 election results
Alabama		
2027	Tommy Tuberville (R); 1/3/2021	
2029	Katie Britt (R); 1/3/2023	
Alaska		
2027	Dan Sullivan (R); 1/6/2015	
2029	Lisa Murkowski (R); 12/20/2002	
Arizona		
2029	Mark Kelly (D); 12/2/2020	
2031	Ruben Gallego (D)	1,113,390
	Kari Lake (R)	1,053,827
Arkansas		
2027	Tom Cotton (R); 1/6/2015	
2029	John Boozman (R); 1/5/2011	
California		
2029	Alex Padilla (D); 1/20/2021	
2031[1]	**Adam Schiff (D)**	**5,462,603**
	Steve Garvey (R)	4,070,790
Colorado		
2027	John Hickenlooper (D); 1/3/2021	
2029	Michael Bennet (D); 1/22/2009	
Connecticut		
2029	Richard Blumenthal (D); 1/5/2011	
2031	**Chris Murphy* (D); 1/3/2013**	**803,586**
	Matthew Corey (R)	587,109
Delaware		
2027	Christopher Coons (D); 11/15/2010	
2031	**Lisa Rochester (D)**	**279,124**
	Eric Hansen (R)	196,252
Florida		
2029	Marco Rubio (R); 1/5/2011	
2031	**Rick Scott* (R); 1/3/2019**	**5,970,772**
	Debbie Mucarsel-Powell (D)	4,594,934
Georgia		
2027	Jon Ossoff (D); 1/20/2021	
2029	Raphael Warnock (D); 1/20/2021	
Hawaii		
2029	Brian Schatz (D); 12/26/2012	
2031	**Mazie Hirono* (D); 1/3/2013**	**294,498**
	Bob McDermott (R)	140,996
Idaho		
2027	Jim Risch (R); 1/6/2009	
2029	Mike Crapo (R); 1/6/1999	
Illinois		
2027	Richard J. Durbin (D); 1/7/1997	
2029	Tammy Duckworth (D); 1/3/2017	
Indiana		
2029	Todd C.Young (R); 1/3/2017	
2031	**Jim Banks (R)**	**1,606,763**
	Valerie McCray (D)	1,049,165
	Andrew Horning (LB)	71,616
Iowa		
2027	Joni Ernst (R); 1/6/2015	
2029	Chuck Grassley (R); 1/5/1981	
Kansas		
2027	Roger Marshall (R); 1/3/2021	
2029	Jerry Moran (R); 1/5/2011	
Kentucky		
2027	Mitch McConnell (R); 1/3/1985	
2029	Rand Paul (R); 1/5/2011	
Louisiana		
2027	Bill Cassidy (R); 1/6/2015	
2029	John Kennedy (R); 1/3/2017	
Maine		
2027	Susan M. Collins (R); 1/7/1997	
2031	**Angus King* (Ind.); 1/3/2013**	**423,059**
	Demi Kouzounas (R)	282,816
	David Costello (D)	86,204
Maryland		
2029	Chris Van Hollen (D); 1/3/2017	
2031	**Angela Alsobrooks (D)**	**1,289,266**
	Larry Hogan (R)	1,119,088
Massachusetts		
2027	Ed Markey (D); 7/16/2013	
2031	**Elizabeth Warren* (D); 1/3/2013**	**1,904,594**
	John Deaton (R)	1,271,221
Michigan		
2027	Gary Peters (D); 1/6/2015	
2031	**Elissa Slotkin (D)**	**2,704,992**
	Mike Rogers (R)	2,685,468
Minnesota		
2027	Tina Smith (DFL); 1/3/2018	
2031	**Amy Klobuchar* (DFL); 1/4/2007**	**1,791,515**
	Royce White (R)	1,290,799
Mississippi		
2027	Cindy Hyde-Smith (R); 4/9/2018	
2031	**Roger Wicker* (R); 12/31/2007**	**668,802**
	Ty Pinkins (D)	393,330
Missouri		
2029	Eric Schmitt (R); 1/3/2023	
2031	**Josh Hawley (R); 1/3/2019**	**1,639,359**
	Lucas Kunce (D)	1,234,159
Montana		
2027	Steve Daines (R); 1/6/2015	
2031	**Tim Sheehy (R)**	**289,228**
	Jon Tester* (D); 1/4/2007	243,761
Nebraska		
2027[2]	**Pete Ricketts* (R); 1/23/2023**	**571,281**
	Preston Love (D)	333,401
2031	**Deb Fischer* (R); 1/3/2013**	**487,661**
	Dan Osborn (Ind.)	417,801
Nevada		
2029	Catherine Cortez Masto (D); 1/3/2017	
2031	**Jacky Rosen* (D); 1/3/2019**	**679,259**
	Sam Brown (R)	658,057
New Hampshire		
2027	Jeanne Shaheen (D); 1/6/2009	
2029	Maggie Hassan (D); 1/3/2017	
New Jersey		
2027	Cory Booker (D); 10/31/2013	
2031	**Andy Kim (D)**	**2,029,223**
	Curtis Bashaw (R)	1,703,079
New Mexico		
2027	Ben Ray Luján (D); 1/3/2021	
2031	**Martin Heinrich* (D); 1/3/2013**	**488,375**
	Nella Domenici (R)	401,930
New York		
2029	Chuck Schumer (D); 1/6/1999	
2031	**Kirsten Gillibrand* (D); 1/27/2009**	**4,426,084**
	Michael Sapraicone (R)	3,116,994
	Diane Sare (Ind.)	
North Carolina		
2027	Thom Tillis (R); 1/6/2015	
2029	Ted Budd (R); 1/3/2023	
North Dakota		
2029	John Hoeven (R); 1/5/2011	
2031	**Kevin Cramer (R); 1/3/2019**	**241,066**
	Katrina Christiansen (D-NPL)	121,291
Ohio		
2029	JD Vance (R); 1/3/2023	
2031	**Bernie Moreno (R)**	**2,803,634**
	Sherrod Brown* (D); 1/4/2007	2,592,539
	Don Kissick (LB)	189,377

Term ends	Senator/candidate (party); service from	2024 election results
Oklahoma		
2027	Markwayne Mullin (R); 1/3/2023	
2029	James Lankford (R); 1/6/2015	
Oregon		
2027	Jeff Merkley (D); 1/6/2009	
2029	Ron Wyden (D); 2/6/1996	
Pennsylvania		
2029	John Fetterman (D) 1/3/2023	
2031	**Dave McCormick (R)**	**3,340,649**
	Bob Casey Jr.* (D); 1/4/2007	3,308,961
	John Thomas (LB)	87,706
Rhode Island		
2027	Jack Reed (D); 1/7/1997	
2031	**Sheldon Whitehouse* (D); 1/4/2007**	**283,877**
	Patricia Morgan (R)	192,226
South Carolina		
2027	Lindsey Graham (R); 1/7/2003	
2029	Tim Scott (R); 1/3/2013	
South Dakota		
2027	Mike Rounds (R); 1/6/2015	
2029	John Thune (R); 1/4/2005	
Tennessee		
2027	Bill Hagerty (R); 1/3/2021	
2031	**Marsha Blackburn* (R); 1/3/2019**	**1,916,591**
	Gloria Johnson (D)	1,026,294
Texas		
2027	John Cornyn (R); 12/2/2002	
2031	**Ted Cruz* (R); 1/3/2013**	**5,965,718**
	Colin Allred (D)	4,990,592
	Ted Brown (LB)	265,673
Utah		
2029	Mike Lee (R); 1/5/2011	
2031	**John Curtis (R)**	**588,181**
	Caroline Gleich (D)	301,317
Vermont		
2029	Peter Welch (D); 1/3/2023	
2031	**Bernie Sanders* (Ind.); 1/4/2007**	**229,917**
	Gerald Malloy (R)	116,137
Virginia		
2027	Mark Warner (D); 1/6/2009	
2031	**Timothy Kaine* (D); 1/3/2013**	**2,303,507**
	Hung Cao (R)	1,955,716
Washington		
2029	Patty Murray (D); 1/3/1993	
2031	**Maria Cantwell* (D); 1/3/2001**	**1,535,231**
	Raul Garcia (R)	1,027,586
West Virginia		
2027	Shelley Moore Capito (R); 1/6/2015	
2031	**Jim Justice (R)**	**508,356**
	Glenn Elliott (D)	203,697
Wisconsin		
2029	Ron Johnson (R); 1/5/2011	
2031	**Tammy Baldwin* (D); 1/3/2013**	1,672,394
	Eric Hovde (R)	1,643,232
Wyoming		
2027	Cynthia Lummis (R); 1/3/2021	
2031	**John Barrasso* (R); 6/22/2007**	**198,366**
	Scott Morrow (D)	63,706

(1) Adam Schiff also won a separate special election to fill the seat for the remainder of Sen. Dianne Feinstein's unexpired term.
(2) Pete Ricketts was appointed to fill the seat vacated by Sen. Ben Sasse (R), who resigned Jan. 8, 2023. Result of special election to fill the seat for the duration of the term.

Members of the 119th Congress: U.S. House of Representatives

Source: 2024 results preliminary as of Nov. 6-9, 2024, © Associated Press, all rights reserved.

Boldface denotes the 2024 election winner. * = Incumbent. ** = Incumbent running in a different district. Candidates receiving fewer than 10,000 votes are not necessarily listed. Terms are for two years ending on Jan. 3, 2025. Annual salary, $174,000; Majority Leader and Minority Leader, $193,400; Speaker of the House, $223,500. To be eligible to serve in the House, a person must be at least 25 years of age, a U.S. citizen for at least seven years, and a resident of the state from which elected.

D = Democrat; R = Republican; C = Conservative; DFL = Dem.-Farmer-Labor; Ind. = Independent; LB = Libertarian; NPA = no party affiliation; WCP = Working Class Party.

Dist.	Representative/candidate (party)	2024 election results
Alabama		
1	**Barry Moore** (R)**	**257,310**
	Tom Holmes (D)	70,451
2	**Shomari Figures (D)**	**157,092**
	Caroleene Dobson (R)	130,847
3	**Mike Rogers* (R)**	**Unopposed**
4	**Robert Aderholt* (R)**	**Unopposed**
5	**Dale Strong* (R)**	**Unopposed**
6	**Gary Palmer* (R)**	**242,709**
	Elizabeth Anderson (D)	101,838
7	**Terri Sewell* (D)**	**186,407**
	Robin Litaker (R)	106,168
Alaska		
	Nick Begich III (R)	124,632
	Mary Sattler Peltola* (D)	113,612
Arizona		
1	David Schweikert* (R)	210,040
	Amish Shah (D)	192,303
2	**Eli Crane* (R)**	**202,474**
	Jonathan Nez (D)	171,110
3	**Yassamin Ansari (D)**	**85,882**
	Jeff Zink (R)	33,323
4	Greg Stanton* (D)	153,737
	Kelly Cooper (R)	134,503
5	**Andy Biggs* (R)**	**197,587**
	Katrina Schaffner (D)	130,926
6	Juan Ciscomani* (R)	173,654
	Kirsten Engel (D)	171,239
7	**Raúl Grijalva* (D)**	**95,730**
	Daniel Butierez (R)	54,161
8	**Abraham Hamadeh (R)**	**159,838**
	Gregory Whitten (D)	126,144
9	**Paul A. Gosar* (R)**	**176,168**
	Quacy Smith (D)	89,125
Arkansas		
1	**Rick Crawford* (R)**	**190,438**
	Rodney Govens (D)	63,092
2	**French Hill* (R)**	**180,196**
	Marcus Jones (D)	125,370
3	**Steve Womack* (R)**	**191,788**
	Caitlin Draper (D)	95,396
	Bobby Wilson (LB)	13,305
4	**Bruce Westerman* (R)**	**196,660**
	Risie Howard (D)	73,004
California		
1	**Doug LaMalfa* (R)**	**106,531**
	Rose Yee (D)	61,184
2	**Jared Huffman* (D)**	**152,931**
	Chris Coulombe (R)	60,311
3	**Kevin Kiley* (R)**	**148,102**
	Jessica Morse (D)	109,302
4	**Mike Thompson* (D)**	**120,621**
	John Munn (R)	62,286
5	**Tom McClintock* (R)**	**149,234**
	Michael Barkley (D)	91,916
6	**Ami Bera* (D)**	**75,484**
	Christine Bish (R)	57,307

Dist.	Representative/candidate (party)	2024 election results
7	**Doris Matsui* (D)**	**90,816**
	Tom Silva (R)	50,055
8	**John Garamendi* (D)**	**122,990**
	Rudy Recile (R)	45,080
9	Josh Harder* (D)	85,528
	Kevin Lincoln (R)	81,504
10	**Mark DeSaulnier* (D)**	**158,448**
	Katherine Piccinini (R)	81,655
11	**Nancy Pelosi* (D)**	**157,744**
	Bruce Lou (R)	38,046
12	**Lateefah Simon (D)**	**82,906**
	Jennifer Tran (D)	47,520
13	John Duarte* (R)	66,675
	Adam Gray (D)	63,414
14	**Eric Swalwell* (D)**	**60,817**
	Vin Kruttiventi (R)	34,754
15	**Kevin Mullin* (D)**	**130,072**
	Anna Kramer (R)	51,244
16	**Sam Liccardo (D)**	**117,905**
	Evan Low (D)	79,079
17	**Ro Khanna* (D)**	**95,200**
	Anita Chen (R)	49,284
18	**Zoe Lofgren* (D)**	**82,483**
	Peter Hernandez (R)	48,198
19	**Jimmy Panetta* (D)**	**163,972**
	Jason Anderson (R)	71,388
20	**Vince Fong* (R)**	**119,720**
	Mike Boudreaux (R)	63,490
21	Jim Costa* (D)	65,967
	Michael Maher (R)	64,664
22	David Valadao* (R)	71,495
	Rudy Salas (D)	61,987
23	**Jay Obernolte* (R)**	**93,524**
	Derek Marshall (D)	62,117
24	**Salud Carbajal* (D)**	**134,028**
	Thomas Cole (R)	80,506
25	**Raul Ruiz* (D)**	**81,541**
	Ian Weeks (R)	63,222
26	**Julia Brownley* (D)**	**132,886**
	Michael Koslow (R)	110,523
27	George Whitesides (D)	134,231
	Mike Garcia* (R)	132,117
28	**Judy Chu* (D)**	**140,011**
	April Verlato (R)	79,409
29	**Luz Rivas (D)**	**95,389**
	Benny Bernal (R)	45,937
30	**Laura Friedman (D)**	**149,244**
	Alex Balekian (R)	73,950
31	**Gil Cisneros (D)**	**101,550**
	Daniel Martinez (R)	76,535
32	**Brad Sherman* (D)**	**154,389**
	Larry Thompson (R)	83,777
33	**Pete Aguilar* (D)**	**70,486**
	Tom Herman (R)	52,272
34	**Jimmy Gomez* (D)**	**71,957**
	David Kim (D)	55,462
35	**Norma Torres* (D)**	**74,475**
	Mike Cargile (R)	57,264
36	**Ted Lieu* (D)**	**174,519**
	Melissa Toomim (R)	86,222
37	**Sydney Kamlager-Dove* (D)**	**105,292**
	Juan Rey (no party preference)	29,707
38	**Linda Sánchez* (D)**	**105,762**
	Eric Ching (R)	80,815
39	Mark Takano* (D)	95,556
	David Serpa (R)	75,067
40	**Young Kim* (R)**	**185,729**
	Joe Kerr (D)	146,612
41	Ken Calvert* (R)	143,621
	Will Rollins (D)	135,741
42	**Robert Garcia* (D)**	**101,105**
	John Briscoe (R)	53,850
43	**Maxine Waters* (D)**	**103,384**
	Steve Williams (R)	37,473
44	**Nanette Barragán* (D)**	**106,962**
	Roger Groh (R)	48,743
45	Michelle Steel* (R)	137,696
	Derek Tran (D)	130,795
46	**Lou Correa* (D)**	**81,939**
	David Pan (R)	54,208
47	Dave Min (D)	151,254
	Scott Baugh (R)	148,541
48	**Darrell Issa* (R)**	**142,834**
	Stephen Houlahan (D)	94,277
49	Mike Levin* (D)	167,787
	Matt Gunderson (R)	156,630
50	**Scott Peters* (D)**	**149,262**
	Peter Bono (R)	88,827
51	**Sara Jacobs* (D)**	**122,245**
	Bill Wells (R)	85,329
52	**Juan Vargas* (D)**	**103,091**
	Justin Lee (R)	57,028
Colorado		
1	**Diana DeGette* (D)**	**174,647**
	Valdamar Archuleta (R)	45,497
2	**Joe Neguse* (D)**	**230,469**
	Marshall Dawson (R)	95,666
3	**Jeff Hurd (R)**	**187,866**
	Adam Frisch (D)	175,160
4	**Lauren Boebert** (R)**	**208,226**
	Trisha Calvarese (D)	168,715
5	**Jeff Crank (R)**	**152,178**
	River Gassen (D)	97,636
6	**Jason Crow* (D)**	**146,777**
	John Fabbricatore (R)	96,177
7	**Brittany Pettersen* (D)**	**229,847**
	Sergei Matveyuk (R)	168,925
8	Yadira Caraveo* (D)	119,438
	Gabe Evans (R)	115,621
Connecticut		
1	**John B. Larson* (D)**	**163,091**
	Jim Griffin (R)	95,979
2	**Joe Courtney* (D)**	**214,378**
	Mike France (R)	155,433
3	**Rosa L. DeLauro* (D)**	**118,286**
	Michael Massey (R)	97,177
4	**Jim Himes* (D)**	**134,027**
	Michael Goldstein (R)	91,651
5	**Jahana Hayes* (D)**	**173,939**
	George Logan (R)	153,529
Delaware		
	Sarah McBride (D)	**283,590**
	John Whalen (R)	207,918
Florida		
1	**Matt Gaetz* (R)**	**273,762**
	Gay Valimont (D)	140,725
2	**Neal Dunn* (R)**	**247,685**
	Yen Bailey (D)	154,010
3	**Kat Cammack* (R)**	**241,007**
	Tom Wells (D)	150,104
4	**Aaron Bean* (R)**	**222,078**
	LaShonda Holloway (D)	165,541
5	**John Rutherford* (R)**	**266,985**
	Jay McGovern (D)	156,172
6	**Michael Waltz* (R)**	**284,179**
	James Stockton (D)	142,850
7	**Cory Mills* (R)**	**233,638**
	Jennifer Adams (D)	179,476
8	**Mike Haridopolos (R)**	**280,075**
	Sandy Kennedy (D)	169,830
9	**Darren Soto* (D)**	**178,320**
	Thomas Chalifoux (R)	137,757
10	**Maxwell Frost* (D)**	**181,175**
	Willie Montague (R)	109,352
11	**Daniel Webster* (R)**	**269,122**
	Barbie Harden Hall (D)	176,508
12	**Gus Bilirakis* (R)**	**306,160**
	Rock Aboujaoude (D)	124,730

Dist.	Representative/candidate (party)	2024 election results
13	**Anna Luna* (R)**	**225,489**
	Whitney Fox (D)	185,756
14	**Kathy Castor* (D)**	**199,030**
	Robert Rochford (R)	145,389
15	**Laurel Lee* (R)**	**195,017**
	Patricia Kemp (D)	152,015
16	**Vern Buchanan* (R)**	**246,989**
	Jan Schneider (D)	167,930
17	**Greg Steube* (R)**	**290,704**
	Manny Lopez (D)	164,257
18	**Scott Franklin* (R)**	**224,935**
	Andrea Kale (D)	119,438
19	**Byron Donalds* (R)**	**275,554**
	Kari Lerner (D)	139,879
20	**Sheila Cherfilus-McCormick* (D)**	**Unopposed**
21	**Brian Mast* (R)**	**277,247**
	Thomas Witkop (D)	171,112
22	**Lois Frankel* (D)**	**201,379**
	Dan Franzese (R)	165,107
23	**Jared Moskowitz* (D)**	**195,910**
	Joe Kaufman (R)	177,835
24	**Frederica Wilson* (D)**	**194,651**
	Jesus Navarro (R)	90,612
25	**Debbie Wasserman Schultz* (D)**	**186,487**
	Chris Eddy (R)	155,957
26	**Mario Díaz-Balart* (R)**	**217,075**
	Joey Atkins (D)	88,926
27	**Maria Elvira Salazar* (R)**	**199,041**
	Lucia Baez-Geller (D)	130,532
28	**Carlos Giménez** (R)**	**209,871**
	Phil Ehr (D)	115,087
Georgia		
1	**Earl L. "Buddy" Carter* (R)**	**218,438**
	Patti Hewitt (D)	132,697
2	**Sanford Bishop* (D)**	**175,476**
	Wayne Johnson (R)	136,289
3	**Brian Jack (R)**	**272,917**
	Maura Keller (D)	139,344
4	**Hank Johnson* (D)**	**228,980**
	Eugene Yu (R)	73,971
5	**Nikema Williams* (D)**	**292,146**
	John Salvesen (R)	48,803
6	**Lucy McBath** (D)**	**275,452**
	Jeff Criswell (R)	93,369
7	**Rich McCormick** (R)**	**274,721**
	Bob Christian (D)	148,362
8	**Austin Scott* (R)**	**225,321**
	Darrius Butler (D)	102,014
9	**Andrew Clyde* (R)**	**270,820**
	Tambrei Cash (D)	121,564
10	**Mike Collins* (R)**	**256,167**
	Lexy Doherty (D)	149,901
11	**Barry Loudermilk* (R)**	**269,532**
	Katy Stamper (D)	130,691
12	**Rick Allen* (R)**	**205,676**
	Elizabeth Johnson (D)	135,209
13	**David Scott* (D)**	**256,612**
	Jonathan Chavez (R)	100,631
14	**Marjorie Taylor Greene* (R)**	**243,200**
	Shawn Harris (D)	134,482
Hawaii		
1	**Ed Case* (D)**	**149,244**
	Patrick Largey (R)	56,154
2	**Jill Tokuda* (D)**	**150,760**
	Steven Bond (R)	66,352
Idaho		
1	**Russ Fulcher* (R)**	**277,905**
	Kaylee Peterson (D)	99,460
2	**Mike Simpson* (R)**	**246,666**
	David Roth (D)	123,892
Illinois		
1	**Jonathan Jackson* (D)**	**184,421**
	Marcus Lewis (R)	105,012
2	**Robin Kelly* (D)**	**184,638**
	Ashley Ramos (R)	92,525
3	**Delia Ramirez* (D)**	**155,694**
	John Booras (R)	81,474
4	**Jesús "Chuy" García* (D)**	**128,232**
	Lupe Castillo (R)	54,013
5	**Mike Quigley* (D)**	**214,961**
	Tommy Hanson (R)	105,734
6	**Sean Casten* (D)**	**185,098**
	Niki Conforti (R)	161,208

Dist.	Representative/candidate (party)	2024 election results
7	**Danny Davis* (D)**	**191,660**
	Chad Koppie (R)	40,803
8	**Raja Krishnamoorthi* (D)**	**163,722**
	Mark Rice (R)	127,136
9	**Jan Schakowsky* (D)**	**202,561**
	Seth Cohen (R)	101,378
10	**Brad Schneider* (D)**	**181,886**
	Jim Carris (R)	125,689
11	**Bill Foster* (D)**	**193,398**
	Jerry Evans (R)	156,791
12	**Mike Bost* (R)**	**264,653**
	Brian Roberts (D)	90,830
13	**Nikki Budzinski* (D)**	**175,402**
	Joshua Loyd (R)	133,580
14	**Lauren Underwood* (D)**	**178,878**
	James Marter (R)	147,491
15	**Mary Miller* (R)**	**Unopposed**
16	**Darin LaHood* (R)**	**Unopposed**
17	**Eric Sorensen* (D)**	**155,811**
	Joe McGraw (R)	134,003
Indiana		
1	**Frank Mrvan* (D)**	**172,100**
	Randy Niemeyer (R)	144,878
2	**Rudy Yakym* (R)**	**163,872**
	Lori Camp (D)	89,784
3	**Martin Stutzman (R)**	**202,437**
	Kiley Adolph (D)	97,464
	Jarrad Lancaster (LB)	10,996
4	**Jim Baird* (R)**	**210,068**
	Derrick Holder (D)	100,027
	Ashley Groff (LB))	13,127
5	**Victoria Spartz* (R)**	**202,549**
	Deborah Pickett (D)	136,180
6	**Jefferson Shreve (R)**	**197,384**
	Cynthia Wirth (D)	96,296
	James Sceniak (LB)	13,488
7	**André Carson* (D)**	**167,904**
	John Schmitz (R)	71,372
8	**Mark Messmer (R)**	**203,497**
	Erik Hurt (D)	85,055
9	**Erin Houchin* (R)**	**220,009**
	Timothy Peck (D)	111,568
Iowa		
1	Mariannette Miller-Meeks* (R)	206,680
	Christina Bohannan (D)	205,884
2	**Ashley Hinson** (R)**	**231,292**
	Sarah Corkery (D)	168,985
3	**Zach Nunn* (R)**	**213,625**
	Lanon Baccam (D)	197,777
4	**Randy Feenstra* (R)**	**245,403**
	Ryan Melton (D)	119,233
Kansas		
1	**Tracey Mann* (R)**	**204,335**
	Paul Buskirk (D)	89,348
2	**Derek Schmidt (R)**	**168,682**
	Nancy Boyda (D)	112,390
	John Hauer (LB)	13,693
3	**Sharice Davids* (D)**	**201,917**
	Prasanth Reddy (R)	162,321
	Steve Roberts (LB)	15,114
4	**Ron Estes* (R)**	**191,618**
	Esau Freeman (D)	101,854
Kentucky		
1	**James Comer* (R)**	**252,534**
	Erin Marshall (D)	85,493
2	**Brett Guthrie* (R)**	**252,826**
	Hank Linderman (D)	93,029
3	**Morgan McGarvey* (D)**	**203,067**
	Mike Craven (R)	124,696
4	**Thomas Massie* (R)**	**Unopposed**
5	**Hal Rogers* (R)**	**Unopposed**
6	**Andy Barr* (R)**	**220,881**
	Randy Cravens (D)	127,535
Louisiana		
1	**Steve Scalise* (R)**	**238,803**
	Mel Manuel (D)	85,880
	Randall Arrington (R)	17,849
	Ross Shales (R)	8,323
2	**Troy Carter* (D)**	**183,897**
	Christy Lynch (R)	41,635
	Devin Graham (R)	39,160
	Devin Davis (D)	32,453

Dist.	Representative/candidate (party)	2024 election results
3	**Clay Higgins* (R)**	**226,264**
	Priscilla Gonzalez (D)	59,826
	Sadi Summerlin (D)	21,322
	Xan John (R)	13,246
4	**Mike Johnson* (R)**	**262,791**
	Joshua Morott (R)	43,422
5	**Julia Letlow* (R)**	**200,990**
	Michael Vallien (D)	82,900
	Vinny Mendoza (R)	35,813
6	Cleo Fields (D)	150,311
	Elbert Guillory (R)	111,731
	Quentin Anderson (D)	23,809
Maine		
1	**Chellie Pingree* (D)**	**201,640**
	Ronald Russell (R)	120,040
	Ethan Alcorn (Ind.)	16,822
2	Jared Golden* (D)	151,306
	Austin Theriault (R)	145,713
Maryland		
1	**Andy Harris* (R)**	**221,368**
	Blane Miller (D)	119,958
	Joshua O'Brien (LB)	11,053
2	**John Olszewski (D)**	**179,085**
	Kim Klacik (R)	136,129
3	**Sarah Elfreth (D)**	**194,493**
	Robert Steinberger (R)	136,667
4	**Glenn Ivey* (D)**	**187,726**
	George McDermott (R)	24,931
5	**Steny Hoyer* (D)**	**230,233**
	Michelle Talkington (R)	119,970
6	**April Delaney (D)**	**182,891**
	Neil Parrott (R)	168,220
7	**Kweisi Mfume* (D)**	**178,344**
	Scott Collier (R)	42,975
8	**Jamie Raskin* (D)**	**220,214**
	Cheryl Riley (R)	64,013
Massachusetts		
1	**Richard Neal* (D)**	**215,416**
	Nadia Donya Milleron (Ind.)	128,288
2	**Jim McGovern* (D)**	**244,483**
	Cornelius Shea (Ind.)	110,933
3	**Lori Trahan* (D)**	**Unopposed**
4	**Jake Auchincloss* (D)**	**Unopposed**
5	**Katherine Clark* (D)**	**Unopposed**
6	**Seth Moulton* (D)**	**Unopposed**
7	**Ayanna Pressley* (D)**	**Unopposed**
8	**Stephen Lynch* (D)**	**249,293**
	Robert Burke (R)	104,497
9	**Bill Keating* (D)**	**235,141**
	Dan Sullivan (R)	180,538
Michigan		
1	**Jack Bergman* (R)**	**274,392**
	Callie Barr (D)	176,806
2	**John Moolenaar* (R)**	**274,152**
	Michael Lynch (D)	133,462
3	**Hillary Scholten* (D)**	**216,865**
	Paul Hudson (R)	177,493
4	**Bill Huizenga* (R)**	**232,079**
	Jessica Swartz (D)	179,233
5	**Tim Walberg* (R)**	**268,777**
	Libbi Urban (D)	133,936
6	**Debbie Dingell* (D)**	**280,133**
	Heather Smiley (R)	158,016
7	**Tom Barrett (R)**	**226,694**
	Curtis Hertel (D)	209,842
	Rachel Dailey (LB)	14,226
8	**Kristen McDonald Rivet (D)**	**217,390**
	Paul Junge (R)	189,238
9	**Lisa McClain* (R)**	**310,239**
	Clinton St. Mosley (D)	137,446
	Jim Walkowicz (WCP)	12,088
10	**John James* (R)**	**217,440**
	Carl Marlinga (D)	191,352
	Andrea Kirby (WCP)	11,152
11	**Haley Stevens* (D)**	**260,489**
	Nick Somberg (R)	177,286

Dist.	Representative/candidate (party)	2024 election results
12	**Rashida Tlaib* (D)**	**248,682**
	James Hooper (R)	92,213
13	**Shri Thanedar* (D)**	**214,428**
	Martell Bivings (R)	78,382
	Simone Coleman (WCP)	12,871
Minnesota		
1	**Brad Finstad* (R)**	**222,954**
	Rachel Bohman (DFL)	158,842
2	**Angie Craig* (DFL)**	**231,773**
	Joe Teirab (R)	175,611
3	**Kelly Morrison (DFL)**	**240,208**
	Tad Jude (R)	170,426
4	**Betty McCollum* (DFL)**	**242,801**
	May Lor Xiong (R)	117,617
5	**Ilhan Omar* (DFL)**	**261,060**
	Dalia Al-Aqidi (R)	86,210
6	**Tom Emmer* (R)**	**257,530**
	Jeanne Hendricks (DFL)	152,700
7	**Michelle Fischbach* (R)**	**274,743**
	AJ Peters (DFL)	114,856
8	**Pete Stauber* (R)**	**247,503**
	Jen Schultz (DFL)	176,729
Mississippi		
1	**Trent Kelly* (R)**	**199,501**
	Dianne Black (D)	86,089
2	**Bennie Thompson* (D)**	**154,233**
	Ron Eller (R)	95,706
3	**Michael Guest* (R)**	**Unopposed**
4	**Mike Ezell* (R)**	**189,103**
	Craig Raybon (D)	64,334
Missouri		
1	**Wesley Bell (D)**	**231,330**
	Andrew Jones (R)	56,009
2	**Ann Wagner* (R)**	**231,954**
	Ray Hartmann (D)	180,660
3	**Bob Onder (R)**	**240,137**
	Bethany Mann (D)	138,106
4	**Mark Alford* (R)**	**259,496**
	Jeanette Cass (D)	96,310
5	**Emanuel Cleaver* (D)**	**198,292**
	Sean Smith (R)	120,350
6	**Sam Graves* (R)**	**264,780**
	Pam May (D)	100,713
7	**Eric Burlison* (R)**	**254,965**
	Missi Hesketh (D)	93,903
8	**Jason Smith* (R)**	**270,813**
	Randi McCallian (D)	77,373
Montana		
1	**Ryan Zinke* (R)**	**143,326**
	Monica Tranel (D)	119,268
2	**Troy Downing (R)**	**174,637**
	John Driscoll (D)	89,787
Nebraska		
1	**Mike Flood* (R)**	**181,865**
	Carol Blood (D)	118,491
2	Don Bacon* (R)	153,191
	Tony Vargas (D)	144,873
3	**Adrian Smith* (R)**	**241,818**
	Daniel Ebers (D)	58,823
Nevada		
1	**Dina Titus* (D)**	**160,218**
	Mark Robertson (R)	138,628
2	**Mark Amodei* (R)**	**188,891**
	Greg Kidd (NPA)	116,145
	Lynn Chapman (Ind. Amer.)	15,301
	Javi Tachiquin (LB)	12,166
3	**Susie Lee* (D)**	**182,388**
	Drew Johnson (R)	174,030
4	**Steven Horsford* (D)**	**163,812**
	John Lee (R)	137,696
New Hampshire		
1	**Chris Pappas* (D)**	**202,258**
	Russell Prescott (R)	170,504
2	**Maggie Goodlander (D)**	**199,740**
	Lily Tang Williams (R)	175,476

Dist.	Representative/candidate (party)	2024 election results
New Jersey		
1	**Donald Norcross* (D)**	**197,487**
	Theodore Liddell (R)	137,783
2	**Jeff Van Drew* (R)**	**210,651**
	Joseph Salerno (D)	147,407
3	**Herb Conaway (D)**	**190,238**
	Rajesh Mohan (R)	161,946
4	**Chris Smith* (R)**	**257,166**
	Matthew Jenkins (D)	119,506
5	**Josh Gottheimer* (D)**	**201,523**
	Mary Jo Guinchard (R)	161,410
6	**Frank Pallone* (D)**	**158,769**
	Scott Fegler (R)	116,340
7	**Thomas Kean Jr.* (R)**	**215,938**
	Sue Altman (D)	188,261
8	**Rob Menendez Jr.* (D)**	**107,871**
	Anthony Valdes (R)	62,986
9	**Nellie Pou (D)**	**124,313**
	Billy Prempeh (R)	113,314
10	**LaMonica McIver* (D)**	**168,501**
	Carmen Bucco (R)	51,168
11	**Mikie Sherrill* (D)**	**208,666**
	Joseph Belnome (R)	158,674
12	**Bonnie Watson Coleman* (D)**	**173,966**
	Darius Mayfield (R)	108,544
New Mexico		
1	**Melanie Stansbury* (D)**	**189,464**
	Steve Jones (R)	147,687
2	**Gabriel Vasquez* (D)**	**136,350**
	Yvette Herrell (R)	126,252
3	**Teresa Leger Fernandez* (D)**	**159,058**
	Sharon Clahchischilliage (R)	124,854
New York		
1	**Nick LaLota* (R)**	**217,461**
	John Avlon (D)	172,700
2	**Andrew Garbarino* (R)**	**197,168**
	Rob Lubin (D)	130,430
3	**Tom Suozzi* (D)**	**177,188**
	Michael LiPetri (R)	168,165
4	**Laura Gillen (D)**	**182,771**
	Anthony D'Esposito* (R)	176,623
5	**Gregory W. Meeks* (D)**	**157,225**
	Paul King (R)	58,380
6	**Grace Meng* (D)**	**111,592**
	Tom Zmich (R)	70,566
7	**Nydia Velázquez* (D)**	**158,015**
	Bill Kregler (R)	45,243
8	**Hakeem Jeffries* (D)**	**155,866**
	John Delaney (R)	52,216
9	**Yvette Clarke* (D)**	**160,481**
	Menachem Raitport (R)	56,614
10	**Dan Goldman* (D)**	**186,991**
	Alexander Dodenhoff (R)	34,577
11	**Nicole Malliotakis* (R)**	**160,908**
	Andrea Morse (D)	87,640
12	**Jerrold Nadler* (D)**	**235,856**
	Michael Zumbluskas (R)	57,403
13	**Adriano Espaillat* (D)**	**164,402**
	Ruben Vargas (R)	32,316
14	**Alexandria Ocasio-Cortez* (D)**	**123,269**
	Tina Forte (R)	55,580
15	**Ritchie Torres* (D)**	**121,318**
	Gonzalo Duran (R)	33,405
16	**George Latimer (D)**	**206,995**
	Miriam Flisser (R)	81,979
17	**Michael Lawler* (R)**	**191,681**
	Mondaire Jones (D)	166,331
18	**Pat Ryan* (D)**	**194,237**
	Alison Esposito (R)	149,002
19	**Josh Riley (D)**	**180,528**
	Marc Molinaro* (R)	176,850
20	**Paul Tonko* (D)**	**211,214**
	Kevin Waltz (R)	138,340
21	**Elise Stefanik* (R)**	**210,099**
	Paula Collins (D)	127,039
22	**John Mannion (D)**	**183,473**
	Brandon Williams* (R)	155,496

Dist.	Representative/candidate (party)	2024 election results
23	**Nick Langworthy* (R)**	**240,610**
	Thomas Carle (D)	123,811
24	**Claudia Tenney* (R)**	**216,826**
	David Wagenhauser (D)	115,409
25	**Joseph Morelle* (D)**	**209,722**
	Gregg Sadwick (R)	137,445
26	**Timothy Kennedy* (D)**	**201,350**
	Anthony Marecki (R)	108,611
North Carolina		
1	**Don Davis* (D)**	**184,993**
	Laurie Buckhout (R)	179,167
2	**Deborah Ross* (D)**	**265,386**
	Alan Swain (R)	126,852
3	**Greg Murphy* (R)**	**245,964**
	Gheorghe Cormos (LB)	71,394
4	**Valerie Foushee* (D)**	**304,963**
	Eric Blankenburg (R)	111,140
5	**Virginia Foxx* (R)**	**237,255**
	Chuck Hubbard (D)	161,302
6	**Addison McDowell (R)**	**231,765**
	Kevin Hayes (Constitution)	102,956
7	**David Rouzer* (R)**	**251,640**
	Marlando Pridgen (D)	176,917
8	**Mark Harris (R)**	**237,024**
	Justin Dues (D)	160,110
9	**Richard Hudson* (R)**	**207,934**
	Nigel Bristow (D)	138,862
	Shelane Etchison (Ind.)	21,800
10	**Pat Harrigan (R)**	**231,425**
	Ralph Scott (D)	152,401
	Steven Feldman (LB)	11,402
11	**Chuck Edwards* (R)**	**243,955**
	Caleb Rudow (D)	185,405
12	**Alma Adams* (D)**	**256,533**
	Addul Ali (R)	90,230
13	**Brad Knott (R)**	**242,208**
	Frank Pierce (D)	170,161
14	**Tim Moore (R)**	**231,696**
	Pam Genant (D)	166,770
North Dakota		
	Julie Fedorchak (R)	**248,572**
	Trygve Hammer (D)	108,974
Ohio		
1	**Greg Landsman* (D)**	**208,650**
	Orlando Sonza (R)	174,621
2	**David Taylor (R)**	**262,843**
	Samantha Meadows (D)	94,751
3	**Joyce Beatty* (D)**	**236,050**
	Michael Young (R)	97,785
4	**Jim Jordan* (R)**	**268,510**
	Tamie Wilson (D)	123,693
5	**Bob Latta* (R)**	**251,824**
	Keith Mundy (D)	120,887
6	**Michael Rulli* (R)**	**242,189**
	Michael Kripchak (D)	120,738
7	**Max Miller* (R)**	**200,962**
	Matthew Diemer (D)	141,741
	Dennis Kucinich (Ind.)	50,321
8	**Warren Davidson* (R)**	**233,439**
	Vanessa Enoch (D)	137,284
9	Marcy Kaptur* (D)	176,228
	Derek Merrin (R)	175,035
	Tom Pruss (LB)	14,799
10	**Mike Turner* (R)**	**209,347**
	Amy Cox (D)	141,567
	Michael Harbaugh (Ind.)	11,232
11	**Shontel Brown* (D)**	**229,628**
	Alan Rapoport (R)	57,779
12	**Troy Balderson* (R)**	**255,587**
	Jerrad Christian (D)	117,229
13	**Emilia Sykes* (D)**	**193,575**
	Kevin Coughlin (R)	185,622
14	**David Joyce* (R)**	**239,054**
	Brian Kenderes (D)	137,727
15	**Mike Carey* (R)**	**192,477**
	Adam Miller (D)	148,045

Dist.	Representative/candidate (party)	2024 election results
Oklahoma		
1	**Kevin Hern* (R)**	**188,529**
	Dennis Baker (D)	107,694
	Mark Sanders (Ind.)	15,723
2	**Josh Brecheen* (R)**	**237,925**
	Brandon Wade (D)	68,789
	Ronnie Hopkins (Ind.)	14,045
3	**Frank Lucas* (R)**	**Unopposed**
4	**Tom Cole* (R)**	**199,784**
	Mary Brannon (D)	86,568
	James Stacy (Ind.)	19,849
5	**Stephanie Bice* (R)**	**207,477**
	Madison Horn (D)	134,364
Oregon		
1	**Suzanne Bonamici* (D)**	**186,075**
	Bob Todd (R)	82,659
2	**Cliff Bentz* (R)**	**209,024**
	Dan Ruby (D)	107,186
	Michael Stettler (Constitution)	10,008
3	**Maxine Dexter (D)**	**154,413**
	Joanna Harbour (R)	56,735
4	**Val Hoyle* (D)**	**182,572**
	Monique DeSpain (R)	151,445
5	Janelle Bynum (D)	176,649
	Lori Chavez-DeRemer* (R)	167,189
	Brett Smith (Ind.)	17,082
6	**Andrea Salinas* (D)**	**155,288**
	Mike Erickson (R)	136,898
Pennsylvania		
1	**Brian Fitzpatrick* (R)**	**256,895**
	Ashley Ehasz (D)	197,957
2	**Brendan Boyle* (D)**	**182,378**
	Aaron Bashir (R)	74,048
3	**Dwight Evans* (D)**	**Unopposed**
4	**Madeleine Dean* (D)**	**263,311**
	David Winkler (R)	183,113
5	**Mary Gay Scanlon* (D)**	**261,153**
	Alfeia Goodwin (R)	140,232
6	**Chrissy Houlahan* (D)**	**226,355**
	Neil Young (R)	179,282
7	**Ryan Mackenzie (R)**	**200,544**
	Susan Wild* (D)	195,004
8	**Robert Bresnahan (R)**	**192,926**
	Matt Cartwright* (D)	185,413
9	**Dan Meuser* (R)**	**272,624**
	Amanda Waldman (D)	112,454
10	**Scott Perry* (R)**	**203,460**
	Janelle Stelson (D)	197,048
11	**Lloyd Smucker* (R)**	**250,813**
	Jim Atkinson (D)	146,390
12	**Summer Lee* (D)**	**228,360**
	James Hayes (R)	178,872
13	**John Joyce* (R)**	**260,826**
	Beth Farnham (D)	89,128
14	**Guy Reschenthaler* (R)**	**266,431**
	Chris Dziados (D)	133,133
15	**Glenn Thompson* (R)**	**272,368**
	Zach Womer (D)	101,356
16	**Mike Kelly* (R)**	**253,194**
	Preston Nouri (D)	143,101
17	**Chris Deluzio* (D)**	**238,775**
	Rob Mercuri (R)	205,894
Rhode Island		
1	**Gabriel Amo* (D)**	**132,213**
	Allen Waters (R)	68,624
	C.D. Reynolds (Ind.)	10,018
2	**Seth Magaziner* (D)**	**149,854**
	Steven Corvi (R)	108,123
South Carolina		
1	**Nancy Mace* (R)**	**227,222**
	Michael Moore (D)	162,308
2	**Joe Wilson* (R)**	**209,492**
	David Robinson (D)	141,587
3	**Sheri Biggs (R)**	**241,605**
	Bryon Best (D)	86,409
4	**William Timmons* (R)**	**206,200**
	Kathryn Harvey (D)	128,460

Dist.	Representative/candidate (party)	2024 election results
5	**Ralph Norman* (R)**	**227,630**
	Evangeline Hundley (D)	130,198
6	**Jim Clyburn* (D)**	**181,544**
	Duke Buckner (R)	112,207
7	**Russell Fry* (R)**	**221,336**
	Mal Hyman (D)	121,515
South Dakota		
	Dusty Johnson* (R)	**280,460**
	Sheryl Johnson (D)	103,550
Tennessee		
1	**Diana Harshbarger* (R)**	**257,530**
	Kevin Jenkins (D)	63,949
2	**Tim Burchett* (R)**	**250,002**
	Jane George (D)	111,094
3	**Chuck Fleischmann* (R)**	**236,258**
	Jack Allen (D)	102,747
4	**Scott DesJarlais* (R)**	**218,980**
	Victoria Broderick (D)	83,758
5	**Andy Ogles* (R)**	**204,807**
	Maryam Abolfazli (D)	142,136
6	**John Rose* (R)**	**225,467**
	Lore Bergman (D)	106,050
7	**Mark Green* (R)**	**191,832**
	Megan Barry (D)	122,593
8	**David Kustoff* (R)**	**240,309**
	Sarah Freeman (D)	84,993
9	**Steve Cohen* (D)**	**159,434**
	Charlotte Bergmann (R)	57,378
Texas		
1	**Nathaniel Moran* (R)**	**Unopposed**
2	**Dan Crenshaw* (R)**	**213,814**
	Peter Filler (D)	111,365
3	**Keith Self* (R)**	**237,030**
	Sandeep Srivastava (D)	141,906
4	**Pat Fallon* (R)**	**240,996**
	Simon Cardell (D)	110,925
5	**Lance Gooden* (R)**	**191,122**
	Ruth Torres (D)	106,431
6	**Jake Ellzey* (R)**	**187,623**
	John Love (D)	97,771
7	**Lizzie Fletcher* (D)**	**147,689**
	Caroline Kane (R)	93,976
8	**Morgan Luttrell* (R)**	**232,848**
	Laura Jones (D)	108,078
9	**Al Green* (D)**	**Unopposed**
10	**Michael McCaul* (R)**	**220,908**
	Theresa Boisseau (D)	117,937
11	**August Pfluger* (R)**	**Unopposed**
12	**Craig Goldman (R)**	**215,112**
	Trey Hunt (D)	123,666
13	**Ronny Jackson* (R)**	**Unopposed**
14	**Randy Weber* (R)**	**209,939**
	Rhonda Hart (D)	95,487
15	**Monica De La Cruz* (R)**	**127,644**
	Michelle Vallejo (D)	95,752
16	**Veronica Escobar* (D)**	**131,144**
	Irene Armendariz Jackson (R)	89,146
17	**Pete Sessions* (R)**	**192,876**
	Mark Lorenzen (D)	97,755
18	**Sylvester Turner (D)**	**150,045**
	Lana Centonze (R)	66,388
19	**Jodey Arrington* (R)**	**214,600**
	Nathan Lewis (Ind.)	27,386
	Bernard Johnson (LB)	23,889
20	**Joaquin Castro* (D)**	**Unopposed**
21	**Chip Roy* (R)**	**263,002**
	Kristin Hook (D)	152,900
22	**Troy Nehls* (R)**	**208,763**
	Marquette Greene-Scott (D)	126,835
23	**Tony Gonzales* (R)**	**180,148**
	S. Limon (D)	108,789
24	**Beth Van Duyne* (R)**	**224,912**
	Sam Eppler (D)	146,647
25	**Roger Williams* (R)**	**Unopposed**

Dist.	Representative/candidate (party)	2024 election results
26	**Brandon Gill (R)**	**240,101**
	Ernest Lineberger (D)	137,530
27	**Michael Cloud* (R)**	**183,570**
	Tanya Lloyd (D)	94,217
28	**Henry Cuellar* (D)**	**125,098**
	Jay Furman (R)	113,750
29	**Sylvia Garcia* (D)**	**98,465**
	Alan Garza (R)	52,599
30	**Jasmine Crockett* (D)**	**194,222**
	Jrmar Jefferson (LB)	34,738
31	**John Carter* (R)**	**226,457**
	Stuart Whitlow (D)	125,458
32	**Julie Johnson (D)**	**137,271**
	Darrell Day (R)	84,525
33	**Marc Veasey* (D)**	**113,048**
	Patrick Gillespie (R)	51,481
34	**Vicente Gonzalez* (D)**	**102,598**
	Mayra Flores (R)	97,465
35	**Greg Casar* (D)**	**169,896**
	Steven Wright (R)	82,354
36	**Brian Babin* (R)**	**205,327**
	Dayna Steele (D)	90,191
37	**Lloyd Doggett* (D)**	**252,442**
	Jenny Garcia Sharon (R)	80,267
38	**Wesley Hunt* (R)**	**213,328**
	Melissa McDonough (D)	125,668
Utah		
1	**Blake Moore* (R)**	**149,315**
	Bill Campbell (D)	76,941
	Daniel Cottam (LB)	10,019
2	**Celeste Maloy* (R)**	**152,139**
	Nathaniel Woodward (D)	84,140
	Cassie Easley (Constitution)	13,315
3	**Mike Kennedy (R)**	**150,141**
	Glenn Wright (D)	80,500
4	**Burgess Owens* (R)**	**128,907**
	Katrina Fallick-Wang (D)	68,019
Vermont		
	Becca Balint* (D)	**218,322**
	Mark Coester (R)	104,409
	Adam Ortiz (Ind.)	19,269
Virginia		
1	**Rob Wittman* (R)**	**266,308**
	Leslie Mehta (D)	203,048
2	**Jen Kiggans* (R)**	**198,708**
	Missy Smasal (D)	181,755
3	**Bobby Scott* (D)**	**209,505**
	John Sitka (R)	90,326
4	**Jennifer McClellan* (D)**	**240,014**
	William Moher (R)	118,189
5	**John McGuire (R)**	**242,557**
	Gloria Witt (D)	178,166
6	**Ben Cline* (R)**	**249,647**
	Ken Mitchell (D)	135,544
7	**Eugene Vindman (D)**	**195,340**
	Derrick Anderson (R)	187,079

Dist.	Representative/candidate (party)	2024 election results
8	**Don Beyer* (D)**	**260,652**
	Jerry Torres (R)	89,753
9	**Morgan Griffith* (R)**	**284,317**
	Karen Baker (D)	105,379
10	**Suhas Subramanyam (D)**	**207,131**
	Mike Clancy (R)	190,227
11	**Gerry Connolly* (D)**	**259,487**
	Mike Van Meter (R)	129,094
Washington		
1	**Suzan DelBene* (D)**	**151,574**
	Jeb Brewer (R)	84,392
2	**Rick Larsen* (D)**	**171,764**
	Cody Hart (R)	94,513
3	**Marie Gluesenkamp Perez* (D)**	**205,425**
	Joe Kent (R)	189,085
4	Dan Newhouse* (R)	127,559
	Jerrod Sessler (D)	115,050
5	**Michael Baumgartner (R)**	**178,179**
	Carmela Conroy (D)	119,142
6	**Emily Randall (D)**	**183,754**
	Drew MacEwen (R)	137,606
7	**Pramila Jayapal* (D)**	**244,150**
	Dan Alexander (R)	42,958
8	**Kim Schrier* (D)**	**213,160**
	Carmen Goers (R)	182,407
9	**Adam Smith* (D)**	**127,694**
	Melissa Chaudhry (D)	53,521
10	**Marilyn Strickland* (D)**	**156,963**
	Don Hewett (R)	111,600
West Virginia		
1	**Carol Miller* (R)**	**227,194**
	Chris Reed (D)	89,355
	Wes Holden (Ind.)	25,476
2	**Riley Moore (R)**	**263,749**
	Steve Wendelin (D)	107,660
Wisconsin		
1	**Bryan Steil* (R)**	**206,218**
	Peter Barca (D)	166,787
2	**Mark Pocan* (D)**	**320,283**
	Erik Olsen (R)	136,349
3	**Derrick Van Orden* (R)**	**211,696**
	Rebecca Cooke (D)	200,556
4	**Gwen Moore* (D)**	**249,919**
	Tim Rogers (R)	74,920
5	**Scott Fitzgerald* (R)**	**300,512**
	Ben Steinhoff (D)	165,638
6	**Glenn Grothman* (R)**	**251,791**
	John Zarbano (D)	160,001
7	**Tom Tiffany* (R)**	**274,110**
	Kyle Kilbourn (D)	156,730
8	**Tony Wied (R)**	**240,519**
	Kristin Lyerly (D)	178,903
Wyoming		
	Harriet Hageman* (R)	**184,626**
	Kyle Cameron (D)	60,763

Nonvoting Members of Congress

Delegate/candidate (party)	2024 election results
American Samoa	
Aumua Amata Coleman Radewagen* (R)	**7,394**
Luisa Kuaea (D)	1,840
Fualaau Tago Lancaster (Ind.)	469
Meleagi Suitonu-Chapman (D)	185
District of Columbia	
Eleanor Holmes Norton* (D)	**167,222**
Kymone Freeman (Green)	14,077
Michael A. Brown (Ind.)	13,012
Myrtle Alexander (R)	12,662
Guam	
Jim Moylan* (R)	**15,422**
Ginger Cruz (D)	13,703
Northern Mariana Islands	
Kimberlyn King-Hinds (R)	**4,931**
Edwin Propst (D)	4,067

Delegate/candidate (party)	2024 election results
John Oliver Delos Reyes Gonzales (Ind.)	**2,282**
James Rayphand (Ind.)	665
Liana Hofschneider (Ind.)	280
Puerto Rico—Resident Commissioner	
(4-year term; begins Jan. 2025)	
Pablo José Hernández Rivera (Popular Democratic)	472,292
William Villafañe (New Progressive)	371,470
Ana Irma Rivera Lassén (Citizen's Victory Movement)	106,025
Roberto Karlo Velázquez Correa (PR Independence Party)	55,383
Viviana Ramírez-Morales (Project Dignity)	55,088
Virgin Islands	
Stacey E. Plaskett* (D)	**9,988**
Ida Smith (Ind.)	2,218
Ronald Pickard (R)	1,311

Presidential Election Results by State and County, 2024

Source: 2024 results preliminary as of Nov. 6, 2024, © Associated Press, all rights reserved. 2020 results are final certified counts from local secretaries of state and/or state elections offices, except New England (CT, ME, MA, NH, RI, VT) vote for select cities and towns provided by AP to allow for comparison with 2024.

Final city, county, and statewide tallies may vary substantially from preliminary 2024 numbers shown due to vast differences in states' vote counting procedures and timelines. Statewide totals may include votes from areas not listed separately.

Alabama

	2020		2024	
County	**Biden (D)**	**Trump (R)**	**Harris (D)**	**Trump (R)**
Autauga	7,503	19,838	7,429	20,447
Baldwin	24,578	83,544	24,763	95,144
Barbour	4,816	5,622	4,120	5,578
Bibb	1,986	7,525	1,617	7,563
Blount	2,640	24,711	2,569	25,271
Bullock	3,446	1,146	2,983	1,099
Butler	3,965	5,458	3,248	5,167
Calhoun	15,216	35,101	13,170	34,841
Chambers	6,365	8,753	5,402	8,704
Cherokee	1,624	10,583	1,550	11,342
Chilton	3,073	16,085	2,697	16,901
Choctaw	3,127	4,296	2,511	4,094
Clarke	5,755	7,324	4,917	6,956
Clay	1,267	5,601	986	5,693
Cleburne	675	6,484	605	6,984
Coffee	5,076	16,899	4,585	17,457
Colbert	8,343	19,203	7,092	19,614
Conecuh	2,966	3,442	2,580	3,423
Coosa	1,796	3,631	1,475	3,750
Covington	2,721	14,586	2,309	14,664
Crenshaw	1,700	4,864	1,453	4,993
Cullman	4,478	36,880	4,033	38,669
Dale	5,170	14,303	4,478	14,473
Dallas	12,230	5,524	10,233	5,188
DeKalb	4,281	24,767	3,757	25,631
Elmore	10,367	30,164	9,764	31,336
Escambia	4,918	10,869	3,956	10,866
Etowah	11,567	35,528	9,969	35,470
Fayette	1,395	7,300	1,141	7,154
Franklin	2,086	10,376	1,566	10,404
Geneva	1,595	10,848	1,389	10,924
Greene	3,884	875	3,131	885
Hale	4,663	3,192	3,861	3,363
Henry	2,606	6,607	2,259	6,983
Houston	12,917	32,618	11,258	32,255
Jackson	3,717	19,670	3,274	20,073
Jefferson	181,688	138,843	161,411	130,272
Lamar	978	6,174	805	6,028
Lauderdale	11,915	31,721	10,299	32,615
Lawrence	3,562	12,322	2,975	12,961
Lee	27,860	42,221	23,857	43,068
Limestone	13,672	34,640	14,452	37,524
Lowndes	4,972	1,836	3,865	1,755
Macon	7,108	1,541	6,069	1,681
Madison	87,286	102,780	87,509	105,149
Marengo	5,488	5,343	4,621	4,990
Marion	1,463	12,205	1,196	12,238
Marshall	5,943	33,191	5,535	34,350
Mobile	79,474	101,243	71,279	99,981
Monroe	4,455	6,147	3,736	5,997
Montgomery	64,529	33,311	57,734	30,404
Morgan	13,234	39,664	12,343	40,310
Perry	3,860	1,339	3,170	1,268
Pickens	4,022	5,594	3,385	5,455
Pike	5,636	8,042	4,882	8,213
Randolph	2,203	8,559	1,919	9,098
Russell	11,228	9,864	10,379	10,047
St. Clair	7,744	36,166	7,184	32,651
Shelby	33,268	79,700	32,947	79,522
Sumter	4,648	1,598	3,722	1,542
Talladega	13,138	22,235	10,878	22,070
Tallapoosa	5,859	14,963	4,974	14,881
Tuscaloosa	37,765	51,117	33,322	50,617
Walker	4,834	26,002	4,092	25,393
Washington	2,258	6,564	1,859	6,526
Wilcox	4,048	1,833	3,449	1,793
Winston	974	10,195	882	10,190
Totals	**849,624**	**1,441,170**	**766,860**	**1,451,948**

Alaska

	2020		2024	
	Biden (D)	**Trump (R)**	**Harris (D)**	**Trump (R)**
Totals	**153,778**	**189,951**	**102,318**	**140,936**

Arizona

	2020		2024	
County	**Biden (D)**	**Trump (R)**	**Harris (D)**	**Trump (R)**
Apache	23,293	11,442	6,975	5,001
Cochise	23,732	35,557	6,301	14,494
Coconino	44,698	27,052	35,605	23,446
Gila	8,943	18,377	7,408	16,227
Graham	4,034	10,749	3,668	10,451
Greenlee	1,182	2,433	909	2,115
La Paz	2,236	5,129	1,610	4,214
Maricopa	1,040,774	995,665	656,716	687,840
Mohave	24,831	78,535	19,607	70,769
Navajo	23,383	27,657	17,781	24,781
Pima	304,981	207,758	181,709	119,526
Pinal	75,106	107,077	61,040	89,505
Santa Cruz	13,138	6,194	9,997	6,878
Yavapai	49,602	91,527	30,471	58,247
Yuma	32,210	36,534	12,322	23,085
Totals	**1,672,143**	**1,661,686**	**1,052,119**	**1,156,579**

Arkansas

	2020		2024	
County	**Biden (D)**	**Trump (R)**	**Harris (D)**	**Trump (R)**
Arkansas	1,818	4,304	1,501	3,948
Ashley	2,125	5,548	1,770	5,741
Baxter	4,635	15,836	4,334	16,235
Benton	42,249	73,965	45,150	79,798
Boone	3,064	13,652	2,850	13,959
Bradley	1,214	2,335	958	2,210
Calhoun	479	1,636	378	1,668
Carroll	4,023	7,424	3,791	7,438
Chicot	2,260	1,752	1,788	1,654
Clark	3,438	4,616	2,938	4,511
Clay	962	4,086	873	3,910
Cleburne	1,988	10,328	1,940	10,592
Cleveland	651	2,867	524	2,803
Columbia	2,814	5,500	2,460	5,362
Conway	2,615	5,694	2,444	5,873
Craighead	11,921	25,558	11,190	25,117
Crawford	4,959	18,607	4,749	18,596
Crittenden	8,514	7,333	7,342	7,011
Cross	1,772	4,946	1,630	4,736
Dallas	963	1,573	797	1,482
Desha	2,016	1,921	1,630	1,803
Drew	2,426	4,349	2,046	4,195
Faulkner	18,347	34,421	17,734	35,322
Franklin	1,300	5,677	1,230	5,562
Fulton	1,035	3,961	906	4,034
Garland	14,045	29,069	12,992	28,322
Grant	1,268	6,794	1,192	6,755
Greene	3,058	12,670	2,933	12,611
Hempstead	2,138	4,470	1,775	4,193
Hot Spring	3,082	9,202	2,816	9,216
Howard	1,340	3,367	1,158	3,246
Independence	2,806	11,250	2,687	11,011
Izard	1,021	4,631	949	4,854
Jackson	1,365	3,593	1,182	3,508
Jefferson	14,981	9,521	12,741	8,432
Johnson	2,283	6,938	2,102	6,734
Lafayette	839	1,757	690	1,579
Lawrence	1,080	4,569	964	4,598
Lee	1,423	1,286	1,253	1,174
Lincoln	1,032	2,729	811	2,501
Little River	1,226	3,715	1,076	3,737
Logan	1,544	6,441	1,464	6,567
Lonoke	6,686	22,884	6,785	23,210
Madison	1,563	5,658	1,491	5,881
Marion	1,531	5,783	1,489	6,215
Miller	4,245	11,920	3,761	11,821
Mississippi	4,558	7,296	3,538	6,935
Monroe	1,147	1,545	1,001	1,385
Montgomery	731	3,046	639	2,974
Nevada	1,076	2,133	844	1,948
Newton	709	3,192	644	3,063
Ouachita	3,995	5,294	3,384	5,047
Perry	1,012	3,479	896	3,528
Phillips	3,623	2,417	2,737	2,081
Pike	644	3,519	560	3,745

	2020		2024	
County	**Biden (D)**	**Trump (R)**	**Harris (D)**	**Trump (R)**
Poinsett	1,424	5,918	1,234	5,714
Polk	1,246	7,035	1,143	6,978
Pope	5,772	18,081	5,481	18,096
Prairie	654	2,786	524	2,628
Pulaski	101,947	63,687	91,633	57,787
Randolph	1,215	5,355	1,135	5,363
St. Francis	3,604	3,242	2,953	2,909
Saline	16,060	39,556	16,601	39,727
Scott	483	2,962	425	2,905
Searcy	588	3,365	510	3,281
Sebastian	14,487	31,198	13,558	30,622
Sevier	1,116	3,884	861	3,767
Sharp	1,398	5,938	1,312	5,969
Stone	1,180	4,616	1,079	4,785
Union	5,584	10,478	5,013	10,190
Van Buren	1,593	6,034	1,435	6,035
Washington	43,824	47,504	43,683	50,181
White	5,978	24,182	5,632	24,495
Woodruff	856	1,543	760	1,511
Yell	1,284	5,226	1,210	5,118
Totals	**423,932**	**760,647**	**394,783**	**754,458**

California

	2020		2024	
County	**Biden (D)**	**Trump (R)**	**Harris (D)**	**Trump (R)**
Alameda	617,659	136,309	164,371	57,089
Alpine	476	244	444	231
Amador	8,153	13,585	6,851	11,795
Butte	50,815	48,819	31,769	32,775
Calaveras	10,046	16,518	7,518	13,200
Colusa	3,239	4,559	1,009	1,765
Contra Costa	416,386	152,877	232,315	104,349
Del Norte	4,677	6,461	2,781	3,717
El Dorado	51,621	61,838	35,900	44,283
Fresno	193,025	164,464	90,474	108,800
Glenn	3,995	7,063	1,753	4,017
Humboldt	44,768	21,770	18,448	11,566
Imperial	34,678	20,847	10,655	8,956
Inyo	4,634	4,620	2,716	2,887
Kern	133,366	164,484	62,390	99,526
Kings	18,699	24,072	10,530	17,821
Lake	14,941	13,123	3,899	3,772
Lassen	2,799	8,970	1,808	5,506
Los Angeles	3,028,885	1,145,530	1,623,052	881,815
Madera	23,168	29,378	14,084	21,823
Marin	128,288	24,612	66,556	15,268
Mariposa	4,088	5,950	3,244	4,918
Mendocino	28,782	13,267	10,110	4,852
Merced	48,991	39,397	16,581	19,185
Modoc	1,150	3,109	865	2,440
Mono	4,013	2,513	2,584	1,723
Monterey	113,953	46,299	56,842	29,165
Napa	49,817	20,676	16,599	8,643
Nevada	36,359	26,779	7,025	7,886
Orange	814,009	676,498	473,741	491,462
Placer	106,869	122,488	71,533	87,638
Plumas	4,561	6,445	3,328	4,781
Riverside	528,340	449,144	265,780	264,064
Sacramento	440,808	259,405	175,509	123,553
San Benito	17,628	10,590	8,112	6,743
San Bernardino	455,859	366,257	186,330	197,819
San Diego	964,650	600,094	535,130	403,378
San Francisco	378,156	56,417	183,040	38,503
San Joaquin	161,137	121,098	71,860	75,626
San Luis Obispo	88,310	67,436	45,386	34,230
San Mateo	291,496	75,584	151,991	52,339
Santa Barbara	129,963	65,736	73,708	42,108
Santa Clara	617,967	214,612	302,165	136,605
Santa Cruz	114,246	26,937	71,532	20,635
Shasta	30,000	60,789	6,287	13,776
Sierra	730	1,142	603	1,020
Siskiyou	9,593	13,290	6,238	8,603
Solano	131,639	69,306	69,224	44,316
Sonoma	199,938	61,825	109,873	38,286
Stanislaus	105,841	104,145	48,135	62,322
Sutter	17,367	24,375	6,988	13,481
Tehama	8,911	19,141	3,754	8,961
Trinity	2,851	3,188	1,579	1,875
Tulare	66,105	77,579	32,278	52,864
Tuolumne	11,978	17,689	9,061	13,441
Ventura	251,388	162,207	144,855	112,572
Yolo	67,598	27,292	32,517	16,109
Yuba	11,230	17,676	5,854	9,923
Totals	**11,110,639**	**6,006,518**	**5,599,564**	**3,906,806**

Colorado

	2020		2024	
County	**Biden (D)**	**Trump (R)**	**Harris (D)**	**Trump (R)**
Adams	134,202	95,657	94,807	75,825
Alamosa	3,759	3,813	3,213	3,998
Arapahoe	213,607	127,323	131,058	83,278
Archuleta	3,738	5,189	3,856	5,158
Baca	317	1,867	271	1,662
Bent	732	1,503	633	1,470
Boulder	159,089	42,501	110,343	26,542
Broomfield	29,077	16,295	28,931	15,740
Chaffee	7,160	6,222	7,909	5,970
Cheyenne	131	993	105	906
Clear Creek	3,604	2,754	3,376	2,390
Conejos	1,959	2,286	1,606	2,333
Costilla	1,311	741	1,132	817
Crowley	437	1,271	419	1,216
Custer	1,112	2,474	1,171	2,560
Delta	5,887	13,081	5,906	12,688
Denver	313,293	71,618	182,175	44,230
Dolores	341	1,089	311	1,049
Douglas	104,653	121,270	104,459	118,103
Eagle	18,588	9,892	16,532	9,892
El Paso	161,941	202,828	108,460	128,225
Elbert	4,490	14,027	3,933	11,923
Fremont	7,369	17,517	7,359	17,024
Garfield	15,427	14,717	14,037	13,329
Gilpin	2,223	1,833	2,191	1,693
Grand	4,710	4,883	4,663	4,765
Gunnison	7,132	3,735	6,824	3,660
Hinsdale	255	353	252	329
Huerfano	2,076	2,203	1,946	2,332
Jackson	175	681	171	624
Jefferson	218,396	148,417	205,319	135,737
Kiowa	98	795	100	741
Kit Carson	662	3,144	546	3,042
La Plata	20,548	14,233	20,470	13,877
Lake	2,303	1,497	2,169	1,538
Larimer	126,120	91,489	107,557	70,135
Las Animas	3,497	4,284	2,431	2,843
Lincoln	470	2,135	425	2,064
Logan	2,218	8,087	2,069	7,775
Mesa	31,536	56,894	31,709	49,774
Mineral	317	427	317	415
Moffat	1,203	5,670	660	3,175
Montezuma	5,836	9,306	4,929	7,698
Montrose	7,687	16,770	7,343	13,576
Morgan	3,876	9,593	3,233	9,742
Otero	3,605	5,756	2,877	4,951
Ouray	2,365	1,577	2,400	1,539
Park	4,903	6,991	4,712	6,632
Phillips	486	1,958	406	1,862
Pitkin	8,989	2,780	6,102	2,224
Prowers	1,458	4,008	1,021	3,264
Pueblo	43,772	42,252	37,140	39,073
Rio Blanco	561	3,061	592	2,748
Rio Grande	2,495	3,660	2,280	3,722
Routt	10,582	5,925	9,717	5,066
Saguache	1,884	1,413	1,673	1,553
San Juan	342	202	356	179
San Miguel	3,924	1,136	3,461	1,121
Sedgwick	301	1,121	281	1,044
Summit	12,631	5,322	11,663	5,181
Teller	5,278	11,241	4,413	8,508
Washington	369	2,595	322	2,402
Weld	66,060	96,145	46,725	68,237
Yuma	785	4,107	708	3,643
Totals	**1,804,352**	**1,364,607**	**1,374,175**	**1,084,812**

Connecticut

	2020		2024	
City	**Biden (D)**	**Trump (R)**	**Harris (D)**	**Trump (R)**
Bridgeport	33,515	8,269	2,997	1,336
Bristol	15,462	13,834	14,038	14,187
Danbury	18,869	12,788	15,871	13,746
East Hartford	14,787	5,524	12,504	5,550
Enfield	11,263	9,298	9,977	9,372

	2020		2024	
City	Biden (D)	Trump (R)	Harris (D)	Trump (R)
Fairfield	22,861	12,052	21,154	12,523
Glastonbury	13,990	7,998	13,185	7,902
Greenwich	22,239	13,264	19,603	14,122
Hamden	21,652	7,139	8,267	4,082
Hartford	28,267	4,118	14,059	3,557
Manchester	19,455	8,530	15,983	7,952
Meriden	14,955	9,981	13,217	9,641
Middletown	15,508	7,611	13,986	7,611
Milford	17,626	13,997	14,420	14,346
New Britain	16,031	7,724	13,503	8,282
New Haven	35,521	6,146	7,728	2,286
Norwalk	29,382	13,311	11,908	8,460
Shelton	10,837	12,747	10,282	12,985
Southington	12,855	13,473	11,365	13,269
Stamford	40,437	18,242	35,570	20,370
Stratford	17,363	10,516	15,708	11,261
Trumbull	11,919	9,175	10,463	9,897
Wallingford	13,560	11,831	15,808	14,565
Waterbury	21,573	14,155	18,327	14,721
West Hartford	27,298	8,451	1,162	785
West Haven	14,245	8,126	12,310	7,949
Other	557,753	445,478	477,845	401,897
Total	**1,080,831**	**714,717**	**790,175**	**635,431**

Delaware

	2020		2024	
County	Biden (D)	Trump (R)	Harris (D)	Trump (R)
Kent	44,552	41,009	41,659	41,390
New Castle	195,034	88,364	178,909	90,196
Sussex	56,682	71,230	64,800	80,960
Totals	**296,268**	**200,603**	**285,368**	**212,546**

District of Columbia

	2020		2024	
	Biden (D)	Trump (R)	Harris (D)	Trump (R)
Totals	**317,323**	**18,586**	**255,899**	**18,669**

Florida

	2020		2024	
County	Biden (D)	Trump (R)	Harris (D)	Trump (R)
Alachua	89,704	50,972	81,454	52,873
Baker	2,037	11,911	1,982	12,925
Bay	25,614	66,097	25,149	71,409
Bradford	3,160	10,334	2,946	10,918
Brevard	148,549	207,883	140,993	216,326
Broward	618,752	333,409	506,294	358,497
Calhoun	1,209	5,274	1,017	5,358
Charlotte	42,273	73,243	40,301	82,039
Citrus	27,092	65,352	26,243	71,271
Clay	38,317	84,480	37,846	87,649
Collier	77,621	128,950	71,652	143,188
Columbia	8,914	23,836	8,244	25,086
DeSoto	4,259	8,313	3,520	8,879
Dixie	1,365	6,759	1,181	6,918
Duval	252,556	233,762	228,800	235,879
Escambia	70,929	96,674	64,475	96,252
Flagler	28,161	43,043	28,406	50,982
Franklin	2,120	4,675	1,870	4,831
Gadsden	16,153	7,465	14,176	7,490
Gilchrist	1,700	7,895	1,660	8,928
Glades	1,385	3,782	1,221	4,033
Gulf	1,985	6,113	1,969	6,675
Hamilton	1,963	3,815	1,722	3,964
Hardee	2,298	6,122	1,746	6,325
Hendry	4,929	7,906	4,092	9,245
Hernando	37,519	70,412	34,308	75,304
Highlands	16,938	34,873	15,204	36,352
Hillsborough	376,367	327,398	320,663	341,323
Holmes	924	8,080	882	8,193
Indian River	37,844	58,872	35,614	62,667
Jackson	6,766	15,488	5,885	16,061
Jefferson	3,897	4,479	3,423	5,006
Lafayette	510	3,128	439	3,290
Lake	83,505	125,859	84,408	140,393
Lee	157,695	233,247	139,084	250,522
Leon	103,517	57,453	94,292	60,305
Levy	6,205	16,749	5,987	18,234
Liberty	694	2,846	563	2,896
Madison	3,747	5,576	3,230	5,867
Manatee	90,166	124,987	86,121	140,132
Marion	74,858	127,826	72,378	140,097
Martin	36,893	61,168	35,518	64,088
Miami-Dade	617,864	532,833	479,732	605,236
Monroe	21,881	25,693	17,807	25,954
Nassau	15,564	42,566	17,101	47,881
Okaloosa	34,248	79,798	31,998	80,214
Okeechobee	4,390	11,470	3,665	12,307
Orange	395,014	245,398	333,392	254,819
Osceola	97,297	73,480	83,863	86,368
Palm Beach	433,572	334,711	372,032	366,521
Pasco	119,073	179,621	117,324	197,624
Pinellas	277,450	276,209	242,229	269,272
Polk	145,049	194,586	136,629	208,777
Putnam	10,527	25,514	9,346	26,683
St. Johns	63,850	110,946	66,669	128,514
St. Lucie	84,137	86,831	83,428	100,208
Santa Rosa	27,612	77,385	26,971	84,214
Sarasota	120,110	148,370	112,496	163,037
Seminole	132,528	125,241	120,364	129,531
Sumter	29,341	62,761	32,532	72,113
Suwannee	4,485	16,410	4,215	17,548
Taylor	2,299	7,751	1,987	7,940
Union	1,053	5,133	971	5,223
Volusia	130,575	173,821	119,917	187,484
Wakulla	5,351	12,874	5,438	14,235
Walton	10,338	32,947	10,277	38,944
Washington	2,347	9,876	2,140	10,369
Totals	**5,297,045**	**5,668,731**	**4,669,481**	**6,099,686**

Georgia

	2020		2024	
County	Biden (D)	Trump (R)	Harris (D)	Trump (R)
Appling	1,784	6,570	1,560	6,761
Atkinson	825	2,300	700	2,350
Bacon	625	4,017	645	4,185
Baker	652	897	582	883
Baldwin	9,140	8,903	9,155	9,573
Banks	932	7,795	1,136	9,353
Barrow	10,453	26,804	12,925	30,674
Bartow	12,091	37,672	13,929	43,240
Ben Hill	2,393	4,111	2,198	4,281
Berrien	1,269	6,419	1,209	6,838
Bibb	43,408	26,559	41,970	26,609
Bleckley	1,312	4,329	1,339	4,685
Brantley	700	6,993	736	7,741
Brooks	2,791	4,261	2,628	4,557
Bryan	6,738	14,240	7,769	16,725
Bulloch	11,248	18,387	11,494	20,960
Burke	5,208	5,400	4,979	6,014
Butts	3,274	8,406	3,544	9,424
Calhoun	1,263	923	1,152	896
Camden	7,967	15,249	8,400	17,805
Candler	1,269	3,133	1,196	3,366
Carroll	16,236	37,476	17,622	42,538
Catoosa	6,932	25,167	7,700	27,140
Charlton	1,105	3,419	1,006	3,606
Chatham	78,247	53,232	79,879	55,521
Chattahoochee	667	880	703	982
Chattooga	1,854	8,064	1,896	8,768
Cherokee	42,779	99,585	48,785	112,075
Clarke	36,055	14,450	36,042	16,008
Clay	791	637	771	663
Clayton	95,466	15,811	94,092	16,854
Clinch	744	2,105	702	2,201
Cobb	221,847	165,436	227,640	168,286
Coffee	4,511	10,578	4,285	11,370
Colquitt	4,190	11,777	4,110	12,445
Columbia	29,232	50,013	31,582	53,610
Cook	2,059	4,900	1,955	5,372
Coweta	24,210	51,501	28,096	57,180
Crawford	1,615	4,428	1,577	4,735
Crisp	2,982	4,985	2,993	5,098
Dade	1,261	6,066	1,342	6,794
Dawson	2,486	13,398	3,346	16,111
Decatur	4,782	6,755	4,367	7,136
DeKalb	308,162	58,377	299,039	62,482
Dodge	2,172	5,843	2,078	6,245
Dooly	1,911	2,159	1,919	2,243
Dougherty	24,568	10,441	23,795	9,893
Douglas	42,814	25,454	46,192	23,970

County	2020 Biden (D)	2020 Trump (R)	2024 Harris (D)	2024 Trump (R)
Early	2,450	2,710	2,156	2,718
Echols	167	1,256	127	1,307
Effingham	7,718	23,361	9,142	26,925
Elbert	2,879	6,226	2,687	6,847
Emanuel	2,886	6,553	2,669	6,910
Evans	1,324	2,888	1,213	3,008
Fannin	2,570	12,169	2,804	13,207
Fayette	33,062	37,956	35,801	38,166
Floyd	11,917	28,906	12,824	31,583
Forsyth	42,208	85,123	45,451	91,210
Franklin	1,593	9,069	1,609	10,355
Fulton	380,212	137,247	380,013	142,912
Gilmer	2,932	13,429	3,396	14,937
Glascock	155	1,402	133	1,534
Glynn	15,882	25,617	16,124	27,546
Gordon	4,384	19,405	4,976	22,481
Grady	3,619	7,034	3,279	7,381
Greene	4,087	7,066	4,514	8,214
Gwinnett	241,994	166,400	242,125	172,819
Habersham	3,562	16,637	4,033	19,133
Hall	25,033	64,183	28,238	72,871
Hancock	2,976	1,154	2,862	1,363
Haralson	1,791	12,330	2,057	14,238
Harris	5,457	14,319	5,971	16,273
Hart	3,157	9,465	3,206	11,064
Heard	824	4,519	858	5,335
Henry	73,443	48,259	83,194	44,962
Houston	32,239	41,540	35,876	45,072
Irwin	1,008	3,134	985	3,340
Jackson	7,642	29,502	10,462	36,477
Jasper	1,761	5,822	1,879	7,195
Jeff Davis	1,028	4,695	924	4,935
Jefferson	4,058	3,537	3,669	3,758
Jenkins	1,266	2,161	1,179	2,217
Johnson	1,222	2,850	1,066	2,913
Jones	4,882	9,940	2,463	5,176
Lamar	2,620	6,331	2,769	7,560
Lanier	1,019	2,509	994	2,726
Laurens	8,074	14,493	7,814	15,454
Lee	4,558	12,007	4,955	12,654
Liberty	13,104	7,959	13,431	9,436
Lincoln	1,432	3,173	1,349	3,556
Long	2,035	3,527	2,478	4,558
Lowndes	20,116	25,692	19,395	28,014
Lumpkin	3,126	12,163	3,350	14,334
Macon	2,858	1,783	2,755	1,916
Madison	3,411	11,326	3,748	12,944
Marion	1,312	2,275	1,253	2,347
McDuffie	4,168	6,169	3,935	6,558
McIntosh	2,612	4,016	2,626	4,745
Meriwether	4,287	6,524	4,371	7,372
Miller	748	2,066	670	2,045
Mitchell	3,993	4,935	3,697	5,147
Monroe	4,385	11,057	4,687	12,949
Montgomery	980	2,960	927	3,031
Morgan	3,353	8,231	3,533	9,587
Murray	2,301	12,944	2,459	14,964
Muscogee	49,446	30,107	49,337	30,573
Newton	29,789	23,869	33,823	24,888
Oconee	8,162	16,595	8,616	18,424
Oglethorpe	2,439	5,592	2,513	6,254
Paulding	29,695	54,517	35,693	58,680
Peach	5,922	6,506	6,276	7,098
Pickens	2,824	14,110	3,499	17,263
Pierce	1,100	7,898	1,089	8,655
Pike	1,505	9,127	1,646	10,846
Polk	3,657	13,587	3,747	15,349
Pulaski	1,230	2,815	1,281	3,036
Putnam	3,448	8,291	3,694	9,130
Quitman	497	604	477	656
Rabun	1,984	7,474	2,221	8,151
Randolph	1,671	1,390	1,601	1,372
Richmond	59,119	26,780	56,545	26,439
Rockdale	31,237	13,014	33,071	11,692
Schley	462	1,800	452	1,970
Screven	2,661	3,915	2,575	4,321
Seminole	1,256	2,613	1,187	2,807
Spalding	11,828	18,104	13,674	19,180
Stephens	2,386	9,367	2,403	10,630
Stewart	1,182	801	1,170	837
Sumter	6,314	5,733	6,127	5,864
Talbot	2,114	1,392	1,888	1,483
Taliaferro	561	360	507	375
Tattnall	2,062	6,054	1,965	6,511
Taylor	1,388	2,420	1,365	2,599
Telfair	1,488	2,825	1,273	2,930
Terrell	2,376	2,004	2,041	2,002
Thomas	8,708	12,969	8,337	13,665
Tift	5,318	10,784	5,435	11,489
Toombs	2,938	7,873	2,670	8,203
Towns	1,550	6,384	1,649	7,154
Treutlen	952	2,101	864	2,250
Troup	11,577	18,142	11,744	19,381
Turner	1,409	2,349	1,363	2,454
Twiggs	2,044	2,370	1,895	2,548
Union	2,800	12,650	3,307	14,470
Upson	4,203	8,606	4,095	9,520
Walker	5,770	23,173	6,432	25,452
Walton	12,683	37,839	15,601	42,394
Ware	4,169	9,903	4,067	10,278
Warren	1,468	1,166	1,353	1,232
Washington	4,743	4,668	4,641	4,824
Wayne	2,688	9,987	2,705	10,807
Webster	640	748	544	788
Wheeler	689	1,583	622	1,648
White	2,411	12,222	2,607	14,134
Whitfield	10,680	25,644	10,949	28,642
Wilcox	861	2,402	845	2,490
Wilkes	2,160	2,823	2,108	2,966
Wilkinson	2,074	2,665	2,012	2,888
Worth	2,395	6,830	2,299	6,989
Totals	**2,473,633**	**2,461,854**	**2,533,821**	**2,651,206**

Hawaii

County	2020 Biden (D)	2020 Trump (R)	2024 Harris (D)	2024 Trump (R)
Hawaii	58,731	26,897	44,580	22,902
Honolulu	238,869	136,259	186,589	112,320
Kauai	21,225	11,582	14,318	8,890
Maui	47,305	22,126	30,809	16,401
Totals	**366,130**	**196,864**	**276,296**	**160,513**

Idaho

County	2020 Biden (D)	2020 Trump (R)	2024 Harris (D)	2024 Trump (R)
Ada	120,539	130,699	116,115	143,759
Adams	591	1,941	577	2,037
Bannock	14,682	23,331	14,306	24,329
Bear Lake	350	2,914	346	2,908
Benewah	977	3,878	934	4,094
Bingham	4,124	15,295	3,390	13,924
Blaine	8,919	4,032	6,478	3,693
Boise	1,204	3,485	1,065	3,627
Bonner	8,310	18,369	4,801	18,649
Bonneville	14,254	37,805	14,458	40,053
Boundary	1,220	4,937	1,145	5,794
Butte	188	1,202	185	1,268
Camas	149	507	153	547
Canyon	25,881	61,759	19,830	64,160
Caribou	431	2,906	445	2,906
Cassia	1,464	7,907	1,359	7,959
Clark	41	264	50	280
Clearwater	877	3,453	774	3,550
Custer	603	2,089	586	1,998
Elmore	2,601	7,246	2,611	7,791
Franklin	657	5,845	703	6,279
Fremont	998	5,548	954	5,645
Gem	1,803	7,951	1,699	8,707
Gooding	1,256	4,659	1,100	4,676
Idaho	1,561	7,826	1,460	8,148
Jefferson	1,661	12,099	1,891	13,481
Jerome	1,893	5,734	1,489	4,971
Kootenai	24,312	62,837	12,924	28,651
Latah	10,236	9,472	6,429	9,666
Lemhi	1,032	3,592	1,038	3,716
Lewis	349	1,489	290	1,503
Lincoln	414	1,469	392	1,466

County	2020 Biden (D)	2020 Trump (R)	2024 Harris (D)	2024 Trump (R)
Madison	2,666	13,559	2,767	13,925
Minidoka	1,550	6,265	1,373	6,401
Nez Perce	6,686	13,738	5,928	13,707
Oneida	249	2,148	253	2,119
Owyhee	816	3,819	756	4,101
Payette	2,161	8,862	2,064	9,457
Power	865	2,116	493	1,580
Shoshone	1,693	4,216	1,472	4,500
Teton	3,318	2,858	3,463	3,005
Twin Falls	9,391	25,897	9,061	27,295
Valley	2,976	3,947	2,869	4,214
Washington	1,073	4,154	1,010	4,429
Totals	**287,021**	**554,119**	**251,486**	**544,968**

Illinois

County	2020 Biden (D)	2020 Trump (R)	2024 Harris (D)	2024 Trump (R)
Adams	8,633	24,220	8,081	23,139
Alexander	1,114	1,486	903	1,340
Bond	2,288	5,625	2,109	5,689
Boone	10,542	13,883	10,070	13,615
Brown	486	1,931	467	1,938
Bureau	6,669	10,411	5,706	9,658
Calhoun	677	2,046	560	2,054
Carroll	2,748	5,105	2,594	5,071
Cass	1,615	3,625	1,438	3,708
Champaign	57,067	35,285	51,321	32,366
Christian	4,335	11,563	3,946	11,195
Clark	1,993	6,226	1,922	6,124
Clay	1,129	5,629	1,050	5,602
Clinton	4,493	14,304	4,355	14,302
Coles	8,067	14,037	7,471	13,595
Cook	1,725,973	558,269	1,267,822	551,986
Crawford	2,202	7,043	2,042	6,723
Cumberland	1,142	4,601	1,057	4,622
DeKalb	24,643	21,905	23,545	22,672
DeWitt	2,191	5,632	2,042	5,509
Douglas	2,335	6,227	2,195	6,067
DuPage	281,222	193,611	245,192	189,159
Edgar	1,887	6,193	1,813	5,944
Edwards	488	2,833	455	2,792
Effingham	3,716	15,006	3,604	15,097
Fayette	1,826	8,055	1,606	7,798
Ford	1,754	5,048	1,636	4,767
Franklin	4,760	13,622	4,240	13,161
Fulton	6,503	9,867	5,970	9,810
Gallatin	622	2,019	558	1,920
Greene	1,349	4,770	1,216	4,716
Grundy	9,626	16,523	9,045	16,927
Hamilton	824	3,432	738	3,380
Hancock	2,315	6,906	1,310	5,220
Hardin	449	1,691	356	1,546
Henderson	1,187	2,394	1,025	2,369
Henry	9,797	15,300	9,199	15,340
Iroquois	2,908	10,877	2,742	10,364
Jackson	11,181	10,890	11,268	10,558
Jasper	1,007	4,494	910	4,446
Jefferson	4,608	12,476	4,226	12,178
Jersey	2,961	8,712	2,807	8,677
Jo Daviess	5,109	7,166	5,013	7,107
Johnson	1,281	5,059	1,239	4,796
Kane	130,166	96,775	117,053	97,983
Kankakee	20,271	28,532	18,308	28,227
Kendall	33,168	29,492	32,762	31,862
Knox	10,703	12,009	9,630	11,804
Lake	204,032	123,594	171,723	116,115
LaSalle	22,442	30,113	20,172	30,211
Lawrence	1,419	4,886	1,282	4,715
Lee	6,407	9,630	6,055	9,654
Livingston	4,615	12,208	4,269	11,926
Logan	3,840	9,136	3,485	8,691
Macon	19,847	28,589	17,929	26,507
Macoupin	7,365	16,153	6,867	16,023
Madison	57,836	76,031	55,971	73,723
Marion	4,524	12,678	4,106	12,380
Marshall	2,005	4,197	1,911	4,119
Mason	1,985	4,654	1,768	4,454
Massac	1,725	4,997	1,678	4,936
McDonough	4,992	7,027	4,607	6,963
McHenry	78,154	82,260	71,783	82,199
McLean	43,933	40,502	43,797	39,891
Menard	2,022	4,764	1,828	4,495
Mercer	3,280	5,418	2,946	5,210
Monroe	6,569	14,142	6,420	14,009
Montgomery	3,905	9,544	3,556	9,370
Morgan	5,076	9,950	4,754	9,555
Moultrie	1,662	4,964	1,600	4,804
Ogle	9,428	16,248	8,796	16,389
Peoria	43,578	38,252	39,772	36,383
Perry	2,612	7,313	2,091	6,894
Piatt	3,329	6,248	3,183	6,084
Pike	1,484	6,332	1,064	5,764
Pope	433	1,722	416	1,698
Pulaski	891	1,699	767	1,579
Putnam	1,338	1,993	1,253	2,010
Randolph	3,592	11,076	3,469	10,645
Richland	1,830	6,089	1,744	5,886
Rock Island	36,691	28,603	34,085	28,037
St. Clair	68,325	57,150	48,048	47,698
Saline	2,789	8,103	2,629	7,827
Sangamon	48,917	53,485	45,853	50,767
Schuyler	1,068	2,773	958	2,718
Scott	572	2,114	488	2,070
Shelby	2,504	9,426	2,223	9,248
Stark	815	2,004	725	1,982
Stephenson	9,055	12,521	8,257	12,328
Tazewell	24,819	42,513	24,145	42,310
Union	2,579	6,161	2,280	5,835
Vermilion	10,323	20,725	9,192	19,712
Wabash	1,253	4,237	1,197	4,089
Warren	3,090	4,676	2,037	4,244
Washington	1,641	6,115	1,557	5,890
Wayne	1,187	7,176	1,151	7,011
White	1,517	5,791	1,388	5,586
Whiteside	12,253	14,527	10,990	14,871
Will	183,915	155,116	157,453	155,142
Williamson	10,206	22,801	9,827	22,639
Winnebago	64,056	60,861	57,911	58,276
Woodford	6,160	14,799	5,939	14,813
Totals	**3,471,915**	**2,446,891**	**2,770,451**	**2,351,499**

Indiana

County	2020 Biden (D)	2020 Trump (R)	2024 Harris (D)	2024 Trump (R)
Adams	3,236	10,686	3,175	10,522
Allen	73,189	92,083	69,527	90,102
Bartholomew	12,934	22,410	12,520	22,215
Benton	1,009	3,007	1,010	2,870
Blackford	1,376	3,841	1,227	3,806
Boone	15,244	22,351	16,425	22,840
Brown	3,036	5,777	2,826	5,632
Carroll	2,224	7,086	2,119	6,897
Cass	4,304	10,552	3,721	10,279
Clark	23,093	33,668	21,284	32,281
Clay	2,552	9,499	2,492	9,328
Clinton	3,361	9,334	3,133	9,100
Crawford	1,355	3,483	1,235	3,668
Daviess	2,169	9,576	1,963	9,322
Dearborn	5,446	19,528	5,327	20,832
Decatur	2,439	9,575	2,406	9,491
DeKalb	4,966	14,237	5,062	14,376
Delaware	20,474	26,827	18,840	26,057
Dubois	6,292	15,033	5,944	14,983
Elkhart	26,108	46,972	10,455	25,411
Fayette	2,237	7,755	2,084	7,625
Floyd	17,511	23,400	17,014	23,386
Fountain	1,629	6,154	1,440	5,622
Franklin	2,137	9,691	2,061	9,810
Fulton	2,280	6,694	2,097	6,633
Gibson	4,023	11,817	3,721	11,885
Grant	8,015	18,543	7,036	17,525
Greene	3,389	11,103	3,270	11,132
Hamilton	88,390	101,587	90,366	102,296
Hancock	12,895	28,996	14,288	29,273
Harrison	5,343	14,565	5,221	14,808
Hendricks	32,604	53,802	31,854	49,638
Henry	5,544	15,043	5,206	15,018
Howard	13,303	26,449	11,921	25,148

County	2020 Biden (D)	2020 Trump (R)	2024 Harris (D)	2024 Trump (R)
Huntington	4,255	13,147	4,416	12,990
Jackson	4,302	14,555	3,666	13,882
Jasper	3,798	11,383	3,489	12,082
Jay	1,926	6,361	1,747	6,217
Jefferson	4,731	9,663	4,442	9,614
Jennings	2,523	9,490	2,328	9,271
Johnson	24,736	51,219	24,869	51,575
Knox	4,067	11,655	3,625	11,236
Kosciusko	8,364	26,499	7,979	26,171
LaGrange	2,355	8,110	2,162	8,073
Lake	124,870	91,760	108,972	97,197
LaPorte	22,427	25,997	19,781	26,546
Lawrence	4,961	15,601	5,003	15,821
Madison	19,524	31,215	19,807	34,813
Marion	247,772	134,175	199,604	114,305
Marshall	5,712	13,844	5,354	13,829
Martin	1,011	4,029	933	3,959
Miami	3,235	10,925	3,046	10,670
Monroe	39,861	22,071	37,180	20,980
Montgomery	4,213	12,659	4,130	12,115
Morgan	7,781	27,512	7,764	26,963
Newton	1,509	4,942	1,368	5,131
Noble	4,660	14,195	4,462	14,209
Ohio	668	2,054	666	2,381
Orange	2,224	6,432	1,988	6,467
Owen	2,420	7,286	2,337	7,344
Parke	1,503	5,400	1,371	5,157
Perry	3,203	5,345	2,966	5,544
Pike	1,415	4,692	1,314	4,609
Porter	39,746	45,008	13,446	21,096
Posey	3,811	9,206	3,569	9,205
Pulaski	1,463	4,246	1,280	4,368
Putnam	3,946	12,278	3,871	12,566
Randolph	2,513	8,312	2,348	8,008
Ripley	2,774	11,261	2,682	11,526
Rush	1,754	6,035	1,675	5,812
St. Joseph	59,896	53,164	55,171	53,546
Scott	2,701	7,331	2,387	7,629
Shelby	5,023	14,568	4,955	14,438
Spencer	3,213	7,357	2,852	7,361
Starke	2,650	7,466	2,433	7,879
Steuben	4,513	11,327	4,957	11,484
Sullivan	2,153	6,691	2,006	6,639
Switzerland	964	3,133	873	3,319
Tippecanoe	35,017	34,581	32,534	32,720
Tipton	1,834	6,110	1,893	5,946
Union	736	2,688	744	2,698
Vanderburgh	34,415	41,844	20,712	25,883
Vermillion	2,145	5,184	1,928	5,174
Vigo	18,123	24,545	16,327	23,731
Wabash	3,494	10,762	3,332	10,422
Warren	974	3,401	898	3,402
Warrick	11,923	21,326	11,290	21,278
Washington	2,784	9,114	2,763	9,737
Wayne	9,524	17,567	8,389	16,741
Wells	2,928	10,855	2,850	11,004
White	3,032	7,957	2,945	7,969
Whitley	4,234	12,862	4,275	13,122
Totals	**1,242,498**	**1,729,857**	**1,069,140**	**1,611,384**

Iowa

County	2020 Biden (D)	2020 Trump (R)	2024 Harris (D)	2024 Trump (R)
Adair	1,198	2,917	1,085	2,916
Adams	590	1,530	576	1,517
Allamakee	2,576	4,735	2,350	4,857
Appanoose	1,891	4,512	1,690	4,704
Audubon	1,071	2,295	970	2,214
Benton	5,160	9,188	4,738	9,544
Black Hawk	35,647	29,640	31,272	30,558
Boone	6,303	8,695	5,894	9,194
Bremer	5,958	8,294	5,552	8,772
Buchanan	4,169	6,420	3,758	6,763
Buena Vista	2,961	5,056	2,460	4,962
Butler	2,424	5,542	2,143	5,781
Calhoun	1,470	3,689	1,327	3,708
Carroll	3,454	7,737	3,151	7,799
Cass	2,201	4,969	2,074	5,006
Cedar	4,337	6,161	4,075	6,388
Cerro Gordo	10,941	12,442	9,949	12,604
Cherokee	1,936	4,495	1,611	4,398
Chickasaw	2,233	4,308	1,918	4,232
Clarke	1,466	3,144	1,264	3,137
Clay	2,662	6,137	2,366	6,044
Clayton	3,340	6,106	3,015	6,245
Clinton	10,812	13,361	9,471	13,960
Crawford	2,220	4,854	1,811	4,648
Dallas	26,879	27,987	29,353	32,329
Davis	1,013	3,032	878	3,027
Decatur	1,120	2,615	957	2,711
Delaware	3,157	6,666	2,975	6,976
Des Moines	8,893	10,592	7,931	10,776
Dickinson	3,661	7,438	3,291	7,770
Dubuque	25,657	27,214	23,697	28,223
Emmet	1,520	3,265	1,315	3,422
Fayette	3,835	6,145	3,332	6,323
Floyd	3,172	4,732	2,781	4,731
Franklin	1,626	3,422	1,393	3,420
Fremont	1,080	2,711	1,023	2,711
Greene	1,769	3,223	1,599	3,210
Grundy	2,206	4,929	2,016	4,996
Guthrie	1,985	4,272	1,973	4,445
Hamilton	2,843	4,956	2,480	5,002
Hancock	1,683	4,390	1,523	4,335
Hardin	2,976	5,850	1,418	3,947
Harrison	2,440	5,569	2,245	5,566
Henry	3,275	6,507	2,994	6,439
Howard	1,772	3,127	1,618	3,157
Humboldt	1,442	3,819	1,232	3,762
Ida	917	2,880	826	2,769
Iowa	3,547	6,009	3,396	6,066
Jackson	4,029	6,940	3,565	7,074
Jasper	7,737	12,084	7,140	12,701
Jefferson	4,319	4,443	3,774	4,350
Johnson	59,177	22,925	58,772	26,069
Jones	4,213	6,572	3,939	6,818
Keokuk	1,414	3,797	1,219	3,869
Kossuth	2,696	6,275	2,280	5,973
Lee	6,541	9,773	5,673	10,148
Linn	70,874	53,364	66,296	54,213
Louisa	1,726	3,500	1,480	3,582
Lucas	1,284	3,287	1,169	3,399
Lyon	1,067	5,707	1,020	5,896
Madison	3,134	6,507	3,005	6,851
Mahaska	2,894	8,297	2,530	8,018
Marion	6,178	12,663	5,928	13,289
Marshall	8,176	9,571	7,134	9,812
Mills	2,508	5,585	2,448	5,647
Mitchell	2,053	3,677	1,929	3,708
Monona	1,407	3,248	1,235	3,331
Monroe	1,078	2,975	1,002	3,104
Montgomery	1,583	3,659	1,507	3,482
Muscatine	9,372	10,823	8,199	11,139
O'Brien	1,569	5,861	1,427	5,995
Osceola	601	2,690	555	2,621
Page	2,086	5,319	2,060	5,153
Palo Alto	1,519	3,370	1,338	3,576
Plymouth	3,494	10,492	3,102	10,654
Pocahontas	933	2,826	794	2,727
Polk	146,250	106,800	139,963	112,181
Pottawattamie	18,575	26,247	17,382	26,266
Poweshiek	4,306	5,657	4,048	5,745
Ringgold	709	1,968	638	2,014
Sac	1,389	4,061	1,288	4,100
Scott	46,926	43,683	42,448	45,947
Shelby	1,959	4,697	1,809	4,592
Sioux	3,019	15,680	2,617	16,022
Story	29,175	20,340	23,909	16,552
Tama	3,577	5,303	3,069	5,379
Taylor	746	2,463	667	2,381
Union	2,061	4,010	1,871	4,038
Van Buren	875	2,859	778	2,785
Wapello	5,821	9,516	4,892	9,470
Warren	12,574	17,782	12,662	19,459
Washington	4,561	6,971	2,027	4,201
Wayne	727	2,338	643	2,426
Webster	6,613	10,938	5,632	10,838
Winnebago	2,135	3,707	1,906	3,636
Winneshiek	5,617	6,235	5,319	6,426

County	2020 Biden (D)	2020 Trump (R)	2024 Harris (D)	2024 Trump (R)
Woodbury	18,704	25,736	16,116	25,923
Worth	1,596	2,738	1,508	2,714
Wright	1,996	4,136	1,770	3,853
Totals	**759,061**	**897,672**	**700,248**	**916,211**

Kansas

County	2020 Biden (D)	2020 Trump (R)	2024 Harris (D)	2024 Trump (R)
Allen	1,570	4,218	1,432	3,984
Anderson	782	2,929	719	2,954
Atchison	2,359	4,906	2,154	4,851
Barber	291	2,014	279	1,801
Barton	2,340	8,608	2,156	8,059
Bourbon	1,541	5,023	1,425	4,915
Brown	1,104	3,262	1,035	3,045
Butler	9,181	22,634	8,840	21,915
Chase	345	1,123	342	1,081
Chautauqua	212	1,402	210	1,287
Cherokee	2,194	6,766	1,926	6,413
Cheyenne	224	1,183	201	1,166
Clark	143	904	128	852
Clay	894	3,177	838	3,056
Cloud	920	3,242	743	3,151
Coffey	964	3,489	927	3,323
Comanche	126	762	127	701
Cowley	4,273	9,656	3,791	9,102
Crawford	6,179	10,045	5,775	9,764
Decatur	218	1,260	197	1,177
Dickinson	2,060	7,126	1,939	6,838
Doniphan	686	2,976	621	2,883
Douglas	40,785	17,286	36,859	16,580
Edwards	271	1,141	210	1,027
Elk	195	1,140	187	1,110
Ellis	3,737	9,758	3,411	9,519
Ellsworth	648	2,148	625	2,014
Finney	4,325	7,236	3,257	6,875
Ford	2,947	5,803	2,354	5,450
Franklin	3,690	8,479	3,603	8,573
Geary	3,983	5,323	3,529	5,099
Gove	166	1,291	147	1,211
Graham	228	1,080	192	979
Grant	518	1,936	384	1,752
Gray	341	1,911	318	1,799
Greeley	78	549	75	509
Greenwood	569	2,444	537	2,287
Hamilton	141	698	127	657
Harper	461	2,168	431	2,017
Harvey	6,747	10,182	6,058	9,366
Haskell	268	1,122	220	1,021
Hodgeman	154	875	131	801
Jackson	1,881	4,517	1,770	4,503
Jefferson	3,194	6,334	2,967	6,538
Jewell	212	1,387	107	926
Johnson	184,259	155,631	175,998	148,756
Kearny	267	1,164	183	1,059
Kingman	752	3,130	746	3,065
Kiowa	156	980	151	930
Labette	2,655	5,735	2,343	5,318
Lane	115	762	107	687
Leavenworth	13,886	21,610	13,565	21,732
Lincoln	266	1,283	247	1,222
Linn	896	4,048	842	3,982
Logan	186	1,249	183	1,183
Lyon	6,055	7,550	5,322	7,215
Marion	1,516	4,465	1,380	4,219
Marshall	1,259	3,729	1,172	3,562
McPherson	4,134	9,964	3,524	9,137
Meade	263	1,523	239	1,390
Miami	5,247	12,308	5,406	12,671
Mitchell	558	2,504	515	2,560
Montgomery	3,228	9,931	2,744	8,637
Morris	729	2,124	712	1,982
Morton	150	1,034	130	879
Nemaha	927	4,664	865	4,555
Neosho	1,796	4,970	1,658	4,842
Ness	149	1,339	128	1,172
Norton	364	2,007	338	1,824
Osage	2,136	5,705	1,909	5,597
Osborne	281	1,629	253	1,442
Ottawa	506	2,610	468	2,417
Pawnee	643	2,045	611	1,970
Phillips	318	2,418	321	2,215
Pottawatomie	3,313	9,452	3,324	9,546
Pratt	933	3,108	941	3,043
Rawlins	214	1,261	173	1,186
Reno	8,886	18,443	8,327	17,384
Republic	424	2,182	391	1,966
Rice	965	3,262	794	3,017
Riley	12,765	11,610	11,595	11,304
Rooks	339	2,325	346	2,126
Rush	295	1,350	263	1,311
Russell	600	2,790	599	2,585
Saline	8,214	15,722	7,562	14,770
Scott	299	2,014	238	1,780
Sedgwick	95,870	122,416	85,918	115,048
Seward	1,833	3,372	1,278	3,034
Shawnee	43,015	40,443	38,995	39,026
Sheridan	147	1,282	122	1,207
Sherman	396	2,269	365	2,112
Smith	336	1,763	291	1,637
Stafford	357	1,645	320	1,516
Stanton	148	614	111	528
Stevens	237	1,760	207	1,558
Sumner	2,591	8,105	2,483	7,624
Thomas	625	3,130	587	2,925
Trego	242	1,363	211	1,326
Wabaunsee	964	2,845	933	2,745
Wallace	44	770	50	659
Washington	475	2,363	394	2,218
Wichita	149	808	105	727
Wilson	723	3,153	641	2,846
Woodson	294	1,228	278	1,181
Wyandotte	36,788	18,934	29,904	18,342
Totals	**570,323**	**771,406**	**523,110**	**735,428**

Kentucky

County	2020 Biden (D)	2020 Trump (R)	2024 Harris (D)	2024 Trump (R)
Adair	1,392	7,276	1,257	7,643
Allen	1,642	7,587	1,505	7,824
Anderson	3,348	9,661	3,226	9,650
Ballard	825	3,356	697	3,331
Barren	5,127	14,654	4,565	15,019
Bath	1,573	3,986	1,278	4,041
Bell	1,789	8,140	1,419	7,831
Boone	20,901	44,814	20,601	45,650
Bourbon	3,296	6,190	3,088	6,284
Boyd	7,083	14,295	6,291	14,363
Boyle	5,298	8,872	4,990	9,159
Bracken	800	3,398	702	3,399
Breathitt	1,301	4,265	1,002	4,036
Breckinridge	2,350	7,701	2,038	7,882
Bullitt	10,552	30,708	10,280	32,299
Butler	1,079	4,960	965	4,905
Caldwell	1,433	4,906	1,256	4,860
Calloway	5,797	11,352	5,111	11,539
Campbell	19,374	28,482	18,952	28,450
Carlisle	463	2,159	408	2,182
Carroll	1,116	2,954	963	3,014
Carter	2,642	8,775	2,305	8,981
Casey	918	6,179	804	6,216
Christian	8,296	15,080	7,055	14,332
Clark	6,004	11,811	5,639	11,950
Clay	831	6,677	692	6,729
Clinton	603	4,280	549	4,276
Crittenden	731	3,451	608	3,349
Cumberland	508	2,769	483	2,922
Daviess	17,286	31,025	15,673	30,705
Edmonson	1,227	4,828	1,118	5,048
Elliott	712	2,246	532	2,335
Estill	1,355	5,100	1,114	5,091
Fayette	90,600	58,860	80,301	56,267
Fleming	1,474	5,534	1,334	5,578
Floyd	3,884	12,250	3,061	12,326
Franklin	12,652	12,900	11,995	13,246
Fulton	794	1,606	636	1,491
Gallatin	822	2,955	761	3,109
Garrard	1,830	6,754	1,719	7,086
Grant	2,205	8,725	1,944	9,372
Graves	3,560	13,206	3,105	13,378

County	2020 Biden (D)	2020 Trump (R)	2024 Harris (D)	2024 Trump (R)
Grayson	2,400	9,453	2,235	9,710
Green	920	4,838	782	5,033
Greenup	4,873	13,064	4,181	12,961
Hancock	1,351	3,145	1,173	3,375
Hardin	18,101	29,832	16,572	30,672
Harlan	1,494	9,367	1,199	9,109
Harrison	2,400	6,334	2,265	6,639
Hart	1,908	6,345	1,642	6,691
Henderson	7,639	12,730	6,837	12,592
Henry	2,142	5,843	1,857	6,093
Hickman	458	1,714	394	1,656
Hopkins	5,439	15,757	4,880	15,174
Jackson	605	5,453	506	5,358
Jefferson	228,358	150,646	203,036	144,537
Jessamine	8,567	17,096	8,303	17,854
Johnson	1,608	8,450	1,350	8,150
Kenton	32,271	48,129	30,580	47,749
Knott	1,412	4,780	1,181	4,732
Knox	2,114	11,012	1,821	11,178
LaRue	1,504	5,685	1,389	5,773
Laurel	4,475	23,237	4,037	23,516
Lawrence	1,238	5,633	1,044	5,464
Lee	481	2,273	406	2,227
Leslie	446	4,321	382	3,908
Letcher	1,799	7,226	1,457	6,848
Lewis	823	4,986	666	4,997
Lincoln	2,254	8,489	2,080	8,833
Livingston	939	4,010	886	4,021
Logan	3,094	9,067	2,734	9,620
Lyon	1,092	3,100	950	3,187
Madison	15,581	27,356	15,180	29,130
Magoffin	1,214	4,174	909	4,288
Marion	2,722	6,113	2,513	6,473
Marshall	4,071	13,297	3,700	13,677
Martin	403	3,496	287	3,343
Mason	2,362	5,477	2,170	5,621
McCracken	11,195	21,820	10,191	21,349
McCreary	725	5,664	641	5,531
McLean	1,074	3,633	989	3,578
Meade	3,632	10,185	3,279	10,630
Menifee	750	2,311	664	2,563
Mercer	3,033	8,506	2,838	8,826
Metcalfe	975	3,959	884	4,197
Monroe	657	4,628	576	4,679
Montgomery	3,630	8,993	3,329	9,302
Morgan	1,175	4,301	939	4,353
Muhlenberg	3,545	10,497	3,048	10,491
Nelson	7,188	15,703	6,515	16,052
Nicholas	955	2,408	824	2,451
Ohio	2,404	8,582	2,094	8,679
Oldham	14,505	22,654	14,402	23,025
Owen	1,098	4,292	988	4,434
Owsley	216	1,671	203	1,625
Pendleton	1,322	5,515	1,210	5,593
Perry	2,356	8,129	1,966	7,913
Pike	4,866	20,284	4,025	19,684
Powell	1,367	4,041	1,174	4,092
Pulaski	5,666	25,442	5,351	26,051
Robertson	253	884	215	915
Rockcastle	1,134	6,577	986	6,635
Rowan	3,880	5,994	3,484	6,224
Russell	1,331	7,519	1,200	7,622
Scott	10,567	17,767	10,501	18,747
Shelby	8,077	15,055	7,822	16,356
Simpson	2,681	5,888	2,403	6,253
Spencer	2,530	8,737	2,415	8,927
Taylor	2,963	9,376	2,576	9,523
Todd	1,205	4,062	1,051	4,009
Trigg	1,791	5,487	1,667	5,436
Trimble	1,012	3,227	923	3,283
Union	1,529	4,965	1,225	4,758
Warren	22,479	31,791	21,065	34,862
Washington	1,644	4,482	1,533	4,720
Wayne	1,700	7,430	1,444	7,203
Webster	1,412	4,506	1,153	4,339
Whitley	2,552	12,567	2,236	12,687
Wolfe	839	2,097	689	2,163
Woodford	6,530	8,362	6,282	8,419
Totals	**772,474**	**1,326,646**	**700,606**	**1,335,516**

Louisiana

Parish	2020 Biden (D)	2020 Trump (R)	2024 Harris (D)	2024 Trump (R)
Acadia	5,443	22,596	4,695	21,783
Allen	2,108	7,574	1,661	7,003
Ascension	20,399	40,687	20,105	41,310
Assumption	3,833	7,271	3,273	6,963
Avoyelles	4,979	12,028	4,460	11,378
Beauregard	2,542	13,575	2,192	13,504
Bienville	3,067	3,891	2,531	3,659
Bossier	15,662	38,074	14,464	37,092
Caddo	55,110	48,021	48,835	44,439
Calcasieu	25,982	55,066	23,911	56,046
Caldwell	745	3,976	580	3,724
Cameron	324	3,671	219	3,119
Catahoula	1,269	3,541	1,060	3,258
Claiborne	2,731	3,770	2,239	3,520
Concordia	3,177	5,550	2,698	4,974
DeSoto	5,457	9,112	4,426	9,356
East Baton Rouge	115,577	88,420	103,783	82,707
East Carroll	1,900	1,080	1,338	931
East Feliciana	4,280	6,064	3,809	6,020
Evangeline	4,158	11,053	3,526	10,483
Franklin	2,658	6,970	2,196	6,524
Grant	1,157	8,117	996	7,925
Iberia	11,027	21,251	9,503	19,511
Iberville	8,514	7,893	7,503	7,616
Jackson	2,143	5,394	1,852	5,291
Jefferson	84,477	105,949	75,675	98,743
Jefferson Davis	3,208	11,423	2,699	11,477
Lafayette	39,685	72,519	37,170	71,999
Lafourche	8,672	36,024	7,860	34,460
LaSalle	638	6,378	546	6,023
Lincoln	7,559	11,311	6,627	11,248
Livingston	9,249	54,877	9,963	55,098
Madison	2,654	1,930	2,094	1,846
Morehouse	4,946	6,510	4,008	5,961
Natchitoches	6,896	9,358	5,740	9,099
Orleans	147,854	26,664	130,578	24,089
Ouachita	25,913	42,255	22,845	40,808
Plaquemines	3,414	7,412	3,023	6,803
Pointe Coupee	4,683	7,503	4,132	7,319
Rapides	19,475	38,347	16,537	36,171
Red River	1,644	2,413	1,321	2,337
Richland	3,225	6,607	2,732	6,354
Sabine	1,731	8,776	1,486	8,611
St. Bernard	6,151	11,179	5,967	11,033
St. Charles	9,800	18,233	8,812	17,443
St. Helena	3,346	2,714	2,848	2,804
St. James	6,510	5,954	5,792	5,902
St. John the Baptist	13,582	7,538	12,043	6,557
St. Landry	17,372	23,171	14,831	21,811
St. Martin	8,439	18,203	7,284	17,466
St. Mary	8,055	14,811	7,010	13,669
St. Tammany	37,746	99,666	37,776	98,375
Tangipahoa	18,887	37,806	16,878	37,482
Tensas	1,329	1,197	1,002	1,093
Terrebonne	11,198	34,339	9,701	31,115
Union	2,654	8,407	2,206	8,176
Vermilion	5,009	21,930	4,637	21,510
Vernon	2,898	14,107	2,513	13,474
Washington	5,970	13,307	5,283	12,809
Webster	6,172	11,830	5,051	10,964
West Baton Rouge	6,200	7,684	6,007	7,625
West Carroll	710	4,317	578	3,986
West Feliciana	2,298	3,863	2,004	3,923
Winn	1,543	4,619	1,291	4,434
Totals	**856,034**	**1,255,776**	**766,405**	**1,208,233**

Maine

City	2020 Biden (D)	2020 Trump (R)	2024 Harris (D)	2024 Trump (R)
Auburn	6,482	5,409	6,449	5,624
Augusta	5,248	4,155	5,386	4,398
Bangor	9,452	6,065	9,332	6,212
Biddeford	7,019	3,703	7,100	4,024
Brunswick	9,708	3,729	10,265	3,736
Gorham	6,460	4,275	6,712	4,420

City	2020 Biden (D)	2020 Trump (R)	2024 Harris (D)	2024 Trump (R)
Lewiston	9,578	7,206	8,764	7,403
Portland	33,784	6,483	31,610	6,107
Saco	7,794	4,497	8,000	5,456
Sanford	5,392	5,182	7,185	6,770
Scarborough	9,487	5,217	9,961	5,117
South Portland	12,075	3,781	11,764	3,621
Westbrook	7,309	3,591	6,941	3,481
Windham	5,780	5,276	5,847	5,399
York	6,117	3,352	6,055	3,337
Other	288,338	287,581	203,997	209,222
Total	**435,072**	**360,737**	**322,848**	**269,391**

Maryland

County	2020 Biden (D)	2020 Trump (R)	2024 Harris (D)	2024 Trump (R)
Allegany	9,158	20,886	7,296	20,295
Anne Arundel	172,823	127,821	145,562	117,781
Baltimore	258,409	146,202	204,027	134,213
Calvert	22,587	25,346	19,093	26,725
Caroline	5,095	10,283	4,026	10,320
Carroll	36,456	60,218	27,241	56,274
Cecil	16,809	29,439	11,541	29,372
Charles	62,171	25,579	50,680	23,166
Dorchester	6,857	8,764	4,822	8,234
Frederick	77,675	63,682	64,035	62,076
Garrett	3,281	12,002	2,469	10,948
Harford	63,095	80,930	49,603	75,708
Howard	129,433	48,390	98,468	43,740
Kent	5,329	5,195	4,145	5,095
Montgomery	419,569	101,222	292,871	93,448
Prince George's	379,208	37,090	267,903	36,175
Queen Anne's	10,709	18,741	8,043	18,146
St. Mary's	23,138	30,826	18,928	30,683
Somerset	4,241	5,739	2,733	5,121
Talbot	11,062	10,946	9,364	10,356
Washington	26,044	40,224	24,371	41,884
Wicomico	22,054	22,944	16,884	21,556
Worcester	12,560	18,571	9,429	17,406
City				
Baltimore	207,260	25,374	141,719	21,671
Totals	**1,985,023**	**976,414**	**1,485,253**	**920,393**

Massachusetts

City	2020 Biden (D)	2020 Trump (R)	2024 Harris (D)	2024 Trump (R)
Arlington	23,024	4,313	21,605	4,098
Barnstable	15,685	10,824	15,025	11,877
Boston	225,368	42,707	187,419	49,654
Brockton	28,087	8,402	23,587	9,261
Brookline	26,046	3,322	23,374	3,442
Cambridge	45,426	3,248	40,371	3,948
Chicopee	14,452	10,622	12,570	11,223
Fall River	17,379	13,409	13,981	14,843
Framingham	23,613	7,705	20,589	8,227
Haverhill	17,880	12,071	16,530	13,356
Lowell	24,492	12,054	20,071	12,313
Lynn	24,123	10,191	18,370	11,613
Medford	22,717	7,412	20,521	7,691
New Bedford	20,805	12,781	18,128	15,440
Newton	39,428	8,165	36,050	8,577
Peabody	16,826	12,688	14,221	13,459
Plymouth	20,780	14,936	21,121	17,559
Quincy	29,956	14,224	24,691	14,934
Somerville	35,392	4,150	32,047	4,435
Springfield	38,849	13,896	33,014	16,187
Taunton	14,704	11,016	13,445	12,753
Waltham	19,847	7,624	17,689	7,742
Weymouth	19,254	12,293	17,100	13,168
Worcester	48,030	21,018	40,476	22,459
Other	1,504,175	869,706	1,208,721	836,299
Total	**2,382,202**	**1,167,202**	**1,923,849**	**1,116,547**

Michigan

County	2020 Biden (D)	2020 Trump (R)	2024 Harris (D)	2024 Trump (R)
Alcona	2,142	4,848	2,140	5,255
Alger	2,053	3,014	2,075	3,116
Allegan	24,449	41,392	23,648	43,072
Alpena	6,000	10,686	6,036	10,965
Antrim	5,960	9,748	6,232	10,083
Arenac	2,774	5,928	2,661	6,379
Baraga	1,478	2,512	1,488	2,778
Barry	11,797	23,471	12,391	25,649
Bay	26,151	33,125	25,725	34,736
Benzie	5,480	6,601	5,767	6,890
Berrien	37,438	43,519	38,288	44,965
Branch	6,159	14,064	5,910	14,847
Calhoun	28,877	36,221	26,078	36,982
Cass	9,130	16,699	8,863	18,251
Charlevoix	6,939	9,841	7,194	10,183
Cheboygan	5,437	10,186	5,539	10,650
Chippewa	6,648	10,681	6,796	11,248
Clare	5,199	10,861	4,880	11,318
Clinton	21,968	25,098	22,439	26,748
Crawford	2,672	5,087	2,751	5,613
Delta	7,606	13,207	6,994	13,433
Dickinson	4,744	9,617	4,761	10,324
Eaton	31,299	31,798	31,038	33,097
Emmet	9,662	12,135	9,995	12,461
Genesee	119,390	98,714	114,632	105,284
Gladwin	4,524	9,893	4,501	10,809
Gogebic	3,570	4,600	3,106	4,274
Grand Traverse	28,683	30,502	30,327	31,409
Gratiot	6,693	12,102	6,679	12,892
Hillsdale	5,883	17,037	5,873	18,627
Houghton	7,750	10,378	7,868	11,178
Huron	5,490	12,731	5,521	13,225
Ingham	94,212	47,639	94,464	50,552
Ionia	10,901	20,657	11,338	22,175
Iosco	5,373	9,759	5,342	10,153
Iron	2,493	4,216	2,441	4,501
Isabella	14,072	14,815	14,003	16,315
Jackson	31,995	47,372	32,327	50,178
Kalamazoo	83,686	56,823	79,482	55,734
Kalkaska	3,002	7,436	3,430	8,149
Kent	187,915	165,741	184,398	167,096
Keweenaw	672	862	689	896
Lake	2,288	3,946	2,298	4,523
Lapeer	16,367	35,482	15,921	36,982
Leelanau	8,795	7,916	8,407	6,392
Lenawee	20,918	31,541	20,782	33,457
Livingston	48,220	76,982	49,484	81,204
Luce	842	2,109	644	1,823
Mackinac	2,632	4,304	2,673	4,476
Macomb	223,952	263,863	204,869	272,646
Manistee	6,107	8,321	6,541	8,627
Marquette	20,465	16,286	20,564	16,849
Mason	6,802	10,207	5,426	7,846
Mecosta	7,375	13,267	7,689	14,444
Menominee	4,316	8,117	4,252	8,645
Midland	20,493	27,675	20,916	28,567
Missaukee	1,967	6,648	1,945	7,066
Monroe	32,975	52,710	32,613	57,402
Montcalm	9,703	21,815	10,362	23,944
Montmorency	1,628	4,171	1,700	4,599
Muskegon	45,643	45,133	45,172	46,358
Newaygo	7,873	18,857	8,129	20,627
Oakland	434,148	325,971	419,121	337,592
Oceana	4,944	8,892	4,530	8,660
Ogemaw	3,475	8,253	2,608	5,983
Ontonagon	1,391	2,358	1,313	2,479
Osceola	3,214	8,928	3,326	9,639
Oscoda	1,342	3,466	1,414	3,716
Otsego	4,743	9,779	4,740	10,371
Ottawa	64,705	100,913	71,573	108,231
Presque Isle	2,911	5,342	3,033	5,569
Roscommon	5,166	9,670	5,290	10,581
Saginaw	51,088	50,785	49,498	52,907
St. Clair	31,363	59,185	30,528	63,312
St. Joseph	9,262	18,127	9,451	19,402
Sanilac	5,966	16,194	5,954	17,080
Schoolcraft	1,589	3,090	1,632	3,195
Shiawassee	15,347	23,149	15,331	24,716
Tuscola	8,712	20,297	8,557	21,764
Van Buren	16,803	21,591	17,172	23,406
Washtenaw	157,136	56,241	156,964	58,798

County	2020 Biden (D)	2020 Trump (R)	2024 Harris (D)	2024 Trump (R)
Wayne	597,170	264,553	500,371	267,492
Wexford	5,838	12,102	6,223	12,968
Totals	**2,804,040**	**2,649,852**	**2,665,126**	**2,756,828**

Minnesota

County	2020 Biden (D)	2020 Trump (R)	2024 Harris (D)	2024 Trump (R)
Aitkin	3,607	6,258	3,524	6,741
Anoka	100,893	104,902	97,666	106,974
Becker	6,589	12,438	6,436	12,967
Beltrami	11,426	12,188	11,493	12,897
Benton	7,280	14,382	7,084	15,260
Big Stone	1,053	1,863	964	1,796
Blue Earth	18,330	16,731	17,558	18,002
Brown	4,753	9,552	4,578	9,692
Carlton	10,098	9,791	9,905	10,435
Carver	30,774	34,009	31,869	35,587
Cass	6,342	11,620	6,300	12,759
Chippewa	2,226	4,250	2,026	4,175
Chisago	11,806	21,916	11,894	23,047
Clay	16,357	15,043	16,122	15,963
Clearwater	1,260	3,372	1,168	3,575
Cook	2,496	1,203	2,416	1,142
Cottonwood	1,834	4,165	1,705	4,157
Crow Wing	13,726	25,676	14,173	27,423
Dakota	146,155	109,638	143,267	109,995
Dodge	4,079	7,783	4,108	8,095
Douglas	7,868	15,799	7,938	16,726
Faribault	2,531	5,191	2,352	5,247
Fillmore	4,551	7,301	4,491	7,638
Freeborn	6,889	9,578	6,449	10,001
Goodhue	11,806	16,052	11,731	16,461
Grant	1,300	2,269	1,187	2,266
Hennepin	532,623	205,973	502,710	197,241
Houston	4,853	6,334	4,667	6,547
Hubbard	4,462	8,202	4,536	8,809
Isanti	7,138	16,491	7,384	18,027
Itasca	10,786	15,239	10,467	15,863
Jackson	1,745	3,948	1,581	3,949
Kanabec	2,774	6,278	2,718	6,819
Kandiyohi	8,440	14,437	7,816	15,015
Kittson	1,006	1,546	911	1,535
Koochiching	2,659	4,131	2,464	4,202
Lac Qui Parle	1,446	2,528	1,314	2,600
Lake	3,647	3,393	3,534	3,265
Lake of the Woods	671	1,704	604	1,710
Le Sueur	5,672	10,775	5,635	11,503
Lincoln	937	2,121	972	2,190
Lyon	4,634	7,979	4,284	8,400
Mahnomen	1,112	1,142	975	1,165
Marshall	1,295	3,721	1,177	3,774
Martin	3,305	7,480	3,171	7,443
McLeod	6,413	13,986	6,374	14,395
Meeker	3,867	9,359	3,802	9,644
Mille Lacs	4,404	9,952	4,374	10,570
Morrison	4,367	14,821	4,306	15,666
Mower	8,899	10,025	10,979	12,202
Murray	1,449	3,363	1,329	3,346
Nicollet	9,622	9,018	9,443	9,540
Nobles	2,933	5,600	2,599	5,541
Norman	1,404	1,953	1,232	1,963
Olmsted	49,491	39,692	49,123	39,467
Otter Tail	11,958	23,800	11,753	24,276
Pennington	2,568	4,532	2,439	4,746
Pine	5,419	10,256	5,333	11,264
Pipestone	1,306	3,553	1,215	3,537
Polk	5,439	9,865	4,967	10,162
Pope	2,477	4,417	2,398	4,676
Ramsey	211,620	77,376	195,165	75,282
Red Lake	691	1,454	642	1,425
Redwood	2,355	5,771	2,300	5,896
Renville	2,496	5,467	2,280	5,610
Rice	17,402	17,464	17,354	18,265
Rock	1,556	3,583	1,585	3,690
Roseau	2,188	6,065	2,093	6,279
St. Louis	67,704	49,017	66,340	50,074
Scott	40,040	45,872	40,242	47,822
Sherburne	18,065	36,222	14,644	33,903
Sibley	2,417	5,864	2,351	6,015
Stearns	31,879	50,959	30,830	53,935
Steele	7,917	12,656	7,650	12,742
Stevens	1,922	3,044	1,826	3,203
Swift	1,784	3,316	1,618	3,340
Todd	3,286	9,753	3,072	10,392
Traverse	661	1,172	596	1,165
Wabasha	4,696	8,153	4,721	8,523
Wadena	2,023	5,520	1,898	6,028
Waseca	3,496	6,624	3,402	6,770
Washington	89,165	73,764	90,195	75,191
Watonwan	1,987	3,103	1,723	3,087
Wilkin	1,026	2,328	986	2,290
Winona	13,333	13,227	12,929	14,292
Wright	28,430	51,973	29,055	54,067
Yellow Medicine	1,688	3,734	1,548	3,738
Totals	**1,717,077**	**1,484,065**	**1,652,867**	**1,509,522**

Mississippi

County	2020 Biden (D)	2020 Trump (R)	2024 Harris (D)	2024 Trump (R)
Adams	7,917	5,696	5,153	3,907
Alcorn	2,782	12,818	1,927	10,808
Amite	2,620	4,503	2,230	4,443
Attala	3,542	5,178	2,311	3,857
Benton	1,679	2,570	1,314	2,526
Bolivar	8,904	4,671	5,890	3,831
Calhoun	1,902	4,625	1,530	4,413
Carroll	1,729	3,924	1,157	3,056
Chickasaw	3,810	4,175	3,054	4,017
Choctaw	1,185	3,001	950	2,847
Claiborne	3,772	603	1,987	424
Clarke	2,838	5,417	2,042	4,367
Clay	5,844	4,181	4,088	3,133
Coahoma	6,020	2,375	4,088	1,539
Copiah	6,470	6,250	4,663	5,170
Covington	3,416	5,854	2,906	5,790
DeSoto	28,265	46,462	23,746	34,685
Forrest	13,755	17,290	10,973	16,106
Franklin	1,480	2,923	1,205	2,780
George	1,218	9,713	1,116	9,712
Greene	966	4,794	821	4,730
Grenada	4,734	6,081	2,878	4,576
Hancock	4,504	16,132	4,247	16,628
Harrison	27,728	46,822	20,433	39,863
Hinds	73,550	25,141	53,953	18,583
Holmes	6,588	1,369	4,638	1,096
Humphreys	3,016	1,118	2,426	982
Issaquena	355	308	278	287
Itawamba	1,249	9,438	1,027	9,522
Jackson	17,375	36,295	13,005	32,360
Jasper	4,341	4,302	3,708	4,097
Jefferson	3,327	531	2,726	539
Jefferson Davis	3,599	2,534	3,003	2,276
Jones	8,517	21,226	6,205	17,889
Kemper	2,887	1,787	1,993	1,489
Lafayette	10,070	12,949	8,768	13,792
Lamar	7,340	20,704	6,958	20,574
Lauderdale	12,960	17,967	8,968	14,418
Lawrence	2,260	4,285	1,881	4,055
Leake	3,897	5,228	3,138	5,095
Lee	12,189	24,207	9,719	22,920
Leflore	7,648	3,129	5,267	2,371
Lincoln	5,040	11,596	4,169	11,250
Lowndes	13,087	13,800	9,453	12,118
Madison	24,440	31,091	18,409	25,031
Marion	3,787	8,273	3,176	7,759
Marshall	8,057	7,566	6,837	7,924
Monroe	5,874	11,177	4,262	9,633
Montgomery	2,121	2,917	1,753	2,675
Neshoba	3,260	8,320	2,595	8,086
Newton	3,075	6,997	2,296	5,824
Noxubee	4,040	1,240	2,616	970

County	2020 Biden (D)	2020 Trump (R)	2024 Harris (D)	2024 Trump (R)
Oktibbeha	10,299	9,004	7,448	7,235
Panola	7,403	8,060	5,025	6,778
Pearl River	4,148	19,595	2,902	16,388
Perry	1,362	4,500	1,059	4,381
Pike	8,646	8,479	5,983	6,426
Pontotoc	2,614	11,550	2,166	11,596
Prentiss	2,153	8,370	1,698	8,487
Quitman	2,150	1,026	1,721	898
Rankin	18,847	50,895	14,425	38,692
Scott	4,330	6,285	3,112	5,449
Sharkey	1,465	688	1,195	549
Simpson	4,037	7,635	3,059	6,407
Smith	1,791	6,458	1,458	6,071
Stone	1,802	5,964	1,286	5,314
Sunflower	6,781	2,799	5,170	2,470
Tallahatchie	3,105	2,488	2,622	2,331
Tate	4,183	8,707	3,082	7,768
Tippah	1,937	8,054	1,500	7,812
Tishomingo	1,059	7,933	917	8,006
Tunica	2,580	926	1,785	782
Union	2,160	10,373	1,498	9,148
Walthall	2,835	4,220	1,945	3,209
Warren	10,442	10,365	8,293	9,145
Washington	12,503	5,300	6,730	3,584
Wayne	3,624	6,307	3,008	5,971
Webster	1,043	4,291	852	4,097
Wilkinson	2,749	1,324	1,817	1,075
Winston	4,040	5,112	3,362	4,892
Yalobusha	2,785	3,671	2,276	3,498
Yazoo	5,496	4,832	3,792	4,193
Totals	**539,398**	**756,764**	**404,063**	**655,094**

Missouri

County	2020 Biden (D)	2020 Trump (R)	2024 Harris (D)	2024 Trump (R)
Adair	3,710	6,413	3,295	6,728
Andrew	2,351	7,255	2,312	7,401
Atchison	564	2,199	529	2,152
Audrain	2,704	7,732	2,684	7,693
Barry	2,948	12,425	2,871	13,130
Barton	844	5,168	820	5,159
Bates	1,672	6,597	1,563	6,695
Benton	2,180	8,109	2,165	8,512
Bollinger	750	5,167	756	5,365
Boone	50,064	38,646	48,165	39,554
Buchanan	13,445	22,450	12,584	22,585
Butler	3,301	14,602	3,160	14,548
Caldwell	897	3,725	888	3,769
Callaway	5,870	14,815	5,918	15,191
Camden	5,652	18,850	5,713	19,568
Cape Girardeau	10,760	28,907	10,538	29,289
Carroll	786	3,706	788	3,702
Carter	418	2,451	364	2,480
Cass	19,052	37,197	19,709	38,691
Cedar	1,145	5,788	1,060	6,058
Chariton	916	3,111	875	3,178
Christian	11,131	34,920	9,540	30,947
Clark	678	2,672	628	2,679
Clay	59,400	64,605	60,186	67,542
Clinton	2,896	7,799	2,848	8,211
Cole	12,694	26,086	12,842	26,649
Cooper	2,249	6,272	2,343	6,388
Crawford	2,113	8,725	2,007	8,742
Dade	656	3,414	671	3,480
Dallas	1,380	6,619	1,454	6,896
Daviess	746	3,102	698	3,149
DeKalb	930	3,828	870	3,883
Dent	1,056	5,987	1,025	6,010
Douglas	1,016	5,898	995	6,242
Dunklin	2,200	8,135	1,884	8,087
Franklin	14,569	38,058	14,666	40,098
Gasconade	1,601	6,222	1,555	6,369
Gentry	613	2,581	616	2,651
Greene	55,068	83,630	55,404	85,404
Grundy	799	3,585	783	3,569
Harrison	597	3,198	534	3,292
Henry	2,619	8,027	2,533	8,285
Hickory	1,056	3,966	977	4,095
Holt	338	1,976	356	1,979
Howard	1,413	3,553	1,338	3,532
Howell	3,218	15,181	3,064	15,716
Iron	945	3,596	824	3,640
Jackson	92,182	100,142	185,341	124,814
Jasper	13,549	37,728	13,856	38,935
Jefferson	37,523	77,046	36,770	80,537
Johnson	6,974	15,489	6,948	16,275
Knox	340	1,486	310	1,473
Laclede	2,780	13,762	2,752	14,147
Lafayette	4,472	12,273	4,294	12,697
Lawrence	3,214	14,426	3,245	14,987
Lewis	984	3,553	866	3,537
Lincoln	6,607	21,848	6,893	24,841
Linn	1,275	4,363	1,182	4,431
Livingston	1,410	5,267	1,422	5,391
Macon	1,662	6,076	1,479	6,286
Madison	1,019	4,584	986	4,721
Maries	814	3,892	755	3,986
Marion	3,202	9,915	3,025	9,985
McDonald	1,439	7,465	1,422	7,826
Mercer	222	1,541	235	1,545
Miller	2,038	10,176	2,066	10,822
Mississippi	1,178	3,537	1,015	3,404
Moniteau	1,308	5,744	1,309	5,870
Monroe	936	3,477	856	3,472
Montgomery	1,208	4,465	1,165	4,759
Morgan	1,924	7,442	1,914	7,725
New Madrid	1,748	5,447	1,561	5,203
Newton	5,818	22,120	5,846	22,889
Nodaway	2,853	6,865	2,663	6,905
Oregon	823	3,847	696	3,882
Osage	1,037	6,425	1,002	6,603
Ozark	752	4,064	698	4,044
Pemiscot	1,560	4,120	1,302	3,870
Perry	1,664	7,657	1,752	7,946
Pettis	4,783	13,854	4,699	13,900
Phelps	5,637	13,480	5,315	13,554
Pike	1,717	5,863	1,614	6,134
Platte	27,179	28,917	27,440	29,306
Polk	2,885	11,850	2,943	12,678
Pulaski	3,740	10,329	3,765	11,579
Putnam	361	1,984	346	2,020
Ralls	1,205	4,396	1,152	4,572
Randolph	2,485	8,018	2,571	8,317
Ray	3,109	8,345	2,927	8,602
Reynolds	529	2,733	471	2,556
Ripley	833	4,839	763	5,000
St. Charles	89,530	128,389	91,980	130,236
St. Clair	988	3,932	959	3,982
St. Francois	7,044	20,511	6,809	21,513
St. Louis Co.	328,151	199,493	302,695	186,266
Ste. Genevieve	2,713	6,630	2,626	7,025
Saline	2,904	6,451	2,718	6,489
Schuyler	373	1,606	334	1,588
Scotland	388	1,560	358	1,537
Scott	3,753	13,769	3,524	13,783
Shannon	706	3,165	624	3,363
Shelby	592	2,700	549	2,690
Stoddard	1,819	11,484	1,724	11,765
Stone	3,506	14,800	3,612	15,330
Sullivan	478	1,974	407	2,039
Taney	5,339	20,508	5,312	21,167
Texas	1,716	9,478	1,589	9,855
Vernon	1,903	7,155	1,773	7,108
Warren	4,769	13,222	4,964	14,912
Washington	1,804	8,047	1,746	8,418
Wayne	845	4,987	781	5,024
Webster	3,573	14,880	3,647	15,951
Worth	215	877	190	904
Wright	1,168	7,453	1,056	7,843
City				
Kansas City	107,660	26,393	94,854	26,031
St. Louis	110,089	21,474	93,799	19,223
Totals	**1,253,014**	**1,718,736**	**1,190,806**	**1,739,020**

Montana

County	2020 Biden (D)	2020 Trump (R)	2024 Harris (D)	2024 Trump (R)
Beaverhead	1,608	3,923	1,515	3,973
Big Horn	2,491	2,207	2,033	2,124
Blaine	1,589	1,469	919	1,082
Broadwater	835	3,173	877	3,724
Carbon	2,421	4,468	1,844	3,565
Carter	74	775	75	760
Cascade	15,456	23,315	12,448	18,327
Chouteau	991	1,891	940	1,885
Custer	1,514	4,205	1,376	4,172
Daniels	195	799	154	776
Dawson	962	3,758	888	3,607
Deer Lodge	2,562	2,186	2,348	2,298
Fallon	172	1,375	163	1,295
Fergus	1,496	4,869	1,522	4,965
Flathead	20,274	38,321	16,732	31,287
Gallatin	37,044	31,696	20,090	17,854
Garfield	41	764	39	756
Glacier	3,610	1,884	2,888	1,914
Golden Valley	78	414	67	440
Granite	638	1,419	576	1,534
Hill	2,981	3,957	2,793	4,121
Jefferson	2,625	5,345	2,504	5,487
Judith Basin	275	1,040	265	1,047
Lake	6,916	9,322	5,885	8,795
Lewis and Clark	19,743	21,409	17,521	18,844
Liberty	249	821	214	752
Lincoln	2,835	8,672	316	1,036
Madison	1,771	4,191	1,673	4,569
McCone	155	956	129	931
Meagher	258	833	256	888
Mineral	686	1,828	682	2,018
Missoula	43,357	26,347	35,103	22,081
Musselshell	413	2,423	394	2,548
Park	5,280	6,025	5,089	5,914
Petroleum	39	298	37	284
Phillips	416	1,936	384	1,752
Pondera	903	2,031	756	1,959
Powder River	154	970	131	963
Powell	752	2,355	729	2,643
Prairie	126	603	122	546
Ravalli	8,763	19,114	8,382	20,121
Richland	875	4,800	776	4,353
Roosevelt	1,910	1,996	1,631	2,037
Rosebud	1,199	2,486	1,089	2,457
Sanders	1,820	5,660	1,687	6,078
Sheridan	574	1,403	509	1,319
Silver Bow	10,392	7,745	8,427	6,819
Stillwater	1,156	4,462	1,053	4,681
Sweet Grass	549	1,840	524	1,785
Teton	1,007	2,608	927	2,528
Toole	467	1,596	410	1,563
Treasure	78	373	57	367
Valley	1,030	3,135	935	3,019
Wheatland	225	823	204	825
Wibaux	77	516	71	463
Yellowstone	30,679	50,772	26,426	46,003
Totals	**244,786**	**343,602**	**195,585**	**297,934**

Nebraska

County	2020 Biden (D)	2020 Trump (R)	2024 Harris (D)	2024 Trump (R)
Adams	4,213	10,085	4,070	9,982
Antelope	452	3,093	396	3,017
Arthur	21	260	17	264
Banner	43	362	34	348
Blaine	35	280	37	250
Boone	499	2,653	495	2,496
Box Butte	1,051	4,002	1,033	3,781
Boyd	135	1,010	132	938
Brown	191	1,470	199	1,422
Buffalo	6,350	16,640	6,325	16,882
Burt	1,063	2,580	982	2,618
Butler	873	3,542	904	3,623
Cass	4,737	10,121	4,693	10,468
Cedar	725	4,174	702	4,141
Chase	226	1,740	200	1,637
Cherry	373	2,844	349	2,676
Cheyenne	855	3,813	778	3,655
Clay	632	2,848	577	2,669
Colfax	1,025	2,636	842	2,634
Cuming	870	3,507	857	3,499
Custer	786	5,090	783	4,996
Dakota	2,744	3,926	2,074	3,891
Dawes	1,082	2,931	986	2,782
Dawson	2,497	6,524	2,090	6,258
Deuel	141	871	151	843
Dixon	651	2,335	573	2,271
Dodge	5,544	10,984	5,367	10,631
Douglas	150,350	119,159	138,905	114,683
Dundy	105	883	96	828
Fillmore	693	2,359	658	2,292
Franklin	276	1,437	235	1,347
Frontier	189	1,229	185	1,206
Furnas	399	2,163	358	2,023
Gage	3,385	7,445	3,232	7,488
Garden	161	1,016	162	949
Garfield	133	933	115	891
Gosper	215	893	203	904
Grant	20	375	15	351
Greeley	229	1,016	192	1,029
Hall	7,681	16,189	6,891	15,413
Hamilton	1,118	4,309	1,065	4,391
Harlan	282	1,615	279	1,506
Hayes	34	494	19	471
Hitchcock	175	1,264	152	1,264
Holt	686	4,769	676	4,670
Hooker	59	376	55	375
Howard	648	2,786	641	2,868
Jefferson	1,016	2,616	965	2,594
Johnson	647	1,518	625	1,494
Kearney	701	2,822	734	2,820
Keith	763	3,544	721	3,386
Keya Paha	49	476	44	498
Kimball	268	1,563	271	1,410
Knox	905	3,721	785	3,588
Lancaster	82,293	70,092	75,163	70,076
Lincoln	3,692	13,071	3,549	12,518
Logan	38	407	25	408
Loup	75	370	73	354
Madison	3,478	11,940	3,283	11,943
McPherson	17	275	12	267
Merrick	743	3,419	721	3,468
Morrill	386	2,113	366	2,026
Nance	359	1,437	351	1,456
Nemaha	921	2,428	907	2,422
Nuckolls	409	1,857	399	1,832
Otoe	2,490	5,649	2,454	5,628
Pawnee	322	1,071	284	1,085
Perkins	199	1,321	187	1,223
Phelps	752	4,157	756	4,144
Pierce	480	3,462	446	3,420
Platte	3,260	12,186	3,132	12,105
Polk	530	2,291	499	2,286
Red Willow	811	4,525	806	4,419
Richardson	996	3,073	911	2,886
Rock	84	744	85	745
Saline	1,986	3,631	1,845	3,719
Sarpy	41,206	51,979	43,510	55,146
Saunders	3,331	9,108	3,547	9,797
Scotts Bluff	4,196	10,952	3,807	10,886
Seward	2,438	6,490	2,378	6,637
Sheridan	340	2,292	357	2,093
Sherman	343	1,322	328	1,337
Sioux	72	642	76	596
Stanton	532	2,561	492	2,536
Thayer	624	2,308	543	2,254
Thomas	45	377	44	348
Thurston	1,122	1,180	919	1,117
Valley	412	1,901	403	1,863
Washington	3,554	8,583	3,527	8,812
Wayne	1,022	3,055	1,006	3,011
Webster	335	1,511	296	1,448
Wheeler	59	438	57	424
York	1,630	5,337	1,637	5,197
Totals	**374,583**	**556,846**	**353,106**	**551,343**

Nevada

County	2020 Biden (D)	2020 Trump (R)	2024 Harris (D)	2024 Trump (R)
Churchill	3,051	9,372	3,062	9,640
Clark	521,852	430,930	460,385	452,812
Douglas	11,571	21,630	9,854	20,808
Elko	4,557	16,741	4,134	16,155

	2020		2024	
County	Biden (D)	Trump (R)	Harris (D)	Trump (R)
Esmeralda	74	400	69	371
Eureka	105	895	97	860
Humboldt	1,689	5,877	1,547	5,664
Lander	496	2,198	383	1,654
Lincoln	330	2,067	295	2,005
Lyon	8,473	20,914	8,399	22,506
Mineral	829	1,423	709	1,517
Nye	7,288	17,528	420	2,146
Pershing	547	1,731	478	1,718
Storey	902	1,908	865	1,983
Washoe	128,128	116,760	98,668	103,333
White Pine	859	3,403	865	3,272
City				
Carson City	12,735	16,113	10,888	14,536
Totals	**703,486**	**669,890**	**601,118**	**660,980**

New Hampshire

	2020		2024	
City	Biden (D)	Trump (R)	Harris (D)	Trump (R)
Bedford	7,521	7,052	1,541	1,565
Concord	15,341	7,836	14,992	8,540
Derry	8,215	9,412	7,730	9,873
Dover	12,508	6,331	12,656	6,650
Exeter	6,820	3,321	6,783	3,385
Goffstown	4,967	5,040	5,037	5,344
Hampton	6,150	5,212	5,522	4,843
Hudson	6,632	7,744	4,039	4,950
Keene	8,950	3,758	8,541	4,183
Londonderry	7,738	7,905	7,510	8,301
Manchester	28,584	21,833	24,654	20,697
Merrimack	8,725	7,669	8,891	8,492
Nashua	26,316	17,699	19,693	15,312
Portsmouth	10,643	3,829	10,289	4,187
Rochester	8,132	8,367	6,806	7,164
Salem	7,638	9,969	7,453	10,943
Other	248,411	232,396	231,232	235,602
Total	**424,937**	**365,660**	**383,369**	**360,031**

New Jersey

	2020		2024	
County	Biden (D)	Trump (R)	Harris (D)	Trump (R)
Atlantic	73,808	64,438	59,293	64,176
Bergen	285,967	204,417	224,863	210,870
Burlington	154,595	103,345	125,504	90,050
Camden	175,065	86,207	145,686	82,527
Cape May	23,941	33,158	20,687	31,127
Cumberland	32,742	28,952	25,666	27,965
Essex	266,820	75,475	208,985	79,744
Gloucester	86,702	83,340	76,179	81,047
Hudson	181,452	65,698	132,987	73,683
Hunterdon	39,457	43,153	36,009	41,670
Mercer	122,532	51,641	98,445	48,608
Middlesex	226,250	143,467	177,291	151,813
Monmouth	181,291	191,808	148,386	191,478
Morris	153,881	141,134	127,545	138,611
Ocean	119,456	217,740	102,079	219,969
Passaic	129,097	92,009	89,086	95,620
Salem	14,479	18,827	11,813	17,894
Somerset	111,173	71,996	82,362	68,376
Sussex	34,481	51,701	30,104	51,371
Union	170,310	80,038	139,025	84,814
Warren	24,901	34,769	21,459	34,349
Totals	**2,608,400**	**1,883,313**	**2,083,454**	**1,885,762**

New Mexico

	2020		2024	
County	Biden (D)	Trump (R)	Harris (D)	Trump (R)
Bernalillo	193,757	116,135	182,267	117,794
Catron	595	1,698	562	1,745
Chaves	6,381	15,656	5,899	15,851
Cibola	4,745	3,975	4,427	4,301
Colfax	2,611	3,271	2,436	3,252
Curry	4,307	10,444	3,872	10,090
De Baca	231	656	206	649
Doña Ana	47,957	32,802	45,056	37,245
Eddy	5,424	17,454	4,966	18,092
Grant	7,590	6,553	7,247	6,555
Guadalupe	1,234	917	959	945
Harding	179	319	128	297
Hidalgo	823	1,120	705	1,138
Lea	4,061	16,531	3,907	16,972
Lincoln	3,194	6,942	3,004	6,906

	2020		2024	
County	Biden (D)	Trump (R)	Harris (D)	Trump (R)
Los Alamos	7,554	4,278	7,575	4,019
Luna	3,563	4,408	3,153	4,688
McKinley	18,029	7,801	15,655	9,341
Mora	1,745	903	1,432	1,007
Otero	8,485	14,521	8,372	14,982
Quay	1,170	2,634	1,047	2,563
Rio Arriba	10,990	5,408	9,323	6,250
Roosevelt	1,802	4,634	1,803	4,670
San Juan	18,083	32,874	17,386	34,202
San Miguel	7,888	3,421	6,937	3,873
Sandoval	40,588	34,174	38,733	35,459
Santa Fe	62,530	18,329	59,327	20,026
Sierra	2,265	3,542	2,321	3,468
Socorro	3,722	3,255	3,344	3,639
Taos	13,121	3,715	11,876	4,115
Torrance	2,344	4,772	2,129	4,872
Union	383	1,388	378	1,245
Valencia	14,263	17,364	13,543	18,997
Totals	**501,614**	**401,894**	**469,975**	**419,248**

New York

	2020		2024	
County	Biden (D)	Trump (R)	Harris (D)	Trump (R)
Albany	99,474	51,081	87,849	52,532
Allegany	6,048	14,135	5,058	13,102
Bronx[1]	355,374	67,740	244,385	91,542
Broome	47,002	43,791	42,093	42,644
Cattaraugus	11,879	22,155	10,914	21,936
Cayuga	16,359	19,632	15,278	19,959
Chautauqua	23,088	34,853	21,076	33,245
Chemung	16,636	21,922	15,032	21,330
Chenango	8,300	13,496	7,948	13,947
Clinton	18,364	16,514	16,930	17,741
Columbia	20,386	14,464	19,472	14,690
Cortland	10,370	10,789	9,842	11,230
Delaware	9,143	13,387	8,845	13,345
Dutchess	81,443	66,872	75,386	68,658
Erie	267,270	197,552	239,485	199,248
Essex	9,950	8,982	9,222	9,294
Franklin	9,253	9,668	8,555	10,291
Fulton	7,931	15,378	7,453	15,872
Genesee	9,625	18,876	9,098	18,580
Greene	10,346	14,271	9,872	14,127
Hamilton	1,178	2,225	1,157	2,190
Herkimer	9,939	18,871	8,814	19,047
Jefferson	17,307	25,629	15,450	25,215
Kings (Brooklyn)[1]	703,310	202,772	551,633	219,335
Lewis	3,823	8,890	3,105	8,786
Livingston	12,477	18,182	11,894	18,482
Madison	14,805	18,409	13,853	18,326
Monroe	225,746	145,661	205,120	141,763
Montgomery	7,977	12,745	7,049	12,929
Nassau	396,504	326,716	322,131	355,276
New York (Manhattan)[1]	603,040	85,185	482,124	103,128
Niagara	46,029	56,068	41,825	57,156
Oneida	41,973	57,860	37,640	58,783
Onondaga	138,991	91,715	124,841	89,582
Ontario	28,749	28,782	28,576	29,415
Orange	84,955	85,068	74,489	89,458
Orleans	5,587	12,126	5,227	12,432
Oswego	21,145	32,142	19,904	32,672
Otsego	12,975	14,382	10,580	13,799
Putnam	24,955	29,283	22,859	30,654
Queens[1]	569,038	212,665	404,126	248,024
Rensselaer	40,969	36,500	38,525	37,772
Richmond (Staten Island)[1]	90,997	123,320	65,872	124,265
Rockland	75,802	73,186	63,151	80,896
St. Lawrence	19,361	24,608	17,502	25,210
Saratoga	68,471	61,305	62,380	61,001
Schenectady	42,465	30,741	38,064	31,086
Schoharie	5,345	9,903	5,176	9,887
Schuyler	3,903	5,621	3,598	5,583

	2020		2024	
County	Biden (D)	Trump (R)	Harris (D)	Trump (R)
Seneca	6,914	8,329	6,396	8,226
Steuben	15,790	29,474	14,938	29,159
Suffolk	381,021	381,253	323,473	402,924
Sullivan	15,489	18,665	13,696	19,256
Tioga	9,634	14,791	8,909	14,365
Tompkins	33,619	11,096	32,181	10,934
Ulster	57,970	37,590	55,349	38,513
Warren	17,642	17,699	16,585	18,080
Washington	11,565	15,941	10,985	16,897
Wayne	17,456	26,204	16,570	26,761
Westchester	312,437	144,731	93,424	68,854
Wyoming	5,073	13,898	4,679	13,181
Yates	4,219	6,208	4,234	5,966
Totals	**5,244,886**	**3,251,997**	**4,151,877**	**3,338,581**

(1) Borough of New York City.

North Carolina

	2020		2024	
County	Biden (D)	Trump (R)	Harris (D)	Trump (R)
Alamance	38,825	46,056	40,180	47,629
Alexander	4,145	15,888	4,043	16,356
Alleghany	1,486	4,527	1,532	4,891
Anson	5,789	5,321	5,209	5,502
Ashe	4,164	11,451	4,490	11,548
Avery	2,191	7,172	2,201	7,087
Beaufort	9,633	16,437	8,962	17,208
Bertie	5,939	3,817	5,212	3,817
Bladen	7,326	9,676	6,582	10,009
Brunswick	33,310	55,850	40,316	67,301
Buncombe	96,515	62,412	97,669	58,544
Burke	13,118	31,019	13,173	32,006
Cabarrus	52,162	63,237	53,794	63,252
Caldwell	10,245	32,119	10,083	32,872
Camden	1,537	4,312	1,513	4,698
Carteret	12,093	30,028	12,699	32,254
Caswell	4,860	7,089	4,486	7,441
Catawba	25,689	56,588	26,425	59,370
Chatham	26,787	21,186	28,818	22,408
Cherokee	3,583	12,628	3,665	13,825
Chowan	3,247	4,471	2,880	4,581
Clay	1,699	5,112	1,893	5,742
Cleveland	16,955	33,798	16,463	34,451
Columbus	9,446	16,832	8,602	17,555
Craven	21,148	31,032	21,747	33,220
Cumberland	84,469	60,032	77,254	59,116
Currituck	4,195	11,657	4,561	13,138
Dare	9,936	13,938	10,010	14,719
Davidson	22,636	64,658	23,841	67,497
Davie	6,713	18,228	6,931	19,284
Duplin	8,767	13,793	8,012	14,622
Durham	144,688	32,459	142,687	32,507
Edgecombe	16,089	9,206	14,824	9,305
Forsyth	113,033	85,064	112,038	86,353
Franklin	15,879	20,901	18,040	23,827
Gaston	40,959	73,033	43,716	73,422
Gates	2,546	3,367	2,251	3,517
Graham	905	3,710	839	3,857
Granville	14,565	16,647	14,235	17,279
Greene	3,832	4,874	3,402	4,931
Guilford	173,086	107,294	170,034	108,610
Halifax	15,545	10,080	13,951	9,727
Harnett	22,093	35,177	23,103	39,057
Haywood	13,144	22,834	13,854	23,280
Henderson	27,211	40,032	29,094	39,193
Hertford	7,097	3,479	6,158	3,546
Hoke	11,804	9,453	11,766	10,441
Hyde	1,046	1,418	924	1,450
Iredell	33,888	67,010	35,394	71,299
Jackson	9,591	11,356	9,658	11,686
Johnston	41,257	68,353	47,728	74,490
Jones	2,197	3,280	1,990	3,393
Lee	12,143	16,469	12,143	17,403
Lenoir	13,605	14,590	12,573	14,465
Lincoln	13,274	36,341	14,787	40,046
Macon	6,230	14,211	6,635	14,871
Madison	4,901	7,979	5,075	8,247
Martin	5,911	6,532	5,328	6,577
McDowell	5,832	16,883	5,872	17,491
Mecklenburg	378,107	179,211	371,871	185,970
Mitchell	1,867	7,090	1,903	6,800
Montgomery	4,327	8,411	4,008	8,991
Moore	20,779	36,764	21,143	39,271
Nash	25,947	25,827	25,316	26,303
New Hanover	66,138	63,331	67,375	66,967
Northampton	6,069	3,989	5,217	3,896
Onslow	24,266	46,078	25,141	54,074
Orange	63,594	20,176	65,094	20,726
Pamlico	2,713	4,849	2,664	5,206
Pasquotank	9,832	9,770	9,456	10,450
Pender	11,723	21,956	12,190	25,707
Perquimans	2,492	4,903	2,259	5,258
Person	8,465	13,184	8,232	13,460
Pitt	47,252	38,982	44,763	39,963
Polk	4,518	7,689	4,818	8,076
Randolph	15,618	56,894	15,319	58,252
Richmond	8,754	11,830	7,749	11,877
Robeson	19,020	27,806	16,538	29,199
Rockingham	15,992	31,301	15,624	33,363
Rowan	23,114	49,297	23,517	50,511
Rutherford	9,135	24,891	8,828	25,313
Sampson	10,966	17,411	9,688	18,062
Scotland	7,186	7,473	6,674	7,697
Stanly	8,129	25,458	8,809	27,407
Stokes	5,286	20,142	5,355	21,472
Surry	8,721	27,538	8,532	28,377
Swain	2,780	4,161	2,605	4,256
Transylvania	8,444	11,636	8,926	11,422
Tyrrell	758	1,044	677	1,052
Union	48,725	80,382	50,700	85,720
Vance	12,431	8,391	11,239	8,596
Wake	393,336	226,197	397,849	234,317
Warren	6,400	3,752	5,841	3,961
Washington	3,396	2,781	3,118	2,753
Watauga	17,122	14,451	17,002	15,117
Wayne	24,215	30,709	22,354	31,390
Wilkes	7,511	27,592	7,151	28,672
Wilson	20,754	19,581	19,811	19,670
Yadkin	3,763	15,933	3,695	16,331
Yancey	3,688	7,516	3,599	7,420
Totals	**2,684,292**	**2,758,773**	**2,683,995**	**2,875,538**

North Dakota

	2020		2024	
County	Biden (D)	Trump (R)	Harris (D)	Trump (R)
Adams	258	981	215	957
Barnes	1,820	3,568	1,652	3,501
Benson	822	1,094	793	1,160
Billings	72	541	92	541
Bottineau	821	2,575	731	2,613
Bowman	228	1,395	207	1,382
Burke	137	994	130	904
Burleigh	14,348	34,744	14,183	36,552
Cass	40,505	42,793	40,169	47,819
Cavalier	474	1,499	491	1,460
Dickey	608	1,742	557	1,827
Divide	265	904	250	882
Dunn	342	1,951	332	1,870
Eddy	383	854	314	860
Emmons	237	1,738	204	1,695
Foster	373	1,362	335	1,323
Golden Valley	137	871	121	842
Grand Forks	12,880	16,987	12,448	18,086
Grant	207	1,145	203	1,069
Griggs	308	907	301	961
Hettinger	196	1,091	191	1,085
Kidder	221	1,215	237	1,134
LaMoure	527	1,645	452	1,602
Logan	128	930	116	895
McHenry	564	2,364	479	2,218
McIntosh	261	1,153	228	1,130
McKenzie	814	4,482	806	4,616
McLean	1,230	4,198	1,093	4,221

County	2020 Biden (D)	2020 Trump (R)	2024 Harris (D)	2024 Trump (R)
Mercer	704	3,856	713	3,802
Morton	3,872	12,243	3,737	12,828
Mountrail	1,256	2,824	1,124	2,872
Nelson	586	1,141	579	1,138
Oliver	129	918	156	908
Pembina	786	2,460	710	2,336
Pierce	497	1,585	439	1,491
Ramsey	1,639	3,577	1,510	3,591
Ransom	945	1,418	920	1,659
Renville	220	1,065	177	993
Richland	2,510	5,072	2,473	5,573
Rolette	2,482	1,257	2,562	1,425
Sargent	738	1,266	661	1,324
Sheridan	104	688	99	640
Sioux	750	240	651	284
Slope	44	380	33	351
Stark	2,499	12,110	2,464	12,303
Steele	392	652	364	622
Stutsman	2,676	6,994	2,688	7,177
Towner	317	830	288	795
Traill	1,493	2,522	1,353	2,647
Walsh	1,333	3,324	1,170	3,167
Ward	7,293	19,974	7,195	20,601
Wells	442	1,893	405	1,815
Williams	2,169	11,739	2,269	12,486
Totals	**115,042**	**235,751**	**112,070**	**246,033**

Ohio

County	2020 Biden (D)	2020 Trump (R)	2024 Harris (D)	2024 Trump (R)
Adams	2,156	9,870	2,073	10,056
Allen	14,149	33,116	12,527	32,679
Ashland	6,541	19,407	6,457	19,444
Ashtabula	16,497	26,890	15,152	27,167
Athens	14,772	10,862	13,399	10,854
Auglaize	4,651	20,798	4,391	20,714
Belmont	9,138	23,560	7,987	22,449
Brown	4,380	16,480	4,012	16,918
Butler	69,613	114,392	65,291	112,440
Carroll	3,251	10,745	3,038	10,447
Champaign	5,062	14,589	4,890	15,132
Clark	24,076	39,032	21,494	39,636
Clermont	34,092	74,570	35,593	75,731
Clinton	4,697	15,488	4,562	15,648
Columbiana	13,359	35,726	11,957	35,100
Coshocton	4,125	12,325	3,782	12,080
Crawford	4,916	15,436	4,617	15,113
Cuyahoga	416,176	202,699	365,761	190,258
Darke	4,731	22,004	4,544	21,875
Defiance	5,981	13,038	5,602	13,098
Delaware	57,735	66,356	60,410	69,057
Erie	17,493	22,160	16,623	22,114
Fairfield	31,224	50,797	31,053	50,878
Fayette	2,975	9,473	2,744	9,545
Franklin	409,144	211,237	370,422	205,133
Fulton	6,664	15,731	6,308	15,627
Gallia	2,990	10,645	2,560	10,135
Geauga	21,201	34,143	20,366	33,328
Greene	34,798	52,072	34,916	52,476
Guernsey	4,577	13,407	4,093	13,058
Hamilton	246,266	177,886	226,763	168,584
Hancock	11,757	26,310	11,336	25,688
Hardin	3,062	9,949	2,844	9,715
Harrison	1,768	5,792	1,542	5,382
Henry	4,062	10,479	3,856	10,707
Highland	3,799	15,678	3,491	15,603
Hocking	3,880	9,737	3,678	9,493
Holmes	1,994	10,796	1,842	10,218
Huron	7,759	18,956	7,410	19,166
Jackson	3,311	11,309	2,906	10,987
Jefferson	10,018	22,828	8,472	22,000
Knox	8,589	22,340	8,525	22,673
Lake	55,514	73,278	53,586	71,622
Lawrence	7,489	20,306	6,411	19,644
Licking	33,055	59,514	32,287	60,112
Logan	5,055	17,964	4,944	17,823
Lorain	75,667	79,520	72,991	81,818
Lucas	115,411	81,763	102,377	79,972
Madison	5,698	13,835	5,647	14,467
Mahoning	57,641	59,903	49,811	60,327
Marion	8,269	19,023	7,717	18,656
Medina	39,800	64,598	39,234	65,288
Meigs	2,492	8,316	2,182	8,002
Mercer	4,030	19,452	3,831	19,483
Miami	15,663	41,371	15,732	41,974
Monroe	1,605	5,463	1,318	5,318
Montgomery	135,064	129,034	123,158	122,645
Morgan	1,725	5,041	1,539	5,083
Morrow	4,048	14,077	4,062	14,413
Muskingum	11,971	27,867	10,716	27,664
Noble	1,170	5,135	1,060	4,988
Ottawa	9,008	14,628	8,763	14,672
Paulding	2,213	7,086	1,964	7,085
Perry	4,098	12,357	3,747	12,811
Pickaway	7,304	20,593	7,282	21,154
Pike	3,110	9,157	2,757	9,113
Portage	35,661	45,990	33,943	46,717
Preble	4,493	17,022	4,294	16,936
Putnam	3,195	16,412	2,962	16,419
Richland	17,640	41,472	16,285	40,557
Ross	10,557	22,278	9,633	22,247
Sandusky	10,596	18,896	9,987	18,978
Scioto	9,080	22,609	7,861	22,320
Seneca	8,266	17,086	7,665	16,927
Shelby	4,465	20,422	4,295	20,348
Stark	75,904	111,097	69,732	109,461
Summit	151,668	124,833	142,188	123,508
Trumbull	44,519	55,194	38,839	54,575
Tuscarawas	12,889	30,458	11,905	30,093
Union	11,141	21,669	12,735	23,611
Van Wert	3,067	11,650	2,976	11,535
Vinton	1,331	4,632	1,158	4,465
Warren	46,069	87,988	46,444	89,676
Washington	9,243	22,307	8,479	21,754
Wayne	16,660	36,759	15,704	36,207
Williams	4,842	13,452	4,599	13,249
Wood	30,617	35,757	29,220	36,066
Wyandot	2,733	8,462	2,694	8,390
Totals	**2,679,165**	**3,154,834**	**2,476,003**	**3,116,579**

Oklahoma

County	2020 Biden (D)	2020 Trump (R)	2024 Harris (D)	2024 Trump (R)
Adair	1,387	5,585	1,285	5,840
Alfalfa	232	1,978	236	1,891
Atoka	765	4,557	778	4,827
Beaver	190	1,968	158	1,937
Beckham	1,048	6,767	1,093	6,470
Blaine	688	3,136	671	3,054
Bryan	3,323	12,344	3,568	13,986
Caddo	2,670	7,013	2,411	6,879
Canadian	16,742	43,550	21,016	50,491
Carter	4,470	14,699	4,277	14,945
Cherokee	6,027	11,223	5,820	11,630
Choctaw	1,082	4,698	942	4,632
Cimarron	70	970	66	860
Cleveland	49,827	66,677	49,364	67,132
Coal	374	2,091	345	2,153
Comanche	13,747	20,905	12,814	20,818
Cotton	393	2,117	392	2,067
Craig	1,217	4,686	1,212	4,739
Creek	6,577	23,294	6,640	24,090
Custer	2,369	8,060	2,278	7,682
Delaware	3,472	13,557	3,471	14,389
Dewey	214	2,124	209	1,984
Ellis	162	1,688	197	1,584
Garfield	4,919	16,970	4,847	16,589
Garvin	1,865	8,878	1,801	9,058

	2020		2024	
County	**Biden (D)**	**Trump (R)**	**Harris (D)**	**Trump (R)**
Grady	4,144	18,538	4,533	20,369
Grant	280	1,916	295	1,787
Greer	328	1,605	304	1,511
Harmon	177	747	165	709
Harper	136	1,327	147	1,283
Haskell	783	4,165	718	4,151
Hughes	919	3,875	831	3,744
Jackson	1,646	6,392	1,601	6,293
Jefferson	319	2,026	319	2,014
Johnston	738	3,441	683	3,460
Kay	4,040	12,834	4,134	12,478
Kingfisher	854	5,521	923	5,743
Kiowa	699	2,673	658	2,565
Latimer	762	3,437	681	3,356
Le Flore	3,299	15,213	3,180	15,316
Lincoln	2,609	12,013	2,708	12,485
Logan	5,455	15,608	5,897	17,733
Love	711	3,305	689	3,510
Major	320	3,084	327	3,082
Marshall	1,100	4,891	1,169	5,348
Mayes	3,581	12,749	3,529	13,511
McClain	3,582	15,295	4,021	16,980
McCurtain	1,858	9,485	1,694	9,471
McIntosh	2,031	6,172	1,936	6,380
Murray	1,156	4,612	1,078	4,686
Muskogee	8,027	16,526	7,395	16,529
Noble	1,003	3,821	1,008	3,852
Nowata	712	3,610	720	3,774
Okfuskee	896	3,058	850	3,069
Oklahoma	141,724	145,050	138,665	143,522
Okmulgee	4,357	9,668	3,976	10,080
Osage	6,002	14,121	5,863	14,398
Ottawa	2,686	8,545	2,510	8,489
Pawnee	1,363	5,267	1,355	5,396
Payne	10,904	17,813	10,546	17,941
Pittsburg	3,768	13,851	3,469	13,824
Pontotoc	4,117	10,805	3,894	10,958
Pottawatomie	7,275	20,240	7,261	20,895
Pushmataha	668	4,016	616	4,025
Roger Mills	168	1,629	160	1,546
Rogers	9,589	34,031	10,140	35,920
Seminole	2,150	6,011	1,951	5,951
Sequoyah	3,035	12,113	2,906	12,488
Stephens	3,154	15,560	3,233	15,084
Texas	894	4,505	793	4,319
Tillman	597	2,076	500	2,005
Tulsa	108,996	150,574	105,881	144,952
Wagoner	8,464	26,165	9,321	28,469
Washington	5,790	17,076	5,788	16,829
Washita	598	4,086	550	4,025
Woods	591	2,993	614	2,954
Woodward	1,005	6,611	967	6,231
Totals	**503,890**	**1,020,280**	**499,043**	**1,035,217**

Oregon

	2020		2024	
County	**Biden (D)**	**Trump (R)**	**Harris (D)**	**Trump (R)**
Baker	2,346	7,352	2,301	6,984
Benton	35,827	14,878	32,294	13,430
Clackamas	139,043	110,509	81,723	65,346
Clatsop	12,916	10,218	11,874	9,418
Columbia	13,835	17,150	12,428	16,720
Coos	14,243	21,829	11,922	17,742
Crook	3,801	11,287	3,378	10,671
Curry	6,058	8,484	5,603	7,820
Deschutes	65,962	55,646	64,036	51,895
Douglas	19,160	43,298	13,497	29,584
Gilliam	324	834	285	794
Grant	929	3,545	805	3,466
Harney	894	3,475	776	3,274
Hood River	8,764	3,955	8,069	3,742
Jackson	59,478	63,869	52,130	59,812
Jefferson	4,393	7,189	3,152	6,254
Josephine	18,451	31,751	14,909	27,365
Klamath	10,388	25,308	8,427	21,447
Lake	792	3,470	621	3,108
Lane	134,366	80,336	98,628	60,717
Lincoln	17,385	12,460	15,861	10,736
Linn	26,512	43,486	24,132	40,804
Malheur	3,260	8,187	2,830	7,593
Marion	80,872	79,002	38,607	40,239
Morrow	1,371	3,586	1,109	3,358
Multnomah	367,249	82,995	219,716	48,052
Polk	22,917	23,732	16,062	17,503
Sherman	260	921	229	877
Tillamook	8,066	8,354	7,210	7,363
Umatilla	10,707	21,270	8,947	20,422
Union	4,254	10,298	3,726	9,107
Wallowa	1,625	3,404	1,437	3,948
Wasco	6,604	7,035	5,870	6,672
Washington	209,940	99,073	150,293	72,300
Wheeler	217	711	208	609
Yamhill	27,174	29,551	18,269	20,633
Totals	**1,340,383**	**958,448**	**941,364**	**729,805**

Pennsylvania

	2020		2024	
County	**Biden (D)**	**Trump (R)**	**Harris (D)**	**Trump (R)**
Adams	18,207	37,523	19,623	40,021
Allegheny	429,065	282,324	419,051	279,292
Armstrong	8,457	27,489	8,442	28,084
Beaver	38,122	54,759	36,795	56,502
Bedford	4,367	23,025	4,316	23,545
Berks	92,895	109,736	89,764	115,676
Blair	17,636	45,306	15,279	42,536
Bradford	8,046	21,600	7,816	22,658
Bucks	204,712	187,367	194,635	195,147
Butler	37,508	74,359	40,046	79,147
Cambria	21,730	48,085	9,413	14,601
Cameron	634	1,771	536	1,650
Carbon	11,212	21,984	11,121	23,383
Centre	40,055	36,372	31,481	34,204
Chester	182,372	128,565	175,686	133,497
Clarion	4,678	14,578	4,529	14,972
Clearfield	9,673	29,203	9,565	30,363
Clinton	5,502	11,902	5,366	12,908
Columbia	10,532	20,098	10,783	20,800
Crawford	12,924	28,559	12,644	29,450
Cumberland	62,245	77,212	65,506	79,784
Dauphin	78,983	66,408	76,899	68,706
Delaware	206,423	118,532	197,225	121,941
Elk	4,522	12,140	4,464	12,506
Erie	68,286	66,869	65,464	67,399
Fayette	20,444	41,227	19,238	43,076
Forest	728	1,882	719	1,897
Franklin	22,422	57,245	22,968	59,105
Fulton	1,085	6,824	1,082	6,984
Greene	4,911	12,579	4,554	12,258
Huntingdon	5,445	17,061	5,332	17,561
Indiana	12,634	28,089	12,610	29,111
Jefferson	4,527	17,960	4,696	18,196
Juniata	2,253	9,649	2,285	9,688
Lackawanna	61,991	52,334	58,956	55,744
Lancaster	115,847	160,209	117,526	164,386
Lawrence	15,978	29,597	15,281	31,164
Lebanon	23,932	46,731	24,265	47,775
Lehigh	98,288	84,259	94,235	89,704
Luzerne	64,873	86,929	59,966	90,370
Lycoming	16,971	41,462	17,012	41,677
McKean	5,098	14,083	5,066	14,323
Mercer	21,067	36,143	19,272	36,679
Mifflin	4,603	16,670	4,675	17,066
Monroe	44,060	38,726	41,258	42,168
Montgomery	319,511	185,460	308,264	193,400
Montour	3,771	5,844	2,351	4,790
Northampton	85,087	83,854	84,291	88,171
Northumberland	12,677	28,952	12,716	29,984
Perry	5,950	18,293	4,058	16,131
Philadelphia	603,790	132,740	526,083	136,088
Pike	13,019	19,213	12,993	21,298
Potter	1,726	7,239	1,664	7,303
Schuylkill	20,727	48,871	20,729	51,416
Snyder	4,910	13,983	5,184	14,592

County	2020 Biden (D)	2020 Trump (R)	2024 Harris (D)	2024 Trump (R)
Somerset	8,654	31,466	8,559	31,884
Sullivan	921	2,619	956	2,697
Susquehanna	6,236	15,207	5,998	15,949
Tioga	4,955	15,742	5,080	16,222
Union	7,475	12,356	7,457	12,594
Venango	7,585	18,569	7,531	18,747
Warren	6,066	14,237	6,164	14,273
Washington	45,088	72,080	43,979	75,084
Wayne	9,191	18,637	9,100	19,911
Westmoreland	72,129	130,218	74,451	134,268
Wyoming	4,704	9,936	4,656	10,183
York	88,114	146,733	89,681	152,793
Totals	**3,458,229**	**3,377,674**	**3,289,390**	**3,445,482**

Rhode Island

City	2020 Biden (D)	2020 Trump (R)	2024 Harris (D)	2024 Trump (R)
Barrington	7,597	2,846	7,250	2,834
Bristol	6,647	4,521	6,504	4,670
Coventry	9,027	10,366	8,461	11,124
Cranston	22,397	17,033	20,661	18,403
Cumberland	10,723	8,329	9,941	8,694
East Providence	14,499	7,832	13,603	8,597
Johnston	6,717	8,126	6,123	9,140
Lincoln	6,492	5,721	6,191	5,946
Newport	7,631	2,609	6,934	2,730
North Kingstown	10,096	6,564	9,892	6,585
North Providence	9,283	7,044	8,447	7,414
Pawtucket	17,626	7,144	11,510	6,138
Portsmouth	6,529	3,955	6,185	3,962
Providence	45,076	9,993	40,735	12,660
Smithfield	5,482	5,688	5,154	6,084
South Kingstown	11,051	4,944	10,560	5,337
Warwick	25,491	19,345	22,983	19,434
West Warwick	7,153	6,427	6,677	7,030
Westerly	7,051	5,400	6,332	5,500
Woonsocket	7,167	6,185	6,381	6,591
Other	56,590	47,349	59,291	56,721
Totals	**307,486**	**199,922**	**273,434**	**209,003**

South Carolina

County	2020 Biden (D)	2020 Trump (R)	2024 Harris (D)	2024 Trump (R)
Abbeville	4,101	8,215	3,396	8,499
Aiken	32,275	51,589	30,455	51,898
Allendale	2,718	835	2,164	811
Anderson	27,169	67,565	23,910	65,305
Bamberg	4,010	2,417	3,243	2,374
Barnwell	4,720	5,492	4,075	5,597
Beaufort	43,419	53,194	43,886	59,002
Berkeley	45,223	57,397	46,358	64,715
Calhoun	3,905	4,305	3,336	4,467
Charleston	121,485	93,297	111,237	99,121
Cherokee	6,983	18,043	5,938	18,687
Chester	6,941	8,660	6,353	9,028
Chesterfield	7,431	11,297	6,520	11,678
Clarendon	8,250	8,361	7,064	9,065
Colleton	8,602	10,440	7,366	10,685
Darlington	15,220	16,832	12,965	17,007
Dillon	6,436	6,582	5,240	6,525
Dorchester	33,824	41,913	32,489	43,839
Edgefield	4,953	8,184	4,432	8,845
Fairfield	7,382	4,625	6,266	4,779
Florence	31,153	32,615	27,692	32,591
Georgetown	15,822	20,487	14,841	22,250
Greenville	103,030	150,021	99,467	157,820
Greenwood	12,145	19,431	10,723	19,655
Hampton	5,323	3,906	4,324	3,799
Horry	59,180	118,821	53,650	122,845
Jasper	7,185	7,078	8,138	9,888
Kershaw	12,699	20,471	11,802	21,252
Lancaster	18,937	30,312	20,062	33,484
Laurens	10,159	20,004	8,741	21,048
Lee	5,329	3,008	4,486	3,073
Lexington	49,301	92,817	47,749	96,836
Marion	8,872	5,711	7,272	5,896
Marlboro	6,290	5,044	5,097	4,853
McCormick	2,687	2,958	2,512	3,562
Newberry	6,958	11,443	5,837	12,065
Oconee	10,414	29,698	9,973	31,722
Orangeburg	27,295	13,603	22,827	13,766
Pickens	13,645	42,907	13,851	45,573
Richland	132,570	58,313	120,171	57,748
Saluda	2,963	6,210	2,454	6,451
Spartanburg	52,926	93,560	50,678	102,843
Sumter	27,379	21,000	23,386	21,192
Union	4,935	8,183	4,083	8,097
Williamsburg	10,289	5,532	8,631	5,523
York	59,008	82,727	59,391	87,931
Totals	**1,091,541**	**1,385,103**	**1,014,531**	**1,453,690**

South Dakota

County	2020 Biden (D)	2020 Trump (R)	2024 Harris (D)	2024 Trump (R)
Aurora	317	1,052	302	1,056
Beadle	2,107	4,808	2,017	4,826
Bennett	466	694	389	676
Bon Homme	721	2,235	697	2,236
Brookings	6,110	8,000	5,978	8,574
Brown	6,538	10,580	6,075	10,642
Brule	673	1,750	666	1,694
Buffalo	352	183	291	164
Butte	939	3,731	935	3,980
Campbell	117	747	120	706
Charles Mix	1,177	2,552	998	2,547
Clark	437	1,373	415	1,382
Clay	3,083	2,456	2,943	2,574
Codington	3,837	8,958	3,840	9,349
Corson	622	647	495	630
Custer	1,522	3,852	1,566	4,309
Davison	2,648	5,613	2,743	6,208
Day	1,052	1,869	1,000	1,876
Deuel	609	1,699	528	1,717
Dewey	1,131	790	1,032	793
Douglas	216	1,468	219	1,419
Edmunds	417	1,538	384	1,618
Fall River	1,053	2,878	1,030	3,132
Faulk	198	964	183	920
Grant	1,056	2,618	946	2,595
Gregory	455	1,771	426	1,790
Haakon	105	1,026	105	1,002
Hamlin	647	2,372	610	2,560
Hand	373	1,433	365	1,375
Hanson	557	1,793	399	1,611
Harding	49	748	48	754
Hughes	2,953	5,522	2,838	5,378
Hutchinson	762	2,944	755	2,911
Hyde	136	564	148	530
Jackson	359	738	358	753
Jerauld	270	721	275	708
Jones	90	498	60	477
Kingsbury	819	1,904	760	1,989
Lake	2,068	3,681	1,978	3,819
Lawrence	4,537	8,753	5,074	9,903
Lincoln	11,981	19,617	12,981	22,621
Lyman	525	1,042	421	993
Marshall	858	1,287	782	1,287
McCook	769	2,068	733	2,227
McPherson	222	1,075	188	1,087
Meade	3,285	9,875	3,420	10,880
Mellette	298	449	285	434
Miner	320	787	293	841
Minnehaha	40,482	49,249	17,500	23,979
Moody	1,179	1,951	1,052	2,068
Oglala Lakota	2,829	297	2,563	406
Pennington	20,606	35,063	20,050	35,005
Perkins	239	1,401	228	1,342
Potter	227	1,139	214	1,059
Roberts	1,828	2,404	1,560	2,513
Sanborn	257	905	259	929
Spink	998	2,104	921	2,145
Stanley	421	1,203	447	1,260

County	2020 Biden (D)	2020 Trump (R)	2024 Harris (D)	2024 Trump (R)
Sully	185	726	168	716
Todd	1,963	532	1,570	497
Tripp	495	2,161	470	2,150
Turner	1,139	3,290	1,044	3,374
Union	2,725	5,944	2,526	6,082
Walworth	565	1,966	481	1,938
Yankton	4,016	6,581	3,850	6,619
Ziebach	481	404	366	388
Totals	**150,471**	**261,043**	**124,363**	**244,023**

Tennessee

County	2020 Biden (D)	2020 Trump (R)	2024 Harris (D)	2024 Trump (R)
Anderson	11,741	23,184	11,510	24,537
Bedford	4,453	14,354	4,119	15,752
Benton	1,529	5,668	1,315	5,880
Bledsoe	971	4,725	891	5,254
Blount	17,932	47,369	17,642	50,646
Bradley	9,851	35,204	9,852	38,818
Campbell	2,441	12,331	2,305	13,111
Cannon	1,261	5,190	1,132	5,682
Carroll	2,559	9,205	2,232	9,535
Carter	4,529	19,584	4,454	20,165
Cheatham	5,514	14,438	5,459	14,977
Chester	1,412	5,952	1,285	6,203
Claiborne	2,202	10,604	1,971	11,462
Clay	735	2,733	614	3,113
Cocke	2,533	12,162	2,414	13,068
Coffee	5,705	17,883	5,437	19,165
Crockett	1,382	4,673	1,196	4,673
Cumberland	6,728	25,168	6,995	27,393
Davidson	199,703	100,218	181,364	101,899
Decatur	904	4,229	819	4,596
DeKalb	1,750	6,672	1,706	7,599
Dickson	6,106	17,643	5,912	18,997
Dyer	3,158	11,768	2,704	11,600
Fayette	7,027	15,690	6,716	16,741
Fentress	1,214	7,441	1,147	8,543
Franklin	4,864	13,987	4,524	15,003
Gibson	5,771	16,259	5,100	16,346
Giles	3,298	9,784	2,974	10,394
Grainger	1,467	8,565	1,432	9,624
Greene	5,199	22,259	5,140	25,524
Grundy	988	4,802	948	5,323
Hamblen	5,500	18,811	5,127	20,130
Hamilton	75,522	92,108	74,349	97,051
Hancock	362	2,372	334	2,558
Hardeman	4,180	5,760	3,526	5,792
Hardin	1,775	9,559	1,703	10,283
Hawkins	4,083	20,405	3,986	22,044
Haywood	4,012	3,343	3,310	3,285
Henderson	2,092	9,797	1,902	10,081
Henry	3,548	11,239	3,285	11,625
Hickman	2,130	7,577	1,968	8,265
Houston	871	2,718	773	2,986
Humphreys	2,017	6,120	1,765	6,387
Jackson	1,135	4,118	1,038	4,577
Jefferson	4,654	18,651	4,499	21,041
Johnson	1,246	6,468	1,211	6,822
Knox	91,422	124,540	87,287	130,134
Lake	526	1,492	429	1,491
Lauderdale	3,193	5,674	2,571	5,633
Lawrence	3,195	15,334	2,939	16,428
Lewis	1,072	4,474	990	4,835
Lincoln	2,919	12,281	2,779	13,190
Loudon	6,948	21,713	7,623	25,209
Macon	1,307	8,096	1,277	8,958
Madison	18,390	23,943	16,114	23,385
Marion	3,177	9,911	3,022	10,770
Marshall	3,605	11,043	3,389	12,414
Maury	14,418	31,464	14,135	37,348
McMinn	4,361	18,198	4,202	19,649
McNairy	1,943	9,093	1,726	9,433
Meigs	1,008	4,467	968	5,082
Monroe	3,764	16,783	3,606	18,508
Montgomery	32,472	42,187	32,723	47,785
Moore	573	2,888	542	3,060
Morgan	1,167	6,930	1,052	7,407
Obion	2,589	10,790	2,221	10,595
Overton	2,033	7,918	1,929	9,035
Perry	615	2,775	558	3,139
Pickett	525	2,381	485	2,437
Polk	1,492	6,792	1,356	7,302
Putnam	9,185	23,759	8,985	25,530
Rhea	2,369	11,050	2,308	11,958
Roane	6,043	19,230	6,071	20,996
Robertson	8,692	24,536	8,428	26,260
Rutherford	59,341	81,480	56,600	88,748
Scott	986	8,004	942	8,608
Sequatchie	1,298	5,855	1,291	6,511
Sevier	8,721	33,783	8,316	35,189
Shelby	246,105	129,815	194,898	116,132
Smith	1,802	7,136	1,594	7,645
Stewart	1,232	4,950	1,160	5,378
Sullivan	17,272	55,860	16,608	58,081
Sumner	27,680	63,454	27,939	68,805
Tipton	6,837	20,070	6,176	20,302
Trousdale	1,012	2,936	856	3,358
Unicoi	1,615	6,599	1,575	6,868
Union	1,249	6,803	1,216	7,380
Van Buren	544	2,342	524	2,712
Warren	3,924	11,850	3,646	13,185
Washington	18,638	40,444	18,099	42,242
Wayne	820	5,795	762	6,016
Weakley	3,020	10,396	2,719	10,528
White	2,143	9,606	2,102	10,698
Williamson	50,161	86,469	47,676	94,539
Wilson	22,254	50,296	23,804	56,338
Totals	**1,143,711**	**1,852,475**	**1,048,303**	**1,961,784**

Texas

County	2020 Biden (D)	2020 Trump (R)	2024 Harris (D)	2024 Trump (R)
Anderson	3,955	15,110	3,621	15,548
Andrews	850	4,943	806	5,204
Angelina	9,143	25,076	8,135	26,034
Aransas	2,916	9,239	2,826	10,073
Archer	446	4,300	519	4,590
Armstrong	75	1,035	77	1,029
Atascosa	5,876	12,039	5,140	13,126
Austin	2,951	11,447	2,809	12,438
Bailey	409	1,434	332	1,393
Bandera	2,505	10,057	2,527	10,929
Bastrop	15,474	20,516	15,941	23,276
Baylor	183	1,494	184	1,467
Bee	3,288	6,006	2,597	6,107
Bell	57,014	67,893	53,800	75,031
Bexar	448,452	308,618	408,981	336,260
Blanco	1,911	5,443	1,952	6,384
Borden	16	397	16	370
Bosque	1,561	7,469	1,519	7,963
Bowie	10,747	27,116	9,237	27,057
Brazoria	62,228	90,433	63,849	95,769
Brazos	35,349	47,530	33,671	56,544
Brewster	2,258	2,461	1,967	2,537
Briscoe	78	639	72	666
Brooks	1,470	998	1,308	1,077
Brown	2,107	13,698	2,131	14,591
Burleson	1,788	6,743	1,703	7,586
Burnet	5,639	18,767	5,464	19,660
Caldwell	6,672	8,031	6,517	8,825
Calhoun	2,148	5,641	1,852	5,936
Callahan	734	6,012	758	6,173
Cameron	64,063	49,032	54,156	60,925
Camp	1,394	3,626	1,200	4,006
Carson	297	2,779	288	2,853
Cass	2,795	11,033	2,398	11,676
Castro	466	1,602	418	1,594
Chambers	3,997	17,353	4,187	20,557
Cherokee	4,210	15,101	3,739	16,580
Childress	310	1,943	263	1,991

County	2020 Biden (D)	2020 Trump (R)	2024 Harris (D)	2024 Trump (R)
Clay	614	5,069	584	5,283
Cochran	177	809	147	736
Coke	178	1,586	179	1,620
Coleman	451	3,641	428	3,711
Collin	230,945	252,318	220,269	278,427
Collingsworth	155	1,048	135	1,066
Colorado	2,420	7,472	2,102	7,819
Comal	24,826	62,740	27,548	74,588
Comanche	853	5,177	739	5,242
Concho	197	1,058	153	1,035
Cooke	3,210	15,596	3,303	16,949
Coryell	7,565	15,438	6,931	16,665
Cottle	113	540	89	565
Crane	241	1,247	186	1,195
Crockett	344	1,220	323	1,085
Crosby	527	1,396	451	1,416
Culberson	438	415	319	451
Dallam	197	1,389	152	1,280
Dallas	598,576	307,076	497,992	316,416
Dawson	808	2,951	667	2,808
Deaf Smith	1,264	3,294	1,013	3,228
Delta	403	2,162	397	2,250
Denton	188,695	222,480	189,949	249,304
DeWitt	1,494	6,567	1,262	6,444
Dickens	130	853	146	843
Dimmit	2,264	1,384	1,750	1,648
Donley	198	1,438	174	1,492
Duval	2,575	2,443	1,993	2,435
Eastland	983	7,237	918	7,397
Ector	11,367	32,697	9,876	32,418
Edwards	168	893	133	867
El Paso	27,565	56,717	142,879	104,966
Ellis	178,126	84,331	33,799	64,706
Erath	2,916	13,684	2,866	15,334
Falls	1,899	4,177	1,709	4,518
Fannin	2,655	12,171	2,602	13,633
Fayette	2,661	10,171	2,510	10,684
Fisher	352	1,448	330	1,487
Floyd	438	1,584	358	1,715
Foard	99	445	92	448
Fort Bend	195,552	157,718	178,134	173,114
Franklin	804	4,161	809	4,461
Freestone	1,635	6,991	1,582	7,588
Frio	2,422	2,823	1,844	3,038
Gaines	576	5,355	538	5,840
Galveston	58,842	93,911	56,520	100,074
Garza	231	1,413	213	1,374
Gillespie	3,176	12,514	3,149	13,175
Glasscock	39	611	38	623
Goliad	877	3,085	778	3,177
Gonzales	1,948	5,627	1,728	5,980
Gray	829	6,840	845	6,688
Grayson	14,506	44,163	14,754	50,468
Gregg	14,796	32,493	13,115	32,829
Grimes	2,833	9,432	2,731	11,175
Guadalupe	28,805	47,553	29,425	54,498
Hale	2,279	7,177	1,899	7,269
Hall	168	995	149	989
Hamilton	641	3,616	624	3,801
Hansford	166	1,849	145	1,840
Hardeman	241	1,330	188	1,210
Hardin	3,474	23,858	3,336	24,669
Harris	918,193	700,630	795,223	716,099
Harrison	7,908	21,466	7,334	22,610
Hartley	195	1,868	163	1,843
Haskell	353	1,840	312	1,915
Hays	59,524	47,680	65,294	58,299
Hemphill	206	1,486	190	1,412
Henderson	7,060	28,911	6,875	31,252
Hidalgo	128,199	90,527	103,952	110,415
Hill	2,860	11,926	2,916	13,646
Hockley	1,482	6,536	1,321	6,610
Hood	5,648	26,496	6,052	30,136
Hopkins	3,046	12,719	2,909	13,682
Houston	2,314	7,060	2,062	7,234
Howard	2,069	8,054	1,754	7,813

County	2020 Biden (D)	2020 Trump (R)	2024 Harris (D)	2024 Trump (R)
Hudspeth	371	779	272	747
Hunt	8,906	29,163	10,195	36,115
Hutchinson	965	7,681	912	7,271
Irion	120	759	105	761
Jack	331	3,418	363	3,817
Jackson	1,033	5,231	904	5,360
Jasper	2,954	12,542	2,606	13,137
Jeff Davis	501	784	450	699
Jefferson	46,073	47,570	38,662	46,453
Jim Hogg	1,197	833	855	725
Jim Wells	6,119	7,453	5,548	7,627
Johnson	16,464	54,628	19,175	60,649
Jones	999	5,660	906	5,981
Karnes	1,234	3,968	1,049	4,000
Kaufman	18,405	37,624	24,686	44,016
Kendall	6,020	20,083	6,340	22,655
Kenedy	65	127	41	115
Kent	47	411	50	390
Kerr	6,524	20,879	6,299	21,594
Kimble	284	1,987	261	2,126
King	8	151	6	129
Kinney	446	1,144	345	1,062
Kleberg	5,314	5,504	4,315	5,572
Knox	265	1,180	214	1,156
La Salle	1,052	1,335	931	1,415
Lamar	4,458	16,760	4,079	17,044
Lamb	840	3,521	716	3,382
Lampasas	2,144	8,086	2,229	8,951
Lavaca	1,333	8,804	1,229	9,199
Lee	1,750	6,255	1,639	6,722
Leon	1,072	7,523	1,028	7,978
Liberty	5,785	23,302	5,923	25,182
Limestone	2,213	6,789	1,920	7,075
Lipscomb	131	1,205	123	1,123
Live Oak	819	4,199	760	4,302
Llano	2,465	10,079	2,605	10,894
Loving	4	60	10	86
Lubbock	40,017	78,861	37,010	86,360
Lynn	428	1,853	367	2,171
Madison	1,088	4,169	960	4,495
Marion	1,339	3,470	1,094	3,550
Martin	288	1,857	247	1,825
Mason	457	1,991	434	2,076
Matagorda	3,733	9,845	3,224	9,951
Maverick	8,332	6,881	6,368	9,282
McCulloch	490	2,904	454	3,024
McLennan	36,688	59,543	33,761	64,522
McMullen	53	460	37	448
Medina	6,773	15,642	6,939	17,450
Menard	197	823	189	859
Midland	12,329	45,624	11,251	46,601
Milam	2,496	7,984	2,315	8,627
Mills	271	2,217	310	2,416
Mitchell	397	2,170	352	2,144
Montague	1,097	8,615	1,204	9,804
Montgomery	74,377	193,382	82,022	221,706
Moore	1,062	4,359	857	4,456
Morris	1,669	3,872	1,305	4,056
Motley	46	604	35	611
Nacogdoches	9,000	17,378	7,680	17,565
Navarro	5,101	13,800	4,687	14,952
Newton	1,173	4,882	952	4,781
Nolan	1,162	4,131	1,018	4,047
Nueces	60,925	64,617	53,015	67,015
Ochiltree	302	2,812	268	2,720
Oldham	81	917	74	894
Orange	6,357	29,186	5,937	30,183
Palo Pinto	2,178	10,179	2,133	11,033
Panola	2,057	9,326	1,902	9,497
Parker	13,017	62,045	14,840	75,091
Parmer	488	2,135	368	2,123
Pecos	1,382	3,215	1,142	3,041
Polk	5,387	18,573	4,868	19,147
Potter	9,921	22,820	8,730	22,966
Presidio	1,463	721	1,288	686
Rains	842	5,155	868	5,638

County	2020 Biden (D)	2020 Trump (R)	2024 Harris (D)	2024 Trump (R)
Randall	12,802	50,796	12,915	53,262
Reagan	172	942	140	800
Real	320	1,643	315	1,625
Red River	1,246	4,517	1,103	4,681
Reeves	1,395	2,254	1,066	2,331
Refugio	1,108	2,210	917	2,131
Roberts	17	529	20	547
Robertson	2,374	5,646	1,916	6,157
Rockwall	16,412	36,726	18,054	43,480
Runnels	552	3,807	452	3,580
Rusk	4,629	16,534	4,327	17,212
Sabine	669	4,784	587	4,969
San Augustine	980	3,007	809	2,913
San Jacinto	2,337	10,161	2,161	10,478
San Patricio	8,988	16,516	8,008	17,323
San Saba	287	2,308	276	2,412
Schleicher	211	940	192	906
Scurry	818	4,983	730	4,908
Shackelford	130	1,484	146	1,565
Shelby	2,068	7,975	1,740	8,155
Sherman	91	886	70	815
Smith	29,615	69,080	27,890	74,657
Somervell	768	4,105	748	4,492
Starr	9,123	8,247	6,845	9,443
Stephens	397	3,385	384	3,354
Sterling	51	584	43	583
Stonewall	116	615	110	604
Sutton	322	1,222	228	1,167
Swisher	478	1,845	403	1,839
Tarrant	411,567	409,741	383,023	425,650
Taylor	14,588	39,547	13,574	41,116
Terrell	119	334	91	314
Terry	757	2,812	587	2,813
Throckmorton	82	806	73	822
Titus	2,856	7,570	2,268	7,849
Tom Green	12,239	32,313	11,508	33,316
Travis	435,860	161,337	398,253	170,613
Trinity	1,323	5,579	1,192	6,124
Tyler	1,403	8,194	1,244	8,265
Upshur	2,877	15,809	2,812	16,925
Upton	170	1,178	146	1,149
Uvalde	4,073	6,174	3,214	6,480
Val Verde	6,771	8,284	5,244	9,130
Van Zandt	3,516	22,270	3,427	24,305
Victoria	10,380	23,358	9,988	24,994
Walker	7,884	15,375	7,451	17,503
Waller	8,191	14,260	10,168	17,057
Ward	764	3,241	627	3,111
Washington	4,261	12,959	4,045	14,012
Webb	41,820	25,898	31,958	33,383
Wharton	4,694	11,926	3,899	12,431
Wheeler	168	2,159	169	2,090
Wichita	13,161	32,069	12,084	31,600
Wilbarger	956	3,524	858	3,562
Willacy	3,108	2,441	2,673	2,856
Williamson	143,795	139,729	147,171	154,853
Wilson	6,350	18,463	6,227	20,881
Winkler	358	1,753	283	1,646
Wise	4,973	27,032	5,597	32,357
Wood	3,509	19,049	3,601	20,568
Yoakum	420	2,174	342	2,039
Young	1,034	7,110	958	7,269
Zapata	1,826	2,033	1,874	2,965
Zavala	2,864	1,490	1,984	1,480
Totals	**5,259,126**	**5,890,347**	**4,792,778**	**6,366,085**

Utah

County	2020 Biden (D)	2020 Trump (R)	2024 Harris (D)	2024 Trump (R)
Beaver	357	2,695	371	2,590
Box Elder	4,473	21,548	3,778	16,068
Cache	16,650	38,032	8,484	17,828
Carbon	2,392	6,693	2,363	6,217
Daggett	111	496	98	414
Davis	57,411	104,135	44,395	73,562
Duchesne	843	7,513	528	3,589
Emery	572	4,207	591	4,220
Garfield	514	2,158	527	2,182
Grand	2,806	2,248	2,794	2,298
Iron	4,892	18,989	4,853	18,355
Juab	645	5,087	696	5,351
Kane	1,083	2,998	1,075	2,976
Millard	624	5,404	462	3,623
Morgan	1,086	5,181	1,191	5,064
Piute	86	773	94	851
Rich	180	1,157	203	1,180
Salt Lake	289,906	230,174	178,736	131,128
San Juan	3,113	3,535	1,822	2,947
Sanpete	1,794	10,459	978	4,819
Sevier	1,084	9,052	997	7,778
Summit	15,244	10,252	7,236	4,621
Tooele	8,943	21,014	7,975	18,172
Uintah	1,663	13,261	1,815	12,839
Utah	76,033	192,812	46,519	105,675
Wasatch	6,187	10,795	3,919	6,553
Washington	20,530	67,294	16,829	53,066
Wayne	365	1,229	372	1,204
Weber	40,695	65,949	28,556	42,515
Totals	**560,282**	**865,140**	**368,257**	**557,685**

Vermont

City	2020 Biden (D)	2020 Trump (R)	2024 Harris (D)	2024 Trump (R)
Bennington	4,369	2,473	4,235	2,690
Brattleboro	5,423	1,052	5,068	1,105
Burlington	19,238	2,292	17,414	2,222
Colchester	6,452	2,852	6,404	2,864
Essex	9,581	3,415	4,965	1,936
Hartford	4,516	1,574	4,363	1,648
Milton	3,344	2,612	3,333	2,774
Montpelier	4,576	468	4,359	491
Rutland City	4,679	3,026	4,264	3,133
Shelburne	4,358	953	4,472	915
South Burlington	10,057	2,271	9,974	2,207
Williston	4,961	1,699	5,029	1,644
Other	161,251	88,001	161,809	95,720
Totals	**242,820**	**112,704**	**235,689**	**119,349**

Virginia

County	2020 Biden (D)	2020 Trump (R)	2024 Harris (D)	2024 Trump (R)
Accomack	7,578	9,172	7,333	9,479
Albemarle	42,466	20,804	42,472	20,721
Alleghany	2,243	5,859	2,065	5,964
Amelia	2,411	5,390	2,163	5,690
Amherst	5,672	11,041	5,354	11,589
Appomattox	2,418	6,702	2,299	7,127
Arlington	105,344	22,318	95,134	23,624
Augusta	10,840	30,714	11,116	31,719
Bath	646	1,834	579	1,933
Bedford	12,176	35,600	12,125	37,232
Bland	532	2,903	519	2,972
Botetourt	5,700	15,099	5,816	15,563
Brunswick	4,552	3,357	4,116	3,475
Buchanan	1,587	8,311	1,331	7,786
Buckingham	3,471	4,544	2,946	4,773
Campbell	8,070	21,245	7,771	22,376
Caroline	7,657	8,336	7,764	9,269
Carroll	2,842	12,659	2,868	12,890
Charles City	2,624	1,761	2,331	1,877
Charlotte	2,317	3,815	957	2,440
Chesterfield	106,935	93,326	108,242	91,840
Clarke	3,920	5,192	3,910	5,520
Craig	587	2,536	533	2,515
Culpeper	10,617	16,012	10,374	17,400
Cumberland	2,227	3,019	2,098	3,282
Dickenson	1,503	5,748	1,298	5,566
Dinwiddie	6,224	8,695	5,815	9,372
Essex	3,038	3,075	2,744	3,220
Fairfax	419,943	168,401	365,654	173,320
Fauquier	17,565	25,106	16,799	26,192
Floyd	3,004	6,225	2,924	6,464
Fluvanna	7,414	8,155	7,592	8,638
Franklin	8,381	20,895	8,230	22,014

County	2020 Biden (D)	2020 Trump (R)	2024 Harris (D)	2024 Trump (R)
Frederick	17,207	30,558	17,842	32,444
Giles	2,156	6,876	2,040	6,982
Gloucester	6,964	14,875	6,937	15,696
Goochland	6,685	9,966	7,763	11,370
Grayson	1,535	6,529	1,482	6,445
Greene	4,163	6,866	4,314	7,233
Greensville	2,627	1,914	2,301	1,913
Halifax	7,666	10,418	6,864	10,591
Hanover	25,307	44,318	26,180	44,850
Henrico	116,572	63,440	110,323	60,774
Henry	9,127	16,725	8,295	16,541
Highland	417	1,092	416	1,083
Isle of Wight	9,399	13,707	9,409	14,353
James City	25,553	23,153	26,211	23,132
King and Queen	1,590	2,450	1,514	2,508
King George	5,404	8,446	5,545	9,325
King William	3,260	7,320	3,333	7,960
Lancaster	3,368	3,697	3,313	3,821
Lee	1,489	8,365	1,370	8,484
Loudoun	138,372	82,088	124,796	89,108
Louisa	8,269	13,294	9,597	15,793
Lunenburg	2,418	3,537	2,193	3,534
Madison	2,698	5,300	2,643	5,568
Mathews	1,825	3,901	1,757	4,062
Mecklenburg	6,803	9,266	6,132	9,402
Middlesex	2,491	4,196	2,418	4,291
Montgomery	23,218	20,629	21,382	20,575
Nelson	4,327	4,812	4,210	4,891
New Kent	4,621	9,631	5,553	10,805
Northampton	3,667	2,955	3,547	3,132
Northumberland	3,252	4,485	3,146	4,877
Nottoway	2,971	4,027	1,196	2,136
Orange	7,995	12,426	8,111	13,484
Page	3,007	9,345	2,910	9,923
Patrick	1,954	7,485	1,849	7,614
Pittsylvania	10,115	23,751	9,387	23,916
Powhatan	5,320	14,055	5,593	14,679
Prince Edward	4,973	4,434	4,396	4,595
Prince George	7,103	10,103	6,571	10,320
Prince William	142,863	81,222	124,465	85,951
Pulaski	4,925	12,127	4,740	12,498
Rappahannock	2,096	2,812	2,020	2,901
Richmond	1,513	2,547	1,414	2,661
Roanoke	21,801	34,268	21,236	33,821
Rockbridge	4,086	8,088	4,085	8,304
Rockingham	12,644	30,349	12,960	31,204
Russell	2,373	10,879	2,134	11,108
Scott	1,692	9,063	1,555	9,165
Shenandoah	6,836	16,463	6,861	16,955
Smyth	3,008	10,963	2,717	11,207
Southampton	3,969	5,730	3,561	6,053
Spotsylvania	34,307	39,411	34,799	41,553
Stafford	40,245	37,636	39,616	39,331
Surry	2,397	2,025	2,150	2,175
Sussex	2,827	2,219	2,406	2,226
Tazewell	3,205	16,731	2,970	16,321
Warren	6,603	14,069	6,702	15,000
Washington	6,617	21,679	6,688	22,036
Westmoreland	4,501	5,318	4,390	5,884
Wise	3,110	13,366	2,997	13,557
Wythe	3,143	11,733	3,017	12,026
York	17,683	20,241	17,768	20,130
Alexandria	66,240	14,544	58,433	15,122
Bristol	2,313	5,347	2,175	5,070
Buena Vista	825	1,863	736	1,928
Charlottesville	20,696	3,094	18,024	2,952
Chesapeake	66,377	58,180	63,274	58,948
Colonial Heights	2,972	6,007	2,873	5,752
Covington	964	1,580	802	1,594
Danville	11,710	7,428	10,411	6,795
Emporia	1,612	754	1,402	736
Fairfax	9,174	4,007	8,523	4,168
Falls Church	7,146	1,490	7,017	1,576
Franklin	2,525	1,487	2,304	1,433
Fredericksburg	8,517	4,037	8,401	4,295
Galax	777	1,838	735	1,896
Hampton	46,220	18,430	40,956	17,690
Harrisonburg	11,022	5,591	9,327	5,244
Hopewell	5,430	4,020	4,919	3,753
Lexington	1,791	906	1,648	874
Lynchburg	18,048	17,097	15,994	17,687
Manassas	10,356	6,256	8,726	6,446
Manassas Park	3,992	1,979	3,298	2,190
Martinsville	3,766	2,165	3,378	2,117
Newport News	53,099	26,377	46,413	25,449
Norfolk	64,440	23,443	56,172	22,891
Norton	464	1,109	449	1,145
Petersburg	12,389	1,584	10,829	1,630
Poquoson	2,054	5,605	2,043	5,654
Portsmouth	30,948	12,755	27,481	11,985
Radford	3,358	2,786	2,965	2,962
Richmond	92,175	16,603	82,798	15,941
Roanoke	26,773	15,607	24,930	15,333
Salem	5,148	7,683	5,102	7,586
Staunton	6,981	5,695	7,285	5,614
Suffolk	28,676	20,082	29,649	21,433
Virginia Beach	117,393	105,087	102,819	97,887
Waynesboro	4,961	5,507	5,117	5,737
Williamsburg	4,790	1,963	5,247	1,984
Winchester	6,610	5,221	6,224	5,112
Totals	**2,413,568**	**1,962,430**	**2,226,241**	**2,000,728**

Washington

County	2020 Biden (D)	2020 Trump (R)	2024 Harris (D)	2024 Trump (R)
Adams	1,814	3,907	713	2,094
Asotin	4,250	7,319	3,472	5,886
Benton	38,706	60,365	22,241	36,252
Chelan	19,349	22,746	13,913	17,138
Clallam	24,721	23,062	18,984	15,352
Clark	140,324	126,303	104,923	88,187
Columbia	668	1,754	632	1,645
Cowlitz	23,938	34,424	15,276	22,197
Douglas	7,811	12,955	4,092	7,704
Ferry	1,486	2,771	1,112	2,276
Franklin	13,340	18,039	8,191	14,313
Garfield	366	1,069	313	931
Grant	11,819	24,764	4,998	11,405
Grays Harbor	17,354	19,877	11,824	13,036
Island	29,213	22,746	12,170	7,636
Jefferson	17,204	6,931	12,172	3,782
King	907,310	269,167	575,457	171,568
Kitsap	90,277	61,563	57,588	36,427
Kittitas	11,421	14,105	5,742	7,866
Klickitat	5,959	7,237	2,649	3,378
Lewis	14,520	29,391	11,998	24,465
Lincoln	1,713	5,150	1,268	3,836
Mason	17,269	18,710	14,180	14,315
Okanogan	8,900	11,840	5,774	8,031
Pacific	6,794	6,953	5,102	4,993
Pend Oreille	2,593	5,728	2,316	5,411
Pierce	249,506	197,730	172,081	138,618
San Juan	9,725	3,057	7,288	2,120
Skagit	38,252	32,762	20,399	16,007
Skamania	3,192	3,885	2,692	3,367
Snohomish	256,728	166,428	153,956	101,208
Spokane	135,765	148,576	97,756	106,118
Stevens	7,839	19,808	2,989	6,874
Thurston	96,608	65,277	58,155	35,852
Wahkiakum	1,165	1,741	1,032	1,452
Walla Walla	13,690	16,400	6,164	7,363
Whatcom	83,660	50,489	66,243	39,679
Whitman	11,184	9,067	5,748	5,343
Yakima	43,179	50,555	16,224	25,021
Totals	**2,369,612**	**1,584,651**	**1,527,827**	**1,019,146**

West Virginia

County	2020 Biden (D)	2020 Trump (R)	2024 Harris (D)	2024 Trump (R)
Barbour	1,457	5,116	1,161	5,007
Berkeley	17,186	33,279	14,675	34,473
Boone	2,041	6,816	1,632	6,253
Braxton	1,457	4,120	1,224	3,956
Brooke	2,947	7,545	2,599	6,922
Cabell	14,994	21,721	13,356	21,103

County	2020 Biden (D)	2020 Trump (R)	2024 Harris (D)	2024 Trump (R)
Calhoun	568	2,364	488	2,386
Clay	641	2,679	578	2,592
Doddridge	435	2,619	371	2,519
Fayette	5,063	11,580	4,360	10,834
Gilmer	599	2,012	484	1,808
Grant	607	4,871	550	4,993
Greenbrier	4,655	10,925	4,180	10,507
Hampshire	1,939	8,033	1,885	8,408
Hancock	3,790	9,806	3,348	9,415
Hardy	1,381	4,859	1,284	4,947
Harrison	9,215	20,683	8,358	20,358
Jackson	3,207	10,093	2,680	9,838
Jefferson	12,127	15,033	11,894	16,505
Kanawha	34,344	46,398	28,984	42,443
Lewis	1,538	5,782	1,364	5,496
Lincoln	1,711	6,012	1,273	5,744
Logan	2,333	10,534	1,838	9,480
Marion	8,901	16,300	8,167	15,843
Marshall	3,455	10,435	3,169	9,741
Mason	2,526	8,491	2,094	8,177
McDowell	1,333	5,148	1,029	4,293
Mercer	5,556	19,237	4,813	18,298
Mineral	2,660	10,040	2,449	10,159
Mingo	1,397	8,544	1,022	7,198
Monongalia	20,282	20,803	19,160	20,984
Monroe	1,345	5,068	1,149	5,031
Morgan	1,998	6,537	1,940	6,991
Nicholas	2,226	8,279	1,919	7,960
Ohio	7,223	12,354	6,676	11,511
Pendleton	820	2,782	680	2,679
Pleasants	699	2,742	653	2,614
Pocahontas	1,047	2,895	920	2,866
Preston	3,163	11,190	2,948	11,152
Putnam	7,878	20,034	7,064	19,729
Raleigh	7,982	24,673	6,743	23,396
Randolph	3,362	8,673	3,005	8,343
Ritchie	586	3,649	517	3,464
Roane	1,455	4,213	1,215	4,172
Summers	1,448	4,074	1,221	3,916
Taylor	1,796	5,477	1,687	5,407
Tucker	938	2,841	889	2,664
Tyler	631	3,226	549	2,952
Upshur	2,256	7,771	2,026	7,607
Wayne	4,088	12,585	3,520	11,870
Webster	610	2,759	478	2,457
Wetzel	1,539	4,993	1,290	4,685
Wirt	466	2,134	408	2,115
Wood	10,926	27,202	10,261	26,256
Wyoming	1,157	7,353	977	6,487
Totals	**235,984**	**545,382**	**209,204**	**527,004**

Wisconsin

County	2020 Biden (D)	2020 Trump (R)	2024 Harris (D)	2024 Trump (R)
Adams	4,329	7,362	4,434	7,750
Ashland	4,801	3,841	4,612	4,190
Barron	9,194	15,803	8,941	16,744
Bayfield	6,147	4,617	6,107	4,860
Brown	65,511	75,871	67,910	79,115
Buffalo	2,860	4,834	2,765	5,213
Burnett	3,569	6,462	3,676	7,005
Calumet	12,116	18,156	12,922	19,474
Chippewa	13,983	21,317	14,575	23,414
Clark	4,524	10,002	4,509	10,485
Columbia	16,410	16,927	16,386	17,988
Crawford	3,953	4,620	3,850	5,081
Dane	260,121	78,794	273,954	85,449
Dodge	16,356	31,355	16,520	33,071
Door	10,044	9,752	10,564	10,098
Douglas	13,218	10,923	13,072	11,729
Dunn	9,897	13,173	10,637	14,727
Eau Claire	31,620	25,341	34,395	27,724
Florence	781	2,133	783	2,356
Fond du Lac	20,588	35,754	20,494	37,270
Forest	1,721	3,285	1,681	3,382
Grant	10,998	14,142	10,965	15,923
Green	10,851	10,169	10,903	10,842
Green Lake	3,344	7,168	3,448	7,454
Iowa	7,828	5,909	7,730	6,571
Iron	1,533	2,438	1,487	2,562
Jackson	4,256	5,791	4,157	6,204
Jefferson	19,904	27,208	20,343	28,567
Juneau	4,746	8,749	4,854	9,525
Kenosha	42,193	44,972	41,823	47,471
Kewaunee	3,976	7,927	4,058	8,266
La Crosse	37,846	28,684	39,003	32,243
Lafayette	3,647	4,821	3,469	5,256
Langlade	3,704	7,330	3,738	7,767
Lincoln	6,261	10,017	6,306	10,631
Manitowoc	16,818	27,218	17,398	28,203
Marathon	30,808	44,624	31,721	46,684
Marinette	7,366	15,304	7,415	16,670
Marquette	3,239	5,719	3,252	6,023
Menominee	1,303	278	1,266	296
Milwaukee	317,527	134,482	310,078	132,104
Monroe	8,433	13,775	8,430	14,448
Oconto	6,715	16,226	6,967	17,670
Oneida	10,105	13,671	10,079	14,455
Outagamie	47,667	58,385	49,435	60,824
Ozaukee	26,517	33,912	27,873	34,501
Pepin	1,489	2,584	1,523	2,798
Pierce	9,796	12,815	10,168	14,416
Polk	9,370	16,611	9,567	18,295
Portage	20,428	19,299	21,501	20,986
Price	3,032	5,394	3,005	5,763
Racine	50,159	54,479	49,716	56,347
Richland	3,995	4,871	3,982	5,207
Rock	46,658	37,138	46,642	40,217
Rusk	2,517	5,257	2,516	5,761
St. Croix	23,190	32,199	23,870	35,532
Sauk	18,108	17,493	18,170	18,795
Sawyer	4,498	5,909	4,599	6,422
Shawano	7,131	15,173	7,276	15,668
Sheboygan	27,101	37,609	27,733	38,758
Taylor	2,693	7,657	2,823	8,209
Trempealeau	6,285	8,833	6,217	9,661
Vernon	7,457	8,218	7,478	8,760
Vilas	5,903	9,261	6,119	9,837
Walworth	22,789	33,851	23,139	36,574
Washburn	3,867	6,334	3,869	6,966
Washington	26,650	60,237	28,505	61,606
Waukesha	103,906	159,649	108,460	162,751
Waupaca	9,703	18,952	9,932	20,057
Waushara	4,388	9,016	4,527	9,554
Winnebago	44,060	47,796	40,559	46,608
Wood	16,365	24,308	16,595	24,995
Totals	**1,630,866**	**1,610,184**	**1,657,476**	**1,688,828**

Wyoming

County	2020 Biden (D)	2020 Trump (R)	2024 Harris (D)	2024 Trump (R)
Albany	9,092	8,579	8,362	8,913
Big Horn	788	4,806	742	4,867
Campbell	1,935	16,975	2,004	15,999
Carbon	1,427	5,014	1,274	4,952
Converse	861	5,917	845	5,756
Crook	378	3,651	443	3,804
Fremont	5,519	12,007	5,179	11,552
Goshen	1,203	4,878	1,156	4,893
Hot Springs	482	1,999	488	2,082
Johnson	897	3,881	847	3,936
Laramie	15,217	27,891	14,146	28,047
Lincoln	1,509	8,643	1,623	8,957
Natrona	8,530	25,271	8,336	24,668
Niobrara	155	1,118	112	1,108
Park	3,410	12,813	3,259	13,079
Platte	890	3,898	780	3,873
Sheridan	4,043	11,843	3,920	12,039
Sublette	882	3,957	920	3,905
Sweetwater	3,823	12,229	3,730	12,539
Teton	9,848	4,341	8,747	4,132
Uinta	1,591	7,496	1,561	7,281
Washakie	651	3,245	656	3,125
Weston	360	3,107	378	3,069
Totals	**73,491**	**193,559**	**69,508**	**192,576**

Governors of the 50 States

Boldface denotes the 2024 election winner. * = Incumbent. Third-party or independent candidates receiving fewer than 50,000 votes are not necessarily listed. Governors of states not holding elections in Nov. 2024 are shown for reference. Unless otherwise noted, terms are for four years—with the exception of two-year terms for governors of New Hampshire and Vermont—ending in Jan. of year listed. D = Democrat; R = Republican; DFL = Dem.-Farmer-Labor; LB = Libertarian.

Term expires	Governor/candidate	2024 election results
Alabama		
2027	Kay Ivey (R)	
Alaska		
Dec. 2026	Mike Dunleavy (R)	
Arizona		
2027	Katie Hobbs (D)	
Arkansas		
2027	Sarah Huckabee Sanders (R)	
California		
2027	Gavin Newsom (D)	
Colorado		
2027	Jared Polis (D)	
Connecticut		
2027	Ned Lamont (D)	
Delaware		
2029	**Matt Meyer (D)**	**275,530**
	Michael Ramone (R)	217,325
Florida		
2027	Ron DeSantis (R)	
Georgia		
2027	Brian Kemp (R)	
Hawaii		
Dec. 2026	Josh Green (D)	
Idaho		
2027	Brad Little (R)	
Illinois		
2027	JB Pritzker (D)	
Indiana		
2029	**Mike Braun (R)**	**1,520,235**
	Jennifer McCormick (D)	1,138,589
	Donald Rainwater (LB)	127,434
Iowa		
2027	Kim Reynolds (R)	
Kansas		
2027	Laura Kelly (D)	
Kentucky		
Dec.2027	Andy Beshear (D)	
Louisiana		
2028	Jeff Landry (R)	
Maine		
2027	Janet Mills (D)	
Maryland		
2027	Wes Moore (D)	
Massachusetts		
2027	Maura Healey (D)	
Michigan		
2027	Gretchen Whitmer (D)	
Minnesota		
2027	Tim Walz (DFL)	
Mississippi		
2028	Tate Reeves (R)	
Missouri		
2029	**Mike Kehoe (R)**	**1,738,063**
	Crystal Quade (D)	1,136,999
Montana		
2029	**Greg Gianforte* (R)**	**321,525**
	Ryan Busse (D)	205,022
Nebraska		
2027	Jim Pillen (R)	
Nevada		
2027	Joe Lombardo (R)	
New Hampshire		
2027	**Kelly Ayotte (R)**	**402,154**
	Joyce Craig (D)	336,879
New Jersey		
2026	Phil Murphy (D)	
New Mexico		
2027	Michelle Lujan Grisham (D)	
New York		
2027	Kathy Hochul (D)	
North Carolina		
2029	**Josh Stein (D)**	**3,036,034**
	Mark K. Robinson (R)	2,224,955
	Mike Ross (LB)	174,306
	Vinny Smith (Constitution)	54,033
North Dakota		
Dec. 2028	**Kelly Armstrong (R)**	**246,562**
	Merrill Piepkorn (D)	93,862
Ohio		
2027	Mike DeWine (R)	
Oklahoma		
2027	Kevin Stitt (R)	
Oregon		
2027	Tina Kotek (D)	
Pennsylvania		
2027	Josh Shapiro (D)	
Rhode Island		
2027	Dan McKee (D)	
South Carolina		
2027	Henry McMaster (R)	
South Dakota		
2027	Kristi Noem (R)	
Tennessee		
2027	Bill Lee (R)	
Texas		
2027	Greg Abbott (R)	
Utah		
2029	**Spencer J. Cox* (R)**	**508,034**
	Brian Smith King (D)	275,932
	Phil Lyman (write-in)	77,291
Vermont		
2027	**Phil Scott* (R)**	**266,317**
	Esther Charlestin (D)	79,183
Virginia		
2026	Glenn Youngkin (R)	
Washington		
2029	**Bob Ferguson (D)**	**1,460,746**
	Dave Reichert (R)	1,129,854
West Virginia		
2029	**Patrick Morrisey (R)**	**454,021**
	Steve Williams (D)	230,238
Wisconsin		
2027	Tony Evers (D)	
Wyoming		
2027	Mark Gordon (R)	

Governors of U.S. Commonwealths and Territories

Term expires	Governor/candidate	2024 election results
American Samoa		
2029[1]	Nikolao Pula	4,284
	Lemanu Palepoi Mauga	3,660
	Vaitautolu I'aulualo	2,169
Guam		
2027	Lou Leon Guerrero (D)	
Northern Mariana Islands		
2027	Arnold Palacios (I)	
Puerto Rico		
2029	Jenniffer González-Colón (New Progressive)	438,183
	Juan Dalmau Ramírez (PR Ind./Citizen Victory Movement)	364,145
	Jesús Manuel Ortiz González (Popular Democratic)	233,470
	Javier Jiménez Pérez (Project Dignity)	73,613
Virgin Islands		
2027	Albert Bryan (D)	

(1) A runoff between the top two candidates was expected to be held.

CHRONOLOGY OF EVENTS

Nov. 1, 2023, to Oct. 31, 2024

The Chronology of Events reports the top National, International, and General news stories, month by month.

November 2023

National

Hollywood Actors End Strike; Union Autoworkers Ratify New Contracts—SAG-AFTRA, the union representing about 160,000 actors, reached a tentative labor agreement Nov. 8 with major Hollywood film and TV studios, ending a historic 118-day strike that halted most productions in tandem with an earlier Writers Guild of America work stoppage that ended in late Sept. Officially ratified in early Dec. by 78% of voting members, the three-year contract provided new compensation minimums including wages, benefits, and streaming bonuses and, for the first time, some protections against the use of actors' likenesses with AI without consent.

On Nov. 20, the United Auto Workers (UAW) announced its workers at the "Big Three" U.S. auto manufacturers of Ford, GM, and Stellantis (parent company of Dodge, Chrysler, and Jeep) had ratified new contracts that ended a six-week-long targeted strike, the longest auto strike in 25 years. The agreements notably secured raises of at least 25% over 4.5 years. Earlier in Nov., non-union employer Hyundai matched that increase after Honda and Toyota announced smaller wage hikes.

Republican Presidential Field Debates; Trump Draws Ire Over "Vermin" Rhetoric; Democrats Notch Off-Cycle Election Wins—A field of five Republican presidential primary candidates qualified for and appeared in the third GOP debate Nov. 8 in Miami, FL. Poll frontrunner and former Pres. Donald Trump again declined to participate and held a rally in nearby Hialeah. The debate's major focus was foreign policy, and though all candidates unequivocally backed Israel in its war against Hamas, they differed over continuing support for Ukraine against Russia's invasion.

Trump at a political rally in Claremont, NH, on Nov. 11 pledged to "root out" adversaries, who he said "live like vermin" and were more dangerous to the U.S. than its foreign enemies. The rhetoric drew attention and rebuke from some who said his dehumanizing language echoed that used by authoritarian dictators including Hitler and Mussolini.

Ohio voters Nov. 7 overwhelmingly passed a state constitutional amendment securing access to abortion, a notable win for Democrats in the Republican-leaning state. Pro-choice candidates also prevailed in a few key races—Kentucky Gov. Andy Beshear secured reelection, and Virginia Democrats retook the state's House and maintained their Senate majority.

Supreme Court Adopts Code of Conduct—Beset by breach-of-ethics allegations since an Apr. 2023 ProPublica report focused on gifts and vacations accepted by Associate Justice Clarence Thomas, the U.S. Supreme Court Nov. 13 announced it had adopted its first-ever formal code of conduct. The code reportedly reflected accepted practice and largely mirrored existing provisions for lower court judges, with formalized recusal requirements and limits on gifts and engagement in political activities. The code lacked any enforcement mechanism.

Biden Signs Short-Term Spending Bill, Preventing Shutdown—Pres. Joe Biden Nov. 16 signed a temporary spending bill that narrowly averted a government shutdown for the second time in less than two months but set up another funding showdown in Congress in early 2024. Though the bill maintained federal funding at current levels, it did not include a nearly $106 bil emergency package that included additional aid to Ukraine and Israel as well as U.S. southern border operation funding. The GOP-controlled House Nov. 14 passed the measure 336-95 with the support of only 127 Republicans, as far-right members rejected newly installed House Speaker Mike Johnson's (R, LA) plan due to the lack of spending cuts.

FTX Head Convicted of Fraud; OpenAI CEO Ousted, Reinstated; Other Business, Economic News—On Nov. 2, a New York federal jury found Sam Bankman-Fried, founder and CEO of the bankrupt cryptocurrency exchange FTX, guilty of fraud, conspiracy, and money laundering. During the more than four-week trial, U.S. prosecutors offered evidence that Bankman-Fried had plundered $8 bil from customer accounts to purchase real estate and make political donations and high-risk investments; he was sentenced Mar. 28, 2024, to 25 years in prison and ordered to forfeit more than $11 bil. In another blow to the crypto sector, Changpeng Zhao, founder of Binance, the world's largest crypto exchange, pleaded guilty in Nov. to U.S. money laundering charges and agreed to pay $50 mil and step down as CEO. Binance agreed to pay another $4.3 bil in fines. Rideshare tech giants Uber and Lyft agreed in early Nov. to pay $290 mil and $38 mil, respectively, to settle New York State wage theft accusations.

Sam Altman was reinstated Nov. 21 as CEO of the San Francisco-based artificial intelligence firm OpenAI, capping a brief but chaotic power struggle that began after the OpenAI board of directors unexpectedly ousted Altman, an OpenAI cofounder, five days earlier. In the interim, roughly 95% of the company—developer of pioneering tool ChatGPT—signed an open letter threatening to resign.

Inflation fell in Oct. to an annualized 3.2%, according to a Bureau of Labor Statistics (BLS) Consumer Price Index report released Nov. 14; gas prices fell 40 cents Oct. 1-Nov.1 to $3.40/gal, according to the Energy Information Admin. The BLS's monthly employment report Nov. 3 showed the U.S. economy added 150,000 jobs in Oct., as the unemployment rate ticked up 0.1 point to 3.9%. The Dow Jones Industrial Average closed Nov. at 35,950.89, up 8.8% as the S&P 500 similarly grew 8.9% to close the month at 4,567.80; the Nasdaq Composite Index finished Nov. at 14,226.22, a 10.7% gain.

NY Court Reimposes Gag Order on Trump—A New York State appellate court Nov. 30 restored a Manhattan Supreme Court judge's gag order barring former Pres. Donald Trump and his counsel from issuing public statements about court staff in a civil case against him and his company for fraudulent business practices. Before the gag order was suspended Nov. 16, the presiding judge had fined Trump multiple times over disparaging remarks and social media posts Trump made about the court's clerk. According to a court officer, the judge and the clerk had received hundreds of "serious and credible" threats as a result of the posts. Trump had testified in the proceedings Nov. 6, with his witness statement characterized as both meandering and belligerent.

On Dec. 8, an appeals court narrowed but mostly upheld a gag order against Trump in a separate federal election interference case.

International

Militia Forces Kill Hundreds of Non-Combatants in Sudan's Darfur—The UN Refugee Agency (UNHCR) accused the Sudanese paramilitary group Rapid Support Forces (RSF) and other Arab militias battling Sudanese government forces of massacring more than 800 mostly unarmed civilians in an unprovoked multiday attack after taking control Nov. 4 of an army base outside Geneina, capital of Sudan's West Darfur state. Local monitors estimated that collectively 1,300-2,000 people from the Masalit and other non-Arab ethnic groups were killed. Some were attacked while attempting to flee to neighboring Chad, where at least 450,000 had sought refuge from the RSF in recent months. Recent RSF seizure of Darfur territory by early Nov. had secured it de facto control of every state in the region except North Darfur.

Fighting between the RSF and Sudan's military had killed at least 9,000 people and displaced some 5.8 mil, according to the UN, since erupting in Apr. 2023.

Israel's War on Hamas and Gaza Intensifies—The Israeli military's campaign to destroy the terror group Hamas in the Gaza Strip, launched in retaliation for Hamas's Oct. 7 cross-border attack that killed about 1,200 Israelis, had killed more than 10,000 mostly civilians—including more than 4,100 children—in less than a month, Gaza's health ministry said Nov. 6. That same day, the Israel Defense Forces (IDF) said it had completely surrounded Gaza's capital, Gaza City. Gaza's death toll included 15 killed by Nov. 3 airstrikes on an ambulance convoy, which Israeli officials said was actually being used for military purposes (Human Rights Watch said it could not verify Israel's intelligence). A record 101 UN workers were also killed in Gaza by Nov. 13, and health administrators said that 40 patients had died Nov. 11-17 due to lack of power at Al-Shifa hospital, where thousands of displaced Gazans were sheltering. In mid-Nov., IDF troops and tanks raided Al-Shifa, which Israeli officials said Hamas was using as a command center with an underground tunnel network, a claim backed by U.S. intelligence officials. Condemning the raid, the World Health Org. by Nov. 12 had recorded nearly 140 IDF attacks on Gaza health facilities. According to the UN-affiliated NGO Shelter Cluster, airstrikes by Nov. 24 had destroyed or damaged more than 60% of housing structures in Gaza.

Out of some 1.1 mil residents in northern Gaza, 807,000 remained, as of Nov. 11, despite Israel's order to move to southern Gaza to avoid military operations, according to the Palestinian Central Bureau of Statistics. Israel on Nov. 9 began daily four-hour pauses during which it suspended northern military operations to allow safe passage south. However, reports persisted of IDF strikes on areas to which civilians had been ordered to relocate.

As part of a deal negotiated by Egypt, Qatar, and the U.S. that paused fighting for four days beginning Nov. 24 (later extended through Nov. 30), Israel and Hamas released 105 and 240 hostages, respectively. Though UN and aid groups increased humanitarian aid and fuel deliveries during that time, UN officials said far more was needed. Ahead of the truce, the UN said just 10% of needed food supplies were entering from Egypt and that Gazans were drinking contaminated water due to treatment plant shutdowns. Numerous aid organizations and heads of state called for an immediate cease-fire to end the fighting. At the end of Nov., the UN reported that more than 1.8 mil residents—some 80% of Gaza's population—were displaced.

Activists continued to stage protests around the globe; in Washington, DC, tens of thousands advocating for Israel assembled at the National Mall Nov. 14, a week after pro-Palestinian demonstrators gathered there. More than 100 demonstrators demanding a cease-fire were arrested in Chicago Nov. 13. The U.S. House voted Nov. 8 to censure Congress's sole Palestinian American Rep. Rashida Tlaib (D, MI) over perceived anti-Israel rhetoric. Later in Nov., three Palestinian students were injured in Burlington, VT, in what was thought to be a targeted shooting.

Biden-Xi Meeting Produces Military, Fentanyl Deals, But No Breakthrough—U.S. Pres. Joe Biden and Chinese Pres. Xi Jinping met Nov. 15 near San Francisco for four hours of closed-door talks that generated only minor progress toward defusing heightened tensions between the two countries. The leaders' first face-to-face meeting in more than a year facilitated resumption of some communications between their respective militaries (suspended by China in Aug. 2022 after then-House Speaker Nancy Pelosi's visit to Taiwan), a pledge by Xi to curb exports of raw ingredients of the drug fentanyl, and a joint promise to cooperate on lowering emissions of the greenhouse gas methane and to foster global renewable energy. Biden reportedly admonished Xi over China's recent heavy military buildup around Taiwan and repeated the U.S.'s commitment to arm Taiwan against forcible reunification with China.

The talks came as China's economy faced a rare period of stagnation, heightened by high youth unemployment, plummeting foreign investment, and a housing glut.

Right-Wing Populist Wins Argentinian Presidency—Ultraconservative economist Javier Milei easily defeated center-left economy minister Sergio Massa in runoff voting Nov. 19 amid soaring inflation exceeding 140% and a nationwide poverty rate of 40% for the first half of 2023. The bombastic Milei, who drew 55.7% support, had vowed to slash taxes and spending, abolish the country's central bank, switch the national currency to the U.S. dollar, relax gun laws, and work to repeal access to abortion. Milei was sworn in Dec. 10, and by late Dec., demonstrations against his austerity reforms were staged in Buenos Aires.

Russia Restarts Attacks on Kyiv, Putin Pulls Out of Nuclear-Test-Ban Treaty; Other Developments—Russia's bloody invasion of Ukraine continued, with the UN declaring Nov. 21 that more than 10,000 civilians had been killed in the country since Feb. 2022. (The agency advised the actual civilian death toll was likely much higher.) On Nov. 10, Russia's military carried out its first missile attacks against Kyiv in 52 days; most of the projectiles were downed by Ukrainian defenses. Pushing back against Ukraine's largely stalled five-month-old counteroffensive, Russia by late Nov. had increased its push on the industrial city of Avdiivka in Donetsk province, at the cost of heavy troop losses, and on Bakhmut, which it had occupied previously. Despite infighting in U.S. Congress that left continuing financial assistance for Ukraine out of a temporary spending bill, the Pentagon on Nov. 20 announced $100 mil in additional military aid that brought the total since the start of the invasion to more than $44 bil, alongside $35 bil from other allies. Russian Pres. Vladimir Putin on Nov. 2 rescinded Russia's ratification of the Comprehensive Nuclear-Test-Ban Treaty, but Foreign Minister Sergei Ryabkov said Russia would not conduct nuclear weapon tests unless the U.S. did.

Far-Right Achieves Election Win in Netherlands—The far-right party of anti-Islamist lawmaker Geert Wilders pulled off a decisive upset victory Nov. 22 in Dutch snap elections called after the coalition government collapsed in July in a dispute over refugee and asylum-seeker entry policies. Wilders's Freedom Party (PVV), which campaigned on an anti-EU, anti-immigrant stance, secured 37 of 150 seats in Parliament, up 20 from 2021 voting; the runner-up leftist Labour-Green coalition won 25 seats—one more than the conservative People's Party for Freedom and Democracy of incumbent Prime Min. Mark Rutte—and the new center-right New Social Contract (NSC) party won 20. Though analysts remained skeptical that Wilders could assemble a governing coalition, the results nevertheless were seen as a continuation of the far-right's recent rise in Europe, which also included election successes in Finland and Italy.

Iran-Allied Attacks on U.S. Troops in Middle East Force Response—Iranian-backed militias launched more than 70 drone, rocket, and missile attacks against U.S. troops in Iraq and Syria Oct. 17-Nov. 30. Most attacks were reportedly intercepted by the U.S.'s military or did not attain their targets, but a small number inflicted mostly minor injuries on more than 60 personnel. In retaliation, the U.S. directed fighter jet and other strategic attacks against militants and targets in those two countries, including some linked to Iran's Islamic Revolutionary Guard. Iran-backed Houthi rebels in Yemen, who had fired multiple attack drones across the Red Sea at Israel since Oct. 19, claimed responsibility for downing an unmanned U.S. Reaper drone Nov. 8 in international waters off the Yemeni coast. Houthi rebels on Nov. 19 seized a cargo ship reportedly partially owned by an Israeli billionaire; the UK-registered ship was taken to a Yemeni port, and its 25-member, non-Israeli crew was taken hostage.

General

Texas Rangers Win World Series—The Texas Rangers won the World Series over the Arizona Diamondbacks in a 5-0 Game 5 shutout Nov. 1 at Chase Field in Phoenix, AZ, in just the third-ever World Series matchup between two wild card teams. The victory brought the Rangers their first championship in the franchise's 63 seasons, ending MLB's second-longest active title drought behind only the Cleveland Guardians (75 seasons). Rangers shortstop Corey Seager, who hit 6 for 21 with three home runs and six RBI, was named World Series MVP, making him the fourth player to claim the award multiple times.

Nepal Earthquake Kills Over 150—A magnitude 5.6 earthquake struck northwestern Nepal's Karnali Province late evening, Nov. 3, killing at least 157 people and injuring more than 300 others. Epicentered in Jajarkot District—where more than 100 of the deaths occurred—at the relatively shallow depth of

11 mi, the quake generated tremors that could reportedly be felt in India's capital over 500 miles away.

December 2023

National

House Expels GOP Rep. Santos; Campus Antisemitism Committee Hearings Draw Attention; Other Congress News—The U.S. House of Representatives on Dec. 1 expelled Rep. George Santos (R, NY), ending an 11-month tenure marred by scandal since post-election reporting revealed he largely fabricated his biography including his education, work, and financial history. In May, Santos was indicted on 13 federal counts stemming from accusations he embezzled from his campaign, fraudulently obtained unemployment funds, and lied on House financial disclosure forms. Ten charges were added in Oct., following allegations he stole campaign donors' identities and charged their credit cards without their knowledge or consent. The House Ethics Committee Nov. 16 released a damning report of his alleged wrongdoing. The bipartisan 311-114 vote to expel Santos reduced the GOP's already thin majority and made him only the sixth House member to be expelled in U.S. history. The House Dec. 7 also voted to censure Rep. Jamaal Bowman (D, NY) for setting off a fire alarm in the Capitol complex in late Sept. before a scheduled vote on a spending bill. Bowman said he did so accidentally.

During a heated House committee hearing Dec. 5, the presidents of Harvard, the Univ. of Pennsylvania, and MIT condemned antisemitism but drew criticism for indirect, legalistic responses to questioning over their administrations' response to activist behavior on campus since the Israel-Hamas war began in Oct. Penn president M. Elizabeth Magill resigned four days later; Harvard's first Black president, Claudine Gay, who also faced plagiarism accusations from conservative critics, resigned Jan. 2, 2024.

Sen. Tommy Tuberville (R, AL) Dec. 5 ended a roughly 10-month blockade of promotions for senior military officers—by then numbering about 440—triggered by his opposition to the Pentagon's payment of travel costs for abortions. Though he said he would continue to delay the promotion of 11 four-star officers, the Senate confirmed them by voice vote Dec. 19.

Japan's Nippon Steel to Acquire U.S. Steel; Tesla Faces Mammoth EV Recall; Other Economic News—Capping a four-month-long auction process, 122-year-old U.S. Steel agreed Dec. 18 to acquisition by Japan's largest steel producer, Nippon Steel, for $14.9 bil. Nippon executives said they would maintain U.S. Steel's brand and its Pittsburgh headquarters and abide by existing labor agreements, but the United Steelworkers Union (USW) leadership voiced opposition to the deal and implored U.S. regulators to scrutinize it.

Following a two-year investigation, federal regulators Dec. 13 announced EV maker Tesla had agreed to recall more than 2 mil vehicles—nearly all its cars on the road in the U.S.—over inadequate protections against driver misuse of Tesla's so-called Autopilot system.

The U.S.'s annual inflation rate dropped slightly in Nov. to 3.1% according to a Bureau of Labor Statistics report released Dec. 12. The Federal Reserve Bank on Dec. 13 said it would maintain its benchmark interest rate at 5.25%-5.5% but forecast three rate cuts in 2024. That same day, the Dow Jones Industrial Average closed above 37,000 (37,090.24) for the first time. The Dow closed Dec. at 37,689.54, up 4.8% from Nov. as the S&P 500 gained 4.4% to finish the month at 4,769.83; the Nasdaq Composite Index closed Dec. at 15,011.35, a 5.5% gain. Though U.S. stocks overall dipped on their final day of trading, they rebounded strongly over the year from 2022, with the Dow up 13.7%; tech-heavy Nasdaq up 43.4%; and the S&P 500 up 24.2% in 2023.

The U.S. economy added 199,000 jobs in Nov., exceeding expectations, with the unemployment rate at 3.7%. In its third and final estimate for the third quarter of 2023, the Bureau of Economic Analysis said that U.S. GDP grew at an annualized rate of 4.9%, compared to a 2.1% increase in the previous quarter.

Colorado Supreme Court Declares Trump Ineligible for Primary Ballot—Colorado's Supreme Court Dec. 19 deemed former president and current Republican frontrunner Donald Trump constitutionally ineligible to run in the state's presidential primary after determining that his role in the attack on the U.S. Capitol on Jan. 6, 2021, constituted insurrection. The 4-3 decision among the justices, all appointed by Democratic governors, was reportedly the first to bar a presidential candidate under an anti-insurrectionist clause in the 14th Amendment adopted post-Civil War to prevent secessionists from returning to office. The court, however, stayed the decision awaiting its certain appeal to the U.S. Supreme Court. By the end of Feb. 2024, challenges against Trump's candidacy were filed in at least 36 other states.

Jury Finds Giuliani Owes Nearly $150 Million Over False Election Claims—A federal judge Dec. 20 ordered Rudy Giuliani, ex-lawyer and adviser to former Pres. Trump, to immediately pay $146 mil (down only slightly from the more than $148 mil awarded by a jury) for publicly accusing two Fulton County, GA, poll workers of manipulating ballots during the 2020 election. Giuliani's unsupported claims, repeated by then-Pres. Trump, had quickly drawn a barrage of racist and violent threats against the pair, a Black mother and daughter, by Trump supporters. Giuliani filed for bankruptcy Dec. 21.

The U.S. Supreme Court Dec. 22 declined special counsel Jack Smith's request to expedite its ruling on Trump's claim of presidential immunity for actions pertaining to the Justice Dept.'s election obstruction case against him.

International

Guinea-Bissau's President Dissolves Parliament, Citing Attempted Coup; Deadly Gunmen and Drone Attacks in Nigeria; Other West Africa News—Guinea-Bissau's Pres. Umaro Sissoco Embaló dissolved the opposition-dominated parliament Dec. 4 in the wake of violence Nov. 30-Dec.1 between National Guard and presidential forces that killed two people, which Embaló labeled a failed coup. Later in the month, he dismissed his prime minister and appointed a replacement. Embaló previously dissolved parliament in May 2022, three months after withstanding an attempt to overthrow him.

On Dec. 3, Nigeria's army carried out what it said was an accidental drone strike on a Muslim celebration in the north-central state of Kaduna, killing at least 85 civilians in Tudun Biri village. Gunmen struck 17 isolated communities in Nigeria's north-central Plateau state Dec. 23-24, burning homes and killing at least 140 villagers, according to the country's Amnesty International office. Though no group claimed responsibility for the attacks in the state's mainly Christian Bokkos and Barkin-Ladi areas, local officials blamed predominantly Muslim Fulani ethnic herders, who were increasingly in conflict with farmers over land and water resources.

The military junta ruling Nigeria's northern neighbor, Niger, Dec. 4 terminated two EU defense and security missions over economic sanctions from the EU and U.S. Around the same time, it reportedly agreed to increase military cooperation with Russia, and in mid-Mar. 2024, formally ended its military relationship with the U.S. The UN on Dec. 11 ended its 10-year-long peacekeeping mission in adjoining Mali—the agency's second-deadliest mission ever after Lebanon, with some 310 fatalities—roughly six months after the military government ordered its departure.

Israel Broadens Attack on Hamas in Gaza—Israel's military campaign against Hamas in the Gaza Strip expanded to southern areas of the enclave Dec. 4 with heavy airstrikes around the city of Khan Yunis—previously a "safe zone" for fleeing northern residents—as Israel Defense Forces (IDF) advanced. Residents heeding IDF warnings hastily fled to the southernmost city of Rafah, sparking an observation from UN Sec.-Gen. António Guterres that Gazans have "nowhere safe to go and very little to survive on."

Casualties continued to mount following the collapse of a seven-day truce ending early Dec. 1—strikes across the territory along with fighting killed at least 316 people over just 24 hours Dec. 2-3, Gaza's Ministry of Health said. By Dec. 20, the ministry said Gaza's death toll since the start of the conflict had surpassed 20,000, and critics decried the IDF's targeting of residential neighborhoods, refugee camps, and hospitals. The World Health Org. said that only 4 of 24 northern Gaza hospitals were even partially operating as of Dec. 27. The U.S. on Dec. 8 was the sole UN Security Council member to vote against a resolution calling for an immediate cease-fire in Gaza (the UK abstained), claiming that a cease-fire would allow Hamas to regroup and re-arm. Nevertheless, U.S. Pres. Joe Biden the following week said Israel was losing support over its "indiscriminate bombing," a position bolstered Dec. 14 by U.S. reports that 40%-45% of the 29,000 air-to-ground munitions Israel had fired into Gaza since Oct. were unguided "dumb bombs."

The IDF, which in early Dec. claimed to have killed at least 5,000 Hamas militants since Oct. 7, drew backlash after admitting to accidentally fatally shooting three Israeli hostages as they waved a white flag in Gaza City Dec. 15. That same day, Israel agreed to open a second border crossing into Gaza to accommodate additional aid trucks; according to a UN report released Dec. 21, over 576,000 people, more than a quarter of Gaza's population, were starving. The UN decried a "rapidly deteriorating human rights situation" in the occupied West Bank, where it said IDF and settlers had killed some 300 Palestinians since Oct. 7. By Dec. 24 more than 150 IDF troops had been killed in Gaza since the start of the ground operation in late Oct. Citing Israeli officials, the UN in late Dec. said 128 hostages remained captive in Gaza.

Ukraine Pleas for Aid Amid Lagging International Support; Other Ukraine-Russia Developments—Ukrainian Pres. Volodymyr Zelenskyy on Dec. 12 made his third visit to Washington, DC, to plead Congress for passage of additional military aid to thwart Russia's ongoing invasion; a $61 bil aid package was blocked by Senate Republicans demanding concessions over U.S. southern border security and immigration policy. Pres. Biden Dec. 27 announced $250 mil in additional Ukraine military assistance, bringing the total since Feb. 2022 to more than $44 bil. In mid-Dec., Hungary's right-wing president Viktor Orbán blocked $54 bil in nonmilitary aid from the EU after the bloc's leaders agreed to open accession negotiations with Ukraine.

Though analysts noted that Ukraine's roughly six-month-old counteroffensive had essentially stalled, with its military reclaiming roughly 200 sq mi in 2023, Russia continued to suffer heavy fatalities; a declassified U.S. intelligence report made public Dec. 12 stated that Russia had lost—due to deaths or injuries—87% of the 360,000 troops it had at the start of the invasion along with two-thirds of its tanks. Adding to a string of recent successful attacks on Russia's Black Sea fleet, a late-night missile strike by Ukraine Dec. 26 sank the large landing ship *Novocherkaask*, injuring 23 sailors on board and leaving 33 others missing, according to the independent Russian media outlet Astra.

Former high-ranking FBI counterintelligence agent Charles McGonigal was sentenced Dec. 14 to 4+ years in prison for conspiring with a Russian oligarch in violation of U.S. sanctions. In Feb. 2024, he was sentenced to an additional 28 months for hiding at least $225,000 that he received from an Albanian agent, bringing his total sentence to 6.5 years.

UN Climate Delegates Agree to "Transition Away" From Fossil Fuels—Diplomats representing nearly 200 countries at the 2023 UN Climate Change Conference in Dubai, United Arab Emirates, reached a historic yet contentious agreement Dec. 13 for nations to move away from fossil fuels to prevent the most extreme effects of climate change. It was the first time nations collectively made such a pledge in the UN's 28 years of global climate negotiations. Though the deal requires "transitioning away" from fossil fuels in "a just, orderly, and equitable manner" that will achieve net-zero emissions of greenhouse gases by 2050, it fell short of a complete "phase-out" sought by over 100 countries, including the U.S.

The summit's agreement came as the world ended its warmest year on record, at 2.12°F over the 20th-century average of 57.0°F, according to NOAA.

Houthi Actions Disrupt Shipping in Retaliation for Israeli War on Hamas—Military officials said U.S. Navy helicopters on Dec. 31 sunk three Iranian-backed Houthi boats in the Red Sea while responding to a distress call from a large cargo ship—operated by Denmark's Maersk—that was under attack by the rebels. The action, which killed at least 10 Houthi fighters according to the Yemen-based Islamist group, appeared to mark the first deadly confrontation between U.S. forces and Houthis in the latter's ongoing disruption of the heavily trafficked trade route since Israel's military campaign against Gaza began. Houthi rebels by Dec. 19 had carried out 100 or more maritime attacks by drones or missiles on at least a dozen different merchant or commercial ships, the Pentagon said. According to Germany's Kiel Institute for World Economy, the quantity of shipping containers passing through the Suez Canal via the Red Sea fell by more than half in Dec.; some 12% of global trade passes through the Suez Canal annually. A U.S.-led coalition aimed at protecting Red Sea shipping was announced Dec. 18, though only the U.S. and the UK had committed ships by the end of the month.

General

FDA Approves First CRISPR Gene Editing Treatment—The FDA on Dec. 8 greenlit the first gene editing therapy for use in humans, to potentially serve as a treatment to manage symptoms of sickle cell disease, a group of inherited and often debilitating red blood cell disorders that primarily affects Black individuals. The breakthrough treatment, developed jointly by Vertex Pharmaceuticals and Switzerland's CRISPR Therapeutics, utilizes the Nobel Prize-winning gene-editing tool known as CRISPR and will be marketed under the brand name Casgevy. Casgevy's current reported price tag of $2.2 mil per patient would likely make it inaccessible to many.

Columbus Takes MLS Cup—The Columbus Crew edged defending champion Los Angeles FC, 2-1, at Lower.com Field in Columbus, OH, Dec. 9, to win their third MLS Cup. Crew forward Cucho Hernández scored the opening goal of the match in the 33rd min., followed just four min. later by midfielder teammate Yaw Yeboah; LAFC remained scoreless until the 74th min. Earning MLS Cup MVP, Hernández notched five goals over six postseason matches—tying him for most in an MLS playoff series—and two assists.

China Quake Kills Over 140—Just before midnight Dec. 18, a moderately powerful earthquake jolted a remote and mountainous area of northwest China, killing at least 149 people, the highest quake-related death toll in the country since 2013. Epicentered in Gansu province about 60 mi SW of Lanzhou City, the earthquake was measured at magnitude 5.9 according to the U.S. Geological Survey, versus the 6.2 magnitude recorded by the China Earthquake Networks Center.

Shooter Kills 14 at Czech University—A lone gunman opened fire at Charles University in Prague Dec. 21, fatally shooting 14 people, including two staff, before dying by suicide in what was reportedly Czechia's deadliest mass killing since it became an independent state in 1993. Police believed the shooter, 24-year-old postgraduate student David Kozák, also killed his father that same day and murdered a man and his two-month-old daughter in a wooded park Dec. 15, according to a handwritten confession found in Kozák's home. In Mar. 2024, Czech Pres. Petr Pavel signed new legislation requiring more frequent medical examinations for gun owners. Kozák reportedly held a permit for eight firearms and had no criminal record.

January 2024

National

Boeing Plane Door Blows off Midflight, Prompting Investigation—An Alaska Airlines Boeing 737 Max 9 made an emergency landing at Portland Intl. Airport in Portland, OR, Jan. 5

after a door panel fell off the plane about 20 min. after takeoff. The aircraft door was found to be missing four bolts, and more than 170 Boeing planes were temporarily grounded by the FAA to undergo inspections. No injuries were reported among passengers, but the incident intensified scrutiny of the aerospace giant, which had previously admitted responsibility for faulty control systems that led to two 737 Max 8 aircraft crashes that killed 346 people total in Indonesia (2018) and Ethiopia (2019). Later in Jan., an engine on a Boeing 747-8 cargo jet caught fire shortly after takeoff, and a Delta Boeing 757 lost its nose tire while taxiing in Atlanta.

Responding to pressure from federal regulators, Boeing in late Mar. 2024 announced a leadership overhaul—CEO Dave Calhoun, in the position since Jan. 2020, would leave before the end of 2024; board chair Larry Kellner would not seek reelection; and the head of the commercial plane unit would depart immediately.

Trump Dominates Early Republican Presidential Contests; Biden Wins New Hampshire; More Election Developments—Former Pres. Donald Trump formalized his status as the frontrunner for the 2024 GOP presidential nomination Jan. 15, handily winning the Iowa caucuses with 51.0% support over closest competitors Florida Gov. Ron DeSantis (21.3%) and former UN Ambassador Nikki Haley (19.1%). Entrepreneur Vivek Ramaswamy, who drew 7.6%, suspended his campaign that same day, followed by DeSantis on Jan. 21; both endorsed Trump. On Jan. 23, Trump came out on top in the New Hampshire primary, securing a 54.3%-43.2% win over Haley, the only other remaining major candidate from an initial field of 13. Others formerly vying for the GOP nomination who had already exited the race included former Vice Pres. Mike Pence, Oct. 28, 2023; Sen. Tim Scott (SC), Nov. 12; North Dakota Gov. Doug Burgum, Dec. 4; former New Jersey Gov. Chris Christie, Jan. 10; and former Arkansas Gov. Asa Hutchinson, Jan. 16.

Though Pres. Joe Biden's name did not appear on the ballot for New Hampshire's Democratic primary, also held on Jan. 23, he nevertheless drew 63.9% of write-in votes, beating Rep. Dean Phillips (MN), who received 19.6%. Biden chose not to submit his name for the ballot after state party officials refused to abide by the national party's new primary schedule, which had the first nominating contest taking place in South Carolina in Feb.

Federal Judge Blocks JetBlue-Spirit Merger; Other Business, Economic News—Citing reduced competition, a Massachusetts federal judge Jan. 17 sided with the Justice Dept. in preventing JetBlue's planned $3.8 bil acquisition of Spirit Airlines. JetBlue formally scrapped the proposed deal in early Mar.

The U.S.'s annualized inflation rate was 3.4% in Dec. 2023, according to a Bureau of Labor Statistics (BLS) report released Jan. 11. Despite the slight increase over Nov. (3.1%), it was a significant drop from Dec. 2022's year-over-year inflation rate of 6.5%.

Finishing Jan. at 4,845.65, the S&P 500 gained 1.6% from Dec. The Dow Jones Industrial Average closed the month at 38,150.30, up 1.2% from Dec., and the Nasdaq Composite Index ended Jan. at 15,164.01, a 1.0% gain. The BLS reported Jan. 5 that the U.S. added a better-than-forecast 216,000 jobs in Dec. as the unemployment rate held at 3.7%, bringing the total number of jobs created in 2023 to roughly 2.7 mil.

Jury Orders Trump to Pay $83 Million to Sex Assault Accuser—A federal jury in New York on Jan. 26 ordered former Pres. Donald Trump to pay writer E. Jean Carroll $83.3 mil in total damages for repeatedly defaming her on social media after she publicly accused him—in 2019, while he was president—of raping her in a Manhattan department store in the mid-1990s. Trump has been accused of sexual assault or misconduct by at least 25 other women. The judgment followed a federal civil jury's verdict in May 2023 that found Trump liable for assaulting Carroll and separate charges of defaming her in the lead up to the trial; it awarded her $5 mil. Both cases remained under appeal.

International

ISIS Bombings Kill More Than 80 in Iran—Iranian officials said two blasts killed at least 84 people in Kerman during a Jan. 3 ceremony commemorating the fourth anniversary of the death of Maj. Gen. Qassem Soleimani, a senior commander in Iran's Islamic Revolutionary Guard, by a targeted U.S. drone strike. The next day, the Sunni extremist group Islamic State claimed responsibility for the pair of suicide bombings, which an Iranian official said occurred roughly 20 min. apart near Soleimani's grave. Later in the month, the *Wall Street Journal* reported that a U.S. official, speaking anonymously, said the U.S. had privately warned Iran of an imminent attack by Islamic State's Afghan affiliate, ISIS-Khorasan.

U.S., UK Launch Attacks on Houthis in Yemen, Citing Hostile Disruption of Shipping—The U.S. and UK on Jan. 11 carried out their first direct strikes against Iran-backed Houthi rebel targets in Yemen in response to Houthi drone and missile attacks on international commercial ships in the Red Sea and Gulf of Aden—numbering at least 27 since Nov. 19, according to the White House—in ostensible protest of Israel's war on Gaza. (U.S. Navy ships intercepted most of the Houthi strikes.) The U.S.-UK strikes on 28 targets were supported by Australia, Bahrain, Canada, and the Netherlands in the form of logistics and intelligence. According to a Houthi spokesperson, who vowed revenge, at least five people were killed. A lesser number of joint U.S.-UK strikes on Jan. 22 hit anti-ship missiles and radars, among other targets, in what was reportedly the U.S.'s eighth round of strikes against the Houthis that month. According to the Biden administration, more than 2,000 ships had rerouted thousands of miles to avoid the region due to the threat of attacks.

Progressive Guatemalan President Inaugurated Amid Strong Resistance—Liberal anti-corruption candidate Bernardo Arévalo was sworn in as Guatemala's president shortly after midnight Jan. 15 following a nine-hour delay. Instigated by the country's opposition-dominated Congress, this delay capped repeated attempts to suspend Arévalo's progressive Movimiento Semilla (Seed Movement) party and block him from office despite his decisive electoral win in an Aug. 2023 runoff. Among other maneuvers, anti-Arévalo lawmakers in early Dec. attempted to remove top electoral court judges in an apparent effort to install replacements opposed to his election, and the attorney general accused Arévalo, without evidence, of committing election fraud.

Palestinian Death Toll Surpasses 25,000 as IDF Surrounds Khan Younis; Israel Supreme Court Overturns Disputed Judiciary Reforms; Other Israel-Gaza News—The Israel Defense Forces (IDF) said 21 IDF soldiers were killed in central Gaza, Jan. 22, after a grenade launched by Hamas triggered explosives the soldiers had rigged in two buildings. The buildings were being demolished as part of a plan to create a controversial "buffer zone"—intended to protect Israel from future assaults—inside the enclave. The attack, along with three other soldiers killed in other fighting in Gaza, marked the deadliest day for Israel since Hamas's bloody Oct. 7 assault, and brought the number of Israeli soldiers killed since the start of their ground operation to 221. Prime Min. Benjamin Netanyahu vowed Israel would continue until it had achieved "absolute victory" over Hamas, and the IDF announced it had surrounded the southern city of Khan Younis.

Outcry over collateral devastation from Israeli's ongoing offensive against Hamas continued as Gaza's health ministry reported Jan. 24 that at least 210 people were killed in Gaza in the last 24 hours, bringing the total since Oct. 7 to at least 25,700, including at least 10,000 children. A UN official said Israeli tank fire hit a UN training center in Khan Younis, where at least 800 displaced persons had sought shelter, killing nine. Expressing their frustration with the Israeli government's failure to free roughly 130 hostages still held by Hamas, some 120,000 people—according to organizers—participated in a 24-hour mass demonstration in Tel Aviv beginning Jan. 13, the 100th day of the war.

Hezbollah militants allied with Hamas in neighboring Lebanon continued to trade airstrikes with Israel's military, intensifying fears of a wider war in the region. A drone strike not claimed by Israel killed Saleh al-Arouri, deputy leader of Hamas, and six others in a Beirut neighborhood, Jan. 2. By Jan. 21, strikes on southern Lebanon had killed at least 25 civilians, according to the UN.

On Jan. 1, Israel's Supreme Court narrowly overturned a controversial law passed in July 2023 that limited the court's own power to block government appointments or decisions. The law in question generated months of angry protests in Israel and criticism from Western allies.

Russia Faults Ukraine in Aircraft Crash; Ukraine Strikes Infrastructure Targets Inside Russia; Other Ukraine Invasion News—Russia's defense ministry accused Ukraine of shooting down an Ilyushin Il-76 military transport aircraft Jan. 24 in Russia's Belgorod region, killing all 74 people onboard, including 65 Ukrainian prisoners of war. Ukraine did not confirm or deny it downed the plane and appeared to dispute the assertion regarding the POWs; credible media outlets also could not confirm it. On Jan. 3, 230 Ukrainian POWs had reportedly been swapped for 248 Russians in what was said to be the largest exchange since the start of Russia's invasion in Feb. 2022.

Ukraine reported it had employed a drone strike Jan. 18 on an oil terminal outside of St. Petersburg, roughly 530 mi north of the Ukrainian border; Russia countered that it had downed the drone, the remnants of which started the facility ablaze. Suspected Ukrainian drone attacks also hit, Jan. 19, an oil storage center in Klintsy, about 40 mi over the Russian border, and Jan. 20, a natural gas terminal 70 mi west of St. Petersburg that ignited a large fire. Ukraine denied responsibility for an attack Jan. 21 on a market in the Russian-controlled city of Donetsk that killed at least 27 people.

Iran-Backed Strike Kills Three U.S. Troops in Jordan—A drone strike in Jordan on the Syrian border killed three U.S. soldiers and injured more than 40 other service members early morning Jan. 28. According to the Pentagon, roughly 160 attacks by Iran-linked militia on U.S. military had occurred since the start of the Israel-Gaza War Oct. 7. The U.S. launched 85 retaliatory airstrikes Feb. 2 against the Iranian Islamic Revolutionary Guard Corps and other affiliated targets in Syria and Iraq. The U.S. also carried out strikes against militia in Iraq following a large missile and rocket attack Jan. 20 on Al-Asad Airbase in western Iraq that left at least four U.S. troops with brain injuries.

Iraqi Prime Min. Mohammed Shia al-Sudani in early Jan. called for an end to the U.S.-led military coalition in Iraq formed in 2014 to help fight the Sunni extremist group ISIS. The first formal talks with U.S. military officials over the matter were held Jan. 27 in Baghdad. (There were about 2,500 U.S. troops deployed in Iraq and 900 in Syria as of Jan.)

General

Japan Quake Kills Over 200—A magnitude 7.6 earthquake struck central Japan's Noto Peninsula Jan. 1, killing more than 230 people and shifting parts of the coast upward as much as 13 ft. Epicentered less than 5 mi north of Suzu, the quake was the most powerful to impact mainland Japan since 2011. Japan estimated infrastructure damage at up to $17.6 bil.

***Oppenheimer*, *Poor Things* Big Winners at Golden Globes**—International journalists awarded best drama film to biopic *Oppenheimer* at a revamped 81st Golden Globe Awards ceremony in Beverly Hills, CA, Jan. 7. *Oppenheimer* drew four other trophies, including best dramatic film actor, won by Cillian Murphy. Lily Gladstone became the first Indigenous woman to receive the award for best dramatic film actress, for *Killers of the Flower Moon*. Best musical/comedy motion picture went to *Poor Things*, and its star Emma Stone took home best actress; Paul Giamatti in *The Holdovers* won the corresponding best actor trophy. HBO's *Succession* won best TV drama, and FX's *The Bear* earned best musical/comedy series.

Hosted by comedian Jo Koy, the ceremony was under new ownership after controversy over financial improprieties and a lack of diversity among the Hollywood Foreign Press Association (HFPA). Dissolved in 2023, the HFPA was replaced by a notably more diverse group of 300 journalists.

Michigan Wins College Football Championship—The Univ. of Michigan Wolverines vanquished the Univ. of Washington Huskies, 34-13, at NRG Stadium in Houston, TX, Jan. 9, to win the College Football Playoff title. Wolverines running back Blake Corum was named the game's offensive MVP after rushing for 134 yards and two touchdowns. The Michigan victory—their 12th national championship and first since 1997—capped an undefeated season tested by head coach Jim Harbaugh's cumulative six-game suspension over a sign-stealing scandal and allegations that staff violated an NCAA-imposed ban on in-person recruiting activities during the COVID-19 pandemic.

***Succession*, *The Bear* Win Big at Strike-Delayed Emmys**—HBO's *Succession* won its third Emmy for outstanding TV drama series at the 75th Primetime Emmy Awards held in Los Angeles on Jan. 15, delayed by four months due to the writers' and actors' strikes. *Succession* stars Kieran Culkin and Sarah Snook also won outstanding actor and actress in a drama series, respectively. FX's *The Bear* took home outstanding comedy series, and its star Jeremy Allen White won outstanding lead actor in a comedy series.

Japan Lands First Lunar Probe—Japan's space agency (JAXA) successfully soft-landed an unmanned spacecraft on the moon Jan. 19, making it just the fifth country to achieve a moon landing. JAXA was lauded for landing its truck-size craft just 180 feet from its target—albeit upside down—reportedly the most precise lunar touchdown ever.

U.S. Winter Storms Kill Scores—Severe winter weather killed 95 people across the U.S., many due to hypothermia and vehicle accidents, according to a CBS News tally for the week ending Jan. 22. Tennessee officials that same day revised their own death toll up to 36 deaths, the most of any state, pushing the total over 100. Frigid temperatures caused water pipes to burst in Memphis, and a boil-water advisory was put in place for over 600,000 people.

Baseball Hall of Fame Elects Four—The Baseball Writers' Assn. of America elected Adrián Beltré, Joe Mauer, and Todd Helton to the Baseball Hall of Fame Jan. 23. Beltré, with 477 home runs and five Gold Glove awards at third base, was selected nearly unanimously in his first year of eligibility. Six-time All-Star Mauer, only the third catcher elected to Cooperstown on the first ballot, amassed 2,123 hits over 15 seasons with the Minnesota Twins. Colorado Rockies power hitter Helton was chosen in his sixth year of eligibility. Three-time Manager of the Year Jim Leyland was elected Dec. 3 by the Hall's Contemporary Baseball Era Non-Players Committee.

Sabalenka, Sinner Take Australian Open Titles—No. 2-seed defending champion Aryna Sabalenka of Belarus overwhelmed China's Zheng Qinwen, the No. 12-seed, in just 76 min. (6-3, 6-2) in the Australian Open women's singles final at Rod Laver Arena in Melbourne, Jan. 27. It was the second Grand Slam singles title for Sabalenka. The next evening, No. 4-seed Jannik Sinner outlasted No. 3-seed Daniil Medvedev of Russia (3-6, 3-6, 6-4, 6-4, 6-3), rallying from two sets down to win his first Grand Slam singles title. The 22-year-old became the first Italian man to secure a Grand Slam since 1976.

February 2024

National

Special Counsel's Biden Mishandled Documents Probe Finds Charges Not Warranted; Other Related Developments—The special counsel appointed after aides to Pres. Joe Biden reported they had found classified documents at his Delaware residence and his private office in Washington, DC, released its final report Feb. 8. The yearlong probe did not recommend charges against Biden but cast the president's actions in a negative light, concluding that he had "willfully" improperly retained classified documents related to national security and shared classified information with his ghostwriter. The report also noted "significant limitations" in the 81-year-old Biden's memory during interviews, which the president hotly denied in a press conference that same day. Nevertheless, the special counsel's report highlighted differences between Biden's case and former Pres. Donald Trump's own alleged mishandling of classified documents, including the latter's repeated refusal to turn over those files when requested.

U.S. Special Counsel David Weiss, a Trump appointee, announced charges Feb. 15 against former FBI informant Alexander Smirnov, whom Weiss accused of fabricating false allegations that the Bidens received bribes from a Ukrainian energy company.

House Republicans Impeach Homeland Security Secretary Amid Border Policy Debate; Other Congress News—In their second attempt, the GOP-controlled House impeached Homeland Security Sec. Alejandro Mayorkas Feb. 13 by a razor-thin 214-213 margin, making him the first cabinet official to be impeached since 1876. The impeachment articles charged Mayorkas with failing to enforce laws deterring undocumented migrants from entering the U.S. and with lying to Congress when he said the Southern border was "secure." Democrats and other critics dismissed the charges as representing partisan policy disagreements that did not meet the constitutional impeachment threshold of "high crimes and misdemeanors." The Senate in mid-Apr. rejected the articles by a 51-49 vote.

The House's action followed a record 2.48 mil U.S. Customs and Border Protection encounters with migrants at the U.S.-Mexico border in FY2023. A handful of Democratic-run cities far removed from the border continued to see high numbers of arriving migrants and asylum seekers, some of whom were sent there by Texas Gov. Greg Abbott (R) or other border state governors. For example, New York City had received some 175,000 migrants since spring 2022, and Chicago had received 37,000 since Aug. 2022. The Senate's long-negotiated, bipartisan border deal was blocked in early Feb. by Republican lawmakers after former Pres. Donald Trump, the GOP's presumptive presidential nominee, voiced his opposition to it.

Tom Suozzi (D) won a special election Feb. 13 for the House seat vacated when Rep. George Santos (R, NY) was expelled, shrinking Republicans' majority. In late Feb., 82-year-old Sen. Mitch McConnell (R, KY), the chamber's longest-serving party leader, announced he would step down from leadership in Nov.

New York Judge Imposes $355 Million Fine on Trump—A New York Supreme Court judge Feb. 16 ordered former Pres. Donald Trump to pay $354.9 mil in penalties (plus nearly $100 mil in pre-judgment interest) related to charges he and his Trump Organization vastly inflated the values of real estate assets to secure more favorable loans. The judge added more than $9 mil in fines total to be paid by Trump's adult sons Eric and Donald Jr. and former Trump Org. CFO Allen Weisselberg. Trump was also barred from serving as an officer of any New York company for three years, and his sons were banned for two years each. The 11-week trial featured testimony from 40 witnesses, including Trump, who was fined twice by the judge for his conduct during the trial.

Alabama High Court Declares Frozen Embryos Children, Endangering Access to Fertility Services—Alabama's Supreme Court drew immediate criticism after it ruled Feb. 16 that frozen fertilized embryos are legally children. The ruling held potential for broad and immediate impacts on the legal and medical systems, including leaving medical personnel criminally liable if they destroyed unwanted embryos, a common practice at fertility clinics as part of in vitro fertilization (IVF) treatments. Less than a week later, clinics in the state suspended IVF services. On Mar. 6, Alabama Gov. Kay Ivey (R) signed a bill that provided clinics with immunity from criminal and civil prosecution but did not address frozen embryos' legal rights.

Capital One Plans to Acquire Discover; FTC Seeks to Block Supermarket Merger; Other Business News—Banking giant Capital One Feb. 19 made public its proposed acquisition of Discover Financial for more than $35 bil. Expected to face heavy scrutiny from federal regulators, the merger would create the country's largest credit card lender if approved. The Federal Trade Commission cited antitrust concerns when it filed suit Feb. 26 to block supermarket chain Kroger's planned $24.6 bil buyout of Albertsons.

The S&P 500 closed above 5,000 for the first time Feb. 9, at 5,026.61; analysts credited optimism over artificial intelligence (AI) stocks. Finishing the month at 5,096.27, the S&P 500 gained 5.2% from Jan. as the Dow Jones Industrial Average closed Feb. at 38,996.39, up 2.2%; the Nasdaq Composite Index finished at 16,091.92, a 6.1% gain.

According to industry analysts, companies' prioritization of AI, along with rising interest rates, resulted in continuing job cuts in the tech sector; nearly 40,000 tech jobs were shed over the first two months of 2024 after more than 262,000 jobs had been cut in 2023, according to layoffs.fyi. The Bureau of Labor Statistics reported Feb. 2 that the U.S. economy added 353,000 jobs in Jan. as the unemployment rate held at 3.7%, the 24th straight month under 4%. The U.S.'s annualized inflation rate was 3.1% in Jan., compared to 3.4% in Dec. 2023, according to a BLS report released Feb. 13.

International

Pakistani Opposition Wins Election Amid Violence, Vote Rigging Allegations; Other Pakistan News—Opposition candidates in Pakistan allied with jailed former Prime Min. Imran Khan secured the most seats in elections held Feb. 8. Even so, Khan's PTI party was excluded from the fragile governing coalition that returned military-backed Shehbaz Sharif to the prime minister position in early Mar. PTI candidates—running as independents after a decision by Pakistan's election commission—won 93 of 266 seats under contention, besting Sharif's PML-N and the center-left PPP, which claimed 75 and 54 seats, respectively. PTI's gains came despite credible allegations of vote tampering to favor the PML-N. Violence also marred the voting, with bomb attacks on two political offices in Balochistan killing at least 30 people Feb. 7 and 9 people on election day. Khan, imprisoned since Aug. 2023 on corruption charges, was sentenced Jan. 30 to 10 more years for exposing state secrets; he also faced more than 170 legal charges that he denounced as politically motivated.

Iran on Jan. 16 had launched a reportedly unprovoked attack on Pakistan's border province of Balochistan, claiming that it had targeted members of the Baloch separatist group Jaish al-Adl. Pakistan recalled its ambassador to Iran and on Jan. 18 carried out retaliatory airstrikes against another Baloch separatist group allegedly operating in Iran's border region, killing nine people.

Putin Critic Navalny Dies in Siberian Prison—Alexei Navalny, prominent critic of Russian Pres. Vladimir Putin, died in mid-Feb. in an isolated Arctic prison camp. The 47-year-old Navalny had in 2020 survived nerve agent poisoning, which he blamed on the Kremlin. Navalny's supporters accused prison staff of torturing Navalny; authorities said he died of natural causes but delayed releasing his body to his family for more than a week. According to the independent Russian monitoring group OVD-Info, Russian police arrested more than 400 people around the country at events held Feb. 16-17 in Navalny's honor.

Russia Seizes Eastern Ukrainian City of Avdiivka—After four months of intense fighting, Russia's military on Feb. 19 said it had seized complete control of the eastern Ukrainian city of Avdiivka, Donetsk, after Ukrainian forces withdrew, for Russia's largest territorial gain since Bakhmut in May 2023. Ukraine's loss amid its stalled counteroffensive prompted U.S. Pres. Joe Biden to renew calls for Congress to pass an additional $60 bil in security assistance, the continued delay of which had resulted in Ukrainian troops having to "ration ammunition." (The EU on Feb. 1 approved $54 bil in nonmilitary aid after Hungary lifted its veto.)

On Feb. 25, Ukrainian Pres. Volodymyr Zelenskyy said 31,000 Ukrainian troops had been killed since the start of the invasion, his first public estimate and well below an Aug. 2023 U.S. assessment of 70,000 Ukrainian troop deaths. Zelenskyy also claimed 180,000 Russian personnel had been killed; in late Feb., Russian independent news outlet Mediazona put Russian troop deaths in Ukraine in 2022 and 2023 at roughly 75,000, while a U.S. report declassified in mid-Dec. 2023 estimated roughly 315,000 Russian troops were dead/injured. The UN's human rights office reported 10,582 civilians killed in Ukraine as of Feb. 15, but cautioned the actual number could be much higher.

After French Pres. Emmanuel Macron openly discussed deploying forces in Ukraine, Russian Pres. Vladimir Putin in his annual state of the nation speech Feb. 29 threatened to use nuclear weapons against NATO countries if they sent troops.

Biden Administration Opposes UN Consensus on Gaza as Death Toll Exceeds 30,000; Other Israel-Hamas War Developments—The total number of people killed in the Gaza Strip in Israel's ongoing offensive surpassed the grim milestone of 30,000, roughly 70% of them women and children, Gaza's health ministry said Feb. 29. Israel claimed that about a third of those killed were militants. The tally by Gaza officials did not include at least 112 people killed that same day when a crowd rushed an aid convoy in Gaza City. Hamas accused Israeli troops of shooting at the crowd, while Israel said its troops only fired warning shots and that a stampede was responsible for most of the deaths. According to UN observers, however, a large number of those receiving hospital treatment had bullet wounds.

The incident came amid growing warnings of humanitarian crises, including an acute malnutrition rate of more than 15% among young children in northern Gaza according to UNICEF. The U.S. on Feb. 20 cast the only vote against a UN Security Council resolution demanding an immediate cease-fire. In a setback for negotiations, Israeli Prime Min. Benjamin Netanyahu earlier in the month rejected as "delusional" a cease-fire proposal from Hamas that would have released hostages in three phases but left the group in power.

Israel's military Feb. 12 said it rescued two hostages during a raid and strikes upon the southern city of Rafah, where roughly 1.5 mil Palestinians had taken refuge. According to the UN, 1.7 mil Gazans were displaced across the territory as of Feb. 25. The Biden administration on Feb. 23 declared Israeli settlements in occupied Palestinian territories illegal following reports of planned settlement expansion in the West Bank. The move, which restored a long-held U.S. policy reversed by former Pres. Trump, came the same day Netanyahu unveiled a post-war plan that would establish indefinite Israeli military control of Gaza, at odds with the White House and allies favoring a two-state solution.

General

Chile Wildfires Kill Over 130; Texas's Smokehouse Creek Fire Sets State Record—Chile's deadliest wildfires on record Feb. 2-7 swept the coastal region of Valparaíso and killed at least 134 people, largely in the hard-hit coastal resort city of Viña del Mar. Chile's interior minister on Feb. 17 said that winds had restarted fires in south-central Chile, pushing the number of active blazes in the country above 250; the fires had thus far burned more than 1,660 sq mi.

Aided by gusty and dry conditions, the Smokehouse Creek Fire that ignited Feb. 26 in Texas's Panhandle region grew into the state's largest wildfire on record, charring more than 1 mil acres in Hemphill, Hutchinson, and Roberts Counties before it was fully contained Mar. 16. Officials said the fire, which killed at least two people, started near Stinnett as a result of a downed power line. The Smokehouse fire along with several other smaller simultaneous blazes caused more than $123 mil in agricultural damage, according to a preliminary assessment by Texas A&M's AgriLife Extension Service.

Taylor Swift Wins Again at Grammy Awards—Pop superstar Taylor Swift won album of the year for *Midnights* at the 66th Grammy Awards ceremony held Feb. 4 at Crypto.com Arena in Los Angeles, making her the first artist to win in that category four times. Miley Cyrus brought home record of the year, her first Grammy, for "Flowers." Billie Eilish and her brother Finneas O'Connell won song of the year for "What Was I Made For?" and R&B singer-songwriter Victoria Monét was named best new artist.

Kansas City Edges San Francisco in Super Bowl LVIII—The defending champion Kansas City Chiefs edged the San Francisco 49ers, 25-22, in an overtime nailbiter at Allegiant Stadium in Paradise, NV, Feb. 11, to win Super Bowl LVIII, their third NFL championship in the last five years and fourth overall. Kansas City QB Patrick Mahomes was named Super Bowl MVP for the third time after completing 34 of 46 passes for 333 yards with one interception and two touchdowns, including the winning three-yard toss with just 3 sec. left in overtime. The broadcast, which included a halftime show headlined by Usher, was the most watched ever, drawing an average 123.7 mil viewers, above the previous high of 115.1 mil in 2023.

Scientists Discover Ancient Stone Wall Under Baltic Sea—German researchers detected a 10,000 to 11,000-year-old stone wall in nearly 70 ft of water off the country's northern Baltic coast that they said may be one of Europe's oldest known human-created "megastructures," according to a study published Feb. 12 in *Proceedings of the National Academy of Sciences*. The half-mile-long "Blinkerwall" structure was found accidentally in 2021; researchers believed it was originally constructed on dry land to corral reindeer.

Byron Wins Daytona 500—After a one-day rain delay, William Byron prevailed in the 66th Daytona 500 Feb. 19 in Daytona Beach, FL, edging Alex Bowman under a caution flag due to a crash involving the then-second and third place drivers on the race's final lap. His win capped a chaotic race that saw 41 lead changes among 20 drivers. A 23-car crash in lap 192 of 200 eliminated past winner Joey Logano, who led for a race-high 45 laps.

First Private Spacecraft Lands on Moon; Other Space News—Intuitive Machines' Nova-C lander touched down on the moon Feb. 22 in the first commercial lunar landing; it was also the first U.S. spacecraft to return to the surface since 1972. The Houston-based firm's six-legged lander, *Odysseus*, was tasked with evaluating the environment near the moon's south pole prior to a crewed NASA surface mission planned for 2025-26.

On Feb. 23, the International Astronomical Union announced that researchers utilizing powerful ground-based telescopes in Hawaii and Chile had discovered another moon orbiting the planet Uranus and two around Neptune, bringing their known totals to 28 and 16, respectively.

According to research published Feb. 19 in *Nature Astronomy*, Australian astronomers identified the most luminous object observed thus far in the universe, the black hole-powered quasar named J0529-4351.

March 2024

National

Supreme Court Sides With Trump on 14th Amendment Ballot Issue—The U.S. Supreme Court on Mar. 4 unanimously ruled that Colorado lacked the authority to exclude former Pres. Donald Trump from the 2024 presidential primary ballot. Colorado's Supreme Court in Dec. 2023 had ruled that the Jan. 6, 2021, attack on the U.S. Capitol disqualified Trump based on a 14th Amendment (1868) clause barring from public office candidates who had previously sworn an oath to defend the Constitution and then engaged in insurrection or rebellion. The U.S. Supreme Court ruled that only Congress had the power to enforce the clause in an unsigned *per curiam* opinion.

Biden Presents State of the Union; EPA's Vehicle Pollution Rules Aim to Cut Greenhouse Gases; Other Biden Administration Developments—Pres. Joe Biden delivered his third State of the Union address to a joint session of Congress Mar. 7 amid lackluster approval ratings and persistent concern over Biden's age and fitness for a second term. The 67-min. speech contrasted Biden's policies on taxes, abortion, and immigration with those of former Pres. Trump and highlighted economic indicators of post-pandemic recovery, even as opinion polling showed many respondents faulted Biden for persistent high costs of groceries, housing, and other essentials. On foreign policy, the president reasserted his support for Ukraine and for Israel to defend itself after the Oct. 7, 2023, attack by Hamas but said Israel must protect Palestinian civilians.

The federal Environmental Protection Agency (EPA) Mar. 20 announced the U.S.'s strictest vehicle emissions standards to date. The EPA estimated automakers could meet the new requirements if 56% of all new vehicles sold in the U.S. by 2032 were fully electric—up from just 7.6% of new auto sales in 2023.

The White House on Mar. 21 canceled $5.8 bil in student loan debt for nearly 77,700 public-service workers, including teachers and firefighters, bringing total student debt canceled by the Biden administration to $143.6 bil held by almost 4 mil borrowers.

Trump and Biden Secure Parties' Presidential Nominations—The Associated Press announced that former Pres. Donald Trump won Washington State's presidential primary Mar. 12, securing him the required number of pledged delegates to formally be named the presumptive Republican presidential nominee. Trump, who also notched lopsided wins that day in Georgia and Mississippi primaries and in Hawaii's caucus, soundly won 14 of 15 contests held Mar. 5, Super Tuesday, before his remaining rival, former UN Ambassador Nikki Haley, suspended her campaign Mar. 6. Haley on Feb. 24 had lost to Trump in her home state of South Carolina and won only two primary contests, Washington, DC (Mar. 3) and Vermont (Mar. 5).

Incumbent Pres. Joe Biden also easily clinched the Democratic Party's nomination Mar. 12 after winning sufficient delegates in Georgia's primary. He faced no serious challengers and lost only one contest, the caucus in American Samoa, to entrepreneur Jason Palmer on Mar. 5.

Federal Court Blocks Texas Immigration Law—A divided U.S. appeals court Mar. 19 blocked Texas from enforcing a strict new immigration law, SB4, that would have allowed local and state police to arrest migrants who cross its southern border illegally, after which state judges could deport them. The controversial law, signed by Gov. Greg Abbott (R) in Dec. 2023, would circumvent federal control over immigration, and some critics argued it could increase racial profiling.

In a 5-4 order handed down Jan. 22, the U.S. Supreme Court allowed federal border agents to cut and clear away razor wire in an Eagle Pass public park, which Texas National Guard soldiers had installed as part of Abbott's three-year-old Operation Lone Star initiative to stem unauthorized immigration. Within days, Abbott announced he would defy the White House and the high court, ordered more razor wire installed, and said Guard soldiers would block agents' access to the park.

Realtors Group Agrees to Landmark Settlement; Justice Dept. Sues Apple; Other Economic News—The National Assn. of Realtors in a landmark $418 mil settlement with home sellers reached in mid-Mar. agreed to rules eliminating seller-paid fees to buying agents that had facilitated standard 5%-6% commissions. Preliminarily approved by a federal judge the following month, the changes could greatly reduce realtors' home-sale commissions.

The Justice Dept., 15 states, and the District of Columbia filed an antitrust suit Mar. 21, accusing tech giant Apple of using its dominance in the smartphone sector to increase costs to consumers and illegally stifle competition by restricting access to its iPhone platforms and designing systems to unfairly favor Apple's own products. On Mar. 4, the European Union had fined Apple almost $2 bil for thwarting music streaming competition. AT&T on Mar. 30 announced it was investigating a data breach that leaked personal details of 7.6 mil current and 65.4 mil former account holders to the so-called dark web.

The Dow Jones Industrial Average closed Mar. at 39,807.37, up 2.1% from Feb., as the S&P 500 index finished at 5,254.35, a 3.1% gain. Closing at 16,379.46, the Nasdaq Composite Index increased 1.8% in Mar. The annual U.S. inflation rate was 3.2% in Feb., according to a Bureau of Labor Statistics (BLS) report released Mar. 12. Though far below the peak rate of 9.1% in June 2022, it remained above the Federal Reserve's 2% target. According to a BLS report released Mar. 8, the economy added 275,000 jobs in Feb. as the unemployment rate rose 0.2%, to 3.9%. The Bureau of Economic Analysis's revised third estimate, released Mar. 28, showed that in the fourth quarter of 2023, real GDP grew at an annualized rate of 3.4% after increasing by 4.9% in the third quarter.

Biden Signs Bill Funding Government, Ending Shutdown Drama—Narrowly staving off a federal government shutdown, Pres. Biden early Mar. 23 signed a long-overdue, $1.2-trillion spending package funding about three-quarters of the government through Sept. The agreement raised defense spending by roughly $29 bil (3.5%) but did not include the deep cuts to nonmilitary spending demanded by far-right House Republicans during the six-month impasse. While Republicans touted funding for 2,000 more border patrol agents, Democrats' wins included increases of $1 bil for Head Start and childcare for military families, and more funding for cancer and Alzheimer's research. Though the legislation included $300 mil in military assistance to Ukraine, a larger security package remained bogged down in Congress. Approved Mar. 23 by the Senate, 74-24 (with the support of 25 Republicans), the GOP-led House passed it Mar. 22, 286-134, triggering a failed effort by Rep. Marjorie Taylor Greene (R, GA) to oust Speaker Mike Johnson (R, LA).

International

U.S. Commences Humanitarian Aid Drops in Gaza; UN Security Council Adopts Cease-Fire Resolution—In coordination with Jordan, the U.S. military Mar. 2 began airdropping much-needed food assistance along the coastline of the Gaza Strip. The aid was intended to supplement the limited freight quantities that had been allowed through a single border crossing with Egypt since the start of Israel's wide-ranging offensive against Hamas nearly five months prior. According to the UN, 140 aid trucks per day were currently entering Gaza compared to some 500 daily before the start of the siege, amid increasingly alarming reports by aid agencies of food shortages and impending famine. U.S. Pres. Joe Biden on Mar. 7 announced the U.S. would construct a temporary pier on Gaza's coast to facilitate sea deliveries. On Mar. 28, the UN's International Court of Justice unanimously ordered Israel to allow humanitarian aid unhindered, arguing that famine was already taking place.

On Mar. 25, the UN Security Council, with the U.S. abstaining, passed a resolution calling for an immediate cease-fire in Gaza for the duration of Ramadan and for Hamas's unconditional release of remaining hostages. The U.S. abstention, amid high rates of civilian deaths in Gaza—the total number of Palestinians killed surpassed 32,000 by Mar. 22, according to Gaza's health ministry—and Israeli Prime Min. Benjamin Netanyahu's vow to invade Rafah appeared to widen a growing rift between Biden and Netanyahu, who canceled a White House visit.

According to media reports and monitoring groups, Israeli airstrikes in Aleppo, Syria, killed at least 40 people Mar. 29, including six Hezbollah militants. Two days earlier, Israeli airstrikes killed 16 people in southern Lebanon, including at least two Hezbollah fighters.

Houthi Sea Attack Kills Three—Houthi militants fired missiles at a Liberian-owned cargo ship off the coast of Yemen Mar. 6, killing three crew members in what was thought to be the first fatal attack on a merchant vessel in retaliation for Israel's ongoing military campaign in Gaza. The following week, Yemen's internationally recognized government said U.S. airstrikes on Houthi rebel targets in port cities and elsewhere in the country killed at least 11 people. According to the Congressional Research Service, Houthis attacked commercial ships at least 53 times between Oct. 17, 2023, and May 1, 2024, including the UK-owned *Rubymar*, which sank Mar. 2 after it was struck about two weeks earlier.

Vietnamese President Resigns—Vietnam's president Vo Van Thuong resigned Mar. 20 just a year into his term, according to the ruling Communist Party, which cited unspecified violations and shortcomings by Thuong. Some observers believed the investigation of Thuong was at least partially motivated by the party's longstanding and publicly popular anti-corruption campaign. In Jan. 2023, Thuong predecessor Nguyen Xuan Phuc and two deputy ministers resigned following COVID-19-related scandals. Though Vietnam's president holds a largely ceremonial position, the apparent forced resignations of Thuong and Phuc in such a short span rattled those concerned about the country's overall political stability. In late Apr., the head of Vietnam's parliament, Vuong Dinh Hue, was also forced to resign.

Moscow Terror Attack Kills Over 140; Putin Wins Another Six-Year Term—At least four gunmen opened fire with automatic weapons on a packed rock concert audience in a Moscow suburb Mar. 22, killing at least 144 in what was said to be the deadliest attack in Russia in 20 years. The masked gunmen also set fire to the venue, Crocus City Hall, where more than 6,000 people were in attendance. ISIS-Khorasan, the Afghan branch of the Sunni terrorist group, claimed responsibility immediately after the attack, but Russian Pres. Vladimir Putin said that Ukraine played a role, which U.S. intelligence officials disputed. The *Washington Post* reported that the U.S. two weeks before the attack had warned the Kremlin that ISIS was planning hostilities on the specific site. Four suspects, all Tajik nationals, were charged Mar. 25; eight others accused of aiding them were arrested by the end of Apr.

Putin won a fifth six-year term in office, claiming about 88% support in voting Mar. 15-17 participated in by 77.5% of the electorate but devoid of any credible opposition candidates. Significantly, Putin's most prominent one-time rivals—anticorruption activist Alexei Navalny and Wagner mercenary chief Yevgeny Prigozhin—both died under suspicious circumstances within the past seven months. The 71-year-old Putin, in power since 2000, was Russia's longest-serving leader since Soviet-era dictator Joseph Stalin.

Russian Airstrikes Damage Ukrainian Infrastructure; Ukraine Drones Strike Oil Facilities in Russia; Other Developments—Russia overnight Mar. 21-22 carried out one of its largest attacks on Ukraine's infrastructure since the start of its invasion more than two years earlier. A combined 150+ drones and missiles killed at least five people and left more than a million without electricity. Pres. Putin the next week signed a decree to conscript roughly 150,000 citizens into military service. The U.S.-based Institute for the Study of War on Mar. 28 said Russia's military had gained just 195 sq mi since Oct. 2023 at a cost of up to 1,000 troops injured or killed daily. In mid-Mar., a missile strike on Odesa killed at least 21 people.

Reportedly running low on ammunition due to stalled U.S. military aid, Ukraine continued to launch airstrikes on targets inside Russia and Russian-occupied Crimea. Drone attacks impacted multiple oil facilities, causing major damage Mar. 12 to a refinery in Nizhniy Novgorod, over 600 mi from Ukraine's border, and setting fire to others, including one about 120 mi southeast of Moscow. Strikes in Russia's Belgorod region also killed at least two people Mar. 16. On Mar. 12, hundreds of pro-Ukranian Russian fighters launched an attack and claimed to take temporary control of the village of Tyotkino in Russia's Kursk region; Russian defense officials said its military prevented the incursion. After missile strikes on four Russian vessels, Ukraine Mar. 26 claimed it had sunk or disabled a third of Russia's Black Sea fleet since the start of the invasion.

Turkish Local Elections Strike Major Blow to Erdogan and Ruling Party; Nightclub Fire Kills Two Dozen in Istanbul—Turkey's center-left Republican People's Party (CHP) triumphed in local elections held Mar. 31, delivering Islamist Pres. Recep Tayyip Erdogan and the conservative Justice and Development Party (AKP) their worst result in more than two decades. Winning 35 of 81 provinces to 24 for Erdogan's AKP, the CHP made large gains in eastern provinces, including in Adiyaman, devastated by a Feb. 2023 earthquake. With more than 78% of eligible voters participating, the election took place amid an ongoing crisis of runaway inflation that reached 67% annually in Feb.

At least 29 people were killed in a nightclub fire in central Istanbul Apr. 2. The club, known as Masquerade, was undergoing renovation without acquiring the proper permits; all of the victims were reportedly construction workers trapped by the blaze.

General

***Oppenheimer*, *Poor Things* Win Big at Oscars**—The biographical thriller *Oppenheimer* picked up the best picture Academy Award and six other trophies, including best director for Christopher Nolan, at the 96th Academy Awards ceremony held Mar. 10 at the Dolby Theatre in Los Angeles. *Oppenheimer*'s Cillian Murphy and Robert Downey Jr. won best actor and best supporting actor, respectively, while best actress went to Emma Stone for the absurdist comedy *Poor Things*, which won three other awards, and best supporting actress to Da'Vine Joy Randolph for *The Holdovers*.

Michigan School Shooter's Parents Convicted of Manslaughter—James Crumbley, whose 15-year-old son shot and killed four classmates in the Detroit, MI, suburb of Oxford Township in 2021, was found guilty of involuntary manslaughter by a jury Mar. 14. Prosecutors presented evidence that Crumbley had failed to secure the gun he and his wife had recently purchased for their son and ignored signs of his son's declining mental health. The shooter's mother, Jennifer Crumbley, was convicted on the same charges in Feb., making the Crumbleys the first U.S. parents to be held criminally responsible for their child's mass shooting. Both were sentenced in Apr. to 10-15 years in prison. (The shooter had been sentenced in Dec. 2023 to life without parole.)

Cargo Ship Collapses Baltimore Bridge, Killing Six—Six construction workers doing overnight maintenance were killed in Baltimore, MD, early Mar. 26 after a large container ship struck a supporting pier of the city's Francis Scott Key Bridge, partially collapsing the 47-year-old structure and sending the workers' vehicles into the Patapsco River 185 ft below. The 947-ft-long, Singapore-registered vessel *Dali* lost power—and thereby steering capability—minutes before impact, after which its operators issued a mayday call that provided officials just enough time to halt auto traffic entering the bridge from both directions. The boat was refloated and returned to port May 20; its uninjured crew had been confined on board since the crash. Removal of the collapsed portion of the 1.6-mi-long bridge was not completed until June 4. The Baltimore port, the U.S.'s tenth largest, fully reopened six days later. Replacing the bridge was expected to cost up to $1.9 bil.

April 2024

National

Norfolk Southern Settles Chemical Spill Suit; Tesla Announces Major Layoffs; Other Business, Economic News—Rail freight company Norfolk Southern (NS) agreed Apr. 9 to pay $600 mil to settle a class action lawsuit over the fiery Feb. 2023 derailment of a train in East Palestine, OH, that leaked tons of toxic chemicals. The settlement class would reportedly cover about 100,000 people, including those within a 20-mi radius of the derailment and personal injury claims for individuals within 10 mi. NS had already spent more than $800 mil in cleanup-related costs but did not admit fault or wrongdoing; the company May 23 agreed to pay another $310 mil to settle charges filed by the Justice Dept. and Environmental Protection Agency (EPA). A National Transportation Safety Board report in June 2024 confirmed that an overheated wheel bearing caused the derailment and said the company "misinterpreted and disregarded" evidence that venting and intentionally burning multiple chemical tank cars post-derailment was not necessary to prevent an explosion.

Facing lagging sales amid a massive recall in early 2024, Tesla CEO Elon Musk in a company-wide email publicly reported Apr. 15 by Electrek announced that more than 10% of Tesla's global workforce—around 14,000 employees—would be laid off.

According to a Bureau of Labor Statistics (BLS) report released Apr. 10, the annual U.S. inflation rate increased to 3.5% in Mar. compared with Feb.'s year-over-year rate of 3.2%. The U.S. economy added 303,000 jobs in Mar. as the unemployment rate ticked down a tenth of a point to 3.8%, the BLS said Apr. 5. Wall Street experienced a down month, with the Dow Jones Industrial Average closing Apr. at 37,815.92, down 5.0% from Mar., as the S&P 500 finished at 5,035.69, a 4.2% drop. Closing at 15,657.82, the Nasdaq Composite Index lost 4.4%.

State Courts Rule on Abortion Bans—Arizona's Supreme Court on Apr. 9 upheld a 160-year-old ban on all abortions except to save a mother's life, drawing national attention. Arizona Gov. Katie Hobbs (D) and the Biden administration condemned the court's 4-2 ruling, which superseded a ban beginning at 15 weeks of pregnancy passed in Mar. 2022. Just three Republican representatives and two senators joined all Democrats in voting to pass a repeal, which Hobbs signed into law May 2. On Apr. 1 Florida's Supreme Court upheld a 15-week abortion ban and permitted a 6-week ban to go into effect in 30 days. The same day, the court allowed a proposed ballot initiative that would enshrine abortion access in the state constitution to appear before Florida voters in Nov. The Florida ballot measure was one of around a dozen state constitutional amendment efforts related to abortion, including one in Arizona.

Campus Protests Draw Attention, Arrests—Amid a global wave of protests over Israel's ongoing offensive in Gaza, police at New York City's Columbia Univ. Apr. 18 arrested at least 108 pro-Palestinian student demonstrators on trespassing charges at the request of the university's president. At least 282 more protesters were detained at Columbia and City University of New York Apr. 30; CNN reported that fewer than 150 of those arrested were affiliated with either of the two institutions. CNN also reported that police by May 7 had arrested more than 2,400 student and non-affiliated protesters at more than 50 college and university campuses in at least 25 states since the initial detainments at Columbia.

While campus administrators said the protests compromised campus safety, the U.S.-based Armed Conflict Location and Event Data Project (ACLED), in its tracking, reported fewer than 20 instances of violence during 553 related demonstrations Apr. 18-May 3 and at least 70 forceful police interventions over the same period. Many of the charges against protesters were later dropped, though some institutions suspended, expelled, or banned students from campus. Notably, some institutions did not take action against protesters, including Wesleyan Univ. in Connecticut and the University of California-Berkeley.

By early May, student-led protests calling for an end to the offensive in Gaza and frequently for school divestment from Israeli holdings had been reported in Australia, Canada, Egypt, France, India, Mexico, and the UK.

Biden Signs Bill Banning TikTok, Funding Ukraine and Israel Assistance—Pres. Joe Biden signed bipartisan legislation Apr. 24 that requires ByteDance, the Chinese parent company of TikTok, to either sell the popular short-form video app's U.S. operations by Jan. 19, 2025, or face a ban on operating in the U.S. Passed by wide margins in the House and Senate, the legislation was criticized by free-speech advocates, including the ACLU. TikTok in mid-May filed a lawsuit arguing the potential ban violated users' First Amendment rights. Lawmakers who supported the measure cited risks of China's authoritarian government using the app to spread misinformation and to access private user data from TikTok's roughly 170 mil U.S. users.

The measure was part of a larger package of national security bills that included $95 bil in foreign military aid, including roughly $61 bil in new aid to Ukraine, $14 bil to Israel, $8 bil to Taiwan and other Indo-Pacific U.S. allies, and $9 bil in humanitarian relief, including in Gaza.

New Federal Rules Proposed on Marijuana, Gun Background Checks, LGBTQ Students, and More—The Justice Dept. Apr. 30 submitted a formal recommendation to the White House to reclassify marijuana from a highly controlled Schedule I drug (on the same level as heroin) to Schedule III alongside less addictive substances. The reclassification would not legalize marijuana federally, but it would lessen constraints on its production and on marijuana-related scientific research. At the time of the recommendation, 24 states had decriminalized recreational marijuana, and 38 states and DC had approved it for medical use.

The Justice Dept. earlier in Apr. finalized rules closing a loophole that allowed firearm sales online and at gun shows without a federal background check; a federal judge temporarily blocked the rule's enforcement in May.

The EPA Apr. 10 mandated that municipalities remove industrial PFAS—so-called forever chemicals linked to serious health problems—from their drinking water systems. The White House on Apr. 19 issued new Title IX rules protecting LGBTQ students from discrimination on campus and rolled back Trump-era rules affecting students accused of sexual misconduct. Federal judges issued injunctions temporarily blocking the expanded LGBTQ protections in at least 15 states by mid-July.

International

Israel Bombs Iranian Target in Syria, Sees Retaliatory Attack; IDF Airstrike Kills Aid Workers; Other Israel-Hamas War Developments—Israel on Apr. 1 launched an airstrike against Iran's embassy complex in Damascus, Syria, that killed two generals, including a top commander in Iran's Revolutionary Guard Corps. In retaliation, Iran Apr. 13 fired more than 300 drones and missiles from Iran into Israel. Those strikes that were not intercepted reportedly caused only limited damage to an Israeli base.

The Israel Defense Forces (IDF) accepted responsibility for a widely condemned Apr. 1 bombing in Gaza on a World Central Kitchen aid convoy that killed seven workers. The incident brought the total number of aid workers killed since Oct. 2023 to over 200, according to a UN official, the most ever for a single conflict. Israeli Prime Min. Benjamin Netanyahu Apr. 4 committed to opening more routes into Gaza for humanitarian relief after U.S. Pres. Joe Biden reportedly threatened to condition future U.S. military assistance on Israel facilitating safe delivery of desperately needed aid.

The IDF carried out frequent air raids on Rafah in Apr., including an overnight attack Apr. 20-21 that killed at least 22 people including 18 children. More than 34,500 Palestinians had been killed in Gaza since the start of Israel's offensive, according to Gaza's health ministry as of Apr. 30. Netanyahu at the end of Apr. said "with or without a [cease-fire] deal," he planned to launch a controversial ground offensive against Rafah. The U.S. remained opposed to ground operations in Rafah absent a plan to protect the estimated 1.5 mil of Gaza's 2.3 mil residents sheltering there. On Apr. 18, the U.S. cast the sole vote against a UN Security Council resolution recommending full UN membership to a State of Palestine; both the UK and Switzerland abstained.

Deadly Attacks Continue in Sudan Civil War—Militias aligned with Sudan's rebel paramilitary Rapid Support Forces (RSF) killed at least 100 civilians in multiple villages in South Kordofan state Apr. 5-6, according to a report by the Sudanese media outlet Dabanga Radio. The incidents followed failed diplomatic efforts to end the civil war between the RSF and the military government's Sudanese Armed Forces (SAF) that broke out in mid-Apr. 2023 amid disagreement over absorption of the RSF into the military as part of a power-sharing deal after a 2021 coup. Clashes between the RSF and SAF in North Darfur's capital of El Fasher increased significantly after Apr. 1, with the city by mid-June reportedly the only remaining substantial Darfur area under SAF control. Tallies of casualties from fighting over the past year varied greatly. U.S.-based ACLED called its figure of over 15,500 deaths as of Apr. 5, 2024, a substantial undercount. A UN panel estimated 10,000-15,000 people were killed in 2023 in West Darfur's capital of El Geneina, where Human Rights Watch in May 2024 accused the RSF and allied militias of carrying out an ethnic cleansing campaign against non-Arabs. According to the UN, by mid-Apr. 2024 about 10 mil in Sudan—roughly 20% of the country's population—qualified as internally displaced persons (IDP). At the same time, the agency said that 750,000 people were suffering "catastrophic" food insecurity.

Ukraine Receives New Military Aid; Other Ukraine Invasion News—Months into a stymied counteroffensive, Ukraine received a boost in the form of a U.S. foreign aid package Apr. 24 that allocated $61 bil in military assistance to outgunned Ukraine. A week earlier, Ukraine's military for the first time employed U.S.-provided long-range ballistic missiles, striking both an airfield in occupied Crimea and Russian troops elsewhere. The UK on Apr. 23 announced its largest-to-date military assistance package for Ukraine, worth $620 mil, which brought the UK's total contribution in the current financial year to $3.7 bil.

Russian strikes on Chernihiv killed at least 18 people and injured dozens of others on Apr. 17. Earlier in the month, a missile demolished a Doctors Without Borders office in Pokrovsk, Donetsk, injuring five. Russia continued its assault on Ukrainian energy facilities, and Ukraine continued to launch air attacks at targets within Russia, including a refinery and drone factory in Tatarstan in early Apr. Ukrainian Pres. Volodymyr Zelenskyy signed two laws aimed at addressing troop shortages, one by lowering the minimum age of conscription from 27 to 25, and a separate mobilization bill that increased punishments on draft dodgers.

Haitian Prime Minister Steps Down Amid Heavy Gang Violence—Haitian Prime Min. Ariel Henry signed a resignation letter Apr. 24, ceding power to a transitional council. Henry's move followed months of violence in Port-au-Prince, where gangs were estimated to collectively control up to 80% of territory by late Feb. On Feb. 29, gangs seized control of two police stations near the National Palace, killing at least four officers, and attacked Haiti's international airport, prompting its closure until May 20. By Mar. 3, gang members reportedly released more than 4,000 inmates from the country's two largest prisons, triggering a month-long state of emergency. The closure, Mar. 7, of Haiti's main port due to sabotage and looting also prevented humanitarian shipments from reaching the impoverished island nation's 11 mil residents.

According to the UN, more than 360,000 Haitians were displaced as of Mar. 9, including some 15,000 since Feb. 29. The UN said that more than 2,500 people had been killed or injured in Haiti in the first three months of 2024. The transitional council May 28 unanimously selected UN aid official and former Prime Min. Garry Conille as interim prime minister until presidential elections are held by early 2026.

General

Boat Accidents Kill 150+ in Mozambique and Central African Republic—More than 100 people died Apr. 7 off the northern coast of Mozambique after the boat in which they were traveling from Lunga to Mozambique Island sank. Many of those aboard the fishing vessel, which was not licensed to carry passengers, were reportedly attempting to flee after receiving disinformation about a cholera outbreak.

In the Central African Republic's capital, Bangui, an overloaded riverboat with more than 300 people reportedly on board capsized on the Mpoko River Apr. 19, killing at least 58.

South Carolina, Connecticut Win NCAA Basketball Tournaments—The Univ. of South Carolina Gamecocks came back from a first-quarter deficit to defeat the Iowa Hawkeyes, 87-75, and win the school's third NCAA women's basketball championship at Rocket Mortgage FieldHouse in Cleveland, OH, Apr. 7, capping an undefeated (38-0) season. Kamilla Cardoso was named most outstanding player of the women's Final Four with 15 points, 17 rebounds, and 3 blocks in the final. Iowa guard Caitlin Clark, credited with drawing crowds and TV ratings all season on her way to establishing a handful of new NCAA scoring records, had 30 points in the final to finish her collegiate career with 3,951 points, the most for any Division I basketball player. Clark on Mar. 3 had surpassed Pete Maravich's 54-year-old record of 3,667 points.

The Univ. of Connecticut Huskies defeated the Purdue Boilermakers, 75-60, at State Farm Stadium in Glendale, AZ, Apr. 8, securing their second straight men's NCAA tournament title and tying with two other schools for most championships overall (six). Racking up 20 points and 7 assists in the final and averaging 14.5 points and 7.2 assists in the tournament, Huskies guard Tristen Newton was named the men's Final Four's most outstanding player.

Millions Witness Dramatic Solar Eclipse; Other Space News—On Apr. 8, millions traveled or simply stepped outside to witness a dramatic total solar eclipse viewable across a wide swath of North America, from Mexico to Canada. NASA estimated that 31.6 mil people lived within the 115-mi wide path of totality, and an additional 150 mil people resided within 200 mi. A partial eclipse could be seen in all contiguous U.S. states, provided the sun was not blocked by clouds.

On Apr. 4, researchers at Arizona's Kitt Peak Natl. Observatory released the largest-ever 3-D map of the universe, created by the facility's Dark Energy Spectroscopic Instrument (DESI), which measured 11 bil years of expansion of the universe with unprecedented accuracy. For the first time in five months, NASA Apr. 20 received readable data from the 46-year-old *Voyager 1* space probe.

Scheffler Victorious at Masters Tournament—No. 1-ranked Scottie Scheffler bested rookie Ludvig Aberg of Sweden by four strokes at Augusta Natl. Golf Club in Augusta, GA, Apr. 14, to win his second Masters tournament. Leading by one shot at the start of the final round, the 27-year-old American sank seven birdies to finish 11-under-277.

Eight Officers Shot, Four Fatally, Serving Warrant in North Carolina—Four law enforcement officers were fatally shot in Charlotte, NC, Apr. 29 by a male suspect they were attempting to serve with two warrants. Injuring four other officers, the attack was the single deadliest on U.S. law enforcement since 2016, when a sniper killed five officers in Dallas. According to the Fraternal Order of Police, a record 378 officers were shot in 2023, of whom 46 were killed, 20 in ambush-style attacks.

May 2024

National

White House Cancels $7.7 Billion in Student Loans, Imposes New Tariffs on Chinese Imports—Pres. Joe Biden May 22 announced another round of student debt forgiveness, canceling $7.7 bil in federal loans to 160,000 borrowers. The action brought total student debt canceled by his administration's proposed policies thus far to $167 bil for some 4.75 mil borrowers. In early Apr., the White House had unveiled a new student debt relief plan—yet to be finalized or implemented—intended to replace the student loan forgiveness plan blocked by the Supreme Court in June 2023. On Aug. 28, the Supreme Court refused a Biden administration request to allow it to reinstate its Saving on a Valuable Education (SAVE) plan affecting more than 8 mil enrollees while two separate, Republican-led legal challenges progress through federal courts. SAVE capped borrowers' monthly payments based on their earnings and family size, and canceled the remainder of the loans after a set number of payments.

Citing Chinese government subsidies that he said unfairly benefit manufacturing in that country, Biden on May 14 imposed steep tariff increases on $18 bil in Chinese imports including electric vehicles, solar cell and computer chips, and steel and aluminum products.

Dept. of Justice Lawsuit Seeks to Break Up Ticketmaster; Major Health Care Co. Hacked; EU Investigates Meta; Other Economic News—The U.S. Dept. of Justice, joined by the attorneys general of 29 states and Washington, DC, filed suit May 23 against Ticketmaster and parent company Live Nation, alleging monopolistic practices that have negatively impacted performers, concertgoers, and other live-event patrons. A consumer class-action lawsuit was filed against Live Nation and Ticketmaster that same day.

On May 8, St. Louis-based health care provider Ascension detected a ransomware attack, which ultimately affected all of its 142 hospitals across 19 states and Washington, DC. The EU May 16 announced an investigation into Meta for aspects of Facebook and Instagram that regulators said were potentially addictive to children and thus violated the bloc's Digital Services Act, which went into full effect in Feb. 2024. In early May, the Federal Trade Commission approved ExxonMobil's $60 bil acquisition of Texas-based Pioneer Natural Resources.

The U.S. economy added a lower-than-forecast 175,000 jobs in Apr. as the unemployment rate ticked up 0.1 point to 3.9%, according to a Bureau of Labor Statistics (BLS) report released May 3. A BLS report released May 15 showed that annual inflation rose 3.4% in Apr., down 0.1% from Mar. The Dow Jones Industrial Average May 16 topped 40,000 for the first time ever, reaching 40,051.05 before closing at 39,869.38. The index closed the month at 38,686.32, up 2.3% from Apr. The S&P 500 finished May at 5,277.51, a 4.8% gain, and the Nasdaq Composite Index closed at 16,735.02, up 6.9% from Apr.

Trump Found Guilty in New York Hush Money Trial—A New York State Supreme Court jury May 30 found former Pres. Donald Trump guilty of all 34 felony counts of falsifying business records to conceal hush-money payments—made to an adult-film star who claimed a prior affair with Trump—in order to influence the 2016 presidential election. The verdict, which came after hours of jury deliberation over two days, made Trump the first current or former U.S. president to be convicted of a felony (no previous president had been charged with one). The proceedings spanned 22 days over six weeks and featured testimony from 22 witnesses, including Stormy Daniels (legal name: Stephanie Clifford), who detailed her one-night sexual encounter with Trump in 2006, and Trump's former personal attorney and fixer Michael Cohen, himself convicted in 2018 on multiple charges, including campaign-finance violations, tax and bank fraud, and lying to Congress. Trump's sentencing was initially scheduled for Sept. 2024.

On May 6, the judge overseeing the trial had found Trump in contempt for defying the court's gag order for the 10th time and threatened to jail the former president. Trump had repeatedly violated the order against referring to jurors, witnesses, prosecutors, court staff, and their relatives in his social media posts, statements to the press, and on his campaign website. Republican lawmakers echoed their party's presumptive presidential nominee's assertion that the trial was politically motivated, with House Speaker Mike Johnson outside the courthouse dismissing it as a "sham trial" from a corrupt court. Trump faced three other criminal cases, including the federal indictment over his alleged attempt to overturn the 2020 election.

International

Chad's Military Ruler Wins Disputed Election—Gen. Mahamat Idriss Déby was elected president of Chad in voting held May 6, a little over three years after he seized power following the death of his father, Idriss Déby Itno, who had ruled the resource-rich but impoverished central African nation for three decades. Chadian rights groups accused Déby's transitional government of committing election fraud and voter intimidation, and main opposition challenger Prime Min. Succès Masra alleged the regime threatened him and arbitrarily arrested some of his supporters. Masra, who received 18.5% of the vote compared with more than 61% for Déby, resigned May 22.

Russia Stages Assault on Ukraine's Kharkiv Border Region; Other Russian Invasion News—Opening what appeared to be a new front in its ongoing invasion of Ukraine, Russia launched a sweeping attack May 10 across its southern border and claimed control by the next day of five villages north of Kharkiv. Russian troops had also seized villages in recent weeks along the roughly 600-mi battlefront in Ukraine's east and south. According to the Institute for the Study of War and the American Enterprise Institute, Russia as of May 7 controlled about 17.5% of Ukraine's territory (about 41,000 sq mi). Amid Russia's gains, the U.S. and other NATO allies gave Ukraine long-sought permission to use arms they supplied to strike targets inside Russia, although the use was limited to targets close to Kharkiv. Ukraine continued to target Russian oil infrastructure in May, including in Luhansk and at the port of Novorossiysk.

Russia and Ukraine at the end of the month exchanged 75 prisoners each in a swap mediated by the UAE. It was the first exchange in three months and the 52nd since Russia's invasion began in 2022.

Slovakian Prime Minister Gravely Injured in Assassination Attempt—Slovakian Prime Min. Robert Fico was shot multiple times May 15 in an assassination attempt that critically injured the 59-year-old populist. Police arrested a 71-year-old suspect and said his attack was politically motivated. Fico's pro-Russia Smer party won Oct. 2023 parliamentary elections on a polarizing platform that included pledges to halt aid to Ukraine and to block its prospective NATO membership. Fico, who had served previously as prime minister in 2006-10 and 2012-18, was released from the hospital May 30.

Iranian President Killed in Helicopter Crash—Iran's conservative president Ebrahim Raisi, foreign minister Hossein Amir-Abdollahian, and six others died May 19 in a helicopter crash during heavy fog near the mountainous northern border with Azerbaijan. Since his 2021 election by a low-turnout vote, Raisi had clashed with the U.S. and allies over Iran's uranium enrichment program, supplying drones to Russia, and its support of Hamas, Hezbollah, and the Yemen-based Houthi rebels attacking commercial shipping. Domestically, Raisi's government faced protests over women's civil rights and an economy slowed by U.S.-led international sanctions. First Vice Pres. Mohammad Mokhber became interim president; elections for a new president were mandated within 50 days.

DRC's Military Foils Coup Attempt—The Democratic Republic of the Congo's military said it thwarted a coup attempt May 19 that included attacks in Kinshasa on the palace of Pres. Felix Tshisekedi and on an ally's residence. Six people were killed, including suspected instigator Christian Malanga, a little-known opposition leader. Three U.S. citizens, including Malanga's son, were among 37 people sentenced to death in Sept. 2024 over their alleged roles in the plot.

ICC Seeks Arrest Warrant for Netanyahu; Israeli Military Enters Central Rafah; Other Gaza Offensive News—The International Criminal Court's (ICC's) chief prosecutor May 20 requested an arrest warrant for Israeli Prime Min. Benjamin Netanyahu and Defense Min. Yoav Gallant over the war on the militant group Hamas in the Gaza Strip that had killed more than 35,000 Palestinians since Oct. 2023, according to Gaza's health ministry. The request, on charges of war crimes and crimes against humanity, came amid continuing international calls for a cease-fire in the territory. The prosecutor also requested warrants for three Hamas leaders over the Oct. 7, 2023, attacks that killed 1,200 Israelis.

On May 26, an Israeli airstrike in the southern city of Rafah on a tent camp for displaced Gazans—which Israel said targeted a Hamas compound—started a fire that killed at least 45 people in the camp, sparking fresh outrage. Netanyahu called it a "tragic error." Netanyahu on May 6 had ordered 100,000 Gazans in eastern parts of Rafah to evacuate; the next day, Israel Defense Forces (IDF) took control of the city's crucial border crossing with Egypt, and on May 9 Israeli forces carried out strikes there. Despite increased tension with the U.S. over Netanyahu's vow to invade the city, Biden in mid-May approved more than $1 bil in arms to Israeli after pausing shipment of heavy bombs a week earlier. By the end of May, Israel's military confirmed it was operating in densely populated central Rafah. Roughly 1 mil Palestinians had fled the city, in which many of them had taken refuge from earlier strikes elsewhere.

In early May, the head of the UN's World Food Program said that northern Gaza was facing a "full-blown famine." Pressured by humanitarian organizations, Israel May 1 reopened northern Gaza's Erez-Beit Hanoun crossing to aid convoys. However, a UN official in a May 8 post on X (formerly Twitter) said that aid was still not entering the crossing. Sea-based aid deliveries began for the first time May 17 at a U.S.-constructed floating pier in Gaza. On May 28, Norway, Ireland, and Spain formally recognized Palestine as a sovereign state.

U.S.-UK Strikes Kill at Least 16 in Yemen Amid Ongoing Houthi Shipping Disruption—U.S. officials reported the U.S. and UK cooperated on strikes targeting 13 additional Houthi military targets in Yemen on May 30 amid ongoing attacks by the militants on commercial ships mostly in the Red Sea and Gulf of Aden in apparent protest of Israel's ongoing offensive in Gaza. The strikes killed at least 16 people according to Houthi media and marked the fifth joint counterattack against Houthi targets since Jan. 12. Houthis claimed responsibility for attacks on multiple merchant ships and two U.S. destroyers in May, reportedly among more than 50 such attacks since Nov. 2023, according to the U.S. Maritime Admin.

Houthis May 26, in coordination with the International Committee of the Red Cross, released 113 prisoners held in connection with the country's nearly 10-year-old civil war.

General

United Methodist Church Lifts Ban on LGBTQ Clergy—United Methodist Church (UMC) delegates at their international general conference in Charlotte, NC, voted overwhelmingly on May 1 to repeal the denomination's 40-year-old ban on LGBTQ persons being ordained or appointed as clergy. The 692-51 vote occurred without any debate; 7,600 UMC congregations—25% of those in the U.S.—had departed the organization in 2019-23, reportedly over UMC leaders not enforcing LGBTQ-related bans. The conference also voted to prohibit local officials from punishing ministers or churches for either holding or refusing to hold same-sex weddings.

Mystik Dan Wins Photo-Finish Kentucky Derby; Seize the Grey Claims Preakness—Longshot Mystik Dan, at 18-1 odds, held off Sierra Leone by a nose and Forever Young by another nose to win the 150th Kentucky Derby May 4 at Churchill Downs in Louisville, KY. The tightest three-horse finish since 1947 necessitated a minutes-long review before officials declared the three-year-old bay colt the victor. It was the first Derby win for both jockey Brian Hernandez Jr. and trainer Kenny McPeek.

At the 149th Preakness Stakes at Pimlico Race Course in Baltimore two weeks later, Seize the Grey, at 9-1 odds, won out over runner-up Mystik Dan by 2¼ lengths after leading the entire race. Running on the first muddy track conditions at Preakness in 85 years, Seize the Grey finished in 1:56.82.

U.S. Overdose Deaths Decrease Slightly—Fatal drug overdoses decreased in the U.S. in 2023 for the first time since 2018 in the wake of the sharp escalation of overdoses that began in 2020, according to preliminary data released May 15 by the CDC. The agency's provisional number of 107,543 overdose deaths represented a 3% drop from the 111,029 reported in 2022, with more than two-thirds (69%) of deaths attributed to synthetic opioids like fentanyl.

Schauffele Prevails at PGA Championship; Tour Golfer Scheffler Arrested, Released—Xander Schauffele won the 106th PGA championship, his first major title, at Valhalla Golf Club in Louisville, KY, May 19. Leading the entire tournament, Schauffele scored four birdies on the final round's front nine and three more on the remaining half to finish with a 21-under-263, just one shot ahead of fellow American Bryson DeChambeau.

Louisville police arrested No. 1-ranked golfer Scottie Scheffler May 17 after an officer accused Scheffler of dragging him with his vehicle when Scheffler came upon an accident scene en route to the course. Released an hour before his second-round teetime, Scheffler finished tied for eighth place, eight strokes behind Schauffele. He was cleared of charges after multiple witnesses disputed the claims of the officer, who had failed to turn on his bodycam.

Spate of Tornadoes Kills More Than Two Dozen—Hundreds of tornadoes impacted more than 10 states May 19-26, killing at least 21 people and injuring more than 150. On May 21, an EF-4 rated twister traveled a 40+ mi path southwest of Des Moines, IA, killing four in Greenfield. It was the strongest tornado in 2024, with peak estimated winds of 175-185 mph (based on damages caused); however, mobile radar measured max ground-level winds at more than 315 mph. The highest death toll occurred in northern Texas's Cooke County, where seven people, including four children, were killed. An earlier outbreak May 6-9 affected more than a dozen states, killing at least five. NOAA confirmed 476 tornadoes in May and 325 in Apr.

NCAA, Conferences Pave Way for Directly Paying Student Athletes—The NCAA and its richest athletic conferences reached a settlement May 23 that set the stage for each college or university to directly distribute about $20 mil annually among its student athletes beginning as early as fall 2025. The settlement also called for the NCAA to pay over $2.75 bil total over 10 years to student athletes who had participated before July 2021, when athletes were first permitted to earn money for their name, image, and likeness rights. The settlement still required the approval of the overseeing federal judge.

Landslide in Papua New Guinea Kills Hundreds—A massive landslide in Papua New Guinea's mountainous Enga province May 24 buried more than 2,000 people, according to a national disaster official three days after the tragedy. The UN had earlier estimated 670+ had been killed, based on the more than 150 homes in Yambali village that local administrators estimated were covered. The slide buried 650 ft of a major roadway under 20-26 ft of earth, complicating relief efforts.

Newgarden Wins Second Straight Indy 500—American driver Josef Newgarden passed Mexico's Pato O'Ward with less than a half lap remaining to clinch the 108th Indianapolis 500 at Indianapolis Motor Speedway May 26, making the 23-year-old Indy's first back-to-back champion in 22 years. Swapping the lead with O'Ward four times over the final laps, Newgarden led 26 laps total of the rain-delayed race, second to Scott McLaughlin of New Zealand, who led 64 laps and finished sixth.

June 2024

National

Biden Limits Asylum at Southern Border; Other Immigration Developments—Pres. Joe Biden signed an executive order June 4 that would effectively turn back any asylum-seeking migrants who made their way over the southern border illegally. The directive immediately suspended asylum claims processing during periods in which the seven-day average of unauthorized crossings surpassed 2,500. The order exempted unaccompanied children, trafficking victims, those experiencing serious medical conditions or facing safety threats, and those utilizing legal pathways. Border patrol encounters with unauthorized migrants fell by 40% over the three weeks following the order, according to the Dept. of Homeland Security. The order drew swift legal challenge by the ACLU; a federal court in 2018 struck down a similar ban by then-Pres. Donald Trump.

On June 18, Biden announced an executive order shielding the undocumented spouses and children of U.S. citizens from deportation; a Texas federal judge in late Aug. temporarily blocked it from taking effect.

Georgia Court Suspends Election Interference Case Against Trump; Hunter Biden Convicted of Felony Gun Charges; Other Legal News—The Georgia Court of Appeals on June 5 halted the state's 2020 election interference case against presumptive Republican nominee Donald Trump and eight other defendants. The indefinite hold awaited the ruling of a panel considering whether to remove Fulton County District Attorney Fani Willis over a potential conflict of interest posed by her romantic relationship with special prosecutor Nathan Wade.

Pres. Joe Biden's son Hunter Biden was found guilty June 11 of all three federal charges he faced related to possessing a gun while under the influence of illegal drugs.

A federal judge June 6 ordered former Trump adviser Steve Bannon to report to prison by July 1 to serve a four-month sentence for refusing to testify before the select House committee investigating the Jan. 6, 2021, Capitol riot. The Republican-led House narrowly voted, 216-207, on June 12 to find Atty. Gen. Merrick Garland in contempt for refusing to turn over an audio recording of an interview concerning Pres. Joe Biden's handling of classified documents.

Federal Reserve Maintains 23-Year-High Interest Rates; Other Economic News—With inflation (3.3% in May) still above its 2% annual target rate, the Federal Reserve Bank on June 12 announced it would maintain the historically high benchmark interest rate of 5.25%-5.5% and indicated it would trim the rate only once before the end of 2024. The European Central Bank on June 6 lowered its benchmark rate a quarter point from a record-high 4.0%. Revised figures released June 27 by the Bureau of Economic Analysis showed that in the first quarter of 2024, real U.S. GDP decreased at an annual rate of 1.4%, compared to a 3.4% gain the prior quarter. The U.S. economy added a better-than-expected 272,000 jobs in May according to a Bureau of Labor Statistics report issued June 7, as the unemployment rate ticked upward to 4.0%.

With its stock up more than ninefold since the end of 2022, American tech component giant Nvidia surpassed Microsoft as the world's most valuable publicly traded company June 18 after its market cap reached $3.34 tril. The Dow Jones Industrial Average closed June at 39,118.86, up 1.1% from May, while the S&P 500 index finished at 5,460.48, a 3.5% gain; the Nasdaq Composite Index ended June at 17,732.60, up 6.0%.

Biden Alarms Supporters With Disastrous Presidential Debate Performance—Pres. Joe Biden (D) and former Pres. Donald Trump (R), the presumptive presidential nominees of their respective parties, held their first 2024 debate on June 27, hosted by CNN in Atlanta, GA. Their microphones muted if either candidate tried to interject out of turn, the 81-year-old Biden and 78-year-old Trump addressed questions on issues including abortion, foreign policy, immigration, and inflation. Biden delivered frequently meandering and faltering remarks in a raspy voice that immediately deepened concerns about his fitness for office and ability to win a second term, while Trump repeatedly made false assertions and accusations. More than 51.3 mil viewers watched the debate according to Nielsen Media Research.

Supreme Court Nears End of Term With Rulings on Federal Powers, Homelessness, Jan. 6 Rioters, and More—The U.S. Supreme Court June 28 announced a major 6-3 ruling that overturned a frequently cited, 40-year-old precedent known as "Chevron deference," which empowered federal agencies to interpret laws passed by Congress in their purview. Writing for the majority, Chief Justice John Roberts said that such deference was inconsistent with federal law, which he said instead directs courts to "decide legal questions by applying their own judgment." Justices Jackson, Kagan, and Sotomayor, the threesome usually described as the Court's liberal wing, dissented in the ruling, which legal experts said would impact a wide array of government regulations.

The same 6-3 majority June 28 issued a closely watched ruling in *City of Grants Pass v. Johnson* that permitted an Oregon city to continue ticketing homeless people for sleeping outside. The Court that same day in *Fischer v. United States* sided with a Jan. 6 Capitol rioter when it said the Justice Dept. had overstepped in pursuing obstruction charges against him. Writing for a slightly different 6-3 majority (with Sotomayor, Kagan, and Barrett in dissent), Roberts said the obstruction law applied only when the defendant's actions impaired "records, documents, or objects" used in the disrupted proceeding of Congress. The decision would impact charges against more than 350 other Jan. 6 defendants and potentially those against Trump himself.

International

South Africa's ANC Loses Three-Decade Parliamentary Majority—Election results in South Africa announced June 1 showed the African National Congress (ANC) had lost the majority it had held since the end of apartheid and election of Nelson Mandela in 1994. The ANC drew less than 40.2% support, a roughly 17-point drop from 2019, in voting May 29 with 58.6% of the electorate participating. South Africans cited disillusionment with persistent corruption within the party, economic inequality, crime, and frequent power outages. On June 14, the ANC formed an unlikely governing coalition that included the Democratic Alliance, the ANC's main opposition party, which won nearly 22% of the vote. The coalition June 14 elected Pres. Cyril Ramaphosa of the ANC to a second term.

Modi Fails to Preserve Indian Governing Majority—India's ruling Bharatiya Janata Party (BJP) unexpectedly lost its parliamentary majority following voting June 1 in the seventh and final phase of the country's 2024 general elections, shedding 63 seats to finish with 240 of 543 lower house seats. Though Prime Min. Narendra Modi won a rare third term in office, the loss of the BJP's 10-year majority meant it would need to govern with a coalition that might moderate the BJP's Hindu nationalist stance. Critics had frequently accused Modi of enflaming religious tensions and stifling journalists and other news media.

Mexico Elects First Woman President—Mexico elected its first woman and first Jewish president on June 2, with climate scientist and former Mexico City mayor Claudia Sheinbaum leading the vote 61.2%-28.1% over tech entrepreneur Xóchitl Gálvez. Receiving a record-high 39.5 mil votes, Sheinbaum—a member of the ruling leftist Morena Party founded by term-limited incumbent Pres. Andrés Manuel López Obrador—had pledged to maintain López Obrador's emphasis on economic austerity and to continue popular social programs. Sheinbaum's challenges upon her swearing-in Oct. 1 will include persistent violence from cartels and gangs—more than three dozen candidates were assassinated in the lead-up to voting—and ongoing U.S.-Mexico immigration and trade issues.

Though Morena and its allies won a comfortable supermajority in Congress's lower house (364 of 500 seats), it fell just short of a two-thirds majority in the Senate needed to approve a spate of amendments sought by López Obrador, including the popular election of federal judges.

Right Surges in European Union Elections—Far-right parties made large gains in direct elections for European Parliament seats held in the bloc's 27 countries June 6-9. Though the center-right European People's Party and its largely centrist pro-EU coalition partners maintained a weak majority, right-wing parties won around 150 seats, mostly in France, Germany, and Italy where liberal and green parties saw substantial defeats.

Israeli Hostage-Rescue Operation Sees High Casualties; Netanyahu Rejects Cease-Fire Deal—Israel Defense Forces (IDF) in a daytime operation June 8 rescued four hostages from two apartment buildings in central Gaza's Nuseirat refugee camp. Involving heavy ground and air attacks, the action was condemned by the UN. Gaza's health ministry reported it had killed more than 270 Palestinians and injured almost 700; the IDF said fewer than 100 were killed. The recovery of the hostages, all kidnapped from the Nova music festival Oct. 7, increased the total number of living hostages rescued to 7. About 120 hostages of 250 originally seized by Hamas remained missing, roughly one-third of whom were presumed dead. The operation took place two days after an Israeli airstrike on a UN-run school in central Gaza killed at least 40 Palestinians.

With Russia abstaining, the UN Security Council on June 10 voted 14-0 to approve a three-phase plan—the first Gaza cease-fire plan passed by the body—that called for Hamas to release hostages in exchange for Palestinian prisoners and for Israeli's military to withdraw from populated areas in Gaza. Israeli Prime Min. Benjamin Netanyahu rejected the plan later in June, asserting again that Israel would not end the offensive until Hamas was eliminated. On June 22, more than 150,000 Israelis, by one estimate, protested in Tel Aviv in favor of a cease-fire and against Netanyahu.

Houthis Sink Another Merchant Ship—Iran-backed Houthi rebels attacked Greek-owned, Liberian-flagged cargo ship MV *Tutor* in the Red Sea June 12, killing one crew member and causing it to sink six days later. The assault, in protest of Israel's ongoing offensive in Gaza, was the second to result in the sinking of a targeted commercial vessel, after the UK-owned *Rubymar* sank in early Mar. Following the attack, U.S. military strikes destroyed seven radar facilities in Houthi-controlled Yemen.

Ukraine Rejects Russia's Cease-Fire-for-Territory Offer; Other Ukraine-Russia Developments—Russian Pres. Vladimir Putin June 14 proposed an immediate cease-fire if Ukraine scrapped plans to join the NATO alliance and gave up its claims to four regions that Russia forcibly annexed in 2022. Ukraine Pres. Volodymyr Zelenskyy immediately rejected the offer. Russia continued to seize villages and launch air strikes across Ukraine. Ukrainian forces meanwhile claimed they largely halted Russian progress in the Kharkiv region over the latter half of the month. On June 17, U.S. Natl. Security Adviser Jake Sullivan told PBS News that the U.S.'s agreement with Ukraine to allow limited use of U.S.-supplied weapons against targets inside Russia from across the Kharkiv front applied to anywhere Russia attacks Ukraine inside its border to try to seize additional Ukrainian territory. The use of U.S.-provided long-range weapons remained prohibited.

At their 2024 summit in Apulia, Italy, leaders of the G7 nations agreed June 13 to loan Ukraine $50 bil backed by frozen Russian assets. Zelenskyy and U.S. Pres. Joe Biden June 13 signed a 10-year bilateral security agreement to fortify Ukraine's military capacity. Putin on June 19 made his first official visit to North Korea in 24 years; North Korea was suspected of supplying Russia with weapons in exchange for military expertise and economic aid.

Terrorist gunmen June 23 killed 21 people—including at least 15 police officers—in the majority-Muslim Dagestan region of Russia. The attackers targeted a synagogue and Orthodox church in Derbent and another church and a police station in Makhachkala.

WikiLeaks' Assange Strikes Plea Deal, Returns to Australia—Julian Assange, founder of the controversial website WikiLeaks, pleaded guilty June 26 in federal court in the U.S. territory of the Northern Mariana Islands to a single Espionage Act count of conspiracy to obtain or disclose national defense information. The 52-year-old Assange was then allowed to return home to his native Australia due to time already served—five years (2019-24) in a London prison on charges of bail breach. Beginning in 2012, Assange sought asylum in the Ecuadorian embassy in London to avoid both a rape charge brought against him in Sweden (dropped in Nov. 2019) and extradition to the U.S., over charges that WikiLeaks had published unredacted classified files in 2010 that detailed U.S. military involvement in Iraq and Afghanistan and endangered U.S. troops.

General

Boeing Starliner Strands Crew at ISS; Other Space News—After multiple technical delays, the first crewed Boeing Starliner capsule launched into space June 5 from Florida's Cape Canaveral to the Intl. Space Station. The two-person NASA crew was scheduled to return about a week later, but Starliner malfunctions—reportedly helium leaks and thruster failure—resulted in their indefinite stay at the station. NASA Aug. 24 announced astronauts Barry Wilmore and Sunita Williams would instead return on a SpaceX capsule in Feb. 2025. The Starliner returned to Earth without passengers and without incident Sept. 7.

On June 25, the return capsule from China's *Chang'e 6* unmanned lunar mission successfully touched down via parachute in Mongolia with the first-ever samples of soil and rocks from the far, or "dark side," of the moon.

Swiatek and Alcaraz Claim French Open Titles—Top-ranked Iga Swiatek of Poland overwhelmed Italian Jasmine Paolini (6-2, 6-1) in just 1 hr., 8 min., to win her third straight French Open women's singles title June 8 at Roland Garros in Paris, France. The following night, No. 1-ranked Carlos Alcaraz outlasted Germany's Alexander Zverev (6-3, 2-6, 5-7, 6-1, 6-2) to claim his first French Open and third Grand Slam title.

Dornoch Wins Belmont Stakes—Dornoch, at 17-1 odds, won the 156th Belmont Stakes June 8, held for the first time at Saratoga Race Course in Saratoga Springs, NY, because of renovations at New York's Belmont Park. Ridden by Panamanian jockey Luis Saez, Dornoch took the lead in the final corner to finish the shortened (1¼-mile) race in 2:01.64.

Heat Kills 1,300+ at Hajj; Earth Marks 12 Straight Months of Record-Breaking Temps—More than 1,300 participants died from heat exhaustion during the annual Hajj pilgrimage to Mecca, according to the Saudi government. About 1.8 mil pilgrims took part in the event June 14-19, 2024, amid a heat wave with temperatures exceeding 120°F.

European researchers June 5 announced that record-high monthly global average temperatures were sustained for the previous 12 months through May, averaging 2.9°F (1.6°C) over preindustrial levels.

DeChambeau Wins Dramatic U.S. Open, Saso Wins Women's Open—American Bryson DeChambeau won the 124th U.S. Open at Pinehurst Resort and Country Club in Pinehurst, NC, on June 16. DeChambeau held a three-shot lead at the start of the final round, but Rory McIlroy racked up five birdies that gave him a two-shot advantage on the 14th tee before committing three bogeys over the remaining four holes. DeChambeau finished with a 6-under-274, one stroke ahead of McIlroy.

On June 2, Japan's Yuka Saso claimed the 79th U.S. Women's Open at Lancaster Country Club in Lancaster, PA. Saso finished in 4-under-276, three strokes ahead of Hinako Shibuno, and claimed a $2.4-mil payout, the largest ever in women's golf.

Boston Celtics Win NBA Championship—The Boston Celtics prevailed in Game 5, 106-88, over the Dallas Mavericks at TD Garden in Boston, MA, June 17, for a record-setting 18th NBA championship. The Celtics were up 21 points at the end of the first half after guard Payton Pritchard sunk a 49-foot half-court buzzer-beater. Boston center Jaylen Brown earned Finals MVP, averaging 20.8 points, 5.4 rebounds, and 5 assists over the five games.

Florida Panthers Take Home Stanley Cup—Rallying after three straight losses, the Florida Panthers edged the Edmonton Oilers, 2-1, in Game 7 at Amerant Bank Arena in Sunrise, FL, on June 24 to win the franchise's first Stanley Cup in its 30-year history. For the first time in 21 years, the Conn Smythe Trophy for playoff MVP went to a player on the losing team—center Connor McDavid, who had 8 goals and 34 assists in 25 games.

July 2024

National

Supreme Court Grants Presidential Immunity for "Official" Acts—The U.S. Supreme Court ended its 2023-24 term July 1 with a landmark 6-3 ruling in the highly anticipated case *Trump v. U.S.* that determined former Pres. Donald Trump may claim legal immunity for some of his actions while in office. Rejecting a federal appeals court's Feb. decision, Chief Justice John Roberts in his majority opinion wrote that a former president enjoys absolute immunity "for actions within his conclusive and preclusive constitutional authority ... and at least presumptive immunity from prosecution for all his official acts. There is no immunity for unofficial acts." In Justice Sonia Sotomayor's strong dissent, she argued, "In every use of official power, the President is now a king above the law."

The court ultimately issued 60 opinions during the 2023-24 term, including a rare Aug. *per curiam* ruling supporting injunctions in several states that blocked federal regulations to prevent gender-identity and sexual-orientation discrimination in schools.

Pres. Joe Biden in late July proposed term limits for Supreme Court justices and a binding code of ethics following recent well-publicized ethical lapses by individual justices; neither proposal was likely to be taken up by Congress.

Trump Injured in Assassination Attempt—Former Pres. Donald Trump survived an apparent assassination attempt July 13, less than 10 min. into his speech at an outdoor rally in Butler, PA. The 20-year-old gunman fired eight rounds from an AR-15-style rifle from atop the roof of a building located about 450 ft from Trump's location onstage. Killing one audience member and injuring two others besides Trump, the shooter, identified as Thomas Matthew Crooks, was fatally shot by a Secret Service sniper. Investigators said that the shooter acted alone and speculated Trump was a "target of opportunity." Pres. Joe Biden in an Oval Office address July 14 condemned the violence and urged unity; he also ordered an independent review of the event's security.

The Secret Service drew immediate criticism over the close call and especially its failure to secure the rooftop. After facing heated bipartisan questioning in front of the House Committee on Oversight and Accountability, agency director Kimberly Cheatle resigned July 23.

Trump Selects Ohio Senator Vance as Running Mate; Milwaukee Hosts Republican National Convention—Former Pres. Trump July 15 named first-term Ohio Sen. JD Vance as his vice-presidential running mate on the first day of the GOP's four-day convention in Milwaukee, WI. Once openly critical of Trump, the 39-year-old veteran and bestselling author had publicly become one of Trump's staunchest defenders.

Trump, with his right ear still bandaged from injuries sustained in the assassination attempt days earlier, formally accepted the Republican presidential nomination for the third straight cycle on July 18. Trump delivered a nearly 93-min. speech during which he pledged to be a president "for all of America," before criticizing Democrats over inflation and a migrant "invasion" and accusing them of rigging the 2020 election.

In late July, Trump appeared to contest Vice Pres. Kamala Harris's racial identity at a conference of Black journalists in Chicago. Trump said, "She was Indian all the way then all of the sudden she made a turn and she became a Black person."

Federal Judge Halts Trump's Classified Documents Case—Florida Federal District Judge Aileen Cannon on July 15 dismissed the Justice Dept's criminal case against former Pres. Donald Trump over his alleged mishandling of classified documents. Cannon argued in her decision that Atty. Gen. Merrick Garland's appointment of Special Counsel Jack Smith was unlawful because it was not confirmed by the Senate. The decision was questioned by many legal experts, who said Cannon ignored long-standing legal precedent. Smith appealed the ruling in Aug.

New Jersey Democratic Senator Convicted of Bribery Resigns—A Manhattan federal jury July 16 convicted three-term Sen. Bob Menendez (D, NJ) on all 16 charges against him including bribery and fraud stemming from allegations Menendez and/or his wife accepted gold bars, hundreds of thousands of dollars in cash, and other bribes in exchange for steering military aid to Egypt and other favors. The first U.S. senator to be found guilty of serving as a foreign agent, Menendez had resigned as chair of the Foreign Relations Committee in Sept. 2023 following his indictment. He resigned his Senate seat effective Aug. 20. New Jersey Gov. Murphy appointed George Helmy to the seat in a caretaker capacity until the winner of the 2024 election could be certified; Helmy took office Sept. 9.

CrowdStrike Computer Glitch Induces Major Outage; Other Economic News—A botched software update by cybersecurity firm CrowdStrike July 19 triggered what many media outlets reported may be the largest global IT outage in history. Though Microsoft estimated less than 1% of Windows-based machines worldwide were affected, the outage froze operations at an array of key service providers including hospitals, 911 dispatch centers, supermarkets, public transit, and airlines. Though CrowdStrike said it put a fix in place 78 min. after the faulty update, industry experts said it could take weeks to fully recover.

On July 7, Boeing agreed to plead guilty to one felony conspiracy charge in connection with two fatal crashes involving its 737 MAX aircraft in 2018 and 2019 that killed 346 people total. Skydance Media July 7 agreed to acquire Paramount Global (including TV network CBS) for approx. $28 bil. AT&T on July 12 disclosed that a data breach exposed phone and text records covering a six-month period in 2022 for nearly all of its 110 mil customers.

According to a Bureau of Labor Statistics (BLS) report released July 11, the annual inflation rate ticked down to 3.0% in June. In a separate report July 5, the BLS announced that the U.S. economy added 206,000 jobs in June as the unemployment rate rose one-tenth of a point to 4.1%. The Dow Jones Industrial Average closed July at 40,842.79, up 4.4% from June, while the S&P 500 index finished at 5,522.30, a 1.1% gain; the Nasdaq Composite Index ended July at 17,599.40, down 0.8%.

Biden Drops Out of Presidential Race, Endorses Harris—Pres. Joe Biden, the presumptive Democratic presidential nominee, announced July 21 that he was ending his campaign and endorsing his 59-year-old Vice Pres. Kamala Harris to replace him, resetting the 2024 presidential race less than four months before Election Day. Calls from Democratic officials and donors to reconsider his candidacy had reached a fever pitch in the four weeks since Biden's unsteady debate performance refocused attention on the 81-year-old's fitness for a second term.

Harris drew immediate, widespread support, including from those thought to be potential competitors if an open convention or mini primary were to be held. Her campaign said it raised over $81 mil in donations in the first 24 hours after Biden bowed out.

International

Labour Party Claims British Election in a Landslide Victory—The center-left Labour Party pulled off a huge win in general elections held July 4 in the UK, ending 14 years of Conservative government rule that oversaw Brexit and the coronavirus pandemic. Led by Keir Starmer, Labour secured 411 of 650 seats, up 211 from 2019, while Conservatives, led by outgoing Prime Min. Rishi Sunak since Oct. 2022, won just 121 seats, a staggering loss of 251 seats. Critics of the UK's first-past-the-post system noted that Labour won 63% of Parliament's seats with only 33.7% of the popular vote. The new Labour government faced a stagnant economy and discontent over public services (incl. health care, mass transit, and schools), among other voter concerns.

French Leftists Secure Election Victory But Not Power—In France, a coalition of leftist parties known as New Popular Front (NFP) won the most seats in snap general elections held over two rounds June 30 and July 7, thwarting a far-right takeover but failing to reach the absolute majority required to govern. French Pres. Emmanuel Macron called for the vote three years early to "clarify" the results of EU's June parliamentary election that saw France's far-right surge. The vote left the NFP with 180 of 577 seats, the centrist Ensemble—including Macron's Renaissance Party—with 159, and the far-right National Rally (RN) and its allies with 142. Macron in mid-July accepted the resignation of his alliance's government, and after nearly two months of political stalemate, Sept. 5 appointed conservative former Brexit negotiator Michel Barnier as prime minister, directing him to establish a unity government. Barnier on Sept. 21 announced a new government, which was comprised primarily of centrists and conservatives and did not include any RN or NFP lawmakers in defiance of the election results.

Moderate Pezeshkian Wins Iranian Presidency—Centrist candidate Masoud Pezeshkian won presidential runoff voting held July 5 to replace Iran's conservative Pres. Ebrahim Raisi, killed in a helicopter crash in May. A longtime lawmaker and former cardiac surgeon, Pezeshkian won nearly 55% support to just over 45% for his hardline opponent, Saeed Jalili; dozens of other candidates were reportedly prevented from running by Iran's powerful Guardian Council. Though Pezeshkian vowed to relax enforcement of a law requiring women to wear headscarves and work toward better relations with the West in the face of continually burdensome economic sanctions, he had not committed to any major changes to Iran's ruling theocracy.

Israel Expands War; Other Related Developments—Israel blamed the Lebanese militant group Hezbollah for a rocket strike July 27 on southwestern Syria's Israeli-occupied Golan Heights that killed 12 children and teens playing on a soccer field, increasing fears of a widening war in the Middle East. In retribution for the assault, Israel struck southern Beirut, killing several, including Fuad Shukr, a Hezbollah leader alleged to have played a central role in the 1983 Beirut bombing that killed 241 U.S. service personnel. Hamas political leader Ismail Haniyeh was assassinated July 31 in Tehran, Iran; Hamas and Iran both blamed Israel. Earlier in July, a drone attack in Tel Aviv claimed by Yemen-based Houthi rebels killed one person, prompting Israel's first confirmed strikes on Yemen.

Venezuelan Opposition Accuses Maduro of Rigged Election as Protests Spur Crackdown—Venezuela's authoritarian socialist Pres. Nicolás Maduro Moros was declared the winner of disputed elections held July 28, sparking protests attended by thousands throughout the country. Police and security forces responded with force, killing at least 11 civilians by July 30 according to Foro Penal, a Venezuelan NGO. Human Rights Watch, in a report released Sept. 4, alleged pro-Maduro authorities and armed groups carried out a "brutal crackdown" against the largely peaceful demonstrations, resulting in at least 24 deaths. By the end of July, Maduro's forces had detained at least 670 people according to Foro Penal. In early Aug., the EU joined the U.S. and at least five Latin American countries in refusing to recognize the reelection of Maduro, president since 2013.

Within Gaza, Israeli's military continued to carry out high casualty strikes, including on UN-run schools serving as displaced persons' shelters, which Israel said were utilized by Hamas. By the end of July, Israel's offensive had killed around 39,400 Palestinians according to Gaza's health ministry. On July 9, the U.S. said it would permanently remove a floating pier it had installed to deliver humanitarian aid; it was frequently out of service due to weather conditions. Prime Min. Benjamin Netanyahu on July 24 addressed a joint session of the U.S. Congress, during which he pledged to continue the war until "total victory" was achieved; roughly half of Democratic lawmakers did not attend.

The anti-settlement group Peace Now said the Israeli government in late June had approved its largest land seizure in the Palestinian territories in over 30 years, taking 4.9 sq mi of the West Bank. On July 19, the UN's top court declared Israeli settlements in the Palestinian territories illegal and called for new construction to cease immediately.

General

Hurricane Beryl Lashes Grenada, Mexico, Texas—Category 4 Hurricane Beryl made landfall July 1 at Grenada's Carriacou Island before strengthening to Category 5 with winds up to 165 mph. The slowly weakening storm made landfall again July 5 on Mexico's Yucatán Peninsula, and on July 8 as a

Category 1 storm near Matagorda, TX. Beryl ultimately dumped up to 10-15 in. of rain on southeast Texas, causing flash flooding and knocking out power to more than 2.7 mil residents. Officials faulted the storm for at least 40 deaths, including at least a dozen due to heat exposure after prolonged power outages, in the Houston region. Other Beryl-related fatalities included at least six in Venezuela and at least a dozen in the Caribbean.

Stampede at Religious Festival Kills Over 120 in India—At least 121 people, reportedly mostly women, died July 2 in a crowd crush in northern India after a Hindu religious gathering. Held in a large tent amid sweltering temperatures, the event in Hathras, Uttar Pradesh, drew some 250,000 people despite obtaining permits for less than one-third that number to attend. Media accounts indicated attendees rushed over muddy ground in pursuit of the preacher as he left. One official also said there was an insufficient number of exits.

World's Oldest Cave Art Found in Indonesia—A team of Australian and Indonesian researchers identified a cave painting—dated to at least 51,200 years ago on Indonesia's Sulawesi Island—as the world's oldest known cave art, according to a study published July 3 in *Nature*. The painting is thought to show three humanlike forms engaging with a pig, which the study's authors said also made it the oldest-known narrative art.

Alec Baldwin Set Shooting Case Dismissed—A New Mexico trial judge July 12 dismissed involuntary manslaughter charges against actor and producer Alec Baldwin for the accidental shooting death in 2021 of cinematographer Halyna Hutchins on the set of *Rust*, partially filmed in Santa Fe, NM. The judge ruled prosecutors had intentionally and unlawfully withheld key evidence from Baldwin's attorneys. In Apr., the film's armorer, Hannah Gutierrez-Reed, was sentenced to 18 months in prison after she was found guilty on related charges.

Krejcikova, Alcaraz Claim Wimbledon Titles—The 31-seed Barbora Krejcikova of Czechia took down No. 7-seed Jasmine Paolini of Italy (6-2, 2-6, 6-4) to win the Wimbledon women's singles championship at London's All England Club, July 13. The next day, 21-year-old No. 3-seed defending champion Carlos Alcaraz of Spain overcame No. 2-seed Novak Djokovic of Serbia, 16 years Alcaraz's senior, in straight sets (6-2, 6-2, 7-6). It was Alcaraz's fourth Grand Slam title.

Pogacar Wins Third Tour de France—Tadej Pogacar won the 111th edition of the world's premiere bicycle race July 21 in Nice, finishing the grueling 2,174-mi, 21-stage course in 83 hrs., 38 min., 56 sec. For the first time in its 121-year history, the Tour did not conclude in Paris, due to Olympic Games preparations. The 25-year-old Slovenian claimed victory of six stages on his way to his third Tour win, besting two-time defending champion Jonas Vingegaard of Denmark by 6 min., 17 sec. Eritrea's Biniam Girmay claimed the green sprinter's jersey after winning three stages. Belgian rider Remco Evenepoel, who placed third in his first Tour appearance, won the white jersey (best young rider).

Schauffele Triumphs at British Open—Xander Schauffele won the 152nd Open Championship and his second major title at Royal Troon Golf Club in Troon, Scotland, July 21. Though the 30-year-old American and five others trailed Billy Horschel by one shot at the close of the third round, Schauffele achieved a bogey-free final 18 holes with six birdies to finish atop the leaderboard at 9-under-275, two ahead of Horschel and England's Justin Rose.

August 2024

National

Judge Rules Google Has Illegal Search Monopoly; Annual Inflation Falls to Lowest Level in Three Years; Other Economic News—In a landmark decision, a federal judge on Aug. 5 ruled that Google's online search business violated antitrust law through its use of restrictive contracts that made Google the default search engine on many devices. The Dept. of Justice Aug. 2 filed suit against TikTok, alleging the video app and parent company ByteDance violated a 2019 Federal Trade Commission settlement by permitting children under age 13 to create accounts without parental consent, collecting data from child users, and not complying with parents' requests to delete children's accounts. Chip giant Intel announced Aug. 1 that it was cutting its workforce by over 15% (an estimated 15,000+ jobs) as part of a $10 bil cost-reduction plan.

The Bureau of Labor Statistics (BLS) announced Aug. 2 that the U.S. economy added 114,000 jobs in July as the unemployment rate increased 0.2% to 4.3%. The BLS in a separate report released Aug. 21 revised its estimates for Apr. 2023-Mar. 2024, reporting that the economy had added 818,000 fewer jobs than previously thought. The Dow Jones Industrial Average closed Aug. at 41,563.08, up 1.8% from July, while the S&P 500 index finished at 5,648.40, a 2.3% gain; the Nasdaq Composite Index ended Aug. at 17,713.62, up 0.6%. Annual inflation fell to 2.9% in July, according to a BLS report released Aug. 14—under 3.0% for the first time since Mar. 2021.

Harris Names Minnesota Governor Walz as Running Mate; Chicago Hosts Democratic National Convention—Vice Pres. Kamala Harris named two-term Minnesota Gov. Tim Walz (D) as her vice-presidential running mate Aug. 6, just weeks after Pres. Joe Biden dropped his reelection bid. Relatively unknown nationally, the 60-year-old Walz had served six terms in Congress and 24 years with the Army National Guard and was a former high school teacher.

Harris and Walz formally accepted the party's nomination at the Democratic Natl. Convention, held Aug. 19-22 in Chicago, IL, that featured an emotional opening night address by Pres. Biden, followed in the next days by speeches from former Pres. Barack Obama and first lady Michelle Obama, former Pres. Bill Clinton, other party leaders, and Harris and Walz.

Harris's nomination was made official by a virtual delegate roll call held Aug. 1-5, prior to the in-person convention. On Aug. 2, the 59-year-old former U.S. senator passed the necessary threshold, winning the support of 2,350 delegates. Harris, the first Black woman and first South Asian person to head a major party's ticket, ultimately received 99% of delegate votes according to the Democratic National Committee. The virtual roll call was held before the convention to ensure Harris's nomination ahead of all states' ballot deadlines.

Trump Campaign Hacked; RFK Jr. Endorses Trump; Other Trump Campaign News—The Trump presidential campaign on Aug. 10 announced that foreign agents had illegally accessed its internal digital communications; the FBI later in the month publicly blamed the hack on Iran. Investigators Sept. 18 said that Iranian hackers had sent emails containing excerpts of breached files to Biden campaign associates before he dropped out of the race. The Justice Dept. charged three Iranians in connection with the hacking by the end of the month. The FBI said it believed Iran had also tried to hack the Democratic presidential campaign.

On Aug. 23, longshot independent candidate Robert F. Kennedy Jr. announced he was suspending his presidential campaign and endorsing former Pres. Donald Trump. Though he sought to remove his name from the ballot in key battleground states, he was not able to do so in Michigan and Wisconsin.

The Trump campaign drew media attention Aug. 26 when two Trump staffers reportedly berated and physically pushed an Arlington Natl. Cemetery worker who tried to prevent them from taking photos or videos near servicemembers' graves. Campaign activity is prohibited by federal law at military cemeteries.

International

***Wall Street Journal* Reporter Among Two Dozen Freed in Major Russia-U.S. Prisoner Swap**—On Aug. 1, Evan Gershkovich of the *Wall Street Journal* was among 24 people freed in the largest U.S.-Russian prisoner swap in post–Cold War history. Detained by Russian authorities since Mar. 2023, Gershkovich had been sentenced to 16 years in prison on espionage charges the U.S. denounced as fabricated. Besides Gershkovich, the deal also freed former U.S. Marine Paul Whelan, whom the U.S. had also deemed "wrongfully detained," and 14 others including Kremlin critics, for 8 Russians.

Al-Shabab Beach Attack Kills Close to 40 in Somalia—The al-Qaeda-linked terrorist group al-Shabab claimed responsibility for an Aug. 2 attack on a popular beach near Mogadishu,

Somalia, that killed at least 37 civilians; security forces said all attackers were killed or captured. For more than 17 years, al-Shabab has carried out an insurgency aimed at overthrowing the internationally recognized Somali government. According to Armed Conflict Location & Event Data (ACLED) in Sept., Somalia in 2024 experienced 127 violent events targeting civilians perpetrated by al-Shabab and 187 reported fatalities.

Bangladesh Prime Minister Resigns After Deadly Protests—Bangladesh's Prime Min. Sheikh Hasina resigned and retreated to India Aug. 5 after a month of protests and related violence killed hundreds of demonstrators and more than 40 police officers. Mostly peaceful demonstrations began in early July in Dhaka, with university students speaking out against the reinstatement of a quota reserving 30% of civil service jobs for relatives of veterans of the war for independence. Protests spread and turned violent by mid-July, when students affiliated with Hasina's Awami League party attacked the anti-quota students in multiple cities. By July 18, police had opened fire—including with live bullets—on student protesters and their allies, killing at least 30, and authorities imposed a countrywide internet blackout as government buildings, vehicles, and a state-run TV center in Dhaka were set on fire.

Although Bangladesh's supreme court July 21 largely rescinded the quota, protests continued as students demanded the government be held accountable for use of excessive force. By early Aug., additional supporters, angered by slow economic growth, official corruption, and authoritarianism, joined the movement calling for Hasina to step down after 15 years in power. At least 95 people were reportedly killed in protests on Aug. 4 alone.

A 17-member interim government took control on Aug. 8, three days after Hasina resigned and protesters stormed her residence and the national parliament building. Estimates for the total death toll since July varied, with the interim health minister claiming more than 1,000 people killed and the UN Human Rights Office reporting almost 650 deaths, including security personnel.

Drones Target Rohingya Fleeing Myanmar—Dozens or hundreds of ethnic Muslim Rohingya were reportedly killed Aug. 5 by targeted drone strikes as they were waiting to cross from Myanmar's Rakhine State into neighboring Bangladesh. Though the death toll could not be verified, multiple survivors said they saw more than 200 bodies on the banks of the Naf River separating the two countries. Witnesses blamed the attack on Myanmar's ethnic Arakan Army (AA). Fighting between the AA and Myanmar military had resumed in Nov. 2023, exposing the stateless Rohingya to repeated violence from both sides and displacing more than 320,000 people in Rakhine State and southern Chin State, according to Human Rights Watch.

Ukraine Captures Russian Territory in Surprise Incursion—Ukraine's military Aug. 6 initiated an offensive on Russia's Kursk region, marking the largest incursion into Russia since WWII. A top Ukrainian commander Aug. 27 said the military had thus far seized control of about 100 Russian settlements within some 500 sq mi it controlled in Kursk. According to another Ukrainian commander, Russia Aug. 26 carried out its largest air assault on Ukraine since the invasion in Feb. 2022, consisting of more than 230 drones and missiles targeting critical energy infrastructure; it launched a second wave the next morning. Fierce fighting also continued in eastern Ukraine, particularly in the strategic Donbas region city of Pokrovsk. Pres. Volodymyr Zelenskyy in early Aug. announced Ukraine's military had received its first U.S.-made F-16 fighter jets from NATO countries.

Misinformation Sparks Anti-Immigrant Riots in UK—A week of riots in the UK against immigrants in roughly 30 cities and towns led to the arrest of more than 400 by Aug. 7. Authorities linked the protests to social media disinformation that falsely claimed a Muslim migrant was responsible for the stabbing deaths of three young children in Southport, England, on July 29. Police arrested a 17-year-old Black suspect in the attack who was neither a migrant nor Muslim. Unrest quickly escalated in Southport beginning July 30 as participants targeted mosques, minority-owned businesses, and hotels used by asylum seekers. Rioters also clashed with police in multiple cities including Liverpool and Manchester, as well as in Belfast, Northern Ireland, where they attacked police with Molotov cocktails. More than 100 officers from among nearly 6,000 reportedly mobilized were injured.

Militants Massacre Hundreds in Burkina Faso—Suspected al-Qaeda-linked jihadists shot dead hundreds of civilians in north-central Burkina Faso on Aug. 24. The civilians were reportedly targeted as they were digging a trench around remote Barsalogho to help safeguard the town against attacks, increasingly common in the West African country since militants linked to the group and to the Islamic State spilled into Burkina Faso from Mali. Though the UN had reported a death toll of about 200, CNN reported that a French government assessment estimated the number of fatalities at up to 600, which, if confirmed, would make the attack one of the deadliest in Africa in decades.

Israel Recovers Hostages' Bodies; Protesters Increase Calls for Cease-Fire—Israel's military Aug. 31 recovered the bodies of six Israeli hostages from Hamas's tunnel network in Rafah, Gaza. Taken in Hamas's Oct. 7 attack, the six hostages included 23-year-old Israeli-American Hersh Goldberg-Polin and were said to have been killed just 2-3 days before forces reached them. Hundreds of thousands of Israelis participated in protests Sept. 1 calling for an immediate cease-fire agreement, making an impassioned case that those six hostages would still be alive had Prime Min. Benjamin Netanyahu done so earlier. Israel's largest trade union called for a general strike the following day. The hostages' deaths left 97 other Oct. 7 hostages missing, including 33 presumed dead. On Aug. 20, the Israeli military said it had recovered the bodies of six other hostages, five of whom had previously been declared deceased, in an operation in southern Gaza's tunnel network.

In mid-Aug., Gaza's health ministry reported that Israel's ongoing offensive had killed more than 40,000 Palestinians in Gaza, including more than 16,000 children. Health officials there also reported Gaza's first case of polio in 25 years, in a paralyzed baby. By the end of the month, Israel and Hamas agreed to three separate three-day pauses in fighting to vaccinate more than 640,000+ children against polio. On Aug. 28, Israel launched its largest military operation in the Palestinian-occupied West Bank since 2002, targeting alleged militants in Jenin, Tulkarem, and Tubas.

General

U.S., China Win Big at XXXIII Olympic Summer Games—More than 10,700 athletes from 206 nations and dependencies competed in 329 medal events in 32 sports at the XXXIII Summer Olympic Games, hosted July 26-Aug. 11 in Paris, France. The U.S. dominated the total medal count, with 126: 40 gold, 44 silver, 42 bronze. China was second overall, with 91 medals (40-27-24), and Japan third with 45 (20-12-13).

Four-time U.S. Olympic swimmer Katie Ledecky won four medals, including two gold, to give her a U.S. women's record 14 Olympic medals. U.S. gymnast Simone Biles claimed gold in the women's all-around event, the team event, and in vault, as well as a silver medal that brought her career medal count after three Olympic Games to 11. U.S. sprinter Noah Lyles claimed the 100-m gold in a memorable photo finish but tested positive for COVID-19 prior to the 200-m final, in which he settled for bronze. Both the U.S. men's and women's basketball squads claimed gold, and the U.S. women edged Brazil (1-0) to claim the team's first soccer Olympic gold since 2012.

France's Olympic venues also hosted the Paralympic Games, Aug. 28-Sept. 8, at which some 4,400 athletes with disabilities from 167 countries competed in 549 events across 22 sports. The Chinese team finished first in the total medal count, with 220 (94 gold, 76 silver, 50 bronze), followed by Great Britain (124; 49-44-31), and the U.S. (105; 36-42-27).

Arson-Sparked "Park Fire" Becomes California's Fourth Largest—Just nine days after igniting, Northern California's Park Fire Aug. 2 became the state's fourth-largest wildfire on record and went on to burn more than 429,600 acres in Butte and Tehama Counties before it was fully extinguished in late Sept. The blaze began in Chico's Bidwell Park after a man allegedly intentionally pushed a burning car down a gully.

Plane Crash in Brazil Kills 62—Brazilian regional airline Voepass Flight 2283 crashed Aug. 9 outside São Paulo, killing all 58 passengers and 4 crew on board. The twin-engine turboprop ATR 72-500 plummeted 17,000 ft into a residential area and burst into flames; no one on the ground was reportedly hurt. Though officials had not yet announced a definitive cause for the crash, an early report showed accumulation of ice on the plane's wings due to a potentially malfunctioning deicing system.

Scientists Report Large Underground Water Deposits on Mars—Based on an analysis of data from NASA's InSight lander (active Nov. 2018-Dec. 2022), researchers in findings published Aug. 12 in *Proceedings of the National Academy of Sciences* said they had located liquid water on Mars, in subsurface reservoirs vast enough to cover the entire planet in water up to about a mile deep. Experts noted that the reservoirs, located at a depth of 7-12 mi below the surface, is far too deep for current technology to access.

Superyacht Sinks Off Italian Coast, Killing Seven—*Bayesian*, a 184-ft luxury sailing superyacht owned by British tech entrepreneur Mike Lynch, capsized and sank in a storm early Aug. 19 while anchored off northern Sicily. Lynch, his 18-year-old daughter, and five others including one crewmember drowned in the roughly 165-ft-deep water; 15 others escaped via life raft. Italian authorities initiated an investigation into why the $40 mil boat, said to be "unsinkable" by Italian yacht maker Perini Navi, sank so quickly.

Boeing Malfunction Extends Astronauts' Eight-Day ISS Stay to Eight Months—In a major blow to Boeing, NASA Aug. 24 announced that it would use rival SpaceX's Dragon spacecraft to bring two of its astronauts back to Earth. Sunita Williams and Barry Wilmore, both NASA veterans, had been stranded at the International Space Station (ISS) since June after Boeing's Starliner, on its first crewed mission, experienced helium leaks and thruster issues enroute. Though Boeing argued its craft was safe to bring back the astronauts, NASA declined, and the Starliner returned crewless to Earth in early Sept. Williams and Wilmore were scheduled to return on a Dragon flight in Feb. 2025.

September 2024

National

Hunter Biden Pleads Guilty on Tax Charges—Pres. Joe Biden's son, Hunter Biden, offered a last-minute guilty plea Sept. 5 to all nine federal tax charges against him, which included failure to pay at least $1.4 mil in taxes from 2016-19. Sentencing was scheduled for Dec. 16; he faced up to 17 years in prison. On Sept. 26, sentencing on his prior federal gun charges conviction was delayed until Dec. 12.

Trump's Sentencing Delayed; Other Trump Legal Developments—A New York judge Sept. 6 pushed back the sentencing date in former president and current Republican nominee Donald Trump's "hush money" case until Nov. 26. The judge said the delay was intended to ward off accusations "that the proceeding has been affected by or seeks to affect the approaching presidential election." Found guilty on 34 criminal counts in May, Trump faced up to four years in prison.

On Sept. 12, an Atlanta-area judge dismissed two charges against Trump related to the filing of false documents in the Georgia election interference case against him and 18 other defendants; Trump still faced eight felony counts.

Harris and Trump Face Off in Presidential Debate; Other Campaign News—Vice Pres. Kamala Harris and former Pres. Trump verbally tussled Sept. 10 in the two candidates' first and only debate, moderated by ABC News at the National Constitution Center in Philadelphia, PA. Over the course of 90 min., Harris critiqued Trump on his criminal conviction, tax policy that favors top earners and large corporations, alleged incitement of the Jan. 6, 2021, insurrection, and nomination of judges who overturned the right to an abortion. Trump in turn called Harris a radical, and repeatedly linked her to the surge in inflation and increased unauthorized migrant crossings during the Biden administration. Trump also repeated a debunked claim that Haitian migrants in Springfield, OH, were eating pets. (By the following week, authorities had recorded 30 fake bomb threats targeting Springfield government buildings and officials' residences, forcing evacuations and cancelation of public events.)

The Teamsters on Sept. 18 declined to endorse a presidential candidate; the powerful union had endorsed Democrats' presidential candidates in every race since 2000.

Thwarting another possible assassination attempt as Trump golfed at his West Palm Beach, FL, club Sept. 15, a Secret Service agent shot at a 58-year-old suspect who was spotted with a rifle in nearby shrubbery. The man, who himself did not fire at Trump, was apprehended uninjured and charged on Sept. 16.

Federal Reserve Cuts Interest Rates; Hotel, Boeing Workers Strike; Other Business News—For the first time since 2020, the Federal Reserve Sept. 18 lowered its key interest rate by a half point to a rate of 4.75%-5%, one week after the Bureau of Labor Statistics (BLS) announced that the U.S.'s annual inflation rate in Aug. was 2.5%. On Sept. 6, the BLS in a separate report said the U.S. economy added 142,000 jobs in Aug. with an unemployment rate of 4.2%. The Bureau of Economic Analysis Sept. 26 in its third and final estimate for the second quarter of 2024, said that U.S. GDP grew at an annualized rate of 3.0%, up from 1.6% the previous quarter. The Dow Jones Industrial Average closed Sept. at 42,330.15, up 1.8% from Aug.; the S&P 500 index finished at 5,762.48, a 2.0% gain, and the Nasdaq Composite Index ended Sept. at 18,189.17, up 2.7%.

Roughly 10,000 workers at more than two dozen hotels across the U.S. initiated a rolling strike beginning Sept. 1 over issues including better pay and working conditions. On Sept. 13, machinists at beleaguered aerospace giant Boeing went on strike; workers rejected a tentative agreement reached Oct. 18 in an Oct. 23 vote, and the strike continued.

On Sept 5, the U.S., UK, EU, and seven other countries signed the first legally binding international treaty to ensure the use of AI does not encroach on human rights, democracy, and rule of law. The EU's high court Sept. 10 ruled that Apple must pay $14.3 bil for tax breaks Ireland's government unlawfully granted it in 1991-2014. The same court also upheld a $2.7 bil fine against Google for boosting its own shopping search results over those of its rivals.

New York City Mayor Indicted on Federal Charges—First-term New York City Mayor Eric Adams was indicted Sept. 26 on federal charges of bribery, fraud, and soliciting illegal foreign donations to his 2021 election campaign. According to the indictment's allegations, Adams improperly channeled foreign campaign contributions through straw donors and accepted luxury international travel from a Turkish official. Adams was the first sitting New York mayor to be criminally charged.

International

Jihadists Carry Out Mass Killing in Nigeria; U.S. Withdraws From Niger—On Sept. 1 suspected terrorists attacked Mafa, Yobe State, Nigeria, killing up to 170 people, according to local sources. Local media reported that the Boko Haram splinter group Islamic State West Africa Province (ISWAP) claimed responsibility. Riding motorcycles and reportedly numbering well over 50, the assailants also burned homes and businesses and planted roadside bombs. The killings were allegedly in retribution for residents apprising authorities of the militants' activities. The UN said Boko Haram and its factions had killed roughly 35,000 people between 2009 and 2020 and displaced between 2 and 3 mil from northeast Nigeria.

In mid-Sept., the U.S. military completed withdrawal of roughly 1,000 troops it had stationed in Niger to combat al-Qaeda and Islamic State in the region. Niger's military government, which seized power in a 2023 coup, ended a 2013 agreement that allowed U.S. troops to operate there.

Jailbreak Attempt Kills 120+ in DRC—At least 129 people were killed Sept. 2 during a failed attempt by inmates to break out of the Democratic Republic of the Congo's severely overcrowded Makala prison in Kinshasa. According to officials, most of those killed died in a stampede, but a DRC prison activist put the number of dead at over 200 and said many had been shot.

Israeli Strikes on Hezbollah Kill Hundreds in Lebanon as War's Scope Widens—Israel Defense Forces (IDF) targeting

Hezbollah Sept. 23 carried out more than 1,300 airstrikes against suspected targets in southern Lebanon that killed more than 550 people, according to Lebanon's health ministry. In retaliation, the Iran-backed Hezbollah launched some 200 rockets at Israel, most of which were intercepted. On Sept. 27, a precision Israeli strike on a Beirut suburb killed Hezbollah leader and co-founder Hassan Nasrallah; another Hezbollah official was killed by a strike the next day, making him reportedly the seventh senior-level Hezbollah leader killed by Israel in just over a week.

On Sept. 17, hundreds of electronic pagers belonging to Hezbollah members simultaneously detonated, followed the next day by members' walkie-talkies. Israel was blamed for the attacks, which killed at least 37 people and injured more than 3,000, many of whom were bystanders. By the end of the month, at least 100,000 people from Lebanon had moved into Syria to escape Israeli strikes, according to the UN. Though U.S. Defense Sec. Lloyd Austin on Sept. 26 confirmed that the U.S. would continue to aid Israel militarily, he cautioned against a full-scale war against Hezbollah.

In southern Gaza, an IDF airstrike on a humanitarian area for displaced Palestinians in Al-Mawasi killed at least 19 people early Sept. 10. The IDF claimed Hamas terrorists were operating in the area, which Hamas denied. U.S. Sec. of State Antony Blinken Sept. 10 called for "fundamental changes" in the IDF's operations in the West Bank after Israel admitted IDF forces the previous week had likely fatally shot 26-year-old U.S. citizen Aysenur Eygi while she was protesting Israeli settlements there.

Sudan Military Attempts to Retake Khartoum—The Sudanese Armed Forces (SAF) Sept. 26 launched an operation to retake the country's capital, Khartoum, and adjoining Omdurman and Bahri from paramilitary Rapid Support Forces (RSF). RSF had gained control of the greater capital area at the start of Sudan's civil war more than 17 months earlier. The SAF offensive started hours before Sudan's de facto head and military leader Gen. Abdel Fattah al-Burhan addressed the UN in New York City. Accusing area countries of supporting the "terrorist" RSF, al-Burhan said he would support a peace plan if the RSF moved out of areas it occupied and gave up arms.

On Aug. 1, USAID confirmed famine was occurring in the Zamzam camp near El Fasher, North Darfur, which sheltered more than 400,000 displaced persons. In a report released Sept. 6, UN-supported human rights investigators called for an "independent and impartial force" to intercede on civilians' behalf, blaming both the SAF and RSF for murder, mutilation, torture, and other "harrowing human rights violations." A UN official Sept. 8 said the war had killed more than 20,000; as of Sept. 17, 10.9 mil people—which incl. 8.1 mil since fighting began in Apr. 2023—were displaced in Sudan.

Far-Right Populists Win Austrian Election—Austria's far-right Freedom Party (FPO) won the most parliamentary seats in general elections held Sept. 29 but fell short of the majority required to govern. The FPO, led by Herbert Kickl, secured 57 out of 183 seats, the largest share won by a far-right party in Austria since WWII. Chancellor Karl Nehammer's center-right Austrian People's Party secured 51 seats, and its coalition partner, the environmentalist Greens, won just 16; the opposition center-left Social Democrats took 41. The FPO had called for ending migrants' right to seek asylum and for scrapping sanctions against Russia and additional aid to Ukraine.

General

Mass Shootings Kill Four in Georgia School, Chicago Train—A 14-year-old student killed two students and two teachers and injured nine others Sept. 4 at Apalachee High School in Winder, GA. The suspect, Colt Gray, surrendered to school-based police and was charged as an adult. His father, Colin Gray, who allegedly gave his son the AR-15-style rifle used in the attack, also faced criminal charges, including involuntary manslaughter and second-degree murder.

Four people sleeping on a Chicago CTA Blue Line subway train were fatally shot in an early-morning attack Sept. 2; a suspect was charged the following day.

Sabalenka, Sinner Win U.S. Open—No. 2-ranked Aryna Sabalenka of Belarus overcame No. 6-ranked American Jessica Pegula in straight sets (7-5, 7-5) in a 1 hr., 53 min. match Sept. 7 to win the U.S. Open women's singles title and her third Grand Slam at Arthur Ashe Stadium in Flushing, NY. The next day, 23-year-old top-ranked Jannik Sinner of Italy dominated American Taylor Fritz, (6-3, 6-4, 7-5) to win the men's title and his second Grand Slam.

Typhoon Yagi Kills 700 in Southeast Asia—Super Typhoon Yagi made landfall Sept. 7 in northern Vietnam's Quang Ninh province with 127 mph winds—the equivalent of a Category 3 hurricane—and brought a deluge of rain that caused heavy flooding and landslides, killing close to 300 people. Yagi's remnants generated flooding and landslides in Myanmar that killed at least 380 there, then caused more than 40 deaths in Thailand. More than 20 were killed in the Philippines, where Yagi first made landfall on Sept. 2 as a tropical storm.

Summer 2024 Sets New Heat Record; Other Climate News—NOAA scientists Sept. 12 announced that June-Aug. 2024 represented the Northern Hemisphere's hottest summer on record (1850-present), at 2.74°F above average temperature, and the Southern Hemisphere's warmest winter, at 1.73°F above average. Aug. 2024 capped a record 15-month streak of record-setting average global temperatures, and July 22 was Earth's hottest day on record. Palm Springs, CA, recorded an all-time high 124°F on July 5; Las Vegas, NV, reached a record 120°F on July 7; and Phoenix, AZ, reported a record 113 straight days over 100°F, beginning May 27.

Primed by heat and drought, 7,184 wildfires in California had burned 1,014,375 acres in 2024 as of Oct. 28. Wildfires in Brazil, including in its Amazon rain forest region, burned more than 91 mil acres (roughly the size of Montana) in 2024 through mid-Oct. according to the EU's Global Wildfire Information System (GWIS).

Billionaire Becomes First Civilian to "Walk" in Space—Tech entrepreneur Jared Isaacman performed the first spacewalk by a non-astronaut Sept. 12 for about 10 min. while tethered to SpaceX's Crew Dragon spacecraft as it orbited at up to 435 mi above Earth. SpaceX engineer Sarah Gillis followed soon after. An accomplished pilot, Isaacman self-funded the all-civilian, four-person SpaceX Polaris Dawn mission, which over five days reached a peak altitude of 875 mi.

***Shogun* Wins Big at Emmys**—FX's historical drama *Shogun* won the Emmy for outstanding TV drama series at the 76th Primetime Emmy Awards Sept. 15 in Los Angeles; *Shogun* stars Hiroyuki Sanada and Anna Sawai won outstanding lead actor and actress in a drama series trophies. *Hacks* (HBO Max) won outstanding comedy series and its star, Jean Smart, won best actress in a comedy series, while Jeremy Allen White claimed the corresponding best actor award, for FX's *The Bear*. Netflix's *Baby Reindeer* won outstanding limited or anthology series.

Sean "Diddy" Combs Charged With Sex Trafficking Amid Wave of Assault Accusations—Federal agents Sept. 16 arrested rapper, mogul, and actor Sean "Diddy" Combs in New York on charges of racketeering and sex trafficking in what the Justice Dept. alleged was a long-standing plot to use his vast business enterprise to exploit and sexually assault women. The 54-year-old, three-time Grammy winner was held without bail; the charges carried a possible combined sentence of life in prison. An attorney Oct. 1 said he was representing 120 people accusing Combs of sexual assault, including 25 who were minors at the time of the alleged abuse.

Hurricane Helene Kills More Than 200, Devastates North Carolina—Hurricane Helene severely impacted the southeastern U.S. Sept. 26-29, killing around 220 people in the deadliest hurricane to strike the U.S. since Katrina in 2005. Rapidly intensifying to a powerful Category 4 hurricane, the 200-mi-wide storm made landfall near Perry in the Big Bend region of Florida late Sept. 26, killing at least 25 with sustained winds of 140 mph and storm surge up to 15 ft. Though Helene weakened to a Category 2 hurricane by the time it reached Georgia (more than 30 dead in the state) the next morning, it brought strong winds and heavy rainfall to South Carolina (at least 49 dead) and hardest-hit western North Carolina (at least 101 dead). The Swannanoa River through

Asheville, NC, saw catastrophic flooding after 14 in. of rain fell on the city Sept. 25-27. Tennessee recorded at least 17 deaths, including five workers in Erwin fleeing a factory overcome by floodwaters; five other workers were rescued, and one remained missing.

Rescue and cleanup efforts were partially hindered in North Carolina by numerous washed-out bridges and roads. Following Pres. Joe Biden's early approval of national disaster declarations in all aforementioned states plus Virginia, former Pres. Trump falsely asserted that the Biden administration had spent FEMA's disaster funding on housing migrants and was intentionally withholding aid from areas that vote Republican. Gov. Roy Cooper (D, NC), joined by Sen. Thom Tillis (R, NC) and Republican governors Brian Kemp (GA), Henry McMaster (SC), and Glenn Youngkin (VA), publicly refuted Trump's claim by thanking Pres. Biden for the swift assistance and praising FEMA's response.

October 2024

National

Vice Presidential Candidates Debate; Other Campaign Developments—The nominees for vice president, Minnesota Gov. Tim Walz (D) and Sen. JD Vance (R, OH), squared off Oct. 1 for 90 min. in their first and only debate at the CBS Broadcast Center in New York City. Largely cordial with one another amid an otherwise vitriolic campaign season, the two clashed over abortion, immigration, gun violence, and foreign policy. Vance repeatedly tied Vice Pres. Kamala Harris to unpopular policies of the current administration, and Walz pressed Vance on his and Donald Trump's refusal to accept the outcome of the 2020 presidential election and misinformation about Haitian immigrants in Springfield, OH.

Both campaigns in Oct. targeted prospective voters in seven closely contested states—Arizona, Georgia, Michigan, Nevada, North Carolina, Pennsylvania, and Wisconsin. Harris's on-the-ground campaigning included stops in Houston, where she appeared with pop superstar Beyoncé and highlighted her support for abortion rights; former Pres. Barack Obama and first lady Michelle Obama also made campaign appearances on her behalf. Delivering her "closing argument" Oct. 29 in front of 75,000 people at the Ellipse in Washington, DC, Harris labeled Trump "unstable" and "consumed with grievance," and vowed to pursue "common sense solutions" to help Americans.

Trump booster and billionaire Elon Musk Oct. 19 announced he would give away $1 mil daily to registered voters in battleground states who sign his political action committee's petition for gun rights and free speech, drawing warnings from the Justice Dept. John Kelly, Trump's former chief of staff, in an interview published Oct. 22 with the *NY Times*, said Trump "falls into the general definition" of a fascist, and *The Atlantic* reported the same day that Kelly said Trump "praised aspects of Hitler's leadership." At a rally for Trump in New York's Madison Square Garden Oct. 27, a comedian disparaged Puerto Rico as a "floating island of garbage," and insulted Latinos, drawing widespread disapproval; other speakers levied ungrounded personal attacks against Harris.

National polling averages by RealClearPolitics showed Americans were closely split between the two candidates leading up to Nov. 5 voting. The average Oct. 1 had Harris with 49.3% support, 2 points ahead of Trump; Trump led Harris, 48.4%-48.1%, as of Oct. 31.

Biden Administration Expands Protections on Lead; Supreme Court Allows New Emissions Rules Amid Legal Challenges—Pres. Joe Biden on Oct. 8 announced a 10-year deadline—starting in three years—for cities nationwide to identify and remove all lead pipes used to distribute municipal drinking water, a major source of lead poisoning, particularly for children, that drew greater attention following the massive water crisis in Flint, MI, a decade ago. Biden said the EPA would make $2.6 bil in funding available to help cities comply. On Oct. 24, the EPA finalized stricter limits on lead paint dust in homes and child care facilities built before 1978. Under the new rules, any amount of lead dust detected would be considered hazardous.

On Oct. 16, the Supreme Court allowed the EPA to enforce, at least temporarily, new regulations requiring new natural gas plants and all coal-fired plants in operation beyond 2039 to slash or capture 90% of carbon emissions.

Panel Finds Secret Service Needs Fundamental Reform—A bipartisan independent panel of former law enforcement officials—commissioned by Pres. Biden to review the Secret Service's failure to prevent the attempted assassination of former Pres. Donald Trump in July—released a blistering report Oct. 17 that called for new leadership from outside the agency to overhaul its culture, including its "present sense of complacency." The panel criticized agents' "troubling lack of critical thinking" that resulted in oversights such as failure to secure the event site, including the roof from which the gunman took his shots, and not adequately communicating with local law enforcement, which had reported the man as suspicious approx. 90 min. prior to the shooting.

McDonalds *E. coli* Outbreak Sickens at Least 75; Inflation Decline Continues; Other Economic News—The CDC Oct. 22 issued a food safety alert over an outbreak of *E. coli* illnesses linked to McDonald's Quarter Pounder sandwiches; it later determined the outbreak was likely caused by contaminated onions. As of Oct. 25, at least 75 people in 13 states had been sickened and 22 were hospitalized, including one person who died.

Year-over-year inflation in the U.S. continued to cool to 2.4% in Sept. according to a Bureau of Labor Statistics (BLS) report released Oct. 10. A separate BLS report released Oct. 4 showed the U.S. economy added 254,000 jobs in Sept. as the unemployment rate fell a tenth of a point to 4.1%.

At midnight Oct. 1, some 45,000 dockworkers seeking higher pay and protection from automation went on strike against East and Gulf Coast ports; the walkout was suspended two days later after a tentative agreement was reached. The Dow Jones Industrial Average closed Oct. at 41,763.46, down 1.3% from Sept., while the S&P 500 index finished at 5,705.45, a decrease of 1.0%. The Nasdaq Composite Index ended Oct. at 18,095.15, a 0.5% drop.

Biden Issues Formal Apology for Native American Boarding Schools—Pres. Joe Biden Oct. 25 issued the first-ever public apology by a sitting U.S. president for the federal government's role in compelling Native American children to attend boarding schools where they were subject to abuse and coerced to abandon their culture, languages, and religion. Biden described the practice as "horribly, horribly wrong" and "a sin on our souls." An Interior Dept. report released in July 2024 had identified 973 American Indian, Alaska Native, and Native Hawaiian children who died within the system of more than 400 schools operated or supported by the federal government, 1819-1969, in 37 states or then-territories; the agency said the real number was likely larger and that many students were also sexually and physically abused. Biden spoke on the Gila River Indian Reservation in Laveen Village, AZ, in his first official visit as president to a Native community.

International

Gang Attack on Haiti Town Kills Dozens—A gang early Oct. 3 killed at least 70 people (local officials reported 115 dead) in the small central Haiti town of Pont Sondé, according to the United Nations High Commissioner for Human Rights (OHCHR). The assailants, who reportedly set fire to at least 45 houses then shot residents escaping the flames, had accused Pont Sondé residents of cooperating with a self-protection group. Some 700,000 Haitians were currently displaced due to gang violence, the UN said in early Oct. The OHCHR Sept. 27, reported that violence involving gangs, who controlled an estimated 80% of Port-au-Prince as of early 2024, had killed more than 3,661 people in Haiti in 2024. On Sept. 30, the UN-backed Integrated Food Security Phase Classification said that more than 5.4 mil Haitians—nearly half the population—were experiencing "high levels of acute food insecurity."

Israel Kills Hamas Leader, Launches "Limited" Ground Invasion of Lebanon; Other Developments—Israel Defense Forces (IDF) troops on a routine patrol in Rafah Oct. 16 killed Yahya Sinwar, the leader of militant Palestinian group Hamas in Gaza. Sinwar was believed to have masterminded the Oct. 7, 2023, assault on Israel—in which Hamas killed about 1,200 people and took over 250 hostages, triggering Israel's ongoing war in Gaza—and also to have held up progress on cease-fire talks. Airstrikes on a residential building in Beit Lahia in northern Gaza Oct. 29 killed more than 90 people and was condemned by the UN. According to Gaza's health ministry, the cumulative death toll of Palestinians killed by Israel's offensive stood at more than 43,000 at the end of Oct. The Committee to Project Journalists reported at least 134 journalists and media workers killed, the most on record for a conflict since recordkeeping began in 1992. In mid-Oct., the Biden administration in a letter to the Israeli government demanded that Israel increase the flow of humanitarian aid into Gaza within the next 30 days or risk a halt to military assistance.

On Oct. 3, an Israeli airstrike targeted a cafe in the Tulkarm Refugee Camp in the northern part of the occupied West Bank, killing at least 18 people, one of whom Israel claimed was a local Hamas leader. According to the UN, 736 Palestinians had been killed in the West Bank since Hamas's 2023 attack, as of Oct. 31.

IDF troops reportedly commenced a ground invasion of southern Lebanon's border region early morning Oct. 1 or late the previous day in what Israel claimed to be "limited, localized, and targeted" raids against Iran-backed militant group Hezbollah. Coming after heavy Israeli air attacks against Lebanon in Sept.—including a precision strike that killed Hezbollah's leader—the incursion, Israel's first into Lebanon since 2006, marked a clear expansion of Israel's military operations in the region. Urging residents in Lebanon within 30 mi of the border to evacuate, IDF troops clashed directly with Hezbollah fighters throughout the month. Israel continued to direct airstrikes at alleged Hezbollah targets, including in a densely settled area of Beirut that Lebanese officials said killed 22 people on Oct. 10. According to the Lebanon Ministry of Health, as of Oct. 31, 2,865 people in Lebanon had been killed by Israeli attacks since Oct. 2023, with an estimated 1.2 mil displaced. Iran on Oct. 1 fired almost 180 missiles at Israel in retribution for Israel's killings of Hamas and Hezbollah officials; most were intercepted. In retaliation, Israel on Oct. 26 struck some 20 targets in Iran.

Israel's parliament on Oct. 28 overwhelmingly passed two laws set to take effect in 90 days that would effectively prevent the United Nations Relief and Works Agency for Palestine Refugees (UNRWA) from providing humanitarian aid in Gaza and the West Bank, following accusations of ties to Hamas including sheltering of its members.

Civilian Deaths Spike in Sudan as Fighting Intensifies—Sudan's paramilitary Rapid Support Forces (RSF) killed over 120 civilians in attacks Oct. 20-25 in Al-Sireha, Gezira state, according to local reports. The U.S. State Dept. condemned the killings, which were said to have been triggered by the defection of an area RSF commander. The activists blamed the RSF-rival, government-backed Sudanese Armed Forces (SAF) for that week's airstrike on a mosque in state capital Wad Madani that killed at least 31 civilians. The Armed Conflict Location and Event Data group (ACLED) recorded more than 24,850 fatalities in Sudan, as of Oct. 4, since the civil war between RSF and SAF broke out in Apr. 2023.

North Korea Sends Troops to Fight for Russia; Other Ukraine Invasion News—The U.S. Dept. of Defense confirmed Oct. 28 that North Korea had sent some 10,000 troops to Russia to fight in its war on neighboring Ukraine. Earlier that day, NATO Sec.-Gen. Mark Rutte publicly verified Ukrainian intelligence reports that North Korean troops were already deployed to Russia's southwestern Kursk region, where Ukraine in Aug. had seized nearly 500 sq mi of territory. Calling North Korea's entry a "dangerous expansion" of Russia's 32-month-old invasion, Sec.-Gen. Rutte said it was also a "sign of Putin's growing desperation." On Oct. 24, Russia's parliament had ratified a new mutual military assistance pact Russia and North Korea agreed on in June 2024. Heavy fighting continued in Kursk in Oct. and along Ukraine's eastern front, including over the strategic Donbas city of Pokrovsk.

According to U.S. officials, cumulative Russian fatalities in the war by early Oct. numbered as many as 115,000, with another 500,000 wounded, following heavy losses in Sept., the deadliest month for Russia in Ukraine.

General

Hurricane Milton Batters Florida—Category 3 storm Milton made landfall Oct. 9 in Siesta Key, FL, in the state's southern Gulf Coast region, killing at least 25 people in 12 counties—and damaging some communities battered by Hurricane Helene just 12 days earlier—before it tracked past Orlando and eastern Florida and dissipated in the Atlantic Ocean. Generating max winds of 120 mph and storm surge of 5-10 ft from Siesta Key to Naples, the storm brought heavy rainfall (up to 18 in. in some areas) that caused extensive flash flooding. According to an early AccuWeather estimate, Milton wrought between $160 and $180 billion in economic losses, but damages were not as extensive as forecasters projected in advance of the storm. On Oct. 11, Pres. Joe Biden approved a major disaster declaration for 34 Florida counties.

Before it made landfall, Milton's winds increased by 125 mph in just over 48 hours and then reached a max sustained level of 180 mph on Oct. 7—the shortest amount of time on record for an Atlantic storm to strengthen from a tropical depression to a Category 5 hurricane, according to NASA. Climate change researchers warned that warming ocean temperatures are fueling faster-forming hurricanes.

NASA Europe Clipper Probe Departs for Jupiter's Europa Moon; Other Space News—NASA's uncrewed Europa Clipper probe was launched Oct. 14 from NASA's Kennedy Space Center in Florida to investigate whether a vast, subsurface ocean on ice-covered Europa, one of Jupiter's many moons, is capable of supporting life. The roughly 100-ft-long, 13,000-lb spacecraft launched aboard a SpaceX Falcon Heavy rocket and is scheduled to travel 1.8 bil mi from Earth before reaching Jupiter's orbit by Apr. 2030, then make more than four dozen flybys of Europa before the mission ends in 2034.

SpaceX Oct. 13 launched the uncrewed Starship, using the most powerful rocket system ever built, on its fifth test flight. Its 230-ft "Super Heavy" reusable rocket booster then maneuvered itself back to the company's South Texas launchpad, where it was caught for the first time in midair by large pincers, dubbed "chopsticks."

L.A. Archdiocese Reaches $880 Mil Settlement Over Abuse Allegations—In a settlement announced Oct. 16, the Roman Catholic Archdiocese of Los Angeles agreed to pay $880 mil to 1,353 people who said they were sexually abused by its clergy as children. Though some of the decades-old civil claims against the diocese exceeded the statute of limitations, a state law temporarily opening a three-year "lookback window" allowed their claims to move forward. The agreement was the largest-ever single abuse-related settlement by a Catholic archdiocese and brought the L.A. Archdiocese's total payments in sexual assault claims to over $1.5 bil.

New York Wins First WNBA Championship—The New York Liberty pulled off a thrilling overtime victory in Game 5 over the Minnesota Lynx, 67-62, at Barclays Center in Brooklyn, NY, Oct. 20, to claim the franchise's first WNBA championship in their sixth Finals appearance. The Liberty trailed by 7 points going into halftime but fought back, with a fourth quarter capped by New York forward Breanna Stewart tying the game in two free throws with just five seconds left. Liberty center Jonquel Jones, who scored 17 points in Game 5 and averaged 17.8 points per game in the series, was named Finals MVP.

Flooding in Spain Kills Over 200 People—Flash flooding in southern and eastern Spain killed at least 211 people Oct. 29-30 after up to more than a foot of rain fell on some parts of the drought-stricken area within several hours. Most of the confirmed deaths occurred in the coastal region of Valencia, where flooding upended cars, downed trees and power lines, and necessitated helicopter rescues for some 70 people.

Dodgers Topple Yankees to Win Baseball's World Series—The Los Angeles Dodgers won the World Series over the New York Yankees in a 7-6 Game 5 victory on Oct. 30 at Yankee Stadium in the Bronx, NY. Erasing a five-run deficit in the fifth inning, the Dodgers claimed the eighth title in their franchise's storied 141-year-history. Dodgers first baseman Freddie Freeman, with home runs in each of the first four games and a record-tying 12 RBIs, was named World Series MVP.

OBITUARIES

For those whose deaths occurred Nov. 1, 2023 to Oct. 31, 2024.

A

Aimée, Anouk, 92, Academy Award-nominated French actress known for Fellini films *La Dolce Vita* (1960) and *8½* (1963); Paris, France, June 18, 2024.

Albini, Steve, 61, musician and audio engineer who helped define the sound of alternative music in the 1980s and '90s; Chicago, IL, May 7, 2024.

Alexander, Paul, 78, lawyer and paralytic polio survivor who lived over 70 years in an iron lung; Dallas, TX, Mar. 11, 2024.

Allen, Larry, 52, Hall of Fame offensive lineman, mostly for the Dallas Cowboys (1994-2005); Mexico, June 2, 2024.

Ames, Bruce, 95, biochemist known for developing the Ames test, which could identify chemicals that cause cancer; Berkeley, CA, Oct. 5, 2024.

Amos, John, 84, actor best known for *Good Times* (1974-76) and miniseries *Roots* (1977); Los Angeles, CA, Aug. 21, 2024.

Amos, Wally, 88, founder of Famous Amos chocolate chip cookies (1975); Honolulu, HI, Aug. 13, 2024.

Anders, William, 90, astronaut on *Apollo 8* (1968), the first mission to circle the moon, from which he took the iconic *Earthrise* photograph; San Juan County, WA, June 7, 2024.

Anderson, Terry, 76, Associated Press journalist held hostage by Islamic militants in Lebanon (1985-91); Greenwood Lake, NY, Apr. 21, 2024.

Angelos, Peter, 94, lawyer who owned the Baltimore Orioles (1993-2024); Towson, MD, Mar. 23, 2024.

Apfel, Iris, 102, interior designer whose 2005 Metropolitan Museum of Art Costume Institute exhibit drawn from her wardrobe made her a fashion icon; Palm Beach, FL, Mar. 1, 2024.

Auster, Paul, 77, writer best known for *The New York Trilogy* (1987) and *4 3 2 1* (2017); Brooklyn, NY, Apr. 30, 2024.

B

Barth, John, 93, writer known for *The Sot-Weed Factor* (1960); Bonita Springs, FL, Apr. 2, 2024.

Bartlett, Donald L., 88, Pulitzer Prize-winning *Philadelphia Inquirer* journalist; Philadelphia, PA, Oct. 5, 2024.

Battle, Hinton, 67, three-time Tony Award-winning actor and dancer known for playing the Scarecrow in *The Wiz* (1975); Los Angeles, CA, Jan. 30, 2024.

Bean, Billy, 60, MLB outfielder who in retirement came out as gay; New York, NY, Aug. 6, 2024.

Bean, Linda, 82, an heiress to the L.L. Bean company; Maine, Mar. 23, 2024.

Bell, C. Gordon, 89, computer engineer known as "father of the minicomputer"; Coronado, CA, May 17, 2024.

Berning, Susie, 83, golfer who won the U.S. Women's Open three times (1968, 1972-73); Indio, CA, Oct. 2, 2024.

Beverly, Frankie, 77, singer-songwriter known as leader of the soul-funk band Maze; Walnut Creek, CA, Sept. 10, 2024.

Bishop, Michael, 78, award-winning writer known for *No Enemy But Time* (1982); LaGrange, GA, Nov. 13, 2023.

Bjorken, James, 90, theoretical physicist who discovered "Bjorken scaling," which helped reveal the presence of quarks; Redwood City, CA, Aug. 6, 2024.

Blakemore, Michael, 95, Australian-born director; only person to ever win the Tony for Best Director of a play and of a musical in the same year (2000); Dec. 10, 2023.

Boesky, Ivan, 87, stock trader notorious for an insider trading scheme in 1986; La Jolla, CA, May 20, 2024.

Borman, Frank, 95, NASA astronaut who commanded *Gemini 7* (1965) and *Apollo 8* (1968), first mission to orbit the moon; Billings, MT, Nov. 7, 2023.

Braugher, Andre, 61, Emmy Award-winning actor known for *Homicide: Life on the Street* (1993-98) and *Brooklyn Nine-Nine* (2013-21); Dec. 11, 2023.

Brother Marquis (Mark Ross), 58, rapper known as a member of the Miami hip-hop group 2 Live Crew; Gadsden, AL, June 3, 2024.

Burgess, Janice, 72, children's TV writer and producer who created *The Backyardigans* (2004-13) and oversaw *Blue's Clues* (1996-2002); New York, NY, Mar. 2, 2024.

Butcher, Sam, 85, artist who created the Christian-themed porcelain figurines Precious Moments; Carthage, MO, May 20, 2024.

Byatt, A.S., 87, Booker Prize-winning British writer who became a literary sensation with *Possession* (1990); London, Eng., UK, Nov. 16, 2023.

C

Calley, William, 80, U.S. army lieutenant who was court-martialed over the My Lai massacre (1968), in which his platoon killed hundreds of unarmed Vietnamese civilians; Gainesville, FL, Apr. 28, 2024.

Carr, Caleb, 68, author best known for *The Alienist* (1994); Cherry Plain, NY, May 23, 2024.

Carruthers, Alastair, 79, Canadian dermatologist who with his ophthalmologist wife Jean pioneered cosmetic use of botulinum toxin A (Botox); Vancouver, BC, Can., Aug. 19, 2024.

Carter, Rosalynn, 96, first lady of the U.S. (1977-81) who championed mental health and co-founded the Carter Center (1982) with Pres. Jimmy Carter; Plains, GA, Nov. 19, 2023.

Cassaday, John, 52, comic book artist best known for co-creating *Planetary* (1999-2009); New York, NY, Sept. 9, 2024.

Cavalli, Roberto, 83, Italian fashion designer whose use of animal prints was a trademark; Florence, Italy, Apr. 12, 2024.

Cepeda, Orlando, 86, Puerto Rican Hall of Fame first baseman who in 1967 won MVP and led the Cardinals to a World Series win; Concord, CA, June 28, 2024.

Charlot, Juli Lynne, 101, fashion designer credited with the "poodle skirt" (1947); Tepoztlán, Mexico, Mar. 3, 2024.

Cheng Pei Pei, 78, Shanghai-born actress known as "Queen of Kung Fu" and for role in *Crouching Tiger, Hidden Dragon* (2000); San Francisco, CA, July 17, 2024.

Christensen, Ward, 78, computer scientist who invented the first online bulletin board system; Rolling Meadows, IL, Oct. 11, 2024.

Cleave, Mary, 76, NASA astronaut and engineer who flew on two shuttle missions and researched global climate change; Annapolis, MD, Nov. 27, 2023.

Clements, John A., 101, physiologist who created a drug to treat premature infants struggling to breathe; Tiburon, CA, Sept. 3, 2024.

Coleman, Dabney, 92, Emmy Award-winning actor known for playing bosses in *9 to 5* (1980) and *Tootsie* (1982); Santa Monica, CA, May 16, 2024.

Colvin, Ruth Johnson, 107, philanthropist who founded Literacy Volunteers of America (1962), now known as ProLiteracy; Syracuse, NY, Aug. 18, 2024.

Conter, Lou, 102, naval lieutenant commander and last known survivor of the USS *Arizona*, which sank during the 1941 attack on Pearl Harbor; Grass Valley, CA, Apr. 1, 2024.

Conway, Lynn, 86, scientist who revolutionized computer chip design; fired by IBM in 1968 when she revealed she was transgender; the company offered an apology in 2020; Jackson, MI, June 9, 2024.

Cooper, Leon, 94, Nobel Prize-winning physicist known for work on superconductivity; Providence, RI, Oct. 23, 2024.

Corman, Roger, 98, director and producer known for cult classic movies and launching the careers of major directors and actors; Santa Monica, CA, May 9, 2024.

Creel, Gavin, 48, Olivier and Tony Award-winning theater actor known for *Hello, Dolly!* (2017); New York, NY, Sept. 30, 2024.

Crosby, Kathryn, 90, film actress and singer who stopped performing after marrying crooner Bing Crosby; Hillsborough, CA, Sept. 20, 2024.

D

Darren, James, 88, actor and singer known for Gidget movies and for his song "Goodbye Cruel World" (1961); Los Angeles, CA, Sept. 2, 2024.

Davis, Romay Johnson, 104, Women's Army Corps member who helped service members receive their mail overseas in WWII; Montgomery, AL, June 21, 2024.

de Brunhoff, Laurent, 98, French author and illustrator who continued the Babar the Elephant series originated by his father; Key West, FL, Mar. 22, 2024.

Del Tredici, David, 86, Pulitzer Prize-winning composer who based two decades of work on *Alice's Adventures in Wonderland*; New York, NY, Nov. 18, 2023.

DeMille, Nelson, 81, bestselling suspense novelist who sold over 58 million books, including *Plum Island* (1997); Mineola, NY, Sept. 17, 2024.

Dennett, Daniel, 82, philosopher and cognitive scientist who authored widely read books on consciousness, religion, and free will; Portland, ME, Apr. 19, 2024.

DePrince, Michaela, 29, Sierra Leone-born ballet dancer; New York, NY, Sept. 10, 2024.

Dobbs, Lou, 78, radio and TV host for CNN (1980-99, 2001-09) and Fox Business (2011-21); July 18, 2024.

Doherty, Shannen, 53, actress known for *Beverly Hills, 90210* (1990-94) and *Charmed* (1998-2001); Malibu, CA, July 13, 2024.

Dohlman, Claes, 101, Swedish-born ophthalmologist who developed an artificial cornea; Weston, MA, July 14, 2024.

Donahue, Phil, 88, pioneering host of eponymous daytime TV talk show (1967-96); New York, NY, Aug. 18, 2024.

Driesell, Lefty, 92, Hall of Fame college basketball coach; Virginia Beach, VA, Feb. 17, 2024.

Drossman, Neil, 83, advertising writer who created memorable ads for Air Wick and Meow Mix; Bronx, NY, Nov. 25, 2023.

Dugdale, Rose, 82, British heiress who became a bomb maker, art thief, and hijacker in support of the Irish Republican Army (IRA); Dublin, Ireland, Mar. 18, 2024.

Duvall, Shelley, 75, actress and producer best known for *Nashville* (1975), *The Shining* (1980), and *Popeye* (1980); Blanco, TX, July 11, 2024.

E

Eddy, Duane, 85, Rock and Roll Hall of Fame guitarist and songwriter known for his twangy guitar on 1950s and '60s hits; Franklin, TN, Apr. 30, 2024.

Edelin, Ramona, 78, National Urban Coalition executive who helped popularize the term "African American"; Washington, DC, Feb. 19, 2024.

Edwards, Anne, 96, writer known for bestselling biographies of actresses Vivien Leigh (1977) and Katharine Hepburn (1985); Beverly Hills, CA, Jan. 20, 2024.

Edwards, Bob, 76, Peabody Award-winning radio host for NPR's *All Things Considered* and *Morning Edition*; Arlington, VA, Feb. 10, 2024.

Endo, Akira, 90, Japanese biochemist whose research in the 1970s led to the creation of statins, drugs that lower cholesterol; Tokyo, Japan, June 5, 2024.

Epper, Jeannie, 83, stuntwoman for over 100 films and TV shows, including *Wonder Woman* (1975-79), as the title character's double; Simi Valley, CA, May 5, 2024.

Epstein, Antony, 102. British pathologist who co-discovered Epstein-Barr, the first virus known to cause cancer in humans; London, Eng., UK, Feb. 6, 2024.

Erwitt, Elliott, 95, French-born American photographer whose images included a 1959 face-off between Vice Pres. Nixon and Soviet Premier Khrushchev; New York, NY, Nov. 29, 2023.

F

Ferry, David, 99, National Book Award-winning poet whose translations of *Gilgamesh*, Horace, and Virgil were highly praised; Lexington, MA, Nov. 5, 2023.

Fischetti, Ronald, 87, lawyer who defended high-profile clients including mobsters, NYPD officers accused of misconduct, and former Pres. Trump; Stamford, CT, Nov. 25, 2023.

Flack, Audrey, 93, sculptor and visual artist known for colorful photorealist paintings; Southampton, NY, June 28, 2024.

Friedman, Kinky, 79, musician and writer who formed the satirical country band Kinky Friedman and the Texas Jewboys; Medina, TX, June 27, 2024.

Fujimori, Alberto, 86, Peruvian president (1990-2000) who was removed from power and later imprisoned on corruption and human rights abuse charges; Lima, Peru, Sept. 11, 2024.

G

Garr, Teri, 79, actress known for comedic roles in *Young Frankenstein* (1974) and *Tootsie* (1982); Los Angeles, CA, Oct. 29, 2024.

Gaudreau, Johnny, 31, NHL hockey player who died with his brother when struck by a car while biking; Oldmans Twp., NJ, Aug. 29, 2024.

Gaynor, Mitzi, 93, actress, singer, and dancer best known for movie musical *South Pacific* (1958); Los Angeles, CA, Oct. 17, 2024.

Glock, Gaston, 94, Austrian engineer who invented the Glock handgun (1982); Dec. 27, 2023.

Gossett, Louis, Jr., 87, Academy Award-winning actor known for *An Officer and a Gentleman* (1982) and *Roots* (1977); Santa Monica, CA, Mar. 29, 2024.

Graham, Bob, 87, U.S. sen. (D, FL, 1987-2005) and gov. (1979-87) who voted against the war in Iraq (2003); Gainesville, FL, Apr. 16, 2024.

Graves, Lorraine, 66, ballet dancer with the Dance Theatre of Harlem; Norfolk, VA, Mar. 21, 2024.

Greene, Shecky, 97, comedian known for shows primarily in Las Vegas for over 50 years; Las Vegas, NV, Dec. 31, 2023.

Greenfield, Martin, 95, tailor whose clients ranged from Pres. Eisenhower to LeBron James; Manhasset, NY, Mar. 20, 2024.

Gregg, Arthur J., 96, U.S. Army general who was the first Black officer to reach the rank of lieutenant general (1977); Richmond, VA, Aug. 22, 2024.

Guillemin, Roger, 100, Nobel Prize-winning French-born American neuroscientist who studied hormones produced by the hypothalamus; San Diego, CA, Feb. 21, 2024.

Gülen, Fethullah, 83, Turkish Muslim theologian whose namesake movement sought social and civic reform; PA, Oct. 20, 2024.

H

Halbreich, Betty, 96, personal shopper who assisted celebrities and socialites at New York department store Bergdorf Goodman (1976-2024); New York, NY, Aug. 24, 2024.

Hamilton, Charles V., 94, political scientist and civil rights activist who coauthored *Black Power: The Politics of Liberation* (1967); Chicago, IL, Nov. 18, 2023.

Haniyeh, Ismail, 62, Palestinian-born leader of Hamas; likely assassinated by Israeli agents; Tehran, Iran, July 31, 2024.

Hardy, Françoise, 80, French singer-songwriter and actress who popularized "yé-yé" pop music; Paris, France, June 11, 2024.

Hayes, Bill, 98, actor and singer known for *Days of Our Lives* (1970-2024), and *Billboard* number-one "The Ballad of Davy Crockett" (1955); Los Angeles, CA, Jan. 12, 2024.

Herzog, Whitey, 92, Hall of Fame manager who led the St. Louis Cardinals to 3 pennants and a World Series win (1982); St. Louis, MO, Apr. 15, 2024.

Higgs, Peter, 94, Nobel Prize-winning British theoretical physicist who predicted a fundamental particle, the Higgs boson; Edinburgh, Scotland, UK, Apr. 8, 2024.

Hitchcock, Peggy Mellon, 90, heiress who funded Timothy Leary's psychedelics experimentation; Tucson, AZ, Apr. 9, 2024.

Holman, Bill, 96, Grammy Award-winning jazz saxophonist, composer, and arranger; Los Angeles, CA, May 6, 2024.

Horn, Rebecca, 80, German visual artist whose best-known work was *Einhorn* (Unicorn) (1970); Bad König, Germany, Sept. 6, 2024.

Houston, Cissy, 91, Grammy Award-winning gospel singer who influenced daughter, Whitney Houston, and niece Dionne Warwick; Newark, NJ, Oct. 7, 2024.

Hunt, Richard, 88, abstract sculptor known for public art about the Black experience; Chicago, IL, Dec. 16, 2023.

I

Indiana, Gary, 74, novelist and art critic with the *Village Voice* (1985-88); best known for a true-crime book trilogy; New York, NY, Oct. 23, 2024.

Inhofe, James, 89, U.S. sen. (R, OK, 1994-2023) and rep. (1987-94) who was a vocal opponent of abortion and marriage equality; Tulsa, OK, July 9, 2024.

J

Jackson Lee, Sheila, 74, U.S. rep. (D, TX, 1995-2024) who authored legislation that made Juneteenth a national holiday; Houston, TX, July 19, 2024.

Jackson, Tito, 70, Rock and Roll Hall of Fame musician who with his brothers the Jackson Five had four *Billboard* number-ones; Gallup, NM, Sept. 15, 2024.

James, Mark, 83, Grammy Award-winning songwriter whose hit songs included "Suspicious Minds" (1968) and "Always on My Mind" (1972); Nashville, TN, June 8, 2024.

Jennings, Will, 80, Oscar and Grammy Award-winning lyricist known for movie hits "Up Where We Belong" (1982) and "My Heart Will Go On" (1997); Tyler, TX, Sept. 6, 2024.

Jewison, Norman, 97, Canadian-born film director known for *In the Heat of the Night* (1967), *Fiddler on the Roof* (1971), and *Moonstruck* (1987); Malibu, CA, Jan. 20, 2024.

Johns, Glynis, 100, Tony Award-winning British actress known for *A Little Night Music* (1973); Los Angeles, CA, Jan. 4, 2024.

Johnson, Edward B., 81, CIA officer who helped rescue six U.S. diplomats from Iran in 1980; Fairfax, VA, Aug. 27, 2024.

Jones, Jack, 86, Grammy Award-winning singer and actor known for *The Love Boat* theme song (1977-86); Rancho Mirage, CA, Oct. 23, 2024.

Jones, James Earl, 93, EGOT-winning actor known for stage performances and voicing Darth Vader in Star Wars films and Mufasa in *The Lion King* (1994, 2019); Pawling, NY, Sept. 9, 2024.

Jones, Parnelli, 90, Hall of Fame driver who won the 1963 Indianapolis 500; Torrance, CA, June 4, 2024.

Jordan, V. Craig, 76, American-British pharmacologist who discovered that failed contraceptive tamoxifen was effective in treating breast cancer; Houston, TX, June 9, 2024.

K

Kadare, Ismail, 88, Albanian novelist whose first novel, *The General of the Dead Army* (1963), won international acclaim; Tirana, Albania, July 1, 2024.

Kahneman, Daniel, 90, Nobel Prize-winning Israeli-American psychologist who popularized his work in bestseller *Thinking, Fast and Slow* (2011); Mar. 27, 2024.

Keith, Toby, 62, singer-songwriter known for patriotic country songs including "Courtesy of the Red, White & Blue" (2002); Oklahoma, Feb. 5, 2024.

Kelley, Bob, 96, car dealer who developed his family business of valuating cars into the *Kelley Blue Book*; Indian Wells, CA, May 28, 2024.

Kennedy, Ethel, 96, human rights advocate and widow of Sen. Robert F. Kennedy (D, NY); Boston, MA, Oct. 10, 2024.

King, Dexter, 62, civil rights leader and son of Martin Luther King Jr. who led the King Center for Nonviolent Social Change; Malibu, CA, Jan. 22, 2024.

Kiptum, Kelvin, 24, Kenyan distance runner who at the time of his death held the marathon world record at 2:00:35; Kaptagat, Kenya, Feb. 11, 2024.

Kissinger, Henry, 100, German-born American diplomat who served as sec. of state (1973-77) and national security adviser (1969-75); Kent, CT, Nov. 29, 2023.

Knight, Bobby, 83, Hall of Fame college basketball coach who won 902 NCAA Div. I games, mostly with the Indiana Hoosiers (1971-2000); Bloomington, IN, Nov. 1, 2023.

Knight, Jean, 80, R&B and soul singer known for hit single "Mr. Big Stuff" (1971); Tampa, FL, Nov. 22, 2023.

Kohl, Herbert, 88, U.S. sen. (D, WI, 1989-2013), businessman, and philanthropist; Milwaukee, WI, Dec. 27, 2023.

Kristofferson, Kris, 88, actor and singer-songwriter known for the song "Me and Bobby McGee" (1969) and film *A Star Is Born* (1976); Maui, HI, Sept. 28, 2024.

Kroemer, Herbert, 95, Nobel Prize-winning German-American physicist whose work on semiconductors helped pave the way for cellphones; Mar. 8, 2024.

Krofft, Marty, 86, Canadian-born writer and puppeteer best known for co-creating *H.R. Pufnstuf* (1969) and *Land of the Lost* (1974-76); Los Angeles, CA, Nov. 25, 2023.

L

Landau, Jon, 63, Academy Award-winning producer known for blockbusters, including *Titanic* (1997) and *Avatar* and its sequel (2009 and 2022); Los Angeles, CA, July 5, 2024.

Lapham, Lewis H., 89, editor of *Harper's Magazine* (1976-81, 1983-2006); also founded *Lapham's Quarterly* (2007); Rome, Italy, July 23, 2024.

Lawrence, Mary Wells, 95, first woman to found, run, and own a major ad agency; known for Alka-Seltzer's "Plop, Plop, Fizz, Fizz" ads; London, Eng., UK, May 11, 2024.

Lawrence, Steve, 88, Grammy Award-winning singer who was popular as a duo act with his wife Eydie Gormé; Los Angeles, CA, Mar. 7, 2024.

Lawson, James, Jr., 95, civil rights leader who advocated Gandhi's philosophy of nonviolence; Los Angeles, CA, June 9, 2024.

Lear, Norman, 101, Emmy Award-winning writer and producer who created sitcoms that addressed political issues, including *All in the Family* (1971-79), *Maude* (1972-78), and *Good Times* (1974-79); Los Angeles, CA, Dec. 5, 2023.

Ledbetter, Lilly, 86, activist for equal pay; U.S. Congress passed legislation in her name (2009); Birmingham, AL, Oct. 12, 2024.

Lee, Tsung-Dao, 97, Nobel Prize-winning Chinese-born physicist known for groundbreaking work disproving the principle of parity; San Francisco, CA, Aug. 4, 2024.

Lesh, Phil, 84, Hall of Fame Grateful Dead bass guitarist and songwriter, known for cowriting "Box of Rain" and "Truckin'" (both 1970); Oct. 25, 2024.

Lewis, Richard, 76, comedian whose dark neuroses led to acting roles, including in the HBO series *Curb Your Enthusiasm* (2000-24); Los Angeles, CA, Feb. 27, 2024.

Lieberman, Joseph, 82, U.S. sen. (D/I, CT, 1989-2013) who was the first Jewish nominee on a major party presidential ticket (2000); New York, NY, Mar. 27, 2024.

Lo Bianco, Tony, 87, actor acclaimed for *The French Connection* (1971); Poolesville, MD, June 11, 2024.

M

MacGowan, Shane, 65, English-born Irish singer-songwriter who led the Pogues, best known for "Fairytale of New York" (1987); Dublin, Ireland, Nov. 30, 2023.

MacNeil, Robert, 93, Canadian-American TV journalist who co-hosted the nightly public TV news with Jim Lehrer (1975-95); New York, NY, Apr. 12, 2024.

Maki, Fumihiko, 95, Pritzker Prize-winning Japanese architect whose work included 4 World Trade Center (New York, 2013); Tokyo, Japan, June 6, 2024.

Marshall, Peter, 98, Emmy Award-winning TV host best known for *Hollywood Squares* (1966-81); Encino, CA, Aug. 15, 2024.

Martin, Maria, 72, Mexican-born American radio journalist who in 1993 created public radio program *Latino USA*; Austin, TX, Dec. 2, 2023.

Mayall, John, 90, British Hall of Fame musician who led John Mayall & the Bluesbreakers (1963), an influential blues band; CA, July 22, 2024.

Mayhew, Richard, 100, artist of abstract landscapes that reflected his Black and Native American heritage; Soquel, CA, Sept. 26, 2024.

Mays, Willie, 93, Hall of Fame 24-time All-Star centerfielder, mostly with the NY/San Francisco Giants; 2-time NL MVP (1954, 1965); Palo Alto, CA, June 18, 2024.

McCourt, Malachy, 92, actor and memoirist; New York, NY, Mar. 11, 2024.

McFadden, Mary, 85, fashion designer whose pleated dress designs were influenced by ancient cultures; Southampton, NY, Sept. 13, 2024.

McGee, Patti, 79, first woman National Skateboard Champion (1964); Brea, CA, Oct. 16, 2024.

McGinnis, George, 73, Hall of Fame forward who won two ABA championships with the Indiana Pacers (1972, 1973); Indianapolis, IN, Dec. 14, 2023.

Melanie, 76, singer-songwriter known for the *Billboard* number-one "Brand New Key" (1971); Jan. 23, 2024.

Mendes, Sérgio, 83, Grammy Award-winning Brazilian bossa nova musician; Los Angeles, CA, Sept. 5, 2024.

Mileti, Nick, 93, sports magnate who once owned Cleveland MLB and NBA franchises; Rocky River, OH, Aug. 21, 2024.

Mixner, David, 77, anti-war and LGBT activist and political operative; New York, NY, Mar. 11, 2024.

Momaday, N. Scott, 89, Pulitzer Prize-winning novelist whose *House Made of Dawn* (1968) launched a Native American literary renaissance; Santa Fe, NM, Jan. 24, 2024.

Morgan, Ted, 91, Pulitzer Prize-winning French-American writer known for biographies of Franklin D. Roosevelt and William S. Burroughs; New York, NY, Dec. 13, 2023.

Mortensen, Chris, 72, journalist known for his coverage of the NFL for ESPN; Birmingham, AL, Mar. 3, 2024.

Mothershed Wair, Thelma, 93, civil rights activist who integrated Central High School as a member of the Little Rock Nine in 1957; Little Rock, AR, Oct. 19, 2024.

Mull, Martin, 80, actor known for *Mary Hartman, Mary Hartman* (1976-77), *Roseanne* (1991-97), and *Sabrina the Teenage Witch* (1997-2000); Los Angeles, CA, June 27, 2024.

Mulroney, Brian, 84, Canadian prime minister (1984-93) who negotiated the 1992 North American Free Trade Agreement (NAFTA); Palm Beach, FL, Feb. 29, 2024.

Munger, Charles, 99, investor and vice chairman of Berkshire Hathaway (1978-2023); Santa Barbara, CA, Nov. 28, 2023.

Munro, Alice, 92, Nobel Prize-winning Canadian writer known for exploring complexities in interconnected short stories; Port Hope, ON, Can., May 13, 2024.

Murphy, William P., Jr., 100, physician who invented the vinyl blood bag, which transformed transfusions; Coral Gables, FL, Nov. 30, 2023.

Mutombo, Dikembe, 58, Congolese-born Hall of Fame NBA center known for his defense; Atlanta, GA, Sept. 30, 2024.

Mwinyi, Ali Hassan, 98, second president of Tanzania (1985-95) who dismantled socialist policies; Dar es Salaam, Tanzania, Feb. 29, 2024.

N

Nash, Bette, 88, flight attendant whose 67-year career set a Guinness World Record; May 17, 2024.

Nasrallah, Hassan, 64, Lebanese Shia cleric and leader of militant group Hezbollah since 1992; Dahieh, Lebanon, Sept. 27, 2024.

Navalny, Alexei, 47, Russian opposition leader whose challenge to Pres. Putin led to his imprisonment; he survived an assassination attempt in 2020; Kharp, Russia, Feb. 16, 2024.

Newhart, Bob, 94, Grammy and Emmy Award-winning comedian known for deadpan style and sitcoms *The Bob Newhart Show* (1972-78) and *Newhart* (1982-90); Los Angeles, CA, July 18, 2024.

O

O'Brien, Edna, 93, Irish writer known for her polarizing first novel, *The Country Girls* (1960); London, Eng., UK, July 27, 2024.

O'Connor, Sandra Day, 93, first woman justice on the U.S. Supreme Court (1981-2006); served as a moderating opinion on abortion and affirmative action; Phoenix, AZ, Dec. 1, 2023.

O'Neal, Ryan, 82, actor known for *Love Story* (1970), *What's Up, Doc?* (1972), and *Paper Moon* (1973); Santa Monica, CA, Dec. 8, 2023.

Osgood, Charles, 91, journalist who hosted *CBS News Sunday Morning* (1996-2016) and delivered humorous radio commentaries; Saddle River, NJ, Jan. 23, 2024.

Ostrow, Steve, 91, LGBT rights activist who founded the Continental Baths, a gay men's sex and entertainment club in New York; Sydney, Australia, Feb. 3, 2024.

Otto, Jim, 86, Hall of Fame center with the Oakland Raiders (1960-74); Auburn, CA, May 19, 2024.

Ozawa, Seiji, Chinese-born Japanese conductor known for leading the Boston Symphony Orchestra (1973-2002); Tokyo, Japan, Feb. 6, 2024.

P

Pascal, Francine, 92, author who created the Sweet Valley High young adult series, which sold over 200 million books; New York, NY, July 28, 2024.

Pascrell, Bill, Jr., 87, U.S. rep. (D, NJ, 1997-2024) who focused on infrastructure; Livingston, NJ, Aug. 21, 2024.

Payne, Liam, 31, British singer and songwriter with the popular boy band One Direction; Buenos Aires, Argentina, Oct. 16, 2024.

Penzias, Arno, 90, German-born Nobel Prize-winning physicist who co-discovered cosmic microwave background radiation, confirming the Big Bang Theory; San Francisco, CA, Jan. 22, 2024.

Piñera, Sebastián, 74, Chilean president (2010-14, 2018-22); Lake Ranco, Los Ríos Region, Chile, Feb. 6, 2024.

Post, William, 96, bakery plant manager who helped create Pop-Tarts; Grand Rapids, MI, Feb. 10, 2024.

R

Raisi, Ebrahim, 63, Iranian president (2021-24) known for his role as a prosecutor in sentencing thousands of dissidents to death; Uzi, Iran, May 19, 2024.

Randolph, Joyce, 99, actress known as Trixie Norton in sitcom *The Honeymooners* (1955-56); New York, NY, Jan. 13, 2024.

Reagon, Bernice Johnson, 81, singer and civil rights activist; Washington, DC, July 16, 2024.

Rich Homie Quan (Dequantes Devontay Lamar), 34, Atlanta rapper known for "Flex (Ooh, Ooh, Ooh)" (2015); Atlanta, GA, Sept. 5, 2024.

Riggio, Leonard, 83, executive chairman of the book retailer Barnes & Noble (1971-2019); New York, NY, Aug. 27, 2024.

Ringgold, Faith, 93, multimedia artist known for painted quilts, including *Tar Beach* (1988), on which she also based a children's book (1991); Englewood, NJ, Apr. 13, 2024.

Rivera, Chita, 91, Tony Award-winning actress, singer, and dancer whose shows included *West Side Story* (1957), *Bye Bye Birdie* (1960), *Chicago* (1975), and *Kiss of the Spider Woman* (1993); New York, NY, Jan. 30, 2024.

Robbins, Trina, 85, cartoonist who helped create *It Ain't Me Babe* (1970), the first comic book made exclusively by women; San Francisco, CA, Apr. 10, 2024.

Robinson, James D., III, 88, CEO of American Express (1977-93) who diversified the company; Roslyn, NY, Mar. 18, 2024.

Robinson, Marian, 86, mother of former first lady Michelle Obama, who lived in the White House to help support the family; Chicago, IL, May 31, 2024.

Rockwell, Thomas, 91, children's author known for *How to Eat Fried Worms* (1973); Danbury, CT, Sept. 27, 2024.

Rodriguez, Juan "Chi-Chi," 88, Puerto Rican-born Hall of Fame golfer; Puerto Rico, Aug. 8, 2024.

Rose, Pete, 83, Cincinnati Reds player-manager and MLB's all-time hits leader; ruled "permanently ineligible" for the Hall of Fame due to gambling on his own teams; Las Vegas, NV, Sept. 30, 2024.

Rowlands, Gena, 94, actress who collaborated with her writer-director husband John Cassavetes on ten films, including *A Woman Under the Influence* (1974) and *Gloria* (1980); Indian Wells, CA, Aug. 14, 2024.

Ruddy, Albert S., 94, Canadian-born Academy Award-winning producer known for *The Godfather* (1972) and *Million Dollar Baby* (2004); Los Angeles, CA, May 25, 2024.

Rush, Barbara, 97, actress best known for sci-fi classic *It Came From Outer Space* (1953) and TV series *Peyton Place* (1968-69); Westlake Village, CA, Mar. 31, 2024.

Rutan, Dick, 85, aviator who piloted the first non-stop, non-refueled flight around the world (1986); Coeur d'Alene, ID, May 3, 2024.

S

Samuelsson, Bengt I., 90, Nobel Prize-winning Swedish biochemist who helped explain prostaglandins; Mölle, Sweden, July 5, 2024.

Sanborn, David, 78, Grammy Award-winning saxophonist; Tarrytown, NY, May 12, 2024.

Schally, Andrew, 97, Nobel Prize-winning Polish-born endocrinologist who studied hormones produced by the hypothalamus; Miami Beach, FL, Oct. 17, 2024.

Schickele, Peter, 88, Grammy Award-winning composer and satirist best known as his fictional alter ego, P.D.Q. Bach; Bearsville, NY, Jan. 16, 2024.

Schmidt, Joe, 92, Hall of Fame football player and coach for the Detroit Lions; Palm Beach Gardens, FL, Sept. 11, 2024.

Seidler, David, 86, Academy Award-winning British-born American screenwriter known for *The King's Speech* (2010); New Zealand, Mar. 16, 2024.

Seixas, Vic, 100, Hall of Fame tennis player who won 15 Grand Slam titles, mostly in doubles and mixed doubles, in the 1950s; Mill Valley, CA, July 5, 2024.

Serra, Richard, 85, sculptor known for large-scale steel works; Orient, NY, Mar. 26, 2024.

Shales, Tom, 79, Pulitzer Prize-winning writer and critic for the *Washington Post* (1972-2010); Alexandria, VA, Jan. 13, 2024.

Shaw, Billy, 85, Hall of Fame football player for the Buffalo Bills (1961-69); Toccoa, GA, Oct. 4, 2024.

Sherman, Richard M., 95, Academy Award-winning songwriter who co-wrote "It's A Small World" (1964) and songs for many films including *Mary Poppins* (1964); Beverly Hills, CA, May 25, 2024.

Sikking, James B., 90, actor best known for *Hill Street Blues* (1981-87) and *Doogie Howser, M.D.* (1989-93); Los Angeles, CA, July 13, 2024.

Simkin, Penny, 85, physical therapist and educator who helped popularize the use of doulas; Seattle, WA, Apr. 11, 2024.

Simmons, Richard, 76, fitness guru whose TV appearances made the enthusiastic aerobics instructor a household name; Los Angeles, CA, July 13, 2024.

Simons, Jim, 86, mathematician who studied string theory before becoming a billionaire Wall Street investor; New York, NY, May 10, 2024.

Simpson, O.J., 76, Hall of Fame running back-turned-actor acquitted of murdering his ex-wife and a friend in a high-profile 1995 criminal trial (found liable in a civil suit, 1997); Las Vegas, NV, Apr. 10, 2024.

Sinwar, Yahya, 61, Palestinian Hamas political leader who was the mastermind of the Oct. 7, 2023, attack on Israel; killed in a firefight with Israeli soldiers; Rafah, Gaza, Oct. 16, 2024.

Smith, Maggie, 89, Academy, Emmy, and Tony Award-winning British actress best known for *The Prime of Miss Jean Brodie* (1969), seven Harry Potter films (2001-11), and TV's *Downton Abbey* (2010-15); London, Eng., UK, Sept. 27, 2024.

Smothers, Tom, 86, comedian who was half of comedy duo the Smothers Brothers, known for their eponymous *Comedy Hour* (1967-69) and its political satire; Santa Rosa, CA, Dec. 26, 2023.

Solow, Robert, 99, Nobel Prize-winning economist known for theories on the role of new technologies in economic growth; Lexington, MA, Dec. 21, 2023.

Song Binbin, 77, Chinese student leader of the militant Red Guards; New York, NY, Sept. 16, 2024.

Soul, David, 80, actor and singer known as a police detective on *Starsky & Hutch* (1975-79); London, Eng., UK, Jan. 4, 2024.

Spurlock, Morgan, 53, documentary filmmaker best known for *Super Size Me* (2004); New York, NY, May 23, 2024.

Stafford, Thomas P., 93, NASA astronaut who was commander of first joint U.S.-Soviet rendezvous mission (1975); Satellite Beach, FL, Mar. 18, 2024.

Stella, Frank, 87, abstract and minimalist painter and sculptor who used geometric patterns and shapes in his work; New York, NY, May 4, 2024.

Sternhagen, Frances, 93, Tony Award-winning actress known for *On Golden Pond* (1979) and *Driving Miss Daisy* (1988); New Rochelle, NY, Nov. 27, 2023.

Sutherland, Donald, 88, Canadian-born actor known for *M*A*S*H* (1970), *Klute* (1971), and The Hunger Games films (2012-15); Miami, FL, June 20, 2024.

Sweeney, Maureen, 100, Irish assistant postmistress whose weather observations at her County Mayo office influenced Allied forces to delay D-Day; Belmullet, Ireland, Dec. 17, 2023.

T

Thompson, Dennis, 75, Hall of Fame drummer with punk rock group MC5; Taylor, MI, May 9, 2024.

Tiant, Luis, 83, Cuban-born pitcher; Wells, ME, Oct. 8, 2024.

Toriyama, Akira, 68, Japanese manga artist who created "Dragon Ball," inspiring film, TV, and video games; Japan, Mar. 1, 2024.

Towne, Robert, 89, Academy Award-winning screenwriter known for *Chinatown* (1974) and as an uncredited writer on *The Godfather* (1972); Los Angeles, CA, July 1, 2024.

Trọng, Nguyễn Phú, 80, Vietnamese president (2018-21) and Communist Party general secretary (2011-24); Hanoi, Vietnam, July 19, 2024.

Truly, Richard, 86, astronaut who led NASA (1989-92) following the 1986 *Challenger* disaster; Genesse, CO, Feb. 27, 2024.

V

Valenzuela, Fernando, 63, Mexican-born Cy Young Award-winning pitcher, mostly with the L.A. Dodgers (1980-90); Los Angeles, CA, Oct. 22, 2024.

W

Walsh, Don, 92, oceanographer aboard the submersible *Trieste* as it reached Challenger Deep, the deepest-known point of the Pacific seabed, in 1960; Myrtle Point, OR, Nov. 12, 2023.

Walsh, M. Emmet, 88, character actor best known for his roles in *Blade Runner* (1982) and *Knives Out* (2019); St. Albans, VT, Mar. 19, 2024.

Walton, Bill, 71, Hall of Fame NBA player and broadcaster; won two NCAA titles with UCLA and NBA titles with Portland and Boston; San Diego, CA, May 27, 2024.

Weathers, Carl, 76, NFL player-turned-actor, best remembered as Apollo Creed in four Rocky films; Los Angeles, CA, Feb. 1, 2024.

Weiss, Mary, 75, lead singer for the Shangri-Las, known for their *Billboard* number-one "Leader of the Pack" (1964); Palm Springs, CA, Jan. 19, 2024.

West, Jerry, 86, Hall of Fame point guard, coach, and executive for L.A. Lakers; immortalized in silhouette as the NBA logo; Los Angeles, CA, June 12, 2024.

Westheimer, Ruth, 96, German-born American therapist known for encouraging frank discussion about sex as "Dr. Ruth"; New York, NY, July 12, 2024.

Wilkinson, Tom, 75, Emmy Award-winning British character actor, known for his role in *The Full Monty* (1997); London, Eng., UK, Dec. 30, 2023.

Wojcicki, Susan, 56, CEO of YouTube (2014-23) who was one of Google's earliest employees; Aug. 9, 2024.

Woodwell, George, 95, ecologist who founded a research center to study global climate change; Woods Hole, MA, June 18, 2024.

Wright, Evan, 59, journalist whose work about the Iraq War included the bestseller *Generation Kill* (2004); Los Angeles, CA, July 12, 2024.

Z

Zimbardo, Philip, 91, psychologist known for the controversial Stanford prison experiment (1971); San Francisco, CA, Oct. 14, 2024.

118TH CONGRESS

118th Congress: Key Information

The 118th Congress convened Jan. 3, 2023, with Democrats maintaining control of the Senate (48 Democrats, 49 Republicans, 3 ind. caucusing with Democrats) and Republicans leading the House for the first time in four years (222-212, 1 vacancy). As of Mar. 2023, a record 154 women were serving in Congress, of whom 25 were in the Senate and 129 (including 3 nonvoting delegates and Puerto Rico's Resident Commissioner) in the House. The 118th Congress also had record minority representation, including six Hispanic lawmakers serving in the Senate and 56 (including 2 nonvoting delegates and the resident commissioner) in the House. The Senate included three Black senators, two senators of Asian heritage, and one Native American. The House had 60 Black members (including 2 nonvoting delegates); 19 Asian/South Asian/Pac. Isl. representatives (including 3 nonvoting delegates); and 4 Native Americans. Four lawmakers died during the 118th Congress: Six-term Sen. Dianne Feinstein (D, CA), the longest-serving woman in the Senate, on Sep. 29, 2023; six-term Rep. Donald M. Payne, Jr. (D, NJ), on Apr. 24, 2024; 15-term Rep. Sheila Jackson Lee (D, TX), on July 19, 2024; and 14-term Rep. Bill Pascrell, Jr. (D, NJ), on Aug. 21, 2024. On May 31, 2024, West Virginia Sen. Joe Manchin left the Democratic Party and registered as an independent but continued to caucus with Democrats.

Leadership. Rep. Kevin McCarthy (R, CA), minority leader in the 116th and 117th Congresses, was elected Speaker of the House Jan. 7 only after 15 floor votes, the most to elect a speaker since 1855. To secure the post, McCarthy agreed to major concessions to far-right members, including passing a rule that would make it easier to force out the speaker. Rep. Steve Scalise (R, LA) became majority leader and Rep. Hakeem Jeffries (D, NY) became the first Black representative to lead a major political party in Congress, moving into the role of minority leader and replacing outgoing Speaker Nancy Pelosi (D, CA; Pelosi maintained her seat but had resigned from party leadership). Rep. Tom Emmer (R, MN) became majority whip and Katherine Clark (D, MA) became minority whip. On Oct. 3, 2023, 8 far-right Republicans, joined by House Democrats, voted (216-210) to remove McCarthy, the first time in U.S. history that the chamber stripped the speaker of their gavel. House Republicans on Oct. 25 unanimously elected four-term Rep. Mike Johnson (R, LA) as Speaker; he was the fourth nominee for the position after McCarthy was ousted. McCarthy resigned from Congress effective Dec. 31, 2023.

In the Senate, Majority Leader Chuck Schumer (D, NY), and Minority Leader Mitch McConnell (R, KY) retained their positions; McConnell, the longest-serving party leader in the Senate, in Feb. 2024 announced he would step down from the leadership post he had held since 2007 in Nov. 2024 but serve out his term through 2026. Sen. Richard Durbin (D, IL) and Sen. John Thune (R, SD) continued to serve as Majority and Minority Whip, respectively.

Ethics. The House on its third attempt expelled first-term Rep. George Santos (R, NY) by a 311-114 vote Dec. 1, 2023, over accusations he repeatedly used campaign funds for personal expenses and knowingly filed false financial disclosure reports. At the time of his ouster, he faced 23 federal charges based on these and other allegations, including using campaign donors' credit cards without their knowledge. Santos, who had admitted he fabricated large parts of his biography for his campaign, pleaded guilty Aug. 19, 2024, to wire fraud and identity theft. Santos was the sixth House member to be expelled, and the first since 2002.

On May 3, 2024, ten-term Rep. Henry Cuellar (D, TX) was indicted on federal charges including bribery, money laundering, and working on behalf of a foreign government after allegedly accepting almost $600,000 in bribes from a Mexican bank and a state-owned oil and gas company in Azerbaijan; in late May, the House Ethics Committee initiated an investigation. Three-term Sen. Bob Menendez (D, NJ) resigned July 23, 2024 (effective Aug. 20), one week after he was convicted of 16 federal charges against him stemming from allegations he accepted cash and other bribes in exchange for steering military aid to Egypt, helping Qatar's government, and securing preferential treatment for three New Jersey businessmen.

As of Sept. 18, 2024, the House Ethics Committee was investigating Reps. Troy Nehls, Ronny Jackson, and Wesley Hunt (all R, TX) for possible misuse of campaign funds, and Rep. Sheila Cherfilus-McCormick (D, FL) over allegations she violated campaign finance laws and improperly used office funds.

Censures. The House censured three Democratic lawmakers in 2023, the most in a single year since 1870. On June 21, 2023, it voted 213-209 along party lines to censure 12-term Rep. Adam Schiff (D, CA) over his role in the previous Congress leading investigations into then-Pres. Donald Trump and for alleging Trump's election campaign colluded with Russia. Three-term Rep. Rashida Tlaib (D, MI), the lone Palestinian American in Congress, was censured Nov. 7, 2023, (234-188) over comments she made about Israel amid its ongoing offensive against Hamas. On Dec. 7, 2023, the House censured two-term Rep. Jamaal Bowman (D, NY) for pulling a fire alarm in the Capitol in Sept. before a scheduled vote; charged with a misdemeanor, he pleaded guilty.

For Further Information. Detailed legislative information can be accessed at www.congress.gov.

Major Actions of the 118th Congress

Major actions taken by the 118th Congress through Sept. 18, 2024. Laws are identified by their Public Law (PL) number.

Debt-Ceiling Suspension. The Fiscal Responsibility Act of 2023 suspended the nation's $31.4 tril borrowing limit until Jan. 2025, averting a first-ever federal government default. Also capped non-defense spending in FY2024; rescinded new IRS funding and some $28 bil in unallocated pandemic funds; ended a COVID-19-era student loan repayment moratorium; and raised the work-requirement age ceiling for able-bodied persons without dependents to receive food assistance to 55 from 49. Passed by the House, May 31, 2023, 314-117; passed by the Senate, June 1, 63-36; signed by Pres. Biden, June 3, 2023 (PL 118-5).

Cabinet Secretary Impeachment. On Jan. 28, 2024, the House announced two articles of impeachment charging Dept. of Homeland Security Sec. Alejandro Mayorkas with "willfully and systematically" refusing to enforce immigration laws and "breach of public trust" by testifying to Congress that the U.S. southern border was secure amid a surge in migrant crossings. First impeachment vote, Feb. 6, failed 214-216. House on Feb. 13 impeached Mayorkas by a 214-213 vote with three Republicans joining all Democrats in opposition, making him the first cabinet secretary since 1876. to be impeached. The Senate on Apr. 17, 2024, rejected the articles, on grounds that they did not constitute "high crimes and misdemeanors."

Federal Budget. The Consolidated Appropriations Act, 2024 and Further Consolidated Appropriations Act, 2024 ended roughly six-month impasse over the budget, forestalling a government shutdown. Provided a combined $1.66 tril in discretionary spending through 2024 that raised defense spending by over $26.7 bil (3.4%) and funded 2,000 more border patrol agents but did not include steep cuts to non-military spending demanded by House Republicans. The final act increased by $1 bil Head Start and childcare for military families and added more funding for cancer and Alzheimer's research and $300 mil in military assistance to Ukraine. First act (PL 118-42): passed by the House (as amended), Mar. 6, 339-85; agreed to by the Senate (as amended), Mar. 8, 75-22; signed by Pres. Biden, Mar. 9, 2024. Second act (PL 118-47): passed by the House (as amended), Mar. 22, 286-134; agreed to by the Senate (as amended), Mar. 23, 74-24; signed by Pres. Biden, Mar. 23, 2024.

Foreign Surveillance. Reforming Intelligence and Securing America Act renewed for two years Title VII of the Foreign Intelligence Surveillance Act (1978), including controversial Section 702, which allows U.S. intelligence agencies to monitor, without a warrant, digital communications of non-Americans in other countries, including texts and emails to people in the U.S. A House amendment that would require a warrant to access U.S. citizens' data under Section 702 narrowly failed in a 212-212 vote that crossed party lines. Passed by the House, Apr. 12, 273-147; agreed to by the Senate, Apr. 19, 60-34; signed by Pres. Biden, Apr. 20, 2024 (PL 118-49).

Military Aid to Allies; TikTok Ban. The bill "Making emergency supplemental appropriations for the fiscal year ending Sept. 30, 2024, and for other purposes" allocated $95 bil in foreign military aid, including roughly $61 bil in long-awaited new aid to Ukraine, $14 bil to Israel, $8 bil to Taiwan and other Indo-Pacific U.S. allies, and $9 bil in humanitarian relief, including in Gaza. Also required TikTok's Chinese parent co., ByteDance, to sell its U.S. operations by Jan. 19, 2025, or face a ban on operating in the U.S. Passed by the House as four bills, (H.R. 8034, H.R. 8035, H.R. 8036, H.R. 8038), Apr. 20; passed as package by the Senate, Apr. 23, 79-18; signed by Pres. Biden, Apr. 24, 2024 (PL 118-50).

Stillbirth Reduction. Maternal and Child Health Stillbirth Prevention Act of 2024 adds stillbirth/stillbirth prevention to the Social Security Act's Title V, ensuring that associated funds can be used for programs intended to decrease stillbirths, which currently total about 21,000 nationally according to the CDC. Passed by the House, May 15, 408-3; passed by the Senate, June 11, unanimous consent; signed by Pres. Biden, July 12, 2024 (PL 118-69).

U.S. SUPREME COURT

The U.S. Supreme Court's 2023-24 term began Oct. 2, 2023, and recessed July 1, 2024. The justices decided 59 cases, not including those decided without oral argument. Chief Justice John G. Roberts Jr., nominated by Pres. George W. Bush in 2005, presided over his 19th full term. The eight associate justices, in order of seniority, were Clarence Thomas, Samuel A. Alito Jr., Sonia Sotomayor, Elena Kagan, Neil M. Gorsuch, Brett M. Kavanaugh, Amy Coney Barrett, and Ketanji Brown Jackson.

Notable Supreme Court Decisions, 2023-24

Note: Gray shading in the columns on the right indicate justices who voted with the majority; unshaded boxes indicate justices who dissented. MO = wrote majority opinion; DO = wrote dissenting opinion; CO = wrote concurring opinion; COJ = wrote or co-wrote opinion concurring in judgment but not in its reasoning; COP = wrote opinion concurring in part of the judgment. In some cases a majority opinion was issued *per curiam* ("by the Court"), with no justice signing it.

Abortion Care
In *Food and Drug Administration v. Alliance for Hippocratic Medicine*, a unanimous Court June 13 ruled that the FDA approval of a widely available abortion drug would remain in place, due to a lack of standing, or direct stake, on the part of the interest groups that had sought to overturn the approval.

Civil Immunity
The justices ruled, 5-4, in *Harrington v. Purdue Pharma* on June 27 that OxyContin-manufacturer Purdue Pharma's multiparty bankruptcy settlement agreement could not shield the Sackler family, the company's owners, from future civil lawsuits without all potential claimholders' participation.

Capitol Attack
The Court ruled in *Fischer v. United States*, 6-3, June 28 that a federal criminal obstruction statute could not be used to charge a rioter involved in the Jan. 6, 2021, attack on the Capitol. The ruling could impact the prosecution of hundreds of Jan. 6 defendants, including those already sentenced.

Eighth Amendment
In *City of Grants Pass v. Johnson* June 28, the justices decided 6-3 that an Oregon town's ordinance aimed at preventing homeless people from sleeping outside did not violate the Eighth Amendment's ban on "cruel and unusual punishment."

Federal Powers
In a 6-3 ruling June 14, the justices in *Garland v. Cargill* struck down a Trump administration ban on bump stocks—gun accessories that enable semiautomatic weapons to fire hundreds of bullets per minute—holding that the Bureau of Alcohol, Tobacco, Firearms, and Explosives had overstepped in classifying bump stocks as machine guns.
In a 6-3 ruling in *Securities and Exchange Commission v. Jarkesy* June 27, the Court held that the SEC's use of its own administrative courts, to impose civil penalties for securities fraud violated the right of a defendant to a jury trial. The decision was expected to affect other federal agencies that made use of similar in-house tribunals.
The Court, 6-3, overturned a 40-year-old, frequently cited precedent informally referred to as *Chevron*, June 28, curtailing the powers of federal agencies. *Chevron* had required courts to defer to federal agencies' interpretations of statutes when the law itself was unclear. The wide-reaching decision was known as *Loper Bright Enterprises v. Raimondo*.

First Amendment
The justices unanimously decided in *National Rifle Association of America v. Vullo* May 30 that the NRA could proceed with a lawsuit against a New York government official, who the NRA said had violated the First Amendment by coercing companies to stop working with the NRA after the 2018 school shooting in Parkland, FL.

Second Amendment
The justices ruled, 8-1, in *United States v. Rahimi* on June 21, that a federal law that criminalizes gun ownership for those under domestic violence restraining orders did not violate the Second Amendment, finding it to be analogous to laws that restricted the activities of dangerous individuals (on a temporary basis) in the era of America's founders..

Voting Rights and Elections
In a 6-3 ruling on May 23, the Court overturned a lower court ruling that had declared a South Carolina congressional map an unconstitutional gerrymander that intentionally limited the voting power of Black constituents. The opinion held that courts should assume "good faith" that those overseeing redistricting were motivated by partisanship and not race. The case was *Alexander v. South Carolina State Conference of the NAACP*.
In an unsigned majority opinion in *Trump v. Anderson*, the Court ruled Mar. 4 that states may not act to bar Pres. Donald Trump from running for another term on the basis of Section 3 of the 14th Amendment, which specifies that insurrectionists may not hold office, arguing that Congress was responsible for its enforcement.

Presidential Immunity
The Court in a 6-3 opinion July 1 limited the prosecution of former Pres. Donald J. Trump on 2020 election interference charges, ruling that the president was entitled to at least "presumptive immunity" for his official acts, though not for his private conduct. The dissenting opinions decried the major expansion of presidential powers. The case was *Trump v. United States*.

Case	Jackson	Kagan	Sotomayor	Roberts	Thomas	Alito	Gorsuch	Kavanaugh	Barrett
Food and Drug Administration v. Alliance for Hippocratic Medicine					CO			MO	
Harrington v. Purdue Pharma							MO	DO	
Fischer v. United States	CO			MO					DO
City of Grants Pass v. Johnson			DO		CO		MO		
Garland v. Cargill			DO		MO	CO			
Securities and Exchange Commission v. Jarkesy			DO	MO			CO		
Loper Bright Enterprises v. Raimondo		DO		MO	CO		CO		
National Rifle Association of America v. Vullo	CO		MO				CO		
United States v. Rahimi	CO		CO	MO	DO		CO	CO	CO
Alexander v. South Carolina State Conference of the NAACP		DO			COP	MO			
Trump v. Anderson	COJ	COJ	COJ						COP, COJ
Trump v. United States	DO		DO	MO	CO				COP

NOTABLE QUOTES, 2024

National News

See also Campaign Trail Quotes, p. 9

"I think the border is a very important issue for Donald Trump. And the fact that he would communicate to Republican senators and congresspeople that he doesn't want us to solve the border problem because he wants to blame Biden for it is really appalling."

—**Sen. Mitt Romney** (R, UT), Jan. 25, 2024, on Trump's efforts to sideline immigration legislation with bipartisan support.

"Believe me, I know the politics within my party at this particular time. I have many faults. Misunderstanding politics is not one of them."

—**Senate minority leader Mitch McConnell** (R, KY) in a speech about his imminent departure from leadership, Feb. 28, 2024.

"Arizona was not a state, women and minorities could not vote, and doctors were still sewing up wounds with horsehair and storing their unwashed medical instruments in velvet-lined cases."

—**Heather Cox Richardson**, professor of history at Boston Coll., in response to the Arizona supreme court ruling Apr. 9, 2024, that a 160-year-old near-total ban on abortion could be enforced.

"I'm just curious, just to better understand your ruling. If someone on this committee then starts talking about somebody's bleach blonde bad built butch body, that would not be engaging in personalities, correct?"

—**Rep. Jasmine Crockett** (D, TX) responding May 16, 2024, to a committee chair's admonishment to avoid personal attacks following derogatory comments from Rep. Marjorie Taylor Greene (R, GA) during a House committee hearing.

"My wife is fond of flying flags. I am not."

—**U.S. Supreme Court Justice Samuel Alito** May 29, 2024, commenting on an inverted U.S. flag flown on his property in Jan. 2021, when it was a frequent symbol of the "stop the steal" movement.

"Mother Teresa could not beat these charges. These charges are rigged. The whole thing is rigged."

—**Former Pres. Donald Trump**, May 29, 2024, before a New York jury reached a 34-count guilty verdict in his hush money trial.

"We hold that a semiautomatic rifle equipped with a bump stock is not a 'machine gun' because it cannot fire more than one shot 'by a single function of the trigger.'"

—**U.S. Supreme Court Justice Clarence Thomas**, writing for a 6-3 majority, June 14, 2024.

"If the occupant of that office misuses official power for personal gain, the criminal law that the rest of us must abide will not provide a backstop. With fear for our democracy, I dissent."

—**U.S. Supreme Court Justice Sonia Sotomayor**, July 1, 2024, in her dissenting opinion in *Trump v. U.S.*, in which the Supreme Court ruled that presidents have immunity for "official acts."

"I lied. I lied to my kids today in second period. I told them it was just a drill."

—**Jennifer Carter**, teacher at Apalachee High School, Winder, GA, on how she managed to prevent panic in her classroom while a live shooter was in the building on Sept. 4, 2024.

"He's lying. And the governor told him he was lying…I don't know why he does this. And the reason I get so angry about it … I care what he communicates to the people that are in need. He implies that we're not doing everything possible. We are."

—**Pres. Biden** responding to false comments former Pres. Donald Trump made about federal Hurricane Helene relief efforts, Sept. 30, 2024.

"Kamala spent all her FEMA money, billions of dollars, on housing for illegal migrants, many of whom should not be in our country."

—**Former Pres. Trump** at a campaign rally, Oct. 3, 2024.

"Although the defendant was the incumbent president during the charged conspiracies, his scheme was fundamentally a private one."

—**Special counsel Jack Smith** in 165-page court filing unsealed Oct. 2, 2024, on why former Pres. Trump wasn't immune from prosecution for the events of Jan. 6, 2021, under the Supreme Court decision in *Trump v. U.S.*

Around the World

"What has happened to Navalny is yet more proof of Putin's brutality. No one should be fooled—not in Russia, not at home, not anywhere in the world."

—**Pres. Biden** responding to the death of Alexei Navalny, Feb. 16, 2024.

"I do believe that as a Jewish person, I have a particular responsibility to resist the instrumentalization of my heritage, and to say that I do not believe that genocide in Gaza or occupation and apartheid in greater Palestine is supportive of my personal safety."

—**Ariela Rosenzweig**, 23-year-old student involved in war protest at Brown Univ., as reported by *The Guardian*, Apr. 26, 2024.

"It's a great American value to protest but I don't believe living in a pup tent for Hamas is really helpful."

—**Sen. John Fetterman** (D, PA) commenting on pro-Palestinian campus protesters Apr. 28, 2024.

"We are incredibly lucky to live in a country where decisions like this are made not by bombs or bullets, but by thousands of ordinary citizens peacefully placing crosses in boxes on bits of paper."

—**British politician Jeremy Hunt**, in his concession speech following July 4, 2024, elections that ended 14 years of Conservative Party rule.

"Given the overwhelming evidence, it is clear to the United States and, most importantly, to the Venezuelan people that Edmundo González Urrutia won the most votes in Venezuela's July 28 presidential election."

—**U.S. Sec. of State Antony Blinken**, in an Aug. 1, 2024, statement after Pres. Nicolás Maduro claimed victory for a third term.

"Russia has brought the war to our land and should feel what it has done."

—**Ukrainian Pres. Volodymyr Zelenskyy**, in a video released Aug. 8, 2024, on Ukraine's counteroffensive into Russian territory.

"Instead of saving lives, hostages are being buried. Instead of doing everything to bring them home, Netanyahu is doing all he can to stay in power."

—**Israel opposition leader Yaid Lapid** reacting after the bodies of six hostages were discovered in Gaza, Sept. 1, 2024.

"It's getting so hot that the pieces that hold the concrete and steel, those bridges can literally fall apart like Tinkertoys."

—**Paul Chinowsky**, professor of civil engineering at Univ. of Colorado Boulder, in Sept. 2, 2024, *NY Times* story on the effects of climate change on infrastructure.

People and Culture

"We hope that you will understand that, as a family, we now need some time, space, and privacy while I complete my treatment."

—**Princess Catherine**, Mar. 22, 2024, announcing that she was being treated for cancer.

"Today, in one of the greatest one-day migrations in history, humans flocked by the millions to a swath of North America that was briefly cast in a shadow of darkness and wonder…For a cosmic moment, they were connected across the millennia with every other person who has ever experienced an eclipse, witnessing the light die and then be reborn as a dazzling ring."

—***NY Times* science writer Dennis Overbye**, on the dramatic solar eclipse witnessed by millions Apr. 8, 2024.

"People were worried he was going to hurt the team. And he was the one to [clinch] it in the end. It's like a Cinderella story, fairytale ending."

—**Sam Mikulak**, three-time Olympic gymnast who helped coach pommel horse specialist Stephen Nedoroscik, reported by the *Washington Post*, July 29, 2024.

"Oh shoot, I am incredible."

—**U.S. sprinter Noah Lyles**, who won Olympic gold in the 100-m by 0.005 seconds Aug. 4, 2024.

"It's as if he told the refugees in the camp, 'Nothing is impossible; here I am.'"

—**Ali Adel Asigmani**, who grew up in the same refugee camp as Yahya al Ghotany, a displaced Syrian who competed in the Olympics, as reported Aug. 10, 2024.

"I don't believe in the medical science that says at 40 or 50 years old, you should not do certain things anymore."

—**Leonel Martinez**, who at 60 years old represented Venezuela in shooting in the 2024 Olympic Games.

"I think that those officers should be commended for how they really showed a great level of restraint. It's just unfortunate that innocent people were shot because of that."

—**New York City Mayor Eric Adams** at a Sept. 17, 2024, news conference; two days earlier, NYPD officers shot at an alleged fare evader on a Brooklyn subway platform, striking and injuring four people.

"That has to be the greatest baseball game of all time. It has to be."

—**L.A. Dodgers second baseman Gavin Lux**, summing up the Sept. 19, 2024, game in which teammate Shohei Ohtani went 6 for 6, with two stolen bases, three home runs, four runs scored, five extra-base hits, and 10 RBI.

OFFBEAT NEWS, 2024

The Grass Is Always Greener?

For years after she got divorced, Tasmania's Kathleen Murray intended to replace the lawnmower her ex-husband took when he moved out. But as a single mother of four, she never got around to it. Instead, she watched as her front yard turned brown, as kangaroos and wallabies grazed on any vegetation that survived, and as echidnas and bandicoots thrived on whatever they found in the holes they dug into the ground. For Murray, the visits by the local fauna were a reward—her "own private Disneyland," as she told a reporter. "My backyard looks like a real-life Hungry Hungry Hippo game."

And in Jan. 2024, she garnered an even greater prize: the title of World's Ugliest Lawn. Launched in 2022 as a local effort by the Swedish island community of Gotland to promote water conservation, the competition went global in 2023. Murray's wildlife wonderland beat out more than 30 entries from Canada, the U.S., and a number of countries in Europe. In selecting Murray's lawn from the other "hideous, yet heroic entries," the competition's judges lauded the fact that "not one dust-covered decimeter is wasted on watering."

For her efforts (or lack thereof), Murray won a brown T-shirt proclaiming her the owner of the world's ugliest lawn. And in keeping with the competition's message of sustainability, she will pass on the trophy to next year's winner.

Tempest in a Teapot

Pennsylvania chemistry professor Michelle Francl never had any reason to think she'd cause an international incident, but her book *Steeped: The Chemistry of Tea*, published in Jan. 2024, did exactly that. The Bryn Mawr professor reported in *Steeped* that salt blocks the receptor that can make tea taste bitter, and even found recipes from China's Tang Dynasty (618-906 C.E.) that listed salt as an essential ingredient in the perfect cup of tea. But in England, where an estimated 100 million cuppas daily are consumed, the notion of salting tea bordered on sacrilege. Or maybe it was just the idea of Americans once again telling Brits what they could do with their tea. In any event, the controversy created so much hot water that the U.S. Embassy in London felt compelled to stir the pot.

In a cheeky statement issued Jan. 24, 2024, the embassy assured its host country "that the unthinkable notion of adding salt to Britain's national drink is not official United States policy. And never will be.... The U.S. Embassy will continue to make tea in the proper way—by microwaving it."

That last assertion may be an even bigger sacrilege to tea connoisseurs, Francl included. She strongly discourages using a microwave to heat water for tea because "you end up getting tea scum forming on the surface, and that scum contains some of the antioxidants and taste compounds."

March Meowness

Librarians in Worcester, MA, in Mar. 2024 hit on a novel way to bring people back to the stacks in the wake of the pandemic. They extended "fur-giveness" to any patrons who lost or damaged books or other materials in exchange for a cat picture. For example, when a 7-year-old boy came to seek absolution for failing to return a Captain Underpants book, librarians restored his borrowing privileges after he used crayons to draw a cat. Any cat picture will do—a photo, a magazine clipping, a quick pencil sketch—and it doesn't even have to be funny. For that matter, it doesn't even have to be a cat, said Jason Homer, the library's executive director. "Any ungovernable animal" will do.

Dubbed March Meowness, the initiative proved extraordinarily successful. Days after the launch, the library acquired hundreds of cat photos and drawings, which it posted on a "cat wall" in the city's main library building and on its Facebook page. The library also created additional cat-themed programming for the month, including a lecture from a cat behaviorist, a de-stressing session with cats from the local shelter, and a cat-eye makeup tutorial (for humans, not felines).

In keeping with a nationwide trend, Worcester's library had abolished late fees in 2020, but continued to fine patrons for lost or damaged books. It created the March Meowness program in response to the special circumstances created by the pandemic, noting how many people moved or left books in classrooms that they didn't return to for months.

The Little Engine That Could... Make Commuters Smile

If you can't make the trains run on time, you can at least make them look like they're trying. That was the thinking behind a ragtag effort by commuters in Boston in Apr. 2024, calling on the Massachusetts Bay Transportation Authority to put googly eyes on the front of its train cars. To MBTA patrons' delight, the agency actually did it.

"Our team found a safe way to install these 'googly' eyes on a limited number of vehicles ... as part of our ongoing efforts to bring moments of joy to our riders' daily commutes," MBTA spokesman Joe Pesaturo told Boston.com. The cost, according to another agency executive, was a few dollars, a rounding error compared to the authority's $25 billion backlog of repairs and infrastructure improvements.

Arielle Lok, one of the organizers of the pro-googly eye forces, said she got the idea of giving a face to the city's public transportation system from her hometown of Vancouver, where buses are decked out with red noses and antlers during Christmas to represent Rudolph, the red-nosed reindeer. When informed of the agency's decision, Lok posted photos of one of the newly adorned trains with the note, "Today, the @MBTA and us saw eye to eye."

An Olympic Competition for Mermaids Makes a Splash in Switzerland

Sure, Katie Ledecky can lap the field in the 1,500 meters at any swimming competition. But can she do it in a mermaid's tail, while raising awareness about water and marine conservation? Mia Sim can, and that's exactly what she did in May 2024 at the Swiss Merlympics, a competition held in various European locations since its debut in Germany in 2015. Sim, a 22-year-old from Lehi, UT, broke the Merlympics speed record by swimming 50 meters in just over 38 seconds, all while keeping her head above the water.

In addition to speed, contestants are judged on their skill at swimming like a mermaid (or merman), posing underwater (harder than it looks, Sim said), rescuing drowning victims (actually, submerged dummies), and helping the environment (competing to retrieve the most trash from the bottom of a pool in 90 seconds). And no, they don't have to wear their tails on the medal stand.

So how do the Merlympics promote water conservation? Sim, a former dancer and cheerleader who now makes her living performing as a mermaid, said she talks about Utah's shrinking water supply whenever she does an appearance. And she said her costume encourages kids to care about stewardship of the oceans in ways that books or newspapers never could.

The Greatest Thing Since Sliced Bread

Few things are as quintessentially French as the baguette. More than 6 billion are made each year (or about 16 million per day), usually selling for about 1 euro. The baguette is so tied to French identity that in 2022, UNESCO added it to its "intangible cultural heritage" list.

And since May 2024, even people who have never been to France can get a whiff of this Gallic icon, thanks to a new scratch-and-sniff stamp celebrating "la baguette de pain française." La Poste, the French postal service, issued an initial print run of 594,000 such stamps on May 16, coinciding with the feast day of St. Honoré, the patron saint of bakers. Each stamp costs 1.96 euro (a bit over $2) and can be used as postage on international letters. The stamps were an immediate hit, selling out online and in some local post offices, especially among international visitors sending postcards home from the Paris Olympics in July and Aug. 2024. But not everyone was impressed.

"This smells more like vanilla," said Jeanne Barrère, manager of the Léonie Bakery in Paris. Her chief baker, Harlem Gbodialo, agreed, saying he detected a "sugary, fruity aroma"—not the smell of a real baguette.

HISTORICAL ANNIVERSARIES

1925 — 100 Years Ago

Leon Trotsky is forced to resign his military leadership post in post-revolution Russia Jan. 6.

A dog sled relay transports diphtheria antitoxin across Alaska Jan. 27-Feb. 2 to combat a deadly epidemic.

The so-called Tri-State Tornado Mar. 18 kills nearly 700 people in Illinois, Indiana, and Missouri.

Former military leader Paul von Hindenburg is elected president of Germany Apr. 26.

Druze forces launch a rebellion against French colonial control in Lebanon and Syria.

Legal giants William Jennings Bryan and Clarence Darrow battle over the teaching of evolution in U.S. schools in the Scopes trial July 10-21.

At a major conference in Locarno, Switzerland, Oct. 5-16, European nations negotiate treaties to finalize postwar borders and normalize relations with the defeated Germany.

Reza Pahlavi becomes the shah of Persia (present-day Iran) Dec. 15.

Art. Le Corbusier's polarizing Pavillon de l'Esprit Nouveau is built for the International Exhibition of Modern Decorative and Industrial Arts in Paris, which will give Art Deco style its name; publishes *The Decorative Art of Today* to address critics. Edward Hopper's *House by the Railroad*, Joan Miró's *Head of a Catalan Peasant*, Pablo Picasso's *The Three Dancers*.

Film. *Ben-Hur* starring Ramon Novarro, *The Big Parade*, *Body and Soul* starring Paul Robeson, *The Freshman* starring Harold Lloyd, *The Gold Rush* starring Charlie Chaplin, *The Phantom of the Opera* starring Lon Chaney.

Literature. Franz Kafka's *The Trial* is published posthumously. John Dos Passos's *Manhattan Transfer*, Theodore Dreiser's *An American Tragedy*, T. S. Eliot's "The Hollow Men," F. Scott Fitzgerald's *The Great Gatsby*, Sinclair Lewis's *Arrowsmith*, Anita Loos's *Gentlemen Prefer Blondes*, Virginia Woolf's *Mrs. Dalloway*.

Music. Alban Berg's opera *Wozzeck* premieres in Berlin. Dmitri Shostakovich's *Symphony No. 1 in F minor*, Sergei Prokofiev's *Symphony No. 2*.

Nonfiction. *The New Negro*, an anthology of writings edited by Alain Locke and featuring Countee Cullen, Langston Hughes, Zora Neale Hurston, and others, defines and documents the Harlem Renaissance. First volume of Adolf Hitler's *Mein Kampf* is published in Germany. William Carlos Williams's *In the American Grain*.

Pop music. Gene Austin's "Yes Sir, That's My Baby," Ben Bernie's "Sweet Georgia Brown."

Radio. The weekly country music program later known as *Grand Ole Opry* first airs, as *WSM Barn Dance*.

Science and technology. Wolfgang Pauli publishes his exclusion principle. Erwin Schrödinger proposes the Schrödinger equation, governing quantum wave mechanics.

Sports. The Pittsburgh Pirates recover from a 3-games-to-1 deficit to defeat the Washington Senators in the World Series.

Television. Charles Francis Jenkins achieves "the first public demonstration of radiovision"—synchronized transmission of pictures and sound. Vladimir Zworykin demonstrates the cathode ray tube television to Westinghouse executives.

Theater. *No, No, Nanette* opens on both Broadway and the West End in London after a successful run in Chicago.

Miscellaneous. *The New Yorker* magazine is founded by Harold Ross and Jane Grant. Mount Rushmore is dedicated in South Dakota.

1975 — 50 Years Ago

In what comes to be known as "The Year of Intelligence," the Rockefeller Commission and Church Committee reveal CIA misdeeds, including mind-control research program Project MKUltra and domestic surveillance of political groups.

Former Atty. Gen. John Mitchell and former presidential advisers H. R. Haldeman and John Ehrlichman are found guilty Jan. 1 of charges related to the Watergate cover-up.

Margaret Thatcher takes control of the opposition Conservative Party in the UK Feb. 11.

Dozens are killed in fighting between Palestinian and Christian militias in downtown Beirut Apr. 13, marking the beginning of 15 years of civil war in Lebanon.

In Cambodia, Khmer Rouge forces capture Phnom Penh Apr. 17, effectively beginning a genocide that would eliminate about a quarter of the country's population.

U.S. launches final evacuation from Saigon of Americans and some South Vietnamese Apr. 29 as Communist forces complete takeover of South Vietnam.

Congress appropriates $405 mil funding for South Vietnam refugees May 16; 140,000 such refugees are flown to U.S.

India Prime Min. Indira Gandhi declares a controversial state of emergency June 25.

The UK experiences severe inflation (over 25%), leading the government to impose severe anti-inflation policies in Aug.

Papua New Guinea gains independence from Australia Sept. 16.

Publishing heiress Patty Hearst, kidnapped in Feb. 1974, is taken into FBI custody in San Francisco Sept. 18 with other Symbionese Liberation Army militants.

Communists take control in Laos Dec. 2, forcing the king's abdication.

Art. T.C. Cannon's *Grandmother Gestating Father and the Washita River Runs Ribbon-Like*, Barkley L. Hendricks's *Blood (Donald Formey)*, Lee Krasner's *Free Space*.

Film. Steven Spielberg's *Jaws* sets the bar for summer blockbusters. *Dog Day Afternoon* starring Al Pacino, *Hester Street*, Robert Altman's *Nashville*, *One Flew Over the Cuckoo's Nest* starring Jack Nicholson, *The Rocky Horror Picture Show*, *Shampoo*.

Health and medicine. Lyme disease is first identified at its namesake Connecticut city. Researchers produce monoclonal antibodies for the first time.

Literature. Natalie Babbitt's *Tuck Everlasting*, Saul Bellow's *Humboldt's Gift*, Jorge Luis Borges's *The Book of Sand*, Agatha Christie's *Curtain: Poirot's Last Case*, E. L. Doctorow's *Ragtime*, Carlos Fuentes's *Terra Nostra*, Arthur Hailey's *The Moneychangers*, Judith Rossner's *Looking for Mister Goodbar*, Gayl Jones's *Corregidora*.

Music. Keith Jarrett performs and records *The Köln Concert*.

Nonfiction. Susan Brownmiller's *Against Our Will: Men, Women, and Rape*; Michel Foucault's *Discipline and Punish*; Primo Levi's *The Periodic Table*; Peter Singer's *Animal Liberation*.

Pop music. Glen Campbell's "Rhinestone Cowboy"; Captain and Tennille's "Love Will Keep Us Together"; Bob Dylan's *Blood on the Tracks*; Earth, Wind, & Fire's "Shining Star"; KC and the Sunshine Band's "That's the Way (I Like It)"; Queen's *A Night at the Opera* feat. "Bohemian Rhapsody"; Patti Smith's *Horses*; Bruce Springsteen's *Born to Run*.

Science and technology. The Altair 8800 PC is a commercial success after appearing in *Popular Electronics*. Bill Gates and Paul Allen form Micro-Soft to sell BASIC software for the Altair 8800.

Sports. Muhammad Ali defeats Joe Frazier to retain the heavyweight championship in a bout known as the "Thrilla in Manila." Cincinnati's "Big Red Machine" outlasts Boston in the World Series, four games to three.

Television. New prime-time shows include *The Jeffersons*, *One Day at a Time*, and *Wonder Woman*. Late-night comedy show *Saturday Night Live* debuts on NBC. PBS airs *Opening Soon at a Theater Near You*, the first film review show featuring Chicago newspaper critics Roger Ebert and Gene Siskel.

Theater. New musicals opening on Broadway include *Chicago*, *A Chorus Line*, and *The Wiz*.

Miscellaneous. Sony introduces the Betamax video recording device to the U.S., with a price tag of $2,495.

2000 — 25 Years Ago

Y2K computer glitch caused few problems as celebrations marked changeover from 1999 to year 2000.

In then-record corporate merger, AOL Jan. 10 announces an agreement to acquire Time Warner for $182 billion.

Russian forces capture the capital of Chechnya in Feb. and establish direct rule in May, though resistance continues.

Vermont Gov. Howard Dean (D) Apr. 26 signs the first state law recognizing same-sex civil unions.

The pro-gun-control "Million Mom March" draws more than 500,000 to Washington, DC, on May 14.

Israeli troops withdraw from south Lebanon in June.

Leaders of North Korea and South Korea meet June 13-15 in first summit since the Korean War.

U.S. and British scientists June 26 announce that they had determined the structure of the human genome.

Six-year-old Elián González is returned to his father in Cuba June 28, after his rescue from a tragic refugee boat wreck in which his mother drowned and an ensuing international custody battle.

Mexico July 2 elects as president center-right candidate Vicente Fox, ending more than seven decades of Institutional Revolutionary Party (PRI) rule.

Russian submarine *Kursk* sinks in the Barents Sea Aug. 12, killing all 118 sailors on board.

Israeli politician Ariel Sharon visits the area known as the Temple Mount and Haram al-Sharif Sept. 28, an event retroactively considered to mark the beginning of the Second Intifada.

Seventeen U.S. sailors die Oct. 12 in al-Qaeda bombing of USS *Cole*, in Aden, Yemen.

Florida Supreme Court, Dec. 8, orders partial manual recounts of state's U.S. presidential election ballots; U.S. Supreme Court reverses that order, Dec. 12, leaving Texas Gov. George W. Bush (R) as winner over Vice Pres. Al Gore (D).

Art. Tate Modern art gallery opens in a former power station in London, England. Online art community deviant ART launches. Jake and Dinos Chapman's *Hell*, Lucian Freud's *After Cézanne*, Pepón Osorio's *My Beating Heart/Mi Corazón Latiente*.

Film. First *X-Men* movie helps launch a superhero film renaissance. Cameron Crowe's *Almost Famous*; Spike Lee's *Bamboozled*; *Billy Elliot*; *Cast Away* starring Tom Hanks; *Crouching Tiger, Hidden Dragon* starring Chow Yun-fat and Michelle Yeoh, *Erin Brockovich* starring Julia Roberts; *Gladiator* starring Russell Crowe; *Meet the Parents*; *Mission: Impossible 2*; the Coen Brothers' *O Brother, Where Art Thou?*; *The Perfect Storm*; Steven Soderbergh's *Traffic*.

Health and medicine. FDA approves RU-486 (mifepristone), a pill that induces abortion. Researchers at Harvard identify four types of brain abnormalities associated with childhood abuse and neglect.

Literature. The *NY Times* creates a separate children's bestseller list in response to the dominance of the Harry Potter series. Margaret Atwood's *The Blind Assassin*, T. C. Boyle's *A Friend of the Earth*, Dan Brown's *Angels & Demons*, Michael Chabon's *The Amazing Adventures of Kavalier & Clay*, Barbara Kingsolver's *Prodigal Summer*, Joyce Carol Oates's *Blonde*, Zadie Smith's *White Teeth*, Joy Williams's *The Quick and the Dead*.

Music. John Coolidge Adams's *El Niño*.

Nonfiction. Stephen Ambrose's *Nothing Like It in the World*, *The Beatles Anthology*, James Bradley and Ron Powers's *Flags of Our Fathers*, Dave Eggers's *A Heartbreaking Work of Staggering Genius*, Malcolm Gladwell's *The Tipping Point*, Stephen King's *On Writing*, Bill O'Reilly's *The O'Reilly Factor*.

Pop music. Bon Jovi's "It's My Life," D'Angelo's *Voodoo*, Eminem's *The Marshall Mathers LP*, Madonna's "Music," NSYNC's *No Strings Attached* feat. "Bye Bye Bye," Radiohead's *Kid A*, Britney Spears's "Oops!...I Did It Again," U2's "Beautiful Day."

Science and technology. Scientists at the Human Genome Project announce that human chromosome 21 has been fully decoded; it is the smallest human chromosome. First astronaut and cosmonauts take up residence at the International Space Station.

Sports. A 24-year-old Tiger Woods becomes the youngest player to win all four of golf's majors, July 23. Summer Olympic Games are held in Sydney, Australia. NY Yankees defeat NY Mets in "Subway Series" for third straight World Series win.

Television. Reality TV competition pioneers *Big Brother* and *Survivor* debut. Over 22 million people watch *Who Wants to Marry a Multi-Millionaire? CSI*, *Curb Your Enthusiasm*, and *Gilmore Girls* air first episodes.

Theater. *Aida* and *Proof* debut on Broadway; original Broadway production of *Cats* ends its historic 18-year run.

Miscellaneous. Final *Peanuts* comic strip appears in newspapers, closing out 50 years in the funny pages. Population of India surpasses 1 billion.

WORLD ALMANAC EDITORS' PICKS
2024 Time Capsule

The editors of *The World Almanac* have selected the following items as representative of the year 2024.

- A piece of the Boeing 737 MAX 9 plane that fell off during an Alaska Airlines flight 10 minutes after takeoff Jan. 5, 2024.
- A rainbow spectrum of 40-ounce vacuum-insulated Stanley "Quencher" mugs that flew off of retailers' shelves (despite a $45 price tag) in early 2024.
- Caitlin Clark's #22 Iowa Hawkeyes jersey to commemorate her all-time NCAA scoring record of 3,951 points, surpassing men's star Pete Maravich's 54-year-old record, in her final regular season game Mar. 3, 2024.
- One of Francis Scott Key Bridge's steel support beams that toppled into Baltimore's Patapsco River when a large container ship struck one of the bridge's piers Mar. 26, 2024.
- ISO-certified eclipse glasses, like those that allowed much of North America to safely observe the dramatic solar eclipse on Apr. 8, 2024.
- Tents from the pro-Palestinian protest encampment set up on Columbia Univ.'s campus beginning Apr. 17, 2024—one of dozens of similar campus protests that tested universities nationwide.
- The verdict sheet on which a New York jury recorded finding former Pres. Donald Trump guilty on all 34 counts of falsifying business records May 30, 2024.
- A share of the chip maker Nvidia, which surpassed Microsoft as the world's most valuable publicly traded company June 18, 2024.
- The bandage worn by former Pres. Trump after surviving an assassination attempt at a rally in Butler, PA, July 13, 2024.
- The letter in which Pres. Joe Biden announced July 21, 2024, that he was stepping down from the presidential race, and his follow-up statement endorsing Vice Pres. Kamala Harris shortly thereafter.
- A delayed-flight voucher to compensate two NASA astronauts experiencing a very extended stay on the International Space Station due to technical issues with Boeing's Starliner spacecraft; their return was postponed from June 2024 to Feb. 2025.
- A medal from the Summer Olympics, in Paris, France, July 26-Aug. 11, 2024, all of which contained an original piece of metal from the Eiffel Tower.
- A video of Moo Deng, a baby pygmy hippo, from the Khao Kheow Open Zoo in Si Racha, Chon Buri, Thailand, who became a viral sensation in Sept. 2024.

ECONOMICS

U.S. Gross Domestic Product, 1930-2023

Source: Bureau of Economic Analysis, U.S. Dept. of Commerce
(in billions of current dollars)

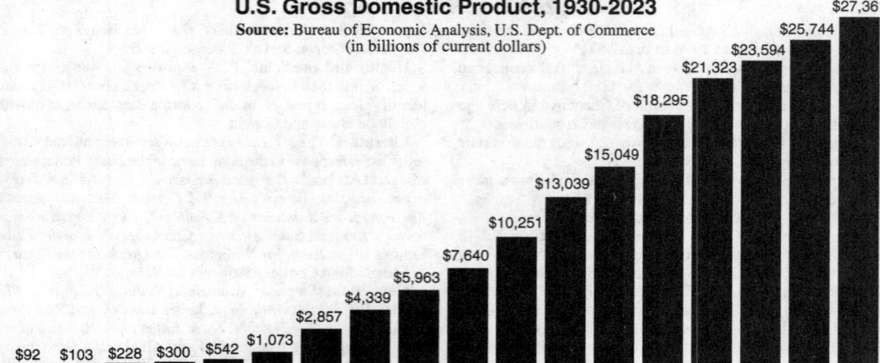

Tracking the U.S. Economy, 1970-2023

Source: Bureau of Economic Analysis, U.S. Dept. of Commerce
(in billions of current dollars, revised)

	1970	1980	1990	2000	2010	2020	2022	2023
Gross domestic product	**$1,073.3**	**$2,857.3**	**$5,963.1**	**$10,251.0**	**$15,049.0**	**$21,323.0**	**$25,744.1**	**$27,360.9**
Gross national product	**1,079.7**	**2,891.5**	**5,997.8**	**10,289.4**	**15,254.6**	**21,537.8**	**25,926.0**	**27,525.1**
Less: Consumption of fixed capital	136.8	428.4	888.5	1,511.2	2,390.4	3,625.5	4,299.9	4,585.8
Equals: Net national product	**942.9**	**2,463.1**	**5,109.3**	**8,778.2**	**12,864.2**	**17,912.3**	**21,626.1**	**22,939.4**
Less: Statistical discrepancy	5.3	44.3	95.4	–95.8	69.4	58.2	–52.3	509.7
Equals: National income	**937.5**	**2,418.8**	**5,014.0**	**8,874.0**	**12,794.8**	**17,854.0**	**21,678.4**	**22,429.6**
Less: Corporate profits with inventory valuation and capital consumption adjustments	86.2	223.1	419.3	826.4	1,774.5	2,383.3	3,208.7	3,258.0
Less: Taxes on production and imports less subsidies[1]	86.6	190.5	398.0	662.7	1,007.3	863.7	1,682.8	1,731.6
Less: Contributions for government social insurance, domestic	46.4	166.2	410.1	705.8	983.7	1,449.3	1,701.7	1,802.6
Less: Net interest and miscellaneous payments on assets	39.5	182.8	432.0	504.0	437.7	529.3	457.4	185.4
Less: Business current transfer payments (net)	4.4	14.0	39.2	85.2	126.3	145.0	216.8	214.5
Less: Current surplus of government enterprises[1]	–1.0	–4.5	3.7	11.5	–18.5	–1.8	4.4	–9.7
Plus: Personal income receipts on assets	114.9	397.7	1,004.8	1,455.6	1,747.7	2,913.7	3,432.0	3,613.4
Plus: Personal current transfer receipts	74.7	280.1	596.9	1,087.3	2,325.2	4,229.9	4,002.1	4,100.7
Equals: Personal income	**865.0**	**2,324.5**	**4,913.3**	**8,621.3**	**12,556.6**	**19,629.0**	**21,840.8**	**22,961.3**
Addenda:								
Gross domestic income	1,068.0	2,813.0	5,867.8	10,346.7	14,979.5	21,264.7	25,796.4	26,851.2
Gross national income	1,074.4	2,847.2	5,902.5	10,385.2	15,185.2	21,479.6	25,978.3	27,015.4

Note: Numbers may not add up to totals due to rounding. (1) Subsidies are included net of the current surplus of government enterprises.

U.S. Gross Domestic Product, 2000-23

Source: Bureau of Economic Analysis, U.S. Dept. of Commerce

	Billions of current dollars					Billions of constant (2017) dollars				
	2000	2010	2020	2022	2023	2000	2010	2020	2022	2023
Gross domestic product	**$10,251**	**$15,049**	**$21,323**	**$25,744**	**$27,361**	**$14,096**	**$16,790**	**$20,234**	**$21,822**	**$22,377**
Personal consumption expenditures	**6,767**	**10,260**	**14,206**	**17,512**	**18,571**	**9,167**	**11,336**	**13,577**	**15,091**	**15,426**
Goods	2,453	3,318	4,713	5,997	6,192	NA	3,300	4,730	5,282	5,388
Durable goods	913	1,049	1,629	2,129	2,199	NA	921	1,683	1,960	2,042
Nondurable goods	1,541	2,269	3,084	3,868	3,993	NA	2,394	3,050	3,328	3,355
Services	4,314	6,942	9,493	11,515	12,379	NA	8,065	8,868	9,836	10,066
Gross private domestic investment	**2,038**	**2,166**	**3,748**	**4,757**	**4,844**	**2,445**	**2,309**	**3,603**	**4,103**	**4,052**
Fixed investment	1,984	2,112	3,786	4,599	4,790	NA	2,270	3,630	3,939	3,965
Nonresidential	1,498	1,735	2,869	3,433	3,716	NA	1,794	2,811	3,132	3,272
Structures	321	380	623	701	840	NA	455	583	553	626
Equipment	766	777	1,111	1,327	1,381	NA	758	1,116	1,249	1,246
Intellectual property products	411	578	1,136	1,405	1,495	NA	586	1,111	1,339	1,399
Residential	485	377	917	1,166	1,074	NA	473	816	823	735
Change in inventories	55	54	–38	157	54	NA	54	–30	128	44
Net exports of goods and services	**–381**	**–532**	**–626**	**–971**	**–799**	**NA**	**–388**	**–663**	**–1,051**	**–928**
Exports	1,096	1,857	2,150	2,995	3,027	1,323	1,907	2,145	2,440	2,504
Goods	795	1,273	1,422	2,063	2,031	NA	1,232	1,453	1,653	1,697
Services	301	584	729	932	996	NA	676	694	790	810
Imports	1,477	2,390	2,777	3,966	3,826	1,733	2,295	2,808	3,491	3,432
Goods	1,251	1,947	2,305	3,262	3,112	NA	1,818	2,358	2,886	2,839
Services	226	443	471	704	714	NA	485	453	607	597
Government consumption expenditures and gross investment	**1,826**	**3,156**	**3,995**	**4,447**	**4,745**	**2,851**	**3,540**	**3,716**	**3,670**	**3,820**
Federal	633	1,300	1,523	1,636	1,772	NA	1,423	1,443	1,421	1,481
National defense	393	828	885	928	995	NA	897	839	800	828
Nondefense	241	472	639	707	777	NA	524	604	621	653
State and local	1,193	1,855	2,471	2,811	2,973	NA	2,117	2,274	2,250	2,339

NA = Not available.

U.S. National Income by Type, 1930-2023

Source: Bureau of Economic Analysis, U.S. Dept. of Commerce
(in billions of current dollars)

	1930	1940	1950	1970	1980	1990	2000	2010	2020	2023
NATIONAL INCOME[1]	**$83.1**	**$91.5**	**$266.6**	**$937.5**	**$2,418.8**	**$5,014.0**	**$8,874.0**	**$12,794.8**	**$17,854.0**	**$22,429.6**
Employee compensation	**47.2**	**52.7**	**158.3**	**623.3**	**1,622.2**	**3,340.4**	**5,847.1**	**7,925.4**	**11,594.7**	**14,234.0**
Wages and salaries	46.2	49.9	147.3	551.6	1,373.4	2,741.2	4,824.9	6,372.5	9,464.6	11,798.1
Government	5.2	8.5	22.6	117.2	261.5	519.0	779.8	1,191.2	1,494.3	1,734.4
Other	41.0	41.4	124.6	434.3	1,112.0	2,222.2	4,045.2	5,181.3	7,970.3	10,063.7
Supplements to wages and salaries	1.0	2.9	11.0	71.8	248.8	599.2	1,022.2	1,552.9	2,130.0	2,436.0
Employer contributions for employee pension and insurance funds	0.9	1.5	7.6	47.9	159.9	392.7	677.0	1,083.9	1,471.5	1,620.7
Employer contributions for government social insurance	0.0	1.4	3.4	23.8	88.9	206.5	345.2	469.0	658.6	815.3
Proprietors' income with inventory valuation and capital consumption adjustments	**10.9**	**12.2**	**37.5**	**77.8**	**171.6**	**353.2**	**753.6**	**1,108.5**	**1,583.8**	**1,848.4**
Farm	3.9	4.1	12.9	12.9	11.7	32.2	31.2	38.7	44.4	54.3
Nonfarm	7.0	8.2	24.6	64.9	159.9	321.0	722.4	1,069.8	1,539.4	1,794.1
Rental income of persons with capital consumption adjustments	**5.4**	**3.8**	**8.8**	**20.7**	**19.0**	**28.2**	**183.5**	**433.7**	**756.1**	**967.3**
Corporate profits with inventory valuation and capital consumption adjustments	**7.5**	**9.9**	**36.1**	**86.2**	**223.1**	**419.3**	**826.4**	**1,774.5**	**2,383.3**	**3,258.0**
Taxes on corporate income	0.8	2.8	17.7	31.3	75.5	121.8	233.4	272.3	307.5	585.2
Profits after tax with inventory valuation and capital consumption adjustments	6.7	7.0	18.3	55.0	147.6	297.5	593.0	1,502.2	2,075.8	2,672.9
Net dividends	5.5	4.0	9.0	27.8	76.0	193.6	413.1	636.0	1,496.7	1,848.8
Undistributed profits with inventory valuation and capital consumption adjustments	1.2	3.0	9.3	27.2	71.6	104.0	179.9	866.2	579.1	824.1
Net interest and miscellaneous payments	**4.8**	**3.3**	**3.1**	**39.5**	**182.8**	**432.0**	**504.0**	**437.7**	**529.3**	**185.4**

Note: Numbers may not add up to totals because of rounding and incomplete enumeration. Income is measured before deduction of taxes. Total national income figures include adjustments not itemized.

U.S. National Income by Industry, 2000-23

Source: Bureau of Economic Analysis, U.S. Dept. of Commerce
(in billions of current dollars)

	2000	2010	2015	2020	2021	2022	2023
NATIONAL INCOME[1]	**$8,782.5**	**$12,724.9**	**$15,607.8**	**$17,571.2**	**$19,601.2**	**$21,560.3**	**$22,476.8**
Domestic industries	**8,744.0**	**12,519.2**	**15,387.6**	**17,356.4**	**19,417.7**	**21,378.4**	**22,312.6**
Private industries	**7,700.8**	**10,866.9**	**13,568.7**	**15,263.5**	**17,267.5**	**19,164.1**	**19,968.9**
Agriculture, forestry, fishing, and hunting	74.1	113.4	147.1	110.5	161.5	200.8	193.1
Mining	90.7	184.1	152.5	86.8	217.2	351.6	285.8
Utilities	135.4	183.7	177.6	213.2	224.4	238.9	248.0
Construction	475.1	534.3	736.2	928.8	988.2	1,096.1	1,157.4
Manufacturing	1,235.6	1,349.1	1,691.1	1,649.1	1,891.0	2,239.0	2,321.0
Durable goods	750.9	751.8	983.2	999.0	1,111.7	1,264.9	1,358.4
Nondurable goods	484.7	597.3	707.9	650.1	779.3	974.1	962.6
Wholesale trade	570.2	728.2	939.5	1,017.5	1,138.6	1,279.4	1,320.8
Retail trade	666.7	863.7	1,066.7	1,253.8	1,431.7	1,522.7	1,636.1
Transportation and warehousing	272.3	384.4	502.6	523.9	658.3	778.2	833.9
Information	304.0	459.1	599.9	674.6	789.1	812.2	826.6
Finance, insurance, real estate, rental, and leasing	1,464.8	2,164.5	2,654.5	3,167.7	3,400.8	3,559.8	3,499.7
Professional and business services[2]	1,100.1	1,729.8	2,218.1	2,690.4	3,039.6	3,370.3	3,605.2
Educational services, health care, and social assistance	688.2	1,303.6	1,554.7	1,853.0	1,999.5	2,149.9	2,333.5
Arts, entertainment, recreation, accommodation, and food services	340.2	495.3	676.5	609.9	799.1	975.5	1,075.1
Other services, except government	283.4	373.8	451.7	484.4	528.5	589.8	632.7
Government	**1,043.2**	**1,652.4**	**1,818.9**	**2,092.9**	**2,150.2**	**2,214.3**	**2,343.7**
Rest of the world	**38.5**	**205.6**	**220.1**	**214.8**	**183.5**	**181.9**	**164.2**

Note: Estimates based on the 2017 North American Industry Classification System (NAICS). (1) Without capital consumption adjustment. (2) Consists of professional, scientific, and technical services; management of companies and enterprises; and administrative and waste management services.

Measuring Inflation: Consumer Price Index

The Consumer Price Index (CPI) is a measure of the change in prices over time of one or more kinds of basic consumer goods and services. The overall CPI is based on the price of food, clothing, shelter, and fuels; transportation fares; charges for doctors' and dentists' services; drug prices; and the cost of other goods and services bought for day-to-day living. Since Jan. 1988, the base period for comparison has been 1982-84, which equals 100.0. The price of apparel, entertainment and recreation, and education and communication have not risen significantly, while the cost of medical care has more than quadrupled since 1982-84. The Consumer Price Index for all urban consumers (CPI-U) covers over 90% of the total U.S. population. The Bureau of Labor Statistics also publishes a separate Consumer Price Index for urban wage earners and clerical workers (CPI-W), which covers about 30% of the total U.S. population.

Distribution of U.S. Total Personal Income, 1930-2023

Source: Bureau of Economic Analysis, U.S. Dept. of Commerce
(in billions of current dollars, except for per capita figures)

Year	Personal income	Personal current taxes	Disposable personal income	Personal outlays	Personal savings	Savings as % of income[1]	Disposable personal income per capita: Current dollars	Disposable personal income per capita: Constant (2017) dollars
1930	$76.5	$1.6	$75.0	$71.6	$3.3	4.5%	$609.0	$7,231.0
1940	79.4	1.7	77.7	72.4	5.3	6.8	588.0	8,418.0
1950	233.7	18.9	214.8	194.8	20.0	9.3	1,416.0	11,306.0
1960	422.1	46.1	376.1	338.2	37.9	10.1	2,080.0	13,387.0
1970	865.0	103.1	762.0	664.4	97.6	12.8	3,715.0	18,797.0
1980	2,324.5	299.5	2,024.9	1,800.1	224.9	11.1	8,892.0	22,842.0
1990	4,913.3	594.7	4,318.6	3,958.0	360.6	8.4	17,262.0	28,878.0
2000	8,621.3	1,236.3	7,385.0	7,068.1	316.8	4.3	26,151.0	35,424.0
2010	12,556.6	1,237.6	11,319.0	10,647.6	671.4	5.9	36,532.0	40,361.0
2015	15,473.7	1,940.9	13,532.9	12,742.3	790.6	5.8	42,013.0	43,179.0
2020	19,629.0	2,256.5	17,372.5	14,694.0	2,678.6	15.4	52,359.0	50,039.0
2021	21,407.7	2,743.3	18,664.4	16,543.9	2,120.5	11.4	56,156.0	51,519.0
2022	21,840.8	3,138.3	18,702.5	18,079.7	622.8	3.3	56,068.0	48,317.0
2023	22,961.3	2,756.3	20,205.0	19,305.1	899.8	4.5	60,276.0	50,069.0

Note: Personal income minus current taxes equals disposable income; disposable income minus outlays equals savings. Figures may not add up to totals because of rounding. (1) Personal savings as a percentage of disposable personal income.

Inflation: U.S. Consumer Price Index, 1915-2023

Source: Bureau of Labor Statistics, U.S. Dept. of Labor

In general, prices as measured by the U.S. Consumer Price Index have risen steadily since World War II. What cost $1.00 in 1982-84 cost about $0.10 in 1915, $0.18 in 1945, and $3.05 in 2023.

(Annual averages of monthly figures, for all urban consumers. **1982-84 = 100**.)

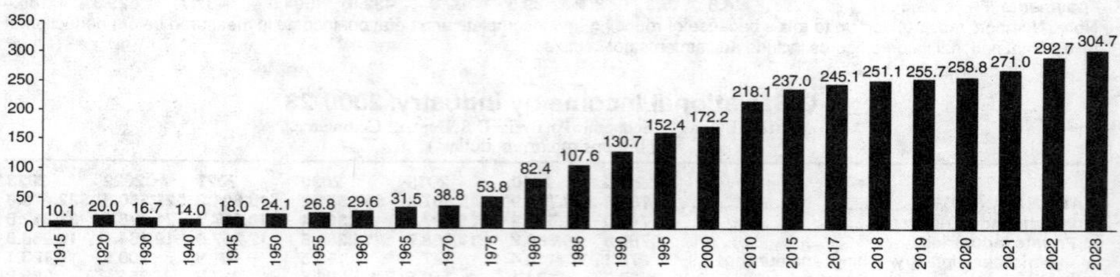

Inflation: U.S. Consumer Price Index by Major Group, 1915-2023

Source: Bureau of Labor Statistics, U.S. Dept. of Labor
For all urban consumers. **1982-84 = 100**, unless otherwise noted.

Year	All items	Apparel	Energy	Food & beverages	Housing	Transportation	Medical care	Entertainment & recreation[1,2]	Educ. & communication[1]	Other goods & services
1915	10.1	15.3	—	—	—	—	—	—	—	—
1920	20.0	43.1	—	—	—	—	—	—	—	—
1930	16.7	24.2	—	—	—	—	—	—	—	—
1940	14.0	21.8	—	—	—	14.2	10.4	—	—	—
1945	18.0	31.4	—	—	—	15.9	11.9	—	—	—
1950	24.1	40.3	—	—	—	22.7	15.1	—	—	—
1955	26.8	42.9	—	—	—	25.8	18.2	—	—	—
1960	29.6	45.7	22.4	—	—	29.8	22.3	—	—	—
1965	31.5	47.8	22.9	—	—	31.9	25.2	—	—	—
1970	38.8	59.2	25.5	40.1	36.4	37.5	34.0	—	—	40.9
1975	53.8	72.5	42.1	60.2	50.7	50.1	47.5	—	—	53.9
1980	82.4	90.9	86.0	86.7	81.1	83.1	74.9	—	—	75.2
1985	107.6	105.0	101.6	105.6	107.7	106.4	113.5	—	—	114.5
1990	130.7	124.1	102.1	132.1	128.5	120.5	162.8	—	—	159.0
1995	152.4	132.0	105.2	148.9	148.5	139.1	220.5	94.5	92.2	206.9
2000	172.2	129.6	124.6	168.4	169.6	153.3	260.8	103.3	102.5	271.1
2005	195.3	119.5	177.1	191.2	195.7	173.9	323.2	109.4	113.7	313.4
2010	218.1	119.5	211.4	220.0	216.3	193.4	388.4	113.3	129.9	381.3
2015	237.0	125.9	202.9	246.8	238.1	199.1	446.8	115.9	138.2	414.9
2020	258.8	118.1	196.9	266.6	271.8	201.3	518.9	122.2	140.3	462.4
2021	271.0	121.0	238.3	276.8	280.7	230.7	525.3	125.2	142.6	476.8
2022	292.7	127.1	298.3	303.3	300.8	266.3	546.6	130.8	143.8	506.4
2023	304.7	130.6	283.3	320.5	320.2	267.0	549.1	136.1	145.2	537.3

— = Comparable data not available. **Note:** Data is not seasonally adjusted. (1) Dec. 1997 = 100. (2) Entertainment was reclassified as Recreation in 1997.

Inflation Rate by Selected Categories, 2022-23

Source: Bureau of Labor Statistics, U.S. Dept. of Labor

For all urban consumers. 1982-84 = 100; change in the Consumer Price Index for selected categories in the 12 months ending Dec. 2022 and Dec. 2023. The following items had the highest rates of inflation and the highest rates of deflation in 2023.

Category	2023	2022
All items	**3.4%**	**6.5%**
Biggest increases		
Motor vehicle insurance	20.3	14.2
Nonprescription drugs	8.3	5.4
Shelter	6.2	7.5
Hospital and related services	5.6	4.6
Food away from home	5.2	8.3
Personal care	5.0	6.6
Electricity	3.3	14.3
Prescription drugs	3.3	1.8
Food	2.7	10.4
Recreation	2.7	5.1

Category	2023	2022
Biggest decreases		
Eggs	–23.8%	59.9%
Fuel oil	–14.7	41.5
Utility (piped) gas service	–13.8	19.3
Airline fares	–9.4	28.5
Energy	–2.0	7.3
Gasoline (all types)	–1.9	–1.5
Communication	–1.7	–1.1
Used cars and trucks	–1.3	–8.8
Dairy and related products	–1.3	15.3
Physicians' services	–0.6	1.7

U.S. Inflation Rate, 1915-2024

Source: Bureau of Labor Statistics, U.S. Dept. of Labor

Inflation is the rate at which the Consumer Price Index increases year over year. If the CPI decreases, as it did during the Great Depression, that is known as deflation.

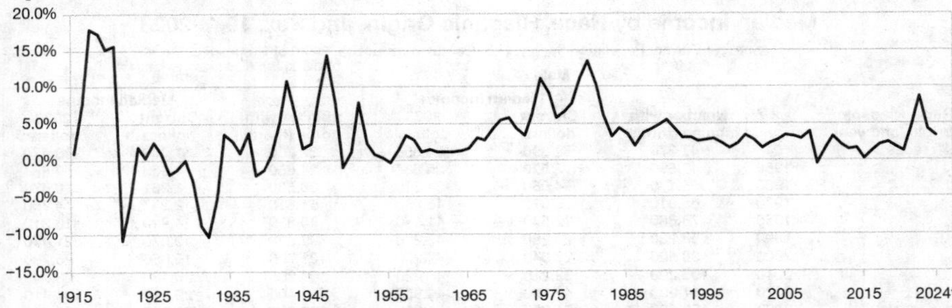

* = 2024 estimate based on the change in the CPI from second quarter 2023 to second quarter 2024.

World's Wealthiest Individuals, 2024

Source: *Forbes* magazine, Apr. 3, 2024

Rank	Name	Source of wealth	Net worth (bil)
1.	Bernard Arnault*	Fashion & Retail	$233.0
2.	Elon Musk	Automotive	195.0
3.	Jeff Bezos	Technology	194.0
4.	Mark Zuckerberg	Technology	177.0
5.	Larry Ellison	Technology	141.0
6.	Warren Buffett	Finance & Investments	133.0
7.	Bill Gates	Technology	128.0
8.	Steve Ballmer	Technology	121.0
9.	Mukesh Ambani	Diversified	116.0
10.	Larry Page	Technology	114.0
11.	Sergey Brin	Technology	110.0
12.	Michael Bloomberg	Finance & Investments	106.0
13.	Amancio Ortega	Fashion & Retail	103.0
14.	Carlos Slim Helu*	Telecom	102.0
15.	Francoise Bettencourt Meyers*	Fashion & Retail	99.5
16.	Michael Dell	Technology	91.0
17.	Gautam Adani	Diversified	84.0
18.	Jim Walton*	Fashion & Retail	78.4
19.	Rob Walton*	Fashion & Retail	77.4
20.	Jensen Huang	Technology	77.0
21.	Alice Walton	Fashion & Retail	72.3
22.	David Thomson*	Media & Entertainment	67.8
23.	Julia Koch*	Diversified	64.3
24.	Zhong Shanshan	Food & Beverage	62.3
25.	Charles Koch*	Diversified	58.5
26.	Giovanni Ferrero	Food & Beverage	43.8
27.	Prajogo Pangestu	Diversified	43.4
27.	Zhang Yiming	Technology	43.4
29.	Tadashi Yanai*	Fashion & Retail	42.8
30.	Phil Knight*	Fashion & Retail	40.9
31.	Mark Mateschitz	Food & Beverage	39.6
32.	Klaus-Michael Kuehne	Logistics	39.2
33.	Colin Huang	Technology	38.9
34.	Stephen Schwarzman	Finance & Investments	$38.8
35.	Jacqueline Mars	Food & Beverage	38.5
35.	John Mars	Food & Beverage	38.5
37.	Dieter Schwarz	Fashion & Retail	38.0
38.	Li Ka-shing	Diversified	37.3
39.	Shiv Nadar	Technology	36.9
40.	Alain Wertheimer	Fashion & Retail	36.8
40.	Gerard Wertheimer	Fashion & Retail	36.8
42.	Ken Griffin	Finance & Investments	36.4
43.	MacKenzie Scott	Technology	35.6
44.	Thomas Peterffy	Finance & Investments	34.0
45.	Reinhold Wuerth*	Manufacturing	33.6
46.	William Ding	Technology	33.5
46.	Savitri Jindal*	Metals & Mining	33.5
48.	Gianluigi Aponte	Logistics	33.1
48.	Rafaela Aponte-Diamant	Logistics	33.1
50.	Changpeng Zhao	Finance & Investments	33.0
51.	Masayoshi Son	Finance & Investments	32.7
52.	Len Blavatnik	Diversified	32.1
53.	Miriam Adelson*	Gambling & Casinos	32.0
54.	François Pinault*	Fashion & Retail	31.6
55.	Jim Simons	Finance & Investments	31.4
56.	Gina Rinehart	Metals & Mining	30.8
57.	Ma Huateng	Technology	30.2
58.	Abigail Johnson	Finance & Investments	29.0
59.	Vagit Alekperov	Energy	28.6
60.	Eduardo Saverin	Technology	28.0
60.	Lukas Walton	Fashion & Retail	28.0
62.	Germán Larrea Mota Velasco*	Metals & Mining	27.9
63.	Lee Shau Kee	Real Estate	27.7
64.	Jeff Yass	Finance & Investments	27.6
65.	Andrea Pignataro	Finance & Investments	27.5

* = Represents wealth held by individual and family members.

Consumer Credit Outstanding, 2010-23

Source: Federal Reserve System
(in billions of dollars, not seasonally adjusted)

	2010	2020	2023
TOTAL	**$2,647.2**	**$4,184.9**	**$5,023.7**
Major holders			
Depository institutions	1,185.5	1,687.5	2,116.9
Finance companies	705.0	551.4	727.3
Credit unions	226.5	505.1	662.6
Federal government[1]	363.8	1,381.0	1,462.2
Nonprofit and educational institutions[2]	71.3	24.1	18.9
Nonfinancial business	44.8	35.8	35.8
Major types of credit, by holder			
Revolving	**839.4**	**974.6**	**1,318.8**
Depository institutions	664.7	875.3	1,195.5
Finance companies	$81.5	$17.1	$20.8
Credit unions	36.3	62.3	82.5
Nonfinancial business	25.5	20.0	19.9
Nonrevolving	**1,807.8**	**3,210.3**	**3,704.9**
Depository institutions	520.8	812.2	921.4
Finance companies	623.5	534.3	706.4
Credit unions	190.1	442.8	580.1
Federal government[1]	363.8	1,381.0	1,462.2
Nonprofit and educational institutions[2]	71.3	24.1	18.9
Nonfinancial business	19.3	15.8	15.8

(1) Includes student loans originated by the Dept. of Education under the Federal Direct Loan Program and the Perkins Loan Program, as well as Federal Family Education Program loans that the government purchased under the Ensuring Continued Access to Student Loans Act. (2) Includes student loans originated under the Federal Family Education Loan Program and held by educational institutions and nonprofit organizations.

Median Income by Race, Hispanic Origin, and Sex, 1948-2023

Source: Current Population Survey, U.S. Census Bureau, U.S. Dept. of Commerce

		Male			Female		
			Median income			Median income	
Race, Hispanic origin, and year		Number with income (thous.)	Current dollars	2023 dollars	Number with income (thous.)	Current dollars	2023 dollars
All races	1948	47,370	$2,396	$24,850	22,730	$1,009	$10,470
	1950	47,590	2,570	26,660	24,650	953	9,884
	1960	55,170	4,080	34,530	36,530	1,261	10,670
	1970	65,010	6,670	43,980	51,650	2,237	14,750
	1980	78,660	12,530	41,550	80,830	4,920	16,310
	1990	88,220	20,290	43,260	92,250	10,070	21,470
	2000	98,500	28,340	47,270	101,700	16,060	26,790
	2010	105,200	32,210	43,620	107,200	20,780	28,140
	2020	117,900	42,700	49,950	118,400	29,410	34,410
	2023	120,600	51,350	51,350	121,200	35,410	35,410
White	1948	NA	2,510	26,030	NA	1,133	11,750
	1950	NA	2,709	28,100	NA	1,060	10,990
	1960	49,790	4,296	36,360	32,000	1,352	11,440
	1970	58,450	7,011	46,220	45,290	2,266	14,940
	1980	69,420	13,330	44,190	70,570	4,947	16,400
	1990	76,480	21,170	45,130	78,570	10,320	21,990
	2000	83,370	29,800	49,690	84,120	16,080	26,810
	2010	86,370	34,370	46,550	85,490	20,900	28,300
	2020	93,390	45,510	53,250	91,210	29,930	35,020
	2023	94,270	52,450	52,450	92,550	35,680	35,680
White, not Hispanic	1980	65,560	13,680	45,360	67,080	4,980	16,510
	1990	69,990	21,960	46,810	72,940	10,580	22,550
	2000	72,530	31,510	52,540	75,210	16,670	27,790
	2010	72,720	37,150	50,320	74,000	21,720	29,410
	2020	75,690	50,190	58,710	75,880	31,490	36,840
	2023	75,250	58,010	58,010	75,840	37,440	37,440
Black	1948	NA	1,363	14,140	NA	492	5,103
	1950	NA	1,471	15,260	NA	474	4,916
	1960	5,384	2,260	19,130	4,525	837	7,083
	1970	5,844	4,157	27,410	5,844	2,063	13,600
	1980	7,387	8,009	26,560	8,596	4,580	15,190
	1990	8,820	12,870	27,430	10,690	8,328	17,750
	2000	9,905	21,340	35,590	12,460	15,880	26,480
	2010	11,430	23,090	31,270	14,210	19,550	26,470
	2020	14,630	31,150	36,440	16,970	26,670	31,200
	2023	15,250	39,670	39,670	17,670	32,230	32,230
Asian	1990	2,235	19,390	41,340	2,333	11,090	23,630
	2000	4,303	30,830	51,420	4,192	17,360	28,940
	2010	5,406	35,120	47,560	5,604	23,550	31,900
	2020	7,548	51,330	60,050	7,930	33,540	39,240
	2023	8,494	62,360	62,360	8,390	40,980	40,980
Hispanic	1980	3,996	9,659	32,030	3,617	4,405	14,610
	1990	6,767	13,470	28,710	5,903	7,532	16,060
	2000	11,340	19,500	32,520	9,431	12,250	20,430
	2010	15,110	22,420	30,360	12,950	16,290	22,060
	2020	19,940	32,080	37,530	17,450	22,910	26,800
	2023	21,410	39,280	39,280	19,090	28,360	28,360

NA = Not available. **Note:** Income for persons 15 years of age and over beginning in Mar. 1980; 14 years of age and over as of Mar. of the following year for previous years. Beginning in 2010, totals for Black and Asian include those who identified themselves as being that race in combination with some other race; totals for white are for those who identified as white alone. Before 2010, Asian category includes Pacific Islanders. Hispanic persons may be of any race.

Poverty Thresholds by Family Size, 1980-2023

Source: U.S. Census Bureau, U.S. Dept. of Commerce

	1980	1990	2000	2010	2023
1 person	$4,190	$6,652	$8,791	$11,140	$15,480
Under age 65	4,290	6,800	8,959	11,340	15,850
Age 65 or older	3,949	6,268	8,259	10,460	14,610
2 people	5,363	8,509	11,240	14,220	19,680
Householder under age 65	5,537	8,794	11,590	14,680	20,490
Householder age 65 or older	4,983	7,905	10,420	13,190	18,430

	1980	1990	2000	2010	2023
3 people	$6,565	$10,420	$13,740	$17,370	$24,230
4 people	8,414	13,360	17,600	22,320	31,200
5 people	9,966	15,790	20,820	26,440	36,990
6 people	11,270	17,840	23,530	29,900	41,860
7 people	12,760	20,240	26,750	34,020	47,670
8 people	14,200	22,580	29,700	37,950	52,850
9 or more people	16,900	26,850	35,150	45,220	62,900

Note: Weighted averages; not used for computing poverty data.

Persons Below Poverty Level by Race and Hispanic Origin, 1960-2023

Source: U.S. Census Bureau, U.S. Dept. of Commerce

	Number below poverty level (thous.)					% of subgroup below poverty level					Avg. income cutoff, family of 4 at poverty level[4]
Year	All races[1]	Asian[2]	Black[2]	White	Hispanic[3]	All races[1]	Asian[2]	Black[2]	White	Hispanic[3]	
1960	39,850	NA	NA	28,310	NA	22.2%	NA	NA	17.8%	NA	$3,022
1970	25,420	NA	7,548	17,480	NA	12.6	NA	33.5%	9.9	NA	3,968
1980	29,270	NA	8,579	19,700	3,491	13.0	NA	32.5	10.2	25.7%	8,414
1990	33,590	858	9,837	22,330	6,006	13.5	12.2%	31.9	10.7	28.1	13,360
2000	31,580	1,258	7,982	21,650	7,747	11.3	9.9	22.5	9.5	21.5	17,600
2010	46,340	2,064	11,600	31,080	13,520	15.1	12.0	27.4	13.0	26.5	22,320
2015	43,120	2,234	10,800	28,570	12,130	13.5	11.1	23.9	11.6	21.4	24,260
2020	37,550	1,827	9,311	25,180	10,520	11.5	8.0	19.3	10.1	17.0	26,500
2021	37,930	2,112	9,298	24,920	10,690	11.6	9.0	19.3	10.0	17.1	27,740
2022	37,920	2,002	8,353	26,050	10,780	11.5	8.2	17.0	10.5	16.9	29,950
2023	36,790	2,192	8,924	24,290	10,890	11.1	8.9	17.8	9.7	16.6	31,200

NA = Not available. **Note:** Because of a change in the definition of poverty, data prior to 1980 are not directly comparable to data since 1980. (1) Includes other races not shown separately. (2) Beginning in 2002, numbers include those who identified themselves as being Asian or Black in combination with some other race. For 1990-2000, Asian includes Pacific Islanders. (3) Persons of Hispanic origin may be of any race. (4) Figures for 1960-80 for nonfarm families only.

Families Below Poverty Level by Status, Race, and Sex, 1980-2023

Source: U.S. Census Bureau, U.S. Dept. of Commerce
(numbers in thousands)

	All families			Married-couple families			Male householder, no spouse present			Female householder, no spouse present		
		Below poverty level			Below poverty level			Below poverty level			Below poverty level	
Year and race	Total	Number	Percent	Total	Number	Percent	Total	Number	Percent	Total	Number	Percent
All races												
1980	60,310	6,217	10.3%	49,290	3,032	6.2%	1,933	213	11.0%	9,082	2,972	32.7%
1990	66,320	7,098	10.7	52,150	2,981	5.7	2,907	349	12.0	11,270	3,768	33.4
2000	73,780	6,400	8.7	56,600	2,637	4.7	4,277	485	11.3	12,900	3,278	25.4
2010	79,560	9,400	11.8	58,670	3,681	6.3	5,649	892	15.8	15,240	4,827	31.7
2020	83,720	7,284	8.7	61,300	2,853	4.7	6,964	797	11.4	15,460	3,634	23.5
2023	84,710	7,009	8.3	62,310	2,883	4.6	7,214	825	11.4	15,180	3,302	21.8
White[1]												
1980	52,710	4,195	8.0	44,860	2,437	5.4	1,584	149	9.4	6,266	1,609	25.7
1990	56,800	4,622	8.1	47,010	2,386	5.1	2,277	226	9.9	7,512	2,010	26.8
2000	61,330	4,333	7.1	49,470	2,181	4.4	3,283	332	10.1	8,574	1,820	21.2
2010	63,980	6,305	9.9	50,020	2,921	5.8	4,176	563	13.5	9,784	2,822	28.8
2020	65,710	4,910	7.5	50,740	2,263	4.5	5,009	481	9.6	9,958	2,166	21.8
2023	65,850	4,650	7.1	50,850	2,194	4.3	5,280	511	9.7	9,713	1,946	20.0
Black[1]												
1980	6,317	1,826	28.9	3,392	474	14.0	291	52	17.7	2,634	1,301	49.4
1990	7,471	2,193	29.3	3,569	448	12.6	472	97	20.6	3,430	1,648	48.1
2000	8,731	1,686	19.3	4,214	266	6.3	732	120	16.3	3,785	1,300	34.3
2010	9,982	2,403	24.1	4,473	407	9.1	979	257	26.3	4,531	1,738	38.4
2020	10,820	1,795	16.6	5,059	306	6.0	1,314	241	18.4	4,446	1,248	28.1
2023	11,080	1,690	15.3	5,496	350	6.4	1,262	216	17.1	4,322	1,124	26.0
Asian[1]												
2002	2,939	218	7.4	2,344	137	5.9	241	30	12.6	354	51	14.3
2010	4,094	379	9.2	3,210	232	7.2	328	32	9.7	556	115	20.7
2020	5,509	347	6.3	4,475	218	4.9	394	30	7.7	641	99	15.4
2023	5,961	383	6.4	4,839	245	5.1	433	43	9.9	690	95	13.8
Hispanic[2]												
1980	3,235	751	23.2	2,365	363	15.3	164	26	16.0	706	362	51.3
1990	4,981	1,244	25.0	3,454	605	17.5	341	66	19.4	1,186	573	48.3
2000	8,017	1,540	19.2	5,426	772	14.2	765	104	13.6	1,826	664	36.4
2010	11,280	2,739	24.3	7,065	1,221	17.3	1,241	248	20.0	2,978	1,270	42.6
2020	13,690	2,028	14.8	8,597	848	9.9	1,686	203	12.1	3,412	976	28.6
2023	14,650	2,113	14.4	9,145	891	9.7	1,986	255	12.9	3,521	966	27.4

Note: The Census Bureau revised race categories in 2002, so data after 2002 are not directly comparable with data for previous years. (1) Beginning in 2010, totals for white include only those who identified themselves as white alone; totals for Black and Asian include those who identified themselves as that race alone or in combination with some other race. (2) Persons of Hispanic origin may be of any race.

Poverty Rates by State, 1990-2023

Source: U.S. Census Bureau, U.S. Dept. of Commerce

The poverty rate is the proportion of the population with income below the government's official poverty level, which is the same nationwide and is adjusted each year for inflation.

State	1990	2000	2010	2020	2023
Alabama	19.2%	13.3%	17.2%	14.9%	14.2%
Alaska	11.4	7.6	12.5	13.4	10.1
Arizona	13.7	11.7	18.8	10.9	11.9
Arkansas	19.6	16.5	15.3	14.1	13.8
California	13.9	12.7	16.3	11.1	11.9
Colorado	13.7	9.8	12.3	9.5	8.5
Connecticut	6.0	7.7	8.6	11.2	8.3
Delaware	6.9	8.4	12.2	10.5	7.8
Dist. of Columbia	21.1	15.2	19.5	16.8	12.7
Florida	14.4	11.0	16.0	13.3	11.6
Georgia	15.8	12.1	18.8	13.3	12.9
Hawaii	11.0	8.9	12.4	10.9	8.2
Idaho	14.9	12.5	13.8	9.1	9.1
Illinois	13.7	10.7	14.1	8.0	9.8
Indiana	13.0	8.5	16.3	12.1	8.3
Iowa	10.4	8.3	10.3	9.2	8.0
Kansas	10.3	8.0	14.5	9.3	8.8
Kentucky	17.3	12.6	17.7	13.9	13.6
Louisiana	23.6	17.2	21.5	15.5	21.5
Maine	13.1	10.1	12.6	8.0	7.4
Maryland	9.9	7.4	10.9	9.4	8.9
Massachusetts	10.7	9.8	10.9	8.4	9.1
Michigan	14.3	9.9	15.7	11.2	12.1
Minnesota	12.0	5.7	10.8	8.5	7.2
Mississippi	25.7	14.9	22.5	17.6	16.0
Missouri	13.4	9.2	15.0	10.7	9.7
Montana	16.3%	14.1%	14.5%	10.9%	8.1%
Nebraska	10.3	8.6	10.2	8.3	9.2
Nevada	9.8	8.8	16.6	12.9	13.9
New Hampshire	6.3	4.5	6.5	6.2	6.1
New Jersey	9.2	7.3	11.1	8.2	9.0
New Mexico	20.9	17.5	18.3	16.6	17.3
New York	14.3	13.9	16.0	11.8	11.0
North Carolina	13.0	12.5	17.4	13.8	13.6
North Dakota	13.7	10.4	12.6	10.7	9.9
Ohio	11.5	10.0	15.4	12.7	11.1
Oklahoma	15.6	14.9	16.3	15.5	12.9
Oregon	9.2	10.9	14.3	9.4	10.3
Pennsylvania	11.0	8.6	12.2	10.7	10.3
Rhode Island	7.5	10.2	14.0	8.5	8.9
South Carolina	16.2	11.1	16.9	13.4	11.7
South Dakota	13.3	10.7	13.6	11.6	7.5
Tennessee	16.9	13.5	16.7	13.1	10.7
Texas	15.9	15.5	18.4	14.0	12.3
Utah	8.2	7.6	10.0	7.4	6.3
Vermont	10.9	10.0	10.8	8.6	6.7
Virginia	11.1	8.3	10.7	7.8	9.4
Washington	8.9	10.8	11.6	8.2	8.7
West Virginia	18.1	14.7	16.8	14.2	13.3
Wisconsin	9.3	9.3	10.1	8.0	9.3
Wyoming	11.0	10.8	9.6	9.7	9.4
United States	**13.5**	**11.3**	**15.1**	**11.5**	**11.1**

Income Inequality in the U.S., 1970-2023

Source: U.S. Census Bureau, U.S. Dept. of Commerce

Top earners' share of income has grown considerably over the past half century. In 1970, the richest 5% of Americans earned 16.6% percent of all income while the share earned by the poorest 20% (or quintile) was 4.1%. By 2023, the top 5% took home 23% of income and the poorest 20% earned just 3.1% of the total. The middle quintile's share declined from 17.4% to 14.1% over the same period.

Income group	Mean income in 2023	Percentage of income earned by each quintile: 1970	1980	1990	1995	2000	2005	2010	2015	2020	2022	2023
Lowest quintile	$17,650	4.1%	4.2%	3.8%	3.7%	3.6%	3.4%	3.3%	3.1%	3.0%	3.0%	3.1%
Second quintile	47,590	10.8	10.2	9.6	9.1	8.9	8.6	8.5	8.2	8.2	8.2	8.3
Middle quintile	80,730	17.4	16.8	15.9	15.2	14.8	14.6	14.6	14.3	14.0	14.0	14.1
Fourth quintile	129,400	24.5	24.7	24.0	23.3	23.0	23.0	23.4	23.2	22.6	22.5	22.6
Highest quintile	297,300	43.3	44.1	46.6	48.7	49.8	50.4	50.3	51.1	52.2	52.1	51.9
Top 5%	526,200	16.6	16.5	18.5	21.0	22.1	22.2	21.3	22.1	23.0	23.5	23.0

Temporary Assistance for Needy Families (TANF), 1997-2022

Source: Office of Family Assistance, Admin. for Children and Families, U.S. Dept. of Health and Human Services

Year	Total TANF expenditures (mil)	Average number of monthly cash beneficiaries: Families	Recipients	Children
1997	$19,010.2	3,936,610	10,935,125	NA
2000	24,780.7	2,229,315	5,833,043	4,303,943
2005	25,580.1	1,901,810	4,495,175	3,428,885
2006	25,593.8	1,789,460	4,179,295	3,207,216
2007	26,922.0	1,697,432	3,957,330	3,047,043
2008	28,129.7	1,726,799	4,041,292	3,084,413
2009	30,577.8	1,847,152	4,364,979	3,280,150
2010	33,255.5	1,847,152	4,364,979	3,280,150
2011	30,264.1	1,921,243	4,599,846	3,435,218
2012	28,867.3	1,876,426	4,476,476	3,351,971
2013	$29,147.1	1,751,067	4,102,491	3,091,076
2014	29,350.9	1,652,996	3,894,213	2,934,582
2015	29,295.9	1,333,707	4,176,387	2,370,198
2016	28,321.2	1,206,820	3,886,868	2,144,955
2017	28,701.0	1,095,368	3,650,293	1,943,028
2018	28,719.7	1,004,923	3,234,514	1,785,278
2019	28,483.0	916,614	2,940,845	1,640,805
2020	28,984.0	885,522	2,027,980	1,573,156
2021	28,037.9	804,117	1,847,644	1,424,759
2022	29,230.4	793,156	1,862,756	1,416,640

NA = Not available.

Adults Receiving TANF Funds by Employment Status, 2022

Source: Office of Family Assistance, Admin. for Children and Families, U.S. Dept. of Health and Human Services

State	Adults	Employed
AL	2,117	38.8%
AK	1,214	29.3
AZ	1,650	13.4
AR	484	13.0
CA	178,995	21.4
CO	7,538	49.2
CT	2,139	17.9
DE	794	23.1
DC	4,443	11.7
FL	8,087	4.4
GA	1,183	19.5
Guam	187	1.2
HI	4,461	24.1
ID	36	7.4
IL	2,482	87.5%
IN	1,286	19.1
IA	2,597	24.9
KS	1,881	33.8
KY	3,353	25.9
LA	1,187	20.0
ME	2,460	19.1
MD	12,000	33.5
MA	22,155	17.0
MI	3,586	29.7
MN	8,381	32.7
MS	291	0.8
MO	2,451	15.2
MT	743	34.0
NE	663	58.2%
NV	4,133	31.2
NH	1,030	26.1
NJ	6,318	6.1
NM	7,788	6.7
NY	51,559	18.8
NC	2,509	10.0
ND	233	45.5
OH	5,817	19.5
OK	884	10.1
OR	10,519	4.3
PA	16,714	24.7
Puerto Rico	3,309	5.1
RI	2,021	11.8
SC	2,586	12.1%
SD	253	20.8
TN	5,164	29.1
TX	2,544	26.7
UT	747	10.3
VT	851	11.9
Virgin Isls.	58	4.7
VA	9,008	18.3
WA	21,623	11.5
WV	1,222	18.0
WI	3,641	25.1
WY	234	20.7
U.S. total	**439,610**	**20.7**

TANF = Temporary Assistance for Needy Families.

Selected Personal Consumption Expenditures in the U.S., 1980-2023

Source: Bureau of Economic Analysis, U.S. Dept. of Commerce
(in billions of dollars)

	1980	1990	2000	2010	2020	2022	2023
Personal consumption expenditures	**$1,750.7**	**$3,809.0**	**$6,767.2**	**$10,260.3**	**$14,206.2**	**$17,511.7**	**$18,570.6**
GOODS	**799.8**	**1,491.3**	**2,453.2**	**3,317.8**	**4,713.1**	**5,997.0**	**6,191.5**
Durable goods	**226.4**	**497.1**	**912.6**	**1,049.0**	**1,628.9**	**2,128.9**	**2,198.8**
Motor vehicles and parts	**84.4**	**205.1**	**363.2**	**344.5**	**547.0**	**730.8**	**768.0**
New motor vehicles	54.3	134.7	210.7	182.3	292.8	374.7	398.2
Net purchases of used motor vehicles	12.2	42.2	110.7	105.6	165.6	242.2	248.5
Motor vehicle parts and accessories	17.9	28.3	41.8	56.6	88.6	113.9	121.3
Furnishings, durable household equipment	**67.8**	**120.9**	**208.1**	**240.9**	**378.5**	**477.4**	**478.3**
Furniture and furnishings	36.9	69.2	121.7	140.5	215.0	277.0	277.5
Household appliances	15.1	23.7	34.1	44.1	69.6	85.9	84.7
Glassware, tableware, and household utensils	10.6	18.4	35.3	36.4	44.6	54.5	56.2
Recreational goods and vehicles	**46.5**	**105.6**	**230.9**	**298.6**	**507.3**	**655.5**	**681.6**
Video, audio, photo, and info-processing equip.	21.9	56.1	127.7	182.8	296.6	385.6	410.7
Sporting equipment, guns, ammunition	8.9	19.9	39.1	52.8	94.6	119.2	124.6
Sports and recreational vehicles	9.8	16.6	34.9	35.8	87.0	113.8	107.1
Recreational books	4.7	10.9	24.4	22.6	23.1	29.0	30.7
Other durable goods	**27.6**	**65.5**	**110.4**	**165.0**	**196.1**	**265.2**	**271.0**
Jewelry and watches	15.0	30.3	49.1	60.9	68.4	99.0	96.9
Therapeutic appliances and equipment	5.1	18.4	32.2	52.4	66.5	83.0	87.9
Nondurable goods	**573.4**	**994.2**	**1,540.6**	**2,268.9**	**3,084.2**	**3,868.1**	**3,992.7**
Food and beverages purchased for off-premises consumption	**239.2**	**391.2**	**540.6**	**786.9**	**1,196.5**	**1,393.5**	**1,442.3**
Food and nonalcoholic beverages	208.0	341.2	463.1	678.6	1,007.4	1,178.9	1,220.1
Alcoholic beverages	30.0	49.3	77.1	107.9	188.5	213.9	221.5
Clothing and footwear	**103.0**	**195.2**	**280.8**	**316.6**	**366.2**	**500.7**	**516.9**
Women's and girls' clothing	48.5	94.5	132.7	149.2	163.3	226.2	234.2
Men's and boys' clothing	30.9	57.4	85.9	83.7	98.5	135.8	140.8
Children's and infants' clothing	3.9	8.1	11.4	18.0	19.3	25.5	25.8
Other clothing materials and footwear	19.7	35.3	50.8	65.8	85.1	113.2	116.2
Gasoline and other energy goods	**101.9**	**124.2**	**184.5**	**336.7**	**258.3**	**510.1**	**471.2**
Other nondurable goods	**129.3**	**283.6**	**534.7**	**828.7**	**1,263.1**	**1,463.8**	**1,562.4**
Pharmaceutical and other medical products	18.7	59.1	159.0	326.1	522.9	575.2	632.5
Recreational items	22.0	50.9	91.9	129.9	225.7	291.6	310.6
Household supplies	29.1	54.2	86.7	108.2	151.3	176.7	183.0
Personal care products	18.7	39.3	68.5	106.0	148.6	181.3	192.3
Tobacco	20.9	41.0	68.5	97.9	120.8	122.4	119.9
Magazines, newspapers, and stationery	18.1	36.5	56.6	52.2	82.7	105.1	112.2
SERVICES	**950.9**	**2,317.7**	**4,314.0**	**6,942.4**	**9,493.1**	**11,514.7**	**12,379.2**
Housing and utilities	**312.5**	**696.5**	**1,198.6**	**1,947.9**	**2,676.0**	**3,053.3**	**3,278.7**
Housing	246.6	570.6	1,010.5	1,648.1	2,324.0	2,618.4	2,842.1
Rental of tenant-occupied nonfarm housing	62.5	150.8	227.9	361.1	529.5	593.5	642.5
Imputed rental of owner-occupied nonfarm housing	178.4	412.8	768.9	1,267.6	1,770.6	1,998.7	2,171.6
Household utilities	65.9	125.9	188.1	299.9	352.1	434.8	436.6
Water supply and sanitation	9.4	27.1	50.4	78.5	110.0	120.9	128.9
Electricity	37.2	71.8	98.4	166.8	191.6	234.8	239.4
Natural gas	19.3	27.0	39.3	54.6	50.5	79.2	68.4
Health care	**171.7**	**506.2**	**918.4**	**1,699.6**	**2,354.8**	**2,776.7**	**2,999.6**
Outpatient services	70.6	232.1	436.6	774.6	1,080.3	1,287.7	1,396.1
Physician services	43.3	134.8	229.2	410.5	570.4	662.0	713.6
Dental services	13.7	32.4	63.6	104.5	119.1	160.6	173.1
Paramedical services	13.6	64.9	143.8	259.6	390.9	465.1	509.4
Hospitals	84.7	228.8	393.9	769.9	1,087.1	1,282.2	1,374.9
Nursing homes	16.4	45.3	87.9	155.1	187.3	206.8	228.7
Transportation services	**55.4**	**126.4**	**261.3**	**305.2**	**358.7**	**562.2**	**604.2**
Motor vehicle services	35.1	87.2	174.4	201.0	275.0	335.6	343.4
Motor vehicle maintenance and repair	31.2	73.9	112.5	136.7	178.4	226.4	235.8
Public transportation	20.2	39.2	86.9	104.2	83.7	226.6	260.8
Recreation services	**40.8**	**121.8**	**254.4**	**403.7**	**468.2**	**654.9**	**716.3**
Membership clubs, sports centers, parks, theaters, museums	20.1	49.7	91.9	146.1	133.1	230.4	264.0
Audio-video, photographic, and information-processing equipment services	10.7	37.9	70.1	106.4	145.1	162.6	164.5
Gambling	6.7	23.7	67.6	109.4	125.4	172.2	185.4
Food services and accommodations	**121.7**	**262.7**	**408.8**	**635.7**	**823.9**	**1,237.2**	**1,367.4**
Purchased meals and beverages	105.9	228.3	344.9	521.8	711.5	1,030.6	1,139.6
Accommodations	10.3	27.6	55.0	98.6	88.6	176.9	194.7
Financial services and insurance	**91.7**	**230.8**	**541.9**	**768.0**	**1,148.9**	**1,252.5**	**1,321.9**
Financial services	47.8	119.0	335.7	479.0	724.0	807.1	852.6
Insurance	43.9	111.7	206.3	289.0	424.9	445.4	469.3
Other services	**127.1**	**297.5**	**572.6**	**887.9**	**1,178.0**	**1,445.8**	**1,540.6**
Telecommunication services	27.6	60.7	126.4	147.6	169.4	183.0	181.9
Internet access	—	0.1	12.0	40.5	84.4	99.7	107.4
Higher education	12.9	34.7	76.8	155.0	188.1	196.4	202.5
Nursery, elementary, and secondary schools	6.7	14.8	24.1	35.6	47.3	55.9	58.7
Commercial and vocational schools	4.2	11.1	24.3	39.9	52.8	66.3	74.4
Professional and other services	24.8	67.7	113.0	158.9	212.3	248.4	263.1
Personal care and clothing services	17.9	44.5	80.4	115.8	118.0	172.4	192.4
Social services and religious activities	14.0	41.2	81.1	139.0	223.9	272.5	295.5
Household maintenance	13.8	25.4	49.2	61.6	91.5	102.3	107.0

— = Not applicable. **Note:** Subtotals may not add up to totals due to rounding or incomplete enumeration.

Leading U.S. Businesses, 2023

Source: *Fortune* magazine, June 2024

(ranked by 2023 revenues, in millions of dollars)

Industry/company (rank)	Revenues
Advertising	
Omnicom Group (287)	$14,692
Interpublic Group (372)	10,889
Aerospace	
Boeing (52)	$77,794
RTX (55)	68,920
Lockheed Martin (57)	67,571
General Dynamics (104)	42,272
Northrop Grumman (109)	39,290
L3Harris Technologies (209)	19,419
Textron (308)	13,683
Huntington Ingalls Industries (357)	11,454
Airlines	
Delta Air Lines (70)	$58,048
United Airlines Holdings (83)	53,717
American Airlines Group (86)	52,788
Southwest Airlines (159)	26,091
Alaska Air Group (385)	10,426
JetBlue Airways (413)	9,615
Apparel	
Nike (88)	$51,217
VF (355)	11,613
PVH (425)	9,218
Skechers U.S.A. (465)	8,000
Automotive Retailing, Services	
Lithia Motors (140)	$31,311
CarMax (141)	31,126
Penske Automotive Group (146)	29,527
AutoNation (155)	26,949
Group 1 Automotive (229)	17,874
Asbury Automotive Group (281)	14,803
Sonic Automotive (296)	14,372
Avis Budget Group (345)	12,008
Carvana (377)	10,771
Hertz Global Holdings (417)	9,371
Rush Enterprises (467)	7,925
Beverages	
Coca-Cola (95)	$45,754
Keurig Dr Pepper (279)	14,814
Molson Coors Beverage (352)	11,702
Constellation Brands (415)	9,453
Monster Beverage (496)	7,140
Building Materials, Glass	
Builders FirstSource (240)	$17,097
Owens Corning (407)	9,677
Vulcan Materials (472)	7,782
UFP Industries (493)	7,218
Chemicals	
Dow (99)	$44,622
3M (134)	32,681
Sherwin-Williams (176)	23,052
PPG Industries (226)	18,246
Ecolab (269)	15,320
Mosaic (307)	13,696
Air Products & Chemicals (322)	12,600
Westlake (326)	12,548
DuPont (327)	12,528
International Flavors & Fragrances (356)	11,479
Celanese (369)	10,940
Albemarle (412)	9,617
Eastman Chemical (426)	9,210
RPM International (492)	7,256
Commercial Banks	
JPMorgan Chase (12)	$239,425
Bank of America (18)	171,912
Citigroup (21)	156,820
Wells Fargo (34)	115,340
Goldman Sachs Group (35)	108,418
Morgan Stanley (41)	96,194
Capital One Financial (91)	49,484
U.S. Bancorp (107)	40,624
Bank of New York Mellon (130)	33,805
Truist Financial (132)	33,246
PNC Financial Services Group (139)	31,882
First Citizens BancShares (182)	22,466
Discover Financial Services (194)	20,606
State Street (225)	18,366
M&T Bank (317)	12,752
Fifth Third Bancorp (321)	12,641
Citizens Financial Group (337)	12,187
Northern Trust (342)	$12,117
Huntington Bancshares (375)	10,837
KeyCorp (386)	10,397
Regions Financial (428)	9,153
New York Community Bancorp (457)	8,178
Computer Software	
Microsoft (13)	$211,915
Oracle (89)	49,954
Salesforce (123)	34,857
Adobe (210)	19,409
Intuit (297)	14,368
ServiceNow (432)	8,971
Workday (490)	7,259
Computers, Office Equipment	
Apple (3)	$383,285
Dell Technologies (48)	88,425
HP (82)	53,718
Hewlett Packard Enterprise (147)	29,135
Western Digital (334)	12,318
Super Micro Computer (498)	7,124
Construction, Farm Machinery	
Caterpillar (59)	$67,060
Deere (64)	61,251
AGCO (295)	14,412
Oshkosh (409)	9,658
Diversified Financials	
Fannie Mae (27)	$141,240
Freddie Mac (36)	108,050
American Express (58)	67,364
StoneX Group (66)	60,856
Marsh & McLennan (180)	22,736
Synchrony (191)	20,999
Ameriprise Financial (254)	16,096
Ally Financial (257)	15,971
Icahn Enterprises (374)	10,847
Arthur J. Gallagher (391)	10,072
Blackstone (464)	8,023
Jefferies Financial Group (480)	7,441
Voya Financial (487)	7,348
Diversified Outsourcing Services	
Aramark (220)	$18,854
Automatic Data Processing (228)	18,012
Jacobs Solutions (249)	16,352
Cintas (437)	8,816
ABM Industries (461)	8,096
Electronics, Electrical Equipment	
Whirlpool (208)	$19,455
Corning (323)	12,588
Rockwell Automation (430)	9,058
Energy	
World Kinect (93)	$47,711
NRG Energy (150)	28,823
Constellation Energy (165)	24,918
Vistra (283)	14,779
Engineering & Construction	
Quanta Services (192)	$20,882
Peter Kiewit Sons' (239)	17,118
Fluor (265)	15,474
AECOM (291)	14,591
EMCOR Group (324)	12,583
MasTec (347)	11,996
Entertainment	
Walt Disney (47)	$88,898
Warner Bros. Discovery (106)	41,321
Netflix (131)	33,723
Paramount Global (142)	30,610
Live Nation Entertainment (179)	22,749
Fox (277)	14,913
Liberty Media (328)	12,525
Electronic Arts (482)	7,426
Equipment Leasing	
United Rentals (298)	$14,332
Financial Data Services	
Visa (135)	$32,653
PayPal Holdings (145)	29,771
Mastercard (164)	25,098
Block (186)	21,916
Fiserv (215)	19,093
Fidelity Natl. Info. Services (288)	14,680
S&P Global (329)	12,497
Global Payments (410)	9,654
Food Consumer Products	
PepsiCo (44)	$91,471
Mondelez International (115)	36,016
Kraft Heinz (156)	26,640
General Mills (203)	20,094
Land O'Lakes (245)	16,795
Kellanova (272)	15,207
Conagra Brands (336)	12,277
Hormel Foods (343)	12,110
Hershey (361)	11,165
Campbell Soup (419)	9,357
J.M. Smucker (446)	8,529
Food Production	
Archer Daniels Midland (43)	$93,935
Tyson Foods (85)	52,881
CHS (97)	45,590
Corteva (238)	17,226
Andersons (285)	14,750
Seaboard (414)	9,562
Ingredion (459)	8,160
Food Services	
Starbucks (116)	$35,976
McDonald's (162)	25,494
Yum China Holdings (368)	10,978
Darden Restaurants (383)	10,488
Chipotle Mexican Grill (399)	9,872
Food & Drug Stores	
Kroger (25)	$150,039
Walgreens Boots Alliance (28)	139,081
Albertsons (53)	77,650
Publix Super Markets (72)	57,534
Rite Aid (171)	24,092
Forest & Paper Products	
Weyerhaeuser (476)	$7,674
General Merchandisers	
Walmart (1)	$648,125
Costco Wholesale (11)	242,290
Target (37)	107,412
Macy's (172)	23,866
BJ's Wholesale Club (205)	19,969
Kohl's (235)	17,476
Nordstrom (286)	14,693
Health Care: Insurance & Managed Care	
UnitedHealth Group (4)	$371,622
Elevance Health (20)	171,340
Centene (22)	153,999
Humana (38)	106,374
Molina Healthcare (128)	34,072
Health Care: Medical Facilities	
HCA Healthcare (61)	$64,968
Tenet Healthcare (195)	20,548
Universal Health Services (299)	14,282
Community Health Systems (330)	12,490
DaVita (341)	12,140
Health Care: Pharmacy & Other Services	
CVS Health (6)	$357,776
Cigna (16)	195,265
IQVIA Holdings (275)	14,984
Labcorp Holdings (309)	13,668
Quest Diagnostics (423)	9,252
BrightSpring Health Services (436)	8,826
Home Equipment & Furnishings	
Stanley Black & Decker (263)	$15,781
Mohawk Industries (364)	11,135
Newell Brands (460)	8,133
Masco (466)	7,967
Homebuilders	
D.R. Horton (120)	$35,460
Lennar (126)	34,233
PulteGroup (255)	16,062
Toll Brothers (394)	9,995
NVR (406)	9,687
Taylor Morrison Home (483)	7,418
Hotels, Casinos, Resorts	
Marriott International (173)	$23,713
MGM Resorts International (251)	16,164
Caesars Entertainment (353)	11,673
Las Vegas Sands (387)	10,372
Hilton Worldwide Holdings (389)	10,235

Industry/company (rank)	Revenues
Household & Personal Products	
Procter & Gamble (50)	$82,006
Kimberly-Clark (198)	20,431
Colgate-Palmolive (207)	19,457
Estée Lauder (259)	15,910
Clorox (485)	7,839
Industrial Machinery	
General Electric (56)	$67,954
Honeywell International (114)	36,662
Cummins (129)	34,065
Carrier Global (184)	22,098
Parker-Hannifin (216)	19,065
Emerson Electric (224)	18,370
Illinois Tool Works (253)	16,107
Otis Worldwide (301)	14,209
Westinghouse Air Brake Technologies (407)	9,677
Dover (448)	8,438
Xylem (486)	7,364
Information Technology Services	
IBM (63)	$61,860
CDW (189)	21,376
Cognizant Technology Solutions (213)	19,353
Kyndryl Holdings (241)	17,026
Leidos Holdings (266)	15,438
DXC Technology (294)	14,430
Booz Allen Hamilton Holding (422)	9,259
Insight Enterprises (427)	9,176
Science Applications International (479)	7,444
Concentrix (499)	7,115
Insurance: Life, Health (Mutual)	
New York Life Insurance (78)	$54,317
TIAA (96)	45,735
Massachusetts Mutual Life Insurance (102)	42,641
Northwestern Mutual (110)	38,788
Guardian Life Ins. Co. of America (252)	16,137
Western & Southern Financial Group (284)	14,775
Mutual of Omaha (306)	13,856
Thrivent Financial for Lutherans (405)	9,720
Insurance: Life, Health (Stock)	
MetLife (60)	$66,905
Prudential Financial (81)	53,979
Aflac (222)	18,701
Reinsurance Group of America (223)	18,567
Pacific Life (282)	14,802
Principal Financial (310)	13,666
Unum Group (332)	12,386
Lincoln National (354)	11,645
Equitable Holdings (381)	10,528
Securian Financial Group (462)	8,067
Genworth Financial (477)	7,488
Insurance: Property & Casualty (Mutual)	
State Farm Insurance (39)	$104,199
Nationwide (75)	54,609
Farmers Insurance Exchange (273)	15,194
Auto-Owners Insurance (314)	12,938
Erie Insurance Group (376)	10,813
Insurance: Property & Casualty (Stock)	
Berkshire Hathaway (5)	$364,482
Progressive (62)	62,109
Allstate (73)	57,094
Liberty Mutual Insurance Group (87)	52,612
AIG (94)	46,802
USAA (103)	42,493
Travelers (105)	41,364
Hartford Financial Services Group (166)	24,527
American Family Insurance Group (243)	17,000
Loews (260)	15,901
Markel Group (262)	15,804
W.R. Berkley (340)	12,143
Fidelity National Financial (351)	11,752
Assurant (365)	11,132
Cincinnati Financial (393)	10,013
FM Global (418)	9,359
American Financial Group (470)	7,827
Old Republic International (491)	7,258

Industry/company (rank)	Revenues
Internet Services & Retailing	
Amazon (2)	$574,785
Alphabet (8)	307,394
Meta Platforms (30)	134,902
Uber Technologies (113)	37,281
Coupang (168)	24,383
Booking Holdings (190)	21,365
Expedia Group (315)	12,839
Wayfair (346)	12,003
Chewy (362)	11,148
Qurate Retail (370)	10,915
Ebay (390)	10,112
Airbnb (396)	9,917
DoorDash (443)	8,635
Mail, Package & Freight Delivery	
United Parcel Service (45)	$90,958
FedEx (46)	90,155
Medical Products & Equipment	
Abbott Laboratories (108)	$40,109
Danaher (153)	27,602
Stryker (197)	20,498
GE HealthCare Technologies (206)	19,552
Becton Dickinson (211)	19,372
Baxter International (270)	15,282
Boston Scientific (300)	14,240
Zimmer Biomet Holdings (484)	7,394
Intuitive Surgical (497)	7,124
Metals	
Nucor (124)	$34,714
Cleveland-Cliffs (185)	21,996
Steel Dynamics (221)	18,795
United States Steel (227)	18,053
Reliance (280)	14,806
Alcoa (380)	10,551
Commercial Metals (438)	8,800
Mining, Crude Oil Production	
ConocoPhillips (68)	$58,574
Occidental Petroleum (149)	28,918
EOG Resources (169)	24,186
Freeport-McMoRan (178)	22,855
Pioneer Natural Resources (212)	19,362
Devon Energy (271)	15,258
Newmont (349)	11,812
Ovintiv (373)	10,883
Hess (378)	10,645
Continental Resources (439)	8,732
Chesapeake Energy (440)	8,721
Diamondback Energy (449)	8,412
APA (455)	8,192
Motor Vehicles & Parts	
Ford Motor (17)	$176,191
General Motors (19)	171,842
Tesla (40)	96,773
Paccar (122)	35,127
Lear (174)	23,467
Goodyear Tire & Rubber (204)	20,066
BorgWarner (258)	15,921
Thor Industries (366)	11,122
Dana (379)	10,555
Autoliv (384)	10,475
Network & Other Communications Equipment	
Cisco Systems (74)	$56,998
Amphenol (325)	12,555
Motorola Solutions (395)	9,978
Oil & Gas Equipment, Services	
Baker Hughes (161)	$25,506
Halliburton (177)	23,018
NOV (444)	8,583
Packaging, Containers	
WestRock (202)	$20,310
International Paper (218)	18,916
Ball (304)	14,029
Berry Global Group (320)	12,664
Crown Holdings (344)	12,010
Graphic Packaging Holding (416)	9,428
Avery Dennison (450)	8,364
Packaging Corp. of America (471)	7,802
O-I Glass (500)	7,105
Petroleum Refining	
Exxon Mobil (7)	$344,582
Chevron (15)	200,949
Marathon Petroleum (24)	150,307
Phillips 66 (26)	149,890
Valero Energy (29)	139,001
PBF Energy (112)	38,325
HF Sinclair (137)	31,964

Industry/company (rank)	Revenues
Delek US Holdings (244)	$16,917
Par Pacific Holdings (454)	8,232
Pharmaceuticals	
Johnson & Johnson (42)	$95,195
Merck (67)	60,115
Pfizer (69)	58,496
AbbVie (77)	54,318
Bristol-Myers Squibb (98)	45,006
Eli Lilly (127)	34,124
Amgen (151)	28,190
Gilead Sciences (154)	27,116
Viatris (267)	15,427
Regeneron Pharmaceuticals (311)	13,117
Vertex Pharmaceuticals (400)	9,869
Biogen (401)	9,836
Zoetis (445)	8,544
Pipelines	
Energy Transfer (51)	$78,586
Enterprise Products Partners (90)	49,715
Plains GP Holdings (92)	48,712
Cheniere Energy (200)	20,394
Oneok (232)	17,677
Targa Resources (256)	16,060
Kinder Morgan (268)	15,334
Williams (371)	10,907
NGL Energy Partners (442)	8,695
Publishing, Printing	
News Corp. (398)	$9,879
Railroads	
Union Pacific (170)	$24,119
CSX (290)	14,657
Norfolk Southern (338)	12,156
Real Estate	
CBRE Group (138)	$31,949
Jones Lang LaSalle (193)	20,761
American Tower (363)	11,144
Equinix (456)	8,188
Prologis (463)	8,024
Scientific, Photographic, & Control Equipment	
Thermo Fisher Scientific (101)	$42,857
Securities	
Apollo Global Management (136)	$32,644
Charles Schwab (160)	25,521
KKR (188)	21,685
BlackRock (231)	17,859
Edward Jones (303)	14,080
Raymond James Financial (312)	12,992
LPL Financial Holdings (392)	10,053
Intercontinental Exchange (397)	9,903
Franklin Resources (468)	7,849
Interactive Brokers Group (473)	7,776
Semiconductors & Other Electronic Components	
Nvidia (65)	$60,922
Intel (79)	54,228
Qualcomm (117)	35,820
Broadcom (118)	35,819
Jabil (125)	34,702
Applied Materials (158)	26,517
Advanced Micro Devices (181)	22,680
Texas Instruments (234)	17,519
Lam Research (237)	17,429
Micron Technology (264)	15,540
Analog Devices (335)	12,306
KLA (382)	10,496
Sanmina (433)	8,935
Microchip Technology (447)	8,439
ON Semiconductor (452)	8,253
Specialty Retailers: Apparel	
TJX (80)	$54,217
Ross Stores (201)	20,377
Gap (278)	14,889
Burlington Stores (404)	9,728
Lululemon athletica (411)	9,619
Foot Locker (458)	8,168
Specialty Retailers: Other	
Home Depot (23)	$152,669
Lowe's (49)	86,377
Best Buy (100)	43,452
Dollar General (111)	38,692
Dollar Tree (143)	30,604
Murphy USA (214)	19,238
AutoZone (236)	17,457
O'Reilly Automotive (261)	15,812
Casey's General Stores (274)	15,095
Tractor Supply (293)	14,556

Industry/company (rank)	Revenues
Dick's Sporting Goods (313)	$12,984
Advance Auto Parts (358)	11,288
Ulta Beauty (360)	11,207
ARKO (453)	8,239
ODP (469)	7,831
Williams-Sonoma (474)	7,751
Bath & Body Works (481)	7,429
Telecommunications	
Verizon Communications (31)	$133,974
AT&T (32)	122,428
Comcast (33)	121,572
Charter Communications (76)	54,607
EchoStar (242)	17,016
Lumen Technologies (292)	14,557
Altice USA (424)	9,237
Temporary Help	
ManpowerGroup (219)	$18,915
Tobacco	
Philip Morris International (121)	$35,174
Altria Group (196)	20,502
Transportation Equipment	
Polaris (431)	$9,015
Transportation & Logistics	
C.H. Robinson Worldwide (233)	$17,596
Ryder System (350)	11,783
GXO Logistics (402)	9,778
Expeditors Intl. of Washington (420)	9,300
XPO (475)	7,744
Trucking, Truck Leasing	
J.B. Hunt Transport Services (316)	$12,830
Knight-Swift Transportation Holdings (495)	$7,142
Utilities: Gas & Electric	
Duke Energy (148)	$28,932
NextEra Energy (152)	28,114
Southern Company (163)	25,253
PG&E (167)	24,428
Exelon (187)	21,727
American Electric Power (217)	18,982
Dominion Energy (230)	17,867
Sempra (246)	16,720
Edison International (250)	16,338
Consolidated Edison (289)	14,663
Xcel Energy (302)	14,206
DTE Energy (318)	12,745
AES (319)	12,668
FirstEnergy (331)	12,450
Entergy (339)	12,147
Eversource Energy (348)	11,911
Public Service Enterprise Group (359)	11,237
UGI (434)	8,928
WEC Energy Group (435)	8,893
CenterPoint Energy (441)	8,696
PPL (451)	8,312
CMS Energy (478)	7,462
Ameren (494)	7,213
Waste Management	
Waste Management (199)	$20,426
Republic Services (276)	14,965
Wholesalers: Diversified	
Genuine Parts (175)	$23,091
WESCO International (183)	22,385
Global Partners (247)	16,492
Grainger (248)	16,478
LKQ (305)	13,866
Graybar Electric (367)	11,042
A-Mark Precious Metals (421)	9,287
Beacon Roofing Supply (429)	9,120
Fastenal (488)	7,347
Watsco (489)	7,284
Wholesalers: Electronics & Office Equipment	
TD Synnex (71)	$57,555
Arrow Electronics (133)	33,107
Avnet (157)	26,537
Wholesalers: Food & Grocery	
Sysco (54)	$76,325
Performance Food Group (84)	53,355
US Foods Holding (119)	35,597
United Natural Foods (144)	30,272
SpartanNash (403)	9,729
Wholesalers: Health Care	
McKesson (9)	$276,711
Cencora (10)	262,173
Cardinal Health (14)	205,012
Henry Schein (333)	12,339
Owens & Minor (388)	10,334

World's Largest Companies, 2023

Source: *Fortune* magazine, July 2024

(ranked by 2023 revenues, in millions of dollars)

Rank	Company (2022 rank), country	Revenue
1.	Walmart (1), U.S.	$648,125
2.	Amazon (4), U.S.	574,785
3.	State Grid (3), China	545,948
4.	Saudi Aramco (2), Saudi Arabia	494,890
5.	Sinopec Group (6), China	429,700
6.	China National Petroleum (5), China	421,714
7.	Apple (8), U.S.	383,285
8.	UnitedHealth Group (10), U.S.	371,622
9.	Berkshire Hathaway (14), U.S.	364,482
10.	CVS Health (11), U.S.	357,776
11.	Volkswagen (15), Germany	348,408
12.	Exxon Mobil (7), U.S.	344,582
13.	Shell (9), UK	323,183
14.	China State Construction Engineering (13), China	320,431
15.	Toyota Motor (19), Japan	312,018
16.	McKesson (18), U.S.	308,951
17.	Alphabet (17), U.S.	307,394
18.	Cencora (24), U.S. (formerly Amerisource Bergen)	262,173
19.	Trafigura Group (12), Singapore	244,280
20.	Costco Wholesale (26), U.S.	242,290
21.	JPMorgan Chase (53), U.S.	239,425
22.	Industrial & Commercial Bank of China (28), China	222,484
23.	TotalEnergies (20), France	218,945
24.	Glencore (21), Switzerland	217,829
25.	BP (22), UK	213,032
26.	Microsoft (30), U.S.	211,915
27.	Cardinal Health (34), U.S.	205,012
28.	Stellantis (31), Netherlands	204,908
29.	Chevron (23), U.S.	200,949
30.	China Construction Bank (29), China	199,826
31.	Samsung Electronics (25), South Korea	198,257
32.	Hon Hai Precision Industry (27), Taiwan	197,876
33.	Cigna (35), U.S.	195,265
34.	Agricultural Bank of China (32), China	192,398
35.	China Railway Engineering Group (39), China	178,563
36.	Ford Motor (46), U.S.	176,191
37.	Bank of China (49), China	172,328
38.	Bank of America (82), U.S.	171,912
39.	General Motors (50), U.S.	171,842
40.	Elevance Health (51), U.S. (formerly Anthem)	171,340
41.	BMW Group (57), Germany	168,103
42.	Mercedes-Benz Group (47), Germany	165,638
43.	China Railway Construction (43), China	160,847
44.	China Baowu Steel Group (44), China	157,216
45.	Citigroup (99), U.S.	156,820
46.	Centene (60), U.S.	153,999
47.	JD.com (52), China	153,217
48.	Home Depot (48), U.S.	152,669
49.	Electricité de France (55), France	151,040
50.	Marathon Petroleum (36), U.S.	150,307
51.	Kroger (58), U.S.	$150,039
52.	Phillips 66 (37), U.S.	149,890
53.	Ping An Insurance (33), China	145,759
54.	Sinochem Holdings (38), China	143,240
55.	China Mobile Communications (62), China	142,832
56.	China National Offshore Oil (42), China	141,732
57.	Honda Motor (70), Japan	141,349
58.	Fannie Mae (75), U.S.	141,240
59.	China Life Insurance (54), China	139,616
60.	Walgreens Boots Alliance (66), U.S.	139,081
61.	Valero Energy (40), U.S.	139,001
62.	Banco Santander (104), Spain	137,245
63.	China Communications Construction (63), China	136,671
64.	BNP Paribas (127), France	136,076
65.	Mitsubishi (45), Japan	135,390
66.	Meta Platforms (81), U.S.	134,902
67.	HSBC Holdings (130), UK	134,901
68.	Verizon Communications (64), U.S.	133,974
69.	China Minmetals (65), China	132,020
70.	Alibaba Group Holding (68), China	131,338
71.	CITIC Group (100), China	131,242
72.	China Resources (74), China	126,170
73.	Hyundai Motor (85), South Korea	124,577
74.	AT&T (78), U.S.	122,428
75.	Shandong Energy Group (72), China	122,383
76.	Comcast (77), U.S.	121,572
77.	Deutsche Telekom (79), Germany	121,046
78.	China Southern Power Grid (83), China	118,814
79.	Uniper (16), Germany	116,663
80.	Wells Fargo (144), U.S.	115,340
81.	Hengli Group (123), China	114,665
82.	Allianz (67), Germany	113,518
83.	China Post Group (86), China	112,779
84.	China Energy Investment (76), China	112,049
85.	Xiamen C&D (69), China	110,666
86.	Reliance Industries (88), India	108,878
87.	Goldman Sachs Group (185), U.S.	108,418
88.	Freddie Mac (133), U.S.	108,050
89.	Rosneft Oil (NA), Russia	107,543
90.	Target (90), U.S.	107,412
91.	Equinor (56), Norway	107,174
92.	Humana (116), U.S.	106,374
93.	SAIC Motor (84), China	105,196
94.	State Farm Insurance (128) U.S.	104,199
95.	Life Insurance Corp. of India (107), India	103,548
96.	Nestlé (106), Switzerland	103,505
97.	Enel (59), Italy	103,311
98.	ENI (61), Italy	102,502
99.	Petrobras (71), Brazil	102,409
100.	SK (92), South Korea	101,969

NA = Not available.

Top U.S. Franchises, 2024

Source: *Entrepreneur* magazine; as of Aug. 2024, unless otherwise noted

Rank	Company (2022 rank)	Type of business	U.S. locations[1]	Startup costs[2]
1.	Taco Bell (1)	Mexican-inspired food	8,565	$611,000-4 mil
2.	Jersey Mike's Subs (3)	Subs, Philly cheesesteaks	2,861	$204,000-1.3 mil
3.	Popeyes Louisiana Kitchen (2)	Fried chicken, seafood, biscuits	4,091[2]	$384,000-3.7 mil
4.	The UPS Store (4)	Shipping, packing, mailboxes, printing	5,693	$101,000-496,000
5.	Ace Hardware (7)	Hardware and home improvement stores	5,965	$602,000-2 mil
6.	Dunkin' (5)	Coffee, doughnuts, baked goods	13,790	$436,000-1.8 mil
7.	Culver's (8)	Frozen custard, specialty burgers	978	$2.8 mil-6.9 mil
8.	Hampton by Hilton (9)	Upper midscale hotels	3,040	$15.2 mil-25.9 mil
9.	Arby's (12)	Sandwiches, fries, shakes	3,613	$645,000-2.5 mil
10.	Kumon (6)	Supplemental education	25,418	$74,000-166,000
11.	Servpro (16)	Fire, water, and other damage cleanup	2,284	$241,000-302,000
12.	KFC (13)	Chicken	28,475[2]	$1.9 mil-3.8 mil
13.	Tropical Smoothie Cafe (11)	Smoothies, salads, wraps, sandwiches	1,464	$300,000-721,000
14.	Wingstop (10)	Chicken wings, tenders, sandwiches, fries	2,046[2]	$326,000-975,000
15.	Smoothie King (17)	Smoothies, smoothie bowls	1,277	$321,000-1.3 mil
16.	Budget Blinds (19)	Window coverings, window film, rugs	1,498	$101,000-211,000
17.	Wendy's (15)	Burgers, chicken, and breakfast sandwiches	7,282	$310,000-2.8 mil
18.	McDonald's (14)	Burgers, chicken, salads, beverages	42,406	$1.5 mil-2.6 mil
19.	IHOP (NA)	Family restaurants	1,832[2]	$1.2 mil-6.6 mil
20.	Snap-on Tools (20)	Professional tools and equipment	4,674	$218,000-482,000
21.	Pet Supplies Plus (22)	Pet food, supplies; bathing/grooming services	732	$498,000-2 mil
22.	DoubleTree by Hilton (25)	Upscale hotels and resorts	524	$30.5 mil-122.5 mil
23.	Stratus Building Solutions (35)	Commercial cleaning and disinfecting	4,182	$4,000-80,000
24.	Papa John's (37)	Pizza	5,968[2]	$189,000-975,000
25.	7-Eleven (18)	Convenience stores	85,134	$142,000-1.4 mil

NA = Not available. **Note:** Franchises are ranked by a combination of factors, including financial strength and stability, growth rate, number of locations, startup costs, and whether the company provides financing. Locations includes company-owned franchises. (1) Includes franchise fees, which vary, and other startup expenses. (2) As of 2023, the latest year available.

Small Businesses in the U.S. Economy, 1978-2022

Source: Business Dynamics Statistics, U.S. Census Bureau; Small Business Administration

Year	Total businesses	Small businesses	Small businesses as % of GDP	Total employed	Small business employees	% employed by small business
1978	3,558,681	3,548,546	NA	70,237,487	37,690,043	53.7%
1980	3,739,254	3,728,394	51.0%	75,047,757	39,794,909	53.0
1985	4,072,945	4,060,884	50.0	81,578,824	44,298,456	54.3
1990	4,445,193	4,430,638	51.0	93,672,444	50,501,813	53.9
1995	4,673,781	4,658,313	50.0	99,007,883	52,579,813	53.1
2000	4,902,688	4,885,367	46.9	113,580,977	57,466,729	50.6
2005	5,167,197	5,149,688	45.5	115,436,631	59,066,170	51.2
2006	5,256,390	5,238,530	45.4	119,273,934	60,752,914	50.9
2007	5,293,177	5,274,559	45.4	119,789,833	60,096,786	50.2
2008	5,232,233	5,212,849	45.0	119,577,841	59,636,080	49.9
2009	5,090,292	5,072,102	44.7	113,691,683	56,194,493	49.4
2010	5,018,813	5,001,137	44.4	111,309,955	55,075,399	49.5
2011	4,995,859	4,978,284	44.3	112,879,366	55,363,093	49.0
2012	5,042,675	5,024,489	44.2	115,353,493	56,342,545	48.8
2013	5,067,524	5,048,717	43.6	117,602,279	57,044,315	48.5
2014	5,104,509	5,085,423	43.5	120,124,783	58,112,906	48.4
2015	5,151,116	5,131,705	NA	123,230,846	59,306,773	48.1
2016	5,216,921	5,196,933	NA	125,746,900	60,278,936	47.9
2017	5,251,809	5,231,563	NA	127,480,852	60,911,671	47.8
2018	5,286,921	5,266,539	NA	129,685,273	61,440,821	47.4
2019	5,335,794	5,314,880	NA	131,880,286	62,051,767	47.1
2020	5,340,972	5,319,769	NA	132,737,246	61,918,141	46.6
2021	5,397,456	5,376,868	NA	127,132,349	59,166,114	46.5
2022	5,535,295	5,514,820	NA	133,689,031	62,837,927	47.0

NA = Not available. **Note:** Small businesses are firms employing fewer than 500 people. Figures include only businesses with paid employees.

Denominations of U.S. Currency

Since 1969 the largest denomination of U.S. currency that has been issued is the $100 bill. As larger-denomination bills reach the Federal Reserve Bank, they are removed from circulation. Because some discontinued currency is expected to be in the hands of holders for many years, the description of the various denominations below is continued.

Note	Portrait	Embellishment on back	Note	Portrait	Embellishment on back
$1	George Washington	Great Seal of U.S.	$500[1]	William McKinley	Ornate denominational marking
2	Thomas Jefferson	Signers of Declaration	1,000[2]	Grover Cleveland	Ornate denominational marking
5	Abraham Lincoln	Lincoln Memorial	5,000	James Madison	Washington resigning as Army commander
10	Alexander Hamilton	U.S. Treasury			
20	Andrew Jackson	White House	10,000	Salmon Chase	Embarkation of the Pilgrims
50	Ulysses S. Grant	U.S. Capitol	100,000[3]	Woodrow Wilson	Ornate denominational marking
100	Benjamin Franklin	Independence Hall			

(1) John Marshall appeared on the earliest version of the $500 bill. (2) Alexander Hamilton appeared on the earliest version of the $1,000 bill, but these were discontinued to avoid confusion with the $10 bill. (3) For use only in transactions between Federal Reserve System and Treasury Department.

The U.S. $1 Bill

Plate position: Shows where on the 32-note plate this bill was printed.

Serial number: Each bill has its own.

Federal Reserve Bank number: Shows which district issued the bill.

Federal Reserve seal: The name of the Federal Reserve Bank that issued the bill is printed in the seal. The letter also tells you which bank distributed the bill. Here are the number and letter codes for the 12 Federal Reserve Banks:

- **1/A:** Boston
- **2/B:** New York
- **3/C:** Philadelphia
- **4/D:** Cleveland
- **5/E:** Richmond
- **6/F:** Atlanta
- **7/G:** Chicago
- **8/H:** St. Louis
- **9/I:** Minneapolis
- **10/J:** Kansas City
- **11/K:** Dallas
- **12/L:** San Francisco

Treasury Department seal: The balancing scales represent justice. The pointed stripe across the middle has 13 stars for the original 13 colonies. The key represents authority.

Plate serial number: Shows which printing plate was used for the face of the bill.

Treasurer of the U.S. signature

Series indicator: Year note's design was first used.

Secretary of the Treasury signature

Plate serial number: Shows which plate was used for the back.

Front of the Great Seal of the United States: The bald eagle is the national bird. The shield has 13 stripes for the 13 original colonies. The eagle holds 13 arrows (symbol of war) and an olive branch with 13 olives and leaves (symbol of peace). Above the eagle is the motto "E Pluribus Unum," Latin for "out of many, one," and a constellation of 13 stars.

Reverse of the Great Seal of the United States: The pyramid symbolizes something that endures for ages. The eye, known as the Eye of Providence, probably comes from an ancient Egyptian symbol. The pyramid has 13 levels; at its base are the Roman numerals for 1776, the year of American independence. "Annuit Coeptis" is Latin for "God has favored our undertaking." "Novus Ordo Seclorum" is Latin for "a new order of the ages." Both phrases are from the works of the Roman poet Virgil.

U.S. Currency and Coin

Source: Bureau of the Fiscal Service, U.S. Dept. of the Treasury

Total Money in Circulation, 1955-2024

Date	Dollars (mil)	Per capita[1]	Date	Dollars (mil)	Per capita[1]	Date	Dollars (mil)	Per capita[1]
June 30, 1955	$30,229	$183	Sept. 30, 1985	$187,337	$782	Sept. 30, 2015	$1,387,552	$4,310
June 30, 1960	32,064	177	Sept. 30, 1990	278,903	1,105	June 30, 2020	1,969,957	5,970
June 30, 1965	39,719	204	Sept. 30, 1995	409,272	1,553	June 30, 2021	2,183,379	6,565
June 30, 1970	54,351	265	Sept. 30, 2000	568,614	2,061	June 30, 2022	2,281,465	6,853
June 30, 1975	81,196	380	Sept. 30, 2005	766,487	2,578	June 30, 2023	2,345,428	6,998
Sept. 30, 1980	129,916	581	Sept. 30, 2010	945,719	3,074	June 30, 2024	2,352,440	6,984

(1) Based on U.S. Census Bureau population estimates.

Money in Circulation by Denomination, 2023

Denomination	Amount in circulation	Denomination	Amount in circulation	Denomination	Amount in circulation
$1	$14,732,206,978	$50	$123,050,738,800	$10,000	$3,430,000
$2	3,271,998,908	$100	1,899,614,388,600	Partial notes[1]	600
$5	17,928,561,515	$500	141,706,000	**Total currency**	**$2,302,185,339,211**
$10	23,567,467,010	$1,000	165,112,000	**Total coins**	**$50,254,549,099**
$20	219,707,963,800	$5,000	1,765,000	**Total currency and coins**	**$2,352,439,888,310**

(1) Represents the value of certain partial denominations not presented for redemption.

U.S. Budget Receipts and Outlays, 1789-1940

Source: U.S. Dept. of the Treasury

(in thousands of dollars; annual statements for years ending June 30, unless otherwise noted)

Yearly average	Receipts	Outlays	Yearly average	Receipts	Outlays	Yearly average	Receipts	Outlays
1789-1800[1]	$5,717	$5,776	1866-1870	$447,301	$377,642	1906-1910	$628,507	$639,178
1801-1810[2]	13,056	9,086	1871-1875	336,830	287,460	1911-1915	710,227	720,252
1811-1820[2]	21,032	23,943	1876-1880	288,124	255,598	1916-1920	3,483,652	8,065,333
1821-1830[2]	21,928	16,162	1881-1885	366,961	257,691	1921-1925	4,306,673	3,578,989
1831-1840[2]	30,461	24,495	1886-1890	375,448	279,134	1926-1930	4,069,138	3,182,807
1841-1850[2]	28,545	34,097	1891-1895	352,891	363,599	1931-1935	2,770,973	5,214,874
1851-1860	60,237	60,163	1896-1900	434,877	457,451	1936-1940	4,960,614	10,192,367
1861-1865	160,907	683,785	1901-1905	559,481	535,559			

(1) Average for period Mar. 4, 1789, to Dec. 31, 1800. (2) Years 1801-42 end Dec. 31; average for 1841-50 is for the period Jan. 1, 1841, to June 30, 1850.

U.S. Budget Receipts and Outlays, Fiscal Years 2000-23

Source: Congressional Budget Office; *Budget of the U.S. Government*, Office of Mgmt. and Budget, Exec. Office of the President

A $236-bil government surplus in 2000 ballooned into a $1.4-tril deficit by 2009. The deficit was reduced by nearly $1 tril, 2009-15, but it began rising again in 2016 and was close to $1 tril again by 2019. In 2020, the deficit soared past $3 tril, in large part because of COVID-19, but by 2022, the shortfall had been cut by more than half.

(in millions of current dollars; numbers may not add up to totals because of independent rounding or omitted subcategories, including some subcategories with negative values)

Function and subfunction	2000	2010	2015	2020	2022	2023
NET RECEIPTS	**$2,025,191**	**$2,162,706**	**$3,249,890**	**$3,421,164**	**$4,897,339**	**$4,440,947**
Individual income taxes	**1,004,462**	**898,549**	**1,540,802**	**1,608,663**	**2,632,146**	**2,176,481**
Corporation income taxes	**207,289**	**191,437**	**343,797**	**211,845**	**424,865**	**419,584**
Social insurance and retirement receipts	**652,852**	**864,814**	**1,065,257**	**1,309,955**	**1,483,527**	**1,614,456**
Employment and general retirement	**620,451**	**815,894**	**1,010,427**	**1,261,651**	**1,410,735**	**1,558,147**
Old-age and survivors insurance (off-budget)	411,677	539,996	658,543	825,307	911,191	1,020,442
Disability insurance (off-budget)	68,907	91,691	111,829	140,121	154,784	173,313
Hospital insurance	135,529	180,068	234,189	291,778	339,145	357,762
Railroad retirement/pension fund (trust funds)	2,688	2,285	3,336	2,717	3,249	3,718
Railroad social security equivalent account	1,650	1,854	2,530	1,728	2,366	2,912
Unemployment insurance	**27,640**	**44,823**	**51,178**	**43,104**	**66,498**	**49,404**
Other retirement	**4,761**	**4,097**	**3,652**	**5,200**	**6,294**	**6,905**
Excise taxes	**68,865**	**66,909**	**98,279**	**86,780**	**87,728**	**75,802**
Federal funds	**22,692**	**18,256**	**37,759**	**29,579**	**24,064**	**5,180**
Alcohol	8,140	9,229	9,639	9,490	10,196	9,501
Tobacco	7,221	17,160	14,453	12,354	11,259	10,299
Telephone	5,670	993	607	370	316	303
Transportation fuels	819	–11,030	–3,394	–6,525	–5,126	–15,234
Trust funds	**46,173**	**48,653**	**60,520**	**57,201**	**63,664**	**70,622**
Transportation	34,972	34,992	40,813	42,764	46,631	42,216
Airport and airway	9,739	10,612	14,268	9,016	11,377	22,277
Black lung disability	518	595	552	301	180	295
Inland waterway	101	74	98	112	124	95
Oil spill liability	182	476	496	400	562	347
Aquatic resources	342	580	574	646	634	575
Leaking underground storage tank	184	169	179	219	245	205
Tobacco assessments	—	937	49	—	1	11
Vaccine injury compensation	133	218	275	310	333	220
Other receipts	**91,723**	**140,997**	**201,755**	**203,921**	**269,073**	**154,624**
OUTLAYS	**1,788,950**	**3,457,079**	**3,691,850**	**6,553,620**	**6,273,259**	**6,134,672**
National defense	**294,363**	**693,485**	**589,659**	**724,588**	**765,649**	**820,263**
Department of Defense—Military	281,029	666,703	562,499	690,363	726,458	775,874
Military personnel	75,950	155,690	145,206	161,424	180,774	183,899
Operation and maintenance	105,812	275,988	247,239	278,867	291,269	317,570
Procurement	51,696	133,603	101,342	139,055	136,176	141,748
Research, development, test, and evaluation	37,602	76,990	64,124	99,875	107,059	121,954
Military construction	5,109	21,169	8,132	8,882	9,726	10,345
Family housing	3,413	3,173	1,198	1,293	1,423	1,469
Atomic energy defense activities	12,138	19,308	18,692	24,479	28,291	32,563
Defense-related activities	1,196	7,474	8,468	9,746	10,900	11,826
International affairs	**17,213**	**45,195**	**52,040**	**67,722**	**71,873**	**69,313**
International development and humanitarian assistance	6,516	19,014	24,087	28,226	34,163	37,576
International security assistance	6,387	11,363	12,907	12,080	26,104	29,260
Conduct of foreign affairs	4,708	13,557	13,246	16,621	14,400	14,610
Foreign information and exchange activities	817	1,485	1,531	1,621	1,969	2,189
International financial programs	–1,215	–224	269	9,174	–4,763	–14,322
General science, space, and technology	**18,594**	**30,100**	**29,412**	**34,022**	**37,404**	**41,276**
General science and basic research	6,167	11,730	11,719	13,301	15,205	16,811
Space flight, research, and supporting activities	12,427	18,370	17,693	20,721	22,199	24,465
Energy	**–761**	**11,618**	**6,841**	**7,083**	**–9,132**	**–406**
Energy supply	–1,818	5,801	4,710	5,498	4,063	4,609
Energy conservation	666	4,997	1,187	1,241	32	1,614
Emergency energy preparedness	162	199	449	–246	–13,844	–7,264
Energy information, policy, and regulation	229	621	495	590	617	635
Natural resources and environment	**25,003**	**43,667**	**36,033**	**42,450**	**41,384**	**47,387**
Water resources	5,078	11,662	7,760	8,909	10,441	10,458
Conservation and land management	6,762	10,783	10,519	13,539	10,144	11,900
Recreational resources	2,540	3,911	3,501	4,195	4,480	4,914
Pollution control and abatement	7,395	10,841	7,240	8,732	9,174	12,465
Agriculture	**36,458**	**21,356**	**18,500**	**47,298**	**33,065**	**33,651**
Farm income stabilization	33,442	16,478	13,424	26,403	16,437	24,633
Agricultural research and services	3,016	4,878	5,076	20,895	16,628	9,018
Commerce and housing credit	**3,207**	**–82,316**	**–37,905**	**572,071**	**–19,075**	**100,765**
Mortgage credit	–3,335	35,804	–35,658	–26,494	–43,386	–22,150
Postal service	2,129	–682	–1,610	–2,346	2,636	5,819
Deposit insurance	–3,053	–32,033	–12,812	–7,238	–11,525	91,205
Transportation	**46,853**	**91,972**	**89,533**	**145,623**	**131,024**	**126,417**
Ground transportation	31,697	60,784	59,126	78,945	89,901	84,228
Air transportation	10,571	21,431	20,033	55,075	28,397	29,165
Water transportation	4,394	9,351	9,994	11,151	12,260	12,496
Community and regional development	**10,623**	**23,894**	**20,669**	**81,878**	**69,963**	**86,553**
Community development	5,480	9,901	7,817	6,368	17,040	11,681
Area and regional development	2,538	3,249	3,861	4,193	6,001	6,334
Disaster relief and insurance	2,605	10,744	8,991	71,317	46,922	68,538
Education, training, employment, and social services	**53,766**	**128,595**	**122,035**	**237,754**	**677,305**	**–2,189**
Elementary, secondary, and vocational education	20,578	73,261	40,022	51,352	122,697	111,403
Higher education	10,117	20,905	51,315	152,971	518,089	–152,600
Research and general education aids	2,543	3,631	3,493	3,909	4,261	4,653

Function and subfunction	2000	2010	2015	2020	2022	2023
Training and employment	$6,777	$9,854	$7,103	$6,594	$7,550	$7,376
Social services	12,557	19,179	18,303	20,974	22,733	24,799
Health	**154,502**	**369,081**	**482,257**	**747,582**	**914,081**	**888,555**
Health care services	136,201	330,710	446,368	703,791	864,578	835,211
Health research and training	15,977	34,227	31,426	38,766	42,642	48,069
Consumer and occupational health and safety	2,324	4,144	4,463	5,025	6,861	5,275
Medicare	**197,113**	**451,636**	**546,202**	**776,225**	**755,094**	**847,544**
Income security	**253,673**	**622,106**	**508,800**	**1,263,639**	**866,097**	**774,655**
General retirement and disability insurance (excl. social security)	5,189	6,564	7,805	2,106	12,078	50,441
Federal employee retirement and disability	77,101	119,763	139,123	153,822	168,692	179,356
Unemployment compensation	23,012	160,145	34,978	475,124	36,802	33,850
Housing assistance	28,949	58,651	47,823	52,997	76,463	67,057
Food and nutrition assistance	32,483	95,110	104,797	115,389	193,932	172,977
Social security	**409,423**	**706,737**	**887,753**	**1,095,816**	**1,218,663**	**1,354,317**
Veterans benefits and services	**47,040**	**108,478**	**159,781**	**218,655**	**274,404**	**301,600**
Income security for veterans	24,958	49,257	76,403	110,055	139,926	151,121
Veterans education, training, and rehabilitation	1,285	8,089	13,383	12,847	11,936	12,582
Hospital and medical care for veterans	19,516	45,714	61,893	90,594	110,706	125,512
Veterans housing	364	540	743	–3,420	1,591	429
Administration of justice	**28,499**	**54,383**	**51,906**	**71,997**	**71,323**	**80,432**
Federal law enforcement activities	12,121	28,713	26,937	37,839	38,203	42,478
Federal litigative and judicial activities	7,762	14,494	14,717	17,865	18,462	19,085
Federal correctional activities	3,707	6,327	7,049	7,764	7,540	8,374
Criminal justice assistance	4,909	4,849	3,203	8,529	7,118	10,495
General government	**13,013**	**23,014**	**20,956**	**180,109**	**133,214**	**38,199**
Legislative functions	2,227	4,100	3,751	4,659	5,058	5,779
Executive direction and management	456	528	510	478	609	655
Central fiscal operations	8,285	11,906	11,096	12,140	14,496	16,140
General property and records management	–32	1,194	–490	76	–991	–538
Central personnel management	184	338	81	231	318	260
General purpose fiscal assistance	2,084	5,082	7,266	155,206	114,902	12,127
Deductions for offsetting receipts	–2,383	–1,721	–4,786	–2,154	–4,312	1,197
Net interest	**222,949**	**196,194**	**223,181**	**345,470**	**475,887**	**658,267**
Undistributed offsetting receipts	**–42,581**	**–82,116**	**–115,803**	**–106,362**	**–234,964**	**–131,927**
TOTAL SURPLUS/DEFICIT	**236,241**	**–1,294,373**	**–441,960**	**–3,132,456**	**–1,375,920**	**–1,693,725**

— = Not available.

Federal Receipts, Outlays, and Surpluses or Deficits, 1901-2026

Source: *Budget of the U.S. Government, Fiscal Year 2025*, Office of Management and Budget, Exec. Office of the President (in millions of current dollars)

Fiscal year	Receipts	Outlays	Surplus or deficit (–)	Fiscal year	Receipts	Outlays	Surplus or deficit (–)	Fiscal year	Receipts	Outlays	Surplus or deficit (–)
1901	$588	$525	**$63**	1943	$24,001	$78,555	–$54,554	1985	$734,037	$946,344	–$212,308
1902	562	485	**77**	1944	43,747	91,304	–47,557	1986	769,155	990,382	–221,227
1903	562	517	**45**	1945	45,159	92,712	–47,553	1987	854,287	1,004,017	–149,730
1904	541	584	–43	1946	39,296	55,232	–15,936	1988	909,238	1,064,416	–155,178
1905	544	567	–23	1947	38,514	34,496	**4,018**	1989	991,104	1,143,743	–152,639
1906	595	570	**25**	1948	41,560	29,764	**11,796**	1990	1,031,958	1,252,993	–221,036
1907	666	579	**87**	1949	39,415	38,835	**580**	1991	1,054,988	1,324,226	–269,238
1908	602	659	–57	1950	39,443	42,562	–3,119	1992	1,091,208	1,381,529	–290,321
1909	604	694	–89	1951	51,616	45,514	**6,102**	1993	1,154,334	1,409,386	–255,051
1910	676	694	–18	1952	66,167	67,686	–1,519	1994	1,258,566	1,461,752	–203,186
1911	702	691	**11**	1953	69,608	76,101	–6,493	1995	1,351,790	1,515,742	–163,952
1912	693	690	**3**	1954	69,701	70,855	–1,154	1996	1,453,053	1,560,484	–107,431
1913	714	715	—	1955	65,451	68,444	–2,993	1997	1,579,232	1,601,116	–21,884
1914	725	726	—	1956	74,587	70,640	**3,947**	1998	1,721,728	1,652,458	**69,270**
1915	683	746	–63	1957	79,990	76,578	**3,412**	1999	1,827,452	1,701,842	**125,610**
1916	761	713	**48**	1958	79,636	82,405	–2,769	2000	2,025,191	1,788,950	**236,241**
1917	1,101	1,954	–853	1959	79,249	92,098	–12,849	2001	1,991,082	1,862,846	**128,236**
1918	3,645	12,677	–9,032	1960	92,492	92,191	**301**	2002	1,853,136	2,010,894	–157,758
1919	5,130	18,493	–13,363	1961	94,388	97,723	–3,335	2003	1,782,314	2,159,899	–377,585
1920	6,649	6,358	**291**	1962	99,676	106,821	–7,146	2004	1,880,114	2,292,841	–412,727
1921	5,571	5,062	**509**	1963	106,560	111,316	–4,756	2005	2,153,611	2,471,957	–318,346
1922	4,026	3,289	**736**	1964	112,613	118,528	–5,915	2006	2,406,869	2,655,050	–248,181
1923	3,853	3,140	**713**	1965	116,817	118,228	–1,411	2007	2,567,985	2,728,686	–160,701
1924	3,871	2,908	**963**	1966	130,835	134,532	–3,698	2008	2,523,991	2,982,544	–458,553
1925	3,641	2,924	**717**	1967	148,822	157,464	–8,643	2009	2,104,989	3,517,677	–1,412,688
1926	3,795	2,930	**865**	1968	152,973	178,134	–25,161	2010	2,162,706	3,457,079	–1,294,373
1927	4,013	2,857	**1,155**	1969	186,882	183,640	**3,242**	2011	2,303,466	3,603,065	–1,299,599
1928	3,900	2,961	**939**	1970	192,807	195,649	–2,842	2012	2,449,990	3,526,563	–1,076,573
1929	3,862	3,127	**734**	1971	187,139	210,172	–23,033	2013	2,775,106	3,454,881	–679,775
1930	4,058	3,320	**738**	1972	207,309	230,681	–23,373	2014	3,021,491	3,506,284	–484,793
1931	3,116	3,577	–462	1973	230,799	245,707	–14,908	2015	3,249,890	3,691,850	–441,960
1932	1,924	4,659	–2,735	1974	263,224	269,359	–6,135	2016	3,267,965	3,852,615	–584,650
1933	1,997	4,598	–2,602	1975	279,090	332,332	–53,242	2017	3,316,184	3,981,634	–665,450
1934	2,955	6,541	–3,586	1976	298,060	371,792	–73,732	2018	3,329,907	4,108,981	–779,074
1935	3,609	6,412	–2,803	1977	355,559	409,218	–53,659	2019	3,463,364	4,446,952	–983,588
1936	3,923	8,228	–4,304	1978	399,561	458,746	–59,185	2020	3,421,164	6,553,620	–3,132,456
1937	5,387	7,580	–2,193	1979	463,302	504,028	–40,726	2021	4,047,111	6,822,461	–2,775,350
1938	6,751	6,840	–89	1980	517,112	590,941	–73,830	2022	4,897,339	6,273,259	–1,375,920
1939	6,295	9,141	–2,846	1981	599,272	678,241	–78,968	2023	4,440,947	6,134,672	–1,693,725
1940	6,548	9,468	–2,920	1982	617,766	745,743	–127,977	2024[1]	5,081,546	6,940,904	–1,859,358
1941	8,712	13,653	–4,941	1983	600,562	808,364	–207,802	2025[1]	5,484,948	7,265,963	–1,781,015
1942	14,634	35,137	–20,503	1984	666,438	851,805	–185,367	2026[1]	5,872,742	7,419,392	–1,546,650

— = $500,000 or less. Figures in **bold** denote annual surplus. **Note:** Budget figures prior to 1933 are based on administrative budget concepts rather than unified budget concepts. Through 1976, fiscal year ends June 30; after 1976, fiscal year ends Sept. 30. Surplus or deficit column may not equal difference between figures because of rounding. (1) Estimate as of Mar. 2024.

Public Debt of the U.S., 1946-2026

Source: *Budget of the U.S. Government, Fiscal Year 2025*, Office of Management and Budget, Exec. Office of the President

	Debt held by public			Interest on public debt as % of—			Debt held by public			Interest on public debt as % of—	
Year	Current dollars (bil)	FY2023 dollars (bil)	As % of GDP	Total federal outlays	GDP	Year	Current dollars (bil)	FY2023 dollars (bil)	As % of GDP	Total federal outlays	GDP
1946	$241.9	$3,034.7	106.1%	7.6%	1.8%	2010	$9,018.9	$12,278.1	60.6%	6.6%	1.5%
1950	219.0	2,220.6	78.6	11.4	1.7	2015	13,116.7	16,414.1	72.5	7.1	1.4
1955	226.6	2,019.4	55.8	7.6	1.3	2016	14,167.6	17,589.0	76.4	7.4	1.5
1960	236.8	1,870.3	44.3	8.5	1.5	2017	14,665.4	17,903.9	76.2	7.8	1.6
1965	260.8	1,930.2	36.8	8.1	1.4	2018	15,749.6	18,810.2	77.6	9.0	1.8
1970	283.2	1,746.7	27.1	7.9	1.5	2019	16,800.7	19,700.7	79.4	9.5	2.0
1975	394.7	1,793.2	24.6	7.5	1.6	2020	21,016.7	24,328.0	99.8	5.9	1.8
1980	711.9	2,248.8	25.5	10.6	2.2	2021	22,284.0	24,934.6	98.4	6.1	1.8
1985	1,507.3	3,628.8	35.3	16.2	3.6	2022	24,253.4	25,364.5	97.0	8.5	2.1
1990	2,411.6	4,987.9	40.9	16.2	3.4	2023	26,235.6	26,235.6	97.3	11.6	2.6
1995	3,604.4	6,575.4	47.7	15.8	3.2	2024[1]	28,156.2	27,243.1	99.6	13.8	3.4
2000	3,409.8	5,732.8	33.7	13.0	2.3	2025[1]	29,983.8	28,577.6	102.2	14.2	3.5
2005	4,592.2	6,898.6	35.8	7.7	1.5	2026[1]	31,639.4	29,540.7	103.6	14.6	3.5

Note: As of end of fiscal year. Through 1976, the fiscal year ended June 30. From 1977 on, the fiscal year ended Sept. 30. (1) Estimate.

State Finances: Revenues, Taxes, Expenditures, and Debt, 2022

Source: U.S. Census Bureau, U.S. Dept. of Commerce

(in thousands of dollars)

	Revenues					
State	Total revenue	General revenue	Intergovernmental revenue	Taxes	Total expenditure	Debt at end of fiscal year
Alabama	$43,976,221	$43,478,927	$18,888,889	$16,324,900	$37,211,367	$11,266,563
Alaska	11,424,674	11,411,167	5,734,271	2,941,280	11,678,662	5,493,142
Arizona	61,445,775	61,422,670	30,803,734	24,410,195	53,482,138	7,016,994
Arkansas	29,686,241	29,686,241	12,489,227	12,768,129	26,657,104	7,608,381
California	467,648,006	467,648,006	135,063,522	283,275,754	446,184,783	159,573,569
Colorado	45,860,107	45,860,107	16,065,607	22,089,402	40,904,355	20,537,521
Connecticut	39,047,228	38,997,961	12,159,819	22,774,523	31,455,478	33,095,934
Delaware	12,879,336	12,867,554	4,158,575	6,310,891	11,974,347	4,093,186
Florida	135,161,251	135,145,207	54,875,559	59,251,311	110,966,804	22,343,571
Georgia	64,878,076	64,876,691	23,510,515	33,933,816	58,649,987	13,828,938
Hawaii	19,615,365	19,615,365	5,518,181	10,279,504	15,546,108	11,922,940
Idaho	15,201,140	14,959,822	5,363,468	7,710,289	12,639,243	929,002
Illinois	117,257,464	117,257,464	43,102,366	62,571,178	109,616,681	41,804,277
Indiana	60,030,807	60,030,807	24,537,146	29,092,294	49,332,797	8,477,908
Iowa	30,352,049	29,920,368	10,301,613	12,908,955	26,014,188	6,906,017
Kansas	27,256,525	27,256,525	8,230,581	12,592,576	23,394,894	7,612,422
Kentucky	44,161,131	44,161,127	20,539,576	16,546,544	40,453,983	10,109,145
Louisiana	40,454,703	40,443,038	21,088,889	14,484,028	41,770,194	16,521,105
Maine	13,530,962	13,274,804	5,450,862	6,439,268	12,695,505	3,899,628
Maryland	59,899,123	59,842,387	22,907,140	29,361,279	58,015,500	25,423,205
Massachusetts	81,671,097	81,037,723	26,326,624	43,492,334	76,485,426	65,553,011
Michigan	88,226,182	86,637,770	34,299,862	37,056,989	83,861,746	26,157,960
Minnesota	60,627,701	60,594,556	20,184,883	34,911,881	53,229,061	17,744,976
Mississippi	25,805,183	25,287,918	11,431,538	10,218,769	22,546,566	7,472,453
Missouri	43,393,135	43,393,104	20,653,471	16,887,389	37,703,688	7,027,362
Montana	10,249,726	10,107,651	4,318,132	4,638,060	8,100,321	2,926,188
Nebraska	15,519,777	15,519,777	6,102,084	7,475,982	13,457,590	2,735,739
Nevada	25,094,336	25,053,780	9,543,112	13,818,086	18,461,084	3,756,918
New Hampshire	10,522,839	9,766,020	4,411,748	3,510,760	10,086,659	7,420,599
New Jersey	96,877,290	96,227,933	29,468,093	52,771,929	92,408,422	57,676,486
New Mexico	35,193,859	35,193,859	12,989,889	12,188,112	28,089,552	6,511,487
New York	267,071,291	259,271,886	101,894,490	132,076,079	226,270,434	153,839,876
North Carolina	83,691,033	83,688,564	32,458,116	38,479,120	77,673,810	14,083,536
North Dakota	11,159,732	11,159,732	2,525,962	5,350,784	8,850,808	3,547,465
Ohio	97,922,872	96,202,106	40,558,394	37,388,627	91,393,368	33,284,334
Oklahoma	34,793,299	33,885,042	14,655,958	13,188,031	28,094,216	10,095,106
Oregon	47,978,640	47,150,807	17,781,001	18,882,848	45,428,607	14,630,471
Pennsylvania	119,857,924	117,452,377	45,307,160	53,700,114	114,420,288	47,544,269
Rhode Island	12,169,713	12,151,840	5,422,624	4,833,177	11,127,619	6,186,615
South Carolina	45,563,433	43,632,096	17,631,339	16,150,255	39,381,977	15,099,061
South Dakota	6,971,925	6,968,459	3,483,768	2,475,394	6,134,617	3,949,806
Tennessee	45,588,575	45,588,575	18,130,559	22,650,165	41,244,710	8,094,851
Texas	206,513,439	206,513,439	83,571,118	81,763,085	185,316,350	63,819,011
Utah	30,227,562	29,730,679	8,707,234	13,491,108	28,361,524	6,091,784
Vermont	9,664,791	9,564,103	4,139,520	4,416,004	8,655,476	2,579,676
Virginia	78,322,673	77,172,602	22,523,231	36,754,617	70,890,105	32,626,248
Washington	70,533,634	70,533,634	24,294,407	36,071,826	67,764,837	29,472,126
West Virginia	17,722,360	17,590,728	8,054,206	7,049,142	17,725,607	20,012,449
Wisconsin	49,023,377	49,023,377	16,450,672	23,363,814	47,018,990	23,645,029
Wyoming	7,365,766	7,211,612	3,555,166	2,441,007	5,870,320	1,194,736
United States	**$3,075,089,348**	**$3,051,467,987**	**$1,131,663,901**	**$1,473,561,604**	**$2,784,697,896**	**$1,113,243,076**

Note: Figures may not add up to totals because of rounding.

State and Local Government Receipts and Current Expenditures, 1960-2023

Source: Bureau of Economic Analysis, U.S. Dept. of Commerce
(in billions of current dollars; as of Aug. 2024)

	1960	1970	1980	1990	2000	2010	2020	2022	2023
Current receipts	**$44.2**	**$119.1**	**$335.9**	**$730.0**	**$1,303.5**	**$1,991.7**	**$3,078.0**	**$3,662.4**	**$3,627.1**
Current tax receipts	37.0	91.3	230.0	519.1	893.2	1,306.4	1,941.0	2,407.6	2,388.8
Personal current taxes	4.2	14.2	48.9	122.6	236.7	294.1	503.0	632.9	570.2
Income taxes	2.5	10.9	42.6	109.6	217.4	265.8	464.0	588.2	524.6
Other	1.7	3.3	6.3	13.0	19.4	28.3	39.0	44.7	45.6
Taxes on production and imports	31.5	73.3	166.7	374.1	621.3	966.3	1,365.2	1,616.0	1,659.3
Sales taxes	5.3	17.0	53.6	125.6	221.4	295.1	443.7	570.8	591.0
Excise taxes	6.8	14.7	29.2	58.7	95.5	154.8	204.2	240.7	246.6
Property taxes	16.2	36.7	68.8	161.5	254.7	438.6	607.6	660.0	686.8
Other	3.1	5.0	15.0	28.2	49.8	77.8	109.7	144.5	134.9
Taxes on corporate income	1.2	3.7	14.5	22.5	35.2	46.1	72.9	158.6	159.4
Contributions for government social insurance	0.5	1.1	3.6	10.0	10.8	17.8	20.0	22.5	21.9
Income receipts on assets	1.3	5.2	26.3	68.4	93.6	80.8	94.8	97.6	100.3
Interest receipts	1.0	4.3	23.1	64.1	86.0	66.3	77.7	78.7	80.7
Dividends	—	—	0.1	0.2	1.4	3.0	6.2	6.6	6.8
Rents and royalties	0.3	0.8	3.1	4.2	6.3	11.4	10.9	12.4	12.7
Current transfer receipts	4.3	20.1	76.9	126.4	299.7	604.4	1,029.3	1,138.0	1,133.6
Federal grants-in-aid	3.8	18.3	69.7	104.4	233.1	505.2	878.8	948.9	952.2
From business (net)	0.2	0.6	2.5	7.1	28.6	40.3	58.1	72.1	69.2
From persons	0.3	1.2	4.7	14.9	38.0	58.8	92.0	109.8	111.8
Current surplus of government enterprises	1.2	1.4	–0.8	6.1	6.1	–17.7	–7.1	–3.2	–17.5
Current expenditures	**41.7**	**117.6**	**341.8**	**766.3**	**1,345.0**	**2,300.6**	**3,129.9**	**3,602.1**	**3,777.2**
Consumption expenditures	33.5	90.4	249.0	544.0	961.9	1,508.1	2,019.7	2,341.1	2,423.5
Government social benefit payments to persons	4.6	16.1	51.2	127.7	271.4	523.9	815.7	1,012.3	1,061.5
Interest payments	3.6	11.1	41.2	94.3	111.1	267.0	293.9	248.0	291.5
Subsidies	0.0	0.0	0.4	0.4	0.5	1.6	0.6	0.7	0.7
Net state and local government saving	**2.5**	**1.4**	**–5.9**	**–36.3**	**–41.5**	**–309.0**	**–51.9**	**60.4**	**–150.1**
Social insurance funds	0.0	0.2	1.3	2.0	2.0	0.9	1.9	4.4	3.4
Other	2.5	1.3	–7.2	–38.2	–43.5	-309.9	–53.8	56.0	–153.5
Addenda:									
Total receipts	**47.2**	**125.3**	**354.5**	**755.0**	**1,347.7**	**2,068.5**	**3,161.8**	**3,894.7**	**3,722.6**
Current receipts	44.2	119.1	335.9	730.0	1,303.5	1,991.7	3,078.0	3,662.4	3,627.1
Capital transfer receipts	3.0	6.2	18.6	25.0	44.2	76.9	83.8	232.3	95.5
Total expenditures	**52.1**	**137.1**	**376.6**	**837.6**	**1,468.4**	**2,446.4**	**3,290.6**	**3,722.4**	**3,953.6**
Current expenditures	41.7	117.6	341.8	766.3	1,345.0	2,300.6	3,129.9	3,602.1	3,777.2
Gross government investment	14.1	29.3	65.7	132.2	231.5	347.3	451.7	470.2	549.9
Net purchases of nonproduced assets	0.9	1.1	2.2	5.7	8.6	12.0	17.4	19.1	19.8
Less: Consumption of fixed capital	4.5	10.9	33.1	66.6	116.6	213.4	308.4	371.5	393.2
Net lending or net borrowing (–)	**–4.9**	**–11.8**	**–22.1**	**–82.5**	**–120.7**	**–377.9**	**–128.8**	**172.3**	**–231.0**

— = Not applicable.

Federal Deposit Insurance Corporation (FDIC)

The Federal Deposit Insurance Corporation (FDIC) was created by Congress during the height of the Depression to maintain stability and public confidence in the nation's banking system. It covered depositors for up to $2,500 in case of bank failure in 1934; the limit today is 100 times that much, or $250,000. In its unique role as deposit insurer of banks and savings associations, and in cooperation with other federal and state regulatory agencies, the FDIC seeks to promote the safety and soundness of insured depository institutions in the U.S. financial system.

The quarterly premiums on deposit insurance are paid by the banks rather than by consumers. The amount of the premium is based on the institution's balance of insured deposits for the preceding quarter and the institution's risk to the insurance fund. In 2009, Congress permanently increased the limit that the FDIC may borrow from the U.S. Treasury from $30 bil to $100 bil.

U.S. Banks, 1935-2024

Source: *Summary of Deposits*, Federal Deposit Insurance Corp. (FDIC)
Comprises all FDIC-insured commercial and savings banks, including savings and loan institutions (S&Ls).

	Number of banks					Deposits (in mil dollars)				
		Commercial banks[2]					Commercial banks[2]			
Year	All banks[1]	National charter	State charter	Non-members	Savings banks, total	All deposits[1]	National charter	State charter	Non-members	Savings banks, total
1935[3]	**15,295**	5,386	1,001	7,735	1,173	**$45,102**	$24,802	$13,653	$5,669	$978
1940	**15,772**	5,144	1,342	6,956	2,330	**67,494**	35,787	20,642	7,040	4,025
1950	**16,500**	4,958	1,912	6,576	3,054	**171,963**	84,941	41,602	19,726	25,694
1960	**17,549**	4,530	1,641	6,955	4,423	**310,262**	120,242	65,487	34,369	90,164
1970	**18,205**	4,621	1,147	7,743	4,694	**686,901**	285,436	101,512	95,566	204,367
1980	**18,763**	4,425	997	9,013	4,328	**1,832,716**	656,752	191,183	344,311	640,470
1990	**15,158**	3,979	1,009	7,355	2,815	**3,637,292**	1,558,915	397,797	693,438	987,142
1995	**12,289**	2,941	995	6,230	2,082	**3,214,678**	1,337,105	439,430	696,108	735,856
2000	**10,119**	2,302	996	5,180	1,622	**4,003,744**	1,792,773	707,562	793,275	706,461
2005	**8,856**	1,864	906	4,779	1,294	**5,933,763**	2,946,589	765,673	1,191,977	1,023,641
2010	**7,821**	1,427	836	4,413	1,135	**7,676,878**	4,305,697	1,002,425	1,464,022	891,159
2015	**6,358**	1,027	816	3,629	876	**10,657,721**	6,393,433	1,573,880	1,823,558	823,906
2020	**5,076**	779	702	2,949	636	**15,590,139**	9,616,766	2,179,212	2,696,151	1,054,195
2021	**4,960**	755	693	2,887	615	**17,235,467**	10,350,965	2,595,643	3,055,213	1,194,327
2022	**4,781**	733	662	2,784	592	**18,141,022**	10,763,034	2,732,220	3,375,272	1,220,165
2023	**4,655**	712	662	2,697	574	**17,269,424**	10,607,385	2,493,974	3,096,490	1,018,763
2024	**4,549**	697	668	2,620	554	**17,405,521**	10,657,782	2,659,399	3,074,532	956,109

Note: Figures are for the end of the year shown through 1990 and for June 30 thereafter. (1) Includes U.S. branches of foreign banks not listed separately. (2) Nonmembers are banks that are not members of the Federal Reserve System; national charter and state charter institutions are Federal Reserve members. (3) Figures for 1935 do not include S&Ls, the data for which are not available.

U.S. Bank Failures, 1934-2024

Source: Federal Deposit Insurance Corp. (FDIC)

Covers all FDIC-insured commercial and savings banks, including savings and loan institutions (S&Ls) 1980 and after. As of Oct. 7, 2024.

Year	Closed or assisted	Year	Closed or assisted	Year	Closed or assisted	Year	Closed or assisted	Year	Closed or assisted
1934	9	1970-79	79	1991	271	2003	3	2015	8
1935	25	1980	22	1992	181	2004	4	2016	5
1936	69	1981	40	1993	50	2005	0	2017	8
1937	75	1982	119	1994	15	2006	0	2018	0
1938	74	1983	99	1995	8	2007	3	2019	4
1939	60	1984	106	1996	6	2008	30	2020	4
1940	43	1985	180	1997	1	2009	148	2021	0
1941	15	1986	204	1998	3	2010	157	2022	0
1942	20	1987	262	1999	8	2011	92	2023	5
1943-49	21	1988	470	2000	7	2012	51	2024	1
1950-59	28	1989	534	2001	4	2013	24	**Total, 1934-2024**	**4,110**
1960-69	44	1990	382	2002	11	2014	18		

Largest U.S. Bank Holding Companies, 2024

Source: National Information Center, Federal Financial Institutions Examination Council
(ranked by total assets, in millions of dollars; as of Mar. 31, 2024)

Rank	Institution, location	Assets	Rank	Institution, location	Assets
1.	JPMorgan Chase & Co., New York, NY	$4,090,727	25.	Huntington Bancshares Inc., Columbus, OH	$193,519
2.	Bank of America Corp., Charlotte, NC	3,273,803	26.	Ally Financial Inc., Detroit, MI	192,877
3.	Citigroup Inc., New York, NY	2,432,510	27.	KeyCorp, Cleveland, OH	187,531
4.	Wells Fargo & Company, San Francisco, CA	1,959,160	28.	Ameriprise Financial, Inc., Minneapolis, MN	179,843
5.	Goldman Sachs Group, Inc., New York, NY	1,698,440	29.	RBC US Group Holdings LLC, Toronto, Canada	166,734
6.	Morgan Stanley, New York, NY	1,228,503	30.	Santander Holdings USA, Inc., Boston, MA	165,766
7.	U.S. Bancorp, Minneapolis, MN	683,606	31.	Northern Trust Corp., Chicago, IL	156,111
8.	PNC Financial Services Group, Inc., Pittsburgh, PA	566,181	32.	Regions Financial Corp., Birmingham, AL	155,227
9.	Truist Financial Corp., Charlotte, NC	534,959	33.	Discover Financial Services, Riverwoods, IL	152,689
10.	TD Group U.S. Holdings LLC, Cherry Hill, NJ	530,324	34.	Synchrony Financial, Stamford, CT	121,173
11.	Capital One Financial Corp., McLean, VA	481,720	35.	DB USA (Deutsche Bank), New York, NY	113,090
12.	Charles Schwab Corp., Westlake, TX	468,784	36.	New York Community Bancorp, Inc., Hicksville, NY	112,900
13.	Bank of New York Mellon Corp., New York, NY	434,728	37.	First Horizon Corp., Memphis, TN	81,800
14.	State Street Corp., Boston, MA	338,003	38.	Raymond James Financial, Inc., St. Petersburg, FL	81,232
15.	BMO Financial Corp., Chicago, IL	295,575	39.	Comerica Inc., Dallas TX	79,660
16.	American Express Co., New York, NY	269,261	40.	Western Alliance Bancorporation, Phoenix, AZ	76,989
17.	HSBC North America Holdings Inc., New York, NY	246,728	41.	Webster Financial Corp., Stamford, CT	76,162
18.	Citizens Financial Group, Inc., Providence, RI	220,862	42.	Mizuho Americas LLC, New York, NY	74,925
19.	First Citizens Bancshares, Inc., Raleigh, NC	217,855	43.	Popular, Inc., San Juan, PR	70,937
20.	United Services Automobile Association, San Antonio, TX	217,199	44.	East West Bancorp, Inc., Pasadena, CA	70,876
21.	M&T Bank Corp., Buffalo, NY	215,137	45.	CIBC Bancorp USA Inc., Chicago, IL	69,640
22.	Fifth Third Bancorp, Cincinnati, OH	214,506	46.	BNP Paribas USA, Inc., New York, NY	64,558
23.	Barclays U.S. LLC, New York, NY	198,127	47.	John Deere Capital Corporation, Middleton, WI	61,071
24.	UBS Americas Holding LLC, New York, NY	194,508	48.	Valley National Bancorp, New York, NY	61,000
			49.	Synovus Financial Corp., Columbus, GA	59,838

Note: Includes foreign-owned banks with a strong presence in the U.S.

Status of Top Recipients of Treasury Department "Bailout" Funds, 2022

Source: ProPublica

Since Oct. 2008, the federal government has spent $635 bil to bail out 987 institutions severely affected by that year's financial crisis. As of Aug. 18, 2022, the government had recouped $390 bil in loans and $353 bil in dividends, interest, and other returns, leading to an overall profit of more than $109 bil. Disbursements to some companies currently appear as losses but may ultimately turn a profit; those investments are listed in *italics*. Companies that failed to repay the government and never will are listed in ***bold italics***.

(in billions of dollars, ranked by amount disbursed)

Recipient	Disbursed	Repaid[1]	Net profit or amount outstanding
Fannie Mae	$119.8	$181.3	$61.5
Freddie Mac	71.6	119.7	48.0
AIG	67.8	72.9	5.0
General Motors	***50.7***	***39.4***	***–11.3***
Bank of America	45.0	49.6	4.6
Citigroup	45.0	58.4	13.4
JPMorgan Chase	25.0	26.7	1.7
Wells Fargo	25.0	27.3	2.3
GMAC (now Ally Financial)	16.3	19.3	3.1
Chrysler	***10.7***	***9.5***	***–1.2***
Goldman Sachs	10.0	11.4	1.4
Morgan Stanley	10.0	11.3	1.3
PNC Financial Services	7.6	8.3	0.7
U.S. Bancorp	6.6	6.9	0.3
PHH Mortgage, subsidiary of Ocwen Financial Corp.	5.0	0.0	–5.0
SunTrust	*4.9*	*5.4*	*0.5*
Capital One Financial Corp.	3.6	3.8	0.3
Regions Financial Corp.	3.5	4.1	0.6
Wellington Management Legacy Securities PPIF Master Fund, LP	3.4	4.2	0.7
Fifth Third Bancorp	3.4	4.0	0.6
Hartford Financial Services	3.4	4.2	0.8
Wells Fargo Bank, NA	3.4	0.0	–3.4
American Express	3.4	3.8	0.4
AG GECC PPIF Master Fund, L.P.	*3.4*	*4.3*	*0.9*
JPMorgan Chase subsidiaries	*3.2*	*0.0*	*–3.2*
AllianceBernstein Legacy Securities Master Fund, L.P.	3.2	3.8	0.6
BB&T	$3.1	$3.3	$0.2
Bank of New York Mellon	3.0	3.2	0.2
KeyCorp	2.5	2.9	0.4
CalHFA Mortgage Assistance Corp.	*2.4*	*0.0*	*–2.4*
CIT Group	***2.3***	—	***–2.3***
Bank of America subsidiaries (incl. Countrywide)	*2.3*	*0.0*	*–2.3*
Comerica Incorporated	2.3	2.6	0.3
State Street	2.0	2.1	0.1
RLJ Western Asset Public/Private Master Fund, L.P.	1.9	2.3	0.5
Select Portfolio Servicing	1.8	0.0	–1.8
Invesco Legacy Securities Master Fund, L.P.	1.7	2.3	0.6
Marshall & Ilsley	1.7	1.9	0.2
Oaktree PPIP Fund, L.P.	*1.7*	*2.0*	*0.3*
Nationstar Mortgage, LLC dba Mr. Cooper	1.6	0.0	–1.6
Blackrock PPIF, L.P.	1.6	2.0	0.4
Northern Trust	*1.6*	*1.7*	*0.1*
Chrysler Financial Services	1.5	1.5	—
Marathon Legacy Securities Public–Private Investment Partnership, L.P.	1.4	1.8	0.4
Zions Bancorp	1.4	1.7	0.3
Huntington Bancshares	1.4	1.6	0.2
Discover Financial Services	1.2	1.5	0.2
Florida Housing Finance Corp.	*1.1*	*0.0*	*–1.1*

— = Less than $0.1 bil. **Note:** Total includes other disbursements not shown. Figures may not add up to totals due to rounding. (1) Amounts repaid include principal, dividends, interest, warrants, and other proceeds.

Federal Reserve System

The Federal Reserve System is the central bank for the U.S. The system was established on Dec. 23, 1913, originally to give the country an elastic currency, provide facilities for discounting commercial paper, and improve the supervision of banking. Since then, the system's responsibilities have been broadened. Over the years, stability and growth of the economy, a high level of employment, stability in the purchasing power of the dollar, and reasonable balance in transactions with other countries have come to be recognized as primary objectives of governmental economic policy.

The Federal Reserve System consists of three key entities: the Board of Governors, 12 District Reserve Banks and their branches, and the Federal Open Market Committee. Several advisory councils help the board meet its varied responsibilities.

The hub of the system is the seven-member **Board of Governors** in Washington, DC. The members of the board are appointed by the president and confirmed by the Senate to 14-year terms. The president also appoints the chair and vice chair of the board from among the board members for four-year terms. As of Oct. 2024, the board members were Jerome H. Powell, chair; Philip N. Jefferson, vice chair; Michael S. Barr, vice chair for supervision; Michelle W. Bowman; Lisa D. Cook; Adriana D. Kugler; and Christopher J. Waller.

The 12 **Federal Reserve Banks** and their branch offices serve as the decentralized portion of the system, carrying out day-to-day operations such as circulating currency and coin and providing fiscal agency functions and payments mechanism services. The 12 Reserve Banks are located in Boston, New York, Philadelphia, Cleveland, Richmond, Atlanta, Chicago, St. Louis, Minneapolis, Kansas City, Dallas, and San Francisco.

The system's principal function is monetary policy, which it controls using three tools: reserve requirements, the discount rate, and open market operations.

Uniform **reserve requirements**, set by the board, are applied to the transaction accounts and nonpersonal time deposits of all depository institutions. Responsibility for setting the **discount rate** (the interest rate at which depository institutions can borrow money from the Reserve Banks) is shared by the Board of Governors and the Reserve Banks. Changes in the discount rate are recommended by the individual boards of directors of the Reserve Banks and are subject to approval by the Board of Governors.

The most important tool of monetary policy is **open market operations**, or the purchase and sale of government securities. Responsibility for influencing the cost and availability of money and credit through the purchase and sale of government securities lies with the **Federal Open Market Committee** (FOMC), which comprises the seven members of the Board of Governors, the president of the Federal Reserve Bank of New York, and four other Federal Reserve Bank presidents, who each serve one-year terms on a rotating basis. The committee bases its decisions on economic and financial developments and outlook, setting yearly growth objectives for key measures of money supply and credit. The decisions of the committee are carried out by the domestic trading desk of the Federal Reserve Bank of New York.

A Federal Advisory Council of banking industry representatives meets with the Federal Reserve Board four times a year to discuss business and financial conditions, as well as to make recommendations.

Website: www.federalreserve.gov

Federal Reserve Board Benchmark Interest Rates, 1955-2024

The interest rate that the Federal Reserve charges its member banks to borrow money overnight, the discount rate, was divided into two categories in 2003: primary credit, for banks in sound financial condition, and secondary credit, for banks that do not qualify for primary credit. The secondary credit rate is ½ a percentage point higher than the primary credit rate shown here for Jan. 9, 2003, and thereafter. Banks typically raise or lower the rates they extend to customers in accordance with changes in these rates.

Effective date	Rate
1955	
Jan. 3	1½
Apr. 15	1¾
Aug. 5	2
Sept. 9	2¼
Nov. 18	2½
1956	
Apr. 13	2¾
Aug. 24	3
1957	
Aug. 23	3½
Nov. 15	3
1958	
Jan. 24	2¾
Mar. 7	2¼
Apr. 18	1¾
Sept. 12	2
Nov. 7	2½
1959	
Mar. 6	3
May 29	3½
Sept. 11	4
1960	
June 10	3½
Aug. 12	3
1963	
July 17	3½
1964	
Nov. 24	4
1965	
Dec. 6	4½
1967	
Apr. 7	4
Nov. 20	4½
1968	
Mar. 22	5
Apr. 19	5½
Aug. 30	5¼
Dec. 18	5½
1969	
Apr. 4	6
1970	
Nov. 13	5¾
Dec. 4	5½
1971	
Jan. 8	5¼
Jan. 22	5
Feb. 19	4¾
1971 (cont.)	
July 16	5
Nov. 19	4¾
Dec. 17	4½
1973	
Jan. 15	5
Feb. 26	5½
May 4	5¾
May 11	6
June 11	6½
July 2	7
Aug. 14	7½
1974	
Apr. 25	8
Dec. 9	7¾
1975	
Jan. 10	7¼
Feb. 5	6¾
Mar. 19	6¼
May 16	6
1976	
Jan. 19	5½
Nov. 22	5¼
1977	
Aug. 31	5¾
Oct. 26	6
1978	
Jan. 9	6½
May 11	7
July 3	7¼
Aug. 21	7¾
Sept. 22	8
Oct. 16	8½
Nov. 1	9½
1979	
July 20	10
Aug. 17	10½
Sept. 19	11
Oct. 8	12
1980	
Feb. 15	13
May 30	12
June 13	11
July 28	10
Sept. 26	11
Nov. 17	12
Dec. 5	13
1981	
May 5	14
Nov. 2	13
Dec. 4	12
1982	
July 20	11½
Aug. 2	11
Aug. 16	10
Aug. 27	10
Oct. 12	9½
Dec. 15	8½
1984	
Apr. 9	9
Nov. 21	8½
Dec. 24	8
1985	
May 20	7½
1986	
Mar. 7	7
Apr. 21	6½
July 11	6
Aug. 21	5½
1987	
Sept. 4	6
1988	
Aug. 9	6½
1989	
Feb. 24	7
1990	
Dec. 18	6½
1991	
Apr. 30	5½
Sept. 13	5
Nov. 6	4½
Dec. 20	3½
1992	
July 2	3
1994	
May 17	3½
Aug. 16	4
Nov. 15	4¾
1995	
Feb. 1	5
1996	
Jan. 31	5
1998	
Oct. 15	4¾
Nov. 17	4½
1999	
Aug. 24	4¾
Nov. 16	5
2000	
Feb. 2	5¼
Mar. 21	5½
May 16	6
2001	
Jan. 3	5¾
Jan. 31	5
Mar. 20	4½
Apr. 18	4
May 15	3½
June 27	3¼
Aug. 21	3
Sept. 17	2½
Oct. 2	2
Dec. 11	1¼
2002	
Nov. 6	¾
2003	
Jan. 9	2¼
June 25	2
2004	
June 30	2¼
Aug. 10	2½
Sept. 21	2¾
Nov. 10	3
Dec. 14	3¼
2005	
Feb. 2	3½
Mar. 22	3¾
May 3	4
June 30	4¼
Aug. 9	4½
Sept. 20	4¾
Nov. 1	5
Dec. 13	5¼
2006	
Jan. 31	5½
Mar. 28	5¾
May 10	6
June 29	6¼
2007	
Aug. 17	5¾
Sept. 18	5¼
Nov. 1	5
Dec. 12	4¾
2008	
Jan. 22	4
Jan. 30	3½
Mar. 17	3¼
Mar. 18	2½
Apr. 30	2¼
Oct. 8	1¾
Oct. 29	1¼
Dec. 16	½
2010	
Feb. 19	¾
2015	
Dec. 17	1
2016	
Dec. 15	1¼
2017	
Mar. 16	1½
June 15	1¾
Dec. 14	2
2018	
Mar. 22	2¼
June 14	2½
Sept. 27	2¾
Dec. 20	3
2019	
Aug. 1	2¾
Sept. 19	2½
Oct. 31	2¼
2020	
Mar. 4	1¾
Mar. 16	¼
2022	
Mar. 17	½
May 5	1
June 16	1¾
July 28	2½
Sept. 22	3¼
Nov. 3	4
Dec. 15	4½
2023	
Feb. 2	4¾
Mar. 23	5
May 4	5¼
July 27	5½
2024	
Sept. 19	5

U.S. Holdings of Foreign Securities, 2005-22

Source: *U.S. Portfolio Holdings of Foreign Securities*, U.S. Dept. of the Treasury
(in billions of dollars; countries ranked by 2022 holdings)

Country	2005	2010	2015	2020	2022
Cayman Islands[1]	$249	$366	$1,216	$2,565	$2,658
United Kingdom	815	1,001	1,239	1,395	1,398
Canada	419	695	705	1,168	1,244
Japan	531	519	822	1,296	1,090
Ireland	75	132	498	698	777
France	274	366	474	698	696
Switzerland	196	327	420	632	591
Netherlands	192	233	404	628	582
Germany	217	299	378	535	454
Australia	128	323	296	378	424
India	33	91	130	234	287
Bermuda	187	160	217	283	249
China[2]	28	102	108	287	243
Taiwan	58	95	108	304	232
South Korea	119	148	171	300	205
Luxembourg	46	100	128	198	201
Sweden	75	122	138	196	180
Denmark	25	49	90	158	173
Jersey[1]	$19	$42	$92	$138	$162
Brazil	90	235	116	168	157
Mexico	86	109	148	153	145
Spain	70	87	115	163	142
Hong Kong	46	135	134	166	127
Italy	79	66	107	148	123
Singapore	36	64	99	92	111
Israel	44	64	80	94	87
Norway	36	56	58	72	86
South Africa	34	78	63	79	65
Indonesia	9	35	47	69	64
British Virgin Islands[1]	8	16	63	65	61
Finland	49	41	38	60	60
Belgium	25	35	68	64	59
Guernsey[1]	6	15	38	53	56
Russia	29	62	40	74	29
Total[3]	**4,609**	**6,763**	**9,451**	**14,387**	**14,013**

(1) Not included in UK totals though it is a territory/dependency. (2) Does not include Hong Kong or Macau. (3) Includes countries not shown.

S&P 500 Index, 1965-2024

Source: S&P Dow Jones Indices
(as of Oct. 7, 2024)

Year	Highest close		Lowest close	
1965	Nov. 15	92.63	June 28	81.60
1970	Jan. 5	93.46	May 26	69.29
1975	July 15	95.61	Jan. 8	70.04
1980	Nov. 28	140.52	Mar. 27	98.22
1985	Dec. 16	212.02	Jan. 4	163.68
1990	July 16	368.95	Oct. 11	295.46
1995	Dec. 13	621.69	Jan. 3	459.11
2000	Mar. 24	1,527.46	Dec. 20	1,264.74
2005	Dec. 14	1,272.74	Apr. 20	1,137.50
2010	Dec. 29	1,259.78	July 2	1,022.58
2011	Apr. 29	1,363.61	Oct. 3	1,099.23
2012	Sept. 14	1,465.77	Jan. 3	1,277.06
2013	Dec. 31	1,848.36	Jan. 8	1,457.15
2014	Dec. 29	2,090.57	Feb. 3	1,741.89
2015	May 21	2,130.82	Aug. 25	1,867.61
2016	Dec. 13	2,271.72	Feb. 11	1,829.08
2017	Dec. 18	2,690.16	Jan. 3	2,257.83
2018	Sept. 20	2,930.75	Dec. 24	2,351.10
2019	Dec. 27	3,240.02	Jan. 3	2,447.89
2020	Dec. 31	3,756.07	Mar. 23	2,237.40
2021	Dec. 29	4,793.06	Jan. 4	3,700.65
2022	Jan. 3	4,796.56	Oct. 12	3,577.03
2023	Dec. 28	4,783.35	Jan. 5	3,808.10
2024	Sept. 30	5,762.48	Jan. 4	4,688.68

Record One-Day Gains and Losses of the Dow Jones Industrial Average

Source: S&P Dow Jones Indices
(ranked by largest one-day losses and gains for two terms; as of Oct. 7, 2024)

Greatest % gains

Rank	Date	Close	Net chg.	% chg.
1.	3/15/1933	62.10	8.26	15.34%
2.	10/6/1931	99.34	12.86	14.87
3.	10/30/1929	258.47	28.40	12.34
4.	3/24/2020	20,704.91	2,112.98	11.37
5.	9/21/1932	75.16	7.67	11.36

Greatest % losses

Rank	Date	Close	Net chg.	% chg.
1.	12/12/1914	54.62	–16.80	–23.52%
2.	10/19/1987	1,738.74	–508.00	–22.61
3.	3/16/2020	20,188.52	–2,997.10	–12.93
4.	10/28/1929	260.64	–38.33	–12.82
5.	10/29/1929	230.07	–30.57	–11.73

Greatest point gains

Rank	Date	Close	Net chg.	% chg.
1.	3/24/2020	20,704.91	2,112.98	11.37%
2.	3/13/2020	23,185.62	1,985.00	9.36
3.	4/6/2020	22,679.99	1,627.46	7.73
4.	3/26/2020	22,552.17	1,351.62	6.38
5.	3/2/2020	26,703.32	1,293.97	5.09

Greatest point losses

Rank	Date	Close	Net chg.	% chg.
1.	3/16/2020	20,188.52	–2,997.10	–12.93%
2.	3/12/2020	21,200.62	–2,352.60	–9.99
3.	3/9/2020	23,851.02	–2,013.76	–7.79
4.	6/11/2020	25,128.17	–1,861.82	–6.90
5.	3/11/2020	23,553.22	–1,464.95	–5.86

Dow Jones Industrial Average, 1965-2024

Source: S&P Dow Jones Indices
(as of Oct. 7, 2024)

Year	Highest close		Lowest close	
1965	Dec. 31	969.26	June 28	840.59
1970	Dec. 29	842.00	May 6	631.16
1975	July 15	881.81	Jan. 2	632.04
1980	Nov. 20	1,000.17	Apr. 21	759.13
1985	Dec. 16	1,553.10	Jan. 4	1,184.96
1990	July 16	2,999.75	Oct. 11	2,365.10
1995	Dec. 13	5,216.47	Jan. 30	3,832.08
1996	Dec. 27	6,560.91	Jan. 10	5,032.94
1997	Aug. 6	8,259.31	Apr. 11	6,391.69
1998	Nov. 23	9,374.27	Aug. 31	7,539.07
1999	Dec. 31	11,497.12	Jan. 22	9,120.67
2000	Jan. 14	11,722.98	Mar. 7	9,796.03
2001	May 21	11,337.92	Sept. 21	8,235.81
2002	Mar. 19	10,635.25	Oct. 9	7,286.27
2003	Dec. 31	10,453.90	Mar. 11	7,524.06
2004	Dec. 28	10,854.54	Oct. 25	9,749.99
2005	Mar. 4	10,940.50	Apr. 20	10,012.36
2006	Dec. 27	12,510.57	Jan. 20	10,667.39
2007	Oct. 9	14,164.53	Mar. 5	12,050.41
2008	Jan. 3	13,056.72	Nov. 20	7,552.29
2009	Dec. 30	10,548.51	Mar. 9	6,547.05
2010	Dec. 29	11,585.38	July 2	9,686.48
2011	Apr. 29	12,810.54	Oct. 3	10,655.30
2012	Oct. 5	13,610.15	June 4	12,101.46
2013	Dec. 31	16,576.66	Jan. 8	13,328.85
2014	Dec. 26	18,053.71	Feb. 3	15,372.80
2015	May 19	18,312.39	Aug. 25	15,666.44
2016	Dec. 20	19,974.62	Feb. 11	15,660.18
2017	Dec. 28	24,837.51	Jan. 19	19,732.40
2018	Oct. 3	26,828.39	Dec. 24	21,792.20
2019	Dec. 27	28,645.26	Jan. 3	22,686.22
2020	Feb. 12	29,551.42	Mar. 23	18,591.93
2021	Dec. 29	36,488.63	Jan. 29	29,982.62
2022	Jan. 4	36,799.65	Sept. 30	28,725.51
2023	Dec. 28	37,710.10	Mar. 13	31,819.14
2024	Oct. 4	42,352.75	Jan. 17	37,266.67

Milestones of the Dow Jones Industrial Average

(as of Oct. 7, 2024)

First close over—		First close over—		First close over—		First close over—		First close over—	
100	Jan. 12, 1906	4,500	June 16, 1995	13,000	Apr. 25, 2007	21,000	Mar. 1, 2017	29,000	Jan. 15, 2020
500	Mar. 12, 1956	5,000	Nov. 21, 1995	14,000	July 19, 2007	22,000	Aug. 2, 2017	30,000	Nov. 24, 2020
1,000	Nov. 14, 1972	6,000	Oct. 14, 1996	15,000	June 27, 2013	23,000	Oct. 17, 2017	31,000	Jan. 7, 2021
1,500	Dec. 11, 1985	7,000	Feb. 13, 1997	16,000	Nov. 21, 2013	24,000	Nov. 30, 2017	32,000	Mar. 10, 2021
2,000	Jan. 8, 1987	8,000	July 16, 1997	17,000	July 3, 2014	25,000	Jan. 4, 2018	33,000	Mar. 17, 2021
2,500	July 17, 1987	9,000	Apr. 6, 1998	18,000	Dec. 23, 2014	26,000	Jan. 16, 2018	34,000	Apr. 15, 2021
3,000	Apr. 17, 1991	10,000	Mar. 29, 1999	19,000	Nov. 22, 2016	27,000	July 11, 2019	35,000	July 23, 2021
3,500	May 19, 1993	11,000	May 3, 1999	20,000	Jan. 25. 2017	28,000	Nov. 15, 2019	36,000	Nov. 2, 2021
4,000	Feb. 23, 1995	12,000	Oct. 19, 2006						

Components of the Dow Jones Averages

(as of Oct. 7, 2024)

Dow Jones Industrial Average

- 3M Co. (MMM)
- Amazon (AMZN)
- American Express Co. (AXP)
- Amgen Inc. (AMGN)
- Apple Inc. (AAPL)
- Boeing Co. (BA)
- Caterpillar Inc. (CAT)
- Chevron Corp. (CVX)
- Cisco Systems Inc. (CSCO)
- Coca-Cola Co. (KO)
- Dow Inc. (DOW)
- Goldman Sachs Group Inc. (GS)
- Home Depot Inc. (HD)
- Honeywell International Inc. (HON)
- Intel Corp. (INTC)
- International Business Machines Corp. (IBM)
- Johnson & Johnson (JNJ)
- JPMorgan Chase & Co. (JPM)
- McDonald's Corp. (MCD)
- Merck & Co. Inc. (MRK)
- Microsoft Corp. (MSFT)
- Nike Inc. (NKE)
- Procter & Gamble Co. (PG)
- Salesforce Inc. (CRM)
- Travelers Companies Inc. (TRV)
- UnitedHealth Group Inc. (UNH)
- Verizon Communications Inc. (VZ)
- Visa Inc. (V)
- Walmart Inc. (WMT)
- Walt Disney Co. (DIS)

Dow Jones Utility Average

- AES Corp. (AES)
- American Electric Power Co. Inc. (AEP)
- American Water Works Co. (AWK)
- Atmos Energy Corp. (ATO)
- Consolidated Edison Inc. (ED)
- Dominion Energy Inc. (D)
- Duke Energy Corp. (DUK)
- Edison International (EIX)
- Exelon Corp. (EXC)
- FirstEnergy Corp. (FE)
- NextEra Energy Inc. (NEE)
- Public Service Enterprise Group Inc. (PEG)
- Sempra (SRE)
- Southern Co. (SO)
- Xcel Energy Inc. (XEL)

Dow Jones Transportation Average

- Alaska Air Group Inc. (ALK)
- American Airlines Group Inc. (AAL)
- Avis Budget Group Inc. (CAR)
- C.H. Robinson Worldwide Inc. (CHRW)
- CSX Corp. (CSX)
- Delta Air Lines Inc. (DAL)
- Expeditors International of Washington Inc. (EXPD)
- FedEx Corp. (FDX)
- J.B. Hunt Transport Services Inc. (JBHT)
- Kirby Corp. (KEX)
- Landstar System Inc. (LSTR)
- Matson Inc. (MATX)
- Norfolk Southern Corp. (NSC)
- Old Dominion Freight Line Inc. (ODFL)
- Ryder System Inc. (R)
- Southwest Airlines Co. (LUV)
- Uber Technologies Inc. (UBER)
- Union Pacific Corp. (UNP)
- United Airlines Holdings Inc. (UAL)
- United Parcel Service Inc. (UPS)

Record One-Day Gains and Losses of the Nasdaq Composite Index

Source: Nasdaq, Inc.

(ranked by largest one-day losses and gains for two terms; as of Oct. 7, 2024)

Greatest point gains			Greatest % gains			Greatest point losses			Greatest % losses		
Rank	Date	Change	Rank	Date	% change	Rank	Date	Change	Rank	Date	% change
1.	11/10/2022	760.97	1.	1/3/2001	14.17%	1.	3/16/2020	–970.28	1.	3/16/2020	–12.32%
2.	3/13/2020	673.07	2.	10/13/2008	11.81	2.	3/12/2020	–750.25	2.	10/19/1987	–11.35
3.	3/24/2020	557.18	3.	12/5/2000	10.48	3.	7/24/2024	–654.94	3.	4/14/2000	–9.67
4.	4/6/2020	540.15	4.	10/28/2008	9.53	4.	5/5/2022	–647.16	4.	3/12/2020	–9.43
5.	3/16/2022	487.93	5.	3/13/2020	9.35	5.	9/13/2022	–632.84	5.	9/29/2008	–9.14
6.	11/30/2022	484.22	6.	4/5/2001	8.92	6.	3/9/2020	–624.94	6.	10/20/1987	–9.00
7.	7/27/2022	469.85	7.	4/18/2001	8.12	7.	9/3/2020	–598.34	7.	10/26/1987	–9.00
8.	1/31/2022	469.31	8.	3/24/2020	8.12	8.	9/3/2024	–577.33	8.	12/1/2008	–8.95
9.	3/9/2021	464.66	9.	5/30/2000	7.94	9.	8/5/2024	–576.08	9.	8/31/1998	–8.56
10.	8/8/2024	464.22	10.	10/13/2000	7.87	10.	5/18/2022	–566.37	10.	10/15/2008	–8.47

Nasdaq Composite Index Closing Prices, 1971-2024

Source: Nasdaq, Inc.; as of Oct. 7, 2024

Year	High	Low	Year	High	Low	Year	High	Low	Year	High	Low
1971	114.12	99.68	**1987**	456.27	288.49	**2000**	5,048.62	2,332.78	**2013**	4,176.59	3,091.81
1975	88.00	60.70	**1988**	397.54	329.00	**2001**	2,892.36	1,387.06	**2014**	4,806.91	3,996.96
1976	97.88	78.06	**1989**	487.60	376.87	**2002**	2,059.38	1,114.11	**2015**	5,218.86	4,506.49
1977	105.05	93.66	**1990**	470.30	322.93	**2003**	2,009.88	1,271.47	**2016**	5,487.44	4,266.84
1978	139.25	99.09	**1991**	586.35	352.85	**2004**	2,178.00	1,752.00	**2017**	6,965.36	5,429.09
1979	152.29	117.84	**1992**	676.95	545.85	**2005**	2,273.37	1,904.18	**2018**	8,109.69	6,192.92
1980	208.29	124.09	**1993**	790.56	645.02	**2006**	2,465.98	2,020.39	**2019**	9,022.39	6,463.50
1981	223.96	170.80	**1994**	803.93	691.23	**2007**	2,811.61	2,340.68	**2020**	12,899.42	6,860.67
1982	241.63	158.92	**1995**	1,072.82	740.53	**2008**	2,609.63	1,505.90	**2021**	16,057.44	12,609.16
1983	329.11	229.88	**1996**	1,328.45	978.17	**2009**	2,167.70	1,265.52	**2022**	15,832.80	10,213.29
1984	288.41	223.91	**1997**	1,748.62	1,194.39	**2010**	2,671.48	2,091.79	**2023**	15,099.18	10,305.24
1985	325.53	245.82	**1998**	2,200.63	1,357.09	**2011**	2,873.54	2,335.83	**2024**	18,647.45	14,510.30
1986	411.21	322.14	**1999**	4,090.61	2,193.13	**2012**	3,183.95	2,648.36			

Average Yields of Treasury, Corporate, and State and Local Bonds, 1977-2024

Source: Office of Market Finance, U.S. Dept. of the Treasury; Federal Reserve System

Year	Treasury 30-year bonds[1]	New Aa corporate bonds[2]	State and local bonds[3]	Year	Treasury 30-year bonds[1]	New Aa corporate bonds[2]	State and local bonds[3]	Year	Treasury 30-year bonds[1]	New Aa corporate bonds[2]	State and local bonds[3]
1977	7.75%	8.02%	5.68%	1993	6.59%	7.22%	5.59%	2009	4.08%	5.31%	4.62%
1978	8.49	8.73	6.03	1994	7.37	7.96	6.19	2010	4.25	4.94	4.30
1979	9.28	9.63	6.52	1995	6.88	7.59	5.95	2011	3.91	4.64	4.50
1980	11.27	11.94	8.55	1996	6.71	7.37	5.76	2012	2.92	3.67	3.73
1981	13.45	14.17	11.34	1997	6.61	7.26	5.52	2013	3.45	4.24	4.26
1982	12.76	13.79	11.64	1998	5.58	6.53	5.09	2014	3.34	4.16	4.24
1983	11.18	12.04	9.51	1999	5.87	7.04	5.43	2015	2.84	3.89	3.65
1984	12.41	12.71	10.10	2000	5.94	7.62	5.71	2016	2.59	3.67	3.14
1985	10.79	11.37	9.11	2001	5.49	7.08	5.15	2017	2.89	3.74	NA
1986	7.78	9.02	7.34	2002	5.43	6.49	5.04	2018	3.11	3.93	NA
1987	8.59	9.38	7.65	2003	4.96	5.67	4.75	2019	2.58	3.39	NA
1988	8.96	9.71	7.68	2004	5.04	5.63	4.68	2020	1.56	2.48	NA
1989	8.45	9.26	7.23	2005	4.64	5.24	4.40	2021	2.06	2.70	NA
1990	8.61	9.32	7.27	2006	4.91	5.59	4.40	2022	3.11	4.07	NA
1991	8.14	8.77	6.92	2007	4.84	5.56	4.40	2023	4.09	4.81	NA
1992	7.67	8.14	6.44	2008	4.28	5.63	4.85	2024[4]	4.18	4.68	NA

NA = Not available. (1) On Feb. 18, 2002, the U.S. Treasury discontinued the 30-year constant maturity yield and reintroduced it on Feb. 9, 2006; rates in the interim are for 20-year yields. (2) Treasury series based on 3-week moving average of reoffering yields of new corporate bonds rated Aa by Moody's Investors Service with an original maturity of at least 20 years. Treasury discontinued yield index after Jan. 31, 2003. Rates thereafter are for Moody's seasoned Aaa corporate bonds as listed by Federal Reserve. (3) Index of new reoffering yields on 20-year general obligations rated Aa by Moody's Investors Service; discontinued by Treasury Jan. 31, 2003; rates thereafter are from Bond Buyer Index of general obligation, 20 years to maturity, mixed quality state and local bonds. (4) Rates are for Sept. 2024.

Ownership of U.S. Treasury Securities, 1990-2023

Source: *Treasury Bulletin, Sept. 2024*, Financial Management Service, U.S. Dept. of the Treasury

In 1990, just over 14% of U.S. treasury securities were held by foreign and international investors. By 2023, the total public debt had grown slightly over tenfold, while the portion held by investors outside the U.S. had grown to 23%.

(in billions of dollars)

	1990	1995	2000	2005	2010	2015	2020	2022	2023
Total public debt	**$3,365**	**$4,989**	**$5,662**	**$8,170**	**$14,025**	**$18,922**	**$27,748**	**$31,420**	**$34,002**
Federal Reserve and intra-governmental holdings	1,060	1,681	2,782	4,200	5,656	7,711	10,809	12,401	11,848
Total privately held	2,305	3,308	2,880	3,971	8,369	11,211	16,939	19,019	22,153
Depository institutions	207	315	261	129	319	547	1,265	1,714	1,647
U.S. savings bonds	126	185	185	205	188	172	147	174	172
Private pension funds[1]	130	142	182	184	207	505	771	815	611
Pension funds of state and local governments	145	192	206	154	154	175	354	327	416
Insurance companies	138	242	117	202	248	310	404	396	444
Mutual funds	163	287	338	254	722	1,318	3,785	2,416	3,649
State and local governments	411	290	246	512	596	681	1,112	1,563	1,680
Foreign and international	487	835	1,201	2,034	4,436	6,146	7,071	7,198	7,933
Other investors[2]	500	821	145	295	1,500	1,357	2,030	4,416	5,601

(1) Includes securities held by the Federal Employees Retirement System Thrift Savings Plan "G Fund." (2) Includes individuals, government-sponsored enterprises, brokers and dealers, bank personal trusts and estates, corporate and noncorporate businesses, and other investors.

Financial Assets of U.S. Families, 1989-2022

Source: Survey of Consumer Finances (triennial), Federal Reserve System

Category	1989	1995	1998	2001	2004	2007	2010	2013	2016	2019	2022
Median net worth (thous.)	**$47.2**	**$66.4**	**$78.0**	**$106.1**	**$107.2**	**$126.4**	**$77.3**	**$83.7**	**$103.5**	**$121.7**	**$192.9**
Average net worth (thous.)	**183.7**	**244.8**	**307.4**	**487.0**	**517.1**	**584.6**	**498.8**	**551.3**	**736.0**	**748.8**	**1,063.7**
Percent of families holding asset											
Any asset	**NA**	**96.3%**	**96.8%**	**96.7%**	**97.9%**	**97.7%**	**97.4%**	**97.9%**	**99.4%**	**99.6%**	**99.7%**
Any financial asset	**88.4%**	**91.0**	**92.9**	**93.1**	**93.8**	**93.9**	**94.0**	**94.5**	**98.5**	**98.7**	**99.0**
Transaction accounts	85.1	87.0	90.5	90.9	91.3	92.1	92.5	93.2	98.0	98.2	98.6
Certificates of deposit	19.4	14.3	15.3	15.7	12.7	16.1	12.2	7.8	6.5	7.7	6.5
Savings bonds	23.8	22.8	19.3	16.7	17.6	14.9	12.0	10.0	8.6	7.5	6.4
Bonds	5.3	3.1	3.0	3.0	1.8	1.6	1.6	1.4	1.2	1.1	1.1
Stocks	16.2	15.2	19.2	21.3	20.7	17.9	15.1	13.8	13.9	15.2	21.0
Pooled investment funds (mutual funds)	7.1	12.3	16.5	17.7	15.0	11.4	8.7	8.2	10.0	9.0	11.5
Retirement accounts	35.4	45.2	48.8	52.2	49.7	52.6	50.4	49.2	52.1	50.5	54.3
Cash value life insurance	34.7	32.0	29.6	28.0	24.2	23.0	19.7	19.2	19.4	19.0	16.1
Other managed assets	3.5	3.9	5.9	6.6	7.3	5.8	5.7	5.2	5.5	5.9	6.2
Other	13.4	11.1	9.4	9.3	10.0	9.3	8.0	6.9	8.1	7.4	9.4
Any nonfinancial asset	**89.1**	**90.9**	**89.9**	**90.7**	**92.5**	**92.0**	**91.3**	**91.0**	**90.8**	**91.4**	**92.3**
Vehicles	83.6	84.1	82.8	84.8	86.3	87.0	86.7	86.3	85.2	85.4	86.6
Primary residence	63.8	64.7	66.2	67.7	69.1	68.6	67.3	65.2	63.7	64.9	66.1
Other residential property	20.0	11.8	12.8	11.3	12.5	13.7	14.3	13.2	13.8	13.1	12.9
Equity in nonresidential property	NA	9.4	8.6	8.3	8.3	8.1	7.7	7.2	6.2	6.7	5.9
Business equity	13.2	11.1	11.5	11.8	11.5	12.0	13.3	11.7	13.0	13.4	14.6
Other	11.9	9.0	8.5	7.6	7.8	7.2	7.0	7.3	6.5	7.9	7.4

NA = Not available.

Characteristics of Mutual Fund Investors, 2023

Source: *Investment Company Fact Book 2024*, Investment Company Institute

Median age of head of household	54
Median annual household income	$100,000
Median household financial assets	$225,000
Median mutual fund assets	$125,000
Median number of funds owned	3
Employed (full- or part-time)	64%
Married or living with a partner	71%
College graduates	54%
Hold more than half their financial assets in mutual funds	67%
Own Individual Retirement Accounts (IRAs)	66%
Own defined contribution retirement plan accounts	82%

Total Assets and New Cash Flow of Mutual Funds by Type, 2000-23

Source: *Investment Company Fact Book 2024*, Investment Company Institute

Sector	2000	2005	2010	2015	2020	2021	2022	2023
				Total net assets (year-end, in mil)				
Consumer	$1,042	$1,405	$3,113	$9,514	$11,230	$12,944	$9,505	$10,514
Financial	16,087	11,837	6,286	10,222	8,692	13,568	10,664	9,704
Health	45,921	45,398	32,507	124,538	135,174	141,862	120,763	112,120
Natural resources	2,885	11,972	22,714	28,988	17,651	22,179	26,659	25,113
Precious metals	1,143	7,003	23,065	4,487	7,242	6,194	5,480	5,522
Real estate	11,675	59,158	55,120	101,459	105,174	149,549	99,372	102,647
Tech./telecom	103,853	34,366	30,738	47,088	115,462	133,585	77,903	118,625
Utilities	22,908	28,390	33,332	32,516	26,535	30,519	36,075	29,426
Other sectors	3,917	3,189	4,597	7,006	7,134	8,995	6,867	7,517
				New net cash flow[1] (annual, in mil)				
Consumer	–$122	–$209	$101	$2,235	–$588	–$291	–$307	–$788
Financial	–534	–1,586	–626	978	–1,532	2,209	–1,049	–1,898
Health	9,256	836	–2,407	11,007	–3,743	–6,168	–7,926	–13,147
Natural resources	248	3,471	1,493	–688	–4,349	–1,464	1,465	–3,951
Precious metals	–214	1,027	2,330	–37	581	–313	47	–138
Real estate	339	3,000	1,746	–4,552	–4,182	2,500	–12,614	–7,753
Tech./telecom	43,837	–8,541	–1,391	288	–1,326	–5,443	–10,796	–1,504
Utilities	1,201	3,311	–848	–2,585	–2,580	–1,434	1,643	–6,099
Other sectors	–187	121	724	–1,510	–867	360	–927	–492

(1) Dollar value of new sales minus redemptions combined with net exchanges.

Mutual Fund Ownership, 1940-2023

Source: *Investment Company Fact Book 2024*, Investment Company Institute

				Households owning mutual funds		Exchange-traded funds (ETFs)	
Year	**Mutual funds**	**Mutual fund accounts (thous.)**	**Total net assets (bil)**	**Number (thous.)**	**Percent of all households**	**Number of funds**	**Total net assets (bil)**
1940	68	296	$0.45	NA	NA	NA	NA
1950	98	939	2.53	NA	NA	NA	NA
1960	161	4,898	17.03	NA	NA	NA	NA
1970	361	10,690	47.62	NA	NA	NA	NA
1980	564	12,088	134.76	4,600	5.7%	NA	NA
1990	3,078	61,948	1,064.34	23,400	25.1	NA	NA
2000	8,134	244,705	6,955.94	48,600	45.7	80	$65.59
2010	7,540	291,299	11,830.53	53,200	45.3	923	991.99
2015	8,115	NA	15,647.73	53,600	43.0	1,597	2,100.68
2016	8,067	NA	16,342.28	54,900	43.6	1,717	2,524.54
2017	7,955	NA	18,748.59	56,200	44.5	1,836	3,401.02
2018	8,093	NA	17,695.41	56,000	43.9	1,989	3,371.15
2019	7,957	NA	21,275.86	58,500	45.5	2,096	4,396.21
2020	7,644	NA	23,830.87	58,700	45.7	2,203	5,449.36
2021	7,500	NA	26,898.89	59,000	45.4	2,570	7,190.51
2022	7,421	NA	22,107.03	68,600	52.0	2,847	6,476.92
2023	7,222	NA	25,519.07	68,700	52.0	3,108	8,085.41

NA = Not available. **Note:** Does not include data for funds that invest primarily in other mutual funds. Mutual fund accounts data include both individual and omnibus accounts.

World's Leading Gold Producers, 1980-2023

Source: *Mineral Commodity Summaries* (series), U.S. Geological Survey, U.S. Dept. of the Interior (ranked by 2023 production; in thousands of troy ounces)

Country	1980	1990	2000	2005	2010	2015	2020	2021	2022	2023[1]
China	225	3,215	5,787	7,234	11,092	14,468	11,735	10,578	11,960	11,896
Australia	548	7,845	9,530	8,423	8,391	8,938	10,545	10,127	10,095	9,967
Russia[2]	8,300	9,710	4,598	5,279	6,173	8,102	9,806	10,288	9,967	9,967
Canada	1,627	5,433	5,022	3,844	2,926	4,919	5,466	7,170	6,623	6,430
United States	970	9,452	11,349	8,231	7,427	6,880	6,205	6,012	5,562	5,466
Kazakhstan	NA	NA	NA	NA	NA	NA	2,025	3,729	3,697	4,180
Mexico	196	311	848	976	2,347	4,340	3,279	3,858	3,858	3,858
Indonesia	60	360	4,006	4,200	3,858	3,119	2,765	2,122	3,376	3,537
South Africa	21,669	19,451	13,767	9,474	6,076	4,662	3,086	3,440	2,861	3,215
Uzbekistan	NA	NA	2,733	2,894	2,894	3,279	3,247	3,215	3,344	3,215
Ghana	353	540	2,318	2,149	2,637	2,829	4,019	2,829	2,829	2,894
Peru	134	293	4,263	6,682	5,273	4,662	2,797	3,119	3,119	2,894
Brazil	NA	NA	NA	NA	1,865	2,604	2,508	1,961	1,961	1,929
Burkina Faso	NA	NA	NA	NA	NA	NA	1,865	2,154	1,865	1,929
Tanzania	NA	NA	NA	NA	NA	NA	1,511	1,929	1,833	1,929
World[3]	**39,197**	**70,089**	**82,949**	**79,412**	**82,306**	**99,667**	**97,417**	**99,346**	**98,381**	**96,452**

NA = Not available. **Note:** One metric ton is equal to 32,150.7 troy ounces. (1) Estimated. (2) Figures for 1980-90 refer to the former USSR. Includes gold recovered as a byproduct but excludes secondary production. (3) Includes countries not shown here.

Gold Owned by the U.S., 2024

Source: *Status Report of U.S. Treasury-Owned Gold*, Bureau of the Fiscal Service, U.S. Dept. of the Treasury (as of Aug. 31, 2024; numbers may not add to totals due to rounding)

	Fine troy ounces	Book value
Total Treasury-owned gold	**261,498,926**	**$11,041,059,958**
Gold bullion	258,641,878	10,920,429,099
Gold coins, blanks, miscellaneous	2,857,048	120,630,859
Held by the U.S. Mint	**248,046,116**	**10,473,052,701**
Denver, CO, deep storage	43,853,707	1,851,599,996
Fort Knox, KY, deep storage	147,341,858	6,221,097,413
West Point, NY, deep storage	54,067,331	2,282,841,677
Gold coins, blanks, miscellaneous	2,783,219	117,513,615
Held by the Federal Reserve Bank	**13,452,811**	**$568,007,257**
Gold bullion	13,378,981	564,890,013
Federal Reserve Banks–NY vault	13,376,988	564,805,851
Federal Reserve Banks–display	1,993	84,162
Gold coins	73,830	3,117,244
Federal Reserve Banks–NY vault	73,452	3,101,308
Federal Reserve Banks–display	377	15,936

Prices of Precious Metals, 1990-2023

Source: *Mineral Commodity Summaries* (series), U.S. Geological Survey, U.S. Dept. of the Interior

	Dollars per troy ounce					Dollars per pound			
Year	Platinum[1]	Palladium[1]	Rhodium[1]	Gold	Silver	Copper[2]	Lead[3]	Tin[4]	Zinc[5]
1990	$467	NA	NA	$385	$4.82	$1.23	$0.46	$3.86	$0.75
1995	425	$153	$463	386	5.15	1.38	0.42	4.16	0.56
2000	549	692	1,990	280	5.00	0.88	0.44	3.70	0.56
2005	900	204	2,060	446	7.34	1.74	0.61	4.83	0.67
2010	1,616	531	2,459	1,228	20.20	3.48	1.09	12.40	1.02
2012	1,555	649	1,275	1,673	31.22	3.67	1.14	12.83	0.96
2013	1,490	730	1,069	1,415	23.87	3.40	1.10	13.52	0.96
2014	1,388	810	1,174	1,269	19.09	3.18	1.06	10.23	1.07
2015	1,056	695	955	1,163	15.72	2.56	0.91	7.56	0.96
2016	990	617	697	1,252	17.20	2.25	0.94	8.39	1.01
2017	951	874	1,113	1,261	17.08	2.85	1.15	9.37	1.39
2018	883	1,036	2,225	1,272	15.73	2.99	1.11	9.36	1.41
2019	867	1,544	3,919	1,395	16.24	2.80	1.00	8.68	1.24
2020	886	2,205	11,205	1,774	20.58	2.87	0.91	7.99	1.11
2021	1,094	2,419	20,254	1,801	25.23	4.32	1.13	15.80	1.46
2022	967	2,134	15,585	1,802	21.88	4.11	1.17	15.46	1.90
2023[E]	1,000	1,500	7,700	1,900	23.40	4.00	1.15	13.00	1.52

NA = Not available. E = Estimated. (1) Average annual dealer prices. (2) U.S. producer price for cathode copper. (3) North American producer price through 2012; North American market price thereafter. (4) *Platts Metals Week* composite price through 2013; New York dealer prices thereafter. (5) *Platts Metals Week* price for North American special high grade zinc except for 1990, which shows average price for high grade zinc.

Who Owns What: Familiar Consumer Products and Services

The following is a partial list of well-known consumer brands with their (U.S.) parent companies as of Sept. 2024. Among brands not listed are many whose parent companies have the same or a similar name (e.g., Colgate is owned by Colgate-Palmolive Co.).

ABC broadcasting: Walt Disney
Ace bandages: 3M
Advil: Haleon
Amana appliances: Whirlpool
American Girl: Mattel
Aquafina water: PepsiCo
Arm & Hammer: Church & Dwight
Athleta clothing: Gap
Band-Aid bandages: Kenvue
Barbie dolls: Mattel
Ben & Jerry's ice cream: Unilever
Benadryl: Kenvue
Ben's Original Rice: Mars
Betty Crocker products: General Mills
Blue Buffalo pet foods: General Mills
Bounty paper towels: Procter & Gamble
Braun appliances: Procter & Gamble
Brita water systems: Clorox
Cadbury chocolates: Mondelēz International
Calphalon cookware: Newell Rubbermaid
Canada Dry ginger ale: Keurig Dr Pepper
Cap'n Crunch cereal: PepsiCo
Cascade dishwasher detergent: Procter & Gamble
Charmin toilet tissue: Procter & Gamble
Cheer detergent: Procter & Gamble
Chips Ahoy!: Mondelēz International
Claritin allergy products: Bayer
Contadina tomatoes: Del Monte
Crest toothpaste: Procter & Gamble
Crisco shortening: B&G Foods
Dairy Queen: Berkshire Hathaway
Dasani water: Coca-Cola
Depends adult diapers: Kimberly-Clark
Dove soap: Unilever
Elmer's glue: Newell Rubbermaid
ESPN networks: Walt Disney
Febreze: Procter & Gamble
Fisher-Price toys: Mattel
Folgers coffee: J.M. Smucker
Frito-Lay's snacks: PepsiCo
Fruit of the Loom apparel: Berkshire Hathaway
Gatorade sports drinks: PepsiCo
GEICO auto insurance: Berkshire Hathaway
Gerber baby food: Nestlé
Gillette: Procter & Gamble
Glad products: Clorox
Glade air fresheners: S.C. Johnson
Green Giant vegetables: B&G Foods
Grey Poupon mustard: Kraft Heinz
Halls cough drops: Mondelēz International
HBO: Warner Bros. Discovery
Head & Shoulders shampoo: Procter & Gamble
Healthy Choice meals: ConAgra
Hebrew National meats: ConAgra
Hellmann's mayonnaise: Unilever
Hidden Valley Salad dressings: Clorox
Hill's Pet Nutrition: Colgate-Palmolive
Hillshire Farm: Tyson Foods
Hostess Twinkies: J.M. Smucker
Hot Pockets: Nestlé
Hot Wheels/Matchbox cars: Mattel
Huggies diapers: Kimberly-Clark
Hulu: Walt Disney
Hunt's tomatoes: ConAgra
Iams pet food: Mars
Irish Spring soap: Colgate-Palmolive
Ivory soap: Procter & Gamble
Jell-O: Kraft Heinz
Jennie-O turkey: Hormel
Jif peanut butter: J.M. Smucker
Jimmy Dean sausages: Tyson Foods
Jolly Rancher candy: Hershey
Keebler cookies: Ferrero
KFC restaurants: Yum! Brands
Kingsford charcoal: Clorox
KitchenAid appliances: Whirlpool
Kiwi shoe products: S.C. Johnson
Knorr soups: Unilever
Kool-Aid: Kraft Heinz
Kotex feminine products: Kimberly-Clark
Lean Cuisine meals: Nestlé
Listerine mouthwash: Kenvue
Maxwell House coffee: Kraft Heinz
Maytag appliances: Whirlpool
Meow Mix pet food: J.M. Smucker
Minute Maid juices: Coca-Cola
Mr. Clean: Procter & Gamble
Mr. Coffee: Newell Rubbermaid
National Geographic: Walt Disney
Mott's applesauce: Keurig Dr Pepper
Neosporin: Kenvue
Neutrogena soap: Kenvue
9Lives cat food: Post Holdings
o.b. tampons: Edgewell Personal Care
OFF! insect repellents: S.C. Johnson
Olay: Procter & Gamble
Old Navy clothing: Gap
Old Spice: Procter & Gamble
Oral-B toothbrushes: Procter & Gamble
Ore-Ida potatoes: Kraft Heinz
Oreo cookies: Mondelēz International
Oscar Mayer meats: Kraft Heinz
Pampers diapers: Procter & Gamble
Pantene shampoo: Procter & Gamble
Paper Mate pens: Newell Rubbermaid
Pepto-Bismol: Procter & Gamble
Perrier water: Nestlé
Peter Pan peanut butter: Post Holdings
Pine-Sol cleaner: Clorox
Pirates' Booty: Hershey
Pizza Hut restaurants: Yum! Brands
Planters nuts: Hormel
Popsicle frozen treats: Unilever
Post-it notes: 3M
Powerade sports drinks: Coca-Cola
Prego pasta sauce: Campbell's
Purina pet foods: Nestlé
Q-tips: Unilever

Quaker Oats: PepsiCo
Raid insecticide: S.C. Johnson
Reese's candy: Hershey
Rice-A-Roni: PepsiCo
Right Guard deodorant: Thriving Brands
Rogaine hair treatment: Kenvue
Roundup herbicide: Bayer
Saran wrap: S.C. Johnson
Schick razors: Edgewell Personal Care
Scope mouthwash: Procter & Gamble
Scotch tape: 3M
Showtime: Paramount
Skippy peanut butter: Hormel
Taco Bell restaurants: Yum! Brands
Tampax tampons: Procter & Gamble
Tang powdered beverages: Mondelēz International
Tide detergent: Procter & Gamble
Timberland apparel: VF Corp.
Tom's of Maine: Colgate-Palmolive
Trident gum: Mondelēz International
Trojan condoms: Church & Dwight
Tubi: Fox
Tums antacids: Haleon
Twitch: Amazon
Tylenol: Kenvue
Vaseline: Unilever
VCA animal hospitals: Mars
V8 vegetable juice: Campbell's
Velveeta cheese products: Kraft Heinz
Vicks cold medicines: Procter & Gamble
Visine eye drops: Kenvue
Windex cleaning products: S.C. Johnson
Wrigley's candy and gum: Mars
Yoplait yogurt: General Mills
Ziploc storage bags: S.C. Johnson

U.S. Home Ownership Rates by Selected Characteristics 1970-2024

Source: U.S. Census Bureau, U.S. Dept. of Commerce

	1970	1980	1990	1995	2000	2010	2015	2020	2022	2023	2024
Region											
Northeast	58.2%	60.8%	62.2%	62.3%	63.4%	64.2%	60.2%	62.4%	62.1%	62.5%	62.5%
Midwest	69.3	69.4	67.4	68.5	72.2	70.8	68.4	69.2	70.1	70.2	69.9
South	66.3	68.6	65.8	66.5	69.2	69.1	64.9	67.6	67.8	67.5	67.2
West	59.4	60.2	57.3	59.8	61.9	61.4	58.5	60.1	60.9	61.7	61.3
Age											
Under 35 years	—	—	—	38.7	40.2	39.0	34.8	37.3	39.1	38.5	37.4
35-44 years	—	—	—	65.1	67.5	65.6	58.0	61.5	61.9	63.1	62.2
45-54 years	—	—	—	75.2	76.7	73.6	69.9	70.3	70.6	70.8	71.1
55-64 years	—	—	—	79.9	80.3	78.7	75.4	76.3	75.1	75.5	75.8
65+ years	—	—	—	78.1	80.3	80.4	78.5	78.7	79.3	78.9	78.6
Race/ethnicity[1]											
White	—	—	—	70.2	73.7	74.4	71.6	73.7	74.6	74.5	74.4
Black	—	—	—	42.6	46.7	46.2	43.0	44.0	45.3	45.7	45.3
Hispanic	—	—	—	42.2	45.4	47.8	45.4	48.9	48.3	49.0	49.9
Other	—	—	—	47.6	54.4	55.7	52.6	56.0	57.3	58.0	58.3
Income[2]											
Median family income or greater	—	—	—	79.5	81.8	81.9	78.3	78.8	79.0	78.8	79.2
Less than median family income	—	—	—	48.6	50.8	51.9	48.6	51.8	52.6	53.0	52.1
Total U.S.	**64.0**	**65.5**	**63.7**	**64.7**	**67.2**	**66.9**	**63.4**	**65.3**	**65.8**	**65.9**	**65.6**

Note: Figures are for 2nd quarter of year shown, except in 2020, which shows 1st-quarter data (COVID-19 impaired completion of the survey for 2nd quarter). Not seasonally adjusted. (1) Hispanic householders may be of any race. "Other" includes householders self-identifying as Asian, Native Hawaiian/Pacific Islander, and American Indian/Alaska Native, as well as combinations of two or more races/ethnicities. (2) Due to a change in survey methodology, data from 2010 and later are not directly comparable with prior years.

U.S. Housing Affordability, 1990-2024

Source: National Association of REALTORS®

Year	Median-priced existing home	Average mortgage rate[1]	Monthly principal & interest payment	Payment as % of median monthly income	Year	Median-priced existing home	Average mortgage rate[1]	Monthly principal & interest payment	Payment as % of median monthly income
1990	$92,000	10.04%	$648	22.0%	2018	$261,600	4.72%	$1,088	17.1%
1995	110,500	7.85	639	18.9	2019	274,600	4.04	1,054	15.7
2000	139,000	8.03	818	19.3	2020	300,200	3.17	1,035	14.7
2005	219,000	5.91	1,040	22.4	2021	357,100	3.01	1,206	16.9
2010	173,100	4.89	734	14.5	2022	392,800	5.40	1,765	23.0
2015	223,900	4.03	858	15.1	2023	394,100	6.88	2,072	25.4
2017	248,800	4.20	973	15.8	2024[2]	432,700	7.00	2,303	26.8

(1) All figures assume a down payment of 20% of the home price. Based on effective rate on loans closed on existing homes for the period shown. (2) Preliminary figure for June 2024, the latest available. All other figures are annual averages.

S&P/Case-Shiller National Home Price Index, 1975-2024

Source: S&P Dow Jones Indices

This index compares the median price of existing U.S. homes over time. The baseline for comparison is Jan. 2000; all numbers before or after reflect home prices in relation to it. For example, the June 2024 index of 325.2 means that home prices were more than triple what they were 23 years earlier, while the Jan. 1975 index of 25.2 means prices then were 25.2% of what they were in 2000.

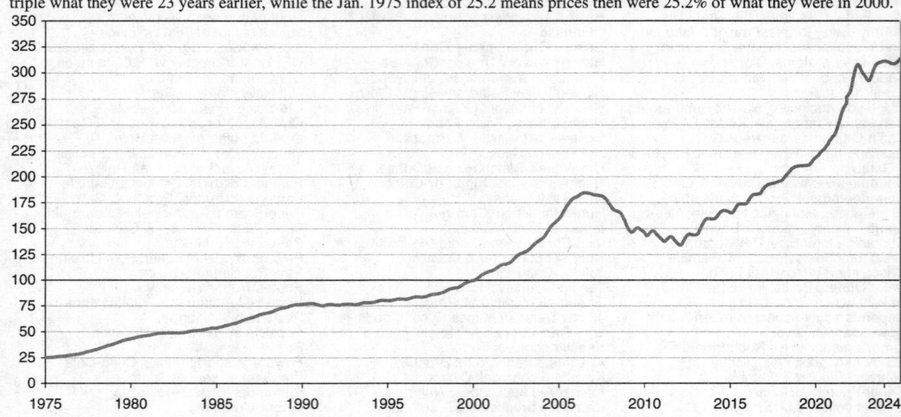

Median Price of Existing Single-Family Homes, by Metropolitan Area, 2010-24

Source: National Association of REALTORS®

Median prices are in thousands of dollars and based on all transactions within time period shown.

Metropolitan area	2010	2020	2024[1]
Akron, OH	$108.9	$168.1	$211.4
Albany-Schenectady-Troy, NY	195.7	232.5	319.7
Albuquerque, NM	178.7	248.1	371.9
Allentown-Bethlehem-Easton, PA-NJ	224.0	234.9	354.4
Anaheim-Santa Ana-Irvine, CA	546.4	900.0	1,437.5
Atlanta-Sandy Springs-Marietta, GA	114.8	260.8	387.8
Atlantic City-Hammonton, NJ	226.4	247.2	352.8
Austin-Round Rock, TX	193.6	367.1	496.5
Baltimore-Columbia-Towson, MD	246.1	328.5	428.6
Baton Rouge, LA	169.6	229.7	271.8
Beaumont-Port Arthur, TX	125.1	180.3	220.6
Birmingham-Hoover, AL	143.0	246.2	324.3
Boise City-Nampa, ID	136.2	353.9	510.7
Boston-Cambridge-Newton, MA-NH	357.3	563.7	793.4
Boulder, CO	358.1	645.9	888.3
Bridgeport-Stamford-Norwalk, CT	408.6	544.0	792.8
Buffalo-Cheektowaga-Niagara Falls, NY	121.2	178.5	261.0
Burlington-South Burlington, VT	261.2	342.9	528.9
Canton-Massillon, OH	90.9	155.4	207.5
Cape Coral-Fort Myers, FL	88.9	289.0	415.0
Champaign-Urbana, IL	141.9	168.6	223.6
Charleston-North Charleston, SC	200.5	324.4	457.0
Charleston, WV	129.1	147.5	193.2
Charlotte-Concord-Gastonia, NC-SC	143.3	296.2	423.7
Chattanooga, TN-GA	121.4	220.1	320.9
Chicago-Naperville-Elgin, IL-IN-WI	191.4	287.6	392.1
Cincinnati, OH-KY-IN	128.0	208.9	309.2
Cleveland-Elyria, OH	114.5	179.5	225.7
Colorado Springs, CO	195.5	361.7	479.6
Columbia, SC	142.6	202.9	281.5
Columbus, OH	136.4	240.8	339.6
Corpus Christi, TX	135.1	225.4	282.4
Crestview-Fort Walton Beach-Destin, FL	NA	339.9	420.0
Cumberland, MD-WV	100.3	120.9	152.8
Dallas-Fort Worth-Arlington, TX	143.8	287.2	391.3
Davenport-Moline-Rock Island, IA-IL	112.2	142.8	179.3
Dayton, OH	103.6	175.8	257.7
Deltona-Daytona Beach-Ormond Beach, FL	115.6	244.9	365.0
Denver-Aurora-Lakewood, CO	232.4	492.7	669.9
Des Moines-West Des Moines, IA	150.9	229.6	310.5
Detroit-Warren-Deaborn, MI	NA	221.3	280.7
Dover, DE	193.3	241.2	341.1
Durham-Chapel Hill, NC	158.3	326.3	477.6
Elmira, NY	101.0	120.4	150.6
El Paso, TX	134.3	177.8	264.4
Erie, PA	107.7	135.1	180.2
Eugene, OR	196.3	354.9	469.1
Fargo, ND-MN	146.4	233.5	310.8
Fayetteville, NC	152.5	163.2	252.4
Fayetteville-Springdale-Rogers, AR-MO	NA	226.3	372.8
Fort Collins, CO	NA	446.0	637.0
Fort Wayne, IN	97.4	169.3	248.6
Fresno, CA	NA	314.0	425.0
Gainesville, FL	161.6	255.0	360.7
Gary-Hammond, IN	122.9	203.4	275.6
Grand Rapids-Wyoming, MI	91.5	230.1	347.2
Green Bay, WI	130.4	204.2	316.1
Greensboro-High Point, NC	129.8	199.2	302.4
Greenville-Anderson-Mauldin, SC	145.3	240.9	338.8
Gulfport-Biloxi-Pascagoulia, MS	125.0	171.3	226.6
Harrisburg-Carlisle, PA	NA	195.8	273.4
Hartford-West Hartford-East Hartford, CT	235.8	264.5	396.1
Honolulu, HI	607.6	851.5	1,101.5
Houston-The Woodlands-Sugar Land, TX	155.0	263.8	351.6
Huntsville, AL	NA	248.0	325.3
Indianapolis-Carmel-Anderson, IN	123.3	227.6	329.7
Jackson, MS	133.2	198.8	239.1
Jacksonville, FL	137.7	279.0	408.0
Kansas City, MO-KS	141.6	237.4	346.6
Knoxville, TN	140.9	229.8	366.4
Lakeland-Winter Haven, FL	NA	230.0	335.0
Lansing-East Lansing, MI	84.4	173.3	240.3
Las Vegas-Henderson-Paradise, NV	$138.0	$331.0	$478.8
Lexington-Fayette, KY	143.2	201.2	280.4
Lincoln, NE	133.6	219.8	298.7
Little Rock-North Little Rock-Conway, AR	132.5	166.9	219.5
Los Angeles-Long Beach-Glendale, CA	323.3	673.1	854.8
Louisville/Jefferson County, KY-IN	134.6	212.1	283.1
Madison, WI	217.7	326.4	470.8
Manchester-Nashua, NH	232.0	357.8	568.7
Memphis, TN-MS-AR	120.2	221.2	289.2
Miami-Fort Lauderdale-West Palm Beach, FL	201.9	398.0	646.0
Milwaukee-Waukesha-West Allis, WI	205.9	291.3	408.9
Minneapolis-St. Paul-Bloomington, MN-WI	170.6	315.2	398.3
Mobile, AL	121.0	167.1	230.5
Montgomery, AL	129.0	171.0	225.8
Myrtle Beach-Conway-North Myrtle Beach, SC-NC	NA	250.2	367.3
Nashville-Davidson–Murfreesboro–Franklin, TN	153.8	298.9	421.0
New Haven-Milford, CT	231.0	265.9	396.3
New Orleans-Metairie, LA	159.7	240.5	290.5
New York-Newark-Jersey City, NY-NJ-PA	393.7	469.1	705.7
North Port-Sarasota-Bradenton, FL	164.6	334.9	525.0
Oklahoma City, OK	145.7	174.9	262.7
Omaha-Council Bluffs, NE-IA	137.3	220.6	313.2
Orlando-Kissimmee-Sanford, FL	134.7	301.6	450.0
Palm Bay-Melbourne-Titusville, FL	103.0	260.4	374.0
Pensacola-Ferry Pass-Brent, FL	141.0	240.0	335.0
Peoria, IL	116.9	128.1	168.5
Philadelphia-Camden-Wilmington, PA-NJ-DE-MD	214.9	272.9	381.2
Phoenix-Mesa-Scottsdale, AZ	139.2	333.0	480.4
Pittsburgh, PA	NA	182.3	236.1
Portland-South Portland, ME	NA	356.2	566.4
Portland-Vancouver-Hillsboro, OR-WA	237.3	451.0	608.5
Providence-Warwick, RI-MA	228.5	347.3	504.8
Raleigh, NC	190.4	325.2	484.9
Reading, PA	153.3	190.8	281.1
Reno, NV	179.5	440.8	620.4
Richmond, VA	NA	303.4	444.4
Riverside-San Bernardino-Ontario, CA	179.3	422.6	600.0
Rochester, NY	118.9	170.4	268.9
Rockford, IL	106.9	141.3	197.7
Sacramento–Roseville–Arden-Arcade, CA	184.2	421.0	555.0
St. Louis, MO-IL	131.1	205.8	279.9
Salem, OR	173.5	353.6	456.1
Salt Lake City, UT	206.5	391.0	583.2
San Antonio-New Braunfels, TX	151.0	254.3	321.8
San Diego-Carlsbad, CA	385.7	710.0	1,050.0
San Francisco-Oakland-Hayward, CA	525.6	1,100.0	1,449.0
San Jose-Sunnyvale-Santa Clara, CA	595.0	1,385.0	2,008.0
Seattle-Tacoma-Bellevue, WA	295.7	596.9	829.6
Shreveport-Bossier City, LA	156.6	179.5	239.8
Spokane-Spokane Valley, WA	172.2	307.4	435.1
Springfield, IL	124.0	148.0	186.6
Springfield, MA	190.0	249.0	364.9
Springfield, MO	109.1	172.1	250.4
Syracuse, NY	125.1	161.4	233.2
Tallahassee, FL	152.8	248.0	342.0
Tampa-St. Petersburg-Clearwater, FL	134.2	272.0	420.0
Toledo, OH	81.5	145.2	188.5
Trenton, NJ	250.7	300.0	467.2
Tucson, AZ	156.6	265.1	396.9
Tulsa, OK	132.3	195.9	273.0
Virginia Beach-Norfolk-Newport News, VA-NC	205.0	275.0	361.0
Washington-Arlington-Alexandria, DC-VA-MD-WV	325.3	475.4	666.6
Wichita, KS	118.7	175.0	224.5
Winston-Salem, NC	134.7	202.4	303.2
Worcester, MA-CT	223.3	325.2	473.4
York-Hanover, PA	158.6	199.3	275.7
Youngstown-Warren-Boardman, OH-PA	67.2	119.0	164.7

NA = Not available. (1) Preliminary figures for second quarter 2024.

Characteristics of American Housing Units, 2011-23

Source: *American Housing Survey, 2011-23*, U.S. Census Bureau, U.S. Dept. of Commerce

Characteristic	2011	2019	2021	2023
Total housing units	**114,833**	**124,135**	**128,504**	**133,231**
	Percentage of all homes			
Units in structure				
1, detached	64.3%	63.9%	63.6%	64.0%
1, attached	5.8	5.2	6.3	6.1
2-4	7.8	7.3	6.6	6.9
5-9	4.8	4.8	4.3	4.3
10-19	4.4	4.2	5.4	4.2
20-49	3.2	3.8	3.5	3.7
50 or more	3.6	5.2	4.9	5.5
Manufactured/mobile home or trailer	6.1	5.4	5.2	5.4
Condominiums	6.4	6.0	6.0	6.5
Year built				
2022-23	NA	NA	NA	0.8
2020-21	NA	NA	0.8	2.3
2015-19	NA	2.8	4.6	4.1
2010-14	NA	4.4	3.9	4.2
2005-09	6.1	6.4	6.0	5.8
2000-04	7.1	7.6	8.0	7.6
1995-99	6.9	7.6	7.1	6.8
1990-94	5.3	5.3	5.3	5.3
1985-89	6.8	7.2	6.8	6.8
1980-84	5.8	6.1	6.3	6.4
1970-79	18.7	14.5	14.4	14.2
1960-69	11.8	10.6	10.3	10.1
1950-59	10.3	10.3	9.6	9.4
1940-49	5.8	4.5	4.5	4.2
1930-39	4.2	2.8	2.5	2.4
1920-29	4.0	3.8	3.8	4.0
1919 or earlier	6.7	6.2	6.0	5.8
Median year built	*1974*	*1978*	*1979*	*1979*
Lot size (single-family homes only)				
Less than 1/8 acre	15.6	10.1	14.4	14.0
1/8-1/4 acre	25.8	23.8	33.5	32.9
1/4-1/2 acre	18.8	14.0	19.5	19.7
1/2-1 acre	12.0	6.9	9.3	9.7
1-5 acres	20.0	11.3	15.1	15.2
5-10 acres	3.2	2.4	3.2	3.4
10+ acres	4.7	3.7	4.9	5.2
Square footage of unit				
Less than 500	2.7	2.4	2.3	2.4
500-749	6.7	6.5	6.4	6.6
750-999	11.1	11.8	11.8	11.7
1,000-1,499	23.0%	23.6%	23.6%	23.3%
1,500-1,999	18.6	18.5	18.6	18.9
2,000-2,499	12.4	12.3	12.3	12.5
2,500-2,999	6.4	6.6	6.5	6.8
3,000-3,999	6.1	6.2	6.2	4.4
4,000 or more	3.9	3.2	3.1	3.2
Number of bedrooms				
None	0.8	0.7	0.8	0.7
1	10.4	11.1	10.9	11.0
2	24.9	24.5	24.5	24.2
3	42.4	39.9	40.1	39.5
4 or more	21.4	23.8	23.7	24.5
Number of complete bathrooms				
1	34.2	31.6	31.0	30.2
1-1/2	13.2	11.4	11.0	10.4
2	52.2[1]	31.0	31.5	32.0
2-1/2	NA	13.5	13.6	13.7
3 or more	NA	12.4	13.0	13.6
Mortgage characteristics				
None, owned free and clear	34.0	26.6	41.9	42.0
One regular mortgage only	56.6	33.2	51.6	51.4
Two or more regular mortgages	8.8	1.2	1.3	1.2
Median outstanding loan amount	*$120,000*	*$136,500*	*$150,000*	*$160,000*
Equipment				
Washing machine	83.2	85.8	85.9	86.9
Clothes dryer	81.0	84.5	84.8	85.8
Dishwasher	67.0	73.9	74.6	75.4
Central air conditioning	65.7	71.4	72.4	74.9
Main heating fuel[2]				
Electricity	35.0	44.0	44.9	44.9
Piped gas	50.6	45.1	44.8	44.8
Bottled gas	4.8	4.3	4.3	4.3
Fuel oil	7.0	4.5	4.0	4.0

NA = Not applicable/not available. (1) Figure is for 2 or more bathrooms. (2) Not all heating fuels are shown here.

Fair Market Rents for Select Metropolitan Areas, 2025

Source: *Fair Market Rents FY 2025*, U.S. Dept. of Housing and Urban Development (HUD)

Metropolitan area	Number of bedrooms 0	1	2	3	4
Atlanta, GA	$1,591	$1,653	$1,830	$2,205	$2,653
Austin, TX	1,549	1,650	1,949	2,484	2,882
Baltimore, MD	1,407	1,604	1,965	2,529	2,826
Birmingham, AL	998	1,144	1,267	1,583	1,791
Boston, MA	2,163	2,288	2,711	3,266	3,594
Buffalo, NY	968	1,001	1,176	1,438	1,625
Charlotte, NC	1,586	1,647	1,824	2,250	2,852
Chicago, IL	1,458	1,560	1,761	2,262	2,657
Cincinnati, OH	883	993	1,287	1,707	1,885
Cleveland, OH	881	995	1,208	1,553	1,667
Columbus, OH	1,104	1,194	1,445	1,741	1,939
Dallas, TX	1,531	1,606	1,884	2,361	3,033
Denver, CO	1,639	1,789	2,140	2,794	3,127
Detroit, MI	991	1,090	1,378	1,688	1,827
Hartford, CT	1,133	1,306	1,653	1,992	2,363
Honolulu, HI	1,887	2,052	2,687	3,765	4,512
Houston, TX	1,226	1,279	1,529	2,038	2,568
Indianapolis, IN	955	1,097	1,283	1,669	2,028
Jacksonville, FL	1,381	1,454	1,730	2,163	2,739
Kansas City, MO	1,074	1,183	1,346	1,756	2,078
Las Vegas, NV	1,316	1,476	1,750	2,452	2,841
Los Angeles, CA	1,856	2,081	2,625	3,335	3,698
Louisville, KY	1,003	1,094	1,330	1,714	1,989
Memphis, TN	1,105	1,207	1,355	1,781	2,086
Miami, FL	1,711	1,898	2,329	3,008	3,527
Milwaukee, WI	$939	$1,056	$1,257	$1,558	$1,701
Minneapolis, MN	1,220	1,381	1,685	2,244	2,513
Nashville, TN	1,589	1,650	1,827	2,308	2,840
New Orleans, LA	1,071	1,236	1,478	1,889	2,217
New York, NY	2,233	2,330	2,580	3,215	3,469
Oklahoma City, OK	886	961	1,180	1,575	1,719
Orlando, FL	1,636	1,727	1,958	2,486	2,960
Philadelphia, PA	1,372	1,512	1,802	2,171	2,468
Phoenix, AZ	1,530	1,679	1,950	2,624	2,934
Pittsburgh, PA	998	1,068	1,280	1,632	1,759
Portland, OR	1,628	1,750	1,997	2,739	3,217
Providence, RI	1,233	1,319	1,614	1,945	2,359
Richmond, VA	1,488	1,545	1,711	2,166	2,677
Riverside, CA	1,776	1,852	2,306	3,079	3,745
Sacramento, CA	1,679	1,777	2,206	2,992	3,455
St. Louis, MO	951	984	1,215	1,570	1,806
Salt Lake City, UT	1,243	1,453	1,748	2,348	2,670
San Antonio, TX	1,116	1,231	1,501	1,907	2,243
San Diego, CA	2,145	2,328	2,881	3,852	4,690
San Francisco, CA	2,275	2,780	3,318	4,138	4,399
San Jose, CA	2,608	2,975	3,446	4,477	4,878
San Juan, PR	552	569	656	861	1,033
Seattle, WA	2,238	2,293	2,671	3,521	4,104
Tampa, FL	1,566	1,686	1,978	2,533	3,082
Washington, DC	2,012	2,056	2,314	2,893	3,413

Note: Figures are projections made in the previous fiscal year. Metropolitan areas include adjacent cities/states not shown here. Fair market rents are primarily used by HUD to determine payment standard amounts for the Housing Choice Voucher program.

Rental Vacancy Rates in U.S. Metropolitan Areas, 1990-2023

Source: *Housing Vacancies and Homeownership, 2024*, U.S. Census Bureau, U.S. Dept. of Commerce

MSA	1990	2000	2010	2020	2023
All metropolitan areas	**7.1%**	**7.7%**	**10.3%**	**6.1%**	**6.5%**
Akron, OH	NA	8.1	12.5	6.1	4.9
Albany, NY	7.2	9.3	8.0	9.5	4.1
Albuquerque, NM	11.6	9.3	5.0	5.4	6.1
Allentown, PA-NJ	NA	4.6	9.1	3.9	7.9
Atlanta, GA	5.2	5.4	13.8	6.4	8.7
Austin, TX	6.6	1.9	11.8	6.6	9.0
Baltimore, MD	5.2	23.3	6.3	7.0	9.4
Baton Rouge, LA	6.0	2.7	11.8	7.4	6.6
Birmingham, AL	3.4	17.5	9.4	18.5	12.2
Boston, MA-NH	5.9	8.8	8.8	4.7	2.5
Bridgeport, CT	6.6	6.9	6.2	3.4	3.0
Buffalo, NY	6.3	10.6	8.7	5.0	9.7
Charleston, SC	5.0	10.5	11.2	27.7	12.0
Charlotte, NC-SC	12.3	9.2	12.1	5.6	6.6
Chicago, IL-IN-WI	5.0	8.2	12.0	7.4	5.6
Cincinnati, OH-KY-IN	8.9	4.6	11.3	7.9	7.2
Cleveland, OH	7.6	8.7	9.4	5.5	4.7
Columbia, SC	NA	8.7	8.0	4.5	8.5
Columbus, OH	8.0	6.2	13.5	5.9	5.8
Dallas-Ft. Worth, TX	8.9	6.9	18.6	7.2	8.4
Dayton, OH	NA	6.9	8.2	4.1	5.3
Denver, CO	7.9	8.9	16.4	4.8	5.3
Detroit, MI	NA	7.6	5.8	5.7	9.3
Fort Myers, FL	7.8	8.4	11.1	15.5	15.3
Fresno, CA	11.2	10.9	10.1	0.8	3.4
Grand Rapids, MI	3.8	4.9	6.9	4.6	3.2
Greensboro NC	9.6	13.4	12.8	7.2	5.7
Hartford, CT	6.1	12.3	11.6	8.1	4.9
Honolulu, HI	NA	10.8	15.9	5.5	6.8
Houston, TX	9.5	9.9	7.2	9.7	10.9
Indianapolis, IN	9.9	8.8	16.2	10.4	8.8
Jacksonville, FL	NA	10.7	14.1	7.5	9.4
Kansas City, MO-KS	6.2	4.7	13.9	9.4	7.6
Knoxville, TN	7.5	7.2	14.0	4.5	4.2
Las Vegas, NV	10.2	7.1	13.8	5.0	7.2
Little Rock, AR	6.3	8.8	6.7	9.1	10.8
Los Angeles, CA	5.2	4.0	9.6	3.6	4.0
Louisville, KY-IN	3.6	5.9	18.5	6.4	3.6
Memphis, TN-AR-MS	6.5	3.9	10.1	6.6	11.4
Miami, FL	8.3%	4.0%	7.6%	5.4%	8.4%
Milwaukee, WI	11.3	3.5	7.4	4.6	4.1
Minneapolis-St. Paul, MN-WI	6.5	2.7	8.2	4.0	8.1
Nashville, TN	13.8	15.5	11.1	7.3	9.3
New Haven, CT	4.7	4.0	15.2	7.8	3.3
New Orleans, LA	4.1	6.2	6.6	6.1	9.2
New York, NY-NJ-PA	9.2	6.8	9.6	4.5	3.9
Oklahoma City, OK	22.6	16.0	19.0	6.4	10.6
Omaha, NE-IA	NA	7.6	6.4	6.5	4.3
Orlando, FL	4.8	2.2	11.6	8.6	7.0
Philadelphia, PA-NJ-DE-MD	10.1	7.4	16.3	5.4	5.2
Phoenix, AZ	9.6	8.3	7.8	4.9	8.0
Pittsburgh, PA	10.3	9.6	4.2	9.3	6.3
Portland, OR-WA	8.3	10.3	9.5	4.3	6.8
Providence, RI-MA	3.3	6.4	7.5	3.5	3.7
Raleigh, NC	9.4	4.8	11.4	2.3	8.8
Richmond, VA	NA	13.8	13.5	2.7	5.2
Riverside-San Bernardino, CA	5.3	6.1	12.3	4.4	3.7
Rochester, NY	5.6	11.6	6.3	2.0	2.0
Sacramento, CA	7.4	5.6	8.4	4.2	4.2
St. Louis, MO-IL	7.8	6.5	11.2	5.3	7.8
Salt Lake City, UT	11.7	7.5	6.0	6.2	6.2
San Antonio, TX	9.9	7.5	14.0	7.2	8.8
San Diego, CA	6.9	4.0	7.8	3.9	4.1
San Francisco, CA	4.2	3.1	6.0	5.3	6.6
San Jose, CA	4.6	3.0	8.2	4.4	3.3
Sarasota, FL	6.3	4.2	10.1	10.3	5.4
Seattle, WA	NA	3.0	7.4	3.6	4.0
Syracuse, NY	3.1	5.4	7.3	11.8	6.4
Tampa, FL	10.7	16.4	10.6	8.9	8.5
Toledo, OH	NA	10.7	12.6	6.2	7.2
Tucson, AZ	10.4	9.5	14.4	8.6	10.2
Tulsa, OK	NA	9.1	11.1	8.6	6.7
Virginia Beach, VA-NC	NA	3.0	8.8	5.5	5.1
Washington, DC-VA-MD-WV	6.7	7.0	8.8	5.5	5.5
Worcester, MA	NA	22.9	7.5	1.3	1.9

MSA = Metropolitan statistical area. NA = Not available.

Affordable Housing Shortages in U.S. Metropolitan Areas, 2023

Source: *The Gap: A Shortage of Affordable Homes, 2024*, National Low Income Housing Coalition

Affordable housing is in short supply in every state in the U.S. and in all of the 50 largest metropolitan areas. The table below shows the number of affordable and available homes per 100 households at two income levels: very low income, defined as earning 20%-50% of the area median income, and extremely low income, those households earning 20% or less of the area median income.

	Affordable and available homes per 100 households		Deficit of affordable and available homes	
Metro area	Very low income	Extremely low income	Very low income	Extremely low income
Atlanta, GA	44	25	161,422	122,791
Austin, TX	46	21	74,883	60,429
Baltimore, MD	57	33	68,527	65,241
Boston, MA	56	46	147,169	117,411
Buffalo, NY	72	37	22,727	33,156
Charlotte, NC	55	35	58,064	45,765
Chicago, IL	58	29	230,890	239,240
Cincinnati, OH	76	41	32,868	49,510
Cleveland, OH	77	38	33,012	56,560
Columbus, OH	62	26	48,343	52,694
Dallas, TX	40	17	244,497	179,108
Denver, CO	41	27	93,256	65,454
Detroit, MI	63	32	85,325	99,583
Hartford, CT	70	34	22,866	32,956
Houston, TX	40	15	230,680	184,283
Indianapolis, IN	67	23	38,789	50,554
Jacksonville, FL	47	29	40,303	32,328
Kansas City, MO	66	36	43,045	46,042
Las Vegas, NV	23	13	91,209	60,344
Los Angeles, CA	27	21	582,884	380,006
Louisville, KY	70	31	20,647	30,218
Memphis, TN	59	36	29,323	29,064
Miami, FL	25	23	226,085	140,763
Milwaukee, WI	75	30	28,174	44,596
Minneapolis, MN	61	28	73,248	79,282
Nashville, TN	53	36	46,507	35,086
New Orleans, LA	43	29	44,558	35,856
New York, NY	46	32	802,969	656,458
Oklahoma City, OK	66	33	28,604	34,735
Orlando, FL	24	18	94,715	56,895
Philadelphia, PA	61	34	142,974	153,236
Phoenix, AZ	34	19	128,908	89,838
Pittsburgh, PA	84	49	21,259	44,088
Portland, OR	39	25	80,971	56,972
Providence, RI	66	49	40,786	39,709
Raleigh, NC	74	37	18,385	23,357
Richmond, VA	60	24	30,226	37,164
Riverside, CA	34	21	113,722	72,055
Rochester, NY	68	35	22,090	29,134
Sacramento, CA	38	23	75,930	56,693
St. Louis, MO	80	35	31,506	63,984
San Antonio, TX	37	28	82,623	55,338
San Diego, CA	27	20	126,617	82,307
San Francisco, CA	48	32	153,670	132,227
San Jose, CA	48	33	57,912	45,752
Seattle, WA	39	26	143,381	101,139
Tampa, FL	36	21	94,696	69,630
Tucson, AZ	45	24	34,568	26,615
Virginia Beach, VA	43	26	54,300	42,532
Washington, DC	53	26	156,133	144,435
United States	**56**	**34**	**7,956,742**	**7,277,489**

U.S. Trade in Goods With Selected Countries and Major Areas, 2023

Source: U.S. Census Bureau and U.S. Bureau of Economic Analysis, U.S. Dept. of Commerce; *World Development Indicators 2023*, The World Bank

Weighted mean tariff rate is the average of tariffs applied to all products weighted by the product's share of the country's imports. A low tariff on a heavily imported product, therefore, has more impact on the weighted mean tariff rate than a high tariff on a product that is rarely imported.

(trade in millions of dollars; top 25 countries as ranked by amount of total trade in goods with U.S.)

Rank	Country	Total trade with U.S.	U.S. exports to (rank)	U.S. imports from (rank)	U.S. trade balance with (rank[1])	Weighted mean tariff rate, 2021
1.	Mexico	$797,959	$322,743 (2)	$475,216 (1)	–$152,474 (2)	NA
2.	Canada	772,975	354,356 (1)	418,619 (3)	–64,263 (7)	2.4%
3.	China[2]	574,663	147,778 (3)	426,885 (2)	–279,107 (1)	2.3
4.	Germany	235,970	76,698 (5)	159,272 (4)	–82,574 (4)	1.4
5.	Japan	222,921	75,683 (6)	147,238 (5)	–71,555 (5)	1.8
6.	South Korea	181,211	65,056 (8)	116,155 (6)	–51,098 (8)	4.9
7.	United Kingdom	138,532	74,315 (7)	64,217 (12)	10,098 (227)	0.7
8.	Taiwan	127,724	39,957 (13)	87,767 (8)	–47,811 (9)	NA
9.	Vietnam	124,269	9,843 (34)	114,426 (7)	–104,583 (3)	1.2
10.	India	124,061	40,375 (12)	83,686 (9)	–43,311 (11)	5.9
11.	Netherlands	119,836	81,310 (4)	38,526 (19)	42,783 (233)	1.4
12.	Italy	101,781	28,860 (16)	72,921 (11)	–44,061 (10)	1.4
13.	France	101,502	43,878 (10)	57,624 (13)	–13,746 (16)	1.4
14.	Ireland	99,115	16,781 (24)	82,334 (10)	–65,554 (6)	1.4
15.	Brazil	83,705	44,639 (9)	39,066 (18)	5,573 (225)	7.8
16.	Singapore	83,370	42,447 (11)	40,924 (17)	1,523 (210)	0.0
17.	Switzerland	80,076	27,780 (18)	52,296 (15)	–24,517 (14)	1.4
18.	Thailand	71,839	15,557 (25)	56,282 (14)	–40,725 (12)	3.2
19.	Malaysia	65,549	19,358 (21)	46,191 (16)	–26,833 (13)	3.6
20.	Belgium	61,644	38,818 (14)	22,826 (22)	15,992 (229)	1.4
21.	Australia	49,508	33,568 (15)	15,940 (27)	17,628 (230)	0.8
22.	Spain	48,283	25,161 (19)	23,122 (21)	2,039 (214)	1.4
23.	Indonesia	36,637	9,838 (35)	26,798 (20)	–16,960 (15)	1.8
24.	Israel	34,795	13,978 (27)	20,817 (23)	–6,838 (23)	2.9
25.	Chile	34,362	18,774 (22)	15,589 (29)	3,185 (221)	0.4
Major area/group						
	North America	$1,570,933	$677,099	$893,835	–$216,736	
	Europe	1,222,290	496,459	725,831	–229,372	
	Euro Area	842,489	333,240	509,249	–176,009	
	EU	943,940	367,626	576,314	–208,688	
	Africa	67,481	28,722	38,760	–10,038	
	OECD	3,291,493	1,370,755	1,920,738	–549,983	
	Pacific Rim Countries	1,407,135	475,884	931,251	–455,367	
	Asia-Near East	129,776	68,304	61,472	6,832	
	Asia-South	144,975	45,131	99,844	–54,713	
	ASEAN	417,862	106,969	310,893	–203,924	
	APEC	3,233,641	1,209,090	2,024,551	–815,460	
	South/Central America	344,918	199,650	145,268	54,382	
	Twenty Latin Amer. Reps.	1,111,945	500,631	611,315	–110,684	
	Latin Amer. Free Trade Association	1,017,589	442,713	574,876	–132,163	
	CAFTA-DR	80,241	45,151	35,090	10,061	
	Central Amer. Common Market	60,175	32,142	28,032	4,110	
	NATO Allies	1,733,759	780,691	953,068	–172,377	
	WORLD TOTAL	**5,098,230**	**2,018,059**	**3,080,170**	**–1,062,111**	

NA = Not available. **Note:** Figures shown are on Census Bureau basis and are not seasonally adjusted. Figures may not equal totals due to rounding. Country grouping data reflect groups at the time of reporting. Rankings include territories as well as nations. (1) Rank by size of U.S. trade deficit. (2) Not incl. Hong Kong and Macau.

Countries With Highest and Lowest Mean Tariff Rates, 2021

Source: *World Development Indicators 2023*, The World Bank

HIGHEST MEAN TARIFF RATES

Rank	Country	Weighted mean tariff rate[1]
1.	Bermuda	23.84%
2.	Cayman Islands	20.39
3.	Belize	17.79
4.	The Gambia	17.69
5.	Solomon Islands	14.31
6.	Sierra Leone	14.22
7.	Nauru	14.07
8.	Venezuela	13.61
9.	Antigua and Barbuda	13.07
10.	Ethiopia	12.66
11.	Guinea	12.26
12.	Barbados	12.24
13.	Nigeria	12.20
14.	Iran	12.09[2]
15.	Nepal	11.99
16.	Rwanda	11.97
17.	Guinea-Bissau	11.82
18.	Zimbabwe	11.37
19.	Angola	11.33
20.	Vanuatu	11.08

LOWEST MEAN TARIFF RATES

Rank	Country	Weighted mean tariff rate[1]
1.	Singapore	0.00%
2.	Sudan	0.00
3.	Macau	0.00
4.	Hong Kong	0.00
5.	Brunei	0.02
6.	Georgia	0.34
7.	Chile	0.43
8.	Peru	0.65
9.	United Kingdom	0.72
10.	Australia	0.81
11.	New Zealand	0.86
12.	Botswana	0.95
13.	Myanmar	1.04
14.	Seychelles	1.07
15.	Laos	1.12
16.	Albania	1.13
17.	Vietnam	1.17
18.	Moldova	1.20
19.	Mauritius	1.27
20.	Namibia	1.32

Note: List only includes countries for which 2020 or 2021 data was available. (1) 2021 unless otherwise noted. (2) 2020.

U.S. Exports and Imports by Principal Commodities, 2023

Source: U.S. Census Bureau and U.S. Bureau of Economic Analysis, U.S. Dept. of Commerce

(in millions of dollars)

Item	Exports	Imports
Total[1]	**$2,018,059**	**$3,080,170**
Manufactured goods	**1,290,332**	**2,667,667**
Agricultural commodities	**174,172**	**195,859**
Food and live animals	**121,236**	**156,260**
Live animals other than fish	1,124	4,016
Meat and preparations	23,724	13,752
Dairy products and birds	6,869	3,526
Fish and preparations	4,637	24,953
Cereals and preparations	28,197	17,520
Vegetables and fruits	23,031	50,139
Sugar, preparations, and honey	2,596	7,254
Coffee, tea, cocoa, and spices	3,370	17,444
Feeding stuff for animals	16,715	5,096
Miscellaneous edible products	10,973	12,560
Beverages and tobacco	**6,638**	**31,605**
Beverages	5,350	29,135
Tobacco and manufactures	1,289	2,470
Crude materials except fuels	**91,439**	**39,553**
Hides, skins, and furskins (raw)	981	28
Oil seeds and oleaginous fruits	30,387	1,471
Crude rubber	2,487	2,753
Cork and wood	6,835	9,392
Pulp and waste paper	8,542	3,905
Textile fibers including waste	8,141	1,321
Crude fertilizers	3,101	3,319
Metalliferous ores and metal scrap	27,668	9,820
Crude animal and vegetable materials	3,297	7,544
Mineral fuels and lubricants	**317,057**	**251,865**
Coal, coke, and briquettes	16,125	1,134
Petroleum products and preparations	233,356	235,236
Gas, natural and manufactured	66,389	12,336
Electric current	1,187	3,159
Animal and vegetable oils	**1,917**	**14,901**
Animal oil and fat	599	1,551
Fixed vegetable fats and oil, crude	917	11,481
Animal or vegetable fats, processed	400	1,870
Chemicals and related products	**269,024**	**361,745**
Organic chemicals	47,604	54,119
Inorganic chemicals	14,202	16,189
Dyeing, tanning, and coloring materials	7,674	4,780
Medicinal and pharmaceutical products	77,247	190,392
Essential oil and retinoids	18,059	23,227
Fertilizers	$4,093	$9,053
Plastics in primary forms	41,718	18,013
Plastics in nonprimary forms	15,491	14,481
Chemical materials and products	42,937	31,490
Manufactured goods by material	**118,661**	**310,449**
Leather and leather manufactures	627	1,176
Rubber manufactures	10,180	27,878
Cork and wood manufactures	2,370	13,326
Paper and paperboard	14,459	19,115
Textile yarn, fabrics	10,899	30,308
Nonmetallic mineral manufactures	15,235	48,531
Iron and steel	17,222	43,384
Nonferrous metals	17,527	57,065
Manufactures of metals	30,142	69,667
Machinery and transport equipment	**545,289**	**1,312,443**
Power-generating machinery	40,087	83,198
Specialized industrial machinery	52,709	79,657
Metalworking machinery	5,436	12,872
General industrial machinery	69,050	137,517
Office machinery	19,957	149,699
Telecommunications equipment	21,411	173,778
Electrical machinery	87,893	273,173
Road vehicles	137,716	366,600
Transport equipment	111,029	35,949
Miscellaneous manufactured articles	**134,135**	**456,383**
Prefabricated buildings	2,247	12,899
Furniture	5,617	53,038
Travel goods	706	11,267
Apparel and clothing accessories	3,245	85,973
Footwear	913	25,728
Scientific and controlling equipment	56,528	80,352
Photographic equipment	6,019	17,440
Miscellaneous manufactured articles	58,859	169,686
Miscellaneous commodities	**83,699**	**144,965**
Special transactions	9,497	100,658
Coin, including gold coin	185	4,062
Coin, other than gold	53	1,320
Gold, nonmonetary	19,809	15,546
Low value estimate	54,155	23,380
Re-exports	**328,966**	**NA**
Agricultural commodities	6,561	NA
Manufactured goods	311,667	NA

NA = Not applicable. **Note:** Numbers may not add up to totals due to rounding. (1) Total on Census Bureau basis; includes re-exports.

Trends in U.S. Foreign Trade, 1790-2023

Source: U.S. Census Bureau and U.S. Bureau of Economic Analysis, U.S. Dept. of Commerce

In 1790, U.S. exports and imports combined came to $43 mil, and there was a $3 mil trade deficit. The trade balance was positive for much of the 20th century, but the U.S. has had a trade deficit every year starting in 1976.

(in millions of dollars)

Year	Exports	Imports	Trade balance	Year	Exports	Imports	Trade balance	Year	Exports	Imports	Trade balance
1790	$20	$23	–$3	1900	$1,394	$850	$545	2000	$1,082,963	$1,452,648	–$369,685
1800	71	91	–20	1905	1,519	1,118	401	2005	1,291,503	2,008,046	–716,543
1810	67	85	–19	1910	1,745	1,557	188	2006	1,463,992	2,227,524	–763,532
1815	53	113	–60	1915	2,769	1,674	1,094	2007	1,660,813	2,371,812	–710,998
1820	70	74	–5	1920	8,228	5,278	2,950	2008	1,849,585	2,561,937	–712,351
1825	91	90	1	1925	4,910	4,227	683	2009	1,592,791	1,987,563	–394,772
1830	72	63	9	1930	3,843	3,061	782	2010	1,872,318	2,375,408	–503,090
1835	115	137	–22	1935	2,283	2,047	235	2011	2,143,551	2,698,074	–554,522
1840	124	98	25	1940	4,021	2,625	1,396	2012	2,247,453	2,773,359	–525,906
1845	106	113	–7	1945	9,806	4,159	5,646	2013	2,313,121	2,759,982	–446,861
1850	144	174	–29	1950	9,997	8,954	1,043	2014	2,392,615	2,876,566	–483,952
1855	219	258	–39	1955	14,298	11,566	2,732	2015	2,280,778	2,771,554	–490,776
1860	334	354	–20	1960	25,939	22,433	3,508	2016	2,240,823	2,720,281	–479,458
1865	166	239	–73	1965	35,285	30,621	4,664	2017	2,394,476	2,911,415	–516,939
1870	393	436	–43	1970	56,640	54,385	2,255	2018	2,542,462	3,121,057	–578,594
1875	513	533	–20	1975	132,585	120,181	12,403	2019	2,546,276	3,105,670	–559,395
1880	836	668	168	1980	271,835	291,242	–19,407	2020	2,160,147	2,813,028	–652,881
1885	742	578	165	1985	289,071	410,951	–121,879	2021	2,567,027	3,408,600	–841,573
1890	858	789	69	1990	535,234	616,098	–80,865	2022	3,018,455	3,969,643	–951,188
1895	808	732	76	1995	794,387	890,771	–96,384	2023	3,053,494	3,826,920	–773,426

Note: Figures shown using balance of payments basis.

World Trade Organization (WTO)

The World Trade Organization is an international body that seeks to promote free trade by lowering barriers among members through negotiations. Founded in 1995, the WTO had grown to 164 member countries as of July 2024, with 25 others, including Belarus, Iran, Iraq, and Vatican City (Holy See), granted observer status. International intergovernmental organizations, such as the International Monetary Fund and the World Bank, have also been granted observer status. With the exception of Vatican City, observers must start accession negotiations within five years of becoming observers.

U.S. Trade in Goods and Services, 2023

Source: U.S. Census Bureau and U.S. Bureau of Economic Analysis, U.S. Dept. of Commerce
(top countries as ranked by amount of total trade with U.S.; in millions of dollars)

Country and category	Food and live animals	Beverages and tobacco	Crude materials, except fuels	Mineral fuels, lubricants	Chemicals	Manufactured goods	Machinery and transport equipment	Misc. manufactured articles	Commodities and transactions[1]	Total[2]
Mexico										
U.S. exports to	$23,729	$326	$9,805	$45,066	$38,456	$39,440	$129,765	$26,311	$9,839	**$323,228**
U.S. imports from	34,276	11,866	2,529	25,012	10,438	33,626	299,168	49,355	13,348	**480,080**
Trade balance	–10,547	–11,541	7,276	20,053	28,018	5,814	–169,403	–23,044	–3,509	**–156,853**
Canada										
U.S. exports to	27,213	1,834	8,329	28,622	42,410	40,795	150,598	32,259	20,008	**352,843**
U.S. imports from	34,713	1,524	14,304	131,909	34,639	52,185	106,676	21,444	27,964	**431,196**
Trade balance	–7,501	310	–5,975	–103,286	7,772	–11,390	43,923	10,814	–7,956	**–78,353**
China										
U.S. exports to	11,539	352	25,045	19,734	27,735	6,055	41,591	13,518	2,191	**147,806**
U.S. imports from	4,666	96	1,367	239	23,682	48,127	229,455	129,479	10,074	**448,036**
Trade balance	6,873	256	23,679	19,495	4,053	–42,072	–187,864	–115,961	–7,883	**–300,230**
Germany										
U.S. exports to	869	128	3,590	5,809	14,012	4,953	35,631	8,361	3,327	**76,699**
U.S. imports from	2,076	338	1,549	407	32,004	13,702	87,710	14,790	10,458	**163,081**
Trade balance	–1,207	–211	2,041	5,402	–17,992	–8,749	–52,079	–6,429	–7,131	**–86,381**
Japan										
U.S. exports to	10,408	268	4,480	12,060	15,386	3,513	18,278	9,874	1,874	**76,165**
U.S. imports from	1,147	277	635	733	15,105	10,250	107,946	11,329	4,089	**151,581**
Trade balance	9,260	–8	3,845	11,327	281	–6,737	–89,668	–1,455	–2,215	**–75,415**
South Korea										
U.S. exports to	6,801	166	2,381	17,214	8,818	2,324	20,315	5,604	1,177	**64,836**
U.S. imports from	1,340	174	569	4,899	13,461	12,616	77,738	7,086	1,817	**119,725**
Trade balance	5,461	–8	1,812	12,315	–4,643	–10,292	–57,423	–1,482	–639	**–54,889**
United Kingdom										
U.S. exports to	1,004	337	2,416	13,340	11,900	4,124	21,614	8,268	11,078	**74,090**
U.S. imports from	949	2,020	586	3,460	11,655	3,925	27,924	8,377	6,558	**65,487**
Trade balance	55	–1,683	1,831	9,880	244	199	–6,310	–110	4,519	**8,603**

Note: Figures for exports are "free alongside ship" values; figures for imports are "cost, insurance, and freight" values. Neither is directly comparable with the Census Bureau basis shown in other tables in this section. Trade balance is with U.S.; subtracting imports from exports may not equal trade balance due to rounding. Total includes categories not shown here. (1) Not classified elsewhere. (2) Total includes animal and vegetable oils, fats, and waxes, not shown separately.

Exchange Rates for Foreign Currencies, 1970-2023

Source: Federal Reserve Board

One U.S. dollar was worth the following amounts in each country's national currency; exchange rates are annual averages.

Country (currency)	1970	1980	1990	2000	2010	2015	2020	2021	2022	2023
Australia (dollar)	0.90	0.88	1.28	1.72	1.09	1.33	1.45	1.33	1.44	1.51
Austria (schilling; euro)	25.88	12.95	11.37	1.08	0.75	0.90	0.88	0.85	0.95	0.92
Belgium (franc; euro)	49.68	29.24	33.42	1.08	0.75	0.90	0.88	0.85	0.95	0.92
Brazil (real)	NA	NA	NA	1.83	1.76	3.34	5.16	5.40	5.16	4.99
Canada (dollar)	1.01	1.17	1.17	1.49	1.03	1.28	1.34	1.25	1.30	1.35
China (yuan)	NA	NA	4.79	8.28	6.77	6.28	6.90	6.45	6.73	7.08
Denmark (krone)	7.49	5.63	6.19	8.10	5.63	6.73	6.54	6.29	7.08	6.89
France (franc; euro)	5.52	4.22	5.45	1.08	0.75	0.90	0.88	0.85	0.95	0.92
Germany[1] (mark; euro)	3.65	1.82	1.62	1.08	0.75	0.90	0.88	0.85	0.95	0.92
Greece (drachma; euro)	30.00	42.62	158.51	365.92	0.75	0.90	0.88	0.85	0.95	0.92
Hong Kong (dollar)	NA	NA	7.79	7.79	7.77	7.75	7.76	7.77	7.83	7.83
India (rupee)	7.58	7.89	17.50	45.00	45.65	64.11	74.14	73.94	78.58	82.57
Ireland (pound; euro)	2.40	2.06	1.66	1.08	0.75	0.90	0.88	0.85	0.95	0.92
Italy (lira; euro)	623.00	856.00	1,198.00	1.08	0.75	0.90	0.88	0.85	0.95	0.92
Japan (yen)	357.60	226.63	144.79	107.80	87.78	121.05	106.78	109.84	131.46	140.50
Malaysia (ringgit)	3.09	2.18	2.71	3.80	3.22	3.90	4.20	4.14	4.40	4.56
Mexico (peso[2])	NA	NA	NA	9.46	12.62	15.87	21.55	20.28	20.12	17.73
Netherlands (guilder; euro)	3.60	2.0	1.82	1.08	0.75	0.90	0.88	0.85	0.95	0.92
Norway (krone)	7.14	4.94	6.26	8.81	6.05	8.07	9.43	8.60	9.61	10.57
Portugal (escudo; euro)	28.75	50.08	142.55	1.08	0.75	0.90	0.88	0.85	0.95	0.92
Singapore (dollar)	3.08	2.14	1.81	1.73	1.36	1.37	1.38	1.34	1.38	1.34
South Korea (won)	310.57	607.43	707.76	1,130.90	1,155.74	1,130.96	1,180.56	1,144.89	1,291.78	1,306.76
Spain (peseta; euro)	69.72	71.76	101.93	1.08	0.75	0.90	0.88	0.85	0.95	0.92
Sweden (krona)	5.17	4.23	5.92	9.17	7.20	8.44	9.22	8.58	10.12	10.61
Switzerland (franc)	4.32	1.68	1.39	1.69	1.04	0.96	0.94	0.91	0.96	0.90
Taiwan (dollar)	NA	NA	26.92	31.26	31.50	31.74	29.46	27.94	29.80	31.15
Thailand (baht)	21.00	20.48	25.58	40.21	31.70	34.24	31.31	32.01	35.05	34.78
United Kingdom (pound)	0.42	0.43	0.56	0.66	0.65	0.65	0.78	0.73	0.81	0.80

NA = Not available. **Note:** The euro, the European Union's single currency, replaced the national currencies in the EU nations shown above. Since 1999 (or 2001 in the case of Greece), the euro has been fixed at the following conversion rates: 13.7603 Austrian schillings, 40.3399 Belgian francs, 6.55957 French francs, 1.95583 German marks, 340.750 Greek drachmas, 0.787564 Irish pounds, 1,936.27 Italian lire, 2.20371 Netherlands guilders, 200.482 Portuguese escudos, and 166.386 Spanish pesetas. (1) West Germany before 1991. (2) Mexico re-based its currency in 1993; earlier values are not comparable.

Top U.S. Trading Partners, 1985-2023

Source: U.S. Census Bureau, U.S. Dept. of Commerce
(in millions of dollars; top five countries as ranked by amount of total trade with U.S. in 2023)

Country/category	1985	1990	1995	2000	2005	2010	2015	2020	2022	2023
Mexico										
U.S. exports to	$13,635	$28,279	$46,292	$111,349	$120,248	$163,665	$236,460	$212,513	$324,310	$323,228
U.S. imports from	19,132	30,157	62,100	135,926	170,109	229,986	296,433	323,477	454,775	475,607
Trade balance	–5,497	–1,878	–15,808	–24,577	–49,861	–66,321	–59,973	–110,964	–130,465	–152,379
Canada										
U.S. exports to	47,251	83,674	127,226	178,941	211,899	249,257	280,855	256,212	356,453	353,235
U.S. imports from	69,006	91,380	144,370	230,838	290,384	277,637	296,305	270,026	436,562	421,096
Trade balance	–21,755	–7,706	–17,144	–51,897	–78,486	–28,380	–15,450	–13,813	–80,109	–67,861
China										
U.S. exports	3,856	4,806	11,754	16,185	41,192	91,911	115,873	124,582	154,012	147,806
U.S. imports from	3,862	15,237	45,543	100,018	243,470	364,953	483,202	432,548	536,307	427,229
Trade balance	–6	–10,431	–33,790	–83,833	–202,278	–273,042	–367,328	–307,967	–382,295	–279,424
Germany										
U.S. exports to	9,050	18,760	22,394	29,448	34,184	48,155	49,979	58,002	72,553	76,699
U.S. imports from	20,239	28,162	36,844	58,513	84,751	82,450	124,888	114,897	146,630	159,720
Trade balance	–11,189	–9,402	–14,450	–29,065	–50,567	–34,295	–74,909	–56,895	–74,077	–83,021
Japan										
U.S. exports to	22,631	48,580	64,343	64,924	54,681	60,472	62,388	64,030	80,180	76,165
U.S. imports from	68,783	89,684	123,479	146,479	138,004	120,552	131,446	119,507	148,064	147,340
Trade balance	–46,152	–41,105	–59,137	–81,555	–83,323	–60,080	–69,058	–55,476	–67,884	–71,175

Note: Figures shown are on Census Bureau basis and are not seasonally adjusted. Data is not directly comparable with other tables in this section.

Busiest U.S. Ports, 2022

Source: U.S. Army Corps of Engineers, Dept. of the Army, U.S. Dept. of Defense
(figures in millions of short tons; ranked by total tonnage handled)

Rank	Port	Domestic	Foreign	Total
1.	Houston, TX	84.2	209.6	293.8
2.	South Louisiana, LA	115.8	110.4	226.2
3.	Corpus Christi, TX	25.7	148.6	174.3
4.	New York, NY-NJ	40.5	100.7	141.3
5.	Long Beach, CA	13.2	79.7	93.0
6.	New Orleans, LA	43.8	39.5	83.3
7.	Beaumont, TX	21.3	53.0	74.3
8.	Baton Rouge, LA	45.8	27.5	73.4
9.	Virginia, VA	4.9	64.5	69.4
10.	Lake Charles, LA	29.3	34.8	64.1
11.	Los Angeles, CA	3.3	56.5	59.8
12.	Plaquemines, LA	30.0	25.3	55.4
13.	Savannah, GA	1.6	52.1	53.7
14.	Mobile, AL	16.7	33.8	50.5
15.	Port Arthur, TX	16.3	31.2	47.5
16.	Baltimore, MD	4.2	36.4	40.6
17.	Texas City, TX	13.1	19.7	32.9
18.	Philadelphia, PA	12.9	18.9	31.8
19.	Freeport, TX	6.2	25.3	31.6
20.	Duluth-Superior, MN-WI	22.9	6.8	29.6
21.	Tampa, FL	17.6	10.4	28.0
22.	Indiana (Southern District), IN	27.7	0.0	27.7
23.	Charleston, SC	1.6	26.1	27.7
24.	Everglades, FL	14.1	11.5	25.6
25.	Indiana (Northern District), IN	25.1	0.4	25.4
26.	Valdez, AK	24.8	0.3	25.1
27.	Pascagoula, MS	11.4	12.6	24.1
28.	Richmond, CA	8.7	14.9	23.6
29.	Portland, OR	10.1	12.8	22.9
30.	South Jersey, NJ	8.2	11.9	20.1
31.	Tacoma, WA	3.2	16.7	19.9
32.	Seattle, WA	2.6	15.9	18.5
33.	Oakland, CA	0.7	17.3	18.0
34.	Jacksonville, FL	8.9	8.9	17.7
35.	Pittsburgh, PA	17.4	0.0	17.4
36.	Kalama, WA	1.5	14.4	15.9
37.	Honolulu, HI	13.7	0.7	14.4
38.	Galveston, TX	8.2	5.3	13.5
39.	Mid-America, IL-IA-MO	13.2	0.0	13.2
40.	Two Harbors, MN	9.8	2.7	12.5
41.	Anacortes, WA	8.2	3.9	12.2
42.	San Juan, PR	5.1	5.6	10.7
43.	New Bourbon, MO	10.3	0.0	10.3
44.	Toledo-Lucas County, OH	7.6	2.6	10.2
45.	Longview, WA	0.6	9.6	10.2
46.	Illinois International, IL	7.6	2.5	10.1
47.	Vancouver, WA	1.9	7.7	9.6
48.	Joliet Regional, IL	9.3	0.0	9.3
49.	Cleveland-Cuyahoga, OH	7.8	1.4	9.2
50.	Brownsville, TX	2.6	6.5	9.1

World's Busiest Ports, 2018-22

Source: Lloyd's List; Shanghai International Shipping Institute
(ranked by throughput volume in 2022 as measured in thousands of twenty-ft equivalent units (TEUs))

		Volume (TEUs)					Percent change			
Rank	Port	2018	2019	2020	2021	2022	2018-19	2019-20	2020-21	2021-22
1.	Shanghai, China	42,010	43,303	43,503	47,030	47,303	3.1%	0.5%	8.1%	0.6%
2.	Singapore	36,599	37,196	36,871	37,470	37,290	1.6	–0.9	1.6	–0.5
3.	Ningbo-Zhoushan, China	26,351	27,530	28,720	31,070	33,351	4.5	4.3	8.2	7.3
4.	Shenzhen, China	25,740	25,770	26,550	28,768	30,036	0.1	3.0	8.4	4.4
5.	Guangzhou, China	19,315	21,010	22,010	23,710	25,670	8.8	4.8	7.7	8.3
6.	Qingdao, China	21,922	23,236	23,505	24,467	24,858	6.0	1.2	4.1	1.6
7.	Busan, South Korea	21,663	21,992	21,824	22,706	22,078	1.5	–0.8	4.0	–2.8
8.	Tianjin, China	15,972	17,264	18,353	20,269	21,021	8.1	6.3	10.4	3.7
9.	Hong Kong, China	19,596	18,361	17,953	17,798	16,685	–6.3	–2.2	–0.9	–6.3
10.	Rotterdam, Netherlands	14,513	14,811	14,349	15,300	14,455	2.1	–3.1	6.6	–5.5
11.	Dubai, United Arab Emirates	14,954	14,111	13,488	13,742	13,970	–5.6	–4.4	1.9	1.7
12.	Antwerp, Belgium	11,100	11,860	12,031	12,020	13,500	6.8	1.4	–0.1	12.3
13.	Port Klang, Malaysia	12,316	13,581	13,244	13,724	13,220	10.3	–2.5	3.6	–3.7
14.	Xiamen, China	10,702	11,122	11,410	12,046	12,435	3.9	2.6	5.6	3.2
15.	Tanjung Pelepas, Malaysia	8,961	9,100	9,800	11,200	10,513	1.6	7.7	14.3	–6.1
16.	Los Angeles, CA, U.S.	9,459	9,338	9,213	10,678	9,912	–1.3	–1.3	15.9	–7.2
17.	New York & New Jersey, U.S.	7,180	7,471	7,586	8,986	9,494	4.1	1.5	18.5	5.7
18.	Kaohsiung, Taiwan	10,446	10,429	9,622	9,864	9,492	–0.2	–7.7	2.5	–3.8
19.	Long Beach, CA, U.S.	8,091	7,632	8,113	9,384	9,134	–5.7	6.3	15.7	–2.7
20.	Suzhou, China[1]	6,360	6,270	6,290	8,110	9,080	–1.4	0.3	28.9	12.0

Note: A TEU is the size of a typical shipping container. (1) Figures are rounded.

Value of Freight Shipments by Transportation Mode, 2017-23

Source: Freight Analysis Framework, U.S. Dept. of Transportation
(value in billions of 2017 dollars)

Mode of transportation	2017 Total	2017 Domestic	2017 Exports	2017 Imports	2023 Total	2023 Domestic	2023 Exports	2023 Imports
Truck	$12,017	$11,297	$368	$353	$12,906	$12,157	$374	$375
Rail	404	227	64	113	403	233	62	107
Water	360	184	55	121	348	182	59	106
Air[1]	1,226	159	496	571	1,288	169	512	607
Multiple modes and mail	3,926	2,362	527	1,037	4,363	2,623	589	1,151
Pipeline	928	851	14	63	976	884	29	63
Other and unknown	45	2	31	12	45	2	31	12
Total	**18,907**	**15,082**	**1,555**	**2,270**	**20,328**	**16,250**	**1,658**	**2,420**

Note: Imports and exports that pass through the U.S. from a foreign origin to a foreign destination by any mode not included. All truck, rail, water, and pipeline movements that involve more than one mode, including exports and imports that change mode at international gateways, are included in multiple modes and mail to avoid double counting. (1) Including truck-air.

Merchant Fleets of the World, 2023

Source: *Review of Maritime Transport, 2023*, United Nations Conference on Trade and Development
(ranked by deadweight tonnage under flag of registration as of Jan. 1, 2023)

Flag of registration	Number of ships	Percent of total world ships	Deadweight tonnage (thous.)	Percent of total world tonnage	Average vessel size (deadweight tons)	Tonnage change, 2022-23
1. Liberia	4,821	4.6%	378,346	16.6%	78,479	12.7%
2. Panama	8,174	7.8	365,096	16.1	44,666	4.2
3. Marshall Islands	4,180	4.0	299,170	13.2	71,572	3.2
4. Hong Kong (China)	2,537	2.4	200,075	8.8	78,863	–3.7
5. Singapore	3,202	3.0	134,985	5.9	42,156	2.7
6. China	8,262	7.8	124,061	5.5	15,016	5.4
7. Malta	1,957	1.9	109,001	4.8	55,698	–5.0
8. The Bahamas	1,274	1.2	72,674	3.2	57,044	–0.9
9. Greece	1,215	1.2	59,016	2.6	48,573	–4.3
10. Japan	5,229	5.0	41,726	1.8	7,980	4.2
11. Cyprus	1,005	1.0	31,164	1.4	31,009	–6.8
12. Indonesia	11,422	10.8	30,171	1.3	2,641	2.5
13. Madeira (Portugal)	729	0.7	26,850	1.2	36,832	3.7
14. Denmark	590	0.6	25,259	1.1	42,811	–3.1
15. Norway	684	0.6	21,271	0.9	31,099	1.0
16. Iran	965	0.9	20,723	0.9	21,475	1.2
17. Isle of Man	269	0.3	20,109	0.9	74,755	–2.5
18. South Korea	2,149	2.0	18,894	0.8	8,792	20.6
19. India	1,859	1.8	18,133	0.8	9,754	7.1
20. Saudi Arabia	433	0.4	13,406	0.6	30,961	–3.5
21. United States	3,531	3.4	12,586	0.6	3,564	0.9
22. Vietnam	1,973	1.9	12,434	0.5	6,302	0.7
23. Russia	2,910	2.8	11,270	0.5	3,873	3.0
24. United Kingdom[1]	866	0.8	11,057	0.5	12,768	–2.5
25. Malaysia	1,750	1.7	9,406	0.4	5,375	2.0
26. Belgium	198	0.2	9,160	0.4	46,261	–6.3
27. Italy	1,276	1.2	9,121	0.4	7,148	–8.6
28. Germany	595	0.6	7,249	0.3	12,183	2.1
29. Cameroon	198	0.2	7,228	0.3	36,503	45.1
30. Bermuda	122	0.1	7,043	0.3	57,731	–10.7
World total[2]	**105,395**	**100.0**	**2,272,772**	**100.0**	**21,564**	**3.2**

Note: List includes only propelled seagoing merchant vessels of 100 gross tons and above. (1) Excludes Channel Islands and Isle of Man. (2) Includes flags of registration not shown.

U.S. International Transactions, 1970-2023

Source: U.S. Bureau of Economic Analysis, U.S. Dept. of Commerce
(in millions of dollars)

	1970	1980	1990	2000	2010	2020	2022	2023
CURRENT ACCOUNT								
Exports of goods and services and income receipts (credits)	**$68,388**	**$344,440**	**$712,128**	**$1,469,648**	**$2,623,991**	**$3,260,095**	**$4,412,523**	**$4,645,183**
Goods	42,469	224,250	387,401	784,940	1,290,279	1,432,218	2,090,339	2,045,221
Services	14,171	47,585	147,833	290,381	562,759	726,433	949,065	1,026,596
Primary income receipts	11,748	72,605	176,894	356,706	680,169	936,236	1,184,423	1,376,721
Imports of goods and services and income payments (debits)	**66,055**	**342,124**	**791,097**	**1,873,098**	**3,055,256**	**3,879,793**	**5,424,621**	**5,550,559**
Goods	39,866	249,750	498,438	1,231,722	1,938,950	2,346,103	3,270,281	3,108,509
Services	14,519	41,492	117,660	216,115	409,313	466,537	713,886	748,198
Primary income payments	5,514	42,533	148,345	338,637	511,948	773,146	1,068,464	1,309,692
Secondary income payments (current transfers)[1]	6,156	8,349	26,654	86,624	195,045	294,008	371,990	384,160
CAPITAL ACCOUNT								
Capital transfer receipts, other credits	NA	NA	0	35	0	372	8,397	82
Capital transfer payments, other debits	NA	NA	7,220	36	157	5,903	8,578	6,402
FINANCIAL ACCOUNT								
Net U.S. acquisition of financial assets[2]	9,336	86,968	103,985	587,682	958,703	943,091	747,109	978,604
Net U.S. incurrence of liabilities[2]	7,226	62,036	162,109	1,066,074	1,391,042	1,634,965	1,535,516	1,887,085
Balance on current account	**2,331**	**2,318**	**–78,969**	**–403,450**	**–431,265**	**–619,698**	**–1,012,098**	**–905,376**
Balance on capital account	**NA**	**NA**	**–7,221**	**–1**	**–157**	**–5,532**	**–181**	**–6,320**
Net lending (+) or net borrowing (–) from financial-acct. transactions[3]	2,331	2,318	–86,190	–403,451	–431,422	–696,980	–869,105	–924,123

NA = Not available or applicable. (1) Includes U.S. government and private transfers, such as U.S. government grants and pensions, fines and penalties, withholding taxes, personal transfers (remittances), insurance-related transfers, and other current transfers. (2) Excludes financial derivatives. (3) Net lending means that U.S. residents are net suppliers of funds to foreign residents, and net borrowing means the opposite. Net lending or net borrowing can be computed from current- and capital-account transactions or from financial-account transactions.

U.S. International Direct Investments, 1990-2023

Source: U.S. Bureau of Economic Analysis, U.S. Dept. of Commerce
(in millions of dollars)

	U.S. direct investment abroad					Foreign direct investment in U.S.				
	1990	**2000**	**2010**	**2020**	**2023**	**1990**	**2000**	**2010**	**2020**	**2023**
All countries[1]	**$430,521**	**$1,316,247**	**$3,741,910**	**$6,063,288**	**$6,676,478**	**$394,911**	**$1,256,867**	**$2,280,044**	**$4,613,481**	**$5,394,095**
Canada	69,508	132,472	295,206	366,880	451,555	29,544	114,309	192,463	487,449	671,671
Europe[1]	**214,739**	**687,320**	**2,034,559**	**3,606,804**	**3,950,153**	**247,320**	**887,014**	**1,659,774**	**2,980,117**	**3,462,655**
Austria	1,113	2,872	11,485	4,296	6,093	625	3,007	4,532	15,346	19,076
Belgium	9,464	17,973	43,975	65,733	66,529	3,900	14,787	69,565	66,093	73,485
Czechia	NA	1,228	5,268	5,025	4,644	NA	NA	65	NA	NA
Denmark	1,726	5,270	11,802	15,376	12,845	819	4,025	7,772	30,173	44,990
Finland	544	1,342	1,597	3,617	5,527	1,504	8,875	4,943	8,082	10,096
France	19,164	42,628	78,320	106,517	100,909	18,650	125,740	189,763	282,257	243,470
Germany	27,609	55,508	103,319	152,278	193,179	28,232	122,412	203,077	347,509	472,851
Greece	282	795	1,775	481	1,824	94	659	–41	NA	NA
Hungary	NA	1,920	4,237	13,866	16,037	NA	5,287	39,266	NA	NA
Ireland	5,894	35,903	158,851	379,886	491,246	1,340	25,523	24,097	249,295	322,614
Italy	14,063	23,484	27,137	27,459	29,025	1,524	6,576	20,142	31,294	42,828
Luxembourg	1,697	27,849	272,206	654,941	532,465	2,195	58,930	170,309	316,922	246,908
Netherlands	19,120	115,429	514,689	827,419	980,403	64,671	138,894	234,408	554,720	717,467
Norway	4,209	4,379	28,541	13,627	15,358	773	2,665	10,478	30,362	42,436
Poland	NA	3,884	13,152	11,956	15,773	29	57	4,386	NA	NA
Portugal	897	2,664	2,612	1,905	2,937	–19	–68	204	NA	NA
Russia	NA	1,147	10,040	12,874	7,669	NA	118	5,689	NA	NA
Spain	7,868	21,236	52,390	37,238	37,850	792	5,068	43,095	84,571	81,386
Sweden	1,787	25,959	23,275	55,608	56,197	5,484	21,991	38,780	59,964	104,853
Switzerland	25,099	55,377	119,891	236,767	238,228	17,674	64,719	180,642	293,461	351,539
Turkey	522	1,826	4,155	6,223	6,254	20	188	749	NA	NA
UK	72,707	230,762	501,247	944,908	1,057,592	98,676	277,613	400,435	535,715	630,551
Latin America[1]	**71,413**	**266,576**	**752,788**	**1,024,534**	**1,065,761**	**20,168**	**53,691**	**62,130**	**209,774**	**210,923**
Argentina	2,531	17,488	11,747	13,325	14,514	420	364	464	NA	NA
The Bahamas	4,004	NA	NA	NA	NA	1,535	1,254	1,753	1,897	3,520
Barbados	252	2,141	7,524	57,819	45,499	191	1,560	706	NA	NA
Bermuda	20,169	60,114	265,524	288,011	219,608	1,550	18,336	365	52,021	41,578
Brazil	14,384	36,717	66,963	69,086	87,909	377	882	1,357	4,480	6,514
Chile	1,896	10,052	30,747	27,152	32,034	5	24	391	NA	NA
Colombia	1,677	3,693	6,181	6,452	8,438	55	2	382	NA	NA
Costa Rica	251	1,716	1,827	3,066	3,810	–2	2	–48	NA	NA
Curaçao[2]	–4,501	NA	NA	NA	NA	12,974	3,807	2,819	1,193	2,189
Dom. Rep.	529	1,143	1,432	2,567	1,893	0	79	–142	NA	NA
Ecuador	280	832	1,283	929	906	6	29	77	NA	NA
Honduras	262	399	936	894	1,391	8	–3	7	NA	NA
Mexico	10,313	39,352	85,751	110,753	144,507	575	7,462	10,970	20,646	38,385
Panama	9,289	30,758	5,156	3,500	4,512	4,188	3,819	952	1,796	1,475
Peru	599	3,130	7,196	7,222	6,646	NA	–13	182	NA	NA
UK isls. in Caribbean[3]	5,929	33,451	191,680	350,988	398,939	–2,979	15,191	38,477	99,194	99,204
Venezuela	1,087	10,531	10,255	3,106	3,268	496	792	3,122	1,381	NA
Africa[1]	**3,650**	**11,891**	**54,816**	**43,808**	**56,291**	**505**	**2,700**	**2,265**	**9,875**	**10,053**
Egypt	1,231	1,998	12,599	10,665	13,691	1	–4	–277	NA	NA
Nigeria	–401	470	5,058	6,786	6,533	–17	NA	23	NA	NA
South Africa	775	3,562	6,017	6,748	7,969	10	704	699	3,552	3,402
Middle East[1]	**3,959**	**10,863**	**34,431**	**80,790**	**80,530**	**4,425**	**6,506**	**16,808**	**41,336**	**50,043**
Israel	746	3,735	9,464	41,329	45,910	640	3,012	8,714	10,487	10,327
Kuwait	NA	NA	NA	NA	NA	NA	NA	NA	1,423	1,195
Lebanon	NA	NA	NA	NA	NA	NA	NA	NA	2	29
Saudi Arabia	1,899	3,661	7,436	11,188	11,311	1,811	NA	NA	6,395	7,519
UAE	409	683	4,935	16,054	16,106	99	64	747	20,409	28,375
Asia and Pacific[1]	**64,718**	**207,125**	**570,111**	**940,473**	**1,072,188**	**92,948**	**192,647**	**346,605**	**884,928**	**988,749**
Australia	15,110	34,838	125,421	178,223	193,340	6,542	18,775	35,632	85,809	110,908
China	354	11,140	58,996	116,508	126,908	NA	277	3,300	36,738	28,043
Hong Kong	6,055	27,447	41,264	94,495	90,564	1,511	1,493	4,440	14,212	18,054
India	372	2,379	24,666	42,291	49,563	NA	96	4,102	1,658	4,664
Indonesia	3,207	8,904	10,558	12,158	15,937	25	16	138	NA	NA
Japan	22,599	57,091	113,523	118,453	63,369	83,091	159,690	255,012	632,079	688,054
Korea, South	2,695	8,968	26,233	37,550	35,642	–1,009	3,110	15,746	60,548	76,689
Malaysia	1,466	7,910	11,791	13,788	10,926	56	310	338	1,034	1,126
New Zealand	3,156	4,271	6,724	11,701	8,547	157	395	584	2,396	2,994
Philippines	1,355	3,638	5,399	5,037	6,359	77	47	103	NA	NA
Singapore	3,975	24,133	102,778	264,188	424,214	1,289	5,087	21,517	28,486	37,468
Taiwan	2,226	7,836	22,188	18,569	19,327	836	3,174	4,642	17,974	15,643
Thailand	1,790	5,824	12,999	15,484	15,138	150	132	158	NA	NA

NA = Not available. **Note:** On a historical cost basis. Direct investment is a category of cross-border investment associated with a resident in one economy having control or a significant degree of influence on the management of an enterprise resident in another economy. Ownership or control of 10% or more of the voting securities of an entity in another economy is the threshold for separating direct investment from other types of investment. (1) Totals and subtotals include countries or territories not shown in table. (2) Curaçao figures before 2010 are for the entire Netherlands Antilles, a confederation that ended in 2010. (3) Incl. British Virgin Islands, Cayman Islands, Montserrat, and Turks and Caicos Islands.

TRANSPORTATION AND TRAVEL

Top Motor Vehicle Producing Nations, 2023

Source: International Organization of Motor Vehicle Manufacturers (OICA)
(in thousands of units; ranked by total production)

Nation	Total motor vehicles	Cars	Commercial vehicles[1]	% change, 2022-23[2]
China	30,160,966	26,123,757	4,037,209	12%
U.S.	10,611,555	1,745,171	8,866,384	6
Japan	8,997,440	7,765,428	1,232,012	15
India	5,851,507	4,783,628	1,067,879	7
South Korea	4,243,597	3,908,747	334,850	13
Germany	4,109,371	4,109,371	0	18
Mexico	4,002,047	903,753	3,098,294	14
Spain	2,451,221	1,907,050	544,171	10
Brazil	2,324,838	1,781,612	543,226	–2
Thailand	1,841,663	580,857	1,260,806	–2
Canada	1,553,026	376,588	1,176,138	26
France	1,505,076	1,026,690	478,386	9
Turkey (Türkiye)	1,468,393	952,667	515,726	9
Czechia	1,404,501	1,397,816	6,685	15
Indonesia	1,395,717	1,180,355	215,362	–5
Slovakia	1,080,000	1,080,000	0	10
UK	1,025,474	905,117	120,357	17
Italy	880,085	541,953	338,132	11
Malaysia	774,600	724,891	49,709	10%
Russia	729,864	526,439	203,425	20
South Africa	633,337	336,980	296,357	14
Poland	612,882	299,300	313,582	27
Argentina	610,725	304,783	305,942	14
Morocco	535,825	471,950	63,875	15
Romania	513,050	513,050	0	1
Hungary	507,225	507,225	0	15
Uzbekistan	425,876	421,414	4,462	25
Belgium	332,103	285,159	46,944	16
Portugal	318,231	243,201	75,030	–1
Taiwan	285,962	221,329	64,633	10
Kazakhstan	146,989	134,054	12,935	30
Austria	114,191	102,291	11,900	–6
Slovenia	60,881	60,881	0	–11
Finland	30,191	30,191	0	–59
Ukraine	1,993	1,993	0	34
Others	2,006,197	877,579	1,128,618	NA
Total	**93,546,599**	**67,133,570**	**26,413,029**	**10**

NA = Not applicable. NAFTA = North American Free Trade Agreement. **Note:** Numbers may not add up to totals due to rounding. (1) Includes light commercial vehicles, heavy trucks, coaches, and buses. (2) Percent change in number of total motor vehicles.

World Motor Vehicle Production, 1950-2023

Source: For 1950-90, American Automobile Manufacturers Assn.; 2000-12, Automotive News Data Center and R.L. Polk; 2013-23, OICA
(in thousands of units)

Year	U.S.	Canada	Europe[1]	Japan	Other	World total	U.S. % of world total
1950	8,006	388	1,991	32	160	10,577	75.7%
1960	7,905	398	6,837	482	866	16,488	47.9
1970	8,284	1,160	13,049	5,289	1,637	29,419	28.2
1980	8,010	1,324	15,496	11,043	2,692	38,565	20.8
1990	9,783	1,928	18,866	13,487	4,496	48,554	20.1
2000	12,832	2,952	17,678	10,145	16,098	59,704	21.5
2010	7,632	2,074	19,371	9,197	35,036	73,311	10.4
2011	8,462	2,127	20,709	7,901	36,828	76,027	11.1
2012	10,142	2,454	22,324	9,448	36,714	81,082	12.5
2013	11,066	2,380	19,923	9,630	44,508	87,507	12.6
2014	11,661	2,394	20,430	9,775	45,536	89,776	12.9
2015	12,100	2,283	21,096	9,278	46,024	90,781	13.3
2016	12,198	2,370	21,700	9,205	49,504	94,977	12.8
2017	11,190	2,200	22,161	9,694	52,058	97,303	11.5
2018	10,986	2,000	21,273	9,201	48,079	91,539	12.0
2019	10,893	1,917	21,269	9,685	48,095	91,858	11.9
2020	8,821	1,376	16,693	8,068	42,481	77,439	11.4
2021	9,157	1,115	16,138	7,837	45,758	80,005	11.4
2022	10,053	1,233	16,033	7,836	49,676	84,830	11.9
2023	10,612	1,553	18,122	8,997	54,262	93,547	11.3

Note: Data may not be fully comparable across all years because they are derived from different sources. Number of units may not add up to totals due to rounding. (1) Prior to 2004, numbers exclude Eastern European production.

Passenger Cars Imported Into the U.S. by Country of Origin, 1970-2023

Source: U.S. Census Bureau, U.S. Dept. of Commerce
(in number of units)

Year	Japan	Mexico	Canada	S. Korea	Germany[1]	Sweden	UK	Italy	France	Total[2]
1970	381,338	NA	692,783	NA	674,945	57,844	76,257	42,523	37,114	2,013,420
1975	695,573	0	733,766	NA	370,012	51,993	67,106	102,344	15,647	2,074,653
1980	1,991,502	1	594,770	NA	338,711	61,496	32,517	46,899	47,386	3,116,448
1985	2,527,467	13,647	1,144,805	NA	473,110	142,640	24,474	8,689	42,882	4,397,679
1990	1,867,794	215,986	1,220,221	201,475	245,286	93,084	27,271	11,045	1,976	3,944,602
1995	1,114,360	462,800	1,552,691	131,718	204,932	82,593	42,450	1,031	14	3,624,428
2000	1,837,631	933,948	2,138,825	568,153	491,704	86,707	81,079	3,129	28,024	6,326,013
2005	1,832,534	693,149	1,967,985	730,500	547,191	93,736	184,716	5,377	412	6,564,844
2010	1,569,220	902,565	1,741,493	515,601	506,053	38,749	96,689	4,298	4,153	5,668,111
2015	1,609,709	1,438,840	1,969,502	1,065,972	639,879	37,789	134,413	132,340	28,034	7,420,613
2017	1,731,889	1,724,526	1,850,765	929,530	502,059	58,492	217,341	159,802	9,801	7,660,401
2018	1,729,301	1,934,412	1,641,534	831,164	458,829	43,359	235,133	153,426	5,091	7,551,409
2019	1,734,743	2,018,770	1,558,959	916,610	413,528	60,147	213,528	102,641	2,413	7,478,857
2020	1,402,501	1,528,214	1,190,967	874,236	286,410	69,719	138,742	91,693	656	5,972,315
2021	1,351,459	1,388,926	952,147	826,761	292,744	78,756	134,262	57,848	453	5,514,272
2022	1,299,937	1,495,356	963,634	872,017	281,465	74,036	82,617	55,064	617	5,541,706
2023	1,296,150	1,234,996	1,035,061	810,730	310,558	84,778	71,668	56,556	1,596	5,241,820

NA = Not available. **Note:** Includes new and used cars. Excludes cars assembled in U.S. foreign trade zones. (1) Figures prior to 1991 are for West Germany. (2) Includes units imported from countries not shown in table.

Passenger Car Production in U.S. Plants, 2021-23

Source: Wards Intelligence

(in number of units; only 2023 models with at least 10,000 produced shown here)

	2023	2022	2021
FORD TOTAL	**61,165**	**65,480**	**65,590**
Ford Mustang	61,165	65,480	65,590
GENERAL MOTORS TOTAL	**233,313**	**233,349**	**97,916**
Cadillac CT5	18,518	20,079	7,510
Chevrolet Camaro	36,076	29,332	22,399
Chevrolet Corvette	41,461	38,686	36,010
Chevrolet Malibu	128,748	132,360	26,860
HONDA TOTAL	**341,546**	**282,878**	**258,489**
Acura Integra	38,304	17,605	—
Acura TLX	18,581	15,344	17,435
Honda Accord	213,318	193,428	174,549
Honda Civic	71,343	42,744	40,352
HYUNDAI TOTAL	**13,674**	**35,748**	**92,590**
Hyundai Elantra	13,674	34,040	49,785
KIA TOTAL	**69,253**	**64,547**	**80,061**
Kia K5	69,253	64,547	80,061

	2023	2022	2021
NISSAN TOTAL	**176,050**	**166,974**	**129,210**
Nissan Altima	154,572	144,622	101,732
Nissan Leaf	12,091	13,150	12,262
SUBARU TOTAL	**43,075**	**55,097**	**54,830**
Subaru Impreza	15,507	32,333	33,176
Subaru Legacy	27,568	22,764	21,654
TESLA TOTAL	**268,102**	**278,011**	**247,896**
Tesla Model 3	243,340	246,246	237,673
Tesla Model S	24,762	31,765	10,223
TOYOTA TOTAL	**511,123**	**500,587**	**489,630**
Lexus ES	44,749	43,187	44,523
Toyota Camry	310,155	307,470	296,936
Toyota Corolla	156,219	132,684	128,297
VOLVO TOTAL	**15,353**	**13,743**	**22,940**
Volvo 60	15,353	13,743	22,940
TOTAL CARS	**1,741,083**	**1,703,608**	**1,564,981**

— = No production. **Note:** Totals may include models not shown.

Light Truck Production in U.S. Plants, 2021-23

Source: Wards Intelligence

(in number of units; only 2023 models with at least 10,000 produced shown here)

	2023	2022	2021
BMW TOTAL	**410,793**	**416,301**	**433,748**
BMW X3	98,815	101,323	118,249
BMW X4	52,552	56,212	55,490
BMW X5	147,514	159,144	170,680
BMW X6	37,743	42,509	38,605
BMW X7	61,859	56,826	50,724
BMW XM	12,310	287	—
FORD TOTAL	**1,787,732**	**1,768,047**	**1,560,582**
Ford Bronco	128,188	139,062	54,562
Ford Econoline	48,114	38,830	40,575
Ford Escape	162,733	187,761	141,385
Ford Expedition	84,783	70,102	82,649
Ford Explorer	214,976	253,370	228,002
Ford F-Series	871,608	807,302	753,853
Ford Ranger	29,558	60,750	98,592
Ford Transit	170,301	129,937	98,536
Lincoln Aviator	23,682	27,008	21,765
Lincoln Corsair	31,285	35,779	20,854
Lincoln Navigator	22,504	18,146	19,809
GENERAL MOTORS TOTAL	**1,486,210**	**1,493,768**	**1,360,989**
Buick Enclave	46,966	41,672	40,836
Cadillac Escalade	33,578	29,664	33,294
Cadillac Escalade ESV	18,121	17,748	18,021
Cadillac Lyriq	20,770	1,028	—
Cadillac XT4	23,979	33,303	8,073
Cadillac XT5	31,006	37,849	25,397
Cadillac XT6	23,008	24,141	18,994
Chevrolet Bolt	24,286	15,365	19,515
Chevrolet Bolt EUV	52,748	29,097	14,911
Chevrolet Colorado	70,317	103,756	85,193
Chevrolet Express	34,606	51,458	29,343
Chevrolet Silverado	316,399	357,566	393,367
Chevrolet Suburban	59,440	60,059	50,741
Chevrolet Tahoe	130,432	130,885	121,863
Chevrolet Traverse	133,768	119,353	114,573
GMC Acadia	75,644	65,888	51,024
GMC Canyon	23,485	36,407	28,620
GMC Savana	17,828	24,285	10,967
GMC Sierra	238,764	207,894	189,935
GMC Yukon	61,162	65,240	65,633
GMC Yukon XL	43,888	40,102	40,560
HONDA TOTAL	**676,716**	**549,030**	**597,835**
Acura MDX	63,384	59,322	50,885
Acura RDX	52,402	31,504	53,792
Honda CR-V	254,143	188,098	209,974
Honda Odyssey	82,613	57,861	59,990
Honda Passport	44,840	47,462	51,014
Honda Pilot	124,400	114,349	130,358
Honda Ridgeline	54,934	50,434	41,822
HYUNDAI TOTAL	**355,326**	**297,084**	**198,816**
Genesis GV70	15,653	—	—
Hyundai Santa Cruz	46,396	41,965	15,025
Hyundai Santa Fe	141,544	121,164	102,084
Hyundai Tucson	151,733	133,955	81,707

	2023	2022	2021
KIA TOTAL	**287,554**	**275,453**	**175,039**
Kia Sorento	75,106	79,384	76,587
Kia Sportage	89,003	89,209	—
Kia Telluride	123,445	106,860	98,452
MERCEDES TOTAL	**354,951**	**316,939**	**294,789**
Mercedes EQE CUV	39,265	—	—
Mercedes EQS CUV	18,375	10,752	—
Mercedes GLE	182,157	195,433	198,362
Mercedes GLS	54,942	55,507	54,569
Mercedes Sprinter	60,212	55,247	41,858
NISSAN TOTAL	**430,131**	**371,776**	**322,578**
Infiniti QX60	37,952	27,164	3,255
Nissan Frontier	71,725	86,316	65,526
Nissan Murano	35,903	35,268	50,791
Nissan Pathfinder	85,636	80,630	32,250
Nissan Rogue	178,047	127,256	138,479
Nissan Titan	20,868	15,142	23,153
RIVIAN TOTAL	**57,232**	**24,338**	**1,015**
Rivian Large Van	17,921	7,268	8
Rivian R1S	21,800	4,190	20
Rivian R1T	17,511	12,880	987
STELLANTIS TOTAL	**1,029,715**	**1,169,830**	**1,171,025**
Dodge Durango	78,669	68,651	67,775
Jeep Cherokee	11,904	58,392	58,542
Jeep Gladiator	63,944	99,454	91,755
Jeep Grand Cherokee	294,909	266,967	301,181
Jeep Wagoneer	50,765	47,452	21,042
Jeep Wrangler	205,941	254,797	249,542
Ram Pickup	323,583	374,117	381,188
SUBARU TOTAL	**307,745**	**231,308**	**214,816**
Subaru Ascent	66,468	68,511	60,522
Subaru Crosstrek	54,403	—	—
Subaru Outback	186,874	162,797	154,294
TESLA TOTAL	**420,487**	**314,631**	**196,691**
Tesla Model X	46,064	39,412	14,166
Tesla Model Y	374,170	275,219	182,525
TOYOTA TOTAL	**623,876**	**554,494**	**641,239**
Lexus TX	11,958	—	—
Toyota Grand Highlander	58,542	—	—
Toyota Highlander	214,680	271,386	292,479
Toyota RAV4	78,944	77,233	76,869
Toyota Sequoia	24,256	6,133	7,436
Toyota Sienna	77,880	79,686	127,270
Toyota Tundra	157,616	120,056	86,546
TOYOTA/MAZDA TOTAL	**154,076**	**104,074**	**12,303**
Mazda CX-50	59,541	29,539	—
Toyota Corolla Cross	94,535	74,535	12,303
VOLKSWAGEN TOTAL	**170,675**	**121,062**	**114,232**
Volkswagen Atlas/ Atlas Cross Sport	121,593	112,236	114,232
Volkswagen ID.4	49,082	8,826	—
LIGHT TRUCK TOTAL	**8,569,053**	**8,029,624**	**7,308,718**

— = No production. **Note:** Totals may include models not shown.

Domestic and Imported Retail Vehicle Sales in the U.S., 1980-2023

Source: Wards Intelligence

(in number of units)

	Cars			Light trucks			All vehicles[1]		
Year	Domestic[2]	Imports	Total cars	Domestic[2]	Imports	Total light trucks	Domestic[2]	Imports	Total vehicles
1980	6,579,778	2,369,457	8,949,235	1,750,735	478,887	2,229,622	8,330,513	2,848,344	11,178,857
1985	8,204,670	2,774,517	10,979,187	3,629,080	832,186	4,461,266	12,109,999	3,615,292	15,725,291
1990	6,916,860	2,384,346	9,301,206	3,956,756	611,941	4,568,697	11,133,504	3,013,865	14,147,369
1995	7,113,902	1,506,257	8,620,159	5,705,708	402,181	6,107,889	13,192,861	1,923,464	15,116,325
2000	6,761,603	2,016,120	8,777,723	7,719,707	852,325	8,572,032	14,922,648	2,889,025	17,811,673
2002	5,816,671	2,225,584	8,042,255	7,707,738	1,066,375	8,774,113	13,829,568	3,309,084	17,138,652
2004	5,333,496	2,149,059	7,482,555	8,138,107	1,246,258	9,384,365	13,880,251	3,418,322	17,298,573
2005	5,473,450	2,186,533	7,659,983	8,072,456	1,215,315	9,287,771	14,020,528	3,423,801	17,444,329
2006	5,416,828	2,344,764	7,761,592	7,396,058	1,346,750	8,742,808	13,334,843	3,714,138	17,048,981
2007	5,197,271	2,365,063	7,562,334	7,138,803	1,388,085	8,526,888	12,687,016	3,773,299	16,460,315
2008	4,490,863	2,278,271	6,769,134	5,329,165	1,096,469	6,425,634	10,107,753	3,385,439	13,493,192
2009	3,558,283	1,843,282	5,401,565	4,116,550	884,242	5,000,792	7,867,766	2,734,277	10,602,043
2010	3,791,499	1,844,240	5,635,739	5,020,441	898,644	5,919,085	9,020,088	2,752,438	11,772,526
2011	4,145,964	1,946,897	6,092,861	5,666,512	982,443	6,648,955	10,108,762	2,939,624	13,048,386
2012	5,119,844	2,125,325	7,245,169	6,127,314	1,060,720	7,188,034	11,581,776	3,197,708	14,779,484
2013	5,433,158	2,153,176	7,586,334	6,704,499	1,239,268	7,943,767	12,479,306	3,403,406	15,882,712
2014	5,609,878	2,098,122	7,708,000	7,384,280	1,359,910	8,744,190	13,388,628	3,471,215	16,859,843
2015	5,595,123	1,933,403	7,528,526	8,097,387	1,782,078	9,879,465	14,127,526	3,729,798	17,857,324
2016	5,145,575	1,737,771	6,883,346	8,436,243	2,157,722	10,593,965	13,969,117	3,909,190	17,878,307
2017	4,592,965	1,496,238	6,089,203	8,651,782	2,409,100	11,060,882	13,644,445	3,920,682	17,565,127
2018	4,086,889	1,223,388	5,310,277	9,153,418	2,761,253	11,914,671	13,711,080	4,001,724	17,712,804
2019	3,543,923	1,175,787	4,719,710	9,621,675	2,619,677	12,241,352	13,676,873	3,811,281	17,488,154
2020	2,559,778	842,060	3,401,838	8,614,605	2,455,405	11,070,010	11,571,020	3,310,336	14,881,356
2021	2,375,728	974,322	3,350,050	9,006,441	2,590,432	11,596,873	11,830,596	3,577,919	15,408,515
2022	2,043,341	815,234	2,858,575	8,815,654	2,080,110	10,895,764	11,325,637	2,904,687	14,230,324
2023	2,252,405	864,242	3,116,647	9,911,144	2,474,688	12,385,832	12,658,257	3,351,011	16,009,268

Note: Vehicles are cars and light trucks belonging to gross vehicle weight (GVW) classes 1-3 (under 14,001 lbs). (1) Except for 1980, "All vehicles" includes medium and heavy trucks. (2) Includes the U.S., Canada, and Mexico.

U.S. Sales of Hybrid, Electric, and Fuel Cell Vehicles, 2000-23

Source: Wards Intelligence; in number of units sold

Power type	2000	2005	2010	2015	2017	2019	2020	2021	2022	2023
Hybrid car	9,350	151,253	231,819	350,753	252,366	230,676	161,078	215,041	186,247	274,853
Hybrid light truck	0	54,575	42,286	22,606	111,363	168,768	293,989	584,005	580,165	900,603
Total hybrid	**9,350**	**205,828**	**274,105**	**373,359**	**363,729**	**399,444**	**455,067**	**799,046**	**766,412**	**1,175,456**
Electric car	463	0	326	72,313	62,208	184,728	119,552	191,006	270,677	325,134
Electric light truck	0	0	0	61	40,172	49,094	118,988	268,418	477,305	839,504
Total electric	**463**	**0**	**326**	**72,374**	**102,380**	**233,822**	**238,540**	**459,424**	**747,982**	**1,164,638**
Fuel cell car	0	6	17	74	2,285	1,822	730	2,911	2,299	2,737
Fuel cell light truck	0	0	0	34	28	267	208	430	408	241
Total fuel cell	**0**	**6**	**17**	**108**	**2,313**	**2,089**	**938**	**3,341**	**2,707**	**2,978**
Plug-in hybrid car	0	0	326	41,739	76,420	58,576	30,860	41,125	24,179	19,744
Plug-in hybrid light truck	0	0	0	2,076	14,607	27,215	38,189	134,992	159,232	273,812
Total plug-in hybrid	**0**	**0**	**326**	**43,815**	**91,027**	**85,791**	**69,049**	**176,117**	**183,411**	**293,556**

U.S. Retail Car Sales by Vehicle Size, 1990-2023

Source: Wards Intelligence; as percent of total U.S. sales

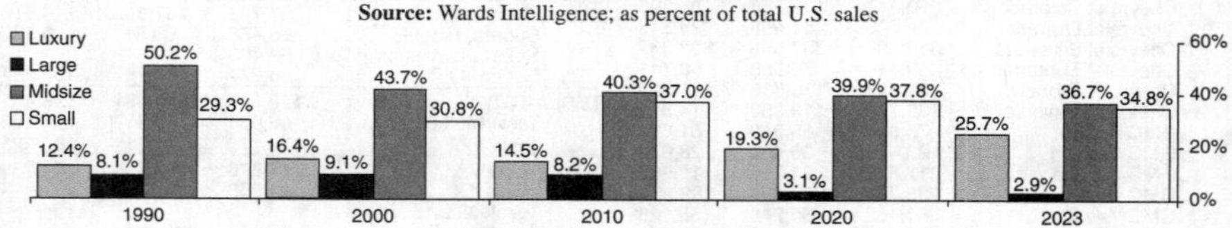

U.S. Light Truck Sales by Type, 1990-2023

Source: Wards Intelligence; as percent of total U.S. sales

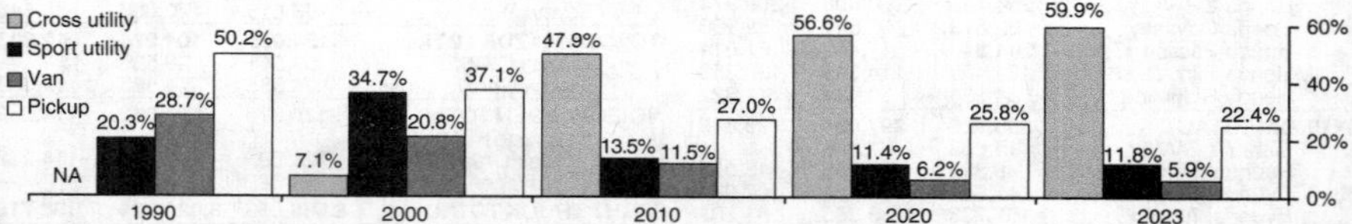

NA = Not applicable. **Note:** Comm. chassis sales (not shown) were 0.8% (for 1990), 0.2% (2000), 0.1% (2010), 0.02% (2020), 0.01% (2023).

Top-Selling Passenger Cars in the U.S., 2021-23

Source: Wards Intelligence; ranked by number of vehicles sold

Car	2023 sales	Car	2022 sales	Car	2021 sales
1. Toyota Camry	290,649	1. Toyota Camry	295,201	1. Toyota Camry	313,795
2. Toyota Corolla	232,370	2. Toyota Corolla	222,216	2. Honda Civic	263,787
3. Tesla Model 3	223,000	3. Tesla Model 3	188,500	3. Toyota Corolla	248,993
4. Honda Civic	200,381	4. Honda Accord	154,612	4. Honda Accord	202,676
5. Honda Accord	197,947	5. Nissan Altima	139,955	5. Tesla Model 3	139,503
6. Hyundai Elantra	134,149	6. Honda Civic	133,932	6. Nissan Sentra	127,861
7. Chevrolet Malibu	130,342	7. Hyundai Elantra	117,177	7. Hyundai Elantra	124,422
8. Nissan Altima	128,030	8. Chevrolet Malibu	115,467	8. Kia Forte	115,929
9. Kia Forte	123,953	9. Kia Forte	108,424	9. Nissan Altima	103,777
10. Nissan Sentra	109,195	10. Dodge Charger	80,074	10. Hyundai Sonata	93,142

Top-Selling Light Trucks in the U.S., 2021-23

Source: Wards Intelligence; ranked by number of vehicles sold

Truck	2023 sales	Truck	2022 sales	Truck	2021 sales
1. Ford F-Series	694,237	1. Ford F-Series	597,020	1. Ford F-Series	656,039
2. Chevrolet Silverado	543,780	2. Chevrolet Silverado	513,354	2. Ram Pickup	544,458
3. Toyota RAV4	434,943	3. Ram Pickup	448,205	3. Chevrolet Silverado	519,774
4. Ram Pickup	423,958	4. Toyota RAV4	399,941	4. Toyota RAV4	407,739
5. Tesla Model Y	382,600	5. GMC Sierra	241,522	5. Honda CR-V	361,271
6. Honda CR-V	361,457	6. Honda CR-V	238,155	6. Nissan Rogue	285,602
7. GMC Sierra	295,737	7. Toyota Tacoma	237,323	7. Jeep Grand Cherokee	264,444
8. Nissan Rogue	262,932	8. Jeep Grand Cherokee	223,345	8. Toyota Highlander	264,128
9. Jeep Grand Cherokee	244,594	9. Toyota Highlander	222,805	9. Toyota Tacoma	252,520
10. Toyota Tacoma	234,768	10. Tesla Model Y	212,600	10. GMC Sierra	248,924

Most Popular Colors by Vehicle Type, 2023

Source: Axalta Coating Systems; for 2023 model year in North America

Luxury cars/SUVs		Intermediate cars/MPVs		Compact/sports cars		Trucks/SUVs	
Color	Percent	Color	Percent	Color	Percent	Color	Percent
Black	29%	White	55%	Gray	27%	White	27%
White	27	Gray	18	White	25	Gray	21
Gray	16	Silver	9	Black	16	Black	18
Blue	6	Black	8	Silver	10	Silver	10
Red	5	Blue	5	Blue	10	Blue	9
Silver	5	Red	3	Red	7	Red	8
Green	4	Brown/beige	<1	Brown/beige	1	Brown/beige	1
Brown/beige	2	Green	<1	Green	<1	Green	1
Yellow/gold	<1	Yellow/gold	<1	Yellow/gold	<1	Yellow/gold	<1
Other	4	Other	<1	Other	<1	Other	<1

Note: SUV = sport utility vehicle; MPV = multipurpose vehicle.

U.S. Light-Duty Vehicle Fuel Efficiency, 1975-2023

Source: Natl. Vehicle and Fuel Emissions Laboratory, Office of Transportation and Air Quality, U.S. Environmental Protection Agency

Cars and light-duty trucks (SUVs, minivans, passenger vans, and pickup trucks) showed significant fuel-efficiency improvements from 1975 through 1987, when the fuel economy for both combined reached a high of 22 miles per gallon (mpg). The fuel economy value mainly declined, 1988-2004, but since 2005, fuel economy has generally increased, reaching a new all-time high of 26.9 mpg in 2023.

Year[1]	Cars (mpg)	Light-duty trucks (mpg)	All light-duty vehicles (mpg)	Year[1]	Cars (mpg)	Light-duty trucks (mpg)	All light-duty vehicles (mpg)
1975	13.5	11.6	13.1	2012	26.9	19.3	23.6
1980	20.0	15.8	19.2	2013	27.6	19.8	24.2
1985	23.0	17.5	21.3	2014	27.6	20.3	24.1
1990	23.3	17.4	21.2	2015	28.2	21.1	24.6
1995	23.3	17.0	20.5	2016	28.5	21.2	24.7
2000	22.5	16.8	19.8	2017	29.2	21.3	24.9
2005	23.1	16.9	19.9	2018	29.9	21.9	25.1
2007	23.7	17.4	20.6	2019	29.9	22.0	24.9
2008	23.9	17.8	21.0	2020	30.7	22.4	25.4
2009	25.0	18.5	22.4	2021	31.8	22.7	25.4
2010	25.7	18.8	22.6	2022	33.3	23.0	26.0
2011	25.4	19.1	22.3	2023[2]	34.9	24.0	26.9

Note: Adjusted mpg composite values (city and highway fuel efficiency combined in a 55%/45% ratio) are used for all vehicles and are intended to reflect real-world use. (1) Because of changes in methodology, mpg figures prior to 1986 are not entirely comparable with later values. (2) Preliminary.

Registered Cars in the U.S., 1900-2022

Source: Office of Highway Policy Information, Federal Highway Administration, U.S. Dept. of Transportation

(number of automobiles for public and private use)

Year	Reg. cars	Year	Reg. cars	Year	Reg. cars	Year	Reg. cars	Year	Reg. cars
1900	8,000	1945	25,796,985	1990	133,700,497	2007	135,932,930	2015	112,864,228
1905	77,400	1950	40,339,077	1995	128,386,775	2008	137,079,843	2016	112,961,266
1910	458,377	1955	52,144,739	2000	133,621,420	2009	134,879,600	2017	111,177,029
1915	2,332,426	1960	61,671,390	2001	137,633,467	2010	130,892,240	2018	111,242,132
1920	8,131,522	1965	75,257,588	2002	135,920,677	2011	125,656,528	2019	108,547,710
1925	17,481,001	1970	89,243,557	2003	135,669,897	2012	111,289,906	2020	105,143,990
1930	23,034,753	1975	106,705,934	2004	136,430,651	2013	113,676,345	2021	102,973,881
1935	22,567,827	1980	121,600,843	2005	136,568,083	2014	113,898,845	2022	99,946,870
1940	27,465,826	1985	127,885,193	2006	135,399,945				

Note: There were no publicly owned vehicles before 1925; statistics also exclude military vehicles for all years. Alaska and Hawaii data included since 1960.

Licensed Drivers by Age and Sex, 1980-2022

Source: Office of Highway Policy Information, Federal Highway Administration, U.S. Dept. of Transportation
(numbers in thousands)

	1980	1990	2000	2010			2022			
Age (years)	**Total**	**Total**	**Total**	**Male**	**Female**	**Total**	**Male**	**Female**	**Total**	**% total drivers**
Under 16	**93**	**43**	**27**	**199**	**198**	**398**	**59**	**59**	**118**	**0.1%**
16	1,823	1,443	1,470	608	605	1,213	538	539	1,077	0.5
17	2,790	2,132	2,331	1,025	1,004	2,028	932	912	1,844	0.8
18	3,247	2,595	2,839	1,408	1,323	2,731	1,334	1,253	2,587	1.1
19	3,542	3,037	3,077	1,641	1,546	3,187	1,528	1,423	2,951	1.3
19 and under	**11,496**	**9,249**	**9,744**	**4,880**	**4,676**	**9,556**	**4,391**	**4,186**	**8,576**	**3.6**
20	3,636	3,229	3,140	1,744	1,682	3,426	1,646	1,557	3,203	1.4
21	3,733	3,249	3,172	1,756	1,717	3,474	1,760	1,666	3,426	1.5
22	3,811	3,262	3,182	1,757	1,725	3,483	1,804	1,717	3,521	1.5
23	3,938	3,398	3,247	1,767	1,748	3,515	1,845	1,762	3,607	1.5
24	3,915	3,758	3,225	1,792	1,779	3,571	1,904	1,832	3,736	1.6
20-24	**19,032**	**16,897**	**15,966**	**8,817**	**8,651**	**17,469**	**8,958**	**8,533**	**17,492**	**7.4**
25-29	18,925	19,895	17,586	9,179	9,253	18,431	9,946	9,748	19,694	8.4
30-34	17,369	20,578	19,155	8,934	8,915	17,849	10,550	10,573	21,123	9.0
35-39	13,696	19,055	21,059	9,079	9,082	18,161	10,191	10,275	20,465	8.7
40-44	11,134	16,905	21,093	9,613	9,565	19,178	9,738	9,898	19,636	8.4
45-49	10,076	13,020	19,154	10,381	10,433	20,814	8,972	9,131	18,103	7.7
50-54	10,090	10,484	16,868	10,241	10,388	20,628	9,540	9,717	19,257	8.2
55-59	9,770	9,438	12,760	9,127	9,313	18,440	9,612	9,886	19,498	8.3
60-64	8,232	9,235	9,915	7,847	8,011	15,858	9,635	10,083	19,718	8.4
65-69	6,580	8,375	8,386	5,652	5,816	11,468	8,449	9,046	17,495	7.4
70-74	NA	NA	7,468	4,029	4,202	8,231	6,729	7,334	14,064	6.0
75-79	NA	NA	5,911	2,966	3,192	6,158	4,712	5,183	9,894	4.2
80-84	NA	NA	3,511	2,090	2,373	4,464	2,702	3,052	5,755	2.4
85 and over	**NA**	**NA**	**2,050**	**1,541**	**1,870**	**3,411**	**1,997**	**2,319**	**4,316**	**1.8**
Total	**145,295**	**167,015**	**190,625**	**104,374**	**105,740**	**210,115**	**116,122**	**118,964**	**235,086**	**100.0**

NA = Not available. **Note:** Numbers may not add up to totals due to rounding.

Mobile Device Handheld Phone and Texting Laws for Drivers, 2024

Source: Governors Highway Safety Association; as of June 2024

State	Handheld ban	Enforce-ment	Texting ban[1]	State	Handheld ban	Enforce-ment	Texting ban[1]	State	Handheld ban	Enforce-ment	Texting ban[1]
AL	Yes	S[2]	Yes	KY	No[4]	P	Yes	ND	No[4]	P	Yes
AK	No	P	Yes	LA	No[4,8]	P	Yes	OH	Yes	P	Yes
AZ	Yes	P[3]	Yes	ME	Yes	P	Yes	OK	No[8]	P	Yes
AR	No[4]	P	Yes	MD	Yes	P	Yes	OR	Yes	P	Yes
CA	Yes	P[5]	Yes	MA	Yes	P	Yes	PA	No[11]	P	Yes
CO	No[6]	P	Yes	MI	Yes	P	Yes	RI	Yes	P	Yes
CT	Yes	P	Yes	MN	Yes	P	Yes	SC	No	P	Yes
DE	Yes	P	Yes	MS	No	P	Yes	SD	No[8]	S	Yes
DC	Yes	P	Yes	MO	Yes	S	Yes	TN	Yes	P	Yes
FL	No	P	Yes	MT	No	NA	No	TX	No[4]	P	Yes
GA	Yes	P	Yes	NE	No[9]	S	Yes	UT	No[4]	P	Yes
HI	Yes	P	Yes	NV	Yes	P	Yes	VT	Yes	P	Yes
ID	Yes	P	Yes	NH	Yes	P	Yes	VA	Yes	P	Yes
IL	Yes	P	Yes	NJ	Yes	P	Yes	WA	Yes	P	Yes
IN	Yes	P	Yes	NM	No[10]	P	Yes	WV	Yes	P	Yes
IA	No[7]	P	Yes	NY	Yes	P	Yes	WI	No[8]	P	Yes
KS	No[8]	P	Yes	NC	No[4]	P	Yes	WY	No	P	Yes

NA = Not applicable. P = Officer may stop vehicle for violation (primary); S = Officer may issue citation only when vehicle is stopped for another moving violation (secondary). **Note:** Laws shown for licensed passenger car drivers. Different laws and regulations apply to school bus, municipal transit, and other mass transit operators. Different laws may apply in school zones, construction zones, or other such areas. (1) Of the 49 states and DC that ban text messaging for all drivers, all but 4 (MO [except for drivers 21 years of age and under], NE, OK, SD) have primary enforcement. (2) Primary for 16-year-old drivers and for 17-year-old drivers who have held an intermediate license for fewer than 6 months. (3) Secondary for cellphone use by instruction and intermediate permit holders under 18 years of age. (4) Yes for drivers under 18 years of age. (5) Secondary for cellphone use by drivers under 18 years of age. (6) Yes for all drivers as of Jan. 1, 2025. (7) Yes for restricted or intermediate license holders. (8) Yes for drivers with learner's permit or intermediate license. (9) Yes for learner's permit and intermediate license holders under 18. (10) Yes for learner's permit and provisional license holders. (11) Yes for all drivers as of June 5, 2025.

Selected Motor Vehicle Statistics

Source: Federal Highway Admin., U.S. Dept. of Transportation; Insurance Inst. for Highway Safety; U.S. Energy Information Admin.

Driver's license age requirements, state gas tax, and safety belt use laws (incl. laws passed, but not in effect) as of 2024. Other figures are for 2022.

	Driver's license age requirements				Licensed drivers				Annual miles driven		
STATE	Learner's permit	Regular[1]	Gas taxes (cents/gal)[6]	Safety belt use law[7]	Per 1,000 resident pop.	Per reg. motor vehicle	Reg. motor vehicles per 1,000 pop.	Fuel use per reg. motor vehicle (gal)	Per gal used	Per reg. vehicle	Per lic. driver
Alabama	15	17	48.60	P(a)	806	0.75	1,077	770	17.02	13,109	17,523
Alaska	14	16y, 6m	27.35	P	711	0.79	926	624	12.93	8,067	10,510
Arizona	15y, 6m	16y, 6m	37.40	S	795	0.98	828	671	18.64	12,505	13,024
Arkansas	14	18	43.40	P	757	0.66	1,172	638	16.91	10,794	16,702
California	15y, 6m	17	86.50	P	708	0.91	797	545	18.58	10,130	11,409
Colorado	15	17	47.64	S	767	0.89	876	791	13.33	10,541	12,046
Connecticut	16	18[2,3,4]	43.40	P(a)	725	0.94	769	641	16.58	10,635	11,285
Delaware	16	17[2]	41.40	P	847	1.88	459	1,241	17.03	21,128	11,451
Dist. of Columbia	16	18[4]	53.30	P	761	1.48	567	316	28.43	8,983	6,694
Florida	15	18	57.00	P	742	0.85	884	582	19.91	11,583	13,807
Georgia	15	18[2]	51.45	P	674	0.82	839	666	21.13	14,079	17,508
Hawaii	15y, 6m	17[2]	36.90	P	651	0.77	863	386	21.45	8,275	10,980
Idaho	14y, 6m	16[2]	51.40	S	718	0.69	1,048	620	15.22	9,431	13,756
Illinois	15	18[2]	84.90	P	676	0.83	821	560	17.92	10,039	12,193
Indiana	15	18	70.10	P	681	0.75	916	704	21.71	15,294	20,560
Iowa	14	17[2]	48.40	P	736	0.63	1,181	644	13.44	8,655	13,896
Kansas	14	16y, 6m	43.43	P(a)	699	0.80	881	717	16.88	12,106	15,266
Kentucky	16	17[2]	48.50	P	663	0.71	951	717	15.62	11,195	16,050
Louisiana	15	17[4]	39.33	P	741	0.76	1,001	654	18.81	12,303	16,612
Maine	15	16y, 9m[2]	49.80	P	765	0.82	934	674	16.79	11,320	13,816
Maryland	15y, 9m	18[2]	65.59	P(a)	714	0.91	798	638	18.07	11,536	12,900
Massachusetts	16	18[2]	45.77	S	700	0.95	743	576	19.08	10,985	11,648
Michigan	14y, 9m	17[2]	66.40	P	775	0.84	937	587	17.37	10,198	12,331
Minnesota	15	16y, 6m	47.00	P	720	0.73	992	575	17.63	10,130	13,957
Mississippi	15	16y, 6m	36.80	P	696	0.90	782	1,072	16.21	17,378	19,517
Missouri	15	17y, 11m	43.37	S(b)	694	0.80	870	799	18.49	14,781	18,514
Montana	14y, 6m	16[2]	52.15	S	776	0.39	2,003	386	15.56	6,007	15,517
Nebraska	15	17	48.40	S	737	0.75	1,000	733	14.74	10,813	14,671
Nevada	15y, 6m	18[2]	42.21	S	696	0.84	841	624	16.57	10,346	12,506
New Hampshire	15y, 6m[5]	18[2]	42.23	None	842	0.83	1,030	579	15.97	9,241	11,304
New Jersey	16	18	60.75	P(a)	716	1.12	648	720	17.42	12,549	11,349
New Mexico	15	16y, 6m[2]	37.28	P	714	0.84	885	898	15.98	14,345	17,786
New York	16	17[2]	44.08	P	614	1.33	463	759	16.68	12,664	9,548
North Carolina	15	16y, 6m[2]	59.05	P(a)	746	0.90	841	697	19.03	13,271	14,960
North Dakota	14	16[2]	41.43	P	723	0.53	1,403	643	13.06	8,395	16,300
Ohio	15y, 6m	18[2]	56.90	S	715	0.77	938	578	17.35	10,026	13,155
Oklahoma	15y, 6m	16y, 6m	38.40	P	636	0.77	832	867	15.37	13,322	17,432
Oregon	15	17[2,3]	58.40	P	732	0.76	976	518	17.07	8,836	11,780
Pennsylvania	16	17	77.10	S(b)	703	0.85	838	568	16.19	9,193	10,950
Rhode Island	16	17y, 6m[2]	56.52	P	695	0.96	737	554	16.85	9,342	9,903
South Carolina	15	16y, 6m	47.15	P	775	0.85	993	700	16.06	11,245	14,417
South Dakota	14	16	48.40	S	747	0.52	1,500	556	13.41	7,453	14,962
Tennessee	15	17	45.80	P	718	0.76	968	678	17.98	12,188	16,442
Texas	15[2]	18	38.40	P	624	0.82	776	893	13.98	12,489	15,523
Utah	15	17[2]	55.55	P	666	0.80	851	630	18.93	11,936	15,243
Vermont	15	16y, 6m[2]	51.01	S	739	0.78	967	552	20.64	11,392	14,899
Virginia	15y, 6m	18[2]	57.50	S	672	0.77	894	642	16.46	10,573	14,062
Washington	15	17[2]	71.22	P	765	0.78	1,006	433	17.22	7,464	9,819
West Virginia	15	17	54.10	P	647	0.71	931	780	11.88	9,264	13,334
Wisconsin	15[2]	16y, 9m[2]	51.30	P	742	0.78	964	634	18.37	11,646	15,125
Wyoming	15	16y, 6m[2]	42.40	S	743	0.49	1,531	789	13.27	10,473	21,589
U.S. AVERAGE			**50.84**		**705**	**0.84**	**850**	**655**	**17.22**	**11,278**	**13,596**

Note: Most states have graduated licensing systems that phase in full driving privileges. During the learner's stage, driving generally is not permitted without adult supervision. In an intermediate stage, young licensees may be allowed to drive unsupervised under certain conditions. (1) Min. age at which all restrictions may be lifted on private passenger car operation. (2) Applicants under a specified age (typically between 17 and 19) must complete driver education. (3) Home training (CT) or more hours of supervised driving (OR) may be substituted for driver ed. (4) Learner's stage mandatory for all license applicants regardless of age. (5) NH does not issue learner's permits. At age 15 years, 6 months, a person can drive while supervised by a licensed driver 25 years or older. (6) Includes 18.4 cents per gallon in federal excise taxes. (7) P = Officer may stop vehicle for violation (primary); S = Officer may issue seat belt citation only when vehicle is stopped for another moving violation (secondary). (a) Secondary enforcement for rear seat occupants; (b) Primary enforcement for children under a specified age.

International Tourism Receipts, 2000-23

Source: World Tourism Organization (UNWTO), © UNWTO; as of June 2024
(in billions of U.S. dollars; ranked by 2023 figures)

Rank	Country	2000	2010	2019	2020	2021	2023
1.	U.S.	$100.2	$130.3	$199.0	$72.5	$71.4	$175.9
2.	Spain	30.9	58.8	79.7	18.5	34.5	92.0
3.	UK	22.2	38.6	58.4	26.7	33.0	73.9
4.	France	33.0	57.1	63.5	32.6	40.8	68.6
5.	Italy	27.5	38.4	49.5	19.9	25.0	55.9
6.	United Arab Emirates	1.1	8.6	38.4	24.6	34.4	51.9
7.	Turkey	7.6	22.6	34.3	13.3	26.6	49.5
8.	Australia	9.4	32.6	45.5	25.8	17.0	46.6
9.	Canada	10.8	17.6	29.8	13.9	15.3	39.2
10.	Japan	3.4	13.2	46.1	10.7	4.9	38.6
11.	Germany	18.7	34.7	41.8	22.1	22.3	37.4
12.	Saudi Arabia	NA	6.7	16.4	4.0	3.8	36.0
13.	Macau	3.2	22.3	40.1	9.2	15.2	32.6
14.	India	3.5	14.5	30.7	13.0	8.7	32.2
15.	Mexico	8.3	12.0	24.6	11.0	19.8	30.8
16.	Thailand	7.5	20.1	59.8	13.4	5.1	29.7
17.	Portugal	5.2	10.1	20.5	8.8	11.9	27.2
18.	Austria	9.8	18.6	22.9	13.8	10.4	25.0
19.	China[1]	16.2	45.8	35.8	10.0	11.3	24.8
20.	Greece	9.2	12.5	20.3	5.0	12.4	22.3
21.	Switzerland	6.6	14.8	18.1	10.2	12.2	21.1
22.	Hong Kong	5.9	22.2	28.9	2.9	1.9	21.1
23.	Singapore	5.1	14.2	20.3	5.4	4.0	21.1
24.	Netherlands	7.2	11.7	18.6	9.7	9.4	20.2
25.	Croatia	2.8	7.2	11.8	5.5	10.8	15.8
26.	South Korea	$6.8	$10.3	$20.9	$10.3	$10.8	$15.3
27.	Poland	5.7	9.4	14.0	8.2	9.1	15.0
28.	Malaysia	5.0	18.1	19.8	3.0	0.1	14.8
29.	Egypt	NA	12.5	13.0	4.4	8.9	14.1
30.	Indonesia	5.0	7.0	16.9	3.4	0.5	14.0
31.	Morocco	2.0	6.7	8.2	3.8	3.8	10.3
32.	Denmark	3.7	5.9	8.7	4.0	4.5	10.3
33.	Sweden	4.1	8.3	9.2	4.3	6.1	9.8
34.	Dom. Rep.	2.9	4.2	7.5	2.7	5.7	9.8
35.	Vietnam	NA	4.5	11.8	2.5	0.1	9.2
36.	Philippines	2.2	2.6	9.8	1.8	0.6	9.1
37.	Qatar	0.1	0.6	5.4	3.6	4.3	8.8
38.	Taiwan	3.7	8.7	14.4	1.8	0.7	8.7
39.	Hungary	3.8	5.6	7.3	3.2	4.2	8.0
40.	New Zealand	2.9	6.5	10.5	5.8	2.9	7.9
41.	Czechia	3.0	7.2	7.3	3.6	3.1	7.9
42.	Ireland	2.6	4.1	6.5	2.4	2.7	7.6
43.	Belgium	6.6	11.4	8.8	6.2	6.3	7.6
44.	Colombia	1.0	2.8	5.7	1.6	2.7	7.6
45.	Jordan	NA	3.6	5.8	1.4	2.8	7.4
46.	Brazil	1.8	5.3	6.0	3.0	2.9	6.9
47.	Russia	3.4	8.8	11.0	3.9	4.0	6.7
48.	Luxembourg	NA	5.7	5.3	4.4	5.6	6.3
49.	Norway	2.2	4.7	5.9	1.8	2.0	6.2
50.	Israel	4.4	4.9	7.5	2.5	2.1	6.0
	World[2]	**495**	**968**	**1,460**	**549**	**627**	**1,483**

NA = Not available. (1) Not including Hong Kong and Macau. (2) Includes countries not shown.

International Tourist Arrivals by Country of Destination, 2000-23

Source: World Tourism Organization (UNWTO), © UNWTO; as of Sept. 2024
(visitors in millions; ranked by most recent data available)

Rank	Country	2000	2010	2019	2020	2022	2023	% change, 2000-23
1.	France	77.2	77.7	90.9	41.7	93.2	100.0	29.5%
2.	Spain	46.4	52.7	83.5	18.9	71.7	85.2	83.6
3.	U.S.	51.2	60.0	79.4	19.2	50.9	66.5	29.8
4.	Italy	41.2	43.6	64.5	25.2	49.8	57.3	39.3
5.	Turkey	9.6	31.4	51.2	15.9	50.5	55.2	474.6
6.	Mexico	20.6	23.3	45.0	24.8	38.3	42.0	104.6
7.	UK	23.2	28.9	39.4	10.7	30.7	37.2	60.4
8.	Germany	19.0	26.9	39.6	12.5	28.5	34.8	83.2
9.	Greece	13.1	15.0	31.4	7.4	27.8	32.7	149.9
10.	Austria	18.0	22.0	31.9	15.1	26.2	30.9	71.7
11.	Thailand	9.6	15.9	39.9	6.7	11.1	28.2	193.2
12.	United Arab Emirates	3.1[1]	NA	21.6	7.2	22.7	28.2	808.1
13.	Saudi Arabia	6.6	10.9	17.5	4.1	16.6	27.4	315.5
14.	Portugal	5.7	6.8	24.6	6.5	22.3	26.5	365.6
15.	Japan	4.8	8.6	31.9	4.1	3.8	25.1	422.3
16.	Netherlands	10.0	10.9	20.1	7.3	16.1	20.3	103.0
17.	Malaysia	10.2	24.6	26.1	4.3	10.1	20.1	97.5
18.	Poland	17.4	12.5	21.2	8.4	16.0	19.0	9.1
19.	Canada	19.6	16.2	22.2	3.0	12.8	18.3	–6.4
20.	Hong Kong	8.8	20.1	23.8	1.4	0.6	17.2	95.0
21.	Croatia	5.3	9.1	17.4	5.6	15.3	NA	NA
22.	Egypt	NA	14.1	12.9	3.6	11.7	14.9	NA
23.	Morocco	4.3	9.3	12.9	2.8	10.9	14.5	237.7
24.	India	2.6	5.8	17.9	6.3	14.3	NA	NA
25.	Macau	5.2	11.9	18.6	2.8	2.5	14.2	173.7
26.	Denmark	3.5	9.4	14.7	6.2	14.2	NA	NA
27.	Hungary	3.0	9.5	16.9	7.4	12.7	12.9	331.0%
28.	Vietnam	2.1	5.1	18.0	3.8	3.7	12.6	500.0
29.	South Korea	5.3	8.8	17.5	2.5	3.2	11.0	108.1
30.	Albania	NA	2.2	6.2	2.6	7.2	9.7	NA
31.	Tunisia	5.1	7.8	9.4	2.0	6.4	9.4	83.7
32.	Switzerland	7.8	8.6	11.8	3.7	9.2	NA	NA
33.	South Africa	5.9	8.1	10.2	2.8	5.7	8.5	43.7
34.	Belgium	6.5	7.2	9.3	2.6	8.2	NA	NA
35.	Dominican Rep.	3.0	4.1	6.5	2.4	7.2	8.1	168.7
36.	Sweden	3.8	5.2	7.6	2.0	6.6	7.5	98.2
37.	Argentina	2.9	6.8	7.4	2.1	3.9	7.3	151.4
38.	Australia	4.9	5.8	9.5	1.8	3.7	7.2	46.7
39.	Uzbekistan	NA	1.0	6.8	1.6	5.2	6.6	NA
40.	Taiwan	2.6	5.6	11.9	1.4	0.9	6.5	149.6
41.	Ireland	6.6	7.1	11.0	NA	NA	6.3	–4.5
42.	Brazil	5.3	5.2	6.4	2.2	3.6	5.9	11.5
43.	Iran	NA	2.9	9.1	1.6	4.1	5.9	NA
44.	China[2]	31.2	55.7	65.7	8.0	NA	NA	NA
45.	Colombia	NA	2.4	4.2	1.3	4.5	5.6	NA
46.	Bahrain	NA	NA	3.9	0.8	3.7	5.6	NA
47.	Cambodia	NA	2.5	6.6	1.3	2.3	5.5	NA
48.	Jordan	NA	4.2	4.5	1.1	4.3	5.4	NA
49.	Puerto Rico	NA	3.2	3.2	2.6	4.2	5.1	NA
50.	Philippines	2.0	3.5	8.3	1.5	2.7	5.0	150.0
	World[3]	**674**	**973**	**1,465**	**406**	**975**	**1,305**	**92.9**

NA = Not available. (1) Dubai only. (2) Not including Hong Kong and Macau. (3) Includes countries not shown.

World Tourism Receipts, 1990-2023

Source: World Tourism Organization (UNWTO), © UNWTO; as of July 2024
(in billions of U.S. dollars)

Year	Receipts[1]	Year	Receipts[1]	Year	Receipts[1]	Year	Receipts[1]	Year	Receipts[1]	Year	Receipts[1]
1990	$271	1999	$475	2004	$652	2009	$901	2014	$1,258	2019	$1,460
1995	415	2000	495	2005	704	2010	968	2015	1,195	2020	549
1996	449	2001	481	2006	766	2011	1,082	2016	1,225	2021	627
1997	449	2002	501	2007	883	2012	1,117	2017	1,319	2022	1,105
1998	457	2003	549	2008	968	2013	1,208	2018	1,431	2023	1,483

(1) Total of all transactions made by or on behalf of visitors for the duration of their visit. Does not include receipts from international passenger transport contracted from companies outside a traveler's country of residence.

International Travel to the U.S., 1990-2023

Source: National Travel and Tourism Office, Intl. Trade Admin., U.S. Dept. of Commerce
(number of visitors in millions)

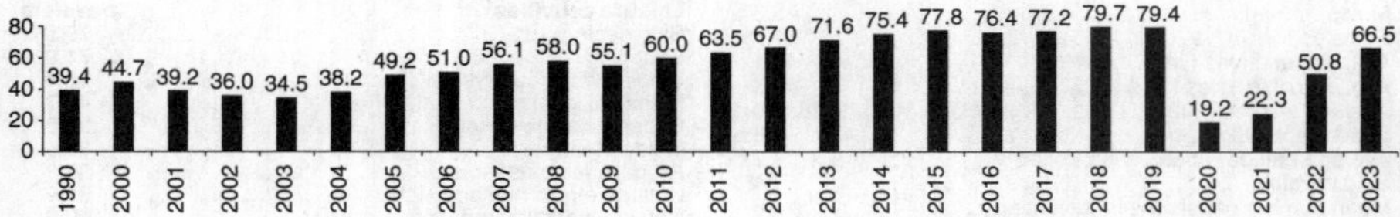

U.S. Domestic Leisure Travel Volume, 2000-23

Source: U.S. Travel Assn.
(in billions of person-trips of 50 mi or more, one-way)

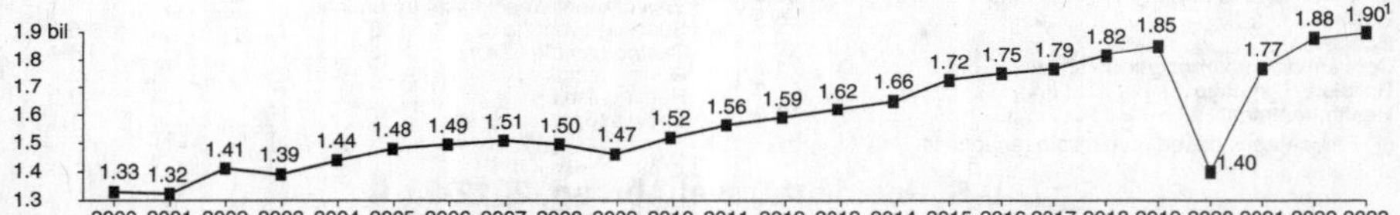

Note: Method of collecting travel data has been revised; data for earlier years have been adjusted to maintain comparability. (1) Forecast.

Top 10 U.S. States by Traveler Spending, 2022

Source: U.S. Travel Assn.
(domestic and international traveler spending within state, in billions of dollars)

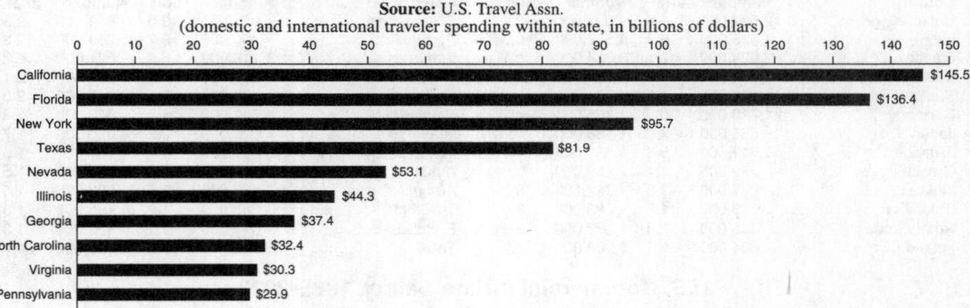

International Visitors to the U.S. by Top Countries of Origin, 2023

Source: National Travel and Tourism Office, Intl. Trade Admin., U.S. Dept. of Commerce
(ranked by number of visitors)

Country of origin	Visitors	Expenditures (mil)	Expenditures per visitor
1. Canada	20,514,314	$24,085	$1,174
2. Mexico	14,499,093	21,362	1,473
3. United Kingdom	3,897,534	13,998	3,592
4. Germany	1,838,481	7,536	4,099
5. India	1,762,369	20,196	11,460
6. Brazil	1,624,719	8,348	5,138
7. South Korea	1,600,400	8,327	5,203
8. France	1,592,934	5,964	3,744
9. Japan	1,518,522	7,161	4,716
10. China[1]	1,078,056	20,990	19,470
11. Italy	976,952	4,271	4,372
12. Australia	954,481	$6,569	$6,882
13. Colombia	932,060	3,513	3,769
14. Spain	825,790	3,327	4,029
15. Argentina	596,155	2,812	4,717
16. Netherlands	572,271	2,305	4,028
17. Dominican Republic	504,319	2,026	4,017
18. Ecuador	468,419	NA	NA
19. Ireland	454,988	1,726	3,794
20. Chile	414,551	1,706	4,115
All countries	**66,481,888**	**225,881**	**3,398**

NA = Not available. **Note:** Expenditures include passenger fares. (1) Does not include Hong Kong.

Traveler Spending in the U.S., 1987-2023

Source: National Travel and Tourism Office, Intl. Trade Admin., U.S. Dept. of Commerce; U.S. Travel Assn.
(in billions of dollars by origin of traveler)

Year	Domestic	International
1987	$235	$31
1990	291	43
1995	360	63
2000	503	82
2001	484	72
2002	478	67
2003	496	65
2004	532	75
2005	572	82
2006	$610	$86
2007	641	97
2008	662	110
2009	606	94
2010	644	104
2011	694	119
2012	728	127
2013	751	135
2014	792	136
2015	$814	$157
2016	837	156
2017	882	156
2018	933	156
2019	992	181
2020	681	41
2021	868	41
2022	918	98
2023[1]	943	131

(1) Forecast.

Characteristics of U.S. Travelers Visiting Overseas Destinations, 2022

Source: Survey of Intl. Air Travelers, National Travel and Tourism Office, Intl. Trade Admin., U.S. Dept. of Commerce

Total U.S. resident travelers	**38,101,000**
Males	45.3%
Females	54.7%
Avg. age of males (yrs.)	45.1
Avg. age of females (yrs.)	43.8
Average income (2021)	$148,000
Used prepaid package	8%
Average number of countries visited	1.2
Solo travelers	64%
Mean number of persons in travel party	1.58
Average number of nights	17.92

Main purpose of trip	**% of travelers**
Vacation/holiday	54.7%
Visit friends/relatives	32.6
Business	5.3
Education	3.1
Convention/conference/trade show	1.7
Religion/pilgrimage	1.0
Health treatment	0.8

Leisure activities[1]	**% of travelers**
Sightseeing	79.5%
Shopping	71.0
Small towns/countryside	47.4
Historical locations	40.7
Experience fine dining	36.9
Guided tour(s)	35.6
Art galleries/museums	35.2
Cultural/ethnic heritage sights	31.9
National parks/monuments	30.9
Nightclubbing/dancing	20.2
Water sports	15.5
Concert/play/musical	11.3
Amusement/theme parks	10.6
Camping/hiking	9.1
Environmental/ecological excursions	7.1
Sporting event	6.1
Casino/gamble	4.4
Golfing/tennis	2.4
Hunting/fishing	2.2
Snow sports	1.1

(1) Percentages based on multiple responses.

U.S. Resident Travel Abroad, 2012-23

Source: Intl. Trade Admin., U.S. Dept. of Commerce
(ranked by number of travelers in 2023)

Country	2012 Number	2012 % of total	2023 Number	2023 % of total
United Kingdom	2,537,000	8.9	4,033,000	10.8
Italy	1,938,000	6.8	3,547,000	9.5
France	2,024,000	7.1	3,024,000	8.1
Dominican Republic	2,252,000	7.9	2,614,000	7.0
Spain	1,140,000	4.0	2,054,000	5.5
Germany	1,710,000	6.0	1,755,000	4.7
Japan	855,000	3.0	1,568,000	4.2
Jamaica	1,511,000	5.3	1,531,000	4.1
Greece	399,000	1.4	1,269,000	3.4
India	941,000	3.3	1,232,000	3.3
Colombia	513,000	1.8	1,083,000	2.9
Netherlands	656,000	2.3	1,083,000	2.9
Ireland	684,000	2.4	1,008,000	2.7
Costa Rica	855,000	3.0	859,000	2.3
Portugal	200,000	0.7	859,000	2.3
Bahamas	1,112,000	3.9	821,000	2.2
Switzerland	570,000	2.0	784,000	2.1
Philippines	599,000	2.1	747,000	2.0
South Korea	542,000	1.9	672,000	1.8
Israel	627,000	2.2	635,000	1.7
Turkey	399,000	1.4	597,000	1.6
Austria	456,000	1.6	560,000	1.5
Aruba	456,000	1.6	523,000	1.4
Thailand	342,000	1.2	485,000	1.3
El Salvador	314,000	1.1	485,000	1.3
Total	**28,502,000**	**100.0**	**37,338,000**	**100.0**

U.S. Commercial Airline Safety, 1985-2022

Source: National Transportation Safety Board; Federal Aviation Administration, U.S. Dept. of Transportation

Year	Departures (mil)	Fatal accidents	Fatalities[1]	Rate of fatal accidents[2]
1985	6.1	4	197	0.066
1990	7.8	4	11	0.051
1995	8.1	1	160	0.012
2000	11.1	2	89	0.018
2001[3]	10.6	6	531	0.019
2005	10.9	3	22	0.027
2006	10.6	2	50	0.019
2008	10.3	0	0	—
2009	9.6	1	50	0.010
2010	9.5	0	0	—
2011	9.4	0	0	—
2012	9.2	0	0	—
2013	9.3	0	0	—
2014	9.0	0	0	—
2015	9.0	0	0	—
2016	9.1	0	0	—
2017	9.1	0	0	—
2018	9.4	1	1	0.011
2019	9.6	1	1	0.010
2020	5.8	0	0	—
2021	7.6	0	0	—
2022	8.4	1	1	0.012

— = Not applicable. **Note:** Statistics are for scheduled commercial carriers. (1) Includes deaths that occurred on the ground as a result of an accident, except for fatalities resulting from the Sept. 11, 2001, terrorist attacks. (2) Per 100,000 departures. (3) The Sept. 11, 2001, terrorist attacks have been included among the number of fatal accidents but have been excluded when calculating the fatal accident rate.

U.S. Airline Statistics, 1995-2023

Source: Airlines for America

	1995	2000	2005	2010	2015	2020	2021	2022	2023
Passengers enplaned (mil)[1]	547.8	666.1	738.6	720.5	798.2	369.4	666.2	852.5	941.6
Revenue passenger miles (bil)[1,2]	540.7	692.8	779.0	798.0	902.2	378.0	687.9	947.9	1,077.9
Available seat miles (bil)[1,3]	807.1	957.0	1,003.4	972.6	1,077.0	643.2	932.9	1,141.2	1,293.2
Cargo revenue ton miles (mil)[1,2]	16,921	23,888	28,039	27,885	27,062	28,742	32,421	32,339	29,906
% of seating utilized[1]	67.0%	72.4%	77.6%	82.1%	83.8%	58.8%	73.7%	83.1%	83.4%
Passenger revenue (mil)[4]	$70,132	$94,307	$94,340	$104,431	$126,880	$49,888	$86,705	$155,155	$179,129
Net profit (mil)[4]	$2,001	$2,238	–$28,647	$2,245	$24,794	–$35,047	–$2,801	$1,630	$7,828
Total employment (thous.)[5]	595.6	739.6	619.6	564.4	605.3	707.9	715.7	763.9	788.5

(1) Scheduled service only. (2) One fare-paying passenger or one ton of revenue cargo transported one mile. (3) One seat transported one mile. (4) Passenger carriers only. (5) Figures are of the sum of full-time and part-time employees.

Top 25 U.S. Passenger Airlines, 2023

Source: Airlines for America

In 2023, 99.7% of all passengers enplaned flew on the top 25 U.S. passenger airlines.
(in millions; ranked by number of passengers enplaned in scheduled service in 2023)

	Airline	Passengers
1.	Southwest Airlines	171.8
2.	American Airlines	164.4
3.	Delta Air Lines	161.6
4.	United Air Lines	134.0
5.	Spirit Air Lines	44.0
6.	JetBlue Airways	42.8
7.	SkyWest Airlines	38.4
8.	Alaska Airlines	35.2
9.	Frontier Airlines	30.1
10.	Republic Airlines	17.6
11.	Allegiant Air	17.2
12.	Envoy Air	14.3
13.	Endeavor Air	12.8
14.	PSA Airlines	11.6
15.	Hawaiian Airlines	10.9
16.	Mesa Airlines	6.2
17.	Horizon Air	4.4
18.	Piedmont Airlines	4.3
19.	Sun Country Airlines	4.1
20.	Commutair	3.1
21.	Breeze Airways	2.8
22.	Air Wisconsin Airlines	2.5
23.	Avelo Airlines	2.3
24.	GoJet Airlines	1.9
25.	Silver Airways	0.8

Note: Includes domestic and international passengers on U.S. airlines.

Top North American Airports by Passenger Traffic, 2023

Top World Airports by Passenger Traffic, 2023

Source: Annual World Airport Traffic Report, 2024 Edition, Airports Council Intl.

City/airport name (airport code)	Total passengers[1]
1. Hartsfield-Jackson Atlanta Intl. (ATL)	104,653,451
2. Dallas/Ft. Worth Intl. (DFW)	81,755,538
3. Denver Intl. (DEN)	77,837,917
4. Los Angeles Intl. (LAX)	75,050,875
5. Chicago O'Hare Intl. (ORD)	73,894,226
6. New York John F. Kennedy Intl. (JFK)	62,464,331
7. Orlando Intl. (MCO)	57,735,726
8. Las Vegas McCarran Intl. (LAS)	57,666,456
9. Charlotte Douglas Intl. (CLT)	53,445,770
10. Miami Intl. (MIA)	52,340,934
11. Seattle-Tacoma Intl. (SEA)	50,877,260
12. San Francisco Intl. (SFO)	50,196,094
13. Newark Liberty Intl. (EWR)	49,084,774
14. Phoenix Sky Harbor Intl. (PHX)	48,654,432
15. Mexico City Benito Juárez Intl. (MEX)	48,415,693
16. Houston George Bush Intercontinental (IAH)	46,192,499
17. Toronto Pearson Intl. (YYZ)	44,761,805
18. Boston Logan Intl. (BOS)	40,861,658
19. Ft. Lauderdale-Hollywood Intl. (FLL)	35,115,485
20. Minneapolis/St. Paul Intl. (MSP)	34,770,800

City/airport name (country; airport code)	Total passengers[1]
1. Dubai Intl. (United Arab Emirates; DXB)	86,994,365
2. London Heathrow (UK; LHR)	79,183,364
3. Tokyo Haneda Intl. (Japan; HND)	78,719,302
4. Istanbul Intl. (Turkey; IST)	76,027,321
5. Delhi Indira Gandhi Intl. (India; DEL)	72,214,841
6. Paris Charles de Gaulle (France; CDG)	67,421,316
7. Guangzhou Bai Yun Intl. (China; CAN)	63,169,169
8. Amsterdam Schiphol (Netherlands; AMS)	61,889,586
9. Adolfo Suárez Madrid-Barajas (Spain; MAD)	60,181,604
10. Flughafen Frankfurt/Main (Germany; FRA)	59,355,389
11. Singapore Changi (Singapore; SIN)	58,946,000
12. Incheon Intl. (South Korea; ICN)	56,235,412
13. Shanghai Pudong Intl. (China; PVG)	54,476,397
14. Beijing Capital Intl. (China; PEK)	52,879,156
15. Shenzhen Baoan Intl. (China; SZX)	52,734,934
16. Bangkok Suvarnabhumi Intl. (Thailand; BKK)	51,699,104
17. Mumbai Chhatrapati Shivaji Intl. (India; BOM)	51,589,040
18. Barcelona-El Prat (Spain; BCN)	49,883,928
19. Jakarta Soekarno-Hatta Intl. (Indonesia; CGK)	49,080,532
20. Kuala Lumpur Intl. (Malaysia; KUL)	47,242,468

Note: World list excludes North American airports and airports that do not participate in Airports Council Intl.'s Airport Traffic Statistics collection. (1) Arriving and departing passengers and direct transit passengers counted once.

Busiest Amtrak Stations, 2023

Source: Amtrak

(in thous.; ranked by total ridership)

Station	Tickets from	Tickets to	Total ridership
New York (Penn Sta.), NY	5,101	5,149	10,250
Washington, DC	2,373	2,378	4,751
Philadelphia (30th Street Sta.), PA	2,103	2,094	4,197
Chicago (Union Sta.), IL	1,348	1,374	2,722
Boston (South Sta.), MA	750	788	1,539
Baltimore (Penn Sta.), MD	545	536	1,081
Los Angeles, CA	505	495	1,000
New Haven (Union Sta.), CT	399	394	793
Albany-Rensselaer, NY	397	393	791
Boston (Back Bay Sta.), MA	363	387	750
Sacramento, CA	392	349	741
BWI Airport Sta., MD	344	367	711
Providence (Amtrak/MBTA), RI	347	362	709
Seattle (King Street Sta.), WA	353	337	690
Newark (Penn Sta.), NJ	331	340	672
Bakersfield, CA	331	327	658
Wilmington, DE	315	311	625
Portland (Union Sta.), OR	260	266	526
Milwaukee-Downtown (Intermodal Sta.), WI	265	244	509
Emeryville, CA	220	251	472
Route 128 (Westwood), MA	199	209	408
Richmond (Staples Mill Rd.), VA	207	197	404
Boston (North Sta.), MA	192	208	400
Stockton (San Joaquin St.), CA	199	200	399
Lancaster, PA	204	177	380

U.S. Public Transportation Usage, 1996-2022

Source: Federal Transit Administration, U.S. Dept. of Transportation

Public transportation usage is measured in unlinked passenger trips (UPT), which counts the number of passengers who board public transportation vehicles each time they board.

(UPT in millions)

Number of passengers by year

Year	UPT	Year	UPT	Year	UPT
1996	7,565	2007	10,054	2015	10,496
1997	7,982	2008	10,367	2016	10,369
1998	8,115	2009	10,252	2017	10,063
1999	8,522	2010	10,082	2018	9,863
2000	8,720	2011	10,209	2019	9,880
2003	8,876	2012	10,472	2020	5,938
2005	9,175	2013	10,528	2021	4,469
2006	9,379	2014	10,633	2022	5,959

Number of passengers by mode of transportation

Mode	2012 UPT	2021 UPT	% change, 2012-21
Bus	5,212	2,234	–57.1%
Heavy rail[1]	3,743	1,607	–57.1
Commuter rail[2]	469	148	–68.4
Light rail[3]	449	177	–60.6
Other	347	156	–55.0
Demand response[4]	102	63	–38.3
Vanpool	36	16	–55.5

(1) An electric railway with the ability to carry a heavy volume of passengers and characterized by high-speed and rapid-acceleration passenger railcars operating singly or in multicar trains on fixed rails. (2) An electric- or diesel-propelled railway for urban passenger travel that operates between a central city and outlying areas. (3) An electric railway that operates singly on fixed rails and is powered by overhead electric lines. (4) Includes passenger cars, vans, or small buses dispatched by request to pick up passengers and transport them to their destinations.

Transportation Expenditures by Level of Government, 2007-21

Source: Bureau of Transportation Statistics, U.S. Dept. of Transportation
(in millions of current dollars)

	2007	2010	2015	2016	2017	2018	2019	2020	2021
Federal, total	**25,470**	**32,046**	**32,296**	**35,134**	**37,144**	**33,734**	**35,094**	**41,781**	**40,616**
Highways	2,284	3,580	2,706	4,980	5,082	3,328	3,573	3,384	3,051
Air	14,021	16,269	16,840	16,610	17,943	18,535	19,329	25,097	21,820
Transit	215	148	125	150	138	174	262	155	149
Water	6,543	8,024	8,500	8,124	8,490	8,693	9,266	9,345	10,082
Rail	1,472	2,661	2,723	3,765	4,601	2,446	2,262	3,344	5,052
Pipeline	57	65	50	52	40	40	46	56	56
General support	878	1,299	1,352	1,453	850	518	356	400	406
State and local, total	**243,373**	**271,470**	**297,255**	**304,305**	**318,231**	**337,150**	**349,118**	**362,014**	**358,148**
Highways	172,524	187,771	204,201	208,113	219,062	232,155	236,015	248,532	244,060
Air	20,086	24,209	22,490	23,759	25,968	28,418	30,991	33,308	33,356
Transit	45,968	54,097	64,136	66,380	66,723	69,977	75,146	73,188	73,861
Water	4,758	5,341	6,355	5,966	6,405	6,532	6,889	6,892	6,786
Rail	5	0	0	0	0	0	0	0	0
Pipeline	19	30	50	60	49	47	55	64	64
General support	13	22	23	27	23	21	22	29	21

Note: Numbers may not add to totals due to rounding.

Record-Breaking Roller Coasters

Source: Roller Coaster DataBase; World Almanac research; as of Aug. 2024

Steel-Tracked Roller Coasters

Fastest	Roller coaster	Theme park, location
128.0	Kingda Ka	Six Flags Great Adventure, Jackson, NJ
111.8	Red Force	Ferrari Land, Salou, Spain
100.0	SUPERMAN: Escape from Krypton	Six Flags Magic Mountain, Valencia, CA
95.0	Steel Dragon 2000	Nagashima Spa Land, Kuwana, Japan
95.0	Fury 325	Carowinds, Charlotte, NC
Tallest		
456 ft	Kingda Ka	Six Flags Great Adventure, Jackson, NJ
415	SUPERMAN: Escape from Krypton	Six Flags Magic Mountain, Valencia, CA
367.3	Red Force	Ferrari Land, Salou, Spain
325	Fury 325	Carowinds, Charlotte, NC
318.2	Steel Dragon 2000	Nagashima Spa Land, Kuwana, Japan
Largest drop		
418 ft	Kingda Ka	Six Flags Great Adventure, Jackson, NJ
328.1	SUPERMAN: Escape from Krypton	Six Flags Magic Mountain, Valencia, CA
320	Fury 325	Carowinds, Charlotte, NC
306.8	Steel Dragon 2000	Nagashima Spa Land, Kuwana, Japan
306	Leviathan	Canada's Wonderland, Vaughan, ON, Canada
Longest		
8,133.2 ft	Steel Dragon 2000	Nagashima Spa Land, Kuwana, Japan
6,708.7	Fujiyama	Fuji-Q Highland, Fujiyoshida, Japan
6,602	Fury 325	Carowinds, Charlotte, NC
6,595	Millennium Force	Cedar Point, Sandusky, OH
6,072	Incredicoaster	Disney California Adventure Park, Anaheim, CA
Inversions		
14	Smiler	Alton Towers, Alton, UK
10	Colossus	Thorpe Park, Chertsey, UK
10	10 Inversion Roller Coaster	Chimelong Paradise, Panyu, China
10	Crazy Coaster	Loca Joy Holiday Theme Park, Yongchuan, China
10	Altair	Cinecittà World, Rome, Italy
10	Velikolukskiy Myasokombinat-2	Wonder Island, St. Petersburg, Russia
10	Sik	Flamingo Land, Malton, UK

Wood-Tracked Roller Coasters

Fastest	Roller coaster	Theme park, location
72.0	Goliath	Six Flags Great America, Gurnee, IL
71.5	Wildfire	Kolmården Wildlife Park, Norrköping, Sweden
70.0	El Toro	Six Flags Great Adventure, Jackson, NJ
68.4	Colossos - Kampf der Giganten	Heide Park Resort, Soltau, Germany
68.0	Outlaw Run	Silver Dollar City, Branson, MO
Tallest		
183.8 ft	Wildfire	Kolmården Wildlife Park, Norrköping, Sweden
183.8	T Express	Everland, Yongin-si, S. Korea
181	El Toro	Six Flags Great Adventure, Jackson, NJ
165	Goliath	Six Flags Great America, Gurnee, IL
164	Colossos - Kampf der Giganten	Heide Park Resort, Soltau, Germany
Largest drop		
180 ft	Goliath	Six Flags Great America, Gurnee, IL
176	El Toro	Six Flags Great Adventure, Jackson, NJ
162	Outlaw Run	Silver Dollar City, Branson, MO
160.8	Wildfire	Kolmården Wildlife Park, Norrköping, Sweden
159.1	Colossos - Kampf der Giganten	Heide Park Resort, Soltau, Germany
Longest		
7,361 ft	The Beast	Kings Island, Mason, OH
6,442	The Voyage	Holiday World, Santa Claus, IN
5,383.8	T Express	Everland, Yongin-si, S. Korea
5,383	Shivering Timbers	Michigan's Adventure, Muskegon, MI
5,249.3	Jupiter	Kijima Kogen, Beppu, Japan
Inversions		
3	Outlaw Run	Silver Dollar City, Branson, MO
3	Wildfire	Kolmården Wildlife Park, Norrköping, Sweden
2	Goliath	Six Flags Great America, Gurnee, IL
1	Hades 360	Mt. Olympus Water & Theme Park, Wisconsin Dells, WI
1	Jungle Trailblazer	Oriental Heritage, Jiujiang, China
1	Jungle Trailblazer	Oriental Heritage, Huaiyin, China
1	Jungle Trailblazer	Oriental Heritage, Cixi, China
1	Mine Blower	Fun Spot America, Kissimmee, FL

Most Visited Amusement/Theme Parks, 2019-23

Source: Themed Entertainment Association
(visitors in thousands; ranked by 2023 figures)

North America

Rank	Park, location	2019 visitors	2023 visitors
1.	Magic Kingdom[1], FL	20,963	17,720
2.	Disneyland, CA	18,666	17,250
3.	Epcot[1], FL	12,444	11,980
4.	Disney's Hollywood Studios[1], FL	11,483	10,300
5.	Islands of Adventure[2], FL	10,375	10,000
	Disney California Adventure, CA	9,861	10,000
7.	Universal Studios Florida[2], FL	10,922	9,750
8.	Universal Studios Hollywood, CA	9,147	9,660
9.	Disney's Animal Kingdom[1], FL	13,888	8,770
10.	SeaWorld Orlando, FL	4,640	4,342

World

Rank	Park, location	2019 visitors	2023 visitors
1.	Universal Studios Japan, Osaka, Japan	14,500	16,000
2.	Tokyo Disneyland, Tokyo, Japan	17,910	15,100
3.	Shanghai Disneyland, Shanghai, China	11,210	14,000
4.	Chimelong Ocean Kingdom, Zhuhai, China	11,736	12,520
5.	Tokyo DisneySea, Tokyo, Japan	14,650	12,400
6.	Disneyland Park at Disneyland Paris, Marne-La-Vallée, France	9,745	10,400
7.	Universal Studios Beijing, Beijing, China	NA	9,000
8.	Hong Kong Disneyland, Hong Kong, China	5,695	6,400
9.	Europa-Park, Rust, Germany	5,750	6,000
10.	Everland, Gyeonggi-do, South Korea	6,606	5,880

NA = Not available. **Note:** World list excludes North American parks. (1) Located at Walt Disney World. (2) Located at Universal Orlando.

Passports, Foreign Travel, and Regulations for Air Travel

Source: Bureau of Consular Affairs, U.S. Dept. of State; Centers for Disease Control and Prevention (CDC), U.S. Dept. of Health and Human Services; Transportation Security Administration (TSA), U.S. Dept. of Homeland Security

Passports, Visas

Passports are issued by the Dept. of State to U.S. citizens and nationals to provide documentation for foreign travel. As of Aug. 2024, the fees for a new passport book and passport card for persons ages 16 and over total $195. For a passport book alone, fees are $165 for a new passport and $130 for passport renewal. For expedited service, there is a $60 fee.

In 2008, the U.S. government began issuing passport cards. Travelers arriving by land or sea from Canada, Mexico, the Caribbean, and Bermuda may present a passport card to enter the U.S. Passport cards may not be used for air travel, however. The fees for a new passport card for persons ages 16 and over total $65 ($30 to renew).

As of Aug. 2024, the processing time for passport applications was 6-8 weeks, and expedited processing time was 2-3 weeks.

Persons who must travel to a foreign country within 14 calendar days because of a life-or-death emergency (e.g., death of an immediate family member) or some other reason may make an appointment with a passport agency to process their application.

A U.S. passport is often sufficient for U.S. citizens to gain admission for a limited stay in another country. Some countries also require an entry visa. Each country has its own specific guidelines concerning length and purpose of visit, among other considerations. Visitors may need to provide proof of sufficient funds for their intended stay, onward/return tickets, and/or at least six months remaining validity on their U.S. passports.

All persons traveling by air outside of the U.S. (excluding direct travel to and from a U.S. territory) are required to present a passport or other valid document upon reentering the U.S.

For up-to-date passport and international travel information, visit the State Dept.'s Consular Affairs website (travel.state.gov) or call U.S. Passports at 1-877-487-2778.

COVID-19 Impact on Foreign Travel

The COVID-19 pandemic had a devastating effect on international travel in 2020, although travel had returned to pre-pandemic levels by 2023. As of Aug. 2024, travelers were recommended to follow safety precautions related to the COVID-19 pandemic while traveling, including not traveling when sick, wearing face masks in crowded areas, and taking additional precautions if recently exposed to someone with COVID-19.

Summary of TSA Regulations

Airplane carry-ons. TSA promotes the liquids (or 3-1-1) rule regarding carry-on items. Containers with liquids, gels, aerosols, creams, or pastes must hold **3.4** oz (100 mL) or less; these containers should be packed inside a single **1**-quart, clear plastic, resealable bag; and this **1** bag must go through checkpoint security. Exceptions to the liquids rule include medication, baby formula and food, and breast milk; these items must be removed and screened separately.

Security checkpoint identification. Adult travelers (18 years of age and over) must present a photo ID. Acceptable documents include a U.S. passport or passport card; foreign government-issued passport; state-issued driver's license; permanent resident card; or U.S. Dept. of Defense ID, among others. Starting May 7, 2025, travelers using a state-issued driver's license must have the enhanced version or one that is compliant with the REAL ID Act.

Screening process. Travelers may wear loose fitting or religious garments (incl. head coverings) through security. They may be subject to additional screening if clothing could conceal prohibited items. Travelers may request a private area if selected for personal screening. Travelers will be screened by someone of the same gender.

In Dec. 2011, the TSA began the TSA PreCheck program, allowing expedited screening at airport security for preapproved passengers; the 5-year membership costs $78-$85. As of Aug. 2024, this was available at more than 200 U.S. airports and by more than 90 participating airlines.

Disability-related permitted carry-on items:

- Wheelchairs, mobility scooters
- Crutches, canes, and walkers
- Portable oxygen concentrators (permitted by some airlines, and only if they meet specific FAA criteria)
- Medications and associated supplies
- Service animals

Permitted carry-on items:

- Disposable and electric razors (blades not allowed)
- Eye drops and contact lens solution (3.4 oz or less)
- Strollers, baby carriers, child car seats
- Beverages (any size) purchased after security screening

Prohibited carry-on items:

- Knives (except plastic or round-bladed butter knives), incl. pocket knives and knives that are religious objects
- Firearms or realistic firearm replicas, ammunition
- Screwdrivers, wrenches, pliers, and other tools more than 7 in. in length; hammers
- Self-defense sprays

For complete travel information, visit www.tsa.gov/travel

EMPLOYMENT

Employment and Unemployment in the U.S., 1900-2023

Source: Bureau of Labor Statistics, U.S. Dept. of Labor

(civilian labor force, persons 16 years of age and older unless otherwise noted; annual averages, in thousands)

Year	Employed	Unemployed		Year	Employed	Unemployed		Year	Employed	Unemployed	
		Number	Rate			Number	Rate			Number	Rate
1900[1]	26,956	1,420	5.0%	1996	126,708	7,236	5.4%	2010	139,064	14,825	9.6%
1910[1]	34,599	2,150	5.9	1997	129,558	6,739	4.9	2011	139,869	13,747	8.9
1920[1]	39,208	2,132	5.2	1998	131,463	6,210	4.5	2012	142,469	12,506	8.1
1930[1]	44,183	4,340	8.9	1999	133,488	5,880	4.2	2013	143,929	11,460	7.4
1940[1]	47,520	8,120	14.6	2000	136,891	5,692	4.0	2014	146,305	9,617	6.2
1950	58,918	3,288	5.3	2001	136,933	6,801	4.7	2015	148,834	8,296	5.3
1960	65,778	3,852	5.5	2002	136,485	8,378	5.8	2016	151,436	7,751	4.9
1965	71,088	3,366	4.5	2003	137,736	8,774	6.0	2017	153,337	6,982	4.4
1970	78,678	4,093	4.9	2004	139,252	8,149	5.5	2018	155,761	6,314	3.9
1975	85,846	7,929	8.5	2005	141,730	7,591	5.1	2019	157,538	6,001	3.7
1980	99,303	7,637	7.1	2006	144,427	7,001	4.6	2020	147,795	12,947	8.1
1985	107,150	8,312	7.2	2007	146,047	7,078	4.6	2021	152,581	8,623	5.3
1990	118,793	7,047	5.6	2008	145,362	8,924	5.8	2022	158,291	5,996	3.6
1995	124,900	7,404	5.6	2009	139,877	14,265	9.3	2023	161,037	6,080	3.6

Note: Because of revisions in population controls, data for a given year may not be strictly comparable to other years. **Other selected unemployment rates (1905-55)**, persons 14 years of age and older: 1905, 4.3%; 1915, 8.5%; 1925, 3.2%; 1935, 20.3%; 1936, 16.9%; 1937, 14.3%; 1938, 19.0%; 1939, 17.2%; 1945, 1.9%; 1955, 4.4%. (1) Persons 14 years of age and older.

Unemployment Rate and Benefits Data by State, 2023

Source: Employment and Training Admin., U.S. Dept. of Labor; state programs only

State/ terr.	Unemployment rate	Monetarily eligible claimants	Number of first payments	Number of final payments	Initial claims	Benefits paid	Average weekly benefit	Employers subject to state law
AL	2.5%	80,572	12,008	3,205	36,711	$57,924,136	$290.10	112,506
AK	4.2	22,748	35,061	10,551	124,959	61,071,063	257.40	21,079
AZ	3.9	120,156	25,409	8,448	82,492	69,682,447	307.04	172,786
AR	3.3	59,480	66,353	25,842	184,088	287,221,662	308.37	83,385
CA	4.8	1,077,179	1,021,193	497,543	2,325,099	6,324,785,835	368.48	1,635,460
CO	3.2	164,149	85,218	25,500	193,881	632,429,047	587.40	224,992
CT	3.8	158,822	87,426	18,732	208,040	514,662,878	473.82	127,499
DE	4.0	23,456	14,410	3,804	29,822	79,980,878	403.58	42,564
DC	4.9	25,396	11,771	3,265	31,768	57,857,331	334.69	42,534
FL	2.9	213,837	159,629	82,349	299,377	1,668,754,052	260.84	708,602
GA	3.2	202,507	118,881	44,761	306,659	325,721,084	339.87	306,434
HI	3.0	34,989	26,037	4,667	78,530	186,834,926	615.31	40,053
ID	3.1	38,677	28,627	7,869	62,947	105,516,972	433.42	80,996
IL	4.5	326,931	264,825	75,166	501,017	1,894,497,524	495.21	343,366
IN	3.3	123,247	74,957	10,922	196,586	238,106,642	321.14	150,504
IA	2.9	68,990	55,395	13,327	115,270	251,734,567	501.72	89,162
KS	2.7	43,151	28,433	7,947	69,756	99,412,026	441.68	86,162
KY	4.2	70,583	26,315	9,293	125,598	152,136,676	453.40	110,639
LA	3.7	61,135	31,502	9,022	92,140	117,221,048	245.19	110,440
ME	2.9	23,638	18,342	4,708	31,982	98,719,386	446.81	55,384
MD	2.1	182,474	51,417	17,386	139,462	353,179,127	383.51	155,374
MA	3.4	401,675	192,538	51,729	483,863	1,837,238,489	682.76	254,087
MI	3.9	245,865	176,732	54,790	364,975	614,816,545	346.88	243,755
MN	2.8	196,891	137,398	38,632	257,885	997,385,668	552.76	156,714
MS	3.2	36,979	18,116	3,705	57,709	34,638,732	221.75	66,399
MO	3.0	107,170	60,990	18,358	174,788	192,457,017	286.31	192,124
MT	2.9	23,647	16,323	5,109	31,287	95,327,381	483.38	53,711
NE	2.3	32,065	15,911	2,804	36,442	70,663,260	423.06	63,896
NV	5.1	89,386	64,385	19,326	124,579	340,925,260	451.32	98,952
NH	2.2	16,923	9,706	1,060	22,956	40,903,090	363.06	54,104
NJ	4.4	315,473	245,097	102,501	487,559	2,297,507,773	576.88	277,092
NM	3.8	36,446	24,602	9,326	50,913	153,245,553	423.83	56,260
NY	4.2	536,205	410,870	143,801	859,496	2,265,088,605	418.92	543,423
NC	3.5	140,790	71,846	36,506	183,585	195,272,342	300.08	300,246
ND	1.9	14,480	10,416	3,971	17,322	33,356,333	521.13	28,232
OH	3.5	427,715	132,729	27,077	613,079	746,990,325	460.23	250,739
OK	3.2	74,466	34,324	16,357	79,595	151,066,493	393.88	105,005
OR	3.7	141,752	85,830	25,821	238,543	715,998,914	543.41	149,229
PA	3.4	349,250	282,347	43,588	555,047	1,581,320,887	453.22	334,483
PR	5.9	52,226	45,588	17,719	74,776	147,717,883	209.29	59,674
RI	3.0	35,381	27,681	6,993	54,987	168,057,975	449.28	44,456
SC	3.0	81,692	46,545	14,299	117,098	140,986,948	296.66	144,928
SD	2.0	7,481	4,479	552	9,948	25,424,171	431.99	34,250
TN	3.3	99,374	53,419	13,068	137,240	175,577,128	253.86	165,360
TX	3.9	617,210	376,525	138,826	818,861	2,347,784,964	479.13	661,277
UT	2.6	72,760	37,870	10,204	100,499	248,080,452	542.36	108,683
VT	2.0	14,025	11,662	1,272	21,194	44,987,546	501.09	28,964
VA	2.9	96,083	15,443	15,254	138,166	229,311,490	340.08	262,122
VI	NA	986	730	229	1,584	1,276,788	448.75	4,512
WA	4.1	217,056	161,153	44,866	359,944	1,439,661,546	703.79	271,083
WV	3.9	34,824	25,960	5,968	43,010	122,125,591	397.82	41,912
WI	3.0	132,562	87,548	12,626	233,209	314,828,154	340.35	170,792
WY	2.9	10,608	7,604	1,721	14,879	39,633,177	460.75	26,808
U.S.	**3.6**	**7,781,563**	**5,135,576**	**1,772,365**	**12,001,202**	**31,387,105,782**	**438.68**	**9,995,641**

NA = Not available.

Weekly Unemployment Insurance Claims, 2000-24

Source: Employment and Training Admin., U.S. Dept. of Labor

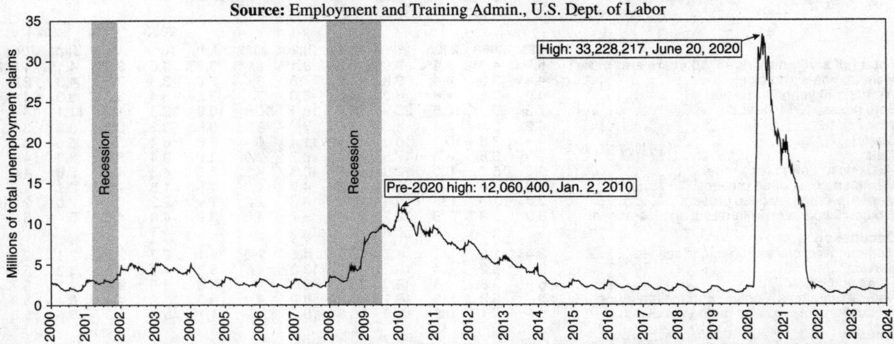

Note: Total includes state programs, programs for federal employees and ex-service members, extended and emergency programs, short-time compensation, Pandemic Unemployment Assistance, and Pandemic Emergency Unemployment Compensation.

U.S. Unemployment Duration by Industry and Occupation, 2023

Source: Bureau of Labor Statistics, U.S. Dept. of Labor

	Number of unemployed persons (thous.)					Weeks of unemployment	
Occupation	**Total**	**Less than 5 weeks**	**5 to 14 weeks**	**15 to 26 weeks**	**27 weeks and over**	**Average (mean) duration**	**Median duration**
Management, professional, and related	1,432	450	466	235	281	21.0	9.6
Management, business, and financial operations	604	174	199	107	125	21.3	10.3
Professional and related	828	277	267	128	156	20.8	9.1
Service	1,240	463	387	161	230	20.0	8.0
Sales and office	1,146	377	346	178	245	21.9	9.5
Sales and related	581	200	172	87	122	21.9	9.1
Office and administrative support	565	176	175	91	123	21.9	9.9
Natural resources, construction, and maintenance	659	266	188	95	111	18.0	7.6
Farming, fishing, and forestry	74	31	20	10	12	18.7	7.2
Construction and extraction	480	199	139	69	72	16.8	7.1
Installation, maintenance, and repair	105	35	28	15	26	23.3	10.5
Production, transportation, and material moving	1,030	371	288	173	198	20.4	9.0
Production	328	127	91	50	60	18.8	8.0
Transportation and material moving	702	244	197	123	137	21.2	9.4
Industry[1]							
Agriculture and related industries	92	35	29	13	15	19.1	8.4
Mining, quarrying, and oil and gas extraction	16	5	4	4	2	—	—
Construction	487	195	147	71	75	16.9	7.7
Manufacturing	450	157	127	78	88	20.5	9.2
Durable goods	260	88	77	48	47	20.0	9.3
Nondurable goods	190	69	50	30	41	21.1	8.9
Wholesale and retail trade	840	285	253	133	170	20.2	9.2
Transportation and utilities	374	125	112	61	76	20.7	9.6
Information	94	30	29	18	17	17.0	9.1
Financial activities	228	67	67	40	55	24.5	11.1
Professional and business services	711	217	235	125	135	20.1	9.7
Education and health services	817	298	260	103	156	20.6	8.2
Leisure and hospitality	762	289	242	96	135	19.8	7.8
Other services	210	75	62	36	37	21.2	8.9
Public administration	121	34	36	21	30	25.2	11.0
No previous work experience	556	180	187	83	106	21.2	9.0
Total unemployed[2]	**6,080**	**2,112**	**1,866**	**925**	**1,177**	**20.6**	**8.9**

(1) Industry data refer to wage and salary workers. Persons who were unpaid family workers or self-employed, unincorporated, on their last job are included in the unemployed total, but not shown separately. (2) Persons whose last job was in the U.S. Armed Forces are included in the unemployed total, but not shown separately.

U.S. Displaced Workers, 2024

Source: Bureau of Labor Statistics, U.S. Dept. of Labor

		Reason for job loss (% distrib.)		
	Number (thous.)	**Plant or company closed down or moved**	**Insufficient work**	**Position or shift abolished**
Total displaced workers	**2,578**	**36.5%**	**26.0%**	**37.5%**
Age: 20 to 24 years	92	35.9	31.1	32.9
25 to 54 years	1,524	38.4	25.8	35.9
55 to 64 years	710	30.6	27.6	41.8
65 years and over	253	41.6	21.0	37.3
Sex: Men	1,428	35.8	29.0	35.1
Women	1,151	37.3	22.2	40.5
Race: White	2,052	36.5	25.1	38.4
Black	298	29.6	33.4	37.0
Asian	155	43.9	25.5	30.6
Hispanic or Latino	454	42.0	25.3	32.7

Note: As of Jan. 2024. Displaced workers are persons age 20 or older who lost or left jobs they had held for at least three years. Workers in this table were displaced between Jan. 2021 and Dec. 2023. Hispanic or Latino persons may be of any race.

U.S. Unemployment Rates by Selected Characteristics, 1995-2024

Source: Bureau of Labor Statistics, U.S. Dept. of Labor

	1995	2000	2005	2010	2015	2020	2022	2023			2024	
								Jan.	June	Yr.	Jan.	June
Total (all civilian workers, 16 years and older)	**5.6%**	**4.0%**	**5.1%**	**9.6%**	**5.3%**	**8.1%**	**3.6%**	**3.9%**	**3.8%**	**3.6%**	**4.1%**	**4.3%**
Men, 20 years and older	4.8	3.3	4.4	9.8	4.9	7.5	3.4	3.9	3.3	3.5	4.3	3.6
Women, 20 years and older	4.9	3.6	4.6	8.0	4.8	8.0	3.3	3.2	3.4	3.2	3.3	4.0
Both sexes, 16 to 19 years	17.3	13.1	16.5	25.9	16.9	18.1	10.8	10.9	13.3	11.2	11.1	14.4
White	4.9	3.5	4.4	8.7	4.6	7.3	3.2	3.5	3.3	3.3	3.8	3.7
Black	10.4	7.6	10.0	16.0	9.6	11.4	6.1	5.6	6.4	5.5	5.5	6.7
Asian	—	3.6	4.0	7.5	3.8	8.7	2.8	3.0	3.4	3.0	3.0	4.4
Hispanic or Latino (any race)	9.3	5.7	6.0	12.5	6.6	10.4	4.3	5.5	4.3	4.6	5.8	4.9
Married men, spouse present[1]	3.3	—	—	6.8	2.8	4.9	1.9	1.8	1.8	1.9	2.1	1.9
Married women, spouse present[1]	3.9	—	—	5.9	3.1	6.3	2.2	1.9	2.2	2.1	2.0	2.3
Women who maintain families, spouse absent[2]	8.0	5.9	7.8	12.3	7.4	9.7	4.8	3.8	4.8	4.6	5.4	6.2
Occupation												
Management, professional, and related	2.4	1.8	2.3	4.7	2.5	4.5	2.0	2.1	2.2	2.0	2.1	2.6
Service	7.5	5.2	6.4	10.3	6.7	13.0	4.8	5.3	4.3	4.5	5.2	5.0
Sales and office	5.0	3.8	4.8	9.0	5.1	8.0	3.7	3.8	3.5	3.6	4.1	3.7
Natural resources, constr., and maintenance	—	5.3	6.5	16.1	7.2	8.9	4.4	6.0	3.3	4.4	6.4	3.9
Production, transp., and material moving	—	5.1	6.5	12.8	6.3	10.2	4.9	4.7	5.2	4.9	5.4	5.8
Industry												
Nonagricultural private wage and salary workers	5.8	4.1	5.2	9.9	5.1	8.4	3.6	3.9	3.3	3.6	4.1	3.9
Mining, quarrying, oil and gas extraction	5.2	4.4	3.1	9.4	8.6	11.3	3.0	0.3	1.3	2.7	3.0	1.3
Construction	11.5	6.2	7.4	20.6	7.3	8.7	4.6	6.9	3.6	4.6	6.9	3.3
Manufacturing	4.9	3.5	4.9	10.6	4.3	6.8	3.0	2.6	2.6	2.8	3.4	3.1
Durable goods	4.4	3.2	4.6	11.2	4.1	6.7	2.9	2.3	2.4	2.6	2.9	2.8
Nondurable goods	5.7	4.0	5.3	9.6	4.6	6.8	3.1	3.1	2.9	3.4	4.2	3.6
Wholesale and retail trade	6.5	4.3	5.4	9.5	5.5	8.3	4.1	5.1	4.4	4.2	4.6	5.1
Transportation and utilities	4.5	3.4	4.1	8.4	4.4	9.3	4.1	4.2	3.1	4.1	4.3	4.5
Information	—	3.2	5.0	9.7	3.9	7.5	2.9	3.9	3.1	3.2	5.5	5.9
Financial activities	3.3	2.4	2.9	6.9	2.6	3.8	1.9	2.3	2.2	2.2	2.1	2.7
Professional and business services	—	4.8	6.2	10.8	5.6	6.7	3.5	3.5	3.3	3.7	4.3	3.7
Education and health services	—	2.5	3.4	5.8	3.6	5.7	2.7	2.4	2.8	2.4	2.6	3.1
Leisure and hospitality	—	6.6	7.8	12.2	7.9	19.4	5.8	6.0	5.1	5.3	6.0	5.2
Other services	8.4	3.9	4.8	8.5	5.2	9.8	3.1	3.3	2.1	3.1	4.0	3.9
Agriculture and related private wage and salary workers	11.1	9.0	8.3	13.9	9.4	8.1	5.6	4.9	5.1	5.6	8.0	4.3
Government workers	2.9	2.1	2.6	4.4	2.7	4.8	2.1	1.9	3.0	2.0	1.8	2.9
Self-employed and unpaid family workers	—	2.1	2.7	5.9	3.9	6.4	3.2	3.5	3.3	3.0	3.5	3.5

— = Not available. **Note:** All monthly rates are unadjusted, except for married men and women, which are seasonally adjusted. (1) Beginning in Jan. 2020, data refers to persons in both opposite-sex and same-sex married couples. Data for prior years refers to persons in opposite-sex married couples only. (2) Beginning in 2020, data refers to female householders residing with one or more family members without a spouse of either sex. Data for prior years refers to female householders residing with one or more family members, without an opposite-sex spouse.

U.S. Workers by Industry and Type, 2013, 2023

Source: Bureau of Labor Statistics, U.S. Dept. of Labor; in thousands

	2013				2023			
Industry	**Total employed**	**Private industry workers[1]**	**Govt. workers**	**Self-employed workers[2]**	**Total employed**	**Private industry workers[1]**	**Govt. workers**	**Self-employed workers[2]**
Mining[3]	1,065	1,046	3	16	590	576	3	11
Construction	9,271	7,326	407	1,530	11,896	9,956	370	1,562
Manufacturing	14,869	14,484	106	275	15,570	15,144	115	308
Durable goods	9,391	9,134	88	166	10,065	9,770	93	199
Nondurable goods	5,478	5,349	18	109	5,506	5,374	22	110
Wholesale and retail trade	19,653	18,696	111	825	19,787	18,937	83	759
Wholesale trade	3,646	3,482	16	146	3,259	3,152	12	94
Retail trade	16,007	15,215	95	679	16,528	15,785	70	664
Transportation and utilities	7,415	5,728	1,344	340	9,949	7,990	1,274	684
Transportation and warehousing	6,228	4,858	1,028	340	8,452	6,828	950	673
Utilities	1,187	870	317	—	1,497	1,162	324	—
Information	2,960	2,666	168	126	2,971	2,680	151	140
Financial activities	9,849	8,957	236	651	11,018	10,051	198	765
Finance and insurance	6,984	6,615	147	221	7,746	7,396	119	231
Real estate and rental and leasing	2,865	2,343	89	430	3,272	2,654	79	535
Professional and business services	16,793	14,270	455	2,057	20,735	18,284	521	1,923
Professional and technical services	10,110	8,708	267	1,129	13,726	12,370	313	1,041
Management, administrative, and waste services	6,682	5,562	189	929	7,009	5,915	208	881
Education and health services	32,535	21,222	10,232	1,072	36,378	24,980	10,400	990
Educational services	12,974	4,260	8,477	234	14,029	5,124	8,710	195
Health care and social assistance	19,562	16,962	1,755	838	22,348	19,856	1,689	795
Hospitals	6,274	5,494	771	10	7,467	6,651	802	14
Health services, except hospitals	10,215	9,334	488	389	11,201	10,361	403	435
Social assistance	3,072	2,134	496	439	3,680	2,845	484	345
Leisure and hospitality	13,554	12,433	443	671	14,288	13,123	408	753
Arts, entertainment, and recreation	3,205	2,391	369	444	3,529	2,702	328	499
Accommodation and food services	10,349	10,042	74	226	10,759	10,421	80	254
Other services	7,127	6,035	32	1,055	7,605	6,432	32	1,136
Other services, except private households	6,404	5,312	32	1,055	6,932	5,759	32	1,136
Private households	723	723	—	—	673	673	—	—
Public administration	6,708	—	6,708	—	7,984	—	7,984	—

— = No data or data that do not meet publication criteria. (1) Includes self-employed workers whose businesses are incorporated. (2) Unincorporated. (3) Includes quarrying and oil and gas extraction.

Persons Not in the U.S. Labor Force, 2023

Source: Bureau of Labor Statistics, U.S. Dept. of Labor

The Labor Dept.'s unemployment rate, based on its household survey, shows the number of people out of work as a percentage of adults age 16 and older in the labor force. That rate excludes the millions of adults considered to be not in the labor force.

(in thousands)

	Number	Age in years			Sex	
		16 to 24	25 to 54	55 and over	Men	Women
Total not in the labor force	**99,826**	**17,210**	**21,400**	**61,215**	**41,599**	**58,227**
Do not want a job now[1]	94,496	15,574	19,172	59,749	39,072	55,424
Want a job[1]	5,330	1,636	2,228	1,466	2,527	2,803
Did not search for work in previous year	3,277	943	1,280	1,054	1,514	1,763
Searched in previous year but not previous four weeks[2]	2,053	693	948	412	1,013	1,040
Not available to work now	595	253	252	90	261	333
Available to work now	1,458	440	696	322	752	706
Reason not currently looking[3]						
Discouraged over job prospects[4]	370	101	186	83	226	144
Reasons other than discouragement	1,088	339	510	239	526	562
Family responsibilities	151	17	102	31	56	95
In school or training	146	115	28	3	71	75
Ill health or disability	124	16	52	56	55	69
Other[5]	667	191	327	149	344	323

(1) Includes some persons who are not asked if they want a job. (2) Persons who had a job in the prior 12 months must have searched since the end of that job to be considered unemployed. (3) Of those available to work now. (4) Includes believing no work is available, not being able to find work, lacking necessary schooling or training, thought of as too young or old by employers, and other types of discrimination. (5) Includes those who did not actively look for work in the prior four weeks for such reasons as child-care and transportation problems, as well as a small number for which reason for nonparticipation was not ascertained.

U.S. Small Business Employment by Industry, 2021

Source: U.S Census Bureau, U.S. Dept. of Commerce

Industry	Small business employment	Total private employment	% small business employment
Health care and social assistance	9,037,964	20,681,593	43.7%
Accommodation and food services	7,491,128	12,142,327	61.7
Construction	5,760,866	7,062,022	81.6
Professional, scientific, and technical services	5,406,594	9,531,475	56.7
Other services (excl. public administration)	4,357,196	5,105,104	85.3
Administrative, support, waste management, and remediation services	3,710,444	12,509,600	29.7
Wholesale trade	3,179,732	5,925,945	53.7
Finance and insurance	1,874,788	6,738,309	27.8
Educational services	1,631,945	3,488,028	46.8
Real estate, rental and leasing	1,477,942	2,180,602	67.8
Arts, entertainment, and recreation	1,217,971	1,858,669	65.5
Information	931,406	3,414,629	27.3
Management of companies and enterprises	364,519	3,484,154	10.5
Mining, quarrying, and oil and gas extraction	222,976	474,877	47.0
Agriculture, forestry, fishing and hunting	137,082	165,688	82.7
Utilities	114,353	633,738	18.0
Industries not classified	14,844	14,844	100.0
Total employed	**58,951,278**	**128,346,299**	**45.9**

Note: A small business is defined here as a firm employing fewer than 500 employees.

U.S. Occupations Projected to Grow Most, 2023-33

Source: Employment Projections Program, Bureau of Labor Statistics, U.S. Dept. of Labor

(ranked by greatest positive change in number of jobs; numbers in thousands)

Occupation	Employment		Change, 2023-33		Median annual wage, 2023[1]
	2023	2033	Number	Percent	
Total, all occupations	**167,849.8**	**174,589.0**	**6,739.2**	**4.0%**	**$48,060**
Home health and personal care aides	3,961.9	4,782.4	820.5	20.7	33,530
Software developers	1,692.1	1,995.7	303.7	17.9	132,270
Cooks, restaurant	1,434.2	1,678.6	244.5	17.0	35,780
Fast food and counter workers	3,734.1	3,946.5	212.5	5.7	29,540
General and operations managers	3,630.1	3,840.5	210.4	5.8	101,280
Registered nurses	3,300.1	3,497.3	197.2	6.0	86,070
Stockers and order fillers	2,864.7	3,033.3	168.6	5.9	36,390
Medical and health services managers	562.7	723.3	160.6	28.5	110,680
Financial managers	837.1	975.3	138.3	16.5	156,100
Nurse practitioners	292.5	427.9	135.5	46.3	126,260
Laborers and freight, stock, and material movers, hand	3,004.8	3,130.6	125.7	4.2	37,660
Medical assistants	783.9	901.9	118.0	15.0	42,000
Construction laborers	1,401.2	1,516.6	115.4	8.2	45,300
Management analysts	1,018.3	1,126.2	107.9	10.6	99,410
Computer and information systems managers	613.5	720.4	106.9	17.4	169,510
Heavy and tractor-trailer truck drivers	2,211.3	2,313.4	102.0	4.6	54,320
Light truck drivers	1,092.6	1,188.9	96.3	8.8	42,470
Accountants and auditors	1,562.0	1,653.4	91.4	5.8	79,880
Substance abuse, behavioral disorder, and mental health counselors	449.8	534.3	84.5	18.8	53,710
Electricians	779.8	864.1	84.3	10.8	61,590
Maintenance and repair workers, general	1,616.5	1,698.3	81.8	5.1	46,700
First-line supervisors of food preparation and serving workers	1,211.4	1,288.2	76.8	6.3	38,520
Janitors and cleaners, except maids and housekeeping cleaners	2,431.6	2,507.3	75.8	3.1	35,020
Market research analysts and marketing specialists	903.4	978.3	74.9	8.3	74,680
Human resources specialists	933.7	1,007.9	74.2	7.9	67,650
Industrial machinery mechanics	429.5	503.3	73.8	17.2	61,420

(1) Wage data cover nonfarm wage and salary workers and do not cover the self-employed, owners and partners in unincorporated firms, or household workers.

U.S. Occupations Projected to Decline Most, 2023-33

Source: Employment Projections Program, Bureau of Labor Statistics, U.S. Dept. of Labor

(ranked by greatest negative change in number of jobs; numbers in thousands)

Occupation	Employment 2023	Employment 2033	Change, 2023-33 Number	Change, 2023-33 Percent	Median annual wage, 2023[1]
Total, all occupations	**167,849.8**	**174,589.0**	**6,739.2**	**4.0%**	**$48,060**
Cashiers	3,338.8	2,985.7	−353.1	−10.6	29,720
Customer service representatives	2,954.6	2,805.8	−148.8	−5.0	39,680
Office clerks, general	2,645.8	2,498.2	−147.5	−5.6	40,480
Cooks, fast food	682.2	588.5	−93.7	−13.7	29,260
First-line supervisors of retail sales workers	1,407.4	1,316.9	−90.5	−6.4	46,730
Bookkeeping, accounting, and auditing clerks	1,663.8	1,579.9	−83.9	−5.0	47,440
First-line supervisors of office and administrative support workers	1,570.5	1,501.4	−69.1	−4.4	63,450
Shipping, receiving, and inventory clerks	848.7	784.2	−64.4	−7.6	39,780
Tellers	350.3	298.8	−51.4	−14.7	37,640
Data entry keyers	163.9	122.8	−41.0	−25.0	37,790
Food preparation workers	904.8	870.8	−34.0	−3.8	32,420
Packers and packagers, hand	641.3	614.3	−26.9	−4.2	34,830
Correctional officers and jailers	370.9	346.0	−24.8	−6.7	53,300
Payroll and timekeeping clerks	160.3	136.2	−24.2	−15.1	52,240
Cutting, punching, and press machine setters, operators, and tenders, metal and plastic	181.3	161.0	−20.3	−11.2	42,400

(1) Wage data cover nonfarm wage and salary workers and do not cover the self-employed, owners and partners in unincorporated firms, or household workers.

Projected Employment by Typical Entry-Level Education, 2023-33

Source: Employment Projections Program, Bureau of Labor Statistics, U.S. Dept. of Labor

Typical entry-level education	Employment, 2023 Number (thous.)	Employment, 2023 Percent distribution	% change in employment, 2023-33	Median annual wage, 2023[1]
Total, all occupations	**167,849.8**	**100.0%**	**4.0%**	**$48,060**
Doctoral or professional degree	4,486.5	2.7	7.1	124,550
Master's degree	3,668.6	2.2	12.1	79,840
Bachelor's degree	41,431.7	24.7	7.2	86,460
Associate's degree	3,438.3	2.0	6.3	62,180
Postsecondary nondegree award	10,383.2	6.2	6.0	47,740
Some college, no degree	4,241.4	2.5	−1.7	44,130
High school diploma or equivalent	63,066.5	37.6	2.5	45,040
No formal educational credential	37,133.6	22.1	1.8	34,430

Note: The occupational employment and growth rates shown include projected growth in all jobs, not just entry-level jobs. (1) Wage data cover nonfarm wage and salary workers and do not cover the self-employed, owners and partners in unincorporated firms, or household workers.

Highest Average Weekly Wages by County, 2023

Source: Bureau of Labor Statistics, U.S. Dept. of Labor

County	Avg. weekly wage	% change, 2022-23	County	Avg. weekly wage	% change, 2022-23
Santa Clara, CA	$3,699	11.3%	Fairfax, VA	$2,146	4.4%
San Mateo, CA	3,469	17.2	Fairfield, CT	2,088	2.6
San Francisco, CA	3,202	7.6	Middlesex, MA	2,047	−0.2
New York, NY	3,028	3.3	Somerset, NJ	1,929	4.7
Suffolk, MA	2,491	−0.1	Morris, NJ	1,909	1.4
Washington, DC	2,385	4.1	Lake, IL	1,863	6.0
Arlington, VA	2,379	9.2	Denver, CO	1,859	3.4
King, WA	2,356	7.2	Fulton, GA	1,837	3.0

Note: Figures shown are for the 4th quarter, from among the 360 largest U.S. counties, which comprise 73.0% of total covered workers. Hidalgo County, TX, recorded the lowest average weekly earnings among the largest counties, with an average of $842. It was followed by Cameron, TX ($865); Harrison, MS ($909); Webb, TX ($909); Horry, SC ($931); Washington, UT ($955); El Paso, TX ($961); Baldwin, AL ($984); Cleveland, OK ($990); and Canyon, ID ($993). Data include all workers covered by state and federal unemployment insurance programs.

Fatal Occupational Injuries, 2022

Source: Census of Fatal Occupational Injuries, Bureau of Labor Statistics, U.S. Dept. of Labor

Event or exposure	Fatalities Number	%
Total	**5,486**	**100%**
Violence and other injuries by persons or animals	**849**	**15**
Intentional injury by person	791	14
Homicides	524	10
Shooting by other person—intentional	435	8
Stabbing, cutting, slashing, piercing	44	1
Suicides	267	5
Transportation incidents	**2,066**	**38**
Aircraft incidents	101	2
Rail vehicle incidents	43	1
Pedestrian vehicular incident	325	6
Pedestrian struck by vehicle in work zone	30	1
Water vehicle incident	31	1
Roadway incident involving motorized land vehicle	1,369	25
Roadway collision with other vehicle	763	14
Roadway collision moving in same direction	207	4
Roadway collision moving in opposite directions, oncoming	252	5
Roadway collision moving perpendicularly	164	3
Roadway collision with object other than vehicle	352	6
Vehicle struck object or animal on side of roadway	314	6
Roadway noncollision incident	249	5
Jack-knifed or overturned, roadway	181	3
Nonroadway incident involving motorized land vehicle	185	3%
Nonroadway noncollision incident	128	2
Jack-knifed or overturned, nonroadway	77	1
Fire or explosion	**107**	**2**
Fall, slip, trip	**865**	**16**
Fall on same level	144	3
Fall to lower level	700	13
Fall from collapsing structure or equipment	33	1
Fall through surface or existing opening	90	2
Exposure to harmful substances or environments	**839**	**15**
Exposure to electricity	145	3
Exposure to temperature extremes	51	1
Exposure to other harmful substances	586	11
Inhalation of harmful substance	49	1
Contact with objects and equipment	**738**	**13**
Struck by object or equipment	484	9
Struck by powered vehicle, nontransport	181	3
Struck by falling object or equipment	238	4
Struck by discharged or flying object	19	0
Caught in or compressed by equipment or objects	142	3
Caught in running equipment or machinery	102	2
Struck, caught, or crushed in collapsing structure, equipment, or material	95	2

Note: Percentages show incidence rate per total fatalities.

U.S. Occupational Injuries and Illnesses Involving Days Away From Work, 2021-22

Source: Bureau of Labor Statistics, U.S. Dept. of Labor

Characteristic	Total cases[2]	Percent of days-away-from-work cases[1] involving— 1 day	2 days	3-5 days	6-10 days	11-20 days	21-30 days	31 days or more	Median days away from work
Total	**2,246,900**	**10.2%**	**7.8%**	**18.4%**	**20.5%**	**14.7%**	**5.1%**	**23.3%**	**10**
Male	1,191,770	11.0	8.3	17.7	16.5	13.6	5.8	27.1	10
Female	1,022,230	9.4	7.3	19.4	24.4	16.1	4.4	19.1	9
Age									
14-15 years	680	14.7	19.1	29.4	16.2	8.8	—	7.4	3
16-19 years	79,990	14.2	11.6	20.1	19.5	19.2	4.8	10.7	7
20-24 years	239,030	13.7	9.4	21.0	21.3	16.7	4.3	13.6	7
25-34 years	493,180	11.7	8.6	19.7	21.9	15.3	4.6	18.2	8
35-44 years	439,560	9.5	7.6	18.6	20.9	14.9	5.0	23.5	10
45-54 years	432,390	8.5	7.3	16.8	19.5	14.1	5.5	28.4	10
55-64 years	386,870	8.3	6.7	16.4	17.9	13.5	6.0	31.3	11
65 years and over	99,760	8.5	6.1	16.6	17.4	12.8	6.5	32.0	11
Age group not reported	75,440	10.7	5.2	19.7	31.9	12.1	3.5	16.9	10
Occupation									
Management, business, financial	101,460	11.6	8.5	22.0	26.6	13.7	3.0	14.5	7
Computer, engineering, science	18,210	13.5	10.8	20.0	23.0	10.8	4.0	18.0	7
Education, legal, community service, arts, media	54,400	13.8	9.5	25.2	21.5	10.5	3.3	16.1	6
Health-care practitioners, technical	223,680	6.6	5.1	19.9	33.2	16.9	4.0	14.2	9
Service	538,380	10.8	8.1	21.2	24.2	13.7	4.7	17.3	8
Sales and related	146,310	10.4	8.4	17.7	20.7	19.4	4.1	19.3	10
Office and administrative support	101,970	9.0	7.0	18.0	24.6	19.2	3.6	18.6	10
Farming, fishing, forestry	27,500	13.0	11.4	19.8	15.3	12.1	5.0	23.3	7
Construction, extraction	136,570	11.8	8.5	16.7	13.0	10.1	7.6	32.3	10
Installation, maintenance, repair	163,140	11.3	8.8	18.0	15.3	12.3	5.7	28.5	10
Production	223,840	13.3	9.3	17.5	15.4	14.8	5.8	23.9	9
Transportation, material moving	503,610	8.1	6.7	14.3	15.1	15.6	6.2	33.9	14

— = Data do not meet publication guidelines or may be too small to be displayed. **Note:** Because of rounding and data exclusion of nonclassifiable responses, data may not sum to the totals. (1) Cases include those that resulted in days away from work, some of which also included job transfer or restriction. (2) Number of nonfatal occupational injuries and illnesses involving days away from work for private industry workers.

Federal Minimum Hourly Wage Rates

Source: Bureau of Labor Statistics, U.S. Dept. of Labor; as of May 2024

Effective date	Minimum wage	% avg. earnings[1]	In 2024 dollars
Oct. 24, 1938	$0.25	40%	$5.61
Oct. 24, 1939	0.30	48	6.73
Oct. 24, 1945	0.40	39	6.94
Jan. 25, 1950	0.75	52	10.02
Mar. 1, 1956	1.00	51	11.72
Sept. 3, 1961	1.15	50	12.04
Sept. 3, 1963	1.25	51	12.79
Feb. 1, 1967	1.40	49	13.36
Feb. 1, 1968	1.60	53	14.69
May 1, 1974	2.00	45	12.92
Jan. 1, 1975	2.10	43	12.66
Jan. 1, 1976	2.30	44	12.99
Jan. 1, 1978	$2.65	43%	$13.32
Jan. 1, 1979	2.90	43	13.34
Jan. 1, 1980	3.10	43	12.51
Jan. 1, 1981	3.35	42	12.09
Apr. 1, 1990	3.80	35	9.26
Apr. 1, 1991	4.25	38	9.87
Oct. 1, 1996	4.75	37	9.42
Sept. 1, 1997	5.15	39	10.03
July 24, 2007	5.85	34	8.82
July 24, 2008	6.55	37	9.35
July 24, 2009	7.25	40	10.57

Note: Before 1961, minimum wage applied mainly to employees engaged in, or producing goods for, interstate commerce. The 1961 amendments extended coverage mainly to employees in large retail and service enterprises and to local transit, construction, and gas station employees. The 1966 and subsequent amendments extended coverage to farm workers; government employees; workers in various retail and service trades; and certain domestic workers. Starting in 1978, minimum wage applied equally to all covered, nonexempt workers. Exceptions apply to certain workers with disabilities, full-time students, persons under age 20 in their first 90 days of employment, tipped employees, and student-learners. (1) Percent of gross hourly earnings of production workers in manufacturing.

Civilian Employment of the Federal Government, 1940-2025

Source: U.S. Office of Personnel Management; Office of Management and Budget

(numbers in thousands)

Year	Total executive branch	Dept. of Defense	Civilian agencies/depts. Total employees	Agriculture	HHS, Education, Social Sec.[1]	Homeland Sec.	Interior	Justice	Transportation	Treasury	Veterans Affairs	Other
1940	699	256	443	98	9	18	46	11	NA	45	40	176
1945	3,370	2,635	736	82	11	20	45	19	NA	84	65	409
1950	1,439	753	686	84	13	20	66	20	NA	76	188	219
1955	1,860	1,187	673	86	40	21	54	24	NA	65	178	206
1960	1,808	1,047	761	99	62	21	56	24	NA	62	172	265
1965	1,901	1,034	867	113	87	21	71	27	NA	74	167	307
1970	2,203	1,219	983	118	112	23	75	33	62	84	169	308
1975	2,149	1,042	1,107	121	147	31	80	47	69	101	213	297
1980	2,161	960	1,201	129	163	40	77	48	66	102	228	346
1985	2,112	1,029	1,084	107	137	39	72	51	55	106	221	294
1990	2,174	1,006	1,168	111	122	48	71	66	59	130	214	347
1995	1,970	822	1,148	104	129	54	72	82	57	129	228	292
2000	1,814	660	1,153	95	128	67	67	95	57	113	203	328
2005	1,830	653	1,177	100	128	143	70	103	56	110	222	244
2010	2,128	741	1,386	96	137	173	71	113	57	112	285	342
2015	2,042	725	1,317	86	139	179	64	114	54	95	335	251
2020	2,180	777	1,403	79	139	198	61	114	53	91	389	279
2022	2,186	772	1,413	85	142	203	62	115	53	94	412	248
2025[2]	2,328	795	1,532	94	152	218	66	123	58	107	448	267

NA = Not available. HHS = Health and Human Services. **Note:** End-of-fiscal-year count; U.S. Postal Service excluded. All years are not directly comparable, as 1940-80 is civilian employment of full-time permanent, temporary, part-time, and intermittent employees; 1985-2024 is full-time equivalent employees. (1) Estimated, 1940-50. (2) Estimated.

Unemployment Rates and Earnings by Education, 2023

Source: Bureau of Labor Statistics, U.S. Dept. of Labor

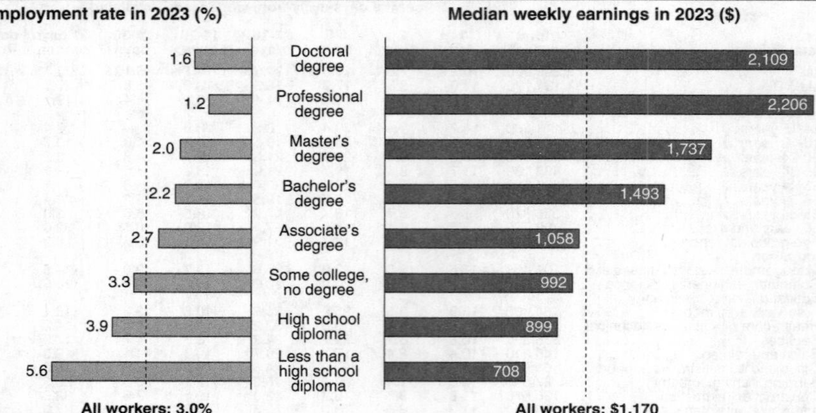

Note: Data for persons age 25 and over. Earnings are for full-time wage and salary workers.

Median Earnings by Industry and Sex, 2022

Source: American Community Survey (ACS), U.S. Census Bureau, U.S. Dept. of Commerce

	Employed			Median earnings			
Industry	**Total**	**% men**	**% women**	**Total**	**Men**	**Women**	**Women's as % of men's**
Total	**162,590,221**	**52.7%**	**47.3%**	**$45,937**	**$52,612**	**$39,688**	**75.4%**
Agriculture, forestry, fishing and hunting, and mining	2,546,743	77.9	22.1	41,787	45,775	29,520	64.5
Construction	11,213,024	88.9	11.1	49,033	49,883	43,414	87.0
Manufacturing	16,096,892	70.8	29.2	54,404	59,585	44,777	75.1
Wholesale trade	3,502,056	70.5	29.5	53,903	57,942	45,666	78.8
Retail trade	18,073,795	52.3	47.7	30,326	34,373	25,833	75.2
Transportation and warehousing, and utilities	9,779,768	74.4	25.6	49,372	52,776	38,552	73.0
Information	3,137,801	59.6	40.4	68,061	77,718	55,285	71.1
Finance and insurance, and real estate and rental and leasing	10,967,381	46.9	53.1	64,873	81,699	54,898	67.2
Professional, scientific, and management, administrative and waste management services	20,474,027	57.1	42.9	61,426	71,860	50,689	70.5
Educational services, and health care and social assistance	37,480,570	26.3	73.7	46,271	56,611	42,763	75.5
Arts, entertainment, and recreation, and accommodation and food services	14,097,318	49.0	51.0	21,787	25,848	19,181	74.2
Other services, except public administration	7,675,317	47.0	53.0	32,499	41,518	26,642	64.2
Public administration	7,545,529	54.7	45.3	65,570	74,796	56,571	75.6

Note: For the civilian employed population 16 years of age and over including workers not employed full-time.

Net Productivity and Workers' Hourly Compensation, 1948-2022

Source: Economic Policy Institute (EPI), based on U.S. Bureau of Economic Analysis and U.S. Bureau of Labor Statistics data

This graph shows the cumulative percent change since 1948 in net productivity and hourly compensation in the U.S. Net productivity is the growth of goods and services produced minus depreciation per hour worked. Hourly compensation is average wages and benefits for private sector production and nonsupervisory workers, who make up around 80% of private payroll employment.

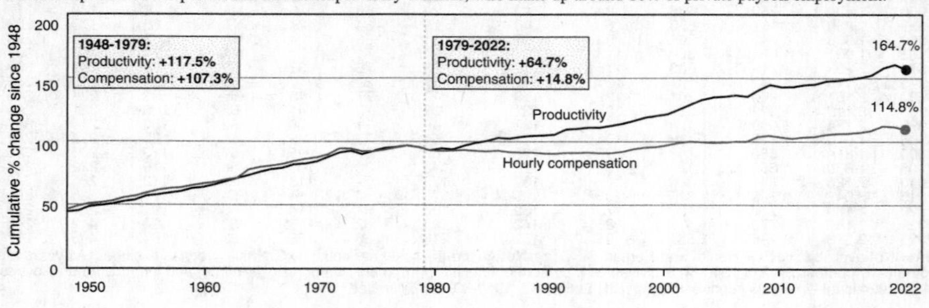

U.S. Median Weekly Earnings, 2024

Source: Bureau of Labor Statistics, U.S. Dept. of Labor

	Total		Men		Women	
AGE, RACE, AND ETHNICITY	Number of workers (thous.)	Median weekly earnings	Number of workers (thous.)	Median weekly earnings	Number of workers (thous.)	Median weekly earnings
TOTAL						
16 years and over	119,937	$1,143	66,023	$1,253	53,915	$1,017
16 to 24 years	10,904	727	6,021	771	4,884	695
16 to 19 years	1,595	626	899	693	696	579
20 to 24 years	9,309	752	5,122	786	4,188	716
25 years and over	109,033	1,201	60,002	1,338	49,031	1,078
25 to 54 years	84,107	1,205	46,310	1,338	37,797	1,091
25 to 34 years	29,392	1,103	16,155	1,171	13,237	1,007
35 to 44 years	29,266	1,247	16,288	1,379	12,978	1,114
45 to 54 years	25,449	1,316	13,867	1,470	11,581	1,151
55 years and over	24,926	1,188	13,692	1,337	11,234	1,037
55 to 64 years	19,588	1,197	10,711	1,361	8,877	1,048
65 years and over	5,338	1,154	2,980	1,251	2,357	1,000
White						
16 years and over	90,152	1,167	50,834	1,281	39,318	1,037
16 to 24 years	8,424	735	4,693	780	3,732	701
25 years and over	81,727	1,236	46,141	1,369	35,586	1,105
25 to 54 years	62,026	1,236	35,078	1,361	26,949	1,113
55 years and over	19,701	1,236	11,063	1,390	8,638	1,071
Black						
16 years and over	16,570	941	7,962	979	8,607	906
16 to 24 years	1,445	691	767	717	678	626
25 years and over	15,125	985	7,196	1,064	7,929	936
25 to 54 years	11,967	988	5,711	1,093	6,256	937
55 years and over	3,158	971	1,485	1,001	1,673	931
Asian						
16 years and over	8,581	1,500	4,774	1,608	3,807	1,337
16 to 24 years	416	954	244	1,050	172	852
25 years and over	8,165	1,543	4,530	1,668	3,635	1,390
25 to 54 years	6,697	1,595	3,715	1,756	2,982	1,465
55 years and over	1,468	1,182	815	1,380	653	994
Hispanic[1]						
16 years and over	23,649	903	14,072	963	9,577	831
16 to 24 years	2,977	700	1,752	726	1,225	668
25 years and over	20,673	948	12,320	1,001	8,353	878
25 to 54 years	17,027	957	10,142	1,003	6,885	885
55 years and over	3,646	920	2,178	988	1,467	824
OCCUPATION						
Management, professional, and related	55,612	1,579	26,641	1,877	28,971	1,389
Management, business, and financial operations	24,018	1,721	12,245	1,899	11,773	1,527
Professional and related	31,594	1,505	14,396	1,843	17,198	1,287
Service	16,195	742	7,520	809	8,675	706
Sales and office	21,061	958	8,901	1,157	12,160	875
Sales and related	9,041	1,042	5,212	1,321	3,828	876
Office and administrative support	12,021	914	3,688	1,012	8,332	874
Natural resources, construction, and maintenance	11,437	1,024	10,867	1,053	570	790
Farming, fishing, and forestry	626	700	487	699	138	705
Construction and extraction	6,668	1,007	6,396	1,016	272	804
Installation, maintenance, and repair	4,144	1,147	3,984	1,168	160	850
Production, transportation, and material moving	15,632	884	12,094	951	3,538	741
Production	6,963	921	5,210	998	1,753	739
Transportation and material moving	8,669	848	6,883	901	1,786	742

Note: Not seasonally adjusted; figures are median usual weekly earnings of full-time wage and salary workers for second quarter 2024. Total includes races not shown here. (1) May be of any race.

Average Hours and Earnings of U.S. Production Workers, 1969-2023

Source: Bureau of Labor Statistics, U.S. Dept. of Labor; annual averages

Year	Weekly hours	Hourly earnings	Weekly earnings	Year	Weekly hours	Hourly earnings	Weekly earnings	Year	Weekly hours	Hourly earnings	Weekly earnings
1969	37.5	$3.22	$120.80	1988	34.6	$9.44	$326.50	2006	33.9	$16.75	$567.00
1970	37.0	3.41	125.91	1989	34.5	9.81	338.42	2007	33.8	17.41	589.09
1971	36.7	3.63	133.35	1990	34.3	10.20	349.63	2008	33.6	18.06	607.10
1972	36.9	3.91	143.99	1991	34.1	10.51	358.46	2009	33.1	18.60	615.82
1973	36.9	4.14	152.71	1992	34.2	10.77	368.17	2010	33.4	19.04	635.86
1974	36.4	4.44	161.76	1993	34.3	11.04	378.80	2011	33.6	19.43	652.75
1975	36.0	4.74	170.45	1994	34.5	11.33	391.11	2012	33.7	19.73	665.56
1976	36.0	5.06	182.36	1995	34.3	11.65	399.93	2013	33.7	20.13	677.62
1977	35.9	5.44	195.34	1996	34.3	12.04	413.17	2014	33.7	20.60	694.74
1978	35.8	5.88	210.17	1997	34.5	12.51	431.67	2015	33.7	21.03	708.73
1979	35.6	6.34	225.46	1998	34.5	13.01	448.47	2016	33.6	21.53	723.20
1980	35.2	6.84	240.83	1999	34.3	13.48	463.07	2017	33.7	22.05	742.42
1981	35.2	7.43	261.29	2000	34.3	14.01	480.90	2018	33.8	22.71	767.01
1982	34.7	7.86	272.98	2001	33.9	14.54	493.53	2019	33.6	23.51	790.64
1983	34.9	8.20	286.34	2002	33.9	14.96	506.48	2020	33.9	24.68	837.39
1984	35.1	8.49	298.08	2003	33.7	15.36	517.65	2021	34.2	25.90	886.54
1985	34.9	8.73	304.37	2004	33.7	15.68	528.65	2022	34.0	27.56	937.44
1986	34.7	8.92	309.69	2005	33.8	16.11	543.91	2023	33.9	28.94	979.95
1987	34.7	9.14	317.33								

Note: Not seasonally adjusted; data refer to production workers and nonsupervisory employees.

Elderly in U.S. Labor Force, 1900-2023

Source: U.S. Census Bureau, U.S. Dept. of Commerce

(percent of persons age 65 and older who participated in the labor force; 1910 figures not available)

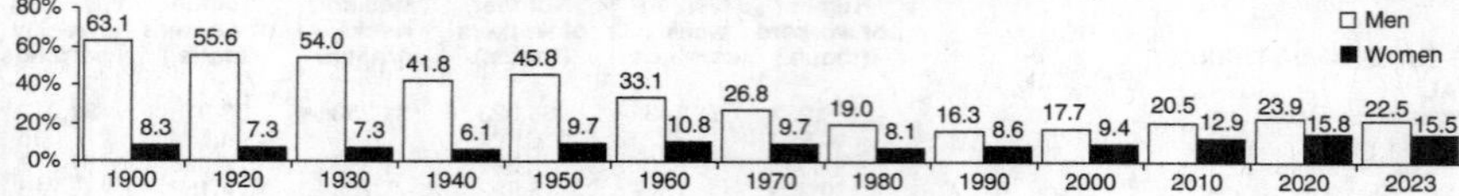

U.S. Union Membership, 1930-2023

Source: Bureau of Labor Statistics, U.S. Dept. of Labor

(numbers in thousands)

Year	Total employed[1]	% in union	Union members[2]	Year	Total employed[1]	% in union	Union members[2]	Year	Total employed[1]	% in union	Union members[2]
1930	29,424	11.6%	3,401	1975	76,945	25.5%	19,611	2015	133,743	11.1%	14,795
1935	27,053	13.2	3,584	1980	90,564	21.9	19,843	2016	136,101	10.7	14,555
1940	32,376	26.9	8,717	1985	94,521	18.0	16,996	2017	137,890	10.7	14,817
1945	40,394	35.5	14,322	1990	103,905	16.1	16,740	2018	140,099	10.5	14,744
1950	45,222	31.5	14,267	1995	110,038	14.9	16,360	2019	141,737	10.3	14,574
1955	50,675	33.2	16,802	2000	120,786	13.5	16,258	2020	132,174	10.8	14,253
1960	54,234	31.4	17,049	2005	125,889	12.5	15,685	2021	136,393	10.3	14,012
1965	60,815	28.4	17,299	2010	124,073	11.9	14,715	2022	141,673	10.1	14,285
1970	70,920	27.3	19,381	2012	127,577	11.3	14,366	2023	144,541	10.0	14,424

(1) Prior to 1985, total labor force figure, which includes unemployed persons. From 1985 on, does not include self-employed workers. (2) From 1930 to 1980, includes dues-paying members of traditional trade unions, regardless of employment status; after 1980, includes employed only. From 1985 on, includes members of employee associations similar to a union.

Median Weekly Earnings of U.S. Workers by Union Affiliation, 2000, 2023

Source: Bureau of Labor Statistics, U.S. Dept. of Labor

	2000				2023			
Sex and age	Total	Union members[1]	Represented by unions[2]	Non-union	Total	Union members[1]	Represented by unions[2]	Non-union
Total, 16 years and older	**$576**	**$696**	**$691**	**$542**	**$1,117**	**$1,263**	**$1,253**	**$1,090**
16 to 24 years	361	437	436	355	714	809	810	709
25 years and older	611	709	705	592	1,170	1,294	1,284	1,155
25 to 34 years	550	627	624	529	1,045	1,160	1,150	1,027
35 to 44 years	631	716	712	614	1,250	1,375	1,374	1,232
45 to 54 years	671	755	752	639	1,255	1,390	1,381	1,232
55 to 64 years	617	727	723	592	1,217	1,289	1,280	1,205
65 years and older	442	577	565	422	1,080	1,152	1,150	1,064
Men, 16 years and older	**646**	**739**	**737**	**620**	**1,202**	**1,341**	**1,333**	**1,180**
16 to 24 years	376	458	457	370	736	813	812	729
25 years and older	700	753	752	682	1,273	1,374	1,367	1,258
25 to 34 years	603	678	675	591	1,107	1,212	1,209	1,090
35 to 44 years	731	776	774	718	1,364	1,448	1,452	1,347
45 to 54 years	777	801	799	769	1,396	1,465	1,445	1,385
55 to 64 years	738	755	757	729	1,380	1,397	1,384	1,380
65 years and older	537	613	613	514	1,181	1,191	1,185	1,181
Women, 16 years and older	**491**	**616**	**613**	**472**	**1,005**	**1,174**	**1,165**	**983**
16 to 24 years	342	406	405	339	691	784	797	685
25 years and older	515	627	623	497	1,060	1,197	1,186	1,034
25 to 34 years	493	579	578	483	985	1,120	1,094	971
35 to 44 years	520	605	604	506	1,136	1,266	1,260	1,112
45 to 54 years	565	697	692	522	1,115	1,317	1,312	1,079
55 to 64 years	505	659	647	481	1,065	1,148	1,147	1,043
65 years and older	378	485	484	365	977	1,118	1,115	960

Note: Data refer to the sole or principal job of full-time wage and salary workers. Excludes self-employed workers regardless of whether their businesses are incorporated. (1) Includes members of an employee association similar to a union. (2) Includes members of a labor union as well as those whose jobs are covered by a union or an employee-association contract.

Work Stoppages (Strikes and Lockouts) in the U.S., 1950-2023

Source: Bureau of Labor Statistics, U.S. Dept. of Labor; involving 1,000 workers or more

Year	No.	Workers (thous.)	Days idle (thous.)	Year	No.	Workers (thous.)	Days idle (thous.)	Year	No.	Workers (thous.)	Days idle (thous.)
1950	424	1,698	30,390	1992	35	364	3,989	2008	15	72	1,954
1955	363	2,055	21,180	1993	35	182	3,981	2009	5	13	124
1960	222	896	13,260	1994	45	322	5,021	2010	11	45	302
1965	268	999	15,140	1995	31	192	5,771	2011	19	113	1,020
1970	381	2,468	52,761	1996	37	273	4,889	2012	19	148	1,131
1975	235	965	17,563	1997	29	339	4,497	2013	15	55	290
1980	187	795	20,844	1998	34	387	5,116	2014	11	34	200
1983	81	909	17,461	1999	17	73	1,996	2015	12	47	740
1984	62	376	8,499	2000	39	394	20,419	2016	15	99	1,543
1985	54	324	7,079	2001	29	99	1,151	2017	7	25	440
1986	69	533	11,861	2002	19	46	660	2018	20	485	2,815
1987	46	174	4,481	2003	14	129	4,091	2019	25	426	3,244
1988	40	118	4,381	2004	17	171	3,344	2020	8	27	966
1989	51	452	16,996	2005	22	100	1,736	2021	16	81	1,552
1990	44	185	5,926	2006	20	70	2,688	2022	23	121	2,195
1991	40	392	4,584	2007	21	189	1,265	2023	33	459	16,673

Note: Numbers cover stoppages that began in the year indicated. Workers are counted more than once if they are involved in more than one stoppage during the year. For work stoppages ongoing at the end of a calendar year, days idle include only the days for the calendar year.

U.S. Energy Overview, 1960-2023

Source: *Monthly Energy Review*, July 2024, Energy Information Administration (EIA), U.S. Dept. of Energy; in quadrillion Btu

	1960	1970	1980	1990	2000	2010	2015	2020	2021	2022	2023
Production	**41.69**	**61.68**	**65.16**	**68.49**	**69.26**	**72.54**	**85.37**	**91.86**	**93.84**	**98.53**	**102.76**
Fossil fuels	39.86	59.15	58.98	58.52	57.31	58.16	70.19	76.15	77.90	82.16	86.23
Coal[1]	10.82	14.61	18.60	22.49	22.74	22.04	17.95	10.70	11.60	12.04	11.75
Natural gas (dry)	12.66	21.67	19.91	18.33	19.66	21.81	28.07	35.06	35.81	37.66	39.25[E]
Crude oil[2]	14.94	20.40	18.25	15.57	12.36	11.61	19.70	23.58	23.40	24.71	26.84[E]
Natural gas plant liquids (NGPL)	1.45	2.48	2.23	2.14	2.55	2.71	4.48	6.81	7.10	7.74	8.39
Nuclear electric power	0.01	0.24	2.74	6.10	7.86	8.43	8.34	8.25	8.13	8.06	8.10
Renewable energy	1.83	2.29	3.45	3.86	4.09	5.94	6.85	7.47	7.81	8.31	8.43
Conventional hydroelectric power[3]	0.51	0.86	0.95	1.00	0.94	0.89	0.85	0.97	0.86	0.87	0.82
Biomass[4]	1.32	1.43	2.48	2.74	3.01	4.55	5.03	4.71	4.91	5.07	5.16
Geothermal energy	(s)	—	0.02	0.06	0.07	0.11	0.12	0.12	0.12	0.12	0.12
Solar	NA	NA	NA	0.06	0.06	0.07	0.20	0.51	0.63	0.77	0.88
Wind	NA	NA	NA	0.01	0.02	0.32	0.65	1.15	1.29	1.48	1.45
Imports	**4.19**	**8.34**	**15.80**	**18.82**	**28.87**	**29.87**	**23.79**	**19.99**	**21.46**	**21.51**	**21.70**
Coal	0.01	—	0.03	0.07	0.31	0.48	0.26	0.11	0.11	0.14	0.09
Natural gas	0.16	0.85	1.01	1.55	3.87	3.83	2.79	2.62	2.88	3.10	3.00
Petroleum[5]	4.00	7.47	14.66	17.12	24.42	25.36	20.41	16.98	18.20	18.00	18.36
Crude oil[2]	2.20	2.81	11.20	12.77	19.78	20.14	16.30	13.04	13.54	13.95	14.40
Petroleum products[6]	1.80	4.66	3.46	4.35	4.64	5.22	4.11	3.94	4.66	4.05	3.95
Biomass[7]	NA	NA	NA	NA	(s)	—	0.08	0.07	0.08	0.07	0.11
Electricity	0.02	0.02	0.09	0.06	0.17	0.15	0.26	0.21	0.18	0.19	0.13
Exports	**1.48**	**2.63**	**3.70**	**4.75**	**3.96**	**8.18**	**12.90**	**23.46**	**25.07**	**27.33**	**29.50**
Coal	1.02	1.94	2.42	2.77	1.53	2.10	1.85	1.73	2.06	2.09	2.41
Natural gas	0.01	0.07	0.05	0.09	0.25	1.15	1.80	5.33	6.71	6.97	7.68
Petroleum	0.43	0.55	1.16	1.82	2.11	4.78	9.12	16.11	15.95	17.89	19.02
Crude oil[2]	0.02	0.03	0.61	0.23	0.11	0.09	0.96	6.70	6.19	7.47	8.49
Petroleum products[6]	0.41	0.52	0.55	1.59	2.00	4.69	8.15	9.41	9.76	10.42	10.54
Biomass[8]	NA	NA	NA	NA	NA	0.05	0.08	0.23	0.25	0.28	0.29
Electricity	—	0.01	0.01	0.06	0.05	0.07	0.03	0.05	0.05	0.05	0.07
Consumption	**43.94**	**66.04**	**76.04**	**82.26**	**96.69**	**95.14**	**94.48**	**88.85**	**93.36**	**94.79**	**93.58**
Fossil fuels	42.09	63.50	69.78	72.28	84.62	80.72	79.09	73.14	77.45	78.50	77.17
Coal	9.84	12.27	15.42	19.17	22.58	20.83	15.55	9.18	10.55	9.89	8.17
Natural gas[9]	12.39	21.80	20.24	19.60	23.82	24.58	28.19	31.64	31.71	33.35	33.61
Petroleum[10]	19.87	29.50	34.16	33.50	38.15	35.32	35.37	32.33	35.24	35.32	35.43
Nuclear electric power	0.01	0.24	2.74	6.10	7.86	8.43	8.34	8.25	8.13	8.06	8.10
Renewable energy	1.83	2.29	3.45	3.86	4.10	5.90	6.83	7.30	7.64	8.09	8.25
Conventional hydroelectric power[3]	0.51	0.86	0.95	1.00	0.94	0.89	0.85	0.97	0.86	0.87	0.82
Biomass[4]	1.32	1.43	2.48	2.74	3.01	4.51	5.02	4.55	4.75	4.86	4.98
Geothermal energy	(s)	—	0.02	0.06	0.07	0.11	0.12	0.12	0.12	0.12	0.12
Solar	NA	NA	NA	0.06	0.06	0.07	0.20	0.51	0.63	0.77	0.88
Wind	NA	NA	NA	0.01	0.02	0.32	0.65	1.15	1.29	1.48	1.45

NA = Not available. — = Less than 0.005 quadrillion Btu. (s) = Less than 0.5 trillion Btu. E = Estimate. **Note:** Numbers may not add up to totals because of rounding. (1) Incl. waste coal supplied beginning in 1989 and refuse recovery beginning in 2001. (2) Incl. lease condensate. Imports incl. crude oil for the Strategic Petroleum Reserve, which began in 1977. (3) Starting in 1990, pumped storage was removed and expanded coverage of industrial use of hydroelectric power was included. (4) Category known as "wood, waste, and alcohol" for years prior to 2000. Includes wood, waste, and alcohol fuels (ethanol blended into motor gasoline). Ethanol is included in both Petroleum and Biomass categories but is only counted once in totals. (5) Imports incl. crude oil for the Strategic Petroleum Reserve, which began in 1977. Imports/exports excl. biofuels. (6) Incl. unfinished oils, natural gasoline, and gasoline blending components; excl. biofuels. (7) Beginning in 1993, incl. fuel ethanol (minus denaturant); also incl. biodiesel (beginning in 2001), renewable diesel fuel (beginning in 2011), and other biofuels (beginning in 2021). (8) Beginning in 2001, incl. biodiesel; beginning in 2010, also incl. fuel ethanol (minus denaturant); beginning in 2016, also incl. wood and wood-derived fuels. (9) Excl. supplemental gaseous fuels. (10) Petroleum products supplied; excl. biofuels.

U.S. Energy Consumption by Source, 1950-2023

Source: *Monthly Energy Review*, July 2024, Energy Information Administration (EIA), U.S. Dept. of Energy

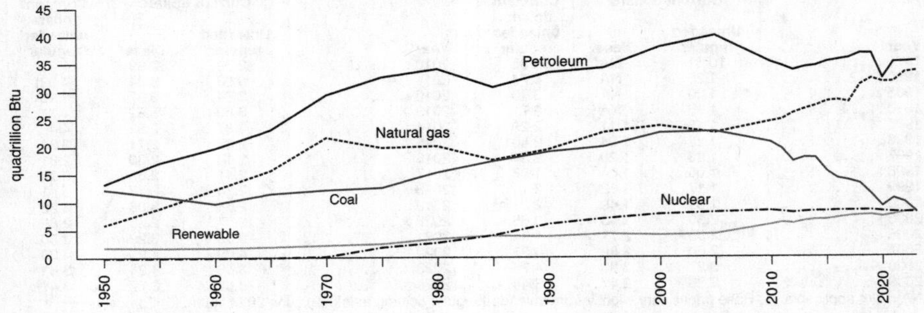

World's Largest Energy Producers and Consumers, 1980-2022

Source: Energy Information Administration (EIA), U.S. Dept. of Energy
(primary energy in quadrillion Btu; ranked by 2022 data as of June 11, 2024)

Production	1980	1990	2000	2010	2015	2016	2018	2020	2021	2022
1. China	14.59	30.99	39.78	92.31	106.50	99.65	108.19	116.31	123.17	137.83
2. United States	65.16	68.49	69.26	72.54	85.37	81.05	91.96	91.86	93.84	98.53
3. Russia	NA	NA	41.20	53.10	56.69	57.83	62.39	59.03	62.89	59.94
4. Saudi Arabia	0.35	15.78	20.72	23.33	28.15	29.16	29.18	26.65	26.58	29.65
5. India	2.12	5.90	8.15	13.23	14.53	15.31	16.51	16.50	17.44	21.89
6. Canada	4.87	10.65	14.74	15.97	18.51	18.71	21.23	20.17	20.83	21.55
7. Australia	2.75	6.50	9.54	13.10	15.48	15.90	17.16	18.40	17.68	17.82
8. Iran	0.31	7.63	10.35	14.59	14.49	17.03	18.17	15.76	16.99	17.64
9. Indonesia	0.74	5.10	7.20	12.69	14.16	14.08	15.77	15.35	16.37	16.50
10. United Arab Emirates	0.21	5.74	6.80	7.71	9.73	9.97	9.55	9.82	9.85	10.88
11. Brazil	0.68	2.61	4.51	7.58	8.94	9.22	9.69	10.57	10.33	10.82
12. Iraq	0.07	4.45	5.61	5.24	8.79	9.68	10.31	9.11	9.17	10.02
13. Qatar	0.19	1.14	2.77	7.78	9.78	9.85	9.74	9.72	9.84	9.96
14. Norway	1.29	4.96	9.32	8.72	8.71	8.80	8.66	8.68	8.87	8.91
15. Kazakhstan	NA	NA	3.89	7.08	7.49	7.29	8.06	7.64	7.47	7.71
16. Kuwait	0.26	2.50	4.36	5.63	7.12	7.37	7.15	6.51	6.44	7.13
17. Algeria	0.49	4.72	6.12	6.93	6.69	6.91	6.75	5.97	6.73	6.72
18. South Africa	2.53	3.86	5.17	5.77	5.82	5.82	5.77	5.61	5.34	6.03
19. Mexico	1.15	7.49	9.06	8.64	7.44	7.09	5.99	5.69	5.81	5.92
20. Nigeria	0.05	3.91	4.88	6.37	6.49	5.74	5.97	5.73	5.06	4.45
21. United Kingdom	5.12	8.99	11.53	6.25	4.85	4.91	5.09	4.86	4.17	4.27
22. Malaysia	0.06	1.85	3.02	3.80	3.91	3.96	4.22	3.87	4.00	4.19
23. Egypt	0.06	2.30	2.26	3.81	3.23	3.10	3.83	3.74	4.00	3.89
24. Colombia	0.28	1.73	2.78	4.16	5.04	4.90	4.73	3.61	3.74	3.77
25. Oman	0.03	1.57	2.39	2.83	3.19	3.26	3.39	3.32	3.47	3.75
Consumption	**1980**	**1990**	**2000**	**2010**	**2015**	**2016**	**2018**	**2020**	**2021**	**2022**
1. China	18.71	27.50	40.97	107.25	129.11	129.35	137.27	145.35	151.90	173.96
2. United States	76.04	82.26	96.69	95.14	94.48	94.09	97.40	88.85	93.36	94.79
3. India	3.43	6.92	11.69	21.41	27.07	28.09	30.63	30.13	30.66	35.26
4. Russia	NA	NA	25.67	29.24	29.97	29.94	31.30	30.01	32.03	32.54
5. Japan	15.19	18.60	21.65	20.98	18.69	18.79	18.58	16.96	16.92	16.89
6. Iran	1.56	2.97	5.12	8.97	10.57	10.78	11.79	11.98	13.02	13.50
7. Canada	7.84	8.66	10.15	11.44	12.32	12.15	12.79	11.68	11.76	12.27
8. South Korea	1.87	4.03	8.07	10.83	11.86	12.22	12.33	11.98	12.44	12.20
9. Saudi Arabia	1.65	3.34	5.10	9.86	9.86	12.27	11.66	9.07	10.63	11.43
10. Germany	NA	NA	14.19	13.70	12.84	12.93	12.84	11.13	11.83	11.09
11. Brazil	3.00	4.43	6.44	8.88	10.34	10.00	9.99	9.41	10.21	10.77
12. Indonesia	1.14	2.26	4.05	6.02	6.56	6.63	7.39	7.12	7.92	9.10
13. France	8.17	8.87	10.44	10.52	9.91	9.74	9.73	8.47	9.13	8.29
14. Mexico	3.77	4.59	6.22	7.34	7.53	7.63	7.54	6.96	7.14	7.56
15. United Kingdom	8.97	9.26	9.86	9.10	8.04	7.99	7.81	6.65	6.77	6.74
16. Australia	2.95	3.62	4.56	5.43	5.48	5.67	5.80	5.59	5.72	6.17
17. Turkey (Türkiye)	0.92	1.78	2.97	4.16	5.28	5.53	5.85	5.64	6.20	6.02
18. Italy	5.87	6.48	7.24	7.25	6.25	6.20	6.28	5.54	6.03	5.81
19. South Africa	2.62	3.81	4.63	5.61	5.56	5.52	5.46	5.54	5.27	5.72
20. Spain	2.98	3.83	5.28	5.63	5.07	5.18	5.32	4.61	4.92	5.05
21. Thailand	0.49	1.21	2.53	4.38	5.11	5.24	5.44	4.95	4.91	5.02
22. Taiwan	1.07	1.99	3.57	4.63	4.66	4.75	4.68	4.56	4.83	4.92
23. United Arab Emirates	0.28	1.23	2.09	3.64	4.70	4.72	4.10	4.34	4.48	4.69
24. Poland	4.75	4.26	3.69	4.08	4.05	4.13	4.30	3.99	4.12	4.05
25. Egypt	0.65	1.35	1.91	3.41	3.64	3.68	3.99	3.60	4.05	4.05

NA = Not applicable or not available.

Average U.S. Gasoline Prices, 1976-2024

Source: *Monthly Energy Review*, July 2024; *Short-Term Energy Outlook*, July 2024; Energy Information Administration (EIA), U.S. Dept. of Energy

(in dollars per gallon, including taxes; constant dollars is price in July 2024 dollars)

Year	Current dollars: Unleaded regular	Current dollars: Diesel	Constant dollars, unleaded regular[1]
1976	$0.61	NA	$3.38
1980	1.25	NA	4.74
1985	1.20	NA	3.40
1990	1.16	NA	2.71
1995	1.15	$1.11	2.29
1996	1.23	1.24	2.40
1997	1.23	1.20	2.34
1998	1.06	1.04	1.98
1999	1.17	1.12	2.15
2000	1.51	1.49	2.71
2005	2.30	2.40	3.65
2006	2.59	2.71	4.01
2007	2.80	2.89	4.25
2008	3.27	3.80	4.75
2009	2.35	2.47	3.44
2010	$2.79	$2.99	$4.00
2011	3.53	3.84	4.92
2012	3.64	3.97	4.96
2013	3.53	3.92	4.72
2014	3.37	3.83	4.46
2015	2.45	2.71	3.21
2016	2.14	2.30	2.81
2017	2.41	2.65	3.09
2018	2.74	3.18	3.41
2019	2.64	3.06	3.20
2020	2.17	2.55	2.65
2021	3.05	3.29	3.50
2022	4.09	4.99	4.26
2023	3.66	4.21	3.63
2024	3.60[2]	3.72[2]	3.41[3]

NA = Not applicable. (1) Base prices vary slightly from unleaded regular column at left. (2) June 2024 figure. (3) Forecast.

Energy Consumption by State, 2022

Source: State Energy Data System, Energy Information Administration (EIA), U.S. Dept. of Energy

Total Consumption

Rank, state	Btu (tril)	Rank, state	Btu (tril)
1. Texas	13,780.6	27. Massachusetts	1,315.2
2. California	6,882.4	28. Maryland	1,202.8
3. Florida	4,325.0	29. Mississippi	1,099.8
4. Louisiana	4,246.0	30. Arkansas	1,052.5
5. Pennsylvania	3,736.9	31. Kansas	1,000.7
6. Illinois	3,675.6	32. Oregon	857.3
7. Ohio	3,503.2	33. Utah	848.7
8. New York	3,452.7	34. Nebraska	846.4
9. Georgia	2,836.2	35. West Virginia	835.5
10. Michigan	2,706.8	36. Alaska	724.1
11. Indiana	2,618.9	37. Connecticut	707.6
12. North Carolina	2,568.8	38. Nevada	706.1
13. Virginia	2,427.8	39. New Mexico	687.6
14. Tennessee	2,101.8	40. North Dakota	670.6
15. New Jersey	2,014.4	41. Idaho	519.0
16. Alabama	1,902.4	42. Wyoming	496.2
17. Wisconsin	1,768.6	43. Montana	395.3
18. Minnesota	1,759.9	44. South Dakota	358.4
19. Missouri	1,733.4	45. Maine	335.3
20. Kentucky	1,673.2	46. New Hampshire	297.2
21. South Carolina	1,623.4	47. Delaware	274.8
22. Washington	1,571.4	48. Hawaii	270.3
23. Arizona	1,526.9	49. Rhode Island	186.6
24. Oklahoma	1,526.4	50. District of Columbia	141.0
25. Colorado	1,464.0	51. Vermont	124.8
26. Iowa	1,423.2	**United States**	**94,773.7**[1]

Consumption per Capita

Rank, state	Btu (mil)	Rank, state	Btu (mil)
1. Alaska	987.4	27. Virginia	279.7
2. Louisiana	925.4	28. Michigan	269.8
3. North Dakota	861.0	29. Delaware	269.6
4. Wyoming	853.1	30. Idaho	267.7
5. West Virginia	471.0	31. Georgia	259.9
6. Texas	458.9	32. Utah	251.0
7. Iowa	444.8	33. Colorado	250.6
8. Nebraska	430.1	34. Maine	241.4
9. South Dakota	393.9	35. North Carolina	240.2
10. Indiana	383.3	36. Nevada	222.2
11. Oklahoma	379.8	37. New Jersey	217.5
12. Alabama	374.9	38. New Hampshire	212.5
13. Mississippi	374.2	39. District of Columbia	210.2
14. Kentucky	370.9	40. Arizona	207.3
15. Montana	352.0	41. Oregon	202.2
16. Arkansas	345.5	42. Washington	201.9
17. Kansas	340.8	43. Connecticut	196.1
18. New Mexico	325.3	44. Maryland	195.1
19. Minnesota	308.0	45. Florida	194.4
20. South Carolina	307.3	46. Vermont	192.8
21. Wisconsin	300.2	47. Massachusetts	188.3
22. Tennessee	298.2	48. Hawaii	187.8
23. Ohio	297.9	49. California	176.3
24. Illinois	292.1	50. New York	175.5
25. Pennsylvania	288.1	51. Rhode Island	170.6
26. Missouri	280.6	**United States**	**284.4**

(1) Includes –55.8 trillion Btu of net imports of coal coke that are not allocated to the states.

U.S. Production of Crude Oil by State, 1990-2023

Source: Energy Information Administration (EIA), U.S. Dept. of Energy

Oil production in North Dakota nearly quadrupled between 2010 and 2023 through the use of hydraulic fracturing, or fracking, a process by which water, sand, and chemicals are injected at high pressure to create fractures in shale rock, releasing the oil or natural gas within. Fracking accounted for just 2% of U.S. oil production in 2000 but grew to 64% by 2023.

(in thousands of barrels; ranked by 2023 production)

Rank, state	1990	2000	2010	2020	2023
1. TX	678,478	443,397	426,767	1,773,072	2,011,995
2. NM	67,250	67,198	65,569	375,419	667,535
3. ND	36,717	32,719	112,555	433,563	432,735
4. CO	30,453	18,481	33,068	171,635	165,714
5. OK	112,273	69,976	70,196	172,804	157,244
6. AK	647,309	355,199	218,904	163,852	155,465
7. CA	320,868	271,132	200,370	142,221	112,189
8. WY	103,856	60,726	53,890	89,076	97,235
9. UT	27,604	15,636	24,663	31,001	56,196
10. LA	147,582	105,425	67,590	36,420	34,515
11. OH	10,008	6,575	4,772	23,864	30,701
12. KS	55,428	34,463	40,470	28,261	27,432
13. MT	19,810	15,428	25,332	19,082	23,235
14. WV	2,143	1,400	1,842	19,484	19,109
15. MS	27,034	19,844	23,981	14,166	12,571
16. IL	19,954	12,206	9,067	7,150	6,900
17. PA	2,641	1,500	3,238	5,532	4,802
18. MI	19,676	7,907	6,980	4,181	4,537
19. AR	10,386	7,154	5,733	4,143	4,326
20. AL	18,538	10,457	7,155	4,295	3,546
21. KY	5,409	3,465	2,519	2,265	1,876
22. IN	3,000	2,098	1,835	1,402	1,527
23. NE	5,889	2,957	2,331	1,673	1,480
24. FL	5,675	4,626	1,777	1,488	1,026
25. SD	1,648	1,170	1,607	1,047	929
26. NY	415	210	381	238	266
27. NV	4,011	621	426	196	211
28. TN	506	346	257	152	115
29. MO	146	94	146	62	66
30. ID	NA	NA	0	1	33
31. AZ	121	59	37	5	6
32. VA	16	9	12	5	4
Federal offshore	**299,835**	**558,242**	**588,335**	**614,750**	**682,908**
U.S. total	**2,684,687**	**2,130,707**	**2,001,805**	**4,142,504**	**4,718,434**

NA = Not available. **Note:** One barrel is equal to 42 U.S. gallons.

Dry Shale Gas Production in the U.S., 2000-24

Source: Energy Information Administration (EIA), U.S. Dept. of Energy

(production in billions of cubic ft per day; ranked by 2024 production)

Site name (primary location)	2000	2005	2010	2015	2018	2020	2021	2022	2023	2024
Marcellus (PA, WV, OH, NY)	—	—	0.44	15.09	18.59	23.40	25.39	25.68	25.69	25.10
Permian (TX, NM)	0.20	0.19	0.27	1.71	4.60	9.95	10.95	12.73	15.03	16.27
Haynesville (LA,TX)	0.14	0.10	2.44	3.86	5.58	9.60	10.25	12.43	14.39	14.23
Utica (OH, PA, WV)	—	—	—	2.03	6.04	6.98	6.61	6.24	5.40	4.47
Eagle Ford (TX)	—	—	0.11	4.46	3.95	4.67	3.65	3.84	4.22	3.48
Niobrara-Codell (CO, WY)	0.26	0.36	0.54	1.24	1.85	2.80	2.50	2.49	2.55	2.82
Woodford (OK)	0.01	0.02	0.97	1.97	2.75	2.90	2.61	2.70	3.18	2.64
Bakken (ND, MT)	0.01	0.02	0.11	0.89	1.33	2.19	2.10	2.09	2.10	2.47
Mississippian (OK)	0.69	0.77	0.65	1.28	2.19	2.76	2.17	2.16	2.38	1.93
Barnett (TX)	0.13	0.97	4.13	3.92	2.54	2.29	2.00	1.89	1.86	1.63
Fayetteville (AR)	—	—	1.81	2.64	1.41	1.18	1.09	0.99	0.94	0.78
Other U.S. shale locations	1.16	1.10	3.13	4.40	3.21	2.82	2.55	2.39	2.35	2.09
Total	**2.60**	**3.52**	**14.60**	**43.48**	**54.05**	**71.56**	**71.86**	**75.62**	**80.11**	**77.92**

— = Less than 0.01 billions of cubic ft per day. **Note:** Figures are monthly averages of production per day estimates as of Jan. 1 of year shown. Numbers may not add up to totals because of rounding.

U.S. Petroleum Trade, 1950-2023

Source: *Monthly Energy Review*, July 2024, Energy Information Administration (EIA), U.S. Dept. of Energy
(in thousands of barrels per day; average for the year)

Year	Imports from Persian Gulf[1]	Total imports	Total exports	Net imports[2]	Petroleum products supplied[3]
1950	NA	850	305	545	6,458
1955	NA	1,248	368	880	8,455
1960	326	1,815	202	1,613	9,797
1965	359	2,468	187	2,281	11,512
1970	184	3,419	259	3,161	14,697
1975	1,165	6,056	209	5,846	16,322
1980	1,519	6,909	544	6,365	17,056
1985	311	5,067	781	4,286	15,726
1990	1,966	8,018	857	7,161	16,988
1995	1,573	8,835	949	7,886	17,725
2000	2,488	11,459	1,040	10,419	19,701
2005	2,334	13,714	1,165	12,549	20,802
2010	1,711	11,793	2,353	9,441	19,178
2015	1,507	9,449	4,738	4,711	19,532
2016	1,766	10,055	5,261	4,795	19,692
2017	1,746	10,144	6,376	3,768	19,952
2018	1,578	9,943	7,601	2,341	20,512
2019	963	9,141	8,471	670	20,543
2020	766	7,863	8,498	–635	18,186
2021	691	8,474	8,536	–62	19,890
2022	981	8,329	9,520	–1,191	20,010
2023	861	8,514	10,150	–1,636	20,246

NA = Not available. **Note:** U.S. exports include shipments to U.S. territories; imports include receipts from U.S. territories. Numbers may not add up to totals because of rounding. (1) Bahrain, Iran, Iraq, Kuwait, Qatar, Saudi Arabia, United Arab Emirates, and the Neutral Zone between Kuwait and Saudi Arabia. (2) Total imports minus total exports. (3) Includes field production, refinery production, imports, and unaccounted-for crude oil minus change in stocks, crude oil losses, refinery inputs, and exports.

World Fossil Fuel Reserves

Source: International Energy Statistics Database, Energy Information Administration (EIA), U.S. Dept. of Energy

	Crude oil (bil barrels), 2021	Natural gas (tril cu ft), 2021	Coal (mil short tons), 2022
North America	**222.8[1]**	**543.0[1]**	**283,423**
Canada	170.3	73.0	7,255
Greenland	0.0	0.0	422
Mexico	5.8	6.4	1,335
United States	47.1[1]	465.4[1]	274,410
Central & South America	**331.1**	**268.5**	**17,035**
Argentina	2.5	14.0	882
Bolivia	0.2	10.7	1
Brazil	12.7	12.9	7,271
Chile	0.2	3.5	1,302
Colombia	2.0	3.1	5,020
Cuba	0.1	2.5	0
Ecuador	8.3	0.4	26
Peru	0.9	10.6	1,727
Trinidad & Tobago	0.2	10.5	0
Venezuela	303.8	200.4	806
Europe	**13.5**	**80.9**	**121,276**
Albania	0.2	0.2	575
Bosnia & Herz.	0.0	0.0	2,496
Bulgaria	0.0	0.2	2,608
Czechia	0.0	0.1	3,963
Germany	0.1	0.8	39,573
Greece	0.0	0.0	3,170
Hungary	0.0	0.1	3,207
Kosovo	0.0	0.0	1,724
Montenegro	0.0	0.0	371
Netherlands	0.1	4.7	3,579
North Macedonia	0.0	0.0	366
Norway	8.1	54.5	2
Poland	0.1	3.2	31,450
Romania	0.6	3.7	321
Serbia	0.1	1.7	8,283
Slovakia	0.0	0.5	21
Slovenia	0.0	0.0	105
Spain	0.2	0.1	1,308
Turkey (Türkiye)	0.4	0.1	12,704
United Kingdom	2.5	6.4	29
Eurasia	**118.9**	**2,338.0**	**284,521**
Armenia	0.0	0.0	349
Azerbaijan	7.0	60.0	0
Belarus	0.2	0.1	0
Georgia	0.0	0.3	993
Kazakhstan	30.0	85.0	28,225
Kyrgyzstan	0.0	0.2	31,415
Russia	80.0	1,688.2	178,757
Tajikistan	0.0	0.2	4,492
Turkmenistan	0.6	400.0	882
Ukraine	0.4	39.0	37,892
Uzbekistan	0.6	65.0	1,516
Middle East	**847.8**	**2,843.1**	**1,326**
Bahrain	0.2	2.9	0
Iran	208.6	1,200.3	1,326
Iraq	145.0	131.7	0
Israel	0.0	6.2	0
Kuwait	101.5	63.0	0
Oman	5.4	23.0	0
Qatar	25.2	842.6	0
Saudi Arabia	258.6	332.8	0
Syria	2.5	8.5	0
UAE	97.8	215.1	0
Yemen	3.0	16.9	0
Africa	**125.3**	**624.1[1]**	**29,403**
Algeria	12.2	159.1	246
Angola	7.8	12.1	0
Botswana	0.0	0.0	1,830
Congo, Dem. Rep. of	0.2	0.0	1,089
Congo Rep.	2.9	10.0	0
Egypt	3.3	63.0	201
Eswatini	0.0	0.0	5,119
Libya	48.4	53.1	0
Mozambique	0.0	100.0	1,975
Nigeria	36.9	203.4	2,363
South Africa	0.0	NA	10,905
Sudan	5.0	3.0	0
Tanzania	0.0	0.2	1,554
Zambia	0.0	0.0	1,042
Zimbabwe	0.0	0.0	553
Asia & Oceania	**46.7[1]**	**590.2**	**520,776**
Afghanistan	0.0	1.8	73
Australia	2.4	114.0	165,597
Bangladesh	0.0	4.5	3,594
Brunei	1.1	9.2	0
China	26.0	235.0	157,847
India	4.6	48.8	122,414
Indonesia	2.5	49.7	38,436
Japan	0.0	0.7	386
Korea, North	0.0	0.0	11,684
Korea, South	NA	0.3	359
Laos	0.0	0.0	68
Malaysia	3.6	42.0	249
Mongolia	NA	0.0	2,778
Myanmar	0.1	22.5	278
New Zealand	0.0	1.1	8,350
Pakistan	0.5	20.9	3,377
Philippines	0.1	3.5	398
Thailand	0.3	4.9	1,172
Vietnam	4.4	24.7	3,704
World	**1,661.9[1]**	**7,257.2[1]**	**1,257,760**

NA = Not available. **Note:** Regional and world totals may include countries not shown. Proved reserves only. Some countries omitted for lack of appreciable reserves. (1) As of 2020, the latest year available.

U.S. Crude Oil Imports by Selected Countries, 1975-2023

Source: Energy Information Administration (EIA), U.S. Dept. of Energy

The United States' dependence on foreign oil continued to decline as a consequence of increased U.S. production of crude oil, natural gas, and domestic biofuels like ethanol and biodiesel. Imports stood at just 6.5 mil barrels a day in 2023, down from more than 10.1 mil barrels per day in 2005. Since 2004, Canada has been the largest foreign supplier of U.S. oil. In 2023, it was responsible for about 60% of all U.S. oil imports, nearly four times as much as those from all OPEC countries combined.

(in thousands of barrels per day; ranked by 2023 imports)

Country	1975	1980	1985	1990	1995	2000	2005	2010	2015	2020	2023
Canada	600	199	468	643	1,040	1,348	1,633	1,970	3,169	3,596	3,874
Mexico	70	507	715	689	1,027	1,313	1,556	1,152	688	656	733
*Saudi Arabia	701	1,250	132	1,195	1,260	1,523	1,445	1,082	1,052	498	349
*Iraq	2	28	46	514	0	620	527	415	229	176	213
Colombia	0	0	0	140	207	318	156	338	373	248	202
Brazil	0	1	0	0	0	5	94	255	190	77	185
*Nigeria	746	841	280	784	621	875	1,077	983	54	67	153
*Venezuela	395	156	306	666	1,151	1,223	1,241	912	776	NA	133
Ecuador[1]	0	0	0	0	96	125	276	210	225	169	128
Guyana	NA	NA	NA	NA	NA	NA	NA	NA	NA	27	98
*Libya	223	548	0	0	0	0	44	43	3	9	80
Argentina	NA	NA	NA	NA	44	53	56	29	18	34	53
Ghana	NA	NA	NA	NA	NA	NA	NA	NA	NA	24	38
United Kingdom	0	173	278	155	341	291	224	120	11	28	38
Trinidad and Tobago	115	115	98	76	62	56	64	45	7	38	37
*Angola[2]	71	37	104	236	360	295	456	383	124	28	32
Kazakhstan	NA	NA	NA	NA	NA	NA	12	18	NA	17	32
*Kuwait	4	27	4	79	213	263	227	195	204	21	21
*Algeria	264	456	84	63	27	1	228	328	3	7	19
*United Arab Emirates	117	172	35	9	5	3	9	2	2	5	17
*Congo Republic[3]	NA	NA	NA	NA	20	42	25	70	9	5	8
Norway	12	144	31	96	258	302	119	25	9	14	6
*Iran	278	8	27	0	0	0	NA	NA	NA	NA	5
Qatar[4]	18	22	0	4	0	0	NA	NA	NA	NA	4
*Equatorial Guinea[5]	NA	NA	NA	NA	NA	6	68	50	5	NA	3
Australia	0	0	21	47	16	49	10	10	10	NA	3
Chad	NA	NA	NA	NA	NA	NA	74	18	72	NA	3
Cameroon	NA	NA	NA	NA	2	4	3	50	NA	19	2
Egypt	NA	NA	NA	NA	32	4	4	7	1	3	2
Non-OPEC countries	**NA**	**NA**	**NA**	**NA**	**3,660**	**4,526**	**5,310**	**4,661**	**4,690**	**5,060**	**5,445**
OPEC countries	**3,211**	**3,864**	**1,312**	**3,514**	**3,570**	**4,544**	**4,816**	**4,553**	**2,673**	**815**	**1,034**
Persian Gulf countries[6]	**1,121**	**1,508**	**244**	**1,801**	**1,479**	**2,409**	**2,207**	**1,694**	**1,487**	**700**	**609**
TOTAL	**4,105**	**5,263**	**3,201**	**5,894**	**7,230**	**9,071**	**10,126**	**9,213**	**7,363**	**5,875**	**6,478**

* = OPEC member, as of 2023. NA = Not available. **Note:** Subtotals and totals include countries not shown here. For years of OPEC membership, see footnotes on individual countries. (1) Suspended its OPEC membership in Dec. 1992, rejoined in Oct. 2007, and again withdrew in Jan. 2020. Imports in 1995-2005 and 2020-23 appear in non-OPEC totals, and imports in 2010-15 appear in OPEC totals. (2) Became a member of OPEC as of 2007 and is not included in OPEC totals from before that year. (3) Member of OPEC as of 2018; not included in OPEC totals before that year. (4) Withdrew from OPEC in Jan. 2019. Imports in 1975-2015 appear in OPEC totals, and imports in 2020-23 appear in non-OPEC totals. (5) Joined OPEC in May 2017 and is not included in OPEC totals from before that year. (6) Bahrain, Iran, Iraq, Kuwait, Qatar, Saudi Arabia, and United Arab Emirates.

U.S. Coal Production and Consumption, 1950-2023

Source: *Monthly Energy Review*, July 2024; *Annual Coal Report 2022*; Energy Information Administration (EIA); U.S. Dept. of Energy

(in thousand short tons)

	Coal production[1]			Coal consumption				
Year	Surface mining	Underground mining	Total production	Residential[2]	Commercial	Industrial	Electric power[3]	Total consumption
1950	139,388	421,000	560,388	51,562	63,021	224,637	91,871	494,102
1960	141,745	292,584	434,329	24,159	16,789	177,402	176,685	398,081
1970	272,131	340,530	612,661	9,024	7,090	186,637	320,182	523,231
1975	361,174	293,467	654,641	2,823	6,587	147,244	405,962	562,640
1980	492,192	337,508	829,700	1,355	5,097	127,004	569,274	702,730
1985	532,838	350,800	883,638	1,711	6,068	116,429	693,841	818,049
1990	604,529	424,546	1,029,076	1,345	5,379	115,207	782,567	904,498
1995	636,725	396,249	1,032,974	755	5,052	106,067	850,230	962,104
2000	699,953	373,659	1,073,612	454	3,673	94,147	985,821	1,084,095
2005	762,887	368,612	1,131,498	378	4,342	83,774	1,037,485	1,125,978
2010	747,214	337,155	1,084,368	NA	3,081	70,381	975,052	1,048,514
2015	590,119	306,821	896,941	NA	1,503	58,167	738,444	798,115
2020	339,905	195,530	535,434	NA	793	40,073	435,827	476,693
2021	356,834	220,597	577,431	NA	811	43,434	501,435	545,679
2022	372,012	222,143	594,155	NA	800	41,900	472,834	515,534
2023	NA	NA	577,485	NA	668	38,081	387,170	425,919

NA = Not available. (1) A small amount of refuse recovery has been included in coal production figures since 2001. (2) Beginning in 2008, residential coal consumption data no longer collected by the EIA. (3) Electricity-only and combined-heat-and-power (CHP) plants whose primary business is to sell electricity or electricity and heat to the public. Through 1988, data are for electric utilities only; beginning in 1989, data are for electric utilities and independent power producers.

World Nuclear Power Summary, 2023

Source: *Nuclear Power Reactors in the World*, International Atomic Energy Agency (IAEA); as of Dec. 31, 2023

	Reactors in operation		Reactors under construction[1]		Nuclear electricity supplied in 2023		Total operating experience[3]	
Country	**No. of units**	**Total MW(e)**	**No. of units**	**Total MW(e)**	**TW·h[2]**	**% of nation's total**	**Years**	**Months**
Argentina	3	1,641	1	25	9.0	6.3%	100	2
Armenia	1	416	0	—	2.5	31.1	49	8
Belarus	2	2,220	0	—	11.0	28.6	3	10
Belgium	5	3,908	0	—	31.3	41.2	329	5
Brazil	2	1,884	1	1,340	13.7	2.2	65	3
Bulgaria	2	2,006	0	—	15.5	40.5	175	3
Canada	19	13,699	0	—	83.5	13.7	845	6
China	55	53,152	24	24,948	406.5	4.9	568	2
Czechia	6	3,934	0	—	28.7	40.0	194	10
Finland	5	4,394	0	—	32.8	42.0	181	2
France	56	61,370	1	1,630	323.8	64.8	2,505	0
Hungary	4	1,916	0	—	15.1	48.8	154	2
India	19	6,290	8	6,028	44.6	3.1	585	6
Iran	1	915	1	974	6.1	1.7	12	4
Japan	12	11,046	2	2,653	77.5	5.5	1,734	6
Korea, South	26	25,825	2	2,680	171.6	31.5	669	10
Mexico	2	1,552	0	—	12.0	4.9	63	11
Netherlands	1	482	0	—	3.8	3.4	79	0
Pakistan	6	3,262	0	—	22.4	17.4	104	9
Romania	2	1,300	0	—	10.3	18.9	43	11
Russia	37	27,727	3	2,700	204.0	18.4	1,484	7
Slovakia	5	2,308	1	440	17.0	61.3	189	7
Slovenia	1	688	0	—	5.3	36.8	42	3
South Africa	2	1,854	0	—	8.2	4.4	78	3
Spain	7	7,123	0	—	54.4	20.3	371	1
Sweden	6	6,944	0	—	46.6	28.6	492	0
Switzerland	4	2,973	0	—	23.4	32.4	240	11
Taiwan	2	1,874	NA	NA	17.2	6.9	241	11
Ukraine	15	13,107	2	2,070	NA	NA	578	6
United Arab Emirates	3	4,011	1	1,310	31.2	19.7	7	0
United Kingdom	9	5,883	2	3,260	37.3	12.5	1,667	9
United States	93	95,835	1	1,117	779.2	18.5	4,879	7
TOTAL	**413**	**371,539**	**59**	**61,091**	**2,545.5**	—	**19,751**	**7**

— = Not applicable. NA = Not available. MW(e) = Megawatt electricity. (1) Bangladesh, Egypt, and Turkey (Türkiye) have reactors under construction, which are included in totals but not listed separately. (2) 1 terawatt-hour (TW·h) = 10^6 megawatt-hour (MW·h). For an average power plant, 1 TW·h = 0.39 megaton of coal equivalent (input) and 0.23 megaton of oil equivalent (input). (3) Total includes shutdown plants for countries not listed here: Germany (862 years), Italy (80 years, 8 months), Kazakhstan (25 years, 10 months), and Lithuania (43 years, 6 months).

Nuclear Reliance by Nation, 2023

Source: *Nuclear Power Reactors in the World*, International Atomic Energy Agency (IAEA)
(nuclear electricity generation as % of total electricity generated within country; as of Dec. 31, 2023)

Rank	Country	Nuclear share	Rank	Country	Nuclear share	Rank	Country	Nuclear share	Rank	Country	Nuclear share
1.	France	64.8%	9.	Switzerland	32.4%	17.	United States	18.6%	25.	Mexico	4.9%
2.	Slovakia	61.3	10.	South Korea	31.5	18.	Russia	18.4	26.	China	4.9
3.	Hungary	48.8	11.	Armenia	31.1	19.	Pakistan	17.4	27.	South Africa	4.4
4.	Finland	42.0	12.	Belarus	28.6	20.	Canada	13.7	28.	Netherlands	3.4
5.	Belgium	41.2	13.	Sweden	28.6	21.	United Kingdom	12.5	29.	India	3.1
6.	Bulgaria	40.4	14.	Spain	20.3	22.	Taiwan	6.9	30.	Brazil	2.2
7.	Czechia	40.0	15.	UAE	19.7	23.	Argentina	6.3	31.	Iran	1.7
8.	Slovenia	36.8	16.	Romania	18.9	24.	Japan	5.6	32.	Germany	1.4

U.S. Nuclear Generation, 1957-2023

Source: *Monthly Energy Review*, July 2024, Energy Information Administration (EIA), U.S. Dept. of Energy

Years	Total operable units[1]	Net summer capacity (mil kW)[2]	Nuclear electricity net generation (mil kWh)	Nuclear share of electricity net generation	Capacity factor[3]
1957	1	0.055	10	—	NA
1958	1	0.055	165	—	NA
1959	2	0.055	188	—	NA
1960	3	0.411	518	0.1%	NA
1965	13	0.793	3,657	0.3	NA
1970	20	7.004	21,804	1.4	NA
1975	57	37.267	172,505	9.0	55.9%
1980	71	51.810	251,116	11.0	56.3
1985	96	79.397	383,691	15.5	58.0
1990	112	99.624	576,862	19.0	66.0
1995	109	99.515	673,402	20.1	77.4
2000	104	97.860	753,893	19.8	88.1
2005	104	99.988	781,986	19.3	89.3
2007	104	100.266	806,425	19.4	91.8
2008	104	100.755	806,208	19.6	91.1
2009	104	101.004	798,855	20.2%	90.3%
2010	104	101.167	806,968	19.6	91.1
2011	104	101.419	790,204	19.3	89.1
2012	104	101.885	769,331	19.0	86.1
2013	100	99.240	789,016	19.4	90.8
2014	99	98.569	797,166	19.5	91.7
2015	99	98.672	797,178	19.5	92.3
2016	99	99.565	805,694	19.8	92.3
2017	99	99.629	804,950	19.9	92.3
2018	98	99.433	807,084	19.3	92.5
2019	96	98.119	809,409	19.6	93.5
2020	94	96.501	789,879	19.7	92.5
2021	93	95.546	779,645	19.0	92.8
2022	92	94.659	771,537	18.2	92.7
2023	93	95.746[E]	775,347	18.6	93.1[E]

NA = Not available. — = Less than 0.05%. E = Estimate. (1) Total of nuclear generating units holding full-power licenses, or equivalent permission to operate. (2) The maximum output that generating equipment can supply to system load, as demonstrated by a multi-hour test, at the time of summer peak demand (June 1 through Sept. 30). (3) Beginning in 2008, capacity factor data calculated using a new methodology.

U.S. Nuclear Reactors Generating the Most Electricity, 2023

Source: Energy Information Administration (EIA), U.S. Dept. of Energy
(in megawatt hours)

Rank	Reactor, location	Electricity generated	Capacity[1]
1.	Grand Gulf-1, Port Gibson, MS	11,749,621	97.0%
2.	Peach Bottom-2, Delta, PA	11,469,213	103.5
3.	Palo Verde-3, Wintersburg, AZ	11,448,890	99.6
4.	South Texas-2, Bay City, TX	11,434,161	102.0
5.	Nine Mile Point-2, Scriba, NY	10,838,275	97.3
6.	Browns Ferry-1, Athens, AL	10,750,377	100.0
7.	Peach Bottom-3, Delta, PA	10,694,880	95.0
8.	Braidwood-1, Braceville, IL	10,562,931	101.9
9.	Donald C. Cook-2, Bridgman, MI	10,361,300	101.3
10.	South Texas-1, Bay City, TX	10,352,983	90.9
11.	Wolf Creek-1, Burlington, KS	10,301,865	96.0
12.	Browns Ferry-3, Athens, AL	10,256,994	95.5
13.	Catawba-2, York, SC	10,177,428	101.0
14.	Sequoyah-1, Soddy-Daisy, TN	10,112,904	100.2
15.	Palo Verde-1, Wintersburg, AZ	10,103,346	88.0%
16.	LaSalle-1, Marseilles, IL	10,095,999	101.9
17.	Palo Verde-2, Wintersburg, AZ	9,970,354	86.6
18.	Limerick-1, Limerick, PA	9,955,706	101.5
19.	Hope Creek-1, Hancocks Bridge, NJ	9,938,423	96.8
20.	Byron-1, Byron, IL	9,835,728	96.5
21.	Browns Ferry-2, Athens, AL	9,813,139	92.8
22.	Susquehanna-1, Salem Township, PA	9,791,524	89.6
23.	Byron-2, Byron, IL	9,629,860	96.8
24.	Braidwood-2, Braceville, IL	9,550,665	94.5
25.	Comanche Peak-1, Glen Rose, TX	9,543,807	90.4

Note: Data is preliminary. (1) The ratio of power generated to the maximum potential generation expressed as a percentage.

Renewable Energy Sources

Source: U.S. Dept. of Energy

Concern over the environmental impact of burning fossil fuels has helped spur interest in alternative fuels that are less polluting. And because the supply of fossil fuels is finite and diminishing, there is interest in "renewable" sources that do not deplete existing supplies. However, renewable energy sources still make up only a small share of U.S. domestic energy production (about 8.2% in 2023). The main reason for this is their relatively higher cost (in some cases two to four times that of power obtained from traditional fuels). The following are the major renewable energy sources available.

Biomass is plant- and animal-derived material usable as an energy source. It includes wood and wood processing waste; agricultural crops and waste materials; food, yard, and wood waste in garbage; and animal manure and human sewage. As of July 2024, biomass was the most common renewable energy source in the U.S. Biomass such as wood can be burned to produce heat and generate electricity. Agricultural crops can be burned as a fuel or converted to liquid biofuels such as ethanol and biodiesel; these are usually blended with petroleum fuels but can also be used on their own. Second-generation biofuels are made from nonfood crops. While biomass fuels provide some benefits to the environment, such as reduced waste in landfills, they still produce carbon dioxide and other pollutants.

Geothermal energy is generated from heat inside the Earth. This form of energy is both clean and renewable. The technology has caught on in countries with substantial geothermal activity such as Iceland, where it accounts for approximately two-thirds of primary energy use. In the U.S., the best sources for geothermal power are in the West, Alaska, and in Hawaii, where geothermal energy resources are close to the Earth's surface. Drilling wells and testing the temperature deep underground is the most reliable method for locating geothermal reservoirs, which are largely undetectable above ground.

Hydrogen is the most abundant element in the universe. It does not naturally occur on Earth as a pure gas or liquid but is always combined with other elements (such as oxygen, to form water). If hydrogen is to be used for energy, it must be separated from these other elements. The two most common methods for producing hydrogen are steam-methane reforming and electrolysis (water splitting).

NASA began using liquid hydrogen in the 1950s as a rocket fuel and used hydrogen fuel cells to power electrical systems on spacecraft. Fuel cells produce electricity by combining hydrogen and oxygen atoms. Hydrogen use in vehicles is a major focus of fuel cell research and development, and several vehicle manufacturers have begun making light-duty hydrogen fuel cell electric vehicles available in regions where hydrogen fueling stations have been built.

Hydropower, or hydroelectric power, is generated by water flowing through turbines. Along with biomass fuels, wind power, and solar energy, it is one of the most common renewable energy sources in the U.S. today by amount of energy produced. A dam on a river is a common hydropower producer. No harmful air pollutants are produced, but the dams needed to generate power can harm river ecosystems. Researchers are working on technologies to maximize use of hydropower and reduce adverse environmental effects.

Ocean energy can be generated in two ways. Ocean thermal energy conversion uses heat that the ocean absorbs from the sun to power generators, sometimes producing drinkable desalinated water as a byproduct. Mechanical ocean energy is generated by the movement of tides and waves through turbines. In both cases, power generation is not very efficient with current technology. New methods of capturing this energy are under development. Mechanical ocean energy requires the building of large dams or breakwater-type structures called tidal barrages, which could harm coastal ecosystems.

Solar energy is generated using light from the sun. Solar energy is increasingly used to generate electricity. Photovoltaic (PV) cells, also called solar cells, are made of semiconducting materials that can directly convert sunlight to electricity without producing any harmful waste. Arrays of mirrors can concentrate the sun's rays onto PV panels, making solar collectors more efficient. Solar thermal systems can use sunlight to heat water. According to the Dept. of Energy, homes incorporating solar heating designs can save 50%-80% on water heating bills. Solar energy is limited by its dependence on a range of factors, including location, time of day, time of year, and weather conditions.

Wind energy uses wind turbines to produce energy. It is one of the most common renewable energy sources in the U.S. today. Wind turbines typically are perched on towers 100 ft tall or higher; they are often placed in large groups ("farms"), which are sometimes located offshore. Farmers and homeowners sometimes use stand-alone turbines to generate supplemental electricity. Tax credits for wind energy producers and government incentives for homeowners have lowered the price of wind power. But some object to wind farms because of their appearance or the noise the turbines make. Wind power raises few other environmental problems, but the turbines can pose a danger to birds. In addition, because weather is involved, consistent energy generation can be a challenge.

CRIME

Crime in the U.S., 2003-22

Source: *Crime in the United States, 2022*, Uniform Crime Reporting (UCR) Program, Federal Bureau of Investigation (FBI), Dept. of Justice

Reported offenses are classified as **violent crimes** if they involve force or the threat of force: murder and nonnegligent manslaughter, rape, robbery, and aggravated assault. The following offenses are considered **property crimes**: burglary, larceny-theft, motor vehicle theft, and arson (excluded from this table because of insufficient data to make estimates).

	Violent crime					Property crime			
Year(s)	**All violent crime**	**Murder and nonnegligent manslaughter**	**Rape[1]**	**Robbery**	**Aggravated assault[2]**	**All property crime**	**Burglary**	**Larceny-theft[3]**	**Motor vehicle theft**
NUMBER OF OFFENSES									
2003	1,459,416	17,716	92,024	451,480	898,196	10,755,844	2,221,300	7,217,863	1,316,681
2005	1,460,666	17,750	92,002	453,165	897,749	10,413,836	2,209,340	6,916,776	1,287,720
2007	1,437,800	17,374	87,624	455,900	876,902	9,968,661	2,213,816	6,644,814	1,110,031
2009	1,333,418	15,511	86,290	414,441	817,176	9,405,612	2,223,277	6,379,794	802,541
2011	1,213,343	14,754	84,630	356,845	757,114	9,073,857	2,196,509	6,153,892	723,456
2013	1,170,770	14,322	80,775	346,749	728,924	8,674,132	1,935,614	6,034,252	704,266
2015	1,197,119	15,894	88,949	326,567	765,709	7,974,900	1,579,920	5,684,715	710,265
2017	1,230,368	18,206	95,945	311,447	804,770	7,692,710	1,397,148	5,526,199	769,363
2018	1,221,594	16,937	103,852	282,180	818,625	7,398,241	1,267,920	5,363,735	766,586
2019	1,194,626	16,952	101,823	263,474	812,377	6,999,989	1,112,338	5,162,288	725,363
2020	1,269,217	22,414	92,721	240,837	913,245	6,470,751	1,026,234	4,628,945	815,572
2021	1,253,716	22,536	109,733	217,550	903,897	6,083,874	899,369	4,334,764	849,741
2022	1,232,428	21,156	96,842	220,450	893,980	6,513,829	899,293	4,672,363	942,173
PERCENT CHANGE: NUMBER OF OFFENSES									
2021-22	−1.7%	−6.1%	−11.7%	1.3%	−1.1%	7.1%	0.0%	7.8%	10.9%
2018-22	0.9	24.9	−6.7	−21.9	9.2	−12.0	−29.1	−12.9	22.9
2013-22	5.3	47.7	19.9	−36.4	22.6	−24.9	−53.5	−22.6	33.8
CRIME RATE PER 100,000 INHABITANTS									
2003	501.8	6.1	31.6	155.2	308.9	3,698.6	763.8	2,482.0	452.8
2005	492.8	6.0	31.0	152.9	302.9	3,513.3	745.4	2,333.5	434.4
2007	476.7	5.8	29.1	151.1	290.7	3,305.0	734.0	2,203.0	368.0
2009	434.3	5.1	28.1	135.0	266.2	3,063.7	724.2	2,078.1	261.4
2011	389.4	4.7	27.2	114.5	243.0	2,912.1	704.9	1,975.0	232.2
2013	370.3	4.5	25.6	109.7	230.6	2,743.9	612.3	1,908.8	222.8
2015	372.4	4.9	27.7	101.6	238.2	2,481.2	491.5	1,768.6	221.0
2017	377.7	5.6	29.5	95.6	247.1	2,361.8	428.9	1,696.6	236.2
2018	373.4	5.2	31.7	86.2	250.2	2,261.3	387.5	1,639.4	234.3
2019	363.9	5.2	31.0	80.3	247.5	2,132.6	338.9	1,572.7	221.0
2020	385.2	6.8	28.1	73.1	277.2	1,963.9	311.5	1,404.9	247.5
2021	377.6	6.8	33.0	65.5	272.2	1,832.3	270.9	1,305.5	255.9
2022	369.8	6.3	29.1	66.1	268.2	1,954.4	269.8	1,401.9	282.7
PERCENT CHANGE: CRIME RATE PER 100,000 INHABITANTS									
2021-22	−2.1%	−6.5%	−12.1%	1.0%	−1.5%	6.7%	−0.4%	7.4%	10.5%
2018-22	−1.0	22.6	−8.5	−23.3	7.2	−13.6	−30.4	−14.5	20.6
2013-22	−0.2	40.1	13.7	−39.7	16.3	−28.8	−55.9	−26.6	26.9

(1) In 2013, the FBI began collecting rape data under a revised definition; the reporting of rape data using the legacy definition was discontinued beginning in 2017. For comparison purposes, this table presents data under the legacy definition of rape ("carnal knowledge of a female forcibly and against her will"), which does not include statutory rape, other types of sexual offenses, or attacks with male victims. (2) Attack or attempted attack upon another with the intent of doing serious bodily harm; usually accompanied by the use of a weapon or other means likely to produce death or great bodily harm. (3) The unlawful taking of another's property not involving force or fraud (e.g., theft of motor vehicle parts, shoplifting). Excludes crimes such as embezzlement and check fraud.

Violent Crime Rates in the U.S., 1985-2022

Source: *Crime in the United States, 2022*, Uniform Crime Reporting (UCR) Program, Federal Bureau of Investigation (FBI), Dept. of Justice

After rising throughout the 1970s and 1980s, the violent crime rate dropped sharply, from a historic high of 758.2 reported offenses per 100,000 population in 1991 to nearly half that in 2022 (380.7; or 369.8 under the legacy definition of rape). The rates of aggravated assault and robbery decreased even more precipitously over that same time period. The UCR Program began collecting rape data under a revised definition in 2013; the reporting of rape data using the legacy definition was discontinued beginning in 2017.

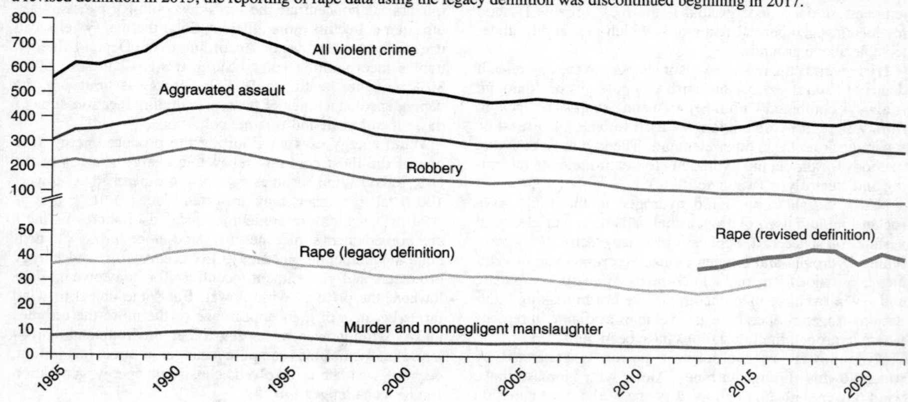

U.S. Crime Rates by Region and State, 2022

Source: *Crime in the United States, 2022*, Uniform Crime Reporting (UCR) Program, Federal Bureau of Investigation (FBI), Dept. of Justice (per 100,000 inhabitants, based on U.S. Census Bureau estimates as of July 1)

	Violent crime					Property crime[1]			
Area	All violent crime	Murder and nonnegligent manslaughter	Rape[2]	Robbery	Aggravated assault[3]	All property crime	Burglary	Larceny-theft[4]	Motor vehicle theft
Total U.S.	**380.7**	**6.3**	**40.0**	**66.1**	**268.2**	**1,954.4**	**269.8**	**1,401.9**	**282.7**
Northeast	**305.0**	**4.3**	**27.2**	**70.6**	**202.9**	**1,484.8**	**148.3**	**1,194.1**	**142.4**
New England	**227.6**	**2.5**	**28.7**	**32.9**	**163.5**	**1,220.6**	**130.2**	**969.3**	**121.1**
Connecticut	150.0	3.8	18.1	44.9	83.3	1,494.0	130.1	1,168.1	195.8
Maine	103.3	2.2	32.0	10.0	59.0	1,213.5	115.9	1,026.8	70.9
Massachusetts	322.0	2.1	29.1	37.7	253.1	1,070.1	142.8	827.6	99.7
New Hampshire	125.6	1.8	39.6	16.1	68.1	1,010.9	73.5	871.0	66.5
Rhode Island	172.3	1.5	38.0	24.6	108.3	1,285.3	128.1	997.6	159.6
Vermont	221.9	3.4	36.8	13.3	168.5	1,671.1	152.1	1,425.5	93.5
Middle Atlantic	**333.0**	**5.0**	**26.7**	**84.2**	**217.2**	**1,580.2**	**154.9**	**1,275.2**	**150.1**
New Jersey	202.9	3.1	16.8	47.6	135.4	1,416.7	148.0	1,109.1	159.6
New York	429.3	4.0	29.5	112.0	283.8	1,721.6	162.5	1,422.0	137.1
Pennsylvania[5]	279.9	7.9	29.5	68.1	174.5	1,482.5	148.2	1,171.2	163.0
Midwest	**340.3**	**6.2**	**47.8**	**50.9**	**235.4**	**1,728.9**	**227.6**	**1,231.2**	**270.1**
East North Central	**329.8**	**6.7**	**48.3**	**54.8**	**220.0**	**1,619.2**	**217.1**	**1,151.2**	**250.9**
Illinois[5]	287.3	7.8	48.1	84.7	146.7	1,682.7	208.5	1,192.7	281.6
Indiana	306.2	6.2	32.8	43.0	224.2	1,544.2	226.1	1,118.6	199.4
Michigan	461.0	6.9	64.8	36.6	352.7	1,536.8	214.3	1,055.3	267.2
Ohio	293.6	6.1	48.4	53.1	185.9	1,782.7	255.3	1,292.9	234.5
Wisconsin	297.0	5.3	38.6	39.4	213.7	1,385.0	153.7	981.0	250.3
West North Central	**362.9**	**5.2**	**46.5**	**42.5**	**268.8**	**1,967.1**	**250.4**	**1,404.9**	**311.8**
Iowa	286.5	1.7	42.5	21.6	220.7	1,331.5	218.6	965.4	147.4
Kansas	414.6	4.6	45.5	29.2	335.4	1,992.2	273.4	1,488.7	230.2
Minnesota	280.6	3.2	40.7	57.0	179.7	1,966.8	214.2	1,464.8	287.9
Missouri	488.0	10.1	48.9	54.8	374.2	2,340.1	295.8	1,557.2	487.1
Nebraska	282.8	3.2	55.3	29.1	195.2	1,888.8	182.5	1,431.4	275.0
North Dakota	279.6	3.5	56.7	27.6	191.8	1,994.8	357.9	1,381.3	255.6
South Dakota	377.4	4.3	55.8	25.3	292.0	1,737.0	263.0	1,231.8	242.2
South	**390.5**	**7.8**	**38.9**	**54.3**	**289.6**	**1,974.9**	**283.7**	**1,452.8**	**238.5**
South Atlantic	**335.2**	**7.3**	**32.3**	**50.1**	**245.5**	**1,763.5**	**222.4**	**1,359.6**	**181.5**
Delaware	383.5	4.8	22.0	57.0	299.8	1,964.1	203.1	1,591.1	169.9
District of Columbia[6]	812.3	29.3	41.5	357.5	383.9	3,561.5	201.2	2,783.0	577.3
Florida[5]	258.9	5.0	30.2	33.6	190.1	1,566.2	173.5	1,254.7	138.0
Georgia	367.0	8.2	36.4	43.6	278.8	1,690.8	217.8	1,266.5	206.5
Maryland[5]	398.5	8.5	30.6	114.2	245.2	1,635.4	190.2	1,225.4	219.8
North Carolina	405.1	8.1	30.5	54.9	311.6	2,064.1	370.8	1,494.0	199.3
South Carolina	491.3	11.2	38.2	40.6	401.3	2,308.2	352.7	1,706.3	249.2
Virginia	234.0	7.3	30.2	38.4	158.1	1,695.7	124.6	1,410.4	160.7
West Virginia	277.9	4.6	44.4	10.0	218.9	1,230.1	190.2	951.2	88.7
East South Central	**416.1**	**8.7**	**34.3**	**45.7**	**327.4**	**1,876.2**	**297.5**	**1,320.2**	**258.4**
Alabama	409.1	10.9	29.6	34.5	334.1	1,739.0	283.9	1,252.7	202.3
Kentucky	214.1	6.8	33.8	38.1	135.4	1,448.8	244.8	989.8	214.2
Mississippi	245.0	7.8	33.7	25.6	178.0	1,746.8	350.2	1,222.6	173.9
Tennessee	621.6	8.6	38.2	67.1	507.6	2,302.3	319.1	1,620.9	362.3
West South Central	**468.0**	**8.0**	**51.8**	**65.0**	**343.1**	**2,363.5**	**376.3**	**1,665.9**	**321.3**
Arkansas	645.3	10.2	76.0	39.7	519.4	2,451.5	466.4	1,734.4	250.7
Louisiana	628.6	16.1	43.0	67.3	502.1	2,748.2	497.8	1,940.0	310.3
Oklahoma	419.7	6.7	57.5	40.6	314.8	2,332.4	482.6	1,535.7	314.0
Texas	431.9	6.7	50.0	70.5	304.7	2,299.9	334.3	1,634.4	331.2
West	**454.9**	**5.6**	**44.2**	**95.6**	**309.4**	**2,458.0**	**372.1**	**1,618.4**	**467.6**
Mountain	**431.7**	**6.0**	**54.5**	**62.5**	**308.8**	**2,300.8**	**325.3**	**1,571.2**	**404.3**
Arizona	431.5	6.8	44.1	70.1	310.5	2,057.6	271.0	1,542.4	244.2
Colorado	492.5	6.4	63.4	72.6	350.1	3,147.6	395.2	1,966.7	785.7
Idaho	241.4	2.7	48.7	8.2	181.7	926.9	158.6	677.1	91.2
Montana	417.9	4.5	54.4	23.3	335.7	1,918.6	200.3	1,495.7	222.6
Nevada	454.0	6.8	58.9	86.1	302.3	2,380.1	436.1	1,453.5	490.5
New Mexico	780.5	12.0	54.6	110.6	603.3	2,984.0	604.0	1,838.4	541.7
Utah	241.8	2.0	59.5	29.6	150.7	1,895.1	201.7	1,485.1	208.4
Wyoming	201.9	2.6	62.8	7.9	128.7	1,636.8	209.5	1,264.9	162.4
Pacific	**465.9**	**5.5**	**39.3**	**111.5**	**309.6**	**2,533.4**	**394.5**	**1,641.0**	**497.9**
Alaska	758.9	9.5	134.0	75.1	540.2	1,789.0	269.0	1,274.6	245.5
California	499.5	5.7	37.4	123.5	332.8	2,343.2	371.9	1,499.3	471.9
Hawaii	259.6	2.1	37.9	66.1	153.5	2,434.7	260.0	1,767.7	407.0
Oregon	342.4	4.5	40.6	68.6	228.7	2,935.3	360.7	2,023.0	551.5
Washington	375.6	5.0	39.2	86.8	244.7	3,356.4	563.0	2,154.0	639.3

Note: Offense totals are based on all law enforcement agencies in the UCR Program and include estimates for agencies that submitted less than 12 months of data. Only the most serious offense in a multiple-offense incident is used in calculating crime rates. (1) Excl. arson because of insufficient data to make estimates. (2) Unless otherwise noted, figures estimated using FBI definition of rape (revised 2013): "penetration, no matter how slight, of the vagina or anus with any body part or object, or oral penetration by a sex organ of another person, without the consent of the victim." (3) Attack or attempted attack upon another with the intent of doing serious bodily harm; usually accompanied by the use of a weapon or other means likely to produce death or great bodily harm. (4) The unlawful taking of another's property not involving force or fraud (e.g., theft of motor vehicle parts, shoplifting). Excl. crimes such as embezzlement and check fraud. (5) Limited data available for state. (6) Incl. offenses reported by Metro Transit Police and DC Fire and Emergency Medical Services Arson Investigation Unit.

Crime Rates in the Largest U.S. Metropolitan Areas, 2022

Source: *Crime in the United States, 2022*, Uniform Crime Reporting Program (UCR), Federal Bureau of Investigation (FBI), Dept. of Justice

Data are for Metropolitan Statistical Areas (MSAs) with sufficient law enforcement agency participation and 12 months of data from the principal city/cities.

(per 100,000 inhabitants based on U.S. Census Bureau estimates as of July 1)

Metropolitan Statistical Area (MSA)	MSA pop. (mil)	Violent crime: All violent crime	Murder[1]	Rape[2]	Robbery	Aggravated assault	All property crime[3]
Atlanta-Sandy Springs-Alpharetta, GA	6.2	375.8	8.8	36.4	50.0	280.6	1,721.7
Austin-Round Rock-Georgetown, TX	2.4	349.6	4.7	49.6	51.1	244.3	2,253.2
Baltimore-Columbia-Towson, MD[4]	2.8	539.3	12.5	33.4	156.2	337.3	1,833.7
Boston-Cambridge-Newton, MA-NH	4.9	272.4	1.8	25.8	34.0	210.8	1,029.2
Charlotte-Concord-Gastonia, NC-SC	2.7	434.4	7.5	25.5	68.7	332.7	2,243.3
Cincinnati, OH-KY-IN	2.3	218.2	4.8	34.0	43.0	136.4	1,601.1
Cleveland-Elyria, OH	2.1	401.0	9.3	38.3	93.2	260.3	1,624.4
Columbus, OH	2.2	279.0	7.0	68.5	72.3	131.3	2,337.9
Dallas-Fort Worth-Arlington, TX	7.9	349.2	5.2	41.9	58.6	243.4	2,186.5
Denver-Aurora-Lakewood, CO	3.0	602.2	7.0	65.8	104.4	424.9	3,964.1
Detroit-Warren-Dearborn, MI	4.3	529.0	10.0	46.0	51.7	421.3	1,667.9
Houston-The Woodlands-Sugar Land, TX	7.3	585.2	9.5	48.0	132.5	395.3	2,825.6
Indianapolis-Carmel-Anderson, IN	2.1	500.8	11.0	39.9	87.4	362.4	2,019.0
Jacksonville, FL[4]	1.7	420.2	8.3	31.3	43.2	337.4	1,757.6
Las Vegas-Henderson-Paradise, NV	2.3	470.5	7.6	55.2	96.4	311.3	2,628.8
Memphis, TN-MS-AR	1.3	1,342.6	23.9	48.3	190.6	1,079.8	4,338.2
Milwaukee-Waukesha, WI	1.6	619.5	14.6	38.3	116.9	449.7	2,134.1
Minneapolis-St. Paul-Bloomington, MN-WI	3.7	332.9	4.2	40.5	82.7	205.5	2,328.2
Nashville-Davidson—Murfreesboro—Franklin, TN	2.0	556.4	6.0	38.2	70.3	441.8	2,040.0
New York-Newark-Jersey City, NY-NJ-PA[4]	11.3	152.0	2.1	11.6	38.1	100.3	1,182.0
Oklahoma City, OK	1.5	429.7	5.6	58.2	53.1	312.9	2,475.0
Philadelphia-Camden-Wilmington, PA-NJ-DE-MD[4]	6.2	418.9	11.2	26.4	125.9	255.5	2,243.7
Portland-Vancouver-Hillsboro, OR-WA	2.5	396.9	6.1	45.0	91.7	254.2	3,411.8
Providence-Warwick, RI-MA	1.7	257.3	1.4	35.0	32.7	188.2	1,198.6
Raleigh-Cary, NC	1.5	251.8	3.8	21.4	42.8	183.7	1,573.9
Richmond, VA	1.3	252.5	11.5	20.9	42.6	177.5	1,954.5
Riverside-San Bernardino-Ontario, CA	4.7	442.2	6.3	29.3	89.3	317.2	2,119.9
Sacramento-Roseville-Folsom, CA	2.4	439.9	5.3	31.7	102.1	300.9	2,067.3
St. Louis, MO-IL[4]	2.8	404.4	11.6	34.0	53.4	305.3	2,165.7
San Antonio-New Braunfels, TX	2.7	584.4	9.8	70.7	73.9	430.0	3,495.8
San Diego-Chula Vista-Carlsbad, CA	3.3	392.8	3.3	23.7	84.2	281.6	1,668.6
San Jose-Sunnyvale-Santa Clara, CA	1.9	399.5	2.3	64.4	96.4	236.4	2,532.2
Seattle-Tacoma-Bellevue, WA	4.0	457.6	5.4	34.9	119.8	297.5	3,857.4
Virginia Beach-Norfolk-Newport News, VA-NC	1.8	357.2	12.9	27.8	63.2	253.3	2,341.8
Washington-Arlington-Alexandria, DC-VA-MD-WV[4]	5.7	204.7	3.5	23.7	59.5	117.9	1,389.6

(1) Data in category includes nonnegligent manslaughter. (2) Based on aggregate totals of data submitted using both the legacy and revised definitions of rape. (3) Includes burglary, larceny-theft, and motor vehicle theft but not arson because of insufficient data to make estimates. (4) Limited data were available for Florida, Illinois, Maryland, and Pennsylvania.

Criminal Victimization, 2018-22

Source: National Crime Victimization Survey, Bureau of Justice Statistics (BJS), U.S. Dept. of Justice

A crime committed against an individual or single household—whether threatened, attempted, or completed—counts as one **victimization**. Because more than one person may be victimized during a criminal incident, the number of victimizations may be greater than the number of personal crime incidents. **Victimization rates** measure the frequency with which victimizations occurred per 1,000 persons age 12 or older or per 1,000 households.

Crime type	Number (in thousands) 2018	2019	2020	2021	2022	Rate 2018	2019	2020	2021	2022
Violent crime[1]	**6,385.5**	**5,813.4**	**4,558.2**	**4,598.3**	**6,625.0**	**23.2**	**21.0**	**16.4**	**16.5**	**23.5**
Rape/sexual assault	734.6	459.3	320.0	324.5	531.8	2.7	1.7	1.2	1.2	1.9
Robbery	573.1	534.4	437.3	464.3	694.9	2.1	1.9	1.6	1.7	2.5
Assault	5,077.8	4,819.7	3,801.0	3,809.5	5,398.3	18.4	17.4	13.7	13.6	19.1
Aggravated assault	1,058.0	1,019.5	812.2	766.3	1,540.1	3.8	3.7	2.9	2.7	5.5
Simple assault	4,019.8	3,800.2	2,988.8	3,043.2	3,858.2	14.6	13.7	10.7	10.9	13.7
Violent crime excl. simple assault[2]	2,365.8	2,013.2	1,569.4	1,555.1	2,766.8	8.6	7.3	5.6	5.6	9.8
Selected characteristics of violent crime										
Domestic violence[3]	1,333.1	1,164.5	856.8	910.9	1,370.4	4.8	4.2	3.1	3.3	4.9
Intimate partner violence[4]	847.2	695.1	484.8	473.7	951.9	3.1	2.5	1.7	1.7	3.4
Stranger violence	2,493.8	2,254.7	1,973.2	2,056.2	2,994.3	9.1	8.1	7.1	7.4	10.6
Violent crime with an injury	1,449.5	1,265.7	1,160.9	975.3	1,412.3	5.3	4.6	4.2	3.5	5.0
Violent crime with a weapon	1,329.7	1,119.1	938.7	895.6	1,798.2	4.8	4.0	3.4	3.2	6.4
Property crime	**13,502.8**	**12,818.0**	**12,085.2**	**11,682.1**	**13,373.3**	**108.2**	**101.4**	**94.5**	**90.3**	**101.9**
Burglary/trespassing[5]	2,639.6	2,178.4	1,741.3	1,800.4	1,919.9	21.1	17.2	13.6	13.9	14.6
Burglary[6]	1,867.6	1,484.7	1,210.6	1,142.9	1,324.0	15.0	11.7	9.5	8.8	10.1
Trespassing[7]	772.0	693.7	530.6	657.4	595.9	6.2	5.5	4.1	5.1	4.5
Motor vehicle theft	534.0	495.7	545.8	558.7	716.7	4.3	3.9	4.3	4.3	5.5
Other theft[8]	10,329.2	10,143.9	9,798.1	9,323.0	10,736.8	82.7	80.2	76.6	72.1	81.8

Note: Details may not add up to totals due to rounding. (1) Excl. homicide because survey is based on interviews with victims. (2) Incl. rape or sexual assault, robbery, and aggravated assault. (3) Committed by current or former intimate partners or family members. (4) Committed by current or former spouses, boyfriends, or girlfriends. (5) Incl. unlawful, forcible, or attempted entry of places, incl. a permanent residence, other residence (e.g., hotel room), or other structure (e.g., garage). Excl. trespassing on land. (6) Incl. only crimes where the offender committed or attempted a theft. (7) Incl. crimes where the offender did not commit or attempt a theft. Excl. trespassing on land. (8) Incl. other unlawful or attempted unlawful taking of property or cash without personal contact with victim.

Prison Population by State, 2000-22

Source: National Prisoner Statistics Program, Bureau of Justice Statistics (BJS), U.S. Dept. of Justice

As of Dec. 31, 2022, 1,230,143 prisoners were under the jurisdiction, or legal authority, of state (87.0%) or federal (13.0%) correctional authorities, a 23.9% decrease from a peak total U.S. prison population of 1,615,487 in 2009. The prison population in 2022 increased, ending eight consecutive years of declines. Jails, which are locally operated, typically hold persons awaiting trial or sentencing as well as those sentenced to one year or less.

Jurisdiction	2000	2021	2022	% change, 2021-22
U.S. total	**1,394,231**	**1,205,087**	**1,230,143**	**2.1%**
Federal[1,2]	**145,416**	**157,314**	**159,309**	**1.3**
State	**1,248,815**	**1,047,773**	**1,070,834**	**2.2**
Alabama	26,406	25,032	26,421	5.5
Alaska[3]	4,173	4,639	4,778	3.0
Arizona	26,510	33,914	33,865	–0.1
Arkansas	11,915	17,022	17,625	3.5
California	163,001	101,441	97,608	–3.8
Colorado	16,833	15,865	17,168	8.2
Connecticut[3]	18,355	9,889	10,506	6.2
Delaware[3]	6,921	4,810	4,954	3.0
Dist. of Columbia[2]	10,352	NA	NA	NA
Florida	71,319	80,417	84,678	5.3
Georgia	44,232	47,010	48,439	3.0
Hawaii[3]	5,053	4,102	4,149	1.1
Idaho	5,535	8,907	9,110	2.3
Illinois	45,281	28,980	29,634	2.3
Indiana	20,125	24,972	25,286	1.3
Iowa	7,955	8,562	8,473	–1.0
Kansas	8,344	8,521	8,709	2.2
Kentucky	14,919	18,560	19,744	6.4
Louisiana	35,207	26,074	27,296	4.7
Maine	1,679	1,577	1,675	6.2
Maryland	23,538	15,134	15,637	3.3
Massachusetts	10,722	6,148	6,001	–2.4
Michigan	47,718	32,186	32,374	0.6
Minnesota	6,238	8,003	8,636	7.9
Mississippi	20,241	17,332	19,802	14.3%
Missouri[4]	27,543	23,422	23,911	2.1
Montana	3,105	4,313	4,691	8.8
Nebraska	3,895	5,600	5,649	0.9
Nevada	10,063	10,202	10,304	1.0
New Hampshire	2,257	2,127	2,086	–1.9
New Jersey	29,784	12,506	12,657	1.2
New Mexico	5,342	5,154	4,970	–3.6
New York	70,199	30,338	31,148	2.7
North Carolina	31,266	28,995	29,627	2.2
North Dakota	1,076	1,689	1,817	7.6
Ohio	45,833	45,029	45,313	0.6
Oklahoma[5]	23,181	22,391	22,941	2.5
Oregon	10,580	13,198	12,518	–5.2
Pennsylvania	36,847	37,194	37,910	1.9
Rhode Island[3]	3,286	2,238	2,393	6.9
South Carolina	21,778	15,759	16,318	3.5
South Dakota	2,616	3,353	3,444	2.7
Tennessee	22,166	21,995	23,735	7.9
Texas	166,719	133,772	139,631	4.4
Utah	5,637	5,911	6,009	1.7
Vermont[3]	1,697	1,287	1,360	5.7
Virginia	30,168	30,357	27,162	–10.5
Washington	14,915	13,674	13,772	0.7
West Virginia	3,856	5,847	5,873	0.4
Wisconsin	20,754	20,202	20,873	3.3
Wyoming	1,680	2,123	2,154	1.5

NA = Not applicable. (1) Incl. adult prisoners held in nonsecure community-corrections facilities and adults and persons age 17 or younger held in privately operated facilities. (2) DC has not operated a prison system since year-end 2001. 2000 figure incl. jail and prison population. Persons sentenced for a felony under DC's criminal code are currently housed in federal facilities. (3) Prisons and jails form one integrated system. Data incl. total jail and prison populations. (4) State does not incl. persons held in federal or other state prisons in its jurisdiction count. (5) Incl. persons waiting in county jail to be moved to state prison.

Death Penalty by State, 1930-2024

Source: *Capital Punishment*, Natl. Prisoner Statistics Program, BJS, USDOJ; Death Penalty Information Center (DPIC)

In 2022, six states executed 18 inmates while 2,382 prisoners remained under sentence of death at year-end 2021, according to the most recent data available from the Bureau of Justice Statistics (BJS). The death row population has decreased every year since 2000.

As of mid-2024, 27 states and the federal government authorized the death penalty. According to the DPIC, five states executed 24 inmates in 2023; in Jan.-Aug. 2024, 12 executions took place. Of the 23 states without the death penalty, 8 that did not execute anyone after 1930 are not shown here (Alaska, Hawaii, Maine, Michigan, Minnesota, North Dakota, Rhode Island, and Wisconsin). More recently, capital punishment was abolished in New Mexico (2009), Illinois (2011), Connecticut (2012), Maryland (2013), New Hampshire (2019; one person remains on state's death row as repeal was not retroactive), Colorado (2020), and Virginia (2021). State supreme courts struck down the death penalty as unconstitutional in Delaware (2016) and Washington (2018), though neither state's legislature has taken action to amend, revise, or repeal their death penalty statutes. Governors issued moratoriums on executions in Oregon (2011), Pennsylvania (2015), California (2019), Ohio (2020), and Arizona (2023). In 2022, Oregon's governor granted clemency to the state's remaining death row prisoners and commuted their sentences to life without the possibility of parole. Nebraska voters, in a 2016 referendum, overturned their state's ban on capital punishment. The federal government resumed executions in 2020, after a nearly 17-year hiatus, but the Biden administration imposed a moratorium July 1, 2021.

All death penalty states and the federal government authorized lethal injection as their primary method of execution. Some states also permitted execution by electrocution, lethal gas (including nitrogen hypoxia), hanging, and firing squad.

Jurisdiction	Prisoners under death sentence, 2021	Executions[2]			
		2022[3]	2021	1977-2022	1930-2022
U.S. total	**2,382**	**18**	**11**	**1,558**	**5,411**
Federal[1]	**42**	**0**	**3**	**16**	**42**
State	**2,340**	**18**	**8**	**1,542**	**5,369**
Alabama	169	2	1	70	205
Arizona	114	3	0	40	78
Arkansas	28	0	0	31	149
California	690	0	0	13	305
Colorado	—	—	—	1	48
Connecticut	—	—	—	1	22
Delaware	0	0	0	16	28
Dist. of Columbia	—	—	—	0	40
Florida	324	0	0	99	269
Georgia	38	0	0	76	441
Idaho	8	0	0	3	6
Illinois	—	—	—	12	102
Indiana	8	0	0	20	61
Iowa	—	—	—	0	18
Kansas	9	0	0	0	15
Kentucky	26	0	0	3	106
Louisiana	62	0	0	28	161
Maryland	—	—	—	5	73
Massachusetts	—	—	—	0	27
Mississippi	36	1	1	23	178
Missouri	19	2	1	93	155
Montana	2	0	0	3	9
Nebraska	12	0	0	4	8
Nevada	61	0	0	12	41
New Hampshire	1	0	0	0	1
New Jersey	—	—	—	0	74
New Mexico	—	—	—	1	9
New York	0	0	0	0	329
North Carolina	136	0	0	43	306
Ohio	132	0	0	56	228
Oklahoma	44	5	2	119	181
Oregon[4]	23	0	0	2	21
Pennsylvania	111	0	0	3	155
South Carolina	34	0	0	43	205
South Dakota	1	0	0	5	6
Tennessee	47	0	0	13	105
Texas	198	5	3	578	875
Utah	7	0	0	7	20
Vermont	—	—	—	0	4
Virginia	—	0	0	113	205
Washington	0	0	0	5	52
West Virginia	—	—	—	0	40
Wyoming	0	0	0	1	8

— = Not available or applicable. (1) As of year end. Excludes persons held under Armed Forces jurisdiction with a military death sentence for murder. (2) Excludes 160 executions carried out by military authorities between 1930 and 1961. (3) BJS advance count. (4) In 2022, Oregon's governor commuted all death sentences to life without the possibility of parole.

U.S. Prison Population, 1925-2022

Source: National Prisoner Statistics Program, Bureau of Justice Statistics (BJS), U.S. Dept. of Justice

As recently as 1970, the U.S. had fewer than 200,000 people behind bars nationwide, or less than 1 in 1,000 residents. That number rose steadily from the 1970s on, reaching an all-time high of 1.62 mil prisoners in 2009. The imprisonment rate has generally declined since its high of 506 prisoners per 100,000 residents in 2008 though it increased slightly between 2021 and 2022.

Year	Prisoners	Imprisonment rate	Year	Prisoners	Imprisonment rate	Year	Prisoners	Imprisonment rate
1925	91,669	79	1980	329,821	138	2015	1,526,603	459
1930	129,453	104	1990	773,919	295	2017	1,489,189	442
1940	173,706	131	1995	1,125,874	411	2019	1,430,165	419
1950	166,165	109	2000	1,394,231	470	2020	1,221,164	357
1960	212,953	117	2005	1,525,910	492	2021	1,205,087	350
1970	196,441	96	2010	1,613,803	500	2022	1,230,143	355

Note: Imprisonment rate is per 100,000 U.S. residents of all ages at year end based on U.S. Census Bureau resident pop. ests. Since 1971, the rate is of prisoners sentenced to more than one year. Data for 1940-70 include all adult felons serving sentences in state and federal institutions. In 1977, the BJS began to include persons under state jurisdiction but not in a state's physical custody, such as persons in private prisons, local jails, and other facilities. Figures may not be directly comparable over time.

Prison Situation Under Correctional Authorities' Jurisdiction, 2022

Source: *Prisoners in 2022*, National Prisoner Statistics Program, Bureau of Justice Statistics (BJS), U.S. Dept. of Justice

Largest prison populations		% change in prison population, 2021-22		Imprisonment rate of sentenced prisoners		Prison population as % of maximum estimated capacity	
Jurisdiction	Number	Jurisdiction	% change	Jurisdiction	Rate[1]	Jurisdiction	% max. capacity[2]
U.S. total	**1,230,143**	**U.S. total**	**2.08%**	**U.S. total**	**355**	**U.S. total**	**NA**
Federal[3]	**159,309**	**Federal[3]**	**1.27**	**Federal[3]**	**44**	**Federal**	**106.86%**
State	**1,070,834**	**State**	**2.20**	**State**	**311**	**State**	**NA**
1. Texas	139,631	1. Mississippi	14.25	1. Mississippi	661	1. Nebraska	114.69
2. California	97,608	2. Montana	8.76	2. Louisiana	596	2. Idaho[7]	108.01
3. Florida	84,678	3. Colorado	8.21	3. Arkansas	574	3. Colorado	103.47
4. Georgia	48,439	4. Tennessee	7.91	4. Oklahoma[5]	563	4. Iowa	99.38
5. Ohio	45,313	5. Minnesota	7.91	5. Idaho[4]	460	5. Arkansas	98.91
6. Pennsylvania	37,910	6. North Dakota	7.58	6. Texas	452	6. Florida	98.02
7. Arizona	33,865	7. Rhode Island[6]	6.93	7. Arizona	446	7. North Dakota	97.88
8. Michigan	32,374	8. Kentucky	6.38	8. Kentucky	437	8. Oregon	94.98
9. New York	31,148	9. Connecticut[6]	6.24	9. Georgia	435	9. Wisconsin	94.96
10. Illinois	29,634	10. Maine	6.21	10. Montana	414	10. Virginia[7]	94.26
11. North Carolina	29,627	11. Vermont[6]	5.67	11. Alabama	390	11. Oklahoma	93.70
12. Louisiana	27,296	12. Alabama	5.55	12. Ohio	385	12. Tennessee	93.49
13. Virginia	27,162	13. Florida	5.30	13. Missouri[4]	381	13. Texas	93.03
14. Alabama	26,421	14. Louisiana	4.69	14. Florida	377	14. Alabama	92.90
15. Indiana	25,286	15. Texas	4.38	15. South Dakota[1]	370	15. Michigan	92.54
16. Missouri[4]	23,911	16. South Carolina	3.55	16. Wyoming	369	16. Hawaii	90.96
17. Tennessee	23,735	17. Arkansas	3.54	17. Indiana	349	17. Washington	90.41
18. Oklahoma[5]	22,941	18. Maryland	3.32	18. Tennessee	334	18. South Dakota[7]	86.08
19. Wisconsin	20,873	19. Wisconsin	3.32	19. West Virginia	331	19. Minnesota	85.55
20. Mississippi	19,802	20. Georgia	3.04	20. Michigan	323	20. Georgia[7]	85.48

NA = Not applicable. **Note:** Jurisdiction refers to the legal authority of state or federal correctional officials over a prisoner, regardless of where the prisoner is held, at year end. Persons sentenced for a felony under DC's criminal code are the responsibility of the Federal Bureau of Prisons. (1) Prisoners sentenced to more than one year per 100,000 U.S. residents based on Census Bureau pop. figures except SD, which incl. a small number of prisoners sentenced to one year or less. (2) Based on custody counts, not jurisdiction population. Excl. inmates held in local jails, other states, or private facilities unless otherwise noted. As % of rated, operational, or design capacity. Some states define capacity differently from BJS. Rankings do not incl. CT, MO, or OH, for which capacity data was not available. (3) Incl. adult prisoners held in nonsecure community-corrections facilities and adults and persons age 17 or younger held in privately operated facilities. (4) State does not incl. persons held in federal or other state prisons in its jurisdiction count. (5) Incl. persons waiting in county jails to be moved to state prison. (6) Prisons and jails form integrated system. Data incl. total jail and prison pops. (7) Incl. persons in private facilities.

Imprisonment Rates by Gender, Race, Hispanic Origin, and Age, 2022

Source: *Prisoners in 2022*, Bureau of Justice Statistics (BJS), U.S. Dept. of Justice

(per 100,000 U.S. residents in a given category at year end)

		MALE							FEMALE						
Age	All prisoners	All male	White	Black	Hispanic	AIAN	Asian[1]	Other[2]	All female	White	Black	Hispanic	AIAN	Asian[1]	Other[2]
Total[3]	**355**	**666**	**337**	**1,826**	**794**	**1,443**	**141**	**2,831**	**49**	**40**	**64**	**49**	**173**	**5**	**269**
18-19	50	92	30	340	85	158	13	109	5	2	12	7	8	1	23
20-24	328	600	229	1,842	663	1,197	95	1,064	43	28	73	49	134	4	187
25-29	674	1,217	514	3,320	1,462	2,351	225	3,239	105	83	145	105	372	10	479
30-34	829	1,498	732	3,722	1,774	3,171	255	5,519	138	118	154	136	507	12	531
35-39	832	1,504	813	3,828	1,747	3,576	279	7,843	139	125	145	137	509	11	671
40-44	784	1,438	776	3,779	1,634	3,312	275	7,767	115	105	126	103	395	9	588
45-49	619	1,154	617	3,106	1,326	2,550	245	10,256	80	73	97	67	260	8	654
50-54	486	910	512	2,446	1,023	1,892	194	8,231	60	53	77	49	163	6	584
55-59	387	740	407	2,045	849	1,453	164	7,604	41	33	61	34	115	5	487
60-64	258	505	277	1,406	650	1,000	106	6,444	22	17	35	20	70	3	698
65 or older	87	188	106	545	317	417	42	2,813	6	4	9	6	24	1	130
Total no. (thous.)[3]	**1,185.6**	**1,103.2**	**328.4**	**370.7**	**258.5**	**17.3**	**14.4**	**113.9**	**82.5**	**39.4**	**14.0**	**15.5**	**2.1**	**0.6**	**11.0**

Note: Rates are based on prisoners with a sentence of more than one year under state or federal jurisdiction. Resident pop. ests. are from the U.S. Census Bureau. White, Black, American Indian and Alaska Native (AIAN), Asian, and Other excl. persons of Hispanic origin. Hispanics may be of any race. (1) Incl. Asians, Native Hawaiians, and Other Pacific Islanders. (2) Incl. persons of two or more races and other races not broken out here. (3) Persons of all ages, including those age 17 or younger.

Prisoners and Incarceration Rates in Selected Countries, 2005-22

Source: UN Crime Trends Survey, United Nations (UN) Office on Drugs and Crime; World Prison Brief, Inst. for Crime & Justice Policy Research

Incarceration rates are per 100,000 population. For years given unless otherwise noted.

Country	Number of prisoners 2022	2015	2010	2005
Argentina	105,906	72,693	59,227	55,423
Azerbaijan	22,334	23,311[4]	21,971	17,845
Brazil	839,672	698,618	513,954	361,402
China	—	1,604,394	1,630,000	—
Colombia	98,242	120,444	86,028	66,829
Dominican Rep.	26,238	24,602	20,743	12,657
El Salvador	39,538	33,258	26,214	12,901
Ethiopia	110,000[2]	—	104,467	72,211[6]
India	573,220	419,623	368,998	358,368
Indonesia	275,518	173,572	117,863	97,691
Kazakhstan	35,228	42,114	55,140	52,203
Malaysia	67,038[3]	51,109	38,387	35,644
Mexico	226,116	221,439	188,013	208,272
Morocco	97,204	74,039	64,877	50,933
Myanmar (Burma)	100,324[2]	79,668[4]	66,000[5]	—
Panama	22,355	17,790	12,542	12,262
Peru	93,137	79,185	45,464	33,010
Philippines	180,826	139,469	95,390	91,200[6]
Poland	71,723	72,695	82,372	84,875
Russia	439,453	646,085	819,280	823,444
South Africa	144,938	159,771	163,312	157,402
Thailand	270,819	323,473	210,855	162,293
Turkey (Türkiye)	341,294	177,262	120,194	55,966
UK[1]	80,659	86,193	85,002	75,121
U.S.	1,767,300[3]	2,172,800	2,279,100	2,200,400
Venezuela	67,200	49,664	40,825	19,257[6]

Country	Incarceration rates 2022	2015	2010	2005
Antigua and Barbuda	248.5	409.7[4]	344.2	242.9
Bahamas, The	321.7	—	342.4	832.9
Barbados	280.1	343.1	331.3	370.0
Belize	295.9	516.7[4]	720.9	492.2
Brazil	390.0	340.5	261.7	193.5
Costa Rica	291.2	286.0	229.3	204.3
Dominica	519.7	258.5	429.1	410.6
El Salvador	624.0	533.7	428.8	213.7
Eswatini	283.4	318.4	340.5[5]	248.8
Fiji	257.3[3]	169.5	121.2	127.2
Grenada	341.2	421.9	384.1	215.0
Iran	216.5[2]	267.7[4]	327.5[5]	191.5
Palau	427.2[3]	404.6	504.4[5]	489.1
Panama	507.1	449.6	346.1	370.9
Peru	273.5	257.8	155.5	117.3
Russia	303.7	446.6	572.0	572.6
Rwanda	565.3[3]	466.2	533.5	—
St. Kitts and Nevis	526.7	460.4[4]	594.9	505.6[6]
St. Vincent and the Grenadines	542.6	937.1[4]	950.5	973.7[6]
Seychelles	295.9	695.5[4]	467.5	188.6
Thailand	377.7	460.2	308.9	246.6
Trinidad and Tobago	249.2[3]	—	261.7	275.4
Turkey (Türkiye)	399.9	222.6	164.2	81.5
U.S.	524.4[3]	669.4	732.4	741.3
Uruguay	419.2	293.8	259.5	187.2

— = Not available. **Note:** Use caution when making comparisons because of differences in each country's legal definitions and methods of offense counting and reporting. (1) England and Wales. (2) 2020. (3) 2021. (4) 2016. (5) 2011. (6) 2006.

Law Enforcement Officers and Civilian Employees, 2023

Source: *Crime in the United States, Law Enforcement Officers Killed and Assaulted*; FBI; U.S. Dept. of Justice

As of Oct. 31, 2023, city, county, state, college and university, and tribal agencies around the country collectively employed 1,041,688 full-time law enforcement workers. About 69.2% of these employees were sworn officers. The FBI defines a law enforcement officer as a person who ordinarily carries a firearm and badge, has full arrest powers, and is paid from specific dedicated government funds. Civilians (e.g., clerks, radio dispatchers, correctional officers) made up the remainder.

Altogether, they provided service to an estimated 310.7 mil people around the country, meaning there were 3.4 full-time law enforcement employees and 2.3 sworn officers per 1,000 residents.

The great majority of officers (86.2%) were men, while women made up 59.9% of civilian employees. The most populous state, California, employed the greatest number of full-time law enforcement workers (117,185). Washington, DC, had the highest rate, with 6.9 full-time law enforcement employees per 1,000 residents, followed by New Jersey (5.2) and Wyoming (4.7). Washington state had the lowest, with 2.0 per 1,000 residents.

Nationwide, 60 law enforcement officers were killed feloniously (that is, willfully and intentionally by the offender) in the line of duty in 2023, according to preliminary statistics, compared to 61 officers in 2022. Of the 60 officers, 45 were killed with firearms and 11 by vehicles. On average, the officers were 39 years of age and had served in law enforcement for 11 years when killed. An additional 35 officers were killed accidentally in 2023 while on the job, 23 of them in motor vehicle crashes. Also in 2023 (preliminary), 79,091 assaults of officers were reported by law enforcement agencies that had submitted 12 months of data. That comes out to a rate of 13.2 assaults per 100 officers.

Sentenced State Prisoners by Offense and Selected Characteristics, 2021

Source: *Prisoners in 2022*, Bureau of Justice Statistics (BJS), U.S. Dept. of Justice

Most serious offense	All prisoners[1]	Male	Female	White	Black	Hispanic	AIAN	Asian[2]
No. sentenced prisoners (thous.)	**1,021.3**	**952.0**	**69.3**	**321.7**	**332.0**	**224.3**	**15.6**	**12.5**
	Percent of total or subset of prisoners by most serious offense							
Violent	**62.9%**	**64.2%**	**45.5%**	**54.8%**	**68.4%**	**71.3%**	**59.7%**	**64.2%**
Murder[3]	15.2	15.2	14.5	11.5	18.7	14.2	13.5	16.5
Negligent manslaughter	1.8	1.7	3.9	1.7	1.1	1.4	1.5	1.3
Rape/sexual assault	15.7	16.6	3.2	19.8	9.8	19.1	13.9	15.6
Robbery	12.0	12.3	7.3	6.3	18.6	11.9	7.4	9.4
Aggravated/simple assault	14.4	14.5	11.8	11.8	15.9	21.0	17.9	15.9
Other	3.9	3.8	4.8	3.7	4.2	3.8	5.5	5.5
Property	**13.0**	**12.6**	**18.6**	**17.9**	**10.4**	**8.5**	**13.5**	**14.9**
Burglary	7.3	7.5	5.8	9.1	6.6	5.2	7.4	6.6
Larceny/theft	2.4	2.2	5.5	4.0	1.8	1.1	1.9	3.0
Motor vehicle theft	0.7	0.7	0.9	0.9	0.4	0.7	1.2	2.0
Fraud	1.1	0.9	4.3	1.8	0.7	0.5	1.5	1.4
Other	1.5	1.4	2.0	2.2	0.8	0.9	1.5	1.9
Drug[4]	**12.5**	**11.6**	**24.6**	**15.0**	**10.2**	**10.1**	**9.3**	**9.3**
Public order[5]	**11.0**	**11.0**	**10.3**	**11.4**	**10.6**	**9.8**	**16.9**	**10.9**
Other/unspecified[6]	**0.7**	**0.6**	**1.0**	**0.9**	**0.5**	**0.3**	**0.6**	**0.7**

Note: Counts based on persons with a prison sentence of more than one year under the jurisdiction, or legal authority, of state correctional officials at year end. Details may not add up to totals due to rounding and missing offense data. White, Black, American Indian and Alaska Native (AIAN), and Asian excl. persons of Hispanic origin. Hispanics may be of any race. (1) Incl. persons of two or more races and other races not broken out here. (2) Incl. Asians, Native Hawaiians, and Other Pacific Islanders. (3) Incl. nonnegligent manslaughter. (4) Incl. possession, trafficking, and other and unspecified drug offenses. (5) Incl. weapons, DUI/DWI, and court offenses; commercialized vice, morals, and decency offenses; liquor law violations; probation and parole violations; and other public order offenses. (6) Incl. juvenile offenses and other unspecified offense categories.

Arrests by Race and Ethnicity, 2022

Source: *Crime in the United States, 2022*, Uniform Crime Reporting (UCR) Program, Federal Bureau of Investigation (FBI), Dept. of Justice

Each instance in which a person is arrested, cited, or summoned for an offense is counted as one arrest. Some arrest data could represent multiple arrests of the same person. Ests. based on statistics from agencies reporting 12 months of arrest data.

Offense charged	Arrests by race: Total number[1]	White	Black/ African Amer.	AIAN	Asian	Native Hawaiian/ Other Pacific Isl.	Arrests by ethnicity: Total number[1]	Hispanic/ Latino
Total arrests	**5,780,699**	**67.9%**	**28.1%**	**2.3%**	**1.3%**	**0.4%**	**4,936,217**	**20.7%**
Violent crime	**344,113**	**57.1**	**39.1**	**1.9**	**1.6**	**0.4**	**300,106**	**25.5**
Murder and nonnegligent manslaughter	9,941	40.6	56.6	1.3	1.1	0.3	8,377	21.3
Rape[2]	15,502	69.5	26.5	1.8	1.9	0.3	13,067	28.6
Robbery	47,252	44.4	52.8	1.2	1.1	0.5	41,264	24.9
Aggravated assault	271,418	59.2	36.8	2.0	1.6	0.4	237,398	25.6
Property crime	**626,674**	**66.1**	**30.5**	**1.8**	**1.2**	**0.3**	**532,540**	**17.7**
Burglary	96,412	67.9	29.1	1.6	1.1	0.3	83,213	20.1
Larceny-theft	460,139	65.8	30.7	1.9	1.3	0.3	389,177	15.8
Motor vehicle theft	62,525	65.3	31.6	1.8	1.0	0.3	53,705	26.9
Arson	7,598	72.3	23.6	1.9	1.9	0.2	6,445	23.3
Other assaults (simple)	751,509	63.3	32.5	2.1	1.5	0.5	642,657	20.9
Forgery and counterfeiting	22,842	65.9	31.1	0.9	1.7	0.3	20,320	21.0
Fraud	60,830	63.2	33.4	1.7	1.4	0.3	52,559	15.6
Embezzlement	7,609	58.8	38.5	1.1	1.4	0.2	6,418	14.9
Stolen property; buying/receiving/possessing	66,628	60.5	35.8	1.4	1.6	0.7	56,837	21.3
Vandalism	129,439	66.4	29.6	2.4	1.3	0.3	111,575	20.6
Weapons; carrying, possessing, etc.	144,681	47.2	50.5	0.9	1.1	0.3	121,657	24.2
Prostitution and commercialized vice	12,333	51.7	40.6	0.5	7.0	0.3	11,638	25.8
Sex offenses (except rape and prostitution)	19,382	72.5	22.7	2.0	2.3	0.5	16,927	30.4
Drug abuse violations	714,442	70.0	27.3	1.6	1.0	0.2	630,635	20.5
Gambling	1,071	55.1	31.9	0.5	11.2	1.3	900	37.1
Offenses against the family and children	37,250	68.4	25.3	5.1	1.0	0.3	31,657	15.2
Driving under the influence	598,932	80.0	15.4	2.2	2.1	0.4	503,985	30.0
Liquor laws	73,191	77.5	15.3	4.9	1.6	0.6	57,728	18.1
Drunkenness[3]	14,324	87.1	10.2	0.8	1.6	0.3	14,257	44.4
Disorderly conduct	189,364	66.4	27.9	4.3	1.1	0.3	155,365	18.2
Vagrancy	12,524	58.9	23.9	15.3	1.2	0.7	10,082	14.6
All other offenses (except traffic)	1,948,006	69.6	26.3	2.5	1.1	0.4	1,654,021	18.0
Suspicion[3]	62	48.4	51.6	0.0	0.0	0.0	62	11.3
Curfew and loitering law violations	5,493	65.6	29.7	3.2	0.7	0.9	4,291	21.0

AIAN = American Indian or Alaska Native. (1) Not all agencies provide ethnicity data so total arrests by race will not equal total arrests by ethnicity. Hispanic or Latino persons may be of any race. (2) Aggregate totals based on both the legacy and revised UCR definitions of rape. (3) Incl. only Summary Reporting System data, submitted by agencies that have not yet transitioned to the new reporting system.

Foreign Nationals Removed From the U.S. by Criminal Status and Nationality, 2013-22

Source: *Immigration Enforcement Actions*, Office of Homeland Security Statistics, U.S. Dept. of Homeland Security

(countries ranked by total foreign nationals removed in 2022)

Country of nationality	2013 Total removed	2013 % criminal[1]	2015 Total removed	2015 % criminal[1]	2017 Total removed	2017 % criminal[1]	2019 Total removed	2019 % criminal[1]	2021 Total removed	2021 % criminal[1]	2022 Total removed	2022 % criminal[1]
Total	**432,334**	**45.9%**	**324,428**	**37.9%**	**284,365**	**38.2%**	**347,090**	**48.9%**	**85,783**	**71.2%**	**108,733**	**58.1%**
Mexico	306,901	47.6	232,435	38.2	181,962	40.3	202,587	48.5	50,650	75.0	62,047	65.7
El Salvador	21,132	44.8	21,823	32.9	18,339	35.0	18,038	48.8	2,790	72.9	7,325	27.5
Guatemala	47,021	32.8	33,350	31.4	32,850	33.6	53,346	43.3	7,723	57.1	6,802	51.6
Honduras	36,640	45.3	20,243	42.1	22,070	41.8	40,651	44.3	5,053	63.3	6,545	56.7
Colombia	1,479	62.8	1,589	49.8	2,029	30.4	2,879	89.1	3,021	90.1	5,823	46.4
Nicaragua	1,340	51.6	929	47.4	903	41.7	2,262	46.7	1,034	39.2	2,680	16.9
Brazil	1,579	23.7	1,019	27.8	1,718	23.6	2,403	61.8	1,965	22.8	2,507	38.8
Ecuador	1,512	38.3	1,430	34.1	1,376	36.3	2,485	59.5	1,854	42.3	1,821	37.0
Dominican Rep.	2,325	78.3	1,885	80.6	2,021	74.7	2,203	73.5	1,728	79.2	1,722	63.9
Haiti	534	85.8	466	57.5	5,723	5.9	728	58.9	398	51.0	1,543	8.0
All other countries[2]	11,871	50.3	9,259	42.9	15,374	31.0	19,508	66.7	9,567	79.1	9,918	72.4

Note: Fiscal year (Oct. 1-Sept. 30) data. Excl. removals by Customs and Border Protection, which does not identify whether foreign nationals have criminal convictions. (1) Of total number removed by country, percent of persons with a prior criminal conviction. (2) Incl. unknown.

Gun Violence Incidents and Deaths, 2014-24

Source: Gun Violence Archive (GVA)

The Gun Violence Archive is an independent data collection and research group with no affiliation with any advocacy organization. Since 2013, it has maintained an online archive of gun violence (GV) incidents, which it collects daily from more than 7,500 media, law enforcement, government, and commercial sources.

(number of actual deaths, injuries, or GV incidents verified as of Aug. 14, 2024; 2024 data are for partial year)

	2014	2017	2020	2023	2024
Total GV deaths, all causes	—	—	**43,947**	**43,178**	—
Deaths[1]	12,368	15,771	19,655	19,088	10,637
Injuries	22,000	31,346	39,520	36,507	20,495
Children (age 0-11) killed/injured	580	722	1,003	943	520
Teens (age 12-17) killed/injured	2,288	3,263	4,162	5,294	2,840
Total GV incidents	**34,862**	**58,116**	—	—	—
Murder/suicides	—	—	569	682	426

	2014	2017	2020	2023	2024
Mass shootings[2]	272	347	611	655	348
Mass murders[2]	—	—	21	40	19
Home invasion	1,884	2,569	—	—	—
Defensive use	1,447	2,117	1,547	1,268	785
Unintentional shooting	1,589	2,067	2,327	1,603	854
Officer-involved incidents[3]					
Officer killed/injured	229	302	405	421	273
Subject-suspect killed/injured	1,854	2,148	2,226	2,256	1,447

— = Not available. **Note:** All numbers are subject to change or incidents recategorized. The GVA previously published trend data from the Centers for Disease Control and Prevention (CDC) on suicides by firearm; it is currently working with the CDC to come up with more accurate, timely numbers. (1) From 2020 on, includes homicide, murder, unintentional shootings, and defensive gun use. (2) Four or more people shot and/or killed in a single event, at the same general time and location, not including the shooter. (3) Numbers for 2014 and 2017 are of reported and verified incidents. Numbers for 2019-24 are of source verified deaths and injuries.

Hate Crimes by Offense Type and Bias Motivation, 2022

Source: *Supplemental Hate Crime Statistics, 2022,* Uniform Crime Reporting (UCR) Program, FBI, U.S. Dept. of Justice

Hate crimes are defined as crimes motivated in whole or in part by the offender's bias against a characteristic such as race, religion, or sexual orientation. The Hate Crime Statistics Act of 1990 led to the collection of hate crime data as part of the FBI's UCR program. Not all law enforcement agencies that participate in the UCR program submit hate crime data, so the data presented is not representative of the nation as a whole. In 2022, 14,631 agencies, representing 305.3 mil inhabitants, participated in the Hate Crime Statistics Program.

Bias motivation	Total offenses	Crimes against persons				Crimes against property					Crimes against society[3]
		Aggravated assault	Simple assault	Intimidation	Other[1]	Robbery	Burglary	Larceny-theft	Destruction/ damage/ vandalism	Other[2]	
Total	**13,337**	**1,561**	**3,111**	**4,023**	**115**	**169**	**169**	**562**	**3,088**	**257**	**282**
Single-bias incidents	**12,913**	**1,525**	**3,042**	**3,846**	**113**	**168**	**164**	**555**	**2,965**	**254**	**281**
Race/ethnicity/ancestry	**7,677**	**1,019**	**1,924**	**2,514**	**50**	**112**	**84**	**249**	**1,421**	**136**	**168**
Anti-white	1,102	155	323	259	10	31	20	97	119	46	42
Anti-Black or African American	4,000	501	875	1,482	24	29	30	67	888	36	68
Anti-American Indian or Alaska Native	209	21	31	20	2	1	6	43	29	25	31
Anti-Asian	579	79	190	191	2	19	8	12	72	1	5
Anti-Native Hawaiian or Other Pacific Isl.	29	5	5	5	0	0	4	2	1	3	4
Anti-multiple races, group	271	13	44	75	2	2	3	4	121	4	3
Anti-Arab	105	15	29	47	0	1	1	2	7	1	2
Anti-Hispanic or Latino	937	190	306	297	7	23	9	9	77	12	7
Anti-other race/ethnicity/ancestry	445	40	121	138	3	6	3	13	107	8	6
Religion	**2,199**	**103**	**223**	**497**	**14**	**10**	**47**	**125**	**1,037**	**78**	**65**
Anti-Jewish	1,194	36	103	322	5	2	5	13	704	2	2
Anti-Catholic	110	2	6	7	0	0	2	7	75	10	1
Anti-Islamic (Muslim)	179	19	41	76	4	1	7	1	26	3	1
Anti-Sikh	192	19	24	6	2	4	8	48	32	27	22
Anti-other religion[4]	460	23	46	80	2	3	23	45	174	30	34
Anti-multiple religions, group	48	2	1	4	1	0	2	5	26	3	4
Anti-atheism/agnosticism/etc.	16	2	2	2	0	0	0	6	0	3	1
Sexual orientation	**2,210**	**288**	**646**	**644**	**32**	**33**	**15**	**106**	**411**	**17**	**18**
Anti-gay (male)	1,194	168	421	344	11	30	7	25	174	8	6
Anti-lesbian	211	23	57	84	3	1	2	6	31	0	4
Anti-lesbian, gay, bisexual, or transgender (mixed group)	745	86	152	203	14	2	5	70	199	9	5
Anti-heterosexual	23	4	5	4	2	0	1	1	3	0	3
Anti-bisexual	37	7	11	9	2	0	0	4	4	0	0
Gender	**121**	**19**	**27**	**41**	**3**	**0**	**2**	**8**	**13**	**3**	**5**
Anti-male	22	2	7	2	0	0	1	3	4	1	2
Anti-female	99	17	20	39	3	0	1	5	9	2	3
Gender identity	**515**	**72**	**160**	**120**	**13**	**12**	**8**	**44**	**62**	**8**	**16**
Anti-transgender	374	60	123	95	11	11	5	24	37	3	5
Anti-gender non-conforming	141	12	37	25	2	1	3	20	25	5	11
Disability	**191**	**24**	**62**	**30**	**1**	**1**	**8**	**23**	**21**	**12**	**9**
Anti-physical disability	83	5	30	12	0	1	3	10	11	6	5
Anti-mental disability	108	19	32	18	1	0	5	13	10	6	4
Multiple-bias incidents[5]	**424**	**36**	**69**	**177**	**2**	**1**	**5**	**7**	**123**	**3**	**1**

(1) Incl. murder/nonnegligent manslaughter, rape (revised or legacy definition), and human trafficking (commercial sex acts and involuntary servitude). (2) Incl. motor vehicle theft and arson. (3) Incl. animal cruelty, drug/narcotic offenses, gambling offenses, prostitution offenses, and weapon law violations, where society as a whole is considered the victim. (4) Incl. offenses against religions not shown. (5) Incidents in which one or more offense types are motivated by two or more biases.

Federal Sentence Length by Type of Crime, 2023

Source: *Sourcebook of Federal Sentencing Statistics*, U.S. Sentencing Commission

Data based on court documentation for federal cases involving felonies and misdemeanors (excluding petty misdemeanors) in which the offender was sentenced in the fiscal year (Oct. 1-Sept. 30). Excl. cases where data was missing or indeterminable.

Type of crime[1]	Mean months	Median months	Number of cases
Total	**53**	**24**	**63,704**
Administration of justice	17	10	643
Antitrust	6	6	18
Arson	58	57	106
Assault	72	48	837
Bribery/corruption	21	14	366
Burglary/trespass	17	8	83
Child pornography	115	97	1,408
Commercialized vice	21	12	84
Drug possession	2	0	124
Drug trafficking	82	63	19,000
Environmental	4	0	145
Extortion/racketeering	31	24	129
Firearms	49	40	8,756
Food and drug	11	0	51
Forgery/counterfeiting/copyright	18	12	112
Fraud/theft/embezzlement	22	12	5,157
Immigration	12	8	19,141
Individual rights[2]	57	18	110
Kidnapping	199	168	151
Manslaughter	75	69	86
Money laundering	63	36	1,312
Murder	285	276	489
National defense	39	24	230
Obscenity/other sex offenses	23	18	325
Prison offenses	14	12	451
Robbery	110	96	1,502
Sexual abuse	213	180	1,393
Stalking/harassing	29	20	240
Tax	15	12	445
Other[3]	4	0	810

Note: Sentences of 470 months or greater (including life) and probation were incl. in avg. computations as 470 months and 0 months, respectively. (1) Obtained from the presentence report or judgment and commitment order. In cases of multiple counts, the offense with the highest statutory sentencing range becomes the type. (2) For example, obstructing an election or registration, or intercepting communications or eavesdropping. (3) For example, interference with a flight crew or the unlawful sale, transportation, possession, etc., of drug paraphernalia, among other felony and misc. offenses not listed or covered separately.

Active Shooter Incidents, 2019-23

Source: *Active Shooter Incidents in the U.S., 2023*, Federal Bureau of Investigation (FBI), U.S. Dept. of Justice and Advanced Law Enforcement Rapid Response Training (ALERRT) Center at Texas State University

The FBI defines an active shooter as "one or more individuals actively engaged in killing or attempting to kill people in a populated area." FBI researchers identify active shooter incidents through the agency's internal holdings and repositories, official law enforcement reports, and open-source data. Gun-related incidents that are the result of circumstances like self-defense, gang violence, and drug-related violence, among others, are excluded. In 2023, 48 active shooter incidents took place in 26 states. Data valid as of Feb. 16, 2024.

	2023	2022	2021	2020	2019
Total incidents	**48**	**50**	**61**	**40**	**30**
Casualties (excluding shooters)	**244**	**313**	**243**	**164**	**258**
Number killed	105	100	103	38	103
Law enforcement officers killed	2	1	2	1	2
Number wounded	139	213	140	126	155
Law enforcement officers wounded	12	21	5	11	15
Met "mass killing" definition[1]	15	13	12	5	13
Incidents where law enforcement engaged shooters	12	9	17	8	11
Shooters	**49**	**50**	**61**	**42**	**33**
Shooter resolution[2]					
Shooter died by suicide	7	9	11	7	6
Shooter killed by law enforcement	12	7	14	4	9
Shooter killed by citizen	0	2	4	2	1
Shooter apprehended by law enforcement	30	29	30	24	17
Shooter wore body armor	5	4	2	1	4

(1) "Three or more killings in a single incident," as defined by the federal government. The FBI does not include the shooter in its mass killing statistics. (2) Number of shooter resolutions may not add up to total because of shooters who are at large or who otherwise do not fit into any category shown here.

Notable Terrorist Incidents Worldwide Since 1971

Source: U.S. Dept. of State; *Facts On File World News Digest*; World Almanac research

Selected noteworthy incidents, excluding most assassinations, kidnappings, and military targets. Does not include all incidents in Iraq or Afghanistan, 2001-present; see also Chronology of the Year's Events.

1971—Mar. 1: Senate wing of U.S. Capitol Building in Wash., DC, bombed by Weather Underground; no deaths.

1972—July 21: "Bloody Friday." Provisional IRA exploded 20+ bombs across Belfast, N. Ireland; 9 killed, hundreds injured. **Sept. 5:** Palestinian group Black September killed 2 Israeli athletes and seized 9 others at Olympic Village in Munich, W. Germany, during Summer Olympics; 9 hostages, 5 militants, 1 Ger. officer died in botched rescue.

1973—Dec. 17: Palestinian gunmen attacked Rome airport and bombed plane on tarmac; hijacked Lufthansa plane with 5 Italian hostages to Athens, Greece, then to Kuwait; 31 killed.

1974—June 17: Houses of Parliament in London, England, bombed by Provisional IRA; 11 injured.

1975—Jan. 27: Puerto Rican FALN nationalists bombed Fraunces Tavern in New York City; 4 killed, 53 injured. **Jan. 29:** U.S. State Dept. building in Wash., DC, bombed by Weather Underground; no deaths.

1976—June 27: Palestinian and Baader-Meinhof militants forced Air France jet to land in Entebbe, Uganda. Israeli army rescued 103 hostages from airport terminal in battle with terrorists and Ugandan troops, July 3-4; 32 killed in all.

1978—Mar. 11: Palestinian militants shot civilians and hijacked bus with hostages from Haifa to Tel Aviv, Israel. Bus exploded during firefight with police at a roadblock; 38 killed.

1979—Nov. 4: Iranian radicals seized U.S. embassy in Tehran, taking 66 Americans hostage. 52 were held until Jan. 20, 1981. **Nov. 20:** Around 200 Islamic fundamentalists opposed to the Saudi monarchy seized Grand Mosque in Mecca, Saudi Arabia, and held hundreds of pilgrims hostage. Saudi forces retook mosque Dec. 4; about 270 died.

1980—Feb. 27: Members of leftist guerrilla group April 19 Movement (M-19) seized Dominican Republic embassy in Bogota, Colombia; 80 hostages taken, 18 held until Apr. 27.

1983—Apr. 18: Hezbollah suicide truck bomb at U.S. embassy in Beirut, Lebanon, killed 63. **Oct. 9:** N. Korean agents ambushed a S. Korean govt. delegation in Rangoon, Burma, killing 21. **Oct. 23:** Hezbollah suicide truck bombings of U.S. and French military bases, Beirut, Lebanon; 242 Americans, 58 French killed.

1984—Sept. 20: U.S. embassy annex nr. Beirut, Lebanon, bombed, killing approx. 20. **Sept. 20:** In worst bioterrorism attack in U.S. history, members of Rajneesh cult contaminated an Oregon salsa bar with salmonella, sickening 751.

1985—Apr. 12: Bomb blast at restaurant nr. U.S. air base in Torrejon, Spain; 18 killed. **June 14:** Hezbollah members hijacked TWA Flight 847 with 153 passengers and crew to Beirut, Lebanon; 39 held for 17 days, 1 U.S. Navy sailor killed. **June 23:** Air India Flight 182 destroyed by bomb off coast of Ireland; 329 killed. Blamed on Sikh terrorists. **Oct. 7:** Four Palestinians hijacked Italian cruise ship *Achille Lauro*; 1 passenger killed. **Nov. 23:** EgyptAir Flight 648 from Athens, Greece, to Cairo hijacked to Malta by Palestinian group Abu Nidal; 60 killed in rescue. **Dec. 27:** Palestinian militants opened fire at El-Al (Isr.) airline counters at Rome and Vienna airports; 19 killed.

1986—Apr. 5: Nightclub in Berlin, W. Germany, bombed; 3 killed, incl. 2 U.S. service personnel, 200+ hurt. 3 Libyan embassy workers in Germany convicted.

1987—Apr. 17: Bomb in Sri Lankan capital killed 100+; blamed on Tamil rebels who, 4 days later, attacked Sinhalese travelers on highway, killing 127. **June 19:** Basque group ETA bombed supermarket garage in Barcelona, Spain; 21 killed. **Nov. 29:** Bomb planted by N. Korean agents exploded on Korean Air Lines Flight 858 over Indian Ocean; 115 killed.

1988—Dec. 21: Pan Am Flight 103 exploded over Lockerbie, Scotland, killing all 259 aboard and 11 on ground; Libya took responsibility for bombing in Aug. 2003.

1989—Sept. 19: French UTA Flight 722 from Congo Republic to Paris destroyed by bomb in midair over Niger; 170 killed.

1992—Mar. 17: Israeli embassy in Buenos Aires, Argentina, bombed; 28 killed, 200+ injured. Hezbollah suspected.

1993—Feb. 26: Truck bomb exploded in World Trade Center garage in New York City; 6 killed. Blast later linked to al-Qaeda. **Mar. 12-19:** At least 11 bombs ripped through Bombay and Calcutta, India; 300+ killed.

1994—Feb. 25: U.S.-born Israeli settler Baruch Goldstein opened fire in mosque in Hebron, West Bank; about 30 Muslim worshippers killed. **July 18:** Buenos Aires, Argentina, Jewish center bombed; 87 killed. Blamed on Hezbollah.

1995—Mar. 20: Twelve killed and over 5,000 injured when Japanese cult members released sarin nerve gas in Tokyo subway cars. **Apr. 19:** Murrah Federal Building in Oklahoma City bombed, killing 168. Timothy McVeigh and Terry Nichols convicted. McVeigh executed in 2001; Nichols sentenced to life in prison. **Nov. 13:** U.S. military compound in Riyadh, Saudi Arabia, bombed by Islamic Movement of Change; 7 killed.

1996—Jan. 31: Tamil Tigers drove explosives-laden truck into Central Bank in Colombo, Sri Lanka; 90 killed. **June 25:** Fuel truck exploded outside Khobar Towers, U.S. military complex in Dhahran, Saudi Arabia; killed 19. **July 27:** Bomb exploded in Atlanta, GA, during Olympic Games; killed 2, injured 100+. Extremist Eric Robert Rudolph sentenced to life in prison, 2005. **Dec. 3:** Bomb exploded on subway in Paris; 4 killed, 86 injured. Algerian Islamic extremist group suspected.

1997—Nov. 17: Gamaa al-Islamiya militants killed 58 tourists and 4 Egyptians in Valley of the Kings nr. Luxor, Egypt.

1998—Aug. 7: U.S. embassies in Nairobi, Kenya, and Dar-es-Salaam, Tanzania, bombed; 257 people killed. Al-Qaeda claimed responsibility. **Aug. 15:** IRA car bomb outside courthouse in Omagh, N. Ireland, killed 29. **Oct. 18:** National Liberation Army of Colombia blew up Ocensa oil pipeline; about 71 killed.

1999—Sept. 9-16: Three buildings bombed in Moscow and Volgodonsk, Russia; about 300 killed. Chechen rebels blamed.

2000—Oct. 12: Small boat assisting in docking of USS *Cole* exploded alongside it in Aden, Yemen; 17 U.S. sailors killed. Blamed on al-Qaeda.

2001—Sept. 11: 19 al-Qaeda terrorists hijacked 4 U.S. domestic flights, including 2 planes that crashed into New York City's World Trade Center towers and 1 into Pentagon. Total dead minus hijackers: 2,977; deadliest terrorist attack yet on U.S. soil. **Sept.-Nov. 7:** Letters tainted with deadly anthrax bacteria mailed through U.S. postal system killed 5, sickened 17; investigation concluded in 2010 that government-employed microbiologist Bruce Ivins, who died by suicide in 2008, was responsible.

2002—Mar. 27: Suicide bombing at hotel in Netanya, Israel, during Passover celebration; 27 killed. **Oct. 12:** Resort in Bali, Indonesia, bombed; 202 dead. Jemaah Islamiah blamed. **Oct. 23:** Chechen guerrillas seized theater in Moscow, held 700+ hostages. Russian authorities gassed theater; most guerrillas and about 128 hostages killed. **Dec. 27:** Chechen rebels plowed truck bomb into pro-Russian govt. headquarters in Grozny, Chechnya; 80 killed, 152 injured.

2003—May 12-13: Al-Qaeda militants detonated car bombs at 3 residential complexes used by Westerners in Riyadh, Saudi Arabia; 34 killed. **May 16:** Five explosions in Casablanca, Morocco; 44 killed. Blamed on al-Qaeda. **Aug. 19:** UN headquarters in Baghdad bombed by truck; 22 killed, incl. UN envoy to Iraq. **Aug. 25:** 2 bombs exploded in taxis in Mumbai, India; 46 killed. Islamic militants suspected. **Nov. 15:** Two synagogues in Istanbul, Turkey, bombed; 25 killed. **Nov. 20:** British consulate and offices of HSBC bombed in Istanbul, Turkey; 27 killed. Blamed on al-Qaeda. **Dec. 5:** Suicide bombing on commuter train in Yessentuki, Russia; 44 killed. Blamed on Chechen rebels.

2004—Feb. 6: Bomb exploded in Moscow subway; 39 killed, 130 injured. Chechen rebels blamed. **Mar. 11:** Al-Qaeda cell bombed 4 commuter trains during morning rush hour in Madrid, Spain; 191 killed, about 1,200 injured. **May 29:** Al-Qaeda militants stormed foreigner compound in Khobar, Saudi Arabia, taking hostages; 22 killed. **Aug. 24:** Chechen suicide bombers caused crash of two Russian passenger planes in diff. parts of Russia; 90 killed. **Sept. 1:** Chechen militants seized school in Beslan, in North Ossetia, Russia; held 1,000+ hostage for 3 days before Russian troops stormed school. About 330 killed, incl. 27 hostage-takers.

2005—July 7: Four bombs exploded on 3 separate subways and 1 bus in London, Eng.; 52 killed, about 700 injured. **July 23:** Three car bombs explode nr. Sharm el-Sheik, Egypt, resorts; about 90 killed. **Nov. 9:** 3 suicide bombings targeted hotels in Amman, Jordan; killed 56. Al-Qaeda in Iraq took responsibility.

2006—July 11: 8 explosions struck 7 different trains and 1 station of public commuter rail system in Mumbai, India; 207 killed. Lashkar-e-Qahhar (Army of Terror) claimed responsibility.

2007—Feb. 19: Train traveling between New Delhi and border with Pakistan caught fire, 68 killed; Indian ministers blamed Muslim militants for trying to disrupt peace talks between India and Pakistan. **Dec. 11:** Two coordinated car bombs went off outside govt. building and UN office building in Algiers, Algeria; 41 killed, incl. 17 UN employees, 170 wounded.

2008—Sept. 20: Suicide bomber in truck set off explosion outside of Marriott Hotel in Islamabad, Pakistan; 53 killed, 271 wounded. **Nov. 26-29:** Series of attacks and bombings on luxury hotels and high-profile targets in Mumbai, India; 171 killed, 300 injured.

2009—Feb. 20: Suicide bomber targeted Shiite funeral in Dera Ismail Khan, Pakistan; 30 killed. **Nov. 5:** U.S. Army major opened fire on Fort Hood (TX) military base, killing 13 and wounding 30+. **Dec. 25:** A Nigerian man failed to blow up a flight from Amsterdam to Detroit with bomb hidden in his underpants.

2010—Jan. 1: Taliban suicide bomber killed more than 100 on playground in NW Pakistan. **Mar. 29:** Two female Chechen separatists detonated suicide bombs at two landmark Moscow subway stations, killing at least 40. **July 9:** Suicide bombers targeted tribal elders in Mohmand, Pakistan, killing more than 100. **July 11:** Several bombs claimed by al-Shabab exploded simultaneously in Kampala, Uganda, killing more than 70 people who had gathered to watch the World Cup final broadcast.

2011—Jan. 24: Suicide bomber killed 35 in Moscow's Domodedovo Airport, location chosen to maximize deaths of foreigners. **July 22:** Anders Behring Breivik, right-wing Norwegian extremist, set off a bomb in van outside govt. buildings in Oslo, then massacred dozens of young people at a summer camp on Tyrifjorden Lake, bringing death toll to 77.

2012—Jan. 21: Series of attacks by Islamist extremist group Boko Haram killed more than 185 in Kano, Nigeria. **May 21:** Suicide bomber claimed by al-Qaeda in the Arabian Peninsula (AQAP) killed more than 100 soldiers during military parade rehearsal nr. Yemeni presidential palace. **Aug. 5:** White supremacist fatally shot 6 worshippers at a Sikh temple before killing himself, Oak Creek, WI. **Sept. 11:** Terrorists stormed U.S. embassy in Benghazi, Libya, killing 4 Americans, including U.S. Amb. J. Christopher Stevens.

2013—Apr. 15: Two bombs exploded nr. Boston Marathon finish line, killing 3 and injuring 264; 4-day search ended in death of suspect Tamerlan Tsarnaev and capture of his brother, Dzhokhar, a naturalized Chechen immigrant. **Sept. 21:** Al-Shabab, a Somali militant group, killed up to 70 people and wounded at least 175 at a Nairobi, Kenya, shopping mall.

2014—Apr.-May: Islamist extremist group Boko Haram kidnapped more than 250 girls from schools in Nigeria; killed more than 150 villagers in Gamboru. **Dec. 15:** Nine Taliban gunmen attacked military-affiliated school in Peshawar, Pakistan, executing about 150, including 132 children.

2015—Jan. 7: Gunmen stormed Paris offices of *Charlie Hebdo*, a satirical newspaper, killing 12. Two days later, French police killed suspects, brothers who identified themselves as belonging to AQAP. **Mar. 18:** Gunmen killed 21 tourists and a police officer at Tunisia's National Bardo Museum. Several terrorist groups claimed credit. **Apr. 2:** Al-Shabab militants killed 147 students at Kenya's Garissa Univ. after separating Christian and Muslim students. **June 17:** Lone white-supremacist gunman killed 9, incl. a state senator, in a historically Black church in Charleston, SC. **Oct. 31:** Terrorists downed a Russian charter flight shortly after takeoff from Egyptian resort, killing all 224 onboard. Egyptian affiliate of the Sunni extremist group the Islamic State in Iraq and Syria (ISIS) said it smuggled a soda-can bomb onto plane. **Nov. 13:** Series of coordinated suicide bombings and other attacks by ISIS on Paris cafes, a soccer stadium, and a concert hall killed 137 (incl. 7 attackers); wounded 350+. **Dec. 2:** A heavily armed married couple opened fire on the husband's coworkers at a holiday party for San Bernardino (CA) County Health Dept., killing 14, wounding 21.

2016—Mar. 22: Three explosions in Brussels, two at the airport and one at a busy subway station, killed 35 people (incl. 3 bombers) and injured 300+. ISIS claimed credit; investigators linked perpetrators to 2015 Paris attacks. **June 12:** Lone gunman killed 49 people and wounded 53 at a gay nightclub in Orlando, FL. **July 7:** A heavily armed man shot and killed five police officers and wounded seven other officers and two civilians in downtown Dallas, TX, during peaceful protest. **July 14:** Tunisian-born man drove rented truck into Bastille Day crowds in Nice, France, killing 86 and injuring 400+. **Dec. 19:** Tunisian man on Germany's terror watch list drove hijacked truck through outdoor market in Berlin, killing 12; 56+ injured.

2017—May 22: Suicide bomber detonated in entrance hall of Manchester, England, arena as fans left a concert by U.S. singer Ariana Grande, killing 22; 800 injured. ISIS claimed responsibility. **June 3:** Three assailants in a van hit pedestrians on London Bridge before exiting vehicle and attacking people with knives; 8 killed and 48+ injured. **Aug. 18:** A Moroccan man killed 2 and injured 8 with a knife in Turku, Finland; country's first terror attack. **Oct. 14:** Two truck bombs detonated in Mogadishu, Somalia, leaving 512 dead, 300+ injured. Blamed on al-Shabab. **Nov. 24:** Attack on Sufi mosque in Bir al-Abed, Egypt, by extremists affiliated with ISIS, killed 311 people and injured 100+ others.

2018—Oct. 27: Man opened fire inside Tree of Life Congregation synagogue in Pittsburgh, PA, killing 11 worshippers.

2019—Mar. 15: Australian gunman attacked two mosques in Christchurch, New Zealand, killing 51. **Apr. 21:** Nine Muslim extremists with alleged links to Islamic State staged suicide bombings in churches and hotels on Easter Sunday in Sri Lanka, killing more than 250. **Aug. 3:** White nationalist targeting Hispanic immigrants killed 23, injured 20+ at Walmart store in El Paso, TX. **Aug. 18:** Suicide bomber killed at least 80 people and injured 180+ at a wedding party in Kabul, Afghanistan. ISIS claimed responsibility. **Dec. 28:** Al-Shabab claimed credit for truck bombing at a Mogadishu, Somalia, police checkpoint that killed 85.

2021—Aug. 26: ISIS-K claimed responsibility for attack outside Kabul, Afghanistan, airport that killed at least 170 Afghans and 13 U.S. service personnel.

2022—Mar. 4: ISIS-K claimed suicide bombing at Shiite mosque that killed at least 65 in Peshawar, Pakistan. **May 14:** White supremacist fatally shot 10 Black people in predominantly Black neighborhood of Buffalo, NY.

2023—Oct. 7: Palestinian militants from Hamas and other armed groups launched a coordinated assault across the Gaza-Israel border, killing around 1,200 Israeli soldiers and civilians.

2024—Mar. 22: ISIS-K gunmen opened fire inside Moscow concert venue before setting it on fire, killing 145 and injuring hundreds.

Notable Assassinations Since 1865

1865—Apr. 14: U.S. Pres. Abraham Lincoln shot by John Wilkes Booth, well-known actor with Confederate sympathies, at Ford's Theater in Washington, DC; died Apr. 15.

1881—Mar. 13: Alexander II of Russia. **July 2:** U.S. Pres. James A. Garfield shot by Charles J. Guiteau, disappointed office seeker, in Washington, DC; died Sept. 19.

1894—June 24: French Pres. Sadi Carnot by Sante Caserio, Italian anarchist, in Lyon.

1898—Sept. 10: Empress Elizabeth of Austria stabbed by Luigi Luccheni, Italian anarchist.

1900—July 29: Umberto I, king of Italy, shot by an anarchist.

1901—Sept. 6: U.S. Pres. William McKinley shot by Leon Czolgosz, anarchist, in Buffalo, NY; died Sept. 14.

1908—Feb. 1: King Carlos I of Portugal and his son Luís Filipe, in Lisbon.

1913—Feb. 23: Mexican Pres. Francisco I. Madero and Vice Pres. José María Pino Suárez. **Mar. 18:** King George of Greece, by an anarchist.

1914—June 28: Archduke Franz Ferdinand of Austria-Hungary and his wife shot by Gavrilo Princip, Serb nationalist, in Sarajevo, Bosnia.

1916—Dec. 30: Grigory Rasputin, Russian mystic and court figure, by group of aristocrats.

1918—July 12: Grand Duke Michael of Russia, at Perm. **July 16:** Nicholas II, former (abdicated) czar of Russia; his wife, Czarina Alexandra; their son, Czarevitch Alexis; their daughters, Grand Duchesses Olga, Tatiana, Marie, Anastasia; and 4 members of household executed by Bolsheviks at Ekaterinburg.

1920—May 20: Mexican Pres. Gen. Venustiano Carranza, in Tlaxcalantongo.

1922—Aug. 22: Michael Collins, Irish revolutionary, in West Cork. **Dec. 16:** Polish Pres. Gabriel Narutowicz in Warsaw.
1923—July 20: Gen. Francisco "Pancho" Villa, ex-rebel leader, in Parral, Mexico.
1928—July 17: Gen. Alvaro Obregon, president-elect of Mexico, in San Angel.
1932—May 6: French Pres. Paul Doumer shot by Russian émigré, Pavel Gorgulov, in Paris.
1934—July 25: Austrian Chancellor Engelbert Dollfuss by Nazis, in Vienna.
1935—Sept. 8: Sen. Huey P. Long, former Louisiana governor, shot by Dr. Carl Austin Weiss, son-in-law of political opponent, in Baton Rouge; died Sept. 10.
1940—Aug. 20: Leon Trotsky (Lev Bronstein), exiled Soviet commissar of war, fatally wounded with ice ax by Soviet agent nr. Mexico City.
1948—Jan. 30: Leader of movement for Indian independence Mohandas K. Gandhi (Mahatma) shot by Hindu fanatic in New Delhi. **Sept. 17:** Count Folke Bernadotte, UN mediator for Palestine, by Jewish extremists in Jerusalem.
1951—July 20: Jordanian King Abdullah ibn Hussein. **Oct. 16:** Prime Min. Liaquat Ali Khan of Pakistan shot, in Rawalpindi.
1956—Sept. 21: Pres. Anastasio Somoza of Nicaragua shot in León by a young poet; died Sept. 29.
1957—July 26: Guatemalan Pres. Carlos Castillo Armas, in Guatemala City by one of his guards.
1958—July 14: King Faisal of Iraq, Crown Prince Abdullah, and **July 15**, Prem. Nuri as-Said, by rebels in Baghdad.
1959—Sept. 25: Prime Min. Solomon Bandaranaike of Ceylon (Sri Lanka), by Buddhist monk in Colombo.
1961—Jan. 17: First elected prime min. of Dem. Rep. of the Congo, Patrice Lumumba, in Katanga Prov. by political rivals. **May 30:** Dominican dictator Rafael Trujillo, nr. Ciudad Trujillo.
1963—June 12: Medgar Evers, NAACP's Mississippi field secretary, shot by Byron De La Beckwith in Jackson, MS. **Nov. 2:** Pres. Ngo Dinh Diem of South Vietnam and his brother, Ngo Dinh Nhu, in military coup. **Nov. 22:** U.S. Pres. John F. Kennedy shot while riding in motorcade through downtown Dallas, TX; accused gunman Lee Harvey Oswald murdered by nightclub owner Jack Ruby while awaiting trial.
1965—Jan. 21: Iranian Prem. Hassan Ali Mansour, in Tehran. **Feb. 21:** Malcolm X, Black nationalist leader, shot by 3 men linked to Nation of Islam at New York City rally.
1966—Sept. 6: Prime Min. Hendrik F. Verwoerd of South Africa stabbed to death in parliament at Cape Town.
1968—Apr. 4: Rev. Martin Luther King Jr. fatally shot in Memphis, TN; James Earl Ray convicted of crime. **June 5:** Sen. Robert F. Kennedy (D, NY) shot in Los Angeles; died June 6. Sirhan Sirhan convicted of crime.
1971—Nov. 28: Jordanian Prime Min. Wasfi Tal by Palestinian guerrillas, in Cairo, Egypt.
1973—Mar. 2: U.S. Amb. Cleo A. Noel Jr., U.S. Charge d'Affaires George C. Moore, and Belgian Charge d'Affaires Guy Eid by Palestinian guerrillas, in Khartoum, Sudan. **Dec. 20:** Spanish Prem. Luis Carrero Blanco in car bombing by Basque separatist group ETA, in Madrid.
1974—Aug. 19: U.S. Amb. to Cyprus, Rodger P. Davies, by sniper's bullet in Nicosia.
1975—Feb. 11: Pres. Richard Ratsimandrava of Madagascar shot in Antananarivo. **Mar. 25:** Saudi Arabian King Faisal shot by nephew Prince Musad Abdel Aziz, in Riyadh. **Aug. 15:** Bangladesh Pres. Sheik Mujibur Rahman killed in coup.
1976—Feb. 13: Nigerian head of state, Gen. Murtala Ramat Mohammed, by self-styled young revolutionaries.
1977—Mar. 16: Kamal Jumblatt, Lebanese Druze chieftain, shot nr. Beirut. **Mar. 18:** Rep. of the Congo Pres. Marien Ngouabi shot in Brazzaville.
1978—May 9: Former Italian Prem. Aldo Moro killed by Red Brigades terrorists who had abducted him Mar. 16 in Rome and held him hostage. **July 9:** Former Iraqi Prem. Abdul Razzak al-Naif shot in London.
1979—Aug. 27: Lord Mountbatten and 3 others died from an IRA bomb on his boat off coast of Co. Sligo, Ireland. **Oct. 26:** S. Korean Pres. Park Chung Hee and 6 bodyguards fatally shot by Kim Jae Kyu, head of S. Korean intelligence agency.
1980—Apr. 12: Liberian Pres. William R. Tolbert, in military coup. **Sept. 17:** Former Nicaraguan Pres. Anastasio Somoza Debayle shot in Paraguay.
1981—Oct. 6: Egyptian Pres. Anwar al-Sadat shot by commandos while reviewing military parade in Cairo; 7 others killed.
1982—Sept. 14: Lebanese Pres.-elect Bashir Gemayel killed by bomb in east Beirut.
1983—Aug. 21: Philippine opposition leader Benigno Aquino Jr. shot at Manila Intl. Airport.
1984—Oct. 31: Indian Prime Min. Indira Gandhi shot by 2 Sikh bodyguards in New Delhi.
1986—Feb. 28: Swedish Prime Min. Olof Palme shot on Stockholm street; case officially closed in 2020 when a prosecutor identified the assassin as Stig Engström (died by suicide, 2000).
1987—June 1: Lebanese Prem. Rashid Karami killed when bomb exploded aboard helicopter.
1988—Apr. 16: PLO military chief Khalil Wazir (Abu Jihad) gunned down by Israeli commandos in Tunisia.
1989—Aug. 18: Colombian pres. candidate Luis Carlos Galán killed by Medellín cartel drug traffickers at campaign rally in Bogotá. **Nov. 22:** Lebanese Pres. Rene Moawad killed when bomb exploded next to his motorcade.
1990—Mar. 22: Colombian pres. candidate Bernardo Jaramillo Ossa shot at airport in Bogotá.
1991—May 21: Former Indian Prime Min. Rajiv Gandhi killed by bomb during election rally in Madras.
1992—June 29: Algerian Pres. Mohamed Boudiaf shot in Annaba.
1993—May 1: Sri Lankan Pres. Ranasinghe Premadasa killed by suicide bomber in Colombo.
1994—Apr. 6: Burundian Pres. Cyprien Ntaryamira and Rwandan Pres. Juvénal Habyarimana killed with 8 others when their plane was shot down, precipitating Rwandan genocide.
1995—Nov. 4: Israeli Prime Min. Yitzhak Rabin shot by Jewish extremist at peace rally in Tel Aviv.
1996—Oct. 2: Andrei Lukanov, former Bulgarian prime min., shot outside of Sofia home.
1998—Apr. 26: Guatemalan Roman Catholic Bishop Juan José Gerardi Conedera, human rights champion, beaten to death in Guatemala City.
1999—Apr. 9: Niger Pres. Ibrahim Bare Mainassara killed by dissident soldiers. **Oct. 27:** Armenian Prime Min. Vazgen Sarkissian, with 7 others, shot during session of parliament.
2001—Jan. 16: Dem. Rep. of Congo Pres. Laurent Kabila shot to death by bodyguard at pres. palace in Kinshasa. **June 1:** Nepal's King Birendra, Queen Aiswarya, and 7 other royals fatally shot by Crown Prince Dipendra, who then killed self.
2002—July 6: Afghan Vice Pres. Haji Abdul Qadir shot outside his office in Kabul.
2003—Mar. 12: Serbian Prime Min. Zoran Djindjic shot by paramilitary snipers outside govt. headquarters in Belgrade.
2004—Feb. 13: Former Chechen Pres. Zelimkhan Yandarbiyev killed after car exploded in Qatar. **Mar. 22:** Sheik Ahmed Yassin, spiritual leader of Hamas, by Israeli missile attack in Gaza City. **May 9:** Chechen Pres. Akhmad Kadyrov by bomb at WWII memorial service in Grozny. **Nov. 2:** Filmmaker Theo van Gogh, critic of Islam and great-grandnephew of painter Vincent van Gogh, shot and stabbed by Muslim militant in Amsterdam.
2005—Jan. 4: Baghdad Gov. Ali al-Haidari gunned down by insurgents in Baghdad, Iraq.
2007—Aug. 2: *Oakland Post* editor Chauncey Bailey, who was investigating financial status of Your Black Muslim Bakery, shot in Oakland, CA. **Dec. 27:** Benazir Bhutto, former Pakistani prime min. and first female elected leader of a Muslim state, by bomb and gunman later linked to then-Pres. Pervez Musharraf.
2008—Feb. 12: Imad Mughniyeh, top Hezbollah commander and reputed mastermind of the 1983 bombing of U.S. embassy in Beirut, by car bomb in Damascus, Syria. **Oct. 23:** Ivo Pukanic, editor-in-chief of Croatian political newspaper *Nacional*, killed in Zagreb when bomb exploded nr. his car.
2009—Mar. 2: Guinea-Bissau's longtime Pres. João Bernardo Vieira shot by army troops outside his home in Bissau. **May 31:** Dr. George Tiller, one of the few doctors in the U.S. to perform abortions late in pregnancy, shot to death in his Wichita, KS, church by anti-abortion extremist.
2011—Sept. 20: Burhanuddin Rabbani, leader of Afghanistan's High Peace Council and a former pres., killed in his Kabul home by assassin with explosives hidden in his turban.
2012—Jan. 11: Iranian nuclear scientist Mostafa Ahmadi Roshan killed by car bomb.
2014—Sept. 1: U.S. airstrikes killed Ahmed Abdi Godane, leader of Somalia-based Islamist militant group al-Shabab.
2015—Feb. 27: Boris Y. Nemtsov, Russian opposition leader and former first deputy prime minister, shot near Red Square.
2016—June 16: UK Labour MP Jo Cox shot and stabbed in West Yorkshire by far-right assailant. **Dec. 20:** Turkish police officer shot Russian ambassador to Turkey, Andrei Karlov, in Ankara.
2017—Feb. 13: Kim Jong Nam, half-brother to N. Korean leader Kim Jong Un, killed in chemical nerve agent attack at Kuala Lumpur airport. Two women, charged in attack by Malaysian authorities, blamed coercion by N. Korean agents. **Oct. 16:** Maltese investigative journalist Daphne Caruana Galizia killed in a car bombing.
2018—Feb. 21: Slovak journalist Ján Kuciak and fiancée shot dead in their home. **Oct. 2:** Saudi journalist Jamal Khashoggi, a U.S. resident, murdered inside Saudi consulate in Istanbul, Turkey; U.S., other intelligence agencies pointed to Saudi crown prince Mohammed bin Salman's involvement.
2020—Jan. 3: Iranian Gen. Qassem Soleimani killed by U.S. airstrike in Baghdad.
2021—July 7: Haitian Pres. Jovenel Moïse killed by mercenaries in his home.
2022—July 8: Japanese former prime min. Shinzo Abe fatally shot while campaigning for his party. **July 31:** Egyptian Ayman al-Zawahiri, al-Qaeda cofounder and successor to Osama bin Laden, killed in U.S. drone strike in Kabul, Afghanistan.
2023—Aug. 9: Ecuadorian anticorruption pres. candidate Fernando Villavicencio shot after campaign event in Quito. **Aug. 23:** Russian Yevgeny Prigozhin, chief of Wagner mercenary group and one-time Putin ally, in a plane crash caused by an intentional explosion/sabotage.
2024—July 31: Ismail Haniyeh, Hamas political leader, in an explosion in Iranian capital of Tehran.

MILITARY AFFAIRS

Chairmen of the Joint Chiefs of Staff, 1949-2024

Chairman	Service
Gen. of the Army Omar N. Bradley, USA	8/16/1949-8/15/1953
Adm. Arthur W. Radford, USN	8/15/1953-8/15/1957
Gen. Nathan F. Twining, USAF	8/15/1957-9/30/1960
Gen. Lyman L. Lemnitzer, USA	10/1/1960-9/30/1962
Gen. Maxwell D. Taylor, USA	10/1/1962-7/1/1964
Gen. Earle G. Wheeler, USA	7/3/1964-7/2/1970
Adm. Thomas H. Moorer, USN	7/2/1970-7/1/1974
Gen. George S. Brown, USAF	7/1/1974-6/20/1978
Gen. David C. Jones, USAF	6/21/1978-6/18/1982
Gen. John W. Vessey Jr., USA	6/18/1982-9/30/1985
Adm. William J. Crowe Jr., USN	10/1/1985-9/30/1989
Gen. Colin L. Powell, USA	10/1/1989-9/30/1993
Gen. John M. Shalikashvili, USA	10/25/1993-9/30/1997
Gen. Henry H. Shelton, USA	10/1/1997-9/30/2001
Gen. Richard B. Myers, USAF	10/1/2001-9/30/2005
Gen. Peter Pace, USMC	10/1/2005-9/30/2007
Adm. Michael G. Mullen, USN	10/1/2007-9/30/2011
Gen. Martin E. Dempsey, USA	10/1/2011-9/30/2015
Gen. Joseph F. Dunford Jr., USMC	10/1/2015-9/30/2019
Gen. Mark A. Milley, USA	10/1/2019-9/30/2023
Gen. Charles Q. Brown Jr., USAF	10/1/2023-

Chief Commanding Officers of the U.S. Military

Chairman, Joint Chiefs of Staff: Gen. Charles Q. Brown Jr. (USAF). **Vice Chairman:** Adm. Christopher W. Grady (USN)

Date of rank is date when the individual achieved his or her current rank. While serving in any of these positions, or as commander of a unified or specified combatant command, basic pay is $18,491.70 per month. Officers below hold positions listed as of Oct. 1, 2024.

Army

Chief of Staff (CSA)	Date of rank
George, Randy A.	Aug. 5, 2022
Other Generals	
Brito, Gary M.	Sept. 8, 2022
Cavoli, Christopher G.	Oct. 1, 2020
Fenton, Bryan P.	Aug. 30, 2022
Flynn, Charles A.	June 4, 2021
Kurilla, Michael E.	Apr. 1, 2022
LaCamera, Paul J.	Nov. 18, 2019
Mingus, James J.	Jan. 4, 2024
Poppas, Andrew P.	July 8, 2022
Rainey, James E.	Oct. 4, 2022
Richardson, Laura J.	Oct. 29, 2021
Williams, Darryl A.	June 27, 2022

Marine Corps

Commandant of the Marine Corps (CMC)	Date of rank
Smith, Eric M.	Oct. 8, 2021
Other Generals	
Langley, Michael E.	Aug. 6, 2022
Mahoney, Christopher J.	Nov. 3, 2024

Coast Guard

Commandant, with rank of Admiral	Date of rank
Fagan, Linda L.	June 18, 2021
Vice Commandant, with rank of Admiral	
Lunday, Kevin E.	June 13, 2024

Air Force

Chief of Staff (CSAF or AF/CC)	Date of rank
Allvin, David W.	Nov. 12, 2020
Other Generals	
Brown, Charles Q.	July 26, 2018
Bussiere, Thomas A.	Dec. 7, 2022
Cotton, Anthony J.	Aug. 27, 2021
Guillot, Gregory M	Feb. 4, 2024
Haugh, Timothy D.	Feb. 2, 2024
Hecker, James B.	June 27, 2022
Lamontagne, John D.	Sept. 7, 2024
Richardson, Duke Z.	June 13, 2022
Schneider, Kevin B.	Feb. 9, 2024
Slife, James C.	Dec. 19, 2023
Van Ovost, Jacqueline D.	Aug. 20, 2020
Wilsbach, Kenneth S	July 8, 2020

Navy

Chief of Naval Operations (CNO)	Date of rank
Franchetti, Lisa M. (surface warfare)	Sept. 2, 2022
Other Admirals	
Caudle, Daryl L. (submariner)	Dec. 7, 2021
Grady, Christopher W. (surface warfare)	May 4, 2018
Houston, William J. (submariner)	Jan. 10, 2024
Koehler, Stephen T. (aviator)	Apr. 4, 2024
Kilby, James W. (surface warfare)	Jan. 5, 2024
Munsch, Stuart B. (submariner)	June 27, 2022
Paparo, Samuel J., Jr. (aviator)	May 5, 2021

Space Force

Name	Date of rank
Guetlein, Michael A.	Dec. 21, 2023
Saltzman, B. Chance	Nov. 2, 2022
Whiting, Stephen N.	Jan. 10, 2024

Commanders of the Unified Combatant Commands

U.S. European Command, Stuttgart-Vaihingen, Germany: Gen. Christopher G. Cavoli (U.S. Army)
U.S. Indo-Pacific Command, Honolulu, Hawaii: Adm. Samuel J. Paparo (USN)
U.S. Special Operations Command, MacDill AFB, Florida: Gen. Bryan P. Fenton (U.S. Army)
U.S. Transportation Command, Scott AFB, Illinois: Gen. Jacqueline Van Ovost (USAF)
U.S. Central Command, MacDill AFB, Florida: Gen. Michael E. Kurilla (U.S. Army)
U.S. Southern Command, Doral, Florida: Gen. Laura J. Richardson (U.S. Army)
U.S. Northern Command, Peterson AFB, Colorado: Gen. Gregory M. Guillot (USAF)
U.S. Strategic Command, Offutt AFB, Nebraska: Gen. Anthony J. Cotton (USAF)
U.S. Africa Command, Kelley Barracks, Stuttgart, Germany: Gen. Michael E. Langley (USMC)
U.S. Cyber Command, Fort George G. Meade, Maryland: Gen. Timothy D. Haugh (USAF)
U.S. Space Command, Peterson AFB, Colorado: Gen. Stephen M. Whiting (USSF)

North Atlantic Treaty Organization (NATO) International Commands

NATO Headquarters: Chairman, NATO Military Committee: Admiral Rob Bauer (Royal Netherlands Navy)

Strategic Commands:
- Allied Command Operations (ACO): Gen. Christopher G. Cavoli (U.S. Army), Supreme Allied Commander Europe
- Allied Command Transformation (ACT): Gen. Philippe Lavigne (French Air and Space Force), Supreme Allied Commander Transformation

ACO Operational Level Commands:
- Joint Force Command Brunssum (JFC Brunssum): Gen. Guglielmo Luigi Miglietta (Italian Army), Commander
- Joint Force Command Naples (JFC Naples): Adm. Stuart B. Munsch (USN), Commander
- Joint Force Command Norfolk (JFC Norfolk): Vice Adm. Douglas G. Perry (USN), Commander

Directors of the Central Intelligence Agency, 1946-2024

In 1942, Pres. Franklin D. Roosevelt established the Office of Strategic Services (OSS); it was disbanded in 1945. In 1946, Pres. Harry Truman established the Central Intelligence Group (CIG) to operate under the National Intelligence Authority (NIA). A 1947 law replaced the NIA with the National Security Council (NSC) and the CIG with the Central Intelligence Agency (CIA).

Director	Served	Appointed by President
Adm. Sidney W. Souers	1946	Truman
Gen. Hoyt S. Vandenberg	1946-1947	Truman
Adm. Roscoe H. Hillenkoetter	1947-1950	Truman
Gen. Walter Bedell Smith	1950-1953	Truman
Allen W. Dulles	1953-1961	Eisenhower
John A. McCone	1961-1965	Kennedy
Adm. William F. Raborn Jr.	1965-1966	Johnson, L. B.
Richard Helms	1966-1973	Johnson, L. B.
James R. Schlesinger	1973	Nixon
William E. Colby	1973-1976	Nixon
George H. W. Bush	1976-1977	Ford
Adm. Stansfield Turner	1977-1981	Carter
William J. Casey	1981-1987	Reagan
William H. Webster	1987-1991	Reagan
Robert M. Gates	1991-1993	Bush, G. H. W.
R. James Woolsey	1993-1995	Clinton
John M. Deutch	1995-1996	Clinton
George J. Tenet	1997-2004	Clinton
Porter Goss	2004-2006	Bush, G. W.
Gen. Michael V. Hayden	2006-2009	Bush, G. W.
Leon E. Panetta	2009-2011	Obama
Gen. David H. Petraeus	2011-2012	Obama
John O. Brennan	2013-2017	Obama
Michael R. Pompeo	2017-2018	Trump
Gina Haspel	2018-2021	Trump
William J. Burns	2021-	Biden

U.S. Military Personnel Strength on Active Duty Worldwide, 2024

Source: U.S. Dept. of Defense
(as of Mar. 31, 2024)

Area	Personnel
TOTAL WORLDWIDE[1]	**1,288,549**
U.S., TERRITORIES, AND SPEC. LOCATIONS	
Regional total	**1,126,733**
OTHER WESTERN HEMISPHERE	
The Bahamas	63
Brazil	61
Canada	152
Colombia	64
Cuba (Guantánamo)	616
El Salvador	54
Haiti	54
Honduras	365
Mexico	88
Regional total	**1,848**
SUB-SAHARAN AFRICA	
Djibouti	406
Kenya	72
Somalia	60
Regional total	**1,075**
EAST ASIA AND PACIFIC	
Australia	732
British Indian Ocean Territory	223
China	64
Japan	54,774
Korea, South	24,234
Palau	83
Philippines	310
Singapore	229
Thailand	111
Regional total	**81,015**
NORTH AFRICA, NEAR EAST, AND SOUTH ASIA	
Bahrain	3,479
Egypt	176
Israel	115
Jordan	120
Kuwait	533
Pakistan	74
Qatar	303
Saudi Arabia	258
United Arab Emirates	177
Regional total	**5,474**
FORMER SOVIET UNION	
Russia	41
Regional total	**208**
EUROPE	
Belgium	1,106
France	81
Germany	35,068
Greece	402
Greenland	135
Hungary	84
Italy	12,375
Netherlands	418
Norway	1,438
Poland	299
Portugal	247
Romania	139
Spain	3,292
Turkey (Türkiye)	1,690
United Kingdom	10,058
Regional total	**67,203**

Note: Most countries and areas with fewer than 100 assigned U.S. military members not listed; regional totals include personnel stationed in countries and areas not shown. (1) Includes other personnel; some may be undistributed. Does not include all personnel on temporary duty or deployed on contingency operations.

U.S. Military Personnel on Active Duty in U.S. States and Territories, 2024

Source: U.S. Dept. of Defense
(as of Mar. 31, 2024)

State/area	Active personnel	Reserve personnel
Alabama	8,518	18,325
Alaska	20,784	4,528
Arizona	16,819	14,393
Arkansas	3,711	10,435
California	157,367	53,015
Colorado	36,111	13,470
Connecticut	6,510	6,388
Delaware	3,397	4,721
Dist. of Columbia	11,096	3,470
Florida	66,039	37,717
Georgia	63,391	26,710
Hawaii	44,423	9,517
Idaho	3,412	5,128
Illinois	17,197	22,211
Indiana	951	16,297
Iowa	202	10,738
Kansas	19,769	9,699
Kentucky	30,755	12,159
Louisiana	14,403	15,996
Maine	824	3,259
Maryland	28,059	18,017
Massachusetts	3,474	13,564
Michigan	1,810	13,691
Minnesota	567	17,090
Mississippi	11,363	14,233
Missouri	13,632	16,555
Montana	3,335	3,933
Nebraska	6,329	5,778
Nevada	11,687	7,720
New Hampshire	1,244	3,941
New Jersey	7,843	16,203
New Mexico	13,338	4,582
New York	18,262	28,680
North Carolina	91,077	20,073
North Dakota	7,065	4,401
Ohio	6,694	24,969
Oklahoma	19,084	12,950
Oregon	1,493	8,146
Pennsylvania	2,317	25,522
Rhode Island	4,141	4,355
South Carolina	32,897	17,703
South Dakota	3,226	4,476
Tennessee	2,364	17,625
Texas	111,005	55,676
Utah	4,376	11,412
Vermont	125	2,940
Virginia	126,145	25,424
Washington	56,572	16,766
West Virginia	183	7,248
Wisconsin	972	12,424
Wyoming	3,053	2,896
Unknown[1]	4	501
U.S. total[2]	**1,119,432**	**737,687**
American Samoa	4	14
Guam	6,593	929
N. Mariana Isls.	15	3
Puerto Rico	671	4,249
U.S. Virgin Isls.	31	102
Wake Island	4	0
Territorial total	**7,318**	**5,297**

(1) Includes other personnel; some may be undistributed. (2) Includes Armed Forces (AF) Europe and AF Pacific—deployed primarily at sea or not at fixed-duty stations (17 active duty, 17 reserve).

U.S. Army Personnel on Active Duty, 1940-2024

Source: Dept. of the Army, U.S. Dept. of Defense
(as of midyear, except where noted)

Date	Total strength[1]	Commissioned officers			Warrant officers[3]		Enlisted personnel		
		Total	Male	Female[2]	Male	Female	Total	Male	Female
1940	267,767	17,563	16,624	939	763	—	249,441	249,441	—
1942	3,074,184	203,137	190,662	12,475	3,285	—	2,867,762	2,867,762	—
1943	6,993,102	557,657	521,435	36,222	21,919	—	6,413,526	6,358,200	55,325
1944	7,992,868	740,077	692,351	47,726	36,893	10	7,215,888	7,144,601	71,287
1945	8,266,373	835,403	772,511	62,892	56,216	44	7,374,710	7,283,930	90,780
1946	1,889,690	257,300	240,658	16,642	9,826	18	1,622,546	1,605,847	16,699
1950	591,487	67,784	63,375	4,409	4,760	22	518,921	512,370	6,551
1960	871,348	91,056	86,832	4,224	10,141	39	770,112	761,833	8,279
1965	967,049	101,812	98,029	3,783	10,285	23	854,929	846,409	8,520
1970	1,319,735	143,704	138,469	5,235	23,005	13	1,153,013	1,141,537	11,476
1975	781,316	89,756	85,184	4,572	13,214	22	678,324	640,621	37,703
1980 (Sept. 30)	772,661	85,339	77,843	7,496	13,265	113	673,944	612,593	61,351
1990 (Mar. 31)	746,220	91,330	79,520	11,810	15,177	470	639,713	567,015	72,698
2000	471,633	66,344	56,391	9,953	10,608	781	393,900	333,947	59,953
2005 (Sept. 30)	492,728	69,174	57,675	11,499	11,506	976	406,923	346,194	57,354
2010 (Sept. 30)	566,045	78,588	64,952	13,636	14,106	1,434	467,248	406,871	60,377
2015 (Dec. 31)	482,264	78,586	64,223	14,363	13,577	1,421	384,301	331,620	52,681
2018	468,331	77,850	63,184	14,666	12,987	1,378	372,667	319,270	53,397
2019	472,209	78,883	63,733	15,150	12,905	1,395	375,600	321,500	54,100
2020	476,306	78,739	63,388	15,351	12,818	1,433	379,993	323,683	56,310
2021	486,141	79,795	63,878	15,917	13,171	1,457	387,170	329,761	57,409
2022	465,239	79,204	63,141	16,063	13,434	1,479	366,655	312,765	53,890
2023 (July)	452,689	77,814	61,638	16,176	13,823	1,528	354,980	302,426	52,554
2024	443,444	77,264	60,911	16,353	14,087	1,564	347,212	295,015	52,197

— = Not applicable. **Note:** Represents strength of active Army, including Philippine Scouts (1940-46), ret. Regular Army personnel on extended active duty, and National Guard and Reserve personnel on extended active duty; excl. those (e.g., U.S. Military Academy cadets, contract surgeons, and National Guard and Reserve personnel) not on extended active duty. (1) Includes categories not listed, e.g., West Point cadets. Data for 1940-46 include personnel in the Army Air Forces and its predecessors (Air Service and Air Corps). (2) Includes Army Nurse Corps for all years, Women's Army Corps (1942-78), and Medical Specialists Corps (1949 and after). (3) Act of Congress approved Apr. 27, 1926, directed the appointment as warrant officers of field clerks still in active service. Includes flight officers as follows: 1943, 5,700; 1944, 13,615; 1945, 31,117; 1946, 2,580.

U.S. Navy Personnel on Active Duty, 1940-2024

Source: U.S. Dept. of Defense
(as of midyear, except where noted)

Year	Officers	Nurses[1]	Enlisted	Officer candi-dates[1]	Total[2]	Year	Officers	Nurses[1]	Enlisted	Officer candi-dates[1]	Total[2]
1940	13,162	442	144,824	2,569	160,997	2013	54,062	—	263,647	—	322,242
1945	320,293	11,086	2,988,207	61,231	3,380,817	2014	54,852	—	265,622	—	323,792
1950	42,687	1,964	331,860	5,037	381,538	2015	54,770	—	268,408	—	326,504
1960	67,456	2,103	544,040	4,385	617,984	2016	54,973	—	271,100	—	330,556
1970	78,488	2,273	605,899	6,000	692,660	2017	55,047	—	264,404	—	323,938
1980	63,100	—	464,100	—	527,200	2018	55,401	—	268,340	—	328,244
1990 (Sept.)	74,429	—	530,133	—	604,562	2019	55,475	—	275,474	—	335,444
1995 (May)	61,075	—	402,626	—	463,701	2020	56,248	—	279,147	—	339,782
2000 (Oct.)	53,698	—	320,212	—	373,910	2021	56,698	—	288,547	—	349,769
2005	54,039	—	305,368	—	363,858	2022	57,105	—	282,481	—	344,022
2010	53,071	—	273,609	—	330,065	2023	56,373	—	272,729	—	333,544
2012	53,799	—	262,975	—	321,300	2024	55,793	—	268,521	—	328,774

— = Not applicable. (1) Starting in 1980, "Nurses" are included with "Officers," and "Officer candidates" are included with "Enlisted." (2) May include categories not shown, e.g., midshipmen.

U.S. Air Force Personnel on Active Duty, 1918-2024

Source: U.S. Dept. of Defense
(as of midyear)

Year	Total	Year	Total	Year	Total	Year	Total	Year	Total	Year	Total
1918	195,023	1944	2,372,292	1995	400,051	2006	352,620	2013	333,506	2019	331,332
1920	9,050	1945	2,282,259	2000	357,777	2007	340,596	2014	328,791	2020	333,559
1930	13,531	1950	411,277	2001	351,935	2008	328,771	2015	312,195	2021	336,329
1940	51,165	1960	814,213	2002	369,721	2009	333,423	2016	315,786	2022	333,455
1941	152,125	1970	791,078	2003	373,116	2010	337,505	2017	322,559	2023	329,286
1942	764,415	1980	557,969	2004	379,887	2011	333,729	2018	325,222	2024	326,065
1943	2,197,114	1990	535,233	2005	358,705	2012	333,487				

Note: Prior to 1950, data are for U.S. Army Air Corps and Air Service of the Signal Corps. For 2021 and on, data includes Space Force personnel.

U.S. Marine Corps Personnel on Active Duty, 1940-2024

Source: U.S. Dept. of Defense
(as of midyear)

Year	Officers	Enlisted	Total	Year	Officers	Enlisted	Total	Year	Officers	Enlisted	Total
1940	1,800	26,545	28,345	2000	17,897	154,744	172,641	2017	21,296	163,234	184,530
1945	37,067	437,613	474,680	2005	19,118	159,113	178,231	2018	21,582	163,637	185,219
1950	7,254	67,025	74,279	2010	21,680	179,446	201,126	2019	21,769	165,045	186,814
1960	16,203	154,418	170,621	2012	22,380	174,748	197,128	2020	21,941	160,788	182,729
1970	24,941	234,796	259,737	2013	22,045	173,048	195,093	2021	22,062	158,074	180,136
1980	18,198	170,271	188,469	2014	21,507	169,327	190,834	2022	21,997	152,487	174,484
1990	19,958	176,694	196,652	2015	21,144	163,144	184,587	2023	21,691	147,830	169,521
1995	18,017	153,929	171,946	2016	20,827	162,543	183,370	2024	21,499	146,533	168,032

U.S. Coast Guard Personnel on Active Duty, 1970-2024

Source: U.S. Dept. of Defense
(as of midyear, except where noted)

Year	Officers	Cadets	Enlisted	Total	Year	Officers	Cadets	Enlisted	Total
1970	5,512	653	31,524	37,689	2014	8,572	676	31,233	40,481
1980	6,463	877	32,041	39,381	2015	8,550	623	30,896	40,069
1985	6,775	733	31,087	38,595	2016	8,550	623	30,896	40,069
1990	6,475	820	29,860	37,308	2017	8,483	623	32,015	41,121
1995	7,489	841	28,401	36,731	2018	8,578	807	32,719	42,104
2000	7,154	863	27,695	35,712	2019	8,361	809	32,406	41,576
2005	7,908	1,006	31,900	40,814	2020	9,144	814	31,791	41,749
2010	8,678	744	33,713	43,135	2021	9,031	801	31,705	41,537
2011	8,659	1,053	33,615	43,327	2022	8,941	789	30,823	40,553
2012 (Mar.)	8,316	988	33,758	43,062	2023	9,023	828	29,720	39,571
2013 (Jan.)	8,376	1,010	32,971	42,357	2024	9,166	851	30,341	40,358

Women in the U.S. Armed Forces

Source: U.S. Dept. of Defense; U.S. Census Bureau, U.S. Dept. of Commerce; U.S. Coast Guard, U.S. Dept. of Homeland Security; U.S. Dept. of Veterans Affairs

All enlisted jobs were opened to women when the draft ended June 30, 1973. Admission to service academies began in 1976. Under rules instituted in 1993, women began to fly combat aircraft and serve aboard warships. By the mid-1990s, 80% of all jobs and more than 90% of all career fields had been opened to women. A woman first achieved the rank of four-star general in 2009. In 2010, the Navy removed its ban on women serving on submarine crews. The Pentagon in 2013 lifted its ban on women serving in direct ground combat units. In 2015, the first two women graduated from the Army's Ranger School. Adm. Linda Fagan was sworn in as commandant of the Coast Guard in June 2022, making her the first woman to lead a U.S. military branch. Adm. Lisa Franchetti became chief of naval operations Nov. 2, 2023; the first woman to hold the post, she was also the first to serve on the Joint Chiefs of Staff.

Women Active Duty Troops, 2024[1]

Service	% women
Army	16.0%
Navy	21.1
Marines	9.8
Air Force (incl. Space Force)	21.6
Coast Guard (May 2024)	16.8

Women on Active Duty, All DOD[2] Services, 1973-2024[3]

Year	% women	Year	% women
1973	2.5%	2017	16.3%
1981	8.9	2018	16.6
1987	10.2	2019	17.0
1993	11.6	2020	17.3
2000	14.4	2021	17.4
2005	14.6	2022	17.6
2010	14.5	2023	17.8
2015	15.6	2024 (June)	17.9

Women Veterans by Period of Service, 2024

Period of service	% of women vets[4]
Gulf War era[5]	68.2%
Vietnam era	12.0
Korean War	1.1
World War II	0.2
Peacetime only	20.0

Note: (1) As of 2024, except where noted. (2) Does not include Coast Guard. (3) As of Sept. 30 for all years, except where noted. (4) Projected pop. Some women served in multiple periods. (5) Includes women who served both pre- and post-9/11 but not in peacetime only.

African American Service in U.S. Wars

Source: U.S. Dept. of Defense; U.S. Census Bureau, U.S. Dept. of Commerce

American Revolution. About 5,000 served in the Continental Army, mostly in integrated units, some in all-black combat units.

Civil War. Some 180,000 served in 163 units of the Union Army's U.S. Colored Troops, and 200,000 worked in service units—10% of the Union Army in all; about 37,000 died, 31,000 wounded.

World War I. 350,000-400,000 served in the armed forces, 100,000 in France. Some 40,000 fought.

World War II. Some 1 mil served in the armed forces—8% of all troops—mostly in Army service units; all-black fighter and bomber Army Air Force units and infantry divisions gave distinguished service.

Korean War. More than 600,000 served in the military; 3,075 lost their lives in combat. By 1954, armed forces were completely desegregated.

Vietnam War. 274,937 served in the armed forces (1965-74)—9.8% of all troops; 7,243 were killed in combat.

Persian Gulf War. About 104,000 served in the Kuwaiti theater—20% of all U.S. troops; 66 died in combat.

Operation Enduring Freedom/Freedom's Sentinel. 204 military deaths and 1,458 wounded in Afghanistan and elsewhere.

Operation Iraqi Freedom/Operation New Dawn/Operation Inherent Resolve. 469 military deaths and 2,809 wounded.

U.S. Military Personnel by Race and Ethnicity, 2022

Source: *2022 Demographics: Profile of the Military Community*, U.S. Dept. of Defense

	Active-duty personnel					Selected reserve personnel				
	Hispanic or Latino		Not Hispanic or Latino			Hispanic or Latino		Not Hispanic or Latino		
Race	No.	%	No.	%	Total	No.	%	No.	%	Total
American Indian/AK Native	3,964	28.2	10,095	71.8	14,059	1,142	19.0	4,856	81.0	5,998
Asian	2,204	3.3	65,250	96.7	67,454	655	1.8	36,689	98.2	37,344
Black or African American	14,149	6.3	212,144	93.7	226,293	5,467	4.4	120,177	95.6	125,644
Native Hawaiian/other Pac. Isl.	1,630	10.4	14,107	89.6	15,737	989	14.3	5,940	85.7	6,929
White	189,118	21.1	708,222	78.9	897,340	99,507	17.7	463,859	82.3	563,366
Multi-racial[1]	6,700	16.4	34,261	83.6	40,961	2,005	13.5	12,800	86.5	14,805
Unknown	22,829	53.2	20,047	46.8	42,876	9,642	51.2	9,182	48.8	18,824
Total	**240,594**	**18.4**	**1,064,126**	**81.6**	**1,304,720**	**119,407**	**15.4**	**653,503**	**84.6**	**772,910**

Note: As of Sept. Percentages may not add up to 100% due to rounding. (1) The Army and Army Reserve do not report "multi-racial."

U.S. Military Reserve Personnel by Service Branch, 2022

Source: *2022 Demographics: Profile of the Military Community*, U.S. Dept. of Defense

Reserve component	Enlisted	Officers	Total	Pct. of total reserve personnel
Army National Guard	282,764	46,941	329,705	42.7%
Army Reserve	137,184	38,987	176,171	22.8
Navy Reserve	41,496	13,728	55,224	7.1
Marine Corps Reserve	28,216	4,383	32,599	4.2
Air National Guard	88,731	16,253	104,984	13.6
Air Force Reserve	53,060	14,988	68,048	8.8
Total Dept. of Defense	**631,451**	**135,280**	**766,731**	**99.2**
Coast Guard Reserve	5,121	1,058	6,179	0.8
Total Selected Reserve	**636,572**	**136,338**	**772,910**	**100.0**

Note: As of Sept. Percentages may not add up to 100% due to rounding.

Monthly Military Pay Scale, 2024

Source: U.S. Dept. of Defense

(effective Jan. 1, 2024; salaries rounded to nearest dollar)

	Cumulative years of service														
	<2	2	3	4	6	8	10	12	14	16	18	20	22	24	26
Commissioned officers															
O-10	NA	NA	NA	NA	NA	NA	NA	NA	NA	NA	NA	18,492	18,492	18,492	18,492
O-9	NA	NA	NA	NA	NA	NA	NA	NA	NA	NA	NA	18,096	18,357	18,492	18,492
O-8	12,804	13,224	13,502	13,579	13,927	14,507	14,642	15,193	15,351	15,826	16,513	17,146	17,569	17,569	17,569
O-7	10,639	11,133	11,362	11,544	11,873	12,198	12,574	12,949	13,325	14,507	15,504	15,504	15,504	15,504	15,584
O-6	8,068	8,863	9,445	9,445	9,481	9,887	9,941	9,941	10,506	11,505	12,091	12,677	13,011	13,349	14,003
O-5	6,726	7,577	8,101	8,200	8,527	8,723	9,153	9,470	9,878	10,502	10,799	11,093	11,427	11,427	11,427
O-4	5,803	6,717	7,166	7,265	7,682	8,128	8,684	9,116	9,417	9,590	9,689	9,689	9,689	9,689	9,689
O-3	5,102	5,784	6,242	6,806	7,133	7,491	7,722	8,102	8,301	8,301	8,301	8,301	8,301	8,301	8,301
O-2	4,409	5,021	5,783	5,978	6,101	6,101	6,101	6,101	6,101	6,101	6,101	6,101	6,101	6,101	6,101
O-1	3,826	3,983	4,815	4,815	4,815	4,815	4,815	4,815	4,815	4,815	4,815	4,815	4,815	4,815	4,815
Commisioned officers with over 4 years of active duty service as enlisted member or warrant officer															
O-3E	NA	NA	NA	6,806	7,133	7,491	7,722	8,102	8,423	8,608	8,859	8,859	8,859	8,859	8,859
O-2E	NA	NA	NA	5,978	6,101	6,295	6,623	6,877	7,065	7,065	7,065	7,065	7,065	7,065	7,065
O-1E	NA	NA	NA	4,815	5,141	5,331	5,526	5,717	5,978	5,978	5,978	5,978	5,978	5,978	5,978
Warrant officers															
W-5	NA	NA	NA	NA	NA	NA	NA	NA	NA	NA	NA	9,376	9,851	10,206	10,597
W-4	5,273	5,672	5,834	5,995	6,271	6,544	6,820	7,235	7,600	7,947	8,231	8,508	8,915	9,249	9,630
W-3	4,816	5,016	5,222	5,289	5,504	5,929	6,371	6,579	6,820	7,067	7,514	7,815	7,995	8,186	8,447
W-2	4,261	4,664	4,788	4,873	5,149	5,579	5,792	6,001	6,257	6,458	6,639	6,856	6,999	7,112	7,112
W-1	3,740	4,143	4,251	4,480	4,750	5,148	5,334	5,595	5,851	6,052	6,238	6,463	6,463	6,463	6,463
Enlisted members															
E-9	NA	NA	NA	NA	NA	NA	6,371	6,515	6,697	6,911	7,127	7,472	7,765	8,073	8,544
E-8	NA	NA	NA	NA	NA	5,215	5,446	5,588	5,759	5,945	6,279	6,449	6,737	6,897	7,291
E-7	3,625	3,956	4,108	4,308	4,466	4,735	4,886	5,155	5,379	5,532	5,695	5,758	5,970	6,083	6,516
E-6	3,136	3,451	3,603	3,751	3,905	4,253	4,388	4,650	4,730	4,788	4,856	4,856	4,856	4,856	4,856
E-5	2,872	3,066	3,214	3,366	3,602	3,849	4,052	4,076	4,076	4,076	4,076	4,076	4,076	4,076	4,076
E-4	2,634	2,768	2,918	3,066	3,197	3,197	3,197	3,197	3,197	3,197	3,197	3,197	3,197	3,197	3,197
E-3	2,378	2,527	2,680	2,680	2,680	2,680	2,680	2,680	2,680	2,680	2,680	2,680	2,680	2,680	2,680
E-2	2,261	2,261	2,261	2,261	2,261	2,261	2,261	2,261	2,261	2,261	2,261	2,261	2,261	2,261	2,261
E-1[1]	2,017	2,017	2,017	2,017	2,017	2,017	2,017	2,017	2,017	2,017	2,017	2,017	2,017	2,017	2,017

NA = Not applicable. **Note:** Basic pay rate for Academy cadets/midshipmen and ROTC members/applicants is $1,340. See Dept. of Defense Financial Management Regulations for details on pay-scale limitations and eligibility requirements. (1) Applicable to E-1 with 4 months or more of active duty. Basic pay for an E-1 with less than 4 months of active duty is $1,865.

U.S. Veteran Population, 2024

Source: U.S. Dept. of Veterans Affairs
(projected population, in thousands, as of Sept. 30)

Period of service	Vet. pop.
Total peacetime veterans[1]	**3,840**
Service between Vietnam War era and Gulf War era	2,768
Service between Korean War and Vietnam War era	1,045
Service between WWII and Korean War	26
Total wartime veterans[2]	**14,077**
Total World War II[3]	84
WWII only	73
Total Korean War[3]	660
Korean War with no other wartime service	589
Korean War with service in WWII	8
Total Vietnam War era[3]	5,422
Vietnam War era with no other wartime service	4,997
Vietnam War era with service in Korea	60
Vietnam War era with service in Korea and WWII	4
Total Gulf War era[3]	8,346
Gulf War era pre-9/11 with service in Vietnam era	250
Gulf War era pre-9/11, post-9/11, and with service in Vietnam War era	55
Gulf War era pre-9/11 only	2,582
Gulf War era pre-9/11 and post-9/11	1,535
Gulf War era post-9/11 only	3,868
TOTAL VETERANS IN CIVILIAN LIFE	**17,917**

Note: Figures are for U.S. veterans worldwide. Includes those who served on active duty in Army, Navy, Air Force, Marines, Coast Guard, uniformed Public Health Service and NOAA, and reservists called to federal active duty. According to Dept. of Veterans Affairs projections, as of Sept. 30 there were 216 living veterans who served prior to WWII. Excludes those dishonorably discharged, those whose only active duty was training, and those currently on active duty. (1) Veterans with both wartime and peacetime service are counted only as "wartime veterans." (2) Veterans serving in more than one period are counted only once in total. (3) Total includes veterans who also served in other periods.

Outlays for Individual Payments to Veterans, 1940-2025

Source: White House Office of Management and Budget
(in millions of dollars)

Year	Total	Compensation	Pensions	Hospital, medical	Education	Insurance & burial
1940	$574	$244	$185	$69	—	$76
1950	8,613	1,533	476	764	$2,739	3,101
1960	5,300	2,049	1,263	931	392	665
1970	8,883	2,980	2,255	1,798	1,002	848
1980	21,153	7,446	3,585	6,513	2,421	1,188
1990	28,801	10,735	3,594	12,281	791	1,400
2000	46,835	20,777	2,969	20,090	1,636	1,363
2010	106,454	43,498	4,359	48,506	8,773	1,318
2011	122,524	52,780	4,664	52,681	11,112	1,287
2012	119,544	50,058	4,537	52,972	10,734	1,243
2013	134,083	59,393	5,173	55,067	13,220	1,230
2014	143,412	64,360	5,251	58,906	13,729	1,166
2015	$153,506	$69,725	$5,299	$63,652	$13,605	$1,225
2016	167,046	79,907	5,824	65,810	14,579	926
2017	167,399	79,839	5,505	67,949	13,520	586
2018	170,949	79,986	4,796	72,899	12,703	565
2019	194,241	95,599	4,940	79,661	13,433	608
2020	214,200	105,615	4,751	90,330	13,120	384
2021	230,039	112,134	4,156	101,018	12,245	486
2022	264,668	135,658	4,114	112,412	12,071	413
2023	291,009	148,428	3,513	126,839	12,659	–430
2024*	326,074	161,213	2,990	147,843	13,401	627
2025*	354,319	187,132	3,013	147,547	16,053	574

— = Not available. * = Estimate. **Note:** Compensation is service-connected; pension is not.

Race and Ethnicity of U.S. Veterans, 2022

Source: U.S. Census Bureau, American Community Survey, 2022

Age/gender		White, not Hispanic or Latino	Black or African-American	Amer. Ind. or AK Native	Asian	Native Hawaiian or other Pac. Isl.	Some other race	Two or more races	Hispanic or Latino
Male	18 to 34	672,378	146,641	11,857	41,200	4,223	60,779	135,309	191,949
	35 to 54	2,084,347	442,167	29,632	88,974	9,328	134,714	351,519	422,486
	55 to 64	1,780,890	423,940	21,735	45,432	6,506	74,057	196,061	212,332
	65 to 74	2,607,397	406,834	25,697	49,398	6,238	69,877	212,921	220,590
	75 and over	3,567,282	248,013	16,768	62,325	3,935	54,921	166,095	184,602
Female	18 to 34	118,717	48,554	3,032	11,337	1,367	14,374	34,790	46,812
	35 to 54	345,095	142,763	7,196	19,663	2,517	24,498	68,418	73,745
	55 to 64	247,695	95,233	3,487	6,520	653	11,090	30,200	26,434
	65 to 74	185,291	48,039	1,989	5,463	366	5,180	17,924	16,181
	75 and over	105,976	11,851	1,186	2,937	468	1,375	4,903	5,701

Employment Status of Veterans With Service-Connected Disabilities, 2023

Source: Bureau of Labor Statistics, U.S. Dept. of Labor; as of Aug. 2023

Veteran status, presence of disability, and period of service	Employed (thous.)			Unemployed (thous.)			Unemployment rate (%)			Not in labor force (thous.)		
	Total	Men	Women	Total	Men	Women	Total	Men	Women	Total	Men	Women
Total veterans	**8,268**	**7,221**	**1,046**	**335**	**270**	**65**	**3.9%**	**3.6%**	**5.9%**	**9,276**	**8,345**	**931**
With service-connected disability	2,475	2,111	364	157	106	51	6.0	4.8	12.3	2,646	2,369	276
Without service-connected disability	5,390	4,745	645	173	159	14	3.1	3.2	2.1	6,180	5,569	611
Gulf War era, total	5,922	5,048	874	252	196	56	4.1	3.7	6.0	1,844	1,402	443
With service-connected disability	2,126	1,796	330	140	92	49	6.2	4.9	12.9	1,003	791	212
Without service-connected disability	3,516	3,004	512	106	99	7	2.9	3.2	1.4	730	525	205
Gulf War era II	3,881	3,281	600	196	154	42	4.8	4.5	6.5	1,030	737	293
With service-connected disability	1,614	1,331	283	110	68	42	6.4	4.9	12.8	638	495	143
Without service-connected disability	2,049	1,755	294	86	86	NA	4.0	4.7	NA	324	197	128
Gulf War era I	2,041	1,767	274	56	42	14	2.7	2.3	4.9	814	665	150
With service-connected disability	512	465	47	30	23	7	5.6	4.8	NA	365	296	69
Without service-connected disability	1,467	1,249	218	21	14	7	1.4	1.1	3.1	405	328	77
WWII, Korean War, and Vietnam era	709	686	23	29	29	NA	3.9	4.0	NA	5,204	4,974	229
With service-connected disability	146	142	4	5	5	NA	3.6	3.7	NA	1,271	1,245	26
Without service-connected disability	540	521	18	23	23	NA	4.1	4.3	NA	3,685	3,491	194
Other service periods	1,637	1,487	150	55	45	10	3.3	3.0	6.0	2,228	1,969	259
With service-connected disability	203	173	3	12	9	3	5.5	5.1	NA	372	334	38
Without service-connected disability	1,334	1,220	115	43	36	7	3.1	2.9	5.8	1,765	1,553	212

NA = Not available. **Note:** Veterans in survey were on active duty in the U.S. Armed Forces during these periods of service: Gulf War era II (Sept. 2001-present), Gulf War era I (Aug. 1990-Aug. 2001), Vietnam era (Aug. 1964-Apr. 1975), Korean War (July 1950-Jan. 1955), World War II (Dec. 1941-Dec. 1946), and other service periods. Veterans who served in more than one wartime period are classified in the most recent period only. A service-connected disability is a health condition or impairment caused or made worse by military service.

U.S. Foreign Military Sales, 1950-2022

Source: Defense Security Cooperation Agency (DSCA), Dept. of Defense

Listed are the top 50 foreign government purchasers of military articles, services, and/or training in fiscal years 1950-2022 through the DSCA-administered Foreign Military Sales (FMS) program for the Dept. of Defense. Transfers may in some cases be completed through grants/leases.

(in millions)

	1950-2022	2021	2022		1950-2022	2021	2022
Saudi Arabia	$164,229.4	$1,564.8	$1,512.3	Iran	$10,715.4	$0.0	$0.0
Israel	53,483.7	1,478.5	2,428.3	Belgium	10,494.2	109.2	61.6
Japan	52,957.8	3,903.5	2,803.5	Switzerland	10,061.9	36.9	5,698.6
Taiwan	49,683.0	2,678.0	2,057.1	Morocco	9,888.6	53.5	–9.5
Australia	45,795.6	937.5	6,668.6	Lebanon	9,859.2	67.1	144.1
South Korea	44,418.7	1,902.0	947.3	Norway	9,460.5	36.8	162.5
Egypt	43,625.9	2,027.9	1,492.1	Jordan	9,385.0	153.6	1,731.6
Qatar	39,401.3	–68.4	5.4	Thailand	8,878.5	297.8	83.3
United Kingdom	34,899.3	2,861.1	869.0	France	8,877.2	1,516.4	665.1
United Arab Emirates	29,634.7	359.7	203.3	Bahrain	5,910.1	452.0	170.2
Iraq	26,319.2	386.4	449.9	Italy	5,855.9	935.6	114.8
Turkey	21,581.0	256.9	196.6	Denmark	4,632.3	35.2	41.8
Germany	20,764.2	1,097.4	440.0	Ukraine	4,093.8	333.1	2,119.4
Kuwait	20,763.6	1,256.7	240.2	Romania	3,812.1	986.4	103.8
Finland	17,243.4	90.6	11,830.6	Kosovo	3,573.3	22.4	16.2
Poland	16,841.2	126.6	4,825.8	Oman	3,519.4	–41.6	–4.5
Afghanistan	16,428.2	1,263.9	–553.2	Colombia	3,154.2	71.6	24.1
Greece	15,741.8	314.6	728.6	Indonesia	2,890.1	27.6	75.9
Netherlands	15,258.6	522.2	83.3	Armenia	2,747.0	0.0	1.3
Canada	14,711.6	2,555.8	381.4	Brazil	2,739.9	101.7	21.5
Seychelles	14,279.1	0.0	0.3	Philippines	2,487.4	90.3	134.7
India	13,394.9	320.2	–254.0	Benin	2,431.8	0.0	0.0
Spain	12,254.2	186.5	199.1	Slovakia	2,425.0	119.9	43.4
Singapore	11,853.5	24.8	800.6	Chile	2,021.7	585.6	41.5
Pakistan	11,141.4	73.2	35.1	New Zealand	2,002.6	58.6	39.0
				World total	**$1,037,178.3**	**$34,809.7**	**$51,924.8**

Note: World total includes countries not listed. International organizations including NATO and the United Nations are also recipients of the program.

Leading Defense Contract Recipients, 2023

Source: U.S. Dept. of Defense; Federal Procurement Data System, U.S. General Services Administration

Listed are the 50 companies or organizations receiving the largest dollar volume of prime contract awards from the U.S. Dept. of Defense during fiscal year 2023 (Oct. 1, 2022-Sept. 30, 2023), as of Aug. 5, 2024.

Rank	Recipient	Funds awarded	Rank	Recipient	Funds awarded
1.	Lockheed Martin Corp.	$69,429,735,804	26.	Pfizer Inc.	$1,865,674,055
2.	RTX Corporation (fmr. Raytheon Technologies Corp.)	30,525,265,482	27.	Dell Technologies Inc.	1,708,790,125
3.	General Dynamics Corp.	23,543,638,090	28.	Idemitsu Kosan Co., Ltd.	1,679,632,596
4.	The Boeing Co.	22,130,773,553	29.	Fluor Corp.	1,672,569,280
5.	Northrop Grumman Corp.	15,989,339,956	30.	Jacobs Engineering Group Inc.	1,509,143,997
6.	Huntington Ingalls Industries, Inc.	9,456,500,284	31.	Leonardo S.p.A.	1,466,829,564
7.	Humana Inc.	7,779,551,423	32.	Johns Hopkins University	1,466,627,942
8.	BAE Systems PLC	7,531,904,836	33.	Massachusetts Institute of Technology	1,377,229,101
9.	L3Harris Technologies, Inc.	6,802,255,793	34.	Peraton Corp.	1,321,515,555
10.	Atlantic Diving Supply Inc.	4,479,569,444	35.	Microsoft Corp.	1,278,294,684
11.	Leidos Holdings, Inc.	4,307,711,001	36.	KBR Technical Services Inc	1,246,008,557
12.	General Electric Co.	4,076,514,228	37.	Sierra Nevada Company, LLC	1,237,423,569
13.	Centene Corp.	3,601,081,144	38.	The Mitre Corporation.	1,207,423,663
14.	Analytic Services Inc.	3,561,511,729	39.	Valero Energy Corporation	1,165,966,340
15.	Science Applications International Corp.	3,068,945,357	40.	Weston Solutions Holdings, Inc.	1,152,575,973
16.	Amentum Services, Inc.	2,726,208,893	41.	AM General LLC	1,144,492,136
17.	Bechtel Corp.	2,710,304,818	42.	United Launch Alliance, LLC	1,118,135,118
18.	Booz Allen Hamilton Holding Corp.	2,601,520,491	43.	The Aerospace Corporation	1,110,325,737
19.	Cencora, Inc. (fmr. AmerisourceBergen)	2,252,438,705	44.	The British Petroleum Co. PLC	1,089,670,200
20.	General Atomics	2,243,770,845	45.	Rolls-Royce Holdings PLC	1,089,458,347
21.	Vectrus Federal Services GmbH	2,192,458,266	46.	KBR, Inc.	1,077,283,569
22.	AmerisourceBergen Holding Corp.	2,139,999,295	47.	FedEx Corp.	1,076,489,888
23.	CACI International Inc.	2,094,989,557	48.	National Security Technology Accelerator	1,046,254,059
24.	Oshkosh Corp.	2,029,049,671	49.	Noble Sales Co., Inc.	1,029,015,131
25.	Textron Inc	1,964,534,570	50.	AECOM	1,005,029,329

Nations With Largest Armed Forces, 2023

Source: *The Military Balance 2024*, International Institute for Strategic Studies, published by Routledge Journals, Taylor & Francis, UK
(ranked by active-duty troop strength as of 2023)

Rank	Country	Active troops (thous.)	Reserve troops (thous.)	Defense expend. (mil)	Tanks (MBT) (army only)	Cruisers/ frigates/ destroyers	Sub-marines	Combat aircraft (air force only) FGA	Combat aircraft (air force only) FTR
1.	China	2,035	510	219,455	4,700	8C/49F/42D*	59	1,339+	466
2.	India	1,476	1,155	73,582	3,740	16F/11D*	16	455	61
3.	United States	1,326	807	905,458	2,640	15C/23F/73D*	66	1,075	185
4.	North Korea	1,280	600	—	3,500+	2F	71	30	401+
5.	Russia	1,100	1,500	74,761	1,750	3C/18F/11D*	50	433+	188
6.	Ukraine	800	400	30,896	937	0	0	0	49
7.	Pakistan	660	0	11,057	2,537	10F	8	253	151
8.	Iran	610	350	7,408	1,513+	0	19	73	138
9.	Ethiopia	503	0	1,540	220	0	0	6+	11
10.	South Korea	500	3,100	43,844	2,115	3C/16F/6D	20	347	173
11.	Vietnam[1]	450	5,000	7,390	1,379	0	8	72	0
12.	Egypt	439	479	3,582	2,480	13F	8	257	32
13.	Indonesia	405	400	8,782	103	7F	4	40	9
14.	Brazil	367	1,340	24,249	292	7F	5	30	47
15.	Thailand	361	200	5,670	394	7F*	0	11	75
16.	Turkey	355	379	9,692	2,378	16F	12	279	15
17.	Eritrea	302	—		270	0	0	2	8
18.	Sri Lanka	266	6	1,267	62	0	0	1	5
19.	Saudi Arabia	257	0	69,067	1,085	10F	0	220	68
20.	Colombia	257	35	5,412	0	0	4	22	0
21.	Japan	247	56	49,038	449	4C/10F/34D*	24	128	200
22.	Mexico	216	82	7,834	0	1F	0	0	5
23.	France	204	37	59,973	215	17F/4D*	9	155	34
24.	Myanmar	201	0	3,051	195+	5F	2	14	64
25.	Morocco	196	150	6,478	703	4F	0	48	22
26.	Iraq	193	0	10,264	401+	0	0	32	0
27.	Germany	181	35	63,696	313	8F/3D	6	0	138
28.	Bangladesh	171	0	4,021	276	5F	2	0	53
29.	Israel	170	465	19,175	400	0	5	310	0
30.	Taiwan	169	1,657	18,889	650	22F/4D	4	267	97
31.	Syria	169	0	—	—	0	0	79	55

— = Not available. * = Navy with aircraft carrier(s), as follows: China 2, France 1, India 2, Japan 4, Russia 1, Thailand 1, U.S. 11. FGA = Fighter, ground attack. FTR = Fighter. MBT = Main battle tank. (1) Estimates.

Conventional Arms Transfer Agreements With the World by Supplier, 2010-23

Source: Stockholm International Peace Research Institute (SIPRI); as of Mar. 11, 2024
(in millions of SIPRI trend-indicator values [TIVs]; ranked by 2010-23 totals)

Supplier	2010	2013	2014	2015	2016	2017	2018	2019	2020	2021	2022	2023	2010-23
United States . .	8,389	7,694	9,490	9,868	9,465	11,444	9,576	10,908	9,532	11,074	15,592	11,287	**142,298**
Russia.	6,240	7,780	5,335	5,788	6,706	6,376	6,901	5,051	3,523	2,315	2,603	1,269	**76,960**
France.	884	1,799	1,768	2,271	2,141	2,315	1,879	3,724	2,387	3,892	3,268	2,012	**31,914**
China	1,511	2,061	1,327	1,814	2,445	1,625	1,358	1,593	700	1,310	2,083	2,432	**23,042**
Germany.	2,357	729	1,822	1,812	2,509	1,841	1,110	997	1,161	857	1,481	3,287	**21,897**
United Kingdom	1,152	1,493	1,658	1,183	1,324	1,107	680	919	637	717	1,665	1,204	**15,562**
Italy	580	886	674	687	621	705	537	383	825	1,650	1,716	1,437	**12,450**
Israel.	660	417	400	570	1,236	1,193	1,147	384	395	619	870	1,159	**10,061**
Spain	273	450	962	982	481	820	705	308	981	619	970	940	**9,752**
Netherlands . . .	366	384	643	469	484	1,067	466	302	462	357	323	258	**6,993**
South Korea . . .	177	350	220	94	437	702	1,049	682	772	510	204	621	**6,349**
Total	**25,937**	**27,126**	**27,023**	**28,353**	**30,784**	**31,200**	**27,380**	**27,219**	**23,758**	**26,352**	**33,544**	**29,104**	**395,791**

Note: SIPRI data on arms transfers relate to actual deliveries of major conventional weapons, using TIV. TIV is based on the known unit production costs of a core set of weapons and is intended to represent the military capability of the weapons transferred rather than the financial value of the transfer. A weapon that has been in service in another armed force is valued at 40% of a new weapon. A significantly refurbished or modified used weapon is valued at 66% of that of a new weapon. Total includes suppliers/countries not shown here.

Timeline of Major Wars Since 1066

Norman Conquest 1066-71	William I, duke of Normandy, landed on the English coast near Hastings on Sept. 28, 1066, and defeated Harold II, Saxon king of England, at Battle of Hastings Oct. 14. William crowned king Dec. 25 in Westminster Abbey. Most revolts were suppressed by 1071. **Conquest linked England's interests with those of the continent and led to its rise as a powerful monarchy.**
Crusades 1095-1270/1291	Military expeditions undertaken by **Western European Christians**, usually at the behest of the **papacy**, to recover **Jerusalem** and other Biblical places of pilgrimage from **Muslim** control. In the long term, stimulated trade and flow of ideas between East and West. Pope Urban II called Nov. 27, 1095, for the **First Crusade**; Crusaders took Jerusalem on July 15, 1099, massacred inhabitants, and founded four temporary states: Antioch, Edessa, Jerusalem, and Tripoli. The failed **Second Crusade** was prompted by Muslims' capture of Edessa in 1144. Jerusalem was captured by Ayyubid sultan Saladin on Oct. 2, 1187, leading to the **Third Crusade**, which involved the Holy Roman emperor, Frederick I (Barbarossa); the French king, Philip II (Augustus); and the English king, Richard I (Lion-Heart) but did not lead to a Crusader victory. The **Fourth Crusade** sacked Constantinople on Apr. 13, 1204. The **Fifth Crusade** began with capture of Damietta in Egypt (1219) but failed at Cairo. A **Sixth Crusade** led to the Treaty of Jaffa in 1229, giving Jerusalem to the Crusaders until 1244, when its seizure by the Khwarezmians led to the launch of a **Seventh Crusade**. The last crusade abruptly ended when its leader, French King Louis IX, died in 1270. The last major Crusader stronghold, Acre, was lost on May 18, 1291.
Hundred Years War 1337-1453	Series of armed conflicts over rival claims to the French throne, broken by a number of truces and peace treaties. Edward III declared self king of France in 1338 and invaded, with victories at Crécy (1346) and Poitiers (1356). **Treaty of Brétigny** signed May 8, 1360, but French king Charles V renewed fighting in 1369. Truce from 1396 until **Henry V** of England invaded in 1415 and **defeated French army at Agincourt**, capturing land north of Loire River, including Paris. **Treaty of Troyes** in 1420 made Henry VI heir of both thrones. The siege of French stronghold Orléans, lifted in 1429 with help from **Joan of Arc**, turned tide in favor of French, who won last battle (1453). **War ended English claims to France, paved way for French absolute monarchy.**
Wars of the Roses 1455-85	Series of dynastic civil wars for the throne in England fought by the **rival houses of Lancaster and York**. Richard, third duke of York, in conflict with the Lancastrian King **Henry VI**, won victories at St. Albans (1455) and Northampton (1460); Richard died at Battle of Wakefield on Dec. 30, 1460, before coronation, leaving his son to become King Edward IV. Henry VI imprisoned in Tower of London, 1465. Edward died in 1483; his brother became **Richard III** after usurping throne from Edward V, nephew. Henry Tudor defeated Richard III at the Battle of Bosworth Field (1485). As Henry VII, he married Edward IV's daughter Elizabeth, 1486, **uniting the houses**.
Thirty Years' War 1618-48	A series of religious and political conflicts involving **most countries of Western Europe**; majority of fighting in Germany, devastating it. Protestants stormed Habsburg palace in the "Defenestration of Prague" (May 23, 1618). Major conflicts included defeat of King Christian IV of Denmark and Norway by Catholic League (1626); victories by Lutheran King Gustav II Adolph of Sweden at Breitenfeld (1631) and Lützen (1632). France, under cardinal and statesman **Richelieu**, chief minister of King Louis XIII, declared war on the Habsburgs in May 1635; defeated Austro-Bavarian army (Aug. 3, 1645), leading to Truce of Ulm. **Peace of Westphalia** signed at Münster on Oct. 24, 1648, bringing peace by recognizing the rulers' sovereignty within their lands and their right to determine the religious beliefs of their subjects.
English Civil Wars 1638-60	Series of conflicts between followers of King Charles (Cavaliers) and of Parliament (Roundheads), over divine right of king versus Parliament's right to control national finances. Presbyterian Scots, allied with Parliament, rioted and in 1640 occupied the northern counties of England. **Oliver Cromwell**, second in command of Parliament's New Model Army, destroyed the king's army at Battle of Naseby (June 14, 1645); first civil war ended May 1646 when Charles surrendered to the Scots. Charles later allied with Scots but was defeated by Cromwell at Preston Aug. 17-19, 1648, and executed Jan. 30, 1649. Parliament abolished monarchy and House of Lords. Cromwell suppressed Irish and Scottish rebellions, was briefly succeeded by son Richard after death (1658). **Charles II restored to the throne** by the "Long Parliament," May 1660.
War of the Spanish Succession 1701-14	War fought by the Grand Alliance (originally England, Netherlands, Denmark, and Austria; later also Portugal), against coalition of France, Spain, and a number of small Italian and German principalities to preserve balance of power after death of Spanish king Charles II. Opened with invasion of Italy, via Venice, by an Austrian army under Prince Eugène of Savoy in May 1701. French forced to withdraw from Netherlands and Italy in 1706 and were finally defeated in 1709 in bloodiest battle of the war at French village of Malplaquet. Treaties of Rastatt and Baden signed in 1714; **Austria given control of Spanish Netherlands, and peace settled between Austria and France**.
War of the Austrian Succession 1740-48	Conflict over rival claims for the **hereditary dominions of the Habsburg family**, following death (1740) of Charles VI, Holy Roman emperor and archduke of Austria. An alliance of Bavaria, France, Spain, Sardinia, Prussia, and Saxony fought against Austria, allied with Holland and Great Britain. King Frederick the Great of Prussia captured Silesia from Austria in the First (1740-42) and Second (1744-45) Silesian Wars. British king George II defeated French army at Battle of Dettingen am Main (June 27, 1743). French conquered Austrian Netherlands (1745-46). Treaty of Aix-la-Chapelle Oct. 18, 1748, **restored most original borders; Prussia became significant force**.
Seven Years' War 1756-63	Worldwide conflicts fought for **control of Germany** and for **supremacy in colonial N America and India**. French defeated British Gen. Edward Braddock in Battle of Monongahela in 1754, leading to formal declaration of **French-Indian War**, May 1756. Frederick II of Prussia invaded Saxony on Aug. 29, 1756; defeated French at Rossbach (1757), Austrians at Leuthen (1757), Russians at Zorndorf (1758). By 1760, British conquered French Canada. Peter III of Russia signed armistice with Prussia, 1762. Treaty of Paris signed Feb. 10, 1763; Peace of Hubertusburg Feb. 15, 1763, between Prussia and Austria. **England emerged as leading world naval power.**
American Revolution 1775-83	Conflict between Great Britain and 13 British colonies in eastern N America. George Washington took command of the Continental Army, July 3, 1775, and King George III declared colonies traitors on Aug. 23. **Declaration of Independence of colonies adopted July 4, 1776.** France recognized the colonies' independence Feb. 6, 1778, followed by Spain on June 21, 1779; both pledged support. French fleet drove British fleet under Adm. Thomas Graves from Chesapeake Bay on Sept. 5, 1781. French and Americans laid siege to Yorktown, VA, Sept. 28-Oct. 19, forcing British Gen. Cornwallis to surrender. **Treaty of Paris** (Sept. 3, 1783) recognized U.S. independence.
Wars of French Revolution and Napoleonic Wars 1792-1815	Large-scale wars fought between France and two multinational coalitions. France declared war on the Austrian part of the Holy Roman Empire, Apr. 20, 1792. Newly created French Republic declared war on monarchs of Britain and Holland, Feb. 1, 1793, and of Spain, Mar. 7. **Napoleon Bonaparte** defeated Austria in N Italy (1796-97), captured Egypt from Britain (1798-99; Battle of the Pyramids, July 21, 1798), and became First Consul after coup d'état of Nov. 9-10, 1799. French Grande Armée later swept through Europe using innovative and aggressive tactics. French navy defeated by British under Adm. Horatio Nelson at **Trafalgar** (Oct. 21, 1805), but Napoleon defeated Austro-Russian forces at Austerlitz (Dec. 2) and controlled most of Europe except Russia and Great Britain by 1808. France suffered its first major defeat by Austria at Aspern-Essling, May 21-22, 1809. **Napoleon invaded Russia**, captured Moscow Sept. 14, 1812, but fled the bitter Russian winter and abandoned Germany after defeat at Leipzig, Oct. 16-19, 1813. Paris captured by Allied armies Mar. 30-31, 1814. Napoleon exiled to Elba May 4 but returned for "Hundred Days" reign, Mar. 20-June 28, 1815; **final defeat at Waterloo** by British and Prussian troops (June 18). The **Bourbon monarchy was restored under Louis XVIII**, and Britain, Prussia, Russia, and Austria maintained European peace.
Crimean War 1853-56	Conflict between **Russia** and coalition of **Great Britain, France, Sardinia, and Turkey for influence over Balkans** and the straits between the Black Sea and Mediterranean. Russia destroyed Turkish fleet at Sinope on Nov. 30, 1853. Britain and France declared war in Mar. 1854 and with Turkish troops defeated Russians at Battle of Alma River, Sept. 20. Lord Lucan of Britain prevented Russia from capturing Balaklava on Oct. 25 ("Charge of the Light Brigade" led by Lord Cardigan). Siege of Sevastopol ended when Russia evacuated Sept. 8, 1855. Treaty of Paris signed Mar. 30, 1856; **curbed Russian expansion and loosened European power alignments.**

American Civil War 1861-65	Conflict between the U.S. (the Union) and 11 secessionist Southern states (the Confederate States of America). Union garrison at Fort Sumter in harbor of Charleston, SC, surrendered to Brig. Gen. P.G.T. Beauregard (Apr. 12-13, 1861). Under Beauregard, 22,000 Confederates repelled 35,000 Union troops under Gen. Irvin McDowell along Bull Run stream near Manassas, VA (July 21). The *Merrimack* (renamed *Virginia*) battled the *Monitor* Mar. 9, 1862. In **Battle of Antietam**, MD (Sept. 17), some 12,000 Northerners and 12,700 Southerners were killed or wounded. Pres. Abraham Lincoln announced **Emancipation Proclamation** Sept. 22. Confederate Gen. Robert E. Lee's 75,000 forces battled 88,000 Union troops under Gen. George Meade at **Gettysburg**, PA, July 1-3, 1863; Lee's army forced across the Potomac R. Lee surrendered to Ulysses S. Grant at **Appomattox Court House** in Virginia (Apr. 9, 1865). **The Union was preserved and slavery subsequently abolished.**
Franco-Prussian War 1870-71	German states led by Prussia defeated France, seizing Alsace and part of Lorraine. French defeated in several major battles, culminating at **Sedan** Sept. 1, 1870, when Prussian forces decisively defeated the French army and captured emperor Napoleon III. Prussian king William I was made emperor of unified Germany, Jan 18, 1871. **France surrendered** Jan. 28. Final treaty signed May 10; set the stage for later **German imperialistic expansion**.
Spanish-American War 1898	War waged by the U.S. to **liberate Cuba from Spanish rule**. A mysterious explosion, blamed on Spain by American newspapers, sank the U.S. battleship *Maine* in Havana's harbor (Feb. 15, 1898), killing 260. The U.S. called for Spain's withdrawal from Cuba, and Spain declared war (Apr. 24). William Rufus Shafter led 17,000 U.S. troops from Daiquirí to Santiago de Cuba, taking **San Juan Hill** with help of the Rough Riders under Teddy Roosevelt. Santiago de Cuba surrendered July 17. The Treaty of Paris (Dec. 10, 1898) provided for the **independence of Cuba** and the cession by Spain to the U.S. of **Puerto Rico, Guam, and for a $20 mil payment, the Philippine Islands**.
World War I 1914-18	Local European war that grew into a global war involving 32 nations: the Allies and the Associated Powers—28 nations including Great Britain, France, Russia, Italy, and the U.S.—versus the Central Powers of Germany, Austria-Hungary, Turkey, and Bulgaria. Archduke Francis Ferdinand of Austria assassinated in Sarajevo, Bosnia (June 28, 1914). Germany invaded France through Belgium; advance on Paris halted by the French under Gen. Joseph Jacques Césaire Joffre at the **First Battle of the Marne**, Sept. 5-12. Germany checked the Russian army at the Battle of Tannenberg, Aug. 26-30. The British suffered 57,470 casualties (19,240 dead) in the opening day of the **First Battle of the Somme** (July 1-Nov. 18, 1916), first of 12 battles that forced Germany back to Hindenburg Line. **U.S. declared war on Germany Apr. 6, 1917.** Russian involvement ended when Bolshevik party seized power on Nov. 7; signed armistice Dec. 15. German offensive halted by U.S. and French troops at **Second Battle of the Marne** (July 15-Aug. 5, 1918), turning point of the war. Allied counteroffensive broke the fortified defensive Hindenburg Line, and an armistice was signed Nov. 11.
World War II 1939-45	Global military conflict stemming from European unrest after World War I and Japan's aggressive expansion into Asia and the Pacific. **War in Europe:** Nazi-Soviet nonaggression pact (Aug. 23, 1939) freed Germany and the Soviet Union to attack Poland in Sept. **Britain and France declared war on Germany** Sept. 3. German forces raced through Europe (Apr.-June 1940), captured Paris June 14. **Italy declared war on France and Britain** June 10. German-Italian campaigns won the Balkans and N Africa by June 1941. U.S. entered war Dec. 1941. Three million Axis troops invaded Russia June 22, 1941, but Russian counterthrusts stopped the German advance (**Stalingrad**, Aug. 20, 1942-Feb. 2, 1943), and Allies took N Africa (Nov. 8, 1942-May 13, 1943), Italy (July 10, 1943-May 2, 1945). Normandy invaded on **D-Day**, June 6, 1944; Paris liberated Aug. 25. Leaders at Yalta Conference (Feb. 4-11, 1945) discussed defeat and division of Germany into four. Adolf Hitler committed suicide Apr. 30. **Germany surrendered unconditionally** May 7. **War in the Pacific:** Japan invaded China (July 7, 1937), joined alliance with Germany and Italy (Sept. 27, 1940), and signed nonaggression pact with Russia (Apr. 13, 1941); attacked Hawaii's Pearl Harbor, Dec. 7, 1941; U.S. declared war on Japan Dec. 8. **Battle of Midway** (June 4-7, 1942) repulsed Japanese advance. Marines landed on Guadalcanal Aug. 7. Navy defeated Japanese fleet at **Leyte Gulf**, Oct. 23-26, 1944. B-29 bombing raids on Japan began in Nov. Marines invaded Iwo Jima (Feb. 19-Mar. 16, 1945) with heavy casualties, then Okinawa (Apr. 1-June 21). **U.S. atom bombs dropped** on Hiroshima (Aug. 6) and Nagasaki (Aug. 9) and Soviet invasion of Manchuria (Aug. 8) **forced Japan to agree, on Aug. 14, to surrender**; formal surrender on Sept. 2.
Korean War 1950-53	Military struggle fought on the Korean Peninsula between the Democratic Peoples' Republic of Korea (N Korea) and the Republic of Korea (S Korea) that developed into an international war involving China allied with N Korea against the U.S. and other nations under the UN flag. DPRK army crossed the 38th parallel and invaded S Korea (June 25, 1950), entering Seoul (June 26). Amphibious assault launched at **Inchon** by Gen. Douglas MacArthur (Sept. 15) helped U.S. forces rout DPRK close to Yalu River by Nov. 24. The Chinese, in counterattack, retook Seoul (Jan. 4, 1951) but were forced back to the 38th parallel by Apr. 22. Armistice was signed (July 27, 1953) by the UN, DPRK, and China, but not ROK, **leaving the peninsula partitioned at about the 38th parallel**.
Vietnam War 1959-75	Struggle primarily in S Vietnam that widened into a war between S Vietnam supported mainly by the U.S. and N Vietnam supported by the USSR and China. Viet Minh, led by Communist leader Ho Chi Minh, formed the Democratic Republic of Vietnam (Sept. 2, 1945). Colonial power France withdrew after fortress at Dien Bien Phu fell (May 8, 1954). Pres. John F. Kennedy pledged U.S. commitment to S Vietnamese independence Dec. 14, 1961. USS *Maddox* destroyer damaged in **Gulf of Tonkin** (Aug. 2, 1964), prompting Congress to increase involvement. Regular bombing of N Vietnam began (Feb. 24, 1965), and the first U.S. combat ground forces arrived (Mar. 6). N Vietnamese Army siege of **Khe Sanh** (Jan. 21-Apr. 7, 1968) and the **"Tet" offensive** (Jan. 30) aimed to cause insurrection in the S. **My Lai Massacre** by U.S. soldiers of civilians (Mar. 16, 1968) created scandal, fueled U.S. disaffection with war. U.S. forces peaked at 543,400 in Apr. 1969. NVA **"Easter Offensive"** (Mar. 30, 1972) rebuffed, and U.S. responded with aerial bombings in May and Dec. U.S. withdrew after cease-fire, Jan. 1973. **NVA offensive captured Saigon, Apr. 30, 1975, and unified Vietnam under Communist rule.**
Persian Gulf Wars 1991, 2003-10	Conflicts fought principally between Iraq and the U.S. concerning Iraq's influence in the Middle East and its development of weapons of mass destruction. **First Gulf War:** Iraq under dictator Saddam Hussein invaded Kuwait Aug. 2, 1990, and annexed it; UN Security Council ordered Iraqi forces to withdraw by Jan. 15, 1991. Beginning Jan. 17, a U.S.-led multinational force (**Operation Desert Storm**) bombed military targets in Iraq and Kuwait. A coordinated air-land offensive (**Operation Desert Sabre**, begun Feb. 24) retook Kuwait City Feb. 26, and permanent cease-fire was signed on Apr. 6. Iraq was ordered to pay reparations to Kuwait, reveal locations of biological and chemical weapons, and eliminate weapons of mass destruction. **Second Gulf War:** The U.S. and UK mistakenly asserted that Iraq was still producing WMDs and posed an imminent threat. The UN passed Resolution 1441, Nov. 8, 2002, warning Iraq of "serious consequences" if it failed to cooperate fully and unconditionally with UN weapons inspectors. Iraq rejected a Mar. 17, 2003, U.S. ultimatum demanding Hussein and his sons leave Iraq. U.S. launched **Operation Iraqi Freedom** Mar. 19, 2003, with support from UK and other allies, but without full UN Security Council support. Baghdad fell Apr. 9, and major combat operations declared over May 1. Hussein was captured Dec. 13, 2003, but guerrilla opposition to U.S. troops and insurgent violence continued. U.S. combat operations in Iraq formally ended Aug. 31, 2010.
Russian-Ukraine War Feb. 24, 2022-	Russia launched full-scale invasion by air, ground, and sea into Ukraine, condemned by U.S. and mostly Western allies. Ukraine thwarted an initial Russian takeover of its capital, Kyiv, after which Russia launched an offensive in eastern Ukraine, including regions in which pro-Russia separatists sparked fighting following Russia's annexation of Crimea in 2014. By May 2024, Ukraine had retaken more than half of territory seized, though Russia occupied roughly 18 percent of Ukraine and continued to launch widespread air and drone strikes against infrastructure and other targets. By Nov. 2023, the UN documented at least 10,000 civilian deaths.
Israel-Hamas War Oct. 7, 2023-	Conflict began when Hamas militants in the Palestinian-occupied Gaza Strip launched a surprise assault on Israel, killing more than 1,200 mostly Israeli citizens and taking more than 250 hostages. After the attack, the deadliest on the country since its 1948 independence, Israeli military launched an ongoing offensive against Hamas in Gaza that has killed more than 39,000 Palestinians as of Aug. 1, 2024, according to the territory's health ministry, displaced an estimated 1.9 mil of Gaza's approx. 2.1 mil residents, and triggered a humanitarian crisis.

Casualties in Principal Wars of the U.S.

Source: U.S. Dept. of Defense; U.S. Coast Guard, U.S. Dept. of Homeland Security

Data prior to World War I are based on incomplete records in many cases. Casualty data are confined to dead and wounded personnel and, therefore, exclude personnel captured or missing in action who were subsequently returned to military control.

	Branch of service	Number serving	CASUALTIES Battle deaths	Other deaths	Wounds not mortal[1]	Total[2]
Revolutionary War 1775-83	**Total**	**184,000 to 250,000**[13]	**4,435**	—	**6,188**	**10,623**
War of 1812 1812-15	**Total**	**286,730**[14]	**2,260**	—	**4,505**	**6,765**
	Army	—	1,950	—	4,000	5,950
	Navy	—	265	—	439	704
	Marines	—	45	—	66	111
Mexican War 1846-48	**Total**	**78,718**[14]	**1,733**	**11,550**	**4,152**	**17,435**
	Army	—	1,721	11,550	4,102	17,373
	Navy	—	1	—	3	4
	Marines	—	11	—	47	58
	Coast Guard[8]	71 off.	—	—	—	—
Civil War 1861-65						
Union forces[3]	**Total**	**2,213,363**	**140,414**	**224,097**	**281,881**	**646,392**
	Army	2,128,948[14]	138,154	221,374	280,040	639,568
	Navy	84,415	2,112	2,411	1,710	6,233
	Marines	(in Navy total)	148	312	131	591
	Coast Guard[8]	219 off.	1	—	—	1
Confederate forces (estimate)[3]	**Total**	**600,000 to 1.5 mil**	**74,524**	**59,297**	—	**133,821**
Spanish-American War 1898	**Total**	**306,760**	**385**	**2,061**	**1,662**	**4,108**
	Army[9]	280,564	369	2,061	1,594	4,024
	Navy	22,875	10	—	47	57
	Marines	3,321	6	—	21	27
	Coast Guard[8]	660	0	—	—	—
World War I Apr. 6, 1917-Nov. 11, 1918	**Total**	**4,734,991**	**53,402**	**63,114**	**204,002**	**320,518**
	Army[10]	4,057,101	50,510	55,868	193,663	300,041
	Navy	599,051	431	6,856	819	8,106
	Marines	78,839	2,461	390	9,520	12,371
	Coast Guard	8,835	30	81	—	111
World War II[4] Dec. 7, 1941-Dec. 31, 1946	**Total**	**16,112,566**	**291,557**	**113,842**	**670,846**	**1,076,245**
	Army[11]	11,260,000	234,874	83,400	565,861	884,135
	Navy[12]	4,183,466	36,950	25,664	37,778	100,392
	Marines	669,100	19,733	4,778	67,207	91,718
	Coast Guard	241,093	574	1,343	—	1,917
Korean War[5] June 25, 1950-July 27, 1953	**Total**	**5,720,000**	**33,739**	**2,835**	**103,284**	**139,858**
	Army	2,834,000	27,731	2,125	77,596	107,452
	Navy	1,177,000	503	154	1,576	2,233
	Marines	424,000	4,267	242	23,744	28,253
	Air Force	1,285,000	1,238	314	368	1,920
	Coast Guard	44,143	—	—	—	—
Vietnam War[6] Aug. 4, 1964-Jan. 27, 1973	**Total**	**8,744,000**	**47,434**	**10,786**	**153,303**	**211,523**
	Army	4,368,000	30,963	7,261	96,802	135,026
	Navy	1,842,000	1,631	935	4,178	6,744
	Marines	794,000	13,095	1,749	51,392	66,236
	Air Force	1,740,000	1,745	841	931	3,517
	Coast Guard	8,000	7	2	60	69
Persian Gulf War 1991	**Total**	**2,225,000**	**147**	**235**	**467**	**849**
	Army	782,000	98	126	354	578
	Navy	669,000	5	50	12	67
	Marines	213,000	24	44	92	160
	Air Force	561,000	20	15	9	44
	Coast Guard	400	—	—	—	—
Iraq War[7] Mar. 19, 2003-Dec. 15, 2011	**Total**	**269,363**[15]	**3,519**	**973**	**32,292**	**36,784**
	Army	99,664[15]	2,574	727	22,543	25,844
	Navy	61,018[15]	63	49	672	784
	Marines	66,166[15]	852	171	8,625	9,648
	Air Force	42,515[15]	29	26	452	507
	Coast Guard	1,250[15]	1	—	1	2

— = Not available. Off. = Officers. **Note:** As of Aug. 2024, there were 1,845 battle deaths, 504 non-hostile deaths, and 20,149 wounded in Op. Enduring Freedom (Oct. 7, 2001-Dec. 31, 2014), mostly in Afghanistan and the Persian Gulf area; 77 battle deaths, 32 non-hostile deaths, and 620 wounded in Operation Freedom's Sentinel (Jan. 1, 2015-Aug. 30, 2021) in Afghanistan, including 13 killed in attack on Kabul's airport in Aug. 2021 during U.S. withdrawal; 23 battle deaths, 92 non-hostile deaths, and 478 wounded in Operation Inherent Resolve (Aug. 8, 2014-) against ISIS in Iraq and Syria. (1) Marine Corps data for Iraq War, World War II, Spanish-American War, and prior wars represent the number of individuals wounded, whereas all other data in this column represent the total number (incidence) of wounds. (2) Totals for all branches do not include categories for which no data are listed. (3) From the final report of the Provost Marshal General, 1863-66. Authoritative statistics for the Confederate forces are not available. In addition, an estimated 26,000-31,000 Confederate personnel died in Union prisons. New estimates published in *Civil War History* in 2012 recalculated the death toll for both sides and determined that it was 20% higher than previously thought, at 750,000. (4) Data are for Dec. 1, 1941, through Dec. 31, 1946, when hostilities were officially terminated by presidential proclamation; few battle deaths or wounds not mortal were incurred after Japanese acceptance of Allied peace terms on Aug. 14, 1945. Numbers serving Dec. 1, 1941-Aug. 31, 1945: Total—14,903,213; Army—10,420,000; Navy—3,883,520; Marine Corps—599,693. (5) As a result of an ongoing Dept. of Defense review of available Korean War casualty record information, updates have been made to previously reported figures for battle deaths and other deaths. (6) Number serving Aug. 5, 1964-Jan. 27, 1973 (date of cease-fire). Includes casualties incurred in Mayaguez incident. Wounds not mortal exclude 150,341 persons not requiring hospital care. (7) Military deaths during the invasion phase, which ended Apr. 30, 2003, totaled 115 combat-related and 23 other. (8) Then known as the U.S. Revenue Cutter Services, predecessor to the U.S. Coast Guard. (9) Number serving Apr. 21-Aug. 13, 1898, while dead and wounded data are for May 1-Aug. 31, 1898. Active hostilities ceased on Aug. 13, 1898, but the U.S. and Spain did not exchange ratifications of the treaty of peace until Apr. 11, 1899. (10) Includes Army Air Forces battle deaths and wounds not mortal, as well as casualties suffered by American forces in northern Russia to Aug. 25, 1919, and in Siberia to Apr. 1, 1920. Other deaths cover Apr. 1, 1917-Dec. 31, 1918. (11) Includes Army Air Forces. (12) Battle deaths and wounds not mortal include casualties incurred in Oct. 1941 due to hostile action. (13) Estimated. (14) As reported by Commissioner of Pensions in his Annual Report for Fiscal Year 1903. (15) Number serving as of Mar. 31, 2003, i.e., does not include numbers of troops deployed since then.

Medal of Honor

Source: Congressional Medal of Honor Society; U.S. Army, U.S. Dept. of Defense; as of Aug. 2024

The Medal of Honor is the highest military award for individual bravery in the U.S. On Dec. 21, 1861, Pres. Abraham Lincoln signed a bill to create the Navy Medal of Honor. Lincoln, on July 14, 1862, approved a resolution providing for the presentation of Medals of Honor to enlisted men of the Army and Voluntary Forces. The law was amended on Mar. 3, 1863, so that officers as well as enlisted men were eligible. The first Army Medals of Honor were awarded on Mar. 25, 1863; the first Navy medals went to sailors and Marines on Apr. 3, 1863.

The Medal of Honor is awarded in the name of Congress to a person who, while a member of the armed forces, distinguishes himself or herself conspicuously by gallantry and intrepidity at the risk of life above and beyond the call of duty while engaged in an action against any enemy of the U.S.; while engaged in military operations involving conflict with an opposing foreign force; or while serving with friendly foreign forces engaged in an armed conflict against an opposing armed force in which the U.S. is not a belligerent party.

The deed performed must have been one of personal bravery or self-sacrifice so conspicuous as to clearly distinguish the individual above his or her comrades and must have involved risk of life. Incontestable proof of the performance of service is required, and each recommendation for award of this decoration is considered on the standard of extraordinary merit.

Prior to World War I, the 2,625 Army Medal of Honor awards up to that time were reviewed to determine which met new stringent criteria. The Army removed 911 names from the list, most of them former members of a Civil War volunteer infantry group who had been induced to extend their enlistments when they were promised the medal. However, the medal was restored to Dr. Mary Walker in 1977 and to Buffalo Bill Cody and seven other scouts in 1989. Of the 3,538 medals issued as of Sept. 12, 2024, 1,525 were awarded for valor in the Civil War; 126 for actions during WWI, 472 in WWII, 146 in the Korean War, 268 in the Vietnam War, 20 for actions in Afghanistan, and 8 for Iraq.

Medal of Honor Recipients From Recent Conflicts

Honoree	Rank[1]	Branch of service	Date of action	Date of award
Somalia Campaign				
Gordon, Gary I.*	Master Sgt.	U.S. Army	10/3/1993	5/23/1994
Shughart, Randall D.*	Sgt. First Class	U.S. Army	10/3/1993	5/23/1994
War in Iraq				
Atkins, Travis W.*	Staff Sgt.	U.S. Army	6/1/2007	3/27/2019
Bellavia, David G.	Staff Sgt.	U.S. Army	11/10/2004	6/25/2019
Cashe, Alwyn C.*	Sgt. First Class	U.S. Army	10/17/2005	12/16/2021
Dunham, Jason L.*	Corporal	USMC	4/14/2004	1/11/2007
McGinnis, Ross A.*	Pvt. First Class/Specialist*	U.S. Army	12/4/2006	6/5/2008
Monsoor, Michael A.*	Petty Officer Second Class	U.S. Navy	9/29/2006	4/8/2008
Payne, Thomas P.	Sgt. Major	U.S. Army	10/22/2015	9/11/2020
Smith, Paul R.*	Sgt. First Class	U.S. Army	4/4/2003	4/5/2005
War in Afghanistan				
Byers, Edward C., Jr.	Senior Chief	U.S. Navy	12/8-9/2012	2/29/2016
Carpenter, William Kyle	Lance Cpl.	USMC	11/21/2010	6/19/2014
Carter, Ty M.	Staff Sgt.	U.S. Army	10/3/2009	8/26/2013
Celiz, Christopher A.*	Sgt. First Class	U.S. Army	7/12/2018	12/16/2021
Chapman, John A.*	Technical Sgt.	USAF	3/4/2002	8/22/2018
Giunta, Salvatore A.	Staff Sgt.	U.S. Army	10/25/2007	11/16/2010
Groberg, Florent A.	Capt.	U.S. Army	8/8/2012	11/12/2015
Meyer, Dakota	Sgt.	USMC	9/8/2009	9/15/2011
Miller, Robert J.*	Staff Sgt.	U.S. Army	1/25/2008	10/6/2010
Monti, Jared C.*	Sgt. First Class	U.S. Army	6/21/2006	9/17/2009
Murphy, Michael P.*	Lt.	U.S. Navy	6/28/2005	10/22/2007
Petry, Leroy A.	Sgt. First Class	U.S. Army	5/26/2008	7/12/2011
Pitts, Ryan M.	Staff Sgt.	U.S. Army	7/13/2008	7/21/2014
Plumlee, Earl D.	Master Sgt.	U.S. Army	8/28/2013	12/16/2021
Romesha, Clinton L.	Staff Sgt.	U.S. Army	10/3/2009	2/11/2013
Shurer, Ronald J., II	Staff Sgt.	U.S. Army	4/6/2008	10/1/2018
Slabinski, Britt K.	Master Chief	U.S. Navy	3/4/2002	5/24/2018
Swenson, William D.	Capt.	U.S. Army	9/8/2009	10/15/2013
White, Kyle J.	Sgt.	U.S. Army	11/9/2007	5/13/2014
Williams, Matthew O.	Master Sgt.	U.S. Army	4/6/2008	10/30/2019

* = Awarded posthumously. (1) Rank at date of award.

Other Selected Awards

Source: The Institute of Heraldry, U.S. Army; Navy Department Awards Web Service; Air Force Personnel Center

Distinguished Service Cross

Established by Congress July 9, 1918, on recommendation of Gen. John J. "Black Jack" Pershing, and awarded for extraordinary heroism not justifying the award of a Medal of Honor. The act or acts of heroism must have been so notable and have involved risk of life so extraordinary as to set the individual apart from his or her comrades. The Navy Cross and Air Force Cross are equivalent.

Silver Star

Third-highest military combat honor. An earlier version of this award, the Citation Star, was established by Congress on July 19, 1918, and retroactively awarded to soldiers for "gallantry in action," back to the Spanish-American War. The Silver Star medal replaced the Citation Star in 1932 and is awarded for gallantry in action which, while of a lesser degree than that required for award of the Distinguished Service Cross, must nevertheless have been performed with marked distinction.

Distinguished Flying Cross

Established by Congress July 2, 1926, and awarded for heroism or extraordinary achievement while participating in aerial flight. Awards are made only to recognize single acts of heroism or extraordinary achievement, not sustained operational activities against an armed enemy. Initial awards were given to persons who made record-breaking long-distance and endurance flights or who set altitude records.

Soldier's Medal

Established by Congress July 2, 1926, to recognize acts of heroism not involving actual conflict with an enemy. The same degree of heroism is required as for the award of the Distinguished Flying Cross. The performance must have involved personal hazard or danger and the voluntary risk of life under conditions not involving conflict with an armed enemy. Awards are not made solely on the basis of having saved a life.

Bronze Star

Established by executive order Feb. 4, 1944, largely to raise the morale of ground troops in WWII, on the recommendation of Gen. George C. Marshall. It is awarded to any person who, while serving in any capacity in or with the U.S. military, distinguishes himself or herself by heroic or meritorious achievement or service not involving participation in aerial flight.

Purple Heart

The original Purple Heart, designated as the Badge of Military Merit, was established by Gen. George Washington on Aug. 7, 1782. Following the American Revolution, the badge fell into disuse until 1932, the 200th anniversary of Washington's birth. During WWII, the Order of the Purple Heart was awarded for both wounds received in action and for meritorious service. Following the introduction of the Legion of Merit, the Purple Heart was awarded only for combat wounds. Today, it is awarded to any armed forces member who, while serving with the U.S. Armed Services, has been wounded or killed, or who has died or may hereafter die after being wounded in action against an enemy of the U.S. or in an armed conflict in which the U.S. or friendly foreign forces are engaged; as the result of an act of any hostile foreign force; as a result of an international terrorist attack against the U.S. or a friendly foreign nation; or as a result of military operations outside the U.S. as part of a peacekeeping force. Wounds must be inflicted directly by enemy action, including while held as a prisoner of war or while being taken captive.

U.S. Army, Navy, Air Force, Marine Corps, and Coast Guard Insignia

Source: Dept. of the Army, Dept. of the Navy, Dept. of the Air Force, U.S. Dept. of Defense; U.S. Coast Guard, U.S. Dept. of Homeland Security

Army

General of the Armies—Gen. John J. Pershing (1860-1948), the only person to have held this rank while living, was authorized to prescribe his own insignia but never wore in excess of four stars. Congress established the rank in 1799 to be bestowed on George Washington; Washington was finally promoted to the rank by joint resolution of Congress, approved by Pres. Gerald Ford, Oct. 19, 1976.

General of the Army—Five silver stars fastened together in a circle and the coat of arms of the U.S. in gold color metal with shield and crest enameled. Reserved for wartime use only.

Rank	Insignia
General of the Army*	Five silver stars
General	Four silver stars
Lieutenant General	Three silver stars
Major General	Two silver stars
Brigadier General	One silver star
Colonel	Silver eagle
Lieutenant Colonel	Silver oak leaf
Major	Gold oak leaf
Captain	Two silver bars
First Lieutenant	One silver bar
Second Lieutenant	One gold bar

Warrant Officers

Grade Five—Silver bar with enamel black line.

Grade Four—Silver bar with 4 enamel black squares.

Grade Three—Silver bar with 3 enamel black squares.

Grade Two—Silver bar with 2 enamel black squares.

Grade One—Silver bar with 1 enamel black square.

Noncommissioned Officers

Sergeant Major of the Army (E-9)—Three chevrons above 3 arcs, with a U.S. coat of arms centered on the chevrons, flanked by 2 stars—1 star on each side of the eagle. Also distinctive red-and-white shield collar insignia.

Command Sergeant Major (E-9)—Three chevrons above 3 arcs with a 5-pointed star with a wreath around the star between the chevrons and arcs.

Sergeant Major (E-9)—Three chevrons above 3 arcs with a 5-pointed star between the chevrons and arcs.

First Sergeant (E-8)—Three chevrons above 3 arcs with a lozenge between the chevrons and arcs.

Master Sergeant (E-8)—Three chevrons above 3 arcs.

Sergeant First Class (E-7)—Three chevrons above 2 arcs.

Staff Sergeant (E-6)—Three chevrons above 1 arc.

Sergeant (E-5)—Three chevrons.

Corporal (E-4)—Two chevrons.

Specialists

Specialist (E-4)—Eagle device only.

Other Enlisted

Private First Class (E-3)—One chevron above 1 arc.

Private (E-2)—One chevron.

Private (E-1)—None.

*Rank reserved for wartime use only.

Air Force

Insignia for Air Force officers are identical to those of the Army. Insignia for enlisted personnel are worn on both sleeves and consist of 1 star and an appropriate number of rockers. Chevrons appear above 5 rockers for the top three noncommissioned officer ranks, as follows (in ascending order): Master Sergeant, 1 chevron; Senior Master Sergeant, 2 chevrons; Chief Master Sergeant, 3 chevrons. The insignia of the Chief Master Sergeant of the Air Force has 3 chevrons and a wreath around the star design, while the Command Chief Master Sergeant insignia features an additional star. General of the Air Force is reserved for wartime use only.

Navy

The following stripes are worn on the lower sleeves of the Service Dress Blue uniform. They are of gold embroidery.

Rank	Insignia
Fleet Admiral*	1 two inch with 4 one-half inch
Admiral	1 two inch with 3 one-half inch
Vice Admiral	1 two inch with 2 one-half inch
Rear Admiral (upper half)	1 two inch with 1 one-half inch
Rear Admiral (lower half)	1 two inch
Captain	4 one-half inch
Commander	3 one-half inch
Lieutenant Commander	2 one-half inch with 1 one-quarter inch between
Lieutenant	2 one-half inch
Lieutenant (jr. grade)	1 one-half inch with 1 one-quarter inch above
Ensign	1 one-half inch
Warrant Officer W-5	½" stripe under ⅛" blue strip with 1 break
Warrant Officer W-4	½" stripe with 1 break
Warrant Officer W-3	½" stripe with 2 breaks, 2" apart
Warrant Officer W-2	½" stripe with 3 breaks, 2" apart

Enlisted personnel (noncommissioned petty officers)—Rating badge worn on the upper left sleeve consisting of a spread eagle, appropriate number of chevrons, and centered specialty mark.

* = Rank reserved for wartime use only.

Marine Corps

Marine Corps' distinctive cap and collar ornament is the Marine Corps emblem—a combination of the American eagle, a globe, and an anchor. Marine Corps and Army officer insignia are similar. Marine Corps enlisted insignia, although basically similar to the Army's, feature crossed rifles beneath the chevrons. Marine Corps enlisted rank insignia are as follows:

Sergeant Major of the Marine Corps (E-9)—Same as Sergeant Major (below) but with Marine Corps emblem in the center with a 5-pointed star on both sides of the emblem.

Sergeant Major (E-9)—Three chevrons above 4 rockers with a 5-pointed star in the center.

Master Gunnery Sergeant (E-9)—Three chevrons above 4 rockers with a bursting bomb insignia in the center.

First Sergeant (E-8)—Three chevrons above 3 rockers with a diamond in the middle.

Master Sergeant (E-8)—Three chevrons above 3 rockers with crossed rifles in the middle.

Gunnery Sergeant (E-7)—Three chevrons above 2 rockers with crossed rifles in the middle.

Staff Sergeant (E-6)—Three chevrons above 1 rocker with crossed rifles in the middle.

Sergeant (E-5)—Three chevrons above crossed rifles.

Corporal (E-4)—Two chevrons above crossed rifles.

Lance Corporal (E-3)—One chevron above crossed rifles.

Private First Class (E-2)—One chevron.

Private (E-1)—None.

Coast Guard

Coast Guard insignia follow Navy custom, with certain minor changes such as the officer cap insignia. The Coast Guard shield is worn on both sleeves of officers and on the right sleeve of all enlisted personnel.

Federal Service Academies

U.S. Military Academy, West Point, NY. Founded 1802. Awards B.S. degree and Army commission for a 5-year service obligation. **Website:** www.usma.edu

U.S. Naval Academy, Annapolis, MD. Founded 1845. Awards B.S. degree and Navy or Marine Corps commission for a 5-year service obligation. **Website:** www.usna.edu

U.S. Air Force Academy, Colorado Springs, CO. Founded 1954. Awards B.S. degree and Air Force commission for a 6-year service obligation. **Website:** www.usafa.af.mil

U.S. Coast Guard Academy, New London, CT. Founded 1876. Awards B.S. degree and Coast Guard commission for a 5-year service obligation. **Website:** www.cga.edu

U.S. Merchant Marine Academy, Kings Point, NY. Founded 1943. Awards B.S. degree; a license as a deck, engineer, or dual officer; and a U.S. Naval Reserve commission. Service obligations vary according to options taken by the graduate. **Website:** www.usmma.edu

Number and Acreage of Farms by State, 2000, 2023

Source: National Agricultural Statistics Service, U.S. Dept. of Agriculture

State	No. of farms (thous.) 2023	No. of farms (thous.) 2000	Acreage in farms (mil) 2023	Acreage in farms (mil) 2000	Acreage per farm 2023	Acreage per farm 2000
AL	37.1	47.0	8.6	9.0	232	191
AK	1.2	0.6	0.9	0.9	725	1,569
AZ	16.4	10.7	25.0	26.9	1,524	2,518
AR	37.4	48.0	13.7	14.6	366	304
CA	62.9	83.1	23.8	28.0	378	337
CO	35.9	30.0	30.0	31.6	836	1,060
CT	5.1	4.2	0.4	0.4	73	86
DE	2.2	2.6	0.5	0.6	242	215
FL	44.4	44.0	9.7	10.4	218	238
GA	39.0	49.1	10.0	10.9	256	223
HI	6.6	5.5	1.1	1.4	159	251
ID	22.6	24.5	11.5	11.9	509	486
IL	70.7	77.0	26.3	27.5	372	357
IN	53.3	63.4	14.6	15.2	274	240
IA	86.8	94.0	30.0	32.5	346	346
KS	55.5	64.5	44.8	47.5	807	736
KY	69.1	90.0	12.4	13.7	179	152
LA	24.8	29.0	8.0	8.0	323	277
ME	7.0	7.1	1.2	1.4	171	190
MD	12.6	12.4	2.0	2.1	159	172
MA	7.1	6.1	0.5	0.5	66	89
MI	45.3	53.0	9.5	10.2	210	192
MN	65.3	81.0	25.4	27.9	389	344
MS	31.1	42.0	10.3	11.2	331	266
MO	87.6	109.0	27.0	30.2	308	277
MT	24.3	27.8	57.6	59.3	2,370	2,133
NE	44.4	46.1	44.0	46.1	991	887
NV	3.1	3.1	5.9	6.4	1,903	2,065
NH	4.0	3.3	0.4	0.4	106	133
NJ	10.0	9.7	0.7	0.8	70	86
NM	20.9	18.0	39.1	44.9	1,871	2,494
NY	30.7	37.5	6.5	7.7	212	205
NC	42.5	55.5	8.1	9.2	191	166
ND	24.8	30.8	38.5	39.4	1,552	1,279
OH	75.8	79.0	13.7	14.8	181	187
OK	70.3	84.5	32.9	33.8	468	401
OR	35.5	40.0	15.3	17.3	431	433
PA	49.0	59.0	7.1	7.7	145	130
RI	1.1	0.8	0.1	0.1	57	75
SC	22.6	24.2	4.6	4.9	204	203
SD	28.3	32.4	42.3	44.0	1,495	1,358
TN	63.1	88.0	10.7	11.8	170	134
TX	231.0	228.3	125.0	130.9	541	573
UT	17.4	15.5	10.5	11.6	603	747
VT	6.5	6.6	1.2	1.3	185	192
VA	39.0	48.5	7.3	8.7	187	180
WA	32.0	37.0	13.9	15.6	434	420
WV	22.8	20.8	3.5	3.6	154	173
WI	58.5	77.5	13.8	16.0	236	206
WY	10.5	9.2	28.8	34.5	2,743	3,750
U.S.	**1,895.0**	**2,166.8**	**878.6**	**945.1**	**464**	**436**

Supplemental Nutrition Assistance Program (SNAP), 1969-2023

Source: Food and Nutrition Service (FNS), U.S. Dept. of Agriculture

Fiscal year	Avg. participation (thous.)	Avg. monthly benefit per person	Total benefits (mil)	All other costs (mil)[1]	Total costs (mil)
1969	2,878	$6.63	$228.8	$21.7	$250.5
1970	4,340	10.55	549.7	27.2	576.9
1975	17,064	21.40	4,385.5	233.2	4,618.7
1980	21,082	34.47	8,720.9	485.6	9,206.5
1985	19,899	44.99	10,743.6	959.6	11,703.2
1990	20,049	58.78	14,142.8	1,304.5	15,447.3
1995	26,619	71.27	22,764.1	1,856.3	24,620.4
2000	17,194	72.62	14,983.3	2,070.7	17,054.0
2003	21,250	83.94	21,404.3	2,412.0	23,816.3
2005	25,628	92.89	28,567.9	2,504.1	31,072.0
2006	26,549	94.75	30,187.4	2,715.7	32,903.1
2007	26,316	96.18	30,373.3	2,800.3	33,173.5
2008	28,223	102.19	34,608.4	3,031.3	37,639.6
2009	33,490	125.31	50,359.9	3,260.0	53,619.9
2010	40,302	$133.79	$64,702.2	$3,581.3	$68,283.5
2011	44,709	133.85	71,810.9	3,875.6	75,686.5
2012	46,609	133.41	74,619.3	3,791.8	78,411.1
2013	47,636	133.07	76,066.3	3,792.7	79,859.0
2014	46,664	125.01	69,998.8	4,061.5	74,060.3
2015	45,767	126.81	69,645.1	4,301.6	73,946.8
2016	44,220	125.40	66,539.3	4,372.9	70,912.1
2017	42,317	125.47	63,711.1	4,464.0	68,175.0
2018	40,776	124.50	60,916.9	4,531.8	65,448.7
2019	35,702	129.83	55,622.3	4,760.1	60,382.4
2020	39,853	155.06	74,156.7	5,005.9	79,162.6
2021	41,604	216.19	107,931.5	5,238.4	113,169.9
2022	41,208	230.48	113,973.3	5,598.0	119,571.3
2023	42,153	211.66	107,061.8	5,948.4	113,010.2

(1) Includes the federal share of state administrative expenses, nutrition education, and employment and training programs, in addition to other federal costs (e.g., benefit and retailer redemption and monitoring, payment accuracy, EBT [electronic benefit transfer] systems, program evaluation and modernization, program access, health and nutrition pilot projects).

U.S. Federal Food Assistance Programs, 1990-2023

Source: Food and Nutrition Service (FNS), U.S. Dept. of Agriculture
(in millions of dollars; for fiscal years ending on Sept. 30)

Program	1990	1995	2000	2005	2010	2015	2020	2022	2023
Supplemental Nutrition Assistance Program (SNAP)[1]	$15,491	$24,620	$17,054	$31,073	$68,284	$73,946	$79,163	$119,574	$113,047
Puerto Rico nutrition assistance[2]	937	1,131	1,268	1,495	2,001	1,951	1,938	2,502	2,816
Natl. school lunch[3]	3,834	5,160	6,149	8,031	10,880	13,003	10,317	22,977	17,311
School breakfast[3,4]	596	1,048	1,393	1,927	2,859	3,892	3,548	6,504	5,276
WIC (Women, Infants, and Children)[5]	2,122	3,440	3,982	4,994	6,690	6,241	5,017	5,761	6,698
Summer food service[6]	164	237	267	267	359	488	4,310	601	517
Child and adult care[7]	813	1,464	1,683	2,111	2,638	3,307	3,023	3,930	3,886
Special milk[4]	19	17	15	16	12	11	4	4	5
Nutrition for the elderly (NSIP)[8]	142	148	137	4	3	3	2	1	2
Food distrib. on Indian reserv.[9]	66	65	76	76	95	120	174	118	127
Commodity supplemental food[9]	85	99	98	156	165	193	286	351	387
Food distrib. to charitable insts.[10]	104	64	2	4	1	0	0	0	0
Emergency food assistance (TEFAP)[11]	334	135	225	373	631	525	769	1,045	1,314
Total[12]	**24,707**	**37,628**	**32,349**	**50,527**	**94,618**	**103,680**	**108,551**	**163,368**	**151,386**

Note: 2023 data are preliminary. All data subject to revision by the FNS. (1) Formerly known as the Food Stamp Program. Includes benefits and admin. expenses. (2) Provides benefits analogous to SNAP. (3) Nine-month averages (summer months are excluded). (4) Cash payments based on federal reimbursement rates to states. (5) Includes food benefits, nutrition services and admin. funds, Farmers' Market Nutrition Program, infrastructure, breastfeeding promotion and peer counseling, program evaluation, and technical assistance. (6) Includes cash payments, entitlement and bonus commodities, and the federal share of state and sponsor admin. costs. (7) Includes cash payments, entitlement and bonus commodities, cash-in-lieu of commodities, sponsor admin. costs, start-up costs, and audits. (8) For 2003 and on, Nutrition Services Incentive Program administered by the Agency on Aging, Dept. of Health and Human Services; FNS costs limited to value of commodities distributed. (9) Includes cost of commodity distrib. (entitlement and bonus) and federal share of state admin. expenses. (10) Includes summer camps. (11) Includes cost of commodities to hunger relief orgs. (e.g., food banks, soup kitchens) and federal share of state admin. expenses. (12) Does not include federal share of state admin. costs for some programs not shown.

U.S. Cost of Food, 2024

Source: Center for Nutrition Policy and Promotion (CNPP), U.S. Dept. of Agriculture (USDA)
(costs for individuals are for those in four-person households)

Age-gender group	Thrifty plan[1] Weekly	Thrifty plan[1] Monthly	Low-cost plan[2] Weekly	Low-cost plan[2] Monthly	Moderate-cost plan[2] Weekly	Moderate-cost plan[2] Monthly	Liberal plan[2] Weekly	Liberal plan[2] Monthly
Individual child								
1 year	$25.20	$109.10	$36.10	$156.30	$40.80	$176.80	$49.30	$213.80
2-3 years	37.80	163.80	37.80	163.90	45.50	197.10	55.30	239.50
4-5 years	41.20	178.70	39.20	169.90	48.30	209.40	58.40	253.10
6-8 years	46.00	199.30	56.10	242.90	66.50	288.30	77.60	336.50
9-11 years	53.20	230.50	59.30	256.80	76.30	330.60	88.90	385.20
Individual male								
12-13 years	56.90	246.60	69.40	300.80	86.10	373.10	100.70	436.40
14-18 years	71.80[3]	311.20[3]	70.50	305.50	88.20	382.40	102.50	444.10
19-50 years	70.10[3]	303.80[3]	69.50	301.30	87.20	377.80	106.20	460.10
51-70 years	61.90	268.10	65.40	283.40	82.00	355.20	97.90	424.30
71+ years	58.90	255.40	64.90	281.20	79.80	345.90	97.80	423.90
Individual female								
12-13 years	49.20	213.00	59.00	255.60	70.20	304.20	87.20	378.00
14-18 years	57.10[3]	247.20[3]	59.20	256.50	70.60	305.90	87.30	378.40
19-50 years	55.90[3]	242.20[3]	60.30	261.10	73.70	319.20	93.90	406.80
51-70 years	51.90	224.80	58.80	254.80	72.60	314.80	87.00	376.90
71+ years	57.10	247.40	58.80	254.60	72.10	312.30	86.10	373.10
4-person family:[4]	225.20	975.70						

Note: As of June 2024. A basis of all four food plans is that all meals and snacks are prepared at home. All costs are rounded to nearest 10 cents. Monthly costs are calculated by multiplying the weekly costs by 4.333. (1) Represents a nutritious, practical, cost-effective diet. The nutritional bases are the Dietary Reference Intakes and the *Dietary Guidelines for Americans, 2020-2025*. For specific foods and quantities, see *Thrifty Food Plan, 2021*. Plan is based on 2013-16 consumption and 2015-16 price data and updated to current dollars by using the Consumer Price Index for specific food items. (2) Represents a nutritious diet at three different cost levels. The nutritional bases of the food plans are the 1997-2005 Dietary Reference Intakes, 2005 Dietary Guidelines for Americans, and 2005 MyPyramid food intake recommendations. In addition to cost, differences among plans are in specific foods and quantities of foods. For specific foods and quantities of foods in the food plans, see *The Low-Cost, Moderate-Cost, and Liberal Food Plans, 2007*. All three food plans are based on 2001-02 data and updated to current dollars by using the Consumer Price Index for specific food items. (3) Age range varies slightly from standard: 14-19 years and 20-50 years, replacing 14-18 years and 19-50 years, respectively. (4) Defined as a couple (male and female), 20-50 years old, and two children ages 6-8 and 9-11 years.

U.S. Household Food Security by Selected Characteristics, 2022

Source: Economic Research Service, U.S. Dept. of Agriculture
(in thousands of households)

	Total[1]	Food secure No.	Food secure %	With low food security No.	With low food security %	With very low food security No.	With very low food security %
All households	**132,730**	**115,750**	**87.2%**	**10,187**	**7.7%**	**6,793**	**5.1%**
Household composition							
With children under 18 years old	37,235	30,798	82.7	4,404	11.8	2,033	5.5
With children under 6 years old	15,551	12,948	83.3	1,769	11.3	834	5.4
Married-couple families	24,152	21,572	89.3	1,965	8.2	615	2.5
Female head, no spouse	9,207	6,160	66.9	1,890	20.5	1,157	12.6
Male head, no spouse	3,437	2,708	78.8	488	14.2	241	7.0
Other household with child[2]	439	358	81.5	NA	NA	NA	NA
With no children under 18 years old	95,494	84,951	89.0	5,783	6.0	4,760	5.0
More than one adult	55,904	51,110	91.4	2,712	4.9	2,082	3.7
Women living alone	21,247	18,037	84.9	1,759	8.3	1,451	6.8
Men living alone	18,344	15,805	86.2	1,311	7.1	1,228	6.7
With adults ages 65+	42,670	38,775	90.9	2,438	5.7	1,457	3.4
Adults aged 65+ living alone	16,381	14,509	88.6	1,119	6.8	753	4.6
Race/ethnicity of households							
White, non-Hispanic	85,603	77,682	90.7	4,522	5.3	3,399	4.0
Black, non-Hispanic	17,271	13,406	77.6	2,283	13.2	1,582	9.2
Other, non-Hispanic	10,348	9,208	89.0	700	6.7	440	4.3
Hispanic[3]	19,507	15,453	79.2	2,682	13.8	1,372	7.0
Area of residence[4]							
Inside metropolitan area	114,666	100,347	87.5	8,592	7.5	5,727	5.0
In principal cities[5]	38,197	32,359	84.7	3,495	9.2	2,343	6.1
Not in principal cities	59,281	53,079	89.5	3,703	6.3	2,499	4.2
Outside metropolitan area	18,063	15,401	85.3	1,595	8.8	1,067	5.9

NA = Not reported. **Note:** Low food security households report food acquisition problems and reduced diet quality but typically few, if any, indications of reduced food intake. The very low food security category identifies households in which the food intake of one or more members was reduced and eating patterns disrupted because of insufficient money and other resources for food. (1) Totals exclude households of unknown food security status. Exclusions represented 0.2% of all households in 2022. (2) Households with children in complex living arrangements, e.g., children of other relatives or unrelated roommate or boarder. (3) Hispanics may be of any race. (4) Based on 2013 Office of Management and Budget delineations of metropolitan areas. (5) Households within incorporated areas of the largest cities in each metropolitan area. Residence inside or outside of principal cities unknown for about 15% of households in metropolitan statistical areas.

Trends in U.S. Food Insecurity in U.S. Households, 1998-2022

Source: Economic Research Service, U.S. Dept. of Agriculture

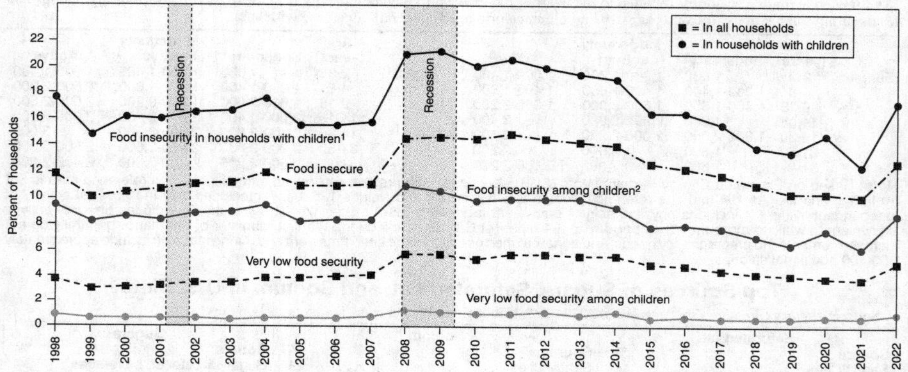

(1) Those with low or very low food security among adults or children or both. (2) In some food-insecure households with children, only adults were food insecure. Households with food-insecure children are those with low or very low food security among children.

U.S. Annual Per Capita Consumption of Selected Foods, 1970-2021

Source: Economic Research Service, U.S. Dept. of Agriculture; Distilled Spirits Council of the U.S.; Beer Institute; Wine Institute

(fruits and vegetables in pounds, beverages in gallons)

	1970	1990	2021	% change, 1970-2021
Fresh fruit	**100.6**	**117.1**	**138.7**	**37.9%**
Apples	17.2	19.8	15.8	–8.2
Avocados	0.5	1.4	8.4	1,769.1
Bananas	17.4	24.3	26.9	54.5
Grapes	2.9	7.9	8.5	190.6
Oranges	16.1	12.4	8.1	–49.4
Peaches/nectarines	5.8	5.5	2.4	–59.2
Strawberries	1.7	3.2	7.3	320.9
Processed vegetables[1]	**115.1**	**130.9**	**112.7**	**–2.1**
Asparagus	0.9	0.4	0.1	–84.9
Broccoli	1.0	2.2	2.6	169.4
Carrots	3.5	3.5	2.2	–37.6
Cauliflower	0.5	0.8	0.7	43.8
Green peas	5.1	4.2	1.7	–66.7
Mushrooms	1.0	1.7	1.2	16.1
Spinach	1.5	0.6	0.6	–62.4
Sweet corn	20.0	19.5	11.4	–43.3
Tomatoes	62.1	75.3	59.4	–4.4

	1970	1990	2021	% change, 1970-2021
Fresh vegetables	**154.4**	**176.4**	**176.2**	**14.1%**
Broccoli	0.5	3.4	5.1	849.7
Carrots	6.0	8.3	8.1	35.7
Cucumbers	2.8	4.7	8.0	183.0
Garlic	0.4	1.4	1.7	289.3
Lettuce head	22.4	27.7	10.6	–52.7
Onions	10.1	15.1	20.8	105.2
Potatoes	61.8	46.7	28.6	–53.8
Tomatoes	12.1	15.5	18.8	54.7
Beverages				
Orange juice	3.6	3.7	2.2	–38.3
Coffee	33.4	26.8	26.2[2]	–21.5[3]
Beer	18.5	23.9	19.6	5.7
Wine	1.3	2.0	3.1	141.5
Sweeteners	**119.1**	**132.5**	**127.3**	**6.9**
Sugar (refined)	101.8	64.4	69.7	–31.5
Honey	1.0	0.8	1.5	44.5
High fructose corn syrup	0.5	49.6	39.5	7,111.9

Note: All figures are rounded; percent change is calculated based on unrounded original data. Per capita consumption based on total population. Alcoholic beverage consumption would be higher if based on legal drinking age population. (1) Canned and frozen. (2) As of 2015. (3) Percent change, 1970-2015.

U.S. Meat Production and Consumption, 1940-2024

Source: Economic Research Service, U.S. Dept. of Agriculture

(in millions of pounds)

	Beef		Veal		Lamb and mutton		Pork		All red meats[1]		All poultry[2]	
Year	Prod.	Cons.	Prod.	Cons.	Prod.	Cons.	Prod.	Cons.	Prod.	Cons.	Prod.	Cons.
1940	7,175	7,257	981	981	876	873	10,044	9,701	19,076	18,812	NA	NA
1950	9,534	9,825	1,230	1,206	597	602	10,714	10,612	22,075	22,279	3,174	3,097
1960	14,753	15,490	1,109	1,118	768	856	13,905	14,057	30,535	31,521	6,310	6,168
1970	21,684	23,451	588	613	551	669	14,699	14,957	37,522	39,689	10,193	9,981
1980	21,643	23,560	400	420	318	351	16,617	16,838	38,978	41,170	14,173	13,525
1990	22,743	24,030	327	325	363	397	15,354	16,025	38,787	40,778	23,468	22,152
2000	26,888	27,338	225	225	234	354	18,952	18,643	46,299	46,560	36,073	30,508
2010	26,412	26,392	145	150	168	317	22,437	19,072	49,180	45,931	43,058	35,201
2015	23,760	24,771	88	88	155	357	24,517	20,656	48,520	45,872	45,769	38,785
2016	25,221	25,673	81	73	155	381	24,941	20,891	50,388	47,019	47,225	39,577
2017	26,187	26,492	80	78	150	396	25,584	21,035	51,991	48,000	48,178	40,236
2018	26,872	26,762	81	89	158	415	26,315	21,491	53,417	48,757	49,018	40,975
2019	27,155	27,272	79	81	153	422	27,638	22,188	55,015	49,963	50,251	42,081
2020	27,174	27,561	69	66	143	435	28,303	22,121	55,680	50,199	50,876	42,670
2024*	26,655	28,007	NA	NA	NA	NA	28,139	22,131	54,973	50,664	52,564	45,069

NA = Not available. * = July projection. (1) Includes beef, veal, lamb and mutton, and pork. May not add up to totals because of rounding. (2) Includes broilers, turkeys, and mature chicken.

Estimated Calorie Requirements

Source: *Dietary Guidelines for Americans, 2020-2025*, U.S. Dept. of Agriculture and U.S. Dept. of Health and Human Services

Estimated amount of calories, rounded to the nearest 200, needed to maintain energy balance by sex, for various age groups and levels of physical activity. In adults ages 19 and older, calorie needs generally decrease with age.

	Age (years)	Sedentary[1]	Moderately active[2]	Active[3]
Female[4]	2-3	1,000	1,000-1,200	1,000-1,400
	4-8	1,200-1,400	1,400-1,600	1,400-1,800
	9-13	1,400-1,600	1,600-2,000	1,800-2,200
	14-18	1,800	2,000	2,400
	19-30	1,800-2,000	2,000-2,200	2,400
	31-50	1,800	2,000	2,200
	51+	1,600	1,800	2,000-2,200
Male	2-3	1,000	1,000-1,400	1,000-1,400
	4-8	1,200-1,400	1,400-1,600	1,600-2,000
	9-13	1,600-2,000	1,800-2,200	2,000-2,600
	14-18	2,000-2,400	2,400-2,800	2,800-3,200
	19-30	2,400-2,600	2,600-2,800	3,000
	31-50	2,200-2,400	2,400-2,600	2,800-3,000
	51+	2,000-2,200	2,200-2,400	2,400-2,800

Note: Based on Estimated Energy Requirements (EER) equations, using reference heights and weights. The reference man is 5 ft 10 in. tall and weighs 154 lbs. The reference woman is 5 ft 4 in. tall and weighs 126 lbs. (1) Includes only the physical activity of independent living. (2) Includes physical activity equivalent to walking 1.5-3 mi per day at 3-4 mph. (3) Includes physical activity equivalent to walking more than 3 mi per day at 3-4 mph. (4) Calorie needs during the first trimester of pregnancy generally do not increase compared to prepregnancy needs. Additional calories needed for the later trimesters and during lactation include approximately 300-400 additional calories.

Top Sources of Sugars, Saturated Fat, and Sodium in U.S. Diets

Source: *Dietary Guidelines for Americans, 2020-2025*; National Health and Nutrition Examination Survey, 2013-16

Saturated fat

Source	%
Sandwiches	19
Desserts, sweet snacks	11
Rice, pasta, other grain-based mixed dishes	7
Higher-fat milk, yogurt	6
Pizza	5
Cheese	4
Chips, crackers, savory snacks	4
Meat, poultry, seafood mixed dishes	4
Poultry, excl. deli and mixed dishes	4
Vegetables, excl. starchy	4
Eggs	3
Meats, excl. deli and mixed dishes	3
Spreads	3
Starchy vegetables	3
Other	20

Sodium

Source	%
Sandwiches	21
Rice, pasta, other grain-based mixed dishes	8
Vegetables, excl. starchy	7
Meat, poultry, seafood mixed dishes	5
Pizza	5
Poultry, excl. deli and mixed dishes	5
Chips, crackers, savory snacks	4
Desserts, sweet snacks	4
Soups	4
Starchy vegetables	4
Breakfast cereals, bars	3
Condiments, gravies	3
Deli, cured products	3
Eggs	3
Yeast breads, tortillas	3
Other	19

Sugars

Source	%
Sugar-sweetened beverages	24
Desserts, sweet snacks	19
Coffee, tea	11
Candy, sugars	9
Breakfast cereals, bars	7
Sandwiches	7
Higher-fat milk, yogurt	4
Other	19

Note: Data are for people ages 1 and older.

Understanding Food Components

Water dissolves and transports other nutrients throughout the body, aiding in the processes of digestion, absorption, circulation, and excretion. It helps regulate body temperature.

Macronutrients

Carbohydrates, of which sugars, fibers, and starches are the major types, are the most important source of energy for the body. The digestive system changes carbohydrates into glucose, which the body uses for energy for cells, tissues, and organs. The body stores extra sugar in the liver and muscles. Best sources: grains, beans, vegetables, fruits.

Fats provide energy by furnishing calories to the body. They also help the body absorb vitamins A, D, E, and K. Best sources of polyunsaturated and monounsaturated fats: olive, canola, and peanut oils; nuts and nut butters; fatty fish; olives; avocado. Sources of saturated fats: meats, cheeses, butter, cream, milk, lard.

Fiber is the portion of plant foods that our bodies cannot digest. There are two basic types: insoluble and soluble. Insoluble fibers help move food materials through the digestive tract; soluble fibers tend to slow them down. Both types absorb water, thus preventing constipation. Soluble fibers are also helpful in reducing blood cholesterol levels. Best sources: beans, bran, fruits, whole grains, vegetables, nuts.

Proteins, composed of amino acids, are essential to good nutrition. They build, maintain, and repair the body. Proteins from animal sources (eggs, meat, fish, milk) supply adequate amounts of all indispensable amino acids and are thus called complete. Proteins from plants, legumes, nuts, seeds, and vegetables can be combined to complete protein needs.

Vitamins

Vitamin A promotes good eyesight; plays a role in bone growth, reproduction, the immune system. Best sources: liver, sweet potatoes, carrots, kale, cantaloupe, fortified milk.

Vitamin B_1 (thiamin) is essential to energy metabolism and the growth, development, and function of cells. Best sources: whole grains, fortified bread and cereal, pork, fish.

Vitamin B_2 (riboflavin) is essential to growth, red blood cell production, energy production, and metabolism of fats. Best sources: eggs, dairy products, organ meats, lean meats, bread products, fortified cereal, spinach.

Vitamin B_6 (pyridoxine and related compounds) is important in making antibodies and hemoglobin, maintaining normal nerve function, and protein metabolism. Best sources: fish, organ meats, beans, poultry, fruits, chickpeas, fortified cereal.

Vitamin B_{12} (cobalamin) is needed to form red blood cells. Best sources: beef liver, clams, meat, fish, poultry, eggs.

Folate (vitamin B_9; folic acid is a synthetic form used in supplements and fortified foods) is required for making DNA and other genetic material and for cell division. Best sources: liver, dark green leafy vegetables, fruit, fruit juice, peanuts, beans, enriched breads, fortified cereals.

Niacin (vitamin B_3) helps turn food into energy and is important for cell development and function. Best sources: poultry, nuts, fish.

Other B vitamins include pantothenic acid and biotin.

Vitamin C (ascorbic acid) acts as an antioxidant; also needed to make collagen, a protein necessary for wound healing. Best sources: citrus fruits, broccoli, strawberries, cantaloupe, kiwi, Brussels sprouts, potatoes, tomatoes, red and green peppers.

Vitamin D is important for bone development. Best sources: sunlight, fortified dairy products, tuna, salmon.

Vitamin E is an antioxidant and enhances immune function. Best sources: vegetable oils, nuts, seeds, green leafy vegetables.

Vitamin K is necessary for formation of prothrombin, which helps blood to clot. Best dietary sources: green leafy vegetables, plant oils. Also made by intestinal bacteria.

Minerals

Calcium is needed to build and maintain bones and teeth. Best sources: dairy, leafy green vegetables.

Iron is a component of hemoglobin, which transports oxygen within blood, and myoglobin, which supplies oxygen to the muscles. Best sources: lean meats, beans, green leafy vegetables, seafood, whole grains, fortified cereal.

Phosphorus is present in every cell of the body, and the majority of it can be found in bones and teeth. Best sources: cheese, milk, meats, poultry, fish.

Other minerals include chloride, chromium, copper, fluoride, iodine, magnesium, manganese, molybdenum, potassium, selenium, sodium, zinc.

Understanding Food Label Claims

Source: Center for Food Safety and Applied Nutrition, U.S. Food and Drug Admin. (FDA), U.S. Dept. of Health and Human Services; Food Safety and Inspection Service, Agricultural Marketing Service, U.S. Dept. of Agriculture (USDA)

Nutrition Packaging Terms

Manufacturers can make certain claims on processed food labels only if they meet the definitions specified here.

SUGAR. Sugar free: less than 0.5 g per serving; **No added sugar; Without added sugar:** no sugars or sugar-containing ingredients added during processing; must state if food is not "low calorie" or "reduced calorie"; **Unsweetened; No added sweeteners:** factual statements; **Reduced sugar:** at least 25% less sugar per serving than reference food.

FAT. Fat free: less than 0.5 g of total fat per serving; **Saturated fat free:** less than 0.5 g of saturated fat and less than 0.5 g of trans fatty acids per serving; **Low fat:** 3 g or less of total fat per serving (and per 50 g if the serving size is small, i.e., 30 g or less, 2 tbs or less); **Low saturated fat:** 1 g or less per serving and not more than 15% of calories from saturated fat; **Reduced fat; Less fat:** at least 25% less total fat per serving than reference food.

FIBER. High fiber: 20% or more of the daily value per serving; **Good source of fiber:** 10%-19% of the daily value per serving; **More fiber; Added fiber:** 10% or more of the daily value per serving than reference food.

SODIUM. Sodium free: less than 5 mg per serving; **Low sodium:** 140 mg or less per serving (and per 50 g if the serving size is small, i.e., 30 g or less, 2 tbs or less); **Very low sodium:** 35 mg or less per serving (and per 50 g if the serving size is small); **Reduced sodium; Less sodium:** at least 25% less per serving than reference food.

CALORIES. Calorie free: less than 5 calories per serving; **Low calorie:** 40 calories or less per serving (and per 50 g if the serving size is small, i.e., 30 g or less, 2 tbs or less); **Reduced calorie; Fewer calories:** at least 25% fewer calories per serving than reference food.

CHOLESTEROL. Cholesterol claims are only permitted when food contains 2 g or less saturated fat per serving. **Cholesterol free:** less than 2 mg of cholesterol; **Low cholesterol:** 20 mg or less of cholesterol (and per 50 g of food if the serving size is small, i.e., 30 g or less, 2 tbs or less); **Reduced cholesterol; Less cholesterol:** at least 25% less per serving than reference food.

Other Packaging Terms

The FDA allows food producers and marketers to use language on their packaging that advertises the health benefits and production methods of their products. Products marked "certified" have been formally evaluated by a USDA National Organic Program-authorized certifying agent. Below are some common packaging terms and their meanings.

Organic: Organic operations must demonstrate that their practices foster cycling of resources, promote ecological balance, maintain and improve soil and water quality, minimize the use of synthetic materials, and conserve biodiversity. Before a product can be labeled organic, a farm or business must pass a site inspection by a USDA-accredited certifying agent. Organic foods must be produced without genetic engineering, ionizing radiation, or sewage sludge.

Foods that contain all organic ingredients may advertise "100 percent organic" on the "principal display panel" (generally the front of the packaging) along with the USDA organic seal. Foods with at least 95% organic ingredients may be called "organic" and may place the official seal on their packaging. Products with at least 70% organic ingredients may display "made with organic ____" but may not use the organic seal. Products with less than 70% organic ingredients may not make any organic claims on the principal display panel but may list organic ingredients on the information panel.

Natural: Product contains no artificial ingredient or added color and is only minimally processed (i.e., does not fundamentally alter the product).

Free range or **free roaming:** Producers must demonstrate that poultry has been allowed access to the outside.

Fresh poultry: Whole poultry and cuts that have never been below 26°F.

Frozen poultry: Temperature of raw, frozen poultry is 0°F or below.

Gluten free: Products with a gluten limit of 20 parts per million.

Halal and **Zabiah Halal:** Produced in federally inspected meat packing plants and handled in accordance with Islamic law and under Islamic authority.

Kosher: Meat and poultry products prepared under rabbinical supervision.

No hormones: Hormones are not allowed in the raising of hogs or poultry, so those products may not make this claim. If sufficient documentation is provided to the USDA, this term may appear on packages of beef.

No antibiotics: Claim may be made on a package (red meat and poultry) if sufficient documentation is provided to the USDA showing that the animals were raised without antibiotics.

Dietary Guidelines for Americans, 2020-25: Key Recommendations

Source: *Dietary Guidelines for Americans, 2020-2025*, U.S. Dept. of Agriculture and U.S. Dept. of Health and Human Services

The government revises its dietary guidelines every five years. The most recent edition marks the first time the guidelines provide recommendations by life stage, from birth through older adulthood. Each stage of life is distinct and has unique needs that affect health and disease risk. Early food preferences influence food and beverage choices later. And the science has evolved to focus on the importance of a healthy dietary pattern over time. The science also shows it is never too late to start and maintain a healthy dietary pattern, which can yield health benefits in the short term and cumulatively over years.

Core elements of a healthy dietary pattern:

- **Vegetables** of all types—dark green; red and orange; beans, peas, and lentils; starchy; and other vegetables.
- **Fruits**, especially whole fruit.
- **Grains**, at least half of which are whole grain.
- **Dairy**, including fat-free or low-fat milk, yogurt, and cheese, and/or lactose-free versions and fortified soy beverages and yogurt as alternatives.
- **Protein foods**, including lean meats, poultry, and eggs; seafood; beans, peas, and lentils; and nuts, seeds, and soy products.
- **Oils**, including vegetable oils and oils in food, such as seafood and nuts.

Dietary components to limit:

- **Added sugars**—Less than 10% of calories per day starting at age 2. Avoid foods and beverages with added sugars for those younger than age 2.
- **Saturated fat**—Less than 10% of calories per day starting at age 2.
- **Sodium**—Less than 2,300 milligrams per day, and even less for children younger than age 14.
- **Alcoholic beverages**—Adults of legal drinking age can choose not to drink, or to drink in moderation by limiting intake to 2 drinks or less in a day for men and 1 drink or less in a day for women, when alcohol is consumed. Drinking less is better for health than drinking more. There are some adults who should not drink alcohol, such as people who are pregnant.

U.S. Annual Per Capita Consumption of Meat and Dairy, 1910-2021

Source: Economic Research Service, U.S. Dept. of Agriculture
(in pounds per capita per year, unless otherwise noted)

Meat	1910	1930	1950	1970	1990	2000	2010	2015	2018	2021	% change, 1910-2021
Beef	48.5	33.7	44.6	79.8	63.9	64.5	56.7	51.4	54.6	56.2	15.8%
Chicken	11.0	11.1	14.3	27.4	42.4	54.2	58.0	62.6	65.2	68.1	520.4
Fish/shellfish	11.2	10.2	11.9	11.7	16.7	16.6	17.4	18.6	18.8	NA	68.0[1]
Pork	38.2	41.1	43.0	48.5	46.4	47.8	44.4	46.3	47.4	47.5	24.2
Total red meat[2]	96.0	83.6	95.8	132.5	112.2	113.7	102.0	98.6	103.0	104.8	9.2
Dairy											
Butter	18.4	17.6	10.9	5.4	4.3	4.5	4.9	5.6	6.0	6.5	–64.9
Cheese, American	2.8	3.2	5.5	7.0	11.1	12.7	13.3	14.0	15.4	16.1	481.9
Cheese, other than American	1.5	1.5	2.2	4.4	13.5	16.9	19.4	21.1	22.6	23.1	1,422.5
Ice cream	1.9	9.3	16.4	16.7	15.4	16.1	14.0	12.9	12.0	12.0	522.0
Milk, skim/lower fat (gallons)	7.1	5.0	2.9	5.8	15.2	14.5	14.8	12.4	10.8	9.3	31.4
Milk, whole (gallons)	25.2	28.2	34.3	25.5	10.5	8.2	5.7	5.5	5.9	5.9	–76.8

NA = Not available. (1) Percent change, 1910-2018. (2) Includes beef, veal, lamb, and pork.

Organic Agriculture, 2017, 2022

Source: National Agricultural Statistics Service, U.S. Dept. of Agriculture

	2022	2017
Number of farms with organic sales		
Organic product sales	17,321	18,166
Average per farm	$553,380	$400,603
By value of sales—		
$1 to $4,999	3,051	3,867
$5,000 to $9,999	1,042	1,470
$10,000 to $24,999	1,896	2,137
$25,000 to $49,999	1,765	1,862
$50,000 or more	9,567	8,830
Value of sales (in thous.)		
Organic product sales	9,585,089	7,277,350
By value of sales—		
$1 to $4,999	5,960	7,585
$5,000 to $9,999	7,333	10,163
$10,000 to $24,999	30,964	35,192
$25,000 to $49,999	62,257	66,544
$50,000 or more	9,478,575	7,157,866
Producer characteristics		
Male	25,461	25,026
Female	14,045	14,660
Primary occupation		
Farming	24,104	25,225
Other	15,402	14,461
Place of residence		
On farm operated	27,085	29,845
Not on farm operated	12,421	9,841
Days worked off farm		
None	17,901	19,098
Any	21,605	20,588
1 to 49 days	4,839	4,800
50 to 99 days	2,211	2,081
100 to 199 days	3,407	3,391
200 days or more	11,148	10,316
Years on present farm		
2 years or less	2,153	3,172
3 or 4 years	3,800	4,451
5 to 9 years	9,525	8,037
10 years or more	24,028	24,026
Average years on present farm	17.8	16.9
Age group		
Under 25 years	1,256	1,320
25 to 34 years	4,878	5,586
35 to 44 years	7,564	7,099
45 to 54 years	6,572	7,082
55 to 64 years	8,203	10,071
65 to 74 years	7,928	6,532
75 years and over	3,105	1,996
Average age	52.7	51.3

Note: Data for farms producing certified or exempt organic commodities only. Data were collected for a maximum of four producers per farm.

Livestock on Farms in the U.S., 1900-2024

Source: National Agricultural Statistics Service, U.S. Dept. of Agriculture
(in thousands as of Jan. 1, unless otherwise noted)

Year	All cattle[1]	Milk cows	Sheep and lambs	Hogs and pigs[2]
1900	59,739	16,544	48,105	51,055
1910	58,993	19,450	50,239	48,072
1920	70,400	21,455	40,743	60,159
1930	61,003	23,032	51,565	55,705
1940	68,309	24,940	52,107	61,165
1950	77,963	23,853	29,826	58,937
1960	96,236	19,527	33,170	59,026
1970	112,369	12,091	20,423	57,046
1975	132,028	11,220	14,515	54,693
1980	111,242	10,758	12,699	67,318
1985	109,582	10,777	10,716	54,073
1990	95,816	10,015	11,358	53,788
1995	102,785	9,482	8,886	57,150
2000	98,199	9,183	7,036	59,335
2005	95,018	9,004	6,135	60,975
2010	93,881	9,086	5,620	65,327
2013	89,300	9,218	5,335	66,373
2014	88,526	9,208	5,245	64,775
2015	89,143	9,307	5,280	66,145
2016	91,918	9,310	5,300	68,919
2017	93,705	9,346	5,250	71,545
2018	94,298	9,432	5,265	73,145
2019	94,805	9,353	5,230	74,550
2020	93,793	9,343	5,200	78,658
2021	93,790	9,442	5,170	77,312
2022	92,077	9,377	5,065	74,446
2023	88,841	9,398	5,130	73,119
2024	87,157	9,357	5,030	75,816

(1) For 1970 and on, includes milk cows and heifers that have calved. (2) As of Dec. 1 of preceding year.

Production of Principal U.S. Crops, 1990-2023

Source: National Agricultural Statistics Service, U.S. Dept. of Agriculture

Year	Corn for grain (1,000 bu)	Oats (1,000 bu)	Barley (1,000 bu)	Sorghum for grain (1,000 bu)	All wheat (1,000 bu)	Rye (1,000 bu)	Canola (1,000 lb)	Cotton (upland) (1,000 b)	Cottonseed (1,000 t)
1990	7,934,028	357,654	422,196	573,303	2,729,778	10,176	NA	15,505.4	5,968.5
1995	7,373,876	162,027	359,562	460,373	2,182,591	10,064	548,447	17,532.2	6,848.7
2000	9,915,051	149,545	318,728	470,526	2,232,460	8,386	1,998,310	16,799.2	6,435.6
2005	11,114,082	114,878	211,896	392,933	2,104,690	7,537	1,580,985	23,259.7	8,172.1
2010	12,446,865	81,190	180,268	345,625	2,206,916	7,431	2,447,628	17,600.0	6,098.1
2013	13,828,964	64,642	216,745	392,331	2,134,979	7,626	2,210,505	12,275.0	4,203.0
2015	13,601,964	89,535	218,187	596,751	2,061,939	11,616	2,878,470	12,455.0	4,043.0
2016	15,148,038	64,770	199,914	480,261	2,308,723	13,451	3,086,340	16,601.0	5,369.0
2017	14,609,407	49,585	143,258	361,871	1,740,910	10,252	3,055,410	20,223.0	6,422.0
2018	14,340,369	56,130	153,527	364,986	1,885,156	8,432	3,615,440	17,566.0	5,631.0
2019	13,619,928	53,258	172,499	341,460	1,932,017	10,622	3,400,865	19,227.0	5,945.0
2020	14,111,449	65,694	170,813	372,960	1,828,043	11,532	3,453,062	14,061.0	4,435.0
2021	15,017,788	39,836	120,593	447,810	1,646,254	9,808	2,715,050	17,523.0	5,323.0
2022	13,650,531	57,669	173,920	187,785	1,649,713	12,453	3,814,823	14,468.0	4,415.0
2023	15,341,595	57,045	185,036	317,745	1,811,977	10,375	4,157,420	12,434.0	3,788.0

Year	Tobacco (1,000 lb)	All hay (1,000 t)	Beans, dry edible (1,000 cwt)	Peas, dry edible (1,000 cwt)	Peanuts (1,000 lb)	Soybeans[1] (1,000 bu)	Potatoes (1,000 cwt)	Sweet potatoes (1,000 cwt)
1990	1,626,380	146,212	32,379	2,372	3,602,770	1,925,947	402,110	12,594
1995	1,268,538	154,166	30,812	4,765	4,247,455	2,176,814	443,606	12,906
2000	1,052,999	151,921	26,409	3,474	3,265,505	2,757,810	513,621	13,794
2005	645,015	151,017	26,772	14,003	4,869,860	3,063,237	423,926	15,730
2010	718,190	145,624	31,801	14,221	4,156,840	3,329,181	404,273	23,845
2013	723,579	135,002	24,576	15,620	4,173,170	3,357,984	434,652	24,785
2015	719,171	134,502	30,057	18,283	6,001,357	3,926,339	441,205	31,016
2016	628,720	134,995	28,703	27,762	5,581,570	4,296,086	441,411	31,546
2017	710,161	128,207	35,961	14,195	7,115,410	4,411,633	450,921	35,646
2018	533,241	123,600	37,745	15,929	5,495,935	4,428,150	450,020	27,378
2019	467,956	128,864	20,756	22,210	5,466,487	3,551,908	424,419	31,973
2020	372,877	126,812	32,665	21,629	6,158,350	4,216,302	420,020	30,128
2021	456,423	119,764	22,407	9,161	6,359,190	4,464,492	412,639	30,048
2022	437,775	111,738	25,734	15,517	5,541,772	4,270,381	402,054	27,740
2023	432,452	118,769	23,910	18,086	5,890,020	4,164,677	440,750	25,086

Year	Rice (1,000 cwt)	Sugarcane (1,000 t)	Sugar beets (1,000 t)	Pecans[2] (1,000 lb)	Apples (1,000 t)	Grapes (1,000 t)	Peaches (1,000 t)	Oranges[3] (1,000 bx)	Grapefruit[3] (1,000 bx)
1990	156,088	28,136	27,513	205,000	4,828	5,660	1,121	184,415	49,300
1995	173,871	30,944	27,954	268,000	5,293	5,922	1,150	263,605	71,050
2000	190,872	36,114	32,541	209,850	5,291	7,688	1,276	299,760	66,980
2005	223,235	26,606	27,433	280,250	4,853	7,814	1,185	216,500	25,640
2010	243,104	27,360	32,034	293,740	4,646	7,471	1,150	192,835	30,400
2013	189,953	30,761	32,789	266,330	5,216	8,632	904	189,893	28,950
2015	193,148	32,122	35,371	254,290	5,023	7,621	847	146,602	21,950
2016	224,145	32,118	36,920	268,770	5,689	7,697	796	141,891	19,400
2017	178,228	33,238	35,317	304,850	5,777	7,384	701	118,520	16,960
2018	223,833	34,542	33,282	240,930	5,120	7,596	652	91,130	12,480
2019	185,104	31,937	28,650	255,600	5,543	6,961	681	126,550	14,810
2020	227,514	36,100	33,610	304,050	5,143	6,040	653	122,840	13,950
2021	191,052	32,838	36,772	266,150	5,036	6,034	702	103,000	10,700
2022	160,041	34,671	32,644	288,350	4,988	5,963	648	80,500	9,130
2023	218,291	32,956	35,226	306,750	5,679	5,910	589	60,130	8,060

b = bale; bu = bushel; bx = box; cwt = hundred weight; lb = pound; t = ton. **Note:** Some 2023 figures are preliminary estimates. (1) Harvested for beans. (2) Utilized production only. (3) Crop year ending in year cited.

Animal Products: Average Prices Received by U.S. Farmers, 1940-2023

Source: National Agricultural Statistics Service, U.S. Dept. of Agriculture

Figures represent dollars per 100 lb for veal calves, beef cattle, hogs, lambs, milk (wholesale), and sheep; dollars per head for milk cows; cents per lb for broilers, chickens, turkeys, and wool; and cents per dozen for eggs. Weighted calendar year prices for livestock and livestock products other than wool. For 1943-63, wool prices were weighted on marketing year basis. The marketing year was changed in 1964 from a calendar year to a Dec.-Nov. basis for broilers, chickens, eggs, and hogs.

Year	Broilers	Calves (veal)	Cattle (beef)	Chickens (excl. broilers)	Eggs	Hogs	Lambs[1]	Milk	Milk cows	Sheep[1]	Turkeys	Wool
1940	17.3	8.83	7.56	13.0	18.0	5.39	8.10	1.82	61	3.95	15.2	28.4
1950	27.4	26.30	23.30	22.2	36.3	18.00	25.10	3.89	198	11.60	32.8	62.1
1960	16.9	22.90	20.40	12.2	36.1	15.30	17.90	4.21	223	5.61	25.4	42.0
1970	13.6	34.50	27.10	9.1	39.1	22.70	26.40	5.71	332	7.51	22.6	35.4
1980	27.7	76.80	62.40	11.0	56.3	38.00	63.60	13.05	1,190	21.30	41.3	88.1
1990	32.6	95.60	74.60	9.3	70.9	53.70	55.50	13.74	1,160	23.20	39.4	80.0
2000	33.6	104.00	68.60	5.7	61.8	42.30	79.80	12.40	1,340	34.30	40.7	33.0
2005	43.6	135.00	89.70	6.5	54.0	50.20	110.00	15.19	1,770	45.10	44.9	71.0
2010	48.2	117.00	92.20	8.1	85.7	54.10	125.00	16.35	1,330	49.70	61.5	115.0
2012	50.0	168.00	122.00	8.8	101.1	64.20	NA	18.56	1,430	NA	72.1	153.0
2014	63.7	261.00	152.00	10.1	122.1	76.50	NA	24.07	1,830	NA	73.5	146.0
2015	53.8	247.00	147.00	10.3	168.0	55.30	NA	17.21	1,990	NA	81.1	145.0
2016	47.8	158.00	119.00	8.1	76.3	49.30	NA	16.34	1,760	NA	82.6	145.0
2017	54.4	168.00	120.00	4.7	85.6	53.10	NA	17.69	1,620	NA	64.6	147.0

Year	Broilers	Calves (veal)	Cattle (beef)	Chickens (excl. broilers)	Eggs	Hogs	Lambs[1]	Milk	Milk cows	Sheep[1]	Turkeys	Wool
2018	55.9	170.00	115.00	4.8	116.1	50.20	NA	16.28	1,360	NA	51.0	175.0
2019	48.6	159.00	116.00	3.7	77.7	51.40	NA	18.63	1,200	NA	57.9	189.0
2020	35.8	161.00	109.00	1.8	93.1	46.90	NA	18.16	1,300	NA	70.9	166.0
2021	53.2	171.00	121.00	1.5	93.9	67.30	NA	18.54	1,360	NA	82.1	170.0
2022	85.0	195.00	142.00	7.6	212.1	72.20	NA	25.39	1,590	NA	106.7	153.0
2023	71.3	261.00	173.00	5.9	195.7	62.70	NA	20.38	1,760	NA	94.0	156.0

NA = Not available. (1) Prices not calculated after 2010.

Crops: Average Prices Received by U.S. Farmers, 1940-2023

Source: National Agricultural Statistics Service, U.S. Dept. of Agriculture

Figures represent cents per lb for apples, cotton, and peanuts; dollars per bushel for barley, corn, oats, soybeans, and wheat; dollars per 100 lb for potatoes, rice, and sorghum; and dollars per ton for cottonseed and hay. Weighted crop year prices. The marketing year is described as follows: apples and potatoes, July-June; barley, oats, and wheat, June-May; corn, sorghum, and soybeans, Sept.-Aug.; cottonseed, Aug.-Feb.; cotton, peanuts, and rice, Aug.-July; and hay, May-Apr.

Year	Apples	Barley	Corn	Cotton-seed	Cotton (upland)	Hay	Oats	Peanuts	Pota-toes	Rice	Sor-ghum	Soy-beans	Wheat
1940	NA	0.39	0.62	21.70	9.8	9.78	0.30	3.7	0.85	1.80	0.87	0.89	0.67
1950	NA	1.19	1.52	86.60	39.9	21.10	0.79	10.9	1.50	5.09	1.88	2.47	2.00
1960	2.7	0.84	1.00	42.50	30.1	21.70	0.60	10.0	2.00	4.55	1.49	2.13	1.74
1970	6.5	0.97	1.33	56.40	21.9	26.10	0.62	12.8	2.21	5.17	2.04	2.85	1.33
1980	12.1	2.86	3.11	129.00	74.4	71.00	1.79	25.1	6.55	12.80	5.25	7.57	3.91
1990	20.9	2.14	2.28	121.00	67.1	80.60	1.14	34.7	6.08	6.68	3.79	5.74	2.61
2000	17.8	2.11	1.85	105.00	49.8	84.60	1.10	27.4	5.08	5.61	3.37	4.54	2.62
2005	24.4	2.53	2.00	96.00	47.7	98.20	1.63	17.3	7.06	7.65	3.33	5.66	3.42
2010	25.1	3.86	5.18	161.00	81.5	114.00	2.52	22.5	9.20	12.70	8.96	11.30	5.70
2012	37.1	6.43	6.89	252.00	72.5	191.00	3.89	30.1	8.63	15.10	11.30	14.40	7.77
2014	25.7	5.30	3.70	194.00	61.3	172.00	3.21	22.0	8.88	13.40	7.20	10.10	5.99
2015	33.6	5.52	3.61	227.00	61.2	145.00	2.12	19.3	8.76	12.20	5.91	8.95	4.89
2016	31.6	4.96	3.36	195.00	68.0	129.00	2.06	19.7	9.08	10.40	4.98	9.47	3.89
2017	32.1	4.47	3.36	142.00	68.6	142.00	2.59	22.9	9.17	12.90	5.75	9.33	4.72
2018	29.9	4.62	3.61	155.00	70.3	166.00	2.66	21.5	8.90	12.60	5.82	8.48	5.16
2019	25.8	4.69	3.56	161.00	59.6	163.00	2.82	20.5	9.94	13.60	5.96	8.57	4.58
2020	29.6	4.75	4.53	194.00	66.3	156.00	2.77	21.0	9.30	14.40	9.00	10.80	5.05
2021	29.6	5.31	6.00	243.00	91.4	193.00	4.55	24.3	10.20	16.10	10.60	13.30	7.63
2022	32.1	7.40	6.54	306.00	84.8	239.00	4.57	26.8	12.90	19.80	11.40	14.20	8.83
2023[1]	27.4	7.50	4.80	225.00	73.6	211.00	3.70	27.0	12.80	18.40	8.65	12.70	7.20

NA = Not available. (1) Preliminary.

World Meat Production, 2000, 2022

Source: UN Food and Agriculture Organization; in thousands of metric tons; ranked by top producers in 2022

Top beef producers				Top pork producers				Top poultry producers			
Rank	Country	2000	2022	Rank	Country	2000	2022	Rank	Country	2000	2022
1.	U.S.	12,017	12,890	1.	China[1]	39,660	55,410	1.	China[1]	11,890	23,400
2.	Brazil	6,579	10,350	2.	U.S.	8,597	12,252	2.	U.S.	16,575	22,030
3.	China[1]	5,131	7,836	3.	Brazil	2,600	5,186	3.	Brazil	6,125	14,691
4.	India	1,525	4,350	4.	Spain	2,905	5,066	4.	Russia	775	5,308
5.	Argentina	2,718	3,133	5.	Russia	1,578	4,532	5.	India	904	4,951
6.	Pakistan	886	2,454	6.	Germany	3,982	4,492	6.	Indonesia	818	4,083
7.	Mexico	1,409	2,176	7.	Vietnam	1,029	3,102	7.	Mexico	1,849	3,800
8.	Australia	1,988	1,878	8.	Canada	1,640	2,263	8.	Poland	589	2,734
9.	Russia	1,898	1,621	9.	France	2,312	2,152	9.	Egypt	592	2,638
10.	Türkiye	359	1,586	10.	Poland	1,923	1,805	10.	Türkiye	668	2,476
11.	Canada	1,263	1,379	11.	Mexico	1,030	1,730	11.	Japan	1,195	2,372
12.	France	1,528	1,361	12.	Netherlands	1,623	1,684	12.	Argentina	1,000	2,361
13.	Uzbekistan	390	1,028	13.	Denmark	1,625	1,609	13.	Iran	815	2,101
14.	South Africa	582	1,008	14.	South Korea	916	1,419	14.	Pakistan	332	1,982
15.	Germany	1,304	995	15.	Japan	1,256	1,293	15.	South Africa	821	1,958
16.	UK	705	925	16.	Italy	1,479	1,255	16.	UK	1,513	1,952
17.	Spain	651	732	17.	Philippines	1,213	1,216	17.	Thailand	1,149	1,913
18.	New Zealand	587	728	18.	UK	899	1,043	18.	Colombia	504	1,820
19.	Zimbabwe	642	725	19.	Belgium	1,042	1,032	19.	Peru	510	1,802
20.	Colombia	745	718	20.	Thailand	693	891	20.	Malaysia	714	1,678
21.	Ireland	577	621	21.	Taiwan	921	805	21.	Spain	992	1,585
22.	Uruguay	453	616	22.	Argentina	214	723	22.	Canada	1,065	1,531
23.	Egypt	570	611	23.	Ukraine	676	659	23.	Germany	790	1,507
24.	Poland	349	541	24.	Chile	261	576	24.	France	2,148	1,478
25.	Kazakhstan	306	533	25.	Colombia	105	517	25.	Philippines	557	1,459
Africa		4,692	7,045	Africa		927	2,101	Africa		2,962	8,190
Asia		12,168	22,385	Asia		47,319	65,872	Asia		22,907	54,534
Central America		1,766	2,813	Central America		1,132	1,902	Central America		2,351	5,156
Europe		11,771	10,264	Europe		25,283	29,596	Europe		11,861	22,341
North America		13,280	14,269	North America		10,237	14,515	Northern America		17,640	23,561
Oceania		2,591	2,621	Oceania		487	583	Oceania		767	1,674
South America		11,846	16,657	South America		3,646	7,705	South America		9,696	23,125
World total		**58,337**	**76,250**	**World total**		**89,240**	**122,585**	**World total**		**68,659**	**139,219**

(1) Not including Hong Kong or Macau.

World Corn, Rice, and Wheat Production, 2000, 2022

Source: UN Food and Agriculture Organization; in millions of metric tons; ranked by top producers in 2022

Top corn producers

Rank	Country	2000	2022
1.	U.S.	251.9	348.8
2.	China	106.0	277.2
3.	Brazil	32.3	109.4
4.	Argentina	16.8	59.0
5.	India	12.0	33.7
6.	Mexico	17.6	26.6
7.	Ukraine	3.8	26.2
8.	Indonesia	9.7	23.6
9.	South Africa	11.4	16.1
10.	Russia	1.5	15.9
11.	Canada	7.0	14.5
12.	Nigeria	4.1	12.9
13.	France	16.0	10.9
14.	Ethiopia	2.7	10.2
15.	Pakistan	1.6	10.2
16.	Türkiye	2.3	8.5
17.	Poland	0.9	8.3
18.	Philippines	4.5	8.3
19.	Romania	4.9	8.0
20.	Egypt	6.5	7.5
21.	Paraguay	0.6	6.2
22.	Tanzania	2.0	5.9
23.	Thailand	4.5	4.9
24.	Italy	10.1	4.7
25.	Vietnam	2.0	4.4
	Africa	43.8	92.8
	Asia	149.1	389.9
	Central America	20.3	30.7
	Europe	63.1	102.7
	North America	258.8	363.3
	Oceania	0.6	0.6
	South America	55.8	183.0
	World total	**592.0**	**1,163.5**

Top rice producers

Rank	Country	2000	2022
1.	China	187.9	208.5
2.	India	127.5	196.2
3.	Bangladesh	37.6	57.2
4.	Indonesia	51.9	54.7
5.	Vietnam	32.5	42.7
6.	Thailand	25.8	34.3
7.	Myanmar	21.3	24.7
8.	Philippines	12.4	19.8
9.	Cambodia	4.0	11.6
10.	Pakistan	7.2	11.0
11.	Brazil	11.1	10.8
12.	Japan	11.9	10.4
13.	Nigeria	3.3	8.5
14.	U.S.	8.7	7.3
15.	Egypt	6.0	5.8
16.	Nepal	4.2	5.5
17.	South Korea	7.2	5.0
18.	Madagascar	2.5	4.6
19.	Laos	2.2	3.6
20.	Peru	1.9	3.4
21.	Sri Lanka	2.9	3.4
22.	Mali	0.7	2.9
23.	Tanzania	0.8	2.9
24.	Colombia	2.2	2.6
25.	Guinea	1.1	2.5
	Africa	17.5	39.9
	Asia	545.5	698.8
	Central America	1.3	1.4
	Europe	3.2	3.1
	North America	8.7	7.3
	Oceania	1.1	0.7
	South America	20.5	23.9
	World total	**598.9**	**776.5**

Top wheat producers

Rank	Country	2000	2022
1.	China	99.6	137.7
2.	India	76.4	107.7
3.	Russia	34.5	104.2
4.	U.S.	60.6	44.9
5.	Australia	24.8	36.2
6.	France	37.4	34.6
7.	Canada	26.5	34.3
8.	Pakistan	21.1	26.2
9.	Germany	21.6	22.6
10.	Argentina	15.5	22.2
11.	Ukraine	10.2	20.7
12.	Türkiye	21.0	19.8
13.	Kazakhstan	9.1	16.4
14.	UK	16.7	15.5
15.	Poland	8.5	13.2
16.	Brazil	1.7	10.3
17.	Iran	8.1	10.0
18.	Egypt	6.6	9.7
19.	Romania	4.4	8.7
20.	Ethiopia	1.2	7.0
21.	Italy	7.5	6.6
22.	Spain	7.3	6.5
23.	Bulgaria	2.8	6.4
24.	Uzbekistan	3.7	6.3
25.	Czechia	4.1	5.2
	Africa	14.3	27.3
	Asia	254.7	342.8
	Central America	3.5	3.6
	Europe	183.4	282.7
	North America	87.2	79.2
	Oceania	25.1	36.6
	South America	19.6	36.2
	World total	**587.6**	**808.4**

Value of U.S. Agricultural Trade, 1935-2023

Source: Economic Research Service, U.S. Dept. of Agriculture
(in millions of dollars)

Year	Agric. exports	Agric. imports	Agric. trade balance	Total agric. trade
1935	$669	$934	–$265	$1,603
1940	738	1,239	–501	1,977
1945	2,191	1,729	462	3,920
1950	2,986	3,177	–191	6,163
1955	3,144	3,781	–637	6,925
1960	4,519	4,010	509	8,529
1965	6,097	3,986	2,111	10,083
1970	7,115	5,433	1,682	12,548
1975	22,220	9,132	13,088	31,352
1980	41,738	16,526	25,212	58,264
1985	32,509	19,194	13,315	51,702
1990	45,348	23,816	21,531	69,164
1995	60,958	30,480	30,479	91,438
2000	55,294	41,646	13,648	96,940
2002	55,964	44,457	11,507	100,422
2004	64,896	56,127	8,770	121,023
2005	64,859	61,567	3,292	126,426
2006	71,231	68,868	2,363	140,099
2007	$85,227	$75,171	$10,056	$160,398
2008	117,951	84,227	33,724	202,178
2009	98,644	78,241	20,403	176,886
2010	111,239	82,934	28,304	194,173
2011	142,090	97,465	44,625	239,554
2012	141,200	108,342	32,858	249,542
2013	145,082	111,002	34,081	256,084
2014	156,849	115,888	40,961	272,737
2015	144,068	121,611	22,456	265,679
2016	133,719	121,083	12,635	254,802
2017	144,781	127,151	17,630	271,932
2018	148,620	136,478	12,142	285,098
2019	140,094	141,437	–1,343	281,530
2020	139,724	143,403	–3,679	283,127
2021	171,816	163,335	8,481	335,151
2022	196,138	194,174	1,964	390,313
2023	178,747	195,373	–16,626	374,119

Note: Data for 1935-65 are for July-June fiscal year; data for 1970-2023 are for Oct.-Sept. fiscal year.

Crop Consumption Per Capita in Selected Nations, 1980-2021

Source: UN Food and Agriculture Organization
(in kilograms per capita per year)

	Corn					Rice					Wheat				
Country	1980	1990	2010	2020	2021	1980	1990	2010	2020	2021	1980	1990	2010	2020	2021
Afghanistan	33	24	2	3	5	20	17	25	25	22	162	140	175	161	156
Argentina	6	5	11	12	12	2	6	12	16	18	115	114	109	119	115
Australia	2	4	5	4	4	8	8	17	14	14	81	70	78	91	89
Bangladesh	<1	<1	1	1	1	144	159	259	260	261	29	21	15	18	18
Brazil	22	22	27	28	30	39	41	46	38	40	50	44	60	53	54
Canada	4	3	19	20	24	3	5	15	17	15	76	78	88	92	87
China[1]	5	4	7	8	8	75	82	129	132	129	59	78	67	71	72
Congo Rep.	5	3	3	5	3	2	5	22	16	17	33	33	37	43	48
Cuba	0	0	27	29	30	51	47	63	152	157	78	74	63	56	55
Egypt	49	57	61	57	57	26	31	54	47	47	129	151	140	137	134
France	2	13	12	12	13	4	4	8	11	10	95	92	108	105	105
Germany	3	6	9	8	5	2	2	5	7	8	69	67	89	72	74
India	8	8	7	5	5	64	78	103	105	105	45	41	59	63	64
Indonesia	24	29	24	1	1	125	131	205	191	183	10	9	22	35	39
Iran	1	1	3	3	3	30	30	42	39	38	154	164	147	153	152
Iraq	<1	3	<1	1	2	31	37	55	59	58	144	185	136	137	138

Country	Corn 1980	Corn 1990	Corn 2010	Corn 2020	Corn 2021	Rice 1980	Rice 1990	Rice 2010	Rice 2020	Rice 2021	Wheat 1980	Wheat 1990	Wheat 2010	Wheat 2020	Wheat 2021
Israel	12	23	22	17	14	6	8	23	24	24	138	124	118	108	102
Italy	5	3	4	3	3	5	5	8	8	9	174	149	147	139	144
Japan	15	19	13	13	13	73	65	81	73	74	44	44	48	46	42
Kenya	114	88	75	68	61	2	2	14	22	20	20	23	41	40	48
Korea, North	43	56	45	68	72	71	70	112	91	90	32	22	21	12	4
Korea, South	2	13	13	17	16	138	97	129	84	81	49	48	53	53	54
Mexico	118	124	117	124	123	5	4	9	10	8	42	42	36	34	36
New Zealand	1	3	4	6	5	2	4	14	17	15	78	69	81	90	91
Nigeria	6	33	31	34	34	15	21	44	34	33	16	3	25	28	29
Pakistan	7	6	12	16	12	23	14	20	19	19	114	128	108	102	104
Philippines	22	19	23	37	38	97	94	172	188	190	17	20	23	45	43
Russia	NA	NA	1	1	1	NA	NA	8	8	8	NA	NA	133	137	138
Saudi Arabia	11	13	23	26	24	33	18	51	55	54	88	104	84	97	98
South Africa	120	108	94	81	76	4	8	22	22	22	56	56	57	56	56
Thailand	5	5	9	10	11	137	114	183	163	171	4	4	13	16	14
Türkiye	8	21	18	17	19	3	6	15	17	13	210	223	182	164	164
Ukraine	NA	NA	12	22	23	NA	NA	4	5	3	NA	NA	112	92	97
UAE	1	1	1	2	3	43	34	71	43	38	63	65	82	115	117
UK	3	3	3	5	5	2	2	17	14	14	82	82	105	123	124
U.S.	8	13	13	12	12	4	7	11	11	12	70	81	83	88	88
Venezuela	55	54	58	50	42	21	13	49	54	55	50	51	47	28	38
Vietnam	7	7	8	19	17	128	133	250	238	232	17	3	11	17	15
Africa	38	41	45	43	42	15	17	34	34	37	45	47	48	47	47
Asia	8	9	9	9	9	77	82	120	119	118	53	60	64	68	69
Central America	107	113	103	108	108	8	7	16	19	16	38	38	36	35	37
Europe	4	5	6	6	6	5	4	8	9	8	118	117	112	111	113
North America	7	12	13	13	14	4	7	11	12	12	71	81	83	88	88
Oceania	2	4	4	3	3	9	10	20	22	26	79	69	65	76	75
South America	22	23	28	29	30	29	32	42	41	42	58	53	62	60	60
World	**13**	**15**	**17**	**18**	**18**	**50**	**54**	**83**	**82**	**81**	**64**	**68**	**67**	**68**	**69**

NA = Not available or not applicable. **Note:** All figures are rounded. Data for 2010, 2020, and 2021 are not directly comparable to earlier years because of a change in methodology. (1) Not including Hong Kong or Macau.

Meat Consumption Per Capita in Selected Nations, 1980-2021

Source: UN Food and Agriculture Organization
(in kilograms per capita per year)

Country	Beef 1980	Beef 1990	Beef 2010	Beef 2020	Beef 2021	Pork 1980	Pork 1990	Pork 2010	Pork 2020	Pork 2021	Poultry 1980	Poultry 1990	Poultry 2010	Poultry 2020	Poultry 2021
Afghanistan	5	7	5	3	3	NA	NA	NA	<1	<1	1	1	2	2	2
Argentina	85	64	51	51	48	9	4	8	14	16	11	11	34	46	48
Australia	53	47	39	37	26	15	18	22	24	25	21	24	47	48	49
Bangladesh	1	1	1	1	1	0	0	0	0	0	1	1	1	2	2
Brazil	22	28	38	35	35	8	7	12	14	13	10	14	38	48	51
Canada	40	36	29	28	26	35	28	25	21	18	22	28	37	41	41
China[1]	<1	1	5	7	8	11	19	38	30	34	1	3	12	17	17
Congo Rep.	4	1	3	2	3	1	2	1	8	9	2	5	7	23	26
Cuba	15	13	7	8	4	5	10	19	22	9	9	12	16	39	33
Egypt	7	8	12	8	6	<1	<1	<1	<1	<1	4	4	11	20	21
France	33	33	26	23	23	37	34	35	33	33	16	21	24	26	27
Germany	23	22	13	15	14	60	60	55	44	43	10	11	18	18	18
India	2	2	1	2	2	<1	<1	<1	<1	<1	<1	<1	2	3	3
Indonesia	2	2	3	3	3	1	3	1	1	1	1	3	7	14	14
Iran	6	6	8	3	4	0	0	0	0	0	6	7	22	28	24
Iraq	5	7	3	3	4	0	0	0	<1	<1	9	11	12	16	13
Israel	13	14	29	30	32	2	2	3	2	1	35	39	66	72	69
Italy	26	27	23	16	16	25	32	42	33	36	18	20	18	21	21
Japan	5	8	9	10	10	13	15	20	22	22	10	14	17	23	25
Kenya	12	9	11	5	5	<1	<1	<1	<1	<1	2	1	1	1	2
Korea, North	2	2	1	1	1	10	11	5	5	4	2	3	2	2	2
Korea, South	3	6	13	19	20	8	13	31	38	38	2	6	15	23	22
Mexico	11	14	17	15	15	18	9	17	20	20	6	10	32	37	38
New Zealand	57	39	21	18	18	12	14	22	24	27	10	17	23	25	24
Nigeria	5	2	2	2	2	1	1	1	1	2	2	2	2	1	1
Pakistan	5	6	8	9	10	0	0	0	0	0	1	1	4	6	6
Philippines	3	2	5	3	4	9	12	18	14	14	5	4	11	16	15
Russia	NA	NA	18	14	13	NA	NA	22	28	28	NA	NA	22	31	31
Saudi Arabia	6	4	6	5	6	NA	NA	NA	NA	NA	24	29	42	42	41
South Africa	20	17	17	17	17	3	4	4	5	6	8	15	33	40	44
Thailand	6	6	3	1	1	6	9	13	13	13	7	9	12	12	11
Türkiye	3	7	10	16	17	<1	<1	0	0	0	6	8	18	20	20
Ukraine	NA	NA	9	7	6	NA	NA	16	17	18	NA	NA	24	25	24
UAE	14	13	3	18	18	NA	NA	NA	2	3	43	39	19	50	49
UK	23	21	20	20	18	26	25	25	25	25	14	19	29	34	34
U.S.	47	43	39	37	38	33	28	28	30	30	26	39	51	58	58
Venezuela	22	18	19	12	13	6	5	8	5	6	17	13	45	16	16
Vietnam	2	2	3	4	5	5	10	25	27	27	2	2	12	16	20
Africa	7	6	6	5	5	1	1	1	2	2	2	3	6	7	7
Asia	2	3	4	6	6	6	9	15	12	13	2	3	9	12	12
Central America	10	12	15	13	14	14	8	13	16	17	6	9	28	34	36
Europe	23	25	16	14	14	32	35	35	34	35	12	15	22	26	26
North America	47	43	38	37	37	33	28	28	29	29	26	38	50	56	56
Oceania	50	43	27	25	18	14	17	19	20	21	18	22	33	34	35
South America	28	27	31	28	28	7	6	10	12	12	9	12	34	41	43
World	**11**	**10**	**9**	**9**	**9**	**12**	**13**	**15**	**13**	**14**	**6**	**8**	**14**	**17**	**17**

NA = Not available or not applicable. **Note:** All figures are rounded. Data for 2010, 2020, and 2021 are not directly comparable to earlier years because of a change in methodology. (1) Not including Hong Kong or Macau.

World Capture of Fish, Crustaceans, and Mollusks, 2000-21

Source: UN Food and Agriculture Organization

(in thousands of metric tons; ranked by 2021 captures)

Country	2000	2010	2015	2020	2021
China[1]	13,915	13,643	14,632	12,067	11,607
Indonesia	4,023	5,236	6,260	6,586	6,852
Peru	10,576	3,923	4,284	5,131	6,007
Russia	3,898	3,994	4,390	4,930	5,059
India	3,570	4,579	4,630	4,469	4,835
U.S.	4,580	4,229	4,930	4,194	4,194
Vietnam	1,435	2,024	2,525	3,146	3,181
Japan	4,302	3,742	3,180	3,044	2,981
Norway	2,699	2,680	2,305	2,472	2,396
Bangladesh	1,004	1,727	1,624	1,920	1,982
Chile	4,241	2,444	1,607	1,678	1,911
Philippines	1,862	2,435	2,091	1,862	1,788
Myanmar	1,092	1,959	1,969	1,976	1,664
Mexico	1,232	1,456	1,378	1,413	1,525
Morocco	753	1,082	1,263	1,260	1,288
Thailand	2,680	1,646	1,339	1,442	1,288
Malaysia	1,198	1,353	1,402	1,314	1,251
South Korea	1,392	1,457	1,309	1,238	1,210
Iceland	1,983	1,058	1,318	1,018	1,038
Oman	118	154	252	777	908

(1) Does not include Hong Kong or Macau.

World Aquaculture Production, 2000-21

Source: UN Food and Agriculture Organization; ranked by 2021 production volume

	Metric tons (thous.)					Value (mil)				
Country	**2000**	**2010**	**2015**	**2020**	**2021**	**2000**	**2010**	**2015**	**2020**	**2021**
China[1]	21,522	35,513	43,748	49,620	51,221	$21,292	$70,830	$126,350	$157,029	$164,186
India	1,943	3,786	5,341	8,636	9,403	2,512	7,073	10,496	15,564	17,262
Indonesia	789	2,305	4,342	5,227	5,515	2,246	4,894	7,900	10,301	11,756
Vietnam	499	2,683	3,462	4,668	4,736	991	5,980	8,885	12,677	13,257
Bangladesh	657	1,309	2,060	2,584	2,639	1,039	2,840	5,140	6,303	6,552
Norway	491	1,020	1,381	1,490	1,665	1,385	5,081	5,811	7,300	9,363
Egypt	340	920	1,175	1,592	1,576	815	1,554	2,230	3,042	3,086
Chile	392	701	1,046	1,486	1,427	1,250	3,753	6,834	8,219	8,821
Thailand	738	1,286	921	1,013	990	2,514	2,813	2,327	3,050	2,994
Myanmar	99	851	997	1,145	929	781	956	1,645	1,889	1,367
Philippines	394	745	782	854	929	681	1,562	1,869	2,090	2,542
Ecuador	61	273	427	775	896	322	1,251	2,305	3,285	3,235
Brazil	172	411	578	629	649	271	1,307	1,228	1,056	1,173
Japan	763	718	705	601	622	3,499	4,042	3,537	3,978	4,078
South Korea	293	476	479	573	582	573	1,480	1,719	2,138	2,493
Iran	41	220	346	481	479	121	638	1,029	1,719	1,739
Turkey (Türkiye)	79	168	240	421	472	220	708	945	1,549	2,088
U.S.	457	497	426	448	448	848	1,023	1,150	1,211	1,211
Cambodia	14	60	143	399	347	28	113	267	1,208	1,050
Russia	74	120	152	270	295	198	397	532	1,295	1,458
World total[2]	**32,420**	**57,759**	**72,893**	**87,630**	**90,862**	**47,834**	**131,188**	**206,912**	**263,274**	**280,931**

Note: Does not include production of aquatic plants or marine mammals. (1) Does not include Hong Kong. (2) Includes nations not shown.

U.S. Commercial Landings of Fish and Shellfish, 2002-22

Source: Natl. Marine Fisheries Service, Natl. Oceanic and Atmospheric Admin., U.S. Dept. of Commerce

	Landings for human food		Landings for industrial purposes[1]		Total	
Year	**Weight (lbs)**	**Value**	**Weight (lbs)**	**Value**	**Weight (lbs)**	**Value**
2002	7,049,246,187	$2,890,955,208	2,153,425,076	$148,955,631	9,202,671,263	$3,039,910,839
2005	7,874,565,447	3,763,245,440	1,681,946,018	116,389,034	9,556,511,465	3,879,634,474
2006	7,903,279,001	4,026,097,205	1,699,733,151	115,978,109	9,603,012,152	4,142,075,314
2007	7,508,644,417	4,011,288,403	1,818,864,175	175,860,243	9,327,508,592	4,187,148,646
2008	6,670,713,867	4,264,740,589	1,709,579,936	154,679,710	8,380,293,803	4,419,420,299
2009	6,237,021,795	3,695,809,954	1,842,021,981	158,006,474	8,079,043,776	3,853,816,428
2010	6,562,399,064	4,388,014,461	1,713,009,592	163,867,760	8,275,408,656	4,551,882,221
2011	7,955,700,600	5,320,710,750	1,951,772,127	187,271,393	9,907,472,727	5,507,982,143
2012	7,540,288,313	5,334,093,426	2,176,578,070	193,464,528	9,716,866,383	5,527,557,954
2013	7,974,755,064	5,322,227,736	1,810,220,475	198,755,393	9,784,975,539	5,520,983,129
2014	7,879,928,272	5,370,603,404	1,671,499,936	194,788,725	9,551,428,208	5,565,392,129
2015	7,769,924,163	5,110,250,834	1,979,039,655	235,199,829	9,748,963,818	5,345,450,663
2016	7,507,809,045	5,161,629,090	2,142,331,116	311,996,668	9,650,140,161	5,473,625,758
2017	8,261,418,212	5,543,183,378	1,692,097,706	249,066,756	9,953,515,918	5,792,250,134
2018	7,528,648,300	5,334,473,514	1,893,940,311	251,362,626	9,422,588,611	5,585,836,140
2019	7,595,825,921	5,251,172,643	1,770,173,982	305,623,805	9,365,999,903	5,556,796,448
2020	6,717,804,859	4,509,461,049	1,679,451,215	318,655,706	8,397,256,074	4,828,116,755
2021	7,115,238,527	6,183,321,481	1,457,338,012	332,296,518	8,572,576,539	6,515,617,999
2022	6,786,496,687	5,604,658,164	1,560,977,713	282,587,807	8,347,474,400	5,887,245,971

Note: Does not include aquaculture products, except for clams, mussels, and oysters. Landings reported in round (live) weight for all items except univalve and bivalve mollusks (e.g., clams, mussels, oysters, scallops), which are reported in weight of meats (excluding the shell). (1) Processed into meal, oil, solubles, and shell products or used as bait or animal food.

U.S. Domestic Landings by Region, 2021-22

Source: Natl. Marine Fisheries Service, Natl. Oceanic and Atmospheric Admin., U.S. Dept. of Commerce

	2021		2022	
Region	**Weight (lbs)**	**Value**	**Weight (lbs)**	**Value**
Alaska	5,272,136,213	$2,049,565,003	4,818,006,376	$1,894,105,630
Gulf	1,139,956,130	920,087,400	1,369,522,647	891,242,935
Hawaii	29,637,142	129,108,461	29,183,551	135,188,833
Middle Atlantic	569,089,553	568,361,150	518,799,591	424,756,431
New England	501,143,142	1,968,086,375	415,935,344	1,405,335,181
Pacific Coast	962,983,605	740,528,871	1,038,485,525	668,169,958
South Atlantic	97,650,203	206,698,970	86,852,572	165,492,140
Total[1]	**8,572,598,676**	**6,582,448,469**	**8,276,790,227**	**5,584,323,553**

Note: Landings reported in round (live) weight for all items except univalve and bivalve mollusks (e.g., clams, oysters, scallops), which are reported in weight of meats (excluding the shell). (1) Includes data for categories not shown.

HEALTH

U.S. Health Expenditures, 1960-2022

Source: Office of the Actuary, Centers for Medicare & Medicaid Services, U.S. Dept. of Health and Human Services

Type of expenditure	1960	1970	1980	1990	2000	2010	2020	2022
			Amount in billions (current dollars)					
NATIONAL HEALTH EXPENDITURES	**$27.1**	**$74.1**	**$253.2**	**$718.7**	**$1,366.0**	**$2,589.6**	**$4,156.3**	**$4,464.6**
				Percent distribution				
Health consumption expenditures	**90.5%**	**89.5%**	**91.9%**	**93.2%**	**93.7%**	**94.1%**	**95.3%**	**95.1%**
Personal health care	85.3	84.2	84.6	85.1	84.7	84.2	81.2	83.0
Hospital care	33.1	36.7	39.7	34.8	30.4	31.2	30.5	30.4
Professional services	29.2	26.7	25.5	28.9	28.3	26.6	25.9	26.7
Physician and clinical services	20.5	19.3	18.8	22.1	21.1	19.8	19.7	19.8
Other professional services	1.4	1.0	1.4	2.4	2.7	2.7	2.8	3.1
Dental services	7.3	6.4	5.3	4.4	4.5	4.1	3.4	3.7
Other health, residential, personal care	1.6	1.8	3.3	3.3	4.6	4.9	5.1	5.5
Home health care[1]	0.2	0.3	0.9	1.7	2.4	2.7	3.0	3.0
Nursing care facilities and continuing care retirement communities[1]	3.0	5.4	6.0	6.2	6.2	5.4	4.7	4.3
Retail outlet sales of medical products	18.1	13.3	9.2	10.1	12.7	13.3	12.0	13.2
Prescription drugs	9.9	7.4	4.8	5.6	8.9	9.8	8.4	9.1
Durable medical equipment	2.7	2.4	1.6	1.9	1.9	1.5	1.3	1.5
Other nondurable medical products	5.5	3.5	2.8	2.6	1.8	2.0	2.3	2.6
Government administration[2]	0.2	1.0	1.1	1.0	1.3	1.2	1.2	1.2
Net cost of health insurance	3.7	2.5	3.6	4.3	4.7	5.8	7.1	6.3
Government public health activities	1.4	1.8	2.5	2.8	3.2	2.9	5.8	4.7
Investment	**9.5**	**10.5**	**8.1**	**6.8**	**6.3**	**5.9**	**4.7**	**4.9**
Research[3]	2.6	2.6	2.1	1.8	1.9	1.9	1.4	1.5
Structures and equipment	6.9	7.8	6.0	5.0	4.4	4.0	3.2	3.4
			Average annual percent change from previous year shown					
NATIONAL HEALTH EXPENDITURES	—	**10.6%**	**13.1%**	**11.0%**	**6.6%**	**6.6%**	**4.8%**	**3.6%**
Health consumption expenditures	—	**10.4**	**13.4**	**11.2**	**6.7**	**6.7**	**5.0**	**3.5**
Personal health care	—	10.4	13.1	11.1	6.6	6.5	4.5	4.8
Hospital care	—	11.7	14.0	9.6	5.2	6.9	4.6	3.4
Professional services	—	9.6	12.6	12.4	6.4	5.9	4.6	5.2
Physician and clinical services	—	9.9	12.8	12.8	6.1	5.9	4.8	4.0
Other professional services	—	6.3	17.0	17.4	7.8	6.7	5.4	9.1
Dental services	—	9.0	10.9	9.0	7.0	5.5	2.8	8.9
Other health, residential, personal care	—	11.5	20.5	11.0	10.3	7.2	5.2	8.2
Home health care[1]	—	14.5	26.9	18.1	9.9	8.1	5.9	3.1
Nursing care facilities and continuing care retirement communities[1]	—	17.4	14.2	11.4	6.6	5.2	3.4	−1.3
Retail outlet sales of medical products	—	7.3	8.9	12.1	9.1	7.1	3.8	8.6
Prescription drugs	—	7.5	8.2	12.8	11.7	7.6	3.3	7.6
Durable medical equipment	—	9.0	8.8	13.0	6.6	4.4	3.0	11.7
Other nondurable medical products	—	5.9	10.5	10.0	3.1	7.5	6.2	10.4
Government administration[2]	—	30.0	14.1	10.0	9.1	5.8	4.8	6.0
Net cost of health insurance	—	6.4	17.2	13.0	7.4	9.0	7.0	−3.0
Government public health activities	—	13.8	16.9	12.0	8.0	5.8	12.3	−7.2
Investment	—	**11.7**	**10.3**	**9.0**	**5.8**	**5.9**	**2.5**	**5.9**
Research[3]	—	10.9	10.8	8.9	7.2	6.8	2.0	3.8
Structures and equipment	—	11.9	10.1	9.0	5.3	5.5	2.7	6.8

— = Not applicable. **Note:** Numbers may not add up to totals due to rounding. (1) Incl. freestanding facilities only. Additional services of this type provided in hospital-based facilities are counted as hospital care. (2) Incl. all administrative costs (e.g., employee salaries) associated with insuring individuals enrolled in federally managed health insurance programs. (3) Research and development expenditures of drug companies and other mfrs. and providers of med. equip. and supplies are included in the expenditure class in which a product falls instead of here.

Health Coverage for Persons Under 65, 1984-2019

Source: National Health Interview Survey, National Center for Health Statistics, CDC, U.S. Dept. of Health and Human Services (percent of population)

	Private insurance				Medicaid[1]				Uninsured[2]			
Characteristic	**1984**	**2000**	**2010**	**2019**	**1984**	**2000**	**2010**	**2019**	**1984**	**2000**	**2010**	**2019**
Total	**76.8%**	**71.5%**	**61.7%**	**64.3%**	**6.8%**	**9.5%**	**16.9%**	**20.5%**	**14.5%**	**17.0%**	**18.2%**	**12.0%**
Age												
Under 18 years	72.6	66.6	54.1	55.6	11.9	19.6	36.4	37.9	13.9	12.6	7.8	5.1
18-44 years	76.5	70.5	60.0	65.5	5.1	5.6	10.9	15.4	17.1	22.4	27.1	17.0
45-64 years	83.3	78.7	71.3	70.3	3.4	4.5	6.8	12.3	9.6	12.6	15.7	11.1
Race and Hispanic origin												
White only, non-Hispanic	82.4	79.5	72.0	73.8	3.7	6.1	11.0	13.7	11.9	12.5	13.7	8.8
Black only, non-Hispanic	58.2	56.0	45.1	49.8	20.7	21.0	30.0	34.8	19.7	19.5	20.7	11.2
Hispanic or Latino, any race	55.7	47.8	36.8	44.6	13.3	15.5	28.6	30.9	29.5	35.6	32.0	22.5
Percent of poverty level												
Below 100%	32.2	25.2	16.0	18.4	33.0	38.4	50.8	60.1	33.9	34.2	30.3	19.2
100%-199%	70.3	50.1	34.8	35.8	5.3	16.2	28.5	39.6	21.8	31.0	32.4	20.7
200%-399%[3]	89.3	78.1	70.7	70.4	0.8	4.0	8.4	12.6	7.6	15.4	17.4	13.0
400% or more	95.4	91.9	89.9	90.8	0.2	0.9	2.0	2.7	3.2	5.9	5.6	4.0
Geographic region												
Northeast	80.5	76.3	68.2	67.8	8.6	10.6	17.9	23.2	10.2	12.2	12.4	7.0
Midwest	80.6	78.8	66.7	71.3	7.4	8.0	17.3	17.4	11.3	12.3	14.1	9.3
South	74.3	66.8	57.5	59.4	5.1	9.4	16.0	19.2	17.7	20.5	21.9	16.6
West	71.9	66.5	58.9	63.4	7.0	10.4	17.1	23.3	18.2	20.7	20.6	10.6

Note: Data based on household interviews of a sample of the civilian noninstitutionalized population. Totals incl. groups not shown separately. Because of questionnaire redesigns, data for 1984 are not strictly comparable with data for later years; data for 2019 have not been fully evaluated for comparability with earlier years. (1) Incl. persons who had a state-sponsored health plan or Children's Health Insurance Program (CHIP). (2) Incl. persons who had only Indian Health Service coverage.

Spending on Health in the 50 Most Populous Countries, 2021

Source: Global Health Expenditure Database, World Health Organization (WHO)

Country	As % of GDP	Per capita[1]	Country	As % of GDP	Per capita[1]	Country	As % of GDP	Per capita[1]	Country	As % of GDP	Per capita[1]
Afghanistan	21.8%	$81.3	France	12.3%	$5,380.9	Mexico	6.1%	$610.6	Spain	10.7%	$3,234.3
Algeria	5.5	204.6	Germany	12.9	6,626.0	Morocco	5.7	221.1	Sudan	2.8	21.6
Angola	3.0	64.2	Ghana	4.2	100.0	Mozambique	9.1	44.5	Tanzania	3.4	37.2
Argentina	9.7	1,044.8	India	3.3	74.0	Myanmar	5.6	65.2	Thailand	5.2	364.4
Bangladesh	2.4	57.9	Indonesia	3.7	160.6	Nepal	5.4	65.3	Turkey (Türkiye)	4.6	441.1
Brazil	9.9	761.3	Iran	5.8	392.5	Nigeria	4.1	83.8	Uganda	4.7	43.4
Canada	12.3	6,470.1	Iraq	5.2	248.9	Pakistan	2.9	43.1	Ukraine	8.0	368.0
China	5.4	670.5	Italy	9.4	3,349.6	Peru	6.2	412.2	UK	12.4	5,738.5
Colombia	9.0	557.5	Japan	10.8	4,347.3	Philippines	5.9	203.2	U.S.	17.4	12,012.2
Congo, Dem. Rep. of	3.8	22.3	Kenya	4.5	94.7	Poland	6.4	1,159.3	Uzbekistan	7.7	157.2
Egypt	4.6	179.7	Korea, South	9.3	3,260.4	Russia	7.4	935.7	Venezuela	4.0	160.1
Ethiopia	3.2	26.5	Madagascar	3.5	17.6	Saudi Arabia	6.0	1,442.0	Vietnam	4.6	172.6
			Malaysia	4.4	487.0	South Africa	8.3	583.7	**World[2]**	**10.3**	—

(1) At average exchange rate. (2) Per capita health spending ranged from $45 in low income countries up to $4,001 in high income countries.

Population Not Covered by Health Insurance by State, 1990-2023

Source: American Community Survey and Current Population Survey, U.S. Census Bureau, U.S. Dept. of Commerce
(numbers in thousands; civilian noninstitutionalized population)

	1990		2000		2023			1990		2000		2023	
	No. not covered	% pop. not covered	No. not covered	% pop. not covered	No. not covered	% pop. not covered		No. not covered	% pop. not covered	No. not covered	% pop. not covered	No. not covered	% pop. not covered
AL	710	17.4%	547	12.5%	426	8.5%	MT	115	14.0%	144	16.1%	94	8.4%
AK	77	15.4	108	17.4	73	10.4	NE	138	8.5	134	7.9	119	6.1
AZ	547	15.5	853	16.4	727	9.9	NV	201	16.5	321	15.7	341	10.8
AR	421	17.4	373	14.1	269	8.9	NH	107	9.9	97	7.9	66	4.8
CA	5,683	19.1	5,956	17.5	2,458	6.4	NJ	773	10.0	857	10.2	662	7.2
CO	495	14.7	559	12.9	387	6.7	NM	339	22.2	415	23.0	189	9.1
CT	226	6.9	300	8.9	205	5.7	NY	2,176	12.1	2,730	14.5	938	4.8
DE	96	13.9	66	8.5	66	6.5	NC	883	13.8	964	12.1	981	9.2
DC	109	19.2	71	12.8	18	2.7	ND	40	6.3	61	9.8	34	4.5
FL	2,376	18.0	2,591	16.2	2,381	10.7	OH	1,123	10.3	1,101	9.8	713	6.1
GA	971	15.3	1,126	13.9	1,233	11.4	OK	574	18.6	587	17.4	450	11.3
HI	81	7.3	95	7.9	44	3.2	OR	360	12.4	398	11.6	230	5.5
ID	159	15.2	198	15.4	172	8.9	PA	1,218	10.1	915	7.6	692	5.4
IL	1,272	10.9	1,474	12.0	763	6.2	RI	105	11.1	71	6.9	48	4.4
IN	587	10.7	608	10.1	464	6.9	SC	550	16.2	426	10.7	480	9.1
IA	225	8.1	233	8.1	159	5.0	SD	81	11.6	80	10.8	74	8.2
KS	272	10.8	256	9.6	240	8.3	TN	673	13.7	603	10.7	654	9.3
KY	480	13.2	509	12.7	241	5.4	TX	3,569	21.1	4,555	22.0	4,917	16.4
LA	797	19.7	736	16.8	310	6.9	UT	156	9.0	243	10.8	270	8.0
ME	139	11.2	131	10.4	81	5.9	VT	54	9.5	44	7.4	22	3.4
MD	601	12.7	473	9.0	381	6.3	VA	996	15.7	670	9.6	543	6.4
MA	530	9.1	450	7.1	179	2.6	WA	557	11.4	767	13.1	481	6.3
MI	865	9.4	767	7.8	448	4.5	WV	249	13.8	239	13.4	103	5.9
MN	389	8.9	393	8.0	238	4.2	WI	321	6.7	378	7.1	284	4.9
MS	531	19.9	368	13.2	297	10.3	WY	58	12.5	71	14.7	61	10.6
MO	665	12.7	474	8.6	458	7.5	**U.S.**	**34,719**	**13.9**	**36,586**	**13.1**	**26,170**	**7.9**

Persons Not Covered by Health Insurance by Selected Characteristics, 2023

Source: Annual Social and Economic Supplement, Current Population Survey, U.S. Census Bureau, U.S. Dept. of Commerce
(numbers without health insurance coverage for entire calendar year, in thousands)

Characteristic	No. not covered	Percent[1]
Total	**26,440**	**8.0%**
Race and Hispanic origin[2]		
White	19,970	8.0
White, not Hispanic	9,642	5.0
Black	3,641	8.1
Asian	1,203	5.5
Hispanic (any race)	11,430	17.5
Age[3]		
Under 65 years	25,900	9.5
Under 19 years[4]	4,439	5.8
19 to 64 years	21,470	10.9
19 to 25 years[5]	4,258	14.1
26 to 34 years	5,064	12.6
35 to 44 years	5,183	11.7
45 to 64 years	6,961	8.6
65 years and over	532	0.9
Nativity		
Native-born	16,820	6.0
Foreign-born	9,621	18.8
Not a citizen	7,836	29.7
Work experience[6]		
All workers	15,690	9.8
Worked full-time, year-round	10,230	8.9
Less than full-time, year-round	5,462	12.2
Did not work at least one week	6,867	12.6
Education[7]		
No high school diploma	3,931	29.5
H.S. graduate (incl. equivalency)	6,712	15.1
Some college, no degree	2,080	9.3
Associate's degree	1,467	7.9
Bachelor's degree	2,233	5.3
Graduate degree or higher	785	3.1
Marital status[8]		
Married	7,917	7.9
Widowed	331	10.5
Divorced	2,079	11.6
Separated	709	18.1
Never married	10,430	14.7

(1) Of the pop. with selected characteristic at left. (2) Numbers are for one race alone unless otherwise noted. (3) People aged 65 and older and certain people under age 65 with long-term disabilities are eligible for Medicare. (4) Eligible for Medicaid/Children's Health Insurance Program (CHIP). (5) May be eligible to be a dependent on a parent's health insurance. (6) Aged 15 to 64 only. (7) Aged 26 to 64 years only. (8) Aged 19 to 64 only.

Health Insurance Marketplace Plan Enrollment by Selected Characteristics, 2024

Source: Centers for Medicare & Medicaid Services (CMS), U.S. Dept. of Health and Human Services
(cumulative enrollment-related activity for Nov. 1, 2023-Jan. 16, 2024; exact dates vary for state-based marketplaces)

	Marketplace total		Federal marketplace[1]		State marketplaces[2]	
	Number	Percent	Number	Percent	Number	Percent
Consumers who have selected a plan	**21,446,150**	**100.0%**	**16,363,133**	**100.0%**	**5,083,017**	**100.0%**
Under 18 years of age	2,158,619	10.1	1,733,414	10.6	425,205	8.4
18-25 years of age	2,190,838	10.2	1,737,891	10.6	452,947	8.9
26-34 years of age	3,534,216	16.5	2,670,288	16.3	863,928	17.0
35-44 years of age	3,979,300	18.6	3,119,284	19.1	860,016	16.9
45-54 years of age	4,088,389	19.1	3,160,456	19.3	927,933	18.3
55-64 years of age	5,136,885	24.0	3,678,763	22.5	1,458,122	28.7
65+ years of age	357,890	1.7	263,037	1.6	94,853	1.9
Consumers receiving financial assistance[3]	19,771,819	92.2	15,541,871	95.0	4,229,948	83.2
With advance premium tax credits	19,743,689	92.1	15,524,292	94.9	4,219,397	83.0
With cost-sharing reductions	10,646,618	49.6	8,666,891	53.0	1,979,727	38.9

Note: Figures may not add up to totals due to rounding. (1) For the 32 states using HealthCare.gov, the federally facilitated marketplace, including 3 states that run their own marketplaces but use the federal platform for eligibility determinations, enrollment, and related functions. (2) For the 18 states and the Dist. of Columbia with their own marketplaces. (3) Advance premium tax credit (APTC) only, cost-sharing reduction (CSR) only (except for New York due to reporting limitations), or both APTC and CSR.

Health Insurance Marketplace Average Monthly Premiums, 2024

Source: Centers for Medicare & Medicaid Services, U.S. Dept. of Health and Human Services

For the 2023 open enrollment period, 32 states used HealthCare.gov, the eligibility and enrollment platform run by the federal government. That number includes 3 states that run their own marketplaces but use HealthCare.gov (state-based marketplaces on the federal platform, or SBM-FPs). Eighteen states and the Dist. of Columbia ran their own exchanges (state-based marketplaces, or SBMs).

(based on enrollment-related activity for Nov. 1, 2023-Jan. 16, 2024; exact dates vary for state-based marketplaces)

State	Avg. premium[1]	Avg. premium after tax credits[1,2]	Avg. tax credits[3]
Alabama	$706	$75	$656
Alaska	967	230	865
Arizona	523	121	452
Arkansas[4]	555	116	476
California[5]	655	195	526
Colorado[5]	556	204	455
Connecticut[5]	897	233	766
Delaware	723	196	585
Dist. of Columbia[5]	894	775	561
Florida	617	65	568
Georgia[4]	583	75	531
Hawaii	696	248	544
Idaho[5]	462	121	395
Illinois	676	189	545
Indiana	532	129	452
Iowa	585	132	507
Kansas	634	111	561
Kentucky[5]	621	206	497
Louisiana	710	90	647
Maine[5]	707	229	564
Maryland[5]	475	179	388
Massachusetts[5]	507	197	385
Michigan	518	137	426
Minnesota[5]	501	297	351
Mississippi	616	36	592
Missouri	650	92	594
Montana	604	162	504
Nebraska	$670	$120	$580
Nevada[5]	530	154	438
New Hampshire	453	202	350
New Jersey[5]	661	201	521
New Mexico[5]	604	151	551
New York[5]	714	410	455
North Carolina	609	77	558
North Dakota	520	132	433
Ohio	581	136	498
Oklahoma	632	79	575
Oregon[4]	655	231	524
Pennsylvania[5]	641	180	530
Rhode Island[5]	545	152	454
South Carolina	599	69	553
South Dakota	695	114	611
Tennessee	622	73	580
Texas	566	50	536
Utah	468	67	421
Vermont[5]	874	243	702
Virginia[5]	473	119	405
Washington[5]	595	271	453
West Virginia	1,119	118	1,035
Wisconsin	671	166	572
Wyoming	937	118	863
Total HC.gov	**602**	**81**	**548**
Total SBMs	**615**	**207**	**492**
Total marketplace	**605**	**111**	**536**

(1) For all consumers, incl. those who did not receive any tax credits. (2) Does not reflect any state-provided premium subsidies. (3) For consumers who elected to receive any tax credits. (4) SBM-FPs. (5) SBM.

Health Care Visits by Selected Characteristics, 1997-2018

Source: National Health Interview Survey, National Center for Health Statistics, CDC, U.S. Dept. of Health and Human Services

Characteristic	No visits			1-3 visits			4-9 visits			10 visits or more		
	1997	2010	2018	1997	2010	2018	1997	2010	2018	1997	2010	2018
	Percent distribution											
All persons[1]	**16.5%**	**15.6%**	**14.5%**	**46.2%**	**45.4%**	**49.2%**	**23.6%**	**25.8%**	**23.4%**	**13.7%**	**13.2%**	**12.9%**
Age												
Under 6 years	5.0	3.7	4.9	44.9	48.9	52.7	37.0	36.8	33.9	13.0	10.6	8.4
6-17 years	15.3	10.4	8.6	58.7	59.1	63.9	19.3	23.6	21.4	6.8	6.9	6.2
18-44 years	21.7	24.2	21.9	46.7	43.9	47.6	19.0	20.6	18.7	12.6	11.3	11.7
45-64 years	16.9	14.8	14.2	42.9	42.8	45.5	24.7	26.1	24.7	15.5	16.4	15.7
65-74 years	9.8	6.3	6.4	36.9	36.1	40.1	31.6	35.7	31.8	21.6	21.9	21.7
75 years and over	7.7	4.1	4.1	31.8	31.0	34.8	33.8	38.0	33.6	26.6	27.0	27.6
Sex												
Male	21.3	20.4	18.7	47.1	46.4	49.7	20.6	22.7	21.2	11.0	10.5	10.3
Female	11.8	10.9	10.3	45.4	44.4	48.8	26.5	28.8	25.6	16.3	15.9	15.4
Health insurance status[2]												
Insured continuously	14.1	12.1	12.9	49.2	48.6	51.9	23.6	26.2	23.1	13.0	13.0	12.1
Uninsured up to 12 mos.	18.9	18.5	21.2	46.0	47.8	48.4	20.8	22.0	20.9	14.4	11.6	9.5
Uninsured 12+ mos.	39.0	43.8	45.3	41.4	39.7	41.6	13.2	12.6	9.9	6.4	3.9	3.1

Note: Totals incl. visits to hospital emergency departments, doctor offices, and clinics as well as home visits by a health care professional during a 12-month period. (1) Incl. persons of unknown health insurance status. (2) Prior to interview, for persons under age 65 only.

Reasons Given by Patients for Physician Office Visits, 2019

Source: National Ambulatory Medical Care Survey, National Center for Health Statistics (NCHS), Centers for Disease Control and Prevention, U.S. Dept. of Health and Human Services

Rank	Principal reason	Number of visits (thous.)	% of all visits
1.	Progress visit, not otherwise specified	221,258	21.3%
2.	General medical examination	60,352	5.8
3.	Postoperative visit	28,479	2.7
4.	Gynecological examination	25,218	2.4
5.	Counseling, not otherwise specified	22,685	2.2
6.	Medication, other and unspecified kinds	18,491	1.8
7.	Shoulder symptoms	16,436	1.6
8.	Hypertension	15,194	1.5
9.	Well-baby examination	15,141	1.5
10.	Cough	15,048	1.5
11.	Diabetes mellitus	13,393	1.3
12.	Prenatal examination, routine	12,565	1.2%
13.	For other and unspecified test results	12,465*	1.2
14.	Cancer, breast	NA*	NA
15.	Knee symptoms	10,370	1.0
16.	Skin lesion	10,295*	1.0
17.	Diagnostic endoscopies	10,264*	NA
18.	Stomach and abdominal pain, cramps, and spasms	10,098	1.0
19.	Other special examination	9,939*	1.0
20.	Preoperative visit for specified and unspecified types of surgery	9,328	0.9
	All other reasons	**488,995**	**47.2**
	All visits	**1,036,484**	**100.0**

* = Estimate does not meet NCHS standards of reliability. NA = Not available. **Note:** Based on nationally representative sample survey of visits to nonfederal office-based patient care physicians. Numbers may not add to totals because of rounding.

Visits to Physician Offices and Hospital Outpatient and Emergency Departments, 1995-2018

Source: National Ambulatory Medical Care Survey and National Hospital Ambulatory Medical Care Survey, National Center for Health Statistics, Centers for Disease Control and Prevention, U.S. Dept. of Health and Human Services

(number of visits per 100 persons)

Sex and age	All places[1] 1995	2000	2011	Physician offices 1995	2000	2011	2018	Hospital outpatient depts. 1995	2000	2011	Hospital emergency depts. 1995	2000	2011	2018
Total	**334**	**374**	**400**	**271**	**304**	**314**	**250**	**26**	**31**	**40**	**37**	**40**	**45**	**41**
Male	290	325	354	232	261	280	214	21	26	32	37	38	42	37
Under 18	273	302	372	209	231	294	179	25	29	37	40	41	41	40
18-44	190	203	208	139	148	145	103	14	17	20	37	38	43	33
45-54	275	316	322	229	260	250	234	20	26	34	26	30	38	35
55-64	351	428	430	300	367	351	277	26	32	45	25	30	34	35
65-74	508	614	655	445	539	566	459	29	38	52	34	36	37	35
75 and over	711	771	869	616	670	758	681	34	42	49	61	59	62	56
Female	377	420	444	309	345	348	286	31	35	48	37	41	48	44
Under 18	277	285	341	217	221	265	172	25	29	38	35	35	39	40
18-44	336	377	393	265	298	286	243	31	33	47	40	46	59	49
45-54	400	451	459	339	384	364	308	32	36	53	29	31	41	39
55-64	446	529	520	382	453	436	383	38	45	54	26	31	31	37
65-74	603	692	707	534	609	611	509	36	46	60	32	37	37	36
75 and over	666	763	790	571	645	657	617	34	49	61	61	69	72	62

(1) Incl. visits to physician offices and hospital outpatient and emergency departments. Prior to 2006, visits to community health centers were not included in survey.

Most Frequently Mentioned Drugs at Office Visits, 2019

Source: National Ambulatory Medical Care Survey, National Center for Health Statistics (NCHS), Centers for Disease Control and Prevention, U.S. Dept. of Health and Human Services

Rank	Therapeutic drug category[1]	No. of mentions (thous.)	% of total[2]
1.	Analgesics[3]	350,354	9.8%
2.	Antihyperlipidemic agents	193,096	5.4
3.	Vitamins	170,853	4.8
4.	Antidepressants	155,241	4.3
5.	Antidiabetic agents	145,757	4.1
6.	Antiplatelet agents	132,183	3.7
7.	Anticonvulsants	125,822	3.5
8.	Dermatological agents	124,561	3.5
9.	Anxiolytics, sedatives, and hypnotics	122,610	3.4
10.	Beta-adrenergic blocking agents	119,291	3.3
11.	Bronchodilators	112,383	3.1%
12.	Proton pump inhibitors	94,277	2.6
13.	Vitamin and mineral combinations	93,902	2.6
14.	Diuretics	92,379	2.6
15.	Immunostimulants	88,972	2.5
16.	Ophthalmic preparations	83,646*	2.3
17.	Antihistamines	76,167	2.1
18.	Minerals and electrolytes	74,588	2.1
19.	Thyroid drugs	74,477	2.1
20.	Calcium channel blocking agents	67,442	1.9

* = Estimate does not meet NCHS standards of reliability. **Note:** A mention is documentation in a patient's record of a drug provided, prescribed, or continued at a visit to a nonfederal office-based patient care physician. (1) Based on the Multum Lexicon second-level therapeutic drug category. (2) Based on an estimated 3,583,272,000 drug mentions. (3) Incl. narcotic and nonnarcotic analgesics and nonsteroidal anti-inflammatory drugs.

U.S. Organ Transplants

Source: Organ Procurement and Transplantation Network (OPTN), United Network for Organ Sharing (UNOS)

Waiting List, July 2024

Type of transplant	Candidates	% of total
All organs	**103,777**	**100.0%**
Kidney	89,455	86.2
Liver	9,515	9.2
Heart	3,401	3.3
Kidney/pancreas	2,177	2.1
Lung	904	0.9
Pancreas	856	0.8
Intestine	192	0.2
Heart/lung	41	0.04
VCA—uterus	9	0.009
VCA—head and neck	3	0.003
VCA—upper limb	3	0.003
Abdominal wall	2	0.002

Transplants Performed, 2023

Type of transplant	Number	% of total
All organs	**46,629**	**100.0%**
Kidney	27,332	58.6
Liver	10,659	22.9
Heart	4,545	9.7
Lung	3,026	6.5
Kidney/pancreas	812	1.7
Pancreas	102	0.2
Intestine	95	0.2
Heart/lung	54	0.1
Genitourinary: uterus	3	0.006
Head and neck: craniofacial	1	0.002
Abdominal wall	0	—

VCA = Vascularized composite allograft. **Note:** Waiting list as of July 23, 2024; numbers may not add up to total because of patients waiting for multiple organs. Total transplants performed include organs not shown separately.

Illicit Drug Use Among Persons Age 12 or Older, 2005-22

Source: National Survey on Drug Use and Health, SAMHSA, U.S. Dept. of Health and Human Services

Of all those age 12 or older who used an illicit drug in the past month in 2022, approximately 1.9 mil were adolescents aged 12-17 (making 7.3% of that age group current drug users). About 9.5 mil current users were young adults aged 18-25 (or 27.2% of that age group).

(numbers in thousands)

Substance	2005 No.	%	2010 No.	%	2015 No.	%	2020 No.	%	2021 No.	%	2022 No.	%
USED IN LIFETIME												
Illicit drugs[1,2]	—	—	—	—	**130,610**	**48.8**	**138,543**	**50.0**	**139,677**	**49.9**	**143,116**	**50.7**
Marijuana	97,545	40.1	1,06,613	42.0	117,865	44.0	126,504	45.7	128,961	46.1	132,296	46.9
Cocaine	33,673	13.8	37,361	14.7	38,744	14.5	39,261	14.2	41,371	14.8	42,231	15.0
Crack	7,928	3.3	9,208	3.6	9,035	3.4	9,356	3.4	10,625	3.8	10,167	3.6
Heroin	3,534	1.5	4,144	1.6	5,099	1.9	6,252	2.3	6,684	2.4	6,558	2.3
Hallucinogens	—	—	—	—	40,915	15.3	43,949	15.9	46,474	16.6	48,850	17.3
LSD	22,433	9.2	23,375	9.2	25,324	9.5	28,123	10.2	30,114	10.8	31,074	11.0
PCP	6,603	2.7	6,255	2.5	6,323	2.4	6,141	2.2	6,570	2.3	6,394	2.3
Ecstasy	—	—	—	—	18,328	6.8	20,478	7.4	21,436	7.7	22,103	7.8
Inhalants	—	—	—	—	25,765	9.6	26,749	9.7	25,436	9.1	27,242	9.7
Methamphetamine	—	—	—	—	14,511	5.4	15,397	5.6	17,461	6.2	16,588	5.9
Opioids including IMF[2]	—	—	—	—	—	—	—	—	—	—	—	—
Illegally made fentanyl	—	—	—	—	—	—	—	—	—	—	1,607	0.6
USED IN PAST YEAR												
Illicit drugs[1,2]	—	—	—	—	**47,730**	**17.8**	**59,277**	**21.4**	**61,995**	**22.2**	**70,338**	**24.9**
Marijuana	25,375	10.4	29,301	11.6	36,043	13.5	49,634	17.9	53,181	19.0	61,901	22.0
Cocaine	5,523	2.3	4,533	1.8	4,828	1.8	5,172	1.9	4,760	1.7	5,274	1.9
Crack	1,381	0.6	885	0.3	833	0.3	657	0.2	1,003	0.4	918	0.3
Heroin	379	0.2	621	0.2	828	0.3	902	0.3	1,089	0.4	1,049	0.4
Hallucinogens	—	—	—	—	4,692	1.8	7,133	2.6	7,572	2.7	8,509	3.0
LSD	563	0.2	881	0.3	1,535	0.6	2,637	1.0	2,579	0.9	2,322	0.8
PCP	164	0.1	96	0.0	120	0.0	95	0.0	198	0.1	204	0.1
Ecstasy	—	—	—	—	2,560	1.0	2,622	0.9	2,228	0.8	2,109	0.7
Inhalants	—	—	—	—	1,759	0.7	2,390	0.9	2,119	0.8	2,254	0.8
Methamphetamine	—	—	—	—	1,713	0.6	2,550	0.9	2,640	0.9	2,705	1.0
Misuse of Rx psychotherapeutics[3]	—	—	—	—	18,942	7.1	16,073	5.8	14,529	5.2	14,204	5.0
Opioids[2]	—	—	—	—	12,693	4.7	9,490	3.4	9,420	3.4	8,918	3.2
Opioids including IMF[2]	—	—	—	—	—	—	—	—	—	—	**9,062**	**3.2**
Illegally made fentanyl	—	—	—	—	—	—	—	—	—	—	686	0.2
USED IN PAST MONTH												
Illicit drugs[1,2]	—	—	—	—	**27,080**	**10.1**	**37,309**	**13.5**	**40,564**	**14.5**	**46,603**	**16.5**
Marijuana	14,626	6.0	17,409	6.9	22,226	8.3	32,784	11.8	36,950	13.2	42,317	15.0
Cocaine	2,397	1.0	1,472	0.6	1,876	0.7	1,831	0.7	1,846	0.7	2,015	0.7
Crack	682	0.3	378	0.1	394	0.1	335	0.1	519	0.2	573	0.2
Heroin	136	0.1	239	0.1	329	0.1	513	0.2	590	0.2	709	0.3
Hallucinogens	—	—	—	—	1,240	0.5	1,761	0.6	2,301	0.8	2,289	0.8
LSD	104	0.0	155	0.1	352	0.1	649	0.2	569	0.2	423	0.1
PCP	48	0.0	36	0.0	25	0.0	24	0.0	106	0.0	89	0.0
Ecstasy	—	—	—	—	557	0.2	681	0.2	603	0.2	389	0.1
Inhalants	—	—	—	—	527	0.2	904	0.3	787	0.3	842	0.3
Methamphetamine	—	—	—	—	897	0.3	1,722	0.6	1,630	0.6	1,685	0.6
Misuse of Rx psychotherapeutics[3]	—	—	—	—	6,365	2.4	5,278	1.9	4,288	1.5	4,612	1.6
Opioids[2]	—	—	—	—	3,963	1.5	2,885	1.0	2,817	1.0	2,944	1.0
Opioids including IMF[2]	—	—	—	—	—	—	—	—	—	—	**3,052**	**1.1**
Illegally made fentanyl	—	—	—	—	—	—	—	—	—	—	330	0.1

— = Not comparable or not reported. **Note:** Misuse is defined as use in any way not directed by a doctor, including use without a prescription or in greater amounts, more often, or for a longer period of time. Because of methodological changes, data for 2015 and 2020 are not comparable with estimates for other years. 2021 estimates are only comparable with 2022. (1) Includes marijuana, cocaine (including crack), heroin, hallucinogens, inhalants, methamphetamine, the misuse of prescription (Rx) psychotherapeutics (lifetime use ests. not given separately due to potential underreporting), and opioids. (2) Opioids refer to heroin and prescription pain relievers, whether use or misuse. Category does not include the use of illegally made fentanyl (IMF) unless specifically noted. (3) Includes four categories of prescription drugs (pain relievers, stimulants, tranquilizers, sedatives) but not over-the-counter drugs.

Daily Use of Cigarettes by 8th, 10th, and 12th Graders, 1995-2023

Source: Monitoring the Future study, Univ. of Michigan Inst. for Social Research; Natl. Inst. on Drug Abuse, Natl. Insts. of Health

(percent who smoked daily in last 30 days)

	8th grade					10th grade					12th grade				
	1995	2000	2005	2015	2023	1995	2000	2005	2015	2023	1995	2000	2005	2015	2023
Total	**9.3**	**7.4**	**4.0**	**1.3**	**0.4**	**16.3**	**14.0**	**7.5**	**3.0**	**1.0**	**21.6**	**20.6**	**13.6**	**5.5**	**0.7**
Gender															
Male	9.2	7.0	3.9	1.1	0.5	16.3	13.7	7.2	2.8	1.0	21.7	20.9	14.6	6.6	0.8
Female	9.2	7.5	4.0	1.4	0.4	16.1	14.1	7.7	2.8	0.7	20.8	19.7	11.9	3.9	0.2
College plans															
None/ under 4 yrs.	22.5	21.7	14.4	5.9	0.9	32.7	28.8	19.2	10.8	2.5	33.7	31.7	24.9	14.1	1.4
Complete 4 yrs.	7.5	5.6	2.9	0.9	0.2	13.3	11.6	5.9	2.0	0.5	17.4	16.6	10.5	3.5	0.3
Region															
Northeast	9.2	6.9	3.2	0.7	0.8	15.8	14.1	7.6	2.7	0.4	22.5	22.8	13.3	5.4	1.1
Midwest	11.0	9.0	4.8	1.6	0.4	17.6	16.3	8.6	2.8	1.2	25.7	23.6	16.3	6.6	1.2
South	9.4	7.8	5.0	1.5	0.3	19.3	15.7	8.8	3.6	1.1	21.7	19.4	15.4	6.1	0.5
West	7.0	4.9	2.4	1.1	0.3	9.4	7.8	4.0	2.3	1.2	14.5	16.9	7.6	3.5	0.5
Race/ethnicity[1]															
White	10.5	9.0	4.6	1.4	0.5	17.6	17.7	9.1	3.5	1.0	23.9	25.7	17.1	7.3	0.5
Black	2.8	3.2	2.1	0.9	0.3	4.7	5.2	3.9	2.1	0.7	6.1	8.0	5.6	4.1	1.1
Hispanic	9.2	7.1	3.1	1.0	0.2	9.9	8.8	5.9	2.1	0.7	11.6	15.7	7.7	3.7	0.9

HS = high school. **Note:** Figures may not add up to totals because of rounding. (1) For each of these groups, data for the specified year and previous year have been combined to increase sample size and thus provide more stable estimates.

Lifetime Prevalence of Drug Use in 12th Graders, 1975-2023

Source: Monitoring the Future study, Univ. of Michigan Inst. for Social Research; Natl. Inst. on Drug Abuse, Natl. Insts. of Health
(percent who have ever used)

Drug	1975	1980	1985	1990	1995	2000	2005	2010	2015	2020	2021	2022	2023	2022-23 change
Any illicit drug[1]	55.2%	65.4%	60.6%	47.9%	48.4%	54.0%	50.4%	48.2%	48.9%	46.6%	41.3%	41.0%	39.9%	−1.2%
Marijuana/hashish	47.3	60.3	54.2	40.7	41.7	48.8	44.8	43.8	44.7	43.7	38.6	38.3	36.5	−1.8
Inhalants[2]	—	17.3	18.1	18.5	17.4	14.2	11.4	9.0	5.7	3.8	5.0	5.8	6.3	0.4
Nitrites	—	11.1	7.9	2.1	1.5	0.8	1.1	—	—	—	—	—	—	—
Hallucinogens[3]	—	15.6	12.1	9.7	12.7	13.0	8.8	8.6	6.4	7.5	7.1	7.1	6.6	−0.5
LSD	11.3	9.3	7.5	8.7	11.7	11.1	3.5	4.0	4.3	5.9	4.9	4.4	3.1	−1.4
PCP	—	9.6	4.9	2.8	2.7	3.4	2.4	1.8	—	—	—	—	—	—
MDMA[4]	—	—	—	—	—	11.0	5.4	7.3	5.9	3.6	2.8	3.0	1.6	−1.3
Cocaine	9.0	15.7	17.3	9.4	6.0	8.6	8.0	5.5	4.0	4.1	2.5	2.4	1.3	−1.1
Crack	—	—	—	3.5	3.0	3.9	3.5	2.4	1.7	1.6	1.5	1.3	0.8	−0.5
Heroin	2.2	1.1	1.2	1.3	1.6	2.4	1.5	1.6	0.8	0.4	0.4	0.5	0.2	−0.3
Other narcotics[5]	9.0	9.8	10.2	8.3	7.2	10.6	12.8	13.0	8.4	5.3	2.3	3.2	2.4	−0.8
Amphetamines[5]	22.3	26.4	26.2	17.5	15.3	15.6	13.1	11.1	10.8	7.3	4.9	5.3	4.3	−1.0
Methamphetamine	—	—	—	—	—	7.9	4.5	2.3	1.0	1.7	0.6	1.1	0.6	−0.5
Crystal meth (ice)	—	—	—	2.7	3.9	4.0	4.0	1.8	1.2	0.2	0.7	0.8	0.9	0.2
Sedatives[5,6]	18.2	14.9	11.8	7.5	7.4	9.2	10.5	7.5	5.9	4.4	3.5	3.6	2.9	−0.7
Methaqualone[5]	8.1	9.5	6.7	2.3	1.2	0.8	1.3	0.4	—	—	—	—	—	—
Tranquilizers[5]	17.0	15.2	11.9	7.2	7.1	8.9	9.9	8.5	6.9	7.0	3.3	3.3	2.7	−0.6
Alcohol	90.4	93.2	92.2	89.5	80.7	80.3	75.1	71.0	64.0	61.5	54.1	61.6	52.8	−8.9
Cigarettes	73.6	71.0	68.8	64.4	64.2	62.5	50.0	42.2	31.1	24.0	17.8	16.8	15.0	−1.8
Smokeless tobacco	—	—	—	—	30.9	23.1	17.5	17.6	13.2	—	8.6	10.3	7.8	−2.5
Any vaping[7]	—	—	—	—	—	—	—	—	35.5	47.2	40.5	40.7	35.7	−5.0
Steroids[5]	—	—	—	2.9	2.3	2.5	2.6	2.0	2.3	2.0	0.8	1.5	0.9	−0.6

— = Not available. **Note:** Because of changes to question wording, some data may not be directly comparable across years. (1) Incl. marijuana, LSD, other hallucinogens, crack, cocaine other than crack, or heroin; or any use of narcotics other than heroin, amphetamines, sedatives (barbiturates), or tranquilizers not under a doctor's orders. (2) Unadjusted for underreporting of amyl and butyl nitrites. (3) Unadjusted for underreporting of PCP. (4) Ecstasy, Molly. (5) Incl. only drug use not under a doctor's orders. (6) Barbiturates. (7) Incl. vaping nicotine, marijuana, or just flavoring.

Cigarette Use in the U.S., 1985-2022

Source: National Survey on Drug Use and Health, SAMHSA, U.S. Dept. of Health and Human Services
(percentage of persons age 12 or older, unless otherwise noted, reporting use in the month prior to the survey)

	1985	2000	2005	2010	2015	2020	2022
Total	**38.7**	**24.9**	**24.9**	**23.0**	**19.4**	**15.0**	**14.6**
Sex							
Male	43.4	26.9	27.4	25.4	21.8	16.4	16.5
Female	34.5	23.1	22.5	20.7	17.1	13.6	12.7
Age							
12-17 years	29.4	13.4	10.8	8.4	4.2	1.4	1.2
18-25 years	47.4	38.3	39.0	34.3	26.7	13.9	10.7
26 years or older[1]	45.7	24.2	24.3	22.8	20.0	16.7	16.7

	1985	2000	2005	2010	2015	2020	2022
Race/Hispanic origin							
White, not Hispanic	38.9	25.9	26.0	24.3	20.7	15.7	15.9
Black, not Hispanic	38.0	23.3	24.5	22.6	21.3	17.3	15.8
Hispanic, any race	40.0	20.7	22.1	20.1	15.3	11.5	11.0
Education[2]							
Non-HS graduate	37.3	32.4	34.8	34.3	28.1	25.3	27.8
HS graduate	37.0	31.1	31.8	29.6	27.4	23.3	22.4
Some college	32.6	27.7	28.1	25.8	23.5	16.1	16.6
College graduate	23.0	13.9	13.8	12.8	9.6	6.8	6.5

HS = High school. **Note:** Because of methodological changes in 2002, 2015, 2020, and 2022, data may not be comparable across years. (1) Persons age 26 to 34 only in 1985. (2) Persons age 18 or older.

Tobacco Use by High School and Middle School Students, 2023

Source: National Youth Tobacco Survey, Centers for Disease Control and Prevention, U.S. Dept. of Health and Human Services

In 2023, 10.0% of high school and middle school students in the U.S. reported current use—defined as use on one or more days in the past 30 days—of a tobacco product. While the use of cigarettes, cigars, and smokeless tobacco has declined significantly among students since 2011, electronic cigarette (e-cigarette) use has increased over the same time period. Since 2014, e-cigarettes have been the most commonly used tobacco product among students in grades 6 through 12.

	High school students using tobacco				Middle school students using tobacco			
Tobacco product	**Female**	**Male**	**All students**	**Estimated no. of users[1]**	**Female**	**Male**	**All students**	**Estimated no. of users[1]**
E-cigarettes	26.0%	19.5%	22.6%	3,550,000	11.0%	8.2%	9.7%	1,170,000
Cigarettes	8.8	8.3	8.5	1,310,000	4.6	4.0	4.3	510,000
Cigars	4.8	7.9	6.4	980,000	2.4	2.9	2.6	310,000
Hookahs	4.0	3.5	3.7	560,000	—	1.7	2.1	240,000
Other oral nicotine products	2.8	4.0	3.5	520,000	2.4	2.1	2.2	260,000
Smokeless tobacco (composite)	2.2	4.3	3.3	500,000	2.3	2.7	2.4	290,000
Nicotine pouches	2.0	4.1	3.1	430,000	—	—	—	—
Pipe tobacco	1.7	2.4	2.1	310,000	1.1	1.1	1.1	120,000
Heated tobacco products	1.7	1.6	1.6	230,000	1.2	—	1.2	130,000
Any tobacco product[2]	**30.1**	**25.9**	**27.9**	**4,390,000**	**15.4**	**13.8**	**14.7**	**1,780,000**
Any combustible tobacco[3]	13.6	14.9	14.2	2,190,000	7.5	7.2	7.3	870,000
Multiple tobacco products	12.8	12.6	12.7	1,990,000	6.7	5.5	6.1	740,000

— = Not available. (1) Rounded down to nearest 10,000. (2) Incl. e-cigarettes, cigars, cigarettes, smokeless tobacco (composite) (i.e., chewing tobacco, snuff, dip, snus), hookahs, nicotine pouches, heated tobacco products, pipe tobacco, or bidis, not shown separately here, or other oral nicotine products (i.e., lozenges, discs, tablets, gums, dissolvable tobacco products). (3) Cigarettes, cigars, hookahs, pipe tobacco, or bidis.

Alcohol Use by 8th and 12th Graders, 1980-2023

Source: Monitoring the Future study, Univ. of Michigan Inst. for Social Research; Natl. Inst. on Drug Abuse, Natl. Insts. of Health

	1980	1990	1995	2000	2005	2010	2015	2021	2022	2023	% change, 2022-23
Alcohol use[1]	Percent using in the 30 days before the survey										
All 8th graders	—	—	**24.6%**	**22.4%**	**17.1%**	**13.8%**	**9.7%**	**7.3%**	**6.0%**	**5.9%**	**−0.1%**
Male	—	—	25.0	22.5	16.2	13.2	9.1	5.9	5.2	6.0	0.8
Female	—	—	24.0	22.0	17.9	14.3	9.9	8.5	6.0	5.2	−0.8
White	—	—	25.4	24.7	17.9	13.9	8.9	9.2	7.6	3.5	−4.1
Black	—	—	18.7	16.0	14.9	11.8	8.2	6.9	4.5	6.8	2.3
Hispanic	—	—	32.4	26.7	20.6	18.1	10.4	6.2	4.8	4.5	−0.3
All 12th graders	**72.0%**	**57.1%**	**51.3**	**50.0**	**47.0**	**41.2**	**35.3**	**25.8**	**28.4**	**24.3**	**−4.1**
Male	77.4	61.3	55.7	54.0	50.7	44.2	36.0	23.1	28.2	23.4	−4.8
Female	66.8	52.3	47.0	46.1	43.3	37.9	35.0	28.6	28.3	24.9	−3.4
White	75.4	63.8	54.5	55.1	52.3	45.4	40.9	35.3	33.8	13.5	−20.3
Black	47.6	35.8	35.2	30.0	29.0	31.4	24.0	18.2	13.6	33.7	20.1
Hispanic	63.6	49.1	48.7	51.2	43.3	40.1	36.3	21.8	19.3	20.0	0.7
Heavy alcohol use[2]	Percent heavily using in the two weeks before the survey										
All 8th graders	—	—	**12.3%**	**11.7%**	**8.4%**	**7.2%**	**4.6%**	**2.8%**	**2.2%**	**2.0%**	**−0.2%**
Male	—	—	12.5	11.7	8.2	6.5	4.6	2.0	2.1	2.1	0.0
Female	—	—	12.1	11.3	8.6	7.8	4.6	3.2	1.7	1.3	−0.4
White	—	—	12.1	13.0	9.0	7.1	4.0	3.6	2.6	1.0	−1.6
Black	—	—	8.3	7.3	6.1	5.3	4.1	3.4	1.6	2.3	0.7
Hispanic	—	—	18.4	16.0	12.1	10.8	5.4	2.4	2.1	1.9	−0.2
All 12th graders	**41.2%**	**32.2%**	**29.8**	**30.0**	**27.1**	**23.2**	**17.2**	**11.8**	**12.6**	**10.2**	**−2.4**
Male	52.1	39.1	36.9	36.7	32.6	28.0	19.3	11.1	14.3	12.0	−2.3
Female	30.5	24.4	23.0	23.5	21.6	18.4	14.9	12.6	11.2	8.5	−2.7
White	44.3	36.6	32.3	34.6	32.5	27.6	21.2	17.2	16.0	4.8	−11.2
Black	17.7	14.4	14.9	11.5	11.3	13.1	9.8	5.8	4.5	16.0	11.5
Hispanic	33.1	25.6	26.6	31.0	23.9	22.1	18.5	9.8	8.1	7.5	−0.6

— = Not available. **Note:** To derive percentages for each race/ethnicity subgroup, data for the specified year and previous year have been combined to increase sample size and thus provide more stable estimates. There was insufficient data for 2020 estimates. (1) In 1993, the alcohol question was changed slightly to indicate that a "drink" is defined as "more than a few sips." (2) Five or more drinks in a row (binge drinking) on one or more occasions.

Acquired Immune Deficiency Syndrome (AIDS)

Source: Centers for Disease Control and Prevention (CDC), U.S. Dept. of Health and Human Services

AIDS (Acquired Immune Deficiency Syndrome) is caused by the human immunodeficiency virus (HIV). HIV disables or kills crucial immune cells known as CD4 cells (also called T cells, or T-lymphocyte or T-helper cells), progressively destroying the body's ability to fight disease.

HIV is commonly spread through unprotected sexual contact with an infected partner's semen or vaginal fluids. It is also spread through contact with infected blood. Modern screening techniques make HIV transmission through transfusions or organ/tissue transplants, rare, but HIV can spread among intravenous drug users who share syringes and similar equipment. HIV can also be spread to a fetus during gestation or delivery or through breastfeeding after a baby's birth. With treatment, the transmission rate can be reduced from about 25% to less than 1%. There is no evidence HIV can spread through saliva or casual contact such as shaking hands or the sharing of food utensils, towels and bedding, or toilet seats.

About two-thirds of people experience flu-like symptoms within 2-4 weeks of being infected with HIV in what is called the acute HIV infection stage. The second stage is chronic infection, also referred to as asymptomatic HIV infection or clinical latency. Even though a person may not have any symptoms, the HIV continues to multiply, infect, and kill CD4 cells.

The term AIDS applies to the final (third) stage of HIV infection. According to the CDC's official case definition, an HIV-infected person 6 years of age or older with fewer than 200 CD4 cells per cubic millimeter of blood can be said to have AIDS. (Healthy adults usually have 500-1,600 CD4 cells per cu mm.) An HIV-infected person who develops an AIDS-defining opportunistic infection (OI) can also be diagnosed with AIDS. In the U.S., the most common OIs include the herpes simplex virus 1, salmonella, candidiasis, and toxoplasmosis.

Months or years prior to the onset of AIDS, people may experience such symptoms as swollen glands, lack of energy, fevers and sweats, and memory loss or other neurologic disorders. Children with AIDS may have delayed development or fail to thrive.

No test can detect HIV immediately after infection. The window period—or time between infection and accurate detection—varies by the type of HIV test used. An antibody test looks for antibodies, disease-fighting proteins of the immune system, to HIV in blood or oral fluid. It can take 23-90 days after exposure for this test to detect HIV antibodies. An antigen/antibody test looks for both HIV antibodies and parts of the virus (antigens); it can detect an infection after 18-90 days. A nucleic acid test (NAT) can detect the presence of HIV in blood 10-33 days following exposure. Most rapid tests and the self-test are antibody tests.

Since 1987, when the U.S. Food and Drug Administration (FDA) approved a drug called zidovudine (or AZT) for the treatment of HIV, more than 40 drugs and drug combinations (fixed doses of two or more medications in a single pill) have received approval. These drugs are grouped into classes: nucleoside reverse transcriptase inhibitors (NRTIs), non-nucleoside reverse transcriptase inhibitors (NNRTIs), protease inhibitors (PIs), fusion inhibitors, CCR5 antagonists, integrase strand transfer inhibitors (INSTIs), attachment inhibitors, post-attachment inhibitors, and capsid inhibitors. Each class of drug attacks the virus at a different point in its life cycle. Patients generally take three different HIV medicines from at least two different classes as part of antiretroviral therapy (ART), which extends the period between HIV infection and the development of serious illness.

Without a vaccine or cure for AIDS, the best way to prevent HIV infection is to avoid activities that carry a risk. The CDC recommends abstinence, mutual monogamy with an uninfected partner, limiting the number of sexual partners, never sharing needles, and using condoms correctly and consistently. People who do not have HIV but are at high risk of exposure can take medication daily to prevent HIV infection, called pre-exposure prophylaxis (PrEP). Daily PrEP reduces the risk of getting HIV from sex and from injection drug use. Post-exposure prophylaxis (PEP) is the emergency use of HIV medicines after a single high-risk event. PEP must be started within 72 hours of exposure to HIV, and it is not always effective.

New AIDS Diagnoses in the U.S., by Transmission Category, 1985-2022

Source: National Center for HIV/AIDS, Viral Hepatitis, STD, and TB Prevention; CDC

Transmission category	All years[1]	1985	1990	1995	2000	2005	2010	2015	2020	2022
All persons 13 years of age and older	**1,350,998**	**11,808**	**47,387**	**64,353**	**38,049**	**33,956**	**27,328**	**18,539**	**14,353**	**16,687**
All males 13 years of age and older	**1,060,857**	**10,948**	**41,435**	**51,476**	**28,068**	**24,890**	**20,495**	**14,054**	**11,097**	**13,040**
Male-to-male sexual contact (MMSC)	651,296	7,718	26,708	28,843	15,409	15,138	14,001	10,123	8,203	9,698
Injection drug use	198,680	1,762	8,791	12,975	5,905	3,515	1,820	923	716	886
MMSC and injection drug use	98,594	1,067	4,009	5,534	2,818	2,460	1,558	912	726	774
Heterosexual contact[2]	100,102	99	1,048	3,619	3,762	3,643	3,003	2,002	1,397	1,594
Other[3]	12,185	302	880	505	174	135	114	94	55	88
All females 13 years of age and older	**280,091**	**860**	**5,952**	**12,877**	**9,981**	**9,066**	**6,833**	**4,485**	**3,256**	**3,647**
Injection drug use	97,419	508	3,408	5,979	3,427	2,427	1,409	821	605	691
Heterosexual contact[2]	176,024	241	2,230	6,660	6,430	6,517	5,285	3,580	2,592	2,871
Other[3]	6,648	110	314	239	124	122	139	85	59	85
All children, under 13 years of age	**10,050**	—	—	—	—	—	—	—	—	—

— = Not available. **Note:** Table shows number of persons diagnosed with an HIV infection at stage 3 (AIDS) in the 50 states, DC, 6 territories, and freely associated states. The definition of AIDS cases has expanded over time. Because of the COVID-19 pandemic, 2020 data should be interpreted with caution. (1) Incl. diagnoses for years not shown, from beginning of epidemic (1981) through 2022. Incl. 6 dependent areas. (2) Sexual contact with a person known to have, or with a risk factor for, HIV infection. (3) Incl. hemophilia, blood transfusion, perinatal exposure (13 years of age or older at time of diagnosis), and risk factor not reported or not identified.

New HIV Diagnoses in the U.S., 2018-22

Source: *HIV Surveillance Report*, 2022, vol. 35; National Center for HIV/AIDS, Viral Hepatitis, STD, and TB Prevention; CDC

	Number of diagnoses					Diagnoses per 100,000 pop.				
Characteristic	**2018**	**2019**	**2020**	**2021**	**2022**	**2018**	**2019**	**2020**	**2021**	**2022**
All persons	**37,217**	**36,408**	**30,375**	**35,724**	**37,663**	**11.4**	**11.1**	**9.2**	**10.8**	**11.3**
Gender										
Male	29,453	28,762	24,203	28,268	29,728	—	—	—	—	—
Female	6,999	6,847	5,386	6,476	6,942	—	—	—	—	—
Transgender woman/girl[1]	691	720	719	873	868	—	—	—	—	—
Transgender man/boy[2]	48	45	41	60	59	—	—	—	—	—
Additional gender identity[3]	26	34	26	47	66	—	—	—	—	—
Age at diagnosis										
Under 13 years	85	58	58	53	62	0.2	0.1	0.1	0.1	0.1
13-14 years	20	21	14	15	22	0.2	0.3	0.2	0.2	0.3
15-19 years	1,722	1,654	1,280	1,467	1,350	8.2	7.9	5.8	6.8	6.2
20-24 years	6,140	6,005	4,873	5,528	5,677	28.1	27.7	22.1	24.6	25.0
25-29 years	7,670	7,401	6,088	6,722	7,190	32.6	31.4	26.7	30.0	32.4
30-34 years	5,627	5,635	5,219	6,346	6,841	25.4	25.1	22.9	27.5	29.4
35-39 years	4,154	4,088	3,384	4,383	4,761	19.3	18.8	15.3	19.7	21.4
40-44 years	2,935	2,919	2,462	3,130	3,522	14.9	14.7	11.9	14.9	16.4
45-49 years	2,743	2,568	2,044	2,284	2,416	13.2	12.6	10.1	11.6	12.3
50-54 years	2,409	2,272	1,828	2,098	2,100	11.6	11.1	8.8	10.1	10.1
55-59 years	1,814	1,824	1,564	1,768	1,743	8.3	8.3	7.1	8.2	8.3
60-64 years	1,031	1,101	875	1,103	1,107	5.1	5.4	4.2	5.2	5.2
65-69 years	483	500	423	538	503	2.8	2.9	2.4	2.9	2.7
70-74 years	247	229	166	186	234	1.8	1.6	1.1	1.2	1.5
75 years and over	137	133	97	103	135	0.6	0.6	0.4	0.5	0.6
Race/ethnicity[4]										
Amer. Indian/Alaska Native	166	181	178	211	217	6.9	7.5	7.4	8.7	9.0
Asian	844	718	599	731	796	4.5	3.8	3.1	3.7	3.9
Black/African American	15,434	15,161	12,566	14,335	14,582	37.7	36.8	30.1	34.2	34.7
Native Hawaiian/other Pac. Isl.	53	56	60	73	83	8.9	9.3	9.7	11.7	13.1
White	9,230	8,894	7,655	8,986	9,110	4.7	4.5	3.9	4.6	4.6
Multiracial	1,546	1,466	1,144	1,241	1,061	21.5	19.9	15.0	15.9	13.3
Hispanic/Latino (any race)	9,944	9,932	8,173	10,147	11,814	16.7	16.4	13.2	16.2	18.6

— = Not available. **Note:** Data shown are for the 50 states and DC. They reflect reports to the CDC as of Dec. 31, 2023, of persons who have been diagnosed with an HIV infection, regardless of the stage of disease. 2020 data should be interpreted with caution due to the impact of the COVID-19 pandemic. (1) Incl. individuals assigned male sex at birth who have ever identified as female gender. (2) Incl. individuals assigned female sex at birth who have ever identified as male gender. (3) Incl., e.g., bigender, gender queer, and two-spirit. (4) Not Hispanic/Latino unless otherwise noted.

Deaths of Persons in the U.S. With HIV Ever Classified as AIDS, 1981-2022

Source: National Center for HIV/AIDS, Viral Hepatitis, STD, and TB Prevention; CDC

Age at death	Number	% of total
Under 13 years	5,195	0.6%
13-14 years	305	0.04
15-19 years	1,393	0.2
20-24 years	11,074	1.4
25-29 years	51,541	6.4
30-34 years	109,964	13.6
35-39 years	138,387	17.1
40-44 years	133,469	16.5
45-49 years	109,902	13.6
50-54 years	86,107	10.6
55-59 years	64,556	8.0
60-64 years	44,605	5.5
65 years and over	53,868	6.6
Race/ethnicity		
American Indian/Alaska Native	2,240	0.3
Asian (incl. Asian/Pac. Isl. legacy)	4,120	0.5
Black/African American	324,391	40.0
Native Hawaiian/other Pac. Islander	451	0.1
White	305,807	37.7
Multiracial	22,848	2.8
Hispanic/Latino (any race)	150,464	18.6

Transmission category[1]	Number	% of total
Male 13 years of age or older	650,668	80.3%
Male-to-male sexual contact (MMSC)	367,550	45.4
Injection drug use	156,721	19.3
MMSC and injection drug use	64,842	8.0
Heterosexual contact[2]	51,537	6.4
Perinatal[3]	810	0.1
Other[4]	9,208	1.1
Female 13 years of age or older	154,503	19.1
Injection drug use	69,170	8.5
Heterosexual contact[2]	80,484	9.9
Perinatal[3]	908	0.1
Other[4]	3,941	0.5
Region of residence		
Northeast	232,232	28.7
Midwest	84,961	10.5
South	316,868	39.1
West	148,588	18.3
U.S. dependent areas	27,717	3.4
Total[5]	**810,366**	**100.0**

Note: Deaths of persons with HIV infection, stage 3 (AIDS) may be due to any cause. Numbers cumulative from beginning of epidemic (1981) through 2022 in the 50 states, DC, 6 dependent areas, and freely associated states. Numbers may not add up to totals. (1) Based on sex assigned at birth. Classified based on risk factor most likely responsible for HIV transmission. (2) Sexual contact with a person known to have, or with a risk factor for, HIV infection. (3) Person 13 years of age or older at time of death. (4) Incl. hemophilia, blood transfusion, and risk factor not reported/identified. (5) Incl. persons of unknown race/ethnicity.

Allergies and Asthma

Source: Asthma and Allergy Foundation of America (AAFA), Centers for Disease Control and Prevention (CDC)

An estimated one in three adults and one in four children in the U.S. suffer from allergies. People with allergies have immune systems that overreact to a normally harmless substance, called an allergen. Common allergens include tree, grass, and weed pollens; dust mites, mold spores, animal dander, latex, and insect venom; plants like poison ivy; and drugs such as penicillin. The U.S. Food and Drug Administration recognizes the following as major food allergens, which must be specially manufactured and labeled: milk, eggs, fish, crustacean shellfish, tree nuts, peanuts, wheat, soybeans, and sesame.

The tendency to develop allergies is usually inherited. Though allergies typically manifest in childhood, they can show up at any age. Food allergies and eczema (inflamed or irritated skin) are common allergies among infants. Older children and adults may develop allergic rhinitis, or hay fever, in reaction to an inhaled allergen. Allergic rhinitis symptoms include nasal congestion, runny nose, and sneezing.

People with allergies should avoid contact with an allergen, if feasible. Medications, such as antihistamines and nasal corticosteroids, may be used to decrease an allergic reaction. Other effective allergy treatments include decongestants, eye drops, and ointments. Allergy shots, a form of immunotherapy, aim to desensitize a patient to an allergen through gradual exposure to increasingly higher doses of it. People at risk of anaphylaxis—a severe, whole-body allergic reaction that occurs rapidly—should have access to injectable epinephrine, an emergency medication.

Some allergy sufferers also have asthma. Asthma is a chronic inflammation disease that can develop at any age. It affects the passageways that carry air into and out of the lungs. During an asthma attack, these airways become inflamed and fill with mucus. A person may experience wheezing, tightening of the chest, and coughing. Asthma can become life-threatening if not controlled in its early stages. The following symptoms may be indicative of an emergency: the patient shows no improvement minutes after initial treatment; struggles to breathe while hunched with chest and neck pulled in; has trouble walking or talking; and develops gray or blue lips or fingernails.

Exposure to an allergen can set off an asthma attack. Tobacco smoke, cold air, and expressing strong emotion can also trigger an attack, as can respiratory infections and physical exercise. An accurate diagnosis by a physician is important.

Website: www.aafa.org

Persons With Asthma in the U.S., 2021

Source: National Health Interview Survey, NCHS, CDC

Characteristic	Number (thous.)	Percent
Total	**24,964**	**7.7%**
Children (under age 18)	4,675	6.5
Adults	20,288	8.0
Age		
0-4 years	370	1.9
5-14 years	3,124	7.7
15-19 years	1,862	9.0
20-24 years	1,970	9.5
25-34 years	3,508	7.8
35-64 years	10,080	8.2
65 years and over	4,034	7.2
Sex		
Males	10,274	6.5
Under age 18	2,695	7.3
Age 18 and over	7,579	6.2
Females	14,690	8.9
Under age 18	1,980	5.6
Age 18 and over	12,710	9.7
Race/ethnicity[1]		
White non-Hispanic	14,806	7.6
Black non-Hispanic	4,207	10.9
Asian non-Hispanic	744	4.1
Amer. Ind./Alaska Native non-Hispanic	566	12.3
Hispanic (any race)	3,917	6.4
Mexican	1,968	5.4
Other Hispanic	1,897	8.0

Note: Includes only those with a current asthma diagnosis. Numbers may not add up to totals due to rounding. (1) Data are for 2019-21.

Alzheimer's Disease

Source: Alzheimer's Association

Alzheimer's disease is a degenerative disease in which nerve cells in the brain deteriorate and die. It is the most common cause of dementia. Early symptoms include forgetting newly learned information and apathy or depression. As the disease advances, a person may exhibit disorientation and behavior changes; confusion about events, time, and place; and suspicion towards family, friends, and caregivers.

The rate of the disease's progression varies. Changes to the brain might begin 20 or more years before they are measurable in a stage researchers call preclinical Alzheimer's disease. For example, decreased glucose metabolism, a known biological marker for Alzheimer's disease, can be picked up by a brain scan. In the next stage—mild cognitive impairment (MCI) due to Alzheimer's disease—a person can still perform everyday activities without significant trouble. The disease's third stage, dementia due to Alzheimer's disease, can range from mild to moderate to severe. While a person could remain independent with assistance early on, they ultimately lose the ability to perform basic bodily functions, such as walking or swallowing, making them susceptible to infections of the lungs, urinary tract, and other organs. The average length of time from diagnosis of Alzheimer's dementia until death is 4-8 years for those age 65 and older.

An estimated 6.9 mil persons in the U.S., or 10.9% of the population age 65 and older, were living with Alzheimer's dementia in 2024; 33.4% of those age 85 and older have Alzheimer's dementia. Because women on average live longer than men, and age is the greatest risk factor for Alzheimer's disease, women make up almost two-thirds of Americans with Alzheimer's. Alzheimer's dementia has a higher prevalence in older adults in the non-Hispanic Black and Hispanic populations, which may be explained by disparities caused by marginalization of those communities. Growing research suggests older adults who identify as being part of a sexual and gender minority (e.g., LGBTQ+) may also be at higher risk of Alzheimer's because of systematic discrimination.

Diagnosis involves a comprehensive evaluation that may include a complete health history, physical examination, neurological and mental status assessments, and other tests. Depression, drug interactions, nutritional imbalances, and excessive alcohol consumption can cause symptoms that look similar to dementia. Parkinson's disease, frontotemporal lobar degeneration, and cerebrovascular disease can also cause dementia.

Treatments for cognitive and behavioral symptoms are available, and clinical trials are ongoing. The U.S. Food and Drug Administration (FDA) has approved multiple drugs in two categories: drugs that temporarily treat symptoms and drugs that target the underlying disease process in order to slow its progression.

Having the e4 form of the APOE (apolipoprotein E) gene and a family history of the disease are also risk factors. Staying physically and mentally active and socially connected may be associated with a lower risk for the disease.

The U.S. cost in 2024 of diagnosing, treating, and providing long-term care for persons age 65 and older with Alzheimer's or other dementias was an estimated $360 bil. That figure does not include the hours of unpaid care that family members, friends, and others provide, valued at around $346.6 bil in 2023. The lifetime cost of caring for a dementia patient was estimated to be almost $400,000 (2023 dollars).

Website: www.alz.org

Warning Signs of Alzheimer's Disease

- Memory loss that disrupts daily life
- Challenges in planning or solving problems
- Difficulty completing familiar tasks at home, at work, or at leisure
- Confusion with time or place
- Trouble understanding visual images and spatial relationships
- New problems with words in speaking or writing
- Misplacing things and losing the ability to retrace steps
- Decreased or poor judgment
- Withdrawal from work or social activities
- Changes in mood and personality

Arthritis

Source: Arthritis Foundation; Centers for Disease Control and Prevention (CDC), U.S. Dept. of Health and Human Services

The term arthritis refers to more than 100 different diseases that cause pain, aching, stiffness, and swelling in or around the joints. An estimated 21.2% of the adult population aged 18 and over reported having diagnosed arthritis in 2023. The cause of most types of arthritis is unknown; scientists are studying the role of genetics, lifestyle, and environment.

Of the three most prevalent forms of arthritis, **osteoarthritis** (OA), also called degenerative arthritis, is the most common, affecting about 33 mil Americans. With OA, protective cartilage at a joint breaks down. When the bones of the joint thus rub together, pain and stiffness may result. The most commonly affected joints are in the lower back, hips, knees, hands, and feet.

Fibromyalgia, another common arthritis condition, affects about 6.4% of American adults, with women (7.7%) more likely than men (4.9%) to have it. People suffering from fibromyalgia experience widespread pain, abnormal pain processing, sleep disturbance, and psychological distress. Other symptoms include tingling or numbness in hands and feet and problems with thinking and memory.

Rheumatoid arthritis (RA) is an autoimmune disease that affects an estimated 1.3 mil U.S. adults (or 0.6%-1% of the adult population). It is one of the most serious and disabling forms of arthritis, which women experience at two to three times the rate of men. With RA, the body's immune system attacks healthy cells in the joints, causing inflammation that can lead to cartilage and bone damage.

Other forms of arthritis and related conditions include lupus, gout, scleroderma, and Sjögren's syndrome. To diagnose arthritis, a doctor will record a patient's symptoms and look for any swelling or limited movement during a physical. Other signs of arthritis include rashes, mouth sores, and dry eyes. A doctor may test a patient's blood, urine, or joint fluid or take joint X-rays.

Medications that relieve pain and swelling, such as analgesics and anti-inflammatory drugs, can be used to treat arthritis. Regular physical activity, in particular low-impact sports like walking or swimming, can improve mood and ease pain. Maintaining a healthy weight puts less stress on joints. Surgery to replace a joint is an option if OA gets to be too severe.

Website: www.arthritis.org

Attention-Deficit/Hyperactivity Disorder (ADHD)

Source: CDC; Natl. Institute of Mental Health; Children and Adults with Attention-Deficit/Hyperactivity Disorder (CHADD)

Attention-deficit/hyperactivity disorder, or ADHD, is one of the most common neurodevelopmental disorders of childhood, when it is usually first diagnosed. Individuals with ADHD may have trouble paying attention and controlling impulsive behaviors.

Signs and Symptoms of ADHD

Inattention

- Often has trouble paying attention to details, resulting in careless mistakes
- Often loses focus, failing to finish tasks or duties
- Often loses things necessary for tasks (e.g., school materials, eyeglasses, keys)

Hyperactivity and impulsivity

- Often fidgets with hands or feet or squirms while seated
- Often talks too much
- Often has trouble waiting their turn

ADHD may manifest in one of three ways. A person who is **predominantly inattentive** is easily distracted or forgets details of daily routines. Someone who is **predominantly hyperactive-impulsive** may feel restless and impulsive. In the third type, **combined presentation**, an individual displays symptoms of both inattentiveness and hyperactivity-impulsivity. The cause of ADHD is unknown, but current research shows that genetics plays a significant role. Alcohol and tobacco use during pregnancy; low birth weight; and brain injury are being studied as other possible risk factors.

According to the 2021-22 National Survey of Children's Health, 10.1% of children age 3-17 years in the U.S. have a current diagnosis of ADHD. Boys are more likely to be diagnosed because girls with ADHD tend to present more inattentive symptoms. At least one-third of children with ADHD will continue to have it as adults. Studies have found that young adults with ADHD are more likely than those who have never been diagnosed with it to drop out of high school, to be unemployed, or to work an unskilled job.

As no single test exists for diagnosing ADHD, it is usually diagnosed through a checklist of symptoms and patient history. In most cases, ADHD is treated with a combination of medication (stimulants and nonstimulants) and behavior therapy.

Breast Cancer

Source: American Cancer Society, Inc.; National Cancer Institute, National Institutes of Health

In 2024, an estimated 310,720 women and 2,790 men in the U.S. will be newly diagnosed with breast cancer, and about 42,250 women and 530 men will die from it. More than 4 mil women live with a history of breast cancer, but mortality rates have been declining, especially among older women, probably because of earlier detection and improved treatment.

The risk for breast cancer is higher for women and increases with age. It is higher for women with a personal or family history of cancer (particularly breast cancer), a longer menstrual history (menstrual periods that started early and ended later in life), recent use of hormonal birth control, use of menopausal hormone therapy, and in those who have no children or had no live birth until after age 30. Other risk factors include alcohol consumption, physical inactivity, and being overweight or obese. About 5%-10% of breast cancers are probably due to inherited mutations, the most common being those in the *BRCA1* and *BRCA2*. Most women who develop breast cancer have no family history of it.

Breast cancer often manifests first as a new lump or mass. Other symptoms include swelling, distortion, tenderness, skin irritation, redness, scaliness, or nipple abnormalities, such as ulceration, retraction, or spontaneous discharge.

Studies show that early detection increases survival and treatment options. Although most detected breast lumps are noncancerous, any suspicious lump should be biopsied.

Treatment for breast cancer may involve breast-conserving surgery (removal of the tumor and surrounding tissue), mastectomy (surgical removal of the breast), radiation, chemotherapy, hormone therapy, and/or targeted therapy. The five-year relative survival rate for female breast cancer patients has improved from 74.8% in 1975-77 to 91.2% in 2014-20; for women diagnosed with localized breast cancer (cancer that has not spread to lymph nodes or other locations outside the breast), survival is 99.6%.

Website: www.cancer.org

Prostate Cancer

Source: Prostate Cancer Foundation (PCF); American Cancer Society, Inc.; National Cancer Institute, National Institutes of Health

The prostate is a male gland located between the bladder and scrotum that secretes seminal fluid. Among men in the U.S., prostate cancer is the most commonly diagnosed non-skin cancer and the second-most common cause, after lung and bronchus cancer, of cancer deaths. In 2024, an estimated 299,010 men will be newly diagnosed with prostate cancer, and about 35,250 will die from the disease. More than 3.3 mil men in the U.S. are living with a history of prostate cancer today.

The most identifiable risk factors for prostate cancer are age, family history, and African ancestry. The average age at diagnosis is about 67, and the chances of developing the disease rise dramatically with age. Black men in the U.S. and Caribbean have the world's highest documented incidence rate of prostate cancer. The cause for this disparity remains unclear.

Usually, the disease has no symptoms in its early stages. As the disease advances, a man may experience weak or interrupted urine flow; inability to urinate or difficulty starting or stopping the urine flow; the need to urinate frequently, especially at night; blood in the urine; or pain or burning with urination. Advanced prostate cancer commonly spreads to the bones, causing pain in areas such as the hips, spine, or ribs.

The American Cancer Society recommends that at age 50, men at average risk of prostate cancer should speak with their health care provider about the benefits and limitations of prostate-specific antigen (PSA) testing. An increased PSA level may indicate a higher chance of having prostate cancer, but older age and the use of certain medications, among other factors, can raise or lower PSA levels. Black men or those with a family history of the disease (a close relative who was diagnosed before age 65) should be aware of their screening options beginning at age 45. Men with more than one close relative with prostate cancer should discuss screening at 40. The U.S. Preventive Services Task Force is currently updating its recommendations on screening. Because prostate cancer is slow-growing, testing is not likely to help men with a life expectancy of less than 10 years. Men under 40 seldom get prostate cancer.

Prostate cancer treatment may include surgery, radiation, hormonal therapy, chemotherapy, or some combination. If caught early on, while tumor cells are localized within the prostate, the five-year relative survival rate approaches 100.0%.

Websites: www.pcf.org; www.cancer.org

Skin Cancer

Source: American Cancer Society, Inc; National Cancer Institute, National Institutes of Health

Skin cancer—the most commonly diagnosed cancer in the U.S.—is generally divided into the following types: **basal and squamous cell skin cancers** (or nonmelanomas) and **melanomas**. Invasive melanoma accounts for only about 1% of all skin cancers but the majority of skin cancer deaths. Risk factors include excess exposure to UV radiation, especially in those with lighter colored skin, atypical or multiple moles (more than 50), family or personal history of skin cancers, advanced age, and a weakened immune system.

Melanomas generally look like abnormal moles on the surface of the skin. Abnormal moles differ from regular skin cells and may be a sign of skin cancer. Changes in the size, shape, or color of a mole should be examined by a doctor as soon as possible.

If caught early, melanoma is highly curable. In 2014-20, the five-year relative survival rate for melanoma at the localized stage was 100.0%; at the regional stage, 74.8%; and 35.0% at the distant stage.

Treatment may include simple removal of the melanoma; amputation if the cancer is found on a finger or toe; or chemotherapy, immunotherapy, and/or radiation if the melanoma has spread to other parts of the body.

Warning Signs of Abnormal Moles

- **A**symmetry: one half does not match the other half
- **B**order irregularity: edges are ragged, notched, or blurred
- **C**olor: not uniform; may be shades of brown or black, and patches of pink, red, blue, or white
- **D**iameter: moles wider than ¼ inch are abnormal (however, melanomas can be smaller)
- **E**volution: mole changes size, shape, or color over time

Website: www.cancer.org

Cancer Risk Factors

Source: American Cancer Society, Inc., www.cancer.org; National Cancer Institute, National Institutes of Health

Alcohol: Alcohol consumption increases the risk of cancers of the mouth, pharynx, larynx, esophagus, liver, colorectum, female breast, and stomach. Alcohol consumption combined with tobacco use increases the risk of cancers of the mouth, pharynx, larynx, and esophagus far more than either drinking or smoking alone.

Body weight, diet, and physical activity: Overweight and obesity are associated with increased risk for developing many cancers, including cancers of the breast in postmenopausal women, colorectum, kidney, pancreas, and esophagus. Overweight and obesity may also be associated with increased risk of fatal prostate cancer, non-Hodgkin lymphoma, and male breast cancer.

Environmental and occupational hazards: Exposure to certain substances, called carcinogens, can increase the risk of various cancers. Carcinogens like arsenic or radon may occur naturally, or they may be manufactured, like vinyl chloride. The risk of lung cancer from asbestos exposure is greatly increased among smokers.

Radon, a form of ionizing radiation, is the second-leading cause of lung cancer in the U.S. Excessive radon exposure in the home may increase lung cancer risk, especially in cigarette smokers.

Examples of occupational hazards, where workers are in contact with carcinogens at higher levels than the public, include diesel engine exhaust, the foams and flame retardants used by firefighters, and pesticides.

Hormones: Menopausal hormone therapy (MHT, formerly called hormone replacement therapy) with estrogen alone can increase the risk of endometrial cancer. Combining progestin with estrogen may reduce that risk, but studies suggest their use may increase the risk of breast and ovarian cancer. The benefits and risks of the use of estrogen should be discussed carefully with one's doctor.

Infectious agents: HPV, the Epstein-Barr virus, the hepatitus B and hepatitus C virus, and *Helicobacter pylori* bacteria are known to cause cancer. Less than 5% of all U.S. cancer cases are due to infections, many of which are treatable and for which vaccines exist.

Tobacco: Smoking is responsible for about 30% of all cancer deaths and 81% of lung cancer deaths in the U.S. Cigarette smoking also increases the risk of the following cancers: oral cavity and pharynx, larynx, lung, esophagus, pancreas, uterine cervix, kidney, bladder, stomach, colorectum, liver, and acute myeloid leukemia. While electronic cigarettes (e-cigarettes) generally have lower carcinogen levels than combustible tobacco products, the long-term risks of use are not yet clear.

Use of smokeless tobacco products—such as chewing tobacco, snuff, and snus—can increase the risk of oral, esophageal, and pancreatic cancers as well as precancerous mouth lesions.

Ultraviolet radiation: Many of the more than 5 mil skin cancers diagnosed annually in the U.S. could have been prevented by protection from the sun's rays and avoidance of indoor tanning. Epidemiological evidence shows that sun exposure duration may be a major factor in increasing incidence rates of melanoma.

Screening Guidelines for Early Detection of Cancer

Cancer site	Population	Test or procedure	Frequency
Breast	Women, age 40+	Mammography	The American Cancer Society (ACS) no longer recommends regular breast self-exams or clinical breast exams; research has not found that they reduce the risk of dying from breast cancer. Women should be familiar with how their breasts look and feel and report any changes to a health care professional. For women at average risk (e.g., lack of strong family history of breast cancer), ages 40-44: annual mammography if desired; for ages 45-54: annual mammograms; for ages 55+: mammograms yearly or every two years for those in good health with a life expectancy of 10+ years. Women at high risk for breast cancer, such as a *BRCA1* or *BRCA2* gene mutation, should get a breast MRI and mammogram yearly.
Cervix	Women, age 21+ or 25+	HPV test, Pap test	The ACS recommends all women begin screening at age 25; the U.S. Preventive Services Task Force (USPSTF) recommends screening start at age 21. For ages 25-65: primary HPV test every 5 years is preferred. If HPV testing alone is not available, then an HPV/Pap co-test every 5 years or a Pap test every 3 years is acceptable. For ages 65+: women who have had regular screenings with normal results in the previous 10 years should no longer be tested; women with a history of abnormal test results or cervical precancers should continue to be tested for at least 25 years after diagnosis. Women who have had a total hysterectomy for reasons unrelated to cervical cancer should not be screened.
Colorectal	Men and women, ages 45-75	Guaiac-based fecal occult blood test (gFOBT) **or** fecal immunochemical test (FIT) **or**	The ACS and USPSTF recommend starting at age 45. Annual, for people with average risk. Testing at home with adherence to instructions for collection and number of samples is recommended. A gFOBT or FIT done during a digital rectal examination in a health care setting is not sufficient for screening as only one stool sample is collected.
		Multitargeted stool DNA test (MT-sDNA) with FIT, **or**	Every 3 years.
		Flexible sigmoidoscopy (FSIG), **or**	Every 5 years, or every 10 years if an FIT is done yearly.
		CT, or virtual, colonography, **or**	Every 5 years.
		Colonoscopy	Every 10 years for people without an increased risk. A colonoscopy should also be done if any of the above tests returns a positive result.
Endometrial	Women, at menopause	Women at average risk should be informed about risks and symptoms of endometrial cancer and encouraged to report any unexpected bleeding or discharge to their physician.	
Lung	Current or former smokers, ages 50-80	Low-dose CT scan (LDCT)	People who smoke or used to smoke with a 20 pack-year or more smoking history (number of packs smoked per day times number of years smoked) should be screened annually. People with serious health problems who have a limited life expectancy should not be screened.
Prostate	Men, age 40+ or 55-69	Prostate-specific antigen test (PSA) and digital rectal exam (DRE)	The ACS recommends men with an average risk and an expected life span of 10+ years should talk with their health care provider at age 50 about the benefits and risks of screening. African Americans—who have a higher rate of prostate cancer—and men with a first-degree relative diagnosed with prostate cancer before age 65 should have this talk at age 45. Men with more than one first-degree relative diagnosed at an early age should have the talk at age 40. The USPSTF is currently updating their recommendation.

New U.S. Cancer Cases and Deaths for Leading Sites, 2024

Source: *Cancer Facts & Figures 2024*, American Cancer Society

The following estimates exclude basal cell and squamous cell skin cancers, also referred to as nonmelanoma skin cancers, and in situ carcinomas (i.e., noninvasive cancers) except of the urinary bladder. In 2024, an estimated 56,500 cases of female breast ductal carcinoma in situ and 99,700 cases of melanoma in situ are expected to be diagnosed. An est. 5.4 mil cases of basal cell and squamous cell skin cancer were diagnosed among 3.3 mil people in 2012 according to the most recent study available.

Estimated New Cases

Both sexes		Male		Female	
Breast	313,510	Prostate	299,010	Breast	310,720
Prostate	299,010	Lung and bronchus	116,310	Lung and bronchus	118,270
Lung and bronchus	234,580	Colon and rectum	81,540	Colon and rectum	71,270
Colon and rectum	152,810	Urinary bladder	63,070	Uterine corpus	67,880
Melanoma of the skin	100,640	Melanoma of the skin	59,170	Melanoma of the skin	41,470
Urinary bladder	83,190	Kidney and renal pelvis	52,380	Non-Hodgkin lymphoma	36,030
Kidney and renal pelvis	81,610	Non-Hodgkin lymphoma	44,590	Pancreas	31,910
Non-Hodgkin lymphoma	80,620	Oral cavity and pharynx	41,510	Thyroid	31,520
Uterine corpus	67,880	Leukemia	36,450	Kidney and renal pelvis	29,230
Pancreas	66,440	Pancreas	34,530	Leukemia	26,320
All sites	**2,001,140**	**All sites**	**1,029,080**	**All sites**	**972,060**

Estimated Deaths

Both sexes		Male		Female	
Lung and bronchus	125,070	Lung and bronchus	65,790	Lung and bronchus	59,280
Colon and rectum	53,010	Prostate	35,250	Breast	42,250
Pancreas	51,750	Colon and rectum	28,700	Pancreas	24,480
Breast	42,780	Pancreas	27,270	Colon and rectum	24,310
Prostate	35,250	Liver and intrahepatic bile duct	19,120	Uterine corpus	13,250
Liver and intrahepatic bile duct	29,840	Leukemia	13,640	Ovary	12,740
Leukemia	23,670	Esophagus	12,880	Liver and intrahepatic bile duct	10,720
Non-Hodgkin lymphoma	20,140	Urinary bladder	12,290	Leukemia	10,030
Brain and other nervous system	18,760	Non-Hodgkin lymphoma	11,780	Non-Hodgkin lymphoma	8,360
Urinary bladder	16,840	Brain and other nervous system	10,690	Brain and other nervous system	8,070
All sites	**611,720**	**All sites**	**322,800**	**All sites**	**288,920**

U.S. Cancer Mortality Rates by Cancer Site, 1975-2022

Source: SEER (Surveillance, Epidemiology, and End Results) Program, National Cancer Institute, National Institutes of Health (mortality rate per 100,000 pop. by year of death; NOS = not otherwise specified)

Cancer site	1975	1980	1985	1990	1995	2000	2005	2010	2015	2020	2022
All cancer sites combined	**199.1**	**207.0**	**211.3**	**214.9**	**209.9**	**198.8**	**185.2**	**171.8**	**160.0**	**145.6**	**142.0**
Anus, anal canal, and anorectum	0.04	0.1	0.2	0.2	0.2	0.2	0.2	0.2	0.3	0.4	0.4
Bones and joints	0.9	0.6	0.5	0.4	0.5	0.4	0.5	0.4	0.5	0.5	0.5
Brain and other nervous system	4.1	4.4	4.6	4.9	4.7	4.5	4.3	4.2	4.4	4.5	4.3
Cervix uteri	5.6	4.5	3.8	3.7	3.2	2.8	2.4	2.3	2.3	2.2	2.1
Colon and rectum	28.1	28.1	26.9	24.6	22.6	20.7	17.6	15.5	14.1	12.7	12.6
Corpus and uterus, NOS	5.3	5.1	4.6	4.3	4.1	4.1	4.1	4.5	4.8	5.2	5.4
Esophagus	3.7	3.8	3.9	4.1	4.3	4.4	4.4	4.3	4.0	3.7	3.7
Eye and orbit	0.2	0.1	0.1	0.1	0.1	0.1	0.1	0.1	0.1	0.1	0.1
Female breast	31.4	31.7	33.0	33.1	30.6	26.6	24.1	21.9	20.5	19.3	18.7
Gallbladder	1.4	1.2	1.1	0.9	0.8	0.7	0.7	0.6	0.6	0.5	0.5
Hodgkin lymphoma	1.3	1.0	0.8	0.7	0.5	0.5	0.4	0.4	0.3	0.3	0.3
Kidney and renal pelvis	3.6	3.7	4.0	4.2	4.3	4.2	4.1	3.9	3.8	3.5	3.4
Larynx	1.7	1.6	1.6	1.6	1.5	1.4	1.2	1.1	1.0	0.9	0.9
Leukemia	8.1	8.4	8.1	8.0	7.9	7.7	7.3	6.9	6.3	5.9	5.7
Liver and intrahepatic bile duct	2.8	2.8	3.1	3.6	4.4	4.6	5.3	5.9	6.6	6.6	6.5
Lung and bronchus	42.6	49.4	54.3	58.9	58.4	55.8	52.9	47.4	41.0	32.2	29.9
Melanoma of the skin	2.1	2.3	2.6	2.8	2.7	2.7	2.8	2.7	2.4	2.0	2.0
Myeloma	2.9	3.3	3.6	3.8	4.0	3.8	3.6	3.3	3.3	3.0	2.8
Non-Hodgkin lymphoma	5.6	6.2	7.1	7.9	8.7	8.2	6.9	6.1	5.5	5.0	4.7
Oral cavity and pharynx	4.3	4.2	3.8	3.6	3.2	2.7	2.5	2.5	2.5	2.6	2.7
Ovary	9.8	9.3	9.1	9.3	9.1	8.9	8.7	7.8	6.8	6.0	5.7
Pancreas	10.7	10.6	10.6	10.7	10.4	10.5	10.8	11.0	11.1	11.2	11.1
Prostate	31.0	33.1	33.9	38.6	37.3	30.4	25.4	21.8	19.3	19.2	18.7
Small intestine	0.3	0.4	0.4	0.4	0.4	0.4	0.4	0.4	0.4	0.4	0.4
Soft tissue including heart	0.9	1.2	1.3	1.4	1.5	1.3	1.3	1.3	1.3	1.3	1.3
Stomach	8.5	7.4	6.5	6.1	5.3	4.5	3.8	3.4	3.1	2.8	2.6
Testis	0.7	0.5	0.4	0.3	0.2	0.2	0.2	0.3	0.2	0.3	0.3
Thyroid	0.5	0.5	0.4	0.4	0.4	0.5	0.5	0.5	0.5	0.5	0.5
Urinary bladder (invasive and in situ)	5.5	5.2	4.7	4.5	4.4	4.3	4.4	4.4	4.4	4.1	4.1
Vagina	0.3	0.3	0.3	0.3	0.3	0.2	0.2	0.2	0.2	0.2	0.2
Vulva	0.5	0.5	0.5	0.4	0.5	0.4	0.5	0.5	0.5	0.6	0.7

U.S. Cancer Survival Rates by Age at Diagnosis, 2014-20

Source: Surveillance, Epidemiology, and End Results (SEER) Program, National Cancer Institute, National Institutes of Health

Age at diagnosis	All races			White			Black		
	Total	Male	Female	Total	Male	Female	Total	Male	Female
All ages	**69.3%**	**67.9%**	**70.7%**	**69.5%**	**67.9%**	**71.2%**	**65.3%**	**67.0%**	**63.6%**
Under age 45	84.9	81.2	87.2	86.0	82.7	88.1	76.2	70.2	79.4
Ages 45-54	77.9	72.5	81.8	78.5	72.8	82.6	72.4	71.0	73.6
Ages 55-64	71.9	70.1	74.1	72.3	70.0	75.1	67.1	69.0	64.5
Ages 65-74	68.9	69.5	68.2	69.2	69.4	68.9	64.7	68.6	59.7
Ages 75 and over	53.4	54.9	52.0	54.2	55.3	53.1	47.4	50.9	44.9

Note: Given percentages are five-year relative (estimated) survival rates for all invasive cancer sites, at all stages of diagnosis; based on follow-up of patients into 2021.

Depression

Source: Substance Abuse and Mental Health Services Admin. and National Institutes of Health, U.S. Dept. of Health and Human Services

Depression is a serious illness that affects thoughts, feelings, and the ability to function in everyday life. It is one of the most common mental disorders in the U.S., affecting all age groups. In 2022, an estimated 22.5 mil adults age 18 and older (or 8.8% of the adult population) in the U.S. had at least one major depressive episode. Over the same 12-month period, 20.1% of persons age 18-25 years experienced at least one major depressive episode versus 4.6% of those 50 or older. More women (13.7 mil) than men (8.8 mil) reported at least one major depressive episode in 2022.

Available treatments can alleviate symptoms. But many depressed people—and those around them—fail to realize that they have an illness or could benefit from medical help.

Symptoms and Types of Depression

- Loss of interest or pleasure in daily activities
- Significant weight loss with appetite and/or weight changes
- Insomnia or hypersomnia (excessive daytime sleepiness or prolonged nighttime sleep)
- Restlessness or moving/talking more slowly
- Fatigue or loss of energy
- Difficulty concentrating, thinking, or making decisions
- Recurrent thoughts of death or suicide, or suicide attempts

A diagnosis of **major depressive disorder** (or **clinical depression**) is made if an individual reports experiencing five or more of these symptoms in the same two-week period.

Bipolar disorder (formerly known as manic-depressive illness), while distinct from depression, is characterized by depressive episodes alternating with manic episodes, when a person may experience an abnormally elevated mood, less need for sleep, increased talkativeness, racing thoughts, and engagement in risky activities (e.g., unprotected sex).

Depression in women who are pregnant or who recently gave birth (**postpartum depression**); **psychotic depression**, where a person also has some type of psychosis, such as delusions or hallucinations; and **seasonal affective disorder** are other forms of depression.

Treatments for Depression

Depression can be treated with medication, psychotherapy, or a combination of the two, which studies have shown to be most effective in treating moderate-to-severe depression. Antidepressants influence the functioning of certain neurotransmitters in the brain. The most popular antidepressants are selective serotonin reuptake inhibitors (SSRIs). Serotonin and norepinephrine reuptake inhibitors (SNRIs) and bupropion are also commonly prescribed as they have fewer side effects than drugs from older classes, such as tricyclics and monoamine oxidase inhibitors (MAOIs). Some people respond better, however, to the older antidepressants.

Research has shown that certain types of psychotherapy, particularly cognitive-behavioral therapy (CBT) and interpersonal therapy (IPT), can help relieve depression. CBT helps patients change the negative thinking and behavior patterns often associated with depression. IPT focuses patients on working through personal relationships that may contribute to depression.

Electroconvulsive therapy (ECT) has been found effective in treating some cases of severe depression, particularly those that have not responded to other treatment. ECT involves using electric currents to produce a seizure in the brain of a patient under general anesthesia. Headaches and memory loss, though common side effects, are typically short-lived. Other types of treatment are being studied.

Website: www.nimh.nih.gov

Diabetes

Source: American Diabetes Association; Centers for Disease Control and Prevention (CDC), U.S. Dept. of Health and Human Services

Diabetes is a chronic disease in which the body does not produce or properly use the hormone **insulin.** Insulin is needed to convert sugar, starches, and other foods into energy. Both genetics and environment appear to play roles in the onset of diabetes. This disease, which has no cure, was the eighth leading cause of death in the U.S. in 2022 (24.1 deaths per 100,000 pop.). In 2022, an est. 24.7 mil Americans (6.4% of the population) had diagnosed diabetes. Diagnosed diabetes in the U.S. cost an estimated $412.9 bil in 2022; of that figure, $306.6 bil were in direct medical costs and $106.3 bil in indirect costs resulting from reduced productivity at or absence from work and premature death. Detection at an earlier stage and modest lifestyle changes, such as a healthier diet and more physical activity, may help prevent or delay complications.

There are two major types of diabetes:

Type 1 (formerly known as insulin-dependent or juvenile diabetes). The body does not produce insulin; the disease is usually diagnosed in children and young adults. People with type 1 diabetes must take daily insulin to stay alive.

Type 2 (formerly known as non-insulin dependent or adult-onset diabetes). The body does not produce enough or cannot properly use insulin. It is the most common form of the disease (90%-95% of all diabetes cases) and often begins later in life.

Prediabetes

In 2021, 97.6 mil Americans age 18 and older (or about 1 in 3 adults) had prediabetes, the state that occurs when a person's blood glucose levels are higher than normal but not high enough for a diagnosis of diabetes. People with prediabetes are at increased risk of developing type 2 diabetes unless lifestyle changes are made.

Complications From Diabetes

People often have diabetes for many years before it is diagnosed. During that time, serious complications may develop. Potential complications include the following:

Diabetic eye disease. High blood glucose can damage blood vessels to the eyes. In 2022, about 28.8% of adults age 18 and older with diagnosed diabetes had severe vision difficulty or blindness. Diabetic retinopathy is the most common cause of vision loss among those with diabetes. People with diabetes are also more likely to develop glaucoma or cataracts.

Kidney disease. In 2021, 60,113 people with diagnosed diabetes (199.0 per 100,000 of the total diabetic population) had end-stage renal disease.

Amputations. Diabetes is the most frequent cause for non-traumatic lower-limb amputations. About 1.2 per 1,000 adults age 18 and older with diabetes were hospitalized in 2020 for amputation below the knee; the rate was 0.5 per 1,000 for amputation above the knee and 2.0 for amputation of the foot.

Heart disease and stroke. Among adults age 35 and older with diabetes, 21.8% had major heart disease or a stroke in 2021.

Common Diabetes Symptoms

- Frequent urination, often at night
- Thirst
- Hunger
- Fatigue
- Blurry vision
- Cuts and bruises that are slow to heal
- Weight loss, nausea, vomiting (type 1)
- Tingling or numbness in hands or feet (type 2)

Gestational Diabetes

Gestational diabetes mellitus (GDM) is a form of diabetes that develops during or is diagnosed during pregnancy. Hormones released during pregnancy can cause insulin resistance, allowing blood glucose levels to rise. Usually there are no symptoms, or the symptoms are mild. Because GDM usually starts around the 24th week, pregnant women should receive a glucose tolerance test between the 24th and 28th week of pregnancy. Diet and exercise can help keep blood glucose levels within normal limits. Treatment may also include daily blood glucose testing and insulin injections.

Women with GDM tend to have larger babies at birth, which can complicate delivery. Glucose levels usually return to normal after delivery, but the odds of recurrence in future pregnancies and development of type 2 diabetes later in life increase. GDM is a common complication, affecting 5%-10% of U.S. pregnancies annually. In 2020, 7.8 of 100 live births in the U.S. were to women with GDM. In the same year, 10.6 of 1,000 live births were to women diagnosed with diabetes before pregnancy, that is, prepregnancy diabetes mellitus (PDM).

Website: www.diabetes.org

Eating Disorders

Source: National Institute of Mental Health (NIMH), National Institutes of Health, U.S. Dept. of Health and Human Services

Eating disorders are medical illnesses that involve serious disturbances in eating behavior. The main types are anorexia nervosa, bulimia nervosa, and binge-eating disorder. Though they can develop at any age, the median age of onset for anorexia nervosa and bulimia nervosa is 18 years old and 21 years old for binge-eating disorder. They may be caused by a combination of genetics, behavioral, psychological, and social factors. Eating disorders often occur with other illnesses such as depression, substance abuse, and anxiety disorders. If not treated, eating disorders can lead to serious complications, which may result in death.

Anorexia nervosa affects an estimated 0.6% of the U.S. adult population and three times as many women as men. It has the highest mortality rate of any mental disorder in the U.S. People with anorexia see themselves as overweight even when they are dangerously thin. In response, they severely restrict their food intake and take extreme measures to lose weight, such as exercising compulsively or purging by means of vomiting or laxatives. While some fully recover after a single episode, others may relapse frequently or experience chronic deterioration. Symptoms that may develop over time include muscle weakness, lethargy, and infertility.

Bulimia nervosa affects an estimated 1.0% of the U.S. adult population. It is five times more prevalent in women than men. It is characterized by recurrent uncontrolled binge-eating episodes followed by what is believed to be compensatory behavior to prevent weight gain, such as self-induced vomiting, use of laxatives or diuretics, exercising excessively, or fasting. Persons with bulimia can weigh within the normal range for their age and height but still fear gaining weight. Symptoms include a chronically inflamed and sore throat, worn tooth enamel, intestinal distress, and severe dehydration.

Binge-eating disorder affects an estimated 2.8% of the U.S. adult population, with women twice as likely than men to have it. As with bulimia, a binge-eating disorder involves episodes of excessive eating during which a person may feel a complete lack of control. Because these episodes are not followed by purging, exercising, or fasting, persons with binge-eating disorder are often overweight or obese.

Early diagnosis and a comprehensive treatment program are essential to recovery. Some patients may need immediate hospitalization. For anorexia, treatment usually follows three established steps: weight restoration, usually in an inpatient hospital setting; treatment of any accompanying psychological disturbances, including the use of medications; and achieving long-term remission or recovery by reducing or eliminating negative thoughts and behaviors.

Heart and Blood Vessel Disease

Source: American Heart Assn. (AHA); Natl. Center for Chronic Disease Prevention and Health Promotion, Centers for Disease Control and Prevention; Natl. Heart, Blood, and Lung Institute, Natl. Institutes of Health (NIH), U.S. Dept. of Health and Human Services

Warning Signs of Heart Attack

- Discomfort in chest. Most heart attacks involve discomfort, such as pressure, squeezing, or pain, in the center of the chest that lasts more than a few minutes or occurs intermittently. Most common symptom in men and women
- Discomfort in other upper body areas, including one or both arms, the back, neck, jaw, or stomach
- Shortness of breath, with or without chest discomfort
- Breaking out in a cold sweat, nausea, or lightheadedness, among other signs

While chest discomfort is the most common symptom of a heart attack, women are more likely to experience the other symptoms, such as abdominal pain, shortness of breath, dizziness, fainting, and extreme fatigue without having any chest pain. The AHA advises calling 911 at onset of symptoms so that emergency medical services can begin treatment on the way to the hospital.

Warning Signs of Stroke

- Face drooping or weakness on one side
- Arm weakness
- Speech difficulty, including slurring
- Time to call 911

Other stroke symptoms, which may appear separately or in combination with F.A.S.T.:

- Sudden numbness or weakness of the face, arm, or leg, especially on one side of the body
- Sudden confusion or trouble speaking or comprehending
- Sudden vision difficulty in one or both eyes
- Sudden trouble walking, dizziness, or loss of coordination
- Sudden severe headache with no known cause

If someone has one or more stroke symptoms, immediately call 911 or the emergency medical service number so an ambulance, ideally one with advanced life support, can be sent. Prompt treatment of a stroke can prevent death or lessen the long-term effects.

A transient ischemic attack (TIA), also referred to as a mini stroke, is when blood flow to the brain is blocked temporarily, with symptoms typically lasting under five minutes. Immediate medical treatment is still necessary as a TIA could signal a future stroke.

Major Modifiable Risk Factors

Major risk factors for heart and blood vessel (cardiovascular) disease are age, gender, and heredity. People 65 years of age or older are more likely to die of coronary heart disease. Men are at greater risk, as well as African Americans and those with a family history of heart disease. Major risk factors that can be modified include the following:

High blood pressure. High blood pressure, or hypertension, increases the risk of stroke, heart attack, kidney failure, and congestive heart failure. It affects men and women of all races, ethnic origins, and ages. But obesity, physical inactivity, and an unhealthy diet can contribute to this often symptomless disease. Everyone 3 years of age and older should have a blood pressure reading at least once a year.

A blood pressure reading consists of two measurements written one above the other, such as 122/78 mm Hg (millimeters of mercury). The upper number (systolic pressure) represents the amount of pressure in the arteries when the heart contracts (beats) and pushes blood through the circulatory system. The lower number (diastolic pressure) represents the pressure in the arteries between beats, when the heart is resting. According to guidelines revised in 2017, a blood pressure reading below 120/80 is considered normal, while a reading of 130/80 or higher indicates hypertension, of which there are two stages:

Stage 1 is 130-139 (systolic) over 80-89 (diastolic);
Stage 2 is 140+ (systolic) over 90+ (diastolic).

The diagnosis can be based on either the systolic or diastolic reading. Any reading higher than 180/120 is a hypertensive crisis that must be addressed by a doctor immediately.

High blood pressure usually cannot be cured, but it can be controlled in a variety of ways, including through diet, exercise, quitting smoking (where applicable), and medication. Treatment should be at the direction and under the supervision of a physician.

High blood cholesterol. Cholesterol is a waxy fatlike substance produced by the liver and found in all cells of the body. Dietary cholesterol exists in animal foods. Excess levels of cholesterol increase the risk of heart disease. High cholesterol in itself usually does not cause symptoms, so many people are unaware that they have a problem.

There are two major kinds of cholesterol: LDL (low-density lipoprotein), often called "bad" cholesterol, can build up on the inside walls of blood vessels, narrowing them. HDL (high-density lipoprotein), known as "good" cholesterol, helps reduce that risk.

NIH guidelines classify healthy total cholesterol levels (determined by a blood test) as less than 170 mg/dL for those age 19 or younger and 125 to 200 mg/dL for persons age 20 or older. LDL levels of less than 100 mg/dL are considered healthy. Healthy levels of HDL are more than 45 mg/dL for those age 19 or younger, 40 mg/dL or higher for men ages 20+, and 50 mg/dL or higher for women ages 20+. Among U.S. adults age 20 and over, 10.0% had high cholesterol (i.e., total cholesterol level equal to or greater than 240 mg/dL) in 2017-20.

As with high blood pressure, high blood cholesterol can be controlled by lifestyle changes and medication and should be treated by a physician.

Triglycerides, another form of fat in the blood, can also raise the risk of heart disease. Levels that are borderline high (150-199 mg/dL), high (200-499 mg/dL), or very high (500 mg/dL or more) may need treatment.

Diabetes. Adults with diabetes mellitus are two to three times more likely to die of heart disease or stroke.

Tobacco smoke. Cigarette smokers and nonsmokers exposed to secondhand smoke are more likely to develop coronary heart disease (CHD).

Obesity. People with excess body fat, especially around the waist (more than 40 in. for men, more than 35 in. for women), are more likely to develop heart and blood vessel disease even without any other risk factors.

Physical inactivity. A sedentary lifestyle is a risk factor for CHD. The risk increase is comparable to that observed for high blood cholesterol, high blood pressure, or cigarette smoking.

Women and Cardiovascular Disease

Heart disease was the number one cause of death for women in the United States in 2022, accounting for 28.4% of all female deaths; stroke (cerebrovascular disease) was the third leading cause, at 8.4%. Many of the major cardiovascular studies were conducted only on men. Researchers are now trying to understand the influence of gender on cardiovascular disease risk and prevention.

One problem in **diagnosis** is that women tend to have heart attacks later in life than men, so symptoms may be masked by other age-related diseases such as arthritis or osteoporosis. Even certain diagnostic tests and procedures such as the exercise stress test may not be as accurate in women, with the result that the disease process leading to heart attack or stroke may not be detected early on, with potentially serious consequences.

Website: www.heart.org

COVID-19

Source: National Center for Immunization and Respiratory Diseases, CDC, U.S. Dept. of Health and Human Services

COVID-19 (coronavirus disease 2019) was discovered in Dec. 2019 in Wuhan, China, and quickly spread around the world. COVID-19 is caused by the SARS-CoV-2 virus. It is part of the coronavirus family, whose viruses cause diseases from the common cold to acute bronchitis to more severe diseases like severe acute respiratory syndrome (SARS) and Middle East respiratory syndrome (MERS). Coronaviruses spread through droplets projected from the mouth or nose when an infected person breathes, coughs, sneezes, or speaks.

The word *corona* means crown and refers to the spike proteins on the surface of coronaviruses. These spike proteins allow the virus to attach to a human cell in order to infect it, replicating inside of the cell and spreading to other cells.

COVID-19 most often causes respiratory symptoms that can feel much like a cold, a flu, or pneumonia. Most experience mild symptoms, but some become severely ill. After infection, some people—even those who experienced minor or no symptoms—may suffer long-term effects, known as post-COVID conditions, or long COVID. Older adults, people with underlying medical conditions, and pregnant people are at increased risk of severe illness from COVID-19. Vaccines against COVID-19 are safe and effective; the first vaccines were made available in the U.S. beginning in Dec. 2020 under emergency authorization.

Symptoms of COVID-19

Symptoms may appear 2-14 days after exposure to the virus. Anyone can have mild to severe symptoms, including the following:

- Fever or chills
- Cough
- Shortness of breath or difficulty breathing
- Fatigue
- Muscle or body aches
- Headache
- New loss of taste or smell
- Sore throat
- Congestion or runny nose
- Nausea or vomiting
- Diarrhea

U.S. COVID-19 Cases, Deaths, and Vaccination Rates

Source: Centers for Disease Control and Prevention, U.S. Dept. of Health and Human Services

The COVID-19 public health emergency in the U.S.—which the Dept. of Health and Human Services first declared on Jan. 31, 2020—expired on May 11, 2023. Authorizations to collect certain public health data also expired on that date. As of May 10, 2023, this data has been archived or will no longer be updated; they may differ from figures elsewhere as the CDC reconciles records. Cumulative totals include confirmed and probable cases and deaths since Jan. 2020. COVID-19 was the third leading cause of death in 2020 and 2021 and the fourth leading cause in 2022.

	Cumulative total		Vaccination rate (% of total pop.)	
State/territory	**Cases**	**Deaths**	**At least one dose**	**Fully vaccinated[1]**
Alabama	1,659,936	21,138	65.1%	53.3%
Alaska	297,588	1,468	73.2	65.3
American Samoa	8,331	34	95.0	89.7
Arizona	2,474,154	33,451	78.4	66.2
Arkansas	995,043	13,115	70.1	57.0
California	12,251,820	101,886	85.1	74.9
Colorado	1,783,663	14,385	84.0	73.8
Connecticut	982,335	12,337	95.0	83.2
Delaware	333,772	3,394	88.5	73.5
Dist. of Columbia	178,904	1,435	95.0	91.3
Florida	7,572,282	88,248	82.9	69.7
Georgia	3,087,729	42,782	68.6	57.5
Guam	61,642	415	94.9	86.0
Hawaii	374,264	1,856	91.7	81.7
Idaho	526,118	5,479	64.1	56.6
Illinois	4,136,659	42,005	79.2	71.5
Indiana	2,076,326	26,446	64.6	57.9
Iowa	908,936	10,797	70.9	64.5
Kansas	945,923	10,214	76.5	65.6
Kentucky	1,743,117	18,623	69.1	59.7
Louisiana	1,600,610	18,971	62.9	55.1
Maine	322,982	3,038	95.0	83.6
Maryland	1,379,385	16,740	92.1	80.0
Massachusetts	2,242,176	24,644	95.0	84.5
Michigan	3,106,362	42,873	69.9	62.6
Minnesota	1,795,771	14,770	79.1	72.4
Mississippi	1,000,415	13,474	61.8	53.8
Missouri	1,790,763	22,931	69.6	59.2
Montana	333,959	3,715	68.4	59.3
Nebraska	575,134	5,089	73.7	66.5
Nevada	898,511	12,008	77.9	63.8
New Hampshire	382,013	3,052	88.5	72.3
New Jersey	3,075,271	36,118	94.9	79.3
New Mexico	681,242	9,236	94.9	75.5
New York[2]	3,572,043	32,341	94.7	81.0
New York City	3,266,726	45,181	NA	NA
North Carolina	3,501,404	29,059	90.2	66.9
North Dakota	291,093	2,513	69.6	58.9
Northern Mariana Islands	13,886	44	90.4	84.9
Ohio	3,441,458	42,207	65.9	60.7
Oklahoma	1,306,350	16,157	74.9	60.6
Oregon	975,856	9,550	82.0	72.7
Pennsylvania	3,559,331	51,047	91.1	73.8
Puerto Rico	1,122,076	5,908	91.0	84.2
Rhode Island	441,466	3,915	95.0	88.0
South Carolina	1,852,019	19,923	71.2	60.1
South Dakota	282,895	3,231	84.3	66.5
Tennessee	2,542,163	29,549	64.6	56.4
Texas	8,508,204	93,780	77.0	63.5
Utah	1,097,475	5,362	75.5	66.9
Vermont	154,243	967	95.0	86.1
Virgin Islands (U.S.)	24,994	131	71.0	55.6
Virginia	2,310,846	23,743	91.3	76.8
Washington	1,957,759	16,186	85.6	76.4
West Virginia	650,556	8,125	67.6	59.8
Wisconsin	2,030,717	16,600	75.3	68.4
Wyoming	187,034	2,031	61.1	53.2
United States[3]	**104,673,730**	**1,133,717**	**81.4**	**69.5**

NA = Not available. (1) Defined as having received two doses on different days of two-dose series or one dose of single-dose vaccine. (2) Excl. New York City, except for vaccination rates, which are for the entire state. (3) U.S. data incl. counts from jurisdictions not shown separately in table, incl. three countries in free association compacts (Marshall Islands, Fed. States of Micronesia, Palau).

Common Infectious Diseases

Source: Centers for Disease Control and Prevention (CDC), U.S. Dept. of Health and Human Services; World Health Organization

State and local officials, in connection with the CDC, monitor certain diseases in the interests of public health. Some diseases must be confirmed in a laboratory while others may be diagnosed based on epidemiologic data (e.g., exposure to a foodborne pathogen linked to confirmed cases of illness in other patients). Statistics may thus appear uneven because of different reporting methods for each disease. This list is meant to be used for reference purposes only and not as a diagnostic tool.

Chickenpox

(Varicella-zoster virus, or VZV) Highly contagious disease commonly associated with children that can be especially serious in babies, adults, pregnant women, and people with weakened immune systems. A person who has had chickenpox may develop shingles later in life if the virus reactivates. **Transmission:** direct contact with rash or through the air when an infected person coughs or sneezes. **Symptoms:** blister-like rash that can last up to 7 days, fever. **Vaccine:** available since 1995. **Treatment:** for relief of symptoms; antivirals only for those at risk of complications. **Annual U.S. cases:** before 1995, about 4 mil, mostly children; 3,496 in 2021; 4,347 in 2022 and 5,773 in 2023 (both provisional).

Chlamydia

(*Chlamydia trachomatis*) One of the most widely spread sexually transmitted infections (STIs), and the most common STI reported to the CDC of the diseases that it tracks. **Transmission:** sexually transmitted. A mother can pass an infection to her baby during delivery. **Symptoms:** Most of those infected show no symptoms. In women, abnormal vaginal discharge, infection of the cervix and urinary tract; can cause pelvic inflammatory disease. In men, infection of urinary tract and pain and swelling in one or both testicles; can also infect the throat, rectum, and eyes. **Treatment:** curable with antibiotics. **Annual U.S. cases:** 1,649,716 in 2022 (or 495.0 per 100,000 pop.).

Common cold

(More than 200 different viruses, rhinoviruses being most common) An upper respiratory viral infection. **Transmission:** touching one's nose, eyes, or mouth after touching something contaminated by the virus; inhalation of airborne virus. **Symptoms:** irritated nose or scratchy throat, sneezing and watery green or yellow nasal discharge, coughing, muscle aches, headaches, postnasal drip (mucus dripping down throat). **Treatment:** no cure. Over-the-counter remedies can relieve symptoms. **Annual U.S. cases:** about 1 bil.

Gonorrhea

(*Neisseria gonorrhoeae*) Very common bacterial STI. **Transmission:** sexually transmitted. Can pass from mother to infant during delivery. **Symptoms:** pain or burning during urination. In men, white, yellow, or green discharge from urethra; in women, increased vaginal discharge, vaginal bleeding between periods. Many men and most women do not present symptoms. **Treatment:** curable with antibiotics, although bacteria has become increasingly resistant. **Annual U.S. cases:** 648,056 in 2022 (or 194.4 per 100,000 pop.).

Hepatitis

A viral disease that causes inflammation of the liver. In the U.S., five forms are endemic: A, B, C, D, and E. Forms A, B, and C are the most common. HBV and HCV can cause chronic disease. **Symptoms:** all forms have generally similar symptoms including jaundice, fatigue, abdominal pain, loss of appetite, nausea, mild flu-like symptoms. Many cases cause no symptoms. In extreme cases, infected persons may develop end-stage liver disease.

Hepatitis A (*Hepatovirus picornaviridae*). **Transmission:** consuming food or water contaminated with feces from infected persons. **Vaccine:** effective. (In developing countries, older children and adults may generally be immune after having been infected when young.) **Treatment:** disease usually resolves on its own; alcohol consumption should be avoided. **Annual U.S. cases:** 2,265 in 2022 (confirmed).

Hepatitis B (*Orthohepadnavirus hepadnaviridae*). **Transmission:** unsterilized needle sharing; contaminated blood transfusions; sexual contact; infants during childbirth. **Vaccine:** highly effective. **Treatment:** for chronic cases, drug treatment is necessary; no cure exists. For acute (short-term) cases, disease usually resolves itself. **Annual U.S. cases:** 2,126 acute and 13 perinatal (pregnant person to child) in 2022 (confirmed).

Hepatitis C (*Hepacivirus flavinviridae*). **Transmission:** unsterilized needle sharing; contaminated blood transfusions; sexual contact; infants during childbirth. **Vaccine:** none. **Treatment:** chronic cases treated with drugs, which can eliminate the virus in more than 95% of patients. For acute cases, the CDC recommends monitoring by a doctor and starting treatment if the infection becomes chronic. **Annual U.S. cases:** 4,848 acute and 197 perinatal in 2022 (confirmed).

HPV

(More than 200 related human papillomaviruses) Most common sexually transmitted infection in U.S.; causes nearly all cases of cervical cancer, over 90% of anal cancers, and 63%-75% of oropharyngeal, vaginal, vulvar, and penile cancers. The CDC estimates most people in the U.S. will acquire HPV at some point in their lives. **Transmission:** sexually transmitted. **Symptoms:** most of those infected have no symptoms though in some cases, low-risk HPVs result in genital warts and precancerous bumps on anus, cervix or vulva, or penis. High-risk HPVs can persist for years and lead to cell changes that become cancerous, possibly producing symptoms. **Vaccine:** currently only protects against certain HPV types but offers most protection when given to children ages 9-12. **Treatment:** while there is no cure, a healthy immune system can usually fight off HPV on its own. Women age 21 and older should be regularly screened for cervical cancer. **Annual U.S. cases:** est. 13 mil new infections, 42.5 mil currently infected in 2018.

Influenza

(Various influenza viruses) Highly contagious viral respiratory infection. **Transmission:** airborne; contact with face after touching infected surface. **Symptoms:** chills, fatigue, fever, headaches, sore throat, sinus congestion, coughing. ("Stomach flu" is not influenza.) **Vaccine:** yearly vaccinations recommended; available as injection or nasal spray. **Treatment:** antiviral drugs; disease normally runs its course in a matter of days. **Annual U.S. cases:** preliminary est. 31 mil symptomatic illnesses, 360,000 flu-related hospitalizations, and 21,000 flu-related deaths during the 2022-23 influenza season, with adults 65 years of age and older making up 72.0% of all deaths from influenza.

Lyme disease

(*Borrelia burgdorferi*) Bacterial inflammatory disease, first identified 1975 in Old Lyme, CT. Most common vector-borne disease in the U.S. Concentrated in the Northeast and mid-Atlantic, north-central states (mostly Wisconsin, Minnesota), and the West Coast, particularly Northern California. **Transmission:** bite from infected blacklegged (or deer) tick. Mice and deer are most common tick hosts. **Symptoms:** mimic those of other diseases. Flu-like symptoms: fatigue, stiff neck, joints. A roughly circular rash may appear at site of tick bite and expand to look like a bull's eye. Untreated Lyme disease can produce symptoms such as fever, rash, facial paralysis, irregular heartbeat, and arthritis. **Treatment:** antibiotics in early stages; anti-inflammatory drugs to relieve symptoms. About 5%-10% of patients continue to experience symptoms after treatment, a condition called Post-Treatment Lyme Disease Syndrome. **Annual U.S. cases:** from 9,465 reported cases in 1991—the first year the CDC began collecting Lyme disease data—to 24,610 cases (16,211 confirmed; 8,399 probable) in 2021. The CDC estimates about 476,000 people are diagnosed and treated for Lyme disease each year.

Malaria

(*Plasmodium* parasite) Mosquito-borne disease that mostly occurs in tropical and subtropical regions. **Transmission:** bite from infected *Anopheles* mosquito. **Symptoms:** high fever, shaking chills, heavy sweating, headaches, fatigue, enlarged spleen. If left untreated, organ damage and death. **Treatment:** antimalarial drugs, such as doxycycline, for treatment and prevention. **Annual cases:** In the U.S., 1,503 in 2021; 1,932 in 2022 and 2,186 in 2023 (both provisional). Worldwide, est. 249 mil cases and 608,000 deaths in 2022, with four African countries accounting for just over half of global malaria deaths.

Measles

(*Rubeola* virus) Declared eliminated in the U.S. in 2000. Spreads mostly via unvaccinated travelers from abroad; MMR coverage among kindergartners in the U.S. is also now below 95% coverage target. **Transmission:** airborne transmission. The virus can survive for up to two hours in the air where an infected person has coughed or sneezed. **Symptoms:** itchy and raised rash, cough, watery eyes, high fever. Complications include ear infections, pneumonia, brain swelling, premature birth, or even death. **Vaccine:** highly effective. **Treatment:** no specific treatment; relief of symptoms. **Annual U.S. cases:** 49 in 2021 and 121 in 2022; 59 in 2023 (preliminary).

Mumps

(Mumps virus) Acute and contagious viral infection. **Transmission:** direct contact with mucus or saliva of infected persons. **Symptoms:** headaches, fever, loss of appetite may precede painful, visible swelling of the salivary glands under one or both ears. In severe cases, inflammation of testes, pancreas, ovaries; brain swelling; deafness. **Vaccine:** MMR (measles, mumps, and rubella) vaccine is effective. **Treatment:** no specific treatment; symptoms may be relieved by applying cold or warm compress to swollen glands. **Annual U.S. cases:** 189 in 2021, 399 in 2022, and 436 in 2023 (all preliminary).

Peptic ulcer

(Most from *Helicobacter pylori* [*H. pylori*] bacteria; also long-term use of aspirin or other anti-inflammatory drugs) Weakening of the stomach or duodenum's protective mucous coating, allowing stomach acid and bacteria to irritate the lining and cause a sore. **Transmission:** *H. pylori* may be transmitted through food and water; possibly through close contact between infected persons. **Symptoms:** indigestion; bloating; dull, transient abdominal pain or discomfort; nausea; vomiting. **Treatment:** antibiotics, drugs to reduce stomach acid. **Annual U.S. cases:** 4.6 mil people.

Pertussis or Whooping cough

(*Bordetella pertussis*) Upper respiratory bacterial infection. **Transmission:** airborne transmission by infected persons; highly contagious. **Symptoms:** initially, mild cold-like symptoms, fever, difficulty breathing; later, violent coughing with characteristic "whooping" sound when patient tries to breathe between coughs, vomiting. Many babies, instead of coughing, may stop breathing and turn blue. **Vaccine:** available as part of Tdap (tetanus, diphtheria, pertussis) combination vaccine. **Treatment:** antibiotics in early cases; otherwise, disease must run its course. **Annual U.S. cases:** 2,116 in 2021; 3,044 in 2022 and 5,611 in 2023 (both provisional).

Salmonella or Salmonellosis

(Most types of *Salmonella*) Bacterial infection. **Transmission:** eating foods contaminated by feces carrying the bacteria or eating undercooked meats or raw eggs contaminated by bacteria. Contact with infected domestic animals. **Symptoms:** fever, diarrhea, abdominal cramps. **Treatment:** no standard treatment. Runs its course in 4-7 days. Antibiotics in severe cases. **Annual U.S. cases:** (excluding *Salmonella* serotype Typhi and Paratyphi infections, which cause typhoid and paratyphoid fevers, respectively) 49,249 in 2021; 56,129 in 2022 and 52,575 in 2023 (both provisional).

Shigellosis

(Four species of *Shigella* bacteria) Diarrheal disease. **Transmission:** swallowing water or consuming food contaminated by infected feces. **Symptoms:** sometimes bloody diarrhea, fever, stomach pain usually lasting 5-7 days. **Treatment:** replacement of fluids and salts to prevent dehydration. Antibiotics in severe cases. Antidiarrheal medicines may make illness worse. **Annual U.S. cases:** 9,999 in 2021; 14,744 in 2022 and 19,130 in 2023 (both provisional).

Syphilis

(*Treponema pallidum*) Bacterial infection that can cause significant health problems if left untreated. **Transmission:** sexually transmitted; pregnant women can transmit during fetal development or at birth. **Symptoms:** primary stage: painless sore, called a chancre, where bacteria entered the body; usually heals in 3-6 weeks with or without treatment. Without treatment, disease enters secondary stage: skin rash as chancre is healing or weeks after it has healed. Without treatment, enters latent stage (no visible symptoms). Very rarely, can move into tertiary stage 10-30 years after infection and cause death. Syphilis can spread to the brain and nervous system (neurosyphilis) or eyes (ocular syphilis) at any stage; symptoms include fever, fatigue, dementia, vision changes. **Treatment:** antibiotics, though reinfection is possible. **Annual U.S. cases:** 207,255 (all stages and congenital syphilis) and 59,016 (primary and secondary) in 2022.

Tetanus or Lockjaw

(*Clostridium tetani*) Bacterial infection. **Transmission:** spores of bacteria commonly found in soil entering body through broken skin. **Symptoms:** muscle stiffness; spasms or "locking" of muscles of the jaw, neck, limbs; seizures, fever. Breathing difficulties may lead to death in 1-2 of every 10 cases. **Vaccine:** four forms of immunization. **Treatment:** tetanus immune globulin to fight infection, drugs to control spasms. **Annual U.S. cases:** 28 in 2021; 26 in 2022 and 15 in 2023 (both provisional).

Tuberculosis

(*Mycobacterium tuberculosis*) Bacterial infection that primarily affects the lungs. **Transmission:** airborne transmission by persons with TB disease. **Symptoms:** no symptoms in person with latent TB infection. Person with TB disease may have weight loss, fever, cough with discharge (sometimes with bloody sputum) lasting 3 or more weeks, night sweats. **Vaccine/treatment:** BCG (bacille Calmette-Guérin) vaccine for children where TB is prevalent. Not recommended for use in the U.S. because of low infection risk and variable effectiveness in adults. Antibiotics to treat TB disease or to prevent latent infection from becoming active. **Annual U.S. cases:** 8,320 in 2022; 9,615 in 2023 (provisional).

Yellow fever

(Yellow fever virus, in *flavivirus* genus) Viral infection endemic in tropical areas of Africa and Central and South America. **Transmission:** bite from virus-carrying mosquito. **Symptoms:** head and body aches, nausea and vomiting, fatigue over 3-4 days. Small percentage may then enter more toxic phase, with fever, jaundice (yellowing skin), organ failure, coma, and death in 7-10 days. Most infected people exhibit no symptoms or only mild symptoms. **Vaccine:** safe and effective, conferring lifetime immunity to most who receive it. **Treatment:** symptoms treated until disease runs its course. **Annual cases:** In the U.S., 1 in 2021; 0 in 2022 and 2023 (both provisional. Worldwide, est. 200,000 cases and 30,000 deaths worldwide (90% in Africa).

Vaccination Coverage for Selected Diseases Among U.S. Adolescents, 2008-19

Source: National Center for Immunization and Respiratory Diseases, CDC, U.S. Dept. of Health and Human Services

(percent of adolescents aged 13-17)

Vaccination coverage	2008	2010	2011	2012	2013	2014	2015	2016	2017	2018	2019
Measles, mumps, rubella (2 doses or more)	89.3%	90.5%	91.1%	91.4%	89.6%	90.7%	90.7%	90.9%	92.1%	91.9%	91.9%
Hepatitis B (3 doses or more)	87.9	91.6	92.3	92.8	91.3	91.4	91.1	91.4	91.9	92.1	91.6
Varicella vaccine (2 doses or more) among those with no history of varicella	34.1	58.1	68.3	74.9	78.5	81.0	83.1	85.6	88.6	89.6	90.6
Tdap (tetanus, diphtheria, pertussis) (1 dose or more)	40.8	68.7	78.2	84.6	84.7	87.6	86.4	88.0	88.7	88.9	90.2
Meningococcal conjugate vaccine (MenACWY) (1 dose or more)	41.8	62.7	70.5	74.0	76.6	79.3	81.3	82.2	85.1	86.6	88.9
HPV (up-to-date among females)[1]	NA	NA	NA	NA	NA	NA	NA	49.5	53.1	53.7	56.8
HPV (3 doses or more among females)[2]	17.9	32.0	34.8	33.4	36.8	39.7	41.9	43.0	44.0	37.9	28.5
HPV (up-to-date among males)[1]	NA	NA	NA	NA	NA	NA	NA	37.5	44.3	48.7	51.8
HPV (3 doses or more among males)[2]	NA	NA	1.3	6.8	13.4	21.6	28.1	31.5	34.8	32.1	26.6

HPV = Human papillomavirus. NA = Category not applicable. **Note:** Based on sample of civilian noninstitutionalized pop., supplemented by survey of vaccination providers to sampled adolescents. Data for 2013 and beyond are not directly comparable with data for earlier years because of changes to data definitions. (1) New recommendations released in Dec. 2016 for full vaccination against HPV (also called up-to-date). (2) Refers to HPV vaccine quadrivalent (2008); HPV vaccine quadrivalent or bivalent (2009-14); or HPV vaccine 9-valent, quadrivalent, or bivalent (2015-). The HPV vaccine was recommended for males in Oct. 2011.

Effectiveness of the Seasonal Flu Vaccine, 2004-24

Source: National Center for Immunization and Respiratory Diseases (NCIRD), CDC, U.S. Dept. of Health and Human Services

The CDC conducts studies to determine vaccine effectiveness (VE), or how well each season's flu vaccine worked among a nationwide sample of patients.

Flu season	VE	Flu season	VE	Flu season	VE
2004-05	10%	2011-12	47%	2018-19	29%
2005-06	21	2012-13	49	2019-20	39
2006-07	52	2013-14	52	2020-21	NA[1]
2007-08	37	2014-15	19	2021-22	36
2008-09	41	2015-16	48	2022-23	30
2009-10	56	2016-17	40	2023-24	42[2]
2010-11	60	2017-18	38		

NA = Not available. (1) VE not estimated due to low influenza virus circulation. (2) Preliminary.

Weight Guidelines

Source: National Center for Health Statistics, CDC, U.S. Dept. of Health and Human Services

Federal clinical guidelines on the identification, evaluation, and treatment of overweight and obesity in adults age 20 and over were first released in 1998. The guidelines define overweight and obese in terms of **body mass index (BMI)**. BMI, based on a person's weight and height, can be an indicator of total body fat. A BMI of 18.5-24.9 is within a healthy weight range. A BMI of less than 18.5 is **underweight** while 25.0-29.9 is considered **overweight**; a BMI of 30.0 or higher indicates **obesity**. Obesity can be further subdivided into three classes, with class 3 obesity (BMI of 40.0 or higher) described as severe obesity. BMI can be calculated at www.nhlbi.nih.gov/health/educational/lose_wt/BMI/bmicalc.htm. (BMI categories for children ages 2 through 19 are based on sex-specific, BMI-for-age percentiles. For example, a 12-year-old girl whose BMI is 26.6 is at the 96th percentile, putting her in the obese category. That means her BMI is the same or higher than 96% of 12-year-old girls in the reference population.)

Waist circumference should be evaluated along with BMI. Men with a waist circumference of more than 40 inches and non-pregnant women with a waist circumference of more than 35 inches may be at increased risk for disease because of excess abdominal fat. BMI and waist circumference are screening tools, not diagnostics. A health-care provider should also perform other assessments to evaluate risk and diagnose disease, taking into consideration such factors as blood pressure, cholesterol levels, and family medical history.

The National Center for Health Statistics notes that 41.9% of American adults (ages 20 and over) and 19.7% of youth (ages 2-19) in 2017-Mar. 2020 were obese. The prevalence of obesity has increased over time, from 30.5% of adults and 13.9% of youth in 1999-2000 to its current levels. Among all age groups, obesity was more prevalent in the non-Hispanic Black and Hispanic population than among non-Hispanic whites and non-Hispanic Asians.

A high prevalence of overweight and obesity is a public health concern because higher body weights increase a person's risk of developing type 2 diabetes, hypertension, dyslipidemia, cardiovascular disease, stroke, gallbladder disease, sleep and respiratory problems, osteoarthritis, and certain cancers.

Adults Meeting U.S. Fitness Guidelines, 1998-2018

Source: National Health Interview Survey, National Center for Health Statistics, CDC, U.S. Dept. of Health and Human Services

	% meeting aerobic activity guidelines					% meeting muscle-strengthening guidelines				
Characteristic	**1998**	**2000**	**2005**	**2010**	**2018**	**1998**	**2000**	**2005**	**2010**	**2018**
Sex and age										
Male, 18-44 years	51.5%	53.6%	50.0%	59.0%	63.6%	27.2%	26.3%	28.7%	35.6%	38.3%
Male, 45-54 years	44.3	45.2	42.6	50.7	56.9	18.8	18.0	19.2	24.8	27.3
Male, 55-64 years	38.3	38.9	38.4	46.0	54.8	12.9	13.8	15.7	22.9	22.7
Male, 65-74 years	38.5	41.8	38.3	40.7	50.3	12.0	12.2	14.5	20.6	22.2
Male, 75 years and over	26.1	30.7	28.6	32.3	39.8	9.5	10.1	12.4	14.5	18.5
Female, 18-44 years	40.0	42.0	43.1	48.5	57.2	17.9	17.9	19.8	22.1	28.2
Female, 45-54 years	36.1	39.1	38.1	44.7	48.6	13.7	16.1	19.8	20.4	21.7
Female, 55-64 years	32.5	33.5	34.1	38.6	46.8	10.3	12.4	15.9	17.5	22.2
Female, 65-74 years	26.2	32.6	30.2	31.8	42.4	7.8	10.5	13.3	15.6	19.8
Female, 75 years and over	14.0	16.8	18.8	18.3	26.8	5.7	6.7	6.7	10.8	12.7
Race or Hispanic origin[1]										
White, not Hispanic	43.1	45.7	45.7	51.5	57.6	18.7	19.3	22.5	26.3	29.4
Black, not Hispanic	30.4	31.7	29.1	37.3	45.8	15.6	16.0	15.7	21.6	24.3
Amer. Indian or AK Native	39.7	29.7	41.6	42.0	54.1	18.2	13.9	20.5	16.7	24.2
Asian	37.1	41.7	37.5	44.2	54.7	17.2	17.2	16.9	21.9	26.7
Two or more races	—	43.9	41.1	50.2	56.6	—	22.2	23.6	30.4	30.0
Hispanic or Latino	29.1	30.8	28.5	36.2	47.8	12.7	11.9	12.9	18.1	24.4
Geographic region										
Northeast	39.6	45.3	43.3	46.9	55.5	17.5	20.0	21.6	24.3	28.6
Midwest	42.0	43.5	43.5	46.1	53.4	18.2	19.3	21.9	24.7	28.4
South	35.3	37.3	36.5	45.0	50.5	15.0	15.1	17.6	22.0	25.0
West	46.7	46.9	44.4	52.0	59.9	22.3	19.7	21.3	27.5	30.8
Total, 18 years and over	**40.0**	**42.2**	**41.1**	**47.3**	**54.3**	**17.7**	**18.0**	**20.2**	**24.4**	**27.8**

— = Not available. **Note:** Measures of physical activity reflect the federal 2008 Physical Activity Guidelines for Americans, which recommend that for substantial health benefits, adults each week perform at least 150 min. of moderate-intensity, 75 min. of vigorous-intensity, or an equivalent combination of moderate- and vigorous-intensity aerobic activity. Aerobic activity should be performed in episodes of at least 10 min., preferably spread throughout the week. The guidelines also recommend that adults perform muscle-strengthening activities that are moderate or high intensity and involve all major muscle groups on two or more days a week. (1) Persons reporting only one race, unless otherwise noted. Persons of Hispanic origin may be of any race.

Obesity Among Adults in the U.S., 2019, 2023

Source: National Health Interview Survey, National Center for Health Statistics, CDC, U.S. Dept. of Health and Human Services

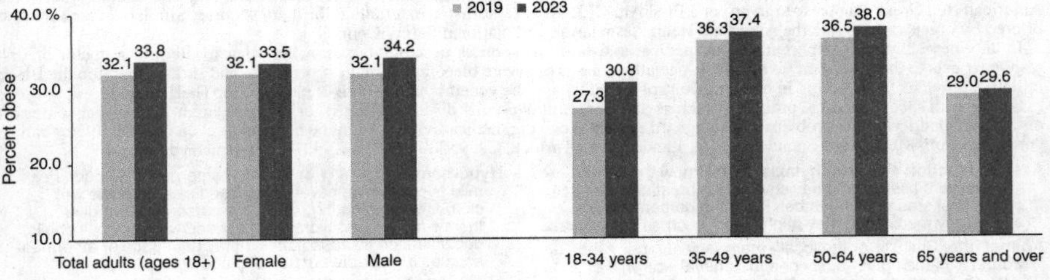

Overweight and Obesity Among U.S. Adults, 1960-2020

Source: National Health and Nutrition Examination Survey, NCHS, CDC, U.S. Dept. of Health and Human Services (as percent of adults age 20-74 in 1960-80 and age 20 and over for all other years shown here)

Survey period	Total			Men			Women		
	Overweight	Obesity	Severe obesity	Overweight	Obesity	Severe obesity	Overweight	Obesity	Severe obesity
1960-62	31.5%	13.4%	0.9%	38.7%	10.7%	0.3%	24.7%	15.8%	1.4%
1971-74	32.7	14.5	1.3	41.7	12.1	0.6	24.3	16.6	2.0
1976-80	32.1	15.0	1.4	39.9	12.7	0.4	24.9	17.0	2.2
1988-94	33.1	22.9	2.8	40.7	20.2	1.7	25.9	25.4	3.9
1999-2000	34.0	30.5	4.7	39.7	27.5	3.1	28.6	33.4	6.2
2001-02	35.1	30.5	5.1	42.2	27.7	3.6	28.2	33.2	6.5
2003-04	34.1	32.2	4.8	39.7	31.1	2.8	28.6	33.2	6.9
2005-06	32.6	34.3	5.9	39.9	33.3	4.2	25.5	35.3	7.4
2007-08	34.3	33.7	5.7	40.1	32.2	4.2	28.6	35.4	7.3
2009-10	33.0	35.7	6.3	38.4	35.5	4.4	27.9	35.8	8.1
2011-12	33.6	34.9	6.4	37.8	33.5	4.4	29.7	36.1	8.3
2013-14	32.5	37.7	7.7	38.7	35.0	5.5	26.5	40.4	9.9
2015-16	31.6	39.6	7.7	36.5	37.9	5.6	26.9	41.1	9.7
2017-18	30.7	42.4	9.2	34.1	43.0	6.9	27.5	41.9	11.5
2017-20[1]	NA	41.9	9.2	NA	41.8	6.6	NA	41.8	11.7

NA = Not available. **Note:** Overweight is body mass index (BMI) of 25 or greater but less than 30; obesity is BMI greater than or equal to 30; extreme obesity is BMI greater than or equal to 40. Does not include pregnant women. (1) 2017-Mar. 2020 prepandemic data set produced by combining full 2017-18 data with partial 2019-20 data.

Benefits of Routine Childhood Immunization Against Selected Diseases, 1994-2023

Source: Morbidity and Mortality Weekly Report 2024, Vol. 73, No. 31, CDC, U.S. Dept. of Health and Human Services

Among the approximately 117 million children born in 1994-2023, routine childhood vaccinations are estimated to have provided direct net savings of $540 billion and societal net savings of $2.7 trillion through the prevention of illnesses, hospitalizations, and deaths. (numbers in thousands)

Vaccine-preventable disease	Illnesses prevented	Hospitalizations prevented	Deaths prevented
Diphtheria	7,528	7,528	752.8
Tetanus	5	5	0.7
Pertussis	80,738	3,646	28.4
Haemophilus influenzae type b	536	495	20.3
Polio	1,847	786	21.9
Measles	104,984	13,172	85.0
Mumps	63,355	2,020	0.3
Rubella	54,225	199	0.4
Congenital rubella syndrome	17	26	1.9
Hepatitis B	6,061	940	90.1
Varicella[1]	106,270	272	1.9
Hepatitis A[1]	4,048	78	1.5
Pneumococcus-related diseases[1,2]	47,804	1,969	123.2
Rotavirus[1]	30,265	819	0.4
Total	**507,683**	**31,955**	**1,128.8**

Note: Data based on 30 annual cohorts of children born in 1994-2023. Since it began in 1994, the U.S. Vaccines for Children (VFC) program has provided vaccines targeting nine diseases for eligible children age 6 and under; seven additional diseases were added to the routine immunization schedule for that age group in 1996-2023. (1) The varicella vaccine for 1996-2023 cohorts, hepatitis A vaccine for 2006-23, pneumococcal conjugate vaccine for 2001-23, and rotavirus vaccine for 2007-23. (2) Incl. invasive pneumococcal disease, otitis media, and pneumonia.

Basic First Aid

Source: Courtesy of the American National Red Cross, www.redcross.org. All rights reserved in all countries.

Note: This information is not intended to be a substitute for formal training. It is recommended that you contact your local American Red Cross chapter to sign up for a First Aid/CPR/AED (automated external defibrillator) course. Similar courses are also offered by organizations like the American Heart Association and National Safety Council.

In an emergency, it is important to get medical assistance as soon as possible, but knowing what to do until a doctor or first responder gets to the scene can save a life, especially in cases of severe bleeding, choking, poisoning, and shock. The Stop the Bleed initiative provides free training in bleeding control techniques to the general public. **Website:** www.StopTheBleed.org

People with special medical problems, such as diabetes, cardiovascular disease, epilepsy, or allergies, are urged to wear some sort of emblem identifying the problem as a safeguard against receiving medication that might be harmful or even fatal. Emblems can be purchased from MedicAlert Foundation, 101 Lander Ave., Turlock, CA 95380; (800) 432-5378; www.medicalert.org.

Allergic reaction and anaphylaxis: If you know the person has a severe allergy or is having difficulty breathing, call 911 or the local emergency number. Have the person use any emergency medication they might carry, such as epinephrine.

Animal bite: Call 911 or the local emergency number if the wound is bleeding seriously or if the animal was wild or a stray or you suspect it of having rabies. Control any bleeding. Wash minor wounds with soap under running water and apply antibiotic ointment and a dressing. In the U.S., people most commonly get rabies through contact with a bat, which may not leave a noticeable bite mark. When possible, proper authorities should test the animal for rabies.

Bleeding: Use a barrier between your hand and the wound to help prevent infection. Cover wound with a sterile dressing. Apply direct pressure until bleeding stops. Cover compress with a bandage. Call 911 or the local emergency number if bleeding is severe.

Burn: Check for life-threatening conditions. If the burn is mild, with skin unbroken and no blisters, flush with cold running water for at least 10 minutes (at least 15 minutes if the burn was caused by a chemical). Gently wash with soap and water and pat dry. Apply a thin layer of antibiotic ointment and then a loose, sterile dry dressing to prevent infection. If the burn is severe, call 911 or the local emergency number. Care for shock (see separate entry). Keep the person from getting chilled or overheated until advanced medical assistance arrives. Do not try to clean a severe burn or break blisters.

Chemical in eye: Call 911 or the local emergency number. Turn the person's head to the side so that the affected eye is lower than the unaffected eye. Flush the affected eye with large amounts of water for at least 20 minutes.

Choking: See **First Aid for Choking** below.

Convulsions (seizures): Ease the person to the floor and roll them onto one side. Place something soft and flat, like a folded jacket, under the person's head. Do not hold the person down or put anything in their mouth. Stay with the person until they are fully conscious. If convulsions last for longer than 5 minutes or the person has a health condition like diabetes or is pregnant, call 911 or the local emergency number.

Cut (minor): Use a clean barrier between your hand and the wound to prevent infection. Apply direct pressure for a few minutes to control any bleeding. Wash the wound thoroughly with soap and water and apply a thin layer of antibiotic ointment or a microthin film dressing. Cover the wound with a sterile dressing and a bandage.

Diabetic emergency: A person experiencing a diabetic emergency might have a headache or even appear intoxicated, slurring their speech and moving with difficulty. Offer the person some form of sugar only if they are conscious and able to swallow. Call 911 if the person is unresponsive.

Foreign object in eye: If an object is embedded in someone's eye, do not remove it. If the object is not embedded, have the person blink several times. If the object doesn't come out, gently flush the eye with saline solution or water. Do not rub the eye. Seek medical attention if the foreign object remains.

Frostbite: Handle the frostbitten area gently. Do not rub. If there is no danger of the affected area refreezing, soak it in warm water (not warmer than 105°F), without allowing it to touch the side of the water container, until normal color returns and it feels warm. Loosely bandage the area with dry, sterile dressings. Put cotton or gauze between any frostbitten fingers or toes. Do not break any blisters. Call 911 or seek emergency help as soon as possible.

Heart attack and stroke: See **Heart and Blood Vessel Disease** earlier in chapter.

Heat stroke: Remove the person from the heat. Loosen any tight clothing. Immerse person in cold water until they become alert. If a large enough source of water is not available, drench the person with cold water and fan constantly. If the person is conscious, have them slowly drink some cool water. Call 911 if the person's condition does not improve.

Hypothermia: Call 911 or the local emergency number. For mild hypothermia, cover all exposed skin. Replace wet clothes with something dry. If the person is alert, give them simple carbohydrates to eat and warm, nonalcoholic, decaffeinated liquids to drink. Apply heat pads or other heat sources if available but do not place against bare skin.

Loss of limb: Call 911 or the local emergency number and care for any life-threatening conditions. If a limb is severed, properly protect it for possible reattachment. After the victim is cared for, the limb should be wrapped in sterile gauze and placed in a plastic bag. Place bag in a larger bag or container of ice and water slurry, not ice alone. Be sure the limb accompanies the victim to the hospital.

Poisoning: Care for any life-threatening conditions. Contact the National Capital Poison Center (800-222-1222, or access their online tool at www.poison.org), 911, or the local emergency number. Do not give the person any food or drink or induce vomiting unless specified to do so by medical professionals. In cases of **alcohol poisoning**, place the person in a position that keeps their airway clear. In cases of **carbon monoxide poisoning**, remove the person from the area if you can do so safely. Naloxone can be administered as a nasal spray or autoinjectable to reverse an **opioid overdose**. All 50 states and DC have enacted naloxone access laws, which allow for it to be dispensed to persons other than a patient. Nonprescription naloxone nasal sprays are also now available.

Shock (injury-related): Monitor breathing and consciousness. Have the person lie down and keep them as comfortable as possible. Do not give the person anything to eat or drink as it increases the risk of vomiting or aspiration. If the weather is cold or damp, place blankets or extra clothing over and under the person; if the weather is hot, provide shade.

Snakebite: Call 911 or the local emergency number immediately if you're not sure whether the snake was venomous. Do not wait for symptoms to appear. Gently wash the injury with soap and water and keep the area below the level of the heart. Have the person remain still if possible. Do not cut, suck at, or apply a tourniquet or ice to a snakebite. Applying an elastic roller bandage may help slow the spread of venom.

Sprains and strains: Splint any injured bone or joint that the person cannot use.

Sting from bee or wasp: If possible, remove the stinger by scraping it away with your finger or a plastic card (like a credit card) or using tweezers. If you use tweezers, grasp the stinger, not the venom sac. Wash the area with soap and water and cover it with a bandage. Apply cold to the area to reduce swelling and pain. Call 911 or the local emergency number immediately if the wound does not stop swelling, the person collapses, or they are known to be allergic to the sting.

Tick bite: Promptly remove any ticks to lower the chance of infection. Use tweezers to grasp it by its head as close to the skin as possible. Pull it slowly and steadily out. Do not use a match or petroleum jelly to remove an embedded tick. Wash and dress the bite area. Seek medical attention if a large rash develops at the site of the bite or you begin to experience flu-like symptoms.

Unconsciousness: Call 911 or the local emergency number immediately. Do not move the person if a spinal injury is suspected.

First Aid for Choking

For a conscious choking victim who is unable to speak, cough, or breathe, deliver a series of five blows to the back followed by five thrusts to the abdomen. Have another person call 911 or the local emergency number. Obtain consent from the victim to treat them. Apply the back blows by leaning the victim forward and striking between the shoulder blades with the heel of your hand. If the victim is still choking, stand or kneel behind the victim and wrap your arms around their waist. Make a fist with one hand and place the thumb side against the middle of the person's abdomen, just above the navel and well below the lower tip of the breastbone. Grasp your fist in your other hand and quickly thrust upwards into the abdomen. Continue back blows and abdominal thrusts until the object is dislodged, and the person can breathe or cough forcefully, or the person loses consciousness.

VITAL STATISTICS

Births and Deaths in the U.S., 1960-2023

Source: National Center for Health Statistics (NCHS), CDC, U.S. Dept. of Health and Human Services

Year	BIRTHS Total number	BIRTHS Rate	DEATHS Total number	DEATHS Rate
1960	4,257,850	23.7	1,711,982	9.5
1970	3,731,386	18.4	1,921,031	9.5
1980	3,612,258	15.9	1,989,841	8.8
1990	4,092,994	16.7	2,148,463	8.6
2000	4,058,814	14.4	2,403,351	8.5
2004	4,112,052	14.0	2,397,615	8.2
2005	4,138,349	14.0	2,448,017	8.3
2006	4,265,555	14.2	2,426,264	8.1
2007	4,316,233	14.3	2,423,712	8.0
2008	4,247,694	14.0	2,471,984	8.1
2009	4,130,665	13.5	2,437,163	7.9
2010	3,999,386	13.0	2,468,435	8.0
2011	3,953,590	12.7	2,515,458	8.1
2012	3,952,841	12.6	2,543,279	8.1
2013	3,932,181	12.4	2,596,993	8.2
2014	3,988,076	12.5	2,626,418	8.2
2015	3,978,497	12.4	2,712,630	8.4
2016	3,945,875	12.2	2,744,248	8.5
2017	3,855,500	11.8	2,813,503	8.6
2018	3,791,712	11.6	2,839,205	8.7
2019	3,747,540	11.4	2,854,838	8.7
2020	3,613,647	10.9	3,383,729	10.3
2021	3,664,292	11.0	3,464,231	10.4
2022	3,667,758	11.0	3,279,857	9.8
2023	3,591,328[1]	10.7[2]	NA	9.2[1]

NA = Not available. **Note:** Rates are per 1,000 population; population counts are enumerated as of Apr. 1 for decennial census years and estimated as of July 1 for all other years. Beginning in 1970, statistics exclude births and deaths among nonresidents of the U.S. (1) Provisional. (2) Not directly comparable to previous years due to difference in calculation.

Marriage and Divorce Rates in the U.S., 1920-2022

Source: National Center for Health Statistics (NCHS), CDC, U.S. Dept. of Health and Human Services

(Per 1,000 total population. Rates for 2000-20 may exclude data and populations from nonreporting states. Some data are provisional.)

The U.S. marriage rate dipped during the Depression and peaked sharply just after World War II; the trend after that has been more gradual. The divorce rate generally rose from the 1920s through 1981, when it peaked at 5.3 per 1,000 population, before declining somewhat. The graph below shows marriage and divorce rates since 1920.

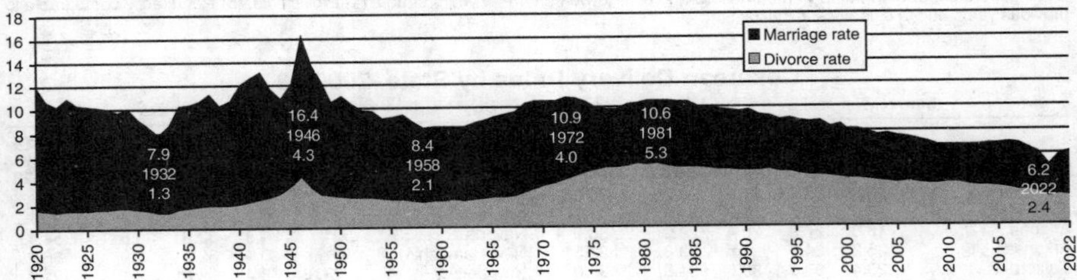

U.S. Median Age at First Marriage, 1890-2023

Source: U.S. Census Bureau, U.S. Dept. of Commerce

Year[1]	Men	Women
1890	26.1	22.0
1900	25.9	21.9
1910	25.1	21.6
1920	24.6	21.2
1930	24.3	21.3
1940	24.3	21.5
1950	22.8	20.3
1960	22.8	20.3
1970	23.2	20.8
1980	24.7	22.0
1990	26.1	23.9
1995	26.9	24.5
2000	26.8	25.1
2005	27.1	25.3
2010	28.2	26.1
2015	29.2	27.1
2016	29.5	27.4
2017	29.5	27.4
2018	29.8	27.8
2019[2]	29.8	28.0
2020	30.5	28.1
2021	30.3	28.6
2022	30.1	28.2
2023	30.2	28.4

(1) Figures for 1947 and on are based on Current Population Survey data; earlier figures based on decennial censuses. (2) Starting in 2019, estimates for marriages include same-sex married couples.

Divorce Rates by State, 2022

Source: National Center for Health Statistics (NCHS), CDC, U.S. Dept. of Health and Human Services

(per 1,000 population, estimated as of July 1)

State	Divorce rate
Alabama	3.2
Alaska	3.0
Arizona	2.3
Arkansas	3.5
California	NA
Colorado	2.9
Connecticut	2.8
Delaware	2.3
District of Columbia	2.0
Florida	3.1
Georgia	2.1
Hawaii	NA
Idaho	3.3
Illinois	1.1
Indiana	NA
Iowa	2.0
Kansas	1.9
Kentucky	3.0
Louisiana	0.7
Maine	2.4
Maryland	2.6
Massachusetts	1.4
Michigan	2.3
Minnesota	NA
Mississippi	3.0
Missouri	2.7
Montana	2.0
Nebraska	2.6
Nevada	4.2
New Hampshire	2.5
New Jersey	2.3
New Mexico	NA
New York	2.3
North Carolina	2.7
North Dakota	2.7
Ohio	2.4
Oklahoma	3.7
Oregon	2.8
Pennsylvania	2.2
Rhode Island	2.4
South Carolina	2.4
South Dakota	2.3
Tennessee	3.0
Texas	1.9
Utah	2.9
Vermont	2.3
Virginia	2.9
Washington	2.8
West Virginia	3.2
Wisconsin	2.1
Wyoming	3.3
United States	**2.4**

NA = Not available. **Note:** Rates based on provisional counts of divorce including annulments and, for certain areas, divorce petitions filed or legal separations.

Birth Rates and Fertility Rates by Age of Mother, 1950-2023

Source: National Center for Health Statistics (NCHS), CDC, U.S. Dept. of Health and Human Services

			Live births per 1,000 women by age of mother									
Year	Birth rate[1]	Fertility rate[2]	10-14 years	15-19 years	15-17 years	18-19 years	20-24 years	25-29 years	30-34 years	35-39 years	40-44 years	45-49 years[3]
1950	24.1	106.2	1.0	81.6	40.7	132.7	196.6	166.1	103.7	52.9	15.1	1.2
1960	23.7	118.0	0.8	89.1	43.9	166.7	258.1	197.4	112.7	56.2	15.5	0.9
1970	18.4	87.9	1.2	68.3	38.8	114.7	167.8	145.1	73.3	31.7	8.1	0.5
1980	15.9	68.4	1.1	53.0	32.5	82.1	115.1	112.9	61.9	19.8	3.9	0.2
1990	16.7	70.9	1.4	59.9	37.5	88.6	116.5	120.2	80.8	31.7	5.5	0.2
2000	14.4	65.9	0.9	47.7	26.9	78.1	109.7	113.5	91.2	39.7	8.0	0.5
2005	14.0	66.7	0.7	40.5	21.4	69.9	102.2	115.5	95.8	46.3	9.1	0.6
2010	13.0	64.1	0.4	34.2	17.3	58.2	90.0	108.3	96.5	45.9	10.2	0.7
2011	12.7	63.2	0.4	31.3	15.4	54.1	85.3	107.2	96.5	47.2	10.3	0.7
2012	12.6	63.0	0.4	29.4	14.1	51.4	83.1	106.5	97.3	48.3	10.4	0.7
2013	12.4	62.5	0.3	26.5	12.3	47.1	80.7	105.5	98.0	49.3	10.4	0.8
2014	12.5	62.9	0.3	24.2	10.9	43.8	79.0	105.8	100.8	51.0	10.6	0.8
2015	12.4	62.5	0.2	22.3	9.9	40.7	76.8	104.3	101.5	51.8	11.0	0.8
2016	12.2	62.0	0.2	20.3	8.8	37.5	73.8	102.1	102.7	52.7	11.4	0.9
2017	11.8	60.3	0.2	18.8	7.9	35.1	71.0	98.0	100.3	52.3	11.6	0.9
2018	11.6	59.1	0.2	17.4	7.2	32.3	68.0	95.3	99.7	52.6	11.8	0.9
2019	11.4	58.3	0.2	16.7	6.7	31.1	66.6	93.7	98.3	52.8	12.0	0.9
2020	10.9	55.7	0.2	15.0	6.1	28.2	63.3	90.9	94.9	51.3	11.8	0.9
2021	11.0	56.3	0.2	13.9	5.6	26.6	61.5	93.0	97.6	53.7	12.0	0.9
2022	11.0	56.0	0.2	13.6	5.6	25.8	57.5	93.5	97.5	55.3	12.6	1.1
2023[4]	10.7[5]	54.4	0.2	13.2	5.6	24.9	55.4	91.1	95.1	54.7	12.6	1.1

(1) Live births per 1,000 population. (2) Live births per 1,000 women 15-44 years of age. (3) Beginning in 1997, rate computed by relating the number of births to women age 45 and over to women 45-49 years of age. (4) Provisional. (5) Not directly comparable to previous years due to difference in calculation.

Cesarean Delivery Rates by State, 2000-23

Source: National Center for Health Statistics (NCHS), CDC, U.S. Dept. of Health and Human Services

State	2000	2010	2020	2023[1]	Percent change, 2000-23
Alabama	26.3%	35.3%	35.0%	34.2%	30.0%
Alaska	17.0	21.5	22.9	24.0	41.2
Arizona	18.6	27.0	28.4	29.0	55.9
Arkansas	26.3	34.8	33.8	33.8	28.5
California	23.4	33.0	30.5	31.6	35.0
Colorado	18.3	25.9	27.2	27.5	50.3
Connecticut	21.6	35.1	34.1	35.1	62.5
Delaware	24.8	33.9	31.7	31.5	27.0
District of Columbia	22.6	33.0	32.3	34.1	50.9
Florida	24.9	37.8	35.9	36.2	45.4
Georgia	22.5	33.8	33.9	35.8	59.1
Hawaii	14.6	27.2	26.3	27.5	88.4
Idaho	18.3	24.8	23.5	24.5	33.9
Illinois	20.9	31.1	30.8	31.0	48.3
Indiana	21.5	30.3	30.1	30.8	43.3
Iowa	20.8	30.3	30.2	30.3	45.7
Kansas	22.2	30.5	30.1	30.3	36.5
Kentucky	23.6	35.4	34.3	34.3	45.3
Louisiana	26.6	39.6	36.8	36.1	35.7
Maine	22.8	29.8	29.7	31.1	36.4
Maryland	24.1	34.5	33.7	35.0	45.2
Massachusetts	23.3	33.0	32.4	33.5	43.8
Michigan	21.9	32.6	32.5	33.3	52.1
Minnesota	19.4	27.1	28.5	30.2	55.7
Mississippi	28.2	37.0	38.2	37.9	34.4
Missouri	22.3	31.9	29.3	30.2	35.4
Montana	19.0%	30.3%	27.6%	26.0%	36.8%
Nebraska	22.5	31.1	28.8	29.4	30.7
Nevada	21.7	34.8	32.9	33.5	54.4
New Hampshire	21.0	30.4	32.1	32.9	56.7
New Jersey	27.3	38.4	33.2	33.1	21.2
New Mexico	17.1	22.8	26.1	28.4	66.1
New York	24.6	34.5	33.6	33.9	37.8
North Carolina	23.0	30.8	29.9	30.8	33.9
North Dakota	20.6	27.7	27.0	26.1	26.7
Ohio	20.0	30.7	31.3	31.5	57.5
Oklahoma	21.0	34.7	32.1	33.1	57.6
Oregon	19.4	29.4	28.8	28.9	49.0
Pennsylvania	21.7	31.3	30.6	31.3	44.2
Rhode Island	21.9	33.0	33.4	33.2	51.6
South Carolina	25.2	35.0	33.5	32.6	29.4
South Dakota	22.8	26.6	24.7	24.4	7.0
Tennessee	24.8	34.2	32.1	32.3	30.2
Texas	24.7	35.1	34.7	34.5	39.7
Utah	16.8	23.1	23.1	24.3	44.6
Vermont	17.3	27.5	26.9	27.5	59.0
Virginia	23.1	34.3	32.6	32.3	39.8
Washington	20.6	29.5	28.5	30.0	45.6
West Virginia	25.4	36.0	34.2	35.0	37.8
Wisconsin	17.5	26.0	26.7	27.3	56.0
Wyoming	19.4	27.9	26.4	28.3	45.9
United States	**22.8**	**32.7**	**31.8**	**32.4**	**42.1**

Note: The cesarean rate is the percentage of all live births by cesarean delivery. (1) Provisional.

Infertility and Use of Infertility Services, by Age and Type of Service, 2015-19

Source: National Survey of Family Growth, National Center for Health Statistics (NCHS), U.S. Dept. of Health and Human Services

A special tabulation in 2015-19 found that for all women 15-49 years of age, 12.2% had ever received any infertility services.

	% of all women who have impaired fecundity[1]		% of all women who have ever received any infertility service	
Age	0 births	1 or more births	0 births	1 or more births
15-29 years	9.2%	12.0%	2.7%	11.5%
30-39 years	22.2	12.2	13.6	15.5
40-49 years	33.4	14.5	21.8	20.0
Total 15-49 years	**13.8**	**13.1**	**6.4**	**16.6**

Type of infertility service	% of women[2]
Medical help to get pregnant	8.9%
Advice	6.7
Tests on woman or man	5.6
Any medical help to prevent miscarriage	5.2
Ovulation drugs	4.0
Artificial insemination	1.7
Surgery to treatment on blocked tubes	0.7
Assisted Reproductive Technology	0.5

(1) Not surgically sterile, and for whom it is difficult or impossible to get pregnant or carry a pregnancy to term. (2) Age 15-49 years.

Numbers of Multiple Births in the U.S., 1990-2022

Source: National Center for Health Statistics (NCHS), CDC, U.S. Dept. of Health and Human Services

Year	Twins	Triplets	Quadruplets	Quintuplets[1]	Year	Twins	Triplets	Quadruplets	Quintuplets[1]
1990	93,865	2,830	185	13	2013	132,324	4,364	270	66
1995	96,736	4,551	365	57	2014	135,336	4,233	246	47
2000	118,916	6,742	506	77	2015	133,155	3,871	228	24
2005	133,122	6,208	418	68	2016	131,723	3,755	217	31
2007	138,961	5,967	369	91	2017	128,310	3,675	193	49
2008	138,660	5,877	345	46	2018	123,536	3,400	115	10
2009	137,217	5,905	355	80	2019	120,291	3,136	114	36
2010	132,562	5,153	313	37	2020	112,437	2,738	108	29
2011	131,269	5,137	239	41	2021	114,161	2,785	133	15
2012	131,024	4,598	276	45	2022	114,483	2,774	108	13

(1) Quintuplets and other multiple births of five or more.

Origin Countries for U.S. Foreign Adoptions, 2000-23

Source: Annual Report on Intercountry Adoption, Bureau of Consular Affairs, U.S. Dept. of State (ranked by fiscal year 2023 adoptions)

Country	2023	2022	2021	2020	2019	2018	2017	2016	2015	2010	2005	2000
India	221	223	245	103	241	302	221	194	138	243	323	503
Colombia	200	235	297	137	244	229	181	131	153	235	291	246
Bulgaria	83	84	108	99	134	134	147	201	185	40	30	214
Haiti	80	79	54	96	130	196	227	178	143	1,332	234	131
Nigeria	62	44	11	83	116	173	176	121	154	189	65	4
Taiwan	59	68	48	42	43	32	44	59	59	285	141	28
Philippines	58	67	68	39	94	105	111	156	150	214	271	173
South Korea	47	141	156	188	166	206	276	260	318	863	1,630	1,794
Thailand	43	49	38	23	38	43	34	45	47	53	71	87
Morocco	26	20	30	17	30	18	31	21	22	32	6	7
Total[1]	**1,275**	**1,517**	**1,785**	**1,622**	**2,971**	**4,059**	**4,714**	**5,372**	**5,648**	**11,059[2]**	**22,710**	**18,120**

(1) Includes countries not shown. (2) Does not reflect approx. 1,090 Haitian children admitted as part of the Special Humanitarian Parole following the 2010 earthquake in Haiti.

Leading Causes of Infant Death in the U.S., 2022

Source: National Vital Statistics System, National Center for Health Statistics (NCHS), CDC, U.S. Dept. of Health and Human Services

Cause of death	Number	Percent of total deaths	Mortality rate[1]
Congenital malformations, deformations, and chromosomal abnormalities	3,970	19.3%	108.2
Disorders related to short gestation and low birth weight, not elsewhere classified	2,884	14.0	78.6
Sudden infant death syndrome	1,529	7.4	41.7
Accidents (unintentional injuries)	1,354	6.6	36.9
Newborn affected by maternal complications of pregnancy	1,215	5.9	33.1
Newborn affected by complications of placenta, cord, and membranes	649	3.2	17.7
Bacterial sepsis[2] of newborn	636	3.1	17.3
Respiratory distress of newborn	455	2.2	12.4
Intrauterine hypoxia and birth asphyxia	362	1.8	9.9
Diseases of the circulatory system	356	1.7	9.7
All other causes	7,143	34.8	—
All causes	**20,553**	**100.0**	**560.4**

— = Not applicable. (1) Deaths of infants under 1 year of age per 100,000 live births. (2) Toxic condition resulting from the spread of bacteria.

Nonmarital Childbearing in the U.S., 1970-2022

Source: National Center for Health Statistics (NCHS), CDC, U.S. Dept. of Health and Human Services

	1970	1975	1980	1985	1990	1995	2000	2005	2010	2015	2020	2022
Live births to unmarried mothers (thous.)	**399**	**448**	**666**	**828**	**1,165**	**1,254**	**1,347**	**1,527**	**1,633**	**1,602**	**1,464**	**1,461**
Percent of live births to unmarried women by race/Hispanic origin of mother												
All races and origins	10.7%	14.3%	18.4%	22.0%	28.0%	32.2%	33.2%	36.9%	40.8%	40.3%	40.5%	39.8%
White	5.5	7.1	11.2	14.7	20.4	25.3	27.1	31.7	35.9	35.8	28.4	27.1
Black	37.5	49.5	56.1	61.2	66.5	69.9	68.5	69.3	72.1	70.1	70.4	69.3
American Indian or Alaska Native	22.4	32.7	39.2	46.8	53.6	57.2	58.4	63.5	65.6	65.8	69.6	68.1
Asian or Pacific Islander[1]	—	—	7.3	9.5	13.2	16.3	14.8	16.2	17.0	16.4	13.9	14.1
Hispanic origin (select states)[2,3]	—	—	23.6	29.5	36.7	40.8	42.7	48.0	53.4	53.0	52.8	53.2
Percent distribution of live births to unmarried women by maternal age												
Under 20 years	50.1%	52.1%	40.8%	33.8%	30.9%	30.9%	28.0%	23.1%	20.1%	12.9%	10.0%	9.1%
20-24 years	31.8	29.9	35.6	36.3	34.7	34.5	37.4	38.3	36.8	35.0	30.8	29.6
25 years and over	18.1	18.0	23.5	29.9	34.4	34.7	34.6	38.7	43.1	52.1	59.2	61.2
Live births per 1,000 unmarried women 15-44 years of age by race/Hispanic origin of mother[4]												
All races and origins	26.4	24.5	29.4	32.8	43.8	44.3	44.0	47.2	47.5	43.4	38.6	37.2
White[5]	13.9	12.4	18.1	22.5	32.9	37.0	38.2	43.2	44.5	40.4	27.6	25.8
Black[5]	95.5	84.2	81.1	77.0	90.5	74.5	70.5	67.2	65.3	59.6	54.9	50.2
Hispanic origin (select states)[2,3]	—	—	—	—	89.6	88.7	87.2	96.2	80.6	67.4	55.8	57.4

— = Not available. (1) For 2020-22, data is for Asian and Native Hawaiian or Other Pacific Islander combined. (2) Hispanic origin data prior to 1995 is not directly comparable with data for more recent years due to differences in reporting area. (3) Hispanics may be of any race. (4) Rates computed by dividing births to unmarried mothers, regardless of mother's age, by the pop. of unmarried women 15-44 years of age. (5) For 1970 and 1975, birth rates are by race of child.

U.S. Teen Birth Rate by State, 2022

Source: National Center for Health Statistics (NCHS), CDC, U.S. Dept. of Health and Human Services

State	Birth rate[1]	State	Birth rate[1]	State	Birth rate[1]	State	Birth rate[1]
Alabama	20.9	Illinois	11.3	Montana	12.2	Rhode Island	8.3
Alaska	16.9	Indiana	16.7	Nebraska	14.1	South Carolina	17.3
Arizona	15.1	Iowa	12.4	Nevada	14.0	South Dakota	17.4
Arkansas	24.6	Kansas	16.2	New Hampshire	4.6	Tennessee	21.0
California	9.8	Kentucky	21.8	New Jersey	8.2	Texas	20.4
Colorado	11.1	Louisiana	23.7	New Mexico	19.7	Utah	9.0
Connecticut	6.4	Maine	8.4	New York	8.6	Vermont	5.8
Delaware	14.7	Maryland	10.9	North Carolina	15.0	Virginia	11.2
Dist. of Columbia	12.5	Massachusetts	5.8	North Dakota	11.7	Washington	9.6
Florida	13.1	Michigan	11.6	Ohio	15.4	West Virginia	19.8
Georgia	16.6	Minnesota	8.2	Oklahoma	21.2	Wisconsin	9.8
Hawaii	11.7	Mississippi	26.4	Oregon	10.1	Wyoming	16.0
Idaho	10.9	Missouri	16.9	Pennsylvania	10.6	**United States**	**13.6**

(1) Number of births per 1,000 females ages 15-19.

Number, Ratio, and Rate of Legal Abortions in U.S., 1970-2021

Source: *Abortion Surveillance—United States, 2021*, Centers for Disease Control and Prevention, U.S. Dept. of Health and Human Services

Year	Legal abortions	Ratio[1]	Rate[2]	Year	Legal abortions	Ratio[1]	Rate[2]	Year	Legal abortions	Ratio[1]	Rate[2]
1970	193,491	52	5	2002	854,122	250	16	2012	699,202	207	13
1971	485,816	137	11	2003	848,163	245	16	2013	664,435	198	12
1972	586,760	180	13	2004	839,226	241	16	2014	652,639	190	12
1973	615,831	196	14	2005	820,151	235	16	2015	638,169	187	12
1974	763,476	242	17	2006	852,385	233	16	2016	623,471	184	12
1975	854,853	272	18	2007	827,609	226	16	2017	612,719	184	11
1980	1,297,606	359	25	2008	825,564	229	16	2018	619,591	188	11
1990	1,429,247	344	24	2009	789,217	224	15	2019	629,898	194	11
1995	1,210,883	311	20	2010	765,651	225	14	2020	620,327	197	11
2000	857,475	251	16	2011	730,322	217	14	2021	625,978	204	12
2001	853,485	249	16								

Note: After 1998, reporting area varies. (1) Number of abortions per 1,000 live births. (2) Number of abortions per 1,000 women aged 15-44 years.

Reported U.S. Abortions by Weeks of Gestation, Age, and Race, 2021

Source: *Abortion Surveillance—United States, 2021*, Centers for Disease Control and Prevention, U.S. Dept. of Health and Human Services

	Weeks of gestation													
	≤6		7-9		10-13		14-15		16-17		18-20		≥21	
Characteristic	No.	%	No.	%	No.	%	No.	%	No.	%	No.	%	No.	%
Age[1]														
Under 15 years	257	24.2%	375	35.3%	223	21.0%	61	5.7%	48	4.5%	61	5.7%	38	3.6%
15-19 years	14,127	37.3	14,214	37.5	6,205	16.4	1,361	3.6	784	2.1	772	2.0	442	1.2
20-24 years	58,488	43.2	50,058	37.0	18,188	13.4	3,723	2.7	2,106	1.6	1,887	1.4	944	0.7
25-29 years	62,433	45.8	49,321	36.2	16,688	12.2	3,339	2.4	1,784	1.3	1,771	1.3	1,012	0.7
30-34 years	45,222	46.8	33,949	35.1	11,462	11.9	2,369	2.5	1,415	1.5	1,329	1.4	893	0.9
35-39 years	23,961	47.0	17,638	34.6	5,775	11.3	1,388	2.7	860	1.7	852	1.7	560	1.1
40 years and over	8,597	50.4	5,471	32.1	1,788	10.5	457	2.7	291	1.7	288	1.7	161	0.9
Total	**213,085**	**44.8**	**171,026**	**36.0**	**60,329**	**12.7**	**12,698**	**2.7**	**7,288**	**1.5**	**6,960**	**1.5**	**4,050**	**0.9**
Race/ethnicity[2]														
Black[3]	68,937	43.4	58,386	36.8	21,661	13.6	4,273	2.7	2,258	1.4	2,274	1.4	1,026	0.6
White[3]	54,371	47.1	39,903	34.6	13,643	11.8	2,958	2.6	1,686	1.5	1,696	1.5	1,076	0.9
Other[3]	11,491	46.8	8,596	35.0	2,784	11.3	641	2.6	378	1.5	365	1.5	294	1.2
Hispanic	41,903	51.3	26,159	32.0	8,887	10.9	1,870	2.3	1, 107	1.4	1,044	1.3	674	0.8
Total	**176,702**	**46.5**	**133,044**	**35.0**	**46,975**	**12.4**	**9,742**	**2.6**	**5,429**	**1.4**	**5,379**	**1.4**	**3,070**	**0.8**

Note: The CDC requests data annually from the central health agencies of 52 reporting areas (all states, DC, and NYC). Reporting is voluntary. Data exclude areas that did not report, did not report weeks of gestation by age, or did not meet reporting standards. (1) Data from 41 reporting areas; excludes 11 (CA, CT, DC, IL, MD, MA, NH, NJ, NY, PA, WI). (2) Data from 31 reporting areas; excludes 21 (CA, CO, CT, DC, HI, IL, IA, LA, MD, MA, NE, NH, NJ, NY, ND, OH, OK, PA, RI, WA, WI). (3) Non-Hispanic.

Adult LGBT and Transgender Population by State

Source: The Williams Institute, UCLA School of Law

(Adult population self-identifying as LGBT and/or transgender as a percentage of overall population.)

State	LGBT, 2017	Transgender, 2022	State	LGBT, 2017	Transgender, 2022	State	LGBT, 2017	Transgender, 2022
Alabama	3.1%	0.5%	Kentucky	3.4%	0.5%	North Dakota	2.7%	0.4%
Alaska	3.7	0.7	Louisiana	3.9	0.4	Ohio	4.3	0.5
Arizona	4.5	0.7	Maine	4.9	0.5	Oklahoma	3.8	0.6
Arkansas	3.3	0.7	Maryland	4.2	0.5	Oregon	5.6	0.6
California	5.3	0.5	Massachusetts	5.4	0.7	Pennsylvania	4.1	0.6
Colorado	4.6	0.6	Michigan	4.0	0.4	Rhode Island	4.5	0.7
Connecticut	3.9	0.5	Minnesota	4.1	0.6	South Carolina	3.5	0.5
Delaware	4.5	0.8	Mississippi	3.5	0.4	South Dakota	3.0	0.4
District of Columbia	9.8	0.9	Missouri	3.8	0.2	Tennessee	3.5	0.5
Florida	4.6	0.6	Montana	2.9	0.4	Texas	4.1	0.4
Georgia	4.5	0.6	Nebraska	3.8	0.5	Utah	3.7	0.6
Hawaii	4.6	0.7	Nevada	5.5	0.3	Vermont	5.2	0.5
Idaho	2.8	0.5	New Hampshire	4.7	0.6	Virginia	3.9	0.5
Illinois	4.3	0.4	New Jersey	4.1	0.6	Washington	5.2	0.6
Indiana	4.5	0.5	New Mexico	4.5	0.7	West Virginia	4.0	0.4
Iowa	3.6	0.3	New York	5.1	0.5	Wisconsin	3.8	0.3
Kansas	3.3	0.6	North Carolina	4.0	0.9	Wyoming	3.3	0.5
						United States	**4.5**	**0.5**

Sexual Orientation and Gender Identity by Age Group, 2024

Source: *Accelerating Acceptance 2024*, a national survey among U.S. adults using sample sourced by research firm Cint on behalf of GLAAD (percent of survey respondents)

Sexual orientation	Age 18-38	39-54	55-73
Strictly straight/heterosexual	69%	86%	91%
Non-heterosexual	31	14	9
Bisexual	16	6	3
Gay or lesbian	5	3	3
Pansexual	4	1	1
Queer	2	1	—
Asexual	1	2	1
Unsure or questioning	3	1	1

Gender identity	Age 18-38	39-54	55-73
Cisgender	83%	91%	95%
Non-cisgender	17	9	5
Transgender	5	2	1
Nonbinary	6	4	1
Unsure or questioning	7	3	4

— = Less than 0.5%. **Note:** Data for ages 74 and older excluded due to low sample comparisons year over year. Percent distributions may not equal 100 due to rounding. **Asexual:** not experiencing sexual attraction; **bisexual:** experiencing sexual or romantic attraction to more than one gender; **cisgender:** strictly identifying with the sex you were assigned at birth; **gay/lesbian:** experiencing sexual attraction to the same gender; **nonbinary:** identifying outside of, or beyond, the binary of male and female gender including gender queer, gender fluid, agender, and bigender; **pansexual:** experiencing sexual or romantic attraction to people of any or all gender identities; **queer:** experiencing sexual or romantic attraction in a way that does not fit into the previously mentioned, dominant norms; **transgender:** identifying with a gender that does not correspond to the sex you were assigned at birth.

Sexual Orientation Among U.S. Adults, 2018

Source: *National Health Interview Survey, 2018*, National Center for Health Statistics (NCHS), U.S. Dept. of Health and Human Services

	Gay or lesbian[1]		Straight[2]		Bisexual	
	Number (thous.)	% of group	Number (thous.)	% of group	Number (thous.)	% of group
Total	**3,955**	**1.6%**	**233,360**	**97.0%**	**3,143**	**1.3%**
Sex						
Men	2,250	1.9	113,250	97.3	895	0.8
Women	1,705	1.4	120,109	96.8	2,248	1.8
Age						
18-44 years	2,113	1.9	105,755	95.8	2,550	2.3
45-64 years	1,484	1.8	78,338	97.6	475	0.6
65 years and older	358	0.7	49,267	99.0	118	0.2

Note: Percent distributions may not equal 100 due to rounding. (1) Response option provided was "gay" for men and "gay or lesbian" for women. (2) Response option provided was "straight, that is, not gay" for men and "straight, that is, not gay or lesbian" for women.

Sexual Behavior of Opposite-Sex and Same-Sex Partners, 2011-19

Source: National Survey of Family Growth, National Center for Health Statistics, U.S. Dept. of Health and Human Services (among population of adults ages 18-49)

	Men			Women		
	Gay	Bisexual	Heterosexual	Lesbian	Bisexual	Heterosexual
Lifetime experience						
Sex with female, ever	51.1%	87.3%	94.4%	91.0%	77.7%	12.3%
Sex with male, ever	94.4	69.5	2.7	74.5	96.6	94.9
Total number of sexual partners in the past 12 months						
None	7.9	9.0	6.8	3.6	5.9	6.9
One	37.3	47.0	73.3	71.8	55.8	77.5
Two	17.4	16.5	9.2	12.7	14.5	8.9
Three or more	36.5	25.9	10.7	11.3	21.1	6.7

Contraceptive Use in the U.S., 2002-19

Source: National Survey of Family Growth, National Center for Health Statistics (NCHS), U.S. Dept. of Health and Human Services

	2002[1]	2006-10[1]	2011-15[1]	2015-17[2]	2017-19[2]	2002[1]	2006-10[1]	2011-15[1]	2015-17[2]	2017-19[2]
Method	Ever used[3]					Currently using[4]				
Any method of contraception	98.2%	99.1%	99.3%	99.2%	99.2%	61.9%	62.2%	61.6%	64.9%	65.3%
Male condom	89.7	93.4	95.0	94.0	94.8	14.7	10.2	9.2	8.7	8.4
Pill	82.3	81.9	79.3	80.5	78.9	19.2	17.1	15.9	12.6	14.0
Withdrawal	56.1	59.6	64.8	65.9	66.0	5.4	3.2	3.9	3.9	3.7
3-month injectable (Depo-Provera)	16.8	23.2	25.4	24.2	25.0	3.3	2.3	2.6	2.1	2.0
Female sterilization	20.7	19.5	17.1	21.5	20.7	16.7	16.5	14.3	18.6	18.1
Calendar rhythm method	16.2	18.1	15.9	18.3	17.1	NA	NA	NA	1.3	1.4
Male sterilization	13.0	13.3	11.4	14.7	14.1	6.3	6.2	4.5	5.9	5.6
Emergency contraception	4.2	10.8	20.0	22.0	25.1	NA	NA	NA	NA	NA
Contraceptive patch	0.9	10.4	10.6	8.7	7.8	NA	NA	NA	NA	NA
Intrauterine device (IUD)	5.8	7.7	15.0	18.9	21.5	1.3	3.5	6.8	7.9	8.4
Not currently using contraception[5]	NA	NA	NA	NA	NA	38.1	37.8	38.4	35.1	34.7

NA = Not available/not applicable. (1) Women ages 15-44. (2) Women ages 15-49. (3) Among women who have ever had intercourse. (4) Percentage of women using specified contraception in month of interview. Women could be using more than one method. Women are classified here according to the one most effective contraceptive method they are using. Additional methods women may be using are not shown. (5) Currently pregnant or postpartum, trying to get pregnant, not having sex, etc.

Sexual Activity of U.S. High School Students, 2021

Source: *Youth Risk Behavior Surveillance—United States, 2021*, CDC, U.S. Dept. of Health and Human Services

(percent of selected population to have engaged in activity)

	Ever had sexual intercourse			First sexual intercourse before age 13			Currently sexually active[1]			Condom use during last sexual intercourse[2]		
Race/ethnicity	**Female**	**Male**	**Total**	**Female**	**Male**	**Total**	**Female**	**Male**	**Total**	**Female**	**Male**	**Total**
Amer. Ind./AK native...	37.2%	29.0%	32.9%	5.5%	2.6%	3.9%	30.7%	11.7%	20.7%	—	—	—
Asian...........	11.1	11.0	11.0	2.0	0.9	1.5	7.0	6.6	6.8	—	—	52.0%
Black or African Amer..	28.7	39.4	33.9	3.2	7.4	5.3	20.7	25.6	23.0	41.4%	55.0%	48.8
Hispanic/Latino.......	31.1	29.8	30.6	3.3	3.5	3.7	22.6	17.9	20.6	42.1	59.6	49.7
Native Hawaiian/other Pac. Isl..........	—	—	28.6	4.2	8.1	6.5	25.9	10.6	16.9	—	—	—
White	32.8	28.0	30.4	2.9	2.2	2.5	24.7	19.3	21.9	52.0	58.1	54.6
Multiple race.........	32.4	34.8	33.5	4.5	4.2	4.3	22.9	20.0	21.6	37.2	51.9	43.2
Grade												
9th.............	15.0	16.4	15.9	4.2	3.6	4.0	9.5	8.7	9.2	47.1	58.4	53.4
10th............	24.4	20.7	22.6	3.6	3.1	3.4	16.7	12.4	14.6	54.8	67.1	59.8
11th............	34.4	34.8	34.6	2.6	3.0	2.8	25.9	23.9	24.9	50.8	59.8	55.0
12th............	49.5	47.3	48.4	1.8	3.0	2.4	38.8	31.9	35.4	41.7	52.4	46.4
Sexual identity												
Heterosexual (straight)	28.9	29.4	29.2	1.2	2.8	2.1	22.8	19.1	20.6	51.1	59.1	55.3
Gay, lesbian, or bisexual	40.0	30.7	38.2	6.9	5.2	6.8	27.3	15.3	25.0	38.8	46.4	39.9
Other/questioning.....	24.1	28.5	25.0	4.7	8.9	5.7	15.3	21.4	16.5	47.7	42.6	45.8
Sex of sexual contacts												
Opposite sex only.....	74.0	72.7	73.3	4.3	6.2	5.4	57.2	48.1	52.2	51.7	59.3	55.5
Same sex only or both sexes...........	66.1	69.4	66.8	14.0	24.5	16.2	43.6	38.1	42.4	39.8	38.5	39.5
All students.......	**30.6**	**29.3**	**30.0**	**3.1**	**3.2**	**3.2**	**22.6**	**18.8**	**20.7**	**47.3**	**57.7**	**51.8**

— = Not available. (1) Sexual intercourse with at least 1 person during the 3 months before the survey. (2) Among the students who were currently sexually active.

Sexual Violence Against U.S. High School Students, 2021

Source: *Youth Risk Behavior Surveillance—United States, 2021*, CDC, U.S. Dept. of Health and Human Services

(as percent of selected population)

	Ever physically forced to have sexual intercourse[1]			Experienced sexual violence by anyone[2]			Experienced sexual dating violence[3]		
Race/ethnicity	**Female**	**Male**	**Total**	**Female**	**Male**	**Total**	**Female**	**Male**	**Total**
Amer. Ind./AK native........	31.7%	7.0%	18.3%	25.5%	6.3%	15.8%	14.3%	7.8%	11.0%
Asian..................	7.5	1.5	4.5	7.7	3.7	5.7	9.7	2.2	5.5
Black or African Amer.......	11.3	3.1	7.1	10.6	4.6	7.4	6.2	4.5	5.3
Hispanic/Latino..........	14.9	3.8	9.5	18.4	4.3	11.3	15.7	3.6	10.0
Native Hawaiian/other Pac. Isl..............	16.2	5.3	9.8	—	1.2	5.4	—	—	5.5
White	13.7	3.4	8.4	20.5	4.4	11.9	17.6	3.7	10.7
Multiple race............	15.7	7.1	11.6	19.1	9.5	14.7	15.3	7.6	11.6
Grade									
9	11.5	2.8	7.1	16.9	3.3	9.9	15.9	1.8	8.9
10	13.7	3.1	8.2	19.6	3.7	11.4	17.5	3.7	10.6
11	12.3	4.1	8.2	19.0	6.1	12.3	15.3	6.1	10.8
12	16.4	4.4	10.2	15.9	5.2	10.4	12.8	4.3	8.7
Sexual identity									
Heterosexual (straight)......	8.6	2.6	5.0	14.1	3.3	7.6	12.1	2.8	6.6
Gay, lesbian, or bisexual.....	24.9	10.1	21.9	26.4	13.4	23.6	21.1	9.9	19.2
Other/questioning..........	16.7	11.6	15.9	20.0	14.4	18.9	19.3	16.5	20.0
Total..................	**13.5**	**3.6**	**8.5**	**17.9**	**4.6**	**11.0**	**15.3**	**4.0**	**9.7**

— = Not available. (1) When they did not want to. (2) Including such things as kissing, touching, or being forced to have sexual intercourse that they did not want to do, one or more times during the 12 months before the survey. (3) Being forced to do sexual things (including kissing, touching, or being physically forced to have sexual intercourse) they did not want to do by someone they were dating or going out with, one or more times during the 12 months before the survey, among students who dated or went out with someone during the 12 months before the survey.

Risky Vehicular Behaviors by U.S. High School Students, 2021

Source: *Youth Risk Behavior Surveillance—United States, 2021*, CDC, U.S. Dept. of Health and Human Services

(percent of selected population to have engaged in activity)

	Did not always wear a seat belt[1]			Rode with a driver who had been drinking alcohol[2]			Drove when drinking alcohol[2,3]			Texted or emailed while driving[2,3]		
Race/ethnicity	**Female**	**Male**	**Total**	**Female**	**Male**	**Total**	**Female**	**Male**	**Total**	**Female**	**Male**	**Total**
Amer. Ind./AK native	41.9%	45.3%	43.6%	20.1%	13.7%	16.6%	—	4.1%	4.1%	—	23.3%	30.8%
Asian	28.5	30.6	29.3	9.4	6.5	7.9	3.0%	3.3	3.1	24.9%	26.2	25.5
Black or African Amer.	57.6	61.4	59.2	16.7	12.9	14.9	1.6	3.1	2.4	24.3	28.4	26.4
Hispanic/Latino	41.3	45.2	43.6	17.7	16.2	16.9	4.6	5.7	5.3	30.4	30.1	30.5
Native Hawaiian/other Pac. Isl.	—	—	42.2	—	21.4	20.4	—	—	—	—	—	—
White	32.6	37.0	34.9	14.7	12.3	13.4	2.9	6.6	4.8	44.6	40.6	42.3
Multiple race	39.9	38.1	39.6	11.7	11.4	11.5	6.3	6.4	6.3	35.5	33.6	34.6
Grade												
9	41.7	47.3	44.5	14.9	12.4	13.7	0.4	3.7	2.2	12.1	12.7	12.4
10	42.1	40.6	41.3	17.1	12.1	14.5	2.5	3.1	2.8	20.2	24.6	22.6
11	35.6	41.1	38.5	14.3	13.3	13.9	4.0	5.9	5.0	39.2	36.3	37.7
12	33.1	36.0	34.6	14.6	14.0	14.3	4.3	8.5	6.3	56.3	52.5	54.3
Total	**38.1**	**41.4**	**39.9**	**15.2**	**13.1**	**14.1**	**3.4**	**5.8**	**4.6**	**37.1**	**35.4**	**36.1**

— = Not available. (1) When riding in a car driven by someone else. (2) In a car or other vehicle, one or more times during the 30 days before the survey. (3) Among students who had driven a car or other vehicle during the 30 days before the survey.

U.S. Motor Vehicle Crashes

Source: National Safety Council (NSC) website: injuryfacts.nsc.org; Natl. Highway Traffic Safety Admin. (NHTSA)

An estimated 46,027 people in the U.S. were killed in motor vehicle crashes in 2022, down 2.0% from the total for 2021. Both the number of licensed drivers (235.1 mil) and vehicle miles driven (3.196 tril) increased in 2022; the death rate per 100 mil vehicle miles decreased 3.6% to 1.33.

Motor vehicle deaths per 10,000 registered vehicles was 1.50 in 2022. In comparison, the death rate was 1.53 in 2021 and 1.44 in 2022, which represents a 4.2% increase over 10 years. The number of fatalities per 100,000 population increased 19.0% between 2012 and 2022 and decreased 2.8% in 2021-22.

In 2022, 6.1 mil male drivers were involved in crashes, whereas 4.4 mil female drivers were involved in crashes. About 72.6% of fatal crashes (or 43,582) involved male drivers, compared with fatal crashes involving female drivers (14,719).

In 2022, 13,524 motor vehicle traffic fatalities (31.8%) involved an alcohol-impaired (blood alcohol concentration of 0.08% or greater) driver or motorcycle operator.

Seat belt use was 91.9% in 2023. The least likely seat belt users were those traveling in light traffic (84.6%) and occupants of pickup trucks (87.0%). In 2022, the most recent year for which data was available, 50% of passenger vehicle occupants killed in traffic crashes were unrestrained.

Crashes, 2022	**Deaths**	**Injuries**
All motor vehicle crashes	46,027	5,200,000
Collision between motor vehicles	19,600	4,060,000
Collision with fixed object	12,200	640,000
Collision with pedestrian	9,200	180,000
Noncollision accidents (e.g., rollovers)	3,400	150,000
Collision with pedalcycle	1,400	130,000
Collision with railroad train	147	0
Collision with animal or animal-drawn vehicle	100	39,000

Note: NSC numbers are estimates.

U.S. Passenger Deaths and Death Rates, 1999-2022

Source: National Safety Council website: injuryfacts.nsc.org

	Passenger vehicles[1]		Vans, SUVs, pickup trucks[1]		Buses[2]		Railroad passenger trains		Scheduled airlines[3]	
Year	**Deaths**	**Rate[4]**	**Deaths**	**Rate[4]**	**Deaths**	**Rate[4]**	**Deaths**	**Rate[4]**	**Deaths**	**Rate[4]**
1999	20,851	0.84	11,295	0.76	40	0.07	14	0.10	23	0.005
2000	20,689	0.81	11,545	0.76	3	0.01	4	0.03	94	0.02
2005	18,509	0.68	13,043	0.76	43	0.07	16	0.10	20	0.003
2010	22,271	0.50	NA	NA	28	0.05	3	0.02	0	0.00
2012	21,773	0.49	NA	NA	25	0.04	5	0.02	0	0.00
2013	21,218	0.47	NA	NA	36	0.06	6	0.03	5	0.001
2014	21,039	0.46	NA	NA	28	0.04	4	0.02	0	0.00
2015	22,362	0.49	NA	NA	28	0.01	15	0.07	1	<0.001
2016	23,776	0.50	NA	NA	47	0.01	2	0.01	6	0.001
2017	23,656	0.49	NA	NA	27	0.01	9	0.04	0	0.00
2018	22,840	0.47	NA	NA	30	0.01	6	0.03	1	<0.001
2019	22,367	0.46	NA	NA	27	0.01	1	0.005	3	<0.001
2020	23,907	0.56	NA	NA	12	0.004	2	0.01	5	0.001
2021	26,452	0.57	NA	NA	6	0.002	6	0.04	0	0.00
2022	25,407	0.54	NA	NA	17	0.004	7	0.03	11	0.001

NA = Not available. (1) From 2007 on, passenger vehicles include passenger cars, light trucks, vans, and SUVs, which were classified separately in previous years. Drivers of light duty vehicles (except taxis) are considered passengers. Includes taxi passengers. (2) Excludes school buses. (3) Excludes charter, cargo, and on-demand services and deaths due to suicide/sabotage. (4) Deaths per 100 mil passenger miles.

Related Factors in Fatal Crashes, 1995-2022

Source: National Highway Traffic Safety Admin. (NHTSA)

Factor	2022 Number	%	2010 Number	%	2005 Number	%	1995 Number	%
Driving too fast for conditions, in excess of posted speed limit, or racing	11,103	18.5%	9,634	21.6%	11,803	20.0%	11,656	20.8%
Under the influence of alcohol, drugs, or medication	6,594	11.0	6,933	15.5	7,441	12.6	—	—
Operating vehicle in a careless manner[1]	5,319	8.9	—	—	2,712	4.6	2,850	5.1
Failure to yield right-of-way	4,432	7.4	3,227	7.2	4,306	7.3	4,868	8.7
Failure to keep in proper lane[2]	3,420	5.7	3,482	7.8	16,551	28.0	15,873	28.3
Distracted (phone, talking, eating, object, etc.)[3]	3,124	5.2	3,064	6.9	3,415	5.8	3,323	5.9
Failure to obey traffic signs, signals, or officer	2,541	4.2	1,933	4.3	2,354	4.0	3,189	5.7
Operating vehicle in erratic, reckless, or negligent manner	2,251	3.7	2,574	5.8	—	—	—	—
Overcorrecting/oversteering	1,708	2.8	2,096	4.7	2,319	3.9	1,328	2.4
Vision obscured (rain, snow, glare, lights, building, trees, etc.)	1,542	2.6	1,440	3.2	1,496	2.5	1,309	2.3
Swerving or avoiding due to wind, slippery surface, etc.	1,334	2.2	1,712	3.8	2,301	3.9	1,926	3.4
Driving wrong way on one-way traffic or wrong side of road	1,282	2.1	1,392	3.1	858	1.5	1,387	2.5
Drowsy, asleep, fatigued, ill, or blackout	1,264	2.1	1,234	2.8	1,552	2.6	1,816	3.2
Making improper turn	485	0.8	990	2.2	1,590	2.7	1,253	2.2
Other factors	6,017	10.0	6,362	14.3	9,304	15.7	9,096	16.2
None reported	8,492	14.1	12,793	28.7	21,265	36.0	20,443	36.4
Unknown	20,263	33.7	5,086	11.4	1,187	2.0	990	1.8
Total drivers	**60,048**	**100.0**	**44,599**	**100.0**	**59,104**	**100.0**	**56,155**	**100.0**

— = Not available or not applicable. **Note:** For each year, the sum of the numbers and percentages is greater than total drivers as more than one factor may be present for the same driver. (1) In 1995 and 2005, the two categories were combined; "careless" not mentioned in factor in 2010. (2) "Failure to keep in proper lane or running off road" in 1995, 2005. (3) "Inattentive (talking, eating, etc.)" in 1995, 2005.

U.S. Death Rates for Suicide at Selected Ages, 1960-2021

Source: *Health, United States, 2020-2021*, National Center for Health Statistics (NCHS), CDC, U.S. Dept. of Health and Human Services (deaths per 100,000 resident population)

Age	2021 Both sexes	Male	Female	2000 Both sexes	Male	Female	1980 Both sexes	Male	Female	1960 Both sexes	Male	Female
15-24 years	NA	23.8	6.1	10.2	17.1	3.0	12.3	20.2	4.3	5.2	8.2	2.2
25-44 years	NA	30.0	7.4	13.4	21.3	5.4	15.6	24.0	7.7	12.2	17.9	6.6
45-64 years	NA	27.1	8.2	13.5	21.3	6.2	15.9	23.7	8.9	22.0	34.4	10.2
65-74 years	NA	26.1	5.6	12.5	22.7	4.0	16.9	30.4	6.5	23.0	39.6	8.4
All ages[1]	**14.1**	**22.8**	**5.7**	**10.4**	**17.7**	**4.0**	**12.2**	**19.9**	**5.7**	**12.5**	**20.0**	**5.6**

(1) Incl. ages not shown separately here.

Leading Causes of Death in the U.S., 2022

Source: National Vital Statistics System, National Center for Health Statistics, CDC, U.S. Dept. of Health and Human Services

Cause of death	Number	% of total deaths	Death rate[1]	Cause of death	Number	% of total deaths	Death rate[1]
All causes	**3,279,857**	**100.0%**	**798.8**	6. Chronic lower respiratory diseases	147,382	4.5%	34.3
1. Heart disease	702,880	21.4	167.2	7. Alzheimer's disease	120,122	3.7	28.9
2. Cancer	608,371	18.5	142.3	8. Diabetes	101,209	3.1	24.1
3. Accidents (unintentional injuries)	227,039	6.9	64.0	9. Kidney disease	57,937	1.8	13.8
4. COVID-19	186,552	5.7	44.5	10. Chronic liver disease and cirrhosis	54,803	1.7	13.8
5. Stroke	165,393	5.0	39.5	All other causes (residual)	908,169	27.7	—

— = Not applicable. (1) Per 100,000 U.S. population.

Overdose Deaths From Selected Drugs in the U.S., 1999-2022

Source: National Center on Health Statistics (NCHS), CDC WONDER, U.S. Dept. of Health and Human Services

	1999	2000	2005	2010	2015	2018	2019	2020	2022	Percent change 1999-2022	Percent change 2020-22
Total overdose deaths	**16,849**	**17,415**	**29,813**	**38,329**	**52,404**	**67,367**	**70,630**	**91,799**	**107,941**	**540.6%**	**17.6%**
Female	5,591	5,852	11,089	15,323	19,447	22,426	22,749	28,071	32,127	474.6	14.4
Male	11,258	11,563	18,724	23,006	32,957	44,941	47,881	63,728	75,814	573.4	19.0
Any opioid	**8,050**	**8,407**	**14,918**	**21,089**	**33,091**	**46,802**	**49,860**	**68,630**	**81,806**	**916.2**	**19.2**
Female	2,057	2,264	5,161	7,734	11,420	14,724	15,225	19,970	23,421	1,038.6	17.3
Male	5,993	6,143	9,757	13,355	21,671	32,078	34,635	48,660	58,385	874.2	20.0
Prescription opioids	3,442	3,785	9,612	14,583	15,281	14,975	14,139	16,416	14,716	327.5	–10.4
Other synthetic opioids[1]	730	782	1,742	3,007	9,580	31,335	36,359	56,516	73,838	10,014.8	30.6
Heroin	1,960	1,842	2,009	3,036	12,989	14,996	14,019	13,165	5,871	199.5	–55.4
Cocaine	3,822	3,544	6,208	4,183	6,784	14,666	15,883	19,447	27,569	621.3	41.8
Psychostimulants[2]	547	578	1,608	1,854	5,716	12,676	16,167	23,837	34,022	6,119.7	42.7
Benzodiazepines	1,135	1,298	3,084	6,497	8,791	10,724	9,711	12,290	10,964	866.0	–10.8
Antidepressants	1,749	1,798	2,861	3,889	4,894	5,064	5,175	5,597	5,863	235.2	4.8

Note: Numbers include all deaths with underlying causes of drug poisoning, regardless of intent. (1) Synthetic opioids other than methadone. This category is dominated by fentanyl-related overdoses. (2) This category, "Psychostimulants with abuse potential," is dominated by methamphetamine-related overdoses.

Drug-Overdose Deaths in the U.S., 2022

Source: National Vital Statistics System, National Center for Health Statistics, CDC, U.S. Dept. of Health and Human Services

State	Number	Rate[1]	State	Number	Rate[1]	State	Number	Rate[1]	State	Number	Rate[1]
Alabama	1,492	31.5	Illinois	3,849	30.0	Montana	208	19.4	Rhode Island	424	38.1
Alaska	254	34.3	Indiana	2,682	41.0	Nebraska	225	11.8	South Carolina	2,279	44.7
Arizona	2,664	37.2	Iowa	469	15.3	Nevada	1,003	30.3	South Dakota	95	11.3
Arkansas	617	21.7	Kansas	754	26.5	New Hampshire	486	36.0	Tennessee	3,825	56.0
California	10,952	26.9	Kentucky	2,271	53.2	New Jersey	2,985	31.6	Texas	5,489	18.2
Colorado	1,811	29.8	Louisiana	2,376	54.5	New Mexico	1,024	50.3	Utah	627	19.8
Connecticut	1,482	40.3	Maine	707	54.3	New York	6,358	31.4	Vermont	276	45.9
Delaware	549	55.3	Maryland	2,573	40.3	North Carolina	4,310	41.8	Virginia	2,496	28.8
Dist. of Columbia	451	64.3	Massachusetts	2,642	37.4	North Dakota	148	19.8	Washington	2,725	33.7
Florida	7,551	35.2	Michigan	2,997	30.7	Ohio	5,144	45.6	West Virginia	1,335	80.9
Georgia	2,687	24.9	Minnesota	1,384	24.8	Oklahoma	1,196	30.7	Wisconsin	1,792	31.8
Hawaii	284	18.6	Mississippi	758	27.6	Oregon	1,363	31.1	Wyoming	126	21.9
Idaho	385	20.7	Missouri	2,192	36.9	Pennsylvania	5,169	40.9	**U.S.**	**107,941**	**32.6**

(1) Number of deaths due to drug overdose per 100,000 population.

Principal Types of Accidental Deaths in the U.S., 1970-2022

Source: National Safety Council website: injuryfacts.nsc.org; National Center for Health Statistics, U.S. Dept. of Health and Human Services

Year[1]	Total[2]	Motor vehicle	Falls	Poisoning	Choking: Inhalation of food, object	Drowning	Fires, flames, smoke	Mechanical suffocation	Firearms
1970	114,638	54,633	16,926	5,299	2,753	7,860	6,718	NA	2,406
1980	105,718	53,172	13,294	4,331	3,249	7,257	5,822	NA	1,955
1985	93,457	45,901	12,001	5,170	3,551	5,316	4,938	NA	1,649
1990	91,983	46,814	12,313	5,803	3,303	4,685	4,175	NA	1,416
1995	93,320	43,363	13,986	9,072	3,185	4,350	3,761	NA	1,225
2000	97,900	43,354	13,322	12,757	4,313	3,482	3,377	1,335	776
2005	117,809	45,343	19,656	23,617	4,386	3,582	3,197	1,514	789
2010	120,859	35,332	26,009	33,041	4,570	3,782	2,782	1,595	606
2013	130,557	35,369	30,208	38,851	4,864	3,391	2,760	1,737	505
2015	146,571	37,757	33,381	47,478	5,051	3,602	2,646	1,863	489
2016	161,374	40,327	34,673	58,335	4,829	3,789	2,730	1,781	495
2017	169,936	40,231	36,338	64,795	5,216	3,709	2,812	1,730	486
2018	167,127	39,404	37,455	62,399	5,084	3,710	2,972	1,617	458
2019	173,040	39,107	39,443	65,773	5,228	3,692	2,692	1,848	486
2020	200,955	42,339	42,114	87,404	4,963	4,177	2,951	1,805	535
2021	224,935	46,980	44,686	102,001	5,325	4,337	3,389	1,857	549
2022	227,039	46,027	46,630	102,958	5,553	4,168	3,478	1,863	463
				Deaths per 100,000 population					
1970	56.2	26.8	8.3	2.6	1.4	3.9	3.3	NA	1.2
1980	46.5	23.4	5.9	1.9	1.4	3.2	2.6	NA	0.9
1985	39.3	19.3	5.0	2.2	1.5	2.2	2.1	NA	0.7
1990	36.9	18.8	4.9	2.3	1.3	1.9	1.7	NA	0.6
1995	35.5	16.5	5.3	3.4	1.2	1.7	1.4	NA	0.5
2000	35.6	15.7	4.8	4.6	1.6	1.3	1.2	0.5	0.3
2005	39.7	15.3	6.6	8.0	1.5	1.2	1.1	0.5	0.3
2010	39.0	11.4	8.4	10.7	1.5	1.2	0.9	0.5	0.2
2013	41.3	11.2	9.6	12.3	1.5	1.1	0.9	0.5	0.2
2015	45.6	11.7	10.4	14.8	1.6	1.1	0.8	0.6	0.2
2016	49.9	12.5	10.7	18.1	1.5	1.2	0.8	0.6	0.2
2017	52.2	12.4	11.2	19.9	1.6	1.1	0.9	0.5	0.2
2018	51.1	12.0	11.4	19.1	1.6	1.1	0.9	0.5	0.1
2019	52.7	11.9	12.0	20.0	1.6	1.1	0.8	0.6	0.1
2020	60.6	12.8	12.7	26.4	1.5	1.3	0.9	0.5	0.2
2021	67.8	14.2	13.5	30.7	1.6	1.3	1.0	0.6	0.2
2022	68.1	13.8	14.0	30.9	1.7	1.3	1.0	0.6	0.1

NA = Not available. **Note:** All figures include on-the-job deaths. (1) Data after 1999 are not comparable with earlier data because of classification changes. (2) Total incl. other accidental deaths not shown in detail here.

Deaths in the U.S. Involving Firearms by Age and Sex, 2022

Source: National Safety Council website: injuryfacts.nsc.org

Type and sex	All ages	Under 5 years	5-14 years	15-24 years	25-44 years	45-54 years	55-64 years	65-74 years	75 years or older
Total firearms deaths	**48,204**	**156**	**628**	**9,363**	**18,340**	**5,981**	**5,625**	**4,030**	**4,081**
Male	41,293	100	463	8,188	15,608	4,979	4,742	3,482	3,731
Female	6,895	40	165	1,175	2,732	1,002	883	548	350
Preventable/accidental	**463**	**49**	**35**	**120**	**124**	**42**	**36**	**31**	**18**
Male	409	37	32	107	113	35	33	28	16
Female	54	12	0	13	0	0	0	0	0
Suicide	**27,032**	**0**	**180**	**3,246**	**7,989**	**3,838**	**4,412**	**3,536**	**3,831**
Male	23,538	0	148	2,872	6,793	3,219	3,782	3,136	3,588
Female	3,494	0	32	374	1,196	619	630	400	243
Assault	**19,651**	**93**	**395**	**5,814**	**9,697**	**1,947**	**1,080**	**422**	**203**
Male	16,419	54	267	5,044	8,235	1,587	844	286	102
Female	3,216	23	128	770	1,462	360	236	136	101

U.S. Infant Mortality Rates by Race and Sex, 1960-2022

Source: National Center for Health Statistics (NCHS), CDC, U.S. Dept. of Health and Human Services
(deaths of infants under 1 year old per 1,000 live births)

	All races[1]			White[2]			Black[2]		
Year	Both sexes	Male	Female	Both sexes	Male	Female	Both sexes	Male	Female
1960	26.0	29.3	22.6	22.9	26.0	19.6	44.3	49.1	39.4
1970	20.0	22.4	17.5	17.8	20.0	15.4	32.7	36.2	29.0
1980	12.6	13.9	11.2	10.9	12.1	9.5	22.2	24.2	20.2
1990	9.2	10.3	8.1	7.6	8.5	6.6	18.0	19.6	16.3
2000	6.9	7.6	6.2	5.7	6.3	5.1	14.1	15.5	12.7
2005	6.9	7.6	6.2	5.7	6.7	4.8	14.3	15.8	12.8
2007	6.8	7.4	6.1	5.6	6.2	5.0	13.8	15.0	12.4
2008	6.6	7.2	6.0	5.5	6.0	5.0	13.1	14.4	11.9
2009	6.4	7.0	5.8	5.3	5.8	4.7	13.1	14.6	11.5
2010	6.1	6.7	5.6	5.1	5.5	4.6	12.0	13.1	10.9
2011	6.1	6.6	5.5	5.1	5.5	4.6	12.0	13.1	10.8
2012	6.0	6.5	5.4	5.0	5.4	4.5	11.6	12.8	10.4
2013	6.0	6.5	5.4	5.0	5.5	4.4	11.6	12.5	10.7
2014	5.8	6.3	5.3	4.8	5.3	4.3	11.4	12.3	10.4
2015	5.9	6.4	5.4	4.8	5.3	4.4	11.7	12.8	10.7
2016	5.9	6.4	5.3	4.8	5.2	4.3	11.8	12.7	10.8
2017	5.8	6.3	5.2	4.7	5.1	4.1	11.0	12.6	10.3
2018	5.7	6.3	5.1	4.6	5.1	4.2	10.8	12.0	9.4
2019	5.6	6.1	5.1	4.4	4.9	4.0	11.0	11.9	10.2
2020	5.4	5.9	5.0	4.4	4.8	4.0	10.4	11.2	9.5
2021	5.4	5.8	5.0	4.4	4.7	4.1	10.6	11.6	9.5
2022	5.6	6.1	5.1	4.5	4.9	4.1	10.9	11.8	10.0

Note: Number of live births is tabulated according to mother's race (1980 and on) or parents' race (before 1980) stated on birth certificate. (1) Incl. races not shown. (2) Non-Hispanic.

Years of Life Expected at Birth in U.S., 1900-2021

Source: National Center for Health Statistics (NCHS), CDC, U.S. Dept. of Health and Human Services

	All races[1]			White[2]			Black[2,3]		
Year	Both sexes	Male	Female	Both sexes	Male	Female	Both sexes	Male	Female
1900[4]	47.3	46.3	48.3	47.6	46.6	48.7	33.0	32.5	33.5
1910[4]	50.0	48.4	51.8	50.3	48.6	52.0	35.6	33.8	37.5
1920[4]	54.1	53.6	54.6	54.9	54.4	55.6	45.3	45.5	45.2
1930	59.7	58.1	61.6	61.4	59.7	63.5	48.1	47.3	49.2
1940	62.9	60.8	65.2	64.2	62.1	66.6	53.1	51.5	54.9
1950	68.2	65.6	71.1	69.1	66.5	72.2	60.8	59.1	62.9
1960	69.7	66.6	73.1	70.6	67.4	74.1	63.6	61.1	66.3
1970	70.8	67.1	74.7	71.7	68.0	75.6	64.1	60.0	68.3
1980	73.7	70.0	77.4	74.4	70.7	78.1	68.1	63.8	72.5
1990	75.4	71.8	78.8	76.1	72.7	79.4	69.1	64.5	73.6
2000	76.8	74.1	79.3	77.3	74.7	79.9	71.8	68.2	75.1
2010	78.7	76.2	81.0	78.8	76.4	81.1	74.7	71.5	77.7
2013	78.8	76.4	81.2	78.8	76.5	81.2	75.1	71.9	78.1
2015	78.7	76.3	81.1	78.7	76.3	81.0	75.1	71.9	78.1
2016	78.7	76.2	81.1	78.6	76.2	81.0	74.9	71.6	78.0
2017	78.6	76.1	81.1	78.5	76.1	81.0	74.9	71.5	78.1
2018	78.7	76.2	81.2	78.6	76.2	81.1	74.7	71.3	78.0
2019	78.8	76.3	81.4	78.8	76.3	81.3	74.8	71.3	78.1
2020	77.0	74.2	79.9	77.4	74.8	80.1	71.5	67.8	75.4
2021	76.4	73.5	79.3	76.7	74.0	79.5	71.2	67.6	75.0

(1) Includes races not shown. (2) Non-Hispanic beginning in 2010. (3) Data for 1900-60 are for the "nonwhite" pop. (4) Data prior to 1930 does not include all states.

U.S. Life Expectancy at Selected Ages, 2022

Source: National Center for Health Statistics (NCHS), CDC, U.S. Dept. of Health and Human Services

Age	All races and origins			Hispanic			White[1]			Black[1]		
(years)	Total	Male	Female	Total	Male	Female	Total	Male	Female	Total	Male	Female
0	77.5	74.8	80.2	80.0	77.0	82.8	77.5	75.1	80.1	72.8	69.1	76.5
1	76.9	74.3	79.6	79.4	76.4	82.2	76.9	74.4	79.4	72.6	68.9	76.3
5	73.0	70.4	75.7	75.4	72.5	78.3	73.0	70.5	75.5	68.8	65.1	72.4
10	68.0	65.4	70.7	70.5	67.6	73.3	68.0	65.6	70.5	63.9	60.2	67.5
15	63.1	60.5	65.8	65.5	62.6	68.4	63.0	60.6	65.6	58.9	55.3	62.6
20	58.3	55.7	60.9	60.7	57.8	63.5	58.2	55.8	60.7	54.3	50.7	57.8
25	53.5	51.1	56.1	56.0	53.2	58.6	53.4	51.1	55.8	49.8	46.4	53.0
30	48.9	46.6	51.3	51.3	48.7	53.8	48.8	46.6	51.0	45.3	42.2	48.4
35	44.3	42.1	46.5	46.7	44.2	49.0	44.2	42.1	46.3	41.0	38.0	43.8
40	39.8	37.7	41.9	42.1	39.8	44.2	39.7	37.7	41.7	36.7	33.8	39.3
45	35.3	33.4	37.3	37.6	35.4	39.5	35.2	33.3	37.1	32.5	29.8	34.9
50	31.0	29.1	32.8	33.1	31.0	34.9	30.8	29.1	32.6	28.4	25.9	30.6
55	26.7	25.0	28.4	28.7	26.8	30.3	26.6	25.0	28.2	24.4	22.1	26.5
60	22.7	21.1	24.2	24.5	22.7	25.9	22.6	21.1	24.0	20.8	18.7	22.6
65	18.9	17.5	20.2	20.5	19.0	21.7	18.8	17.5	20.0	17.4	15.5	19.0
70	15.3	14.2	16.3	16.8	15.4	17.7	15.2	14.1	16.2	14.4	12.8	15.6
75	12.0	11.0	12.8	13.2	12.1	13.9	11.8	10.9	12.6	11.5	10.2	12.4
80	8.9	8.1	9.5	10.0	9.1	10.4	8.8	8.0	9.4	8.9	7.8	9.5
85	6.4	5.8	6.8	7.2	6.5	7.4	6.3	5.7	6.7	6.6	5.8	7.0
90	4.4	3.9	4.6	5.0	4.4	5.0	4.3	3.8	4.5	4.8	4.2	5.0
95	3.0	2.7	3.1	3.4	3.0	3.3	2.9	2.6	3.0	3.4	3.1	3.5
100	2.1	1.9	2.2	2.4	2.2	2.3	2.0	1.8	2.1	2.5	2.3	2.5

Note: Data are provisional. (1) Non-Hispanic.

NOTED PERSONALITIES

Widely Known Americans of the Present

Political leaders, journalists, other prominent living persons. As of Oct. 2024. Excludes most who fall in categories listed elsewhere in Noted Personalities, such as Writers of the Present and Entertainment Personalities of the Present. Includes some figures who are active in American life but are not U.S. citizens.

Greg Abbott, b 11/13/1957 (Wichita Falls, TX), TX gov. (R).
Stacey Abrams, b 12/9/1973 (Madison, WI), former GA House minority leader (D); 2022 GA gov. contender.
Eric Adams, b 9/1/1960 (New York, NY), NYC mayor (D).
Pete Aguilar, b 6/19/1979 (Fontana, CA), U.S. rep. (D, CA); House Dem. Caucus chair.
Edwin "Buzz" Aldrin, b 1/20/1930 (Montclair, NJ), former astronaut, second person to walk on the Moon.
Samuel A. Alito Jr., b 4/1/1950 (Trenton, NJ), U.S. Supreme Court justice.
Gloria Allred, b 7/3/1941 (Philadelphia, PA), civil rights lawyer.
Marin Alsop, b 10/16/1956 (New York, NY), Baltimore Symphony musical dir. laureate.
Christiane Amanpour, b 1/12/1958 (London, Eng., UK), TV journalist.
Marc Andreessen, b 7/9/1971 (New Lisbon, IA), co-author of web browser Mosaic, cofounder of Netscape.
José Andrés, b 7/13/1969 (Mieres, Spain), chef, founder of World Central Kitchen.
Lloyd Austin, b 8/8/1953 (Mobile, AL), defense sec., U.S. Army gen. (ret.).
David Axelrod, b 2/22/1955 (New York, NY), political strategist.
James Baker, b 4/28/1930 (Houston, TX), former sec. of state.
Robert Ballard, b 6/30/1942 (Wichita, KS), oceanographer; found wreck of the *Titanic*.
Steve Ballmer, b 3/24/1956 (Detroit, MI), former Microsoft CEO; L.A. Clippers owner.
Steve Bannon, b 11/27/1953 (Norfolk, VA), former chief strategist to Pres. Trump, Breitbart News exec.
Mike Barnicle, b 10/13/1943 (Worcester, MA), columnist.
William Barr, b 5/23/1950 (New York, NY), U.S. atty. gen. (1991-93, 2019-20).
Mary Barra, b 12/24/1961 (Waterford, MI), General Motors CEO.
Amy Coney Barrett, b 1/28/1972 (New Orleans, LA), U.S. Supreme Court justice.
Dave Barry, b 7/3/1947 (Armonk, NY), humorist.
Glenn Beck, b 2/10/1964 (Mount Vernon, WA), political commentator.
Ben Bernanke, b 12/13/1953 (Augusta, GA), former Federal Reserve chair.
Carl Bernstein, b 2/14/1944 (Washington, DC), journalist; with Bob Woodward cracked Watergate scandal.
Jeff Bezos, b 1/12/1964 (Albuquerque, NM), Amazon founder.
Hunter Biden, b 2/4/1970 (Wilmington, DE), lawyer, son of Pres. Joe Biden.
Jill Biden, b 6/5/1951 (Hammonton, NJ), first lady, professor.
Joseph R. Biden Jr., b 11/20/1942 (Scranton, PA), 46th U.S. president.
Deborah Birx, b 4/4/1956 (Baltimore, MD), physician, fmr. White House coronavirus response coordinator.
Antony Blinken, b 4/16/1962 (Yonkers, NY), sec. of state.
Wolf Blitzer, b 3/22/1948 (Augsburg, Germany), TV journalist.
Michael R. Bloomberg, b 2/14/1942 (Brighton, MA), former NYC mayor, financial information/media entrepreneur.
Charles M. Blow, b 8/11/1970 (Gibsland, LA), columnist.
Cory Booker, b 4/27/1969 (Washington, DC), U.S. sen. (D, NJ), former Newark mayor; 2020 pres. contender.
Andy Borowitz, b 1/4/1958 (Cleveland, OH), humorist.
Alvin Bragg, b 10/21/1973 (New York, NY), Manhattan district attorney.
Donna Brazile, b 12/15/1959 (Kenner, LA), political analyst.
Stephen Breyer, b 8/15/1938 (San Francisco, CA), former U.S. Supreme Court justice.
Sergey Brin, b 8/21/1973 (Moscow, Russia), cofounder of Google.
Tom Brokaw, b 2/6/1940 (Webster, SD), TV journalist, retired anchor.
David Brooks, b 8/11/1961 (Toronto, ON, Can.), columnist, political commentator.
Aaron Brown, b 11/10/1948 (Hopkins, MN), broadcast journalist.
Frank Bruni, b 10/31/1964 (White Plains, NY), columnist.
Warren Buffett, b 8/30/1930 (Omaha, NE), investor, leading philanthropist.
Lonnie Bunch III, b 11/18/1952 (Newark, NJ), Smithsonian Institution sec.
Doug Burgum, b 8/1/1956 (Arthur, ND), ND gov. (R); 2024 pres. contender.
Tarana Burke, b 9/12/1973 (New York, NY), activist who started #metoo movement.
Barbara Bush, b 11/25/1981 (Dallas, TX), daughter of former pres. George W. Bush.
George W. Bush, b 7/6/1946 (New Haven, CT), 43rd U.S. president.
Jeb Bush, b 2/11/1953 (Midland, TX), former FL gov. (R).
Laura Bush, b 11/4/1946 (Midland, TX), former first lady.
Pete Buttigieg, b 1/19/1982 (South Bend, IN), transportation sec.; 2020 pres. contender (D).
Gretchen Carlson, b 6/21/1966 (Anoka, MN), TV journalist.
Tucker Carlson, b 5/16/1969 (San Francisco, CA), news commentator.
Jimmy Carter, b 10/1/1924 (Plains, GA), 39th U.S. president; 2002 Nobel Peace Prize winner.
Joaquin Castro, b 9/16/1974 (San Antonio, TX), U.S. rep. (D, TX).
Julián Castro, b 9/16/1974 (San Antonio, TX), fmr. housing and urban dev. sec.; 2020 pres. contender (D).
Dick Cheney, b 1/30/1941 (Lincoln, NE), former U.S. vice president.
Liz Cheney, b 7/28/1966 (Madison, WI), fmr. U.S. rep. (R, WY).
Lynne Cheney, b 8/14/1941 (Casper, WY), political commentator, wife of former U.S. vice pres. Dick Cheney.
Brian Chesky, b 8/29/1981 (Niskayuna, NY), Airbnb founder, CEO.
Judy Chicago, b 7/20/1939 (Chicago, IL), artist.
Dale Chihuly, b 9/20/1941 (Tacoma, WA), glass sculptor.
Noam Chomsky, b 12/7/1928 (Philadelphia, PA), linguist, activist.
Chris Christie, b 9/6/1962 (Newark, NJ), former NJ gov. (R); 2016, 2024 pres. contender.
Connie Chung, b 8/20/1946 (Washington, DC), former TV journalist.
Katherine Clark, b 7/17/1963 (New Haven, CT), House minority whip (D, MA).
Bill Clinton, b 8/19/1946 (Hope, AR), 42nd U.S. president.
Chelsea Clinton, b 2/27/1980 (Little Rock, AR), daughter of former pres. Bill Clinton and Hillary Clinton.
Hillary Rodham Clinton, b 10/26/1947 (Chicago, IL), former sec. of state, U.S. sen. (D, NY), first lady; 2016 presidential nominee.
Kate Clinton, b 11/9/1947 (Buffalo, NY), political humorist.
Jim Clyburn, b 7/21/1940 (Sumter, SC), U.S. rep. (D, SC).
Kenneth Cole, b 3/23/1954 (Brooklyn, NY), fashion designer.
Gail Collins, b 11/25/1945 (Cincinnati, OH), newspaper columnist, writer.
Jason Collins, b 12/2/1978 (Northridge, CA), first openly gay active NBA player.
James Comey, b 12/14/1960 (Yonkers, NY), former FBI director.
Kellyanne Conway, b 1/20/1967 (Camden, NJ), fmr. counselor to Pres. Trump.
Tim Cook, b 11/1/1960 (Robertdale, AZ), CEO of Apple Inc.
Anderson Cooper, b 6/3/1967 (New York, NY), TV news anchor.
Bob Costas, b 3/22/1952 (Astoria, Queens, NY), TV sports journalist.
Ann Coulter, b 12/8/1961 (New Canaan, CT), political commentator, author.
Katie Couric, b 1/7/1957 (Arlington, VA), TV and online journalist.
Harlan Crow, b 10/17/1949 (Dallas, TX), real estate developer.
Candy Crowley, b 12/12/1948 (Kalamazoo, MI), TV journalist.
Ben Crump, b 10/10/1969 (Lumberton, NC), civil rights attorney.
Ted Cruz, b 12/22/1970 (Calgary, AB, Can.), U.S. sen. (R, TX).

Mark Cuban, b 7/31/1958 (Pittsburgh, PA), entrepreneur, Dallas Mavericks owner.
Andrew Cuomo, b 12/6/1957 (New York, NY), former NY gov. (D), state atty. gen.
Chris Cuomo, b 8/9/1970 (Queens, NY), TV journalist.
Ann Curry, b 11/19/1956 (Guam), TV journalist.
Angela Davis, b 1/26/1944 (Birmingham, AL), political activist, professor.
Bill de Blasio, b 5/8/1961 (New York, NY), former NYC mayor (D); 2020 pres. contender.
Michael Dell, b 2/23/1965 (Houston, TX), founder and CEO of tech giant Dell.
Alan Dershowitz, b 9/1/1938 (Brooklyn, NY), attorney, political commentator.
Ron DeSantis, b 9/14/1978 (Jacksonville, FL), FL gov. (R); 2024 pres. contender.
José Díaz-Balart, b 11/7/1960 (Fort Lauderdale, FL), TV journalist.
John Dickerson, b 7/6/1968 (Washington, DC), TV journalist.
Barry Diller, b 2/2/1942 (San Francisco, CA), media exec.
Jamie Dimon, b 3/13/1956 (New York, NY), chair, CEO of JPMorgan Chase.
James Dobson, b 4/21/1936 (Shreveport, LA), evangelical Christian leader.
Timothy Dolan, b 2/6/1950 (St. Louis, MO), Rom. Cath. cardinal, archbishop of NY.
Jack Dorsey, b 11/19/1976 (St. Louis, MO), Twitter cofounder.
Maureen Dowd, b 1/14/1952 (Washington, DC), columnist.
Elizabeth Drew, b 11/16/1935 (Cincinnati, OH), journalist.
Matt Drudge, b 10/27/1966 (Takoma Park, MD), Drudge Report founder/editor.
Maurice DuBois, b 8/20/1965 (Gordon Heights, NY), TV journalist.
Michael S. Dukakis, b 11/3/1933 (Brookline, MA), former MA gov. (D), 1988 pres. nominee.
David Duke, b 7/1/1950 (Tulsa, OK), white nationalist activist; politician.
Dick Durbin, b 11/21/1944 (East St. Louis, IL), U.S. Senate majority whip (D, IL).
Sylvia Earle, b 8/30/1935 (Gibbstown, NJ), marine biologist.
Marian Wright Edelman, b 6/6/1939 (Bennettsville, SC), Children's Defense Fund founder.
Michael Eisner, b 3/7/1942 (Mt. Kisco, NY), former Disney Co. CEO.
Sarah Kate Ellis, b 11/27/1991 (Staten Island, NY), GLAAD CEO.
Lawrence J. Ellison, b 8/17/1944 (New York, NY), Oracle Corp. cofounder.
Rahm Emanuel, b 11/29/1959 (Chicago, IL), amb. to Japan; fmr. Chicago mayor, Obama chief of staff, U.S. rep. (D, IL).
Doug Emhoff, b 10/13/1964 (Brooklyn, NY), husband of vice pres. Kamala Harris.
Tom Emmer, b 3/3/1961 (South Bend, IN), House majority whip (R, MN).
Myrlie Evers-Williams, b 3/17/1933 (Vicksburg, MS), civil rights activist.
Shawn Fain, b 10/30/1968 (Kokomo, IN), UAW pres.
Louis Farrakhan, b 5/11/1933 (Roxbury, MA), Nation of Islam leader.
Ronan Farrow, b 12/19/1987 (New York, NY), investigative journalist.
Anthony Fauci, b 12/24/1940 (New York, NY), physician, fmr. National Institute of Allergy and Infectious Diseases dir.
John Fetterman, b 8/15/1969 (West Reading, PA), U.S. sen. (D, PA).
Michael Flynn, b 12/1/1958 (Middletown, RI), U.S. Army gen. (ret.); briefly Pres. Trump's natl. security adviser.
Steve (Malcolm) Forbes Jr., b 7/18/1947 (Morristown, NJ), publisher, former pres. contender (R).
Christine Blasey Ford, b 11/28/1966 (Potomac, MD), professor; complainant against U.S. Supreme Court justice Brett Kavanaugh.
Tom Ford, b 8/27/1961 (Austin, TX), fashion designer, director.
Thomas Friedman, b 7/20/1953 (Minneapolis, MN), columnist, author.
Tulsi Gabbard, b 4/12/1981 (Leloaloa, Amer. Samoa), former U.S. rep (D, HI); 2020 pres. contender.
Merrick Garland, b 11/13/1952 (Chicago, IL), U.S. atty. gen.; Supreme Court nominee.
Bill Gates, b 10/28/1955 (Seattle, WA), software pioneer; Microsoft exec.
Henry Louis Gates Jr., b 9/16/1950 (Keyser, WV), African American studies scholar; TV host.
Melinda French Gates, b 8/15/1964 (Dallas, TX), philanthropist.
David Geffen, b 2/21/1943 (Brooklyn, NY), entertainment exec.
Charles Gibson, b 3/4/1943 (Evanston, IL), TV journalist.
Gabrielle Giffords, b 6/8/1970 (Tucson, AZ), former U.S. rep. (D, AZ); shot in 2011 assassination attempt.
Newt Gingrich, b 6/17/1943 (Harrisburg, PA), former House speaker (R, GA); 2012 pres. contender.
Rudolph Giuliani, b 5/28/1944 (Brooklyn, NY), atty. for fmr. Pres. Trump, fmr. NYC mayor (R).
Ira Glass, b 3/3/1959 (Baltimore, MD), radio host.
Roger Goodell, b 2/19/1959 (Jamestown, NY), NFL commissioner.
Ellen Goodman, b 4/11/1941 (Newton, MA), columnist.
Doris Kearns Goodwin, b 1/4/1943 (Brooklyn, NY), historian, TV commentator.
Berry Gordy, b 11/28/1929 (Detroit, MI), Motown record label founder.
Al Gore Jr., b 3/31/1948 (Washington, DC), former U.S. sen. (D, TN), vice pres., 2000 pres. nominee.
Lindsey Graham, b 7/9/1955 (Central, SC), U.S. sen. (R, SC).
Temple Grandin, b 8/29/1947 (Boston, MA), animal behavioral scientist.
Marjorie Taylor Greene, b 5/27/1974 (Milledgeville, GA), U.S. rep. (R, GA).
Jeff Greenfield, b 6/10/1943 (New York, NY), TV journalist.
Alan Greenspan, b 3/6/1926 (New York, NY), former Federal Reserve chair.
Savannah Guthrie, b 12/27/1971 (Melbourne, Vic., Australia), TV journalist.
Jenna Bush Hager, b 11/25/1981 (Dallas, TX), daughter of former pres. George W. Bush; TV host.
Nikki Haley, b 1/20/1972 (Bamberg, SC), fmr. U.S. ambassador to UN, SC gov. (R); 2024 pres. contender.
Nikole Hannah-Jones, b 4/9/1976 (Waterloo, IA), journalist.
Sean Hannity, b 12/30/1961 (New York, NY), radio and TV host, author, political commentator.
Kamala Harris, b 10/20/1964 (Oakland, CA), U.S. vice pres. and 2024 pres. nominee; former U.S. sen. (D, CA).
Jaime Harrison, b 2/5/1976 (Orangeburg, SC), Dem. Natl. Committee chair.
Reed Hastings, b 10/8/1960 (Boston, MA), Netflix cofounder, exec. chair.
Carla Hayden, b 8/10/1952 (Tallahassee, FL), librarian of U.S. Congress.
Tommy Hilfiger, b 3/24/1951 (Elmira, NY), fashion designer.
Anita Hill, b 7/30/1956 (Morris, OK), legal scholar; complainant against U.S. Supreme Court justice Clarence Thomas.
Paris Hilton, b 2/17/1981 (New York, NY), heiress.
Perez Hilton, b 3/23/1978 (Miami, FL), gossip columnist.
James P. Hoffa, b 5/19/1941 (Detroit, MI), fmr. Teamsters Union head.
David Hogg, b 4/12/2000 (Los Angeles, CA), gun control activist.
Eric Holder Jr., b 1/21/1951 (Bronx, NY), former U.S. atty. gen.
Lester Holt, b 3/8/1959 (San Francisco, CA), TV journalist.
David Horowitz, b 1/10/1939 (New York, NY), consumer advocate, columnist, author.
Steny H. Hoyer, b 6/14/1939 (New York, NY), U.S. rep. (D, MD).
Mike Huckabee, b 8/24/1955 (Hope, AR), former AR gov. (R), TV host; 2008, 2016 pres. contender.
Dolores Huerta, b 4/10/1930 (Dawson, NM), labor activist.
Arianna Huffington, b 7/15/1950 (Athens, Greece), political commentator.
Brit Hume, b 6/22/1943 (Washington, DC), TV journalist.
Asa Hutchinson, b 12/3/1950 (Bentonville, AR), fmr. AR gov. (R); 2024 pres. contender.
Carl Icahn, b 2/16/1936 (Brooklyn, NY), financier.
Bob Iger, b 2/10/1951 (Oceanside, NY), Walt Disney Co. CEO.
Jay Inslee, b 2/9/1951 (Seattle, WA), WA gov. (D); 2020 pres. contender.
Jesse Jackson, b 10/8/1941 (Greenville, SC), civil rights leader, former pres. contender (D).
Ketanji Brown Jackson, b 9/14/1970 (Washington, DC), U.S. Supreme Court justice.
Marc Jacobs, b 4/9/1964 (New York, NY), fashion designer.
Letitia James, b 10/18/1958 (Brooklyn, NY), NY atty. gen.
Andy Jassy, b 1/13/1968 (Scarsdale, NY), Amazon CEO.
Karine Jean-Pierre, b 8/13/1974 (Fort-de-France, Martinique), White House press sec.
Hakeem Jeffries, b 8/4/1970 (Brooklyn, NY), House minority leader (D, NY).
Jasper Johns, b 5/15/1930 (Augusta, GA), painter, printmaker.
Mike Johnson, b 1/30/1972 (Shreveport, LA), U.S. rep. (R, LA), U.S. House speaker.
Robert L. Johnson, b 4/8/1946 (Hickory, MS), Black Entertainment Television co-founder.
Sheila Johnson, b 1/25/1949 (PA), Black Entertainment Television co-founder.
Alex Jones, b 2/11/1974 (Dallas, TX), InfoWars creator, radio host.
Cleve Jones, b 10/11/1954 (W. Lafayette, IN), AIDS and LGBTQ rights activist.
Colin Kaepernick, b 11/3/1987 (Milwaukee, WI), football player, activist.
Elena Kagan, b 4/28/1960 (New York, NY), U.S. Supreme Court justice.
Tim Kaine, b 2/26/1958 (St. Paul, MN), U.S. sen. (D, VA), 2016 vice-pres. nominee.
Travis Kalanick, b 8/6/1976 (Los Angeles, CA), Uber cofounder and former CEO.
Donna Karan, b 10/2/1948 (Forest Hills, Queens, NY), fashion designer.
Jeffrey Katzenberg, b 12/21/1950 (New York, NY), entertainment exec.
Brett Kavanaugh, b 2/12/1965 (Washington, DC), U.S. Supreme Court justice.
Garrison Keillor, b 8/7/1942 (Anoka, MN), author, broadcaster.
Mark Kelly, b 2/21/1964 (Orange, NJ), U.S. sen. (D, AZ), former NASA shuttle commander.
Megyn Kelly, b 11/18/1970 (Syracuse, NY), TV commentator, host.
Brian Kemp, b 11/2/1963 (Athens, GA), GA gov. (R).
Anthony M. Kennedy, b 7/23/1936 (Sacramento, CA), former U.S. Supreme Court justice.
Caroline Kennedy, b 11/27/1957 (New York, NY), author, diplomat, daughter of Pres. Kennedy.
Robert F. Kennedy Jr., b 1/17/1954 (Washington, DC), environmental lawyer, activist; 2024 pres. contender.
John Kerry, b 12/11/1943 (Aurora, CO), fmr. U.S. climate envoy, sec. of state, U.S. sen. (D, MA); 2004 pres. nominee.
Gayle King, b 12/28/1954 (Chevy Chase, MD), TV and magazine journalist.
Adam Kinzinger, b 2/27/1978 (Kankakee, IL), fmr. U.S. rep. (R, IL).
Ron Klain, b 8/8/1961 (Indianapolis, IN), fmr. White House chief of staff.
Calvin Klein, b 11/19/1942 (Bronx, NY), fashion designer.

Amy Klobuchar, b 5/25/1960 (Plymouth, MN), U.S. sen. (D, MN); 2020 pres. contender.
Philip H. Knight, b 2/24/1938 (Portland, OR), founder and chair emeritus of Nike.
Charles G. Koch, b 5/3/1940 (Wichita, KS), Koch Industries exec., philanthropist.
Sarah Koenig, b 7/9/1969 (New York, NY), radio journalist.
Jeff Koons, b 1/21/1955 (York, PA), artist.
Ted Koppel, b 2/8/1940 (Lancashire, Eng., UK), former TV journalist.
Michael Kors, b 8/9/1959 (Merrick, NY), fashion designer.
Hoda Kotb, b 8/9/1964 (Norman, OK), TV host.
Nicholas D. Kristof, b 4/27/1959 (Chicago, IL), columnist, author.
William Kristol, b 12/23/1952 (New York, NY), editor, columnist.
Steve Kroft, b 8/22/1945 (Kokomo, IN), TV journalist.
Paul Krugman, b 2/28/1953 (Albany, NY), economist, columnist.
Jared Kushner, b 1/10/1981 (Livingston, NJ), fmr. Trump senior adviser; real estate developer.
Brian Lamb, b 10/9/1941 (Lafayette, IN), cable TV exec., journalist.
Wayne LaPierre Jr., b 11/8/1949 (Schenectady, NY), fmr. National Rifle Assn. exec. VP.
Matt Lauer, b 12/30/1957 (New York, NY), former TV journalist.
Ralph Lauren, b 10/14/1939 (Bronx, NY), fashion designer.
Annie Leibovitz, b 10/2/1949 (Waterbury, CT), photographer.
Monica Lewinsky, b 7/23/1973 (San Francisco, CA), former White House intern.
Shannon Lucid, b 1/14/1943 (Shanghai, China), NASA scientist, astronaut.
Loretta Lynch, b 5/21/1959 (Greensboro, NC), former U.S. atty. gen.
Rachel Maddow, b 4/1/1973 (Castro Valley, CA), TV/radio host, political commentator.
Michelle Malkin, b 10/20/1980 (Philadelphia, PA), political commentator.
Joe Manchin, b 8/24/47 (Farmington, WV), U.S. sen. (D/I, WV).
Rob Manfred, b 9/28/1958 (Rome, NY), MLB commissioner.
Chelsea Manning, b 12/17/1987 (Crescent, OK), Army pvt. convicted on espionage charges.
Ruth Marcus, b 5/15/1958 (Philadelphia, PA), columnist.
Meghan Markle (Duchess of Sussex), b 8/4/1981 (Los Angeles, CA), wife of UK's Prince Harry, actress.
Chris Matthews, b 12/17/1945 (Philadelphia, PA), TV journalist.
Peter Max, b 10/19/1937 (Berlin, Germany), artist.
Kevin McCarthy, b 1/26/1965 (Bakersfield, CA), fmr. U.S. House Speaker (R, CA).
Mitch McConnell, b 2/20/1942 (Tuscumbia, AL), U.S. sen. minority leader (R, KY).
Ronna Romney McDaniel, b 1973 (Austin, TX), fmr. Rep. Natl. Committee chair.
Dr. Phil McGraw, b 9/1/1950 (Vinita, OK), TV host, author.
Mark Meadows, b 7/28/1959 (Verdun, France), fmr. White House chief of staff, fmr. U.S. rep. (R, NC).
Lorne Michaels, b 11/17/44 (Toronto, ON, Canada), creator and producer of *Saturday Night Live*.
Kate Michelman, b 8/4/1942 (NJ), activist.
Michael Moore, b 4/23/1954 (Davison, MI), activist, documentary filmmaker, author.
Bill Moyers, b 6/5/1934 (Hugo, OK), TV journalist, author.
Robert S. Mueller III, b 8/7/1944 (New York, NY), special counsel who investigated Russian interference in 2016 U.S. elections; former FBI director.
David Muir, b 11/8/1973 (Syracuse, NY), TV news anchor.
Rupert Murdoch, b 3/11/1931 (Melbourne, Vic., Austral.), media exec.
Bobby Murphy, b 7/19/1988 (Berkeley, CA), Snapchat cofounder.
Patty Murray, b 10/11/1950 (Bothell, WA), Senate pres. pro tempore (D, WA).
Vivek Murthy, b 7/10/1977 (Huddersfield, Eng., UK), U.S. surgeon gen.
Elon Musk, b 6/28/1971 (Pretoria, S. Afr.), X (fmr. Twitter) owner; SpaceX and Tesla CEO.
Satya Nadella, b 8/19/1967 (Hyderabad, India), Microsoft CEO.
Ralph Nader, b 2/27/1934 (Winsted, CT), consumer advocate, independent pres. cand. (1996, 2000, '04, '08).
Carl Nassib, b 4/12/1993 (West Chester, PA), first openly gay active NFL player.
Craig Newmark, b 12/6/1952 (Morristown, NJ), founder of Craigslist.com.
Gavin Newsom, b 10/10/1967 (San Francisco, CA), CA gov. (D).
Kristi Noem, b 11/30/1971 (Watertown, SD), SD gov. (R).
Peggy Noonan, b 9/7/1950 (Brooklyn, NY), columnist, speechwriter.
Oliver North, b 10/7/1943 (San Antonio, TX), former NRA pres., Natl. Sec. Council aide, figure in Iran-contra scandal.
Eleanor Holmes Norton, b 6/13/1937 (Washington, DC), DC delegate to U.S. House (D).
Barack Obama, b 8/4/1961 (Honolulu, HI), 44th U.S. president, former U.S. sen. (D, IL).
Michelle Obama, b 1/17/1964 (Chicago, IL), former first lady, lawyer.
Soledad O'Brien, b 9/19/1966 (Smithtown, NY), TV journalist.
Alexandria Ocasio-Cortez, b 10/13/1989 (Bronx, NY), U.S. rep. (D, NY).
Norah O'Donnell, b 1/23/1974 (Washington, DC), TV journalist.
Ilhan Omar, b 10/4/1981 (Mogadishu, Somalia), U.S. rep. (D, MN).
Bill O'Reilly, b 9/10/1949 (New York, NY), fmr. TV host.
Suze Orman, b 5/5/1951 (Chicago, IL), financial adviser, TV host.
Beto O'Rourke, b 9/26/1972 (El Paso, TX), former U.S. rep. (D, TX); 2020 pres. contender.
Joel Osteen, b 3/5/1963 (Houston, TX), televangelist, author.
Michael Ovitz, b 12/14/1946 (Encino, CA), entertainment exec.
Candace Owens, b 4/29/1989 (Stamford, CT), political activist.
Mehmet Oz, b 6/11/1960 (Cleveland, OH), surgeon, TV host; 2022 U.S. sen. contender (R, PA).
Clarence Page, b 6/2/1947 (Dayton, OH), journalist, TV commentator.
Lawrence Page, b 3/26/1973 (East Lansing, MI), cofounder of Google.
Camille Paglia, b 4/2/1947 (Endicott, NY), scholar, author.
Sarah Palin, b 2/11/1964 (Sandpoint, ID), former AK gov. (R), 2008 vice-pres. nominee.
Leon E. Panetta, b 6/28/1938 (Monterey, CA), former sec. of defense, CIA director, Obama chief of staff, U.S. rep. (D, CA).
Sean Parker, b 12/3/1979 (Herndon, VA), cofounder of Napster, Facebook.
Rand Paul, b 1/7/1963 (Pittsburgh, PA), U.S. sen. (R, KY).
Jane Pauley, b 10/31/1950 (Indianapolis, IN), TV journalist.
Nancy Pelosi, b 3/26/1940 (Baltimore, MD), fmr. U.S. House Speaker (D, CA).
Karen Pence, b 1/1/1957 (Indianapolis, IN), wife of fmr. U.S. vice pres. Mike Pence.
Mike Pence, b 6/7/1959 (Columbus, IN), fmr. U.S. vice pres., IN gov. (R); 2024 pres. contender.
David Petraeus, b 11/7/1952 (Cornwall-on-Hudson, NY), former CIA director, CENTCOM cmdr.
Alexandra Petri, b 3/15/1988 (WI), columnist.
Sundar Pichai, b 6/10/1972 (Madurai, Tamil Nadu, India), Alphabet/Google CEO.
John Podesta, b 1/8/1949 (Chicago, IL), U.S. climate envoy.
Mike Pompeo, b 12/30/1963 (Orange, CA), former sec. of state, CIA director.
Jerome Powell, b 2/4/1953 (Washington, DC), Federal Reserve chair.
Reince Priebus, b 3/18/1972 (Kenosha, WI), former White House chief of staff, Rep. Natl. Committee chair.
Jen Psaki, b 12/1/1978 (Stamford, CT), former White House press sec; TV commentator.
Dan Quayle, b 2/4/1947 (Indianapolis, IN), former U.S. vice pres., U.S. sen. (R, IN).
Anna Quindlen, b 7/8/1953 (Philadelphia, PA), author, columnist.
Martha Raddatz, b 2/14/1953 (Idaho Falls, ID), TV journalist.
Vivek Ramaswamy, b 8/9/1985 (Cincinnati, OH), biotech entrepreneur, 2024 pres. contender (R).
Jorge Ramos, b 3/15/1958 (Mexico City, Mex.), TV journalist.
Dan Rather, b 10/31/1931 (Wharton, TX), TV journalist, retired anchor.
Robert Redfield, b 7/15/1951, fmr. Centers for Disease Control and Prevention dir.
Ralph Reed Jr., b 6/24/1961 (Portsmouth, VA), political adviser.
Robert B. Reich, b 6/24/1946 (Scranton, PA), economist, author, former labor sec.
Condoleezza Rice, b 11/14/1954 (Birmingham, AL), former sec. of state, natl. security adviser.
Frank Rich, b 6/2/1949 (Washington, DC), essayist, columnist.
John G. Roberts, b 1/27/1955 (Buffalo, NY), U.S. Supreme Court chief justice.
Robin Roberts, b 11/23/1960 (Tuskegee, AL), *Good Morning America* co-host.
Eugene Robinson, b 3/12/1954 (Orangeburg, SC), columnist.
Kelley Robinson, b 1986?, Human Rights Campaign pres.
V. Gene Robinson, b 5/29/1947 (Lexington, KY), first openly gay Episcopal bishop (retired).
Al Roker, b 8/20/1954 (Queens, NY), TV weather person.
Mitt Romney, b 3/12/1947 (Detroit, MI), U.S. sen. (R, UT); 2012 pres. nominee, former MA gov.
Charlie Rose, b 1/5/1942 (Henderson, NC), TV journalist.
Rod Rosenstein, b 1/13/65 (Philadelphia, PA), fmr. U.S. deputy atty. gen.
Karl Rove, b 12/25/1950 (Denver, CO), former adviser to Pres. G. W. Bush, political commentator.
Marco Rubio, b 5/28/1971 (Miami, FL), U.S. sen. (R, FL).
Edward Ruscha, b 12/16/1937 (Omaha, NE), artist.
Paul Ryan, b 1/29/1970 (Janesville, WI), 2012 vice-pres. nominee, former U.S. rep. (R, WI) and House Speaker.
Sheryl Sandberg, b 8/28/1969 (Washington, DC), fmr. Facebook exec., author.
Bernie Sanders, b 9/8/1941 (Brooklyn, NY), U.S. sen. (I, VT); 2016 and 2020 Dem. pres. contender.
Sarah Huckabee Sanders, b 8/13/1982 (Hope, AR), AR gov. (R); fmr. White House press sec.
George Santos, b 7/22/1988 (Queens, NY), expelled fmr. U.S. rep. (R, NY).
Ted Sarandos, b 7/30/1964 (Phoenix, AZ), co-CEO of Netflix.
Diane Sawyer, b 12/22/1945 (Glasgow, KY), TV journalist.
Stephen Scalise, b 10/6/1965 (New Orleans, LA), U.S. rep. (R, LA), House majority leader.
Bob Schieffer, b 2/25/1937 (Austin, TX), TV journalist.
Charles Schumer, b 11/23/1950 (Brooklyn, NY), U.S. Sen. majority leader (D, NY).

Arnold Schwarzenegger, b 7/30/1947 (Thal, Styria, Austria), actor, former CA gov. (R).
Tim Scott, b 9/19/1965 (North Charleston, SC), U.S. sen. (R, SC), 2024 pres. contender.
Al Sharpton, b 10/3/1954 (Brooklyn, NY), activist, civil rights leader, TV personality.
Amy Sherald, b 8/30/1973 (Columbus, GA), artist.
Will Shortz, b 8/26/1952 (Crawfordsville, IN), puzzle editor.
Maria Shriver, b 11/6/1955 (Chicago, IL), TV journalist, former CA first lady.
Liz Shuler, b 1970 (OR), AFL-CIO pres.
Adam Silver, b 4/25/1962 (Rye, NY), NBA commissioner.
Nate Silver, b 1/13/1978 (E. Lansing, MI), statistician.
Russell Simmons, b 10/4/1957 (Queens, NY), music producer.
Jack Smith, b 6/5/1969, U.S. Dept. of Justice special counsel; fmr. war crimes prosecutor.
Edward Snowden, b 6/21/1983 (Elizabeth City, NC), computer specialist accused of leaking classified information.
George Soros, b 8/12/1930 (Budapest, Hung.), financier, philanthropist.
Sonia Sotomayor, b 6/25/1954 (Bronx, NY), U.S. Supreme Court justice.
Evan Spiegel, b 6/4/1990 (Los Angeles, CA), Snapchat cofounder.
Steven Spielberg, b 12/18/1946 (Cincinnati, OH), movie director, producer.
Lesley Stahl, b 12/16/1941 (Swampscott, MA), TV journalist.
Shelby Steele, b 1/1/1946 (Chicago, IL), scholar, critic.
Elise Stefanik, b 7/2/1984 (Albany, NY), House conference chair (R, NY).
Gloria Steinem, b 3/25/1934 (Toledo, OH), author, feminist.
George Stephanopoulos, b 2/10/1961 (Fall River, MA), TV journalist, *Good Morning America* co-host; former pres. adviser.
Howard Stern, b 1/12/1954 (Jackson Heights, NY), radio host.
Jon Stewart, b 11/28/1962 (New York, NY), comedian, news commentator.
Martha Stewart, b 8/3/1941 (Nutley, NJ), homemaking adviser, entrepreneur, TV personality.
Biz Stone, b 3/10/1974 (Boston, MA), cofounder of Twitter.
Roger Stone, b 8/27/1952 (Norwalk, CT), political consultant.
Michael Strahan, b 11/21/1971 (Houston, TX), fmr. NFL player, TV host.
Chesley Sullenberger III, b 1/23/1951 (Denison, TX), pilot who safely landed a passenger jet in the Hudson River.
Andrew Sullivan, b 8/10/1963 (S. Godstone, Eng., UK), political commentator.
A(rthur) G(regg) Sulzberger, b 8/5/1980 (Washington, DC), *NY Times* publisher and NY Times Co. chair.
Arthur Ochs Sulzberger Jr., b 9/22/1951 (Mt. Kisco, NY), fmr. NY Times Co. chair.
Jake Tapper, b 3/12/1969 (New York, NY), TV journalist.
Marc A. Thiessen, b 1/13/1967, columnist.
Clarence Thomas, b 6/23/1948 (Savannah, GA), U.S. Supreme Court justice.
Linda Thomas-Greenfield, b 11/22/1952 (Baker, LA), U.S. amb. to United Nations.
John Thune, b 1/7/1961 (Pierre, SD), U.S. Sen. minority whip (R, SD).
Joseph Tobin, b 5/3/1952 (Detroit, MI), Rom. Cath. cardinal, archbishop of Newark, NJ.
Chuck Todd, b 4/8/1972 (Miami, FL), TV journalist, fmr. *Meet the Press* moderator.
Donald Trump, b 6/14/1946 (Jamaica, Queens, NY), 45th U.S. president; 2024 pres. nominee; real estate exec., TV personality.
Donald Trump Jr., b 12/31/1977 (New York, NY), son of Pres. Trump; Trump Org. exec.
Eric Trump, b 1/6/1984 (New York, NY), son of Pres. Trump; Trump Org. exec.
Ivanka Trump, b 10/30/1981 (New York, NY), daughter of and fmr. adviser to Pres. Trump.
Lara Trump, b 10/12/1982 (Wilmington, NC), Rep. Natl. Committee co-chair.
Melania Trump, b 4/26/1970 (Novo Mesto, [now] Slovenia), fmr. first lady, model.
Ted Turner, b 11/19/1938 (Cincinnati, OH), TV exec., philanthropist.
Neil deGrasse Tyson, b 10/5/1958 (New York, NY), astrophysicist, author, TV host.
Hamdi Ulukaya, b 10/26/1972 (Erzincan, Turkey), Chobani CEO.
Greta Van Susteren, b 6/11/1954 (Appleton, WI), attorney, TV journalist.
J(ames) D(avid) Vance, b 8/2/1984 (Middletown, OH), U.S. sen. (R, OH), 2024 vice pres. nominee.
Meredith Vieira, b 12/30/1953 (Providence, RI), TV journalist/host.
Diane von Fürstenberg, b 12/31/1946 (Brussels, Belgium), fashion designer.
Jimmy Wales, b 8/8/1966 (Huntsville, AL), cofounder of Wikipedia.
Chris Wallace, b 10/12/1947 (Chicago, IL), TV journalist.
Tim Walz, b 4/6/1964 (West Point, NE), MN gov (D); 2024 vice pres. nominee.
Alexander Wang, b 5/17/1984 (San Francisco, CA), fashion designer.
Vera Wang, b 6/27/1949 (New York, NY), fashion designer.
Elizabeth Warren, b 6/22/1949 (Oklahoma City, OK), U.S. sen. (D, MA); 2020 pres. contender.
James Watson, b 4/6/1928 (Chicago, IL), biochemist, DNA pioneer.
Shannon Watts, b 1971?, founder of Moms Demand Action.
Andrew Weil, b 6/8/1942 (Philadelphia, PA), health adviser.
Harvey Weinstein, b 3/19/1952 (Flushing, Queens, NY), movie exec.; convicted in 2020 on rape and sexual abuse charges.
Bill Weld, b 7/31/1945 (Smithtown, NY), fmr. MA gov. (R); 2020 pres. contender.
Kristen Welker, b 7/1/1976 (Philadelphia, PA), TV journalist, *Meet the Press* moderator.
Jann Wenner, b 1/7/1946 (New York, NY), founder of *Rolling Stone*.
Michael Whatley, 1968? (NC), Rep. Nat'l Committee chair.
Cornel West, b 6/23/1953 (Tulsa, OK), academic, critic; 2024 pres. contender (People's Party, Green Party).
Gretchen Whitmer, b 8/23/1971 (Lansing, MI), MI gov. (D).
Kehinde Wiley, b 2/28/1977 (Los Angeles, CA), artist.
George Will, b 5/4/1941 (Champaign, IL), journalist, author.
Brian Williams, b 5/5/1959 (Ridgewood, NJ), TV journalist.
Evan Williams, b 3/31/1972 (Clarks, NE), Twitter cofounder.
Jody Williams, b 10/9/1950 (Brattleboro, VT), peace activist, 1997 Nobel Peace Prize winner.
Marianne Williamson, b 7/8/1952 (Houston, TX), activist and author; 2020, 2024 pres. contender (D).
Oprah Winfrey, b 1/29/1954 (Kosciusko, MS), TV and media personality, entrepreneur, actress.
Anna Wintour, b 11/3/1949 (London, Eng., UK), *Vogue* editor.
Susan Wojcicki, b 7/5/1968 (Santa Clara, CA), former CEO of YouTube.
Judy Woodruff, b 11/20/1946 (Tulsa, OK), TV journalist.
Bob Woodward, b 3/26/1943 (Geneva, IL), journalist; with Carl Bernstein cracked Watergate scandal.
Steve Wozniak, b 8/11/1950 (Sunnyvale, CA), inventor, cofounder of Apple.
Steve Wynn, b 1/27/1942 (New Haven, CT), casino developer.
Andrew Yang, b 1/13/1975 (Schenectady, NY), Venture for America founder; 2020 pres. contender (D).
Janet Yellen, b 8/13/1946 (New York, NY), treasury sec.; former Federal Reserve chair.
David Zaslav, b 1/15/1960 (Brooklyn, NY), CEO of Warner Bros. Discovery.
Jeff Zients, b 11/12/1966 (Washington, DC), White House chief of staff.
Mark Zuckerberg, b 5/14/1984 (Dobbs Ferry, NY), founder of Facebook/Meta.
Mortimer Zuckerman, b 6/4/1937 (Montréal, QC, Can.), publisher, columnist.

Widely Known World Personalities of the Present

Living non-Americans only. Generally excludes current heads of state or government (see Nations of the World) and excludes most others covered elsewhere, such as in Widely Known Americans, Writers, and Entertainment or Sports Personalities.

Mahmoud Abbas (Abu Mazen), b 3/26/1935 (Safed, Palestine [now Israel]), president of the Palestinian National Authority.
Gerry Adams, b 10/6/1948 (Belfast, N. Ireland, UK), fmr. Sinn Fein leader.
Mahmoud Ahmadinejad, b 10/28/1956 (Garmsar, Iran), former Iranian pres.
Ai Weiwei, b 1957 (Beijing, China), visual artist, activist.
Akihito, b 12/23/1933 (Tokyo, Jpn.), Japanese emperor emeritus.
Albert II, b 6/6/1934 (Brussels, Belgium), former king of Belgium (1993-2013).
Prince Andrew (Duke of York), b 2/19/1960 (London, Eng., UK), second son of Queen Elizabeth II.
Princess Anne (Princess Royal), b 8/15/1950 (London, Eng., UK), daughter of Queen Elizabeth II.
Jacinda Ardern, b 7/26/1980 (Hamilton, NZ), former New Zeal. prime min.
Oscar Arias Sánchez, b 9/13/1941 (Heredia, Costa Rica), former Costa Rican pres., 1987 Nobel Peace Prize laureate.
Giorgio Armani, b 7/30/1934 (Piacenza, Italy), fashion designer.
Hanan Ashrawi, b 10/8/1946 (Nablus, Israel), Palestinian activist.
Julian Assange, b 7/3/1971 (Townsville, Qld., Austral.), founder of WikiLeaks media org.
Thomas Bach, b 12/29/1953 (Würzburg, Ger.), president of the Intl. Olympic Cmte.
Ban Ki-moon, b 6/13/1944 (Umsong, [now] South Korea), former UN sec.-gen.
Abdul Ghani Baradar, b 1968? (Yatimak, Afghanistan), Taliban co-founder, leader.
Ehud Barak, b 2/12/1942 (Mishmar Ha-Sharon Kibbutz, Israel), former Israeli min. of defense, prime min.
Beatrix, b 1/31/1938 (Baarn, Netherlands), former Dutch queen (1980-2013).
Jocelyn Bell Burnell, b 7/15/1943 (Belfast, N. Ire.), astrophysicist.
Tim Berners-Lee, b 6/8/1955 (London, Eng., UK), World Wide Web inventor.
Tony Blair, b 5/6/1953 (Edinburgh, Scot., UK), former British prime min.
Hans Blix, b 6/28/1928 (Uppsala, Swed.), former UN weapons inspector.
Bono (Paul David Hewson), b 5/20/1960 (Glasnevin, Dublin, Ire.), musician, social activist, philanthropist.
Richard Branson, b 7/18/1950 (S. London, Eng., UK), British Virgin Records and Airways founder.
Gordon Brown, b 2/20/1951 (Glasgow, Scot., UK), former British prime min.
Tina Brown, b 11/21/1953 (Maidenhead, Eng., UK), journalist, author.
Gisele Bündchen, b 7/20/1980 (Horizontina, Rio Grande do Sul, Braz.), model.
Mark Burnett, b 7/17/1960 (Myland, Eng., UK), reality TV producer.

Rhonda Byrne, b 3/12/1951 (Australia), author, TV writer and producer.
David Cameron, b 10/9/1966 (London, Eng., UK), former British prime min.
Queen Camilla, b 7/17/1947 (London, Eng., UK), wife of King Charles III.
Kim Campbell, b 3/10/1947 (Port Alberni, BC, Can.), former Canadian prime min.
Magnus Carlsen, b 11/30/1990 (Tonsberg, Norway), fmr. world chess champion.
Princess Caroline, b 1/23/1957 (Monte Carlo, Monaco), Monaco royal (eldest daughter of Prince Rainier and Princess Grace).
Raúl Castro Ruz, b 6/3/1931 (Birán, Cuba), former pres. of Cuba.
Catherine (Kate) Middleton (Princess of Wales), b 1/9/1982 (Reading, Eng., UK), wife of Prince William.
Princess Charlotte Elizabeth Diana (of Wales), b 5/2/2015 (London, Eng., UK), daughter of Prince William and Catherine.
Chen Guangcheng, b 11/12/1971 (Dongshigu, China), civil rights activist.
Yao Chen, b 10/5/1979 (Nanping, Fujian, China), actress, microblogger.
Deepak Chopra, b 1946 (New Delhi, India), writer, alternative medicine advocate.
Jean Chrétien, b 1/11/1934 (Shawinigan, QC, Can.), former Canadian prime min.
Joe (Charles Joseph) Clark, b 6/5/1939 (High River, AB, Can.), former Canadian prime min.
Simon Cowell, b 10/7/1959 (Brighton, East Sussex, Eng., UK), music exec., TV producer, former *American Idol* judge.
Dalai Lama, 14th (Tenzin Gyatso), b 7/6/1935 (Taktser, Amdo, Tibet), Buddhist leader; 1989 Nobel Peace Prize winner.
Richard Dawkins, b 3/26/1941 (Nairobi, Kenya), ethologist, evolutionary biologist, author.
Shirin Ebadi, b 6/21/1947 (Hamadan, Iran), human rights activist, 2003 Nobel Peace Prize winner.
Prince Edward (Duke of Edinburgh), b 3/10/1964 (London, Eng., UK), third son of Queen Elizabeth II.
Daniel Ek, b 2/21/1983 (Stockholm, Sweden), Spotify cofounder/CEO.
Mohamed ElBaradei, b 6/17/1942 (Cairo, Egypt), former director general of the International Atomic Energy Agency (IAEA); 2005 Nobel Peace Prize winner.
Francis (Jorge Mario Bergoglio), b 12/17/1936 (Buenos Aires, Argentina), pope of Roman Catholic Church.
Fumihito, Prince Akishino, b 11/30/1965 (Tokyo, Jpn.), crown prince of Japan.
John Galliano, b 11/28/1960 (Gibraltar, UK), fashion designer.
Prince George Alexander Louis (of Wales), b 7/22/2013 (London, Eng., UK), elder son of Prince William and Catherine.
Wael Ghonim, b 12/23/1980 (Cairo, Egypt), computer engineer and internet activist.
Jane Goodall, b 4/3/1934 (London, Eng., UK), anthropologist, primatologist.
Juan Guaidó, b 7/28/1983 (La Guaira, Venezuela), Venezuelan opposition leader.
António Guterres, b 4/30/1949 (Lisbon, Portugal), UN sec.-gen.
Jürgen Habermas, b 6/18/1929 (Dusseldorf, Ger.), philosopher.
Stephen Harper, b 4/30/1959 (Toronto, ON, Can.), former Canadian prime min.
Prince Henry (Harry) (Duke of Sussex), b 9/15/1984 (London, Eng., UK), younger son of King Charles III and Diana.
Damien Hirst, b 6/7/1965 (Bristol, Eng., UK), artist.
David Hockney, b 7/9/1937 (Bradford, Eng., UK), artist.
Hu Jintao, b 12/21/1942 (Shanghai, China), former pres. of China.
Jensen Huang, b 2/17/1963 (Tainan, Taiwan), pres. and CEO of Nvidia.
Boris Johnson, b 6/19/1964 (New York, NY), former British prime min.
Juan Carlos I, b 1/5/1938 (Rome, Italy), former king of Spain (1975-2014).
Hamid Karzai, b 12/24/1957 (Kandahar, Afghanistan), former pres. of Afghanistan.
Garry Kasparov, b 4/13/1963 (Baku, Azerbaijan, USSR), former world chess champion; Russian pro-democracy leader.
Ayatollah Ali Khamenei, b 7/17/1939 (Mashhad, Iran), Supreme Leader, cleric; former president of Iran.
Imram Khan, b 10/5/1952 (Lahore, Pakistan), fmr. Pakistani prime min.
Marie Kondo, b 10/9/1984 (Tokyo, Japan), organizing specialist.
Christine Lagarde, b 1/1/1956 (Paris, Fr.), European Central Bank pres.
Carrie Lam, b 5/13/1957 (Wan Chai, Hong Kong), fmr. chief executive of Hong Kong.
Jean-Marie Le Pen, b 6/20/1928 (La Trinité-sur-Mer, Fr.), French right-wing politician.
Marine Le Pen, b 8/5/1968 (Neuilly-sur-Seine, Fr.), head of France's far-right party (2011-21).
Tzipi Livni, b 7/5/1958 (Tel Aviv, Isr.), attorney, Israeli politician.
Prince Louis Arthur Charles (of Wales), b 4/23/2018 (London, Eng., UK), younger son of Prince William and Catherine.
John Major, b 3/29/1943 (Wimbledon, Eng., UK), former British prime min.
Nouri al-Malaki, b 7/1/1950 (Iraq), former prime min. of Iraq.
Imelda Marcos, b 7/2/1929 (Manila, Philip.), former first lady of the Philippines.
Paul Martin, b 8/28/1938 (Windsor, ON, Can.), former prime min. of Canada.
Empress Masako, b 12/9/1963 (Tokyo, Jpn.), empress of Japan.
Theresa May, b 10/1/1956 (Eastbourne, Eng., UK), former British prime min.
Stella McCartney, b 9/13/1971 (London, Eng., UK), fashion designer.
Dmitry Medvedev, b 9/14/1965 (Leningrad, USSR [now Russia]), fmr. prime min., president of Russia.
Rigoberta Menchú, b 1/9/1959 (Aldea Chimel, Guatemala), human rights activist, 1992 Nobel Peace Prize winner.
Angela Merkel, b 7/17/1954 (Hamburg, Ger.), first woman chancellor of Germany.
Jean-Marie Messier, b 12/13/1956 (Grenoble, Fr.), former CEO of Vivendi Universal.
Michiko, b 10/20/1934 (Tokyo, Japan), empress emerita of Japan.
Kate Moss, b 1/16/1974 (Addiscombe, Surrey, Eng., UK), model.
Archie Harrison Mountbatten-Windsor, b 5/6/2019 (London, Eng., UK), son of Prince Harry and Meghan Markle.
Lilibet Diana Mountbatten-Windsor, b 6/4/2021 (Santa Barbara, CA), daughter of Prince Harry and Meghan Markle.
Renhō Murata, b 11/28/1968 (Tokyo, Japan), first woman leader of Japan's Democratic Party.
Queen Noor (Lisa Halaby), b 8/23/1951 (Washington, DC), American-born widow of Jordan's King Hussein.
Ehud Olmert, b 9/30/1945 (Binyamina, Palestine), former prime min. of Israel.
Daniel Ortega Saavedra, b 11/11/1945 (La Libertad, Nicar.), Nicaraguan pres., Sandinista leader.
Ren Zhengfei, b 10/25/1944 (Guizhou, China), founder and CEO of Huawei Technologies.
Gerhard Richter, b 2/9/1932 (Dresden, Ger.), artist.
Mary Robinson, b 5/21/1944 (Ballina, Co. Mayo, Ire.), former Irish pres., former UN High Commissioner for Human Rights.
Arundhati Roy, b 11/24/1961 (Shillong, Meghalaya, India), author, political activist.
Ségolène Royal, b 9/22/1953 (Dakar, Senegal), French socialist politician.
Muqtada al-Sadr, b 8/4/1974 (Najaf, Iraq), extremist Shiite cleric.
Mohammad bin Salman, b 8/31/1985 (Riyadh, Saudi Arabia), Saudi crown prince.
Nicolas Sarkozy, b 1/28/1955 (Paris, France), former French pres.
Gerhard Schröder, b 4/7/1944 (Mossenburg, Ger.), former German chancellor.
Nawaz Sharif, b 12/25/1949 (Lahore, Pakistan), former Pakistan prime min.
Ayatollah Ali al-Sistani, b 8/4/1930 (Mashhad, Iran), major Iraqi Shiite religious leader.
Carlos Slim Helú, b 1/28/1940 (Mexico City, Mex.), founder of Grupo Carso; former chair of Telmex, América Móvil.
Princess Stephanie, b 2/1/1965 (Monte Carlo, Monaco), youngest child of Prince Rainier and Princess Grace.
Dominique Strauss-Kahn, b 4/25/1949 (Neuilly-sur-Seine, France), former Intl. Monetary Fund managing dir.
Rishi Sunak, b 5/12/1980 (Southampton, Eng., UK), former British prime min.
Aung San Suu Kyi, b 6/19/1945 (Rangoon, Myanmar), political activist, 1991 Nobel Peace Prize winner; deposed Myanmar govt. leader.
Valentina Tereshkova, b 3/6/1937 (Maslennikovo, Russia, USSR), first woman in space.
Greta Thunberg, b 1/3/2003 (Stockholm, Swed.), environmental activist.
Liz Truss, b 7/26/1975 (Oxford, Eng., UK), former British prime min.
Ursula von der Leyen, b 10/8/1958 (Brussels, Belg.), first woman European Commission pres.
Lech Walesa, b 9/29/1943 (Popowo, Pol.), Solidarity leader, former pres. of Poland; 1983 Nobel Peace Prize winner.
Justin Welby, b 1/6/1956 (London, Eng., UK), archbishop of Canterbury.
Prince William (of Wales), b 6/21/1982 (London, Eng., UK), elder son of King Charles III and Diana; heir apparent to British throne.
Rowan Williams, b 6/14/1950 (Ystradgynlais, Wales, UK), former archbishop of Canterbury.
Malala Yousafzai, b 7/12/1997 (Mingora, Pakistan), activist for girls' education, 2014 Nobel Peace Prize winner.
Muhammad Yunus, b 6/28/1940 (Chittagong, Bangladesh), economist, 2006 Nobel Peace Prize winner.
Mohammad Javad Zarif, b 1/8/1960 (Tehran, Iran), former Irani minister of foreign affairs.

Architects

Alvar Aalto, 1898-1976, Säynätsalo Town Hall, Vuoksenniska Church, Finland.
Max Abramovitz, 1908-2004, Avery Fisher Hall, New York, NY; U.S. Steel Tower (Bldg.), Pittsburgh, PA.
Tadao Ando, b 1941, Modern Art Museum, Ft. Worth, TX; Stone Hill Center, MA.
Michael Arad, b 1969, Natl. 9/11 Memorial, New York, NY.
Henry Bacon, 1866-1924, Lincoln Memorial, Washington, DC.
Benjamin Banneker, 1731-1806, African American inventor, astronomer, mathematician; helped design and lay out Washington, DC.
Pietro Belluschi, 1899-1994, Juilliard School, Lincoln Center, Pan Am Bldg.

(now MetLife Bldg.) with Walter Gropius, New York, NY.

Marcel Breuer, 1902-81, Whitney Museum of American Art (now Met Breuer) (with Hamilton Smith), New York, NY.

Filippo Brunelleschi, 1377-1446, Santa Maria del Fiore Cathedral, Florence, Italy.

Charles Bulfinch, 1763-1844, State House, Boston, MA; Capitol (part), Wash., DC.

Gordon Bunshaft, 1909-90, Lever House, New York, NY; Hirshhorn Museum, Washington, DC.

Daniel H. Burnham, 1846-1912, Union Station, Washington, DC; Flatiron Bldg., New York, NY.

Santiago Calatrava, b 1951, World Trade Center transport hub, New York, NY.

Irwin Chanin, 1892-1988, theaters, skyscrapers, New York, NY.

David Childs, b 1941, Washington Mall Master Plan/Constitution Gardens, Washington, DC; One World Trade Center, New York, NY.

Lucio Costa, 1902-98, master plan for city of Brasilia, Brazil (with Oscar Niemeyer).

Ralph Adams Cram, 1863-1942, Cath. of St. John the Divine, New York, NY; U.S. Military Acad. (part), West Point, NY.

Gustave Eiffel, 1832-1923, Eiffel Tower, Paris.

Norman Foster, b 1935, Commerzbank Headquarters, Frankfurt-am-Main, Ger.; London Millennium Bridge, 30 St. Mary Axe ("The Gherkin"), London, Eng., UK.

James Ingo Freed, 1930-2005, Holocaust Memorial Museum, Washington, DC; Jacob K. Javits Center, New York, NY.

R. Buckminster Fuller, 1895-1983, U.S. Pavilion (geodesic domes), Expo 67, Montréal, QC, Can.

Antoni Gaudí, 1852-1926, Basilica and Expiatory Temple of the Sagrada Familia, Barcelona, Spain.

Frank O. Gehry, b 1929, Guggenheim Museum, Bilbao, Spain; Walt Disney Concert Hall, Los Angeles, CA.

Cass Gilbert, 1859-1934, Custom House, Woolworth Bldg., New York, NY; Supreme Court Bldg., Washington, DC.

Bertram G. Goodhue, 1869-1924, Capitol, Lincoln, NE; St. Thomas's Church, St. Bartholomew's Church, New York, NY.

Michael Graves, 1934-2015, Portland Bldg., Portland, OR; Humana Bldg., Louisville, KY.

Walter Gropius, 1883-1969, Pan Am Bldg. (now MetLife Bldg.) (with Pietro Belluschi), New York, NY.

Zaha Hadid, 1950-2016, Rosenthal Center for Contemporary Art, Cincinnati, OH; London Aquatics Centre, Eng., UK.

Lawrence Halprin, 1916-2009, Ghirardelli Sq., San Francisco, CA; Nicollet Mall, Minneapolis, MN; FDR Memorial, Washington, DC.

Peter Harrison, 1716-75, Touro Synagogue, Redwood Library, Newport, RI.

Wallace K. Harrison, 1895-1981, Metropolitan Opera House, Lincoln Center, New York, NY.

Thomas Hastings, 1860-1929, NY Public Library (with John Carrère), Frick Mansion, New York, NY.

James Hoban, 1762-1831, White House, Washington, DC.

Raymond Hood, 1881-1934, Rockefeller Center (part), Daily News Bldg., New York, NY; Tribune Tower, Chicago, IL.

Richard M. Hunt, 1827-95, Metropolitan Museum (part), New York, NY; Biltmore Estate, Asheville, NC.

Arata Isozaki, 1931-2022, Museum of Contemporary Art, Los Angeles, CA.

Toyo Ito, b 1941, Sendai Mediatheque, Sendai, Japan; Tower of Winds, Yokohama, Japan.

Helmut Jahn, 1940-2021, United Airlines Terminal, O'Hare Airport, Chicago, IL.

William Le Baron Jenney, 1832-1907, Home Insurance Bldg. (demolished 1931), Chicago, IL.

Philip C. Johnson, 1906-2005, AT&T Bldg. (now 550 Madison Ave.), New York, NY; Transco (now Williams) Tower, Houston, TX.

Albert Kahn, 1869-1942, General Motors Bldg. (now Cadillac Place), Detroit, MI.

Louis Kahn, 1901-74, Salk Laboratory, La Jolla, CA; Yale Art Gallery, New Haven, CT.

Francis Kéré, b 1965, Centre for Earth Architecture, Mopti, Mali.

Rem Koolhaas, b 1944, Seattle Central Library, Seattle, WA.

Christopher Grant LaFarge, 1862-1938, Roman Catholic Chapel, West Point, NY.

Benjamin H. Latrobe, 1764-1820, Capitol (part), Washington, DC; State Capitol Bldg., Richmond, VA.

Le Corbusier (Charles-Edouard Jeanneret), 1887-1965, Salvation Army Hostel, Swiss Dormitory, Paris, France; master plan for cities of Algiers and Buenos Aires.

William Lescaze, 1896-1969, Philadelphia Savings Fund Society, PA; Borg-Warner Bldg., Chicago, IL.

Daniel Libeskind, b 1946, developed master plan for the rebuilding of World Trade Center site, New York, NY.

Maya Lin, b 1959, Vietnam Veterans Mem., Washington, DC.

Charles Rennie Mackintosh, 1868-1928, Glasgow School of Art; Hill House, Helensburgh, Scot., UK.

Bernard R. Maybeck, 1862-1957, Hearst Hall, Univ. of CA, Berkeley; First Church of Christ Scientist, Berkeley, CA.

Charles F. McKim, 1847-1909, Boston Public Library; Columbia Univ. (part), New York, NY.

Charles M. McKim, 1920-2017, KUHT-TV Transmitter Bldg., Lutheran Church of the Redeemer, Houston, TX.

Richard Meier, b 1934, Getty Center, Los Angeles, CA; High Museum of Art, Atlanta, GA.

Ludwig Mies van der Rohe, 1886-1969, Seagram Bldg. (with Philip C. Johnson), New York, NY; National Gallery, Berlin, Ger.

Robert Mills, 1781-1855, Washington Monument, Washington, DC.

Charles Moore, 1925-93, Sea Ranch, nr. San Francisco, CA; Piazza d'Italia, New Orleans, LA.

Julia Morgan, 1872-1957, Hearst Castle, San Simeon, CA.

John Nash, 1752-1835, Buckingham Palace, London, Eng., UK.

Richard J. Neutra, 1892-1970, Orange Co. Courthouse, Santa Ana, CA.

Oscar Niemeyer, 1907-2012, government buildings, Brasilia Palace Hotel, Brasilia, Braz.

Gyo Obata, 1923-2022, Natl. Air and Space Museum, Smithsonian Inst., Washington, DC; Dallas-Ft. Worth Airport, TX.

Frederick L. Olmsted, 1822-1903, Central Park, New York, NY; Fairmount Park, Philadelphia, PA.

I(eoh) M(ing) Pei, 1917-2019, East Wing, Natl. Gallery of Art, Washington, DC; Pyramid, The Louvre, Paris, Fr.; Rock & Roll Hall of Fame and Museum, Cleveland, OH.

Cesar Pelli, 1926-2019, World Financial Center, Carnegie Hall Tower, New York, NY; Petronas Twin Towers, Malaysia.

William Pereira, 1909-85, Cape Canaveral, FL; Transamerica Pyramid, San Francisco.

Renzo Piano, b 1937, Pompidou Centre, Paris, Fr.; New York Times Bldg., New York, NY; The Shard, London, Eng., UK.

John Russell Pope, 1874-1937, National Gallery, Jefferson Memorial, Wash., DC.

John Portman, 1924-2017, Peachtree Center, Atlanta, GA.

George Browne Post, 1837-1913, NY Stock Exchange, New York, NY; Capitol, Madison, WI.

James Renwick Jr., 1818-95, Grace Church, St. Patrick's Cathedral, New York, NY; Smithsonian Institution (Castle), Washington, DC.

Henry H. Richardson, 1838-86, Trinity Church, Boston, MA.

Kevin Roche, 1922-2019, Oakland Museum, Oakland, CA; Fine Arts Center, Univ. of Massachusetts, Amherst, MA.

James Gamble Rogers, 1867-1947, Columbia-Presbyterian Medical Ctr., New York, NY; Northwestern Univ., Evanston, IL.

John Wellborn Root, 1887-1963, Palmolive Bldg., Chicago, IL; Hotel Statler (now Capital Hilton), Washington, DC.

Paul Rudolph, 1918-97, Jewitt Art Center, Wellesley College, MA; Art & Architecture Bldg., Yale Univ., New Haven, CT.

Eero Saarinen, 1910-61, Gateway to the West Arch, St. Louis, MO; TWA Flight Center, JFK Airport, New York, NY.

Kazuyo Sejima, b 1956, 21st Century Museum of Contemporary Art (with Ryue Nishizawa), Kanazawa, Japan.

Kodja Mimar Sinan, 1489-1588, chief court architect of Ottoman dynasty.

Louis Skidmore, 1897-1962, Atomic Energy Commission town site, Oak Ridge, TN; Terrace Plaza Hotel, Cincinnati, OH.

Norma Merrick Sklarek, 1928-2012, Terminal One, Los Angeles International Airport, CA.

Clarence S. Stein, 1882-1975, Temple Emanu-El, New York, NY.

Edward Durell Stone, 1902-78, interior of Radio City Music Hall, Museum of Modern Art, New York, NY.

Louis H. Sullivan, 1856-1924, Auditorium Bldg., Chicago, IL.

Kenzo Tange, 1913-2005, Hiroshima Peace Park, 1964 Tokyo Olympic stadiums, Japan.

Richard Upjohn, 1802-78, Trinity Church, New York, NY.

Max O. Urbahn, 1912-95, Vehicle Assembly Bldg., Cape Canaveral, FL.

Joern Utzon, 1918-2008, Sydney Opera House, NSW, Australia.

William Van Alen, 1883-1954, Chrysler Building, New York, NY.

Calvert Vaux, 1824-95, Central Park, New York, NY; Prospect Park, Brooklyn, NY.

Robert Venturi, 1925-2018, Gordon Wu Hall, Princeton, NJ; Mielparque Nikko Kirifuri Resort, Japan.

Ralph T. Walker, 1889-1973, NY Telephone (now Verizon) Bldg., Irving Trust Bldg. (now 1 Wall St.), New York, NY.

Wang Shu, b 1963, Ningbo Museum, China.

Roland A. Wank, 1898-1970, Cincinnati Union Terminal, OH; head architect, 1933-44, Tennessee Valley Authority.

Stanford White, 1853-1906, Washington Arch in Washington Square Park, first Madison Square Garden, New York, NY.

Christopher Wren, 1632-1723, St. Paul's Cathedral, London, Eng., UK.

Frank Lloyd Wright, 1867-1959, Imperial Hotel, Tokyo, Japan; Guggenheim Museum, New York, NY; Kaufmann "Fallingwater" house, Mill Run, PA; Taliesin West, Scottsdale, AZ.

Tom Wright, b 1957, Burj Al Arab hotel, Dubai, UAE.

William Wurster, 1895-1973, Ghirardelli Sq., San Francisco, CA.

Minoru Yamasaki, 1912-86, World Trade Center (destroyed 2001), New York, NY.

Artists, Photographers, and Sculptors of the Past

Artists are painters unless otherwise indicated.

Berenice Abbott, 1898-1991, (U.S.) photographer. Documentary of New York City, *Changing New York* (1939).
Ansel Easton Adams, 1902-84, (U.S.) photographer. Landscapes of the American Southwest.
Washington Allston, 1779-1843, (U.S.) landscapist. *Belshazzar's Feast*.
Albrecht Altdorfer, 1480-1538, (Ger.) landscapist.
Fra Angelico, c. 1400-55, (It.) Renaissance muralist. *Madonna of the Linen Drapers' Guild*.
Diane Arbus, 1923-71, (U.S.) photographer. Disturbing images.
Alexsandr Archipenko, 1887-1964, (U.S.) sculptor. *Boxing Match, Medranos*.
Jean Arp, 1887-1966, (Fr.) sculptor and painter. Founder of Dada movement.
Richard Artschwager, 1923-2013, (U.S.) painter and sculptor. *Table With Pink Tablecloth*.
Eugène Atget, 1856-1927, (Fr.) photographer. Paris life.
John James Audubon, 1785-1851, (U.S.) *Birds of America*.
Richard Avedon, 1923-2004, (U.S.) fashion and celebrity photographer.
Hans Baldung-Grien, 1484-1545, (Ger.) *Todentanz*.
Ernst Barlach, 1870-1938, (Ger.) Expressionist sculptor. *Man Drawing a Sword*.
Frédéric-Auguste Bartholdi, 1834-1904, (Fr.) sculptor. *Liberty Enlightening the World* (Statue of Liberty).
Fra Bartolommeo, 1472-1517, (It.) *Vision of St. Bernard*.
Romare Bearden, 1911-88, (U.S.) collage and other media. *The Visitation*.
Aubrey Beardsley, 1872-98, (Br.) illustrator. *Salome, Lysistrata, Morte d'Arthur, Volpone*.
Cecil Beaton, 1904-80, (Br.) fashion and celebrity photographer.
Max Beckmann, 1884-1950, (Ger.) Expressionist. *The Descent From the Cross*.
Gentile Bellini, 1426-1507, (It.) Renaissance. *Procession in St. Mark's Square*.
Giovanni Bellini, 1428-1516, (It.) Renaissance. *St. Francis in Ecstasy*.
Jacopo Bellini, 1400-70, (It.) Renaissance. *Crucifixion*.
George Wesley Bellows, 1882-1925, (U.S.) sports artist, portraitist, landscapist. *Stag at Sharkey's, Edith Clavell*.
Thomas Hart Benton, 1889-1975, (U.S.) American regionalist. *Threshing Wheat, Arts of the West*.
Ruth Bernhard, 1905-2006, (Ger.-U.S.) photographer. Black-and-white studies of female nudes.
Gianlorenzo Bernini, 1598-1680, (It.) Baroque sculptor. *The Assumption*.
Albert Bierstadt, 1830-1902, (U.S.) landscapist. *The Rocky Mountains, Mount Corcoran*.
George Caleb Bingham, 1811-79, (U.S.) American frontier. *Fur Traders Descending the Missouri*.
William Blake, 1757-1827, (Br.) engraver. *Book of Job, Songs of Innocence, Songs of Experience*.
Rosa Bonheur, 1822-99, (Fr.) Realist. *The Horse Fair*.
Pierre Bonnard, 1867-1947, (Fr.) Intimist. *The Breakfast Room, Girl in a Straw Hat*.
Gutzon Borglum, 1867-1941, (U.S.) sculptor. Mt. Rushmore Memorial.
Hieronymus Bosch, 1450-1516, (Flem.) religious allegories. *The Crowning With Thorns*.
Fernando Botero, 1932-2023, (Colombia) figurative painter and sculptor.
Sandro Botticelli, 1444-1510, (It.) Renaissance. *Birth of Venus, Adoration of the Magi, Guiliano de' Medici*.
Louise Bourgeois, 1911-2010, (Fr.) sculptor. *Maman*.
Margaret Bourke-White, 1904-71, (U.S.) photographer, photojournalist. WWII, USSR, rural South during the Depression.
Mathew Brady, c. 1823-96, (U.S.) photographer. Civil War.
Constantin Brancusi, 1876-1957, (Romania-Fr.) Nonobjective sculptor. *Flying Turtle, The Kiss*.
Georges Braque, 1882-1963, (Fr.) Cubist. *Violin and Palette*.
Pieter Bruegel the Elder, c. 1525-69, (Flem.) Renaissance. *The Peasant Dance, Hunters in the Snow, Magpie on the Gallows*.
Pieter Bruegel the Younger, 1564-1638, (Flem.) Baroque. *Village Fair, The Crucifixion*.
Edward Burne-Jones, 1833-98, (Br.) Pre-Raphaelite artist-craftsman. *The Mirror of Venus*.
Alexander Calder, 1898-1976, (U.S.) sculptor. *Lobster Trap and Fish Tail*.
Julia Margaret Cameron, 1815-79, (Br.) photographer, prominent portraitist.
Robert Capa (Endre Friedmann), 1913-54, (Hung.-U.S.) photographer, war photojournalist. Invasion of Normandy.
Michelangelo Merisi da Caravaggio, 1573-1610, (It.) Baroque. *The Supper at Emmaus*.
Emily Carr, 1871-1945, (Can.) landscapist. *Blunden Harbour, Big Raven, Rushing Sea of Undergrowth*.
Carlo Carrà, 1881-1966, (It.) Metaphysical school. *Lot's Daughters, The Enchanted Room*.
Leonora Carrington, 1917-2011, (Br.) Surrealist. *The Inn of the Dawn Horse (Self-Portrait)*.
Henri Cartier-Bresson, 1908-2004, (Fr.) photographer. *Imagenes à la sauvette*.
Mary Cassatt, 1844-1926, (U.S.) Impressionist. *The Cup of Tea, Woman Bathing, The Boating Party*.
George Catlin, 1796-1872, (U.S.) American Indian life. *Gallery of Indians, Buffalo Dance*.
Benvenuto Cellini, 1500-71, (It.) Mannerist sculptor, goldsmith. *Perseus and Medusa*.
Paul Cézanne, 1839-1906, (Fr.) Post-Impressionist. *Card Players, Mont-Sainte-Victoire With Large Pine Trees*.
Marc Chagall, 1887-1985, (Russ.) Jewish life and folklore. *I and the Village, The Praying Jew*.
John Chamberlain, 1927-2011, (U.S.) sculptor of automobile metal.
Jean Simeon Chardin, 1699-1779, (Fr.) still lifes. *The Kiss, The Grace*.
Giorgio de Chirico, 1888-1978, (It.) founded the Metaphysical school. *Enigma of an Autumn Night*.
Christo (Javacheff), 1935-2020, (Bulg.), large-scale environmental installation artist with wife Jeanne-Claude. *The Gates, Surrounded Islands*.
Frederick Church, 1826-1900, (U.S.) Hudson River school. *Niagara, Andes of Ecuador*.
Giovanni Cimabue, 1240-1302, (It.) Byzantine mosaicist. *Madonna Enthroned With St. Francis*.
Claude (Lorrain) (Claude Gellée), 1600-82, (Fr.) Ideal-landscapist. *The Enchanted Castle*.
Chuck Close, 1940-2021, (U.S.) photo-realistic and conceptual portraitist.
Thomas Cole, 1801-48, (U.S.) Hudson River school. *The Ox-Bow, In the Catskills*.
John Constable, 1776-1837, (Br.) landscapist. *Salisbury Cathedral From the Bishop's Grounds*.
John Singleton Copley, 1738-1815, (U.S.) portraitist. *Samuel Adams, Watson and the Shark*.
Lovis Corinth, 1858-1925, (Ger.) Expressionist. *Apocalypse*.
Jean-Baptiste-Camille Corot, 1796-1875, (Fr.) landscapist. *Souvenir de Mortefontaine, Pastorale*.
Correggio, 1494-1534, (It.) Renaissance muralist. *Mystic Marriages of St. Catherine*.
Gustave Courbet, 1819-77, (Fr.) Realist. *The Artist's Studio*.
Lucas Cranach the Elder, 1472-1553, (Ger.) Protestant Reformation portraitist. *Luther*.
Bill Cunningham, 1929-2016, (U.S.) fashion photographer.
Imogen Cunningham, 1883-1976, (U.S.) photographer, portraitist. Plants.
Nathaniel Currier, 1813-88, and **James M. Ives**, 1824-95, (both U.S.) lithographers. *A Midnight Race on the Mississippi, American Forest Scene—Maple Sugaring*.
John Steuart Curry, 1897-1946, (U.S.) Americana, murals. *Baptism in Kansas*.
Edward S. Curtis, 1868-1952, (U.S.) photographer. *The North American Indian*.
Louis Daguerre, 1787-1851, (Fr.) photographer. Invented daguerreotype process.
Salvador Dalí, 1904-89, (Sp.) Surrealist. *Persistence of Memory, The Crucifixion*.
Honoré Daumier, 1808-79, (Fr.) caricaturist. *The Third-Class Carriage*.
Jacques-Louis David, 1748-1825, (Fr.) Neoclassicist. *The Oath of the Horatii*.
Arthur Davies, 1862-1928, (U.S.) Romantic landscapist. *Unicorns, Leda and the Dioscuri*.
Edgar Degas, 1834-1917, (Fr.) Realist/Impressionist. *The Ballet Class*.
Willem de Kooning, 1904-97, (Neth.-U.S.) Abstract Expressionist. *Excavation, Woman I, Door to the River*.
Eugène Delacroix, 1798-1863, (Fr.) Romantic. *Massacre at Chios, Liberty Leading the People*.
Paul Delaroche, 1797-1856, (Fr.) historical themes. *Children of Edward IV*.
Luca Della Robbia, 1400-82, (It.) Renaissance terra-cotta. *Cantoria* (singing gallery), Florence cathedral.
Donatello, 1386-1466, (It.) Renaissance sculptor. *David, Gattamelata*.
Aaron Douglas, 1899-79, (U.S.) Harlem Renaissance illustrator and muralist.
Jean Dubuffet, 1902-85, (Fr.) painter, sculptor, printmaker. *Group of Four Trees*.
Marcel Duchamp, 1887-1968, (Fr.) Dadaist. *Nude Descending a Staircase, No. 2*.
Raoul Dufy, 1877-1953, (Fr.) Fauvist. *Chateau and Horses*.
Asher Brown Durand, 1796-1886, (U.S.) Hudson River school. *Kindred Spirits*.
Albrecht Dürer, 1471-1528, (Ger.) Renaissance painter, engraver, woodcuts. *St. Jerome in His Study, Melencolia I*.
Anthony van Dyck, 1599-1641, (Flem.) Baroque portraitist. *Portrait of Charles I Hunting*.
Thomas Eakins, 1844-1916, (U.S.) Realist. *The Gross Clinic*.
Alfred Eisenstaedt, 1898-1995, (Ger.-U.S.) photographer, photojournalist. Famous photo, V-J Day, Aug. 14, 1945.
Peter Henry Emerson, 1856-1936, (Br.) photographer. Promoted photography as an independent art form.
Jacob Epstein, 1880-1959, (Br.) religious and allegorical sculptor. *Genesis, Ecce Homo*.
Erté (Romain de Tiertoff), 1892-1990, (Fr.) painter, fashion and stage designer.
Walker Evans, 1903-75, (U.S.) photographer. Documented Great Depression.
Jan van Eyck, c. 1390-1441, (Flem.) naturalistic panels. *Adoration of the Lamb*.
Horst Faas, 1933-2012, (Ger.) Vietnam War photographer.
Roger Fenton, 1819-69, (Br.) photographer. Crimean War.
Anselm Feuerbach, 1829-80, (Ger.) Romantic Classicist. *Judgment of Paris, Iphigenia*.
John Bernard Flannagan, 1895-1942, (U.S.) animal sculptor. *Triumph of the Egg*.
Jean-Honoré Fragonard, 1732-1806, (Fr.) Rococo. *The Swing*.
Robert Frank, 1924-2019, (Switz.-U.S.) photographer. *The Americans*.
Helen Frankenthaler, 1928-2011, (U.S.) Abstract Expressionist. *Mountains and Sea*.
Daniel Chester French, 1850-1931, (U.S.) sculptor. *The Minute Man of Concord*; seated *Lincoln*, Lincoln Memorial, Washington, DC.

Lucian Freud, 1922-2011, (Ger.-Br.) portraitist. *Girl With Roses*.
Caspar David Friedrich, 1774-1840, (Ger.) Romantic landscapist. *Man and Woman Gazing at the Moon*.
Thomas Gainsborough, 1727-88, (Br.) portraitist. *The Blue Boy*, *The Watering Place*, *The Parish Clerk*.
Alexander Gardner, 1821-82, (U.S.) photographer. Civil War, railroad construction, Great Plains Indians.
Paul Gauguin, 1848-1903, (Fr.) Post-Impressionist. *The Tahitians*, *Spirit of the Dead Watching*.
Lorenzo Ghiberti, 1378-1455, (It.) Renaissance sculptor. "Gates of Paradise" baptistery doors, Florence, It.
Alberto Giacometti, 1901-66, (Switz.) attenuated sculptures of solitary figures. *Man Pointing*.
Giorgione, c. 1477-1510, (It.) Renaissance. *The Tempest*.
Giotto di Bondone, 1267-1337, (It.) Renaissance. *Presentation of Christ in the Temple*.
François Girardon, 1628-1715, (Fr.) Baroque sculptor of classical themes. *Apollo Tended by the Nymphs*.
Milton Glaser, 1929-2020, (U.S.) graphic designer. I ♥ NY logo.
Edward Gorey, 1925-2000, (U.S.) illustrator. *The Doubtful Guest*.
Arshile Gorky, 1905-48, (U.S.) Surrealist. *The Liver Is the Cock's Comb*.
Francisco de Goya y Lucientes, 1746-1828, (Sp.) painter, printmaker. *The Naked Maja*, *The Disasters of War* (etchings).
El Greco (Domenikos Theotokopoulos), 1541-1614, (Gr.-Sp.) painter, sculptor. *View of Toledo*, *Assumption of the Virgin*.
Horatio Greenough, 1805-52, (U.S.) Neoclassical sculptor.
Matthias Grünewald, 1480-1528, (Ger.) mystical religious themes. *The Resurrection*.
Frans Hals, c. 1580-1666, (Neth.) portraitist. *Laughing Cavalier*, *Gypsy Girl*.
Richard Hamilton, 1922-2011, (Br.) Pop Art. *Just What Is It That Makes Today's Homes So Different, So Appealing?*
Austin Hansen, 1910-96, (U.S.) photographer. Harlem, NY, life.
Keith Haring, 1958-90, (U.S.) painter, muralist. *Crack is Wack*.
Childe Hassam, 1859-1935, (U.S.) Impressionist. *Southwest Wind*, *July 14 Rue Daunon*.
Carmen Herrera, 1915-2022, (Cuba-U.S.) abstract painter.
Edward Hicks, 1780-1849, (U.S.) folk. *The Peaceable Kingdom*.
Lewis Wickes Hine, 1874-1940, (U.S.) photographer. Studies of immigrants, children in industry.
Hans Hofmann, 1880-1966, (U.S.) early Abstract Expressionist. *Spring*, *The Gate*.
William Hogarth, 1697-1764, (Br.) caricaturist. *The Rake's Progress*.
Katsushika Hokusai, 1760-1849, (Jpn.) printmaker. *Crabs*.
Hans Holbein the Elder, 1460-1524, (Ger.) late Gothic. *Presentation of Christ in the Temple*.
Hans Holbein the Younger, 1497-1543, (Ger.) portraitist. *Henry VIII*, *The French Ambassadors*.
Winslow Homer, 1836-1910, (U.S.) naturalist, marine themes. *Marine Coast*, *High Cliff*.
Edward Hopper, 1882-1967, (U.S.) realistic urban scenes. *Nighthawks*, *House by the Railroad*.
Horst P. Horst, 1906-99, (Ger.) fashion, celebrity photographer.
Jean-Auguste-Dominique Ingres, 1780-1867, (Fr.) Classicist. *Valpincon Bather*.
George Inness, 1825-94, (U.S.) luminous landscapist. *Delaware Water Gap*.
William Henry Jackson, 1843-1942, (U.S.) photographer. American West, building of Union Pacific Railroad.
Jeanne-Claude (Javacheff), 1935-2009, (Moroc.), large-scale environmental installation artist with husband Christo. *The Gates*, *Surrounded Islands*.
Frances Benjamin Johnston, 1864-1952, (U.S.) photographer. Historic homes.
Donald Judd, 1928-94, (U.S.) sculptor, major Minimalist.
Frida Kahlo, 1907-54, (Mex.) folkloric stylist. *Self-Portrait With Monkey*.
Wassily Kandinsky, 1866-1944, (Russ.) Abstractionist. *Capricious Forms*, *Improvisation 28 (second version)*.
Ellsworth Kelly, 1923-2015, (U.S.) painter, sculptor. *Red Blue Green*.
Paul Klee, 1879-1940, (Switz.) Abstractionist. *Twittering Machine*, *Pastoral*, *Death and Fire*.
Gustav Klimt, 1862-1918, (Austria) cofounder of Vienna Secession Movement. *The Kiss*.
Oskar Kokoschka, 1886-1980, (Austria) Expressionist. *View of Prague*, *Harbor of Marseilles*.
Käthe Kollwitz, 1867-1945, (Ger.) printmaker, social justice themes. *The Peasant War*.
Gaston Lachaise, 1882-1935, (U.S.) figurative sculptor. *Standing Woman*.
John La Farge, 1835-1910, (U.S.) muralist. *Red and White Peonies*, *The Ascension*.
Edwin (Henry) Landseer, 1802-73, (Br.) painter, sculptor. *Shoeing*, *Rout of Comus*.
Dorothea Lange, 1895-1965, (U.S.) photographer. Great Depression, migrant farm workers.
Fernand Léger, 1881-1955, (Fr.) Machine art. *The Cyclists*.
Saul Leiter, 1923-2013, (U.S) photographer.
Leonardo da Vinci, 1452-1519, (It.) Renaissance. *Mona Lisa*, *Last Supper*, *The Annunciation*.
Emanuel Leutze, 1816-68, (U.S.) historical themes. *Washington Crossing the Delaware*.
Edmonia Lewis, 1844?-1907, (U.S.) sculptor. *The Death of Cleopatra*.
Roy Lichtenstein, 1923-97, (U.S.) Pop Art.
Jacques Lipchitz, 1891-1973, (Fr.) Cubist sculptor. *Harpist*.
Filippino Lippi, 1457-1504, (It.) Renaissance. *Adoration of the Magi*.
Fra Filippo Lippi, 1406-69, (It.) Renaissance. *Coronation of the Virgin*, *Madonna and Child With Angels*.
Morris Louis, 1912-62, (U.S.) Abstract Expressionist. *Signa*, *Stripes*, *Alpha-Phi*.
René Magritte, 1898-1967, (Belg.) Surrealist. *The Descent of Man*, *The Betrayal of Images*.
Aristide Maillol, 1861-1944, (Fr.) sculptor. *L'Harmonie*.
Édouard Manet, 1832-83, (Fr.) forerunner of Impressionism. *Luncheon on the Grass*, *Olympia*.
Andrea Mantegna, 1431-1506, (It.) Renaissance frescoes. *Triumph of Caesar*.
Robert Mapplethorpe, 1946-89, (U.S.) photographer.
Franz Marc, 1880-1916, (Ger.) Expressionist. *Blue Horses*.
John Marin, 1870-1953, (U.S.) Expressionist seascapes. *Maine Island*.
Reginald Marsh, 1898-1954, (U.S.) satire. *Tattoo and Haircut*.
Agnes Martin, 1912-2004, (U.S.) abstract artist. *Night Sea*.
Masaccio, 1401-28, (It.) Renaissance. *The Tribute Money*.
Henri Matisse, 1869-1954, (Fr.) Fauvist. *Woman With the Hat*.
John McCracken, 1934-2011, (U.S.) Minimalist sculptor.
Michelangelo Buonarroti, 1475-1564, (It.) Renaissance. *Pietà*, *David*, *Moses*, *The Last Judgment*, Sistine Chapel ceiling.
Jean-Francois Millet, 1814-75, (Fr.) peasants. *The Gleaners*, *The Man With a Hoe*.
Joan Miró, 1893-1983, (Sp.) exuberant colors, playful images. Catalan landscape, *Dutch Interior*.
Amedeo Modigliani, 1884-1920, (It.) figurative paintings, sculptures. *Reclining Nude*.
Piet Mondrian, 1872-1944, (Neth.) Abstractionist. *Composition With Red, Yellow and Blue*.
Claude Monet, 1840-1926, (Fr.) Impressionist. *The Bridge at Argenteuil*, *Haystacks*, *Bridge Over a Pond of Water Lillies*.
Henry Moore, 1898-1986, (Br.) sculptor of large-scale, abstract works. *Reclining Figure* (several).
Gustave Moreau, 1826-98, (Fr.) Symbolist. *The Apparition (Dance of Salome)*.
James Wilson Morrice, 1865-1924, (Can.) landscapist. *The Ferry*, *Quebec*, *Venice*, *Looking Over the Lagoon*.
William Morris, 1834-96, (Br.) decorative artist, leader of Arts and Crafts movement.
Grandma Moses (Anna Mary Robertson Moses), 1860-1961, (U.S.) folk. *Out for the Christmas Tree*, *Catching the Thanksgiving Turkey*.
Samuel Morse, 1791-1872, (U.S.) portraitist. *Gallery of the Louvre*.
Edvard Munch, 1863-1944, (Nor.) Expressionist. *The Cry*.
Bartolome Murillo, 1618-82, (Sp.) Baroque religious artist. *Vision of St. Anthony*, *The Two Trinities*.
Elizabeth Murray, 1940-2007, (U.S.) abstract colors. *Kitchen Party*.
Eadweard Muybridge, 1830-1904, (Br.-U.S.) photographer. Studies of motion, *Animal Locomotion*.
Nadar (Gaspar-Félix Tournachon), 1820-1910, (Fr.) photographer, caricaturist, portraitist. Invented photo-essay.
LeRoy Neiman, 1921-2012, (U.S.) sports expressionist painter.
Arnold Newman, 1918-2006, (U.S.) portrait photographer.
Barnett Newman, 1905-70, (U.S.) Abstract Expressionist. *Stations of the Cross*.
Isamu Noguchi, 1904-88, (U.S.) abstract sculptor, designer. *Kouros*, *BirdC(MU)*, sculptural gardens.
Kenneth Noland, 1924-2010, (U.S.) Color Field, abstract.
Georgia O'Keeffe, 1887-1986, (U.S.) Southwest motifs. *Cow's Skull: Red, White, and Blue*; *The Shelton With Sunspots*.
Claes Oldenburg, 1929-2022, (Swed.-U.S.) pop-art sculptor. *Spoonbridge and Cherry*.
José Clemente Orozco, 1883-1949, (Mex.) frescoes. *House of Tears*, *Pre-Columbian Golden Age*.
Timothy H. O'Sullivan, 1840-82, (U.S.) Civil War photographer.
Gordon Parks, 1912-2006, (U.S.) African American photographer, filmmaker. *Life* photographer, 1948-68.
Charles Willson Peale, 1741-1827, (U.S.) Amer. Revolutionary portraitist. *The Staircase Group*, U.S. presidents.
Rembrandt Peale, 1778-1860, (U.S.) portraitist. *Thomas Jefferson*.
Irving Penn, 1917-2009, (U.S.) portraitist, fashion photographer.
Pietro Perugino, 1446-1523, (It.) Renaissance. *Delivery of the Keys to St. Peter*.
Pablo Picasso, 1881-1973, (Sp.) painter, sculptor. *Guernica*, *Dove*, *Head of a Woman*, *Head of a Bull*, *Metamorphosis*.
Piero della Francesca, c. 1415-92, (It.) Renaissance. *Duke of Urbino*, *Flagellation of Christ*.
Camille Pissarro, 1830-1903, (Fr.) Impressionist. *Boulevard des Italiens, Morning, Sunlight*; *Bather in the Woods*.
Jackson Pollock, 1912-56, (U.S.) Abstract Expressionist. *Autumn Rhythm*.
Nicolas Poussin, 1594-1665, (Fr.) Baroque pictorial classicism. *St. John on Patmos*.
Maurice B. Prendergast, c. 1860-1924, (U.S.) Postimpressionist watercolorist. *Umbrellas in the Rain*.
Pierre-Paul Prud'hon, 1758-1823, (Fr.) Romanticist. *Crime Pursued by Vengeance and Justice*.
Pierre Cecile Puvis de Chavannes, 1824-98, (Fr.) muralist. *The Poor Fisherman*.
Raphael Sanzio, 1483-1520, (It.) Renaissance. *Disputa*, *School of Athens*, *Sistine Madonna*.
Robert Rauschenberg, 1925-2008, (U.S.) printmaker. *Combine*, *Bed*, *Revolvers*, *Outpost*.

Man Ray (Emmanuel Radnitsky), 1890-1976, (U.S.) Dadaist and Surrealist. *Observing Time*, *The Lovers*, *Marquis de Sade*.
Odilon Redon, 1840-1916, (Fr.) Symbolist painter, lithographer. *In the Dream*, *Vase of Flowers*.
Rembrandt van Rijn, 1606-69, (Neth.) painter, printmaker. *The Bridal Couple*, *The Night Watch*.
Frederic Remington, 1861-1909, (U.S.) painter, sculptor. Portrayer of the American West, *Bronco Buster*.
Pierre-Auguste Renoir, 1841-1919, (Fr.) Impressionist. *The Luncheon of the Boating Party*, *Dance in the Country*.
Joshua Reynolds, 1723-92, (Br.) portraitist. *Mrs. Siddons as the Tragic Muse*.
Faith Ringgold, 1930-2024, (U.S.) painter, creator of narrative quilts.
Herb Ritts, 1952-2002, (U.S.) photographer. Nudes, celebrities.
Diego Rivera, 1886-1957, (Mex.) frescoes. *The Fecund Earth*.
Larry Rivers, 1923-2002, (U.S.) painter, sculptor, often realistic. Dutch Masters series.
Henry Peach Robinson, 1830-1901, (Br.) a leader of "high art" photography.
Norman Rockwell, 1894-1978, (U.S.) painter, illustrator. *Saturday Evening Post* covers.
Auguste Rodin, 1840-1917, (Fr.) sculptor. *The Thinker*.
Milton Rogovin, 1909-2011, (U.S.) documentary photographer.
Willy Ronis, 1910-2009, (Fr.) photographer. Postwar Paris.
Joe Rosenthal, 1911-2006, (U.S.) photojournalist. Photographed six Marines raising the U.S. flag over Iwo Jima in WWII.
Mark Rothko, 1903-70, (U.S.) Abstract Expressionist. *Light, Earth and Blue*.
Georges Rouault, 1871-1958, (Fr.) Expressionist. *Three Judges*.
Henri Rousseau, 1844-1910, (Fr.) primitive exotic themes. *The Snake Charmer*.
Theodore Rousseau, 1812-67, (Switz.-Fr.) landscapist. *Under the Birches*, *Evening*.
Peter Paul Rubens, 1577-1640, (Flem.) Baroque. *Mystic Marriage of St. Catherine*.
Jacob van Ruisdael, c. 1628-82, (Neth.) landscapist. *Jewish Cemetery*.
Charles M. Russell, 1866-1926, (U.S.) Western life.
Salomon van Ruysdael, c. 1600-70, (Neth.) landscapist. *River With Ferry-Boat*.
Albert Pinkham Ryder, 1847-1917, (U.S.) seascapes, allegories. *Toilers of the Sea*.
Augustus Saint-Gaudens, 1848-1907, (U.S.) memorial statues. *Farragut*, *Mrs. Henry Adams (Grief)*.
Niki de Saint Phalle, 1930-2002, (Fr.) paintings, sculptures, prints, large public installations.
Andrea Sansovino, 1460-1529, (It.) Renaissance sculptor. *Baptism of Christ*.
Jacopo Sansovino, 1486-1570, (It.) Renaissance sculptor. *St. John the Baptist*.
John Singer Sargent, 1856-1925, (U.S.) Edwardian society portraitist. *The Wyndham Sisters*, *Madame X*.
Andrea del Sarto, 1486-1530, (It.) frescoes. *Madonna of the Harpies*.
George Segal, 1924-2000, (U.S.) sculptor. Life-sized figures realistically depicting daily life.
Richard Serra, 1938-2024, (U.S.) sculptor.
Georges Seurat, 1859-91, (Fr.) Pointillist. *Sunday Afternoon on the Island of La Grande Jatte*.
Gino Severini, 1883-1966, (It.) Futurist and Cubist. *Dynamic Hieroglyph of the Bal Tabarin*.
Ben Shahn, 1898-1969, (U.S.) social and political themes. Sacco and Vanzetti series, *Seurat's Lunch*, *Handball*.
Charles Sheeler, 1883-1965, (U.S.) abstractionist.
David Alfaro Siqueiros, 1896-1974, (Mex.) political muralist. *March of Humanity*.
David Smith, 1906-65, (U.S.) welded metal sculpture. *Hudson River Landscape*, *Zig*, *Cubi* series.
Edward Steichen, 1879-1973, (U.S.) photographer. Credited with transforming photography into an art form.
Frank Stella, 1936-2024, (U.S.) abstract painter.
Alfred Stieglitz, 1864-1946, (U.S.) photographer, editor. Helped create acceptance of photography as art.
Paul Strand, 1890-1976, (U.S.) photographer. People, nature, landscapes.
Gilbert Stuart, 1755-1828, (U.S.) portraitist. George Washington, Thomas Jefferson, James Madison.
Thomas Sully, 1783-1872, (U.S.) portraitist. *The Passage of the Delaware*.
William Henry Fox Talbot, 1800-77, (Br.) photographer. *Pencil of Nature*, early photographically illustrated book.
George Tames, 1919-94, (U.S.) photographer. Presidents, political leaders.
Yves Tanguy, 1900-55, (Fr.) Surrealist. *Mama, Papa Is Wounded!*
Giovanni Battista Tiepolo, 1696-1770, (It.) Rococo frescoes. *The Crucifixion*.
Louis Comfort Tiffany, 1848-1933, (U.S.) stained glass, decorative arts.
Jacopo Tintoretto, 1518-94, (It.) Mannerist. *The Last Supper*.
Titian (Tiziano Vecellio), c. 1488-1576, (It.) Renaissance. *Venus and the Lute Player*, *The Bacchanal*.
Jose Rey Toledo, 1916-94, (U.S.) Native American life. Tribal dances.
George Tooker, 1920-2011, (U.S.) Magic Realist. *Subway*.
Henri de Toulouse-Lautrec, 1864-1901, (Fr.) Postimpressionist. *At the Moulin Rouge*.
John Trumbull, 1756-1843, (U.S.) historical themes. *The Declaration of Independence*.
Deborah Turbeville, 1937-2013, (U.S.) fashion photographer.
J(oseph) M(allord) W(illiam) Turner, 1775-1851, (Br.) Romantic landscapist. *Snow Storm*.
Cy Twombly, 1928-2011, (U.S.) painter and sculptor. *Leda and the Swan*.
Paolo Uccello, 1397-1475, (It.) Gothic-Renaissance. *The Rout of San Romano*.
Maurice Utrillo, 1883-1955, (Fr.) Impressionist. *Sacré-Coeur de Montmartre*.
Vincent van Gogh, 1853-90, (Neth.) *The Starry Night*, *L'Arlesienne*, *Bedroom at Arles*, *Self-Portrait*.
John Vanderlyn, 1775-1852, (U.S.) Neoclassicist. *Ariadne Asleep on the Island of Naxos*.
Diego Velázquez, 1599-1660, (Sp.) Baroque. *Las Meninas*, *Portrait of Juan de Pareja*.
Jan Vermeer, 1632-75, (Neth.) interior genre subjects. *Young Woman With a Water Jug*.
Paolo Veronese, 1528-88, (It.) Venetian painter. *The Temptation of St. Anthony*.
Andrea del Verrocchio, 1435-88, (It.) sculptor. *Colleoni*.
Maurice de Vlaminck, 1876-1958, (Fr.) Fauvist landscapist. *Red Trees*.
Andy Warhol, 1928-87, (U.S.) Pop Art. *Campbell's Soup Cans*, *Marilyn Diptych*.
Antoine Watteau, 1684-1721, (Fr.) Rococo "scenes of gallantry." *The Embarkation for Cythera*.
George Frederic Watts, 1817-1904, (Br.) painter and sculptor. Grandiose allegorical themes. *Hope*.
Benjamin West, 1738-1820, (U.S.) realistic historical themes. *Death of General Wolfe*.
Edward Weston, 1886-1958, (U.S.) photographer. Landscapes of American West.
James Abbott McNeill Whistler, 1834-1903, (U.S.) *Arrangement in Grey and Black No. 1* (*Portrait of the Artist's Mother*).
Archibald M. Willard, 1836-1918, (U.S.) murals. *The Spirit of '76*.
Grant Wood, 1891-1942, (U.S.) Midwestern regionalist. *American Gothic*, *Daughters of Revolution*.
Andrew Wyeth, 1917-2009, (U.S.), regionalist. *Christina's World*.
Ossip Zadkine, 1890-1967, (Russ.) School of Paris sculptor. *The Destroyed City*, *Musicians*, *Christ*.

Business Leaders and Philanthropists of the Past

Giovanni Agnelli, 1921-2003, (It.) industrialist; principal shareholder of Fiat.
Karl Albrecht, 1920-2014, and **Theo Albrecht**, 1922-2010, (both Ger.) cofounders of Aldi supermarkets.
Paul Allen, 1953-2018, (U.S.) Microsoft cofounder; philanthropist.
Walter Annenberg, 1908-2002, (U.S.) publisher, founder of *TV Guide*, philanthropist.
Elizabeth Arden (F. N. Graham), 1884-1966, (U.S.) Canadian-born founder of cosmetics empire.
Philip D. Armour, 1832-1901, (U.S.) industrialist; streamlined meatpacking.
Brooke Astor, 1902-2007, (U.S.) philanthropist; pres. of Vincent Astor Foundation.
John Jacob Astor, 1763-1848, (U.S.) German-born fur trader, banker, real estate magnate; at death, richest in U.S.
Francis W. Ayer, 1848-1923, (U.S.) ad industry pioneer.
August Belmont, 1816-90, (U.S.) German-born financier.
Liliane Bettencourt, 1922-2017, (Fr.) L'Oreal heiress, philanthropist.
James B. (Diamond Jim) Brady, 1856-1917, (U.S.) financier, philanthropist, legendary bon vivant.
Adolphus Busch, 1839-1913, (U.S.) German-born brewery founder.
Asa Candler, 1851-1929, (U.S.) founded Coca-Cola Co.
Andrew Carnegie, 1835-1919, (U.S.) Scottish-born industrialist, philanthropist; founded Carnegie Steel Co.
Tom Carvel, 1908-89, (Gr.-U.S.) founded ice cream chain.
William Colgate, 1783-1857, (Br.-U.S.) businessman, philanthropist; founded soap-making empire.
Jay Cooke, 1821-1905, (U.S.) financier.
Peter Cooper; 1791-1883, (U.S.) industrialist, inventor, philanthropist; founded Cooper Union college (1859).
Ezra Cornell, 1807-74, (U.S.) businessman, philanthropist; headed Western Union.
Erastus Corning, 1794-1872, (U.S.) financier; headed New York Central Railroad.
Charles Crocker, 1822-88, (U.S.) railroad builder, financier.
Samuel Cunard, 1787-1865, (Can.) pioneered transatlantic steam navigation.
Marcus Daly, 1841-1900, (U.S.) Irish-born copper magnate.
W. Edwards Deming, 1900-93, (U.S.) quality-control expert who revolutionized Japanese manufacturing.
Walt Disney, 1901-66, (U.S.) pioneer in cinema animation; built entertainment empire.
Herbert H. Dow, 1866-1930, (U.S.) founder of chemical co.
Anthony Drexel, 1826-93, (U.S.) banker, philanthropist, university founder.
James Duke, 1856-1925, (U.S.) founded American Tobacco, Duke Univ.
Eleuthere I. du Pont, 1771-1834, (Fr.-U.S.) gunpowder manufacturer.
Thomas C. Durant, 1820-85, (U.S.) railroad official, financier.
William C. Durant, 1861-1947, (U.S.) industrialist; formed General Motors.
George Eastman, 1854-1932, (U.S.) inventor; manufacturer of photographic equipment.
Marshall Field, 1834-1906, (U.S.) founded Chicago's largest department store.
Harvey Firestone, 1868-1938, (U.S.) founded tire company.
Avery Fisher, 1906-94, (U.S.) industrialist, philanthropist; founded Fisher Electronics.
Henry M. Flagler, 1830-1913, (U.S.) financier; helped form Standard Oil, developed FL as resort state.
Malcolm Forbes, 1919-90, (U.S.) magazine publisher.
Henry Ford, 1863-1947, (U.S.) automaker; developed first popular low-priced car.
Henry Ford II, 1917-87, (U.S.) headed auto company founded by grandfather.

Henry C. Frick, 1849-1919, (U.S.) steel and coke magnate; had prominent role in development of U.S. Steel.
Jakob Fugger (Jakob the Rich), 1459-1525, (Ger.) headed leading banking, trading house in 16th-cent. Europe.
Alfred C. Fuller, 1885-1973, (U.S.) Canadian-born businessman; founded brush company.
Elbert H. Gary, 1846-1927, (U.S.) chaired board of U.S. Steel, 1903-27.
Jean Paul Getty, 1892-1976, (U.S.) founded oil empire.
Amadeo Giannini, 1870-1949, (U.S.) founded Bank of America.
Stephen Girard, 1750-1831, (U.S.) French-born financier, philanthropist.
Leonard H. Goldenson, 1905-99, (U.S.) turned ABC into major TV network.
Jay Gould, 1836-92, (U.S.) railroad magnate, financier.
Hetty Green, 1834-1916, (U.S.) financier nicknamed "witch of Wall St."
William Gregg, 1800-67, (U.S.) launched textile industry in the South.
Meyer Guggenheim, 1828-1905, (U.S.) Swiss-born merchant, philanthropist; built merchandising, mining empires.
Armand Hammer, 1898-1990, (U.S.) headed Occidental Petroleum.
Elliot Handler, 1916-2011, (U.S.) cofounder of Mattel; introduced the Barbie doll.
Edward H. Harriman, 1848-1909, (U.S.) railroad financier; headed Union Pacific.
Hugh Hefner, 1926-2017, (U.S.) founded Playboy Enterprises.
Henry J. Heinz, 1844-1919, (U.S.) founded food empire.
Harry, 1909-97, and **Leona Helmsley**, 1920-2007, (both U.S.) real estate magnates, philanthropists.
Milton Snavely Hershey, 1857-1945, (U.S.) chocolate co. founder, philanthropist.
James J. Hill, 1838-1916, (U.S.) Canadian-born railroad magnate, financier; founded Great Northern Railway.
Conrad N. Hilton, 1888-1979, (U.S.) hotel chain founder.
Howard Hughes, 1905-76, (U.S.) industrialist, aviator, filmmaker.
H. L. Hunt, 1889-1974, (U.S.) oil magnate.
Collis P. Huntington, 1821-1900, (U.S.) railroad magnate.
Henry E. Huntington, 1850-1927, (U.S.) railroad builder, philanthropist.
Lee Iacocca, 1924-2019, (U.S.) auto executive (Ford, Chrysler).
Walter L. Jacobs, 1898-1985, (U.S.) founder of the first rental car agency.
Steve Jobs, 1955-2011, (U.S.) Apple cofounder and exec.; Pixar exec.
Howard Johnson, 1896-1972, (U.S.) founded restaurants.
John H. Johnson, 1918-2005, (U.S.) publisher of *Ebony* and *Jet*.
Samuel Curtis Johnson, 1928-2004, (U.S.) headed S.C. Johnson & Sons.
Henry J. Kaiser, 1882-1967, (U.S.) industrialist; built empire in steel, aluminum.
Ingvar Kamprad, 1926-2018, (Swed.) Ikea founder.
Minor C. Keith, 1848-1929, (U.S.) railroad magnate; founded United Fruit Co.
Will K. Kellogg, 1860-1951, (U.S.) businessman, philanthropist; founded breakfast food co.
Kirk Kerkorian, 1917-2015, (U.S.) private equity magnate; real estate developer.
Richard King, 1825-85, (U.S.) cattle farmer; founded King Ranch in Texas.
John W. Kluge, 1914-2010, (Ger.-U.S.) Metromedia chair; philanthropist.
William S. Knudsen, 1879-1948, (U.S.) Danish-born auto industry executive.
David Koch, 1940-2019, (U.S.) businessman, chemical engineer, political activist.
Samuel H. Kress, 1863-1955, (U.S.) businessman, art collector, philanthropist; founded "dime store" chain.
Ray A. Kroc, 1902-84, (U.S.) oversaw vast expansion of McDonald's.
Alfred Krupp, 1812-87, (Ger.) armaments magnate.
Estée Lauder, 1908-2004, (U.S.) cofounder of Estée Lauder companies.
Kenneth L. Lay, 1942-2006, (U.S.), former CEO of Enron; indicted on fraud charges.
William Levitt, 1907-94, (U.S.) industrialist; "suburb maker."
Thomas Lipton, 1850-1931, (Scot.) merchant; tea empire.
James McGill, 1744-1813, (Scot.-Can.) funded Montréal's McGill Univ.
Andrew W. Mellon, 1855-1937, (U.S.) financier, industrialist, philanthropist.
Charles E. Merrill, 1885-1956, (U.S.) financier; developed firm of Merrill Lynch.
J(ohn) P(ierpont) Morgan, 1837-1913, (U.S.) most powerful figure in finance and industry at turn of 20th cent.
Akio Morita, 1921-99, (Jpn.) cofounded Sony Corp.
Malcolm Muir, 1885-1979, (U.S.) created *Business Week*; led *Newsweek*, 1937-61.
Charles Munger, 1924-2023, (U.S.) financier.
Roy Neuberger, 1903-2010, (U.S.) financier, art patron.
Samuel Newhouse, 1895-1979, (U.S.) publishing and broadcasting magnate.
Jean Nidetch, 1923-2015, (U.S.) Weight Watchers cofounder.
Aristotle Onassis, 1906-75, (Gr.) shipping magnate.
William S. Paley, 1901-90, (U.S.) built CBS communications empire.
Frederick D. Patterson, 1901-88, (U.S.) founder of United Negro College Fund, 1944.
George Peabody, 1795-1869, (U.S.) merchant, financier, philanthropist.
James C. Penney, 1875-1971, (U.S.) businessman; developed department store.
Frank Perdue, 1920-2005, (U.S.) founder of Perdue Farms, chicken-processing co.
Ross Perot, 1930-2019, (U.S.) computer services pioneer, philanthropist; 2-time pres. candidate (Ind.)
William C. Procter, 1862-1934, (U.S.) headed soap co.
Sumner Redstone, 1923-2020, (U.S.) National Amusements owner, incl. subsidiaries Viacom, CBS.
David Rockefeller, 1915-2017, (U.S.) banker, philanthropist.
John D. Rockefeller, 1839-1937, (U.S.) industrialist; established Standard Oil.
John D. Rockefeller Jr., 1874-1960, (U.S.) philanthropist; provided land for UN.
Laurance S. Rockefeller, 1910-2004, (U.S.) philanthropist, conservationist.
Meyer A. Rothschild, 1743-1812, (Ger.) founded international banking house.
Thomas Fortune Ryan, 1851-1928, (U.S.) financier; a founder of American Tobacco.
Edmond J. Safra, 1932-99, (U.S.) banker.
David Sarnoff, 1891-1971, (U.S.) broadcasting pioneer; established first radio network, NBC.
Richard Sears, 1863-1914, (U.S.) founded mail-order co.
Werner von Siemens, 1816-92, (Ger.) industrialist, inventor.
Alfred P. Sloan, 1875-1966, (U.S.) industrialist, philanthropist; headed GM.
A. Leland Stanford, 1824-93, (U.S.) railroad official, philanthropist; founded university.
Frank Stanton, 1908-2006, (U.S.) president of CBS network, 1946-71.
Nathan Straus, 1848-1931, (U.S.) German-born merchant, philanthropist; headed Macy's dept. stores.
Levi Strauss, c. 1829-1902, (U.S.) pants manufacturer.
Clement Studebaker, 1831-1901, (U.S.) wagon, carriage maker.
Gustavus Swift, 1839-1903, (U.S.) pioneer meatpacker.
Gerard Swope, 1872-1957, (U.S.) industrialist, economist; headed General Electric.
Dave Thomas, 1932-2002, (U.S.) Wendy's restaurant chain founder.
James Walter Thompson, 1847-1928, (U.S.) ad exec., founder of ad agency.
Alice Tully, 1902-93, (U.S.) arts patron.
Theodore N. Vail, 1845-1920, (U.S.) organized Bell Telephone, led AT&T.
Cornelius Vanderbilt, 1794-1877, (U.S.) financier; established steamship, railroad empires.
Lillian Vernon, 1927-2015, (Ger.-U.S.) catalog merchant, philanthropist.
Henry Villard, 1835-1900, (U.S.) German-born railroad executive, financier.
Charles R. Walgreen, 1873-1939, (U.S.) founded drugstore chain.
Madame C. J. Walker, 1867-1919, (U.S.) African American hair care entrepreneur, philanthropist.
DeWitt, 1889-1981, and **Lila Wallace**, 1889-1984, (both U.S.) cofounders of *Reader's Digest* magazine.
Sam Walton, 1918-92, (U.S.) Walmart founder.
John Wanamaker, 1838-1922, (U.S.) department-store merchandising pioneer.
Aaron Montgomery Ward, 1843-1913, (U.S.) established first mail-order firm.
Thomas J. Watson, 1874-1956, (U.S.) IBM head, 1914-56.
Jack Welch, 1935-2020, (U.S.) General Electric CEO.
George Westinghouse, 1846-1914, (U.S) inventor, manufacturer; organized Westinghouse Electric Co., 1886.
John Hay Whitney, 1905-82, (U.S.) publisher, sportsman, philanthropist.
Chuck Williams, 1915-2015, (U.S.) Williams-Sonoma founder.
Charles E. Wilson, 1890-1961, (U.S.) auto exec., public official.
Frank W. Woolworth, 1852-1919, (U.S.) created five-and-dime chain.
William Wrigley Jr., 1861-1932, (U.S.) founded Wrigley chewing gum co.

American Cartoonists

Reviewed by Lucy Shelton Caswell, Professor and Curator, Cartoon Research Library, Ohio State University.

Scott Adams, b 1957, Dilbert.
Charles Addams, 1912-88, macabre cartoons.
Brad Anderson, 1924-2015, Marmaduke.
Sergio Aragonés, b 1937, (Span.-Mex.) *Mad* magazine.
Peter Arno, 1904-68, *The New Yorker*.
Tex Avery, 1908-80, animator; Bugs Bunny, Porky Pig.
George Baker, 1915-75, The Sad Sack.
Carl Barks, 1901-2000, Donald Duck comic books.
Alison Bechdel, b 1960, graphic novelist.
C. C. Beck, 1910-89, Captain Marvel.
Dave Berg, 1920-2002, *Mad* magazine.
Jim Berry, 1932-2015, Berry's World.
Herb Block (Herblock), 1909-2001, political cartoonist.
George Booth, 1926-2022, *The New Yorker*.
Loren Bouchard, b 1969, Bob's Burgers.
Berkeley Breathed, b 1957, Bloom County.
Dik Browne, 1917-89, Hi & Lois, Hagar the Horrible.
Marjorie Buell, 1904-93, Little Lulu.
Ernie Bushmiller, 1905-82, Nancy.
Milton Caniff, 1907-88, Terry & the Pirates, Steve Canyon.
Al Capp, 1909-79, Li'l Abner.
Roz Chast, b 1954, *The New Yorker*.
Gene Colan, 1926-2011, *Daredevil*.
Paul Conrad, 1924-2010, political cartoonist.
Roy Crane, 1901-77, Captain Easy, Buz Sawyer.
R(obert) Crumb, b 1943, underground cartoonist.
Shamus Culhane, 1908-96, animator.
Jay N. "Ding" Darling, 1876-1962, political cartoonist.
Jack Davis, 1924-2016, *Mad* magazine.
Jim Davis, b 1945, Garfield.
Billy DeBeck, 1890-1942, Barney Google.
Rudolph Dirks, 1877-1968, The Katzenjammer Kids.

Walt Disney, 1901-66, produced animated cartoons; Mickey Mouse, Donald Duck.
Steve Ditko, 1927-2018, Spider-Man.
Mort Drucker, 1929-2020, *Mad* magazine.
Will Eisner, 1917-2005, The Spirit.
Jules Feiffer, b 1929, political cartoonist.
Bud Fisher, 1885-1954, Mutt & Jeff.
Ham Fisher, 1900-55, Joe Palooka.
Max Fleischer, 1883-1972, Betty Boop.
Hal Foster, 1892-1982, Tarzan, Prince Valiant.
Fontaine Fox, 1884-1964, Toonerville Folks.
Isadore "Friz" Freleng, 1905-95, animator; Yosemite Sam, Porky Pig, Sylvester and Tweety Bird.
Rube Goldberg, 1883-1970, Boob McNutt.
Chester Gould, 1900-85, Dick Tracy.
Harold Gray, 1894-1968, Little Orphan Annie.
Matt Groening, b 1954, Life in Hell, The Simpsons.
Cathy Guisewite, b 1950, Cathy.
Bill Hanna, 1910-2001, and **Joe Barbera**, 1911-2006, animators; Tom & Jerry, Yogi Bear, Flintstones.
Oliver Harrington, 1912-95, Bootsie.
Johnny Hart, 1931-2007, B.C., Wizard of Id.
Alfred Harvey, 1913-94, created Casper the Friendly Ghost.
Jimmy Hatlo, 1898-1963, Little Iodine.
John Held Jr., 1889-1958, Jazz Age.
George Herriman, 1881-1944, Krazy Kat.
Harry Hershfield, 1885-1974, Abie the Agent.
Stephen Hillenburg, 1961-2018, SpongeBob SquarePants.
Al Hirschfeld, 1903-2003, *NY Times* theater caricaturist.
Burne Hogarth, 1911-96, Tarzan.
Helen Hokinson, 1900-49, *The New Yorker*.
Nicole Hollander, b 1939, Sylvia.
Al Jaffee, 1921-2023, *Mad* magazine.
Lynn Johnston, b 1947, (Can.) For Better or For Worse.
Oliver Johnston, 1912-2008, Disney animator.
Chuck Jones, 1912-2002, animator; Bugs Bunny, Porky Pig; created Road Runner, Wile E. Coyote.
Mike Judge, b 1962, Beavis and Butt-Head, King of the Hill.
Bob Kane, 1916-98, Batman.
Bil Keane, 1922-2011, The Family Circus.
Walt Kelly, 1913-73, Pogo.
Hank Ketcham, 1920-2001, Dennis the Menace.
Ted Key, 1912-2008, Hazel.
Frank King, 1883-1969, Gasoline Alley.
Jack Kirby, 1917-94, Fantastic Four, The Incredible Hulk.
Rollin Kirby, 1875-1952, political cartoonist.
B(ernard) Kliban, 1935-90, cat books.
Edward Koren, 1935-2023, *The New Yorker*.
Joe Kubert, 1926-2012, Sgt. Rock.
Harvey Kurtzman, 1921-93, *Mad* magazine.
Walter Lantz, 1900-94, Woody Woodpecker.
Gary Larson, b 1950, The Far Side.
Mell Lazarus, 1927-2016, Momma.
Stan Lee, 1922-2018, Marvel Comics.
David Levine, 1926-2009, *NY Review of Books* caricatures.
Seth MacFarlane, b 1973, Family Guy.
Jeff MacNelly, 1947-2000, political cartoonist; Shoe.
Doug Marlette, 1949-2007, political cartoonist; Kudzu.
Don Martin, 1931-2000, *Mad* magazine.
Bill Mauldin, 1921-2003, political cartoonist.
Winsor McCay, 1872-1934, Little Nemo.
John T. McCutcheon, 1870-1949, political cartoonist.
Patrick McDonnell, b 1956, Mutts.
Dwayne McDuffie, 1962-2011, Justice League.
Aaron McGruder, b 1974, The Boondocks.
George McManus, 1884-1954, Bringing Up Father.
Dale Messick, 1906-2005, Brenda Starr.
Wiley Miller, b 1951, Non Sequitur.
Norman Mingo, 1896-1980, Alfred E. Neuman.
Bob Montana, 1920-75, Archie.
Dick Moores, 1909-86, Gasoline Alley.
Willard Mullin, 1902-78, sports cartoonist; Dodgers' "Brooklyn Bum," "Mets Kid."
Randall Munroe, b 1984, xkcd.
Russell Myers, b 1938, Broom Hilda.
Thomas Nast, 1840-1902, political cartoonist; Republican elephant, Democratic donkey.
Pat Oliphant, b 1935, political cartoonist.
Frederick Burr Opper, 1857-1937, Happy Hooligan.
Richard Outcault, 1863-1928, Yellow Kid, Buster Brown.
Brant Parker, 1920-2007, Wizard of Id.
Trey Parker, b 1969, South Park co-creator.
Harvey Pekar, 1939-2010, American Splendor.
Mike Peters, b 1943, Mother Goose & Grimm.
George Price, 1901-95, *The New Yorker*.
Antonio Prohias, 1921-98, Spy vs. Spy.
Alex Raymond, 1909-56, Flash Gordon, Jungle Jim.
Forrest (Bud) Sagendorf, 1915-94, Popeye.
Art Sansom, 1920-91, The Born Loser.
Charles Schulz, 1922-2000, Peanuts.
Elzie C. Segar, 1894-1938, Popeye.
Marie Severin, 1929-2018, Marvel Comics.
Joe Shuster, 1914-92, and **Jerry Siegel**, 1914-96, Superman.
Sidney Smith, 1887-1935, The Gumps.
Otto Soglow, 1900-75, Little King.
Art Spiegelman, b 1948, Raw, Maus.
William Steig, 1907-2003, *The New Yorker*.
Matt Stone, b 1971, South Park co-creator.
James Swinnerton, 1875-1974, Little Jimmy, Canyon Kiddies.
Paul Szep, b 1941, political cartoonist.
Paul Terry, 1887-1971, animator of Mighty Mouse.
Bob Thaves, 1924-2006, Frank and Ernest.
James Thurber, 1894-61, *The New Yorker*.
Garry Trudeau, b 1948, Doonesbury.
Jim Unger, 1937-2012, Herman.
Mort Walker, 1923-2018, Beetle Bailey.
Bill Watterson, b 1958, Calvin and Hobbes.
Russ Westover, 1887-1966, Tillie the Toiler.
Signe Wilkinson, b 1950, political cartoonist.
Frank Willard, 1893-1958, Moon Mullins.
J. R. Williams, 1888-1957, The Willets Family, Out Our Way.
Gahan Wilson, 1930-2019, *The New Yorker*.
Tom Wilson, 1931-2011, Ziggy.
Art Young, 1866-1943, political cartoonist.
Chic Young, 1901-73, Blondie.

Economists, Educators, Historians, and Social Scientists of the Past

For psychologists, see Scientists of the Past.

Brooks Adams, 1848-1927, (U.S.) historian, political theoretician; *The Law of Civilization and Decay*.
Henry Adams, 1838-1918, (U.S.) historian, autobiographer; *The Education of Henry Adams*.
Stephen Ambrose, 1936-2002, (U.S.) historian; *Eisenhower*.
Hannah Arendt, 1906-75, (Ger.) political philosopher; *The Origins of Totalitarianism*.
Francis Bacon, 1561-1626, (Eng.) philosopher, essayist, statesman; championed observation and induction.
George Bancroft, 1800-91, (U.S.) historian; 10-volume *History of the United States*.
Jack Barbash, 1910-94, (U.S.) labor economist; helped create the AFL-CIO.
Henry Barnard, 1811-1900, (U.S.) public school reformer.
Charles A. Beard, 1874-1948, (U.S.) historian; *The Economic Basis of Politics*.
(St.) Bede (the Venerable), c. 673-735, (Br.) scholar, historian; *Ecclesiastical History of the English People*.
Daniel Bell, 1919-2011, (U.S.) sociologist; *The End of Ideology*.
Ruth Benedict, 1887-1948, (U.S.) anthropologist; studied Indian tribes of the Southwest.
Isaiah Berlin, 1909-97, (Br.) philosopher, historian; *The Age of Enlightenment*.
Leonard Bloomfield, 1887-1949, (U.S.) linguist; *Language*.
Franz Boas, 1858-1942, (U.S.) German-born anthropologist; studied American Indians.
Van Wyck Brooks, 1886-1963, (U.S.) historian; critic of New England culture, especially literature.
Edmund Burke, 1729-97, (Ire.) British parliamentarian and political philosopher; *Reflections on the Revolution in France*.
James MacGregor Burns, 1918-2014, (U.S.) historian, political scientist.
Nicholas Murray Butler, 1862-1947, (U.S.) educator; headed Columbia Univ., 1902-45; 1931 Nobel Peace Prize winner.
Joseph Campbell, 1904-87, (U.S.) author, editor, teacher; wrote books on mythology, folklore.
Thomas Carlyle, 1795-1881, (Scot.) historian, critic; *Sartor Resartus*, *Past and Present*, *The French Revolution*.
(Charles) Bruce Catton, 1899-1978, (U.S.) historian; *A Stillness at Appomattox*.
Edward Channing, 1856-1931, (U.S.) historian; 6-volume *History of the United States*.
Henry Steele Commager, 1902-98, (U.S.) historian, educator; *The Growth of the American Republic*.
John R. Commons, 1862-1945, (U.S.) economist, labor historian; *Legal Foundations of Capitalism*.
James B. Conant, 1893-1978, (U.S.) educator, diplomat; *The American High School Today*.
Benedetto Croce, 1866-1952, (It.) philosopher, statesman, historian; *Philosophy of the Spirit*.
Bernard A. De Voto, 1897-1955, (U.S.) historian; wrote trilogy on American West, edited Mark Twain manuscripts.
Melvil Dewey, 1851-1931, (U.S.) devised decimal system of library-book classification.
Donald Herbert Donald, 1920-2009, (U.S.) Pulitzer Prize-winning Civil War and Lincoln historian.
St. Clair Drake, 1911-90, (U.S.) sociologist, Black studies pioneer; *Black Metropolis* (1945), with Horace R. Cayton.
W(illiam) E(dward) B(urghardt) Du Bois, 1868-1963, (U.S.) historian, sociologist; NAACP founder, 1909.
Will(iam), 1885-1981, (U.S.) and **Ariel Durant**, 1898-1981, (Ukraine) historians; *The Story of Civilization*.
Emile Durkheim, 1858-1917, (Fr.) a founder of modern sociology; *The Rules of Sociological Method*.
Charles Eliot, 1834-1926, (U.S.) educator, Harvard president.
Friedrich Engels, 1820-95, (Ger.) political writer; with Karl Marx wrote the *Communist Manifesto*.
Irving Fisher, 1867-1947, (U.S.) economist; contributed to the development of modern monetary theory.

John Fiske, 1842-1901, (U.S.) historian and lecturer; popularized Darwinian theory of evolution.
Charles Fourier, 1772-1837, (Fr.) utopian socialist.
John Hope Franklin, 1915-2009, (U.S.) historian; *From Slavery to Freedom: A History of African Americans*.
James George Frazer, 1854-1941, (Br.) anthropologist; studied myth in religion; *The Golden Bough*.
Milton Friedman, 1912-2006, (U.S.) economist; advocate for free markets.
Paul Fussell, 1924-2012, (U.S.) literary historian; *The Great War and Modern Memory*.
John Kenneth Galbraith, 1908-2006, (Can.-U.S.) economist, author, professor, former amb. to India.
Peter Gay, 1923-2015, (Ger.-U.S.) cultural historian; *The Enlightenment: An Interpretation*.
Giovanni Gentile, 1875-1944, (It.) philosopher, educator; reformed Italian educational system.
Henry George, 1839-97, (U.S.) economist, reformer; led single-tax movement.
Edward Gibbon, 1737-94, (Br.) historian; *The History of the Decline and Fall of the Roman Empire*.
Andrew Greeley, 1928-2013, (U.S.) Rom. Cath. priest; sociologist.
Francesco Guicciardini, 1483-1540, (It.) historian; *Storia d'Italia*, principal historical work of the 16th cent.
Thomas Hobbes, 1588-1679, (Eng.) philosopher, political theorist; *Leviathan*.
Richard Hofstadter, 1916-70, (U.S.) historian; *The Age of Reform*.
Charles Hamilton Houston, 1895-1950, (U.S.) African-American lawyer, Howard Univ. instructor; champion of minority rights.
Samuel Huntington, 1927-2008, (U.S.), political scientist, Harvard University professor; *The Clash of Civilizations*.
Alfred Kahn, 1917-2010, (U.S.) economist; deregulated the U.S. airline industry.
John Keegan, 1934-2012, (Br.) war historian; *The Face of Battle*.
George F. Kennan, 1904-2005, (U.S.) diplomat, historian; main architect of U.S. Cold War "containment" strategy.
John Maynard Keynes, 1883-1946, (Br.) economist; principal advocate of deficit spending.
Alfred Kinsey, 1894-1956, (U.S.) zoologist; pioneering human sex researcher.
Russell Kirk, 1918-94, (U.S.), social philosopher; *The Conservative Mind*.
Alfred L. Kroeber, 1876-1960, (U.S.) cultural anthropologist; studied Indians of North and South America.
Elisabeth Kubler-Ross, 1926-2004, (Switz.) psychiatrist, author; *On Death and Dying*.
Christopher Lasch, 1932-94, (U.S.) social critic, historian; *The Culture of Narcissism*.
James L. Laughlin, 1850-1933, (U.S.) economist; helped establish Federal Reserve System.
Margaret Leech, 1893-1974, (U.S.) historian; *Reveille in Washington, 1860-1865*.
Lucien Lévy-Bruhl, 1857-1939, (Fr.) philosopher; studied the psychology of primitive societies; *Primitive Mentality*.
John Locke, 1632-1704, (Eng.) philosopher, political theorist; *Two Treatises of Government*.
Thomas B. Macaulay, 1800-59, (Br.) historian, statesman.
Niccolò Machiavelli, 1469-1527, (It.) writer, statesman; *The Prince*.
Bronislaw Malinowski, 1884-1942, (Pol.) considered the father of social anthropology.
Thomas R. Malthus, 1766-1834, (Br.) economist; *Essay on the Principle of Population*.
Horace Mann, 1796-1859, (U.S.) pioneered modern public school system.
Karl Mannheim, 1893-1947, (Hung.) sociologist, historian; *Ideology and Utopia*.
Harriet Martineau, 1802-76, (Eng.) writer, feminist; *Society in America*.
Karl Marx, 1818-83, (Ger.) political theorist, proponent of Communism; *Communist Manifesto*, *Das Kapital*.
Benjamin Mays, 1895-1984, (U.S.) minister, educator, civil rights leader; headed Morehouse College, 1940-67.
Giuseppe Mazzini, 1805-72, (It.) political philosopher.
David McCullough, 1933-2022, (U.S.) historian; *John Adams*.
William H. McGuffey, 1800-73, (U.S.) his *Reader* was a mainstay of 19th-cent. U.S. public education.
George H. Mead, 1863-1931, (U.S.) philosopher, social psychologist.
Margaret Mead, 1901-78, (U.S.) cultural anthropologist; popularized field; *Coming of Age in Samoa*.
Alexander Meiklejohn, 1872-1964, (U.S.) Br.-born educator; championed academic freedom and experimental curricula.
James Mill, 1773-1836, (Scot.) philosopher, historian, economist; a proponent of utilitarianism.
John Stuart Mill, 1806-73, (Eng.) philosopher, economist; *Utilitarianism*. Eldest son of James Mill.
Perry G. Miller, 1905-63, (U.S.) historian; interpreted 17th-cent. New England.
Theodor Mommsen, 1817-1903, (Ger.) historian; *The History of Rome*.
Ashley Montagu, 1905-99, (Eng.) anthropologist; *The Natural Superiority of Women*.
Charles-Louis Montesquieu, 1689-1755, (Fr.) social philosopher; *The Spirit of Laws*.
Maria Montessori, 1870-1952, (It.) educator, physician; started Montessori method of student self-motivation.
Samuel Eliot Morison, 1887-1976, (U.S.) historian; chronicled voyages of early explorers.
Edmund Morris, 1940-2019, (Br.-U.S.) historian, presidential biographer (T. Roosevelt, Reagan).
Lewis Mumford, 1895-1990, (U.S.) sociologist, critic; *The Culture of Cities*.
Gunnar Myrdal, 1898-1987, (Swed.) economist, social scientist; *Asian Drama: An Inquiry Into the Poverty of Nations*.
Allan Nevins, 1890-1971, (U.S.) historian, biographer; *The Ordeal of the Union*.
José Ortega y Gasset, 1883-1955, (Sp.) philosopher; advocated control by elite; *The Revolt of the Masses*.
Elinor Ostrom, 1933-2012, (U.S.) political economist.
Robert Owen, 1771-1858, (Br.) political philosopher, reformer; pioneer in cooperative movement.
Thomas Paine, 1737-1809, (Br.-U.S.) political theorist, writer; *Common Sense*.
Vilfredo Pareto, 1848-1923, (It.) economist, sociologist.
Francis Parkman, 1823-93, (U.S.) historian; *France and England in North America*.
Elizabeth P. Peabody, 1804-94, (U.S.) education pioneer; founded first kindergarten in U.S., 1860.
William Prescott, 1796-1859, (U.S.) early American historian; *The Conquest of Peru*.
Pierre Joseph Proudhon, 1809-65, (Fr.) social theorist; father of anarchism; *The Philosophy of Property*.
François Quesnay, 1694-1774, (Fr.) economic theorist.
Robert V. Remini, 1921-2013, (U.S.) historian; *The Life of Andrew Jackson*.
David Ricardo, 1772-1823, (Br.) economic theorist; advocated free international trade.
David Riesman, 1909-2002, (U.S.) sociologist; co-author, *The Lonely Crowd*.
Jacqueline de Romilly, 1913-2010, (Fr.) scholar of Greek civilization and language.
Theodore Roszak, 1933-2011, (U.S.) historian; *The Making of a Counter Culture*.
Jean-Jacques Rousseau, 1712-78, (Fr.) social philosopher; the father of romantic sensibility; *Confessions*.
Paul Samuelson, 1915-2009, (U.S.) economist, famed for modern mathematical approach to economics.
Edward Sapir, 1884-1939, (Ger.-U.S.) anthropologist; studied ethnology and linguistics of American Indian groups.
Ferdinand de Saussure, 1857-1913, (Switz.) a founder of modern linguistics.
Arthur Schlesinger Jr., 1917-2007, (U.S.) historian, author; *The Imperial Presidency*.
Joseph Schumpeter, 1883-1950, (Czech.-U.S.) economist, sociologist.
Elizabeth Seton, 1774-1821, (U.S.) nun; established parochial school education in U.S., first native-born American saint.
Georg Simmel, 1858-1918, (Ger.) sociologist, philosopher; helped establish German sociology.
Robert Sklar, 1936-2011, (U.S.) film scholar.
Adam Smith, 1723-90, (Br.) economist; advocated laissez-faire economy, free trade; *The Wealth of Nations*.
Jared Sparks, 1789-1866, (U.S.) historian, educator, editor; *The Library of American Biography*.
Oswald Spengler, 1880-1936, (Ger.) philosopher, historian; *The Decline of the West*.
Leo Steinberg, 1920-2011, (Russ.-U.S.) art historian.
William G. Sumner, 1840-1910, (U.S.) social scientist, economist; laissez-faire economy, Social Darwinism.
Hippolyte Taine, 1828-93, (Fr.) historian, basis of naturalistic school; *The Origins of Contemporary France*.
A(lan) J(ohn) P(ercivale) Taylor, 1906-90, (Br.) historian; *The Origins of the Second World War*.
Nikolaas Tinbergen, 1907-88, (Neth.-Br.) ethologist; pioneer in study of animal behavior.
Alexis de Tocqueville, 1805-59, (Fr.) political scientist, historian; *Democracy in America*.
Francis E. Townsend, 1867-1960, (U.S.) led old-age pension movement, 1933.
Arnold Toynbee, 1889-1975, (Br.) historian; *A Study of History*, sweeping analysis of hist. of civilizations.
George Trevelyan, 1876-1962, (Br.) historian, statesman; favored "literary" over "scientific" history; *History of England*.
Henri Troyat, 1911-2007, (Russ.-Fr.), biographies of major figures in Russian history.
Frederick J. Turner, 1861-1932, (U.S.) historian, educator; *The Frontier in American History*.
Thorstein B. Veblen, 1857-1929, (U.S.) economist, social philosopher; *The Theory of the Leisure Class*.
Giovanni Vico, 1668-1744, (It.) historian, biographer; regarded by many as first modern historian; *New Science*.
Izaak Walton, 1593-1683, (Eng.) biographer; political-philosophical study of fishing, *The Compleat Angler*.
Booker T. Washington, 1856-1915, (U.S.) founder, 1881, and first pres. of Tuskegee Institute; *Up From Slavery*.
Sidney J., 1859-1947, and **Beatrice Webb**, 1858-1943, (both Br.) leading figures in Fabian Society and Labor Party.
Max Weber, 1864-1920, (Ger.) sociologist; *The Protestant Ethic and the Spirit of Capitalism*.
Walter White, 1893-1955, (U.S.) exec. sec., NAACP, 1931-55.
Roy Wilkins, 1901-81, (U.S.) exec. director, NAACP, 1955-77.
Emma Hart Willard, 1787-1870, (U.S.) pioneered higher education for women.
James Q. Wilson, 1931-2012, (U.S.) political scientist; co-authored broken windows theory.
Carter G. Woodson, 1875-1950, (U.S.) historian; founded Assn. for the Study of Negro Life and History.
C. Vann Woodward, 1908-99, (U.S.) historian; *The Strange Career of Jim Crow*.
Howard Zinn, 1922-2010, (U.S.) historian; *A People's History of the United States*.

American Journalists of the Past

Reviewed by Dean Mills, Dean, Missouri School of Journalism.

See also Business Leaders and Philanthropists, American Cartoonists, and Writers of the Past.

Franklin P. Adams (F.P.A.), 1881-1960, humorist; wrote column "The Conning Tower."

Roger Ailes, 1940-2017, Fox News cofounder and CEO.

Joseph W. Alsop, 1910-89, and **Stewart Alsop**, 1914-74, Washington-based political analysts, columnists.

Jack Anderson, 1922-2006, muckraking Washington, DC, syndicated columnist.

Roger Angell, 1920-2022, *New Yorker* fiction editor; sports essayist.

Brooks Atkinson, 1894-1984, theater critic.

Robert L. Bartley, 1937-2003, editorial-page editor for *Wall Street Journal*.

Jessie Tarbox Beals, 1870-1942, photojournalist.

James Gordon Bennett, 1795-1872, editor and publisher; founded *NY Herald*.

James Gordon Bennett Jr., 1841-1918, succeeded father, financed expeditions, founded afternoon paper.

Nellie Bly (Elizabeth Cochrane), 1864?-1922, pioneer woman journalist, investigative reporter; noted for series on trip around the world.

Elias Boudinot, c. 1803-39, founding editor of first Native American newspaper in U.S., *Cherokee Phoenix* (1828-34).

Benjamin Bradlee, 1921-2014, *Washington Post* exec. editor.

Ed Bradley, 1941-2006, TV journalist (*60 Minutes*).

Andrew Breitbart, 1969-2012, conservative commentator and blogger.

Jimmy Breslin, 1928-2017, *NY Daily News* columnist.

David Brinkley, 1920-2003, co-anchor of NBC's *Huntley-Brinkley Report*, host of ABC's *This Week With David Brinkley*.

Arthur Brisbane, 1864-1936, editor; helped introduce "yellow journalism" with sensational, simply written articles.

David Broder, 1929-2011, political journalist for *Washington Post*.

Joyce Brothers, 1927-2013, psychologist, columnist.

Heywood Broun, 1888-1939, author, columnist; founded American Newspaper Guild.

Helen Gurley Brown, 1922-2012, author; editor-in-chief of *Cosmopolitan* magazine (1965-97).

Art Buchwald, 1925-2007, journalist, humorist, syndicated columnist.

William F. Buckley Jr., 1925-2008, columnist and commentator; founder of *National Review*.

Herb Caen, 1916-97, longtime columnist for *San Francisco Chronicle* and *Examiner*.

John Campbell, 1653-1728, published *Boston News-Letter*, first continuing newspaper in the American colonies.

Jimmy Cannon, 1909-73, syndicated sports columnist.

John Chancellor, 1927-96, NBC reporter, anchor.

Harry Chandler, 1864-1944, *L.A. Times* publisher (1917-41).

Otis Chandler, 1928-2006, *Los Angeles Times* publisher (1960-80).

Marquis Childs, 1903-90, reporter and columnist for *St. Louis Post-Dispatch* and United Feature syndicate.

Craig Claiborne, 1920-2000, *NY Times* food editor and critic; key in internationalizing American tastes.

Alexander Cockburn, 1941-2012, left-wing journalist.

Charles Collingwood, 1917-85, CBS news correspondent.

Alistair Cooke, 1908-2004, Brit. journalist, TV narrator; naturalized American citizen, "Letter From America" series.

Howard Cosell, 1920-95, TV and radio sportscaster.

Gardner Cowles, 1861-1946, founded newspaper chain.

Judith Crist, 1922-2012, film critic.

Walter Cronkite, 1916-2009, CBS evening news anchor, TV journalist.

Evelyn Cunningham, 1916-2010, African-American civil rights reporter.

Cyrus Curtis, 1850-1933, publisher of *Saturday Evening Post*, *Ladies' Home Journal*, *Country Gentleman*.

John Charles Daly, 1914-91, war correspondent, TV journalist; Voice of America head.

Charles Anderson Dana, 1819-97, editor, publisher; made *NY Sun* famous for its news reporting.

Elmer (Holmes) Davis, 1890-1958, *NY Times* editorial writer, radio commentator.

Richard Harding Davis, 1864-1916, war correspondent, travel writer, fiction writer.

Benjamin Day, 1810-89, published *NY Sun* beginning in 1833, introducing penny press to the U.S.

Dorothy Dix (Elizabeth Meriwether Gilmer), 1861-1951, reporter; pioneer of the advice column genre.

Finley Peter Dunne, 1867-1936, humorist, social critic; wrote "Mr. Dooley" columns.

Roger Ebert, 1942-2013, film critic.

Mary Baker Eddy, 1821-1910, founded Christian Science movement and *Christian Science Monitor*.

Rowland Evans Jr., 1921-2001, Washington columnist.

Fanny Fern (Sara Willis Parton), 1811-72, newspaper columnist, author.

Marshall Field III, 1893-1956, retail magnate; *Chicago Sun* founder.

Doris Fleeson, 1901-70, war correspondent, columnist.

Benjamin Franklin, 1706-90, publisher of *Poor Richard's Almanack*.

James Franklin, 1697-1735, printer, pioneer journalist; publisher of *New England Courant* and *Rhode Island Gazette*.

Fred W. Friendly, 1915-98, radio, TV reporter, producer, executive; collaborator with Edward R. Murrow.

Margaret Fuller, 1810-50, social reformer, transcendentalist, critic and foreign correspondent for *NY Tribune*.

Frank E. Gannett, 1876-1957, founded newspaper chain.

Mary Ellen Garber, 1916-2008, sports journalist.

William Lloyd Garrison, 1805-79, abolitionist; publisher of *The Liberator*.

Jack Germond, 1928-2013, political reporter.

Edwin Lawrence Godkin, 1831-1902, founder of *The Nation*, editor of *NY Evening Post*.

Katharine Graham,1917-2001, *Washington Post* publisher.

Sheilah Graham, 1904-89, Hollywood gossip columnist.

Horace Greeley, 1811-72, editor, politician; founded *NY Tribune*.

Meg Greenfield, 1930-99, *Newsweek* columnist, *Washington Post* editorial page editor.

Gilbert Hovey Grosvenor, 1875-1966, longtime editor of *National Geographic* magazine.

John Gunther, 1901-70, *Chicago Daily News* foreign correspondent, author.

David Halberstam, 1934-2007, journalist, sports reporter, author; *The Best and the Brightest*, *Summer of '49*.

Sarah Josepha Buell Hale, 1788-1879, first female magazine editor; *Ladies' Magazine*, later *Godey's Lady's Book*.

Pete Hamill, 1935-2020, NY tabloid journalist.

Paul Harvey, 1918-2009, radio broadcaster and commentator.

William Randolph Hearst, 1863-1951, founder of Hearst newspaper chain, one of the pioneers of yellow journalism.

Gabriel Heatter, 1890-1972, radio commentator.

John Hersey, 1914-98, foreign correspondent for *Time*, *Life*, and *The New Yorker*; author.

Marguerite Higgins, 1920-66, reporter, war correspondent.

Christopher Hitchens, 1949-2011, columnist and literary critic.

Hedda Hopper, 1885-1966, Hollywood gossip columnist.

Tony Horwitz, 1958-2019, author and journalist.

Roy Howard, 1883-1964, editor, executive; Scripps-Howard papers and United Press (later United Press International).

Chet (Chester Robert) Huntley, 1911-74, co-anchor of NBC's *Huntley-Brinkley Report*.

Ada Louise Huxtable, 1921-2013, architecture critic.

Gwen Ifill, 1955-2016, TV journalist.

Ralph Ingersoll, 1900-85, editor; *Fortune*, *Time*, *Life* exec.

Molly Ivins, 1944-2007, author, syndicated political columnist.

Peter Jennings, 1938-2005, ABC correspondent, anchor.

Pauline Kael, 1919-2001, film critic.

H. V. (Hans von) Kaltenborn, 1878-1965, radio commentator, reporter.

Murray Kempton, 1917-97, reporter, columnist for magazines and newspapers, including *NY Post*.

Dorothy Kilgallen, 1913-65, crime reporter, columnist.

James J. Kilpatrick, 1920-2010, political columnist, author and television personality.

John S. Knight, 1894-1981, editor, publisher; founded Knight newspaper group, which merged into Knight-Ridder.

Joseph Kraft, 1942-86, foreign policy columnist.

Irving Kristol, 1920-2009, columnist, commentator.

Arthur Krock, 1886-1974, *NY Times* political writer, Washington bureau chief.

Charles Kuralt, 1934-97, TV anchor; host of CBS "On the Road" featuring stories about life in the U.S.

Ann Landers (Eppie Lederer), 1918-2002, advice columnist.

David Lawrence, 1888-1973, reporter, columnist, publisher; founded *U.S. News & World Report*.

Jim Lehrer, 1934-2020, television journalist.

Frank Leslie, 1821-80, engraver, publisher of newspapers and magazines, notably *Leslie's Illustrated Newspaper*.

Anthony Lewis, 1927-2013, legal journalist.

Alexander Liberman, 1912-99, editorial director for Condé Nast magazines.

A(bbott) J(oseph) Liebling, 1904-63, foreign correspondent, critic; principally with *The New Yorker*.

Walter Lippmann, 1889-1974, political analyst, social critic, columnist, author.

Peter Lisagor, 1915-76, Washington bureau chief, *Chicago Daily News*; broadcast commentator.

David Ross Locke, 1833-88, humorist, satirist under pseudonym P.V. Nasby; owned *Toledo (Ohio) Blade*.

Elijah Parish Lovejoy, 1802-37, abolitionist editor in St. Louis and in Alton, IL; killed by proslavery mob.

Clare Booth Luce, 1903-87, war correspondent for *Life*, diplomat, playwright.

Henry R. Luce, 1898-1967, founded *Time*, *Fortune*, *Life*, *Sports Illustrated*.

Dwight Macdonald, 1906-82, reporter, social critic.

Robert MacNeil, 1931-2024, TV journalist.

Don Marquis, 1878-1937, humor columnist for *NY Sun* and *NY Tribune*; wrote "Archy and Mehitabel" stories.

Nancy Hicks Maynard, 1946-2008, African American publisher, journalist.

Robert Maynard, 1937-97, first African-American editor and then owner of major U.S. paper, the *Oakland Tribune*.

C(harles) K(enny) McClatchy, 1858-1936, founder of McClatchy newspaper chain.

Sarah McClendon, 1910-2003, veteran White House correspondent.
Samuel McClure, 1857-1949, founder (1893) of *McClure's Magazine*, famous for its investigative reporting.
Anne O'Hare McCormick, 1889-1954, foreign correspondent; first woman on *NY Times* editorial board.
Robert R. McCormick, 1880-1955, editor, publisher, executive of *Chicago Tribune* and *NY Daily News*.
Ralph McGill, 1893-1969, crusading editor, publisher of *Atlanta Constitution*.
Mary McGrory, 1918-2004, Washington columnist.
O(scar) O(dd) McIntyre, 1884-1938, feature writer, syndicated columnist on everyday life in New York City.
John McLaughlin, 1927-2016, TV journalist.
Joseph Medill, 1823-99, longtime editor of the *Chicago Tribune*.
H(enry) L(ouis) Mencken, 1880-1956, reporter, editor, columnist with *Baltimore Sun* papers; anti-establishment viewpoint.
Edwin Meredith, 1876-1928, founder of magazine company.
Frank A. Munsey, 1854-1925, owner, editor, and publisher of newspapers and magazines, including *Munsey's Magazine*.
Edward R. Murrow, 1908-65, broadcast reporter, exec.; reported from Britain in WWII; hosted *See It Now*, *Person to Person*.
Allen Neuharth, 1924-2013, *USA Today* founder.
Edwin Newman, 1919-2010, NBC news correspondent.
P. J. O'Rourke, 1947-2022, political satirist.
Louella Parsons, 1881-1972, Hollywood gossip columnist.
Ethel L. Payne, 1911-91, African American civil rights reporter.
Daniel Pearl, 1963-2002, American journalist; kidnapped and murdered in Pakistan.
Drew (Andrew Russell) Pearson, 1897-1969, investigative reporter, columnist.
(James) Westbrook Pegler, 1894-1969, reporter, columnist.
Shirley Povich, 1905-98, sports columnist.
Joseph Pulitzer, 1847-1911, *NY World* publisher; founded Columbia Journalism School, Pulitzer Prizes.
Joseph Pulitzer II, 1885-1955, longtime *St. Louis Post-Dispatch* editor, publisher; built it into major paper.
Ernie Pyle, 1900-45, reporter, war correspondent; killed in WWII.
William Raspberry, 1935-2012, public affairs columnist.
Henry Raymond, 1820-69, cofounder, editor, *NY Times*.
Harry Reasoner, 1923-91, ABC and CBS news reporter, anchor.
John Reed, 1887-1920, reporter; foreign correspondent famous for coverage of Bolshevik Revolution; buried at the Kremlin.
Whitelaw Reid, 1837-1912, longtime editor, *NY Tribune*.
James Reston, 1909-95, *NY Times* political reporter, columnist.
Frank Reynolds, 1923-83, ABC reporter, anchor.
(Henry) Grantland Rice, 1880-1954, sportswriter.
Jacob Riis, 1849-1914, reporter, photographer; exposed slum conditions in *How the Other Half Lives*.
Cokie Roberts, 1943-2019, broadcast journalist.
Max Robinson, 1939-88, first African American to anchor network news (ABC), 1978.
Andy Rooney, 1919-2011, radio and TV commentator (*60 Minutes*).
A. M. Rosenthal, 1922-2006, reporter, editor for *NY Times*, 1943-99.
Harold Ross, 1892-1951, founder, editor, *The New Yorker*.
Carl T. Rowan, 1925-2000, reporter, columnist, author.
Mike Royko, 1932-97, Chicago newspaper columnist; wrote *Boss*, biography of Mayor Richard J. Daley (1902-76).
Louis Rukeyser, 1933-2006, TV journalist, financial analyst; hosted *Wall Street Week* on public television.
(Alfred) Damon Runyon, 1884-1946, sportswriter, columnist; stories collected in *Guys and Dolls*.
Tim Russert, 1950-2008, TV journalist; moderator of *Meet the Press* (NBC).
John B. Russwurm, 1799-1851, cofounded (1827) nation's first Black newspaper, *Freedom's Journal*, in New York, NY.
Morley Safer, 1931-2016, TV journalist (*60 Minutes*).
William Safire, 1929-2009, Pulitzer Prize-winning columnist, *NY Times*.
Adela Rogers St. Johns, 1894-1988, reporter, sportswriter for Hearst newspapers.
Pierre Salinger, 1925-2004, press sec. under Pres. Kennedy and Johnson, foreign correspondent.
Harrison Salisbury, 1908-93, reporter, foreign correspondent; Soviet specialist.
Andrew Sarris, 1928-2012, film critic, *Village Voice*.
Daniel Schorr, 1916-2010, broadcast and print journalist.
E(dward) W(illis) Scripps, 1854-1926, founded first large U.S. newspaper chain, pioneered syndication.
Eric Sevareid, 1912-92, war correspondent, radio newscaster, CBS commentator.
Anthony Shadid, 1968-2012, foreign correspondent.
Randy Shilts, 1951-94, journalist; author of *And the Band Played On*.
William L. Shirer, 1904-93, broadcaster, foreign correspondent; wrote *The Rise and Fall of the Third Reich*.
Howard K. Smith, 1914-2002, ABC news reporter, anchor.
Liz Smith, 1923-2017, gossip columnist.
Red (Walter) Smith, 1905-82, sportswriter.
Edgar P. Snow, 1905-71, correspondent; expert on Chinese Communist movement.
Tony Snow, 1955-2008, columnist, radio/TV journalist, White House press sec.
Tom Snyder, 1936-2007, television journalist.
Lawrence Spivak, 1900-94, co-creator, moderator, producer of *Meet the Press*.
(Joseph) Lincoln Steffens, 1866-1936, muckraking journalist.
I(sidor) F(einstein) Stone, 1907-89, one-man editor of *I. F. Stone's Weekly*.
Arthur Hays Sulzberger, 1891-1968, longtime publisher of *NY Times*, 1935-61.
Arthur Ochs "Punch" Sulzberger, 1926-2012, longtime publisher of *NY Times*, 1963-92.
C(yrus) L(eo) Sulzberger, 1912-93, *NY Times* foreign correspondent, columnist.
David Susskind, 1920-87, TV producer, public affairs talk-show host (*Open End*).
John Cameron Swayze, 1906-95, early TV newscaster (NBC).
Herbert Bayard Swope, 1882-1958, war correspondent, editor of *NY World*.
André Leon Talley, 1949-2022, creative director of *Vogue*.
Ida Tarbell, 1857-1944, muckraking journalist.
Helen Thomas, 1920-2013, White House correspondent, 1959-2010.
Isaiah Thomas, 1750-1831, printer, publisher; cofounder of revolutionary journal, *Massachusetts Spy*.
Lowell Thomas, 1892-1981, radio newscaster, world traveler.
Dorothy Thompson, 1894-1961, foreign correspondent, columnist, radio commentator.
Hunter S. Thompson, 1937-2005, political journalist, author; *Fear and Loathing on the Campaign Trail* (1972).
Kenneth Thompson, 1923-2006, Canadian media magnate; owned Toronto *Globe and Mail* newspaper.
Abigail Van Buren (Pauline Phllips), 1918-2013, advice columnist.
Mike Wallace, 1918-2012, TV journalist (*60 Minutes*).
Barbara Walters, 1929-2022, first woman co-anchor of network evening news (ABC), 1976; co-creator and co-host of *The View*.
Ida Bell Wells-Barnett, 1862-1931, African-American reporter, editor, anti-lynching crusader.
William Allen White, 1868-1944, newspaper editor, publisher.
Tom Wicker, 1926-2011, *NY Times* political reporter, columnist.
Walter Winchell, 1897-1972, reporter, columnist, broadcaster of celebrity news.
John Peter Zenger, 1697-1746, printer, journalist; acquitted in precedent-setting libel suit (1735).

Military and Naval Leaders of the Past

Reviewed by Alan C. Aimone, U.S. Military Academy Library.

Alexander the Great, 356-323 BCE, (Maced.) conquered Persia and much of the world known to Europeans.
Harold Alexander, 1891-1969, (Br.) led Allied invasion of Italy, 1943, WWII.
Ethan Allen, 1738-89, (U.S.) headed Green Mountain Boys; captured Ft. Ticonderoga, 1775, Amer. Rev.
Edmund Allenby, 1861-1936, (Br.) in Boer War, WWI; led Egyptian expeditionary force, 1917-18.
Benedict Arnold, 1741-1801, (U.S.) victorious at Saratoga; tried to betray West Point to British, Amer. Rev.
Henry "Hap" Arnold, 1886-1950, (U.S.) commanded Army Air Force in WWII.
Ashurnasirpal II, 884-859 BCE, (Assyria) king; began Assyrian conquest of Middle East.
John Barry, 1745-1803, (U.S.) won numerous sea battles during Amer. Rev.
Pierre Beauregard, 1818-93, (U.S.) Confed. general; ordered bombardment of Ft. Sumter that began Civil War.
Belisarius, c. 505-565, (Byzant.) won remarkable victories for Byzantine emperor Justinian I.
Black Hawk, 1767-1838, (Amer. Ind.) Sauk war chief.
Gebhard von Blücher, 1742-1819, (Ger.) helped defeat Napoleon at Waterloo.
Simón Bolívar, 1783-1830, (Venez.) S. Amer. revolutionary who liberated much of the continent from Spanish rule.
Edward Braddock, 1695-1755, (Br.) commanded forces in French and Indian War.
Omar N. Bradley, 1893-1981, (U.S.) headed U.S. ground troops in Normandy invasion, 1944, WWII.
John Burgoyne, 1722-92, (Br.) general; defeated at Saratoga, Amer. Rev.
Julius Caesar, 100-44 BCE, (Rom.) general and politician; conquered northern Gaul, overthrew Roman Republic.
Charlemagne, 742-814, (Fr.) king of the Franks, Holy Roman Emperor; conquered most of Western Europe.
Claire Lee Chennault, 1893-1958, (U.S.) headed Flying Tigers in WWII.
El Cid (Rodrigo Diaz de Vivar), 1040-99, (Sp.) renowned knight; captured Valencia (1094), hero of "Song of Cid" epic.
Mark W. Clark, 1896-1984, (U.S.) helped plan N African invasion in WWII; commander of UN forces, Korean War.
Karl von Clausewitz, 1780-1831, (Prus.) military theorist.
Lucius D. Clay, 1897-1978, (U.S.) led Berlin airlift, 1948-49.
Henry Clinton, 1738-95, (Br.) commander of forces in Amer. Rev., 1778-81.
Cochise, c. 1815-74, (Amer. Ind.) chief of Chiricahua band of Apache Indians in Southwest U.S.
Charles Cornwallis, 1738-1805, (Br.) victorious at Brandywine, 1777; surrendered at Yorktown, Amer. Rev.
Hernán Cortés, 1485-1547, (Sp.) led Spanish conquistadors in the defeat of the Aztec empire, 1519-28.

Crazy Horse, 1849-77, (Amer. Ind.) Sioux war chief victorious at Battle of the Little Bighorn.
George Armstrong Custer, 1839-76, (U.S.) army officer defeated and killed at Battle of the Little Bighorn.
Benjamin O. Davis Jr., 1912-2002, (U.S.) leader of WWII Black aviators; first African American general in U.S. Air Force.
Benjamin O. Davis Sr., 1877-1970, (U.S.) first African American general in U.S. Army, 1940.
Moshe Dayan, 1915-81, (Isr.) directed campaigns in the 1967, 1973 Arab-Israeli wars.
Stephen Decatur, 1779-1820, (U.S.) naval hero of Barbary wars, War of 1812.
Anton Denikin, 1872-1947, (Russ.) led White forces in Russian civil war.
George Dewey, 1837-1917, (U.S.) destroyed Spanish fleet at Manila, 1898, Span.-Amer. War.
Karl Doenitz, 1891-1980, (Ger.) submarine cmdr. in chief and naval cmdr., WWII; last pres. of Third Reich.
Jimmy Doolittle, 1896-1993, (U.S.) led 1942 air raid on Tokyo and other Japanese cities in WWII.
Hugh Dowding, 1882-1970, (Br.) headed RAF Fighter Command, 1936-40, WWII.
Jubal Early, 1816-94, (U.S.) Confed. general; led raid on Washington, DC, 1864, Civil War.
Dwight D. Eisenhower, 1890-1969, (U.S.) commanded Allied forces in Europe, WWII.
Erich von Falkenhayn, 1861-1922, (Ger.) minister of war, general, commander at Verdun in WWI.
David Farragut, 1801-70, (U.S.) Union admiral; captured New Orleans, Mobile Bay, Civil War.
John Arbuthnot Fisher, 1841-1920, (Br.) WWI admiral; naval reformer.
Ferdinand Foch, 1851-1929, (Fr.) headed victorious Allied armies, 1918, WWI.
Nathan Bedford Forrest, 1821-77, (U.S.) Confed. general; led raids against Union supply lines, Civil War.
Frederick the Great, 1712-86, (Prus.) led Prussia in Seven Years' War.
Horatio Gates, 1728-1806, (U.S.) commanded army at Saratoga, Amer. Rev.
Genghis Khan, 1162-1227, (Mongol) unified Mongol tribes, subjugated much of Asia, 1206-21.
Geronimo, 1829-1909, (Amer. Ind.) leader of Chiricahua band of Apache Indians.
Vo Nguyen Giap, 1911?-2013, (Viet.) commanded People's Army of Vietnam against U.S.
Charles G. Gordon, 1833-85, (Br.) led forces in China, Crimean War; killed at Khartoum, Sudan.
Ulysses S. Grant, 1822-85, (U.S.) headed Union army, Civil War, 1864-65; forced Robert E. Lee's surrender, 1865.
Nathanael Greene, 1742-86, (U.S.) defeated British in Southern campaign, 1780-81, Amer. Rev.
Heinz Guderian, 1888-1954, (Ger.) tank theorist; led panzer tank forces in Poland, France, Russia, WWII.
Gustavus Adolphus, 1594-1632, (Swed.) king, military tactician, reformer; led forces in Thirty Years' War.
Douglas Haig, 1861-1928, (Br.) led British armies in France, 1915-18, WWI.
William F. Halsey, 1882-1959, (U.S.) defeated Japanese fleet at Leyte Gulf, 1944, WWII.
Hannibal, 247-183 BCE, (Carthage) invaded Rome, crossing Alps, in Second Punic War, 218-201 BCE.
Arthur Travers Harris, 1895-1984, (Br.) led Britain's WWII bomber command.
Paul von Hindenburg, 1847-1934, (Ger.) chief of general staff, WWI; second pres. of Weimar Republic.
Richard Howe, 1726-99, (Br.) commanded navy in Amer. Rev., 1776-78; June 1 victory against French, 1794.
William Howe, 1729-1814, (Br.) commanded forces in Amer. Rev., 1776-78.
Isaac Hull, 1773-1843, (U.S.) sunk British frigate *Guerriere*, War of 1812.
Thomas "Stonewall" Jackson, 1824-63, (U.S.) Confed. general; led Shenandoah Valley campaign, Civil War.
Daniel James Jr., 1920-78, (U.S.) first Black 4-star general, 1975; commander, N. American Air Defense Command.
Joseph Joffre, 1852-1931, (Fr.) headed Allied armies; won Battle of the Marne, 1914, WWI.
John Paul Jones, 1747-92, (U.S.) commanded *Bonhomme Richard* in victory over *Serapis*, Amer. Rev., 1779.
Chief Joseph, c. 1840-1904, (Amer. Ind.) chief of the Nez Percé; forced by U.S. army to retreat and surrender.
Stephen Kearny, 1794-1848, (U.S.) headed Army of the West in Mexican War.
Albert Kesselring, 1885-1960, (Ger.) field marshal who led the defense of Italy in WWII.
Ernest J. King, 1878-1956, (U.S.) key WWII naval strategist.
Horatio H. Kitchener, 1850-1916, (Br.) led forces in Boer War, victorious at Khartoum, organized army in WWI.
Henry Knox, 1750-1806, (U.S.) general in Amer. Rev.; first sec. of war under U.S. Constitution.
Lavrenti Kornilov, 1870-1918, (Russ.) commander-in-chief, 1917; led counter-revolutionary march on Petrograd.
Thaddeus Kosciuszko, 1746-1817, (Pol.) aided Amer. Rev.
Walter Krueger, 1881-1967, (U.S.) led Sixth Army in WWII in Southwest Pacific.
Mikhail Kutuzov, 1745-1813, (Russ.) fought at Borodino, Napol. Wars, 1812; abandoned Moscow, forced French retreat.
Marquis de Lafayette, 1757-1834, (Fr.) fought in, secured French aid for Amer. Rev.
T(homas) E. Lawrence (of Arabia), 1888-1935, (Br.) organized revolt of Arabs against Turks in WWI.
William Daniel Leahy, 1875-1959, (U.S.) chief of staff to Pres. Roosevelt in WWII, Fleet Admiral.
Henry (Light-Horse Harry) Lee, 1756-1818, (U.S.) cavalry officer in Amer. Rev.
Robert E. Lee, 1807-70, (U.S.) Confed. general; defeated at Gettysburg, Civil War; surrendered to Grant, 1865.
Curtis LeMay, 1906-90, (U.S.) Air Force cmdr. in WWII, Korean War, Vietnam War.
Lyman Lemnitzer, 1899-1988, (U.S.) WWII hero; later general, chairman of Joint Chiefs of Staff.
James Longstreet, 1821-1904, (U.S.) aided Lee at Gettysburg, Civil War.
Erich Ludendorff, 1865-1937, (Ger.) general; victor at Tannenberg, WWI.
Douglas MacArthur, 1880-1964, (U.S.) commanded forces in SW Pacific in WWII; headed occupation forces in Japan, 1945-51; UN commander in Korean War.
Carl Gustaf Mannerheim, 1867-1951, (Fin.) army officer and pres. of Finland, 1944-46.
Erich von Manstein, 1887-1973, (Ger.) served WWI, WWII; planned invasion of France (1940); convicted of war crimes.
Francis Marion, 1733-95, (U.S.) led guerrilla actions in South Carolina during Amer. Rev.
Duke of Marlborough, 1650-1722, (Br.) led forces against Louis XIV in War of the Spanish Succession.
George C. Marshall, 1880-1959, (U.S.) chief of staff in WWII; authored Marshall Plan.
Maurice, Count of Nassau, 1567-1625, (Neth.) military innovator; led forces in Thirty Years' War.
George B. McClellan, 1826-85, (U.S.) Union general; commanded Army of the Potomac, 1861-62, Civil War.
George Meade, 1815-72, (U.S.) commanded Union forces at Gettysburg, Civil War.
Doris "Dorie" Miller, 1919-43, (U.S.) Navy hero of Pearl Harbor attack; first African American awarded Navy Cross.
Billy Mitchell, 1879-1936, (U.S.) WWI air-power advocate; court-martialed for insubordination, later vindicated.
Helmuth von Moltke, 1800-91, (Ger.) victorious in Austro-Prussian, Franco-Prussian wars.
Louis de Montcalm, 1712-59, (Fr.) headed troops in Canada, French and Indian War; defeated at Quebec, 1759.
Bernard Law Montgomery, 1887-1976, (Br.) stopped German offensive at Alamein, 1942, WWII; helped plan Normandy invasion.
Daniel Morgan, 1736-1802, (U.S.) victorious at Cowpens, 1781, Amer. Rev.
Louis Mountbatten, 1900-79, (Br.) Supreme Allied Commander of SE Asia, 1943-46, WWII.
Joachim Murat, 1767-1815, (Fr.) led cavalry at Marengo, Austerlitz, and Jena, Napoleonic Wars.
Napoleon Bonaparte, 1769-1821, (Fr.) defeated Russia and Austria at Austerlitz, 1805; invaded Russia, 1812; defeated at Waterloo, 1815.
Horatio Nelson, 1758-1805, (Br.) naval cmdr.; destroyed French fleet at Trafalgar.
Michel Ney, 1769-1815, (Fr.) commanded forces in Switz., Austria, Russ., Napoleonic Wars; defeated at Waterloo.
Chester Nimitz, 1885-1966, (U.S.) cmdr. of naval forces in Pacific in WWII.
Osceola, 1804-38, (Amer. Ind.) war leader of Seminole people of Florida.
George S. Patton, 1885-1945, (U.S.) led assault on Sicily, 1943, Third Army invasion of Europe, WWII.
Oliver Perry, 1785-1819, (U.S.) won Battle of Lake Erie in War of 1812.
John Pershing, 1860-1948, (U.S.) commanded Mexican border campaign, 1916; Amer. Expeditionary Force, WWI.
Henri Philippe Pétain, 1856-1951, (Fr.) defended Verdun, 1916; headed Vichy government in WWII.
George E. Pickett, 1825-75, (U.S.) Confed. general famed for "charge" at Gettysburg, Civil War.
Pontiac, 1720?-69, (Amer. Ind.) Ottawa war chief.
Charles Portal, 1893-1971, (Br.) chief of staff, Royal Air Force, 1940-45; led in Battle of Britain.
Colin Powell, 1937-2021, (U.S.) army general, chair of the Joint Chiefs of Staff; first Black sec. of state.
Manfred Freiherr von Richthofen (Red Baron), 1892-1918, (Ger.) WWI flying ace, led elite fighter squadron.
Hyman Rickover, 1900-86, (U.S.) father of nuclear navy.
Matthew Bunker Ridgway, 1895-1993, (U.S.) commanded Allied ground forces in Korean War.
Erwin Rommel, 1891-1944, (Ger.) headed Afrika Korps, WWII.
Gerd von Rundstedt, 1875-1953, (Ger.) supreme cmdr. in West, 1942-45, WWII.
Saladin, 1138-93, (Kurdish Muslim) recaptured Jerusalem from Crusaders.
Aleksandr Samsonov, 1859-1914, (Russ.) led invasion of E Prussia, WWI; defeated at Tannenberg, 1914.
Antonio López de Santa Anna, 1794-1876, (Mex.) defeated Texans at the Alamo; defeated in Mexican War.
Maurice, Count of Saxe, 1696-1750, (Fr.) general, noted tactician; War of Austrian Succession, War of Pol. Succession.
H. Norman Schwarzkopf, 1934-2012, (U.S.) army general; led Persian Gulf War, 1991.
Scipio Africanus the Elder, 234?-183 BCE, (Roman) hero of Second Punic War; defeated Hannibal, invaded N Africa.
Winfield Scott, 1786-1866, (U.S.) hero of War of 1812; headed forces in Mexican War, took Mexico City.
Philip Sheridan, 1831-88, (U.S.) Union cavalry officer; headed Army of the Shenandoah, 1864-65, Civil War.

William T. Sherman, 1820-91, (U.S.) Union general; sacked Atlanta during "march to the sea," 1864, Civil War.
Sitting Bull, c. 1831-90, (Amer. Ind.) Hunkpapa Lakota chief victorious at Battle of the Little Bighorn.
Carl Spaatz, 1891-1974, (U.S.) directed strategic bombing against Germany, later Japan, in WWII.
Raymond Spruance, 1886-1969, (U.S.) victorious at Midway Island, 1942, WWII.
Joseph W. Stilwell, 1883-1946, (U.S.) headed forces in the China, Burma, India theater in WWII.
J.E.B. Stuart, 1833-64, (U.S.) Confed. cavalry commander, Civil War.
Sun Tzu, 6th? cent. BCE, (China) general; author of *The Art of War*.
Aleksandr Suvorov, 1729-1800, (Russ.) commanded Allied Russian and Austrian armies, Russo-Turkish War.
Tamerlane, 1336-1405, (Turkoman Mongol) conqueror; established empire from India to Mediterranean Sea.
Tecumseh, 1768-1813, (Amer. Ind.) Shawnee chief; led Indian confederation opposing colonists.
George H. Thomas, 1816-70, (U.S.) saved Union army at Chattanooga, 1863; won at Nashville, 1864, Civil War.
Semyon Timoshenko, 1895-1970, (USSR) defended Moscow, Stalingrad, WWII; led winter offensive, 1942-43.
Alfred von Tirpitz, 1849-1930, (Ger.) responsible for submarine blockade in WWI.
Henri de la Tour d'Auvergne, Viscount of Turenne, 1611-75, (Fr.) marshal; Thirty Years' War, Fronde, War of Devolution.
Sebastien Le Prestre de Vauban, 1633-1707, (Fr.) innovative military engineer, theorist.
Jonathan M. Wainwright, 1883-1953, (U.S.) forced to surrender on Corregidor, Philippines, 1942, WWII.
George Washington, 1732-99, (U.S.) led Continental army, 1775-83, Amer. Rev.
Archibald Wavell, 1883-1950, (Br.) commanded forces in N and E Africa, SE Asia in WWII.
Anthony Wayne, 1745-96, (U.S.) captured Stony Point, NY, 1779, Amer. Rev.
Duke of Wellington, 1769-1852, (Br.) defeated Napoleon at Waterloo, 1815.
William Westmoreland, 1914-2005, (U.S.) commanded forces in Vietnam, 1964-68.
William I (The Conqueror), 1027-87, (Br.) victor, Battle of Hastings, 1066; became first Norman king of England.
James Wolfe, 1727-59, (Br.) captured Quebec from French, 1759, French and Indian War.
Isoroku Yamamoto, 1884-1943, (Jpn.) cmdr. in chief of Japanese fleet; naval planner before and during WWII.
Georgi Zhukov, 1895-1974, (Russ.) defended Moscow, 1941; led assault on Berlin, 1945, WWII.

Philosophers and Religious Figures of the Past

Excludes biblical figures and popes (see Religion chapter). For Greeks and Romans, see also Historical Figures chapter.

Lyman Abbott, 1835-1922, (U.S.) clergyman, reformer; advocate of Christian Socialism.
Pierre Abelard, 1079-1142, (Fr.) philosopher, theologian, teacher; used dialectic method to support Christian beliefs.
Felix Adler, 1851-1933, (U.S.) German-born founder of the Ethical Culture Soc.
Mortimer Adler, 1902-2001, (U.S.) philosopher; helped create "Great Books" program.
(St.) Anselm, c. 1033-1109, (It.) philosopher-theologian, church leader; "ontological argument" for God's existence.
(St.) Thomas Aquinas, 1225-74, (It.) preeminent medieval philosopher-theologian; *Summa Theologica*.
Aristotle, 384-322 BCE, (Gr.) pioneering wide-ranging philosopher, logician, ethician, naturalist.
(St.) Augustine, 354-430, (N Africa) philosopher, theologian, bishop; *Confessions*, *City of God*, *On the Trinity*.
J. L. Austin, 1911-60, (Br.) ordinary-language philosopher.
Averroes (Ibn Rushd), 1126-98, (Sp.) Islamic philosopher, physician.
Avicenna (Ibn Sina), 980-1037, (Iran) Islamic philosopher, scientist.
A(lfred) J(ules) Ayer, 1910-89, (Br.) philosopher, logical positivist; *Language, Truth, and Logic*.
Roger Bacon, c. 1214-94, (Eng.) philosopher, scientist.
Bahá'u'lláh (Mirza Husayn Ali), 1817-92, (Pers.) founder of Bahá'í faith.
Karl Barth, 1886-1968, (Switz.) theologian; a leading force in 20th-cent. Protestantism.
Thomas à Becket, 1118-70, (Eng.) archbishop of Canterbury; opposed Henry II, murdered by king's men.
(St.) Benedict, c. 480-547, (It.) founded the Benedictine order.
Jeremy Bentham, 1748-1832, (Br.) philosopher, reformer; enunciated utilitarianism.
Henri Bergson, 1859-1941, (Fr.) philosopher of evolution.
George Berkeley, 1685-1753, (Ire.) idealist philosopher, bishop.
John Biddle, 1615-62, (Eng.) founder of English Unitarianism.
Jakob Boehme, 1575-1624, (Ger.) theosophist, mystic.
Dietrich Bonhoeffer, 1906-45, (Ger.) Lutheran theologian, pastor; executed as opponent of Nazis.
William Brewster, 1567-1644, (Eng.) *Mayflower* passenger, Plymouth Colony leader.
Emil Brunner, 1889-1966, (Switz.) Protestant theologian.
Giordano Bruno, 1548-1600, (It.) philosopher, pantheist.
Martin Buber, 1878-1965, (Ger.) Jewish philosopher, theologian; *I and Thou*.
Buddha (Siddhartha Gautama), c. 563-c. 483 BCE, (India) philosopher; founded Buddhism.
John Calvin, 1509-64, (Fr.) theologian; a key figure in the Protestant Reformation.
Rudolph Carnap, 1891-1970, (U.S.) German-born analytic philosopher; a founder of logical positivism.
William Ellery Channing, 1780-1842, (U.S.) clergyman; early spokesman for Unitarianism.
Auguste Comte, 1798-1857, (Fr.) philosopher; originated positivism.
Confucius, 551-479 BCE, (China) founder of Confucianism.
John Cotton, 1584-1652, (Eng.) Puritan theologian.
Thomas Cranmer, 1489-1556, (Eng.) Anglican churchman; wrote much of *Book of Common Prayer*.
Jacques Derrida, 1930-2004, (Fr.) deconstructionist philosopher.
René Descartes, 1596-1650, (Fr.) philosopher, mathematician; "father of modern philosophy"; *Discourse on Method*, *Meditations on First Philosophy*.
John Dewey, 1859-1952, (U.S.) philosopher, educator; instrumentalist theory of knowledge, progressive education.
Denis Diderot, 1713-84, (Fr.) philosopher, encyclopedist.
John Duns Scotus, c. 1266-1308, (Scot.) Franciscan philosopher, theologian.
Mary Baker Eddy, 1821-1910, (U.S.) founder of Christian Science; *Science and Health*.
Jonathan Edwards, 1703-58, (U.S.) preacher, theologian; "Sinners in the Hands of an Angry God."
(Desiderius) Erasmus, c. 1466-1536, (Neth.) Renaissance humanist; *On the Freedom of the Will*.
Jerry Falwell, 1933-2007, (U.S.) TV evangelist, religious commentator.
Johann Fichte, 1762-1814, (Ger.) idealist philosopher.
Michel Foucault, 1926-84, (Fr.) structuralist philosopher, historian.
George Fox, 1624-91, (Br.) founder of Society of Friends (Quakers).
(St.) Francis of Assisi, 1182-1226, (It.) espoused voluntary poverty, founded Franciscans order.
al-Ghazali, 1058-1111, (Iran) Islamic philosopher.
Billy Graham, 1918-2018, (U.S.) evangelist, adviser to presidents.
Billy James Hargis, 1925-2004, (U.S.) anti-Communist televangelist; founder of the Church of the Christian Crusade.
Georg W. F. Hegel, 1770-1831, (Ger.) idealist philosopher; *Phenomenology of Mind*.
Martin Heidegger, 1889-1976, (Ger.) existentialist philosopher; affected many fields; *Being and Time*.
Johann G. Herder, 1744-1803, (Ger.) philosopher, cultural historian; a founder of German Romanticism.
Thomas Hobbes, 1588-1679, (Eng.) philosopher, political theorist; *Leviathan*.
L. Ron Hubbard, 1911-1986, (U.S.) founder of Scientology.
David Hume, 1711-76, (Scot.) empiricist philosopher; *Enquiry Concerning Human Understanding*.
Jan Hus, 1369-1415, (Czech.) religious reformer.
Edmund Husserl, 1859-1938, (Ger.) philosopher; founded the phenomenological movement.
Thomas Huxley, 1825-95, (Br.) philosopher, educator.
William Ralph Inge, 1860-1954, (Br.) theologian; explored mystic aspects of Christianity.
William James, 1842-1910, (U.S.) philosopher, psychologist, pragmatist; studied religious experience.
Karl Jaspers, 1883-1969, (Ger.) existentialist philosopher.
Joan of Arc, 1412-31, (Fr.) national heroine, a patron saint of France; key figure in the Hundred Years War.
Immanuel Kant, 1724-1804, (Ger.) philosopher; founder of modern critical philosophy; *Critique of Pure Reason*.
Thomas à Kempis, c. 1380-1471, (Ger.) monk, devotional writer; *Imitation of Christ* attributed to him.
Soren Kierkegaard, 1813-55, (Den.) religious philosopher, pre-existentialist; *Either/Or*, *The Sickness Unto Death*.
John Knox, 1505-72, (Scot.) leader of Protestant Reformation in Scotland.
Hans Küng, 1928-2021, (Switz.) Catholic priest and theologian.
Lao-Tzu, 604-531 BCE, (China) philosopher; considered the founder of the Taoist religion.
Gottfried von Leibniz, 1646-1716, (Ger.) rationalistic philosopher, logician, mathematician.
John Locke, 1632-1704, (Eng.) political theorist, empiricist philosopher; *Essay Concerning Human Understanding*.
(St.) Ignatius Loyola, 1491-1556, (Sp.) founder of the Jesuits; *Spiritual Exercises*.
Martin Luther, 1483-1546, (Ger.) leader of the Protestant Reformation; founded Lutheran church.
Jean-Francois Lyotard, 1924-98, (Fr.) postmodern philosopher, lecturer; *The Post-Modern Condition*.
Maimonides, 1135-1204, (Sp.) major Jewish philosopher.
Gabriel Marcel, 1889-1973, (Fr.) Rom. Cath. existentialist philosopher, dramatist.
Jacques Maritain, 1882-1973, (Fr.) neo-Thomist philosopher.
Cotton Mather, 1663-1728, (U.S.) defender of orthodox Puritanism; founded Yale, 1701.

Aimee Semple McPherson, 1890-1944, (Can.-U.S.) Pentecostal evangelist.
Philipp Melanchthon, 1497-1560, (Ger.) theologian, humanist; an important voice in the Reformation.
Maurice Merleau-Ponty, 1908-61, (Fr.) existentialist philosopher; *Phenomenology of Perception*.
Thomas Merton, 1915-68, (U.S.) Trappist monk, spiritual writer; *The Seven Storey Mountain*.
Dwight Moody, 1837-99, (U.S.) evangelist.
Rev. Sun Myung Moon, 1920-2012, (N. Kor.) Unification Church founder.
G(eorge) E(dward) Moore, 1873-1958, (Br.) philosopher; *Principia Ethica*, "A Defense of Common Sense."
Muhammad, c. 570-632, (Arab.) prophet of Islam.
Elijah Muhammad, 1897-1975, (U.S.) founder of Black Muslim group, Nation of Islam.
Heinrich Muhlenberg, 1711-87, (Ger.) organized the Lutheran Church in America.
John H. Newman, 1801-90, (Br.) Rom. Cath. convert, cardinal; led Oxford Movement; *Apologia pro Vita Sua*.
Thích Nhat Hanh, 1926-2022, (Viet.) Buddhist monk ("father of mindfulness").
Reinhold Niebuhr, 1892-1971, (U.S.) Protestant theologian.
Richard Niebuhr, 1894-1962, (U.S.) Protestant theologian.
Friedrich Nietzsche, 1844-1900, (Ger.) philosopher; *The Birth of Tragedy*, *Beyond Good and Evil*, *Thus Spake Zarathustra*.
Robert Nozick, 1938-2002, (U.S.) political philosopher; *Anarchy, State, and Utopia*.
Blaise Pascal, 1623-62, (Fr.) philosopher, mathematician; *Pensées* (Thoughts).
(St.) Patrick, c. 389-c. 461, (Br.) brought Christianity to Ireland.
Norman Vincent Peale, 1898-1993, (U.S.) minister, author; *The Power of Positive Thinking*.
C(harles) S. Peirce, 1839-1914, (U.S.) philosopher, logician; originated concept of pragmatism, 1878.
Plato, c. 428-347 BCE, (Gr.) philosopher; wrote Socratic dialogues; argued for immortality of soul, indep. reality of ideas or forms; *Republic*, *Meno*, *Phaedo*, *Apology*.
Plotinus, 205-70, (Rom.) a founder of neo-Platonism; *Enneads*.
W(illard) V(an) O(rman) Quine, 1908-2001, (U.S.) philosopher, logician; "On What There Is."
John Rawls, 1922-2002, (U.S.) political philosopher; *A Theory of Justice*.
Oral Roberts, 1918-2009, (U.S.) televangelist, university founder.
Pat Robertson, 1930-2023, (U.S.) TV evangelist; founder of Christian Broadcasting Network, Christian Coalition.
Moishe Rosen, 1932-2010, (U.S.) Jews for Jesus founder.
Josiah Royce, 1855-1916, (U.S.) idealist philosopher.
Bertrand Russell, 1872-1970, (Br.) philosopher, logician; one of the founders of modern logic; prolific popular writer.
Charles T. Russell, 1852-1916, (U.S.) founder of Jehovah's Witnesses.
Gilbert Ryle, 1900-76, (Br.) analytic philosopher; *The Concept of Mind*.
George Santayana, 1863-1952, (U.S.) philosopher, writer, critic; *The Sense of Beauty*, *The Realms of Being*.
Jean-Paul Sartre, 1905-80, (Fr.) philosopher, novelist, playwright; *Nausea*, *No Exit*, *Being and Nothingness*.
Friedrich von Schelling, 1775-1854, (Ger.) philosopher of romantic movement.
Friedrich Schleiermacher, 1768-1834, (Ger.) theologian; a founder of modern Protestant theology.
Arthur Schopenhauer, 1788-1860, (Ger.) philosopher; *The World as Will and Idea*.
Robert Schuller, 1926-2015, (U.S.) evangelist; Crystal Cathedral founder.
Albert Schweitzer, 1875-1965, (Ger.) theologian, social philosopher, medical missionary.
Joseph Smith, 1805-44, (U.S.) founded Latter-Day Saints (Mormon) movement, 1830.
Socrates, 469-399 BCE, (Gr.) philosopher immortalized by Plato.
Herbert Spencer, 1820-1903, (Br.) philosopher of evolution.
Herbert Spiegel, 1914-2009, (U.S.) psychiatrist who popularized hypnosis.
Baruch de Spinoza, 1632-77, (Neth.) rationalist philosopher; *Ethics*.
John Stott, 1921-2011, (Br.) evangelical Anglican cleric.
Billy Sunday, 1862-1935, (U.S.) evangelist.
Daisetz Teitaro Suzuki, 1870-1966, (Jpn.) Buddhist scholar.
Emanuel Swedenborg, 1688-1772, (Swed.) philosopher, mystic; *Principia*.
Pierre Teilhard de Chardin, 1881-1955, (Fr.) Jesuit priest, paleontologist, philosopher-theologian; *The Divine Milieu*.
(St.) Therese of Lisieux, 1873-97, (Fr.) Carmelite nun ("Little Flower"), revered for everyday sanctity; *The Story of a Soul*.
Paul Tillich, 1886-1965, (U.S.) German-born philosopher, theologian; brought depth psychology to Protestantism.
John Wesley, 1703-91, (Br.) theologian, evangelist; founded Methodism.
Alfred North Whitehead, 1861-1947, (Br.) philosopher, mathematician; *Process and Reality*.
William of Occam, c. 1285-c. 1349, (Eng.) medieval scholastic philosopher, nominalist.
Roger Williams, c. 1603-83, (U.S.) clergyman; championed religious freedom and separation of church and state.
Ludwig Wittgenstein, 1889-1951, (Austria) philosopher; major influence on contemporary language philosophy; *Tractatus Logico-Philosophicus*, *Philosophical Investigations*.
John Woolman, 1720-72, (U.S.) Quaker social reformer, abolitionist, writer; *The Journal*.
John Wycliffe, 1320-84, (Eng.) theologian, reformer.
(St.) Francis Xavier, 1506-52, (Sp.) Jesuit missionary; "Apostle of the Indies."
Brigham Young, 1801-77, (U.S.) Mormon leader after Joseph Smith's death; colonized Utah.
Huldrych Zwingli, 1484-1531, (Switz.) theologian; led Swiss Protestant Reformation.

Political Leaders of the Past

U.S. presidents, vice presidents, Supreme Court justices, and signers of the Declaration of Independence listed elsewhere. See also Historical Figures.

Shinzo Abe, 1954-2022, (Jpn.) prime minister.
Abu Bakr, 573-634, (Arab.) Muslim leader, first caliph, chosen successor to Muhammad.
Dean Acheson, 1893-1971, (U.S.) sec. of state; architect of Cold War foreign policy.
Samuel Adams, 1722-1803, (U.S.) patriot; Boston Tea Party firebrand.
Konrad Adenauer, 1876-1967, (Ger.) first West German chancellor.
Emilio Aguinaldo, 1869-1964, (Philip.) revolutionary; fought against Spain and the U.S.
Akbar, 1542-1605, Mogul emperor of India.
Madeleine Albright, 1937-2022, (Czech.-U.S.) first woman U.S. sec. of state.
Salvador Allende Gossens, 1908-73, (Chile) Marxist pres., 1970-73; ousted and died in coup.
Idi Amin, 1925-2003, (Uganda) Ugandan ruler, 1971-79; blamed for hundreds of thousands of deaths.
Kofi Annan, 1938-2018, (Ghana) UN sec.- gen.
Corazon Aquino, 1933-2009, (Philip.) pres. of the Philippines, 1986-92.
Yasir Arafat, 1929-2004, (Egypt) leader of the Palestine Liberation Organization (PLO).
Herbert H. Asquith, 1852-1928, (Br.) Liberal prime min.; instituted major social reforms.
Hafez al Assad, 1930-2000, (Syr.) pres. of Syria, 1970-2000.
Atahualpa, 1500?-33, (Inca) last ruling chief of Incan empire (in present-day Peru).
Kemal Atatürk, 1881-1938, (Turk.) founded modern Turkey.
Clement Attlee, 1883-1967, (Br.) Labour leader, prime min.; enacted natl. health service, nationalized many industries.
Stephen F. Austin, 1793-1836, (U.S.) led Texas colonization.
Mikhail Bakunin, 1814-76, (Russ.) revolutionary; leading exponent of anarchism.
Arthur J. Balfour, 1848-1930, (Br.) foreign sec. under Lloyd George; issued Balfour Declaration backing Zionism.
Bernard M. Baruch, 1870-1965, (U.S.) financier, govt. adviser.
Fulgencio Batista y Zaldívar, 1901-73, (Cuba) Cuban pres., 1940-44, 1952-59; overthrown by Castro.
Menachem Begin, 1913-92, (Isr.) Israeli prime min.; shared 1978 Nobel Peace Prize.
Ahmed Ben Bella, 1918-2012, (Alg.) first Algerian pres., 1963-65.
Eduard Benes, 1884-1948, (Czech.) pres. during interwar and post-WWII eras.
David Ben-Gurion, 1886-1973, (Isr.) first prime min. of Israel, 1948-53, 1955-63.
Thomas Hart Benton, 1782-1858, (U.S.) MO senator; championed agrarian interests and westward expansion.
Ernest Bevin, 1881-1951, (Br.) Labour party leader, foreign minister; helped lay foundation for NATO.
King Bhumibol Adulyadej, 1927-2016, (Thai.) monarch, 1946-2016.
Benazir Bhutto, 1953-2007, (Pak.) Pakistan prime min.; first elected woman leader of a majority-Muslim country.
Otto von Bismarck, 1815-98, (Ger.) statesman known as the Iron Chancellor; uniter of Germany, 1870.
Black Kettle, 1803?-68, (Amer. Ind.) Cheyenne peace chief.
James G. Blaine, 1830-93, (U.S.) Republican politician, diplomat; influential in Pan-American movement.
Léon Blum, 1872-1950, (Fr.) socialist leader, writer; headed first Popular Front government.
William E. Borah, 1865-1940, (U.S.) isolationist senator (R, ID); helped block U.S. membership in League of Nations.
Cesare Borgia, 1476-1507, (It.) soldier, politician; Italian Renaissance figure who partly inspired Machiavelli's *The Prince*.
P. W. Botha, 1916-2006, (S. Afr.) S. African president, prime min.
Boutros Boutros-Ghali, 1922-2016, (Egypt), UN sec.-gen.
Willy Brandt, 1913-92, (Ger.) statesman, chancellor of West Germany, 1969-74; promoted East/West peace, *Ostpolitik*.
Joseph Brant, 1742-1807, (Amer. Ind.) Mohawk chief.
Leonid Brezhnev, 1906-82, (USSR) Soviet leader, 1964-82.
Aristide Briand, 1862-1932, (Fr.) foreign min.; chief architect of Locarno Pact and anti-war Kellogg-Briand Pact.
William Jennings Bryan, 1860-1925, (U.S.) Democratic, populist leader, orator; three times lost race for presidency.
Ralph Bunche, 1904-71, (U.S.) first Black person to win the Nobel Peace Prize, 1950; undersecretary of the UN, 1950.
Robert Byrd, 1917-2010, (U.S.) longest serving U.S. senator (D, WV), 1959-2010.

John C. Calhoun, 1782-1850, (U.S.) political leader; champion of states' rights and a symbol of the Old South.

James Callaghan (Baron Callaghan), 1912-2005, (Br.) Labour party politician, prime min., 1976-79.

Robert Castlereagh, 1769-1822, (Br.) foreign sec.; guided Grand Alliance against Napoleon.

Fidel Castro, 1926-2016, (Cuba) prime min./pres., 1959-2008; led Communist revolution.

Camillo Benso Cavour, 1810-61, (It.) statesman; largely responsible for uniting Italy under the House of Savoy.

Nicolae Ceausescu, 1918-89, (Rom.) Communist leader, head of state, 1967-89; executed.

Neville Chamberlain, 1869-1940, (Br.) Conservative prime min. whose appeasement of Hitler led to Munich Pact.

Hugo Chávez, 1954-2013, (Venez.) socialist Venezuelan pres., 1999-2013.

Chiang Kai-shek, 1887-1975, (China) Nationalist Chinese pres. whose govt. was driven from mainland to Taiwan.

Madame Chiang Kai-shek (Mayling Soong), 1898-2003, (China) highly influential wife of Nationalist Chinese leader Chiang Kai-shek.

Jacques Chirac, 1932-2019, (Fr.) pres. of France, 1995-2007.

Shirley Chisholm, 1924-2005, (U.S.) first Black woman elected to U.S. House (1968, D, NY); pres. contender, 1972.

Winston Churchill, 1874-1965, (Br.) prime min., soldier, author; guided Britain through WWII.

Galeazzo Ciano, 1903-44, (It.) Fascist foreign minister; helped create Rome-Berlin Axis; executed by Benito Mussolini.

Henry Clay, 1777-1852, (U.S.) "The Great Compromiser"; one of the most influential pre-Civil War political leaders.

Georges Clemenceau, 1841-1929, (Fr.) twice prem.; Woodrow Wilson's antagonist at Paris Peace Conference after WWI.

DeWitt Clinton, 1769-1828, (U.S.) political leader; promoted Erie Canal.

Robert Clive, 1725-74, (Br.) first administrator of Bengal; laid foundation for British Empire in India.

Jean Baptiste Colbert, 1619-83, (Fr.) statesman; influential under Louis XIV; created the French navy.

David Crockett, 1786-1836, (U.S.) frontiersman, congressman; died defending the Alamo.

Oliver Cromwell, 1599-1658, (Br.) Lord Protector of England; led parliamentary forces during Civil War.

Curzon of Kedleston, 1859-1925, (Br.) viceroy of India, foreign sec.; major force in post-WWI world.

Édouard Daladier, 1884-1970, (Fr.) Radical Socialist politician; arrested by Vichy government, interned by Germans.

Richard J. Daley, 1902-76, (U.S.) Chicago mayor, 1955-76.

Georges Danton, 1759-94, (Fr.) leading French Rev. figure.

Jefferson Davis, 1808-89, (U.S.) pres. of the Confederacy.

Charles G. Dawes, 1865-1951, (U.S.) statesman, banker; advanced plan to stabilize post-WWI German finances.

Alcide De Gasperi, 1881-1954, (It.) prime min.; founder of Christian Democratic party.

Charles De Gaulle, 1890-1970, (Fr.) general, statesman; first pres. of the Fifth Republic.

F. W. (Frederik Willem) de Klerk, 1936-2021, (S. Afr.) S. Afr. pres., 1989-94; 1993 Nobel Peace Prize winner.

Deng Xiaoping, 1904-97, (China) "paramount leader" of China; backed economic modernization.

Eamon De Valera, 1882-1975, (Ire.-U.S.) statesman; led fight for Irish independence.

Thomas E. Dewey, 1902-71, (U.S.) NY governor (R); twice lost in try for presidency.

Ngo Dinh Diem, 1901-63, (Viet.) South Vietnamese pres.; assassinated in government takeover.

John Dingell Jr., 1926-2019, (U.S.) longest-serving U.S. rep (D, MI), 1955-2015.

Benjamin Disraeli, 1804-81, (Br.) prime min.; considered founder of modern Conservative party.

Anatoly Dobrynin, 1919-2010, (Russ.) diplomat and Soviet amb. to U.S. (1962-86).

Engelbert Dollfuss, 1892-1934, (Austria) chancellor; assassinated by Nazis.

Andrea Doria, 1466-1560, (It.) Genoese admiral, statesman; called "Father of Peace" and "Liberator of Genoa."

Stephen A. Douglas, 1813-61, (U.S.) Democratic leader, orator; ran against Lincoln for IL sen. seat, presidency.

Alexander Dubcek, 1921-92, (Czech.) statesman whose attempted liberalization was crushed, 1968.

John Foster Dulles, 1888-1959, (U.S.) sec. of state under Eisenhower; Cold War policy maker.

Friedrich Ebert, 1871-1925, (Ger.) Social Democratic movement leader; first pres., Weimar Republic, 1919-25.

Anthony Eden, 1897-1977, (Br.) foreign sec., prime min. during Suez invasion of 1956.

Ludwig Erhard, 1897-1977, (Ger.) economist, West German chancellor; led nation's economic rise after WWII.

King Fahd, 1923-2005, (Saudi Arabia) monarch from 1982 but inactive after 1995 stroke; encouraged U.S. relations.

Geraldine Ferraro, 1935-2011, (U.S.) U.S. rep. (D, NY), first woman vice-pres. nominee (1984).

João Baptista de Figueiredo, 1918-99, (Braz.) pres. of Brazil; restored nation's democracy after military rule.

Hamilton Fish, 1808-93, (U.S.) sec. of state; successfully mediated disputes with Great Britain, Latin America.

James V. Forrestal, 1892-1949, (U.S.) sec. of navy, first sec. of defense.

Francisco Franco, 1892-1975, (Sp.) leader of rebel forces during Spanish Civil War, longtime ruler of Spain.

Benjamin Franklin, 1706-90, (U.S.) printer, publisher, author, inventor, scientist, diplomat.

Louis de Frontenac, 1620-98, (Fr.) governor of New France (Canada).

J. William Fulbright, 1905-95, (U.S.) U.S. senator (D, AR); leading figure in U.S. foreign policy during Cold War years.

Hugh Gaitskell, 1906-63, (Br.) Labour party leader; major force in reversing its stand for unilateral disarmament.

Albert Gallatin, 1761-1849, (U.S.) sec. of treasury; instrumental in negotiating end of War of 1812.

Léon Gambetta, 1838-82, (Fr.) statesman, politician; one of the founders of the Third Republic.

Indira Gandhi, 1917-84, (India) daughter of Jawaharlal Nehru; prime min. of India, 1966-77, 1980-84; assassinated.

Mohandas K. Gandhi, 1869-1948, (India) political leader, ascetic; led movement against British rule; assassinated.

Giuseppe Garibaldi, 1807-82, (It.) patriot, soldier; a leader in the Risorgimento, Italian unification movement.

Valéry Giscard d'Estaing, 1926-2020, (Fr.) pres. of France, 1974-81.

William E. Gladstone, 1809-98, (Br.) prime min.; dominant force of Liberal party, 1868-94.

Paul Joseph Goebbels, 1897-1945, (Ger.) Nazi propagandist; master of mass psychology.

Barry Goldwater, 1909-98, (U.S.) conservative U.S. senator (R, AZ), 1964 pres. nominee.

Mikhail Gorbachev, 1931-2022, (USSR) reformist Soviet leader; 1990 Nobel Peace Prize winner.

Klement Gottwald, 1896-1953, (Czech.) Communist leader.

Haile Selassie (Tafari Makonnen), 1892-1975, (Ethiopia) emperor of Ethiopia.

Alexander Hamilton, 1755-1804, (U.S.) first treasury sec.; champion of strong central government.

Dag Hammarskjöld, 1905-61, (Swed.) statesman; UN sec.-general.

King Hassan II, 1929-99, (Moroc.) ruler of Morocco, 1962-99.

Vaclav Havel, 1936-2011, (Czech.) first president of Czech Republic, 1989-92.

John Hay, 1838-1905, (U.S.) sec. of state; primarily associated with Open Door Policy toward China.

Edward Heath, 1916-2005, (Br.) Conservative prime min., 1970-74; promoted European unity.

Patrick Henry, 1736-99, (U.S.) major Revolutionary War figure, orator.

Édouard Herriot, 1872-1957, (Fr.) Radical Socialist leader; twice prem., pres. of National Assembly.

Theodor Herzl, 1860-1904, (Hung.) founded modern Zionism.

Heinrich Himmler, 1900-45, (Ger.) head of Nazi SS and Gestapo.

Paul von Hindenburg, 1847-1934, (Ger.) field marshal, WWI; second pres. of Weimar Republic, 1925-34.

Adolf Hitler, 1889-1945, (Ger.) dictator; built Nazism, launched WWII, presided over the Holocaust.

Ho Chi Minh, 1890-1969, (Viet.) N. Vietnamese pres., Communist leader.

Harry L. Hopkins, 1890-1946, (U.S.) New Deal administrator; closest adviser to Franklin D. Roosevelt during WWII.

Edward M. House, 1858-1938, (U.S.) diplomat; confidential adviser to Woodrow Wilson.

Samuel Houston, 1793-1863, (U.S.) leader of struggle for Texas independence.

Cordell Hull, 1871-1955, (U.S.) sec. of state, 1933-44; initiated reciprocal trade to lower tariffs, helped organize UN.

John Hume, 1937-2020, (N. Ire.) nationalist party leader; 1998 Nobel Peace Prize winner.

Hubert H. Humphrey, 1911-78, (U.S.) U.S. senator (D, MN), vice pres., pres. nominee (1968).

King Hussein, 1935-99, (Jordan) peacemaker; ruler of Jordan, 1952-99.

Saddam Hussein, 1937-2006, (Iraq) Iraqi ruler; put to death for crimes against humanity.

Muhammad Ali Jinnah, 1876-1948, (Pak.) founder, first gov.-gen. of Pakistan.

Barbara Jordan, 1936-96, (U.S.) U.S. rep. (D, TX), orator, educator; first Black woman to win a seat in the TX state senate, 1966.

Benito Juarez, 1806-72, (Mex.) rallied his country against foreign threats; sought to create democratic, federal republic.

Betty Mae Tiger Jumper, 1923-2011, (Amer. Ind.) first woman Seminole chief.

Constantine Karamanlis, 1907-98, (Gr.) Greek prime min.; restored democracy, later president.

Frank B. Kellogg, 1856-1937, (U.S.) sec. of state; negotiated Kellogg-Briand Pact to outlaw war.

Edward M. Kennedy, 1932-2009, (U.S.) senator (D, MA); championed progressive causes.

Robert F. Kennedy, 1925-68, (U.S.) attorney general, U.S. sen. (D, NY); assassinated while seeking presidency.

Aleksandr Kerensky, 1881-1970, (Russ.) headed provisional government after Feb. 1917 revolution.

Ayatollah Ruhollah Khomeini, 1900-89, (Iran), religious-political leader; spearheaded overthrow of Shah, 1979.

Nikita Khrushchev, 1894-1971, (USSR) prem., first sec. of Communist party; initiated de-Stalinization.

Kim Dae-jung, 1925-2009, (Korea) S. Korean dissident, opposition leader, pres.; 2000 Nobel Peace Prize winner.

Kim Il Sung, 1912-94, (Korea) N. Korean dictator, 1948-94.
Kim Jong Il, 1942-2011, (Korea) N. Korean dictator, 1994-2011.
Henry Kissinger, 1923-2023, (Ger.-U.S.) U.S. sec. of state (1973-77).
Edward I. Koch, 1924-2013, (U.S.) New York City mayor, 1978-89.
Helmut Kohl, 1930-2017, (Ger.) chancellor, 1982-98; reunified Germany.
Lajos Kossuth, 1802-94, (Hung.) principal figure in 1848 Hungarian revolution.
Pyotr Kropotkin, 1842-1921, (Russ.) anarchist; championed the peasants but opposed Bolshevism.
Kublai Khan, c. 1215-94, (Mongol) emperor; founder of Yuan dynasty in China.
Béla Kun, 1886-c. 1939, (Hung.) member of Third Communist International; tried to foment worldwide revolution.
Robert M. LaFollette, 1855-1925, (U.S.) Wisconsin public official; leader of progressive movement.
Fiorello La Guardia, 1882-1947, (U.S.) New York City reform mayor, 1933-45.
Pierre Laval, 1883-1945, (Fr.) politician, Vichy foreign min.; executed for treason.
Andrew Bonar Law, 1858-1923, (Can.) Conservative party politician, British prime min.; led opposition to Irish home rule.
Vladimir Ilyich Lenin (Ulyanov), 1870-1924, (Russ.) revolutionary; founded Bolshevism; Soviet leader, 1917-24.
Ferdinand de Lesseps, 1805-94, (Fr.) diplomat, engineer; conceived idea of Suez Canal.
René Lévesque, 1922-87, (Can.) prem. of Quebec, 1976-85; led unsuccessful separatist campaign.
Trygve Lie, 1896-1968, (Nor.) first UN sec.-gen.
Maxim Litvinov, 1876-1951, (Pol.-Russ.) revolutionary, commissar of foreign affairs; favored cooperation with West.
David Lloyd George, 1863-1945, (Br.) Liberal party prime min.; laid foundations for modern welfare state.
Henry Cabot Lodge, 1850-1924, (U.S.) U.S. senator (R, MA); led opposition to participation in League of Nations.
Huey P. Long, 1893-1935, (U.S.) Louisiana political demagogue, governor, U.S. senator (D); assassinated.
Rosa Luxemburg, 1871-1919, (Ger.) revolutionary; leader of the German Social Democratic party and Spartacus party.
J. Ramsay MacDonald, 1866-1937, (Br.) first Labour party prime min. of Great Britain.
Harold Macmillan, 1895-1986, (Br.) prime min. of Great Britain, 1957-63.
Makarios III, 1913-77, (Cyprus) Greek Orthodox archbishop; first pres. of Cyprus.
Nelson Mandela, 1918-2013, (S. Afr.) anti-apartheid leader; first Black pres. of S. Africa, 1994-99.
Wilma Mankiller, 1945-2010, (Amer. Ind.) first female chief of the Cherokee Nation.
Mao Zedong, 1893-1976, (China) chief Chinese Marxist theorist, revolutionary, political leader; led revolution establishing his nation as Communist state.
Jean Paul Marat, 1743-93, (Fr.) revolutionary, politician; identified with radical Jacobins; assassinated.
Thurgood Marshall, 1908-93, (U.S.) first Black U.S. solicitor general, 1965; first Black justice of U.S. Supreme Court, 1967-91.
José Martí, 1853-95, (Cuba) patriot, poet; independence leader.
Jan Masaryk, 1886-1948, (Czech.) foreign min.; died under mysterious circumstances, allegedly by suicide, following Communist coup.
Thomas G. Masaryk, 1850-1937, (Czech.) statesman, philosopher; first pres. of Czechoslovakia.
Jules Mazarin, 1602-61, (Fr.) cardinal, statesman; prime min. under Louis XIII and queen regent Anne of Austria.
Giuseppe Mazzini, 1805-72, (It.) reformer dedicated to Risorgimento movement for renewal of Italy.
Tom Mboya, 1930-69, (Kenya) political leader; instrumental in securing independence for Kenya.
John McCain, 1936-2018, (U.S.) U.S. sen. (R, AZ), 2008 pres. nominee.
Eugene McCarthy, 1916-2005, (U.S.) political leader, author; 1968 Dem. presidential contender.
Joseph R. McCarthy, 1908-57, (U.S.) senator (R, WI); extremist in searching out alleged Communists and pro-Communists.
Cosimo I de' Medici, 1519-74, (It.) Duke of Florence, grand duke of Tuscany.
Lorenzo de' Medici (the Magnificent), 1449-92, (It.) merchant prince; a towering figure in Italian Renaissance.
Catherine de Médicis, 1519-89, (Fr.) queen consort of Henry II, regent of France; influential in Catholic-Huguenot wars.
Golda Meir, 1898-1978, (Ukr.-Isr.) a founder of the state of Israel; prime min., 1969-74.
Klemens W. N. L. Metternich, 1773-1859, (Austria) statesman; arbiter of post-Napoleonic Europe.
Slobodan Milosevic, 1941-2006, (Serb./Yugo.) former Yugoslav pres.; tried for genocide, crimes against humanity.
François Mitterrand, 1916-96, (Fr.) pres. of France, 1981-95.
Mobutu Sese Seko, 1930-97, (Zaire) longtime ruler of Zaire (now Dem. Rep. of Congo), 1965-97; exiled after rebellion.
Guy Mollet, 1905-75, (Fr.) socialist politician, resistance leader.
Walter Mondale, 1928-2021, (U.S.) U.S. senator (D, MN), vice pres., pres. nominee (1984).
Henry Morgenthau Jr., 1891-1967, (U.S.) sec. of treasury; fundraiser for New Deal and U.S. WWII activities.
Gouverneur Morris, 1752-1816, (U.S.) statesman, diplomat, financial expert; helped plan decimal coinage.
Mohammed Morsi, 1951-2019, (Egypt) first democratically elected pres. of Egypt, 2012; deposed 2013.
Daniel Patrick Moynihan, 1927-2003, (U.S.) senator (D, NY), diplomat, social scientist, author.
Hosni Mubarak, 1928-2020, (Egy.) Egyptian president deposed in 2011 uprising.
Robert Mugabe, 1924-2019, (Zimb.) prime min. and pres. of Zimbabwe.
Benito Mussolini, 1883-1945, (It.) leader of the Italian fascist state; assassinated.
Imre Nagy, c. 1896-1958, (Hung.) Communist prem.; assassinated after Soviets crushed 1956 uprising.
Gamal Abdel Nasser, 1918-70, (Egypt) leader of Arab unification; second Egyptian pres.
Alexei Navalny, 1976-2024, (Rus.) opposition leader.
Jawaharlal Nehru, 1889-1964, (India) prime min.; guided India through its early years of independence.
Kwame Nkrumah, 1909-72, (Ghana) first prime min., 1957-60; pres., 1960-66, of Ghana.
Manuel Noriega, 1934-2017, (Pan.) dictator, 1983-89; military officer, CIA informant.
Frederick North, 1732-92, (Br.) prime min.; his policies led to loss of American colonies.
Julius K. Nyerere, 1922-99, (Tanz.) founding father; first pres., 1962-85, of Tanzania.
Daniel O'Connell, 1775-1847, (Ire.) nationalist political leader; known as The Liberator.
Omar, c. 581-644, (Arab.) Muslim leader; second caliph, led Islam to become an imperial power.
Thomas P. (Tip) O'Neill Jr., 1912-94, (U.S.) U.S. rep. (D, MA), speaker of the House, 1977-86.
Ignace Paderewski, 1860-1941, (Pol.) statesman, pianist, composer, briefly prime min.; ardent patriot.
Ian Paisley, 1926-2014, (Ire.) Unionist Party leader who agreed to power sharing in N. Ireland.
Viscount Palmerston, 1784-1865, (Br.) Whig-Liberal prime min., foreign min.; embodied British nationalism.
Andreas George Papandreou, 1919-96, (Gr.) leftist politician; served as prem., 1981-89, 1993-96.
Georgios Papandreou, 1888-1968, (Gr.) Republican politician; served three times as prime min.
Franz von Papen, 1879-1969, (Ger.) politician; major role in overthrow of Weimar Republic and rise of Hitler.
Charles Stewart Parnell, 1846-91, (Ire.) nationalist leader; "uncrowned king of Ireland."
Lester Pearson, 1897-1972, (Can.) diplomat, Liberal party leader, prime min.
Robert Peel, 1788-1850, (Br.) reformist prime min.; founder of Conservative party.
Shimon Peres, 1922-2016, (Bela.-Isr.) Israel prime min., 1984-86, 1995-96; president, 2007-14.
Javier Pérez de Cuéllar, 1920-2020 (Per.) UN sec.-gen.
Frances Perkins, 1882-1965, (U.S.) first female cabinet member (sec. of labor).
Eva (Evita) Perón, 1919-52, (Arg.) highly influential second wife of Juan Perón.
Juan Perón, 1895-1974, (Arg.) dynamic pres. of Argentina, 1946-55, 1973-74.
H. Ross Perot, 1930-2019, (U.S.) entrepreneur; pres. contender, 1992, 1996.
Joseph Pilsudski, 1867-1935, (Pol.) statesman; instrumental in reestablishing Polish state in the 20th cent.
Charles Pinckney, 1757-1824, (U.S.) founding father; his Pinckney plan largely incorporated into Constitution.
Christian Pineau, 1905-95, (Fr.) leader of French Resistance during WWII; foreign min., 1956-58.
Augusto Pinochet (Ugarte), 1915-2006, (Chile) former Chilean ruler; indicted for human rights abuses while in office.
William Pitt the Elder, 1708-78, (Br.) statesman; the "Great Commoner," transformed Britain into imperial power.
William Pitt the Younger, 1759-1806, (Br.) prime min. during French Revolutionary wars.
Georgi Plekhanov, 1857-1918, (Russ.) revolutionary, social philosopher; called "father of Russian Marxism."
Raymond Poincaré, 1860-1934, (Fr.) French pres.; advocated harsh punishment of Germany after WWI.
Pol Pot, 1925-98, (Camb.) leader of Khmer Rouge; ruled Cambodia, 1975-79; responsible for mass deaths.
Georges Pompidou, 1911-74, (Fr.) Gaullist political leader; pres., 1969-74.
Grigori Potemkin, 1739-91, (Russ.) field marshal; favorite of empress Catherine II.
Adam Clayton Powell Jr., 1908-72, (U.S.) civil rights leader; U.S. rep. (D, NY), 1945-69.
Muammar al-Qaddafi, 1942-2011, (Libya) Libyan ruler, 1969-2011.
Yitzhak Rabin, 1922-95, (Isr.) military, political leader; prime min. of Israel, 1974-77, 1992-95; assassinated.
Joseph H. Rainey, 1832-87, (U.S.) first Black person elected to U.S. House (1869), from SC.
Edmund Randolph, 1753-1813, (U.S.) attorney; prominent in drafting, ratification of Constitution.
John Randolph, 1773-1833, (U.S.) Southern planter; strong advocate of states' rights.
Jeannette Rankin, 1880-1973, (U.S.) pacifist; first woman member of U.S. Congress (R, MT).
Walt(h)er Rathenau, 1867-1922, (Ger.) industrialist, statesman.
Sam Rayburn, 1882-1961, (U.S.) U.S. rep. (D, TX) for 47 years, House speaker for 17.
Red Cloud, 1822?-1909, (Amer. Ind.) leader of the Oglala Lakota.
Janet Reno, 1938-2016, (U.S.) first U.S. woman attorney general.

Hiram R. Revels, 1822-1901, (U.S.) first African American U.S. senator (R); elected in MS, served 1870-71.
Paul Reynaud, 1878-1966, (Fr.) statesman; prem. in 1940 at time of France's defeat by Germany.
Syngman Rhee, 1875-1965, (Korea) first pres. of S. Korea.
Cecil Rhodes, 1853-1902, (Br.) imperialist, industrial magnate; established Rhodes scholarships in his will.
Ann Richards, 1933-2006, (U.S.) former TX gov. (D).
Cardinal de Richelieu, 1585-1642, (Fr.) statesman, known as "red eminence"; chief minister to Louis XIII.
Maximilien Robespierre, 1758-94, (Fr.) leading figure in French Revolution and Reign of Terror.
Eleanor Roosevelt, 1884-1962, (U.S.) influential first lady, humanitarian, UN diplomat.
Elihu Root, 1845-1937, (U.S.) lawyer, statesman, diplomat; leading Republican supporter of the League of Nations.
John Ross, 1790-1866, (Amer. Ind.) longest-serving principal chief of Cherokee Nation (1828-66).
Dean Rusk, 1909-95, (U.S.) statesman; sec. of state, 1961-69.
John Russell, 1792-1878, (Br.) Liberal prime min. during the Irish potato famine.
Anwar al-Sadat, 1918-81, (Egypt) pres., 1970-81; promoted peace with Israel; Nobel laureate; assassinated.
António de Oliveira Salazar, 1889-1970, (Port.) longtime dictator of Portugal.
José de San Martin, 1778-1850, ([now] Arg.) S. Amer. revolutionary; protector of Peru.
Eisaku Sato, 1901-75, (Jpn.) prime min.; presided over Japan's post-WWII emergence as major world power.
Abdul Aziz Ibn Saud, c. 1880-1953, (Saudi Arabia) king of Saudi Arabia, 1932-53.
Helmut Schmidt, 1918-2015, (Ger.) German chancellor, 1974-82.
Robert Schuman, 1886-1963, (Fr.) statesman; founded European Coal and Steel Community.
Carl Schurz, 1829-1906, (Ger.-U.S.) political leader, journalist, orator, reformer.
Kurt Schuschnigg, 1897-1977, (Austria) chancellor; unsuccessful in stopping Austria's annexation by Germany.
William H. Seward, 1801-72, (U.S.) anti-slavery activist; as U.S. sec. of state purchased Alaska.
Carlo Sforza, 1872-1952, (It.) foreign min. of Italy, anti-Fascist.
Yitzhak Shamir, 1915-2012, (Russ.-Isr.) prime min. of Israel, 1983-84, 1986-92.
Ariel Sharon, 1928-2014, (Isr.) prime min. of Israel, 2001-06.
Eduard Shevardnadze, 1928-2014, (Geo.) Georgian pres., 1995-2003.
George Shultz, 1920-2021, (U.S.) sec. of state.
Norodom Sihanouk, 1922-2012, (Camb.) king of Cambodia, 1941-55, 1993-2004.
Sitting Bull, c. 1831-90, (Amer. Ind.) Hunkpapa Lakota leader; defeated Custer at Battle of the Little Bighorn.
Alfred E. Smith, 1873-1944, (U.S.) NY Democratic governor; first Roman Catholic to run for president (1928).
Margaret Chase Smith, 1897-1995, (U.S.) U.S. rep., senator (R, ME); first woman elected to both houses of Congress.
Jan C. Smuts, 1870-1950, (S. Afr.) statesman, philosopher, soldier, prime min.
Paul Henri Spaak, 1899-1972, (Belg.) statesman, socialist leader.
Joseph Stalin, 1879-1953, (USSR) Soviet dictator, 1924-53; instituted forced collectivization, massive purges, and labor camps, causing millions of deaths.
Edwin M. Stanton, 1814-69, (U.S.) sec. of war, 1862-68.
Alexander Stephens, 1812-83, (U.S.) vice pres. of the Confederacy.
Edward R. Stettinius Jr., 1900-49, (U.S.) industrialist; sec. of state who coordinated aid to WWII allies.
Adlai E. Stevenson, 1900-65, (U.S.) Democratic leader, diplomat, governor (IL), presidential nominee (1952, '56).
Henry L. Stimson, 1867-1950, (U.S.) statesman; served in five administrations, foreign policy adviser in 1930s and 1940s.
Carl Stokes, 1927-96, (U.S.) first Black mayor of a major American city (Cleveland, 1967-72).
Suharto, 1921-2008, (Indon.) former longtime Indonesian ruler.
Sukarno, 1901-70, (Indon.) dictatorial first pres. of the Indonesian republic.
Sun Yat-sen, 1866-1925, (China) revolutionary; leader of Kuomintang political party, regarded as father of modern China.
Robert A. Taft, 1889-1953, (U.S.) conservative Senate leader (OH); called "Mr. Republican."
Charles de Talleyrand, 1754-1838, (Fr.) statesman, diplomat; the major force of the Congress of Vienna of 1814-15.
U Thant, 1909-74, (Burma) statesman, UN sec.-general.
Margaret Thatcher, 1925-2013, (Br.) conservative British prime min., 1979-90; first woman UK prime min.
Norman M. Thomas, 1884-1968, (U.S.) social reformer; six times Socialist party presidential candidate.
Josip Broz Tito, 1892-1980, (Yugo.) pres. of Yugoslavia, 1953-80; WWII guerrilla chief, postwar rival of Stalin.
Palmiro Togliatti, 1893-1964, (It.) major Italian Communist leader.
Hideki Tojo, 1885-1948, (Jpn.) statesman, soldier; prime min. during most of WWII.
François Toussaint L'Ouverture, c. 1744-1803, (Haiti) patriot, martyr; thwarted French colonial aims.
Leon Trotsky, 1879-1940, (Russ.) revolutionary; founded Red Army, expelled from party in conflict with Stalin; assassinated.
Pierre Elliott Trudeau, 1919-2000, (Can.) longtime liberal prime min. of Canada, 1968-79, 1980-84; achieved native Canadian constitution.
Rafael L. Trujillo Molina, 1891-1961, (Dom. Rep.) dictator of Dominican Republic, 1930-61; assassinated.
Moise K. Tshombe, 1919-69, (Congo) pres. of secessionist Katanga prov., prem. of Congo (now Dem. Rep. of the Congo).
William M. Tweed, 1823-78, (U.S.) political boss of Tammany Hall, New York City's Democratic political machine.
Walter Ulbricht, 1893-1973, (Ger.) Communist leader of German Democratic Republic.
Arthur H. Vandenberg, 1884-1951, (U.S.) senator (R, MI); proponent of bipartisan anti-Communist foreign policy.
Eleutherios Venizelos, 1864-1936, (Gr.) most prominent Greek statesman of early 20th cent.
Hendrik F. Verwoerd, 1901-66, (S. Afr.) prime min.; rigorously applied apartheid policy despite protest.
Kurt Waldheim, 1918-2007, (Austria) UN sec.-gen., Austrian pres.
George Wallace, 1919-98, (U.S.) former segregationist governor of Alabama, pres. candidate.
Robert Walpole, 1676-1745, (Br.) statesman; generally considered Britain's first prime min.
Nancy Ward (Nan'yehi), 1738?-1824?, (Amer. Ind.) Cherokee peace leader.
Robert C. Weaver, 1907-97, (U.S.) first African American appointed to cabinet; sec. of Housing and Urban Development.
Daniel Webster, 1782-1852, (U.S.) orator, politician; advocate of business interests during Jacksonian agrarianism.
Chaim Weizmann, 1874-1952, (Russ.-Isr.) Zionist leader, scientist; first Israeli pres.
Kevin White, 1929-2012, (U.S.) Boston mayor, 1967-84.
Wendell L. Willkie, 1892-1944, (U.S.) Republican who tried to unseat Franklin D. Roosevelt when he ran for his third term.
Harold Wilson, 1916-95, (Br.) Labour party leader; prime min., 1964-70, 1974-76.
Boris Yeltsin, 1931-2007, (Russ.) first freely elected pres. of post-Soviet Russia.
Emiliano Zapata, c. 1879-1919, (Mex.) revolutionary; major influence on modern Mexico.
Todor Zhivkov, 1911-98, (Bulg.) Communist ruler of Bulgaria from 1954 until ousted in a 1989 coup.
Zhou Enlai, 1898-1976, (China) diplomat, prime min.; a leading figure of the Chinese Communist party.

Scientists of the Past

Revised by Peter Barker, Prof. and Chair, Dept. of the History of Science, Univ. of Oklahoma.

For pre-modern scientists, see also Philosophers and Religious Figures of the Past and the Historical Figures chapter.

Albertus Magnus, c. 1200-80, (Ger.) theologian, philosopher; helped found medieval study of natural science.
Alhazen (Ibn al-Haytham), c. 965-c. 1040, (Arab.) mathematician, astronomer, optical theorist.
Andre-Marie Ampère, 1775-1836, (Fr.) mathematician, chemist; founder of electrodynamics.
Mary Anning, 1799-1847, (Br.) paleontologist.
Neil Armstrong, 1930-2012, (U.S.) astronaut; first man to walk on the Moon.
John V. Atanasoff, 1903-95, (U.S.) physicist; co-invented Atanasoff-Berry electronic digital computer (1939-41).
Amedeo Avogadro, 1776-1856, (It.) chemist, physicist; proposed that equal volumes of gas contain equal numbers of molecules, permitting determination of molecular weights.
John Bardeen, 1908-91, (U.S.) double Nobel laureate in physics (transistor, 1956; superconductivity, 1972).
A. H. Becquerel, 1852-1908, (Fr.) physicist; discovered radioactivity in uranium (1896).
Alexander Graham Bell, 1847-1922, (U.S.) inventor; first to patent and commercially exploit the telephone (1876).
Daniel Bernoulli, 1700-82, (Switz.) mathematician; developed fluid dynamics and kinetic theory of gases.
Clifford Berry, 1918-63, (U.S.) collaborated with John V. Atanasoff on the ABC electronic digital computer (1939-41).
Jöns Jakob Berzelius, 1779-1848, (Swed.) chemist; developed modern chemical symbols and formulas.
Henry Bessemer, 1813-98, (Br.) engineer; invented Bessemer steel-making process.
Hans Bethe, 1906-2005, (Ger.-U.S.) physicist; won Nobel Prize in 1967 for describing how stars generate energy.
Bruno Bettelheim, 1903-90, (Austria-U.S.) psychoanalyst; studied disturbed children; *Uses of Enchantment* (1976).
Louis Blériot, 1872-1936, (Fr.) engineer; monoplane pioneer.
Franz Boas, 1858-1942, (Ger.-U.S.) founded modern anthropology; studied Pacific Coast tribes.
Niels Bohr, 1885-1962, (Den.) atomic and nuclear physicist; founded quantum mechanics.
Norman Borlaug, 1914-2009, (U.S.) plant pathologist and geneticist; father of "green" (agricultural) revolution.
Max Born, 1882-1970, (Ger.) atomic and nuclear physicist; helped develop quantum mechanics.

Satyendranath Bose, 1894-1974, (India) physicist; forerunner of modern quantum theory for integral-spin particles.

Louis de Broglie, 1892-1987, (Fr.) physicist; proposed quantum wave-particle duality.

Robert Bunsen, 1811-99, (Ger.) chemist; pioneered spectroscopic analysis; discovered rubidium, caesium.

Luther Burbank, 1849-1926, (U.S.) naturalist; developed plant breeding into a modern science.

Vannevar Bush, 1890-1974, (U.S.) electrical engineer; developed differential analyzer, an early analogue computer; led WWII Office of Scientific Res. and Dev.

Marvin Camras, 1916-95, (U.S.) inventor, electrical engineer; invented magnetic tape recording.

Alexis Carrel, 1873-1944, (Fr.) surgeon, biologist; developed methods of suturing blood vessels, transplanting organs.

Rachel Carson, 1907-64, (U.S.) marine biologist, environmentalist; *Silent Spring* (1962).

George Washington Carver, 1864-1943, (U.S.) chemist and botanist; promoted alternative crops.

James Chadwick, 1891-1974, (Br.) physicist; discovered the neutron (1932); led Brit. team on Manhattan Project in U.S.

Eugenie Clark, 1922-2015, (U.S.) ichthyologist and oceanographer.

Albert Claude, 1898-1983, (Belg.-U.S.) a founder of modern cell biology; determined role of mitochondria.

Samuel Cohen, 1921-2010, (U.S.) physicist who invented the neutron bomb.

Barry Commoner, 1917-2012, (U.S.) biologist; noted environmentalist.

Nicolaus Copernicus, 1473-1543, (Pol.) first modern astronomer to propose Sun as center of the planets' motions.

Jacques Yves Cousteau, 1910-97, (Fr.) oceanographer; co-inventor, with Emile Gagnan (Fr.), of the Aqualung (1943).

Seymour Cray, 1925-96, (U.S.) computer industry pioneer; developed supercomputers.

Francis Crick, 1916-2004, (Br.) biophysicist; co-discoverer of genetic code; shared 1962 Nobel Prize in Physiology/Medicine.

Marie, 1867-1934, (Pol.-Fr.) and **Pierre Curie**, 1859-1906, (Fr.) physical chemists; pioneer investigators of radioactivity; discovered radium and polonium (1898).

Gottlieb Daimler, 1834-1900, (Ger.) engineer, inventor; pioneer automobile manufacturer.

John Dalton, 1766-1844, (Br.) chemist, physicist; formulated atomic theory, made first table of atomic weights.

Charles Darwin, 1809-82, (Br.) naturalist; established theory of organic evolution; *Origin of Species* (1859).

Lee De Forest, 1873-1961, (U.S.) inventor of triode; pioneer in wireless telegraphy, sound pictures, television.

Pierre-Gilles de Gennes, 1932-2007, (Fr.) physicist whose research aided development of liquid-crystal display (LCD); awarded 1991 Nobel Prize for Physics.

Max Delbrück, 1906-81, (Fr.-Ger.-U.S.) a founder of molecular biology.

Rudolf Diesel, 1858-1913, (Ger.) mechanical engineer; patented Diesel engine (1892).

Theodosius Dobzhansky, 1900-75, (Russ.-U.S.) biologist; reconciled genetics and natural selection.

Christian Doppler, 1803-53, (Austria) physicist; showed change in wave frequency caused by motion of source, now known as Doppler effect.

J. Presper Eckert Jr., 1919-95, (U.S.) co-inventor, with John W. Mauchly, of the ENIAC computer (1943-45).

Thomas A. Edison, 1847-1931, (U.S.) inventor; held more than 1,000 patents, including incandescent electric lamp.

Robert Edwards, 1925-2013, (Br.) physiologist; pioneered in vitro fertilization.

Paul Ehrlich, 1854-1915, (Ger.) medical researcher in immunology and bacteriology; pioneered antitoxin production.

Albert Einstein, 1879-1955, (Ger.-U.S.) theoretical physicist; founded relativity theory.

John F. Enders, 1897-1985, (U.S.) virologist; helped discover vaccines against polio, measles, mumps, and chicken pox.

Erik Erikson, 1902-94, (U.S.) psychoanalyst, author; theory of developmental stages of life; *Childhood and Society* (1950).

Leonhard Euler, 1707-83, (Switz.) mathematician, physicist; pioneer of calculus, revived ideas of Fermat.

Gabriel Fahrenheit, 1686-1736, (Ger.) physicist; improved thermometers and introduced Fahrenheit temperature scale.

Michael Faraday, 1791-1867, (Br.) chemist, physicist; discovered electrical induction and invented dynamo (1831).

Philo T. Farnsworth, 1906-71, (U.S.) inventor; built first television system (San Francisco, 1928).

Pierre de Fermat, 1601-65, (Fr.) mathematician; founded modern theory of numbers.

Enrico Fermi, 1901-54, (It.-U.S.) nuclear physicist; demonstrated first controlled chain reaction (Chicago, 1942).

Richard Feynman, 1918-88, (U.S.) theoretical physicist, author; founder of Quantum Electrodynamics (QED).

Alexander Fleming, 1881-1955, (Br.) bacteriologist; discovered penicillin (1928).

Dian Fossey, 1932-85, (U.S.) primatologist.

Jean B. J. Fourier, 1768-1830, (Fr.) introduced Fourier Series, method of analysis in math and physics.

Sigmund Freud, 1856-1939, (Austria) psychiatrist; founder of psychoanalysis; *Interpretation of Dreams* (1901).

Erich Fromm, 1900-80, (U.S.) psychoanalyst; *Man for Himself* (1947).

Galileo Galilei, 1564-1642, (It.) physicist; used telescope to vindicate Copernicus, founded modern science of motion.

Carl Friedrich Gauss, 1777-1855, (Ger.) mathematician; completed work of Fermat and Euler in number theory.

Josiah W. Gibbs, 1839-1903, (U.S.) theoretical physicist, chemist; founded chemical thermodynamics.

John Glenn, 1921-2016, (U.S.) astronaut, first American to orbit Earth (1962).

Robert H. Goddard, 1882-1945, (U.S.) physicist; invented liquid fuel rocket (1926).

George W. Goethals, 1858-1928, (U.S.) chief engineer who completed Panama Canal (1907-14).

William C. Gorgas, 1854-1920, (U.S.) physician; pioneer in prevention of yellow fever and malaria.

Stephen Jay Gould, 1941-2002, (U.S.) paleontologist, evolutionary biologist, writer.

Ernest Haeckel, 1834-1919, (Ger.) zoologist, evolutionist; early Darwinist, introduced concept of "ecology."

Otto Hahn, 1879-1968, (Ger.) chemist; with Lise Meitner discovered nuclear fission (1938).

Edmund Halley, 1656-1742, (Br.) astronomer; predicted return of 1682 comet (Halley's Comet) in 1759.

William Harvey, 1578-1657, (Br.) physician, anatomist; discovered circulation of the blood (1628).

Stephen Hawking, 1942-2018, (Br.) physicist; explored gravity, black holes; *A Brief History of Time* (1988).

Werner Heisenberg, 1901-76, (Ger.) physicist; developed matrix mechanics and uncertainty principle (1927).

Hermann von Helmholtz, 1821-94, (Ger.) physicist, physiologist; formulated principle of conservation of energy.

Caroline Herschel, 1750-1848, (Ger.-Br.) astronomer.

William Herschel, 1738-1822, (Ger.-Br.) astronomer; discovered Uranus (1781).

Heinrich Hertz, 1857-94, (Ger.) physicist; discovered radio waves and photo-electric effect (1886-87).

Peter Higgs, 1929-2024, (Br.) theoretical physicist.

David Hilbert, 1862-1943, (Ger.) mathematician; contributed to algebra, calculus, and foundational studies (formalism).

Albert Hofmann, 1906-2008, (Switz.) chemist; inventor of LSD.

Edwin P. Hubble, 1889-1953, (U.S.) astronomer; discovered observational evidence of expanding universe.

Alexander von Humboldt, 1769-1859, (Ger.) naturalist; explored Central, S. America, ideated ecology.

Edward Jenner, 1749-1823, (Br.) physician; pioneered vaccination, introduced term "virus."

Katherine Johnson, 1918-2020, (U.S.) NASA mathematician.

James Joule, 1818-89, (Br.) physicist; found relation between heat and mechanical energy (conservation of energy).

Carl Jung, 1875-1961, (Switz.) psychiatrist; founder of analytical psychology.

Ernest Everett Just, 1883-1941, (U.S.) marine biologist; studied egg development; *Biology of Cell Surfaces* (1941).

Johannes Kepler, 1571-1630, (Ger.) astronomer; discovered laws of planetary motion.

Al-Khwarizmi, early 9th cent., (Arab.) mathematician; regarded as founder of algebra.

Robert Koch, 1843-1910, (Ger.) bacteriologist; isolated bacterial causes of tuberculosis and other diseases.

Georges Köhler, 1946-95, (Ger.) immunologist; with César Milstein, developed monoclonal antibody technique.

Willem Kolff, 1911-2009, (Neth.-U.S.) physician, biomedical engineer; developed first practical kidney dialysis machine; considered the "father of artificial organs."

Jacques Lacan, 1901-81, (Fr.) influential psychoanalyst.

Joseph Lagrange, 1736-1813, (Fr.) geometer, astronomer; showed that gravity of Earth and Moon cancel, creating stable points in space around them.

Jean B. Lamarck, 1744-1829, (Fr.) naturalist; forerunner of Darwin in evolutionary theory.

Pierre Simon de Laplace, 1749-1827, (Fr.) astronomer, physicist; proposed nebular origin for solar system.

Lewis H. Latimer, 1848-1928, (U.S.) African American scientist; associate of Edison; supervised installation of first electric street lighting in New York City.

Antoine Lavoisier, 1743-94, (Fr.) a founder of modern chemistry.

Ernest O. Lawrence, 1901-58, (U.S.) physicist; invented the cyclotron.

Louis, 1903-72, and **Mary Leakey**, 1913-96, (both Br.) early hominid paleoanthropologists; discovered remains in Africa.

Richard Leakey, 1944-2022, (Kenya) anthropologist, paleontologist, conservationist.

Anton van Leeuwenhoek, 1632-1723, (Neth.) founder of microscopy.

Jerome Lejeune, 1927-94, (Fr.) geneticist; discovered chromosomal cause of Down syndrome (1959).

Claude Lévi-Strauss, 1908-2009, (Belg.-Fr.) cultural anthropologist, sociologist, philosopher.

Kurt Lewin, 1890-1947, (Ger.-U.S.) social psychologist; studied human motivation and group dynamics.

Justus von Liebig, 1803-73, (Ger.) founded quantitative organic chemistry.

Joseph Lister, 1827-1912, (Br.) physician; pioneered antiseptic surgery.

Hendrik Lorentz, 1853-1928, (Neth.) physicist; developed electron theory of matter, contributed to relativity theory.

Konrad Lorenz, 1903-89, (Austria) ethologist; pioneer in study of animal behavior.

Bernard Lovell, 1913-2012, (Br.) physicist and radio astronomer.

Percival Lowell, 1855-1916, (U.S.) astronomer; predicted the existence of Pluto.

Louis, 1864-1948, and **Auguste Lumière**, 1862-1954, (both Fr.) invented cinematograph, made first motion picture (1895).

Theodore H. Maiman, 1927-2007, (U.S.) physicist; invented the first workable laser, which he displayed in 1960.
Guglielmo Marconi, 1874-1937, (It.) physicist; developed wireless telegraphy.
John W. Mauchly, 1907-80, (U.S.) co-inventor, with J. Presper Eckert Jr., of computer ENIAC (1943-45).
James Clerk Maxwell, 1831-79, (Br.) physicist; unified electricity and magnetism, electromagnetic theory of light.
Maria Goeppert Mayer, 1906-72, (Ger.-U.S.) physicist; developed shell model of atomic nuclei.
Barbara McClintock, 1902-92, (U.S.) geneticist; showed that some genetic elements are mobile.
Lise Meitner, 1878-1968, (Austria) co-discoverer, with Otto Hahn, of nuclear fission (1938).
Gregor J. Mendel, 1822-84, (Austria) botanist, monk; his experiments became the foundation of modern genetics.
Dmitri Mendeleyev, 1834-1907, (Russ.) chemist; established Periodic Table of the Elements.
Bruce R. Merrifield, 1921-2006, (U.S.) chemist; discovered how to synthesize proteins quickly and efficiently.
Franz Mesmer, 1734-1815, (Ger.) physician; introduced hypnotherapy.
Albert A. Michelson, 1852-1931, (U.S.) physicist; invented interferometer.
Robert A. Millikan, 1868-1953, (U.S.) physicist; measured electronic charge.
Thomas Hunt Morgan, 1866-1945, (U.S.) geneticist, embryologist; established role of chromosomes in heredity.
John F. Nash Jr., 1928-2015, (U.S.) mathematician; Nobel Prize winner (1994) in economics for work on game theory.
Isaac Newton, 1642-1727, (Br.) natural philosopher; discovered laws of gravitation, motion; with Gottfried Wilhelm von Leibniz, founded calculus.
Robert N. Noyce, 1927-90, (U.S.) invented microchip.
J. Robert Oppenheimer, 1904-67, (U.S.) physicist; scientific director of Manhattan Project.
Wilhelm Ostwald, 1853-1932, (Ger.) chemist, philosopher; main founder of modern physical chemistry.
Louis Pasteur, 1822-95, (Fr.) chemist; showed that germs cause disease and fermentation; originated pasteurization.
Linus C. Pauling, 1901-94, (U.S.) chemist; studied chemical bonds; campaigned for nuclear disarmament.
Jean Piaget, 1896-1980, (Switz.) psychologist; four-stage theory of intellectual development in children.
Max Planck, 1858-1947, (Ger.) physicist; introduced quantum hypothesis (1900).
Jules Henri Poincaré, 1854-1912, (Fr.) mathematician; founded algebraic topology, many other discoveries.
Walter S. Reed, 1851-1902, (U.S.) Army physician; proved mosquitoes transmit yellow fever.
Theodor Reik, 1888-1969, (Austria-U.S.) psychoanalyst; major Freudian disciple.
Sally Ride, 1951-2012, (U.S.) astronaut; 1st U.S. woman in space.
Bernhard Riemann, 1826-66, (Ger.) mathematician; developed non-Euclidean geometry used by Einstein.
Norbert Rillieux, 1806-94, (U.S.) African American inventor of a vacuum pan evaporator (1846); revolutionized sugar-refining industry.
Wilhelm Roentgen, 1845-1923, (Ger.) physicist; discovered X-rays (1895).
Carl Rogers, 1902-87, (U.S.) psychotherapist, author; originated nondirective therapy.
Ernest Rutherford, 1871-1937, (Br.) physicist; pioneer investigator of radioactivity, identified the atomic nucleus.
Albert B. Sabin, 1906-93, (Russ.-U.S.) developed oral polio live-virus vaccine.
Carl Sagan, 1934-96, (U.S.) astronomer, author.
Jonas Salk, 1914-95, (U.S.) developed first successful polio vaccine, widely used in U.S. after 1955.
Allan Sandage, 1926-2010, (U.S.) astronomer; refined the Hubble Constant, a measure of the universe's expansion.
Frederick Sanger, 1918-2013, (Br.) biochemist; detailed molecular structure of insulin.
Giovanni Schiaparelli, 1835-1910, (It.) astronomer; reported canals on Mars.
Erwin Schrödinger, 1887-1961, (Austria) physicist; developed wave equation for quantum systems.
Glenn T. Seaborg, 1912-99, (U.S.) chemist; Nobel Prize winner (1951); co-discoverer of plutonium.
Harlow Shapley, 1885-1972, (U.S.) astronomer; mapped galactic clusters and position of Sun in Milky Way Galaxy.
Norman E. Shumway, 1923-2006, (U.S.) surgeon; performed world's first successful heart-lung transplant.
B. F. Skinner, 1904-90, (U.S.) psychologist; leading advocate of behaviorism.
Richard E. Smalley, 1943-2005, (U.S.) chemist; with three other scientists, discovered buckminsterfullerenes, a previously unknown class of carbon molecules.
Roger W. Sperry, 1913-94, (U.S.) neurobiologist; established different functions of right and left sides of brain.
Benjamin Spock, 1903-98, (U.S.) pediatrician, child care expert; *Common Sense Book of Baby and Child Care*.
Charles P. Steinmetz, 1865-1923, (Ger.-U.S.) electrical engineer; developed basic ideas on alternating current.
Ernst Stuhlinger, 1913-2008, (Ger.) rocket scientist; electric propulsion for NASA in early space age.
Leo Szilard, 1898-1964, (Hung.-U.S.) physicist; helped on Manhattan Project, later opposed nuclear weapons.
Edward Teller, 1908-2003, (Hung.-U.S.) physicist; aided on Manhattan Project, had key role in development of H-bomb.
Nikola Tesla, 1856-1943, (Serb.-U.S.) invented electrical devices including AC dynamos, transformers, and motors.
William Thomson (Lord Kelvin), 1824-1907, (Br.) physicist; aided in success of transatlantic telegraph cable (1865); proposed Kelvin absolute temperature scale.
Alan Turing, 1912-54, (Br.) mathematician; helped develop basis for computers.
James Van Allen, 1914-2006, (U.S.) physicist; discovered the presence of radiation belts around Earth (Van Allen belts).
Rudolf Virchow, 1821-1902, (Ger.) pathologist; pioneered the modern theory that diseases affect the body through cells.
Alessandro Volta, 1745-1827, (It.) physicist; electricity pioneer.
Wernher von Braun, 1912-77, (Ger.-U.S.) aerospace engineer; developed rockets for warfare and space exploration.
John von Neumann, 1903-57, (Hung.-U.S.) mathematician; originated game theory; basic design for modern computers.
Alfred Russell Wallace, 1823-1913, (Br.) naturalist; proposed concept of evolution independently of Darwin.
John B. Watson, 1878-1958, (U.S.) psychologist; a founder of behaviorism.
James E. Watt, 1736-1819, (Br.) mechanical engineer, inventor; invented modern steam engine (1765).
Alfred L. Wegener, 1880-1930, (Ger.) meteorologist, geophysicist; postulated continental drift.
Norbert Wiener, 1894-1964, (U.S.) mathematician; founder of cybernetics.
Daniel Hale Williams, 1858-1931, (U.S.) African American surgeon; performed one of first two open-heart operations (1893).
Sewall Wright, 1889-1988, (U.S.) evolutionary theorist; helped found population genetics.
Wilhelm Wundt, 1832-1920, (Ger.) founder of experimental psychology.
Qian Xuesen, 1911-2009, (China) rocket scientist; helped found Jet Propulsion Lab, father of China's space program.
Rosalyn Yalow, 1921-2011, (U.S.), physicist; co-developer of radioimmunoassay.
Chuck Yeager, 1923-2020, (U.S.) test pilot, broke the sound barrier.
Ferdinand von Zeppelin, 1838-1917, (Ger.) soldier, aeronaut, airship designer.

Social Reformers, Activists, and Humanitarians of the Past

Ralph David Abernathy, 1926-90, (U.S.) Black civil rights activist; pres., 1968, Southern Christian Leadership Conf.
Jane Addams, 1860-1935, (U.S.) cofounder of Hull House; won Nobel Peace Prize, 1931.
Susan B. Anthony, 1820-1906, (U.S.) a leader in temperance, antislavery, and woman suffrage movements.
Dennis Banks, 1937-2017, (Amer. Ind.) civil rights activist.
Thomas Barnardo, 1845-1905, (Br.) social reformer; pioneer in care of destitute children.
Clara Barton, 1821-1912, (U.S.) organized American Red Cross.
Daisy Bates, 1914-99, (U.S.) Black civil rights leader who fought for integration; advocate for the "Little Rock 9" during Arkansas desegregation crisis in 1957.
Henry Ward Beecher, 1813-87, (U.S.) clergyman, abolitionist.
Peter Benenson, 1921-2005, (Br.) activist; founded Amnesty International, 1961.
Mary McLeod Bethune, 1875-1955, (U.S.) Black educator, civil rights activist; adviser to FDR and Truman; founder, pres., Bethune-Cookman College.
Elizabeth Blackwell, 1821-1910, (Br.) first female physician in the U.S.
Amelia Bloomer, 1818-94, (U.S.) suffragette, social reformer.
Julian Bond, 1940-2015, (U.S.) civil rights leader, NAACP chair, 1998-2015.
Yelena Bonner, 1923-2011, (Russ.) human rights activist in former Soviet Union.
William Booth, 1829-1912, (Br.) founded Salvation Army.
James Brady, 1940-2014, (U.S.) gun control advocate; Reagan press sec.
John Brown, 1800-59, (U.S.) abolitionist who led murder of five pro-slavery men; hanged.
Linda Brown, 1943-2018, (U.S.) civil rights activist; daughter of *Brown v. Board of Education* (1954) plaintiff.
Frances Xavier (Mother) Cabrini, 1850-1917, (It.-U.S.) nun; founded charitable institutions; first American canonized as a saint, 1946.
Stokely Carmichael (Kwame Ture), 1941-98, (Trinidad-U.S.) Black power activist; major proponent of Pan-Africanism; prime min. of Black Panthers.
Carrie Chapman Catt, 1859-1947, (U.S.) suffragette.
Cesar Chavez, 1927-93, (U.S.) labor leader; helped establish United Farm Workers of America.
Eldridge Cleaver, 1935-98, (U.S.) revolutionary social critic; former minister of information for Black Panthers; *Soul on Ice*.
Clarence Darrow, 1857-1938, (U.S.) lawyer; defender of underdog, opponent of capital punishment.
Ossie Davis, 1917-2005, (U.S.) Black civil rights activist, actor, director.
Dorothy Day, 1897-1980, (U.S.) founder of Catholic Worker movement.
Eugene V. Debs, 1855-1926, (U.S.) labor leader; led Pullman Strike, 1894; four-time Socialist presidential candidate.

Vine Deloria Jr., 1933-2005, (U.S.) Native American activist, author; *Custer Died for Your Sins*.
Dorothea Dix, 1802-87, (U.S.) crusader for mentally ill.
Thomas Dooley, 1927-61, (U.S.) "jungle doctor"; noted for efforts to supply medical aid to developing countries.
Marjory Stoneman Douglas, 1890-1998, (U.S.) writer, environmentalist; campaigned to save Florida Everglades.
Frederick Douglass, 1817-95, (U.S.) author, editor, orator, diplomat; edited abolitionist weekly *The North Star*.
Andrea Dworkin, 1946-2005, (U.S.) radical feminist, antipornography crusader.
Medgar Evers, 1925-63, (U.S.) Black civil rights leader; campaigned to register Black voters; assassinated.
James Farmer, 1920-99, (U.S.) Black civil rights leader; founded Congress of Racial Equality (CORE).
Betty Friedan, 1921-2006, (U.S.) author, feminist; *The Feminine Mystique*.
Millard Fuller, 1935-2009, (U.S.) founder of Habitat for Humanity.
William Lloyd Garrison, 1805-79, (U.S.) abolitionist.
Miep Gies, 1909-2010, (Neth.) protector of Anne Frank and her family during WWII.
Emma Goldman, 1869-1940, (Russ.-U.S.) published anarchist *Mother Earth*; birth-control advocate.
Samuel Gompers, 1850-1924, (U.S.) labor leader; first pres. of the American Federation of Labor (AFL).
Juliette Gordon Low, 1860-1927, (U.S.) Girl Scouts founder.
Prince Hall, 1735-1807, (U.S.) activist; founded Black Freemasonry; served in American Revolutionary War.
Michael Harrington, 1928-89, (U.S.) exposed poverty in affluent U.S. in *The Other America*, 1963.
Dorothy Height, 1912-2010, (U.S.) civil rights activist; pres. of the National Council of Negro Women, 1957-97.
Sidney Hillman, 1887-1946, (Lith.-U.S.) labor leader; helped organize CIO.
Benjamin Hooks, 1925-2010, (U.S.) civil rights activist; exec. dir. NAACP, 1977-92.
Samuel G. Howe, 1801-76, (U.S.) social reformer; changed public attitudes toward the blind, deaf, mentally challenged.
Marsha P. Johnson, 1945-92, (U.S.) LGBT rights activist.
Vernon Jordan, 1935-2021, (U.S.) civil rights activist.
Franklin Kameny, 1925-2011, (U.S.) gay rights activist.
Helen Keller, 1880-1968, (U.S.) crusader for better treatment for the disabled; deaf and blind herself.
Jack Kevorkian 1928-2011, (U.S.) pathologist; assisted-suicide activist.
Coretta Scott King, 1927-2006, (U.S.) Black civil rights leader; wife of Rev. Martin Luther King Jr.
Rev. Martin Luther King Jr., 1929-68, (U.S.) civil rights leader; led 1955-56 Montgomery, AL, boycott; founder, pres., Southern Christian Leadership Conference, 1957; Nobel peace laureate, 1964; assassinated.
Larry Kramer, 1935-2020, (U.S.) HIV/AIDS activist.
Maggie Kuhn, 1905-95, (U.S.) founded Gray Panthers, 1970.
William Kunstler, 1919-95, (U.S.) civil liberties attorney.
John Lewis, 1940-2020, (U.S.) U.S. rep. (D, GA), Black civil rights activist.
John L. Lewis, 1880-1969, (U.S.) labor leader; headed United Mine Workers, 1920-60.
Belva Lockwood, 1830-1917, (U.S.) lawyer; first woman to argue before U.S. Supreme Court.
Almena Lomax, 1915-2011, (U.S.) civil rights activist; journalist who founded *The Los Angeles Tribune*.
Rev. Joseph Lowery, 1921-2020, (U.S.) Black civil rights activist.
Clara Luper, 1923-2011, (U.S.) civil rights activist.
Wangari Maathai, 1940-2011, (Kenya) environmental activist; 2004 Nobel Peace Prize winner.
Robert Macauley, 1923-2010, (U.S.) founder of AmeriCares.
Malcolm X (Little), 1925-65, (U.S.) Black Muslim, Black nationalist leader; promoted Black pride; assassinated.
Russell Means, 1939-2012, (Amer. Ind.) civil rights activist.
Karl Menninger, 1893-1990, (U.S.) with brother **William Menninger** (1899-1966), founded Menninger Clinic and Menninger Foundation.
Harvey Milk, 1930-78, (U.S.) LGBT rights activist; assassinated.
Kate Millett, 1934-2017, (U.S.) writer, feminist; *Sexual Politics*.
David Mixner, 1946-2024, (U.S.) LGBT rights activist.
Lucretia Mott, 1793-1880, (U.S.) reformer, pioneer feminist.
Philip Murray, 1886-1952, (U.S.) Scottish-born labor leader.
Huey P. Newton, 1942-89, (U.S.) co-founded Black Panther Party, 1966.
Florence Nightingale, 1820-1910, (Br.) founder of modern nursing.
Emmeline Pankhurst, 1858-1928, (Br.) suffragette.
Rosa Parks,1913-2005, (U.S.) Black civil rights activist; her actions sparked 1955-56 Montgomery, AL, bus boycott.
A. Philip Randolph, 1889-1979, (U.S.) organized Brotherhood of Sleeping Car Porters, 1925; an organizer of 1941 and 1963 March on Washington movements.
Walter Reuther, 1907-70, (U.S.) labor leader; headed United Auto Workers.
Jacob Riis, 1849-1914, (Den.-U.S.) crusader for urban reforms.
Sylvia Rivera, 1951-2002, (U.S.) LGBT rights activist.
Paul Robeson, 1898-1976, (U.S.) actor, singer, Black civil rights activist.
Bayard Rustin, 1910-87, (U.S.) Black and LGBT civil rights activist; an organizer of the 1963 March on Washington.
Margaret Sanger, 1883-1966, (U.S.) social reformer; pioneered the birth-control movement.
Phyllis Schlafly, 1924-2016, (U.S.) anti-Equal Rights Amendment activist.
Earl of Shaftesbury (A. A. Cooper), 1801-85, (Br.) social reformer.
Eunice Kennedy Shriver, 1921-2009, (U.S.) cofounder of Special Olympics for athletes with intellectual disabilities.
Sargent Shriver, 1915-2011, (U.S.) founding director of Peace Corps; founder of Job Corps, Head Start.
Fred Shuttlesworth, 1922-2011, (U.S.) civil rights activist.
Albertina Sisulu, 1918-2011, (S. Africa) anti-apartheid activist.
Elizabeth Cady Stanton, 1815-1902, (U.S.) woman suffrage pioneer.
Lucy Stone, 1818-93, (U.S.) feminist, abolitionist.
Mother Teresa of Calcutta, 1910-97, (Alban.) nun; founded order to care for sick, dying poor; 1979 Nobel Peace Prize winner; canonized 2016.
Mamie Till-Mobley, 1921-2003, (U.S.) civil rights activist.
Willard Townsend, 1895-1957, (U.S.) organized the United Transport Service Employees (Red Caps), 1935.
Sojourner Truth (Isabella Baumfree), 1797-1883, (U.S.) preacher, abolitionist; worked for Black educ. opportunity.
Harriet Tubman, 1823-1913, (U.S.) prominent figure in the Underground Railroad; nurse, spy for Union Army in the Civil War.
Nat Turner, 1800-31, (U.S.) slave who led the most significant of more than 200 slave revolts in U.S., in Southampton, VA; hanged.
Desmond Tutu, 1931-2021, (S. Afr.) former S. African archbishop; 1984 Nobel Peace Prize winner.
Philip Vera Cruz, 1905-94, (Philip.-U.S.) helped found the United Farm Workers Union.
Rev. C(ordy) T(indell) Vivian, 1924-2020, (U.S.) Black civil rights activist.
Edgar Wayburn, 1906-2010, (U.S.) conservationist; Sierra Club pres.
Elie Wiesel, 1928-2016, (Rom.-U.S.) Holocaust survivor, author, and activist; 1986 Nobel Peace Prize winner.
William Wilberforce, 1759-1833, (Br.) social reformer; prominent in struggle to abolish slave trade.
Frances E. Willard, 1839-98, (U.S.) temperance, women's rights leader.
Betty Williams, 1944-2020, (N. Ire.) peace activist; 1976 Nobel Peace Prize winner.
Edith Windsor, 1929-2007, (U.S.) LGBT civil rights activist.
Mary Wollstonecraft, 1759-97, (Br.) *Vindication of the Rights of Women*.
Victoria Woodhull, 1838-1927, (U.S.) suffragist, first woman to run for president (1872).

Sports Personalities of the Past and Present

Note: In May 2024, MLB incorporated statistics from seven different Negro Leagues (1920-48) into players' historical records.

Henry (Hank) Aaron, 1934-2021, Milwaukee-Atlanta outfielder; hit then-record 755 home runs, record 2,297 RBI.
Kareem Abdul-Jabbar, b 1947, Milwaukee, L.A. Lakers center; MVP 6 times; second all-time leading NBA scorer, 38,387 pts.
Andre Agassi, b 1970, tennis player; 8 Grand Slam singles titles.
Troy Aikman, b 1966, quarterback; led Dallas Cowboys to Super Bowl wins in 1993-94, '96; Super Bowl MVP, 1993.
Ben Ainslie, b 1977, (Br.) most decorated Olympic sailor; gold, 2000, '04, '08, '12; silver, 1996.
Michelle Akers, b 1966, soccer player; led U.S. to victory in World Cup (1991, '99).
Grover Cleveland "Pete" Alexander, 1887-1950, pitcher; won 373 NL games; pitched 16 shutouts, 1916.
Muhammad Ali, 1942-2016, 3-time heavyweight champion, activist.
Morten Andersen, b 1960, (Den.) NFL kicker, career leader in games played (382).
Sparky Anderson, 1934-2010, first manager to win World Series in the NL (Cincinnati, 1975-76) and AL (Detroit, 1984).
Mario Andretti, b 1940, (It.) race-car driver; won Daytona 500 (1967), Indy 500 (1969); Formula 1 world title (1978).
Giannis Antetokounmpo, b 1994, (Gr.-Nigeria) Milwaukee Bucks forward; NBA MVP 2019, '20.
Earl Anthony, 1938-2001, bowler; 6 PBA Championships (1973-75, '81-'83), 43 career PBA tournaments.
Eddie Arcaro, 1916-97, only jockey to win racing's Triple Crown twice, 1941, '48; rode to 4,779 wins in his career.
Henry Armstrong, 1912-88, first boxer to hold world title in three weight classes simultaneously (1938).
Lance Armstrong, b 1971, cyclist; record 7-time winner of Tour de France (1999-2005); stripped of victories in 2012 for use of performance-enhancing drugs.
Arthur Ashe, 1943-93, tennis player; first Black man to win U.S. Open (1968), Austral. Open (1970), Wimbledon (1975).

Evelyn Ashford, b 1957, sprinter; won 100m gold (1984) and silver (1988); member of 5 U.S. Olympic teams.
Red Auerbach, 1917-2006, coached Boston to 9 NBA titles.
Geno Auriemma, b 1954, (It.) UConn women's basketball coach; record 11 NCAA women's basketball titles.
Tracy Austin, b 1962, tennis player; youngest to win U.S. Open (age 16 in 1979).
Ernie Banks, 1931-2015, Chicago Cubs slugger; hit 512 NL homers; twice MVP.
Roger Bannister, 1929-2018, (Br.) physician; ran 1st sub-4-min. mile, May 6, 1954 (3 min., 59.4 sec.).
Charles Barkley, b 1963, NBA MVP, 1993; 4th player ever to surpass 20,000 pts., 10,000 rebounds, 4,000 assists.
Rick Barry, b 1944, NBA scoring leader, 1967; ABA scoring leader, 1969.
Sammy Baugh, 1914-2008, Washington Redskins quarterback, punter, defensive back.
Elgin Baylor, 1934-2021, L.A. Lakers forward; 11-time all-star.
Bob Beamon, b 1946, Olympic long jump gold medalist, 1968; world record jump of 29 ft 2½ in. stood until 1991.
Boris Becker, b 1967, (Ger.) tennis player; 6 Grand Slam singles titles.
David Beckham, b 1975, (Br.) soccer midfielder; joined L.A. Galaxy, 2007-12, with record-breaking $250-mil contract.
Bill Belichick, b 1952, NFL coach; led New England to 6 Super Bowl wins.
Jean Béliveau, 1931-2014, (Can.) Montréal Canadiens center; scored 507 career goals; twice MVP.
Johnny Bench, b 1947, Cincinnati Reds catcher; twice MVP; led league in home runs twice, RBIs 3 times.
Patty Berg, 1918-2006, won a record 15 LPGA majors.
Chris Berman, b 1955, sportscaster.
Yogi Berra, 1925-2015, NY Yankees catcher (1946-63); 3-time MVP.
Mookie Betts, b 1992, All-Star right-fielder and shortstop; AL MVP (2018).
Abebe Bikila, 1932-73, (Eth.) runner; won consecutive Olympic marathon gold medals in 1960 (barefoot), '64.
Simone Biles, b 1997, gymnast; won 11 Olympic medals, including 7 gold; record 30 world championship medals.
Matt Biondi, b 1965, swimmer; won 5 golds, 1988 Olympics.
Larry Bird, b 1956, Boston Celtics forward (1979-92); NBA MVP, 1984-86; 1998 coach of the year with Indiana Pacers.
Sue Bird, b 1980, point guard; 4-time WNBA champion (2004, '10, '18, '20); Olympic gold (2004, '08, '12, '16, '20).
Bonnie Blair, b 1964, speed skater; won 5 individual gold medals in 3 Olympics (1988, '92, '94).
George Blanda, 1927-2010, quarterback, kicker; 26 years as active player, scored 2,002 career points.
Fanny Blankers-Koen, 1918-2004, (Neth.) track and field athlete; won 4 Olympic gold medals (1948).
Wade Boggs, b 1958, AL batting champ, 1983, '85-'88; reached 3,000 career hits, 1999 (3,010).
Usain Bolt, b 1986, (Jam.) Olympic sprinter, gold medalist, 2008, '12, '16; world record for men's 100-m, 200-m runs.
Barry Bonds, b 1964, outfielder; hit record 73 homers, 2001; record 7-time NL MVP; 1st all-time in HRs (762); indicted in steroid scandal, 2007.
Björn Borg, b 1956, (Swed.) tennis player; 11 Grand Slam singles titles.
Ray Bourque, b 1960, (Can.) leads NHL defensemen in career goals, assists, points; 5-time Norris Trophy winner.
Bill Bradley, b 1943, led NY Knicks to 2 NBA titles (1970, '73); U.S. senator (NJ), 1979-97.
Donald Bradman, 1908-2001, (Austral.) widely regarded as greatest cricketer ever; set several batting records.
Terry Bradshaw, b 1948, quarterback; led Pittsburgh to 4 Super Bowl wins, 1975-76, '79-'80; NFL MVP, 1978.
Tom Brady, b 1977, quarterback; 7 Super Bowl titles; 5-time Super Bowl MVP; 3-time NFL MVP.
Drew Brees, b 1979, New Orleans Saints quarterback; Super Bowl MVP, 2010.
Christine Brennan, b 1958, sports journalist for *USA Today*, radio and TV commentator specializing in figure skating.
George Brett, b 1953, Kansas City Royals infielder; led AL in batting, 1976, '80, '90; MVP, 1980.
Lou Brock, 1939-2020, St. Louis Cardinals outfielder; stole NL single-season record 118 bases, 1974; led NL 8 times.
Jim Brown, 1936-2023, Cleveland fullback; 12,312 career yds; 3-time NFL MVP.
Paul Brown, 1908-91, football team owner, coach; led eponymous Cleveland Browns to 3 NFL championships.
Bob Bryan, b 1978, tennis player; won 16 Grand Slam doubles titles; Olympic gold, 2012.
Mike Bryan, b 1978, tennis player; won 18 Grand Slam doubles titles; Olympic gold, 2012.
Kobe Bryant, 1978-2020, NBA guard; won 5 titles with Lakers (2000-02, '09, '10); NBA MVP, 2008; NBA Finals MVP, 2009, '10.
Paul "Bear" Bryant, 1913-83, college football coach with 323 wins; led Alabama to 6 national titles (1961, '64-'65, '73, '78-'79).
Sergei Bubka, b 1963, (Ukr.) pole vaulter; first to clear 20 ft; gold medal, 1988 Olympics.
Joe Buck, b 1969, sportscaster.
Don Budge, 1915-2000, won numerous amateur and pro tennis titles; Grand Slam, 1938.
Dick Butkus, 1942-2023, Chicago Bears linebacker; NFL defensive player of the year (1969-70).
Dick Button, b 1929, figure skater; won 1948, '52 Olympic gold medals; world titleholder, 1948-52.
Miguel Cabrera, b 1983, (Venez.) 12-time MLB All-Star; won AL triple crown (2012); AL MVP 2012, '13.
Walter Camp, 1859-1925, Yale football player, coach, athletic director; established many rules for modern football.
Roy Campanella, 1921-93, Brooklyn Dodgers catcher (1948-57); 3-time NL MVP.
Earl Campbell, b 1955, NFL running back; MVP 1978-79.
Jose Canseco, b 1964, outfielder; led Oakland A's to the World Series, 1988; wrote book about steroids in baseball, 2005.
Eric Cantona, b 1966, (Fr.) soccer forward; Manchester United (1992-97).
Rod Carew, b 1945, AL infielder; 7 batting titles, 1977 MVP.
Steve Carlton, b 1944, NL pitcher; 4-time Cy Young winner; 4,136 career strikeouts.
Pete Carroll, b 1951, football coach; NCAA champion (2003, '04); won Super Bowl XLVIII.
Billy Casper, 1931-2015, PGA Player of the Year 2 times; U.S. Open champ twice.
Tamika Catchings, b 1979, basketball forward, WNBA MVP, 2011; 4-time Olympic gold medalist.
Tracy Caulkins, b 1963, swimmer; 3-time Olympic gold medalist.
Wilt Chamberlain, 1936-99, center; 7-time NBA leading scorer, 4-time MVP; scored 100 pts. in a game, 1962.
Oscar Charleston, 1896-1954, Negro League center fielder; .363 lifetime batting average.
Nathan Chen, b 1999, figure skater; 2022 Olympic gold medalist; U.S. champion, 2017-22; world champion, 2018-19, '21.
Caitlin Clark, b 2002, basketball player; NCAA Division I all-time leading scorer.
Bobby Clarke, b 1949, (Can.) Philadelphia Flyers center; led team to 2 Stanley Cup championships; 3-time MVP.
Roger Clemens, b 1962, pitcher; 1986 AL MVP; only 7-time Cy Young winner; 354 wins, 4,672 Ks (3rd all-time); accused of lying to Congress about steroids, 2010.
Roberto Clemente, 1934-72, Pittsburgh Pirates outfielder; won 4 batting titles; MVP, 1966; 3,000 career hits; killed in plane crash on aid mission.
Kim Clijsters, b 1983, (Belg.) tennis player; 4 Grand Slam singles titles.
Ty Cobb, 1886-1961, Detroit Tigers outfielder; .367 lifetime batting average, 12 batting titles.
Sebastian Coe, b 1956, (Br.) runner; won Olympic 1,500m gold medal and 800m silver medal in both 1980, '84.
Nadia Comaneci, b 1961, (Rom.) gymnast; won 3 gold medals, achieved 7 perfect scores, 1976 Olympics; 9 Olympic medals overall.
Maureen Connolly, 1934-69, tennis player; 9 Grand Slam singles titles.
Jimmy Connors, b 1952, tennis player; 8 Grand Slam singles titles.
Alberto Contador, b 1982, (Sp.) cyclist; won Tour de France 2007, '09; stripped of 2010 title because of doping offense.
Cynthia Cooper-Dyke, b 1963, WNBA player; 4-time finals MVP; 2-time league MVP.
James J. Corbett, 1866-1933, heavyweight champion, 1892-97; credited with being the first "scientific" boxer.
Angel Cordero Jr., b 1942, jockey; leading money winner, 1976, '82-'83; rode 3 Kentucky Derby winners.
Margaret Smith Court, b 1942, (Austral.) tennis player; won 24 Grand Slam singles titles (11 in Open Era).
Bob Cousy, b 1928, Boston guard; 6 NBA titles, 1957 MVP.
Sidney Crosby, b 1987, (Can.) hockey player; Art Ross, Hart Trophies (2007, '14), Olympic gold medal (2010, '14).
Mark Cuban, b 1958, Dallas Mavericks owner; known for outspokenness.
Stephen Curry, b 1988, NBA point guard; 4 NBA titles; NBA MVP, 2015, '16; Olympic gold medalist, 2024.
Bjoern Daehlie, b 1967, (Nor.) cross-country skier; 8 Olympic gold medals.
Al Davis, 1929-2011, Oakland Raiders owner, former coach.
Oscar De La Hoya, b 1973, boxer; won IBF lightweight (1995), WBC super lightweight (1996) and welterweight (1997-99, 2000) titles.
Donna de Varona, b 1947, swimmer; won 2 Olympic golds, 1964; 1st female sportscaster at a major network, 1965.
Dizzy Dean, 1910-74, pitcher; St. Louis Cardinals' "Gashouse Gang" in the '30s.
Mary Decker Slaney, b 1958, middle-distance runner; numerous U.S./world records.
Frank Deford, 1938-2017, writer for *Sports Illustrated*; author, commentator.
Jack Dempsey, 1895-1983, heavyweight champ, 1919-26.
Gail Devers, b 1966, Olympic 100m gold medalist (1992, '96).
Joe DiMaggio, 1914-99, NY Yankees outfielder; hit safely in record 56 consecutive games, 1941; AL MVP 3 times.
Novak Djokovic, b 1987, (Serb.) tennis player; 24 Grand Slam singles titles; Olympic gold medalist (2024).
Landon Donovan, b 1982, soccer forward.
Tony Dorsett, b 1954, Heisman winner who led the Dallas Cowboys to an NFL title in his rookie year, 1977.
Gabrielle Douglas, b 1995, gymnast; Olympic gold in all-around (2012), team (2012, '16).
Caeleb Dressel, b 1996, swimmer; 9-time Olympic gold medalist (2016, '20, '24).
Tim Duncan, b 1976, San Antonio center; NBA MVP, 2002, '03; 3-time Finals MVP.
Margaret Osborne duPont, 1918-2012, tennis player; 6-time Grand Slam singles champion.
Roberto Duran, b 1951, (Pan.) boxer; held titles at 3 weights; lost 1980 "no mas" fight to Sugar Ray Leonard.
Kevin Durant, b 1988, NBA forward; NBA MVP, 2014; Finals MVP, 2017, '18; 4-time Olympic gold medalist.
Leo Durocher, 1905-91, manager; won 3 NL pennants (Brooklyn, 1941; NY Giants, 1951, '54), 1954 World Series.

Dale Earnhardt Jr., b 1974, stock car racer; Daytona 500 winner (2004, '14).
Dale Earnhardt Sr., 1951-2001, 7-time NASCAR Winston Cup champ; died in a last-lap crash at 2001 Daytona 500.
Ashton Eaton, b 1988, Olympic decathlon gold medalist, 2012, '16.
Stefan Edberg, b 1966, (Swed.) tennis player; 6 Grand Slam singles titles.
Gertrude Ederle, 1905-2003, first woman to swim English Channel (1926).
Teresa Edwards, b 1964, 5-time basketball Olympian; gold medalist, 1984, '88, '96, 2000; bronze medalist, 1992.
Hicham El Guerrouj, b 1974, (Morocco) runner; holds world records in mile (3:43.13) and 1,500m (3:26); won gold medals in 1,500m and 5,000m, 2004 Olympics.
John Elway, b 1960, quarterback; led Denver Broncos to 2 Super Bowl wins, 1998-99; NFL MVP, 1987; Super Bowl MVP, 1999.
Roy Emerson, b 1936, (Austral.) tennis player; 12 Grand Slam singles titles.
Julius "Dr. J" Erving, b 1950, 3-time ABA MVP, 1981 NBA MVP.
Phil Esposito, b 1942, (Can.) NHL scoring leader 5 times.
Janet Evans, b 1971, 4 Olympic swimming golds, 1988, '92.
Lee Evans, 1947-2021, Olympic 400m gold medalist in 1968 with 43.86-sec. world record not broken until 1988.
Chris Evert, b 1954, tennis player; 18 Grand Slam singles titles.
Ray Ewry, 1873-1937, track and field athlete; won 8 Olympic gold medals (1900, '04, '08).
Nick Faldo, b 1957, (Br.) golfer; won Masters, British Open 3 times each.
Juan Manuel Fangio, 1911-95 (Arg.), 5-time World Grand Prix driving champ (1951, '54-'57).
Marshall Faulk, b 1973, 2000 NFL MVP; scored then-record 26 TDs, 2001; 3-time Off. Player of the Year (1999-2001).
Brett Favre, b 1969, quarterback; led Green Bay to Super Bowl win, 1997; 3-time NFL MVP.
Roger Federer, b 1981, (Switz.) tennis player; 20 Grand Slam singles titles.
Allyson Felix, b 1985, sprinter; 7-time Olympic gold medalist (2008, '12, '16, '20).
Bob Feller, 1918-2010, Cleveland Indians pitcher; won 266 games; pitched 3 no-hitters, 12 one-hitters.
Rollie Fingers, b 1946, pitcher; 341 career saves; AL MVP, Cy Young, 1981; World Series MVP, 1974.
Peggy Fleming, b 1948, world figure skating champion, 1966-68; gold medalist, 1968 Olympics.
Whitey Ford, 1928-2020, NY Yankees pitcher; won 10 World Series games.
George Foreman, b 1949, heavyweight champion, 1973-74, '94-'95; at 45, oldest to win a heavyweight title; gold medalist, 1968 Olympics.
Dick Fosbury, 1947-2023, high jumper; won 1968 Olympic gold medal; developed the "Fosbury Flop."
Jimmie Foxx, 1907-67, Red Sox, Athletics slugger; MVP 3 times; triple crown, 1933.
A. J. Foyt, b 1935, won Indy 500 4 times; U.S. Auto Club champ 7 times.
Dario Franchitti, b 1973, (Scot.) 3-time Indy 500 winner, 2007, '10, '12.
Missy Franklin, b 1995, swimmer; 5-time Olympic gold medalist (2012, '16).
Joe Frazier, 1944-2011, heavyweight champion, 1970-73; gold medalist, 1964 Olympics.
Walt Frazier, b 1945, guard for NY Knicks' NBA championship teams (1970, '73).
Chris Froome, b 1985, (Kenya) 4-time Tour de France winner (2013, '15-'17).
Peter Gammons, b 1945, sportswriter, broadcaster.
Lou Gehrig, 1903-41, NY Yankees 1st baseman; MVP, 1927, '36; triple crown, 1934; played 2,130 straight games (1925-39).
Althea Gibson, 1927-2003, tennis player; first Black woman to compete and win at Wimbledon, U.S. Open; 5 Grand Slam singles titles.
Bob Gibson, 1935-2020, St. Louis Cardinals pitcher; won Cy Young twice; struck out 3,117 batters.
Josh Gibson, 1911-47, Negro Leagues catcher; all-time career leader in batting avg. (.372) and slugging pct. (.718).
Marc Girardelli, b 1963, (Lux.) skier; won 5 World Cup titles.
Raúl González, b 1977, (Sp.) soccer player; led Real Madrid to 3 Champions League titles (1998, 2000, '02).
Jeff Gordon, b 1971, race-car driver; youngest to win NASCAR title 4 times (1995, '97-'98, 2001).
Steffi Graf, b 1969, (Ger.) tennis player; 22 Grand Slam singles titles (3rd all-time).
Otto Graham, 1921-2003, Cleveland quarterback; 4-time all-pro.
Red Grange, 1903-91, All-American at Univ. of Illinois, 1923-25; played for Chicago Bears, 1925-35.
"Mean" Joe Greene, b 1946, Pittsburgh Steelers lineman; twice NFL outstanding defensive player.
Wayne Gretzky, b 1961, (Can.) top scorer in NHL history with record 894 goals, 1,963 assists, 2,857 pts.; MVP, 1980-87, '89.
Bob Griese, b 1945, All-Pro quarterback; led Miami Dolphins to 17-0 season, 1972, 2 Super Bowl titles, 1973-74.
Ken Griffey Jr., b 1969, outfielder; led AL in homers 1994, '97-'99; 1997 AL MVP; 10 gold gloves.
Archie Griffin, b 1954, Ohio State running back; only 2-time winner of the Heisman Trophy (1974-75).
Florence Griffith Joyner, 1959-98, sprinter; won 3 gold medals at 1988 Olympics; world records for 100m and 200m.
Brittney Griner, b 1990, WNBA center, 3-time Olympic gold medalist.
Lefty Grove, 1900-75, pitcher; won 300 AL games.
Janet Guthrie, b 1938, 1st woman driver in Indy 500 (1977).
Tony Gwynn, 1960-2014, 8-time NL batting champ; 3,141 career hits.
Walter Hagen, 1892-1969, golfer; 5 PGA, 4 British Open titles.
Mika Hakkinen, b 1968, (Fin.) Formula One racing driver; Formula One champion, 1998-99.
George Halas, 1895-1983, founder/player/coach of Chicago Bears; won 6 NFL championships as coach.
Roy Halladay, 1977-2017, pitcher; Cy Young, 2003, '10; perfect game, 2010.
Dorothy Hamill, b 1956, figure skater; Olympic gold medalist, 1976.
Lewis Hamilton, b 1985, (Br.) race-car driver; 7-time Formula 1 world champ (2008, '14-'15, '17-'20).
Scott Hamilton, b 1958, U.S. and world figure skating champion, 1981-84; Olympic gold medalist, 1984.
Mia Hamm, b 1972, soccer player; led U.S. teams to World Cup victories (1991, '99) and Olympic gold (1996, 2004).
Yuzuru Hanyu, b 1994, (Jpn.) figure skater; Olympic gold medalist, 2014, '18.
James Harden, b 1989, NBA shooting guard; NBA MVP, 2018.
Franco Harris, 1950-2022, running back; 4 Super Bowls with Steelers (1975-76, '79-'80); 1,000+ season yds. 8 times.
Marvin Harrison, b 1972, Indianapolis Colts wide receiver; 143 single-season receptions, 2002.
Bill Hartack, 1932-2007, jockey; rode 5 Kentucky Derby winners.
Dominik Hasek, b 1965, (Czech.) NHL goaltender; 6 Vezina Trophies; NHL MVP, 1997-98.
John Havlicek, 1940-2019, Boston Celtics forward; scored 26,395 career pts.
Elvin Hayes, b 1945, 12-time NBA All-Star; scored 27,313 career pts.
Eric Heiden, b 1958, speed skater; won 5 Olympic golds, 1980.
Rickey Henderson, b 1958, outfielder; 1990 AL MVP; record 130 stolen bases, 1982; all-time leader in steals, runs.
Sonja Henie, 1912-69, (Nor.) world champion figure skater, 1927-36; Olympic gold medalist, 1928, '32, '36.
Martina Hingis, b 1980, (Switz.) 5 Grand Slam singles titles; youngest number-one player (16 yrs., 6 mos.), 1997.
Ben Hogan, 1912-97, golfer; won 4 U.S. Open titles, 2 PGA Championships, 2 Masters.
Larry Holmes, b 1949, World Heavyweight Champion, 1978-85.
Evander Holyfield, b 1962, 4-time heavyweight champion.
Rogers Hornsby, 1896-1963, NL 2nd baseman; batted .424, 1924; twice won triple crown.
Paul Hornung, 1935-2020, Green Bay running back, kicker; Heisman Trophy winner, 1956.
Gordie Howe, 1928-2016, (Can.) hockey forward; NHL MVP 6 times; scored 801 goals in 26 NHL seasons.
Carl Hubbell, 1903-88, NY Giants pitcher; 20-game winner 5 consecutive seasons, 1933-37.
Bobby Hull, 1939-2023, (Can.) NHL all-star 10 times; MVP, 1965-66.
Brett Hull, b 1964, (Can.) St. Louis Blues forward; led NHL in goals, 1990-92; MVP, 1991.
Catfish Hunter, 1946-99, pitched perfect game, 1968; 20-game winner 5 times.
Don Hutson, 1913-97, Packers receiver; caught 99 TD passes; 2-time NFL MVP.
Juli Inkster, b 1960, golfer; won 7 career LPGA major titles.
Bo Jackson, b 1962, NFL running back (1987-90) and MLB outfielder (1986-91, '93-'94); 1985 Heisman Trophy winner.
Phil Jackson, b 1945, won 11 NBA titles as coach of Bulls and Lakers; 1970, '73 title as player with NY Knicks.
Reggie Jackson, b 1946, slugger; led AL in home runs 4 times; MVP, 1973; hit 5 World Series home runs, 1977.
"Shoeless" Joe Jackson, 1889-1951, outfielder; .356 career batting average; one of the "Black Sox" banned for allegedly throwing 1919 World Series.
Jaromír Jágr, b 1972, (Czech.) hockey player; NHL MVP, 1999; 5 Art Ross Trophies.
LeBron James, b 1984, NBA forward; 4-time NBA MVP; 4 NBA titles; all-time leading NBA scorer; Olympic gold medalist, 2008, '12, '24.
Ron Jaworski, b 1951, NFL quarterback (1974-89), analyst.
Sally Jenkins, b 1960, sports journalist and writer for *Washington Post*.
Caitlyn Jenner, b 1949, Olympic men's decathlon gold medalist, 1976; came out as transgender woman, 2015.
Lynn Jennings, b 1960, runner; 3-time World, 9-time U.S. cross country champ; bronze (10,000m), 1992 Olympics.
Derek Jeter, b 1974, shortstop; led NY Yankees to 5 World Series titles; World Series MVP, 2000.
Earvin "Magic" Johnson, b 1959, 3-time NBA MVP; 5 NBA titles; 3-time Finals MVP.
Jack Johnson, 1878-1946, heavyweight champion, 1908-15.
Jimmie Johnson, b 1975, 7-time NASCAR Cup Series champ.
Michael Johnson, b 1967, sprinter; 4-time Olympic gold medalist (1992, '96, 2000).
Rafer Johnson, 1934-2020, Olympic decathlon gold medalist (1960).
Randy Johnson, b 1963, MLB pitcher with 4,875 strikeouts (2nd all-time), perfect game, 2004; 5-time Cy Young winner.
Walter Johnson, 1887-1946, Washington Senators pitcher; won 417 games; record 110 shutouts.
Bobby Jones, 1902-71, won golf's Grand Slam, 1930; U.S. amateur champ 5 times, U.S. Open champ 4 times.
Cobi Jones, b 1970, soccer player; most U.S. national team appearances with 164.

David "Deacon" Jones, 1938-2013, 5-time All-Pro with L.A. Rams (1965-69); "sack" specialist credited with inventing the term.

Marion Jones, b 1975, multi-event Olympic medalist; stripped of medals in 2007 after admitting use of PEDs.

Roy Jones Jr., b 1969, light heavyweight champ, 1999-2004.

Michael Jordan, b 1963, guard; 10-time leading NBA scorer; 5-time MVP; 6-time Finals MVP.

Jackie Joyner-Kersee, b 1962, Olympic gold medalist in heptathlon (1988, '92), long jump (1988).

Dorothy Kamenshek, 1925-2010, 4 All-American Girls Baseball League titles, 1940s.

Mary Keitany, b 1982, (Ken.) distance runner; 4-time NYC marathon winner.

Travis Kelce, b 1989, NFL tight end; 3 Super Bowl wins.

Clayton Kershaw, b 1988, pitcher; NL Cy Young winner (2011, '13, '14).

Harmon Killebrew, 1936-2011, Minnesota Twins slugger; led AL in home runs 6 times; 573 career home runs.

Jean-Claude Killy, b 1943, (Fr.) skier; 3 Olympic golds, 1968.

Ralph Kiner, 1922-2014, Pittsburgh Pirates slugger; led NL in home runs 7 consecutive years, 1946-52.

Billie Jean King, b 1943, 12 Grand Slam singles titles (8 in Open Era); beat Bobby Riggs, 1973.

Peter King, b 1957, sportswriter.

Bob Knight, 1940-2023, NCAA basketball coach; led Indiana to men's title in 1976, '81, '87.

Brooks Koepka, b 1990, golfer; won U.S. Open, 2017-18; PGA championship, 2018-19, 2023.

Olga Korbut, b 1955, (Belarus) gymnast; 4 Olympic gold medals, 1972, '76.

Sandy Koufax, b 1935, 3-time Cy Young winner; lowest ERA in NL, 1962-66; pitched 4 no-hitters, 1 perfect game.

Jack Kramer, 1921-2009, world's number one tennis player, 1946-53; first at Wimbledon to compete in shorts.

Ingrid Kristiansen, b 1956, (Nor.) only runner to have held simultaneous world records in 5,000m, 10,000m, and marathon.

Julie Krone, b 1963, winningest female jockey; first woman to ride a winner in a Triple Crown race (Belmont, 1993).

Mike Krzyzewski, b 1947, basketball coach; 5 NCAA championships with Duke; led 3 Olympic gold medal teams (2008, '12, '16).

Michelle Kwan, b 1980, figure skater; 9 U.S., 5 World titles; silver medalist at 1998 Olympics, bronze in 2002.

Guy Lafleur, 1951-2022, (Can.) 3-time NHL scoring leader; 1977-78 MVP.

Alexi Lalas, b 1970, soccer player; first modern-era American to play in Italian League Serie A.

Kenesaw Mountain Landis, 1866-1944, 1st commissioner of baseball (1920-44); banned the 8 "Black Sox" involved in fixing 1919 World Series.

Tom Landry, 1924-2000, Dallas Cowboys head coach, 1960-88; won 2 Super Bowls (1972, '78); 270 career wins.

Dick "Night Train" Lane, 1928-2002, defensive back; NFL season record 14 interceptions (1952).

Don Larsen, 1929-2020, as NY Yankee, pitched only World Series perfect game, Oct. 8, 1956—2-0 win over Brooklyn.

Rod Laver, b 1938, (Austral.) tennis player; 11-time Grand Slam singles champion (5 in Open era).

Katie Ledecky, b 1997, swimmer; 14 Olympic medals, incl. 9 gold (2012, '16, '20, '24).

Sunisa Lee, b 2003, gymnast; 6 Olympic medals, incl. 2 gold (2020, '24).

Mario Lemieux, b 1965, (Can.) 6-time NHL leading scorer; 3-time MVP; playoff MVP, 1991-92.

Greg LeMond, b 1961, cyclist; 3-time Tour de France winner (1986, '89-'90); first American to win the event.

Ivan Lendl, b 1960, (Czech.) tennis player; 8 Grand Slam singles titles.

Sugar Ray Leonard, b 1956, boxer; held titles in 5 different weight classes.

Lisa Leslie, b 1972, L.A. Sparks center; 3-time WNBA MVP.

Carl Lewis, b 1961, track and field athlete; won 10 Olympic medals (9 gold) in sprinting and long jump.

Lennox Lewis, b 1965, (Br.) heavyweight champ, 1994, 1997-2004; Olympic gold medalist, 1988.

Ray Lewis, b 1975, linebacker for the Baltimore Ravens; Super Bowl MVP, 2001.

Tara Lipinski, b 1982, youngest figure skater to win world championships, 1997, and Winter Olympic gold, 1998.

Carli Lloyd, b 1982, soccer midfielder; Olympic gold medalist (2008, '12); World Cup champion (2015, '19).

Ryan Lochte, b 1984, swimmer; 12-time Olympic medalist, incl. 6 gold (2004, '08, '12, '16).

Vince Lombardi, 1913-70, Green Bay Packers coach; led team to 5 NFL championships, 2 Super Bowl victories.

Nancy Lopez, b 1957, golfer; 4-time LPGA Player of the Year; 3-time winner of the LPGA Championship.

Greg Louganis, b 1960, won Olympic gold medals in both springboard and platform diving, 1984, '88.

Joe Louis, 1914-81, heavyweight champion, 1937-49.

Sid Luckman, 1916-98, Chicago Bears quarterback; led team to 4 NFL championships; MVP, 1943.

Connie Mack, 1862-1956, Philadelphia Athletics manager, 1901-50; won 9 pennants, 5 championships.

John Madden, 1936-2021, won Super Bowl as coach of Oakland Raiders (1977); NFL TV analyst.

Greg Maddux, b 1966, pitcher; won 4 Cy Young awards, 1992-95; 355 career wins.

Patrick Mahomes, b 1995, youngest QB to win a Super Bowl; 2-time NFL MVP.

Karl Malone, b 1963, Utah Jazz, L.A. Lakers forward; MVP, 1997, '99; 36,928 career pts. (3rd all-time).

Moses Malone, 1955-2015, NBA center; 3-time MVP.

Eli Manning, b 1981, NY Giants quarterback; Super Bowl MVP, 2008, '12.

Peyton Manning, b 1976, quarterback; record 5 NFL MVP awards; Super Bowl MVP, 2007; single-season passing yards record (5,477), 2013.

Mickey Mantle, 1931-95, NY Yankees outfielder; triple crown, 1956; 18 World Series home runs; MVP 3 times.

Diego Maradona, 1960-2020, (Arg.) soccer player; led Argentina to World Cup, 1986.

Pete Maravich, 1947-88, guard; scored NCAA record 44.2 ppg during collegiate career; led NBA in scoring, 1977.

Rocky Marciano, 1923-69, heavyweight champion, 1952-56; retired undefeated.

Dan Marino, b 1961, Miami quarterback; NFL MVP, 1984; 5-time passing yards leader.

Roger Maris, 1934-85, NY Yankees outfielder; hit AL record 61 home runs, 1961, record held 37 years; MVP, 1960-61.

Marta (Marta Vieira da Silva), b 1986, (Braz.) soccer forward; FIFA World Player of the Year a record 6 times.

Eddie Mathews, 1931-2001, Milwaukee-Atlanta Braves 3rd baseman; hit 512 career home runs.

Christy Mathewson, 1880-1925, pitcher; won 373 games.

Bob Mathias, 1930-2006, decathlon gold, 1948, '52 Olympics.

Misty May-Treanor, b 1977, beach volleyball player; 3-time Olympic gold medalist with Kerri Walsh Jennings (2004, '08, '12).

Willie Mays, 1931-2024, NY-S.F. Giants center fielder; hit 660 home runs, led NL 4 times; had 3,293 hits; twice MVP.

Floyd Mayweather Jr., b 1977, boxer with 50-0 record.

Willie McCovey, 1938-2018, S.F. Giants slugger; hit 521 home runs; led NL 3 times; MVP, 1969.

John McEnroe, b 1959, tennis player; 7 Grand Slam singles titles.

John McGraw, 1873-1934, NY Giants manager; led team to 10 pennants, 3 championships.

Conor McGregor, b 1988, (Ire.) mixed martial artist.

Mark McGwire, b 1963, hit then-record 70 home runs in 1998; 583 career home runs; admitted PED use, 2010.

Rory McIlroy, b 1989, (N. Ire.) golfer; won U.S. Open, 2011; PGA Championship, 2012, '14; British Open, 2014.

Tamara McKinney, b 1962, 1st U.S. skier to win overall Alpine World Cup championship (1983).

Sydney McLaughlin-Levrone, b 1999, hurdler and sprinter; 4-time Olympic gold medalist (2020, '24).

Andrea Mead Lawrence, 1932-2009, skier; first woman to win 2 gold medals in alpine skiing at one Olympics (1952).

Lionel Messi, b 1987, (Arg.) soccer forward; 8-time Ballon d'Or winner; led Argentina to World Cup win, 2022.

Mark Messier, b 1961, (Can.) center; NHL MVP, 1990, '92; Conn Smythe Trophy, 1984.

Debbie Meyer, b 1952, 1st swimmer to win 3 individual Olympic golds (1968).

Al Michaels, b 1944, sportscaster.

Phil Mickelson, b 1970, golfer; 6 career major titles.

George Mikan, 1924-2005, Minn. Lakers center; considered the best basketball player of first half of 20th cent.

Stan Mikita, 1940-2018, (Czech.) Chicago Blackhawks center; led NHL in scoring 4 times; MVP twice.

Billy Mills, b 1938, runner; upset winner of the 1964 Olympic 10,000m; only American man ever to win the event.

Joe Montana, b 1956, S.F. 49ers quarterback; 3-time Super Bowl MVP.

Archie Moore, 1913-98, light-heavyweight champ, 1952-62.

Howie Morenz, 1902-37, (Can.) Montréal Canadiens forward; considered best hockey player of first half of 20th cent.

Alex Morgan, b 1989, soccer forward; women's World Cup champion (2015, '19); Olympic gold medalist (2012).

Edwin Moses, b 1955, undefeated in 122 consecutive 400m hurdles races, 1977-87; Olympic gold medalist, 1976, '84.

Shirley Muldowney, b 1940, 1st woman to race Natl. Hot Rod Assn. Top Fuel dragsters; 3-time NHRA points champ.

Andy Murray, b 1987, (Br.) tennis player; 3-time Grand Slam singles champion; Olympic gold medal in men's singles (2012, '16).

Eddie Murray, b 1956, 3rd MLB player with both 3,000+ hits and 500+ home runs.

Stan Musial, 1920-2013, St. Louis Cardinals hitter who won 7 NL batting titles; MVP 3 times.

Rafael Nadal, b 1986, (Sp.) tennis player; 22-time Grand Slam singles champion; Olympic gold medal in men's singles (2008).

Bronko Nagurski, 1908-90, (Can.) Chicago Bears fullback and tackle; gained more than 4,000 yds rushing.

Joe Namath, b 1943, Jets quarterback; 1969 Super Bowl MVP.

Rosie Napravnik, b 1988, jockey.

Steve Nash, b 1974, (Can.) Phoenix Suns point guard; NBA MVP, 2005, '06.

Martina Navratilova, b 1956, (Czech.) tennis player; won 18 Grand Slam singles titles.

Byron Nelson, 1912-2006, won 11 consecutive golf tournaments in 1945; twice Masters and PGA titlist.

Ernie Nevers, 1903-76, Stanford fullback; early pro football star.

Paula Newby-Fraser, b 1962, ([now] Zimbabwe) 8-time Ironman Triathlon world champ.
John Newcombe, b 1944, (Austral.) tennis player; 7 Grand Slam singles and 17 Grand Slam men's doubles titles.
Neymar (Neymar da Silva Santos Júnior), b 1992, (Braz.) soccer forward; led Brazil to Olympic gold, 2016.
Jack Nicklaus, b 1940, PGA Player of the Year, 1967, '72; leading money winner 8 times; won 18 majors (6 Masters).
Chuck Noll, 1932-2014, Pittsburgh Steelers coach; won 4 Super Bowls.
Dirk Nowitzki, b 1978, (Ger.) NBA forward; led Mavericks to NBA title, 2011; NBA MVP, 2007.
Paavo Nurmi, 1897-1973, (Fin.) distance runner; won 9 Olympic gold medals, 1920, '24, '28.
Lorena Ochoa, b 1981, (Mex.) LPGA Player of the Year, 2006-09, money leader 2006-08.
Al Oerter, 1936-2007, discus thrower; won gold medal at 4 consecutive Olympics, 1956, '60, '64, '68.
Apolo Ohno, b 1982, short-track speed skater; most decorated U.S. Winter Olympic athlete with 2 gold, 2 silver, 4 bronze (2002, '06, '10).
Shohei Ohtani, b 1994, (Jpn.) MLB pitcher and designated hitter; AL MVP, 2021, '23.
Hakeem Olajuwon, b 1963, (Nigeria) Houston center; NBA MVP, 1994; playoff MVP, 1994-95; career blocked shots leader (3,830).
Barney Oldfield, 1878-1946, pioneer auto racer; was first to drive a car 60 mph, 1903.
Shaquille O'Neal, b 1972, center; led L.A. Lakers to NBA titles, 2000-02, and Miami Heat to NBA title, 2006; Finals MVP 2000-02; NBA MVP 2000.
Bobby Orr, b 1948, (Can.) Boston Bruins defenseman; 8-time Norris Trophy winner; led NHL in scoring twice, assists 5 times.
Naomi Osaka, b 1997, (Jpn.) tennis player; won U.S. Open (2018, '20), Austral. Open (2019, '21).
Mel Ott, 1909-58, NY Giants right fielder; hit 511 home runs; led NL 6 times.
Alexander Ovechkin, b 1985, (Russ.) hockey player; NHL MVP, 2008, '09, '13.
Jesse Owens, 1913-80, track-and-field athlete; 4 1936 Olympic golds.
Terrell Owens, b 1973, NFL wide receiver.
Satchel Paige, 1906-82, pitcher; starred in Negro Leagues, 1924-48; entered major leagues at age 42.
Arnold Palmer, 1929-2016, golf's first $1 mil winner; won 4 Masters, 2 British Opens.
Jim Palmer, b 1945, Baltimore Orioles pitcher; won Cy Young award 3 times; 20-game winner 8 times.
Inbee Park, b 1988, (S. Kor.) golfer; 2nd woman ever to win first 3 majors of season (2013).
Candace Parker, b 1986, WNBA forward; WNBA MVP (2008, '13); Olympic gold medalist (2008, '12).
Joe Paterno, 1926-2012, Penn St. football coach; national title-winner, 1982, '86; most wins in NCAA Div. I coaching history (409); legacy complicated by child sex abuse scandal at Penn St.
Danica Patrick, b 1982, race car driver; 1st woman to lead Indy 500 and to win NASCAR Sprint Cup series pole.
Floyd Patterson, 1935-2006, 2-time heavyweight champion; first to ever regain the title after losing it.
Walter Payton, 1954-99, Chicago Bears running back; 2nd most rushing yards in NFL history; top NFC rusher, 1976-80.
Pelé (Edson Arantes do Nascimento), 1940-2022, (Braz.) soccer player; led Brazil to 3 World Cups (1958, '62, '70); scored 1,281 goals.
Bob Pettit, b 1932, first NBA player to score 20,000 pts.; twice NBA scoring leader.
Richard Petty, b 1937, NASCAR national champ 7 times; 7-time Daytona 500 winner.
Michael Phelps, b 1985, Olympic swimmer; record-holder, most Olympic medals (28) and gold medals (23) won by a single athlete.
Oscar Pistorius, b 1986, (S. Afr.) sprinter, 1st double-leg amputee to compete in Olympics, 2012; convicted (2015) of murder in girlfriend's death.
Jacques Plante, 1929-86, (Can.) NHL goaltender; 7 Vezina trophies; first goalie to wear mask in a game.
Gary Player, b 1935, (S. Afr.) golfer; won 3 Masters, 3 British Opens, 2 PGA Championships, and U.S. Open.
Mike Powell, b 1963, track-and-field athlete; holds world record for long jump (29 ft 4.5 in.).
Steve Prefontaine, 1951-75, runner; 1st to win 4 NCAA titles in same event (5,000m, 1970-73).
Kirby Puckett, 1960-2006, Minnesota center fielder with .318 career avg.; World Series titles, 1987, '91.
Albert Pujols, b 1980, MLB slugger; NL MVP, 2005, '08-'09.
Paula Radcliffe, b 1973, British runner; fmr. marathon world record holder.
Manny Ramirez, b 1972, (Dom. Rep.) outfielder; 2004 World Series MVP; suspended for violating MLB performance-enhancing drug policy, 2009, '11.
Megan Rapinoe, b 1985, soccer forward; World Cup champion (2015, '19); won Golden Boot, Golden Ball (2019).
Willis Reed, 1942-2023, NY Knicks center; MVP, 1970; playoff MVP, 1970, '73.
Mary Lou Retton, b 1968, gymnast; won all-around gold medal at 1984 Olympics; also won 2 silvers, 2 bronzes.
Jerry Rice, b 1962, receiver; 1989 Super Bowl MVP; NFL record for career touchdowns (208), receptions (1,549).
Maurice Richard, 1921-2000, (Can.) Montréal Canadiens forward; scored 544 regular season goals, 82 playoff goals.
Branch Rickey, 1881-1965, MLB exec. helped break baseball's color barrier, 1947; initiated farm system, 1919.
Cal Ripken Jr., b 1960, Baltimore shortstop; AL MVP, 1983, '91; most consecutive games played (2,632).
Mariano Rivera, b 1969, (Pan.) relief pitcher; helped NY Yankees to 5 World Series titles; World Series MVP, 1999; all-time MLB leader in regular season and postseason saves.
Oscar Robertson, b 1938, NBA guard; averaged career 25.7 pts. per game; MVP, 1964.
Brooks Robinson, 1937-2023, Baltimore Orioles 3rd baseman; played in 4 World Series; MVP, 1964; 16 gold gloves.
Frank Robinson, 1935-2019, MVP in both NL and AL; triple crown, 1966; 586 career home runs; first Black manager in majors.
Jackie Robinson, 1919-72, broke baseball's color barrier with Brooklyn Dodgers, 1947; NL MVP, 1949.
Sugar Ray Robinson, 1921-89, boxer; middleweight champion 5 times; welterweight champion, 1946-51.
Knute Rockne, 1888-1931, Notre Dame football coach, 1918-31; revolutionized game by stressing forward pass.
Aaron Rodgers, b 1983, NFL quarterback; led Packers to victory in Super Bowl XLV; Super Bowl MVP, 2011; NFL MVP, 2011, '14, '20, '21.
Bill Rodgers, b 1947, runner; won Boston and New York City marathons 4 times each between 1975 and 1980.
Alex Rodriguez, b 1975, MLB infielder; 3-time AL MVP; admitted steroid use 2001-03; suspended 162 games for PED use, 2013-14.
Juan "Chi Chi" Rodriguez, 1935-2024, champion golfer; 8 PGA tour wins, 22 Champions tour wins.
Ben Roethlisberger, b 1982, Pittsburgh Steelers quarterback; youngest QB to win Super Bowl, 2005.
Ronaldinho (Ronaldo de Assis Moreira), b 1980, (Braz.) soccer midfielder; FIFA World Player of the Year, 2004, '05.
Ronaldo (Ronaldo Luiz Nazario de Lima), b 1976, (Braz.) soccer forward; led Brazil to 2002 World Cup title; 3-time FIFA world player of the year.
Cristiano Ronaldo, b 1985, (Port.) soccer forward; FIFA player of the year, 2008; UEFA career scoring leader (141).
Art Rooney, 1901-88, NFL owner; bought Pittsburgh Pirates in 1933, renamed Steelers, 1940.
Pete Rose, 1941-2024, won 3 NL batting titles; hit in 44 consecutive games, 1978; most career hits, 4,256; banned for gambling, 1989; admitted betting on his team, 2004.
Ken Rosewall, b 1934, (Austral.) tennis player; 8 Grand Slam singles titles.
Ronda Rousey, b 1987, judoka and mixed martial arts fighter.
Patrick Roy, b 1965, (Can.) Montréal-Colorado goalie; only 3-time NHL playoffs MVP, 1986, '93, 2001.
Wilma Rudolph, 1940-94, sprinter; won 3 1960 Olympic golds.
Adolph Rupp, 1901-77, NCAA basketball coach; led Kentucky to 4 national titles, 1948-49, '51, '58.
Bill Russell, 1934-2022, Boston Celtics center; led team to 11 NBA titles; MVP 5 times; first Black coach of major pro sports team.
Babe Ruth, 1895-1948, NY Yankees outfielder; hit 60 home runs, 1927, 714 lifetime (3rd all-time); led AL 12 times.
Johnny Rutherford, b 1938, auto racer; won 3 Indy 500s.
Nolan Ryan, b 1947, pitcher; holds season (383), career (5,714) strikeout records; won 324 games (7 no-hitters).
Pete Sampras, b 1971, tennis player; 14 Grand Slam singles wins.
Joan Benoit Samuelson, b 1957, won 1st Olympic women's marathon (1984), Boston Marathon (1979, '83).
Barry Sanders, b 1968, running back; won Heisman Trophy, 1988; NFL MVP, 1997.
Deion Sanders, b 1967, NFL cornerback (1989-2000, '04-'05) and MLB outfielder (1989-95, '97, 2005).
Gale Sayers, 1943-2020, Chicago running back; twice led NFL in rushing.
Mike Schmidt, b 1949, Phillies 3rd baseman; led NL in home runs 8 times; 548 lifetime; 3-time NL MVP.
Michael Schumacher, b 1969, (Ger.) race-car driver; 7-time Formula 1 world champ (1994-95, 2000-04).
Vin Scully, 1927-2022, Dodgers broadcaster, 1950-2016.
Tom Seaver, 1944-2020, pitcher; won NL Cy Young award 3 times; won 311 major league games.
Monica Seles, b 1973, (Yugo.) tennis player; won 9 Grand Slam singles titles; stabbed on court by spectator, 1993.
Maria Sharapova, b 1987, (Russ.) tennis player; 5 Grand Slam singles titles.
Patty Sheehan, b 1956, golfer; 3 LPGA Championships (1983-84, '93).
Willie Shoemaker, 1931-2003, jockey; rode 4 Kentucky Derby, 5 Belmont Stakes winners.
Frank Shorter, b 1947, runner; only American to win men's Olympic marathon (1972) since 1908; silver medalist (1976).
Don Shula, 1930-2020, all-time winningest NFL coach (347 games).
Bill Simmons, b 1969, columnist; podcast, TV host; Grantland and theringer.com founder.
O. J. Simpson, 1947-2024, running back; rushed for 2,003 yds, 1973; AFC leading rusher 4 times; acquitted of murder, 1995; found guilty of robbery and kidnapping, imprisoned 2008-17.

Charlie "Chino" Smith, 1901-32, Negro Leagues second baseman.
Dean Smith, 1931-2015, basketball coach; 879 Division I wins; led North Carolina to 2 NCAA titles (1982, '93).
Emmitt Smith, b 1969, running back; NFL and Super Bowl MVP, 1993; rushed for career record 18,355 yds.
Conn Smythe, 1895-1980, (Can.) won 7 Stanley Cups as Toronto GM (1929-61); playoff MVP award named in his honor.
Sam Snead, 1912-2002, PGA and Masters champ 3 times each; 82 PGA tournament victories.
Annika Sorenstam, b 1970, (Swed.) golfer; set LPGA 18-hole record of 59 (–13); won 10 LPGA majors, including career Grand Slam.
Sammy Sosa, b 1968, (Dom. Rep.) MLB slugger; NL MVP, 1998; 1st to hit 60+ HR 3 times (1998-99, 2001).
Warren Spahn, 1921-2003, pitcher; won 363 NL games; 20-game winner 13 times; Cy Young winner, 1957.
Tris Speaker, 1888-1958, AL outfielder; batted .345 over 22 seasons; hit record 792 career doubles.
Jordan Spieth, b 1993, golfer; won Masters, 2015; U.S. Open, 2015; British Open, 2017.
Mark Spitz, b 1950, swimmer; won 7 golds at 1972 Olympics.
Amos Alonzo Stagg, 1862-1965, football innovator; Univ. of Chicago football coach for 41 years, 5 undefeated seasons.
Bart Starr, 1934-2019, Green Bay Packers quarterback; led team to 5 NFL titles, 2 Super Bowl victories.
Roger Staubach, b 1942, Dallas Cowboys quarterback; 2-time Super Bowl champ.
George Steinbrenner, 1930-2010, NY Yankees owner.
Casey Stengel, 1890-1975, managed Yankees to 10 pennants, 7 World Series wins between 1949 and 1960.
Breanna Stewart, b 1994, forward; WNBA champion and Finals MVP (2018, '20); WNBA MVP, 2018, '23; Olympic gold medalist, 2016, '20, '24.
Jackie Stewart, b 1939, (Scot.) auto racer; 27 Grand Prix wins.
John Stockton, b 1962, Utah Jazz guard; NBA career leader in assists, steals; NBA assists leader, 1988-96.
Picabo Street, b 1971, skier; 2-time World Cup downhill champion (1995-96); Olympic super G gold medalist, 1998.
Louise Suggs, 1923-2015, golfer; U.S. Women's Open champ, 1949, '52; 11 major victories.
John L. Sullivan, 1858-1918, last bare-knuckle heavyweight champion, 1882-92.
Pat Summerall, 1930-2013, NFL kicker, radio and TV sportscaster who announced 26 Super Bowls.
Pat Summitt, 1952-2016, women's basketball coach; led Tennessee to 8 NCAA titles; 1,098 career wins.
Ichiro Suzuki, b 1973, (Jpn.) outfielder; AL MVP, 2001; single-season hits record (262), 2004; 3,000th U.S. hit, 2016.
Sheryl Swoopes, b 1971, guard/forward; 1st 3-time WNBA MVP (2000, '02, '05); Olympic gold medalist (1996, 2000, '04).
Fran Tarkenton, b 1940, Minnesota, NY Giants quarterback; 342 career TD passes; 1975 Player of the Year.
Diana Taurasi, b 1982, WNBA guard, leading all-time scorer; 6-time Olympic gold medalist; WNBA MVP, 2009.
Lawrence Taylor, b 1959, linebacker; led NY Giants to 2 Super Bowl titles; played in 10 Pro Bowls.
Daley Thompson, b 1958, (Br.) decathlete; Olympic gold medalist in 1980, '84.
Jenny Thompson, b 1973, swimmer; 12 Olympic medals (8 gold) in 1992, '96, 2000, '04.
Bobby Thomson, 1923-2010, MLB utility player known for pennant-clinching "Shot Heard 'Round the World" for the NY Giants, 1951.
Jim Thorpe, 1888-1953, football All-American, 1911-12; won pentathlon and decathlon, 1912 Olympics.
Bill Tilden, 1893-1953, tennis player; won 7 U.S. Open titles, 3 Wimbledon.
Y. A. Tittle, 1926-2017, NY Giants quarterback; MVP, 1961, '63.
Alberto Tomba, b 1966, (It.) alpine skier; 5 Olympic medals (3 golds, 2 silver) in 1988, '92, '94.
LaDainian "L.T." Tomlinson, b 1979, running back; NFL single-season record for rushing touchdowns (28).
Joe Torre, b 1940, MLB player, manager; NL MVP, 1971; won 4 World Series in 5 years as NY Yankees manager.
Lee Trevino, b 1939, golfer; 6-time PGA major winner.
Bryan Trottier, b 1956, (Can.) Islanders, Penguins center for 6 Stanley Cup champs.
Mike Trout, b 1991, MLB outfielder; 3-time AL MVP, 2014, '16, '19.
Gene Tunney, 1897-1978, heavyweight champion, 1926-28.
Mike Tyson, b 1966, undisputed heavyweight champ, 1987-90; at 20, youngest to win a heavyweight title (WBC, 1986).
Wyomia Tyus, b 1945, Olympic 100m gold medalist, 1964, '68.
Johnny Unitas, 1933-2002, Baltimore Colts quarterback; passed for more than 40,000 yds; MVP, 1957, '67.
Al Unser, 1939-2021, Indy 500 winner 4 times.
Bobby Unser, 1934-2021, Indy 500 winner 3 times.
Norm Van Brocklin, 1926-83, quarterback; passed for game record 554 yds, 1951; MVP, 1960.
Amy Van Dyken, b 1973, swimmer; first American woman to win 4 gold medals in one Olympics (1996).
Justin Verlander, b 1983, pitcher; won AL MVP, 2011, and Cy Young, 2011, '19, '22.
Sebastian Vettel, b 1987, (Ger.) Formula 1 race car driver.
Michael Vick, b 1980, quarterback; suspended and convicted (2007) of illegal dog fighting, gambling activities.
Lasse Viren, b 1949, (Fin.) runner; Olympic 5,000m and 10,000m gold medalist in 1972, '76.
Lindsey Vonn, b 1984, skier; Olympic gold, 2010; 4 overall World Cup titles 2008-10, '12.
Dwyane Wade, b 1982, guard; led Miami Heat to NBA title, 2006, '12-'13; finals MVP, 2006; NBA scoring title, 2009.
Honus Wagner, 1874-1955, Pittsburgh Pirates shortstop; 8 NL batting titles.
Grete Waitz, 1953-2011, (Nor.) distance runner; 9-time winner of the New York City Marathon (1978-80, '82-'86, '88).
"Jersey" Joe Walcott, 1914-94, boxer; became heavyweight champion at age 37, 1951-52.
Kerri Walsh Jennings, b 1978, beach volleyball player; 3-time Olympic gold medalist with Misty May-Treanor (2004, '08, '12).
Bill Walton, 1952-2024, center; led Portland Trail Blazers to 1977 NBA title; MVP, 1978; TV commentator.
Abby Wambach, b 1980, soccer player; 2 gold medals in Olympics (2004, '12).
Kurt Warner, b 1971, quarterback; NFL MVP, 1999, 2001; Super Bowl MVP, 2000.
Gerry "Bubba" Watson, b 1978, golfer; won Masters, 2012, '14.
Tom Watson, b 1949, golfer; 6-time PGA Player of the Year; won 5 British Opens, 2 Masters, U.S. Open.
Stan Wawrinka, b 1985, (Switz.) tennis player; won Austral. Open (2014), French Open (2015), U.S. Open (2016).
Karrie Webb, b 1974, (Austral.) golfer; youngest woman (26 yrs., 6 mos.) to win career Grand Slam, 1999-2001.
Johnny Weissmuller, 1903-84, swimmer; won 52 national championships, 5 Olympic gold medals.
Jerry West, 1938-2024, L.A. Lakers guard; career averaged 27 pts. per game.
Dan Wheldon, 1978-2011, (Br.) race-car driver; 2-time Indy 500 winner (2005, '11).
Byron "Whizzer" White, 1917-2002, running back; led NCAA in scoring and rushing at Colorado, 1937; led NFL in rushing twice, 1938, '40; Supreme Court justice, 1962-93.
Shaun White, b 1986, snowboarder/skateboarder, Olympic gold medalist in half-pipe (2006, '10, '18).
Kathy Whitworth, 1939-2022, 7-time LPGA Player of the Year; 88 tour wins, most on LPGA or PGA tour.
Michelle Wie West, b 1989, golfer; in 2002 became youngest-ever qualifier for LPGA event; turned pro at age 15.
Bradley Wiggins, b 1980, (Br.) cyclist; Tour de France winner, 2012; 8 Olympic medals (5 gold) over 5 Games.
Michael Wilbon, b 1958, commentator/analyst for ESPN.
Lenny Wilkens, b 1937, 3rd winningest coach in NBA history; Hall of Fame player and coach.
Serena Williams, b 1981, tennis player; 23-time Grand Slam singles champion; Olympic gold medals in singles (2012) and doubles (2000, '08, '12) with sister Venus.
Ted Williams, 1918-2002, Boston Red Sox outfielder; won 6 batting titles, 2 triple crowns; hit .406 in 1941.
Venus Williams, b 1980, tennis player; 7-time Grand Slam singles champion; Olympic gold medals in singles (2000) and doubles with sister Serena (2000, '08, '12).
Helen Wills Moody, 1905-98, tennis player; won U.S. Open 7 times, Wimbledon 8 times.
Katarina Witt, b 1965, (Ger.) figure skater; won Olympic gold medal, 1984, '88; world champ, 1984-85, '87-'88.
John Wooden, 1910-2010, UCLA basketball coach; 10 NCAA titles.
Tiger Woods, b 1975, golfer; youngest to win career Grand Slam, at age 24 (1997-2000); 15 career major titles.
Mickey Wright, 1935-2020, golfer; won LPGA and U.S. Open championship 4 times; 82 career wins, including 13 majors.
Eric Wynalda, b 1969, soccer player; scored 1st goal in major league soccer history (1996).
Kristi Yamaguchi, b 1971, figure skater; won national, world, Olympic titles, in 1992.
Yao Ming, b 1980, (China) center for Houston Rockets; 8-time NBA All-Star.
Carl Yastrzemski, b 1939, Boston Red Sox slugger; won 3 batting titles; triple crown, 1967.
Cy Young, 1867-1955, pitcher; won record 511 games.
Steve Young, b 1961, 49ers quarterback; NFL MVP, 1992, '94; 3 Super Bowl titles, Super Bowl MVP, 1995.
Babe Didrikson Zaharias, 1911-56, all-around athlete; 3 track-and-field medals (2 golds), 1932 Olympics; won 10 golf majors; also played baseball; 6-time AP Female Athlete of the Year.
Emil Zátopek, 1922-2000, (Czech.) runner; won 3 gold medals at 1952 Olympics (5,000m, 10,000m, marathon).
Zinedine Zidane, b 1972, (Fr.) soccer midfielder; led France to 1998 World Cup title; named top player in 2006; 3-time FIFA world player of the year (1998, 2000, '03).

Writers of the Present

Name	Birthplace	Birthdate
Chimamanda Ngozi Adichie	Enugu, Nigeria	9/15/1977
Mitch Albom	Passaic, NJ	5/23/1958
Elizabeth Alexander	New York, NY	5/30/1962
Sherman Alexie	Wellpinit, WA	10/7/1966
Isabel Allende	Lima, Peru	8/2/1942
Dorothy Allison	Greenville, SC	4/11/1949
Piers Anthony	Oxford, England, UK	8/6/1934
Jeffrey Archer	Somerset, England, UK	4/15/1940
Margaret Atwood	Ottawa, ON, Canada	11/18/1939
David Auburn	Chicago, IL	11/30/1969
Jean Auel	Chicago, IL	2/18/1936
Alan Ayckbourn	Hampstead, England, UK	4/12/1939
Fredrik Backman	Stockholm, Sweden	6/2/1981
Nicholson Baker	New York, NY	1/7/1957
David Baldacci	Richmond, VA	8/5/1960
Julian Barnes	Leicester, Eng., UK	1/19/1946
Sebastian Barry	Dublin, Ireland	7/5/1955
Ann Beattie	Washington, DC	9/8/1947
Alan Bennett	Leeds, England, UK	5/9/1934
John Berendt	Syracuse, NY	12/5/1939
Elizabeth Berg	St. Paul, MN	12/2/1948
Wendell Berry	Henry County, KY	8/5/1934
Judy Blume	Elizabeth, NJ	2/12/1938
T. Coraghessan Boyle	Peekskill, NY	12/2/1948
Barbara Taylor Bradford	Leeds, England, UK	5/10/1933
Christopher Bram	Buffalo, NY	2/22/1952
Geraldine Brooks	Sydney, NSW, Australia	9/14/1955
Dan Brown	Exeter, NH	6/22/1964
Rita Mae Brown	Hanover, PA	11/28/1944
Christopher Buckley	New York, NY	9/28/1952
James Lee Burke	Houston, TX	12/5/1936
Augusten Burroughs	Pittsburgh, PA	10/23/1965
Robert Olen Butler	Granite City, IL	1/20/1945
Ethan Canin	Ann Arbor, MI	7/19/1960
Peter Carey	Bacchus-Marsh, Vic., Australia	5/7/1943
Robert A. Caro	New York, NY	10/30/1935
Michael Chabon	Washington, DC	5/24/1963
Tracy Chevalier	Washington, DC	10/19/1962
Lee Child	Coventry, England, UK	10/29/1954
Sandra Cisneros	Chicago, IL	12/20/1954
Ta-Nehisi Coates	Baltimore, MD	9/30/1975
Harlan Coben	Newark, NJ	1/4/1962
Paulo Coelho	Rio de Janeiro, Brazil	8/24/1947
J(ohn) M(axwell) Coetzee	Capetown, South Africa	2/9/1940
Billy Collins	New York, NY	3/22/1941
Suzanne Collins	Hartford, CT	8/10/1962
Michael Connelly	Philadelphia, PA	7/21/1956
Robin Cook	New York, NY	5/4/1940
Patricia Cornwell	Miami, FL	6/9/1956
S. A. Crosby	Newport News, VA	8/4/1973
Michael Cunningham	Cincinnati, OH	11/6/1952
Don DeLillo	Bronx, NY	11/20/1936
Hernán Díaz	Buenos Aires, Argentina	1973
Junot Díaz	Santo Domingo, Dominican Republic	12/31/1968
Annie Dillard	Pittsburgh, PA	4/30/1945
Anthony Doerr	Cleveland, OH	10/27/1973
Emma Donoghue	Dublin, Ireland	10/24/1969
Rita Dove	Akron, OH	8/28/1952
Roddy Doyle	Dublin, Ireland	5/8/1958
Carol Ann Duffy	Glasgow, Scotland, UK	12/23/1955
Jennifer Egan	Chicago, IL	9/7/1962
Timothy Egan	Seattle, WA	11/8/1954
Dave Eggers	Boston, MA	3/12/1970
Jonathan Eig	Brooklyn, NY	4/26/1964
Bret Easton Ellis	Los Angeles, CA	3/7/1964
James Ellroy	Los Angeles, CA	3/4/1948
Louise Erdrich	Little Falls, MN	6/7/1954
Laura Esquivel	Mexico City, Mexico	9/30/1950
Jeffrey Eugenides	Detroit, MI	3/8/1960
Janet Evanovich	South River, NJ	4/22/1943
Percival Everett	Fort Gordon, GA	12/22/1956
Helen Fielding	Morley, Yorkshire, Eng., UK	2/19/1958
Fannie Flagg	Birmingham, AL	9/21/1944
Gillian Flynn	Kansas City, MO	2/24/1971
Jonathan Safran Foer	Washington, DC	2/21/1977
Ken Follett	Cardiff, Wales, UK	6/5/1949
Richard Ford	Jackson, MS	2/16/1944
Frederick Forsyth	Ashford, England, UK	8/25/1938
Jonathan Franzen	Western Springs, IL	8/17/1959
Michael Frayn	London, England, UK	9/8/1933
Charles Frazier	Asheville, NC	11/4/1950
Neil Gaiman	Portchester, England, UK	11/10/1960
Roxane Gay	Omaha, NE	10/15/1974
Malcolm Gladwell	Fareham, Hampshire, Eng., UK	9/3/1963
Robert Goddard	Fareham, Hampshire, Eng., UK	11/13/1954
Gail Godwin	Birmingham, AL	6/18/1937
Mary Gordon	Far Rockaway, NY	12/8/1949
Amanda Gorman	Los Angeles, CA	3/7/1998
David Grann	New York, NY	3/10/1967
John Green	Indianapolis, IN	8/24/1977
Andrew Sean Greer	Washington, DC	11/21/1970
John Grisham	Jonesboro, AR	2/8/1955
John Guare	New York, NY	2/5/1938
Matt Haig	Sheffield, England, UK	7/3/1975
Daniel Handler	San Francisco, CA	2/28/1970
David Handler	Los Angeles, CA	9/14/1952
Kristin Hannah	Garden Grove, CA	9/25/1960
Paul Harding	Wenham, MA	12/19/1967
David Hare	St. Leonards, Sussex, Eng., UK	6/5/1947
Robert Hass	San Francisco, CA	3/1/1941
Paula Hawkins	Harare, Zimbabwe	8/28/1972
Mark Helprin	New York, NY	6/28/1947
Carl Hiaasen	Plantation, FL	3/12/1953
Laura Hillenbrand	Fairfax, VA	5/15/1967
S. E. Hinton	Tulsa, OK	7/22/1948
Alice Hoffman	New York, NY	3/16/1952
Alan Hollinghurst	Stroud, Gloucestershire, England, UK	5/26/1954
Colleen Hoover	Sulphur Springs, TX	12/11/1979
Khaled Hosseini	Kabul, Afghanistan	3/4/1965
John Irving	Exeter, NH	3/2/1942
Walter Isaacson	New Orleans, LA	5/20/1952
Kazuo Ishiguro	Nagasaki, Japan	11/8/1954
E. L. James	London, England, UK	7/3/1963
Elfriede Jelinek	Mürzzuschlag, Austria	10/20/1946
N. K. Jemisin	Iowa City, IA	9/19/1972
Ha Jin	Liaoning, China	2/21/1956
Adam Johnson	South Dakota	7/12/1967
Edward P. Jones	Washington, DC	10/5/1950
Erica Jong	New York, NY	3/26/1942
Sebastian Junger	Boston, MA	1/17/1962
Jan Karon	Lenoir, NC	3/14/1937
Garrison Keillor	Anoka, MN	8/7/1942
Thomas Keneally	Sydney, NSW, Australia	10/7/1935
William Kennedy	Albany, NY	1/16/1928
Sue Monk Kidd	Sylvester, GA	8/12/1948
Jamaica Kincaid	St. John's, Antigua and Barbuda	5/25/1949
Stephen King	Portland, ME	9/21/1947
Barbara Kingsolver	Annapolis, MD	4/8/1955
Maxine Hong Kingston	Stockton, CA	10/27/1940
Jeff Kinney	Andrews Air Force Base, MD	2/19/1971
Dean Koontz	Everett, PA	7/9/1945
Ted Kooser	Ames, IA	4/25/1939
Jon Krakauer	Brookline, MA	4/12/1954
R. F. Kuang	Guangzhou, China	5/29/1996
Tony Kushner	New York, NY	7/16/1956
Jhumpa Lahiri	London, England, UK	7/11/1967
Erik Larson	Brooklyn, NY	1/3/1954
Jean Marie Gustave Le Clézio	Nice, France	4/13/1940
David Leavitt	Pittsburgh, PA	6/23/1961
Jonathan Lethem	Brooklyn, NY	2/19/1964
Tracy Letts	Tulsa, OK	7/4/1965
David Lodge	South London, England, UK	1/28/1935
Gregory Maguire	Albany, NY	6/9/1954
Thomas Mallon	Glen Cove, NY	11/2/1951
David Malouf	Brisbane, Qld., Australia	3/20/1934
David Mamet	Chicago, IL	11/30/1947
Emily St. John Mandel	Merville, BC, Canada	1979
Yann Martel	Salamanca, Spain	6/25/1963
George R. R. Martin	Bayonne, NJ	9/20/1948
Bobbie Ann Mason	nr. Mayfield, KY	5/1/1940
Armistead Maupin	Washington, DC	4/13/1944
James McBride	New York, NY	9/4/1957
Colum McCann	Dublin, Ireland	2/28/1965
Alice McDermott	Brooklyn, NY	6/27/1953
Ian McEwan	Aldershot, England, UK	6/21/1948
Thomas McGuane	Wyandotte, MI	12/11/1939
Jay McInerney	Hartford, CT	1/13/1955
Terry McMillan	Port Huron, MI	10/18/1951
John McPhee	Princeton, NJ	3/8/1931
Stephenie Meyer	Hartford, CT	12/24/1973
Steven Millhauser	New York, NY	8/3/1943
Liane Moriarty	Sydney, NSW, Australia	11/15/1966
Walter Mosley	Los Angeles, CA	1/12/1952
Andrew Motion	London, England, UK	10/26/1952
Jojo Moyes	Maidstone, England, UK	8/4/1969
Herta Müller	Nitzkydorf, Banat, Romania	8/17/1953
Haruki Murakami	Kyoto, Japan	1/12/1949
Celeste Ng	Pittsburgh, PA	7/30/1980
Viet Thanh Nguyen	Buon Me Thuot, Vietnam	3/13/1971
Lynn Nottage	Brooklyn, NY	11/2/1964
Joyce Carol Oates	Lockport, NY	6/16/1938
Tim O'Brien	Austin, MN	10/1/1946
Michael Ondaatje	Colombo, Sri Lanka	9/12/1943
Delia Owens	GA	4/4/1949?
Cynthia Ozick	New York, NY	4/17/1928
Chuck Palahniuk	Pasco, WA	2/21/1962
Orhan Pamuk	Istanbul, Turkey	6/7/1952
Suzan-Lori Parks	Fort Knox, KY	5/10/1963
Ann Patchett	Los Angeles, CA	12/2/1963
James Patterson	Newburgh, NY	3/22/1947
Louise Penny	Toronto, ON, Canada	7/1/1958
Jodi Picoult	New York, NY	5/19/1966

Name	Birthplace	Birthdate
Marge Piercy	Detroit, MI	3/31/1936
Dav Pilkey	Cleveland, OH	3/4/1966
Robert Pinsky	Long Branch, NJ	10/20/1940
Michael Pollan	New York, NY	2/6/1955
Richard Powers	Evanston, IL	6/18/1957
Richard Price	Bronx, NY	10/12/1949
E. Annie Proulx	Norwich, CT	8/22/1935
Philip Pullman	Norwich, England, UK	10/19/1946
Thomas Pynchon	Glen Cove, NY	5/8/1937
David Rabe	Dubuque, IA	3/10/1940
Ishmael Reed	Chattanooga, TN	2/22/1938
Taylor Jenkins Reid	Ocean City, MD	12/20/1983
Rick Riordan	San Antonio, TX	6/5/1964
Mary Roach	Etna, NH	3/20/1959
Nora Roberts	Silver Spring, MD	10/10/1950
Marilynne Robinson	Sandpoint, IL	11/26/1943
Veronica Roth	New York, NY	8/19/1988
J. K. Rowling	Chipping Sodbury, Eng., UK	7/31/1965
Norman Rush	San Francisco, CA	10/24/1933
Salman Rushdie	Bombay, India	6/19/1947
Richard Russo	Johnstown, NY	7/15/1949
George Saunders	Amarillo, TX	12/2/1958
Alice Sebold	Madison, WI	9/6/1963
David Sedaris	Johnson City, NY	12/26/1956
Vikram Seth	Calcutta, India	6/20/1952
John Patrick Shanley	Bronx, NY	10/13/1950
Lionel Shriver	Gastonia, NC	5/18/1957
Jane Smiley	Los Angeles, CA	9/26/1949
Zadie Smith	London, Eng., UK	10/25/1975
Wole Soyinka	Abeokuta, Nigeria	7/13/1934
Nicholas Sparks	Omaha, NE	12/31/1965
Danielle Steel	New York, NY	8/14/1947
R(obert) L(awrence) Stine	Columbus, OH	10/8/1943
Kathryn Stockett	Jackson, MS	5/17/1969
Tom Stoppard	Zlin, Czechoslovakia	7/3/1937
Elizabeth Strout	Portland, ME	1/6/1956
Amy Tan	Oakland, CA	2/19/1952
Donna Tartt	Greenwood, MS	12/23/1963
Paul Theroux	Medford, MA	4/10/1941
Olga Tokarczuk	Sulechow, Poland	1/29/1962
Justin Torres	Baldwinsville, NY	1/13/1980
Amor Towles	Boston, MA	10/24/1964
Calvin Trillin	Kansas City, MO	12/5/1935
Scott F. Turow	Chicago, IL	4/12/1949
Anne Tyler	Minneapolis, MN	10/25/1941
Mario Vargas Llosa	Arequipa, Peru	3/28/1936
Abraham Verghese	Addis Ababa, Ethiopia	5/30/1955
Paula Vogel	Washington, DC	11/16/1951
Sarah Vowell	Muskogee, OK	12/27/1969
Ocean Vuong	Ho Chi Minh City, Vietnam	10/14/1988
Alice Walker	Eatonton, GA	2/9/1944
Joseph Wambaugh	East Pittsburgh, PA	1/22/1937
Jesmyn Ward	DeLisle, MS	4/1/1977
Andy Weir	Davis, CA	6/16/1972
Edmund White	Cincinnati, OH	1/13/1940
Colson Whitehead	New York, NY	11/6/1969
Tobias Wolff	Birmingham, AL	6/19/1945
Rebecca Yarros	Washington, DC	4/14/1981
Markus Zusak	Sydney, NSW, Australia	6/23/1975

Writers of the Past

See also Journalists, and Greeks and Romans in Historical Figures chapter.

Chinua Achebe, 1930-2013, (Nigeria) novelist. *Things Fall Apart*.

Alice Adams, 1926-99, (U.S.) novelist, short-story writer. *Superior Woman*.

Richard Adams, 1920-2016, (Br.) novelist. *Watership Down*.

James Agee, 1909-55, (U.S.) novelist. *A Death in the Family*.

S(hmuel) Y(osef) Agnon, 1888-1970, (Isr.) Hebrew novelist. *Only Yesterday*.

Conrad Aiken, 1889-1973, (U.S.) poet, critic. *Ushant*.

Anna Akhmatova, 1889-1966, (Russ.) poet. *Requiem*.

Edward Albee, 1928-2016, (U.S.) playwright. *Who's Afraid of Virginia Woolf?*

Louisa May Alcott, 1832-88, (U.S.) novelist. *Little Women*.

Sholom Aleichem, 1859-1916, (Russ.) Yiddish writer. *Tevye's Daughters*, *The Old Country*.

Vicente Aleixandre, 1898-1984, (Sp.) poet. *La destrucción o el amor*, *Dialogolos del conocimiento*.

Horatio Alger, 1832-99, (U.S.) "rags-to-riches" books.

Jorge Amado, 1912-2001, (Brazil) novelist. *Dona Flor and Her Two Husbands*, *The Violent Land*.

Eric Ambler, 1909-98, (Br.) suspense novelist. *A Coffin for Dimitrios*.

Kingsley Amis, 1922-95, (Br.) novelist, critic. *Lucky Jim*.

Martin Amis, 1949-2023, (Br.) novelist, essayist. *Money*, *London Fields*.

Hans Christian Andersen, 1805-75, (Den.) author of fairy tales. *The Ugly Duckling*.

Maxwell Anderson, 1888-1959, (U.S.) playwright. *What Price Glory?*, *High Tor*, *Winterset*, *Key Largo*.

Sherwood Anderson, 1876-1941, (U.S.) short-story writer. "Death in the Woods," *Winesburg, Ohio*.

Maya Angelou, 1928-2014, (U.S.) poet, memoirist. *I Know Why the Caged Bird Sings*.

Reinaldo Arenas, 1943-90, (Cuba) short-story writer, novelist. *Before Night Falls*.

Ludovico Ariosto, 1474-1533, (It.) poet. *Orlando Furioso*.

Matthew Arnold, 1822-88, (Br.) poet, critic. "Thyrsis," "Dover Beach," "Culture and Anarchy."

John Ashbery, 1927-2007, (U.S.) poet. *Self-Portrait in a Convex Mirror*.

Isaac Asimov, 1920-92, (U.S.) versatile writer, espec. of science fiction. *I Robot*.

Miguel Angel Asturias, 1899-1974, (Guat.) novelist. *El Señor Presidente*.

Louis Auchincloss, 1917-2010, (U.S.) novelist, memoirist, short-story writer. *The Rector of Justin*.

W(ystan) H(ugh) Auden, 1907-73, (Br.) poet, playwright, literary critic. "The Age of Anxiety."

Jane Austen, 1775-1817, (Br.) novelist. *Pride and Prejudice*, *Sense and Sensibility*, *Emma*, *Mansfield Park*.

Paul Auster, 1947-2024, (U.S.) writer. *The New York Trilogy*.

Ba Jin (Li Yaotang), 1904-2005, (China) novelist of pre-revolutionary China.

Isaac Babel, 1894-1941, (Russ.) short-story writer, playwright. *Odessa Tales*, *Red Cavalry*.

Russell Baker, 1925-2019, (U.S.) columnist, essayist. *Growing Up*.

James Baldwin, 1924-87, (U.S.) author, playwright. *The Fire Next Time*, *Blues for Mister Charlie*.

Honoré de Balzac, 1799-1850, (Fr.) novelist. *Le Père Goriot*, *Cousine Bette*, *Eugénie Grandet*.

Russell Banks, 1940-2023, (U.S.) novelist. *Continental Drift*.

James M. Barrie, 1860-1937, (Br.) playwright, novelist. *Peter Pan*, *Dear Brutus*, *What Every Woman Knows*.

John Barth, 1930-2024, (U.S.) novelist. *The Sot-Weed Factor*.

Charles Baudelaire, 1821-67, (Fr.) poet. *Les Fleurs du Mal*.

L(yman) Frank Baum, 1856-1919, (U.S.) Wizard of Oz series.

Simone de Beauvoir, 1908-86, (Fr.) novelist, essayist. *The Second Sex*, *Memoirs of a Dutiful Daughter*.

Samuel Beckett, 1906-89, (Ire.) novelist, playwright. *Waiting for Godot*, *Endgame* (plays); *Murphy*, *Watt*, *Molloy* (novels).

Brendan Behan, 1923-64, (Ire.) playwright. *The Quare Fellow*, *The Hostage*, *Borstal Boy*.

Saul Bellow, 1915-2005, (U.S.) novelist. *The Adventures of Augie March*, *Humboldt's Gift*.

Robert Benchley, 1889-1945, (U.S.) humorist.

Stephen Vincent Benét, 1898-1943, (U.S.) poet, novelist. *John Brown's Body*.

Jan Berenstain, 1923-2012, and **Stan Berenstain**, 1923-2005, (both U.S.) co-writers and illustrators of Berenstain Bears series of children's books.

Thomas Berger, 1924-2014, (U.S.) novelist. *Little Big Man*.

John Berryman, 1914-72, (U.S.) poet. *Homage to Mistress Bradstreet*.

Ambrose Bierce, 1842-1914, (U.S.) short-story writer, journalist. *In the Midst of Life*, *The Devil's Dictionary*.

Maeve Binchy, 1940-2012, (Ire.) novelist, short-story writer. *Circle of Friends*, *Tara Road*.

Elizabeth Bishop, 1911-79, (U.S.) poet. *North and South—A Cold Spring*.

William Blake, 1757-1827, (Br.) poet, artist. *Songs of Innocence*, *Songs of Experience*.

Aleksandr Blok, 1880-1921, (Russ.) poet. "The Twelve," "The Scythians."

Harold Bloom, 1930-2019, (U.S.) literary critic. *The Anxiety of Influence*.

Enid Blyton, 1897-1968, (Br.) children's writer. Famous Five series.

Giovanni Boccaccio, 1313-75, (It.) poet. *Decameron*.

Heinrich Böll, 1917-85, (Ger.) novelist, short-story writer. *Group Portrait With Lady*.

Jorge Luis Borges, 1900-86, (Arg.) short-story writer, poet, essayist. *Labyrinths*.

James Boswell, 1740-95, (Scot.) biographer. *The Life of Samuel Johnson*.

Pierre Boulle, 1913-94, (Fr.) novelist. *The Bridge Over the River Kwai*, *Planet of the Apes*.

Paul Bowles, 1910-99, (U.S.) novelist, short-story writer. *The Sheltering Sky*.

Ray Bradbury, 1920-2012, (U.S.) novelist, short-story writer. *Fahrenheit 451*, *The Martian Chronicles*.

Anne Bradstreet, c. 1612-72, (U.S.) poet. *The Tenth Muse Lately Sprung Up in America*.

Bertolt Brecht, 1898-1956, (Ger.) dramatist, poet. *The Threepenny Opera*, *Mother Courage and Her Children*.

Joseph Brodsky, 1940-96, (Russ.-U.S.) poet. *A Part of Speech*, *Less Than One*, *To Urania*.

Charlotte Brontë, 1816-55, (Br.) novelist. *Jane Eyre*.

Emily Brontë, 1818-48, (Br.) novelist. *Wuthering Heights*.

Sterling A. Brown, 1901-89, (U.S.) poet, literature professor. *Southern Road*.

William Wells Brown, 1815-84, (U.S.) writer, memoirist; first novel by an African American, *Clotel*, 1853.

Elizabeth Barrett Browning, 1806-61, (Br.) poet. *Sonnets From the Portuguese*, *Aurora Leigh*.

Robert Browning, 1812-89, (Br.) poet. "My Last Duchess," "Fra Lippo Lippi," *The Ring and the Book*.

Pearl S. Buck, 1892-1973, (U.S.) novelist. *The Good Earth*.

Charles Bukowski, 1920-94, (U.S.) novelist, poet. *Ham on Rye*, *Women*.

Mikhail Bulgakov, 1891-1940, (Russ.) novelist, playwright. *The Heart of a Dog*, *The Master and Margarita*.

John Bunyan, 1628-88, (Br.) writer. *Pilgrim's Progress*.
Anthony Burgess, 1917-93, (Br.) author. *A Clockwork Orange*.
Frances Hodgson Burnett, 1849-1924, (Br.-U.S.) novelist. *The Secret Garden*.
Robert Burns, 1759-96, (Scot.) poet. "Flow Gently, Sweet Afton," "My Heart's in the Highlands," "Auld Lang Syne."
Edgar Rice Burroughs, 1875-1950, (U.S.) writer; created Tarzan, John Carter.
William S. Burroughs, 1914-97, (U.S.) novelist. *Naked Lunch*.
Octavia Butler, 1947-2006, (U.S.) science-fiction writer. *Kindred*.
A. S. Byatt, 1936-2023, (Br.) novelist. *Possession*.
George Gordon, Lord Byron, 1788-1824, (Br.) poet. *Don Juan*, *Childe Harold*, *Manfred*, *Cain*.
Pedro Calderon de la Barca, 1600-81, (Sp.) playwright. *Life Is a Dream*.
Hortense Calisher, 1911-2009, (U.S.) novelist, short-story writer. *False Entry*.
Italo Calvino, 1923-85, (It.) novelist, short-story writer. *If on a Winter's Night a Traveler*.
Luís Vaz de Camões, 1524?-80 (Port.) poet. *The Lusiads*.
Albert Camus, 1913-60, (Fr.) writer. *The Stranger*, *The Fall*.
Elias Canetti, 1905-94, (Bulg.) novelist, essayist. *Auto-Da-Fe*.
Karel Capek, 1890-1938, (Czech.) playwright, novelist, essayist. *R.U.R. (Rossum's Universal Robots)*.
Truman Capote, 1924-84, (U.S.) author. *Other Voices, Other Rooms*; *Breakfast at Tiffany's*; *In Cold Blood*.
Eric Carle, 1929-2021, (U.S.) children's author and illustrator. *The Very Hungry Caterpillar*.
Caleb Carr, 1955-2024, (U.S.) novelist, historian. *The Alienist*.
Lewis Carroll (Charles Dodgson), 1832-98, (Br.) writer, mathematician. *Alice's Adventures in Wonderland*.
Barbara Cartland 1901-2000, (Br.) romance novelist.
Giacomo Casanova, 1725-98, (It.) adventurer, memoirist.
Willa Cather, 1873-1947, (U.S.) novelist. *O Pioneers!*, *My Ántonia*, *Death Comes for the Archbishop*.
Constantine Cavafy, 1863-1933, (Gr.) poet. "Ithaka," "Sensual Pleasures."
Camilo Jose Cela, 1916-2001, (Sp.) novelist. *The Family of Pascual Duarte*, *The Hive*.
Miguel de Cervantes Saavedra, 1547-1616, (Sp.) novelist, dramatist, poet. *Don Quixote*.
Raymond Chandler, 1888-1959, (U.S.) writer of detective fiction. Philip Marlowe series.
Geoffrey Chaucer, c. 1340-1400, (Br.) poet. *The Canterbury Tales*, *Troilus and Criseyde*.
John Cheever, 1912-82, (U.S.) novelist, short-story writer. *The Wapshot Scandal*, "The Country Husband."
Anton Chekhov, 1860-1904, (Russ.) short-story writer, dramatist. *Uncle Vanya*, *The Cherry Orchard*, *The Three Sisters*.
Charles Waddell Chesnutt, 1858-1932, (U.S.) author known for his short stories. *The Conjure Woman*.
G(ilbert) K(eith) Chesterton, 1874-1936, (Br.) critic, novelist, relig. apologist. Father Brown series of mysteries.
Kate Chopin, 1851-1904, (U.S.) writer. *The Awakening*.
Agatha Christie, 1890-1976, (Br.) mystery writer; created Miss Marple, Hercule Poirot. *Murder on the Orient Express*, *Murder of Roger Ackroyd*.
Tom Clancy, 1947-2013, (U.S.) novelist. *The Hunt for Red October*.
Mary Higgins Clark, 1927-2020, (U.S.) novelist. *Where Are the Children?*
Arthur C. Clarke, 1917-2008, (Br.) science-fiction writer. *2001: A Space Odyssey*.
James Clavell, 1924-94, (Br.-U.S.) novelist. *Shogun*, *King Rat*.
Beverly Cleary, 1916-2021, (U.S.) children's author. Ramona Quimby books.
Jean Cocteau, 1889-1963, (Fr.) writer, visual artist, filmmaker. *The Beauty and the Beast*, *Les Enfants Terribles*.
Samuel Taylor Coleridge, 1772-1834, (Br.) poet, critic. "Kubla Khan," "The Rime of the Ancient Mariner."
(Sidonie) Colette, 1873-1954, (Fr.) novelist. *Claudine*, *Gigi*.
Wilkie Collins, 1824-89, (Br.) novelist. *The Moonstone*.
Evan S. Connell, 1924-2013, (Br.) novelist, short-story writer. *Mrs. Bridge*.
Joseph Conrad, 1857-1924, (Br.) novelist. *Lord Jim*, *Heart of Darkness*, *The Secret Agent*.
Pat Conroy, 1945-2016, (U.S.) novelist. *The Prince of Tides*, *The Great Santini*.
James Fenimore Cooper, 1789-1851, (U.S.) novelist. *Leatherstocking Tales*, *The Last of the Mohicans*.
Pierre Corneille, 1606-84, (Fr.) dramatist. *Medeé*, *Le Cid*.
Hart Crane, 1899-1932, (U.S.) poet. "The Bridge."
Stephen Crane, 1871-1900, (U.S.) novelist, short-story writer. *The Red Badge of Courage*, "The Open Boat."
Harry Crews, 1935-2012, (U.S.) novelist. *A Feast of Snakes*.
Michael Crichton, 1942-2008, (U.S.) writer. *The Andromeda Strain*, *Jurassic Park*.
Countee Cullen, 1903-46, (U.S.) poet, prominent in the Harlem Renaissance of the 1920s. *The Black Christ*.
E. E. Cummings, 1894-1962, (U.S.) poet. *Tulips and Chimneys*.
Roald Dahl, 1916-90, (Br.-U.S.) writer. *Charlie and the Chocolate Factory*, *James and the Giant Peach*.
Gabriele D'Annunzio, 1863-1938, (It.) poet, novelist, dramatist. *The Child of Pleasure*, *The Intruder*, *The Victim*.
Dante Alighieri, 1265-1321, (It.) poet. *The Divine Comedy*.
Robertson Davies, 1913-95, (Can.) novelist, playwright, essayist. Salterton, Deptford, and Cornish trilogies.
Daniel Defoe, 1660-1731, (Br.) writer. *Robinson Crusoe*, *Moll Flanders*, *Journal of the Plague Year*.
Nelson DeMille, 1943-2024, (U.S.) novelist. *Plum Island*.
Philip K. Dick, 1928-82, (U.S.) science-fiction writer. *Do Androids Dream of Electric Sheep?*
Charles Dickens, 1812-70, (Br.) novelist. *David Copperfield*, *Oliver Twist*, *Great Expectations*, *A Tale of Two Cities*.
James Dickey, 1923-97, (U.S.) poet, novelist. *Deliverance*.
Emily Dickinson, 1830-86, (U.S.) poet. "Because I could not stop for Death …," "Success is counted sweetest …"
Joan Didion, 1934-2021, (U.S.) essayist, novelist. *The Year of Magical Thinking*.
Isak Dinesen (Karen Blixen), 1885-1962, (Den.) author. *Out of Africa*, *Seven Gothic Tales*, *Winter's Tales*.
E(dgar) L(awrence) Doctorow, 1931-2015, (U.S.) novelist. *Ragtime*, *Billy Bathgate*.
John Donne, 1573-1631, (Br.) poet. *Songs and Sonnets*.
José Donoso, 1924-96, (Chile) surreal novelist and short-story writer. *The Obscene Bird of Night*.
John Dos Passos, 1896-1970, (U.S.) novelist. *U.S.A.*
Fyodor Dostoyevsky, 1821-81, (Russ.) novelist. *Crime and Punishment*, *The Brothers Karamazov*, *The Possessed*.
Arthur Conan Doyle, 1859-1930, (Br.) novelist. Sherlock Holmes mystery stories.
Theodore Dreiser, 1871-1945, (U.S.) novelist. *An American Tragedy*, *Sister Carrie*.
John Dryden, 1631-1700, (Br.) poet, dramatist, critic. *All for Love*, *Mac Flecknoe*, *Absalom and Achitophel*.
Alexandre Dumas (père), 1802-70, (Fr.) novelist, dramatist. *The Three Musketeers*, *The Count of Monte Cristo*.
Alexandre Dumas (fils), 1824-95, (Fr.) dramatist, novelist. *La Dame aux Camélias*, *Le Demi-Monde*.
Paul Laurence Dunbar, 1872-1906, (U.S.) poet, novelist. *Lyrics of Lowly Life*.
Lawrence Durrell, 1912-90, (Br.) novelist, poet. *Alexandria Quartet*.
Umberto Eco, 1932-2016, (It.) novelist. *The Name of the Rose*.
Ilya G. Ehrenburg, 1891-1967, (Russ.) writer. *The Thaw*.
George Eliot (Mary Ann or Marian Evans), 1819-80, (Br.) novelist. *Silas Marner*, *Middlemarch*.
T(homas) S(tearns) Eliot, 1888-1965, (Br.) poet, critic. *The Waste Land*, "The Love Song of J. Alfred Prufrock."
Stanley Elkin, 1930-95, (U.S.) novelist, short-story writer. *George Mills*.
Ralph Ellison, 1914-94, (U.S.) writer. *Invisible Man*.
Ralph Waldo Emerson, 1803-82, (U.S.) poet, essayist. "Brahma," "Nature," "The Over-Soul," "Self-Reliance."
James T. Farrell, 1904-79, (U.S.) novelist. *Studs Lonigan*.
Howard Fast, 1914-2003, (U.S.) novelist. *Spartacus*, *The Immigrants*.
William Faulkner, 1897-1962, (U.S.) novelist. *Sanctuary*; *Light in August*; *The Sound and the Fury*; *Absalom, Absalom!*
Edna Ferber, 1887-1968, (U.S.) novelist, short-story writer, playwright. *So Big*, *Cimarron*, *Show Boat*.
Lawrence Ferlinghetti, 1919-2021, (U.S.) poet. *A Coney Island of the Mind*.
Henry Fielding, 1707-54, (Br.) novelist. *Tom Jones*.
F(rancis) Scott Fitzgerald, 1896-1940, (U.S.) short-story writer, novelist. *The Great Gatsby*, *Tender Is the Night*.
Gustave Flaubert, 1821-80, (Fr.) novelist. *Madame Bovary*.
Ian Fleming, 1908-64, (Br.) novelist. James Bond spy thrillers: *Dr. No*, *Goldfinger*.
Horton Foote, 1916-2009, (U.S.) playwright, screenwriter. *The Trip to Bountiful*.
Ford Madox Ford, 1873-1939, (Br.) novelist, critic, poet. *The Good Soldier*.
C(ecil) S(cott) Forester, 1899-1966, (Br.) writer. Horatio Hornblower books.
E(dward) M(organ) Forster, 1879-1970, (Br.) novelist. *A Passage to India*, *Howards End*.
Anatole France, 1844-1924, (Fr.) writer. *Penguin Island*, *My Friend's Book*, *The Crime of Sylvestre Bonnard*.
Dick Francis, 1920-2010, (Br.) crime novelist.
Marilyn French, 1929-2009, (U.S.) novelist. *The Women's Room*.
Brian Friel, 1929-2015, (N. Ire.) playwright. *Dancing at Lughnasa*.
Robert Frost, 1874-1963, (U.S.) poet. "Birches," "Fire and Ice," "Stopping by Woods on a Snowy Evening."
Carlos Fuentes, 1928-2012, (Pan.) novelist, essayist. *The Old Gringo*.
William Gaddis, 1922-98, (U.S.) novelist. *The Recognitions*.
Ernest J. Gaines, 1933-2019, (U.S.) novelist. *The Autobiography of Miss Jane Pittman*.
John Galsworthy, 1867-1933, (Br.) novelist, dramatist. *The Forsyte Saga*.
Federico García Lorca, 1898-1936, (Sp.) poet, dramatist. *Blood Wedding*.
Gabriel García Márquez, 1927-2014, (Col.) novelist. *One Hundred Years of Solitude*.
Erle Stanley Gardner, 1889-1970, (U.S.) mystery writer; created Perry Mason.
Jean Genet, 1911-86, (Fr.) playwright, novelist. *The Maids*.
Kahlil Gibran, 1883-1931, (Leban.-U.S.) mystical novelist, essayist, poet. *The Prophet*.
André Gide, 1869-1951, (Fr.) writer. *The Immoralist*, *The Pastoral Symphony*, *Strait Is the Gate*.
Allen Ginsberg, 1926-97, (U.S.) Beat poet. "Howl."
Jean Giraudoux, 1882-1944, (Fr.) novelist, dramatist. *Electra*, *The Madwoman of Chaillot*, *Ondine*, *Tiger at the Gate*.
Johann Wolfgang von Goethe, 1749-1832, (Ger.) poet, dramatist, novelist. *Faust*, *Sorrows of Young Werther*.
Nikolai Gogol, 1809-52, (Russ.) short-story writer, dramatist, novelist. *Dead Souls*, *The Inspector General*.

William Golding, 1911-93, (Br.) novelist. *Lord of the Flies*.
William Goldman, 1931-2018, (U.S.) novelist, screenwriter. *The Marathon Man*, *The Princess Bride*.
Oliver Goldsmith, 1728-74, (Br.-Ire.) dramatist, novelist. *The Vicar of Wakefield*, *She Stoops to Conquer*.
Nadine Gordimer, 1923-2014, (S. Afr.) novelist. *Burger's Daughter*.
Maxim Gorky, 1868-1936, (Russ.) dramatist, novelist. *The Lower Depths*.
Sue Grafton, 1940-2017, (U.S.) crime novelist; Kinsey Millhone "alphabet mysteries."
Günter Grass, 1927-2015, (Ger.) novelist, poet. *The Tin Drum*.
Shirley Ann Grau, 1929-2020, (U.S.) novelist. *The Keepers of The House*.
Robert Graves, 1895-1985, (Br.) poet, classical scholar, novelist. *I, Claudius*; *The White Goddess*.
Thomas Gray, 1716-71, (Br.) poet. "Elegy Written in a Country Churchyard," "The Progress of Poesy."
Julien Green, 1900-98, (U.S.-Fr.) expatriate American novelist. *Moira*, *Each Man in His Darkness*.
Graham Greene, 1904-91, (Br.) novelist. *The Power and the Glory*, *The Heart of the Matter*, *The Ministry of Fear*.
Zane Grey, 1872-1939, (U.S.) writer of Western stories.
Jakob Grimm, 1785-1863, philologist, folklorist; with brother **Wilhelm Grimm**, 1786-1859, (both Ger.) collected *Grimm's Fairy Tales*.
Alex Haley, 1921-92, (U.S.) author. *Roots*.
Dashiell Hammett, 1894-1961, (U.S.) detective-story writer; created Sam Spade. *The Maltese Falcon*.
Jupiter Hammon, c. 1720-1800, (U.S.) poet; first African American to have his works published, 1761.
Knut Hamsun, 1859-1952, (Nor.) novelist. *Hunger*.
Lorraine Hansberry, 1930-65, (U.S.) playwright. *A Raisin in the Sun*.
Thomas Hardy, 1840-1928, (Br.) novelist, poet. *The Return of the Native*, *Tess of the D'Urbervilles*, *Jude the Obscure*.
E. Lynn Harris, 1955-2009, (U.S.) novelist. *Invisible Life*, *Basketball Jones*.
Joel Chandler Harris, 1848-1908, (U.S.) writer. Uncle Remus stories.
Jim Harrison, 1937-2016, (U.S.) novelist and essayist. *Legends of the Fall*.
Moss Hart, 1904-61, (U.S.) playwright. *Once in a Lifetime*, *You Can't Take It With You*, *The Man Who Came to Dinner*.
Bret Harte, 1836-1902, (U.S.) short-story writer, poet. *The Luck of Roaring Camp*.
Jaroslav Hasek, 1883-1923, (Czech.) writer, playwright. *The Good Soldier Schweik*.
Vaclav Havel, 1936-2011, (Czech.) essayist, poet, playwright. *The Power of the Powerless*.
John Hawkes, 1925-98, (U.S.) experimental fiction writer. *The Goose on the Grave*, *Blood Oranges*.
Nathaniel Hawthorne, 1804-64, (U.S.) novelist, short-story writer. *The Scarlet Letter*, "Young Goodman Brown."
Seamus Heaney, 1939-2013, (Ire.) poet. *Death of a Naturalist*.
Heinrich Heine, 1797-1856, (Ger.) poet. *Book of Songs*.
Robert Heinlein, 1907-88, (U.S.) science-fiction writer. *Stranger in a Strange Land*.
Joseph Heller, 1923-99, (U.S.) novelist. *Catch-22*.
Lillian Hellman, 1905-84, (U.S.) playwright, memoirist. *The Little Foxes*, *An Unfinished Woman*, *Pentimento*.
Ernest Hemingway, 1899-1961, (U.S.) novelist, short-story writer. *A Farewell to Arms*, *For Whom the Bell Tolls*.
O. Henry (W. S. Porter), 1862-1910, (U.S.) short-story writer. "The Gift of the Magi."
George Herbert, 1593-1633, (Br.) poet. "The Altar," "Easter Wings."
Zbigniew Herbert, 1924-98, (Pol.) poet. "Apollo and Marsyas."
Robert Herrick, 1591-1674, (Br.) poet. "To the Virgins to Make Much of Time."
John Hersey, 1914-93, (U.S.) novelist, journalist. *Hiroshima*, *A Bell for Adano*.
Hermann Hesse, 1877-1962, (Ger.) novelist, poet. *Death and the Lover*, *Steppenwolf*, *Siddhartha*.
Georgette Heyer, 1902-74, (Br.) Regency romance novelist.
Jack Higgins, 1929-2022, (Br.) novelist. *The Eagle Has Landed*.
Oscar Hijuelos, 1951-2013, (U.S.) novelist. *The Mambo Kings Play Songs of Love*.
Tony Hillerman, 1925-2008, (U.S.) novelist. *Dance Hall of the Dead*.
James Hilton, 1900-54, (Br.) novelist. *Lost Horizon*.
Chester Himes, 1909-84, (U.S.) novelist. *Cotton Comes to Harlem*.
Oliver Wendell Holmes, 1809-94, (U.S.) poet, novelist. *The Autocrat of the Breakfast-Table*.
bell hooks, 1952-2021, (U.S.) writer, critic. *All About Love*.
Gerard Manley Hopkins, 1844-89, (Br.) poet. "Pied Beauty," "God's Grandeur."
A(lfred) E. Housman, 1859-1936, (Br.) poet. *A Shropshire Lad*.
William Dean Howells, 1837-1920, (U.S.) novelist, critic. *The Rise of Silas Lapham*.
Langston Hughes, 1902-67, (U.S.) poet, lyric writer, author; a major influence in 1920s Harlem Renaissance.
Ted Hughes, 1930-98, (Br.) British poet laureate, 1984-98. *Crow*.
Victor Hugo, 1802-85, (Fr.) poet, dramatist, novelist. *Notre Dame de Paris*, *Les Misérables*.
Zora Neale Hurston, 1891-1960, (U.S.) novelist, folklorist. *Their Eyes Were Watching God*, *Mules and Men*.
Aldous Huxley, 1894-1963, (Br.) writer. *Brave New World*.
Henrik Ibsen, 1828-1906, (Nor.) dramatist, poet. *A Doll's House*, *Ghosts*, *The Wild Duck*, *Hedda Gabler*.
William Inge, 1913-73, (U.S.) playwright. *Picnic*, *Bus Stop*.
Eugene Ionesco, 1910-94, (Fr.) surrealist dramatist. *The Bald Soprano*, *The Chairs*.
Washington Irving, 1783-1859, (U.S.) writer. "Rip Van Winkle," "The Legend of Sleepy Hollow."
Christopher Isherwood, 1904-86, (Br.) novelist, playwright. *The Berlin Stories*.
Shirley Jackson, 1916-65, (U.S.) short-story writer. "The Lottery."
John Jakes, 1932-2023, (U.S.) novelist. The Kent Family Chronicles.
Henry James, 1843-1916, (U.S.) novelist, short-story writer, critic. *The Portrait of a Lady*, *The Ambassadors*, *Daisy Miller*.
P(hyllis) D(orothy) James, 1920-2014, (Br.) mystery novelist.
Robinson Jeffers, 1887-1962, (U.S.) poet, dramatist. *Tamar and Other Poems*, *Medea*.
James Weldon Johnson, 1871-1938, (U.S.) poet, novelist, diplomat; lyricist for *Lift Every Voice and Sing*.
Samuel Johnson, 1709-84, (Br.) author, scholar, critic. *Dictionary of the English Language*, *Vanity of Human Wishes*.
Ben Jonson, 1572-1637, (Br.) dramatist, poet. *Volpone*.
James Joyce, 1882-1941, (Ire.) writer. *Ulysses*, *Dubliners*, *A Portrait of the Artist as a Young Man*, *Finnegans Wake*.
Ernst Junger, 1895-1998, (Ger.) novelist, essayist. *The Peace*, *On the Marble Cliff*.
Franz Kafka, 1883-1924, (Austria-Hung./Czech.) novelist, short-story writer. *The Trial*, *The Castle*, "The Metamorphosis."
George S. Kaufman, 1889-1961, (U.S.) playwright. *The Man Who Came to Dinner*, *You Can't Take It With You*.
Yasunari Kawabata, 1899-1972, (Jpn.) novelist. *The Sound of the Mountains*.
Nikos Kazantzakis, 1883-1957, (Gr.) novelist. *Zorba the Greek*, *A Greek Passion*.
Alfred Kazin, 1915-98 (U.S.) author, critic. *On Native Grounds*.
John Keats, 1795-1821, (Br.) poet. "Ode on a Grecian Urn," "Ode to a Nightingale," "La Belle Dame Sans Merci."
Jack Kerouac, 1922-69, (U.S.) author, Beat poet. *On the Road*, *The Dharma Bums*, "Mexico City Blues."
Joyce Kilmer, 1886-1918, (U.S.) poet. "Trees."
Galway Kinnell, 1927-2014, (U.S.) poet.
Rudyard Kipling, 1865-1936, (Br.) author, poet. "The White Man's Burden," "Gunga Din," *The Jungle Book*.
Larry Kramer, 1935-2020, (U.S.) playwright. *The Normal Heart*.
Judith Krantz, 1928-2019, (U.S.) novelist. *Scruples*.
Maxine Kumin, 1925-2014, (U.S.) poet, author. *Up Country: Poems of New England*.
Milan Kundera, 1929-2023, (Czech.) novelist. *The Unbearable Lightness of Being*.
Jean de la Fontaine, 1621-95, (Fr.) poet. *Fables choisies* (Selected Fables).
Pär Lagerkvist, 1891-1974, (Swed.) poet, dramatist, novelist. *Barabbas*, *The Sybil*.
Selma Lagerlöf, 1858-1940, (Swed.) novelist. *Jerusalem*, *The Ring of the Lowenskolds*.
Alphonse de Lamartine, 1790-1869, (Fr.) poet, novelist, statesman. *Méditations poétiques*.
Charles Lamb, 1775-1834, (Br.) essayist. *Specimens of English Dramatic Poets*, *Essays of Elia*.
Louis L'Amour, 1908-88, (U.S.) Western author, screenwriter. *Hondo*, *The Cherokee Trail*.
Giuseppe di Lampedusa, 1896-1957, (It.) novelist. *The Leopard*.
William Langland, c. 1332-1400, (Br.) poet. *Piers Plowman*.
Ring Lardner, 1885-1933, (U.S.) short-story writer, humorist.
Steig Larsson, 1954-2004, (Swed.) novelist. *The Girl With the Dragon Tattoo*.
Arthur Laurents, 1917-2011, (U.S.) playwright and director. *West Side Story*.
D(avid) H(erbert) Lawrence, 1885-1930, (Br.) novelist. *Sons and Lovers*, *Women in Love*, *Lady Chatterley's Lover*.
Halldór Laxness, 1902-98, (Iceland) novelist. *Iceland's Bell*.
John le Carré, 1931-2020, (Br.) novelist. *The Spy Who Came in From the Cold*, *Tinker Tailor Soldier Spy*.
Harper Lee, 1926-2016, (U.S.) novelist. *To Kill a Mockingbird*.
Ursula K. Le Guin, 1929-2018, (U.S.) science-fiction writer. *The Left Hand of Darkness*.
Madeleine L'Engle, 1918-2007, (U.S.) young-adult novelist. *A Wrinkle in Time*.
Elmore Leonard, 1925-2013, (U.S.) novelist. *Get Shorty*.
Mikhail Lermontov, 1814-41, (Russ.) novelist, poet. "Demon," *Hero of Our Time*.
Alain-René Lesage, 1668-1747, (Fr.) novelist. *Gil Blas de Santillane*.
Doris Lessing, 1919-2013, (Br.) writer. *The Golden Notebook*.
Gotthold Lessing, 1729-81, (Ger.) dramatist, philosopher, critic. *Miss Sara Sampson*, *Minna von Barnhelm*.
Ira Levin, 1929-2007, (U.S.) novelist, playwright. *Deathtrap*, *Rosemary's Baby*.
C(live) S(taples) Lewis, 1898-1963, (Br.) critic, novelist, religious writer. *Allegory of Love*; *The Lion, the Witch and the Wardrobe*; *Out of the Silent Planet*.
Sinclair Lewis, 1885-1951, (U.S.) novelist. *Babbitt*, *Main Street*, *Dodsworth*.
Li Po, 701-762, (China) poet. "Song Before Drinking," "She Spins Silk."
Vachel Lindsay, 1879-1931, (U.S.) poet. *General William Booth Enters Into Heaven*, *The Congo*.
Hugh Lofting, 1886-1947, (Br.) writer. Dr. Doolittle series.
Jack London, 1876-1916, (U.S.) novelist, journalist. *Call of the Wild*, *The Sea-Wolf*, *White Fang*.
Henry Wadsworth Longfellow, 1807-82, (U.S.) poet. *Evangeline*, *The Song of Hiawatha*.
Lope de Vega, 1562-1635, (Sp.) playwright. *Noche de San Juan*, *Maestro de Danzar*.

H(oward) P(hillips) Lovecraft, 1890-1937, (U.S.) novelist, short-story writer. "At the Mountains of Madness."
Amy Lowell, 1874-1925, (U.S.) poet, critic. "Lilacs."
James Russell Lowell, 1819-91, (U.S.) poet, editor. *Poems*, *The Biglow Papers*.
Robert Lowell, 1917-77, (U.S.) poet. "Lord Weary's Castle."
Alison Lurie, 1926-2020, (U.S.) novelist. *Foreign Affairs*.
Joaquim Maria Machado de Assis, 1839-1908, (Brazil) novelist, poet. *The Posthumous Memoirs of Bras Cubas*.
Archibald MacLeish, 1892-1982, (U.S.) poet. *Conquistador*.
Naguib Mahfouz, 1911-2006, (Egypt) novelist; first Arabic-language writer to win the Nobel Prize for Literature. *Cairo Trilogy*.
Norman Mailer, 1923-2007, (U.S.) novelist, essayist, journalist. *The Naked and the Dead*.
Bernard Malamud, 1914-86, (U.S.) short-story writer, novelist. "The Magic Barrel," *The Assistant*, *The Fixer*.
Stéphane Mallarmé, 1842-98, (Fr.) poet. *Poésies*.
Thomas Malory, c. 1410-71, (Br.) writer. *Morte d'Arthur*.
Andre Malraux, 1901-76, (Fr.) novelist. *Man's Fate*.
Osip Mandelstam, 1891-1938, (Russ.) poet. *Stone*, *Tristia*.
Thomas Mann, 1875-1955, (Ger.) novelist, essayist. *Buddenbrooks*, *The Magic Mountain*, "Death in Venice."
Katherine Mansfield, 1888-1923, (Br.) short-story writer. "Bliss."
Hilary Mantel, 1952-2022, (Br.) novelist. *Wolf Hall*, *Bring Up the Bodies*.
Christopher Marlowe, 1564-93, (Br.) dramatist, poet. *Tamburlaine the Great*, *Dr. Faustus*, *The Jew of Malta*.
Andrew Marvell, 1621-78, (Br.) poet. "To His Coy Mistress."
John Masefield, 1878-1967, (Br.) poet. "Sea Fever," "Cargoes," *Salt Water Ballads*.
Edgar Lee Masters, 1869-1950, (U.S.) poet, biographer. *Spoon River Anthology*.
Peter Matthiessen, 1927-2014, (U.S.) novelist. *The Snow Leopard*.
W(illiam) Somerset Maugham, 1874-1965, (Br.) author. *Of Human Bondage*, *The Moon and Sixpence*.
Guy de Maupassant, 1850-93, (Fr.) novelist, short-story writer. "A Life," "Bel-Ami," "The Necklace."
François Mauriac, 1885-1970, (Fr.) novelist, dramatist. *Viper's Tangle*, *The Kiss to the Leper*.
Vladimir Mayakovsky, 1893-1930, (Russ.) poet, dramatist. *The Cloud in Trousers*.
Cormac McCarthy, 1933-2023, (U.S.) novelist. *All the Pretty Horses*, *The Road*.
Mary McCarthy, 1912-89, (U.S.) critic, novelist, memoirist. *Memories of a Catholic Girlhood*.
Frank McCourt, 1930-2009, (U.S.) memoirist. *Angela's Ashes*, *'Tis*.
Carson McCullers, 1917-67, (U.S.) novelist. *The Heart Is a Lonely Hunter*, *Member of the Wedding*.
Colleen McCullough, 1937-2015, (Austral.) novelist. *The Thorn Birds*.
David McCullough, 1933-2022, (U.S.) historian, biographer. *Truman*, *John Adams*.
Larry McMurtry, 1936-2021, (U.S.) novelist. *Lonesome Dove*.
Terrence McNally, 1939-2020, (U.S.) playwright. *Love! Valour! Compassion!*
Herman Melville, 1819-91, (U.S.) novelist, poet. *Moby-Dick*, *Typee*, *Billy Budd*.
George Meredith, 1828-1909, (Br.) novelist, poet. *The Ordeal of Richard Feverel*, *The Egoist*.
Prosper Mérimée, 1803-70, (Fr.) author. *Carmen*.
James Merrill, 1926-95, (U.S.) poet. *Divine Comedies*.
W(illiam) S(tanley) Merwin, 1927-2019, (U.S.) poet. *The Lice*.
James Michener, 1907-97, (U.S.) novelist. *Tales of the South Pacific*.
Edna St. Vincent Millay, 1892-1950, (U.S.) poet. *The Harp Weaver and Other Poems*.
Arthur Miller,1915-2005, (U.S.) playwright. *The Crucible*, *After the Fall*, *Death of a Salesman*.
Henry Miller, 1891-1980, (U.S.) novelist. *Tropic of Cancer*.
A(lan) A(lexander) Milne, 1882-1956, (Br.) author. *Winnie-the-Pooh*.
Czeslaw Milosz, 1911-2004, (Pol.) essayist, poet. "Esse," "Encounter."
John Milton, 1608-74, (Br.) poet, writer. *Paradise Lost*, *Comus*, *Lycidas*, *Areopagitica*.
Mishima Yukio (Hiraoka Kimitake) 1925-70, (Jpn.) writer. *Confessions of a Mask*.
Gabriela Mistral, 1889-1957, (Chile) poet. *Sonnets of Death*.
Margaret Mitchell, 1900-49, (U.S.) novelist. *Gone With the Wind*.
Jean Baptiste Molière, 1622-73, (Fr.) dramatist. *Tartuffe*, *Le Misanthrope*, *Le Bourgeois Gentilhomme*.
Ferenc Molnár, 1878-1952, (Hung.) dramatist, novelist. *Liliom*, *The Swan*.
Michel de Montaigne, 1533-92, (Fr.) essayist. *Essais*.
Eugenio Montale, 1896-1981, (It.) poet.
Brian Moore, 1921-99, (Ire.-U.S.) novelist. *The Lonely Passion of Judith Hearne*.
Clement C. Moore, 1779-1863, (U.S.) poet, educator. "A Visit From Saint Nicholas."
Marianne Moore, 1887-1972, (U.S.) poet.
Alberto Moravia, 1907-90, (It.) novelist, short-story writer. *The Time of Indifference*.
Thomas More, 1478-1535, (Br.) writer, statesman, saint. *Utopia*.
Wright Morris, 1910-98, (U.S.) novelist. *My Uncle Dudley*.
Toni Morrison, 1931-2019, (U.S.) novelist. *Song of Solomon*, *Beloved*.
Bharati Mukherjee, 1940-2017, (India-U.S.) novelist, short-story writer. *Jasmine*.
Alice Munro, 1931-2024, (Can.) short-story writer.
Murasaki Shikibu, c. 978-1026, (Jpn.) novelist. *The Tale of Genji*.
Iris Murdoch, 1919-99, (Br.) novelist, philosopher. *The Sea, the Sea*.
Alfred de Musset, 1810-57, (Fr.) poet, dramatist. *La Confession d'un Enfant du Siècle*.
Vladimir Nabokov, 1899-1977, (Russ.-U.S.) novelist. *Lolita*, *Pale Fire*.
V. S. Naipaul, 1932-2018, (Trinidad) novelist, travel writer. *A House for Mr. Biswas*.
R. K. Narayan, 1906-2001, (India) novelist. *The Guide*.
Ogden Nash, 1902-71, (U.S.) poet.
Irène Némirovsky, 1903-42, (Ukraine) novelist. *David Golder*, *Suite Française*.
Pablo Neruda, 1904-73, (Chile) poet. *Twenty Love Poems and One Song of Despair*, *Toward the Splendid City*.
Patrick O'Brian, 1914-2000, (Br.) historical novelist. *Master and Commander*, *Blue at the Mizzen*.
Edna O'Brien, 1930-2024, (Ire.) novelist, short-story writer. *The Country Girls*.
Sean O'Casey, 1884-1964, (Ire.) dramatist. *Juno and the Paycock*, *The Plough and the Stars*.
Flannery O'Connor, 1925-64, (U.S.) novelist, short-story writer. *Wise Blood*, "A Good Man Is Hard to Find."
Frank O'Connor (Michael Donovan), 1903-66, (Ire.) short-story writer. "Guests of a Nation."
Clifford Odets, 1906-63, (U.S.) playwright. *Waiting for Lefty*, *Awake and Sing*, *Golden Boy*, *The Country Girl*.
Kenzaburo Oe, 1935-2023, (Jpn.) novelist and essayist. *A Personal Matter*.
John O'Hara, 1905-70, (U.S.) novelist, short-story writer. *From the Terrace*, *Appointment in Samarra*, *Pal Joey*.
Omar Khayyam, c. 1028-1122, (Per.) poet. *Rubaiyat*.
Eugene O'Neill, 1888-1953, (U.S.) playwright. *Emperor Jones*, *Anna Christie*, *Long Day's Journey Into Night*.
George Orwell (Eric Arthur Blair), 1903-50, (Br.) novelist, essayist. *Animal Farm*, *Nineteen Eighty-Four*.
John Osborne, 1929-95, (Br.) dramatist, novelist. *Look Back in Anger*, *The Entertainer*.
Wilfred Owen, 1893-1918, (Br.) poet. "Dulce et Décorum Est."
Grace Paley, 1922-2007, (U.S.) short-story writer, poet. *The Little Disturbances of Man*.
Dorothy Parker, 1893-1967, (U.S.) poet, short-story writer. *Enough Rope*, *Laments for the Living*.
Robert B. Parker, 1932-2010, (U.S.) crime novelist. Spenser novels.
Boris Pasternak, 1890-1960, (Russ.) poet, novelist. *Doctor Zhivago*.
Alan Paton, 1903-88, (S. Africa) novelist. *Cry, the Beloved Country*.
Gary Paulsen, 1939-2021, (U.S.) young-adult novelist. *Hatchet*, *Dogsong*.
Octavio Paz, 1914-98, (Mex.) poet, essayist. *The Labyrinth of Solitude*, *They Shall Not Pass!*, *The Sun Stone*.
Samuel Pepys, 1633-1703, (Br.) public official, diarist.
S(idney) J(oseph) Perelman, 1904-79, (U.S.) humorist. *The Road to Miltown*, *Under the Spreading Atrophy*.
Charles Perrault, 1628-1703, (Fr.) writer. *Tales From Mother Goose* (*Sleeping Beauty*, *Cinderella*).
Petrarch (Francesco Petrarca), 1304-74, (It.) poet. *Africa*, *Trionfi*, *Canzoniere*.
Harold Pinter, 1930-2008, (Br.) playwright. *The Birthday Party*, *The Caretaker*, *The Homecoming*.
Luigi Pirandello, 1867-1936, (It.) novelist, dramatist. *Six Characters in Search of an Author*.
Sylvia Plath, 1932-63, (U.S.) author, poet. *The Bell Jar*, *The Colossus*.
Edgar Allan Poe, 1809-49, (U.S.) poet, short-story writer, critic. "Annabel Lee," "The Raven," "The Purloined Letter."
Alexander Pope, 1688-1744, (Br.) poet. *The Rape of the Lock*, *The Dunciad*, *An Essay on Man*.
Katherine Anne Porter, 1890-1980, (U.S.) novelist, short-story writer. *Ship of Fools*.
Chaim Potok, 1929-2002, (U.S.) novelist. *The Chosen*.
Ezra Pound, 1885-1972, (U.S.) poet. *Cantos*.
Anthony Powell, 1905-2000, (Br.) novelist. A Dance to the Music of Time series.
Terry Pratchett, 1948-2015 (Br.) fantasy novelist. Discworld series.
Reynolds Price, 1933-2011, (U.S.) novelist, short-story writer, poet. *A Long and Happy Life*.
J(ohn) B(oynton) Priestley, 1894-1984, (Br.) novelist, dramatist. *The Good Companions*.
Marcel Proust, 1871-1922, (Fr.) novelist. *Remembrance of Things Past*.
Aleksandr Pushkin, 1799-1837, (Russ.) poet, novelist. *Boris Godunov*, *Eugene Onegin*.
Mario Puzo, 1920-99, (U.S.) novelist. *The Godfather*.
François Rabelais, 1495-1553, (Fr.) writer. *Gargantua*.
Jean Racine, 1639-99, (Fr.) dramatist. *Andromaque*, *Phèdre*, *Bérénice*, *Britannicus*.
David Rakoff, 1964-2012, (Can.-U.S.) essayist. *Fraud*, *Don't Get Too Comfortable*.
Ayn Rand, 1905-82, (Russ.-U.S.) novelist, moral theorist. *The Fountainhead*, *Atlas Shrugged*.
Terence Rattigan, 1911-77, (Br.) playwright. *Separate Tables*, *The Browning Version*.
Erich Maria Remarque, 1898-1970, (Ger.-U.S.) novelist. *All Quiet on the Western Front*.
Mary Renault, 1905-83, (Br.) novelist. *The Last of the Wine*.
Ruth Rendell, 1930-2015, (Br.) novelist. Chief Inspector Reginald Wexford mysteries.
Anne Rice, 1941-2021, (U.S.) novelist. *Interview With the Vampire*.
Adrienne Rich, 1929-2012, (U.S.) poet. *Diving Into the Wreck: Poems, 1971-1972*.
Samuel Richardson, 1689-1761, (Br.) novelist. *Pamela; or Virtue Rewarded*.
Rainer Maria Rilke, 1875-1926, (Ger.) poet. *Life and Songs*, *Duino Elegies*, *Poems From the Book of Hours*.
Arthur Rimbaud, 1854-91, (Fr.) poet. *A Season in Hell*.

Harold Robbins, 1916-97, (U.S.) novelist, *The Carpetbaggers*.
Edwin Arlington Robinson, 1869-1935, (U.S.) poet. "Richard Cory," "Miniver Cheevy," *Merlin*.
Theodore Roethke, 1908-63, (U.S.) poet. *Open House*, *The Waking*, *The Far Field*.
Romain Rolland, 1866-1944, (Fr.) novelist, biographer. *Jean-Christophe*.
Pierre de Ronsard, 1524-85, (Fr.) poet. *Sonnets pour Hélène*, *La Franciade*.
Christina Rossetti, 1830-94, (Br.) poet. "When I Am Dead, My Dearest."
Dante Gabriel Rossetti, 1828-82, (Br.) poet, painter. "The Blessed Damozel."
Edmond Rostand, 1868-1918, (Fr.) poet, dramatist. *Cyrano de Bergerac*.
Philip Roth, 1933-2018, (U.S.) novelist. *Portnoy's Complaint*.
Damon Runyon, 1880-1946, (U.S.) short-story writer, journalist. *Guys and Dolls*, *Blue Plate Special*.
John Ruskin, 1819-1900, (Br.) critic, social theorist. *Modern Painters*, *The Seven Lamps of Architecture*.
Oliver Sacks, 1933-2015, (Br.) neurologist, writer. *The Man Who Mistook His Wife for a Hat*.
François Sagan (Françoise Quoirez), 1935-2004, (Fr.) novelist. *Bonjour Tristesse*.
Antoine de Saint-Exupéry, 1900-44, (Fr.) writer. *Wind, Sand and Stars*; *The Little Prince*.
Saki (or H[ector] H[ugh] Munro), 1870-1916, (Br.) writer. *The Chronicles of Clovis*.
J. D. Salinger, 1919-2010, (U.S.) novelist. *The Catcher in the Rye*.
George Sand (Amandine Lucie Aurore Dupin), 1804-76, (Fr.) novelist. *Indiana*, *Consuelo*.
Carl Sandburg, 1878-1967, (U.S.) poet. *The People, Yes*; *Chicago Poems*; *Smoke and Steel*; *Harvest Poems*.
José Saramago, 1922-2010, (Port.) novelist. *Blindness*.
William Saroyan, 1908-81, (U.S.) playwright, novelist. *The Time of Your Life*, *The Human Comedy*.
Nathalie Sarraute, 1900-99, (Fr.) Nouveau Roman novelist. *Tropismes*.
May Sarton, 1914-95, (Belg.-U.S.) poet, novelist. *Encounter in April*, *Anger*.
Dorothy L. Sayers, 1893-1957, (Br.) mystery writer; created Lord Peter Wimsey.
Richard Scarry, 1920-94, (U.S.) author and illustrator of children's books. *Richard Scarry's Best Story Book Ever*.
Friedrich von Schiller, 1759-1805, (Ger.) dramatist, poet, historian. *Don Carlos*, *Maria Stuart*, *Wilhelm Tell*.
Walter Scott, 1771-1832, (Scot.) novelist, poet. *Ivanhoe*.
Gil Scott-Heron, 1949-2011, (U.S.) poet. "The Revolution Will Not Be Televised."
Jaroslav Seifert, 1902-86, (Czech.) poet.
Maurice Sendak, 1928-2012, (U.S.) children's book author and illustrator. *Where the Wild Things Are*.
Dr. Seuss (Theodor Seuss Geisel), 1904-91, (U.S.) children's book author and illustrator. *The Cat in the Hat*.
William Shakespeare, 1564-1616, (Br.) dramatist, poet. *Romeo and Juliet*, *Hamlet*, *King Lear*, *Julius Caesar*, sonnets.
Karl Shapiro, 1913-2000, (U.S.) poet. "Elegy for a Dead Soldier."
George Bernard Shaw, 1856-1950, (Ire.-Br.) playwright, critic. *St. Joan*, *Pygmalion*, *Major Barbara*, *Man and Superman*.
Sidney Sheldon, 1917-2007, (U.S.) screenwriter, novelist. *Rage of Angels*, *Memories of Midnight*.
Mary Wollstonecraft Shelley, 1797-1851, (Br.) novelist, feminist. *Frankenstein*, *The Last Man*.
Percy Bysshe Shelley, 1792-1822, (Br.) poet. *Prometheus Unbound*, *Adonais*, "Ode to the West Wind," "To a Skylark."
Sam Shepard, 1943-2017, (U.S.) playwright. *Buried Child*, *True West*.
Richard B. Sheridan, 1751-1816, (Br.) dramatist. *The Rivals*, *School for Scandal*.
Robert Sherwood, 1896-1955, (U.S.) playwright, biographer. *The Petrified Forest*, *Abe Lincoln in Illinois*.
Mikhail Sholokhov, 1906-84, (Russ.) writer. *The Silent Don*.
Anne Rivers Siddons, 1936-2019, (U.S.) novelist. *Peachtree Road*.
Shel Silverstein, 1932-99, (U.S.) poet, writer. *The Giving Tree*, *Where the Sidewalk Ends*.
Georges Simenon (Georges Sims), 1903-89, (Belg.-Fr.) mystery writer; created Inspector Maigret.
Neil Simon, 1927-2018, (U.S.) playwright. *The Odd Couple*, *Brighton Beach Memoirs*.
Upton Sinclair, 1878-1968, (U.S.) novelist. *The Jungle*.
Isaac Bashevis Singer, 1904-91, (Pol.-U.S.) novelist, short-story writer, in Yiddish. *The Magician of Lublin*.
C(harles) P(ercy) Snow, 1905-80, (Br.) novelist, scientist. *Strangers and Brothers*, *Corridors of Power*.
Aleksandr Solzhenitsyn, 1918-2008, (Russ.) novelist, dramatist. *One Day in the Life of Ivan Denisovich*.
Susan Sontag, 1933-2004, (U.S.) critic, essayist, novelist. *Notes on Camp*, *The Volcano Lover*, *In America*.
Stephen Spender, 1909-95, (Br.) poet, critic, novelist. *Twenty Poems*, "Elegy for Margaret."
Edmund Spenser, 1552-99, (Br.) poet. *The Faerie Queene*.
Mickey Spillane, 1918-2006, (U.S.) novelist; Mike Hammer detective novels. *The Killing Man*.
Johanna Spyri, 1827-1901, (Switz.) children's author. *Heidi*.
Christina Stead, 1903-83, (Austral.) novelist, short-story writer. *The Man Who Loved Children*.
Richard Steele, 1672-1729, (Br.) essayist, playwright; began the *Tatler* and *Spectator*. *The Conscious Lovers*.
Gertrude Stein, 1874-1946, (U.S.) writer. *Three Lives*.
John Steinbeck, 1902-68, (U.S.) novelist. *The Grapes of Wrath*, *Of Mice and Men*, *The Winter of Our Discontent*.
Stendhal (Marie Henri Beyle), 1783-1842, (Fr.) novelist. *The Red and the Black*, *The Charterhouse of Parma*.
Laurence Sterne, 1713-68, (Br.) novelist. *Tristram Shandy*.
Wallace Stevens, 1879-1955, (U.S.) poet. *Harmonium*, *The Man With the Blue Guitar*, *Notes Toward a Supreme Fiction*.
Robert Louis Stevenson, 1850-94, (Br.) novelist, poet, essayist. *Treasure Island*, *A Child's Garden of Verses*.
Mary Stewart, 1916-2014, (Br.) novelist. Merlin trilogy.
Bram Stoker, 1847-1912, (Br.) writer. *Dracula*.
Rex Stout, 1886-1975, (U.S.) mystery writer; created Nero Wolfe.
Harriet Beecher Stowe, 1811-96, (U.S.) novelist. *Uncle Tom's Cabin*.
Lytton Strachey, 1880-1932, (Br.) biographer, critic. *Eminent Victorians*, *Queen Victoria*, *Elizabeth and Essex*.
Mark Strand, 1934-2014, (Can.-U.S.) poet. *Blizzard of One*.
August Strindberg, 1849-1912, (Swed.) dramatist, novelist. *The Father*, *Miss Julie*, *The Creditors*.
William Styron, 1925-2006, (U.S.) novelist, essayist. *The Confessions of Nat Turner*, *Sophie's Choice*, *Darkness Visible: A Memoir of Madness*.
Jonathan Swift, 1667-1745, (Br.) satirist, poet. *Gulliver's Travels*, "A Modest Proposal."
Algernon C. Swinburne, 1837-1909, (Br.) poet, dramatist. *Atalanta in Calydon*.
John M. Synge, 1871-1909, (Ire.) poet, dramatist. *Riders to the Sea*, *The Playboy of the Western World*.
Wislawa Szymborska, 1923-2012, (Pol.) poet. "Cat in an Empty Apartment."
Rabindranath Tagore, 1861-1941, (India) author, poet. *Sadhana, The Realization of Life*, *Gitanjali*.
Booth Tarkington, 1869-1946, (U.S.) novelist. *The Magnificent Ambersons*.
Peter Taylor, 1917-94, (U.S.) novelist. *A Summons to Memphis*.
Sara Teasdale, 1884-1933, (U.S.) poet. *Helen of Troy and Other Poems*, *Rivers to the Sea*.
Alfred, Lord Tennyson, 1809-92, (Br.) poet. *Idylls of the King*, *In Memoriam*, "The Charge of the Light Brigade."
William Makepeace Thackeray, 1811-63, (Br.) novelist. *Vanity Fair*, *Henry Esmond*, *Pendennis*.
Dylan Thomas, 1914-53, (Wales) poet. *Under Milk Wood*, *A Child's Christmas in Wales*.
Hunter S. Thompson, 1937-2005, (U.S.) author, journalist. *Hell's Angels*, *Fear and Loathing in Las Vegas*.
Henry David Thoreau, 1817-62, (U.S.) writer, philosopher, naturalist. *Walden*, "Civil Disobedience."
James Thurber, 1894-1961, (U.S.) humorist. "The Secret Life of Walter Mitty," *My Life and Hard Times*.
J(ohn) R(onald) R(euel) Tolkien, 1892-1973, (Br.) writer. *The Hobbit*, Lord of the Rings trilogy.
Leo Tolstoy, 1828-1910, (Russ.) novelist, short-story writer. *War and Peace*, *Anna Karenina*, "The Death of Ivan Ilyich."
Lionel Trilling, 1905-75, (U.S.) critic, author. *The Liberal Imagination*.
Anthony Trollope, 1815-82, (Br.) novelist. *The Warden*, *Barchester Towers*, the Palliser novels.
Ivan Turgenev, 1818-83, (Russ.) novelist, short-story writer. *Fathers and Sons*, *First Love*, *A Month in the Country*.
Amos Tutuola, 1920-97, (Nigeria) novelist. *The Palm-Wine Drunkard*, *My Life in the Bush of Ghosts*.
Mark Twain (Samuel Clemens), 1835-1910, (U.S.) novelist, humorist. *The Adventures of Huckleberry Finn*.
Sigrid Undset, 1881-1949, (Nor.) novelist. *Kristin Lavransdatter*.
John Updike, 1932-2009, (U.S.) novelist, literary critic. *Rabbit Is Rich*, *The Witches of Eastwick*.
Paul Valéry, 1871-1945, (Fr.) poet, critic. *La Jeune Parque*, *The Graveyard by the Sea*.
Paul Verlaine, 1844-96, (Fr.) Symbolist poet. *Songs Without Words*.
Jules Verne, 1828-1905, (Fr.) novelist. *Twenty Thousand Leagues Under the Sea*.
Gore Vidal, 1925-2012, (U.S.) novelist. *The City and the Pillar*.
François Villon, 1431-c. 1463, (Fr.) poet. *The Lays*, *The Grand Testament*.
Voltaire (F. M. Arouet), 1694-1778, (Fr.) writer of "philosophical romances"; philosopher, historian. *Candide*.
Kurt Vonnegut Jr., 1922-2007, (U.S.) novelist, essayist. *Cat's Cradle*, *Slaughterhouse-Five*, *Breakfast of Champions*.
Derek Walcott, 1930-2016, (St. Lucia) poet. "Omeros."
David Foster Wallace, 1962-2008, (U.S.) novelist, essayist. *Infinite Jest*, *A Supposedly Fun Thing I'll Never Do Again*.
Robert Penn Warren, 1905-89, (U.S.) novelist, poet, critic. *All the King's Men*.
Wendy Wasserstein, 1950-2006, (U.S.) playwright. *The Heidi Chronicles*.
Evelyn Waugh, 1903-66, (Br.) novelist. *The Loved One*, *Brideshead Revisited*, *A Handful of Dust*.
H(erbert) G(eorge) Wells, 1866-1946, (Br.) novelist. *The Time Machine*, *The Invisible Man*, *The War of the Worlds*.
Eudora Welty, 1909-2001, (U.S.) Southern short-story writer, novelist. "Why I Live at the P.O.," "The Ponder Heart."
Rebecca West, 1893-1983, (Br.) novelist, critic, journalist. *Black Lamb and Grey Falcon*.
Edith Wharton, 1862-1937, (U.S.) novelist. *The Age of Innocence*, *The House of Mirth*, *Ethan Frome*.
Phillis Wheatley, c. 1753-84, (U.S.) poet; 2nd American woman and first Black woman to be published, 1770.
E(lwyn) B(rooks) White, 1899-1985, (U.S.) essayist, novelist. *Charlotte's Web*, *Stuart Little*.
Patrick White, 1912-90, (Austral.) novelist. *The Tree of Man*.

T(erence) H(anbury) White, 1906-64, (Br.) author. *The Once and Future King*, *A Book of Beasts*.
Walt Whitman, 1819-92, (U.S.) poet. *Leaves of Grass*.
John Greenleaf Whittier, 1807-92, (U.S.) poet, journalist. *Snow-Bound*.
Elie Wiesel, 1928-2016, (Rom.) memoirist, novelist. *Night*.
Oscar Wilde, 1854-1900, (Ire.) novelist, playwright. *The Picture of Dorian Gray*, *The Importance of Being Earnest*.
Laura Ingalls Wilder, 1867-1957, (U.S.) novelist. Little House on the Prairie series of children's books.
Thornton Wilder, 1897-1975, (U.S.) playwright. *Our Town*, *The Skin of Our Teeth*, *The Matchmaker*.
Tennessee Williams, 1911-83, (U.S.) playwright. *A Streetcar Named Desire*, *Cat on a Hot Tin Roof*, *The Glass Menagerie*.
William Carlos Williams, 1883-1963, (U.S.) poet, physician. *The Tempers*, *Al Que Quiere! Paterson*, "This Is Just to Say."
Edmund Wilson, 1895-1972, (U.S.) critic, novelist. *Axel's Castle*, *To the Finland Station*.
Lanford Wilson, 1937-2011, (U.S.) playwright. *Talley's Folly*, *Fifth of July*.
P(elham) G(renville) Wodehouse, 1881-1975, (Br.-U.S.) humorist. Jeeves novels, *Anything Goes*.
Thomas Wolfe, 1900-38, (U.S.) novelist, journalist. *Look Homeward, Angel*; *You Can't Go Home Again*.
Tom Wolfe, 1930-2018, (U.S.) novelist, journalist. *Bonfire of the Vanities*, *The Right Stuff*.
Virginia Woolf, 1882-1941, (Br.) novelist, essayist. *Mrs. Dalloway*, *To the Lighthouse*, *A Room of One's Own*.
William Wordsworth, 1770-1850, (Br.) poet. "Tintern Abbey," "Ode: Intimations of Immortality," *The Prelude*.
Herman Wouk, 1915-2019, (U.S.) novelist. *The Caine Mutiny*.
Richard Wright, 1908-60, (U.S.) novelist, short-story writer. *Native Son*, *Black Boy*, *Uncle Tom's Children*.
Elinor Wylie, 1885-1928, (U.S.) poet. *Nets to Catch the Wind*.
William Butler Yeats, 1865-1939, (Ire.) poet, playwright. "The Second Coming," *The Wild Swans at Coole*.
Frank Yerby, 1916-91, (U.S.) first best-selling African American novelist. *The Foxes of Harrow*.
Yevgeny Yevtushenko, 1933-2017, (Russ.) poet. "Babi Yar."
Émile Zola, 1840-1902, (Fr.) novelist. *Nana*, *Thérèse Raquin*.

Poets Laureate

In England, Henry III (1216-72) reportedly had a Versificator Regis, or King's Poet, paid 100 shillings per year. Other poets said to have filled the role of poet laureate include Geoffrey Chaucer (d 1400), Edmund Spenser (d 1599), Ben Jonson (d 1637), and William d'Avenant (d 1668). The first official English poet laureate was John Dryden, appointed 1668, for life. Then came Thomas Shadwell, in 1689; Nahum Tate, 1692; Nicholas Rowe, 1715; Rev. Laurence Eusden, 1718; Colley Cibber, 1730; William Whitehead, 1757; Rev. Thomas Warton, 1785; Henry James Pye, 1790; Robert Southey, 1813; William Wordsworth, 1843; Alfred, Lord Tennyson, 1850; Alfred Austin, 1896; Robert Bridges, 1913; John Masefield, 1930; C. Day Lewis, 1968; John Betjeman, 1972; Ted Hughes, 1984; Andrew Motion, 1999; Carol Ann Duffy, 2009; and Simon Armitage, 2019.

In the U.S., appointment is by the Librarian of Congress to a term of one year, which may be renewed: Robert Penn Warren, appointed 1986; Richard Wilbur, 1987; Howard Nemerov, 1988; Mark Strand, 1990; Joseph Brodsky, 1991; Mona Van Duyn, 1992; Rita Dove, 1993; Robert Hass, 1995; Robert Pinsky, 1997; Stanley Kunitz, 2000; Billy Collins, 2001; Louise Glück, 2003; Ted Kooser, 2004; Donald Hall, 2006; Charles Simic, 2007; Kay Ryan, 2008; W. S. Merwin, 2010; Philip Levine, 2011; Natasha Trethewey, 2012; Charles Wright, 2014; Juan Felipe Herrera, 2015; Tracy K. Smith, 2017; Joy Harjo, 2019; Ada Limón, 2022.

Composers of Classical and Avant-Garde Music

John Adams, b 1947, (U.S.) *Nixon in China*, *The Death of Klinghoffer*.
Milton Babbitt, 1916-2011, (U.S.) serial and electronic music.
Carl Philipp Emanuel Bach, 1714-88, (Ger.) cantatas, passions, numerous keyboard and instrumental works.
Johann Christian Bach, 1735-82, (Ger.) concertos, operas, sonatas. Known as the "English" Bach.
Johann Sebastian Bach, 1685-1750, (Ger.) *St. Matthew Passion*, *The Well-Tempered Clavier*.
Samuel Barber, 1910-81, (U.S.) *Adagio for Strings*, *Vanessa*.
Béla Bartók, 1881-1945, (Hung.) *Concerto for Orchestra*, *The Miraculous Mandarin*.
Amy Beach (Mrs. H. H. A. Beach), 1867-1944, (U.S.) *The Year's at the Spring*, *Fireflies*, *The Chambered Nautilus*.
Ludwig van Beethoven, 1770-1827, (Ger.) concertos (*Emperor*), sonatas (*Moonlight*, *Pathétique*), 9 symphonies.
Vincenzo Bellini, 1801-35, (It.) *I Puritani*, *La Sonnambula*, *Norma*.
Alban Berg, 1885-1935, (Austria) *Wozzeck*, *Lulu*.
Hector Berlioz, 1803-69, (Fr.) *Damnation of Faust*, *Symphonie Fantastique*, *Requiem*.
Leonard Bernstein, 1918-90, (U.S.) *Chichester Psalms*, *Jeremiah Symphony*, *Mass*.
Georges Bizet, 1838-75, (Fr.) *Carmen*, *Pearl Fishers*.
Ernest Bloch, 1880-1959, (Switz.-U.S.) *Macbeth* (opera), *Schelomo*, *Voice in the Wilderness*.
Luigi Boccherini, 1743-1805, (It.) chamber music and guitar pieces.
Alexander Borodin, 1833-87, (Russ.) *Prince Igor*, *In the Steppes of Central Asia*, *Polovtzian Dances*.
Pierre Boulez, 1925-2016, (Fr.) *Le Visage nuptial*, *Éclat/Multiples*, *Domaines*.
Johannes Brahms, 1833-97, (Ger.) Liebeslieder Waltzes, *Academic Festival Overture*, chamber music, 4 symphonies.
Henry Brant, 1913-2008, (Can.) spatial music.
Benjamin Britten, 1913-76, (Br.) *Peter Grimes*, *Turn of the Screw*, *A Ceremony of Carols*, *War Requiem*.
Anton Bruckner, 1824-96, (Austria) 9 symphonies.
Dietrich Buxtehude, 1637-1707, (Den.) organ works, vocal music.
William Byrd, 1543-1623, (Br.) masses, motets.
John Cage, 1912-92, (U.S.) *Winter Music*, *Fontana Mix*.
Elliott Carter, 1908-2012, (U.S.) *Second String Quartet*, *Third String Quartet*.
Emmanuel Chabrier, 1841-94, (Fr.) *Le Roi Malgré Lui*, *España*.
Gustave Charpentier, 1860-1956, (Fr.) *Louise*.
Frédéric Chopin, 1810-49, (Pol.) mazurkas, waltzes, etudes, nocturnes, polonaises, sonatas.
Aaron Copland, 1900-90, (U.S.) *Appalachian Spring*, *Fanfare for the Common Man*, *Lincoln Portrait*.
John Corigliano, b 1938, (U.S.) *Symphony No. 2*.
Paul Creston, 1906-85, (U.S.) *Walt Whitman*.
Claude Debussy, 1862-1918, (Fr.) *Pelleas et Melisande*, *La Mer*, *Prelude to the Afternoon of a Faun*.
David Del Tredici, 1937-2023, (U.S.) *Child Alice*, *In Memory of a Summer Day*.
Gaetano Donizetti, 1797-1848, (It.) *Elixir of Love*, *Lucia di Lammermoor*, *Daughter of the Regiment*.
Paul Dukas, 1865-1935, (Fr.) *Sorcerer's Apprentice*.
Antonín Dvořák, 1841-1904, (Czech.) *Songs My Mother Taught Me*, *Symphony in E Minor (From the New World)*.
Edward Elgar, 1857-1934, (Br.) *Enigma Variations*, *Pomp and Circumstance*.
Manuel de Falla, 1876-1946, (Sp.) *El Amor Brujo*, *La Vida Breve*, *The Three-Cornered Hat*.
Louise Farrenc, 1804-75, (Fr.) Nonet in E flat, Op. 38.
Gabriel Faurè, 1845-1924, (Fr.) *Requiem*, Elègie for Cello and Piano.
Cesar Franck, 1822-90, (Belg.) Symphony in D minor, Violin Sonata.
George Gershwin, 1898-1937, (U.S.) *Rhapsody in Blue*, *An American in Paris*, *Porgy and Bess*.
Philip Glass, b 1937, (U.S.) *Einstein on the Beach*, *The Voyage*.
Mikhail Glinka, 1804-57, (Russ.) *A Life for the Tsar*, *Ruslan and Ludmilla*.
Christoph W. Gluck, 1714-87, (Ger.) *Alceste*, *Iphigènie en Tauride*.
Henryk Gorecki, 1933-2010, (Pol.) Symphony no. 3 (*Symphony of Sorrowing Songs*).
Charles Gounod, 1818-93, (Fr.) *Faust*, *Romeo and Juliet*.
Percy Grainger, 1882-1961, (Austral.) *Country Gardens*.
Edvard Grieg, 1843-1907, (Nor.) *Peer Gynt Suite*, Concerto in A minor for piano.
George Frideric Handel, 1685-1759, (Ger.-Br.) *Messiah*, *Water Music*.
Howard Hanson, 1896-1981, (U.S.) Symphonies No. 1 (Nordic) and No. 2 (Romantic).
Roy Harris, 1898-1979, (U.S.) symphonies.
(Franz) Joseph Haydn, 1732-1809, (Austria) symphonies (*Clock*, *London*, *Toy*), chamber music, oratorios.
Hildegard von Bingen, 1098-1179, (Ger.) *Ordo virtutum*.
Paul Hindemith, 1895-1963, (U.S.) *Mathis der Maler*.
Gustav Holst, 1874-1934, (Br.) *The Planets*.
Arthur Honegger, 1892-1955, (Fr.) *Judith*, *Le Roi David*, *Pacific 231*.
Alan Hovhaness, 1911-2000, (U.S.) symphonies, *Magnificat*.
Engelbert Humperdinck, 1854-1921, (Ger.) *Hansel and Gretel*.
Charles Ives, 1874-1954, (U.S.) *Concord Sonata*, symphonies.
Aram Khachaturian, 1903-78, (Russ.) ballets, piano pieces, *Sabre Dance*.
Zoltán Kodaly, 1882-1967, (Hung.) *Háry János*, *Psalmus Hungaricus*.
Fritz Kreisler, 1875-1962, (Austria) *Caprice Viennois*, *Tambourin Chinois*.
Edouard Lalo, 1823-92, (Fr.) *Symphonie Espagnole*.
David Lang, b 1957, (U.S.) *The Little Match Girl Passion*.
Morten Lauridsen, b 1943, (U.S.) *Lux Aeterna*.
Ruggero Leoncavallo, 1857-1919, (It.) *Pagliacci*.
György Ligeti, 1923-2006, (Rom.) *Atmosphères*, *Requiem*.
Franz Liszt, 1811-86, (Hung.) 20 Hungarian rhapsodies, symphonic poems.
Edward MacDowell, 1861-1908, (U.S.) *To a Wild Rose*.
Gustav Mahler, 1860-1911, (Austria) *Das Lied von der Erde*; 9 complete symphonies.
Pietro Mascagni, 1863-1945, (It.) *Cavalleria Rusticana*.
Jules Massenet, 1842-1912, (Fr.) *Manon*, *Le Cid*, *Thaïs*.

Felix Mendelssohn, 1809-47, (Ger.) *A Midsummer Night's Dream*, *Songs Without Words*, violin concerto.
Gian Carlo Menotti, 1911-2007, (It.-U.S.) *The Medium*, *The Consul*, *Amahl and the Night Visitors*.
Olivier Messiaen, 1908-1992, (Fr.) *Apparition de l'Église Éternelle*.
Claudio Monteverdi, 1567-1643, (It.) opera, masses, madrigals.
Wolfgang Amadeus Mozart, 1756-91, (Austria) chamber music, concertos, operas (*Magic Flute*, *Marriage of Figaro*), 41 symphonies.
Modest Mussorgsky, 1839-81, (Russ.) *Boris Godunov*, *Pictures at an Exhibition*.
Carl Nielsen, 1865-1931, (Den.) *Saul og David*.
Jacques Offenbach, 1819-80, (Fr.) *Tales of Hoffmann*.
Carl Orff, 1895-1982, (Ger.) *Carmina Burana*.
Johann Pachelbel, 1653-1706, (Ger.) Canon and Fugue in D major.
Ignacy Paderewski, 1860-1941, (Pol.) Minuet in G.
Niccolò Paganini, 1782-1840, (It.) Caprices for violin solo.
Giovanni Palestrina, c. 1525-94, (It.) masses, madrigals.
Arvo Pärt, b 1935, (Eston.) sacred music. *Fratres*, *Cantus in memoriam Benjamin Britten*, *Tabula Rasa*.
Krzysztof Penderecki, 1933-2020, (Pol.) *Psalmus*, *Polymorphia*, *De natura sonoris*.
Francis Poulenc, 1899-1963, (Fr.) *Dialogues des Carmèlites*.
Mel Powell, 1923-98, (U.S.) *Duplicates: A Concerto for Two Pianos and Orchestra*, *Cantilena Concertante*.
Sergei Prokofiev, 1891-1953, (Russ.) Classical Symphony, *Love for Three Oranges*, *Peter and the Wolf*.
Giacomo Puccini, 1858-1924, (It.) *La Boheme*, *Manon Lescaut*, *Tosca*, *Madama Butterfly*.
Henry Purcell, 1659-95, (Br.) *Dido and Aeneas*.
Sergei Rachmaninoff, 1873-1943, (Russ.) concertos, preludes (Prelude in C sharp minor), symphonies.
Maurice Ravel, 1875-1937, (Fr.) *Bolèro*, *Daphnis et Chloè*, Piano Concerto in D for Left Hand Alone.
Steve Reich, b 1936, (U.S.) *Double Sextet*, *Three Tales*.
Nikolai Rimsky-Korsakov, 1844-1908, (Russ.) *Golden Cockerel*, *Scheherazade*, *Flight of the Bumblebee*.
Ned Rorem, 1923-2022, (U.S.) "Evidence of Things Not Seen."
Gioachino Rossini, 1792-1868, (It.) *Barber of Seville*, *Otello*, *William Tell*.
John Rutter, b 1945, (Br.) *Magnificat*, *Requiem*.
Camille Saint-Saëns, 1835-1921, (Fr.) *Carnival of Animals (The Swan)*, *Samson and Delilah*, *Danse Macabre*.
Alessandro Scarlatti, 1660-1725, (It.) cantatas, oratorios, operas.
Domenico Scarlatti, 1685-1757, (It.) harpsichord works.
Alfred Schnittke, 1934-98 (Russ.-Ger.) *Life With an Idiot*.
Arnold Schoenberg, 1874-1951, (Austria) *Pelleas and Melisande*, *Pierrot Lunaire*, *Verklärte Nacht*.
Franz Schubert, 1797-1828, (Austria) chamber music (*Trout Quintet*), lieder, symphonies ("Unfinished").
Robert Schumann, 1810-56, (Ger.) *Die Frauenliebe und Leben*, *Träumerei*.
Dmitri Shostakovich, 1906-75, (Russ.) symphonies, *Lady Macbeth of the District Mzensk*.
Jean Sibelius, 1865-1957, (Fin.) *Finlandia*.
Bedrich Smetana, 1824-84, (Czech.) *The Bartered Bride*.
Karlheinz Stockhausen, 1928-2008, (Ger.) *Kontra-Punkte*, *Kontakte for Electronic Instruments*.
Richard Strauss, 1864-1949, (Ger.) *Salome*, *Elektra*, *Der Rosenkavalier*, *Thus Spake Zarathustra*.
Igor Stravinsky, 1882-1971, (Russ.) *Noah and the Flood*, *The Rake's Progress*, *The Rite of Spring*.
Toru Takemitsu, 1930-96, (Jpn.) *Requiem for Strings*, *Dorian Horizon*.
Thomas Tallis, c. 1505-85, (Br.) anthems, motets.
Peter I. Tchaikovsky, 1840-93, (Russ.) *Nutcracker*, *Swan Lake*, *The Sleeping Beauty*.
Georg Philipp Telemann, 1681-1767, (Ger.) church music, orchestral suites, chamber music.
Virgil Thomson, 1896-1989, (U.S.) opera, film music, *Four Saints in Three Acts*.
Dmitri Tiomkin, 1894-1979, (Russ.-U.S.) film scores, including *High Noon*.
Michael Tippett, 1905-98, (Br.) *A Child of Our Time*, *The Midsummer Marriage*, *The Knot Garden*.
Michael Torke, b 1961, (U.S.) *Bright Blue Music*, *Ecstatic Orange*.
Eric Whitacre, b 1970, (U.S.) *Cloudburst*.
Ralph Vaughan Williams, 1872-1958, (Br.) *Fantasia on a Theme by Thomas Tallis*, symphonies, vocal music.
Giuseppe Verdi, 1813-1901, (It.) *Aida*, *Rigoletto*, *Don Carlo*, *Il Trovatore*, *La Traviata*, *Falstaff*, *Macbeth*.
Heitor Villa-Lobos, 1887-1959, (Braz.) *Bachianas Brasileiras*.
Antonio Vivaldi, 1678-1741, (It.) Concerto grossos (*The Four Seasons*).
Richard Wagner, 1813-83, (Ger.) *Rienzi*, *Tannhäuser*, *Lohengrin*, *Tristan und Isolde*.
William Walton, 1902-83, (Br.) *Façade*, *Belshazzar's Feast*.
Carl Maria von Weber, 1786-1826, (Ger.) *Der Freischutz*.
Judith Weir, b. 1954, (Br.) *King Harald's Saga*.

Composers of Operettas, Musicals, and Popular Music

Richard Adler, 1921-2012, (U.S.) *Pajama Game*; *Damn Yankees*.
Milton Ager, 1893-1979, (U.S.) "I Wonder What's Become of Sally"; "Hard-Hearted Hannah"; "Ain't She Sweet?"
Leroy Anderson, 1908-75, (U.S.) "Sleigh Ride"; "Blue Tango"; "Syncopated Clock."
Paul Anka, b 1941, (Can.) "My Way"; *Tonight Show* theme.
Harold Arlen, 1905-86, (U.S.) "Stormy Weather"; "Over the Rainbow"; "Blues in the Night"; "That Old Black Magic."
Burt Bacharach, 1928-2023, (U.S.) "Raindrops Keep Fallin' on My Head"; "Walk on By"; "What the World Needs Now Is Love."
Ernest Ball, 1878-1927, (U.S.) "Mother Machree"; "When Irish Eyes Are Smiling."
John Barry, 1933-2011, (U.S.) *Born Free*; *Lion in Winter*; *Out of Africa*.
Irving Berlin, 1888-1989, (U.S.) *Annie Get Your Gun*; *Call Me Madam*; "God Bless America"; "White Christmas."
Alan Bergman, b 1925, and **Marilyn Bergman**, 1928-2022, (both U.S.) "The Way We Were"; "You Don't Bring Me Flowers."
Leonard Bernstein, 1918-90, (U.S.) *On the Town*; *Wonderful Town*; *Candide*; *West Side Story*.
Eubie Blake, 1883-1983, (U.S.) *Shuffle Along*; "I'm Just Wild About Harry."
Jerry Bock, 1928-2010, (U.S.) *Mr. Wonderful*; *Fiorello*; *Fiddler on the Roof*; *The Rothschilds*.
Carrie Jacobs Bond, 1862-1946, (U.S.) "I Love You Truly."
Nacio Herb Brown, 1896-1964, (U.S.) "Singing in the Rain"; "You Were Meant for Me"; "All I Do Is Dream of You."
Hoagy Carmichael, 1899-1981, (U.S.) "Stardust"; "Georgia on My Mind"; "Old Buttermilk Sky."
James Cleveland, 1931-91, (U.S.) composer, musician, singer; first Black gospel artist to appear at Carnegie Hall.
George M. Cohan, 1878-1942, (U.S.) "Give My Regards to Broadway"; "You're a Grand Old Flag"; "Over There."
Cy Coleman, 1929-2004, (U.S.) *Sweet Charity*; "Witchcraft."
John Frederick Coots, 1895-1985, (U.S.) "Santa Claus Is Coming to Town"; "You Go to My Head"; "For All We Know."
Noël Coward, 1899-1973, (Br.) *Bitter Sweet*; "Mad Dogs and Englishmen"; "Mad About the Boy."
Neil Diamond, b 1941, (U.S.) "I'm a Believer"; "Sweet Caroline."
Walter Donaldson, 1893-1947, (U.S.) "My Buddy"; "Carolina in the Morning"; "Makin' Whoopee."
Vernon Duke, 1903-69, (U.S.) "April in Paris."
Bob Dylan, b 1941, (U.S.) "Blowin' in the Wind"; "Like a Rolling Stone."
Gus Edwards, 1879-1945, (U.S.) "School Days"; "By the Light of the Silvery Moon"; "In My Merry Oldsmobile."
Sherman Edwards, 1919-81, (U.S.) "See You in September"; "Wonderful! Wonderful!"
Duke Ellington, 1899-1974, (U.S.) "Sophisticated Lady"; "Satin Doll"; "It Don't Mean a Thing"; "Solitude."
Sammy Fain, 1902-89, (U.S.) "I'll Be Seeing You"; "Love Is a Many-Splendored Thing."
Fred Fisher, 1875-1942, (U.S.) "Peg O' My Heart"; "Chicago."
Stephen Collins Foster, 1826-64, (U.S.) "My Old Kentucky Home"; "Old Folks at Home"; "Beautiful Dreamer."
Rudolf Friml, 1879-1972, (Czech.-U.S.) *The Firefly*; *Rose Marie*; *Vagabond King*; *Bird of Paradise*.
John Gay, 1685-1732, (Br.) *The Beggar's Opera*.
George Gershwin, 1898-1937, (U.S.) "Someone to Watch Over Me"; "I've Got a Crush on You"; "Embraceable You."
João Gilberto, 1931-2019, (Brazil) bossa nova pioneer.
Morton Gould, 1913-96, (U.S.) "Fall River Suite"; "Holocaust Suite"; "Spirituals for Orchestra"; "Stringmusic."
Ferde Grofe, 1892-1972, (U.S.) "Grand Canyon Suite."
Marvin Hamlisch, 1944-2012, (U.S.) "The Way We Were"; "Nobody Does It Better"; *A Chorus Line*.
Ray Henderson, 1896-1970, (U.S.) *George White's Scandals*; "That Old Gang of Mine"; "Five Foot Two, Eyes of Blue."
Victor Herbert, 1859-1924, (Ire.-U.S.) *Mlle. Modiste*; *Babes in Toyland*; *The Red Mill*; *Naughty Marietta*; *Sweethearts*.
Jerry Herman, 1931-2019, (U.S.) *Hello, Dolly!*; *Mame*.
Brian Holland, b 1941, **Lamont Dozier**, 1941-2022, and **Eddie Holland**, b 1939, (all U.S.) "Heat Wave"; "Stop! In the Name of Love"; "Baby, I Need Your Loving."
Rupert Holmes, b 1947, (Br.-U.S.) *The Mystery of Edwin Drood*; *Curtains*.
James Horner, 1953-2015, (U.S.) *Titanic*; "Somewhere Out There"; "My Heart Will Go On."
Antonio Carlos Jobim, 1927-94, (Brazil) "The Girl From Ipanema"; "Desafinado"; "One Note Samba."
Billy Joel (William Martin), b 1949, (U.S.) "Just the Way You Are"; "Honesty"; "Piano Man."
Elton John, b 1947, (Br.) *The Lion King*; "Candle in the Wind"; "Your Song."
Scott Joplin, 1868-1917, (U.S.) Maple Leaf Rag; *Treemonisha*.
John Kander, b 1927, (U.S.) *Cabaret*; *Chicago*; *Funny Lady*.
Jerome Kern, 1885-1945, (U.S.) *Sally*; *Sunny*; *Show Boat*.
Carole King, b 1942, (U.S.) "Will You Love Me Tomorrow?"; "Natural Woman"; "One Fine Day"; "Up on the Roof."
Burton Lane, 1912-97, (U.S.) *Finian's Rainbow*.
Jonathan Larson, 1960-96, (U.S.) *tick, tick... BOOM!*; *Rent*.
Franz Lehar, 1870-1948, (Hung.) *Merry Widow*.

Jerry Leiber, 1933-2011, and **Mike Stoller**, b 1933, (both U.S.) "Hound Dog"; "Searchin'"; "Yakety Yak"; "Love Me Tender."
Mitch Leigh, 1928-2014, (U.S.) *Man of La Mancha*.
John Lennon, 1940-80, and **Paul McCartney**, b 1942, (both Br.) "I Want to Hold Your Hand"; "She Loves You."
Jay Livingston, 1915-2001, (U.S.) "Mona Lisa"; "Que Sera, Sera."
Andrew Lloyd Webber, b 1948, (Br.) *Jesus Christ Superstar*; *Evita*; *Cats*; *The Phantom of the Opera*.
Frank Loesser, 1910-69, (U.S.) *Guys and Dolls*; *Where's Charley?*; *The Most Happy Fella*; *How to Succeed in Business....*
Frederick Loewe, 1901-88, (Austria-U.S.) *Brigadoon*; *Paint Your Wagon*; *My Fair Lady*; *Camelot*.
Robert Lopez, b 1975, (U.S.) *Avenue Q*; *The Book of Mormon*; *Frozen*.
Henry Mancini, 1924-94, (U.S.) "Moon River"; "Days of Wine and Roses"; "Pink Panther Theme."
Barry Mann, b 1939, and **Cynthia Weil**, 1940-2023, (both U.S.) "You've Lost That Loving Feeling."
Hugh Martin, 1914-2011, (U.S.) "Have Yourself a Merry Little Christmas"; "The Trolley Song."
Jimmy McHugh, 1894-1969, (U.S.) "Don't Blame Me"; "I'm in the Mood for Love"; "I Feel a Song Coming On."
Christine McVie, 1943-2022, (Br.) "Don't Stop"; "Songbird."
Alan Menken, b 1949, (U.S.) *Little Shop of Horrors*; *Beauty and the Beast*.
Joseph Meyer, 1894-1987, (U.S.) "If You Knew Susie"; "California, Here I Come"; "Crazy Rhythm."
Lin-Manuel Miranda, b 1980, (U.S.) *In the Heights*; *Hamilton*.
Joni Mitchell, b 1943, (Can.) "Both Sides Now"; "Big Yellow Taxi."
Ennio Morricone, 1928-2020, (It.) *The Good, the Bad and the Ugly*; *The Untouchables*.
Willie Nelson, b 1933, (U.S.) "Crazy"; "On the Road Again."
Chauncey Olcott, 1858-1932, (U.S.) "Mother Machree."
Dolly Parton, b 1946, (U.S.) "I Will Always Love You"; "Jolene"; "9 to 5."
Jerome "Doc" Pomus, 1925-91, (U.S.) "Save the Last Dance for Me"; "A Teenager in Love."
Cole Porter, 1891-1964, (U.S.) *Anything Goes*; *Kiss Me Kate*; *Can Can*; *Silk Stockings*.
Smokey Robinson, b 1940, (U.S.) "Shop Around"; "My Guy"; "My Girl"; "Get Ready."
Richard Rodgers, 1902-79, (U.S.) *Oklahoma!*; *Carousel*; *South Pacific*; *The King and I*; *The Sound of Music*.
Sigmund Romberg, 1887-1951, (Hung.) *Maytime*; *The Student Prince*; *Desert Song*; *Blossom Time*.
Harold Rome, 1908-93, (U.S.) *Pins and Needles*; *Call Me Mister*; *Wish You Were Here*; *Fanny*; *Destry Rides Again*.
Vincent Rose, 1880-1944, (U.S.) "Avalon"; "Whispering"; "Blueberry Hill."
Harry Ruby, 1895-1974, (U.S.) "Three Little Words"; "Who's Sorry Now?"
Arthur Schwartz, 1900-84, (U.S.) *The Band Wagon*; "Dancing in the Dark"; "By Myself"; "That's Entertainment."
Stephen Schwartz, b 1948, (U.S.) *Godspell*; *Pippin*; *Wicked*.
Neil Sedaka, b 1939, (U.S.) "Breaking Up Is Hard to Do."
Marc Shaiman, b 1959, (U.S.) *Hairspray*.
Richard M. Sherman, 1928-2024, and **Robert B. Sherman**, 1925-2012, (both U.S.) *Mary Poppins*; *The Jungle Book*.
Paul Simon, b 1942, (U.S.) "Sounds of Silence"; "I Am a Rock"; "Mrs. Robinson"; "Bridge Over Troubled Waters."
Stephen Sondheim, 1930-2021, (U.S.) *A Little Night Music*; *Company*; *Sweeney Todd*; *Sunday in the Park With George*.
John Philip Sousa, 1854-1932, (U.S.) *El Capitan*; "Stars and Stripes Forever."
Oskar Straus, 1870-1954, (Austria) *Chocolate Soldier*.
Johann Strauss, 1825-99, (Austria) *Gypsy Baron*; *Die Fledermaus*; waltzes: Blue Danube; Artist's Life.
Charles Strouse, b 1928, (U.S.) *Bye Bye, Birdie*; *Annie*.
Jule Styne, 1905-94, (Br.-U.S.) *Gentlemen Prefer Blondes*; *Bells Are Ringing*; *Gypsy*; *Funny Girl*.
Arthur S. Sullivan, 1842-1900, (Br.) *H.M.S. Pinafore*; *Pirates of Penzance*; *The Mikado*.
Deems Taylor, 1885-1966, (U.S.) *Peter Ibbetson*.
Jeanine Tesori, b 1971, (U.S.) *Fun Home*; *Shrek the Musical*; *Kimberly Akimbo*.
Harry Tobias, 1905-94, (U.S.) *I'll Keep the Lovelight Burning*.
Egbert van Alstyne, 1882-1951, (U.S.) "In the Shade of the Old Apple Tree"; "Memories"; "Pretty Baby."
Jimmy Van Heusen, 1913-90, (U.S.) "Moonlight Becomes You"; "Swinging on a Star"; "All the Way"; "Love and Marriage."
Albert von Tilzer, 1878-1956, (U.S.) "I'll Be With You in Apple Blossom Time"; "Take Me Out to the Ball Game."
Harry von Tilzer, 1872-1946, (U.S.) "Only a Bird in a Gilded Cage"; "Wait 'til the Sun Shines, Nellie."
Fats Waller, 1904-43, (U.S.) "Honeysuckle Rose"; "Ain't Misbehavin'."
Harry Warren, 1893-1981, (U.S.) "You're My Everything"; "We're in the Money"; "I Only Have Eyes for You."
Jimmy Webb, b 1946, (U.S.) "Up, Up and Away"; "By the Time I Get to Phoenix"; "Didn't We?"; "Wichita Lineman."
Kurt Weill, 1900-50, (Ger.-U.S.) *Threepenny Opera*; *Lady in the Dark*; *Knickerbocker Holiday*; *One Touch of Venus*.
Percy Wenrich, 1887-1952, (U.S.) "When You Wore a Tulip"; "Moonlight Bay"; "Put On Your Old Gray Bonnet."
Richard A. Whiting, 1891-1938, (U.S.) "Till We Meet Again"; "Sleepytime Gal"; "Beyond the Blue Horizon"; "My Ideal."
Frank Wildhorn, b 1959, (U.S.) *Jekyll and Hyde*; *Victor/Victoria*; *The Civil War*.
John Williams, b 1932, (U.S.) *Jaws*; *E.T.*; *Star Wars* series; *Raiders of the Lost Ark* series.
Meredith Willson, 1902-84, (U.S.) *The Music Man*.
Stevie Wonder, b 1950, (U.S.) "You Are the Sunshine of My Life"; "Signed, Sealed, Delivered, I'm Yours."
Vincent Youmans, 1898-1946, (U.S.) *No, No, Nanette*; "Tea for Two"; "I Want to Be Happy."

Lyricists

Howard Ashman, 1950-91, (U.S.) *Little Shop of Horrors*; *The Little Mermaid*.
Johnny Burke, 1908-84, (U.S.) "Misty"; "Imagination."
Irving Caesar, 1895-1996, (U.S.) "Swanee"; "Tea for Two"; "Just a Gigolo."
Sammy Cahn, 1913-93, (U.S.) "High Hopes"; "Love and Marriage"; "The Second Time Around"; "It's Magic."
Leonard Cohen, 1934-2016, (Can.) "Suzanne"; "Hallelujah."
Betty Comden, 1917-2006, and **Adolph Green**, 1915-2002, (both U.S.) "The Party's Over"; "New York, New York."
Hal David, 1921-2012, (U.S.) "What the World Needs Now Is Love."
Buddy De Sylva, 1895-1950, (U.S.) "When Day Is Done"; "Look for the Silver Lining"; "April Showers."
Howard Dietz, 1896-1983, (U.S.) "Dancing in the Dark"; "That's Entertainment."
Al Dubin, 1891-1945, (U.S.) "Tiptoe Through the Tulips"; "Lullaby of Broadway."
Fred Ebb, 1936-2004, (U.S.) *Cabaret*; *Zorba*; *Woman of the Year*; *Chicago*.
Ray Evans, 1915-2007, (U.S.) "Mona Lisa"; "Que Sera, Sera."
Dorothy Fields, 1905-74, (U.S.) "On the Sunny Side of the Street"; "Don't Blame Me"; "The Way You Look Tonight."
Ira Gershwin, 1896-1983, (U.S.) "The Man I Love"; "S'Wonderful"; "Embraceable You."
William S. Gilbert, 1836-1911, (Br.) *H.M.S. Pinafore*; *Pirates of Penzance*.
Gerry Goffin, 1939-2014, (U.S.) "Will You Love Me Tomorrow"; "Take Good Care of My Baby"; "Up on the Roof."
Mack Gordon, 1905-59, (Pol.-U.S.) "You'll Never Know"; "The More I See You"; "Chattanooga Choo-Choo."
Oscar Hammerstein II, 1895-1960, (U.S.) *Show Boat*; *Oklahoma!*; *Carousel*.
E.Y. (Yip) Harburg, 1898-1981, (U.S.) "Brother, Can You Spare a Dime"; "April in Paris"; "Over the Rainbow."
Sheldon Harnick, 1924-2023, (U.S.) *Fiddler on the Roof*; *She Loves Me*.
Lorenz Hart, 1895-1943, (U.S.) "Isn't It Romantic"; "Blue Moon"; "Lover"; "Manhattan"; "My Funny Valentine."
DuBose Heyward, 1885-1940, (U.S.) "Summertime."
Gus Kahn, 1886-1941, (U.S.) "Memories"; "Ain't We Got Fun."
Alan J. Lerner, 1918-86, (U.S.) *Brigadoon*; *My Fair Lady*; *Camelot*; *Gigi*; *On a Clear Day You Can See Forever*.
Johnny Mercer, 1909-76, (U.S.) "Blues in the Night"; "Come Rain or Come Shine"; "Laura"; "That Old Black Magic."
Bob Merrill, 1921-98, (U.S.) "People"; "(How Much Is That) Doggie in the Window."
Jack Norworth, 1879-1959, (U.S.) "Take Me Out to the Ball Game"; "Shine On Harvest Moon."
Mitchell Parish, 1901-93, (U.S.) "Stardust"; "Stairway to the Stars."
Andy Razaf, 1895-1973, (U.S.) "Honeysuckle Rose"; "Ain't Misbehavin."
Tim Rice, b 1944, (Br.) *Jesus Christ Superstar*; *Evita*; *The Lion King*.
Leo Robin, 1900-84, (U.S.) "Thanks for the Memory"; "Diamonds Are a Girl's Best Friend."
Bernie Taupin, b 1947 (Br.) "Rocket Man"; "Your Song."
Paul Francis Webster, 1907-84, (U.S.) "Secret Love"; "The Shadow of Your Smile"; "Love Is a Many-Splendored Thing."
Jack Yellen, 1892-1991, (U.S.) "Ain't She Sweet"; "Happy Days Are Here Again."

Blues and Jazz Artists of the Past

Julian "Cannonball" Adderley, 1928-75, alto sax.
Nat Adderley, 1931-2000, cornet.
Henry "Red" Allen, 1908-67, trumpet.
Mose Allison, 1927-2016, piano.
Louis "Satchmo" Armstrong, 1901-71, trumpet, singer, bandleader.
Albert Ayler, 1936-70, tenor sax, alto sax.
Mildred Bailey, 1907-51, singer.
Chet Baker, 1929-88, trumpet, singer.
Ray Barretto, 1930-2006, conga drummer.
William "Count" Basie, 1904-84, bandleader, piano, composer.
Sidney Bechet, 1897-1959, soprano sax, clarinet.
Bix Beiderbecke, 1903-31, cornet, composer, piano.
Rowland "Bunny" Berigan, 1908-42, trumpet.
Barney Bigard, 1906-80, clarinet.
Eubie Blake, 1883?-1983, composer, piano.
Art Blakey, 1919-90, drums, bandleader.
Jimmy Blanton, 1921-42, bass.
Charles "Buddy" Bolden, 1877-1931, cornet, pioneer bandleader.
Lester Bowie, 1941-99, trumpet, composer, bandleader.
Michael Brecker, 1949-2007, saxophone.
Big Bill Broonzy, 1893-1958, blues singer, guitar.
Clarence "Gatemouth" Brown, 1924-2005, guitar, singer.
Clifford Brown, 1930-56, trumpet.
Ray Brown, 1926-2002, bass.
Dave Brubeck, 1920-2012, piano, bandleader.
Don Byas, 1912-72, tenor sax.

Charlie Byrd, 1925-99, guitar; popularized bossa nova.
Cab Calloway, 1907-94, bandleader, singer.
Harry Carney, 1910-74, baritone sax, clarinet.
Benny Carter, 1907-2003, alto sax.
Betty Carter, 1930-98, jazz singer.
Sidney "Big Sid" Catlett, 1910-51, drums.
Adolphus Anthony "Doc" Cheatham, 1905-97, trumpet.
Don Cherry, 1936-95, trumpet.
Charlie Christian, 1916-42, guitar.
Kenny "Klook" Clarke, 1914-85, drums.
Buck Clayton, 1911-91, trumpet.
Al Cohn, 1925-88, tenor sax.
Nat "King" Cole, 1919-65, piano, singer.
William "Cozy" Cole, 1909-81, drums.
Ornette Coleman, 1930-2015, alto sax, composer.
Alice Coltrane, 1937-2007, piano, composer.
John Coltrane, 1926-67, tenor sax, soprano sax, composer.
Eddie Condon, 1905-73, guitar, bandleader.
Tadd Dameron, 1917-65, piano, composer.
Eddie "Lockjaw" Davis, 1921-86, tenor sax.
Miles Davis, 1926-91, trumpet, composer.
Wild Bill Davison, 1906-89, cornet.
Blossom Dearie, 1924-2009, singer.
Paul Desmond, 1924-77, alto sax.
Vic Dickenson, 1906-84, trombone.
Willie Dixon, 1915-92, composer, bass.
Johnny Dodds, 1892-1940, clarinet.
Warren "Baby" Dodds, 1898-1959, drums.
Eric Dolphy, 1928-64, alto sax, bass clarinet, flute.
Jimmy Dorsey, 1904-57, alto sax, bandleader.
Tommy Dorsey, 1905-56, trombone, bandleader.
Billy Eckstine, 1914-93, singer, bandleader.
Harry "Sweets" Edison, 1915-99, trumpet.
David "Honeyboy" Edwards, 1915-2011, guitar, singer.
Roy Eldridge, 1911-89, trumpet, singer.
Duke Ellington, 1899-1974, piano, bandleader, composer.
Bill Evans, 1929-80, piano.
Gil Evans, 1912-88, composer, arranger, piano.
Art Farmer, 1928-99, trumpet, flugelhorn.
Maynard Ferguson, 1926-2006, trumpet, bandleader.
Ella Fitzgerald, 1917-96, singer.
Tommy Flanagan, 1930-2001, piano.
Pete Fountain, 1930-2016, clarinetist.
Erroll Garner, 1921-77, piano, composer.
Stan Getz, 1927-91, tenor sax.
Dizzy Gillespie, 1917-93, trumpet, composer, singer.
Jimmy Giuffre, 1921-2008, clarinetist, composer.
Benny Goodman, 1909-86, clarinet, bandleader.
Dexter Gordon, 1923-90, tenor sax.
Stéphane Grappelli, 1908-97, violin.
Bobby Hackett, 1915-76, trumpet, cornet.
Lionel Hampton, 1908-2002, vibraphone, bandleader.
W. C. Handy, 1873-1958, composer.
Jimmy Harrison, 1900-31, trombone.
Coleman Hawkins, 1904-69, tenor sax.
Percy Heath, 1923-2005, bass.
Fletcher Henderson, 1898-1952, bandleader, arranger.
Woody Herman, 1913-87, clarinet, alto sax, bandleader.
Jay C. Higginbotham, 1906-73, trombone.
Ruiz Hilton, 1952-2006, piano, composer.
Earl "Fatha" Hines, 1903-83, piano.
Milt Hinton, 1910-2000, bass.
Al Hirt, 1922-99, trumpet.
Johnny Hodges, 1906-70, alto sax.
Billie Holiday, 1915-59, singer.
John Lee Hooker, 1917-2001, blues guitar, singer.
Sam "Lightnin'" Hopkins, 1912-82, blues singer, guitar.
Shirley Horn, 1934-2005, piano, singer.
Howlin' Wolf (Chester Burnett), 1910-76, blues singer, harmonica, guitar.
Alberta Hunter, 1895-1984, singer.
Mahalia Jackson, 1911-72, gospel singer.
Milt Jackson, 1923-99, vibraphone.
Elmore James, 1918-63, blues singer, guitar.
Etta James, 1938-2012, blues singer.
Al Jarreau, 1940-2017, jazz singer.
"Blind" Lemon Jefferson, 1897-1929, blues singer, guitar.
J. J. Johnson, 1924-2001, trombone.
James P. Johnson, 1891-1955, piano, composer.
Robert Johnson, 1912-38, blues singer, guitar.
William "Bunk" Johnson, 1879-1949, trumpet.
Elvin Jones, 1927-2004, drums.
Jo Jones, 1911-85, drums.
Philly Joe Jones, 1923-85, drums.
Thad Jones, 1923-86, cornet, bandleader, composer.
Scott Joplin, 1868-1917, ragtime composer.
Louis Jordan, 1908-75, singer, alto sax.
Stan Kenton, 1911-79, bandleader, composer, piano.
Barney Kessel, 1923-2004, guitar.
Albert King, 1923-92, blues guitar.
B. B. King, 1925-2015, blues guitar, singer.
John Kirby, 1908-52, bandleader, bass.
Rahsaan Roland Kirk, 1936-77, saxophone, composer.
Gene Krupa, 1909-73, drums, bandleader.
Scott LaFaro, 1936-61, bass.
Lead Belly (Huddie Ledbetter), 1888-1949, folk and blues singer, guitar.
Peggy Lee, 1920-2002, singer.
John Lewis, 1920-2001, piano, Modern Jazz Quartet founder.
Mel Lewis, 1929-90, drums, bandleader.
Jimmie Lunceford, 1902-47, bandleader.
Machito (Frank Grillo), 1908-84, Latin percussion, singer, bandleader.
Shelly Manne, 1920-84, drums, bandleader.
Ellis Marsalis Jr., 1934-2020, piano.
Jackie McLean, 1931-2006, saxophone, composer.
Jimmy McPartland, 1907-91, trumpet.
Marian McPartland, 1918-2013, pianist.
Carmen McRae, 1920-94, singer.
Glenn Miller, 1904-44, trombone, bandleader.
Charles Mingus, 1922-79, bass, composer, bandleader.
Thelonious Monk, 1917-82, piano, composer.
Wes Montgomery, 1925-68, guitar.
James Moody, 1925-2010, saxophone.
Ferdinand "Jelly Roll" Morton, 1885-1941, composer, piano.
Bennie Moten, 1894-1935, piano, bandleader.
Gerry Mulligan, 1927-96, baritone sax, composer.
Theodore "Fats" Navarro, 1923-50, trumpet.
Red Nichols, 1905-65, cornet, bandleader.
Red Norvo, 1908-99, vibraphone, xylophone, bandleader.
Anita O'Day, 1919-2006, singer.
Arturo "Chico" O'Farrill, 1921-2001, Latin composer, arranger.
King Oliver, 1885-1938, cornet, bandleader.
Sy Oliver, 1910-88, arranger, composer.
Edward "Kid" Ory, 1886-1973, trombone, bandleader.
Johnny Otis, 1921-2012, blues singer.
Oran "Hot Lips" Page, 1908-54, trumpet, singer.
Charlie "Bird" Parker, 1920-55, alto sax, composer.
Joe Pass, 1929-94, guitar.
Jaco Pastorius, 1951-87, bass guitarist.
Art Pepper, 1925-82, alto sax.
Pinetop Perkins, 1913-2011, piano.
Oscar Peterson, 1925-2007, piano.
Oscar Pettiford, 1922-60, bass.
Earl "Bud" Powell, 1924-66, piano.
Chano Pozo, 1915-48, percussionist, singer.
Louis Prima, 1911-78, singer, bandleader.
Tito Puente, 1923-2000, Latin percussion, bandleader.
Gertrude "Ma" Rainey, 1886-1939, blues singer.
Lou Rawls, 1933-2006, singer.
Dewey Redman, 1931-2006, tenor sax.
Don Redman (Robert Rodney Chudnick), 1900-64, composer, arranger.
Django Reinhardt, 1910-53, guitar.
Buddy Rich, 1917-87, drums.
Max Roach, 1924-2007, drums, composer.
Red Rodney (Robert Chudnick), 1927-94, trumpet.
Jimmy Rowles, 1918-96, piano.
Jimmy Rushing, 1903-72, blues and jazz singer.
Charles "Pee Wee" Russell, 1906-69, clarinet.
Artie Shaw, 1910-2004, swing-era bandleader, clarinet.
George Shearing, 1919-2011, piano.
Wayne Shorter, 1933-2023, tenor and soprano sax.
Nina Simone (Eunice Waymon), 1933-2003, singer.
John "Zoot" Sims, 1925-85, tenor sax.
Zutty Singleton, 1898-1975, drums.
Bessie Smith, 1894-1937, blues singer.
Clarence "Pinetop" Smith, 1904-29, piano, singer, boogie woogie pioneer.
Willie "The Lion" Smith, 1897-1973, piano, composer.
Francis "Muggsy" Spanier, 1906-67, cornet.
Edward "Sonny" Stitt, 1924-82, tenor sax, alto sax.
Billy Strayhorn, 1915-67, composer, piano, Duke Ellington collaborator.
Sun Ra (Herman Blount), 1915?-93, bandleader, piano, composer.
Art Tatum, 1910-56, piano.
Art Taylor, 1929-95, drums.
Billy Taylor, 1921-2010, piano.
Jack Teagarden, 1905-64, trombone, singer.
Clark Terry, 1920-2015, trumpet.
Mel Tormé, 1925-99, singer ("The Velvet Fog").
Dave Tough, 1908-48, drums.
Lennie Tristano, 1919-78, piano, composer.
Joe Turner, 1911-85, blues singer.
Sarah Vaughan, 1924-90, singer.
Joe Venuti, 1903-78, violin.
Aaron "T-Bone" Walker, 1910-75, blues guitar.
Thomas "Fats" Waller, 1904-43, piano, singer, composer.
Dinah Washington (Ruth Jones), 1924-63, singer.
Grover Washington Jr., 1943-99, pop-jazz sax, composer.
Ethel Waters, 1896-1977, jazz and blues singer.
Muddy Waters (McKinley Morganfield), 1915-83, blues singer, songwriter.
Julius Watkins, 1921-77, French horn.
William "Chick" Webb, 1902-39, bandleader, drums.
Ben Webster, 1909-73, tenor sax.
Junior Wells (Amos Blackmore), 1934-98, blues singer, harmonica.
Paul Whiteman, 1890-1967, bandleader.
Margaret Whiting, 1924-2011, singer.
Charles "Cootie" Williams, 1910-85, trumpet, bandleader.
Joe Williams, 1918-99, singer.
Mary Lou Williams, 1910-81, piano, composer.
Tony Williams, 1945-97, drums.
John Lee "Sonny Boy" Williamson, 1914-48, blues singer, harmonica.
Sonny Boy Williamson (Aleck "Rice" Miller), 1900?-65, blues singer, harmonica.
Teddy Wilson, 1912-86, piano.
Kai Winding, 1922-83, trombone.
Jimmy Yancey, 1894-1951, piano.
Lester "Pres" Young, 1909-59, tenor sax.

Country Music Artists of the Past and Present

* = Inducted into Country Music Hall of Fame (Nashville, TN) as performer between 1961 and 2024.

***Roy Acuff**, 1903-92, fiddler, singer, songwriter; "Wabash Cannon Ball."

***Alabama** (Jeff Cook, 1949-2022; Teddy Gentry, b 1952; Mark Herndon, b 1955; Randy Owen, b 1949); "Feels So Right."

Jason Aldean, b 1977, singer; "Don't You Wanna Stay."

***James "Whispering Bill" Anderson**, b 1937, singer, songwriter; "Make Mine Night Time."

***Eddy Arnold**, 1918-2008, singer, guitarist, known as the Tennessee Plowboy.

***Chet Atkins**, 1924-2001, guitarist, composer, producer; helped create the "Nashville sound."

***Gene Autry**, 1907-98, singing movie cowboy; "Back in the Saddle Again."

Clint Black, b 1962, singer, songwriter; "Killin' Time."

***Garth Brooks**, b 1962, singer, songwriter; "Friends in Low Places."

***Brooks & Dunn** (Kix Brooks, b 1955; Ronnie Dunn, b 1953); "Hard Workin' Man."

Kane Brown, b 1993, singer, songwriter; "Lose It."

Luke Bryan, b 1976, singer, songwriter; "Someone Else Calling You Baby."

***Boudleaux**, 1920-87, and **Felice Bryant**, 1925-2003, songwriting team; "Hey Joe."

***Glen Campbell**, 1936-2017, singer, guitarist; "Gentle on My Mind."

Brandi Carlile, b 1981, singer, songwriter; "The Joke."

Mary Chapin Carpenter, b 1958, singer, songwriter; "I Feel Lucky."

***Carter Family** (original members A. P., 1891-1960; "Mother" Maybelle, 1909-78; Sara, 1898-1979); "Wildwood Flower."

***Johnny Cash**, 1932-2003, singer, songwriter; "I Walk the Line," "Ring of Fire," "Folsom Prison Blues."

Kenny Chesney, b 1968, guitarist, singer, songwriter; "You Had Me From Hello."

The Chicks (fmr. Dixie Chicks) (Natalie Maines, b 1974; Emily Strayer, b 1972; Martie Maguire, b 1969); *Wide Open Spaces*.

Eric Church, b 1977, singer, songwriter, guitarist; "Record Year."

***Roy Clark**, 1933-2018, guitarist, banjoist, singer, co-host of *Hee Haw*; "Yesterday, When I Was Young."

***Patsy Cline**, 1932-63, singer; "Walkin' After Midnight," "Crazy," "Sweet Dreams."

Luke Combs, b 1990, singer, songwriter; "Beautiful Crazy."

Billy Ray Cyrus, b 1961, singer, songwriter; "Achy Breaky Heart."

***Charlie Daniels**, 1936-2020, guitarist, fiddler; "The Devil Went Down to Georgia."

***Jimmy Dean**, 1928-2010, singer; "Big Bad John."

John Denver, 1943-97, singer, songwriter; "Rocky Mountain High."

Dale Evans, 1912-2001, singer, actress, married Roy Rogers.

Sara Evans, b 1971, singer, songwriter; "Born to Fly."

***Flatt & Scruggs** (Lester Flatt, 1914-79; Earl Scruggs, 1924-2012), guitar-banjo duo and soloists; "Foggy Mountain Breakdown."

***Red Foley**, 1910-68, singer; "Chattanoogie Shoe Shine Boy."

***Tennessee Ernie Ford**, 1919-91, singer, TV host; "Sixteen Tons."

***William "Lefty" Frizzell**, 1928-75, singer, guitarist; "Long Black Veil."

***Vince Gill**, b 1957, singer, songwriter; "When I Call Your Name."

***Merle Haggard**, 1937-2016, singer, songwriter; "Okie From Muskogee."

***Emmylou Harris**, b 1947, singer, songwriter, folk-country crossover artist; "If I Could Only Win Your Love."

Hunter Hayes, b 1991, singer; "Wanted."

Faith Hill, b 1967, singer, songwriter; "Breathe."

***Alan Jackson**, b 1958, singer, songwriter; "Where Were You (When the World Stopped Turning)."

***Waylon Jennings**, 1937-2002, singer, songwriter, outlaw country pioneer; "Luckenbach, Texas."

***George Jones**, 1931-2013, singer; "He Stopped Loving Her Today."

***The Judds** (Naomi, 1946-2022; Wynonna, b 1964), mother-daughter duo; Wynonna also a solo act.

***Toby Keith**, 1961-2024, singer, songwriter, guitarist; "Should've Been a Cowboy."

Alison Krauss, b 1971, bluegrass fiddler, singer, bandleader; "When You Say Nothing at All."

***Kris Kristofferson**, b 1936, singer, songwriter, actor; "Me and Bobby McGee."

Lady A (fmr. Lady Antebellum) (Dave Haywood, b 1982; Charles Kelley, b 1981; Hillary Scott, b 1984); *Need You Now*.

Miranda Lambert, b 1983, singer, guitarist; "The House That Built Me."

***Louvin Brothers** (Charlie, 1927-2011; Ira, 1924-65), singers; "If I Could Only Win Your Love."

***Patty Loveless**, b 1957, singer, songwriter; "How Can I Help You Say Goodbye."

Lyle Lovett, b 1957, singer, songwriter, bandleader, actor; "Cowboy Man."

***Loretta Lynn**, 1932-2022, singer; "Coal Miner's Daughter."

***Barbara Mandrell**, b 1948, singer; "I Was Country When Country Wasn't Cool."

Kathy Mattea, b 1959, singer, songwriter; "Eighteen Wheels and a Dozen Roses."

Martina McBride, b 1966, singer, songwriter; "Independence Day."

***Reba McEntire**, b 1955, singer, songwriter, actress; "Whoever's in New England."

Tim McGraw, b 1967, singer; "It's Your Love," "I Like It, I Love It."

***Roger Miller**, 1936-92, singer, songwriter; "King of the Road."

***Ronnie Milsap**, b 1943, singer, songwriter; "There's No Gettin' Over Me."

***Bill Monroe**, 1911-96, singer, songwriter, mandolin player, "father of bluegrass music"; "Mule Skinner Blues."

Maren Morris, b 1990, singer, songwriter; "My Church."

Anne Murray, b 1945, singer; "You Needed Me."

Kacey Musgraves, b 1988, singer, songwriter; "Space Cowboy."

***Willie Nelson**, b 1933, singer, songwriter, actor; "On the Road Again."

Mark O'Connor, b 1961, fiddler, country-classical crossover composer.

***Buck Owens**, 1929-2006, singer, guitarist; "Act Naturally."

Brad Paisley, b 1972, singer, songwriter; "Whiskey Lullaby," "When I Get Where I'm Going."

***Dolly Parton**, b 1946, singer, songwriter, actress; "Here You Come Again," "9 to 5."

Johnny Paycheck (Don Lytle), 1938-2003, singer, guitarist; "Take This Job and Shove It."

***Minnie Pearl**, 1912-96, comedian, Grand Ole Opry star.

Kellie Pickler, b 1986, singer, songwriter.

***Ray Price**, 1926-2013, country singer, guitarist, songwriter; "Crazy Arms."

***Charley Pride**, 1934-2020, singer, first major Black country star; "Kiss an Angel Good Mornin'."

John Prine, 1946-2020, singer, songwriter; "Angel From Montgomery."

Eddie Rabbitt, 1941-98, singer, songwriter; "I Love a Rainy Night."

Rascal Flatts (Jay DeMarcus, b 1971; Gary LeVox, b 1970; Joe Don Rooney, b 1975); "Life Is a Highway"; "Rewind."

***Jim Reeves**, 1923-64, singer, songwriter; "Four Walls."

Thomas Rhett, b 1990, singer, songwriter.

Charlie Rich, 1932-95, singer, songwriter called the "Silver Fox"; "The Most Beautiful Girl."

LeAnn Rimes, b 1982, singer; *Blue*.

***Tex Ritter**, 1905-74, singer, songwriter; "Jingle, Jangle, Jingle."

***Marty Robbins**, 1925-82, singer, songwriter; "A White Sport Coat and a Pink Carnation."

***Jimmie Rodgers**, 1897-1933, singer, songwriter; "T for Texas."

***Kenny Rogers**, 1938-2020, singer, songwriter; "The Gambler."

***Roy Rogers** (Leonard Slye), 1911-98, singer, actor, "King of the Cowboys," sang with Sons of the Pioneers.

***Fred Rose**, 1898-1954, songwriter, singer, producer; "Blue Eyes Cryin' in the Rain."

Blake Shelton, b 1976, singer; "Home."

***Ricky Skaggs**, b 1954, singer, songwriter, bandleader; "Don't Cheat in Our Hometown."

Ralph Stanley, 1927-2016, singer, banjo player; "Man of Constant Sorrow."

Chris Stapleton, b 1978, singer, songwriter; *Traveller*.

***George Strait**, b 1952, singer, bandleader; "Ace in the Hole."

Sugarland (Kristian Bush, b 1970; Jennifer Nettles, b 1974); "Stay."

Taylor Swift, b 1989, singer, songwriter; "You Belong With Me."

***Lonnie "Mel" Tillis**, 1932-2017, singer, songwriter, bandleader; "I Ain't Never."

***Merle Travis**, 1917-83, singer, guitarist, songwriter; "Divorce Me C.O.D."

***Randy Travis**, b 1959, singer, songwriter; "Forever and Ever, Amen."

***Ernest Tubb**, 1914-84, singer, songwriter, guitarist; "Walking the Floor Over You."

***Tanya Tucker**, b 1958, singer, songwriter; "Delta Dawn."

Josh Turner, b 1977, singer; "Why Don't We Just Dance."

Shania Twain, b 1965, singer, songwriter; "You're Still the One."

***Conway Twitty**, 1933-93, singer, songwriter; "Hello Darlin'."

Carrie Underwood, b 1983, singer, songwriter; *American Idol* winner.

Keith Urban, b 1967, guitarist, singer, songwriter; "Somebody Like You."

***Porter Wagoner**, 1927-2007, singer, songwriter, guitarist; "Soul of a Convict."

***Kitty Wells** (Ellen Deason), 1919-2012, singer, songwriter; "It Wasn't God Who Made Honky-Tonk Angels."

***Dottie West**, 1932-91, singer, songwriter; "Here Comes My Baby."

***Hank Williams Jr.**, b 1949, singer, songwriter; "Bocephus"; "All My Rowdy Friends (Have Settled Down)."

***Hank Williams Sr.**, 1923-53, singer, songwriter; "Your Cheatin' Heart."

***Bob Wills**, 1905-75, Western Swing fiddler, singer, bandleader, songwriter; "New San Antonio Rose."

Lainey Wilson, b 1992, singer, songwriter; "Things a Man Oughta Know."

Lee Ann Womack, b 1966, singer, songwriter; "I Hope You Dance."

***Tammy Wynette**, 1942-98, singer; "Stand By Your Man."

Trisha Yearwood, b 1964, singer, songwriter; "How Do I Live."

Dwight Yoakam, b 1957, singer, songwriter, actor; "Ain't That Lonely Yet."

Zac Brown Band (Coy Bowles, b 1979; Zac Brown, b 1978; Clay Cook, b 1978; Jimmy De Martini, b 1976; Chris Fryar, b 1970; John Driskell Hopkins, b 1971); "Chicken Fried."

Dance Figures of the Past

Alvin Ailey, 1931-89, (U.S.) modern dancer, choreographer; melded modern dance and Afro-Caribbean techniques.
Alicia Alonso, 1920-2019, (Cuba) ballerina, founder of National Ballet of Cuba.
Frederick Ashton, 1904-88, (Br.) ballet choreographer; director of Great Britain's Royal Ballet, 1963-70.
Fred Astaire, 1899-1987, dancer, actor; teamed with dancer/actress **Ginger Rogers**, 1911-95, (both U.S.) in movie musicals.
George Balanchine, 1904-83, (Russ.-U.S.) ballet choreographer, teacher; most influential exponent of neoclassical style; founded, with Lincoln Kirstein, School of American Ballet and New York City Ballet.
Pina Bausch, 1940-2009, (Ger.) modern dance choreographer influencing the Tanztheater style of dance.
Carlo Blasis, 1795-1878, (It.) ballet dancer, choreographer, writer; his teaching methods are standards of classical dance.
August Bournonville, 1805-79, (Den.) ballet dancer, choreographer, teacher; exuberant, light style.
Fernando Bujones, 1955-2005, (Cuba-U.S.) ballet dancer.
Gisella Caccialanza, 1914-98, (U.S.) ballerina; charter member of Balanchine's American Ballet.
Irene, 1893-1969, (U.S.) and **Vernon Castle**, 1887-1918, (Br.) husband-and-wife ballroom dancers.
Enrico Cecchetti, 1850-1928, (It.) ballet dancer, leading dancer of Russia's Imperial Ballet; his technique was basis for Britain's Imperial Soc. of Teachers of Dancing.
Gower, 1921-80, dancer, choreographer, director; with wife **Marge Champion**, 1919-2020, (both U.S.) choreographed, danced in Broadway musicals and films.
John Cranko, 1927-73, (S. Afr.) choreographer; created narrative ballets based on literary works.
Merce Cunningham, 1919-2009, (U.S.) dancer, choreographer of avant-garde dance.
Jacques d'Amboise, 1934-2021, (U.S.) ballet dancer, choreographer.
Alexandra Danilova, 1903-97, (Russ.) ballerina; noted teacher at the School of American Ballet.
Agnes de Mille, 1905-93, (U.S.) ballerina, choreographer; known for using American themes, she choreographed the ballet *Rodeo* and the musical *Oklahoma!*
Dame Ninette De Valois, 1898-2001, (Br.) choreographer, founding director of London's Royal Ballet; *The Rake's Progress*.
Sergei Diaghilev, 1872-1929, (Russ.) impresario; founded Les Ballet Russes; saw ballet as art unifying dance, drama, music, and decor.
Isadora Duncan, 1877-1927, (U.S.) expressive dancer who united free movement with serious music; one of the founders of modern dance.
Katherine Dunham, 1910-2006, (U.S.) dancer, choreographer; internationally known for African, Caribbean, and African American dance forms.
Fanny Elssler, 1810-84, (Austria) ballerina of the Romantic era; known for dramatic skill, sensual style.
Michel Fokine, 1880-1942, (Russ.) ballet dancer, choreographer, teacher; rejected strict classicism in favor of dramatically expressive style.
Margot Fonteyn, 1919-91, (Br.) prima ballerina, Royal Ballet of Great Britain; famed performance partner of Rudolf Nureyev.
Bob Fosse, 1927-87, (U.S.) jazz dancer, choreographer, director; Broadway musicals and film.
Serge Golovine, 1924-98, (Fr.) ballet dancer with Grand Ballet du Marquis de Cuevas, choreographer.
Martha Graham, 1894-1991, (U.S.) modern dancer, choreographer; created and codified her own dramatic technique.
Melissa Hayden, 1923-2006, (Can.) ballet dancer.
Martha Hill, 1900-95, (U.S.) educator; leading figure in modern dance; founded American Dance Festival.
Gregory Hines, 1946-2003, (U.S.) tap-dance innovator; master of improvisation.
Doris Humphrey, 1895-1958, (U.S.) modern dancer, choreographer, writer, teacher.
Michael Jackson, 1958-2009, (U.S.) singer and dancer who perfected the "moonwalk."
Robert Joffrey, 1930-88, ballet dancer, choreographer; cofounded with **Gerald Arpino**, 1928-2008, (both U.S.) the Joffrey Ballet.
Kurt Jooss, 1901-79, (Ger.) choreographer, teacher; created expressionist works using modern and classical techniques.
Tamara Karsavina, 1885-1978, (Russ.) prima ballerina of Russia's Imperial Ballet and Diaghilev's Ballets Russes; partner of Nijinsky.
Nora Kaye, 1920-87, (U.S.) ballerina with Metropolitan Opera Ballet and Ballet Theater (now American Ballet Theatre).
Gene Kelly, 1912-96, (U.S.) dancer, actor in movie musicals.
Michael Kidd, 1915-2003, (U.S.) dancer, film and theater choreographer.
Lincoln Kirstein, 1907-96, (U.S.) brought ballet as an art form to U.S.; founded, with George Balanchine, School of American Ballet and New York City Ballet.
Serge Lifar, 1905-86, (Russ.-Fr.) prem. danseur, choreographer; director of dance at Paris Opera, 1930-45, 1947-58.
José Limón, 1908-72, (Mex.-U.S.) modern dancer, choreographer, teacher; developed technique based on Humphrey.
Catherine Littlefield, 1908-51, (U.S.) ballerina, choreographer, teacher; pioneer of American ballet.
Kenneth MacMillan, 1929-92, (Br.) dancer, choreographer; directed Royal Ballet of Great Britain, 1970-77.
Dame Alicia Markova, 1910-2004, (Br.) ballerina known for title role in *Giselle*; helped popularize ballet in U.S. and Britain.
Léonide Massine, 1896-1979, (Russ.-U.S.) ballet dancer, choreographer; known for his "symphonic ballet."
Arthur Mitchell, 1934-2018, (U.S.) dancer, choreographer; cofounded Dance Theatre of Harlem.
Fayard Nicholas, 1914-2006, tap dancer, choreographer, actor; together with brother **Harold Nicholas**, 1921-2000, (both U.S.) formed the Nicholas Brothers.
Vaslav Nijinsky, 1890-50, (Russ.) prem. danseur, choreographer; leading member of Diaghilev's Ballets Russes; his ballets were revolutionary for their time.
Alwin Nikolais, 1910-93, (U.S.) modern choreographer; created dance theater utilizing mixed media effects.
Jean-George Noverre, 1727-1810, (Fr.) ballet choreographer, teacher, writer; "Shakespeare of the Dance."
Rudolf Nureyev, 1938-93, (Russ.) prem. danseur, choreographer; leading male dancer of his generation; director of dance at Paris Opera, 1983-89.
Ruth Page, 1899-1991, (U.S.) ballerina, choreographer; danced, directed ballet at Chicago Lyric Opera.
Anna Pavlova, 1881-1931, (Russ.) prima ballerina; toured with her own company to world acclaim.
Marius Petipa, 1818-1910, (Fr.) ballet dancer, choreographer; ballet master of the Imperial Ballet; established Russian classicism as leading style of late 19th cent.
Roland Petit, 1924-2011, (Fr.) dancer, choreographer; founder of Les Ballets de Paris.
Pearl Primus, 1919-95, (Trinidad-U.S.) modern dancer, choreographer, scholar; combined African, Caribbean, and African American styles.
Jerome Robbins, 1918-98, (U.S.) choreographer, director, dancer; *The King and I*, *West Side Story*, *Fiddler on the Roof*.
Bill "Bojangles" Robinson, 1878-1949, (U.S.) famed tap dancer; called "King of Tapology" on stage and screen.
Ruth St. Denis, 1877-1968, (U.S.) influential interpretive dancer, choreographer, teacher.
Ted Shawn, 1891-1972, (U.S.) modern dancer, choreographer; formed dance company and school with Ruth St. Denis; established Jacob's Pillow Dance Festival.
Marie Taglioni, 1804-84, (It.) ballerina, teacher; in title role of *La Sylphide* established image of the ethereal ballerina.
Maria Tallchief, 1925-2013, (U.S.) prima ballerina, 1st of Amer. Indian descent.
Marjorie Tallchief, 1926-2021, (U.S.) prima ballerina.
Paul Taylor, 1930-2018, (U.S.) dancer, choreographer, teacher.
Glen Tetley, 1926-2007, (U.S.) dancer, choreographer, ballet director; fused elements of modern dance with ballet.
Antony Tudor, 1908-87, (Br.) choreographer, teacher; exponent of the "psychological ballet."
Galina Ulanova, 1910-98, (Russ.) revered ballerina with Bolshoi Ballet.
Agrippina Vaganova, 1879-1951, (Russ.) ballet teacher, director called "queen of variations"; codified Soviet ballet technique.
Mary Wigman, 1886-1973, (Ger.) modern dancer, choreographer, teacher; influenced European expressionist dance.

Opera Singers of the Past

Licia Albanese, 1909-2014, (It.) soprano.
Frances Alda, 1879-1952, (N.Z.) soprano.
Pasquale Amato, 1878-1942, (It.) baritone.
Marian Anderson, 1897-1993, (U.S.) contralto.
Charles Anthony, 1929-2012, (U.S.) tenor.
Jussi Björling, 1911-60, (Swed.) tenor.
Lucrezia Bori, 1887-1960, (It.) soprano.
Grace Bumbry, 1937-2023, (U.S.) mezzo-soprano.
Montserrat Caballé, 1933-2018, (Sp.) soprano.
Maria Callas, 1923-77, (U.S.) soprano.
Emma Calvé, 1858-1942, (Fr.) soprano.
Enrico Caruso, 1873-1921, (It.) tenor.
Feodor Chaliapin, 1873-1938, (Russ.) bass.
Lili Chookasian, 1921-2012, (U.S.) contralto.
Boris Christoff, 1914-93, (Bulg.) bass.
Franco Corelli, 1921-2003, (It.) tenor.
Hughes Cuenod, 1902-2010, (Switz.) tenor.
Victoria De Los Angeles, 1923-2005, (Sp.) soprano.
Giuseppe De Luca, 1876-1950, (It.) baritone.
Fernando De Lucia, 1860-1925, (It.) tenor.
Edouard De Reszke, 1853-1917, (Pol.) bass.
Jean De Reszke, 1850-1925, (Pol.) tenor.
Emmy Destinn, 1878-1930, (Czech.) soprano.
Mattiwilda Dobbs, 1925-2015, (U.S.) coloratura soprano.
Emma Eames, 1865-1952, (U.S.) soprano.
(Carlo Broschi) Farinelli, 1705-82, (It.) castrato.
Geraldine Farrar, 1882-1967, (U.S.) soprano.
Eileen Farrell, 1920-2002, (U.S.) soprano.
Kathleen Ferrier, 1912-53, (Eng.) contralto.
Dietrich Fischer-Dieskau, 1925-2012, (Ger.) baritone.
Kirsten Flagstad, 1895-1962, (Nor.) soprano.

2024 YEAR *in* PICTURES

WORLD

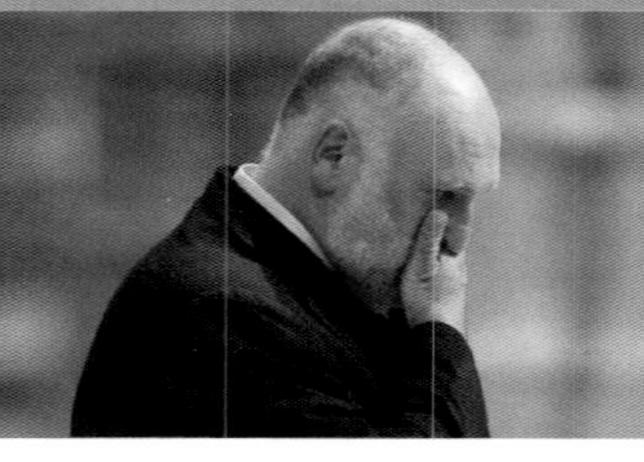

DAMAGES DONE
According to the UN as of Aug. 19, 2024, more than 280 aid workers had died in Gaza since Oct. 7, 2023, including seven hunger-relief workers with chef José Andrés's World Central Kitchen, killed by Israeli airstrikes Apr. 1, 2024.

FORCE TO RECKON WITH The Israeli offensive in Gaza, aimed at dismantling Hamas after its shock attack on Israel killed more than 1,200 people in Oct. 2023, left thousands dead and major cities like Khan Yunis all but destroyed by Apr. 2024.

RELIEF NEEDED With millions of Gaza residents internally displaced and humanitarian aid deliveries limited by the ongoing war, by May 2024, parts of Gaza were facing "full-blown famine," according to the leader of the UN's World Food Program.

DANGER ZONE
Israeli strikes on Hezbollah in Lebanon expanded and accelerated in late Sept. 2024, raising fears of an even broader regional conflict.

RUSSIAN OPPOSITION MOURNS Thousands attended the Mar. 1, 2024, funeral of Russian opposition leader Alexei Navalny, who had survived a prior assassination attempt but died at an Arctic Circle penal colony in Feb. 2024.

ONCE IN A LIFETIME North America witnessed a dramatic total solar eclipse Apr. 8, 2024; NASA estimated that 31.6 mil people lived within the 115-mi wide path of totality and another 150 million people within 200 miles.

TAIWAN DISASTER A powerful, 7.4 magnitude earthquake destroyed parts of eastern Taiwan Apr. 3, 2024.

TERRORISM IN MOSCOW An affilitate of the Sunni terror group ISIS claimed responsibility for a Mar. 22, 2024, attack on a Moscow concert venue that killed more than 140 people.

WORLD

MAKING HISTORY Mexico elected its first woman and first Jewish president, Claudia Sheinbaum, by a wide margin on June 2, 2024.

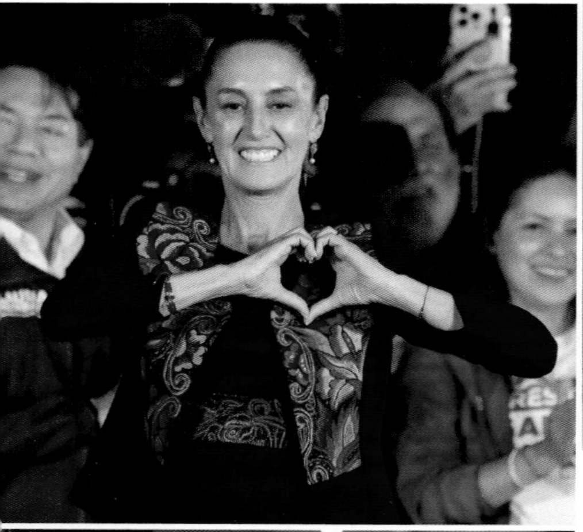

CHANGING OF THE GUARD The Labour Party's victory in July 4, 2024, elections ended 14 years of Conservative government in the UK; Labour leader Keir Starmer replaced Rishi Sunak as prime minister July 5.

NEW IRANIAN LEADER Reformist candidate Masoud Pezeshkian secured Iran's presidency in runoff voting July 5, 2024, replacing Pres. Ebrahim Raisi, who died in a May 2024 helicopter crash.

HOMECOMING DAY WikiLeaks founder Julian Assange returned to his native Australia June 26, 2024; following years in custody over U.S. Espionage Act and other charges, he pleaded guilty and was sentenced to time served and released.

UKRAINE FIGHT CONTINUES Ukrainian forces made a surprise incursion into Russia's Kursk region beginning Aug. 6, 2024, marking the first time since World War II that Russian territory had been occupied.

NEITHER FREE NOR FAIR Opposition leader Maria Corina Machado (barred from running) and presidential candidate Edmundo González campaigned to oust incumbent Pres. Nicolás Maduro in Venezuela's July 28, 2024, elections.

CLOSING RANKS A late alliance of left-wing parties prevented the far-right National Rally party from taking power in France's snap legislative elections held June 30 and July 7, 2024.

MANY HAPPY RETURNS *Wall Street Journal* reporter Evan Gershkovich returned to the U.S. Aug. 1, 2024, in a 26-person prisoner swap after 16 months in Russian custody.

NATIONAL

GUILTY VERDICT A New York jury returned a guilty verdict for former Pres. Donald Trump May 30, 2024, on 34 counts of falsifying business records related to hush-money payments, making him the first U.S. president ever convicted of a felony.

FALLING DOWN
A large container ship Mar. 26, 2024, struck a supporting pier of Baltimore's Francis Scott Key Bridge, collapsing the 47-year-old structure and killing six workers.

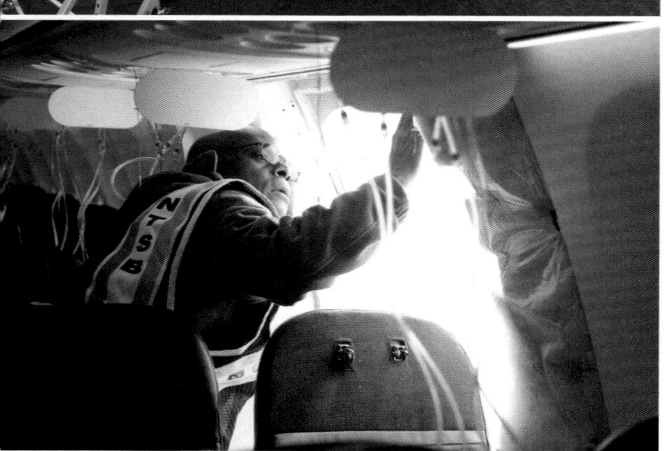

FLIGHT RISK
A door-sized section of a Boeing 737 MAX 9 blew off 10 minutes after takeoff from Portland, OR, on Jan. 5, 2024; similar models were grounded by federal regulators amid ongoing investigations into the aerospace giant.

MASTER OF THE SENATE Senate Minority Leader Mitch McConnell (R, KY) announced Feb. 28, 2024, that he would step down as Republican leader following the Nov. elections, after 18 years of party leadership.

CROSSING OVER Even as border crossing numbers fell dramatically after new asylum restrictions were announced in mid-2024, U.S. immigration policy remained a topic of high interest in the election year.

LODGE A PROTEST Pro-Palestinian protesters at Columbia Univ. in New York City set up an encampment beginning Apr. 17, 2024; according to CNN, more than 2,400 protesters at over 50 campuses were arrested in similar protests by May 7.

FLOODED OUT Hurricane Helene swept across the southeast U.S. Sept. 26-29, 2024, leaving high water, destruction, and more than 230 people dead in communities from coastal Florida to mountainous North Carolina and Tennessee.

SMOKING GUN A federal jury in Delaware June 11, 2024, convicted Hunter Biden, son of Pres. Joe Biden, on three counts related to a gun purchase in 2018.

"THANK YOU, JOE"
Just weeks after Pres. Joe Biden announced he would withdraw from the race, he appeared on the first night of the Democratic National Convention, Aug. 19, 2024, in Chicago, to restate his endorsement of Vice Pres. Kamala Harris.

THE DEMOCRATIC TICKET
Vice Pres. Kamala Harris named Minnesota Gov. Tim Walz her vice presidential pick on Aug. 6, 2024; the ticket came together with fewer than 100 days left before Election Day.

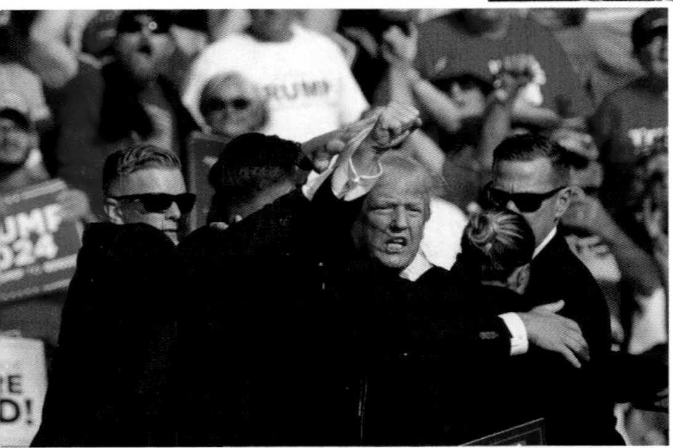

CLOSE CALL A shooter targeted former Pres. Donald Trump July 13, 2024, at a campaign rally in Butler, PA; one spectator and the shooter were killed, and Trump and two rally attendees were injured.

THE REPUBLICAN TICKET
Former Pres. Donald Trump named Sen. JD Vance (R, OH) his vice presidential pick on July 15, 2024, the first day of the Republican National Convention in Milwaukee, WI.

Olive Fremstad, 1871-1951, (Swed.-U.S.) soprano.
Amelita Galli-Curci, 1882-1963, (It.) soprano.
Mary Garden, 1874-1967, (Br.) soprano.
Nicolai Gedda, 1925-2017, (Swed.) tenor.
Nicolai Ghiaurov, 1929-2004, (Bulg.) bass.
Beniamino Gigli, 1890-1957, (It.) tenor.
Tito Gobbi, 1913-84, (It.) baritone.
Giulia Grisi, 1811-69, (It.) soprano.
Frieda Hempel, 1885-1955, (Ger.) soprano.
Jerome Hines, 1921-2003, (U.S.) bass.
Hans Hotter, 1909-2003, (Ger.) bass-baritone.
Maria Jeritza, 1887-1982, (Czech.) soprano.
Sena Jurinac, 1921-2011, (Yugo.) soprano.
Alexander Kipnis, 1891-1978, (Russ.-U.S.) bass.
Dorothy Kirsten, 1910-92, (U.S.) soprano.
Alfredo Kraus, 1927-99, (Sp.) tenor.
Luigi Lablache, 1794-1858, (It.) bass.
Lilli Lehmann, 1848-1929, (Ger.) soprano.
Lotte Lehmann, 1888-1976, (Ger.-U.S.) soprano.
Jenny Lind, 1820-87, (Swed.) soprano.
Christa Ludwig, 1924-2021, (Ger.) mezzo-soprano.
Cornell MacNeil, 1922-2011, (U.S.) baritone.
Maria Malibran, 1808-36, (Sp.) mezzo-soprano.
Giovanni Martinelli, 1885-1969, (It.) tenor.
John McCormack, 1884-1945, (Ire.) tenor.
Nellie Melba, 1861-1931, (Austral.) soprano.
Lauritz Melchior, 1890-1973, (Den.) tenor.
Robert Merrill, 1919-2004, (U.S.) baritone.
Zinka Milanov, 1906-89, (Yugo.) soprano.
Patrice Munsel, 1925-2015, (U.S.) coloratura soprano.
Patricia Neway, 1919-2012, (U.S.) soprano.
Birgit Nilsson, 1918-2005, (Swed.) soprano.
Lillian Nordica, 1857-1914, (U.S.) soprano.
Jessye Norman, 1945-2019, (U.S.) soprano.
Magda Olivero, 1910-2014, (It.) soprano.
Giuditta Pasta, 1797-1865, (It.) soprano.
Adelina Patti, 1843-1919, (It.) soprano.
Luciano Pavarotti, 1935-2007, (It.) tenor.
Peter Pears, 1910-86, (Eng.) tenor.
Jan Peerce, 1904-84, (U.S.) tenor.
Roberta Peters, 1930-2017, (U.S.) soprano.
Ezio Pinza, 1892-1957, (It.) bass.
Lily Pons, 1898-1976, (Fr.) soprano.
Rosa Ponselle, 1897-1981, (U.S.) soprano.
Hermann Prey, 1929-98, (Ger.) baritone.
Margaret Price, 1941-2011, (Br.) soprano.
Regina Resnik, 1922-2013, (U.S.) soprano turned mezzo-soprano.
Elisabeth Rethberg, 1894-1976, (Ger.) soprano.
Giovanni Battista Rubini, 1794-1854, (It.) tenor.
Leonie Rysanek, 1926-98, (Austria) soprano.
Dorothy Sarnoff, 1914-2008, (U.S.) soprano.
Bidú Sayão, 1902-99, (Braz.) soprano.
Friedrich Schorr, 1888-1953, (Hung.) bass-baritone.
Elisabeth Schwarzkopf, 1915-2006, (Ger.) soprano.
Renata Scotto, 1934-2023, (It.) soprano.
Marcella Sembrich, 1858-1935, (Pol.) soprano.
Cesare Siepi, 1923-2010, (It.) bass.
Beverly Sills, 1929-2007, (U.S.) soprano.
Elisabeth Söderström, 1927-2009, (Swed.) soprano.
Eleanor Steber, 1914-90, (U.S.) soprano.
Risë Stevens, 1913-2013, (U.S.) mezzo-soprano.
Joan Sutherland, 1926-2010, (Austral.) soprano.
Ferrucio Tagliavini, 1913-95, (It.) tenor.
Renata Tebaldi, 1922-2004 (It.) soprano.
Luisa Tetrazzini, 1871-1940, (It.) soprano.
Lawrence Tibbett, 1896-1960, (U.S.) baritone.
Giorgio Tozzi, 1923-2011, (U.S.) bass-baritone.
Tatiana Troyanos, 1938-93, (U.S.) mezzo-soprano.
Richard Tucker, 1913-75, (U.S.) tenor.
Shirley Verrett, 1931-2010, (U.S.) mezzo-soprano.
Pauline Viardot, 1821-1910, (Fr.) mezzo-soprano.
Jon Vickers, 1926-2015, (Can.) tenor.
William Warfield, 1920-2002, (U.S.) bass-baritone.
Leonard Warren, 1911-60, (U.S.) baritone.
Ljuba Welitsch, 1913-96, (Bulg.) soprano.
Camilla Williams, 1919-2012, (U.S.) soprano.
Wolfgang Windgassen, 1914-74, (Ger.) tenor.

Rock 'n' Roll, Rhythm and Blues, and Rap Artists

Titles in quotation marks are singles; others are albums. * = Inducted into Rock & Roll Hall of Fame as performer between 1986 and 2024; year is in parentheses.

***ABBA** (2010): "Dancing Queen"
Paula Abdul: "Straight Up"
***AC/DC** (2003): "Back in Black"
Bryan Adams: "Cuts Like a Knife"
Adele: "Rolling in the Deep"
***Aerosmith** (2001): "Sweet Emotion"
Christina Aguilera: "What a Girl Wants"
Alice in Chains: "Heaven Beside You"
***The Allman Brothers Band** (1995): "Ramblin' Man"
***The Animals** (1994): "House of the Rising Sun"
Paul Anka: "Lonely Boy"
Fiona Apple: "Criminal"
Frankie Avalon: "Venus"
Iggy Azalea: "Fancy"
The B-52s: "Love Shack"
Bachman Turner Overdrive: "Takin' Care of Business"
Backstreet Boys: "I Want It That Way"
Bad Company: "Can't Get Enough"
Erykah Badu: "On and On"
***Joan Baez** (2017): "The Night They Drove Old Dixie Down"
***La Vern Baker** (1991): "I Cried a Tear"
***Hank Ballard[1] and the Midnighters** (1990): "Work With Me, Annie"
***The Band** (1994): "The Weight"
Barenaked Ladies: "One Week"
***The Beach Boys** (1988): "Good Vibrations"
***Beastie Boys** (2012): "(You Gotta) Fight for Your Right (to Party)"
***The Beatles** (1988): *Sgt. Pepper's Lonely Hearts Club Band*
Beck: "Loser"
***Jeff Beck** (2009): "Escape"
***The Bee Gees** (1997): "Stayin' Alive"
***Pat Benatar** (2022): "Hit Me With Your Best Shot"
***Chuck Berry** (1986): "Johnny B. Goode"
Beyoncé: "Crazy in Love"
The Big Bopper: "Chantilly Lace"
Björk: "Human Behavior"
The Black Crowes: "Hard to Handle"
Black Eyed Peas: *Elephunk*
***Black Sabbath** (2006): "Paranoid"
***Bobby "Blue" Bland** (1992): "Turn On Your Love Light"
***Mary J. Blige** (2024): *My Life*
Blind Faith: "Can't Find My Way Home"
Blink-182: "All the Small Things"
***Blondie** (2006): "Heart of Glass"
Blood, Sweat, and Tears: "Spinning Wheel"
Blues Traveler: "Run-Around"
Gary "U.S." Bonds: "Quarter to Three"
***Bon Jovi** (2018): "Livin' on a Prayer"
***Booker T. and the M.G.'s** (1992): "Green Onions"
Boston: "More Than a Feeling"
***David Bowie** (1996): "Space Oddity"
Boyz II Men: "I'll Make Love to You"
Toni Braxton: "Un-Break My Heart"
Chris Brown: "Kiss Kiss"
***James Brown** (1986): "Papa's Got a Brand New Bag"
***Ruth Brown** (1993): "Lucky Lips"
***Jackson Browne** (2004): "Doctor My Eyes"
***Buffalo Springfield** (1997): "For What It's Worth"
***Jimmy Buffett** (2024): "Margaritaville"
***Solomon Burke** (2001): "Over and Over (Huggin' and Lovin')"
***The Paul Butterfield Blues Band** (2015): "Born in Chicago"
***The Byrds** (1991): "Turn! Turn! Turn!"
Cardi B: "Bodak Yellow"
Mariah Carey: "Always Be My Baby"
The Carpenters: "(They Long to Be) Close to You"
***The Cars** (2018): "Shake It Up"
***Johnny Cash** (1992): "I Walk the Line"
***Ray Charles** (1986): "Georgia on My Mind"
***Cheap Trick** (2016): "Surrender"
Chubby Checker: "The Twist"
***Cher** (2024): "Believe"
***Chicago** (2016): "Saturday in the Park"
***Eric Clapton** (2000): "Layla"
Kelly Clarkson: "Since U Been Gone"
***The Clash** (2003): "Rock the Casbah"
***Jimmy Cliff** (2010): "I Can See Clearly Now"
***The Coasters** (1987): "Yakety Yak"
***Eddie Cochran** (1987): "Summertime Blues"
Joe Cocker: "With a Little Help From My Friends"
***Leonard Cohen** (2008): "Suzanne"
Coldplay: "Clocks"
Collective Soul: "The World I Know"
Phil Collins: "Against All Odds"
***Sam Cooke** (1986): "You Send Me"
Coolio: "Gangsta's Paradise"
***Alice Cooper** (2011): "School's Out"
***Elvis Costello and the Attractions** (2003): "Alison"
Counting Crows: "Mr. Jones"
***Cream** (1993): "Sunshine of Your Love"
Creed: "Arms Wide Open"
***Creedence Clearwater Revival** (1993): "Proud Mary"
***Crosby, Stills and Nash** (1997): "Suite: Judy Blue Eyes"
***Sheryl Crow** (2023): "All I Want to Do"
The Crystals: "Da Doo Ron Ron"
***The Cure** (2019): "Boys Don't Cry"
Daft Punk: "Get Lucky"
Danny and the Juniors: "At the Hop"
***Bobby Darin** (1990): "Splish Splash"
Daughtry: "It's Not Over"
***The Dave Clark Five** (2008): "Glad All Over"
***Dave Matthews Band** (2024): "Don't Drink the Water"
***Miles Davis** (2006): *Bitches Brew*
Spencer Davis Group: "Gimme Some Lovin'"
***Deep Purple** (2016): "Smoke on the Water"
***Def Leppard** (2019): "Photograph"
***The Dells** (2004): "Oh, What a Night"
***Depeche Mode** (2020): "Strange Love"
Destiny's Child: "Survivor"
***Neil Diamond** (2011): "Cracklin' Rosie"
***Bo Diddley** (1987): "Who Do You Love?
***Dion[1] and the Belmonts** (1989): "A Teenager in Love"
Celine Dion: "Because You Loved Me"
***Dire Straits** (2018): "Money for Nothing"
DMX: "What's My Name"
Doja Cat: "Kiss Me More"
***Fats Domino** (1986): "Blueberry Hill"
***Donovan** (2012): "Mellow Yellow"
***The Doobie Brothers** (2020): "What a Fool Believes"
***The Doors** (1993): "Light My Fire"
Dr. Dre: "Nothin' But a 'G' Thang"
***Dr. John** (2011): "Right Place, Wrong Time"
Drake: "Hotline Bling"
***The Drifters** (1988): "Save the Last Dance for Me"
***Duran Duran** (2022): "Hungry Like the Wolf"
***Bob Dylan** (1988): "Like a Rolling Stone"
***The Eagles** (1998): "Hotel California"
***Earth, Wind, and Fire** (2000): "Shining Star"
***Duane Eddy** (1994): "Rebel-Rouser"
Billie Eilish: "Bad Guy"
***Electric Light Orchestra** (2017): "Don't Bring Me Down"
***Missy Elliott** (2023): "Sock It 2 Me"
***Eminem** (2022): "The Real Slim Shady"
En Vogue: "Hold On"
***The Eurythmics** (2022): "Sweet Dreams (Are Made of This)"
Everclear: "Father Of Mine"
***The Everly Brothers** (1986): "Wake Up, Little Susie"
50 Cent (Curtis Jackson): *Get Rich or Die Tryin'*
The Five Satins: "In the Still of the Night"
Roberta Flack: "The First Time Ever I Saw Your Face"
***The Flamingos** (2001): "I Only Have Eyes for You"
***Fleetwood Mac** (1998): *Rumours*
***The Foo Fighters** (2021): "I'll Stick Around"
***Foreigner** (2024): "Double Vision"
***The Four Seasons** (1990): "Sherry"

***The Four Tops** (1990): "I Can't Help Myself (Sugar Pie, Honey Bunch)"
***Peter Frampton** (2024): *Frampton Comes Alive!*
***Aretha Franklin** (1987): "Respect"
fun.: "We Are Young"
Nelly Furtado: "I'm Like a Bird"
***Peter Gabriel** (2014): "Shock the Monkey"
***Gamble (Kenny) and Huff (Leon)** (2008): "If You Don't Know Me by Now"
***Marvin Gaye** (1987): "I Heard It Through the Grapevine"
***Genesis** (2010): "No Reply at All"
***The Go-Go's** (2021): "We Got the Beat"
Goo Goo Dolls: "Iris"
Grand Funk Railroad: "We're an American Band"
***Grandmaster Flash and the Furious Five** (2007): "The Message"
***The Grateful Dead** (1994): "Uncle John's Band"
***Al Green** (1995): "Let's Stay Together"
***Green Day** (2015): "Boulevard of Broken Dreams"
The Guess Who: "American Woman"
***Guns N' Roses** (2012): "Sweet Child o' Mine"
***Buddy Guy** (2005): *A Man and His Blues*
***Bill Haley[1] and His Comets** (1987): "Rock Around the Clock"
***Hall (Darryl) and Oates (John)** (2014): "Kiss on My List"
***George Harrison** (2004): "My Sweet Lord"
***Isaac Hayes** (2002): "Theme From 'Shaft'"
***Heart** (2013): "Barracuda"
***Jimi Hendrix** (1992): "Purple Haze"
Lauryn Hill: "Doo-Wop (That Thing)"
***The Hollies** (2010): "Long Cool Woman (In a Black Dress)"
***Buddy Holly** (1986): "Peggy Sue"
***John Lee Hooker** (1991): "Boogie Chillen"
Hootie and the Blowfish: *Cracked Rear View*
***Whitney Houston** (2020): "I Will Always Love You"
***The Impressions** (1991): "For Your Precious Love"
Indigo Girls: "Closer to Fine"
INXS: "Need You Tonight"
***The Isley Brothers** (1992): "It's Your Thing"
Ja Rule: *Venni, Vetti, Vecci*
***The Jackson Five** (1997): "ABC"
***Janet Jackson** (2019): *Rhythm Nation*
***Michael Jackson** (2001): *Thriller*
***Etta James** (1993): "At Last"
Tommy James and the Shondells: "Crimson and Clover"
Jane's Addiction: "Jane Says"
Jay and the Americans: "This Magic Moment"
***Jay Z** (2021): "99 Problems"
***Jefferson Airplane** (1996): "White Rabbit"
Jethro Tull: *Aqualung*
***Joan Jett and the Blackhearts** (2015): "I Love Rock 'n' Roll"
Jewel: "You Were Meant for Me"
***Billy Joel** (1999): "Piano Man"
***Elton John** (1994): "Candle in the Wind"
***Little Willie John** (1996): "Sleep"
Norah Jones: *Come Away With Me*
***Janis Joplin** (1995): "Me and Bobby McGee"
***Journey** (2017): "Don't Stop Believin'"
K.C. and the Sunshine Band: "Get Down Tonight"
R. Kelly: "I Can't Sleep Baby (If I)"
Alicia Keys: "Fallin'"
Kid Rock: "Cowboy"
***B. B. King** (1987): "The Thrill Is Gone"
***Carole King** (2021): *Tapestry*
***The Kinks** (1990): "You Really Got Me"
***Kiss** (2014): "Rock 'n' Roll All Night"
***Gladys Knight and the Pips** (1996): "Midnight Train to Georgia"
***Kool & the Gang** (2024): "Celebration"
Korn: "Blind"
Lenny Kravitz: "Are You Gonna Go My Way?"
Lady Gaga: "Poker Face"
Kendrick Lamar: *DAMN*.
***Led Zeppelin** (1995): "Stairway to Heaven"
***Brenda Lee** (2002): "I'm Sorry"
John Legend: "Ordinary People"
***John Lennon** (1994): "Imagine"
***Jerry Lee Lewis** (1986): "Whole Lotta Shakin' Going On"
Lil' Kim: "No Matter What They Say"
Lil Nas X: "Old Town Road"
Lil Wayne: *Tha Block Is Hot*
Limp Bizkit: "Break Stuff"
Linkin Park: "One Step Closer"
Dua Lipa: "Levitating"
***Little Anthony and the Imperials** (2009): "Tears on My Pillow"
***Little Richard** (1986): "Tutti Frutti"
***Little Walter** (2008): "Juke"
Lizzo: "Truth Hurts"
LL Cool J: "Mama Said Knock You Out"
Jennifer Lopez: "Love Don't Cost a Thing"
***Darlene Love** (2011): "He's a Rebel"
***The Lovin' Spoonful** (2000): "Summer in the City"
Ludacris: "Money Maker"
***Frankie Lymon and the Teenagers** (1993): "Why Do Fools Fall in Love?"
***Lynyrd Skynyrd** (2006): "Free Bird"
***Madonna** (2008): "Material Girl"
***The Mamas and the Papas** (1998): "Monday, Monday"
Marilyn Manson: "Beautiful People"
***Bob Marley** (1994): *Exodus*
Maroon 5: "Moves Like Jagger"
Bruno Mars: "Just the Way You Are"
***Martha and the Vandellas** (1995): "Dancin' in the Streets"
The Marvelettes: "Please, Mr. Postman"
Matchbox 20: "Push"
John Mayer: "Daughters"
***Curtis Mayfield** (1999): "Superfly"
***Paul McCartney** (1999): "Band on the Run"
Don McLean: "American Pie"
***Clyde McPhatter** (1987): "A Lover's Question"
Meat Loaf: "Paradise by the Dashboard Light"
Megan Thee Stallion: "Savage"
***John (Cougar) Mellencamp** (2008): "Jack and Diane"
Men at Work: "Who Can It Be Now?"
***Metallica** (2009): "Enter Sandman"
***George Michael** (2023): "Faith"
***Steve Miller** (2016): "Take the Money and Run"
Nicki Minaj: *Pink Friday*
***Joni Mitchell** (1997): *Blue*
Moby: "Bodyrock"
Janelle Monáe: "Make Me Feel"
The Monkees: "I'm a Believer"
***Moody Blues** (2018): "Nights in White Satin"
***The Moonglows** (2000): "Blue Velvet"
Alanis Morissette: "Ironic"
***Van Morrison** (1993): "Brown-Eyed Girl"
Mötley Crüe: "Live Wire"
Motörhead: "Ace of Spades"
Jason Mraz: "I'm Yours"
Mumford & Sons: "Little Lion Man"
Nelly: *Country Grammar*
***Ricky Nelson** (1987): "Hello, Mary Lou"
***Stevie Nicks** (2019): "Edge of Seventeen"
***Nine Inch Nails** (2020): "Closer"
***Nirvana** (2014): *Nevermind*
No Doubt: *Rock Steady*
***The Notorious B.I.G.** (2020): "Mo Money Mo Problems"
NSYNC: "Bye, Bye, Bye"
Ted Nugent: "Stranglehold"
***N.W.A.** (2016): "Straight Outta Compton"
***The O'Jays** (2005): "Back Stabbers"
One Direction: "What Makes You Beautiful"
***Roy Orbison** (1987): "Oh, Pretty Woman"
***Ozzy Osbourne** (2024): "Crazy Train"
OutKast: *Speakerboxxx/The Love Below*
***Parliament/Funkadelic** (1997): "One Nation Under a Groove"
***Pearl Jam** (2017): *Ten*
***Carl Perkins** (1987): "Blue Suede Shoes"
Katy Perry: "Firework"
Peter, Paul, and Mary: "Leaving on a Jet Plane"
***Tom Petty and the Heartbreakers** (2002): "Refugee"
Liz Phair: *Exile in Guyville*
Phish: "Sample in a Jar"
***Wilson Pickett** (1991): "Land of 1,000 Dances"
Pink: *Missundaztood*
***Pink Floyd** (1996): *The Wall*
***Gene Pitney** (2002): "Only Love Can Break a Heart"
***The Platters** (1990): "The Great Pretender"
The Pointer Sisters: "I'm So Excited"
***The Police** (2003): "Every Breath You Take"
Iggy Pop: "Lust for Life"
***Elvis Presley** (1986): "Love Me Tender"
***The Pretenders** (2005): "Back on the Chain Gang"
***Lloyd Price** (1998): "Stagger Lee"
***Prince** (2004): "Purple Rain"
***Public Enemy** (2013): "Fight the Power"
Puff Daddy and the Family: *No Way Out*
***Queen** (2001): "Bohemian Rhapsody"
***Radiohead** (2019): *OK Computer*
***Rage Against the Machine** (2023): "Bulls on Parade"
***Bonnie Raitt** (2000): "Something to Talk About"
***The Ramones** (2002): "I Wanna Be Sedated"
***Red Hot Chili Peppers** (2012): "Under the Bridge"
***Otis Redding** (1989): "(Sittin' on) The Dock of the Bay"
***Jimmy Reed** (1991): "Ain't That Loving You, Baby?"
***Lou Reed** (2015): "Walk on the Wild Side"
***R.E.M.** (2007): "Losing My Religion"
REO Speedwagon: "Can't Fight This Feeling"
Busta Rhymes: "What's It Gonna Be?"
***The Righteous Brothers** (2003): "You've Lost That Lovin' Feelin' "
Rihanna: "Umbrella"
Johnny Rivers: "Poor Side of Town"
***Smokey Robinson[1] and the Miracles** (1987): "Shop Around"
***The Rolling Stones** (1989): "Satisfaction"
***The Ronettes** (2007): "Be My Baby"
***Linda Ronstadt** (2014): "You're No Good"
Diana Ross: "I'm Coming Out"
***Roxy Music** (2019): "Love Is the Drug"
***Todd Rundgren** (2021): "Hello It's Me"
***Run-DMC** (2009): "Raisin' Hell"
***Rush** (2013): "Tom Sawyer"
Sade: "Smooth Operator"
Salt-N-Pepa: "Shoop"
***Sam and Dave** (1992): "Soul Man"
***Santana** (1998): "Black Magic Woman"
Seal: "Kiss From a Rose"
Neil Sedaka: "Breaking Up Is Hard to Do"
***Bob Seger** (2004): "Old Time Rock & Roll"
***Sex Pistols** (2006): "Anarchy in the UK"
Shakira: "Whenever, Wherever"
***Tupac Shakur** (2017): "How Do U Want It"
***Del Shannon** (1999): "Runaway"
Ed Sheeran: "Thinking Out Loud"
***The Shirelles** (1996): "Soldier Boy"
***Carly Simon** (2022): "You're So Vain"
***Paul Simon** (2001): "50 Ways to Leave Your Lover"
***Simon and Garfunkel** (1990): "Bridge Over Troubled Water"
***Nina Simone** (2018): "Mississippi Goddamn"
***Percy Sledge** (2005): "When a Man Loves a Woman"
***Sly and the Family Stone** (1993): "Everyday People"
Smashing Pumpkins: "Today"
***Patti Smith** (2007): "Because the Night"
Sam Smith: "Stay With Me"
Will Smith: "Gettin' Jiggy With It"
The Smiths: "This Charming Man"
Snoop Dogg (a.k.a. Snoop Lion, Snoopzilla): "Gin and Juice"
Sonic Youth: "Bull in the Heather"
Soundgarden: "Black Hole Sun"
Britney Spears: "Hit Me Baby One More Time"
Spice Girls: "Wannabe"
***Dusty Springfield** (1999): "I Only Want to Be With You"
***Bruce Springsteen** (1999): "Born to Run"
***Staple Singers** (1999): "I'll Take You There"
***Steely Dan** (2001): "Rikki Don't Lose That Number"
Gwen Stefani: "Hollaback Girl"
Steppenwolf: "Born to Be Wild"
***Cat Stevens** (2014): "Wild World"
***Rod Stewart** (1994): "Maggie Mae"
Sting: "If You Love Somebody, Set Them Free"
Stone Temple Pilots: "Plush"
***The Stooges** (2010): "I Wanna Be Your Dog"
Styx: "Come Sail Away"
The Sugar Hill Gang: "Rapper's Delight"
***Donna Summer** (2013): "Bad Girls"
***The Supremes** (1988): "Stop! In the Name of Love"
Taylor Swift: "Shake It Off"
***Talking Heads** (2002): "Once in a Lifetime"
***James Taylor** (2001): "You've Got a Friend"
***The Temptations** (1989): "My Girl"
Robin Thicke: "Blurred Lines"
Three Dog Night: "Joy to the World"
Justin Timberlake: "SexyBack"
TLC: "Waterfalls"
***Traffic** (2004): *Traffic*
***T. Rex** (2020): "Bang a Gong (Get It On)"
***A Tribe Called Quest** (2024): "Check the Rhime"
***Big Joe Turner** (1987): "Shake, Rattle & Roll"
***Ike and Tina Turner** (1991): "Proud Mary"
***Tina Turner** (2021): "What's Love Got to Do With It"

The Turtles: "Happy Together"
***U2** (2005): "With or Without You"
Usher: "You Make Me Wanna"
***Ritchie Valens** (2001): "La Bamba"
***Van Halen** (2007): "Running With the Devil"
***Stevie Ray Vaughan & Double Trouble** (2015): "Change It"
***The Velvet Underground** (1996): "Sweet Jane"
***The Ventures** (2008): "Walk, Don't Run"
***Gene Vincent** (1998): "Be-Bop-A-Lula"
***Tom Waits** (2011): "Downtown Train"
The Wallflowers: "One Headlight"
***Dionne Warwick** (2024): "I Say a Little Prayer"
***Muddy Waters** (1987): "I Can't Be Satisfied"
Mary Wells: "My Guy"
Kanye West: "Gold Digger"
The White Stripes: "Seven Nation Army"
Whitesnake: "Here I Go Again"
***The Who** (1990): *Tommy*
Pharrell Williams: "Happy"
***Jackie Wilson** (1987): "That's Why"
***Bill Withers** (2015): "Lean on Me"
***Bobby Womack** (2009): "Lookin' for a Love"
***Stevie Wonder** (1989): "You Are the Sunshine of My Life"
Wu-Tang Clan: "Protect Ya Neck"
***The Yardbirds** (1992): "For Your Love"
***Yes** (2017): "Owner of a Lonely Heart"
***Neil Young** (1995): "Down by the River"
***The Young Rascals/The Rascals** (1997): "Good Lovin'"
***Frank Zappa[1]/Mothers of Invention** (1995): *Hot Rats*
***The Zombies** (2019): "She's Not There"
***ZZ Top** (2004): "Legs"

(1) Only individual performer is in Rock and Roll Hall of Fame.

Entertainment Personalities of the Present

Living actors, musicians, dancers, singers, producers, directors, and radio-TV performers.

Name	Birthplace	Birthdate
Abdul, Paula	San Fernando, CA	6/19/1962
Abraham, F. Murray	Pittsburgh, PA	10/24/1939
Abrams, J(effrey) J(acob)	New York, NY	6/27/1966
Adams, Amy	Vicenza, Italy	8/20/1974
Adams, Bryan	Kingston, ON, Canada	11/5/1959
Adams, Yolanda	Houston, TX	8/27/1961
Adele	London, England, UK	5/5/1988
Adjani, Isabelle	Paris, France	6/27/1955
Ad-Rock	South Orange, NJ	10/31/1966
Aduba, Uzo	Boston, MA	2/10/1981
Affleck, Ben	Berkeley, CA	8/15/1972
Affleck, Casey	Falmouth, MA	8/12/1975
Aghdashloo, Shohreh	Tehran, Iran	5/11/1952
Aguilera, Christina	Staten Island, NY	12/18/1980
Ahmed, Riz	Wembley, Eng., UK	12/1/1982
Aiken, Clay	Raleigh, NC	11/30/1978
Alba, Jessica	Pomona, CA	4/28/1981
Alberghetti, Anna Maria	Pesaro, Italy	5/15/1936
Albert, Marv	Brooklyn, NY	6/12/1941
Alda, Alan	New York, NY	1/28/1936
Alexander, Jane	Boston, MA	10/28/1939
Alexander, Jason	Newark, NJ	9/23/1959
Ali, Mahershala	Oakland, CA	2/16/1974
Allen, Debbie	Houston, TX	1/16/1950
Allen, Joan	Rochelle, IL	8/20/1956
Allen, Karen	Carrollton, IL	10/5/1951
Allen, Tim	Denver, CO	6/13/1953
Allen, Woody	Bronx, NY	12/1/1935
Alpert, Herb	Los Angeles, CA	3/31/1935
Almodóvar, Pedro	Calzada de Calatrava, Spain	9/24/1949
Ambrose, Lauren	New Haven, CT	2/20/1978
Amos, Tori	Newton, NC	8/22/1963
Anderson, Anthony	Los Angeles, CA	8/15/1970
Anderson, Gillian	Chicago, IL	8/9/1968
Anderson, Ian	Dunfermline, Scotland, UK	8/10/1947
Anderson, Loni	St. Paul, MN	8/5/1945
Anderson, Melissa Sue	Berkeley, CA	9/26/1962
Anderson, Pamela	Ladysmith, BC, Canada	7/1/1967
Anderson, Richard Dean	Minneapolis, MN	1/23/1950
Anderson, Wes	Houston, TX	5/1/1969
André 3000	Atlanta, GA	5/27/1975
Andress, Ursula	Bern, Switzerland	3/19/1936
Andrews, Julie	Walton-on-Thames, Surrey, England, UK	10/1/1935
Andrews, Naveen	London, England, UK	1/17/1969
Aniston, Jennifer	Sherman Oaks, CA	2/11/1969
Anka, Paul	Ottawa, ON, Canada	7/30/1941
Ann-Margret	Stockholm, Sweden	4/28/1941
Ansari, Aziz	Columbia, SC	2/23/1983
Anthony, Marc	New York, NY	9/16/1968
Apatow, Judd	Syosset, NY	12/6/1967
Apple, Fiona	New York, NY	9/13/1977
Applegate, Christina	Los Angeles, CA	11/25/1971
Archer, Anne	Los Angeles, CA	8/24/1947
Arkin, Adam	Brooklyn, NY	8/19/1956
Armisen, Fred	Hattiesburg, MS	12/4/1966
Armitage, Iain	Savannah, GA	7/15/2008
Arnaz, Desi, Jr.	Hollywood, CA	1/19/1953
Arnaz, Lucie	Hollywood, CA	7/17/1951
Arnett, Will	Toronto, ON, Canada	5/4/1970
Arnold, Tom	Ottumwa, IA	3/6/1959
Arquette, David	Winchester, VA	9/8/1971
Arquette, Patricia	Chicago, IL	4/8/1968
Arquette, Rosanna	New York, NY	8/10/1959
Arroyo, Martina	New York, NY	2/2/1937
Ashanti (Douglas)	Glen Cove, NY	10/13/1980
Ashford, Annaleigh	Denver, CO	6/25/1985
Ashley, Elizabeth	Ocala, FL	8/30/1939
Assante, Armand	New York, NY	10/4/1949
Astin, John	Baltimore, MD	3/30/1930
Astin, Sean	Santa Monica, CA	2/25/1971
Atkins, Eileen	London, England, UK	6/16/1934
Atkinson, Rowan	Newcastle upon Tyne, Eng., UK	1/6/1955
Austin, Patti	New York, NY	8/10/1948
Avalon, Frankie	Philadelphia, PA	9/18/1940
Awkwafina	Stony Brook, NY	6/2/1988
Aykroyd, Dan	Ottawa, ON, Canada	7/1/1952
Azalea, Iggy	Sydney, NSW, Australia	6/7/1990
Azaria, Hank	Forest Hills, Queens, NY	4/25/1964
Babyface	Indianapolis, IN	4/10/1959
Baccarin, Morena	Rio de Janeiro, Brazil	6/2/1979
Bacon, Kevin	Philadelphia, PA	7/8/1958
Bad Bunny	Almirante Sur, PR	3/10/1994
Badalucco, Michael	Brooklyn, NY	12/20/1954
Bader, Diedrich	Alexandria, VA	12/24/1966
Badu, Erykah	Dallas, TX	2/26/1971
Baez, Joan	Staten Island, NY	1/9/1941
Bailey, Jonathan	Wallingford, Eng., UK	4/25/1988
Baio, Scott	Brooklyn, NY	9/22/1960
Baker, Anita	Toledo, OH	1/26/1958
Baker, Carroll	Johnstown, PA	5/28/1931
Baker, Diane	Hollywood, CA	2/25/1938
Baker, Joe Don	Groesbeck, TX	2/12/1936
Baker, Kathy	Midland, TX	6/8/1950
Baker, Simon	Launceston, Tas., Australia	7/30/1969
Bakula, Scott	St. Louis, MO	10/9/1954
Baldwin, Alec	Massapequa, NY	4/3/1958
Baldwin, Daniel	Massapequa, NY	10/5/1960
Baldwin, Stephen	Massapequa, NY	5/12/1966
Baldwin, William	Massapequa, NY	2/21/1963
Bale, Christian	Pembrokeshire, Wales, UK	1/30/1974
Balfe, Caitriona	Dublin, Ireland	10/4/1979
Ballas, Mark	Houston, TX	5/24/1986
Bana, Eric	Melbourne, Vic., Australia	8/9/1968
Banderas, Antonio	Málaga, Spain	8/10/1960
Banks, Elizabeth	Pittsfield, MA	2/10/1974
Banks, Jonathan	Washington, DC	1/31/1947
Banks, Tyra	Los Angeles, CA	12/4/1973
Baranski, Christine	Buffalo, NY	5/2/1952
Barbeau, Adrienne	Sacramento, CA	6/11/1945
Bardem, Javier	Las Palmas, Canary Islands, Spain	3/1/1969
Bardot, Brigitte	Paris, France	9/28/1934
Barkin, Ellen	Bronx, NY	4/16/1955
Barrie, Barbara	Chicago, IL	5/23/1931
Barrino, Fantasia	High Point, NC	6/30/1984
Barrymore, Drew	Los Angeles, CA	2/22/1975
Bartlett, Murray	Sydney, NSW, Australia	3/20/1971
Bartoli, Cecilia	Rome, Italy	6/4/1966
Barton, Mischa	London, England, UK	1/24/1986
Baryshnikov, Mikhail	Riga, Latvia	1/28/1948
Basinger, Kim	Athens, GA	12/8/1953
Bass, Lance	Laurel, MS	5/4/1979
Bassett, Angela	New York, NY	8/16/1958
Bassey, Shirley	Cardiff, Wales, UK	1/8/1937
Bateman, Jason	Rye, NY	1/14/1969
Bateman, Justine	Rye, NY	2/19/1966
Bates, Kathy	Memphis, TN	6/28/1948
Batiste, Jon	New Orleans, LA	11/11/1986
Batt, Bryan	New Orleans, LA	3/1/1963
Battle, Kathleen	Portsmouth, OH	8/13/1948
Baxter, Meredith	South Pasadena, CA	6/21/1947
Bean, Sean	Sheffield, England, UK	4/17/1959
Beatty, Warren	Richmond, VA	3/30/1937
Beauvais, Garcelle	St. Marc, Haiti	11/26/1966
Beck	Los Angeles, CA	7/8/1970
Beckham, Victoria	Hertfordshire, England, UK	4/17/1974
Beckinsale, Kate	London, England, UK	7/26/1973
Bedelia, Bonnie	New York, NY	3/25/1948
Bee, Samantha	Toronto, ON, Canada	10/25/1969
Begley, Ed, Jr.	Los Angeles, CA	9/16/1949
Behar, Joy	Brooklyn, NY	10/7/1942
Bell, Kristen	Huntington Woods, MI	7/18/1980
Bello, Maria	Norristown, PA	4/18/1967

Name	Birthplace	Birthdate
Belushi, Jim	Chicago, IL	6/15/1954
Benanti, Laura	Kinnelon, NJ	7/15/1979
Benatar, Pat	Brooklyn, NY	1/10/1953
Benedict, Dirk	Helena, MT	3/1/1945
Benigni, Roberto	Misericordia, Italy	10/27/1952
Bening, Annette	Topeka, KS	5/29/1958
Benjamin, Richard	New York, NY	5/22/1938
Bennett, Alan	Leeds, England, UK	5/9/1934
Benson, George	Pittsburgh, PA	3/22/1943
Benson, Robby	Dallas, TX	1/21/1956
Berenger, Tom	Chicago, IL	5/31/1950
Bergen, Candice	Beverly Hills, CA	5/9/1946
Bergeron, Tom	Haverhill, MA	5/6/1955
Bernard, Crystal	Garland, TX	9/30/1961
Bernhard, Sandra	Flint, MI	6/6/1955
Bernsen, Corbin	North Hollywood, CA	9/7/1954
Bernthal, Jon	Washington, DC	9/20/1976
Berry, Halle	Cleveland, OH	8/14/1966
Bertinelli, Valerie	Wilmington, DE	4/23/1960
Best, Eve	London, England, UK	7/31/1971
Bettany, Paul	London, England, UK	5/27/1971
Bialik, Mayim	San Diego, CA	12/12/1975
Bichir, Demián	Mexico City, Mexico	8/1/1963
Bieber, Justin	Stratford, ON, Canada	3/1/1994
Biel, Jessica	Ely, MN	3/3/1982
Big Boi	Savannah, GA	2/1/1975
Bigelow, Kathryn	San Carlos, CA	11/27/1951
Biggs, Jason	Pompton Plains, NJ	5/12/1978
Bilson, Rachel	Los Angeles, CA	8/25/1981
Binoche, Juliette	Paris, France	3/9/1964
Birch, Thora	Beverly Hills, CA	3/11/1982
Bisset, Jacqueline	Weybridge, England, UK	9/13/1944
Björk (Gudmundsdottir)	Reykjavik, Iceland	11/21/1965
Black, Clint	Long Branch, NJ	2/4/1962
Black, Jack	Santa Monica, CA	8/28/1969
Black, Lewis	Washington, DC	8/30/1948
Blades, Ruben	Panama City, Panama	7/16/1948
Blair, Linda	St. Louis, MO	1/22/1959
Blanchett, Cate	Melbourne, Vic., Australia	5/14/1969
Bledel, Alexis	Houston, TX	9/16/1981
Bledsoe, Tempestt	Chicago, IL	8/1/1973
Bleeth, Yasmine	New York, NY	6/14/1968
Blethyn, Brenda	Ramsgate, Kent, Eng., UK	2/20/1946
Blige, Mary J.	Bronx, NY	1/11/1971
Bloom, Claire	London, England, UK	2/15/1931
Bloom, Orlando	Canterbury, England, UK	1/13/1977
Bloom, Rachel	Manhattan Beach, CA	4/3/1987
Blunt, Emily	London, England, UK	2/23/1983
Blyth, Ann	Mt. Kisco, NY	8/16/1928
Bocelli, Andrea	Lajatico, Italy	9/22/1958
Bogosian, Eric	Woburn, MA	4/24/1953
Bolton, Michael	New Haven, CT	2/26/1953
Bomer, Matt	Spring, TX	10/11/1977
Bon Jovi, Jon	Sayreville, NJ	3/2/1962
Bonaduce, Danny	Broomall, PA	8/13/1959
Bonet, Lisa	San Francisco, CA	11/16/1967
Bonham Carter, Helena	London, England, UK	5/26/1966
Bonneville, Hugh	London, England, UK	11/10/1963
Bono	Dublin, Ireland	5/10/1960
Boone, Debby	Hackensack, NJ	9/22/1956
Boone, Pat	Jacksonville, FL	6/1/1934
Boreanaz, David	Buffalo, NY	5/16/1969
Borstein, Alex	Chicago, IL	2/15/1971
Bostwick, Barry	San Mateo, CA	2/24/1945
Bosworth, Kate	Los Angeles, CA	1/2/1983
Bottoms, Timothy	Santa Barbara, CA	8/30/1951
Bow Wow	Columbus, OH	3/9/1987
Bowen, Julie	Baltimore, MD	3/3/1970
Boxleitner, Bruce	Elgin, IL	5/12/1950
Boy George	Bexleyheath, England, UK	6/14/1961
Boyle, Danny	Manchester, England, UK	10/20/1956
Boyle, Lara Flynn	Davenport, IA	3/24/1970
Boyle, Susan	Blackburn, Scotland, UK	4/1/1961
Bracco, Lorraine	Brooklyn, NY	10/2/1955
Brady, Wayne	Orlando, FL	6/2/1972
Braff, Zach	South Orange, NJ	4/6/1975
Branagh, Kenneth	Belfast, N. Ireland, UK	12/10/1960
Brand, Russell	Grays, Essex, UK	6/4/1975
Brandauer, Klaus Maria	Steiermark, Austria	6/22/1944
Brandy (Norwood)	McComb, MS	2/11/1979
Bratt, Benjamin	San Francisco, CA	12/16/1963
Braxton, Toni	Severn, MD	10/7/1966
Bremner, Ewen	Edinburgh, Scotland, UK	1/23/1972
Brendon, Nicholas	Los Angeles, CA	4/12/1971
Brenneman, Amy	Glastonbury, CT	6/22/1964
Bridges, Beau	Los Angeles, CA	12/9/1941
Bridges, Jeff	Los Angeles, CA	12/4/1949
Brightman, Sarah	Berkhamsted, England, UK	8/14/1960
Brinkley, Christie	Monroe, MI	2/2/1954
Britton, Connie	Boston, MA	3/6/1967
Broadbent, Jim	Lincolnshire, England, UK	5/24/1949
Broderick, Matthew	New York, NY	3/21/1962
Brody, Adam	San Diego, CA	12/15/1979
Brody, Adrien	New York, NY	4/14/1973

Name	Birthplace	Birthdate
Brolin, James	Los Angeles, CA	7/18/1940
Brolin, Josh	Los Angeles, CA	2/12/1968
Brooks, Albert	Beverly Hills, CA	7/22/1947
Brooks, Garth	Tulsa, OK	2/7/1962
Brooks, James L.	North Bergen, NJ	5/9/1940
Brooks, Mel	Brooklyn, NY	6/28/1926
Brosnahan, Rachel	Milwaukee, WI	12/15/1990
Brosnan, Pierce	Navan, Co. Meath, Ireland	5/16/1953
Brown, Blair	Washington, DC	4/23/1946
Brown, Bobby	Roxbury, MA	2/5/1969
Brown, Bryan	Panania, NSW, Australia	6/23/1947
Brown, Chris	Tappahannock, VA	5/5/1989
Brown, Foxy	Brooklyn, NY	9/6/1979
Brown, Millie Bobby	Marbella, Spain	2/19/2004
Brown, Sterling K.	St. Louis, MO	4/5/1976
Browne, Jackson	Heidelberg, Germany	10/9/1948
Bruckheimer, Jerry	Detroit, MI	9/21/1943
Brunson, Quinta	Philadelphia, PA	12/21/1989
Bryan, Luke	Leesburg, GA	7/17/1976
Bryson, Peabo	Greenville, SC	4/13/1951
Bublé, Michael	Burnaby, BC, Canada	9/9/1975
Buckley, Betty	Big Spring, TX	7/3/1947
Bujold, Genevieve	Montréal, QC, Canada	7/1/1942
Bullock, Sandra	Arlington, VA	7/26/1964
Bündchen, Gisele	Horizontina, Brazil	7/20/1980
Burgess, Tituss	Athens, GA	2/21/1979
Burghoff, Gary	Bristol, CT	5/24/1943
Burke, Cheryl	San Francisco, CA	5/3/1984
Burke, Delta	Orlando, FL	7/30/1956
Burnett, Carol	San Antonio, TX	4/26/1933
Burns, Edward	Woodside, Queens, NY	1/29/1968
Burns, Ken	New York, NY	7/29/1953
Burrell, Ty	Grants Pass, OR	8/22/1967
Burstyn, Ellen	Detroit, MI	12/7/1932
Burton, LeVar	Landstuhl, Germany	2/16/1957
Burton, Tim	Burbank, CA	8/25/1958
Buscemi, Steve	Brooklyn, NY	12/13/1957
Busey, Gary	Goose Creek, TX	6/29/1944
Busfield, Timothy	Lansing, MI	6/12/1957
Bush, Kate	Welling, England, UK	7/30/1958
Butler, Austin	Anaheim, CA	8/17/1991
Butler, Brett	Montgomery, AL	1/30/1958
Butler, Dan	Fort Wayne, IN	12/2/1954
Butler, Gerard	Glasgow, Scotland, UK	11/13/1969
Butz, Norbert Leo	St. Louis, MO	1/30/1967
Buzzi, Ruth	Westerly, RI	7/24/1936
Bynes, Amanda	Thousand Oaks, CA	4/3/1986
Byrne, David	Dumbarton, Scotland, UK	5/14/1952
Byrne, Gabriel	Dublin, Ireland	5/12/1950
Byrne, Rose	Sydney, NSW, Australia	7/24/1979
Cage, Nicolas	Long Beach, CA	1/7/1964
Cain, Dean	Mt. Clemens, MI	7/31/1966
Caine, Michael	London, England, UK	3/14/1933
Callies, Sarah Wayne	LaGrange, IL	6/1/1977
Callow, Simon	London, England, UK	6/15/1949
Cameron, James	Kapuskasing, ON, Can.	8/16/1954
Cameron, Kirk	Panorama City, CA	10/12/1970
Campbell, Bruce	Royal Oak, MI	6/22/1958
Campbell, Naomi	South London, Eng., UK	5/22/1970
Campbell, Neve	Guelph, ON, Canada	10/3/1973
Campion, Jane	Waikanae, New Zealand	4/30/1954
Cannavale, Bobby	Union City, NJ	5/3/1971
Cannon, Dyan	Tacoma, WA	1/4/1937
Cannon, Nick	San Diego, CA	10/8/1980
Caplan, Lizzy	Los Angeles, CA	6/30/1982
Capshaw, Kate	Ft. Worth, TX	11/3/1953
Cardellini, Linda	Redwood City, CA	6/25/1975
Cardi B	New York, NY	10/11/1992
Cardinale, Claudia	Tunis, Tunisia	4/15/1938
Carell, Steve	Concord, MA	8/16/1962
Carey, Drew	Cleveland, OH	5/23/1958
Carey, Mariah	Huntington, NY	3/27/1970
Cariou, Len	St. Boniface, MB, Can.	9/30/1939
Carlile, Brandi	Ravensdale, WA	6/1/1981
Carlton, Vanessa	Milford, PA	8/16/1980
Caron, Leslie	Boulogne, France	7/1/1931
Carpenter, John	Carthage, NY	1/16/1948
Carpenter, Mary Chapin	Princeton, NJ	2/21/1958
Carr, Vikki	El Paso, TX	7/19/1941
Carreras, Jose	Barcelona, Spain	12/5/1946
Carrere, Tia	Honolulu, HI	1/2/1967
Carrey, Jim	Newmarket, ON, Canada	1/17/1962
Carter, Jim	Harrogate, Yorkshire, England, UK	8/19/1948
Carter, Lynda	Phoenix, AZ	7/24/1951
Carter, Nick	Jamestown, NY	1/28/1980
Carter, Ron	Ferndale, MI	5/4/1937
Cartwright, Nancy	Kettering, OH	10/25/1957
Caruso, David	Forest Hills, Queens, NY	1/17/1956
Carvey, Dana	Missoula, MT	6/2/1955
Cash, Rosanne	Memphis, TN	5/24/1955
Castellaneta, Dan	Chicago, IL	10/29/1957

Name	Birthplace	Birthdate
Castle-Hughes, Keisha	Donnybrook, WA, Australia	3/24/1990
Cates, Phoebe	New York, NY	7/16/1963
Cattrall, Kim	Liverpool, England, UK	8/21/1956
Cavanagh, Tom	Ottawa, ON, Canada	10/26/1963
Cavett, Dick	Gibbon, NE	11/19/1936
Caviezel, Jim	Mount Vernon, WA	9/26/1968
Cavill, Henry	Jersey, Channel Isls., UK	5/5/1983
Cedric the Entertainer	Jefferson City, MO	4/24/1964
Cera, Michael	Brampton, ON, Canada	6/7/1988
Chalamet, Timothée	New York, NY	12/27/1995
Chalke, Sarah	Ottawa, ON, Canada	8/27/1976
Chamberlain, Richard	Beverly Hills, CA	3/31/1934
Chambers, Justin	Springfield, OH	7/11/1970
Chan, Jackie	Hong Kong	4/7/1954
Chance the Rapper	Chicago, IL	4/16/1993
Chandler, Kyle	Buffalo, NY	9/17/1965
Channing, Stockard	New York, NY	2/13/1944
Chaplin, Geraldine	Santa Monica, CA	7/31/1944
Chapman, Tracy	Cleveland, OH	3/30/1964
Chappelle, Dave	Washington, DC	8/24/1973
Charles, Josh	Baltimore, MD	9/15/1971
Charo	Murcia, Spain	1/15/1951?
Chase, Chevy	New York, NY	10/8/1943
Chasez, JC (Joshua)	Washington, DC	8/8/1976
Chastain, Jessica	Sacramento, CA	3/29/1977
Cheadle, Don	Kansas City, MO	11/29/1964
Checker, Chubby	Spring Gulley, SC	10/3/1941
Chen Moonves, Julie	New York, NY	1/6/1970
Chenoweth, Kristin	Broken Arrow, OK	7/24/1968
Cher	El Centro, CA	5/20/1946
Chesney, Kenny	Lutrelle, TN	3/26/1968
Chianese, Dominic	Bronx, NY	2/24/1931
Chiklis, Michael	Lowell, MA	8/30/1963
Chlumsky, Anna	Chicago, IL	12/3/1980
Chmerkovskiy, Maksim	Odessa, Ukraine	1/17/1980
Cho, Margaret	San Francisco, CA	12/5/1968
Chong, Thomas	Edmonton, AB, Canada	5/24/1938
Chopra, Priyanka	Jamshedpur, India	7/18/1982
Chow Yun-Fat	Lamma Island, Hong Kong	5/18/1955
Christensen, Hayden	Vancouver, BC, Canada	4/19/1981
Christie, Julie	Chukua, Assam, India	4/14/1940
Chuck D	Roosevelt, NY	8/1/1960
Church, Charlotte	Llandaff, Cardiff, Wales, UK	2/21/1986
Church, Thomas Haden	El Paso, TX	6/17/1960
Clapton, Eric	Ripley, Surrey, Eng., UK	3/30/1945
Clark, Petula	Epson, Surrey, Eng., UK	11/15/1932
Clarke, Emilia	London, Eng., UK	10/23/1986
Clarkson, Kelly	Burleson, TX	4/24/1982
Clarkson, Patricia	New Orleans, LA	12/29/1959
Clay, Andrew Dice	Brooklyn, NY	9/29/1957
Cleese, John	Weston-super-Mare, Eng., UK	10/27/1939
Clooney, George	Lexington, KY	5/6/1961
Close, Glenn	Greenwich, CT	3/19/1947
Coen, Ethan	St. Louis Park, MN	9/21/1957
Coen, Joel	St. Louis Park, MN	11/29/1954
Cohen, Andy	St. Louis, MO	6/2/1968
Cohen, Sacha Baron	London, England, UK	10/13/1971
Colbert, Stephen	Washington, DC	5/13/1964
Cole, Gary	Park Ridge, IL	9/20/1956
Colfer, Chris	Fresno, CA	5/27/1990
Collette, Toni	Blacktown, NSW, Australia	11/1/1972
Collins, Joan	London, England, UK	5/23/1933
Collins, Judy	Seattle, WA	5/1/1939
Collins, Pauline	Exmouth, England, UK	9/3/1940
Collins, Phil	London, England, UK	1/30/1951
Collins, Stephen	Des Moines, IA	10/1/1947
Colman, Olivia	Norfolk, Eng., UK	1/30/1974
Columbus, Chris	Spangler, PA	9/10/1958
Colvin, Shawn	Vermillion, SD	1/10/1956
Combs, Sean	New York, NY	11/4/1969
Comer, Jodie	Liverpool, Eng., UK	3/11/1993
Connelly, Jennifer	Round Top, NY	12/12/1970
Connick, Harry, Jr.	New Orleans, LA	9/11/1967
Connolly, Kevin	Patchogue, NY	3/5/1974
Conroy, Frances	Monroe, GA	11/13/1953
Consuelos, Mark	Zaragoza, Spain	3/30/1971
Conti, Tom	Paisley, Scotland, UK	11/22/1941
Coogler, Ryan	Oakland, CA	5/23/1986
Coolidge, Jennifer	Brookline, MA	8/28/1961
Coolidge, Rita	Nashville, TN	5/1/1945
Coon, Carrie	Copley, OH	1/24/1981
Cooper, Alice	Detroit, MI	2/4/1948
Cooper, Bradley	Philadelphia, PA	1/5/1975
Cooper, Chris	Kansas City, MO	7/9/1951
Copeland, Misty	Kansas City, MO	9/10/1982
Copperfield, David	Metuchen, NJ	9/16/1956
Coppola, Francis Ford	Detroit, MI	4/7/1939
Coppola, Sofia	New York, NY	5/14/1971
Corbett, John	Wheeling, WV	5/9/1961
Corbin, Barry	Lamesa, TX	10/16/1940
Corden, James	Hillingdon, England, UK	8/22/1978
Corgan, Billy	Elk Grove, IL	3/17/1967
Corwin, Jeff	Norwell, MA	7/11/1967
Cosby, Bill	Philadelphia, PA	7/12/1937

Name	Birthplace	Birthdate
Cosgrove, Miranda	Los Angeles, CA	5/14/1993
Costas, Bob	Astoria, Queens, NY	3/22/1952
Costello, Elvis	London, England, UK	8/25/1954
Costner, Kevin	Compton, CA	1/18/1955
Cotillard, Marion	Paris, France	9/30/1975
Cowell, Simon	London, England, UK	10/7/1959
Cox, Brian	Dundee, Scotland, UK	6/1/1946
Cox, Courteney	Birmingham, AL	6/15/1964
Cox, Laverne	Mobile, AL	5/29/1972
Cox, Ronny	Cloudcroft, NM	7/23/1938
Coyote, Peter	New York, NY	10/10/1941
Craig, Daniel	Chester, England, UK	3/2/1968
Cranston, Bryan	San Fernando Valley, CA	3/7/1956
Crawford, Cindy	DeKalb, IL	2/20/1966
Crawford, Michael	Salisbury, England, UK	1/19/1942
Criss, Darren	San Francisco, CA	2/5/1987
Cromwell, James	Los Angeles, CA	1/27/1940
Cross, Marcia	Marlborough, MA	3/25/1962
Crow, Sheryl	Kennett, MO	2/11/1962
Crowe, Cameron	Palm Springs, CA	7/13/1957
Crowe, Russell	Wellington, New Zealand	4/7/1964
Crudup, Billy	Manhasset, NY	7/8/1948
Cruise, Tom	Syracuse, NY	7/3/1962
Cruz, Penelope	Madrid, Spain	4/28/1974
Cryer, Jon	New York, NY	4/16/1965
Crystal, Billy	Long Beach, NY	3/14/1948
Cuarón, Alfonso	Mexico City, Mexico	11/28/1961
Culkin, Kieran	New York, NY	9/30/1982
Culkin, Macaulay	New York, NY	8/26/1980
Cullum, John	Knoxville, TN	3/2/1930
Cumberbatch, Benedict	London, England, UK	7/19/1976
Cumming, Alan	Aberfeldy, Perthshire, Scotland, UK	1/27/1965
Cuoco, Kaley	Camarillo, CA	11/30/1985
Curry, Tim	Grappenhall, Cheshire, England, UK	4/19/1946
Curtin, Jane	Cambridge, MA	9/6/1947
Curtis, Jamie Lee	Los Angeles, CA	11/22/1958
Cusack, Joan	New York, NY	10/11/1962
Cusack, John	Evanston, IL	6/28/1966
Cyrus, Billy Ray	Flatwoods, KY	8/25/1961
Cyrus, Miley	Nashville, TN	11/23/1992
Dafoe, Willem	Appleton, WI	7/22/1955
Dale, Jim	Rothwell, England, UK	8/15/1935
Dalton, Timothy	Colwyn Bay, Wales, UK	3/21/1946
Daltrey, Roger	London, England, UK	3/1/1944
Daly, Carson	Santa Monica, CA	6/22/1973
Daly, Timothy	New York, NY	3/1/1956
Daly, Tyne	Madison, WI	2/21/1946
Damon, Matt	Cambridge, MA	10/8/1970
Dane, Eric	San Francisco, CA	11/9/1972
Danes, Claire	New York, NY	4/12/1979
D'Angelo	Richmond, VA	2/11/1974
D'Angelo, Beverly	Columbus, OH	11/15/1954
Daniels, Anthony	Salisbury, England, UK	2/21/1946
Daniels, Jeff	Athens, GA	2/19/1955
Daniels, Lee	Philadelphia, PA	12/24/1959
Daniels, William	Brooklyn, NY	3/31/1927
Danner, Blythe	Rosemont, PA	2/3/1943
Danson, Ted	San Diego, CA	12/29/1947
Danza, Tony	Brooklyn, NY	4/21/1951
Darby, Kim	Hollywood, CA	7/8/1948
Daughtry, Chris	Roanoke Rapids, NC	12/26/1979
David, Larry	Brooklyn, NY	7/2/1947
Davidson, John	Pittsburgh, PA	12/13/1941
Davidson, Pete	Staten Island, NY	11/16/1993
Davis, Clifton	Chicago, IL	10/4/1945
Davis, Geena	Wareham, MA	1/21/1956
Davis, Hope	Englewood, NJ	3/23/1964
Davis, Judy	Perth, WA, Australia	4/23/1955
Davis, Kristin	Boulder, CO	2/24/1965
Davis, Viola	Saint Matthews, SC	8/11/1965
Dawber, Pam	Farmington Hills, MI	10/18/1951
Dawson, Rosario	New York, NY	5/9/1979
Day, Andra	Edmonds, WA	12/30/1984
Day-Lewis, Daniel	London, England, UK	4/29/1957
de Armas, Ana	Havana, Cuba	4/30/1988
De Mornay, Rebecca	Santa Rosa, CA	8/29/1962
De Niro, Robert	New York, NY	8/17/1943
De Rossi, Portia	Melbourne, Vic., Australia	1/31/1973
Debicki, Elizabeth	Paris, France	8/24/1990
DeBose, Ariana	New Hanover, NC	1/25/1991
DeGeneres, Ellen	Metairie, LA	1/26/1958
DeGraw, Gavin	Middletown, NY	2/4/1977
Del Toro, Benicio	Santurce, Puerto Rico	2/19/1967
Del Toro, Guillermo	Guadalajara, Jalisco, Mexico	10/9/1964
Delaney, Kim	Philadelphia, PA	11/29/1961
Delany, Dana	New York, NY	3/13/1956
Dempsey, Patrick	Lewiston, ME	1/13/1966
Dench, Judi	York, England, UK	12/9/1934
Deneuve, Catherine	Paris, France	10/22/1943
DePalma, Brian	Newark, NJ	9/11/1940
Depardieu, Gerard	Chateauroux, France	12/27/1948
Depp, Johnny	Owensboro, KY	6/9/1963

Name	Birthplace	Birthdate
Derek, Bo	Long Beach, CA	11/20/1956
Dern, Bruce	Winnetka, IL	6/4/1936
Dern, Laura	Santa Monica, CA	2/10/1967
Deschanel, Zooey	Los Angeles, CA	1/17/1980
De Shields, André	Baltimore, MD	1/12/1946
Devine, Loretta	Houston, TX	8/21/1949
DeVito, Danny	Neptune, NJ	11/17/1944
DeWitt, Joyce	Wheeling, WV	4/23/1949
Dey, Susan	Pekin, IL	12/10/1952
Diamond, Neil	Brooklyn, NY	1/24/1941
Diaz, Cameron	San Diego, CA	8/30/1972
Diaz, Guillermo	New Jersey	3/22/1975
Diaz, Justino	San Juan, PR	1/29/1940
DiCaprio, Leonardo	Hollywood, CA	11/11/1974
Dick, Andy	Charleston, SC	12/21/1965
Dickens, Kim	Huntsville, AL	6/18/1965
Dickinson, Angie	Kulm, ND	9/30/1931
Diesel, Vin	New York, NY	7/18/1967
Diggs, Daveed	Oakland, CA	1/24/1982
Diggs, Taye	Newark, NJ	1/2/1972
Dillahunt, Garret	Castro Valley, CA	11/24/1964
Dillon, Kevin	Mamaroneck, NY	8/19/1965
Dillon, Matt	New Rochelle, NY	2/18/1964
Dinklage, Peter	Morristown, NJ	6/11/1969
Dion (DiMucci)	Bronx, NY	7/18/1939
Dion, Celine	Charlemagne, QC, Canada	3/30/1968
Djalili, Omid	London, England, UK	9/30/1965
Dobrev, Nina	Sofia, Bulgaria	1/9/1989
Dockery, Michelle	Barking, Essex, Eng., UK	12/15/1981
Dolenz, Micky	Los Angeles, CA	3/8/1945
Domingo, Colman	Philadelphia, PA	11/28/1969
Domingo, Placido	Madrid, Spain	1/21/1941
D'Onofrio, Vincent	Brooklyn, NY	6/30/1959
Donovan (Leitch)	Glasgow, Scotland, UK	5/10/1946
Donovan, Tate	New York, NY	9/25/1963
Dorn, Michael	Luling, TX	12/9/1952
Douglas, Michael	New Brunswick, NJ	9/25/1944
Dourdan, Gary	Philadelphia, PA	12/11/1966
Dovolani, Tony	Pristina, Kosovo	7/17/1973
Dowd, Ann	Holyoke, MA	1/30/1956
Down, Lesley-Anne	London, England, UK	3/17/1954
Downey, Robert, Jr.	New York, NY	4/4/1965
Downey, Roma	Derry, N. Ireland, UK	5/6/1960
Drake	Toronto, ON, Canada	10/24/1986
Drescher, Fran	Flushing, Queens, NY	9/30/1957
Dreyfuss, Richard	Brooklyn, NY	10/29/1947
Driver, Adam	San Bernardino, CA	11/19/1983
Driver, Minnie	London, England, UK	1/31/1970
Duchovny, David	New York, NY	8/7/1960
Duff, Hilary	Houston, TX	9/28/1987
Duffy (Aimee Anne)	Bangor, Gwynedd, Wales, UK	6/23/1984
Duffy, Julia	Minneapolis, MN	6/27/1951
Duffy, Patrick	Townsend, MT	3/17/1949
Duhamel, Josh	Minot, ND	11/14/1972
Dujardin, Jean	Rueil-Malmaison, France	6/19/1972
Dullea, Keir	Cleveland, OH	5/30/1936
Dunaway, Faye	Bascom, FL	1/14/1941
Duncan, Lindsay	Edinburgh, Scotland, UK	11/7/1950
Duncan, Sandy	Henderson, TX	2/20/1946
Dunham, Lena	New York, NY	5/13/1986
Dunne, Griffin	New York, NY	6/8/1955
Dunst, Kirsten	Point Pleasant, NJ	4/30/1982
Dussault, Nancy	Pensacola, FL	6/30/1936
Dutton, Charles S.	Baltimore, MD	1/30/1951
Duvall, Robert	San Diego, CA	1/5/1931
DuVernay, Ava	Los Angeles, CA	8/24/1972
Dylan, Bob	Duluth, MN	5/24/1941
Dylan, Jakob	New York, NY	12/9/1969
Dzundza, George	Rosenheim, Germany	7/19/1945
Eads, George	Fort Worth, TX	3/1/1967
Easton, Sheena	Bellshill, Scotland, UK	4/27/1959
Eastwood, Clint	San Francisco, CA	5/31/1930
Ebersole, Christine	Chicago, IL	2/21/1953
Eckhart, Aaron	Cupertino, CA	3/12/1968
Eden, Barbara	Tucson, AZ	8/23/1931
Edwards, Anthony	Santa Barbara, CA	7/19/1962
Efron, Zac	San Luis Obispo, CA	10/18/1987
Egerton, Taron	Birkenhead, England, UK	11/10/1989
Eggold, Ryan	Lakewood, CA	8/10/1984
Ehle, Jennifer	Winston-Salem, NC	12/29/1969
Eichner, Billy	New York, NY	9/18/1978
Eikenberry, Jill	New Haven, CT	1/21/1947
Eilish, Billie	Los Angeles, CA	12/18/2001
Eisenberg, Jesse	Bayside, NY	10/5/1983
Ejiofor, Chiwetel	London, England, UK	7/10/1974
Ekland, Britt	Stockholm, Sweden	10/6/1942
Elba, Idris	London, England, UK	9/6/1972

Name	Birthplace	Birthdate
Electra, Carmen	Cincinnati, OH	4/20/1972
Elfman, Jenna	Los Angeles, CA	9/30/1971
Elgort, Ansel	New York, NY	3/14/1994
Elizondo, Hector	New York, NY	12/22/1936
Elliott, Chris	New York, NY	5/31/1960
Elliott, Missy	Portsmouth, VA	7/1/1971
Elliott, Sam	Sacramento, CA	8/9/1944
Elvira	Manhattan, KS	9/17/1951
Emerson, Michael	Cedar Rapids, IA	9/7/1954
Eminem	St. Joseph, MO	10/17/1972
Englund, Robert	Glendale, CA	6/6/1949
Enya	Gweedore, Ireland	5/17/1961
Epps, Omar	Brooklyn, NY	7/23/1973
Erivo, Cynthia	London, England, UK	1/8/1987
Esposito, Giancarlo	Copenhagen, Den.	4/26/1958
Estefan, Gloria	Havana, Cuba	9/1/1957
Estevez, Emilio	New York, NY	5/12/1962
Estrada, Erik	New York, NY	3/16/1949
Etheridge, Melissa	Leavenworth, KS	5/29/1961
Evans, Chris	Framingham, MA	6/13/1981
Evans, Linda	Hartford, CT	11/18/1942
Evans, Luke	Pontypool, Wales, UK	4/15/1979
Everett, Rupert	Norfolk, England, UK	5/29/1959
Evigan, Greg	South Amboy, NJ	10/14/1953
Fabares, Shelley	Santa Monica, CA	1/19/1944
Fabian	Philadelphia, PA	2/6/1943
Fabio (Lanzoni)	Milan, Italy	3/15/1959
Fabolous	Brooklyn, NY	11/18/1977
Facinelli, Peter	Queens, NY	11/26/1973
Fairchild, Morgan	Dallas, TX	2/3/1950
Faison, Donald	New York, NY	6/22/1974
Falana, Lola	Philadelphia, PA	9/11/1942
Falco, Edie	Brooklyn, NY	7/5/1963
Fallon, Jimmy	Brooklyn, NY	9/19/1974
Fanning, Dakota	Conyers, GA	2/23/1994
Fanning, Elle	Conyers, GA	4/9/1998
Fargo, Donna	Mt. Airy, NC	11/10/1949
Faris, Anna	Baltimore, MD	11/29/1976
Farmiga, Vera	Clifton, NJ	8/6/1973
Farr, Jamie	Toledo, OH	7/1/1934
Farrell, Colin	Dublin, Ireland	5/31/1976
Farrell, Mike	St. Paul, MN	2/6/1939
Farrell, Perry	Bayside, Queens, NY	3/29/1959
Farrell, Suzanne	Cincinnati, OH	8/16/1945
Farrelly, Bobby	Cumberland, RI	6/17/1958
Farrelly, Peter	Phoenixville, PA	12/17/1956
Farrow, Mia	Los Angeles, CA	2/9/1945
Fassbender, Michael	Heidelberg, Germany	4/2/1977
Fatone, Joey	Brooklyn, NY	1/28/1977
Feinstein, Michael	Columbus, OH	9/7/1956
Feldman, Corey	Los Angeles, CA	7/16/1971
Feldon, Barbara	Bethel Park, PA	3/12/1933
Feldshuh, Tovah	New York, NY	12/27/1952
Feliciano, Jose	Lares, Puerto Rico	9/10/1945
Fenn, Sherilyn	Detroit, MI	2/1/1965
Fergie	Hacienda Heights, CA	3/27/1975
Ferguson, Craig	Glasgow, Scotland, UK	5/17/1962
Ferguson, Jesse Tyler	Missoula, MT	10/22/1975
Ferrara, Jerry	Brooklyn, NY	11/29/1979
Ferrell, Conchata	Charleston, WV	3/28/1943
Ferrell, Will	Irvine, CA	7/16/1967
Ferrera, America	Los Angeles, CA	4/18/1984
Feuerstein, Mark	New York, NY	6/8/1971
Fey, Tina	Upper Darby, PA	5/18/1970
Field, Sally	Pasadena, CA	11/6/1946
Fiennes, Joseph	Salisbury, England, UK	5/27/1970
Fiennes, Ralph	Suffolk, England, UK	12/22/1962
Fierstein, Harvey	Brooklyn, NY	6/6/1954
50 Cent	Jamaica, Queens, NY	7/6/1976
Fillion, Nathan	Edmonton, AB, Canada	3/27/1971
Fincher, David	Denver, CO	8/28/1962
Firth, Colin	Grayshott, England, UK	9/10/1960
Firth, Peter	Bradford, Yorkshire, Eng., UK	10/27/1953
Fischer, Jenna	Ft. Wayne, IN	3/7/1974
Fishburne, Laurence	Augusta, GA	7/30/1961
Flack, Roberta	Black Mountain, NC	2/10/1939
Flanagan, Fionnula	Dublin, Ireland	12/10/1941
Flavor Flav	Roosevelt, NY	3/16/1959
Fleetwood, Mick	Redruth, Cornwall, Eng., UK	6/24/1942
Fleming, Renée	Indiana, PA	2/14/1959
Flockhart, Calista	Freeport, IL	11/11/1964
Florek, Dann	Flat Rock, MI	5/1/1950
Fogerty, John	Berkeley, CA	5/28/1945
Foley, Dave	Etobicoke, ON, Canada	1/4/1963
Foley, Scott	Kansas City, KS	7/15/1972
Fonda, Bridget	Los Angeles, CA	1/27/1964
Fonda, Jane	New York, NY	12/21/1937
Ford, Faith	Alexandria, LA	9/14/1964

Name	Birthplace	Birthdate
Ford, Harrison	Chicago, IL	7/13/1942
Forte, Will	Alameda Co., CA	6/17/1970
Foster, Jodie	Los Angeles, CA	11/19/1962
Foster, Sutton	Statesboro, GA	3/18/1975
Fox, Jorja	New York, NY	7/7/1968
Fox, Matthew	Abington, PA	7/14/1966
Fox, Megan	Rockwood, TN	5/16/1986
Fox, Michael J.	Edmonton, AB, Canada	6/9/1961
Fox, Vivica A.	South Bend, IN	7/30/1964
Foxworth, Robert	Houston, TX	11/1/1941
Foxworthy, Jeff	Atlanta, GA	9/6/1958
Foxx, Jamie	Terrell, TX	12/13/1967
Foy, Claire	Stockport, England, UK	4/16/1984
Frampton, Peter	Kent, England, UK	4/22/1950
Francis, Connie	Newark, NJ	12/12/1938
Franco, Dave	Palo Alto, CA	6/12/1985
Franco, James	Palo Alto, CA	4/19/1978
Franken, Al	New York, NY	5/21/1951
Franz, Dennis	Maywood, IL	10/28/1944
Fraser, Brendan	Indianapolis, IN	12/3/1968
Freeman, Martin	Aldershot, Hampshire, Eng., UK	9/8/1971
Freeman, Morgan	Memphis, TN	6/1/1937
French, Dawn	Holyhead, Wales, UK	10/11/1957
Fricker, Brenda	Dublin, Ireland	2/17/1945
Froggatt, Joanne	Littlebeck, North Yorkshire, England, UK	8/21/1980
Fry, Stephen	London, England, UK	8/24/1957
Fuentes, Daisy	Havana, Cuba	11/17/1966
Fuller, Robert	Troy, NY	7/29/1933
Furlong, Edward	Pasadena, CA	8/2/1977
Furtado, Nelly	Victoria, BC, Canada	12/2/1978
Gabriel, Peter	Surrey, England, UK	2/13/1950
Gaines, Boyd	Atlanta, GA	5/11/1953
Galecki, Johnny	Bree, Belgium	4/30/1975
Galifianakis, Zach	Wilkesboro, NC	10/1/1969
Gallagher, Peter	Armonk, NY	8/19/1955
Gallo, Vincent	Buffalo, NY	4/11/1961
Galway, James	Belfast, N. Ireland, UK	12/8/1939
Garber, Victor	London, ON, Canada	3/16/1949
Garcia, Andy	Havana, Cuba	4/12/1956
Garfield, Andrew	Los Angeles, CA	8/20/1983
Garfunkel, Art	Forest Hills, Queens, NY	11/5/1941
Garlin, Jeff	Chicago, IL	6/5/1962
Garner, Jennifer	Houston, TX	4/17/1972
Garner, Julia	Bronx, NY	2/1/1994
Garofalo, Janeane	Newton, NJ	9/28/1964
Garr, Teri	Lakewood, OH	12/11/1944
Garrett, Brad	Woodland Hills, CA	4/14/1960
Garth, Jennie	Urbana, IL	4/3/1972
Gatlin, Larry	Seminole, TX	5/2/1948
Gayle, Crystal	Paintsville, KY	1/9/1951
Gaynor, Mitzi	Chicago, IL	9/4/1931
Geary, Anthony	Coalville, UT	5/29/1947
Gellar, Sarah Michelle	New York, NY	4/14/1977
Gere, Richard	Philadelphia, PA	8/31/1949
Gervais, Ricky	Reading, England, UK	6/25/1961
Gerwig, Greta	Sacramento, CA	8/4/1983
Giamatti, Paul	New Haven, CT	6/6/1967
Giannini, Giancarlo	La Spezia, Italy	8/1/1942
Gibb, Barry	Isle of Man, England, UK	9/1/1946
Gibbons, Leeza	Hartsville, SC	3/26/1957
Gibbs, Marla	Chicago, IL	6/14/1931
Gibson, Debbie	Brooklyn, NY	8/31/1970
Gibson, Mel	Peekskill, NY	1/3/1956
Gibson, Thomas	Charleston, SC	7/3/1962
Gifford, Kathie Lee	Neuilly-sur-Seine, France	8/16/1953
Gilbert, Melissa	Los Angeles, CA	5/8/1964
Gilbert, Sara	Santa Monica, CA	1/29/1975
Gill, Vince	Norman, OK	4/12/1957
Gillette, Anita	Baltimore, MD	8/16/1936
Gilliam, Terry	Minneapolis, MN	11/22/1940
Gilmour, David	Cambridge, England, UK	3/6/1946
Gilpin, Peri	Waco, TX	5/27/1961
Givens, Robin	New York, NY	11/27/1964
Gladstone, Lily	Kalispell, Montana	8/2/1986
Glaser, Paul Michael	Cambridge, MA	3/25/1943
Gleeson, Brendan	Belfast, N. Ireland, UK	3/29/1955?
Glenn, Scott	Pittsburgh, PA	1/26/1941
Gless, Sharon	Los Angeles, CA	5/31/1943
Glover, Crispin	New York, NY	4/20/1964
Glover, Danny	San Francisco, CA	7/22/1947
Glover, Donald	Edwards Air Force Base, CA	9/25/1983
Glover, Julian	London, England, UK	3/27/1935
Glover, Savion	Newark, NJ	11/19/1973
Goldberg, Whoopi	New York, NY	11/13/1955
Goldblum, Jeff	Pittsburgh, PA	10/22/1952
Goldthwait, Bobcat	Syracuse, NY	5/26/1962
Goldwyn, Tony	Los Angeles, CA	5/20/1960
Gomez, Selena	Grand Prairie, TX	7/22/1992
Gooding, Cuba, Jr.	Bronx, NY	1/2/1968
Goodman, John	Affton, MO	6/20/1952
Gordon-Levitt, Joseph	Los Angeles, CA	2/17/1981
Gosling, Ryan	London, ON, Canada	11/12/1980
Gosselaar, Mark-Paul	Panorama City, CA	3/1/1974
Gould, Elliott	Brooklyn, NY	8/29/1938
Grace, Topher	New York, NY	7/12/1978
Graham, Heather	Milwaukee, WI	1/29/1970
Graham, Lauren	Honolulu, HI	3/16/1967
Grammer, Kelsey	St. Thomas, U.S. Virgin Isls.	2/21/1955
Grande, Ariana	Boca Raton, FL	6/26/1993
Grant, Amy	Augusta, GA	11/25/1960
Grant, Hugh	London, England, UK	9/9/1960
Grant, Lee	Bronx, NY	10/31/1925
Gray, Linda	Santa Monica, CA	9/12/1940
Gray, Macy	Canton, OH	9/6/1969
Green, Al	Forrest City, AR	4/13/1946
Green, Cee Lo	Atlanta, GA	5/30/1974
Green, Seth	Philadelphia, PA	2/8/1974
Green, Tom	Pembroke, ON, Canada	7/30/1971
Greene, Graham	Six Nations Reserve, ON, Canada	6/22/1952
Greenfield, Max	Dobbs Ferry, NY	9/4/1980
Greenwood, Bruce	Noranda, QC, Canada	8/12/1956
Gregory, Cynthia	Los Angeles, CA	7/8/1946
Grenier, Adrian	Santa Fe, NM	7/10/1976
Grey, Jennifer	New York, NY	3/26/1960
Grey, Joel	Cleveland, OH	4/11/1932
Grier, David Alan	Detroit, MI	6/30/1955
Grier, Pam	Winston-Salem, NC	5/26/1949
Griffin, Kathy	Oak Park, IL	11/4/1961
Griffith, Melanie	New York, NY	8/9/1957
Griffiths, Rachel	Melbourne, Vic., Australia	12/18/1968
Grint, Rupert	Walton-at-Stone, Hertfordshire, Eng., UK	8/24/1988
Groban, Josh	Los Angeles, CA	2/27/1981
Groff, Jonathan	Lancaster, PA	3/26/1985
Grohl, Dave	Warren, OH	1/14/1969
Gross, Michael	Chicago, IL	6/21/1947
Guest, Christopher	New York, NY	2/5/1948
Gumbel, Bryant	New Orleans, LA	9/29/1948
Gumbel, Greg	New Orleans, LA	5/3/1946
Gunn, Anna	Santa Fe, NM	8/11/1968
Gunn, Tim	Washington, DC	7/29/1953
Guthrie, Arlo	Brooklyn, NY	7/10/1947
Guttenberg, Steve	Brooklyn, NY	8/24/1958
Guy, Buddy	Lettsworth, LA	7/30/1936
Guy, Jasmine	Boston, MA	3/10/1964
Gyllenhaal, Jake	Los Angeles, CA	12/19/1980
Gyllenhaal, Maggie	New York, NY	11/16/1977
Haas, Shira	Tel Aviv, Israel	5/11/1995
Hackman, Gene	San Bernardino, CA	1/30/1930
Haddish, Tiffany	Los Angeles, CA	12/3/1979
Hader, Bill	Tulsa, OK	6/7/1978
Hagerty, Julie	Cincinnati, OH	6/15/1955
Hahn, Kathryn	Westchester, IL	7/23/1973
Hale, Tony	West Point, NY	9/30/1970
Hall, Anthony Michael	West Roxbury, MA	4/14/1968
Hall, Arsenio	Cleveland, OH	2/12/1955
Hall, Daryl	Pottstown, PA	10/11/1946
Hall, Deidre	Milwaukee, WI	10/31/1947
Hall, Michael C.	Raleigh, NC	2/1/1971
Hall, Tamron	Luling, TX	9/16/1970
Halliwell, Geri	Watford, England, UK	8/6/1972
Hamill, Mark	Oakland, CA	9/25/1951
Hamilton, George	Memphis, TN	8/12/1939
Hamilton, Linda	Salisbury, MD	9/26/1956
Hamlin, Harry	Pasadena, CA	10/30/1951
Hamm, Jon	St. Louis, MO	3/10/1971
Hammer, Armie	Los Angeles, CA	8/28/1986
Hammer (M.C.)	Oakland, CA	3/30/1963
Hammond, Darrell	Melbourne, FL	10/8/1955
Hancock, Herbie	Chicago, IL	4/12/1940
Handler, Chelsea	Livingston, NJ	2/25/1975
Hanks, Colin	Sacramento, CA	11/24/1977
Hanks, Tom	Concord, CA	7/9/1956
Hannah, Daryl	Chicago, IL	12/3/1960
Hannigan, Alyson	Washington, DC	3/24/1974
Hanson, Isaac	Tulsa, OK	11/17/1980
Hanson, Taylor	Tulsa, OK	3/14/1983
Hanson, Zac	Tulsa, OK	10/22/1985
Harden, Marcia Gay	La Jolla, CA	8/14/1959
Hardy, Tom	London, England, UK	9/15/1977
Harewood, Dorian	Dayton, OH	8/6/1950
Hargitay, Mariska	Los Angeles, CA	1/23/1964
Harington, Kit	London, Eng., UK	12/26/1986
Harlow, Jack	Louisville, KY	3/13/1998
Harmon, Angie	Highland Park, TX	8/10/1972
Harmon, Mark	Burbank, CA	9/2/1951
Harper, Ben	Claremont, CA	10/28/1969
Harper, Tess	Mammoth Spring, AR	8/15/1950
Harrelson, Woody	Midland, TX	7/23/1961
Harris, Ed	Tenafly, NJ	11/28/1950
Harris, Emmylou	Birmingham, AL	4/2/1947
Harris, Jared	London, Eng., UK	8/24/1961
Harris, Neil Patrick	Albuquerque, NM	6/15/1973

Name	Birthplace	Birthdate
Harris, Rosemary	Ashby, England, UK	9/19/1927?
Harris, Steve	Chicago, IL	12/3/1965
Harrison, Gregory	Avalon, CA	5/31/1950
Harry, Deborah	Miami, FL	7/1/1945
Hart, Kevin	Philadelphia, PA	7/3/1980
Hart, Mary	Madison, SD	11/8/1950
Hart, Melissa Joan	Smithtown, NY	4/18/1976
Hartley, Mariette	New York, NY	6/21/1940
Hartman, David	Pawtucket, RI	5/19/1935
Hartman Black, Lisa	Houston, TX	6/1/1956
Hartnett, Josh	San Francisco, CA	7/21/1978
Harvey, P. J.	Yeovil, Somerset, Eng., UK	10/9/1969
Harvey, Steve	Welch, WV	1/17/1956
Hasselbeck, Elisabeth	Cranston, RI	5/28/1977
Hasselhoff, David	Baltimore, MD	7/17/1952
Hatcher, Teri	Sunnyvale, CA	12/8/1964
Hatfield, Juliana	Wiscasset, ME	7/27/1967
Hathaway, Anne	Brooklyn, NY	11/12/1982
Hawke, Ethan	Austin, TX	11/6/1970
Hawn, Goldie	Washington, DC	11/21/1945
Hayek, Salma	Coatzacoalcos, Mexico	9/2/1966
Hayes, Hunter	Breaux Bridge, LA	9/9/1991
Hayes, Sean	Glen Ellyn, IL	6/26/1970
Hays, Robert	Bethesda, MD	7/24/1947
Haysbert, Dennis	San Mateo, CA	6/2/1955
Head, Anthony	Camden Town, Eng., UK	2/20/1954
Headey, Lena	Hamilton, Bermuda	10/3/1973
Hearn, George	St. Louis, MO	6/18/1934
Heaton, Patricia	Bay Village, OH	3/4/1958
Heder, Jon	Fort Collins, CO	10/26/1977
Hedges, Lucas	New York, NY	12/12/1996
Hedren, Tippi	New Ulm, MN	1/19/1930
Heigl, Katherine	Washington, DC	11/24/1978
Helberg, Simon	Los Angeles, CA	12/9/1980
Helfgott, David	Melbourne, Vic., Australia	5/19/1947
Helgenberger, Marg	Fremont, NE	11/16/1958
Helms, Ed	Atlanta, GA	1/24/1974
Hemingway, Mariel	Mill Valley, CA	11/22/1961
Hemsworth, Chris	Melbourne, Vic., Australia	8/11/1983
Hemsworth, Liam	Melbourne, Vic., Australia	1/13/1990
Hemsworth, Luke	Melbourne, Vic., Australia	11/5/1980
Hendricks, Christina	Knoxville, TN	5/3/1975
Henley, Don	Gilmer, TX	7/22/1947
Henner, Marilu	Chicago, IL	4/6/1952
Hennessy, Jill	Edmonton, AB, Canada	11/25/1968
Henson, Taraji P.	Washington, DC	9/11/1970
Hershey, Barbara	Hollywood, CA	2/5/1948
Hetfield, James	Downey, CA	8/3/1963
Hewitt, Jennifer Love	Waco, TX	2/21/1979
Hickey, John Benjamin	Piano, TX	6/25/1963
Hicks, Catherine	Scottsdale, AZ	8/6/1951
Hiddleston, Tom	London, England, UK	2/9/1981
Higgins, John Michael	Boston, MA	2/12/1963
Hightower, Chelsie	Las Vegas, NV	7/21/1989
Hill, Dulé	Orange, NJ	5/3/1975
Hill, Faith	Jackson, MS	9/21/1967
Hill, Jonah	Los Angeles, CA	12/20/1983
Hill, Lauryn	South Orange, NJ	5/26/1975
Hines, Cheryl	Miami Beach, FL	9/21/1965
Hirsch, Emile	Palms, CA	3/13/1985
Hirsch, Judd	Bronx, NY	3/15/1935
Hodgman, John	Cambridge, MA	6/3/1971
Hoffman, Dustin	Los Angeles, CA	8/8/1937
Hogan, Hulk	Augusta, GA	8/11/1953
Hogan, Paul	Lightning Ridge, NSW, Australia	10/8/1939
Holliday, Polly	Jasper, AL	7/2/1937
Holland, Tom	Kingston upon Thames, Eng., UK	6/1/1996
Hollander, Tom	Bristol, Eng., UK	8/25/1967
Holloway, Josh	San Jose, CA	7/20/1969
Holly, Lauren	Bristol, PA	10/28/1963
Holmes, Katie	Toledo, OH	12/18/1978
Hopkins, Anthony	Port Talbot, South Wales, UK	12/31/1937
Hopkins, Telma	Louisville, KY	10/28/1948
Horne, Marilyn	Bradford, PA	1/16/1934
Hornsby, Bruce	Williamsburg, VA	11/23/1954
Horsley, Lee	Muleshoe, TX	5/15/1955
Hough, Derek	Salt Lake City, UT	5/17/1985
Hough, Julianne	Salt Lake City, UT	7/20/1988
Hounsou, Djimon	Cotonou, Benin	4/24/1964
Howard, Clint	Burbank, CA	4/20/1959
Howard, Ron	Duncan, OK	3/1/1954
Howard, Terrence	Chicago, IL	3/11/1969
Howell, C. Thomas	Van Nuys, CA	12/7/1966
Hudgens, Vanessa	Salinas, CA	12/14/1988
Hudson, Ernie	Benton Harbor, MI	12/17/1945
Hudson, Jennifer	Chicago, IL	9/12/1981
Hudson, Kate	Los Angeles, CA	4/19/1979
Huffman, Felicity	Bedford, NY	12/9/1962

Name	Birthplace	Birthdate
Hughley, D. L.	Los Angeles, CA	3/6/1963
Hulce, Tom	Detroit, MI	12/6/1953
Humperdinck, Engelbert	Madras, India	5/2/1936
Hunt, Bonnie	Chicago, IL	9/22/1964
Hunt, Helen	Culver City, CA	6/15/1963
Hunt, Linda	Morristown, NJ	4/2/1945
Hunter, Holly	Conyers, GA	3/20/1958
Hurley, Elizabeth	Hampshire, England, UK	6/10/1965
Hurt, Mary Beth	Marshalltown, IA	9/26/1948
Huston, Anjelica	Santa Monica, CA	7/8/1951
Hutcherson, Josh	Union, KY	10/12/1992
Hutton, Lauren	Charleston, SC	11/17/1943
Hutton, Timothy	Malibu, CA	8/16/1960
Ian, Janis	Bronx, NY	4/7/1951
Ice Cube	Los Angeles, CA	6/15/1969
Ice-T	Newark, NJ	2/16/1958
Idle, Eric	S. Shields, England, UK	3/29/1943
Idol, Billy	Middlesex, England, UK	11/30/1955
Iglesias, Enrique	Madrid, Spain	5/8/1975
Iglesias, Julio	Madrid, Spain	9/23/1943
Iler, Robert	New York, NY	3/2/1985
Iman	Mogadishu, Somalia	7/25/1955
Imbruglia, Natalie	Sydney, NSW, Australia	2/4/1975
Imperioli, Michael	Mount Vernon, NY	3/26/1966
Iñárritu, Alejandro G.	Mexico City, Mexico	8/15/1963
Innes, Laura	Pontiac, MI	8/16/1957?
Ireland, Kathy	Glendale, CA	3/20/1963
Irons, Jeremy	Cowes, Isle of Wight, Eng., UK	9/19/1948
Irving, Amy	Palo Alto, CA	9/10/1953
Irwin, Bill	Santa Monica, CA	4/11/1950
Isaac, Oscar	Guatemala	3/9/1979
Ivanek, Željko	Ljubljana, Yugo. (Slovenia)	8/15/1957
Ivey, Judith	El Paso, TX	9/4/1951
Ivory, James	Berkeley, CA	6/7/1928
Izzard, Eddie	Aden, Yemen	2/7/1962
Ja Rule	Hollis, Queens, NY	2/29/1976
Jackée (Harry)	Winston-Salem, NC	8/14/1956
Jackman, Hugh	Sydney, NSW, Australia	10/12/1968
Jackson, Cheyenne	Newport, WA	7/12/1975
Jackson, Janet	Gary, IN	5/16/1966
Jackson, Jermaine	Gary, IN	12/11/1954
Jackson, Jonathan	Orlando, FL	5/11/1982
Jackson, Joshua	Vancouver, BC, Canada	6/11/1978
Jackson, Kate	Birmingham, AL	10/29/1948
Jackson, La Toya	Gary, IN	5/29/1956
Jackson, Peter	Wellington, New Zealand	10/31/1961
Jackson, Samuel L.	Washington, DC	12/21/1948
Jacobi, Derek	London, England, UK	10/22/1938
Jagger, Mick	Dartford, England, UK	7/26/1943
James, Brian d'Arcy	Saginaw, MI	6/29/1968
James, Kevin	Mineola, NY	4/26/1965
James, Lily	Esher, England, UK	4/5/1989
James, Theo	Oxford, England, UK	12/16/1984
Jamison, Judith	Philadelphia, PA	5/10/1943
Janney, Allison	Dayton, OH	11/19/1959
Janssen, Famke	Amsterdam, Netherlands	11/5/1965
Jardine, Al	Lima, OH	9/3/1942
Jarmusch, Jim	Akron, OH	1/22/1953
Jarrett, Keith	Allentown, PA	5/8/1945
Jay-Z	Brooklyn, NY	12/4/1969
Jenkins, Barry	Miami, FL	11/19/1979
Jenkins, Richard	DeKalb, IL	5/4/1947
Jenner, Caitlyn	Mount Kisco, NY	10/28/1949
Jenner, Kendall	Los Angeles, CA	9/3/1995
Jenner, Kris	San Diego, CA	11/5/1955
Jenner, Kylie	Los Angeles, CA	8/10/1997
Jennings, Ken	Edmonds, WA	5/23/1974
Jepsen, Carly Rae	Mission, BC, Canada	11/21/1985
Jett, Joan	Philadelphia, PA	9/22/1958
Jewel (Kilcher)	Payson, UT	5/23/1974
Jillette, Penn	Greenfield, MA	3/5/1955
Jillian, Ann	Cambridge, MA	1/29/1950
Joel, Billy	Bronx, NY	5/9/1949
Johansson, Scarlett	New York, NY	11/22/1984
John, Elton	Pinner, Middlesex, Eng., UK	3/25/1947
Johnson, Beverly	Buffalo, NY	10/13/1952
Johnson, Don	Flatt Creek, MO	12/15/1949
Johnson, Dwayne "The Rock"	Hayward, CA	5/2/1972
Johnston, Bruce	Los Angeles, CA	6/24/1942
Johnston, Kristen	Washington, DC	9/20/1967
Jolie, Angelina	Los Angeles, CA	6/4/1975
Jonas, Joe	Casa Grande, AZ	8/15/1989
Jonas, Kevin	Teaneck, NJ	11/5/1987
Jonas, Nick	Dallas, TX	9/16/1992
Jones, Angus T.	Austin, TX	10/8/1993
Jones, Bill T.	Bunnell, FL	2/15/1952
Jones, Cherry	Paris, TN	11/21/1956
Jones, Gemma	London, England, UK	12/4/1942

Name	Birthplace	Birthdate
Jones, Grace	Spanish Town, Jamaica	5/19/1948
Jones, Jack	Hollywood, CA	1/14/1938
Jones, John Paul	Sidcup, England, UK	1/3/1946
Jones, January	Sioux Falls, SD	1/5/1978
Jones, Leslie	Memphis, TN	9/7/1967
Jones, Mick	London, England, UK	6/26/1955
Jones, Norah	New York, NY	3/30/1979
Jones, Quincy	Chicago, IL	3/14/1933
Jones, Shirley	Charleroi, PA	3/31/1934
Jones, Star	Badin, NC	3/24/1962
Jones, Tom	Pontypridd, Wales, UK	6/7/1940
Jones, Tommy Lee	San Saba, TX	9/15/1946
Jonze, Spike	Rockville, MD	10/22/1969
Jordan, Michael B.	Santa Ana, CA	2/9/1987
Jovovich, Milla	Kiev, Ukraine	12/17/1975
Judd, Ashley	Granada Hills, CA	4/19/1968
Judd, Wynonna	Ashland, KY	5/30/1964
Kaczmarek, Jane	Milwaukee, WI	12/21/1955
Kaling, Mindy	Cambridge, MA	6/24/1979
Kaluuya, Daniel	London, Eng., UK	2/24/1989
Kanaly, Steve	Burbank, CA	3/14/1946
Kane, Carol	Cleveland, OH	6/18/1952
Kaplan, Gabe	Brooklyn, NY	3/31/1945
Kardashian, Khloe	Los Angeles, CA	6/27/1984
Kardashian, Kim	Los Angeles, CA	10/21/1980
Kardashian, Kourtney	Los Angeles, CA	4/18/1979
Karn, Richard	Seattle, WA	2/17/1956
Katic, Stana	Hamilton, ON, Canada	4/26/1978
Kattan, Chris	Sherman Oaks, CA	10/19/1970
Kaufmann, Jonas	Munich, Germany	1/10/1969
Kavner, Julie	Burbank, CA	9/7/1951
Kaye, Judy	Phoenix, AZ	12/11/1948
Kazan, Lainie	New York, NY	5/15/1940
Keach, Stacy	Savannah, GA	6/2/1941
Keaton, Diane	Santa Ana, CA	1/5/1946
Keaton, Michael	Coraopolis, PA	9/5/1951
Keener, Catherine	Miami, FL	3/23/1959
Keillor, Garrison	Anoka, MN	8/7/1942
Keitel, Harvey	Brooklyn, NY	5/13/1939
Keith, David	Knoxville, TN	5/8/1954
Keith, Penelope	Sutton, Surrey, Eng., UK	4/2/1940
Kelly, Minka	Los Angeles, CA	6/24/1980
Kelly, R(obert)	Chicago, IL	1/8/1967
Kemper, Ellie	Kansas City, MO	5/2/1980
Kendrick, Anna	Portland, ME	8/9/1985
Kennedy, Jamie	Upper Darby, PA	5/25/1970
Kenny G	Seattle, WA	6/5/1956
Kent, Allegra	Santa Monica, CA	8/11/1937
Keoghan, Phil	Christchurch, New Zealand	5/31/1967
Kerns, Joanna	San Francisco, CA	2/12/1953
Kesha	Los Angeles, CA	3/1/1987
Key, Keegan-Michael	Southfield, MI	3/22/1971
Keys, Alicia	New York, NY	1/25/1981
Khaled, DJ	New Orleans, LA	11/26/1975
Khalifa, Wiz	Minot, ND	9/8/1987
Khan, Chaka	Great Lakes, IL	3/23/1953
Kid Rock	Romeo, MI	1/17/1971
Kidman, Nicole	Honolulu, HI	6/20/1967
Kilborn, Craig	Kansas City, KS	8/24/1962
Kilmer, Val	Los Angeles, CA	12/31/1959
Kim, Daniel Dae	Pusan, South Korea	8/4/1968
Kimmel, Jimmy	Brooklyn, NY	11/13/1967
King, Aja Naomi	Los Angeles, CA	1/11/1985
King, Carole	Brooklyn, NY	2/9/1942
King, Gayle	Chevy Chase, MD	12/28/1954?
King, Perry	Alliance, OH	4/30/1948
King, Regina	Los Angeles, CA	1/15/1971
Kingsley, Ben	Scarborough, England, UK	12/31/1943
Kingston, Alex	London, England, UK	3/11/1963
Kinnear, Greg	Logansport, IN	6/17/1963
Kinney, Kathy	Stevens Point, WI	11/3/1954
Kinski, Nastassja	Berlin, W. Germany	1/24/1960
Kirkland, Gelsey	Bethlehem, PA	12/29/1952
Kirkpatrick, Chris	Clarion, PA	10/17/1971
Kirshner, Mia	Toronto, ON, Canada	1/25/1975
Kitsch, Taylor	Kelowna, BC, Canada	4/8/1981
Klein, Robert	Bronx, NY	2/8/1942
Kline, Kevin	St. Louis, MO	10/24/1947
Klum, Heidi	Bergish-Gladbach, Germany	6/1/1973
Knight, Gladys	Atlanta, GA	5/28/1944
Knight, T. R.	Minneapolis, MN	3/26/1973
Knight, Wayne	New York, NY	8/7/1955
Knightley, Keira	Teddington, England, UK	3/26/1985
Knopfler, Mark	Glasgow, Scotland, UK	8/12/1949
Knowles, Beyoncé	Houston, TX	9/4/1981
Knoxville, Johnny	Knoxville, TN	3/11/1971
Kopell, Bernie	Brooklyn, NY	6/21/1933
Krakowski, Jane	Parsippany, NJ	10/11/1968
Krasinski, John	Newton, MA	10/20/1979
Krause, Peter	Aleandria, MN	8/12/1965
Kravitz, Lenny	Brooklyn, NY	5/26/1964

Name	Birthplace	Birthdate
Kravitz, Zoë	Los Angeles, CA	12/1/1988
Kressley, Carson	Allentown, PA	11/11/1969
Kretschmann, Thomas	Dessau, E. Germany	9/8/1962
Kudrow, Lisa	Encino, CA	7/30/1963
Kunis, Mila	Kiev, Ukraine	8/14/1983
Kurtz, Swoosie	Omaha, NE	9/6/1944
Kutcher, Ashton	Cedar Rapids, IA	2/7/1978
Kwan, Daniel	Westborough, MA	2/10/1988
Kwan, Nancy	Hong Kong	5/19/1939
LaBelle, Patti	Philadelphia, PA	5/24/1944
LaBeouf, Shia	Los Angeles, CA	6/11/1986
Lachey, Nick	Harlan, KY	11/9/1973
Ladd, Cheryl	Huron, SD	7/12/1951
Ladd, Diane	Meridian, MS	11/29/1932
Lady Gaga	New York, NY	3/28/1986
Lagasse, Emeril	Fall River, MA	10/15/1959
Lahti, Christine	Birmingham, MI	4/4/1950
Laine, Cleo	Southall, England, UK	10/28/1927
Lake, Ricki	Hastings-on-Hudson, NY	9/21/1968
Lakshmi, Padma	Chennai, India	9/1/1970
Lamar, Kendrick	Compton, CA	6/17/1987
Lamas, Lorenzo	Santa Monica, CA	1/20/1958
Lambert, Adam	Indianapolis, IN	1/29/1982
Lambert, Christopher	Great Neck, NY	3/29/1957
Lambert, Miranda	Longview, TX	11/10/1983
Landis, John	Chicago, IL	8/3/1950
Lane, Diane	New York, NY	1/22/1965
Lane, Nathan	Jersey City, NJ	2/3/1956
lang, k.d.	Consort, AB, Canada	11/2/1961
Lang, Stephen	Jamaica Estates, Queens, NY	7/11/1952
Lange, Jessica	Cloquet, MN	4/20/1949
Langella, Frank	Bayonne, NJ	1/1/1938
LaPaglia, Anthony	Adelaide, SA, Australia	1/31/1959
Larroquette, John	New Orleans, LA	11/25/1947
Larson, Brie	Sacramento, CA	10/1/1989
LaSalle, Eriq	Hartford, CT	6/23/1962
Lauper, Cyndi	Ozone Park, Queens, NY	6/22/1953
Laurie, Hugh	Oxford, England, UK	6/11/1959
Lautner, Taylor	Grand Rapids, MI	2/11/1992
Lavigne, Avril	Belleville, ON, Canada	9/27/1984
Lavin, Linda	Portland, ME	10/15/1937
Law, Jude	London, England, UK	12/29/1972
Lawless, Lucy	Mount Albert, New Zealand	3/29/1968
Lawrence, Carol	Melrose Park, IL	9/5/1934
Lawrence, Jennifer	Louisville, KY	8/15/1990
Lawrence, Joey	Montgomery, PA	4/20/1976
Lawrence, Martin	Frankfurt, Germany	4/16/1965
Lawrence, Vicki	Inglewood, CA	3/26/1949
Learned, Michael	Washington, DC	4/9/1939
Leary, Denis	Worcester, MA	8/18/1957
LeBlanc, Matt	Newton, MA	7/25/1967
LeBon, Simon	Bushey, England, UK	10/27/1958
Lee, Ang	Pingtung, Taiwan	10/23/1954
Lee, Brenda	Lithonia, GA	12/11/1944
Lee, Jason	Huntington Beach, CA	4/25/1970
Lee, Michele	Los Angeles, CA	6/24/1942
Lee, Spike	Atlanta, GA	3/20/1957
Leeves, Jane	Ilford, England, UK	4/18/1961
Legend, John	Springfield, OH	12/28/1978
Leguizamo, John	Bogotá, Colombia	7/22/1964
Leigh, Jennifer Jason	Hollywood, CA	2/5/1962
Leighton, Laura	Iowa City, IA	7/24/1968
Lennox, Annie	Aberdeen, Scotland, UK	12/25/1954
Leno, Jay	New Rochelle, NY	4/28/1950
Leo, Melissa	New York, NY	9/14/1960
Leonard, Robert Sean	Westwood, NJ	2/28/1969
Leoni, Tea	New York, NY	2/25/1966
Leto, Jared	Bossier City, LA	12/26/1971
Letterman, David	Indianapolis, IN	4/12/1947
Leung, Tony	Hong Kong	6/27/1962
Levin, Harvey	Los Angeles, CA	9/2/1960
Levine, Adam	Los Angeles, CA	3/18/1979
Levine, Ted	Bellaire, OH	5/29/1957
Levinson, Barry	Baltimore, MD	4/6/1942
Levy, Daniel	Toronto, ON, Canada	8/9/1983
Levy, Eugene	Hamilton, ON, Canada	12/17/1946
Lewis, Damian	London, Eng., UK	2/11/1971
Lewis, Huey	New York, NY	7/5/1950
Lewis, Jason	Newport Beach, CA	6/25/1971
Lewis, Juliette	Los Angeles, CA	6/21/1973
Lewis, Leona	London, England, UK	4/3/1985
Li, Jet	Beijing, China	4/26/1963
Light, Judith	Trenton, NJ	2/9/1949
Lil' Kim	Brooklyn, NY	7/11/1975
Lil Nas X	Lithia Springs, GA	4/9/1999
Lil' Romeo	New Orleans, LA	8/19/1989
Lil Wayne	New Orleans, LA	9/27/1982
Lilly, Evangeline	Fort Saskatchewan, AB, Can.	8/3/1979
Lincoln, Andrew	London, England, UK	9/14/1973

Name	Birthplace	Birthdate
Linden, Hal	Bronx, NY	3/20/1931
Ling, Lisa	Sacramento, CA	8/30/1973
Linn-Baker, Mark	St. Louis, MO.	6/17/1954
Linney, Laura	New York, NY	2/5/1964
Lipa, Dua	London, England, UK	8/22/1995
Lithgow, John	Rochester, NY	10/19/1945
Little, Rich	Ottawa, ON, Canada	11/26/1938
Littrell, Brian	Lexington, KY	2/20/1975
Liu, Lucy	Jackson Heights, Queens, NY	12/2/1968
Liu, Simu	Harbin, China	4/19/1989
Lively, Blake	Tarzana, CA.	8/25/1987
LL Cool J	St. Albans, Queens, NY	1/14/1968
Lloyd, Christopher	Stamford, CT	10/22/1938
Lloyd Webber, Andrew	London, England, UK	3/22/1948
Lockhart, June	New York, NY	6/25/1925
Locklear, Heather	Westwood, CA.	9/25/1961
Loggins, Kenny	Everett, WA	1/7/1948
Lohan, Lindsay	New York, NY	7/2/1986
Lonergan, Kenneth	New York, NY	10/16/1962
Long, Nia	Brooklyn, NY	10/30/1970
Long, Shelley	Ft. Wayne, IN	8/23/1949
Longoria, Eva	Corpus Christi, TX	3/15/1975
Lopez, George	Mission Hills, CA	4/23/1961
Lopez, Jennifer	Bronx, NY	7/24/1969
Lopez, Mario	San Diego, CA.	10/10/1973
Lorde	Takapuna, New Zealand	11/7/1996
Loren, Sophia	Rome, Italy	9/20/1934
Louis C.K.	Washington, DC	9/12/1967
Louis-Dreyfus, Julia	New York, NY	1/13/1961
Lovato, Demi	Albuquerque, NM.	8/20/1992
Love, Courtney	San Francisco, CA	7/9/1964
Love, Mike	Baldwin Hills, CA	3/15/1941
Loveless, Patty	Pikeville, KY	1/4/1957
Lovett, Lyle	Klein, TX	11/1/1957
Lovitz, Jon	Tarzana, CA.	7/21/1957
Lowe, Rob	Charlottesville, VA	3/17/1964
Lucas, George	Modesto, CA	5/14/1944
Lucci, Susan	Scarsdale, NY	12/23/1946
Luckinbill, Laurence	Ft. Smith, AR	11/21/1934
Ludacris	Champaign, IL.	9/11/1977
Luhrmann, Baz	Sydney, NSW, Australia	9/17/1962
LuPone, Patti	Northport, NY	4/21/1949
Lynch, David	Missoula, MT.	1/20/1946
Lynch, Jane	Dolton, IL.	7/14/1960
Lynne, Shelby	Quantico, VA	10/22/1968
Lyonne, Natasha	New York, NY	4/4/1979
Ma, Yo-Yo	Paris, France	10/7/1955
Macchio, Ralph	Huntington, NY	11/4/1961
MacDonald, Kelly	Glasgow, Scotland, UK	2/23/1976
MacDowell, Andie	Gaffney, SC	4/21/1958
MacFarlane, Seth	Kent, CT	10/26/1973
MacGowan, Shane	Tunbridge, Kent, Eng., UK	12/25/1957
MacGraw, Ali	Pound Ridge, NY.	4/1/1939
Macklemore	Seattle, WA	6/19/1983
MacLachlan, Kyle	Yakima, WA.	2/22/1959
MacLaine, Shirley	Richmond, VA	4/24/1934
MacNicol, Peter	Dallas, TX	4/10/1954
MacPherson, Elle	Sydney, NSW, Australia	3/29/1964
Macy, William H.	Miami, FL	3/13/1950
Madden, Richard	Elderslie, Scot., UK	6/18/1986
Madigan, Amy	Chicago, IL	9/11/1950
Madonna (Ciccone)	Bay City, MI	8/16/1958
Madsen, Michael	Chicago, IL	9/25/1959
Maguire, Tobey	Santa Monica, CA	6/27/1975
Maher, Bill	New York, NY	1/20/1956
Majors, Lee	Wyandotte, MI	4/23/1939
Makarova, Natalia	Leningrad, Russia	11/21/1940
Malek, Rami	Los Angeles, CA	5/12/1981
Malick, Terrence	Ottawa, IL	11/30/1943
Malick, Wendie	Buffalo, NY	12/13/1950
Malina, Joshua	New York, NY	1/17/1966
Malkovich, John	Christopher, IL.	12/9/1953
Mamet, David	Chicago, IL	11/30/1947
Manchester, Melissa	Bronx, NY	2/15/1951
Mandel, Howie	Toronto, ON, Canada	11/29/1955
Mandrell, Barbara	Houston, TX	12/25/1948
Mangione, Chuck	Rochester, NY	11/29/1940
Manheim, Camryn	Caldwell, NJ	3/8/1961
Manilow, Barry	Brooklyn, NY	6/17/1943
Mann, Aimee	Richmond, VA	8/9/1960
Manoff, Dinah	New York, NY	1/25/1958
Manson, Marilyn	Canton, OH	1/5/1969
Mantegna, Joe	Chicago, IL	11/13/1947
Mantello, Joe	Rockford, IL.	12/27/1962
Mara, Kate	Bedford, NY.	2/27/1983
Mara, Rooney	Bedford, NY.	4/17/1985
Margulies, Julianna	Spring Valley, NY	6/8/1966
Marie, Constance	Hollywood, CA.	9/9/1965
Marin, Cheech	Los Angeles, CA	7/13/1946
Marinaro, Ed	New York, NY	3/31/1950
Maron, Marc	Jersey City, NJ.	9/27/1963
Mars, Bruno	Honolulu, HI	10/8/1985
Marsalis, Branford	Breaux Bridge, LA	8/26/1960
Marsalis, Wynton	New Orleans, LA	10/18/1961
Marsh, Jean	London, England, UK	7/1/1934
Martin, Chris	Devon, England, UK	3/2/1977
Martin, Jesse L.	Rocky Mount, VA	1/18/1969
Martin, Kellie	Riverside, CA.	10/16/1975
Martin, Ricky	San Juan, Puerto Rico	12/24/1971
Martin, Steve	Waco, TX.	8/14/1945
Martindale, Margo	Jacksonville, TX.	7/18/1951
Martins, Peter	Copenhagen, Denmark	10/27/1946
Maslany, Tatiana	Regina, SK, Canada	9/22/1985
Mason, Marsha	St. Louis, MO.	4/3/1942
Masterson, Mary Stuart	New York, NY	6/28/1966
Mastrantonio, Mary Elizabeth	Lombard, IL.	11/17/1958
Masur, Richard	New York, NY	11/20/1948
Mathers, Jerry	Sioux City, IA	6/2/1948
Matheson, Tim	Glendale, CA.	12/31/1947
Mathis, Johnny	Gilmer, TX	9/30/1935
Matlin, Marlee	Morton Grove, IL	8/24/1965
Matthews, Dave	Johannesburg, South Africa	1/9/1967
May, Elaine	Philadelphia, PA	4/21/1932
Mayer, John	Bridgeport, CT.	10/16/1977
Mays, Jayma	Bristol, TN	7/16/1979
Mazar, Debi	Jamaica, Queens, NY	8/13/1964
McAdams, Rachel	London, ON, Canada	11/17/1978
McArdle, Andrea	Abington, PA	11/5/1963
McAvoy, James	Glasgow, Scotland, UK	4/21/1979
McBride, Patricia	Teaneck, NJ	8/23/1942
McCarthy, Andrew	Westfield, NJ	11/29/1962
McCarthy, Jenny	Chicago, IL	11/1/1972
McCarthy, Melissa	Plainfield, IL.	8/26/1970
McCartney, Paul	Liverpool, England, UK	6/18/1942
McConaughey, Matthew	Uvalde, TX.	11/4/1969
McCoo, Marilyn	Jersey City, NJ.	9/30/1943
McCormack, Eric	Toronto, ON, Canada	4/18/1963
McCormack, Mary	Plainsfield, NJ	2/8/1969
McCrane, Paul	Philadelphia, PA	1/19/1961
McDaniel, James	Washington, DC	3/25/1958
McDermott, Dylan	Waterbury, CT	10/26/1961
McDiarmid, Ian	Carnoustie, Tayside, Scot., UK	4/17/1944?
McDonald, Audra	Berlin, Germany	7/3/1970
McDonnell, Mary	Wilkes-Barre, PA	4/28/1952
McDormand, Frances	Chicago, IL	6/23/1957
McDowell, Malcolm	Leeds, England, UK	6/13/1943
McEntire, Reba	McAlester, OK	3/28/1955
McFerrin, Bobby	New York, NY	3/11/1950
McGillis, Kelly	Newport Beach, CA	7/9/1957
McGovern, Elizabeth	Evanston, IL	7/18/1961
McGovern, Maureen	Youngstown, OH	7/27/1949
McGraw, Tim	Delhi, LA	5/1/1967
McGregor, Ewan	Crieff, Scotland, UK	3/31/1971
McHale, Joel	Rome, Italy	11/20/1971
McHale, Kevin	Plano, TX.	6/14/1988
McKean, Michael	New York, NY	10/17/1947
McKechnie, Donna	Pontiac, MI	11/16/1942
McKellen, Ian	Burnley, England, UK	5/25/1939
McKenzie, Ben	Austin, TX	9/12/1978
McKidd, Kevin	Elgin, Scotland, UK	8/9/1973
McKinnon, Kate	Sea Cliff, NY	1/6/1984
McLachlan, Sarah	Halifax, NS, Canada	1/28/1968
McLean, A. J.	West Palm Beach, FL	1/9/1978
McNichol, Kristy	Los Angeles, CA	9/11/1962
McRaney, Gerald	Collins, MS	8/19/1947
McQueen, Steve	London, England, UK	10/9/1969
McQueen, Steven R.	Los Angeles, CA	7/13/1988
McShane, Ian	Blackburn, England, UK	9/29/1942
Meester, Leighton	Marco Island, FL	4/9/1986
Megan Thee Stallion	Bexar County, TX.	2/15/1995
Mehta, Zubin	Bombay, India	4/29/1936
Mellencamp, John	Seymour, IN	10/7/1951
Meloni, Christopher	Washington, DC	4/2/1961
Mendes, Sam	Redding, England, UK	8/1/1965
Mendes, Shawn	Toronto, ON, Canada	8/8/1998
Menzel, Idina	Syosset, NY.	5/30/1971
Menzies, Tobias	London, England, UK	3/7/1974
Merchant, Natalie	Jamestown, NY	10/26/1963
Merkerson, S. Epatha	Saginaw, MI.	11/28/1952
Messing, Debra	Brooklyn, NY	8/15/1968
Metcalf, Laurie	Carbondale, IL.	6/16/1955
Meyers, Seth	Bedford, NH.	12/28/1973
Michaels, Al	Brooklyn, NY	11/12/1944
Michaels, Bret	Butler, PA	3/15/1963
Michaels, Lorne	Toronto, ON, Canada	11/17/1944
Michele, Lea	Bronx, NY	8/29/1986

Name	Birthplace	Birthdate
Midler, Bette	Honolulu, HI	12/1/1945
Midori (Goto)	Osaka, Japan	10/25/1971
Miguel, Luis	San Juan, PR	4/19/1970
Mike D	Brooklyn, NY	11/20/1965
Milano, Alyssa	Brooklyn, NY	12/19/1972
Miles, Vera	nr. Boise City, OK.	8/23/1930
Miller, Dennis	Pittsburgh, PA	11/3/1953
Miller, Jonny Lee	Kingston upon Thames, England, UK	11/15/1972
Miller, Penelope Ann	Santa Monica, CA	1/13/1964
Mills, Donna	Chicago, IL	12/11/1943
Mills, Hayley	London, England, UK	4/18/1946
Milnes, Sherrill	Downers Grove, IL	1/10/1935
Milsap, Ronnie	Robinsville, NC	1/16/1943
Minaj, Nicki	St. James, Trinidad and Tobago	12/8/1982
Ming-Na (Wen)	Coloane Island, Macao	11/20/1963
Minhaj, Hasan	Davis, CA	9/23/1985
Minnelli, Liza	Los Angeles, CA	3/12/1946
Minogue, Kylie	Melbourne, Vic., Australia	5/28/1968
Miranda, Lin-Manuel	New York, NY	1/16/1980
Mirren, Helen	London, England, UK	7/26/1945
Mitchell, Brian Stokes	Seattle, WA	10/31/1957
Mitchell, Elizabeth	Los Angeles, CA	3/27/1970
Mitchell, Jerry	Paw Paw, MI	1/15/1960
Mitchell, Joni	Fort McLeod, AB, Canada	11/7/1943
Moby	New York, NY	9/11/1965
Modine, Matthew	Loma Linda, CA	3/22/1959
Molina, Alfred	London, England, UK	5/24/1953
Moloney, Janel	Woodland Hills, CA	10/3/1969
Monáe, Janelle	Kansas City, KS	12/1/1985
Monaghan, Dominic	Berlin, Germany	12/8/1976
Monica (Arnold)	College Park, GA	10/24/1980
Mo'Nique	Woodlawn, MD	12/11/1967
Moore, Demi	Roswell, NM	11/11/1962
Moore, Julianne	Fort Bragg, NC	12/3/1960
Moore, Mandy	Nashua, NH	4/10/1984
Moore, Melba	New York, NY	10/29/1945
Moore, Michael	Flint, MI	4/23/1954
Moore, Terry	Los Angeles, CA	1/7/1929
Morales, Esai	Brooklyn, NY	10/1/1962
Moranis, Rick	Toronto, ON, Canada	4/18/1953
Moreno, Rita	Humacao, Puerto Rico	12/11/1931
Morgan, Jeffrey Dean	Seattle, WA	4/22/1966
Morgan, Piers	Guildford, Surrey, UK	3/30/1965
Morgan, Tracy	Bronx, NY	11/10/1968
Moriarty, Michael	Detroit, MI	4/5/1941
Morris, Garrett	New Orleans, LA	2/1/1937
Morissette, Alanis	Ottawa, ON, Canada	6/1/1974
Morrison, Matthew	Fort Ord, CA	10/30/1978
Morrison, Van	Belfast, N. Ireland, UK	8/31/1945
Morrissey (Steven Patrick)	Manchester, England, UK	5/22/1959
Morrow, Rob	New Rochelle, NY	9/21/1962
Morse, David	Beverly, MA	10/11/1953
Mortensen, Viggo	New York, NY	10/20/1958
Mortimer, Emily	London, England, UK	12/1/1971
Morton, Joe	New York, NY	10/18/1947
Morton, Samantha	Nottingham, England, UK	5/13/1977
Moses, William	Los Angeles, CA	11/17/1959
Moss, Carrie-Anne	Vancouver, BC, Canada	8/21/1967
Moss, Elisabeth	Los Angeles, CA	7/24/1982
Moss, Kate	Croydon, Surrey, Eng., UK	1/16/1974
Moss-Bachrach, Ebon	Amherst, MA	3/19/1977
Moyer, Stephen	Brentwood, UK	10/11/1969
Moynahan, Bridget	Binghamton, NY	4/28/1971
Mueller-Stahl, Armin	Tilsit, E. Prussia	12/17/1930
Mulaney, John	Chicago, IL	8/26/1982
Muldaur, Diana	Brooklyn, NY	8/19/1938
Mulgrew, Kate	Dubuque, IA	4/29/1955
Mullally, Megan	Los Angeles, CA	11/12/1958
Mullan, Peter	Peterhead, Scotland, UK	11/2/1959
Mulligan, Carey	London, England, UK	5/28/1985
Mulroney, Dermot	Alexandria, VA	10/31/1963
Muniz, Frankie	Wood-Ridge, NJ	12/5/1985
Murphy, Annie	Ottawa, ON, Canada	12/19/1986
Murphy, Ben	Jonesboro, AR	3/6/1942
Murphy, Cillian	Cork, Ireland	5/25/1976
Murphy, Donna	Corona, Queens, NY	3/7/1958
Murphy, Eddie	Brooklyn, NY	4/3/1961
Murphy, Michael	Los Angeles, CA	5/5/1938
Murphy, Ryan	Indianapolis, IN	11/30/1965
Murray, Anne	Springhill, NS, Canada	6/20/1945
Murray, Bill	Wilmette, IL	9/21/1950
Musburger, Brent	Portland, OR	5/26/1939
Muti, Riccardo	Naples, Italy	7/28/1941
Myers, Mike	Scarborough, ON, Canada	5/25/1963
Nagra, Parminder	Leicester, England, UK	10/5/1975

Name	Birthplace	Birthdate
Nanjiani, Kumail	Karachi, Pakistan	2/21/1978
Nash, Graham	Blackpool, England, UK	2/2/1942
Nash, Niecy	Palmdale, CA	2/23/1970
Naughton, James	Middletown, CT	12/6/1945
Navarro, Dave	Santa Monica, CA	6/7/1967
Nealon, Kevin	St. Louis, MO	11/18/1953
Neeson, Liam	Ballymena, N. Ireland, UK	6/7/1952
Neill, Sam	Ulster, N. Ireland, UK	9/14/1947
Nelligan, Kate	London, ON, Canada	3/16/1951
Nelly	Austin, TX	11/2/1974
Nelson, Craig T.	Spokane, WA	4/4/1944
Nelson, Judd	Portland, ME	11/28/1959
Nelson, Tracy	Santa Monica, CA	10/25/1963
Nelson, Willie	Abbott, TX	4/30/1933
Netrebko, Anna	Krasnodar, Russia	9/18/1971
Neuwirth, Bebe	Newark, NJ	12/31/1958
Neville, Aaron	New Orleans, LA	1/24/1941
Newman, Randy	New Orleans, LA	11/28/1943
Newton, Thandiwe	London, England, UK	11/6/1972
Newton, Wayne	Norfolk, VA	4/3/1942
Nicholas, Denise	Detroit, MI	7/12/1944
Nicholson, Jack	Neptune, NJ	4/22/1937
Nicks, Stevie	Phoenix, AZ	5/26/1948
Nighy, Bill	Caterham, Surrey, Eng., UK	12/12/1949
Nixon, Cynthia	New York, NY	4/9/1966
Noah, Trevor	Soweto, South Africa	2/20/1984
Noble, John	Port Pirie, S. Austral., Australia	8/20/1948
Nolan, Christopher	London, England, UK	7/30/1970
Nolte, Nick	Omaha, NE	2/8/1941
Noone, Peter	Manchester, England, UK	11/5/1947
Norris, Chuck	Ryan, OK	3/10/1940
Northam, Jeremy	Cambridge, England, UK	12/1/1961
Norton, Edward	Boston, MA	8/18/1969
Noth, Christopher	Madison, WI	11/13/1954
Novak, Kim	Chicago, IL	2/13/1933
Nuyen, France	Marseilles, France	7/31/1939
Nyong'o, Lupita	Mexico City, Mexico	3/1/1983
Oates, John	New York, NY	4/7/1949
O'Brien, Conan	Brookline, MA	4/18/1963
O'Brien, Margaret	San Diego, CA	1/15/1937
Ocean, Billy	Fyzabad, Trinidad and Tobago	1/21/1950
Ocean, Frank	Long Beach, CA	10/28/1987
O'Connell, Finneas	Los Angeles, CA	7/30/1997
O'Connor, Josh	Cheltenham, England, UK	5/20/1990
Odenkirk, Bob	Berwyn, IL	10/22/1962
Odom, Leslie, Jr.	Queens, NY	8/6/1981
O'Donnell, Chris	Winnetka, IL	6/26/1970
O'Donnell, Rosie	Commack, NY	3/21/1962
Offerman, Nick	Joliet, IL	6/26/1970
O'Grady, Gail	Detroit, MI	1/23/1963
Oh, Sandra	Nepean, ON, Canada	7/20/1971
O'Hara, Catherine	Toronto, ON, Canada	3/4/1954
O'Hare, Denis	Kansas City, MO	1/17/1962
Oka, Masi	Tokyo, Japan	12/27/1974
Oldman, Gary	South London, Eng., UK	3/21/1958
Olin, Ken	Chicago, IL	7/30/1954
Olin, Lena	Stockholm, Sweden	3/22/1955
Oliver, Jamie	Clavering, England, UK	5/27/1975
Oliver, John	Birmingham, England, UK	4/23/1977
Olmos, Edward James	E. Los Angeles, CA	2/24/1947
Olsen, Ashley	Sherman Oaks, CA	6/13/1986
Olsen, Elizabeth	Sherman Oaks, CA	2/16/1989
Olsen, Mary-Kate	Sherman Oaks, CA	6/13/1986
Olson, Nancy	Milwaukee, WI	7/14/1928
Olyphant, Timothy	Honolulu, HI	5/20/1968
O'Malley, Mike	Boston, MA	10/31/1966
O'Neal, Tatum	Los Angeles, CA	11/5/1963
O'Neill, Ed.	Youngstown, OH	4/12/1946
Ontkean, Michael	Vancouver, BC, Canada	1/24/1946
O'Quinn, Terry	Newbury, MI	7/15/1952
Orlando, Tony	New York, NY	4/3/1944
Ormond, Julia	Epsom, England, UK	1/4/1965
Osbourne, Jack	London, England, UK	11/8/1985
Osbourne, Kelly	London, England, UK	10/27/1984
Osbourne, Ozzy	Birmingham, England, UK	12/3/1948
Osbourne, Sharon	London, England, UK	10/9/1952
Osment, Haley Joel	Los Angeles, CA	4/10/1988
Osmond, Donny	Ogden, UT	12/9/1957
Osmond, Marie	Ogden, UT	10/13/1959
Oswalt, Patton	Portsmouth, VA	1/27/1969
O'Toole, Annette	Houston, TX	4/1/1951
Owen, Clive	Keresley, England, UK	10/3/1964
Oyelowo, David	Oxford, England, UK	4/1/1976
Oz, Frank	Herford, England, UK	5/25/1944
Pacino, Al	New York, NY	4/25/1940
Page, Elliot	Halifax, NS, Canada	2/21/1987

Name	Birthplace	Birthdate
Page, Jimmy	Heston, England, UK	1/9/1944
Paisley, Brad	Glen Dale, WV	10/28/1972
Palin, Michael	Sheffield, England, UK	5/5/1943
Palmer, Keke	Harvey, IL	8/26/1993
Palminteri, Chazz	Bronx, NY	5/15/1951
Paltrow, Gwyneth	Los Angeles, CA	9/27/1972
Panettiere, Hayden	Palisades, NY	8/21/1989
Panjabi, Archie	Edgware, England, UK	5/31/1972
Pantoliano, Joe	Hoboken, NJ	9/12/1951
Paquin, Anna	Winnipeg, MB, Canada	7/24/1982
Parker, Jameson	Baltimore, MD	11/18/1947
Parker, Mary-Louise	Fort Jackson, SC	8/2/1964
Parker, Sarah Jessica	Nelsonville, OH	3/25/1965
Parsons, Estelle	Marblehead, MA	11/20/1927
Parsons, Jim	Houston, TX	3/24/1973
Parton, Dolly	Sevierville, TN	1/19/1946
Pascal, Pedro	Santiago, Chile	4/2/1975
Pasdar, Adrian	Pittsfield, MA	4/30/1965
Patel, Dev	London, England, UK	4/23/1990
Patinkin, Mandy	Chicago, IL	11/30/1952
Patric, Jason	Flushing, Queens, NY	6/17/1966
Pattinson, Robert	London, England, UK	5/13/1986
Patton, Will	Charleston, SC	6/14/1954
Paul, Aaron	Emmett, ID	8/27/1979
Paul, Adrian	London, England, UK	5/29/1959
Paulson, Sarah	Tampa, FL	12/17/1975
Pearce, Guy	Ely, England, UK	10/5/1967
Peele, Jordan	New York, NY	2/21/1979
Peet, Amanda	New York, NY	1/11/1972
Penn, Kal	Montclair, NJ	4/23/1977
Penn, Sean	Burbank, CA	8/17/1960
Pepper, Barry	Campbell River, BC, Can.	4/4/1970
Perez, Rosie	Brooklyn, NY	9/6/1964
Perkins, Elizabeth	Flushing, Queens, NY	11/18/1960
Perlman, Itzhak	Tel Aviv, Israel	8/31/1945
Perlman, Rhea	Brooklyn, NY	3/31/1948
Perlman, Ron	New York, NY	4/13/1950
Perrine, Valerie	Galveston, TX	9/3/1943
Perry, Katy	Santa Barbara, CA	10/25/1984
Perry, Tyler	New Orleans, LA	9/13/1969
Pesci, Joe	Newark, NJ	2/9/1943
Peters, Bernadette	Ozone Park, Queens, NY	2/28/1948
Peters, Evan	St. Louis, MO	1/20/1987
Petty, Lori	Chattanooga, TN	3/23/1963
Pfeiffer, Michelle	Santa Ana, CA	4/29/1958
Phair, Liz	New Haven, CT	4/17/1967
Phillippe, Ryan	New Castle, DE	9/10/1974
Phillips, Lou Diamond	Subic Bay, Philippines	2/17/1962
Phillips, Mackenzie	Alexandria, VA	11/10/1959
Phillips, Michelle	Long Beach, CA	6/4/1944
Phillips, Sian	Bettws, Wales, UK	5/14/1934
Phoenix, Joaquin	San Juan, Puerto Rico	10/28/1974
Pierce, David Hyde	Albany, NY	4/3/1959
Pike, Rosamund	London, England, UK	1/27/1979
Pinchot, Bronson	New York, NY	5/20/1959
Pink	Doylestown, PA	9/8/1979
Pinkett Smith, Jada	Baltimore, MD	9/18/1971
Pirner, Dave	Green Bay, WI	4/16/1964
Piscopo, Joe	Passaic, NJ	6/17/1951
Pitbull	Miami, FL	1/15/1981
Pitt, Brad	Shawnee, OK	12/18/1963
Piven, Jeremy	New York, NY	7/26/1965
Plant, Robert	W. Bromwich, Eng., UK	8/20/1948
Platt, Ben	Los Angeles, CA	9/24/1993
Plaza, Aubrey	Wilmington, DE	6/26/1984
Plimpton, Martha	New York, NY	11/16/1970
Plowright, Joan	Brigg, England, UK	10/28/1929
Plummer, Amanda	New York, NY	3/23/1957
Poehler, Amy	Newton, MA	9/16/1971
Polanski, Roman	Paris, France	8/18/1933
Pompeo, Ellen	Everett, MA	11/10/1969
Pop, Iggy	Muskegon, MI	4/21/1947
Porter, Billy	Pittsburgh, PA	9/21/1969
Portman, Natalie	Jerusalem, Israel	6/9/1981
Posey, Parker	Baltimore, MD	11/8/1968
Potts, Annie	Nashville, TN	10/28/1952
Povich, Maury	Washington, DC	1/17/1939
Powers, Stefanie	Hollywood, CA	11/2/1942
Pratt, Chris	Virginia, MN	6/21/1979
Prentiss, Paula	San Antonio, TX	3/4/1939
Prepon, Laura	Watchung, NJ	3/7/1980
Presley, Priscilla	Brooklyn, NY	5/24/1945
Pressly, Jaime	Kinston, NC	7/30/1977
Price, Leontyne	Laurel, MS	2/10/1927
Priestley, Jason	Vancouver, BC, Canada	8/28/1969
Prince, Faith	Augusta, GA	8/5/1957
Principal, Victoria	Fukuoka, Japan	1/3/1950
Probst, Jeff	Wichita, KS	11/4/1962
Proctor, Emily	Raleigh, NC	10/8/1968
Pryce, Jonathan	Holywell, N. Wales, UK	6/1/1947
Puck, Wolfgang	St. Veit, Austria	1/8/1949
Pulliam, Keshia Knight	Newark, NJ	4/9/1979
Pullman, Bill	Hornell, NY	12/17/1953
Purcell, Sarah	Richmond, IN	10/8/1948
Purefoy, James	Taunton, England, UK	6/3/1964
Quaid, Dennis	Houston, TX	4/9/1954
Quaid, Randy	Houston, TX	10/1/1950
Quan, Ke Huy	Saigon, Vietnam	8/20/1971
Queen Latifah	Newark, NJ	3/18/1970
Quinn, Aidan	Chicago, IL	3/8/1959
Quinn, Colin	Brooklyn, NY	6/6/1959
Quinn, Martha	Albany, NY	5/11/1959
Quinto, Zachary	Pittsburgh, PA	6/2/1977
Rachins, Alan	Cambridge, MA	10/3/1942
Radcliffe, Daniel	London, England, UK	7/23/1989
Radnor, Josh	Columbus, OH	7/29/1974
Rae, Issa	Los Angeles, CA	1/12/1985
Raffi (Cavoukian)	Cairo, Egypt	7/8/1948
Rainbow, Randy	Plantation, FL	7/6/1981
Raitt, Bonnie	Burbank, CA	11/8/1949
Ralph, Sheryl Lee	Waterbury, CT	12/30/1956
Ramey, Samuel	Colby, KS	3/28/1942
Ramirez, Sara	Mazatlan, Mexico	8/31/1975
Ramos, Anthony	Brooklyn, NY	11/1/1991
Rampling, Charlotte	Sturmer, MA	2/5/1946
Ramsay, Gordon	Elderslie, Scotland, UK	11/8/1966
Ramsey, Bella	Nottingham, Eng., UK	9/30/2003
Rancic, Giuliana	Naples, Italy	8/17/1975
Randolph, Da'Vine Joy	Philadelphia, PA	5/21/1986
Raphael, Sally Jessy	Easton, PA	2/25/1935
Rashad, Phylicia	Houston, TX	6/19/1948
Ratzenberger, John	Bridgeport, CT	4/6/1947
Raver, Kim	New York, NY	3/15/1969
Ray, Rachael	Glen Falls, NY	8/25/1968
Redford, Robert	Santa Monica, CA	8/18/1936
Redgrave, Vanessa	London, England, UK	1/30/1937
Redmayne, Eddie	London, England, UK	1/6/1982
Reed, Rex	Ft. Worth, TX	10/2/1938
Reeves, Keanu	Beirut, Lebanon	9/2/1964
Reeves, Martha	Eufaula, AL	7/18/1941
Regalbuto, Joe	New York, NY	8/24/1949
Reid, Tara	Wyckoff, NJ	11/8/1975
Reid, Tim	Norfolk, VA	12/19/1944
Reid, Vernon	London, England, UK	8/22/1958
Reilly, John C.	Chicago, IL	5/24/1965
Reiner, Rob	Bronx, NY	3/6/1947
Reinhold, Judge	Wilmington, DE	5/21/1957
Reiser, Paul	New York, NY	3/30/1957
Remini, Leah	Brooklyn, NY	6/15/1970
Renner, Jeremy	Modesto, CA	1/7/1971
Reynolds, Ryan	Vancouver, BC, Canada	10/23/1976
Reznor, Trent	Mercer, PA	5/17/1965
Rhames, Ving	New York, NY	5/12/1959
Rhimes, Shonda	Chicago, IL	1/13/1970
Rhymes, Busta	Brooklyn, NY	5/20/1972
Rhys, Matthew	Cardiff, Wales, UK	11/4/1974
Rhys Meyers, Jonathan	Dublin, Ireland	7/27/1977
Ribisi, Giovanni	Los Angeles, CA	12/17/1974
Ricci, Christina	Santa Monica, CA	2/12/1980
Richards, Denise	Downers Grove, IL	2/17/1971
Richards, Keith	Dartford, Kent, Eng., UK	12/18/1943
Richards, Michael	Culver City, CA	7/24/1949
Richardson, Kevin	Lexington, KY	10/3/1971
Richardson, Miranda	Lancashire, Eng., UK	3/3/1958
Richardson, Patricia	Bethesda, MD	2/23/1951
Richie, Lionel	Tuskegee, AL	6/20/1949
Richie, Nicole	Berkeley, CA	9/21/1981
Richter, Andy	Grand Rapids, MI	10/28/1966
Riegert, Peter	New York, NY	4/11/1947
Rihanna	St. Michael, Barbados	2/20/1988
Riley, Amber	Long Beach, CA	2/15/1986
Rimes, LeAnn	Jackson, MS	8/28/1982
Ringwald, Molly	Roseville, CA	2/18/1968
Ripa, Kelly	Stratford, NJ	10/2/1970
Rivera, Geraldo	New York, NY	7/4/1943
Robbie, Margot	Dalby, Qld., Australia	7/2/1990
Robbins, Tim	W. Covina, CA	10/16/1958
Roberts, Eric	Biloxi, MS	4/18/1956
Roberts, Julia	Smyrna, GA	10/28/1967
Roberts, Tony	New York, NY	10/22/1939
Robinson, Smokey	Detroit, MI	2/19/1940
Rock, Chris	Andrews, SC	2/7/1965
Rockwell, Sam	Daly City, CA	11/5/1968
Rodrigo, Olivia	Temecula, CA	2/20/2003
Rodriguez, Michelle	Bexar County, TX	7/12/1978
Rogan, Joe	Newark, NJ	8/11/1967
Rogen, Seth	Vancouver, BC, Canada	4/15/1982
Rogers, Mimi	Coral Gables, FL	1/27/1956

Name	Birthplace	Birthdate
Rohm, Elisabeth	Dusseldorf, Germany	4/28/1973
Rollins, Henry	Washington, DC	2/13/1961
Rollins, Sonny	New York, NY	9/7/1930
Romano, Ray	Forest Hills, Queens, NY	12/21/1957
Romijn, Rebecca	Berkeley, CA	11/6/1972
Ronan, Saoirse	New York, NY	4/12/1994
Ronson, Mark	London, England, UK	9/4/1975
Ronstadt, Linda	Tucson, AZ	7/15/1946
Root, Stephen	Sarasota, FL	11/17/1951
Rose, Axl	Lafayette, IN	2/6/1962
Roseanne	Salt Lake City, UT	11/3/1952
Ross, Diana	Detroit, MI	3/26/1944
Ross, Katharine	Hollywood, CA	1/29/1940
Ross, Marion	Albert Lea, MN	10/25/1928
Ross, Tracee Ellis	Los Angeles, CA	10/29/1972
Rossdale, Gavin	London, England, UK	10/30/1965
Rossellini, Isabella	Rome, Italy	6/18/1952
Rossum, Emmy	New York, NY	9/12/1986
Roth, David Lee	Bloomington, IN	10/10/1955
Rotten, Johnny	London, England, UK	1/31/1956
Rourke, Mickey	Schenectady, NY	9/16/1952
Routh, Brandon	Des Moines, IA	10/9/1979
Routledge, Patricia	Birkenhead, England, UK	2/17/1929
Rowan, Kelly	Ottawa, ON, Canada	10/26/1965
Rubinstein, John	Beverly Hills, CA	12/8/1946
Rudd, Paul	Passaic, NJ	4/6/1969
Rudner, Rita	Miami, FL	9/17/1955?
Rudolph, Maya	Gainesville, FL	7/27/1972
Ruehl, Mercedes	Jackson Heights, Queens, NY	2/28/1948
Ruffalo, Mark	Kenosha, WI	11/22/1967
RuPaul	San Diego, CA	11/17/1960
Rupp, Debra Jo	Glendale, CA	2/24/1951
Rush, Geoffrey	Toowoomba, Qld., Australia	7/6/1951
Russell, Keri	Fountain Valley, CA	3/23/1976
Russell, Kurt	Springfield, MA	3/17/1951
Russo, Rene	Burbank, CA	2/17/1954
Ruttan, Susan	Oregon City, OR	9/16/1950
Ryan, Meg	Fairfield, CT	11/19/1961
Ryan, Roz	Detroit, MI	7/7/1951
Ryder, Winona	Winona, MN	10/29/1971
Rylance, Mark	Ashford, England, UK	1/18/1960
Sabato, Antonio, Jr.	Rome, Italy	2/29/1972
Sade (Adu)	Ibadan, Nigeria	1/16/1959
Sagal, Katey	Hollywood, CA	1/19/1954
Saint, Eva Marie	Newark, NJ	7/4/1924
St. James, Susan	Hollywood, CA	8/14/1946
St. John, Jill	Los Angeles, CA	8/19/1940
St. Patrick, Mathew	Philadelphia, PA	3/17/1968
Sajak, Pat	Chicago, IL	10/26/1946
Saldana, Zoë	Passaic, NJ	6/19/1978
Salonga, Lea	Manila, Philippines	2/22/1971
Samberg, Andy	Berkeley, CA	8/18/1978
Samms, Emma	London, England, UK	8/28/1960
San Giacomo, Laura	Hoboken, NJ	11/14/1962
Sandler, Adam	Brooklyn, NY	9/9/1966
Santana, Carlos	Autlan, Mexico	7/20/1947
Sara, Mia	Brooklyn, NY	6/19/1967
Sarandon, Susan	New York, NY	10/4/1946
Savage, Ben	Highland Park, IL	9/13/1980
Savage, Fred	Highland Park, IL	7/9/1976
Sawa, Devon	Vancouver, BC, Canada	9/7/1978
Sayles, John	Schenectady, NY	9/28/1950
Scacchi, Greta	Milan, Italy	2/18/1960
Scaggs, Boz	Canton, OH	6/8/1944
Scales, Prunella	Sutton Abinger, Eng., UK	6/22/1932
Scalia, Jack	Brooklyn, NY	11/10/1951
Scheinert, Daniel	Birmingham, AL	6/7/1987
Schiff, Richard	Bethesda, MD	5/27/1955
Schiffer, Claudia	Rheinbach, Germany	8/25/1970
Schneider, John	Mt. Kisco, NY	4/8/1960
Schneider, Rob	San Francisco, CA	10/31/1963
Schreiber, Liev	San Francisco, CA	10/4/1967
Schroder, Rick	Staten Island, NY	4/13/1970
Schumer, Amy	New York, NY	6/1/1981
Schwarzenegger, Arnold	Thal, Austria	7/30/1947
Schwimmer, David	Astoria, Queens, NY	11/2/1966
Sciorra, Annabella	Wethersfield, CT	3/24/1964
Scorsese, Martin	Flushing, Queens, NY	11/17/1942
Scott, Adam	Santa Cruz, CA	4/3/1973
Scott, Andrew	Dublin, Ireland	10/21/1976
Scott, Ridley	South Shields, Eng., UK	11/30/1937
Scott, Seann William	Cottage Grove, MN	10/3/1976
Scott Thomas, Kristin	Redruth, England, UK	5/24/1960
Seacrest, Ryan	Atlanta, GA	12/24/1974
Seagal, Steven	Lansing, MI	4/10/1951
Secor, Kyle	Tacoma, WA	5/31/1957
Sedaka, Neil	Brooklyn, NY	3/13/1939
Sedgwick, Kyra	New York, NY	8/19/1965
Seehorn, Rhea	Norfolk, VA	5/12/1972
Segel, Jason	Los Angeles, CA	1/18/1980
Seidelman, Susan	Abington, PA	12/11/1952
Seinfeld, Jerry	Brooklyn, NY	4/29/1954
Sellecca, Connie	Bronx, NY	5/25/1955
Selleck, Tom	Detroit, MI	1/29/1945
Severinsen, Doc	Arlington, OR	7/7/1927
Sevigny, Chloë	Springfield, MA	11/18/1974
Sewell, Rufus	Twickenham, Middlesex, England, UK	10/29/1967
Seyfried, Amanda	Allentown, PA	12/3/1985
Seymour, Jane	Hillingdon, England, UK	2/15/1951
Shackelford, Ted	Oklahoma City, OK	6/23/1946
Shaffer, Paul	Thunder Bay, ON, Canada	11/28/1949
Shakira (Mebarak Ripoll)	Barranquilla, Colombia	2/2/1977
Shalhoub, Tony	Green Bay, WI	10/9/1953
Shannon, Molly	Shaker Heights, OH	9/16/1964
Shatner, William	Montréal, QC, Canada	3/22/1931
Shaughnessy, Charles	London, England, UK	2/9/1955
Shaw, Fiona	Cork, Ireland	7/10/1958
Shawkat, Alia	Riverside, CA	4/18/1989
Shea, John	North Conway, NH	4/14/1949
Shearer, Harry	Los Angeles, CA	12/23/1943
Sheedy, Ally	New York, NY	6/13/1962
Sheen, Charlie	Los Angeles, CA	9/3/1965
Sheen, Martin	Dayton, OH	8/3/1940
Sheen, Michael	Newport, Wales, UK	2/5/1969
Sheeran, Ed	Hebden Bridge, West Yorkshire, Eng., UK	2/17/1991
Sheindlin, Judy	Brooklyn, NY	10/21/1942
Shelton, Blake	Ada, OK	6/18/1976
Shepherd, Cybill	Memphis, TN	2/18/1950
Shepherd, Sherri	Chicago, IL	4/22/1967
Sheridan, Nicollette	Worthing, England, UK	11/21/1963
Shields, Brooke	New York, NY	5/31/1965
Shire, Talia	Lake Success, NY	4/25/1946
Short, Martin	Hamilton, ON, Canada	3/26/1950
Shortz, Will	Crawfordsville, IN	8/26/1952
Show, Grant	Detroit, MI	2/27/1962
Shue, Andrew	South Orange, NJ	2/20/1967
Shue, Elisabeth	Wilmington, DE	10/6/1963
Shyamalan, M. Night	Pondicherry, India	8/6/1970
Sidibe, Gabourey	Brooklyn, NY	5/6/1983
Sigler, Jamie-Lynn	Jericho, NY	5/15/1981
Silverman, Jonathan	Beverly Hills, CA	8/5/1966
Silverman, Sarah	Bedford, NH	12/1/1970
Silverstone, Alicia	San Francisco, CA	10/4/1976
Simmons, Gene	Haifa, Israel	8/25/1949
Simmons, Henry	Stamford, CT	7/1/1970
Simon, Carly	New York, NY	6/25/1945
Simon, Paul	Newark, NJ	10/13/1941
Simpson, Ashlee	Waco, TX	10/3/1984
Simpson, Jessica	Abilene, TX	7/10/1980
Sinatra, Nancy	Jersey City, NJ	6/8/1940
Sinbad	Benton Harbor, MI	11/10/1956
Sinise, Gary	Blue Island, IL	3/17/1955
Sisto, Jeremy	Grass Valley, CA	10/6/1974
Skarsgard, Alexander	Stockholm, Sweden	8/25/1976
Skarsgard, Stellan	Gothenburg, Sweden	6/13/1951
Skerritt, Tom	Detroit, MI	8/25/1933
Slater, Christian	New York, NY	8/18/1969
Slater, Helen	Massapequa, NY	12/15/1963
Slattery, John	Boston, MA	8/13/1962
Slezak, Erika	Hollywood, CA	8/5/1946
Slick, Grace	Evanston, IL	10/30/1939
Smart, Jean	Seattle, WA	9/13/1951
Smirnoff, Karina	Kharkiv, Ukraine	1/2/1978
Smirnoff, Yakov	Odessa, Ukraine	1/24/1951
Smith, Allison	New York, NY	12/9/1969
Smith, Jaclyn	Houston, TX	10/26/1945
Smith, Jaden	Malibu, CA	7/8/1998
Smith, Kevin	Red Bank, NJ	8/2/1970
Smith, Lois	Topeka, KS	11/3/1930
Smith, Patti	Chicago, IL	12/30/1946
Smith, Robert	Blackpool, England, UK	4/21/1959
Smith, Sam	London, England, UK	5/19/1992
Smith, Will	Philadelphia, PA	9/25/1968
Smith, Willow	Los Angeles, CA	10/31/2000
Smits, Jimmy	Brooklyn, NY	7/9/1955
Smothers, Dick	Governor's Island, NY	11/20/1938
Smulders, Cobie	Vancouver, BC, Canada	4/3/1982
Snipes, Wesley	Orlando, FL	7/31/1962
Snooki (Nicole Polizzi)	Santiago, Chile	11/23/1987

Name	Birthplace	Birthdate
Snoop Dogg	Long Beach, CA	10/20/1971
Soderbergh, Steven	Atlanta, GA	1/14/1963
Soloway, Joey	Chicago, IL	9/26/1965
Somerhalder, Ian	Covington, LA	12/8/1978
Sommer, Elke	Berlin, Germany	11/5/1940
Sorbo, Kevin	Mound, MN	9/24/1958
Sorkin, Aaron	New York, NY	6/9/1961
Sorvino, Mira	Tenafly, NJ	9/28/1967
Spacek, Sissy	Quitman, TX	12/25/1949
Spacey, Kevin	South Orange, NJ	7/26/1959
Spade, David	Birmingham, MI	7/22/1964
Spader, James	Boston, MA	2/7/1960
Spalding, Esperanza	Portland, OR	10/18/1984
Spano, Joe	San Francisco, CA	7/7/1946
Spears, Britney	Kentwood, LA	12/2/1981
Spears, Jamie-Lynn	McComb, MS	4/4/1991
Spelling, Tori	Los Angeles, CA	5/16/1973
Spencer, Octavia	Montgomery, AL	5/25/1972
Spielberg, Steven	Cincinnati, OH	12/18/1946
Spiner, Brent	Houston, TX	2/2/1949
Springfield, Rick	Sydney, NSW, Australia	8/23/1949
Springsteen, Bruce	Long Branch, NJ	9/23/1949
Squibb, June	Vandalia, IL	11/6/1929
Stahl, Nick	Harlingen, TX	12/5/1979
Stallone, Sylvester	New York, NY	7/6/1946
Stamos, John	Cypress, CA	8/19/1963
Stamp, Terence	Stepney, England, UK	7/22/1938
Staples, Mavis	Chicago, IL	7/10/1939
Stapleton, Chris	Lexington, KY	4/15/1978
Starr, Ringo	Liverpool, England, UK	7/7/1940
Statham, Jason	Shirebrook, England, UK	7/26/1967
Staunton, Imelda	London, Eng., UK	1/9/1956
Steenburgen, Mary	Newport, AR	2/8/1953
Stefani, Gwen	Fullterton, CA	10/3/1969
Stein, Ben	Washington, DC	11/25/1944
Stern, Daniel	Bethesda, MD	8/28/1957
Stern, Howard	Roosevelt, NY	1/12/1954
Stevens, Andrew	Memphis, TN	6/10/1955
Stevens, Cat (Yusef Islam)	London, England, UK	7/21/1948
Stevens, Connie	Brooklyn, NY	8/8/1938
Stevenson, Parker	Philadelphia, PA	6/4/1952
Stewart, French	Albuquerque, NM	2/20/1964
Stewart, Jon	New York, NY	11/28/1962
Stewart, Kristen	Los Angeles, CA	4/9/1990
Stewart, Patrick	Mirfield, England, UK	7/13/1940
Stewart, Rod	London, England, UK	1/10/1945
Stiles, Julia	New York, NY	3/28/1981
Stiller, Ben	New York, NY	11/30/1965
Stills, Stephen	Dallas, TX	1/3/1945
Sting	Newcastle upon Tyne, England, UK	10/2/1951
Stipe, Michael	Decatur, GA	1/4/1960
Stoltz, Eric	Whittier, CA	9/30/1961
Stone, Dee Wallace	Kansas City, KS	12/14/1948
Stone, Emma	Scottsdale, AZ	11/6/1988
Stone, Oliver	New York, NY	9/15/1946
Stone, Sharon	Meadville, PA	3/10/1958
Stonestreet, Eric	Kansas City, KS	9/9/1971
Stookey, Paul	Baltimore, MD	12/30/1937
Stowe, Madeleine	Eagle Rock, CA	8/18/1958
Strahan, Michael	Houston, TX	11/21/1971
Strait, George	Pearsall, TX	5/18/1952
Strasser, Robin	New York, NY	5/7/1945
Strathairn, David	San Francisco, CA	1/26/1949
Strauss, Peter	Croton-on-Hudson, NY	2/20/1947
Streep, Meryl	Summit, NJ	6/22/1949
Streisand, Barbra	Brooklyn, NY	4/24/1942
Stringfield, Sherry	Colorado Springs, CO	6/24/1967
Stroman, Susan	Wilmington, DE	10/17/1954
Strong, Jeremy	Boston, MA	12/25/1978
Struthers, Sally	Portland, OR	7/28/1948
Styles, Harry	Holmes Chapel, Cheshire, Eng., UK	2/1/1994
Suchet, David	London, England, UK	5/2/1946
Sudeikis, Jason	Fairfax, VA	9/18/1975
Sullivan, Susan	New York, NY	11/18/1942
Sunjata, Daniel	Evanston, IL	12/30/1971
Sutherland, Kiefer	London, England, UK	12/21/1966
Suvari, Mena	Newport, RI	2/9/1979
Swank, Hilary	Lincoln, NE	7/30/1974
Swift, Taylor	Wyomissing, PA	12/13/1989
Swinton, Tilda	London, England, UK	11/5/1960
Swit, Loretta	Passaic, NJ	11/4/1937
Sykes, Wanda	Portsmouth, VA	3/7/1964
Szmanda, Eric	Milwaukee, WI	7/24/1975
T, Mr.	Chicago, IL	5/21/1952
Takei, George	Los Angeles, CA	4/20/1937
Tamblyn, Amber	Santa Monica, CA	5/14/1983
Tamblyn, Russ	Los Angeles, CA	12/30/1934
Tambor, Jeffrey	San Francisco, CA	7/8/1944
Tarantino, Quentin	Knoxville, TN	3/27/1963
Tatum, Channing	Cullman, AL	4/26/1980
Tautou, Audrey	Beaumont, France	8/9/1976?
Taylor, Buck	Hollywood, CA	5/13/1938
Taylor, Holland	Philadelphia, PA	1/14/1943
Taylor, James	Boston, MA	3/12/1948
Taylor, Lili	Glencoe, IL	2/20/1967
Taylor-Joy, Anya	Miami, FL	4/16/1996
Taymor, Julie	Newton, MA	12/15/1952
Te Kanawa, Kiri	Gisborne, New Zealand	3/6/1944
Teigen, Chrissy	Delta, Utah	11/30/1985
Teller	Philadelphia, PA	2/14/1948
Tennant, David	Bathgate, West Lothian, Scotland, UK	4/18/1971
Tennant, Victoria	London, England, UK	9/30/1950
Tennille, Toni	Montgomery, AL	5/8/1940
Tesh, John	Garden City, NY	7/9/1952
Tharp, Twyla	Portland, IN	7/1/1941
The Weeknd	Toronto, ON, Canada	2/16/1990
Theron, Charlize	Benoni, South Africa	8/7/1975
Thicke, Robin	Los Angeles, CA	3/10/1977
Thiessen, Tiffani	Long Beach, CA	1/23/1974
Thomas, Jonathan Taylor	Bethlehem, PA	9/8/1981
Thomas, Marlo	Deerfield, MI	11/21/1937
Thomas, Michael Tilson	Hollywood, CA	12/21/1944
Thomas, Philip Michael	Columbus, OH	5/26/1949
Thomas, Richard	New York, NY	6/13/1951
Thomas, Sean Patrick	Wilmington, DE	12/17/1970
Thompson, Emma	London, England, UK	4/15/1959
Thompson, Jack	Sydney, NSW, Australia	8/31/1940
Thompson, Kenan	Atlanta, GA	5/10/1978
Thompson, Lea	Rochester, MN	5/31/1961
Thorne-Smith, Courtney	San Francisco, CA	11/8/1967
Thornton, Billy Bob	Hot Springs, AR	8/4/1955
Thurman, Uma	Boston, MA	4/29/1970
Tiegs, Cheryl	Breckenridge, MN	9/25/1947
Tierney, Maura	Boston, MA	2/3/1965
Tilly, Jennifer	Harbor City, CA	9/16/1958
Tilly, Meg	Long Beach, CA	2/14/1960
Timberlake, Justin	Memphis, TN	1/31/1981
Tisdale, Ashley	West Deal, NJ	7/2/1985
Tomei, Marisa	Brooklyn, NY	12/4/1964
Tomlin, Lily	Detroit, MI	9/1/1939
Tonioli, Bruno	Ferrara, Italy	11/25/1955
Tovey, Russell	Billericay, Essex, Eng., UK	11/14/1981
Townsend, Robert	Chicago, IL	2/6/1957
Townshend, Peter	Chiswick, England, UK	5/19/1945
Travanti, Daniel J.	Kenosha, WI	3/7/1940
Travis, Nancy	Astoria, Queens, NY	9/21/1961
Travis, Randy	Marshville, NC	5/4/1959
Travolta, John	Englewood, NJ	2/18/1954
Trejo, Danny	Los Angeles, CA	5/16/1944
Tripplehorn, Jean	Tulsa, OK	6/10/1963
Tritt, Travis	Marietta, GA	2/9/1963
Tucci, Stanley	Peekskill, NY	1/11/1960
Tucker, Chris	Decatur, GA	8/31/1972
Tucker, Michael	Baltimore, MD	2/6/1944
Tucker, Tanya	Seminole, TX	10/10/1958
Tune, Tommy	Wichita Falls, TX	2/28/1939
Turlington, Christy	Walnut Creek, CA	1/2/1969
Turner, Janine	Lincoln, NE	12/6/1962
Turner, Kathleen	Springfield, MO	6/19/1954
Turner, Sophie	Northampton, Eng., UK	2/21/1996
Turturro, John	Brooklyn, NY	2/28/1957
Tveit, Aaron	Middletown, NY	10/21/1983
Twain, Shania	Windsor, ON, Canada	8/28/1965
Twiggy (Lawson)	London, England, UK	9/19/1949
Tyler, Liv	New York, NY	7/1/1977
Tyler, Steven	Yonkers, NY	3/26/1948
Uecker, Bob	Milwaukee, WI	1/26/1934
Uggams, Leslie	New York, NY	5/25/1943
Ullman, Tracey	Slough, England, UK	12/30/1959
Ullmann, Liv	Tokyo, Japan	12/16/1938
Ulrich, Skeet	Lynchburg, VA	1/20/1970
Underwood, Blair	Tacoma, WA	8/25/1964
Underwood, Carrie	Muskogee, OK	3/10/1983
Urban, Keith	Whangarei, North Island, New Zealand	10/26/1967
Urie, Michael	Dallas, TX	8/8/1980
Usher (Raymond IV)	Dallas, TX	10/14/1978

Name	Birthplace	Birthdate
Vaccaro, Brenda	Brooklyn, NY	11/18/1939
Valley, Mark	Ogdensburg, NY	12/24/1964
Valli, Frankie	Newark, NJ	5/3/1934
Van Ark, Joan	New York, NY	6/16/1943
Van Damme, Jean-Claude	Brussels, Belgium	10/18/1960
Van Der Beek, James	Cheshire, CT	3/8/1977
Van Doren, Mamie	Rowena, SD	2/6/1931
Van Dyke, Dick	West Plains, MO	12/13/1925
Van Peebles, Mario	Mexico City, Mexico	1/15/1957
Van Sant, Gus	Louisville, KY	7/24/1952
Van Zandt, Steven	Winthrop, MA	11/22/1950
VanCamp, Emily	Port Perry, ON, Canada	5/12/1986
Vance, Courtney B.	Detroit, MI	3/12/1960
Vardalos, Nia	Winnipeg, MB, Canada	9/24/1962
Vaughn, Vince	Minneapolis, MN	3/28/1970
Vedder, Eddie	Evanston, IL	12/23/1964
Ventimiglia, Milo	Anaheim, CA	7/8/1977
Vereen, Ben	Miami, FL	10/10/1946
Vergara, Sofía	Barranquilla, Colombia	7/10/1972
Vieira, Meredith	Providence, RI	12/30/1953
Vikander, Alicia	Gothenburg, Sweden	10/3/1988
Villella, Edward	Long Island, NY	10/1/1936
Vinton, Bobby	Canonsburg, PA	4/16/1935
Visnjic, Goran	Sibenik, Yugo. (Croatia)	9/9/1972
Vitale, Dick	East Rutherford, NJ	6/9/1939
Voight, Jon	Yonkers, NY	12/29/1938
Von Stade, Frederica	Somerville, NJ	6/1/1945
Von Trier, Lars	Copenhagen, Denmark	4/30/1956
Waddingham, Hannah	London, England, UK	7/28/1974
Wagner, Jack	Washington, MO	10/3/1959
Wagner, Lindsay	Los Angeles, CA	6/22/1949
Wagner, Robert	Detroit, MI	2/10/1930
Wahl, Ken	Chicago, IL	10/31/1954
Wahlberg, Donnie	Dorchester, MA	8/17/1969
Wahlberg, Mark	Dorchester, MA	6/5/1971
Waititi, Taika	Raukokore, New Zealand	8/16/1975
Waits, Tom	Pomona, CA	12/7/1949
Walden, Robert	New York, NY	9/25/1943
Walken, Christopher	Astoria, Queens, NY	3/31/1943
Waller-Bridge, Phoebe	London, England, UK	7/14/1985
Wallis, Quvenzhané	Houma, LA	8/23/2008
Walsh, Kate	San Jose, CA	10/13/1967
Waltz, Christoph	Vienna, Austria	10/4/1956
Warburton, Patrick	Paterson, NJ	11/14/1964
Ward, Fred	San Diego, CA	12/30/1942
Ward, Sela	Meridian, MS	7/11/1956
Warfield, Marsha	Chicago, IL	3/5/1954
Warner, Malcolm-Jamal	Jersey City, NJ	8/18/1970
Warren, Lesley Ann	New York, NY	8/16/1946
Warwick, Dionne	East Orange, NJ	12/12/1940
Washington, Denzel	Mt. Vernon, NY	12/28/1954
Washington, Isaiah	Houston, TX	8/3/1963
Washington, Kerry	Bronx, NY	1/31/1977
Wasikowska, Mia	Canberra, Australia	10/14/1989
Watanabe, Ken	Koide, Niigata, Japan	10/21/1959
Waters, John	Baltimore, MD	4/22/1946
Waters, Roger	Great Bookham, Eng., UK	9/6/1943
Waterston, Sam	Cambridge, MA	11/15/1940
Watson, Emily	London, England, UK	1/14/1967
Watson, Emma	Paris, France	4/15/1990
Watts, Naomi	Shoreham, England, UK	9/28/1968
Wayans, Damon	New York, NY	9/4/1960
Wayans, Keenen Ivory	Brooklyn, NY	6/8/1958
Wayans, Marlon	New York, NY	7/23/1972
Wayans, Shawn	New York, NY	1/19/1971
Weaver, Sigourney	New York, NY	10/8/1949
Weir, Peter	Sydney, NSW, Australia	8/21/1944
Weisz, Rachel	London, England, UK	3/7/1971
Weld, Tuesday	New York, NY	8/27/1943
Weller, Peter	Stevens Point, WI	6/24/1947
Welling, Tom	Putnam Valley, NY	4/26/1977
Wendt, George	Chicago, IL	10/17/1948
Wentz, Pete	Wilmette, IL	6/5/1979
West, Dominic	Sheffield, Eng., UK	10/15/1969
West, Kanye	Atlanta, GA	6/8/1977
West, Shane	Baton Rouge, LA	6/10/1978
Wettig, Patricia	Cincinnati, OH	12/4/1951
Whalley, Joanne	Manchester, England, UK	8/25/1964
Wheaton, Wil	Burbank, CA	7/29/1972
Whishaw, Ben	Clifton, Eng., UK	10/14/1980
Whitaker, Forest	Longview, TX	7/15/1961
White, Jack	Detroit, MI	7/9/1975
White, Jaleel	Pasadena, CA	11/27/1976
White, Jeremy Allen	Brooklyn, NY	2/17/1991
White, Vanna	N. Myrtle Beach, SC	2/18/1957
Whitford, Bradley	Madison, WI	10/10/1959

Name	Birthplace	Birthdate
Whittaker, Jodie	Skelmanthorpe, West Yorkshire, England, UK	6/17/1982
Wiest, Dianne	Kansas City, MO	3/28/1948
Wiig, Kristen	Canandaigua, NY	8/22/1973
Wilde, Olivia	New York, NY	3/10/1984
Wiley, Samira	Washington, DC	4/15/1987
Williams, Armstrong	Marion, SC	2/5/1959
Williams, Barry	Santa Monica, CA	9/30/1954
Williams, Billy Dee	New York, NY	4/6/1937
Williams, Hal	Columbus, OH	12/14/1938
Williams, Hank, Jr.	Shreveport, LA	5/26/1949
Williams, Jesse	Chicago, IL	8/5/1981
Williams, JoBeth	Houston, TX	12/6/1948
Williams, Lucinda	Lake Charles, LA	1/26/1953
Williams, Maisie	Bristol, Eng., UK	4/15/1997
Williams, Michelle	Kalispell, MT	9/9/1980
Williams, Montel	Baltimore, MD	7/3/1956
Williams, Paul	Omaha, NE	9/19/1940
Williams, Pharrell	Virginia Beach, VA	4/5/1973
Williams, Tyler James	New York, NY	10/9/1992
Williams, Vanessa	Millwood, NY	3/18/1963
Williamson, Kevin	New Bern, NC	3/14/1965
Willis, Bruce	Idar-Oberstein, W. Germany	3/19/1955
Wilmore, Larry	Los Angeles, CA	10/30/1961
Wilson, Brian	Inglewood, CA	6/20/1942
Wilson, Cassandra	Jackson, MS	12/4/1955
Wilson, Chandra	Houston, TX	8/27/1969
Wilson, Demond	Valdosta, GA	10/13/1946
Wilson, Luke	Dallas, TX	9/21/1971
Wilson, Owen	Dallas, TX	11/18/1968
Wilson, Rainn	Seattle, WA	1/20/1966
Wilson, Rebel	Sydney, NSW, Australia	2/3/1980
Winfrey, Oprah	Kosciusko, MS	1/29/1954
Winger, Debra	Cleveland, OH	5/16/1955
Winkler, Henry	New York, NY	10/30/1945
Winningham, Mare	Phoenix, AZ	5/16/1959
Winslet, Kate	Reading, England, UK	10/5/1975
Winwood, Steve	Birmingham, Eng., UK	5/12/1948
Witherspoon, Reese	New Orleans, LA	3/22/1976
Witt, Alicia	Worcester, MA	8/21/1975
Wolf, Scott	Boston, MA	6/4/1968
Wonder, Stevie	Saginaw, MI	5/13/1950
Wong, Ali	San Francisco, CA	4/19/1982
Wong, B. D.	San Francisco, CA	10/24/1962
Wong, Faye	Beijing, China	8/8/1969
Woo, John	Guangzhou, China	5/1/1946
Wood, Elijah	Cedar Rapids, IA	1/28/1981
Wood, Evan Rachel	Raleigh, NC	9/7/1987
Woodard, Alfre	Tulsa, OK	11/8/1952
Woodley, Shailene	Simi Valley, CA	11/15/1991
Woods, James	Vernal, UT	4/18/1947
Woodward, Joanne	Thomasville, GA	2/27/1930
Wopat, Tom	Lodi, WI	9/9/1951
Worthington, Sam	Godalming, Surrey, Eng., UK	8/2/1976
Wright, Jeffrey	Washington, DC	12/7/1965
Wright, Robin	Dallas, TX	4/8/1966
Wright, Steven	New York, NY	12/6/1955
Wu, Constance	Richmond, VA	3/22/1982
Wyle, Noah	Hollywood, CA	6/4/1971
Wyman, Bill	London, England, UK	10/24/1936
Yang, Bowen	Brisbane, Qld., Australia	11/6/1990
Yankovic, Weird Al	Lynwood, CA	10/23/1959
Yanni (Chrysomallis)	Kalamata, Greece	11/14/1954
Yarrow, Peter	New York, NY	5/31/1938
Yearwood, Trisha	Monticello, GA	9/19/1964
Yeoh, Michelle	Ipoh, Malaysia	8/6/1962
Yeun, Steven	Seoul, South Korea	12/21/1983
Yoakam, Dwight	Pikesville, KY	10/23/1956
York, Michael	Fulmer, England, UK	3/27/1942
Young, Burt	New York, NY	4/30/1940
Young, Neil	Toronto, ON, Canada	11/12/1945
Young, Sean	Louisville, KY	11/20/1959
Youssef, Ramy	Queens, NY	3/26/1991
Zane, Billy	Chicago, IL	2/24/1966
Zellweger, Renée	Katy, TX	4/25/1969
Zemeckis, Robert	Chicago, IL	5/14/1952
Zendaya	Oakland, CA	9/1/1996
Zerbe, Anthony	Long Beach, CA	5/20/1936
Zeta-Jones, Catherine	Swansea, Wales, UK	9/25/1969
Zhang Ziyi	Beijing, China	2/9/1979
Zhao, Chloé	Beijing, China	3/31/1982
Zimbalist, Stephanie	New York, NY	10/8/1956
Zimmer, Constance	Seattle, WA	10/11/1970
Zimmer, Kim	Grand Rapids, MI	2/2/1955
Zukerman, Pinchas	Tel Aviv, Israel	7/16/1948
Zuniga, Daphne	Berkeley, CA	10/28/1962

Entertainment Personalities of the Past

See also other lists for some deceased entertainers not included here.

Name	Born	Died
Aaliyah (Haughton)	1979	2001
Abbado, Claudio	1933	2014
Abbott, Bud	1895	1974
Abbott, George	1887	1995
Acuff, Roy	1903	1992
Adams, Don	1923	2005
Adams, Edie	1927	2008
Adams, Joey	1911	1999
Adams, Maude	1872	1953
Adler, Jacob P.	1855	1926
Adler, Stella	1902	1992
Adoree, Renee	1898	1933
Agar, John	1921	2002
Aherne, Brian	1902	1986
Aiello, Danny	1933	2019
Ailey, Alvin	1931	1989
Aimée, Anouk	1932	2024
Akins, Claude	1918	1994
Albert, Eddie	1906	2005
Albertson, Jack	1907	1981
Alda, Robert	1914	1986
Allen, Fred	1894	1956
Allen, Gracie	1906	1964
Allen, Mel	1913	1996
Allen, Peter	1944	1992
Allen, Steve	1921	2000
Alley, Kirstie	1951	2022
Allgood, Sara	1883	1950
Allman, Gregg	1947	2017
Allyson, June	1917	2006
Altman, Robert	1925	2006
Ameche, Don	1908	1993
Ames, Ed	1927	2023
Ames, Leon	1903	1993
Amos, John	1939	2024
Amsterdam, Morey	1908	1996
Anderson, G. M. "Bronco Billy"	1882	1971
Anderson, Harry	1952	2018
Anderson, Judith	1897	1992
Anderson, Louie	1953	2022
Anderson, Marian	1897	1993
Anderson, Richard	1926	2017
Andersson, Bibi	1935	2019
Andre the Giant	1946	1993
Andrews, Dana	1909	1992
Andrews, Laverne	1913	1967
Andrews, Maxene	1916	1995
Andrews, Patty	1918	2013
Angeli, Pier	1932	1971
Antonioni, Michelangelo	1912	2007
Arbuckle, Fatty (Roscoe)	1887	1933
Archerd, Army	1922	2009
Arden, Eve	1908	1990
Arkin, Alan	1934	2023
Arlen, Richard	1900	1976
Arliss, George	1868	1946
Armstrong, Louis	1901	1971
Arnaz, Desi	1917	1986
Arness, James	1923	2011
Arnold, Eddy	1918	2008
Arnold, Edward	1890	1956
Arquette, Cliff	1905	1974
Arthur, Beatrice	1922	2009
Arthur, Jean	1900	1991
Arzner, Dorothy	1897	1979
Ashcroft, Peggy	1907	1991
Asner, Ed	1929	2021
Astaire, Fred	1899	1987
Astor, Mary	1906	1987
Atkins, Chet	1924	2001
Attenborough, Richard	1923	2014
Atwill, Lionel	1885	1946
Auberjonois, René	1940	2019
Autry, Gene	1907	1998
Avildsen, John	1935	2017
Ayres, Lew	1908	1996
Aznavour, Charles	1924	2018
Bacall, Lauren	1924	2014
Backus, Jim	1913	1989
Bailey, Pearl	1918	1990
Bain, Conrad	1923	2013
Bainter, Fay	1892	1968
Baker, Josephine	1906	1975
Balanchine, George	1904	1983
Ball, Lucille	1911	1989
Ballard, Kaye	1925	2019
Balsam, Martin	1919	1996
Bancroft, Anne	1931	2005
Bankhead, Tallulah	1902	1968
Bara, Theda	1885?	1955
Barker, Bob	1923	2023
Barnum, Phineas T.	1810	1891
Barrett, Syd	1946	2006
Barry, Gene	1919	2009
Barrymore, Ethel	1879	1959
Barrymore, John	1882	1942
Barrymore, Lionel	1878	1954
Barrymore, Maurice	1848	1905
Barthelmess, Richard	1895	1963
Bartholomew, Freddie	1924	1992
Barty, Billy	1924	2000
Basehart, Richard	1914	1984
Basie, Count	1904	1984
Bates, Alan	1934	2003
Bavier, Frances	1902	1989
Baxter, Anne	1923	1985
Baxter, Warner	1889	1951
Beatty, Ned	1937	2021
Beaumont, Hugh	1909	1982
Beavers, Louise	1902	1962
Beck, Jeff	1944	2023
Beery, Noah, Jr.	1913	1994
Beery, Noah, Sr.	1884	1946
Beery, Wallace	1885	1949
Begley, Ed	1901	1970
Bel Geddes, Barbara	1922	2005
Belafonte, Harry	1927	2023
Bell, Art	1945	2018
Bellamy, Ralph	1904	1991
Belmondo, Jean-Paul	1933	2021
Belushi, John	1949	1982
Belzer, Richard	1944	2023
Benaderet, Bea	1906	1968
Bendix, William	1906	1964
Bennett, Constance	1904	1965
Bennett, Joan	1910	1990
Bennett, Michael	1943	1987
Bennett, Tony	1926	2023
Benny, Jack	1894	1974
Berg, Gertrude	1899	1966
Bergen, Edgar	1903	1978
Bergen, Polly	1930	2014
Bergman, Ingmar	1918	2007
Bergman, Ingrid	1915	1982
Berkeley, Busby	1895	1976
Berle, Milton	1908	2002
Berlin, Irving	1888	1989
Berman, Shelley	1925	2017
Bernardi, Herschel	1923	1986
Bernhardt, Sarah	1844	1923
Bernstein, Leonard	1918	1990
Berry, Chuck	1926	2017
Berry, Ken	1933	2018
Bertolucci, Bernardo	1941	2018
Bessell, Ted	1939	1996
Bickford, Charles	1889	1967
Big Bopper, The	1930	1959
Bikel, Theodore	1924	2015
Billingsley, Barbara	1915	2010
Bing, Rudolf	1902	1997
Bishop, Joey	1918	2007
Bitzer, Billy	1872	1944
Bixby, Bill	1934	1993
Black, Karen	1939	2013
Blackstone, Harry, Jr.	1934	1997
Blackstone, Harry, Sr.	1885	1965
Blaine, Vivian	1921	1995
Blake, Amanda	1931	1989
Blake, Eubie	1887	1983
Blake, Robert	1933	2023
Blanc, Mel	1908	1989
Blocker, Dan	1928	1972
Blondell, Joan	1909	1979
Blondin, Charles	1824	1897
Blyden, Larry	1925	1975
Bogarde, Dirk	1921	1999
Bogart, Humphrey	1899	1957
Bogdanovich, Peter	1939	2022
Boland, Mary	1880	1965
Boles, John	1895	1969
Bolger, Ray	1904	1987
Bologna, Joseph	1934	2017
Bond, Ward	1903	1960
Bondi, Beulah	1888	1981
Bono, Sonny	1935	1998
Boone, Richard	1917	1981
Booth, Edwin	1833	1893
Booth, John Wilkes	1838	1865
Booth, Junius Brutus	1796	1852
Booth, Shirley	1898	1992
Borge, Victor	1909	2000
Borgnine, Ernest	1917	2012
Borzage, Frank	1893	1962
Bosco, Philip	1930	2018
Boseman, Chadwick	1976	2020
Bosley, Tom	1927	2010
Bourdain, Anthony	1956	2018
Bow, Clara	1905	1965
Bowes, Maj. Edward	1874	1946
Bowie, David	1947	2016
Bowman, Lee	1914	1979
Boxcar Willie	1931	1999
Boyd, Stephen	1928	1977
Boyd, William	1898	1972
Boyer, Charles	1899	1978
Boyle, Peter	1935	2006
Bracken, Eddie	1915	2002
Brady, Alice	1892	1939
Brando, Marlon	1924	2004
Branigan, Laura	1957	2004
Braugher, Andre	1962	2023
Brazzi, Rossano	1916	1994
Brennan, Eileen	1932	2013
Brennan, Walter	1894	1974
Brenner, David	1936	2014
Brent, George	1904	1979
Brett, Jeremy	1935	1995
Brewer, Teresa	1931	2007
Brice, Fanny	1891	1951
Bridges, Lloyd	1913	1998
Brimley, Wilford	1934	2020
Broderick, Helen	1891	1959
Bronson, Charles	1921	2003
Brooks, Foster	1912	2001
Brooks, Louise	1906	1985
Brown, Clarence	1890	1987
Brown, James	1933	2006
Brown, Joe E.	1892	1973
Brown, Johnny Mack	1904	1974
Brown, Les	1912	2001
Browne, Roscoe Lee	1925	2007
Browning, Tod	1882	1962
Brubeck, Dave	1920	2012
Bruce, Lenny	1925	1966
Bruce, Nigel	1895	1953
Bruce, Virginia	1910	1982
Brynner, Yul	1915	1985
Buchanan, Edgar	1903	1979
Buffett, Jimmy	1946	2023
Bumbry, Grace	1937	2023
Buñuel, Luis	1900	1983
Buono, Victor	1938	1982
Burke, Billie	1885	1970
Burnette, Smiley	1911	1967
Burns, George	1896	1996
Burr, Raymond	1917	1993
Burton, Richard	1925	1984
Busch, Mae	1897	1946
Bushman, Francis X.	1883	1966
Buttons, Red	1919	2006
Byington, Spring	1893	1971
Caan, James	1940	2022
Caballé, Montserrat	1933	2018
Cabot, Bruce	1904	1972
Cabot, Sebastian	1918	1977
Caesar, Sid	1922	2014
Cagney, James	1899	1986
Caldwell, Sarah	1924	2006
Caldwell, Zoe	1933	2020
Calhern, Louis	1895	1956
Calhoun, Rory	1922	1999
Callas, Charlie	1927	2011
Callas, Maria	1923	1977
Calloway, Cab	1907	1994
Cambridge, Godfrey	1933	1976
Campanella, Joseph	1924	2018
Campbell, Glen	1936	2017
Campbell, Mrs. Patrick	1865	1940
Candy, John	1950	1994
Canova, Judy	1916	1983
Cantinflas	1911	1993
Cantor, Eddie	1892	1964
Capra, Frank	1897	1991
Cara, Irene	1959	2022
Carey, Harry	1878	1947
Carey, Harry, Jr.	1921	2012
Carlin, George	1937	2008
Carlisle Hart, Kitty	1910	2007
Carmen, Eric	1949	2024
Carney, Art	1918	2003
Carpenter, Karen	1950	1983
Carradine, David	1936	2009
Carradine, John	1906	1988
Carrillo, Leo	1880	1961
Carroll, Diahann	1935	2019
Carroll, Leo G.	1892	1972
Carroll, Madeleine	1906	1987
Carroll, Pat	1927	2022
Carson, Jack	1910	1963
Carson, Johnny	1925	2005
Carter, Benny	1907	2003
Carter, Dixie	1939	2010

Name	Born	Died
Carter, Jack	1923	2015
Carter, Nell	1948	2003
Caruso, Enrico	1873	1921
Casals, Pablo	1876	1973
Cash, Johnny	1932	2003
Cash, June Carter	1929	2003
Cass, Peggy	1924	1999
Cassavetes, John	1929	1989
Cassidy, David	1950	2017
Cassidy, Jack	1927	1976
Castle, Irene	1893	1969
Castle, Vernon	1887	1918
Champion, Gower	1919	1980
Chandler, Jeff	1918	1961
Chaney, Lon	1883	1930
Chaney, Lon, Jr.	1905	1973
Channing, Carol	1921	2019
Chapin, Harry	1942	1981
Chaplin, Charles	1889	1977
Chapman, Graham	1941	1989
Charisse, Cyd	1922	2008
Charles, Ray	1930	2004
Chase, Ilka	1905	1978
Chatterton, Ruth	1893	1961
Cherrill, Virginia	1908	1996
Chevalier, Maurice	1888	1972
Chiba, Sonny	1939	2021
Child, Julia	1912	2004
Christopher, William	1932	2016
Cimino, Michael	1939	2016
Clair, René	1898	1981
Clark, Dick	1929	2012
Clark, Roy	1933	2018
Clayburgh, Jill	1944	2010
Clayton, Jan	1917	1983
Clemons, Clarence	1942	2011
Cliburn, Van	1934	2013
Clift, Montgomery	1920	1966
Cline, Patsy	1932	1963
Clooney, Rosemary	1928	2002
Cobain, Kurt	1967	1994
Cobb, Lee J.	1911	1976
Coburn, Charles	1877	1961
Coburn, James	1928	2002
Coca, Imogene	1908	2001
Cocker, Joe	1944	2014
Coco, James	1930	1987
Cody, Buffalo Bill	1846	1917
Cody, Iron Eyes	1907	1999
Cohan, George M.	1878	1942
Cohen, Leonard	1934	2016
Cohen, Myron	1902	1986
Colbert, Claudette	1903	1996
Cole, Nat "King"	1919	1965
Cole, Natalie	1950	2015
Coleman, Dabney	1932	2024
Coleman, Gary	1968	2010
Coleman, Ornette	1930	2015
Collins, Gary	1938	2012
Collins, Ray	1890	1965
Colman, Ronald	1891	1958
Columbo, Russ	1908	1934
Comden, Betty	1917	2006
Como, Perry	1912	2001
Conklin, Chester	1888	1971
Connery, Sean	1930	2020
Conniff, Ray	1916	2002
Connors, Chuck	1921	1992
Connors, Mike	1925	2017
Conrad, Robert	1935	2020
Conrad, William	1920	1994
Conried, Hans	1917	1982
Constantine, Michael	1927	2021
Conte, Richard	1911	1975
Convy, Bert	1933	1991
Conway, Tim	1933	2019
Coogan, Jackie	1914	1984
Cook, Barbara	1927	2017
Cook, Elisha, Jr.	1904	1995
Cooke, Alistair	1908	2004
Cooke, Sam	1931	1964
Coolio	1963	2022
Cooper, Gary	1901	1961
Cooper, Gladys	1888	1971
Cooper, Jackie	1922	2011
Copland, Aaron	1900	1990
Corby, Ellen	1913	1999
Corea, Chick	1941	2021
Corelli, Franco	1921	2003
Corey, Jeff	1914	2002
Corio, Ann	1914	1999
Corley, Pat	1930	2006
Cornelius, Don	1936	2012

Name	Born	Died
Cornell, Chris	1964	2017
Cornell, Katharine	1893	1974
Correll, Charles	1890	1972
Costello, Dolores	1905	1979
Costello, Lou	1906	1959
Cotten, Joseph	1905	1994
Coward, Noel	1899	1973
Cox, Wally	1924	1973
Crabbe, Buster	1908	1983
Crain, Jeanne	1925	2003
Crane, Bob	1928	1978
Craven, Wes	1939	2015
Crawford, Broderick	1911	1986
Crawford, Joan	1904	1977
Crenna, Richard	1926	2003
Crews, Laura Hope	1880	1942
Crisp, Donald	1880	1974
Crisp, Quentin	1908	1999
Croce, Jim	1942	1973
Cronyn, Hume	1911	2003
Crosby, Bing	1903	1977
Crosby, David	1941	2023
Cross, Ben	1947	2020
Crothers, Scatman	1910	1986
Cruz, Celia	1925	2003
Cugat, Xavier	1900	1990
Cukor, George	1899	1983
Cullen, Bill	1920	1990
Culp, Robert	1930	2010
Cummings, Constance	1910	2005
Cummings, Robert	1908	1990
Curtis, Tony	1925	2010
Curtiz, Michael	1888	1962
Cushing, Peter	1913	1994
Da Silva, Howard	1909	1986
Dahl, Arlene	1925	2021
Dailey, Dan	1915	1978
Damone, Vic	1928	2018
Dandridge, Dorothy	1923	1965
Dangerfield, Rodney	1921	2004
Daniell, Henry	1894	1963
Daniels, Bebe	1901	1971
Daniels, Charlie	1936	2020
Darin, Bobby	1936	1973
Darnell, Linda	1923	1965
Darren, James	1936	2024
Darwell, Jane	1879	1967
Davenport, Harry	1866	1949
Davies, Marion	1897	1961
Davis, Ann B.	1926	2014
Davis, Bette	1908	1989
Davis, Joan	1907	1961
Davis, Mac	1942	2020
Davis, Ossie	1917	2005
Davis, Sammy, Jr.	1925	1990
Dawson, Richard	1932	2012
Day, Dennis	1917	1988
Day, Doris	1922	2019
Day, Laraine	1920	2007
De Carlo, Yvonne	1922	2007
De Havilland, Olivia	1916	2020
De Laurentiis, Dino	1919	2010
de Mille, Agnes	1905	1993
De Mille, Cecil B.	1881	1959
De Wilde, Brandon	1942	1972
De Wolfe, Billy	1907	1974
Dean, James	1931	1955
Dean, Jimmy	1928	2010
Dearie, Blossom	1924	2009
Dee, Frances	1907	2004
Dee, Ruby	1922	2014
Dee, Sandra	1942	2005
Defore, Don	1917	1993
DeFranco, Buddy	1923	2014
DeHaven, Gloria	1925	2016
Dekker, Albert	1905	1968
Del Rio, Dolores	1905	1983
Delon, Alain	1935	2024
DeLuise, Dom	1933	2009
Demarest, William	1892	1983
Demme, Jonathan	1944	2017
Dennehy, Brian	1938	2020
Dennis, Sandy	1937	1992
Denny, Reginald	1891	1967
Denver, Bob	1935	2005
Denver, John	1943	1997
Derek, John	1926	1998
DeSica, Vittorio	1901	1974
Devine, Andy	1905	1977
Dewhurst, Colleen	1924	1991
Diamond, Selma	1920	1985
Diddley, Bo	1928	2008

Name	Born	Died
Dietrich, Marlene	1901	1992
Diller, Phyllis	1917	2012
Disney, Walt	1901	1966
Dix, Richard	1894	1949
Dmytryk, Edward	1908	1999
Dobson, Kevin	1943	2020
Doherty, Shannen	1971	2024
Domino, Fats	1928	2017
Donahue, Phil	1935	2024
Donahue, Troy	1936	2001
Donat, Robert	1905	1958
Donen, Stanley	1924	2019
Donlevy, Brian	1901	1972
Dors, Diana	1931	1984
Dorsey, Jimmy	1904	1957
Dorsey, Tommy	1905	1956
Dotrice, Roy	1923	2017
Douglas, Kirk	1916	2020
Douglas, Melvyn	1901	1981
Dove, Billie	1900	1998
Dow, Tony	1945	2022
Downey, Morton, Jr.	1933	2001
Downs, Hugh	1921	2020
Doyle, David	1929	1997
Drake, Alfred	1914	1992
Draper, Ruth	1884	1956
Dressler, Marie	1869	1934
Drew, Ellen	1915	2003
Drew, Mrs. John	1820	1897
Duchin, Eddy	1909	1951
Duff, Howard	1917	1990
Duggan, Andrew	1923	1988
Dukakis, Olympia	1931	2021
Duke, Patty	1946	2016
Dumbrille, Douglass	1890	1974
Dumont, Margaret	1889	1965
Duncan, Isadora	1878	1927
Duncan, Michael Clarke	1957	2012
Dunham, Katherine	1910	2006
Dunn, James	1905	1967
Dunne, Irene	1898	1990
Dunnock, Mildred	1901	1991
Durante, Jimmy	1893	1980
Durbin, Deanna	1921	2013
Durning, Charles	1923	2012
Duryea, Dan	1907	1968
Duse, Eleanora	1858	1924
Duvall, Shelley	1949	2024
Dvorak, Ann	1912	1979
Dysart, Richard	1929	2015
Eagels, Jeanne	1894	1929
Ebert, Roger	1942	2013
Ebsen, Buddy	1908	2003
Eckstine, Billy	1914	1993
Eddy, Nelson	1901	1967
Edelman, Herb	1933	1996
Edwards, Blake	1922	2010
Edwards, Cliff	1895	1971
Edwards, Ralph	1913	2005
Edwards, Vince	1928	1996
Egan, Richard	1923	1987
Eisenstein, Sergei	1898	1948
Ekberg, Anita	1931	2015
Elam, Jack	1916	2003
Ellington, Duke	1899	1974
Elliot, Cass	1941	1974
Elliott, Bob	1923	2016
Elliott, Denholm	1922	1992
Elman, Mischa	1891	1967
Ephron, Nora	1941	2012
Evans, Dale	1912	2001
Evans, Edith	1888	1976
Evans, Maurice	1901	1989
Evans, Robert	1930	2019
Everett, Chad	1937	2012
Everly, Don	1937	2021
Everly, Phil	1939	2014
Ewell, Tom	1909	1994
Fabray, Nanette	1920	2018
Fairbanks, Douglas	1883	1939
Fairbanks, Douglas, Jr.	1909	2000
Falk, Peter	1927	2011
Farentino, James	1938	2012
Farina, Dennis	1944	2013
Farley, Chris	1964	1997
Farmer, Frances	1913	1970
Farnsworth, Richard	1920	2000
Farnum, Dustin	1874	1929
Farnum, William	1876	1953
Farrar, Geraldine	1882	1967
Farrell, Charles	1901	1990
Farrell, Eileen	1920	2002

Name	Born	Died
Fassbinder, Rainer Werner	1946	1982
Fawcett, Farrah	1947	2009
Faye, Alice	1915	1998
Fazenda, Louise	1895	1962
Feld, Fritz	1900	1993
Feldman, Marty	1933	1982
Fell, Norman	1924	1998
Fellini, Federico	1920	1993
Fenneman, George	1919	1997
Ferrer, Jose	1912	1992
Ferrer, Mel	1917	2008
Fetchit, Stepin	1898	1985
Fiedler, Arthur	1894	1979
Fiedler, John	1925	2005
Fields, Gracie	1898	1979
Fields, Totie	1930	1978
Fields, W. C.	1879	1946
Finch, Peter	1916	1977
Fine, Larry	1902	1975
Finney, Albert	1936	2019
Fisher, Carrie	1956	2016
Fisher, Eddie	1928	2010
Fiske, Minnie Maddern	1865	1932
Fitzgerald, Barry	1888	1961
Fitzgerald, Ella	1917	1996
Fitzgerald, Geraldine	1913	2005
Fleming, Art	1924	1995
Fleming, Rhonda	1923	2020
Fleming, Victor	1889	1949
Fletcher, Louise	1934	2022
Flynn, Errol	1909	1959
Flynn, Joe	1925	1974
Foch, Nina	1924	2008
Fogelberg, Dan	1951	2007
Foley, Red	1910	1968
Fonda, Henry	1905	1982
Fonda, Peter	1940	2019
Fontaine, Joan	1917	2013
Fontanne, Lynn	1887	1983
Fonteyn, Margot	1919	1991
Ford, Glenn	1916	2006
Ford, John	1894	1973
Ford, Paul	1901	1976
Ford, Tennessee Ernie	1919	1991
Forman, Milos	1932	2018
Forrest, Edwin	1806	1872
Forrest, Helen	1917	1999
Forsythe, John	1918	2010
Fosse, Bob	1927	1987
Foster, Preston	1901	1970
Foxx, Redd	1922	1991
Foy, Eddie	1856	1928
Franchi, Sergio	1926	1990
Franciosa, Anthony	1928	2006
Francis, Anne	1930	2011
Francis, Arlene	1907	2001
Francis, Kay	1905	1968
Franciscus, James	1934	1991
Frankenheimer, John	1930	2002
Franklin, Aretha	1942	2018
Franklin, Bonnie	1944	2013
Frawley, William	1887	1966
Freed, Alan	1921	1965
Freeman, Al, Jr.	1934	2012
Freeman, Mona	1926	2014
French, Victor	1934	1989
Frey, Glenn	1948	2016
Friganza, Trixie	1870	1955
Froman, Jane	1907	1980
Frost, David	1939	2013
Funicello, Annette	1942	2013
Funt, Allen	1914	1999
Furness, Betty	1916	1994
Gabin, Jean	1904	1976
Gable, Clark	1901	1960
Gabor, Eva	1920	1995
Gabor, Zsa Zsa	1917	2016
Gandolfini, James	1961	2013
Garagiola, Joe	1926	2016
Garbo, Greta	1905	1990
Garcia, Jerry	1942	1995
Gardenia, Vincent	1922	1992
Gardner, Ava	1922	1990
Garfield, John	1913	1952
Garland, Beverly	1926	2008
Garland, Judy	1922	1969
Garner, James	1928	2014
Garrett, Betty	1919	2011
Garson, Greer	1904	1996
Gassman, Vittorio	1922	2000
Gavin, John	1931	2018
Gaye, Marvin	1939	1984
Gaynor, Janet	1906	1984
Gazzara, Ben	1930	2012
Gebel-Williams, Gunther	1934	2001
Geer, Will	1902	1978

Name	Born	Died
Gershwin, George	1898	1937
Getty, Estelle	1923	2008
Ghostley, Alice	1926	2007
Gibb, Andy	1958	1988
Gibb, Maurice	1949	2003
Gibb, Robin	1949	2012
Gibson, Henry	1935	2009
Gibson, Hoot	1892	1962
Gielgud, John	1904	2000
Gifford, Frank	1930	2015
Gilbert, Billy	1894	1971
Gilbert, John	1895	1936
Gilberto, Astrud	1940	2023
Gilford, Jack	1907	1990
Gillespie, Dizzy	1917	1993
Gillette, William	1853	1937
Gilley, Mickey	1936	2022
Gingold, Hermione	1897	1987
Gish, Dorothy	1898	1968
Gish, Lillian	1893	1993
Gleason, Jackie	1916	1987
Gleason, James	1886	1959
Gluck, Alma	1884	1938
Gobel, George	1919	1991
Godard, Jean-Luc	1930	2022
Goddard, Paulette	1905?	1990
Godfrey, Arthur	1903	1983
Godunov, Alexander	1949	1995
Goldwyn, Samuel	1882	1974
Goodman, Benny	1909	1986
Goodman, Len	1944	2023
Gorcey, Leo	1917	1969
Gordon, Gale	1906	1995
Gordon, Ruth	1896	1985
Gorme, Eydie	1932	2013
Gorshin, Frank	1934	2005
Gosden, Freeman	1899	1982
Gossett, Louis, Jr.	1936	2024
Gottfried, Gilbert	1955	2022
Gottschalk, Louis	1829	1869
Gould, Glenn	1932	1982
Gould, Harold	1923	2010
Gould, Morton	1913	1996
Goulet, Robert	1933	2007
Grable, Betty	1916	1973
Graham, Martha	1894	1991
Graham, Virginia	1912	1998
Grahame, Gloria	1925	1981
Granger, Farley	1925	2011
Granger, Stewart	1913	1993
Grant, Cary	1904	1986
Granville, Bonita	1923	1988
Grapewin, Charley	1869	1956
Graves, Peter	1926	2010
Gray, Dolores	1924	2002
Gray, Spalding	1941	2004
Grayson, Kathryn	1922	2010
Greco, Jose	1918	2000
Green, Adolph	1915	2002
Greene, Lorne	1915	1987
Greene, Shecky	1926	2023
Greenstreet, Sydney	1879	1954
Greenwood, Charlotte	1890	1978
Gregory, Dick	1932	2017
Gregory, James	1911	2002
Griffin, Merv	1925	2007
Griffith, Andy	1926	2012
Griffith, D. W.	1874	1948
Griffith, Hugh	1912	1980
Griffiths, Richard	1947	2013
Grimes, Tammy	1934	2016
Grizzard, George	1928	2007
Grodin, Charles	1935	2021
Guardino, Harry	1925	1995
Guillaume, Robert	1927	2017
Guinness, Alec	1914	2000
Guthrie, Woody	1912	1967
Guy-Blaché, Alice	1873	1968
Gwenn, Edmund	1875	1959
Gwynne, Fred	1926	1993
Hackett, Buddy	1924	2003
Hackett, Joan	1934	1983
Hagen, Jean	1923	1977
Hagen, Uta	1919	2004
Haggard, Merle	1937	2016
Hagman, Larry	1931	2012
Haines, William	1900	1973
Hale, Alan, Jr.	1918	1990
Hale, Alan, Sr.	1892	1950
Hale, Barbara	1922	2017
Haley, Bill	1925	1981
Haley, Jack	1899	1979
Hall, Huntz	1919	1999
Hall, Jon	1915	1979
Hall, Monty	1921	2017
Hamilton, Margaret	1902	1985
Hammerstein, Oscar	1847	1919
Hammerstein, Oscar, II	1895	1960

Name	Born	Died
Hampton, Lionel	1908	2002
Hardwicke, Cedric	1893	1964
Hardy, Oliver	1892	1957
Harlow, Jean	1911	1937
Harper, Valerie	1939	2019
Harrington, Pat, Jr.	1929	2016
Harris, Julie	1925	2013
Harris, Phil	1904	1995
Harris, Richard	1930	2002
Harrison, George	1943	2001
Harrison, Rex	1908	1990
Hart, William S.	1864	1946
Hartman, Phil	1948	1998
Harvey, Laurence	1928	1973
Harvey, Paul	1918	2009
Harwell, Ernie	1918	2010
Hatfield, Bobby	1940	2003
Hauer, Rutger	1944	2019
Havens, Richie	1941	2013
Havoc, June	1912	2010
Hawkins, Jack	1910	1973
Hawkins, Screamin' Jay	1929	2000
Hawks, Howard	1896	1977
Hawthorne, Nigel	1929	2001
Hayakawa, Sessue	1890	1973
Hayden, Sterling	1916	1986
Hayes, Gabby	1885	1969
Hayes, Helen	1900	1993
Hayes, Isaac	1942	2008
Haymes, Dick	1917	1980
Hayward, Leland	1902	1971
Hayward, Louis	1909	1985
Hayward, Susan	1917	1975
Hayworth, Rita	1918	1987
Head, Edith	1897	1981
Healy, Ted	1896	1937
Heard, John	1945	2017
Heche, Anne	1969	2022
Heckart, Eileen	1919	2001
Heflin, Van	1910	1971
Heifetz, Jascha	1901	1987
Held, Anna	1873	1918
Helm, Levon	1940	2012
Helmond, Katherine	1929	2019
Hemingway, Margaux	1955	1996
Hemsley, Sherman	1938	2012
Henderson, Florence	1934	2016
Henderson, Skitch	1918	2005
Hendrix, Jimi	1942	1970
Henie, Sonja	1912	1969
Henreid, Paul	1908	1992
Henry, Buck	1930	2020
Henson, Jim	1936	1990
Hepburn, Audrey	1929	1993
Hepburn, Katharine	1907	2003
Herrmann, Edward	1943	2014
Hersholt, Jean	1886	1956
Hesseman, Howard	1940	2022
Heston, Charlton	1923	2008
Hickey, William	1928	1997
Hickman, Dwayne	1934	2022
Hickson, Joan	1906	1998
Hildegarde	1906	2005
Hill, Arthur	1922	2006
Hill, Benny	1925	1992
Hill, George Roy	1921	2002
Hiller, Wendy	1912	2003
Hillerman, John	1932	2017
Hines, Gregory	1946	2003
Hingle, Pat	1924	2009
Hirt, Al	1922	1999
Hitchcock, Alfred	1899	1980
Ho, Don	1930	2007
Hodiak, John	1914	1955
Hoffman, Philip Seymour	1967	2014
Holbrook, Hal	1925	2021
Holden, William	1918	1981
Holder, Geoffrey	1930	2014
Holiday, Billie	1915	1959
Holliday, Judy	1921	1965
Holloway, Sterling	1905	1992
Holly, Buddy	1936	1959
Holm, Celeste	1919	2012
Holm, Ian	1931	2020
Holt, Jack	1888	1951
Holt, Tim	1918	1973
Homolka, Oscar	1898	1978
Hooker, John Lee	1917	2001
Hope, Bob	1903	2003
Hopkins, Miriam	1902	1972
Hopper, Dennis	1936	2010
Hopper, DeWolf	1858	1935
Hopper, Hedda	1885	1966
Horowitz, Vladimir	1904	1989
Horne, Lena	1917	2010
Horton, Edward Everett	1886	1970
Hoskins, Bob	1942	2014
Houdini, Harry	1874	1926

Name	Born	Died
Houseman, John	1902	1988
Houston, Whitney	1963	2012
Howard (Horwitz), Curly	1903	1952
Howard, Ken	1944	2016
Howard, Leslie	1890	1943
Howard (Horwitz), Moe	1897	1975
Howard (Horwitz), Shemp	1895	1955
Howard, Trevor	1916	1988
Howes, Sally Ann	1930	1921
Hudson, Rock	1925	1985
Hughes, Bernard	1915	2006
Hughes, John	1950	2009
Hull, Henry	1890	1977
Hull, Josephine	1886	1957
Humphries, Barry	1934	2023
Hunter, Jeffrey	1926	1969
Hunter, Kim	1922	2002
Hunter, Tab	1931	2018
Hurt, John	1940	2017
Hurt, William	1950	2022
Hussey, Ruth	1911	2005
Huston, John	1906	1987
Huston, Walter	1884	1950
Hutton, Betty	1921	2007
Hutton, Jim	1934	1979
Hyde-White, Wilfrid	1903	1991
Hyman, Earle	1926	2017
Imus, Don	1940	2019
Ingram, James	1952	2019
Ingram, Rex	1895	1969
Ireland, Jill	1936	1990
Ireland, John	1915	1992
Irving, George S.	1922	2016
Irving, Henry	1838	1905
Ives, Burl	1909	1995
Irwin, Steve	1962	2006
Iturbi, Jose	1895	1980
Jackson, Anne	1926	2016
Jackson, Glenda	1936	2023
Jackson, Mahalia	1911	1972
Jackson, Michael	1958	2009
Jackson, Milt	1923	1999
Jaeckel, Richard	1926	1997
Jaffe, Sam	1891	1984
Jagger, Dean	1903	1991
Jam Master Jay	1965	2002
James, Dennis	1917	1997
James, Etta	1938	2012
James, Harry	1916	1983
James, Rick	1948	2004
Janis, Conrad	1928	2022
Janis, Elsie	1889	1956
Jannings, Emil	1886	1950
Janssen, David	1930	1980
Jarreau, Al	1940	2017
Jeffreys, Anne	1923	2017
Jenkins, Allen	1900	1974
Jennings, Waylon	1937	2002
Jessel, George	1898	1981
Jeter, Michael	1952	2003
Jewison, Norman	1926	2024
Johns, Glynis	1923	2024
Johnson, Arte	1929	2019
Johnson, Ben	1918	1996
Johnson, Celia	1908	1982
Johnson, Chic	1892	1962
Johnson, J.J.	1924	2001
Johnson, Robert	1911	1938
Johnson, Van	1916	2008
Jolson, Al	1886	1950
Jones, Brian	1942	1969
Jones, Buck	1889	1942
Jones, Carolyn	1933	1983
Jones, Davy	1945	2012
Jones, Dean	1931	2015
Jones, George	1931	2013
Jones, Henry	1912	1999
Jones, James Earl	1931	2024
Jones, Jennifer	1919	2009
Jones, Spike	1911	1965
Joplin, Janis	1943	1970
Joplin, Scott	1868	1917
Jordan, Leslie	1955	2022
Jordan, Richard	1937	1993
Jory, Victor	1902	1982
Jourdan, Louis	1921	2015
Judd, Naomi	1946	2022
Julia, Raul	1940	1994
Jump, Gordon	1932	2003
Jurado, Katy	1924	2002
Kahn, Madeline	1942	1999
Kane, Helen	1904	1966
Kanin, Garson	1912	1999
Karlen, John	1933	2020
Karloff, Boris	1887	1969
Karras, Alex	1935	2012

Name	Born	Died
Kasem, Casey	1932	2014
Kaufman, Andy	1949	1984
Kaye, Danny	1911	1987
Kaye, Stubby	1918	1997
Kazan, Elia	1909	2003
Kean, Charles	1811	1868
Kean, Mrs. Charles	1806	1880
Kean, Edmund	1787	1833
Keaton, Buster	1895	1966
Keel, Howard	1919	2004
Keeler, Ruby	1910	1993
Keeshan, Bob (Captain Kangaroo)	1927	2004
Keith, Brian	1921	1997
Kellaway, Cecil	1893	1973
Kellerman, Sally	1937	2022
Kelley, DeForest	1920	1999
Kelly, Emmett	1898	1979
Kelly, Gene	1912	1996
Kelly, Grace	1929	1982
Kelly, Jack	1927	1992
Kelly, Patsy	1910	1981
Kennedy, Arthur	1914	1990
Kennedy, Edgar	1890	1948
Kennedy, George	1925	2016
Kercheval, Ken	1935	2019
Kerr, Deborah	1921	2007
Kibbee, Guy	1886	1956
Kidder, Margot	1948	2018
Kiel, Richard	1939	2014
Kilbride, Percy	1888	1964
Kiley, Richard	1922	1999
King, Alan	1927	2004
King, B. B.	1925	2015
King, Henry	1896	1982
King, Larry	1933	2021
Kinski, Klaus	1926	1991
Kirby, Bruno	1949	2006
Kirby, Durward	1912	2000
Kirby, George	1923	1995
Kitt, Eartha	1927	2008
Klemperer, Werner	1920	2000
Klugman, Jack	1922	2012
Knievel, Evel	1938	2007
Knight, Shirley	1936	2020
Knight, Ted	1923	1986
Knotts, Don	1924	2006
Korman, Harvey	1927	2008
Kostelanetz, Andre	1901	1980
Kotto, Yaphet	1939	2021
Kovacs, Ernie	1919	1962
Kramer, Stanley	1913	2001
Kristofferson, Kris	1936	2024
Kubrick, Stanley	1928	1999
Kulp, Nancy	1921	1991
Kurosawa, Akira	1910	1998
Kyser, Kay	1906	1985
Ladd, Alan	1913	1964
Lahr, Bert	1895	1967
Laine, Frankie	1913	2007
Lake, Arthur	1905	1987
Lake, Veronica	1919	1973
LaLanne, Jack	1914	2011
Lamarr, Hedy	1913	2000
Lamas, Fernando	1915	1982
Lamour, Dorothy	1914	1996
Lancaster, Burt	1913	1994
Lanchester, Elsa	1902	1986
Landau, Martin	1928	2017
Landis, Carole	1919	1948
Landon, Michael	1936	1991
Lane, Priscilla	1917	1995
Lang, Fritz	1890	1976
Langdon, Harry	1884	1944
Lange, Hope	1931	2003
Langford, Frances	1914	2005
Langtry, Lillie	1853	1929
Lansbury, Angela	1925	2022
Lanza, Mario	1921	1959
LaRue, Lash (Alfred)	1917	1996
Lauder, Harry	1870	1950
Laughton, Charles	1899	1962
Laurel, Stan	1890	1965
Laurie, Piper	1932	2023
Lawford, Peter	1923	1984
Lawrence, Florence	1886	1938
Lawrence, Gertrude	1898	1952
Lawrence, Steve	1935	2024
Leach, Robin	1941	2018
Leachman, Cloris	1926	2021
Lean, David	1908	1991
Lear, Norman	1922	2023
Ledger, Heath	1979	2008
Lee, Bernard	1908	1981
Lee, Bruce	1940	1973
Lee, Canada	1907	1952
Lee, Christopher	1922	2015
Lee, Gypsy Rose	1914	1970
Lee, Peggy	1920	2002

Name	Born	Died
LeGallienne, Eva	1899	1991
Legrand, Michel	1932	2019
Leibman, Ron	1937	2019
Leigh, Janet	1927	2004
Leigh, Vivien	1913	1967
Leighton, Margaret	1922	1976
Lemmon, Jack	1925	2001
Lennon, John	1940	1980
Lenya, Lotte	1898	1981
Leonard, Eddie	1870	1941
Leonard, Sheldon	1907	1997
Leone, Sergio	1929	1989
LeRoy, Mervyn	1900	1987
Leslie, Joan	1925	2015
Levant, Oscar	1906	1972
Levene, Sam	1905	1980
Levine, James	1943	2021
Lewis, Al	1923	2006
Lewis, Jerry	1926	2017
Lewis, Jerry Lee	1935	2022
Lewis, Joe E.	1902	1971
Lewis, Richard	1947	2024
Lewis, Shari	1934	1998
Lewis, Ted	1892	1971
Liberace	1919	1987
Lightfoot, Gordon	1938	2023
Lillie, Beatrice	1894	1989
Lincoln, Elmo	1889	1952
Lind, Jenny	1820	1887
Lindfors, Viveca	1920	1995
Lindley, Audra	1918	1997
Linkletter, Art	1912	2010
Linville, Larry	1939	2000
Liotta, Ray	1954	2022
Little, Cleavon	1939	1992
Little Richard	1932	2020
Llewelyn, Desmond	1914	1999
Lloyd, Harold	1893	1971
Lloyd, Marie	1870	1922
Lloyd, Norman	1914	2021
Locke, Sandra	1944	2018
Lockhart, Gene	1891	1957
Loggia, Robert	1930	2015
Lollobrigida, Gina	1927	2023
Lom, Herbert	1917	2012
Lombard, Carole	1908	1942
Lombardo, Guy	1902	1977
Long, Richard	1927	1974
Lopes, Lisa	1971	2002
Lopez, Vincent	1895	1975
Lord, Jack	1920	1998
Lorne, Marion	1888	1968
Lorre, Peter	1904	1964
Loudon, Dorothy	1925	2003
Lowe, Edmund	1890	1971
Loy, Myrna	1905	1993
Lubitsch, Ernst	1892	1947
Ludden, Allen	1918	1981
Lugosi, Bela	1882	1956
Lukas, Paul	1894	1971
Lumet, Sidney	1924	2011
Lunt, Alfred	1892	1977
Lupino, Ida	1918	1995
Lymon, Frankie	1942	1968
Lynde, Paul	1926	1982
Lynley, Carol	1942	2019
Lynn, Loretta	1932	2022
Lynn, Vera	1917	2020
Maazel, Lorin	1930	2014
Mabley, Jackie "Moms"	1894	1975
Mac, Bernie	1957	2008
MacArthur, James	1937	2010
MacCorkindale, Simon	1952	2010
MacDonald, Jeanette	1903	1965
Macdonald, Norm	1959	2021
Mack, Ted	1904	1976
MacKenzie, Gisele	1927	2003
MacLane, Barton	1902	1969
MacLeod, Gavin	1931	2021
MacMurray, Fred	1908	1991
MacNee, Patrick	1922	2015
MacRae, Gordon	1921	1986
Macy, Bill	1922	2019
Madden, John	1936	2021
Madison, Guy	1922	1996
Magnani, Anna	1908	1973
Mahoney, John	1940	2018
Mancini, Henry	1924	1994
Main, Marjorie	1890	1975
Malden, Karl	1912	2009
Malle, Louis	1932	1995
Malone, Dorothy	1925?	2018
Mamoulian, Rouben	1897	1987
Mankiewicz, Joseph	1909	1993
Mann, Herbie	1930	2003
Mansfield, Jayne	1932	1967
Marais, Jean	1913	1998
March, Fredric	1897	1975

Name	Born	Died
March, Hal	1920	1970
Marchand, Nancy	1928	2000
Markova, Alicia	1910	2004
Marley, Bob	1945	1981
Marriner, Neville	1924	2016
Marsh, Mae	1895	1968
Marshall, Garry	1934	2016
Marshall, Herbert	1890	1966
Marshall, Penny	1943	2018
Marshall, Peter	1926	2024
Martin, Dean	1917	1995
Martin, Dick	1922	2008
Martin, Mary	1913	1990
Martin, Ross	1920	1981
Martin, Tony	1913	2012
Marvin, Lee	1924	1987
Marx, Harpo (Arthur)	1888	1964
Marx, Zeppo (Herbert)	1901	1979
Marx, Groucho (Julius)	1890	1977
Marx, Chico (Leonard)	1887	1961
Marx, Gummo (Milton)	1893	1977
Mason, Jackie	1928	2021
Mason, James	1909	1984
Massey, Raymond	1896	1983
Mastroianni, Marcello	1924	1996
Masur, Kurt	1927	2015
Matthau, Walter	1920	2000
Mature, Victor	1913	1999
Maxwell, Marilyn	1921	1972
Mayer, Louis B.	1885	1957
Mayfield, Curtis	1942	1999
Mayo, Virginia	1920	2005
Mazursky, Paul	1930	2014
MCA (Adam Yauch)	1964	2012
McCallum, David	1933	2023
McCambridge, Mercedes	1916	2004
McCarey, Leo	1898	1969
McCarthy, Kevin	1914	2010
McCartney, Linda	1941	1998
McCarver, Tim	1941	2023
McClanahan, Rue	1934	2010
McClure, Doug	1935	1995
McCormack, John	1884	1945
McCrea, Joel	1905	1990
McDaniel, Hattie	1895	1952
McDowall, Roddy	1928	1998
McFarland, Spanky (George)	1928	1993
McGoohan, Patrick	1928	2009
McGuire, Al	1931	2001
McGuire, Dorothy	1916	2001
McHugh, Frank	1898	1981
McIntire, John	1907	1991
McLaglen, Victor	1886	1959
McMahon, Ed	1923	2009
McPartland, Marian	1918	2013
McQueen, Butterfly	1911	1995
McQueen, Steve	1930	1980
Meader, Vaughn	1936	2004
Meadows, Audrey	1924	1996
Meadows, Jayne	1919	2015
Meara, Anne	1929	2015
Meat Loaf	1947	2022
Meek, Donald	1880	1946
Méliès, Georges	1861	1938
Mendes, Sergio	1941	2024
Menjou, Adolphe	1890	1963
Menuhin, Yehudi	1916	1999
Mercer, Marian	1935	2011
Mercouri, Melina	1925	1994
Mercury, Freddie	1946	1991
Meredith, Burgess	1909	1997
Merman, Ethel	1908	1984
Merrick, David	1911	2000
Merrill, Dina	1925	2017
Merrill, Gary	1915	1990
Michael, George	1963	2016
Mifune, Toshiro	1920	1997
Milland, Ray	1905	1986
Miller, Ann	1923	2004
Miller, Glenn	1904	1944
Miller, Marilyn	1898	1936
Miller, Mitch	1911	2010
Miller, Roger	1936	1992
Mills, John	1908	2005
Milner, Martin	1931	2015
Mimieux, Yvette	1942	2022
Mineo, Sal	1939	1976
Minghella, Anthony	1954	2008
Mingus, Charles	1922	1979
Minnelli, Vincente	1903	1986
Miranda, Carmen	1909	1955
Mitchell, Thomas	1892	1962
Mitchum, Robert	1917	1997
Mix, Tom	1880	1940
Moffat, Donald	1930	2018
Molinaro, Al	1919	2015
Moll, Richard	1943	2023
Monroe, Marilyn	1926	1962
Monroe, Vaughn	1911	1973

Name	Born	Died
Montalban, Ricardo	1920	2009
Montand, Yves	1921	1991
Monteith, Cory	1982	2013
Montgomery, Elizabeth	1933	1995
Montgomery, George	1916	2000
Montgomery, Robert	1904	1981
Moody, Ron	1924	2015
Moore, Clayton	1914	1999
Moore, Colleen	1900	1988
Moore, Dudley	1935	2002
Moore, Garry	1915	1993
Moore, Grace	1898	1947
Moore, Mary Tyler	1936	2017
Moore, Roger	1927	2017
Moorehead, Agnes	1906	1974
Moreau, Jeanne	1928	2017
Morgan, Dennis	1910	1994
Morgan, Frank	1890	1949
Morgan, Harry	1915	2011
Morgan, Helen	1900	1941
Morgan, Henry	1915	1994
Morita, Pat	1932	2005
Morley, Robert	1908	1992
Morris, Chester	1901	1970
Morris, Greg	1934	1996
Morrison, Jim	1943	1971
Morrow, Vic	1929	1982
Morse, Robert	1931	2022
Morton, Jelly Roll	1885	1941
Mostel, Zero	1915	1977
Mowbray, Alan	1897	1969
Mulhare, Edward	1923	1997
Mull, Martin	1943	2024
Mulligan, Gerry	1927	1996
Mulligan, Richard	1932	2000
Muni, Paul	1895	1967
Murnau, F. W.	1888	1931
Murphy, Audie	1924	1971
Murphy, Brittany	1977	2009
Murphy, George	1902	1992
Murray, Arthur	1895	1991
Murray, Kathryn	1906	1999
Murray, Mae	1889	1965
Nabors, Jim	1930	2017
Nagel, Conrad	1897	1970
Naish, J. Carroll	1900	1973
Naldi, Nita	1898	1961
Nance, Jack	1943	1996
Natwick, Mildred	1908	1994
Nazimova, Alla	1879	1945
Neal, Patricia	1926	2010
Negri, Pola	1897	1987
Nelson, David	1936	2011
Nelson, Ed	1928	2014
Nelson, Harriet (Hilliard)	1909	1994
Nelson, Ozzie	1906	1975
Nelson, Rick	1940	1985
Nero, Peter	1934	2023
Nesbit, Evelyn	1884	1967
Nesmith, Michael	1942	2021
Nettleton, Lois	1927	2008
Newhart, Bob	1929	2024
Newley, Anthony	1931	1999
Newman, Edwin	1919	2010
Newman, Paul	1925	2008
Newton-John, Olivia	1948	2022
Nicholas, Fayard	1914	2006
Nicholas, Harold	1924	2000
Nichols, Mike	1931	2014
Nielsen, Leslie	1926	2010
Nijinsky, Vaslav	1890	1950
Nilsson, Anna Q.	1888	1974
Nimoy, Leonard	1931	2015
Niven, David	1910	1983
Nolan, Lloyd	1902	1985
Norman, Jessye	1945	2019
Normand, Mabel	1894	1930
North, Sheree	1933	2005
Notorious B.I.G.	1972	1997
Novarro, Ramon	1899	1968
Nureyev, Rudolf	1938	1993
Oakie, Jack	1903	1978
Oakley, Annie	1860	1926
Oates, Warren	1928	1982
Oberon, Merle	1911	1979
O'Brien, Edmond	1915	1985
O'Brien, George	1900	1985
O'Brien, Pat	1899	1983
O'Connell, Arthur	1908	1981
O'Connell, Helen	1921	1993
O'Connor, Carroll	1924	2001
O'Connor, Donald	1925	2003
O'Connor, Sinead	1966	2023
O'Connor, Una	1880	1959
Odetta (Holmes)	1930	2008
O'Hara, Maureen	1920	2015
O'Herlihy, Daniel	1919	2005
O'Keefe, Dennis	1908	1968
Oland, Warner	1880	1938

Name	Born	Died
Olcott, Chauncey	1860	1932
Oliveira, Manoel de	1908	2015
Oliver, Edna May	1883	1942
Olivier, Laurence	1907	1989
Olsen, Merlin	1940	2010
O'Neal, Ron	1937	2004
O'Neal, Ryan	1941	2023
O'Neill, James	1849	1920
Ophüls, Max	1902	1957
Orbach, Jerry	1935	2004
Orbison, Roy	1936	1988
Ormandy, Eugene	1899	1985
O'Shea, Milo	1926	2013
O'Sullivan, Maureen	1911	1998
O'Toole, Peter	1932	2013
Ouspenskaya, Maria	1876	1949
Owen, Reginald	1887	1972
Owens, Buck	1929	2006
Ozawa, Seiji	1935	2024
Paar, Jack	1918	2004
Paderewski, Ignace	1860	1941
Page, Bettie	1923	2008
Page, Geraldine	1924	1987
Page, Patti	1927	2013
Pakula, Alan	1928	1998
Palance, Jack	1919	2006
Pallette, Eugene	1889	1954
Palmer, Betsy	1926	2015
Palmer, Lilli	1914	1986
Palmer, Robert	1949	2003
Pangborn, Franklin	1894	1958
Papas, Irene	1926	2022
Pardo, Don	1918	2014
Parker, Alan	1944	2020
Parker, Eleanor	1922	2013
Parker, Fess	1925	2010
Parker, Jean	1915	2005
Parks, Bert	1914	1992
Parks, Larry	1914	1975
Pasternack, Josef A.	1881	1940
Pastor, Tony (vaudevillian)	1837	1908
Pastor, Tony (bandleader)	1907	1969
Patrick, Gail	1911	1980
Patti, Adelina	1843	1919
Patti, Carlotta	1840	1889
Paul, Les	1915	2009
Pavarotti, Luciano	1935	2007
Pavlova, Anna	1885	1931
Paxton, Bill	1955	2017
Paycheck, Johnny	1938	2003
Payne, John	1912	1989
Pearl, Minnie	1912	1996
Peck, Gregory	1916	2003
Peckinpah, Sam	1925	1984
Pendergrass, Teddy	1950	2010
Penn, Arthur	1922	2010
Penner, Joe	1905	1941
Peppard, George	1928	1994
Perkins, Anthony	1932	1992
Perkins, Carl	1932	1998
Perkins, Marlin	1905	1986
Perry, Luke	1965	2019
Perry, Matthew	1969	2023
Persoff, Nehemiah	1919	2022
Peters, Brock	1927	2005
Peters, Jean	1926	2000
Peters, Roberta	1930	2017
Petersen, Wolfgang	1941	2022
Peterson, Oscar	1925	2007
Petty, Tom	1950	2017
Philbin, Regis	1931	2020
Phillips, John	1935	2001
Phoenix, River	1970	1993
Piaf, Edith	1915	1963
Pickens, Slim	1919	1983
Pickett, Wilson	1941	2006
Pickford, Mary	1892	1979
Pidgeon, Walter	1897	1984
Pinza, Ezio	1892	1957
Pitney, Gene	1941	2006
Pitts, Zasu	1898	1963
Plato, Dana	1964	1999
Pleasence, Donald	1919	1995
Pleshette, Suzanne	1937	2008
Plummer, Christopher	1929	2021
Poitier, Sidney	1927	2022
Pollack, Sydney	1934	2008
Pons, Lily	1904	1976
Ponselle, Rosa	1897	1981
Ponti, Carlo	1912	2007
Porter, Edwin S.	1870	1941
Postlethwaite, Pete	1946	2011
Poston, Tom	1921	2007
Powell, Dick	1904	1963
Powell, Eleanor	1912	1982
Powell, Jane	1929	2021
Powell, William	1892	1984
Power, Tyrone	1914	1958
Preminger, Otto	1905	1986

Name	Born	Died
Presley, Elvis	1935	1977
Preston, Billy	1946	2006
Preston, Robert	1918	1987
Previn, Andre	1929	2019
Price, Ray	1926	2013
Price, Vincent	1911	1993
Pride, Charley	1934	2020
Prima, Louis	1911	1978
Prince	1958	2016
Prince, Hal	1928	2019
Prinze, Freddie	1954	1977
Prosky, Robert	1930	2008
Provine, Dorothy	1937	2010
Prowse, Juliet	1936	1996
Pryor, Richard	1940	2005
Puente, Tito	1923	2000
Pyle, Denver	1920	1997
Quayle, Anthony	1913	1989
Questel, Mae	1908	1998
Quinn, Anthony	1915	2001
Quintero, José	1924	1999
Rabb, Ellis	1930	1998
Rabbitt, Eddie	1941	1998
Radner, Gilda	1946	1989
Rae, Charlotte	1926	2018
Rafferty, Gerry	1947	2011
Raft, George	1895	1980
Rainer, Luise	1910	2014
Rains, Claude	1889	1967
Raitt, John	1917	2005
Ralston, Esther	1902	1994
Ramis, Harold	1944	2014
Ramone, Dee Dee	1952	2002
Ramone, Joey	1951	2001
Ramone, Johnny	1948	2004
Ramone, Tommy	1949	2014
Rampal, Jean-Pierre	1922	2000
Randall, Tony	1920	2004
Randolph, John	1915	2004
Randolph, Joyce	1924	2024
Rathbone, Basil	1892	1967
Ratoff, Gregory	1897	1960
Rawls, Lou	1933	2006
Ray, Aldo	1926	1991
Ray, Johnnie	1927	1990
Ray, Nicholas	1911	1979
Rayburn, Gene	1917	1999
Raye, Martha	1916	1994
Raymond, Gene	1908	1998
Reagan, Ronald	1911	2004
Redding, Otis	1941	1967
Reddy, Helen	1941	2020
Redgrave, Corin	1939	2010
Redgrave, Lynn	1943	2010
Redgrave, Michael	1908	1985
Reed, Donna	1921	1986
Reed, Lou	1942	2013
Reed, Oliver	1938	1999
Reed, Robert	1932	1992
Rees, Roger	1944	2015
Reese, Della	1931	2017
Reeve, Christopher	1952	2004
Reeves, George	1914	1959
Reeves, Steve	1926	2000
Reid, Wallace	1891	1923
Reilly, Charles Nelson	1931	2007
Reiner, Carl	1922	2020
Reinhardt, Max	1873	1943
Reinking, Ann	1949	2020
Reitman, Ivan	1946	2022
Remick, Lee	1935	1991
Renaldo, Duncan	1904	1980
Rennie, Michael	1909	1971
Renoir, Jean	1894	1979
Rettig, Tommy	1941	1996
Reubens, Paul	1952	2023
Reynolds, Burt	1936	2018
Reynolds, Debbie	1932	2016
Rich, Charlie	1932	1995
Richardson, Ian	1934	2007
Richardson, Natasha	1963	2009
Richardson, Ralph	1902	1983
Rickles, Don	1926	2017
Rickman, Alan	1946	2016
Riddle, Nelson	1921	1985
Riefenstahl, Leni	1902	2003
Rigg, Diana	1938	2020
Ripperton, Minnie	1947	1979
Ritchard, Cyril	1898	1977
Ritter, John	1948	2003
Ritter, Tex	1905	1974
Ritter, Thelma	1905	1969
Ritz, Al	1901	1965
Ritz, Harry	1906	1986
Ritz, Jimmy	1903	1985
Rivera, Chita	1933	2024
Rivers, Joan	1933	2014
Roach, Hal	1892	1992

Name	Born	Died
Roach, Max	1924	2007
Robards, Jason	1922	2000
Robbins, Jerome	1918	1998
Robbins, Marty	1925	1982
Roberts, Doris	1925	2016
Roberts, Pernell	1928	2010
Roberts, Rachel	1927	1980
Robertson, Cliff	1925	2011
Robertson, Dale	1923	2013
Robeson, Paul	1898	1976
Robinson, Bill	1878	1949
Robinson, Edward G.	1893	1973
Robson, Flora	1902	1984
Roche, Eugene	1928	2004
Rochester (Eddie Anderson)	1905	1977
Roddenberry, Gene	1921	1991
Rodgers, Jimmie	1897	1933
Rodgers, Jimmie F.	1933	2021
Rogers, Buddy	1904	1999
Rogers, Fred	1928	2003
Rogers, Ginger	1911	1995
Rogers, Kenny	1938	2020
Rogers, Roy	1911	1998
Rogers, Wayne	1933	2015
Rogers, Will	1879	1935
Rohmer, Eric	1920	2010
Roland, Gilbert	1905	1994
Rolle, Esther	1920	1998
Rollins, Howard	1950	1996
Roman, Ruth	1924	1999
Romero, Cesar	1907	1994
Rooney, Mickey	1920	2014
Rose Marie	1923	2017
Rose, Billy	1899	1966
Rossellini, Roberto	1906	1977
Rostropovich, Mstislav	1927	2007
Roundtree, Richard	1942	2023
Rowan, Dan	1922	1987
Rowlands, Gena	1930	2024
Rubinstein, Artur	1887	1982
Rubenstein, Zelda	1933	2010
Ruggles, Charles	1886	1970
Rush, Barbara	1927	2024
Russell, Harold	1914	2002
Russell, Jane	1921	2011
Russell, Ken	1927	2011
Russell, Leon	1942	2016
Russell, Lillian	1861	1922
Russell, Mark	1932	2023
Russell, Nipsey	1923	2005
Russell, Rosalind	1911	1976
Rutherford, Ann	1917	2012
Rutherford, Margaret	1892	1972
Ryan, Irene	1903	1973
Ryan, Robert	1909	1973
Rydell, Bobby	1942	2022
Sabu (Dastagir)	1924	1963
Saget, Bob	1956	2022
Sahl, Mort	1927	2021
St. Cyr, Lili	1917	1999
St. Denis, Ruth	1877	1968
Sakall, S. Z.	1883	1955
Saks, Gene	1921	2015
Sale (Chic), Charles	1885	1936
Sales, Soupy	1926	2009
Sanders, George	1906	1972
Sands, Julian	1958	2023
Sanford, Isabel	1917	2004
Sargent, Dick	1933	1994
Sarrazin, Michael	1940	2011
Savalas, Telly	1922	1994
Saxon, John	1936	2020
Schallert, William	1922	2016
Scheider, Roy	1935	2008
Schell, Maria	1926	2005
Schell, Maximilian	1930	2014
Schenkel, Chris	1923	2005
Schiavelli, Vincent	1948	2005
Schildkraut, Joseph	1896	1964
Schlesinger, John	1926	2003
Schnabel, Artur	1882	1951
Schneider, Maria	1952	2011
Schneider, Romy	1938	1982
Schwartzkopf, Elizabeth	1915	2006
Scofield, Paul	1922	2008
Scolari, Peter	1955	2021
Scott, George C.	1927	1999
Scott, Gordon	1926	2007
Scott, Hazel	1920	1981
Scott, Lizabeth	1922	2015
Scott, Martha	1914	2003
Scott, Randolph	1898	1987
Scott, Stuart	1965	2015
Scott, Zachary	1914	1965
Scott-Heron, Gil	1949	2011
Scott-Siddons, Mrs.	1843	1896
Scully, Vin	1927	2022
Seberg, Jean	1938	1979

Name	Born	Died
Seeger, Pete	1919	2014
Seeley, Blossom	1892	1974
Segal, George	1934	2021
Segovia, Andres	1893	1987
Seldes, Marian	1928	2014
Selena (Quintanilla)	1971	1995
Sellers, Peter	1925	1980
Selznick, David O.	1902	1965
Sennett, Mack	1880	1960
Señor Wences	1896	1999
Serkin, Rudolph	1903	1991
Serling, Rod	1924	1975
Shakur, Tupac	1971	1996
Shandling, Garry	1949	2016
Shankar, Ravi	1920	2012
Sharif, Omar	1932	2015
Shaw, Artie	1910	2004
Shaw, Robert (actor)	1927	1978
Shaw, Robert (conductor)	1916	1999
Shawn, Ted	1891	1972
Shearer, Moira	1926	2006
Shearer, Norma	1902	1983
Shearing, George	1919	2011
Shelley, Carole	1939	2018
Shepard, Sam	1943	2017
Sheppard, Bob	1910	2010
Sheridan, Ann	1915	1967
Shore, Dinah	1917	1994
Short, Bobby	1924	2005
Shorter, Wayne	1933	2023
Shubert, Lee	1875	1953
Shull, Richard B.	1929	1999
Siddons, Sarah	1755	1831
Sidney, Sylvia	1910	1999
Siegel, Don	1912	1991
Signoret, Simone	1921	1985
Sills, Beverly	1929	2007
Silver, Ron	1946	2009
Silverheels, Jay	1912	1980
Silvers, Phil	1912	1985
Sim, Alastair	1900	1976
Simmons, Jean	1929	2010
Simmons, Richard	1948	2024
Simone, Nina	1933	2003
Sinatra, Frank	1915	1998
Sinclair, Madge	1938	1995
Singleton, John	1968	2019
Singleton, Penny	1908	2003
Sirico, Tony	1942	2022
Sirk, Douglas	1900	1987
Siskel, Gene	1946	1999
Sizemore, Tom	1961	2023
Sjostrom, Victor	1879	1960
Skelton, Red	1913	1997
Skinner, Otis	1858	1942
Sledge, Percy	1940	2015
Smith, Alexis	1921	1993
Smith, Bessie	1894?	1937
Smith, Buffalo Bob	1917	1998
Smith, C. Aubrey	1863	1948
Smith, Elliott	1969	2003
Smith, Kate	1907	1986
Smith, Keely	1928	2017
Smith, Maggie	1934	2024
Smothers, Tom	1937	2023
Snodgress, Carrie	1946	2004
Snow, Hank	1914	1999
Snyder, Tom	1936	2007
Solti, George	1912	1997
Somers, Suzanne	1946	2023
Sondergaard, Gale	1899	1985
Sorvino, Paul	1939	2022
Sothern, Ann	1909	2001
Soul, David	1943	2024
Sousa, John Philip	1854	1932
Spector, Phil	1940	2021
Spector, Ronnie	1943	2022
Spelling, Aaron	1923	2006
Spencer, John	1946	2005
Sperber, Wendie Jo	1958	2005
Springer, Jerry	1944	2023
Springfield, Dusty	1939	1999
Stack, Robert	1919	2003
Stafford, Jo	1917	2008
Stander, Lionel	1908	1994
Stang, Arnold	1918	2009
Stanley, Kim	1925	2001
Stanton, Harry Dean	1926	2017
Stanwyck, Barbara	1907	1990
Stapleton, Jean	1923	2013
Stapleton, Maureen	1925	2006
Steiger, Rod	1925	2002
Sterling, Jan	1921	2004
Stern, Isaac	1920	2001
Sternhagen, Frances	1930	2023
Stevens, Craig	1918	2000
Stevens, George	1904	1975
Stevens, Inger	1934	1970

Name	Born	Died
Stevens, Mark	1916	1994
Stevens, Risë	1913	2013
Stevens, Stella	1938	2023
Stevenson, McLean	1929	1996
Stewart, James	1908	1997
Stickney, Dorothy	1896	1998
Stiers, David Ogden	1942	2018
Stiller, Jerry	1927	2020
Stockwell, Dean	1936	2021
Stokowski, Leopold	1882	1977
Stone, Lewis	1879	1953
Stone, Milburn	1904	1980
Storch, Larry	1923	2022
Storm, Gale	1922	2009
Straight, Beatrice	1918	2001
Strasberg, Lee	1901	1982
Strasberg, Susan	1938	1999
Stritch, Elaine	1925	2014
Strummer, Joe	1952	2002
Stuart, Gloria	1910	2010
Stuarti, Enzo	1919	2005
Sturges, Preston	1898	1959
Sullavan, Margaret	1911	1960
Sullivan, Barry	1912	1994
Sullivan, Ed	1902	1974
Sumac, Yma	1922	2008
Summer, Donna	1948	2012
Summerville, Slim	1892	1946
Sutherland, Donald	1935	2024
Sutherland, Joan	1926	2010
Swanson, Gloria	1899	1983
Swayze, Patrick	1952	2009
Sweet, Blanche	1896	1986
Switzer, Carl "Alfalfa"	1927	1959
Talbot, Lyle	1902	1996
Tallchief, Maria	1925	2013
Talmadge, Constance	1900	1973
Talmadge, Norma	1893	1957
Tamiroff, Akim	1899	1972
Tandy, Jessica	1909	1994
Tanguay, Eva	1878	1947
Tati, Jacques	1908	1982
Taylor, Billy	1921	2010
Taylor, Dub	1907	1994
Taylor, Elizabeth	1932	2011
Taylor, Estelle	1899	1958
Taylor, Laurette	1887	1946
Taylor, Paul	1930	2018
Taylor, Rip	1931	2019
Taylor, Robert	1911	1969
Taylor, Rod	1930	2015
Temple Black, Shirley	1928	2014
Terry, Ellen	1847	1928
Thalberg, Irving	1899	1936
Thaw, John	1942	2002
Thaxter, Phyllis	1919	2012
Thicke, Alan	1947	2016
Thigpen, Lynne	1948	2003
Thomas, Danny	1912	1991
Thomas, Jay	1948	2017
Thompson, Sada	1927	2011
Thorndike, Sybil	1882	1976
Thulin, Ingrid	1926	2004
Tierney, Gene	1920	1991
Tillis, Mel	1932	2017
Tiny Tim	1932	1996
Todd, Michael	1909	1958
Todd, Richard	1919	2009
Tomlinson, David	1917	2000
Tone, Franchot	1905	1968
Tork, Peter	1942	2019
Torme, Mel	1925	1999
Torn, Rip	1931	2019
Toscanini, Arturo	1867	1957
Tracy, Lee	1898	1968
Tracy, Spencer	1900	1967
Travers, Henry	1874	1965
Travers, Mary	1936	2009
Treacher, Arthur	1894	1975
Trebek, Alex	1940	2020
Tree, Herbert Beerbohm	1853	1917
Trevor, Claire	1909	2000
Truffaut, Francois	1932	1984

Name	Born	Died
Tucker, Forrest	1919	1986
Tucker, Richard	1913	1975
Tucker, Sophie	1884	1966
Turner, Big Joe	1911	1985
Turner, Ike	1931	2008
Turner, Lana	1920?	1995
Turner, Tina	1939	2023
Turpin, Ben	1869	1940
Twitty, Conway	1933	1993
Tyson, Cicely	1924	2021
Urich, Robert	1946	2002
Ustinov, Peter	1921	2004
Valens, Ritchie	1941	1959
Valentino, Rudolph	1895	1926
Vallee, Rudy	1901	1986
Van, Bobby	1928	1980
Van Cleef, Lee	1925	1989
Van Fleet, Jo	1922	1996
Van Halen, Eddie	1955	2020
Van Patten, Dick	1928	2015
Vance, Vivian	1912	1979
Vandross, Luther	1951	2005
Varney, Jim	1949	2000
Vaughan, Sarah	1924	1990
Vaughn, Robert	1932	2016
Veidt, Conrad	1893	1943
Velez, Lupe	1908	1944
Vera-Ellen (Rohe)	1926	1981
Verdon, Gwen	1925	2000
Verrett, Shirley	1931	2010
Vicious, Sid	1957	1979
Vickers, Jon	1926	2015
Vidor, King	1894	1982
Vigoda, Abe	1921	2016
Villechaize, Herve	1943	1993
Vincent, Gene	1935	1971
Vincent, Jan-Michael	1944	2019
Von Stroheim, Erich	1885	1957
Von Sydow, Max	1929	2020
Von Zell, Harry	1906	1981
Wain, Bea	1917	2017
Waite, Ralph	1928	2014
Walker, Clint	1927	2018
Walker, Junior	1942	1995
Walker, Nancy	1922	1992
Walker, Paul	1973	2013
Walker, Robert	1918	1951
Wallace, Marcia	1942	2013
Wallach, Eli	1915	2014
Wallenda, Karl	1905	1978
Walsh, J. T.	1943	1998
Walsh, Raoul	1887	1980
Walston, Ray	1914	2001
Walter, Bruno	1876	1962
Walter, Jessica	1941	2021
Walters, Barbara	1929	2022
Ward, Simon	1941	2012
Warden, Jack	1920	2006
Waring, Fred	1900	1984
Warner, H. B.	1876	1958
Warrick, Ruth	1915	2005
Washington, Dinah	1924	1963
Waters, Ethel	1896	1977
Waters, Muddy	1913?	1983
Waxman, Al	1935	2001
Wayne, David	1914	1995
Wayne, John	1907	1979
Weathers, Carl	1948	2024
Weaver, Dennis	1924	2006
Weaver, Fritz	1926	2016
Webb, Clifton	1891	1966
Webb, Jack	1920	1982
Weems, Ted	1901	1963
Weiland, Scott	1967	2015
Weissmuller, Johnny	1904	1984
Welch, Raquel	1940	2023
Welk, Lawrence	1903	1992
Welles, Orson	1915	1985
Wellman, William	1896	1975
Wells, Kitty	1919	2012
Werner, Oskar	1922	1984
Wertmüller, Lina	1928	2021
West, Adam	1928	2017
West, Mae	1893	1980

Name	Born	Died
Weston, Jack	1924	1996
Whale, James	1889	1957
White, Barry	1944	2003
White, Betty	1922	2021
White, Jesse	1919	1997
White, Pearl	1889	1938
Whiteman, Paul	1891	1967
Whiting, Margaret	1924	2011
Whitmore, James	1921	2009
Whitty, May	1865	1948
Wickes, Mary	1910	1995
Widmark, Richard	1914	2008
Wilde, Cornel	1915	1989
Wilder, Billy	1906	2002
Wilder, Gene	1933	2016
Wilding, Michael	1912	1979
Wilkinson, Tom	1948	2023
Willard, Fred	1939	2020
Williams, Andy	1927	2012
Williams, Bert	1874	1922
Williams, Cindy	1947	2023
Williams, Esther	1921	2013
Williams, Guy	1924	1989
Williams, Hank, Sr.	1923	1953
Williams, Michael K.	1966	2021
Williams, Robin	1951	2014
Williams, Treat	1951	2023
Williamson, Nicol	1936	2011
Wills, Bob	1905	1975
Wills, Chill	1902	1978
Wilson, Carl	1946	1998
Wilson, Dennis	1944	1983
Wilson, Dooley	1894	1953
Wilson, Elizabeth	1921	2015
Wilson, Flip	1933	1998
Wilson, Jackie	1934	1984
Wilson, Marie	1917	1972
Wilson, Nancy	1937	2018
Windom, William	1923	2012
Winehouse, Amy	1983	2011
Winfield, Paul	1941	2004
Winston, George	1949	2023
Winter, Johnny	1944	2014
Winters, Jonathan	1925	2013
Winters, Shelley	1920	2006
Wise, Robert	1914	2005
Wiseman, Joseph	1918	2009
Withers, Bill	1938	2020
Wolfman Jack	1938	1995
Wong, Anna May	1907	1961
Wood, Ed	1924	1978
Wood, Natalie	1938	1981
Wood, Peggy	1892	1978
Wood, Sam	1884	1949
Woodward, Edward	1930	2009
Wooley, Sheb	1921	2003
Woolley, Monty	1888	1963
Worth, Irene	1916	2002
Wray, Fay	1907	2004
Wright, Teresa	1918	2005
Wyatt, Jane	1910	2006
Wyler, William	1902	1981
Wyman, Jane	1917	2007
Wynette, Tammy	1942	1998
Wynn, Ed	1886	1966
Wynn, Keenan	1916	1986
York, Dick	1928	1992
York, Susannah	1939	2011
Young, Alan	1919	2016
Young, Clara Kimball	1890	1960
Young, Gig	1913	1978
Young, Loretta	1913	2000
Young, Robert	1907	1998
Young, Roland	1887	1953
Youngman, Henny	1906	1998
Zanuck, Darryl F.	1902	1979
Zappa, Frank	1940	1993
Zeffirelli, Franco	1923	2019
Zevon, Warren	1947	2003
Ziegfeld, Florenz	1869	1932
Zimbalist, Efrem, Jr.	1918	2014
Zinneman, Fred	1907	1997
Zukor, Adolph	1873	1976

Original Names of Selected Entertainers

Adele: Adele Laurie Blue Adkins
Ad-Rock: Adam Horovitz
Clay Aiken: Clayton Grissom
Alan Alda: Alphonso D'Abruzzo
Jason Alexander: Jay Greenspan
Woody Allen: Allen Konigsberg
André 3000: Andre Benjamin
Julie Andrews: Julia Wells
Criss Angel: Christopher Sarantakos
Beatrice Arthur: Bernice Frankel
Fred Astaire: Frederick Austerlitz
Awkwafina: Nora Lum
Babyface: Kenneth Edmonds
Lauren Bacall: Betty Joan Perske
Erykah Badu: Erica Wright
Eric Bana: Eric Banadinovich
Anne Bancroft: Anna Maria Italiano
Theda Bara: Theodosia Goodman
Beck: Bek David Campbell
Pat Benatar: Patricia Andrejewski
Tony Bennett: Anthony Benedetto
Jack Benny: Benjamin Kubelsky
Milton Berle: Mendel Berlinger
Irving Berlin: Israel Baline
Sarah Bernhardt: Henriette-Rosine Bernard
Jello Biafra: Eric Reed Boucher
Big Boi: Antwan Patton
The Big Bopper: Jiles Perry "J.P." Richardson
Robert Blake: Michael James Vijencio Gubitosi
Jon Bon Jovi: John Francis Bongiovi
Bono: Paul Hewson
David Bowie: David Robert Jones
Boy George: George Alan O'Dowd
Fanny Brice: Fanny Borach

Charles Bronson: Charles Buchinski
Albert Brooks: Albert Einstein
Mel Brooks: Melvin Kaminsky
Foxy Brown: Inga Marchand
George Burns: Nathan Birnbaum
Ellen Burstyn: Edna Gilhooley
Richard Burton: Richard Jenkins
Red Buttons: Aaron Chwatt
Nicolas Cage: Nicholas Coppola
Michael Caine: Maurice Micklewhite
Maria Callas: Maria Kalogeropoulos
Cardi B: Belcalis Marlenis Almánza
Jackie Chan: Chan Kwong-Sung
Cyd Charisse: Tula Finklea
Ray Charles: Ray Charles Robinson
Charo: María Rosario Pilar Martínez Molina Baeza
Chubby Checker: Ernest Evans
Cher: Cherilyn Sarkisian
Chuck D: Carlton Ridenhour
Patsy Cline: Virginia Patterson Hensley
Claudette Colbert: Lily Chauchoin
Coolio: Artis Leon Ivey Jr.
Alice Cooper: Vincent Furnier
David Copperfield: David Kotkin
Howard Cosell: Howard Cohen
Elvis Costello: Declan McManus
Lou Costello: Louis Cristillo
Peter Coyote: Peter Cohon
Joan Crawford: Lucille LeSueur
Quentin Crisp: Denis Pratt
Tom Cruise: Thomas Cruise Mapother IV
Tony Curtis: Bernard Schwartz
Miley Cyrus: Destiny Hope Cyrus
D'Angelo: Michael D'Angelo Archer
Rodney Dangerfield: Jacob Cohen
Bobby Darin: Walden Robert Cassotto
Andra Day: Cassandra Monique Batie
Doris Day: Doris von Kappelhoff
Yvonne De Carlo: Peggy Middleton
Portia de Rossi: Amanda Lee Rogers
Sandra Dee: Alexandra Zuck
John Denver: Henry John Deutschendorf Jr.
Bo Derek: Mary Cathleen Collins
Danny DeVito: Daniel Michaeli
Angie Dickinson: Angeline Brown
Bo Diddley: Elias Bates
Vin Diesel: Mark Vincent
Phyllis Diller: Phyllis Driver
Divine: Harris Glenn Milstead
DMX: Earl Simmons
Troy Donahue: Merle Johnson Jr.
Kirk Douglas: Issur Danielovitch
Drake: Aubrey Drake Graham
Bob Dylan: Robert Zimmerman
Barbara Eden: Barbara Huffman
Elvira: Cassandra Peterson
Eminem: Marshall Mathers
Enya: Eithne Ni Bhraonain
Dale Evans: Frances Smith
Chad Everett: Raymon Cramton
Fabian: Fabian Anthony Forte
Fabolous: John David Jackson
Douglas Fairbanks: Douglas Ullman
Morgan Fairchild: Patsy McClenny
Jamie Farr: Jameel Farah
Fergie: Stacy Ferguson
Stepin Fetchit: Lincoln Perry
W. C. Fields: William Claude Dukenfield
50 Cent: Curtis Jackson
Flavor Flav: William Drayton
Joan Fontaine: Joan de Havilland
Jodie Foster: Alicia Christian Foster
Jamie Foxx: Eric Bishop
Redd Foxx: John Sanford
Arlene Francis: Arlene Kazanjian
Connie Francis: Concetta Franconero
Greta Garbo: Greta Gustafsson
Judy Garland: Frances Gumm
James Garner: James Bumgarner
Crystal Gayle: Brenda Gail Webb
George Gershwin: Jacob Gershowitz
Kathie Lee Gifford: Kathie Epstein
Whoopi Goldberg: Caryn Johnson
Cary Grant: Archibald Leach
Lee Grant: Lyova Rosenthal
Robert Guillaume: Robert Williams
Buddy Hackett: Leonard Hacker
Hammer: Stanley Kirk Burrell
Jean Harlow: Harlean Carpenter
Helen Hayes: Helen Brown
Susan Hayward: Edythe Marrener
Rita Hayworth: Margarita Cansino
Pee-Wee Herman: Paul Reubenfeld
Charlton Heston: John Charles Carter
Perez Hilton: Mario Lavandeira Jr.
Hulk Hogan: Terry Gene Bollea
Billie Holiday: Eleanora Fagan
Judy Holliday: Judith Tuvim
Bob Hope: Leslie Townes Hope
Harry Houdini: Erik Weisz
Howlin' Wolf: Chester Burnett
Rock Hudson: Roy Scherer Jr. (later Fitzgerald)
Engelbert Humperdinck: Arnold Dorsey
Kim Hunter: Janet Cole
Ice Cube: O'Shea Jackson
Ice-T: Tracy Morrow
Billy Idol: William Broad
Etta James: Jamesetta Hawkins
Ja Rule: Jeffrey Atkins
Jay-Z: Shawn Carter
Elton John: Reginald Dwight
Al Jolson: Asa Yoelson
Jennifer Jones: Phylis Isley
Tom Jones: Thomas Woodward
Spike Jonze: Adam Spiegel
Wynonna Judd: Christina Ciminella
Mindy Kaling: Vera Mindy Chokalingam
Boris Karloff: William Henry Pratt
Diane Keaton: Diane Hall
Michael Keaton: Michael Douglas
Kesha: Kesha Rose Sebert
Alicia Keys: Alicia Augello Cook
Chaka Khan: Yvette Stevens
Kid Rock: Robert Ritchie
Carole King: Carole Klein
Larry King: Larry Zeiger
Ben Kingsley: Krishna Banji
Ted Knight: Tadewurz Wladziu Konopka
Cheryl Ladd: Cheryl Stoppelmoor
Lady Gaga: Stefani Germanotta
Veronica Lake: Constance Ockleman
Kendrick Lamar: Kendrick Lamar Duckworth
Hedy Lamarr: Hedwig Kiesler
Dorothy Lamour: Mary Leta Dorothy Slaton
Michael Landon: Eugene Orowitz
Mario Lanza: Alfredo Cocozza
Queen Latifah: Dana Owens
Stan Laurel: Arthur Jefferson
Brenda Lee: Brenda Mae Tarpley
Gypsy Rose Lee: Rose Louise Hovick
Peggy Lee: Norma Egstrom
Janet Leigh: Jeanette Morrison
Vivien Leigh: Vivian Hartley
Huey Lewis: Hugh Cregg
Jerry Lewis: Joseph Levitch
Lil' Kim: Kimberly Denise Jones
Lil Nas X: Montero Lamar Hill
Little Richard: Richard Penniman
LL Cool J: James Todd Smith
Carole Lombard: Jane Peters
Lorde: Ella Yelich-O'Connor
Sophia Loren: Sophia Scicolone
Peter Lorre: Laszlo Lowenstein
Louis C.K.: Louis Szekely
Myrna Loy: Myrna Williams
Bela Lugosi: Bela Ferenc Blasko
Moms Mabley: Loretta Mary Aiken
Macklemore: Ben Haggerty
Shirley MacLaine: Shirley Beaty
Elle Macpherson: Eleanor Gow
Madonna: Madonna Louise Veronica Ciccone
Lee Majors: Harvey Lee Yeary
Karl Malden: Mladen Sekulovich
Barry Manilow: Barry Alan Pincus
Jayne Mansfield: Vera Jane Palmer
Marilyn Manson: Brian Warner
Bruno Mars: Peter Gene Hernandez
Dean Martin: Dino Crocetti
Ricky Martin: Enrique Jose Martin Morales
MCA: Adam Yauch
Meat Loaf: Marvin Lee Aday
Megan Thee Stallion: Megan Jovon Ruth Pete
Freddie Mercury: Farrokh Bulsara
Ethel Merman: Ethel Zimmermann
George Michael: Georgios Panayiotou
Mike D: Michael Diamond
Nicki Minaj: Onika Tanya Maraj
Helen Mirren: Ilynea Lydia Mironoff
Joni Mitchell: Roberta Joan Anderson
Moby: Richard Melville Hall
Mo'Nique: Monique Imes
Marilyn Monroe: Norma Jean Mortenson (later Baker)
Yves Montand: Ivo Livi
Demi Moore: Demetria Guynes
Rita Moreno: Rosita Alverio
Harry Morgan: Harry Bratsburg
Morrissey: Steven Patrick Morrissey
Mr. T: Lawrence Tureaud
Paul Muni: Mehilem Weisenfreund
Nelly: Cornell Haynes Jr.
Mike Nichols: Michael Igor Peschowsky
Chuck Norris: Carlos Ray Norris
Notorious B.I.G.: Christopher Wallace
Hugh O'Brian: Hugh Krampke
Maureen O'Hara: Maureen FitzSimons
Jack Palance: Vladimir Palanuik
Minnie Pearl: Sarah Ophelia Cannon
Katy Perry: Kathryn Hudson
Bernadette Peters: Bernadette Lazzara
Joaquin Phoenix: Joaquin Bottom
Edith Piaf: Edith Gassion
Slim Pickens: Louis Lindley
Mary Pickford: Gladys Smith
Pink: Alecia Moore
Pitbull: Armando Christian Pérez
Iggy Pop: James Newell Osterberg
Natalie Portman: Natalie Hershlag
Prince: Prince Rogers Nelson
Dee Dee Ramone: Douglas Colvin
Joey Ramone: Jeffrey Hyman
Johnny Ramone: John Cummings
Tommy Ramone: Tom Erdelyi
Tony Randall: Leonard Rosenberg
Della Reese: Delloreese Patricia Early
Busta Rhymes: Trevor Smith Jr.
Joan Rivers: Joan Sandra Molinsky
Edward G. Robinson: Emmanuel Goldenberg
The Rock: Dwayne Johnson
Ginger Rogers: Virginia McMath
Roy Rogers: Leonard Franklin Slye
Mickey Rooney: Joe Yule Jr.
Johnny Rotten: John Lydon
Lillian Russell: Helen Leonard
Meg Ryan: Margaret Hyra
Winona Ryder: Winona Horowitz
Sade: Helen Folsade Abu
Soupy Sales: Milton Supman
Susan Sarandon: Susan Tomaling
Seal: Seal Henry Olusegun Olumide Adeola Samuel
Jane Seymour: Joyce Frankenberg
Omar Sharif: Michael Shalhoub
Charlie Sheen: Carlos Irwin Estevez
Martin Sheen: Ramon Estevez
Talia Shire: Talia Coppola
Beverly Sills: Belle Silverman
Phil Silvers: Philip Silversmith
Gene Simmons: Chaim Witz
Sinbad: David Adkins
Anna Nicole Smith: Vickie Lynn Hogan
Snoop Dogg: Calvin Broadus
Barbara Stanwyck: Ruby Stevens
Jean Stapleton: Jeanne Murray
Ringo Starr: Richard Starkey
Cat Stevens: Stephen Demetre Georgiou
Connie Stevens: Concetta Ingolia
Jon Stewart: Jonathan Stuart Leibowitz
Sting: Gordon Sumner
Joe Strummer: John Graham Mellor
Donna Summer: La Donna Gaines
Rip Taylor: Charles Elmer Taylor Jr.
Robert Taylor: Spangler Brugh
The Weeknd: Abel Makkonen Tesfaye
Danny Thomas: Muzyad Yakhoob (later Amos Jacobs)
Tiny Tim: Herbert Khaury
Rip Torn: Elmore Rual Torn Jr.
Randy Travis: Randy Traywick
Tina Turner: Annie Mae Bullock
Shania Twain: Eilleen Regina Edwards
Twiggy: Lesley Hornby
Conway Twitty: Harold Lloyd Jenkins
Steven Tyler: Stephen Tallarico
Rudolph Valentino: Rudolpho D'Antonguolla
Frankie Valli: Frank Castelluccio
Eddie Vedder: Edward Louis Seversen III
Sid Vicious: John Simon Ritchie
John Wayne: Marion Morrison
Raquel Welch: Raquel Tejada
Gene Wilder: Jerome Silberman
Shelley Winters: Shirley Schrift
Jane Wyman: Sarah Jane Mayfield
Loretta Young: Gretchen Michaels Young
Buckwheat Zydeco: Stanley Dural Jr.

Worldwide Top-Grossing American Movies, 2000-24

Source: Box Office Mojo

Year	Title	Gross (mil)	Year	Title	Gross (mil)
2000	Mission: Impossible II	$546.4	2013	Frozen	$1,280.8
2001	Harry Potter and the Sorcerer's Stone	974.8	2014	Transformers: Age of Extinction	1,104.1
2002	The Lord of the Rings: The Two Towers	923.3	2015	Star Wars: Episode VII—The Force Awakens	2,068.2
2003	The Lord of the Rings: The Return of the King	1,140.7	2016	Captain America: Civil War	1,153.3
2004	Shrek 2	928.8	2017	Star Wars: Episode VIII—The Last Jedi	1,332.5
2005	Harry Potter and the Goblet of Fire	896.0	2018	Avengers: Infinity War	2,048.4
2006	Pirates of the Caribbean: Dead Man's Chest	1,066.2	2019	Avengers: Endgame	2,797.8
2007	Pirates of the Caribbean: At World's End	961.0	2020	Bad Boys for Life	426.5
2008	The Dark Knight	1,003.0	2021	Spider-Man: No Way Home	1,905.3
2009	Avatar	2,744.3	2022	Avatar: The Way of Water	2,320.3
2010	Toy Story 3	1,067.0	2023	Barbie	1,404.2
2011	Harry Potter and the Deathly Hallows: Part 2	1,341.5	2024	Inside Out 2	1,676.1
2012	The Avengers	1,518.8			

Note: Box-office grosses worldwide through Sept. 13, 2024.

All-Time Top-Grossing American Movies

Source: Box Office Mojo

Rank	Title (original release date)	Gross (mil)	Rank	Title (original release date)	Gross (mil)
1.	Star Wars: Episode VII—The Force Awakens (2015)	$936.7	26.	Star Wars: Episode IV—A New Hope (1977)	$461.0
2.	Avengers: Endgame (2019)	858.4	27.	Avengers: Age of Ultron (2015)	459.0
3.	Spider-Man: No Way Home (2021)	814.8	28.	Black Panther: Wakanda Forever (2022)	453.8
4.	Avatar (2009)	785.2	29.	The Dark Knight Rises (2012)	448.1
5.	Top Gun: Maverick (2022)	718.7	30.	Shrek 2 (2004)	444.9
6.	Black Panther (2018)	700.4	31.	E.T. the Extra-Terrestrial (1982)	439.5
7.	Avatar: The Way of Water (2022)	684.1	32.	Toy Story 4 (2019)	434.0
8.	Avengers: Infinity War (2018)	678.8	33.	Captain Marvel (2019)	426.8
9.	Titanic (1997)	674.3	34.	The Lion King (1994)	425.0
10.	Jurassic World (2015)	653.4	35.	The Hunger Games: Catching Fire (2013)	424.7
11.	Inside Out 2 (2024)	652.1	36.	Pirates of the Caribbean: Dead Man's Chest (2006)	423.3
12.	Barbie (2023)	636.2	37.	Jurassic World: Fallen Kingdom (2018)	417.7
13.	The Avengers (2012)	623.4	38.	Toy Story 3 (2010)	415.0
14.	Star Wars: Episode VIII—The Last Jedi (2017)	620.2	39.	Wonder Woman (2017)	412.8
15.	Deadpool & Wolverine (2024)	615.7	40.	Doctor Strange in the Multiverse of Madness (2022)	411.3
16.	Incredibles 2 (2018)	608.6	41.	Iron Man 3 (2013)	409.0
17.	The Super Mario Bros. Movie (2023)	574.9	42.	Captain America: Civil War (2016)	408.1
18.	The Lion King (2019)	543.6	43.	The Hunger Games (2012)	408.0
19.	The Dark Knight (2008)	535.0	44.	Spider-Man (2002)	407.8
20.	Rogue One: A Star Wars Story (2016)	533.5	45.	Jurassic Park (1993)	407.2
21.	Star Wars: The Rise of Skywalker	515.2	46.	Jumanji: Welcome to the Jungle (2017)	404.5
22.	Beauty and the Beast (2017)	504.5	47.	Transformers: Revenge of the Fallen (2009)	402.1
23.	Star Wars: Episode I—The Phantom Menace (1999)	487.6	48.	Frozen (2013)	401.0
24.	Finding Dory (2016)	486.3	49.	Spider-Man: Far From Home (2019)	391.3
25.	Frozen 2 (2019)	477.4	50.	Guardians of the Galaxy Vol. 2 (2017)	389.8

Note: Box-office grosses in the U.S. and Canada through Sept. 13, 2024, in absolute dollars. Rising ticket prices favor newer films. Revenues from rereleases are included.

Top-Grossing American Movies (Adjusted Lifetime Gross)

Source: Box Office Mojo

Rank	Title (original release date)	Adj. gross (mil)	Rank	Title (original release date)	Adj. gross (mil)
1.	Gone With the Wind (1939)	$1,895.4	24.	Fantasia (1940)	$778.1
2.	Star Wars: Episode IV—A New Hope (1977)	1,669.0	25.	The Godfather (1972)	739.5
3.	The Sound of Music (1965)	1,335.1	26.	Forrest Gump (1994)	736.8
4.	E.T. the Extra-Terrestrial (1982)	1,329.2	27.	Mary Poppins (1964)	732.6
5.	Titanic (1997)	1,270.1	28.	Grease (1978)	722.4
6.	The Ten Commandments (1956)	1,227.5	29.	The Avengers (2012)	720.4
7.	Jaws (1975)	1,200.9	30.	Jurassic World (2015)	719.6
8.	Doctor Zhivago (1965)	1,163.1	31.	Black Panther (2018)	715.0
9.	The Exorcist (1973)	1,036.3	32.	Thunderball (1965)	700.9
10.	Snow White and the Seven Dwarfs (1937)	1,021.3	33.	The Dark Knight (2008)	697.7
11.	Star Wars: Episode VII—The Force Awakens (2015)	1,013.0	34.	The Jungle Book (1967)	690.4
12.	101 Dalmatians (1961)	936.2	35.	Sleeping Beauty (1959)	681.0
13.	Star Wars: Episode V—The Empire Strikes Back (1980)	920.8	36.	Avengers: Infinity War (2018)	678.6
14.	Ben-Hur (1959)	918.7	37.	Ghostbusters (1984)	667.9
15.	Avatar (2009)	911.8	38.	Shrek 2 (2004)	665.7
16.	Avengers: Endgame (2019)	892.7	39.	Spider-Man (2002)	661.8
17.	Star Wars: Episode VI—Return of the Jedi (1983)	881.3	40.	Butch Cassidy and the Sundance Kid (1969)	661.1
18.	Jurassic Park (1993)	860.2	41.	Love Story (1970)	656.0
19.	Star Wars: Episode I—The Phantom Menace (1999)	846.2	42.	Independence Day (1996)	649.0
20.	The Lion King (1994)	835.3	43.	Home Alone (1990)	634.7
21.	The Sting (1973)	835.3	44.	Star Wars: Episode VIII—The Last Jedi (2017)	633.4
22.	Raiders of the Lost Ark (1981)	829.7	45.	Pinocchio (1940)	631.6
23.	The Graduate (1967)	801.9	46.	Cleopatra (1963)	629.5
			47.	Beverly Hills Cop (1984)	629.2
			48.	Goldfinger (1964)	621.2
			49.	Incredibles 2 (2018)	621.2
			50.	Airport (1970)	619.5

Note: Adjusted lifetime gross is in 2022 dollars, as of Aug. 15, 2022, and adjusts for ticket price inflation using estimated number of tickets sold.

50 Top-Grossing Movies, 2024

Source: Comscore, Inc.

Rank	Title	Gross (mil)
1.	Inside Out 2	$652.0
2.	Deadpool & Wolverine	613.8
3.	Despicable Me 4	357.9
4.	Dune: Part Two	282.1
5.	Twisters	264.5
6.	Godzilla x Kong: The New Empire	196.4
7.	Kung Fu Panda 4	193.6
8.	Bad Boys: Ride or Die	193.6
9.	Kingdom of the Planet of the Apes	171.1
10.	It Ends With Us	141.3
11.	A Quiet Place: Day One	138.9
12.	Ghostbusters: Frozen Empire	113.4
13.	IF	111.4
14.	Beetlejuice Beetlejuice	111.0
15.	Alien: Romulus	97.2
16.	Bob Marley: One Love	96.9
17.	The Fall Guy	92.9
18.	The Garfield Movie	92.0
19.	Wonka	85.3
20.	Longlegs	74.0
21.	Migration	73.2
22.	Mean Girls	72.4
23.	Civil War	68.6
24.	Furiosa: A Mad Max Saga	67.5
25.	The Beekeeper	66.2
26.	Anyone But You	$63.5
27.	Challengers	50.1
28.	Aquaman and the Lost Kingdom	48.0
29.	Argylle	45.2
30.	Madame Web	43.8
31.	Trap	41.6
32.	The Strangers: Chapter 1	35.2
33.	Coraline 15th Anniversary	32.6
34.	Night Swim	32.5
35.	The Boys in the Boat	30.6
36.	Horizon: An American Saga, Chapter 1	29.0
37.	Imaginary	28.0
38.	Abigail	25.9
39.	Monkey Man	25.1
40.	Arthur the King	25.0
41.	Poor Things	24.3
42.	The Bikeriders	21.7
43.	The Forge	20.8
44.	The Ministry of Ungentlemanly Warfare	20.5
45.	Fly Me to the Moon	20.5
46.	Unsung Hero	20.3
47.	Blink Twice	20.2
48.	The First Omen	20.1
49.	The Iron Claw	19.6
50.	Cabrini	19.5

Note: Preliminary box-office grosses in the U.S. and Canada, Jan. 1-Aug. 31, 2024; some films had 2023 release dates.

50 Top-Grossing Movies, 2023

Source: Comscore, Inc.

Rank	Title	Gross (mil)
1.	Barbie	$636.2
2.	The Super Mario Bros. Movie	574.9
3.	Spider-Man: Across the Spider-Verse	381.3
4.	Guardians of the Galaxy Vol. 3	359.0
5.	Oppenheimer	326.1
6.	The Little Mermaid (2023)	298.2
7.	Avatar: The Way of Water	283.1
8.	Ant-Man and the Wasp: Quantumania	214.5
9.	John Wick: Chapter 4	187.1
10.	Sound of Freedom	184.2
11.	Taylor Swift: The Eras Tour	180.6
12.	Indiana Jones and the Dial of Destiny	174.5
13.	Mission: Impossible—Dead Reckoning Part One	172.6
14.	The Hunger Games: The Ballad of Songbirds & Snakes	159.7
15.	Transformers: Rise of the Beasts	157.3
16.	Creed III	156.2
17.	Elemental	154.4
18.	Fast X	146.1
19.	Five Nights at Freddy's	137.3
20.	Wonka	133.1
21.	Puss in Boots: The Last Wish	130.4
22.	Teenage Mutant Ninja Turtles: Mutant Mayhem	118.7
23.	Scream VI	108.4
24.	The Flash	108.2
25.	Trolls Band Together	97.5
26.	M3GAN	$95.2
27.	Dungeons & Dragons: Honor Among Thieves	93.5
28.	The Equalizer 3	92.4
29.	The Nun II	86.3
30.	The Marvels	84.5
31.	Meg 2: The Trench	82.6
32.	Insidious: The Red Door	82.2
33.	Aquaman and the Lost Kingdom	76.5
34.	Blue Beetle	72.5
35.	Haunted Mansion	67.7
36.	Evil Dead Rise	67.4
37.	Killers of the Flower Moon	67.3
38.	The Exorcist: Believer	65.5
39.	Paw Patrol: The Mighty Movie	65.3
40.	Cocaine Bear	64.7
41.	A Man Called Otto	64.2
42.	Wish	60.6
43.	Napoleon	60.5
44.	Shazam! Fury of the Gods	57.7
45.	Migration	54.1
46.	Saw X	53.6
47.	Air (2023)	52.5
48.	Jesus Revolution	52.1
49.	No Hard Feelings	50.5
50.	Godzilla Minus One	45.6

Note: Box-office grosses in the U.S. and Canada, Jan. 1, 2023-Dec. 31, 2023; some films had 2022 releases.

National Film Registry, 2023

Source: National Film Registry, Library of Congress

The National Film Registry adds 25 "culturally, historically, or aesthetically significant" American films annually.

A Movie Trip Through Filmland (1921)
Dinner at Eight (1933)
Bohulano Family Film Collection (1950s-1970s)
Helen Keller: In Her Story (1954)
Lady and the Tramp (1955)
Edge of the City (1957)
We're Alive (1974)
Cruisin' J-Town (1975)
¡Alambrista! (1977)
Passing Through (1977)
Fame (1980)
Desperately Seeking Susan (1985)
The Lighted Field (1987)
Matewan (1987)
Home Alone (1990)
Queen of Diamonds (1991)
Terminator 2: Judgment Day (1991)
The Nightmare Before Christmas (1993)
The Wedding Banquet (1993)
Maya Lin: A Strong Clear Vision (1994)
Apollo 13 (1995)
Bamboozled (2000)
Love & Basketball (2000)
12 Years a Slave (2013)
20 Feet From Stardom (2013)

Movie Theaters, 1946-2021

Source: Motion Picture Association of America (MPAA); Comscore, Inc.

Year	Box office (mil)	Admissions (mil)	Admissions per week (mil)	Screens	Avg. ticket price	Films produced	Films released
1946	$1,692.0	4,067.3	78.2	NA	$0.42	NA	400
1950	1,379.0	3,017.5	58.0	NA	0.46	NA	483
1955	1,204.0	2,072.3	39.9	NA	0.58	NA	319
1960	984.4	1,304.5	25.1	NA	0.76	NA	248
1965	1,041.8	1,031.5	19.8	NA	1.01	NA	279
1970	1,429.2	920.6	17.7	NA	1.55	279	306
1975	2,114.8	1,032.8	19.9	15,030	2.03	258	233
1980	2,748.5	1,021.5	19.6	17,590	2.69	214	233
1985	3,749.4	1,056.1	20.3	21,147	3.55	264	470
1990	5,021.8	1,188.6	22.9	23,689	4.22	346	410
1995	5,269.0	1,211.0	23.3	27,805	4.35	631	411
2000	7,468.0	1,383.0	26.6	37,396	5.39	683	475
2005	8,832.0	1,376.0	26.5	38,852	6.41	920	507
2010	10,741.0	1,341.0	25.8	39,547	7.89	795	563
2012	10,774.5	1,358.0	26.0	39,918	7.96	476[1]	690
2013	10,919.7	1,340.0	25.8	42,814	8.13	455[1]	681
2014	10,329.0	1,267.6	24.4	41,518	8.17	482[1]	762
2015	11,081.2	1,321.0	25.4	42,552	8.43	495[1]	753
2016	11,573.4	1,315.0	25.3	42,659	8.65	511[1]	799
2017	11,072.7	1,240.0	23.8	43,216	8.97	549[1]	872
2018	11,852.1	1,304.0	25.1	43,459	9.11	576[1]	862
2019	11,375.3	1,242.0	23.9	43,679	9.16	601[1,2]	987
2020[3]	2,200.0	240.0	4.6	42,623	9.37	341[1,2]	338
2021	4,500.0	470.0	9.0	41,882	9.57	696[1,2]	387

NA = Not available. **Note:** The MPAA's 2022 Theme Report was delayed due to the Writers Guild of America strike. (1) Non-MPAA members with est. budget under $1 mil were not tracked. (2) Incl. Netflix as a member studio. (3) Box office numbers were down 80% in 2020 due to the COVID-19 pandemic.

Best American Movies of All Time

Source: American Film Institute

First unveiled in 1998 based on ballots sent to 1,500 individuals, mostly from the film world, in 1997. Updated in 2007 (the version shown here) to include newly eligible films and reflect shifting cultural perspectives. Criteria for judging included historical significance, cultural impact, critical recognition and awards, and popularity. The year each film was first released is in parentheses.

1. Citizen Kane (1941)
2. The Godfather (1972)
3. Casablanca (1942)
4. Raging Bull (1980)
5. Singin' in the Rain (1952)
6. Gone With the Wind (1939)
7. Lawrence of Arabia (1962)
8. Schindler's List (1993)
9. Vertigo (1958)
10. The Wizard of Oz (1939)
11. City Lights (1931)
12. The Searchers (1956)
13. Star Wars (1977)
14. Psycho (1960)
15. 2001: A Space Odyssey (1968)
16. Sunset Boulevard (1950)
17. The Graduate (1967)
18. The General (1927)
19. On the Waterfront (1954)
20. It's a Wonderful Life (1946)
21. Chinatown (1974)
22. Some Like It Hot (1959)
23. The Grapes of Wrath (1940)
24. E.T. the Extra-Terrestrial (1982)
25. To Kill a Mockingbird (1962)
26. Mr. Smith Goes to Washington (1939)
27. High Noon (1952)
28. All About Eve (1950)
29. Double Indemnity (1944)
30. Apocalypse Now (1979)
31. The Maltese Falcon (1941)
32. The Godfather Part II (1974)
33. One Flew Over the Cuckoo's Nest (1975)
34. Snow White and the Seven Dwarfs (1937)
35. Annie Hall (1977)
36. The Bridge on the River Kwai (1957)
37. The Best Years of Our Lives (1946)
38. The Treasure of the Sierra Madre (1948)
39. Dr. Strangelove (1964)
40. The Sound of Music (1965)
41. King Kong (1933)
42. Bonnie and Clyde (1967)
43. Midnight Cowboy (1969)
44. The Philadelphia Story (1940)
45. Shane (1953)
46. It Happened One Night (1934)
47. A Streetcar Named Desire (1951)
48. Rear Window (1954)
49. Intolerance (1916)
50. The Lord of the Rings: The Fellowship of the Ring (2001)

Film and TV Content Ratings

The Motion Picture Association of America (MPAA) established a ratings system in 1968. It was revised in 1984 and in 1990. The MPAA, Natl. Cable Television Assn., and Natl. Assn. of Broadcasters developed the TV ratings system in 1997, in accordance with the Telecommunications Act of 1996; it was implemented in Oct. 1997.

Film Ratings

G: General Audience. All ages admitted. Does not contain themes, language, nudity, sex, or violence that the MPAA ratings board believes would offend parents whose younger children see the film. Does not necessarily denote a certificate of approval nor children's movie. No nudity, sex scenes, or drug use depicted.

PG: Parental Guidance Suggested. Some material may not be suited for children. The MPAA ratings board recommends that parents determine whether the content of the film is appropriate for their children. The film may contain more mature themes, some profanity, violence, or brief nudity. No drug use depicted.

PG-13: Parents Strongly Cautioned. Some material may be inappropriate for children under 13. Any movie depicting drug use or more than brief nudity is automatically rated at least PG-13. Violence is permitted, though it is generally not both realistic or extreme and persistent violence. The single use of one sexually-derived expletive rates a PG-13; more than one use requires at least an R rating.

R: Restricted. Under 17 requires accompanying parent or adult guardian. Movies given R ratings contain some adult material, defined as adult themes or activity, hard language, intense or persistent violence, sexually-oriented nudity, or drug abuse.

NC-17: No One 17 and Under Admitted. Those films that most parents would consider too adult for children under 17. An NC-17 rating does not mean the film is obscene or pornographic. The rating can be based on violence, sex, aberrational behavior, drug abuse, or any other element.

TV Ratings

TV-Y: All Children. Program designed to be acceptable for children of all ages. Its themes and elements are designed for a very young audience.

TV-Y7: Directed to Older Children. Program designed for children ages 7 and older, and more appropriate for those who have the skills to distinguish between make-believe and reality. May include mild fantasy/comedic violence. Programs with more than mild fantasy violence are denoted TV-Y7-FV.

TV-G: General Audience. Program not necessarily designed for children, but most parents would find it suitable for all ages. Little or no violence, no strong language, and little or no sexual dialogue or situations.

TV-PG: Parental Guidance Suggested. Program might contain material that parents would consider inappropriate for children, such as an adult theme or one or more of the following: suggestive dialogue (D), infrequent coarse language (L), some sexual situations (S), or moderate violence (V).

TV-14: Parents Strongly Cautioned. Program contains material that many parents would consider inappropriate for children under 14, such as one or more of the following: intensely suggestive dialogue (D), strong coarse language (L), intense sexual situations (S), or intense violence (V).

TV-MA: Mature Audience Only. Program specifically designed for adults and may be unsuitable for children under 17. Contains one or more of the following: crude indecent language (L), explicit sexual activity (S), or graphic violence (V).

Most Popular YouTubers, 2024

Source: SocialBlade

Rank	Name	Subscribers (mil)
1.	MrBeast	309.0
2.	T-Series	271.0
3.	YouTube Movies	182.0
4.	Cocomelon - Nursery Rhymes	180.0
5.	SET India	176.0
6.	Kids Diana Show	124.0
7.	Vlad and Niki	123.0
8.	Like Nastya	119.0
9.	PewDiePie	111.0
10.	Zee Music Company	109.0
11.	WWE	103.0
12.	Goldmines	99.0
13.	Sony SAB	94.7
14.	BLACKPINK	94.5
15.	ChuChu TV Nursery Rhymes & Kids Songs	92.4
16.	Stokes Twins	84.0
17.	Zee TV	83.0
18.	5-Minute Crafts	80.7
19.	BANGTANTV	78.8
20.	Pinkfong Baby Shark - Kids' Songs & Stories	76.9
21.	HYBE LABELS	75.5
22.	Colors TV	75.1
23.	Justin Bieber	73.3
24.	Shemaroo Filmi Gaane	69.2
25.	T-Series Bhakti Sagar	69.1
26.	Tips Official	67.9
27.	Canal KondZilla	67.2
28.	Aaj Tak	66.6
29.	A4	65.4
30.	El Reino Infantil	65.4
31.	Infobells - Hindi	63.7
32.	ZamZam Electronics Trading	63.0
33.	Wave Music	62.6
34.	Movieclips	61.9
35.	EminemMusic	61.5
36.	Sony Music India	61.4
37.	YRF	61.1
38.	Dude Perfect	60.4
39.	Toys and Colors	60.0
40.	Taylor Swift	59.7
41.	Har Pal Geo	57.6
42.	LooLoo Kids - Nursery Rhymes and Children's Songs	57.5
43.	Marshmello	57.3
44.	Billion SurpriseToys	57.1
45.	Mark Rober	55.9
46.	ARY Digital HD	55.8
47.	Panda Boi	55.4
48.	Alan Chikin Chow	55.4
49.	Ed Sheeran	55.0
50.	Fede Vigevani	54.9

Note: Ranked by channel subscribers as of Aug. 15, 2024.

Most Popular Podcasts, 2024

Source: Podtrac

Rank	Podcast	Publisher
1.	The Daily	New York Times
2.	NPR News Now	NPR
3.	Up First	NPR
4.	Dateline NBC	NBC News
5.	The Dan Bongino Show	Dan Bongino
6.	The Ben Shapiro Show	The Daily Wire
7.	Morbid	Wondery
8.	FOX News Hourly Update	FOX News Podcasts
9.	SmartLess	Wondery
10.	Pardon My Take	Barstool Sports
11.	Stuff You Should Know	iHeart Podcasts
12.	Smosh Reads Reddit Stories	Smosh
13.	Shawn Ryan Show	Cumulus Podcast Network
14.	Matt and Shane's Secret Podcast	Matt McCusker & Shane Gillis
15.	My Favorite Murder With Karen Kilgariff and Georgia Hardstark	Exactly Right
16.	This American Life	This American Life
17.	Huberman Lab	Scicomm Media
18.	20/20	The Walt Disney Company
19.	MrBallen Podcast: Strange, Dark, & Mysterious Stories	Wondery
20.	Today Explained	Vox Media

Note: Rankings based on U.S. unique monthly audience for July 2024.

Top-Selling Video Games, 2023

Source: The NPD Group, Inc.

The U.S. video game industry generated $58.1 bil in revenue in 2023: $9.41 bil on hardware, including peripherals, and $48.7 bil on software, including in-game purchases and subscriptions. Overall spending was up 2% from $57.0 bil in 2022.

Ranked by combined dollar sales of game in physical/digital formats unless noted. Reporting period: Jan. 1, 2023-Dec. 29, 2023.

Rank	Game (console)
1.	Hogwarts Legacy (PC, PS4, PS4P, PS5, XBO, XBSX, Switch)
2.	Call of Duty: Modern Warfare III (2023) (PC, PS4, PS5, XBO, XBSX)
3.	Grand Theft Auto V (PC, PS4, PS5, XBO, XBSS, XBSX)
4.	Madden NFL 24 (PC, PS4, PS5, XBO, XBSX)
5.	NBA 2K24 (Apple Arcade, PC, PS4, PS5, Switch, XBO, XBSS, XBSX)
6.	Marvel's Spider-Man 2 (PS5)
7.	The Legend of Zelda: Tears of the Kingdom* (Switch)
8.	NBA 2K23 (PC, PS4, PS4P, PS5, XBO, XBSS, XBSX, Switch)
9.	Red Dead Redemption II (PC, PS4, Stadia, XBO)
10.	Call of Duty: Modern Warfare 2 (2022) (PC, PS4, PS5, XBO, XBSS, XBSX)
11.	EA Sports FC 24 (PC, PS4, PS5, Switch, XBO, XBSS, XBSX)
12.	Star Wars: Jedi: Survivor (PC, PS4, PS5, XBO, XBSS, XBSX)
13.	Minecraft (Android, iOS, macOS, Nintendo 3DS, PC, PS3, PS4, PS Vita, Switch, XBO, XBO 360, Wii U)
14.	Diablo IV (PC, PS4, PS5, XBO, XBSS, XBSX)
15.	Super Mario Bros. Wonder* (Switch)
16.	Mortal Kombat 1 (PC, PS5, Switch, XBSS, XBSX)
17.	Resident Evil 4 (2023) (PC, PS4, PS5, XBSS, XBSX)
18.	FIFA 23 (PC, PS4, PS5, Switch, XBO, XBSS, XBSX)
19.	MLB: The Show 23** (PS4, PS5, Switch, XBO, XBSS, XBSX)
20.	Starfield (PC, XBSS, XBSX)

* = Digital sales not included. ** = Xbox & Switch digital sales not included. **Note:** Includes bundled, collector's, or game-of-the-year editions, except those bundled with hardware. iOS = iPhone operating system; PC = personal computer; PS = PlayStation; PS4P = PlayStation 4 Pro; XBO = Microsoft Xbox One; XBSS = Xbox Series S; XBSX = Xbox Series X.

Profiles of Video Gamers, 2023

Source: Entertainment Software Association

	Age of gamer							
Gamers who said they played—	**8-12**	**13-17**	**18-24**	**25-34**	**35-44**	**45-54**	**55-64**	**65+**
On a smartphone	61%	70%	70%	73%	75%	73%	74%	61%
On a console	66	76	57	63	57	47	19	9
On a computer	53	54	57	51	43	40	38	46
On mobile gaming network	78	77	76	77	78	80	84	77
On a tablet	38	26	19	18	21	23	30	37
On a virtual reality device	14	22	13	16	17	9	3	1
On only one type of device	33	28	39	37	46	53	67	72
Action games	41	38	40	33	30	20	8	5
Arcade games	45	35	23	25	24	19	15	11
Fighting games	13	15	18	16	12	7	2	1
Puzzle games	24	26	19	30	40	49	69	72
Racing games	16	15	16	11	10	11	4	3
Shooter games	21	37	33	31	23	18	8	4
Simulation games	16	15	18	17	14	11	10	8
Skill and chance games	5	6	10	11	13	22	43	49
Sports games	13	23	19	22	18	10	6	2
Strategy games	15	14	19	18	13	12	10	8
Role playing & narrative games	11	11	15	21	20	18	8	5

Longest-Running Broadway Shows

Source: The Broadway League

Rank	Title (run)[1]	Performances[2]
1.	The Phantom of the Opera (1988-2023)	13,981
2.	*Chicago (revival) (1996-)	10,793
3.	*The Lion King (1997-)	10,413
4.	*Wicked (2003-)	7,952
5.	Cats (1982-2000)	7,485
6.	Les Misérables (1987-2003)	6,680
7.	A Chorus Line (1975-90)	6,137
8.	Oh! Calcutta! (revival) (1976-89)	5,959
9.	Mamma Mia! (2001-15)	5,758
10.	Beauty and the Beast (1994-2007)	5,462
11.	Rent (1996-2008)	5,123
12.	*The Book of Mormon (2011-)	4,807
13.	Jersey Boys (2005-17)	4,642
14.	Miss Saigon (1991-2001)	4,092
15.	*Aladdin (2014-)	3,579
16.	42nd Street (1980-89)	3,486
17.	Grease (1972-80)	3,388
18.	Fiddler on the Roof (1964-72)	3,242
19.	Life With Father (1939-47)	3,224
20.	Tobacco Road (1933-41)	3,182
21.	*Hamilton (2015-)	3,021
22.	Hello, Dolly! (1964-70)	2,844
23.	My Fair Lady (1956-62)	2,717
24.	Hairspray (2002-09)	2,642
25.	Mary Poppins (2006-13)	2,619
26.	Avenue Q (2003-09)	2,534
27.	Kinky Boots (2013-19)	2,505
28.	The Producers (2001-07)	2,502
29.	Beautiful: The Carole King Musical (2014-19)	2,416
30.	Cabaret (revival) (1998-2004)	2,377
	Annie (1977-83)	2,377
32.	Rock of Ages (2009-15)	2,328
	Man of La Mancha (1965-71)	2,328
34.	Abie's Irish Rose (1922-27)	2,327
35.	Oklahoma! (1943-48)	2,212
36.	Smokey Joe's Café (1995-2000)	2,036
37.	Pippin (1972-77)	1,944
38.	South Pacific (1949-54)	1,925
39.	The Magic Show (1974-78)	1,920
40.	Aida (2000-04)	1,852
41.	Gemini (1977-81)	1,819
42.	*Harry Potter and the Cursed Child (2018-)	1,793
	Deathtrap (1978-82)	1,793
44.	Harvey (1944-49)	1,775
45.	Dancin' (1978-82)	1,774
46.	La Cage aux Folles (1983-87)	1,761
47.	Hair (1968-72)	1,750
48.	Dear Evan Hansen (2016-22)	1,672
	The Wiz (1975-79)	1,672
50.	Come From Away (2017-22)	1,669

* = Still running as of Sept. 2024. (1) Unless noted, listings reflect a show's first run on Broadway. (2) Number of performances through May 20, 2024. **Note:** Broadway was shut down as a result of the COVID-19 pandemic beginning Mar. 12, 2020. Shows began officially reopening Sept. 14, 2021.

Broadway Season Statistics, 1959-2024

Source: The Broadway League

Season	Gross (mil $)	Attendance (mil)	Playing weeks	New productions	Avg. ticket price
1959-1960	$46	7.9	1,156	58	$5.82
1964-1965	51	8.2	1,250	67	6.20
1969-1970	53	7.1	1,047	62	7.46
1974-1975	57	6.6	1,101	54	8.64
1979-1980	146	9.6	1,540	61	15.21
1984-1985	209	7.3	1,078	33	28.47
1989-1990	282	8.0	1,070	39	35.07
1994-1995	406	9.0	1,120	33	44.91
1999-2000	603	11.4	1,460	37	52.99
2004-2005	769	11.5	1,494	39	66.70
2005-2006	862	12.0	1,501	39	71.83
2006-2007	939	12.3	1,509	35	76.28
2007-2008	938	12.3	1,560	36	76.45
2008-2009	943	12.2	1,548	43	77.61
2009-2010	$1,020	11.9	1,464	39	$85.79
2010-2011	1,081	12.5	1,588	42	86.27
2011-2012	1,139	12.3	1,522	41	92.38
2012-2013	1,139	11.6	1,430	46	98.42
2013-2014	1,269	12.2	1,496	44[1]	103.88
2014-2015	1,365	13.1	1,626	37	104.18
2015-2016	1,373	13.3	1,648	39	103.11
2016-2017	1,449	13.3	1,580	45[2]	109.21
2017-2018	1,697	13.8	1,624	33	123.07
2018-2019	1,829	14.8	1,737	38	123.87
2019-2020[3]	1,358	11.1	1,282	33	121.99
2021-2022[3]	845	6.7	946	39[4]	125.63
2022-2023	1,578	12.3	1,474	40	128.43
2023-2024	1,539	12.3	1,471	39	125.27

(1) Includes one return engagement. (2) Includes two return engagements. (3) Broadway shut down Mar. 12, 2020, due to the COVID-19 pandemic. Broadway shows began reopening on Sept. 14, 2021. (4) Includes five return engagements.

Notable U.S. Museums

This unofficial list of some of the largest museums in the U.S., by budget, was compiled with the assistance of the American Association of Museums (AAM). Zoos, aquariums, arboretums, botanical gardens, and planetariums may be AAM members but are not included here.

Museum	City	State
Academy Museum of Motion Pictures	Los Angeles	CA
American Museum of Natural History	New York	NY
Amon Carter Museum of Western Art	Ft. Worth	TX
The Art Institute of Chicago	Chicago	IL
Boston Children's Museum	Boston	MA
Brooklyn Museum of Art	Brooklyn	NY
Busch-Reisinger Museum	Cambridge	MA
California Academy of Sciences	San Francisco	CA
California Science Center	Los Angeles	CA
Carnegie Museums of Pittsburgh	Pittsburgh	PA
Children's Museum of Indianapolis	Indianapolis	IN
Cincinnati Art Museum	Cincinnati	OH
Cincinnati Museum Center	Cincinnati	OH
Cleveland Museum of Art	Cleveland	OH
Colonial Williamsburg	Williamsburg	VA
Corning Museum of Glass	Corning	NY
Crystal Bridges Museum of American Art	Bentonville	AR
Dallas Museum of Art	Dallas	TX
Denver Art Museum	Denver	CO
Denver Museum of Nature and Science	Denver	CO
Detroit Institute of Arts	Detroit	MI
Exploratorium	San Francisco	CA
The Field Museum	Chicago	IL
Fine Arts Museums of San Francisco	San Francisco	CA
Franklin Institute	Philadelphia	PA
The Frick Collection	New York	NY
J. Paul Getty Museum	Los Angeles	CA
Solomon R. Guggenheim Museum of Art	New York	NY
Harvard University Art Museums	Cambridge	MA
Henry F. DuPont Winterthur Museum	Winterthur	DE
Henry Ford Museum/Greenfield Village	Dearborn	MI
High Museum of Art	Atlanta	GA
Houston Museum of Natural Science	Houston	TX
Jamestown-Yorktown Foundation	Williamsburg	VA
Jewish Museum	New York	NY
L.A. County Museum of Art	Los Angeles	CA
Liberty Science Center, Liberty State Park	Jersey City	NJ
Maryland Science Center	Baltimore	MD
Mashantucket Pequot Museum and Research Center	Mashantucket	CT
Metropolitan Museum of Art	New York	NY
Milwaukee Public Museum	Milwaukee	WI
Minneapolis Institute of Arts	Minneapolis	MN
Museum of African American History	Detroit	MI
Museum of the American Arts and Crafts Movement	St. Petersburg	FL
Museum of the American West	Los Angeles	CA
Museum of Broadway	New York	NY
Museum of Contemporary Art	Los Angeles	CA
Museum of Fine Arts	Boston	MA
Museum of Fine Arts	Houston	TX
Museum of Modern Art	New York	NY

Museum	City	State
Museum of New Mexico	Santa Fe	NM
Museum of Science	Boston	MA
Museum of Science and Industry	Chicago	IL
Musical Instrument Museum	Phoenix	AZ
Mystic Seaport Museum	Mystic	CT
National Air and Space Museum	Washington	DC
National Baseball Hall of Fame and Museum, Inc.	Cooperstown	NY
National Civil Rights Museum	Memphis	TN
National Constitution Center	Philadelphia	PA
National Gallery of Art	Washington	DC
National Museum of African American History and Culture	Washington	DC
National Museum of American History	Washington	DC
National Museum of the American Indian	Washington	DC
National Museum of Natural History	Washington	DC
National 9/11 Memorial & Museum	New York	NY
National World War II Museum	New Orleans	LA
Nelson-Atkins Museum of Art	Kansas City	MO
New-York Historical Society	New York	NY
New York State Museum	Albany	NY
Peabody Essex Museum	Salem	MA
Philadelphia Museum of Art	Philadelphia	PA
Rock and Roll Hall of Fame and Museum, Inc.	Cleveland	OH
St. Louis Science Center	St. Louis	MO
San Diego Museum of Art	San Diego	CA
San Francisco Museum of Modern Art	San Francisco	CA
Science Museum of Minnesota	St. Paul	MN
Toledo Museum of Art	Toledo	OH
U.S. Holocaust Memorial Museum	Washington	DC
Univ. of Pennsylvania Museum of Archaeology and Anthropology	Philadelphia	PA
Virginia Museum of Fine Arts	Richmond	VA
Wadsworth Atheneum	Hartford	CT
Walker Art Center	Minneapolis	MN
Whitney Museum of American Art	New York	NY

Characteristics of Public Libraries by State, 2019

Source: Public Libraries Survey, Institute of Museum and Library Services

State	Libraries[1]	Operating revenue[2] (thous.)	Library visits Total (thous.)	Library visits Per capita	Circulation[3] Total (thous.)	Circulation[3] Per capita	Internet use[4] Total (thous.)	Internet use[4] Per capita
AL	220	$112,525	14,450	3.0	20,606	4.3	3,415	0.7
AK	64	39,837	3,062	4.8	5,036	7.8	551	0.9
AZ	89	210,027	23,446	3.3	49,272	6.9	4,246	0.6
AR	60	88,522	9,236	3.4	14,013	5.1	1,449	0.5
CA	185	1,745,727	139,011	3.5	215,768	5.4	24,393	0.6
CO	112	346,011	29,582	5.3	64,123	11.4	5,122	0.9
CT	180	201,517	19,014	5.8	24,927	7.6	3,419	1.0
DE	21	31,574	4,056	4.2	5,593	5.8	509	0.5
DC	1	60,828	3,820	5.4	4,865	6.9	944	1.3
FL	81	673,322	63,289	3.0	103,314	4.9	13,401	0.6
GA	62	214,026	26,003	2.4	35,986	3.3	10,964	1.0
HI	1	40,263	3,436	2.4	5,625	4.0	793	0.6
ID	103	65,518	8,290	5.5	16,379	10.9	1,397	0.9
IL	623	878,783	60,853	5.2	105,752	9.0	9,656	0.8
IN	236	397,598	30,247	5.0	65,173	10.7	4,764	0.8
IA	535	138,270	16,434	5.4	24,515	8.0	2,468	0.8
KS	318	153,380	13,459	5.4	25,225	10.1	2,379	0.9
KY	120	209,295	16,157	3.6	28,888	6.5	3,628	0.8
LA	67	278,802	15,934	3.5	21,990	4.8	4,471	1.0
ME	228	50,760	6,602	5.4	7,993	6.6	693	0.6
MD	24	325,864	24,905	4.1	56,180	9.3	4,979	0.8
MA	367	336,325	39,202	5.8	54,839	8.0	5,195	0.8
MI	396	472,794	43,741	4.4	75,915	7.7	6,976	0.7
MN	136	243,046	21,902	3.9	51,248	9.1	3,875	0.7
MS	53	51,306	6,983	2.3	6,690	2.2	1,712	0.6
MO	149	300,794	24,159	4.4	51,838	9.5	4,237	0.8
MT	82	31,134	4,053	4.1	6,121	6.2	829	0.8
NE	236	64,814	7,158	4.5	13,682	8.6	1,626	1.0
NV	22	104,543	9,391	3.1	17,397	5.7	2,526	0.8
NH	220	66,333	6,836	5.1	10,037	7.5	673	0.5
NJ	296	509,762	42,036	4.8	51,097	5.9	7,398	0.8
NM	88	54,180	6,811	4.6	9,350	6.2	1,529	1.0
NY	756	1,543,388	95,175	4.9	110,536	5.7	15,728	0.8
NC	82	247,597	30,188	2.9	51,051	4.9	4,903	0.5
ND	73	21,436	2,064	3.0	3,542	5.2	393	0.6
OH	251	918,327	67,938	5.9	178,937	15.6	12,598	1.1
OK	119	132,466	13,169	4.1	25,524	7.9	2,793	0.9
OR	132	265,822	19,623	5.6	54,174	15.4	2,652	0.8
PA	452	296,888	40,276	3.2	64,084	5.2	5,218	0.4
RI	48	55,027	5,171	4.9	6,675	6.3	762	0.7
SC	42	158,533	13,592	2.9	24,546	5.3	3,116	0.7
SD	111	28,420	3,693	4.8	5,822	7.5	947	1.2
TN	186	140,358	18,036	2.7	28,621	4.3	4,166	0.6
TX	544	589,149	65,948	2.5	116,451	4.4	11,373	0.4
UT	70	129,792	14,822	4.8	35,488	11.5	1,957	0.6
VT	162	26,035	3,416	5.9	4,201	7.2	427	0.7
VA	93	308,421	33,548	4.0	60,979	7.3	5,759	0.7
WA	60	500,216	36,055	4.8	86,800	11.7	6,109	0.8
WV	97	42,286	4,667	2.5	6,413	3.5	730	0.4
WI	381	266,993	29,071	5.0	54,093	9.3	3,485	0.6
WY	23	32,097	3,124	5.4	4,506	7.8	621	1.1
U.S.	**9,057**	**14,200,729**	**1,243,130**	**3.9**	**2,171,880**	**6.9**	**223,956**	**0.7**

(1) Includes central libraries only. (2) Some operating revenues may be estimated. (3) The total annual circulation of all library materials of all types, including renewals. (4) Total number of sessions accessing the internet using the library's devices.

Opera: Most Performed Works, 2023-24

Source: OPERA America

Title	Composer	Librettist	Productions	Performances
La bohème	Giacomo Puccini	Giuseppe Giacosa, Luigi Illica	21	86
Don Giovanni	Wolfgang Mozart	Lorenzo Da Ponte	13	49
Carmen	Georges Bizet	Henri Meilhac, Ludovic Halévy	12	60
Madama Butterfly	Giacomo Puccini	Giuseppe Giacosa, Luigi Illica	12	57
The Barber of Seville	Gioachino Rossini	Cesare Sterbini	12	56
La traviata	Giuseppe Verdi	Francesco Maria Piave	12	47
The Marriage of Figaro	Wolfgang Mozart	Lorenzo Da Ponte	12	32
Tosca	Giacomo Puccini	Giuseppe Giacosa, Luigi Illica	10	20
Romeo and Juliet	Charles Gounod	Jules Barbier, Michel Carré	9	37
The Elixir of Love	Gaetano Donizetti	Felice Romani	9	30

Note: Scheduled productions of a given work during the 2023-24 season (Sept. 1, 2023-Aug. 31, 2024), by members of OPERA America's professional company members. List includes Canadian performances.

Best-Selling U.S. Magazines, 2024

Source: Alliance for Audited Media (AAM)

General magazines, exclusive of comics; also excludes magazines that failed to file reports to AAM. Based on total average paid and verified circulation during the six months ending June 30, 2024; ranked by paid circulation size.

Publication	Paid circ.
1. AARP The Magazine	22,279,401
2. AARP Bulletin	22,215,966
3. Costco Connection	15,368,081
4. Better Homes and Gardens	3,022,239
5. Southern Living	2,813,989
6. People	2,541,473
7. Reader's Digest	2,014,420
8. Real Simple	1,996,486
9. Texas Co-op Power	1,956,609
10. Us Weekly	1,950,401
11. Golf Digest	1,656,316
12. National Geographic	1,525,841
13. American Legion Magazine	1,487,749
14. American Rifleman	1,389,907
15. The New Yorker	1,282,027
16. Vogue	1,244,760
17. Vanity Fair	1,241,029
18. Taste of Home	1,229,872
19. Golf Magazine	1,207,234
20. Good Housekeeping	1,192,508
21. The Atlantic	1,107,293
22. Allrecipes	1,106,877
23. Time	1,075,018
24. Smithsonian	1,064,247
25. AMAC Magazine	1,048,112
26. Elle	1,042,986
27. Food Network Magazine	1,027,753
28. Magnolia Journal	1,014,639
29. Essence	974,153
30. Travel + Leisure	971,624
31. TV Guide Magazine	963,789
32. Food & Wine	934,228
33. GQ	932,580
34. First for Women	851,047
35. Architectural Digest	840,982
36. Bon Appétit	839,846
37. Midwest Living	833,961
38. Woman's World	801,682
39. Outside	792,923
40. HGTV Magazine	792,106
41. The Family Handyman	773,672
42. Woman's Day	769,706
43. Carolina Country	767,205
44. Star Magazine	750,163
45. The Elks Magazine	741,063
46. Harper's Bazaar	740,653
47. Condé Nast Traveler	724,850
48. American Hunter	716,860
49. The Tennessee Magazine	713,317
50. Esquire	645,725

Best-Selling Digital Replica U.S. Magazines, 2024

Source: Alliance for Audited Media (AAM)

General magazines, exclusive of comics; also excludes magazines that failed to file reports to AAM. Based on total average paid and verified circulation during the six months ending June 30, 2024; ranked by paid circulation size.

Publication	Paid circ.
1. Us Weekly	1,685,547
2. Golf Digest	884,281
3. Star Magazine	637,756
4. People	632,051
5. The Atlantic	612,237
6. Outside	563,647
7. Better Homes and Gardens	561,872
8. Golf Magazine	553,447
9. Southern Living	549,497
10. The New Yorker	548,552
11. National Geographic	472,731
12. First for Women	455,423
13. Woman's World	434,361
14. Real Simple	399,885
15. Rolling Stone	309,497
16. Wired	307,219
17. New York	292,759
18. Vanity Fair	278,095
19. Economist (North America)	277,673
20. Vogue	274,934
21. Good Housekeeping	264,099
22. Taste of Home	262,946
23. Wine Enthusiast	256,147
24. Time	246,379
25. Reader's Digest	236,017
26. Elle	219,680
27. Food Network Magazine	215,745
28. HGTV Magazine	211,869
29. Bon Appétit	206,358
30. Women's Health	203,849
31. In Touch Weekly	202,182
32. IEEE Spectrum	198,139
33. Travel + Leisure	197,968
34. Luxe Interiors + Design	197,855
35. TV Guide Magazine	197,375
36. Architectual Digest	197,289
37. GQ	192,953
38. Cosmopolitan	189,345
39. Popular Mechanics	188,817
40. Fortune (North America)	181,665
41. Food & Wine	180,647
42. The Family Handyman	174,424
43. Woman's Day	174,336
44. Esquire	166,513
45. Allrecipes	165,024
46. The Knot	163,921
47. Prevention	156,207
48. Entrepreneur	155,750
49. Harper's Bazaar	151,790
50. Men's Health	150,426

Some Notable New Books, 2024

Source: Reference and User Services Association, American Library Association (ALA)

Fiction

Biography of X, Catherine Lacey
Chain-Gang All-Stars, Nana Kwame Adjei-Brenyah
Dearborn, Ghassan Zeineddine
Hangman, Maya Binyam
In Memoriam, Alice Winn
North Woods, Daniel Mason
Open Throat, Henry Hoke
Same Bed Different Dreams, Ed Park
The Heaven and Earth Grocery Store, James McBride
The Reformatory, Tananarive Due
Y/N, Esther Yi

Poetry

Promises of Gold / Promesas de Oro, José Olivarez
Side Notes From the Archivist, Anastacia-Renee
Trace Evidence, Charif Shanahan

Nonfiction

A Fever in the Heartland: The Ku Klux Klan's Plot to Take Over America, and the Woman Who Stopped Them, Timothy Egan
Dyscalculia: A Love Story of Epic Miscalculation, Camonghne Felix
How to Say Babylon: A Memoir, Safiya Sinclair
King: A Life, Jonathan Eig
Master, Slave, Husband, Wife: An Epic Journey From Slavery to Freedom, Ilyon Woo
Mott Street: A Chinese American Family's Story of Exclusion and Homecoming, Ava Chin
Our Migrant Souls: A Meditation on Race and the Meanings and Myths of "Latino," Héctor Tobar
Poverty, by America, Matthew Desmond
The Exceptions: Nancy Hopkins, MIT, and the Fight for Women in Science, Kate Zernike
The Great Displacement: Climate Change and the Next American Migration, Jake Bittle
The Talk, Darrin Bell
The Wager: A Tale of Shipwreck, Mutiny, and Murder, David Grann

Best-Selling Books, 2023

Source: NPD BookScan

Hardcover Fiction

1. *Fourth Wing*, Rebecca Yarros
2. *Iron Flame*, Rebecca Yarros
3. *Lessons in Chemistry*, Bonnie Garmus
4. *Happy Place*, Emily Henry
5. *Demon Copperhead*, Barbara Kingsolver
6. *The Exchange: After the Firm*, John Grisham
7. *Holly*, Stephen King
8. *Tomorrow, and Tomorrow, and Tomorrow*, Gabrielle Zevin
9. *The Covenant of Water*, Abraham Verghese
10. *Fourth Wing* (Special Edition), Rebecca Yarros

Hardcover Nonfiction

1. *The Woman in Me*, Britney Spears
2. *The Creative Act: A Way of Being*, Rick Rubin
3. *The Wager: A Tale of Shipwreck, Mutiny, and Murder*, David Grann
4. *Outlive: The Science and Art of Longevity*, Peter Attia
5. *I'm Glad My Mom Died*, Jennette McCurdy
6. *Magnolia Table, Volume 3: A Collection of Recipes for Gathering*, Joanna Gaines
7. *Elon Musk*, Walter Isaacson
8. *Friends, Lovers, and the Big Terrible Thing: A Memoir*, Matthew Perry
9. *Baking Yesteryear: The Best Recipes From the 1900s to the 1980s*, B. Dylan Hollis
10. *The Democrat Party Hates America*, Mark R. Levin

Trade Paperback

1. *It Ends With Us*, Colleen Hoover
2. *It Starts With Us*, Colleen Hoover
3. *Verify*, Colleen Hoover
4. *A Court of Thorns and Roses*, Sarah J. Maas
5. *The Seven Husbands of Evelyn Hugo*, Taylor Jenkins Reid
6. *Icebreaker*, Hannah Grace
7. *The Housemaid*, Freida McFadden
8. *Twisted Love*, Ana Huang
9. *Ugly Love*, Colleen Hoover
10. *The 48 Laws of Power*, Robert Greene

Mass Market Fiction

1. *Without a Trace*, Danielle Steel
2. *Tom Clancy Red Winter*, Marc Cameron
3. *Reacher: Bad Luck and Trouble*, Lee Child
4. *3 Days to Live*, James Patterson
5. *Gabriel's Angel*, Nora Roberts
6. *Livid: A Scarpetta Novel*, Patricia Cornwell
7. *Payback in Death: An Eve Dallas Novel*, J. D. Robb
8. *Tracking Stolen Treasures*, Lisa Phillips
9. *An Amish Mother for His Child*, Patricia Johns
10. *Her Scandalous Amish Secret*, Jocelyn McClay

Children's and Young Adult Hardcover

1. *Dog Man: Twenty Thousand Fleas Under the Sea: A Graphic Novel* (Dog Man #11), Dav Pilkey
2. *No Brainer* (Diary of a Wimpy Kid #18), Jeff Kinney
3. *Taylor Swift: A Little Golden Book Biography*, Wendy Loggia
4. *Percy Jackson and the Olympians: The Chalice of the Gods*, Rick Riordan
5. *Cat Kid Comic Club: Influencers: A Graphic Novel* (Cat Kid Comic Club #5), Dav Pilkey
6. *Murtagh: The World of Eragon*, Christopher Paolini
7. *From the World of Percy Jackson: The Sun and the Star*, Rick Riordan
8. *Don't Let the Pigeon Drive the Sleigh!* Mo Willems
9. *Harry Potter and the Prisoner of Azkaban: MinaLima Edition* (Harry Potter, Book 3), J. K. Rowling
10. *Dr. Seuss's How the Grinch Lost Christmas!* Alastair Heim

Note: Hardcover bestsellers include 2022 and 2023 releases. Trade paperback bestsellers are for overall 2023 sales of paperback editions for titles first published in any year. Mass market fiction and children's and young adult bestsellers include frontlist/2023 releases only.

Most Challenged Books, 2023

Source: Office for Intellectual Freedom, American Library Association (ALA)

A challenge is a formal, written complaint filed with a library or school requesting that materials be removed because of content or appropriateness. The ALA reported that 65% more unique titles were challenged in 2023 compared to 2022. The common reasons given for challenges follow each book's title and author.

1. *Gender Queer*, Maia Kobabe. LGBTQIA+ content, explicit images.
2. *All Boys Aren't Blue*, George M. Johnson. LGBTQIA+ content, profanity, sexually explicit.
3. *This Book Is Gay*, Juno Dawson. LGBTQIA+ content, sex education, sexually explicit.
4. *The Perks of Being a Wallflower*, Stephen Chbosky. LGBTQIA+ content, drug use, profanity, sexually explicit.
5. *Flamer*, Mike Curato. LGBTQIA+ content, sexually explicit.
6. *The Bluest Eye*, Toni Morrison. Sexually explicit.
7. *Me and Earl and the Dying Girl*, Jesse Andrews. Profanity, sexually explicit.

   Tricks, Ellen Hopkins. LGBTQIA+ content, drug use, sexuality explicit.
9. *Let's Talk About It: The Teen's Guide to Sex, Relationships, and Being a Human*, Erika Moen and Matthew Nolan. LGBTQIA+ content, sex education, sexually explicit.
10. *Sold*, Patricia McCormick. Sexually explicit.

U.S. Daily Newspapers, 2023

Source: *Press Gazette* analysis of Alliance for Audited Media data
(in thousands)

Rank	Newspaper	Avg. circulation	% change, 2022-23	Rank	Newspaper	Avg. circulation	% change, 2022-23
1.	Wall Street Journal	555.2	−14%	14.	Dallas Morning News	52.2	−13%
2.	New York Times	267.6	−13	15.	San Francisco Chronicle	50.8	−6
3.	New York Post	131.2	−8	16.	Houston Chronicle	48.1	−17
4.	Washington Post	127.7	−13	17.	Arizona Republic	46.7	−14
5.	USA Today	121.6	−16	18.	Philadelphia Inquirer	45.3	−19
6.	Los Angeles Times	105.7	−17	19.	Daily News	41.5	−18
7.	Star Tribune	86.9	−12	20.	Buffalo News[1]	38.4	−32
8.	Newsday	83.5	−10	21.	The San Diego Union-Tribune	37.8	−14
9.	Chicago Tribune	73.0	−16	22.	Plain Dealer/Plain Dealer Sunday	37.0	−21
10.	Seattle Times	71.7	−13	23.	Denver Post	36.7	−25
11.	Honolulu Star-Advertiser	71.6	−7	24.	Las Vegas Review Journal	35.8	−12
12.	Tampa Bay Times	62.6	−24	25.	The Star-Ledger	34.4	−15
13.	Boston Globe	56.9	−11				

Note: Print circulation is average Mon.-Fri. figure for six months prior to Sept. 2023. Where this data was not available, Wednesday circulation data was used. (1) Print circulation for the six months prior to Mar. 2023.

Daily Circulation and Revenues for U.S. Daily Newspapers, 1960-2022

Source: Pew Research Center
(in thousands)

Year	Circulation Weekday	Circulation Sunday	Revenues from— Advertising	Revenues from— Circulation	Year	Circulation Weekday	Circulation Sunday	Revenues from— Advertising	Revenues from— Circulation
1960	58.9	47.7	$3,681	$1,604	2009	45.7	46.2	$27,564	$10,067
1970	62.1	49.2	5,704	2,634	2010	NA	NA	25,838	10,049
1980	62.2	54.7	14,794	5,470	2011	44.4	48.5	27,078	9,989
1990	62.3	62.6	32,280	NA	2012	43.4	44.8	25,316	10,449
1995	58.2	61.2	36,092	9,720	2013	40.7	43.3	23,587	10,642
2000	55.8	59.4	48,670	10,541	2014	40.4	42.8	22,078	10,744
2001	55.6	59.1	44,305	10,783	2015	37.7	41.0	20,362	10,870
2002	55.2	58.8	44,102	11,026	2016	34.7	37.8	18,275	10,910
2003	55.2	58.5	46,156	11,224	2017	30.9	34.0	16,476	11,211
2004	54.6	57.8	48,244	10,989	2018	28.6	30.8	14,346	10,995
2005	53.3	55.3	49,435	10,747	2019	26.0	27.4	12,864	11,017
2006	52.3	53.2	49,275	10,548	2020	24.3	25.8	9,601	11,054
2007	50.7	51.2	45,375	10,295	2021	22.7	23.4	10,264	11,525
2008	48.6	49.1	37,848	10,087	2022	20.9	20.9	9,761	11,606

NA = Not available. **Note:** Circulation figures from 2015 on and revenue figures after 2013 are estimates and may not be directly comparable to previous years.

U.S. News Consumption by Selected Characteristics, 2023

Source: Pew Research Center
(percent of U.S. adults in each group that get news at least sometimes from each platform)

Characteristic	Television	Radio	Print publications	Digital devices: Total digital	Digital devices: News websites or apps	Digital devices: Social media	Search	Podcasts
Total	**62%**	**52%**	**37%**	**86%**	**67%**	**49%**	**71%**	**30%**
Men	61	51	35	86	68	44	71	33
Women	65	53	38	86	66	54	72	27
Age								
18-29	41	37	24	89	59	69	77	41
30-49	53	52	29	90	70	55	74	35
50-64	72	62	39	86	72	40	71	26
65+	85	52	55	77	63	34	62	17
Race/ethnicity								
White	62	54	38	86	68	46	69	28
Black	76	54	39	80	64	53	71	33
Asian	52	42	32	93	83	61	82	43
Hispanic	62	48	32	87	60	56	74	31
Education level								
High school or less	67	53	37	77	57	48	65	24
Some college	63	51	35	89	69	52	75	30
College+	57	51	37	93	76	49	74	36
Income level								
Less than $30,000	61	48	34	80	56	52	70	28
$30,000-$79,999	64	53	37	88	70	49	73	30
More than $80,000	60	52	38	92	81	46	72	37
Political affiliation								
Republican/Lean Rep.	63	54	35	85	66	48	70	29
Democratic/Lean Dem.	63	50	38	87	69	50	73	32

Note: White, Black, and Asian adults include those who report being only one race and are not Hispanic; Hispanics are of any race.

National Recording Registry, 2024

Source: Library of Congress

Each year since 2002, the National Recording Registry at the Library of Congress adds 25 recordings showcasing the "range and diversity of American recorded sound heritage."

"Clarinet Marmalade," Jim Europe's 369th Band (1919)
"Kauhavan Polkka," Viola Turpeinen & John Rosendahl (1928)
Wisconsin Folksong Recordings (1937-46)
"Rose Room," Benny Goodman Sextet with Charlie Christian (1939)
"Rudolph, the Red-Nosed Reindeer," Gene Autry (1949)
"Tennessee Waltz," Patti Page (1950)
"Rocket '88,'" Jackie Brenston and His Delta Cats (1951)
"Catch a Falling Star" / "Magic Moments," Perry Como (1957)
"Chances Are," Johnny Mathis (1957)
The Sidewinder, Lee Morgan (1964)
Surrealistic Pillow, Jefferson Airplane (1967)
"Ain't No Sunshine," Bill Withers (1971)
This Is a Recording, Lily Tomlin (1971)
J.D. Crowe & the New South, J.D. Crowe & the New South (1975)
Arrival, ABBA (1976)
Parallel Lines, Blondie (1978)
The Cars, The Cars (1978)
"El Cantante," Héctor Lavoe (1978)
"La Di Da Di," Doug E. Fresh & Slick Rick (1985)
"Don't Worry, Be Happy," Bobby McFerrin (1988)
"Amor Eterno," Juan Gabriel (1990)
Pieces of Africa, Kronos Quartet (1992)
Dookie, Green Day (1994)
Ready to Die, Notorious B.I.G. (1994)
Wild Open Spaces, The Chicks (1998)

U.S. Commercial Radio Stations by Format, 2014-24

Source: Inside Radio (www.insideradio.com)
(as of July 2024; ranked by 2024 numbers)

Format	2014	2015	2016	2017	2018	2019	2020	2021	2022	2023	2024
1. Country	2,053	2,112	2,126	2,121	2,143	2,157	2,147	2,150	2,135	2,136	2,122
2. News/Talk	1,409	1,360	1,355	1,330	1,296	1,268	1,241	1,267	1,246	1,225	1,204
3. Classic Hits	754	805	881	965	1,001	1,046	1,081	1,115	1,143	1,138	1,130
4. Spanish	844	862	878	858	865	867	886	889	912	899	912
5. Classic Rock	486	486	492	519	522	548	558	571	606	606	611
6. Sports	788	788	780	752	726	702	687	653	629	624	610
7. Top 40	577	579	583	594	595	591	582	579	561	550	550
8. Adult Contemporary	597	609	608	592	581	575	567	551	539	540	534
9. Hot AC	465	462	464	451	452	447	471	452	450	446	428
10. Religion (Teaching, Variety)	324	318	318	332	351	365	392	394	393	402	394
11. Rock	302	304	304	291	285	289	291	290	265	265	264
12. Oldies	476	413	343	293	295	278	262	249	240	231	224
13. Contemporary Christian	157	168	173	193	172	195	201	210	228	216	194
14. R&B	131	143	148	155	158	152	152	160	168	173	172
15. Urban AC	167	166	163	170	170	164	168	171	171	173	166
16. Inspirational Gospel	211	218	213	206	198	198	182	178	171	168	165
17. Ethnic	152	161	168	163	165	159	156	153	151	148	141
18. Soft Adult Contemporary	131	121	108	114	118	122	130	130	121	119	112
19. Alternative Rock	105	103	112	115	117	111	109	110	116	111	106
20. Modern Rock	100	101	107	106	114	111	109	107	104	102	106
Total stations	**11,386**	**11,314**	**11,386**	**11,412**	**11,365**	**11,297**	**11,215**	**11,133**	**11,240**	**10,902**	**10,810**

Note: Totals include stations that are changing or did not report format, as well as formats not listed here.

Top-Selling Albums of All Time

Source: Recording Industry Assn. of America (RIAA)

Sales figures represent RIAA multi-platinum certifications; albums ranked by latest sales certification. As of Aug. 16, 2024.

Rank	Title, artist	Unit sales (mil)
1.	*Their Greatest Hits (1971-1975)*, Eagles	38.0
2.	*Thriller*, Michael Jackson	34.0
3.	*Back in Black*, AC/DC	26.0
4.	*Hotel California*, Eagles	26.0
5.	*Led Zeppelin IV*, Led Zeppelin	24.0
6.	*The Beatles*, The Beatles	24.0
7.	*Greatest Hits Volume I & Volume II*, Billy Joel	23.0
8.	*Double Live*, Garth Brooks	23.0
9.	*The Wall*, Pink Floyd	23.0
10.	*Cracked Rear View*, Hootie & the Blowfish	22.0
11.	*Rumours*, Fleetwood Mac	21.0
12.	*Come on Over*, Shania Twain	20.0
13.	*No Fences*, Garth Brooks	18.0
14.	*Appetite for Destruction*, Guns N' Roses	18.0
15.	*Greatest Hits*, Journey	18.0
16.	*The Bodyguard* (soundtrack), Whitney Houston	18.0
17.	*Jagged Little Pill*, Alanis Morissette	17.0
18.	*Boston*, Boston	17.0
19.	*Born in the U.S.A.*, Bruce Springsteen	17.0
20.	*Greatest Hits*, Elton John	17.0
21.	*The Beatles 1967-1970*, The Beatles	17.0
22.	*Saturday Night Fever* (soundtrack), Bee Gees	16.0
23.	*Physical Graffiti*, Led Zeppelin	16.0
24.	*Metallica*, Metallica	16.0
25.	*Legend*, Bob Marley and the Wailers	15.0
26.	*Slippery When Wet*, Bon Jovi	15.0
27.	*Dark Side of the Moon*, Pink Floyd	15.0
28.	*Supernatural*, Santana	15.0
29.	*Greatest Hits 1974-1978*, Steve Miller Band	15.0
30.	*The Beatles 1962-1966*, The Beatles	15.0
31.	*21*, Adele	14.0
32.	*Backstreet Boys*, Backstreet Boys	14.0
33.	*...Baby One More Time*, Britney Spears	14.0
34.	*Tapestry*, Carole King	14.0
35.	*Ropin' the Wind*, Garth Brooks	14.0
36.	*Bat Out of Hell*, Meat Loaf	14.0
37.	*Simon & Garfunkel's Greatest Hits*, Simon & Garfunkel	14.0
38.	*Dirty Dancing* (soundtrack)	14.0
39.	*Confessions*, Usher	14.0
40.	*Whitney Houston*, Whitney Houston	14.0
41.	*Millennium*, Backstreet Boys	13.0
42.	*Bruce Springsteen & E Street Band Live 1975-'85*, Bruce Springsteen	13.0
43.	*Speakerboxxx/The Love Below*, OutKast	13.0
44.	*Ten*, Pearl Jam	13.0
45.	*Purple Rain* (soundtrack), Prince & The Revolution	13.0
46.	*Wide Open Spaces*, The Chicks	13.0

Top Musical Artists All-Time by Digital Sales

Source: Recording Industry Assn. of America (RIAA)

Units represent digital singles certified as sold, including streaming-equivalent, as of Aug. 16, 2024.

Artist	Units (mil)	Artist	Units (mil)	Artist	Units (mil)	Artist	Units (mil)
Drake	244.0	Lady Gaga	82.5	A Boogie wit da Hoodie	54.0	Red Hot Chilli Peppers	45.0
Rihanna	183.0	Luke Bryan	82.5	Flo Rida	54.0	Thomas Rhett	44.5
Eminem	167.0	Usher	82.5	Blake Shelton	52.0	Tyler, the Creator	44.5
Kanye West	160.5	Youngboy Never Broke Again	82.0	Harry Styles	52.0	50 Cent	44.0
Taylor Swift	137.5	J. Cole	78.0	Pitbull	52.0	Linkin Park	44.0
Post Malone	136.0	Lil Baby	76.0	Sam Smith	51.0	Rae Sremmurd	43.5
The Weeknd	126.0	XXXTentacion	76.0	DJ Khaled	49.5	Tim McGraw	43.5
Justin Bieber	122.5	Twenty One Pilots	70.0	Nicki Minaj	49.5	Original Broadway Cast of *Hamilton*	43.0
Katy Perry	121.5	Michael Jackson	65.5	Carrie Underwood	49.0	NF	42.5
Beyoncé	114.5	Mariah Carey	64.0	Journey	48.5	Queen	42.5
Morgan Wallen	106.5	SZA	62.0	Kenny Chesney	48.0	Kane Brown	42.0
Imagine Dragons	103.5	Miley Cyrus	61.5	Billie Eilish	47.5	Lil Uzi Vert	42.0
Luke Combs	95.5	Britney Spears	58.0	Big Sean	47.0	Shawn Mendes	41.5
Ed Sheeran	95.0	Cardi B	58.0	Lana Del Rey	47.0	Train	41.5
Future	95.0	Khalid	58.0	Kate Gates	46.5	Demi Lovato	41.0
Chris Brown	94.5	Fall Out Boy	57.0	The Chainsmokers	46.5	Kendrick Lamar	41.0
Lil Wayne	92.0	Polo G	57.0	Sam Hunt	45.5	George Strait	40.5
Bruno Mars	91.5	Chris Stapleton	56.5	Doja Cat	45.0	AC/DC	40.0
Ariana Grande	88.5	Florida Georgia Line	54.5	Eric Church	45.0	Alicia Keys	39.0
Maroon 5	87.5	Panic! at the Disco	54.5	Halsey	45.0		
Juice Wrld	84.0						

Top Musical Artists All-Time by Album Sales

Source: Recording Industry Assn. of America (RIAA)

Certified album sales in millions, including streaming equivalent where applicable, as of Aug. 16, 2024.

Artist	Certified sales (mil)	Artist	Certified sales (mil)	Artist	Certified sales (mil)
The Beatles	183.0	Eminem	61.5	Guns N' Roses	44.5
Garth Brooks	162.0	Whitney Houston	61.0	Santana	43.5
Elvis Presley	146.5	Van Halen	56.5	Queen	43.0
The Eagles	120.0	Fleetwood Mac	55.5	Bon Jovi	41.0
Led Zeppelin	112.5	Celine Dion	53.0	Reba McEntire	41.0
Michael Jackson	89.0	Journey	52.5	Eric Clapton	40.0
Billy Joel	86.0	U2	52.0	Tim McGraw	40.0
AC/DC	83.0	Taylor Swift	51.0	Chicago	39.0
Elton John	80.0	Neil Diamond	49.5	Britney Spears	38.5
Mariah Carey	75.0	Alabama	49.0	Simon & Garfunkel	38.5
Pink Floyd	75.0	Kenny G	48.0	Foreigner	38.0
Bruce Springsteen	71.0	Shania Twain	48.0	Rod Stewart	38.0
Aerosmith	69.5	Drake	47.5	Backstreet Boys	37.0
George Strait	69.5	Kenny Rogers	47.5	2Pac	36.5
Barbra Streisand	68.5	Alan Jackson	44.5	Bob Dylan	36.0
The Rolling Stones	66.5	Bob Seger & the Silver Bullet Band	44.5	Def Leppard	35.5
Madonna	65.5			Kevin Chesney	35.0
Metallica	63.0			Dave Matthews Band	34.5

Multi-Platinum Awards for Recorded Music, 2023-24

Source: Recording Industry Assn. of America (RIAA)

To be certified platinum, an **album** must sell 1 mil units (LPs, CDs, or digital) with a manufacturer's dollar volume of at least $2 mil based on one-third of the suggested retail list price for each copy sold. To achieve multi-platinum status, an album must reach minimum total sales of at least 2 mil units with a manufacturer's dollar volume of at least $4 mil based on one-third of the list price. RIAA began including streaming in their award formulas in 2018; 1,500 streams count as the equivalent of 10 track sales or 1 album sale. **Digital singles** must sell 2 mil to achieve a multi-platinum award. For digital singles award formulas, 150 streams equal one download sold.

Awards listed here are for albums and digital singles (released Sept. 1, 2022-Aug. 16, 2024) that were certified Sept. 2023-Aug. 16, 2024. Number in parentheses represents millions sold. Alphabetized by artist name.

Albums

Stick Season, Noah Kahan (2)
One Thing at a Time, Morgan Wallen (5)

Digital Singles

"Beautiful Things" (3), Benson Boone
"I Remember Everything" (2), Zach Bryan feat. Kacey Musgraves
"Fast Car" (5), Luke Combs
"Tomorrow 2" (2), Glorilla with Cardi B
"Fukumean" (3), Gunna
"Truck Bed" (2), Hardy
"Too Sweet" (2), Hozier
"Dial Drunk" (2), Noah Kahan with Post Malone
"Daylight" (2), David Kushner
"All My Life" (2), Lil Durk feat. J Cole
"Just Wanna Rock" (4), Lil Uzi Vert
"Superhero (Heroes & Villains)" (2), Metro Boomin, Future, Chris Brown
"Creepin'" (2), Metro Boomin, The Weeknd, 21 Savage
"Tennessee Orange" (2), Megan Moroney
"Wild Ones" (2), Jessie Murph & Jelly Roll
"Escapism." (2), Raye feat. 070 Shake
"A Bar Song (Tipsy)" (2), Shaboozey
"Unholy" (2), Sam Smith feat. Kim Petras
"Lose Control" (2), Teddy Swims
"Kill Bill" (5), "Shirt" (2), "Snooze" (4), SZA
"Favorite Song" (2), Toosii
"Water" (2), Tyla
"Last Night" (7), "Thinkin' Bout Me" (3), Morgan Wallen
"Peaches & Eggplants" (2), Young Nudy feat. 21 Savage
"Pretty Little Poison" (2), Warren Zeiders
"Religiously" (2), Bailey Zimmerman

Top-Grossing North American Concert Tours, 2005-23

Source: Pollstar

Rank	Artist (year)	Total gross[1]	Cities/ shows
1.	Taylor Swift (2023)	$905.4	20/53
2.	Beyoncé (2023)	438.0	25/35
3.	Bad Bunny (2022)	356.5	43/63
4.	Taylor Swift (2018)	277.3	27/40
5.	Morgan Wallen (2023)	277.1	43/43
6.	Elton John (2022)	201.8	38/50
7.	Taylor Swift (2015)	199.4	41/62
8.	Drake (2023)	184.9	27/43
9.	Pink (2023)	182.6	30/33
10.	Bruce Springsteen & the E Street Band (2023)	179.5	31/35
11.	The Rolling Stones (2019)	177.8	14/16
12.	Def Leppard / Mötley Crüe (2022)	177.4	35/36
13.	U2 (2017)	176.1	26/30
14.	Ed Sheeran (2023)	172.3	28/31
15.	Beyoncé (2016)	169.4	30/32
16.	Jay-Z and Beyoncé (2018)	$166.4	24/30
17.	Eagles (2018)	166.0	45/53
18.	The Rolling Stones (2005)	162.0	38/42
19.	Harry Styles (2022)	160.4	12/47
20.	Elton John (2019)	157.4	57/81
21.	U2 (2011)	156.0	21/25
22.	George Strait (2023)	148.7	11/14
23.	Karol G (2023)	144.6	13/18
24.	U2 (2005)	138.9	43/78
25.	The Rolling Stones (2006)	138.5	35/39
26.	Kenny Chesney (2022)	135.3	38/41
27.	Madonna (2012)	133.7	31/45
28.	The Police (2007)	133.2	41/54
29.	Guns N' Roses (2016)	130.8	24/31
30.	RBD (2023)	130.5	21/30

(1) In millions. Not adjusted for inflation.

Music Sales by Format and Value, 1995-2023

Source: Recording Industry Assn. of America (RIAA)
(in millions, net after returns)

	1995	2000	2005	2010	2015	2020	2022	2023	% change, 2022-23
Physical units shipped	**1,112.7**	**1,079.2**	**748.8**	**267.7**	**135.0**	**56.8**	**79.8**	**81.7**	**2.4%**
Dollar value	**$12,320.3**	**14,323.7**	**11,195.0**	**3,663.7**	**1,862.2**	**1,163.3**	**1,731.0**	**1,912.0**	**10.5**
Compact discs (CDs)	722.9	942.5	705.4	253.0	117.1	31.6	37.7	37.0	–1.9
Dollar value	$9,377.4	13,214.5	10,520.2	3,389.4	1,445.0	483.3	482.6	537.1	11.3
LPs/EPs	2.2	2.2	1.0	4.2	13.7	23.7	40.5	43.2	6.6
Dollar value	$25.1	27.7	14.2	88.9	333.4	643.9	1,224.4	1,350.2	10.3
Music videos	12.6	18.2	33.8	9.1	3.1	1.0	0.8	0.6	–26.1
Dollar value	$220.3	281.9	602.2	177.6	70.4	27.4	11.3	10.7	–5.7
Other physical[1]	375.0	116.3	8.6	1.4	1.1	0.5	0.7	0.9	17.2
Dollar value	$2,697.5	799.6	58.4	7.8	13.4	8.8	12.7	14.0	10.5
Digital formats: number downloaded	—	—	**553.1**	**1,471.8**	**1,120.5**	**314.0**	**202.4**	**167.3**	**17.4**
Digital formats: dollar value	—	—	**$925.3**	**2,699.8**	**2,314.3**	**664.7**	**494.7**	**434.1**	**–12.2**
Albums downloaded	—	—	13.6	85.8	106.8	33.1	24.5	20.5	–16.3
Dollar value	—	—	$135.7	872.4	1,064.4	319.3	241.9	204.7	–15.4
Singles downloaded	—	—	366.9	1,177.4	986.3	249.3	172.5	142.0	–17.7
Dollar value	—	—	$363.3	1,336.4	1,185.2	303.3	214.1	190.8	–10.9
Ringtones and ringbacks	—	—	170.0	188.5	21.9	8.1	4.4	4.1	–8.0
Dollar value	—	—	$421.6	448.0	54.6	20.2	11.0	10.1	–8.0
Other digital downloads[2]	—	—	2.6	20.1	5.5	1.6	1.0	0.8	–20.4
Dollar value	—	—	$4.7	43.0	10.1	21.9	27.7	28.5	3.1
Subscription and streaming dollar value	—	—	**$169.6**	**461.6**	**2,331.3**	**10,051.3**	**13,667.5**	**14,769.0**	**8.1**
Subscription formats[3]	—	—	1.3	1.5	10.8	75.5	91.6	96.8	5.7
Dollar value	—	—	$149.2	212.4	1,156.7	6,972.7	9,179.0	10,149.7	10.6
Limited tier paid subscriptions	—	—	—	—	—	719.9	1,063.0	1,021.4	–3.9
SoundExchange distribution[4]	—	—	$20.4	249.2	802.6	947.4	959.4	1,004.8	4.7
On-demand streaming (ad supported)[5]	—	—	—	—	$372.0	1,200.1	1,822.1	1,864.5	2.3
Other ad-supported streaming[6]	—	—	—	—	—	211.2	261.5	317.7	21.5
Synchronization royalties[7]	—	—	—	$188.7	202.9	265.2	382.5	410.9	7.4
Total physical and digital[8]	**1,112.7**	**1,079.2**	**1,301.9**	**1,739.5**	**1,255.5**	**348.9**	**282.1**	**249.0**	**–11.7**
Total value physical and digital	**$12,320.3**	**14,323.7**	**12,289.9**	**7,013.8**	**6,710.8**	**12,144.7**	**15,893.2**	**17,115.1**	**7.7**

— = Not available or not applicable. (1) Includes CD singles, cassettes, vinyl singles, DVD audio, and SACD. (2) Includes kiosk and music video downloads. (3) Streaming, tethered, and other paid subscription services not operating under statutory licenses. Subscription volume is annual average number of subscriptions (excluding limited tier). (4) Estimated payments to performers/copyright holders for digital and customized radio services under statutory licenses. (5) Ad-supported audio and music video services not operating under statutory licenses. (6) Revenues for statutory services that are not distributed by SoundExchange or included in other streaming categories. (7) Includes fees and royalties from sound recordings used in other media. Not included in subscription and streaming dollar value. (8) Units total includes physical and downloaded albums and singles but not streaming, subscriptions, or royalties.

Top Basic Cable TV Networks, 2023

Source: Kagan, a media research group within S&P Global Market Intelligence

Rank	Network (year began)	Subscribers (mil)
1.	C-SPAN (1979)	76.0
2.	HGTV (1994)	75.0
3.	Food Network (1993)	74.7
4.	TLC (1972)	73.2
5.	TBS (1976)	73.1
6.	TNT (1988)	73.0
7.	FX (1994)	72.8
8.	USA (1980)	72.8
9.	Discovery Channel (1985)	71.9
10.	National Geographic Channel (2001)	71.7
11.	Disney Channel (1983)	70.9
12.	Animal Planet (1996)	70.7
13.	AMC (1984)	70.5
14.	CNN (1980)	70.3
15.	E! (1987)	70.3
16.	Syfy (1992)	70.0
17.	Bravo (1980)	69.9
18.	truTV (2008)	69.6
19.	The Weather Channel (1982)	69.3
20.	ESPN (1979)	69.1

Most Watched Original Streaming Shows, 2024

Source: © 2024 Nielsen, licensed for use in this publication

Shows ranked by estimated total number of minutes the program was viewed using the streaming platform shown by persons aged 2-99 in the U.S., Sept. 1, 2023-Aug. 31, 2024.

Rank	Series, provider	Mins. (mil)
1.	Bridgerton, Netflix	20,631
2.	Love Is Blind, Netflix	15,008
3.	Reacher, Amazon	14,550
4.	The Boys, Amazon	14,028
5.	Virgin River, Netflix	13,755
6.	The Crown, Netflix	12,256
7.	Futurama, Hulu	11,719
8.	Fallout, Amazon	11,267
9.	Gabby's Dollhouse, Netflix	10,945
10.	Fool Me Once, Netflix	10,186
11.	The Bear, Hulu	9,496
12.	The Great British Baking Show, Netflix	9,030
13.	Evil, Paramount Plus	8,833
14.	Stranger Things, Netflix	8,627
15.	Avatar: The Last Airbender, Netflix	7,969

Most Watched Acquired Streaming Shows, 2024

Source: © 2024 Nielsen, licensed for use in this publication

Shows ranked by estimated total number of minutes the program was viewed using the streaming platform shown by persons aged 2-99 in the U.S., Sept. 1, 2023-Aug. 31, 2024.

Rank	Series, provider	Mins. (mil)
1.	Bluey, multiple distributors	55,716
2.	Grey's Anatomy, multiple distributors	49,960
3.	Suits, multiple distributors	41,438
4.	NCIS, multiple distributors	39,227
5.	Family Guy, multiple distributors	37,435
6.	Young Sheldon, multiple distributors	36,754
7.	The Big Bang Theory, multiple distributors	29,318
8.	Criminal Minds, multiple distributors	28,670
9.	Law & Order: SVU, multiple distributors	25,514
10.	Cocomelon, multiple distributors	25,207
11.	Spongebob Squarepants, multiple distributors	24,511
12.	Bob's Burgers, multiple distributors	24,282
13.	Gilmore Girls, multiple distributors	24,082
14.	Friends, multiple distributors	23,962
15.	Supernatural, multiple distributors	21,907

Most Watched Streaming Movies, 2024

Source: © 2024 Nielsen, licensed for use in this publication

Feature-length films ranked by estimated total number of minutes the movie was viewed using the streaming platform shown by persons aged 2-99 in the U.S., Sept. 1, 2023-Aug. 31, 2024.

Rank	Movie, provider	Mins. (mil)
1.	The Super Mario Bros. Movie, multiple distributors	16,285
2.	Elemental, multiple distributors	12,975
3.	Moana, multiple distributors	12,375
4.	Encanto, multiple distributors	7,908
5.	Leave the World Behind, Netflix	7,907
6.	Minions, multiple distributors	7,012
7.	Frozen, multiple distributors	6,811
8.	Leo, Netflix	6,632
9.	Cars, multiple distributors	5,674
10.	Trolls, multiple distributors	5,547
11.	Trolls Band Together, multiple distributors	5,503
12.	Inside Out, multiple distributors	5,430
13.	The Boss Baby, multiple distributors	5,221
14.	Shrek, multiple distributors	5,178
15.	Spider-Man: Across the Spider-Verse, multiple distributors	5,019

Highest-Rated Syndicated Programs, 2023-24

Source: © 2024 Nielsen, licensed for use in this publication

Average audience percentages, or ratings, are estimates of the percentage of all TV-owning households watching a program live or on DVR within seven days of broadcast, Sept. 1, 2023-Aug. 31, 2024.

Rank	Program	Avg. audience
1.	Jeopardy	5.0%
2.	Family Feud	4.7
3.	Wheel of Fortune	4.4
4.	Judge Judy	4.0
5.	Dateline Weekly	3.6
6.	Litton's Weekend Adventure	2.2
7.	Inside Edition	2.0
8.	Entertainment Tonight	1.9
9.	Family Feud (weekend)	1.7
10.	America's Test Kitchen	1.6
11.	Live With Kelly and Mark	1.5
12.	Law & Order: Special Victims Unit	1.5
13.	Wheel of Fortune (weekend)	1.4
14.	Access Hollywood (weekend)	1.4
15.	Hot Bench	1.3
16.	Dateline	1.3%
17.	The Big Bang Theory	1.3
18.	Jeopardy (weekend)	1.2
19.	Chicago Fire	1.0
20.	The Kelly Clarkson Show	0.9
21.	Cook's Country From America's Test Kitchen	0.9
22.	Chicago P.D.	0.8
23.	Last Man Standing	0.8
24.	This Old House	0.8
25.	Modern Family (weekend)	0.8
26.	Lidia's Italian Kitchen	0.8
27.	The Rookie	0.7
28.	Ask This Old House	0.7
29.	Access Hollywood	0.7
30.	The Drew Barrymore Show	0.7

Highest-Rated Prime-Time Television Programs, 2023-24

Source: © 2024 Nielsen, licensed for use in this publication

Data are for regularly scheduled network programs airing at least twice Sept. 1, 2023-Aug. 31, 2024. Ranked by average audience percentages, or ratings, which are estimates of the percentage of all TV-owning households watching a particular program live or on DVR within seven days of broadcast.

Rank	Program, network	Avg. audience
1.	Sunday Night Football, NBC	10.4%
2.	NFL National Post Game Show, CBS	10.0
3.	Sunday Night Football, FOX	8.1
4.	Sunday Night Football Pre-Kick, NBC	7.9
5.	Monday Night Football, ABC	6.4
6.	Tracker, CBS	6.3
7.	NCIS, CBS	5.7
8.	The OT, FOX	5.6
9.	Football Night in America, NBC	5.5
10.	Young Sheldon, CBS	5.4
11.	Chicago Fire, NBC	5.3
12.	FBI, CBS	5.3
13.	Blue Bloods, CBS	5.0
14.	60 Minutes, CBS	4.9
15.	Chicago Med, NBC	4.9
16.	Ghosts, CBS	4.8
17.	Chicago P.D., NBC	4.8
18.	The Equalizer, CBS	4.7
19.	NCIS: Hawai'i, CBS	4.7
20.	Elsbeth, CBS	4.6
21.	FBI: Most Wanted, CBS	4.5
22.	60 Minutes Presents, CBS	4.3
23.	Fire Country, CBS	4.3
24.	FBI International, CBS	4.3
25.	Law & Order: SVU, NBC	4.2
26.	The Voice, NBC	4.2%
27.	911, ABC	4.1
28.	The Voice-Tuesday, NBC	4.0
29.	Will Trent, ABC	4.0
30.	Monday Night Football Kickoff, ABC	4.0
31.	NCIS: Sydney, CBS	3.8
32.	The Golden Bachelor, ABC	3.8
33.	America's Got Talent-Tuesday, NBC	3.8
34.	So Help Me Todd, CBS	3.7
35.	CSI: Vegas, CBS	3.7
36.	Irrational, NBC	3.7
37.	S.W.A.T., CBS	3.7
38.	Dancing With the Stars, ABC	3.6
39.	Law & Order, NBC	3.6
40.	Survivor, CBS	3.6
41.	The Rookie, ABC	3.5
42.	The Neighborhood, CBS	3.4
43.	America's Got Talent-Wednesday, NBC	3.4
44.	American Idol, ABC	3.3
45.	Bob Hearts Abishola, CBS	3.2
46.	Law & Order: Organized Crime, NBC	3.2
47.	Grey's Anatomy, ABC	3.2
48.	The Good Doctor, ABC	3.2
49.	Found, NBC	3.1
50.	American Idol-Monday, ABC	3.1

Highest-Rated Basic Cable Programs, 2023-24

Source: © 2024 Nielsen, licensed for use in this publication

Excl. children's series, miniseries, movies, news events, and program durations under 20 min. Average audience percentages, or ratings, are estimates of the percentage of all TV-owning households watching a program live or within seven days of broadcast, Sept. 1, 2023-Aug. 31, 2024.

Highest-Rated Series

Rank	Program, channel	Avg. audience
1.	The Five, Fox News Channel	2.0%
2.	Curse of Oak Island, History	2.0
3.	When Calls the Heart, Hallmark Channel	1.8
4.	Jesse Walters Primetime, Fox News Channel	1.8
5.	Rachel Maddow Show, MSNBC	1.7
6.	Hannity, Fox News Channel	1.6
7.	Sister Wives, TLC	1.6
8.	Gutfeld!, Fox News Channel	1.5
9.	Sister Wives: Christine and David's Wedding, TLC	1.5
10.	The Ingraham Angle, Fox News Channel	1.5
11.	Special Report With Bret Baier, Fox News Channel	1.4
12.	The Way Home, Hallmark Channel	1.3
13.	90 Day Fiancé: Before the 90 Days Tell All, TLC	1.3
14.	The Secret of Skinwalker Ranch, History	1.3
15.	90 Day: The Last Resort, TLC	1.2
16.	Gold Rush, Discovery Channel	1.2
17.	Real Housewives of Beverly Hills, Bravo	1.2
18.	Rock the Block, HGTV	1.1
19.	90 Day Fiancé: Happily Ever After No Limits, TLC	1.1
20.	Outnumbered, Fox News Channel	1.1
21.	Home Town, HGTV	1.1
22.	The Last Word With Lawrence O'Donnell, MSNBC	1.1
23.	America's Newsroom , Fox News Channel	1.1
24.	The Faulkner Focus, Fox News Channel	1.1

Highest-Rated Sports Programs

Rank	Program, channel	Avg. audience
1.	College Football Playoff National Semifinal-Monday (1/1/2024, Alabama-Michigan), ESPN	12.2%
2.	College Football Playoff National Championship, ESPN	12.0
3.	College Football Playoff National Semifinal-Monday (1/1/2024, Texas-Washington), ESPN	8.9
4.	NFL Game-Monday (11/20/2023), ESPN	5.8
5.	NFL Game-Saturday (12/30/2023), ESPN	5.5
6.	NFL Divisional Round Game-Saturday (1/20/2024), ESPN	5.4
7.	Orange Bowl, ESPN	5.2
8.	Cotton Bowl, ESPN	5.0
9.	NFL Game-Monday (9/11/2023), ESPN	5.0
10.	NFL Game-Sunday (11/5/2023), NFL Network	4.9
11.	NFL Wildcard-Monday (1/15/2024), ESPN	4.7
12.	MLB NLCS Game 7-Tuesday (10/24/2023), TBS	4.7
13.	NFL Game-Saturday (12/16/2023) Game 2, NFL Network	4.7
14.	NFL Game-Monday (10/16/2023), ESPN	4.6
15.	NFL Game-Saturday (12/16/2023) Game 3, NFL Network	4.5
16.	Peach Bowl, ESPN	4.3
17.	NFL Game-Monday (9/25/2023), ESPN	4.2
18.	NFL Game-Monday (12/18/2023), ESPN	4.2
19.	NFL Game-Sunday (12/24/2023), NFL Network	4.1
20.	NFL Game-Monday (11/27/2023), ESPN	4.1
21.	NFL Game-Monday (12/11/2023), ESPN	4.1
22.	NFL Game-Monday (11/13/2023), ESPN	3.9
23.	NFL Game-Saturday (12/16/2023) Game 1, NFL Network	3.9
24.	NFL Game-Monday (10/23/2023), ESPN	3.9
25.	NFL Game-Saturday (1/6/2024), ESPN	3.8

Highest-Rated Premium Cable Programs, 2023-24

Source: © 2024 Nielsen, licensed for use in this publication

Average audience percentages, or ratings, are estimates of the percentage of all TV-owning households watching a program live or on DVR within seven days of broadcast, Sept. 19, 2023-Aug. 31, 2024.

Highest-Rated Original Series

Rank	Program, channel	Avg. audience
1.	House of the Dragon, HBO	1.0%
2.	True Detective, HBO	0.8
3.	Real Time With Bill Maher, HBO	0.7
4.	The Gilded Age, HBO	0.6
5.	Last Week Tonight With John Oliver, HBO	0.6
6.	Curb Your Enthusiasm, HBO	0.5
7.	Power Book IV: Force, Starz	0.3
8.	Billions, Showtime (Season 7)	0.3
9.	Winning Time, HBO	0.3
10.	Power Book III: Raising Kanan, Starz	0.3
11.	Power Book II: Ghost, Starz	0.3
12.	Hard Knocks, HBO (Season 23)	0.2
13.	BMF, Starz	0.2
14.	The Regime, HBO	0.2
15.	Hightown, Starz	0.2
16.	The Chi, Showtime (Season 6)	0.2
17.	The Serpent Queen, Starz	0.1
18.	The Circus, Showtime (Season 8)	0.1
19.	Murder in Boston, HBO	0.1
20.	Hard Knocks, HBO (Season 24)	0.1

Highest-Rated Movies

Rank	Program, channel	Avg. audience
1.	Aquaman and the Lost Kingdom, HBO	0.3%
2.	Barbie, HBO	0.3
3.	Meg 2: The Trench, HBO	0.3
4.	Wonka, HBO	0.3
5.	Dune: Part Two, HBO	0.2
6.	Horizon: An American Saga—Chapter One, HBO	0.2
7.	The Last Voyage of the Demeter, Showtime	0.2
8.	Furiosa: A Mad Max Saga, HBO	0.2
9.	Blue Beetle, HBO	0.2
10.	Godzilla x Kong: The New Empire, HBO	0.2
11.	Skyfall, HBO	0.2
12.	The Color Purple (2023), HBO	0.2
13.	Albert Brooks: Defending My Life, HBO	0.2
14.	Priscilla, HBO	0.2
15.	The Iron Claw, HBO	0.2
16.	Elizabeth Taylor: The Lost Tapes, HBO	0.1
17.	Jurassic World Dominion, Starz	0.1
18.	The Nun II, HBO	0.1
19.	The Truth vs. Alex Jones, HBO	0.1
20.	Knox Goes Away, HBO	0.1

Highest-Rated Television Programs by Season, 1950-2024

Source: © 2024 Nielsen, licensed for use in this publication; regular series programs (excl. sports), Sept.-May season

Rating is percentage of all TV-owning households tuned in to the program. Data prior to 1988-89 exclude Alaska and Hawaii.

Season	Program	Rating	TV-owning households (thous.)
1950-51	Texaco Star Theatre	61.6%	10,320
1951-52	Godfrey's Talent Scouts	53.8	15,300
1952-53	I Love Lucy	67.3	20,400
1953-54	I Love Lucy	58.8	26,000
1954-55	I Love Lucy	49.3	30,700
1955-56	$64,000 Question	47.5	34,900
1956-57	I Love Lucy	43.7	38,900
1957-58	Gunsmoke	43.1	41,920
1958-59	Gunsmoke	39.6	43,950
1959-60	Gunsmoke	40.3	45,750
1960-61	Gunsmoke	37.3	47,200
1961-62	Wagon Train	32.1	48,555
1962-63	Beverly Hillbillies	36.0	50,300
1963-64	Beverly Hillbillies	39.1	51,600
1964-65	Bonanza	36.3	52,700
1965-66	Bonanza	31.8	53,850
1966-67	Bonanza	29.1	55,130
1967-68	The Andy Griffith Show	27.6	56,670
1968-69	Rowan & Martin's Laugh-In	31.8	58,250
1969-70	Rowan & Martin's Laugh-In	26.3	58,500
1970-71	Marcus Welby, M.D.	29.6	60,100
1971-72	All in the Family	34.0	62,100
1972-73	All in the Family	33.3	64,800
1973-74	All in the Family	31.2	66,200
1974-75	All in the Family	30.2	68,500
1975-76	All in the Family	30.1	69,600
1976-77	Happy Days	31.5	71,200
1977-78	Laverne & Shirley	31.6	72,900
1978-79	Laverne & Shirley	30.5	74,500
1979-80	60 Minutes	28.2	76,300
1980-81	Dallas	31.2	79,900
1981-82	Dallas	28.4	81,500
1982-83	60 Minutes	25.5	83,300
1983-84	Dallas	25.7	83,800
1984-85	Dynasty	25.0	84,900
1985-86	The Cosby Show	33.8	85,900
1986-87	The Cosby Show	34.9	87,400
1987-88	The Cosby Show	27.8%	88,600
1988-89	Roseanne	25.5	90,400
1989-90	Roseanne	23.4	92,100
1990-91	Cheers	21.6	93,100
1991-92	60 Minutes	21.7	92,100
1992-93	60 Minutes	21.6	93,100
1993-94	Home Improvement	21.9	94,200
1994-95	Seinfeld	20.5	95,400
1995-96	E.R.	22.0	95,900
1996-97	E.R.	21.2	97,000
1997-98	Seinfeld	22.0	98,000
1998-99	E.R.	17.8	99,400
1999-2000	Who Wants to Be a Millionaire	18.6	100,800
2000-01	Survivor II	17.4	102,200
2001-02	Friends	15.3	105,500
2002-03	CSI	16.3	106,700
2003-04	CSI	15.9	108,400
2004-05	CSI	16.5	106,900
2005-06	American Idol-Tuesday	17.6	110,200
2006-07	American Idol-Wednesday	17.3	112,800
2007-08	American Idol-Tuesday	15.5	113,050
2008-09	American Idol-Wednesday	14.4	114,900
2009-10	American Idol-Tuesday	13.7	114,900
2010-11	American Idol-Wednesday	14.5	115,900
2011-12	NCIS	12.3	114,700
2012-13	NCIS	13.5	114,200
2013-14	NCIS	12.6	115,800
2014-15	The Big Bang Theory	11.6	116,400
2015-16	NCIS	12.8	116,400
2016-17	The Big Bang Theory	11.5	118,400
2017-18	The Big Bang Theory	11.3	119,600
2018-19	The Big Bang Theory	10.9	119,900
2019-20	NCIS	9.5	120,600
2020-21	NCIS	7.7	121,000
2021-22	NCIS	6.6	122,400
2022-23	NCIS	6.0	123,800
2023-24	Tracker	6.3	125,000

All-Time Most Watched Television Programs

Source: © 2024 Nielsen, licensed for use in this publication; Jan. 1961-Aug. 2024

Estimates exclude unsponsored or joint network telecasts (e.g., presidential addresses) and programs under 30 minutes. Ranked by number of households tuned in to the program (avg. audience). Rating is percentage of all TV-owning households tuned in.

Rank	Program	Telecast date	Network	Rating	Avg. audience (thous.)
1.	Super Bowl XLIX	2/1/2015	NBC	48.1%	55,948
2.	Super Bowl 50	2/7/2016	CBS	47.1	54,775
3.	Super Bowl XLVIII	2/2/2014	FOX	47.1	54,585
4.	Super Bowl LI	2/5/2017	FOX	45.8	54,180
5.	Super Bowl XLVI	2/5/2012	NBC	47.0	53,910
6.	Super Bowl XLV	2/6/2011	FOX	46.1	53,435
7.	Super Bowl XLVII	2/3/2013	CBS	46.7	53,363
8.	Super Bowl LVIII	2/11/2024	CBS	42.5	53,156
9.	Super Bowl LII	2/4/2018	NBC	43.5	52,017
10.	Super Bowl XLIV	2/7/2010	CBS	45.2	51,873
11.	Super Bowl XLVII Delay	2/3/2013	CBS	44.5	50,861
12.	Super Bowl LIV	2/2/2020	FOX	42.1	50,726
13.	Super Bowl LVII	2/12/2023	FOX	40.8	50,519
14.	M*A*S*H (last episode)	2/28/1983	CBS	60.2	50,150
15.	Super Bowl LIII	2/3/2019	CBS	41.4	49,595
16.	Super Bowl XLII	2/3/2008	FOX	43.2	48,721
17.	Super Bowl XLIII	2/1/2009	NBC	42.0	48,139
18.	Super Bowl XLI	2/4/2007	CBS	42.7	47,535
19.	Super Bowl LV	2/7/2021	CBS	38.4	46,446
20.	Super Bowl XL	2/5/2006	ABC	41.6	45,869
21.	XVII Winter Olympics (women's figure skating)	2/23/1994	CBS	48.5	45,690
22.	Super Bowl LVI	2/13/2022	CBS	37.2	45,533
23.	Super Bowl XXXIX	2/6/2005	FOX	41.1	45,080
24.	Super Bowl XXXVIII	2/1/2004	CBS	41.4	44,910
25.	Super Bowl XXX	1/28/1996	NBC	46.0	44,150
26.	Super Bowl XXXII	1/25/1998	NBC	44.5	43,630
27.	Super Bowl XXXIV	1/30/2000	ABC	43.3	43,620
28.	Super Bowl XXXVII	1/26/2003	ABC	40.7	43,430
29.	Super Bowl XXVIII	1/30/1994	NBC	45.5	42,860
30.	Super Bowl XXXVI	2/3/2002	FOX	40.4	42,660
31.	Cheers (last episode)	5/20/1993	NBC	45.5	42,360

All-Time Highest-Rated Television Programs

Source: © 2024 Nielsen, licensed for use in this publication; Jan. 1961-Aug. 2024

Estimates exclude unsponsored or joint network telecasts (e.g., presidential addresses) and programs under 30 minutes long. Ranked by rating (percentage of all TV-owning households tuned in to the program). Average audience is number of TV-owning households tuned in.

Rank	Program	Telecast date	Network	Rating	Avg. audience (thous.)
1.	M*A*S*H Special (last episode)	2/28/1983	CBS	60.2%	50,150
2.	Dallas ("Who Shot J.R.?" episode)	11/21/1980	CBS	53.3	41,470
3.	Roots Part VIII	1/30/1977	ABC	51.1	36,380
4.	Super Bowl XVI	1/24/1982	CBS	49.1	40,020
5.	Super Bowl XVII	1/30/1983	NBC	48.6	40,480
6.	XVII Winter Olympics (women's figure skating)	2/23/1994	CBS	48.5	45,690
7.	Super Bowl XX	1/26/1986	NBC	48.3	41,490
8.	Super Bowl XLIX	2/1/2015	NBC	48.1	55,948
9.	Gone With the Wind Part 1	11/7/1976	NBC	47.7	33,960
10.	Gone With the Wind Part 2	11/8/1976	NBC	47.4	33,750
11.	Super Bowl XII	1/15/1978	CBS	47.2	34,410
12.	Super Bowl XLVIII	2/2/2014	FOX	47.1	54,585
13.	Super Bowl XIII	1/21/1979	NBC	47.1	35,090
14.	Super Bow 50	2/7/2016	CBS	47.1	54,775
15.	Super Bowl XLVI	2/5/2012	NBC	47.0	53,910
16.	Super Bowl XLVII	2/3/2013	CBS	46.7	53,363
17.	Bob Hope Christmas Show	1/15/1970	NBC	46.6	27,260
18.	Super Bowl XVIII	1/22/1984	CBS	46.4	38,880
19.	Super Bowl XIX	1/20/1985	ABC	46.4	39,390
20.	Super Bowl XIV	1/20/1980	CBS	46.3	35,330
21.	Super Bowl XLV	2/6/2011	FOX	46.1	53,435
22.	Super Bowl XXX	1/28/1996	NBC	46.0	44,150
23.	ABC Sunday Night Movie (The Day After)	11/20/1983	ABC	46.0	38,550
24.	Roots Part VI	1/28/1977	ABC	45.9	32,680
25.	The Fugitive (last episode)	8/29/1967	ABC	45.9	25,700
26.	Super Bowl LI	5/2/2017	FOX	45.8	54,180
27.	Super Bowl XXI	1/25/1987	CBS	45.8	40,030
28.	Roots Part V	1/27/1977	ABC	45.7	32,540
29.	Super Bowl XXVIII	1/30/1994	NBC	45.5	42,860
30.	Cheers (last episode)	5/20/1993	NBC	45.5	42,360
31.	The Ed Sullivan Show (first live U.S. appearance of The Beatles)	2/9/1964	CBS	45.3	23,240
32.	Super Bowl XLIV	2/7/2010	CBS	45.2	51,873
33.	Super Bowl XXVII	1/31/1993	NBC	45.1	41,990
34.	Bob Hope Christmas Show	1/14/1971	NBC	45.0	27,050
35.	Roots Part III	1/25/1977	ABC	44.8	31,900
36.	Super Bowl XXXII	1/25/1998	NBC	44.5	43,630
37.	Super Bowl XLVII Delay	2/3/2013	CBS	44.5	50,861
38.	Super Bowl XI	1/9/1977	NBC	44.4	31,610
39.	Super Bowl XV	1/25/1981	NBC	44.4	34,540
40.	Super Bowl VI	1/16/1972	CBS	44.2	27,450
41.	XVII Winter Olympics (women's figure skating)	2/25/1994	CBS	44.1	41,540
42.	Roots Part II	1/24/1977	ABC	44.1	31,400
43.	Beverly Hillbillies ("The Giant Jackrabbit" episode)	1/8/1964	CBS	44.0	22,570

AWARDS — MEDALS — PRIZES

Alfred B. Nobel Prizes, 1901-2024

Alfred B. Nobel (1833-96) bequeathed $9 mil, the interest on which was to be distributed yearly to those judged to have most benefited humankind in chemistry, literature, promotion of peace, physics, and physiology or medicine. Prizes were first awarded in 1901. The prize in economics, funded by Sweden's central bank, was first awarded in 1969. Each prize is now worth 11 mil Swedish kronor (about $1.07 mil in 2024). If year is omitted, no award was given. The Royal Swedish Academy selects prize winners for chemistry, economics, and physics; the Nobel Assembly at Karolinska Institutet, physiology or medicine; the Swedish Academy, literature; and the Norwegian Nobel Committee, the peace prize. Winners sharing a prize are generally listed in alphabetical order, except when the awarding body has given a larger proportion of a shared prize to one or more recipients.

Physics

1901 Wilhelm C. Röntgen, Ger.
1902 Hendrik A. Lorentz, Pieter Zeeman, Neth.
1903 Antoine Henri Becquerel, Pierre Curie, Fr.; Marie Curie, Pol.-Fr.
1904 Lord Rayleigh (John W. Strutt), UK
1905 Philipp E. A. von Lenard, Ger.
1906 Joseph J. Thomson, UK
1907 Albert A. Michelson, U.S.
1908 Gabriel Lippmann, Fr.
1909 Carl F. Braun, Ger.; Guglielmo Marconi, Ital.
1910 Johannes D. van der Waals, Neth.
1911 Wilhelm Wien, Ger.
1912 Nils G. Dalén, Swed.
1913 Heike Kamerlingh Onnes, Neth.
1914 Max von Laue, Ger.
1915 William H. Bragg, William L. Bragg, UK
1917 Charles G. Barkla, UK
1918 Max K. E. L. Planck, Ger.
1919 Johannes Stark, Ger.
1920 Charles E. Guillaume, Fr.-Switz.
1921 Albert Einstein, Ger.-U.S.
1922 Niels Bohr, Den.
1923 Robert A. Millikan, U.S.
1924 Karl M. G. Siegbahn, Swed.
1925 James Franck, Gustav Hertz, Ger.
1926 Jean B. Perrin, Fr.
1927 Arthur H. Compton, U.S.; Charles T. R. Wilson, UK
1928 Owen W. Richardson, UK
1929 Prince Louis-Victor de Broglie, Fr.
1930 Chandrasekhara V. Raman, India
1932 Werner Heisenberg, Ger.
1933 Paul A. M. Dirac, UK; Erwin Schrödinger, Austria
1935 James Chadwick, UK
1936 Carl D. Anderson, U.S.; Victor F. Hess, Austria
1937 Clinton J. Davisson, U.S.; George P. Thomson, UK
1938 Enrico Fermi, Ital.-U.S.
1939 Ernest O. Lawrence, U.S.
1943 Otto Stern, U.S.
1944 Isidor Isaac Rabi, U.S.
1945 Wolfgang Pauli, U.S.-Austria
1946 Percy W. Bridgman, U.S.
1947 Edward V. Appleton, UK
1948 Patrick M. S. Blackett, UK
1949 Hideki Yukawa, Jpn.
1950 Cecil F. Powell, UK
1951 John D. Cockcroft, UK; Ernest T. S. Walton, Ire.
1952 Felix Bloch, Edward M. Purcell, U.S.
1953 Frits Zernike, Neth.
1954 Max Born, UK; Walter Bothe, Ger.
1955 Polykarp Kusch, Willis E. Lamb, U.S.
1956 John Bardeen, Walter H. Brattain, William Shockley, U.S.
1957 Tsung-Dao Lee, Chen Ning Yang, U.S.-China
1958 Pavel Cherenkov, Il'ja Frank, Igor Y. Tamm, USSR
1959 Owen Chamberlain, Emilio G. Segre, U.S.
1960 Donald A. Glaser, U.S.
1961 Robert Hofstadter, U.S.; Rudolf L. Mossbauer, Ger.
1962 Lev D. Landau, USSR
1963 Maria Goeppert-Mayer, Eugene P. Wigner, U.S.; J. Hans D. Jensen, Ger.
1964 Nicolay G. Basov, Aleksandr M. Prokhorov, USSR; Charles H. Townes, U.S.
1965 Sin-Itiro Tomonaga, Jpn.; Julian S. Schwinger, Richard P. Feynman, U.S.
1966 Alfred Kastler, Fr.
1967 Hans A. Bethe, U.S.
1968 Luis W. Alvarez, U.S.
1969 Murray Gell-Mann, U.S.
1970 Hannes Alfvén, Swed.; Louis Néel, Fr.
1971 Dennis Gabor, UK
1972 John Bardeen, Leon N. Cooper, John R. Schrieffer, U.S.
1973 Brian D. Josephson, UK; Leo Esaki, Jpn.; Ivar Giaever, U.S.
1974 Antony Hewish, Martin Ryle, UK
1975 Aage Bohr, Den.; Ben Mottelson, U.S.-Den.; Leo James Rainwater, U.S.
1976 Burton Richter, Samuel C. C. Ting, U.S.
1977 Philip W. Anderson, John H. van Vleck, U.S.; Nevill F. Mott, UK
1978 Pyotr Kapitsa, USSR; Arno Penzias, Robert Wilson, U.S.
1979 Sheldon L. Glashow, Steven Weinberg, U.S.; Abdus Salam, Pakistan
1980 James W. Cronin, Val L. Fitch, U.S.
1981 Nicolaas Bloembergen, Arthur Schawlow, U.S.; Kai M. Siegbahn, Swed.
1982 Kenneth G. Wilson, U.S.
1983 Subramanyan Chandrasekhar, William A. Fowler, U.S.
1984 Carlo Rubbia, Ital.; Simon van der Meer, Neth.
1985 Klaus von Klitzing, Ger.
1986 Ernest Ruska, Gerd Binnig, Ger.; Heinrich Rohrer, Switz.
1987 J. Georg Bednorz, Ger.; K. Alex Müller, Switz.
1988 Leon M. Lederman, Melvin Schwartz, Jack Steinberger, U.S.
1989 Norman F. Ramsey, U.S.; Hans G. Dehmelt, Ger.-U.S.; Wolfgang Paul, Ger.
1990 Jerome I. Friedman, Henry W. Kendall, U.S.; Richard E. Taylor, Can.
1991 Pierre-Gilles de Gennes, Fr.
1992 Georges Charpak, Pol.-Fr.
1993 Russell A. Hulse, Joseph H. Taylor, U.S.
1994 Bertram N. Brockhouse, Can.; Clifford G. Shull, U.S.
1995 Martin Perl, Frederick Reines, U.S.
1996 David M. Lee, Douglas D. Osheroff, Robert C. Richardson, U.S.
1997 Steven Chu, William D. Phillips, U.S.; Claude Cohen-Tannoudji, Fr.
1998 Robert B. Laughlin, U.S.; Horst L. Störmer, Ger.-U.S; Daniel C. Tsui, China-U.S.
1999 Gerardus 't Hooft, Martinus J. G. Veltman, Neth.
2000 Jack S. Kilby, U.S.; Herbert Kroemer, Ger.-U.S.; Zhores I. Alferov, Russ.
2001 Eric A. Cornell, Carl E. Wieman, U.S.; Wolfgang Ketterle, Ger.
2002 Raymond Davis Jr., Riccardo Giacconi, U.S.; Masatoshi Koshiba, Jpn.
2003 Alexei A. Abrikosov, Vitaly L. Ginzburg, Russ.; Anthony J. Leggett, UK
2004 David J. Gross, H. David Politzer, Frank Wilczek, U.S.
2005 Roy J. Glauber, John L. Hall, U.S.; Theodor W. Hänsch, Ger.
2006 John C. Mather, George F. Smoot, U.S.
2007 Albert Fert, Fr.; Peter Grünberg, Ger.
2008 Yoichiro Nambu, U.S.; Makoto Kobayashi, Toshihide Maskawa, Jpn.
2009 Charles K. Kao, U.S.-UK; Willard S. Boyle, U.S.-Can.; George E. Smith, U.S.
2010 Andre Geim, Russ.-Neth.; Konstantin Novoselov, Russ.-UK
2011 Saul Perlmutter, Adam G. Riess, U.S.; Brian P. Schmidt, Austral.-U.S.
2012 Serge Haroche, Fr.; David J. Wineland, U.S.
2013 François Englert, Belg.; Peter W. Higgs, UK
2014 Isamu Akasaki, Hiroshi Amano, Jpn.; Shuji Nakamura, Jpn.-U.S.
2015 Takaaki Kajita, Jpn.; Arthur B. McDonald, Can.
2016 David J. Thouless, UK-U.S.; F. Duncan M. Haldane, J. Michael Kosterlitz, UK-U.S.
2017 Rainer Weiss, Ger.-U.S.; Barry C. Barish, Kip S. Thorne, U.S.
2018 Arthur Ashkin, U.S.; Gérard Mourou, Fr.; Donna Strickland, Can.
2019 James Peebles, Can.-U.S.; Michel Mayor, Didier Queloz, Switz.
2020 Roger Penrose, UK; Reinhard Genzel, Ger.; Andrea Ghez, U.S.
2021 Giorgio Parisi, Ital.; Klaus Hasselmann, Ger.; Syukuro Manabe, U.S.
2022 Alain Aspect, Fr.; John F. Clauser, U.S.; Anton Zeilinger, Austria
2023 Pierre Agostini, Anne L'Huillier, Fr.; Ferenc Krausz, Hung.-Austria
2024 Geoffrey E. Hinton, UK-Can.; John J. Hopfield, U.S.

Chemistry

1901 Jacobus H. van 't Hoff, Neth.
1902 Emil Fischer, Ger.
1903 Svante A. Arrhenius, Swed.
1904 William Ramsay, UK
1905 Adolf von Baeyer, Ger.
1906 Henri Moissan, Fr.
1907 Eduard Buchner, Ger.
1908 Ernest Rutherford, UK
1909 Wilhelm Ostwald, Ger.
1910 Otto Wallach, Ger.
1911 Marie Curie, Pol.-Fr.
1912 Victor Grignard, Paul Sabatier, Fr.
1913 Alfred Werner, Switz.
1914 Theodore W. Richards, U.S.
1915 Richard M. Willstätter, Ger.
1918 Fritz Haber, Ger.
1920 Walther H. Nernst, Ger.
1921 Frederick Soddy, UK
1922 Francis W. Aston, UK
1923 Fritz Pregl, Austria
1925 Richard A. Zsigmondy, Ger.
1926 Theodor Svedberg, Swed.
1927 Heinrich O. Wieland, Ger.
1928 Adolf O. R. Windaus, Ger.
1929 Arthur Harden, UK; Hans von Euler-Chelpin, Swed.
1930 Hans Fischer, Ger.
1931 Friedrich Bergius, Carl Bosch, Ger.
1932 Irving Langmuir, U.S.
1934 Harold C. Urey, U.S.
1935 Frédéric Joliot, Irène Joliot-Curie, Fr.
1936 Peter J. W. Debye, Neth.
1937 Walter N. Haworth, UK; Paul Karrer, Switz.
1938 Richard Kuhn, Ger.
1939 Adolf F. J. Butenandt, Ger.; Leopold Ruzicka, Switz.
1943 George de Hevesy, Hung.
1944 Otto Hahn, Ger.
1945 Artturi I. Virtanen, Fin.
1946 James B. Sumner, John H. Northrop, Wendell M. Stanley, U.S.
1947 Robert Robinson, UK
1948 Arne W. K. Tiselius, Swed.
1949 William F. Giauque, U.S.
1950 Kurt Alder, Otto P. H. Diels, Ger.
1951 Edwin M. McMillan, Glenn T. Seaborg, U.S.
1952 Archer J. P. Martin, Richard L. M. Synge, UK
1953 Hermann Staudinger, Ger.
1954 Linus C. Pauling, U.S.
1955 Vincent du Vigneaud, U.S.
1956 Cyril N. Hinshelwood, UK; Nikolay N. Semenov, USSR
1957 Lord (Alexander R.) Todd, UK
1958 Frederick Sanger, UK
1959 Jaroslav Heyrovsky, Czech.
1960 Willard F. Libby, U.S.
1961 Melvin Calvin, U.S.
1962 John C. Kendrew, Max F. Perutz, UK
1963 Giulio Natta, Ital.; Karl Ziegler, Ger.
1964 Dorothy C. Hodgkin, UK
1965 Robert B. Woodward, U.S.
1966 Robert S. Mulliken, U.S.
1967 Manfred Eigen, Ger.; Ronald G. W. Norrish, George Porter, UK
1968 Lars Onsager, U.S.
1969 Derek H. R. Barton, UK; Odd Hassel, Nor.
1970 Luis F. Leloir, Arg.
1971 Gerhard Herzberg, Can.
1972 Christian B. Anfinsen, Stanford Moore, William H. Stein, U.S.
1973 Ernst Otto Fischer, Ger.; Geoffrey Wilkinson, UK
1974 Paul J. Flory, U.S.
1975 John Cornforth, Austral.-UK; Vladimir Prelog, Bosnia-Switz.
1976 William N. Lipscomb, U.S.
1977 Ilya Prigogine, Belg.
1978 Peter Mitchell, UK
1979 Herbert C. Brown, U.S.; Georg Wittig, Ger.
1980 Paul Berg, Walter Gilbert, U.S.; Frederick Sanger, UK
1981 Kenichi Fukui, Jpn.; Roald Hoffmann, U.S.
1982 Aaron Klug, UK-Lith.
1983 Henry Taube, Can.
1984 Robert Bruce Merrifield, U.S.
1985 Herbert A. Hauptman, Jerome Karle, U.S.
1986 Dudley Herschbach, Yuan T. Lee, U.S.; John C. Polanyi, Can.
1987 Donald J. Cram, Charles J. Pedersen, U.S.; Jean-Marie Lehn, Fr.
1988 Johann Deisenhofer, Robert Huber, Hartmut Michel, Ger.
1989 Sidney Altman, Thomas R. Cech, U.S.
1990 Elias James Corey, U.S.
1991 Richard R. Ernst, Switz.
1992 Rudolph A. Marcus, Can.-U.S.
1993 Kary B. Mullis, U.S.; Michael Smith, UK-Can.
1994 George A. Olah, U.S.
1995 Paul Crutzen, Neth.; Mario Molina, Mex.-U.S.; Sherwood Rowland, U.S.
1996 Robert F. Curl Jr., Richard E. Smalley, U.S.; Harold W. Kroto, UK
1997 Paul D. Boyer, U.S.; John E. Walker, UK; Jens C. Skou, Den.
1998 Walter Kohn, U.S.; John A. Pople, UK
1999 Ahmed H. Zewail, U.S.
2000 Alan J. Heeger, U.S.; Alan G. MacDiarmid, N.Z.-U.S.; Hideki Shirakawa, Jpn.
2001 K. Barry Sharpless, William S. Knowles, U.S.; Ryoji Noyori, Jpn.
2002 John B. Fenn, U.S.; Koichi Tanaka, Jpn.; Kurt Wüthrich, Switz.
2003 Peter Agre, Roderick MacKinnon, U.S.
2004 Aaron Ciechanover, Avram Hershko, Isr.; Irwin Rose, U.S.
2005 Yves Chauvin, Fr.; Robert H. Grubbs, Richard R. Schrock, U.S.
2006 Roger D. Kornberg, U.S.
2007 Gerhard Ertl, Ger.
2008 Martin Chalfie, Osamu Shimomura, Roger Y. Tsien, U.S.
2009 Venkatraman Ramakrishnan, UK; Thomas A. Steitz, U.S.; Ada E. Yonath, Isr.
2010 Richard F. Heck, U.S.; Ei-ichi Negishi, Jpn.-U.S.; Akira Suzuki, Jpn.
2011 Dan Shechtman, Isr.
2012 Brian K. Kobilka, Robert J. Lefkowitz, U.S.
2013 Martin Karplus, Austria-U.S.; Michael Levitt, S. Afr.-U.S.; Arieh Warshel, Isr.-U.S.
2014 Eric Betzig, William E. Moerner, U.S.; Stefan W. Hell, Ger.
2015 Tomas Lindahl, Swed.-UK; Paul Modrich, U.S.; Aziz Sancar, Turk.-U.S.
2016 Bernard L. Feringa, Neth.; Jean-Pierre Sauvage, Fr.; J. Fraser Stoddart, UK-U.S.
2017 Jacques Dubochet, Switz.; Joachim Frank, Ger.-U.S.; Richard Henderson, UK
2018 Frances H. Arnold, George P. Smith, U.S.; Gregory P. Winter, UK
2019 John B. Goodenough, Ger.-U.S.; M. Stanley Whittingham, UK-U.S.; Akira Yoshino, Jpn.
2020 Emmanuelle Charpentier, Fr.; Jennifer Doudna, U.S.
2021 Benjamin List, Ger.; David W.C. MacMillan, UK-U.S.
2022 Carolyn R. Bertozzi, K. Barry Sharpless, U.S.; Morten Meldal, Den.
2023 Moungi Bawendi, Fr.-U.S.; Louis Brus, U.S.; Alexei Ekimov, Russ.
2024 David Baker, John M. Jumper, U.S.; Demis Hassabis, UK

Physiology or Medicine

1901 Emil A. von Behring, Ger.
1902 Ronald Ross, UK
1903 Niels R. Finsen, Den.
1904 Ivan P. Pavlov, Russ.
1905 Robert Koch, Ger.
1906 Camillo Golgi, Ital.; Santiago Ramón y Cajal, Spain
1907 Charles L. A. Laveran, Fr.
1908 Paul Ehrlich, Ger.; Ilya Mechnikov, Fr.
1909 Emil T. Kocher, Switz.
1910 Albrecht Kossel, Ger.
1911 Allvar Gullstrand, Swed.
1912 Alexis Carrel, Fr.
1913 Charles R. Richet, Fr.
1914 Robert Bárány, Austria
1919 Jules Bordet, Belg.
1920 Schack A. S. Krogh, Den.
1922 Archibald V. Hill, UK; Otto F. Meyerhof, Ger.
1923 Frederick G. Banting, Can.; John J. R. Macleod, UK
1924 Willem Einthoven, Neth.
1926 Johannes A. G. Fibiger, Den.
1927 Julius Wagner-Jauregg, Austria
1928 Charles J. H. Nicolle, Fr.
1929 Christiaan Eijkman, Neth.; Frederick G. Hopkins, UK
1930 Karl Landsteiner, U.S.
1931 Otto H. Warburg, Ger.
1932 Edgar D. Adrian, Charles S. Sherrington, UK
1933 Thomas H. Morgan, U.S.
1934 George R. Minot, William P. Murphy, G. H. Whipple, U.S.
1935 Hans Spemann, Ger.
1936 Henry H. Dale, UK; Otto Loewi, U.S.
1937 Albert Szent-Gyorgyi, Hung.-U.S.
1938 Corneille J. F. Heymans, Belg.
1939 Gerhard Domagk, Ger.
1943 Henrik C. P. Dam, Den.; Edward A. Doisy, U.S.
1944 Joseph Erlanger, Herbert S. Gasser, U.S.
1945 Ernst B. Chain, Alexander Fleming, Howard W. Florey, UK
1946 Hermann J. Muller, U.S.
1947 Carl F. Cori, Gerty T. Cori, U.S.; Bernardo A. Houssay, Arg.
1948 Paul H. Müller, Switz.
1949 Walter R. Hess, Switz.; Antonio Egas Moniz, Port.
1950 Philip S. Hench, Edward C. Kendall, U.S.; Tadeus Reichstein, Switz.
1951 Max Theiler, U.S.
1952 Selman A. Waksman, U.S.
1953 Hans A. Krebs, UK; Fritz A. Lipmann, U.S.
1954 John F. Enders, Frederick C. Robbins, Thomas H. Weller, U.S.
1955 Alex H. T. Theorell, Swed.
1956 André F. Cournand, Dickinson W. Richards, U.S.; Werner Forssmann, Ger.
1957 Daniel Bovet, Ital.
1958 George W. Beadle, Edward L. Tatum, Joshua Lederberg, U.S.
1959 Arthur Kornberg, Severo Ochoa, U.S.
1960 Frank Macfarlane Burnet, Austral.; Peter B. Medawar, UK
1961 Georg von Békésy, U.S.
1962 Francis H. C. Crick, Maurice H. F. Wilkins, UK; James D. Watson, U.S.
1963 John C. Eccles, Austral.; Alan L. Hodgkin, Andrew F. Huxley, UK
1964 Konrad E. Bloch, U.S.; Feodor Lynen, Ger.
1965 François Jacob, André Lwoff, Jacques Monod, Fr.
1966 Charles B. Huggins, Peyton Rous, U.S.
1967 Ragnar Granit, Swed.; Haldan Keffer Hartline, George Wald, U.S.
1968 Robert W. Holley, H. Gobind Khorana, Marshall W. Nirenberg, U.S.
1969 Max Delbrück, Alfred D. Hershey, Salvador Luria, U.S.
1970 Julius Axelrod, U.S.; Bernard Katz, UK; Ulf von Euler, Swed.
1971 Earl W. Sutherland Jr., U.S.
1972 Gerald M. Edelman, U.S.; Rodney R. Porter, UK
1973 Konrad Lorenz, Austria; Nikolaas Tinbergen, UK; Karl von Frisch, Ger.

1974 Albert Claude, Lux.-U.S.; Christian de Duve, Belg.; George Emil Palade, Rom.-U.S.
1975 David Baltimore, Howard Temin, U.S.; Renato Dulbecco, Ital.-U.S.
1976 Baruch S. Blumberg, Daniel Carleton Gajdusek, U.S.
1977 Rosalyn S. Yalow, Roger Guillemin, Andrew V. Schally, U.S.
1978 Werner Arber, Switz.; Daniel Nathans, Hamilton O. Smith, U.S.
1979 Allan M. Cormack, U.S.; Godfrey N. Hounsfield, UK
1980 Baruj Benacerraf, George Snell, U.S.; Jean Dausset, Fr.
1981 Roger W. Sperry, David H. Hubel, Torsten N. Wiesel, U.S.
1982 Sune K. Bergström, Bengt I. Samuelsson, Swed.; John R. Vane, UK
1983 Barbara McClintock, U.S.
1984 Niels K. Jerne, UK-Den.; Georges J. F. Köhler, Ger.; César Milstein, UK-Arg.
1985 Michael S. Brown, Joseph L. Goldstein, U.S.
1986 Stanley Cohen, U.S.; Rita Levi-Montalcini, Ital.-U.S.
1987 Susumu Tonegawa, Jpn.
1988 James W. Black, UK; Gertrude B. Elion, George H. Hitchings, U.S.
1989 J. Michael Bishop, Harold E. Varmus, U.S.
1990 Joseph E. Murray, E. Donnall Thomas, U.S.
1991 Edwin Neher, Bert Sakmann, Ger.
1992 Edmond H. Fisher, Edwin G. Krebs, U.S.
1993 Richard J. Roberts, UK; Phillip A. Sharp, U.S.
1994 Alfred G. Gilman, Martin Rodbell, U.S.
1995 Edward B. Lewis, Eric F. Wieschaus, U.S.; Christiane Nüsslein-Volhard, Ger.
1996 Peter C. Doherty, Austral.; Rolf M. Zinkernagel, Switz.
1997 Stanley B. Prusiner, U.S.
1998 Robert F. Furchgott, Louis J. Ignarro, Ferid Murad, U.S.
1999 Günter Blobel, U.S.
2000 Arvid Carlsson, Swed.; Paul Greengard, U.S.; Eric R. Kandel, Austria-U.S.
2001 Leland H. Hartwell, U.S.; R. Timothy (Tim) Hunt, Paul M. Nurse, UK
2002 Sydney Brenner, John E. Sulston, UK; H. Robert Horvitz, U.S.
2003 Paul C. Lauterbur, U.S.; Peter Mansfield, UK
2004 Richard Axel, Linda B. Buck, U.S.
2005 Barry J. Marshall, J. Robin Warren, Austral.
2006 Andrew Z. Fire, Craig C. Mello, U.S.
2007 Mario R. Capecchi, Oliver Smithies, U.S.; Martin J. Evans, UK
2008 Harald zur Hausen, Ger.; Françoise Barré-Sinoussi, Luc Montagnier, Fr.
2009 Elizabeth H. Blackburn, Carol W. Greider, Jack W. Szostak, U.S.
2010 Robert G. Edwards, UK
2011 Bruce A. Beutler, U.S.; Jules A. Hoffmann, Fr.; Ralph M. Steinman, Can.-U.S.
2012 John B. Gurdon, UK; Shinya Yamanaka, Jpn.-U.S.
2013 James E. Rothman, Randy W. Schekman, U.S.; Thomas C. Südhof, Ger.-U.S.
2014 John O'Keefe, U.S.-UK; May-Britt Moser, Edvard I. Moser, Nor.
2015 William C. Campbell, Ire.-U.S.; Satoshi Omura, Jpn.; Youyou Tu, China
2016 Yoshinori Ohsumi, Jpn.
2017 Jeffrey C. Hall, Michael Rosbash, Michael W. Young, U.S.
2018 James P. Allison, U.S.; Tasuku Honjo, Jpn.
2019 William G. Kaelin Jr., Gregg L. Semenza, U.S.; Peter J. Ratcliffe, UK
2020 Harvey J. Alter, Charles M. Rice, U.S.; Michael Houghton, UK
2021 David Julius, Ardem Patapoutian, U.S.
2022 Svante Pääbo, Swed.
2023 Katalin Karikó, Hung.-U.S.; Drew Weissman, U.S.
2024 Victor Ambros, Gary Ruvkun, U.S.

Literature

1901 Rene F. A. Sully Prudhomme, Fr.
1902 Theodor Mommsen, Ger.
1903 Bjørnstjerne Bjørnson, Nor.
1904 José Echegaray y Eizaguirre, Spain; Fréderic Mistral, Fr.
1905 Henryk Sienkiewicz, Pol.
1906 Giosuè Carducci, Ital.
1907 Rudyard Kipling, UK
1908 Rudolf C. Eucken, Ger.
1909 Selma Lagerlöf, Swed.
1910 Paul J. L. Heyse, Ger.
1911 Maurice Maeterlinck, Belg.
1912 Gerhart Hauptmann, Ger.
1913 Rabindranath Tagore, India
1915 Romain Rolland, Fr.
1916 Verner von Heidenstam, Swed.
1917 Karl A. Gjellerup, Henrik Pontoppidan, Den.
1919 Carl F. G. Spitteler, Switz.
1920 Knut Hamsun, Nor.
1921 Anatole France, Fr.
1922 Jacinto Benavente, Spain
1923 William Butler Yeats, Ire.
1924 Wladyslaw S. Reymont, Pol.
1925 George Bernard Shaw, Ire.-UK
1926 Grazia Deledda, Ital.
1927 Henri Bergson, Fr.
1928 Sigrid Undset, Nor.
1929 Thomas Mann, Ger.
1930 Sinclair Lewis, U.S.
1931 Erik A. Karlfeldt, Swed.
1932 John Galsworthy, UK
1933 Ivan A. Bunin, USSR
1934 Luigi Pirandello, Ital.
1936 Eugene O'Neill, U.S.
1937 Roger Martin du Gard, Fr.
1938 Pearl S. Buck, U.S.
1939 Frans E. Sillanpää, Fin.
1944 Johannes V. Jensen, Den.
1945 Gabriela Mistral, Chile
1946 Hermann Hesse, Ger.-Switz.
1947 André Gide, Fr.
1948 T. S. Eliot, UK
1949 William Faulkner, U.S.
1950 Bertrand Russell, UK
1951 Pär F. Lagerkvist, Swed.
1952 François Mauriac, Fr.
1953 Winston Churchill, UK
1954 Ernest Hemingway, U.S.
1955 Halldór K. Laxness, Ice.
1956 Juan Ramón Jiménez, Spain
1957 Albert Camus, Fr.
1958 Boris L. Pasternak, USSR (declined)
1959 Salvatore Quasimodo, Ital.
1960 Saint-John Perse, Fr.
1961 Ivo Andric, Yugo.
1962 John Steinbeck, U.S.
1963 Giorgos Seferis, Greece
1964 Jean-Paul Sartre, Fr. (declined)
1965 Mikhail Sholokhov, USSR
1966 Shmuel Yosef Agnon, Isr.; Nelly Sachs, Swed.
1967 Miguel Angel Asturias, Guat.
1968 Yasunari Kawabata, Jpn.
1969 Samuel Beckett, Ire.
1970 Aleksandr I. Solzhenitsyn, USSR
1971 Pablo Neruda, Chile
1972 Heinrich Böll, Ger.
1973 Patrick White, Austral.
1974 Eyvind Johnson, Harry Edmund Martinson, Swed.
1975 Eugenio Montale, Ital.
1976 Saul Bellow, U.S.
1977 Vicente Aleixandre, Spain
1978 Isaac Bashevis Singer, U.S.
1979 Odysseus Elytis, Greece
1980 Czeslaw Milosz, Pol.-U.S.
1981 Elias Canetti, Bulg.-UK
1982 Gabriel García Márquez, Colombia
1983 William Golding, UK
1984 Jaroslav Siefert, Czech.
1985 Claude Simon, Fr.
1986 Wole Soyinka, Nigeria
1987 Joseph Brodsky, USSR-U.S.
1988 Naguib Mahfouz, Egypt
1989 Camilo José Cela, Spain
1990 Octavio Paz, Mex.
1991 Nadine Gordimer, S. Afr.
1992 Derek Walcott, St. Lucia
1993 Toni Morrison, U.S.
1994 Kenzaburō Oe, Jpn.
1995 Seamus Heaney, Ire.
1996 Wislawa Szymborska, Pol.
1997 Dario Fo, Ital.
1998 José Saramago, Por.
1999 Günter Grass, Ger.
2000 Gao Xingjian, China-Fr.
2001 V. S. Naipaul, UK
2002 Imre Kertész, Hung.
2003 J. M. Coetzee, S. Afr.
2004 Elfriede Jelinek, Austria
2005 Harold Pinter, UK
2006 Orhan Pamuk, Turk.
2007 Doris Lessing, UK
2008 Jean-Marie Gustave Le Clézio, Fr.
2009 Herta Müller, Ger.
2010 Mario Vargas Llosa, Peru
2011 Tomas Tranströmer, Swed.
2012 Mo Yan, China
2013 Alice Munro, Can.
2014 Patrick Modiano, Fr.
2015 Svetlana Alexievich, Belarus
2016 Bob Dylan, U.S.
2017 Kazuo Ishiguro, Jpn.-UK
2018 Olga Tokarczuk, Pol.
2019 Peter Handke, Austria
2020 Louise Glück, U.S.
2021 Abdulrazak Gurnah, Tanzania
2022 Annie Ernaux, Fr.
2023 Jon Fosse, Nor.
2024 Han Kang, S. Kor.

Peace

1901 Jean H. Dunant, Switz.; Frédéric Passy, Fr.
1902 Élie Ducommun, Charles A. Gobat, Switz.
1903 William R. Cremer, UK
1904 Institute of International Law, Belg.
1905 Baroness Bertha von Suttner, Austria
1906 Theodore Roosevelt, U.S.
1907 Ernesto T. Moneta, Ital.; Louis Renault, Fr.
1908 Klas P. Arnoldson, Swed.; Fredrik Bajer, Den.
1909 Auguste M. F. Beernaert, Belg.; Paul H. B. B. d'Estournelles de Constant, Fr.
1910 Permanent Intl. Peace Bureau
1911 Tobias M. C. Asser, Neth.; Alfred H. Fried, Austria
1912 Elihu Root, U.S.
1913 Henri La Fontaine, Belg.
1917 Intl. Committee of the Red Cross
1919 Woodrow Wilson, U.S.
1920 Léon V. A. Bourgeois, Fr.
1921 Karl H. Branting, Swed.; Christian L. Lange, Nor.
1922 Fridtjof Nansen, Nor.
1925 Austen Chamberlain, UK; Charles G. Dawes, U.S.
1926 Aristide Briand, Fr.; Gustav Stresemann, Ger.
1927 Ferdinand E. Buisson, Fr.; Ludwig Quidde, Ger.
1929 Frank B. Kellogg, U.S.
1930 Nathan Söderblom, Swed.
1931 Jane Addams, Nicholas Murray Butler, U.S.
1933 Norman Angell, UK
1934 Arthur Henderson, UK
1935 Carl von Ossietzky, Ger.
1936 Carlos Saavedra Lamas, Arg.
1937 Lord Robert Cecil, UK
1938 Nansen Intl. Office for Refugees
1944 Intl. Committee of the Red Cross
1945 Cordell Hull, U.S.
1946 Emily G. Balch, John R. Mott, U.S.

1947 Friends Service Council, UK; Amer. Friends Service Committee, U.S.
1949 Lord John Boyd Orr of Brechin, UK
1950 Ralph J. Bunche, U.S.
1951 Léon Jouhaux, Fr.
1952 Albert Schweitzer, Fr.
1953 George C. Marshall, U.S.
1954 Office of UN High Commissioner for Refugees
1957 Lester B. Pearson, Can.
1958 Georges Pire, Belg.
1959 Philip J. Noel-Baker, UK
1960 Albert J. Lutuli, S. Afr.
1961 Dag Hammarskjöld, Swed.
1962 Linus C. Pauling, U.S.
1963 Intl. Committee of the Red Cross, League of Red Cross Societies
1964 Martin Luther King Jr., U.S.
1965 UN Children's Fund (UNICEF)
1968 René Cassin, Fr.
1969 Intl. Labor Organization, Switz.
1970 Norman E. Borlaug, U.S.
1971 Willy Brandt, Ger.
1973 Henry Kissinger, U.S.; Le Duc Tho, N. Viet. (Tho declined)
1974 Seán MacBride, Ire.; Eisaku Sato, Jpn.
1975 Andrei Sakharov, USSR
1976 Mairead Corrigan, Betty Williams, N. Ire.
1977 Amnesty International, UK
1978 Anwar al-Sadat, Egypt; Menachem Begin, Isr.
1979 Mother Teresa of Calcutta, Alb.-India
1980 Adolfo Pérez Esquivel, Arg.
1981 Office of UN High Commissioner for Refugees
1982 Alfonso García Robles, Mex.; Alva Myrdal, Swed.
1983 Lech Walesa, Pol.
1984 Bishop Desmond Tutu, S. Afr.
1985 Intl. Physicians for the Prevention of Nuclear War, U.S.
1986 Elie Wiesel, Rom.-U.S.
1987 Oscar Arias Sánchez, Costa Rica
1988 UN Peacekeeping Forces
1989 Dalai Lama (Tenzin Gyatso), Tibet
1990 Mikhail S. Gorbachev, USSR
1991 Aung San Suu Kyi, Burma
1992 Rigoberta Menchú Tum, Guat.
1993 Frederik W. de Klerk, Nelson Mandela, S. Afr.
1994 Yasser Arafat, Pal.; Shimon Peres, Yitzhak Rabin, Isr.
1995 Joseph Rotblat, Pol.-UK; Pugwash Conferences, Can.
1996 Bishop Carlos Ximenes Belo, José Ramos-Horta, Timor-Leste
1997 Jody Williams, U.S.; Intl. Campaign to Ban Landmines
1998 John Hume, David Trimble, N. Ire.
1999 Médecins Sans Frontières (Doctors Without Borders), Fr.
2000 Kim Dae Jung, S. Kor.
2001 UN; Kofi Annan, Ghana
2002 Jimmy Carter, U.S.
2003 Shirin Ebadi, Iran
2004 Wangari Maathai, Kenya
2005 Mohamed ElBaradei, Egypt; Intl. Atomic Energy Agency, Austria
2006 Muhammad Yunus, Grameen Bank, Bangl.
2007 Intergovernmental Panel on Climate Change, Switz.; Al Gore, U.S.
2008 Martti Ahtisaari, Fin.
2009 Barack H. Obama, U.S.
2010 Liu Xiaobo, China
2011 Leymah Gbowee, Ellen Johnson Sirleaf, Liberia; Tawakkol Karman, Yemen
2012 European Union
2013 Organization for the Prohibition of Chemical Weapons (OPCW)
2014 Kailash Satyarthi, India; Malala Yousafzai, Pakistan
2015 National Dialogue Quartet, Tunisia
2016 Juan Manuel Santos, Colombia
2017 Intl. Campaign to Abolish Nuclear Weapons
2018 Denis Mukwege, Congo; Nadia Murad, Iraq
2019 Abiy Ahmed, Ethiopia
2020 World Food Programme
2021 Dmitry A. Muratov, Russ.; Maria Ressa, Phil.
2022 Ales Bialiatski, Bela.; Memorial, Russ.; Center for Civil Liberties, Ukr.
2023 Narges Mohammadi, Iran
2024 Nihon Hidankyo, Jpn.

Nobel Memorial Prize in Economic Sciences

1969 Ragnar Frisch, Nor.; Jan Tinbergen, Neth.
1970 Paul A. Samuelson, U.S.
1971 Simon Kuznets, U.S.
1972 Kenneth J. Arrow, U.S.; John R. Hicks, UK
1973 Wassily Leontief, U.S.
1974 Gunnar Myrdal, Swed.; Friedrich A. von Hayek, Austria
1975 Leonid Kantorovich, USSR; Tjalling C. Koopmans, Neth.-U.S.
1976 Milton Friedman, U.S.
1977 James E. Meade, UK; Bertil Ohlin, Swed.
1978 Herbert A. Simon, U.S.
1979 Arthur Lewis, UK; Theodore W. Schultz, U.S.
1980 Lawrence R. Klein, U.S.
1981 James Tobin, U.S.
1982 George J. Stigler, U.S.
1983 Gerard Debreu, Fr.-U.S.
1984 Richard Stone, UK
1985 Franco Modigliani, Ital.-U.S.
1986 James M. Buchanan, U.S.
1987 Robert M. Solow, U.S.
1988 Maurice Allais, Fr.
1989 Trygve Haavelmo, Nor.
1990 Harry M. Markowitz, Merton H. Miller, William F. Sharpe, U.S.
1991 Ronald H. Coase, UK-U.S.
1992 Gary S. Becker, U.S.
1993 Robert W. Fogel, Douglass C. North, U.S.
1994 John C. Harsanyi, John F. Nash, U.S.; Reinhard Selten, Ger.
1995 Robert E. Lucas Jr., U.S.
1996 James A. Mirrlees, UK; William Vickrey, Can.-U.S.
1997 Robert C. Merton, U.S.; Myron S. Scholes, Can.-U.S.
1998 Amartya Sen, India
1999 Robert A. Mundell, Can.
2000 James J. Heckman, Daniel L. McFadden, U.S.
2001 George A. Akerlof, A. Michael Spence, Joseph E. Stiglitz, U.S.
2002 Daniel Kahneman, U.S.-Isr.; Vernon L. Smith, U.S.
2003 Robert F. Engle, U.S.; Clive W. J. Granger, UK
2004 Finn E. Kydland, Nor.; Edward C. Prescott, U.S.
2005 Robert J. Aumann, Isr.-U.S.; Thomas C. Schelling, U.S.
2006 Edmund S. Phelps, U.S.
2007 Leonid Hurwicz, Eric S. Maskin, Roger B. Myerson, U.S.
2008 Paul Krugman, U.S.
2009 Elinor Ostrom, Oliver E. Williamson, U.S.
2010 Peter A. Diamond, Dale T. Mortensen, U.S.; Christopher A. Pissarides, Cyprus-UK
2011 Thomas J. Sargent, Christopher A. Sims, U.S.
2012 Alvin E. Roth, Lloyd S. Shapley, U.S.
2013 Eugene F. Fama, Lars Peter Hansen, Robert J. Shiller, U.S.
2014 Jean Tirole, Fr.
2015 Angus Deaton, UK-U.S.
2016 Oliver Hart, U.S.; Bengt Holmström, Fin.-U.S.
2017 Richard H. Thaler, U.S.
2018 William D. Nordhaus, Paul M. Romer, U.S.
2019 Abhijit Banerjee, India-U.S.; Esther Duflo, Fr.-U.S.; Michael Kremer, U.S.
2020 Paul R. Milgrom, Robert B. Wilson, U.S.
2021 David Card, Joshua D. Angrist, Guido W. Imbens, U.S.
2022 Ben S. Bernanke, Douglas W. Diamond, Philip H. Dybvig, U.S.
2023 Claudia Goldin, U.S.
2024 Daron Acemoglu, Turk.-U.S.; Simon Johnson, James A. Robinson, UK-U.S.

Pulitzer Prizes in Journalism, Letters, and Music

Endowed by Joseph Pulitzer (1847-1911), publisher of the *New York World*, in a bequest to Columbia Univ. and awarded annually.

Pulitzer Prizes in Journalism, 2024

Public Service: ProPublica, for the work of Joshua Kaplan, Justin Elliott, Brett Murphy, Alex Mierjeski, and Kirsten Berg, revealing how politically influential billionaires wooed Supreme Court justices with gifts and travel.

Breaking News Reporting: Lookout Santa Cruz (CA) staff, for community-focused coverage of catastrophic flooding and mudslides.

Investigative Reporting: Hannah Dreier, *NY Times*, for series revealing the reach of migrant child labor in the U.S.

Explanatory Reporting: Sarah Stillman, *The New Yorker*, for indictment of the legal system's reliance on the felony murder charge and its disparate consequences.

Local Reporting: Sarah Conway, City Bureau, and Trina Reynolds-Tyler, Invisible Institute, for investigative series on Chicago's missing Black girls and women and how systemic racism and police neglect contributed to the crisis.

National Reporting: Reuters staff, for series on Elon Musk's automobile and aerospace businesses; and *Washington Post* staff, for examination of the AR-15 semi-automatic rifle, the weapon most often used for mass shootings.

International Reporting: *NY Times* staff, for coverage of Hamas's Oct. 7 attack on Israel, Israel's intelligence failures, and the Israeli military's deadly response in Gaza.

Feature Writing: Katie Engelhart, *NY Times* contributing writer, for portrait of a family's legal and emotional struggles with its matriarch's progressive dementia.

Commentary: Vladimir Kara-Murza, *Washington Post* contributor, for columns written under great risk from his prison cell on the consequences of dissent in Putin's Russia.

Criticism: Justin Chang, *L.A. Times*, for genre-spanning film criticism.

Editorial Writing: David E. Hoffman, *Washington Post*, for series on new technologies, tactics authoritarian regimes use to suppress dissent, and how they can be fought.

Illustrated Reporting and Commentary: Medar de la Cruz, *The New Yorker* contributor, for visually driven story set inside Rikers Island jail.

Breaking News Photography: Reuters photography staff, for raw and urgent images documenting the Oct. 7 attack in Israel by Hamas and first weeks of the Israeli assault on Gaza.

Feature Photography: Associated Press photography staff, for photos chronicling the journey of migrants from Colombia to the U.S. border.

Audio Reporting: Invisible Institute staff and USG Audio, for *You Didn't See Nothin*, an investigative series that revisits a 1990s Chicago hate crime.

Pulitzer Prizes in Letters, 1918-2024

Other Pulitzer Prize Winners, 2024: Biography: Jonathan Eig, *King: A Life*; Ilyon Woo, *Master Slave Husband Wife: An Epic Journey from Slavery to Freedom*. Memoir/autobiography: Cristina Rivera Garza, *Liliana's Invincible Summer: A Sister's Search for Justice*. History: Jacqueline Jones, *No Right to an Honest Living: The Struggles of Boston's Black Workers in the Civil War Era*. Poetry: Brandon Som, *Tripas: Poems*.

Fiction

1918 Ernest Poole, *His Family*
1919 Booth Tarkington, *The Magnificent Ambersons*
1921 Edith Wharton, *The Age of Innocence*
1922 Booth Tarkington, *Alice Adams*
1923 Willa Cather, *One of Ours*
1924 Margaret Wilson, *The Able McLaughlins*
1925 Edna Ferber, *So Big*
1926 Sinclair Lewis, *Arrowsmith* (refused)
1927 Louis Bromfield, *Early Autumn*
1928 Thornton Wilder, *The Bridge of San Luis Rey*
1929 Julia Peterkin, *Scarlet Sister Mary*
1930 Oliver La Farge, *Laughing Boy*
1931 Margaret Ayer Barnes, *Years of Grace*
1932 Pearl S. Buck, *The Good Earth*
1933 T. S. Stribling, *The Store*
1934 Caroline Miller, *Lamb in His Bosom*
1935 Josephine W. Johnson, *Now in November*
1936 Harold L. Davis, *Honey in the Horn*
1937 Margaret Mitchell, *Gone With the Wind*
1938 John P. Marquand, *The Late George Apley*
1939 Marjorie Kinnan Rawlings, *The Yearling*
1940 John Steinbeck, *The Grapes of Wrath*
1942 Ellen Glasgow, *In This Our Life*
1943 Upton Sinclair, *Dragon's Teeth*
1944 Martin Flavin, *Journey in the Dark*
1945 John Hersey, *A Bell for Adano*
1947 Robert Penn Warren, *All the King's Men*
1948 James A. Michener, *Tales of the South Pacific*
1949 James Gould Cozzens, *Guard of Honor*
1950 A. B. Guthrie Jr., *The Way West*
1951 Conrad Richter, *The Town*
1952 Herman Wouk, *The Caine Mutiny*
1953 Ernest Hemingway, *The Old Man and the Sea*
1955 William Faulkner, *A Fable*
1956 MacKinlay Kantor, *Andersonville*
1958 James Agee, *A Death in the Family*
1959 Robert Lewis Taylor, *The Travels of Jaimie McPheeters*
1960 Allen Drury, *Advise and Consent*
1961 Harper Lee, *To Kill a Mockingbird*
1962 Edwin O'Connor, *The Edge of Sadness*
1963 William Faulkner, *The Reivers*
1965 Shirley Ann Grau, *The Keepers of the House*
1966 Katherine Anne Porter, *Collected Stories*
1967 Bernard Malamud, *The Fixer*
1968 William Styron, *The Confessions of Nat Turner*
1969 N. Scott Momaday, *House Made of Dawn*
1970 Jean Stafford, *Collected Stories*
1972 Wallace Stegner, *Angle of Repose*
1973 Eudora Welty, *The Optimist's Daughter*
1975 Michael Shaara, *The Killer Angels*
1976 Saul Bellow, *Humboldt's Gift*
1978 James Alan McPherson, *Elbow Room*
1979 John Cheever, *The Stories of John Cheever*
1980 Norman Mailer, *The Executioner's Song*
1981 John Kennedy Toole, *A Confederacy of Dunces*
1982 John Updike, *Rabbit Is Rich*
1983 Alice Walker, *The Color Purple*
1984 William Kennedy, *Ironweed*
1985 Alison Lurie, *Foreign Affairs*
1986 Larry McMurtry, *Lonesome Dove*
1987 Peter Taylor, *A Summons to Memphis*
1988 Toni Morrison, *Beloved*
1989 Anne Tyler, *Breathing Lessons*
1990 Oscar Hijuelos, *The Mambo Kings Play Songs of Love*
1991 John Updike, *Rabbit at Rest*
1992 Jane Smiley, *A Thousand Acres*
1993 Robert Olen Butler, *A Good Scent From a Strange Mountain*
1994 E. Annie Proulx, *The Shipping News*
1995 Carol Shields, *The Stone Diaries*
1996 Richard Ford, *Independence Day*
1997 Steven Millhauser, *Martin Dressler: The Tale of an American Dreamer*
1998 Philip Roth, *American Pastoral*
1999 Michael Cunningham, *The Hours*
2000 Jhumpa Lahiri, *Interpreter of Maladies*
2001 Michael Chabon, *The Amazing Adventures of Kavalier & Clay*
2002 Richard Russo, *Empire Falls*
2003 Jeffrey Eugenides, *Middlesex*
2004 Edward P. Jones, *The Known World*
2005 Marilynne Robinson, *Gilead*
2006 Geraldine Brooks, *March*
2007 Cormac McCarthy, *The Road*
2008 Junot Díaz, *The Brief Wondrous Life of Oscar Wao*
2009 Elizabeth Strout, *Olive Kitteridge*
2010 Paul Harding, *Tinkers*
2011 Jennifer Egan, *A Visit From the Goon Squad*
2013 Adam Johnson, *The Orphan Master's Son*
2014 Donna Tartt, *The Goldfinch*
2015 Anthony Doerr, *All the Light We Cannot See*
2016 Viet Thanh Nguyen, *The Sympathizer*
2017 Colson Whitehead, *The Underground Railroad*
2018 Andrew Sean Greer, *Less*
2019 Richard Powers, *The Overstory*
2020 Colson Whitehead, *The Nickel Boys*
2021 Louise Erdrich, *The Night Watchman*
2022 Joshua Cohen, *The Netanyahus*
2023 Barbara Kingsolver, *Demon Copperhead*; Hernan Diaz, *Trust*
2024 Jayne Anne Phillips, *Night Watch*

Drama

1918 Jesse Lynch Williams, *Why Marry?*
1920 Eugene O'Neill, *Beyond the Horizon*
1921 Zona Gale, *Miss Lulu Bett*
1922 Eugene O'Neill, *Anna Christie*
1923 Owen Davis, *Icebound*
1924 Hatcher Hughes, *Hell-Bent Fer Heaven*
1925 Sidney Howard, *They Knew What They Wanted*
1926 George Kelly, *Craig's Wife*
1927 Paul Green, *In Abraham's Bosom*
1928 Eugene O'Neill, *Strange Interlude*
1929 Elmer Rice, *Street Scene*
1930 Marc Connelly, *The Green Pastures*
1931 Susan Glaspell, *Alison's House*
1932 George S. Kaufman, Morrie Ryskind, and Ira Gershwin, *Of Thee I Sing*
1933 Maxwell Anderson, *Both Your Houses*
1934 Sidney Kingsley, *Men in White*
1935 Zoe Akins, *The Old Maid*
1936 Robert E. Sherwood, *Idiot's Delight*
1937 George S. Kaufman and Moss Hart, *You Can't Take It With You*
1938 Thornton Wilder, *Our Town*
1939 Robert E. Sherwood, *Abe Lincoln in Illinois*
1940 William Saroyan, *The Time of Your Life*
1941 Robert E. Sherwood, *There Shall Be No Night*
1943 Thornton Wilder, *The Skin of Our Teeth*
1945 Mary Chase, *Harvey*
1946 Russel Crouse and Howard Lindsay, *State of the Union*
1948 Tennessee Williams, *A Streetcar Named Desire*
1949 Arthur Miller, *Death of a Salesman*
1950 Richard Rodgers, Oscar Hammerstein II, and Joshua Logan, *South Pacific*
1952 Joseph Kramm, *The Shrike*
1953 William Inge, *Picnic*
1954 John Patrick, *The Teahouse of the August Moon*
1955 Tennessee Williams, *Cat on a Hot Tin Roof*
1956 Frances Goodrich and Albert Hackett, *The Diary of Anne Frank*
1957 Eugene O'Neill, *Long Day's Journey Into Night*
1958 Ketti Frings, *Look Homeward, Angel*
1959 Archibald MacLeish, *J.B.*
1960 George Abbott, Jerome Weidman, Sheldon Harnick, and Jerry Bock, *Fiorello!*
1961 Tad Mosel, *All the Way Home*
1962 Frank Loesser and Abe Burrows, *How to Succeed in Business Without Really Trying*
1965 Frank D. Gilroy, *The Subject Was Roses*
1967 Edward Albee, *A Delicate Balance*
1969 Howard Sackler, *The Great White Hope*
1970 Charles Gordone, *No Place to Be Somebody*
1971 Paul Zindel, *The Effect of Gamma Rays on Man-in-the-Moon Marigolds*
1973 Jason Miller, *That Championship Season*
1975 Edward Albee, *Seascape*
1976 Michael Bennett, James Kirkwood, Nicholas Dante, Marvin Hamlisch, and Edward Kleban, *A Chorus Line*
1977 Michael Cristofer, *The Shadow Box*
1978 Donald L. Coburn, *The Gin Game*
1979 Sam Shepard, *Buried Child*
1980 Lanford Wilson, *Talley's Folly*
1981 Beth Henley, *Crimes of the Heart*
1982 Charles Fuller, *A Soldier's Play*
1983 Marsha Norman, *'night, Mother*
1984 David Mamet, *Glengarry Glen Ross*
1985 Stephen Sondheim and James Lapine, *Sunday in the Park With George*
1987 August Wilson, *Fences*
1988 Alfred Uhry, *Driving Miss Daisy*
1989 Wendy Wasserstein, *The Heidi Chronicles*
1990 August Wilson, *The Piano Lesson*

1991 Neil Simon, *Lost in Yonkers*
1992 Robert Schenkkan, *The Kentucky Cycle*
1993 Tony Kushner, *Angels in America: Millennium Approaches*
1994 Edward Albee, *Three Tall Women*
1995 Horton Foote, *The Young Man From Atlanta*
1996 Jonathan Larson, *Rent*
1998 Paula Vogel, *How I Learned to Drive*
1999 Margaret Edson, *Wit*
2000 Donald Margulies, *Dinner With Friends*
2001 David Auburn, *Proof*
2002 Suzan-Lori Parks, *Topdog/Underdog*
2003 Nilo Cruz, *Anna in the Tropics*
2004 Doug Wright, *I Am My Own Wife*
2005 John Patrick Shanley, *Doubt, a parable*
2007 David Lindsay-Abaire, *Rabbit Hole*
2008 Tracy Letts, *August: Osage County*
2009 Lynn Nottage, *Ruined*
2010 Tom Kitt and Brian Yorkey, *Next to Normal*
2011 Bruce Norris, *Clybourne Park*
2012 Quiara Alegría Hudes, *Water by the Spoonful*
2013 Ayad Akhtar, *Disgraced*
2014 Annie Baker, *The Flick*
2015 Stephen Adly Guirgis, *Between Riverside and Crazy*
2016 Lin-Manuel Miranda, *Hamilton*
2017 Lynn Nottage, *Sweat*
2018 Martyna Majok, *Cost of Living*
2019 Jackie Sibblies Drury, *Fairview*
2020 Michael R. Jackson, *A Strange Loop*
2021 Katori Hall, *The Hot Wing King*
2022 James Ijames, *Fat Ham*
2023 Sanaz Toossi, *English*
2024 Eboni Booth, *Primary Trust*

General Nonfiction

1962 Theodore H. White, *The Making of the President 1960*
1963 Barbara W. Tuchman, *The Guns of August*
1964 Richard Hofstadter, *Anti-Intellectualism in American Life*
1965 Howard Mumford Jones, *O Strange New World*
1966 Edwin Way Teale, *Wandering Through Winter*
1967 David Brion Davis, *The Problem of Slavery in Western Culture*
1968 Will and Ariel Durant, *Rousseau and Revolution*
1969 Norman Mailer, *The Armies of the Night*; Rene Jules Dubos, *So Human an Animal: How We Are Shaped by Surroundings and Events*
1970 Eric H. Erikson, *Gandhi's Truth*
1971 John Toland, *The Rising Sun*
1972 Barbara W. Tuchman, *Stilwell and the American Experience in China, 1911-1945*
1973 Frances FitzGerald, *Fire in the Lake: The Vietnamese and the Americans in Vietnam*; Robert Coles, *Children of Crisis, Vols. II and III*
1974 Ernest Becker, *The Denial of Death*
1975 Annie Dillard, *Pilgrim at Tinker Creek*
1976 Robert N. Butler, *Why Survive? Being Old in America*
1977 William W. Warner, *Beautiful Swimmers*
1978 Carl Sagan, *The Dragons of Eden*
1979 Edward O. Wilson, *On Human Nature*
1980 Douglas R. Hofstadter, *Gödel, Escher, Bach: An Eternal Golden Braid*
1981 Carl E. Schorske, *Fin-de-Siècle Vienna: Politics and Culture*
1982 Tracy Kidder, *The Soul of a New Machine*
1983 Susan Sheehan, *Is There No Place on Earth for Me?*
1984 Paul Starr, *Social Transformation of American Medicine*
1985 Studs Terkel, *The Good War*
1986 Joseph Lelyveld, *Move Your Shadow*; J. Anthony Lukas, *Common Ground*
1987 David K. Shipler, *Arab and Jew: Wounded Spirits in a Promised Land*
1988 Richard Rhodes, *The Making of the Atomic Bomb*
1989 Neil Sheehan, *A Bright Shining Lie: John Paul Vann and America in Vietnam*
1990 Dale Maharidge and Michael Williamson, *And Their Children After Them*
1991 Bert Holldobler and Edward O. Wilson, *The Ants*
1992 Daniel Yergin, *The Prize: The Epic Quest for Oil, Money, and Power*
1993 Garry Wills, *Lincoln at Gettysburg*
1994 David Remnick, *Lenin's Tomb: The Last Days of the Soviet Empire*
1995 Jonathan Weiner, *The Beak of the Finch: A Story of Evolution in Our Time*
1996 Tina Rosenberg, *The Haunted Land: Facing Europe's Ghosts After Communism*
1997 Richard Kluger, *Ashes to Ashes: America's Hundred-Year Cigarette War, the Public Health, and the Unabashed Triumph of Philip Morris*
1998 Jared Diamond, *Guns, Germs, and Steel: The Fates of Human Societies*
1999 John McPhee, *Annals of the Former World*
2000 John W. Dower, *Embracing Defeat: Japan in the Wake of World War II*
2001 Herbert P. Bix, *Hirohito and the Making of Modern Japan*
2002 Diane McWhorter, *Carry Me Home: Birmingham, Alabama: The Climactic Battle of the Civil Rights Revolution*
2003 Samantha Power, *A Problem From Hell: America and the Age of Genocide*
2004 Anne Applebaum, *Gulag: A History*
2005 Steve Coll, *Ghost Wars*
2006 Caroline Elkins, *Imperial Reckoning: The Untold Story of Britain's Gulag in Kenya*
2007 Lawrence Wright, *The Looming Tower: Al-Qaeda and the Road to 9/11*
2008 Saul Friedländer, *The Years of Extermination: Nazi Germany and the Jews, 1939-1945*
2009 Douglas A. Blackmon, *Slavery by Another Name: The Re-Enslavement of Black Americans From the Civil War to World War II*
2010 David E. Hoffman, *The Dead Hand: The Untold Story of the Cold War Arms Race and Its Dangerous Legacy*
2011 Siddhartha Mukherjee, *The Emperor of All Maladies: A Biography of Cancer*
2012 Stephen Greenblatt, *The Swerve: How the World Became Modern*
2013 Gilbert King, *Devil in the Grove: Thurgood Marshall, the Groveland Boys, and the Dawn of a New America*
2014 Dan Fagin, *Toms River: A Story of Science and Salvation*
2015 Elizabeth Kolbert, *The Sixth Extinction: An Unnatural History*
2016 Joby Warrick, *Black Flags: The Rise of ISIS*
2017 Matthew Desmond, *Evicted: Poverty and Profit in the American City*
2018 James Forman Jr., *Locking up Our Own: Crime and Punishment in Black America*
2019 Eliza Griswold, *Amity and Prosperity: One Family and the Fracturing of America*
2020 Greg Grandin, *The End of the Myth: From the Frontier to the Border Wall in the Mind of America*; Anne Boyer, *The Undying: Pain, Vulnerability, Mortality, Medicine, Art, Time, Dreams, Data, Exhaustion, Cancer, and Care*
2021 David Zucchino, *Wilmington's Lie: The Murderous Coup of 1898 and the Rise of White Supremacy*
2022 Andrea Elliott, *Invisible Child: Poverty, Survival, & Hope in an American City*
2023 Robert Samuels and Toluse Olorunnipa, *His Name Is George Floyd: One Man's Life and the Struggle for Racial Justice*
2024 Nathan Thrall, *A Day in the Life of Abed Salama: Anatomy of a Jerusalem Tragedy*

Special Citation in Letters

1944 Richard Rodgers and Oscar Hammerstein II, for *Oklahoma!*
1957 Kenneth Roberts, for his historical novels
1960 *The Armada*, by Garrett Mattingly
1961 *American Heritage Picture History of the Civil War*
1973 *George Washington, Vols. I-IV*, by James Thomas Flexner
1977 Alex Haley, for *Roots*
1978 E. B. White
1984 Theodor Seuss Geisel (Dr. Seuss)
1992 Art Spiegelman, for *Maus*
2006 Edmund S. Morgan
2007 Ray Bradbury

Pulitzer Prizes in Music, 1943-2024

1943 William Schuman, *Secular Cantata No. 2, A Free Song*
1944 Howard Hanson, *Symphony No. 4, Op. 34*
1945 Aaron Copland, *Appalachian Spring*
1946 Leo Sowerby, *The Canticle of the Sun*
1947 Charles Ives, *Symphony No. 3*
1948 Walter Piston, *Symphony No. 3*
1949 Virgil Thomson, *Louisiana Story*
1950 Gian-Carlo Menotti, *The Consul*
1951 Douglas Moore, *Giants in the Earth*
1952 Gail Kubik, *Symphony Concertante*
1954 Quincy Porter, *Concerto for Two Pianos and Orchestra*
1955 Gian-Carlo Menotti, *The Saint of Bleecker Street*
1956 Ernest Toch, *Symphony No. 3*
1957 Norman Dello Joio, *Meditations on Ecclesiastes*
1958 Samuel Barber, *Vanessa*
1959 John LaMontaine, *Concerto for Piano and Orchestra*
1960 Elliott Carter, *Second String Quartet*
1961 Walter Piston, *Symphony No. 7*
1962 Robert Ward, *The Crucible*
1963 Samuel Barber, *Piano Concerto No. 1*
1966 Leslie Bassett, *Variations for Orchestra*
1967 Leon Kirchner, *Quartet No. 3*
1968 George Crumb, *Echoes of Time and the River*
1969 Karel Husa, *String Quartet No. 3*
1970 Charles Wuorinen, *Time's Encomium*
1971 Mario Davidovsky, *Synchronisms No. 6*
1972 Jacob Druckman, *Windows*
1973 Elliott Carter, *String Quartet No. 3*

1974 Donald Martino, *Notturno*
1975 Dominick Argento, *From the Diary of Virginia Woolf*
1976 Ned Rorem, *Air Music*
1977 Richard Wernick, *Visions of Terror and Wonder*
1978 Michael Colgrass, *Deja Vu for Percussion and Orchestra*
1979 Joseph Schwantner, *Aftertones of Infinity*
1980 David Del Tredici, *In Memory of a Summer Day*
1982 Roger Sessions, *Concerto for Orchestra*
1983 Ellen Taaffe Zwilich, *Symphony No. 1*
1984 Bernard Rands, *Canti del Sole*
1985 Stephen Albert, *Symphony, RiverRun*
1986 George Perle, *Wind Quintet IV*
1987 John Harbison, *The Flight Into Egypt*
1988 William Bolcom, *12 New Etudes for Piano*
1989 Roger Reynolds, *Whispers Out of Time*
1990 Mel Powell, *Duplicates: A Concerto for Two Pianos and Orchestra*
1991 Shulamit Ran, *Symphony*
1992 Wayne Peterson, *The Face of the Night, The Heart[2] of the Dark*
1993 Christopher Rouse, *Trombone Concerto*
1994 Gunther Schuller, *Of Reminiscences and Reflections*
1995 Morton Gould, *Stringmusic*
1996 George Walker, *Lilacs for Voice and Orchestra*
1997 Wynton Marsalis, *Blood on the Fields*
1998 Aaron Jay Kernis, *String Quartet No. 2 (musica instrumentalis)*
1999 Melinda Wagner, *Concerto for Flute, Strings, and Percussion*
2000 Lewis Spratlan, *Life is a Dream, Opera in Three Acts: Act II, Concert Version*
2001 John Corigliano, *Symphony No. 2 for String Orchestra*
2002 Henry Brant, *Ice Field*
2003 John Adams, *On the Transmigration of Souls*
2004 Paul Moravec, *Tempest Fantasy*
2005 Steven Stucky, *Second Concerto for Orchestra*
2006 Yehudi Wyner, *Piano Concerto: "Chiavi in Mano"*
2007 Ornette Coleman, *Sound Grammar*
2008 David Lang, *The Little Match Girl Passion*
2009 Steve Reich, *Double Sextet*
2010 Jennifer Higdon, *Violin Concerto*
2011 Zhou Long, *Madame White Snake*
2012 Kevin Puts, *Silent Night: Opera in Two Acts*
2013 Caroline Shaw, *Partita for 8 Voices*
2014 John Luther Adams, *Become Ocean*
2015 Julia Wolfe, *Anthracite Fields*
2016 Henry Threadgill, *In for a Penny, In for a Pound*
2017 Du Yun, *Angel's Bone*
2018 Kendrick Lamar, *DAMN.*
2019 Ellen Reid, *p r i s m*
2020 Anthony Davis, *The Central Park Five*
2021 Tania León, *Stride*
2022 Raven Chacon, *Voiceless Mass*
2023 Rhiannon Giddens and Michael Abels, *Omar*
2024 Tyshawn Sorey, *Adagio (For Wadada Leo Smith)*

Special Citation in Music

1974 Roger Sessions
1976 Scott Joplin
1982 Milton Babbitt
1985 William Schuman
1998 George Gershwin
1999 Edward Kennedy "Duke" Ellington
2006 Thelonious Monk
2007 John Coltrane
2008 Bob Dylan
2010 Hank Williams
2019 Aretha Franklin

Booker Prize for Fiction, 1969-2023

The Booker Prize for fiction, named the Man Booker Prize, 2002-18, is £50,000, awarded annually to the author of the best new full-length novel written in English.

Year Author, book
1969 P. H. Newby, *Something to Answer For*
1970 Bernice Rubens, *The Elected Member*
1971 V. S. Naipaul, *In a Free State*
1972 John Berger, *G*
1973 J. G. Farrell, *The Siege of Krishnapur*
1974 Nadine Gordimer, *The Conservationist*; Stanley Middleton, *Holiday*
1975 Ruth Prawer Jhabvala, *Heat and Dust*
1976 David Storey, *Saville*
1977 Paul Scott, *Staying On*
1978 Iris Murdoch, *The Sea, the Sea*
1979 Penelope Fitzgerald, *Offshore*
1980 William Golding, *Rites of Passage*
1981 Salman Rushdie, *Midnight's Children*[1]
1982 Thomas Keneally, *Schindler's Ark*
1983 J. M. Coetzee, *Life and Times of Michael K*
1984 Anita Brookner, *Hotel du Lac*
1985 Keri Hulme, *The Bone People*
1986 Kingsley Amis, *The Old Devils*
1987 Penelope Lively, *Moon Tiger*
1988 Peter Carey, *Oscar and Lucinda*
1989 Kazuo Ishiguro, *The Remains of the Day*
1990 A. S. Byatt, *Possession*
1991 Ben Okri, *The Famished Road*
1992 Michael Ondaatje, *The English Patient*[2]; Barry Unsworth, *Sacred Hunger*
1993 Roddy Doyle, *Paddy Clarke Ha Ha Ha*
1994 James Kelman, *How Late It Was, How Late*
1995 Pat Barker, *The Ghost Road*
1996 Graham Swift, *Last Orders*

Year Author, book
1997 Arundhati Roy, *The God of Small Things*
1998 Ian McEwan, *Amsterdam*
1999 J. M. Coetzee, *Disgrace*
2000 Margaret Atwood, *The Blind Assassin*
2001 Peter Carey, *True History of the Kelly Gang*
2002 Yann Martel, *Life of Pi*
2003 DBC Pierre, *Vernon God Little*
2004 Alan Hollinghurst, *The Line of Beauty*
2005 John Banville, *The Sea*
2006 Kiran Desai, *The Inheritance of Loss*
2007 Anne Enright, *The Gathering*
2008 Aravind Adiga, *The White Tiger*
2009 Hilary Mantel, *Wolf Hall*
2010 Howard Jacobson, *The Finkler Question*
2011 Julian Barnes, *The Sense of an Ending*
2012 Hilary Mantel, *Bring up the Bodies*
2013 Eleanor Catton, *The Luminaries*
2014 Richard Flanagan, *The Narrow Road to the Deep North*
2015 Marlon James, *A Brief History of Seven Killings*
2016 Paul Beatty, *The Sellout*
2017 George Saunders, *Lincoln in the Bardo*
2018 Anna Burns, *Milkman*
2019 Margaret Atwood, *The Testaments*; Bernardine Evaristo, *Girl, Woman, Other*
2020 Douglas Stuart, *Shuggie Bain*
2021 Damon Galgut, *The Promise*
2022 Shehan Karunatilaka, *The Seven Moons of Maali Almeida*
2023 Paul Lynch, *Prophet Song*

(1) Rushdie's *Midnight's Children* also won the Booker of Bookers prize in 1993 and the Best of the Booker prize in 2008.
(2) Ondaatje's *The English Patient* also won the Golden Man Booker prize in 2018.

Newbery Medal, 1922-2024

The Newbery Medal is awarded annually by the Association for Library Service to Children, a division of the American Library Association, to the most distinguished contribution to American children's literature published in the previous year.

Year Book, author
1922 *The Story of Mankind*, Hendrik Willem van Loon
1923 *The Voyages of Dr. Dolittle*, Hugh Lofting
1924 *The Dark Frigate*, Charles Boardman Hawes
1925 *Tales From Silver Lands*, Charles J. Finger
1926 *Shen of the Sea*, Arthur Bowie Chrisman
1927 *Smoky, the Cowhorse*, Will James
1928 *Gay-Neck: The Story of a Pigeon*, Dhan Gopal Mukerji
1929 *The Trumpeter of Krakow*, Eric P. Kelly
1930 *Hitty, Her First Hundred Years*, Rachel Field
1931 *The Cat Who Went to Heaven*, Elizabeth Coatsworth
1932 *Waterless Mountain*, Laura Adams Armer
1933 *Young Fu of the Upper Yangtze*, Elizabeth Foreman Lewis
1934 *Invincible Louisa*, Cornelia Meigs
1935 *Dobry*, Monica Shannon

Year Book, author
1936 *Caddie Woodlawn*, Carol Ryrie Brink
1937 *Roller Skates*, Ruth Sawyer
1938 *The White Stag*, Kate Seredy
1939 *Thimble Summer*, Elizabeth Enright
1940 *Daniel Boone*, James Daugherty
1941 *Call It Courage*, Armstrong Sperry
1942 *The Matchlock Gun*, Walter D. Edmonds
1943 *Adam of the Road*, Elizabeth Janet Gray
1944 *Johnny Tremain*, Esther Forbes
1945 *Rabbit Hill*, Robert Lawson
1946 *Strawberry Girl*, Lois Lenski
1947 *Miss Hickory*, Carolyn Sherwin Bailey
1948 *The Twenty-One Balloons*, William Pène du Bois
1949 *King of the Wind*, Marguerite Henry

Year	Book, author
1950	*The Door in the Wall*, Marguerite de Angeli
1951	*Amos Fortune, Free Man*, Elizabeth Yates
1952	*Ginger Pye*, Eleanor Estes
1953	*Secret of the Andes*, Ann Nolan Clark
1954	*... And Now Miguel*, Joseph Krumgold
1955	*The Wheel on the School*, Meindert DeJong
1956	*Carry On, Mr. Bowditch*, Jean Lee Latham
1957	*Miracles on Maple Hill*, Virginia Sorensen
1958	*Rifles for Watie*, Harold Keith
1959	*The Witch of Blackbird Pond*, Elizabeth George Speare
1960	*Onion John*, Joseph Krumgold
1961	*Island of the Blue Dolphins*, Scott O'Dell
1962	*The Bronze Bow*, Elizabeth George Speare
1963	*A Wrinkle in Time*, Madeleine L'Engle
1964	*It's Like This, Cat*, Emily Cheney Neville
1965	*Shadow of a Bull*, Maia Wojciechowska
1966	*I, Juan de Pareja*, Elizabeth Borton de Trevino
1967	*Up a Road Slowly*, Irene Hunt
1968	*From the Mixed-Up Files of Mrs. Basil E. Frankweiler*, E. L. Konigsburg
1969	*The High King*, Lloyd Alexander
1970	*Sounder*, William H. Armstrong
1971	*The Summer of the Swans*, Betsy Byars
1972	*Mrs. Frisby and the Rats of NIMH*, Robert C. O'Brien
1973	*Julie of the Wolves*, Jean Craighead George
1974	*The Slave Dancer*, Paula Fox
1975	*M. C. Higgins, the Great*, Virginia Hamilton
1976	*The Grey King*, Susan Cooper
1977	*Roll of Thunder, Hear My Cry*, Mildred D. Taylor
1978	*Bridge to Terabithia*, Katherine Paterson
1979	*The Westing Game*, Ellen Raskin
1980	*A Gathering of Days*, Joan Blos
1981	*Jacob Have I Loved*, Katherine Paterson
1982	*A Visit to William Blake's Inn: Poems for Innocent and Experienced Travelers*, Nancy Willard
1983	*Dicey's Song*, Cynthia Voigt
1984	*Dear Mr. Henshaw*, Beverly Cleary
1985	*The Hero and the Crown*, Robin McKinley
1986	*Sarah, Plain and Tall*, Patricia MacLachlan
1987	*The Whipping Boy*, Sid Fleischman
1988	*Lincoln: A Photobiography*, Russell Freedman
1989	*Joyful Noise: Poems for Two Voices*, Paul Fleischman
1990	*Number the Stars*, Lois Lowry
1991	*Maniac Magee*, Jerry Spinelli
1992	*Shiloh*, Phyllis Reynolds Naylor
1993	*Missing May*, Cynthia Rylant
1994	*The Giver*, Lois Lowry
1995	*Walk Two Moons*, Sharon Creech
1996	*The Midwife's Apprentice*, Karen Cushman
1997	*The View From Saturday*, E. L. Konigsburg
1998	*Out of the Dust*, Karen Hesse
1999	*Holes*, Louis Sachar
2000	*Bud, Not Buddy*, Christopher Paul Curtis
2001	*A Year Down Yonder*, Richard Peck
2002	*A Single Shard*, Linda Sue Park
2003	*Crispin: The Cross of Lead*, Avi
2004	*The Tale of Despereaux*, Kate DiCamillo
2005	*Kira-Kira*, Cynthia Kadohata
2006	*Criss Cross*, Lynne Rae Perkins
2007	*The Higher Power of Lucky*, Susan Patron
2008	*Good Masters! Sweet Ladies! Voices From a Medieval Village*, Laura Amy Schlitz
2009	*The Graveyard Book*, Neil Gaiman
2010	*When You Reach Me*, Rebecca Stead
2011	*Moon Over Manifest*, Clare Vanderpool
2012	*Dead End in Norvelt*, Jack Gantos
2013	*The One and Only Ivan*, Katherine Applegate
2014	*Flora & Ulysses: The Illuminated Adventures*, Kate DiCamillo
2015	*The Crossover*, Kwame Alexander
2016	*Last Stop on Market Street*, Matt de la Peña
2017	*The Girl Who Drank the Moon*, Kelly Barnhill
2018	*Hello, Universe*, Erin Entrada Kelly
2019	*Merci Suárez Changes Gears*, Meg Medina
2020	*New Kid*, Jerry Craft
2021	*When You Trap a Tiger*, Tae Keller
2022	*The Last Cuentista*, Donna Barba Higuera
2023	*Freewater*, Amina Luqman-Dawson
2024	*The Eyes and the Impossible*, Dave Eggers

Caldecott Medal, 1938-2024

The Caldecott Medal is awarded annually by the Association for Library Service to Children, a division of the American Library Association, to the illustrator of the most distinguished American picture book for children.

Year	Book, illustrator
1938	*Animals of the Bible*, Dorothy P. Lathrop
1939	*Mei Li*, Thomas Handforth
1940	*Abraham Lincoln*, Ingri and Edgar Parin d'Aulaire
1941	*They Were Strong and Good*, Robert Lawson
1942	*Make Way for Ducklings*, Robert McCloskey
1943	*The Little House*, Virginia Lee Burton
1944	*Many Moons*, Louis Slobodkin
1945	*Prayer for a Child*, Elizabeth Orton Jones
1946	*The Rooster Crows*, Maude and Miska Petersham
1947	*The Little Island*, Leonard Weisgard
1948	*White Snow, Bright Snow*, Roger Duvoisin
1949	*The Big Snow*, Berta and Elmer Hader
1950	*Song of the Swallows*, Leo Politi
1951	*The Egg Tree*, Katherine Milhous
1952	*Finders Keepers*, Nicolas, pseud. (Nicholas Mordvinoff)
1953	*The Biggest Bear*, Lynd Ward
1954	*Madeline's Rescue*, Ludwig Bemelmans
1955	*Cinderella, or the Little Glass Slipper*, Marcia Brown
1956	*Frog Went A-Courtin'*, Feodor Rojankovsky
1957	*A Tree Is Nice*, Marc Simont
1958	*Time of Wonder*, Robert McCloskey
1959	*Chanticleer and the Fox*, Barbara Cooney
1960	*Nine Days to Christmas*, Marie Hall Ets
1961	*Baboushka and the Three Kings*, Nicolas Sidjakov
1962	*Once a Mouse*, Marcia Brown
1963	*The Snowy Day*, Ezra Jack Keats
1964	*Where the Wild Things Are*, Maurice Sendak
1965	*May I Bring a Friend?*, Beni Montresor
1966	*Always Room for One More*, Nonny Hogrogian
1967	*Sam, Bangs, and Moonshine*, Evaline Ness
1968	*Drummer Hoff*, Ed Emberley
1969	*The Fool of the World and the Flying Ship*, Uri Shulevitz
1970	*Sylvester and the Magic Pebble*, William Steig
1971	*A Story A Story*, Gail E. Haley
1972	*One Fine Day*, Nonny Hogrogian
1973	*The Funny Little Woman*, Blair Lent
1974	*Duffy and the Devil*, Margot Zemach
1975	*Arrow to the Sun*, Gerald McDermott
1976	*Why Mosquitoes Buzz in People's Ears*, Leo and Diane Dillon
1977	*Ashanti to Zulu: African Traditions*, Leo and Diane Dillon
1978	*Noah's Ark*, Peter Spier
1979	*The Girl Who Loved Wild Horses*, Paul Goble
1980	*Ox-Cart Man*, Barbara Cooney
1981	*Fables*, Arnold Lobel
1982	*Jumanji*, Chris Van Allsburg
1983	*Shadow*, Marcia Brown
1984	*The Glorious Flight: Across the Channel With Louis Bleriot*, Alice and Martin Provensen
1985	*Saint George and the Dragon*, Trina Schart Hyman
1986	*The Polar Express*, Chris Van Allsburg
1987	*Hey, Al*, Richard Egielski
1988	*Owl Moon*, John Schoenherr
1989	*Song and Dance Man*, Stephen Grammell
1990	*Lon Po Po: A Red-Riding Hood Story From China*, Ed Young
1991	*Black and White*, David Macaulay
1992	*Tuesday*, David Wiesner
1993	*Mirette on the High Wire*, Emily Arnold McCully
1994	*Grandfather's Journey*, Allen Say
1995	*Smoky Night*, David Diaz
1996	*Officer Buckle and Gloria*, Peggy Rathmann
1997	*Golem*, David Wisniewski
1998	*Rapunzel*, Paul O. Zelinsky
1999	*Snowflake Bentley*, Mary Azarian
2000	*Joseph Had a Little Overcoat*, Simms Taback
2001	*So You Want to be President?*, David Small
2002	*The Three Pigs*, David Wiesner
2003	*My Friend Rabbit*, Eric Rohmann
2004	*The Man Who Walked Between the Towers*, Mordicai Gerstein
2005	*Kitten's First Full Moon*, Kevin Henkes
2006	*The Hello, Goodbye Window*, Chris Raschka
2007	*Flotsam*, David Wiesner
2008	*The Invention of Hugo Cabret*, Brian Selznick
2009	*The House in the Night*, Beth Krommes
2010	*The Lion & the Mouse*, Jerry Pinkney
2011	*A Sick Day for Amos McGee*, Erin E. Stead
2012	*A Ball for Daisy*, Chris Raschka
2013	*This Is Not My Hat*, Jon Klassen
2014	*Locomotive*, Brian Floca
2015	*The Adventures of Beekle: The Unimaginary Friend*, Dan Santat
2016	*Finding Winnie: The True Story of the World's Most Famous Bear*, Sophie Blackall
2017	*Radiant Child: The Story of Young Artist Jean-Michel Basquiat*, Javaka Steptoe
2018	*Wolf in the Snow*, Matthew Cordell
2019	*Hello Lighthouse*, Sophie Blackall
2020	*The Undefeated*, Kadir Nelson
2021	*We Are Water Protectors*, Michaela Goade
2022	*Watercress*, Jason Chin
2023	*Hot Dog*, Doug Salati
2024	*Big*, Vashti Harrison

National Book Awards, 1950-2023

The National Book Awards (known as American Book Awards 1980-86) are administered by the National Book Foundation and have been given annually since 1950. The $10,000 prizes are awarded for works published in the U.S. In some years, multiple awards were given for nonfiction in various categories; in such cases, the history and biography (if any) or biography winner is listed. Selected additional awards in nonfiction are listed in footnotes.

Other National Book Awards, 2023: Poetry: Craig Santos Perez, *from unincorporated territory [åmot]*. Translated Literature: Stênio Gardel, Bruna Dantas Lobato, *The Words That Remain*. Young People's Literature: Dan Santat, *A First Time for Everything*. Distinguished Contribution to American Letters: Rita Dove. Literarian Award: Paul Yamazaki.

Fiction

Year	Author, book
1950	Nelson Algren, *The Man With the Golden Arm*
1951	William Faulkner, *The Collected Stories*
1952	James Jones, *From Here to Eternity*
1953	Ralph Ellison, *Invisible Man*
1954	Saul Bellow, *The Adventures of Augie March*
1955	William Faulkner, *A Fable*
1956	John O'Hara, *Ten North Frederick*
1957	Wright Morris, *The Field of Vision*
1958	John Cheever, *The Wapshot Chronicle*
1959	Bernard Malamud, *The Magic Barrel*
1960	Philip Roth, *Goodbye, Columbus*
1961	Conrad Richter, *The Waters of Kronos*
1962	Walker Percy, *The Moviegoer*
1963	J. F. Powers, *Morte d'Urban*
1964	John Updike, *The Centaur*
1965	Saul Bellow, *Herzog*
1966	Katherine Anne Porter, *The Collected Stories*
1967	Bernard Malamud, *The Fixer*
1968	Thornton Wilder, *The Eighth Day*
1969	Jerzy Kosinski, *Steps*
1970	Joyce Carol Oates, *Them*
1971	Saul Bellow, *Mr. Sammler's Planet*
1972	Flannery O'Connor, *The Complete Stories*
1973	John Barth, *Chimera*
1974	Thomas Pynchon, *Gravity's Rainbow*
1974	Isaac Bashevis Singer, *A Crown of Feathers*
1975	Robert Stone, *Dog Soldiers*
1976	William Gaddis, *JR*
1977	Wallace Stegner, *The Spectator Bird*
1978	Mary Lee Settle, *Blood Ties*
1979	Tim O'Brien, *Going After Cacciato*
1980	William Styron, *Sophie's Choice*
1981	Wright Morris, *Plains Song*
1982	John Updike, *Rabbit Is Rich*
1983	Alice Walker, *The Color Purple*
1984	Ellen Gilchrist, *Victory Over Japan*
1985	Don DeLillo, *White Noise*
1986	E. L. Doctorow, *World's Fair*
1987	Larry Heinemann, *Paco's Story*
1988	Pete Dexter, *Paris Trout*
1989	John Casey, *Spartina*
1990	Charles Johnson, *Middle Passage*
1991	Norman Rush, *Mating*
1992	Cormac McCarthy, *All the Pretty Horses*
1993	E. Annie Proulx, *The Shipping News*
1994	William Gaddis, *A Frolic of His Own*
1995	Philip Roth, *Sabbath's Theater*
1996	Andrea Barrett, *Ship Fever and Other Stories*
1997	Charles Frazier, *Cold Mountain*
1998	Alice McDermott, *Charming Billy*
1999	Ha Jin, *Waiting*
2000	Susan Sontag, *In America*
2001	Jonathan Franzen, *The Corrections*
2002	Julia Glass, *Three Junes*
2003	Shirley Hazzard, *The Great Fire*
2004	Lily Tuck, *The News From Paraguay*
2005	William T. Vollmann, *Europe Central*
2006	Richard Powers, *The Echo Maker*
2007	Denis Johnson, *Tree of Smoke*
2008	Peter Matthiessen, *Shadow Country*
2009	Colum McCann, *Let the Great World Spin*
2010	Jaimy Gordon, *Lord of Misrule*
2011	Jesmyn Ward, *Salvage the Bones*
2012	Louise Erdrich, *The Round House*
2013	James McBride, *The Good Lord Bird*
2014	Phil Klay, *Redeployment*
2015	Adam Johnson, *Fortune Smiles: Stories*
2016	Colson Whitehead, *The Underground Railroad*
2017	Jesmyn Ward, *Sing, Unburied, Sing*
2018	Sigrid Nunez, *The Friend*
2019	Susan Choi, *Trust Exercise*
2020	Charles Yu, *Interior Chinatown*
2021	Jason Mott, *Hell of a Book*
2022	Tess Gunty, *The Rabbit Hutch*
2023	Justin Torres, *Blackouts*

Nonfiction

Year	Author, book
1950	Ralph L. Rusk, *Ralph Waldo Emerson*
1951	Newton Arvin, *Herman Melville*
1952	Rachel Carson, *The Sea Around Us*
1953	Bernard A. De Voto, *The Course of an Empire*
1954	Bruce Catton, *A Stillness at Appomattox*
1955	Joseph Wood Krutch, *The Measure of Man*
1956	Herbert Kubly, *An American in Italy*
1957	George F. Kennan, *Russia Leaves the War*
1958	Catherine Drinker Bowen, *The Lion and the Throne*
1959	J. Christopher Herold, *Mistress to an Age: A Life of Madame De Stael*
1960	Richard Ellman, *James Joyce*
1961	William L. Shirer, *The Rise and Fall of the Third Reich*
1962	Lewis Mumford, *The City in History: Its Origins, Its Transformations, and Its Prospects*
1963	Leon Edel, *Henry James, Vol. II: The Conquest of London* and *Vol. III: The Middle Years*
1964	William H. McNeill, *The Rise of the West: A History of the Human Community*
1965	Louis Fisher, *The Life of Lenin*
1966	Arthur M. Schlesinger Jr., *A Thousand Days: John F. Kennedy in the White House*
1967	Peter Gay, *The Enlightenment, An Interpretation, Vol. I: The Rise of Modern Paganism*
1968	George F. Kennan, *Memoirs: 1925-1950*[1]
1969	Winthrop D. Jordan, *White Over Black: American Attitudes Toward the Negro, 1550-1812*[2]
1970	T. Harry Williams, *Huey Long*[3]
1971	James MacGregor Burns, *Roosevelt: The Soldier of Freedom*
1972	Joseph P. Lash, *Eleanor and Franklin: The Story of Their Relationship, Based on Eleanor Roosevelt's Private Papers*
1973	James Thomas Flexner, *George Washington, Vol. IV: Anguish and Farewell, 1793-1799*[4]
1974	John Clive, *Macaulay, The Shaping of the Historian*; Douglas Day, *Malcolm Lowry: A Biography*[5]
1975	Richard B. Sewall, *The Life of Emily Dickinson*[6]
1976	David Brion Davis, *The Problem of Slavery in the Age of Revolution, 1770-1823*
1977	W. A. Swanberg, *Norman Thomas: The Last Idealist*[7]
1978	W. Jackson Bate, *Samuel Johnson*
1979	Arthur M. Schlesinger Jr., *Robert Kennedy and His Times*
1980	Tom Wolfe, *The Right Stuff*
1981	Maxine Hong Kingston, *China Men*
1982	Tracy Kidder, *The Soul of a New Machine*
1983	Fox Butterfield, *China: Alive in the Bitter Sea*
1984	Robert V. Remini, *Andrew Jackson and the Course of American Democracy, 1833-1845*
1985	J. Anthony Lukas, *Common Ground: A Turbulent Decade in the Lives of Three American Families*
1986	Barry Lopez, *Arctic Dreams*
1987	Richard Rhodes, *The Making of the Atom Bomb*
1988	Neil Sheehan, *A Bright Shining Lie: John Paul Vann and America in Vietnam*
1989	Thomas L. Friedman, *From Beirut to Jerusalem*
1990	Ron Chernow, *The House of Morgan: An American Banking Dynasty and the Rise of Modern Finance*
1991	Orlando Patterson, *Freedom*
1992	Paul Monette, *Becoming a Man: Half a Life Story*
1993	Gore Vidal, *United States: Essays 1952-1992*
1994	Sherwin B. Nuland, *How We Die: Reflections on Life's Final Chapter*
1995	Tina Rosenberg, *The Haunted Land: Facing Europe's Ghosts After Communism*
1996	James Carroll, *An American Requiem: God, My Father, and the War That Came Between Us*
1997	Joseph J. Ellis, *American Sphinx: The Character of Thomas Jefferson*
1998	Edward Ball, *Slaves in the Family*
1999	John W. Dower, *Embracing Defeat: Japan in the Wake of World War II*
2000	Nathaniel Philbrick, *In the Heart of the Sea: The Tragedy of the Whaleship Essex*

Year	Author, book
2001	Andrew Solomon, *The Noonday Demon: An Atlas of Depression*
2002	Robert A. Caro, *Master of the Senate: The Years of Lyndon Johnson*
2003	Carlos Eire, *Waiting for Snow in Havana: Confessions of a Cuban Boy*
2004	Kevin Boyle, *Arc of Justice: A Saga of Race, Civil Rights, and Murder in the Jazz Age*
2005	Joan Didion, *The Year of Magical Thinking*
2006	Timothy Egan, *The Worst Hard Time: The Untold Story of Those Who Survived the Great American Dust Bowl*
2007	Tim Weiner, *Legacy of Ashes: The History of the CIA*
2008	Annette Gordon-Reed, *The Hemingses of Monticello: An American Family*
2009	T. J. Stiles, *The First Tycoon: The Epic Life of Cornelius Vanderbilt*
2010	Patti Smith, *Just Kids*
2011	Stephen Greenblatt, *The Swerve: How the World Became Modern*
2012	Katherine Boo, *Behind the Beautiful Forevers: Life, Death, and Hope in a Mumbai Undercity*
2013	George Packer, *The Unwinding: An Inner History of the New America*
2014	Evan Osnos, *Age of Ambition: Chasing Fortune, Truth, and Faith in the New China*
2015	Ta-Nehisi Coates, *Between the World and Me*
2016	Ibram X. Kendi, *Stamped From the Beginning: The Definitive History of Racist Ideas in America*
2017	Masha Gessen, *The Future Is History: How Totalitarianism Reclaimed Russia*
2018	Jeffrey C. Stewart, *The New Negro: The Life of Alain Locke*
2019	Sarah M. Broom, *The Yellow House*
2020	Les Payne and Tamara Payne, *The Dead Are Arising: The Life of Malcolm X*
2021	Tiya Miles, *All That She Carried: The Journey of Ashley's Sack, a Black Family Keepsake*
2022	Imani Perry, *South to America: A Journey Below the Mason-Dixon to Understand the Soul of a Nation*
2023	Ned Blackhawk, *The Rediscovery of America: Native Peoples and the Unmaking of U.S. History*

(1) Science, Philosophy, & Religion: Jonathan Kozol, *Death at an Early Age*. (2) Arts & Letters: Norman Mailer, *The Armies of the Night: History as a Novel, the Novel as History*. (3) Arts & Letters: Lillian Hellman, *An Unfinished Woman: A Memoir*. (4) Contemp. Affairs: Frances FitzGerald, *Fire in the Lake: The Vietnamese and the Americans in Vietnam*. (5) Arts & Letters: Pauline Kael, *Deeper Into the Movies*. (6) Arts & Letters: Roger Shattuck, *Marcel Proust*; Lewis Thomas, *The Lives of a Cell: Notes of a Biology Watcher*. (7) Contemp. Thought: Bruno Bettelheim, *The Uses of Enchantment: The Meaning and Importance of Fairy Tales*.

Journalism Awards, 2024

National Magazine Awards, by American Society of Magazine Editors and Columbia Univ. Graduate School of Journalism. General Excellence—News, Sports, and Entertainment: *The Atlantic*; Service and Lifestyle: *Highsnobiety*; Special Interest: *The Marshall Project*; Literature, Science, and Politics: *The Yale Review*. Podcasting: *You Didn't See Nothin*, Invisible Institute with USG Audio. Video: *Business Insider*. Design: *Rest of World*. Photography: *New York*. Single-Topic Issue: *New York*. Service Journalism: *NY Times Magazine*. Lifestyle Journalism: *Philadelphia*. Reporting: ProPublica with *Texas Tribune*. Feature Writing: *NY Times Magazine*. Profile Writing: *The Atlantic*. Columns and Essays: *The Atlantic*. Reviews and Criticism: *The Atlantic*. Public Interest: *NY Times Magazine*.

George Foster Peabody Awards, by Univ. of Georgia. Career achievement: Mel Brooks. Global impact: WITNESS. Institutional award: *Star Trek*. Trailblazer award: Quinta Brunson. Arts: *Can You Bring It: Bill T. Jones and D-Man in the Waters*, World Channel/APT; *Judy Blume Forever*, Prime Video. Children's/youth: *Bluey*, Disney+. Documentary: *All That Breathes*, *All the Beauty and the Bloodshed*, and *The Stroll*, HBO Max; *Bobi Wine: The People's President*, National Geographic; "20 Days in Mariupol," *Frontline*, PBS, and Associated Press; "While We Watched," *POV*, PBS. Entertainment: *Jury Duty*, Amazon Freevee; *The Bear* and *Reservation Dogs*, FX; *The Last of Us*, *Last Week Tonight with John Oliver: Israel-Hamas War*, *Reality*, and *Somebody Somewhere*, HBO Max; *Dead Ringers*, Prime Video; *Fellow Travelers*, Showtime. Interactive/immersive: "The Hidden History of Racism in New York City," Instagram; *Pentiment*, Obsidian Entertainment; "We Are OFK," OFK; "You Destroy. We Create | The War on Ukraine's Culture," Meta Quest. News: "It's Bisan from Gaza and I'm Still Alive," Al Jazeera Media Network; "Against All Enemies," NBC 5 / KXAS-TV (Dallas-Fort Worth); "Clarence and Ginni Thomas: Politics, Power and the Supreme Court," *Frontline*, "War in the Holy Land," *PBS NewsHour*, PBS; "Hate Comes to Main Street," WTVF-TV, NewsChannel 5 (Nashville). Public service: "America and the Taliban," *Frontline*, PBS; "The Post Roe Baby Boom: Inside Mississippi's Maternal Health Crisis," *USA Today*. Radio/podcast: *The Big Dig*, GBH-News (Boston); *The Retrievals*, Serial/*NY Times*; *You Didn't See Nothin*, Invisible Institute/USG Audio; *The Empty Grave of Comrade Bishop* and "Post Reports: Surviving to Graduation," *Washington Post*.

Miscellaneous Book Awards, 2024

Coretta Scott King Awards, by American Library Assn., for African American authors and illustrators of outstanding books for children and young adults. Author: *Nigeria Jones*, Ibi Zoboi. Illustrator: *An American Story*, illustrated by Dare Coulter. New talent, author: *There Goes the Neighborhood*, Jade Adia. New talent, illustrator: *We Could Fly*, illustrated by Briana Mukodiri Uchendu.

Edgar Awards, by Mystery Writers of America. Novel: *Flags on the Bayou*, James Lee Burke. First Novel: *The Peacock and the Sparrow*, I.S. Berry. Paperback Original: *Vera Wong's Unsolicited Advice for Murderers*, Jesse Q. Sutanto. Fact Crime: *Crooked: The Roaring '20s Tale of a Corrupt Attorney General, a Crusading Senator, and the Birth of the American Political Scandal*, Nathan Masters. Critical/Biographical: *Love Me Fierce in Danger: The Life of James Ellroy*, Steven Powell. Short Story: "Hallowed Ground," Linda Castillo. Juvenile: *The Ghosts of Rancho Espanto*, Adrianna Cuevas. Young Adult: *Girl Forgotten*, April Henry. TV Episode: "Escape from Shit Mountain," *Poker Face*, Nora Zuckerman and Lilla Zuckerman. Robert L. Fish Memorial Award: "The Body in Cell Two," *Ellery Queen Mystery Magazine*, Kate Hohl. Mary Higgins Clark Award: *Play the Fool*, Lina Chern. Sue Grafton Memorial Award: *An Evil Heart*, Linda Castillo. Lilian Jackson Braun Memorial Award: *Glory Be* by Danielle Arceneaux. Grand Masters: Katherine Hall Page, R.L. Stine. Ellery Queen Award: Michaela Hamilton, Kensington Books.

Golden Kite Awards, by the Society of Children's Book Writers and Illustrators. Picture Book Text: *Nell Plants a Tree*, Anne Wynter. Picture Book Illustration: *Big*, Vashti Harrison. Middle Grade Fiction: *The Lost Year*, Katherine Marsh. Illustrated Book (older readers): *Curlfriends: New in Town*, Sharee Miller. Nonfiction text (younger readers): *Tomfoolery: Randolph Caldecott and the Rambunctious Coming-of-Age of Children's Books*, Michelle Markel. Nonfiction text (older readers): *The 21: The True Story of the Youth Who Sued the U.S. Government Over Climate Change*, Elizabeth Rusch. Young Adult Fiction: *The Blood Years*, Elana K. Arnold. Sid Fleischman Award: *To Catch a Thief*, Martha Brockenbrough.

Lambda Literary Awards. Lesbian Fiction: *Biography of X*, Catherine Lacey. Gay Fiction: *Family Meal*, Bryan Washington. Bisexual Fiction: *Natural Beauty*, Ling Ling Huang. Transgender Fiction: *Wild Geese*, Soula Emmanuel. Bisexual Nonfiction: *Creep: Accusations and Confessions*, Myriam Gurba. Transgender Nonfiction: *Miss Major Speaks: Conversations with a Black Trans Revolutionary*, Toshio Meronek and Miss Major. LGBTQ+ Nonfiction: *Hi Honey, I'm Homo!* Matt Baume.

National Book Critics Circle Awards. Fiction: Lorrie Moore, *I Am Homeless If This Is Not My Home*. Nonfiction: Roxanna Asgarian, *We Were Once a Family: A Story of Love, Death, and Child Removal in America*. Biography: Jonny Steinberg, *Winnie and Nelson: Portrait of a Marriage*. Autobiography: Safiya Sinclair, *How to Say Babylon: A Memoir*. Criticism: Tina Post, *Deadpan: The Aesthetics of Black Inexpression*. Poetry: Kim Hyesoon, trans. by Don Mee Choi, *Phantom Pain Wings*. John Leonard Prize: Tahir Hamut Izgil, trans. by Joshua L. Freeman, *Waiting to Be Arrested at Night: A Uyghur Poet's Memoir of China's Genocide*. Gregg Barrios Book in Translation: Tezer Özlü, trans. by Maureen Freely, *Cold Nights of Childhood*. Ivan Sandrof Lifetime Achievement Award: Judy Blume. Nona Balakian Citation for Excellence in Reviewing: Becca Rothfeld.

Nebula Awards, by the Science Fiction and Fantasy Writers Assn. Novel: *The Saint of Bright Doors*, Vajra Chandrasekera. Novella: *Linghun*, Ai Jiang. Novelette: "The Year Without Sunshine," Naomi Kritzer. Short Story: "Tantie Merle and the Farmhand 4200," R. S. A. Garcia. Ray Bradbury Award: *Barbie*, Greta Gerwig and Noah Baumbach. Andre Norton Award: *To Shape a Dragon's Breath*, Moniquill Blackgoose. Game Writing: *Baldur's Gate 3*, Adam Smith.

Printz Award, for young adult literature: *The Collectors: Stories*, edited by A.S. King.

Spingarn Medal, 1915-2024

The Spingarn Medal has been awarded annually in most years since 1915 by the National Assn. for the Advancement of Colored People for outstanding achievement by an African American.

1915 Ernest E. Just
1916 Charles Young
1917 Harry T. Burleigh
1918 William S. Braithwaite
1919 Archibald H. Grimké
1920 W. E. B. Du Bois
1921 Charles S. Gilpin
1922 Mary B. Talbert
1923 George W. Carver
1924 Roland Hayes
1925 James W. Johnson
1926 Carter G. Woodson
1927 Anthony Overton
1928 Charles W. Chesnutt
1929 Mordecai W. Johnson
1930 Henry A. Hunt
1931 Richard B. Harrison
1932 Robert R. Moton
1933 Max Yergan
1934 William T. B. Williams
1935 Mary McLeod Bethune
1936 John Hope
1937 Walter White
1939 Marian Anderson
1940 Louis T. Wright
1941 Richard Wright
1942 A. Philip Randolph
1943 William H. Hastie
1944 Charles Drew
1945 Paul Robeson
1946 Thurgood Marshall
1947 Dr. Percy L. Julian
1948 Channing H. Tobias
1949 Ralph J. Bunche
1950 Charles H. Houston
1951 Mabel K. Staupers
1952 Harry T. Moore
1953 Paul R. Williams
1954 Theodore K. Lawless
1955 Carl Murphy
1956 Jack R. Robinson
1957 Martin Luther King Jr.
1958 Daisy Bates and the Little Rock Nine
1959 Duke Ellington
1960 Langston Hughes
1961 Kenneth B. Clark
1962 Robert C. Weaver
1963 Medgar W. Evers
1964 Roy Wilkins
1965 Leontyne Price
1966 John H. Johnson
1967 Edward W. Brooke
1968 Sammy Davis Jr.
1969 Clarence M. Mitchell Jr.
1970 Jacob Lawrence
1971 Leon H. Sullivan
1972 Gordon Parks
1973 Wilson C. Riles
1974 Damon Keith
1976 Henry (Hank) Aaron
1977 Alvin Ailey
1977 Alex Haley
1979 Andrew Young
1979 Rosa L. Parks
1980 Dr. Rayford W. Logan
1981 Coleman Young
1982 Dr. Benjamin E. Mays
1983 Lena Horne
1985 Thomas Bradley
1985 Bill Cosby
1986 Dr. Benjamin L. Hooks
1987 Percy E. Sutton
1988 Frederick D. Patterson
1989 Jesse Jackson
1990 L. Douglas Wilder
1991 Gen. Colin L. Powell
1992 Barbara Jordan
1993 Dorothy I. Height
1994 Maya Angelou
1995 John Hope Franklin
1996 A. Leon Higginbotham Jr.
1997 Carl T. Rowan
1998 Myrlie Evers-Williams
1999 Earl G. Graves Sr.
2000 Oprah Winfrey
2001 Vernon E. Jordan Jr.
2002 John Lewis
2003 Constance Baker Motley
2004 Robert L. Carter
2005 Oliver W. Hill
2006 Dr. Benjamin S. Carson
2007 John Conyers Jr.
2008 Ruby Dee
2009 Julian Bond
2010 Cicely Tyson
2011 Frankie Muse Freeman
2012 Harry Belafonte
2013 Jessye Norman
2014 Quincy Jones
2015 Sidney Poitier
2016 Nathaniel R. Jones
2018 Willie L. Brown Jr.
2019 Patrick Gaspard
2021 Cato T. Laurencin
2022 Jim Clyburn
2023 Dr. Hazel N. Dukes
2024 Henry Louis Gates Jr.

Miss America Winners, 1921-2024

Year	Winner, hometown
1921	Margaret Gorman, Washington, DC
1922-23	Mary Campbell, Columbus, Ohio
1924	Ruth Malcolmson, Philadelphia, Pennsylvania
1925	Fay Lamphier, Oakland, California
1926	Norma Smallwood, Tulsa, Oklahoma
1927	Lois Delander, Joliet, Illinois
1933	Marion Bergeron, West Haven, Connecticut
1935	Henrietta Leaver, Pittsburgh, Pennsylvania
1936	Rose Coyle, Philadelphia, Pennsylvania
1937	Bette Cooper, Bertrand Island, New Jersey
1938	Marilyn Meseke, Marion, Ohio
1939	Patricia Donnelly, Detroit, Michigan
1940	Frances Marie Burke, Philadelphia, Pennsylvania
1941	Rosemary LaPlanche, Los Angeles, California
1942	Jo-Caroll Dennison, Tyler, Texas
1943	Jean Bartel, Los Angeles, California
1944	Venus Ramey, Washington, DC
1945	Bess Myerson, New York, New York
1946	Marilyn Buferd, Los Angeles, California
1947	Barbara Walker, Memphis, Tennessee
1948	BeBe Shopp, Hopkins, Minnesota
1949	Jacque Mercer, Litchfield, Arizona
1951	Yolande Betbeze, Mobile, Alabama
1952	Coleen Kay Hutchins, Salt Lake City, Utah
1953	Neva Jane Langley, Macon, Georgia
1954	Evelyn Margaret Ay, Ephrata, Pennsylvania
1955	Lee Meriwether, San Francisco, California
1956	Sharon Ritchie, Denver, Colorado
1957	Marian McKnight, Manning, South Carolina
1958	Marilyn Van Derbur, Denver, Colorado
1959	Mary Ann Mobley, Brandon, Mississippi
1960	Lynda Lee Mead, Natchez, Mississippi
1961	Nancy Fleming, Montague, Michigan
1962	Maria Fletcher, Asheville, North Carolina
1963	Jacquelyn Mayer, Sandusky, Ohio
1964	Donna Axum, El Dorado, Arkansas
1965	Vonda Kay Van Dyke, Phoenix, Arizona
1966	Deborah Irene Bryant, Overland Park, Kansas
1967	Jane Anne Jayroe, Laverne, Oklahoma
1968	Debra Dene Barnes, Moran, Kansas
1969	Judith Anne Ford, Belvidere, Illinois
1970	Pamela Anne Eldred, Birmingham, Michigan
1971	Phyllis Ann George, Denton, Texas
1972	Laurie Lea Schaefer, Bexley, Ohio
1973	Terry Anne Meeuwsen, DePere, Wisconsin
1974	Rebecca Ann King, Denver, Colorado
1975	Shirley Cothran, Denton, Texas
1976	Tawney Elaine Godin, Saratoga Springs, New York
1977	Dorothy Kathleen Benham, Edina, Minnesota
1978	Susan Perkins, Columbus, Ohio
1979	Kylene Barker, Roanoke, Virginia
1980	Cheryl Prewitt, Ackerman, Mississippi
1981	Susan Powell, Elk City, Oklahoma
1982	Elizabeth Ward, Russellville, Arkansas
1983	Debra Maffett, Anaheim, California
1984[1]	Suzette Charles, Mays Landing, New Jersey
1985	Sharlene Wells, Salt Lake City, Utah
1986	Susan Akin, Meridian, Mississippi
1987	Kellye Cash, Memphis, Tennessee
1988	Kaye Lani Rae Rafko, Monroe, Michigan
1989	Gretchen Carlson, Anoka, Minnesota
1990	Debbye Turner, Columbia, Missouri
1991	Marjorie Vincent, Oak Park, Illinois
1992	Carolyn Suzanne Sapp, Honolulu, Hawaii
1993	Leanza Cornett, Jacksonville, Florida
1994	Kimberly Aiken, Columbia, South Carolina
1995	Heather Whitestone, Birmingham, Alabama
1996	Shawntel Smith, Muldrow, Oklahoma
1997	Tara Dawn Holland, Overland Park, Kansas
1998	Kate Shindle, Evanston, Illinois
1999	Nicole Johnson, Roanoke, Virginia
2000	Heather Renee French, Maysville, Kentucky
2001	Angela Perez Baraquio, Honolulu, Hawaii
2002	Katie Harman, Gresham, Oregon
2003	Erika Harold, Urbana, Illinois
2004	Ericka Dunlap, Orlando, Florida
2005	Deidre Downs, Birmingham, Alabama
2006	Jennifer Berry, Tulsa, Oklahoma
2007	Lauren Nelson, Lawton, Oklahoma
2008	Kirsten Haglund, Farmington Hills, Michigan
2009	Katie Stam, Seymour, Indiana
2010	Caressa Cameron, Fredricksburg, Virginia
2011	Teresa Scanlan, Gering, Nebraska
2012	Laura Kaeppeler, Kenosha, Wisconsin
2013	Mallory Hytes Hagen, Brooklyn, New York
2014	Nina Davuluri, Syracuse, New York
2015	Kira Kazantsev, New York, New York
2016	Betty Cantrell, Warner Robins, Georgia
2017	Savvy Shields, Fayetteville, Arkansas
2018	Cara Mund, Bismarck, North Dakota
2019	Nia Franklin, Brooklyn, New York
2020	Camille Schrier, Richmond, Virginia
2022	Emma Broyles, Anchorage, Alaska
2023	Grace Stanke, Wausau, Wisconsin
2024	Madison Marsh, Colorado

(1) Miss New York, Vanessa Williams, resigned July 23, 1984.

Tony (Antoinette Perry) Awards, 2024

Play: *Stereophonic*, David Adjmi
Musical: *The Outsiders*
Book of a musical: *Suffs*, Shaina Taub
Original score: *Suffs*, Shaina Taub
Play revival: *Appropriate*
Musical revival: *Merrily We Roll Along*
Actor, play: Jeremy Strong, *An Enemy of the People*
Actress, play: Sarah Paulson, *Appropriate*
Actor, musical: Jonathan Groff, *Merrily We Roll Along*
Actress, musical: Maleah Joi Moon, *Hell's Kitchen*
Featured actor, play: Will Brill, *Stereophonic*
Featured actress, play: Kara Young, *Purlie Victorious: A Non-Confederate Romp Through the Cotton Patch*
Featured actor, musical: Daniel Radcliffe, *Merrily We Roll Along*
Featured actress, musical: Kecia Lewis, *Hell's Kitchen*
Direction, play: Daniel Aukin, *Stereophonic*
Direction, musical: Danya Taymor, *The Outsiders*
Choreography: Justin Peck, *Illinoise*
Orchestrations: Jonathan Tunick, *Merrily We Roll Along*
Costume design, play: Dede Ayite, *Jaja's African Hair Braiding*
Costume design, musical: Linda Cho, *The Great Gatsby*
Lighting design, play: Jane Cox, *Appropriate*
Lighting design, musical: Brian MacDevitt and Hana S. Kim, *The Outsiders*
Scenic design, play: David Zinn, *Stereophonic*
Scenic design, musical: Tom Scutt, *Cabaret at the Kit Kat Club*
Sound design, play: Ryan Rumery, *Stereophonic*
Sound design, musical: Cody Spencer, *The Outsiders*
Regional theatre: Wilma Theater, Philadelphia
Special Tony Award: Alex Edelman, Abe Jacob, Nikiya Mathis
Special Tony Award, lifetime achievement: Jack O'Brien, George C. Wolfe
Isabelle Stevenson Award: Billy Porter

Tony Awards, 1948-2024

Year	Play	Musical
1948	*Mister Roberts*	No award
1949	*Death of a Salesman*	*Kiss Me Kate*
1950	*The Cocktail Party*	*South Pacific*
1951	*The Rose Tattoo*	*Guys and Dolls*
1952	*The Fourposter*	*The King and I*
1953	*The Crucible*	*Wonderful Town*
1954	*The Teahouse of the August Moon*	*Kismet*
1955	*The Desperate Hours*	*The Pajama Game*
1956	*The Diary of Anne Frank*	*Damn Yankees*
1957	*Long Day's Journey Into Night*	*My Fair Lady*
1958	*Sunrise at Campobello*	*The Music Man*
1959	*J.B.*	*Redhead*
1960	*The Miracle Worker*	*Fiorello!* and *The Sound of Music*
1961	*Becket*	*Bye, Bye Birdie*
1962	*A Man for All Seasons*	*How to Succeed in Business Without Really Trying*
1963	*Who's Afraid of Virginia Woolf?*	*A Funny Thing Happened on the Way to the Forum*
1964	*Luther*	*Hello, Dolly!*
1965	*The Subject Was Roses*	*Fiddler on the Roof*
1966	*Marat/Sade*	*Man of La Mancha*
1967	*The Homecoming*	*Cabaret*
1968	*Rosencrantz and Guildenstern Are Dead*	*Hallelujah, Baby!*
1969	*The Great White Hope*	*1776*
1970	*Borstal Boy*	*Applause*
1971	*Sleuth*	*Company*
1972	*Sticks and Bones*	*Two Gentlemen of Verona*
1973	*That Championship Season*	*A Little Night Music*
1974	*The River Niger*	*Raisin*
1975	*Equus*	*The Wiz*
1976	*Travesties*	*A Chorus Line*
1977	*The Shadow Box*	*Annie*
1978	*Da*	*Ain't Misbehavin'*
1979	*The Elephant Man*	*Sweeney Todd*
1980	*Children of a Lesser God*	*Evita*
1981	*Amadeus*	*42nd Street*
1982	*The Life and Adventures of Nicholas Nickelby*	*Nine*
1983	*Torch Song Trilogy*	*Cats*
1984	*The Real Thing*	*La Cage aux Folles*
1985	*Biloxi Blues*	*Big River*
1986	*I'm Not Rappaport*	*The Mystery of Edwin Drood*
1987	*Fences*	*Les Misérables*
1988	*M. Butterfly*	*Phantom of the Opera*
1989	*The Heidi Chronicles*	*Jerome Robbins' Broadway*
1990	*The Grapes of Wrath*	*City of Angels*
1991	*Lost in Yonkers*	*The Will Rogers Follies*
1992	*Dancing at Lughnasa*	*Crazy for You*
1993	*Angels in America: Millennium Approaches*	*Kiss of the Spider Woman*
1994	*Angels in America: Perestroika*	*Passion*
1995	*Love! Valour! Compassion!*	*Sunset Boulevard*
1996	*Master Class*	*Rent*
1997	*The Last Night of Ballyhoo*	*Titanic*
1998	*Art*	*The Lion King*
1999	*Side Man*	*Fosse*
2000	*Copenhagen*	*Contact*
2001	*Proof*	*The Producers*
2002	*Edward Albee's The Goat or Who Is Sylvia?*	*Thoroughly Modern Millie*
2003	*Take Me Out*	*Hairspray*
2004	*I Am My Own Wife*	*Avenue Q*
2005	*Doubt*	*Monty Python's Spamalot*
2006	*The History Boys*	*Jersey Boys*
2007	*The Coast of Utopia*	*Spring Awakening*
2008	*August: Osage County*	*In the Heights*
2009	*God of Carnage*	*Billy Elliot, The Musical*
2010	*Red*	*Memphis*
2011	*War Horse*	*The Book of Mormon*
2012	*Clybourne Park*	*Once*
2013	*Vanya and Sonia and Masha and Spike*	*Kinky Boots*
2014	*All the Way*	*A Gentleman's Guide to Love & Murder*
2015	*The Curious Incident of the Dog in the Night-Time*	*Fun Home*
2016	*The Humans*	*Hamilton*
2017	*Oslo*	*Dear Evan Hansen*
2018	*Harry Potter and the Cursed Child, Parts One and Two*	*The Band's Visit*
2019	*The Ferryman*	*Hadestown*
2020	*The Inheritance*	*Moulin Rouge!*
2022	*The Lehman Trilogy*	*A Strange Loop*
2023	*Leopoldstadt*	*Kimberly Akimbo*
2024	*Stereophonic*	*The Outsiders*

Selected Prime-Time Emmy Awards, 2023

Drama series: *Succession*, HBO Max
Comedy series: *The Bear*, FX
Limited series: *Beef*, Netflix
Reality competition program: *RuPaul's Drag Race*, MTV
Scripted variety series: *Last Week Tonight With John Oliver*, HBO Max
Talk series: *The Daily Show With Trevor Noah*, Comedy Central
Lead actor, drama: Kieran Culkin, *Succession*, HBO Max
Lead actress, drama: Sarah Snook, *Succession*, HBO Max
Lead actor, comedy: Jeremy Allen White, *The Bear*, FX
Lead actress, comedy: Quinta Brunson, *Abbott Elementary*, ABC
Lead actor, limited series: Steven Yeun, *Beef*, Netflix
Lead actress, limited series: Ali Wong, *Beef*, Netflix
Sup. actor, drama: Matthew Macfadyen, *Succession*, HBO Max
Sup. actress, drama: Jennifer Coolidge, *The White Lotus*, HBO Max
Sup. actor, comedy: Ebon Moss-Bachrach, *The Bear*, FX
Sup. actress, comedy: Ayo Edebiri, *The Bear*, FX
Sup. actor, limited series: Paul Walter Hauser, *Black Bird*, Apple TV+
Sup. actress, limited series: Niecy Nash-Betts, *Dahmer – Monster: The Jeffrey Dahmer Story*, Netflix

Selected Prime-Time Emmy Awards, 2024

Drama series: *Shogun*, FX
Comedy series: *Hacks*, HBO Max
Limited series: *Baby Reindeer*, Netflix
Reality competition program: *The Traitors*, Peacock
Scripted variety series: *Last Week Tonight With John Oliver*, HBO Max
Talk series: *The Daily Show*, Comedy Central
Lead actor, drama: Hiroyuki Sanada, *Shogun*, FX
Lead actress, drama: Anna Sawai, *Shogun*, FX
Lead actor, comedy: Jeremy Allen White, *The Bear*, FX
Lead actress, comedy: Jean Smart, *Hacks*, HBO Max
Lead actor, limited series: Richard Gadd, *Baby Reindeer*, Netflix
Lead actress, limited series: Jodie Foster, *True Detective: Night Country*, HBO Max
Sup. actor, drama: Billy Crudup, *The Morning Show*, Apple TV+
Sup. actress, drama: Elizabeth Debicki, *The Crown*, Netflix
Sup. actor, comedy: Ebon Moss-Bachrach, *The Bear*, FX
Sup. actress, comedy: Liza Colón-Zayas, *The Bear*, FX
Sup. actor, limited series: Lamorne Morris, *Fargo*, FX
Sup. actress, limited series: Jessica Gunning, *Baby Reindeer*, Netflix

Prime-Time Emmy Awards, 1952-2024

The Academy of Television Arts and Sciences presented the first Emmy Awards in 1949. Through the years, award categories have changed, but since 1952, the Academy has given out an outstanding comedy and drama award annually.

Year	Comedy	Drama
1952	*Red Skelton Show*, NBC	*Studio One*, CBS
1953	*I Love Lucy*, CBS	*Robert Montgomery Presents*, NBC
1954	*I Love Lucy*, CBS	*The U.S. Steel Hour*, ABC
1955	*Make Room for Daddy*, ABC	*The U.S. Steel Hour*, ABC
1956	*Phil Silvers Show*, CBS	*Producers' Showcase*, NBC
1957	*Phil Silvers Show*, CBS	"Requiem for a Heavyweight," CBS[1]
1958	*Phil Silvers Show*, CBS	*Gunsmoke*, CBS
1959[2]	*Jack Benny Show*, CBS	2 awards[3]
1960	*Art Carney Special*, NBC	*Playhouse 90*, CBS
1961	*Jack Benny Show*, CBS	*Hallmark Hall of Fame: Macbeth*, NBC
1962	*Bob Newhart Show*, CBS	*The Defenders*, CBS
1963	*Dick Van Dyke Show*, CBS	*The Defenders*, CBS
1964	*Dick Van Dyke Show*, CBS	*The Defenders*, CBS
1965	*Dick Van Dyke Show*, CBS	*Hallmark Hall of Fame: The Magnificent Yankee*, NBC
1966	*Dick Van Dyke Show*, CBS	*The Fugitive*, ABC
1967	*The Monkees*, NBC	*Mission: Impossible*, CBS
1968	*Get Smart*, NBC	*Mission: Impossible*, CBS
1969	*Get Smart*, NBC	*NET Playhouse*, NET
1970	*My World and Welcome to It*, NBC	*Marcus Welby, M.D.*, ABC
1971	*All in the Family*, CBS	*The Bold Ones: The Senator*, NBC
1972	*All in the Family*, CBS	*Masterpiece Theatre: Elizabeth R*, PBS
1973	*All in the Family*, CBS	*The Waltons*, CBS
1974	*M*A*S*H*, CBS	*Masterpiece Theatre: Upstairs, Downstairs*; PBS
1975	*Mary Tyler Moore Show*, CBS	*Masterpiece Theatre: Upstairs, Downstairs*; PBS
1976	*Mary Tyler Moore Show*, CBS	*Police Story*, NBC
1977	*Mary Tyler Moore Show*, CBS	*Masterpiece Theatre: Upstairs, Downstairs*; PBS
1978	*All in the Family*, CBS	*The Rockford Files*, NBC
1979	*Taxi*, ABC	*Lou Grant*, CBS
1980	*Taxi*, ABC	*Lou Grant*, CBS
1981	*Taxi*, ABC	*Hill Street Blues*, NBC
1982	*Barney Miller*, ABC	*Hill Street Blues*, NBC
1983	*Cheers*, NBC	*Hill Street Blues*, NBC
1984	*Cheers*, NBC	*Hill Street Blues*, NBC
1985	*The Cosby Show*, NBC	*Cagney & Lacey*, CBS
1986	*Golden Girls*, NBC	*Cagney & Lacey*, CBS
1987	*Golden Girls*, NBC	*L.A. Law*, NBC
1988	*The Wonder Years*, ABC	*thirtysomething*, ABC
1989	*Cheers*, NBC	*L.A. Law*, NBC
1990	*Murphy Brown*, CBS	*L.A. Law*, NBC
1991	*Cheers*, NBC	*L.A. Law*, NBC
1992	*Murphy Brown*, CBS	*Northern Exposure*, CBS
1993	*Seinfeld*, NBC	*Picket Fences*, CBS
1994	*Frasier*, NBC	*Picket Fences*, CBS
1995	*Frasier*, NBC	*NYPD Blue*, ABC
1996	*Frasier*, NBC	*ER*, NBC
1997	*Frasier*, NBC	*Law & Order*, NBC
1998	*Frasier*, NBC	*The Practice*, ABC
1999	*Ally McBeal*, FOX	*The Practice*, ABC
2000	*Will & Grace*, NBC	*The West Wing*, NBC
2001	*Sex and the City*, HBO	*The West Wing*, NBC
2002	*Friends*, NBC	*The West Wing*, NBC
2003	*Everybody Loves Raymond*, CBS	*The West Wing*, NBC
2004	*Arrested Development*, FOX	*The Sopranos*, HBO
2005	*Everybody Loves Raymond*, CBS	*Lost*, ABC
2006	*The Office*, NBC	*24*, FOX
2007	*30 Rock*, NBC	*The Sopranos*, HBO
2008	*30 Rock*, NBC	*Mad Men*, AMC
2009	*30 Rock*, NBC	*Mad Men*, AMC
2010	*Modern Family*, ABC	*Mad Men*, AMC
2011	*Modern Family*, ABC	*Mad Men*, AMC
2012	*Modern Family*, ABC	*Homeland*, Showtime
2013	*Modern Family*, ABC	*Breaking Bad*, AMC
2014	*Modern Family*, ABC	*Breaking Bad*, AMC
2015	*Veep*, HBO	*Game of Thrones*, HBO
2016	*Veep*, HBO	*Game of Thrones*, HBO
2017	*Veep*, HBO	*The Handmaid's Tale*, Hulu
2018	*The Marvelous Mrs. Maisel*, Amazon	*Game of Thrones*, HBO
2019	*Fleabag*, Amazon	*Game of Thrones*, HBO
2020	*Schitt's Creek*, Pop	*Succession*, HBO
2021	*Ted Lasso*, Apple TV+	*The Crown*, Netflix
2022	*Ted Lasso*, Apple TV+	*Succession*, HBO
2023	*The Bear*, FX	*Succession*, HBO Max
2024	*Hacks*, HBO Max	*Shogun*, FX

(1) Best single program of the year; shown on *Playhouse 90*, which was named best new series. (2) Beginning in 1959, Emmys were awarded for work in the season encompassing the previous and current year. (3) *Playhouse 90* (CBS) was best dramatic series of one hour or longer, *Alcoa-Goodyear Theatre* (NBC) of less than one hour.

Golden Globe Awards, 2024

Film

Drama: *Oppenheimer*
Comedy/musical: *Poor Things*
Actress, drama: Lily Gladstone, *Killers of the Flower Moon*
Actor, drama: Cillian Murphy, *Oppenheimer*
Actress, comedy/musical: Emma Stone, *Poor Things*
Actor, comedy/musical: Paul Giamatti, *The Holdovers*
Supporting actress: Da'Vine Joy Randolph, *The Holdovers*
Supporting actor: Robert Downey Jr., *Oppenheimer*
Director: Christopher Nolan, *Oppenheimer*
Screenplay: Justine Triet, Arthur Harari, *Anatomy of a Fall*
Animated film: *The Boy and the Heron*
Cinematic and box office achievement: *Barbie*
Non-English-language film: *Anatomy of a Fall*
Original score: Ludwig Göransson, *Oppenheimer*
Original song: "What Was I Made For?" *Barbie*, Billie Eilish, Finneas O'Connell

Television

Series, drama: *Succession*, HBO Max
Series, comedy/musical: *The Bear*, FX
Limited series or made-for-TV movie: *Beef*, Netflix
Actress, drama: Sarah Snook, *Succession*, HBO Max
Actor, drama: Kieran Culkin, *Succession*, HBO Max
Actress, comedy/musical: Ayo Edebiri, *The Bear*, FX
Actor, comedy/musical: Jeremy Allen White, *The Bear*, FX
Actress, limited series/TV movie: Ali Wong, *Beef*, Netflix
Actor, limited series/TV movie: Steven Yeun, *Beef*, Netflix
Supporting actress, TV: Elizabeth Debicki, *The Crown*, Netflix
Supporting actor, TV: Matthew Macfadyen, *Succession*, HBO Max
Performance in a Stand-Up Comedy: Ricky Gervais, *Armageddon*

Academy Awards (Oscars), 1927-2023

Year indicates date of film's release; awards ceremony held in subsequent year.

Year	Picture	Actor	Actress	Supporting actor[1]	Supporting actress[1]	Director
1927 -28	*Wings*	Emil Jannings *The Way of All Flesh*	Janet Gaynor *Seventh Heaven*	NA	NA	Frank Borzage *Seventh Heaven*; Lewis Milestone *Two Arabian Knights*
1928 -29	*Broadway Melody*	Warner Baxter *In Old Arizona*	Mary Pickford *Coquette*	NA	NA	Frank Lloyd *The Divine Lady*
1929 -30	*All Quiet on the Western Front*	George Arliss *Disraeli*	Norma Shearer *The Divorcee*	NA	NA	Lewis Milestone *All Quiet on the Western Front*
1930 -31	*Cimarron*	Lionel Barrymore *Free Soul*	Marie Dressler *Min and Bill*	NA	NA	Norman Taurog *Skippy*
1931 -32	*Grand Hotel*	Fredric March *Dr. Jekyll and Mr. Hyde*; Wallace Beery *The Champ*	Helen Hayes *The Sin of Madelon Claudet*	NA	NA	Frank Borzage *Bad Girl*
1932 -33	*Cavalcade*	Charles Laughton *The Private Life of Henry VIII*	Katharine Hepburn *Morning Glory*	NA	NA	Frank Lloyd *Cavalcade*
1934	*It Happened One Night*	Clark Gable *It Happened One Night*	Claudette Colbert *It Happened One Night*	NA	NA	Frank Capra *It Happened One Night*
1935	*Mutiny on the Bounty*	Victor McLaglen *The Informer*	Bette Davis *Dangerous*	NA	NA	John Ford *The Informer*
1936	*The Great Ziegfeld*	Paul Muni *The Story of Louis Pasteur*	Luise Rainer *The Great Ziegfeld*	Walter Brennan *Come and Get It*	Gale Sondergaard *Anthony Adverse*	Frank Capra *Mr. Deeds Goes to Town*
1937	*The Life of Emile Zola*	Spencer Tracy *Captains Courageous*	Luise Rainer *The Good Earth*	Joseph Schildkraut *The Life of Emile Zola*	Alice Brady *In Old Chicago*	Leo McCarey *The Awful Truth*
1938	*You Can't Take It With You*	Spencer Tracy *Boys Town*	Bette Davis *Jezebel*	Walter Brennan *Kentucky*	Fay Bainter *Jezebel*	Frank Capra *You Can't Take It With You*
1939	*Gone With the Wind*	Robert Donat *Goodbye, Mr. Chips*	Vivien Leigh *Gone With the Wind*	Thomas Mitchell *Stage Coach*	Hattie McDaniel *Gone With the Wind*	Victor Fleming *Gone With the Wind*
1940	*Rebecca*	James Stewart *The Philadelphia Story*	Ginger Rogers *Kitty Foyle*	Walter Brennan *The Westerner*	Jane Darwell *The Grapes of Wrath*	John Ford *The Grapes of Wrath*
1941	*How Green Was My Valley*	Gary Cooper *Sergeant York*	Joan Fontaine *Suspicion*	Donald Crisp *How Green Was My Valley*	Mary Astor *The Great Lie*	John Ford *How Green Was My Valley*
1942	*Mrs. Miniver*	James Cagney *Yankee Doodle Dandy*	Greer Garson *Mrs. Miniver*	Van Heflin *Johnny Eager*	Teresa Wright *Mrs. Miniver*	William Wyler *Mrs. Miniver*
1943	*Casablanca*	Paul Lukas *Watch on the Rhine*	Jennifer Jones *The Song of Bernadette*	Charles Coburn *The More the Merrier*	Katina Paxinou *For Whom the Bell Tolls*	Michael Curtiz *Casablanca*
1944	*Going My Way*	Bing Crosby *Going My Way*	Ingrid Bergman *Gaslight*	Barry Fitzgerald *Going My Way*	Ethel Barrymore *None But the Lonely Heart*	Leo McCarey *Going My Way*
1945	*The Lost Weekend*	Ray Milland *The Lost Weekend*	Joan Crawford *Mildred Pierce*	James Dunn *A Tree Grows in Brooklyn*	Anne Revere *National Velvet*	Billy Wilder *The Lost Weekend*
1946	*The Best Years of Our Lives*	Fredric March *The Best Years of Our Lives*	Olivia de Havilland *To Each His Own*	Harold Russell *The Best Years of Our Lives*	Anne Baxter *The Razor's Edge*	William Wyler *The Best Years of Our Lives*
1947	*Gentleman's Agreement*	Ronald Colman *A Double Life*	Loretta Young *The Farmer's Daughter*	Edmund Gwenn *Miracle on 34th Street*	Celeste Holm *Gentleman's Agreement*	Elia Kazan *Gentleman's Agreement*
1948	*Hamlet*	Laurence Olivier *Hamlet*	Jane Wyman *Johnny Belinda*	Walter Huston *The Treasure of the Sierra Madre*	Claire Trevor *Key Largo*	John Huston *The Treasure of the Sierra Madre*
1949	*All the King's Men*	Broderick Crawford *All the King's Men*	Olivia de Havilland *The Heiress*	Dean Jagger *Twelve O'Clock High*	Mercedes McCambridge *All the King's Men*	Joseph L. Mankiewicz *Letter to Three Wives*
1950	*All About Eve*	José Ferrer *Cyrano de Bergerac*	Judy Holliday *Born Yesterday*	George Sanders *All About Eve*	Josephine Hull *Harvey*	Joseph L. Mankiewicz *All About Eve*
1951	*An American in Paris*	Humphrey Bogart *The African Queen*	Vivien Leigh *A Streetcar Named Desire*	Karl Malden *A Streetcar Named Desire*	Kim Hunter *A Streetcar Named Desire*	George Stevens *A Place in the Sun*
1952	*The Greatest Show on Earth*	Gary Cooper *High Noon*	Shirley Booth *Come Back, Little Sheba*	Anthony Quinn *Viva Zapata!*	Gloria Grahame *The Bad and the Beautiful*	John Ford *The Quiet Man*
1953	*From Here to Eternity*	William Holden *Stalag 17*	Audrey Hepburn *Roman Holiday*	Frank Sinatra *From Here to Eternity*	Donna Reed *From Here to Eternity*	Fred Zinnemann *From Here to Eternity*

Year	Picture	Actor	Actress	Supporting actor[1]	Supporting actress[1]	Director
1954	*On the Waterfront*	Marlon Brando *On the Waterfront*	Grace Kelly *The Country Girl*	Edmond O'Brien, *The Barefoot Contessa*	Eva Marie Saint *On the Waterfront*	Elia Kazan *On the Waterfront*
1955	*Marty*	Ernest Borgnine *Marty*	Anna Magnani *The Rose Tattoo*	Jack Lemmon *Mister Roberts*	Jo Van Fleet *East of Eden*	Delbert Mann *Marty*
1956	*Around the World in 80 Days*	Yul Brynner *The King and I*	Ingrid Bergman *Anastasia*	Anthony Quinn *Lust for Life*	Dorothy Malone *Written on the Wind*	George Stevens *Giant*
1957	*The Bridge on the River Kwai*	Alec Guinness *The Bridge on the River Kwai*	Joanne Woodward *The Three Faces of Eve*	Red Buttons *Sayonara*	Miyoshi Umeki *Sayonara*	David Lean *The Bridge on the River Kwai*
1958	*Gigi*	David Niven *Separate Tables*	Susan Hayward *I Want to Live*	Burl Ives *The Big Country*	Wendy Hiller *Separate Tables*	Vincente Minnelli *Gigi*
1959	*Ben-Hur*	Charlton Heston *Ben-Hur*	Simone Signoret *Room at the Top*	Hugh Griffith *Ben-Hur*	Shelley Winters *Diary of Anne Frank*	William Wyler *Ben-Hur*
1960	*The Apartment*	Burt Lancaster *Elmer Gantry*	Elizabeth Taylor *Butterfield 8*	Peter Ustinov *Spartacus*	Shirley Jones *Elmer Gantry*	Billy Wilder *The Apartment*
1961	*West Side Story*	Maximilian Schell *Judgment at Nuremberg*	Sophia Loren *Two Women*	George Chakiris *West Side Story*	Rita Moreno *West Side Story*	Jerome Robbins and Robert Wise *West Side Story*
1962	*Lawrence of Arabia*	Gregory Peck *To Kill a Mockingbird*	Anne Bancroft *The Miracle Worker*	Ed Begley *Sweet Bird of Youth*	Patty Duke *The Miracle Worker*	David Lean *Lawrence of Arabia*
1963	*Tom Jones*	Sidney Poitier *Lilies of the Field*	Patricia Neal *Hud*	Melvyn Douglas *Hud*	Margaret Rutherford *The V.I.P.s*	Tony Richardson *Tom Jones*
1964	*My Fair Lady*	Rex Harrison *My Fair Lady*	Julie Andrews *Mary Poppins*	Peter Ustinov *Topkapi*	Lila Kedrova *Zorba the Greek*	George Cukor *My Fair Lady*
1965	*The Sound of Music*	Lee Marvin *Cat Ballou*	Julie Christie *Darling*	Martin Balsam *A Thousand Clowns*	Shelley Winters *A Patch of Blue*	Robert Wise *The Sound of Music*
1966	*A Man for All Seasons*	Paul Scofield *A Man for All Seasons*	Elizabeth Taylor *Who's Afraid of Virginia Woolf?*	Walter Matthau *The Fortune Cookie*	Sandy Dennis *Who's Afraid of Virginia Woolf?*	Fred Zinnemann *A Man for All Seasons*
1967	*In the Heat of the Night*	Rod Steiger *In the Heat of the Night*	Katharine Hepburn *Guess Who's Coming to Dinner*	George Kennedy *Cool Hand Luke*	Estelle Parsons *Bonnie and Clyde*	Mike Nichols *The Graduate*
1968	*Oliver!*	Cliff Robertson *Charly*	Katharine Hepburn *The Lion in Winter*; Barbra Streisand *Funny Girl*	Jack Albertson *The Subject Was Roses*	Ruth Gordon *Rosemary's Baby*	Carol Reed *Oliver!*
1969	*Midnight Cowboy*	John Wayne *True Grit*	Maggie Smith *The Prime of Miss Jean Brodie*	Gig Young *They Shoot Horses, Don't They?*	Goldie Hawn *Cactus Flower*	John Schlesinger *Midnight Cowboy*
1970	*Patton*	George C. Scott *Patton* (refused)	Glenda Jackson *Women in Love*	John Mills *Ryan's Daughter*	Helen Hayes *Airport*	Franklin Schaffner *Patton*
1971	*The French Connection*	Gene Hackman *The French Connection*	Jane Fonda *Klute*	Ben Johnson *The Last Picture Show*	Cloris Leachman *The Last Picture Show*	William Friedkin *The French Connection*
1972	*The Godfather*	Marlon Brando *The Godfather* (refused)	Liza Minnelli *Cabaret*	Joel Grey *Cabaret*	Eileen Heckart *Butterflies Are Free*	Bob Fosse *Cabaret*
1973	*The Sting*	Jack Lemmon *Save the Tiger*	Glenda Jackson *A Touch of Class*	John Houseman *The Paper Chase*	Tatum O'Neal *Paper Moon*	George Roy Hill *The Sting*
1974	*The Godfather Part II*	Art Carney *Harry and Tonto*	Ellen Burstyn *Alice Doesn't Live Here Anymore*	Robert DeNiro *The Godfather Part II*	Ingrid Bergman *Murder on the Orient Express*	Francis Ford Coppola *The Godfather Part II*
1975	*One Flew Over the Cuckoo's Nest*	Jack Nicholson *One Flew Over the Cuckoo's Nest*	Louise Fletcher *One Flew Over the Cuckoo's Nest*	George Burns *The Sunshine Boys*	Lee Grant *Shampoo*	Milos Forman *One Flew Over the Cuckoo's Nest*
1976	*Rocky*	Peter Finch *Network*	Faye Dunaway *Network*	Jason Robards, *All the President's Men*	Beatrice Straight *Network*	John G. Avildsen *Rocky*
1977	*Annie Hall*	Richard Dreyfuss *The Goodbye Girl*	Diane Keaton *Annie Hall*	Jason Robards *Julia*	Vanessa Redgrave *Julia*	Woody Allen *Annie Hall*
1978	*The Deer Hunter*	Jon Voight *Coming Home*	Jane Fonda *Coming Home*	Christopher Walken *The Deer Hunter*	Maggie Smith *California Suite*	Michael Cimino *The Deer Hunter*
1979	*Kramer vs. Kramer*	Dustin Hoffman *Kramer vs. Kramer*	Sally Field *Norma Rae*	Melvyn Douglas *Being There*	Meryl Streep *Kramer vs. Kramer*	Robert Benton *Kramer vs. Kramer*
1980	*Ordinary People*	Robert DeNiro *Raging Bull*	Sissy Spacek *Coal Miner's Daughter*	Timothy Hutton *Ordinary People*	Mary Steenburgen *Melvin and Howard*	Robert Redford *Ordinary People*
1981	*Chariots of Fire*	Henry Fonda *On Golden Pond*	Katharine Hepburn *On Golden Pond*	John Gielgud *Arthur*	Maureen Stapleton *Reds*	Warren Beatty *Reds*
1982	*Gandhi*	Ben Kingsley *Gandhi*	Meryl Streep *Sophie's Choice*	Louis Gossett Jr. *An Officer and a Gentleman*	Jessica Lange *Tootsie*	Richard Attenborough *Gandhi*
1983	*Terms of Endearment*	Robert Duvall *Tender Mercies*	Shirley MacLaine *Terms of Endearment*	Jack Nicholson *Terms of Endearment*	Linda Hunt *The Year of Living Dangerously*	James L. Brooks *Terms of Endearment*
1984	*Amadeus*	F. Murray Abraham *Amadeus*	Sally Field *Places in the Heart*	Haing S. Ngor *The Killing Fields*	Peggy Ashcroft *A Passage to India*	Milos Forman *Amadeus*
1985	*Out of Africa*	William Hurt *Kiss of the Spider Woman*	Geraldine Page *The Trip to Bountiful*	Don Ameche *Cocoon*	Anjelica Huston *Prizzi's Honor*	Sydney Pollack *Out of Africa*
1986	*Platoon*	Paul Newman *The Color of Money*	Marlee Matlin *Children of a Lesser God*	Michael Caine *Hannah and Her Sisters*	Dianne Wiest *Hannah and Her Sisters*	Oliver Stone *Platoon*

Year	Picture	Actor	Actress	Supporting actor[1]	Supporting actress[1]	Director
1987	*The Last Emperor*	Michael Douglas *Wall Street*	Cher *Moonstruck*	Sean Connery *The Untouchables*	Olympia Dukakis *Moonstruck*	Bernardo Bertolucci *The Last Emperor*
1988	*Rain Man*	Dustin Hoffman *Rain Man*	Jodie Foster *The Accused*	Kevin Kline *A Fish Called Wanda*	Geena Davis *The Accidental Tourist*	Barry Levinson *Rain Man*
1989	*Driving Miss Daisy*	Daniel Day-Lewis *My Left Foot*	Jessica Tandy *Driving Miss Daisy*	Denzel Washington *Glory*	Brenda Fricker *My Left Foot*	Oliver Stone, *Born on the Fourth of July*
1990	*Dances With Wolves*	Jeremy Irons *Reversal of Fortune*	Kathy Bates *Misery*	Joe Pesci *Goodfellas*	Whoopi Goldberg *Ghost*	Kevin Costner *Dances With Wolves*
1991	*The Silence of the Lambs*	Anthony Hopkins *The Silence of the Lambs*	Jodie Foster *The Silence of the Lambs*	Jack Palance *City Slickers*	Mercedes Ruehl *The Fisher King*	Jonathan Demme *The Silence of the Lambs*
1992	*Unforgiven*	Al Pacino *Scent of a Woman*	Emma Thompson *Howards End*	Gene Hackman *Unforgiven*	Marisa Tomei *My Cousin Vinny*	Clint Eastwood *Unforgiven*
1993	*Schindler's List*	Tom Hanks *Philadelphia*	Holly Hunter *The Piano*	Tommy Lee Jones *The Fugitive*	Anna Paquin *The Piano*	Steven Spielberg *Schindler's List*
1994	*Forrest Gump*	Tom Hanks *Forrest Gump*	Jessica Lange *Blue Sky*	Martin Landau *Ed Wood*	Dianne Wiest, *Bullets Over Broadway*	Robert Zemeckis *Forrest Gump*
1995	*Braveheart*	Nicolas Cage *Leaving Las Vegas*	Susan Sarandon *Dead Man Walking*	Kevin Spacey *The Usual Suspects*	Mira Sorvino *Mighty Aphrodite*	Mel Gibson *Braveheart*
1996	*The English Patient*	Geoffrey Rush *Shine*	Frances McDormand *Fargo*	Cuba Gooding Jr. *Jerry Maguire*	Juliette Binoche *The English Patient*	Anthony Minghella *The English Patient*
1997	*Titanic*	Jack Nicholson *As Good As It Gets*	Helen Hunt *As Good As It Gets*	Robin Williams *Good Will Hunting*	Kim Basinger *L.A. Confidential*	James Cameron *Titanic*
1998	*Shakespeare in Love*	Roberto Benigni *Life Is Beautiful*	Gwyneth Paltrow *Shakespeare in Love*	James Coburn *Affliction*	Judi Dench *Shakespeare in Love*	Steven Spielberg *Saving Private Ryan*
1999	*American Beauty*	Kevin Spacey *American Beauty*	Hilary Swank *Boys Don't Cry*	Michael Caine, *The Cider House Rules*	Angelina Jolie *Girl, Interrupted*	Sam Mendes *American Beauty*
2000	*Gladiator*	Russell Crowe *Gladiator*	Julia Roberts *Erin Brockovich*	Benicio Del Toro *Traffic*	Marcia Gay Harden *Pollock*	Steven Soderbergh *Traffic*
2001	*A Beautiful Mind*	Denzel Washington *Training Day*	Halle Berry *Monster's Ball*	Jim Broadbent *Iris*	Jennifer Connelly *A Beautiful Mind*	Ron Howard *A Beautiful Mind*
2002	*Chicago*	Adrien Brody *The Pianist*	Nicole Kidman *The Hours*	Chris Cooper *Adaptation*	Catherine Zeta-Jones, *Chicago*	Roman Polanski *The Pianist*
2003	*The Lord of the Rings: The Return of the King*	Sean Penn *Mystic River*	Charlize Theron *Monster*	Tim Robbins *Mystic River*	Renée Zellweger *Cold Mountain*	Peter Jackson *The Lord of the Rings: The Return of the King*
2004	*Million Dollar Baby*	Jamie Foxx *Ray*	Hilary Swank *Million Dollar Baby*	Morgan Freeman *Million Dollar Baby*	Cate Blanchett *The Aviator*	Clint Eastwood *Million Dollar Baby*
2005	*Crash*	Philip Seymour Hoffman *Capote*	Reese Witherspoon *Walk the Line*	George Clooney *Syriana*	Rachel Weisz *The Constant Gardener*	Ang Lee *Brokeback Mountain*
2006	*The Departed*	Forest Whitaker, *The Last King of Scotland*	Helen Mirren *The Queen*	Alan Arkin *Little Miss Sunshine*	Jennifer Hudson *Dreamgirls*	Martin Scorsese *The Departed*
2007	*No Country for Old Men*	Daniel Day-Lewis *There Will Be Blood*	Marion Cotillard *La Vie en Rose*	Javier Bardem *No Country for Old Men*	Tilda Swinton *Michael Clayton*	Joel Coen and Ethan Coen, *No Country for Old Men*
2008	*Slumdog Millionaire*	Sean Penn *Milk*	Kate Winslet *The Reader*	Heath Ledger *The Dark Knight*	Penelope Cruz, *Vicky Cristina Barcelona*	Danny Boyle *Slumdog Millionaire*
2009	*The Hurt Locker*	Jeff Bridges *Crazy Heart*	Sandra Bullock *The Blind Side*	Christoph Waltz *Inglourious Basterds*	Mo'Nique *Precious*	Kathryn Bigelow *The Hurt Locker*
2010	*The King's Speech*	Colin Firth *The King's Speech*	Natalie Portman *Black Swan*	Christian Bale *The Fighter*	Melissa Leo *The Fighter*	Tom Hooper *The King's Speech*
2011	*The Artist*	Jean Dujardin *The Artist*	Meryl Streep *The Iron Lady*	Christopher Plummer, *Beginners*	Octavia Spencer *The Help*	Michel Hazanavicius *The Artist*
2012	*Argo*	Daniel Day-Lewis *Lincoln*	Jennifer Lawrence *Silver Linings Playbook*	Christoph Waltz *Django Unchained*	Anne Hathaway *Les Misérables*	Ang Lee *Life of Pi*
2013	*12 Years a Slave*	Matthew McConaughey *Dallas Buyers Club*	Cate Blanchett *Blue Jasmine*	Jared Leto *Dallas Buyers Club*	Lupita Nyong'o *12 Years a Slave*	Alfonso Cuarón *Gravity*
2014	*Birdman*	Eddie Redmayne *The Theory of Everything*	Julianne Moore *Still Alice*	J. K. Simmons *Whiplash*	Patricia Arquette *Boyhood*	Alejandro G. Iñárritu *Birdman*
2015	*Spotlight*	Leonardo DiCaprio *The Revenant*	Brie Larson *Room*	Mark Rylance *Bridge of Spies*	Alicia Vikander *The Danish Girl*	Alejandro G. Iñárritu *The Revenant*
2016	*Moonlight*	Casey Affleck *Manchester by the Sea*	Emma Stone *La La Land*	Mahershala Ali *Moonlight*	Viola Davis *Fences*	Damien Chazelle *La La Land*
2017	*The Shape of Water*	Gary Oldman *Darkest Hour*	Frances McDormand *Three Billboards Outside Ebbing, Missouri*	Sam Rockwell *Three Billboards Outside Ebbing, Missouri*	Allison Janney *I, Tonya*	Guillermo del Toro *The Shape of Water*
2018	*Green Book*	Rami Malek *Bohemian Rhapsody*	Olivia Colman *The Favourite*	Mahershala Ali *Green Book*	Regina King *If Beale Street Could Talk*	Alfonso Cuarón *Roma*
2019	*Parasite*	Joaquin Phoenix *Joker*	Renée Zellweger *Judy*	Brad Pitt *Once Upon a Time... in Hollywood*	Laura Dern *Marriage Story*	Bong Joon-ho *Parasite*
2020	*Nomadland*	Anthony Hopkins *The Father*	Frances McDormand *Nomadland*	Daniel Kaluuya *Judas and the Black Messiah*	Yuh-jung Youn *Minari*	Chloé Zhao *Nomadland*
2021	*CODA*	Will Smith *King Richard*	Jessica Chastain *The Eyes of Tammy Faye*	Troy Kotsur *CODA*	Ariana DeBose *West Side Story*	Jane Campion *The Power of the Dog*

Year	Picture	Actor	Actress	Supporting actor[1]	Supporting actress[1]	Director
2022	*Everything Everywhere All at Once*	Brendan Fraser *The Whale*	Michelle Yeoh *Everything Everywhere All at Once*	Ke Huy Quan *Everything Everywhere All at Once*	Jamie Lee Curtis *Everything Everywhere All at Once*	Daniel Kwan and Daniel Scheinert *Everything Everywhere All at Once*
2023	*Oppenheimer*	Cillian Murphy *Oppenheimer*	Emma Stone *Poor Things*	Robert Downey Jr. *Oppenheimer*	Da'Vine Joy Randolph *The Holdovers*	Christopher Nolan *Oppenheimer*

NA = Not applicable. (1) Award not given until 1936.

Other Academy Award Winners, 2023

Animated film: *The Boy and the Heron*
Cinematography: *Oppenheimer*
Costume design: *Poor Things*
Documentary feature: *20 Days in Mariupol*
Film editing: *Oppenheimer*
International feature film: *The Zone of Interest*, UK
Makeup and hairstyling: *Poor Things*
Original score: *Oppenheimer*, Ludwig Görranson
Original song: "What Was I Made For?" *Barbie*, Billie Eilish and Finneas O'Connell
Production design: *Poor Things*
Short films: *War Is Over!* (animated), *The Last Repair Shop* (documentary), *The Wonderful Story of Henry Sugar* (live action)
Sound: *The Zone of Interest*
Visual effects: *Godzilla Minus One*
Writing (adapted screenplay): *American Fiction*, Cord Jefferson
Writing (original screenplay): *Anatomy of a Fall*, Justine Triet and Arthur Harari

Other Film Awards, 2024

British Academy of Film and Television Awards (BAFTAs)

Awarded in 2024 to films released in the UK in 2023.

Best film: *Oppenheimer*
Outstanding British film: *The Zone of Interest*
Outstanding debut by a British writer/director/producer: *Earth Mama*
Director: Christopher Nolan, *Oppenheimer*
Original screenplay: *Anatomy of a Fall*, Justine Triet and Arthur Harari
Adapted screenplay: *American Fiction*, Cord Jefferson
Animated film: *The Boy and the Heron*
Documentary: *20 Days in Mariupol*
Film not in the English language: *The Zone of Interest*
Actor: Cillian Murphy, *Oppenheimer*
Actress: Emma Stone, *Poor Things*
Supporting actor: Robert Downey Jr., *Oppenheimer*
Supporting actress: Da'Vine Joy Randolph, *The Holdovers*

Directors Guild of America Awards

Feature film: Christopher Nolan, *Oppenheimer*
First-time feature film: Celine Song, *Past Lives*
Documentary: Mstyslav Chernov, *20 Days in Mariupol*
TV movie/limited series: Sarah Adina Smith, *Lessons in Chemistry*, "Him and Her"
TV series (drama): Peter Hoar, *The Last of Us*, "Long, Long Time"
TV series (comedy): Christopher Storer, *The Bear*, "Fishes"

Screen Actors Guild Awards

Motion picture cast: *Oppenheimer*
Female actor in a lead role: Lily Gladstone, *Killers of the Flower Moon*
Male actor in a lead role: Cillian Murphy, *Oppenheimer*
Female actor in a supporting role: Da'Vine Joy Randolph, *The Holdovers*
Male actor in a supporting role: Robert Downey Jr., *Oppenheimer*
Drama series ensemble: *Succession*
Female actor in a drama series: Elizabeth Debicki, *The Crown*
Male actor in a drama series: Pedro Pascal, *The Last of Us*
Comedy series ensemble: *The Bear*
Female actor in a comedy series: Ayo Edebiri, *The Bear*
Male actor in a comedy series: Jeremy Allen White, *The Bear*
Female actor in a TV movie/limited series: Ali Wong, *Beef*
Male actor in a TV movie/limited series: Steven Yeun, *Beef*

Academy of Country Music Awards, 2024

Entertainer: Lainey Wilson
Male artist: Chris Stapleton
Female artist: Lainey Wilson
Duo: Dan + Shay
Group: Old Dominion
Album: *Higher*, Chris Stapleton
Single: "Fast Car," Luke Combs
Song: "Next Thing You Know," Jordan Davis
Visual media: "Burn It Down," Parker McCollum
Music event: "Save Me," Jelly Roll with Lainey Wilson
New female artist: Megan Moroney
New male artist: Nate Smith
New duo/group: Tigirlily Gold

Selected Grammy Awards, 2023

Source: The Recording Academy
For albums released Oct. 1, 2022-Sept. 15, 2023, awarded in Feb. 2024.

Record of the year (single): "Flowers," Miley Cyrus
Album of the year: *Midnights*, Taylor Swift
Song of the year: "What Was I Made For?" Billie Eilish, Finneas O'Connell
New artist: Victoria Monét
Pop performance, solo: "Flowers," Miley Cyrus
Pop performance, duo/group: "Ghost in the Machine," SZA feat. Phoebe Bridgers
Pop album, vocal: *Midnights*, Taylor Swift
Pop dance recording: "Padam Padam," Kylie Minogue
Dance/electronic recording: "Rumble," Skrillex, Fred again.., Flowdan
Dance/electronic album: *Actual Life 3 (January 1 - September 9 2022)*, Fred again..
Rock performance: "Not Strong Enough," boygenius
Metal performance: "72 Seasons," Metallica
Rock song: "Not Strong Enough," boygenius (Julien Baker, Phoebe Bridgers, Lucy Dacus, songwriters)
Rock album: *This Is Why*, Paramore
Alternative music album: *The Record*, boygenius
Alternative music performance: "This Is Why," Paramore
R&B performance: "ICU," Coco Jones
R&B performance, traditional: "Good Morning," PJ Morton feat. Susan Carol
R&B song: "Snooze," SZA (Kenny B. Edmonds, Blair Ferguson, Khris Riddick-Tynes, Solána Rowe, Leon Thomas, songwriters)
R&B album: *Jaguar II*, Victoria Monét
R&B album, progressive: *SOS*, SZA
Rap performance: "Scientists & Engineers," Killer Mike feat. André 3000, Future, Eryn Allen Kane
Rap performance, melodic: "All My Life," Lil Durk feat. J. Cole
Rap song: "Scientists & Engineers," Killer Mike feat. André 3000, Future, Eryn Allen Kane (Andre Benjamin, Paul Beauregard, James Blake, Danian Ramel Farmer III, Bryan Jones, Eryn Allen Koehn, Michael Render, Tim Moore, Dion Wilson, songwriters)
Rap album: *Michael*, Killer Mike
Country performance, solo: "White Horse," Chris Stapleton
Country performance, duo/group: "I Remember Everything," Zach Bryan feat. Kacey Musgraves
Country song: "White Horse," Chris Stapleton (Chris Stapleton, Dan Wilson, songwriters)
Country album: *Bell Bottom Country*, Lainey Wilson
Jazz performance: "Tight," Samara Joy
Jazz album, instrumental: *The Winds of Change*, Billy Childs
Jazz album, vocal: *How Love Begins*, Nicole Zuraitis
American roots performance: "Eve Was Black," Allison Russell
American roots song: "Cast Iron Skillet," Jason Isbell and the 400 Unit (Jason Isbell, songwriter)
Americana performance: "Dear Insecurity," Brandy Clark feat. Brandi Carlile
Americana album: *Weathervanes*, Jason Isbell and the 400 Unit
Bluegrass album: *City of Gold*, Molly Tuttle and Golden Highway
Blues album, traditional: *All My Love for You*, Bobby Rush
Contemporary Christian album: *Church Clothes 4*, Lecrae
Folk album: *Joni Mitchell at Newport [Live]*, Joni Mitchell
Gospel album: *All Things New: Live In Orlando*, Tye Tribbett
Latin pop album: *X Mí (Vol. 1)*, Gaby Moreno
Música urbana album: *MAÑANA SERÁ BONITO*, Karol G
New age album: *So She Howls*, Carla Patullo feat. Tonality and the Scorchio Quartet
Comedy album: *What's in a Name?* Dave Chappelle
Soundtrack album, compilation: *Barbie the Album*, Various artists
Soundtrack album, score: *Oppenheimer*, Ludwig Göransson
Song, visual media: "What Was I Made For?" *Barbie* (Billie Eilish, Finneas O'Connell, songwriters)
Music video: "Im Only Sleeping," The Beatles
Music film: *Moonage Daydream*, David Bowie

Grammy Awards, 1958-2023

Record of the Year (single)	Year	Album of the Year
Domenico Modugno, "Nel Blu Dipinto Di Blu (Volare)"	1958	Henry Mancini, *The Music From Peter Gunn*
Bobby Darin, "Mack the Knife"	1959	Frank Sinatra, *Come Dance With Me*
Percy Faith, "Theme From a Summer Place"	1960	Bob Newhart, *Button Down Mind*
Henry Mancini, "Moon River"	1961	Judy Garland, *Judy at Carnegie Hall*
Tony Bennett, "I Left My Heart in San Francisco"	1962	Vaughn Meader, *The First Family*
Henry Mancini, "The Days of Wine and Roses"	1963	Barbra Streisand, *The Barbra Streisand Album*
Stan Getz and Astrud Gilberto, "The Girl From Ipanema"	1964	Stan Getz and João Gilberto, *Getz/Gilberto*
Herb Alpert, "A Taste of Honey"	1965	Frank Sinatra, *September of My Years*
Frank Sinatra, "Strangers in the Night"	1966	Frank Sinatra, *A Man and His Music*
5th Dimension, "Up, Up and Away"	1967	The Beatles, *Sgt. Pepper's Lonely Hearts Club Band*
Simon and Garfunkel, "Mrs. Robinson"	1968	Glen Campbell, *By the Time I Get to Phoenix*
5th Dimension, "Aquarius/Let the Sunshine In"	1969	Blood, Sweat & Tears, *Blood, Sweat & Tears*
Simon and Garfunkel, "Bridge Over Troubled Water"	1970	Simon and Garfunkel, *Bridge Over Troubled Water*
Carole King, "It's Too Late"	1971	Carole King, *Tapestry*
Roberta Flack, "The First Time Ever I Saw Your Face"	1972	George Harrison and Friends, *The Concert for Bangla Desh*
Roberta Flack, "Killing Me Softly With His Song"	1973	Stevie Wonder, *Innervisions*
Olivia Newton-John, "I Honestly Love You"	1974	Stevie Wonder, *Fulfillingness' First Finale*
Captain & Tennille, "Love Will Keep Us Together"	1975	Paul Simon, *Still Crazy After All These Years*
George Benson, "This Masquerade"	1976	Stevie Wonder, *Songs in the Key of Life*
Eagles, "Hotel California"	1977	Fleetwood Mac, *Rumours*
Billy Joel, "Just the Way You Are"	1978	Bee Gees, *Saturday Night Fever*
The Doobie Brothers, "What a Fool Believes"	1979	Billy Joel, *52nd Street*
Christopher Cross, "Sailing"	1980	Christopher Cross, *Christopher Cross*
Kim Carnes, "Bette Davis Eyes"	1981	John Lennon and Yoko Ono, *Double Fantasy*
Toto, "Rosanna"	1982	Toto, *Toto IV*
Michael Jackson, "Beat It"	1983	Michael Jackson, *Thriller*
Tina Turner, "What's Love Got to Do With It"	1984	Lionel Richie, *Can't Slow Down*
USA for Africa, "We Are the World"	1985	Phil Collins, *No Jacket Required*
Steve Winwood, "Higher Love"	1986	Paul Simon, *Graceland*
Paul Simon, "Graceland"	1987	U2, *The Joshua Tree*
Bobby McFerrin, "Don't Worry, Be Happy"	1988	George Michael, *Faith*
Bette Midler, "Wind Beneath My Wings"	1989	Bonnie Raitt, *Nick of Time*
Phil Collins, "Another Day in Paradise"	1990	Quincy Jones, *Back on the Block*
Natalie Cole, with Nat "King" Cole, "Unforgettable"	1991	Natalie Cole, with Nat "King" Cole, *Unforgettable*
Eric Clapton, "Tears in Heaven"	1992	Eric Clapton, *Unplugged*
Whitney Houston, "I Will Always Love You"	1993	Whitney Houston, *The Bodyguard*
Sheryl Crow, "All I Wanna Do"	1994	Tony Bennett, *MTV Unplugged*
Seal, "Kiss From a Rose"	1995	Alanis Morissette, *Jagged Little Pill*
Eric Clapton, "Change the World"	1996	Celine Dion, *Falling Into You*
Shawn Colvin, "Sunny Came Home"	1997	Bob Dylan, *Time Out of Mind*
Celine Dion, "My Heart Will Go On"	1998	Lauryn Hill, *The Miseducation of Lauryn Hill*
Santana feat. Rob Thomas, "Smooth"	1999	Santana, *Supernatural*
U2, "Beautiful Day"	2000	Steely Dan, *Two Against Nature*
U2, "Walk On"	2001	Various artists, *O Brother, Where Art Thou?*
Norah Jones, "Don't Know Why"	2002	Norah Jones, *Come Away With Me*
Coldplay, "Clocks"	2003	OutKast, *Speakerboxxx/The Love Below*
Ray Charles and Norah Jones, "Here We Go Again"	2004	Ray Charles and various artists, *Genius Loves Company*
Green Day, "Boulevard of Broken Dreams"	2005	U2, *How to Dismantle an Atomic Bomb*
Dixie Chicks, "Not Ready to Make Nice"	2006	Dixie Chicks, *Taking the Long Way*
Amy Winehouse, "Rehab"	2007	Herbie Hancock, *River: The Joni Letters*
Robert Plant and Alison Krauss, "Please Read the Letter"	2008	Robert Plant and Alison Krauss, *Raising Sand*
Kings of Leon, "Use Somebody"	2009	Taylor Swift, *Fearless*
Lady Antebellum, "Need You Now"	2010	Arcade Fire, *The Suburbs*
Adele, "Rolling in the Deep"	2011	Adele, *21*
Gotye, "Somebody That I Used to Know"	2012	Mumford & Sons, *Babel*
Daft Punk feat. Pharrell Williams and Nile Rodgers, "Get Lucky"	2013	Daft Punk, *Random Access Memories*
Sam Smith, "Stay With Me"	2014	Beck, *Morning Phase*
Mark Ronson feat. Bruno Mars, "Uptown Funk"	2015	Taylor Swift, *1989*
Adele, "Hello"	2016	Adele, *25*
Bruno Mars, "24K Magic"	2017	Bruno Mars, *24K Magic*
Childish Gambino, "This Is America"	2018	Kacey Musgraves, *Golden Hour*
Billie Eilish, "Bad Guy"	2019	Billie Eilish, *When We All Fall Asleep, Where Do We Go?*
Billie Eilish, "Everything I Wanted"	2020	Taylor Swift, *Folklore*
Silk Sonic, "Leave the Door Open"	2021	Jon Batiste, *We Are*
Lizzo, "About Damn Time"	2022	Harry Styles, *Harry's House*
Miley Cyrus, "Flowers"	2023	Taylor Swift, *Midnights*

MTV Video Music Awards, 2024

Video of the year: "Fortnight," Taylor Swift feat. Post Malone
Artist of the year: Taylor Swift
Song of the year: "Espresso," Sabrina Carpenter
Song of summer: "Fortnight," Taylor Swift feat. Post Malone
Best new artist: Chappell Roan
Best collaboration: "Fortnight," Taylor Swift feat. Post Malone
Push performance of the year: "Easy," Le Sserafim
Video for good: "What Was I Made For?" Billie Eilish
VMAs Most Iconic Performance: "Roar," Katy Perry
Best Afrobeats: "Water," Tyla
Best alternative: "Beautiful Things," Benson Boone
Best hip-hop: "Houdini," Eminem
Best K-pop: "Rockstar," Lisa
Best Latin: "Mil Veces," Anitta
Best pop: Taylor Swift
Best R&B: "Snooze," SZA
Best rock: "Human," Lenny Kravitz
Art direction: "Boa," Megan Thee Stallion
Choreography: "Houdini," Dua Lipa
Cinematography: "We Can't Be Friends (Wait for Your Love)," Ariana Grande
Direction: "Fortnight," Taylor Swift feat. Post Malone
Editing: "Fortnight," Taylor Swift feat. Post Malone
Visual effects: "Houdini," Eminem

SCIENCE

Science and Technology News

The following were some of the developments in science and technology in the previous year, as of Sept. 2024.

Interaction With Light Yields New Phase of Matter

Interactions between light and matter happen extremely quickly, making it difficult to study what happens inside atoms when they occur. In fact, a tiny unit called an attosecond, equal to a billionth of a billionth of a second, is commonly used to measure the time in which they typically take place. In a study published online in *Nature Communications* in Nov. 2023, Spanish researchers reported on their use of attosecond pulses of X-rays to probe how the electrons in an atom respond when a material is subjected to powerful pulses of infrared laser radiation. Using graphite as their test substance, they found that varying the strength of the infrared light could change the electrons' and thus the material's properties (such as conductivity), as the graphite entered a new distinct phase, a sort of light-matter hybrid. This attosecond X-ray spectrometry technology thus proved to be a fruitful means for studying light-matter interactions and could advance future research on such topics as photosynthesis or in such fields as solar cell development and optical computing.

Climate Change

The amount of carbon dioxide (CO_2) in Earth's atmosphere is an important factor in climate change. Knowing the atmospheric concentration of CO_2 in past periods can help scientists clarify the character of current global warming. Samples of ancient air can be found today in bubbles in ice that was formed long ago. But such ice, obtained from polar-ice cores extracted by geologists, generally yields good data for only the past 800,000 years or so. In Dec. 2023 an international group of researchers reported in the journal *Science* on seven years of work analyzing and integrating numerous existing studies of CO_2 concentration that rely on indirect, or "proxy," evidence relating to the Cenozoic period (the most recent 66 million years) of Earth's history. Their results indicated that the current level of CO_2 in the atmosphere is the highest in nearly 15 million years.

In Mar. 2024 the World Meteorological Organization reported that in terms of average global temperature, the year 2023 was the hottest in an observational record starting in 1850.

Entangled Molecules

Entanglement is a key concept in the field of physics known as quantum mechanics. It involves a situation where two or more things are correlated with one another so that a change occurring in a property of one simultaneously occurs in the other(s), no matter how far apart they are. Instances of entanglement were previously observed in atoms and in subatomic particles, but controlled entanglement even of such complex objects as molecules has now been demonstrated, as reported by two papers by American and South Korean researchers in the Dec. 8, 2023, issue of *Science*. The two experiments used pairs of ultracold calcium monofluoride molecules held in a reconfigurable array of optical tweezers (tightly focused laser beams). This achievement is of potentially great significance since it may bolster ongoing efforts to harness quantum mechanics to enhance the capabilities of computer and other technologies.

Car Harm

Invented well over a century ago, automobiles became an essential means of transportation throughout the world. But a review of research on their impact showed that the benefits they provide in modern life have come at a stunning cost. The study, published by British and German scientists in the *Journal of Transport Geography* in early 2024, examined the negative effects of "automobility" with regard to violence (including accidental crashes and intentional violence), ill health, social injustice, and environmental damage. Among the findings: car use has killed some 60-80 million people, is currently responsible for 1 in every 34 deaths, and has injured at least 2 billion individuals. Automobility has worsened social inequity and harmed ecosystems (such as through pollution and resource extraction) in every part of the world. It harms nearly everyone, the researchers contend, even those who live in car-free areas. They suggested that the harm associated with automobility could be reduced by the implementation of various policy and other changes, some of then already being implemented in a number of regions, such as congestion charges, parking reductions, car-free zones, lower traffic speeds, and decreased emissions of pollutants.

Microplastic Harm

Plastics play a key role in modern civilization. But these extraordinarily useful materials can degrade or break down. When this happens, microscopic particles of plastic—known as microplastics and the even tinier nanoplastics (MNPs for short)—enter the environment, ending up in, among other places, the bodies of living organisms, such as animals and human beings. In a 2023 report in *Annals of Global Health*, the Minderoo-Monaco Commission on Plastics and Human Health called for a Global Plastics Treaty regulating the production and use of plastics so as to reduce the risks they pose. The commission acknowledged that much remained to be learned about these risks. A notable advance toward this end, particularly regarding human health, came in an observational study reported by Italian researchers in the Mar. 7, 2024, issue of the *New England Journal of Medicine*. The study enrolled 257 patients with cardiovascular disease who underwent surgical removal of plaque from their carotid arteries. MNPs were detected in plaque from 150. As of some 34 months after the procedure, 30 of those patients (that is, 20% of those studied with exposure to MNPs) had suffered a nonfatal heart attack or nonfatal stroke or had died—compared to only 8 (or 7.5%) of the 107 patients with no evidence of MNPs.

Reproductive Cells and Life Expectancy

In humans and a number of other vertebrate species, females tend to live longer than males. Researchers have previously observed that at least in some invertebrates, germ cells—the cells that develop into eggs in females and sperm in males—play a role in growth and aging. The situation for vertebrates, however, has not been well investigated. In a study published in the online journal *Science Advances* in June 2024, Japanese scientists focused on a short-lived (and thus readily investigated) model, the African turquoise killifish (*Nothobranchius furzeri*). They found evidence suggesting that removing the germ cells led to hormonal changes, which varied according to the sex of the fish but led to an increase in the male lifespan and a decrease in the female.

New Satellite Galaxies of the Milky Way

Since ancient times, sky observers have noticed the existence of the Large and Small Magellanic Clouds, which were eventually found to be satellites of our Milky Way galaxy. By mid-2024, some 60 Milky Way satellite galaxies were known, with Sextans II and Virgo III being the most recently found. The Aug. 2024 issue of *Publications of the Astronomical Society of Japan* published an analysis of the two and of their discovery using the huge Subaru telescope in Hawaii. Their distances from the sun were estimated at 126 kiloparsecs for Sextans II and 151 kiloparsecs for Virgo III. (One kiloparsec is about 3,260 light-years.) Study of the new satellite galaxies, and of any others that may remain to be found, could help astronomers resolve some of the perplexing issues associated with their current standard model of cosmology. That model expects a major galaxy like the Milky Way to have hundreds of satellite galaxies and leaves much unexplained about the so-called dark matter that is suspected to make up much of the universe.

Science Glossary

This glossary covers some concepts that come up frequently in the news, in biology, chemistry, geology, and physics.

Biology

Amino acid: any of a group of organic molecules with a certain structure. About 20 are the building blocks of proteins.

Antibiotic: a substance produced by or derived from a bacterium, fungus, or other organism that battles infections and diseases caused by microorganisms, especially bacteria; it works by killing the microorganism or halting its growth.

Archaeon (plural, archaea): one of a group of single-celled microorganisms; archaea are prokaryotes, like bacteria, but they share some similarities with eukaryotes.

Autoimmunity: a condition in which an individual's immune system reacts against his or her own tissues; leads to diseases such as lupus, some forms of diabetes, inflammatory bowel disease, and rheumatoid arthritis.

Bacterium (plural, bacteria): one of a large, varied class of microscopic and simple, single-celled organisms. Bacteria live almost everywhere; some forms cause disease, while others are useful in digestion and other natural processes.

Biodiversity (biological diversity): richness of variety of life-forms—including plants, animals, and other types—in a given environment.

Cell: the smallest unit of life capable of living independently, or with other cells; usually bounded by a membrane. May include a nucleus and other specialized parts.

Cholesterol: a fatty substance in animal tissues. It is produced by the liver in humans; is found in foods such as butter, eggs, and meat; and is an essential body constituent.

Chromosome: one of the rodlike structures in cell nuclei that carry genetic material (DNA).

Cloning: the process of copying a particular piece of DNA to allow it to be sequenced, studied, or used in some other way; can also refer to producing a genetic copy of an organism.

CRISPR (Clustered Regularly Interspaced Short Palindromic Repeats): a segment of DNA in prokaryotes that helps defend against virus attacks; it contains short genetic sequences that, coupled with a special enzyme, permit recognition and cleavage of like sequences in invading viruses. Term is also applied to a technology based on this approach that provides relatively precise targeting of specific bits of genetic code for such purposes as genetic modification or diagnosis.

DNA (deoxyribonucleic acid): a usually double-stranded molecule that carries genetic information, which determines the form and functioning of all known living things.

Ecosystem: an interdependent community of living organisms and their climatic and geographical habitat.

Enzyme: a protein that promotes a particular chemical reaction in the body.

Estrogen: one of a group of hormones that promote development of female secondary sex characteristics and the growth and health of the female reproductive system; males also produce small amounts of estrogen.

Eukaryote: any of the group of single- or multicelled organisms whose cells have distinct nuclei.

Evolution: the process of gradual change that can occur in a species as it adapts to its environment; natural selection is the process by which evolution occurs.

Gene: a portion of a DNA molecule that provides the blueprint for the assembly of a protein.

Gene pool: the collection and total diversity of genes in an interbreeding population.

Gene therapy: a treatment in which scientists try to implant functioning genes into a person's cells so the genes can produce proteins that the person lacks or that help the person fight disease.

Genetic sequencing: the process of finding the order of subunits in a gene or the order of all an organism's genes.

Genome: the complete set of an organism's genetic material.

Hormone: a substance secreted in one part of an organism that regulates the functioning of other tissues or organs.

Meiosis: the process of cell division that results in gametes (sperm or egg cells), all of which contain half the number of chromosomes as their precursor.

Metabolism: the sum total of the body's chemical processes providing energy for vital functions and enabling new material to be synthesized.

Mitosis: the process by which a cell divides its nucleus and other cell materials into two duplicate daughter cells with the same DNA.

Neuron or **nerve cell:** any of the cells in the nervous system that send electrical and chemical messages to other cells.

Nucleus (plural, nuclei): the center of an atom; or the portion of a eukaryotic cell that contains most of the cell's genetic material. (In most eukaryotic cells, some DNA is also found in the cell's "powerhouses"—tiny components called **mitochondria** that lie outside the nucleus and supply chemical energy.)

Organism: a living entity, capable of growth, metabolism, and usually reproduction.

Phenotype: the observable properties and characteristics of an organism arising at least in part from its genetic makeup.

Pheromone: a chemical secreted by an organism to influence the behavior of other members of its species.

Placebo effect: a phenomenon in which patients show an improvement in their condition after taking a medically inactive substance, called a placebo.

Prokaryote: a single-celled organism that does not have a distinct nucleus, such as a bacterium or archaeon.

Protein: a complex molecule made up of one or more chains of amino acids; essential to the structure and function of all cells.

RNA (ribonucleic acid): a complex molecule similar to the genetic material DNA but usually single-stranded; several forms of RNA translate the genetic code of DNA and use that code to assemble proteins for structural and biological functions in the body. RNA also serves as the genetic material of some viruses.

Species: a population of organisms that breed with each other in nature and produce fertile offspring; other definitions of species exist to accommodate the diversity of life on Earth.

Stem cell: a cell that can develop into other types of cells; for instance, stem cells in bone marrow can differentiate into different types of blood cells.

Steroid: a type of chemical substance with a certain molecular structure. Some steroids are hormones that can suppress immune response or influence stress reaction, blood pressure, or sexual development.

Testosterone: a steroid hormone that stimulates the development and maintenance of male sexual characteristics and the production of sperm; women also produce small amounts of testosterone.

Virus: a microscopic, often disease-causing agent made of genetic material surrounded by a protein shell; can only reproduce inside a living cell. There also exist "subviral" infectious agents, such as **viroids** (which consist of a short, circular strand of RNA without a protein coat) and **prions** (consisting of protein material).

Chemistry

Acid: a class of compounds that contrasts with bases. Acids taste sour, turn litmus red/pink, and often produce hydrogen gas in contact with some metals. Acids donate protons (hydrogen atoms minus the electron) in chemical reactions.

Base: a substance that yields hydroxyl ions (OH-) when dissolved in water; any of a class of compounds whose aqueous solutions taste bitter, feel slippery, turn litmus blue, and react with acids to form salts; also known as **alkaline**.

Carbon fiber: an extremely strong, thin fiber made by pyrolyzing (decomposing by heat) synthetic fibers, such as rayon, until charred; used to make high-strength composites.

Chlorofluorocarbon (CFC): one of a group of industrial chemicals that contain chlorine, fluorine, and carbon and can damage Earth's ozone layer.

Element: a substance that cannot be chemically decomposed into simpler substances; all the atoms of an element have the same number of protons.

Isotope: an atom of a chemical element with the same number of protons in its nucleus as other atoms of that element, but with a different number of neutrons.

Molecule: the basic unit of a chemical compound, composed of two or more atoms bound together.

Noble gases or **inert gases:** a group of gases including helium, neon, argon, krypton, xenon, and radon that are not reactive except in rare and limited instances.

Osmosis: the transfer of a fluid across a semipermeable membrane, usually from an area of higher concentration to one of lower concentration.

Polymer: a huge molecule containing hundreds or thousands of smaller molecules arranged in repeating units.

Salt: a neutral compound produced by the reaction of an acid and a base.

Geology

Anthropocene: a proposed epoch of geologic time marked by a significant influence of human activity on the environment. Suggested starting points include the mid-20th century (when extensive testing of nuclear and thermonuclear bombs began) and the Industrial Revolution of the 19th century.

Fault, tectonic: a crack or break in Earth's crust, often due to the slippage of tectonic plates past or over one another; usually geologically unstable.

Igneous: a type of rock formed by solidification from a molten state, especially from molten magma.

Magma: hot liquid rock material under Earth's surface, from which igneous rock is formed by cooling.

Metamorphic: in geology, the name given to rocks or minerals that have recrystallized under the influence of heat and pressure since their original formation.

Pangaea: a single supercontinent that scientists believe began to break apart at least 200 mil years ago to form the current continents.

Plate tectonics: theory that Earth's lithosphere—the uppermost layer that includes the crust—is made up of many separate rigid plates of rock that float on top of hot semiliquid rock.

Sedimentary: a type of rock formed by the buildup of material at the bottoms of bodies of water.

Physics

Absolute zero: the theoretical temperature at which all motion within a molecule stops, corresponding to −273.15°C (−459.67°F).

Antimatter: matter that consists of antiparticles, such as antiprotons, that have an opposite charge from normal particles; when matter meets antimatter, both are destroyed, and their combined mass is converted to energy. Antimatter is created in certain radioactive decay processes but appears to be present in only small amounts in the universe.

Atom: the basic unit of a chemical element.

Atomic mass: the total mass of an atom of a given element; atoms of the same element with different atomic masses (different numbers of neutrons but not protons) are called **isotopes**.

Atomic number: the number of protons in an atom of a given element of the periodic table; the characteristic that sets atoms of different elements apart.

Axion: a hypothetical subatomic particle with low mass and energy that has been proposed to exist because of the properties of the strong nuclear force. Axions have been suggested as a candidate for dark matter and also as a possible explanation for the imbalance between matter and antimatter in the universe.

Bose-Einstein condensate (BEC): a "super-atom" comprising thousands of atoms super-cooled to within a few hundred millionths of a degree of absolute zero and thus condensed into the lowest energy state. Atoms bound in the BEC behave synchronously, giving the BEC wavelike properties.

Boson: one of the two primary categories of particles in the Standard Model; bosons include the Higgs boson and force-carrying particles such as photons, gluons, and the W and Z particles.

Dark energy: a mysterious, undefined energy leading to a repulsive force pervading all of space-time; proposed by cosmologists as counteracting gravity and accelerating the expansion of the universe; predicted to make up 68.3% of the universe's composition.

Dark matter: hypothetical, invisible matter that some scientists believe makes up 26.8% of the universe (dark matter and ordinary matter together make up 31.7% of the universe). Its existence was proposed to account for otherwise inexplicable gravitational forces observed in space.

Doppler effect: a change in the frequency of sound, light, or radio waves caused by the motion of the source emitting the waves or the motion of the person or instrument perceiving the waves.

Electron: negatively charged particle that (along with its positively charged counterpart, the **positron**) is the least massive electrically charged fundamental particle; one of six **leptons**.

Energy: capacity to perform work. Energy can take various forms, such as potential energy, kinetic energy, and chemical energy.

Entropy: a measure of disorder in a system.

Fermion: any one of a number of matter particles including electrons, protons, neutrons, neutrinos, leptons, and quarks; one of the two primary categories of particles in the Standard Model, the other being bosons.

Field: the existence of physical effects such as forces (gravitational, electric, etc.) is visualized and described mathematically by physicists in terms of fields, which show the strength and direction of a force at a given position.

Fission: a nuclear reaction that occurs when the nuclei of large, unstable atoms break apart, releasing large amounts of energy.

Fluorescence: luminescence that is caused by the absorption of radiation at one wavelength followed by an almost immediate re-radiation, usually at a different wavelength, that stops almost immediately when the causative radiation stops.

Force: in classical physics, something that causes acceleration in a body; can be thought of as a push or pull.

Fusion: a nuclear reaction occurring when light atomic nuclei collide at high temperatures and combine to form one heavier atomic nucleus, releasing a large amount of energy along with, possibly, a subatomic particle in the process.

Gravity: an attractive force between any two objects or particles, proportional to the mass (or energy) of the objects; strength of the force decreases with greater distance; the only fundamental force still unaccounted for by the Standard Model.

Half-life: the time it takes for half of a given amount of a radioactive element to decay.

Hertz (Hz): a measure of frequency, or how many times a given event occurs per second; applied to sound waves, electrical current, and microchip clock speeds.

Higgs boson: a boson associated with a field accounting for the existence of mass in many particles.

Laser: light consisting of a cascade of photons all having the same wavelength; stands for Light Amplification by Stimulated Emission of Radiation.

Light-emitting diode (LED): a semiconductor that emits light when an electrical current is passed through it. The color of the light depends on the material used in making the diode.

Neutrino: a tiny fundamental particle, classed as a fermion, with no electrical charge and very small mass. Neutrinos move very quickly through the universe; they come in three varieties, or flavors: the electron neutrino, muon neutrino, and tau neutrino.

Neutron: a neutral particle, made up of quarks, found in the nuclei of atoms (except the most common isotope of hydrogen).

Particle accelerator: a machine that accelerates charged particles to extremely high speeds around a circular track or along a straight line. Accelerators are used in scientific research, manufacturing, and medical diagnosis and therapy. Those used to study fundamental physics can be enormous—the Large Hadron Collider in Switzerland has a circumference of 16.8 mi (27 km).

Phosphorescence: luminescence that is caused by the absorption of radiation at one wavelength followed by a delayed re-radiation, usually at a different wavelength, that continues for a time after the causative radiation stops.

Photon: the elementary unit, or quantum, of electromagnetic radiation, such as light. It has no mass or electrical charge and is one of the fundamental force-carrying particles described by the Standard Model.

Plasma: a high-energy state of matter different from solid, liquid, or gas in which atomic nuclei and the electrons orbiting them separate from each other.

Proton: a positively charged subatomic particle, made up of quarks, found in the nuclei of atoms.

Quantum: a natural unit of some physically measurable property, such as energy or electrical charge.

Quark: a fundamental matter particle classed as a fermion; there are six different varieties, or flavors, of quarks grouped in pairs: up and down, charm and strange, top and bottom. Each flavor has a corresponding antiquark. Quarks combine to form such particles as neutrons and protons. Quark-antiquark combinations form the composite particles known as **mesons**.

Radiation: energy emitted as rays or particles. Radiation includes heat, light, ultraviolet rays, gamma rays, X-rays, cosmic rays, alpha particles, and beta particles.

Relativity, general theory of: a theory of space-time proposed by Albert Einstein in 1915; it links gravity to the curvature of space-time.

Relativity, special theory of: Albert Einstein's theory of space and time: all laws of physics are valid in all uniformly moving frames of reference, and the speed of light in a vacuum is always the same, so long as the source and the observer are moving uniformly (not accelerating).

Standard Model: prevailing theory of the interaction of subatomic particles. Particles are either fermions—such as electrons, neutrinos, and quarks—or bosons—such as Higgs bosons, gluons, W or Z bosons, and photons. The theory successfully explains three of the four elementary forces acting on particles (strong, weak, electromagnetic) but thus far has not incorporated gravity.

String theory: a theory that seeks to unify quantum mechanics and general relativity, positing that the basic constituents of matter can best be understood not as pointlike particles but as tiny oscillating "strings."

Subatomic particle: a particle smaller than an atom; three important types—proton, neutron, and electron—are found in most atoms.

Superconductivity: the property of certain materials, usually metals and chemically complex ceramics, to conduct electricity without resistance, generally at very cold temperatures.

Thermodynamics: the branch of physics studying the flow and transformation of heat and other forms of energy, often with a focus on temperature.

Ultraviolet radiation: a form of light, invisible to the human eye, that has a shorter wavelength and greater energy than visible light but a longer wavelength and less energy than X-rays.

Virtual particle: subatomic particles that rapidly pop into and out of existence and can exert real forces; usually occur in particle-antiparticle pairs and are rapidly annihilated.

Mohs Scale of Hardness

Hardness is the ability of a solid substance to resist abrasion or deformation on its surface. Soft minerals scratch more easily than hard ones. For example, a diamond will scratch graphite because graphite is softer. In 1812, German mineralogist Friedrich Mohs (1773-1839) created the arbitrary scale shown below to measure relative hardness using 10 minerals that were readily available at that time. The numbers in the Mohs scale are arranged in order of increasing hardness. An item's hardness is obtained by determining which mineral in the Mohs scale can scratch it.

Mohs scale

1	Talc	6	Orthoclase feldspar
2	Gypsum	7	Quartz
3	Calcite	8	Topaz
4	Fluorite	9	Corundum
5	Apatite	10	Diamond

Selected items and their relative hardness

2.5	Fingernail	5.5	Steel knife blade
2.5-3	Gold, silver	6-7	Glass
3	Copper penny	6.5	Iron pyrite
4-4.5	Platinum	7+	Hardened steel file
4-5	Iron		

Chemical Elements, Atomic Numbers, Year Discovered

Source: International Union of Pure and Applied Chemistry (IUPAC)

See Periodic Table of the Elements on the following page for atomic weights.

Element	Symbol	Atomic number	Year discov.
Actinium	Ac	89	1899
Aluminum	Al	13	1825
Americium	Am	95	1944
Antimony	Sb	51	1450
Argon	Ar	18	1894
Arsenic	As	33	13th cent.
Astatine	At	85	1940
Barium	Ba	56	1808
Berkelium	Bk	97	1949
Beryllium	Be	4	1798
Bismuth	Bi	83	15th cent.
Bohrium	Bh	107	1981
Boron	B	5	1808
Bromine	Br	35	1826
Cadmium	Cd	48	1817
Calcium	Ca	20	1808
Californium	Cf	98	1950
Carbon	C	6	BCE
Cerium	Ce	58	1803
Cesium	Cs	55	1860
Chlorine	Cl	17	1774
Chromium	Cr	24	1797
Cobalt	Co	27	1735
Copernicium	Cn	112	1996
Copper	Cu	29	BCE
Curium	Cm	96	1944
Darmstadtium	Ds	110	1995
Dubnium (Hahnium)[1]	Db (Ha)	105	1970
Dysprosium	Dy	66	1886
Einsteinium	Es	99	1952
Erbium	Er	68	1843
Europium	Eu	63	1901
Fermium	Fm	100	1953
Flerovium	Fl	114	1999
Fluorine	F	9	1771
Francium	Fr	87	1939
Gadolinium	Gd	64	1886
Gallium	Ga	31	1875
Germanium	Ge	32	1886
Gold	Au	79	BCE
Hafnium	Hf	72	1923
Hassium	Hs	108	1984
Helium	He	2	1868
Holmium	Ho	67	1878
Hydrogen	H	1	1766
Indium	In	49	1863
Iodine	I	53	1811
Iridium	Ir	77	1804
Iron	Fe	26	BCE
Krypton	Kr	36	1898
Lanthanum	La	57	1839
Lawrencium	Lr	103	1961
Lead	Pb	82	BCE
Lithium	Li	3	1817
Livermorium	Lv	116	2000
Lutetium	Lu	71	1907
Magnesium	Mg	12	1829
Manganese	Mn	25	1774
Meitnerium	Mt	109	1982
Mendelevium	Md	101	1955
Mercury	Hg	80	BCE
Molybdenum	Mo	42	1782
Moscovium	Mc	115	2004
Neodymium	Nd	60	1885
Neon	Ne	10	1898
Neptunium	Np	93	1940
Nickel	Ni	28	1751
Nihonium	Nh	113	2004
Niobium[2]	Nb	41	1801
Nitrogen	N	7	1772
Nobelium	No	102	1958
Oganesson	Og	118	2006
Osmium	Os	76	1804
Oxygen	O	8	1774
Palladium	Pd	46	1803
Phosphorus	P	15	1669
Platinum	Pt	78	1735
Plutonium	Pu	94	1941
Polonium	Po	84	1898
Potassium	K	19	1807
Praseodymium	Pr	59	1885
Promethium	Pm	61	1945
Protactinium	Pa	91	1917
Radium	Ra	88	1898
Radon	Rn	86	1900
Rhenium	Re	75	1925
Rhodium	Rh	45	1803
Roentgenium	Rg	111	1995
Rubidium	Rb	37	1861
Ruthenium	Ru	44	1845
Rutherfordium	Rf	104	1969
Samarium	Sm	62	1879
Scandium	Sc	21	1879
Seaborgium	Sg	106	1974
Selenium	Se	34	1817
Silicon	Si	14	1823
Silver	Ag	47	BCE
Sodium	Na	11	1807
Strontium	Sr	38	1790
Sulfur	S	16	BCE
Tantalum	Ta	73	1802
Technetium	Tc	43	1937
Tellurium	Te	52	1782
Tennessine	Ts	117	2010
Terbium	Tb	65	1843
Thallium	Tl	81	1861
Thorium	Th	90	1828
Thulium	Tm	69	1879
Tin	Sn	50	BCE
Titanium	Ti	22	1791
Tungsten (Wolfram)	W	74	1783
Uranium	U	92	1789
Vanadium	V	23	1830
Xenon	Xe	54	1898
Ytterbium	Yb	70	1878
Yttrium	Y	39	1794
Zinc	Zn	30	BCE
Zirconium	Zr	40	1789

(1) The name Dubnium (Db) was approved by IUPAC for element 105, but the name Hahnium (Ha) was used in most of the scientific literature before 1998 and is still sometimes used in the U.S. (2) Formerly Columbium.

Periodic Table of the Elements

Source: Los Alamos National Laboratory Chemistry Division; International Union of Pure and Applied Chemistry (IUPAC)

Shaded elements are commonly regarded as metals.

Key: atomic number — 14; atomic weight[1] — 28.08-28.09; symbol — Si; name — Silicon

1	2	3	4	5	6	7	8	9	10	11	12	13	14	15	16	17	18
1 1.008 H Hydrogen																	2 4.003 He Helium
3 6.938-6.997 Li Lithium	4 9.012 Be Beryllium											5 10.81-10.82 B Boron	6 12.01 C Carbon	7 14.01 N Nitrogen	8 16.00 O Oxygen	9 19.00 F Fluorine	10 20.18 Ne Neon
11 22.99 Na Sodium	12 24.30-24.31 Mg Magnesium											13 26.98 Al Aluminum	14 28.08-28.09 Si Silicon	15 30.97 P Phosphorus	16 32.06-32.08 S Sulfur	17 35.45-35.46 Cl Chlorine	18 39.79-39.96 Ar Argon
19 39.10 K Potassium	20 40.08 Ca Calcium	21 44.96 Sc Scandium	22 47.87 Ti Titanium	23 50.94 V Vanadium	24 52.00 Cr Chromium	25 54.94 Mn Manganese	26 55.85 Fe Iron	27 58.93 Co Cobalt	28 58.69 Ni Nickel	29 63.55 Cu Copper	30 65.38 Zn Zinc	31 69.72 Ga Gallium	32 72.63 Ge Germanium	33 74.92 As Arsenic	34 78.97 Se Selenium	35 79.90-79.91 Br Bromine	36 83.80 Kr Krypton
37 85.47 Rb Rubidium	38 87.62 Sr Strontium	39 88.91 Y Yttrium	40 91.22 Zr Zirconium	41 92.91 Nb Niobium	42 95.95 Mo Molybdenum	43 [98]* Tc Technetium	44 101.1 Ru Ruthenium	45 102.9 Rh Rhodium	46 106.4 Pd Palladium	47 107.9 Ag Silver	48 112.4 Cd Cadmium	49 114.8 In Indium	50 118.7 Sn Tin	51 121.8 Sb Antimony	52 127.6 Te Tellurium	53 126.9 I Iodine	54 131.3 Xe Xenon
55 132.9 Cs Cesium	56 137.3 Ba Barium	57-71 Lanthanoids	72 178.5 Hf Hafnium	73 180.95 Ta Tantalum	74 183.8 W Tungsten	75 186.2 Re Rhenium	76 190.2 Os Osmium	77 192.2 Ir Iridium	78 195.1 Pt Platinum	79 197.0 Au Gold	80 200.6 Hg Mercury	81 204.4 Tl Thallium	82 206.14-207.94 Pb Lead	83 209.0* Bi Bismuth	84 [209]* Po Polonium	85 [210]* At Astatine	86 [222]* Rn Radon
87 [223]* Fr Francium	88 [226]* Ra Radium	89-103 Actinoids	104 [265]* Rf Rutherfordium	105 [270]* Db Dubnium	106 [269]* Sg Seaborgium	107 [270]* Bh Bohrium	108 [270]* Hs Hassium	109 [278]* Mt Meitnerium	110 [281]* Ds Darmstadtium	111 [281]* Rg Roentgenium	112 [285]* Cn Copernicium	113 [286]* Nh Nihonium	114 [289]* Fl Flerovium	115 [289]* Mc Moscovium	116 [293]* Lv Livermorium	117 [293]* Ts Tennessine	118 [294]* Og Oganesson

Lanthanoid series	57 138.9 La Lanthanum	58 140.1 Ce Cerium	59 140.9 Pr Praseodymium	60 144.2 Nd Neodymium	61 [145]* Pm Promethium	62 150.4 Sm Samarium	63 152.0 Eu Europium	64 157.3 Gd Gadolinium	65 158.9 Tb Terbium	66 162.5 Dy Dysprosium	67 164.9 Ho Holmium	68 167.3 Er Erbium	69 168.9 Tm Thulium	70 173.1 Yb Ytterbium	71 175.0 Lu Lutetium
Actinoid series	89 [227]* Ac Actinium	90 232.0* Th Thorium	91 231.0* Pa Protactinium	92 238.0* U Uranium	93 [237]* Np Neptunium	94 [244]* Pu Plutonium	95 [243]* Am Americium	96 [247]* Cm Curium	97 [247]* Bk Berkelium	98 [251]* Cf Californium	99 [252]* Es Einsteinium	100 [257]* Fm Fermium	101 [258]* Md Mendelevium	102 [259]* No Nobelium	103 [262]* Lr Lawrencium

Note: Atomic weight shown is a weighted average of the atomic masses of normally found isotopes. * = Element has no stable nuclides. A value enclosed in brackets, e.g. [209], indicates the mass number of the longest-lived isotope of the element. However, four such elements (Bi, Th, Pa, and U) do have a characteristic terrestrial isotopic composition, and for these an atomic weight is tabulated. (1) For elements having two or more stable isotopes with a notable variation in atomic-weight values, a range is shown.

Basic Laws of Physics

Newton's Laws of Motion

1. An object in motion moves at a constant velocity in a straight line unless acted upon by a force. Likewise, an object at rest will stay at rest. These two properties are known as inertia.

2. The acceleration of an object is proportional to the force acting on it and inversely proportional to the mass of the object. Force (*F*) equals mass (*m*) times acceleration (*a*):

$$F = ma$$

3. For every action, there is an equal and opposite reaction. For example, if a force of one ton pushes down on an object, the object pushes up with an equal force. As per the second law, the amount of movement (acceleration) produced in the object will depend on the object's mass.

Law of Gravity

In common usage, gravity refers to the gravitational force between planets and objects on or near them. But in scientific parlance, gravitation is one of four basic forces controlling the interactions of matter. (The others are the strong and weak forces, which act on the subatomic level, and the electromagnetic force.) The gravitational force (*F*) between objects is proportional to the product of their masses (m_1 and m_2) and inversely proportional to the square of the distance (*d*) between them. *G* represents the gravitational constant in Newton's law of gravity, a fixed ratio of approximately 6.67430×10^{-11} newton m^2/kg^2.

The basic law of gravity is:

$$F = G\frac{m_1 m_2}{d^2}$$

Near Earth's surface, Earth's gravitational force pulls objects downward at a constant acceleration of 9.8 m/s^2 (*g*). This allows calculation of the vertical velocity (*v*) of an object with an initial vertical velocity of v_0 in free fall at a given point in time (*t*) and calculation of the distance (*d*) of an object from Earth at any given time with a given initial velocity (v_0) and a known initial height (*a*) via the following equations (here, the effects of air resistance are ignored, and downward velocities and directions are negative):

$$v = v_0 - gt$$

$$d = -½g(t^2) + v_0t + a$$

Assuming that height is measured in feet and speeds in feet per second, the maximum height (*H*) reached by an object with a positive (upward) initial velocity is expressed as:

$$H = a + \frac{{v_0}^2}{64}$$

For motion not near Earth's surface, more complicated equations are required. Also, if the object's upward velocity is very great, the object may escape Earth's gravity. Even near Earth's surface, there are slight complications. Gravity is lessened by the centrifugal force of the Earth's rotation. At the poles, where centrifugal force is absent, acceleration due to gravity is greater.

Gravity is weaker on a mountaintop than at sea level because the mountaintop is farther from Earth's center.

Conservation Laws

In physics, laws of conservation state that in a closed system, where neither mass nor energy is added or subtracted, certain measurable quantities remain constant.

Conservation of Mass: Mass is neither created nor destroyed within a closed system except when converted from or to energy.

Conservation of Momentum: All moving objects have momentum, and in a closed system, total momentum is always conserved. Linear momentum is the product of the mass of an object and its velocity. In the following equation, *M* and *V* represent the initial total mass and velocity of objects within a closed system. After a collision between those objects, the mass and velocity of individual objects may change (for example, one object breaks into smaller pieces, each traveling at a different velocity), but the product of the total mass and velocity in the system after the collision (*mv*) will remain the same.

$$MV = mv$$

Any object moving in a circle has another kind of momentum—angular momentum. This is because circular motion requires acceleration toward the center of the circle. The amount of acceleration depends on the speed of the object and the square of the radius of the circle. (Angular momentum is the product of this speed, the mass of the object, and the square of the radius.)

Conservation of Energy: The total amount of energy in a closed system will not change except when converted from or to mass.

Conservation of Mass-Energy: Although mass and energy can be converted into one another, the total amount of mass and energy together must be conserved. This is reflected in Einstein's famous equation, where *m* is mass, *E* is energy, and *c* is the speed of light in a vacuum (which is constant):

$$E = mc^2$$

Relativistic mass can describe how mass increases with velocity. The following equation—where *m* is the mass of a moving object, m_0 is the object's mass when not moving, *v* is the object's velocity in relation to a stationary observer, and *c* is the speed of light—shows the relationship:

$$m = \frac{m_0}{\sqrt{1-\frac{v^2}{c^2}}}$$

The theory that no object can travel faster than the speed of light is based in this equation. As an object approaches *c*, so much energy is converted to mass that it no longer accelerates.

Laws of Thermodynamics

1. Heat is a form of energy. Within a closed system energy must be conserved except in nuclear reactions or other extreme conditions. It is neither created nor destroyed.

2. Within a self-sustaining system, heat can never go from an area of low temperature to an area of high temperature, for that would require added energy. Without added energy, disorder, or entropy, can only increase.

3. Absolute zero cannot be attained by any procedure in a finite number of steps. Although it can be approached asymptotically, it can never be reached.

Laws of Current Electricity

Electric current generally represents the flow of electrons through a conductor. The rate at which electrons flow can be measured in amperes, defined as the number of electrons (measured in a unit called the coulomb, equal to about 6.24 quintillion or 6.24×10^{18} electrons) moving past a particular point every second. One ampere is equal to 1 coulomb of charge passing each second. Like water, electrons tend to move from areas of high pressure to low pressure. The difference between these two pressures, known as potential difference, is measured in volts.

Certain substances, such as copper and carbon, allow electric currents to pass more readily than others—that is, they have greater conductivity. Resistance to conductivity is measured in ohms.

Ohm's Law: Electric current is directly proportional to the potential difference and inversely proportional to the total resistance of the circuit. *I* is electric current (measured in amperes), *V* is the potential difference (measured in volts), and *R* is resistance (measured in ohms):

$$I = \frac{V}{R}$$

Law of Electric Power: Electric power (*P*), measured in watts, represents the rate at which electricity is converted into some other form of energy (such as light, in the case of a lightbulb). For a direct-current circuit, *P* is the product of current and potential difference:

$$P = IV$$

Two Basic Laws of Quantum Physics

1. Heisenberg's uncertainty principle: Certain pairs of observable quantities like energy and time or position and momentum cannot be measured with complete accuracy simultaneously. Also known as the indeterminacy principle.

2. Pauli's exclusion principle: Two electrons in an atom cannot simultaneously occupy the same quantum or energy state. This has since been shown to be true also for other types of the subatomic particles known as fermions.

Breaking the Sound Barrier; Speed of Sound

The prefix **Mach** is used to describe supersonic speed. It was named for Ernst Mach (1838-1916), a Czech-born Austrian physicist. Mach may be defined as the ratio of the velocity of an object to the velocity of sound in a particular medium. A plane moving at the speed of sound moves at Mach 1. At twice the speed of sound, it moves at Mach 2.

When a plane passes the sound barrier—that is, flies faster than the speed at which sound travels—people in the area, though not the people on the plane, hear what seem to be thunderclaps. These sounds are sometimes called sonic booms.

Sound is produced by vibrations of an object. It is transmitted by the alternating increase and decrease in pressure that radiates outward from a source through a material medium of molecules, like waves spreading out on a pond after a rock has been tossed in.

The **frequency of sound** is determined by the number of times the vibrating waves undulate per second. It is measured in cycles per second. The slower the cycle of waves, the lower the frequency. As the frequency increases, the sound becomes higher in pitch. The human ear is sensitive to frequencies between 20 and 20,000 vibrations per second, although this range varies among individuals and decreases with age.

Intensity, or loudness, is the strength of the pressure of these radiating waves and is measured in decibels (dB).

The **speed of sound** varies depending on temperature and the medium through which it travels. It moves faster in water than in air, for example. At sea level and a temperature of 59°F (15°C), the speed of sound is approximately 761 mph, or 1,100 ft per sec.

Light and Colors of the Spectrum

Light, a form of electromagnetic radiation similar to radiant heat, radio waves, and X-rays, is emitted from a source in straight lines and spreads in area as it travels. For emission from a point source, light per unit area diminishes in proportion to the square of the distance.

The English mathematician and physicist Isaac Newton (1642-1727) described light as an **emission of particles**; the Dutch astronomer, mathematician, and physicist Christiaan Huygens (1629-95) and others developed the theory that light travels in a **wave motion**. It is now believed that these two theories are essentially complementary. The development of quantum theory has led to results where light acts like a series of particles in some experiments and like a wave in others.

The first relatively accurate measurement of the **speed of light** was made by French physicist Armand Hippolyte Louis Fizeau (1819-96). Today the speed of light is known precisely as 299,792.458 km per sec (or 186,282.397 mi/sec) in a vacuum. In water the speed of light is about 25% less, and in glass, 33% less.

Color sensations are produced through the excitation of the retina of the eye by light vibrating at different frequencies. The different colors of the visible spectrum may be seen by viewing light refracted by passage through a prism, which separates light into its component wavelengths.

Customarily, the basic colors are taken to be the six monochromatic (single) colors that occupy relatively large areas of the spectrum: red, orange, yellow, green, blue, and violet. So-called primary colors can be combined to produce the sensation of other colors. However, scientists disagree about how many and what primary colors to recognize. The color sensation of **black** is due to complete lack of stimulation of the retina, that of **white** to complete stimulation.

Infrared and **ultraviolet rays**, which are below the red (long) end and above the violet (short) end of the visible spectrum, respectively, are invisible to the naked human eye. Heat is the principal effect of infrared rays, and chemical action that of ultraviolet rays. Some animals can see infrared or ultraviolet light.

Life Cycles of Selected Animals

Information reviewed by Ronald M. Nowak, author of *Walker's Mammals of the World* (6th ed., Johns Hopkins University Press, 1999). Average longevity figures supplied by Ronald T. Reuther. These apply to animals in captivity; the potential lifespan of animals is rarely attained in nature. Figures on gestation and incubation are averages based on estimates.

Animal	Gestation (days)	Average longevity (yrs.)	Maximum longevity (yrs.-mos.)
Ass	365	12	47
Baboon	187	20	45
Bear (black)	219	18	36-10
Bear (grizzly)	225	25	50
Bear (polar)	240	20	45
Beaver	105	5	50
Bison	285	15	40
Camel	406	12	50
Cat (domestic)	63	12	38
Chimpanzee	230	20	60
Chipmunk	31	6	10
Cow	284	15	30
Deer (white-tailed)	201	8	20
Dog (domestic)	61	12	21
Elephant (African)	660	35	70
Elephant (Asian)	645	40	77
Elk	250	15	26-8
Fox (red)	52	7	14
Giraffe	457	10	36-2
Goat (domestic)	151	8	18
Gorilla	258	20	54
Guinea pig	68	4	8
Hippopotamus	238	41	61
Horse	330	20	50
Kangaroo (gray)	36	7	24
Leopard	98	12	23
Lion	100	15	30
Monkey (rhesus)	166	15	37
Moose	240	12	27
Mouse (domestic white)	19	3	6
Mouse (meadow)	21	3	4
Opossum (American)	13	1	5
Pig (domestic)	112	10	27
Puma	90	12	20
Rabbit (domestic)	31	5	18-10
Rhinoceros (black)	450	15	45-10
Rhinoceros (white)	480	20	50
Sea lion (California)	350	12	34
Sheep (domestic)	154	12	23
Squirrel (gray)	44	10	23-6
Tiger	105	16	26-3
Wolf (maned)	63	5	15-8
Zebra (Grant's)	365	15	50

Animal	Incubation time (days)
Chicken	21
Duck	30
Goose	30
Pigeon	18
Turkey	26

Geologic Time Scale

Our understanding of Earth's ancient history is largely a result of geoscientists' study of climate, rock strata, ice samples, mineral deposits, and fossils from around the world; clues to the planet's origin have also been found through the study of extraterrestrial bodies. Geologists divide Earth's history into the following units (MYA = million years ago):

PRECAMBRIAN TIME (4,567-539 MYA)

HADEAN EON (4,567-4,031 MYA) Earth initially has no continents, oceans, or life; surface conditions are defined by intense volcanic activity and widespread meteorite impact. Oldest known minerals and rocks, many of meteoric origin, date to this eon, which may also have seen the first appearance of life.

ARCHEAN EON (4,031-2,500 MYA) Earth's surface cools and water vapor in atmosphere condenses to form early oceans, which define small protocontinents; there is substantial evidence for the existence of single-celled organisms, bacteria and archaea, in these oceans.

PROTEROZOIC EON (2,500-539 MYA) Protocontinents merge into larger landmasses as Earth's crust continues to shift. Atmospheric oxygen levels increase, and first known multicellular life appears. Later, soft-bodied marine animals emerge.

PHANEROZOIC EON (539 MYA-present)

Paleozoic Era (539-252 MYA)

Cambrian Period (539-485 MYA). The supercontinent known as Gondwana, or Gondwanaland, dominates the Southern Hemisphere. Seas experience an explosion of invertebrate animal life, including thousands of species of trilobites; the first known vertebrates appear. There is no life on land.

Ordovician Period (485-444 MYA). Gondwanaland extends from South Pole to tropic regions; Northern Hemisphere is mostly open ocean. Average global temperatures are warmer than in the current era. First primitive land plants, early ancestors of starfish and mollusks, and first armored, jawless fishes appear. The period ends in mass extinction of a majority of species, possibly a result of a global drop in sea level due to glaciation.

Silurian Period (444-419 MYA). South Pole remains covered by supercontinent, but precursors of present-day N America, Europe, and Asia coalesce around the equator and middle latitudes. Appearance of first known vascular land plants, first freshwater fish, first jawed fish, first coral reefs, and first air-breathing animals (certain eurypterids, also called sea scorpions, largest known arthropods).

Devonian Period (419-359 MYA). Collisions between Gondwanaland and ancestral landmasses of N America and Eurasia produce mountains visible today as northern Appalachians. Newly formed ozone layer offers protection from sun's rays, allowing first air-breathing spiders and mites to appear on dry land. Fish with fins and scales and first amphibians emerge. Late Devonian mass extinction.

Carboniferous Period (359-299 MYA). Precursors of modern N America and Northern Europe lie in tropical latitudes N of the equator; warm and humid conditions there facilitate spread of lush forests and peat swamps that later form most of the world's coal and limestone. Later period sees emergence of first true conifers, Lepidodendrales ("scale trees") as tall as 100 ft, and first true reptiles.

Permian Period (299-252 MYA). All major landmasses collide to form the supercontinent Pangaea, surrounded by the world ocean Panthalassa. Gradual warming through much of the Permian allows for initial flourishing of species, including dinosaur precursors (up to 10 ft long) and marine species in shallow inland seas. The period ended with the largest of Earth's five mass extinctions. As much as 95% of all marine species and most land species went extinct in the event, which was likely caused by increased greenhouse gases in atmosphere.

Mesozoic Era (252-66 MYA)

Triassic Period (252-201 MYA). Pangaea separates into supercontinents of Laurasia and Gondwana; subtropical conditions extend as far N as present-day Wyoming and New England. Emergence of icthyosaurs and plesiosaurs (large marine reptiles), pterosaurs (winged reptiles), several species of dinosaurs (up to 15 ft long), first true mammals, and first insects to undergo metamorphosis from larva to pupa to adult. Triassic-Jurassic mass extinction.

Jurassic Period (201-145 MYA). N American continent drifts westward, opening Gulf of Mexico; rift forms between S America and Africa. Warm, moist climate contributes to flourishing of coral reefs and temperate and subtropical forests. Appearance of first angiosperms (flowering plants), the earliest known birds (offshoots of a dinosaur group), and huge dinosaurs such as the carnivorous *Allosaurus* and herbivorous *Apatosaurus*.

Cretaceous Period (145-66 MYA). African continental plate drifts N, creating roots of European Alps; gap between S America and Africa broadens; western movement of N America drives formation of Sierra Nevada and Rocky Mountains, turning the western interior of continent into a vast swamp. Later, sea levels rise and cover about one-third of Earth's present land area. The global climate is warm and mild. The period ends in a mass extinction of plant and animal species (including dinosaurs). Likely causes include an asteroid impact and increased volcanic activity.

Cenozoic Era (66 MYA-present)

Paleogene Period (66-23 MYA)

- Paleocene Epoch (66-56 MYA). Australia begins to separate from Antarctica; N America and Greenland begin to spread apart. Mammalian life predominates, including early marsupials, insectivores, creodonts (carnivorous relatives of cats and dogs), and primitive hoofed mammals.
- Eocene Epoch (56-33.9 MYA). Australia drifts farther from Antarctica; the Indian subcontinent becomes welded to Asia, and tectonic forces drive the upheaval of the Alpine-Himalayan system. Climate in N America and Europe is subtropical and moist, with temperate forests as far N as Greenland and Siberia. Ancestors of modern horses, elephants, rhinoceroses, camels, bats, primates, and squirrel-like rodents emerge; earliest known marine mammals appear in later Eocene.
- Oligocene Epoch (33.9-23 MYA). San Andreas fault develops between N American and Pacific plates. Mammalian species continue to diversify, producing modern horse and multiple rodent, camel, and rhinoceros-like species, as well as first known species of great ape. Long-term cooling trend begins that would later cause Pleistocene ice ages.

Neogene Period (23-2.6 MYA)

- Miocene Epoch (23-5.3 MYA). Crustal plate collisions continue to drive uplift of Alps, Himalayas, and Cordilleran Ranges in Americas; eroded sediment is deposited in shallow marine basins, forming reservoirs for oil fields of California, Romania, and Caspian Sea. Ocean currents prevent Antarctica from receiving warmer waters, fostering growth of Antarctic ice sheet. Northern forests become grassy prairies. Large apes related to the orangutan live in Asia and southern Europe. Oldest hominin fossils from Africa date to this epoch.
- Pliocene Epoch (5.3-2.6 MYA). Alps continue to rise in Europe, and subduction of the Pacific tectonic plate elevates the Sierra Nevada and volcanic Cascade Range. Climate becomes cooler and drier, driving formation of permanent Arctic ice cap. Rapid primate evolution produces *Australopithecus*, an early direct ancestor of modern humans (*Homo sapiens*).

Quarternary Period (2.6 MYA-present)

- Pleistocene Epoch (2.6 MYA-11,700 years ago). Glacier ice covers as much as 25% or more of Earth's land surface, carving numerous present-day features including the Great Lakes; increased rainfall in lower latitudes allows plant and animal life to flourish in northern and eastern Africa. Late Pleistocene brings worldwide extinction of many large mammals, including the mastodon, saber-toothed tiger, and ground sloth. Evidence of Neanderthals, Denisovans, and the small archaic humans *Homo floresiensis* and *Homo luzonensis* dates from the latter part of the Pleistocene.
- Holocene Epoch (11,700 years ago-present). Melting ice caused sea levels to rise 100 ft or more in early Holocene, covering large areas of land and extending continental shelf of N America. Humans proliferate, and civilization begins.

Biological Classification

In biology, classification is the identification, naming, and grouping of organisms into a formal system. The two fields that are most directly concerned with classification are taxonomy and systematics. Although they overlap, taxonomy is more concerned with nomenclature (naming) and with constructing hierarchical systems, and systematics with uncovering evolutionary relationships. Two kingdoms of living forms, Plantae and Animalia, have been recognized since Aristotle established the first taxonomy in the 4th century BCE. Plants and animals are examples of eukaryotes; their cells have nuclei bound by membranes. Two other kingdoms of eukaryotes that have been identified are Protista (mostly one-celled organisms) and Fungi. Single-celled bacteria and archaea lack such nuclei. They are referred to as prokaryotes (or procaryotes) and are commonly placed in separate kingdoms. The seven basic categories of classification (from most general to most specific) are kingdom, phylum (or division), class, order, family, genus, and species. (In addition, many scientists group all eukaryotes in a single "domain," and treat bacteria and archaea as two other domains.) Below are two examples of classification:

ZOOLOGICAL HIERARCHY

Kingdom	Phylum	Class	Order	Family	Genus	Species name	Common name
Animalia	Chordata	Mammalia	Primates	Hominidae	*Homo*	*Homo sapiens*	Human

BOTANICAL HIERARCHY

Kingdom	Division*	Class	Order	Family	Genus	Species name	Common name
Plantae	Magnoliophyta	Magnoliopsida	Magnoliales	Magnoliaceae	*Magnolia*	*M. virginiana*	Sweet bay

*In botany, the division is generally used in place of the phylum.

Selected Endangered or Threatened Animal Species

Source: Fish and Wildlife Service, U.S. Dept. of the Interior

Common name	Scientific name	Range of concern
Albatross, Amsterdam	*Diomedia amsterdamensis*	Amsterdam Island, Indian Ocean
Antelope, giant sable	*Hippotragus niger variani*	Angola
Armadillo, giant	*Priodontes maximus*	Venezuela and Guyana to Argentina
Bandicoot, desert	*Perameles eremiana*	Australia
Bat, gray	*Myotis grisescens*	Central, southeastern U.S.
Bear, grizzly	*Ursus arctos horribilis*	U.S. (mountain-prairie region)
Bobcat, Mexican	*Lynx rufus escuinapae*	Mexico
Bumble bee, rusty patched	*Bombus affinis*	Canada; Eastern, midwestern U.S.
Camel, Bactrian	*Camelus bactrianus*	Mongolia, China
Caribou, woodland	*Rangifer tarandus caribou*	Canada, U.S. (ID, WA)
Cheetah	*Acinonyx jubatus*	Africa to India
Chimpanzee, pygmy	*Pan paniscus*	Dem. Rep. of the Congo
Condor, California	*Gymnogyps californianus*	U.S. (AZ, CA, NV, UT), Mexico (Baja California)
Crane, whooping	*Grus americana*	Canada, central U.S.
Crocodile, American	*Crocodylus acutus*	U.S. (FL); Caribbean; Central, S America
Dolphin, Chinese river	*Lipotes vexillifer*	China
Duck, Hawaiian	*Anas wyvilliana*	U.S. (HI)
Elephant, Asian	*Elephas maximus*	South-central and southeastern Asia
Fox, northern swift	*Vulpes velox hebes*	Canada
Frog, mountain yellow-legged	*Rana muscosa*	U.S. (CA)
Gorilla	*Gorilla gorilla*	Central and western Africa
Hyena, brown	*Parahyaena brunnea*	Southern Africa
Impala, black-faced	*Aepyceros melampus petersi*	Angola, Namibia
Kangaroo, Tasmanian forester	*Macropus giganteus tasmaniensis*	Australia (Tasmania)
Leopard	*Panthera pardus*	Central and Southern Africa, Asia
Monkey, spider	*Ateles geoffroyi frontatus*	Central America
Ocelot	*Leopardus pardalis*	U.S. (AZ, TX), Mexico; Central, S America
Orangutan	*Pongo pygmaeus*	Indonesia
Ostrich, West African	*Struthio camelus spatzi*	Western Sahara
Otter, marine	*Lontra felina*	Peru south to Straits of Magellan
Panda, giant	*Ailuropoda melanoleuca*	China
Panther, Florida	*Puma concolor coryi*	U.S. (FL)
Parrot, imperial	*Amazona imperialis*	Dominica
Penguin, Galapagos	*Spheniscus mendiculus*	Ecuador (Galapagos Islands)
Porpoise, Gulf of California harbor (vaquita)	*Phocoena sinus*	Mexico
Rhinoceros, black	*Diceros bicornis*	Sub-Saharan Africa
Salamander, Chinese giant	*Andrias davidianus*	China
Salmon, sockeye	*Oncorhynchus nerka*	U.S. (OR, WA)
Sea lion, Steller (Western pop.)	*Eumetopias jubatus*	U.S. (AK), Russia
Squirrel, Carolina northern flying	*Glaucomys sabrinus coloratus*	U.S. (NC, TN, VA)
Tiger	*Panthera tigris*	Asia
Tortoise, Galapagos	*Geochelone nigra*	Ecuador (Galapagos Islands)
Whale, gray (Western North Pacific pop.)	*Eschrichtius robustus*	NW Pacific Ocean
Wolf, red	*Canis rufus*	U.S. (FL)
Wolverine, North American	*Gulo gulo luscus*	U.S. (Northern Rocky Mountains, North Cascade Mountains)
Woodpecker, ivory-billed	*Campephilus principalis*	U.S. (AR)
Yak, wild	*Bos mutus*	China (Tibet), India
Zebra, mountain	*Equus zebra zebra*	South Africa

Status of Endangered and Threatened Species, 2024

Source: Fish and Wildlife Service, U.S. Dept. of the Interior; as of July 2024

	Endangered		Threatened			
Group	U.S.	Foreign	U.S.	Foreign	Total species[1]	U.S. species with active recovery plans
Mammals	66	263	30	23	382	65
Birds	68	219	25	22	334	81
Fishes	92	27	78	9	206	108
Reptiles	19	70	31	25	145	43
Clams	75	2	21	0	98	74
Insects	76	4	18	0	98	70
Snails	39	1	13	1	54	43
Amphibians	25	8	18	1	52	31
Crustaceans	25	0	7	0	32	25
Corals	0	3	7	15	25	0
Arachnids	11	5	0	0	16	11
Annelid worms	0	0	0	0	0	0
Flatworms and roundworms	0	0	0	0	0	0
Hydroids	0	0	0	0	0	0
Millipedes	0	0	0	0	0	0
Sponges	0	0	0	0	0	0
Animal subtotals	**496**	**602**	**248**	**96**	**1,442**	**551**
Plant subtotals	**764**	**1**	**174**	**2**	**941**	**839**
Grand totals	**1,260**	**603**	**422**	**98**	**2,383**	**1,390**

(1) 24 animal species are counted more than once in this table, primarily because these animals have distinct population segments, each with its own individual listing status. The U.S. species tallied more than once as endangered or threatened are Atlantic sturgeon, bearded seal, California tiger salamander, Chinook salmon, chum salmon, coho salmon, foothill yellow-legged frog, gray wolf, lesser prairie-chicken, mountain yellow-legged frog, piping plover, roseate tern, sockeye salmon, and steelhead (rainbow trout). The foreign species counted more than once are argali, broad-snouted caiman, humpback whale, leopard, scalloped hammerhead shark, and vicuña. Green sea turtles and loggerhead sea turtles appear on both the U.S. and foreign lists.

Major Venomous Animals

Snakes

Asian pit viper—2 ft to 5 ft long; throughout Asia; reactions and mortality vary, but most bites cause tissue damage; mortality generally low.

Australian brown snake—4 ft to 7 ft long; very slow onset of cardiac or respiratory distress; moderate mortality, but because death can be sudden and unexpected, it is the most dangerous of the Australian snakes; antivenom.

Barba amarilla or fer-de-lance—up to 7 ft long; from tropical Mexico to Brazil; severe tissue damage common; moderate mortality; antivenom.

Black mamba—up to 14 ft long; southern and central Africa; rapid onset of dizziness, difficulty breathing, erratic heartbeat; mortality high, nears 100% without antivenom.

Boomslang—less than 6 ft long; African savannahs; rapid onset of nausea and dizziness, often followed by slight recovery and then sudden death from internal hemorrhaging; bites rare, mortality high; antivenom.

Bushmaster—up to 12 ft long; tropical forests of Central and S America; few bites occur, but mortality high.

Common, or Asian, cobra—4 ft to 8 ft long; throughout S Asia; considerable tissue damage, sometimes paralysis; mortality probably not more than 10%; antivenom.

Copperhead—less than 4 ft long; New England to Texas; pain and swelling; very seldom fatal; antivenom seldom needed.

Coral snake—2 ft to 5 ft long; in Americas S of Canada; bite may be painless; slow onset of paralysis, impaired breathing; mortalities rare but high without antivenom and mechanical respiration.

Cottonmouth water moccasin—up to 5 ft long; wetlands of southern U.S. from Virginia to Texas; rapid onset of severe pain, swelling, tissue destruction can be extensive; mortality low; antivenom.

Death adder—less than 3 ft long; Australia; rapid onset of faintness, cardiac and respiratory distress; at least 50% mortality without antivenom.

Desert horned viper—up to 2 ft long; dry areas of Africa and western Asia; swelling and tissue damage; mortality low; antivenom.

European viper—1 ft to 3 ft long; throughout Europe; bleeding and tissue damage; mortality low; antivenom.

Gaboon viper—more than 6 ft long; S of the Sahara; massive tissue damage, internal bleeding; few recorded bites.

King cobra—up to 16 ft long; throughout S Asia; rapid swelling, dizziness, loss of consciousness, difficulty breathing, erratic heartbeat; mortality varies with amount of venom involved, but most bites involve nonfatal amounts; antivenom.

Krait—up to 5 ft long; SE Asia; rapid onset of sleepiness, numbness; up to 50% mortality even with use of antivenom.

Puff adder—up to 5 ft long, thick; S of the Sahara, throughout the Middle East; rapid large swelling, great pain, dizziness; moderate mortality, often from internal bleeding; antivenom.

Rattlesnake—2 ft to 6 ft long; throughout Western Hemisphere; rapid onset of severe pain, swelling; mortality low, but amputation of affected digits is sometimes necessary; antivenom. Mojave rattler may produce temporary paralysis.

Ringhals, or spitting, cobra—5 ft to 7 ft long; southern Africa; squirts venom through holes in front of fangs as a defense; venom severely irritating and can cause blindness.

Russell's viper or tic-polonga—more than 5 ft long; throughout Asia; internal bleeding; bite reports common; moderate mortality rate; antivenom.

Saw-scaled, or carpet, viper—up to 2 ft long; dry areas from India to Africa; severe bleeding, fever; high mortality, causes more human fatalities than any other snake; antivenom.

Sea snake—3 ft to 10 ft long; throughout Pacific, Indian Oceans except NE Pacific; almost painless bite; variety of muscle pain, paralysis; mortality low, many bites not envenomed; some antivenoms.

Sharp-nosed pit viper or hundred-pace snake—up to 5 ft long; S Vietnam, Taiwan, and China; the most toxic of Asian pit vipers; very rapid onset of swelling and tissue damage, internal bleeding; moderate mortality; antivenom.

Taipan—up to 11 ft long; Australia and New Guinea; rapid paralysis with severe breathing difficulty; mortality nears 100% without antivenom.

Tiger snake—2 ft to 6 ft long; southern Australia; pain, numbness, mental disturbances with rapid paralysis; may be deadliest of all land snakes, but antivenom is quite effective.

Yellow, or cape, cobra—7 ft long; southern Africa; most toxic venom of any cobra; rapid onset of swelling, breathing and cardiac difficulties; mortality is high without treatment; antivenom.

Note: Not all bites by venomous snakes are actually envenomed. Any animal bite, however, carries the danger of tetanus, and anyone suffering a venomous snake bite should seek medical attention. Antivenoms do not cure; they are only an aid in the treatment of bites. Mortality rates above are for envenomed bites: low mortality, c. 2% or less; moderate, 2%-5%; high, 5%-15%.

Lizards

Gila monster—up to 24 in. long, with heavy body and tail; high desert in SW U.S. and northern Mexico; immediate severe pain, transient low blood pressure; no recent mortality.

Mexican beaded lizard—similar to Gila monster; W coast of Mexico; reaction and mortality similar to Gila monster.

Insects

Ants, bees, hornets, wasps—global distribution; usual reaction is piercing pain in area of sting, though many people suffer allergic reactions (swelling, rashes); not directly fatal, except in cases of massive multiple stings, and a few may die within minutes from severe sensitivity to the venom (anaphylactic shock).

Spiders, scorpions

Black widow—small, round-bodied with red hourglass marking; the widow and its relatives are found in tropical and temperate zones; severe musculoskeletal pain, weakness, breathing difficulty, convulsions, which may be more serious in small children; low mortality; antivenom. The **redback** spider of Australia has the hourglass marking on its back, rather than on its front, but otherwise looks almost identical to the black widow.

Brown recluse, or fiddleback, spider—small, oblong body; throughout U.S.; pain with later ulceration, which may last months, at place of bite; fever, nausea, and stomach cramps in severe cases; very low mortality.

Funnel web spider—several varieties, often large; Australia; slow onset of breathing, circulation difficulties; low mortality; antivenom.

Scorpion—crablike body with stinger in tail, various sizes; many varieties throughout tropical and subtropical areas; severe pain spreading from the wound, numbness, severe agitation, cramps, and even respiratory failure; low mortality, usually in children; antivenoms.

Tarantula—large, hairy spider; worldwide; the American tarantula, and probably all other tarantulas, are harmless to humans, though their bite may cause some pain and swelling.

Sea life

Cone shell or cone snail—mollusk in small shell; S Pacific and Indian Oceans; shoots barbs into victims; paralysis; low mortality.

Octopus—global distribution, usually in warm waters; rapid onset of paralysis with breathing difficulty; all varieties produce venom, but only a few can cause death.

Portuguese man-of-war—jellyfish-like siphonophore with tentacles up to 100 ft long; in most warm water areas; immediate severe pain; not directly fatal, though shock may cause death in rare cases.

Sea wasp or box jellyfish—tentacles up to 30 ft long; S Pacific; very rapid onset of circulatory problems; high mortality because of speed of toxic reaction; antivenom.

Stingray—several varieties of differing sizes; tropical and temperate seas and some freshwater; severe pain, rapid onset of nausea, vomiting, breathing difficulties; wound area may ulcerate, gangrene may occur; seldom fatal.

Stonefish—brownish fish that lies motionless on bottom of shallow waters; throughout S Pacific and Indian Oceans; extraordinary pain, rapid paralysis; low mortality; antivenom, warm water relieves pain.

Speeds of Selected Animals

Source: *Natural History* magazine. © American Museum of Natural History

Animal	Speed (mph)	Animal	Speed (mph)	Animal	Speed (mph)
Cheetah	70	Mongolian wild ass	40	Human	27.89
Pronghorn antelope	61	Greyhound	39.35	Elephant	25
Wildebeest	50	Whippet	35.50	Black mamba snake	20
Lion	50	Rabbit (domestic)	35	Six-lined race runner (lizard)	18
Thomson's gazelle	50	Mule deer	35	Wild turkey	15
Quarterhorse	47.5	Jackal	35	Squirrel	12
Elk	45	Reindeer	32	Pig (domestic)	11
Cape hunting dog	45	Giraffe	32	Chicken	9
Coyote	43	White-tailed deer	30	Spider (*Tegenaria atrica*)	1.17
Gray fox	42	Warthog	30	Giant tortoise	0.17
Hyena	40	Grizzly bear	30	Three-toed sloth	0.15
Zebra	40	Cat (domestic)	30	Garden snail	0.03

Note: Most of these measurements are for maximum speeds over approximate quarter-mile distances. Exceptions are the lion and elephant, whose speeds were clocked in the act of charging; the whippet, which was timed over a 200-yd course; the cheetah, timed over a 100-yd distance; a human, timed over a 15-yd segment of a 100-yd run; and the black mamba, six-lined race runner, spider, giant tortoise, three-toed sloth, and garden snail, which were measured over various small distances.

Most Popular Breeds of Pedigreed Cats, 2022-23

Source: The Cat Fanciers' Association

(ranked by total registrations for the period Jan. 1, 2022-Dec. 31, 2023)

Rank	Breed	Rank	Breed	Rank	Breed	Rank	Breed	Rank	Breed
1.	Ragdoll	11.	American Shorthair	20.	Burmese	29.	Toybob	37.	Korat
2.	Maine Coon Cat	12.	Russian Blue	21.	Somali	30.	Turkish Angora	38.	Burmilla
3.	Persian	13.	Norwegian Forest Cat	22.	Tonkinese	31.	Bombay	39.	Singapura
4.	Exotic	14.	Oriental	23.	Ocicat	32.	Balinese/Javanese	40.	Chartreux
5.	Devon Rex	15.	Bengal	24.	Lykoi	33.	American Curl	41.	American Bobtail
6.	British Shorthair	16.	Cornish Rex	25.	Egyptian Mau	34.	Colorpoint Shorthair	42.	Khao Manee
7.	Abyssinian	17.	Siamese	26.	European Burmese	35.	Havana Brown	43.	LaPerm
8.	Scottish Fold	18.	Selkirk Rex	27.	Japanese Bobtail	36.	Manx	44.	American Wirehair
9.	Siberian	19.	Birman	28.	RagaMuffin			45.	Turkish Van
10.	Sphynx								

Most Popular American Kennel Club Dog Breed Registrations, 2020-2023

Source: American Kennel Club (AKC)

(ranked by 2023 registrations)

Breed	Rank 2023	2022	2021	2020
French Bulldog	1	1	2	2
Labrador Retriever	2	2	1	1
Golden Retriever	3	3	3	4
German Shepherd Dog	4	4	4	3
Poodle	5	5	5	6
Dachshund	6	9	10	10
Bulldog	7	6	6	5
Beagle	8	8	7	7
Rottweiler	9	7	8	8
German Shorthaired Pointer	10	10	9	9
Pembroke Welsh Corgi	11	11	11	11
Australian Shepherd	12	12	12	12
Yorkshire Terrier	13	13	13	13
Cavalier King Charles Spaniel	14	14	15	17
Doberman Pinscher	15	15	16	18
Cane Corso	16	18	21	25
Miniature Schnauzer	17	17	18	19
Boxer	18	16	14	14
Great Dane	19	19	17	15
Shih Tzu	20	20	22	20
Bernese Mountain Dog	21	22	20	22
Pomeranian	22	23	24	23
Boston Terrier	23	24	23	21
Siberian Husky	24	21	19	16
Havanese	25	25	25	24
Shetland Sheepdog	26	27	28	27
English Springer Spaniel	27	26	26	26
Brittany	28	28	27	28
Miniature American Shepherd	29	31	30	31
Cocker Spaniel	30	29	29	30

Dog Breeds by Type

Source: American Kennel Club (AKC)

According to the AKC, there are more than 340 dog breeds known throughout the world. As of mid-2024, the AKC recognized about 200 registered breeds and used the following seven groups to classify them, according to functions and other distinctive traits.

Herding Group: Australian Cattle Dog, Australian Shepherd, Bearded Collie, Beauceron, Belgian Laekenois, Belgian Malinois, Belgian Sheepdog, Belgian Tervuren, Bergamasco Sheepdog, Berger Picard, Border Collie, Bouvier des Flandres, Briard, Canaan Dog, Cardigan Welsh Corgi, Collie, Entlebucher Mountain Dog, Finnish Lapphund, German Shepherd Dog, Icelandic Sheepdog, Lancashire Heeler, Miniature American Shepherd, Mudi, Norwegian Buhund, Old English Sheepdog, Pembroke Welsh Corgi, Polish Lowland Sheepdog, Puli, Pumi, Pyrenean Shepherd, Shetland Sheepdog, Spanish Water Dog, Swedish Vallhund.

Hound Group: Afghan Hound, American English Coonhound, American Foxhound, Azawakh, Basenji, Basset Hound, Beagle, Black and Tan Coonhound, Bloodhound, Bluetick Coonhound, Borzoi, Cirneco dell'Etna, Dachshund, English Foxhound, Grand Basset Griffon Vendéen, Greyhound, Harrier, Ibizan Hound, Irish Wolfhound, Norwegian Elkhound, Otterhound, Petit Basset Griffon Vendéen, Pharaoh Hound, Plott Hound, Portuguese Podengo Pequeno, Redbone Coonhound, Rhodesian Ridgeback, Saluki, Scottish Deerhound, Sloughi, Treeing Walker Coonhound, Whippet.

Non-Sporting Group: American Eskimo Dog, Bichon Frise, Boston Terrier, Bulldog, Chinese Shar-Pei, Chow Chow, Coton de Tulear, Dalmatian, Finnish Spitz, French Bulldog, Keeshond, Lhasa Apso, Löwchen, Norwegian Lundehund, Poodle (Standard and Miniature), Schipperke, Shiba Inu, Tibetan Spaniel, Tibetan Terrier, Xoloitzcuintli.

Sporting Group: American Water Spaniel, Barbet, Boykin Spaniel, Bracco Italiano, Brittany, Chesapeake Bay Retriever, Clumber Spaniel, Cocker Spaniel, Curly-Coated Retriever, English Cocker Spaniel, English Setter, English Springer Spaniel, Field Spaniel, Flat-Coated Retriever, German Shorthaired Pointer, German Wirehaired Pointer, Golden Retriever, Gordon Setter, Irish Red and White Setter, Irish Setter, Irish Water Spaniel, Labrador Retriever, Lagotto Romagnolo, Nederlandse Kooikerhondje, Nova Scotia Duck Tolling Retriever, Pointer, Spinone Italiano, Sussex Spaniel, Vizsla, Weimaraner, Welsh Springer Spaniel, Wirehaired Pointing Griffon, Wirehaired Vizsla.

Terrier Group: Airedale Terrier, American Hairless Terrier, American Staffordshire Terrier, Australian Terrier, Bedlington Terrier, Border Terrier, Bull Terrier, Cairn Terrier, Cesky Terrier, Dandie Dinmont Terrier, Glen of Imaal Terrier, Irish Terrier, Kerry Blue Terrier, Lakeland Terrier, Manchester Terrier (Standard), Miniature Bull Terrier, Miniature Schnauzer, Norfolk Terrier, Norwich Terrier, Parson Russell Terrier, Rat Terrier, Russell Terrier, Scottish Terrier, Sealyham Terrier, Skye Terrier, Smooth Fox Terrier, Soft Coated Wheaten Terrier, Staffordshire Bull Terrier, Welsh Terrier, West Highland White Terrier, Wire Fox Terrier.

Toy Group: Affenpinscher, Biewer Terrier, Brussels Griffon, Cavalier King Charles Spaniel, Chihuahua, Chinese Crested, English Toy Spaniel, Havanese, Italian Greyhound, Japanese Chin, Maltese, Manchester Terrier (Toy), Miniature Pinscher, Papillon, Pekingese, Pomeranian, Poodle (Toy), Pug, Russian Toy, Shih Tzu, Silky Terrier, Toy Fox Terrier, Yorkshire Terrier.

Working Group: Akita, Alaskan Malamute, Anatolian Shepherd Dog, Bernese Mountain Dog, Black Russian Terrier, Boerboel, Boxer, Bullmastiff, Cane Corso, Chinook, Doberman Pinscher, Dogo Argentino, Dogue de Bordeaux, German Pinscher, Giant Schnauzer, Great Dane, Great Pyrenees, Greater Swiss Mountain Dog, Komondor, Kuvasz, Leonberger, Mastiff, Neapolitan Mastiff, Newfoundland, Portuguese Water Dog, Rottweiler, Saint Bernard, Samoyed, Siberian Husky, Standard Schnauzer, Tibetan Mastiff.

Discoveries and Innovations: Biology, Chemistry, Medicine, Physics

Discovery	Date	Discoverer(s)	Nationality
Acetylene gas	**1862**	Berthelot	French
ACTH	**1927**	Evans, Long	U.S.
Adrenaline	**1901**	Takamine	Japanese
Aluminum, electrolytic process	**1886**	Hall	U.S.
Aluminum, isolated	**1825**	Oersted	Danish
Anesthesia, ether	**1842**	Long	U.S.
Anesthesia, local	**1885**	Koller	Austrian
Anesthesia, spinal	**1898**	Bier	German
Aniline dye	**1856**	Perkin	English
Anti-rabies	**1885**	Pasteur	French
Antiseptic surgery	**1867**	Lister	English
Antitoxin, diphtheria	**1891**	Von Behring	German
Argyrol	**1897**	Bayer	German
Arsphenamine	**1910**	Ehrlich	German
Aspirin	**1853**	Gerhardt	French
Atabrine	**1932**	Mietzsch, et al.	German
Atomic numbers	**1913**	Moseley	English
Atomic theory	**1803**	Dalton	English
Atomic time clock	**1948**	Lyons	U.S.
Atom-smashing theory	**1919**	Rutherford	English
Bacitracin	**1943**	Johnson, Meleneyl	U.S.
Bacteria, description	**1676**	Leeuwenhoek	Dutch
Bacterial genome, synth.	**2010**	Venter	U.S.
Bleaching powder	**1798**	Tennant	English
Blood, circulation	**1628**	Harvey	English
Bordeaux mixture	**1885**	Millardet	French
Bromine from the sea	**1826**	Balard	French
Calcium carbide	**1888**	Wilson	U.S.
Calculus	**1670**	Newton	English
Camphor synthetic	**1896**	Haller	French
Canning (food)	**1804**	Appert	French
Carbon oxides	**1925**	Fisher	German
Chemotherapy	**1909**	Ehrlich	German
Chloamphenicol	**1947**	Burkholder	U.S.
Chlorine	**1774**	Scheele	Swedish
Chloroform	**1831**	Guthrie	U.S.
Chlortetracycline	**1948**	Duggen	U.S.
Classification of plants and animals	**1735**	Linnaeus	Swedish
Cloning, DNA	**1973**	Boyer, Cohen	U.S.
Cloning, mammal	**1996**	Wilmut, et al.	Scottish
Cocaine	**1860**	Niermann	German
Combustion explained	**1777**	Lavoisier	French
Conditioned reflex	**1914**	Pavlov	Russian
Cortisone	**1936**	Kendall	U.S.
Cortisone, synthesis	**1946**	Sarett	U.S.
Cosmic rays	**1910**	Gockel	Swiss
Cyclotron	**1930**	Lawrence	U.S.
DDT (not applied as insecticide until 1939)	**1874**	Zeidler	German
Denisovan humans (DNA analysis)	**2010**	Krause, et al. Pääbo	German Swedish
Deuterium	**1932**	Urey, Brickwedde, Murphy	U.S.
DNA (as carrier of heredity)	**1943**	Avery, MacLeod, McCarty	U.S.
DNA (structure)	**1953**	Crick Watson Wilkins	English U.S. NZ-Eng.
Electric resistance, law of	**1827**	Ohm	German
Electric waves	**1888**	Hertz	German
Electrolysis	**1852**	Faraday	English
Electromagnetism	**1819**	Oersted	Danish
Electron	**1897**	Thomson, J.	English
Electron diffraction	**1936**	Thomson, G. Davisson	English U.S.
Electroshock treatment	**1938**	Cerletti, Bini	Italian
Erythromycin	**1952**	McGuire	U.S.
Evolution, natural selection	**1858**	Darwin	English
Falling bodies, law of	**1590**	Galileo	Italian
Gases, law of combining volumes	**1808**	Gay-Lussac	French
Geometry, analytic	**1619**	Descartes	French
Gold, cyanidation	**1887**	MacArthur, R. Forrest, W. Forrest	Scottish
Gravitation, law	**1687**	Newton	English
Gravitational waves (det.)	**2015**	LIGO	U.S.-Intl.
Higgs boson	**2012**	CERN	International
HIV (human immuno-deficiency virus)	**1984**	Montagnier Gallo	French U.S.
Holograph	**1948**	Gabor	Hung.-Brit.
Homo floresiensis ("hobbit" humans)	**2003**	Morwood, et al.	New Zea.
Human genome sequence (first draft)	**2001**	Human Genome Project, Celera Genomics Corp.	U.S.-Intl.
In vitro fertilization	**1978**	Steptoe, Edwards	English
Indigo, synthesis of	**1880**	Baeyer	German
Induction, electric	**1830**	Henry	U.S.
Insulin	**1922**	Banting, Best Macleod	Canadian Scottish
Intelligence testing	**1905**	Binet, Simon	French
Isotopes, theory	**1912**	Soddy	English
Laser	**1957**	Gould	U.S.
Light, velocity	**1675**	Roemer	Danish

Discovery	Date	Discoverer(s)	Nationality
Light, wave theory	**1690**	Huygens	Dutch
Lithography	**1796**	Senefelder	Bohemian
Logarithms	**1614**	Napier	Scottish
LSD-25	**1943**	Hoffman	Swiss
Mendelian laws	**1866**	Mendel	Austrian
Mercator projection (map)	**1568**	Mercator (Kremer)	Flemish
Methanol	**1661**	Boyle	Irish
Milk condensation	**1853**	Borden	U.S.
Molecular hypothesis	**1811**	Avogadro	Italian
Motion, laws of	**1687**	Newton	English
Neomycin	**1949**	Waksman, Lechevalier	U.S.
Neutrino	**1956**	Reines, Cowan	U.S.
Neutron	**1932**	Chadwick	English
Nitric acid	**1648**	Glauber	German
Nitric oxide	**1772**	Priestley	English
Nitroglycerin	**1846**	Sobrero	Italian
Oil cracking process	**1891**	Dewar	U.S.
Oxygen	**1774**	Priestley	English
Oxytetracycline	**1950**	Finlay, et al.	U.S.
Ozone	**1840**	Schonbein	German
Paper, sulfite process	**1867**	Tilghman	U.S.
Paper, wood pulp, sulfate process	**1884**	Dahl	German
Penicillin	**1928**	Fleming	Scottish
Penicillin, practical use	**1941**	Florey, Chain	English
Periodic law and table of elements	**1869**	Mendeleev	Russian
Physostigmine synthesis	**1935**	Julian	U.S.
Pill, birth-control	**1954**	Pincus, Rock	U.S.
Planetary motion, laws	**1609**	Kepler	German
Plutonium fission	**1940**	Kennedy, Wahl, Seaborg, Segre	U.S.
Polymyxin	**1947**	Ainsworth	English
Positron	**1932**	Anderson	U.S.
Proton	**1919**	Rutherford	New Zea.
Psychoanalysis	**1900**	Freud	Austrian
Pulsars	**1967**	Bell	English
Quantum theory	**1900**	Planck	German
Quasars	**1963**	Matthews, Sandage	U.S.
Quinine synthetic	**1946**	Woodward, Doering	U.S.
Radioactivity	**1896**	Becquerel	French
Radiocarbon dating	**1947**	Libby	U.S.
Radium	**1898**	Curie, Pierre	French
		Curie, Marie	Pol.-Fr.
Relativity theory	**1905**	Einstein	German
Reserpine	**1949**	Jal Vakil	Indian
Schick test	**1913**	Schick	U.S.
Silicon	**1823**	Berzelius	Swedish
Smallpox eradication	**1979**	World Health Org.	UN
Streptomycin	**1944**	Waksman, et al.	U.S.
Sulfanilamide	**1935**	Bovet, Trefouel	French
Sulfanilamide theory	**1908**	Gelmo	German
Sulfapyridine	**1938**	Ewins, Phelps	English
Sulfathiazole	**1939**	Fosbinder, Walter	U.S.
Sulfuric acid	**1831**	Phillips	English
Sulfuric acid, lead	**1746**	Roebuck	English
Superconductivity	**1911**	Onnes	Dutch
Superconductivity theory	**1957**	Bardeen, Cooper, Schreiffer	U.S.
Superconductors, high-temp.	**1986**	Bednorz	Ger.
		Müller	Swiss
Syphilis test	**1906**	Wassermann	German
Transplant, face	**2005**	Devauchelle, Dubernard	French
Transplant, heart	**1967**	Barnard	S. African
Tuberculin	**1890**	Koch	German
Uranium fission, atomic reactor	**1942**	Fermi, Szilard	U.S.
Uranium fission theory	**1939**	Hahn, Meitner, Strassmann	German
		Bohr	Danish
		Fermi	Italian
		Einstein, Pegram, Wheeler	U.S.
Vaccine, COVID-19[1]	**2020**	Pfizer/BioNTech	U.S., Ger.
Vaccine, Ebola	**2016**	Public Health Agency of Canada	Canadian
Vaccine, malaria (RTS,S)	**2021**	GlaxoSmithKline	British
Vaccine, measles	**1963**	Enders	U.S.
Vaccine, MMR	**1971**	Hilleman	U.S.
Vaccine, meningitis (first conjugate)	**1987**	Gordon, et al., Connaught Labs	U.S.
Vaccine, polio	**1954**	Salk	U.S.
Vaccine, polio, oral	**1960**	Sabin	U.S.
Vaccine, rabies	**1885**	Pasteur	French
Vaccine, smallpox	**1796**	Jenner	English
Vaccine, typhus	**1909**	Nicolle	French
Vaccine, varicella	**1974**	Takahashi	Japanese
Van Allen belts, radiation	**1958**	Van Allen	U.S.
Vitamin A	**1913**	McCollum, Davis	U.S.
Vitamin B	**1916**	McCollum	U.S.
Vitamin C	**1928**	Szent-Gyorgyi	Hungarian
		King	U.S.
Vitamin D	**1922**	McCollum	U.S.
Xerography	**1938**	Carlson	U.S.
X-ray	**1895**	Roentgen	German

(1) Out of more than 150 COVID-19 vaccine candidates under development at the end of 2020, Pfizer/BioNTech's was the first to receive emergency use validation from the World Health Org.

Inventions

Invention	Date	Inventor(s)	Nationality
Adding machine	**1642**	Pascal	French
Adding machine	**1885**	Burroughs	U.S.
Aerosol spray	**1926**	Rotheim	Norwegian
Air brake	**1869**	Westinghouse	U.S.
Air conditioning	**1902**	Carrier	U.S.
Air pump	**1654**	Guericke	German
Airbag	**1952**	Hetrick	U.S.
Airplane, automatic pilot	**1912**	Sperry	U.S.
Airplane, experimental	**1896**	Langley	U.S.
Airplane, hydro	**1911**	Curtiss	U.S.
Airplane jet engine	**1939**	Ohain	German
Airplane with motor	**1903**	Wright Bros.	U.S.
Airship	**1852**	Giffard	French
Aqua-Lung	**1943**	Cousteau, Gagnan	French
Arc welder	**1919**	Thomson	U.S.
Aspartame	**1965**	Schlatter	U.S.
ATM (automated cash-dispensing machine)	**1967**	Shepherd-Barron	Scottish
Autogyro	**1920**	de la Cierva	Spanish
Automobile, diff. gear	**1885**	Benz	German
Automobile, electric	**1892**	Morrison	U.S.
Automobile, exp'mtl	**1864**	Marcus	Austrian
Automobile, gasoline	**1889**	Daimler	German
Automobile, gasoline	**1892**	Duryea	U.S.
Automobile magneto	**1897**	Bosch	German
Automobile muffler	**1904**	Pope	U.S.
Automobile self-starter	**1911**	Kettering	U.S.
Bakelite	**1907**	Baekeland	Belg.-U.S.
Bar code	**1952**	Woodland, Silver	U.S.
Barometer	**1643**	Torricelli	Italian
Bicycle, electric	**1895**	Bolton	U.S.
Bicycle, modern	**1885**	Starley	English
Bifocal lens	**1780**	Franklin	U.S.
Bottle machine	**1895**	Owens	U.S.
Bluetooth	**1994**	Haartsen	Dutch
Braille printing	**1829**	Braille	French
Brassiere, modern	**1913**	Jacob	U.S
Bubble gum	**1928**	Diemer	U.S.
Burner, gas	**1855**	Bunsen	German
Calculator, electronic pocket	**1972**	Merryman, Van Tassel	U.S.
Calculator, mechanical	**1623**	Schickard	German
Camera, digital	**1977**	Lloyd, Sasson	U.S.
Camera, Kodak	**1888**	Eastman, Walker	U.S.
Camera, Polaroid Land	**1948**	Land	U.S.
Can, pop-top	**1959**	Fraze	U.S.
Car coupler	**1873**	Janney	U.S.
Carburetor, gasoline	**1893**	Maybach	German
Carding machine	**1797**	Whittemore	U.S.
Carpet sweeper	**1876**	Bissell	U.S.
Cash register	**1879**	Ritty	U.S.
Cassette, audio	**1963**	Philips Co.	Dutch
Cassette, videotape	**1969**	Sony	Japanese
CAT, or CT, scan	**1973**	Hounsfield	English
Cathode-ray tube	**1897**	Braun	German
Cellophane	**1908**	Brandenberger	Swiss
Celluloid	**1870**	Hyatt	U.S.
Cement, Portland	**1824**	Aspdin	English
Chronometer	**1735**	Harrison	English
Circuit breaker	**1925**	Hilliard	U.S.
Circuit, integrated	**1959**	Kilby, Noyce, Texas Instr.	U.S.
Clock, pendulum	**1657**	Huygens	Dutch
Coaxial cable system	**1929**	Affel, Espensched	U.S.
Coca-Cola	**1885**	Pemberton	U.S.
Coffeemaker, auto drip	**1963**	Bunn Corp.	U.S.
Compressed air rock drill	**1871**	Ingersoll	U.S.
Comptometer	**1887**	Felt	U.S.
Computer, electronic	**1942**	Atanasoff, Berry	U.S.

Invention	Date	Inventor(s)	Nationality
Computer, laptop	1987	Sinclair	English
Computer, large-scale automatic digital	1943	Aiken, et al.	U.S.
Computer, mini	1960	Digital Corp.	U.S.
Condenser microphone (telephone)	1916	Wente	U.S.
Contact lens, corneal	1948	Tuohy	U.S.
Contraceptive, oral	1954	Pincus, Rock	U.S.
Corn, hybrid	1917	Jones	U.S.
Cotton gin	1793	Whitney	U.S.
Cream separator	1878	DeLaval	Swedish
Cultivator, disc	1878	Mallon	U.S.
Cyclotron	1931	Lawrence	U.S.
Cystoscope	1878	Nitze	German
Diapers, disposable	1950	Donovan	U.S.
Diesel engine	1895	Diesel	German
Disc, compact	1972	RCA	U.S.
Disc player, compact	1979	Sony, Philips Co.	Japanese, Dutch
Dishwasher	1893	Cochrane	U.S.
Disk, floppy	1970	IBM	U.S.
Disk, video	1972	Philips Co.	Dutch
Drone (unmanned aircraft, remotely controlled)	1916	Low	English
Dynamite	1866	Nobel	Swedish
Dynamo, contin. current	1871	Gramme	Belgian
Electric battery	1800	Volta	Italian
Electric fan	1882	Wheeler	U.S.
Electrocardiograph	1903	Einthoven	Dutch
Electroencephalograph	1929	Berger	German
Electromagnet	1824	Sturgeon	English
Electron microscope	1931	Ruska, Knoll	German
Electron spectrometer	1944	Deutsch, Elliott, Evans	U.S.
Electron tube multigrid	1913	Langmuir	U.S.
Electronic cigarette (nicotine-based)	2003	Hon (Han)	Chinese
Electronic paper (e-ink)	1974	Sheridon	U.S.
Electroplating	1805	Brugnatelli	Italian
Electrostatic generator	1929	Van de Graaff	U.S.
Elevator brake	1852	Otis	U.S.
Elevator, push button	1922	Larson	U.S.
Engine, automatic transmission	1910	Fottinger	German
Engine, coal-gas 4-cycle	1876	Otto	German
Engine, compression ignition	1883	Daimler	German
Engine, electric ignition	1883	Benz	German
Engine, gas, compound	1926	Eickemeyer	U.S.
Engine, gasoline	1872	Brayton	U.S.
Engine, gasoline	1889	Daimler	German
Engine, jet	1930	Whittle	English
Engine, steam, piston	1705	Newcomen	English
Engine, steam, piston	1769	Watt	Scottish
Engraving, half-tone	1852	Talbot	U.S.
Ferris wheel	1893	Ferris	U.S.
Fiber optic wire	1970	Keck, Maurer, Schultz	U.S.
Fiber optics	1955	Kapany	English
Fiberglass	1938	Owens-Corning	U.S.
Filament, tungsten	1913	Coolidge	U.S.
Flanged rail	1831	Stevens	U.S.
Flatiron, electric	1882	Seely	U.S.
Food, frozen	1923	Birdseye	U.S.
Freon	1930	Midgley, et al.	U.S.
Furnace (for steel)	1858	Siemens	German
Galvanometer	1820	Sweigger	German
Garbage bag, polyethylene	1950	Wasylyk	Canadian
Gas discharge tube	1922	Hull	U.S.
Gas lighting	1792	Murdoch	Scottish
Gas mantle	1885	Welsbach	Austrian
Gasoline, cracked	1913	Burton	U.S.
Gasoline, high octane	1930	Ipatieff	Russian
Gasoline (lead ethyl)	1922	Midgley	U.S.
Geiger counter	1913	Geiger	German
Geodesic dome	1948	Fuller	U.S.
Glass, laminated safety	1909	Benedictus	French
Glider	1853	Cayley	English
Google search software	1996	Brin, Page	U.S.
Gun, breechloader	1811	Thornton	U.S.
Gun, Browning	1897	Browning	U.S.
Gun, magazine	1875	Hotchkiss	U.S.
Gun, silencer	1908	Maxim, H. P.	U.S.
Guncotton (nitrocellulose)	1847	Schoenbein	German
Gyrocompass	1911	Sperry	U.S.
Gyroscope	1852	Foucault	French

Invention	Date	Inventor(s)	Nationality
Hard drive, computer	1955	Johnson	U.S.
Harvester-thresher	1818	Lane	U.S.
Heart, artificial	1982	Jarvik	U.S.
Helicopter	1939	Sikorsky	U.S.
Hovercraft	1955	Cockerell	English
Hydrometer	1768	Baume	French
Iron lung	1928	Drinker, Slaw	U.S.
Jet Ski	1973	Jacobsen	U.S.
Kaleidoscope	1817	Brewster	Scottish
Kevlar	1965	Kwolek, Blades	U.S.
Kidney dialysis machine	1941	Kolff	Dutch
Kinetoscope	1889	Edison	U.S.
Lamp, arc	1847	Staite	English
Lamp, fluorescent	1938	General Electric, Westinghouse	U.S.
Lamp, incandescent	1879	Edison	U.S.
Lamp, incand., gas	1913	Langmuir	U.S.
Lamp, klieg	1911	Kliegl, A. and J.	U.S.
Lamp, mercury vapor	1912	Hewitt	U.S.
Lamp, miner's safety	1816	Davy	English
Lamp, neon	1909	Claude	French
Lathe, turret	1845	Fitch	U.S.
Launderette	1934	Cantrell	U.S.
Lens, achromatic	1758	Dollond	English
Lens, fused bifocal	1908	Borsch	U.S.
Leyden jar (condenser)	1745	von Kleist	German
Lightning rod	1752	Franklin	U.S.
Linoleum	1860	Walton	English
Linotype	1884	Mergenthaler	U.S.
Linux	1991	Torvalds	Finnish
Liquid Paper	c.1951	Graham	U.S.
Lock, cylinder	1851	Yale	U.S.
Locomotive, electric	1851	Vail	U.S.
Locomotive, exp'mtl	1802	Trevithick	English
Locomotive, exp'mtl	1812	Fenton, et al.	English
Locomotive, exp'mtl	1814	Stephenson	English
Locomotive, 1st U.S.	1830	Cooper	U.S.
Locomotive, practical	1829	Stephenson	English
Loom, power	1785	Cartwright	English
Loudspeaker, dynamic	1924	Rice, Kellogg	U.S.
Machine gun	1862	Gatling	U.S.
Machine gun, improved	1872	Hotchkiss	U.S.
Machine gun (Maxim)	1883	Maxim, H. S.	U.S.-Eng.
Magnet, electro	1828	Henry	U.S.
Magnetic Resonance Imaging (MRI)	1971	Damadian	U.S.
Maser	1953	Townes	U.S.
Mason jar	1858	Mason	U.S.
Match, friction	1827	Walker	English
Mercerized textiles	1843	Mercer	English
Meter, induction	1888	Shallenberger	U.S.
Metronome	1816	Malezel	German
Microcomputer	1973	Truong, et al.	French
Micrometer	1636	Gascoigne	English
Microphone	1877	Berliner	U.S.
Microprocessor	1971	Intel Corp.	U.S.
Microscope, compound	1590	Janssen	Dutch
Microscope, electronic	1931	Knoll, Ruska	German
Microscope, field ion	1951	Mueller	German
Microwave oven	1947	Spencer	U.S.
Monitor, warship	1861	Ericsson	U.S.
Monotype	1887	Lanston	U.S.
Motor, AC	1892	Tesla	U.S.
Motor, DC	1837	Davenport	U.S.
Motor, induction	1887	Tesla	U.S.
Motorcycle	1885	Daimler	German
Mouse, computer	1967	Engelbart	U.S.
Movie machine	1894	Jenkins	U.S.
Movie, panoramic	1952	Waller	U.S.
Movie, talking	1927	Warner Bros.	U.S.
Mower, lawn	1831	Budding, Ferrabee	English
Mowing machine	1822	Bailey	U.S.
Neoprene	1930	Carothers	U.S.
Nylon	1937	Carothers, DuPont	U.S.
Oil cracking furnace	1891	Gavrilov	Russian
Oil filled power cable	1921	Emanueli	Italian
Oleomargarine	1869	Mege-Mouries	French
Ophthalmoscope	1851	Helmholtz	German
Pacemaker	1952	Zoll	U.S.
Pacemaker, implantable cardiac	1958	Greatbatch	U.S.
Paper	105	Ts'ai	Chinese
Paper clip	1900	Waaler	Norwegian
Paper machine	1809	Dickinson	U.S.
Parachute	1785	Blanchard	French
Pen, ballpoint	1888	Loud	U.S.
Pen, fountain	1884	Waterman	U.S.
Pen, steel	1780	Harrison	English

Invention	Date	Inventor(s)	Nationality
Pendulum	**1583**	Galileo	Italian
Percussion cap	**1807**	Forsythe	Scottish
Phonograph	**1877**	Edison	U.S.
Photo, color	**1892**	Ives	U.S.
Photo film, celluloid	**1893**	Reichenbach	U.S.
Photo film, transparent	**1884**	Eastman, Goodwin	U.S.
Photocopier	**1938**	Carlson	U.S.
Photoelectric cell	**1895**	Elster	German
Photographic paper	**1835**	Talbot	English
Photography	**1816**	Niepce	French
Photography	**1835**	Daguerre	French
Photography	**1835**	Talbot	English
Photophone	**1880**	Bell	U.S.-Scot.
Phototelegraphy	**1925**	Bell Labs	U.S.
Piano	**1709**	Cristofori	Italian
Piano, player	**1863**	Fourneaux	French
Pin, safety	**1849**	Hunt	U.S.
Pistol (revolver)	**1836**	Colt	U.S.
Plow, cast iron	**1785**	Ransome	English
Plow, disc	**1896**	Hardy	U.S.
Pneumatic hammer	**1890**	King	U.S.
Post-it note	**1980**	Fry, Silver	U.S.
Powder, smokeless	**1884**	Vieille	French
Printing press, rotary	**1845**	Hoe	U.S.
Printing press, web	**1865**	Bullock	U.S.
Propeller, screw	**1804**	Stevens	U.S.
Propeller, screw	**1837**	Ericsson	Swedish
Punch card accounting	**1889**	Hollerith	U.S.
Radar	**1940**	Watson-Watt	Scottish
Radio amplifier	**1906**	De Forest	U.S.
Radio beacon	**1928**	Donovan	U.S.
Radio crystal oscillator	**1918**	Nicolson	U.S.
Radio FM, 2-path	**1933**	Armstrong	U.S.
Radio, magnetic detector	**1902**	Marconi	Italian
Radio receiver, cascade tuning	**1913**	Alexanderson	U.S.
Radio receiver, heterodyne	**1913**	Fessenden	Canadian
Radio, signals	**1895**	Marconi	Italian
Radio transmitter triode modulation	**1914**	Alexanderson	U.S.
Radio tube diode	**1904**	Fleming	English
Radio tube oscillator	**1915**	De Forest	U.S.
Radio tube triode	**1906**	De Forest	U.S.
Rayon (acetate)	**1895**	Cross	English
Rayon (cuprammonium)	**1890**	Despeissis	French
Rayon (nitrocellulose)	**1884**	Chardonnet	French
Razor, electric	**1928**	Schick	U.S.
Razor, safety	**1895**	Gillette	U.S.
Reading machine for the blind	**1976**	Kurzweil	U.S.
Reaper	**1834**	McCormick	U.S.
Record, cylinder	**1887**	Bell, Tainter	U.S.
Record, disc	**1887**	Berliner	U.S.
Record, long playing	**1947**	Goldmark	U.S.
Record, wax cylinder	**1888**	Edison	U.S.
Refrigerator car	**1868**	David	U.S.
Remote control	**1898**	Tesla	U.S.
Resin, synthetic	**1931**	Hill	English
Richter scale	**1935**	Richter	U.S.
Rifle, repeating	**1860**	Henry	U.S.
Rocket, liquid fuel	**1926**	Goddard	U.S.
Rollerblades	**1980**	Olson	U.S.
Rubber, vulcanized	**1839**	Goodyear	U.S.
Saccharin	**1879**	Remsen, Fahlberg	U.S.
Saw, circular	**1777**	Miller	English
Scotch tape	**1930**	Drew	U.S.
Seat belt	**1959**	Volvo	Swedish
Segway human transporter	**2001**	Kamen	U.S.
Seismograph	**1880**	Milne, Ewing, Gray	Eng.-Scot.
Sewing machine	**1790**	Saint	English
Shoe-lasting machine	**1883**	Matzeliger	U.S.
Shoe-sewing machine	**1860**	McKay	U.S.
Shrapnel shell	**1784**	Shrapnel	English
Shuttle, flying	**1733**	Kay	English
Skates, in-line	**1759**	Merlin	Belgian
Sleeping-car	**1865**	Pullman	U.S.
Slide rule	**1620**	Oughtred	English
Slinky	**1943**	James	U.S.
Smoke detector	**1969**	Smith, House	U.S.
Soap, hardwater	**1928**	Bertsch	German
Spectroscope	**1859**	Kirchoff, Bunsen	German
Spectroscope (mass)	**1918**	Dempster	U.S.
Spinning jenny	**c.1764**	Hargreaves	English
Spinning mule	**1779**	Crompton	English
Steam car	**1770**	Cugnot	French
Steam turbine	**1884**	Parsons	English

Invention	Date	Inventor(s)	Nationality
Steamboat, exp'mtl	**1778**	Jouffroy	French
Steamboat, exp'mtl	**1785**	Fitch	U.S.
Steamboat, exp'mtl	**1787**	Rumsey	U.S.
Steamboat, exp'mtl	**1803**	Fulton	U.S.
Steamboat, exp'mtl	**1804**	Stevens	U.S.
Steamboat, practical	**1802**	Symington	Scottish
Steamboat, practical	**1807**	Fulton	U.S.
Steel alloy, high-speed	**1901**	Taylor, White	U.S.
Steel (converter)	**1856**	Bessemer	English
Steel, manganese	**1884**	Hadfield	English
Steel, stainless	**1916**	Brearley	English
Stereoscope	**1838**	Wheatstone	English
Stethoscope	**1819**	Laennec	French
Stethoscope, binaural	**1840**	Cammann	U.S.
Stock ticker	**1870**	Edison	U.S.
Storage battery, rechargeable	**1859**	Plante	French
Stove, electric	**1896**	Hadaway	U.S.
Submarine	**1891**	Holland	U.S.
Submarine, even keel	**1894**	Lake	U.S.
Submarine, torpedo	**1776**	Bushnell	U.S.
Synthesizer	**1964**	Moog	U.S.
Tank, military	**1914**	Swinton	English
Tape recorder, magnetic	**1899**	Poulsen	Danish
Taser	**1974**	Cover	U.S.
Teflon	**1938**	Du Pont	U.S.
Telegraph, magnetic	**1837**	Morse	U.S.
Telegraph, quadruplex	**1864**	Edison	U.S.
Telegraph, railroad	**1887**	Woods	U.S.
Telegraph, wireless high frequency	**1895**	Marconi	Italian
Telephone[1]	**1871**	Meucci	U.S.-Italian
Telephone[1]	**1876**	Bell	U.S.-Scot.
Telephone amplifier	**1912**	De Forest	U.S.
Telephone answering machine (1st practical)	**1954**	Hashimoto	Japanese
Telephone, automatic	**1891**	Strowger	U.S.
Telephone, cellular	**1947**	Bell Labs	U.S.
Telephone, cordless[2]	**1950**	Gross	U.S.
Telephone, radio	**1900**	Poulsen	Danish
		Fessenden	Canadian
Telephone, radio	**1906**	De Forest	U.S.
Telephone, radio, long distance	**1915**	AT&T	U.S.
Telephone, recording	**1898**	Poulsen	Danish
Telescope	**1608**	Lippershey	Dutch
Telescope	**1609**	Galileo	Italian
Telescope, astronomical	**1611**	Kepler	German
Telescope, reflecting	**1668**	Newton	English
Teletype	**1928**	Morkrum, Kleinschmidt	U.S.
Television, color	**1928**	Baird	Scottish
Television, electronic	**1927**	Farnsworth	U.S.
Television, iconoscope	**1923**	Zworykin	U.S.
Television, mech. scanner	**1923**	Baird	Scottish
Tesla coil	**1891**	Tesla	U.S.
Thermometer	**1593**	Galileo	Italian
Thermometer	**1730**	Reaumur	French
Thermometer, mercury	**1714**	Fahrenheit	German
3D printing (stereolithography)	**1984**	Hull	U.S.
Time recorder	**1890**	Bundy	U.S.
Tire, double-tube	**1845**	Thomson	Scottish
Tire, pneumatic	**1888**	Dunlop	Scottish
Toaster, automatic	**1921**	Strite	U.S.
Toilet, flush	**1589**	Harington	English
Torpedo, marine	**1804**	Fulton	U.S.
Tractor, crawler	**1904**	Holt	U.S.
Transformer, AC	**1885**	Stanley	U.S.
Transistor	**1947**	Shockley, Brattain, Bardeen	U.S.
Trolley car, electric	**1884-87**	Van DePoele, Sprague	U.S.
Tungsten, ductile	**1912**	Coolidge	U.S.
Tupperware®	**1945**	Tupper	U.S.
Turbine, gas	**1849**	Bourdin	French
Turbine, hydraulic	**1849**	Francis	U.S.
Turbine, steam	**1884**	Parsons	English
Type, movable	**1447**	Gutenberg	German
Typewriter	**1867**	Sholes, Soule, Glidden	U.S.
Universal Serial Bus (USB)	**1994**	Bhatt, et al.	U.S.
Vacuum cleaner, electric	**1907**	Spangler	U.S.
Vacuum evaporating pan	**1846**	Rillieux	U.S.
Velcro	**1948**	de Mestral	Swiss

Invention	Date	Inventor(s)	Nationality
Video game ("Pong")	**1972**	Bushnell	U.S.
Video home system (VHS)	**1975**	Matsushita, JVC	Japanese
Vinyl	**1926**	Semon	U.S.
Washer, electric	**1901**	Fisher	U.S.
Welding, atomic hydrogen	**1924**	Langmuir, Palmer	U.S.
Welding, electric	**1877**	Thomson	U.S.
Wheelchair, multiterrain	**1986**	Twitchell	U.S.
Wheelchair, stair-climbing	**1962**	Blanco	U.S.
Wiki software	**1995**	Cunningham	U.S.
Wind tunnel	**1912**	Eiffel	French
Windshield wiper	**1903**	Anderson	U.S.
Wire, barbed	**1874**	Glidden	U.S.
World Wide Web	**1989**	Berners-Lee	English
Wrench, double-acting	**1913**	Owen	U.S.
X-ray tube	**1913**	Coolidge	U.S.
Zamboni	**1949**	Zamboni	U.S.
Zeppelin	**1900**	Zeppelin	German
Zipper, early model	**1893**	Judson	U.S.
Zipper, improved	**1913**	Sundback	Canadian

(1) While Alexander Graham Bell has traditionally been credited with invention of the telephone, which he patented, Antonio Meucci developed a working model before Bell. (2) Al Gross held a number of important early patents in the field of wireless communication; other people were also involved in the development of practical cordless telephones.

U.S. Patents by Field of Technology, 2000-22

Source: World Intellectual Property Organization Statistics Database

(ranked by number of utility patents, or patents for inventions, for the top 20 fields in 2022, as of July 2024)

Field	2000	2005	2010	2015	2019	2020	2021	2022	% change 2000-22
Computer technology	12,101	14,246	33,424	46,750	51,574	53,539	52,904	53,270	340.21%
Digital communication	3,679	5,304	9,523	23,459	31,978	32,649	30,703	30,282	723.10
Medical technology	8,040	6,122	10,254	16,289	22,030	21,932	20,755	20,764	158.26
Electrical machinery, apparatus, energy	9,504	9,286	14,256	18,676	23,620	22,118	19,898	19,919	109.59
Semiconductors	9,163	9,986	14,280	18,371	18,743	18,865	17,232	16,874	84.15
Audio-visual technology	7,887	8,139	12,126	15,888	16,851	16,556	15,209	15,374	94.93
Transport	7,207	6,382	6,800	11,089	15,134	15,138	14,097	15,052	108.85
Measurement	6,882	7,577	10,732	12,265	16,537	15,877	14,635	14,779	114.75
Optics	7,502	8,318	10,835	11,676	12,919	12,274	10,944	10,571	40.91
Telecommunications	5,802	6,325	10,916	12,809	12,118	11,196	9,712	9,238	59.22
Other special machines	4,960	3,612	4,647	6,139	8,186	8,380	7,904	7,688	55.00
Control	2,732	2,683	4,418	5,630	8,742	8,652	7,837	7,651	180.05
IT methods for management	739	1,148	3,534	3,490	7,517	7,919	7,783	7,468	910.55
Engines, pumps, turbines	4,143	4,263	4,158	6,300	8,739	8,620	7,531	7,225	74.39
Pharmaceuticals	4,001	2,841	5,118	6,903	7,503	7,820	7,691	7,090	77.21
Civil engineering	4,419	3,481	4,745	6,432	8,275	7,980	7,196	7,015	58.75
Mechanical elements	4,886	3,797	4,337	6,929	8,261	7,988	7,198	6,819	39.56
Handling	4,401	3,137	4,372	5,164	6,382	6,298	5,981	6,049	37.45
Furniture, games	4,949	3,589	5,043	5,911	6,924	6,756	6,255	5,968	20.59
Biotechnology	3,864	2,818	3,979	5,414	6,277	6,286	6,038	5,687	47.18

Patent Offices Granting Most Utility Patents, 2000-22

Source: World Intellectual Property Organization Statistics Database

(ranked by 2022 figures; as of July 2024)

National or regional office	2000	2005	2010	2015	2019	2020	2021	2022
China	13,058	53,305	135,110	359,316	452,804	530,127	695,946	798,347
United States	157,496	143,806	219,614	298,407	354,430	351,993	327,307	323,410
Japan	125,880	122,944	222,693	189,358	179,910	179,383	184,372	201,420
South Korea	34,956	73,512	68,843	101,873	125,661	134,766	145,882	135,180
European Patent Office	27,523	53,258	58,108	68,431	137,782	133,706	108,799	81,086
India	1,263	4,320	7,138	6,022	23,578	26,361	30,721	30,490
Germany	14,707	17,063	13,678	14,795	18,255	17,305	21,113	23,592
Brazil	NA	2,439	3,251	3,411	10,947	20,407	26,872	23,546
Russia	17,592	23,390	30,322	34,706	34,008	28,788	23,662	23,315
Canada	12,125	15,516	19,120	22,201	22,009	21,284	22,687	18,125
Australia	13,548	10,979	14,557	23,098	17,010	17,778	17,155	16,407
France	11,274	11,473	9,899	12,699	13,593	12,874	15,493	12,421
Hong Kong	2,737	6,518	5,353	5,963	6,780	7,658	14,662	11,602
South Africa	3,399	1,831	5,331	4,499	6,162	3,466	6,107	11,267
United Kingdom	8,253	10,159	5,594	5,464	5,948	9,772	10,895	10,578
Indonesia	NA	NA	NA	1,911	10,514	7,981	6,850	9,970
Mexico	5,527	8,098	9,399	9,338	8,702	7,726	10,369	9,698
Italy	5,285	5,534	16,106	7,153	8,617	9,152	7,254	7,348
Malaysia	405	2,508	2,160	2,877	4,106	8,206	6,876	5,957
Israel	2,033	2,269	2,293	4,492	4,197	4,668	5,488	5,358
North Korea	NA	3,583	6,290	NA	4,712	4,227	NA	3,889
Singapore	5,090	7,530	4,442	7,054	4,188	5,386	6,488	3,886
Vietnam	727	668	822	1,388	2,620	4,319	3,691	3,868
Turkey	1,147	823	NA	1,723	1,941	2,063	3,387	3,449
Netherlands	2,820	2,373	1,947	1,377	1,936	1,911	2,264	2,815
World	**516,800**	**632,500**	**915,200**	**1,239,400**	**1,506,100**	**1,596,900**	**1,754,900**	**1,823,200**

NA = Not available.

U.S. Utility Patents, 1790-2020

Source: U.S. Patent and Trademark Office, U.S. Dept. of Commerce

Year	Patent applications	Patents granted	Year	Patent applications	Patents granted	Year	Patent applications	Patents granted
1790	NA	3	1990	164,558	90,365	2010	490,226	219,614
1810	NA	223	2000	295,926	157,494	2011	503,582	224,505
1830	NA	544	2001	326,508	166,035	2012	542,815	253,155
1850	2,193	884	2002	334,445	167,331	2013	571,612	277,835
1870	19,171	12,157	2003	342,441	169,023	2014	578,802	300,677
1890	39,884	25,308	2004	356,943	164,290	2015	589,410	298,408
1910	63,293	35,130	2005	390,733	143,806	2016	605,571	303,049
1930	89,554	45,226	2006	425,967	173,772	2017	606,956	318,828
1950	67,264	43,039	2007	456,154	157,282	2018	597,141	307,759
1970	103,175	64,429	2008	456,321	157,772	2019	621,453	354,430
1980	104,329	61,819	2009	456,106	167,349	2020	597,175	352,066

NA = Not available.

Computer Milestones

1623: German mathematician Wilhelm Schickard developed the first mechanical calculator, capable of adding, subtracting, multiplying, and dividing.

1642: French mathematician Blaise Pascal built the first of more than four dozen copies of an adding and subtracting machine that he invented.

1801: French inventor Joseph Marie Jacquard demonstrated a new control system for looms. He "programmed" the loom, communicating desired weaving operations to the machine via patterns of holes in paper cards.

1833-71: British mathematician and scientist Charles Babbage used the Jacquard punch-card system in his design for a sophisticated, programmable "Analytical Engine" that foreshadowed basic computer features. Babbage's concept was beyond the capabilities of the technology of his time, and the machine remained unfinished at his death in 1871.

1889: American engineer Herman Hollerith patented an electromechanical punch-card tabulating system that facilitated the handling of large amounts of statistical data and quickly found use in censuses in the U.S. and other countries.

1911: Hollerith's Tabulating Machine Company merged with two other enterprises to form the Computing-Tabulating-Recording Company, which was renamed the International Business Machines Corporation (IBM) in 1924.

1941: German engineer Konrad Züse completed the Z3, the first fully functional digital computer to be controlled by a program; the Z3 was not electronic—it was based on electrical switches called relays.

1942: Iowa State Coll. physicist John Vincent Atanasoff and assistant Clifford Berry completed a working model of the first fully electronic computer using vacuum tubes, which could operate much more quickly than relays; the rudimentary machine was not programmable.

1943: IBM and Harvard professor Howard Aiken completed the first large-scale automatic digital computer, the Mark I, a relay-based machine 55-ft long and 8-ft high. British scientists built their first Colossus machine, an electronic computer for breaking German codes during World War II.

1946: ENIAC (Electronic Numerical Integrator and Computer), a 30-ton room-sized electronic computer with more than 18,000 vacuum tubes, was completed by physicist John Mauchly and engineer J. Presper Eckert at the Univ. of Pennsylvania for the U.S. Army. ENIAC could be programmed to do different tasks, but cables had to be plugged in, and switches had to be set by hand.

1951: Eckert and Mauchly's UNIVAC (Universal Automatic Computer) became the first commercially available computer in the U.S. Its first customer was the Census Bureau. CBS-TV used a UNIVAC in 1952 to predict election results.

1955: In the first known use of the term, four U.S. computer scientists proposed a workshop on "artificial intelligence." It took place the next year at Dartmouth Coll.

1959: COBOL, a computer programming language designed for business use, first appeared, based on programming language innovations of American mathematician Grace Hopper.

1967: American computer pioneer Doug Engelbart applied for a patent on the mouse.

1969-71: The powerful Unix operating system was developed at Bell Laboratories; later versions became widely used on large computers and formed the basis for the Macintosh OS X operating system (introduced in 2001).

1971: Intel released the 4004, the first commercial microprocessor (an entire computer processing unit on a chip).

1973: The Alto computer, developed at Xerox's Palo Alto Research Center, became operational, implementing many features of modern commercial personal computers, including a graphical user interface (GUI) featuring windows, icons, and pointers that could be manipulated by a mouse.

1975: The first widely marketed personal computer (PC), the MITS Altair 8800, was introduced in kit form, with no keyboard, video display, or printer, for under $400. Microsoft was founded by Americans Bill Gates and Paul Allen.

1976: The first word-processing program for personal computers, Electric Pencil, was written. Apple Computer Company was founded by Americans Steven Jobs and Stephen Wozniak.

1977: Apple introduced the Apple II; capable of displaying text and graphics in color, the machine enjoyed phenomenal success.

1981: IBM unveiled its Personal Computer (IBM 5150), which used an operating system from Microsoft known as MS-DOS (Disk Operating System).

1984: Apple introduced the first Macintosh. The easy-to-use Macintosh came with a proprietary operating system and was the first popular computer to have a GUI and a mouse.

1990: Microsoft released Windows 3.0, the first workable version of its own GUI. Adobe released the first commercial version of the image-editing software Photoshop.

1991: The Unix-like Linux operating system was invented by Helsinki Univ. student Linus Torvalds and made available for free.

1996: The Palm Pilot, the first widely successful handheld computer and personal information manager, arrived.

1997: The IBM supercomputer Deep Blue beat Russian world chess champion Garry Kasparov in a 6-game match, 2-1, with 3 draws.

2002: The total number of personal computers, including desktop and laptop machines of all types, shipped by manufacturers since 1975 reached 1 bil.

2007: Amazon launched the Kindle, a hardware/software system for displaying books electronically.

2008: Google released the Linux-based Android operating system for mobile devices.

2010: Apple released the iPad tablet computer and sold more than 3 mil devices in the first 80 days.

2012: Microsoft released Windows 8, featuring enhanced support for touchscreens and an interface with a grid of tiles displaying actively updated content and apps.

2015: Microsoft released Windows 10, promising faster startup and improved security, along with features like a personal digital assistant and a new web browser, Microsoft Edge.

2016: Univ. of Maryland scientists developed the first reprogrammable quantum computer; it used lasers to manipulate its five qubits, or bits of quantum information.

2022: Apple became the first company in the world to achieve a stock market value of $3 tril; in 2018, it had become the first company to hit $1 tril. The U.S. supercomputer Frontier became the first "exascale" computer, capable of more than 1 exaflop, or 1 quintillion (billion billion) operations per second.

2024: A faulty update by security company CrowdStrike caused a massive outage affecting millions of Microsoft Windows systems worldwide.

World's Fastest Supercomputers, 2024

Source: Top500.org, as of midyear 2024

Rank	Name	Location	Manufacturer/ vendor	Processors (cores)	Top speed[1]
1.	Frontier	Oak Ridge National Laboratory, TN, U.S	HPE Cray	8,699,904	1,206.00
2.	Aurora	Argonne National Laboratory, IL, U.S.	HPE Cray-Intel	9,264,128	1,012.00
3.	Eagle	Azure cloud, U.S.	Microsoft	2,073,600	561.20
4.	Supercomputer Fugaku	RIKEN Center for Computational Science, Japan	Fujitsu	7,630,848	442.01
5.	LUMI	EuroHPC at CSC Data Center, Kajaani, Finland	HPE Cray	2,752,704	379.70
6.	Alps	Swiss National Supercomputing Centre, Lugano, Switzerland	HPE Cray	1,305,600	270.00
7.	Leonardo	EuroHPC at CINECA, Bologna, Italy	Atos	1,824,768	241.20
8.	MareNostrum 5 ACC	EuroHPC at Barcelona Supercomputing Center, Spain	Atos	663,040	175.30
9.	Summit	Oak Ridge National Laboratory, TN, U.S.	IBM	2,414,592	148.60
10.	Eos NVIDIA DGX SuperPOD	Nvidia, U.S.	Nvidia	485,888	121.40
11.	Venado	Los Alamos National Laboratory, NM, U.S.	HPE Cray	481,440	98.51
12.	Sierra	Lawrence Livermore National Laboratory, CA, U.S.	IBM	1,572,480	94.64
13.	Sunway TaihuLight	National Supercomputing Center, Wuxi, China.	NRCPC[2]	10,649,600	93.01
14.	Perlmutter	National Energy Research Scientific Computing Center, CA, U.S.	HPE Cray	888,832	79.23
15.	Selene	Nvidia, Santa Clara, CA, U.S	Nvidia	555,520	63.46
16.	Tianhe-2A (Milky Way-2A)	National Super Computer Center, Guangzhou, China	NUDT[3]	4,981,760	61.44

Note: The 500 fastest supercomputers use versions of the Linux operating system. (1) Top speed, in petaflops, achieved as measured according to the Linpack Benchmark. 1 petaflop = 1 quadrillion floating-point operations per sec. (2) NRCPC = National Research Center of Parallel Computer Engineering and Technology. (3) NUDT = National University of Defense Technology.

Top Operating Systems Worldwide, 2009-24

Source: StatCounter Global Stats, gs.statcounter.com
(ranked by 2024 figures)

Operating system	% of OS market								
	2009	2012	2015	2017	2019	2020	2021	2023	2024
Android	0.02%	3.29%	25.62%	41.24%	39.91%	39.06%	41.56%	40.12%	45.14%
Windows	93.85	79.14	50.85	35.24	35.12	36.05	30.20	29.34	26.03
iOS	0.36	5.16	11.37	13.20	13.85	14.22	16.55	16.78	18.34
OS X	4.07	6.16	4.90	4.66	5.94	7.91	6.38	8.62	5.39
Unknown	0.37	0.55	2.28	2.99	3.33	1.30	3.36	1.64	2.64
Linux	0.76	0.75	1.12	0.77	0.77	0.87	0.99	1.33	1.61
Chrome OS	—	—	0.15	0.19	0.24	0.31	0.50	1.36	0.51
Samsung	—	0.74	0.36	0.19	0.10	0.11	0.24	0.21	0.22

— = Not available. **Note:** Percent of users accessing the web with a particular operating system (OS), for July of year shown. Includes desktop, laptop, tablet, console, and mobile devices' operating systems.

U.S. Sales and Household Penetration of Selected Hardware, 2021-23

Source: Consumer Technology Association
(factory sales to dealers in thousands of units and millions of dollars; percent of all households for Jan. of year shown)

Hardware	2021			2022			2023		
	Units	Sales	%	Units	Sales	%	Unit	Sales	%
Smartphones	153,808	$74,512	90%	139,196	$74,177	98%	130,033	$70,437	98%
Televisions	46,536	21,530	91	40,843	18,689	87	41,141	17,881	87
Laptop/notebook/netbook PCs[1]	76,517	46,259	73	58,685	39,771	72	50,713	33,681	75
Streaming media players	20,261	928	55	19,507	933	55	18,532	908	63
Tablet computers	52,704	16,176	61	45,918	14,163	59	30,480	9,636	62
Home game consoles	14,549	6,091	53	14,112	5,613	52	14,536	5,493	54
Desktop computers[1,2]	15,339	11,111	53	16,438	12,756	51	14,107	11,056	52
Smartwatches	24,438	6,508	35	24,487	6,587	34	22,038	6,589	36
Digital cameras	3,987	1,480	36	3,829	1,427	34	3,398	1,379	33
E-readers	4,450	294	27	4,494	303	26	4,359	297	25
Action camcorders	2,218	367	10	2,251	367	9	2,318	374	16

Note: Based on sales data tracking and consumer surveys conducted by CTA. (1) Includes commercial and consumer shipments. (2) Includes all-in-one computers.

Device Market Share in the U.S., 2009-24

Source: StatCounter Global Stats, gs.statcounter.com

Device type	% of market								
	2009	2012	2015	2017	2019	2020	2021	2023	2024
Desktops	98.29%	89.93%	61.51%	46.32%	47.84%	49.58%	46.44%	65.72%	46.47%
Mobile devices	1.71	10.07	29.05	44.10	44.22	45.87	49.86	32.52	50.77
Tablets	—	—	9.44	9.58	7.94	4.55	3.70	1.77	2.76

— = Not available. **Note:** Percent of users accessing the web for July of year shown with desktops (including laptops), mobile devices (pocket-sized computing devices typically featuring a display screen with touch input or a miniature keyboard), and tablets (portable computing devices that are larger than a mobile device and have a touchscreen interface).

Device Market Share in the World, 2009-24

Source: StatCounter Global Stats, gs.statcounter.com

Device type	% of market							
	2009	2012	2015	2017	2019	2021	2023	2024
Mobile devices	1.05%	11.09%	37.15%	53.99%	51.11%	55.89%	55.67%	61.74%
Desktops	98.95	88.91	57.00	41.22	45.18	41.36	42.40	36.10
Tablets	—	—	5.85	4.79	3.71	2.74	1.93	2.16

— = Not available. **Note:** Percent of users accessing the web for July of year shown with desktops (including laptops), mobile devices (pocket-sized computing devices typically featuring a display screen with touch input or a miniature keyboard), and tablets (portable computing devices that are larger than a mobile device and have a touchscreen interface).

Individuals Using the Internet by Region and Development Level, 2005-23

Source: ITU World Telecommunication/ICT Indicators Database (estimated data)

	2005	2007	2009	2011	2013	2015	2017	2019	2020	2021	2022	2023
Africa	2.0%	3.2%	4.3%	7.6%	11.3%	15.8%	20.0%	25.4%	28.9%	31.7%	33.9%	37.1%
Americas	35.9	42.7	46.2	51.1	56.0	62.4	71.7	75.9	82.2	83.4	84.6	86.9
Arab States	8.6	14.4	20.3	25.8	31.6	38.4	46.7	55.3	61.6	64.2	66.9	68.9
Asia & Pacific	9.6	13.6	19.0	25.1	29.4	33.7	38.7	48.5	56.1	59.7	62.4	65.9
Commonwealth of Independent States	11.0	18.9	32.8	47.3	57.3	62.2	68.3	76.3	79.6	83.2	86.1	89.1
Europe	42.7	52.1	59.7	64.7	69.4	72.6	76.7	81.7	84.8	87.1	88.6	90.5
Low-income countries	0.8	2.1	3.1	4.2	5.7	8.9	12.1	17.5	18.8	21.6	23.7	27.1
Lower-middle-income countries	3.9	5.9	8.1	13.0	16.5	21.0	26.6	35.8	45.2	48.6	51.6	55.2
Upper-middle-income countries	10.8	17.7	27.6	36.8	43.6	49.4	55.7	65.3	71.0	74.6	77.1	80.5
High-income countries	57.9	66.1	69.5	72.1	76.2	79.4	85.4	88.3	90.7	91.7	92.2	93.2
Least developed countries	0.7	1.8	2.6	3.9	5.9	10.7	16.3	22.9	26.9	29.5	32.0	35.4
World	**15.6**	**20.3**	**25.4**	**31.0**	**35.4**	**39.9**	**45.4**	**53.2**	**59.3**	**62.2**	**64.4**	**67.4**

About the Internet

The internet is not owned or funded by any one institution, organization, or government. It has no CEO and is not a commercial service. Its development is guided by the Internet Society (ISOC), a nonprofit formed in 1992. The Internet Society helps fund the Internet Engineering Task Force (IETF), which deals with short-term issues of standards and the internet's architecture. The Internet Architecture Board (IAB), a committee of the IETF, oversees the latter's work and appoints the chair of the Internet Research Task Force (IRTF). The IAB and IRTF focus on long-term issues.

Major Historical Highlights

1969: ARPANET, an experimental four-computer network, was established by the Advanced Research Projects Agency (ARPA) of the U.S. Defense Dept. Two years later, ARPANET linked about 23 computers ("hosts") at 15 sites, including MIT and Harvard.

1971: Engineer Bob Thomas created Creeper, generally considered the first worm, a virus able to self-replicate over a network.

1976: British evolutionary biologist Richard Dawkins coined the term "meme," referring to an idea or a behavior that persists and may spread "virally."

1978: The first spam, or junk email, was sent over ARPANET.

1982: Author William Gibson coined the term "cyberspace" in the story "Burning Chrome."

1983: The set of communications rules (protocol) known as TCP/IP became the main networking protocol of ARPANET. Its adoption was tantamount to the birth of the internet. The military portion of ARPANET was moved onto MILNET.

1986: The U.S. National Science Foundation (NSF) launched NSFNET, the first large-scale network using internet technology.

1988: Internet Relay Chat (IRC) was developed by Finnish student Jarkko Oikarinen, enabling people to communicate via the internet in "real time."

1988: A worm crafted by Cornell Univ. computer science graduate student Robert Morris Jr. infected thousands of computers, shutting many down and causing millions of dollars of damage—the first known case of large-scale damage caused by a computer virus spread via the internet.

1989: Massachusetts-based The World—the first commercial internet service provider supplying dial-up access—debuted.

1989-90: English scientist Tim Berners-Lee invented the World Wide Web. Created as an environment in which scientists at the European Center for Nuclear Research in Switzerland could share information, it gradually evolved into a medium with text, graphics, audio, animation, and video.

1990: ARPANET was disbanded.

1991: NSFNET was opened to commercial traffic. Berners-Lee introduced the first browser, or software for accessing the web.

1993: The National Center for Supercomputing Applications (U.S.) released versions of Mosaic, the first web browser able to present both text and images on a single page.

1993: A coffee pot at England's Cambridge Univ. became the subject of the first live streaming (and the first webcam).

1994: Netscape Communications released the Netscape Navigator browser.

1995: Microsoft released its Internet Explorer browser. It initially failed to make a dent in Netscape's dominance of the browser market, but Internet Explorer surpassed Netscape by 1999.

1995: Amazon and AuctionWeb (now eBay) began operating online.

1997: The initial version of the WiFi network protocol was released.

1998: Under a contract with the U.S. Dept. of Commerce, the nonprofit Internet Corporation for Assigned Names and Numbers (ICANN) took over the management of assigning domain names and internet protocol (IP) addresses.

1999: Release of the free Napster file-sharing service enabled users to easily exchange files containing music or other content without regard to copyright restrictions.

2000: Estonia became the first country to pass a law declaring internet access a fundamental human right of its citizens.

2004: A group of Harvard students founded social network TheFacebook (later just Facebook).

2004: The Mozilla Foundation released the first official version of the open-source browser Mozilla Firefox.

2006: The microblogging and social networking service Twitter was introduced.

2008: Google introduced its Chrome browser. By 2012, Chrome ranked as the most widely used browser in the world, according to StatCounter.com.

2009: The software for Bitcoin, the world's first "cryptocurrency," was released. It relied on cryptography and a complex decentralized public ledger to secure transactions.

2011: ICANN decided to allow the use of almost any characters in any language for the names of generic top-level domains.

2012: The number of Facebook users surpassed 1 bil.

2014: The number of internet hosts (websites) passed 1 bil.

2014: Estonia became the first country in the world to offer noncitizens "e-residency"—a government-issued transnational digital identity.

2016: The leak of more than 11.5 mil documents from Panamanian law firm Mossack Fonseca, which said it was the victim of a hack, exposed large-scale offshore tax evasion.

2016: Global internet traffic surpassed 1 zettabyte (1 tril gigabytes), according to networking giant Cisco.

2017: The number of Facebook users surpassed 2 bil.

2018: Amid growing concern over the misuse of individuals' personal data, the European Union's General Data Protection Regulation (GDPR) went into effect, providing strong safeguards governing personal data held by any organization worldwide that conducts business in Europe.

2018: By year's end the proportion of the world's population using the internet had passed the 50% mark, according to the Intl. Telecommunications Union.

2021: A ransomware cyberattack caused a multi-day shutdown of the Colonial Pipeline, provider of almost half the fuel supply of the U.S. East Coast.

2022: OpenAI released ChatGPT, a chatbot (software capable of human-like conversation) for public use, quickly setting a record for the fastest-growing user base of a consumer internet application. Trained on massive amounts of existing data, and an example of so-called generative artificial intelligence, ChatGPT could upon request produce text, poetry, computer code, and more.

2022: Tesla CEO Elon Musk acquired Twitter, renaming it X the following year.

2023: An official advisory from the U.S. surgeon general warned of potential harmful effects of social media use on the mental health and well-being of children and adolescents.

2023: Amid growing public and White House concern over the risks of misuse of artificial intelligence, OpenAI and other leading companies agreed to take steps to ensure the safety, security, and trustworthiness of the technology.

2024: The European Union adopted the world's first comprehensive legislation governing artificial intelligence.

Safety and Security on the Internet

Common sense dictates some basic security rules:

- Avoid using the same password for multiple websites. A password manager can generate passwords and then save them.
- Do not give out your phone number, address, credit card number, or other personal information unless needed for a transaction at a site you trust.
- If you feel someone is being threatening or dangerous, inform your internet service provider.
- Use protective firewall, antivirus, and antispyware software to guard your system against attacks by hackers.
- Be careful about opening email and file attachments from unknown correspondents.
- To avoid falling victim to **phishing**—which uses a forged email message, purportedly from a respectable organization, to elicit personal data—do not click on hyperlinks in emails from companies with which you do business. Phishing emails typically contain a link leading to a fabricated website resembling the site of the ostensible sender. If you want to visit a company's website, open your browser and manually enter the site's address.
- Users of so-called **peer-to-peer** (P2P) file-sharing networks or protocols should open up only part of their computer system, not their entire hard drive, to sharing.
- When manufacturers provide **patches** to solve security flaws or other problems with operating systems, web browsers, or other software, it is usually advisable to install these fixes. If a fix is not available for a serious security problem, consider switching to an alternative program.

Internet Addresses

The fundamental part of an address on the internet is called the domain. The final part of a domain name, known as the **top-level domain (TLD)**, is its most basic part. For example, .com is the top-level domain of many mainstream web addresses. So-called generic top-level domains (gTLDs) consist of three or more letters. Domain names with two letters are generally for countries or regions. Country-code TLDs (ccTLDs) are usually managed by an organization within a certain country.

Worst Data Breaches, 2010-22

Source: Upguard, Inc.
(ranked by approximate number of exposed data records, as of Sept. 2024)

Rank	Company	Year	Records exposed (mil)	Rank	Company	Year	Records exposed (mil)
1.	CAM4	2020	10,880	9.	Yahoo	2014	500
2.	Yahoo	2013	3,000		Marriott/Starwood	2018	500
3.	Aadhaar	2018	1,100	11.	Adult Friend Finder	2016	412
	Alibaba	2022	1,100	12.	MySpace	2013	360
5.	First American Financial Corp.	2019	885	13.	Exactis	2018	340
6.	Verifications.io	2019	763	14.	Twitter	2018	330
7.	LinkedIn	2021	700	15.	NetEase	2015	234
8.	Facebook	2019	533	16.	Sociallarks	2021	200

U.S. Internet Crimes by Number of Victims, 2021-23

Source: Internet Crime Complaint Center, Federal Bureau of Investigation (FBI)
(ranked by reported number of victims in 2023)

Rank	Type of crime	2021	2022	2023
1.	Phishing[1]/spoofing[2]	342,494	321,136	298,878
2.	Personal data breach	51,829	58,859	55,851
3.	Non-payment/non-delivery	82,478	51,679	50,523
4.	Extortion	39,360	39,416	48,223
5.	Investment	20,561	30,529	39,570
6.	Tech support	23,903	32,538	37,560
7.	Business email compromise	19,954	21,832	21,489
8.	Identity theft	51,629	27,922	19,778
9.	Confidence fraud/romance	24,299	19,021	17,823
10.	Employment	15,253	14,946	15,443
11.	Government impersonation	11,335	11,554	14,190
12.	Credit card/check fraud	16,750	22,985	13,718
13.	*Harassment/stalking	NA	11,779	9,587
14.	Real estate	11,578	11,727	9,521
15.	Other	12,346	9,966	8,808
16.	Advanced fee	11,034	11,264	8,045
17.	Lottery/sweepstakes/inheritance	5,991	5,650	4,168
18.	Overpayment[3]	6,108	6,183	4,144
19.	Data breach	1,287	2,795	3,727
20.	Ransomware	3,729	2,385	2,825

* = New crime type added in 2022. NA = Not available. (1) The use of unsolicited email, text messages, and telephone calls purportedly from a legitimate company requesting personal, financial, and/or login credentials. (2) Contact information (phone number, email, and/or website) is deliberately falsified to mislead and appear to be from a legitimate source. (3) An individual is sent a payment/commission and is instructed to keep a portion of the payment and send the remainder to another individual or business.

U.S. Internet Crimes by Losses, 2021-23

Source: Internet Crime Complaint Center, Federal Bureau of Investigation (FBI)
(ranked by dollar value of reported 2023 losses)

Rank	Type of crime	2021	2022	2023
1.	Investment	$1,455,943,193	$3,311,742,206	$4,570,275,683
2.	Business email compromise	2,395,953,296	2,742,354,049	2,946,830,270
3.	Tech support	347,657,432	806,551,993	924,512,658
4.	Personal data breach	517,021,289	742,438,136	744,219,879
5.	Confidence fraud/romance	956,039,739	735,882,192	652,544,805
6.	Data breach	151,568,225	459,321,859	534,397,222
7.	Government impersonation	142,643,253	240,553,091	394,050,518
8.	Non-payment/non-delivery	337,493,071	281,770,073	309,648,416
9.	Other	75,837,524	117,686,789	240,053,059
10.	Credit card/check fraud	172,998,385	264,148,905	173,627,614
11.	Real estate	350,328,166	396,932,821	145,243,348
12.	Advanced fee	98,694,137	104,325,444	134,516,577
13.	Identity theft	278,267,918	189,205,793	126,203,809
14.	Lottery/sweepstakes/inheritance	71,289,089	83,602,376	94,502,836
15.	Extortion	60,577,741	54,335,128	74,821,835
16.	Employment	47,231,023	52,204,269	70,234,079
17.	Ransomware[1]	49,207,908	34,353,237	59,641,384
18.	*SIM swap	NA	72,652,571	48,798,103
19.	Overpayment	33,407,671	38,335,772	27,955,195
20.	*Botnet	NA	17,099,378	22,422,708

* = New crime type added in 2022. NA = Not available. (1) Does not include estimates of lost business, time, wages, files, or equipment, or any third-party remediation services acquired by a victim. In some cases, victims do not report any loss amount to the FBI. Figure represents only what victims report to the FBI via the Internet Crime Complaint Center and does not account for victim direct reporting to FBI field offices/agents.

Fixed Broadband Penetration in Selected Countries, 2009-23

Source: Organisation for Economic Co-operation and Development (OECD)
(nonmobile broadband subscriptions per 100 inhabitants; ranked by 2023 figures)

Nation	2009	2011	2013	2015	2017	2018	2019	2020	2021	2022	2023
France	30.69	34.81	37.80	40.40	42.39	43.22	44.05	45.06	46.17	46.67	47.00
Germany	31.03	33.92	35.49	37.59	40.21	41.19	42.35	43.55	44.33	44.77	45.40
Canada	30.60	32.84	34.46	36.73	38.10	38.97	40.25	40.95	41.98	42.05	41.98
United Kingdom	29.48	32.75	35.50	37.88	39.44	40.03	40.28	40.85	41.41	41.52	41.24
Japan	24.72	27.28	28.11	29.77	31.31	31.85	32.70	34.27	35.49	36.83	40.84
United States	26.04	28.28	30.28	31.73	33.10	33.72	34.57	36.33	37.84	38.40	39.10
Italy	20.29	22.52	23.22	24.89	27.55	28.65	29.66	30.78	31.92	32.11	32.11

Note: Includes internet connections with speeds greater than 256 kilobits per second (256 kbps).

Nations With Highest Percentage of Population Using the Internet, 2000-22

Source: © International Telecommunication Union; ranked by 2022 figures

Rank	Nation	2000	2005	2010	2015	2018	2019	2020	2021	2022
1.	Bahrain	6.15%	21.30%	55.00%	93.50%	98.60%	99.70%	99.70%	100.00%	100.00%
	Qatar	4.86	24.70	69.00	92.90	99.70	99.70	99.70	100.00	100.00
	Saudi Arabia	2.21	12.70	41.00	69.60	93.30	95.70	97.90	100.00	100.00
	United Arab Emirates	23.60	40.00	68.00	90.50	98.50	99.20	100.00	100.00	100.00
5.	Iceland	44.50	87.00	93.40	98.20	99.00	99.50	99.50	99.70	99.90
6.	Kuwait	6.73	25.90	61.40	82.00	99.60	99.50	99.10	99.70	99.80
7.	Brunei	9.00	36.50	53.00	71.20	95.00	95.00	95.10	95.60	99.00
	Norway	52.00	82.00	93.40	96.80	96.50	98.00	94.60	99.00	99.00
9.	Monaco	42.20	55.50	75.00	93.40	NA	83.30	98.60	98.40	98.40
10.	Luxembourg	22.90	70.00	90.60	96.40	97.10	97.10	98.50	98.70	98.20
11.	Denmark	39.20	82.70	88.70	96.30	97.30	98.00	96.50	98.90	97.90
12.	Oman	3.52	6.68	35.80	73.50	85.50	90.30	95.20	95.80	97.80
13.	Malaysia	21.40	48.60	56.30	71.10	81.20	84.20	89.60	96.80	97.40
14.	South Korea	44.70	73.50	83.70	89.90	96.00	96.20	96.50	97.60	97.20
15.	United States	43.10	68.00	71.70	74.60	88.50	89.40	96.60	96.80	97.10
16.	Liechtenstein	36.50	63.40	80.00	96.60	NA	93.10	94.30	95.60	96.80
	Switzerland	47.10	70.10	83.90	87.50	91.80	93.10	94.30	95.60	96.80
18.	Singapore	36.00	61.00	71.00	79.00	88.20	88.90	92.00	96.90	96.00
19.	New Zealand	47.40	62.70	80.50	85.20	89.00	89.90	95.20	95.70	95.70
20.	Hong Kong	27.80	56.90	72.00	84.90	90.50	91.70	92.40	93.10	95.60
	Ireland	17.90	41.60	69.90	83.50	87.00	87.00	92.00	94.50	95.60
22.	United Kingdom	26.80	70.00	85.00	92.00	90.70	92.50	94.80	95.30	95.30
23.	Sweden	45.70	84.80	90.00	90.60	89.20	94.50	94.50	94.70	95.00
24.	Australia	46.80	63.00	76.00	84.60	90.00	93.60	94.70	95.00	94.90
25.	Andorra	10.50	37.60	81.00	87.90	NA	90.70	93.20	93.90	94.50
	Spain	13.60	47.90	65.80	78.70	86.10	90.70	93.20	93.90	94.50

NA = Not available.

Nations With the Most Internet Users

Source: *The World Factbook*, Central Intelligence Agency (CIA); estimates for nations as of 2021

Rank	Nation	Internet users[1]	% of worldwide users	Rank	Nation	Internet users[1]	% of worldwide users
1.	China	1,022,000,000	21.11%	14.	Turkey (Türkiye)	68,850,000	1.42%
2.	India	644,000,000	13.30	15.	Bangladesh	66,300,000	1.37
3.	United States	312,800,000	6.46	16.	United Kingdom	64,990,000	1.34
4.	Brazil	170,100,000	3.51	17.	Thailand	61,200,000	1.26
5.	Indonesia	167,400,000	3.46	18.	Philippines	58,300,000	1.20
6.	Russia	132,000,000	2.73	19.	France	55,900,000	1.15
7.	Nigeria	115,500,000	2.39	20.	South Korea	50,960,000	1.05
8.	Japan	99,600,000	2.06	21.	Pakistan	48,300,000	1.00
9.	Mexico	98,800,000	2.04	22.	Italy	44,250,000	0.91
10.	Egypt	79,200,000	1.64	23.	Spain	44,180,000	0.91
11.	Germany	75,530,000	1.56	24.	South Africa	42,480,000	0.88
12.	Vietnam	71,780,000	1.48	25.	Argentina	39,150,000	0.81
13.	Iran	69,520,000	1.44		**World**	**4,840,690,000**	**100.00**

(1) Estimated number of individuals who can access the internet at home, via any device type (computer or mobile) and connection.

Top Web Browsers Worldwide, 2009-24

Source: StatCounter Global Stats, gs.statcounter.com
(ranked by 2024 figures)

Browser	% of browser market							
	2009	2013	2015	2017	2019	2021	2023	2024
Chrome	2.98%	36.63%	45.09%	54.30%	63.37%	65.12%	63.55%	65.39%
Safari	3.35	11.23	13.20	14.15	15.05	18.65	19.95	18.39
Edge	—	—	—	—	—	3.40	5.14	5.25
Firefox	30.18	16.84	9.99	5.73	4.49	3.45	2.79	2.74
Samsung Internet	—	—	—	3.53	3.75	3.13	2.38	2.59
Opera	2.88	3.51	5.48	3.98	2.58	2.13	2.98	2.06
UC	—	1.75	5.61	8.57	3.57	1.18	1.01	1.04
Android	0.02	5.49	6.58	2.47	0.97	0.71	0.60	0.57
QQ	—	0.05	0.19	0.11	0.31	0.27	0.28	0.53
360 Safe	—	0.15	0.09	0.08	0.02	0.29	0.27	0.43
Yandex	—	0.25	0.27	0.29	0.24	0.23	0.27	0.33
Internet Explorer	59.48	20.49	10.81	3.74	2.26	0.57	0.18	0.15

— = Not available. **Note:** Percent of desktop, laptop, tablet, console, and mobile device users accessing the web with a particular browser, for July of year shown.

U.S. Internet Use by Selected Characteristics, 2013-23

Source: Pew Research Center

	% who are users 2013	% who are users 2023		% who are users 2013	% who are users 2023		% who are users 2013	% who are users 2023
All adults[1]	84%	95%	**Race/ethnicity**			**Annual household income**		
Gender			White, non-Hispanic	85%	96%	Less than $30,000	72%	87%
Male	84	94	Black, non-Hispanic	79	91	$30,000-$49,999[3]	86	96
Female	84	96	Hispanic	80	97	$50,000-$74,999[3]	93	98
Age			**Education**			$75,000 or more[3]	97	99
18-29	97	97	No high school diploma	54	90[2]	**Geography**		
30-49	92	98	High school graduate	75	90[2]	Urban	86	95
50-64	81	96	Some college	92	98	Suburban	85	97
65+	56	88	College graduate	96	99	Rural	78	93

Note: Percent of U.S. adults, age 18 and over, who use the internet, email, or access the internet via a mobile device. (1) Includes race categories not shown. (2) Instead of the categories "No high school diploma" and "High school graduate," a single figure was reported for "High school or less." (3) Changes in survey methodology in 2023 included adjustments to income categories: $30,000-$69,999 (96%); $70,000-$99,999 (98%); $100,000+ (99%).

Frequency of Social Media Use by U.S. Teenagers, 2023

Source: Pew Research Center
(percent of teenagers ages 13-17 surveyed)

Site/platform	Almost constantly	Several times a day	About once a day	Several times a week	Less often	Do not use	Daily total
YouTube	16%	38%	17%	14%	8%	6%	71%
TikTok	17	32	9	4	2	36	58
Snapchat	14	29	8	5	4	39	51
Instagram	8	27	12	7	5	41	47
Facebook	3	8	8	6	7	67	19

Social Media Use by U.S. Adults, 2021-23

Source: Pew Research Center
(percent of adult survey respondents who say they ever use)

Site/platform	2021	2023	Site/platform	2021	2023
YouTube	81%	83%	LinkedIn	28%	30%
Facebook	69	68	WhatsApp	23	29
Instagram	40	47	Snapchat	25	27
Pinterest	31	35	X (fmr. Twitter)	23	22
TikTok	21	33	Reddit	18	22

Most-Visited U.S. Websites, 2024

Source: Comscore, Inc.
Some websites represent an aggregation of domain names; examples added in parentheses.

All U.S. Sites Rank	Website	Visitors[1]	Video Sites Rank	Website	Visitors[2]
1.	Google sites (YouTube, Blogger)	278,413	1.	Google sites (YouTube)	254,380
2.	Yahoo (AOL)	249,329	2.	Paramount Global	188,391
3.	Microsoft sites (Bing, LinkedIn, Xbox Network)	245,922	3.	Comcast NBCUniversal	185,565
4.	Paramount Global	241,123	4.	The Walt Disney Company	180,453
5.	The Walt Disney Company (ABC, ESPN)	240,260	5.	Universal Music Group	145,968
6.	Comcast NBCUniversal	239,440	6.	WMX - Warner Music Group	132,517
7.	Facebook	236,515	7.	Hulu	127,820
8.	Amazon sites	236,226	8.	The Orchard Music	111,636
9.	Warner Bros. Discovery	214,745	9.	BroadbandTV	109,745
10.	Raptive (formerly CafeMedia)	183,050	10.	VEVO	96,072
11.	Apple Inc.	178,564	11.	Fox Corporation	94,374
12.	Dotdash Meredith	177,652	12.	Warner Bros. Discovery	84,918
13.	Universal Music Group	175,865	13.	Amazon sites	82,509
14.	PayPal	174,169	14.	Studio71 Network	81,811
15.	Fox Corporation	165,989	15.	Microsoft sites	78,351
16.	Freestar	154,022	16.	USA Today Network	60,963
17.	Hearst	147,085	17.	Yahoo	57,603
18.	Penske Media Corp (PMC)	142,290	18.	Nexstar Inc.	42,958
19.	Twitter (a.k.a. X)	139,914	19.	Spotter	41,548
20.	Bytedance Inc. (TikTok)	136,647	20.	STN Video	40,573
21.	Wal-Mart	135,986	21.	Conde Nast Digital	32,662
22.	Reddit	134,645	22.	Culture Genesis	32,266
23.	Spotify	132,279	23.	Little Dot Studios	32,056
24.	The Orchard Music	127,815	24.	Vox Media	30,970
25.	Nexstar Inc.	124,574	25.	Minute Media/The Players' Tribune	28,874

(1) Number of persons, in thousands, who visited the media property (including website/apps) at least once from any U.S. location in May 2024. Mobile users under age 18 are not measured. (2) Number of persons, in thousands, who visited the media property from a desktop in April 2024. Excludes advertisement videos.

Top Search Engines in the U.S. 2009-24

Source: StatCounter Global Stats, gs.statcounter.com
(ranked by 2024 figures)

Search engine	% of search market 2009	2012	2015	2017	2019	2021	2023	2024
Google	77.54%	80.28%	79.64%	77.45%	80.86%	80.04%	77.52%	74.18%
Bing	9.41	9.50	8.31	12.73	11.86	11.83	15.62	18.24
Yahoo!	10.95	8.22	9.79	8.12	5.49	4.77	3.94	4.31
DuckDuckGo	0.00	0.01	0.32	0.74	1.21	2.71	2.39	2.59
AOL	1.22	0.76	0.88	0.30	0.05	0.04	0.04	0.23

Note: Percent of desktop and laptop computer users utilizing a particular search engine, for July of year shown.

Most Popular U.S. Smartphone Apps, 2024

Source: Comscore, Inc.

Rank	Apps[1]	Reach[2]	Rank	Apps[1]	Reach[2]
1.	YouTube	75%	14.	Cash App	33%
2.	Facebook	66	15.	Walmart	32
3.	Gmail	66	16.	Apple Maps	29
4.	Google Search	63	17.	Google Drive	25
5.	Google Maps	60	18.	Apple News	25
6.	Amazon Mobile	56	19.	Venmo	24
7.	Instagram	39	20.	Snapchat	24
8.	Google Play	39	21.	Yahoo Stocks	23
9.	Spotify	39	22.	Apple Notes	23
10.	TikTok	38	23.	Temu: Team Up, Price Down	22
11.	Facebook Messenger	36	24.	Pinterest	22
12.	Google Photos	35	25.	McDonald's	21
13.	PayPal	34			

(1) Includes applications developed for Android and iOS platforms. (2) Percentage of total U.S. smartphone users age 18 and over who used the app in May 2024.

U.S. Internet Use by Race and Ethnicity, 2003-23

Source: U.S. Census Bureau survey for National Telecommunications and Information Administration, U.S. Dept. of Commerce (number in thousands of civilian individuals, age 3 and older)

	Total U.S.[1]		White, non-Hispanic		African American, non-Hispanic		Asian American, non-Hispanic		American Indian or Alaska Native, non-Hispanic		Hispanic	
Survey date	Number	% with internet use	Number	% with internet use	Number	% with internet use	Number	% with internet use	Number	% with internet use	Number	% with internet use
Oct. 2003	161,636	58.7%	122,243	65.1%	14,898	45.2%	7,043	63.0%	676	48.1%	14,038	37.2%
Oct. 2007	177,987	62.4	130,432	68.9	17,223	50.1	8,686	68.4	793	47.1	17,760	41.6
Oct. 2009	197,941	68.4	141,213	74.3	20,848	59.5	9,243	72.3	1,017	54.9	22,186	49.3
Oct. 2010	209,472	71.7	145,989	76.7	22,389	63.7	9,949	74.2	1,094	62.5	26,246	56.6
July 2011	204,596	69.7	142,827	75.0	21,287	60.2	10,010	73.6	1,142	59.7	25,648	54.4
Oct. 2012	222,038	74.7	149,231	79.1	24,290	68.3	11,643	78.4	1,350	62.5	30,960	62.1
July 2013	213,708	71.4	142,313	75.4	22,996	64.0	11,739	75.3	1,424	61.5	30,771	61.0
July 2015	226,747	74.6	147,408	78.0	25,025	67.8	12,919	77.4	1,423	70.2	34,772	65.8
Nov. 2017	240,270	77.7	151,594	80.2	27,949	73.4	13,993	79.4	1,497	62.7	39,826	72.1
Nov. 2019	248,526	79.4	154,232	81.8	28,814	74.7	14,774	78.3	1,850	73.8	43,129	74.8
Nov. 2021	253,242	80.5	155,071	82.5	29,892	76.9	15,189	80.6	1,885	74.6	45,074	76.7
Nov. 2023	266,466	83.3	158,585	84.5	32,551	81.8	16,644	81.5	1,911	82.7	49,625	80.5

(1) Includes race categories not shown.

Telecommunications Milestones

1753: Scottish surgeon Charles Morrison proposed using 26 electric lines, one for each letter of the alphabet, to make an electric telegraph. A letter would be indicated by charging the corresponding line, causing movement of a light object at the receiving end. Swiss scientist Georges-Louis Lesage built such a 26-line "electrostatic" system in 1774.

1837: In England, Charles Wheatstone and William Fothergill Cooke patented an electromagnetic telegraph. To indicate letters, their system used the magnetic field generated by a current to deflect compass needles. In 1839, they built the first commercial electric telegraph along a 13-mi (21-km) route.

1837: American inventor Samuel Morse filed a provisional patent application for a different type of electric telegraph that indicated letters by making marks of various lengths on paper. In 1844, he completed a 30-mi telegraph line from Washington, DC, to Baltimore, MD.

1866: The first successful transatlantic telegraph cable was laid.

1876: Alexander Graham Bell applied for a U.S. patent on the telephone. In his first successful experiment, on Mar. 10, he used the device to call his assistant.

1901: Italian inventor Guglielmo Marconi successfully transmitted the first transatlantic radio signal—from Cornwall, England, to Newfoundland, Canada.

1927: Commercial transatlantic telephone service (via radio) began between New York and London.

1946: The first commercial mobile phone service was launched, in St. Louis, MO.

1947: U.S. scientists invented the transistor, thereby giving birth to a revolution in telecommunications and electronics.

1948: U.S. mathematician/engineer Claude Shannon's epochal paper "A Mathematical Theory of Communication" laid the foundation for modern information theory. Its treatment of such crucial concepts as data compression and error detection and correction opened the way to digital communication.

1951: The mayors of Englewood, NJ, and Alameda, CA, made the first customer-dialed long-distance telephone call, facilitated by the introduction of area codes.

1956: The first transoceanic telephone cable went into service.

1962: NASA launched the world's first active communications satellite, AT&T's *Telstar 1*.

1978: Trials were conducted in Chicago and Newark, NJ, on a cellular approach to mobile telephony. This divided a region into a multitude of small overlapping areas, or cells, and made possible a significant increase in quality of calls and quantity of callers. Callers could be switched from one cell to another as they moved about.

1983: The first commercial cellular system in the U.S. went into operation in Chicago. A similar system was also launched in the Baltimore, MD-Washington, DC, area.

1984: As a result of a 1982 antitrust settlement with the U.S. government, AT&T, which handled most telephone service in the U.S., was broken up into several separate entities.

1994: The first smartphone, IBM's Simon Personal Communicator, went on the market. A bricklike touchscreen device, it combined a cellular phone with such features as an address book, calendar, calculator, email and faxing capability, and games.

2007: Apple released the iPhone, inaugurating an era of multi-functional smartphones.

2012: By late in the year more than 1 bil smartphones of all types were in use worldwide.

2016: Users of Facebook's messaging app Messenger passed the 1 bil mark.

2016: Total sales of Apple's iPhone reached 1 bil units.

2019: Telecommunications carriers began launching commercial "5G" (fifth generation) super-fast cellular networks, with the first large-scale deployments taking place in South Korea and the U.S.

Nations With the Most Cellphone Use, 2000-23

Source: International Telecommunication Union, ITU DataHub, datahub.itu.int
(millions of subscriptions; estimates reported as of Sept. 2024; ranked by 2022 figures)

Country	2000	2010	2012	2014	2016	2018	2020	2022	2023
China	85	859	1,110	1,290	1,360	1,650	1,720	1,770	1,810
India	4	752	865	944	1,130	1,180	1,150	1,140	1,160
United States	109	285	305	323	338	348	353	373	386
Indonesia	4	211	282	326	386	319	356	343	352
Russia	3	238	208	221	229	229	239	245	NA
Nigeria	—	87	113	139	154	173	204	222	224
Brazil	23	197	248	281	244	209	206	213	213
Japan	67	123	141	158	167	180	195	211	219
Pakistan	—	99	120	136	136	154	176	193	189
Bangladesh	—	68	97	127	136	162	176	186	191
Philippines	6	83	102	111	120	135	150	166	135
Iran	1	54	58	69	80	89	128	146	151
Vietnam	1	112	132	136	121	141	139	137	131
Mexico	14	91	101	105	112	120	123	136	140
Thailand	3	72	85	97	120	125	116	126	121
Germany	48	88	92	100	103	108	107	104	105
Egypt	1	71	97	95	98	94	95	102	106
South Africa	8	50	68	79	82	92	96	100	108
Turkey	16	62	68	72	75	80	82	90	92
United Kingdom	44	77	78	78	79	79	79	82	84
Colombia	2	44	49	55	59	64	68	81	87
Italy	42	94	97	90	86	83	78	78	79
South Korea	27	51	54	57	61	66	70	77	84
France	29	58	62	65	68	70	73	77	77
Ethiopia	—	7	20	30	51	NA	44	71	NA
Kenya	—	25	31	34	39	50	61	66	67
Tanzania	—	21	27	32	40	44	51	60	70
Argentina	6	57	64	61	64	59	55	60	63
Spain	24	51	51	51	52	54	56	59	61
Myanmar	—	1	4	29	51	61	78	58	66

— = Under 500,000 subscriptions. NA = Not available.

U.S. Wireless Industry, 2010-21

Source: CTIA.org; as of Dec. of year shown

Year	Estimated total subscribers	Cell sites	Mobile wireless data traffic (trillion megabytes)	Annual service revenue (thousand dollars)	Cumulative capital expenditures (thousand dollars)
2010	296,285,629	253,086	0.388	$159,929,649	$310,014,851
2011	315,963,848	283,385	0.867	169,767,314	335,331,967
2012	326,475,248	301,779	1.468	185,013,935	365,426,326
2013	335,652,171	304,360	3.230	189,192,812	398,567,671
2014	355,445,472	298,055	4.061	187,848,447	430,642,374
2015	377,921,241	307,626	9.650	191,949,025	462,605,007
2016	395,881,497	308,334	13.719	188,524,256	488,996,535
2017	400,205,829	323,448	15.687	179,091,135	514,625,256
2018	421,793,010	349,344	28.585	182,779,484	542,033,353
2019	442,456,704	395,562	37.060	187,361,982	571,125,121
2020	468,898,212	417,215	42.205	189,912,441	601,018,145
2021	498,910,316	418,887	53.356	204,214,004	635,759,036

U.S. Smartphone-Only Internet Access by Selected Characteristics, 2013-23

Source: Pew Research Center
(percentage of U.S. adults who do not have home broadband but own smartphones)

	% of adults who say they do not have broadband at home but own smartphones	
	2013	2023
All adults	8%	15%
Gender		
Male	9	15
Female	8	14
Age		
18-29	12	20
30-49	9	11
50-64	7	14
65+	3	16
Race/ethnicity		
White, non-Hispanic	6	12
Black, non-Hispanic	10	21
Hispanic	16	20

	% of adults who say they do not have broadband at home but own smartphones	
	2013	2023
Education[1]		
No high school diploma	14%	24%[2]
High school graduate	11	24[2]
Some college	8	13
College graduate	4	6
Annual household income		
Less than $30,000	12	28
$30,000-$49,999[3]	9	19
$50,000-$74,999[3]	5	9
$75,000 or more[3]	5	4
Geography		
Urban	9	17
Suburban	7	11
Rural	9	18

(1) Includes race categories not shown. (2) Instead of the categories "No high school diploma" and "High school graduate," a single figure was reported for "High school or less." (3) Changes in survey methodology in 2023 included adjustments to income categories: $30,000-$69,999 (19%); $70,000-$99,999 (9%); $100,000+ (4%).

ENVIRONMENT

U.S. Greenhouse Gas Emissions From Human Activities, 1990-2022

Source: U.S. Environmental Protection Agency

Gas and major source(s)	1990	2005	2018	2019	2020	2021	2022	% change, 1990-2022
Carbon dioxide (CO_2)	5,131.6	6,126.9	5,362.2	5,234.5	4,689.0	5,017.2	5,053.0	−1.5%
Fossil fuel combustion	4,752.2	5,744.1	4,988.2	4,852.6	4,341.7	4,654.3	4,699.4	−1.1
Methane (CH_4)	871.7	795.4	771.5	754.3	735.3	720.5	702.4	−19.4
Enteric fermentation[1]	183.1	188.2	196.8	197.3	196.3	196.5	192.6	5.2
Natural gas systems	218.8	210.1	190.3	188.7	180.3	174.6	173.1	−20.9
Landfills	197.8	147.7	126.3	128.7	124.1	122.0	119.8	−39.4
Manure management	39.1	55.0	67.7	66.7	66.9	66.4	64.7	65.5
Nitrous oxide (N_2O)	408.2	419.2	439.5	416.4	391.2	398.2	389.7	−4.5
Agricultural soil management	288.8	294.1	333.4	315.6	292.1	298.0	290.8	0.7
Hydrofluorocarbons (HFCs), etc.[2]	125.4	153.1	179.6	185.0	186.3	192.9	198.2	58.1
Total U.S. emissions	**6,536.9**	**7,494.6**	**6,752.7**	**6,590.1**	**6,001.8**	**6,328.8**	**6,343.2**	**−3.0**
Net U.S. emissions[3]	**5,560.2**	**6,586.9**	**5,837.3**	**5,726.6**	**5,097.4**	**5,418.2**	**5,489.2**	**−1.3**

Note: Emissions given in terms of equivalent emissions of carbon dioxide (CO_2), using units of million metric tons of carbon dioxide equivalent (MMT CO_2 eq.). (1) Digestive process of ruminant animals, such as cattle and sheep, producing methane as a byproduct. (2) Includes HFCs, PFCs (perfluorocarbons), SF_6 (sulfur hexafluoride), and NF_3 (nitrogen trifluoride). (3) Total emissions minus the net sum of all emissions (i.e., sources) of greenhouse gases to the atmosphere plus removals of CO_2 (i.e., sinks or negative emissions) from the atmosphere.

U.S. Greenhouse Gas Emissions, 2022

Source: U.S. Environmental Protection Agency

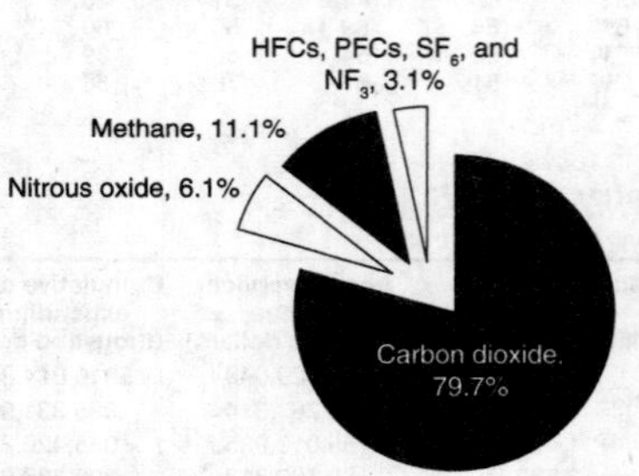

World Carbon Dioxide Emissions From the Use of Fossil Fuels, 2022

Source: U.S. Energy Information Administration

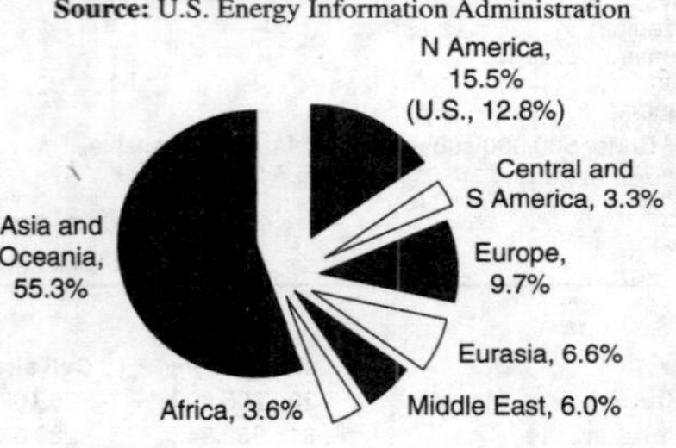

HFC = hydrofluorocarbon; PFC = perfluorocarbon; SF_6 = sulfur hexafluoride; NF_3 = nitrogen trifluoride. **Note:** Emissions sources are independently rounded; percentages may not add up to 100.

Top 20 Nations Producing Carbon Dioxide Emissions, 1980-2022

Source: Energy Information Administration, U.S. Dept. of Energy

(in million metric tons of carbon dioxide emitted from the consumption of energy; ranked by 2022 totals)

Country	1980	1990	2000	2005	2010	2015	2020	2022	% change, 1980-2022	% change, 1990-2022
China	1,597	2,417	3,483	6,120	9,004	10,427	10,850	13,506	745.8%	458.7%
U.S.	4,756	5,038	5,889	6,007	5,594	5,262	4,584	4,941	3.9	−1.9
India	270	541	886	1,119	1,648	2,145	2,339	2,805	939.0	418.1
Russia[1]	3,516	4,024	1,540	1,571	1,661	1,690	1,676	1,840	−47.7	−54.3
Japan	872	1,109	1,233	1,279	1,197	1,215	1,052	1,049	20.4	−5.4
Iran	102	195	303	430	537	613	653	750	638.1	285.5
Indonesia	72	149	256	301	409	461	538	685	848.9	360.9
Germany[2]	736	719	872	844	822	788	631	668	−9.2	−7.1
South Korea	139	264	466	504	612	662	657	643	363.2	144.0
Saudi Arabia	107	199	290	405	497	621	525	638	496.3	221.1
Canada	426	439	515	575	565	592	542	573	34.6	30.5
Brazil	188	243	327	342	410	500	496	517	175.3	112.6
South Africa	229	329	393	446	479	474	469	477	108.6	44.8
Mexico	206	280	382	431	457	465	411	454	119.8	61.8
Australia	221	268	339	370	392	382	376	415	87.6	55.2
Turkey (Türkiye)	62	128	207	233	268	351	372	392	530.2	206.7
UK	613	606	570	585	542	451	331	353	−42.3	−41.7
Italy	337	421	452	473	416	349	288	317	−6.2	−24.7
France	472	385	409	421	388	347	288	312	−34.0	−18.9
Thailand	34	84	158	237	258	296	287	308	817.2	268.0
World[3]	**18,722**	**22,150**	**24,266**	**28,701**	**32,531**	**34,836**	**33,848**	**38,502**	**105.7**	**73.8**

(1) Numbers for 1980-90 are for the former Soviet Union. (2) Numbers for 1980-90 are for former West Germany. (3) Includes nations not listed.

Major Greenhouse Gas Sources, Lifespans, and Added Heat

Source: NASA/JPL-Caltech

Human activities have been emitting greenhouse gases into the atmosphere since at least 1750 (the Industrial Revolution), and this rate is accelerating. When these gases enter the atmosphere, they stay for years, creating a time lag between when they arrive and when we see the consequences, which include sea level rise, Arctic sea ice melt, and extreme events.

This table lists the major greenhouse gases causing today's global warming, their sources, their average lifetimes in the atmosphere, and their possible added heat ("global warming potential") over a 20- and 100-year period.

Greenhouse gas	Sources[1]	Avg. lifetime in the atmosphere	Possible added heat[2] over a 20-yr period	Possible added heat over a 100-yr period
Carbon dioxide (CO_2)	• **human sources (100%):** mostly the burning of fossil fuels, deforestation/land-use change, wildfire/biomass burning • **natural sources (0%)**	hundreds to thousands of years; about 25% of it lasts effectively forever	CO_2 is used as a reference point for other greenhouse gases, so its possible added warming is 1	CO_2 is used as a reference point for other greenhouse gases, so its possible added warming is 1
Methane (CH_4)	• **human sources (60%):** leaks from fossil fuel prod. and trans.; landfills; livestock digestion and manure; rice farming, natural gas; wildfires/biomass burning • **natural sources (40%):** plant-matter breakdown in wetlands, lakes, ponds; wildfires/biomass burning; termites; ocean; sediment; volcanoes; permafrost	about a decade	1 metric ton can trap about 80 times the heat of 1 metric ton of CO_2	1 metric ton can trap about 30 times the heat of 1 metric ton of CO_2
Nitrous oxide (N_2O)	• **human sources (40%):** prod. and use of organic and comm. fertilizer; burning fossil fuels; burning vegetation • **natural sources (60%):** bacteria breaking down nitrogen in soils and the ocean	about 110 years	1 metric ton can trap 273 times the heat of 1 metric ton of CO_2	1 metric ton can trap 273 times the heat of 1 metric ton of CO_2
Chlorofluorocarbons (CFCs)	• **human sources (100%):** refrigerants; solvents; spray-can propellants • **natural sources:** effectively none	about 52-93 years	1 metric ton can trap thousands to tens of thousands of times the heat of 1 metric ton of CO_2	1 metric ton can trap thousands to tens of thousands of times the heat of 1 metric ton of CO_2

(1) Contributions to global warming. (2) Global warming potential.

Atmospheric Concentration of Carbon Dioxide, 1744-2023

Source: Carbon Dioxide Information Analysis Center, U.S. Dept. of Energy; Earth System Research Laboratory, Natl. Oceanic and Atmospheric Admin., U.S. Dept. of Commerce

Year[1]	CO_2 in ppm	Year[1]	CO_2 in ppm	Year[1]	CO_2 in ppm	Year[1]	CO_2 in ppm	Year[1]	CO_2 in ppm
1744	277	1878	290	1960	317	2000	370	2020	414
1791	280	1903	295	1970	326	2005	380	2021	416
1816	284	1915	301	1980	339	2010	390	2022	419
1843	287	1927	306	1990	354	2015	401	2023	421
1869	289	1943	308						

ppm = Parts per million. (1) Measurements for 1744-1943 were derived from a 200-m-deep ice core sample drilled near Siple Station in Antarctica in 1983-84. Measurements for 1960-2021, most of 2022, and part of 2023 were taken directly from the atmosphere at Mauna Loa Observatory in Hawaii; from Dec. 2022 to July 4, 2023, measurements were taken at the Maunakea Observatories, due to the eruption of Mauna Loa Volcano in Nov. 2022.

Emissions of Principal Air Pollutants in the U.S., 1970-2023

Source: U.S. Environmental Protection Agency; in million tons

Pollutant	1970	1980	1990	2000	2005	2010	2015	2020	2022	2023
Carbon monoxide	204.0	185.4	154.2	114.5	86.7	60.2	56.3	62.4	49.8	48.8
Nitrogen oxides[1]	26.9	27.1	25.5	22.6	21.9	15.3	11.1	7.8	7.3	6.9
Particulate matter[2]										
PM10	13.0	7.0	27.8	23.7	17.6	16.2	16.1	16.8	17.5	17.5
PM2.5	NA	NA	7.6	7.3	5.5	4.6	4.7	5.8	6.1	6.1
Sulfur dioxide	31.2	25.9	23.1	16.3	14.6	6.9	3.5	1.8	1.9	1.7
Volatile org. compounds[1]	34.7	31.1	24.1	17.5	16.9	13.6	14.1	16.6	14.6	14.5
Ammonia	NA	NA	4.3	4.9	4.7	4.4	4.5	5.5	5.0	5.0
Black carbon	NA	NA	NA	NA	0.5	0.4	0.3	0.4	0.3	0.3
Organic carbon	NA	NA	NA	NA	1.3	1.2	1.3	2.1	2.3	2.3
Total[3]	**309.8**	**276.5**	**266.6**	**206.8**	**169.7**	**122.8**	**111.9**	**119.2**	**104.8**	**103.1**

NA = Not available. (1) Ozone, a major air pollutant and the primary constituent of smog, is not emitted directly to the air but is formed by sunlight acting on emissions of nitrogen oxides and volatile organic compounds. (2) PM10 = particulates 10 microns or smaller in diameter. PM2.5 = particulates 2.5 microns or smaller in diameter. (3) Totals are rounded, as are components of totals.

Sources of Air Pollutants in the U.S., 1970-2023

Source: U.S. Environmental Protection Agency; in thousand tons

Carbon monoxide sources	1970	1980	1990	2000	2005	2010	2015	2020	2022	2023
Stationary fuel combustion	4,632	7,302	5,511	4,784	4,723	5,007	4,615	4,720	4,764	4,764
Industrial and other processes	16,899	9,250	5,853	4,479	3,844	3,469	3,276	3,075	3,140	3,140
Transportation	174,602	160,512	131,702	92,239	65,632	41,994	34,062	25,955	25,613	24,638
Total carbon monoxide[1]	**204,042**	**185,408**	**154,188**	**114,467**	**86,663**	**60,247**	**56,296**	**62,437**	**49,815**	**48,840**
Nitrogen oxide sources										
Stationary fuel combustion	10,061	11,320	10,894	8,819	6,316	3,955	3,097	2,333	2,322	2,235
Industrial and other processes	1,215	666	891	943	1,353	1,228	1,168	1,068	1,204	1,204
Transportation	15,276	14,846	13,373	12,560	13,920	9,960	6,596	3,988	3,558	3,223
Total nitrogen oxide[1]	**26,882**	**27,080**	**25,527**	**22,598**	**21,865**	**15,340**	**11,114**	**7,816**	**7,339**	**6,916**
Sulfur dioxide sources										
Stationary fuel combustion	23,456	21,391	20,290	14,163	12,585	6,073	2,857	1,112	1,168	1,014
Industrial and other processes	7,101	3,807	1,901	1,418	1,063	609	475	484	482	482
Transportation	551	717	874	697	798	165	53	25	28	29
Total sulfur dioxide[1]	**31,218**	**25,926**	**23,077**	**16,347**	**14,563**	**6,938**	**3,502**	**1,845**	**1,853**	**1,701**

(1) Includes categories not listed.

Average Global Temperature and Atmospheric Carbon Dioxide, 1880-2023

Source: Goddard Institute for Space Studies, National Aeronautics and Space Administration, via Earth Policy Institute; National Centers for Environmental Information, National Oceanic and Atmospheric Admin. (NOAA), U.S. Dept. of Commerce

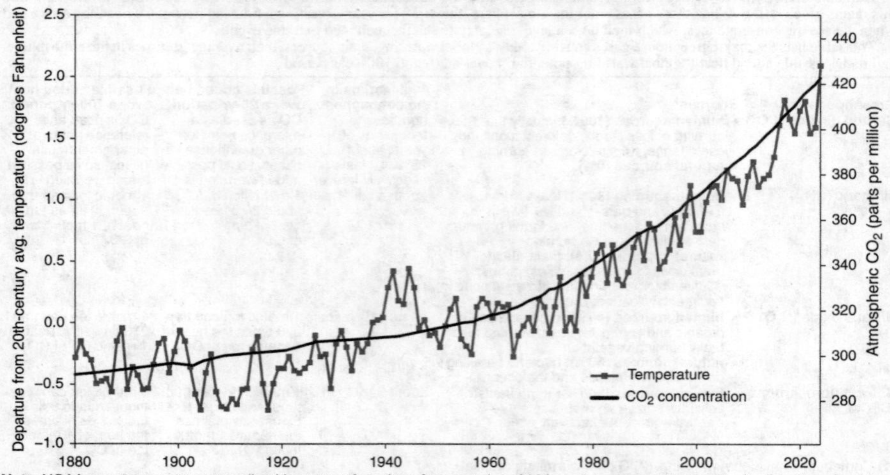

Note: NOAA uses temperature anomalies (departures from the reference value of 20th-century average temperature) rather than absolute temperatures to report average global temperatures.

Climate Change Indicators in the U.S.

Source: U.S. Environmental Protection Agency (EPA)

In May 2021, the EPA's "Climate Change Indicators in the United States" resource (https://www.epa.gov/climate-indicators) relaunched, presenting compelling and clear evidence of changes to climate reflected in rising temperatures, droughts, heat waves, ocean acidity, river flooding, sea level rise, and wildfires, among other indicators. The indicators show:

- Global Temperature: Since 1880, when thermometer-based observations began, 2016 was the warmest year on record, and 2012-21 was the warmest decade.
- Arctic Sea Ice: Sept. 2012 had the lowest sea ice extent ever recorded, 44% below the 1981-2010 average for that month. The Sept. 2023 sea ice extent was the 5th smallest on record.
- Coastal Flooding: Coastal flooding became more frequent at most locations along the East and Gulf Coasts.
- Heat Waves in U.S. Cities: Frequency of heat waves increased steadily, from an average of two heat waves per year during the 1960s to six per year during the 2010s and 2020s.
- Ice Sheets: Since 1992, Greenland and Antarctica both lost more than 100 bil metric tons of ice per year on average.
- Length of Growing Season: The average length of the growing season in the contiguous 48 states increased by more than two weeks since the beginning of the 20th century.
- Marine Species Distribution: In conjunction with warming ocean waters, many marine species off U.S. coasts shifted northward and moved to deeper waters.
- Sea Level: Sea level (relative to the land) rose along much of the U.S. coastline between 1960 and 2021, particularly the Mid-Atlantic coast and parts of the Gulf Coast, where some stations registered increases of more than 8 in.

Ocean Heat Content, 1955-2023

Source: National Oceanic and Atmospheric Admin. (NOAA), U.S. Dept. of Commerce

Rising amounts of greenhouse gases have prevented heat radiated from Earth's surface from escaping as freely as it used to. Most of the excess atmospheric heat has passed back to the ocean, causing the upper ocean heat content to increase significantly. This has contributed to seal level rise, ocean heat waves and coral bleaching, and melting of ocean-terminating glaciers and ice sheets around Greenland and Antarctica. This graph shows the increase in ocean heat from 1955 to 2023, using 1993 as the average for comparison.

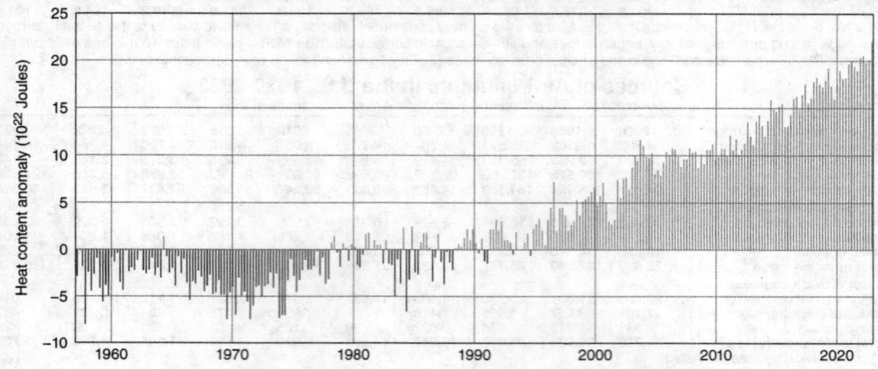

Air Pollution in Selected World Cities, 2017-23

Source: IQAir

Particulate matter refers to extremely small particles and liquid droplets in the air that come from vehicle exhaust, burning of fuels, dust, cooking, tobacco smoke, and chemical reactions in the atmosphere. Particulates 2.5 microns or less in diameter (PM2.5) are capable of reaching deep into the respiratory tract and can cause or worsen heart and lung diseases. The World Health Org. (WHO) estimates that exposure to ambient (outdoor) air pollution causes 4.2 mil deaths worldwide every year. Data in this table show the annual average PM2.5 concentration measured in μg/m³. In 2021, the WHO cut the recommended annual PM2.5 concentration from 10.0 to 5.0, with the goal of preventing millions of deaths; around 99% of the world's population lives in places where air quality levels exceed these limits.

City, country	PM2.5 level (μg/m³) 2023	2020	2017
Addis Ababa, Ethiopia	27.0	14.7	26.9
Amsterdam, Netherlands	9.1	9.9	12.2
Bangkok, Thailand	21.7	20.6	27.6
Beijing, China	34.1	37.5	58.8
Berlin, Germany	10.5	11.8	8.5
Bogotá, Colombia	13.4	14.3	15.7
Chicago, IL, U.S.	13.0	11.1	6.7
Delhi, India	102.1	84.1	108.2
Dhaka, Bangladesh	80.2	77.1	79.7
Dubai, UAE	43.6	32.6	NA
Hong Kong, China	15.5	15.4	21.8
Istanbul, Turkey	18.7	16.7	NA
Johannesburg, South Africa	18.7	22.3	NA
Karachi, Pakistan	56.4	43.8	38.5
Kolkata, India	47.8	46.6	76.7
Lima, Peru	19.7	18.0	27.7
London, England, UK	8.4	9.6	12.7
Los Angeles, CA, U S	9.5	14.6	16.1
Madrid, Spain	9.0	9.0	9.9
Mexico City, Mexico	22.3	18.8	20.4
Montréal, QC, Canada	11.1	9.5	6.8
Moscow, Russia	10.4	10.5	8.4
Mumbai, India	43.8	41.3	54.2
New York, NY, U.S.	11.6	6.5	NA
Oslo, Norway	6.2	6.4	7.4
Paris, France	10.3	12.2	15.4
Prague, Czechia	9.8	10.9	15.6
Rome, Italy	13.1	13.6	NA
Santiago, Chile	21.3	23.6	23.1
São Paulo, Brazil	14.3	14.2	16.0
Seoul, South Korea	19.7	20.9	25.2
Shanghai, China	28.7	31.5	38.9
Sofia, Bulgaria	12.0	27.5	20.8
Sydney, Australia	5.0	7.2	7.1
Tokyo, Japan	9.7	10.1	13.0
Toronto, ON, Canada	10.8	7.0	7.5

NA = Not available.

Municipal Waste Generation in Selected Countries, 2000-21

Source: Organization for Economic Cooperation and Development (OECD)

The OECD definition of municipal waste is waste collected and treated by or for municipalities. It covers waste from households, including bulky waste, similar waste from commerce and trade, office buildings, institutions and small businesses, as well as yard and garden waste, street sweepings, the contents of litter containers, and market cleansing waste if managed as household waste; it excludes waste from municipal sewage networks and treatment, as well as waste from construction and demolition activities. Measured in kg/capita.

Location	2000	2010	2020	2021
Armenia	65.7	131.4	204.3	174.6
Austria	579.9	562.2	834.2	—
Azerbaijan	134.8	174.2	230.1	250.5
Belarus	—	379.2	422.5	414.5
Belgium	471.3	456.3	730.7	761.3
Bulgaria	611.7	553.6	408.0	—
Costa Rica	—	332.2	285.5	313.5
Croatia	264.9	379.5	418.3	439.0
Czechia	334.3	317.0	543.4	570.5
Denmark	664.4	758.7	814.4	786.5
Estonia	453.1	304.9	382.9	394.5
European Union[1]	513.1	502.2	520.8	529.6
Finland	502.3	469.7	609.5	609.3
France	514.3	534.3	538.5	561.3
Germany	642.4	602.1	641.2	646.6
Hungary	445.8	403.3	403.2	416.3
Iceland	462.3	484.2	614.0	—
Ireland	601.4	624.8	644.9	—
Israel	630.9	606.4	648.5	656.9
Italy	508.6	542.3	487.0	—
Japan	432.0	354.2	330.3	—
Latvia	271.2	324.2	478.3	461.1
Lithuania	354.5	399.2	478.7	482.7
Luxembourg	653.2	678.6	790.0	793.7
Moldova	49.7	115.5	226.2	251.1
Netherlands	598.3	570.8	533.4	515.2
Norway	613.5	469.4	603.6	798.8
Peru	—	—	237.4	243.6
Poland	319.6	312.4	342.0	358.3
Portugal	457.2	516.1	512.7	515.7
Romania	354.7	313.3	290.0	301.4
Slovakia	253.5	316.5	478.5	496.5
Slovenia	512.5	489.9	487.6	511.2
South Korea	360.6	362.1	434.9	—
Spain	653.6	510.6	464.3	472.8
Sweden	425.3	441.5	430.8	417.8
Switzerland	658.5	711.2	705.7	704.4
Turkey (Türkiye)	476.4	406.5	414.7	—
United Kingdom	576.6	509.2	462.2	463.8
United States	782.7	736.3	—	—
OECD Europe	**525.6**	**499.8**	**501.4**	—
OECD total	**542.9**	**518.4**	**533.7**	—

— = Not available. (1) 27 member countries in 2020.

Arctic Sea Ice, 1979-2023

Source: National Oceanic and Atmospheric Admin. (NOAA), U.S. Dept. of Commerce

Since satellite-based measurements began in the late 1970s, Arctic sea ice extent has decreased in all months and virtually all regions. Between 1979 and 2021, sea ice cover at the end of summer shrank by 13% per decade relative to the 1981-2010 average. And the ice that survives year-round is thinner and more fragile than it used to be. This graph shows the sea ice extent in the Arctic at the end of the summer melt season each Sept. from 1979-2023.

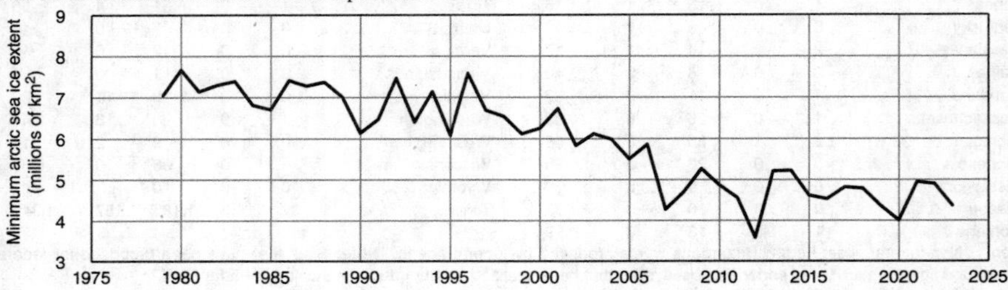

Air Quality of Selected U.S. Urban Areas, 1980-2023

Source: Office of Air Quality Planning and Standards, U.S. Environmental Protection Agency

Data indicate the number of days metropolitan statistical areas or corresponding core-based statistical areas failed to meet acceptable air-quality standards based on monitoring of six common pollutants.

Urban area	1980	1990	2000	2005	2010	2015	2020	2021	2022	2023
Atlanta-Sandy Springs-Roswell, GA	28	59	48	17	7	2	0	0	1	2
Bakersfield, CA	72	91	109	79	40	29	32	30	13	0
Baltimore-Columbia-Towson, MD	62	29	17	20	20	1	0	0	0	4
Baton Rouge, LA	27	30	34	20	3	2	0	1	1	1
Boston-Cambridge-Newton, MA-NH	26	6	1	8	1	1	0	1	0	0
Chicago-Naperville-Elgin, IL-IN-WI	40	28	10	25	2	3	5	2	3	10
Cincinnati, OH-KY-IN	43	22	10	19	4	1	0	0	1	4
Cleveland-Elyria, OH	11	9	8	17	4	0	1	0	2	5
Dallas-Fort Worth-Arlington, TX	43	26	35	40	5	5	3	4	3	2
Denver-Aurora-Lakewood, CO	28	3	1	2	2	2	4	17	1	3
Detroit-Warren-Dearborn, MI	28	10	3	17	2	1	2	0	0	7
Fresno, CA	90	55	106	45	22	24	40	19	3	1
Houston-The Woodlands-Sugar Land, TX	79	55	52	44	17	15	3	9	6	4
Indianapolis-Carmel-Anderson, IN	35	9	9	7	0	1	0	0	1	4
Kansas City, MO-KS	34	2	12	16	0	0	1	0	0	1
Las Vegas-Henderson-Paradise, NV	25	10	1	9	0	1	3	3	4	1
Los Angeles-Long Beach-Anaheim, CA	203	145	66	61	15	38	63	27	30	2
Memphis, TN-MS-AR	29	20	23	13	2	0	1	0	3	0
Miami-Fort Lauderdale-West Palm Beach, FL	19	2	1	1	0	0	0	0	0	2
Minneapolis-St. Paul-Bloomington, MN-WI	11	2	1	7	0	0	1	3	0	6
Nashville-Davidson–Murfreesboro–Franklin, TN	11	30	17	6	1	0	0	0	0	0
New Orleans-Metairie, LA	10	4	13	3	2	0	0	0	0	0
New York-Newark-Jersey City, NY-NJ-PA	83	43	18	22	12	3	0	3	1	7
Philadelphia-Camden-Wilmington, PA-NJ-DE-MD	80	36	20	22	12	2	0	2	0	6
Phoenix-Mesa-Scottsdale, AZ	31	15	19	11	2	3	143	135	23	5
Pittsburgh, PA	38	10	12	27	15	1	0	1	1	4
Riverside-San Bernardino-Ontario, CA	170	154	114	93	71	51	92	81	68	24
Sacramento–Roseville–Arden-Arcade, CA	53	42	42	42	9	4	27	17	8	0
Salt Lake City, UT	21	0	13	8	7	2	2	9	0	1
San Francisco-Oakland-Hayward, CA	11	6	4	2	1	0	13	1	0	0
Seattle-Tacoma-Bellevue, WA	5	8	5	1	0	3	9	2	10	0
Tucson, AZ	2	1	0	2	0	0	1	0	0	0
Washington-Arlington-Alexandria, DC-VA-MD-WV	52	22	12	18	13	1	1	1	0	4
Winston-Salem, NC	0	7	18	3	3	0	0	0	0	1

Hazardous Waste Sites in the U.S., 2024

Source: National Priorities List, U.S. Environmental Protection Agency; as of May 2024

State/territory	Proposed		Final		Total
	Gen.	Fed.	Gen.	Fed.	
Alabama	1	0	9	3	13
Alaska	0	0	1	5	6
Arizona	0	0	8	2	10
Arkansas	0	0	9	0	9
California	2	0	72	24	98
Colorado	1	0	17	3	21
Connecticut	0	0	12	1	13
Delaware	1	0	16	1	18
District of Columbia	0	0	0	1	1
Florida	1	0	46	6	53
Georgia	1	0	15	2	18
Guam	0	0	1	1	2
Hawaii	0	0	1	2	3
Idaho	3	0	4	2	9
Illinois	3	0	42	4	49
Indiana	0	0	40	0	40
Iowa	1	0	12	1	14
Kansas	1	0	13	1	15
Kentucky	0	0	9	1	10
Louisiana	2	0	14	1	17
Maine	0	0	8	2	10
Maryland	1	0	11	10	22
Massachusetts	1	0	26	6	33
Michigan	2	1	65	0	68
Minnesota	0	0	23	2	25
Mississippi	0	0	9	0	9
Missouri	0	0	30	3	33
Montana	1	0	18	0	19
Nebraska	0	0	17	1	18
Nevada	1	0	1	0	2
New Hampshire	1	0	19	1	21
New Jersey	1	0	109	6	116
New Mexico	0	0	14	1	15
New York	0	0	80	4	84
North Carolina	0	0	36	2	38
North Dakota	0	0	0	0	0
Ohio	3	1	34	3	41
Oklahoma	1	0	8	1	10
Oregon	1	0	11	3	15
Pennsylvania	1	0	85	6	92
Puerto Rico	0	0	18	1	19
Rhode Island	0	0	10	2	12
South Carolina	0	0	26	2	28
South Dakota	0	0	1	1	2
Tennessee	0	0	16	3	19
Texas	1	0	51	4	56
Utah	3	0	7	5	15
Vermont	0	0	12	0	12
Virgin Islands	0	0	1	0	1
Virginia	0	0	18	11	29
Washington	1	0	33	13	47
West Virginia	0	0	9	2	11
Wisconsin	1	0	36	0	37
Wyoming	0	0	0	1	1
Total	**37**	**2**	**1,183**	**157**	**1,340**

Gen. = Non-federal sites; Fed. = Hazardous waste produced by federal agency. **Note:** Sites that have been proposed for federal Superfund financing are listed under Proposed; sites that have qualified for Superfund financing are under Final.

Renewable Water Resources, 2021

Source: Food and Agriculture Organization (FAO), United Nations

Globally, water supplies are abundant, but they are unevenly distributed among and within countries. In some areas, water withdrawals are so high, relative to supply, that surface water supplies are shrinking, and groundwater reserves are being depleted faster than they can be replenished by precipitation. According to the FAO, the U.S. (including Alaska and Hawaii) has 8,362 cubic meters per capita and 3,069 cubic kilometers of internal renewable water resources total.

The tables below take into account only countries for which data are available, draw upon studies done over a number of years, and use 2021 population data. Numbers represent each country's internal resources. Countries ranked by per capita figures.

Countries With Greatest Internal Water Resources

Country	Cubic m per capita	Total cubic km
Iceland	459,044	170.0
Guyana	299,540	271.0
Suriname	161,505	99.0
Bhutan	100,323	78.0
Papua New Guinea	80,507	801.0
Canada	74,695	2,902.0
Norway	70,701	393.0
Gabon	70,050	166.0
New Zealand	63,746	327.0
Solomon Islands	63,149	44.7

Countries With Lowest Internal Water Resources

Country	Cubic m per capita	Total cubic km
Kuwait	0.0	0.02
Bahrain	2.73	0.116
Egypt	9.15	57.5
United Arab Emirates	16.02	0.15
Qatar	20.83	0.058
Maldives	57.53	0.03
Jordan	61.18	0.937
Yemen	63.67	2.1
Saudi Arabia	66.76	2.4
Israel	84.27	1.78

Top Countries by Forest Area, 1990-2021

Source: Food and Agriculture Organization, United Nations

(in square kilometers; ranked by 2021 forest area)

Country	Forest area, 1990	Forest area, 2021	% change, 1990-2021	% of land area covered by forest in 2021
Russia	NA	8,153,116	NA	49.8%
Brazil	5,888,980	4,953,914	−15.9%	59.3
Canada	3,482,729	3,468,911	−0.4	39.5
United States	3,024,500	3,097,950	2.4	33.9
China	1,571,406	2,218,578	41.2	23.6
Australia	1,338,822	1,340,051	0.1	17.4
Congo, Dem. Rep. of	1,506,290	1,250,539	−17.0	55.2
Indonesia	1,185,450	915,277	−22.8	48.4
India	639,380	724,264	13.3	24.4
Peru	764,485	721,575	−5.6	56.4
Angola	792,628	660,523	−16.7	53.0
Mexico	705,917	655,643	−7.1	33.7
Colombia	649,581	589,426	−9.3	53.1
Bolivia	578,047	506,208	−12.4	46.7
Venezuela	520,260	461,734	−11.2	52.3
Tanzania	573,900	452,760	−21.1	51.1
Zambia	474,120	446,258	−5.9	60.0
Mozambique	433,780	364,976	−15.9	46.4
Papua New Guinea	363,997	358,222	−1.6	79.1
Argentina	352,040	284,637	−19.1	10.4
Myanmar	392,185	282,542	−28.0	43.3
Sweden	280,630	279,800	−0.3%	68.7%
Japan	249,500	249,350	−0.1	68.4
Gabon	237,616	235,187	−1.0	91.3
Finland	218,753	224,090	2.4	73.7
Turkey (Türkiye)	197,835	223,764	13.1	29.1
Central African Republic	232,030	222,730	−4.0	35.8
Congo	223,150	219,310	−1.7	64.2
Nigeria	265,261	214,637	−19.1	23.6
Cameroon	225,000	202,845	−9.8	42.9
Thailand	193,610	198,370	2.5	38.8
Malaysia	206,185	190,639	−7.5	58.0
Spain	139,047	185,765	33.6	37.2
Guyana	186,022	184,061	−1.1	93.5
Chile	152,461	183,336	20.3	24.7
Sudan	NA	181,874	NA	9.7
Zimbabwe	188,267	173,985	−7.6	45.0
France	144,360	173,364	20.1	31.7
South Africa	181,421	170,137	−6.2	14.0
Ethiopia	204,086	169,955	−16.7	15.1
World	**42,364,334**	**40,539,066**	**−4.3**	**31.1**

NA = Not available. **Note:** World total includes nations not listed individually.

Largest Trees in the U.S., 2021

Source: American Forests

Nearly 900 native and naturalized species of trees grow in the U.S. The trunk of the world's largest known living tree, the General Sherman giant sequoia in California, weighs almost 1,400 tons—about as much as 15 adult blue whales. To determine the country's largest trees (or "national champions"), American Forests uses a point system whereby trunk circumference, or girth at 4.5 ft above ground level (in inches) + height (in feet) + ¼ average crown spread (in feet) = total points.

Tree type	Location	Girth at 4.5 ft (in.)	Height (ft)	Crown spread (ft)	Total points
Giant sequoia (Gen. Sherman tree)	Tulare, CA	1,231	275	107	1,533
Coast	Del Norte, CA	950	321	75	1,290
Sitka spruce	Grays Harbor, WA	740	191	80	951
Western redcedar	Clallam, WA	746	164	48	922
Coast 1	Grays Harbor, WA	581	294	66	891
Coast	Jefferson, WA	640	221	37	870
Port Orford cedar	Coos, OR	522	242	35	773
Bald cypress	West Feliciana, LA	626	91	87	739
California laurel	Curry, OR	601	101	87	724
Monterey cypress	San Mateo, CA	588	102	111	718

National Weather Service Watches and Warnings

Source: National Weather Service, National Oceanic and Atmospheric Admin. (NOAA), U.S. Dept. of Commerce; *Glossary of Meteorology*, American Meteorological Society

The National Weather Service issues watches, warnings, and advisories for specific geographic areas to alert people to the possibility or imminent arrival of severe weather or of flooding. Often the weather hazard is a convective storm (a storm involving upward and downward movement of heat and moisture). A severe thunderstorm or tornado watch is issued when a severe convective storm, covering a relatively small geographic area or moving in a narrow path, is sufficiently intense to threaten life and property. Excessive localized convective rains are not classified as severe storms but are often the product of severe local storms. Such rainfall may result in phenomena, such as flash floods, that threaten life and property. Lightning occurs with all thunderstorms and, along with flash floods, is a leading cause of storm deaths and injuries.

Cyclone: Atmospheric circulation of winds rotating counterclockwise in the Northern Hemisphere and clockwise in the Southern Hemisphere. Tornadoes, hurricanes/typhoons, and the lows shown on weather maps are all examples of cyclones. Cyclones are usually accompanied by precipitation or stormy weather.

Severe thunderstorm: Thunderstorm (a local storm produced by a cumulonimbus cloud) that produces a tornado, winds of at least 50 knots (58 mph), and/or hail at least 1 in. in diameter. A severe thunderstorm watch indicates conditions are favorable for the development of a severe thunderstorm within 4 to 8 hours. A severe thunderstorm warning indicates a severe thunderstorm has been sighted by radar or reported by a spotter.

Tornado: Violently rotating column of air that extends from the base of a thunderstorm to the ground. On a local scale, it is the most destructive of all atmospheric phenomena. A tornado path can exceed 1 mi wide and 50 mi long and is generally less than 1.25 mi in diameter. The average forward speed is 30 mph, and wind speeds can reach 300 mph. A rotating column of air over water is called a **waterspout**.

Tropical storm: Cyclone that develops over tropical or subtropical waters with 1-min. sustained surface winds between 34 and 63 knots (39-73 mph). A tropical storm watch is issued when tropical storm conditions pose a threat to specified coastal areas within 48 hours. A tropical storm warning is issued when such conditions are expected in a specified coastal area within 36 hours.

Hurricane: Tropical cyclone having 1-min. sustained surface winds of 64 knots (74 mph) or more. (In the western North Pacific Ocean, west of the International Date Line, such storms are known as **typhoons**.) The hurricane-force winds form a circle or oval, sometimes as wide as 300 mi in diameter. In the lower latitudes, hurricanes usually move W or NW at 10-15 mph. When the center approaches 25° to 30° N, the direction of motion often changes to the NE, with increased forward speed. In the Atlantic, hurricane season is June 1-Nov. 30. Hurricane season is May 15-Nov. 30 in the eastern Pacific. A hurricane warning is issued when a hurricane is forecast for an area within 36 hours.

Winter storm and **blizzard:** A winter storm watch is issued when there is a potential for heavy snow or significant ice accumulations, usually at least 24-36 hours in advance. A winter storm warning is issued when a winter storm is producing or is forecast to produce heavy snow or significant ice accumulations. A blizzard warning is issued for winter storm conditions in which winds are 35 mph or more, there is sufficient falling and/or blowing snow to frequently reduce visibility to less than ¼ mi, and the conditions are expected to prevail for at least 3 hours.

River flooding: Occurs when rains, sometimes coupled with melting snow, quickly fill river basins with an excess of water. Torrential rains from decaying hurricanes or tropical systems are also a major cause. **Coastal flooding:** Tropical storm and hurricane winds or intense offshore low-pressure systems can drive ocean water inland. Coastal floods can also be produced by sea waves called **tsunamis**, produced by earthquakes or underwater volcanic eruptions or landslides. **Flash flooding:** Usually due to copious amounts of rain falling in a short time. Ice can also cause flash flooding. When ice accumulates at natural or artificial obstructions, it can stop the flow of water. The resulting buildup of water can lead to flooding upstream. If the jam suddenly gives way, a flash flood can happen downstream. Flash flooding typically occurs within 6 hours of the causative event.

Flash floods account for the majority of flood deaths in the U.S. and are the leading cause of deaths associated with thunderstorms. Urbanization significantly increases runoff because less rain is absorbed by the terrain, making flash flooding in urban areas extremely dangerous. Streets can become swift-moving rivers, and basements can fill with water.

A flash flood watch indicates flash flooding is possible within a designated area. A flash flood warning indicates flooding is in progress, imminent, or highly likely.

National Weather Service Marine Warnings and Advisories

Primary sources of dissemination are mobile apps and push notifications, commercial radio, the internet, TV, U.S. Coast Guard radio, and National Oceanic and Atmospheric Admin. (NOAA) VHF radio broadcasts. The NOAA Weather Radio All Hazards (NWR) network broadcasts on seven frequencies between 162.400 and 162.550 MHz. These broadcasts can usually be received within about 40 mi of the transmission site using a special radio receiver. The following are examples of the warnings and advisories that may be addressed to mariners.

Small craft advisory: Alerts mariners to sustained weather and/or sea conditions, present or forecast, potentially hazardous to small boats, including winds 20-33 knots (23-38 mph) and/or dangerous wave conditions. The advisory is also issued when sea or lake ice exists that could be hazardous to small boats. Criteria vary depending on region and type of marine environment.

Special marine warning: Indicates potentially hazardous weather conditions not covered by existing marine warnings. The conditions are usually of short duration (2 hr. or less) and involve wind speeds of 34 knots (39 mph) or more, and/or hail at least ¾ in. in diameter or waterspouts.

Gale warning: Indicates winds of 34-47 knots (39-54 mph) not directly associated with a tropical storm are forecast for the area.

Storm warning: Indicates winds 48-63 knots (55-73 mph) not directly associated with a tropical storm are forecast for the area.

Hurricane and Tornado Classifications

Source: National Weather Service, NOAA, U.S. Dept. of Commerce

The Saffir-Simpson Hurricane Wind Scale, created by Herbert Saffir and expanded upon by Robert Simpson, rates a hurricane's intensity from 1 to 5. The scale, updated in 2012, provides examples of the type of damage and impacts associated with winds of the indicated intensity. The Fujita (or F) Scale was created by T. Theodore Fujita in 1971 to classify tornadoes. The Enhanced Fujita Scale, an update, was implemented in the U.S. in 2007. It uses 3-sec. gusts estimated at the point of damage based on a judgment of eight levels of damage to 28 indicators.

Saffir-Simpson Hurricane Wind Scale

Category	Wind speed[1]	Summary of damage
1	74-95 mph	Very dangerous winds will produce some damage.
2	96-110 mph	Extremely dangerous winds will cause extensive damage.
3	111-129 mph	Devastating damage will occur.
4	130-156 mph	Catastrophic damage will occur.
5	157 mph or higher	Catastrophic damage will occur.

(1) 1-min. sustained winds.

Enhanced Fujita Scale (Tornadoes)

Rank	3-sec. gust
EF-0	65-85 mph
EF-1	86-110 mph
EF-2	111-135 mph
EF-3	136-165 mph
EF-4	166-200 mph
EF-5	Over 200 mph

Monthly Normal Mean Temperatures, Precipitation in U.S. Cities

Source: National Centers for Environmental Information, NESDIS, NOAA, U.S. Dept. of Commerce

Normals are averages covering a 30-year period. The temperature and precipitation normals given here are based on records for 1991-2020. Temperatures listed below represent means of the normal daily maximum and normal daily minimum temperatures for each month. (*) = City station. Other figures are for airport stations. T = Temperature in Fahrenheit; P = Precipitation in inches.

	Jan.		Feb.		Mar.		Apr.		May		June		July		Aug.		Sept.		Oct.		Nov.		Dec.	
Station	T	P	T	P	T	P	T	P	T	P	T	P	T	P	T	P	T	P	T	P	T	P	T	P
Albany, NY	24	2.6	27	2.3	36	3.1	48	3.1	60	3.4	68	4.1	73	4.6	71	3.8	64	3.7	51	3.9	41	3.0	30	3.3
Albuquerque, NM	37	0.4	42	0.4	50	0.5	57	0.5	66	0.4	76	0.6	79	1.6	77	1.3	70	1.2	58	0.9	46	0.6	37	0.5
Anchorage, AK	17	0.8	21	0.9	26	0.7	38	0.4	48	0.7	56	1.0	60	1.8	58	2.9	49	3.1	36	1.8	24	1.2	19	1.2
Asheville, NC	39	4.1	42	3.5	48	3.8	57	4.2	65	4.1	72	4.8	75	4.7	74	5.0	68	4.1	58	3.4	48	3.7	41	4.2
Atlanta, GA	45	4.6	49	4.6	56	4.7	63	3.8	71	3.6	78	4.5	81	4.8	80	4.3	75	3.8	65	3.3	54	4.0	47	4.6
Atlantic City, NJ	34	3.4	36	3.2	43	4.5	53	3.3	62	3.3	71	3.6	77	4.5	75	4.6	68	3.6	57	4.1	47	3.4	39	4.5
Baltimore, MD	34	3.1	37	2.9	44	4.0	55	3.4	64	3.9	74	4.0	78	4.5	76	4.1	69	4.4	57	3.9	47	3.1	39	3.7
Birmingham, AL	45	5.0	49	5.0	56	5.7	64	5.1	72	4.9	78	4.8	82	5.4	81	4.4	76	4.0	65	3.3	54	4.2	47	4.9
Bismarck, ND*	13	0.5	17	0.5	29	0.8	42	1.4	55	2.5	65	3.4	71	3.1	70	2.4	60	1.8	45	1.5	30	0.7	18	0.7
Boise, ID	32	1.4	38	1.0	45	1.3	51	1.2	60	1.5	68	0.8	77	0.2	76	0.2	66	0.4	53	0.8	40	1.2	32	1.5
Boston, MA	30	3.4	32	3.2	38	4.2	49	3.6	58	3.3	68	3.9	74	3.3	73	3.2	66	3.6	55	4.0	45	3.7	36	4.3
Buffalo, NY*	26	3.4	26	2.5	34	2.9	46	3.4	58	3.4	67	3.4	72	3.2	70	3.2	63	4.1	52	4.0	41	3.5	31	3.8
Burlington, VT	21	2.1	23	1.8	32	2.2	46	3.1	58	3.8	68	4.3	72	4.1	71	3.5	63	3.7	50	3.8	39	2.7	28	2.5
Caribou, ME	12	3.0	14	2.4	25	2.8	39	3.0	52	3.5	61	3.9	67	4.2	65	3.6	57	3.4	45	4.0	33	3.4	20	3.6
Charleston, SC	50	3.4	53	3.1	59	3.4	66	3.3	73	3.3	79	6.2	83	6.6	81	7.0	77	6.0	68	4.3	58	2.7	52	3.4
Charleston, WV	35	3.3	38	3.4	46	4.1	57	3.6	65	4.9	72	4.7	76	5.4	75	3.8	68	3.5	57	2.9	46	3.2	39	3.6
Chicago, IL	25	2.0	29	2.0	39	2.5	50	3.8	61	4.5	71	4.1	75	3.7	74	4.3	66	3.2	54	3.4	41	2.4	31	2.1
Cleveland, OH	29	1.8	31	1.5	38	2.4	49	3.1	61	3.5	70	2.8	74	3.7	73	3.5	67	2.9	56	3.2	45	2.9	35	2.0
Columbus, OH	30	3.0	33	2.4	42	3.6	53	3.9	63	4.0	72	4.3	75	4.7	74	3.7	67	3.1	55	2.9	44	2.8	35	3.1
Dallas-Ft. Worth, TX	46	2.5	51	2.8	58	3.3	66	3.2	74	4.8	82	3.7	86	2.1	86	2.2	79	2.7	68	4.4	56	2.5	48	2.8
Denver, CO	32	0.4	33	0.4	41	1.0	47	1.9	56	2.0	67	2.0	73	1.8	71	2.3	63	1.3	50	1.0	39	0.5	31	0.4
Des Moines, IA	22	1.1	27	1.3	39	2.2	51	4.0	62	5.2	72	5.3	76	3.8	74	4.2	66	3.2	53	2.8	39	1.9	28	1.6
Detroit, MI	26	2.2	28	2.1	37	2.4	49	3.3	60	3.7	70	3.3	74	3.5	72	3.3	65	3.2	53	2.5	41	2.6	31	2.3
Dodge City, KS*	33	0.6	36	0.6	45	1.4	54	2.0	65	3.0	75	3.3	80	3.1	78	3.0	70	1.3	57	2.0	44	0.8	34	1.0
Duluth, MN*	11	1.0	15	1.0	27	1.5	40	2.5	52	3.4	61	4.4	67	3.9	66	3.7	57	3.5	44	2.9	30	2.0	17	1.5
Fairbanks, AK	–8	0.6	0	0.5	11	0.4	34	0.3	50	0.5	61	1.5	63	2.3	57	2.1	46	1.4	26	0.8	4	0.7	–4	0.6
Fresno, CA	48	2.2	52	1.9	57	1.9	62	1.0	70	0.4	78	0.2	84	0.0	82	0.0	77	0.1	67	0.6	55	0.9	48	1.8
Galveston, TX	56	4.3	59	2.1	65	3.0	72	2.1	78	3.0	84	4.2	86	3.4	86	4.7	82	6.7	75	5.2	66	4.3	59	4.2
Grand Rapids, MI*	25	2.5	27	2.1	36	2.4	48	4.0	59	4.0	69	3.9	73	3.9	71	3.6	64	3.4	52	4.0	40	3.1	30	2.5
Hartford, CT	27	3.3	30	3.1	38	3.8	50	3.9	60	3.8	69	4.3	74	4.2	73	4.2	65	4.4	53	4.5	42	3.5	33	4.1
Helena, MT	23	0.4	27	0.4	36	0.5	45	1.0	54	2.0	62	2.2	71	1.1	69	1.0	59	1.0	46	0.8	33	0.6	23	0.5
Honolulu, HI	74	1.8	74	1.9	75	2.4	77	0.8	78	0.8	80	0.5	82	0.5	82	0.8	82	0.9	80	1.5	78	2.3	76	2.2
Houston, TX	54	3.8	58	3.0	64	3.5	70	4.0	77	5.0	83	6.0	85	3.8	85	4.8	81	4.7	72	5.5	62	3.9	55	4.0
Huron, SD	16	0.6	21	0.8	33	1.2	46	2.5	58	3.2	68	3.9	74	2.8	71	2.6	63	2.4	48	2.0	33	0.8	21	0.7
Indianapolis, IN	29	2.6	33	2.1	43	3.3	54	4.1	64	4.3	73	5.1	76	4.3	74	3.2	68	2.6	56	3.3	43	3.3	34	2.7
Jackson, MS	47	5.4	51	5.1	58	5.7	65	5.8	73	4.4	80	4.4	82	5.0	82	4.7	77	3.5	66	3.8	55	4.4	49	5.1
Jacksonville, FL	55	3.0	58	2.4	63	3.0	68	2.4	74	3.0	80	6.3	82	6.1	82	6.9	79	7.3	72	6.0	63	2.6	58	2.8
Juneau, AK	29	6.0	30	4.3	33	3.7	41	3.5	49	3.5	55	3.8	57	5.1	56	6.4	50	9.2	42	8.4	34	6.5	30	6.5
Kansas City, MO	29	1.2	34	1.5	45	2.4	55	4.1	65	5.3	74	5.3	78	4.6	77	4.2	68	4.0	56	3.3	44	2.0	33	1.6
Knoxville, TN	39	4.7	43	4.8	51	4.9	60	4.7	68	4.1	75	4.2	79	5.3	78	3.6	72	3.5	60	2.8	49	4.2	42	5.0
Lander, WY	21	0.5	25	0.7	36	1.3	43	2.1	53	2.7	63	1.1	72	0.6	70	0.5	60	1.0	45	1.4	32	0.8	22	0.6
Las Vegas, NV	50	0.6	54	0.8	61	0.4	68	0.2	77	0.1	88	0.0	93	0.4	92	0.3	84	0.3	70	0.3	57	0.3	48	0.5
Lexington, KY	34	3.4	38	3.6	46	4.5	56	4.4	65	5.4	73	5.0	77	5.1	76	3.7	69	3.4	58	3.7	46	3.4	38	4.2
Little Rock, AR	41	3.5	45	4.0	53	5.0	61	5.6	70	5.1	78	3.6	81	3.3	81	3.2	74	3.0	63	4.5	51	4.7	43	5.1
Los Angeles, CA	58	2.9	58	3.0	59	1.7	61	0.6	64	0.3	66	0.1	70	0.0	71	0.0	70	0.1	67	0.5	62	0.8	58	2.2
Louisville, KY	36	3.4	40	3.4	48	4.6	59	4.8	68	5.2	76	4.3	80	4.1	79	3.7	72	3.7	60	3.7	49	3.4	40	4.1
Marquette, MI*	19	1.9	20	1.5	28	1.6	38	2.7	50	2.9	59	3.1	66	3.1	66	2.3	59	3.3	47	3.4	35	2.4	24	2.0
Memphis, TN	42	4.1	46	4.6	54	5.7	63	5.9	72	5.3	80	4.0	83	4.8	82	3.4	76	3.0	65	4.0	53	4.7	45	5.5
Miami, FL	69	1.8	71	2.2	73	2.5	77	3.4	80	6.3	83	10.5	84	7.4	84	9.6	83	10.2	80	7.7	75	3.5	71	2.4
Milwaukee, WI	24	1.8	27	1.7	36	2.2	46	3.9	57	3.5	68	4.4	73	3.4	72	3.7	65	3.2	53	2.8	40	2.2	30	1.9
Minneapolis-St. Paul, MN	16	0.9	21	0.9	33	1.7	47	2.9	60	3.9	70	4.6	74	4.1	72	4.3	64	3.0	50	2.6	35	1.6	22	1.2
Mobile, AL	52	5.2	56	3.8	62	5.1	68	4.9	76	4.4	82	5.8	84	6.6	84	7.1	80	4.5	71	3.8	61	4.1	55	5.3
Moline, IL	23	1.7	28	1.8	40	2.6	51	3.8	63	4.7	72	5.0	76	4.2	73	4.0	66	3.3	54	2.8	40	2.3	29	2.0
Nashua, NH*	24	3.0	27	3.1	35	4.1	47	3.9	58	3.6	67	4.2	73	3.6	71	3.7	64	4.2	51	4.7	40	3.7	30	4.5
Nashville, TN	40	4.0	43	4.5	52	4.5	61	4.7	69	5.0	77	4.4	81	4.2	80	3.8	73	3.8	62	3.4	50	3.9	43	4.4
New Orleans, LA	54	5.2	58	4.1	64	4.4	70	5.2	77	5.6	82	7.6	84	6.8	84	6.9	81	5.1	73	3.7	62	3.9	57	4.8
New York, NY	33	3.2	35	2.8	41	3.9	51	3.6	61	3.7	70	3.9	76	3.9	75	4.1	68	3.6	57	3.7	47	3.1	38	4.0
Newark, NJ	33	3.4	35	3.0	43	4.1	53	3.9	63	4.0	73	4.3	78	4.7	76	4.2	69	3.8	58	3.8	47	3.3	38	4.1
Norfolk, VA	42	3.4	44	2.9	51	3.7	60	3.4	68	3.8	77	4.4	81	6.1	79	5.9	74	5.4	64	3.9	53	3.1	46	3.3
Oklahoma City, OK	38	1.3	42	1.4	51	2.6	59	3.6	68	5.3	77	4.5	82	3.6	81	3.6	73	3.7	61	3.3	49	1.7	40	1.8
Omaha, NE	24	0.8	29	1.0	41	1.8	53	3.2	64	4.7	74	4.4	78	3.6	76	4.6	68	3.0	54	2.3	40	1.5	29	1.2
Philadelphia, PA	34	3.1	36	2.8	44	4.0	55	3.5	64	3.3	74	4.0	79	4.4	77	4.3	70	4.4	58	3.5	47	2.9	39	4.0
Phoenix, AZ	57	0.9	60	0.9	66	0.8	73	0.2	82	0.1	91	0.0	96	0.9	94	0.9	89	0.6	77	0.6	65	0.6	56	0.7
Pittsburgh, PA	29	3.0	31	2.6	40	3.2	52	3.3	61	3.8	69	4.1	73	4.3	72	3.5	65	3.3	53	2.8	43	2.9	34	2.8
Portland, ME	24	3.5	26	3.5	34	4.1	45	4.4	55	3.7	64	4.2	70	3.4	69	3.6	62	3.8	50	5.3	40	4.3	30	4.5
Portland, OR	42	5.0	44	3.7	48	4.0	53	2.9	59	2.5	64	1.6	70	0.5	71	0.5	65	1.5	56	3.4	47	5.5	42	5.8
Providence, RI	30	4.0	32	3.4	39	4.9	49	4.3	59	3.4	68	3.8	74	2.9	73	3.6	66	4.2	54	4.2	45	4.3	36	4.7
Raleigh-Durham, NC	42	3.4	45	2.8	52	4.1	61	3.5	69	3.4	77	3.9	81	5.0	79	4.7	73	5.2	62	3.4	52	3.3	45	3.4
Rapid City, SD	24	0.3	26	0.5	35	0.9	44	2.1	54	3.5	65	2.9	72	2.3	71	1.6	61	1.2	47	1.4	35	0.5	26	0.4
Richmond, VA	38	3.2	41	2.6	48	4.0	58	3.2	67	4.0	75	4.6	79	4.4	78	4.9	71	4.6	60	3.4	50	3.1	42	3.5
St. Louis, MO	32	2.6	37	2.2	47	3.5	58	4.7	68	4.8	77	4.5	80	3.9	79	3.4	71	3.0	59	3.2	47	3.4	37	2.5
Salt Lake City, UT	31	1.4	37	1.3	46	1.8	52	2.2	62	1.8	72	1.0	81	0.5	79	0.6	68	1.1	55	1.3	42	1.3	32	1.4
San Antonio, TX	52	2.0	56	1.7	63	2.3	69	2.4	77	4.4	83	3.3	85	2.4	86	2.2	80	3.9	71	3.8	61	2.1	54	2.0
San Diego, CA	58	2.0	59	2.2	61	1.5	63	0.7	65	0.3	67	0.1	71	0.1	72	0.0	72	0.1	68	0.5	63	0.8	58	1.7
San Francisco, CA	51	3.9	54	4.0	56	2.7	57	1.4	60	0.5	63	0.1	64	0.0	65	0.0	65	0.1	63	0.8	56	2.0	51	4.1
San Juan, PR	78	4.1	78	2.6	79	2.2	80	4.6	82	5.5	83	4.7	83	6.0	84	6.3	83	6.5	83	5.2	81	7.4	79	4.9
Santa Fe, NM	32	0.5	36	0.4	43	0.7	50	0.5	60	0.6	70	0.6	73	1.8	71	2.0	65	1.3	53	1.2	40	0.7	32	0.5
Savannah, GA	51	3.3	54	2.8	60	3.5	67	3.4	74	3.6	80	6.7	83	5.8	82	5.5	78	4.4	69	3.7	59	2.4	53	3.2
Seattle-Tacoma, WA	43	5.8	44	3.8	47	4.2	51	3.2	58	1.9	62	1.5	67	0.6	67	1.0	63	1.6	54	3.9	47	6.3	42	5.7
Spokane, WA	30	2.0	33	1.4	40	1.8	47	1.3	56	1.6	62	1.2	71	0.4	70	0.5	61	0.6	48	1.4	36	2.1	29	2.3
Springfield, MO*	34	2.5	39	2.4	48	3.5	57	4.7	66	5.6	75	4.5	79	3.9	78	3.6	70	4.3	59	3.6	47	3.6	37	2.6
Tampa, FL	62	2.7	65	2.6	69	2.5	74	2.6	80	2.6	83	7.4	84	7.8	84	9.0	83	6.1	77	2.3	70	1.4	65	2.6
Utqiagvik (fmr. Barrow), AK*	–13	0.3	–13	0.3	–12	0.3	3	0.3	21	0.4	34	0.4	40	1.0	39	1.1	34	0.8	21	0.6	5	0.4	–7	0.5
Washington, DC	34	2.9	36	2.6	44	3.5	55	3.5	64	4.7	73	4.3	77	4.2	76	3.5	69	3.9	57	3.7	46	3.1	38	3.3
Wilmington, DE	34	3.2	36	2.8	43	4.2	54	3.5	64	3.6	73	4.7	78	4.4	76	4.0	69	4.4	57	3.7	47	3.1	38	3.9

Normal High and Low Temperatures, Precipitation in U.S. Cities

Source: National Centers for Environmental Information, NESDIS, NOAA, U.S. Dept. of Commerce

The normal temperatures and precipitation data given here are based on records for the period 1991-2020. The extreme temperatures are based on records from the time of each station's installation, through 2023.

		NORMAL TEMPERATURE (°F)				EXTREME TEMPERATURE (°F)		AVG. ANNUAL PRECIPITATION
		January		July				
State	Station	Max.	Min.	Max.	Min.	Highest	Lowest	(in.)
Alabama	Mobile	62	43	92	75	106	3	60.52
Alaska	Anchorage	23	11	66	53	90	–34	16.42
Alaska	Juneau	33	24	64	50	90	–22	66.99
Alaska	Utqiagvik (fmr. Barrow)	–6	–19	46	35	79	–56	6.19
Arizona	Phoenix	68	46	107	85	122	17	7.22
Arkansas	Little Rock	51	31	92	71	114	–5	50.42
California	Los Angeles	66	49	75	64	110	23	12.23
California	San Francisco	58	45	73	55	106	20	19.64
Colorado	Denver	45	19	87	59	105	–24	15.02
Connecticut	Hartford	35	19	85	63	103[1]	–26[1]	47.05
Delaware	Wilmington	41	26	87	68	103	–14	45.33
District of Columbia	Washington-Dulles	43	25	88	67	105	–18	43.24
Florida	Jacksonville	65	45	91	73	105	7	51.82
Florida	Miami	76	61	91	78	98	30	67.41
Georgia	Atlanta	54	36	90	72	106	–8	50.43
Georgia	Savannah	61	40	92	74	105	3	48.12
Hawaii	Honolulu	81	67	88	75	95	53	16.41
Idaho	Boise	39	26	93	62	111	–25	11.51
Illinois	Chicago	32	19	85	66	104	–27	37.86
Indiana	Indianapolis	36	21	85	67	105	–27	40.67
Iowa	Des Moines	31	14	86	66	108	–26	36.55
Kansas	Dodge City	46	20	94	66	111	–21	22.00
Kentucky	Lexington	42	25	87	67	105	–21	49.84
Kentucky	Louisville	44	28	89	71	106	–22	48.34
Louisiana	New Orleans	63	46	91	77	105	11	63.35
Maine	Caribou	21	3	77	56	96	–41	40.70
Maine	Portland	32	16	80	61	103	–39	48.12
Maryland	Baltimore	43	25	89	68	106	–7	45.00
Massachusetts	Boston	37	23	82	66	103	–12	43.59
Michigan	Detroit	32	19	84	64	104	–21	34.32
Michigan	Grand Rapids	31	19	83	63	104	–22	39.40
Michigan	Sault Ste. Marie	24	8	77	55	98	–36	34.46
Minnesota	Duluth	20	2	78	56	97	–39	31.18
Minnesota	Minneapolis-St. Paul	24	9	83	65	105	–34	31.62
Mississippi	Jackson	57	37	92	72	107	2	57.35
Missouri	Kansas City	38	20	88	68	109	–23	39.30
Missouri	St. Louis	40	24	90	71	108	–18	41.70
Montana	Helena	32	14	86	55	105	–42	11.40
Nebraska	Omaha	34	15	88	68	114	–23	31.86
Nevada	Las Vegas	59	41	105	82	117	8	4.18
New Hampshire	Concord	32	13	83	59	102	–37	41.95
New Jersey	Atlantic City	43	25	87	67	106	–11	45.96
New Mexico	Albuquerque	48	26	91	67	107	–17	8.84
New York	Albany	33	16	84	62	100	–28	40.68
New York	Buffalo	32	19	80	63	99	–20	40.68
New York	New York-JFK	40	26	84	69	104	–2	43.29
North Carolina	Raleigh-Durham	52	32	91	70	105	–9	46.07
North Dakota	Bismarck	23	3	84	58	112	–44	19.21
Ohio	Cleveland	35	24	81	68	104	–20	33.34
Ohio	Columbus	37	22	85	65	102	–22	41.57
Oklahoma	Oklahoma City	49	27	93	70	113	–14	36.39
Oregon	Portland	48	36	82	59	116	–3	36.91
Pennsylvania	Philadelphia	41	26	88	70	104	–7	44.11
Pennsylvania	Pittsburgh	36	21	83	63	103	–22	39.61
Puerto Rico	San Juan	83	72	89	78	98	60	59.87
Rhode Island	Providence	38	22	84	65	104	–13	47.54
South Carolina	Charleston	60	39	91	74	105	6	52.51
South Dakota	Huron	26	6	86	62	112	–41	23.32
South Dakota	Rapid City	36	13	86	59	111	–31	17.44
Tennessee	Memphis	51	33	92	74	108	–13	54.94
Tennessee	Nashville	49	30	91	71	109	–17	50.51
Texas	Dallas-Fort Worth	57	36	96	76	113	–2	37.01
Texas	Houston	64	44	95	76	109	7	51.84
Utah	Salt Lake City	39	24	94	68	107	–30	15.52
Vermont	Burlington	29	13	82	62	101	–30	37.53
Virginia	Norfolk	51	34	89	73	105	–3	49.18
Virginia	Richmond	48	29	90	69	105	–12	45.50
Washington	Seattle-Tacoma	48	38	77	57	108	0	39.34
Washington	Spokane	35	25	84	58	109	–25	16.45
West Virginia	Charleston	44	26	86	66	104	–16	46.24
Wisconsin	Milwaukee	31	17	82	65	103	–26	34.57
Wyoming	Lander	33	10	88	55	101	–37	13.23

Mean annual snowfall (in.), selected cities: Based on climate normals 1991-2020: Albany, NY, 59.2; Anchorage, AK, 77.9; Boston, MA, 49.2; Buffalo, NY, 95.4; Burlington, VT, 87.5; Caribou, ME, 118.2; Duluth, MN, 90.2; Lander, WY, 87.6; Sault Ste. Marie, MI, 120.1.

Wettest spot: Mt. Waialeale in Kauai, HI, may be the rainiest place in the U.S. It has a recorded average annual rainfall of 460 in.

Temperature extremes: The highest temperature ever recorded under standard conditions in the U.S. was 134°F in Death Valley, CA, on July 10, 1913. The record low in the U.S. was –80°F at Prospect Creek, AK, Jan. 23, 1971. (1) Record for Windsor Locks, CT.

Annual Climatological Data for U.S. Cities, 2023

Source: National Centers for Environmental Information, NESDIS, NOAA, U.S. Dept. of Commerce

		TEMPERATURE (°F)				PRECIPITATION						FASTEST WIND[2]		NO. OF DAYS	
									Snowfall[1]						
Station	Elev. (ft)	Highest	Date	Lowest	Date	Total (in.)	Greatest in 24 hrs. (in.)	Date	Total snow-fall (in.)	Greatest in 24 hrs. (in.)	Date	MPH	Date	Prec. 0.01 in. or more	Snowfall 1 in. or more
Albany, NY	281	93	9/7+	–13	2/4	48.62	2.45	12/17-18	47.1	9.9	3/14	37	4/1	156	13
Albuquerque, NM	5,308	104	7/17	17	2/17	5.77	0.78	9/12-13	4.1	1.0	2/15	53	2/26	45	1
Anchorage, AK	222	72	8/5+	–6	12/30	24.22	1.70	8/15-16	132.1	9.0	11/8	32	8/31	156	37
Asheville, NC	2,174	94	8/25	18	11/29	38.42	2.90	12/9-10	T	T	12/18	38	8/27	117	0
Atlanta, GA	974	99	8/26	28	11/29	41.04	2.56	1/3-4	0.0	0.0	—	48	8/12	105	0
Atlantic City, NJ	117	97	9/6	12	2/4	44.32	3.67	9/23	0.3	0.2	2/1	43	4/1	112	0
Baltimore, MD	196	100	9/6	14	2/4	42.39	2.82	12/17-18	0.2	0.2	2/1	43	4/1	111	0
Birmingham, AL	630	100	8/25	23	3/20	—	—	—	T	T	12/30+	41	3/3	—	0
Bismarck, ND	1,654	101	7/26	–29	2/24	20.55	1.72	6/24	61.7	8.5	10/26	46	9/4	91	16
Boise, ID	2,861	105	8/16	9	1/30	13.86	1.46	8/26	22.5	3.1	1/19	40	8/7	103	9
Boston, MA	180	93	9/7	–10	2/4	49.76	3.07	7/29	11.6	2.3	1/23	53	12/18	132	4
Buffalo, NY	717	91	7/6	0	2/4	40.52	1.80	9/6-7	40.0	6.2	3/10	44	3/25	169	12
Burlington, VT	348	96	6/1	–15	2/4	44.78	2.95	10/7-8	63.3	9.5	3/14	32	7/9	159	17
Caribou, ME	626	93	6/1	–22	2/1	41.85	1.93	1/12-13	120.2	14.0	2/17	36	12/18	167	32
Charleston, SC	48	98	8/14+	27	12/20	54.64	3.68	7/23	0.0	0.0	—	37	12/10	116	0
Cheyenne, WY	6,128	93	8/21	–19	2/23	20.37	1.39	7/19-20	59.1	5.4	11/24	55	2/19	107	21
Chicago, IL	658	100	8/24	–1	2/3	33.73	3.79	7/1-2	19.8	3.6	1/25	37	7/28	135	6
Cleveland, OH	805	91	9/5	12	2/4+	45.00	2.84	8/23-24	23.0	4.4	1/22	45	3/25	145	9
Columbus, OH	812	94	6/3	12	2/4	41.45	2.49	5/12	6.8	3.0	1/22	49	7/24	129	1
Dallas-Ft. Worth, TX	562	110	9/8	25	1/31	29.31	4.08	10/25-26	1.3	1.3	1/31	53	3/2	71	1
Denver, CO	5,382	99	9/1	–11	2/23	18.94	3.37	5/11-12	36.8	5.3	10/28	43	12/26	92	13
Des Moines, IA	971	100	8/23	–4	1/31	24.93	2.09	7/12	25.9	6.4	3/11	48	6/2	90	7
Detroit, MI	631	90	7/5	5	1/31	36.65	3.51	8/23-24	32.1	6.5	1/25	47	3/25	141	8
Duluth, MN	1,429	97	9/3	–22	2/3	32.99	4.17	9/23-24	85.0	6.6	3/12	46	4/4	129	23
Fairbanks, AK	464	90	7/24	–34	3/4	10.59	0.69	6/22-23	90.7	5.6	2/23	30	4/23	129	31
Fresno, CA	375	109	7/17	31	2/15	13.64	2.81	2/24-25	T	T	2/22	39	2/21	45	0
Grand Rapids, MI	788	91	9/5	2	1/31	36.74	2.02	1/31	46.3	8.7	3/10	43	12/9	145	15
Helena, MT	3,867	103	7/22	–13	2/24	12.47	1.26	9/22	39.5	6.4	10/26	41	8/18	95	11
Honolulu, HI	18	91	9/16+	60	1/9+	13.48	1.81	3/23	—	—	—	37	8/8	95	—
Houston, TX	107	109	8/27+	33	12/11	41.75	4.05	1/24	0.0	0.0	—	47	6/21	87	0
Huron, SD	1,284	104	8/22	–23	2/24	20.14	3.48	10/12-13	42.2	11.9	2/22-23	43	2/14	75	11
Indianapolis, IN	797	94	8/24	10	2/1	34.38	2.24	3/3	5.7	2.8	1/25	51	3/31	121	1
Jackson, MS	296	106	8/24	25	3/20	41.06	2.65	4/13	T	T	6/25	45	6/25	96	0
Jacksonville, FL	34	99	8/14+	29	1/16	58.61	4.45	9/25-26	T	T	1/4	41	6/14	113	0
Kansas City, MO	1,008	103	8/25	8	1/31	37.37	2.91	8/13	10.5	3.7	2-9	44	7/30	107	3
Knoxville, TN	982	94	8/27+	21	11/29	47.51	2.84	6/19	T	T	12/29+	53	1/12	120	0
Las Vegas, NV	2,091	116	7/16	30	2/1	4.59	0.88	9/1	T	T	2/23+	41	2/21	29	0
Lexington, KY	984	98	8/25	16	11/29	41.25	2.59	1/2-3	0.9	0.4	1/26	54	3/3	115	0
Little Rock, AR	292	107	8/26	25	1/14	56.86	4.19	2/24	T	T	2/1	48	6/25	99	0
Los Angeles, CA	326	91	10/5	41	2/26+	25.36	3.14	3/14-15	—	—	—	45	2/21	52	—
Louisville, KY	484	99	8/25	20	2/4	41.09	2.79	3/3	1.3	1.0	1/22	56	3/3	111	1
Marquette, MI	1,415	95	9/4	–11	1/31	44.83	2.98	5/1	195.2	20.0	2/23	—	—	170	38
Memphis, TN	286	102	8/26+	25	3/20+	55.73	4.53	7/21	0.2	0.2	1/31	47	7/5	113	0
Miami, FL	29	98	7/23	44	1/16	83.43	8.16	11/15-16	—	—	—	39	6/19	155	—
Milwaukee, WI	680	101	8/23	–3	1/31	34.01	2.09	8/14-15	49.7	8.9	3/25	38	6/25	125	13
Minneapolis, MN	874	98	9/4	–13	2/3	29.69	1.90	10/12-13	62.4	8.8	1/4	43	6/24	111	14
Mobile, AL	212	106	8/26	29	3/20	56.75	3.42	6/16	0.0	0.0	—	39	1/25	115	0
Moline, IL	607	100	8/24	0	2/3	29.22	1.63	9/16	25.1	7.3	3/25	55	4/4	107	8
Nashville, TN	574	100	8/25+	19	2/4	39.06	2.30	5/7-8	T	T	3/19	38	6/30	121	0
New Orleans, LA	7	105	8/27	36	12/29	39.85	4.17	12/1-2	—	—	—	36	6/20	92	—
New York, NY	161	93	9/7+	3	2/4	59.29	5.85	9/28-29	2.3	0.9	2/28+	29	2/3	123	0
Newark, NJ	28	97	9/6	5	2/4	53.98	3.42	4/28-29	2.6	1.2	2/27	40	4/1	122	1
Norfolk, VA	69	97	7/3	22	2/4	50.55	3.81	12/17-18	T	T	2/2	45	9/22	108	0
Oklahoma City, OK	1,284	107	8/19	16	1/30	37.30	3.23	7/9	2.7	2.1	1/24	56	7/9	87	1
Philadelphia, PA	62	97	9/7	15	2/4	42.19	3.02	12/17-18	0.3	0.3	2/1	47	8/7	117	0
Phoenix, AZ	1,106	119	7/25+	35	2/16	4.21	0.80	3/15-16	—	—	—	51	8/31	27	—
Pittsburgh, PA	1,175	91	9/6+	5	2/4+	32.60	1.39	6/15-16	13.1	2.2	1/22	45	4/1	150	6
Portland, ME	72	89	7/12	–14	2/4	56.67	3.24	9/18-19	52.5	8.5	3/4	40	12/18	141	10
Portland, OR	223	108	8/14	18	2/25	35.75	2.14	12/5-6	10.8	10.8	2/22	39	1/4	146	1
Providence, RI	53	92	9/7	–9	2/4	57.66	3.35	7/16	8.2	4.0	2/28	40	12/18	132	2
Raleigh-Durham, NC	430	102	9/7+	23	11/29	44.94	2.85	12/17	T	T	9/8	48	9/8	114	0
Rapid City, SD	3,153	103	9/2	–24	1/30	19.63	2.38	5/11-12	—	—	—	49	12/26	93	—
Reno, NV	4,407	108	7/16	4	1/31+	10.46	0.84	5/2-3	34.5	4.9	1/16	44	3/28	82	12
Richmond, VA	167	101	9/6	16	2/4	43.47	3.50	12/10-11	0.2	0.2	12/11	45	9/7	114	0
St. Louis, MO	710	104	8/25	11	1/31	33.14	1.99	9/26-27	3.0	2.1	1/25	52	7/29	113	1
Salt Lake City, UT	4,224	106	7/22+	9	1/30	17.64	1.70	4/2-3	66.0	11.5	2/22	45	3/10	105	16
San Antonio, TX	821	106	8/17+	31	12/11	—	—	—	T	T	4/28	43	3/2	—	0
San Diego, CA	81	86	9/11	39	2/16	14.43	1.89	1/15-16	—	—	—	39	2/22	59	—
San Francisco, CA	89	92	10/6+	36	1/31	25.53	1.72	1/4-5	—	—	—	55	3/14	74	—
San Juan, PR	10	96	10/16+	68	4/8	56.19	5.22	10/27-28	0.0	0.0	—	36	8/12	219	0
Sault Ste. Marie, MI	727	89	6/2	–15	2/3	35.04	1.82	4/1	120.0	18.6	4/1	35	11/16	151	31
Savannah, GA	143	99	7/21	27	12/20	41.98	3.41	12/16-17	0.0	0.0	—	40	6/7	108	0
Scottsbluff, NE	3,949	103	8/22	–22	1/31	22.22	1.77	5/10-11	45.3	7.0	1/18	45	3/31	105	15
Seattle, WA	434	95	8/16+	22	2/24	34.97	3.00	12/4-5	2.3	1.6	2/26	37	1/9	149	1
Spokane, WA	2,384	102	8/15	3	2/24	13.75	0.76	12/9-10	40.6	4.8	3/10	40	11/11	103	15
Springfield, MO	1,280	100	8/20	12	2/1	43.05	2.71	8/13-14	7.3	3.7	1/25	51	5/9	108	2
Tampa, FL	40	97	8/13	40	1/16+	37.15	3.34	8/16-17	0.0	0.0	—	38	8/30	93	0
Utqiagvik (fmr. Barrow), AK	38	76	8/5	–38	3/4	—	—	—	—	—	—	44	2/24	—	—
Washington, DC	3	99	9/5	16	2/4	35.68	2.41	12/17-18	0.5	0.4	2/1	46	7/14	116	0
Wilmington, DE	77	97	6/2	13	2/4	52.09	4.72	6/26-27	1.1	0.7	12/7	39	4/1	116	0
Windsor Locks, CT	165	96	4/14	–9	2/4	64.91	4.15	9/29-30	17.1	4.5	4/14	40	12/18	129	5

(+) = Indicates value also occurred on an earlier date(s). (T) = Trace amount. — = Data not available or unreported. (1) Comprises all forms of frozen precipitation, including snow, ice pellets, and hail. (2) Sustained for at least 2 min., not peak gust.

Record Temperatures by State

Source: National Centers for Environmental Information, NOAA, U.S. Dept. of Commerce
(as of Apr. 11, 2024)

	LOWEST TEMPERATURE				HIGHEST TEMPERATURE			
State	°F	Date	Station	Approx. elevation (ft)	°F	Date	Station	Approx. elevation (ft)
Alabama	–27	Jan. 30, 1966	New Market	732	112	Sept. 6, 1925	Centreville	220
Alaska	–80	Jan. 23, 1971	Prospect Creek Camp	955	100	June 27, 1915	Fort Yukon	445
Arizona	–40	Jan. 7, 1971	Hawley Lake	8,180	128	June 29, 1994	Lake Havasu City	449
Arkansas	–29	Feb. 13, 1905	Brook Farm Pond	1,260	120	Aug. 10, 1936	Ozark	390
California	–45	Jan. 20, 1937	Boca	5,575	134	July 10, 1913	Greenland Ranch	–194
Colorado	–61	Feb. 1, 1985	Maybell	5,944	115	July 20, 2019	John Martin Dam	3,814
Connecticut	–32	Jan. 22, 1961[1]	Coventry	480	106	July 15, 1995[1]	Danbury	405
Delaware	–17	Jan. 17, 1893	Millsboro	20	110	July 21, 1930	Millsboro	20
Florida	–2	Feb. 13, 1899	Tallahassee	192	109	June 29, 1931	Monticello	98
Georgia	–17	Jan. 27, 1940	CCC Fire Camp F-16	1,000	112	Aug. 20, 1983[1]	Greenville	960
Hawaii	12	May 17, 1979	Mauna Kea Observ.	13,773	100	Apr. 27, 1931	Pahala	840
Idaho	–60	Jan. 18, 1943	Island Park Dam	6,290	118	July 28, 1934	Orofino	1,320
Illinois	–38	Jan. 31, 2019	Mount Carroll	640	117	July 14, 1954	East St. Louis	410
Indiana	–36	Jan. 19, 1994	New Whiteland	785	116	July 14, 1936	Collegeville	650
Iowa	–47	Feb. 3, 1996[1]	Elkader	788	118	July 20, 1934	Keokuk	651
Kansas	–40	Feb. 13, 1905	Lebanon	1,841	121	July 24, 1936[1]	Alton	1,685
Kentucky	–37	Jan. 19, 1994	Shelbyville	730	114	July 28, 1930	Greensburg	590
Louisiana	–16	Feb. 13, 1899	Minden	185	114	Aug. 10, 1936	Plain Dealing	251
Maine	–50	Jan. 16, 2009	Big Black River	885	105	July 10, 1911[1]	North Bridgton	449
Maryland	–40	Jan. 13, 1912	Oakland	2,420	109	July 10, 1936[2]	Frederick	380
Massachusetts	–35	Jan. 12, 1981[1]	Chester	640	107	Aug. 2, 1975[3]	Chester	640
Michigan	–51	Feb. 9, 1934	Vanderbilt	905	112	July 13, 1936[3]	Stanwood	830
Minnesota	–60	Feb. 2, 1996	Tower	1,430	115	July 29, 1917	Beardsley	1,089
Mississippi	–19	Jan. 30, 1966	Corinth	385	115	July 29, 1930	Holly Springs	502
Missouri	–40	Feb. 13, 1905	Warsaw	705	118	July 14, 1954[3]	Warsaw	705
Montana	–70	Jan. 20, 1954	Rogers Pass	5,545	117	July 5, 1937[1]	Medicine Lake	1,942
Nebraska	–47	Dec. 22, 1989[1]	Oshkosh	3,390	118	July 24, 1936[1]	Minden	2,160
Nevada	–50	Jan. 8, 1937	San Jacinto	5,203	125	June 29, 1994	Laughlin	605
New Hampshire	–50	Jan. 22, 1885	Mt. Washington	6,271	106	July 4, 1911	Nashua	135
New Jersey	–34	Jan. 5, 1904	River Vale	31	110	July 10, 1936	Runyon	20
New Mexico	–50	Feb. 1, 1951	Gavilan	7,425	122	June 27, 1994	Waste Isolat. Pilot Plant	3,411
New York	–52	Feb. 18, 1979	Old Forge	1,748	108	July 22, 1926	Troy	35
North Carolina	–34	Jan. 21, 1985	Mt. Mitchell	6,240	110	Aug. 21, 1983	Fayetteville	186
North Dakota	–60	Feb. 15, 1936	Parshall	1,950	121	July 6, 1936	Steele	1,853
Ohio	–39	Feb. 10, 1899	Milligan	875	113	July 21, 1934	Gallipolis	569
Oklahoma	–31	Feb. 10, 2011	Nowata	NA	120	Aug. 12, 1936[1]	Altus	1,380
Oregon	–54	Feb. 10, 1933[1]	Seneca	4,659	119	June 29, 2021[2]	Pelton Dam	1,410
Pennsylvania	–42	Jan. 5, 1904	Smethport	1,469	111	July 10, 1936[1]	Phoenixville	105
Rhode Island	–28	Jan. 11, 1942	Wood River Junction	49	104	Aug. 2, 1975	Providence	60
South Carolina	–19	Jan. 21, 1985	Caesar's Head	3,200	113	June 29, 2012	Columbia	242
South Dakota	–58	Feb. 17, 1936	McIntosh	2,179	120	July 15, 2006[1]	Fort Pierre	1,590
Tennessee	–32	Dec. 30, 1917	Mountain City	2,503	113	Aug. 9, 1930[1]	Perryville	371
Texas	–23	Feb. 8, 1933[1]	Seminole	3,336	120	June 28, 1994[1]	Monahans	2,547
Utah	–50	Jan. 5, 1913	Strawberry Tunnel (East)	7,615	117	July 10, 2021[1]	Saint George	2,857
Vermont	–50	Dec. 30, 1933	Bloomfield	1,040	107	July 7, 1912	Vernon	226
Virginia	–30	Jan. 21, 1985	Mountain Lake Bio. Station	3,870	110	July 15, 1954[1]	Balcony Falls	732
Washington	–48	Dec. 30, 1968[3]	Winthrop	1,749	120	June 29, 2021	Hanford	NA
West Virginia	–37	Dec. 30, 1917	Lewisburg	2,300	112	July 10, 1936[1]	Martinsburg	534
Wisconsin	–55	Feb. 4, 1996[1]	Couderay	1,300	114	July 13, 1936	Wisconsin Dells	835
Wyoming	–66	Feb. 9, 1933	Riverside Ranger Sta.	6,500	115	July 15, 1988[1]	Diversion Dam	5,590

NA = Not available. (1) Also on earlier dates at the same or other places. (2) Also at other places on the same date and on earlier dates at the same or other places. (3) Also at other places on the same date.

Tropical Cyclone Names in 2025

Source: National Hurricane Center, Central Pacific Hurricane Center, NOAA, U.S. Dept. of Commerce; World Meteorological Org.

NOAA's National Hurricane Center began using name lists in 1953. Presently, six lists, maintained by the World Meteorological Org., are used in rotation. If there are more than 21 named storms in one season, storms take names from supplemental lists, established by the WMO in 2021. Previously, the Greek alphabet had been used if a list was exhausted in a given season (this happened in 2005 and 2020).

Atlantic: Andrea, Barry, Chantal, Dexter, Erin, Fernand, Gabrielle, Humberto, Imelda, Jerry, Karen, Lorenzo, Melissa, Nestor, Olga, Pablo, Rebekah, Sebastien, Tanya, Van, Wendy.

Atlantic (supplemental): Adria, Braylen, Caridad, Deshawn, Emery, Foster, Gemma, Heath, Isla, Jacobus, Kenzie, Lucio, Makayla, Nolan, Orlanda, Pax, Ronin, Sophie, Tayshaun, Viviana, Will.

Eastern North Pacific: Alvin, Barbara, Cosme, Dalila, Erick, Flossie, Gil, Henriette, Ivo, Juliette, Kiko, Lorena, Mario, Narda, Octave, Priscilla, Raymond, Sonia, Tico, Velma, Wallis, Xina, York, Zelda.

Eastern North Pacific (supplemental): Aidan, Bruna, Carmelo, Daniella, Esteban, Flor, Gerardo, Hedda, Izzy, Jacinta, Kenito, Luna, Marina, Nancy, Ovidio, Pia, Rey, Skylar, Teo, Violeta, Wilfredo, Xinia, Yariel, Zoe.

World Temperature and Precipitation

Source: Natl. Centers of Environmental Information, NOAA, U.S. Dept. of Commerce

Data are for the period 1991-2020. Surface elevations are supplied by the WMO and may differ from figures in other sections of *The World Almanac*.

Station	Surface elevation (ft)	Temperature (°F) AVERAGE DAILY January Max.	January Min.	July Max.	July Min.	EXTREME Max.	EXTREME Min.	Avg. annual precipitation (in.)
Abu Dhabi, United Arab Emirates	89	76.1	56.8	108.5	85.5	120.7	41.7	2.0
Amsterdam, Netherlands	–13	43.2	34.2	72.5	57.2	NA	NA	33.5
Auckland, New Zealand	23	75.0	61.0	58.3	45.9	NA	NA	44.1
Bangkok, Thailand	10	90.9	74.1	92.3	79.0	NA	NA	67.0
Barcelona, Spain	13	57.6	43.2	84.2	71.1	NA	NA	22.3
Beijing, China	107	36.1	19.6	89.2	73.4	107.4	1.4	20.8
Berlin, Germany	156	38.5	29.5	77.4	59.2	95.0	69.3	22.5
Bucharest, Romania	295	37.4	23.0	86.7	60.1	108.0	–14.1	25.5
Budapest, Hungary	456	37.4	27.5	82.6	62.1	104.4	0.0	22.5
Buenos Aires, Argentina	82	86.2	68.4	59.9	45.5	NA	NA	49.5
Cairo, Egypt	210	66.1	50.1	95.0	74.8	NA	NA	1.0
Cape Town, South Africa	138	80.6	61.9	64.2	45.3	NA	NA	19.4
Caracas, Venezuela	2,789	80.8	63.1	82.4	68.9	98.8	41.2	43.5
Casablanca, Morocco	184	63.7	48.0	79.0	68.9	104.9	30.2	16.1
Christchurch, New Zealand	121	72.5	53.2	52.2	33.3	NA	NA	24.3
Damascus, Syria	2,001	55.6	33.4	100.0	65.5	NA	10.4	4.9
Dubai, United Arab Emirates	26	75.9	59.6	106.8	88.2	119.8	45.3	3.1
Dublin, Ireland	233	46.4	36.1	67.1	52.3	81.0	10.0	30.4
Geneva, Switzerland	1,348	41.2	30.0	80.1	58.3	NA	NA	37.2
Hamburg, Germany	35	39.6	31.1	73.8	55.9	91.8	66.6	30.3
Helsinki, Finland	10	30.7	21.9	71.4	58.1	91.8	–16.6	25.7
Hong Kong, China	104	65.7	58.3	88.9	80.4	NA	NA	95.7
Islamabad, Pakistan	1,663	63.9	38.5	95.7	76.8	NA	NA	49.7
Jerusalem, Israel	2,657	54.9	44.1	86.0	68.0	108.9	27.5	20.7
Karachi, Pakistan	69	79.3	53.6	92.5	82.2	NA	NA	7.3
Lagos, Nigeria	459	88.7	76.8	83.1	74.8	104.2	56.7	67.1
London, England, UK	16	47.5	38.3	74.5	58.5	NA	NA	24.2
Madrid, Spain	1,998	52.3	33.4	93.2	63.5	108.0	13.1	14.7
Moscow, Russia	482	25.0	16.3	76.5	58.6	NA	NA	28.0
Mumbai, India	35	86.4	66.9	85.8	77.9	106.9	53.1	87.1
Munich, Germany	1,462	37.2	25.3	76.1	55.0	91.6	64.4	29.8
New Delhi, India	694	68.2	45.5	96.1	81.5	117.0	30.9	29.9
Ottawa, Canada	260	22.6	6.8	80.1	60.3	99.1	–26.0	2.8
Paris, France	246	45.7	37.8	78.3	61.2	NA	NA	25.0
Prague, Czech Republic	933	36.1	26.6	76.6	57.7	100.4	–9.6	20.0
Reykjavik, Iceland	171	37.8	28.9	58.8	48.4	78.3	4.8	34.5
Riga, Latvia	10	31.8	23.9	74.8	58.8	93.4	–22.9	26.6
Riyadh, Saudi Arabia	2,034	68.2	48.6	110.1	84.9	118.0	28.0	3.9
Rome, Italy	423	53.6	38.2	87.8	66.7	104.0	19.8	29.6
Sarajevo, Bosnia and Herzegovina	2,067	39.4	26.8	82.0	57.6	101.8	–8.0	37.4
Seoul, South Korea	279	35.8	22.1	84.2	72.1	NA	NA	55.8
Shanghai, China	30	46.8	36.0	90.3	78.6	103.8	18.0	48.7
Stockholm, Sweden	46	33.6	24.6	73.9	56.1	93.6	–12.5	21.2
Sydney, Australia	20	81.9	68.0	63.9	47.5	115.5	37.4	39.1
Tehran, Iran	3,907	47.3	34.3	98.4	77.4	108.7	12.6	9.4
Tokyo, Japan	83	49.6	34.2	85.8	72.3	NA	NA	62.9
Toronto, Canada	369	31.5	19.9	80.6	64.6	100.8	–14.6	NA
Zurich, Switzerland	1,824	38.3	29.5	75.7	57.9	NA	NA	43.6

NA = Not available.

Speed of Winds in the U.S.

Source: National Centers for Environmental Information, NESDIS, NOAA, U.S. Dept. of Commerce

Based on available records through 2023. Maximum speeds are highest 3-sec. wind speeds.

Station	Avg. mph	Max. mph	Station	Avg. mph	Max. mph	Station	Avg. mph	Max. mph
Albuquerque, NM	8.2	89	Helena, MT	6.8	81	Oklahoma City, OK	11.3	87
Anchorage, AK	6.9	71	Honolulu, HI	10.3	49	Omaha, NE	10.0	96
Atlanta, GA	8.2	76	Houston, TX	7.5	97	Philadelphia, PA	9.2	75
Baltimore, MD	7.1	72	Indianapolis, IN	9.5	85	Phoenix, AZ	6.2	86
Birmingham, AL	6.1	75	Jackson, MS	6.1	76	Pittsburgh, PA	7.7	75
Bismarck, ND	9.4	83	Jacksonville, FL	6.6	86	Portland, ME	7.9	72
Boise, ID	7.6	68	Little Rock, AR	7.0	87	Portland, OR	7.3	67
Boston, MA	11.4	76	Los Angeles, CA	7.4	54	Providence, RI	9.2	66
Buffalo, NY	10.2	75	Louisville, KY	7.8	79	Richmond, VA	7.6	72
Burlington, VT	8.2	70	Miami, FL	8.3	104	St. Louis, MO	9.0	79
Charleston, SC	7.8	69	Milwaukee, WI	10.1	79	Salt Lake City, UT	8.3	75
Chicago, IL	9.8	84	Minneapolis, MN	9.6	71	San Francisco, CA	10.5	77
Cleveland, OH	9.6	72	Mobile, AL	7.4	91	San Juan, PR	8.0	93
Dallas-Ft. Worth, TX	10.5	79	Mount Washington, NH	35.3	231	Seattle, WA	7.9	69
Denver, CO	9.9	80	Nashville, TN	7.0	78	Sioux Falls, SD	10.2	87
Des Moines, IA	9.8	77	New Orleans, LA	7.9	88	Washington, DC	8.9	74
Detroit, MI	9.3	78	New York, NY	6.3	68	Wichita, KS	11.5	101
Fairbanks, AK	4.3	59	Newark, NJ	9.7	78	Wilmington, DE	8.5	78

Wind Chill Temperature

Source: National Weather Service, NOAA, U.S. Dept. of Commerce

Temperature and wind combine to cause heat loss from body surfaces. For example, when the air temperature is 5°F, a 10-mph wind can cause body heat loss equal to that which could occur when the air temperature is –10°F with no wind. In other words, a 10-mph wind can make 5°F feel like –10°F. Wind speeds greater than 45 mph have little additional chilling effect. Direct sunlight can increase the wind chill temperature 10°F to 15°F. When the wind chill temperature falls within the shaded areas, frostbite can occur on exposed skin in the times indicated or less.

Wind speed (mph)	Air temperature (°F)																	
Calm	40	35	30	25	20	15	10	5	0	–5	–10	–15	–20	–25	–30	–35	–40	–45
	Wind chill temperature (°F)																	
5	36	31	25	19	13	7	1	–5	–11	–16	–22	–28	–34	–40	–46	–52	–57	–63
10	34	27	21	15	9	3	–4	–10	–16	–22	–28	–35	–41	–47	–53	–59	–66	–72
15	32	25	19	13	6	0	–7	–13	–19	–26	–32	–39	–45	–51	–58	–64	–71	–77
20	30	24	17	11	4	–2	–9	–15	–22	–29	–35	–42	–48	–55	–61	–68	–74	–81
25	29	23	16	9	3	–4	–11	–17	–24	–31	–37	–44	–51	–58	–64	–71	–78	–84
30	28	22	15	8	1	–5	–12	–19	–26	–33	–39	–46	–53	–60	–67	–73	–80	–87
35	28	21	14	7	0	–7	–14	–21	–27	–34	–41	–48	–55	–62	–69	–76	–82	–89
40	27	20	13	6	–1	–8	–15	–22	–29	–36	–43	–50	–57	–64	–71	–78	–84	–91
45	26	19	12	5	–2	–9	–16	–23	–30	–37	–44	–51	–58	–65	–72	–79	–86	–93

30 minutes   10 minutes   5 minutes

Heat Index

Source: National Weather Service, NOAA, U.S. Dept. of Commerce

The heat index, or apparent temperature, is a measure of how hot it feels when the relative humidity is factored in with the actual air temperature. For example, when air temperature is 100°F, and relative humidity is 50%, it can feel as if it's 118°F with no humidity. Full sunlight can make one feel even hotter. On the chart, the shaded areas indicate the likelihood of heat disorders with prolonged exposure or strenuous activity.

Relative humidity (%)	Air temperature (°F)															
	80	82	84	86	88	90	92	94	96	98	100	102	104	106	108	110
	Apparent temperature (°F)															
40	80	81	83	85	88	91	94	97	101	105	109	114	119	124	130	136
45	80	82	84	87	89	93	96	100	104	109	114	119	124	130	137	
50	81	83	85	88	91	95	99	103	108	113	118	124	131	137		
55	81	84	86	89	93	97	101	106	112	117	124	130	137			
60	82	84	88	91	95	100	105	110	116	123	129	137				
65	82	85	89	93	98	103	108	114	121	128	136					
70	83	86	90	95	100	105	112	119	126	134						
75	84	88	92	97	103	109	116	124	132							
80	84	89	94	100	106	113	121	129								
85	85	90	96	102	110	117	126	135								
90	86	91	98	105	113	122	131									
95	86	93	100	108	117	127										
100	87	95	103	112	121	132										

Caution   Extreme caution   Danger   Extreme danger

Ultraviolet (UV) Index Forecast

Source: National Weather Service (NWS), NOAA, U.S. Dept. of Commerce; U.S. Environmental Protection Agency (EPA); World Health Organization (WHO)

The NWS and EPA developed and began offering a UV index in 1994 in response to increasing incidences of skin cancer, cataracts, and other effects from exposure to the sun's harmful rays. In 2004, they adapted their index to the Global Solar UV Index sponsored by the WHO. The UV index is now a regular element of NWS atmospheric forecasts. To see the UV index for a given location, visit https://enviro.epa.gov/envirofacts/uv/search or use WHO's app SunSmart Global UV.

The UV index, ranging from 0 to 11+, is an indication of the expected intensity of UV radiation reaching the Earth's surface during the solar noon hour (the time of day, dependent on location and time of year, when the sun appears to have reached its highest point in the sky). The lower the UV index value, the less the expected radiation. The UV index forecast is produced daily for 58 cities by the NWS Climate Prediction Center.

UV levels are influenced by the following:

Ozone. Ozone, a form of oxygen, the molecules of which consist of three atoms rather than two, absorbs UV radiation. The more ozone, the lower the UV radiation at the surface.

Time of day. UV radiation is highest at midday (when the sun peaks in the sky) and is lower in the early morning and late afternoon.

Cloud cover. UV radiation levels are highest under cloudless skies. Even with cloud cover, UV radiation levels can be high due to the scattering of UV radiation by water molecules and fine particles in the atmosphere.

Ground reflection. Reflective surfaces intensify UV exposure. Water reflects about 10% of UV radiation that reaches it; sand, 15%; and snow, as much as 80%.

Altitude. At higher altitudes, a thinner atmosphere filters less UV radiation. For every 1,000 ft (305 m) one travels above sea level, UV levels increase by 2%.

Latitude. The closer a location is to the equator, the higher the UV radiation level.

Seasons. UV radiation is highest in spring and summer, drops in fall, and is lowest in winter.

Land cover. Structures and trees lessen exposure to UV radiation.

Using the UV Forecast

UV index	Exposure	Protective actions
0-2	Low	Sunglasses on bright days, SPF 15+ sunscreen, cover up if you burn easily
3-5	Moderate	Seek shade during midday hours; hat, sunglasses; SPF 30+ sunscreen
6-7	High	Seek shade during midday hours; protective clothing, hat, sunglasses, sunscreen
8-10	Very high	If outside 10 AM-4 PM, seek shade; wear protective clothing, hat, sunglasses, sunscreen; avoid bright surfaces
11+	Extreme	If outside 10 AM-4 PM, seek shade; wear protective clothing, hat, sunglasses, sunscreen; avoid bright surfaces

Lightning

Source: National Weather Service, NOAA, U.S. Dept. of Commerce

Lightning is a powerful electric discharge, or spark, that can occur in the atmosphere when an imbalance of positive and negative charges develops. It can travel within a cloud, between clouds, between a cloud and clear sky, or between a cloud and the ground. Lightning generally accompanies rainstorms, but it can also be seen with snowstorms, volcano eruption clouds, and violent forest fires. In a common form of cloud-to-ground lightning, a negatively charged area in a thunderstorm sends charges down toward positively charged objects. Lightning can travel miles away from the area of a storm.

The transfer of charges in lightning generates a huge amount of heat, sending the temperature in the channel to 50,000°F or more and causing the air within it to expand rapidly. The sound of that expansion is thunder. Sound travels more slowly than light, so lightning is usually observed before thunder is heard.

An estimated 25 mil cloud-to-ground lightning bolts happen in the U.S. each year. They killed an annual average of 36 people in 1994-2023. This is a small number compared to U.S. deaths from fire (3,670 in 2023) and motor vehicle crashes (about 40,000-46,000 annually in recent years), but it is still significant. In comparison, tornadoes caused an average of 72 deaths a year and hurricanes an average of 48 over the same 30-year time period. According to the National Weather Service, 14 people were struck and killed by lightning in 2023; 10 more were injured.

Most lightning deaths and injuries occur in summer when people are outdoors. If outdoors, one should run to a safe building or vehicle when thunder is first heard, lightning is seen, or dark threatening clouds are observed developing overhead. Even while indoors, one is advised to stay away from windows and doors and to avoid contact with anything conducting electricity, including corded phones, computers and other electrical equipment, and tubs, showers, and other plumbing. One should stay inside until 30 min. after the last occurrence of lightning or thunder.

More information about lightning can be found online at www.weather.gov/safety/lightning

Global Temperature Extremes and Precipitation Records

Source: World Weather & Climate Extremes Archive, World Meteorological Organization (WMO)

(records in each category ranked from most to least extreme; as of May 23, 2024)

Highest Temperature Extremes

Continent/area	Highest temp. (°F)	Place	Elevation (ft)	Date
North America	134	Death Valley, CA, U.S. (Furnace Creek (fmr. Greenland) Ranch)	–179	July 10, 1913
Africa	131[1]	Kebili, Tunisia	125	July 7, 1931
Europe/Middle East/ Greenland	129	Tirat Tsvi, Israel	–722	June 21, 1942
Asia[2]	129.0	Mitribah, Kuwait	398	July 21, 2016
	128.7	Turbat, Pakistan	495	May 28, 2017
Southwest Pacific	123	Oodnadatta, Australia	367	Jan. 2, 1960
South America	120	Rivadavia, Argentina	673	Dec. 11, 1905
Continental Europe	118.4	Athens, Greece (and Elefsina, Greece)	774	July 10, 1977
Antarctica	67.6	Signy Research Station (UK)	23	Jan. 30, 1982

(1) Previous record of 136.4°F set on Sept. 13, 1922, in El Azizia, Libya, was invalidated in 2012; an error had been made in recording the temperature. (2) Record effectively tied due to margin of error in measurement.

Lowest Temperature Extremes

Continent/area	Lowest temp. (°F)	Place	Elevation (ft)	Date
Antarctica	–128.6	Vostok Station (Soviet Union/Russia)	11,220	July 21, 1983
Europe/Middle East/ Greenland	–93.3	Klinck Auto. Weather Sta., Greenland	10,551	Dec. 22, 1991
Asia	–90	Verkhoyansk, Russia	350	Feb. 5 and 7, 1892
	–90	Oimekon, Russia	2,625	Feb. 6, 1933
North America	–81.4	Snag, Yukon, Canada	2,120	Feb. 3, 1947
Continental Europe	–72.6	Ust'-Shchugor, Russia	279	Dec. 31, 1978
South America	–27	Sarmiento, Argentina	879	June 1, 1907
Southwest Pacific	–14	Eweburn (now Ranfurly), New Zealand	1,388	July 17, 1903
Africa	–11	Ifrane, Morocco	5,364	Feb. 11, 1935
Australia	–9.4	Charlotte Pass, New South Wales	5,758	June 29, 1994

Highest Measured Average Annual Precipitation Extremes

Continent/area	Highest avg. (in.)[1]	Place	Elevation (ft)	Years in averaging period
Asia	467.4	Mawsynram, India	4,695	38
Southwest Pacific	460.0	Mt. Waialeale, Kauai, HI, U.S.	5,148	30
Africa	405.0	Debundscha, Cameroon	30	32
South America	354.0[2]	Quibdo, Colombia	230	29
Australia	316.3	Bellenden Ker, Queensland	5,102	34
North America	276	Henderson Lake, British Columbia, Canada	12	15
Europe	180.8	Crkvice, Montenegro	3,461	30
Antarctica	>31.5[3]	Along coast of E and W and over the Antarctic Peninsula		3[4]

(1) Official greatest average annual precipitation. (2) The frequently cited record of 523.6 in. in Lloro, Colombia (14 mi SE and at a higher elevation than Quibdo) is an estimate. (3) Water equivalent. (4) July 1996-June 1999.

Lowest Measured Average Annual Precipitation Extremes

Continent/area	Lowest avg. (in.)[1]	Place	Elevation (ft)	Years in averaging period
South America	0.03	Arica, Chile	213	59
Antarctica	0.08	Amundsen-Scott South Pole Station (U.S.)	9,301	10
Africa	<0.1	Wadi Halfa, Sudan	590	39
North America	1.2	Batagues, Mexico	69	14
Asia	1.8	Aden, Yemen	63	50
Southwest Pacific	4.05	Troudaninna, Australia	46	42
Continental Europe	6.4	Astrakhan, Russia	66	25

(1) Official lowest average annual precipitation.

OCEANOGRAPHY

Tides and Their Causes

Source: National Ocean Service, NOAA, U.S. Dept. of Commerce

The tides are natural phenomena involving the movement of waves in the Earth's large fluid bodies as a result of the gravitational attraction of the sun and moon. These two variable influences combined produce the complex recurrent cycle of the tides. Tides may occur in both oceans and seas; to a limited extent in large lakes and in the atmosphere; and, to a very minute degree, in the Earth itself. The length of time between succeeding tides can vary.

The tide-generating force represents the difference between (1) the centrifugal force produced by Earth's revolution around the common center of gravity of the Earth-moon system and (2) the gravitational attraction of the moon acting upon the Earth's overlying waters. The moon is about 390 times closer to Earth than is the sun. So despite its smaller mass, the moon's tide-raising force is two times greater.

The tide-generating forces of the moon and sun acting tangentially to the Earth's surface tend to cause a maximum accumulation of waters at two diametrically opposite points on the Earth's surface and to withdraw compensating amounts of water from all points 90° removed from these tidal bulges. As the Earth rotates beneath the maxima and minima of these tide-generating forces, a sequence of two high tides, separated by two low tides, is produced each lunar day (24 hr. and 50 min., the time it takes for a specific site on the Earth to rotate from an exact point under the moon to the same point under the moon) in what is called a **semidiurnal tide**. Each ocean basin reacts differently to tidal forces.

Twice each month, when the sun, moon, and Earth are directly aligned—the moon between the Earth and sun (at new moon) or on the opposite side of Earth from the sun (at full moon)—the sun and moon exert gravitational forces in a mutual or additive fashion. The highest high tides and lowest low tides, called **spring tides**, are produced at these times. At two positions 90° in between, the moon and sun's gravitational forces—imposed at right angles—counteract each other to the greatest extent, and the range between high and low tides is reduced, resulting in **neap tides**.

The inclination of the moon's monthly orbit and of the sun to the equator during Earth's yearly passage through its orbit produce a difference in the height of succeeding high and low tides, known as the diurnal inequality. In most cases, this produces a so-called **mixed tide**. In extreme cases, these phenomena may result in a **diurnal tide**, with only one high tide and one low tide each day. There are other monthly and yearly variations in the tides because of the elliptical shape of the orbits.

The range of tides in the open ocean is generally less than in the coastal regions, where the incoming tide can be augmented by the continental shelves, as well as by bays and estuaries. The largest tidal ranges in the world occur in the Bay of Fundy, Canada, where the range of tide reaches 53 ft. The highest tides in the U.S. occur near Anchorage, AK, with tidal ranges that average around 30 ft.

In every case, actual high or low tide can vary considerably from the average as a result of weather conditions such as strong winds, abrupt barometric pressure changes, or prolonged periods of extreme high or low pressure.

Mean Ranges of Tide

Place	Ft	In.	Place	Ft	In.	Place	Ft	In.
Baltimore, MD	1	2	Key West, FL	1	3	Provincetown, MA	9	3
Biloxi, MS	1	6	Los Angeles, CA	3	10	St. Petersburg, FL	1	7
Boston, MA	9	6	Miami Beach, FL	2	6	San Diego, CA	4	1
Charleston, SC	5	3	New London, CT	2	7	San Francisco, CA	4	1
Eastport, ME	18	4	New York, NY	4	6	San Juan, PR	1	1
Ft. Pulaski, GA	6	11	Newport, RI	3	6	Sandy Hook, NJ	4	8
Galveston, TX	1	0	Philadelphia, PA	6	1	Seattle, WA	7	8
Honolulu, HI	1	3	Portland, ME	9	1	Washington, DC	2	9

Note: Mean range is the difference in height between mean high water and mean low water.

El Niño and La Niña

Source: National Weather Service, NOAA, U.S. Dept. of Commerce

El Niño is a climatically significant disruption of the ocean-atmosphere system characterized by large-scale weakening of trade winds and warming of surface layer waters in the central and eastern equatorial Pacific. The term *El Niño*, Spanish for "the little boy" or "the Christ Child," was originally used by fishing crews to refer to a warm ocean current that appeared around Christmas off the west coast of Ecuador and Peru lasting several months. The term has come to be reserved for exceptionally strong warm currents that bring heavy rains.

El Niño events generally occur at irregular intervals of two to seven years, at an average of once every three to four years. They typically last 12 to 18 months. The intensity of El Niño events varies depending on the area encompassed by the abnormally warm ocean temperatures. Some are strong, such as in 1982-83, 1997-98, and 2015-16. Others are considerably weaker, such as the 2018-19 event. The eastward extent of warmer-than-normal water varies from episode to episode.

El Niño influences weather around the globe, and its impacts are most clearly seen in the winter. During El Niño years, winter temperatures in the continental U.S. tend to be warmer than normal in the northern states and on the West Coast and cooler than normal in the Southeast. Conditions tend to be wetter than normal over central and southern California, the Southwest, and across much of the South, and drier than normal over the northern portions of the Rocky Mountains and in the Ohio Valley. Globally, El Niño brings wetter than normal conditions to Peru and Chile and dry conditions to Australia and Indonesia. It should be noted that El Niño is only one of a number of factors influencing seasonal variations of climate.

La Niña ("the little girl") is characterized by colder than normal sea surface temperatures in the equatorial Pacific. La Niña typically brings wetter, cooler conditions to the Pacific Northwest and drier, warmer conditions to much of the southern U.S. El Niño and La Niña are opposite phases of the El Niño-Southern Oscillation (ENSO) cycle, which involves a shift in tropical sea-level pressure between the Eastern and Western Hemispheres.

NOAA and other agencies monitor these events using satellites, weather balloons, and buoys in the Pacific Ocean. Numerical computer models of the ocean and atmosphere use these data to predict the onset and evolution of El Niño and La Niña. ENSO-neutral conditions were expected through late summer 2024, with La Niña favored to emerge Sept.-Nov. and continue through winter 2024-25.

DISASTERS

U.S. Weather and Climate Disasters by Type, 1980-2023

Source: National Centers for Environmental Information, National Oceanic and Atmospheric Admin., U.S. Dept. of Commerce

Does not include disasters causing under $1 billion in 2023 consumer price index-adjusted losses. The worst year for billion-dollar disasters in this period was 2017, with $392.6 billion (CPI-adjusted) in damages from events including Hurricanes Harvey, Irma, and Maria. It easily surpassed the previous U.S. annual record of $266.8 billion, established in 2005. As of June 10, 2024.

Disaster type	Number of events	Losses (bil)	Percent of total losses	Avg. event cost (bil)	Deaths
Drought	31	$360.2	13.3%	$11.6	4,522[1]
Flooding[2]	44	200.2	7.4	4.6	738
Freeze	9	37.3	1.4	4.1	162
Severe storm	186	463.2	17.0	2.5	2,094
Tropical cyclone	62	1,411.2	51.9	22.8	6,897
Wildfire	22	145.7	5.4	6.6	535
Winter storm	22	100.1	3.7	4.6	1,402
All disasters	**376**	**2,717.9**	**100.0**	**7.2**	**16,350**

Note: Tropical cyclones include hurricanes, tropical storms, tropical depressions, and associated storm surges and flooding. (1) Drought-associated deaths are the result of heat waves, which do not always occur with droughts. (2) Does not include inland flood damage caused by tropical cyclone events.

U.S. Weather and Climate Disasters, 2023

Source: National Centers for Environmental Information, National Oceanic and Atmospheric Admin., U.S. Dept. of Commerce

Does not include disasters causing under $1 billion in 2023 consumer price index-adjusted losses.

Date	Location	Event and location	Losses (bil)	Deaths
Dec. 26-Mar. 19	CA	Succession of atmospheric rivers caused severe flooding, record snowfall, copious rainfall across state	$4.7	22
Feb. 2-5	Northeast	Strong winter storm across region; –108°F wind chill temperature observed on Mount Washington, NH	1.8	1
Mar. 2-3	TX, AL, MS, TN, KY, IN, OH	Severe storms	6.1	13
Mar. 24-26	MS, AL, GA, TN; OH, WV, PA	Severe storms incl. more than 40 tornadoes across four states	2.9	23
Mar. 31-Apr. 1	IL, IN, OH, MO, IA, AR, TN, PA	Historic outbreak of at least 145 tornadoes across region	5.9	33
Apr. 1-Sept. 30	TX, LA, OK, KS, IL, MO, NE	Drought conditions; for second straight year, low water levels on Mississippi River impacted river commerce	14.8	247
Apr. 4-6	IL, KY, IA, IN, OH, MO, MI	Large hail, high winds, more than 35 tornadoes	2.9	5
Apr. 12-13	Fort Lauderdale, FL	Flash flooding (over 25 in. of rainfall in less than 24 hours)	1.1	0
Apr. 15	MO, AR, IL, TX, LA, FL Panhandle	Hail, tornadoes, high winds	1.4	0
Apr. 19-20	Central OK; TX, MO, NE, KS, IA, IL, WI	Cluster of tornadoes in one state; severe hail, high winds in seven other states	3.1	1
Apr. 25-27	TX, GA, FL	Severe weather across multiple states	1.4	0
May 6-8	MO, IL, IA, IN; KY, TN, SC, TX	Severe weather across region, with damage in latter four states	2.2	1
May 10-12	Eastern Rockies across central U.S., CO, KS, OK, NE, TX, ND	Dozens of tornadoes, severe hail storms	3.5	1
May 18-19	North-central TX (esp. Collin County)	Hail	1.7	0
May 24-25	Guam	Typhoon Mawar (Category 4)	4.4	2
June 11-14	TX, LA, MS, AL, GA, TN, AR, SC, FL	Hail, tornadoes, high winds	4.2	0
June 15-18	OK, TX, MS, GA, FL, AR, OH	Severe storms; over 70 preliminary tornadoes, incl. an EF-3	3.9	5
June 21-26	CO; WY, CO, MN, IN, KY, AR	Severe hail; more than 60 tornadoes across six other states	5.4	8
June 28-July 2	Central U.S., esp. in MO, IL, IN	Severe storms	2.0	3
July 9-15	Northeast; Montpelier, VT; WI, MN, IL	Flooding, incl. record-breaking 5.28 in. of rain in Vermont city; high wind, hail across three other states	2.2	10
July 19-21	MI, WI, OH, TN, GA	Severe storms across regions	1.9	1
July 28-29	NE, MO, IL, IN, WI	Severe storms across regions	1.5	2
Aug. 5-8	Northeast and East; GA to NY	High wind, severe hail, tornadoes across regions, esp. on Aug. 7, with damage reports spanning multiple states	1.7	4
Aug. 8	Lahaina, Maui Island, HI	Deadliest U.S. wildfire in over a century destroyed historic Hawaii town	5.7	100
Aug. 11	South-central MN	Hail storms	1.8	0
Aug. 29-31	Big Bend, FL; Charleston, SC	Hurricane Idalia, strongest hurricane (Category 3) in more than 125 years to hit Florida region; flooding in Charleston	3.6	5
Sept. 23-24	TX, OK, MO	Hail storms	1.7	0
Dec. 16-18	FL to ME	Storm amplified by record-high temperatures produced heavy rainfall, flooding, high winds, coastal erosion	1.3	5
2023 total		**28 events**	**94.8**	**492**

Note: As of June 10, 2024. Data may be updated as new information becomes available.

Some Notable Aircraft Disasters Since 1937

Source: National Transportation Safety Board; World Almanac research

Particularly notable disasters are in bold. Asterisk (*) indicates number of deaths includes people on ground. As of Sept. 2024.

Date	Aircraft	Incident details, site	Deaths
1937, May 6	**German zeppelin Hindenburg**	**Burned at mooring, Lakehurst, NJ**	**36***
1944, Aug. 23	U.S. Air Force B-24 Liberator bomber	Hit school, Freckleton, England, UK	61*
1945, July 28	U.S. Army B-25	Hit Empire State Building after getting lost in fog, New York, NY	14*
1952, Dec. 20	U.S. Air Force C-124	Crashed at Moses Lake, WA	87
1953, Mar. 3	**Canadian Pacific DH-106 Comet**	**Crashed on takeoff from Karachi, Pakistan; world's first fatal commercial passenger jet crash**	**11**
1953, June 18	U.S. Air Force C-124	Crashed, burned near Tokyo, Japan	129
1955, Oct. 6	United Airlines DC-4	Crashed in Medicine Bow Peak, WY	66
1955, Nov. 1	United Airlines DC-6	Bomb on board exploded near Longmont, CO	44[1]

Date	Aircraft	Incident details, site	Deaths
1956, June 20	LAV (Venezuela) Super Constellation	Crashed into Atlantic off Asbury Park, NJ	74
1956, June 30	TWA Super Const., United DC-7	Collided over Grand Canyon, AZ	128
1960, Dec. 16	United DC-8, TWA Super Const.	Collided over New York, NY, killing all 128 on planes, 6 on ground	134*
1962, Mar. 16	Flying Tiger (U.S.) Super Constellation	Vanished in W Pacific en route to Philippines from Guam	107
1962, June 3	Air France Boeing 707	Crashed on takeoff from Paris, France	130
1962, June 22	Air France Boeing 707	Crashed in storm, Guadeloupe, French W Indies	113
1963, Feb. 1	Lebanese Middle East Airlines Vickers Viscount 754, Turkish Mil. Douglas C-47	Collided over Ankara, Turkey, killing all 17 on planes, 87 on ground	104*
1963, Nov. 29	Trans-Canada Air Lines DC-8	Crashed after takeoff from Montréal, QC, Canada	118
1965, May 20	Pakistani Boeing 720	Crashed at airport in Cairo, Egypt	121
1966, Jan. 24	Air India Boeing 707	Crashed on Mont Blanc, France-Italy	117
1966, Feb. 4	All-Nippon Boeing 727	Plunged into Tokyo Bay, Japan	133
1966, Mar. 5	BOAC (British Overseas Airways Corp.) Boeing 707	Crashed into Mt. Fuji, Japan, after encountering severe turbulence	124
1966, Dec. 24	U.S. military-chartered CL-44	Crashed into village in S Vietnam	129*
1967, Apr. 20	Globe Air Bristol Britannia	Crashed on approach to airport, Nicosia, Cyprus	126
1967, July 19	Piedmont Boeing 727, Cessna 310	Collided over Hendersonville, NC	82
1968, Apr. 20	S. African Airways Boeing 707	Crashed on takeoff from Windhoek, Namibia	122
1968, May 3	Braniff International Electra	Crashed in storm near Dawson, TX	85
1968, May 12	U.S. Air Force Lockheed C-130B	Hit by mortar while evacuating Kham Duc Camp, S Vietnam	155
1969, Mar. 16	VIASA DC-9	Crashed after takeoff from Maracaibo, Venezuela	155[2]
1970, July 3	British-chartered DH-106 Comet	Crashed near Barcelona, Spain	112
1970, July 5	Air Canada DC-8	Crashed near Toronto Intl. Airport, ON, Canada	108
1970, Nov. 14	Southern Airways DC-9	Crashed into mountains near Huntington, WV	75[3]
1971, July 30	All-Nippon Boeing 727, Japan Air Force F-86 fighter	Collided over Morioka, Japan	162[4]
1971, Sept. 4	Alaska Airlines Boeing 727	Crashed into mountain near Juneau, AK	111
1972, May 18	Aeroflot Antonov 10A	Wings separated from fuselage on approach to Kharkov, USSR	122
1972, June 18	British European Airways Trident-1C	Crashed near Staines after takeoff from London, Eng., UK	118
1972, Aug. 14	East German Ilyushin 62	Crashed on takeoff from East Berlin, E Germany	156
1972, Aug. 31	Aeroflot Ilyushin 18V	Crashed in field near Magnitogorsk, USSR	101
1972, Oct. 1	Aeroflot Ilyushin 18V	Crashed into Black Sea, USSR	109
1972, Oct. 13	Aeroflot Ilyushin 62	Crashed near Moscow, USSR	174
1972, Dec. 3	Spanish-chartered Convair CV-990	Crashed on takeoff from Canary Islands, Spain	155
1972, Dec. 29	Eastern Airlines Lockheed L-1011 TriStar	Crashed on approach to Miami Intl. Airport, FL	99
1973, Jan. 22	Nigerian-chartered Boeing 707	Burst into flames upon landing at Kano Airport, Nigeria	176
1973, Feb. 21	**Libyan Arab Boeing 727**	**Flew off course, shot down by Israeli fighter planes over Sinai Desert**	**108**
1973, Apr. 10	Invicta Airlines (UK) Vickers Vanguard	Crashed during snowstorm on approach to Basel, Switzerland	108
1973, June 3	Soviet Supersonic Tu-144	Crashed near Goussainville, France	14[5]
1973, July 11	Varig Airlines (Brazil) Boeing 707	Crashed on approach to Orly Airport, Paris, France	123
1973, July 31	Delta Airlines DC-9	Crashed while attempting landing in fog, Logan Airport, Boston, MA	89
1973, Sept. 30	Aeroflot Tupolev 104B	Crashed after takeoff from Sverdlovsk, USSR	108
1973, Oct. 13	Aeroflot Tupolev 104B	Crashed on approach to Moscow, USSR	122
1973, Dec. 22	Royal Air Maroc SE 210 Caravelle VIN	Flew into side of a mountain near Tangier, Morocco	106
1974, Mar. 3	Turkish DC-10	Improperly closed cargo door caused crash, nr. Paris, France	346
1974, Apr. 22	Pan American (U.S.) Boeing 707	Crashed in Bali, Indonesia	107
1974, Apr. 27	Aeroflot Ilyushin 18V	Crashed after takeoff from Leningrad, USSR	109
1974, Dec. 1	TWA Boeing 727	Crashed on approach in storm, Upperville, VA	92
1974, Dec. 4	Dutch-chartered DC-8	Crashed in storm near Colombo, Sri Lanka	191
1975, Apr. 4	U.S. Air Force Galaxy C-5A	Crashed on takeoff nr. Saigon, S Vietnam; carried orphans	155
1975, June 24	Eastern Airlines 727	Crashed in storm, JFK Airport, New York, NY	113
1975, Aug. 3	Alia Royal Jordanian Boeing 707	Hit mountainside in heavy fog near Agadir, Morocco	188
1975, Aug. 20	Czechoslovakian Air Ilyushin 62	Crashed on approach to Damascus, Syria	126
1976, Mar. 6	Aeroflot Ilyushin 18E	Crashed between Moscow, USSR, and Yerevan, Armenia	111
1976, Sept. 10	British Airways Trident, Inex Adria DC-9	Collided near Zagreb, Yugoslavia	176
1976, Sept. 19	Turkish Boeing 727	Hit mountain in southern Turkey	154
1976, Oct. 6	Cubana Airlines DC-8	Bombs set by anti-Castro Cuban exiles detonated mid-flight	73
1976, Oct. 13	Lloyd Aero Boliviano Boeing 707	Crashed into soccer field after takeoff from Santa Cruz, Bolivia	91[6]
1977, Mar. 27	**KLM (Neth.) 747, Pan Am (U.S.) 747**	**Collided on foggy runway, Tenerife, Canary Islands, Spain**	**583**
1977, Nov. 19	TAP Portugal Boeing 727	Crashed in Madeira, Portugal	131
1977, Dec. 4	Malaysian Airlines Boeing 737	Hijacked and forced to fly to Singapore, crashed near Johor Strait	100
1978, Jan. 1	Air India 747	Crashed into sea after takeoff from Bombay, India	213
1978, Sept. 25	Pacific SW Air Boeing 727, Cessna 172	Collided over San Diego, CA	144*
1978, Nov. 15	Indonesian-chartered DC-8	Crashed on approach to airport, Colombo, Sri Lanka	183
1979, May 25	**American Airlines DC-10**	**Crashed after takeoff from O'Hare Airport, Chicago, IL; highest death toll in U.S. aviation history**	**275***
1979, Aug. 11	Aeroflot/Moldova Tu-134, Aeroflot Tu-134	Collided over Ukraine	178
1979, Nov. 26	Pakistani Boeing 707	Crashed near Jidda, Saudi Arabia	156
1979, Nov. 28	Air New Zealand DC-10	Crashed into Mt. Erebus during Antarctica flyover	257
1980, Mar. 14	PLL LOT Ilyushin 62	Crashed making emergency landing, Warsaw, Poland	87[7]
1980, Apr. 25	Dan-Air Services (UK) Boeing 727	Crashed into mountain, Tenerife, Canary Islands, Spain	146
1980, July 8	Aeroflot Tupolev 154B	Crashed after takeoff from Alma-Ata, USSR	166
1980, Aug. 19	Saudi Arabian Lockheed TriStar	Returned to Riyadh airport after fire on board; evacuation delayed	301
1981, Dec. 1	Inex Adria (Yugoslavia) DC-9	Crashed into mountain on island of Corsica, France	180
1982, Jan. 13	Air Florida Boeing 737	Crashed into bridge, Potomac R. after takeoff from Washington, DC	78*
1982, June 8	VASP (Brazil) Boeing 727	Crashed into mountain near Fortaleza, Brazil	137
1982, June 28	Aeroflot Yakovlev 42	Crashed near Mozyr, USSR	132
1982, July 9	Pan Am Boeing 727	Crashed after takeoff from Kenner, LA, near New Orleans	153*

Date	Aircraft	Incident details, site	Deaths
1983, July 11	Ecuadorean Boeing 737	Inexperienced pilot crashed into hill near Cuenca, Ecuador	119
1983, Sept. 1	**S. Korean Boeing 747**	**Shot down after entering restricted Soviet airspace near Sakhalin; plane apparently misidentified**	**269**
1983, Sept. 23	Gulf Air Boeing 737	Bomb exploded in cargo hold over Mina Jebel Ali, UAE	112
1983, Nov. 27	Avianca Boeing 747	Crashed near Barajas Airport, Madrid, Spain	181
1984, Oct. 11	Aeroflot/East Siberia Tu-154	Crashed into vehicles on runway while landing in poor weather, Omsk, Russia	178*
1985, Feb. 19	Spanish Boeing 727	Crashed into Mt. Oiz, Spain	148
1985, June 23	Air India Boeing 747	Crashed into Atlantic off Ireland after bomb allegedly set by Sikh extremists detonated on board	329
1985, July 10	Aeroflot Tupolev 154B	Crashed after takeoff from Uzbekistan, USSR	200
1985, Aug. 2	Delta Air Lines Lockheed L-1011 TriStar	Crashed after encountering microburst near Dallas-Ft. Worth Airport, TX	135*
1985, Aug. 12	**Japan Air Lines Boeing 747**	**Crashed into Mt. Ogura, Japan; world's worst single-plane disaster**	**520**
1985, Dec. 12	Arrow Air (U.S.) DC-8	Crashed after takeoff from Gander, NL, Canada	256[8]
1986, Mar. 31	Mexican Boeing 727	Crashed NW of Mexico City, Mexico	167
1986, Aug. 31	Aeromexico DC-9, Piper PA-28	Collided over Cerritos, CA	82*
1987, May 9	Polish IL-62M	Crashed after takeoff from Warsaw, Poland	183
1987, Aug. 16	Northwest Airlines MD-82	Crashed after takeoff from Romulus, MI	156
1987, Nov. 28	S. African Boeing 747	Crashed into Indian Ocean near Mauritius	159
1987, Nov. 29	Korean Air Boeing 707	Bomb planted by 2 N. Korean agents exploded while plane over Andaman Sea off Burma	115
1988, Mar. 17	Colombian Boeing 707	Crashed into mountainside near Venezuela border	143
1988, July 3	**Iran Air Airbus A300**	**Misidentified as hostile aircraft, shot down by U.S. Navy warship *Vincennes* over Persian Gulf**	**290**
1988, Oct. 19	Indian Airlines Boeing 737	Exploded after striking trees near runway, Ahmedabad, India	131
1988, Dec. 21	**Pan Am (U.S.) Boeing 747**	**Bomb set by Libyan agent; exploded over Lockerbie, Scotland**	**270[9]**
1989, Feb. 8	U.S.-chartered Boeing 707	Crashed into mountain on Azores Isls., off Portugual	144
1989, June 7	Surinam Airways DC-8	Crashed near Paramaribo Airport, Suriname	176
1989, July 19	United Airlines DC-10	Defect in plane forced emergency landing in Sioux City, IA	111
1989, Sept. 3	Cubana Aviacion Ilyushin 62M	Crashed on takeoff from Havana, Cuba	171*
1989, Sept. 19	**UTA (France) DC-10**	**Bomb set by Libyan agents exploded on board flight from Congo (Brazzaville) to France while over desert in Niger**	**170**
1989, Oct. 21	TAN-SAHSA (Honduras) Boeing 727	Crashed into mountain near Tegucigalpa, Honduras	131
1989, Nov. 27	Avianca (Colombia) Boeing 727	Bomb exploded on flight from Bogotá, Colombia	107
1990, Jan. 25	Avianca (Colombia) Boeing 707	Crashed on landing at JFK Airport, New York, NY	73
1990, Oct. 2	Xiamen Airlines Boeing 737, China Southern Boeing 757	Hijacked after takeoff fr. Xiamen; collided with China Southern aircraft on runway during emergency landing, Guangzhou, China	128
1991, May 26	Lauda Air (Austria) Boeing 767-300	Broke up following takeoff from Bangkok, Thailand	223
1991, July 11	Nigeria Airways DC-8	Crashed on landing at Jidda, Saudi Arabia	261
1991, Oct. 5	U.S. Air Force Lockheed C-130 Hercules	Crashed after takeoff from Jakarta, Indonesia	135*
1992, July 31	Thai Airbus A300-310	Crashed into mountain N of Kathmandu, Nepal	113
1992, Sept. 26	Nigerian Air Force LC-130 Hercules	Transport full of military officers crashed near Lagos, Nigeria	158
1992, Sept. 28	Pakistan Intl. Air Airbus A300	Crashed into hillside near Kathmandu, Nepal	167
1992, Oct. 4	**El Al (Israel) Boeing 747-200F**	**Crashed into 2 apartment bldgs., Amsterdam, Netherlands**	**120***
1992, Nov. 24	China Southern Airlines Boeing 737	Crashed on approach to Giulin, China	141
1992, Dec. 22	Libyan Arab Air Boeing 727	Collided with Libyan Air Force MiG-23 on approach to Tripoli	159
1993, Feb. 8	Iran Air Tu-154, Iranian Air Force jet	Collided after military jet took off from Tehran, Iran	131
1993, May 19	SAM Colombia Boeing 727	Crashed into mountain near Medellín, Colombia	132
1993, Nov. 20	Macedonian Yakovlev 42D	Crashed into mountain near Skopje, Macedonia	116
1994, Jan. 3	Aeroflot Tu-154	Crashed and exploded after takeoff from Irkutsk, Russia	125*
1994, Apr. 26	China Airlines Airbus A300	Crashed on approach to Nagoya Airport, Japan	264
1994, June 6	China Northwest Airlines Tu-154	Crashed near Xian, China	160
1994, Sept. 8	USAir Boeing 737-300	Crashed near Pittsburgh Intl. Airport, Aliquippa, PA	132
1994, Oct. 31	American Eagle ATR-72-210	Crashed in field near Roselawn, IN	68
1995, Dec. 18	Zairean Lockheed L-188C Electra	Overloaded charter crashed in Lunda Norte, Angola	141
1995, Dec. 20	American Airlines Boeing 757	Crashed into mountain N of Cali, Colombia	159
1996, Jan. 8	African Air Antonov-32 cargo plane	Crashed into a market in Kinshasa, Zaire; all deaths on ground	237*
1996, Feb. 6	Alas Nacionales (Dom. Rep.) Boeing 757	Crashed into Atlantic off Dominican Republic	189
1996, Feb. 29	Faucett (Peru) Boeing 737	Crashed into hillside near Arequipa, Peru	123
1996, Apr. 3	U.S. Air Force Boeing T-43A	Crashed into mountain near Dubrovnik, Croatia	35[10]
1996, May 11	ValuJet DC-9	Crashed into Florida Everglades after improper cargo started fire	110
1996, July 17	Trans World Airlines Boeing 747	Exploded and crashed into Atlantic off Long Island, NY	230
1996, Aug. 29	Vnukovo Airlines (Russia) Tu-154	Crashed into mountain on Arctic island of Spitsbergen	141
1996, Nov. 7	ADC Airlines (Nigeria) Boeing 727	Crashed into lagoon SE of Lagos, Nigeria	144
1996, Nov. 12	**Saudi Arabian Boeing 747, Kazakh Ilyushin 76 cargo plane**	**Collided near New Delhi, India; world's worst midair collision**	**349**
1996, Nov. 23	Ethiopian Airlines Boeing 767	Hijacked; crashed into Indian O. off the Comoros (fuel ran out)	127
1997, Aug. 6	Korean Air Boeing 747-300	Crashed into jungle on Guam on approach to airport	228
1997, Sept. 26	Indonesian Airbus A300	Crashed near airport, Medan, Indonesia	234
1998, Feb. 16	China Airlines Airbus A300	Crashed on approach to airport in Taipei, Taiwan	203*
1998, Sept. 2	Swissair MD-11	Crashed into Atlantic off Nova Scotia, Canada, after onboard fire	229
1999, Oct. 31	EgyptAir Boeing 767	Crashed off Nantucket, MA; result of deliberate actions by copilot, motives unknown	217
2000, Jan. 30	Kenya Airways Airbus A310	Crashed into Atlantic after takeoff from Abidjan, Côte d'Ivoire	169
2000, Jan. 31	Alaska Airlines MD-83	Crashed into Pacific off coast of Southern CA	88
2000, Apr. 19	Air Philippines Boeing 737-200	Crashed on approach to airport, Davao, Philippines	131
2000, July 25	**Air France Concorde**	**Crashed into hotel after takeoff from Paris; world's first Concorde crash**	**113***

Date	Aircraft	Incident details, site	Deaths
2000, Aug. 23	Gulf Air Airbus A320	Crashed into Persian Gulf on approach to airport in Bahrain	143
2001, July 3	Vladivostokavia Tu-154	Crashed on approach to airport, Irkutsk, Russia	145
2001, Sept. 11	**2 Boeing 767s, 2 Boeing 757s**	**September 11 terrorist attacks**	**2651[11]**
2001, Oct. 8	Cessna 525A Citation, Scandinavian Airlines System (SAS) MD-87	Collided in heavy fog on takeoff from Milan, Italy	118*
2001, Nov. 12	**American Airlines Airbus A300**	**Crashed after takeoff from JFK Airport, New York, NY**	**265***
2002, Feb. 12	Iran Air Tours Tu-154	Crashed into mountain on approach to airport, Khorramabad, Iran	119
2002, Apr. 15	Air China Boeing 767	Crashed into mountain in rain and fog on approach to airport, Pusan, S. Korea	129
2002, May 4	EAS Airlines BAC 1-11	Crashed shortly after takeoff from Kano, Nigeria	149
2002, May 7	China Northern Airlines MD-82	Plunged into sea, apparently after a passenger started fire in cabin, NE China	112
2002, May 25	China Airlines Boeing 747	Broke apart in midair, plunged into Taiwan Strait en route to Hong Kong airport	225
2002, July 27	**Ukraine Air Force Sukhoi Su-27**	**Crashed while performing, Lviv, Ukraine; world's worst air-show crash**	**77[12]**
2002, Aug. 19	Russian Mi-26 transport helicopter	Hit by Chechen missile near Grozny, Chechnya	127
2003, Jan. 8	Turkish Airlines British Aerospace RJ-100	Crashed on approach to airport in Diyarbakir, Turkey	75
2003, Feb. 19	Iranian Revolutionary Guard Ilyushin 76	Crashed into mountain near Kerman, Iran; passengers were Revolutionary Guard members.	275
2003, May 26	Ukrain.-Medit. Airlines Yak-42	Crashed into mountain in fog approaching Trabzon, Turkey; passengers incl. Spanish peacekeepers returning from Afghan.	75
2003, July 8	Sudan Airways Boeing 737-200	Mechanical problems reported shortly after takeoff; crashed upon return to Port Sudan Airport	115
2003, Dec. 25	Union Transp. Africains Boeing 727	Overloading caused crash on takeoff from Cotonou, Benin	141
2004, Jan. 3	Flash Airlines Boeing 737-300	Crashed into Red Sea after takeoff from Sharm el Sheikh, Egypt	148
2004, Aug. 24	Volga-Aviaexpress Tu-134, Sibir Airlines Tu-154	2 planes that took off from Moscow crashed within minutes of each other; brought down by Chechen suicide bombers	90
2005, Aug. 14	Helios Airways Boeing 737-300	Crashed after air pressure failure on board, near Athens, Greece	121
2005, Aug. 16	W Caribbean Airways (Colombia) MD-82	Crashed after engine failure, near Machiques, Venezuela	160
2005, Sept. 5	Mandala Airlines Boeing 737-200	Crashed shortly after takeoff from Medan, Sumatra, Indonesia	145*
2005, Oct. 22	Bellview Airlines Boeing 737-200	Crashed during heavy electrical storm near Lagos, Nigeria	117
2005, Dec. 6	Islamic Rep. of Iran Air Force Lockheed C-130	Crashed into apartment building after reportedly attempting emergency landing back at airport, Tehran, Iran	116*
2005, Dec. 10	Sosoliso Airlines DC-9-30	Crashed during storm on approach to Port Harcourt, Nigeria	107
2006, May 3	Armavia Airbus A320	Crashed into Black Sea on approach to airport, Sochi, Russia	113
2006, July 9	S7 Airlines Airbus A310	Skidded off runway, crashed into concrete barrier after landing, Irkutsk, Russia	125
2006, Aug. 22	Pulkovo Aviation Tu-154	Crashed after encountering storm, near Donetsk, Ukraine	170
2006, Sept. 29	Gol Airlines Boeing 737	Crashed into Amazon jungle after midair collision with Embraer Legacy jet (which itself landed safely), Brazil	154
2007, May 5	Kenya Airways Boeing 737-800	Crashed shortly after takeoff from Douala, Cameroon	114
2007, July 17	TAM Airlines Airbus 320	Crashed into cargo depot, gas station after skidding off runway, São Paulo, Brazil	199*
2008, Aug. 20	Spanair Boeing-MD-82	Swerved off runway, caught fire on takeoff attempt, Madrid, Spain	154
2009, Feb. 12	Colgan Air Bombardier Dash 8 Q400	Crashed into house after pilot error caused stall near Buffalo, NY	50*
2009, June 1	**Air France Airbus A330**	**Plunged into Atlantic Ocean en route from Rio de Janeiro, Brazil, to Paris, France**	**228**
2009, June 30	Yemenia Airbus A310-300	Crashed into Indian Ocean after stalling on approach to Comoros	152
2009, July 15	Caspian Airlines Tupolev 154	Crashed after takeoff from Tehran, Iran	168
2010, Apr. 10	Polish Air Force Tupolev 154M	Crashed on approach to Smolensk Air Base, killing Polish Pres. Lech Kaczynski, his wife, and several members of parliament	96
2010, May 12	Afriqiyah Airways Airbus A330-200	Crashed short of runway in Tripoli, Libya	103
2010, May 22	Air India Express Boeing 737-800	Overran runway on landing at Mangalore, India	158
2010, July 28	Airblue Airbus 321-231	Crashed into Margalla Hills near Islamabad, Pakistan	152
2012, Apr. 20	Bhoja Airlines Boeing 737-236	Crashed on approach to airport in Islamabad, Pakistan	127
2012, June 3	Dana Air MD-83	Crashed into residential area of Lagos, Nigeria	163*
2014, Mar. 8	Malaysia Airlines Boeing 777	Disappeared over S Indian O. en route fr. Kuala Lumpur to Beijing	239
2014, July 17	Malaysia Airlines Boeing 777	Shot down by Russian missile over disputed eastern Ukraine	298
2014, July 24	Air Algérie Boeing-MD-83	Crashed in desert near Gossi, Mali	116
2014, Dec. 28	Indonesia AirAsia Airbus A320-216	Disappeared over Java Sea between Surabaya and Singapore	162
2015, Mar. 24	Germanwings Airbus A320-211	Copilot deliberately crashed aircraft into French Alps	150
2015, June 30	Indonesian Air Force Lockheed C-130B	Transport plane crashed near Medan Soewondo Air Force Base	139*
2015, Oct. 31	Metrojet Airbus A321-231	Bomb detonated on board after takeoff fr. Sharm el Sheikh, Egypt	224
2016, Nov. 28	LaMia (Bolivia) Avro RJ85	Ran out of fuel and crashed near Medellín, Colombia; passengers incl. Brazilian Chapecoense soccer team	71
2016, Dec. 25	Russian Air Force Tupolev 154B-2	Crashed into Black Sea after takeoff from Sochi, Russia	92
2017, June 7	Myanmar Air Force Shaanxi Y-8-200F	Crashed into Andaman Sea en route to Yangon, Myanmar	122
2018, Apr. 11	Algerian military transport Ilyushin 76	Crashed after takeoff from near Algiers; passengers included Western Sahara separatists, refugees	257
2018, May 18	Cubana de Aviación Boeing 737	Aging aircraft crashed after takeoff from Havana, Cuba	112
2018, Oct. 29	Lion Air Boeing 737 Max 8	Crashed into Java Sea shortly after takeoff from Jakarta, Indonesia	189[13]
2019, Mar. 10	Ethiopian Airlines Boeing 737 Max 8	Crashed minutes after takeoff from Addis Ababa	157[13]
2020, Jan. 8	Ukrainian Airlines Boeing 737-800	Shot down by two Iranian missiles after takeoff from Tehran	176
2020, Jan. 26	Privately-operated Sikorsky S-76B helicopter	Crashed in bad visibility into hillside nr. Calabasas, CA, carrying retired NBA player Kobe Bryant, his daughter, others	9

Date	Aircraft	Incident details, site	Deaths
2022, Mar. 21	China Eastern Boeing 737-800	Suspected deliberate crash into mountainous area near Wuzhou, Guangxi Prov., China	132
2023, Aug. 23	Embraer ERJ-135BJ Legacy 600	Crashed en route to St. Petersburg, Russia, killing all aboard, including Wagner mercenary group chief, in suspected sabotage	10
2024, May 20	Bell 212 helicopter	Crashed in fog in NW Iran with Iranian Pres. Ebrahim Raisi and foreign min. among those on board	8

(1) Bomb planted by Jack G. Graham in insurance plot to kill his mother, Daisie E. King, a passenger. (2) 84 on plane, 71 on ground killed. (3) Incl. 43 Marshall Univ. (WV) football players and coaches. (4) Fighter pilot parachuted to safety. (5) First supersonic plane crash; killed 8 on ground. (6) Crew of 3, 88 on ground killed. (7) Incl. 22 members of U.S. amateur boxing team. (8) Incl. 8 crew and 248 members of U.S. 101st Airborne Division returning from peacekeeping mission in Sinai, Egypt. (9) Incl. 11 on ground. (10) Incl. U.S. Sec. of Commerce Ron Brown. (11) 4 planes were hijacked and crashed, with all on board killed (265, incl. 19 hijackers). American Airlines Flight 11 (Boeing 767-200) with 81 passengers, 11 crew crashed into Tower 1 of World Trade Center (WTC); United Airlines Flight 175 (Boeing 767-200) with 56 passengers, 9 crew crashed into Tower 2 of WTC; American Airlines Flight 77 (Boeing 757-200) with 58 passengers, 6 crew crashed into Pentagon outside Washington, DC; United Airlines Flight 93 (Boeing 757-200), with 37 passengers, 7 crew crashed near Shanksville, PA. The official death toll of 2,997 includes those who died on the ground at the Pentagon and the WTC, and 3 later victims whose deaths the NYC chief medical examiner ruled were caused by exposure to toxic dust created by the disaster. Does not include those with cancers and other medical conditions related to WTC site exposure. (12) The two pilots ejected to safety. All spectator deaths. (13) Two fatal crashes, possibly due to faulty sensors and software, led to worldwide grounding of Boeing 737 Max series.

Some Notable Shipwrecks Since 1854

Does not include most wartime disasters.

Date—vessel(s)	Incident	Deaths
1854, Mar. 1—City of Glasgow	British steamer left Liverpool for Philadelphia, never heard from again	480
1854, Sept. 27—Arctic and Vesta	U.S. Collins Line steamer sunk in collision with French steamer nr. Cape Race, Canada	285-351
1856, Jan. 23—Pacific	U.S. Collins Line steamer went missing in N Atlantic	186-286
1857, Sept. 12—Central America	U.S. mail steamship sank off Florida coast with $1.5 mil in gold	427
1858, Sept. 23—Austria	German steamer destroyed by fire in N Atlantic	471
1863, Apr. 27—Anglo-Saxon	British steamer wrecked at Cape Race, Canada	238
1865, Apr. 27—Sultana	Mississippi R. steamer carrying 2,400 released Union prisoners exploded nr. Memphis, TN. Worst maritime disaster in U.S. history	1,800
1869, Feb. 20—Radetzky	Austrian steam frigate exploded in Adriatic Sea	345
1869, Oct. 27—Stonewall	U.S. steamer burned, Mississippi R. below Cairo, IL	200
1872, Nov. 7—Mary Celeste	U.S. half-brig sailing from New York City to Genoa, Italy, with 10 on board found abandoned	Unknown
1873, Jan. 22—Northfleet	British steamer at anchor struck by Spanish steamer *Murillo* off Dungeness, England, UK	300
1873, Apr. 1—Atlantic	British White Star steamer off Halifax, Nova Scotia, Canada	585
1873, Nov. 23—Ville du Havre and Loch Earn	French steamer sank after collision with British sailing ship	226
1874, Nov. 17—Cospatrick	En route from London to NZ, caught fire off Cape of Good Hope	468
1875, May 7—Schiller	German steamer off Isles of Scilly, UK	312
1875, Nov. 4—Pacific	U.S. steamer sank after collision off Cape Flattery, WA	236
1878, Mar. 24—Eurydice	British frigate sank off Isle of Wight, England, UK	398
1878, Sept. 3—Princess Alice	British steamer sank after collision with *Bywell Castle* in Thames R.	700
1878, Dec. 18—Byzantin and Rinaldo	French and British steamers collided in Dardanelles, off Turkey	210
1883, Jan. 19—Cimbria and Sultan	German steamer sank in collision with British steamer in North Sea	389
1887, Nov. 15—Wah Yeung	Chinese steamer burned in Canton R., Hong Kong	400
1890, Feb. 17—Duburg	British steamer wrecked, China Sea	400
1890, Sept. 16—Ertugrul	Ottoman frigate in typhoon off Japan	587
1891, Mar. 17—Utopia and Anson	British steamer sank in collision with British ironclad off Gibraltar	562
1893, June 22—Victoria	British battleship sank after collision with British warship *Camperdown*, off Syrian coast	358
1895, Jan. 30—Elbe and Craithie	German steamer sank in collision with British steamer in North Sea	332
1895, Mar. 11—Reina Regenta	Spanish cruiser foundered nr. Gibraltar	400
1898, Feb. 15—USS Maine	Explosion caused battleship to sink in Havana Harbor, Cuba	260
1898, July 4—La Bourgogne and Cromartyshire	French steamer sank in collision with British sailing ship off Nova Scotia, Canada	549
1904, May 15—Yoshino	Japanese cruiser sank after collision with cruiser *Kasuga* in fog off Liao-Tung Peninsula, China	329
1904, June 15—General Slocum	Excursion steamer burned off N. Brother Isl., New York, NY	1,021
1904, June 28—Norge	Danish steamer wrecked on Rockall Isl., Scotland, UK	620
1906, Aug. 4—Sirio	Italian steamer wrecked off Cape Palos, Spain	350
1907, Feb. 11—Larchmont	U.S. steamer sank after collision with U.S. schooner *Harry Knowlton* nr. Block Island, RI	131
1908, Mar. 23—Mutsu Maru	Japanese steamer sank in collision with another steamer nr. Hakodate, Japan	300
1909, July 26—Waratah	British steamer vanished en route from Durban to Cape Town, So. Africa	300
1911, Sept. 25—Liberté	French battleship exploded at Toulon	285
1912, Apr. 14-15—Titanic	British White Star steamer hit iceberg in N Atlantic	1,503
1912, Sept. 28—Kichemaru	Japanese steamer sank off Japan coast	1,000
1914, May 29—Empress of Ireland	Canadian Pacific steamer collided with Norwegian coal transporter *Storstad* in St. Lawrence R., Canada	1,014
1914, Nov. 26—Bulwark	British battleship exploded in Sheerness Harbor, England, UK	788
1915, May 7—Lusitania	British Cunard Line steamer torpedoed and sunk by German submarine off Ireland	1,198
1915, July 24—Eastland	Steamer capsized, Chicago R., IL	844
1916, Feb. 26—Provence	French cruiser sank in Mediterranean; then-worst maritime disaster	3,100
1916, Mar. 5—Principe de Asturias	Spanish steamer wrecked nr. Santos, Brazil	558

Date—vessel(s)	Incident	Deaths
1917, Dec. 6—Mont Blanc and Imo	French ammunition ship and Belgian steamer collided in Halifax Harbor, Canada	1,900+
1918, Apr. 25—Kiang-Kwan	Chinese steamer sank after collision with Chinese gunboat *Chutai* off Hankow, China	500
1918, July 12—Kawachi	Japanese battleship blew up in Tokayama Bay	500
1918, Oct. 25—Princess Sophia	Canadian-Pacific steamer sank off Vanderbilt Reef, Alaska	398
1919, Jan. 17—Chaonia	French steamer lost in Straits of Messina, Italy	460
1919, Sept. 9—Valbanera	Spanish steamer lost off FL coast	500
1920, Jan. 11—Afrique	French liner sank nr. La Rochelle, France	553
1921, Mar. 18—Hong Kong	Chinese steamer wrecked, S China Sea	1,000
1922, Aug. 26—Niitaka	Japanese cruiser sank in storm off Kamchatka, USSR	300
1927, Sept. 20—Gentoku Maru	Japanese steamer capsized in Tsingtao Bay, China	278
1927, Oct. 25—Principessa Mafalda	Italian steamer blew up, sank off Porto Seguro, Brazil	314
1934, Sept. 8—Morro Castle	U.S. steamer en route from Havana to NY, burned off Asbury Park, NJ	134
1940, June 17—Lancastria	Nazi forces sank Cunard liner evacuating British troops from France	2,500-6,000
1940, July 24—Meknes	French liner torpedoed by Nazis in English Channel	350
1942, Feb. 18—USS Truxtun and USS Pollux	Destroyer and cargo ship ran aground, sank off Newfoundland, Canada	204
1942, Oct. 2—Curacao and Queen Mary	British cruiser sank off Ireland after collision with liner carrying U.S. troops	338
1943, Nov. 26—HMT Rohna	Transport with U.S. soldiers sunk by German bomber off Algerian coast; largest U.S. troop loss at sea due to enemy action	1,149
1944, Dec. 17-18—Spence, Monaghan, Hull	3 U.S. destroyers sank during typhoon, Philippine Sea	790
1945, Jan. 30—Wilhelm Gustloff	Liner with German refugees, soldiers sunk by Soviet submarine in Baltic	5,000-9,000
1945, Apr. 16—Goya	Cargo ship carrying German refugees, soldiers sunk by Soviet submarine in Baltic	6,000-7,000
1945, May 3—Cap Arcona and Thielbeck	German ocean liner and freighter carrying concentration camp inmates sunk by British warplanes in Lubeck Bay, Germany	7,000-8,000
1947, Jan. 19—Heimara	Greek steamer hit rocks off Athens, Greece	392
1947, Apr. 16—Grandcamp	Ammonium nitrate explosion aboard French freighter caused fires throughout port, Texas City, TX	576+
1948, Dec. 4—Kiangya	Ship with Chinese Civil War refugees hit WWII-era landmine on Huangpu R., S of Shanghai	3,920
1949, Jan. 27—Taiping and Chienyuan	Ship with Chinese Civil War refugees collided with cargo ship near Zhoushan Archipelago	1,500
1954, Sept. 26—Toya Maru	Japanese ferry sank, Tsugaru Strait, Japan	1,172
1956, July 26—Andrea Doria and Stockholm	Italian liner and Swedish liner collided off Nantucket Isl., MA	51
1957, July 14—Eshghabad	Soviet fishing boat ran aground in Caspian Sea	270
1961, Apr. 8—Dara	British liner exploded in Persian Gulf	236
1961, July 8—Save	Portuguese ship ran aground off Mozambique	259
1965, Nov. 13—Yarmouth Castle	Cruise ship burned and sank off Nassau, The Bahamas	89
1970, Dec. 15—Namyong-Ho	S. Korean ferry sank in Korea Strait	308
1975, Nov. 10—Edmund Fitzgerald	U.S. cargo ship sank during storm on Lake Superior	29
1976, Oct. 20—George Prince	Mississippi R. ferry collided with Norwegian tanker *Frosta*, Luling, LA	77
1980, Apr. 22—Don Juan	Sank off Mindoro Isl., Philippines, after colliding with barge	1,000+
1981, Jan. 27—Tamponas II	Indonesian car ferry caught fire and sank in Java Sea	580
1983, May 25—10th of Ramadan	Nile steamer caught fire and sank in Lake Nasser, Egypt	357
1986, May 25—Shamia	Ferry capsized in storm, Meghna R., Bangladesh	500+
1986, Sept. 1—Admiral Nakhimov and Pyotr Vasev	Soviet cruise ship collided with Soviet freighter in Black Sea	425
1987, Dec. 20—Doña Paz and Vector	Philippine ferry and oil tanker collided in Tablas Strait, Philippines	4,385
1988, Aug. 6	Indian ferry capsized on Ganges R.	400+
1988, Oct. 24—Doña Marilyn	Philippine ferry sank by typhoon near Leyte Isl.	350+
1991, Dec. 14—Salem Express	Ferry rammed coral reef nr. Safaga, Egypt	462
1993, Feb. 17—Neptune	Ferry capsized during heavy rainfall off Port-au-Prince, Haiti	500+
1993, Oct. 10—Seohae	S. Korean ferry capsized in Yellow Sea during storm	292
1994, Sept. 28—Estonia	Ferry en route from Estonia to Sweden sank in Baltic Sea off Finland	852
1996, May 21—Bukoba	Overcrowded Tanzanian ferry sank in Lake Victoria	500+
1997, Sept. 8—Pride of la Gonâve	Haitian ferry sank off Montrouis, Haiti	200+
1999, Feb. 6—Harta Rimba	Cargo ship sank off Indonesia	280+
1999, May 1—Miss Majestic	"Duck" boat on tour sank, Lake Hamilton, AR	13
1999, Nov. 24—Dashun	Passenger ferry capsized nr. Yantai, China	280
2000, June 29—Cahaya Bahari	Overloaded ferry carrying refugees from religious strife capsized in storm off Sulawesi Isl., Indonesia	500+
2001, Oct. 19	Fishing boat overloaded with refugees, mainly from Middle East, sank off Indonesia	350+
2002, May 4—Salahuddin-2	Overloaded Bangladesh ferry sank in Meghna R.	300+
2002, Sept. 26—Joola	Overloaded Senegalese ferry capsized in ocean off The Gambia	1,863
2003, July 8—MV-Nasrin 1	Overcrowded ferry sank nr. Chandpur in Bangladesh R.	400
2004, Feb. 27—Superferry 14	Philippine ferry bombed by Islamic militants; deadliest terrorist attack at sea	116
2006, Feb. 3—Al-Salam Boccaccio 98	Ferry caught fire, sank in Red Sea off Egypt	1,000+
2006, Dec. 30—Senopati Nusantara	High waves capsized ferry en route to Java, Indonesia	400+
2007, Nov. 23—Explorer	Canadian cruise ship hit Antarctic iceberg; first commercial passenger ship to sink in region	0
2008, June 23—Princess of the Stars	Philippine ferry capsized during Typhoon *Fengshen* nr. Manila	800
2011, Sept. 10—MV Spice Islander	Overloaded ferry sank off coast of Tanzania	240+
2012, Jan. 17—Costa Concordia	Cruise ship ran aground off Italian coast; captain abandoned ship before evacuating passengers	32
2013, Oct. 3	Boat carrying migrants fleeing Eritrea sank near Lampedusa Isl., Italy	360
2014, Apr. 16—Sewol	Ferry carrying 476 people, most students, Korea's SW coast	304
2015, June 1—Dongfangzhixing (Eastern Star)	Chinese cruise ship sank in Yangtze R. during torrential rains	442
2015, Oct. 1—El Faro	Cargo ship en route from FL to Puerto Rico sailed into hurricane	33
2018, June 18—Sinar Bangun	Overloaded ferry sank in bad weather, Lake Toba, Sumatra, Indonesia	167

Date—vessel(s)	Incident	Deaths
2018, July 19	"Duck" boat sank in a severe storm, Table Rock Lake, nr. Branson, MO	17
2018, Sept. 20—MV Nyerere	Overloaded Tanzanian ferry capsized in Lake Victoria	227+
2019, Sept. 2—Conception	Dive boat caught fire nr. Santa Cruz Isl., CA, while passengers slept	34

Note: Deaths of migrants and refugees trying to cross the Mediterranean Sea began to spike in 2014. The UN's Intl. Organization for Migration reported the following figures for dead and missing in the Mediterranean: 3,538 (2014), 3,771 (2015), 5,096 (2016), 3,139 (2017), 2,277 (2018), 1,510 (2019), 1,881 (2020), 3,231 (2021), 3,017 (2022), 4,110 (2023), and 629 (2024, as of June 9).

Some Notable Railroad Disasters Since 1925

Date	Location	Deaths
1925, June 16	Hackettstown, NJ	50
1933, Dec. 23	Lagny-Pomponne, France	230
1937, July 16	Near Patna, India	107
1938, Dec. 25	Near Kishinev, Romania	150
1939, Dec. 22	Genthin, near Magdeburg, Germany	132
1943, Sept. 6	Frankford Junction, Philadelphia, PA	79
1943, Dec. 16	Between Rennert and Buie, NC	72
1944, Jan. 16	León Province, Spain	500
1944, Mar. 2	Salerno, Italy	521
1944, Dec. 31	Bagley, UT	50
1945, July 16	Munich, Germany	102
1946, Mar. 20	Aracaju, Brazil	185
1949, Oct. 22	Near Nowy Dwór, Poland	200+
1950, Nov. 22	Richmond Hill, Queens, NY	79
1951, Feb. 6	Woodbridge, NJ	84
1952, Mar. 4	Near Rio de Janeiro, Brazil	119
1952, July 9	Rzepin, Poland	160
1952, Oct. 8	Harrow, England, UK	112
1953, Dec. 24	Tangiwai, New Zealand	151
1953, Dec. 24	Sakvice, Czechoslovakia	103
1955, Apr. 3	Guadalajara, Mexico	300
1957, Sept. 1	Kendal, Jamaica	178
1957, Sept. 29	Montgomery, W Pakistan	300
1957, Dec. 4	London, England, UK	90
1958, May 8	Rio de Janeiro, Brazil	128
1960, Nov. 14	Pardubice, Czechoslovakia	117
1962, May 3	Tokyo, Japan	163
1963, Nov. 9	Yokohama, Japan	162
1965, Feb. 27	Near Port Sudan, Sudan	124
1970, Feb. 1	Buenos Aires, Argentina	236
1972, June 16	Near Soissons, France	108
1972, Oct. 6	Near Saltillo, Mexico	204
1974, Aug. 30	Zagreb, Yugoslavia	153
1981, June 6	Bihar, India	268+
1982, Jan. 27	El Asnam, Algeria	120
1982, July 11	Tepic, Mexico	120
1983, Feb. 19	Empalme, Mexico	100
1985, Jan. 13	Awash, Ethiopia	392
1985, Sept. 12	Viseu, Portugal	118
1986, Aug. 6	Bihar, India	202
1987, July 2	Kasumbalesha Shaba, Zaire	125
1987, Aug. 7	Between Moscow and Rostov, USSR	106
1987, Oct. 19	Jakarta, Indonesia	153
1988, June 4	Arzamas, USSR	100
1988, July 8	Kerala, India	108
1989, Jan. 15	Maizdi Khan, Bangladesh	135
1989, June 4	Ufa, USSR	645
1989, Aug. 11	San Rafael R., Sinaloa State, Mexico	112
1990, Jan. 4	Sindh Province, Pakistan	307
1991, Mar. 5	Nacala, Mozambique	109
1991, June 8	Ghotki, Pakistan	100
1991, Sept. 5	Pointe-Noire, Congo Republic	110
1993, Jan. 30	Near Mtito Andei, Kenya	140+
1993, Apr. 25	Near Karachi, Pakistan	150
1994, Sept. 22	Lubango, Angola	300
1994, Dec. 30	Near Namkham, Myanmar	102
1995, Jan. 13	Dinajpur, Bangladesh	150
1995, Aug. 20	Firozabad, Uttar Pradesh, India	350
1995, Nov. 28	Baku, Azerbaijan	337
1997, Mar. 3	Punjab Province, Pakistan	128
1997, May 4	Kisangani, Zaire	100+
1998, Feb. 19	Yaounde, Cameroon	120
1998, June 3	Eschede, Germany	102
1998, Nov. 26	Khanna, India	108
1999, Aug. 2	Gaisal, West Bengal, India	285
2002, Feb. 20	S of Cairo, Egypt	377
2002, May 25	Muamba, Mozambique	195
2002, June 24	Igandu, Tanzania	281
2002, Sept. 10	Bihar, India	112
2004, Feb. 18	Neyshabur, NE Iran	300
2004, Apr. 22	Ryongchon, North Korea	161
2005, Apr. 25	Near Amagasaki, Japan	107
2005, July 13	Ghotki, Pakistan	132
2005, Oct. 29	Veligonda, Andhra Pradesh, India	110
2007, Aug. 2	Nr. Benaleka, Dem. Rep. of Congo	100
2010, May 28	W. Bengal, India	148
2011, July 23	Wenzhou, China	140
2016, Nov. 20	Kanpur, Uttar Pradesh, India	146
2019, Oct. 31	Rahim Yar Khan, Pakistan	75
2021, Apr. 2	Hualien, Taiwan	49
2023, Feb. 28	Tempe, Greece	57
2023, June 2	Odisha, India	293

Notable Droughts

Source: EM-DAT: The International Disaster Database, CRED/UC Louvain, Belgium, www.emdat.be; World Almanac research

Date	Location	Est. deaths
1900	Bengal, India	1,250,000
1900	Cape Verde islands	11,000
1910-14	Zinder Dept., Niger	85,000
1920	China	500,000
1920	Cape Verde islands	24,000
1921	S Ukraine, Volga, USSR	1,200,000
1928-30	Shaanxi, Henan, Gansu, China	3,000,000
1940-44	Cape Verde islands	20,000
1942	Calcutta, Bengal, India	1,500,000
1943	Bangladesh	1,900,000
1946	Cape Verde islands	30,000
1965	Ethiopia	2,000
1965-67	India	1,500,000
1966	Lombok, Indonesia	8,000
1973-78	Ethiopia	100,000
1974-76	Somalia	19,000
1981-85	Mozambique	100,000
1981-85	Chad	3,000
1983	Swaziland	500
1983-84	Eritrea, Ethiopia	300,000
1983-85	N Sudan	150,000
1987	Somalia, Eritrea, Ethiopia	967
1987	NW India	300
1988	Central China	1,400
1991	Jiangxi, Hunan Provinces, China	2,000
1997	Irian Jaya, Indonesia	672
1999-2003	Pakistan	143
2002	Malawi	500
2006	SW China	134
2014-17	Tharparkar, Pakistan	166
2022	Somalia	43,000

Some Notable Miscellaneous Disasters Since 1950

Date	Event	Location	Details	Est. deaths
1952, Dec.	Pollution	London, England, UK	Heavy smog blanketed city; impeded breathing	4,000
1959-61	Famine	China	Govt. policies compounded by flooding and drought	15-40 mil
1980, summer	Extreme heat	Central, eastern U.S.	Combined direct and indirect deaths est. at 10,000	1,260
1984, Dec. 3	Industrial accident	Bhopal, India	Toxic gas leaked from a Union Carbide factory	16,000
1986, Aug. 21	Gas	Nr. Lake Nyos, Cameroon	Volcanic lake released cloud of carbon dioxide gas	1,700
1990, July 2	Stampede	Mecca, Saudi Arabia	Pilgrims panicked in tunnel leading to the holy city	1,426
1995, June 29	Building collapse	Seoul, South Korea	Improperly built and maintained Sampoong Dept. Store failed with shoppers inside	501

Date	Event	Location	Details	Est. deaths
2003, summer	Extreme heat	Europe	Italy (20,089 deaths) and France (19,490) suffered most	72,210
2005, Aug. 31	Stampede	Baghdad, Iraq	Rumors of suicide bomber caused panic among religious pilgrims on al-Aimmah Bridge	965
2010, summer	Extreme heat	Russia	Prolonged heat also triggered wildfires	55,000
2013, Apr. 24	Building collapse	Savar, Bangladesh	Garment factory found to have substandard foundation	1,100+
2015, Sept. 24	Stampede	Mina, Saudi Arabia	Two groups of pilgrims collided during hajj to Mecca	2,411
2017, Aug. 14	Landslide	Freetown, Sierra Leone	Rain, deforestation partially collapsed Sugar Loaf Mt.	1,141
2019, July 21-27	Extreme heat	France	Record temperatures across Europe	868
2021, June 25-July 1	Extreme heat	British Columbia, Canada	Heat dome caused record temperatures	619
2022, summer	Extreme heat	Europe	Europe's hottest summer on record	61,672

Some Notable U.S. Tornadoes Since 1925

Date	Location	Deaths
1925, Mar. 18	Tri-State (MO, IL, IN)	695
1927, Apr. 12	Rocksprings, TX	74
1927, May 9	AR; Poplar Bluff, MO	92
1927, Sept. 29	St. Louis, MO	90
1930, May 6	Hill, Navarro, Ellis Cos., TX	41
1932, Mar. 21	Alabama	268
1936, Apr. 5-6	Tupelo, MS-Gainesville, GA	419+
1938, Sept. 29	Charleston, SC	32
1942, Mar. 16	Central to NE Mississippi	75
1942, Apr. 27	Rogers and Mayes Cos., OK	52
1944, June 23	OH, PA, WV, MD	150
1945, Apr. 12	OK, AR	102
1947, Apr. 9	TX; Woodward, OK; KS	181
1948, Mar. 19	Bunker Hill and Gillespie, IL	33
1949, Jan. 3	LA, AR	58
1952, Mar. 21-22	AR, MO, TN	208
1953, May 11	Waco, TX	114
1953, June 8	Flint-Beecher, MI	116
1953, June 9	Worcester and vicinity, MA	90
1953, Dec. 5	Vicksburg, MS	38
1955, May 25	Udall, KS; MO; Blackwell, OK; TX	115
1957, May 20	KS, MO	48
1958, June 4	NW Wisconsin	30
1959, Feb. 10	St. Louis, MO	21
1960, May 5-6	Southeastern OK, AR	30
1965, Apr. 11	IA, IN, IL, OH, MI, WI	271
1966, Mar. 3	Jackson, MS; AL	57
1967, Apr. 21	IL, MO, IA, MI	33
1968, May 15	Midwest	71
1969, Jan. 23	Mississippi	32
1970, May 11	Lubbock, TX	23
1971, Feb. 21	Mississippi Delta: MS, LA, AR, TN	110
1973, May 26-27	South, Midwest	47
1974, Apr. 3-4	AL; GA; KY; Xenia, OH; other states	315
1977, Apr. 4	AL, MS, GA	22
1979, Apr. 10	TX, OK	60
1984, Mar. 28	NC, SC	57
1985, May 31	NY; PA; OH; Ontario, Can.	75
1987, May 22	Saragosa, TX	30
1989, Nov. 15	Huntsville, AL	18
1990, Aug. 28	Northern IL	25
1991, Apr. 26	KS, OK	23
1992, Nov. 21-23	South, Midwest	26
1994, Mar. 27-28	AL, TN, GA, NC, SC	52
1995, May 6-7	Southern OK, northern TX	23
1997, Mar. 1	Central AR	26
1997, May 27	Jarrell, TX	27
1998, Feb. 22-23	Central FL	42
1998, Apr. 8	AL, GA, MS	39
1999, May 3	OK, KS	54
2000, Feb. 14	SW Georgia	22+
2002, Nov. 10-11	AL, MS, TN, IN, OH, PA	36
2003, May 4-11	TN, MO, KS, IL, OK, WV, AL	48
2005, Nov. 6	KY, IN	22
2007, Mar. 1	AL, GA, MO, Midwest	20
2008, Feb. 25	TN, AR, KY, AL, MO	57
2008, May 10	MS, OK, GA	23
2011, Apr. 14-16	Southeast, Midwest, OK to VA	38
2011, Apr. 25-28	362 funnels from TX to NY	321
2011, May 22	Joplin, MO	161
2012, Mar. 2-3	Southeast, Ohio Valley (AL, GA, IN, KY, OH, TN)	42
2013, May 20	Moore, OK	24
2013, May 31	El Reno, OK	21
2017, Jan. 20-22	AL, FL, GA, LA, MS, SC, TX	20
2021, Dec. 10-11	AR; Edwardsville, IL; Mayfield, KY; MO; TN	90+
2023, Mar. 31-Apr. 1	IL, IN, OH, MO, IA, AR, TN, PA	33

Some Notable Hurricanes, Typhoons, Blizzards, Other Storms

C. = cyclone; H. = hurricane; TS. = tropical storm; T. = typhoon.[1]

Date	Location	Est. deaths
1881, Aug. 24-29	H., GA, SC	700
1888, Mar. 11-14	Blizzard, Eastern U.S.	400
1893, Aug. 15-Sept. 2	H., GA, SC	1,000+
1893, Oct. 1	H., LA	1,100+
1900, Sept. 8	H., Galveston, TX	8,000+
1906, Sept. 18	T., Hong Kong	10,000+
1906, Sept. 19-24	H., LA, MS	350
1909, Sept. 20	H., LA	350+
1915, Aug. 16	H., Galveston, TX	275
1915, Sept. 29	H., LA	275
1919, Sept. 6-14	H., Carib., FL Keys, Gulf, TX	600+[2]
1922, July 27	T., Swatow, China	100,000
1926, Sept. 11-22	H., FL, AL, MS	370+
1926, Oct. 20	H., Cuba	600
1928, Sept. 6-20	H., southern FL	2,500+
1930, Sept. 3	H., Dominican Republic	2,000
1935, Aug. 29-Sept. 10	H., Caribbean, SE U.S.	400+
1937, Sept. 2	T., Hong Kong	10,000+
1938, Sept. 21	H., NY, New England	682
1940, Nov. 11-12	NE, Midwest U.S.	154
1942, Oct.	T., W. Sundarbans, Bangladesh	61,000
1942, Oct. 15-16	H., Bengal, India	40,000
1947, Dec. 26	Blizzard, NYC, N Atl. states	55
1952, Oct. 22	T., Philippines	440
1954, Aug. 30	H. Carol, NE U.S.	68
1954, Oct. 5-18	H. Hazel, E Canada, U.S., Haiti	347
1955, Aug. 7-21	H. Diane, Eastern U.S.	400
1955, Sept. 19	H. Hilda, Mexico	200
1956, Feb. 1-29	Blizzard, W Europe	1,000
1957, June 25-30	H. Audrey, TX to AL	390
1958, Feb. 15-16	Blizzard, NE U.S.	171
1959, Sept. 17-19	T. Sarah, Japan, S. Korea	2,000
1959, Sept. 26-27	T. Vera, Honshu, Japan	4,466
1960, Sept. 4-12	H. Donna, Caribbean, E U.S.	148
1961, Oct. 31	H. Hattie, Brit. Honduras	400
1962, Sept. 1	T. Wanda, Hong Kong	130-200
1963, May 28-29	Windstorm, Bangladesh	22,000
1963, Oct. 4-8	H. Flora, Caribbean	6,000
1964, June 30	T. Winnie, N Philippines	107
1964, Sept. 5	T. Ruby, Hong Kong, China	735
1965, May 11-12	Windstorm, Bangladesh	17,000
1965, June 1-2	Windstorm, Bangladesh	30,000
1965, Sept. 7-12	H. Betsy, FL, MS, LA	74
1965, Dec. 15	Windstorm, Bangladesh	10,000
1966, June 4-10	H. Alma, Honduras, SE U.S.	51
1966, Sept. 24-30	H. Inez, Carib., FL, Mexico	293
1967, July 9	T. Billie, SW Japan	347
1967, Sept. 5-23	H. Beulah, Carib., Mex., TX	54
1967, Dec. 12-20	Blizzard, SW U.S.	51
1969, Aug. 17-18	H. Camille, MS, LA	256
1970, Sept. 15	T. Pitang (Georgia), Philippines	300
1970, Oct. 14	T. Sening (Joan), Philippines	583
1970, Oct. 15	T. Titang (Kate), Philippines	526

Date	Location	Est. deaths
1970, Nov. 13	C. Bhola, Bay of Bengal, Bangladesh.	300,000
1971, Aug. 1	T. Rose, Hong Kong.	130
1972, June 19-29	H. Agnes, FL to NY.	118
1972, Dec. 3	T. Theresa, Philippines.	169
1973, Apr. 26-30	C. Flores, Indonesia	1,650
1973, June-Aug.	Monsoon rains, India	1,217
1974, July 11	T. Gilda, Japan, S. Korea	108
1974, Sept. 19-20	H. Fifi, Honduras.	2,000
1975, Sept. 13-27	H. Eloise, Caribbean, NE U.S.	71
1976, May 20	T. Olga, floods, Philippines.	215
1976, Sept. 25-Oct. 2	H. Liza, western Mexico	630
1978, Oct. 27	T. Rita, Philippines	400
1979, Aug. 30-Sept. 7	H. David, Caribbean, E U.S.	1,100
1980, Aug. 4-11	H. Allen, Caribbean, TX	272
1981, Nov. 25	T. Irma, Luzon Isl., Philippines	176
1983, June	Monsoon, India.	900
1984, Sept. 2	T. Ike, southern Philippines	1,363
1985, May 25	C., Bangladesh.	15,000
1985, Oct. 26-Nov. 6	H. Juan, SE U.S.	97
1987, Nov. 25	T. Nina, Philippines.	650
1988, Sept. 10-17	H. Gilbert, Carib., Gulf of Mex.	260
1989, Sept. 16-22	H. Hugo, Caribbean, SE U.S.	86
1990, May 6-11	C. (mult.), SE India.	450
1991, Apr. 30	C. Gorky, Bangladesh.	139,000
1991, Nov. 5	TS. Thelma, central Philippines	7,000+
1992, Aug. 24-26	H. Andrew, Southern FL, LA	65
1993, Mar. 12-14	Blizzard, Eastern U.S.	270+
1993, June	Monsoon, Bangladesh	2,000
1994, Nov. 8-18	TS. Gordon, Caribbean, FL	830
1995, Oct. 2-4	H. Opal, S Mexico, FL, AL	59
1995, Nov. 2-3	T. Angela, Philippines.	600+
1996, Jan. 7-8	Blizzard, NE U.S.	100
1996, Aug. 22	Blizzard, Himalayas, N India.	239
1996, Aug. 29-Sept. 6	H. Fran, Carib., NC, VA, WV	30
1996, Sept. 9	T. Sally, S China.	114
1996, Nov. 6	C., Andhra Pradesh, India	1,000+
1996, Dec. 25	TS. Greg, eastern Malaysia	100+
1997, May 19	C., Bangladesh.	108
1997, Aug. 18-21	T. Winnie, Taiwan, E China	140+
1997, Oct. 8-10	H. Pauline, SW Mexico.	230
1998, June 9	C., Gujarat, India	1,320
1998, Aug.	Monsoon, Bangladesh	326
1998, Sept. 21-23	H. Georges, Carib., FL, U.S. Gulf	600+
1998, Oct. 27-29	H. Mitch, Central America.	11,000+
1999, Sept. 4-17	H. Floyd, The Bahamas, E U.S.	56
1999, Oct. 29	C., E India.	9,392
1999, Dec. 26-29	Gales, France, Switz., Germany	120
2000, Dec. 27	Winter storm, TX, OK, AR	40+
2001, July 30	T. Toraji, Taiwan.	200
2001, Nov. 6-12	T. Lingling, S Philip., Vietnam.	220+
2002, Aug.-Sept.	T. Rusa, N. and S. Korea	115+
2003, Feb. 16-17	Blizzard, E seaboard U.S.	59
2003, Sept. 7-19	H. Isabel, NC, VA, E seaboard	40+
2003, Sept. 12	T. Maemi, S. Korea.	130
2004, Mar. 7-19	C. Gafilo, Madagascar	198
2004, May 19	C., Myanmar.	220
2004, Aug. 12-15	T. Rananim, eastern China.	164
2004, Aug. 13-14	H. Charley, FL, SC	36
2004, Sept. 5-6	H. Frances, The Bahamas, FL	35
2004, Sept. 7-16	H. Ivan, Barbados, Grenada, U.S. Gulf Coast.	115
2004, Sept. 16-26	H. Jeanne, Dom. Rep., Haiti, FL	2,754
2005, July 7-11	H. Dennis, Jamaica, Haiti, Cuba, FL.	50
2005, Aug. 23-30	H. Katrina, LA, MS, FL, GA, AL	1,392+[3]
2005, Aug. 31-Sept. 1	T. Talim, Taiwan, E China	129+
2005, Sept. 21-24	H. Rita, TX, LA	62[4]
2005, Sept. 21-28	T. Damrey, SE Asia; Philippines; Hainan, China.	145
2005, Oct. 4	H. Stan, Central Amer., Mex.	1,000+[5]
2006, July 14	TS. Bilis, SE China	612
2006, Aug. 10	T. Saomai, SE China	295
2006, Nov. 30	T. Durian, Philippines	450-1,000+
2007, June 6-7	C. Gonu, Oman, Iran	54[6]
2007, Nov. 15	C. Sidr, southern Bangladesh.	3,363
2008, May 2-3	C. Nargis, southern Myanmar.	138,366
2008, June 20-25	T. Fengshen, Philippines, China	233
2008, Aug. 26-Sept. 1	H. Gustav, Haiti, Dom. Rep., U.S.	138
2008, Sept. 1-4	TS. Hanna, Haiti.	529
2008, Sept. 7-13	H. Ike, Haiti; Cuba; TX	164
2009, May 23-26	C. Alia, India, Bangladesh	260
2009, Aug. 7-9	T. Morakot, mudslides, Taiwan	700+
2009, Sept. 23-30	T. Ketsana, Philippines, Vietnam, Cambodia, Laos	498+
2009, Oct. 3-10	T. Parma, Philippines	375
2009, Oct. 30-Nov. 3	T. Mirinae, Philippines, Vietnam	159+
2010, May 29	TS. Agatha, Guatemala, El Salvador, Honduras	184
2010, July 13-17	T. Conson, Philippines.	105+
2011, Oct. 29-30	C., Odisha (Orissa) state, E India	9,893
2011, Dec. 16	TS. Washi, Philippines	1,257
2012, Jan. 24-Feb. 14	Blizzard/cold snap, E Europe	650+
2012, Oct. 22-31	H. Sandy, Cuba, Haiti, Jamaica, Eastern U.S.	245[7]
2012, Dec. 4	T. Bopha, Philippines	1,146
2013, Nov. 8	T. Haiyan, Philippines.	7,986
2013, Nov. 10	C., Puntland, Somalia.	162
2014, July 15	T. Rammasun, Philippines, China, Vietnam.	173
2016, Oct. 4-8	H. Matthew, Haiti, Bahamas, FL, GA, SC, NC.	585
2017, Aug. 25-30	H. Harvey, South TX, LA.	93+[8]
2017, Aug. 31-Sept. 11	H. Irma, Barbuda, Cuba, FL	134
2017, Sept. 16-30	H. Maria, Dominica, Virgin Isls., Puerto Rico	3,056[9]
2019, Mar. 14-15	C. Idai, Zimbabwe, Mozambique	1,303
2019, May 3-4	C. Fani, E India, Bangladesh	81
2019, Aug. 28-Sept. 6	H. Dorian, Bahamas, SE U.S.	84
2020, May 16-21	C. Amphan, E India, Bangladesh	98
2020, Oct. 31-Nov. 13	H. Eta, Nicaragua, Honduras, Guatemala, FL, NC	172
2021, Aug. 26-Sept. 1	H. Ida, LA, MS, AL, PA, NJ, NY	91
2022, Sept. 28-30	H. Ian, FL, SC.	152
2023, Mar. 12-13	C. Freddy, Malawi	1,209
2024, June 28-July 8	H. Beryl, Grenada, St. Vincent and Grenadines, Jamaica, Mexico, TX	18+

(1) "Tropical cyclone" is a generic term for a weather system. When max. sustained winds reach 74 mph, a tropical cyclone is classified as a hurricane, typhoon, or (tropical) cyclone depending on where in the world it originates. (2) Incl. about 500 lost at sea. (3) A Jan. 2023 assessment accounts for 520 direct deaths—341 in LA, 172 in MS, 6 in FL, and 1 in GA—as well as 565 indirect deaths (most of cardiovascular causes), and 307 deaths of indeterminate cause. (4) Incl. 55 indirect deaths. (5) Incl. deaths from floods and landslides. (6) First documented super cyclone in Arabian Sea. (7) Incl. 87 indirect deaths in the U.S. (8) Downgraded to a tropical storm Aug. 26, Harvey nevertheless caused severe flooding. (9) Puerto Rico's government, Aug. 2018, revised its death toll from 64 to 2,975 in line with a report they commissioned from George Washington Univ. public health experts. A separate Harvard study (May 2018) estimated the death toll to be at least 4,645.

Some Notable Floods, Tidal Waves

Source: EM-DAT: The International Disaster Database, CRED/UC de Louvain, Belgium, www.emdat.be; World Almanac research

Date	Location	Est. deaths
1703	Awa, Japan.	100,000+
1889, May 31	Johnstown, PA	2,200+
1903, June 15	Heppner, OR.	325
1911	Chang Jiang (Yangtze) R., China.	100,000
1913, Mar. 25-27	OH, IN.	732
1915, Aug. 17	Galveston, TX.	275
1927, Jan.-July	Mississippi Valley	246+
1927, Nov. 1	Mostagenem, Algeria	3,000
1928, Mar. 13	Dam collapse, Saugus, CA.	450
1928, Sept. 16	Lake Okeechobee, FL	1,770+
1931, Aug.	Huang He R., China	3,700,000
1933	Shandong, China	18,000
1937, Jan. 22	OH, MS valleys.	250
1938, June 9	Huang He R., China	500,000
1946, Apr. 1	HI, AK.	159
1947, Sept. 20	Honshu Isl., Japan	2,000
1949, July	China	57,000
1949, Oct.	Guatemala	40,000
1950	Pakistan	2,900
1951, Aug. 28	Manchuria.	4,800
1953, Jan. 31	Storm surge, Zuiderzee, Netherlands	2,000
1953, June 23	Japan	2,566
1954, Aug.	China	30,000
1954, Aug. 17	Farahzad, Iran	2,000
1955, Oct. 7-12	India, Pakistan	1,700
1959, Nov. 1	Western Mexico	2,000

Date	Location	Est. deaths
1959, Dec. 2	Frejus, France	412
1960, Oct. 10	Bangladesh	6,000
1960, Oct. 31	Bangladesh	4,000
1961, July	N India	2,000
1962, Sept. 27	Barcelona, Spain	445
1963, Oct. 9	Dam collapse, Vaiont, Italy	1,800
1967, Jan. 18-24	Eastern Brazil	894
1967, Mar. 19	Rio de Janeiro, Brazil	436
1967, Nov. 26	Lisbon, Portugal	464
1968, July	Rajasthan, Gujarat states, India	4,892
1968, Oct. 7	NE India	780
1969, Jan. 18-26	Southern CA	100
1969, Aug. 20-22	Western VA	189
1969, Oct. 1-8	Tunisia	500
1970, July 22	Himalayas, India	500
1972, Feb. 26	Buffalo Creek, WV	118
1972, June 9	Rapid City, SD	238
1972, Aug. 7	Luzon Isl., Philippines	454
1972, Aug. 19-31	Pakistan	1,500
1974, Mar. 29	Tubaro, Brazil	1,000
1974, July	Bangladesh	28,700
1974, Aug. 12	Monty-Long, Bangladesh	2,500
1975, Aug. 8	Dam collapse, Henan Prov., China	171,000
1976, July 31	Big Thompson Canyon, CO	140
1978, July	N, NE India	3,800
1979, July 17	Lomblem Isl., Indonesia	539
1979, Aug. 11	Morbi, India	10,000
1980, June	Sichuan, China	6,200
1981, Apr.	N China	550
1981, July	Sichuan, Hubei Prov., China	1,300
1982, Jan. 23	Near Lima, Peru	600
1982, May 12	Guangdong, China	430
1982, Sept. 17-21	El Salvador, Guatemala	1,300+
1984, Aug.-Sept.	South Korea	200+
1987, July 22	Bangladesh	2,055
1987, Aug.-Sept.	Northern Bangladesh	1,000+
1988, June-Sept.	Bangladesh	2,379
1988, Sept.	N India	1,000+
1989, July 14	China	2,000
1994, May-Oct.	Assam, India	2,001
1995, July	NE China	1,200
1995, Sept. 1-20	India	1,479
1996, June-July	Guizhou, Hebei, China	2,775
1997, Oct.-Nov.	Somalia	2,311
1998, July 17	Papua New Guinea	3,000
1998, July-Aug.	Hunan, Sichuan, China	3,656
1998, July-Sept.	Bangladesh	1,441
1998, Aug.	India	1,811
1999, Oct.-Dec.	Central Vietnam	700+
1999, Dec. 15-20	NW Venezuela	30,000
2000, Feb.-Mar.	Mozambique	700
2000, Sept. 19-30	India, Bangladesh	1,000+
2001, Aug. 1-6	Taiwan	100+
2001, Nov. 9-10	Northern Algeria	711+
2002, Apr.-Aug.	China	800+
2002, July-Aug.	India, Nepal, Bangladesh	1,100+
2004, May 23-Jun. 1	Dom. Republic, Haiti	2,665
2004, June-Sept.	Bangladesh, India, Myanmar, Nepal	2,000+
2004, June-Sept.	China	500
2004, Nov.-Dec.	Philippines	1,060+
2004, Dec. 26	Indian Ocean nations	227,898
2005, July 26-Aug. 5	W Maharashtra state, India	1,200
2006, Feb. 17	Leyte Isl., Philippines	1,000
2006, July 17	S of Java, Indonesia	530+
2007, July 21-Aug. 3	Bangladesh	1,110
2007, July-Sept.	India	1,103
2008, June-July	India	1,063
2009, July-Sept.	India	992
2010, May-Aug.	China	1,691
2010, June 13-24	Cenxi, China	377+
2010, July-Aug.	Pakistan	1,985
2010, Aug. 1-4	Zhouqu County, China	1,500+
2011, Jan. 11-12	SE Brazil	900
2011, Mar. 11	NE Japan	20,896
2011, Apr.-May	Northern Colombia	425+
2011, July-Dec.	Thailand	708+
2011, July-Dec.	Philippines, Cambodia, Myanmar	2,000+
2012, July-Oct.	Nigeria	363
2012, Aug.-Oct.	Pakistan	480
2012, Sept.-Oct.	Nigeria	431
2013, June	Uttarakhand, India	6,054
2015, Nov.-Dec.	S India	500
2018, June-Aug.	Kerala, India	504
2018, Dec. 22	Sunda Strait, Indonesia	437
2022, June-Sept.	Pakistan	1,739+
2023, May 2-4	South Kivu Prov., Dem. Rep. of Congo	2,970
2023, Sept. 10	Libya	4,300+

Some Major Earthquakes

Source: Global Volcanism Network, Smithsonian Institution; U.S. Geological Survey, U.S. Dept. of the Interior; World Almanac research Magnitude of earthquakes (mag.) is a relative measurement of an earthquake's energy. Deaths include those in aftershocks or related events.

Date	Location	Deaths	Mag.
526, May 20	Antioch, Syria	250,000	NA
856	Corinth, Greece	45,000	NA
856, Dec. 22	Damghan, Iran	200,000	NA
893, Mar. 23	Ardabil, Iran	150,000	NA
1057	Chihli, China	25,000	NA
1138, Aug. 9	Aleppo, Syria	230,000	NA
1169, Feb. 11	Nr. Mt. Etna, Sicily	15,000	NA[1]
1268	Silicia, Asia Minor	60,000	NA
1290, Sept. 27	Chihli, China	100,000	NA
1293, May 20	Kamakura, Japan	30,000	NA
1531, Jan. 26	Lisbon, Portugal	30,000	NA
1556, Jan. 24	Shaanxi, China	830,000	NA
1667, Nov.	Shemakha, Caucasia (now Azerbaijan)	80,000	NA
1693, Jan. 11	Catania, Italy	60,000	NA
1737, Oct. 11	India, Calcutta	300,000	NA
1755, June 7	N Persia (current-day Iran)	40,000	NA
1755, Nov. 1	Lisbon, Portugal	60,000	8.75[2]
1783, Feb. 4	Calabria, Italy	30,000	NA
1797, Feb. 4	Quito, Ecuador	41,000	NA
1822, Sept. 5	Asia Minor, Aleppo	22,000	NA
1828, Dec. 28	Echigo, Japan	30,000	NA
1868, Aug. 13-16	Peru, Ecuador	40,000	NA
1875, May 16	Venezuela, Colombia	16,000	NA
1886, Aug. 31	Charleston, SC	60	6.6
1896, June 15	Sanriku, Japan (tsunami)	27,120	8.5
1902, Apr. 19	Quezaltenango and San Marcos, Guatemala	2,000	7.5
1902, Dec. 16	Uzbekistan, Russia	4,700	6.4
1903, Apr. 28	Malazgirt, Turkey	3,500	7.0
1905, Apr. 4	Kangra, India	19,000	7.5
1906, Jan. 31	Off coast of Esmeraldas, Ecuador	1,000	8.8
1906, Mar. 16	Chia-i, Taiwan	1,250	6.8
1906, Apr. 18-19	San Francisco, CA	3,000+	7.7[3]
1906, Aug. 17	Valparaiso, Chile	3,882	8.6
1907, Oct. 21	Central Asia	12,000	8.1
1908, Dec. 28	Messina, Italy	72,000	7.2
1909, Jan. 23	Silakhor, Iran	5,000-6,000	7.3
1912, Aug. 9	Murefte, Turkey	2,800	7.4
1914, Oct. 3	Burdur, Turkey	4,000	7.0
1915, Jan. 13	Avezzano, Italy	32,610	7.0
1917, July 30	Yunnan Prov., China	1,800	7.5
1920, Dec. 16	Gansu, China	200,000	7.8[4]
1923, Mar. 24	Sichuan, China	3,500	7.3
1923, Mar. 25	Torbat-e Heydariyeh, Iran	2,200	5.7
1923, Sept. 1	Yokohama, Japan	142,800	7.9
1925, Mar. 16	Yunnan Prov., China	5,800	7.0
1927, Mar. 7	Tango, Japan	3,020	7.6
1927, May 22	Gansu, China	40,900	7.6
1929, May 1	Koppeh Dagh, Iran	3,800	7.2
1930, May 6	Salmas, Iran	2,500	7.2
1930, July 23	Irpinia, Italy	1,404	6.5
1931, Mar. 31	Managua, Nicaragua	2,500	6.0
1931, Apr. 27	Armenia-Azerbaijan border	2,800	5.7

Date	Location	Deaths	Mag.
1931, Aug. 10	Xinjiang, China	10,000	8.0
1933, Mar. 2	Sanriku, Japan (tsunami)	2,990	8.4
1933, Mar. 10	Long Beach, CA	115	6.2
1933, Aug. 25	Sichuan, China	9,300	7.5
1934, Jan. 15	Bihar, India-Nepal	10,700	8.1
1935, Apr. 21	Miao-li, Taiwan	3,270	7.1
1935, May 30	Quetta, Pakistan	30,000	7.6
1939, Jan. 25	Chillan, Chile	28,000	7.8
1939, Dec. 26	Erzincan, Turkey	32,700	7.8
1943, Sept. 10	Tottori, Japan	1,190	7.4
1943, Nov. 26	Ladik, Turkey	4,000	7.6
1944, Jan. 15	San Juan, Argentina	8,000	7.4
1944, Feb. 1	Gerede, Turkey	2,790	7.4
1945, Jan. 12	Mikawa, Japan	1,961	7.1
1945, Nov. 27	Makran Coast, Pakistan	4,000	8.0
1946, May 31	Ustukran, Turkey	1,300	5.9
1946, Nov. 10	Ancash, Peru	1,400	7.3
1946, Dec. 20	Honshu, Japan	1,362	8.1
1948, June 28	Fukui, Japan	3,769	7.3
1948, Oct. 5	Ashgabat, Turkmenistan	110,000	7.3
1949, July 10	Khait, Tajikistan	12,000	7.5
1949, Aug. 5	Pelileo, Ecuador	5,050	6.8
1950, Aug. 15	Assam, India	1,526	8.6
1954, Sept. 9	Orleansville, Algeria	1,250	6.8
1956, June 10-17	Northern Afghanistan	2,000	7.7
1957, July 2	Northern Iran	1,200	7.1
1960, Feb. 29	Agadir, Morocco	12,000	5.7
1960, May 21-30	Southern Chile	1,655	9.5[5]
1962, Sept. 1	NW Iran	12,255	7.1
1964, Mar. 27	Prince Wm. Sound, AK	131	9.2[6]
1966, Aug. 19	Eastern Turkey	2,529	6.8
1968, Aug. 31	NE Iran	12,000	7.3
1969, July 25	Guangdong, China	3,000	5.9
1970, Jan. 5	Yunnan Prov., China	10,000	7.5
1970, May 31	Chimbote, Ancash, Peru	70,000	7.9
1971, Feb. 9	San Fernando Valley, CA	65	6.6
1972, Apr. 10	Southern Iran	5,054	7.1
1972, Dec. 23	Managua, Nicaragua	5,000	6.2
1974, May 10	Zhaotong, China	1,540	6.8
1974, Dec. 28	Northern Pakistan	5,300	6.2
1975, Feb. 4	Haicheng, China	2,000	7.0
1975, Sept. 6	Eastern Turkey	2,300	6.7
1976, Feb. 4	Guatemala	23,000	7.5
1976, May 6	NE Italy	1,000	6.5
1976, June 25	Irian Jaya, New Guinea	422	7.1
1976, July 28	Tangshan, China	242,769	7.5
1976, Aug. 16	Mindanao, Philippines	8,000	7.9
1976, Nov. 24	NW Iran-Turkey border	5,000	7.3
1977, Mar. 4	Romania	1,500	7.2
1978, Sept. 16	NE Iran	15,000	7.8
1980, Oct. 10	NW Algeria	5,000	7.7
1980, Nov. 23	Southern Italy	2,735	6.5
1981, June 11	Southern Iran	3,000	6.9
1981, July 28	Southern Iran	1,500	7.3
1982, Dec. 13	W Arabian Peninsula	2,800	6.0
1983, Oct. 30	Eastern Turkey	1,342	6.9
1985, Sept. 19	Michoacan, Mexico	9,500	8.0
1986, Oct. 10	El Salvador	1,000+	5.5
1987, Mar. 6	Colombia-Ecuador	1,000	7.0
1988, Aug. 20	India-Nepal border	1,000	6.8
1988, Dec. 7	Spitak, Armenia	25,000	6.8
1989, Oct. 17	San Francisco Bay area, CA	63	6.9
1990, June 20	Western Iran	40,000+	7.4
1990, July 16	Luzon, Philippines	1,621	7.7
1991, Feb. 1	Pakistan-Afgh. border	1,200	6.8
1991, Oct. 19	Northern India	2,000	7.0
1992, Dec. 12	Flores Isl., Indonesia	2,500	7.5
1993, Sept. 30	Maharashtra, S India	9,748	6.2
1994, Jan. 17	Northridge, CA	61	6.7
1994, June 6	Cauca, SW Colombia	1,000	6.8
1995, Jan. 16	Kobe, Japan	5,502	6.9
1995, May 27	Sakhalin Isl., Russia	1,989	7.5
1997, Feb. 28	NW Iran	1,000+	6.1
1997, May 10	Northern Iran	1,567	7.3
1998, Feb. 4	Hindu Kush, Afghanistan	2,323	5.9
1998, May 30	Afgh.-Tajikistan border	4,000+	6.6
1998, July 17	Papua New Guinea	2,183	7.0
1999, Jan. 25	Armenia, Colombia	1,185+	6.1
1999, Aug. 17	Izmit, western Turkey	17,118+	7.6
1999, Sept. 20	Taichung, Taiwan	2,400	7.6
2001, Jan. 26	Gujarat, India	20,085	7.6
2002, Mar. 25-26	Hindu Kush, Afghanistan	1,000+	6.1
2003, May 21	Northern Algeria	2,266	6.8
2003, Dec. 26	Bam, SE Iran	31,000	6.6
2004, Dec. 26	Sumatra-Andaman Isls., Indonesia	227,898	9.1[7]
2005, Mar. 28	N Sumatra, Indonesia	1,313	8.6
2005, Oct. 8	Kashmir, Pakistan, India	86,000	7.6
2006, May 26	Java, Indonesia	5,749	6.3
2008, May 12	E Sichuan Prov., China	87,857	7.9
2009, Sept. 30	Sumatra, Indonesia	1,117	7.5
2010, Jan. 12	Haiti	316,000[8]	7.0
2010, Apr. 13	Southern Qinghai, China	2,698+	6.9
2011, Mar. 11	NE Japan	20,896	9.0[9]
2015, Apr. 25	Nepal	8,669+	7.8
2017, Sept. 19	Mexico City, Mexico	369	7.1
2017, Nov. 12	NW Iran-Iraq border	530	7.3
2018, Sept. 28	Sulawesi, Indonesia	4,340	7.5
2021, Aug. 14	Haiti	2,248+	7.2
2022, June 22	SE Afghanistan	1,036	6.2
2023, Feb. 6	Southern Turkey, NW Syria	56,683	7.8
2023, Sept. 8	Morocco	2,946	6.8
2023, Oct. 7-15	Western Afghanistan	1,500+	6.3

NA = Not available. (1) Once thought to have been a volcanic eruption; evidence indicates an earthquake and tsunami occurred on this date. (2) Earthquake caused the most deadly tsunami to date in the Atlantic Ocean. (3) Incl. deaths from resulting fires; revised ests. of magnitude range 7.7-7.9. (4) Commonly referred to as the Gansu quake, actually located within Ningxia autonomous region. (5) Largest recorded earthquake; caused a tsunami that spread across the Pacific Ocean as far as Japan. (6) "Good Friday" earthquake sent a tsunami that hit British Columbia, Canada, and U.S. Pacific coast. (7) Undersea earthquake triggered devastating Indian Ocean tsunamis. (8) Official govt. death toll (Jan. 2011). Ests. from other groups vary widely. (9) The most powerful earthquake in Japan's history set off a tsunami that inundated much of the coast and caused a partial meltdown of the Fukushima nuclear power plant.

Some Notable Fires Since 1940

See also Some Notable Explosions Since 1920.

Date	Location	Deaths
1940, Apr. 23	Nightclub, Natchez, MS	198
1942, Nov. 28	Cocoanut Grove Nightclub, Boston, MA	492
1942, Dec. 12	Hostel, St. John's, NL, Canada	100
1943, Sept. 7	Gulf Hotel, Houston, TX	55
1944, July 6	Ringling Circus, Hartford, CT	168
1946, June 5	LaSalle Hotel, Chicago, IL	61
1946, Dec. 7	Winecoff Hotel, Atlanta, GA	119
1946, Dec. 12	Ice plant, tenement, New York, NY	37
1949, Apr. 5	Hospital, Effingham, IL	77
1950, Jan. 7	Mercy Hospital, Davenport, IA	41
1953, Mar. 29	Nursing home, Largo, FL	35
1953, Apr. 16	Metalworking plant, Chicago, IL	35
1957, Feb. 17	Home for aged, Warrenton, MO	72
1958, Mar. 19	Garment factory, New York, NY	24
1958, Dec. 1	Parochial school, Chicago, IL	95
1958, Dec. 16	Store, Bogotá, Colombia	83
1960, Mar. 12	Chemical plant, Pusan, Korea	68
1960, July 14	Psychiatric hospital, Guatemala City	225
1960, Nov. 13	Movie theater, Amude, Syria	152
1960, Dec. 19	USS *Constellation*, Brooklyn, NY	49
1961, Jan. 6	Thomas Hotel, San Francisco, CA	20
1961, Dec. 17	Circus, Niteroi, Brazil	323
1963, May 4	Theater, Diourbel, Senegal	64
1963, Nov. 18	Surfside Hotel, Atlantic City, NJ	25
1963, Nov. 23	Nursing home, Fitchville, OH	63
1963, Dec. 29	Roosevelt Hotel, Jacksonville, FL	22
1964, Dec. 18	Nursing home, Fountaintown, IN	20
1965, Aug. 11-16	Watts riot fires, Los Angeles, CA	30+
1966, Dec. 7	Barracks, Erzurum, Turkey	68
1967, Feb. 7	Restaurant, Montgomery, AL	25
1967, May 22	Dept. store, Brussels, Belgium	322
1967, July 16	State prison, Jay, FL	37
1967, July 29	USS *Forrestal*, off N Vietnam	134

Date	Location	Deaths
1968, May 11	Wedding hall, Vijayawada, India	58
1969, Dec. 2	Nursing home, Notre Dame, QC, Can.	54
1970, Jan. 9	Nursing home, Marietta, OH	27
1970, Nov. 1	Nightclub, nr. Grenoble, France	146
1970, Dec. 20	Hotel, Tucson, AZ	28
1971, Dec. 25	Hotel, Seoul, S. Korea	162
1972, May 13	Nightclub, Osaka, Japan	116
1973, June 24	Bar, New Orleans, LA	32
1973, Aug. 3	Amusement park, Isle of Man, UK	51
1973, Nov. 29	Dept. store, Kumamoto, Japan	107
1973, Dec. 2	Theater, Seoul, S. Korea	50
1974, Feb. 1	Bank building, São Paulo, Brazil	189
1974, Nov. 3	Hotel, disco, Seoul, S. Korea	88
1975, Dec. 12	Pilgrim camp, Mina, Saudi Arabia	138
1976, Oct. 24	Social club, Bronx, NY	25
1977, Feb. 18	Movie screening, Xinjiang, China	694
1977, Feb. 25	Rossiya Hotel, Moscow, Russia	45
1977, May 28	Nightclub, Southgate, KY	164
1977, June 26	Jail, Columbia, TN	42
1977, Nov. 14	Hotel, Manila, Philippines	47
1978, Aug. 19	Movie theater, Abadan, Iran	425+
1979, July 14	Hotel, Saragossa, Spain	80
1979, Dec. 31	Social club, Chapais, QC, Can.	42
1980, May 20	Nursing home, Kingston, Jamaica	157
1980, Nov. 21	MGM Grand Hotel, Las Vegas, NV	84
1980, Dec. 4	Stouffer's Inn, Harrison, NY	26
1981, Jan. 9	Boarding home, Keansburg, NJ	30
1981, Feb. 14	Discotheque, Dublin, Ireland	44
1982, Nov. 8	County jail, Biloxi, MS	29
1983, Feb. 13	Movie theater, Turin, Italy	64
1983, Feb. 16	"Ash Wednesday" bushfires, S Australia and Victoria, Australia	75
1983, Dec. 17	Discotheque, Madrid, Spain	83
1985, Apr. 21	Movie theaters, Tabaco, Philippines	44
1985, Apr. 26	Hospital, Buenos Aires, Argentina	79
1985, May 11	Soccer stadium, Bradford, Eng., UK	53
1985, May 13	MOVE headquarters, row houses, Philadelphia, PA	11
1986, Dec. 31	Dupont Plaza Hotel, Puerto Rico	96
1987, May 6-June 2	Forest fire, Mohe, China	191
1987, Nov. 17	Subway, London, England	30
1988, Mar. 20	2,000+ buildings, Lashio, Myanmar	134
1990, Mar. 25	Happy Land social club, Bronx, NY	87
1991, Mar. 3	Munitions dump, Addis Ababa, Ethiopia	260+
1991, Aug.-Oct.	Wildfires, Sumatra, Borneo, Indonesia	57
1991, Sept. 3	Chicken-processing plant, Hamlet, NC	25
1993, Apr. 19	Cult compound, Waco, TX	72
1993, May 10	Toy factory, Bangkok, Thailand	213
1993, Nov. 19	Toy factory, Shenzhen, China	87
1994, Nov. 2	Burning fuel flood, Durunka, Egypt	500
1994, Nov. 27	Dance hall, Fuxin, China	233
1994, Dec. 8	Theater, Karamay, China	323
1995, Oct. 28	Subway train, Baku, Azerbaijan	300
1995, Dec. 23	School, Mandi Dabwali, India	500+
1996, Mar. 19	Nightclub, Quezon City, Philippines	150+
1996, Mar. 28	Shopping mall, Bogor, Indonesia	78
1996, Nov. 20	Garley Building, Hong Kong	39
1997, Feb. 23	Worship site, Baripada, India	164
1997, Apr. 15	Encampment, Mina, Saudi Arabia	343
1997, June 7	Temple, Thanjavur, India	60+
1997, June 13	Movie theater, New Delhi, India	60
1997, July 11	Hotel, Pattaya, Thailand	90
1997, Sept.-Nov.	Drought-fueled fire, Sumatra, Indon.	240
1998, Apr.-June	Wildfire, Oaxaca, Mexico	50
1999, Mar. 24	Mt. Blanc Tunnel, France, Italy	40
1999, Oct. 30	Karaoke salon, Inchon, S. Korea	55+
2000, Mar. 17	Church, Kanungu, Uganda	530
2000, Nov. 11	Cable car, Kaprun, Austria	155
2000, Dec. 25	Shopping center, Luoyang, China	309
2001, Mar. 26	School, Machakos, Kenya	64
2001, Aug. 18	Hotel, Quezon City, Philippines	73
2001, Sept. 1	Nightclub, Tokyo, Japan	44
2001, Dec. 29	Fireworks accident, Lima, Peru	291
2003, Feb. 18	Subway train, Taegu, S. Korea	198
2003, Feb. 20	Nightclub pyrotechnics, Warwick, RI	100
2003, Sept. 15	Prison, Riyadh, Saudi Arabia	94
2003, Nov. 24	Students' hostel, Moscow, Russia	36
2004, May 17	Prison, San Pedro Sula, Honduras	104
2004, July 16	Pvt. school, Kumbakonam, India	80+
2004, Aug. 1	Market, Asunción, Paraguay	400+
2004, Dec. 30	Club, Buenos Aires, Argentina	194
2005, Feb. 14	Mosque, Tehran, Iran	59
2005, Mar. 7	Prison, Higuey, Dom. Republic	159
2005, Sept. 5	Theater, Beni Suef, Egypt	32
2006, Dec. 9	Drug treatment center, Moscow, Russ.	45
2007, Mar. 20	Nursing home, Kamyshevatskaya, Russia	62
2007, Aug. 24-Sept. 2	Wildfires (arson), Greece	73
2008, Apr. 26	Factory fire, Casablanca, Morocco	55
2008, Sept.	Wildfires, Mozambique, S. Africa, Swaziland	89
2009, Jan. 1	Nightclub fire, Bangkok, Thailand	67
2009, Jan.-Feb.	"Black Saturday" wildfires (arson), Victoria, Australia	173
2010, July	Bushfires, Nizhiny Novgorod, Russia	53
2010, Dec. 2-5	Grassland fire, Israel	44
2012, Feb. 14	Prison fire, Comayagua, Honduras	360+
2012, Nov. 24	Garment factory, Bagladesh	112
2013, Jan. 27	Nightclub, Santa Maria, Brazil	241
2014, May 2	Trade union building, Odessa, Ukraine	40+
2016, Apr. 10	Temple fireworks, Kerala, India	110+
2016, Dec. 2	"Ghost Ship" warehouse, Oakland, CA	36
2017, June 14	Grenfell Tower apts., London, Eng., UK	72
2017, June 17-18	Forest fires, central Portugal	64
2018, July 23	Wildfires, Attica region, Greece	99
2018, Nov. 8-25	Camp Fire wildfire, Butte Co., CA	85
2019, Oct.-2020, Feb.	"Black Summer" wildfires, Australia	33[1]
2023, Aug. 8	Wildfires, Lahaina, Maui, HI	102
2023, Sept. 28	Wedding venue, Qaraqosh, Iraq	119+
2024, June 12	Foreign workers' housing, Mangaf, Kuwait	50+

(1) Research published in Mar. 2020 found an additional 417 excess deaths from smoke inhalation.

U.S. Fires, 2022

Source: National Fire Protection Association

- Public fire departments responded to an estimated 1.5 mil fires in 2022, including 522,500 structure fires (360,000 in homes), 222,000 vehicle fires, and 760,000 fires outside or other fires.
- An estimated 3,790 civilians died in fires in 2022.
- There were an estimated 13,250 civilian fire injuries reported, 10,320 of them in home structure fires.
- Direct property damage from fires amounted to an estimated $18.0 bil. Structure fires accounted for $15.0 bil of property damage, and property loss associated with home fires came to $10.5 bil.

Some Notable Explosions Since 1920

See also Principal U.S. Mine Disasters Since 1867. Some bombings related to political conflicts and terrorism are not included.

Date	Location	Deaths
1920, Sept. 16	Wall Street, New York, NY	39
1921, Sept. 21	Chem. storage facility, Oppau, Ger.	561
1924, Jan. 3	Food plant, Pekin, IL	42
1927, May 18	School bombing, Bath, MI	45
1928, Apr. 13	Dance hall, West Plains, MO	40
1937, Mar. 18	School, New London, TX	311
1940, Sept. 12	Hercules Powder factory, Kenvil, NJ	55
1942, Apr. 26	Honkeiko (Benxihu) colliery, China	1,549
1942, June 5	Ordnance plant, Elwood, IL	49
1944, Apr. 14	SS *Fort Stikine*, Bombay docks, India	700
1944, July 17	Munitions ships, depot, Port Chicago, CA	322
1944, Oct. 20	Liquid natural gas tanks, Cleveland, OH	130
1947, Apr. 16	Freighter, chemical co. plant, Texas City, TX	576
1948, July 28	Farben works, Ludwigshafen, Ger.	184

Date	Location	Deaths
1950, May 19	Munitions barges, S. Amboy, NJ	30
1954, May 26	USS *Bennington*, off RI	103
1956, Aug. 7	Dynamite trucks, Cali, Colombia	1,100
1958, Apr. 18	Sunken munitions ship, Okinawa, Japan	40
1959, Apr. 10	WWII bomb, Philippines	38
1959, June 28	Rail tank cars, Meldrim, GA	25
1959, Aug. 7	Truck with explosives, Roseburg, OR	14
1959, Nov. 2	Explosives, Jamuri Bazar, India	46
1959, Dec. 13	2 apt. bldgs., Dortmund, Germany	26
1960, Mar. 4	Belgian munitions ship, Havana, Cuba	100
1960, Oct. 24	Rocket on launchpad, Baikonur Cosmodrome, USSR	74+
1962, Oct. 3	New York Telephone Co. office, New York, NY	23
1963, Jan. 2	Packing plant, Terre Haute, IN	17
1963, Mar. 9	Dynamite plant, S. Africa	45
1963, Aug. 13	Explosives dump, Gauhaiti, India	32
1963, Oct. 31	State Fair Coliseum, Indianapolis, IN	73
1963, Nov. 9	Mitsui Miike coal mine, Japan	458
1964, July 23	Harbor munitions, Bone, Algeria	100
1965, Aug. 9	Missile silo, Searcy, AR	53
1965, Oct. 21	Bridge, Tila Bund, Pakistan	80
1965, Nov. 24	Armory, Keokuk, IA	20
1968, Apr. 6	Sports store, Richmond, IN	43
1969, Mar. 31	Coal mine, nr. Barroteran, Mexico	180
1970, Apr. 8	Subway construction, Osaka, Japan	73
1971, June 24	Tunnel under construction, Sylmar, CA	17
1973, Feb. 10	Liquid gas tank, Staten Island, NY	40
1975, Dec. 27	Coal mine, Chasnala, India	431
1976, Apr. 13	Munitions works, Lapua, Finland	40
1977, Nov. 11	Freight train, Iri, S. Korea	57
1977, Dec. 22	Grain elevator, Westwego, LA	35
1978, July 11	Propylene tank truck, Tarragona, Spain	150
1980, Oct. 23	School, Ortuella, Spain	64
1982, Apr. 25	Antiques exhibition, Todi, Italy	33
1982, Nov. 2	Salang Tunnel, Afghanistan	1,000+
1984, Feb. 25	Oil pipeline, Cubatao, Brazil	508
1984, June 21	Naval supply depot, Severomorsk, USSR	200+
1984, Nov. 19	Gas storage area, NE Mexico City	334
1984, Dec. 3	Chemical plant, Bhopal, India	3,849
1984, Dec. 5	Coal mine, Taipei, Taiwan	94
1985, June 25	Fireworks factory, Hallett, OK	21
1988, Apr. 10	Army ammunitions dump nr. Rawalpindi and Islamabad, Pakistan	100
1988, July 6	Oil rig, North Sea off NE Scotland, UK	167
1989, June 3	Gas pipeline, between Ufa, Asha, USSR	650+
1992, Mar. 3	Coal mine, Kozlu, Turkey	270+
1992, Apr. 22	Gas leak in sewers, Guadalajara, Mexico	200+
1992, May 9	Coal mine, Plymouth, Nova Scotia, Can.	26
1993, Feb. 26	World Trade Center, New York, NY	6
1994, July 18	Jewish community center, Buenos Aires, Argentina	100
1995, Apr. 19	Fed. office building, Oklahoma City, OK	168
1995, Apr. 29	Subway construction, S. Korea	110
1996, Jan. 31	Bank, Colombo, Sri Lanka	53
1996, Mar. 3-4	Jerusalem and Tel Aviv, Israel	33
1996, June 25	U.S. military housing complex, nr. Dhahran, Saudi Arabia	19
1996, July 24	Train, Colombo, Sri Lanka	86
1996, Nov. 16	Military apt., Dagestan region, Russia	68
1996, Nov. 21	Propane gas leak in bldg., San Juan, PR	33
1996, Nov. 27	Coal mine, Shanxi Prov., China	91+
1996, Dec. 30	Train, Assam, India	59+
1997, Dec. 2	Coal mine, Novokuznetsk, Russia	68
1998, Feb. 14	2 oil tankers, Yaounde, Cameroon	120
1998, Feb. 14	17 bombs, Coimbatore, India	50
1998, Apr. 4	Coal mine, Donetsk, Ukraine	63
1998, Aug. 7	Bomb, U.S. emb., Nairobi, Kenya	213
1998, Aug. 7	Bomb, U.S. emb., Dar-es-Salaam, Tanzania	11
1998, Sept. 8	2 buses, São Paulo, Brazil	59
1998, Oct. 17	Oil pipeline, Jesse, Nigeria	700+
1999, May 16	Fuel truck, Punjab Prov., Pakistan	75
1999, Sept. 9	Apartment building, Moscow, Russia	94
1999, Sept. 13	Apartment building, Moscow, Russia	118
1999, Sept. 16	Apartment building, Moscow, Russia	18
1999, Sept. 26	Fireworks factory, Celaya, Mexico	56
2000, Feb. 25	Bombs on 2 buses, Ozamis, Philippines	41
2000, Mar. 11	Coal mine, Krasnodon, Ukraine	80
2000, Apr. 16	Airport hangar, Dem. Rep. of Congo	100+
2000, Aug. 12	Flaw in torpedo, *Kursk* submarine, off Russia	118
2000, Sept. 9	Truck explosion, Urumqi, China	60
2000, Oct. 12	USS *Cole*, Yemen	17
2001, Mar. 6	School, Jianxi Prov., China	41
2001, Apr. 21	Coal mine, Shaanxi, China	51
2001, June 1	Dance club, Tel Aviv, Israel	21
2001, July 17	Coal mine, Guanxi, China	76+
2001, Aug. 19	Coal mine, Donetsk region, Ukraine	52
2001, Sept. 21	Chem. plant, Toulouse, France	29
2002, Jan. 21	Volcanic lava caused gas station blast, Goma, Dem. Rep. of Congo	50+
2002, Jan. 27	Munitions dump, Lagos, Nigeria	1,000+
2002, May 9	Land mine at parade, Kaspiisk, Russia	34+
2002, June 14	Car bomb outside U.S. consulate, Karachi, Pakistan	12
2002, June 18	Bomb on bus, Jerusalem, Israel	20
2002, July 5	Bomb in market, Larba, Algeria	35+
2002, Aug. 9	Explosion, Jalalabad, Afghanistan	25+
2002, Sept. 5	Car bomb, Kabul, Afghanistan	30
2002, Oct. 12	Nightclub bombings, Bali, Indonesia	202
2003, Aug. 25	Bombs in 2 taxis, Mumbai, India	52
2003, Dec. 5	Bomb on train, Yessentuki, Russia	45
2003, Dec. 23	Gas well explosion, Chongqing, China	233
2004, Feb. 6	Bomb on subway car, Moscow, Russia	39
2004, Mar. 11	Bombs on commuter trains, Madrid, Spain	191
2005, Feb. 14	Coal mine, NE China	214
2005, Mar. 23	Oil refinery, Texas City, TX	15
2005, July 7	Bombs in mass transit, London, Eng., UK	56
2005, Oct. 1	Bombings of restaurants, Bali, Indonesia	26
2005, Nov. 27	Coal mine, NE China	161+
2006, May 12	Oil pipeline, nr. Lagos, Nigeria	200
2006, July 1	Bombings of trains, station, Mumbai, India	207
2007, Mar. 19	Coal mine, Siberia, Russia	108
2007, Mar. 22	Natl. weapons depot, Maputo, Mozambique	117
2007, June 9	Oil pipeline, Pyongan Prov., N. Korea	110
2007, Nov. 18	Methane gas buildup in coal mine, E Ukraine	90
2008, May 15	Pipeline explosion in Lagos, Nigeria	100+
2008, Sept. 20	Truck bomb outside hotel, Islamabad, Pakistan	40+
2009, Feb. 22	Coal mine, N China	74
2010, May 8-9	Coal mine, Siberia, Russia	91
2010, June 17	Coal mine, Amaga, Colombia	73
2011, Mar. 28	Munitions factory, Abyan, Yemen	150+
2011, July 13	Bombs in 3 locations in Mumbai, India	27
2012, Mar. 4	Arms depot, Brazzaville, Congo Rep.	250+
2013, Apr. 17	Fertilizer plant, West, TX	15
2013, June 3	Poultry plant, Mishzai, China	119+
2013, June 30	Fuel tanker, Kampala, Uganda	30+
2013, July 6	Derailed oil train, Lac-Mégantic, QC, Canada	47
2013, Aug. 1	Weapons cache, Homs, Syria	40
2014, May 13	Coal mine, Soma, Turkey	301
2015, Aug. 12	Chemical warehouse, Tianjin, China	173
2017, Oct. 27	Fireworks factory, Tangerang, Indon.	47+
2020, Aug. 4	Chemicals improperly stored at port, Beirut, Lebanon	211
2021, Mar. 7	Explosions at military base, Bata, Equatorial Guinea	107
2021, Nov. 25	Listvyazhnaya coal mine, Siberia, Russia	51
2022, Apr. 23	Illegal oil refinery, SE Nigeria	100+

Principal U.S. Mine Disasters Since 1867

Source: Bureau of Mines, U.S. Dept. of the Interior; Office of Mine Safety Health Research, Centers for Disease Control
All are bituminous coal mines unless otherwise noted.

Date	Location	Deaths
1867, Apr. 3	Winterpock, VA	69
1869, Sept. 6	Plymouth, PA	110
1883, Feb. 16	Braidwood, IL	69
1884, Mar. 13	Pocahontas, VA	112
1891, Jan. 27	Mt. Pleasant, PA	109
1892, Jan. 7	Krebs, OK	100
1895, Mar. 20	Red Canyon, WY	62
1900, May 1	Scofield, UT	200
1902, May 19	Coal Creek, TN	184
1902, July 10	Johnstown, PA	112
1903, June 30	Hanna, WY	169
1904, Jan. 25	Cheswick, PA	179
1905, Feb. 20	Virginia City, AL	112
1907, Jan. 29	Stuart, WV	84
1907, Dec. 6	Monongah, WV	362
1907, Dec. 19	Van Meter, PA	239
1908, Nov. 28	Marianna, PA	154
1909, Jan. 12	Switchback, WV	67
1909, Nov. 13	Cherry, IL	259
1910, Jan. 31	Primero, CO	75
1910, May 5	Palos, AL	84
1910, Nov. 8	Delagua, CO	79
1911, Apr. 7	Troop, PA	73
1911, Apr. 8	Littleton, AL	128
1911, Dec. 9	Briceville, TN	84
1912, Mar. 20	McCurtain, OK	73
1912, Mar. 26	Jed, WV	81
1913, Apr. 23	Finleyville, PA	98
1913, Oct. 22	Dawson, NM	263
1914, Apr. 28	Eccles, WV	183
1915, Mar. 2	Layland, WV	112
1917, Apr. 27	Hastings, CO	121
1917, June 8	Butte, MT[1]	163
1917, Aug. 4	Clay, KY	62
1919, June 5	Wilkes-Barre, PA	92
1922, Nov. 6	Spangler, PA	79
1922, Nov. 22	Dolomite, AL	90
1923, Feb. 8	Dawson, NM	120
1923, Aug. 14	Kemmerer, WY	99
1924, Mar. 8	Castle Gate, UT	172
1924, Apr. 28	Benwood, WV	119
1926, Jan. 13	Wilburton, OK	91
1927, Apr. 30	Everettville, WV	97
1928, May 19	Mather, PA	195
1929, Dec. 17	McAlester, OK	61
1930, Nov. 5	Millfield, OH	82
1940, Jan. 10	Bartley, WV	91
1940, Mar. 16	St. Clairsville, OH	72
1940, July 15	Portage, PA	63
1943, Feb. 27	Washoe, MT	74
1944, July 5	Powhatan Pt., OH	66
1947, Mar. 25	Centralia, IL	111
1951, Dec. 21	West Frankfort, IL	119
1968, Nov. 20	Farmington, WV	78
1970, Dec. 30	Hyden, KY	38
1972, Feb. 26	Saunders, WV	114
1972, May 2	Kellogg, ID[2]	91
2010, Apr. 5	Montcoal, WV	29

Note: The world's worst mine disaster killed 1,549 workers in Manchuria, China, Apr. 26, 1942. (1) Copper mine. (2) Silver mine.

Notable Nuclear Accidents

Sept. 29, 1957: After cooling system failure, nuclear waste at Chelyabinsk-65 in Kyshtym, Russia, exploded. Residents were evacuated but not informed until 1989 about their exposure to radiation.

Oct. 7, 1957: Fire in the Windscale plutonium production reactor N of Liverpool, England, UK, released radioactive material; later blamed for 39 cancer deaths.

Jan. 3, 1961: Reactor explosion at a federal installation near Idaho Falls, ID, killed 3 workers. Radiation contained.

Oct. 5, 1966: Sodium cooling system malfunction caused a partial core meltdown at the Enrico Fermi demonstration breeder reactor, near Detroit, MI. Radiation contained.

Jan. 21, 1969: Coolant malfunction from an experimental underground reactor at Lucens Vad, Switzerland, released radiation into a cavern, which was then sealed.

Mar. 22, 1975: Fire at the Brown's Ferry reactor in Decatur, AL, caused dangerous lowering of cooling water levels.

Mar. 28, 1979: Worst commercial nuclear accident in the U.S. occurred as equipment failures and human mistakes led to a loss of coolant and a partial core meltdown at the Three Mile Island reactor in Middletown, PA.

Feb. 11, 1981: Eight workers were contaminated when 100,000 gallons of radioactive coolant leaked into the containment building of TVA's Sequoyah 1 plant near Chattanooga, TN.

Apr. 25, 1981: Some 100 workers were exposed to radiation during repairs of a nuclear plant at Tsuruga, Japan.

Jan. 6, 1986: Cylinder of nuclear material burst after being improperly heated at a Kerr-McGee plant in Gore, OK. One worker died; 100 were hospitalized.

Apr. 26, 1986: Fires and resulting explosions at the Chernobyl nuclear power plant near Kiev, USSR (now in Ukraine), left at least 31 dead in the immediate aftermath and spread radioactive material over much of Europe. An estimated 135,000 people were evacuated. Tens of thousands of excess cancer deaths (as well as increased birth defects) were expected.

Sept. 1987: Cesium chloride from an improperly discarded hospital irradiation machine contaminated more than 200 people and killed at least 4 in Goiânia, Brazil.

Mar. 11, 2011: A 9.0 magnitude earthquake caused a tsunami that inundated the Fukushima Daiichi nuclear power plant on Japan's NE coast. Three of the plant's reactors suffered partial meltdowns; more than 12,000 tons of radioactive water was released into the sea.

Record Oil Spills

The exact number of barrels in a metric ton varies with the type of oil, but a general approximation is 7 barrels per metric ton. By custom, 42 gallons constitute a barrel of crude oil.

Name, location	Date	Cause	Est. metric tons
BP *Deepwater Horizon* rig, Gulf of Mexico, U.S.	Apr. 20-July 15, 2010	Explosion	700,000[1]
Ixtoc I oil well, S Gulf of Mexico	June 3, 1979	Blowout	600,000
Nowruz oil field, Persian Gulf	Feb. 1983	Blowout	600,000
Atlantic Empress, off Trinidad and Tobago	July 19, 1979	Collision with *Aegean Captain*	276,000
ABT Summer, off Angola	May 28, 1991	Explosion	260,000
Amoco Cadiz, near Portsall, France	Mar. 16, 1978	Grounding	223,000
Castillo de Bellver, off Cape Town, South Africa	Aug. 6, 1983	Fire	150,000-160,000
Haven, off Genoa, Italy	Apr. 11, 1991	Explosion	144,000
Odyssey, off Nova Scotia, Canada	Nov. 10, 1988	Broke apart in storm	132,000
Torrey Canyon, off Land's End, England, UK	Mar. 18, 1967	Grounding	119,000
Sea Star, Gulf of Oman	Dec. 19, 1972	Collision	115,000
Sanchi, off Shanghai, China	Jan. 6, 2018	Collision with *CF Crystal*	113,000
Urquiola, La Coruna, Spain	May 12, 1976	Grounding	100,000

(1) The Dept. of Energy estimated the spill at 4.9 mil barrels, or more than 200 mil gallons.

Other Notable Oil Spills

Name, location	Date	Cause	Gallons
Persian Gulf	Jan. 21, 1991	Intentional spillage by Iraq	130,000,000[1]
Braer, off Shetland Islands, UK	Jan. 5, 1993	Grounding	26,000,000
Taylor Energy platform, Gulf of Mexico, U.S.	Sept. 2004-present	Broke apart during H. *Ivan*	Up to 25,000,000
Prestige, off N Spain	Nov. 13-19, 2002	Ship broke in half	22,600,000
Aegean Sea, off N Spain	Dec. 3, 1992	Grounding	21,500,000
Sea Empress, off SW Wales, UK	Feb. 15, 1996	Grounding	18,000,000
Newtown Creek, Greenpoint, Brooklyn, NY	Oct. 5, 1950-present	Industrial explosion	17,000,000[2]
Hawaiian Patriot, off Hawaii in Pacific	Feb. 23-24, 1977	Hull cracked; ship exploded	14,700,000
World Glory, off South Africa	June 13, 1968	Hull failure	13,524,000
Exxon Valdez, Prince William Sound, AK	Mar. 24, 1989	Grounding	10,080,000
Ashland Oil facility, Floreffe, PA; Monongahela R.	Jan. 2, 1988	Storage tank collapse	3,850,000

(1) Est. by Saudi Arabia. Some estimates as low as 25 mil gal. (2) Legacy of refinery operations since mid-1800s and leaking storage tanks. Spill estimated at up to 30 mil gal.

AEROSPACE

Notable Human Spaceflight Missions

Source: National Aeronautics and Space Administration (NASA); Congressional Research Service; World Almanac research

The spaceflights listed are a selection of notable crewed U.S. missions by NASA, unless otherwise noted, plus crewed non-U.S. missions (shown with an asterisk). The non-U.S. missions were sponsored by the USSR—later, the Commonwealth of Independent States (CIS) and, from 1997, Russia—or by China. Launch dates are Eastern Standard Time. **EVA** = extravehicular activity. **ASTP** = Apollo-Soyuz Test Project. **STS** = Space Transportation System, NASA's name for the overall shuttle program.

For shuttle flights, mission name is in parentheses following name of orbiter. Duration of flight is listed in hours:minutes for 1961-Apr. 1970; days (d.), hours (hr.), and minutes (min.) thereafter. Number of total flights taken by each crew member is given in parentheses when flight listed is not the person's first.

4/12/1961: ***Vostok 1***; 1:48; Yuri A. Gagarin. **1st human orbital flight.**

5/5/1961: ***Mercury-Redstone 3***; 0:15; Alan B. Shepard Jr. **1st American in space.**

7/21/1961: ***Mercury-Redstone 4***; 0:15; Virgil I. Grissom. Flight successful but spacecraft sank shortly after splashdown; Grissom rescued.

8/6/1961: ***Vostok 2***; 25:18; Gherman S. Titov. 1st spaceflight of more than 24 hours.

2/20/1962: ***Mercury-Atlas 6***; 4:55; John H. Glenn Jr. **1st American in orbit**; three orbits.

5/24/1962: ***Mercury-Atlas 7***; 4:56; M. Scott Carpenter. Manual retrofire error caused 250-mi landing overshoot.

8/11/1962: ***Vostok 3***; 94:22; Andrian G. Nikolayev. *Vostok 3* and *4* made 1st group flight.

8/12/1962: ***Vostok 4***; 70:57; Pavel R. Popovich. On 1st orbit, it came within 3 mi of *Vostok 3*.

10/3/1962: ***Mercury-Atlas 8***; 9:13; Walter M. Schirra Jr. Landed 5 mi from target; six orbits.

5/15/1963: ***Mercury-Atlas 9***; 34:19; L. Gordon Cooper. 1st U.S. evaluation of effects of one day in space on a person; 22 orbits.

6/14/1963: ***Vostok 5***; 119:06; Valery F. Bykovsky. *Vostok 5* and *6* made 2nd group flight.

6/16/1963: ***Vostok 6***; 70:50; Valentina V. Tereshkova. **1st woman in space**; passed within 3 mi of *Vostok 5*.

10/12/1964: ***Voskhod 1***; 24:17; Vladimir M. Komarov, Konstantin P. Feoktistov, Boris B. Yegorov. 1st three-person orbital flight; 1st without space suits.

3/18/1965: ***Voskhod 2***; 26:02; Pavel I. Belyayev, Aleksei A. Leonov. Leonov made **1st spacewalk** (10 min.).

3/23/1965: ***Gemini-Titan 3***; 4:53; Virgil I. Grissom (2), John W. Young. 1st piloted spacecraft to change its orbital path.

6/3/1965: ***Gemini-Titan 4***; 97:56; James A. McDivitt, Edward H. White II. White was **1st American to "walk in space"** (23 min.).

8/21/1965: ***Gemini-Titan 5***; 190:55; L. Gordon Cooper (2), Charles Conrad Jr. Longest-duration human flight to date.

12/4/1965: ***Gemini-Titan 7***; 330:35; Frank Borman, James A. Lovell Jr. Longest-duration *Gemini* flight.

12/15/1965: ***Gemini-Titan 6A***; 25:51; Walter M. Schirra Jr. (2), Thomas P. Stafford. Completed 1st U.S. space rendezvous, with *Gemini 7*.

3/16/1966: ***Gemini-Titan 8***; 10:41; Neil A. Armstrong, David R. Scott. **1st docking of one space vehicle with another**; mission aborted, control malfunction.

6/3/1966: ***Gemini-Titan 9A***; 72:21; Thomas P. Stafford (2), Eugene A. Cernan. Performed simulation of lunar module rendezvous.

7/18/1966: ***Gemini-Titan 10***; 70:47; John W. Young (2), Michael Collins. 1st use of Agena target vehicle's propulsion systems; 1st orbital docking.

9/12/1966: ***Gemini-Titan 11***; 71:17; Charles Conrad Jr. (2), Richard F. Gordon Jr. 1st tethered flight; highest Earth-orbit altitude (850 mi).

11/11/1966: ***Gemini-Titan 12***; 94:34; James A. Lovell Jr. (2), Edwin E. "Buzz" Aldrin Jr. Final *Gemini* mission; 5-hr. EVA.

1/27/1967: ***Apollo 1***; Virgil I. Grissom, Edward H. White II, and Roger B. Chaffee died in a fire on the ground at Cape Canaveral, FL.

4/23/1967: ***Soyuz 1***; 26:40; Vladimir M. Komarov (2). Crashed on reentry, killing Komarov; **1st space fatality**.

10/11/1968: ***Apollo-Saturn 7***; 260:09; Walter M. Schirra Jr. (3), Donn F. Eisele, R. Walter Cunningham. **1st piloted flight of *Apollo*** spacecraft command-service module only; live TV footage of crew.

12/21/1968: ***Apollo-Saturn 8***; 147:00; Frank Borman (2), James A. Lovell Jr. (3), William A. Anders. **1st lunar orbit** and piloted lunar return reentry (command-service module only); views of lunar surface televised to Earth.

1/14/1969: ***Soyuz 4***; 71:21; Vladimir A. Shatalov. Docked with *Soyuz 5*.

1/15/1969: ***Soyuz 5***; 72:54; Boris V. Volyanov, Aleksei S. Yeliseyev, Yevgeny V. Khrunov. Docked with *Soyuz 4*; Yeliseyev and Khrunov transferred to *Soyuz 4* via a spacewalk.

3/3/1969: ***Apollo-Saturn 9***; 241:00; James A. McDivitt (2), David R. Scott (2), Russell L. Schweickart. 1st piloted flight of lunar module.

5/18/1969: ***Apollo-Saturn 10***; 192:03; Thomas P. Stafford (3), John W. Young (3), Eugene A. Cernan (2). 1st lunar module orbit of moon, 50,000 ft from moon's surface.

7/16/1969: ***Apollo-Saturn 11***; 195:18; Neil A. Armstrong (2), Michael Collins (2), Edwin E. "Buzz" Aldrin Jr. (2). **1st moon landing** made by Armstrong and Aldrin (7/20); collected 47.5 lbs of soil, rock samples; lunar stay time 21:36.

10/11/1969: ***Soyuz 6***; 118:43; Georgi S. Shonin, Valery N. Kubasov. 1st welding of metals in space.

10/12/1969: ***Soyuz 7***; 118:40; Anatoly V. Flipchenko, Vladislav N. Volkov, Viktor V. Gorbatko. Space lab construction test made; *Soyuz 6*, *7*, and *8*: 1st time three spacecraft, seven crew members orbited the Earth at once.

10/13/1969: ***Soyuz 8***; 118:51; Vladimir A. Shatalov (2), Aleksei S. Yeliseyev (2). Part of space lab construction team.

11/14/1969: ***Apollo-Saturn 12***; 244:36; Charles Conrad Jr. (3), Richard F. Gordon Jr. (2), Alan L. Bean. Conrad and Bean made **2nd moon landing** (11/18); collected 75 lbs of samples; lunar stay time 31:31.

4/11/1970: ***Apollo-Saturn 13***; 142:54; James A. Lovell Jr. (4), Fred W. Haise Jr., John L. Swigert Jr. Aborted after service module oxygen tank ruptured; crew returned in lunar module.

6/1/1970: ***Soyuz 9***; 17 d., 16 hr., 59 min.; Andrian G. Nikolayev (2), Vitaly I. Sevastyanov. Longest human spaceflight to date.

1/31/1971: ***Apollo-Saturn 14***; 9 d., 2 min.; Alan B. Shepard Jr. (2), Stuart A. Roosa, Edgar D. Mitchell. Shepard and Mitchell made **3rd moon landing** (2/5); collected 94 lbs of lunar samples; lunar stay 33:31.

4/19/1971: ***Salyut 1***; launched without crew. **1st space station.**

4/22/1971: ***Soyuz 10***; 1 d., 23 hr., 46 min.; Vladimir A. Shatalov (3), Aleksei S. Yeliseyev (3), Nikolay N. Rukavishnikov. **1st successful docking with a space station**; failed to enter space station.

6/6/1971: ***Soyuz 11***; 23 d., 28 hr., 22 min.; Georgi T. Dobrovolskiy, Vladislav N. Volkov (2), Viktor I. Patsayev. Docked and entered *Salyut 1* space station; **crew died** during reentry from loss of pressurization.

7/26/1971: ***Apollo-Saturn 15***; 12 d., 17 hr., 12 min.; David R. Scott (3), James B. Irwin, Alfred M. Worden. Scott and Irwin made **4th moon landing** (7/30). 1st lunar rover use; 1st deep spacewalk; collected 170 lbs of samples; lunar stay 66:55.

4/16/1972: ***Apollo-Saturn 16***; 11 d., 1 hr., 51 min.; John W. Young (4), Charles M. Duke Jr., Thomas K. Mattingly II. Young and Duke made **5th moon landing** (4/20); collected 209 lbs of lunar samples; lunar stay 71:02.

12/7/1972: ***Apollo-Saturn 17***; 12 d., 13 hr., 52 min.; Eugene A. Cernan (3), Ronald E. Evans, Harrison H. Schmitt. Cernan and Schmitt made 6th and **final crewed lunar landing** (12/11); collected 243 lbs of samples; record lunar stay over 75 hr.

5/14/1973: ***Skylab 1***; launched without crew. **1st U.S. space station**; fell out of orbit 7/11/1979.

5/25/1973: ***Skylab 2***; 28 d., 49 min.; Charles Conrad Jr. (4), Joseph P. Kerwin, Paul J. Weitz. 1st U.S.-piloted orbiting space station; crew repaired damage caused in boost.

7/28/1973: ***Skylab 3***; 59 d., 11 hr., 1 min.; Alan L. Bean (2), Owen K. Garriott, Jack R. Lousma. Crew systems and operational tests; scientific activities; three EVAs, 13:44.

11/16/1973: ***Skylab 4***; 84 d., 1 hr., 16 min.; Gerald P. Carr, Edward G. Gibson, William R. Pogue. Final *Skylab* mission.

7/15/1975: ***Soyuz 19 (ASTP)***; 6 d., 11 hr., 31 min.; Aleksei A. Leonov (2), Valery N. Kubasov (2). U.S.-USSR joint flight; crews linked up in space (7/17), conducted experiments, shared meals, held a joint news conference.

7/15/1975: ***Apollo (ASTP)***; 9 d., 7 hr., 28 min.; Vance D. Brand, Thomas P. Stafford (4), Donald K. Slayton. Joint flight with *Soyuz 19*.

12/10/1977: *Soyuz 26*; 96 d., 10 hr.; Yuri V. Romanenko, Georgiy M. Grechko (2). 1st multiple docking at a space station (*Soyuz 26* and *27* docked at *Salyut 6*).

1/10/1978: *Soyuz 27*; 5 d., 22 hr., 59 min.; Vladimir A. Dzhanibekov. See *Soyuz 26*.

3/2/1978: *Soyuz 28*; 7 d., 22 hr., 16 min.; Aleksei A. Gubarev (2), Vladimir Remek. 1st international crew launch; Remek was 1st Czech in space.

4/12/1981: *Columbia (STS-1)*; 2 d., 6 hr., 21 min.; John W. Young (5), Robert L. Crippen. **1st reusable space shuttle** to fly into Earth's orbit.

11/12/1981: *Columbia (STS-2)*; 3 days; Joe H. Engle, Richard H. Truly. 1st scientific payload; 1st reuse of space shuttle.

11/11/1982: *Columbia (STS-5)*; 6 days; Vance D. Brand (2), Robert F. Overmyer, Joseph P. Allen, William B. Lenoir. 1st four-person crew.

6/18/1983: *Challenger (STS-7)*; 7 days; Robert L. Crippen (2), Frederick H. Hauck, John M. Fabian, Sally K. Ride, Norman E. Thagard. Ride was **1st U.S. woman in space**; 1st 5-person crew.

6/27/1983: *Soyuz T-9*; 150 days; Vladimir A. Lyakhov (2), Aleksandr Pavlovich. Docked at *Salyut 7*. 1st construction in space.

8/30/1983: *Challenger (STS-8)*; 7 days; Richard H. Truly (2), Daniel C. Brandenstein, Dale A. Gardner, Guion S. Bluford Jr., William E. Thornton. Bluford was **1st African-American in space; 1st night launch**.

11/28/1983: *Columbia (STS-9)*; 11 days; John W. Young (6), Brewster H. Shaw Jr., Owen K. Garriott (2), Robert A.R. Parker, Byron K. Lichtenberg, Ulf Merbold. 1st six-person crew; 1st Spacelab mission.

2/3/1984: *Challenger (41-B)*; 8 days; Vance Brand (3), Robert L. Gibson, Ronald E. McNair, Bruce McCandless II, Robert L. Stewart. 1st untethered EVA.

2/8/1984: *Soyuz T-10B*; 63 days; Leonid Kizim, Vladimir Solovyov, Oleg Atkov. Docked with *Salyut 7*; crew set space duration record of 237 days (since eclipsed).

4/3/1984: *Soyuz T-11*; 182 days; Yury Malyshev (2), Gennady Strekalov (3), Rakesh Sharma. Docked with *Salyut 7*; Sharma was 1st Indian in space.

4/6/1984: *Challenger (41-C)*; 7 days; Robert L. Crippen (3), Francis R. Scobee, George D. Nelson, Terry J. Hart, James D. van Hoften. 1st in-orbit satellite repair.

8/30/1984: *Discovery (41-D)*; 7 days; Henry W. Hartsfield Jr. (2), Michael L. Coats, Richard M. Mullane, Steven A. Hawley, Judith A. Resnik, Charles D. Walker. 1st flight of non-astronaut (payload specialist Walker).

10/5/1984: *Challenger (41-G)*; 9 days; Robert L. Crippen (4), Jon A. McBride, Kathryn D. Sullivan, Sally K. Ride (2), David C. Leestma, Marc Garneau, Paul D. Scully-Power. 1st seven-person crew.

11/8/1984: *Discovery (51-A)*; 8 days; Frederick H. Hauck (2), David M. Walker, Anna L. Fisher, Dale A. Gardner (2), Joseph P. Allen (2). 1st satellite retrieval/repair.

4/12/1985: *Discovery (51-D)*; 7 days; Karol J. Bobko, Donald E. Williams, Charles D. Walker (2), M. Rhea Seddon, Jeffrey A. Hoffman, S. David Griggs, E. Jake Garn. Garn (R, UT) was **1st U.S. senator in space**.

6/17/1985: *Discovery (51-G)*; 8 days; Daniel C. Brandenstein (2), John O. Creighton, Shannon W. Lucid, John M. Fabian (2), Steven R. Nagel, Prince Sultan Salman al-Saud, Patrick Baudry. Launched three satellites; Salman al-Saud was 1st Arab in space; Baudry was 1st French person on U.S. mission.

10/3/1985: *Atlantis (51-J)*; 5 days; Karol J. Bobko (3), Ronald J. Grabe, David C. Hilmers, Robert L. Stewart (2), William A. Pailes. 1st *Atlantis* flight.

10/30/1985: *Challenger (61-A)*; 8 days; Henry W. Hartsfield Jr. (3), Steven R. Nagel (2), James F. Buchli (2), Guion S. Bluford Jr. (2), Bonnie J. Dunbar, Wubbo J. Ockels, Richard Furrer, Ernst Messerschmid. 1st eight-person crew; 1st German Spacelab mission.

1/12/1986: *Columbia (61-C)*; 7 days; Robert L. Gibson (2), Charles F. Bolden Jr., Franklin R. Chang Díaz, Steven A. Hawley (2), George D. Nelson (2), Robert J. Cenker, Bill Nelson. B. Nelson (D, FL) was **1st U.S. representative in space**.

1/28/1986: *Challenger (51-L)*; 73 seconds; Francis R. Scobee (2), Michael J. Smith, Judith A. Resnik (2), Ellison S. Onizuka (2), Ronald E. McNair, Gregory B. Jarvis, Christa McAuliffe. **Exploded 73 seconds after liftoff; all aboard were killed**, including McAuliffe, a New Hampshire schoolteacher who won competition to become 1st private citizen in space.

2/20/1986: *Mir*[1]; launched without crew. **Space station** with six docking ports launched.

3/13/1986: *Soyuz T-15*; 125 days; Leonid Kizim (3), Vladimir Solovyov (2). Ferry between stations; docked at *Mir*.

9/29/1988: *Discovery (STS-26)*; 4 days; Frederick H. Hauck (3), Richard O. Covey (2), George D. Nelson (3), John M. Lounge (2), David C. Hilmers (2). **1st shuttle flight since *Challenger* explosion** 1/28/1986.

5/4/1989: *Atlantis (STS-30)*; 4 days; David M. Walker (2), Ronald J. Grabe (2), Norman E. Thagard (3), Mary L. Cleave (2), Mark C. Lee. Launched Venus orbiter *Magellan*.

10/18/1989: *Atlantis (STS-34)*; 5 days; Donald E. Williams (2), Michael J. McCulley, Shannon W. Lucid (2), Franklin R. Chang Díaz (2), Ellen S. Baker. Launched Jupiter probe and orbiter *Galileo*.

4/24/1990: *Discovery (STS-31)*; 6 days; Loren J. Shriver (2), Charles F. Bolden Jr. (2), Steven A. Hawley (3), Bruce McCandless (2), Kathryn D. Sullivan (2). **Launched Hubble Space Telescope.**

10/6/1990: *Discovery (STS-41)*; 5 days; Richard N. Richards (2), Robert D. Cabana, Bruce E. Melnick, William M. Shepherd (2), Thomas D. Akers. Launched *Ulysses* spacecraft to investigate interstellar space and the sun.

9/12/1992: *Endeavour (STS-47)*; 8 days; Robert L. Gibson (4), Curtis L. Brown Jr., Mark C. Lee (2), N. Jan Davis, Jay Apt (2), Mae Carol Jemison, Mamoru Mohri. Jemison was **1st black woman in space**; Lee and Davis were **1st married couple to travel together in space**; 1st Japanese Spacelab.

6/21/1993: *Endeavour (STS-57)*; 10 days; Ronald J. Grabe (4), Brian J. Duffy (2), G. David Low (3), Nancy J. Sherlock, Janice E. Voss, Peter J. K. Wisoff. Carried Spacelab commercial payload module.

12/2/1993: *Endeavour (STS-61)*; 11 days; Richard O. Covey (3), Kenneth D. Bowersox (2), F. Story Musgrave (5), Kathryn Thornton (3), Claude Nicollier (2), Jeffrey A. Hoffman (4), Thomas D. Akers (3). Hubble Space Telescope repaired; Akers set new U.S. EVA duration record (29 hr., 40 min.).

3/14/1995: *Soyuz TM-21*; 112 days; Norman E. Thagard (5), Vladimir Dezhurov, Gennady Strekalov (5). Docked with *Mir* 3/16. Thagard was 1st American on board Russian spacecraft; Valery Polyakov returned to Earth, 3/22/1995, after record stay in space (439 days).

6/27/1995: *Atlantis (STS-71)*; 10 days; Robert L. Gibson (5), Charles J. Precourt (2), Ellen S. Baker (3), Bonnie J. Dunbar (4), Gregory J. Harbaugh (3), Anatoly Solovyev (4) (to *Mir*), Nikolai M. Budarin (to *Mir*), Norman E. Thagard (5) (from *Mir*), Gennady Strekalov (from *Mir*), Vladimir Dezhurov (from *Mir*). **1st shuttle-*Mir* docking**; exchanged crew members with *Mir*.

11/12/1995: *Atlantis (STS-74)*; 9 days; Kenneth D. Cameron (3), James D. Halsell Jr. (2), Jerry L. Ross (5), William S. McArthur Jr. (2), Chris A. Hadfield. 2nd shuttle-*Mir* docking (11/15-11/18); erected a 15-ft permanent docking tunnel to *Mir* for future use by U.S. orbiters.

9/16/1996: *Atlantis (STS-79)*; 11 days; William F. Readdy (3), Terry W. Wilcutt (2), Thomas D. Akers (4), John E. Blaha (5) (to *Mir*), Jay Apt (4), Carl E. Walz (3), Shannon W. Lucid (5) (from *Mir*). Docked with *Mir* 9/18; exchanged crew members; Lucid set **U.S. and women's duration in space record** (188 days).

11/19/1996: *Columbia (STS-80)*; 18 days; Kenneth D. Cockrell (3), Kent V. Rominger (2), Tamara E. Jernigan (4), Thomas D. Jones (3), F. Story Musgrave (6). Longest-duration shuttle flight; Musgrave, 61, oldest thus far to fly in space; two science satellites deployed, retrieved.

8/5/1997: *Soyuz TM-26*; 198 days; Anatoly Solovyev (5), Pavel Vinogradov. Docked with *Mir* 8/7; repaired damaged space station.

8/7/1997: *Discovery (STS-85)*; 12 days; Curtis L. Brown Jr. (4), Kent V. Rominger (3), N. Jan Davis (3), Robert L. Curbeam Jr., Stephen K. Robinson, Bjarni V. Tryggvason. Deployed and retrieved satellite designed to study Earth's middle atmosphere; demonstrated robotic arm.

4/17/1998: *Columbia (STS-90)*; 16 days; Richard A. Searfoss (3), Scott D. Altman, Richard M. Linnehan (2), Dave R. Williams, Kathryn P. Hire, Jay C. Buckey, James A. Pawelczyk. Studied effects of microgravity on the nervous systems of the crew and more than 2,000 live animals; 1st surgery in space on animals meant to survive.

6/2/1998: ***Discovery (STS-91)***; 10 days; Charles J. Precourt (4), Dominic L. Gorie, Wendy B. Lawrence (3), Franklin R. Chang Díaz (6), Janet L. Kavandi, Valery V. Ryumin (4), Andrew S. W. Thomas (2) (from *Mir*). Final docking mission with *Mir*; Thomas from *Mir*, 141 days in space.

10/29/1998: ***Discovery (STS-95)***; 10 days; Curtis L. Brown Jr. (5), Steven W. Lindsey (2), Scott E. Parazynski (3), Stephen K. Robinson (2), Pedro Duque, Chiaki Mukai (2), John H. Glenn Jr. (2). The 77-year-old Glenn, one of the original *Mercury* astronauts, and at that point a senator (D, OH), became **oldest person to fly in space**; Duque was 1st Spaniard in space; experiments to study aging performed on Glenn.

12/4/1998: ***Endeavour (STS-88)***; 12 days; Robert D. Cabana (4), Frederick W. Sturckow, Nancy J. Currie (3), Jerry L. Ross (6), James H. Newman (3), Sergei K. Krikalev (4). **1st assembly of International Space Station (ISS)**; attached U.S.-built *Unity* connecting module to Russian-built *Zarya* control module; 1st crew to enter ISS.

7/23/1999: ***Columbia (STS-93)***; 5 days; Eileen M. Collins (3), Jeffrey S. Ashby, Steven A. Hawley (5), Catherine G. Coleman (2), Michel Tognini (2). Collins was **1st woman space shuttle commander**; deployed Chandra X-ray Observatory telescope.

2/11/2000: ***Endeavour (STS-99)***; 12 days; Kevin R. Kregel (4), Dominic L. Gorie (2), Janet L. Kavandi (2), Janice E. Voss (5), Mamoru Mohri (2), Gerhard P.J. Thiele. Used radar to make most complete topographic map of Earth's surface ever produced.

10/31/2000: ****Soyuz TM-31***; William M. Shepherd (4), Yuri Gidzenko (2), Sergei Krikalev (5). Established **1st permanent manning of ISS** with three-person crew for a 4-month stay.

7/12/2001: ***Atlantis (STS-104)***; 13 days; Steven W. Lindsey (3), Charles O. Hobaugh, Michael L. Gernhardt (4), Janet L. Kavandi (3), James F. Reilly II (2). Installed the Joint Airlock, with nitrogen and oxygen tanks to permit future spacewalks from the ISS; three EVAs.

10/30/2002: ****Soyuz TMA-1***[1]; Sergei Zalyotin (2), Frank De Winne, Yuri Lonchakov (2). 1st launch of *Soyuz TMA* (crew returned 11/10/2002 on *Soyuz TM-34* already docked at ISS).

1/16/2003: ***Columbia (STS 107)***; 16 days; Rick D. Husband (2), William C. McCool, Michael P. Anderson (2), David M. Brown, Kalpana Chawla (2), Laurel B. Clark, Ilan Ramon. **Entire crew lost when *Columbia* broke apart** upon reentry, 2/1, due to heat shield damage; Ramon was 1st Israeli astronaut.

10/15/2003: ****Shenzhou 5***; 21 hr.; Yang Liwei. **1st Chinese manned spacecraft.**

6/21/2004: ***SpaceShipOne***[2]; 90 min.; Mike Melvill. **1st privately funded manned spaceflight.**

7/26/2005: ***Discovery (STS-114)***; 14 days; Eileen M. Collins (4), James M. Kelly (2), Charles J. Camarda, Wendy B. Lawrence (4), Soichi Noguchi, Stephen K. Robinson (3), Andrew S.W. Thomas (3). **1st space shuttle flight since *Columbia* disaster**; tested new safety modifications to craft.

6/8/2007: ***Atlantis (STS-117)***; 14 days; Frederick W. Sturckow (3), Lee J. Archambault, Patrick G. Forrester (2), John "Danny" Olivas, James F. Reilly (3), Steven R. Swanson, Clayton C. Anderson (to ISS), Sunita L. Williams (from ISS). Delivered truss segments and solar arrays to ISS; Williams set new record for **longest spaceflight by a woman (195 days)**.

8/8/2007: ***Endeavour (STS-118)***; 13 days; Scott J. Kelly (2), Charles O. Hobaugh (2), Alvin B. Drew, Barbara R. Morgan, Tracy Caldwell Dyson, Rick A. Mastracchio (2), Dave R. Williams (2). Brought **Teacher in Space** project participant Morgan to ISS; attached new truss.

10/10/2007: ****Soyuz TMA-11***[1]; Yuri I. Malenchenko (3), Sheikh Muszaphar Shukor (to ISS), Peggy A. Whitson (2) (from ISS), Yi So-yeon (from ISS). Delivered and installed components of ISS; malfunctioned on return to Earth, landing short of its touchdown area but causing no fatalities.

3/11/2008: ***Endeavour (STS-123)***; 16 days; Dominic L. Gorie (4), Gregory H. Johnson, Richard M. Linnehan (4), Robert L. Behnken, Michael J. Foreman, Takao Doi (2), Garrett E. Reisman (to ISS), Léopold Eyharts (from ISS). Delivered components of the Japanese Kibo science laboratory.

4/8/2008: ****Soyuz TMA-12***[1]; Oleg Kononenko, Sergei Volkov, Yi So-yeon (to ISS), Richard Garriott (from ISS). Yi became **1st S. Korean in space.**

9/25/2008: ****Shenzhou 7***; 68 hr.; Jing Haipeng, Liu Boming, Zhai Zhigang. Zhai completed **1st Chinese spacewalk.**

5/11/2009: ***Atlantis (STS-125)***; 13 days; Scott D. Altman (4), Gregory C. Johnson, Andrew J. Feustel, Michael T. Good, John M. Grunsfeld (5), Michael J. Massimino (2), K. Megan McArthur. Final Hubble Space Telescope servicing mission.

6/15/2010: ****Soyuz TMA-19***[1]; Fyodor Yurchikhin (3), Shannon Walker, Douglas H. Wheelock (2). 100th mission since launching of the International Space Station.

7/8/2011: ***Atlantis (STS-135)***; 13 days; Christopher Ferguson (3), Doug Hurley (2), Sandy H. Magnus (3), Rex J. Walheim (3). **Final space shuttle mission.**

5/30/2020: ***SpaceX Demo-2***; Robert L. Behnken (3), Douglas G. Hurley (3). **1st commercially operated crewed spaceflight** to carry Americans into orbit.

Note: Four Soviet cosmonauts have died during spaceflight: one person was killed on *Soyuz 1* (1967) when parachute lines tangled during descent; the three-person *Soyuz 11* crew (1971) was asphyxiated. Three Americans died in the *Apollo 1* (1967) fire on the ground at Cape Canaveral, FL; seven Americans died in the *Challenger* (1986) explosion; and six Americans and an Israeli astronaut died aboard *Columbia* (2003). (1) *Soyuz* crew often return from the ISS on spacecraft that launched and were docked at the station before their arrival. (2) Date of first successful flight; later, *SpaceShipOne* flew at least 100 km (62 mi) into space, 9/29/2004, piloted by Mike Melvill, and 10/4/2004, piloted by Brian Binnie, winning the $10-mil Ansari Prize for first private venture to accomplish this feat twice within two weeks.

U.S. Space Shuttles

Source: National Aeronautics and Space Administration (NASA)

After 135 launches, the United States ended its space shuttle program with the safe landing of the *Atlantis* shuttle on July 21, 2011, at Florida's Kennedy Space Center. Two shuttles—*Challenger* in 1986 and *Columbia* in 2003—were destroyed in flight. The surviving shuttles are now on display at museums. *Enterprise* performed atmospheric test flights but never flew in space.

***Atlantis*:** Kennedy Space Center, Merritt Island, FL; www.kennedyspacecenter.com

***Discovery*:** Udvar-Hazy Center, Smithsonian National Air and Space Museum, Chantilly, VA; discovery.si.edu

***Endeavour*:** California Science Center, Los Angeles, CA. Reinstalled in vertical position in Jan. 2024 at Samuel Oschin Air and Space Center, under construction; www.californiasciencecenter.org

***Enterprise*:** Intrepid Museum, New York, NY; www.intrepidmuseum.org/Space_Shuttle_Pavilion

International Space Station

Source: National Aeronautics and Space Administration (NASA)

Construction on the International Space Station (ISS) began in 1998 and was completed in 2011. It has been inhabited continuously since 2000 and visited by more than 280 crew members from 23 countries as of July 2024. In 2023, Russia announced it would leave the partnership in 2028. The entire station is scheduled to be de-orbited in 2030, when it will land in a remote part of the ocean.

Cooperating nations: Belgium, Canada, Denmark, France, Germany, Italy, Japan, Netherlands, Norway, Russia, Spain, Sweden, Switzerland, United Kingdom, and U.S. As of July 2024, individuals from all of these countries (except Norway and Switzerland) have flown to the ISS, as have visitors from Belarus, Brazil, Israel, Kazakhstan, Malaysia, Saudi Arabia, South Africa, South Korea, Turkey, and the United Arab Emirates.

About the ISS

- It has a mass of 924,739 lbs and is about as long as a football field at 357.5 ft.
- It is entirely powered by an acre of solar panels.
- It requires three people to keep it running but has room for up to 10 people to live aboard.
- Astronauts typically spend 4-6 months aboard.

ISS Research

- Effects of long-term exposure to reduced gravity on humans, plants, crystals, cells, and pathogens
- Recording large-scale long-term changes in Earth's environment by observing the planet from orbit
- Testing recycling technologies for human life support

Summary of Worldwide Successful Launches, 1957-2023

Source: National Aeronautics and Space Administration (NASA); Space Launch Report

Year	1957-59	1960-69	1970-79	1980-89	1990-99	2000-09	2010-19	2020	2021	2022	2023	Total
Russia[1]	6	399	1,028	1,132	542	246	240	17	23	22	19	3,674
U.S.	18	614	247	191	300	206	209	32	41	73	100	2,031
China	—	—	8	16	33	52	194	35	52	62	66	518
ESA[2]	—	2	5	14	55	63	71	4	6	4	3	227
Ukraine	—	—	—	—	59	57	24	2	2	2	1	147
Japan	—	—	18	26	23	18	36	4	3	0	2	130
India	—	—	1	9	11	13	42	2	1	4	7	90
France[2]	—	4	14	5	16	0	0	0	0	0	0	39
New Zealand	—	—	—	—	—	—	7	6	5	9	8	35
UK[2]	—	1	6	4	7	0	0	0	0	0	0	18
Germany[2]	—	—	3	7	6	0	0	0	0	0	0	16
Canada	—	—	4	5	4	0	0	0	0	0	0	13
Israel	—	—	—	—	—	3	3	1	0	0	1	8
Iran	—	—	—	—	—	1	3	1	0	1	1	7
South Korea	—	—	—	—	—	1	0	0	0	1	2	4
North Korea	—	—	—	—	—	—	1	0	0	0	1	2
Total	**24**	**1,020**	**1,334**	**1,409**	**1,056**	**660**	**830**	**104**	**133**	**178**	**211**	**6,959**

— = Not applicable. (1) Data for 1957-91 apply to the Soviet Union, for 1992-96 to the Commonwealth of Independent States, after 1996 to Russia. (2) ESA = European Space Agency, which includes France, Germany, and UK after 2009.

Notable Lunar and Planetary Science Missions

Source: National Aeronautics and Space Administration (NASA)

Spacecraft	Launch date[1]	Mission	Mission notes
Mariner 2	Aug. 27, 1962	Venus	Passed within 22,000 mi of Venus 12/14/1962; confirmed high surface temperature on planet; contact lost 1/3/1963 at 54 mil mi.
Ranger 7	July 28, 1964	Moon	Yielded over 4,000 photos of lunar surface.
Mariner 4	Nov. 28, 1964	Mars	1st probe to fly by Mars; passed behind planet 7/14/1965.
Ranger 8	Feb. 17, 1965	Moon	Yielded over 7,000 photos of lunar surface.
Venera 3	Nov. 16, 1965	Venus	Soviet probe; 1st artificial probe to impact on the surface of another planet, 3/1/1966; probe failed to send back data.
Surveyor 3	Apr. 17, 1967	Moon	Scooped and tested lunar soil.
Mariner 5	June 14, 1967	Venus	In solar orbit; closest Venus flyby 10/19/1967; allowed scientists to obtain accurate readings on the composition of the Venusian atmosphere.
Mariner 6	Feb. 24, 1969	Mars	Came within 2,000 mi of Mars 7/31/1969; collected data, photos.
Mariner 7	Mar. 27, 1969	Mars	Came within 2,000 mi of Mars 8/5/1969.
Venera 7	Aug. 17, 1970	Venus	Soviet probe; 1st probe to land safely on the surface of another planet.
Mariner 9	May 30, 1971	Mars	1st craft to orbit Mars 11/13/1971; sent back over 7,000 photos.
Pioneer 10	Mar. 2, 1972	Jupiter	Passed Jupiter 12/4/1973; took readings on Jupiter's composition. Exited planetary system 6/13/1983; last signal received 1/23/2003 from 7.6 bil mi.
Pioneer 11	Apr. 5, 1973	Jupiter, Saturn	Passed Jupiter 12/3/1974, Saturn 9/1/1979; discovered an additional ring and 2 moons around Saturn. Transmission ended 9/30/1995.
Mariner 10	Nov. 3, 1973	Venus, Mercury	Passed Venus 2/5/1974, arrived at Mercury 3/29/1974. 1st time gravity of a planet (Venus) used to whip spacecraft toward another (Mercury); 1st probe to visit 2 planets.
Viking 1	Aug. 20, 1975	Mars	Landed on Mars 7/20/1976; 1st probe to land safely on Mars; performed chemical analysis of soil; functioned 6 years.
Viking 2	Sept. 9, 1975	Mars	Sister probe of *Viking 1*; landed on Mars 9/3/1976; functioned 3 years.
Voyager 2	Aug. 20, 1977	Jupiter, Saturn, Uranus, Neptune	Encountered Jupiter 7/9/1979, Saturn 8/25/1981, Uranus 1/24/1986, Neptune 8/25/1989. Confirmed existence of rings around Neptune. As of 9/2023 it was 12.5 bil mi from sun and still returning data to Earth.
Voyager 1	Sept. 5, 1977	Jupiter, Saturn	Encountered Jupiter 3/5/1979; provided evidence of rings around Jupiter; passed Saturn 11/12/1980; became most distant human-made object 2/17/1998. As of 9/2023 it was nearly 15.0 bil mi from sun and still returning data to Earth.
Pioneer Venus 1	May 20, 1978	Venus	Entered Venus orbit 12/4/1978; studied atmosphere, magnetic field, weather, and surface; fuel ran out; probe was destroyed in atmospheric entry, 8/1992.
Pioneer Venus 2 (multiprobe)	Aug. 8, 1978	Venus	Consisted of a "bus" carrying 1 large and 3 small atmospheric probes. All 4 probes entered the Venus atmosphere 12/9/1978.
Magellan	May 4, 1989	Venus	Landed on Venus 8/10/1990; monitored geological activity; mapped more than 99% of planet surface, showed that about 85% is covered by volcanic flows; ceased operating 10/11/1994.
Galileo	Oct. 18, 1989	Jupiter	Used Earth's gravity to propel itself towards Jupiter; encountered Venus 2/10/1990, Jupiter 12/7/1995; encountered moons. Released probe into Jovian atmosphere; intentionally flown into Jupiter 9/21/2003.
Mars Global Surveyor	Nov. 7, 1996	Mars	Began orbiting Mars 9/11/1997; began mapping entire surface 3/9/1999; discovered a weak magnetic field on planet; observed Martian moon Phobos; found evidence of liquid water in past 6/22/2000.
Mars Pathfinder	Dec. 4, 1996	Mars	Landed on Mars 7/4/1997; rover *Sojourner* measured climate and soil composition, sent surface images; ceased operating 9/27/1997.
Cassini-Huygens	Oct. 15, 1997	Saturn	Began orbiting Saturn 6/30/2004; spotted evidence of a subterranean ocean and hot spots region on moon Titan; detected an atmosphere on moon Enceladus. Intentionally destroyed 9/15/2017. *Huygens* probe landed on Titan 1/14/2005; found possible water ice, channels carved by liquid methane springs.

Spacecraft	Launch date[1]	Mission	Mission notes
Lunar Prospector	Jan. 6, 1998	Moon	Began orbiting moon 1/11/1998; mapped abundance of 11 elements on moon's surface; discovered evidence of water ice at both lunar poles.
Deep Space 1	Oct. 24, 1998	Comet Borrelly	Flew within 1,500 mi of comet; sent back photos showing 6-mi-long nucleus.
Stardust	Feb. 7, 1999	Comet Wild 2	Reached comet 1/2/2004; gathered dust samples, capsule returned to Earth 1/15/2006. Spacecraft, on new mission Stardust-NExT (follow-up for Deep Impact), reached comet Tempel 1, 2/14/2011.
2001 Mars Odyssey	Apr. 7, 2001	Mars	Reached Mars 10/24/2001; detected evidence of water ice near south pole; primary mission to study climate and geologic history completed 8/2004; began extended mission, aiming to identify minerals on Mars.
Genesis	Aug. 8, 2001	Sun	Orbited sun, collected particles from solar wind; capsule containing specimens crashed to Earth 9/8/2004; some samples survived.
Mars Express/ Beagle 2 lander	June 3, 2003	Mars	1st European Space Agency probe to another planet; arrived at Mars 12/2003; performed remote sensing including photography in search of subsurface water. *Beagle 2* lander was deployed 12/19/2003, but contact was lost.
Mars Exploration Rovers	June 7 and July 10, 2003	Mars	Rovers *Spirit* and *Opportunity* landed on Mars 1/2004, found further evidence that water existed on surface; *Spirit* took 1st photo of a Martian meteor; survived severe dust storms in 2007. *Opportunity* explored massive Victoria Crater 2007-08, set record for most distance driven off-Earth (25 mi) 7/2014.
MESSENGER	Mar. 2, 2004	Mercury	Began returning images of Mercury during initial flyby 1/14/2008; entered orbit 3/17/2011; delivered 100,000th image 5/3/2012; impacted Mercury 4/30/2015.
Deep Impact	Jan. 12, 2005	Comet Tempel 1	Reached Tempel 1; deployed impact probe that slammed into comet 7/4/2005 with force roughly equivalent to 5 tons of TNT. Flyby spacecraft, on supplemental mission EPOXI, reached comet Hartley 2, 11/4/2010.
Mars Reconnaissance Orbiter	Aug. 12, 2005	Mars	Reached Mars 3/10/2006 and began taking detailed images of Martian surface; in 3/2008, found salt deposits suggesting ancient water supplies; in 6/2008, found largest known impact crater in solar system.
New Horizons (Pluto)	Jan. 19, 2006	Pluto, Charon	Flew past Jupiter 7/2007 on its way to Pluto and its largest moon, Charon. Returned first-ever photographs of Pluto 7/14/2015. Began examining other objects in the Kuiper Belt in 2019.
Phoenix Mars Lander	Aug. 4, 2007	Mars	Landed on Mars 5/25/2008; examined northern polar region, analyzed weather/minerals; water ice verified 7/31/2008; lost contact 11/2/2008.
Dawn	Sept. 27, 2007	Asteroid Belt (bet. Jupiter and Mars)	Compared evolution of dwarf planet Ceres with Vesta, an asteroid, in an effort to shed light on formation of the solar system. Departed Vesta 8/2012; reached Ceres 3/6/2015.
Kepler/K2	Mar. 9, 2009	Extrasolar planets	Detected potentially habitable Earth-size planets around other Milky Way stars. Kepler confirmed existence of more than 2,600 exoplanets before running out of fuel in Oct. 2018.
Lunar Crater Observation and Sensing Satellite	June 18, 2009	Moon	Impacted the Cabeus crater; detected presence of water ice in moon's surface 10/9/2009. Lunar Reconnaissance Orbiter (LRO), launched with LCROSS, mapped moon's surface.
Juno	Aug. 5, 2011	Jupiter	Entered Jupiter's orbit 7/4/2016; began returning data and color images that improve understanding of the formation of the planet and solar system.
Mars Science Laboratory	Nov. 26, 2011	Mars	*Curiosity* rover landed on Mars 8/6/2012 and began assessing Mars's past and present ability to support life.
Lunar Atmosphere and Dust Environment Explorer	Sept. 6, 2013	Moon	Studied the fragile lunar atmosphere from orbit for 100 days; impacted with lunar surface 4/17/2014.
Mars Atmosphere and Volatile EvolutioN (MAVEN)	Nov. 18, 2013	Mars	Entered orbit 9/21/2014; exploring Mars's upper atmosphere to determine how planet's loss of atmospheric gas changed its climate from a warmer, wetter environment to a cold desert.
OSIRIS-REx	Sept. 8, 2016	Bennu (asteroid)	First mission to return a sample from an asteroid, aiming to better understand potential asteroid-Earth impacts and the source of Earth's organic materials and water. Entered orbit around Bennu 12/31/2018; returned to Earth 9/24/2023.
Transiting Exoplanet Survey Satellite	Apr. 18, 2018	Extrasolar planets	Survey 200,000 of the brightest nearby stars in search of planets outside our solar system.
InSight	May 5, 2018	Mars	Landed 11/26/2018; began drilling in 2019 beneath surface to investigate how rocky planets form and develop.
Parker Solar Probe	Aug. 12, 2018	Sun	First spacecraft to reach Sun's upper atmosphere 12/14/2021.
ICESat-2	Sept. 15, 2018	Earth	Initiated ultra-precise measurements of Earth's ice sheets and glaciers and how changes are affecting rising sea levels.
Mars Perseverance	July 30, 2020	Mars	Landed 2/18/2021 and began searching for signs of ancient microbial life to evaluate the past habitability of Mars.
Double Asteroid Redirection Test (DART)	Nov. 24, 2021	Dimorphos (asteroid)	Crashed into asteroid 9/26/2022 to assess human ability to alter its speed and orbit in order to prevent an asteroid or comet from hitting Earth.
James Webb Space Telescope	Dec. 25, 2021	Universe	Replaced Hubble Space Telescope as the world's premier astronomical observatory. Returned first high-resolution color images 7/2022.
Europa Clipper	Oct. 2024	Europa	Assess if Europa, Jupiter's icy, ocean-bearing moon, is suitable for life.
Quesst	2024	Suborbital	First flight of the X-59, aircraft that can travel at supersonic speed without causing thunderous sonic boom.
SPHEREx	Before Apr. 2025	Milky Way galaxy and beyond	Spectro-Photometer for the History of the Universe, Epoch of Reionization and Ices Explorer will collect data on more than 450 million galaxies and 100 million stars to explore the origins of the universe.
Artemis III	Sept. 2026 or later	Moon	First human moon landing in more than 50 years. Explore lunar surface in preparation for human flight to Mars and study potential for habitation of the moon.
Martian Moons eXploration (MMX)	Nov. 2026	Phobos, Deimos	Japanese Aerospace Exploration Agency mission to determine the origin of two Martian moons.

Note: U.S./NASA missions unless otherwise noted. (1) In Coordinated Universal Time.

General Aviation and Air Taxi Active Aircraft, 2022

Source: Federal Aviation Administration; aircraft not associated with major airlines or the military

Aircraft Type	Total active	Personal	Business	Instructional	Aerial apps.	Aerial observation	Other work	Sightseeing	Air medical	Other	On-demand operations
Fixed Wing	**164,567**	**108,396**	**22,413**	**15,600**	**2,547**	**2,174**	**882**	**247**	**187**	**5,611**	**6,503**
Piston	137,728	103,424	10,589	15,440	525	1,898	519	241	164	3,802	1,113
Turboprop	10,713	2,298	3,356	81	1,950	270	319	0	—	628	1,792
Turbojet	16,126	2,674	8,468	78	73	—	45	—	—	1,181	3,583
Rotorcraft	**9,769**	**1,459**	**492**	**1,248**	**1,024**	**1,978**	**458**	**168**	**89**	**481**	**2,372**
Piston	2,748	1,090	165	812	216	191	—	113	0	31	111
Turbine	7,021	369	320	436	808	1,788	445	55	89	450	2,260
Other Aircraft	**4,476**	**3,082**	**55**	**464**	**0**	**0**	**52**	**716**	**0**	**48**	**58**
Gliders	1,628	1,236	—	367	0	0	0	—	0	—	0
Lighter-than-air	2,848	1,846	—	98	0	0	52	714	0	44	58
Experimental	**28,062**	**26,442**	**721**	**315**	—	**30**	**54**	—	0	**443**	—
Amateur	22,127	21,176	603	185	—	—	0	0	0	155	0
Exhibition	1,819	1,549	44	38	0	—	39	—	0	131	5
Experimental light-sport	3,457	3,271	44	78	0	—	0	—	0	54	0
Other	658	447	30	—	—	21	—	0	0	103	0
Special Light-sport	**2,666**	**2,206**	**55**	**342**	**0**	—	—	—	**0**	**37**	**0**
ALL AIRCRAFT	**209,540**	**141,586**	**23,749**	**17,969**	**3,596**	**4,198**	**1,462**	**1,144**	**276**	**6,619**	**8,938**

— = Insufficient data. **Note:** Columns may not add to totals due to rounding. Totals include some categories not shown. **Personal**—Flying for personal reasons; **Business**—Individual or group use for business transportation with or without a professional crew (includes fractional ownership); **Instructional**—Flying under the supervision of a flight instructor; **Aerial applications**—Includes agriculture, forestry, public health, fire fighting, and other applications; **Aerial observation**—Includes aerial mapping/photography, patrol, search and rescue, hunting, traffic advisory, ranching, surveillance, oil and mineral exploration, etc.; **Other work**—Construction work, parachuting, aerial advertising, towing gliders, external load, etc.; **Sightseeing**—Commercial sightseeing; **Air medical services**—Air ambulance services, rescue, human organ transportation, emergency medical services; **Other**—Positioning flights, proficiency flights, training, ferrying, sales demos; **On-demand operations**—On-demand air taxi, air tours, commuter, and air medical services.

Estimated Active Airmen Certificates Held, 2023

Source: Federal Aviation Administration, U.S. Dept. of Transportation

Category	Certificates	Category	Certificates	Category	Certificates
Pilot total	**806,940**	Rotorcraft (helicopters only)	13,428	**Nonpilot total**	**749,618**
Student	316,470	Glider (only)	21,292	Mechanic	329,156
Recreational (only)	71	**Flight Instructor Certificates**	**131,577**	Repairmen	39,141
Sport (only)	7,144	**Instrument Ratings**	**332,313**	Parachute Rigger	7,775
Airplane[1]		**Remote Pilots[2]**	**368,633**	Ground Instructor	78,691
Private	167,711			Dispatcher	25,562
Commercial	106,711			Flight Navigator	23
Airline Transport	174,113			Flight Attendant	245,353
				Flight Engineer	23,917

Note: The term *airmen* includes men and women certified as pilots, mechanics, or other aviation technicians. (1) Includes pilots with an airplane-only certificate as well as those with an airplane and a helicopter and/or glider certificate. (2) Remote pilot certification began in Aug. 2016. These numbers are not included in pilot totals.

World's Most Commonly Flown Aircraft, 2024

Source: Forecast International; World Almanac research

Manufacturer, headquarters, and model	Number in operation	Avg. age (years)
Airbus, Netherlands		
A220-300	244	3.0
A319-100	1,062	18.6
A320-200	3,578	13.7
A320 neo	1,779	4.0
A321-200	1,530	11.4
A321 neo	1,225	2.8
A330-200	424	15.3
A330-300	645	13.4
A330-900 neo	115	3.2
A350-900XWB	470	5.0
A380-800[1]	229	10.2
ATR, France		
ATR-42-300 (Turboprop)	147	34.0
ATR-72-500 (Turboprop)	255	17.8
ATR-72-600 (Turboprop)	485	7.6
Boeing, U.S.		
717-200	125	22.3
737 MAX 8	1,214	3.7
737 MAX 9	211	2.8
737-200 Adv	139	42.0
737-300	344	31.5
737-400	241	31.0
737-500	188	29.9
737-700	868	19.0
737-800	4,544	13.1
737-900ER	444	10.2
747-400[1]	149	28.9
747-400F[1]	129	24.6
757-200	424	29.6
767-300ER	396	25.6
767-300F	240	10.7
777-200ER	293	22.4
777-300ER	765	11.4
Boeing (continued)		
777F	257	7.7
787-8	371	9.2
787-9 Dreamliner	609	6.3
Bombardier, Canada		
RJ200ER	245	22.6
RJ200LR	111	22.6
RJ700	279	18.8
RJ900	404	12.1
British Aerospace, UK		
Jetstream 31 (Turboprop)	184	35.4
Cessna, U.S.		
208B	413	31.9
De Havilland, Canada		
DHC-6-300 (Turboprop)	258	47.3
DHC-8-102 (Turboprop)	127	35.7
DHC-8-400Q[2] (Turboprop)	423	13.1
Fairchild, U.S.		
SA-227AC (Turboprop)	173	38.6
Embraer, Brazil		
Embraer 175	165	10.1
Embraer 175LR	525	8.0
Embraer 190AR	199	15.4
Embraer 190LR	188	13.4
ERJ 145LR	265	22.8
Fokker, Netherlands		
Fokker 50	111	33.6
Fokker 100	151	32.0
Raytheon, U.S.		
1900D (Turboprop)	322	27.7
Saab, Sweden		
SF.340B (Turboprop)	192	30.7
Sukhoi, Russia		
Superjet 100-95	176	7.6

Note: All aircraft are two-engine planes except where indicated. (1) Four-engine. (2) Manufactured by Bombardier since 1992.

Milestones in Aviation History

Source: National Aeronautics and Space Administration (NASA); Smithsonian National Air and Space Museum; Air Transport Association of America; National Museum of the U.S. Air Force (USAF); National Park Service, U.S. Dept. of the Interior

1903, Dec. 17: Brothers Wilbur and Orville Wright (U.S.) made the first human-carrying, powered flight near Kitty Hawk, NC. Each brother made two flights; the longest, about 852 ft, lasted 59 sec.

1908, May 14: Charles Furnas (U.S.), worker for Wright brothers, became first American airplane passenger.

1911, Feb.: The Burgess Company and Curtiss, Inc. receive authorization to build Wright planes, becoming the first licensed airplane manufacturer in the U.S.

1911, Sept. 23: First transportation of mail by airplane officially approved by the U.S. Postal Service.

1914, Jan. 1: First scheduled passenger airline service began.

1914, June 18: Lawrence Burst Sperry (U.S.) released the controls and stood in his airborne plane, successfully demonstrating his gyrostabilizer, the first autopilot system.

1918, Mar. 6: The Curtiss-Sperry "Flying Bomb" (U.S.) made its first successful flight. The first radio-controlled plane led to the development of cruise missiles.

1918, May 15: First scheduled airmail service began, between New York and Washington, DC, with intermediate stop in Philadelphia. In 1921, scheduled transcontinental airmail service began between New York City and San Francisco.

1919, June 14-15: Capt. John Alcock (UK) and Lt. Arthur W. Brown (U.S.) completed the first nonstop flight across the Atlantic Ocean. They traveled from Newfoundland, Canada, to Ireland in 16 hr., 12 min.

1923, Aug.: Rotating beacons enabled the first U.S. night flights.

1924, Apr. 6-Sept. 28: Two U.S. Army planes landed in Seattle, completing the first circumnavigation of the globe. They completed the 26,000-mi journey in 371 hours of flying time.

1926, May 12-13: Roald Amundsen (Norway), Umberto Nobile (Italy), Lincoln Ellsworth (U.S.), and Oscar Wisting (Norway) made the first flight over the North Pole, in a dirigible that flew between Spitsbergen, Norway, and Teller, AK. Two weeks earlier, Adm. Richard E. Byrd and Floyd Bennett (both U.S.) claimed to have made the first flight over the Pole (May 9, 1926) in a Fokker F-VII. But when Byrd's diary was released to the public in 1996, some historians began to question whether his plane had reached the Pole.

1927, May 20-21: Charles Lindbergh (U.S.) completed the first solo transatlantic flight in the *Spirit of St. Louis*. "Lucky Lindy" traveled 3,610 mi from New York to Paris in 33 hr., 29 min., 30 sec.

1929, Aug. 8-29: Hugo Eckener (Germany) piloted the *Graf Zeppelin* around the world in record time: 20,373 mi in 21 days, 5 hr., 31 min.

1929, Nov. 28: Richard E. Byrd, Harold June, Ashley McKinley (all U.S.) and Bernt Balchen (Norway) became first to fly over the South Pole, in 18 hr., 41 min. round trip from Ross Ice Shelf base.

1930, May 15: Ellen Church (U.S.) became first flight attendant.

1931, June 23-July 1: Wiley Post (U.S.) and Harold Gatty (Austral.-U.S.) broke the speed record for around-the-world flight, traveling 15,474 mi in 8 days, 15 hr., 51 min., in the monoplane *Winnie Mae*.

1931, Oct. 3-5: Clyde Pangborn and Hugh Herndon (both U.S.) completed the first nonstop transpacific flight. They traveled 4,558 mi from Misawa, Japan, to East Wenatchee, WA, in 41 hr., 34 min.

1932, May 20-21: Amelia Earhart (U.S.) completed first solo transoceanic flight by a woman, making the 2,026-mi journey from Newfoundland, Canada, to Ireland in 14 hr., 56 min.

1933, July 15-22: Wiley Post completed the first solo circumnavigation of the globe. His 15,596-mi trip took 7 days, 18 hr., 49 min.

1936, June 25: American Airlines began scheduled passenger service of the first Douglas DC-3 aircraft. The DC-3 was the first aircraft with a kitchen onboard and hence offered the first in-flight hot meal service.

1937, May 6: German *Hindenburg* zeppelin exploded in Lakehurst, NJ, killing 35 of the 97 people aboard (and one on the ground). The airship had made 34 transatlantic flights in 1936.

1938, July 10-13: Howard Hughes (U.S.) and four assistants established a new speed record for circumnavigating the globe: 14,824 mi in 3 days, 9 hr., 17 min.

1939, Aug. 27: The German-made Heinkel He 178 made the first successful flight powered by a jet engine.

1947, Oct. 14: Chuck Yeager (U.S.) broke the sound barrier, reaching Mach 1 in a Bell X-1 rocket-powered aircraft.

1947, Nov. 2: Howard Hughes piloted a Hughes H-4 Hercules on its only flight. The largest plane ever built at the time, the so-called *Spruce Goose* could carry 750 troops or two Sherman tanks.

1949, Mar. 2: James Gallagher (U.S.) piloted the first round-the-world flight refueled in midair. The *Lucky Lady* USAF B-50 covered 23,452 mi in 94 hr., 1 min. and refueled four times.

1950, Sept. 22: Col. David Schilling (USAF) made the first nonstop transatlantic jet flight, covering 3,300 mi in 10 hr., 1 min.

1952, Aug. 26: The UK bomber Canberra made the first round-trip transatlantic crossing on the same day, from Northern Ireland to Newfoundland, Canada, and back in 7 hr., 59 min.

1953, May 18: Jacqueline Cochran (U.S.) became the first woman to fly faster than the speed of sound.

1956, Mar. 10: Britain's Fairey FD-2 aircraft set a world speed record of 1,132 mph.

1956, Nov. 11: Convair B-58 (USAF), the first supersonic bomber, was introduced.

1957, Jan. 15-18: Three USAF B-52 Stratofortresses made the first nonstop global flight by jet planes. They were refueled in flight by KC-97 aerial tankers.

1958, Oct. 24: A Mirage III-A achieved Mach 2 (twice the speed of sound) in level flight, first European plane to do so.

1962, Nov. 29: Britain and France signed an agreement to jointly develop the Concorde, a supersonic plane that could fly twice as fast as most U.S. jets.

1969, June 5: The Soviet Tupolev Tu-144 became the first passenger airliner to break the sound barrier.

1970, May 26: The Tupolev Tu-144 became first passenger airline to exceed Mach 2 with a top speed of about 1,335 mph at 53,475 ft.

1976, Aug. 23: The Concorde began the first scheduled supersonic commercial service.

1977, Aug. 23: The *Gossamer Condor*, built by aeronautical engineer Paul MacCready (U.S.), successfully demonstrated human-powered flight through pedalling.

1979, June 12: MacCready's human-powered *Gossamer Albatross* crossed the English Channel in 2 hr., 49 min.

1981, July 7: MacCready-developed *Solar Challenger* became first solar-powered airplane to cross the English Channel.

1995, Aug. 15-16: The Concorde set a new around-the-world speed record for a passenger plane of 31 hr., 27 min., 49 sec.

1999, Mar. 1-21: Bertrand Piccard (Switz.) and Brian Jones (UK) completed the first around-the-world flight in a hot-air balloon. Their 29,055-mi journey lasted 19 days, 21 hr., 55 min.

2001, Aug. 13: Solar-powered, propeller-driven plane *Helios* (NASA) reached 96,863 ft, breaking altitude record for non-rocket-powered aircraft.

2002, June 19-July 4: Steve Fossett (U.S.) completed the first nonstop solo circumnavigation of globe in a balloon.

2003, Nov. 26: The Concorde flew its final flight.

2005, Mar. 1-3: Steve Fossett achieved the first nonstop solo circumnavigation in an airplane without refueling.

2011, Feb. 4: Northrop Grumman and the U.S. Navy reported the first successful flight for the unmanned X-47B fighter jet.

2012, May 22-31: SpaceX became the first private company to successfully launch (and later recover) a spacecraft to the International Space Station.

2016, July 26: *Solar Impulse 2* became first fuel-free plane to circumnavigate the globe. The 17-leg journey began in Mar. 2015.

2019, Apr. 13: *Stratolaunch* aircraft, with world's longest wingspan, made its maiden voyage. Its design enabled it to launch satellites into space from 35,000 ft, saving rocket fuel.

2020, May 31: A SpaceX Crew Dragon capsule safely delivered two NASA astronauts to the ISS, marking the first time a private spacecraft carried passengers into orbit without government involvement.

ASTRONOMY

Edited by Laurence A. Marschall, Prof. Emeritus, Dept. of Physics and Astronomy, Gettysburg College

Celestial Events Summary, 2025

There will be four eclipses in 2025: two partial solar eclipses and two total lunar eclipses. The most accessible of the solar eclipses, on Mar. 29, will only be visible from NW Europe and Africa, N Russia, Greenland, and far NE Canada. The solar eclipse of Sept. 21 will only be visible from the South Pacific, New Zealand, and W Antarctica. The two total lunar eclipses, Mar. 14 and Sept. 7, will be widely visible, the former from most of the western hemisphere (the Americas, W Europe and W Africa), the latter from the eastern hemisphere (Europe, Africa, Asia, and Australia).

Many of the meteor showers in 2025 are likely to peak under dark skies after midnight, unhampered by much moonlight, making it a favorable year for meteor shower watchers. Among the best may be the Orionids in Oct. and the Leonids in Nov., and the Geminids in Dec. The Quarantids in Jan. also occur in dark skies. The Perseids in Aug., however, will peak near full moon, which will reduce their visibility, though some activity will be visible, especially from dark rural sites.

Venus will be visible in the evening sky Jan.-Feb., until it approaches inferior conjunction with the sun in Mar. and reappears in the morning sky in Apr. until Nov. as it approaches superior conjunction with the sun in Jan. 2026. Mars is the evening star from Jan. until Oct. Jupiter is visible in the evening sky Jan.-May, reaching conjunction with the sun in June, and reappearing in the morning sky in July, where it will be visible through Dec. Saturn is an evening object at the start of the year, reaching conjunction in Mar. then visible in the morning sky in Apr., becoming visible all night around opposition in Sept. and then appearing as an evening object for the remainder of the year. Mercury, frequently too close to the sun for easy viewing, begins the year in the morning sky. It is in the morning sky in Apr., May, and Dec. and in the evening in Feb., Mar., June, July, and Oct. The best opportunities for seeing Mercury in the morning sky are near western elongation Apr. 21, Aug. 19, and Dec. 7, while the best opportunities to see it in the evening sky occur at eastern elongation Mar. 8, July 4, and Oct. 29.

The crescent moon, with its subdued light, regularly pairs with the two brightest planets, Venus and Jupiter. Waxing crescent pairings are visible in the early evening soon after sunset, while waning crescent pairings are visible in the early morning before sunrise. In 2025 the waxing crescent moon pairs with Venus in Jan.-Feb. and with Jupiter in Jan.-Apr. The waning crescent pairs with Venus in Apr.-Oct. and with Jupiter in Aug.-Dec. The moon will occult four bright planets this year: Mars on Jan. 14 and Feb. 9; Mercury on Mar. 1; Venus on Sept. 19; and Saturn on Jan. 4. The most noticeable planetary conjunction of the year occurs when Venus and Jupiter pass close to each other on Aug. 12.

Astronomical Positions and Constants

Two celestial bodies are in **conjunction** when they are due north and south of each other, either in **right ascension** (with respect to the north celestial pole) or in **celestial longitude** (with respect to the north ecliptic pole). Celestial bodies in conjunction will rise and set at nearly the same time. For the inner planets—Mercury and Venus—**inferior conjunction** occurs when either planet passes between Earth and the sun, while **superior conjunction** occurs when either Mercury or Venus is on the far side of the sun. Celestial bodies are in **opposition** when their right ascensions differ by exactly 12 hours, or when their celestial longitudes differ by 180°. In this case one of the two objects in opposition will rise while the other is setting. **Quadrature** refers to the arrangement where the coordinates of two bodies differ by exactly 90°. These terms may refer to the relative positions of any two bodies as seen from Earth, but one of the bodies is so frequently the sun that mention of the sun is omitted in that case.

When objects are in conjunction, the alignment is not perfect, and one usually passes above or below the other. The geocentric angular separation between the sun and an object is termed **elongation**. Elongation is limited only for Mercury and Venus; the greatest elongation for each of these bodies is approximately the time for longest observation. **Perihelion** is the point in an object's orbit when it is nearest to the sun, and **aphelion** is the point when it is farthest from the sun. **Perigee** is the point in an orbit where an object is nearest Earth, **apogee** the point when it is farthest from Earth. An **occultation** of a planet or a star is an eclipse of it by some other body, usually the moon. A **transit** of the sun occurs when Mercury or Venus passes directly between Earth and the sun, appearing to cross the sun's disk.

The following were adopted as part of the International Astronomical Union System of Astronomical Constants (1976/2009): **Speed of light**, 299,792.458 km per sec., or about 186,282 statute mi per sec.; **solar parallax**, 8".794143; **astronomical unit** (AU or au, mean distance between the Earth and sun), 149,597,870,700 m, or 92,955,807 mi; **constant of nutation**, 9".2025; and **constant of aberration**, 20".49552.

Celestial Events Highlights, 2025

(In Coordinated Universal Time, or UTC, the standard time of the prime meridian.)

January

Mercury is visible low in the E just before sunrise.
Mars is visible all night, in the E in the evening and setting in the W near sunrise.
Venus, Jupiter, Saturn, Uranus, and **Neptune** are visible in the W in the early evening.

Jan. 3: Venus 1.4°N of moon; Quarantid meteor shower
Jan. 4: Earth at perihelion; Saturn 0.7°S of moon; occultation of Saturn by moon
Jan. 5: Moon at ascending node
Jan. 6: First quarter moon
Jan. 7: Moon at perigee
Jan. 10: Pleiades 0.3°S of moon; Venus at greatest elongation: 47.2°E of sun
Jan. 13: Pollux 2.1°N of moon; full moon
Jan. 14: Mars 0.2°S of moon; occultation of Mars by moon
Jan. 16: Mars at opposition; Regulus 2.2°S of moon
Jan. 18: Venus 2.2°N of Saturn
Jan. 19: Moon at descending node; Mercury at aphelion
Jan. 21: Spica 0.1°N of moon; moon at apogee; last quarter moon
Jan. 23: Mars 2.3°S of Pollux
Jan. 24: Antares 0.3°N of moon
Jan. 29: New moon

February

Mercury is too close to the sun to be visible, moving into the evening sky late in the month.
Venus, Jupiter, and **Uranus** are visible in the W in the early evening.
Mars is visible in the E in the evening and in the W in the early morning.
Saturn and **Neptune** are low in the W early in the month and later are too close to the sun for easy visibility.

Feb. 1: Saturn 1.1°S of moon; Venus 2.3°N of moon; moon at ascending node
Feb. 2: Moon at perigee
Feb. 5: First quarter moon
Feb. 6: Pleiades 0.5°S of moon
Feb. 9: Mercury at superior conjunction; Mars 0.8°S of moon; occultation of Mars by moon
Feb. 10: Pollux 2.1°N of moon
Feb. 12: Full moon; Regulus 2.2°S of moon

Feb. 15: Moon at descending node
Feb. 17: Spica 0.3°N of moon
Feb. 18: Moon at apogee
Feb. 19: Venus at aphelion
Feb. 20: Last quarter moon
Feb. 21: Antares 0.4°N of moon
Feb. 28: New moon

March

Mercury is visible low in the W just after sunset.
Venus is visible low in the W in the evening early in the month, later moving too close to the sun for easy visibility.
Mars, Jupiter, and **Uranus** are visible in the W in the evening.
Saturn and **Neptune** are too close to the sun for easy visibility.

Mar. 1: Mercury 0.4°N of moon; occultation of Mercury by moon; moon at ascending node; moon at perigee
Mar. 4: Mercury at perihelion
Mar. 5: Pleiades 0.6°S of moon
Mar. 6: First quarter moon
Mar. 8: Mercury at greatest elongation: 18.2°E of sun
Mar. 9: Mars 1.7°S of moon; Pollux 2.0°N of moon
Mar. 12: Regulus 2.2°S of moon; Saturn in conjunction with sun
Mar. 14: Full moon; total lunar eclipse; moon at descending node
Mar. 16: Spica 0.3°N of moon
Mar. 17: Moon at apogee
Mar. 19: Neptune in conjunction with sun
Mar. 20: Vernal equinox, 9:01 UTC; Antares 0.5°N of moon
Mar. 22: Last quarter moon
Mar. 23: Venus at inferior conjunction; Saturn ring plane crossing as seen from Earth
Mar. 24: Mercury at inferior conjunction
Mar. 28: Moon at ascending node
Mar. 29: Partial solar eclipse; new moon; Mars 3.9°S of Pollux
Mar. 30: Moon at perigee

April

Mercury is visible in the E just before sunrise.
Venus is visible in the E before sunrise.
Mars is visible in the W after sunset.
Jupiter and **Uranus** are visible low in the W after sunset.
Saturn and **Neptune** are too close to the sun for easy visibility, moving to the dawn sky late in the month.

Apr. 1: Pleiades 0.6°S of moon
Apr. 5: First quarter moon; Pollux 2.0°N of moon; Mars 2.2°S of moon
Apr. 8: Regulus 2.2°S of moon
Apr. 10: Mercury 2.1°N of Saturn; moon at descending node
Apr. 13: Full moon; Spica 0.3°N of moon; moon at apogee
Apr. 16: Mars at aphelion; Antares 0.4°N of moon
Apr. 21: Last quarter moon; Mercury at greatest elongation: 27.4°W of sun
Apr. 22: Lyrid meteor shower
Apr. 25: Venus 2.4°N of moon; moon at ascending node; Saturn 2.3°S of moon
Apr. 26: Mercury 4.4°S of moon
Apr. 27: Moon at perigee; new moon
Apr. 28: Venus 3.7°N of Saturn
Apr. 29: Pleiades 0.5°S of moon

May

Mercury is visible in the E just before sunrise early in the month and is too close to the sun for easy visibility at the end of the month.
Mars is visible in the W after sunset.
Venus is visible in the E before sunrise.
Jupiter and **Uranus** are too close to the sun for easy visibility.
Saturn and **Neptune** are visible low in the E just before sunrise.

May 3: Pollux 2.1°N of moon; Mars 2.1°S of moon
May 4: First quarter moon
May 5: Eta-Aquarid meteor shower; Regulus 2.0°S of moon
May 7: Moon at descending node
May 10: Spica 0.4°N of moon
May 11: Moon at apogee
May 12: Full moon
May 14: Antares 0.3°N of moon
May 18: Uranus in conjunction with sun
May 20: Last quarter moon
May 22: Moon at ascending node; Saturn 2.8°S of moon
May 23: Venus 4.0°S of moon
May 26: Moon at perigee
May 27: New moon
May 30: Mercury at superior conjunction; Pollux 2.3°N of moon
May 31: Mercury at perihelion

June

Mercury is too close to the sun for easy visibility early in the month, visible in the W after sunset late in the month.
Venus is visible in the E before sunrise.
Mars is visible in the W in the evening.
Jupiter and **Uranus** are too close to the sun for easy visibility.
Saturn and **Neptune** are visible in the E before sunrise.

June 1: Venus at greatest elongation: 45.9°W of sun; Mars 1.4°S of moon
June 2: Regulus 1.8°S of moon
June 3: First quarter moon
June 4: Moon at descending node
June 6: Spica 0.5°N of moon
June 7: Moon at apogee
June 10: Antares 0.3°N of moon
June 11: Full moon
June 12: Venus at perihelion
June 17: Mars 0.7°N of Regulus
June 18: Moon at ascending node; last quarter moon
June 19: Saturn 3.4°S of moon
June 21: Summer solstice, 2:42 UTC; Mercury 4.8°S of Pollux
June 23: Pleiades 0.6°S of moon; moon at perigee
June 24: Jupiter in conjunction with sun
June 25: New moon
June 26: Pollux 2.5°N of moon
June 27: Mercury 2.9°S of moon
June 29: Regulus 1.5°S of moon
June 30: Mars 0.2°S of moon

July

Mercury and **Mars** are visible low in the W just after sunset.
Venus is visible in the E before sunrise.
Jupiter is too close to the sun for easy visibility early in the month, visible in the E just before dawn later in the month.
Saturn, Uranus, and **Neptune** are visible low in the E before sunrise.

July 1: Moon at descending node
July 2: First quarter moon
July 3: Earth at aphelion; Spica 0.8°N of moon
July 4: Mercury at greatest elongation: 25.9°E of sun
July 5: Moon at apogee
July 7: Antares 0.4°N of moon
July 10: Full moon
July 13: Venus 3.1°N of Aldebaran
July 14: Mercury at aphelion
July 15: Moon at ascending node
July 16: Saturn 3.8°S of moon
July 18: Last quarter moon
July 20: Pleiades 0.7°S of moon; moon at perigee
July 23: Jupiter 4.9°S of moon
July 24: New moon
July 26: Regulus 1.4°S of moon
July 28: Delta-Aquarid meteor shower; moon at descending node; Mars 1.3°N of moon
July 31: Spica 1.0°N of moon

August

Mercury is too close to the sun for easy visibility early in the month, visible low in the E just before dawn late in the month.
Venus is visible in the E before sunrise.
Mars is visible low in the W just after sunset.
Jupiter, Saturn, Uranus, and **Neptune** are visible in the E before sunrise.

Aug. 1: Mercury at inferior conjunction; first quarter moon; moon at apogee
Aug. 4: Antares 0.6°N of moon
Aug. 9: Full moon

Aug. 11: Moon at ascending node
Aug. 12: Venus 0.9°S of Jupiter; Saturn 4.0°S of moon; Perseid meteor shower
Aug. 14: Moon at perigee
Aug. 16: Last quarter moon; Pleiades 0.9°S of moon
Aug. 19: Mercury at greatest elongation: 18.6°W of sun; Jupiter 4.8°S of moon
Aug. 20: Pollux 2.4°N of moon
Aug. 21: Mercury 3.7°S of moon
Aug. 23: New moon
Aug. 24: Moon at descending node
Aug. 26: Mars 2.8°N of moon
Aug. 27: Mercury at perihelion; Spica 1.1°N of moon
Aug. 29: Moon at apogee
Aug. 31: First quarter moon; Antares 0.7°N of moon

September

Mercury is too close to the sun for easy visibility.
Venus is visible low in the E just before sunrise.
Mars is visible low in the W just after sunset.
Jupiter and **Uranus** are visible in the E after midnight.
Saturn and **Neptune** are visible all night, rising in the E after sunset and near the meridian at midnight.

Sept. 7: Full moon; total lunar eclipse; moon at ascending node
Sept. 8: Saturn 4.0°S of moon
Sept. 10: Moon at perigee
Sept. 12: Pleiades 1.0°S of moon
Sept. 13: Mars 2.0°N of Spica; Mercury at superior conjunction
Sept. 14: Last quarter moon
Sept. 16: Jupiter 4.6°S of moon; Pollux 2.4°N of moon
Sept. 19: Venus 0.4°N of Regulus; Regulus 1.3°S of moon; Venus 0.8°S of moon; occultation of Venus by moon
Sept. 20: Moon at descending node
Sept. 21: Saturn at opposition; partial solar eclipse; new moon
Sept. 22: Autumnal equinox, 18:19 UTC
Sept. 23: Neptune at opposition; Spica 1.1°N of moon
Sept. 24: Mars 3.9°N of moon
Sept. 26: Moon at apogee
Sept. 27: Antares 0.6°N of moon
Sept. 29: First quarter moon

October

Mercury is too close to the sun for easy visibility early in the month, visible low in the W after sunset late in the month.
Venus is visible low in the E just before sunrise.
Mars is too close to the sun for easy visibility.
Jupiter and **Uranus** are visible in the E after midnight.
Saturn and **Neptune** are visible in the W after sunset.

Oct. 2: Venus at perihelion
Oct. 5: Moon at ascending node
Oct. 6: Saturn 3.8°S of moon
Oct. 7: Full moon
Oct. 8: Moon at perigee
Oct. 10: Pleiades 0.9°S of moon
Oct. 13: Last quarter moon; Jupiter 4.3°S of moon; Pollux 2.5°N of moon
Oct. 16: Regulus 1.3°S of moon
Oct. 18: Moon at descending node
Oct. 19: Mercury 2.0°S of Mars; Venus 3.7°N of moon
Oct. 21: Orionid meteor shower; new moon
Oct. 23: Mercury 2.3°N of moon; moon at apogee
Oct. 25: Antares 0.5°N of moon
Oct. 29: First quarter moon; Mercury at greatest elongation: 23.9°E of sun

November

Mercury is visible low in the W just after sunset early in the month, too close to the sun for easy visibility later in the month.
Venus is visible low in the E just before sunrise early in the month, too close to the sun for easy visibility later in the month.
Mars is too close to the sun for easy visibility.
Jupiter is visible in the E after midnight.
Saturn and **Neptune** are visible in the W after sunset.
Uranus is visible most of the night, rising in the E after sunset and near the meridian at midnight.

Nov. 1: Moon at ascending node
Nov. 3: Venus 3.3°N of Spica; Saturn 3.7°S of moon
Nov. 5: S Taurid meteor shower; full moon; moon at perigee
Nov. 6: Pleiades 0.8°S of moon
Nov. 9: Mercury 2.6°N of Antares
Nov. 10: Pollux 2.7°N of moon; Jupiter 4.0°S of moon
Nov. 12: Last quarter moon; N Taurid meteor shower; Regulus 1.1°S of moon
Nov. 13: Mercury 1.2°S of Mars
Nov. 14: Moon at descending node
Nov. 17: Spica 1.2°N of moon; Leonid meteor shower
Nov. 20: Moon at apogee; new moon; Mercury at inferior conjunction
Nov. 21: Uranus at opposition
Nov. 23: Mercury at perihelion
Nov. 28: First quarter moon; moon at ascending node
Nov. 29: Saturn 3.7°S of moon

December

Mercury is visible in the E just before sunrise early in the month, too close to the sun for easy visibility later in the month.
Venus and **Mars** are too close to the sun for easy visibility.
Jupiter is visible most of the night, rising in the E after sunset and near the meridian at midnight.
Saturn, Uranus, and **Neptune** are visible in the W after sunset.

Dec. 4: Pleiades 0.8°S of moon; moon at perigee; full moon
Dec. 7: Jupiter 3.7°S of moon; Pollux 2.9°N of moon; Mercury at greatest elongation: 20.7°W of sun
Dec. 10: Regulus 0.8°S of moon
Dec. 11: Moon at descending node; last quarter moon
Dec. 14: Geminid meteor shower; Spica 1.4°N of moon
Dec. 17: Moon at apogee
Dec. 18: Antares 0.4°N of moon
Dec. 20: New moon
Dec. 21: Winter solstice, 15:03 UTC
Dec. 22: Ursid meteor shower
Dec. 25: Moon at ascending node
Dec. 27: Saturn 4.0°S of moon; first quarter moon
Dec. 31: Pleiades 0.9°S of moon

Moon Phases, 2025

(In Coordinated Universal Time, or UTC, the standard time of the prime meridian.)

New Moon			Waxing Quarter			Full Moon			Waning Quarter		
Date	Hr.	Min.	Date	Hr.	Min.	Date	Hr.	Min.	Date	Hr.	Min.
Jan. 29	12	36	Jan. 6	23	56	Jan. 13	22	27	Jan. 21	20	31
Feb. 28	0	45	Feb. 5	8	02	Feb. 12	13	53	Feb. 20	17	32
Mar. 29	10	58	Mar. 6	16	32	Mar. 14	6	55	Mar. 22	11	29
Apr. 27	19	31	Apr. 5	2	15	Apr. 13	0	22	Apr. 21	1	36
May 27	3	02	May 4	13	52	May 12	16	56	May 20	11	59
June 25	10	32	June 3	3	41	June 11	7	44	June 18	19	19
July 24	19	11	July 2	19	30	July 10	20	37	July 18	0	38
Aug. 23	6	06	Aug. 1	12	41	Aug. 9	7	55	Aug. 16	5	12
Sept. 21	19	54	Aug. 31	6	25	Sept. 7	18	09	Sept. 14	10	33
Oct. 21	12	25	Sept. 29	23	54	Oct. 7	3	48	Oct. 13	18	13
Nov. 20	6	47	Oct. 29	16	21	Nov. 5	13	19	Nov.12	5	28
Dec. 20	1	43	Nov. 28	6	59	Dec. 4	23	14	Dec. 11	20	52
			Dec. 27	19	10						

Meteorites and Meteor Showers

When a chunk of material, ice or rock, plunges into Earth's atmosphere and burns up in a fiery display, the event is a **meteor**. While the chunk of material is still in space, it is a **meteoroid**. If a portion of the material survives passage through the atmosphere and reaches the ground, the remnant on the ground is a **meteorite**.

Meteorites found on Earth are classified into types, depending on their composition: **irons**, those composed chiefly of iron, a small percentage of nickel, and traces of other metals such as cobalt; **stones**, stony meteors consisting of silicates; and **stony irons**, containing varying proportions of both iron and stone.

Serious study of meteorites as non-Earth objects began in the 20th century. Scientists use sophisticated chemical analysis, X-rays, and mass spectrography in determining their origin and composition. Although most meteorites are now believed to be fragments of asteroids or comets, geochemical studies have shown that a few Antarctic stones came from the moon or from Mars, presumably ejected by the explosive impact of asteroids.

The largest known meteorite, estimated to weigh about 55 metric tons, is the Hoba meteorite near Grootfontein, Namibia. The Manicouagan impact crater in Quebec, Canada, with an estimated diameter of 60 mi, is one of the largest crater structures still visible on the surface of the Earth. Not obvious to the eye because of erosion, larger impact craters identified include the Vredefort crater in South Africa at 185 mi across and the Sudbury crater in Ontario, Canada (125 mi). The Bedout impact site off the NW coast of Australia gained attention in 2004 when scientists identified further evidence in support of the idea that it may be linked to the Permian extinction event 250 mil years ago. A 2019 study of the Chicxulub impact crater (93 mi across) in Yucatán Peninsula and the Gulf of Mexico gave evidence of an associated mass extinction event at the end of the Mesozoic Era (66 mil years ago).

Meteor showers vary in strength, but usually the three most visible meteor showers of the year are the **Perseids**, around Aug. 13, the **Orionids**, around Oct. 21, and the **Geminids**, around Dec. 14. These showers feature meteors at the rate of about 60 per hour. Best observing conditions occur in the absence of moonlight, usually when the moon's phase is between waning crescent and waxing quarter.

For most meteor showers the cometary debris is relatively uniformly scattered along the comet's orbit. However, in the case of the **Leonid** meteor shower, which occurs every year around Nov. 17-18, the debris from Comet Temple-Tuttle seems to be bunched up in one stretch. Hence, the meteor shower produced in most years is relatively weak. However, about every 33 years, Earth encounters the bunched-up debris when it crosses the comet's orbit. Sometimes the expected shower is a disappointment, as in 1899 and 1933; at other times, the dense debris provides a spectacular show, as in 1833 and 1866. The Leonids stormed again more recently, producing rates of 1,000-3,000 meteors per hour in 2001.

Morning and Evening "Stars," 2025

(In Coordinated Universal Time, or UTC, the standard time of the prime meridian.)

	Morning	Evening
Jan.	Mercury Mars to Jan. 16	Venus Mars from Jan. 17 Jupiter Saturn Uranus Neptune
Feb.	Mercury to Feb. 9	Mercury from Feb. 10 Venus Mars Jupiter Saturn Uranus Neptune
Mar.	Mercury from Mar. 25 Venus from Mar. 24 Saturn from Mar. 13 Neptune from Mar. 20	Mercury to Mar. 24 Venus to Mar. 23 Mars Jupiter Saturn to Mar. 12 Uranus Neptune to Mar. 19
Apr.	Mercury Venus Saturn Neptune	Mars Jupiter Uranus
May	Mercury to May 30 Venus Saturn Uranus from May 19 Neptune	Mercury from May 31 Mars Jupiter Uranus to May 18
June	Venus Jupiter from June 25 Saturn Uranus Neptune	Mercury Mars Jupiter to June 24
July	Venus Jupiter Saturn Uranus Neptune	Mercury Mars
Aug.	Mercury from Aug. 2 Venus Jupiter Saturn Uranus Neptune	Mercury to Aug. 1 Mars
Sept.	Mercury to Sept.13 Venus Jupiter Saturn to Sept. 21 Uranus Neptune to Sept. 23	Mercury from Sept. 14 Mars Saturn from Sept. 22 Neptune from Sept. 24
Oct.	Venus Jupiter Uranus	Mercury Mars Saturn Neptune
Nov.	Mercury from Nov. 21 Venus Jupiter Uranus to Nov. 21	Mercury to Nov. 20 Mars Saturn Uranus from Nov. 22 Neptune
Dec.	Mercury Venus Jupiter	Mars Saturn Uranus Neptune

Greenwich Sidereal Time for 0h UTC, 2025

UTC = Coordinated Universal Time. Add 12 hours to obtain right ascension of mean sun.

Date	Hr.	Min.	Date	Hr.	Min.	Date	Hr.	Min.	Date	Hr.	Min.
Jan. 1	6	43.6	Apr. 1	12	38.4	July 10	19	12.7	Oct. 8	1	7.5
Jan. 11	7	23.0	Apr. 11	13	17.9	July 20	19	52.1	Oct.18	1	46.9
Jan. 21	8	2.5	Apr. 21	13	57.3	July 30	20	31.5	Oct. 28	2	26.4
Jan. 31	8	41.9	May 1	14	36.7	Aug. 9	21	10.1	Nov. 7	3	5.8
Feb. 10	9	21.3	May 11	15	16.1	Aug. 19	21	50.4	Nov. 17	3	45.2
Feb. 20	10	0.7	May 21	15	55.6	Aug. 29	22	29.8	Nov. 27	4	24.7
Mar. 2	10	40.2	May 31	16	34.1	Sept. 8	23	9.2	Dec. 7	5	4.1
Mar. 12	11	19.6	June 10	17	14.4	Sept. 18	23	48.7	Dec. 17	5	43.5
Mar. 22	11	59.0	June 20	17	53.8	Sept. 28	0	28.1	Dec. 27	6	22.9
			June 30	18	33.3						

Largest Telescopes

Astronomers indicate the size of telescopes not by length or magnification but by the diameter of the primary light-gathering component, such as the lens or mirror. The larger the diameter of the mirror or lens, the fainter the objects that can be detected. In principle, larger telescopes also have better resolving power—the ability to discern small details—than smaller telescopes. However, the Earth's atmosphere limits the details that can be seen using ground-based telescopes. That is why the Hubble Space Telescope, which orbits the Earth outside of its atmosphere, can achieve higher resolutions with its 2.4-m (7.9-ft) mirror than much larger telescopes on Earth. Adaptive optics systems can compensate for the blurring effects of the Earth's atmosphere, allowing ground-based telescopes to achieve higher levels of detail. Telescopes to detect infrared, ultraviolet, X-ray, and gamma radiation must be placed in space or high-altitude balloons because the atmosphere absorbs most of these types of radiation; as a result, such telescopes are generally much smaller than optical, infrared, and radio telescopes.

Refracting (lens) telescopes are currently not made with lens diameters of more than 40 in. Because **reflecting telescopes** can be made less expensively and with more precision than refracting telescopes, all modern large optical telescopes are made with mirrors. **Radio telescopes** are larger than optical telescopes because larger diameters are required to obtain equivalent resolution of radio's longer wavelengths. A technique called interferometry, originally developed for radio telescopes, uses arrays of telescopes to achieve better resolution.

Largest refracting (lens) optical telescope: Yerkes Observatory, 1 m (40 in.), at Williams Bay, WI

Largest reflecting (mirror) optical/infrared telescope: Gran Telescopio Canarias, 10.4 m (34 ft), on La Palma, Canary Islands (segmented mirror)

Largest infrared interferometer: Four 8.2-m (27-ft) telescopes of the Very Large Telescope Interferometer (VLTI) with a 200-m (656-ft) baseline on Cerro Paranal in Chile

Largest fully steerable radio dish: Robert Byrd Green Bank Telescope (GBT), 100 m (328 ft), in Green Bank, WV

Largest single radio dish: Five-hundred-meter Aperture Spherical Telescope (FAST), 500 m (1,640 ft), in Guizhou, China

Largest baseline radio interferometer: 10 25-m (82-ft) diameter telescopes of the Very Long Baseline Array (VLBA), dispersed from Hawaii to the Virgin Islands with a resolution equal to a radio dish of 8,600 km (5,000 mi), making it the highest resolution telescope in the solar system

Largest submillimeter interferometer: 54 12-m (39-ft) and 12 7-m (23-ft) antennas of the Atacama Large Millimeter Array (ALMA), located at a site above 5,000 m (16,400 ft) in the Atacama Desert in Chile. The antennas can be spread out over a 16-km (10-mi) distance to increase the resolving power of the array.

Largest airborne telescope: Stratospheric Observatory for Infrared Astronomy (SOFIA), 2.5-m (8.2-ft) infrared telescope aboard a NASA 747. Retired in 2022.

Largest space telescope: The James Webb Space Telescope (JWST), 6.5-m (21-ft) infrared reflecting telescope was successfully launched by NASA on Dec. 25, 2021, and began observations at the sun-earth L_2 point, in 2022.

Constellations

Culturally, constellations are imagined patterns among the stars that, in some cases, have been recognized through millennia. Knowledge of constellations was once necessary in order to function as an astronomer. For today's astronomers, constellations are simply areas of the sky in which objects await observation and interpretation.

Because Western culture has dominated much of modern scientific discourse, constellations and celestial traditions of other cultures are not widely known outside their regions of origin. Even the patterns with which we are most familiar today have undergone considerable change over the centuries.

Today, **88 constellations** are officially recognized. Although many have ancient origins, some are modern, devised out of unclaimed stars by astronomers a few centuries ago. Unclaimed stars were those too faint or inconveniently placed to be included in the more prominent constellations. Stars in a constellation are not necessarily near each other; they are just located in the same direction on the celestial sphere.

Common names of stars often referred to parts of the traditional figures they represented, such as Deneb, the tail of the swan, and Betelgeuse, the giant's shoulder. Astronomers may avoid traditional names by labeling stars with Greek letters, generally to denote order of brightness. The "alpha star" would typically be the brightest in a constellation. The "of" implies possession, so the genitive (possessive) form of the constellation name is used, e.g., Alpha Orionis (the first star of Orion) for Betelgeuse. (While Rigel is brighter than Betelgeuse, its designation is Beta Orionis, possibly because Betelgeuse appeared brighter when they were named.)

Asterisms are widely recognized patterns of stars. The so-called Big Dipper is a small part of the constellation Ursa Major, the big bear; the three stars of the Summer Triangle are each in a different constellation, with Vega in Lyra the lyre, Deneb in Cygnus the swan, and Altair in Aquila the eagle. The northeast star of the asterism Great Square of Pegasus is Alpha Andromedae.

Name	Abbr.	Meaning
Andromeda	And	Chained Maiden
Antlia	Ant	Air Pump
Apus	Aps	Bird of Paradise
Aquarius	Aqr	Water Bearer
Aquila	Aql	Eagle
Ara	Ara	Altar
Aries	Ari	Ram
Auriga	Aur	Charioteer
Boötes	Boo	Herder
Caelum	Cae	Chisel
Camelopardalis	Cam	Giraffe
Cancer	Cnc	Crab
Canes Venatici	CVn	Hunting Dogs
Canis Major	CMa	Greater Dog
Canis Minor	CMi	Littler Dog
Capricornus	Cap	Sea-Goat
Carina	Car	Keel
Cassiopeia	Cas	Queen
Centaurus	Cen	Centaur
Cepheus	Cep	King
Cetus	Cet	Whale
Chamaeleon	Cha	Chameleon
Circinus	Cir	Compass (drawing)
Columba	Col	Dove
Coma Berenices	Com	Berenice's Hair
Corona Australis	CrA	Southern Crown
Corona Borealis	CrB	Northern Crown
Corvus	Crv	Crow
Crater	Crt	Cup
Crux	Cru	Cross (southern)
Cygnus	Cyg	Swan
Delphinus	Del	Dolphin
Dorado	Dor	Dolphinfish
Draco	Dra	Dragon
Equuleus	Equ	Little Horse
Eridanus	Eri	River
Fornax	For	Furnace
Gemini	Gem	Twins
Grus	Gru	Crane (bird)
Hercules	Her	Hercules
Horologium	Hor	Clock
Hydra	Hya	Water Snake (female)
Hydrus	Hyi	Water Snake (male)
Indus	Ind	Indian
Lacerta	Lac	Lizard
Leo	Leo	Lion
Leo Minor	LMi	Littler Lion
Lepus	Lep	Hare
Libra	Lib	Balance
Lupus	Lup	Wolf
Lynx	Lyn	Lynx
Lyra	Lyr	Lyre
Mensa	Men	Table Mountain
Microscopium	Mic	Microscope
Monoceros	Mon	Unicorn
Musca	Mus	Fly
Norma	Nor	Square (rule)
Octans	Oct	Octant
Ophiuchus	Oph	Serpent Bearer
Orion	Ori	Hunter
Pavo	Pav	Peacock
Pegasus	Peg	Flying Horse
Perseus	Per	Hero
Phoenix	Phe	Phoenix
Pictor	Pic	Painter
Pisces	Psc	Fishes
Piscis Austrinus	PsA	Southern Fish
Puppis	Pup	Stern (deck)
Pyxis	Pyx	Compass (sea)
Reticulum	Ret	Reticle
Sagitta	Sge	Arrow
Sagittarius	Sgr	Archer
Scorpius	Sco	Scorpion
Sculptor	Scl	Sculptor
Scutum	Sct	Shield
Serpens	Ser	Serpent
Sextans	Sex	Sextant
Taurus	Tau	Bull
Telescopium	Tel	Telescope
Triangulum	Tri	Triangle
Triangulum Australe	TrA	Southern Triangle
Tucana	Tuc	Toucan
Ursa Major	UMa	Greater Bear
Ursa Minor	UMi	Littler Bear
Vela	Vel	Sail
Virgo	Vir	Maiden
Volans	Vol	Flying Fish
Vulpecula	Vul	Fox

Eclipses, 2025

(In Coordinated Universal Time, or UTC, the standard time of the prime meridian.)

There will be four eclipses in 2025: two partial solar eclipses and two total lunar eclipses. Neither solar eclipse will be particularly accessible to a wide audience. The partial solar eclipse of Mar. 29 will be visible from the North Atlantic, NW Europe and Africa, and N Russia. The partial solar eclipse of Sept. 21 will only be visible from the far South Pacific, New Zealand, and W Antarctica. The two lunar eclipses, however, will be notably dark over wide regions of the globe. The total lunar eclipse of Mar. 14 will be visible from the E Pacific, North America, South America, W Europe, and W Africa. The total lunar eclipse of Sept. 7 will be visible from Europe, Africa, Asia, and Australia.

The tables below give the times in UTC of when the moon or sun will reach certain phases of each event. In the case of the lunar eclipses, the times are relevant for any observer who can see the moon. In the case of solar eclipses, the tabulated times refer to when the given event begins or ends from specific points along the eclipse path; as the moon's shadow sweeps quickly across the Earth, the observed duration and degree of eclipse depends on the observer's precise location. Interactive maps are available on the internet to calculate times for specific locations.

I. Total Eclipse of the Moon: Mar. 14

This eclipse, with the moon's center passing just over one lunar radius north of the center of Earth's shadow, promises a relatively dark eclipse of the moon. It will be visible from the E Pacific, North America, South America, W Europe, and W Africa.

Event	Date	Hr.	Min.
Penumbral eclipse begins	Mar. 14	3	57.3
Umbral eclipse begins	Mar. 14	5	9.4
Total umbral eclipse begins	Mar. 14	6	26.1
Greatest eclipse	Mar. 14	6	58.4
Total umbral eclipse ends	Mar. 14	7	31.3
Umbral eclipse ends	Mar. 14	8	47.4
Penumbral eclipse ends	Mar. 14	10	0.1

II. Partial Eclipse of the Sun: Mar. 29

This eclipse is a relatively deep partial eclipse with 94% of the sun blocked by the moon at maximum. But maximum occurs in far NE Canada, at latitude 61° 6.0' N, longitude 77° 5.1' W, at which site the sun will be at the horizon. The partial eclipse will only be visible above the horizon from extreme NW Africa, NW Europe, N Russia, Greenland, and far NE Canada.

Event	Date	Hr.	Min.
Partial eclipse begins	Mar. 29	8	50.7
Greatest eclipse	Mar. 29	10	47.4
Partial eclipse ends	Mar. 29	12	43.7

III. Total Eclipse of the Moon: Sept. 7

This eclipse, with the moon's center passing almost exactly one lunar radius south of the center of Earth's shadow, promises a relatively dark eclipse of the moon and will be similar to the total lunar eclipse of Mar. 14, 2025. It will be visible from Europe, Africa, Asia, and Australia.

Event	Date	Hr.	Min.
Penumbral eclipse begins	Sept. 7	15	28.3
Umbral eclipse begins	Sept. 7	16	26.9
Total umbral eclipse begins	Sept. 7	17	30.6
Greatest eclipse	Sept. 7	18	11.8
Total umbral eclipse ends	Sept. 7	18	53.3
Umbral eclipse ends	Sept. 7	19	56.9
Penumbral eclipse ends	Sept. 7	20	55.5

IV. Partial Eclipse of the Sun: Sept. 21

This eclipse is a deep partial eclipse with 86% of the sun blocked by the moon at maximum. But maximum occurs in the far South Pacific near Antarctica, at latitude 60° 54.1' S, longitude 153° 29.9' E, at which site the sun will be at the horizon. The partial eclipse will only be visible from the South Pacific, New Zealand, and portions of W Antarctica.

Event	Date	Hr.	Min.
Partial eclipse begins	Sept. 21	17	29.6
Greatest eclipse	Sept. 21	19	41.9
Partial eclipse ends	Sept. 21	21	53.7

Total Solar Eclipses, 2025-46

Total solar eclipses take place nearly as often as total lunar eclipses. Total lunar eclipses are visible over at least half of the Earth, while total solar eclipses can be seen only along a very narrow path up to a few hundred miles wide and a few thousand miles long. Observing a total solar eclipse is thus a rarity for most people, though the experience is so memorable that many enthusiasts travel long distances just to see totality.

Solar eclipses can be dangerous to observe. This is not because the sun emits more potent rays, but because the sun is always dangerous to observe directly, and people are particularly likely to stare at it during a solar eclipse.

Date	Duration[1] min.	sec.	Width (mi)	Path of totality
2026, Aug. 12	2	18	183	Greenland, Iceland, Spain
2027, Aug. 2	6	24	160	Spain, N Africa, Arabian Peninsula
2028, July 22	5	10	140	Indian Ocean, Australia, New Zealand
2030, Nov. 25	3	45	105	Namibia, Botswana, South Africa, Indian Ocean, E Australia
2033, Mar. 30	2	37	485	Alaska, E Russia, Arctic
2034, Mar. 20	4	9	100	Central and NE Africa, Arabian Peninsula, Central and E Asia
2035, Sept. 2	2	54	72	China, Korea, Japan, Pacific Ocean
2037, July 13	3	58	125	Australia, New Zealand
2038, Dec. 26	2	18	96	Australia, New Zealand, South Pacific
2039, Dec. 15	1	51	236	Antarctica
2041, Apr. 30	1	51	45	Angola, Congo, Uganda, Kenya, Somalia
2042, Apr. 20	4	51	130	Malaysia, Indonesia, Philippines, N Pacific
2044, Aug. 23	2	4	281	Greenland, N. Canada, Montana, North Dakota
2045, Aug. 12	6	6	159	U.S., Caribbean, NE S. America
2046, Aug. 2	4	51	146	Brazil, Angola, E Namibia, Botswana

(1) Length of time at optimal viewing area.

Total Solar Eclipses in the U.S. in the 21st Century

During the 21st century, there are eight total solar eclipses visible somewhere in the continental U.S. The first came after a long gap, in 2017. The last total solar eclipse before that had been on Feb. 26, 1979, in the northwestern U.S.

Date	Path of totality	Date	Path of totality
Aug. 21, 2017	Oregon to South Carolina	Mar. 30, 2052	Florida to Georgia
Apr. 8, 2024	Mexico to Texas and N through Maine	May 11, 2078	Louisiana to North Carolina
Aug. 23, 2044	Montana to North Dakota	May 1, 2079	New Jersey to the lower edge of New England
Aug. 12, 2045	Northern California to Florida	Sept. 14, 2099	North Dakota to Virginia

Beginnings of the Universe

One of the dominating astronomical discoveries of the 20th century was that the galaxies of the universe all seem to be moving away from Earth. Doppler redshifts were observed for spiral nebulae around 1920 even though they were not yet known to be galaxies. By the early 1930s, Edwin Hubble and M. L. Humason had established that the more distant a galaxy, the faster it was receding. It turned out that they were moving away not just from the Earth but from one another—that is, the **universe is expanding**. Scientists conclude that the universe must once, very long ago, have been extremely compact and dense, and a rapid expansion caused the energy and matter to rapidly expand. The beginning of this expansion is referred to as the **Big Bang**.

On the subatomic level, according to this theory, there were vast changes of energy and matter and the way physical laws operated during the first few minutes after the Big Bang. After those early minutes the percentages of the basic matter of the universe—hydrogen, helium, and lithium—were set. Everything was so compact and hot that radiation dominated the early universe and there were no stable, unionized atoms. The universe was opaque, in the sense that any energy emitted was quickly absorbed and then re-emitted. As the universe expanded, density and temperature continued to drop. A few hundred thousand years after the Big Bang, the temperature dropped far enough that electrons and nuclei could combine to form stable atoms as the universe became transparent. Once that occurred, the radiation that had been trapped was free to escape.

In the 1940s, George Gamow and others predicted that remnants of this escaped radiation should be observable. They had started to search for this background radiation when physicists Arno Penzias and Robert Wilson, using a radio telescope, inadvertently found it, for which they won the 1978 Nobel Prize in Physics.

In 2003, NASA's Wilkinson Microwave Anisotropy Probe made measurements of the temperature of this **cosmic microwave background radiation** to within millionths of a degree. From these measurements, scientists were able to deduce that our universe is 13.7 billion years old and that first-generation stars began to form a mere 200 mil years after the Big Bang.

In 2014, scientists operating a telescope in Antarctica claimed to have found direct evidence for cosmic inflation, the rapid expansion of the universe during the 10-32 sec. after the Big Bang that helps explain why variations of the cosmic background radiation are so small. Follow-up observations cast doubt on this, and higher precision measurements are planned.

A related mystery is evidence suggesting hidden matter and hidden energy that cannot be directly observed. The presence of dark matter is indicated by the rotation curves of galaxies and the dynamics of clusters of galaxies. **Dark matter** may be composed of gas; large numbers of cool, compact objects like dead stars; or even subatomic particles. Evidence for **dark energy** is derived from studies of distant Type Ia supernovae indicating that the expansion of the universe is accelerating rather than slowing. Dark energy seems to work on the very fabric of the universe, acting as a force that increases the rate at which space expands. Visible matter seems to constitute only about 4% of the total mass of the universe while the rest of the universe's mass is in the form of dark matter (27%) and dark energy (68%).

Galaxies

By the 20th century, more than 10,000 **nebulae**—cloud-like luminous objects in the sky—had been discovered. Some were correctly identified as star clusters and others as clouds of gas and dust. Those nebulae which were spiral or elliptical in shape were found in regions of the sky far from the glowing band that is our own Milky Way galaxy. Philosopher Immanuel Kant had written in 1775 that some of these fuzzy objects might be **"island universes"** apart from our own. But the idea remained speculative until 1923-24, when Edwin Hubble discovered variable stars—stars whose varying brightness makes their distance from Earth calculable—in some of these nebulae. This provided conclusive evidence that these systems were far enough away to be outside our own island universe, the Milky Way galaxy.

Galaxies range in size from small dwarf elliptical ones, with perhaps 1 million stars, to spiral galaxies containing 300 billion stars, to giant elliptical galaxies that may be home to more than 10 trillion stars. The diameters of galaxies range from 3,000 light-years in dwarf elliptical galaxies to over 500,000 light-years in giant elliptical galaxies. It is estimated that the Milky Way galaxy is about 100,000 light-years in diameter with about 400 billion stars.

Galaxies also congregate into **clusters**. The smallest are poor clusters of only a few dozen galaxies, while the largest rich clusters may contain thousands. The Milky Way is part of a poor cluster of about three dozen galaxies called the **Local Group**. The largest galaxy of the Local Group is Andromeda, a spiral galaxy visible to the unaided eye in the constellation of Andromeda on a very dark night. The Milky Way is the second largest galaxy in this group; most of the others are small.

The Solar System

The major planets of the solar system, in order of mean distance from the sun, are **Mercury**, **Venus**, **Earth**, **Mars**, **Jupiter**, **Saturn**, **Uranus**, and **Neptune**. The dwarf planets in order of average distance from the sun are **Ceres** (located between Mars and Jupiter), **Pluto**, **Haumea**, **Makemake**, **2007 OR10**, and **Eris**. All planets orbit counterclockwise around the sun as viewed from above the Earth's North Pole.

Because Mercury and Venus are nearer to the sun than is Earth, their motions about the sun appear from Earth as wide swings first to one side of the sun then to the other, though both planets move around the sun in almost circular orbits. When their passage takes them between Earth and the sun or beyond the sun in relation to Earth, they cannot be seen.

The planets that lie farther from the sun than does Earth may be seen for longer periods. They are invisible only when so located in the sky that they rise and set at about the same time as the sun and are thus overwhelmed by the sun's light. Mercury and Venus, because they are between Earth and the sun, show phases much as the moon does. The planets farther from the sun are always seen as full, although Mars does occasionally present a slightly gibbous phase, like the moon when it is not quite full.

The planets appear to move rapidly among the stars because they are relatively closer to Earth. The stars are also in motion, some at tremendous speeds, but they are so far away that their motion does not change their apparent positions in the heavens enough to be perceived. The nearest star is about 9,000 times farther away than Neptune. The count for identified **moons** in the solar system orbiting the 8 major planets and Pluto stood at 293 as of 2024. In addition, 470 satellites of dwarf planets, asteroids, and Kuiper Belt Objects (KBOs) have been discovered as of 2024—they are called "small body satellites."

Planet Superlatives

Largest, most massive planet	Jupiter	Smallest, least massive planet	Mercury
Fastest orbiting planet	Mercury	Slowest orbiting planet	Neptune
Fastest sidereal rotation	Jupiter	Slowest sidereal rotation	Venus
Longest (synodic) day	Mercury	Shortest (synodic) day	Jupiter
Rotational pole closest to ecliptic	Uranus	Hottest planet	Venus
Most moons	Saturn	No moons	Mercury, Venus
Planet with largest moon	Jupiter	Planet with moon with most eccentric orbit	Neptune
Greatest average density	Earth	Lowest average density	Saturn
Tallest mountain	Mars	Deepest oceans	Jupiter
Strongest magnetic fields	Jupiter	Greatest amount of liquid water on surface	Earth
Most circular orbit	Venus		

Selected Characteristics of the Sun and Planets

Object	Radius— at unit distance[1] ″	Radius— at mean least distance[2] ″	Radius— in mi mean radius	Volume[3]	Mass[3]	Density[3]	Sidereal period d.	hr.	min.	sec.	Gravity at surface[3]	Reflecting power[4]	Daytime surface temp. (° F)
Sun	959.5	976.0	432,500	1,304,000	333,000	0.26	25	9	7		28.00	—	9,941
Mercury	3.36	6.5	1,516	0.0562	0.0553	0.98	58	15	36		0.38	0.11	845
Venus	8.34	33.0	3,760	0.857	0.815	0.95	243		30R		0.91	0.65	867
Earth	8.78	—	3,959	1.000	1.000	1.00		23	56	4.2	1.00	0.37	59
Moon	2.40	986.2	1,079	0.0203	0.0123	0.61	27	7	43	40	0.16	0.12	260
Mars	4.67	12.8	2,106	0.151	0.107	0.71		24	37	22	0.38	0.15	–24
Jupiter	96.40	24.5	43,441	1,321.30	317.83	0.24		9	55	30	2.53	0.52	–162
Saturn	80.29	10.05	36,184	763.6	95.16	0.12		10	39	20	1.06	0.47	–218
Uranus	34.97	2.05	15,759	63.1	14.54	0.23		17	14	20R	0.90	0.51	–323
Neptune	33.95	1.2	15,301	57.7	17.15	0.3		16	6	40	1.14	0.41	–330

R = Retrograde rotation. (1) Angular radius, in seconds of arc, if object were seen at a distance of 1 astronomical unit. (2) Angular radius, in seconds of arc, when object is closest to Earth. (3) Earth = 1. (4) A value of 1 would indicate a perfect reflector.

Planets of the Solar System

The International Astronomical Union (IAU) on Aug. 24, 2006, at their General Assembly in Prague, Czech Republic, agreed on a new definition for planet, and in the process effectively removed Pluto's planet status. The ruling came after years of debate as to whether Pluto, discovered in 1930, should still be considered the ninth planet in our solar system because of its size, orbit, and other characteristics. New discoveries of other Pluto-like objects in the solar system, such as the 2003 discovery of Eris, a **Kuiper Belt object** (KBO) comparable in size to Pluto, also contributed to the debate.

Under the IAU's new definition, Mercury, Venus, Earth, Mars, Jupiter, Saturn, Uranus, and Neptune are regarded as "classical" planets. A **planet** is now defined as a celestial body that (a) is in orbit around the sun, (b) has sufficient mass for its self-gravity to overcome rigid body forces so that it assumes a hydrostatic equilibrium (nearly round) shape, and (c) has cleared the neighborhood around its orbit.

Pluto, Eris, Ceres, Makemake, 2007 OR10, and Haumea are regarded as dwarf planets, with the status of Pluto's largest moon, Charon, still to be determined. A **dwarf planet** is a celestial body that (a) is in orbit around the sun, (b) has sufficient mass for its self-gravity to overcome rigid body forces so that it assumes a hydrostatic equilibrium (nearly round) shape, (c) has not cleared the neighborhood around its orbit, and (d) is not a satellite.

The IAU also created a new category, **small solar system bodies**, for all other objects orbiting the sun, including comets, asteroids, KBOs, and other small objects. It has not yet established a process by which other solar system objects will be classified.

Note: AU = astronomical unit (92.96 mil mi, mean distance of Earth from the sun); **d.** = 1 Earth synodic (solar) day (24 hours); **synodic day** = rotation period of a planet measured with respect to the sun (the "true" day, i.e., the time from midday to midday, or from sunrise to sunrise); **sidereal day** = rotation period of a planet with respect to the stars.

Mercury

Distance from the sun
- Perihelion .... 28.6 mil mi
- Semi-major axis (mean distance).... 36 mil mi (0.387 AU)
- Aphelion........ 43.4 mil mi

Period of revolution around sun .... 87.97 d.
Orbital eccentricity 0.2056
Orbital inclination .... 7.00°
Synodic day (midday to midday) .... 175.94 d.
Sidereal day .... 58.65 d.
Rotational inclination .... 0.01°
Mass (Earth = 1) 0.0553
Mean radius .... 1,516 mi
Mean density (Earth = 1) 0.984
Natural satellites 0
Average surface temperature .... 333°F

Mercury, named for the Roman gods' messenger, is the closest planet to the sun and the smallest planet in the solar system. Mercury orbits so close to the sun that it can never be observed against a dark sky; it is always seen during morning or evening twilights. In 2008, the *Messenger* spacecraft made the first flybys of Mercury since the 1970s. *Messenger* went into orbit about Mercury in Mar. 2011 for a reconnaissance mission; the original one-year science program was extended in 2012. The goals of the mission included mapping, imaging, and measuring the surface composition of Mercury, as well as probing the planet's interior structure and interactions with the sun. Among the discoveries were that at least part of Mercury's metallic core is liquid, that there may be water ice in shadowed craters near the poles, and that the planet's magnetic field is offset from the planet's center.

Orbit and rotation. Mercury moves with great speed around the sun, averaging about 30 mi per second to complete its orbit, which takes about 88 Earth days. Mercury takes nearly 59 days to rotate on its axis. Because its orbital period is only about 50% longer than its sidereal rotation, the time from one sunrise to the next on Mercury is about 176 days—twice as long as a Mercurial year. Oddly, Mercury has a magnetic field, albeit a very weak one. It has been held that both a fluid core and rapid rotation—neither of which Mercury was believed to have—are necessary for the generation of a planetary magnetic field. Mercury may demonstrate the contrary.

Atmosphere. Mercury's atmosphere is almost nonexistent. What very little it has is composed of 42% oxygen, 29% sodium, 22% hydrogen, 6% helium, 0.5% potassium, and 0.5% other particles. Because of Mercury's lack of atmosphere, the surface during the day may reach a temperature of about 845°F, while the temperature at night may fall as low as –300°F. Earth-based observation has provided evidence of water ice near the poles.

Surface and composition. Mercury's surface is rocky and cratered similar to that of the Earth's moon. The most imposing feature on Mercury, the Caloris Basin, is a huge impact crater more than 800 mi in diameter. Mercury has a huge iron core that extends out to about 75% of the planet's radius; it has a higher percentage of iron than any other planet in the solar system.

Venus

Distance from the sun
- Perihelion .... 66.8 mil mi
- Semi-major axis (mean distance).. 67.2 mil mi (0.723 AU)
- Aphelion........ 67.7 mil mi

Period of revolution around sun .... 224.7 d.
Orbital eccentricity 0.0067
Orbital inclination .... 3.39°
Synodic day (midday to midday) ..... 116.75 d. (retrograde)
Sidereal day .... 243.02 d. (retrograde)
Rotational inclination .... 177.4°
Mass (Earth = 1) 0.815
Mean radius .... 3,760 mi
Mean density (Earth = 1) 0.951
Natural satellites 0
Average surface temperature .... 867°F

Venus, named for the Roman goddess of love, is the second planet out from the sun. Because Venus is almost the same size as Earth, it is believed that the two planets were formed at the same time by the same general process and from the same mixture of chemical elements. Venus can easily be seen from Earth with the naked eye; it is the third-brightest object in the sky, exceeded only by the sun and the moon.

Orbit and rotation. It takes Venus 225 Earth days to complete its orbit around the sun. Its synodic revolution—the amount of time it takes for Venus to return to the same position relative to Earth and the sun, which is a result of the combination of its own motion with that of Earth—is 584 days. Because of this, every 19 months Venus is closer to Earth than to any other planet. The rotation period of Venus appears to be 243 days clockwise. In other words, its rotation is counter to the rotation of the other planets and counter to its own motion around the sun. This rate and sense of rotation make for a solar day (sunrise to sunrise) on Venus of 116.8 Earth days. Night lasts 58 days, and day lasts 58 days. Venus has no detectable magnetic field.

Atmosphere. The Venusian atmosphere is very thick and toxic. It is composed primarily of 96.5% carbon dioxide, 3.5% nitrogen, and trace concentrations of sulfur dioxide, argon, water, carbon monoxide, helium, and neon. In addition, it exerts an atmospheric pressure at the surface more than 90 times Earth's normal sea-level pressure. The planet is covered with a dense, white, cloudy atmosphere that conceals whatever is below. These clouds are believed to contain sulfuric acid, meaning that it rains sulfuric acid on Venus. Due to the thickness of the atmosphere and resulting extreme greenhouse effect, the temperature is essentially the same day and night; the planet has an average surface temperature of about 867°F, making it the hottest planet in the solar system. Winds of about 200 mph in the clouds may account for the consistency in temperature despite the low rotation speed of the planet. However, at the surface, the winds are very slow.

Surface and composition. Radar-produced maps of the planet show large craters, continent-sized highlands, and extensive dry lowlands. No tectonic activity has been found similar to Earth's moving tectonic plates, but a system of global rift zones and numerous broad, low, dome-like structures, called coronae, may have been produced by the upwelling and subsidence of magma from the mantle. Volcanic surface features, such as vast lava plains, fields of small lava domes, and large shield volcanoes, are common. About 1,600 volcanoes and volcanic features appear on the Venusian surface; more than 85% of the surface is covered by volcanic flows. Theia Mons, a huge shield volcano, has a diameter of over 600 mi and a height of over 3.5 mi. (The largest Hawaiian volcano is only about 125 mi in diameter but rises nearly 5.5 mi from the ocean floor.) In recent years, evidence of continuous volcanic activity has been noted by astronomers. Aside from volcanoes, there are highly deformed mountain belts across Venus along with a few meteor-impact craters more than 20 mi wide. Erosion is a very slow process on Venus due to the lack of water. There are indications of some wind movement of dust and sand. The few impact craters on Venus suggest that the surface is generally geologically young—less than 800 mil years old. Despite the fact that probes have landed on Venus, there are very few pictures from the surface because the probes couldn't withstand the high temperature and atmospheric pressure for more than a few hours.

Mars

Distance from the sun	
Perihelion	128.4 mil mi
Semi-major axis (mean distance)	141.6 mil mi (1.524 AU)
Aphelion	154.9 mil mi
Period of revolution around sun	686.98 d. (1.88 yr.)
Orbital eccentricity	0.0935
Orbital inclination	1.85°
Synodic day (midday to midday)	24 hr., 39 min., 35 sec.
Sidereal day	24 hr., 37 min., 22 sec.
Rotational inclination	25.19°
Mass (Earth = 1)	0.107
Mean radius	2,106 mi
Mean density (Earth = 1)	0.713
Natural satellites	2
Average surface temperature	–81°F

Named for the Roman god of war, the Red Planet has some features much like Earth. Mars has climate, seasons, volcanoes, and possibly once had liquid water flowing across its surface. Mars can easily be seen with the naked eye on most clear nights, which is why it was one of the first planets to be studied by ancient astronomers. Later, when telescopes came into use, many observers claimed that canals made by Martians existed on the planet's surface, which led to speculation as to whether there was intelligent life there. Unmanned probes have since put all those theories to rest; the canals turned out to be topographic patterns and dust storms.

Mars is currently being explored by a number of robotic craft, both on the surface and in orbit. The *Curiosity*/Mars Science Laboratory, an SUV-sized robot, landed on the surface in Aug. 2012. Its mission was to understand the history of the Martian geology and climate, search for the presence of organic matter, and assess the planet's past suitability for life. An Indian orbiter is currently using remote sensing to study the Martian surface and atmosphere, while NASA's *MAVEN* spacecraft is studying the upper atmosphere of Mars and its interaction with the solar wind. The European Space Agency *Trace Gas Orbiter* (TGO) began orbiting Mars in Oct. 2016. NASA's *InSight* mission, which landed in 2018, was relaying seismic data that is being used to map the interior of Mars. In 2020, three spacecraft were launched to the red planet, all arriving successfully in 2021: NASA's *Perseverance* lander, equipped with a helicopter named *Ingenuity*, and Mars missions by China and by the United Arab Emirates.

Orbit and rotation. Although Mars's orbital path is nearly circular, it is somewhat more eccentric than that of most other planets. Mars is more than 26 mil mi farther from the sun at its most distant point compared to its closest approach. Its orbit and speed in relation to Earth's bring it fairly close to Earth, at opposition, about every two years. Mars was at opposition on Dec. 8, 2022, and will be close again on Jan. 16, 2025. Every 15-17 years the close approaches are especially favorable for observation. The July 27, 2018, opposition was the last one that was particularly close, and the next such favorable opposition occurs on Sept. 15, 2035.

Mars rotates in 24 hr. and 37 min., almost the same period of time as Earth. Mars's mean distance from the sun is 142 mil mi. Because Mars's axis of rotation is inclined by about 25° from the vertical to the plane of its solar orbit about the sun, the planet has seasons.

Unlike Earth's global magnetic field, the Martian magnetic field is small, weak, and localized and may be the remnant of a stronger field from the planet's past.

Atmosphere. The Martian atmosphere is composed primarily of 95.32% carbon dioxide, 2.7% nitrogen, 1.6% argon, 0.13% oxygen, 0.08% carbon monoxide, and, in very minor quantities, water, hydrogen oxide, and neon. The atmosphere on Mars is very thin. It has an atmospheric pressure between 1% and 2% of Earth's (if Earth's atmosphere were that thin, there would not be enough oxygen to breathe). Because the Martian atmosphere is so thin and because of the planet's weak magnetic field, its surface is bombarded by cosmic radiation about 100 times as intense as on Earth.

Martian weather systems consist mainly of huge dust storms. On the poles, white caps (believed to be both water ice and carbon dioxide ice) grow in winter and shrink in summer. It is mainly the carbon dioxide that comes and goes with the seasons. The water ice is apparently in many layers with dust between them, indicating climatic cycles.

Surface and composition. Mars is an alien world with rust-red sand and pink skies. In the planet's beginning stages when it was much hotter, Mars's surface melted to a sufficient extent to separate into dense and lighter layers. Mars later cooled enough to allow liquid water to possibly flow across its surface. NASA scientists announced in Sept. 2015 the most convincing evidence to date that liquid water flows on the present-day Martian surface. Using imaging and spectroscopy instruments on the Mars Reconnaissance Orbiter, they showed that seasonal flows on Martian slopes contain hydrated minerals that can only form in the presence of liquid water.

Natural satellites. Mars has two small satellites called Phobos and Deimos, each discovered in 1877 by American astronomer Asaph Hall. (Phobos measures about 11 by 17 mi and Deimos about 7 by 9 mi.) Deimos, the outer satellite, revolves around the planet in about 31 hours. Phobos, the inner satellite, whips around Mars in a little more than 7 hours, making three orbits each Martian day. Since it orbits Mars faster than the planet rotates, Phobos rises in the west and sets in the east, opposite to what other bodies appear to do in the Martian sky. Both moons are irregularly shaped and pitted with numerous craters. Their origins are not known; however, some astronomers consider them to be asteroid-like objects that were captured by Mars very early in its history.

Jupiter

Distance from the sun	
Perihelion	460.1 mil mi
Semi-major axis (mean distance)	483.8 mil mi (5.204 AU)
Aphelion	507.4 mil mi
Period of revolution around sun	11.862 yr.
Orbital eccentricity	0.0489
Orbital inclination	1.304°
Synodic day (midday to midday)	9 hr., 55 min., 33 sec.
Sidereal day	9 hr., 55 min., 30 sec.
Rotational inclination	3.13°
Mass (Earth = 1)	317.8
Mean radius	43,441 mi
Mean density (Earth = 1)	0.24
Natural satellites	95
Average temperature*	–162°F

*i.e., temperature where atmospheric pressure equals 1 Earth atmosphere.

Jupiter, named for the Roman ruler of the gods, is the largest planet in the solar system (11 times the diameter of Earth). Its mass is more than twice the mass of all the other planets, moons, and asteroids put together. Visible to the naked eye and known to the ancients, it was a focus of the Italian scientist Galileo Galilei, who viewed the planet and its four largest moons through a homemade telescope.

Orbit and rotation. Jupiter is at an average distance of 484 mil mi from the sun and takes almost 12 Earth years to make a complete revolution. The largest of the planets, Jupiter has an equatorial diameter of 88,846 mi; its polar diameter is more than 5,700 mi shorter. This noticeable oblateness is a result of the liquidity of the planet and its extremely rapid rotation rate—a Jupiter day is less than 10 Earth hours long. A point on Jupiter's equator moves at a speed of 22,000 mph, as compared with 1,000 mph for a point on Earth's equator. Jupiter's magnetic field is by far the strongest of any planet. Electrical activity caused by this field is so strong that it discharges trillions of watts into Jupiter's environment daily. In July 2016, NASA's *Juno* spacecraft entered orbit around the planet to begin a study of Jupiter's composition, magnetic field, and auroras, including close-up views of the poles of the planet. In 2021, it began sending back images of Jupiter's satellites as well as the planet itself. Originally planned for one-year operation, in 2021 the mission was extended until Sept. 2025 or until the spacecraft ceases to function.

Atmosphere. Jupiter's atmosphere is primarily composed of 90% molecular hydrogen and 10% helium. Minor constituents include methane, ammonia, hydrogen deuteride, ethane, and water. Jupiter has a turbulent atmosphere characterized by thick clouds, high winds, and huge lightning storms many times larger than those on Earth. The atmospheric temperature varies, but the temperature at the tops of clouds may be about –280°F. The Great Red Spot seen prominently on Jupiter is a huge hurricane-like storm that is three times the diameter of Earth. In 2006, the Hubble Space Telescope detected the appearance of a second, smaller red spot.

Surface and composition. Gas giant planets like Jupiter, Saturn, and Neptune do not have a surface like Earth or any of the other rocky planets. The gases become denser with depth, until they may turn into a slush or slurry. Jupiter has a liquid hydrogen ocean more than 35,000 mi deep. It likely has a rocky core about the size of Earth, but 13 times more massive. There is no sharp interface between the gaseous atmosphere and the hydrogen ocean that accounts for most of Jupiter's volume. At lower depths, under enormous pressure, the liquid hydrogen takes on the properties of a metal. It is likely that this liquid metallic hydrogen is the source for both Jupiter's persistent radio noise and for its improbably strong magnetic field.

Natural satellites. Jupiter has 95 known satellites, the latest discovered in 2023. Four of the moons (in order of distance from Jupiter), Io, Europa, Ganymede, and Callisto—all discovered by Galileo in 1610—are large and bright and are close in diameter to Earth's moon and Mercury. Because they move so rapidly around Jupiter, their change in position from night to night can be seen from Earth using binoculars.

Io is one of the most volcanically active bodies in the solar system. A gaseous, doughnut-shaped ring, or torus, enveloping Io's orbit around Jupiter may have been formed by material ejected from Io's active volcanoes. (This is not to be confused with Jupiter's rings.) These volcanoes, hotter than Earth's volcanoes, erupt mainly molten sulfur and result in a constantly changing surface appearance.

Europa may have a 30-mi-deep salty, liquid ocean beneath its icy crust, perhaps a small metallic core, and a very tenuous atmosphere. Ganymede is the biggest moon in the solar system. With a diameter of 3,120 mi, it is bigger than both Mercury and Pluto. Ganymede also has its own magnetic field produced by a molten core of perhaps iron sulfide. Callisto has the oldest, most heavily cratered surface in the solar system, a very thin atmosphere of carbon dioxide, and possibly a subsurface liquid ocean.

The other known satellites are much smaller, with four closer to Jupiter than Io, five between Ganymede and Callisto, and the rest farther out. Most of Jupiter's moons orbit the planet at high inclinations from the equator, unlike the innermost satellites. These moons may be captured asteroids.

Rings. Jupiter has a diffuse, dark set of rings that were discovered by the *Voyager 1* spacecraft and cannot be seen from Earth without powerful telescopes. They are composed of small dust grains blasted off the four innermost moons by meteoroid impacts.

Saturn

Saturn, named for the Roman ruler of the Titans, is the sixth planet from the sun and most distant of the planets visible to the unaided eye. Saturn is second in size to Jupiter, but its mass is much smaller. Saturn is the only planet less dense than water, meaning that Saturn would float if there were a pool of water gigantic enough to hold it.

Orbit and rotation. Saturn's diameter is almost 74,900 mi at the equator, while its polar diameter is more than 7,300 mi shorter. Like Jupiter, its noticeable oblateness is a result of the liquidity of the planet and its extremely rapid rate of rotation; a day is little more than 10 Earth hours long.

Distance from the sun	
Perihelion	840.44 mil mi
Semi-major axis (mean distance)	890.8 mil mi (9.582 AU)
Aphelion	941.07 mil mi
Period of revolution around sun	29.458 yr.
Orbital eccentricity	0.0565
Orbital inclination	2.485°
Synodic day (midday to midday)	10 hr., 39 min., 23 sec.
Sidereal day	10 hr., 39 min., 22 sec.
Rotational inclination	26.73°
Mass (Earth = 1)	95.159
Mean radius	36,184 mi
Mean density (Earth = 1)	0.125
Natural satellites	146
Average temperature*	–218°F

*i.e., temperature where atmospheric pressure equals 1 Earth atmosphere.

Atmosphere. Saturn's atmosphere is composed primarily of 96.3% hydrogen, 3.3% helium, and traces of methane, ammonia, hydrogen deuteride, ethane, and water. Saturn's atmosphere is much like that of Jupiter, except that the temperature at the top of its cloud layer is at least 50°F colder.

Surface and composition. Saturn's atmosphere resembles Jupiter's; it likely has a small dense center surrounded by a deep ocean of hydrogen.

Natural satellites. Saturn has 146 known natural satellites, the discovery of the latest 63 announced in 2023. Saturn's moon Mimas has an impact crater 81 mi across (the moon itself is only 249 mi across). Enceladus has an atmosphere and shows evidence of geysers that spit water ice and vapor. Two tiny moons orbit within the rings, plowing through and making gaps in the rings along their orbits. Pan, the innermost satellite, creates the Encke Gap of Saturn's A-ring. Daphnis creates the Keeler Gap. The most intriguing Saturnian moon is Titan. The second-biggest moon in the solar system, Titan is bigger than Mercury. Its atmosphere is similar to Earth's atmosphere of long ago; it is made up of approximately 95% nitrogen with traces of methane. Titan's atmosphere extends about 360 mi into space whereas most of Earth's atmosphere lies within 37 mi of the surface. Photographs from Titan's surface, taken by the *Huygens* lander in 2005, show a muddy terrain, with possible deposits of water ice, channels carved by liquid methane springs, and an interesting boundary between light and dark material on the surface. In 2006, scientists found sand dunes on Titan's surface. The "sand" is believed to be tiny water ice crystals or organic compounds. Surface phenomena such as sand dunes are signs of erosion and wind. Unlike winds on Earth or Mars, Titan's winds are not the result of uneven solar heating on the moon's surface but rather Saturn's gravitational pull (similar to how the moon acts on the Earth's oceans).

Rings. Saturn's ring system is the planet's most recognizable feature. It begins about 4,000 mi above the visible disk of Saturn lying above its equator and extends about 260,000 mi into space. The diameter of the ring system visible from Earth is about 170,000 mi; the rings are estimated to be about 700 ft thick. Because they are so thin, roughly every 15 years when the ring plane is seen edge-on from Earth, the rings disappear from sight. In 2025 this will occur on Mar. 23, but at that time Saturn will be too close to the sun to be observable. The next time this phenomenon will be visible is Oct. 15, 2038. The rings are composed of rock and ice and range in size from tiny particles to large chunks of material the size of a bus. There are several divisions in the rings. The 2,920-mi Cassini divi-sion, the gap between the A and B rings, is the largest division.

Uranus

Uranus, discovered by Sir William Herschel in 1781, was the first planet discovered using a telescope. It was named for the father of the Titans in Roman mythology.

Orbit and rotation. Uranus has a diameter of over 31,000 mi and spins once in approximately 17.23 hours, according to magnetic data collected by *Voyager 2*. One of the most fascinating features of Uranus is how far over it is tipped. Its north pole lies 98° from its orbital plane. Thus, its seasons are extreme. Over its 84-year orbit, when the sun rises at the north pole, it shines there for about 42 Earth years; then it sets, and the north pole is in darkness for 42 Earth years. In addition to its rotational tilt, Uranus's magnetic field axis is tipped 58.6° from its rotational axis and is displaced about 30% of its radius away from the planet's center.

Distance from the sun	
Perihelion	1,703.4 mil mi
Semi-major axis (mean distance)	1,784.8 mil mi (19.201 AU)
Aphelion	1,866.4 mil mi
Period of revolution around sun	84.01 yr.
Orbital eccentricity	0.0457
Orbital inclination	0.772°
Synodic day (midday to midday)	17 hr., 14 min., 23 sec. (retrograde)
Sidereal day	17 hr., 14 min., 24 sec. (retrograde)
Rotational inclination	97.77°
Mass (Earth = 1)	14.536
Mean radius	15,759 mi
Mean density (Earth = 1)	0.23
Natural satellites	28
Average temperature*	–323°F

*i.e., temperature where atmospheric pressure equals 1 Earth atmosphere.

Atmosphere. The atmosphere is composed primarily of 82.5% hydrogen, 15.2% helium, and 2.3% methane, with small amounts of hydrogen deuteride, ammonia ice, water ice, ammonia hydrosulfide, and methane ice.

Surface and composition. Uranus has no solid surface, and likely no rocky core but rather a mixture of rocks and assorted ices with about 15% hydrogen and some helium.

Natural satellites. Uranus has 28 known moons, which have orbits lying in the plane of the planet's equator. Five moons are relatively large, while 22 are very small and were only discovered with the *Voyager 2* mission or in later observations. Miranda has grooved markings, reminiscent of Jupiter's Ganymede, but often arranged in a chevron pattern. Rifts and channels on Ariel provide evidence of liquid flowing over its surface in the past. Umbriel is extremely dark, prompting some observers to regard its surface as among the oldest in the system. Titania has rifts and fractures but not the evidence of flow found on Ariel. Oberon's main feature is its surface saturated with craters, unrelieved by other formations.

Rings. In the equatorial plane there is also a complex of 11 rings, 9 of which were discovered in 1978 by observers watching Uranus pass before a star.

Neptune

Named for the Roman god of the sea, Neptune was the first planet discovered through mathematical predictions before it was directly observed. Its approximate orbit and position were first calculated independently by British astronomer John Couch Adams and French astronomer Urbain Le Verrier in 1845. In 1846, German astronomer Johann Galle first observed Neptune through a telescope.

Orbit and rotation. Neptune orbits the sun in 164.8 Earth years in a nearly circular orbit. Its magnetic field is considerably asymmetric to the planet's structure, similar to, but not so extreme as, Uranus's magnetic field. Neptune's magnetic field axis is tipped 46.9° from its rotational axis and is displaced more than 55% of its radius away from the planet's center.

Distance from the sun	
Perihelion	2,761.7 mil mi
Semi-major axis (mean distance)	2,793.1 mil mi (30.047 AU)
Aphelion	2,824.5 mil mi
Period of revolution around sun	164.79 yr.
Orbital eccentricity	0.0113
Orbital inclination	1.769°
Synodic day (midday to midday)	16 hr., 6 min., 37 sec.
Sidereal day	16 hr., 6 min., 36 sec.
Rotational inclination	28.32°
Mass (Earth = 1)	17.147
Mean radius	15,301 mi
Mean density (Earth = 1)	0.297
Natural satellites	16
Average temperature*	–330°F

*i.e., temperature where atmospheric pressure equals 1 Earth atmosphere.

Atmosphere. The Neptunian atmosphere is composed primarily of 80% hydrogen, 19% helium, 1.5% methane, and small amounts of hydrogen deuteride, ethane, ammonia ice, water ice, ammonia hydrosulfide, and methane ice. Neptune's atmosphere is quite blue, with quickly changing white clouds often suspended high above an apparent surface. A Great Dark Spot, reminiscent of Jupiter's Great Red Spot, was discovered in 1989 when *Voyager 2* visited the planet. Observations with the Hubble Space Telescope have shown that the Great Dark Spot originally seen by *Voyager* has apparently dissipated, but a new dark spot has since appeared. Lightning and auroras have been found on other giant planets, but only the aurora phenomenon has been seen on Neptune. As with the other giant planets, Neptune emits more energy than it receives from the sun. The excess has been found to be 2.7 times the solar contribution.

Surface and composition. As with the other giant planets, Neptune may have no solid surface or exact diameter. However, a mean value of 30,600 mi may be assigned to a diameter between atmosphere levels where the pressure is about the same as sea level on Earth.

Natural satellites. The largest of Neptune's 16 satellites is Triton. It is the only large moon in a retrograde orbit, which suggests that it was captured rather than having formed along with the planet. Triton's large size, sufficient to raise significant tides on the planet, may one day, billions of years from now, bring Triton close enough to Neptune for Triton to be torn apart. Triton has a tenuous atmosphere of nitrogen with a trace of hydrocarbons and evidence of active geysers injecting material into it. Triton is the coldest object yet measured in the solar system with a surface temperature of –391°F. Only about half of Triton has been observed, but its terrain shows cratering and a strange regional feature described as resembling the skin of a cantaloupe. Nereid has the highest orbital eccentricity (0.75) of any moon. Its long looping orbit suggests that it was also captured. In 2003, two more moons, which orbit farther from their parent planet than any other moons in the solar system, were discovered. In July 2013, archival Hubble Space Telescope images were used to discover the existence of a 14th natural satellite of Neptune. At less than 20 km diameter, it is the smallest of Neptune's known moons. The *Voyager 2* probe in 1989 confirmed the existence of six rings around Neptune composed of very fine particles. There may be some clumps in the rings' structure. It is not known whether Neptune's satellites influence the formation or maintenance of the rings.

Dwarf Planets

Ceres

Distance from the sun	
Perihelion	237 mil mi (2.55 AU)
Semi-major axis (mean distance)	257 mil mi (2.77 AU)
Period of revolution around sun	4.6 yr.
Orbital eccentricity	0.0756
Orbital inclination	10.59°
Sidereal day	9.074 hr.
Mass (Earth = 1)	0.00015
Mean radius	292 mi

Ceres was the first asteroid discovered; Italian astronomer Giuseppe Piazzi first observed it on Jan. 1, 1801. In the 1800s, it was considered a planet but lost that designation. Ceres is the largest object in the asteroid belt, comprising nearly one third of all the mass of asteroids. In Aug. 2006, it was designated a dwarf planet by the Intl. Astronomical Union (IAU).

After a journey of over seven years, the *Dawn* spacecraft entered into orbit around Ceres in Mar. 2015, making *Dawn* the first spacecraft to visit a dwarf planet. Astronomers are particularly interested in asteroids since they are thought to be rocky protoplanets, examples of the building blocks from which planets formed early in the history of the solar system. *Dawn*'s scientific instrumentation consists of cameras for surface imaging, a spectrometer for measuring surface mineralogy, and a neutron detector for measuring elemental composition of Ceres. *Dawn* has produced high-resolution maps of the entire surface and the most accurate measurements of Ceres's size and mass. The images show a heavily cratered surface with features such as extremely reflective spots within a crater—thought to be freshly exposed water ice—and at least one mountain several miles high.

Orbit and rotation. Ceres orbits the sun in the asteroid belt region between Mars and Jupiter.

Surface and composition. Ceres's composition is similar to that of the stony meteorites known as carbonaceous chondrites. These are considered to be the oldest materials in the solar system, with a composition reflecting that of the primitive solar nebula. Extremely dark in color, probably because of their hydrocarbon content, they show evidence of having absorbed water. Thus, unlike the Earth and the moon, they have never melted nor been reheated since they first formed. *Dawn* observations suggest that the surface of Ceres consists largely of water ice, though its interior is mostly rock. Up to 25% of Ceres's mass may be water ice. There is evidence for hydrothermal vents at the surface of Ceres, perhaps indicating that liquid water existed below the surface in the recent past. Further study using *Dawn* will try to confirm observations suggesting that water evaporates from the surface and produces a diffuse atmosphere.

Pluto

Distance from the sun	
Perihelion	2,756.9 mil mi
Semi-major axis (mean distance)	3,670.1 mil mi (39.482 AU)
Aphelion	4,583.2 mil mi
Period of revolution around sun	247.74 yr.
Orbital eccentricity	0.2502
Orbital inclination	17.09°
Synodic day (midday to midday)	6 d., 9 hr., 17 min. (retrograde)
Sidereal day	6 d., 9 hr., 18 min. (retrograde)
Rotational inclination	119.59°
Mass (Earth = 1)	0.0022
Mean radius	736.5 mi
Mean density (Earth = 1)	0.339
Natural satellites	5
Average surface temperature	–369°F

Pluto, named for the Roman god of the underworld, is the largest Kuiper Belt object (KBO) by radius, and the second largest by mass. It was first discovered in 1930 by American astronomer Clyde Tombaugh and classified as a planet until 2006, when the IAU changed its designation to dwarf planet. In 2008, Pluto was designated by the IAU as the prototype for a class of objects called **plutoids**, bodies that (a) have an average distance from the sun greater than Neptune's; (b) are large enough that gravity determines their shape; and (c) have not cleared their orbit of other objects. Haumea, Makemake, and Eris are also plutoids. The *New Horizons* spacecraft, launched on a voyage to Pluto and beyond in 2006, made the first flyby of Pluto on July 14, 2015, and traveled on to a flyby of Kuiper belt object 2014 MU69 (Arrokoth), nicknamed Ultima Thule, on Jan. 1, 2019.

Orbit and rotation. Pluto's orbit is highly eccentric; although its average distance from the sun is 3.7 billion mi, it may get as close as 2.76 billion mi and as far as 4.58 billion mi. For about 20 years of its 248-year orbit, it is closer to the sun than Neptune. Currently, it is beyond Neptune's orbit.

Atmosphere and surface. Before the *New Horizons* flyby, all observations of Pluto had been made with telescopes nearly 3 billion mi away, so the mission brought new data to light. The mass and density of Pluto suggests that it is composed of a rocky core with an overlying water-ice mantle. Close-up observations of Pluto from *New Horizons* revealed a mixed surface, with some ancient, heavily cratered terrain and other younger, smoother plains with no craters. The smooth terrain, estimated to be no more than 100 mil years old, is much younger than scientists expected and may indicate that geologic processes continue to modify Pluto. Nitrogen ice on the smooth plains appears to be flowing, like glaciers on Earth, onto the more heavily cratered surface. Compositional evidence shows that the smooth areas contain nitrogen, methane, and carbon monoxide ices. Scientists also found several mountain ranges rising more than 2 mi above the smooth plains; they speculated that the mountains are made of water ice thrust up from below Pluto's nitrogen-rich icy surface.

New Horizons also provided the first close-up measurements of Pluto's atmosphere, confirming earlier measurements of methane, nitrogen, and carbon monoxide, the same molecules that form ice on Pluto's surface. Scientists speculate that the atmosphere forms from evaporation of surface ices when the dwarf planet is closer to the sun. The new measurements also revealed hydrocarbon hazes as much as 50 mi above Pluto's surface. The hazes are thought to form when Pluto's tenuous atmosphere is exposed to the sun's ultraviolet rays. Dark regions on Pluto's surface likely result from these hydrocarbons settling. Knowledge of Pluto will continue to improve as more data is analyzed.

Natural satellites. Pluto has five known natural satellites. Charon, the biggest, has a diameter of 750 mi—about half of Pluto's diameter of 1,474 mi. No other planet or dwarf planet has a moon so close to its size. Discovered in 1978, Charon orbits Pluto at a distance of 12,200 mi and takes 6.39 days to move around the dwarf planet. In this same length of time, Pluto and Charon both rotate once on their axes, meaning that the Pluto-Charon system appears to rotate as virtually a rigid body. Both worlds are roughly spherical and have comparable densities. Because of these similarities and their peculiar relationship, there is debate as to whether Charon should one day be designated a dwarf planet. *New Horizons* provided the first detailed look at Charon, revealing a surface with less color and likely dominated by water ice. New evidence suggests Charon may have had a water ocean in the past. Much of Charon's surface is smoother than expected, with few craters, implying that Charon has an active geology capable of resurfacing. The images also reveal fractures extending hundreds of miles and a canyon around 5 mi deep.

Two other moons, discovered in 2005 and 2006, were officially named Nix and Hydra. Two additional moons, discovered in 2011 and 2012, were officially named Kerberos and Styx by the IAU in 2013. In late 2015, NASA released *New Horizons*-sourced images of Nix and Hydra, revealing irregularly shaped objects about 25 and 35 mi across, respectively. Astronomers examining *New Horizons* data have been surprised to find no additional moons, down to the roughly 1-mi-diameter limit of detectability by the spacecraft.

Haumea

Distance from the sun	
Semi-major axis (mean distance)	43.355 AU
Period of revolution around sun	285.48 yr.
Orbital eccentricity	0.189
Orbital inclination	28.20°
Mass (Earth = 1)	0.0007
Mean radius	420 mi
Natural satellites	2

Haumea was discovered in 2004 and was accepted as a dwarf planet by the IAU in 2008.

Orbit and rotation. Haumea has a moderately eccentric orbit and takes about 285 years to go around the sun.

Surface and composition. Spectra of Haumea indicate the presence of almost pure crystalline water ice. The surface reflects about 60% of the sunlight that reaches it. Haumea has a very oblong shape, twice as long as it is wide.

Natural satellites. Haumea has two natural satellites, Hi'iake and Namaka.

Makemake

Distance from the sun	
Semi-major axis (mean distance)	45.715 AU
Period of revolution around sun	309.1 yr.
Orbital eccentricity	0.155
Orbital inclination	28.99°
Mass (Earth = 1)	0.0007
Mean radius	450 mi
Natural satellites	1

Makemake was discovered in 2005 and was accepted as a dwarf planet by the IAU in 2008.

Orbit and rotation. Makemake has a moderately eccentric orbit and takes about 310 years to go around the sun.

Surface and composition. Spectra of Makemake indicate the presence of frozen methane, as well as several organic compounds. The surface is highly reflective and appears similar to that of Pluto.

Natural satellites. Makemake has one natural satellite.

Gonggong (2007 OR10)

Distance from the sun	
Semi-major axis (mean distance)	67.143 AU
Period of revolution around sun	550.19 yr.
Orbital eccentricity	0.505
Orbital inclination	30.87°
Mass (Earth = 1)	0.0006
Mean radius	950 mi
Natural satellites	1

2007 OR10 was discovered in 2007 and was named Gonggong in 2020 pending final approval by the IAU.

Orbit and rotation. 2007 OR10 has a highly elliptical orbit and takes about 550 years to go around the sun.

Surface and composition. Spectra of 2007 OR10 indicate the presence of frozen methane and water ice. The surface is highly reflective and appears similar to that of Pluto.

Natural satellites. One natural satellite of 2007 OR10 was discovered by astronomers using the Hubble Space Telescope in 2017.

Eris

Distance from the sun	
Semi-major axis (mean distance)	67.6497 AU
Period of revolution around sun	556.43 yr.
Orbital eccentricity	0.44171
Orbital inclination	44.204°
Mass (Earth = 1)	0.0027
Mean radius	723 mi
Natural satellites	1

Discovered in 2003 by astronomers at the California Institute of Technology, Eris is the largest dwarf planet by mass, about 27% larger than Pluto, although Pluto has a slightly larger radius.

Orbit and rotation. Eris has a highly elliptical orbit and takes about 560 years to go around the sun—more than twice the time it takes Pluto. Its inclination is steep, tilted at 44° to the planetary plane. It also has an extremely eccentric orbit. It will be at its closest to the sun, actually coming inside part of Pluto's orbit, in about 280 years.

Surface and composition. Eris, with a surface covered in frozen methane, may be similar to Pluto and the Neptunian moon Triton. Observations made by the Hubble Space Telescope show that Eris's surface is almost white and uniform, reflecting 86% of the light that hits it. This makes it the most reflective body in the solar system. The dwarf planet's interior is likely a mixture of rock and ice.

Natural satellites. Eris has one moon, Dysnomia.

Small Solar System Bodies

Asteroids

Besides planets and moons, many smaller objects orbit the sun. In 2006, the International Astronomical Union (IAU) officially designated these objects "small solar system bodies." Asteroids or minor planets are found mainly in a belt between the orbits of Mars and Jupiter. Within this belt there may be millions of asteroids of varying sizes. Most asteroids are very small. Ceres, which can be classified both as an asteroid and a dwarf planet, is 588 mi in diameter, about one-quarter the diameter of our moon.

Some of these asteroids are gravitationally locked with Jupiter and the sun so that they have roughly the same orbit as Jupiter but are either 60° ahead or behind the planet. These are the **Trojan asteroids**. Many of the smaller moons of the solar system, especially those in retrograde orbits, may be captured asteroids. Asteroids whose orbits either cross or come close to the Earth's orbit are labeled **Near Earth asteroids**, or NEAs. A handful of asteroids have actually been imaged by the Arecibo and Goldstone radio telescopes and by the NEAR Shoemaker space probe. The *Galileo* spacecraft imaged the asteroids Gaspra and Ida (including Ida's moon Dactyl) on its way to Jupiter. The Japanese *Hayabusa 2*, after orbiting asteroid Ryugu, returned a sample to Earth in Dec. 2020. NASA's OSIRIS-REx mission, after orbiting asteroid Bennu, returned a sample to Earth on Sept. 24, 2023, after which it moved on to rendezvous with the asteroid Apophis in 2029. On Sept. 26, 2022, a NASA mission called the Double Asteroid Redirection Test (DART) fired a projectile at Dimorphos, the small moon of the binary asteroid Didymos, successfully altering the orbital by period by over 30 minutes, in a demonstration of how Earth might de-fend itself against collisions with asteroids. As of 2024, 18 asteroids had been visited by spacecraft.

Comets

Comets are small icy bodies that orbit the sun. When one approaches the sun, the energy from the sun boils off material from the comet's icy nucleus, producing an enlarged head (or **coma**), and in many cases an extended tail. Because of that, comets are brighter when near the sun. For large comets, the head may be 100,000 mi across and the tail more than a million mi long, though both are mainly empty space.

Comets have been known since ancient times. British astronomer Edmund Halley (1656-1742) ultimately realized that a group of historical reports were just repeated visits of the same object. Comets are the only astronomical objects named after their discoverers. In 1986, the European spacecraft *Giotto* took the first close-up images of a comet's nucleus, specifically of Comet Halley, showing it had a peanut-shaped nucleus with a longest dimension of about 10 mi.

In 1995, U.S. observers Alan Hale (1958-) and Thomas Bopp (1949-2018) independently discovered a comet that was then beyond the orbit of Jupiter. It is one of the brightest comets of all time. It also holds the record for length of time visible to the naked eye—19 months—and is the most photographed comet in history. In July 2009, an amateur astronomer discovered a large impact scar in the upper atmosphere of Jupiter, likely the result of another cometary impact. In Mar. 2020, astronomers using the *NEOWISE* mission of the Wide-field Infrared Survey Explorer (*WISE*) discovered a comet, which in July 2020 was widely visible to the naked eye. Comet *NEOWISE* is the brightest comet since Hale-Bopp. In 2014, the *Rosetta* spacecraft became the first spacecraft to orbit a comet, 67P/Churyumov-Gerasimenko. *Rosetta* also deployed a lander onto the comet surface. As of summer 2024, eight comets have been studied directly by spacecraft.

Kuiper Belt

The Kuiper Belt is a doughnut-shaped region that extends to about 50 AU (astronomical units) from the sun and is thought to be the source of short-period comets such as Comets Halley or Swift-Tuttle. It is filled with icy bodies that are in solar orbit. The more than 1,000 objects found in this region in recent years are called Kuiper Belt objects (KBOs). It is estimated that there are more than 70,000 objects 60 mi in diameter or larger within the Kuiper Belt. Dwarf planets Pluto and Eris are considered KBOs. There are at least six KBOs larger than 300 mi in diameter.

On Jan. 1, 2019, *New Horizons* made the first close study of a KBO when it flew by the object 2014 MU 69, originally nicknamed Ultima Thule but now provisionally named Arrokoth by the IAU. In the first images sent back to Earth, Arrokoth appears to be a "contact binary," composed of two smaller bodies, 14 mi and 9 mi across, in close contact with each other. No satellite of Arrokoth was observed.

Arrokoth (2014 MU 69)

Distance from the sun	
Semi-major axis (mean distance)	44.539 AU
Period of revolution around sun	298 yr.
Orbital eccentricity	0.04172
Orbital inclination	2.451°
Mass (Earth = 1)	Unknown
Mean radius	14 mi ("Ultima") and 9 mi ("Thule")

Oort Cloud

The Oort Cloud is a vast spherical region hypothesized to exist around the sun and populated by comets. Dutch astronomer Jan Oort (1900-92) proposed its existence as the origin for long-period comets that enter the inner part of the solar system where the planets orbit. Current technology is not sufficient to detect any members of the Oort Cloud other than observed comets whose orbits may reach out as far as 50,000 AU. Recent examples of such long-period comets are Comets Hale-Bopp and Hyakutake.

The Sun

Distance from Earth, mean	92.96 mil mi (1 AU)
Sidereal day (rotation period)	25.38 d.
Mass (Earth = 1)	332,900
Mean radius	432,200 mi
Mean density (Earth = 1)	0.255
Average surface temperature	9,941°F

The sun is the Earth's primary source of light and heat and its closest star. The biggest object in the solar system, the sun is 332,900 times more massive than Earth and contains 99.86% of the mass of the entire solar system. On the whole, the sun is made up of about 92.1% hydrogen and 7.8% helium, with trace amounts of other elements. It has a mass and luminosity greater than that of 90% of the stars in the Milky Way galaxy. Although most of the stars that can be easily seen on a clear night are bigger and brighter than the sun, its proximity to Earth makes it appear tremendously large and bright. The sun is 400,000 times as bright as the full moon, and it gives Earth 6 mil times as much light as do all the other stars put together. Because of the great distance between the sun and Earth, it takes about 499 sec., or slightly more than 8 min., for light from the sun to reach Earth.

Composition. The sun has six regions. The first three from the inside out are the core, the radiative zone, and the convective zone. Together they form the interior. The others, which comprise the visible surface, are the photosphere, the chromosphere, and the outermost region, the corona.

The sun's heat and energy are produced in its core. Through a series of nuclear fusion reactions, hydrogen nuclei are converted to helium nuclei, releasing energy in the process. Temperatures in the core are theorized to be 28 mil °F. In 2017 astronomers discovered that the core rotates nearly four times faster than the surface, a rapidity left over from the time when the sun was formed. From the core, photons transport the energy outward through the radiative zone. It can take photons several million years to pass through this area. In the convective zone, gases move energy outward at a faster rate. Like a boiling pot, bubbles of gas bring energy to the surface.

The photosphere is the visible surface of the sun, that is, the light that we see as sunlight. When sunlight is analyzed with a spectroscope, it is found to consist of a continuous spectrum composed of all the colors of the rainbow, crossed by many dark lines. The dark "absorption lines" are produced by gaseous materials in the outer layers of the sun. More than 60 of the natural terrestrial elements have been identified in the sun, all in gaseous form because of the sun's intense heat.

Just above the photosphere is the chromosphere, which is visible to the naked eye only in total solar eclipses, during which it appears to be a pinkish-violet layer with occasional great prominences projecting above its general level. With proper instruments, the chromosphere can be seen or photographed whenever the sun is visible. Above the chromosphere is the corona, also visible to the naked eye only at times of total eclipse or with instruments that permit the brighter portions of the corona to be seen. The corona surges millions of miles from the sun; its atoms are all in a state of extreme excitation and high ionization that indicates temperatures nearly 2 mil °F.

Sunspots. These dark, irregularly shaped regions may reach diameters of thousands of miles. There is an intimate connection between sunspots and the corona. At times of low sunspot activity, the fine streamers of the corona are longer above the sun's equator than over the polar regions of the sun; during periods of high sunspot activity, the corona extends fairly evenly outward from all regions of the sun but to a much greater distance in space. The average life of a sunspot group is two months, but some have lasted for more than a year. Sunspots reach a low point, on average, every 11.3 years, with a peak of activity occurring irregularly between two successive periods of minimal activity. The sun experienced an unusually quiet period in 2008 and 2009; its latest period of maximum activity occurred in 2014, though this was among the weakest maximums ever recorded.

Solar wind and magnetic field. Magnetic arches, called prominences, may extend tens of thousands of miles into the corona and may release enormous amounts of energy heating the corona. Coronal mass ejections are enormous releases of solar energy. Coronal holes are regions where the corona appears dark in X-rays, and are associated with open magnetic field lines, where the magnetic field lines project out into space instead of back toward the sun. It is in these regions where the high-speed solar wind originates.

The solar wind carries the sun's magnetic field, which extends beyond the planets. This is called the interplanetary magnetic field (IMF). Far past Pluto and the Kuiper Belt, the solar wind and the IMF lose their influence. The boundary between them and interstellar space is called the heliopause. In 2013, NASA announced that the *Voyager 1* spacecraft, launched in 1977, seemed at last to have reached the heliopause, at a distance 18 billion km (11 billion mi) from the sun.

Searching for Extrasolar Planets

The sun is a typical star in many respects and—with over 400 billion stars in the Milky Way—it is plausible that many other stars might have planets. Since 1995, astronomers have gathered evidence of thousands of planets orbiting stars other than the sun. Astronomers have not directly observed most of these objects but inferred their existence from observations of their parent stars.

Astronomers have used two main techniques to detect planets. The first, called the radial-velocity method, uses the Doppler effect to detect periodic changes in the motion of a star caused by the gravitational tug of an unseen planet. The magnitude of the star's motion and the time it takes to repeat can be used to infer the planet's mass and distance from its host star. This technique is most sensitive to high-mass planets orbiting close to their stars because that situation produces more noticeable changes in a star's motion.

The second technique, the transit method, relies on the dimming of a star's light as an unseen planet repeatedly passes in front of it. Astronomers are able to infer the diameter of the planet and the distance at which the planet orbits the star. When combined with the mass determined from the radial-velocity method, astronomers can determine the density of the unseen planet and begin to infer its similarity to planets in our solar system.

Astronomers have also used optical gravitational lensing to detect extrasolar planets. This technique, which detects the observed brightening of a distant background star as a planet passes in front of it, has allowed Southern Hemisphere astronomers to find the most distant planet yet detected, about halfway to the center of our own Milky Way galaxy.

The first planets to be discovered outside the solar system tended to be massive "hot Jupiters," orbiting close to their parent stars (closer than Mercury's orbit around the sun) and comparable in mass to the gas giant Jupiter. But as detection instruments and techniques have improved, smaller and more distant planets have been discovered. The planets discovered so far seem to fall into several groups: rocky planets as massive as 1.75 times that of Earth; mini-Neptunes, 2-3.5 times as massive as Earth, with gas surrounding a rocky core; "super Earths" more massive than the mini-Neptunes; and gas giants, as massive or more massive than Jupiter.

In 2005, astronomers obtained the first direct image of an extrasolar planet around a normal star called GQ Lupi, which is like Earth's sun but younger. The planet is about 100 AU (astronomical units) away from the star and estimated to be about twice as massive as Jupiter.

In 2006, astronomers discovered what they call a "super Earth" orbiting a red dwarf 9,000 light-years away. The planet appears to have about 13 times Earth's mass and may be composed of rock and ice, but it is believed not to have liquid on its surface. Such super Earths appear to be common in extrasolar planetary systems. In 2007, astronomers detected water in the atmosphere of an extrasolar planet for the first time.

In 2009, NASA launched Kepler, the first telescope sensitive enough to detect Earth-sized planets around other stars. Kepler's first-released data in 2010 indicated that small planets are more common than large planets. Kepler has now detected a large number of planets with diameters similar to that of Earth. Some of the planets are known to orbit within the host star's habitable zone, meaning that the conditions are such that liquid water could exist on the planetary surface. As of July 2024, astronomers had confirmed over 2,773 planets discovered by Kepler and nearly 2,000 unconfirmed candidates; an extension of the Kepler Mission, K2, discovered another 548 confirmed planets and 976 candidates requiring further confirmation.

Planets with masses much less than Jupiter's are now regularly discovered. A team of astronomers announced, Aug. 2016, the discovery of a possibly Earth-like planet, Proxima b, in orbit around Proxima Centauri, the star closest to the sun. About 4.2 light-years away, it is the closest known exoplanet. In Feb. 2017, astronomers announced the discovery of at least seven Earth-sized planets orbiting a small star, Trappist-1, located about 40 light-years away. They appear similar in mass and composition to Earth, and three of the planets are in the habitable zone of the star. In June 2017, the Kepler mission announced the discovery of 10 Earth-sized planets, probably rocky in composition, that might support liquid water and could be potentially habitable.

NASA successfully launched the Transiting Exoplanet Survey Satellite (TESS) mission on Apr. 18, 2018, aboard a SpaceX Falcon 9 rocket. This landmark mission was conducting an all-sky survey of extrasolar planets, including those orbiting bright nearby stars, which can be investigated in further detail by large Earth-based and space telescopes. By July 2020, it had finished its primary mission, covering about 75% of space. By 2024, TESS had found 542 confirmed exoplanets as well as over 7,000 candidates needing further detailed observation for confirmation. In Dec. 2019, the European Space Agency launched a complementary mission, Cheops (CHaracterising ExOPlanet Satellite), which is also targeting planets around bright nearby stars, and is designed to characterize the nature of planets discovered orbiting them.

Earth: Size, Computation of Time, Seasons

Distance from the sun	
Perihelion	91.4 mil mi
Semi-major axis (mean distance)	93 mil mi (1.0000 AU)
Aphelion	94.5 mil mi
Period of revolution	365.256 d.
Orbital eccentricity	0.0167
Orbital inclination	0°
Synodic day (midday to midday)	24 hr., 0 min., 0 sec.
Sidereal day (rotation period)	23 hr., 56 min., 4.2 sec.
Rotational inclination	23.45°
Mass (Earth = 1)	1
Mean radius	3,958.8 mi
Mean density (Earth = 1)	1
Natural satellites	1
Average surface temperature	59°F

Earth is the fifth-largest planet and the third from the sun. Its mass is 5.9736×10^{24} kg. Earth's equatorial diameter is 7,926 mi while its polar diameter is only 7,900 mi.

Size and dimensions. Earth is considered a solid mass, yet it has a large, liquid iron, **magnetic core** with a radius of about 2,160 mi. Surprisingly, it has a solid **inner core** that may be a large iron crystal, with a radius of 760 mi. Around the core is a thick shell, or **mantle**, of dense rock. This mantle is composed of materials rich in iron and magnesium. It is somewhat plastic-like, and under slow steady pressure, it can flow like a liquid. The mantle, in turn, is covered by a thin **crust** forming the solid granite and basalt base of the continents and ocean basins. Over broad areas of Earth's surface, the crust has a thin cover of sedimentary rock such as sandstone, shale, and limestone formed by weathering and by deposits of sands, clays, and plant and animal remains.

The temperature inside the Earth increases about 1°F with every 100 to 200 ft in depth, in the upper 100 km (62 mi) of Earth. It reaches nearly 8,000°F-9,000°F at the center. The heat is believed to come from radioactivity in rocks, pressures within Earth, and the original heat of formation.

Atmosphere. Earth's atmosphere is a blanket composed of 78% nitrogen, 21% oxygen, and 1% argon. Present in minute quantities are carbon dioxide, hydrogen, neon, helium, krypton, and xenon. Water vapor displaces other gases and varies from nearly zero to about 4% by volume. The atmosphere rests on Earth's surface with a weight equivalent to a layer of water 34 ft deep. For about 300,000 ft upward, the gases remain in the proportions stated. Gravity holds the gases to Earth. The weight of the air compresses it at the bottom so that the greatest density is at Earth's surface. Pressure and density decrease as height increases.

The lowest layer of the atmosphere extending up from the Earth's surface about 7.5 mi is the **troposphere**, which contains 90% of the air. This is also where most weather phenomena occur. The temperature drops with increasing height through this layer. The **stratosphere** extends about 23 mi above the troposphere; the temperature generally increases with height within this layer. The stratosphere contains **ozone**, which prevents ultraviolet rays from reaching Earth's surface. Since there is very little convection in the stratosphere, jets regularly cruise in the lower parts to provide a smoother ride for passengers.

Above the stratosphere is the **mesosphere**, where the temperature again decreases with height for another 19 mi. Extending above the mesosphere to the outer fringes of the atmosphere is the **thermosphere**, a region where temperature once more increases with height to a value measured in thousands of degrees Fahrenheit. The lower portion of this region, extending from 50 to about 400 mi in altitude, is characterized by high ion density and is thus called the **ionosphere**. Most meteors are in the lower thermosphere or the mesosphere at the time they are observed.

Longitude and latitude. Position on the globe is measured by meridians and parallels. Meridians, which are imaginary lines drawn around Earth through the poles, determine **longitude**. The meridian running through Greenwich, England, is the **prime meridian** of longitude; all others are either E or W. Parallels, which are imaginary circles parallel with the equator, determine **latitude**. The length of a degree of longitude varies as the cosine of the latitude. At the equator a degree of longitude is 69.171 statute mi; this is gradually reduced toward the poles. Value of a longitude degree at the poles is zero.

Latitude is reckoned by the number of degrees N or S of the **equator**, an imaginary circle on Earth's surface everywhere equidistant between the two poles. According to the International Astronomical Union, the length of a degree of latitude is 68.708 statute mi at the equator and varies slightly N and S because of the oblate form of the globe. At the poles, it is 69.403 statute mi.

Definitions of time. Earth rotates on its axis and follows an elliptical orbit around the sun. The rotation makes the sun appear to move across the sky from E to W. This rotation determines day and night, and the complete rotation, in relation to the sun, is called the **apparent or true solar day**. A sundial thus measures **apparent solar time**. This length of time varies, but an average determines a mean solar day of 24 hours.

The mean solar day and **mean solar time** are in universal use for civil purposes. Mean solar time may be obtained from apparent solar time by correcting observations of the sun for the **equation of time**. Mean solar time may be up to 16 min. different from apparent solar time.

Sidereal time is the measure of time defined by the diurnal motion of the vernal equinox and is determined from observation of the meridian transits of stars. One complete rotation of Earth relative to the equinox is called the **sidereal day**. The **mean sidereal day** is 23 hr., 56 min., 4.2 sec. of mean solar time.

The interval required for Earth to make one absolute revolution around the sun is a **sidereal year**; it consisted of 365 days, 6 hr., 9 min., and 9.5 sec. of mean solar time (approximately 24 hr. per day) in 1900 and has been increasing at the rate of 0.0001 second annually.

The **tropical year**, upon which our calendar is based, is the interval between two consecutive returns of the sun to the vernal equinox. The tropical year consisted of 365 days, 5 hr., 48 min., and 46 sec. in 1900. It has been decreasing at the rate of 0.53 sec. per century. The **calendar year** begins at midnight precisely, local clock time, on the night of Dec. 31-Jan. 1. The day and the calendar month also begin at midnight by the clock.

On Jan. 1, 1972, the Bureau International des Poids et Mesures in Paris introduced **International Atomic Time** (TAI) as the most precisely determined time scale for astronomical usage. The fundamental unit of TAI in the international system of units is the second, defined as the duration of 9,192,631,770 periods of the radiation corresponding to the transition between two hyperfine levels of the ground state of the cesium-133 atom. **Coordinated Universal Time** (UTC), which serves as the basis for civil timekeeping and is the standard time of the prime meridian, is officially defined by a formula which relates UTC to mean sidereal time in Greenwich, England. (UTC replaced Greenwich Mean Time as the basis for standard time for the world.)

Zones and seasons. The five zones of Earth's surface are the Torrid, lying between the Tropics of Cancer and Capricorn; the N Temperate, between Cancer and the Arctic Circle; the S Temperate, between Capricorn and the Antarctic Circle; and the two Frigid Zones, between the Polar Circles and the Poles.

The inclination, or tilt, of Earth's axis, 23°45′ away from a perpendicular to Earth's orbit of the sun, determines the seasons. These are commonly marked in the N Temperate Zone, where spring begins at the vernal equinox, summer at the summer solstice, autumn at the autumnal equinox, and winter at the winter solstice. In the S Temperate Zone, the seasons are reversed. Spring begins at the autumnal equinox, summer at the winter solstice, and so on.

The points at which the sun crosses the equator are the **equinoxes**, when day and night are most nearly equal. The points at which the sun is at a maximum distance from the equator are the **solstices**, when days and nights are most unequal. However, at the equator, day and night are equal throughout the year.

In June, the North Pole is tilted 23°27′ toward the sun, and the days in the Northern Hemisphere are longer than the nights, while the days in the Southern Hemisphere are shorter than the nights. In Dec., the North Pole is tilted 23°27′ away from the sun, and the situation is reversed.

Seasons in 2025. In 2025, the four seasons begin in the Northern Hemisphere as shown. (Add 1 hour to Eastern Standard Time for Atlantic Time; subtract 1 hour for Central, 2 for Mountain, 3 for Pacific, 4 for Alaska, 5 for Hawaii-Aleutian. Also shown is Coordinated Universal Time.)

Season	Date	UTC	EST/EDT
Vernal Equinox (spring)	Mar. 20	9:01	5:01 EDT
Northern Solstice (summer)	June 21	2:42	22:42 EDT June 20
Autumnal Equinox (fall)	Sept. 22	18:19	14:19 EDT
Southern Solstice (winter)	Dec. 21	15:03	10:03 EST

Poles. The geographic (rotation) poles, or points where Earth's axis of rotation cuts the surface, are not absolutely fixed in the body of Earth. The pole of rotation describes an irregular curve about its mean position.

Two periods have been detected in this motion: (1) an annual period due to seasonal changes in barometric pressure, to load of ice and snow on the surface, and to other seasonal phenomena; (2) a period of about 14 months due to the shape and constitution of Earth. In addition, there are small but as yet unpredictable irregularities. The whole motion is so small that the actual pole at any time remains within a circle of 30 or 40 ft in radius centered at the mean position of the pole.

The pole of rotation for the time being is, of course, the pole having a latitude of 90° and an indeterminate longitude.

Magnetic poles. Although Earth's magnetic field resembles that of an ordinary bar magnet, this magnetic field is probably produced by electric currents in the liquid currents of the Earth's outer core. The **north magnetic pole** of Earth is that region where the magnetic force is downward, and the **south magnetic pole** is that region where the magnetic force is upward. A compass placed at the magnetic poles experiences no directive force in azimuth (i.e., direction).

There are slow changes in the distribution of Earth's magnetic field. This slow temporal change is referred to as the secular change of the main magnetic field, and the magnetic poles shift due to this. The location of the N magnetic pole was first measured in 1831 at Cape Adelaide on the W coast of Boothia Peninsula in Canada's Northwest Territories (about latitude 70°N and longitude 96°W). Since then it has moved over 500 mi. As of 2024 it was estimated to be at latitude 85.98°N, longitude 142.29°E, in the Arctic Ocean far north of Siberia. Measurement for several decades by Canadian scientists indicates the motion of the pole has accelerated, now averaging about 34 mi per year.

The direction of the horizontal components of the magnetic field at any point is known as magnetic N at that point, and the angle by which it deviates E or W of true N is known as the magnetic declination.

A compass without error points in the direction of magnetic north. (In general, this is not the direction of the true rotational North Pole.) If you follow the direction indicated by the N end of the compass, you will go along an irregular curve that eventually reaches the north magnetic pole (though not usually by a great-circle route). However, the action of the compass should not be thought of as due to any influence of the distant pole, but simply as an indication of the distribution of Earth's magnetism at the place of observation.

Rotation. The speed of Earth's rotation about its axis is slightly variable. The variations may be classified as:

(A) **Secular.** Tidal friction acts as a brake on the rotation and causes a slow secular increase in the length of the day, about 1 millisecond per century.

(B) **Irregular.** The speed of rotation may increase for a number of years (about 5 to 10) and then start decreasing. The maximum difference from the mean in the length of the day during a century is about 5 milliseconds. The accumulated difference in time has amounted to approximately 44 seconds since 1900. The cause is probably motion in the interior of Earth.

(C) **Periodic.** Seasonal variations exist with periods of 1 year and 6 months. The cumulative effect is such that each year, Earth is late about 30 milliseconds near June 1 and is ahead about 30 milliseconds near Oct. 1. The maximum seasonal variation in the length of the day is about 0.5 millisecond. It is believed that the principal cause of the annual variation is the seasonal change in the wind patterns of the Northern and Southern Hemispheres. The semiannual variation is due chiefly to tidal action of the sun, which distorts the shape of Earth slightly.

The Moon

Distance from Earth	
Perigee	225,744 mi
Semi-major axis (mean distance)	238,855 mi
Apogee	251,966 mi
Period of revolution	27.322 d.
Orbital eccentricity	0.0549
Orbital inclination	5.145°
Synodic orbital period (period of phases)	29.53 d.
Sidereal day (rotation period)	27.322 d.
Rotational inclination	6.68°
Mass (Earth = 1)	0.0123
Mean radius	1,079 mi
Mean density (Earth = 1)	0.607
Average surface temperature	–100°F

The moon is the second-brightest object in the sky (the sun is the first). Earth's only natural satellite, the moon is the force behind the rising and falling of tides, and it helps to regulate Earth's inclination as they orbit the sun. Many probes have been sent to the moon, and between 1969 and 1972, 12 U.S. astronauts walked on its surface. The moon is the subject of renewed international interest. In 2007, Japan and China orbited satellites around the moon, India orbited a spacecraft in fall 2008, and the U.S. sent an orbiter and impactor in 2009. In Sept. 2009, American scientists announced the discovery of a thin layer of water ice near the lunar poles. Since 2009, NASA has been mapping and measuring the surface composition and other properties of the moon using the Lunar Reconnaissance Orbiter. In Sept. 2013, NASA launched *LADEE*, a mission to study the ephemeral lunar atmosphere and lunar dust from a low orbit. In Dec. 2013, China became the third nation to land a spacecraft on the moon when *Chang'e 3* set down on Mare Imbrium. *Chang'e 3* released the *Yutu* rover to study the lunar surface. On July 22, 2019, India successfully launched the *Chandrayaan-2* mission. Scheduled to land a rover near the south pole of the moon on Sept. 7, 2019, mission control lost contact with the lander 1.3 mi from the surface, though an orbiter remained operational. The *Chandrayaan-3* follow-on mission landed a rover near the south pole of the moon on Aug. 23, 2023. On June 1, 2024, China's *Chang'e 6* spacecraft landed on the far side of the moon, successfully deploying a mini rover. Most notably, the lander's robotic scoop took samples with a total mass of 1,935.3 grams from the surface of the moon and a return module transported the sample to a module in orbit around the moon. The sample was then transferred to a capsule, which landed the sample by parachute in Inner Mongolia on June 25, 2024, marking the first robotic return of samples from the lunar far side.

Orbit and rotation. The moon completes a circuit around Earth in a period that averages 27 days, 7 hr., 43.2 min. This is the moon's sidereal period. Because of the motion of the moon in common with Earth around the sun, the mean duration of the lunar month—the period from one new moon to the next new moon—is 29 days, 12 hr., 44.05 min. This is the moon's synodic period.

The mean distance of the moon from Earth is 238,855 mi, but its orbit about Earth is elliptical, and thus the actual distance varies considerably. The maximum distance from Earth that the moon may reach is 251,966 mi and the least distance is 225,744 mi.

The moon rotates on its axis in a period of time that is exactly equal to its sidereal revolution about Earth—27.322 days. Thus the backside, or farside, of the moon always faces away from Earth. But this does not mean that the backside is always dark. The farside of the moon gets as much direct sunlight as the nearside; at new moon phase, the farside of the moon is fully lit but not visible from Earth.

The moon's revolution about Earth is irregular because of its elliptical orbit. The moon's rotation, however, is regular, and this, together with the irregular revolution, produces what is called libration in longitude, which permits an observer on Earth to see first farther around the eastern side and then farther around the western side of the moon. The moon's variation north or south of the ecliptic permits one to see farther over first one pole of the moon and then the other; this is called libration in latitude. These two libration effects permit observers on Earth to see a total of about 60% of the moon's surface over a period of time.

Atmosphere and surface. The moon, like the planet Mercury, has no real atmosphere to speak of. What little exists is variable and tenuous. With its long day and night, the daytime temperature can reach 260°F. The coldest nighttime temperature is –280°F. This day-to-night contrast is exceeded only by that on Mercury. The lunar surface has not changed much since humans began observing it. The side visible from Earth has large craters and vast dark areas called maria that were once lava. The farside has almost no maria but is pockmarked with craters; it was first photographed in 1959 by the Soviet space probe *Lunik III*.

Recent findings show that up to 300 mil metric tons of water ice may exist in craters at the lunar poles. In its interior, the moon may have a small core, which supports the idea that most of the moon's mass was ripped away from the early Earth when a Mars-sized object collided with Earth.

Harvest moon and hunter's moon. The harvest moon, the full moon nearest the autumnal equinox, ushers in a period of several days when the moon rises soon after sunset. This phenomenon gives farmers in temperate latitudes extra hours of light in which to harvest their crops. The 2025 harvest moon falls on Sept. 7. Harvest moon in the Southern Hemisphere temperate latitudes in 2025 falls on Mar. 14.

The next full moon after harvest moon is called the hunter's moon; it is accompanied by a similar but less marked phenomenon. In 2025, the hunter's moon occurs on Oct. 7 in the Northern Hemisphere and on Apr. 13 in the Southern Hemisphere.

CALENDAR

Western Calendars

The **Julian calendar**, under which all Western nations measured time until 1582 CE, was authorized by Julius Caesar in 46 BCE. It called for a year of 365¼ days, starting in Jan., with every fourth year being a **leap year** of 366 days. St. Bede, an Anglo-Saxon monk also known as the Venerable Bede, announced in 730 CE that the Julian year was 11 min., 14 sec. too long, a cumulative error of about a day every 128 years, but nothing was done about this for centuries.

By 1582 the accumulated error was estimated at 10 days. In that year, Pope Gregory XIII decreed that the day following Oct. 4, 1582, should be called Oct. 15, thus dropping 10 days and initiating the **Gregorian calendar**.

The Gregorian calendar perpetuated a chronological system devised by the monk Dionysius Exiguus (fl. 6th cent.). His chronology started with the first year following the birth of Jesus Christ, which he inaccurately took to be year 753 in the Roman calendar. Leap years were continued, but, to prevent further displacements, centesimal years (years ending in 00) were made common years, not leap years, unless divisible by 400. Under this plan, 1600 and 2000 were leap years; 1700, 1800, and 1900 were not.

The Gregorian calendar was adopted at once by France, Italy, Spain, Portugal, and Luxembourg. Within two years, most German Catholic states, Belgium, and parts of Switzerland and the Netherlands were brought under the new calendar, and Hungary followed in 1587. The rest of the Netherlands, along with Denmark and the German Protestant states, made the change in 1699-1700.

The British government adopted the Gregorian calendar and imposed it on all its possessions, including the American colonies, in 1752, decreeing that the day following Sept. 2, 1752, should be called Sept. 14, a loss of 11 days. All dates preceding were marked OS, for Old Style. In addition, New Year's Day was moved to Jan. 1 from Mar. 25. (Under the old reckoning, for example, Mar. 24, 1700, was followed by Mar. 25, 1701.) Thus George Washington's birth date, which was Feb. 11, 1731, OS, became Feb. 22, 1732, NS (New Style). In 1753, Sweden also went Gregorian.

In 1793, the French revolutionary government adopted a calendar of 12 months of 30 days each with five extra days in Sept. of each common year and six extra days every fourth year. Napoleon reinstated the Gregorian calendar in 1806.

The Gregorian system later spread to non-European regions, replacing traditional calendars at least for official purposes. Japan in 1873, Egypt in 1875, China in 1912, and Turkey in 1925 made the change, usually in conjunction with political upheaval. In China, the republican government began reckoning years from its 1911 founding. After 1949, the People's Republic adopted the Common (or Christian) Era year count, even for the traditional lunar calendar, which it retained. In 1918, the Soviet Union decreed that the day after Jan. 31, 1918, OS, would be Feb. 14, 1918, NS. Greece changed over in 1923. The Russian Orthodox church and some other Christian sects retained the Julian calendar. Saudi Arabia switched to the Gregorian calendar in 2016.

As of 2024, several nations officially used non-Gregorian calendars. Ethiopia used a calendar similar to the Julian system, and Afghanistan and Iran used the traditional Persian, or Solar Hijri, calendar.

To convert from the Julian to the Gregorian calendar, add 10 days to dates Oct. 5, 1582, through Feb. 28, 1700; after that date, add 11 days through Feb. 28, 1800; 12 days through Feb. 28, 1900; and 13 days through Feb. 28, 2100.

A **century** consists of 100 consecutive years. The 1st century CE may be said to have run from the years 1 through 100. The 20th century by this reckoning consisted of the years 1901 through 2000 and ended Dec. 31, 2000, as did the 2nd millennium CE. The 21st century thus technically began on Jan. 1, 2001.

For a **perpetual calendar**, see pages 384-85.

Gregorian Calendar

Choose the desired year from the table below or from the perpetual calendar (for years 1803 to 2080). The number after each year designates which calendar to use for that year, as shown in the perpetual calendar. (The Gregorian calendar was inaugurated Oct. 15, 1582. From that date through Dec. 31, 1582, use calendar 6.)

1583-1802

1583	7	1603	4	1623	1	1643	5	1663	2	1683	6	1703	2	1723	6	1743	3	1763	7	1783	4
1584	8	1604	12	1624	9	1644	13	1664	10	1684	14	1704	10	1724	14	1744	11	1764	8	1784	12
1585	3	1605	7	1625	4	1645	1	1665	5	1685	2	1705	5	1725	2	1745	6	1765	3	1785	7
1586	4	1606	1	1626	5	1646	2	1666	6	1686	3	1706	6	1726	3	1746	7	1766	4	1786	1
1587	5	1607	2	1627	6	1647	3	1667	7	1687	4	1707	7	1727	4	1747	1	1767	5	1787	2
1588	13	1608	10	1628	14	1648	11	1668	8	1688	12	1708	8	1728	12	1748	9	1768	13	1788	10
1589	1	1609	5	1629	2	1649	6	1669	3	1689	7	1709	3	1729	7	1749	4	1769	1	1789	5
1590	2	1610	6	1630	3	1650	7	1670	4	1690	1	1710	4	1730	1	1750	5	1770	2	1790	6
1591	3	1611	7	1631	4	1651	1	1671	5	1691	2	1711	5	1731	2	1751	6	1771	3	1791	7
1592	11	1612	8	1632	12	1652	9	1672	13	1692	10	1712	13	1732	10	1752	14	1772	11	1792	8
1593	6	1613	3	1633	7	1653	4	1673	1	1693	5	1713	1	1733	5	1753	2	1773	6	1793	3
1594	7	1614	4	1634	1	1654	5	1674	2	1694	6	1714	2	1734	6	1754	3	1774	7	1794	4
1595	1	1615	5	1635	2	1655	6	1675	3	1695	7	1715	3	1735	7	1755	4	1775	1	1795	5
1596	9	1616	13	1636	10	1656	14	1676	11	1696	8	1716	11	1736	8	1756	12	1776	9	1796	13
1597	4	1617	1	1637	5	1657	2	1677	6	1697	3	1717	6	1737	3	1757	7	1777	4	1797	1
1598	5	1618	2	1638	6	1658	3	1678	7	1698	4	1718	7	1738	4	1758	1	1778	5	1798	2
1599	6	1619	3	1639	7	1659	4	1679	1	1699	5	1719	1	1739	5	1759	2	1779	6	1799	3
1600	14	1620	11	1640	8	1660	12	1680	9	1700	6	1720	9	1740	13	1760	10	1780	14	1800	4
1601	2	1621	6	1641	3	1661	7	1681	4	1701	7	1721	4	1741	1	1761	5	1781	2	1801	5
1602	3	1622	7	1642	4	1662	1	1682	5	1702	1	1722	5	1742	2	1762	6	1782	3	1802	6

Julian Period

How many days have you lived? To determine this, multiply your age by 365, add the number of days since your last birthday, and account for all leap years. Chances are your calculations will go wrong somewhere. Astronomers, however, find it convenient to express dates and time intervals in days rather than in years, months, and days. This is done by placing events within the Julian period.

The Julian period was devised in 1583 by the French classical scholar Joseph Scaliger (1540-1609). Some sources postulate Scaliger named it after his father, Julius Caesar Scaliger; others cite Scaliger's references to the Julian calendar.

Scaliger began with a zero hour, or starting time, of noon on Jan. 1, 4713 BCE (on the Julian calendar). This was the most recent time that three major chronological cycles began on the same day: (1) the 28-year solar cycle, after which dates in the Julian calendar return to the same days of the week (e.g., Feb. 11 falls on a Monday); (2) the 19-year lunar cycle, after which the phases of the moon return to the same dates of the year; and (3) the 15-year indiction cycle, used in ancient Rome to regulate taxes.

It will take 7,980 years to complete the period, the product of the numbers 28, 19, and 15, which have no common factors.

Noon (Universal Time) of Jan. 1, 2025, will be Julian date (JD) 2,460,677; that many days will have passed since the start of the current Julian period. The JD at noon of any date in 2025 may be found by adding to that number the day of the year for that date and subtracting one.

Julian Calendar

To find which of the 14 calendars of the perpetual calendar (pages 384-85) applies to any year under the Julian system, find the century for the desired year in the three leftmost columns below. Locate the desired year from among the four top rows. The number at the intersection of that row and column is the calendar designation for that year. For some years and countries, the Julian new year did not start Jan. 1; to find the correct perpetual calendar for Britain and its possessions, you can generally add one year for dates from Jan. 1 to Mar. 24. For example, to look up Feb. 2, 1705, Old Style, use the year 1706.

Year (last 2 digits of desired year)

				01	**02**	**03**	**04**	**05**	**06**	**07**	**08**	**09**	**10**	**11**	**12**	**13**	**14**	**15**	**16**	**17**	**18**	**19**	**20**	**21**	**22**	**23**	**24**	**25**	**26**	**27**	**28**
				29	**30**	**31**	**32**	**33**	**34**	**35**	**36**	**37**	**38**	**39**	**40**	**41**	**42**	**43**	**44**	**45**	**46**	**47**	**48**	**49**	**50**	**51**	**52**	**53**	**54**	**55**	**56**
				57	**58**	**59**	**60**	**61**	**62**	**63**	**64**	**65**	**66**	**67**	**68**	**69**	**70**	**71**	**72**	**73**	**74**	**75**	**76**	**77**	**78**	**79**	**80**	**81**	**82**	**83**	**84**
Century			**00**	**85**	**86**	**87**	**88**	**89**	**90**	**91**	**92**	**93**	**94**	**95**	**96**	**97**	**98**	**99**													
0	**700**	**1400**	12	7	1	2	10	5	6	7	8	3	4	5	13	1	2	3	11	6	7	1	9	4	5	6	14	2	3	4	12
100	**800**	**1500**	11	6	7	1	9	4	5	6	14	2	3	4	12	7	1	2	10	5	6	7	8	3	4	5	13	1	2	3	11
200	**900**	**1600**	10	5	6	7	8	3	4	5	13	1	2	3	11	6	7	1	9	4	5	6	14	2	3	4	12	7	1	2	10
300	**1000**	**1700**	9	4	5	6	14	2	3	4	12	7	1	2	10	5	6	7	8	3	4	5	13	1	2	3	11	6	7	1	9
400	**1100**	**1800**	8	3	4	5	13	1	2	3	11	6	7	1	9	4	5	6	14	2	3	4	12	7	1	2	10	5	6	7	8
500	**1200**	**1900**	14	2	3	4	12	7	1	2	10	5	6	7	8	3	4	5	13	1	2	3	11	6	7	1	9	4	5	6	14
600	**1300**	**2000**	13	1	2	3	11	6	7	1	9	4	5	6	14	2	3	4	12	7	1	2	10	5	6	7	8	3	4	5	13

Signs of the Zodiac

The zodiac is the apparent yearly path of the sun among the stars as viewed from Earth and was divided by the ancients into 12 equal sections or signs, each named for the constellation situated within its limits in ancient times. Astrologers claim that the temperament and destiny of each individual depend on the zodiac sign under which the person was born and the relationships between the planets at that time and throughout the person's life.

Below are the 12 traditional signs and the traditional range of dates pertaining to each:

♈ **Aries** (Ram), March 21-April 19

♉ **Taurus** (Bull), April 20-May 20

♊ **Gemini** (Twins), May 21-June 21

♋ **Cancer** (Crab), June 22-July 22

♌ **Leo** (Lion), July 23-August 22

♍ **Virgo** (Virgin), August 23-September 22

♎ **Libra** (Scales), September 23-October 23

♏ **Scorpio** (Scorpion), October 24-November 21

♐ **Sagittarius** (Archer), November 22-December 21

♑ **Capricorn** (Goat), December 22-January 19

♒ **Aquarius** (Water Bearer), January 20-February 18

♓ **Pisces** (Fishes), February 19-March 20

Chinese Calendar and Asian Festivals

The Chinese calendar, like the Jewish and Islamic calendars (see the Religion chapter), is a lunisolar calendar. It is divided into 12 months of 29 or 30 days (compensating for the lunar month's mean duration of 29 days, 12 hr., 44.05 min.). This calendar is synchronized with the solar year by the addition of extra months at fixed intervals.

The Chinese calendar runs on a 60-year cycle. The last 24 years of the cycle 1864-1923 along with the cycles 1924-83 and 1984-2043, and the first 24 years of the cycle 2044-2103 are shown below grouped by their association with 1 of 12 animals in the Chinese zodiac. Jan. 29, 2025, marks the beginning of the year 4723 in the Chinese calendar and is designated the Year of the Snake.

Both the Western (Gregorian) and traditional lunar calendars are used publicly in China and in North and South Korea, and two New Year's celebrations are held. In Taiwan and Vietnam and in overseas Chinese communities, the lunar calendar is used only to set the dates for traditional festivals, with the Gregorian system in general use.

The 4-day Chinese New Year; the 3-day Vietnamese New Year festival, Tet; and the 3-to-4-day Korean festival, Suhl, begin at the second new moon after the winter solstice. The new moon in East Asia, which is west of the international date line, may be a day later than the new moon in the U.S. The festivals may start, therefore, anywhere between Jan. 21 and Feb. 19 of the Gregorian calendar.

Rat	Ox	Tiger	Hare (Rabbit)	Dragon	Snake	Horse	Sheep (Goat)	Monkey	Rooster	Dog	Pig (Boar)
1900	1901	1902	1903	1904	1905	1906	1907	1908	1909	1910	1911
1912	1913	1914	1915	1916	1917	1918	1919	1920	1921	1922	1923
1924	1925	1926	1927	1928	1929	1930	1931	1932	1933	1934	1935
1936	1937	1938	1939	1940	1941	1942	1943	1944	1945	1946	1947
1948	1949	1950	1951	1952	1953	1954	1955	1956	1957	1958	1959
1960	1961	1962	1963	1964	1965	1966	1967	1968	1969	1970	1971
1972	1973	1974	1975	1976	1977	1978	1979	1980	1981	1982	1983
1984	1985	1986	1987	1988	1989	1990	1991	1992	1993	1994	1995
1996	1997	1998	1999	2000	2001	2002	2003	2004	2005	2006	2007
2008	2009	2010	2011	2012	2013	2014	2015	2016	2017	2018	2019
2020	2021	2022	2023	2024	2025	2026	2027	2028	2029	2030	2031
2032	2033	2034	2035	2036	2037	2038	2039	2040	2041	2042	2043
2044	2045	2046	2047	2048	2049	2050	2051	2052	2053	2054	2055
2056	2057	2058	2059	2060	2061	2062	2063	2064	2065	2066	2067

Note: The first 3-7 weeks of each Western year belong to the previous Chinese year.

Perpetual Calendar

The number shown for each year indicates which Gregorian calendar to use. For 1583-1802, see "Gregorian Calendar" on page 382. For 1803-20, use numbers for 1983-2000, respectively. The years in the calendar labels are the last and next occurrences of each calendar.

1821....2	1847....6	1873....4	1899....1	1925....5	1951....2	1977....7	2003....4	2029....2	2055....6
1822....3	1848...14	1874....5	1900....2	1926....6	1952...10	1978....1	2004...12	2030....3	2056...14
1823....4	1849....2	1875....6	1901....3	1927....7	1953....5	1979....2	2005....7	2031....4	2057....2
1824...12	1850....3	1876...14	1902....4	1928....8	1954....6	1980...10	2006....1	2032...12	2058....3
1825....7	1851....4	1877....2	1903....5	1929....3	1955....7	1981....5	2007....2	2033....7	2059....4
1826....1	1852...12	1878....3	1904...13	1930....4	1956....8	1982....6	2008...10	2034....1	2060...12
1827....2	1853....7	1879....4	1905....1	1931....5	1957....3	1983....7	2009....5	2035....2	2061....7
1828...10	1854....1	1880...12	1906....2	1932...13	1958....4	1984....8	2010....6	2036...10	2062....1
1829....5	1855....2	1881....7	1907....3	1933....1	1959....5	1985....3	2011....7	2037....5	2063....2
1830....6	1856...10	1882....1	1908...11	1934....2	1960...13	1986....4	2012....8	2038....6	2064...10
1831....7	1857....5	1883....2	1909....6	1935....3	1961....1	1987....5	2013....3	2039....7	2065....5
1832....8	1858....6	1884...10	1910....7	1936...11	1962....2	1988...13	2014....4	2040....8	2066....6
1833....3	1859....7	1885....5	1911....1	1937....6	1963....3	1989....1	2015....5	2041....3	2067....7
1834....4	1860....8	1886....6	1912....9	1938....7	1964...11	1990....2	2016...13	2042....4	2068....8
1835....5	1861....3	1887....7	1913....4	1939....1	1965....6	1991....3	2017....1	2043....5	2069....3
1836...13	1862....4	1888....8	1914....5	1940....9	1966....7	1992...11	2018....2	2044...13	2070....4
1837....1	1863....5	1889....3	1915....6	1941....4	1967....1	1993....6	2019....3	2045....1	2071....5
1838....2	1864...13	1890....4	1916...14	1942....5	1968....9	1994....7	2020...11	2046....2	2072...13
1839....3	1865....1	1891....5	1917....2	1943....6	1969....4	1995....1	2021....6	2047....3	2073....1
1840...11	1866....2	1892...13	1918....3	1944...14	1970....5	1996....9	2022....7	2048...11	2074....2
1841....6	1867....3	1893....1	1919....4	1945....2	1971....6	1997....4	2023....1	2049....6	2075....3
1842....7	1868...11	1894....2	1920...12	1946....3	1972...14	1998....5	2024....9	2050....7	2076...11
1843....1	1869....6	1895....3	1921....7	1947....4	1973....2	1999....6	2025....4	2051....1	2077....6
1844....9	1870....7	1896...11	1922....1	1948...12	1974....3	2000...14	2026....5	2052....9	2078....7
1845....4	1871....1	1897....6	1923....2	1949....7	1975....4	2001....2	2027....6	2053....4	2079....1
1846....5	1872....9	1898....7	1924...10	1950....1	1976...12	2002....3	2028...14	2054....5	2080....9

1 2023/2034

JANUARY

S	M	T	W	T	F	S
1	2	3	4	5	6	7
8	9	10	11	12	13	14
15	16	17	18	19	20	21
22	23	24	25	26	27	28
29	30	31				

FEBRUARY

S	M	T	W	T	F	S
			1	2	3	4
5	6	7	8	9	10	11
12	13	14	15	16	17	18
19	20	21	22	23	24	25
26	27	28				

MARCH

S	M	T	W	T	F	S
			1	2	3	4
5	6	7	8	9	10	11
12	13	14	15	16	17	18
19	20	21	22	23	24	25
26	27	28	29	30	31	

APRIL

S	M	T	W	T	F	S
						1
2	3	4	5	6	7	8
9	10	11	12	13	14	15
16	17	18	19	20	21	22
23	24	25	26	27	28	29
30						

MAY

S	M	T	W	T	F	S
	1	2	3	4	5	6
7	8	9	10	11	12	13
14	15	16	17	18	19	20
21	22	23	24	25	26	27
28	29	30	31			

JUNE

S	M	T	W	T	F	S
				1	2	3
4	5	6	7	8	9	10
11	12	13	14	15	16	17
18	19	20	21	22	23	24
25	26	27	28	29	30	

JULY

S	M	T	W	T	F	S
						1
2	3	4	5	6	7	8
9	10	11	12	13	14	15
16	17	18	19	20	21	22
23	24	25	26	27	28	29
30	31					

AUGUST

S	M	T	W	T	F	S
		1	2	3	4	5
6	7	8	9	10	11	12
13	14	15	16	17	18	19
20	21	22	23	24	25	26
27	28	29	30	31		

SEPTEMBER

S	M	T	W	T	F	S
					1	2
3	4	5	6	7	8	9
10	11	12	13	14	15	16
17	18	19	20	21	22	23
24	25	26	27	28	29	30

OCTOBER

S	M	T	W	T	F	S
1	2	3	4	5	6	7
8	9	10	11	12	13	14
15	16	17	18	19	20	21
22	23	24	25	26	27	28
29	30	31				

NOVEMBER

S	M	T	W	T	F	S
			1	2	3	4
5	6	7	8	9	10	11
12	13	14	15	16	17	18
19	20	21	22	23	24	25
26	27	28	29	30		

DECEMBER

S	M	T	W	T	F	S
					1	2
3	4	5	6	7	8	9
10	11	12	13	14	15	16
17	18	19	20	21	22	23
24	25	26	27	28	29	30
31						

2 2018/2029

JANUARY

S	M	T	W	T	F	S
	1	2	3	4	5	6
7	8	9	10	11	12	13
14	15	16	17	18	19	20
21	22	23	24	25	26	27
28	29	30	31			

FEBRUARY

S	M	T	W	T	F	S
				1	2	3
4	5	6	7	8	9	10
11	12	13	14	15	16	17
18	19	20	21	22	23	24
25	26	27	28			

MARCH

S	M	T	W	T	F	S
				1	2	3
4	5	6	7	8	9	10
11	12	13	14	15	16	17
18	19	20	21	22	23	24
25	26	27	28	29	30	31

APRIL

S	M	T	W	T	F	S
1	2	3	4	5	6	7
8	9	10	11	12	13	14
15	16	17	18	19	20	21
22	23	24	25	26	27	28
29	30					

MAY

S	M	T	W	T	F	S
		1	2	3	4	5
6	7	8	9	10	11	12
13	14	15	16	17	18	19
20	21	22	23	24	25	26
27	28	29	30	31		

JUNE

S	M	T	W	T	F	S
					1	2
3	4	5	6	7	8	9
10	11	12	13	14	15	16
17	18	19	20	21	22	23
24	25	26	27	28	29	30

JULY

S	M	T	W	T	F	S
1	2	3	4	5	6	7
8	9	10	11	12	13	14
15	16	17	18	19	20	21
22	23	24	25	26	27	28
29	30	31				

AUGUST

S	M	T	W	T	F	S
			1	2	3	4
5	6	7	8	9	10	11
12	13	14	15	16	17	18
19	20	21	22	23	24	25
26	27	28	29	30	31	

SEPTEMBER

S	M	T	W	T	F	S
						1
2	3	4	5	6	7	8
9	10	11	12	13	14	15
16	17	18	19	20	21	22
23	24	25	26	27	28	29
30						

OCTOBER

S	M	T	W	T	F	S
	1	2	3	4	5	6
7	8	9	10	11	12	13
14	15	16	17	18	19	20
21	22	23	24	25	26	27
28	29	30	31			

NOVEMBER

S	M	T	W	T	F	S
				1	2	3
4	5	6	7	8	9	10
11	12	13	14	15	16	17
18	19	20	21	22	23	24
25	26	27	28	29	30	

DECEMBER

S	M	T	W	T	F	S
						1
2	3	4	5	6	7	8
9	10	11	12	13	14	15
16	17	18	19	20	21	22
23	24	25	26	27	28	29
30	31					

3 2019/2030

JANUARY

S	M	T	W	T	F	S
		1	2	3	4	5
6	7	8	9	10	11	12
13	14	15	16	17	18	19
20	21	22	23	24	25	26
27	28	29	30	31		

FEBRUARY

S	M	T	W	T	F	S
					1	2
3	4	5	6	7	8	9
10	11	12	13	14	15	16
17	18	19	20	21	22	23
24	25	26	27	28		

MARCH

S	M	T	W	T	F	S
					1	2
3	4	5	6	7	8	9
10	11	12	13	14	15	16
17	18	19	20	21	22	23
24	25	26	27	28	29	30
31						

APRIL

S	M	T	W	T	F	S
	1	2	3	4	5	6
7	8	9	10	11	12	13
14	15	16	17	18	19	20
21	22	23	24	25	26	27
28	29	30				

MAY

S	M	T	W	T	F	S
			1	2	3	4
5	6	7	8	9	10	11
12	13	14	15	16	17	18
19	20	21	22	23	24	25
26	27	28	29	30	31	

JUNE

S	M	T	W	T	F	S
						1
2	3	4	5	6	7	8
9	10	11	12	13	14	15
16	17	18	19	20	21	22
23	24	25	26	27	28	29
30						

JULY

S	M	T	W	T	F	S
	1	2	3	4	5	6
7	8	9	10	11	12	13
14	15	16	17	18	19	20
21	22	23	24	25	26	27
28	29	30	31			

AUGUST

S	M	T	W	T	F	S
				1	2	3
4	5	6	7	8	9	10
11	12	13	14	15	16	17
18	19	20	21	22	23	24
25	26	27	28	29	30	31

SEPTEMBER

S	M	T	W	T	F	S
1	2	3	4	5	6	7
8	9	10	11	12	13	14
15	16	17	18	19	20	21
22	23	24	25	26	27	28
29	30					

OCTOBER

S	M	T	W	T	F	S
		1	2	3	4	5
6	7	8	9	10	11	12
13	14	15	16	17	18	19
20	21	22	23	24	25	26
27	28	29	30	31		

NOVEMBER

S	M	T	W	T	F	S
					1	2
3	4	5	6	7	8	9
10	11	12	13	14	15	16
17	18	19	20	21	22	23
24	25	26	27	28	29	30

DECEMBER

S	M	T	W	T	F	S
1	2	3	4	5	6	7
8	9	10	11	12	13	14
15	16	17	18	19	20	21
22	23	24	25	26	27	28
29	30	31				

4 2014/2025

JANUARY

S	M	T	W	T	F	S
			1	2	3	4
5	6	7	8	9	10	11
12	13	14	15	16	17	18
19	20	21	22	23	24	25
26	27	28	29	30	31	

FEBRUARY

S	M	T	W	T	F	S
						1
2	3	4	5	6	7	8
9	10	11	12	13	14	15
16	17	18	19	20	21	22
23	24	25	26	27	28	

MARCH

S	M	T	W	T	F	S
						1
2	3	4	5	6	7	8
9	10	11	12	13	14	15
16	17	18	19	20	21	22
23	24	25	26	27	28	29
30	31					

APRIL

S	M	T	W	T	F	S
		1	2	3	4	5
6	7	8	9	10	11	12
13	14	15	16	17	18	19
20	21	22	23	24	25	26
27	28	29	30			

MAY

S	M	T	W	T	F	S
				1	2	3
4	5	6	7	8	9	10
11	12	13	14	15	16	17
18	19	20	21	22	23	24
25	26	27	28	29	30	31

JUNE

S	M	T	W	T	F	S
1	2	3	4	5	6	7
8	9	10	11	12	13	14
15	16	17	18	19	20	21
22	23	24	25	26	27	28
29	30					

JULY

S	M	T	W	T	F	S
		1	2	3	4	5
6	7	8	9	10	11	12
13	14	15	16	17	18	19
20	21	22	23	24	25	26
27	28	29	30	31		

AUGUST

S	M	T	W	T	F	S
					1	2
3	4	5	6	7	8	9
10	11	12	13	14	15	16
17	18	19	20	21	22	23
24	25	26	27	28	29	30
31						

SEPTEMBER

S	M	T	W	T	F	S
	1	2	3	4	5	6
7	8	9	10	11	12	13
14	15	16	17	18	19	20
21	22	23	24	25	26	27
28	29	30				

OCTOBER

S	M	T	W	T	F	S
			1	2	3	4
5	6	7	8	9	10	11
12	13	14	15	16	17	18
19	20	21	22	23	24	25
26	27	28	29	30	31	

NOVEMBER

S	M	T	W	T	F	S
						1
2	3	4	5	6	7	8
9	10	11	12	13	14	15
16	17	18	19	20	21	22
23	24	25	26	27	28	29
30						

DECEMBER

S	M	T	W	T	F	S
	1	2	3	4	5	6
7	8	9	10	11	12	13
14	15	16	17	18	19	20
21	22	23	24	25	26	27
28	29	30	31			

5 2015/2026

JANUARY

S	M	T	W	T	F	S
				1	2	3
4	5	6	7	8	9	10
11	12	13	14	15	16	17
18	19	20	21	22	23	24
25	26	27	28	29	30	31

FEBRUARY

S	M	T	W	T	F	S
1	2	3	4	5	6	7
8	9	10	11	12	13	14
15	16	17	18	19	20	21
22	23	24	25	26	27	28

MARCH

S	M	T	W	T	F	S
1	2	3	4	5	6	7
8	9	10	11	12	13	14
15	16	17	18	19	20	21
22	23	24	25	26	27	28
29	30	31				

APRIL

S	M	T	W	T	F	S
			1	2	3	4
5	6	7	8	9	10	11
12	13	14	15	16	17	18
19	20	21	22	23	24	25
26	27	28	29	30		

MAY

S	M	T	W	T	F	S
					1	2
3	4	5	6	7	8	9
10	11	12	13	14	15	16
17	18	19	20	21	22	23
24	25	26	27	28	29	30
31						

JUNE

S	M	T	W	T	F	S
	1	2	3	4	5	6
7	8	9	10	11	12	13
14	15	16	17	18	19	20
21	22	23	24	25	26	27
28	29	30				

JULY

S	M	T	W	T	F	S
			1	2	3	4
5	6	7	8	9	10	11
12	13	14	15	16	17	18
19	20	21	22	23	24	25
26	27	28	29	30	31	

AUGUST

S	M	T	W	T	F	S
						1
2	3	4	5	6	7	8
9	10	11	12	13	14	15
16	17	18	19	20	21	22
23	24	25	26	27	28	29
30	31					

SEPTEMBER

S	M	T	W	T	F	S
		1	2	3	4	5
6	7	8	9	10	11	12
13	14	15	16	17	18	19
20	21	22	23	24	25	26
27	28	29	30			

OCTOBER

S	M	T	W	T	F	S
				1	2	3
4	5	6	7	8	9	10
11	12	13	14	15	16	17
18	19	20	21	22	23	24
25	26	27	28	29	30	31

NOVEMBER

S	M	T	W	T	F	S
1	2	3	4	5	6	7
8	9	10	11	12	13	14
15	16	17	18	19	20	21
22	23	24	25	26	27	28
29	30					

DECEMBER

S	M	T	W	T	F	S
		1	2	3	4	5
6	7	8	9	10	11	12
13	14	15	16	17	18	19
20	21	22	23	24	25	26
27	28	29	30	31		

6 2021/2027

JANUARY

S	M	T	W	T	F	S
					1	2
3	4	5	6	7	8	9
10	11	12	13	14	15	16
17	18	19	20	21	22	23
24	25	26	27	28	29	30
31						

FEBRUARY

S	M	T	W	T	F	S
	1	2	3	4	5	6
7	8	9	10	11	12	13
14	15	16	17	18	19	20
21	22	23	24	25	26	27
28						

MARCH

S	M	T	W	T	F	S
	1	2	3	4	5	6
7	8	9	10	11	12	13
14	15	16	17	18	19	20
21	22	23	24	25	26	27
28	29	30	31			

APRIL

S	M	T	W	T	F	S
				1	2	3
4	5	6	7	8	9	10
11	12	13	14	15	16	17
18	19	20	21	22	23	24
25	26	27	28	29	30	

MAY

S	M	T	W	T	F	S
						1
2	3	4	5	6	7	8
9	10	11	12	13	14	15
16	17	18	19	20	21	22
23	24	25	26	27	28	29
30	31					

JUNE

S	M	T	W	T	F	S
		1	2	3	4	5
6	7	8	9	10	11	12
13	14	15	16	17	18	19
20	21	22	23	24	25	26
27	28	29	30			

JULY

S	M	T	W	T	F	S
				1	2	3
4	5	6	7	8	9	10
11	12	13	14	15	16	17
18	19	20	21	22	23	24
25	26	27	28	29	30	31

AUGUST

S	M	T	W	T	F	S
1	2	3	4	5	6	7
8	9	10	11	12	13	14
15	16	17	18	19	20	21
22	23	24	25	26	27	28
29	30	31				

SEPTEMBER

S	M	T	W	T	F	S
			1	2	3	4
5	6	7	8	9	10	11
12	13	14	15	16	17	18
19	20	21	22	23	24	25
26	27	28	29	30		

OCTOBER

S	M	T	W	T	F	S
					1	2
3	4	5	6	7	8	9
10	11	12	13	14	15	16
17	18	19	20	21	22	23
24	25	26	27	28	29	30
31						

NOVEMBER

S	M	T	W	T	F	S
	1	2	3	4	5	6
7	8	9	10	11	12	13
14	15	16	17	18	19	20
21	22	23	24	25	26	27
28	29	30				

DECEMBER

S	M	T	W	T	F	S
			1	2	3	4
5	6	7	8	9	10	11
12	13	14	15	16	17	18
19	20	21	22	23	24	25
26	27	28	29	30	31	

7 2022/2033

JANUARY

S	M	T	W	T	F	S
						1
2	3	4	5	6	7	8
9	10	11	12	13	14	15
16	17	18	19	20	21	22
23	24	25	26	27	28	29
30	31					

FEBRUARY

S	M	T	W	T	F	S
		1	2	3	4	5
6	7	8	9	10	11	12
13	14	15	16	17	18	19
20	21	22	23	24	25	26
27	28					

MARCH

S	M	T	W	T	F	S
		1	2	3	4	5
6	7	8	9	10	11	12
13	14	15	16	17	18	19
20	21	22	23	24	25	26
27	28	29	30	31		

APRIL

S	M	T	W	T	F	S
					1	2
3	4	5	6	7	8	9
10	11	12	13	14	15	16
17	18	19	20	21	22	23
24	25	26	27	28	29	30

MAY

S	M	T	W	T	F	S
1	2	3	4	5	6	7
8	9	10	11	12	13	14
15	16	17	18	19	20	21
22	23	24	25	26	27	28
29	30	31				

JUNE

S	M	T	W	T	F	S
			1	2	3	4
5	6	7	8	9	10	11
12	13	14	15	16	17	18
19	20	21	22	23	24	25
26	27	28	29	30		

JULY

S	M	T	W	T	F	S
					1	2
3	4	5	6	7	8	9
10	11	12	13	14	15	16
17	18	19	20	21	22	23
24	25	26	27	28	29	30
31						

AUGUST

S	M	T	W	T	F	S
	1	2	3	4	5	6
7	8	9	10	11	12	13
14	15	16	17	18	19	20
21	22	23	24	25	26	27
28	29	30	31			

SEPTEMBER

S	M	T	W	T	F	S
				1	2	3
4	5	6	7	8	9	10
11	12	13	14	15	16	17
18	19	20	21	22	23	24
25	26	27	28	29	30	

OCTOBER

S	M	T	W	T	F	S
						1
2	3	4	5	6	7	8
9	10	11	12	13	14	15
16	17	18	19	20	21	22
23	24	25	26	27	28	29
30	31					

NOVEMBER

S	M	T	W	T	F	S
		1	2	3	4	5
6	7	8	9	10	11	12
13	14	15	16	17	18	19
20	21	22	23	24	25	26
27	28	29	30			

DECEMBER

S	M	T	W	T	F	S
				1	2	3
4	5	6	7	8	9	10
11	12	13	14	15	16	17
18	19	20	21	22	23	24
25	26	27	28	29	30	31

8 2012/2040

JANUARY

S	M	T	W	T	F	S
1	2	3	4	5	6	7
8	9	10	11	12	13	14
15	16	17	18	19	20	21
22	23	24	25	26	27	28
29	30	31				

FEBRUARY

S	M	T	W	T	F	S
			1	2	3	4
5	6	7	8	9	10	11
12	13	14	15	16	17	18
19	20	21	22	23	24	25
26	27	28	29			

MARCH

S	M	T	W	T	F	S
				1	2	3
4	5	6	7	8	9	10
11	12	13	14	15	16	17
18	19	20	21	22	23	24
25	26	27	28	29	30	31

APRIL

S	M	T	W	T	F	S
1	2	3	4	5	6	7
8	9	10	11	12	13	14
15	16	17	18	19	20	21
22	23	24	25	26	27	28
29	30					

MAY

S	M	T	W	T	F	S
		1	2	3	4	5
6	7	8	9	10	11	12
13	14	15	16	17	18	19
20	21	22	23	24	25	26
27	28	29	30	31		

JUNE

S	M	T	W	T	F	S
					1	2
3	4	5	6	7	8	9
10	11	12	13	14	15	16
17	18	19	20	21	22	23
24	25	26	27	28	29	30

JULY

S	M	T	W	T	F	S
1	2	3	4	5	6	7
8	9	10	11	12	13	14
15	16	17	18	19	20	21
22	23	24	25	26	27	28
29	30	31				

AUGUST

S	M	T	W	T	F	S
			1	2	3	4
5	6	7	8	9	10	11
12	13	14	15	16	17	18
19	20	21	22	23	24	25
26	27	28	29	30	31	

SEPTEMBER

S	M	T	W	T	F	S
						1
2	3	4	5	6	7	8
9	10	11	12	13	14	15
16	17	18	19	20	21	22
23	24	25	26	27	28	29
30						

OCTOBER

S	M	T	W	T	F	S
	1	2	3	4	5	6
7	8	9	10	11	12	13
14	15	16	17	18	19	20
21	22	23	24	25	26	27
28	29	30	31			

NOVEMBER

S	M	T	W	T	F	S
				1	2	3
4	5	6	7	8	9	10
11	12	13	14	15	16	17
18	19	20	21	22	23	24
25	26	27	28	29	30	

DECEMBER

S	M	T	W	T	F	S
						1
2	3	4	5	6	7	8
9	10	11	12	13	14	15
16	17	18	19	20	21	22
23	24	25	26	27	28	29
30	31					

9 2024/2052

JANUARY

S	M	T	W	T	F	S
	1	2	3	4	5	6
7	8	9	10	11	12	13
14	15	16	17	18	19	20
21	22	23	24	25	26	27
28	29	30	31			

FEBRUARY

S	M	T	W	T	F	S
				1	2	3
4	5	6	7	8	9	10
11	12	13	14	15	16	17
18	19	20	21	22	23	24
25	26	27	28	29		

MARCH

S	M	T	W	T	F	S
					1	2
3	4	5	6	7	8	9
10	11	12	13	14	15	16
17	18	19	20	21	22	23
24	25	26	27	28	29	30
31						

APRIL

S	M	T	W	T	F	S
	1	2	3	4	5	6
7	8	9	10	11	12	13
14	15	16	17	18	19	20
21	22	23	24	25	26	27
28	29	30				

MAY

S	M	T	W	T	F	S
			1	2	3	4
5	6	7	8	9	10	11
12	13	14	15	16	17	18
19	20	21	22	23	24	25
26	27	28	29	30	31	

JUNE

S	M	T	W	T	F	S
						1
2	3	4	5	6	7	8
9	10	11	12	13	14	15
16	17	18	19	20	21	22
23	24	25	26	27	28	29
30						

JULY

S	M	T	W	T	F	S
	1	2	3	4	5	6
7	8	9	10	11	12	13
14	15	16	17	18	19	20
21	22	23	24	25	26	27
28	29	30	31			

AUGUST

S	M	T	W	T	F	S
				1	2	3
4	5	6	7	8	9	10
11	12	13	14	15	16	17
18	19	20	21	22	23	24
25	26	27	28	29	30	31

SEPTEMBER

S	M	T	W	T	F	S
1	2	3	4	5	6	7
8	9	10	11	12	13	14
15	16	17	18	19	20	21
22	23	24	25	26	27	28
29	30					

OCTOBER

S	M	T	W	T	F	S
		1	2	3	4	5
6	7	8	9	10	11	12
13	14	15	16	17	18	19
20	21	22	23	24	25	26
27	28	29	30	31		

NOVEMBER

S	M	T	W	T	F	S
					1	2
3	4	5	6	7	8	9
10	11	12	13	14	15	16
17	18	19	20	21	22	23
24	25	26	27	28	29	30

DECEMBER

S	M	T	W	T	F	S
1	2	3	4	5	6	7
8	9	10	11	12	13	14
15	16	17	18	19	20	21
22	23	24	25	26	27	28
29	30	31				

10 2008/2036

JANUARY

S	M	T	W	T	F	S
		1	2	3	4	5
6	7	8	9	10	11	12
13	14	15	16	17	18	19
20	21	22	23	24	25	26
27	28	29	30	31		

FEBRUARY

S	M	T	W	T	F	S
					1	2
3	4	5	6	7	8	9
10	11	12	13	14	15	16
17	18	19	20	21	22	23
24	25	26	27	28	29	

MARCH

S	M	T	W	T	F	S
						1
2	3	4	5	6	7	8
9	10	11	12	13	14	15
16	17	18	19	20	21	22
23	24	25	26	27	28	29
30	31					

APRIL

S	M	T	W	T	F	S
		1	2	3	4	5
6	7	8	9	10	11	12
13	14	15	16	17	18	19
20	21	22	23	24	25	26
27	28	29	30			

MAY

S	M	T	W	T	F	S
				1	2	3
4	5	6	7	8	9	10
11	12	13	14	15	16	17
18	19	20	21	22	23	24
25	26	27	28	29	30	31

JUNE

S	M	T	W	T	F	S
1	2	3	4	5	6	7
8	9	10	11	12	13	14
15	16	17	18	19	20	21
22	23	24	25	26	27	28
29	30					

JULY

S	M	T	W	T	F	S
		1	2	3	4	5
6	7	8	9	10	11	12
13	14	15	16	17	18	19
20	21	22	23	24	25	26
27	28	29	30	31		

AUGUST

S	M	T	W	T	F	S
					1	2
3	4	5	6	7	8	9
10	11	12	13	14	15	16
17	18	19	20	21	22	23
24	25	26	27	28	29	30
31						

SEPTEMBER

S	M	T	W	T	F	S
	1	2	3	4	5	6
7	8	9	10	11	12	13
14	15	16	17	18	19	20
21	22	23	24	25	26	27
28	29	30				

OCTOBER

S	M	T	W	T	F	S
			1	2	3	4
5	6	7	8	9	10	11
12	13	14	15	16	17	18
19	20	21	22	23	24	25
26	27	28	29	30	31	

NOVEMBER

S	M	T	W	T	F	S
						1
2	3	4	5	6	7	8
9	10	11	12	13	14	15
16	17	18	19	20	21	22
23	24	25	26	27	28	29
30						

DECEMBER

S	M	T	W	T	F	S
	1	2	3	4	5	6
7	8	9	10	11	12	13
14	15	16	17	18	19	20
21	22	23	24	25	26	27
28	29	30	31			

11 2020/2048

JANUARY

S	M	T	W	T	F	S
			1	2	3	4
5	6	7	8	9	10	11
12	13	14	15	16	17	18
19	20	21	22	23	24	25
26	27	28	29	30	31	

FEBRUARY

S	M	T	W	T	F	S
						1
2	3	4	5	6	7	8
9	10	11	12	13	14	15
16	17	18	19	20	21	22
23	24	25	26	27	28	29

MARCH

S	M	T	W	T	F	S
1	2	3	4	5	6	7
8	9	10	11	12	13	14
15	16	17	18	19	20	21
22	23	24	25	26	27	28
29	30	31				

APRIL

S	M	T	W	T	F	S
			1	2	3	4
5	6	7	8	9	10	11
12	13	14	15	16	17	18
19	20	21	22	23	24	25
26	27	28	29	30		

MAY

S	M	T	W	T	F	S
					1	2
3	4	5	6	7	8	9
10	11	12	13	14	15	16
17	18	19	20	21	22	23
24	25	26	27	28	29	30
31						

JUNE

S	M	T	W	T	F	S
	1	2	3	4	5	6
7	8	9	10	11	12	13
14	15	16	17	18	19	20
21	22	23	24	25	26	27
28	29	30				

JULY

S	M	T	W	T	F	S
			1	2	3	4
5	6	7	8	9	10	11
12	13	14	15	16	17	18
19	20	21	22	23	24	25
26	27	28	29	30	31	

AUGUST

S	M	T	W	T	F	S
						1
2	3	4	5	6	7	8
9	10	11	12	13	14	15
16	17	18	19	20	21	22
23	24	25	26	27	28	29
30	31					

SEPTEMBER

S	M	T	W	T	F	S
		1	2	3	4	5
6	7	8	9	10	11	12
13	14	15	16	17	18	19
20	21	22	23	24	25	26
27	28	29	30			

OCTOBER

S	M	T	W	T	F	S
				1	2	3
4	5	6	7	8	9	10
11	12	13	14	15	16	17
18	19	20	21	22	23	24
25	26	27	28	29	30	31

NOVEMBER

S	M	T	W	T	F	S
1	2	3	4	5	6	7
8	9	10	11	12	13	14
15	16	17	18	19	20	21
22	23	24	25	26	27	28
29	30					

DECEMBER

S	M	T	W	T	F	S
		1	2	3	4	5
6	7	8	9	10	11	12
13	14	15	16	17	18	19
20	21	22	23	24	25	26
27	28	29	30	31		

12 2004/2032

JANUARY

S	M	T	W	T	F	S
				1	2	3
4	5	6	7	8	9	10
11	12	13	14	15	16	17
18	19	20	21	22	23	24
25	26	27	28	29	30	31

FEBRUARY

S	M	T	W	T	F	S
1	2	3	4	5	6	7
8	9	10	11	12	13	14
15	16	17	18	19	20	21
22	23	24	25	26	27	28
29						

MARCH

S	M	T	W	T	F	S
	1	2	3	4	5	6
7	8	9	10	11	12	13
14	15	16	17	18	19	20
21	22	23	24	25	26	27
28	29	30	31			

APRIL

S	M	T	W	T	F	S
				1	2	3
4	5	6	7	8	9	10
11	12	13	14	15	16	17
18	19	20	21	22	23	24
25	26	27	28	29	30	

MAY

S	M	T	W	T	F	S
						1
2	3	4	5	6	7	8
9	10	11	12	13	14	15
16	17	18	19	20	21	22
23	24	25	26	27	28	29
30	31					

JUNE

S	M	T	W	T	F	S
		1	2	3	4	5
6	7	8	9	10	11	12
13	14	15	16	17	18	19
20	21	22	23	24	25	26
27	28	29	30			

JULY

S	M	T	W	T	F	S
				1	2	3
4	5	6	7	8	9	10
11	12	13	14	15	16	17
18	19	20	21	22	23	24
25	26	27	28	29	30	31

AUGUST

S	M	T	W	T	F	S
1	2	3	4	5	6	7
8	9	10	11	12	13	14
15	16	17	18	19	20	21
22	23	24	25	26	27	28
29	30	31				

SEPTEMBER

S	M	T	W	T	F	S
			1	2	3	4
5	6	7	8	9	10	11
12	13	14	15	16	17	18
19	20	21	22	23	24	25
26	27	28	29	30		

OCTOBER

S	M	T	W	T	F	S
					1	2
3	4	5	6	7	8	9
10	11	12	13	14	15	16
17	18	19	20	21	22	23
24	25	26	27	28	29	30
31						

NOVEMBER

S	M	T	W	T	F	S
	1	2	3	4	5	6
7	8	9	10	11	12	13
14	15	16	17	18	19	20
21	22	23	24	25	26	27
28	29	30				

DECEMBER

S	M	T	W	T	F	S
			1	2	3	4
5	6	7	8	9	10	11
12	13	14	15	16	17	18
19	20	21	22	23	24	25
26	27	28	29	30	31	

13 2016/2044

JANUARY

S	M	T	W	T	F	S
					1	2
3	4	5	6	7	8	9
10	11	12	13	14	15	16
17	18	19	20	21	22	23
24	25	26	27	28	29	30
31						

FEBRUARY

S	M	T	W	T	F	S
	1	2	3	4	5	6
7	8	9	10	11	12	13
14	15	16	17	18	19	20
21	22	23	24	25	26	27
28	29					

MARCH

S	M	T	W	T	F	S
		1	2	3	4	5
6	7	8	9	10	11	12
13	14	15	16	17	18	19
20	21	22	23	24	25	26
27	28	29	30	31		

APRIL

S	M	T	W	T	F	S
					1	2
3	4	5	6	7	8	9
10	11	12	13	14	15	16
17	18	19	20	21	22	23
24	25	26	27	28	29	30

MAY

S	M	T	W	T	F	S
1	2	3	4	5	6	7
8	9	10	11	12	13	14
15	16	17	18	19	20	21
22	23	24	25	26	27	28
29	30	31				

JUNE

S	M	T	W	T	F	S
			1	2	3	4
5	6	7	8	9	10	11
12	13	14	15	16	17	18
19	20	21	22	23	24	25
26	27	28	29	30		

JULY

S	M	T	W	T	F	S
					1	2
3	4	5	6	7	8	9
10	11	12	13	14	15	16
17	18	19	20	21	22	23
24	25	26	27	28	29	30
31						

AUGUST

S	M	T	W	T	F	S
	1	2	3	4	5	6
7	8	9	10	11	12	13
14	15	16	17	18	19	20
21	22	23	24	25	26	27
28	29	30	31			

SEPTEMBER

S	M	T	W	T	F	S
				1	2	3
4	5	6	7	8	9	10
11	12	13	14	15	16	17
18	19	20	21	22	23	24
25	26	27	28	29	30	

OCTOBER

S	M	T	W	T	F	S
						1
2	3	4	5	6	7	8
9	10	11	12	13	14	15
16	17	18	19	20	21	22
23	24	25	26	27	28	29
30	31					

NOVEMBER

S	M	T	W	T	F	S
		1	2	3	4	5
6	7	8	9	10	11	12
13	14	15	16	17	18	19
20	21	22	23	24	25	26
27	28	29	30			

DECEMBER

S	M	T	W	T	F	S
				1	2	3
4	5	6	7	8	9	10
11	12	13	14	15	16	17
18	19	20	21	22	23	24
25	26	27	28	29	30	31

14 2000/2028

JANUARY

S	M	T	W	T	F	S
						1
2	3	4	5	6	7	8
9	10	11	12	13	14	15
16	17	18	19	20	21	22
23	24	25	26	27	28	29
30	31					

FEBRUARY

S	M	T	W	T	F	S
		1	2	3	4	5
6	7	8	9	10	11	12
13	14	15	16	17	18	19
20	21	22	23	24	25	26
27	28	29				

MARCH

S	M	T	W	T	F	S
			1	2	3	4
5	6	7	8	9	10	11
12	13	14	15	16	17	18
19	20	21	22	23	24	25
26	27	28	29	30	31	

APRIL

S	M	T	W	T	F	S
						1
2	3	4	5	6	7	8
9	10	11	12	13	14	15
16	17	18	19	20	21	22
23	24	25	26	27	28	29
30						

MAY

S	M	T	W	T	F	S
	1	2	3	4	5	6
7	8	9	10	11	12	13
14	15	16	17	18	19	20
21	22	23	24	25	26	27
28	29	30	31			

JUNE

S	M	T	W	T	F	S
				1	2	3
4	5	6	7	8	9	10
11	12	13	14	15	16	17
18	19	20	21	22	23	24
25	26	27	28	29	30	

JULY

S	M	T	W	T	F	S
						1
2	3	4	5	6	7	8
9	10	11	12	13	14	15
16	17	18	19	20	21	22
23	24	25	26	27	28	29
30	31					

AUGUST

S	M	T	W	T	F	S
		1	2	3	4	5
6	7	8	9	10	11	12
13	14	15	16	17	18	19
20	21	22	23	24	25	26
27	28	29	30	31		

SEPTEMBER

S	M	T	W	T	F	S
					1	2
3	4	5	6	7	8	9
10	11	12	13	14	15	16
17	18	19	20	21	22	23
24	25	26	27	28	29	30

OCTOBER

S	M	T	W	T	F	S
1	2	3	4	5	6	7
8	9	10	11	12	13	14
15	16	17	18	19	20	21
22	23	24	25	26	27	28
29	30	31				

NOVEMBER

S	M	T	W	T	F	S
			1	2	3	4
5	6	7	8	9	10	11
12	13	14	15	16	17	18
19	20	21	22	23	24	25
26	27	28	29	30		

DECEMBER

S	M	T	W	T	F	S
					1	2
3	4	5	6	7	8	9
10	11	12	13	14	15	16
17	18	19	20	21	22	23
24	25	26	27	28	29	30
31						

Calendar for the Year 2025

January

S	M	T	W	T	F	S
			1	2	3	4
5	6	7	8	9	10	11
12	13	14	15	16	17	18
19	**20**	21	22	23	24	25
26	27	28	29	30	31	

February

S	M	T	W	T	F	S
						1
2	3	4	5	6	7	8
9	10	11	12	13	14	15
16	**17**	18	19	20	21	22
23	24	25	26	27	28	

March

S	M	T	W	T	F	S
						1
2	3	4	5	6	7	8
9	10	11	12	13	14	15
16	17	18	19	20	21	22
23	24	25	26	27	28	29
30	31					

April

S	M	T	W	T	F	S
		1	2	3	4	5
6	7	8	9	10	11	12
13	14	15	16	17	18	19
20	21	22	23	24	25	26
27	28	29	30			

May

S	M	T	W	T	F	S
				1	2	3
4	5	6	7	8	9	10
11	12	13	14	15	16	17
18	19	20	21	22	23	24
25	**26**	27	28	29	30	31

June

S	M	T	W	T	F	S
1	2	3	4	5	6	7
8	9	10	11	12	13	14
15	16	17	18	**19**	20	21
22	23	24	25	26	27	28
29	30					

July

S	M	T	W	T	F	S
		1	2	3	**4**	5
6	7	8	9	10	11	12
13	14	15	16	17	18	19
20	21	22	23	24	25	26
27	28	29	30	31		

August

S	M	T	W	T	F	S
					1	2
3	4	5	6	7	8	9
10	11	12	13	14	15	16
17	18	19	20	21	22	23
24	25	26	27	28	29	30
31						

September

S	M	T	W	T	F	S
	1	2	3	4	5	6
7	8	9	10	11	12	13
14	15	16	17	18	19	20
21	22	23	24	25	26	27
28	29	30				

October

S	M	T	W	T	F	S
			1	2	3	4
5	6	7	8	9	10	11
12	**13**	14	15	16	17	18
19	20	21	22	23	24	25
26	27	28	29	30	31	

November

S	M	T	W	T	F	S
						1
2	3	4	5	6	7	8
9	10	**11**	12	13	14	15
16	17	18	19	20	21	22
23	24	25	26	**27**	28	29
30						

December

S	M	T	W	T	F	S
	1	2	3	4	5	6
7	8	9	10	11	12	13
14	15	16	17	18	19	20
21	22	23	24	**25**	26	27
28	29	30	31			

Federal Holidays and Other Notable Dates, 2025

Some dates may be subject to change.

The dates in bold in the calendar above and named below in italics are U.S. federal holidays, designated by the president or Congress and applicable to federal employees and in the District of Columbia. Most U.S. states also observe these holidays, and many states observe others; practices vary by state. In most states the secretary of state's office can provide details.

January

1 *New Year's Day*; Rose Bowl, Sugar Bowl
9 Orange Bowl
10 Cotton Bowl
12-26 Australian Open tennis tournament
20 *Martin Luther King Jr. Day*; Inauguration Day; College Football Playoff national championship game (Atlanta, GA)
27 Australia Day (observed)
29 Chinese New Year

February

2 Groundhog Day
9 Super Bowl LIX (New Orleans, LA)
10-11 Westminster Dog Show
12 Lincoln's Birthday
14 Valentine's Day
16 NBA All-Star Game (San Francisco); Daytona 500
17 *Washington's Birthday* (observed), a.k.a. Presidents' Day, or Washington-Lincoln Day (3rd Mon. in Feb.)
28-Mar. 5 Carnival, Brazil

March

1 Ramadan (Islamic month of fasting), 1st full day; Iditarod Trail Sled Dog Race begins
2 Academy Awards
4 Mardi Gras
5 Ash Wednesday
9 Daylight saving time begins in U.S.
14 Purim (Feast of Lots) begins previous night
17 St. Patrick's Day
20 First day of spring (Northern Hemisphere)
21 Benito Juárez's Birthday, Mexico

April

1 April Fools' Day
4, 6 NCAA Women's Basketball Final Four (Tampa, FL)
5, 7 NCAA Men's Basketball Final Four (San Antonio, TX)
10-13 Masters golf tournament
13 Passover, 1st full day
15 Tax Day (IRS filing deadline)
18 Good Friday
20 Easter; Orthodox Easter
21 Patriots' Day; Boston Marathon (3rd Mon. in Apr.)
22 Earth Day
24 Take Our Daughters and Sons to Work Day
25 Arbor Day

May

1 May Day (International Workers' Day)
3 Kentucky Derby
5 Cinco de Mayo (Battle of Puebla Day), Mexico; Buddha's Birthday, Hong Kong, South Korea
11 Mother's Day
12-18 PGA Championship (Charlotte, NC)
17 Armed Forces Day; Preakness Stakes
19 Victoria Day, Canada
25-June 8 French Open tennis tournament
26 *Memorial Day*, or Decoration Day (last Mon. in May)
29-June 1 U.S. Women's Open golf tournament (Erin, WI)
31 Dragon Boat Festival, China

June

7 Belmont Stakes
12-15 U.S. Open golf tournament (Oakmont, PA)
14 Flag Day
15 Father's Day
19 *Juneteenth*
20 First day of summer (Northern Hemisphere)
27 Islamic New Year (Muharram 1) begins previous night
30-July 13 Wimbledon tennis tournament

July

1 Canada Day
4 *Independence Day*
7-14 Running of the Bulls (Pamplona, Spain)
14 Bastille Day, France
17-20 British Open golf tournament (Portrush, Northern Ireland, UK)

September

1 *Labor Day*, U.S., Canada (1st Mon. in Sept.)
7 National Grandparents Day, U.S.
16 Independence Day, Mexico (celebration begins previous night)
17 Constitution Day and Citizenship Day, U.S.
22 First day of autumn (Northern Hemisphere)
23 Rosh Hashanah (New Year), 1st full day

October

2 Yom Kippur (Day of Atonement) begins previous night
6 U.S. Supreme Court session begins
12 Día de la Raza, Spain, Mexico
13 *Columbus Day* (2nd Monday in Oct.); Thanksgiving Day, Canada
31 Halloween

November

1 All Saints' Day
2 Daylight saving time ends in U.S.; New York City Marathon
4 Election Day (1st Tues. after 1st Mon. in Nov.)
9 Remembrance Sunday, UK
11 *Veterans Day*; Remembrance Day, Canada
27 *Thanksgiving Day*

December

10 Nobel Prizes awarded (winners announced in Oct.)
12 Día de la Virgen de Guadalupe, Mexico
15-22 Hanukkah (Festival of Lights) begins previous night
21 First day of winter (Northern Hemisphere)
25 *Christmas Day*
26 Boxing Day, Australia, Canada, New Zealand, UK
26-Jan. 1 Kwanzaa
31 Cotton Bowl

Other Calendars: Year and New Year's Day, 2025

Era	Year	Begins in 2025	Era	Year	Begins in 2025
Byzantine	7534	Sept. 14	Islamic/Muslim (Hijra)	1447	June 27[1]
Chinese (Year of the Snake)	4723	Jan. 29	Japanese[2]	7	May 1
Diocletian	1742	Sept. 11	Jewish	5786	Sept. 23[1]
Grecian (Seleucidae)	2337	Sept. 14 or Oct. 14	Nabonassar (Babylonian)	2774	Apr. 23
Indian (Saka)	1947	Mar. 22	Roman (Ab Urbe Condita)	2778	Jan. 14

(1) Year begins the previous night. (2) Era starts at 0 with new emperor.

Chronological Cycles, 2025

Dominical Letter	E	Roman Indiction	3	Solar Cycle	18
Golden Number (lunar cycle)	XII	Epact	0	Julian Period (year of)	6738

Special Months

There are many thousands of special months, days, and weeks because of anniversaries, official proclamations, and promotional events, both trivial and serious. Here are a few of the special months:

January: Get Organized Month, National Mentoring Month, National Poverty in America Awareness Month

February: Black History Month, American Heart Month, Library Lovers' Month, Youth Leadership Month

March: Irish-American Heritage Month, National Women's History Month, Red Cross Month, National Frozen Food Month, National Colorectal Cancer Awareness Month

April: National Child Abuse Prevention Month, National Humor Month, Stress Awareness Month, Grange Month, Sexual Assault Awareness and Prevention Month

May: Clean Air Month, Get Caught Reading Month, National Barbecue Month, Asian American and Pacific Islander Heritage Month, National Inventors Month, National Mental Health Month

June: Great Outdoors Month; Lesbian, Gay, Bisexual, and Transgender Pride Month; National Safety Month

July: Cell Phone Courtesy Month, National Hot Dog Month, National Make a Difference to Children Month, Women's Motorcycle Month

August: National Black Business Month, Happiness Happens Month, National Immunization Awareness Month

September: Library Card Sign-Up Month, National Hispanic Heritage Month (Sept. 15-Oct. 15), National Biscuit Month

October: Adopt-A-Shelter-Dog Month, National Domestic Violence Awareness Month, National Breast Cancer Awareness Month, Global Diversity Awareness Month, National Popcorn Poppin' Month

November: National American Indian Heritage Month, National Adoption Month, American Diabetes Month, National Peanut Butter Lovers' Month

December: Safe Toys and Gifts Month, National Impaired Driving Prevention Month, National Tie Month

Standard Time Differences: World Cities

The time indicated in the table is fixed by law and is called the legal time or, more generally, standard time. Use of daylight saving time varies widely. An asterisk (*) indicates morning of the following day. At 12:00 noon, Eastern Standard Time, the standard time (in 24-hour time) in selected cities is as shown.

City	Time	City	Time	City	Time	City	Time
Abu Dhabi	21 00	Denver	10 00	Lisbon	17 00	St. Petersburg	20 00
Addis Ababa	20 00	Dhaka	23 00	London	17 00	Santiago	13 00
Amsterdam	18 00	Dublin	17 00	Los Angeles	9 00	São Paulo	14 00
Ankara	20 00	Edinburgh	17 00	Madrid	18 00	Sarajevo	18 00
Athens	19 00	Geneva	18 00	Manila	1 00*	Seoul	2 00*
Auckland	5 00*	Helsinki	19 00	Mecca	20 00	Shanghai	1 00*
Baghdad	20 00	Ho Chi Minh City	0 00*	Melbourne	3 00*	Singapore	1 00*
Bangkok	0 00*	Hong Kong	1 00*	Montevideo	14 00	Stockholm	18 00
Beijing	1 00*	Honolulu	7 00	Moscow	20 00	Sydney	3 00*
Belfast	17 00	Houston	11 00	Mumbai (Bombay)	22 30	Taipei	1 00*
Belgrade	18 00	Islamabad	22 00	Munich	18 00	Tashkent	22 00
Berlin	18 00	Istanbul	20 00	Nagasaki	2 00*	Tehran	20 30
Bogotá	12 00	Jakarta	0 00*	Nairobi	20 00	Tel Aviv	19 00
Brussels	18 00	Jerusalem	19 00	New Delhi	22 30	Tokyo	2 00*
Bucharest	19 00	Johannesburg	19 00	New York	12 00	Toronto	12 00
Budapest	18 00	Kabul	21 30	Oslo	18 00	Vancouver	9 00
Buenos Aires	14 00	Karachi	22 00	Paris	18 00	Vienna	18 00
Cairo	19 00	Kathmandu	22 45	Prague	18 00	Vladivostok	3 00*
Cape Town	19 00	Kiev	19 00	Pyongyang	2 00*	Warsaw	18 00
Caracas	13 00	Kinshasa	18 00	Quito	12 00	Wellington	5 00*
Casablanca	17 00	Kolkata (Calcutta)	22 30	Rio de Janeiro	14 00	Yangon (Rangoon)	23 30
Chicago	11 00	Lagos	18 00	Riyadh	20 00	Yokohama	2 00*
Copenhagen	18 00	Lima	12 00	Rome	18 00	Zurich	18 00

Wedding Anniversary Gifts

The traditional names for wedding anniversaries go back many years in social usage and have been used to suggest types of appropriate anniversary gifts. Traditional products for gifts are listed here in capital letters, with allowable revisions in parentheses, followed by common modern gifts for each anniversary.

Anniversary	Gift	Anniversary	Gift	Anniversary	Gift
1st	PAPER, clocks	**9th**	POTTERY (CHINA), leather goods	**25th**	SILVER, sterling silver
2nd	COTTON, china	**10th**	TIN, ALUMINUM, diamond	**30th**	PEARL, diamond
3rd	LEATHER, crystal, glass	**11th**	STEEL, fashion jewelry	**35th**	CORAL (JADE), jade
4th	LINEN (SILK), appliances	**12th**	SILK, pearls, colored gems	**40th**	RUBY, ruby
5th	WOOD, silverware	**13th**	LACE, textiles, furs	**45th**	SAPPHIRE, sapphire
6th	IRON, wood objects	**14th**	IVORY, gold jewelry	**50th**	GOLD, gold
7th	WOOL (COPPER), desk sets	**15th**	CRYSTAL, watches	**55th**	EMERALD, emerald
8th	BRONZE, linens, lace	**20th**	CHINA, platinum	**60th**	DIAMOND, diamond

Birthstones

Source: American Gem Society

Birth month	Ancient[1] birthstone	Modern birthstone
January	Garnet	Garnet
February	Amethyst	Amethyst
March	Jasper	Bloodstone or Aquamarine
April	Sapphire	Diamond
May	Agate, Chalcedony, or Carnelian	Emerald
June	Emerald	Pearl, Moonstone, or Alexandrite
July	Onyx	Ruby
August	Carnelian	Sardonyx or Peridot
September	Chrysolite	Sapphire
October	Aquamarine	Opal or Tourmaline
November	Topaz	Topaz
December	Ruby	Turquoise, Tanzanite, or Zircon

(1) Varied by region and culture. Birthstones listed here are those of ancient Hebrew tradition.

Standard Time and Daylight Saving Time

Source: National Institute of Standards and Technology, U.S. Dept. of Commerce

See also Time Zone map, page 492.

Standard Time

Standard time is reckoned from the prime meridian of longitude in Greenwich, England. The world is divided into 24 zones, each 15 deg of arc, or one hour in time apart. The Greenwich meridian (0 deg) extends through the center of the initial zone. Each zone extends 7.5 deg on either side of its central meridian. Zones to the east are numbered from 1 to 12, with the prefix "minus" indicating the number of hours to be subtracted to obtain Greenwich Time.

Westward zones are similarly numbered, but prefixed "plus," showing the number of hours that must be added to get Greenwich Time. The standard time maintained in many countries does not coincide with zone time. For example, China extends across five time zones, but the entire country is on Greenwich Time plus 8 hours.

The U.S. and possessions are divided into nine standard time zones. All places in each zone use, instead of their local time, the time counted from the transit of the mean sun across the standard time meridian that passes near the middle of that zone. These time zones are designated as Atlantic, Eastern, Central, Mountain, Pacific, Alaska, Hawaii-Aleutian, Samoa, and Chamorro (Guam and Northern Mariana Isls.); the time in these zones is reckoned from the 60th, 75th, 90th, 105th, 120th, 135th, 150th, and 165th meridians west of Greenwich and the 150th meridian east of Greenwich. The time zone line wanders to conform to local geography. The time in the various zones in the U.S. and U.S. territories west of Greenwich is earlier than Greenwich Time by 4, 5, 6, 7, 8, 9, 10, and 11 hours, respectively. However, Chamorro crosses the international date line and is 10 hours later than Greenwich Time.

24-Hour Time

With the 24-hour system, the day begins at midnight, and times are designated 00:00 through 23:59. Twenty-four-hour time is widely used in scientific work throughout the world. In the U.S., it is also used in operations of the armed forces. In Europe, it is frequently used by the transportation networks in preference to the 12-hour AM and PM system.

International Date Line

The date line, approximately coinciding with the 180th meridian, separates the calendar dates. The date must be advanced one day when crossing in a westerly direction and set back one day when crossing in an easterly direction. The date line frequently deviates from the 180th meridian because of decisions by affected nations. The line is deflected eastward through the Bering Strait and westward of the Aleutians to prevent separating the islands by date. The line is deflected eastward of the Tonga and New Zealand islands in the South Pacific. In 1995, Kiribati announced that its islands east of the date line would observe the same date as islands to the west, though most maps do not depict this deviation in the date line. In 2011, Samoa moved west of the date line to ease its relationship with Australia and New Zealand. The line is established by international custom; there is no international authority prescribing its exact course.

Daylight Saving Time

Daylight saving time is achieved by advancing the clock one hour. Since 2007, daylight saving time has begun at 2 AM on the second Sunday in Mar. and has ended at 2 AM on the first Sunday in Nov. **In 2025, daylight saving time begins at 2 AM on Mar. 9 and ends at 2 AM on Nov. 2.** Prior to 2007, daylight saving time traditionally ran from the first Sunday in Apr. to the last Sunday in Oct.

Daylight saving time was first observed in the U.S. during World War I and again during World War II. In 1966, Congress passed the Uniform Time Act, which provided that any state or territory choosing to observe daylight saving time must begin and end on the dates established by federal law. Any state could, by law, exempt itself; a 1972 amendment to the act authorized states in more than one time zone to exempt the entire state or one time zone only. Currently, most of Arizona, Hawaii, Puerto Rico, the U.S. Virgin Islands, Guam, American Samoa, and Northern Mariana Isls. do not observe daylight saving time. All of Indiana, which is in two time zones, observed daylight saving time for the first time in 2006.

Congress and the secretary of transportation both have authority to change time zone boundaries, which they have done on a number of occasions since 1966. In 2018, Florida passed legislation that would keep the state on daylight saving time year-round, but either Congress or the Transportation Dept. was required to act before the new law could go into effect. By mid 2023, 17 other U.S. states had also passed laws/regulations maintaining year-round DST. The Senate—but not yet the House—in Mar. 2022 unanimously passed legislation to make DST permanent beginning in 2023; following the bill's expiration, it was reintroduced in the Senate and House in Mar. 2023.

Daylight Saving Time: International Usage

Canada, which extends over six time zones, generally observes daylight saving time during the same period as the U.S. Most provincial governments observe the four-week extension to daylight saving time that went into effect in 2007. Most of Saskatchewan remains on standard time year-round; communities elsewhere in Canada may also exempt themselves from daylight saving time. Beginning in Mar. 2020, the territory Yukon began observing Pacific Daylight Saving Time year-round. Mexico in late Oct. 2022 stopped observing daylight saving time, with the exception of in cities bordering the U.S.

Member nations of the European Union observe a "summer-time period," a version of daylight saving time, from the last Sunday of Mar. until the last Sunday in Oct. Although the EU Parliament in Mar. 2019 voted to end mandatory DST starting in 2021 and instead allow member countries to follow permanent standard time if they choose, European Council negotiations to do so had not started as of May 2024.

Turkey stopped observing daylight saving time in 2016, maintaining its "summer hours." Russia, which uses 11 time zones, moved to permanent standard time in 2014 after a three-year experiment to maintain year-round "summer hours" proved unpopular. The country observed "winter hours" year-round beginning in Oct. 2014. Morocco abandoned daylight saving time in Oct. 2018, with a Ramadan exception, and officials in both Jordan and Syria in Oct. 2022 independently announced the countries would remain permanently on daylight saving time, with exceptions within Syria. After an eight-year lapse, Egypt reintroduced daylight saving time in Apr. 2023.

China does not observe daylight saving time. Mongolia discontinued daylight saving time in 2017, two years after it was reintroduced. Japan, which lies within one time zone, also does not modify its legal time during the summer months. Samoa scrapped DST in 2021, after adopting it in 2010, and Fiji last observed it in 2021.

Many countries in the Southern Hemisphere maintain daylight saving time generally from Oct. to Mar. (Brazil, mostly south of the equator, scrapped daylight saving time in 2019.) However, most countries near the equator do not deviate from standard time.

WEIGHTS AND MEASURES

Source: National Institute of Standards and Technology (NIST), U.S. Dept. of Commerce

International System of Units (SI)

Two systems of weights and measures coexist in the U.S. today: the **U.S. Customary System** and the **International System of Units** (SI, for Système International d'Unités). The SI is a more complete, coherent version of the **metric system**. Throughout U.S. history, the customary system—parts of which were inherited but are now different from the British Imperial System—has been generally used. Federal and state legislation gave it, through implication, standing as the primary weights and measures system. The metric system, however, is the only system that Congress has ever specifically sanctioned, dating back to an 1866 law. The U.S. was one of the original 17 countries to sign the International Metric Convention (or Treaty of the Meter) May 20, 1875, which established several intergovernmental organizations to oversee and refine the SI. The U.S. is represented at these organizations by the Natl. Institute of Standards and Technology (NIST).

Since that time, use of the metric system in the U.S. has slowly increased, particularly in the scientific community, the pharmaceutical industry, and the manufacturing sector—the last motivated by the predominant use of the metric system in international commerce.

On Dec. 23, 1975, Pres. Gerald R. Ford signed the Metric Conversion Act of 1975. It defined the "metric system of measurement" as the SI, as established in 1960 by the General Conference on Weights and Measures and interpreted in the U.S. by the secretary of commerce, who delegated that authority to the director of the NIST. The Trade and Competitiveness Act of 1988 declared the metric system the preferred system of weights and measures for U.S. trade and commerce, but explicitly permitted "the continued use of traditional systems of weights and measures in nonbusiness activities." The Code of Federal Regulations made the use of metric units mandatory for federal agencies in 1991. However, the metric system has not yet become the system of choice for most Americans' daily use.

The following are the seven base SI units: **length**—meter; **mass**—kilogram; **time**—second; **electric current**—ampere; **thermodynamic temperature**—kelvin; **amount of substance**—mole; and **luminous intensity**—candela. All seven were redefined as of May 20, 2019, to emphasize the dependence of base unit definitions on physical constants with fixed numerical values and on the other base units.

Frequently Used Conversions

Boldface indicates exact values. For greater accuracy, use the "multiply by" number in parentheses. For weights, avoirdupois (avdp) weight is the system applied to all goods except medicines, precious metals, and precious stones.

U.S. Customary to Metric

	If you have:	Multiply by:		To get:
Length	inches	**25.4**		millimeters
	inches	**2.54**		centimeters
	inches	**0.0254**		meters
	feet	0.3	(**0.3048**)	meters
	yards	0.9	(**0.9144**)	meters
	miles[1]	1.6	(**1.609344**)	kilometers
Area	sq inches	6.5	(**6.4516**)	sq cm
	sq feet	0.09	(**0.09290304**)	sq meters
	sq yards	0.84	(**0.83612736**)	sq meters
	acres	0.4	(0.4046873)	hectares
	sq miles[1]	2.6	(2.58998811)	sq kilometers
Weight	ounces (avdp)	28	(28.34952)	grams
	pounds (avdp)	454	(**453.59237**)	grams
	pounds (avdp)	0.45	(**0.45359237**)	kilograms
	short tons[2]	0.91	(**0.90718474**)	metric tons
	long tons[3]	1	(1.016047)	metric tons
Liquid	ounces	0.03	(0.02957353)	liters
	cups	0.24	(0.23658824)	liters
	pints	0.47	(0.473176473)	liters
	quarts	0.95	(0.946352946)	liters
	gallons	3.79	(3.785412)	liters

Metric to U.S. Customary

	If you have:	Multiply by:		To get:
Length	millimeters	0.04	(0.03937)	inches
	centimeters	0.4	(0.3937)	inches
	meters	39	(39.37)	inches
	meters	3.3	(3.280840)	feet
	meters	1.1	(1.093613)	yards
	kilometers	0.6	(0.621371)	miles[1]
Area	sq cm	0.16	(0.15500)	sq inches
	sq meters	10.8	(10.76391)	sq feet
	sq meters	1.2	(1.195990)	sq yards
	hectares	2.5	(2.471044)	acres
	sq kilometers	0.39	(0.386102)	sq miles[1]
Weight	grams	0.035	(0.03527396)	ounces (avdp)
	grams	0.002	(0.00220462)	pounds (avdp)
	kilograms	2.2	(2.204623)	pounds (avdp)
	metric tons	1.1	(1.102311)	short tons[2]
	metric tons	0.98	(0.9842065)	long tons[3]
Liquid	liters	33.8	(33.81402)	ounces
	liters	4.2	(4.226752)	cups
	liters	2.1	(2.113376)	pints
	liters	1.1	(1.056688)	quarts
	liters	0.26	(0.264172)	gallons

(1) Survey mile. (2) A short ton is 2,000 pounds. (3) A long ton is 2,240 pounds.

Temperature Conversions

The left-hand column below gives a temperature according to the **Celsius** scale, and the right-hand gives the same temperature according to the **Fahrenheit** scale. The lowest number on each scale is equivalent to absolute zero, the theoretical temperature at which all molecular motion would stop.

For temperatures not shown: To convert Fahrenheit to Celsius, subtract 32 degrees and divide by 1.8; to convert Celsius to Fahrenheit, multiply by 1.8 and add 32 degrees.

Celsius	Fahrenheit	Celsius	Fahrenheit	Celsius	Fahrenheit	Celsius	Fahrenheit	Celsius	Fahrenheit
−273.15	−459.67	−45.6	−50	−1.1	30	30	86	65.6	150
−250	−418	**−40**	**−40**	**0**	**32**	32.2	90	70	158
−200	−328	−34.4	−30	4.4	40	35	95	80	176
−184.4	−300	−30	−22	10	50	**37**	**98.6**	90	194
−156.7	−250	−28.9	−20	15.6	60	37.8	100	93.3	200
−150	−238	−23.3	−10	**20**	**68**	40	104	**100**	**212**
−128.9	−200	−20	−4	21.1	70	43.3	110	121.1	250
−101.1	−150	−17.8	0	23.9	75	48.9	120	148.9	300
−100	−148	−12.2	10	25	77	50	122	150	302
−73.3	−100	−10	14	26.7	80	54.4	130	200	392
−50	−58	−6.7	20	29.4	85	60	140	300	572

Note: Although the term *centigrade* is still frequently used, the International Committee on Weights and Measures and the National Institute of Standards and Technology have recommended since 1948 that this scale be called *Celsius*.

Boiling and Freezing Points

Water boils at 212°F (100°C) at sea level. For every 550 feet above sea level, the boiling point of water is lower by about 1°F. Methyl alcohol (wood alcohol) boils at 148.5°F. Average human oral temperature is 98.6°F. **Water freezes** at 32°F (0°C).

Selected Geometric Formulas

The value of π (the Greek letter pi) is approximately 3.14159265 (equal to the ratio of the circumference of a circle to its diameter). The equivalence is typically rounded further to 3.1416 or 3.14.

Calculating Circumference

Circle: Multiply the diameter by π.

Calculating Area

Circle: Multiply the square of the radius (equal to ½ the diameter) by π.
Rectangle: Multiply the length of the base by the height.
Sphere (surface): Multiply the square of the radius by π and multiply by 4.
Square: Square the length of one side.
Trapezoid: Add the length of the two parallel sides, multiply by the height, and divide by 2.
Triangle: Multiply the base by the height and divide by 2.

Calculating Volume

Cone: Multiply the square of the radius of the base by π, multiply by the height, and divide by 3.
Cube: Cube the length of one edge.
Cylinder: Multiply the square of the radius of the base by π and multiply by the height.
Pyramid: Multiply the area of the base by the height and divide by 3.
Rectangular prism: Multiply the length by the width by the height.
Sphere: Multiply the cube of the radius by π, multiply by 4, and divide by 3.

Playing Cards and Dice Chances

5-Card Poker Hands

Hand	Number possible	Odds against
Royal flush	4	649,739 to 1
Other straight flush	36	72,192 to 1
Four of a kind	624	4,164 to 1
Full house	3,744	693 to 1
Flush	5,108	508 to 1
Straight	10,200	254 to 1
Three of a kind	54,912	46 to 1
Two pairs	123,552	20 to 1
One pair	1,098,240	4 to 3 (1.37 to 1)
Nothing	1,302,540	1 to 1
Total	**2,598,960**	

Bridge

The odds—against suit distribution in a hand of 4-4-3-2 are about 4 to 1; against 5-4-2-2 about 8 to 1; against 6-4-2-1 about 20 to 1; against 7-4-1-1 about 254 to 1; against 8-4-1-0 about 2,211 to 1; and against 13-0-0-0 about 158,753,389,899 to 1.

Dice

(probabilities on 2 dice)

Total	Odds against (single toss)	Total	Odds against (single toss)
2	35 to 1	8	31 to 5
3	17 to 1	9	8 to 1
4	11 to 1	10	11 to 1
5	8 to 1	11	17 to 1
6	31 to 5	12	35 to 1
7	5 to 1		

Large Numbers

No. of zeros	U.S. term	British[1], French, German	No. of zeros	U.S. term	British[1], French, German
6	million	million	42	tredecillion	septillion
9	billion	milliard	45	quattuordecillion	1,000 septillion
12	trillion	billion	48	quindecillion	octillion
15	quadrillion	1,000 billion	51	sexdecillion	1,000 octillion
18	quintillion	trillion	54	septendecillion	nonillion
21	sextillion	1,000 trillion	57	octodecillion	1,000 nonillion
24	septillion	quadrillion	60	novemdecillion	decillion
27	octillion	1,000 quadrillion	63	vigintillion	1,000 decillion
30	nonillion	quintillion	100	googol	googol
33	decillion	1,000 quintillion	303	centillion	NA
36	undecillion	sextillion	600	NA	centillion
39	duodecillion	1,000 sextillion	googol	googolplex	googolplex

NA = Not available. (1) In recent years, it has become more common in Britain to use U.S. terminology for large numbers.

Prime Numbers to 1,009

A prime number is any positive integer greater than 1 that is divisible only by two positive integers—1 and itself.

	2	3	5	7	11	13	17	19	23
29	31	37	41	43	47	53	59	61	67
71	73	79	83	89	97	101	103	107	109
113	127	131	137	139	149	151	157	163	167
173	179	181	191	193	197	199	211	223	227
229	233	239	241	251	257	263	269	271	277
281	283	293	307	311	313	317	331	337	347
349	353	359	367	373	379	383	389	397	401
409	419	421	431	433	439	443	449	457	461
463	467	479	487	491	499	503	509	521	523
541	547	557	563	569	571	577	587	593	599
601	607	613	617	619	631	641	643	647	653
659	661	673	677	683	691	701	709	719	727
733	739	743	751	757	761	769	773	787	797
809	811	821	823	827	829	839	853	857	859
863	877	881	883	887	907	911	919	929	937
941	947	953	967	971	977	983	991	997	1,009

Common Fractions Converted to Decimals

8ths	16ths	32nds	64ths	8ths	16ths	32nds	64ths	8ths	16ths	32nds	64ths	8ths	16ths	32nds	64ths
			1 = 0.015625				17 = 0.265625				33 = 0.515625				49 = 0.765625
		1	2 = 0.03125			9	18 = 0.28125			17	34 = 0.53125			25	50 = 0.78125
			3 = 0.046875				19 = 0.296875				35 = 0.546875				51 = 0.796875
	1	2	4 = 0.0625		5	10	20 = 0.3125		9	18	36 = 0.5625		13	26	52 = 0.8125
			5 = 0.078125				21 = 0.328125				37 = 0.578125				53 = 0.828125
		3	6 = 0.09375			11	22 = 0.34375			19	38 = 0.59375			27	54 = 0.84375
			7 = 0.109375				23 = 0.359375				39 = 0.609375				55 = 0.859375
1	2	4	8 = 0.125	3	6	12	24 = 0.375	5	10	20	40 = 0.625	7	14	28	56 = 0.875
			9 = 0.140625				25 = 0.390625				41 = 0.640625				57 = 0.890625
		5	10 = 0.15625			13	26 = 0.40625			21	42 = 0.65625			29	58 = 0.90625
			11 = 0.171875				27 = 0.421875				43 = 0.671875				59 = 0.921875
	3	6	12 = 0.1875		7	14	28 = 0.4375		11	22	44 = 0.6875		15	30	60 = 0.9375
			13 = 0.203125				29 = 0.453125				45 = 0.703125				61 = 0.953125
		7	14 = 0.21875			15	30 = 0.46875			23	46 = 0.71875			31	62 = 0.96875
			15 = 0.234375				31 = 0.484375				47 = 0.734375				63 = 0.984375
2	4	8	16 = 0.25	4	8	16	32 = 0.5	6	12	24	48 = 0.75	8	16	32	64 = 1.0

Roman Numerals

I — 1	IV — 4	VII — 7	X — 10	XX — 20	L — 50	C — 100	D — 500
II — 2	V — 5	VIII — 8	XI — 11	XXX — 30	LX — 60	CC — 200	CM — 900
III — 3	VI — 6	IX — 9	XIX — 19	XL — 40	XC — 90	CD — 400	M — 1,000

Note: The numerals V, X, L, C, D, or M shown with a horizontal line on top denote 1,000 times the original value.

Ancient Measures

Biblical		**Greek**		**Roman**	
Cubit	= 21.8 inches	Cubit	= 18.3 inches	Cubit	= 17.5 inches
Omer	= 0.45 peck	Stadion	= 607.2 or 622 feet	Stadium	= 202 yards
	= 3.964 liters	Obolos	= 715.38 milligrams	As, libra,	
Ephah	= 10 omers	Drachma	= 4.2923 grams	pondus	= 325.971 grams
Shekel	= 0.497 ounce	Mina	= 0.9463 pound		= 0.71864 pound
	= 14.1 grams	Talent	= 60 mina		

Metric System Prefixes

The following prefixes, in combination with the basic unit names, provide the multiples and submultiples in the metric system. For example, the unit name *meter*, with the prefix *kilo* added, produces *kilometer*, meaning "1,000 meters."

Prefix	**Symbol**	**Multiples**	**Equivalent**	**Prefix**	**Symbol**	**Multiples**	**Equivalent**
yotta	Y	10^{24}	septillionfold	deci	d	10^{-1}	tenth part
zetta	Z	10^{21}	sextillionfold	centi	c	10^{-2}	hundredth part
exa	E	10^{18}	quintillionfold	milli	m	10^{-3}	thousandth part
peta	P	10^{15}	quadrillionfold	micro	μ	10^{-6}	millionth part
tera	T	10^{12}	trillionfold	nano	n	10^{-9}	billionth part
giga	G	10^{9}	billionfold	pico	p	10^{-12}	trillionth part
mega	M	10^{6}	millionfold	femto	f	10^{-15}	quadrillionth part
kilo	k	10^{3}	thousandfold	atto	a	10^{-18}	quintillionth part
hecto	h	10^{2}	hundredfold	zepto	z	10^{-21}	sextillionth part
deka	da	10^{1}	tenfold	yocto	y	10^{-24}	septillionth part

Weight and Measurement Equivalents

The international foot, defined in 1959 as exactly equal to 0.3048 meter, is shorter than the survey foot by exactly 2 parts in 1 million. This means that a mile, also known as an international mile, is about ⅛ inch shorter than the survey mile. The NIST discouraged the use of the survey foot or survey mile for any purposes after Jan. 1, 2023.

When the name of a unit is enclosed in brackets, e.g., [1 hand], either (1) the unit is not in general current use in the U.S. or (2) the unit is believed to be based on custom and usage rather than on formal definition.

Equivalents involving decimals are, in most instances, rounded to the third decimal place; exact equivalents are so designated.

Lengths

1 angstrom (Å)	= 0.1 nanometer (exactly)
	= 0.0001 micrometer (exactly)
	= 0.0000001 millimeter (exactly)
	= 0.000000004 inch
1 cable's length	= 120 fathoms (exactly)
	= 720 feet (exactly)
	= 219 meters
1 centimeter (cm)	= 0.3937 inch
1 chain (ch) (engineer's)	= 30.48 meters (exactly)
	= 100 feet
1 chain (Gunter's or surveyor's)	= 66 feet (exactly)
	= 20.1168 meters
1 decimeter (dm)	= 3.937 inches
1 degree (geographical)	= 364,566.929 feet
	= 69.047 miles (avg.)
	= 111.123 kilometers (avg.)
of latitude	= 68.708 miles at equator
	= 69.403 miles at poles
of longitude	= 69.171 miles at equator
1 dekameter (dam)	= 32.808 feet
1 fathom (fath)	= 6 feet (exactly)
	= 1.8288 meters
1 foot (ft)	= 12 inches (exactly)
	= 0.3048 meters (exactly)
	= 0.015 chains (surveyor's)
1 furlong (fur)	= 660 feet (exactly)
	= ⅛ mile (exactly)
	= 201.168 meters
[1 hand (height measure for horses, from ground to top of their shoulders)]	= 4 inches
1 inch (in.)	= 2.54 centimeters (exactly)
1 kilometer (km)	= 0.621371 mile
	= 3,280.8 feet
1 league (land)	= 3 miles (exactly)
	= 4.828 kilometers
1 link (engineer's)	= 1 foot
	= 0.305 meter
1 link (Gunter's or surveyor's)	= 7.92 inches (exactly)
	= 0.201 meter

1 meter (m) = 39.37 inches
= 1.09361 yards

1 micrometer (μm) = 0.001 millimeter (exactly)
= 0.00003937 inch

1 mil = 0.001 inch (exactly)
= 0.0254 millimeter (exactly)

1 mile (mi) (statute or land) = 5,280 feet (exactly)
= 1.609344 kilometers (exactly)

1 mile (nmi) (international nautical) = 1.852 kilometers (exactly)
= 1.151 miles
= 6,076.1 feet

1 millimeter (mm) = 0.03937 inch

1 nanometer (nm) = 0.001 micrometer (exactly)
= 0.00000003937 inch

1 pica (typography) = 12 points

1 point (pt) (typography) = 0.013837 inch (exactly)
= 0.351 millimeter

1 rod (rd), pole, or perch = 16½ feet (exactly)
= 5.029 meters

1 yard (yd) = 3 feet (exactly)
= 0.9144 meter (exactly)

Areas or Surfaces

1 acre (A) = 43,560 square feet (exactly)
= 4,840 square yards
= 0.405 hectare

1 are (a) = 119.599 square yards
= 0.025 acre

1 bolt (cloth measure):
length = 100 yards
width = 45 or 60 inches

1 hectare (ha) = 2.471 acres

[1 square (building)] = 100 square feet

1 square centimeter (cm^2) = 0.155 square inch

1 square decimeter (dm^2) = 15.500 square inches

1 square foot (ft^2) = 929.030 square centimeters

1 square inch ($in.^2$) = 6.4516 square centimeters (exactly)

1 square kilometer (km^2) = 247.104 acres
= 0.386102 square mile

1 square meter (m^2) = 1.196 square yards
= 10.764 square feet

1 square mile (mi^2) = 640 acres (exactly)
= 258.999 hectares

1 square millimeter (mm^2) = 0.002 square inch

1 square rod (rd^2), square pole, or square perch = 25.293 square meters

1 square yard (yd^2) = 0.836127 square meter

Capacities or Volumes

1 barrel (bbl), liquid = 31 to 42 gallons*

*There are a variety of "barrels" established by law or usage. For example, federal taxes on fermented liquors are based on a barrel of 31 gallons. Many state laws fix the "barrel for liquids" as 31½ gallons; one state fixes a 36-gallon barrel for cistern measurement. Federal law recognizes a 40-gallon barrel for "proof spirits." By custom, 42 gallons constitute a barrel of crude oil or petroleum products for statistical purposes, and this equivalent is recognized "for liquids" by some states.

1 barrel (bbl), standard for fruits, vegetables, and other dry commodities except dry cranberries = 7,056 cubic inches
= 105 dry quarts
= 3.281 bushels, struck measure

1 barrel, standard, cranberry = $86\frac{45}{64}$ dry quarts
= 2.709 bushels, struck measure
= 5,826 cubic inches

1 board foot (lumber measure) = a foot-square board 1 inch thick

1 bushel (U.S.) (struck measure) = 2,150.42 cubic inches (exactly)
= 35.239 liters

[1 bushel, heaped (U.S.)] = 2,747.715 cubic inches
= 1.278 bushels, struck measure**

**Frequently recognized as 1¼ bushels, struck measure.

[1 bushel (bu) (British Imperial) (struck measure)] = 1.032 U.S. bushels, struck measure
= 2,219.36 cubic inches

1 cord (cd) (firewood) = 128 cubic feet (exactly)

1 cubic centimeter (cm^3) = 0.061 cubic inch

1 cubic decimeter (dm^3) = 61.024 cubic inches

1 cubic foot (ft^3) = 7.481 gallons
= 28.317 cubic decimeters

1 cubic inch ($in.^3$) = 0.554 fluid ounce
= 4.433 fluid drams
= 16.387 cubic centimeters

1 cubic meter (m^3) = 1.308 cubic yards

1 cubic yard (yd^3) = 0.765 cubic meter

1 cup, measuring = 8 fluid ounces (exactly)
= ½ liquid pint (exactly)

1 dekaliter (daL) = 2.642 gallons
= 1.135 pecks

[1 dram, fluid (fl dr) (British)] = 0.961 U.S. fluid dram
= 0.217 cubic inch
= 3.552 milliliters

1 gallon (gal) (U.S.) = 4 quarts, liquid (exactly)
= 231 cubic inches (exactly)
= 3.785 liters
= 0.833 British gallon
= 128 U.S. fluid ounces (exactly)

[1 gallon (British Imperial)] = 277.42 cubic inches
= 1.201 U.S. gallons
= 4.546 liters
= 160 British fluid ounces (exactly)

1 gill (gi) = 7.219 cubic inches
= 4 fluid ounces (exactly)
= 0.118 liter

1 hectoliter (hL) = 26.418 gallons
= 2.838 bushels

1 liter (L) (1 cubic decimeter exactly) = 1.057 liquid quarts
= 0.908 dry quart
= 61.024 cubic inches

1 milliliter (mL) (1 cu cm exactly) = 0.271 fluid dram
= 16.231 minims
= 0.061 cubic inch

1 ounce, liquid (U.S.) = 1.805 cubic inches
= 29.573 milliliters
= 1.041 British fluid ounces

[1 ounce, fluid (fl oz) (British)] = 0.961 U.S. fluid ounce
= 1.734 cubic inches
= 28.412 milliliters

1 peck (pk) = 8.810 liters

1 pint (pt), dry = 33.600 cubic inches
= 0.551 liter

1 pint, liquid = 28.875 cubic inches (exactly)
= 0.473 liter

1 quart (qt), dry (U.S.) = 67.201 cubic inches
= 1.101 liters
= 0.969 British quart

1 quart, liquid (U.S.) = 2 pints, liquid (exactly)
= 4 cups (exactly)
= 57.75 cubic inches (exactly)
= 0.946 liter
= 0.833 British quart

[1 quart (British)] = 69.354 cubic inches
= 1.032 U.S. dry quarts
= 1.201 U.S. liquid quarts

1 tablespoon (T., Tbs, tbsp.) = 3 teaspoons (exactly)
= 4 fluid drams
= ½ fluid ounce (exactly)

1 teaspoon (t., tsp.) = $\frac{1}{3}$ tablespoon (exactly)
= $1\frac{1}{3}$ fluid drams***

***The equivalent "1 teaspoon = $1\frac{1}{3}$ fluid drams" has been found to correspond more closely with the actual capacities of teaspoons in use than the equivalent "1 teaspoon = 1 fluid dram" given by many dictionaries.

Weights or Masses

1 assay ton* (AT) = 29.167 grams

*Used in assaying. The assay ton bears the same relation to the milligram that a ton of 2,000 pounds avoirdupois bears to the ounce troy; hence, the weight in milligrams of precious metal obtained from one assay ton of ore gives directly the number of troy ounces to the net ton.

1 carat (c) = 200 milligrams (exactly)
= 3.086 grains

1 dram avoirdupois (dr avdp) = $27\frac{11}{32}$ (= 27.344) grains
= 1.772 grams

1 gamma (γ) = 1 microgram (exactly)

1 grain (gr) = 64.79891 milligrams (exactly)

1 gram (g) .... = 15.432 grains
= 0.035 ounce, avoirdupois

1 hundredweight, gross (or long)** (gross cwt) .... = 112 pounds (exactly)
= 50.802 kilograms

**The gross (or long) ton and hundredweight are used commercially in the U.S. to only a limited extent, usually in restricted industrial fields. These units are the same as the British ton and hundredweight.

1 hundredweight, gross or short (cwt or net cwt) ...... = 100 pounds (exactly)
= 45.359 kilograms

1 kilogram (kg) .... = 2.20462 pounds

1 microgram (μg) .... = 0.000001 gram (exactly)

1 milligram (mg) .... = 0.015 grain

1 ounce, avoirdupois (oz avdp) = 437.5 grains (exactly)
= 0.911 troy ounce
= 28.3495 grams

1 ounce, troy (oz t) .... = 480 grains (exactly)
= 1.097 avoirdupois ounces
= 31.103 grams

1 pennyweight (dwt) .... = 1.555 grams

1 pound, avoirdupois (lb avdp) = 7,000 grains (exactly)
= 1.215 troy pounds
= 453.59237 grams (exactly)

1 pound, troy (lb t) .... = 5,760 grains (exactly)
= 0.823 avoirdupois pound
= 373.242 grams

1 stone (st) .... = 14 pounds avdp (exactly)
= 6.350 kilograms

1 ton, gross or long. .... = 2,240 pounds (exactly)
= 1.12 net tons (exactly)
= 1.016 metric tons

1 ton, metric (t) .... = 2,204.623 pounds
= 0.984 gross ton
= 1.102 net tons

1 ton, net or short (tn). .... = 2,000 pounds (exactly)
= 0.893 gross ton
= 0.907 metric ton

Electrical Units

The **watt** (W) is the unit of power (electrical, mechanical, thermal). Electrical power is given by the product of the voltage and the current.

Energy is sold by the **joule** (J), but in common practice the billing of electrical energy is expressed in terms of the **kilowatt-hour** (kWh), which is 3,600,000 joules, or 3.6 megajoules.

The **horsepower** (hp) is a nonmetric unit sometimes used in mechanics. It is equal to 746 watts.

The **ohm** (Ω) is the unit of electrical resistance and represents the physical property of a conductor that offers a resistance to the flow of electricity, permitting just 1 ampere to flow at 1 volt of pressure.

Measures of Force and Pressure

Dyne (dyn) = force necessary to accelerate a 1-gram mass 1 centimeter per second squared = 0.000072 poundal

Poundal (pdl) = force necessary to accelerate a 1-pound mass 1 foot per second squared = 13,825.5 dynes = 0.138255 newton

Newton (N) = force needed to accelerate a 1-kilogram mass 1 meter per second squared = 100,000 dynes (exactly)

Pascal (pressure) (Pa) = 1 newton per square meter = 0.020885 pound per square foot

Atmosphere (air pressure at sea level) (atm) = 2,116.217 pounds per square foot = 14.6959 pounds per square inch = 1.0332 kilograms per square centimeter = 101,325 newtons per square meter

Measures of Alcohol

Pony .... = 1.0 fluid ounce

Shot .... = varies, usu. 1.0-1.5 fluid ounces

Jigger .... = 1.5 fluid ounces

Pint (pt)........... = 16 fluid ounces
= 0.625 fifth

Fifth.............. = 25.6 fluid ounces
= 1.6 pints
= 0.8 quart
= 0.757 liter

Quart (qt) .... = 32 fluid ounces
= 1.25 fifths

Wine bottle (standard)........ = 0.75 liter
= 25.4 fluid ounces

Magnum .... = 1.5 liters

For champagne and brandy:

Jeroboam .... = 2 magnums
= 3 liters
= 101 fluid ounces

For champagne:

Rehoboam .... = 3 magnums

Methuselah......... = 4 magnums

Salmanazar .... = 6 magnums

Balthazar .... = 8 magnums

Nebuchadnezzar ... = 10 magnums

Miscellaneous Measures

Caliber (cal)—the diameter of a gun bore. In the U.S., caliber is traditionally expressed in hundredths of inches, e.g., .22. In Britain, caliber is often expressed in thousandths of inches, e.g., .270. Now it is commonly expressed in millimeters, e.g., the 5.56 mm M16 rifle. The caliber of heavier weapons has long been expressed in millimeters, e.g., the 155 mm howitzer.

Naval guns' caliber refers to the barrel length as a multiple of the bore diameter. For example, a 5-inch, 50-caliber naval gun has a 5-inch bore and a barrel length of 250 inches.

Decibel (dB)—a measure of the relative intensity of sound. The threshold of hearing is given as 0 decibels. A 20-decibel sound is 10 times more intense than a 10-decibel sound; 30 decibels is 100 times more intense. (A 10-decibel increase corresponds generally to the perception of a sound being twice as loud.)

One decibel is the smallest difference between sounds detectable by the human ear. Long or repeated exposure to an 85-decibel-or-higher sound can damage hearing.

10 decibels	breathing
20	rustling leaves
30	whisper
40	refrigerator humming
50	quiet conversation
60	conversation, laughter
70	vacuum cleaner
80	city traffic
90	subway, lawn mower
100	chainsaw

Em—a printer's measure designating the width of any given type size. For example, an em of 10-point type is 10 points. An en is half an em.

Gauge (ga)—the diameter of a shotgun bore. Gauge numbers originally referred to the number of lead balls—of equal diameter as the gun barrel—required to make a pound. Thus, a 16-gauge shotgun's bore was smaller than a 12-gauge shotgun's. Today, an international agreement assigns millimeter measures to each gauge.

Gauge	Bore diameter (mm)	Gauge	Bore diameter (mm)
6	23.34	14	17.60
10	19.67	16	16.81
12	18.52	20	15.90

Horsepower (hp)—the power needed to lift 550 pounds 1 foot in 1 second or to lift 33,000 pounds 1 foot in 1 minute. Equivalent to 746 watts or 2,546 British thermal units per hour.

Karat or carat (k or c)—a measure of fineness for gold equal to 1/24 part of pure gold in an alloy. 24-karat gold is pure; 18-karat gold is ¼ alloy. The carat is also used as a unit of weight for precious stones; it is equal to 200 milligrams or 3.086 grains.

Knot (kn or kt)—a measure of the speed of ships. A knot equals 1 nautical mile (about 1.151 statute miles) per hour.

Quire (qr)—25 sheets of paper of the same size and quality.

Ream (rm)—500 sheets of paper of the same size and quality.

POSTAL INFORMATION

Administration of the U.S. Postal Service

The Postal Reorganization Act, creating a government-owned postal service under the executive branch and replacing the old executive Post Office Department, was signed into law Aug. 12, 1970. The service officially came into being on July 1, 1971. The U.S. Postal Service is governed by an 11-person board. Nine members are appointed by the president, with Senate approval. These nine choose a postmaster general. The board and the postmaster general choose the 11th member, who serves as deputy postmaster general.

The Postal Service Reform Act of 2022 was signed into law Apr. 6, 2022, altering budget requirements imposed by 2006 legislation and eliminating a provision requiring USPS to pre-fund retiree benefits for 50 years, which had incurred massive annual deficits. (The Postal Service last received a public service subsidy, i.e., taxpayer dollars, in 1982.)

Historical Postage Rates, 1851-2024

Postage cost for a prepaid, 1-oz. letter (the first-class standard after July 1, 1885).

Effective date	Rate	2024 dollars	Effective date	Rate	2024 dollars	Effective date	Rate	2024 dollars
July 1, 1851	$0.06[1]	$2.54	Mar. 22, 1981	$0.18	$0.64	Jan. 22, 2012	$0.45	$0.62
July 1, 1863	0.06	1.55	Nov. 1, 1981	0.20	0.67	Jan. 27, 2013	0.46	0.63
Oct. 1, 1883	0.04	1.29	Feb. 17, 1985	0.22	0.65	Jan. 26, 2014	0.49[3]	0.66
July 1, 1885	0.02	0.67	Apr. 3, 1988	0.25	0.67	Apr. 10, 2016	0.47	0.62
Nov. 2, 1917	0.03[2]	0.70	Feb. 3, 1991	0.29	0.68	Jan. 22, 2017	0.49	0.63
July 1, 1919	0.02[2]	0.36	Jan. 1, 1995	0.32	0.67	Jan. 21, 2018	0.50	0.63
July 6, 1932	0.03	0.69	Jan. 10, 1999	0.33	0.63	Jan. 27, 2019	0.55	0.69
Aug. 1, 1958	0.04	0.43	Jan. 7, 2001	0.34	0.61	Aug. 29, 2021	0.58	0.67
Jan. 7, 1963	0.05	0.52	June 30, 2002	0.37	0.65	July 10, 2022	0.60	0.64
Jan. 7, 1968	0.06	0.55	Jan. 8, 2006	0.39	0.62	Jan. 22, 2023	0.63	0.66
May 16, 1971	0.08	0.62	May 14, 2007	0.41	0.62	July 9, 2023	0.66	0.68
Mar. 2, 1974	0.10	0.66	May 12, 2008	0.42	0.61	Jan. 21, 2024	0.68	—
Dec. 31, 1975	0.13	0.74	May 11, 2009	0.44	0.65	July 14, 2024	0.73	—
May 29, 1978	0.15	0.73						

— = Not applicable. **Note:** 2024 dollars are as of May. (1) For prepaid domestic letters traveling under 3,000 miles. (2) The price increased one cent during World War I; Congress restored its prewar rate in 1919. (3) The Postal Regulatory Commission approved a 6% total price increase: a 1.7% increase for inflation and an additional 4.3% temporary increase to compensate for USPS losses during the 2008-09 recession.

Status of the U.S. Postal Service, 2001-23

Source: *Postal Facts*, U.S. Postal Service

	2001	2005	2010	2015	2018	2019	2020	2021	2022	2023
Total mail items (bil)	207.5	211.7	170.9	154.3	146.4	142.6	129.2	128.9	127.3	116.2
First-class mail items (bil)	103.7	98.1	77.6	62.6	56.7	54.9	52.6	50.7	48.9	46.0
Stamped mail items (bil)	53.6	45.9	28.9	20.7	17.5	16.5	15.2	13.9	12.9	11.8
Marketing mail items (bil)	89.9	100.9	81.8	80.0	77.3	75.7	64.0	66.2	67.1	59.4
Shipping/package volume (bil)	NA	NA	3.1	4.5	6.2	6.2	7.3	7.6	7.2	7.1
Annual revenue (bil)	$65.8	$69.9	$67.1	$68.8	$70.6	$71.1	$73.1	$77.0	$78.8	$78.2
Total retail revenue (bil)	$14.8	$17.3	$17.5	$19.2	$12.7	$12.7	$12.7	$13.0	$12.2	$11.6
Total customer visits (bil)	1.4	1.3	1.1	0.9	0.8	0.8	0.8	0.7	0.7	0.7
Delivery points (mil)	137.7	144.3	150.9	155.0	158.6	160.0	161.4	163.1	164.9	166.6
Total delivery routes	242,600	243,000	230,600	226,777	231,843	231,807	231,579	233,171	233,585	234,344
Total retail offices	38,123	37,142	36,222	35,520	34,772	34,613	34,451	34,223	33,641	33,904
Career employees	775,903	704,716	583,908	491,863	497,157	496,934	495,941	516,636	516,750	525,469

U.S. Domestic Mail Rates

Source: *Price List* (Notice 123), U.S. Postal Service. Effective July 14, 2024. Rates are for retail customers unless noted. Domestic rates apply to the U.S., its territories and possessions, APOs, FPOs, and Freely Associated States.

First-Class Mail

Includes written matter such as letters, postcards, bills, account statements, and any matter sealed or closed against inspection up to 13 oz. In most cases, delivery is within 2-3 business days.

Letters measuring up to 6⅛ by 11½ in. and not more than ¼ in. thick cost 73¢ for the first oz., 28¢ for each additional oz. or fraction thereof, up to 3.5 oz. Nonmachinable letters (such as those in square, oversized, or unusually shaped envelopes) start at $1.19. Postcard postage is 56¢. Large envelopes up to 12 by 15 in. (or letters over 3.5 oz.) cost $1.50 for the first oz. and 27¢ for each additional oz. or fraction thereof. Presort- and automation-compatible mail can qualify for lower rates if certain piece minimums, mailing permits, and other requirements are met.

Forever Stamps. The USPS introduced the nondenominational "Forever" stamp Apr. 12, 2007, at an initial cost of 41¢. The Forever stamp can be purchased at the current First-Class standard rate and will always be valid as First-Class postage on standard envelopes weighing 1 oz. or less, even after rates increase.

Priority Mail

Priority Mail is delivered within 1-3 business days in most cases, with no additional charge for Saturday deliveries. Can be any mailable article up to 70 lbs and not over 108 in. in length and girth combined.

Priority Mail Flat Rate: $9.85, $10.15, $10.60, regardless of weight, if matter fits into designated USPS flat-rate envelopes. $10.40, $18.40, $24.75 if it fits into flat-rate boxes.

Priority Mail Forever Prepaid Flat Rate packaging can be purchased online at the current priority mail flat rate and remains valid for use after future price increases.

Priority Mail Express

Provides guaranteed expedited service for any mailable article up to 70 lbs and not over 108 in. in combined length and girth. Offers next-day delivery to most destinations; $12.50 additional charge for Sunday or holiday delivery. Includes insurance up to $100, mailing receipt, proof of delivery signature record, and tracking.

Priority Mail Express Flat Rate: $30.45, $30.65, $31.20, regardless of weight, if matter fits into designated USPS flat-rate envelopes.

Domestic Mail Services and Fees

Adult signature required: $9.35 per piece; person 21 years of age or older must sign for shipment.

Adult signature restricted delivery: $9.65 per piece; specific addressee or agent 21 years of age or older must sign for shipment.

Certificate of mailing: $2.20 per piece.

Certified mail: $4.85 per piece; provides proof of mailing and electronic verification of delivery or delivery attempt.

Certified mail restricted delivery: $12.75 per piece.

Collect on delivery (COD): $12.10 for amount to be collected/insurance desired up to $50; $14.95 for $50.01-$100; $3.35 for each additional $100.

Domestic money order: $2.35 for money orders $0.01 to $500; $3.40 for $500.01 to $1,000.

Pickup on demand: $26.50 per pickup; available for Priority Mail, Priority Mail Express, and USPS Retail Ground.

Restricted delivery: $7.70 per item when purchased in combination with COD, Insured Mail, or Registered Mail.

Return receipt: If requested at time of mailing, $4.10 for a receipt by mail, $2.62 for email receipt.

Signature confirmation: $3.70 online, $4.55 at post office.

Sunday/holiday delivery: Available for Priority Mail Express only. Fee: $12.50.

Tracking

Formerly known as Delivery Confirmation, tracking can be used with First-Class Mail parcels, Priority Mail, USPS Retail Ground, and Package Services (Bound Printed Matter, Media Mail, and Library Mail). Available free of charge at time of mailing, except for USPS Marketing Mail parcels ($0.32).

Change of Address

The USPS will forward mail to another address provided a Change of Address (COA) form has been filed in person or mailed to a post office or submitted online at moversguide.usps.com ($1.10 credit card authentication fee). The form can be picked up at any post office or requested by phone at (800) ASK-USPS.

P.O. Box Service

Private P.O. boxes can be rented in five sizes at most post offices. Prices depend on box size and location, ranging from $18.00-$367.00 per 3-month period or $28.00-$639.00 per 6-month period. Keys at most locations require a $5.00 deposit.

Registered Mail

The most secure service provided by the USPS. Full value of item must be declared at time of registration and mailing. Fee: $18.60 for a declared value of $0, up to $35.70 for articles with a declared value of $4,000.01 to $5,000. For each additional $1,000 or fraction thereof above $5,000, add $2.70.

International Mail Rates

Source: *Price List* (Notice 123), U.S. Postal Service. Effective July 14, 2024. Refer to www.usps.com for USPS price groups not shown here and weight limits by country.

First-Class Mail International

Letter-post items weighing up to 1 oz. and single postcards can be sent airmail for $1.65 to all countries.

Priority Mail International

Delivery is in 6-10 business days in many markets. Items must not be more than 108 in. in length and girth combined; max. weight is 70 lbs, though the limit varies by country.

Priority Mail International Flat Rate: $30.90-$52.40, depending on country price group, if matter fits into designated USPS flat-rate envelope (max. weight 4 lbs). Flat-rate boxes are $32.20-$152.05, depending on country price group and box size.

Priority Mail Express International

Priority Mail Express International Flat Rate: $59.50-$87.05, depending on country price group, if matter fits into flat-rate envelope (max. weight 4 lbs).

Global Express Guaranteed

Provides international expedited delivery, in partnership with FedEx, to certain countries. Item to be mailed must not weigh more than 70 lbs nor measure more than 108 in. in combined length and girth. Rate: Starts at $74.95 and $83.50 to Canada and Mexico, respectively, up to $163.90 to countries in price group 4, for items not over 0.5 lb in weight.

International Mail Services and Fees

Business reply: Card: $2.30; envelope (up to 2 oz.): $2.85.

Customs clearance and delivery: $8.85 per inbound letters and flats.

Insurance: Available to many countries for loss of or damage to items. Consult USPS for each country's indemnity limits.

Registered mail: Fee: $21.75 or $20.75 per First-Class mail or package piece.

Return receipt: Shows to whom and when item is delivered. Fee: $5.80 or $6.10 per mail piece.

Postal money order: $49.65 per money order. Only accepted in certain countries.

U.S. Postal Abbreviations

The abbreviations below are approved by the U.S. Postal Service for use in addresses.

State	Abbr.	State	Abbr.	State	Abbr.	State	Abbr.
Alabama	AL	Illinois	IL	Missouri	MO	Pennsylvania	PA
Alaska	AK	Indiana	IN	Montana	MT	Puerto Rico	PR
American Samoa	AS	Iowa	IA	Nebraska	NE	Rhode Island	RI
Arizona	AZ	Kansas	KS	Nevada	NV	South Carolina	SC
Arkansas	AR	Kentucky	KY	New Hampshire	NH	South Dakota	SD
California	CA	Louisiana	LA	New Jersey	NJ	Tennessee	TN
Colorado	CO	Maine	ME	New Mexico	NM	Texas	TX
Connecticut	CT	Marshall Islands[1]	MH	New York	NY	Utah	UT
Delaware	DE	Maryland	MD	North Carolina	NC	Vermont	VT
District of Columbia	DC	Massachusetts	MA	North Dakota	ND	Virgin Islands	VI
Florida	FL	Michigan	MI	Northern Mariana Isls.	MP	Virginia	VA
Georgia	GA	Micronesia, Federated States of[1]	FM	Ohio	OH	Washington	WA
Guam	GU			Oklahoma	OK	West Virginia	WV
Hawaii	HI	Minnesota	MN	Oregon	OR	Wisconsin	WI
Idaho	ID	Mississippi	MS	Palau[1]	PW	Wyoming	WY

(1) Although an independent nation, this country is subject to domestic rates and fees.

Canadian Province and Territory Postal Abbreviations

Source: Canada Post

Province/Territory	Abbr.	Province/Territory	Abbr.	Province/Territory	Abbr.	Province/Territory	Abbr.
Alberta	AB	Newfoundland and Labrador	NL	Nunavut	NU	Quebec	QC
British Columbia	BC	Northwest Territories	NT	Ontario	ON	Saskatchewan	SK
Manitoba	MB	Nova Scotia	NS	Prince Edward Island	PE	Yukon	YT
New Brunswick	NB						

SOCIAL SECURITY AND MEDICARE

Social Security Coverage

Source: Social Security Administration; World Almanac research; provisions shown are as under current law, Aug. 2024.

Social Security Benefits

Social Security's **Old-Age, Survivors, and Disability Insurance (OASDI)** program benefits are based on a worker's **primary insurance amount (PIA)**, which is related by law to the average indexed monthly earnings (AIME) on which Social Security contributions have been paid. The full PIA is payable to a worker who retires at full retirement age (FRA), which is 65-67 depending on birth year, and to an entitled disabled worker at any age. Spouses and children of retired or disabled workers and survivors of deceased workers receive set proportions of the PIA subject to a family maximum amount. The PIA is calculated by applying varying percentages to succeeding parts of the AIME. The formula is adjusted annually to reflect changes in average annual wages.

Increases in Social Security benefits are initiated for December of each year, assuming the Consumer Price Index (CPI) for the third calendar quarter of the year increased relative to the base quarter (i.e., the third calendar quarter of the year in which an increase last took effect). The size of the benefit increase is determined by the percentage rise of the CPI between the quarters measured.

The **average monthly benefit** payable to all retired workers amounted to $1,905 in Dec. 2023. The average benefit for disabled workers in that month was $1,537.

Maximum Monthly Retired-Worker Benefits Payable to Individuals Who Retired at Full Retirement Age (FRA)[1]

Retirement year[1]	Maximum benefit— Payable at retirement	Payable effective Dec. 2023
1990	$975	$2,379
1995	1,199	2,464
2000	1,435	2,636
2005	1,939	3,155
2010	2,346	3,281
2015	2,663	3,425
2017	2,687	3,444
2018	2,788	3,504
2019	2,861	3,497
2020	3,011	3,623
2021	3,148	3,739
2022	3,345	3,753
2023	3,627	3,743
2024	3,822	3,822

(1) Benefits in 2000 and earlier are for retirement at age 65 at beginning of a given year. Benefits in 2005 through 2008 are for starting benefits at exact FRA during the year. Benefits in 2009 through 2020 are for retirement at age 66 at beginning of year. Benefits in 2021-23 are for starting benefits at exact FRA during the year. Beneficiaries born in 1938 through 1942 are born in years where the FRA is transitioning from age 65 to age 66, and beneficiaries born in 1955 through 1959 are born in years where the FRA is transitioning from age 66 to age 67.

Amount of Work Required

To qualify for benefits, the worker generally must have worked a certain length of time in covered employment. Just how long depends on when the worker reaches age 62 or, if earlier, when he or she dies or becomes disabled. A person born after 1929 who dies, becomes disabled, or reaches 62 after 1991 must generally have had at least 10 years of work credit to qualify for benefits.

Contribution and Benefit Base

(annual limit on the amount of earnings subject to taxation under OASDI)

Calendar year	OASDI[1]	Calendar year	OASDI[1]	Calendar year	OASDI[1]
1995	$61,200	2009	$106,800	2017	$127,200
2000	76,200	2010	106,800	2018	128,400
2003	87,000	2011	106,800	2019	132,900
2004	87,900	2012	110,100	2020	137,700
2005	90,000	2013	113,700	2021	142,800
2006	94,200	2014	117,000	2022	147,000
2007	97,500	2015	118,500	2023	160,200
2008	102,000	2016	118,500	2024	168,600

(1) Old-Age, Survivors, and Disability Insurance.

A person is **fully insured** when he or she has one quarter of coverage for every year after age 21 is reached (or 1950, if later) up to but not including the year the worker reaches 62, dies, or becomes disabled. In 2024, a person earns one credit, or "quarter of coverage" for each $1,730 of annual earnings in covered employment, up to four credits (or quarters) per year.

To receive **disability benefits**, the worker, in addition to being fully insured, must generally have credit for 20 quarters of coverage out of the 40 calendar quarters before he or she became disabled. A disabled blind worker need meet only the fully insured requirement. Persons disabled before age 31 can qualify with a briefer period of coverage. Certain survivor benefits are payable if the deceased worker had 6 quarters of coverage in the 13 quarters preceding death.

Tax Rate Schedule

(percentage of covered earnings)

Year	Total	OASDI[1]	HI[2]
	(for employees and employers, each)		
1979-80	6.13%	5.08%	1.05%
1981	6.65	5.35	1.30
1982-83	6.70	5.40	1.30
1984	7.00	5.70	1.30
1985	7.05	5.70	1.35
1986-87	7.15	5.70	1.45
1988-89	7.51	6.06	1.45
1990 and after[3]	7.65	6.20	1.45
Year	(for self-employed)		
1979-80	8.10%	7.05%	1.05%
1981	9.30	8.00	1.30
1982-83	9.35	8.05	1.30
1984	14.00	11.40	2.60
1985	14.10	11.40	2.70
1986-87	14.30	11.40	2.90
1988-89	15.02	12.12	2.90
1990 and after[3]	15.30	12.40	2.90

(1) Old-Age, Survivors, and Disability Insurance. (2) Hospital Insurance (Medicare). (3) Public Law (PL) 111-147 exempted most employers from paying the employer share of OASDI payroll tax on wages paid Mar. 19-Dec. 31, 2010, to certain qualified individuals hired after Feb. 3, 2010. PL 111-312 reduced the OASDI payroll tax rate for 2011 by 2 percentage points for employees and for self-employed workers. PL 112-96 extended the 2011 rate reduction through 2012. The laws required that the general fund of the Treasury reimburse the OASI and DI Trust Funds for these temporary reductions.

What Aged Workers Receive

A person may receive monthly old-age benefits when he or she has enough work in covered employment and has reached retirement age—age 62 for reduced benefits or the age below for full benefits.

Full Retirement Age (FRA) by Birth Year

Year of birth	FRA	Year of birth	FRA
1937 or earlier	65	1955	66 and 2 mos.
1938	65 and 2 mos.	1956	66 and 4 mos.
1939	65 and 4 mos.	1957	66 and 6 mos.
1940	65 and 6 mos.	1958	66 and 8 mos.
1941	65 and 8 mos.	1959	66 and 10 mos.
1942	65 and 10 mos.	1960 or later	67
1943-54	66		

Note: If born on Jan. 1, refer to the previous birth year.

In 2000, the retirement earnings test was eliminated beginning with the month when the beneficiary reaches **full retirement age (FRA)**. A person at or above FRA no longer receives reduced benefits because of earnings. However, a person's benefits are reduced $1 for every $3 of earnings above the limit allowed by law ($59,520 for 2024) if he or she retires in the same calendar year but months prior to FRA. For retirees who have not yet reached the calendar year in which they will attain FRA, the reduction is $1 for every $2 of earnings over the exempt amount ($22,320 for 2024).

For workers who reached age 65 between 1982 and 1989, Social Security benefits are raised by 3% for each year in which the worker did not receive benefits between FRA and 70 (72 before 1984), whether because of earnings from work, because the worker did not apply for benefits, or because the worker declined benefits after entitlement. The **delayed retirement credit** is 1% per year for workers who reached age 65 before 1982. The rate for workers who reached age 65 in 1998-99 is 5.5%; 2000-01, 6.0%; 2002-03, 6.5%; 2004-05, 7.0%; and 2006-07, 7.5%. The delayed retirement credit rose to 8% per year for 2008 and years after.

For workers retiring early, benefits are permanently reduced 5/9 of 1% for each month before the FRA, up to 36 months. If the number of months exceeds 36, then the benefit is further reduced 5/12 of 1% per month.

For example, workers who retire at exactly age 62 have a total of 60 months of reduction if their FRA is 67. The reduction for the first 36 months is 5/9 of 36%, or 20%. The reduction for the remaining 24 months is 5/12 of 24%, or 10%. These workers would see their benefits reduced by 30% by retiring early. The nearer to FRA a person is when he or she begins collecting a benefit, the larger the monthly benefit will be.

Benefits for Worker's Spouse

The spouse of a worker who is getting Social Security retirement or disability payments may become entitled to an insurance benefit of **one-half of the worker's PIA** if claiming benefits at full retirement age. Reduced spouse's benefits are available at age 62 and are permanently reduced 25/36 of 1% for each month before FRA, up to 36 months. If the number of months exceeds 36, then the benefit is further reduced 5/12 of 1% per month. Benefits are also payable to the aged divorced spouse of an insured worker if he or she was married to the worker for at least 10 years. To qualify for divorced spouse benefits, the insured worker does not have to be receiving benefits if the divorce occurred at least two years earlier. Benefits received as a spouse are reduced by the amount of one's PIA.

Benefits for Children of Workers

If a retired or disabled worker has a child under age 18, the **child** will usually get a benefit equal to **one-half of the worker's unreduced benefit**. So will the worker's spouse, regardless of age, if he or she is **caring for an entitled child** of the worker, and the child is under 16 or became disabled before age 22. However, total benefits paid on a worker's earnings record are subject to a family maximum. Total monthly benefits paid to the family of a worker who retired in 2024 at age 66 and 8 months and always had the maximum earnings creditable under Social Security cannot exceed $6,648.

Entitled children generally stop receiving benefits at age 18, though they can continue receiving benefits until age 19 if they attend elementary or secondary school full-time. A child disabled before age 22 may get a benefit as long as the disability meets the definition in the law.

Benefits may also be paid to a grandchild or step-grandchild of a worker or of his or her spouse, in special circumstances.

OASDI Beneficiaries

Beneficiaries	May 2010	May 2020	May 2023	May 2024
Total (in thous.)[1]	**53,349**	**64,697**	**66,665**	**67,851**
Age 65 and over, total	36,914	49,199	52,727	54,274
Retired workers	30,734	43,034	46,828	48,451
Disabled workers	339	550	780	814
Survivors/ dependents	5,841	5,615	5,119	5,009
Under age 65, total	16,435	15,497	13,938	13,577
Retired workers	3,314	2,699	2,560	2,594
Disabled workers	7,628	7,781	6,720	6,415
Survivors/ dependents	5,492	5,017	4,659	4,568
Total monthly benefits (in mil)	**$56,966**	**$89,936**	**$113,287**	**$120,655**

OASDI = Old-Age, Survivors, and Disability Ins. (1) Numbers may not add up to totals due to rounding or incomplete enumeration.

What Disabled Workers Receive

A worker who becomes unable to work may be eligible for a monthly disability benefit. Benefits continue until it is determined that the individual is no longer disabled. When a disabled-worker beneficiary reaches FRA (see table on previous page), the disability benefit becomes a retired-worker benefit.

Benefits—like those for dependents of retired-worker beneficiaries generally—may be paid to dependents of disabled beneficiaries. However, the maximum family benefit in disability cases is generally lower than in retirement cases.

Survivor Benefits

If an insured worker should die, one or more types of benefits may be payable to survivors, again subject to a maximum family benefit described above.

1. If claiming benefits at FRA, the **surviving spouse** will receive a benefit equal to 100% of the deceased worker's benefit. Benefits claimed before FRA are reduced, with a maximum reduction of 28.5% at age 60. However, if the deceased worker claimed benefits before FRA, the surviving spouse's benefits are limited to the reduced amount the worker would be getting if alive, but not less than 82.5% of the worker's PIA. Remarriage after the worker's death ends the surviving spouse's benefit rights. However, if the widow(er) marries, and the marriage later ends, he or she regains benefit rights. (A marriage after age 60, or age 50 if disabled, is deemed not to have occurred for benefit purposes.) Survivor benefits may also be paid to a divorced spouse if the marriage lasted for at least 10 years.

Disabled widows and widowers may under certain circumstances qualify for benefits after attaining age 50 at the rate of 71.5% of the deceased worker's PIA. The widow or widower must have become totally disabled before or within seven years after the spouse's death or the last month in which he or she received mother's or father's insurance benefits.

2. There is a benefit for each **child under age 18**. The monthly benefit for a child of a deceased worker is 3/4 of the PIA, subject to the family maximum. A child who became disabled before age 22 may also receive benefits. Also, a child can receive benefits until age 19 if he or she is in full-time attendance at an elementary or secondary school.

3. There is a **mother's or father's benefit** for the widow(er) if children of the worker who are under age 16 are in his or her care. The benefit is 75% of the PIA (subject to the family maximum), and it continues until the youngest child reaches age 16, at which time payments stop even if the child's benefit continues. Benefits may continue if the widow(er) has a disabled child beneficiary age 16 or over in his or her care.

4. Dependent parents may be eligible for benefits if they have been receiving at least half their support from the worker before his or her death, have reached age 62, and (except in certain circumstances) have not remarried since the worker's death. Each parent gets 75% of the worker's PIA; if only one parent survives, the benefit is 82% (could be reduced for the family maximum).

5. A **lump sum** cash payment of **$255** is made if the worker was living with a spouse or has a child who is eligible for immediate monthly survivor benefits.

Self-Employed Workers

A self-employed person who has **net earnings of $400 or more** in a year must report such earnings for Social Security tax and credit purposes. Income from real estate, savings, dividends, loans, pensions, or insurance policies are not included unless it is part of a person's business.

A self-employed person receives one credit (also known as a "quarter of coverage") for each $1,730 for 2024, up to a maximum of four credits (or "quarters") per year.

The nonfarm self-employed have the option of reporting their earnings as 2/3 of their gross income from self-employment. This option can be used only if actual net earnings from self-employment income are less than $1,600 and less than 2/3 of their gross income. The option may be used only five times. Also, the self-employed person must have actual net earnings of $400 or more in two of the three taxable years immediately preceding the year in which he or she uses the option.

When a person has both taxable wages and earnings from self-employment, wages are credited for Social Security purposes first; only as much self-employment income as brings total earnings up to the current taxable maximum becomes subject to the self-employment tax.

Farm Owners and Workers

Self-employed farmers whose gross annual earnings from farming are **$8,460** or less, or whose net farm profits were less than $6,107, may report 2/3 of their gross earnings instead of net earnings, up to $5,640, for Social Security purposes, and pay the self-employment tax on that amount. Cash or crop shares received from a tenant or share farmer count if the owner participated materially in production or management. The self-employed farmer pays contributions at the same rate as other self-employed persons.

Agricultural employees. A worker's earnings from farm work count toward benefits if (1) the employer pays the worker $150 or more in cash during the year or (2) the employer spends $2,500 or more in the year for agricultural labor. Under these rules, a person gets credit for one calendar quarter for each $1,730 in cash pay in 2024.

Foreign farm workers admitted to the U.S. on a temporary basis are not covered.

Household Workers

If an employer pays a household worker (e.g., cleaning person, cook, babysitter, nanny, gardener) who is age 18 or older **$2,700 or more** in wages in 2024, the wages are covered under Social Security. This includes transportation costs paid for in cash. The job need not be regular or full-time. The employee should get a Social Security card at the Social Security office and show it to the employer. The employer deducts the amount of the employee's Social Security tax from the worker's pay, adds an identical amount as the employer's Social Security tax, and sends the total amount to the federal government.

Medicare Coverage

Source: Centers for Medicare & Medicaid Services, U.S. Dept. of Health and Human Services

The Medicare health insurance program provides acute-care coverage for Social Security and Railroad Retirement beneficiaries age 65 and over; workers and spouses age 65 and over with sufficient Medicare-only coverage in federal, state, or local government employment; certain persons entitled to receive Social Security or Railroad Retirement disability benefits; certain disabled persons with Medicare-only coverage through government employment; certain persons with end-stage kidney disease; and certain persons in the vicinity of Libby, MT, with asbestos-related conditions. What follows is a basic description that may not cover all circumstances.

The **basic Medicare plan**, available nationwide, is a fee-for-service arrangement where the beneficiary may use any provider accepting Medicare. Some services are not covered, and there are some out-of-pocket costs.

Hospital insurance (Part A). The basic hospital insurance program pays covered services for hospital and post-hospital care, including:

- All necessary inpatient hospital care for the first 60 days of each benefit period, except for a deductible ($1,632 in 2024). For days 61-90, Medicare pays for services over and above the coinsurance ($408 per day in 2024). After 90 days, the beneficiary has 60 lifetime reserve days for which Medicare helps pay. The coinsurance amount for reserve days was $816 in 2024.
- Up to 100 days of care in a skilled-nursing facility in each benefit period. Hospital insurance pays for all covered services for the first 20 days; for days 21-100, the beneficiary pays coinsurance ($204 per day in 2024).
- Part-time home health care provided by a home health agency (but, as of Jan. 1, 1998, limited to the first 100 visits after a hospital or skilled nursing facility stay of at least 3 days).
- Coverage of hospice care for certain terminally ill beneficiaries.

There is a premium for Part A insurance in certain—but not most—cases.

Medical insurance (Part B). Eligible elderly and disabled persons can receive benefits under this supplementary program only if they sign up and agree to a monthly premium. As of 2007, the monthly premium is tied to annual income. Individuals with an income of $103,000 or less and couples with an income of $206,000 or less pay $174.70 per person if they sign up upon becoming eligible in 2024. Part B covers certain medical services and supplies, including:

- Physicians' and surgeons' services, as well as some services furnished by certain other medical professionals and Medicare-approved practitioners.
- Services in an emergency room, outpatient clinic, ambulatory surgical center, or rural emergency hospital.
- Home health care not covered under Part A.
- Laboratory tests, X-rays, and other diagnostic radiology services.
- Certain preventative care services and screening tests.
- Most physical and occupational therapy and speech pathology services.
- Comprehensive outpatient rehabilitation facility services.
- Mental health care in a partial hospitalization psychiatric program, if inpatient care would otherwise be required.
- Radiation therapy; renal (kidney) dialysis and transplants; and heart, lung, heart-lung, liver, pancreas, bone marrow, and intestinal transplants.
- Approved durable medical equipment for home use.
- Drugs and biologicals that are not usually self-administered. (Certain self-administered drugs, such as some anti-cancer drugs, are also covered.)
- Certain services for diabetes.
- Ambulance services when other transportation methods are contraindicated.

Part B services are generally subject to a deductible ($240 in 2024), coinsurance (generally 20% of the remaining allowed charges with certain exceptions), a deductible for blood, and amounts above the allowed charge if a doctor or supplier does not accept the Medicare-approved rate as payment in full. For outpatient hospital services, coinsurance varies by service, usually falling between 20% and 50% of allowed charges. There are no deductibles or coinsurance for certain services, such as lab tests paid under the clinical lab fee schedule, home health agency services (except some durable medical equipment, which is subject to 20% coinsurance), and some preventative care services. Payments for certain physical, speech, and occupational therapy services are subject to certain limits. Dental care, hearing aids, and routine eye care are generally not covered under the basic plan.

To get medical insurance (Part B), persons approaching age 65 may enroll during the seven-month initial enrollment period, which includes the month of their 65th birthday as well as the three months before and after. Persons desiring coverage to begin in the month they reach age 65 must enroll in the three months before their birthday. Persons who enroll after their initial enrollment period may be subject to late-enrollment premiums.

The monthly premium is deducted from the cash benefit for persons receiving Social Security, Railroad Retirement, or Civil Service Retirement benefits. Income from the medical premiums and the federal matching payments are put in the Part B Account of the Supplementary Medical Insurance Trust Fund, from which benefits and administrative expenses are paid.

Effective Jan. 2023, there was a new basis for Part B eligibility, for post-kidney-transplant immunosuppressive drug coverage only, upon payment of a monthly premium determined solely for this coverage.

Medicare Advantage (Part C) (formerly Medicare+ Choice). Persons eligible for Medicare may have the option of getting services through a Medicare-certified local coordinated care plan, such as a health maintenance organization (HMO), local preferred provider organization (PPO), provider-sponsored organization (PSO), or other local Medicare-certified **managed care** plan; a regional preferred provider organization (RPPO); a private fee-for-service plan; or, in certain cases, a special-needs plan. Any such plan must provide at least the same benefits as Parts A and B, except for hospice services. They may provide added benefits (such as vision or hearing coverage) or reduce cost sharing or premiums. Enrollees may be required to use the plan's network of participating providers or pay higher out-of-pocket costs to go outside the network.

Prescription Drug Coverage (Part D). Effective Jan. 1, 2006, an optional Medicare prescription drug plan provides insurance coverage for prescription drugs. Medicare recipients pay a monthly premium (averaging about $34.50 in 2024 for basic coverage, depending on the provider) and a portion of drug costs. As of 2011, the monthly premium was tied to annual income; in 2024, individuals with an income greater than $103,000 and couples with an income greater than $206,000 pay more. The open enrollment period is Oct. 15-Dec. 7. Coverage varies depending on the drug plan selected.

Further details are available on the Internet at www.medicare.gov or by calling 1-800-MEDICARE (1-800-633-4227).

Medicare card. Persons qualifying for hospital insurance under Social Security receive a health insurance card. The card indicates whether the individual has taken out medical insurance protection. It is to be shown to the hospital, skilled-nursing facility, home health agency, doctor, or other provider of covered services.

Payments are generally made only in the 50 states, District of Columbia, Puerto Rico, U.S. Virgin Isls., Guam, American Samoa, and Northern Mariana Isls.

Social Security Financing

Social Security is paid for by a tax on certain earnings (for 2024, on earnings up to $168,600) for **Old-Age, Survivors, and Disability Insurance (OASDI)** and on all earnings (no upper limit) for hospital insurance with the **Medicare** program; the taxable earnings base for OASDI is adjusted annually to reflect changes in average wages. The employed worker and his or her employer share Social Security taxes equally.

Employers remit amounts withheld from employee wages for Social Security and income taxes to the Internal Revenue Service; employer Social Security taxes are also payable at the same time. (Self-employed workers pay Social Security taxes when filing their regular income tax forms.) The Social Security taxes (along with revenues arising from partial taxation of the Social Security benefits of certain high-income people) are transferred to the Social Security Trust Funds; they can be used only to pay benefits, the cost of rehabilitation services, and administrative expenses. By law, money not immediately needed for those purposes is invested in obligations of the federal government, which must pay interest on the money borrowed and must repay the principal when the obligations are redeemed or mature.

On Jan. 1, 1974, the **Supplemental Security Income (SSI)** program, established by the Social Security Amendments of 1972, replaced federal grants to the states to aid the needy aged, blind, and disabled. The program provides for federal payments, based on uniform national standards and eligibility requirements, and for state supplementary payments. The Social Security Administration administers the federal payments—financed by general funds of the Treasury—as well as the state supplement for those states that choose to have it federally administered. States may supplement the federal payment of all recipients and must supplement it for persons otherwise adversely affected by the transition from the former public assistance programs. In May 2024, the number of persons receiving federally administered SSI payments was 7,394,584; the payments totaled about $5.4 bil.

The **maximum monthly federal SSI payment** for individuals without an eligible spouse and with no other countable income, living in their own household, was $914 in 2023. For couples where both members were eligible, the maximum payment was $1,371.

For further information, contact the Social Security Administration toll-free at 1-800-772-1213 or visit its website at www.ssa.gov.

Examples of Monthly Social Security Benefits Available, 2024

Benefit or beneficiary	For low earnings ($29,813)[1]	For med. earnings ($66,251)[1]	For max. earnings ($163,084)[1,2]
Primary insurance amount (worker retiring at 66 years, 8 months)	$1,433.30	$2,367.20	$3,822.80
Maximum family benefit (worker retiring at 66 years, 8 months)	2,150.10	4,311.50	6,690.30
Maximum family disability benefit (worker disabled at 55; in 2024)	2,033.20	3,573.00	5,795.10
Disabled worker (worker disabled at 55):			
Worker alone	1,446.00	2,382.00	3,863.00
Worker, spouse, and 1 child	2,032.00	3,572.00	5,793.00
Retired worker claiming benefits at age 62:			
Worker alone[3]	1,009.00	1,662.00	2,694.00
Worker with spouse claiming benefits at—			
FRA or over	1,730.00	2,849.00	4,618.00
Age 62[3]	1,477.00	2,433.00	3,944.00
Widow or widower claiming benefits at—			
Age 66 or over[4]	1,433.00	2,367.00	3,822.00
Age 60[4]	1,024.00	1,692.00	2,733.00
Disabled widow or widower claiming benefits at age 50-59[5]	1,024.00	1,692.00	2,733.00
1 surviving child[4]	1,074.00	1,775.00	2,867.00
Widow or widower at FRA or over and 1 child[4]	2,149.00	4,142.00	6,689.00
Widowed mother or father and 1 child[4]	2,148.00	3,550.00	5,734.00
Widowed mother or father and 2 children[4]	2,148.00	4,311.00	6,690.00

FRA = Full retirement age. **Note:** Effective Jan. 2024. (1) Career average earnings: an average of lifetime earnings indexed to the year prior to entitlement (2023 in this case). (2) Assumes work beginning at age 22. (3) Assumes maximum reduction. (4) Assumes worker lived and worked until FRA without receiving reduced benefits. (5) Effective Jan. 1984, disabled widow(er) claiming a benefit at ages 50-59 receive a benefit equal to 71.5% of the PIA.

Social Security Recipients by Age, Sex, Race, and Hispanic Origin, 2023

Source: Social Security Administration

Characteristic/benefit	Total	White	Black	American Indian, Alaska Native	Asian	Native Hawaiian/ other Pacific Isl.	Hispanic
Social Security beneficiaries (thous.)[1]	**56,330**	**46,924**	**6,468**	**930**	**2,567**	**180**	**5,062**
Sex							
Male	25,432	21,284	2,807	421	1,174	87	2,296
Female	30,898	25,640	3,662	509	1,392	93	2,766
Age							
15-54 years	4,155	3,095	865	136	152	31	619
55-64 years	5,948	4,634	1,037	155	227	24	689
65-74 years	25,147	21,049	2,671	430	1,214	82	2,178
75 years or older	21,080	18,145	1,896	210	974	43	1,576
Supplemental Security Income recipients (thous.)[1]	**5,711**	**3,837**	**1,539**	**151**	**280**	**31**	**983**
Sex							
Male	2,778	1,833	819	62	99	18	474
Female	2,933	2,004	720	89	181	12	509
Age							
15-54 years	2,613	1,793	735	79	62	13	464
55-64 years	1,658	1,162	453	33	26	6	199
65-74 years	902	535	259	32	101	3	172
75 years or older	538	346	91	7	91	9	148
Average annual benefit in 2022 (dollars)							
Social Security	$18,540	$18,932	$16,488	$16,619	$16,843	$16,390	$15,931
Supplemental Security Income	9,219	9,308	9,020	11,285	8,597	NA	8,846

NA = Not available. **Note:** Race categories include people who reported being of that race, alone or in combination with another race. Persons of Hispanic origin may be of any race. The sum of the individual categories may not add up to totals because of rounding and because the totals include persons who reported being of more than one race. (1) Persons 15 or older receiving Social Security benefits or Supplemental Security Income in Mar. 2023.

Old-Age, Survivors, and Disability Insurance Beneficiaries, 2022

Source: Social Security Administration

State or area	Total benefits (thous.)	Total benefi-ciaries	Retirement (old-age)			Survivors		Disability		
			Retired workers	Spouses	Children	Widow(er)s and parents	Children	Disabled workers	Spouses	Children
Alabama	$1,889,214	1,168,912	778,722	26,153	12,426	74,058	45,430	197,520	2,275	32,328
Alaska	183,662	112,221	84,579	2,666	2,094	5,470	4,882	10,603	133	1,794
Arizona	2,569,996	1,468,715	1,135,622	41,810	15,352	77,814	41,492	135,085	1,614	19,926
Arkansas	1,113,085	712,122	477,621	13,461	7,402	42,796	26,599	122,160	1,370	20,713
California	10,436,876	6,251,295	4,769,219	268,490	79,402	355,097	160,623	539,044	7,939	71,481
Colorado	1,650,988	939,291	732,528	29,529	7,820	48,865	25,314	83,080	765	11,390
Connecticut	1,334,885	708,390	546,322	17,511	7,505	34,507	18,687	72,936	618	10,304
Delaware	439,772	234,539	182,497	4,671	1,674	11,383	6,445	24,568	173	3,128
Dist. of Columbia	138,711	83,476	61,434	1,623	812	3,537	3,304	11,547	21	1,198
Florida	8,490,838	4,986,213	3,832,752	139,472	48,385	265,699	122,778	498,785	5,958	72,384
Georgia	3,205,178	1,945,822	1,400,931	42,482	20,638	110,163	73,130	253,596	2,767	42,115
Hawaii	503,166	291,053	236,828	7,692	3,749	14,091	6,330	18,954	309	3,100
Idaho	647,993	385,393	292,182	10,673	4,054	19,776	10,852	40,481	531	6,844
Illinois	3,952,153	2,285,265	1,713,244	66,311	23,057	134,035	71,205	240,755	2,544	34,114
Indiana	2,435,324	1,401,813	1,010,170	31,532	12,815	82,494	50,208	185,000	1,981	27,613
Iowa	1,161,578	677,020	516,300	14,216	6,488	36,905	19,349	73,109	552	10,101
Kansas	1,018,122	580,532	434,744	13,504	6,062	31,992	18,946	64,502	567	10,215
Kentucky	1,592,922	1,014,477	661,892	26,618	10,071	70,696	40,974	174,569	3,017	26,640
Louisiana	1,430,357	933,612	600,241	35,732	10,238	78,857	43,614	139,242	2,346	23,342
Maine	584,809	363,772	266,516	8,317	3,411	18,121	9,566	49,412	452	7,977
Maryland	1,913,753	1,048,952	798,028	25,654	9,927	53,215	34,049	111,702	673	15,704
Massachusetts	2,303,138	1,306,185	966,118	34,591	13,825	61,975	35,495	166,264	1,099	26,818
Michigan	4,006,249	2,269,413	1,638,924	58,839	22,859	129,976	71,430	297,020	3,825	46,540
Minnesota	1,979,069	1,100,951	856,950	24,564	10,737	50,889	28,308	111,495	731	17,277
Mississippi	1,051,669	685,446	456,819	13,156	8,558	43,566	32,384	110,558	1,535	18,870
Missouri	2,215,715	1,341,389	959,137	27,406	12,252	76,106	48,115	189,232	1,872	27,269
Montana	414,265	253,030	196,144	6,049	2,512	13,495	7,211	23,922	293	3,404
Nebraska	626,556	364,735	277,705	8,083	3,613	19,560	11,239	38,098	246	6,191
Nevada	972,786	579,563	449,101	14,081	5,825	29,245	15,624	57,412	595	7,680
New Hampshire	602,248	326,752	245,379	6,498	2,600	14,184	7,884	41,813	256	8,138
New Jersey	3,147,563	1,669,244	1,274,772	48,721	18,326	87,604	44,893	167,868	1,714	25,346
New Mexico	732,866	461,134	335,665	13,643	4,206	26,005	16,933	55,907	672	8,103
New York	6,440,333	3,710,827	2,745,712	122,422	44,582	195,704	97,156	433,997	5,064	66,190
North Carolina	3,794,228	2,234,888	1,658,163	41,284	19,704	113,752	70,759	286,368	2,811	42,047
North Dakota	237,884	143,329	109,380	3,510	1,233	8,808	4,807	13,517	82	1,992
Ohio	3,993,516	2,427,966	1,727,949	71,481	20,228	162,931	86,001	313,017	3,573	42,786
Oklahoma	1,345,413	824,838	575,991	19,602	8,362	53,428	31,560	116,636	1,407	17,852
Oregon	1,582,498	917,497	710,755	24,187	8,885	46,975	20,462	93,286	1,009	11,938
Pennsylvania	5,085,579	2,898,240	2,135,246	74,020	25,206	167,698	84,559	356,858	3,732	50,921
Rhode Island	405,624	233,253	172,134	4,184	2,606	10,475	5,936	32,460	213	5,245
South Carolina	2,121,373	1,238,565	915,425	23,771	11,027	66,838	40,652	155,753	1,555	23,544
South Dakota	320,010	193,088	151,144	3,929	1,638	10,106	5,910	17,547	136	2,678
Tennessee	2,513,871	1,516,343	1,070,692	34,101	14,388	91,252	56,722	214,317	2,434	32,437
Texas	7,502,621	4,568,465	3,268,859	183,344	49,276	314,843	163,638	495,459	7,191	85,855
Utah	784,010	447,459	330,823	18,644	5,472	23,870	17,489	42,865	532	7,764
Vermont	275,700	159,575	120,203	3,424	1,666	7,356	3,919	19,667	113	3,227
Virginia	2,844,152	1,618,643	1,207,649	41,998	15,202	89,194	47,256	187,134	2,097	28,113
Washington	2,577,039	1,428,764	1,098,757	43,820	14,441	72,027	33,854	144,360	1,492	20,013
West Virginia	759,139	474,159	306,268	18,512	5,399	38,144	18,267	74,772	1,774	11,023
Wisconsin	2,292,436	1,307,526	1,007,263	25,217	11,741	62,969	35,474	142,054	1,128	21,680
Wyoming	216,533	123,325	94,686	3,001	1,041	6,574	3,711	12,468	138	1,706
American Samoa	5,463	5,960	2,694	191	236	574	646	1,194	35	390
Guam	22,592	19,707	13,490	1,065	487	1,591	1,197	1,426	44	407
N. Mariana Isls.	3,153	3,647	2,279	143	178	335	344	283	6	79
Puerto Rico	909,495	824,394	505,211	60,168	9,180	71,789	23,114	133,312	4,594	17,026
U.S. Virgin Isls.	32,089	21,921	17,477	794	370	1,205	613	1,238	22	202
Foreign countries	610,556	700,808	450,156	116,311	11,048	100,153	12,474	7,829	347	2,490
Unknown	855	543	391	21	4	60	14	42	0	11
All areas	**111,421,667**	**65,994,457**	**48,587,883**	**2,022,892**	**682,295**	**3,840,827**	**2,019,827**	**7,604,098**	**90,972**	**1,145,663**

Outcomes of Applications for Disability Benefits, 2000-21

Source: Social Security Administration

Year of application	Total	Pending final decision	Technical denials[1]	Medical denials		Medical allowances		Award rate[3]	Allowance rate[4]
				Medical	Subsequent nonmedical[2]	Awards	Subsequent denials[2]		
2000	1,364,323	0	136,054	456,467	3,817	766,047	1,938	56.1%	62.6%
2005	2,087,733	0	528,760	642,170	6,964	907,877	1,962	43.5	58.4
2010	2,981,615	0	978,627	861,506	19,094	1,120,313	2,075	37.6	56.0
2011	2,952,112	0	981,930	872,759	20,762	1,074,600	2,061	36.4	54.6
2012	2,955,946	0	1,024,469	867,276	23,847	1,038,076	2,278	35.1	53.9
2013	2,790,688	0	971,042	827,173	24,973	965,255	2,245	34.6	53.2
2014	2,687,365	0	936,820	804,035	27,025	917,203	2,282	34.1	52.5
2015	2,547,682	2,916	904,248	758,791	27,516	851,912	2,299	33.5	52.1
2016	2,430,102	3,911	875,652	715,998	27,361	805,195	1,985	33.2	52.1
2017	2,306,263	6,474	834,165	674,477	28,140	761,070	1,937	33.1	52.1
2018	2,226,343	17,624	811,182	630,861	29,773	734,825	2,078	33.3	52.7
2019	2,183,465	42,882	774,847	614,839	28,877	720,139	1,881	33.6	52.9
2020	1,999,612	128,426	713,878	526,008	28,778	600,986	1,536	32.1	52.1
2021	1,793,096	218,869	719,173	407,663	24,301	421,837	1,253	26.8	49.5

Note: Data as of June 2022. Applications for more recent years may still be pending; award and allowance rates will change. Does not include Supplemental Security Income-only applications. (1) Application denied for non-medical reason. (2) Denied for non-medical reasons after medical criteria were adjudicated. (3) Percent of all applications, minus pending claims, in which benefits were awarded. (4) Percent of all medical decisions that resulted in an allowance.

OASDI Recipients and Monthly Payments, 1940-2023

Source: Social Security Administration

		Monthly benefits					Monthly benefits		
Year	Total recipients	Total (thous.)	Avg.[1]	Avg. (2023 dollars)[2]	Year	Total recipients	Total (thous.)	Avg.[1]	Avg. (2023 dollars)[2]
1940	222,488	$4,070	$18.29	$387.60	**2000**	45,414,794	$34,848,920	$767.35	$1,357.74
1945	1,288,107	23,801	18.48	305.25	**2005**	48,434,445	44,351,772	915.71	1,432.88
1950	3,477,243	126,857	36.48	450.64	**2010**	54,032,097	58,048,364	1,074.33	1,501.24
1955	7,960,616	411,613	51.71	573.41	**2015**	59,963,425	73,642,029	1,228.12	1,584.05
1960	14,844,589	936,321	63.07	633.51	**2016**	60,907,307	75,917,962	1,246.45	1,592.12
1965	20,866,767	1,516,802	72.69	685.09	**2017**	61,903,360	79,732,580	1,288.02	1,610.97
1970	26,228,629	2,628,326	100.21	767.37	**2018**	62,906,222	84,419,840	1,342.00	1,636.76
1975	32,085,372	5,727,903	178.52	985.49	**2019**	64,064,496	88,523,452	1,381.79	1,657.73
1980	35,618,840	10,694,022	300.23	1,081.91	**2020**	64,850,867	92,197,039	1,421.68	1,685.11
1985	37,058,353	15,901,643	429.10	1,199.36	**2021**	65,228,238	99,804,910	1,530.09	1,723.03
1990	39,832,125	21,686,763	544.45	1,260.81	**2022**	65,994,457	111,421,667	1,688.35	1,752.88
1995	43,387,259	28,148,078	648.76	1,294.55	**2023**	67,076,966	118,527,109	1,767.03	1,767.03

OASDI = Old-Age, Survivors, and Disability Insurance. **Note:** Disability insurance payments began in 1957. (1) Avg. monthly benefit does not necessarily reflect individual payments to OASDI recipients. (2) Adjusted for inflation.

Social Security Trust Funds

Source: Social Security Administration

Old-Age and Survivors Insurance (OASI) Trust Fund, 1940-2023

(in millions)

	INCOME					DISBURSEMENTS					
Fiscal year[1]	Total	Net payroll tax contribs.	Income from taxing benefits	General fund reimbursements[2]	Net interest[3]	Total	Benefit pymts.[4]	Admin. expenses	Transfers to Railroad Retirement program	Net increase in fund[5]	Year-end balance
1940	$592	$550	—	—	$42	$28	$16	$12	—	$564	$1,745
1950	2,367	2,106	—	$4	257	784	727	57	—	1,583	12,893
1960	10,360	9,843	—	—	517	11,073	10,270	202	$600	–713	20,829
1970	31,746	29,955	—	442	1,350	27,321	26,268	474	579	4,425	32,616
1980	100,051	97,608	—	557	1,886	103,228	100,626	1,160	1,442	–3,177	24,566
1990	278,607	260,069	$2,924	1,471	14,143	223,481	218,948	1,564	2,969	55,126	203,445
1995	326,067	289,525	5,114	11	31,417	294,456	288,607	1,797	4,052	31,611	447,946
2000	484,228	418,219	12,476	1	53,532	353,396	347,868	1,990	3,538	130,832	893,003
2005	599,992	502,998	15,332	—	81,662	436,919	430,439	2,900	3,579	163,073	1,615,623
2010	682,448	552,037	21,068	737	108,606	579,907	572,515	3,462	3,930	102,541	2,398,377
2015	795,319	672,246	29,627	211	93,235	741,464	733,711	3,496	4,258	53,855	2,766,554
2017	822,442	702,123	35,416	15	84,888	798,961	791,094	3,551	4,316	23,481	2,820,101
2018	822,440	706,127	34,718	11	81,583	841,474	833,034	3,672	4,769	–19,034	2,801,066
2019	900,075	785,576	34,896	15	79,589	896,829	888,068	3,881	4,880	3,246	2,804,312
2020	955,571	841,664	37,910	7	75,990	948,702	940,200	3,658	4,844	6,869	2,811,181
2021	935,985	831,124	34,323	2	70,536	991,367	982,673	3,902	4,792	–55,383	2,755,799
2022	1,041,093	929,042	46,970	—	65,081	1,073,262	1,063,896	4,050	5,316	–32,169	2,723,629
2023	1,152,222	1,039,004	49,765	183	63,269	1,202,065	1,192,148	4,341	5,576	–49,843	2,673,786

— = Not applicable. **Note:** Numbers may not add up to totals due to rounding. (1) Fiscal years 1977 and later consist of the 12 months ending on Sept. 30 of each year. Fiscal years prior to 1977 consisted of the 12 months ending on June 30 of each year. (2) Includes reimbursements from the general fund of the Treasury to the OASI Trust Fund for certain legislated measures since 1957. (3) Includes net profits or losses on marketable investments. Beginning in 1967, the trust fund paid administrative expenses on an estimated basis, with a final adjustment including interest made in the following fiscal year. Net interest includes these interest adjustments. Beginning in Oct. 1973, figures include relatively small gifts to the fund. (4) Beginning in 1967, includes payments for vocational rehabilitation services furnished to disabled persons receiving benefits because of their disabilities; beginning in 1983, includes reimbursements paid from the general fund to the trust fund for unnegotiated benefit checks. (5) Net change in assets during fiscal year, including amounts borrowed or repaid by other funds.

Disability Insurance (DI) Trust Fund, 1960-2023

(in millions)

	INCOME					DISBURSEMENTS					
Fiscal year[1]	Total	Net payroll tax contribs.	Income from taxing benefits	General fund reimbursements[2]	Net interest[3]	Total	Benefit pymts.[4]	Admin. expenses	Transfers to Railroad Retirement program	Net increase in fund[5]	Year-end balance
1960	$1,034	$987	—	—	$47	$533	$528	$32	–$27	$501	$2,167
1970	4,380	4,141	—	$16	223	2,954	2,795	149	10	1,426	5,104
1980	17,376	16,805	—	118	453	15,320	14,998	334	–12	2,056	7,680
1990	28,215	27,154	$158	138	766	25,124	24,327	717	80	3,091	11,455
1995	70,209	67,986	335	—	1,888	41,374	40,234	1,072	68	28,835	35,206
2000	77,023	70,001	756	—	6,266	56,008	54,244	1,608	159	21,014	113,752
2005	96,765	85,418	1,164	—	10,183	86,360	83,721	2,301	338	10,405	193,298
2010	105,513	93,739	1,745	125	9,904	126,344	122,935	2,947	462	–20,831	186,946
2015	150,978	146,848	1,209	2	2,918	147,710	144,893	2,751	66	3,267	96,409
2017	144,392	141,195	479	—	2,719	143,393	140,742	2,543	107	999	98,063
2018	170,272	167,043	1,000	2	2,227	146,575	143,642	2,759	174	23,698	93,141
2019	150,978	146,848	1,209	2	2,918	147,710	144,893	2,751	66	3,267	96,409
2020	147,387	142,898	1,671	1	2,817	146,733	144,084	2,505	144	655	97,063
2021	144,392	141,195	479	—	2,719	143,393	140,742	2,543	107	999	98,063
2022	162,007	157,816	1,533	—	2,658	145,379	142,459	2,764	156	16,628	114,691
2023	180,726	176,465	1,021	—	3,241	152,500	149,643	2,798	60	28,226	142,917

— = Not applicable. **Note:** Numbers may not add up to totals due to rounding. (1) Fiscal years 1977 and later consist of the 12 months ending on Sept. 30 of each year. Fiscal years prior to 1977 consisted of the 12 months ending on June 30 of each year. (2) Includes reimbursements from the general fund of the Treasury to the DI Trust Fund for certain legislated measures since 1957. (3) Includes net profits or losses on marketable investments. Beginning in 1967, the trust fund paid administrative expenses on an estimated basis, with a final adjustment including interest made in the following fiscal year. Net interest includes these interest adjustments. The 1970 report describes the accounting for administrative expenses for years prior to 1967. Beginning in July 1974, figures include relatively small gifts to the fund. (4) Beginning in 1967, includes payments for vocational rehabilitation services furnished to persons receiving benefits because of a disability; beginning in 1983, includes reimbursements paid from the general fund to the trust fund for unnegotiated benefit checks. (5) Net change in assets during fiscal year, including amounts borrowed or repaid by other funds.

Supplementary Medical Insurance Trust Fund (Medicare SMI), 1975-2023

Source: Centers for Medicare & Medicaid Services, U.S. Dept. of Health and Human Services

(in millions)

	INCOME					DISBURSEMENTS				
Fiscal year[1]	Total	Premium from participants[2]	Govt. contribs.[3]	Transfers from states[4]	Interest and other income[5,6]	Total	Benefit pymts.[6,7,8]	Admin. expenses	Net change	Year-end balance
1975	$4,322	$1,887	$2,330	—	$106	$4,170	$3,765	$404	$152	$1,424
1980	10,275	2,928	6,932	—	416	10,737	10,144	593	–462	4,532
1990	46,138	11,494	33,210	—	1,434	43,022	41,498	1,524	3,115	14,527
2000	89,239	20,515	65,561	—	3,164	88,992	87,212[9]	1,780	247	45,896
2005	152,505	35,939	115,200	—	1,366	152,735	149,820[10]	2,914	–230	16,885
2010	282,734	61,364[11]	213,709	4,493	3,168	272,224	268,710[11]	3,514	10,510	71,976
2012	290,864	66,067[11]	210,508	8,324	5,965	291,907	287,777[11]	4,130	–1,043	71,783
2013	313,158	71,300[11]	227,208	8,666	5,985	315,123	311,367[11]	3,756	–1,965	69,818
2014	334,943	75,887[11]	244,351	8,727	5,978	333,438	329,141[11]	4,297	1,504	71,323
2015	357,511	79,379[11]	263,484	8,797	5,851	359,393	355,787[11]	3,606	–1,882	69,441
2016	400,623	86,063[11]	299,491	9,755	5,315	403,877	399,456[11]	4,421	–3,254	66,187
2017	422,441	94,794[11]	309,647	11,072	6,928	414,122	409,261[11]	4,861[12]	8,319	74,506
2018	441,569	106,179[11]	316,746	11,670	6,974	414,092	409,408[11]	4,684	27,477	101,983
2019	463,569	113,507[11]	331,830	12,154	6,077	458,358	453,480[11]	4,878	5,210	107,193
2020	497,597	121,972[11]	357,467	11,720	6,439	514,798	509,599[11,13]	5,199	–17,201	89,993
2021	594,893	129,172[11]	448,194[14]	11,859	5,668	511,079	505,734[11,13]	5,345	83,814	173,807
2022	570,784	144,292[11]	406,385[14]	13,330	6,778	573,434	567,774[11,13]	5,659	–2,650	171,158
2023	611,645	149,357[11]	438,976[14]	15,106	8,206	621,621	615,671[11,13]	5,949	–9,975	161,182

— = Not applicable. **Note:** Numbers may not add up to totals because of rounding. (1) Fiscal year 1975 ended June 30, 1975; fiscal years 1980 and after ended on Sept. 30 of each year. (2) For Part D, premiums include both amounts withheld from Social Security benefits (and certain other federal benefit payments) and amounts paid directly to Part D plans (estimated). (3) For Part B, includes matching payments from the Treasury's general fund, plus certain interest-adjustment items. For Part D, includes all federal govt. transfers. (4) For full-benefit dually eligible individuals, states pay 90% of estimated costs in 2006, phasing down to 75% in 2015 and after. (5) Other income includes recoveries of amounts reimbursed from the trust fund that are not trust fund obligations and other miscellaneous income. (6) Values after 2005 include additional premiums for Medicare Advantage (MA) plans that are deducted from beneficiaries' Social Security benefits, transferred to HI and SMI trust funds, and then transferred to the plans. (7) Includes costs of Peer Review Organizations in 1983-2001 and costs of Quality Review Organizations beginning in 2002. (8) For Part D, includes payments to plans, subsidies to employer-sponsored retiree drug plans, payments to states for low-income eligibility determinations, and Part D drug premiums (the amount collected from beneficiaries and transferred to plans and an estimated amount for premiums paid directly by enrollees to plans). Includes amounts for transitional assistance benefits in 2004-06. (9) Benefit payments less monies transferred from the HI trust fund for home health agency costs. (10) Certain HI hospice costs were misallocated to, and paid from, the Part B account of the SMI trust fund. (11) Includes an estimated $4.221 bil (2010), $4.843 bil (2011), $5.222 bil (2012), $6.306 bil (2013), $7.450 bil (2014), $8.445 bil (2015), $9.084 bil (2016), $10.175 bil (2017), $10.513 bil (2018), $10.567 bil (2019), $10.464 bil (2020), $11.466 bil (2021), $12.199 bil (2022), and $12.802 bil (2023) for premiums paid directly to Part D plans. (12) Reflects a larger-than-usual and upward adjustment for the reallocation of prior-year HI and SMI expenses. (13) Includes $38.4 bil in net Part B payments made through the Medicare Accelerated and Advance Payments (AAP) Program in fiscal year 2020, in light of the COVID-19 public health emergency, and subsequent net repayments of $14.5 bil, $22.0 bil, and $1.7 bil in fiscal years 2021, 2022, and 2023, respectively. (14) Includes (i) a transfer of $37.8 bil in fiscal year 2021 from the general fund of the Treasury to the Part B account, which occurred in Nov. 2020 for the Part B outstanding balance of the Medicare AAP Program, as required by Public Law 116-159, and (ii) subsequent recoveries from Part B providers and suppliers that were transferred from Part B to the Treasury's general fund in the amounts of $8.5 bil, $26.5 bil, and $2.7 bil in fiscal years 2021, 2022, and 2023, respectively.

Hospital Insurance Trust Fund (Medicare HI), 1975-2023

Source: Centers for Medicare & Medicaid Services, U.S. Dept. of Health and Human Services

(in millions)

	INCOME								DISBURSEMENTS				
Fiscal year[1]	Total	Payroll taxes	Taxation of benefits	Transfers from Railroad Retire-ment acct.	Reimb. for uninsured persons	Premiums from voluntary enrollees	Pymts. for military wage credits	Interest and other income[2,3]	Total	Benefit pymts.[3,4]	Admin. expenses[5]	Net change	Year-end balance
1975	$12,568	$11,291	—	$132	$481	$6	$48	$609	$10,612	$10,353	$259	$1,956	$9,870
1980	25,415	23,244	—	244	697	17	141	1,072	24,288	23,790	497	1,127	14,490
1990	79,563	70,655	—	367	413	113	107	7,908	66,687	65,912	774	12,876	95,631
2000	159,681	137,738	$8,787	465	470	1,392	2	10,827	130,284	127,934[6]	2,350	29,397	168,084
2005	196,921	168,954	8,765	445	286	2,303	0	16,168	184,142	181,292[7]	2,850	12,779	277,723
2010	218,004	183,603	13,760	535	–142	3,314	0	16,933	248,978	245,650	3,328	–30,975	278,939
2012	241,730	204,752	18,643	511	262	3,400	0	14,162	258,155	254,459	3,696	–16,425	229,372
2013	243,560	212,901	14,310	577	0	3,397	0	12,375	266,546	262,411	4,135	–22,986	206,386
2014	262,753	227,579	18,066	612	432	3,259	0	12,805	266,853	262,520	4,332	–4,100	202,286
2015	272,359	237,697	20,208	595	187	3,277	0	10,396	278,736	273,248	5,488	–6,377	195,909
2016	287,106	250,472	23,022	657	158	3,232	0	9,566	290,648	285,574	5,075	–3,542	192,367
2017	298,524	259,740	24,206	637	147	3,492	0	10,302	293,265	290,279	2,986	5,259	197,626
2018	302,839	264,566	24,192	597	132	3,533	0	9,819	297,168	292,078	5,090	5,671	203,297
2019	319,256	281,441	23,781	570	127	3,823	0	9,513	323,726	318,371	5,355	–4,470	198,826
2020	336,116	295,913	26,941	606	109	3,975	0	8,571	400,646	395,823[8]	4,823	–64,530	134,296
2021	333,744	299,147	24,975	568	95	4,141	0	4,819	331,938	326,812[8]	5,126	1,806	136,102
2022	386,619	343,729	32,775	516	82	4,467	0	5,050	344,743	339,554[8]	5,189	41,876	177,979
2023	410,093	362,511	34,968	588	52	4,651	0	7,322	396,329	390,683[8]	5,646	13,764	191,743

— = Not applicable. **Note:** Numbers may not add up to totals because of rounding. (1) Fiscal year 1975 ended June 30, 1975; fiscal years 1980 and later ended Sept. 30 of each year. (2) Other income includes recoveries of amounts reimbursed from the trust fund that are not trust fund obligations, receipts from the fraud and abuse control program, and other small amounts of miscellaneous income. In 2008, includes an adjustment of –$853 mil for interest inadvertently earned as a result of HI hospice costs that were misallocated to, and paid from, the Part B account of the Supplementary Medical Insurance (SMI) trust fund from May 2005 to Sept. 2007. (3) Values after 2005 include additional premiums for Medicare Advantage (MA) plans that are deducted from beneficiaries' Social Security benefits, transferred to the HI and SMI trust funds, and then transferred to the plans. (4) Includes costs of Peer Review Organizations in 1983-2001 and costs of Quality Review Organizations beginning in 2002. (5) Includes costs of experiments and demonstration projects. Beginning in 1997, includes fraud and abuse control expenses. (6) Includes monies transferred to the SMI trust fund for home health agency costs. (7) Certain HI hospice costs were misallocated to, and paid from, the Part B account of the SMI trust fund. (8) Includes $65.5 bil in net HI payments made through the Medicare Accelerated and Advance Payments Program in fiscal year 2020, in light of the COVID-19 public health emergency, and subsequent net repayments of $21.9 bil, $40.4 bil, and $3.0 bil in fiscal years 2021, 2022, and 2023, respectively.

TAXES

Federal Personal Income Tax Return Facts, 2025

Source: Jessica A. Newport, CPA, Senior Accountant, Andrews Hooper Pavlik PLC

Deadlines. The deadline for filing a 2024 U.S. individual income tax return (Form 1040) is Apr. 15, 2025.

Extensions. Taxpayers who cannot file a 2024 individual income tax return by the deadline can apply for a six-month extension to Oct. 15, 2025. To qualify for an extension, Form 4868 must be filed no later than Apr. 15, 2025.

E-Filing. The electronic filing program began as a pilot program in 1986; by 2011, 1 bil individual tax returns had been e-filed. As of May 10, 2024, 137.4 mil returns for income tax year 2023 had been e-filed, compared to 134.9 mil as of May 12, 2023.

Penalties. The IRS can levy two potential penalties after the filing due date when there is a balance owed. One penalty is for failing to file a timely tax return; the other is for failure to pay the tax when due. In addition, interest is charged on any unpaid tax balance.

Refunds. As of May 10, 2024, the average refund for the 2024 tax filing season was $2,869, compared to $2,812 as of May 12, 2023. The IRS refunded $269.5 bil, of which $256.6 bil was refunded with direct deposit.

Statute of limitations. Taxpayers who have not yet filed their 2021 federal tax return have until three years after the deadline to file and claim their refund. After that date, any refunds for 2021 income tax or withholding tax, including the earned income tax credit, will be lost.

Federal Income Tax Rates for Taxable-Income Brackets, 2024

Tax rate	Unmarried individuals	Married filing jointly or surviving spouses	Married filing separately	Head of household other than surviving spouses
10%	$0 to $11,600	$0 to $23,200	$0 to $11,600	$0 to $16,550
12%	$11,601 to $47,150	$23,201 to $94,300	$11,601 to $47,150	$16,551 to $63,100
22%	$47,151 to $100,525	$94,301 to $201,050	$47,151 to $100,525	$63,101 to $100,500
24%	$100,526 to $191,950	$201,051 to $383,900	$100,526 to $191,950	$100,501 to $191,950
32%	$191,951 to $243,725	$383,901 to $487,450	$191,951 to $243,725	$191,951 to $243,700
35%	$243,726 to $609,350	$487,451 to $731,200	$243,726 to $365,600	$243,701 to $609,350
37%	Over $609,350	Over $731,200	Over $365,600	Over $609,350

Standard Deduction, 2024

The standard deduction is a flat amount subtracted from the adjusted gross income of taxpayers who do not itemize deductions.

Single	$14,600
Married filing jointly or qualifying widow(er) ...	$29,200
Married filing separately	$14,600
Head of household	$21,900

Additional standard deduction. Elderly and/or blind, single or head of household: $1,950. Elderly and/or blind, married or qualifying widow(er): $1,550.

Personal exemption. The deduction for personal exemptions was suspended until Jan. 1, 2026, under the Tax Cuts and Jobs Act of 2017.

FICA and Medicare tax. For Social Security, wages paid in 2024 are taxable up to $168,600. For Medicare, all wages are taxable.

Common Income Tax Errors

Periodically, the IRS issues a list of the most commonly made income tax errors.

1. Filing too early. Taxpayers should wait to file until they are certain they have received all their tax reporting documents.
2. Wrong or missing Social Security numbers.
3. Wrong names.
4. Filing status errors, such as Head of Household instead of Single.
5. Math mistakes, for example, when adding or subtracting items on a form or worksheet.
6. Errors in credits or deductions, like the Earned Income Tax Credit, Child and Dependent Care Credit, and standard deductions.
7. Wrong bank and/or account numbers for direct deposit of any tax refund.
8. Forms not signed or dated. An unsigned tax return is not valid. Both spouses must sign a joint return.
9. E-file PIN errors. E-filed returns can be signed electronically with a personal identification number (PIN). Usually, last year's PIN can be used, but if it is unknown, adjusted gross income information from last year's original return needs to be entered for verification.

Retirement Savings Plans and Income Tax

401(k) plan. The maximum amount that an individual can contribute to a 401(k) plan for 2024 is $23,000. Individuals born before 1975 can put away an additional $7,500, for a total of $30,500.

IRAs. Contributions to IRAs and Roth IRAs were limited to $7,000 in 2024. Anyone born before 1975 can contribute an extra $1,000. Funds may be deposited into a traditional IRA for 2024 until Apr. 15, 2025. Contributions after Apr. 15, 2025 will automatically be considered funds deposited for 2025.

Roth IRA. Contributions paid into a Roth IRA are not tax deductible. Distributions of funds including investment earnings held in the account for five years or longer and distributed after age 59½ are free of both income tax and the 10% early-withdrawal penalty. Withdrawals from the account in less than five years can be subject to tax and a 10% withdrawal penalty regardless of age. There are income limitations on contributions.

Distributions. There is a 10% penalty for IRA distributions before age 59½. Distributions paid to a beneficiary due to disability/death of the owner are not subject to this penalty, nor are payments used for certain unreimbursed medical expenses, higher-education expenses, or first-time home buyer acquisition costs (up to $10,000).

The owner of a traditional IRA (or a SIMPLE plan, pension, or profit-sharing plan account) must begin receiving distributions by Apr. 1 of the calendar year following the year in which he or she reaches age 72 (73 if the owner reaches age 72 after Dec. 31, 2022). Any employee who works beyond 72 (73 if the owner reaches age 72 after Dec. 31, 2022) and is not a 5% or more owner of the business can continue to defer profit-sharing and pension plan distributions.

Tax Credits

A tax deduction reduces a taxpayer's taxable income whereas tax credits reduce the amount of tax owed.

Adoption credit. The adoption credit in 2024 for qualified expenses is $16,810. The credit limit is per child and is adjusted annually for inflation. The credit is not refundable and phases out for taxpayers at higher income levels.

American Opportunity Tax Credit. This education credit provides up to $2,500 per student per year in the first four years of a student's postsecondary education.

Child and dependent care credit. This credit is for expenses for the care of taxpayers' qualifying children under age 13 or care of a disabled spouse or dependent, while the taxpayer works or looks for work.

Child tax credit. The maximum child tax credit is $2,000 for each qualifying child dependent age 16 and under. The credit is subject to income limitations.

Earned Income Credit. Lower-income workers who maintain a household may be eligible for an Earned Income Credit. This credit is based on total earned income such as wages, commissions, and tips. Military personnel can include tax-free combat pay in income to compute the credit.

Energy credits. There are many energy-related credits—from the purchase of an alternative fuel vehicle and the installation of solar/fuel cell property in a residence, to the production of biodiesel or ethanol.

Alternative Minimum Tax

The Alternative Minimum Tax (AMT) was established in 1969 to prevent individuals with very high incomes from using special tax breaks to pay little or no tax. The AMT 2024 exemption for a single taxpayer is $85,700 and $133,300 for married filing jointly. For married taxpayers filing separate returns, the exemption is $66,650.

Estate and Gift Taxes

Estate tax. The Tax Relief Act of 2010 reinstated the estate tax with a 35% flat rate and increased the exemptions to $5 mil in 2011 and $5.12 mil in 2012. The estate tax rate was increased to 40% for 2013 and subsequent years. The Tax Cuts and Jobs Act of 2017 set the 2024 exemption at $13.61 mil per person, $27.22 mil for married couples.

Gifting. For 2024 U.S. citizens, residents, and non-resident aliens have an annual gift tax exclusion of up to $18,000 per individual to as many individuals as he or she chooses. For married couples the exclusion is $36,000, even if only one spouse does all the gifting.

International property. All property owned worldwide by American citizens is subject to U.S. estate tax rules and regulations.

Resident aliens. Aliens residing in the U.S. are subject to the same rules as American citizens.

Tax Rates for Estates and Trusts

If taxable income is	The tax is
Not over $3,100	10% of the taxable income
Over $3,100 but not over $11,150	$310 plus 24% of the excess over $3,100
Over $11,150 but not over $15,200	$2,242 plus 35% of the excess over $11,150
Over $15,200	$3,660 plus 37% of the excess over $15,200

Taxable Social Security Benefits

Earnings limitations. Social Security recipients who have not reached their full retirement age of 67 in 2024 will lose $1 of their benefits for every $2 of earned income over $22,320. Recipients who reached full retirement age in 2024 will not lose any benefits if they earned $59,520 or less. Recipients will have to pay back some benefits if their income exceeded that amount.

Taxable benefits. Up to 50% of Social Security benefits may be taxable if the person's total income is more than $25,000 but less than $34,000 for a single individual, head of household, qualifying widow(er), or a married person who is filing separately if spouses lived apart all year; or more than $32,000 but less than $44,000 for married individuals filing jointly. For higher incomes, 85% of Social Security benefits may become taxable.

If the only income received during the year was Social Security, these benefits are not taxable, and the recipient probably does not have to file a tax return.

Retention of Income Tax Records

Federal tax returns generally can be audited for up to three years after filing or six years if the IRS suspects underreported income, so it's wise to keep copies of an income tax return and records for at least seven years after filing a return.

Tax Audits

Audit odds. The IRS audit rate for individual income tax returns in tax year 2021 was 0.58%. The odds of an audit generally trend upward with higher taxpayer income, especially on certain types of income. For taxpayers with incomes of $50,000-$75,000, the audit rate was 0.10%. For taxpayers with gross income of $1 mil-$5 mil, the rate was 0.50%. The audit rate was 0.20% for all incomes under $200,000.

The audit selection process is not random. It is based on a set of formulas that are designed to spot questionable returns. If the IRS concludes that a person owes more tax, and he or she disagrees with the findings, the taxpayer can meet with a supervisor.

If the taxpayer still does not agree, he or she can appeal to a separate Appeals Office or take it to the U.S. Tax Court, Federal District Court, or the U.S. Court of Federal Claims.

Tax Court. The U.S. Tax Court is a federal court where taxpayers can dispute tax deficiencies as determined by the Commissioner of Internal Revenue before payment of the disputed amounts. The Tax Court is composed of presidentially appointed members. Many taxpayers choose the Tax Court because they are not required to pay the contested tax up front.

Appeals. For more information about audits, call the IRS at (800) TAX-FORM (829-3676) for its free Publication 556, *Examination of Returns, Appeal Rights, and Claims for Refund* or visit www.irs.gov.

IRS Contact Information

Website: www.irs.gov
Tax questions: (800) 829-1040
Forms/publications: (800) TAX-FORM (829-3676)

Taxpayers can view and download tax forms and publications in Spanish from www.irs.gov/es. The IRS site also offers help in Chinese, Korean, Vietnamese, and Russian.

Hearing impaired: (800) 829-4059 (TTY/TDD)

Additional services: The Volunteer Income Tax Assistance (VITA) program offers free tax return preparation help to people who generally make $64,000 or less, persons with disabilities, and taxpayers who speak limited English. Visit www.irs.gov/individuals/free-tax-return-preparation-for-qualifying-taxpayers or (800) 906-9887.

Report wrongdoing: Report misconduct, waste, fraud, or abuse by an IRS employee to the Treasury Inspector General for Tax Administration at (800) 366-4484.

Working With a Tax Preparer

The following are some suggestions when using a tax preparer:

- **Choose** wisely. Regulations require all paid tax return preparers including attorneys, certified public accountants, and IRS-enrolled agents to have a Preparer Tax Identification Number. Check the preparer's qualifications and history. Ask about service fees in advance.
- **Review** last year's tax return. Make note of any changes since then such as marriage, divorce, number of dependents, retirement, job changes, additional income, or new deductions.
- **Organize** your records with income items first, followed by itemized deductions (medical, taxes, interest, and charitable and other miscellaneous deductions), followed by gains, losses, rentals, or other items.
- **Time** spent with your preparer may affect your bill. If you provide disorganized records and deductions, there may be an additional cost to have your tax preparer organize your information.
- **Prepare** a list of questions in advance. Ask about any invoices or bills that you are not sure apply.
- **Alert** your preparer if you're waiting to receive additional information. He or she can begin preparing your tax return and include the missing data later to finalize your return. Amending a return after it is completed may incur additional fees.
- **Review** your tax return before signing it. Ask questions about any item you don't understand. Even though your preparer is required to sign the return, you are responsible for its contents.

Total U.S. Tax Collections by Type of Tax, 1960-2023

Source: *Internal Revenue Service Data Book, 2023*, Internal Revenue Service, U.S. Dept. of the Treasury
(as percent of total gross collection or total income taxes)

Fiscal year	Total IRS collections (bil)[1]	Income taxes: Total	Business[2]	Individual[3]	Estate and trust[3]	Employment taxes[4]	Estate taxes	Gift taxes	Excise taxes[5]
1960	$92	73.1%	33.0%	67.0%	—	12.2%	1.6%	0.20%	12.9%
1965	114	69.7	32.7	67.3	—	14.9	2.1	0.25	12.9
1970	196	70.9	25.3	74.7	—	19.1	1.7	0.22	8.1
1975	294	68.8	22.6	77.4	—	23.9	1.5	0.13	5.7
1980	519	69.3	20.1	79.9	—	24.7	1.2	0.04	4.7
1985	743	63.8	16.3	83.7	—	30.3	0.8	0.04	5.0
1990	1,056	61.6	16.9	83.1	—	34.8	0.9	0.20	2.6
1995	1,376	61.8	20.5	79.5	—	33.8	1.0	0.13	3.3
2000	2,097	65.5	17.2	82.8	—	30.5	1.2	0.20	2.6
2005	2,269	62.3	21.7	78.3	—	34.0	1.0	0.09	2.5
2010	2,345	62.0	19.1	80.0	0.8%	35.1	0.7	0.12	2.0
2015	3,303	66.1	17.9	80.6	1.5	31.0	0.5	0.06	2.3
2018	3,465	64.5	11.8	86.5	1.7	32.7	0.7	0.03	2.1
2019	3,565	63.4	12.3	86.0	1.7	33.9	0.4	0.04	2.3
2020	3,493	61.1	12.3	86.1	1.6	36.3	0.5	0.03	2.1
2021	4,112	67.3	15.1	82.9	2.0	30.6	0.6	0.11	1.4
2022	4,902	69.0	14.1	83.4	2.5	28.9	0.6	0.09	1.4
2023	4,694	64.3	15.1	83.1	1.7	33.4	0.7	0.04	1.6

— = Not available. **Note:** Numbers may not add up to totals because of rounding. (1) Credits to taxpayer accounts excluded beginning with fiscal year 2009. (2) Incl. taxes on corporation income and unrelated business income from tax-exempt organizations. (3) Income tax reported for estates and trusts is included in individual income tax in FY1960-2007. Estate and trust income tax is reported separately from FY2008 on. (4) Incl. taxes for Old-Age, Survivors, Disability, and Hospital Insurance; federal unemployment insurance; and Railroad Retirement. (5) Excl. excise taxes collected by the U.S. Customs and Border Protection and the Alcohol and Tobacco Tax and Trade Bureau. The IRS collected taxes on alcohol and tobacco until FY1988 and taxes on firearms until FY1991.

Taxes Collected by State Governments, 2023

Source: Annual Survey of State Government Tax Collections, U.S. Census Bureau, U.S. Dept. of Commerce
(as percent of total taxes collected or total sales and gross receipts taxes)

State	Total taxes collected in dollars (mil)[1]	Property taxes	Sales and gross receipts taxes: Total	General	Selective[2]	License taxes[3]	Individual income taxes	Corporation net income taxes	Other taxes[4]
Alabama	$16,713.1	3.3%	47.6%	57.9%	42.1%	3.7%	35.4%	9.3%	0.7%
Alaska	3,271.4	3.9	8.9	—	100.0	3.3	—	13.6	70.2
Arizona	23,363.4	5.6	63.6	84.2	15.8	2.9	20.5	6.6	0.8
Arkansas	12,758.8	11.2	52.3	74.7	25.3	3.4	24.7	6.6	1.9
California	220,591.3	1.5	34.2	71.0	29.0	6.0	43.7	13.6	1.0
Colorado	18,131.7	—	44.0	57.7	42.3	3.7	37.4	12.9	1.9
Connecticut	21,894.7	—	39.9	63.6	36.4	1.6	40.4	16.0	2.2
Delaware	6,563.5	—	9.9	—	100.0	40.4	37.0	8.7	4.1
District of Columbia	10,337.5	29.5	23.0	80.8	19.2	2.3	29.5	10.9	4.8
Florida	61,902.7	—	80.2	80.5	19.5	3.7	—	8.9	7.2
Georgia	33,702.0	2.5	34.5	77.1	22.9	2.3	49.4	10.8	0.6
Hawaii	10,187.6	—	61.4	75.6	24.4	3.3	30.4	3.4	1.5
Idaho	7,384.9	—	50.7	81.9	18.1	6.2	29.0	14.0	0.1
Illinois	62,987.2	0.1	42.5	57.9	42.1	6.1	34.6	15.7	1.1
Indiana	30,323.4	0.1	54.4	66.7	33.3	2.9	38.6	4.1	0.0
Iowa	12,967.4	0.0	48.1	74.6	25.4	8.7	35.7	6.5	0.9
Kansas	13,139.6	6.7	43.2	76.8	23.2	3.4	34.3	11.9	0.5
Kentucky	17,217.1	4.6	48.5	68.4	31.6	3.5	35.1	7.0	1.3
Louisiana	15,498.2	0.6	51.2	60.6	39.4	4.6	30.2	7.9	5.4
Maine	6,439.6	0.7	47.5	73.9	26.1	5.0	38.5	7.0	1.3
Maryland	29,693.9	3.6	42.6	54.0	46.0	3.5	40.9	6.9	2.6
Massachusetts	41,603.1	0.0	29.9	75.3	24.7	3.2	52.7	11.0	3.3
Michigan	37,125.3	7.3	48.8	71.2	28.8	6.1	31.0	5.5	1.2
Minnesota	34,473.2	2.2	37.6	61.9	38.1	4.3	40.6	13.5	1.8
Mississippi	10,329.5	0.3	63.8	76.2	23.8	4.1	23.4	7.9	0.5
Missouri	17,355.8	0.2	40.2	70.2	29.8	4.2	50.0	5.3	0.1
Montana	4,710.1	8.3	19.6	—	100.0	10.9	48.6	6.5	6.1
Nebraska	7,326.7	0.0	46.4	80.8	19.2	2.7	41.0	9.5	0.4
Nevada	14,177.5	10.5	76.9	73.0	27.0	5.2	—	—	7.4
New Hampshire	3,546.9	8.6	29.3	—	100.0	16.2	4.2	35.8	5.8
New Jersey	51,673.4	0.0	40.2	71.0	29.0	4.5	35.8	16.8	2.6
New Mexico	14,267.4	0.8	37.2	78.8	21.2	2.4	18.5	3.1	38.0
New York	125,188.2	—	26.3	57.9	42.1	1.5	46.9	19.4	5.8
North Carolina	38,940.9	—	45.3	67.5	32.5	6.9	43.3	4.2	0.3
North Dakota	6,048.5	0.1	30.2	69.6	30.4	3.8	8.2	5.4	52.4
Ohio	38,747.0	—	65.1	65.2	34.8	5.5	29.2	0.0	0.2
Oklahoma	13,844.8	—	39.7	69.1	30.9	8.5	31.7	5.6	14.5
Oregon	20,877.7	0.1	19.6	32.8	67.2	7.5	63.6	7.8	1.5
Pennsylvania	55,074.5	0.1	49.2	56.9	43.1	5.3	30.9	10.4	4.2
Rhode Island	4,738.5	0.1	54.6	60.4	39.6	3.9	34.0	5.5	1.9
South Carolina	15,649.3	0.6	47.7	68.7	31.3	4.8	36.9	8.7	1.3
South Dakota	2,629.1	—	84.7	75.4	24.6	13.2	—	1.8	0.3
Tennessee	23,817.2	—	74.1	78.5	21.5	10.9	0.0	13.3	1.7
Texas	86,776.2	—	84.6	73.1	26.9	4.5	—	—	11.0
Utah	13,490.5	—	41.4	81.6	18.4	3.0	48.2	6.4	1.0
Vermont	4,498.7	26.9	33.2	39.2	60.8	3.3	26.9	6.7	3.0
Virginia	37,124.1	0.1	37.8	52.9	47.1	3.7	44.8	11.8	1.8
Washington	38,025.4	11.8	74.0	81.1	18.9	5.5	2.2	—	6.5
West Virginia	7,638.8	0.1	45.3	52.4	47.6	2.5	35.3	5.5	11.4
Wisconsin	23,745.9	0.4	43.6	72.0	28.0	5.5	38.7	11.2	0.5
Wyoming	3,346.9	14.3	44.7	86.7	13.3	6.6	—	—	34.5
United States	**1,431,860.0**	**1.8**	**46.4**	**69.3**	**30.7**	**4.8**	**33.0**	**10.0**	**3.9**

— = Tax not collected by state. **Note:** For fiscal year 2023 (July 1, 2022-June 30, 2023) for all states except AL and MI (ends Sept. 30), NY (Mar. 31), and TX (Aug. 31). (1) Incl. taxes not shown separately. (2) Imposed on sales of particular commodities/services, e.g., alcohol and tobacco, motor fuels, public utilities. (3) Related to the exercise of a privilege, such as owning/operating a motor vehicle. (4) Incl. death and gift taxes and severance taxes (on removal of natural resources).

State Government Personal Income Tax Rates, 2024

Source: Reproduced with permission from *CCH State Tax Guide*, published and copyrighted by CCH Inc., a Wolters Kluwer business

Alaska, Florida, Nevada, South Dakota, Texas, Washington, and **Wyoming** did not have state income taxes and are thus not listed. Tax rates apply in stages—for example, a single person in Connecticut making $60,000 in taxable income would pay 2% on the first $10,000 of income, 4.5% on the next $40,000, and 5.5% on the last $10,000. For further details on some states, see notes at end of table.

Alabama

Single, Head of household, or Married filing separately
- $0 to $500 .... 2%
- $501 to $3,000 .... 4%
- $3,001 and over 5%

Married filing jointly
- $0 to $1,000 .... 2%
- $1,001 to $6,000 .... 4%
- $6,001 and over 5%

Arizona[1]

2.5% flat tax rate

Arkansas[2]

For net income less than $89,601:
- $0 to $5,299 .... 0%
- $5,300 to $10,599 .... 2%
- $10,600 to $15,099 .... 3%
- $15,100 to $24,999 .... 3.4%
- $25,000 to $89,600 .... 3.9%

For net income greater than $89,600:
- $0 to $4,500 .... 2.0%
- $4,501 and over 3.9%

For net income over $89,600 but not over $92,700, the amount of tax is reduced by a specified bracket adjustment amount.

California[1,2]

Single or Married/registered domestic partner filing separately
- $0 to $10,756 .... 1%
- $10,757 to $25,499 .... 2%
- $25,500 to $40,245 .... 4%
- $40,246 to $55,866 .... 6%
- $55,867 to $70,606 .... 8%
- $70,607 to $360,659 .... 9.3%
- $360,660 to $432,787 .... 10.3%
- $432,788 to $721,314 .... 11.3%
- $721,315 and over 12.3%

Head of household
- $0 to $21,527 .... 1%
- $21,528 to $51,000 .... 2%
- $51,001 to $65,744 .... 4%
- $65,745 to $81,364 .... 6%
- $81,365 to $96,107 .... 8%
- $96,108 to $490,493 .... 9.3%
- $490,494 to $588,593 .... 10.3%
- $588,594 to $980,987 .... 11.3%
- $980,988 and over 12.3%

Married/registered domestic partner filing jointly or Qualifying widow(er)
- $0 to $21,512 .... 1%
- $21,513 to $50,998 .... 2%
- $50,999 to $80,490 .... 4%
- $80,491 to $111,732 .... 6%
- $111,733 to $141,212 .... 8%
- $141,213 to $721,318 .... 9.3%
- $721,319 to $865,574 .... 10.3%
- $865,575 to $1,442,628 .... 11.3%
- $1,442,629 and over 12.3%

Colorado

4.25% of federal taxable income

Connecticut

Single or Married filing separately
- $0 to $10,000 .... 2%
- $10,001 to $50,000 .... 4.5%
- $50,001 to $100,000 .... 5.5%
- $100,001 to $200,000 .... 6%
- $200,001 to $250,000 .... 6.5%
- $250,001 to $500,000 .... 6.9%
- $500,001 and over 6.99%

Head of household
- $0 to $16,000 .... 2%
- $16,001 to $80,000 .... 4.5%
- $80,001 to $160,000 .... 5.5%
- $160,001 to $320,000 .... 6%
- $320,001 to $400,000 .... 6.5%
- $400,001 to $800,000 .... 6.9%
- $800,001 and over 6.99%

Married filing jointly or Qualifying widow(er)
- $0 to $20,000 .... 2%
- $20,001 to $100,000 .... 4.5%
- $100,001 to $200,000 .... 5.5%
- $200,001 to $400,000 .... 6%
- $400,001 to $500,000 .... 6.5%
- $500,001 to $1,000,000 .... 6.9%
- $1,000,001 and over 6.99%

Delaware
- $0 to $2,000 .... 0%
- $2,001 to $5,000 .... 2.2%
- $5,001 to $10,000 .... 3.9%
- $10,001 to $20,000 .... 4.8%
- $20,001 to $25,000 .... 5.2%
- $25,001 to $60,000 .... 5.55%
- $60,001 and over 6.6%

District of Columbia
- $0 to $10,000 .... 4%
- $10,001 to $40,000 .... 6%
- $40,001 to $60,000 .... 6.5%
- $60,001 to $250,000 .... 8.5%
- $250,001 to $500,000 .... 9.25%
- $500,001 to $1,000,000 .... 9.75%
- $1,000,001 and over 10.75%

Georgia

5.39% of Georgia taxable net income

Hawaii

Single or Married filing separately
- $0 to $2,400 .... 1.4%
- $2,401 to $4,800 .... 3.2%
- $4,801 to $9,600 .... 5.5%
- $9,601 to $14,400 .... 6.4%
- $14,401 to $19,200 .... 6.8%
- $19,201 to $24,000 .... 7.2%
- $24,001 to $36,000 .... 7.6%
- $36,001 to $48,000 .... 7.9%
- $48,001 to $150,000 .... 8.25%
- $150,001 to $175,000 .... 9%
- $175,001 to $200,000 .... 10%
- $200,001 and over 11%

Head of household
- $0 to $3,600 .... 1.4%
- $3,601 to $7,200 .... 3.2%
- $7,201 to $14,400 .... 5.5%
- $14,401 to $21,600 .... 6.4%
- $21,601 to $28,800 .... 6.8%
- $28,801 to $36,000 .... 7.2%
- $36,001 to $54,000 .... 7.6%
- $54,001 to $72,000 .... 7.9%
- $72,001 to $225,000 .... 8.25%
- $225,001 to $262,500 .... 9%
- $262,501 to $300,000 .... 10%
- $300,001 and over 11%

Married filing jointly or Surviving spouse
- $0 to $4,800 .... 1.4%
- $4,801 to $9,600 .... 3.2%
- $9,601 to $19,200 .... 5.5%
- $19,201 to $28,800 .... 6.4%
- $28,801 to $38,400 .... 6.8%
- $38,401 to $48,000 .... 7.2%
- $48,001 to $72,000 .... 7.6%
- $72,001 to $96,000 .... 7.9%
- $96,001 to $300,000 .... 8.25%
- $300,001 to $350,000 .... 9%
- $350,001 to $400,000 .... 10%
- $400,001 and over 11%

Idaho[1,2,3]

Single
- 5.695% of taxable income over $2,500

Married filing jointly
- 5.695% of taxable income over $5,000

Illinois

4.95% of federal AGI

Indiana

3.05% of AGI

Iowa[2]

Single, Head of household, or Married filing separately
- $0 to $6,210 .... 4.4%
- $6,211 to $31,050 .... 4.82%
- $31,051 and over 5.7%

Married filing jointly
- $0 to $12,420 .... 4.4%
- $12,421 to $62,100 .... 4.82%
- $62,101 and over 5.7%

Kansas

Single, Head of household, or Married filing separately
- $0 to $23,000 .... 5.2%
- $23,001 and over 5.58%

Married filing jointly
- $0 to $46,000 .... 5.2%
- $46,001 and over 5.58%

Kentucky

4% of taxable income

Louisiana[1]

Single, Head of household, or Married filing separately
- $0 to $12,500 .... 1.85%
- $12,501 to $50,000 .... 3.5%
- $50,001 and over 4.25%

Married filing jointly
- $0 to $25,000 .... 1.85%
- $25,001 to $100,000 .... 3.5%
- $100,001 and over 4.25%

Maine[2,3]

Single or Married filing separately
- $0 to $24,499 .... 5.8%
- $24,500 to $58,049 .... 6.75%
- $58,050 and over 7.15%

Head of household
- $0 to $36,749 .... 5.8%
- $36,750 to $87,099 .... 6.75%
- $87,100 and over 7.15%

Married filing jointly or Surviving spouse
- $0 to $49,049 .... 5.8%
- $49,050 to $116,099 .... 6.75%
- $116,100 and over 7.15%

Maryland

Single, Married filing separately, or Dependent taxpayer
- $0 to $1,000 .... 2%
- $1,001 to $2,000 .... 3%
- $2,001 to $3,000 .... 4%
- $3,001 to $100,000 .... 4.75%
- $100,001 to $125,000 .... 5%
- $125,001 to $150,000 .... 5.25%
- $150,001 to $250,000 .... 5.5%
- $250,001 and over 5.75%

Head of household, Married filing jointly, or Qualifying widow(er)
- $0 to $1,000 .... 2%
- $1,001 to $2,000 .... 3%
- $2,001 to $3,000 .... 4%
- $3,001 to $150,000 .... 4.75%
- $150,001 to $175,000 .... 5%
- $175,001 to $225,000 .... 5.25%
- $225,001 to $300,000 .... 5.5%
- $300,001 and over 5.75%

Massachusetts
- Part A income (short-term capital gains) 8.5%
- Part A income (long term capital gains from collectibles and pre-1996 installment sales) 12%
- Part A income (interest and dividends) 5%
- Part B income 5%
- Part C income 5%

Michigan

4.25% of taxable income

Minnesota[2]

Single
- $0 to $31,690 .... 5.35%
- $31,691 to $104,090 .... 6.8%
- $104,091 to $193,240 .... 7.85%
- $193,241 and over 9.85%

Head of household
- $0 to $39,010 .... 5.35%
- $39,011 to $156,760 .... 6.8%
- $156,761 to $256,880 .... 7.85%
- $256,881and over 9.85%

Married filing jointly
- $0 to $46,330 .... 5.35%
- $46,331 to $184,040 .... 6.8%
- $184,041 to $321,450 .... 7.85%
- $321,451 and over 9.85%

Married filing separately
- $0 to $23,165 .... 5.35%
- $23,166 to $92,020 .... 6.8%
- $92,021 to $160,725 .... 7.85%
- $160,726 and over 9.85%

Mississippi

4.7% on taxable income over $10,000

Missouri[2,3]
- $0 to $1,207 .... 0%
- $1,208 to $2,414 .... 2%
- $2,415 to $3,621 .... 2.5%
- $3,622 to $4,828 .... 3%
- $4,829 to $6,035 .... 3.5%
- $6,036 to $7,242 .... 4%
- $7,243 to $8,449 .... 4.5%
- $8,450 and over 4.95%

Montana[2]

Single or Married filing separately

$0 to $20,500 .... 4.7%
$20,501 and over 5.9%

Head of household

$0 to $30,750 .... 4.7%
$30,751 and over 5.9%

Married filing jointly or Surviving spouse

$0 to $41,000 .... 4.7%
$41,001 and over 5.9%

Nebraska[2]

Single or Married filing separately

$0 to $3,900 .... 2.46%
$3,901 to $23,370 ...... 3.51%
$23,371 to $37,670 ..... 5.01%
$37,671 and over 5.84%

Head of household

$0 to $7,270 .... 2.46%
$7,271 to $37,400 ...... 3.51%
$37,401 to $55,850 ..... 5.01%
$55,851 and over 5.84%

Married filing jointly or Surviving spouse

$0 to $7,790 .... 2.46%
$7,791 to $46,760 ...... 3.51%
$46,761 to $75,340 ..... 5.01%
$75,341 and over 5.84%

New Hampshire

3% on interest and dividends only

New Jersey

Single or Married/civil-union partner filing separately

$0 to $20,000 .... 1.4%
$20,001 to $35,000 ..... 1.75%
$35,001 to $40,000 ...... 3.5%
$40,001 to $75,000 .... 5.525%
$75,001 to $500,000 .... 6.37%
$500,001 to $1,000,000 .. 8.97%
$1,000,001 and over .. 10.750%

Head of household, Married/civil-union couple filing jointly, or Qualifying widow(er)/Surviving civil-union partner

$0 to $20,000 .... 1.4%
$20,001 to $50,000 ..... 1.75%
$50,001 to $70,000 ..... 2.45%
$70,001 to $80,000 ...... 3.5%
$80,001 to $150,000 ... 5.525%
$150,001 to $500,000 ... 6.37%
$500,001 to $1,000,000 .. 8.97%
$1,000,001 and over .. 10.750%

New Mexico[1]

Single

$0 to $5,500 .... 1.7%
$5,501 to $11,000 .... 3.2%
$11,001 to $16,000 ...... 4.7%
$16,001 to $210,000 ..... 4.9%
$210,001 and over 5.9%

Head of household, Married filing jointly, or Qualifying widow(er)

$0 to $8,000 .... 1.7%
$8,001 to $16,000 ...... 3.2%
$16,001 to $24,000 ..... 4.7%
$24,001 to $315,000 .... 4.9%
$315,001 and over 5.9%

Married filing separately

$0 to $4,000 .... 1.7%
$4,001 to $8,000 .... 3.2%
$8,001 to $12,000 ...... 4.7%
$12,001 to $157,500 .... 4.9%
$157,501 and over 5.9%

New York

Single or Married filing separately

$0 to $8,500 .... 4%
$8,501 to $11,700 ...... 4.5%
$11,701 to $13,900 ..... 5.25%
$13,901 to $80,650 ...... 5.5%
$80,651 to $215,400 .... 6%
$215,401 to $1,077,550 .. 6.85%
$1,077,551 to $5,000,000 9.65%
$5,000,001 to $25,000,000 10.3%
$25,000,001 and over ... 10.9%

Head of household

$0 to $12,800 .... 4%
$12,801 to $17,650 ...... 4.5%
$17,651 to $20,900 ..... 5.25%
$20,901 to $107,650 ..... 5.5%
$107,651 to $269,300 ...... 6%
$269,301 to $1,616,450 .. 6.85%
$1,616,451 to $5,000,000 9.65%
$5,000,001 to $25,000,000 10.3%
$25,000,001 and over ... 10.9%

Married filing jointly or Qualifying widow(er)

$0 to $17,150 .... 4%
$17,151 to $23,600 ...... 4.5%
$23,601 to $27,900 ..... 5.25%
$27,901 to $161,550 ..... 5.5%
$161,551 to $323,200 ...... 6%
$323,201 to $2,155,350 .. 6.85%
$2,155,351 to $5,000,000 9.65%
$5,000,001 to $25,000,000 10.3%
$25,000,001 and over ... 10.9%

North Carolina

4.5% on state taxable income

North Dakota[2]

Single

$0 to $47,150 .... 0%
$47,151 to $238,200 .... 1.95%
$238,201 and over 2.5%

Head of household

$0 to $63,175 .... 0%
$63,176 to $264,100 .... 1.95%
$264,101 and over 2.5%

Married filing jointly or Surviving spouse

$0 to $78,775 .... 0%
$78,776 to $289,975 ... 1.95%
$289,976 and over 2.5%

Married filing separately

$0 to $39,375 .... 0%
$39,376 to $144,975 .... 1.95%
$144,976 and over 2.5%

Ohio

$26,051 to $100,000 ... 2.75%
$100,001 and over 3.5%

Oklahoma

Single or Married filing separately

$0 to $1,000 .... 0.25%
$1,001 to $2,500 .... 0.75%
$2,501 to $3,750 .... 1.75%
$3,751 to $4,900 .... 2.75%
$4,901 to $7,200 .... 3.75%
$7,201 and over 4.75%

Head of household, Married filing jointly, or Qualifying widow(er)

$0 to $2,000 .... 0.25%
$2,001 to $5,000 .... 0.75%
$5,001 to $7,500 .... 1.75%
$7,501 to $9,800 .... 2.75%
$9,801 to $14,400 ...... 3.75%
$14,401 and over 4.75%

Oregon[2,3]

Single or Married filing separately

$0 to $4,050 .... 4.75%
$4,051 to $10,200 ...... 6.75%
$10,201 to $125,000 .... 8.75%
$125,001 and over 9.9%

Married filing jointly, Head of household, or Qualifying widow(er)

$0 to $8,100 .... 4.75%
$8,101 to $20,400 ...... 6.75%
$20,401 to $250,000 .... 8.75%
$250,001 and over 9.9%

Pennsylvania

3.07% of taxable compensation, net profits, net gains from the sale of property, rent, royalties, patents or copyrights, income from estates or trusts, dividends, interest, and winnings

Rhode Island[2]

$0 to $77,450 .... 3.75%
$77,451 to $176,050 .... 4.75%
$176,051 and over 5.99%

South Carolina[2]

$0 to $3,459 .... 0%
$3,460 to $17,329 .... 3%
$17,330 and over 6.2%

Tennessee

0% on interest and dividend income of individuals as of tax year 2021

Utah

4.55% on state taxable income

Vermont[2]

Single

$0 to $47,900 .... 3.35%
$47,901 to $116,000 ..... 6.6%
$116,001 to $242,000 ... 7.6%
$242,001 and over 8.75%

Head of household

$0 to $64,150 .... 3.35%
$64,151 to $165,700 ..... 6.6%
$165,701 to $268,350 .... 7.6%
$268,351 and over 8.75%

Married or Civil union filing jointly

$0 to $79,950 .... 3.35%
$79,951 to $193,350 ..... 6.6%
$193,351 to $294,650 .... 7.6%
$294,651 and over 8.75%

Married or Civil union filing separately

$0 to $39,975 .... 3.35%
$39,976 to $96,675 ...... 6.6%
$96,676 to $147,325 ..... 7.6%
$147,326 and over 8.75%

Virginia

$0 to $3,000 .... 2%
$3,001 to $5,000 .... 3%
$5,001 to $17,000 .... 5%
$17,001 and over 5.75%

West Virginia

Single, Head of household, Married filing jointly, or Widow(er) with dependent child

$0 to $10,000 .... 2.36%
$10,001 to $25,000 ..... 3.15%
$25,001 to $40,000 ..... 3.54%
$40,001 to $60,000 ..... 4.72%
$60,001 and over 5.12%

Married filing separately

$0 to $5,000 .... 2.36%
$5,001 to $12,500 ...... 3.15%
$12,501 to $20,000 ..... 3.54%
$20,001 to $30,000 ..... 4.72%
$30,001 and over 5.12%

Wisconsin[1,2]

Single or Head of household

$0 to $14,320 .... 3.5%
$14,321 to $28,640 ...... 4.4%
$28,641 to $315,310 .... 5.30%
$315,311 and over 7.65%

Married filing jointly

$0 to $19,090 .... 3.5%
$19,091 to $38,190 ...... 4.4%
$38,191 to $420,420 .... 5.30%
$420,421 and over 7.65%

Married filing separately

$0 to $9,550 .... 3.5%
$9,551 to $19,090 .... 4.4%
$19,091 to $210,210 .... 5.30%
$210,211 and over 7.65%

AGI = Adjusted gross income; AMT = Alternative minimum tax. (1) Community property state in which, in general, one-half of the community income is taxable to each spouse. (2) Brackets indexed for inflation annually. (3) 2024 adjusted brackets were not available. Bracketed rates listed are for 2023. Other notes, by state: **California:** An additional 1% tax is imposed on taxable income in excess of $1 mil. **Colorado:** Individual taxpayers are subject to an AMT equal to the amount by which 3.47% of their Colorado alternative minimum taxable income exceeds their Colorado normal tax. **Connecticut:** Resident estates and trusts are subject to a 6.99% rate on all income. **Illinois:** Surcharge is imposed on income from the sale or exchange of certain assets. **Indiana:** Counties may impose an AGI tax on residents or on nonresidents, or a county option income tax. **Massachusetts:** An additional 4% tax is imposed on taxable income in excess of $1 mil. Part A income represents either interest and dividends or short-term capital gains, long-term capital gains from collectibles, and long-term capital gains from pre-1996 installment sales. Part B income represents wages, salaries, tips, pensions, business income, rents, etc. Part C income represents gains from the sale of capital assets held for more than one year. 5.85% optional rate may be elected for Part A interest and dividend income, Part B income after exemptions, and Part C income. **Minnesota:** A 6.75% AMT is imposed. **New Mexico:** Qualified nonresident taxpayers may pay an alternative tax of 0.75% of gross receipts from sales in New Mexico. **New York:** A supplemental tax is imposed to recapture the tax table benefit. **Vermont:** The tax amount is increased by 24% for certain items.

EDUCATION STATISTICS

U.S. Public Schools: Students, Staff, Spending, 1899-2022

Source: National Center for Education Statistics, U.S. Dept. of Education

	1899-1900	1919-20	1939-40	1959-60	1979-80	1999-2000	2009-10	2019-20	2021-22[1]
Population (thous.)									
Total U.S. population[2]	75,995	104,514	131,028	177,830	225,055	279,040	306,772	328,330	331,894
Population 5-17 years of age	21,573	27,571	30,151	43,881	48,043	52,811	53,890	53,517	54,739
Percentage 5-17 years of age	28.4%	26.4%	23.0%	24.7%	21.3%	18.9%	17.6%	16.3%	16.5%
Enrollment (thous.)									
Elementary and secondary[3]	15,503	21,578	25,434	35,182	41,651	46,857	49,361	50,796	49,433
Prekindergarten through grade 8	14,984	19,378	18,832	26,911	28,034	33,486	34,409	35,551	33,998
Grades 9-12	519	2,200	6,601	8,271	13,616	13,371	14,952	15,246	15,436
Percent of pop. ages 5-17 enrolled	71.9%	78.3%	84.4%	80.2%	86.7%	88.7%	91.6%	94.9%	90.3%
Grades 9-12 as percent of all enrolled	3.3%	10.2%	26.0%	23.5%	32.7%	28.5%	30.3%	30.0%	31.2%
High school graduates	62	231	1,143	1,627	2,748	2,554	3,128	3,371	3,420
Instructional staff (thous.)									
Total instructional staff	*	678	912	1,449	2,406	3,819	4,279	4,434	4,419
Teachers, librarians, and other nonsupervisory instructional staff	423	657	875	1,385	2,300	3,682	4,111	4,240	4,225
Revenue and expenditures (mil)									
Total revenue	$220	$970	$2,261	$14,747	$96,881	$372,944	$599,929	$794,568	$909,221
Total expenditures	215	1,036	2,344	15,613	95,962	381,838	608,065	793,719	880,677
Current expenditures[4]	180	861	1,942	12,329	86,984	323,889	518,886	682,217	767,840
Capital outlay	35	154	258	2,662	6,506	43,357	59,843	81,335	81,745
Interest on school debt	*	18	131	490	1,874	9,135	17,720	21,428	21,507
Other programs[5]	*	3	13	133	598	5,457	NA	8,739	9,585
Salaries and pupil cost									
Avg. annual salary of instruct. staff[6]	$325	$871	$1,441	$4,995	$15,970	$41,807	$55,370	$64,172	$66,397
Expenditure per capita total pop.	3	10	18	88	426	1,368	1,982	2,417	2,653
Current expenditure per pupil ADA[4]	17	53	88	375	2,272	7,394	11,427	14,427	16,190

* = Data not collected. NA = Not available. ADA = Average daily attendance. **Note:** Because of rounding, details may not add up to totals. Prior to 1959-60, data do not include Alaska and Hawaii. (1) Revenues and expenditures are provisional data; high school graduates, and expenditure per pupil ADA are projected. (2) Data for 1899-1900 are based on total population from the decennial census. From 1919-20 to 1959-60, total population includes armed forces overseas, as of July 1 preceding the school year. Data for later years are for resident population excluding armed forces overseas. (3) Data for 1899-1940 are school year enrollment; data for later years are fall enrollment. (4) Because of changes in the definition of "current expenditures," data for 1959-60 and later years are not entirely comparable with prior years. (5) Incl. expenditures for community services, adult education, community colleges, private schools, and other progs. not part of public and secondary education. (6) Data prior to 1959-60 include supervisors, principals, teachers, and nonsupervisory instructional staff.

U.S. Public High School Graduation Rates, 2021-22

Source: National Center for Education Statistics, U.S. Dept. of Education

State	Rate[1]	Rank	State	Rate[1]	Rank	State	Rate[1]	Rank	State	Rate[1]	Rank
Alabama	88.2%	13	Illinois	87.3%	19	Montana	85.8%	30	Rhode Island	83.3%	37
Alaska	77.8	47	Indiana	87.7	17	Nebraska	87.1	21	South Carolina	83.8	34
Arizona	77.3	48	Iowa	89.9	6	Nevada	81.7	43	South Dakota	82.1	41
Arkansas	88.2	13	Kansas	89.1	9	New Hampshire	87.7	17	Tennessee	90.4	2
California	87.0	22	Kentucky	90.1	4	New Jersey	85.2	31	Texas	89.7	8
Colorado	82.3	40	Louisiana	83.1	38	New Mexico	—	—	Utah	88.2	13
Connecticut	88.9	11	Maine	86.1	28	New York	86.7	24	Vermont	82.8	39
Delaware	87.8	16	Maryland	86.3	26	North Carolina	86.4	25	Virginia	89.1	9
Dist. of Columbia	76.4	49	Massachusetts	90.1	4	North Dakota	85.1	32	Washington	83.6	35
Florida	87.3	19	Michigan	81.0	45	Ohio	86.2	27	West Virginia	91.2	1
Georgia	84.1	33	Minnesota	83.6	35	Oklahoma	—	—	Wisconsin	90.3	3
Hawaii	86.0	29	Mississippi	88.9	11	Oregon	81.3	44	Wyoming	81.8	42
Idaho	79.9	46	Missouri	89.8	7	Pennsylvania	87.0	22	**Total U.S.**	**86.6**	—

— Not available or applicable. (1) The 4-year adjusted cohort graduation rate (ACGR) is the number of students who graduate in 4 years with a regular high school diploma divided by the number of students who form the adjusted cohort for the graduating class. From the beginning of 9th grade (or the earliest high school grade), students who are entering that grade for the first time form a cohort that is "adjusted" by adding any students who subsequently transfer into the cohort and subtracting any students who subsequently transfer out, emigrate to another country, or die.

High School Dropouts by Sex, Race, and Ethnicity, 1960-2022

Source: National Center for Education Statistics, U.S. Dept. of Education

(data for Oct. of year shown unless otherwise noted)

	Total dropout rate				Male dropout rate				Female dropout rate			
Year[1]	All races[2]	White	Black	Hispanic	All races[2]	White	Black	Hispanic	All races[2]	White	Black	Hispanic
1960[3]	27.2%	NA	NA	NA	27.8%	NA	NA	NA	26.7%	NA	NA	NA
1970[4]	15.0	13.2%	27.9%	NA	14.2	12.2%	29.4%	NA	15.7	14.1%	26.6%	NA
1980	14.1	11.4	19.1	35.2%	15.1	12.3	20.8	37.2%	13.1	10.5	17.7	33.2%
1990	12.1	9.0	13.2	32.4	12.3	9.3	11.9	34.3	11.8	8.7	14.4	30.3
2000	10.9	6.9	13.1	27.8	12.0	7.0	15.3	31.8	9.9	6.9	11.1	23.5
2005	9.4	6.0	10.4	22.4	10.8	6.6	12.0	26.4	8.0	5.3	9.0	18.1
2010	7.4	5.1	8.0	15.1	8.5	5.9	9.5	17.3	6.3	4.2	6.7	12.8
2015	5.9	4.6	6.5	9.2	6.3	5.0	6.4	9.9	5.4	4.1	6.5	8.4
2017	5.8	4.6	5.7	9.5	6.6	5.0	7.0	11.5	5.0	4.3	4.4	7.4
2019	5.2	4.5	5.6	7.5	5.9	5.3	6.6	7.8	4.6	3.8	4.6	7.1
2020	5.3	4.8	4.2	7.4	6.2	5.4	5.6	8.9	4.4	4.1	2.9	5.9
2021	5.1	4.4	3.9	8.2	5.7	4.7	4.6	9.2	4.6	4.2	3.3	7.2
2022	5.0	4.1	5.7	7.0	5.5	4.4	5.1	8.7	4.4	3.8	6.2	5.2

NA = Not available. **Note:** Table shows "status" dropouts, defined as 16- to 24-year-olds who are not enrolled in school and who have not completed a high school program, regardless of when they left school. People who have received GED credentials are not shown. Excludes persons in the military and persons living in institutions (e.g., prisons or nursing facilities). Race categories exclude persons of Hispanic ethnicity unless otherwise noted. (1) Because of changes in data collection procedures, data for years prior to 1992 may not be comparable to later years. For 2005 and after, white and Black data exclude persons identifying themselves as being of two or more races. (2) Includes other racial/ethnic groups not separately shown. (3) Based on the Apr. 1960 decennial census. (4) White and Black data include persons of Hispanic ethnicity.

Overview of U.S. Public Schools, 2022-23

Source: National Center for Education Statistics, U.S. Dept. of Education; National Education Association (NEA)

State	Local school districts	Elementary schools[1]	Middle schools[1]	Secondary schools[1]	Classroom teachers	Total enrollment[2]	Pupils per teacher	Teachers' avg. pay	Expend. per pupil[2]
AL	149	702	261	411	47,386	727,685	15.4	$60,441	$12,536
AK	54	172	38	76	7,030	131,212	18.7	76,371	20,535
AZ	660	1,232	238	768	49,565	1,132,361	22.8	60,275	11,321
AR	259	510	209	331	31,138	476,318	15.3	54,309	12,482
CA	1,018	5,972	1,394	2,234	292,378	5,852,544	20.0	95,160	17,869
CO	185	1,052	291	442	58,083	883,264	15.2	60,775	15,751
CT	201	600	181	196	42,184	513,513	12.2	83,400	24,053
DE	45	118	38	44	10,144	141,729	14.0	68,787	17,048
DC	70	145	41	42	8,052	91,001	11.3	84,882	26,766
FL	75	2,232	587	922	138,399	2,870,507	20.7	53,098	12,488
GA	226	1,310	482	487	120,414	1,750,888	14.5	64,461	14,083
HI	1	184	42	43	10,969	170,209	15.5	70,947	20,040
ID	183	389	115	212	17,922	318,979	17.8	56,365	9,599
IL	852	2,343	717	967	134,897	1,859,663	13.8	73,916	20,861
IN	417	1,062	334	426	61,323	1,034,151	16.9	57,015	12,732
IA	328	685	250	343	38,190	511,327	13.4	61,231	13,366
KS	286	724	225	371	34,821	490,483	14.1	56,481	14,221
KY	171	725	221	436	40,180	660,029	16.4	56,296	13,599
LA	169	718	224	284	48,299	685,606	14.2	54,248	16,297
ME	205	354	85	118	14,714	173,931	11.8	59,964	20,838
MD	24	887	228	243	62,686	889,971	14.2	79,420	18,018
MA	398	1,050	319	375	76,978	912,117	11.8	92,307	23,941
MI	832	1,660	507	1,001	82,718	1,383,889	16.7	67,011	14,289
MN	559	1,036	346	1,001	57,057	870,019	15.2	70,005	16,460
MS	152	442	184	321	32,092	440,285	13.7	53,354	12,258
MO	556	1,221	394	667	73,653	861,535	11.7	53,999	13,414
MT	401	429	225	173	11,036	150,573	13.6	55,909	14,042
NE	244	540	138	318	24,929	309,709	12.4	58,763	15,329
NV	20	433	119	147	19,059	484,240	25.4	61,719	11,516
NH	168	285	99	97	15,609	167,298	10.7	64,169	21,082
NJ	691	1,508	436	489	116,698	1,371,921	11.8	81,102	24,719
NM	89	459	165	223	23,094	316,660	13.7	63,580	13,424
NY	731	2,555	798	1,205	215,761	2,403,931	11.1	92,696	30,867
NC	115	1,495	487	601	92,681	1,379,811	14.9	56,559	13,173
ND	168	276	45	175	9,244	115,385	12.5	56,792	16,970
OH	989	1,767	673	937	102,323	1,756,830	17.2	66,390	15,059
OK	509	930	369	478	42,763	701,258	16.4	55,505	11,089
OR	222	716	207	271	31,781	552,380	17.4	72,476	15,773
PA	789	1,639	523	716	122,324	1,686,844	13.8	74,945	20,264
RI	66	176	59	67	10,785	137,452	12.7	79,289	20,754
SC	82	688	251	299	54,569	789,231	14.5	57,778	13,488
SD	149	333	174	199	10,038	138,075	13.8	53,153	12,549
TN	146	1,025	346	420	65,781	968,313	14.7	55,369	12,111
TX	1,209	4,729	1,767	2,100	371,802	5,518,432	14.8	60,716	11,833
UT	157	635	145	207	31,087	691,075	22.2	63,481	10,282
VT	184	207	27	63	7,924	83,654	10.6	66,536	26,749
VA	131	1,147	348	328	105,025	1,247,121	11.9	63,103	16,177
WA	318	1,226	378	653	63,629	1,065,190	16.7	86,804	19,427
WV	59	409	110	163	19,250	250,049	13.0	52,870	15,370
WI	449	1,127	400	563	56,429	822,804	14.6	62,524	15,654
WY	48	191	60	89	7,277	91,640	12.6	61,979	19,622
Total U.S.	**16,209**	**52,450**	**16,300**	**23,742**	**3,222,170**	**49,033,092**	**15.2**	**69,544**	**16,281**

(1) 2021-22 estimates. (2) Fall enrollment.

Mathematics and Reading Scores of U.S. Students, 1971-2023

Source: National Assessment of Educational Progress, National Center for Education Statistics (NCES), U.S. Dept. of Education

Average scores for 9-year-olds in 2022 declined 5 points in reading and 7 points in mathematics compared to 2020. Average scores for 13-year-olds in 2023 declined 4 points in reading and 9 points in math compared to 2020.

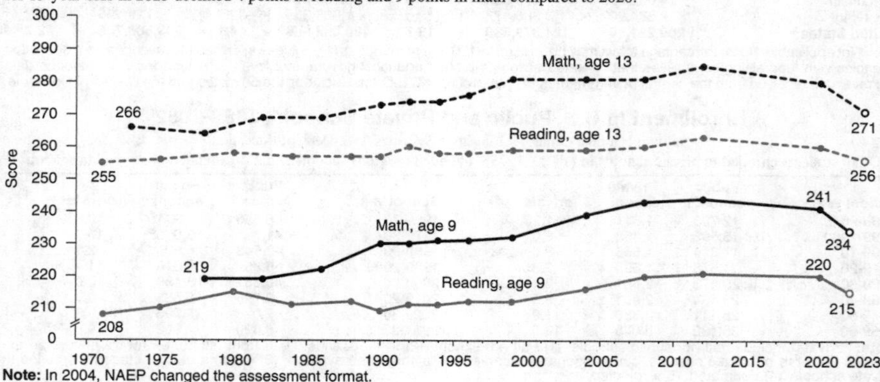

Note: In 2004, NAEP changed the assessment format.

Revenues for Public Elementary and Secondary Schools by State, 2021-22

Source: National Center for Education Statistics, U.S. Dept. of Education; amounts in thousands

		Federal		State		Local and intermediate[1]	
State/territory	Total	Amount	% of tot. rev.	Amount	% of tot. rev.	Amount	% of tot. rev.
Alabama	$10,792,202	$1,931,155	17.9%	$5,556,327	51.5%	$3,304,721	30.6%
Alaska	2,773,741	574,870	20.7	1,604,694	57.9	594,177	21.4
American Samoa	167,604	144,056	86.0	23,548[2]	14.0	0	0.0
Arizona	14,672,339	2,784,806	19.0	7,011,647	47.8	4,875,885	33.2
Arkansas	6,651,819	1,433,935	21.6	2,856,142	42.9	2,361,743	35.5
California	121,355,886	16,847,268	13.9	66,101,993	54.5	38,406,625	31.6
Colorado	14,420,051	1,520,172	10.5	5,679,461	39.4	7,220,419	50.1
Connecticut	13,239,291	1,087,244	8.2	4,771,384	36.0	7,380,663	55.7
Delaware	2,865,156	377,366	13.2	1,646,054	57.5	841,735	29.4
District of Columbia	2,929,959	388,612	13.3	NA	NA	2,541,347	86.7
Florida	39,273,621	6,718,759	17.1	14,045,015	35.8	18,509,848	47.1
Georgia	28,379,630	4,565,056	16.1	11,464,480	40.4	12,350,094	43.5
Guam	389,230	162,268	41.7	NA	NA	226,961	58.3
Hawaii	3,564,706	517,246	14.5	3,019,578	84.7	27,882	0.8
Idaho	3,625,661	660,819	18.2	2,201,523	60.7	763,320	21.1
Illinois	43,096,693	4,572,058	10.6	14,935,423	34.7	23,589,212	54.7
Indiana	15,704,938	2,035,177	13.0	9,081,115	57.8	4,588,646	29.2
Iowa	8,323,604	1,131,442	13.6	4,155,915	49.9	3,036,246	36.5
Kansas	7,772,650	772,764	9.9	5,040,683	64.9	1,959,204	25.2
Kentucky	10,484,757	2,098,713	20.0	4,922,194	46.9	3,463,850	33.0
Louisiana	11,578,806	2,252,851	19.5	4,248,786	36.7	5,077,170	43.8
Maine	3,572,182	360,138	10.1	1,475,710	41.3	1,736,335	48.6
Maryland	18,821,341	2,140,259	11.4	7,704,198	40.9	8,976,883	47.7
Massachusetts	21,970,717	2,138,805	9.7	8,441,887	38.4	11,390,024	51.8
Michigan	25,399,046	3,730,050	14.7	14,123,026	55.6	7,545,970	29.7
Minnesota	16,201,682	1,961,992	12.1	9,930,488	61.3	4,309,202	26.6
Mississippi	5,798,181	1,345,720	23.2	2,557,895	44.1	1,894,566	32.7
Missouri	14,094,582	2,120,955	15.0	3,971,830	28.2	8,001,797	56.8
Montana	2,362,676	498,309	21.1	942,787	39.9	921,580	39.0
Nebraska	5,357,134	663,676	12.4	1,605,972	30.0	3,087,486	57.6
Nevada	6,734,655	1,092,504	16.2	4,605,898	68.4	1,036,254	15.4
New Hampshire	3,646,234	323,491	8.9	1,072,086	29.4	2,250,656	61.7
New Jersey	39,545,314	3,063,098	7.7	18,279,946	46.2	18,202,270	46.0
New Mexico	5,353,522	914,876	17.1	3,472,738	64.9	965,909	18.0
New York	84,359,192	6,179,944	7.3	30,084,073	35.7	48,095,175	57.0
North Carolina	19,783,607	3,938,564	19.9	11,212,921	56.7	4,632,121	23.4
North Dakota	2,208,876	413,225	18.7	1,082,225	49.0	713,426	32.3
Northern Mariana Islands	131,445	106,887	81.3	24,558[2]	18.7	0	0.0
Ohio	29,997,293	4,378,599	14.6	10,886,151	36.3	14,732,542	49.1
Oklahoma	8,913,854	1,730,723	19.4	3,921,713	44.0	3,261,418	36.6
Oregon	10,707,493	1,159,893	10.8	5,628,093	52.6	3,919,507	36.6
Pennsylvania	38,213,766	5,204,437	13.6	13,405,446	35.1	19,603,882	51.3
Puerto Rico	2,705,072	1,303,342	48.2	1,401,671[2]	51.8	59	0.0
Rhode Island	3,077,564	379,005	12.3	1,292,244	42.0	1,406,315	45.7
South Carolina	13,474,785	2,043,698	15.2	6,184,537	45.9	5,246,550	38.9
South Dakota	2,011,553	438,813	21.8	618,551	30.7	954,190	47.4
Tennessee	13,314,504	2,561,387	19.2	5,492,640	41.3	5,260,478	39.5
Texas	79,559,851	14,589,067	18.3	26,966,566	33.9	38,004,218	47.8
Utah	8,016,314	1,018,052	12.7	4,152,684	51.8	2,845,578	35.5
Vermont	2,067,775	240,653	11.6	1,786,828	86.4	40,294	1.9
Virgin Islands (U.S.)	390,034	219,804	56.4	NA	NA	170,230	43.6
Virginia	21,015,780	2,546,987	12.1	8,199,624	39.0	10,269,170	48.9
Washington	21,905,230	2,717,228	12.4	13,928,583	63.6	5,259,419	24.0
West Virginia	4,114,694	779,035	18.9	1,939,544	47.1	1,396,115	33.9
Wisconsin	14,062,023	1,669,555	11.9	6,455,274	45.9	5,937,194	42.2
Wyoming	2,054,207	266,477	13.0	1,068,335	52.0	719,395	35.0
United States[3]	**909,221,141**	**124,879,530**	**13.7**	**400,832,906**	**44.1**	**383,508,706**	**42.2**

NA = Not applicable. **Note:** Percentage totals may not add up to 100 due to rounding. (1) Includes intermediate revenues from education agencies with fundraising capabilities that operate between the state and local government levels. (2) Reported state revenue data are revenues received from the central government of the jurisdiction. (3) U.S. total includes the 50 states and the District of Columbia.

Enrollment in U.S. Public and Private Schools, 1889-2032

Source: National Center for Education Statistics, U.S. Dept. of Education

Of all students enrolled in private schools in fall 2021, 75% attended religious schools and 25% attended nonsectarian schools.

School year[1]	Public school[2]	Private school[2]	% private[3]	School year[1]	Public school[2]	Private school[2]	% private[3]
1889-90	12,723	1,611	11.2%	1969-70	45,550	5,500[4]	10.8%
1899-1900	15,503	1,352	8.0	1979-80	41,651	5,000[4]	10.7
1909-10	17,814	1,558	8.0	1989-90	40,543	5,599	12.1
1919-20	21,578	1,699	7.3	1999-2000	46,857	6,018	11.4
1929-30	25,678	2,651	9.4	2009-10	49,361	5,488	10.0
1939-40	25,434	2,611	9.3	2019-20	50,796	5,486	9.7
1949-50	25,111	3,380	11.9	2029-30[5]	47,028	5,096	9.8
1959-60	35,182	5,675	13.9	2031-32[5]	46,890	4,902	9.5

Note: "Private" includes all nonpublic schools. (1) Fall enrollment. (2) In thousands. Data from fall 1980 onward covers an expanded universe of private schools; comparisons with earlier years should be avoided. (3) Percent of U.S. students enrolled in private schools. (4) Estimated. (5) Projected.

Program for International Student Assessment (PISA) Scores, 2009-22

Source: National Center for Education Statistics, U.S. Dept. of Education

Scores are reported on a scale from 0 to 1,000. The PISA test is administered to 15-year-old students.

Education system	Mathematics		Reading		Science	
	2009	2022	2009	2022	2009	2022
Albania	377	368	385	358	391	376
Argentina	388	378	398	401	401	406
Australia*	514	487	515	498	527	507
Austria*	496	487	470	480	494	491
Baku (Azerbaijan)[1]	—	397	—	365	—	380
Belgium*	515	489	506	479	507	491
Brazil	386	379	412	410	405	403
Brunei	—	442	—	429	—	446
Bulgaria	428	417	429	404	439	421
Cambodia[2]	—	336	—	329	—	347
Canada*	527	497	524	507	529	515
Chile*	421	412	449	448	447	444
Colombia[1]*	381	383	413	409	402	411
Costa Rica*	—	385	—	415	—	411
Croatia	460	463	476	475	486	483
Cyprus	—	418	—	381	—	411
Czechia*	493	487	478	489	500	498
Denmark*	503	489	495	489	499	494
Dominican Republic[1]	—	339	—	351	—	360
El Salvador[1]	—	343	—	365	—	373
Estonia*	512	510	501	511	528	526
Finland*	541	484	536	490	554	511
France*	497	474	496	474	498	487
Georgia	—	390	—	374	—	384
Germany*	513	475	497	480	520	492
Greece*	466	430	483	438	470	441
Guatemala[2]	—	344	—	374	—	373
Hong Kong (China)	555	540	533	500	549	520
Hungary*	490	473	494	473	503	486
Iceland*	507	459	500	436	496	447
Indonesia	371	366	402	359	383	383
Ireland*	487	492	496	516	508	504
Israel*	447	458	474	474	455	465
Italy*	483	471	486	482	489	477
Jamaica[1]	—	377	—	410	—	403
Japan*	529	536	520	516	539	547
Jordan	387	361	405	342	415	375
Kazakhstan	405	425	390	386	400	423
Korea, South*	546	527	539	515	538	528
Kosovo	—	355	—	342	—	357
Latvia*	482	483	484	475	494	494
Lithuania*	477	475	468	472	491	484
Macau (China)	525	552	487	510	511	543
Malaysia[1]	—	409	—	388	—	416
Malta	—	466	—	445	—	466
Mexico[1]*	419	395	425	415	416	410
Moldova	—	414	—	411	—	417
Mongolia	—	425	—	378	—	412
Montenegro	403	406	408	405	401	403
Morocco	—	365	—	339	—	365
Netherlands*	526	493	508	459	522	488
New Zealand*	519	479	521	501	532	504
North Macedonia	—	389	—	359	—	380
Norway*	498	468	503	477	500	478
Palestinian Authority	—	366	—	349	—	369
Panama[1]	360	357	371	392	376	388
Paraguay[1]	—	338	—	373	—	368
Peru	365	391	370	408	369	408
Philippines	—	355	—	347	—	356
Poland*	495	489	500	489	508	499
Portugal*	487	472	489	477	493	484
Qatar	368	414	372	419	379	432
Romania	427	428	424	428	428	428
Saudi Arabia	—	389	—	383	—	390
Serbia	442	440	442	440	443	447
Singapore	562	575	526	543	542	561
Slovakia*	497	464	477	447	490	462
Slovenia*	501	485	483	469	512	500
Spain*	483	473	481	474	488	485
Sweden*	494	482	497	487	495	494
Switzerland*	534	508	501	483	517	503
Taiwan	543	547	495	515	520	537
Thailand[1]	419	394	421	379	425	409
Turkey[1]*	445	453	464	456	454	476
Ukraine[1,3]	—	441	—	428	—	450
UAE	—	431	—	417	—	432
UK*	492	489	494	494	514	500
U.S.*	487	465	500	504	502	499
Uruguay	427	409	426	430	427	435
Uzbekistan	—	364	—	336	—	355
Vietnam[1]	—	469	—	462	—	472
OECD average	**496**	**472**	**493**	**476**	**501**	**485**

— = Not available. * = Organization for Economic Cooperation and Development (OECD) nation as of 2022. (1) 50-75% of the 15-year-old population is covered by the PISA sample. (2) Less than 50% of the 15-year-old population is covered by the PISA sample. (3) 18 of 27 regions.

Mathematics, Reading, and Science Achievement of U.S. Students, 1998-2022

Source: National Assessment of Educational Progress, National Center for Education Statistics, U.S. Dept. of Education

(percent of public school students in a grade who scored at or above basic levels in national tests)

	4th grade				8th grade					
	Math		Reading		Math		Reading		Science	
State	2000	2022	1998	2022	2000	2022	1998	2022	2000	2015
AL	55	71	56	59	53	53	67	61	53	54
AK	—	65	—	51	—	59	—	63	—	—
AZ	57	70	51	61	60	58	72	68	55	61
AR	55	69	54	58	49	55	68	64	53	62
CA	50	67	48	58	50	56	63	67	38	56
CO	—	75	67	68	—	63	77	73	—	—
CT	76	74	76	64	70	63	81	72	64	70
DE	—	64	53	53	—	51	64	62	—	62
DC	24	57	27	50	23	46	44	57	—	—
FL	—	81	53	71	—	58	67	69	—	66
GA	57	75	54	61	54	59	68	69	52	65
HI	55	77	45	64	51	58	59	68	40	58
ID	68	76	—	61	70	71	—	74	71	76
IL	63	76	—	62	67	62	—	71	59	63
IN	77	78	—	63	74	66	—	70	66	70
IA	75	80	67	64	—	67	—	71	—	75
KS	76	75	70	60	76	61	81	67	—	71
KY	59	75	62	62	60	57	74	68	60	73
LA	57	69	44	57	47	53	63	66	44	—
ME	73	75	72	60	73	61	83	66	72	77
MD	60	65	58	56	62	54	70	67	57	67
MA	77	79	70	70	70	70	79	77	70	75
MI	71	71	62	58	68	60	—	68	68	69
MN	76	78	67	61	80	69	78	72	72	76
MS	45	74	47	63	42	54	62	63	41	51
MO	71	72	61	60	64	61	75	67	66	75
MT	72	80	72	65	79	68	83	72	79	78
NE	65	80	—	65	73	68	—	70	71	75
NV	60	69	51	57	55	56	70	68	52	62
NH	—	80	74	67	—	70	—	73	—	81
NJ	—	77	—	67	—	67	—	77	—	71
NM	50	60	51	48	48	45	71	57	48	55
NY	66	66	62	58	63	60	76	70	58	63
NC	73	75	58	61	67	61	74	66	54	64
ND	73	81	—	65	76	69	—	69	72	79
OH	73	76	—	65	73	64	—	71	72	72
OK	67	71	66	55	62	52	80	62	60	66
OR	65	66	58	56	71	57	78	67	68	72
PA	—	76	—	64	—	62	—	68	—	—
RI	65	74	64	62	59	58	76	68	58	64
SC	59	74	53	61	53	56	66	63	48	65
SD	—	80	—	65	—	72	—	73	—	77
TN	59	76	57	59	52	60	71	67	55	71
TX	76	78	59	58	67	61	74	66	52	70
UT	69	78	62	67	66	70	77	75	67	82
VT	73	74	—	62	73	66	—	73	71	79
VA	71	75	62	60	65	65	78	69	61	74
WA	—	74	64	61	—	64	76	71	—	70
WV	65	67	60	52	58	48	75	60	57	63
WI	—	79	69	63	—	70	78	72	—	75
WY	71	84	64	71	69	72	76	71	69	79
U.S.	**64**	**74**	**58**	**61**	**62**	**60**	**71**	**68**	**57**	**67**

— = Not available.

Fighting, Bullying, and Safety Concerns of High School Students, 2021

Source: *Youth Risk Behavior Surveillance–United States, 2021*, CDC, U.S. Dept. of Health and Human Services

	In a physical fight on school property[1]			Bullied on school property[2]			Electronically bullied[2,3]			Did not go to school because of safety concerns[4]		
	Female	Male	Total	Female	Male	Total	Female	Male	Total	Female	Male	Total
Race/ethnicity												
Amer. Ind./AK native	1.8%	4.4%	3.1%	23.5%	12.8%	17.8%	24.2%	18.1%	20.9%	15.9%	11.1%	13.3%
Asian	0.4	3.1	1.7	9.6	12.0	10.8	13.5	13.2	13.3	6.4	2.8	4.5
Black or African Amer.	5.7	11.3	8.5	11.6	5.5	8.5	12.1	6.6	9.5	14.6	9.6	12.1
Hispanic/Latino	3.3	7.1	5.4	14.1	10.1	12.4	16.0	9.8	13.2	13.0	8.9	11.3
Native Hawaiian/other Pac. Isl.	—	—	0.9	4.6	11.8	8.9	15.6	5.5	9.7	7.3	9.0	8.5
White	2.4	8.0	5.4	20.5	15.3	17.9	25.8	12.2	18.8	8.7	4.7	6.6
Multiple race	6.0	9.6	7.6	17.6	17.0	17.5	18.0	15.2	16.9	8.6	8.0	8.2
Grade												
9	5.0	11.7	8.5	19.2	14.8	17.1	22.2	11.1	16.6	11.8	7.1	9.3
10	3.3	7.2	5.3	19.1	12.3	15.9	21.9	11.0	16.5	11.9	6.1	9.0
11	2.8	6.3	4.6	15.7	12.8	14.2	19.8	11.5	15.5	9.0	7.0	8.0
12	1.8	6.3	4.1	13.7	10.8	12.2	17.8	11.0	14.4	8.9	5.6	7.3
Sexual identity												
Heterosexual (straight)	2.3	6.9	5.1	13.7	10.8	12.0	16.7	9.8	12.7	8.0	5.6	6.6
Gay, lesbian, or bisexual	5.2	3.4	5.0	23.7	26.7	24.9	28.5	23.3	27.6	14.6	11.7	14.1
Other/questioning	3.3	8.9	4.5	19.9	23.4	21.1	23.8	25.0	24.8	12.7	11.8	12.6
Total	**3.2**	**8.1**	**5.8**	**17.0**	**12.8**	**15.0**	**20.5**	**11.2**	**15.9**	**10.5**	**6.6**	**8.6**

(1) One or more times during the 12 months before the survey. (2) During the 12 months before the survey. (3) Including being bullied through texting, Instagram, Facebook, or other social media. (4) On at least one day during the 30 days before the survey.

Characteristics of Public Charter Schools and Students, 2009-23

Source: National Center for Education Statistics, U.S. Dept. of Education

	2009-10	2011-12	2013-14	2015-16	2017-18	2019-20	2021-22	2022-23
Number of charter school students	**1,610,285**	**2,057,599**	**2,519,065**	**2,845,322**	**3,143,269**	**3,431,230**	**3,674,712**	**3,717,857**
	Percentage of charter school students who were—							
Sex								
Male	49.5%	49.6%	49.6%	49.6%	49.6%	49.7%	49.8%	49.8%
Female	50.5	50.4	50.4	50.4	50.4	50.3	50.2	50.2
Race/ethnicity								
Hispanic	26.0	28.0	30.0	31.7	33.1	35.3	36.1	36.8
White	37.3	35.6	34.9	33.1	32.1	30.4	29.4	28.6
Black	30.3	28.7	27.1	26.8	25.8	24.9	24.4	24.4
Asian/Pacific Islander	3.9	4.0	4.1	4.3	4.4	4.5	4.7	4.7
American Ind./Alaska Native	1.0	0.9	0.8	0.7	0.7	0.8	0.7	0.7
Two or more races	1.4	2.8	3.0	3.4	3.9	4.2	4.7	4.8
Number of charter schools	**4,952**	**5,696**	**6,465**	**6,855**	**7,193**	**7,547**	**7,847**	**7,998**
	Percentage of charter schools that were—							
School level								
Prekindergarten	0.5%	0.5%	0.3%	0.4%	0.3%	0.5%	0.3%	0.3%
Elementary	43.6	44.7	45.9	46.0	46.6	47.0	47.2	47.0
Middle	11.6	12.2	11.5	11.2	10.7	10.5	10.4	10.2
Secondary and high	30.9	28.7	28.2	28.3	28.3	27.7	27.3	27.5
Other[1]	13.5	13.9	14.0	14.1	14.0	14.4	14.8	15.0
Locale[2]								
City	54.8	55.4	56.5	56.5	56.1	56.6	56.3	56.4
Suburban	21.1	21.2	26.1	25.9	26.3	25.7	25.7	25.7
Town	8.0	7.4	7.0	6.7	6.1	6.0	6.0	5.9
Rural	16.1	16.0	10.4	10.9	11.5	11.7	12.0	12.0

Note: Race categories exclude persons of Hispanic ethnicity, who may be of any race. (1) Includes other, ungraded, and not applicable/not reported. (2) Excludes schools with missing locale information.

Homeschooled Students, 2019

Source: National Center for Education Statistics, U.S. Dept. of Education

A total of 1,456,586 U.S. students in grades K-12 were homeschooled in 2019, down from 1,689,726 in 2016, 1,772,987 in 2012, and 1,520,140 in 2007, and up from 1,095,652 in 2003 and 850,171 in 1999. In a 2019 U.S. Dept. of Education survey of parents who homeschool their children, the reason they gave as most important in their decision to homeschool was concern over the school environment, with such factors as safety, drugs, or negative peer pressure (25%); dissatisfaction with academic instruction in schools (15%); desire to provide religious instruction (13%); emphasis on family life together (8%); desire to provide a nontraditional approach to education (8%); the child has other special needs (7%); desire to provide moral instruction (7%); and the child has a physical or mental health problem (3%). In all, 80% cited concern over school environment as one of their reasons, 75% cited moral instruction, 75% cited emphasis on family life together, 73% cited dissatisfaction with academic instruction, and 59% cited religious instruction.

Characteristic	No. of students (thous.)	% distrib.	Home-schooling rate[1]
Household locale			
City	399	27%	2.5%
Suburban	532	37	2.4
Town	102	7	2.2
Rural	423	29	4.7
Race/ethnicity[2]			
White	1,014	71	4.0
Black	84	6	1.2
Other[3]	83	6	2.7
Hispanic	250	17	1.9

Characteristic	No. of students (thous.)	% distrib.	Home-schooling rate[1]
Parents' education			
High school diploma or less	330	23%	2.2%
Vocational/technical, assoc. degree, or some college	376	26	2.9
Bachelor's degree/some graduate school	449	31	3.3
Graduate/professional degree	302	21	3.1
Total	**1,457**	**NA**	**2.8**

NA = Not applicable. **Note:** Numbers may not add up to totals because of rounding. Homeschooled students are school-age children in a grade equivalent to K-12 who receive instruction at home all or most of the time. Excludes students enrolled in public or private school more than 25 hours per week or homeschooled because of temporary illness only. (1) Percentage of total subgroup (e.g., all "City" students) that is homeschooled. (2) Race categories exclude persons of Hispanic ethnicity, who may be of any race. (3) Includes two or more races and race/ethnicity not reported.

Students With Disabilities Receiving Educational Services, 1976-2023

Source: Office of Special Education Programs, U.S. Dept. of Education

Students served by federally funded educational programs for disabled students include children and young adults 3-21 years old. (numbers served in thousands)

Type of disability	1976 -77	1980 -81	1990 -91	2000 -01	2010 -11	2015 -16	2017-18[1,3]	2018 -19[1]	2019 -20[1,4]	2020 -21[4,5]	2021 -22[4,6]	2022 -23[4]
Autism	—	—	—	93	417	617	710	762	803	828	882	980
Deaf-blindness	—	3	1	1	2	1	1	2	2	2	2	2
Developmental delay	—	—	—	213	382	434	461	479	502	487	487	518
Emotional disturbance	283	347	389	480	390	347	353	358	365	353	334	327
Hearing impairment	88	79	58	77	78	75	75	74	73	72	71	70
Intellectual disability	961	830	534	624	448	425	436	439	442	429	426	434
Multiple disabilities	—	68	96	131	130	131	132	133	133	128	125	126
Orthopedic impairment	87	58	49	82	63	47	41	39	37	35	33	32
Other health impairment[7]	141	98	55	303	716	909	1,002	1,049	1,094	1,096	1,116	1,150
Specific learning disability	796	1,462	2,129	2,860	2,361	2,298	2,342	2,368	2,405	2,346	2,355	2,408
Speech/lang. impairment	1,302	1,168	985	1,388	1,396	1,337	1,357	1,378	1,374	1,357	1,378	1,430
Traumatic brain injury	—	—	—	16	26	27	27	27	27	25	25	25
Visual impairment	38	31	23	29	28	27	27	27	27	26	25	25
All disabilities	**3,694**	**4,144**	**4,710[8]**	**6,296**	**6,436**	**6,677**	**6,964**	**7,134**	**7,282**	**7,183**	**7,259**	**7,526**

— = Not available. **Note:** Details may not add up to totals because of rounding and/or incomplete enumeration. (1) Includes Wisconsin's 2015-16 student data (2016-17, 2017-18, 2018-19, and 2019-20 data were not available). (2) Includes Nebraska's 2015-16 data for 3-to-5-year-old students (2016-17 data were not available). (3) Includes 2016-17 data for 3-to-5-year-old students in Minnesota and 6-to-21-year-old students in Maine and Vermont because 2017-18 data were not available. (4) Data by disability type for Iowa are imputed. (5) Includes 2019-20 data for 5-to-21-year-old students in Louisiana (2020-21 data were not available). (6) Includes 2020-21 data for 3-to-5-year-old students in Louisiana (2021-22 data were not available). (7) Includes limited strength, vitality, or alertness due to chronic or acute health problems such as a heart condition, tuberculosis, rheumatic fever, nephritis, asthma, sickle cell anemia, hemophilia, epilepsy, lead poisoning, leukemia, or diabetes. (8) Total includes 390 preschool disabled students. For all other years, preschool children were included in the counts by disability condition.

Population With Upper Secondary Education in Selected Countries, 2022

Source: Organization for Economic Cooperation and Development

Sorted by percentage of the population ages 25-64 that have received at least an upper secondary (senior high school) education.

Country	%	Country	%	Country	%	Country	%	Country	%
Japan	100%	Australia	69%	Poland	64%	Latvia	58%	Spain	47%
South Korea	87	Austria	68	Bulgaria	63	Germany	57	Turkey (Türkiye)	45
United States	78	France	67	Colombia	62	Lithuania	57	Costa Rica	43
Czechia	75	Hungary	67	Netherlands	62	Ireland	56	Indonesia	43
Israel	73	Norway	66	Belgium	61	United Kingdom	54	South Africa	43
Canada	71	Slovakia	66	Greece	61	Romania	54	Mexico	42
Finland	71	Switzerland	66	New Zealand	60	Iceland	52	Portugal	38
Slovenia	71	Denmark	65	Estonia	59	Luxembourg	48	China (2020)	36
Chile (2020)	70	Argentina (2021)	65	Sweden	59	Italy	47	Brazil	20
								India	18

Financial Aid to U.S. Undergraduate Students, 2000-22

Source: National Center for Education Statistics, U.S. Dept. of Education

				Percent of enrolled students in student aid programs				Average award[1]			
Type of institution/ year	Number enrolled	Number receiving financial aid	Percent receiving aid	Federal grants	State/ local grants	Institu- tional grants	Student loans[2]	Federal grants	State/ local grants	Institu- tional grants	Student loans[2]
All institutions											
2000-01	1,976,600	1,390,527	70.3%	31.6%	31.2%	31.1%	40.1%	$4,256	$3,490	$8,112	$6,443
2021-22	2,282,669	1,991,973	87.3	56.0	33.2	54.0	38.6	5,295	4,374	13,282	7,956
Public											
2000-01	1,333,236	872,109	65.4	30.0	33.5	22.7	30.7	4,121	2,921	3,893	5,220
2021-22	1,617,365	1,401,935	86.7	60.1	39.1	47.6	31.4	5,229	4,238	6,435	7,462
4-year											
2000-01	804,793	573,430	71.3	26.6	36.5	29.6	40.7	4,398	3,539	4,478	5,497
2021-22	1,183,279	1,030,951	87.1	55.9	36.7	57.6	37.7	5,085	5,012	6,949	7,774
2-year											
2000-01	528,443	298,679	56.5	35.2	28.8	12.1	15.3	3,804	1,728	1,718	4,101
2021-22	434,086	370,984	85.5	71.3	45.7	20.1	14.3	5,535	2,549	2,422	5,221
Private nonprofit											
2000-01	439,369	363,044	82.6	28.4	31.8	68.1	57.7	4,927	5,131	12,611	6,880
2021-22	521,768	467,215	89.5	40.4	22.5	81.9	52.3	5,612	5,155	26,359	8,739
4-year											
2000-01	419,499	347,638	82.9	27.4	32.2	70.1	58.1	5,016	5,137	12,765	6,846
2021-22	505,005	453,137	89.7	39.3	22.9	83.9	51.8	5,577	5,167	26,532	8,924
2-year											
2000-01	19,870	15,406	77.5	49.2	23.9	25.7	49.5	3,884	4,950	3,710	7,718
2021-22	16,763	14,078	84.0	73.0	8.9	22.8	66.7	6,187	4,243	7,229	4,424
Private for-profit											
2000-01	203,995	155,374	76.2	49.3	15.2	6.2	63.5	3,958	4,268	2,635	9,443
2021-22	143,536	122,823	85.6	67.2	5.8	25.3	70.3	5,271	3,679	4,344	8,322
4-year											
2000-01	81,075	51,739	63.8	36.1	11.9	8.3	57.7	3,929	4,944	2,766	9,839
2021-22	48,566	42,396	87.3	62.6	8.2	38.1	68.7	5,619	3,730	6,547	8,314
2-year											
2000-01	122,920	103,635	84.3	58.0	17.3	4.8	67.3	3,969	3,961	2,486	9,220
2021-22	94,970	80,427	84.7	69.5	4.5	18.8	71.1	5,111	3,632	2,059	8,326

Note: Data for full-time, first-time, degree/certificate-seeking undergraduate students. (1) Average amounts for students participating in indicated programs, in constant 2022-23 dollars. (2) Includes only loans made directly to students, not parents.

Charges at U.S. Institutions of Higher Education, 1969-2023

Source: National Center for Education Statistics, U.S. Dept. of Education

Data are for the entire academic year and are average charges, in current dollars, for full-time students at degree-granting postsecondary institutions. Room and board based on full-time students. For 1989-90 on, board is based on 20 meals per week.

	Tuition and fees			Board rates			Dormitory charges		
	All institutions	2-yr	4-yr	All institutions	2-yr	4-yr	All institutions	2-yr	4-yr
Public (in-state)									
1969-70	$323	$178	$358	$508	$465	$510	$366	$308	$369
1979-80	583	355	738	867	893	865	715	574	725
1989-90	1,356	756	1,780	1,635	1,581	1,638	1,513	962	1,557
1999-2000	2,504	1,348	3,349	2,364	1,834	2,406	2,440	1,549	2,519
2009-10	4,763	2,283	6,717	3,655	2,571	3,755	4,401	2,854	4,564
2010-11	5,075	2,441	7,132	3,845	2,683	3,956	4,646	2,955	4,832
2011-12	5,563	2,651	7,713	3,946	2,866	4,042	4,849	3,100	5,031
2012-13	5,899	2,792	8,070	4,061	2,888	4,163	5,062	3,247	5,241
2013-14	6,120	2,881	8,312	4,205	2,955	4,308	5,304	3,448	5,479
2014-15	6,370	2,955	8,543	4,313	3,072	4,412	5,504	3,559	5,677
2015-16	6,612	3,038	8,778	4,469	3,118	4,576	5,686	3,759	5,850
2016-17	6,818	3,156	8,804	4,562	3,111	4,666	5,859	3,823	6,018
2017-18	7,051	3,242	9,036	4,682	3,204	4,785	6,060	3,834	6,227
2018-19	7,248	3,312	9,212	4,843	3,582	4,927	6,290	4,057	6,459
2019-20	7,410	3,377	9,349	4,943	3,578	5,031	6,483	4,105	6,655
2020-21	7,635	3,503	9,374	5,107	3,649	5,189	6,630	4,408	6,774
2021-22	7,869	3,563	9,596	5,207	3,613	5,292	6,798	4,428	6,944
2022-23	7,998	3,598	9,750	5,386	3,790	5,472	7,017	4,566	7,167
Private (nonprofit and for-profit)									
1969-70	$1,533	$1,034	$1,562	$560	$546	$561	$434	$413	$436
1979-80	3,130	2,062	3,225	955	923	957	827	766	831
1989-90	8,147	5,196	8,396	1,948	1,811	1,953	1,923	1,663	1,935
1999-2000	14,100	8,225	14,616	2,877	2,753	2,879	3,236	3,067	3,242
2009-10	21,764	14,862	22,269	4,329	4,390	4,329	5,248	5,211	5,248
2010-11	22,042	13,687	22,677	4,430	4,475	4,430	5,403	4,939	5,410
2011-12	22,850	13,961	23,464	4,586	4,475	4,586	5,622	5,169	5,627
2012-13	23,943	14,149	24,523	4,709	3,977	4,712	5,831	5,228	5,837
2013-14	25,110	14,170	25,707	4,864	4,211	4,866	6,021	5,489	6,026
2014-15	26,182	14,261	26,739	5,019	4,560	5,021	6,221	5,506	6,228
2015-16	27,436	14,528	27,942	5,123	4,181	5,128	6,457	5,666	6,464
2016-17	28,945	14,589	29,476	5,268	4,350	5,273	6,710	5,949	6,717
2017-18	30,274	14,894	30,723	5,437	4,645	5,440	6,961	6,057	6,968
2018-19	31,527	15,720	31,883	5,616	6,909	5,608	7,171	5,951	7,179
2019-20	32,411	15,831	32,764	5,756	4,587	5,760	7,397	6,326	7,401
2020-21	32,351	15,473	32,728	5,903	4,619	5,907	7,573	5,571	7,580
2021-22	33,700	16,588	34,051	6,046	4,819	6,049	7,824	5,942	7,830
2022-23	34,923	17,408	35,248	6,279	5,148	6,282	8,118	6,236	8,124

U.S. Student Loan Balances by Age, 2004-22

Source: *2022 Student Loan Update*, Federal Reserve Bank of New York; Equifax

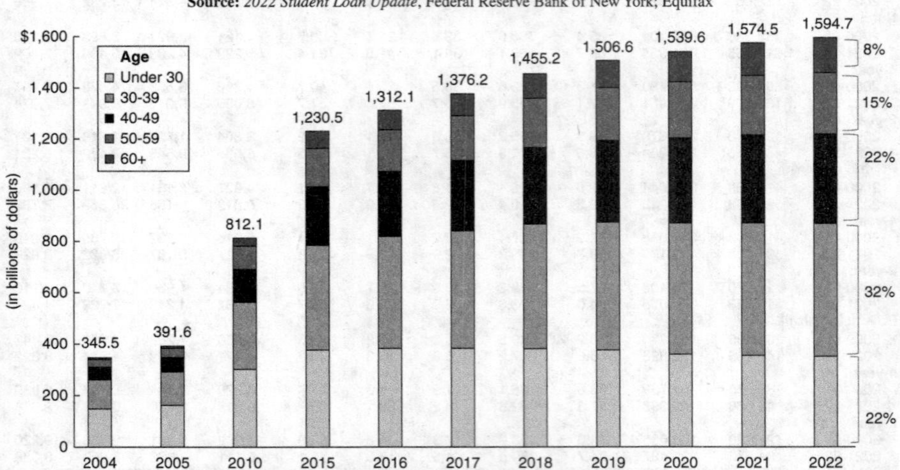

Note: Total annual balances include loans held by persons of unknown ages. Percentages may not add up to 100 due to rounding.

Student Loan Debt by State, 2004-20

Source: *Student Debt and the Class of 2020*, Project on Student Debt, Institute for College Access & Success

State[1]	Average debt 2004	Average debt 2014	Average debt 2020	% with debt 2004	% with debt 2020
Alabama	$18,042	$29,425	$30,996	57%	51%
Alaska	15,648	26,742	26,356	48	47
Arizona	18,147	22,609	24,298	48	47
Arkansas	16,210	25,344	27,319	59	54
California	16,071	21,382	21,125	49	46
Colorado	16,352	25,064	26,424	53	49
Connecticut	18,906	29,750	35,853	57	57
Delaware	14,780	33,808	39,705	45	60
District of Columbia	19,357	—	32,966	58	46
Florida	18,857	24,947	24,454	51	47
Georgia	15,354	26,518	27,759	53	56
Hawaii	13,509	24,554	24,926	29	45
Idaho	22,273	26,091	24,983	68	58
Illinois	15,650	28,984	28,552	56	57
Indiana	19,425	29,222	28,521	54	57
Iowa	24,204	29,732	29,560	76	60
Kansas	16,266	25,521	26,002	57	60
Kentucky	14,250	25,939	28,356	52	61
Louisiana	18,993	23,025	26,284	61	53
Maine	19,410	30,908	32,764	64	63
Maryland	12,597	27,457	30,461	52	55
Massachusetts	17,021	29,391	33,457	60	56
Michigan	18,754	29,450	29,863	58	58
Minnesota	19,580	31,579	32,012	72	64
Mississippi	15,503	26,177	29,714	60	58
Missouri	$15,511	$25,844	$28,713	59%	56%
Montana	18,019	26,946	27,114	68	55
Nebraska	17,384	26,278	26,781	62	60
Nevada	14,144	20,211	21,357	46	46
New Hampshire	21,441	33,410	39,928	65	70
New Jersey	16,223	28,318	35,117	58	63
New Mexico	—	18,969	20,868	—	45
New York	18,857	27,822	30,951	62	54
North Carolina	16,863	25,218	29,681	51	55
North Dakota	22,409	—	31,939	73	66
Ohio	19,182	29,353	30,605	62	59
Oklahoma	16,942	23,430	27,876	55	50
Oregon	17,267	26,106	26,504	63	53
Pennsylvania	19,556	33,264	39,375	69	64
Rhode Island	19,328	31,841	36,791	68	64
South Carolina	16,775	29,163	32,635	55	60
South Dakota	19,023	26,023	32,029	82	73
Tennessee	16,905	25,510	26,852	41	53
Texas	17,170	26,250	26,273	51	52
Utah	12,362	18,921	18,344	43	39
Vermont	20,706	29,060	34,866	56	57
Virginia	15,831	26,432	29,616	57	55
Washington	17,415	24,804	23,993	56	47
West Virginia	18,246	26,854	29,208	69	66
Wisconsin	16,560	28,810	30,270	60	63
Wyoming	15,352	23,708	23,510	44	48
U.S.	**18,550**	**28,950**	**NA**	**65**	**NA**

— = Usable cases covered less than 30% of bachelor's degree recipients, or underlying data showed a state-level change of 30% or more in average debt from previous year. NA = Not available. (1) Location of surveyed colleges (not necessarily location of degree recipient).

College Enrollment by Selected Characteristics, 1947-2022

Source: National Center for Education Statistics, U.S. Dept. of Education
(numbers in thousands)

Year	Total enrollment[1]	Attendance status: Full-time	Part-time	% part-time	Sex of student: Male	Female	Control of institution: Public	Private: Total	Private: Nonprofit	Private: For-profit
1947[2]	2,338	NA	NA	NA	1,659	679	1,152	1,186	NA	NA
1950[2]	2,281	NA	NA	NA	1,560	721	1,140	1,142	NA	NA
1955[2]	2,653	NA	NA	NA	1,733	920	1,476	1,177	NA	NA
1965	5,921	4,096	1,825[3]	30.8%	3,630	2,291	3,970	1,951	NA	NA
1970	8,581	5,816	2,765	32.2	5,044	3,537	6,428	2,153	2,134	18
1975	11,185	6,841	4,344	38.8	6,149	5,036	8,835	2,350	2,311	39
1980	12,097	7,098	4,999	41.3	5,874	6,223	9,457	2,640	2,528	112[4]
1985	12,247	7,075	5,172	42.2	5,818	6,429	9,479	2,768	2,572	196
1990	13,819	7,821	5,998	43.4	6,284	7,535	10,845	2,974	2,760	214
1995	14,262	8,129	6,133	43.0	6,343	7,919	11,092	3,169	2,929	240
2000	15,312	9,010	6,303	41.2	6,722	8,591	11,753	3,560	3,109	450
2005	17,487	10,797	6,690	38.3	7,456	10,032	13,022	4,466	3,455	1,011
2007	18,258	11,271	6,987	38.3	7,820	10,438	13,501	4,757	3,571	1,186
2008	19,082	11,735	7,347	38.5	8,178	10,904	13,971	5,111	3,661	1,450
2009	20,314	12,605	7,708	37.9	8,733	11,581	14,811	5,503	3,768	1,735
2010	21,019	13,087	7,932	37.7	9,046	11,974	15,142	5,877	3,854	2,023
2011	21,011	13,003	8,008	38.1	9,034	11,976	15,116	5,894	3,927	1,967
2012	20,644	12,734	7,910	38.3	8,919	11,725	14,885	5,760	3,951	1,808
2013	20,377	12,597	7,780	38.2	8,861	11,515	14,747	5,630	3,971	1,658
2014	20,209	12,454	7,755	38.4	8,798	11,412	14,655	5,554	3,997	1,557
2015	19,988	12,288	7,701	38.5	8,724	11,264	14,573	5,415	4,066	1,349
2016	19,847	12,125	7,722	38.9	8,638	11,208	14,586	5,261	4,079	1,182
2017	19,778	12,076	7,702	38.9	8,571	11,207	14,572	5,206	4,108	1,098
2018	19,651	11,990	7,662	39.0	8,445	11,207	14,539	5,112	4,132	980
2019	19,630	11,954	7,676	39.1	8,364	11,266	14,504	5,127	4,135	991
2020	19,027	11,609	7,418	39.0	7,885	11,142	13,884	5,143	4,101	1,042
2021	18,659	11,326	7,332	39.3	7,768	10,891	13,546	5,113	4,112	1,001
2022	18,580	11,286	7,294	39.3	7,815	10,765	13,494	5,086	4,108	978

NA = Not available. **Note:** Data for 1947-95 are for institutions of higher education, while later data are for degree-granting institutions. Degree-granting institutions grant associate's or higher degrees and participate in Title IV federal financial aid programs. The degree-granting classification is very similar to the earlier higher education classification, but it includes more two-year colleges and excludes a few higher education institutions that do not grant degrees. (1) Fall enrollment. (2) Degree-credit enrollment only. (3) Includes part-time resident students and all extension students (students attending courses at sites separate from the primary reporting campus). In later years, part-time student enrollment was collected as a distinct category. (4) Large increases are due to the addition of schools accredited by the Accrediting Commission of Career Schools and Colleges of Technology.

U.S. Bachelor's Degrees Conferred, 1899-2032

Source: National Center for Education Statistics, U.S. Dept. of Education
(*) figures are projected.

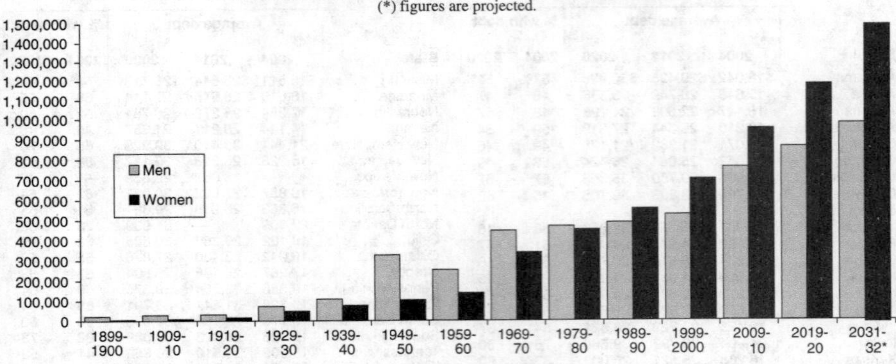

Financial Aid for College and Other Postsecondary Education

Reviewed by the National Association of Student Financial Aid Administrators; as of May 2024

The cost of postsecondary education in the U.S. continues to increase, but financial aid—in the form of **grants** (no repayment needed), **loans**, and/or **work-study** programs—is widely available to help families meet these expenses. Most federal aid is limited to families that demonstrate financial need as determined by standard formulas and is designed to help students attend the college of their choice regardless of their ability to pay. Financial aid personnel at each school can provide information about all aid programs (federal, state, institutional, and private) available to students, how to apply, and deadlines.

All applicants for federal aid must file a Free Application for Federal Student Aid (**FAFSA**), generally as soon as possible after Oct. 1 for the academic year starting the following Aug. or Sept. This change from Jan. in prior years allows students to apply for aid earlier. Applicants can file a FAFSA form online at fafsa.gov or by completing a printed-out form and mailing it.

The figures provided should match federal income tax forms filed for the previous year. (The use of tax data that has already been filed ensures timely processing.) Thus, the 2024-25 academic year application, expected to be available Oct. 1, 2023 (but actually delayed until Dec.), should have been filed with 2022 tax information. For the 2024-25 cycle, the Dept. of Education made significant changes to the online form. Many other sources of aid—state governments, employers and unions, civic organizations, and the institutions themselves—also use the FAFSA to determine eligibility for aid. Some federal programs pay for postsecondary education in return for service: AmeriCorps, Reserve Officers' Training Corps (Army, Navy, and Air Force), the G.I. Bill, and the National Health Service Corps. A student must reapply for aid annually.

All students, parents, and borrowers are required to use an **FSA ID**, which consists of a username and password, to access certain U.S. Dept. of Education websites. An FSA ID is used to confirm identity when accessing financial aid information and electronically signing federal student aid documents. Part of the change in the application allows for direct data transfer from the IRS into the FAFSA application. The FSA ID ensures the appropriate matches are made with the IRS for this process. The FSA ID also allows any contributors represented on the FAFSA application to provide consent to transfer any information found in IRS records for the associated year.

The **federal formula** is based on information provided on the FAFSA and takes into account factors such as family income in the preceding calendar year, parental and student assets, and the length of time to parents' retirement. Financial aid personnel have the authority to consider unusual expenses, such as very high medical expenses, which are not reported on the FAFSA. Outside scholarships are also considered in determining eligibility for federal, institutional, and state financial aid programs.

The formula determines a student's **SAI, or student aid index**. The SAI is subtracted from the total cost of attending college for each person. The difference determines financial need and the maximum federal aid for which the family may be eligible. Federal Pell Grants are also determined using some data elements on the form in conjunction with U.S. Poverty Guidelines that are published annually. Note: Some institutions will require an additional form for admitted students. Schools try to cover a student's financial need using a combination of tools but may not be able to fully meet need because of a lack of funds.

The **aid package** offered by each school may include one or more of the following: Federal Pell Grants, for those who demonstrate sufficient financial need; Federal Supplemental Educational Opportunity Grants, for those who still have significant need after receiving Federal Pell Grants; grants from the school; Federal Work-Study or other work programs; and federal Direct Subsidized and Unsubsidized Loans (often referred to as Direct Loans). Parents of undergraduates and students in graduate or professional school may apply for a PLUS Loan. Direct Unsubsidized Loans and Direct PLUS Loans are available regardless of financial need, but students and parents must still complete the FAFSA to get these loans. Professional judgment, which allows an institution to consider current financial circumstances not reflected in the FAFSA, is also available. Students and families that have incurred a loss of income or job elimination can work directly with their chosen institution's financial aid office to accurately reflect their current financial situation.

Loans have varying interest rates and other requirements. Repayment of Direct Subsidized Loans and Direct Unsubsidized Loans generally does not begin until after graduation; deferments, income-based repayment plans, and loan forgiveness are available on federal loans for students who meet certain requirements. For PLUS Loans, parents and graduate-level students must pass a credit check and may need to begin repayment of both principal and interest while the student is still in school.

Terms may vary, but federal student loans must be repaid, even if financial circumstances change, education is incomplete or not as expected, or post-graduation income is less than expected. The loan servicer or lender is required to provide a loan repayment schedule that states the first payment due date, the number and frequency of payments, and the amount due. Some loans have a grace period, a set period (in most cases six months) after graduation before repayment begins. Direct loans have several repayment plan options—including graduated repayments, extended repayment, and income-based repayment—or loan consolidation. In most cases, student loan debt cannot be discharged in bankruptcy. Certain federal income **tax credits and refunds** are available to families who meet requirements.

The **rules for financial aid** are complex and changeable. Comprehensive resources on financial aid from the U.S. Dept. of Education, including fact sheets, videos, worksheets, and other tools, are available online at studentaid.gov/resources.

Further information is available from the Federal Student Aid Information Center: 1-800-4-FED-AID, Mon., 8 AM-9 PM ET; Tue.-Wed., 8 AM-8 PM; Thu.-Fri., 8 AM-6 PM; studentaid.gov; web chat is also available.

Endowment Assets of Colleges and Universities, 2023

Source: *2023 NACUBO-Commonfund Study of Endowments*, National Association of College and University Business Officers (NACUBO)

Rank	College/university	Endowment assets[1]	% change, 2022-23
1.	Harvard University	$49,495,108	0.1%
2.	University of Texas System	44,967,186	5.4
3.	Yale University	40,746,900	–1.5
4.	Stanford University	36,495,000	0.4
5.	Princeton University	34,058,774	–4.8
6.	Massachusetts Institute of Technology	23,453,446	–5.2
7.	University of Pennsylvania	20,962,965	1.2
8.	Texas A&M University System	19,285,472	5.7
9.	University of Michigan	17,875,691	3.0
10.	University of California	17,689,324	14.7
11.	University of Notre Dame	16,616,524	–0.7
12.	Northwestern University	13,699,895	–3.0
13.	Columbia University	13,642,667	2.7
14.	Duke University	13,237,963	9.3
15.	Washington University	11,467,279	–6.4
16.	Johns Hopkins University	10,538,865	27.8
17.	Emory University	10,239,776	2.4
18.	Cornell University	10,035,558	2.0
19.	University of Chicago	9,869,725	–0.5
20.	University of Virginia	9,799,870	–0.6
21.	Vanderbilt University	$9,684,196	–5.1%
22.	Dartmouth College	7,930,125	–1.7
23.	University of Southern California	7,463,051	2.0
24.	The Ohio State University	7,383,676	6.1
25.	Rice University	7,240,020	–0.7
26.	Brown University	6,201,434	1.0
27.	New York University	5,877,433	14.2
28.	University of Minnesota	5,501,497	2.5
29.	University of Pittsburgh	5,489,296	–0.7
30.	University of North Carolina at Chapel Hill	5,200,812	–2.2
31.	University of Washington	4,940,534	5.6
32.	Pennsylvania State University	4,443,874	3.8
33.	Michigan State University	4,054,000	4.5
34.	Carnegie Mellon University	3,888,140	0.8
35.	UCLA	3,873,061	8.8
36.	University of Wisconsin	3,838,022	9.8
37.	Purdue University	3,793,601	3.2
38.	California Institute of Technology	3,665,200	0.8
39.	Indiana University	3,557,620	1.2
40.	Williams College	3,486,558	–1.4

Note: Market value of endowment assets in the fiscal year. (1) In thousands.

Average ACT Scores and Characteristics of College-Bound Students, 1990-2023

Source: ACT, Inc. (formerly American College Testing)

SCORES[1]	Unit	1990	1995	2000	2005	2010	2015	2017	2019	2020	2021	2022	2023
Composite score	**Points**	**20.6**	**20.8**	**21.0**	**20.9**	**21.0**	**21.0**	**21.0**	**20.7**	**20.6**	**20.3**	**19.8**	**19.5**
Male	Points	21.0	21.0	21.2	21.1	21.2	21.1	21.0	20.6	20.5	20.3	19.7	19.4
Female	Points	20.3	20.7	20.9	20.9	20.9	21.0	21.1	20.8	20.8	20.6	20.0	19.7
English score	**Points**	**20.5**	**20.2**	**20.5**	**20.4**	**20.5**	**20.4**	**20.3**	**20.1**	**19.9**	**19.6**	**19.0**	**18.6**
Male	Points	20.1	19.8	20.0	20.0	20.1	20.0	19.9	19.6	19.3	19.1	18.5	18.2
Female	Points	20.9	20.6	20.9	20.8	20.8	20.8	20.8	20.6	20.5	20.2	19.6	19.2
Math score	**Points**	**19.9**	**20.2**	**20.7**	**20.7**	**21.0**	**20.8**	**20.7**	**20.4**	**20.2**	**19.9**	**19.3**	**19.0**
Male	Points	20.7	20.9	21.4	21.3	21.6	21.3	21.2	20.8	20.6	20.4	19.7	19.4
Female	Points	19.3	19.7	20.2	20.2	20.5	20.4	20.4	20.0	20.0	19.7	19.1	18.8
PARTICIPANTS													
Total number	**(Thous.)**	**817**	**945**	**1,065**	**1,186**	**1,569**	**1,924**	**2,030**	**1,783**	**1,670**	**1,295**	**1,350**	**1,386**
Male	Percent	46%	44%	43%	44%	45%	47%	46%	46%	46%	46%	47%	49%
White	Percent	79	80	72	66	62	55	52	52	52	54	53	52
Black	Percent	9	9	10	12	14	13	13	12	12	12	11	12
Hispanic[2]	Percent	4	5	5	7	10	16	17	16	17	14	16	17
Composite score													
27 or above	Percent	12	13	14	14	16	18	18	18	18	17	15	14
18 or below	Percent	35	34	32	34	35	37	38	41	42	44	48	50

Note: Minimum score, 1; maximum score, 36. Test scores and characteristics of college-bound students are based on the performance of all ACT-tested students who graduated in the spring of a given school year and took the ACT assessment during junior or senior year of high school. (1) For 2020-23, ACT reported a category of "other responses" for gender that included "another gender" and "prefer not to respond," as well as missing values. (2) Persons of Hispanic origin may be of any race.

Average ACT Composite Scores by State, 2023

Source: ACT, Inc. (formerly American College Testing)

State	Avg. comp. score	% grads taking ACT
Alabama	18.0	100%
Alaska	20.2	15
Arizona	17.7	98
Arkansas	18.6	96
California	25.7	4
Colorado	24.5	9
Connecticut	26.4	8
Delaware	24.8	4
District of Columbia	26.0	17
Florida	18.9	46
Georgia	21.3	28
Hawaii	17.9	64
Idaho	23.0	12
Illinois	24.5	16
Indiana	22.9	8
Iowa	20.8	48
Kansas	19.4	74
Kentucky	18.7	100
Louisiana	18.2	100%
Maine	24.8	2
Maryland	24.5	7
Massachusetts	26.4	8
Michigan	24.4	7
Minnesota	20.8	68
Mississippi	17.6	100
Missouri	19.8	66
Montana	18.8	98
Nebraska	19.2	96
Nevada	17.2	100
New Hampshire	25.2	5
New Jersey	24.4	10
New Mexico	20.2	14
New York	25.3	9
North Carolina	18.5	90
North Dakota	19.6	89
Ohio	19.2	82%
Oklahoma	17.8	100
Oregon	20.9	13
Pennsylvania	23.9	6
Rhode Island	24.5	5
South Carolina	18.8	40
South Dakota	21.1	59
Tennessee	18.4	100
Texas	19.3	23
Utah	19.9	90
Vermont	23.6	6
Virginia	24.6	8
Washington	24.5	6
West Virginia	20.3	26
Wisconsin	19.4	95
Wyoming	19.0	100
U.S.	**19.5**	**37**

Mean SAT Scores of College-Bound Seniors, 1975-2023

Source: The College Board
(for school year ending in year shown)

	1975	1980	1990	2000	2005	2010	2015	2016[2,6]	2017[3]	2018[3]	2019[3]	2020[3,4]	2021[3,4]	2022[3,4]	2023[3,4]
Reading and writing[1]	**512**	**502**	**500**	**505**	**508**	**500**	**495**	**494**	**533**	**536**	**531**	**528**	**533**	**529**	**520**
Male	515	506	505	507	513	502	497	495	532	534	529	523	530	526	517
Female	509	498	496	504	505	498	493	493	534	539	534	532	535	531	523
Math score	**498**	**492**	**501**	**514**	**520**	**515**	**511**	**508**	**527**	**531**	**528**	**523**	**528**	**521**	**508**
Male	518	515	521	533	538	533	527	524	538	542	537	531	537	530	515
Female	479	473	483	498	504	499	496	494	516	522	519	516	519	512	500
Writing score	**NA**	**NA**	**NA**	**NA**	**NA**	**491**	**484**	**482**	**NA**	**NA**	**NA**	**NA**	**NA**	**NA**	**NA**
Male	NA	NA	NA	NA	NA	485	478	475	NA	NA	NA	NA	NA	NA	NA
Female	NA	NA	NA	NA	NA	497	490	487	NA	NA	NA	NA	NA	NA	NA

NA = Not applicable. **Note:** In 1995, the College Board recentered the scoring scale for the SAT. Earlier scores have been adjusted to account for this recentering. (1) Verbal section, 1975-2005; critical reading, 2006-16. (2) Through Jan. 2016. (3) Beginning in Mar. 2016, students took a redesigned SAT. The College Board advised against comparing 2016-23 SAT results with earlier data. (4) For 2020, 2021, 2022, and 2023, 0.1%, 0.2%, 0.4%, and 0.6% of test takers, respectively, responded "another/no response" for gender.

Mean SAT Scores by State, 1990-2023

Source: The College Board; National Center for Education Statistics, U.S. Dept. of Education
(for school year ending in year shown; V = Verbal, M = Math, CR = Critical reading, W = Writing, ERW = Evidence-based reading and writing)

	1990		2000		2010			2020		% grads	2023[1]		% grads
State	**V**	**M**	**V**	**M**	**CR**	**M**	**W**	**ERW**	**M**	**taking SAT[1]**	**ERW**	**M**	**taking SAT[2]**
Alabama	545	534	559	555	556	550	544	576	551	7%	592	570	3%
Alaska	514	501	519	515	518	515	491	555	543	37	553	529	30
Arizona	521	520	521	523	519	525	500	571	568	29	596	587	11
Arkansas	545	532	563	554	566	566	552	590	567	4	610	582	2
California	494	508	497	518	501	516	500	527	522	67	546	536	25
Colorado	533	534	534	537	568	572	555	511	501	100	508	488	90
Connecticut	506	496	508	509	509	514	513	527	512	100	512	495	93
Delaware	510	496	502	496	493	495	481	497	481	100	489	469	95
District of Columbia	483	467	494	486	474	464	466	498	482	100	495	474	100
Florida	495	493	498	500	496	498	479	512	479	100	503	463	90
Georgia	478	473	488	486	488	490	475	537	516	68	539	515	53
Hawaii	480	505	488	519	483	505	470	549	546	51	565	549	30
Idaho	542	524	540	541	543	541	517	500	484	100	494	476	95
Illinois	542	547	568	586	585	600	577	504	503	98	492	478	96
Indiana	486	486	498	501	494	505	477	540	534	64	489	482	100
Iowa	584	588	589	600	603	613	582	611	609	3	610	598	2
Kansas	566	563	574	580	590	595	567	617	620	4	626	619	2
Kentucky	548	541	548	550	575	575	563	609	598	4	616	592	2
Louisiana	551	537	562	558	555	550	547	597	573	5	611	583	3
Maine	501	490	504	500	468	467	454	504	491	98	551	529	38
Maryland	506	502	507	509	501	506	495	522	507	88	515	493	71
Massachusetts	503	498	511	513	512	526	509	560	559	80	560	551	57
Michigan	529	534	557	569	585	605	576	503	495	100	493	474	97
Minnesota	552	558	581	594	594	607	580	624	633	4	601	599	3
Mississippi	552	538	562	549	566	548	552	610	593	3	601	583	1
Missouri	548	541	572	577	593	595	580	610	603	4	603	588	3
Montana	540	542	543	546	538	538	517	598	587	10	607	586	5
Nebraska	559	562	560	571	585	593	568	615	614	3	631	621	1
Nevada	511	511	510	517	496	501	473	579	571	17	591	576	6
New Hampshire	518	510	520	519	520	524	510	531	524	93	526	508	82
New Jersey	495	498	498	513	495	514	497	541	540	82	538	528	64
New Mexico	554	546	549	543	553	549	534	533	522	19	458	444	94
New York	489	496	494	506	484	499	478	528	530	79	522	516	62
North Carolina	478	470	492	496	497	511	477	553	544	48	570	557	24
North Dakota	579	578	588	609	580	594	559	615	617	2	652	634	1
Ohio	526	522	533	539	538	548	522	536	534	21	525	519	18
Oklahoma	553	542	563	560	569	568	547	490	481	20	486	468	18
Oregon	515	509	527	527	523	524	499	557	547	51	574	551	24
Pennsylvania	497	490	498	497	492	501	480	543	534	67	547	531	48
Rhode Island	498	488	505	500	494	495	488	501	489	100	489	468	95
South Carolina	475	467	484	482	484	495	468	524	503	68	527	501	50
South Dakota	580	570	587	588	592	603	571	609	610	3	605	602	1
Tennessee	558	544	563	553	576	571	565	601	585	7	606	585	4
Texas	490	489	493	500	484	505	473	510	500	73	497	481	71
Utah	566	555	570	569	568	559	547	601	603	3	621	618	2
Vermont	507	493	513	508	519	521	506	559	545	63	563	536	45
Virginia	501	496	509	500	512	512	497	567	549	65	569	544	49
Washington	513	511	526	528	524	532	508	539	534	69	549	532	37
West Virginia	520	514	526	511	515	507	500	480	456	98	478	445	90
Wisconsin	552	559	584	597	595	604	579	615	628	3	615	621	2
Wyoming	534	538	545	545	570	567	546	614	606	2	604	596	1
National average	**500**	**501**	**505**	**514**	**501**	**516**	**492**	**528**	**523**	**NA**	**520**	**508**	**NA**

NA = Not available. **Note:** In 1995, the College Board recentered the scoring scale for the SAT. In 2005, the Verbal portion became Critical reading, and a writing test was added. In 2016, this portion became Evidence-based reading and writing. (1) Beginning in Mar. 2016, students took a redesigned SAT test. The College Board advised against comparing 2020 and 2023 SAT results with earlier data. (2) Percentage of students from the class of 2023 who took the SAT during high school.

EDUCATION: COLLEGES AND UNIVERSITIES

Four-Year Colleges and Universities

Note: These listings include only accredited degree-granting institutions in the U.S. and U.S. territories with a total enrollment of 1,200 or more. Only four-year colleges and universities that award a bachelor's degree as their highest undergraduate degree are included. Data reported for institutions that provided updated information on Peterson's Annual Survey of Undergraduate Institutions for the 2023-24 academic year, with some exceptions where the previous academic year was the most recent available.

All institutions are coeducational except those where the ZIP code is followed directly by a number in parentheses: (1) = men only; (2) = primarily men; (3) = women only; (4) = primarily women; (5) undergraduate: men only, graduate: coed; (6) undergraduate: women only, graduate: coed.

The **Tuition & fees** column shows the annual tuition and required fees for full-time students or, where indicated, the tuition and standard fees per unit for part-time students. Where tuition varies according to residence, the figure is given for the most local resident and is coded as follows: (A) = area residents; (S) = state residents; all other figures apply to all students regardless of residence. Where annual expenses are expressed as a lump sum (including full-time tuition, mandatory fees, and room and board), the figure is entered under Tuition & fees and coded (C) = comprehensive fee. **Room & board** is the typical cost for one academic year.

Control: (1) independent (nonprofit); (2) independent-religious; (3) proprietary (profit-making); (4) federal; (5) state; (6) commonwealth (Puerto Rico); (7) territory (U.S. territories); (8) county; (9) district; (10) city; (11) state and local; (12) state-related; (13) private—unspecified; (14) public—unspecified. **Degree** means the highest degree offered: B = bachelor's, M = master's, D = doctorate.

Enrollment is the total number of matriculated undergraduate and (if applicable) graduate students.

Faculty is the total number of full-time and part-time faculty members teaching courses.

Grad. rate is the percentage of full-time, first-time bachelor's (or equivalent) degree-seeking undergraduate students entering school in 2017 (or most recent available year prior) who obtained their degrees within six years.

NA indicates category is inapplicable, or data is not available from a consistent source.

Name, address	Year founded	Tuition & fees	Room & board	Control, degree	Enroll-ment	Faculty	Grad. rate
Abilene Christian Univ., Abilene, TX 79699	1906	$44,200	$14,540	2-D	5,057	463	61%
Abraham Baldwin Agr. Coll., Tifton, GA 31793	1933	$3,268 (A)	$9,800	5-B	3,327	NA	NA
Acad. of Art Univ., San Francisco, CA 94105-3410	1929	$29,896	NA	3-M	6,823	621	NA
Adams State Univ., Alamosa, CO 81101	1921	$8,959 (A)	$10,440	14-D	3,141	245	33
Adelphi Univ., Garden City, NY 11530-0701	1896	$49,110	$20,028	1-D	7,406	1,136	69
Adrian Coll., Adrian, MI 49221-2575	1859	$39,396	$12,870	2-M	1,871	194	52
Adventist Univ. of Health Scis., Orlando, FL 32803	1992	$21,420	$22,320	1-D	1,692	292	NA
Alabama Agr. & Mech. Univ., Huntsville, AL 35811	1875	$8,860 (A)	$5,130	5-D	5,969	363	27
Alabama State Univ., Montgomery, AL 36101-0271	1867	$11,068 (A)	$7,052	5-D	3,964	226	29
Albany State Univ., Albany, GA 31705-2717	1903	$6,700 (A)	$9,476	5-M	6,615	158	34
Albion Coll., Albion, MI 49224-1831	1835	$56,950	$13,500	13-B	1,354	126	57
Albright Coll., Reading, PA 19612-5234	1856	$28,794	$13,954	2-M	1,530	NA	NA
Alcorn State Univ., Lorman, MS 39096-7500	1871	$8,549 (A)	$10,255	5-D	2,933	221	46
Allegheny Coll., Meadville, PA 16335	1815	$53,610	$13,796	13-B	1,233	176	71
Alliant Intl. Univ.–San Diego, San Diego, CA 92131	1952	$17,370	$19,431	1-D	3,200	520	NA
Alma Coll., Alma, MI 48801-1599	1886	$47,430	$13,128	2-M	1,260	907	62
Alvernia Univ., Reading, PA 19607-1799	1958	$45,000	$19,400	2-D	2,560	NA	61
Alverno Coll., Milwaukee, WI 53234-3922 (6)	1887	$32,794	$9,508	1-D	1,596	103	52
Amer. InterContinental Univ. Atlanta, Atlanta, GA 30328	1970	$14,910	$8,057	3-M	1,311	55	NA
Amer. InterContinental Univ. Online, Schaumburg, IL 60173	1970	$12,860	$8,057	3-M	12,637	NA	NA
Amer. Intl. Coll., Springfield, MA 01109-3189	1885	$42,970	$16,260	1-D	3,283	NA	NA
Amer. Publ. Univ. System, Charles Town, WV 25414	1991	$8,400	NA	3-D	50,047	NA	NA
Amer. Univ., Washington, DC 20016-8001	1893	$58,771	$17,960	1-D	13,019	1,662	78
AmeriTech Coll., Draper, UT 84020-6545	NA	$18,900	NA	3-M	1,309	NA	NA
Amherst Coll., Amherst, MA 01002-5000	1821	$67,280	$17,560	13-B	1,910	313	93
Anderson Univ., Anderson, IN 46012	1917	$35,640	$12,250	2-D	1,255	174	50
Anderson Univ., Anderson, SC 29621	1911	$33,520	$11,940	1-D	4,346	422	66
Andrews Univ., Berrien Springs, MI 49104	1874	$33,710	$10,050	1-D	2,867	171	71
Angelo State Univ., San Angelo, TX 76909	1928	$9,443 (A)	$12,140	14-D	11,250	412	41
Anna Maria Coll., Paxton, MA 01612	1946	$43,064	$16,240	2-D	1,448	26	42
Antelope Valley Coll., Lancaster, CA 93536-5426	1929	$1,104 (A)	NA	9-B	11,105	352	NA
Appalachian State Univ., Boone, NC 28608	1899	$7,541 (A)	$6,630	5-D	21,253	1,477	73
Aquinas Coll., Grand Rapids, MI 49506	1886	$40,218	$15,310	2-M	1,265	163	60
Arapahoe Comm. Coll., Littleton, CO 80160-9002	1965	$4,435 (A)	$14,679	5-B	12,636	507	NA
Arcadia Univ., Glenside, PA 19038-3295	1853	$49,610	$14,380	2-D	3,142	377	NA
Arkansas State Univ., State University, AR 72467	1909	$8,378 (A)	NA	5-D	13,024	669	51
Arizona State Univ. at the Tempe campus, Tempe, AZ 85287	1885	$12,223 (A)	$16,712	14-D	79,593	4,661	69
Arkansas Tech Univ., Russellville, AR 72801	1909	$10,635 (A)	$9,852	5-D	9,487	474	50
Art Ctr. Coll. of Design, Pasadena, CA 91103	1930	$54,170	NA	1-M	2,382	NA	83
Asbury Univ., Wilmore, KY 40390-1198	1890	$33,640	$10,804	13-M	1,942	183	65
Ashford Univ., San Diego, CA 92123	1918	$11,960	NA	3-D	24,832	748	20
Ashland Univ., Ashland, OH 44805-3702	1878	$28,910	$11,960	1-D	6,201	389	61
Aspen Univ., Denver, CO 80246-1930	1960	$4,968	NA	1-D	6,373	NA	NA
Assumption Coll., Worcester, MA 01609-1296	1904	$49,414	$9,586	1-M	2,044	213	75
Athens State Univ., Athens, AL 35611	1822	$10,020 (A)	$11,313	5-M	2,955	188	NA
Atlantic Univ. Coll., Guaynabo, PR 00970	1983	$5,420	NA	1-M	1,489	NA	NA
Auburn Univ. at Montgomery, Montgomery, AL 36124-4023	1967	$9,772 (A)	$12,762	14-D	5,190	331	36
Auburn Univ., Auburn University, AL 36849	1856	$12,176 (A)	$16,124	5-D	33,015	1,726	79
Augsburg Coll., Minneapolis, MN 55454-1351	1869	$45,452	$15,149	1-D	3,161	313	52
Augusta Univ., Augusta, GA 30912	1828	$8,414 (A)	NA	5-D	3,891	NA	NA
Augustana Coll., Rock Island, IL 61201-2296	1860	$49,834	$12,166	2-M	2,484	253	79
Augustana Univ., Sioux Falls, SD 57197	1860	$39,190	$9,470	2-D	2,158	216	76
Aurora Univ., Aurora, IL 60506-4892	1893	$29,170	$7,520	13-D	5,935	550	58
Austin Comm. Coll. District, Austin, TX 78752-4390	1973	$8,580 (A)	NA	11-B	39,896	444	NA
Austin Peay State Univ., Clarksville, TN 37044	1927	$9,023 (A)	$13,462	14-D	9,945	687	43

Name, address	Year founded	Tuition & fees	Room & board	Control, degree	Enroll-ment	Faculty	Grad. rate
Averett Univ., Danville, VA 24541-3692	1859	$38,550	$14,530	13-M	1,317	209	46%
Azusa Pacific Univ., Azusa, CA 91702-7000	1899	$44,458	$14,056	2-D	7,131	751	61
Babson Coll., Babson Park, MA 02457-0310	1919	$57,152	$21,496	1-M	3,943	275	92
Baker Coll., Flint, MI 48507	1911	$13,900	$4,600	1-D	3,898	608	25
Baldwin Wallace Univ., Berea, OH 44017-2088	1845	$39,832	$13,774	13-M	3,308	430	69
Ball State Univ., Muncie, IN 47306	1918	$11,082 (A)	$12,334	5-D	20,440	1,207	63
Bard Coll., Annandale-on-Hudson, NY 12504	1860	$66,084	$18,852	1-D	2,303	281	72
Barnard Coll., New York, NY 10027-6598 (3)	1889	$69,888	$21,714	1-B	3,223	388	93
Barry Univ., Miami Shores, FL 33161-6695	1940	$33,950	$12,820	1-D	6,836	1,021	37
Barton Coll., Wilson, NC 27893-7000	1902	$37,006	$12,024	13-M	1,259	137	52
Baruch Coll. of the City Univ. of New York, New York, NY 10010-5585	1919	$7,461 (A)	NA	11-D	19,698	704	72
Bay Path Univ., Longmeadow, MA 01106-2292 (6)	1897	$37,527	$13,316	1-D	1,689	NA	NA
Baylor Univ., Waco, TX 76798	1845	$58,280	$15,878	13-D	20,824	1,583	80
Belhaven Univ., Jackson, MS 39202-1789	1883	$29,195	$9,400	13-D	3,613	557	51
Bellarmine Univ., Louisville, KY 40205	1950	$48,770	$10,850	1-D	2,993	375	68
Bellevue Coll., Bellevue, WA 98007-6484	1966	$4,205 (A)	NA	5-B	10,617	746	NA
Bellevue Univ., Bellevue, NE 68005-3098	1965	$8,636	$10,683	1-D	9,665	NA	NA
Belmont Abbey Coll., Belmont, NC 28012-1802	1876	$19,900	$12,142	2-M	1,501	91	47
Belmont Univ., Nashville, TN 37212	1890	$42,540	$15,010	13-D	8,862	923	72
Bemidji State Univ., Bemidji, MN 56601-2699	1919	$10,224 (A)	NA	5-M	4,577	NA	NA
Benedict Coll., Columbia, SC 29204	1870	$18,308	$7,146	13-D	1,731	133	21
Benedictine Coll., Atchison, KS 66002-1499	1859	$36,350	$14,220	2-M	2,334	189	62
Benedictine Univ., Lisle, IL 60532	1887	$35,940	$10,850	2-D	3,123	299	53
Bentley Univ., Waltham, MA 02452-4705	1917	$61,480	$20,140	13-D	5,264	502	88
Berea Coll., Berea, KY 40404	1855	$45,058	$8,208	1-B	1,487	199	62
Berkeley Coll.–New York City Campus, New York, NY 10017	1936	$29,600	$7,680	13-M	1,902	140	42
Berkeley Coll.–Woodland Park Campus, Woodland Park, NJ 07424	1931	$28,600	$7,680	3-M	2,078	96	43
Berklee Coll. of Mus, Boston, MA 02215-3693	1945	$52,040	$19,930	1-M	8,448	1,311	67
Berry Coll., Mount Berry, GA 30149	1902	$40,366	$14,230	13-M	2,370	243	74
Beth Medrash Govoha, Lakewood, NJ 08701-2797 (1)	1943	$23,656	NA	2-M	5,788	NA	NA
Bethel Coll., Mishawaka, IN 46545-5591	1947	$33,320	$10,250	2-M	1,292	67	57
Bethel Univ., McKenzie, TN 38201	1842	$18,168	$10,324	2-D	3,779	445	75
Bethel Univ., St. Paul, MN 55112-6999	1871	$44,226	$12,170	13-D	3,521	410	75
Bethune-Cookman Univ., Daytona Beach, FL 32114-3099	1904	$14,794	$10,396	2-M	2,516	196	29
Big Bend Comm. Coll., Moses Lake, WA 98837-3299	1962	$4,358 (A)	NA	5-B	3,518	96	NA
Binghamton Univ., State Univ. of New York, Binghamton, NY 13902-6000	1946	$10,363 (A)	$18,809	5-D	18,312	1,107	82
Biola Univ., La Mirada, CA 90639-0001	1908	$48,984	$12,780	2-D	5,296	457	69
Bismarck State Coll., Bismarck, ND 58506-5587	1939	$5,247 (A)	NA	5-B	3,771	28	NA
Black Hills State Univ., Spearfish, SD 57799	1883	$9,911 (A)	$7,302	5-M	3,425	NA	42
Bloomsburg Univ. of Pennsylvania, Bloomsburg, PA 17815-1301	1839	$11,169 (A)	$11,326	5-D	7,438	195	56
Bluefield State Coll., Bluefield, WV 24701-2198	1895	$9,700 (A)	$10,200	5-M	1,298	109	38
Bob Jones Univ., Greenville, SC 29614	1927	$24,470	$9,990	13-D	2,893	223	71
Boise State Univ., Boise, ID 83725-0399	1932	$9,048 (A)	$7,442	5-D	26,727	NA	61
Boston Coll., Chestnut Hill, MA 02467-3800	1863	$71,418	$17,930	13-D	14,694	1,474	91
Boston Univ., Boston, MA 02215	1839	$68,102	$19,020	1-D	36,624	2,829	90
Bowdoin Coll., Brunswick, ME 04011	1794	$67,832	$18,488	13-B	1,850	235	96
Bowie State Univ., Bowie, MD 20715-9465	1865	$9,217 (A)	$12,441	5-D	6,408	560	38
Bowling Green State Univ., Bowling Green, OH 43403	1910	$13,390 (A)	$11,784	14-D	17,027	1,106	62
Bowling Green State Univ.–Firelands Coll., Huron, OH 44839-9791	1968	$5,337 (A)	NA	5-B	1,970	102	NA
Bradley Univ., Peoria, IL 61625-0002	1897	$39,680	$12,850	1-D	5,217	613	72
Brandeis Univ., Waltham, MA 02454-9110	1948	$67,680	$19,944	1-D	5,302	553	86
Brenau Univ., Gainesville, GA 30501 (4)	1878	$33,757	$12,600	13-D	2,420	271	37
Bridgewater Coll., Bridgewater, VA 22812-1599	1880	$16,090	$14,850	13-M	1,436	146	49
Bridgewater State Univ., Bridgewater, MA 02325	1840	$11,734 (A)	$14,078	5-M	9,604	456	56
Brigham Young Univ., Provo, UT 84602-1001	1875	$13,376	$10,396	1-D	35,074	1,921	79
Brigham Young Univ.–Hawaii, Laie, HI 96762-1294	1955	$6,438	$9,916	2-B	3,107	NA	NA
Brigham Young Univ.–Idaho, Rexburg, ID 83460	1888	$4,536	$4,676	2-B	43,660	NA	44
Brookline Coll., Phoenix, AZ 85021	1979	NA	NA	3-M	1,511	27	NA
Brooklyn Coll. of the City Univ. of New York, Brooklyn, NY 11210-2889	1930	$7,450 (A)	$22,260	5-M	13,935	1,250	57
Brown Univ., Providence, RI 02912	1764	$71,312	$17,444	1-D	11,516	1,099	96
Bryan Coll., Dayton, TN 37321	1930	$18,900	$8,550	1-M	1,587	64	58
Bryant & Stratton Coll.–Orchard Park Campus, Orchard Park, NY 14127	1854	$20,080	NA	1-D	1,206	75	NA
Bryant & Stratton Coll.–Virginia Beach Campus, Virginia Beach, VA 23462	1854	$30,120	NA	1-D	1,504	15	NA
Bryant & Stratton Coll.–Wauwatosa Campus, Wauwatosa, WI 53226	1854	$30,570	NA	1-D	1,453	NA	NA
Bryant Univ., Smithfield, RI 02917	1863	$52,677	$17,860	1-M	3,591	286	81
Bryn Mawr Coll., Bryn Mawr, PA 19010-2899 (6)	1885	$65,510	$19,400	1-D	1,666	212	86
Bucknell Univ., Lewisburg, PA 17837	1846	$67,812	$16,924	1-M	3,892	429	86
Buena Vista Univ., Storm Lake, IA 50588	1891	$41,798	$11,330	13-M	1,309	97	47
Buffalo State Coll., State Univ. of New York, Buffalo, NY 14222-1095	1867	$8,486 (A)	$16,716	5-M	6,405	572	NA
Butler Univ., Indianapolis, IN 46208-3485	1855	$47,560	$17,250	1-D	5,763	654	80
Caldwell Univ., Caldwell, NJ 07006-6195	1939	$39,452	$13,800	1-D	2,092	127	59
California Baptist Univ., Riverside, CA 92504-3206	1950	$41,228	$12,140	13-D	11,483	791	58
California Coll. of the Arts, San Francisco, CA 94107	1907	$57,946	$21,075	1-M	1,225	NA	NA

Name, address	Year founded	Tuition & fees	Room & board	Control, degree	Enroll-ment	Faculty	Grad. rate
California Inst. of Integral Stds, San Francisco, CA 94103	1968	$44,472	NA	13-D	2,047	175	NA
California Inst. of Tech., Pasadena, CA 91125-0001	1891	$65,898	$20,283	13-D	2,463	356	93%
California Inst. of the Arts, Valencia, CA 91355-2340	1961	$56,724	$12,820	1-D	1,520	238	61
California Lutheran Univ., Thousand Oaks, CA 91360-2787	1959	$50,670	$16,210	1-D	3,410	444	74
California Polytechnic State Univ., San Luis Obispo, San Luis Obispo, CA 93407	1901	$12,721 (A)	$18,225	5-M	22,279	1,469	86
California State Polytechnic Univ., Pomona, Pomona, CA 91768-2557	1938	$7,438 (A)	$16,682	14-D	26,415	1,515	67
California State Univ., Bakersfield, Bakersfield, CA 93311	1965	$8,090 (A)	$15,076	5-D	9,787	624	NA
California State Univ., Channel Islands, Camarillo, CA 93012	2002	$7,148 (A)	$14,200	5-D	6,938	NA	NA
California State Univ., Chico, Chico, CA 95929-0722	1887	$7,972 (A)	$12,489	5-M	13,999	895	64
California State Univ., Dominguez Hills, Carson, CA 90747-0001	1960	$8,376 (A)	$16,200	5-M	14,299	1,013	48
California State Univ., East Bay, Hayward, CA 94542-3000	1957	$6,084 (A)	$17,831	5-D	13,041	882	NA
California State Univ., Fresno, Fresno, CA 93740-8027	1911	$7,341 (A)	NA	5-D	21,462	1,377	NA
California State Univ., Fullerton, Fullerton, CA 92831-3599	1957	$7,470 (A)	$18,898	5-D	41,962	2,203	69
California State Univ., Long Beach, Long Beach, CA 90840	1949	$7,378 (A)	$15,222	5-D	38,190	2,547	70
California State Univ., Los Angeles, Los Angeles, CA 90032-8530	1947	$7,158 (A)	$19,696	5-D	25,080	NA	52
California State Univ., Monterey Bay, Seaside, CA 93955-8001	1994	$7,437 (A)	$14,102	5-M	6,742	535	63
California State Univ., Northridge, Northridge, CA 91330	1958	$7,095 (A)	$20,306	5-D	40,564	1,980	NA
California State Univ., Sacramento, Sacramento, CA 95819	1947	$8,018 (A)	$19,174	5-D	30,946	126	55
California State Univ., San Bernardino, San Bernardino, CA 92407	1965	$8,076 (A)	$15,002	5-D	18,510	1,166	55
California State Univ., San Marcos, San Marcos, CA 92096-0001	1990	$8,086 (A)	$15,388	14-M	15,431	868	54
California State Univ., Stanislaus, Turlock, CA 95382	1957	$8,246 (A)	$12,728	5-D	9,845	698	58
Calvin Coll., Grand Rapids, MI 49546-4388	1876	$39,350	$12,120	13-M	3,364	313	77
Cambridge Coll., Boston, MA 02129	1971	$19,691	$11,000	1-D	2,356	231	NA
Cameron Univ., Lawton, OK 73505-6377	1908	$6,900 (A)	$9,410	5-M	3,559	213	28
Campbell Univ., Buies Creek, NC 27506	1887	$40,820	$15,200	2-D	5,272	500	56
Campbellsville Univ., Campbellsville, KY 42718-2799	1906	$27,998	$8,988	1-D	12,249	253	NA
Canisius Coll., Buffalo, NY 14208-1098	1870	$34,500	$15,150	13-M	2,545	265	71
Capella Univ., Minneapolis, MN 55402	1993	$14,990	NA	3-D	11,773	NA	NA
Capital Univ., Columbus, OH 43209-2394	1830	$41,788	$13,446	13-D	2,388	337	66
Carleton Coll., Northfield, MN 55057-4001	1866	$68,892	$17,586	1-B	2,019	271	91
Carlow Univ., Pittsburgh, PA 15213-3165 (4)	1929	$35,874	$13,808	2-D	2,310	608	55
Carnegie Mellon Univ., Pittsburgh, PA 15213-3891	1900	$65,374	$20,850	1-D	16,779	1,237	NA
Carroll Coll., Helena, MT 59625-0002	1909	$40,352	$11,212	2-B	1,330	NA	69
Carson-Newman Univ., Jefferson City, TN 37760	1851	$34,700	$10,507	1-D	2,735	248	45
Cascadia Coll., Bothell, WA 98011	1994	$4,210 (A)	NA	5-B	2,044	129	NA
Case Western Reserve Univ., Cleveland, OH 44106	1826	$66,674	$18,762	1-D	12,266	1,016	87
Castleton Univ., Castleton, VT 05735	1787	$13,078 (A)	$12,404	5-M	2,210	187	NA
Cecil Coll., North East, MD 21901-1999	1968	$4,770 (A)	NA	8-B	2,090	160	NA
Cedar Crest Coll., Allentown, PA 18104-6196 (4)	1867	$44,934	$12,722	2-D	1,440	108	74
Cedarville Univ., Cedarville, OH 45314	1895	$37,150	$9,574	2-D	5,374	463	74
Central Connecticut State Univ., New Britain, CT 06050-4010	1849	$13,050 (A)	$13,086	5-D	9,712	867	49
Central Michigan Univ., Mount Pleasant, MI 48859	1892	$14,790 (A)	NA	5-D	14,423	900	62
Central State Univ., Wilberforce, OH 45384	1887	$7,824 (A)	$11,390	5-M	5,434	147	25
Central Washington Univ., Ellensburg, WA 98926	1891	$9,402 (A)	$16,480	5-M	9,257	488	54
Centre Coll., Danville, KY 40422-1394	1819	$48,070	$12,300	13-B	1,356	140	87
Chadron State Coll., Chadron, NE 69337	1911	$8,294 (A)	$9,700	5-M	2,649	NA	NA
Chamberlain Coll. of Nurs., Addison, IL 60101	1889	$22,050	NA	3-D	23,964	1,055	NA
Chamberlain Coll. of Nurs., Atlanta, GA 30342	NA	$22,690	$14,540	3-B	1,330	NA	NA
Chamberlain Coll. of Nurs., Houston, TX 77041	NA	$22,990	$14,540	3-B	1,558	NA	NA
Chaminade Univ. of Honolulu, Honolulu, HI 96816-1578	1955	$194 (C)	NA	1-D	2,039	118	63
Champlain Coll., Burlington, VT 05402-0670	1878	$47,850	$17,600	1-M	2,228	266	63
Chapman Univ., Orange, CA 92866	1861	$64,984	$20,454	13-D	9,961	1,301	80
Charleston Southern Univ., Charleston, SC 29423-8087	1964	$30,505	$13,866	2-D	3,551	186	35
Charter Coll., Anchorage, AK 99508	1985	$17,208	NA	3-B	2,120	NA	NA
Charter Oak State Coll., New Britain, CT 06053-2142	1973	$8,506 (A)	NA	5-M	1,471	182	NA
Chatham Univ., Pittsburgh, PA 15232-2826 (4)	1869	$44,626	$13,600	1-D	2,319	349	67
Chestnut Hill Coll., Philadelphia, PA 19118-2693	1924	$40,100	$13,100	2-D	1,420	700	63
Chicago State Univ., Chicago, IL 60628	1867	$11,756 (A)	$8,724	5-D	2,366	219	21
Chipola Coll., Marianna, FL 32446-3065	1947	$3,450 (A)	NA	5-D	1,340	NA	NA
Christian Brothers Univ., Memphis, TN 38104-5581	1871	$38,420	$9,410	1-M	2,043	231	60
Christopher Newport Univ., Newport News, VA 23606-3072	1960	$16,828 (A)	$12,460	14-M	4,503	456	75
City Coll. of the City Univ. of New York, New York, NY 10031-9198	1847	$7,340 (A)	$13,536	14-D	14,628	1,334	55
Claflin Univ., Orangeburg, SC 29115	1869	$8,238	$4,740	2-M	1,886	NA	NA
Claremont McKenna Coll., Claremont, CA 91711	1946	$67,980	$20,830	1-M	1,384	198	95
Clark Atlanta Univ., Atlanta, GA 30314	1988	$28,310	$18,106	2-D	4,000	314	46
Clark Univ., Worcester, MA 01610-1477	1887	$57,867	$12,500	13-D	3,801	336	77
Clayton State Univ., Morrow, GA 30260-0285	1969	$5,180 (A)	NA	5-M	7,052	NA	31
Clemson Univ., Clemson, SC 29634	1889	$15,554 (S)	$12,872	5-D	28,747	1,989	88
Coastal Carolina Univ., Conway, SC 29528-6054	1954	$11,820 (A)	$9,100	5-D	10,829	831	51
Coe Coll., Cedar Rapids, IA 52402-5092	1851	$52,576	$11,336	13-B	1,278	143	59
Colby Coll., Waterville, ME 04901-8840	1813	$69,600	$17,890	1-B	2,282	238	90
Colgate Univ., Hamilton, NY 13346-1386	1819	$70,306	$17,610	1-M	3,146	376	91
Coll. for Creative Stds, Detroit, MI 48202-4034	1906	$51,365	$8,350	1-M	1,517	296	64
Coll. of Central Florida, Ocala, FL 34474	1957	$3,613 (A)	$8,046	11-B	5,492	52	NA
Coll. of Charleston, Charleston, SC 29424-0001	1770	$12,978 (A)	$14,091	5-D	11,729	926	65
Coll. of Coastal Georgia, Brunswick, GA 31520	1961	$4,594 (A)	$14,012	5-B	3,232	49	23
Coll. of Mount St. Vincent, Riverdale, NY 10471-1093	1911	$44,540	$14,900	1-M	2,877	260	57
Coll. of St. Benedict, Saint Joseph, MN 56374 (3)	1913	$53,884	$12,160	2-D	1,470	105	78
Coll. of Southern Idaho, Twin Falls, ID 83303-1238	1964	$4,200 (A)	$6,360	5-B	8,775	334	NA

Name, address	Year founded	Tuition & fees	Room & board	Control, degree	Enroll-ment	Faculty	Grad. rate
Coll. of Staten Island of the City Univ. of New York, Staten Island, NY 10314-6600	1976	$7,500 (A)	NA	11-D	10,657	932	50%
Coll. of the Holy Cross, Worcester, MA 01610-2395	1843	$64,500	$18,820	13-B	3,219	348	90
Coll. of the Ozarks, Point Lookout, MO 65726	1906	$22,320	$8,500	13-B	1,427	129	61
Collin Cty. Comm. Coll. District, McKinney, TX 75069	1985	$2,010 (A)	$9,379	5-B	37,776	2,029	NA
Colorado Christian Univ., Lakewood, CO 80226	1914	$41,342	$13,488	2-B	1,565	153	62
Colorado Mesa Univ., Grand Junction, CO 81501-3122	1925	$8,508 (A)	$13,146	14-D	8,995	597	45
Colorado Mountain Coll., Glenwood Springs, CO 81601	1965	$3,270 (A)	$12,680	9-B	5,185	NA	NA
Colorado Sch. of Mines, Golden, CO 80401-1887	1874	$21,186 (S)	$16,820	5-D	7,608	437	80
Colorado State Univ., Fort Collins, CO 80523	1870	$13,382 (A)	$16,817	5-D	33,361	2,170	68
Colorado State Univ.–Global Campus, Greenwood Village, CO 80111	2007	$8,400 (S)	NA	5-M	9,507	521	NA
Colorado State Univ.–Pueblo, Pueblo, CO 81001-4901	1933	$9,720 (A)	$10,350	5-D	6,617	339	35
Colorado Tech Univ. Colorado Springs, Colorado Springs, CO 80907	1965	$12,240	NA	3-D	24,504	NA	NA
Columbia Basin Coll., Pasco, WA 99301-3397	1955	$5,686 (A)	$17,868	5-B	5,640	NA	NA
Columbia Coll., Columbia, SC 29203-5998 (4)	1854	$21,250	$8,400	2-M	1,514	78	55
Columbia Coll. Chicago, Chicago, IL 60605-1996	1890	$33,782	$23,400	13-M	6,529	815	49
Columbia Intl. Univ., Columbia, SC 29203	1923	$27,900	$11,950	1-D	2,849	141	68
Columbia Southern Univ., Orange Beach, AL 36561	1993	$6,224	$9,548	13-D	18,487	562	NA
Columbia Univ., New York, NY 10027	1754	$68,400	$17,058	1-D	29,661	196	95
Columbia Univ., Sch. of General Studies, New York, NY 10027-6939	1754	$67,310	$20,628	1-D	28,114	3,270	92
Columbus State Univ., Columbus, GA 31907-5645	1958	$5,898 (A)	$11,720	5-D	7,191	522	45
Concord Univ., Athens, WV 24712-1000	1872	$10,664 (A)	$11,526	14-M	1,798	131	42
Concordia Coll., Moorhead, MN 56562	1891	$29,916	$9,800	2-D	2,042	160	72
Concordia Univ. Chicago, River Forest, IL 60305-1499	1864	$37,488	$11,510	2-D	5,029	397	47
Concordia Univ. Irvine, Irvine, CA 92612-3299	1972	$43,480	$13,870	2-D	3,734	462	63
Concordia Univ. Nebraska, Seward, NE 68434	1894	$40,640	$10,850	2-M	1,203	253	NA
Concordia Univ. St. Paul, St. Paul, MN 55104-5494	1893	$25,600	$11,500	13-D	5,819	485	57
Concordia Univ. Texas, Austin, TX 78726	1926	$36,690	$13,700	2-D	1,733	181	NA
Concordia Univ. Wisconsin, Mequon, WI 53097-2402	1881	$35,470	$13,200	1-D	5,063	504	64
Connecticut Coll., New London, CT 06320	1911	$67,242	$18,558	1-B	1,995	257	84
Converse Coll., Spartanburg, SC 29302 (6)	1889	$21,410	$12,664	1-D	1,319	NA	NA
Coppin State Univ., Baltimore, MD 21216-3698	1900	$7,100 (A)	$12,155	5-D	3,800	312	NA
Cornell Univ., Ithaca, NY 14853	1865	$69,314	$19,428	1-D	26,284	744	100
Cornerstone Univ., Grand Rapids, MI 49525-5897	1941	$31,210	$11,360	2-D	1,781	167	NA
Creighton Univ., Omaha, NE 68178-0001	1878	$48,856	$13,652	1-D	8,255	875	80
Cumberland Univ., Lebanon, TN 37087	1842	$27,840	$10,340	1-M	1,481	NA	NA
Curry Coll., Milton, MA 02186-9984	1879	$47,570	$18,310	1-M	2,053	276	52
Daemen Coll., Amherst, NY 14226-3592	1947	$35,218	$14,230	13-D	2,642	253	58
Dakota State Univ., Madison, SD 57042-1799	1881	$9,633 (A)	$7,862	14-D	3,509	138	48
Dallas Baptist Univ., Dallas, TX 75211-9299	1898	$40,190	$11,400	13-D	4,201	461	61
Dalton State Coll., Dalton, GA 30720	1963	$3,990 (A)	$10,419	5-B	4,366	NA	NA
Dartmouth Coll., Hanover, NH 03755	1769	$65,511	$18,759	1-D	6,746	928	96
Davenport Univ., Grand Rapids, MI 49512	1866	$30,220	NA	1-M	6,429	610	NA
Davidson Coll., Davidson, NC 28035	1837	$64,160	$17,666	1-B	1,904	222	92
Daytona State Coll., Daytona Beach, FL 32114	1957	$3,610 (A)	NA	5-B	12,728	746	NA
Delaware State Univ., Dover, DE 19901-2277	1891	$9,688 (A)	$12,035	5-D	5,797	NA	45
Delaware Valley Univ., Doylestown, PA 18901-2697	1896	$44,850	$15,076	1-D	2,189	258	52
Delta State Univ., Cleveland, MS 38733-0001	1924	$8,605 (A)	$8,731	5-D	2,716	253	47
Denison Univ., Granville, OH 43023	1831	$67,000	$16,400	1-B	2,406	312	80
DePaul Univ., Chicago, IL 60604-2287	1898	$45,999	$19,095	13-D	21,348	1,722	70
DePauw Univ., Greencastle, IN 46135	1837	$59,070	$15,330	2-B	1,819	228	80
DeSales Univ., Center Valley, PA 18034-9568	1964	$46,800	$13,800	1-D	2,929	409	71
DeVry Univ. Online, Addison, IL 60101	1997	$18,860	$16,232	3-M	22,298	991	41
Dickinson Coll., Carlisle, PA 17013-2896	1773	$65,650	$17,100	1-M	2,217	259	83
Dickinson State Univ., Dickinson, ND 58601-4896	1918	$9,118 (A)	$8,564	5-M	1,453	148	43
Dixie State Univ., St. George, UT 84770-3876	1911	$6,074 (A)	$9,308	5-M	12,567	661	35
Dominican Coll., Orangeburg, NY 10962-1210	1952	$33,060	$14,790	1-D	1,378	188	57
Dominican Univ. of California, San Rafael, CA 94901-2298	1890	$52,161	$16,191	13-D	1,889	285	76
Dominican Univ., River Forest, IL 60305-1099	1901	$38,828	$11,600	2-D	3,424	406	58
Dordt Coll., Sioux Center, IA 51250-1697	1955	$35,960	$11,430	2-M	1,737	NA	75
Drake Univ., Des Moines, IA 50311-4516	1881	$52,130	$12,452	1-D	4,504	454	77
Drew Univ., Madison, NJ 07940-1493	1867	$45,060	$16,404	2-D	2,196	191	74
Drexel Univ., Philadelphia, PA 19104-2875	1891	$62,412	$18,096	1-D	21,573	1,906	77
Drury Univ., Springfield, MO 65802	1873	$36,955	$11,379	1-M	1,595	109	66
Duke Univ., Durham, NC 27708	1838	$68,953	$19,053	2-D	17,112	1,897	96
Duquesne Univ., Pittsburgh, PA 15282-0001	1878	$48,986	$23,940	13-D	8,137	938	75
D'Youville Coll., Buffalo, NY 14201-1084	1908	$34,600	$11,800	1-D	2,554	141	58
East Carolina Univ., Greenville, NC 27858-4353	1907	$7,170 (A)	$11,541	5-D	26,785	1,490	62
East Central Univ., Ada, OK 74820	1909	$7,405 (A)	$7,640	5-M	4,650	99	31
East Georgia State Coll., Swainsboro, GA 30401-2699	1973	$2,900 (A)	$11,318	5-B	3,001	125	NA
East Stroudsburg Univ. of Pennsylvania, East Stroudsburg, PA 18301-2999	1893	$11,236 (A)	$10,804	14-D	5,463	313	44
East Tennessee State Univ., Johnson City, TN 37614	1911	$9,486 (A)	$10,270	5-D	13,166	1,118	55
East Texas Baptist Univ., Marshall, TX 75670-1498	1912	$28,760	$10,145	2-M	1,771	91	42
Eastern Connecticut State Univ., Willimantic, CT 06226-2295	1889	$13,928 (A)	$16,006	5-M	4,082	403	60
Eastern Florida State Coll., Cocoa, FL 32922-6597	1960	$2,496 (A)	NA	5-B	10,590	NA	NA
Eastern Illinois Univ., Charleston, IL 61920	1895	$13,658 (A)	$12,520	14-M	8,804	510	45
Eastern Kentucky Univ., Richmond, KY 40475-3102	1906	$11,280 (A)	$12,268	5-D	14,565	485	52
Eastern Mennonite Univ., Harrisonburg, VA 22802-2462	1917	$86,140	$13,170	2-D	1,292	177	47
Eastern Michigan Univ., Ypsilanti, MI 48197	1849	$15,792 (A)	$13,652	5-D	13,352	976	46

Name, address	Year founded	Tuition & fees	Room & board	Control, degree	Enroll-ment	Faculty	Grad. rate
Eastern New Mexico Univ., Portales, NM 88130	1934	$7,074 (A)	$8,698	14-M	5,398	252	34%
Eastern Oregon Univ., La Grande, OR 97850-2899	1929	$10,709 (A)	$11,590	5-M	2,798	198	37
Eastern Univ., St. Davids, PA 19087-3696	1952	$38,400	$13,498	13-D	6,980	392	57
Eastern Washington Univ., Cheney, WA 99004-2431	1882	$8,586 (A)	$15,574	5-D	10,273	NA	47
Eckerd Coll., St. Petersburg, FL 33711	1958	$51,884	$14,734	13-B	1,986	185	68
ECPI Univ., Virginia Beach, VA 23462	1966	$18,484	NA	3-M	11,745	902	31
Edgewood Coll., Madison, WI 53711-1997	1927	$35,860	$13,250	2-D	1,339	NA	NA
EDP Univ. of Puerto Rico, Hato Rey, PR 00918	1968	$7,050	$10,320	1-M	1,375	144	27
Elizabeth City State Univ., Elizabeth City, NC 27909-7806	1891	$6,956 (A)	$11,986	5-M	2,149	154	42
Elizabethtown Coll., Elizabethtown, PA 17022-2298	1899	$37,950	$13,340	1-D	2,152	250	77
Elmhurst Coll., Elmhurst, IL 60126-3296	1871	$41,628	$11,858	13-D	3,850	474	65
Elms Coll., Chicopee, MA 01013-2839	1928	$43,325	$15,605	2-D	1,332	162	65
Elon Univ., Elon, NC 27244-2010	1889	$44,536	$17,051	13-D	7,207	623	83
Embry-Riddle Aeron Univ.–Daytona, Daytona Beach, FL 32114-3900	1926	$44,074	$16,894	1-D	7,945	44	NA
Embry-Riddle Aeron Univ.–Prescott, Prescott, AZ 86301-3720	1926	$43,974	$14,928	1-D	3,162	192	71
Emerson Coll., Boston, MA 02116-4624	1880	$55,392	$20,810	1-D	3,702	NA	NA
Emmanuel Coll., Boston, MA 02115	1919	$48,690	$18,280	13-M	2,059	197	66
Emory & Henry Coll., Emory, VA 24327-0947	1836	$35,150	$14,060	2-D	1,230	NA	54
Emory Univ., Atlanta, GA 30322-1100	1836	$64,280	$20,220	2-D	14,830	1,327	92
Emporia State Univ., Emporia, KS 66801-5415	1863	$7,356 (A)	$10,542	5-D	4,658	207	54
Endicott Coll., Beverly, MA 01915-2096	1939	$40,650	$17,806	1-D	4,381	751	78
Eugene Lang Coll. of Lib. Arts, New York, NY 10011-8601	1972	$51,900	$27,050	13-B	1,555	231	56
Evangel Univ., Springfield, MO 65802	1955	$28,548	$8,948	1-D	2,495	297	64
Everglades Univ., Boca Raton, FL 33431	1989	$21,680	NA	1-M	2,718	362	58
Excelsior Coll., Albany, NY 12203-5159	1970	$17,340	$8,200	1-M	14,633	313	NA
Fairfield Univ., Fairfield, CT 06824	1942	$58,350	$19,838	2-D	6,289	729	84
Fairmont State Univ., Fairmont, WV 26554	1865	$8,454 (A)	$9,326	5-M	3,298	NA	NA
Farmingdale State Coll., Farmingdale, NY 11735	1912	$8,576 (A)	$8,836	5-M	9,541	793	59
Fashion Inst. of Tech., New York, NY 10001-5992 (4)	1944	$7,793 (A)	$25,458	5-M	8,108	928	NA
Faulkner Univ., Montgomery, AL 36109-3398	1942	$23,920	$8,230	1-D	3,350	NA	NA
Fayetteville State Univ., Fayetteville, NC 28301-4298	1867	$5,507 (A)	$9,440	5-D	6,847	331	35
Feather River Coll., Quincy, CA 95971-9124	1968	$1,496 (A)	$12,691	9-B	1,821	108	NA
Felician Univ., Lodi, NJ 07644-2117	1942	$39,300	$14,740	1-D	2,205	97	52
Ferris State Univ., Big Rapids, MI 49307	1884	$15,256 (A)	$10,660	5-D	9,918	621	54
FIDM/Fashion Inst. of Design & Merchandising, Los Angeles Campus, Los Angeles, CA 90015-1421	1969	$33,771	NA	3-M	1,764	251	74
Fisher Coll., Boston, MA 02116-1500	1903	$35,689	$18,041	1-M	1,421	193	32
Fitchburg State Univ., Fitchburg, MA 01420-2697	1894	$11,160 (A)	$14,225	5-M	6,296	388	53
Flagler Coll., St. Augustine, FL 32085-1027	1968	$29,800	$16,660	13-M	2,441	164	56
Florida Agr. & Mech. Univ., Tallahassee, FL 32307-3200	1887	$5,785 (A)	$11,644	5-D	9,265	708	52
Florida Atlantic Univ., Boca Raton, FL 33431-0991	1961	$6,099 (A)	$15,860	5-D	30,849	1,441	64
Florida Gateway Coll., Lake City, FL 32025	1947	$3,610 (A)	$6,700	5-B	2,912	188	NA
Florida Gulf Coast Univ., Fort Myers, FL 33965-6565	1991	$8,045 (A)	$9,142	5-D	16,230	892	56
Florida Inst. of Tech., Melbourne, FL 32901-6975	1958	$45,900	$13,520	1-D	8,585	487	65
Florida Intl. Univ., Miami, FL 33199	1972	$6,566 (A)	$11,600	5-D	54,085	2,387	70
Florida Memorial Univ., Miami-Dade, FL 33054	1879	$19,110	$7,972	2-M	1,669	NA	NA
Florida Natl. Univ., Hialeah, FL 33012	1982	$17,368	NA	3-M	2,638	144	42
Florida Southern Coll., Lakeland, FL 33801-5698	1883	$43,220	$13,600	2-D	3,386	348	68
Florida Southwestern State Coll., Fort Myers, FL 33919	1962	$3,772 (A)	$10,044	11-B	13,797	500	NA
Florida State Coll. at Jacksonville, Jacksonville, FL 32202-4030	1965	$2,976 (A)	$8,052	5-B	19,053	1,014	NA
Florida State Univ., Tallahassee, FL 32306	1851	$5,654 (A)	$13,474	5-D	43,234	2,028	83
Fordham Univ., New York, NY 10458	1841	$62,990	$18,660	2-D	16,556	1,928	83
Fort Hays State Univ., Hays, KS 67601-4099	1902	$5,924 (A)	$9,079	5-D	15,033	NA	46
Fort Lewis Coll., Durango, CO 81301-3999	1911	$11,780 (A)	$11,334	5-M	3,425	238	43
Fort Valley State Univ., Fort Valley, GA 31030	1895	$5,526 (A)	$11,080	5-M	2,776	NA	28
Framingham State Univ., Framingham, MA 01701-9101	1839	$11,920 (A)	$15,310	5-M	4,111	290	55
Francis Marion Univ., Florence, SC 29502-0547	1970	$11,160 (A)	$9,432	5-D	4,017	331	43
Franciscan Univ. of Steubenville, Steubenville, OH 43952-1763	1946	$32,530	$9,540	1-D	3,039	141	77
Franklin & Marshall Coll., Lancaster, PA 17604-3003	1787	$68,580	$15,568	1-B	1,911	244	86
Franklin Pierce Univ., Rindge, NH 03461-0060	1962	$44,963	$15,911	1-D	1,434	NA	NA
Franklin Univ., Columbus, OH 43215-5399	1902	$9,577	$8,540	1-M	3,738	NA	NA
Freed-Hardeman Univ., Henderson, TN 38340-2399	1869	$25,000	$8,540	1-D	2,320	108	65
Fresno Pacific Univ., Fresno, CA 93702-4709	1944	$35,558	$8,800	1-M	2,711	NA	NA
Friends Univ., Wichita, KS 67213	1898	$32,578	$9,874	2-M	1,694	NA	40
Front Range Comm. Coll., Westminster, CO 80031	1968	$4,740 (A)	NA	5-B	21,096	1,086	NA
Frostburg State Univ., Frostburg, MD 21532-1099	1898	$10,220 (A)	$11,750	5-D	4,090	NA	NA
Full Sail Univ., Winter Park, FL 32792-7437 (2)	1979	$53,813	NA	13-M	26,421	735	NA
Galen Coll. of Nurs., Louisville, KY 40207	1989	$15,300	$15,660	3-M	4,369	197	NA
Galen Coll. of Nurs., San Antonio, TX 78229	1989	$415/quarter hr.	$15,660	3-B	3,732	186	NA
Galen Coll. of Nurs., St. Petersburg, FL 33716	1989	$15,300	$15,660	3-B	2,374	132	NA
Gallaudet Univ., Washington, DC 20002-3625	1864	$19,654	$14,775	1-D	1,246	259	44
Galveston Coll., Galveston, TX 77550	1967	$2,546 (A)	$7,926	11-B	2,119	132	NA
Gannon Univ., Erie, PA 16541-0001	1925	$39,496	$15,960	2-D	4,565	423	70
Gardner-Webb Univ., Boiling Springs, NC 28017	1905	$33,620	$10,690	2-D	3,884	NA	NA
Geneva Coll., Beaver Falls, PA 15010-3599	1848	$32,460	$10,980	1-M	1,251	179	61
George Fox Univ., Newberg, OR 97132-2697	1891	$42,750	$14,060	2-D	4,083	300	69
George Mason Univ., Fairfax, VA 22030	1972	$13,405 (A)	$13,120	5-D	39,528	2,960	69
Georgetown Univ., Washington, DC 20057	1789	$68,017	$22,994	1-D	20,392	2,023	94
Georgia Coll. & State Univ., Milledgeville, GA 31061	1889	$9,186 (A)	NA	5-D	6,811	443	62
Georgia Gwinnett Coll., Lawrenceville, GA 30043	2006	$4,948 (A)	$16,018	5-B	11,918	512	20

Name, address	Year founded	Tuition & fees	Room & board	Control, degree	Enroll-ment	Faculty	Grad. rate
Georgia Highlands Coll., Rome, GA 30161	1970	$3,048 (A)	NA	5-B	6,168	NA	NA
Georgia Inst. of Tech., Atlanta, GA 30332-0001	1885	$11,764 (A)	$15,570	14-D	47,946	1,284	92%
Georgia Military Coll., Milledgeville, GA 31061-3398	1879	$6,638 (A)	$5,325	5-D	6,765	628	NA
Georgia Southern Univ., Statesboro, GA 30458	1906	$6,998 (A)	$11,228	14-D	26,106	1,104	53
Georgia Southwestern State Univ., Americus, GA 31709-4693	1906	$5,996 (A)	$4,700	5-M	3,415	180	32
Georgia State Univ., Atlanta, GA 30302-3083	1915	$10,500 (A)	$16,002	14-D	7,385	1,626	53
Georgian Court Univ., Lakewood, NJ 08701-2697	1908	$70,720	$12,910	2-D	1,910	234	55
Gettysburg Coll., Gettysburg, PA 17325-1483	1832	$66,640	$16,110	13-M	2,216	260	83
Glenville State Coll., Glenville, WV 26351-1200	1872	$9,412 (A)	$11,484	5-M	1,577	NA	NA
Golden Gate Univ., San Francisco, CA 94105-2968	1901	$11,258	$13,200	1-D	2,685	153	NA
Gonzaga Univ., Spokane, WA 99258	1887	$55,480	$15,730	1-D	7,306	830	87
Goodwin Coll., East Hartford, CT 06118	1999	$39,976	$6,500	1-M	3,034	259	NA
Gordon Coll., Wenham, MA 01984-1899	1889	$30,700	$13,300	1-M	1,610	178	68
Goucher Coll., Baltimore, MD 21204-2794	1885	$53,350	$17,190	1-M	1,501	212	60
Governors State Univ., University Park, IL 60484	1969	$10,800 (A)	NA	5-D	4,338	524	17
Grace Coll., Winona Lake, IN 46590-1294	1948	$30,034	$10,712	2-D	1,381	NA	NA
Graceland Univ., Independence, MO 64050-3434	NA	$20,950	$11,000	1-D	1,204	127	39
Graceland Univ., Lamoni, IA 50140	1895	$20,950	$11,000	1-D	1,204	127	39
Grambling State Univ., Grambling, LA 71245	1901	$7,683 (A)	$11,706	5-D	4,153	NA	NA
Grand Canyon Univ., Phoenix, AZ 85017-1097	1949	$17,600	$10,400	2-D	62,424	NA	NA
Grand Valley State Univ., Allendale, MI 49401-9403	1960	$15,140 (A)	$10,420	5-D	22,269	1,812	69
Grand View Univ., Des Moines, IA 50316-1599	1896	$34,308	$11,032	2-M	1,649	83	52
Grantham Univ., Lenexa, KS 66219	1951	$8,280	NA	3-M	5,435	NA	NA
Green River Coll., Auburn, WA 98092-3699	1965	$4,808 (A)	NA	5-D	6,252	436	NA
Grinnell Coll., Grinnell, IA 50112-1690	1846	$64,862	$15,878	1-B	1,759	615	88
Grove City Coll., Grove City, PA 16127-2104	1876	$21,700	$12,230	13-M	2,394	239	80
Guam Comm. Coll., Mangilao, GU 96913	1977	$3,414 (A)	$10,800	7-B	1,690	194	NA
Gulf Coast State Coll., Panama City, FL 32401-1058	1957	$2,370 (A)	$13,482	5-B	4,847	257	NA
Gurnick Acad. of Med. Arts, San Mateo, CA 94403	2004	$17,708	$15,076	3-B	2,462	NA	NA
Gustavus Adolphus Coll., St. Peter, MN 56082-1498	1862	$55,746	$11,804	2-B	2,088	199	78
Gwynedd Mercy Univ., Gwynedd Valley, PA 19437-0901	1948	$40,122	$13,850	1-D	2,165	335	66
Hamilton Coll., Clinton, NY 13323-1296	1812	$68,960	$17,510	1-B	2,053	265	91
Hamline Univ., St. Paul, MN 55104-1284	1854	$48,311	$12,030	2-D	3,113	251	65
Hampton Univ., Hampton, VA 23668	1868	$30,842	$14,308	1-D	3,249	NA	53
Hardin-Simmons Univ., Abilene, TX 79698-0001	1891	$31,686	$10,634	2-D	2,128	206	55
Harding Univ., Searcy, AR 72149-0001	1924	$25,962	$9,060	2-D	4,805	360	69
Harris-Stowe State Univ., St. Louis, MO 63103-2136	1857	$6,442 (A)	$9,828	5-B	1,400	161	12
Harrisburg Univ. of Sci. & Tech., Harrisburg, PA 17101	2001	$24,400	$11,040	1-D	3,082	286	32
Harvard Univ., Cambridge, MA 02138	1636	$60,084	$21,190	13-D	11,865	1,078	98
Haverford Coll., Haverford, PA 19041-1392	1833	$70,398	$19,170	13-B	1,424	189	89
Hawai'i Pacific Univ., Honolulu, HI 96813	1965	$34,392	$21,050	1-D	4,748	321	41
Henderson State Univ., Arkadelphia, AR 71999-0001	1890	$8,244 (A)	$8,400	5-M	2,603	NA	NA
Herzing Univ., Madison, WI 53718	1948	$14,200	$12,324	1-M	1,642	NA	NA
High Point Univ., High Point, NC 27268	1924	$41,916	$16,524	2-D	5,860	326	70
Hillsdale Coll., Hillsdale, MI 49242-1298	1844	$33,189	$13,180	1-D	1,823	285	87
Hobart & William Smith Colls., Geneva, NY 14456	1822	$64,842	$17,768	1-M	1,669	182	73
Hofstra Univ., Hempstead, NY 11549	1935	$55,450	$18,560	1-D	10,393	1,281	67
Holy Family Univ., Philadelphia, PA 19114	1954	$33,968	$16,480	2-D	3,081	NA	55
Hood Coll., Frederick, MD 21701-8575	1893	$47,700	$16,200	1-D	2,078	240	55
Hope Coll., Holland, MI 49422-9000	1866	$38,530	$14,330	1-B	3,369	368	82
Houston Baptist Univ., Houston, TX 77074-3298	1960	$38,100	$9,585	13-D	4,257	314	44
Howard Univ., Washington, DC 20059-0002	1867	$35,810	$17,322	1-D	12,886	1,350	79
Humboldt State Univ., Arcata, CA 95521-8299	1913	$7,864 (A)	$12,540	5-M	5,976	531	47
Hunter Coll. of the City Univ. of New York, New York, NY 10065-5085	1870	$7,380 (A)	NA	5-D	22,970	1,094	56
Huntington Univ., Huntington, IN 46750-1299	1897	$29,982	$9,880	2-D	1,364	185	69
Husson Univ., Bangor, ME 04401-2999	1898	$22,072	$12,882	1-D	3,131	271	57
Idaho State Univ., Pocatello, ID 83209	1901	$8,610 (A)	$7,200	5-D	12,319	796	36
Illinois Inst. of Tech., Chicago, IL 60616	1890	$52,386	$17,356	1-D	8,563	660	72
Illinois State Univ., Normal, IL 61790	1857	$16,144 (A)	$11,754	5-D	20,989	1,233	66
Illinois Wesleyan Univ., Bloomington, IL 61702-2900	1850	$57,704	$13,370	1-B	1,576	197	83
Immaculata Univ., Immaculata, PA 19345	1920	$28,980	$13,150	2-D	2,426	291	65
Indian River State Coll., Fort Pierce, FL 34981-5596	1959	$3,078 (A)	$8,670	5-B	11,093	NA	NA
Indiana State Univ., Terre Haute, IN 47809	1865	$9,978 (A)	NA	14-D	8,305	537	41
Indiana Tech., Fort Wayne, IN 46803-1297	1930	$30,446	$11,268	1-D	2,307	212	40
Indiana Univ. Bloomington, Bloomington, IN 47405-7000	1820	$11,790 (A)	$13,380	5-D	47,526	2,530	81
Indiana Univ. East, Richmond, IN 47374-1289	1971	$8,179 (A)	NA	5-M	2,985	243	45
Indiana Univ. Kokomo, Kokomo, IN 46902-9003	1945	$8,179 (A)	NA	5-M	2,892	227	44
Indiana Univ. Northwest, Gary, IN 46408-1197	1959	$8,179 (A)	NA	5-M	3,045	268	36
Indiana Univ. of Pennsylvania, Indiana, PA 15705	1875	$11,290 (A)	$10,920	14-D	9,246	439	53
Indiana Univ.–Purdue Univ. Fort Wayne, Fort Wayne, IN 46805-1499	1917	$10,798 (A)	$11,669	5-M	8,874	568	32
Indiana Univ.–Purdue Univ. Indianapolis, Indianapolis, IN 46202	1969	$10,448 (A)	$13,010	5-D	25,497	4,528	54
Indiana Univ. South Bend, South Bend, IN 46615	1922	$8,179 (A)	$11,216	5-M	4,446	346	36
Indiana Univ. Southeast, New Albany, IN 47150-6405	1941	$8,179 (A)	$11,654	5-M	3,752	343	33
Indiana Wesleyan Univ., Marion, IN 46953-4974	1920	$31,168	$10,554	2-D	3,071	267	NA
Inter Amer. Univ. of Puerto Rico, Aguadilla Campus, Aguadilla, PR 00605	1957	$5,542	NA	1-D	3,517	199	37
Inter Amer. Univ. of Puerto Rico, Arecibo Campus, Arecibo, PR 00614-4050	1957	$5,542	NA	1-D	2,955	NA	NA
Inter Amer. Univ. of Puerto Rico, Bayamón Campus, Bayamón, PR 00957	1912	$5,542	NA	1-D	4,440	248	NA

Name, address	Year founded	Tuition & fees	Room & board	Control, degree	Enroll-ment	Faculty	Grad. rate
Inter Amer. Univ. of Puerto Rico, Fajardo Campus, Fajardo, PR 00738-7003	1965	$5,542	NA	1-D	1,407	98	NA
Inter Amer. Univ. of Puerto Rico, Guayama Campus, Guayama, PR 00785	1958	$5,542	NA	1-D	1,927	164	NA
Inter Amer. Univ. of Puerto Rico, Metropolitan Campus, San Juan, PR 00919-1293	1962	$5,542	NA	1-D	5,001	231	NA
Inter Amer. Univ. of Puerto Rico, Ponce Campus, Mercedita, PR 00715-1602	1962	$5,542	NA	1-D	3,359	284	NA
Inter Amer. Univ. of Puerto Rico, San Germán Campus, San Germán, PR 00683-5008	1912	$5,580	NA	1-D	3,299	233	NA
Iona Coll., New Rochelle, NY 10801-1890	1940	$88,740	$18,820	13-M	3,720	315	58%
Iowa State Univ. of Sci. & Tech., Ames, IA 50011	1858	$10,497 (A)	$9,726	5-D	30,177	1,678	75
Ithaca Coll., Ithaca, NY 14850	1892	$52,155	$16,192	1-D	4,828	542	74
Jackson State Univ., Jackson, MS 39217	1877	$8,965 (A)	$11,722	5-D	6,564	535	NA
Jacksonville State Univ., Jacksonville, AL 36265-1602	1883	$12,894 (A)	$9,524	5-B	9,632	545	52
Jacksonville Univ., Jacksonville, FL 32211	1934	$47,830	$13,730	1-D	3,957	441	57
James Madison Univ., Harrisonburg, VA 22807	1908	$13,966 (A)	$12,916	5-D	22,760	1,405	81
John Brown Univ., Siloam Springs, AR 72761-2121	1919	$32,176	$10,189	1-M	2,151	95	64
John Carroll Univ., University Heights, OH 44118	1886	$50,500	$14,520	13-M	2,773	315	76
John Jay Coll. of Criminal Justice of the City Univ. of New York, New York, NY 10019	1964	$7,470 (A)	NA	5-M	13,319	1,153	NA
Johns Hopkins Univ., Baltimore, MD 21218	1876	$64,730	$21,520	1-D	30,363	1,531	95
Johnson & Wales Univ., Providence, RI 02903-3703	1914	$41,982	$19,800	1-D	5,334	477	52
Johnson State Coll., Johnson, VT 05656	2018	$12,838 (A)	$12,404	5-M	1,555	64	36
Juniata Coll., Huntingdon, PA 16652-2119	1876	$56,402	$13,346	1-M	1,293	151	69
Kalamazoo Coll., Kalamazoo, MI 49006-3295	1833	$60,900	$12,549	2-B	1,210	127	80
Kansas State Univ., Manhattan, KS 66506	1863	$11,221 (A)	NA	5-D	19,745	1,022	70
Kean Univ., Union, NJ 07083	1855	$13,426 (A)	$15,562	5-D	13,352	531	43
Keene State Coll., Keene, NH 03435	1909	$14,784 (A)	$13,766	5-M	2,890	136	59
Keiser Univ., Fort Lauderdale, FL 33309	1977	$39,058	$13,328	1-D	19,019	4,104	36
Kennesaw State Univ., Kennesaw, GA 30144	1963	$6,948 (A)	$13,287	14-D	43,268	2,139	48
Kent State Univ., Kent, OH 44242-0001	1910	$13,054 (A)	$13,440	5-D	26,106	1,688	66
Kent State Univ. at Ashtabula, Ashtabula, OH 44004-2299	1958	$8,053 (A)	$13,990	14-B	1,762	86	9
Kent State Univ. at Geauga, Burton, OH 44021-9500	1964	$8,053 (A)	$13,990	5-M	2,154	88	28
Kent State Univ. at Salem, Salem, OH 44460-9412	1966	$8,053 (A)	$13,990	5-B	1,463	68	22
Kent State Univ. at Stark, Canton, OH 44720-7599	1946	$8,053 (A)	$13,990	14-M	3,433	180	34
Kent State Univ. at Trumbull, Warren, OH 44483-1998	1954	$8,053 (A)	$13,990	5-B	2,029	59	21
Kent State Univ. at Tuscarawas, New Philadelphia, OH 44663-9403	1962	$8,053 (A)	$13,990	5-B	1,885	116	32
Kentucky State Univ., Frankfort, KY 40601	1886	$8,923 (A)	$9,186	5-D	1,689	135	28
Kenyon Coll., Gambier, OH 43022	1824	$71,520	$15,640	13-B	2,147	205	85
Kettering Univ., Flint, MI 48504	1919	$48,470	$10,400	1-M	1,605	160	71
Keuka Coll., Keuka Park, NY 14478	1890	$39,332	$13,670	1-M	1,284	119	49
Keystone Coll., La Plume, PA 18440	1868	$17,850	$12,000	1-M	1,386	151	44
King Univ., Bristol, TN 37620-2699	1867	$36,194	$10,880	1-D	1,299	179	46
King's Coll., Wilkes-Barre, PA 18711-0801	1946	$42,600	$15,086	2-D	1,932	180	60
Kutztown Univ. of Pennsylvania, Kutztown, PA 19530-0730	1866	$11,372 (A)	$11,110	5-D	7,466	398	56
La Salle Univ., Philadelphia, PA 19141-1199	1863	$37,500	$17,840	13-D	3,554	343	58
La Sierra Univ., Riverside, CA 92505	1922	$35,910	$11,670	1-D	2,278	NA	58
Lackawanna Coll., Scranton, PA 18509	1894	$17,950	$12,110	1-B	1,859	195	NA
Lafayette Coll., Easton, PA 18042	1826	$64,648	$19,866	13-B	2,729	304	88
Lake Forest Coll., Lake Forest, IL 60045	1857	$56,402	$12,700	1-M	1,818	190	1
Lake Superior State Univ., Sault Sainte Marie, MI 49783	1946	$14,218 (A)	$11,633	5-B	1,669	140	56
Lakeland Univ., Plymouth, WI 53073	1862	$31,890	$11,258	2-M	2,964	NA	NA
Lamar Univ., Beaumont, TX 77710	1923	$8,905 (A)	NA	5-D	17,482	523	37
Lancaster Bible Coll., Lancaster, PA 17601	1933	$30,690	$11,640	2-D	1,967	32	60
Lander Univ., Greenwood, SC 29649-2099	1872	$11,700 (A)	$12,260	5-M	3,049	249	NA
Lane Coll., Jackson, TN 38301-4598	1882	$11,090	$7,610	2-B	1,267	41	NA
Langston Univ., Langston, OK 73050	1897	$6,509 (A)	$11,100	5-D	2,222	147	NA
Laramie Cty. Comm. Coll., Cheyenne, WY 82007-3299	1968	$4,613 (A)	$8,300	9-B	3,779	244	NA
Lasell Coll., Newton, MA 02466-2709	1851	$42,630	$16,500	1-M	1,639	156	61
Lawrence Tech Univ., Southfield, MI 48075-1058	1932	$44,760	$11,930	1-D	3,277	352	66
Lawrence Univ., Appleton, WI 54911	1847	$56,982	$12,342	13-B	1,410	215	76
Le Moyne Coll., Syracuse, NY 13214	1946	$40,330	$16,200	13-D	3,166	337	71
Lebanon Valley Coll., Annville, PA 17003-1400	1866	$52,080	$14,350	1-D	2,142	294	73
Lee Univ., Cleveland, TN 37320-3450	1918	$22,690	$9,340	2-D	3,680	433	60
Lehigh Univ., Bethlehem, PA 18015	1865	$64,760	$17,220	13-D	7,590	727	89
Lehman Coll. of the City Univ. of New York, Bronx, NY 10468-1589	1931	$7,410 (A)	$17,928	14-D	12,947	984	128
Lenoir-Rhyne Univ., Hickory, NC 28601	1891	$43,900	$12,900	2-D	2,355	291	48
Lesley Univ., Cambridge, MA 02138-2790 (4)	1909	$33,040	$20,360	1-D	4,509	NA	NA
LeTourneau Univ., Longview, TX 75607-7001	1946	$72,680	$11,120	13-M	3,398	299	67
Lewis & Clark Coll., Portland, OR 97219-7899	1867	$64,828	$15,648	1-D	3,526	449	71
Lewis Univ., Romeoville, IL 60446	1932	$39,200	$12,140	2-D	6,636	630	62
Lewis-Clark State Coll., Lewiston, ID 83501-2698	1893	$8,558 (A)	$12,330	5-B	3,710	212	32
Liberty Univ., Lynchburg, VA 24515	1971	$24,600	$13,828	2-D	15,822	NA	71
Life Univ., Marietta, GA 30060-2903	1974	$15,036	$8,240	1-D	2,712	186	27
LIM Coll., New York, NY 10022-5268 (4)	1939	$30,610	$18,625	3-M	1,309	104	51
Limestone Coll., Gaffney, SC 29340-3799	1845	$27,800	$11,210	1-M	1,786	184	27
Lincoln Memorial Univ., Harrogate, TN 37752-1901	1897	$26,938	$12,222	1-D	5,418	505	50
Lincoln Univ., Jefferson City, MO 65101	1866	$9,246 (A)	$8,832	5-M	1,799	101	22
Lincoln Univ., Lincoln University, PA 19352	1854	$13,364 (A)	$11,616	14-M	1,848	194	52
Lindenwood Univ., St. Charles, MO 63301-1695	1832	$21,600	$11,700	1-D	7,288	880	50
Lindsey Wilson Coll., Columbia, KY 42728	1903	$27,808	$10,178	13-D	4,055	230	38

Name, address	Year founded	Tuition & fees	Room & board	Control, degree	Enroll-ment	Faculty	Grad. rate
Lipscomb Univ., Nashville, TN 37204-3951	1891	$40,572	$15,424	1-D	4,796	633	69%
Lock Haven Univ. of Pennsylvania, Lock Haven, PA 17745-2390	1870	$11,169 (A)	$11,954	5-M	11,088	164	54
Logan Univ., Chesterfield, MO 63017	1935	$9,100	$5,924	1-D	1,878	125	NA
Long Island Univ.–LIU Post, Brookville, NY 11548-1300	1954	$42,282	$17,846	1-D	15,737	761	47
Longwood Univ., Farmville, VA 23909	1839	$15,740 (A)	$14,601	5-M	4,358	332	66
Lorain County Comm. Coll., Elyria, OH 44035	1963	$4,265 (A)	NA	11-B	10,138	605	NA
Loras Coll., Dubuque, IA 52004-0178	1839	$39,824	$11,000	2-M	1,232	117	70
Los Angeles Film Sch, Hollywood, CA 90028	1999	NA	NA	3-B	4,900	171	NA
Louisiana State Univ. & Agr. & Mech. Coll., Baton Rouge, LA 70803	1860	$11,954 (A)	$14,296	14-D	39,418	1,997	71
Louisiana State Univ. at Alexandria, Alexandria, LA 71302-9121	1960	$6,961 (A)	$8,330	5-B	3,208	68	33
Louisiana State Univ. Health Scis. Ctr., New Orleans, LA 70112-2223	1931	$7,785 (A)	NA	5-D	2,804	NA	NA
Louisiana State Univ. in Shreveport, Shreveport, LA 71115-2399	1967	$7,519 (A)	NA	14-D	9,736	281	33
Louisiana Tech Univ., Ruston, LA 71272	1894	$12,332 (A)	$9,447	5-D	11,612	966	57
Lourdes Univ., Sylvania, OH 43560-2898	1958	$28,910	$12,120	2-D	1,387	65	22
Lower Columbia Coll., Longview, WA 98632-0310	1934	$4,625 (A)	$17,310	5-B	2,435	169	NA
Loyola Marymount Univ., Los Angeles, CA 90045	1911	$61,862	$22,026	13-D	10,256	1,224	80
Loyola Univ. Chicago, Chicago, IL 60660	1870	$53,710	$17,010	1-D	17,397	1,516	76
Loyola Univ. Maryland, Baltimore, MD 21210-2699	1852	$57,150	$17,670	2-D	5,107	474	80
Loyola Univ. New Orleans, New Orleans, LA 70118-6195	1912	$49,440	$15,600	1-D	4,399	415	67
Lubbock Christian Univ., Lubbock, TX 79407-2099	1957	$26,988	$8,460	2-D	1,589	162	49
Luther Coll., Decorah, IA 52101	1861	$52,120	$11,530	2-B	1,454	168	75
Lynchburg Coll., Lynchburg, VA 24501-3199	1903	$36,750	$13,700	13-D	2,592	251	62
Lynn Univ., Boca Raton, FL 33431-5598	1962	$43,450	$13,750	1-D	3,520	265	52
Macalester Coll., St. Paul, MN 55105-1899	1874	$68,104	$15,760	13-B	2,142	246	90
Madonna Univ., Livonia, MI 48150-1173	1937	$27,360	$12,840	1-D	2,066	266	58
Maharishi Univ. of Mgmt, Fairfield, IA 52557	1971	$17,060	$7,400	1-D	2,015	NA	43
Manhattan Coll., Riverdale, NY 10471	1853	$48,850	$18,440	13-M	3,495	419	66
Mansfield Univ. of Pennsylvania, Mansfield, PA 16933	1857	$11,169 (A)	$11,326	5-M	1,791	36	54
Marian Univ., Fond du Lac, WI 54935-4699	1936	$33,000	$9,718	2-D	1,284	NA	NA
Marian Univ., Indianapolis, IN 46222-1997	1851	$40,664	$13,850	2-D	3,928	143	64
Marist Coll., Poughkeepsie, NY 12601-1387	1929	$47,620	$18,330	13-D	6,452	600	80
Marquette Univ., Milwaukee, WI 53201-1881	1881	$51,170	$16,490	2-D	11,373	1,186	80
Marshall Univ., Huntington, WV 25755	1837	$9,162 (A)	$12,596	14-D	11,269	671	150
Mary Baldwin Univ., Staunton, VA 24401-3610 (4)	1842	$33,157	$10,630	1-D	1,654	NA	NA
Maryland Inst. Coll. of Art, Baltimore, MD 21217	1826	$55,170	$16,380	1-M	1,327	NA	NA
Marymount Manhattan Coll., New York, NY 10021-4597	1936	$41,870	$21,054	13-B	1,641	365	50
Marymount Univ., Arlington, VA 22207-4299	1950	$38,250	$16,188	2-D	3,711	312	61
Maryville Univ. of St. Louis, St. Louis, MO 63141-7299	1872	$27,166	$11,200	1-D	9,883	1,074	72
Marywood Univ., Scranton, PA 18509-1598	1915	$39,570	$15,100	13-D	2,850	360	76
Massachusetts Coll. of Art & Design, Boston, MA 02115-5882	1873	$14,960 (A)	$18,000	5-M	1,986	326	69
Massachusetts Inst. of Tech., Cambridge, MA 02139-4307	1861	$62,396	$20,280	1-D	11,858	939	95
Massachusetts Maritime Acad, Buzzards Bay, MA 02532-1803	1891	$10,776 (A)	$14,048	5-M	1,426	150	79
McDaniel Coll., Westminster, MD 21157-4390	1867	$52,081	$14,638	13-M	2,882	560	64
McKendree Univ., Lebanon, IL 62254-1299	1828	$34,070	$11,300	2-D	1,958	97	56
McNeese State Univ., Lake Charles, LA 70609	1939	$8,832 (A)	$11,188	5-D	7,287	427	NA
MCPHS Univ., Boston, MA 02115-5896	1823	$38,850	$20,400	1-D	3,950	NA	NA
Medgar Evers Coll. of the City Univ. of New York, Brooklyn, NY 11225-2298	1969	$7,353 (A)	NA	11-B	3,640	398	25
Mercer Univ., Macon, GA 31207	1833	$42,312	$15,156	1-D	9,124	1,861	73
Mercy Coll., Dobbs Ferry, NY 10522-1189	1950	$22,880	$19,350	1-D	8,774	925	48
Mercy Coll. of Ohio, Toledo, OH 43604 (4)	1993	$18,825	NA	2-M	1,561	NA	NA
Mercyhurst Univ., Erie, PA 16546	1926	$45,770	$12,958	13-M	2,668	164	68
Meredith Coll., Raleigh, NC 27607-5298 (6)	1891	$45,630	NA	1-M	1,576	216	65
Merrimack Coll., North Andover, MA 01845-5800	1947	$51,017	$18,295	1-M	5,688	476	72
Methodist Univ., Fayetteville, NC 28311-1498	1956	$39,664	$13,586	2-D	1,916	241	38
Metropolitan State Univ., St. Paul, MN 55106-5000	1971	$9,780 (A)	$15,864	5-D	6,155	NA	NA
Metropolitan State Univ. of Denver, Denver, CO 80204	1963	$11,124 (A)	NA	5-M	16,995	1,156	29
Miami Dade Coll., Miami, FL 33132	1960	$3,054 (A)	$24,052	11-B	39,161	2,301	NA
Miami Univ., Oxford, OH 45056	1809	$18,162 (A)	$16,750	5-D	18,618	1,102	82
Miami Univ. Hamilton, Hamilton, OH 45011-3399	1968	$7,278 (A)	NA	5-M	2,450	101	36
Miami Univ. Middletown, Middletown, OH 45042-3497	1966	$7,278 (A)	NA	5-M	1,585	45	28
Michigan State Univ., East Lansing, MI 48824	1855	$16,711 (A)	$10,860	5-D	51,316	3,016	83
Michigan Tech Univ., Houghton, MI 49931	1885	$19,122 (A)	$13,050	14-D	7,324	452	69
Mid-America Christian Univ., Oklahoma City, OK 73170-4504	1953	$19,896	$9,064	2-M	1,935	NA	NA
MidAmerica Nazarene Univ., Olathe, KS 66062-1899	1966	$37,174	$11,554	2-M	1,508	187	43
Middle Georgia State Univ., Macon, GA 31206	2015	$5,038 (A)	NA	5-D	7,843	396	26
Middle Tennessee State Univ., Murfreesboro, TN 37132	1911	$10,006 (A)	$12,242	5-D	20,183	1,185	54
Middlebury Coll., Middlebury, VT 05753-6002	1800	$67,600	$19,250	13-D	2,857	337	93
Midway Univ., Midway, KY 40347-1120	1847	$27,200	$9,800	13-M	1,945	153	48
Midwestern State Univ., Wichita Falls, TX 76308	1922	$9,950 (A)	$11,124	5-D	5,784	362	41
Miles Coll., Fairfield, AL 35064	1905	$12,464	$7,570	2-B	1,438	147	NA
Millikin Univ., Decatur, IL 62522-2084	1901	$26,792	$13,106	1-D	1,659	230	59
Minnesota State Univ. Mankato, Mankato, MN 56001	1868	$9,944 (A)	$10,606	5-D	14,482	661	52
Minnesota State Univ. Moorhead, Moorhead, MN 56563	1887	$10,428 (A)	$10,994	5-D	4,681	236	55
Minot State Univ., Minot, ND 58707-0002	1913	$8,632 (A)	$8,058	5-D	2,741	279	48
MiraCosta Coll., Oceanside, CA 92056	1934	$1,162 (A)	$34,328	9-B	11,707	698	NA
Misericordia Univ., Dallas, PA 18612-1098	1924	$40,370	$15,426	1-D	2,107	298	69
Mississippi Coll., Clinton, MS 39058	1826	$42,000	$11,520	13-D	4,117	364	63
Mississippi State Univ., Mississippi State, MS 39762	1878	$10,202 (A)	$12,902	5-D	22,657	1,458	NA
Mississippi Univ. for Women, Columbus, MS 39701-9998	1884	$8,092 (A)	$8,275	5-D	2,673	NA	NA

Name, address	Year founded	Tuition & fees	Room & board	Control, degree	Enroll-ment	Faculty	Grad. rate
Mississippi Valley State Univ., Itta Bena, MS 38941-1400	1946	$7,294 (A)	$8,180	5-M	1,879	84	27%
Missouri Baptist Univ., St. Louis, MO 63141-8660	1964	$17,306	NA	13-D	5,641	407	48
Missouri Southern State Univ., Joplin, MO 64801-1595	1937	$9,600 (A)	$8,444	5-M	4,090	269	35
Missouri State Univ., Springfield, MO 65897	1905	$9,582 (A)	$10,230	5-D	23,418	725	57
Missouri Univ. of Sci. & Tech., Rolla, MO 65409	1870	$10,815 (A)	$11,792	5-D	7,156	627	64
Missouri Valley Coll., Marshall, MO 65340-3197	1889	$23,700	$11,300	2-B	1,305	129	22
Missouri Western State Univ., St. Joseph, MO 64507-2294	1915	$9,690 (A)	$12,311	5-M	4,024	217	42
Molloy Coll., Rockville Centre, NY 11571-5002	1955	$39,790	$17,500	13-D	4,970	741	73
Monmouth Univ., West Long Branch, NJ 07764-1898	1933	$46,552	$16,268	13-D	4,981	633	70
Monroe Coll., Bronx, NY 10468	1933	$18,464	$11,500	3-M	7,011	573	69
Montana State Univ., Bozeman, MT 59717	1893	$8,083 (A)	$13,446	5-D	16,978	1,003	57
Montana State Univ. Billings, Billings, MT 59101	1927	$6,706 (A)	$9,000	5-M	4,147	223	25
Montana Tech of The Univ. of Montana, Butte, MT 59701-8997	1900	$9,280 (A)	$11,530	5-D	1,602	131	57
Montcalm Comm. Coll., Sidney, MI 48885	1965	$4,890 (A)	NA	11-B	1,832	5	NA
Montclair State Univ., Montclair, NJ 07043-1624	1908	$13,762 (A)	$16,822	5-D	22,570	2,042	1
Moody Bible Inst., Chicago, IL 60610-3284	1886	$15,786	$13,990	2-M	2,407	187	61
Moravian Coll., Bethlehem, PA 18018-6650	1742	$53,500	$15,812	2-D	2,658	363	71
Morehead State Univ., Morehead, KY 40351	1887	$10,024 (A)	$9,300	5-D	8,619	400	49
Morehouse Coll., Atlanta, GA 30314 (1)	1867	$32,893	$14,778	1-B	2,567	NA	59
Morgan State Univ., Baltimore, MD 21251	1867	$8,228 (A)	$13,320	5-D	8,564	307	44
Morrisville State Coll., Morrisville, NY 13408	1908	$8,676 (A)	$15,310	5-M	2,040	184	35
Mount Aloysius Coll., Cresson, PA 16630-1999	1939	$27,072	$13,788	2-M	2,752	164	NA
Mount Holyoke Coll., South Hadley, MA 01075 (3)	1837	$67,018	$19,684	13-M	2,330	272	85
Mount Marty Coll., Yankton, SD 57078-3724	1936	$34,600	$9,800	13-D	1,314	46	60
Mount Mercy Univ., Cedar Rapids, IA 52402-4797	1928	$39,070	$11,030	2-D	1,526	72	57
Mount St. Joseph Univ., Cincinnati, OH 45233-1670	1920	$34,950	$11,200	2-D	2,105	255	51
Mount St. Mary Coll., Newburgh, NY 12550-3494	1960	$41,370	$18,820	13-M	2,246	191	66
Mount St. Mary's Univ., Emmitsburg, MD 21727-7799	1808	$48,630	$7,650	2-M	2,499	245	58
Mount St. Mary's Univ., Los Angeles, CA 90049 (4)	1925	$49,564	$15,618	2-D	2,311	452	55
Muhlenberg Coll., Allentown, PA 18104-5586	1848	$62,804	$13,682	1-M	18,848	300	80
Murray State Univ., Murray, KY 42071	1922	$10,100 (A)	$11,112	14-D	9,841	566	63
Muskingum Univ., New Concord, OH 43762	1837	$31,862	$12,550	2-D	2,169	NA	51
Natl. Univ., La Jolla, CA 92037-1011	1971	$26,568	NA	1-D	30,442	3,281	60
Natl. Univ. Coll., Bayamón, PR 00960	NA	$7,314 (A)	NA	3-M	22,080	43	5
Navajo Tech Univ., Crownpoint, NM 87313	1979	$3,800	NA	1-M	1,600	136	14
Nazareth Coll. of Rochester, Rochester, NY 14618	1924	$42,210	$16,250	1-D	2,442	508	73
Nebraska Wesleyan Univ., Lincoln, NE 68504-2796	1887	$41,652	$12,184	1-M	1,690	152	69
Neumann Univ., Aston, PA 19014-1298	1965	$39,070	$15,840	1-D	2,171	224	46
Nevada State Coll., Henderson, NV 89002	2002	$6,840 (A)	$11,819	5-B	3,747	267	15
New England Coll., Henniker, NH 03242-3293	1946	$80,356	$16,280	13-D	2,856	246	33
New England Inst. of Tech., East Greenwich, RI 02818	1940	$35,440	$16,800	13-D	1,895	40	NA
New Jersey City Univ., Jersey City, NJ 07305-1597	1927	$14,460 (A)	$8,422	5-D	7,550	708	36
New Jersey Inst. of Tech., Newark, NJ 07102	1881	$19,022 (A)	$15,000	5-D	13,007	1,010	72
New Mexico Highlands Univ., Las Vegas, NM 87701	1893	$7,140 (A)	$9,302	5-M	2,815	289	16
New Mexico Inst. of Mining & Tech., Socorro, NM 87801	1889	$9,058 (A)	$9,614	5-D	1,671	246	56
New Mexico State Univ., Las Cruces, NM 88003-8001	1888	$8,504 (A)	$11,252	5-D	14,779	1,039	52
New York City Coll. of Tech of the City Univ. of New York, Brooklyn, NY 11201-2983	1946	$7,331 (A)	NA	11-B	13,087	1,533	30
New York Inst. of Tech., Old Westbury, NY 11568-8000	1955	$44,360	$17,360	1-D	7,230	995	53
New York Univ., New York, NY 10012-1019	1831	$62,796	$24,652	13-D	57,335	6,644	89
Newberry Coll., Newberry, SC 29108-2197	1856	$33,100	$13,908	2-M	1,242	135	43
Newman Univ., Wichita, KS 67213-2097	1933	$37,500	$10,279	2-M	2,053	233	NA
Niagara Univ., Niagara University, NY 14109	1856	$37,920	$12,980	13-D	4,221	447	72
Nicholls State Univ., Thibodaux, LA 70310	1948	$8,890 (A)	$10,574	5-M	5,664	329	NA
Nichols Coll., Dudley, MA 01571-5000	1815	$40,475	$14,950	1-M	1,553	NA	59
Norfolk State Univ., Norfolk, VA 23504	1935	$9,910 (A)	$11,290	5-D	4,977	NA	NA
North Carolina Agr. & Tech State Univ., Greensboro, NC 27411	1891	$6,748 (A)	$10,988	5-D	12,142	NA	NA
North Carolina Central Univ., Durham, NC 27707-3129	1910	$6,629 (A)	$11,912	14-D	7,965	518	46
North Carolina State Univ., Raleigh, NC 27695	1887	$9,105 (A)	$14,332	14-D	37,314	2,239	86
North Carolina Wesleyan Coll., Rocky Mount, NC 27804-8677	1956	$69,872	$13,348	13-M	1,344	161	39
North Central Coll., Naperville, IL 60566-7063	1861	$45,726	$14,688	13-D	2,856	308	71
North Dakota State Univ., Fargo, ND 58102	1890	$10,910 (S)	$4,850	5-D	11,952	755	64
North Park Univ., Chicago, IL 60625-4895	1891	$35,025	$10,765	2-D	3,138	NA	NA
North Seattle Coll., Seattle, WA 98103-3599	1970	$4,205 (A)	NA	5-B	2,873	NA	NA
Northeastern Illinois Univ., Chicago, IL 60625-4699	1961	$12,383 (A)	$10,390	5-M	5,736	495	NA
Northeastern State Univ., Tahlequah, OK 74464-2399	1846	$7,737 (A)	$8,120	5-D	6,409	374	37
Northeastern Univ., Boston, MA 02115-5096	1898	$65,506	$21,620	1-D	38,760	2,564	90
Northern Arizona Univ., Flagstaff, AZ 86011	1899	$13,010 (A)	$11,728	5-D	28,194	1,607	57
Northern Illinois Univ., De Kalb, IL 60115-2854	1895	$13,249 (A)	$14,160	14-D	15,504	1,097	50
Northern Kentucky Univ., Highland Heights, KY 41099	1968	$11,088 (A)	NA	5-D	14,964	1,003	50
Northern Marianas Coll., Saipan, MP 96950	1981	$5,188 (A)	$10,200	7-B	1,230	99	NA
Northern Michigan Univ., Marquette, MI 49855-5301	1899	$13,304 (A)	$12,582	5-D	7,197	423	53
Northern State Univ., Aberdeen, SD 57401-7198	1901	$8,844 (A)	$10,600	5-M	3,521	140	55
Northwest Coll., Powell, WY 82435-1898	1946	$4,962 (A)	$7,180	11-B	1,379	87	NA
Northwest Florida State Coll., Niceville, FL 32578-1295	1963	$3,678 (A)	$8,930	11-B	3,465	266	NA
Northwest Missouri State Univ., Maryville, MO 64468-6001	1905	$13,263 (A)	$12,282	5-M	7,870	296	53
Northwest Nazarene Univ., Nampa, ID 83686-5897	1913	$40,794	$12,070	2-D	1,774	196	60
Northwestern Coll., Orange City, IA 51041-1996	1882	$36,710	$10,700	1-M	1,665	208	63
Northwestern Michigan Coll., Traverse City, MI 49686-3061	1951	$4,650 (A)	$9,350	11-B	4,609	280	NA
Northwestern Oklahoma State Univ., Alva, OK 73717-2799	1897	$7,463 (A)	$5,700	5-D	1,833	153	26
Northwestern State Univ. of Louisiana, Natchitoches, LA 71497	1884	$8,864 (A)	$10,617	5-D	8,847	445	44
Northwestern Univ., Evanston, IL 60208	1851	$68,322	$21,126	1-D	22,801	1,771	96

Name, address	Year founded	Tuition & fees	Room & board	Control, degree	Enroll-ment	Faculty	Grad. rate
Northwood Univ., Michigan Campus, Midland, MI 48640-2398	1959	$33,000	$12,500	1-D	1,344	148	58%
Norwich Univ., Northfield, VT 05663	1819	$49,560	$15,800	1-M	3,425	115	61
Notre Dame Coll., South Euclid, OH 44121-4293	1922	$32,595	$12,492	2-M	1,444	160	42
Nova Southeastern Univ., Fort Lauderdale, FL 33314-7796	1964	$38,700	$16,840	1-D	20,877	1,664	64
Oakland Univ., Rochester, MI 48309-4401	1957	$15,262 (A)	$10,932	5-D	15,922	1,085	57
Oakwood Univ., Huntsville, AL 35896	1896	$21,890	$10,690	2-M	1,824	NA	NA
Oberlin Coll., Oberlin, OH 44074	1833	$64,618	$18,942	1-M	2,983	NA	83
Occidental Coll., Los Angeles, CA 90041-3314	1887	$66,274	$19,252	13-M	1,854	277	85
Oglala Lakota Coll., Kyle, SD 57752-0490	1970	$2,684 (A)	$7,200	11-M	1,300	119	NA
Oglethorpe Univ., Atlanta, GA 30319-2797	1835	$45,806	$17,020	1-M	1,446	132	58
Ohio Christian Univ., Circleville, OH 43113	1948	$26,460	$9,950	2-M	1,483	161	49
Ohio Dominican Univ., Columbus, OH 43219-2099	1911	$35,770	$12,882	13-M	1,258	125	49
Ohio Northern Univ., Ada, OH 45810-1599	1871	$37,600	$13,800	2-D	3,015	214	67
Ohio Univ., Athens, OH 45701-2979	1804	$14,374 (A)	$14,162	5-D	24,640	1,155	66
Ohio Wesleyan Univ., Delaware, OH 43015	1842	$53,888	$14,684	2-B	1,452	188	62
Oklahoma Baptist Univ., Shawnee, OK 74804	1910	$34,050	$8,300	13-M	1,526	120	54
Oklahoma Christian Univ., Oklahoma City, OK 73136-1100	1950	$25,900	$8,280	2-M	2,017	NA	57
Oklahoma City Univ., Oklahoma City, OK 73106-1402	1904	$34,754	$13,596	2-D	2,550	344	69
Oklahoma Panhandle State Univ., Goodwell, OK 73939-0430	1909	$6,814 (A)	$6,154	5-B	1,245	91	NA
Oklahoma State Univ., Stillwater, OK 74078	1890	$9,243 (A)	$9,560	5-D	26,008	1,441	66
Oklahoma State Univ. Inst. of Tech., Okmulgee, OK 74447-3901	1946	$5,774 (A)	$7,880	5-B	2,483	148	42
Oklahoma State Univ. Oklahoma City, Oklahoma City, OK 73107-6120	1961	$5,339 (A)	$5,344	5-B	4,189	355	NA
Old Dominion Univ., Norfolk, VA 23529	1930	$12,276 (A)	$14,934	5-D	22,541	1,643	44
Olivet Nazarene Univ., Bourbonnais, IL 60914	1907	$37,940	$10,590	2-D	3,462	382	64
Olympic Coll., Bremerton, WA 98337-1699	1946	$4,344 (A)	$8,592	5-B	11,617	475	NA
Oral Roberts Univ., Tulsa, OK 74171	1963	$35,470	$9,960	2-D	5,577	196	54
Oregon Inst. of Tech., Klamath Falls, OR 97601-8801	1947	$13,260 (A)	$10,008	5-D	5,103	304	58
Oregon State Univ., Corvallis, OR 97331	1868	$14,535 (A)	$16,386	5-D	34,292	1,817	70
Otis Coll. of Art & Design, Los Angeles, CA 90045-9785	1918	$50,040	$15,300	1-M	1,312	55	62
Otterbein Univ., Westerville, OH 43081	1847	$35,548	$12,724	2-D	2,357	326	69
Ouachita Baptist Univ., Arkadelphia, AR 71998-0001	1886	$34,500	$9,720	13-M	1,792	180	70
Our Lady of the Lake Univ., San Antonio, TX 78207-4689	1895	$32,106	$8,957	2-D	2,326	307	38
Pace Univ., New York, NY 10038	1906	$53,290	$23,800	13-D	14,092	1,372	61
Pace Univ., Pleasantville Campus, Pleasantville, NY 10570	1906	$53,290	$19,240	1-D	4,366	455	70
Pacific Lutheran Univ., Tacoma, WA 98447	1890	$50,292	$13,008	1-D	2,737	281	71
Pacific Univ., Forest Grove, OR 97116-1797	1849	$56,374	$15,620	1-D	3,479	426	65
Palm Beach Atlantic Univ., West Palm Beach, FL 33416-4708	1968	$40,650	$13,800	2-D	3,875	380	58
Palm Beach State Coll., Lake Worth, FL 33461-4796	1933	$3,050 (A)	$12,825	5-B	30,052	1,170	NA
Park Univ., Parkville, MO 64152-3795	1875	$17,500	$10,200	1-M	10,165	397	27
Parsons Sch. of Design, New York, NY 10011	1896	$59,318	$25,930	13-M	5,566	151	81
Pasco-Hernando State Coll., New Port Richey, FL 34654-5199	1977	$2,945 (A)	NA	5-B	7,476	377	NA
Peninsula Coll., Port Angeles, WA 98362-2779	1961	$4,205 (A)	$18,507	5-B	3,321	116	NA
Penn State Abington, Abington, PA 19001	1950	$14,684 (A)	$14,474	5-B	3,095	291	59
Penn State Altoona, Altoona, PA 16601	1939	$15,388 (A)	$14,474	5-B	2,421	225	64
Penn State Berks, Reading, PA 19610	1924	$15,388 (A)	$14,474	5-B	1,944	169	60
Penn State Erie, The Behrend Coll., Erie, PA 16563	1948	$15,388 (A)	$14,474	5-M	3,323	309	69
Penn State Harrisburg, Middletown, PA 17057	1966	$15,388 (A)	$14,474	5-D	4,651	403	68
Penn State Univ. Park, University Park, PA 16802	1855	$20,644 (A)	$14,474	5-D	49,135	3,435	86
Pennsylvania Coll. of Health Scis., Lancaster, PA 17601	1903	$21,440	$21,500	1-D	1,793	213	64
Pennsylvania Coll. of Tech., Williamsport, PA 17701-5778	1965	$18,240 (A)	$12,560	12-M	4,307	375	54
Pensacola State Coll., Pensacola, FL 32504-8998	1948	$2,510 (A)	$10,226	5-B	7,771	324	74
Pepperdine Univ., Malibu, CA 90263	1937	$69,918	$21,750	13-D	9,545	926	85
Peru State Coll., Peru, NE 68421	1867	$7,320 (A)	$10,464	5-M	1,286	NA	NA
Piedmont Coll., Demorest, GA 30535	1897	$31,700	$12,900	2-D	1,870	132	40
Pima Med. Inst., Tucson, AZ 85716	1972	NA	NA	3-B	1,970	NA	NA
Pittsburg State Univ., Pittsburg, KS 66762	1903	$8,330 (A)	$10,243	5-D	5,732	266	NA
Plymouth State Univ., Plymouth, NH 03264-1595	1871	$14,558 (A)	$12,104	5-D	3,839	329	47
Point Loma Nazarene Univ., San Diego, CA 92106-2899	1902	$46,250	$13,650	2-D	4,494	527	74
Point Park Univ., Pittsburgh, PA 15222-1984	1960	$39,570	$13,440	1-D	3,299	466	60
Point Univ., West Point, GA 31833	1937	$22,300	$8,000	2-M	1,666	NA	NA
Polk State Coll., Winter Haven, FL 33881-4299	1964	$3,366 (A)	NA	5-B	7,491	93	NA
Polytechnic Univ. of Puerto Rico, Hato Rey, PR 00918	1966	$9,222	$11,928	1-D	4,388	221	24
Pomona Coll., Claremont, CA 91711	1887	$65,420	$21,394	1-B	1,761	278	93
Pontifical Catholic Univ. of Puerto Rico–Mayaguez Campus, Mayaguez, PR 00680	NA	$5,443	NA	2-M	1,273	80	24
Pontifical Catholic Univ. of Puerto Rico, Ponce, PR 00717-0777	1948	$5,545	$5,199	2-D	6,614	190	46
Portland State Univ., Portland, OR 97207-0751	1946	$11,769 (A)	$13,443	5-D	20,519	1,425	53
Post Univ., Waterbury, CT 06723-2540	1890	$32,525	$13,640	1-D	13,844	959	27
Pratt Inst., Brooklyn, NY 11205-3899	1887	$61,445	$17,336	1-M	5,232	1,244	73
Princeton Univ., Princeton, NJ 08544-1019	1746	$62,400	$20,250	1-D	8,922	1,232	97
Providence Coll., Providence, RI 02918	1917	$63,550	$17,840	1-M	4,807	568	88
Pueblo Comm. Coll., Pueblo, CO 81004-1499	1933	$4,058 (A)	$14,679	5-B	6,481	289	NA
Purchase Coll., State Univ. of New York, Purchase, NY 10577-1400	1967	$9,016 (A)	$17,850	5-M	3,257	409	62
Purdue Univ. Northwest, Hammond, IN 46323-2094	2016	$8,672 (A)	$8,907	14-D	6,606	406	44
Purdue Univ., West Lafayette, IN 47907	1869	$9,992 (A)	$10,030	5-D	52,211	2,974	84
Queens Coll. of the City Univ. of New York, Queens, NY 11367-1597	1937	$7,538 (A)	$15,546	5-M	16,481	1,319	60
Queens Univ. of Charlotte, Charlotte, NC 28274-0002	1857	$45,846	$17,496	2-M	1,846	285	66
Quinnipiac Univ., Hamden, CT 06518-1940	1929	$55,480	$17,900	1-D	8,788	1,091	77
Radford Univ., Radford, VA 24142	1910	$12,548 (A)	$12,733	5-D	7,531	703	50
Ramapo Coll. of New Jersey, Mahwah, NJ 07430-1680	1969	$15,978 (A)	$13,922	5-D	5,521	496	72

Name, address	Year founded	Tuition & fees	Room & board	Control, degree	Enroll-ment	Faculty	Grad. rate
Randolph-Macon Coll., Ashland, VA 23005-5505	1830	$49,466	$14,540	13-M	1,523	204	75%
Rasmussen Coll. Ocala, Ocala, FL 34474	1984	$13,338	$9,936	3-D	1,422	NA	NA
Reed Coll., Portland, OR 97202-8199	1908	$69,350	$9,050	13-M	1,458	164	76
Regent Univ., Virginia Beach, VA 23464-9800	1977	$21,650	$8,010	1-D	10,168	851	53
Regis Coll., Weston, MA 02493	1927	$50,490	$17,080	1-D	2,801	677	69
Regis Univ., Denver, CO 80221-1099	1877	$45,990	$14,974	2-D	4,668	659	67
Rensselaer Polytechnic Inst., Troy, NY 12180-3590	1824	$64,081	$18,120	1-D	7,015	495	83
Rhode Island Coll., Providence, RI 02908-1991	1854	$11,320 (A)	$13,719	5-D	5,768	618	46
Rhode Island Sch. of Design, Providence, RI 02903-2784	1877	$62,688	$16,626	13-M	2,540	526	88
Rhodes Coll., Memphis, TN 38112-1690	1848	$57,110	$13,620	1-M	1,952	204	82
Rice Univ., Houston, TX 77251-1892	1912	$60,709	$18,100	13-D	8,556	982	96
Ringling Coll. of Art & Design, Sarasota, FL 34234-5895	1931	$57,900	$17,350	1-B	1,705	170	71
Rivier Univ., Nashua, NH 03060	1933	$37,642	$16,856	2-D	1,274	NA	49
Roanoke Coll., Salem, VA 24153-3794	1842	$36,510	$15,366	2-B	1,826	143	71
Robert Morris Univ., Moon Township, PA 15108-1189	1921	$35,760	$13,100	1-D	3,770	248	65
Roberts Wesleyan Coll., Rochester, NY 14624-1997	1866	$38,826	$12,976	2-D	1,606	260	64
Rochester Inst. of Tech., Rochester, NY 14623-5603	1829	$59,274	$16,142	1-D	16,863	3,513	73
Rockhurst Univ., Kansas City, MO 64110-2561	1910	$43,420	$11,540	2-D	3,496	154	76
Rocky Mountain Coll. of Art + Design, Lakewood, CO 80214	1963	$19,448	NA	3-M	1,625	69	48
Roger Williams Univ., Bristol, RI 02809	1956	$44,418	$17,112	13-D	4,344	468	72
Rogers State Univ., Claremore, OK 74017-3252	1909	$7,920 (A)	$9,452	5-M	3,216	181	41
Rollins Coll., Winter Park, FL 32789-4499	1885	$60,580	$16,820	13-D	2,740	228	77
Roosevelt Univ., Chicago, IL 60605	1945	$33,398	$12,350	1-D	4,127	469	44
Rose-Hulman Inst. of Tech., Terre Haute, IN 47803-3999 (2)	1874	$54,174	$18,753	1-M	2,250	203	82
Rowan Univ., Glassboro, NJ 08028-1701	1923	$15,700 (A)	$14,390	5-D	19,738	1,921	68
Russell Sage Coll., Troy, NY 12180	1916	$36,756	$13,790	1-D	2,064	249	66
Rutgers Univ.–Camden, Camden, NJ 08102-1401	1926	$17,079 (A)	$13,389	5-D	5,776	606	66
Rutgers Univ.–New Brunswick, Piscataway, NJ 08854-8097	1766	$17,239 (A)	$14,715	5-D	50,617	3,870	85
Rutgers Univ.–Newark, Newark, NJ 07102	1908	$16,586 (A)	$15,060	5-D	10,809	974	68
Sacred Heart Univ., Fairfield, CT 06825	1963	$50,404	$20,370	2-D	11,179	1,052	75
Saginaw Valley State Univ., University Center, MI 48710	1963	$12,240 (A)	$11,700	14-D	6,889	644	54
St. Ambrose Univ., Davenport, IA 52803-2898	1882	$36,658	$13,378	2-D	2,703	313	63
St. Anselm Coll., Manchester, NH 03102-1310	1889	$48,920	$17,020	2-M	2,078	210	83
St. Bonaventure Univ., St. Bonaventure, NY 14778-2284	1858	$41,735	$15,450	13-D	2,618	242	70
St. Catherine Univ., St. Paul, MN 55105 (6)	1905	$51,454	$12,188	13-D	3,539	429	64
St. Cloud State Univ., St. Cloud, MN 56301-4498	1869	$10,182 (A)	$10,596	5-D	10,093	564	41
St. Edward's Univ., Austin, TX 78704	1885	$51,384	$14,010	1-M	3,009	NA	NA
St. Francis Coll., Brooklyn Heights, NY 11201-4398	1884	$27,571	$18,000	2-M	2,735	157	54
St. Francis Univ., Loretto, PA 15940-0600	1847	$42,220	$12,668	1-D	2,856	213	77
St. John Fisher Coll., Rochester, NY 14618-3597	1948	$39,666	$14,342	13-D	3,680	426	74
St. John's Univ., Collegeville, MN 56321 (5)	1857	$53,942	$11,922	2-M	1,645	116	76
St. John's Univ., Queens, NY 11439	1870	$52,770	$20,430	2-D	19,663	670	69
St. Joseph's Coll., Long Island Campus, Patchogue, NY 11772-2399	1916	$36,550	NA	1-M	3,036	387	65
St. Joseph's Univ., Philadelphia, PA 19131-1395	1851	$53,260	$15,856	2-D	7,201	787	80
St. Lawrence Univ., Canton, NY 13617	1856	$65,890	$17,000	1-M	2,089	199	80
St. Leo Univ., Saint Leo, FL 33574-6665	1889	$29,500	$16,550	2-D	2,788	200	47
St. Louis Univ., St. Louis, MO 63103	1818	$55,760	$15,280	2-D	14,079	1,194	80
St. Martin's Univ., Lacey, WA 98503	1895	$45,205	$14,796	2-D	1,466	289	57
St. Mary's Coll., Notre Dame, IN 46556 (3)	1844	$53,230	$14,260	2-D	1,517	139	77
St. Mary's Coll. of California, Moraga, CA 94575	1863	$57,803	$17,600	2-D	2,775	101	69
St. Mary's Coll. of Maryland, St. Mary's City, MD 20686-3001	1840	$15,298 (A)	$15,244	5-M	1,611	207	68
St. Mary's Univ. of Minnesota, Winona, MN 55987-1399	1912	$45,000	$11,200	2-D	2,756	355	67
St. Mary's Univ., San Antonio, TX 78228	1852	$37,434	$12,894	13-D	3,419	363	66
St. Michael's Coll., Colchester, VT 05439	1904	$51,450	$17,070	1-M	1,370	154	69
St. Norbert Coll., De Pere, WI 54115-2099	1898	$45,580	$14,004	2-M	2,165	175	74
St. Olaf Coll., Northfield, MN 55057-1098	1874	$73,390 (C)	NA	13-B	3,074	313	84
St. Peter's Univ., Jersey City, NJ 07306-5997	1872	$42,552	$18,808	2-D	3,430	327	60
St. Petersburg Coll., St. Petersburg, FL 33733-3489	1927	$2,682 (A)	$17,911	11-B	24,543	1,298	NA
St. Thomas Aquinas Coll., Sparkill, NY 10976	1952	$39,450	$17,080	1-M	1,950	119	62
St. Thomas Univ., Miami Gardens, FL 33054-6459	1961	$34,720	$12,460	2-D	3,100	NA	43
St. Vincent Coll., Latrobe, PA 15650-2690	1846	$41,576	$13,252	2-D	1,552	78	76
St. Xavier Univ., Chicago, IL 60655-3105	1847	$36,840	$12,480	2-M	3,066	211	52
Salem State Univ., Salem, MA 01970-5353	1854	$12,338 (A)	$15,336	5-M	6,239	NA	55
Salisbury Univ., Salisbury, MD 21801-6837	1925	$11,084 (A)	$13,900	5-D	7,030	604	67
Salve Regina Univ., Newport, RI 02840-4192	1934	$47,930	$17,500	13-D	2,836	316	75
Sam Houston State Univ., Huntsville, TX 77341	1879	$11,370 (A)	$11,720	5-D	21,403	1,034	56
Samford Univ., Birmingham, AL 35229	1841	$40,150	$13,056	1-D	5,790	550	80
San Diego Mesa Coll., San Diego, CA 92111-4998	1964	$1,144 (A)	$30,736	9-B	17,661	723	NA
San Diego State Univ., San Diego, CA 92182	1897	$8,728 (A)	$22,824	5-D	37,539	2,154	78
San Francisco State Univ., San Francisco, CA 94132-1722	1899	$7,950 (A)	$22,266	5-D	25,046	1,700	54
San Jacinto Coll. District, Pasadena, TX 77504-3323	1961	$2,490 (A)	$18,971	11-B	26,135	1,042	NA
San Jose State Univ., San Jose, CA 95192-0001	NA	$7,992 (A)	$12,641	5-D	36,062	1,937	64
Santa Clara Univ., Santa Clara, CA 95053	1851	$61,293	$19,893	2-D	9,326	988	88
Santa Fe Coll., Gainesville, FL 32606	1966	$2,563 (A)	$10,367	11-B	11,043	157	NA
Sarah Lawrence Coll., Bronxville, NY 10708-5999	1926	$66,862	$18,426	1-M	1,744	297	70
Savannah Coll. of Art & Design, Savannah, GA 31402-3146	1978	$41,630	$18,123	1-M	11,398	629	69
Savannah State Univ., Savannah, GA 31404	1890	$6,794 (A)	$15,008	5-M	4,827	NA	NA
Sch. of the Art Inst. of Chicago, Chicago, IL 60603-3103	1866	$56,420	$16,100	13-M	3,401	729	67
Sch. of Visual Arts, New York, NY 10010-3994	1947	$49,140	$24,200	3-M	4,016	1,098	74
Seattle Pacific Univ., Seattle, WA 98119-1997	1891	$40,407	$16,491	1-D	3,114	326	63
Seattle Univ., Seattle, WA 98122-1090	1891	$56,721	$15,702	13-D	7,121	806	73
Seminole State Coll. of Florida, Sanford, FL 32773-6199	1966	$2,871 (A)	$25,391	11-B	17,706	175	NA

Name, address	Year founded	Tuition & fees	Room & board	Control, degree	Enroll-ment	Faculty	Grad. rate
Seton Hall Univ., South Orange, NJ 07079-2697	1856	$52,520	$17,970	13-D	9,494	1,002	71%
Seton Hill Univ., Greensburg, PA 15601	1883	$42,944	$14,222	2-D	1,989	235	72
Sewanee: The Univ. of the South, Sewanee, TN 37383-1000	1857	$56,120	$16,028	13-D	1,693	231	82
Shawnee State Univ., Portsmouth, OH 45662	1986	$9,341 (A)	$11,624	14-D	3,206	378	48
Shenandoah Univ., Winchester, VA 22601-5195	1875	$36,930	$12,390	2-D	4,343	426	70
Shepherd Univ., Shepherdstown, WV 25443	1871	$8,282 (A)	$11,308	5-D	3,159	166	49
Shippensburg Univ. of Pennsylvania, Shippensburg, PA 17257-2299	1871	$13,510 (A)	$13,340	5-D	5,162	313	50
Shorter Univ., Rome, GA 30165	1873	$23,944	$9,784	2-M	1,410	NA	43
Siena Coll., Loudonville, NY 12211-1462	1937	$44,805	$17,085	2-M	3,623	369	76
Siena Heights Univ., Adrian, MI 49221-1796	1919	$29,778	$13,240	2-M	1,966	190	50
Simmons Coll., Boston, MA 02115 (6)	1899	$45,884	$17,618	1-D	5,053	1,004	71
Skidmore Coll., Saratoga Springs, NY 12866	1922	$64,880	$17,340	1-B	2,776	403	82
Skyline Coll., San Bruno, CA 94066-1698	1969	$1,424 (A)	$31,288	9-B	14,900	333	NA
Slippery Rock Univ. of Pennsylvania, Slippery Rock, PA 16057-1383	1889	$10,507 (A)	$10,584	5-D	8,362	422	66
Smith Coll., Northampton, MA 01063 (6)	1871	$65,178	$22,570	1-D	2,830	313	90
Sonoma State Univ., Rohnert Park, CA 94928-3609	1960	$8,624 (A)	$16,802	5-M	6,578	234	60
South Carolina State Univ., Orangeburg, SC 29117-0001	1896	$11,060 (A)	$9,890	5-D	2,626	59	34
South Coll., Knoxville, TN 37917 (4)	1882	$17,985	NA	3-D	4,151	NA	NA
South Dakota Sch. of Mines & Tech., Rapid City, SD 57701-3995	1885	$10,168 (A)	$8,800	5-D	2,043	NA	NA
South Dakota State Univ., Brookings, SD 57007	1881	$9,299 (A)	$8,804	14-D	11,505	651	59
South Florida State Coll., Avon Park, FL 33825-9356	1965	$3,165 (A)	$6,403	5-B	2,796	123	NA
South Georgia State Coll., Douglas, GA 31533-5098	1906	$3,314 (A)	$9,788	5-B	1,717	115	NA
South Univ., Savannah, GA 31406	1899	$15,826	$8,925	1-D	9,955	NA	NA
Southeast Missouri State Univ., Cape Girardeau, MO 63701-4799	1873	$9,495 (A)	$13,126	5-M	9,686	496	56
Southeastern Baptist Theol Sem, Wake Forest, NC 27587	1950	$10,072	$7,026	2-D	2,764	79	54
Southeastern Louisiana Univ., Hammond, LA 70402	1925	$8,373 (A)	$9,530	14-D	13,888	587	44
Southeastern Oklahoma State Univ., Durant, OK 74701-0609	1909	$7,450 (A)	$8,210	5-M	4,783	83	34
Southeastern Univ., Lakeland, FL 33801-6099	1935	$32,950	$5,565	2-D	10,534	470	49
Southern Adventist Univ., Collegedale, TN 37315-0370	1892	$25,590	$8,460	2-D	3,477	172	NA
Southern Arkansas Univ.–Magnolia, Magnolia, AR 71753	1909	$9,640 (A)	$8,028	5-D	5,126	328	41
Southern Connecticut State Univ., New Haven, CT 06515-1355	1893	$13,438 (A)	$14,938	5-D	8,820	987	48
Southern Illinois Univ. Carbondale, Carbondale, IL 62901-4701	1869	$13,334 (A)	$12,341	5-D	11,359	984	54
Southern Illinois Univ. Edwardsville, Edwardsville, IL 62026	1957	$12,923 (A)	$10,951	5-D	13,010	612	49
Southern Methodist Univ., Dallas, TX 75275	1911	$67,038	$19,064	1-D	11,842	1,125	83
Southern Nazarene Univ., Bethany, OK 73008	1899	$29,600	$8,370	2-M	1,526	NA	NA
Southern New Hampshire Univ., Manchester, NH 03106-1045	1932	$15,450	$12,800	1-D	3,305	200	68
Southern Oregon Univ., Ashland, OR 97520	1926	$12,762 (A)	$16,968	5-M	5,506	208	35
Southern Univ. & Agr. & Mech. Coll., Baton Rouge, LA 70813	1880	$9,922 (A)	$9,260	5-D	6,917	392	31
Southern Univ. at New Orleans, New Orleans, LA 70126-1009 (4)	1959	$8,054 (A)	NA	5-M	1,439	NA	5
Southern Utah Univ., Cedar City, UT 84720-2498	1897	$6,962 (A)	$9,236	5-D	15,033	672	51
Southwest Baptist Univ., Bolivar, MO 65613-2597	1878	$28,319	$8,953	2-D	2,761	99	48
Southwest Minnesota State Univ., Marshall, MN 56258	1963	$10,361 (A)	NA	5-M	6,531	249	40
Southwest Univ. at El Paso, El Paso, TX 79925	1999	$16,000	NA	3-B	1,558	NA	NA
Southwestern Assemblies of God Univ., Waxahachie, TX 75165-5735	1927	$23,808	$8,100	2-M	1,591	56	NA
Southwestern Univ., Georgetown, TX 78626	1840	$53,613	$16,230	2-B	1,457	154	69
Spelman Coll., Atlanta, GA 30314-4399 (3)	1881	$30,333	$16,293	1-B	2,588	303	76
Spring Arbor Univ., Spring Arbor, MI 49283-9799	1873	$32,580	$10,960	2-D	1,233	NA	NA
Springfield Coll., Springfield, MA 01109-3797	1885	$44,382	$14,614	1-D	2,785	419	68
Stanbridge Univ., Irvine, CA 92612	NA	NA	NA	3-M	1,508	NA	NA
Stanford Univ., Stanford, CA 94305-2004	1885	$65,880	$19,922	1-D	18,446	2,082	93
State Coll. of Florida Manatee-Sarasota, Bradenton, FL 34206-7046	1957	$3,114 (A)	NA	5-B	8,744	338	NA
State Univ. of New York at Fredonia, Fredonia, NY 14063-1136	1826	$8,831 (A)	$15,590	5-M	3,526	227	61
State Univ. of New York at New Paltz, New Paltz, NY 12561	1828	$8,572 (A)	$16,684	5-M	7,027	635	69
State Univ. of New York at Oswego, Oswego, NY 13126	1861	$8,769 (A)	$16,440	5-M	6,756	540	60
State Univ. of New York at Plattsburgh, Plattsburgh, NY 12901-2681	1889	$9,035 (A)	$17,300	5-M	4,474	353	65
State Univ. of New York Coll. at Cortland, Cortland, NY 13045	1868	$8,874 (A)	$15,560	5-M	6,780	636	68
State Univ. of New York Coll. at Geneseo, Geneseo, NY 14454-1401	1871	$8,999 (A)	$15,962	14-M	3,957	344	72
State Univ. of New York Coll. at Old Westbury, Old Westbury, NY 11568-0210	1965	$8,422 (A)	$13,972	5-M	4,543	201	43
State Univ. of New York Coll. at Oneonta, Oneonta, NY 13820-4015	1883	$8,775 (A)	$16,284	14-M	5,457	465	70
State Univ. of New York Coll. at Potsdam, Potsdam, NY 13676	1816	$8,712 (A)	$15,480	5-M	2,501	301	48
State Univ. of New York Coll. of Agr. & Tech at Cobleskill, Cobleskill, NY 12043	1916	$8,676 (A)	$16,568	5-B	1,783	156	50
State Univ. of New York Coll. of Environmental Sci. & Forestry, Syracuse, NY 13210-2779	1911	$9,206 (A)	$18,080	5-D	1,976	118	71
State Univ. of New York Coll. of Tech at Alfred, Alfred, NY 14802	1908	$8,862 (A)	$14,180	5-B	3,525	256	45
State Univ. of New York Coll. of Tech at Canton, Canton, NY 13617	1906	$8,689 (A)	$16,700	5-B	2,930	221	51
State Univ. of New York Coll. of Tech at Delhi, Delhi, NY 13753	1913	$8,772 (A)	$15,270	5-M	2,615	63	59
State Univ. of New York Empire State Coll., Saratoga Springs, NY 12866-4391	1971	$7,630 (A)	NA	5-D	9,462	NA	NA
State Univ. of New York Maritime Coll., Throggs Neck, NY 10465-4198	1874	$8,665 (A)	$15,274	5-M	1,350	117	76
Stetson Univ., DeLand, FL 32723	1883	$57,410	$17,728	1-D	3,669	426	63
Stevens Inst. of Tech., Hoboken, NJ 07030	1870	$63,462	$19,124	1-D	8,842	538	90
Stockton Univ., Galloway, NJ 08205-9441	1969	$15,998 (A)	$15,834	5-D	8,788	714	72
Stonehill Coll., Easton, MA 02357	1948	$54,300	$15,300	2-M	2,542	NA	82
Stony Brook Univ., State Univ. of New York, Stony Brook, NY 11794	1957	$10,560 (A)	$17,662	5-D	25,865	1,659	77
Strayer Univ.–Arlington Campus, Arlington, VA 22201	NA	$13,920	$9,438	3-M	3,801	NA	NA
Strayer Univ.–Birmingham Campus, Birmingham, AL 35243	NA	$13,920	$9,438	3-M	1,534	NA	NA

Name, address	Year founded	Tuition & fees	Room & board	Control, degree	Enroll-ment	Faculty	Grad. rate
Strayer Univ.–Greenville Campus, Greenville, SC 29607	NA	$13,920	NA	3-M	2,459	NA	NA
Strayer Univ.–Lower Bucks Cty. Campus, Trevose, PA 19053	NA	$13,920	$9,438	3-M	1,971	NA	NA
Suffolk Univ., Boston, MA 02108-2770	1906	$47,550	$21,326	1-D	6,780	649	59%
Sul Ross State Univ., Alpine, TX 79832	1920	$9,004 (A)	$10,892	5-M	1,942	159	27
Sullivan Univ., Louisville, KY 40205	1962	$15,480	$10,485	3-D	2,500	162	NA
Susquehanna Univ., Selinsgrove, PA 17870	1858	$59,850	$16,100	2-M	2,191	229	74
Swarthmore Coll., Swarthmore, PA 19081-1397	1864	$65,494	$20,308	1-B	1,644	220	94
Syracuse Univ., Syracuse, NY 13244	1870	$61,338	$19,188	1-D	22,698	1,817	81
Tallahassee Comm. Coll., Tallahassee, FL 32304-2895	1966	$3,365 (A)	$11,100	11-B	11,935	149	NA
Tarleton State Univ., Stephenville, TX 76402	1899	$4,798 (A)	NA	5-D	14,092	352	46
Taylor Univ., Upland, IN 46989-1001	1846	$40,464	$11,528	13-M	2,396	206	77
Temple Univ., Philadelphia, PA 19122-6096	1884	$18,060 (A)	$12,366	12-D	30,205	2,534	75
Tennessee State Univ., Nashville, TN 37209-1561	1912	$8,336 (A)	$8,716	14-D	8,198	542	34
Tennessee Tech Univ., Cookeville, TN 38505	1915	$11,376 (A)	$13,302	14-D	9,006	NA	NA
Texas A&M Intl. Univ., Laredo, TX 78041	1970	$7,845 (A)	$9,650	5-D	8,525	412	47
Texas A&M Univ., College Station, TX 77843	1876	$12,413 (A)	$13,008	14-D	76,633	4,336	84
Texas A&M Univ.–Central Texas, Killeen, TX 76549	2009	$7,012 (A)	$9,136	14-M	2,253	122	NA
Texas A&M Univ.–Commerce, Commerce, TX 75429	1889	$10,026 (A)	$9,808	5-D	11,500	790	41
Texas A&M Univ.–Corpus Christi, Corpus Christi, TX 78412	1947	$10,533 (A)	$12,308	5-D	10,855	573	34
Texas A&M Univ.–Kingsville, Kingsville, TX 78363	1925	$9,892 (A)	$11,200	5-D	6,562	672	46
Texas A&M Univ.–San Antonio, San Antonio, TX 78224	2009	$13,220 (A)	$10,760	5-M	6,010	NA	NA
Texas A&M Univ.–Texarkana, Texarkana, TX 75503	1971	$8,689 (A)	$12,082	5-D	2,138	88	24
Texas Christian Univ., Fort Worth, TX 76129-0002	1873	$61,740	$16,700	13-D	12,273	1,256	86
Texas Lutheran Univ., Seguin, TX 78155-5999	1891	$34,920	$11,880	2-D	1,441	193	55
Texas Southern Univ., Houston, TX 77004-4584	1947	$7,170 (A)	$10,914	5-D	7,524	325	23
Texas State Univ., San Marcos, TX 78666	1899	$12,206 (A)	$12,630	5-D	38,722	1,912	56
Texas Tech Univ., Lubbock, TX 79409	1923	$11,852 (A)	$10,742	14-D	40,773	2,199	64
Texas Wesleyan Univ., Fort Worth, TX 76105	1890	$37,934	$13,024	2-D	2,619	NA	NA
Texas Woman's Univ., Denton, TX 76204 (4)	1901	$10,540 (A)	$11,000	14-D	15,585	961	44
The Catholic Univ. of America, Washington, DC 20064	1887	$58,378	$19,490	13-D	5,171	674	81
The Citadel, The Military Coll. of South Carolina, Charleston, SC 29409 (2)	1842	$17,354 (A)	$9,791	5-M	3,727	313	NA
The Coll. at Brockport, State Univ. of New York, Brockport, NY 14420-2997	1867	$8,698 (A)	$16,530	5-D	6,931	502	57
The Coll. of New Jersey, Ewing, NJ 08628	1855	$18,546 (A)	$16,140	5-M	7,652	151	85
The Coll. of St. Rose, Albany, NY 12203-1419	1920	$37,452	$14,394	1-D	3,314	264	59
The Coll. of St. Scholastica, Duluth, MN 55811-4199	1912	$41,778	$11,830	2-D	3,512	377	65
The Coll. of William & Mary, Williamsburg, VA 23187-8795	1693	$25,734 (A)	$16,182	5-D	9,762	NA	NA
The Coll. of Wooster, Wooster, OH 44691-2363	1866	$61,640	$14,490	1-B	1,876	202	74
The Colorado Coll., Colorado Springs, CO 80903-3294	1874	$70,734	$16,020	13-M	2,173	285	86
The Culinary Inst. of America, Hyde Park, NY 12538-1499	1946	$38,670	$15,660	13-M	3,104	210	NA
The Evergreen State Coll., Olympia, WA 98505	1967	$8,988 (A)	NA	5-M	2,116	150	41
The George Washington Univ., Washington, DC 20052	1821	$67,580	$19,700	1-D	25,568	2,570	85
The Master's Univ., Santa Clarita, CA 91321-1200	1927	$32,870	$14,110	2-D	2,606	232	65
The Ohio State Univ., Columbus, OH 43210	1870	$12,485 (S)	$13,966	5-D	60,046	6,327	88
The Ohio State Univ.–Newark Campus, Newark, OH 43055-1797	1957	$8,944 (S)	$14,240	5-M	2,422	148	5
The Univ. of Akron, Akron, OH 44325	1870	$13,136 (A)	$11,904	5-D	13,518	1,070	53
The Univ. of Akron Wayne Coll., Orrville, OH 44667-9192	1972	$6,959 (A)	$11,490	5-B	2,353	43	NA
The Univ. of Alabama, Tuscaloosa, AL 35487	1831	$11,900 (A)	$13,316	5-D	6,187	2,036	74
The Univ. of Alabama at Birmingham, Birmingham, AL 35294	1969	$11,040 (A)	$12,630	5-D	21,639	461	64
The Univ. of Alabama in Huntsville, Huntsville, AL 35899	1950	$11,878 (A)	$11,540	5-D	8,743	537	62
The Univ. of Arizona, Tucson, AZ 85721	1885	$13,277 (A)	$14,400	5-D	53,187	2,628	66
The Univ. of Findlay, Findlay, OH 45840-3653	1882	$39,486	$11,200	1-D	5,057	381	62
The Univ. of Iowa, Iowa City, IA 52242-1316	1847	$11,283 (S)	$12,920	5-D	30,042	1,801	1
The Univ. of Kansas, Lawrence, KS 66045	1866	$11,700 (A)	$10,818	5-D	28,406	1,774	69
The Univ. of Montana Western, Dillon, MT 59725-3598	1893	$6,670 (A)	$10,046	5-B	1,424	89	47
The Univ. of North Carolina at Chapel Hill, Chapel Hill, NC 27599	1789	$8,998 (A)	$13,016	5-D	32,496	2,419	92
The Univ. of North Carolina at Charlotte, Charlotte, NC 28223-0001	1946	$7,214 (A)	$5,759	5-D	30,298	1,553	68
The Univ. of North Carolina at Greensboro, Greensboro, NC 27412-5001	1891	$7,594 (A)	$10,136	14-D	17,743	1,036	58
The Univ. of North Carolina at Pembroke, Pembroke, NC 28372-1510	1887	$2,571 (A)	$11,016	5-D	7,630	423	45
The Univ. of North Carolina Wilmington, Wilmington, NC 28403-3297	1947	$7,277 (A)	$14,268	5-D	17,843	1,232	74
The Univ. of Scranton, Scranton, PA 18510	1888	$53,708	$17,380	2-D	4,825	433	81
The Univ. of South Dakota, Vermillion, SD 57069	1862	$9,432 (A)	$9,060	5-D	9,868	666	61
The Univ. of Tampa, Tampa, FL 33606-1490	1931	$34,408	$14,612	13-D	11,054	888	62
The Univ. of Tennessee, Knoxville, TN 37996	1794	$13,484 (A)	$13,356	5-D	36,304	2,206	73
The Univ. of Tennessee at Chattanooga, Chattanooga, TN 37403-2598	1886	$10,448 (A)	NA	5-D	11,380	779	53
The Univ. of Tennessee at Martin, Martin, TN 38238	1900	$10,560 (A)	$9,195	5-M	6,950	NA	NA
The Univ. of Texas at Arlington, Arlington, TX 76019	1895	$11,404 (A)	$10,582	5-D	34,726	NA	NA
The Univ. of Texas at Austin, Austin, TX 78712-1111	1883	$13,576 (A)	$14,964	14-D	53,082	3,244	88
The Univ. of Texas at Dallas, Richardson, TX 75080	1969	$14,644 (A)	$14,566	14-D	30,885	1,391	75
The Univ. of Texas at El Paso, El Paso, TX 79968-0001	1913	$9,200 (A)	$9,582	5-D	23,880	1,299	47
The Univ. of Texas at San Antonio, San Antonio, TX 78249-0617	1969	$10,550 (A)	$9,328	5-D	34,864	1,339	51
The Univ. of Texas at Tyler, Tyler, TX 75799-0001	1971	$9,736 (A)	$13,756	14-D	9,678	571	47
The Univ. of Texas of the Permian Basin, Odessa, TX 79762-0001	1973	$9,235 (A)	$14,098	5-M	5,899	306	43
The Univ. of Texas Rio Grande Valley, Edinburg, TX 78539	1927	$9,541 (A)	$7,726	5-D	31,559	1,544	53
The Univ. of the Arts, Philadelphia, PA 19102-4944	1876	$54,190	$19,028	1-D	1,313	105	66
The Univ. of Toledo, Toledo, OH 43606-3390	1872	$12,159 (A)	$14,830	5-D	14,939	933	58
The Univ. of Tulsa, Tulsa, OK 74104-3189	1894	$48,340	$15,544	13-D	3,559	378	73
The Univ. of Virginia's Coll. at Wise, Wise, VA 24293	1954	$10,546 (A)	$12,357	5-B	1,712	103	43
The Univ. of West Alabama, Livingston, AL 35470	1835	$10,990 (A)	$9,006	5-D	5,594	273	39

Name, address	Year founded	Tuition & fees	Room & board	Control, degree	Enroll-ment	Faculty	Grad. rate
Thomas Edison State Univ., Trenton, NJ 08608	1972	$6,838 (A)	NA	14-D	10,632	NA	NA
Thomas Jefferson Univ., Philadelphia, PA 19107	1824	$47,355	$15,834	1-D	8,315	930	68%
Thomas More Coll., Crestview Hills, KY 41017-3495	1921	$40,150	$9,530	2-M	1,506	NA	NA
Tiffin Univ., Tiffin, OH 44883-2161	1888	$33,690	$12,298	1-D	3,595	258	NA
Toccoa Falls Coll., Toccoa Falls, GA 30598	1907	$47,900	$8,600	2-M	2,532	192	46
Touro Coll., New York, NY 10010	1971	$19,820	$22,396	1-D	11,953	1,416	73
Touro Univ. Worldwide, Los Alamitos, CA 90720	NA	$14,600	NA	1-D	2,251	115	NA
Towson Univ., Towson, MD 21252-0001	1866	$11,728 (A)	$15,802	14-D	19,527	1,678	71
Trevecca Nazarene Univ., Nashville, TN 37210-2877	1901	$29,790	$9,900	2-D	3,327	131	61
Trine Univ., Angola, IN 46703-1764	1884	$36,560	$10,870	1-D	3,839	208	65
Trinity Coll., Hartford, CT 06106-3100	1823	$70,770	$18,890	1-M	2,205	290	84
Trinity Univ., San Antonio, TX 78212-7200	1869	$106,704	$14,750	13-M	2,694	354	82
Trinity Washington Univ., Washington, DC 20017-1094 (3)	1897	$26,110	$12,160	2-M	1,415	NA	NA
Trocaire Coll., Buffalo, NY 14220-2094 (4)	1958	$19,820	NA	1-B	1,271	172	NA
Troy Univ., Troy, AL 36082	1887	$12,720 (A)	$9,500	5-D	13,923	1,104	47
Truckee Meadows Comm. Coll., Reno, NV 89512-3901	1971	$3,342 (A)	$19,728	5-B	9,651	658	NA
Truett McConnell Univ., Cleveland, GA 30528	1946	$24,440	$8,856	2-M	2,796	184	44
Truman State Univ., Kirksville, MO 63501-4221	1867	$10,602 (A)	$11,752	5-M	3,636	279	68
Tufts Univ., Medford, MA 02155	1852	$67,844	$17,660	1-D	13,274	288	93
Tulane Univ., New Orleans, LA 70118-5669	1834	$68,678	$18,868	1-D	12,285	1,318	89
Tusculum Coll., Greeneville, TN 37743-9997	1794	$28,150	$10,750	2-M	1,303	80	34
Tuskegee Univ., Tuskegee, AL 36088	1881	$23,440	$10,680	1-D	2,995	173	46
Tyler Jr Coll., Tyler, TX 75711-9020	1926	$2,544 (A)	NA	11-B	9,290	82	NA
Union Coll., Schenectady, NY 12308-2311	1795	$69,039	$17,010	1-B	2,082	228	85
Union Univ., Jackson, TN 38305-3697	1823	$39,850	$12,280	2-D	2,674	198	71
United States Air Force Acad., USAF Academy, CO 80840-5025	1954	NA	NA	4-B	4,124	679	89
United States Military Acad., West Point, NY 10996	1802	NA	NA	14-B	4,508	764	88
United States Naval Acad., Annapolis, MD 21402-5000	1845	NA	NA	4-B	4,450	376	90
Unity Coll., Unity, ME 04988	1965	$18,035	$9,780	1-M	1,429	165	47
Univ. at Albany, State Univ. of New York, Albany, NY 12222-0001	1844	$10,701 (A)	$16,423	5-D	16,880	1,282	64
Univ. at Buffalo, the State Univ. of New York, Buffalo, NY 14260	1846	$10,782 (A)	$16,754	5-D	31,887	2,137	73
Univ. of Alaska Anchorage, Kenai Peninsula Coll., Soldotna, AK 99669-9798	1964	$6,511 (A)	$13,335	5-B	2,142	NA	NA
Univ. of Alaska Fairbanks, Fairbanks, AK 99775-7520	1917	$10,016 (A)	$10,450	5-D	6,710	978	33
Univ. of Alaska Southeast, Juneau, AK 99801	1972	$10,260 (A)	$12,820	14-M	1,918	170	33
Univ. of Alaska Southeast, Sitka Campus, Sitka, AK 99835-9418	1962	$7,652 (A)	$9,800	5-M	1,552	45	NA
Univ. of Arkansas, Fayetteville, AR 72701	1871	$10,104 (A)	$14,244	5-D	32,140	NA	70
Univ. of Arkansas at Little Rock, Little Rock, AR 72204-1099	1927	$8,937 (A)	NA	5-D	8,266	NA	37
Univ. of Arkansas at Monticello, Monticello, AR 71656	1909	$9,301 (A)	$8,600	5-M	2,048	NA	NA
Univ. of Arkansas at Pine Bluff, Pine Bluff, AR 71601-2799	1873	$8,476 (A)	$8,722	5-D	2,658	106	26
Univ. of Arkansas for Med. Scis., Little Rock, AR 72205-7199	1879	$8,236 (A)	NA	5-D	3,240	989	NA
Univ. of Arkansas–Fort Smith, Fort Smith, AR 72913-3649	1928	$9,128 (A)	NA	11-M	5,887	337	44
Univ. of Baltimore, Baltimore, MD 21201-5779	1925	$9,992 (A)	$19,350	5-D	1,856	405	NA
Univ. of Bridgeport, Bridgeport, CT 06604	1927	$34,190	$16,350	1-D	2,338	NA	NA
Univ. of California, Berkeley, Berkeley, CA 94720	1868	$15,553 (A)	$22,402	5-D	46,128	NA	93
Univ. of California, Davis, Davis, CA 95616	1908	$16,757 (A)	$19,785	5-D	39,075	2,284	NA
Univ. of California, Irvine, Irvine, CA 92697	1965	$18,541 (A)	$18,991	5-D	36,587	1,711	86
Univ. of California, Los Angeles, Los Angeles, CA 90095	1919	$17,102 (A)	$18,369	14-D	48,046	2,821	93
Univ. of California, Merced, Merced, CA 95343	NA	$14,610 (A)	$21,445	5-D	9,148	445	69
Univ. of California, Riverside, Riverside, CA 92521-0102	1954	$14,921 (A)	$20,691	5-D	26,426	1,167	77
Univ. of California, San Diego, La Jolla, CA 92093	1959	$16,131 (A)	$18,522	5-D	42,376	1,714	88
Univ. of California, Santa Barbara, Santa Barbara, CA 93106-2014	1909	$15,460 (A)	$19,947	5-D	26,068	1,241	86
Univ. of California, Santa Cruz, Santa Cruz, CA 95064	1965	$15,097 (A)	$19,948	5-D	19,764	1,006	74
Univ. of Central Arkansas, Conway, AR 72035-0001	1907	$10,523 (A)	$10,640	14-D	9,790	686	53
Univ. of Central Florida, Orlando, FL 32816	1963	$8,132 (A)	$10,410	5-D	69,320	2,304	75
Univ. of Central Missouri, Warrensburg, MO 64093	1871	$10,050 (A)	NA	5-M	11,637	543	49
Univ. of Central Oklahoma, Edmond, OK 73034-5209	1890	$8,522 (A)	$9,050	5-M	12,661	352	35
Univ. of Charleston, Charleston, WV 25304-1099	1888	$32,842	$11,162	1-D	2,926	239	43
Univ. of Chicago, Chicago, IL 60637-1513	1890	$69,006	$19,053	1-D	15,763	1,805	95
Univ. of Cincinnati, Cincinnati, OH 45221	1819	$13,976 (A)	$16,178	5-D	43,976	3,621	72
Univ. of Cincinnati Blue Ash Coll., Cincinnati, OH 45236-1007	1967	$7,200 (A)	NA	5-B	16,098	1,080	NA
Univ. of Cincinnati Clermont Coll., Batavia, OH 45103-1785	1972	$6,750 (A)	NA	5-B	2,242	284	NA
Univ. of Colorado Boulder, Boulder, CO 80309	1876	$12,466 (A)	$16,950	5-D	39,089	94	75
Univ. of Colorado Colorado Springs, Colorado Springs, CO 80918	1965	$12,111 (A)	NA	5-D	11,374	1,006	45
Univ. of Colorado Denver, Denver, CO 80217-3364	1912	$12,723 (A)	NA	14-D	9,382	6,194	47
Univ. of Connecticut, Storrs, CT 06269	1881	$21,044 (A)	$14,380	5-D	25,842	258	83
Univ. of Dallas, Irving, TX 75062-4736	1956	$53,930	$15,010	1-D	2,180	215	67
Univ. of Dayton, Dayton, OH 45469	1850	$49,140	$16,800	2-D	11,304	968	82
Univ. of Delaware, Newark, DE 19716	1743	$16,810 (A)	$8,740	12-D	23,568	1,801	81
Univ. of Denver, Denver, CO 80208	1864	$61,434	$17,759	1-D	13,384	1,455	78
Univ. of Detroit Mercy, Detroit, MI 48221	1877	$32,946	$10,652	1-D	5,528	635	73
Univ. of Dubuque, Dubuque, IA 52001-5099	1852	$40,065	$11,470	13-D	1,817	333	41
Univ. of Evansville, Evansville, IN 47722	1854	$42,676	$14,270	2-D	1,763	179	NA
Univ. of Florida, Gainesville, FL 32611	1853	$6,380 (A)	$12,120	14-D	54,814	3,581	91
Univ. of Georgia, Athens, GA 30602	1785	$11,440 (A)	$10,194	5-D	41,615	2,794	88
Univ. of Guam, Mangilao, GU 96923	1952	$6,374 (A)	$5,128	7-M	2,962	163	41
Univ. of Hartford, West Hartford, CT 06117-1599	1877	$49,075	$14,532	1-D	5,913	763	66
Univ. of Hawaii at Hilo, Hilo, HI 96720-4091	1970	$7,838 (A)	$11,586	5-D	3,924	NA	NA
Univ. of Hawaii at Manoa, Honolulu, HI 96822	1907	$12,186 (A)	$14,936	5-D	19,256	1,302	63
Univ. of Hawaii Maui Coll., Kahului, HI 96732	1967	$3,284 (A)	$22,501	5-B	4,071	117	NA
Univ. of Hawaii–West Oahu, Kapolei, HI 96707	1976	$7,584 (A)	$17,358	14-B	2,863	176	47
Univ. of Houston–Clear Lake, Houston, TX 77058-1002	1971	$9,054 (A)	$9,440	5-D	8,210	530	NA

Name, address	Year founded	Tuition & fees	Room & board	Control, degree	Enroll-ment	Faculty	Grad. rate
Univ. of Houston–Downtown, Houston, TX 77002	1974	$8,889 (A)	NA	5-M	14,105	761	34%
Univ. of Houston–Victoria, Victoria, TX 77901-4450	1973	$7,149 (A)	NA	5-M	4,407	161	NA
Univ. of Houston, Houston, TX 77204	1927	$11,882 (A)	$10,830	5-D	46,676	3,137	65
Univ. of Idaho, Moscow, ID 83844-2282	1889	$9,084 (A)	$11,243	14-D	11,849	609	61
Univ. of Illinois at Chicago, Chicago, IL 60607-7128	1965	$14,338 (A)	$14,600	5-D	33,522	1,922	60
Univ. of Illinois at Springfield, Springfield, IL 62703-5407	1969	$12,262 (A)	$12,242	5-D	4,661	342	62
Univ. of Illinois at Urbana–Champaign, Champaign, IL 61820	1867	$17,640 (A)	$14,522	5-D	56,563	943	85
Univ. of Indianapolis, Indianapolis, IN 46227-3697	1902	$37,200	$15,542	13-D	5,447	509	56
Univ. of Kentucky, Lexington, KY 40506-0032	1865	$12,859 (A)	$14,676	5-D	32,703	2,305	70
Univ. of La Verne, La Verne, CA 91750-4443	1891	$48,870	$15,094	13-D	4,171	732	63
Univ. of Louisiana at Lafayette, Lafayette, LA 70504	1898	$10,418 (S)	$11,988	5-D	15,345	831	52
Univ. of Louisiana at Monroe, Monroe, LA 71209-0001	1931	$9,190 (A)	NA	5-D	8,565	438	54
Univ. of Louisville, Louisville, KY 40292-0001	1798	$9,578 (A)	NA	14-D	22,139	1,603	61
Univ. of Maine, Orono, ME 04469	1865	$13,326 (A)	$13,410	5-D	11,262	815	57
Univ. of Maine at Augusta, Augusta, ME 04330-9410	1965	$8,888 (A)	$11,996	5-B	4,683	95	NA
Univ. of Maine at Farmington, Farmington, ME 04938	1863	$11,308 (A)	$11,298	5-M	1,950	149	53
Univ. of Maine at Fort Kent, Fort Kent, ME 04743-1292	1878	$9,405 (A)	$9,590	5-B	1,517	80	45
Univ. of Maine at Presque Isle, Presque Isle, ME 04769-2888	1903	$9,401 (A)	$10,710	5-M	1,590	72	35
Univ. of Mary Hardin-Baylor, Belton, TX 76513	1845	$59,080	$13,224	2-D	3,520	212	53
Univ. of Mary, Bismarck, ND 58504-9652	1959	$21,034	$9,770	2-D	3,789	284	64
Univ. of Mary Washington, Fredericksburg, VA 22401-5358	1908	$14,640 (A)	$14,250	5-M	3,808	307	67
Univ. of Maryland, Baltimore Cty., Baltimore, MD 21250	1963	$12,952 (A)	$14,203	5-D	14,148	949	NA
Univ. of Maryland, Coll. Park, College Park, MD 20742	1856	$11,505 (A)	$15,057	5-D	40,813	2,659	88
Univ. of Maryland Eastern Shore, Princess Anne, MD 21853	1886	$9,076 (A)	$12,646	5-D	2,648	162	40
Univ. of Maryland Univ. Coll., Adelphi, MD 20783	1947	$8,136 (A)	$16,754	5-D	58,526	2,146	NA
Univ. of Massachusetts Amherst, Amherst, MA 01003	1863	$17,772 (A)	$16,709	5-D	31,810	1,781	83
Univ. of Massachusetts Boston, Boston, MA 02125-3393	1964	$15,691 (A)	$17,512	5-D	15,671	1,149	51
Univ. of Massachusetts Dartmouth, North Dartmouth, MA 02747-2300	1895	$15,612 (A)	$18,566	14-D	7,759	578	49
Univ. of Massachusetts Lowell, Lowell, MA 01854	1894	$16,966 (A)	$16,148	5-D	16,959	1,043	70
Univ. of Memphis, Memphis, TN 38152	1912	$10,728 (A)	$6,448	5-D	21,736	1,334	49
Univ. of Miami, Coral Gables, FL 33124	1925	$62,616	$23,790	13-D	19,593	1,643	84
Univ. of Michigan, Ann Arbor, MI 48109	1817	$19,309 (S)	$14,460	5-D	52,065	3,776	93
Univ. of Michigan–Dearborn, Dearborn, MI 48128	1959	$15,640 (A)	$2,262	5-D	8,037	493	56
Univ. of Michigan–Flint, Flint, MI 48502-1950	1956	$14,190 (A)	$12,276	5-D	6,130	452	45
Univ. of Minnesota, Crookston, Crookston, MN 56716-5001	1966	$13,288 (A)	$11,024	14-B	2,518	110	50
Univ. of Minnesota, Duluth, Duluth, MN 55812-2496	1947	$14,610 (A)	$11,110	5-D	9,350	557	64
Univ. of Minnesota, Twin Cities Campus, Minneapolis, MN 55455-0213	1851	$15,148 (A)	$13,878	14-D	54,890	3,567	85
Univ. of Mississippi, University, MS 38677	1844	$9,412 (A)	$12,040	5-D	24,043	1,410	69
Univ. of Missouri–Kansas City, Kansas City, MO 64110-2499	1929	$13,371 (A)	$12,384	14-D	15,327	1,213	55
Univ. of Missouri–St. Louis, St. Louis, MO 63121	1963	$12,648 (A)	$10,920	5-D	14,815	450	57
Univ. of Missouri, Columbia, MO 65211	1839	$14,830 (A)	$13,700	5-D	31,041	1,646	76
Univ. of Mobile, Mobile, AL 36613	1961	$26,910	$11,470	2-D	2,055	136	NA
Univ. of Montana, Missoula, MT 59812	1893	$8,546 (A)	NA	5-D	7,223	577	49
Univ. of Montevallo, Montevallo, AL 35115	1896	$13,710 (A)	$11,006	14-M	2,942	228	49
Univ. of Mount Olive, Mount Olive, NC 28365	1951	$25,950	$11,212	2-M	2,154	NA	NA
Univ. of Mount Union, Alliance, OH 44601-3993	1846	$35,400	$11,500	2-D	2,133	263	68
Univ. of Nebraska at Kearney, Kearney, NE 68849-0001	1903	$8,564 (A)	$11,910	5-M	6,017	475	60
Univ. of Nebraska at Omaha, Omaha, NE 68182	1908	$8,370 (A)	$11,998	5-D	15,015	378	NA
Univ. of Nebraska–Lincoln, Lincoln, NE 68588	1869	$9,579 (A)	$12,430	5-D	23,986	1,606	66
Univ. of Nevada, Las Vegas, Las Vegas, NV 89154	1957	$9,142 (A)	$12,072	5-D	31,093	2,377	50
Univ. of Nevada, Reno, Reno, NV 89557	1874	$9,172 (A)	$14,496	5-D	21,791	1,644	62
Univ. of New England, Biddeford, ME 04005-9526	1996	$44,210	$17,250	1-D	6,473	565	63
Univ. of New Hampshire, Durham, NH 03824	1866	$19,202 (A)	$15,642	5-D	13,679	789	77
Univ. of New Haven, West Haven, CT 06516	1920	$47,332	$19,808	1-D	9,830	795	58
Univ. of New Mexico, Albuquerque, NM 87131-2039	1889	$10,298 (A)	$12,328	5-D	22,389	1,076	1
Univ. of New Orleans, New Orleans, LA 70148	1958	$9,172 (A)	$11,292	5-D	5,985	263	NA
Univ. of North Alabama, Florence, AL 35632-0001	1830	$12,950 (A)	$8,700	5-D	10,529	655	1
Univ. of North Carolina at Asheville, Asheville, NC 28804-3299	1927	$7,461 (A)	$11,814	5-M	2,925	285	55
Univ. of North Dakota, Grand Forks, ND 58202	1883	$12,665 (A)	$10,914	5-D	14,172	839	63
Univ. of North Florida, Jacksonville, FL 32224	1965	$6,398 (A)	$10,192	5-D	16,406	928	63
Univ. of North Georgia, Dahlonega, GA 30597	1873	$6,898 (A)	$12,770	5-D	18,086	939	52
Univ. of North Texas at Dallas, Dallas, TX 75241	2001	$9,590 (A)	$9,954	5-D	3,797	246	44
Univ. of North Texas, Denton, TX 76203	1890	$11,615 (A)	$10,680	5-D	47,507	2,051	60
Univ. of Northern Colorado, Greeley, CO 80639	1890	$12,010 (A)	$15,230	14-D	9,067	679	51
Univ. of Northern Iowa, Cedar Falls, IA 50614	1876	$9,728 (A)	$9,534	5-D	9,021	544	69
Univ. of Northwestern Ohio, Lima, OH 45805-1498	1920	$12,930	$8,421	1-M	3,848	4	57
Univ. of Northwestern–St. Paul, St. Paul, MN 55113-1598	1902	$36,830	$12,082	13-M	3,262	299	67
Univ. of Notre Dame, Notre Dame, IN 46556	1842	$65,025	$17,900	13-D	13,174	1,526	96
Univ. of Oklahoma, Norman, OK 73019-0390	1890	$9,595 (A)	$12,188	5-D	29,166	1,645	75
Univ. of Oregon, Eugene, OR 97403	1876	$15,320 (A)	$16,611	14-D	23,786	1,505	71
Univ. of Pennsylvania, Philadelphia, PA 19104	1740	$68,686	$19,174	1-D	23,790	1,669	97
Univ. of Phoenix–Online Campus, Phoenix, AZ 85034-7209	1989	$9,552	$7,460	3-D	236,109	2,283	NA
Univ. of Phoenix–Phoenix Campus, Tempe, AZ 85282-2371	1976	$9,552	$7,700	3-M	66,294	253	NA
Univ. of Pikeville, Pikeville, KY 41501	1889	$24,850	$9,000	2-D	2,578	115	41
Univ. of Pittsburgh, Pittsburgh, PA 15260	1787	$21,524 (A)	$13,420	12-D	29,488	2,473	84
Univ. of Portland, Portland, OR 97203-5798	1901	$57,300	$10,400	2-D	3,457	458	80
Univ. of Puerto Rico in Aguadilla, Aguadilla, PR 00604	1972	$5,540 (A)	NA	6-B	3,139	155	46
Univ. of Puerto Rico in Arecibo, Arecibo, PR 00614	1967	$4,164 (A)	NA	6-B	3,378	231	NA
Univ. of Puerto Rico in Bayamón, Bayamón, PR 00959	1971	$4,970 (A)	$11,161	6-B	2,967	185	31
Univ. of Puerto Rico in Carolina, Carolina, PR 00984-4800	1974	$7,515 (A)	NA	6-B	3,392	222	NA

Name, address	Year founded	Tuition & fees	Room & board	Control, degree	Enroll-ment	Faculty	Grad. rate
Univ. of Puerto Rico in Cayey, Cayey, PR 00736	1967	$4,940 (A)	NA	6-B	3,830	83	42%
Univ. of Puerto Rico in Humacao, Humacao, PR 00792	1962	$4,940 (A)	$11,161	6-B	2,634	134	40
Univ. of Puerto Rico in Ponce, Ponce, PR 00732-7186	1970	$5,324 (A)	NA	6-B	2,382	85	48
Univ. of Puerto Rico in Utuado, Utuado, PR 00641-2500	1979	$4,940 (A)	NA	6-B	1,623	38	NA
Univ. of Puerto Rico, Rio Piedras Campus, San Juan, PR 00931-3300	1903	$5,210 (A)	$11,155	6-D	3,610	1,271	47
Univ. of Puget Sound, Tacoma, WA 98416	1888	$62,898	$15,670	1-D	1,914	241	68
Univ. of Redlands, Redlands, CA 92373-0999	1907	$57,614	$17,624	1-D	2,371	NA	NA
Univ. of Rhode Island, Kingston, RI 02881	1892	$16,942 (A)	$15,607	5-D	16,585	1,134	70
Univ. of Richmond, University of Richmond, VA 23173	1830	$65,230	$17,140	13-D	3,776	626	88
Univ. of Rio Grande, Rio Grande, OH 45674	1876	$20,560	$10,500	1-M	2,161	49	43
Univ. of Rochester, Rochester, NY 14627	1850	$67,034	$19,570	1-D	12,160	320	84
Univ. of St. Francis, Fort Wayne, IN 46808-3994	1890	$36,460	$11,580	2-D	1,852	262	60
Univ. of St. Francis, Joliet, IL 60435-6169	1920	$38,110	$11,980	2-D	3,426	139	65
Univ. of St. Joseph, West Hartford, CT 06117-2700 (4)	1932	$47,924	$13,588	1-D	2,002	177	61
Univ. of St. Mary, Leavenworth, KS 66048-5082	1923	$33,890	$10,032	2-D	1,414	87	44
Univ. of St. Thomas, Houston, TX 77006-4696	1947	$33,660	$10,248	13-D	3,890	396	69
Univ. of St. Thomas, St. Paul, MN 55105-1096	1885	$54,398	$14,969	2-D	6,402	610	NA
Univ. of San Diego, San Diego, CA 92110-2492	1949	$59,486	$17,270	13-D	9,106	1,012	82
Univ. of San Francisco, San Francisco, CA 94117	1855	$60,492	$19,764	1-D	9,212	1,107	71
Univ. of Sioux Falls, Sioux Falls, SD 57105-1699	1883	$20,690	$8,960	1-D	1,509	131	60
Univ. of South Alabama, Mobile, AL 36688-0002	1963	$11,620 (A)	$8,830	5-D	13,768	911	52
Univ. of South Carolina, Columbia, SC 29208	1801	$12,688 (A)	$15,708	5-D	36,579	2,500	78
Univ. of South Carolina Aiken, Aiken, SC 29801	1961	$11,126 (A)	$9,182	5-M	3,855	163	40
Univ. of South Carolina Beaufort, Bluffton, SC 29909	1959	$11,080 (A)	$12,260	5-M	2,037	157	NA
Univ. of South Carolina Lancaster, Lancaster, SC 29721-0889	1959	$7,558 (A)	NA	5-B	1,729	46	NA
Univ. of South Carolina Sumter, Sumter, SC 29150-2498	1962	$7,558 (A)	NA	5-B	1,206	42	NA
Univ. of South Carolina Upstate, Spartanburg, SC 29303-4999	1967	$11,922 (A)	$11,460	5-D	4,923	371	43
Univ. of South Florida, Tampa, FL 33620-9951	1956	$6,410 (A)	$12,622	5-D	48,566	2,405	75
Univ. of Southern Indiana, Evansville, IN 47712-3590	1965	$9,330 (A)	$11,548	5-D	7,361	592	NA
Univ. of Southern Maine, Portland, ME 04103	1878	$12,090 (A)	$11,370	5-D	7,528	NA	46
Univ. of Southern Mississippi, Hattiesburg, MS 39406-0001	1910	$9,618 (A)	$12,014	5-D	13,110	869	41
Univ. of the Cumberlands, Williamsburg, KY 40769-1372	1888	$9,875	$9,300	2-D	4,014	378	NA
Univ. of the District of Columbia, Washington, DC 20008-1175	1976	$6,152 (A)	NA	9-D	4,803	576	14
Univ. of the Incarnate Word, San Antonio, TX 78209-6397	1881	$37,090	$14,296	13-D	7,251	714	52
Univ. of the Pacific, Stockton, CA 95211-0197	1851	$57,080	$17,190	1-D	6,755	829	66
Univ. of the Sacred Heart, San Juan, PR 00914-0383	1935	$6,290	$3,650	2-M	4,067	112	NA
Univ. of the Virgin Islands, St. Thomas, VI 00802	1962	$6,268 (A)	$10,650	5-D	1,739	207	28
Univ. of Utah, Salt Lake City, UT 84112-1107	1850	$10,625 (A)	$15,800	5-D	35,262	2,308	64
Univ. of Vermont, Burlington, VT 05405	1791	$19,058 (A)	$13,776	5-D	13,926	66	76
Univ. of Virginia, Charlottesville, VA 22903	1819	$19,434 (A)	$15,862	5-D	26,228	1,628	95
Univ. of Washington, Bothell, Bothell, WA 98011	1990	$12,919 (A)	$17,538	5-M	5,809	329	68
Univ. of Washington, Seattle, WA 98195	1861	$12,973 (A)	$18,405	5-D	55,230	2,666	84
Univ. of Washington, Tacoma, Tacoma, WA 98402-3100	1990	$14,332 (A)	$16,371	5-D	4,777	329	62
Univ. of West Florida, Pensacola, FL 32514-5750	1963	$8,400 (A)	$12,432	5-D	12,389	220	53
Univ. of West Georgia, Carrollton, GA 30118	1906	$7,064 (A)	$10,912	5-D	12,769	722	43
Univ. of Wisconsin–Eau Claire, Eau Claire, WI 54702-4004	1916	$9,277 (A)	$9,651	14-D	9,482	619	68
Univ. of Wisconsin–Green Bay, Green Bay, WI 54311-7001	1968	$8,700 (A)	NA	5-D	6,568	795	NA
Univ. of Wisconsin–La Crosse, La Crosse, WI 54601-3742	1909	$9,774 (A)	$7,345	14-D	10,307	596	71
Univ. of Wisconsin–Madison, Madison, WI 53706-1380	1848	$12,739 (A)	$14,124	5-D	50,633	3,232	89
Univ. of Wisconsin–Milwaukee, Milwaukee, WI 53201-0413	1956	$10,086 (A)	$11,220	5-D	22,920	1,577	51
Univ. of Wisconsin–Oshkosh, Oshkosh, WI 54901	1871	$9,632 (A)	$8,940	5-D	13,114	533	NA
Univ. of Wisconsin–Parkside, Kenosha, WI 53141-2000	1968	$7,466 (A)	$8,526	5-M	4,030	268	40
Univ. of Wisconsin–Platteville, Platteville, WI 53818-3099	1866	$8,644 (A)	NA	5-M	6,757	494	NA
Univ. of Wisconsin–River Falls, River Falls, WI 54022	1874	$8,135 (A)	$7,434	5-D	5,184	337	59
Univ. of Wisconsin–Stevens Point, Stevens Point, WI 54481-3897	1894	$8,790 (A)	$8,500	5-D	8,018	282	56
Univ. of Wisconsin–Stout, Menomonie, WI 54751	1891	$10,701 (A)	$9,008	5-D	6,938	402	53
Univ. of Wisconsin–Superior, Superior, WI 54880-4500	1893	$8,812 (A)	NA	5-M	2,721	229	44
Univ. of Wisconsin–Whitewater, Whitewater, WI 53190-1790	1868	$9,491 (A)	$8,682	5-D	11,522	558	64
Univ. of Wyoming, Laramie, WY 82071	1886	$6,938 (A)	$13,340	5-D	10,913	732	60
Universidad del Este, Carolina, PR 00984	1949	$5,460	NA	1-M	6,574	NA	NA
Universidad del Turabo, Gurabo, PR 00778-3030	1972	$5,920	NA	1-D	10,896	NA	19
Universidad Metropolitana, San Juan, PR 00928-1150	1980	$5,920	NA	1-D	7,003	NA	26
Upper Iowa Univ., Fayette, IA 52142-1857	1857	$33,639	$8,290	1-M	3,031	343	38
Ursinus Coll., Collegeville, PA 19426	1869	$61,010	$17,128	1-B	1,492	198	77
Utah State Univ., Logan, UT 84322	1888	$8,560 (S)	$9,076	5-D	28,063	895	55
Utah Valley Univ., Orem, UT 84058-5999	1941	$6,270 (A)	$9,234	5-M	44,653	1,804	37
Utica Coll., Utica, NY 13502-4892	1946	$26,686	$15,720	1-D	3,861	363	58
Valdosta State Univ., Valdosta, GA 31698	1906	$6,124 (A)	$9,530	5-D	10,180	578	42
Valley City State Univ., Valley City, ND 58072	1890	$8,513 (A)	$7,280	5-M	1,754	154	48
Valparaiso Univ., Valparaiso, IN 46383	1859	$48,450	$13,618	1-D	2,849	293	67
Vanderbilt Univ., Nashville, TN 37240-1001	1873	$67,498	$22,054	1-D	13,456	1,316	93
Vanguard Univ. of Southern California, Costa Mesa, CA 92626	1920	$39,950	$11,030	2-M	2,268	226	61
Vassar Coll., Poughkeepsie, NY 12604	1861	$71,030	$18,240	1-M	2,456	357	89
Vermont Tech Coll., Randolph Center, VT 05061-0500	1866	$16,539 (A)	$9,877	5-M	1,368	41	33
Villanova Univ., Villanova, PA 19085-1699	1842	$67,346	$17,694	2-D	10,383	1,218	91
Vincennes Univ., Vincennes, IN 47591	1801	$6,812 (A)	$11,966	5-B	16,775	750	29
Virginia Commonwealth Univ., Richmond, VA 23284-9005	1838	$17,291 (A)	$18,254	14-D	28,238	2,109	65
Virginia Military Inst., Lexington, VA 24450	1839	$21,046 (A)	$11,310	5-B	1,560	201	82
Virginia Polytechnic Inst. & State Univ., Blacksburg, VA 24061	1872	$15,948 (A)	$16,550	14-D	38,293	2,415	86
Virginia State Univ., Petersburg, VA 23806-0001	1882	$6,755 (A)	$11,890	5-D	3,653	NA	44

Name, address	Year founded	Tuition & fees	Room & board	Control, degree	Enroll-ment	Faculty	Grad. rate
Virginia Union Univ., Richmond, VA 23220-1170	1865	$14,730	$9,798	2-D	1,640	161	42%
Virginia Wesleyan Univ., Virginia Beach, VA 23455	1961	$73,100	$11,449	13-M	1,711	123	49
Viterbo Univ., La Crosse, WI 54601-4797	1890	$34,250	NA	1-D	2,302	NA	65
Wagner Coll., Staten Island, NY 10301-4495	1883	$53,200	$16,485	1-D	1,947	298	62
Wake Forest Univ., Winston-Salem, NC 27109	1834	$67,670	$18,494	1-D	8,660	932	90
Walden Univ., Minneapolis, MN 55401	1970	$10,200	NA	1-D	7,595	NA	NA
Waldorf Univ., Forest City, IA 50436	1903	$25,220	$9,448	2-M	2,457	NA	NA
Walla Walla Univ., College Place, WA 99324	1892	$34,227	$9,648	2-M	1,357	NA	29
Walsh Coll. of Accountancy & Bus. Admin., Troy, MI 48083	1922	$14,654	$8,636	1-D	1,811	64	NA
Walsh Univ., North Canton, OH 44720-3396	1958	$33,020	$11,810	1-D	2,246	NA	58
Wartburg Coll., Waverly, IA 50677-0903	1852	$51,040	$11,062	2-M	1,450	146	67
Washburn Univ., Topeka, KS 66621	1865	$9,578 (A)	$10,759	5-D	5,663	455	52
Washington & Lee Univ., Lexington, VA 24450	1749	$64,525	$17,685	1-D	2,277	312	95
Washington State Univ., Pullman, WA 99164	1890	$13,391 (A)	$13,622	5-D	17,050	1,796	63
Washington State Univ.–Global Campus, Pullman, WA 99164-5220	NA	$11,678 (A)	NA	5-M	3,750	NA	NA
Washington Univ. in St. Louis, St. Louis, MO 63130-4899	1853	$65,144	$21,854	1-D	16,500	1,587	94
Wayland Baptist Univ., Plainview, TX 79072-6998	1908	$23,782	$9,782	2-D	2,861	220	19
Wayne State Coll., Wayne, NE 68787	1910	$8,171 (A)	$9,020	5-M	4,807	231	56
Wayne State Univ., Detroit, MI 48202	1868	$16,268 (A)	$12,392	5-D	23,702	1,657	57
Waynesburg Univ., Waynesburg, PA 15370-1222	1849	$29,460	$12,300	2-D	1,315	119	59
Weatherford Coll., Weatherford, TX 76086	1869	$4,950 (A)	NA	11-B	5,637	220	NA
Weber State Univ., Ogden, UT 84408-1001	1889	$6,391 (A)	$9,900	5-D	30,536	1,594	40
Webster Univ., St. Louis, MO 63119-3194	1915	$31,750	$12,318	1-D	4,324	401	61
Wellesley Coll., Wellesley, MA 02481 (3)	1870	$67,176	$10,904	1-B	2,417	342	91
Wentworth Inst. of Tech., Boston, MA 02115-5998	1904	$42,884	$19,355	13-M	4,018	338	69
Wesleyan Univ., Middletown, CT 06459	1831	$70,042	$19,872	1-B	3,271	467	92
West Chester Univ. of Pennsylvania, West Chester, PA 19383	1871	$10,687 (A)	$10,326	14-D	17,076	912	70
West Coast Univ., Anaheim, CA 92802	NA	$36,084	$9,920	3-B	2,990	NA	NA
West Coast Univ., North Hollywood, CA 91606	1909	$37,434	$9,920	3-M	2,413	NA	NA
West Coast Univ., Ontario, CA 91761	NA	$36,084	$9,920	3-B	2,408	NA	NA
West Liberty Univ., West Liberty, WV 26074	1837	$9,116 (A)	$12,054	5-M	2,315	118	58
West Texas A&M Univ., Canyon, TX 79015	1909	$9,204 (A)	$8,030	5-D	8,963	448	51
West Virginia State Univ., Institute, WV 25112-1000	1891	$8,833 (A)	$12,886	5-M	2,102	149	26
West Virginia Univ. at Parkersburg, Parkersburg, WV 26104	1961	$6,026 (A)	$7,200	5-B	1,760	NA	NA
West Virginia Univ., Morgantown, WV 26506	1867	$10,368 (A)	$13,020	5-D	21,086	NA	NA
West Virginia Wesleyan Coll., Buckhannon, WV 26201	1890	$34,090	$12,988	2-M	1,449	72	50
Western Carolina Univ., Cullowhee, NC 28723	1889	$4,630 (A)	$6,790	5-D	11,628	533	59
Western Connecticut State Univ., Danbury, CT 06810-6885	1903	$13,401 (A)	$14,932	5-D	5,247	560	51
Western Governors Univ., Salt Lake City, UT 84107	1998	$7,744	$8,100	1-M	150,116	4,059	64
Western Illinois Univ., Macomb, IL 61455-1390	1899	$13,142 (A)	$11,320	5-D	7,073	515	45
Western Kentucky Univ., Bowling Green, KY 42101	1906	$11,436 (A)	$12,043	5-D	16,759	939	56
Western Michigan Univ., Kalamazoo, MI 49008	1903	$14,594 (A)	$11,713	5-D	17,559	1,190	58
Western Nevada Coll., Carson City, NV 89703-7316	1971	$3,983 (A)	$14,156	5-B	3,528	226	NA
Western New England Univ., Springfield, MA 01119	1919	$47,820	$15,570	1-D	3,574	219	64
Western New Mexico Univ., Silver City, NM 88062-0680	1893	$6,998 (A)	$11,498	5-M	3,570	234	26
Western Oregon Univ., Monmouth, OR 97361	1856	$11,514 (A)	$12,528	5-M	3,951	298	45
Western State Colorado Univ., Gunnison, CO 81231	1901	$10,771 (A)	$10,286	5-M	3,551	141	47
Western Washington Univ., Bellingham, WA 98225-5996	1893	$9,582 (A)	$15,747	14-D	14,747	1,007	66
Western Wyoming Comm. Coll., Rock Springs, WY 82901	1959	$3,384 (A)	$5,720	11-B	2,423	218	NA
Westfield State Univ., Westfield, MA 01086	1839	$12,364 (A)	$14,018	14-M	4,555	442	55
Westminster Coll., Salt Lake City, UT 84105-3697	1875	$86,016	$12,372	13-D	1,214	231	69
Westmont Coll., Santa Barbara, CA 93108-1099	1937	$53,584	$16,960	13-B	1,319	176	70
Wheaton Coll., Norton, MA 02766	1834	$63,960	$16,200	1-M	1,752	189	76
Wheeling Jesuit Univ., Wheeling, WV 26003-6295	1954	$29,290	$11,700	2-D	1,289	79	58
Whitman Coll., Walla Walla, WA 99362-2083	1859	$63,922	$15,080	1-B	1,523	185	86
Whitworth Univ., Spokane, WA 99251-0001	1890	$50,920	$10,800	2-D	2,417	190	76
Wichita State Univ., Wichita, KS 67260	1895	$7,917 (A)	$12,020	5-D	17,548	860	52
Widener Univ., Chester, PA 19013-5792	1821	$55,730	$15,730	1-D	5,610	709	64
Wilkes Univ., Wilkes-Barre, PA 18766-0002	1933	$43,496	$16,166	13-D	5,198	412	59
Willamette Univ., Salem, OR 97301-3931	1842	$51,156	$16,150	2-D	1,883	228	76
William Carey Univ., Hattiesburg, MS 39401	1906	$14,550	$7,310	2-M	2,101	NA	NA
William Paterson Univ. of New Jersey, Wayne, NJ 07470-8420	1855	$15,704 (A)	NA	5-D	9,368	381	53
William Penn Univ., Oskaloosa, IA 52577-1799	1873	$58,500	$8,222	1-M	1,536	231	30
Williams Coll., Williamstown, MA 01267	1793	$68,560	$17,260	1-M	2,153	348	97
Wilmington Univ., New Castle, DE 19720-6491	1967	$12,570	NA	1-D	8,713	2,466	NA
Wingate Univ., Wingate, NC 28174	1896	$42,576	$6,770	2-D	3,322	347	47
Winona State Univ., Winona, MN 55987	1858	$9,528 (A)	$9,654	5-D	6,127	451	61
Winston-Salem State Univ., Winston-Salem, NC 27110-0003	1892	$6,079 (A)	$11,058	5-M	4,560	NA	NA
Winthrop Univ., Rock Hill, SC 29733	1886	$14,748 (A)	$10,894	5-M	4,694	450	61
Wittenberg Univ., Springfield, OH 45501-0720	1845	$45,940	$6,052	2-M	1,343	135	54
Wofford Coll., Spartanburg, SC 29303-3663	1854	$56,005	$9,490	13-B	1,823	182	81
Worcester Polytechnic Inst., Worcester, MA 01609-2280	1865	$60,765	$17,906	1-D	7,308	567	88
Worcester State Univ., Worcester, MA 01602-2597	1874	$11,286 (A)	$13,104	14-M	5,611	442	56
Wright State Univ., Dayton, OH 45435	1964	$9,907 (A)	$9,732	5-D	9,884	NA	46
Xavier Univ. of Louisiana, New Orleans, LA 70125	1925	$28,979	$11,310	13-D	3,181	313	48
Xavier Univ., Cincinnati, OH 45207	1831	$50,640	$13,820	1-D	6,016	470	71
Yale Univ., New Haven, CT 06520	1701	$67,375	$19,900	1-D	15,081	2,036	96
Yeshiva Univ., New York, NY 10033-3201	1886	$51,800	$11,250	1-D	6,068	701	85
York Coll. of Pennsylvania, York, PA 17403-3651	1787	$25,588	$13,290	1-D	3,656	429	64
York Coll. of the City Univ. of New York, Jamaica, NY 11451	1967	$7,357 (A)	NA	5-M	6,161	537	30
Youngstown State Univ., Youngstown, OH 44555-0001	1908	$12,463 (A)	$10,384	5-D	6,338	527	47

Associations and Organizations

Source: World Almanac research

Selected list, generally by category and first distinctive key word in each title. Listed by acronym when that is the official name. Year established is in parentheses. Entries for religious organizations include addresses and leadership information for 2024.

Academic and Educational

Academies, Natl. (1863): (202) 334-2000; www.nationalacademies.org
African American Life and History, Assn. for the Study of (1915): (202) 238-5910; www.asalh.org
Alpha Delta Kappa (1947): (816) 363-5525; www.alphadeltakappa.org
AMIDEAST (America-Mideast Educational and Training Services, Inc.) (1951): (202) 776-9600; www.amideast.org
Anthropological Assn., American (1902): (703) 528-1902; www.americananthro.org
Archaeological Institute of America (1879): (857) 305-9350; www.archaeological.org
Arts, Americans for the (1960): (202) 371-2830; www.americansforthearts.org
Arts and Sciences, American Academy of (1780): (617) 576-5000; www.amacad.org
Beta Gamma Sigma Inc. (1913): (314) 432-5650; www.betagammasigma.org
Beta Sigma Phi Intl. (1931): (816) 444-6800; www.bspinternational.org
Biological Sciences, American Institute of (1947): (703) 674-2500; www.aibs.org
Classical Studies, Society for (fmr. American Philological Assn.) (1869): (212) 992-7828; www.classicalstudies.org
College Board (1900): (212) 713-8000; www.collegeboard.org
Colleges and Universities, American Assn. of (1915): (202) 387-3760; www.aacu.org
Community Colleges, American Assn. of (1920): (202) 728-0200; www.aacc.nche.edu
Consumer Interests, American Council on (1953): (727) 940-2658 ext. 2002; www.consumerinterests.org
Delta Kappa Gamma Society Intl. (1929): (512) 478-5748; www.dkg.org
Education, American Council on (1918): (202) 939-9300; www.acenet.edu
Education, Council for Advancement and Support of (1974): (202) 328-2273; www.case.org
Education of Young Children, Natl. Assn. for the (1926): (202) 232-8777; www.naeyc.org
Educators for World Peace, Intl. Assn. of (1973): (256) 534-5501
English-Speaking Union of the U.S. (1920): (212) 818-1200; www.esuus.org
Entomological Society of America (1889): (301) 731-4535; www.entsoc.org
Family Relations, Natl. Council on (1938): (888) 781-9331; www.ncfr.org
Foreign Study, American Institute for (1964): (866) 906-2437; www.aifs.com
Freedom of Information Coalition, Natl. (1989): (757) 276-1413; www.nfoic.org
French Institute/Alliance Française (1898): (212) 355-6100; www.fiaf.org
Genealogical Society, Natl. (1903): (703) 525-0050; www.ngsgenealogy.org
Genetic Assn., American (1914): (541) 264-5612; www.theaga.org
Geological Society of America (1888): (303) 357-1000; www.geosociety.org
Hemispheric Affairs, Council on (1975): (202) 223-4975; www.coha.org
Industrial and Applied Mathematics, Society for (1952): (215) 382-9800; www.siam.org
Intl. Education, Institute of (1919): (212) 883-8200; www.iie.org
Intl. Educational Exchange, Council on (1947): (207) 553-4000; www.ciee.org
Intl. Law, American Society of (1906): (202) 939-6001; www.asil.org
Irish American Cultural Inst. (1962): (973) 605-1991; www.iaci-usa.org
IRTS Foundation (fmr. Intl. Radio and TV Society Foundation) (1939): (212) 867-6650; www.irtsfoundation.org
Law Libraries, American Assn. of (1906): (312) 939-4764; www.aallnet.org
Learned Societies, American Council of (1919): (212) 697-1505; www.acls.org
Libraries Assn., Special (1909): (703) 647-4900; www.sla.org
Linguistic Society of America (1924): (202) 835-1714; www.lsadc.org
Literacy Assn., Intl. (fmr. Intl. Reading Assn.) (1956): (302) 731-1600; www.literacyworldwide.org
Mathematical Society, American (1888): (401) 455-4000; www.ams.org
Mensa, American (1960): (817) 607-0060; www.us.mensa.org
Meteorological Society, American (1919): (617) 227-2425; www.ametsoc.org
Metric Assn., Inc., U.S. (1916): www.usma.org
Microbiology, American Society for (1899): (202) 737-3600; www.asm.org
Modern Language Assn. of America (1883): (646) 576-5000; www.mla.org
Museums, American Alliance of (1906): (202) 289-1818; www.aam-us.org
Music Education, Natl. Assn. for (fmr. Music Educators Natl. Conference) (1907): (703) 860-4000; www.nafme.org
Musicological Society, American (1934): (212) 992-6340; www.amsmusicology.org
Negro College Fund, United (1944): (800) 331-2244; www.uncf.org
Oriental Society, American (1842): (734) 347-1259; www.aos-site.org
ORT America (1922): (212) 505-7700; www.ortamerica.org
PEN America (1922): (212) 334-1660; www.pen.org
Phi Beta Kappa Society (1776): (202) 265-3808; www.pbk.org
Phi Theta Kappa Honor Society (1918): (800) 946-9995; www.ptk.org
Philosophical Assn., American (1900): (302) 831-1112; www.apaonline.org
Physics, American Inst. of (1931): (301) 209-3100; www.aip.org
Physiological Society, American (1887): (844) 526-1700; www.physiology.org
Poetry Society of America (1910): (212) 254-9628; www.poetrysociety.org
Poets, Academy of American (1934): (212) 274-0343; www.poets.org
Political Science, Academy of (1880): (212) 870-2500; www.psqonline.org
Religion, American Academy of (1909): (404) 727-3049; www.aarweb.org
Science, American Assn. for the Advancement of (1848): (202) 326-6400; www.aaas.org
Science Fiction Society, World (1939): www.wsfs.org
Sciences, Natl. Academy of (1863): (202) 334-2000; www.nasonline.org
Sigma Beta Delta (1994): (984) 200-8027; www.sigmabetadelta.org
Sociological Assn., American (1905): (202) 383-9005; www.asanet.org
Tau Beta Pi Assn. (1885): (865) 546-4578; www.tbp.org
Teach For America (1990): (212) 279-2080; www.teachforamerica.org
Theological Schools, Assn. of (1918): (412) 788-6505; www.ats.edu
Theosophical Society in America (1875): (630) 668-1571; www.theosophical.org
Universities, Assn. of American (1900): (202) 408-7500; www.aau.edu
World Learning, Inc. (1932): (202) 408-5420; www.worldlearning.org

Animal Welfare and Environment

Animal Welfare Institute (1951): (202) 337-2332; www.awionline.org
Animals, American Society for the Prevention of Cruelty to (ASPCA) (1866): (212) 876-7700; www.aspca.org
Animals, People for the Ethical Treatment of (PETA) (1980): (757) 622-7382; www.peta.org
Appalachian Trail Conservancy (1925): (304) 535-6331; www.appalachiantrail.org
Audubon Society, Natl. (1905): (212) 979-3196; www.audubon.org
Cat Fanciers' Assn., Inc., The (1906): (330) 680-4070; www.cfa.org
Conservation Intl. (1987): (703) 341-2400; www.conservation.org
Defenders of Wildlife (1947): (800) 385-9712; www.defenders.org
Ducks Unlimited (1937): (901) 758-3825; www.ducks.org
Forest History Society (1946): (919) 682-9319; www.foresthistory.org
Foresters, Society of American (1900): (202) 938-3910; www.eforester.org
Friends of the Earth (1969): (202) 783-7400; www.foe.org
Garden Club of America (1913): (212) 753-8287; www.gcamerica.org
Garden Clubs, Inc., Natl. (1929): (314) 776-7574; www.gardenclub.org
Geographic Society, Natl. (1888): (202) 857-7000; www.nationalgeographic.org
Green Mountain Club (1910): (802) 244-7037; www.greenmountainclub.org
Greenpeace (1971): (202) 462-1177; www.greenpeace.org
Hiking Society, American (1976): (301) 565-6704; www.americanhiking.org
Horse Council, American (1969): (202) 296-4031; www.horsecouncil.org
Humane Society of the U.S., The (1954): (202) 452-1100; www.humanesociety.org
Natural Resources Defense Council (1970): (212) 727-2700; www.nrdc.org
Nature Conservancy, The (1951): (703) 841-5300; www.nature.org
Ocean Conservancy (1972): (202) 429-5609; www.oceanconservancy.org
Ornithological Society, American (fmr. Amer. Ornithologists' Union) (1883): (312) 665-7936; www.americanornithology.org
Recreation and Park Assn., Natl. (1965): (703) 858-0784; www.nrpa.org
Recycling Coalition, Inc., Natl. (1978): www.nrcrecycles.org
Rose Society, American (1892): (318) 938-5402; www.rose.org
Save the Redwoods League (1918): (415) 362-2352; www.savetheredwoods.org
Sierra Club (1892): (415) 977-5500; www.sierraclub.org
Water Environment Federation (1928): (800) 666-0206; www.wef.org
Wildflower Center, Lady Bird Johnson (1982): (512) 232-0100; www.wildflower.org
Wildlife Federation, Natl. (1936): (800) 822-9919; www.nwf.org
World Wildlife Fund (1961): (202) 293-4800; www.worldwildlife.org

Children and Social Services

Big Brothers Big Sisters of America (1904): (813) 720-8778; www.bbbs.org
Boy Scouts of America: see Scouts BSA
Boys & Girls Clubs of America (1906): (404) 487-5700; www.bgca.org
Camp Fire (fmr. Camp Fire Boys & Girls) (1910): (816) 285-2010; www.campfire.org
Child Welfare League of America (1920): (202) 688-4200; www.cwla.org
Children's Book Council, The (1944-45): (212) 966-1990; www.cbcbooks.org
Feeding America (fmr. America's Second Harvest) (1979): (800) 771-2303; www.feedingamerica.org
FFA Organization, Natl. (fmr. Future Farmers of America) (1928): (888) 332-2668; www.ffa.org
4-H Council, Natl. (1914): (301) 961-2800; www.4-h.org
Future Business Leaders of America (1942): (800) 325-2946; www.fbla.org
Gifted Children, Natl. Assn. for (1954): (202) 785-4268; www.nagc.org
Girl Scouts of the USA (1912): (212) 852-8000; www.girlscouts.org
Honor Society, Natl. (1921): (703) 860-0200; www.nhs.us
Junior Achievement USA® (1919): (719) 540-8000; jausa.ja.org
Junior Auxiliaries, Inc., Natl. Assn. of (1941): (662) 332-3000; www.najanet.org
Junior Chamber Intl. USA (1914): (636) 778-3010; www.jciusa.org
Junior Honor Society, Natl. (1929): (703) 860-0200; www.njhs.us

Missing and Exploited Children, Natl. Center for (1984): (703) 224-2150; www.missingkids.com
Pilot Intl. (1921): (478) 477-1208; www.pilotinternational.org
Scouts BSA (fmr. Boy Scouts of America) (1910): (972) 580-2000; www.scouting.org
Student Council, Natl. (1931): (703) 860-0200; www.natstuco.org

Fraternal

Eagles, Fraternal Order of (1898): (614) 883-2200; www.foe.com
Eastern Star, General Grand Chapter, Order of the (1876): (202) 667-4737; www.easternstar.org
Elks of the USA, Benevolent and Protective Order of (1868): (773) 755-4700; www.elks.org
Freemasonry, Scottish Rite of, Supreme Council, 33° Northern Masonic Jurisdiction (1813): (781) 862-4410; www.scottishritenmj.org
Freemasonry, Scottish Rite of, Supreme Council, 33° Southern Jurisdiction (1802): (202) 232-3579; www.scottishrite.org
Kiwanis Intl. (1915): (317) 875-8755; www.kiwanis.org
Knights of Columbus (1882): (203) 752-4000; www.kofc.org
Knights of Pythias, Order of (1864): (781) 341-2422; www.pythias.org
Lions Clubs Intl. (1917): (630) 571-5466; www.lionsclubs.org
Moose Intl., Inc. (1888): (630) 859-2000; www.mooseintl.org
Odd Fellows, Independent Order of (1819): (336) 725-5955; www.odd-fellows.org
Rotary Intl. (1905): (847) 866-3000; www.rotary.org
Shriners Intl. (1872): (813) 281-0300; www.shrinersinternational.org
Sons and Daughters of Italy in America, Order (1905): (202) 547-2900; www.osia.org
Sons of Norway (1895): (612) 827-3611; www.sofn.com
Woodmen of America, Modern (1883): (309) 558-3077; www.modernwoodmen.org

Historical

American Battlefield Trust (1987): (202) 367-1861; www.battlefields.org
Colonial Dames XVII Century, Natl. Soc. (1915): (202) 293-1700; www.colonialdames17c.org
Daughters of the American Revolution (1890): (202) 628-1776; www.dar.org
Daughters of the Confederacy, United (1894): (804) 355-1636; www.hqudc.org
Historic Preservation, Natl. Trust for (1949): (202) 588-6000; www.savingplaces.org
Historical Assn., American (1884): (202) 544-2422; www.historians.org
Lewis and Clark Trail Heritage Foundation (1969): (406) 454-1234; www.lewisandclark.org
Mayflower Descendants, General Soc. of (1897): (508) 746-3188; www.themayflowersociety.org
Pilgrims, Natl. Soc. Sons and Daughters of the (1908): www.societyofthepilgrims.com
Railway Historical Society, Inc., Natl. (1935): (215) 557-6606; www.nrhs.com
Sons of the American Revolution, Natl. Soc. of the (1889): (502) 589-1776; www.sar.org
Sons of Confederate Veterans (1896): (931) 380-1844; www.scv.org
State and Local History, American Assn. for (1940): (615) 320-3203; www.aaslh.org
Supreme Court Historical Society (1974): (202) 543-0400; www.supremecourthistory.org
Theodore Roosevelt Assn. (1920): (516) 921-6319; www.theodoreroosevelt.org
Thoreau Society (1941): (978) 369-5310; thoreausociety.org
Titanic Historical Society, Inc. (1963): (413) 543-4770; www.titanichistoricalsociety.org
Victorian Society in America (1966): (856) 216-8124; www.victoriansociety.org

Industrial and Trade

Aerospace Industries Assn. (1919): (703) 358-1000; www.aia-aerospace.org
Better Business Bureaus, Intl. Assn. of (1912): (703) 276-0100; www.bbb.org
Chamber of Commerce, U.S. (1912): (202) 659-6000; www.uschamber.com
Chemistry Council, American (1872): (202) 249-7000; www.americanchemistry.com
Construction Specifications Institute (1948): (800) 689-2900; www.csiresources.org
CropLife America (1933): (202) 296-1585; www.croplifeamerica.org
Electrical Manufacturers Assn., Natl. (1926): (703) 841-3200; www.nema.org
Fire Protection Assn., Natl. (NFPA) (1896): (617) 770-3000; www.nfpa.org
Fisheries Soc., American (1870): (301) 897-8616; www.fisheries.org
Foreign Trade Council, Natl. (1914): (202) 887-0278; www.nftc.org
Funeral Consumers Alliance (1963): (802) 865-8300; www.funerals.org
Hotel & Lodging Assn., American (1910): (202) 289-3100; www.ahla.com
Insurance Assn., American Property Casualty (1866): (847) 297-7800; www.apci.org
Manufacturers, Natl. Assn. of (1895): (202) 637-3000; www.nam.org
News/Media Alliance (fmr. Newspaper Assn. of America; merged with Assn. of Magazine Media, 2022) (1992): (571) 366-1000; www.newsmediaalliance.org
Nuclear Society, American (1954): (708) 352-6611; www.ans.org
Orchestras, League of American (1942): (212) 262-5161; www.americanorchestras.org
Petroleum Institute, American (1919): (202) 682-8000; www.api.org
PRINTING United Alliance (2020, from merger of Printing Industries of America and Specialty Graphic Imaging Assn.): (703) 385-1335; www.printing.org
Publishers, Assn. of American (1970): (202) 347-3375; www.publishers.org
Retail Federation, Natl. (1911): (202) 626-8100; www.nrf.com
Safety Council, Natl. (1913): (630) 285-1121; www.nsc.org
Shipbuilders Council of America (1920): (202) 737-3234; www.shipbuildersusa.org
Small Business Assn., Natl. (1937): (800) 345-6728; www.nsba.biz
Software & Information Industry Assn. (1999): (202) 289-7442; www.siia.net
Tall Buildings and Urban Habitat, Council on (1969): (312) 283-5599; www.ctbuh.org
Toy Assn., Inc. (1916): (212) 675-1141; www.toyassociation.org
Water Works Assn., American (1881): (303) 794-7711; www.awwa.org
Zoos & Aquariums, Assn. of (1924): (301) 562-0777; www.aza.org

Lifestyle and Travel

AAA (American Automobile Assn.) (1902): (407) 444-7000; www.aaa.com
AARP (fmr. American Assn. of Retired Persons) (1958): (888) 687-2277; www.aarp.org
AFS Intercultural Programs USA (1947): (800) 237-4636; www.afsusa.org
Aircraft Owners and Pilots Assn. (1939): (301) 695-2000; www.aopa.org
Appalachian Mountain Club (1876): (617) 523-0636; www.outdoors.org
Boat Owners Assn. of the U.S. (1966): (800) 395-2628; www.boatus.com
Camp Assn., American (1910): (765) 342-8456; www.acacamps.org
Consumer Federation of America (1968): (202) 387-6121; www.consumerfed.org
Consumer Reports, Inc. (fmr. Consumers Union) (1936): (914) 378-2000; www.consumerreports.org
Green America (fmr. Co-op America) (1982): (800) 584-7336; www.greenamerica.org
Hostelling Intl. USA (1934): (240) 650-2100; www.hiusa.org
Jewish Community Centers Assn. of North America (1917): (212) 532-4949; www.jcca.org
Motorcyclist Assn., American (1924): (614) 856-1900; www.americanmotorcyclist.com
Planetary Society (1980): (626) 793-5100; www.planetary.org
Rail Passengers Assn. (1967): (202) 408-8362; www.railpassengers.org
SCRABBLE® Players Assn., N. American (2009): (214) 810-2439; www.scrabbleplayers.org
Sports Car Club of America (1944): (785) 357-7222; www.scca.com
Toastmasters Intl. (1924): (720) 439-5050; www.toastmasters.org
Vertical Flight Society (fmr. American Helicopter Society Intl.) (1943): (703) 684-6777; www.vtol.org
YMCA (Young Men's Christian Assn.) of the USA (1851): (800) 872-9622; www.ymca.org
YWCA (fmr. Young Women's Christian Assn.) USA (1858): (202) 467-0801; www.ywca.org

Military and Veterans

Air & Space Forces Assn. (fmr. Air Force Assn.) (1946): (703) 247-5800; www.afa.org
American Legion (1919): (317) 630-1200; www.legion.org
American Legion Auxiliary (1919): (317) 569-4500; member.legion-aux.org
AMVETS (American Veterans) (1944): (301) 459-9600; www.amvets.org
Army, Assn. of the United States (1950): (703) 841-4300; www.ausa.org
Blinded Veterans Assn. (1945): (800) 669-7079; www.bva.org
Civil Air Patrol (1941): (877) 227-9142; www.gocivilairpatrol.com
Coast Guard Combat Veterans Assn. (1985): (410) 690-8000; www.coastguardcombatvets.org
Disabled American Veterans (1920): (877) 426-2838; www.dav.org
82nd Airborne Division Assn., Inc. (1944): (910) 223-1182; www.82ndairborneassociation.org
Ex-Prisoners of War, American (1942): (817) 649-2979; www.axpow.org
Fleet Reserve Assn. (1924): (703) 683-1400; www.fra.org
Iraq and Afghanistan Veterans of America (2004): (212) 982-9699; www.iava.org
Jewish War Veterans of the U.S.A. (1896): (202) 265-6280; www.jwv.org
Marine Corps League (1937): (703) 207-9588; www.mclnational.org
Military Officers Assn. of America (1929): (703) 549-2311; www.moaa.org
Military Order of the World Wars (1919): (703) 683-4911; www.moww.org
National Guard Assn. of the U.S. (1878): (202) 789-0031; www.ngaus.org
Naval Institute, U.S. (1873): (410) 268-6110; www.usni.org
Navy League of the United States (1902): (703) 528-1775; www.navyleague.org
Ninety-Nines, Inc. (Intl. Org. of Women Pilots) (1929): (405) 685-7969; www.ninety-nines.org
Non Commissioned Officers Assn. (1960): (210) 653-6161; www.ncoausa.org
Paralyzed Veterans of America (1946): (800) 424-8200; www.pva.org
POW/MIA Families, Natl. League of (1970): (703) 465-7432; www.pow-miafamilies.org
Purple Heart, Military Order of the (1932): (703) 642-5360; www.purpleheart.org
Reserve Org. of America (fmr. Reserve Officers Assn. of the U.S.) (1922): (202) 479-2200; www.roa.org
Sons of the American Legion (1932): (317) 630-1200; www.legion.org/sons
Tin Can Sailors (Natl. Assn. of Destroyer Veterans) (1976): (800) 223-5535; www.destroyers.org
Uniformed Services Foundation (2021): (800) 638-0594; www.hqafsa.org
USO, Inc. (United Service Orgs.) (1941): (888) 484-3876; www.uso.org
USS *Missouri* Memorial Assn., Inc. (1994): (808) 455-1600; www.ussmissouri.org
Veterans Memorial Museum (Home of the Legion of Valor) (1991): (559) 498-0510; www.fresnovetsmuseum.com
Veterans of Foreign Wars (1899): (816) 756-3390; www.vfw.org
Veterans of Foreign Wars Auxiliary (1914): (816) 561-8655; vfwauxiliary.org
Vietnam Veterans of America (1978): (301) 585-4000; www.vva.org

Women's Army Corps Veterans' Assn.-Army Women United (1946): (256) 820-6824; www.armywomen.org
Wounded Warrior Project (2003): (877) 832-6997; www.woundedwarriorproject.org

Political

Abortion Federation, Natl. (1977): (202) 667-5881; prochoice.org
Action Network, American (2010): (202) 559-6420; americanactionnetwork.org
Advancement and Support of Education, Council for (1974): (202) 328-2273; www.case.org
American Indians, Natl. Congress of (1944): (202) 466-7767; www.ncai.org
American-Islamic Relations, Council on (1994): (202) 488-8787; www.cair.com
Black Lives Matter (2013): (779) 256-5463; www.blacklivesmatter.com
Brady: United Against Gun Violence (1974): (202) 370-8100; www.bradyunited.org
Cities, Natl. League of (1924): (202) 626-3000; www.nlc.org
Civil Liberties Union, American (ACLU) (1920): (212) 549-2500; www.aclu.org
Coalition to Stop Gun Violence (1974): (202) 408-0061; www.csgv.org
Common Cause (1970): (202) 833-1200; www.commoncause.org
Concerned Women for America (1979): (202) 488-7000; concernedwomen.org
Congress of Racial Equality (CORE) (1942): (702) 637-7968; www.the congressofracialequality.org
Conservation Voters, League of (1969): (202) 785-8683; www.lcv.org
Constitution Party (1992): (717) 390-1993; www.constitutionparty.com
Counties, Natl. Assn. of (1935): (202) 393-6226; www.naco.org
Crossroads GPS (Grassroots Policy Strategies) (2010): (202) 706-7051; www.crossroadsgps.org
Democratic Natl. Committee (1848): (202) 863-8000; www.democrats.org
Democratic Socialists of America (1982): (212) 727-8610; www.dsausa.org
Everytown for Gun Safety (2013): (646) 324-8250; www.everytown.org
Evident Change (fmr. Natl. Council on Crime and Delinquency) (1907): (800) 306-6223; www.evidentchange.org
Feminists for Life of America (1972): (703) 836-3354; feministsforlife.org
GLAAD (fmr. Gay & Lesbian Alliance Against Defamation) (1985): (212) 629-3322; www.glaad.org
Governors Assn., Natl. (1908): (202) 624-5300; www.nga.org
Grange of the Order of Patrons of Husbandry, Natl. (1867): (202) 628-3507; www.nationalgrange.org
Gray Panthers (1970): (202) 737-6637
Green Party of the U.S. (1984): (202) 319-7191; www.gp.org
Homeless, Natl. Coalition for the (1984): (202) 462-4822; www.nationalhomeless.org
Human Rights Campaign (1980): (202) 628-4160; www.hrc.org
Immigration Equality (1994): (212) 714-2904; immigrationequality.org
Immigration Reform, Federation for American (FAIR) (1979): (202) 328-7004; www.fairus.org
Japanese American Citizens League (1929): (202) 223-1240; jacl.org
Jewish Committee, American (1906): (212) 751-4000; www.ajc.org
John Birch Society (1958): (920) 749-3780; jbs.org
LGBTQ Task Force, Natl. (fmr. Natl. Gay and Lesbian Task Force) (1973): (202) 393-5177; www.thetaskforce.org
Libertarian Natl. Committee, Inc. (1971): (202) 333-0008; www.lp.org
Mayors, U.S. Conference of (1932): (202) 293-7330; www.usmayors.org
Men, Natl. Coalition for (1977): (619) 231-1909; www.ncfm.org
NAACP (Natl. Assn. for the Advancement of Colored People) (1909): (410) 580-5777; www.naacp.org
NRA (National Rifle Assn.) (1871): (800) 672-3888; www.nra.org
OpenSecrets (2021, from merger of Center for Responsive Politics and National Inst. on Money in Politics): (202) 857-0044; www.opensecrets.org
Parliamentarians, Natl. Assn. of (1930): (816) 833-3892; www.parliamentarians.org
Patriot Majority (2005): www.patriot majority.org
National Popular Vote (2006): (650) 472-1587; www.nationalpopularvote.com
Progress, Center for American (2003): (202) 682-1611; www.americanprogress.org
Reform Party Natl. Committee (1995): (972) 275-9297; www.reformparty.org
Republican Natl. Committee (1854): (202) 863-8500; www.gop.com
Southern Christian Leadership Conference (1957): (404) 522-1420; nationalsclc.org
Southern Poverty Law Center (1971): (334) 956-8200; www.splcenter.org
State Governments, Council of (1933): (859) 244-8000; www.csg.org
Tax Foundation (1937): (202) 464-6200; www.taxfoundation.org
Tax Reform, Americans for (1985): (202) 785-0266; www.atr.org
Taxpayers Union, Natl. (1969): (703) 683-5700; www.ntu.org
Tea Party Patriots (2009): (877) 748-3277; www.teapartypatriots.org
Term Limits, U.S. (1991): (202) 261-3532; www.termlimits.com
Urban League, Natl. (1910): (212) 558-5300; www.nul.org
Woman's Christian Temperance Union (1874): (847) 864-1396; www.wctu.org
Women, Natl. Organization for (NOW) (1966): (202) 628-8669; www.now.org
Women and Families, Natl. Partnership for (1971): (202) 986-2600; www.national partnership.org
Women Voters, League of (1920): (202) 429-1965; www.lwv.org
Zionist Organization of America (1897): (212) 481-1500; www.zoa.org

Religious

African Methodist Episcopal Church (1787): 900 13th Ave. S., Ste. 340, Nashville, TN 37212; (615) 254-0911; www.ame-church.com; Gen. Sec., Dr. Jeffery B. Cooper
African Methodist Episcopal Zion Church (1796): 3225 Sugar Creek Rd., Charlotte, NC 28269; (704) 599-4630; www.amez.org; Chief Operating Officer, Rev. Julius Walls Jr.
American Baptist Churches USA (1907): P.O. Box 851, Valley Forge, PA 19482; (610) 768-2000; www.abc-usa.org; Gen. Sec., Rev. Dr. Gina Jacobs-Strain
Antiochian Orthodox Christian Archdiocese of North America (1895): 358 Mountain Rd., Englewood, NJ 07631; (201) 871-1355; www.antiochian.org; Primate, Archbishop of New York and Metropolitan Saba Isper
Armenian Apostolic Church of America: *Eastern Prelacy* (1958): 138 E. 39th St., NY, NY 10016; (212) 689-7810; www.armenian prelacy.org; Prelate, Archbishop Anoushavan Tanielian; *Western Prelacy* (1973): 6252 Honolulu Ave., La Crescenta, CA 91214; (818) 248-7737; www.westernprelacy.org; Prelate, Bishop Torkom Donoyan
Assemblies of God USA (1914): 1445 N. Boonville Ave., Springfield, MO 65802; (417) 862-2781; www.ag.org; Gen. Supt., Doug Clay
Atheists, American (1963): 225 Cristiani St., Cranford, NJ 07016; (908) 276-7300; www.atheists.org; Board Chair, Jen Scott
Bahá'ís of the U.S., Natl. Spiritual Assembly of the (1909): 1233 Central St., Evanston, IL 60201; (847) 733-3400; www.bahai.us; Sec., Kenneth E. Bowers
Baptist Bible Fellowship Intl. (1950): 720 E. Kearney St., Springfield, MO 65803; (417) 862-5001; www.bbfi.org; Pres., Jon Haley
Baptist Convention, Southern (1845): 901 Commerce St., Nashville, TN 37203; (615) 244-2355; www.sbc.net; Pres., Clint Pressley
Baptist Convention, USA, Inc., Natl. (1886): 1700 Baptist World Center Dr., Nashville, TN 37207; (615) 228-6292; www.national baptist.com; Pres., Dr. Jerry Young
Baptist Convention of America Intl., Inc., Natl. (1880): 550 W. Kentucky St., Louisville, KY 40203; (844) 610-6222; www.nbcainc.com; Pres., Rev. Samuel C. Tolbert Jr.
Baptist Convention of America, Natl. Missionary (1880): 6925 Wofford Dr., Dallas, TX 75227; (214) 381-3734; www.nmbca.org; Pres., Dr. Anthony E. Sharp
Bible Society, American (1816): 101 N. Independence Mall East FL8, Philadelphia, PA 19106; (215) 309-0900; www.americanbible.org; Pres. and CEO, Dr. Jennifer Holloran
Biblical Literature, Society of (1880): 825 Houston Mill Rd., Atlanta, GA 30329; (404) 727-3100; www.sbl-site.org; Exec. Dir., Steed Vernyl Davidson
B'nai B'rith Intl. (1843): 1120 20th St. NW, Ste. 300 N, Washington, DC 20036; (202) 857-6600; www.bnaibrith.org; Pres., Seth J. Riklin
Brethren in Christ Church (c. 1778): 431 Grantham Rd., Mechanicsburg, PA 17055; (717) 697-2634; www.bicus.org; Natl. Dir., Dr. Alan Robinson
Buddhist Churches of America (1899): 1710 Octavia St., San Francisco, CA 94109; (415) 776-5600; www.buddhist churchesofamerica.org; Pres., Steven Terusaki
Catholic Bishops, U.S. Conference of (2001): 3211 4th St. NE, Washington, DC 20017; (202) 541-3000; www.usccb.org; Pres., Rev. Timothy P. Broglio
Christian Church (Disciples of Christ) (1832): Disciples Center, P.O. Box 1986, Indianapolis, IN 46206; (317) 635-3100; www.disciples.org; Gen. Min. and Pres., Rev. Teresa Hord Owens
Christian Methodist Episcopal Church (1870): 4466 Elvis Presley Blvd., Memphis, TN 38116; (901) 345-0580; www.the cmechurch.org; Senior Bishop, Lawrence L. Reddick III
Church of the Brethren (1708): General Offices, 1451 Dundee Ave., Elgin, IL 60120; (847) 742-5100; www.brethren.org; Gen. Sec., David A. Steele
Church of Christ (1830): P.O. Box 472, Independence, MO 64051; (816) 206-0147; www.churchofchrist1830.org; Sec., Council of Apostles, Duane L. Ely
Church of God (Anderson, IN) (1881): P.O. Box 2420, Anderson, IN 46018; (765) 642-0256; www.jesusisthesubject.org; Gen. Dir., Jim Lyon
Church of God (Cleveland, TN) (1886): 2490 Keith St., P.O. Box 2430, Cleveland, TN 37320; (423) 472-3361; www.churchof god.org; Gen. Overseer, Tim Hill
Church of God in Christ (1897): Mason Temple, 930 Mason St., Memphis, TN 38126; (901) 947-9300; www.cogic.org; Presiding Bishop, Bishop John Drew Sheard
Church of Jesus Christ (1862): World Operations Ctr., 110 Walton Tea Room Rd., Greensburg, PA 15601; (724) 837-4425; www.thechurchofjesuschrist.org; Pres., Apostle Joel Gehly
Church of the Nazarene (1908): Global Ministry Center, 17001 Prairie Star Pkwy., Lenexa, KS 66220; (913) 577-0500; www.nazarene.org; Gen. Sec., Gary Hartke
Community of Christ (reorganized Church of Jesus Christ of Latter-day Saints) (1830): Intl. Headquarters, 1001 W. Walnut, Independence, MO 64050; (816) 833-1000; www.cofchrist.org; Pres., Stephen M. Veazey
Community Churches, International Council of (1950): P.O. Box 846, Longmont, CO 80502; (815) 464-5690; www.icccnow.org; Exec. Dir., Rev. Phil Tom
Conservative Judaism, United Synagogue of (1913): 3080 Broadway, Ste. B208, NY, NY 10027; (212) 533-7800; www.uscj.org; CEO, Rabbi Jacob Blumenthal
Converge (fmr. Baptist General Conference) (1852): 11002 Lake Hart Dr., Mail Code 200, Orlando, FL 32832; (800) 323-4215; www.converge.org; Pres., John K. Jenkins Sr.
Cumberland Presbyterian Church (1810): 8207 Traditional Pl., Cordova, TN 38016; (901) 276-4572; www.cumberland.org

Episcopal Church (1789): 815 Second Ave., NY, NY 10017; (212) 716-6000; www.episcopalchurch.org; Presiding Bishop and Primate, Most Rev. Michael B. Curry

Evangelical Lutheran Church in America (1988): 8765 W. Higgins Rd., Chicago, IL 60631; (773) 380-2700; www.elca.org; Presiding Bishop, Rev. Elizabeth A. Eaton

First Church of Christ, Scientist, The (1879): 210 Massachusetts Ave., Boston, MA 02115; (617) 450-2000; www.christianscience.com; Pres., Lindsey J. Taylor, C.S.B.

Free Methodist Church USA (1860): 5235 Decatur Blvd., Indianapolis, IN 46241; (317) 244-3660; www.fmcusa.org; COO, Mark Dowley

Freedom From Religion Foundation (1978): P.O. Box 750, Madison, WI 53701; (608) 256-8900; www.ffrf.org; Pres., Annie Laurie Gaylor and Dan Barker

Friends General Conference (1900): 1216 Arch St., #2B, Philadelphia, PA 19107; (215) 561-1700; www.fgcquaker.org; Gen. Sec., Barry Crossno

Gideons Intl., The (1899): P.O. Box 140800, Nashville, TN 37214; (615) 564-5000; www.gideons.org; Exec. Dir., Dan Heighway

Greek Orthodox Archdiocese of America (1922): 8 E. 79th St., NY, NY 10075; (212) 570-3500; www.goarch.org; Primate, Archbishop Elpidophoros

Hadassah, the Women's Zionist Organization of America, Inc. (1912): 40 Wall St., NY, NY 10005; (800) 664-5646; www.hadassah.org; Exec. Dir. and CEO, Naomi Adler

Interfaith Alliance (1994): 110 Maryland Ave., NE, Ste. 509, Washington, DC 20002; (202) 466-0567; www.interfaith alliance.org; Pres., Rev. Paul Brandeis Raushenbush

Islamic Society of North America: 6555 S. County Rd. 750 East, Plainfield, IN 46168; (317) 839-8157; www.isna.net; Pres., Safaa Zarzour

Jehovah's Witnesses (1931): 900 Red Mills Rd., Wallkill, NY 12589; (845) 744-6000; www.jw.org

Jewish Congress, American (1918): 654 Madison Ave., 9th Fl., NY, NY 10065; (212) 879-4500; www.ajcongress.org; Pres., Jack Rosen

Jewish Women, Natl. Council of (1893): 2055 L St. NW, Ste. 650, Washington, D.C. 20036; (202) 296-2588; www.ncjw.org; Pres., Dana Gershon

Latter-day Saints, The Church of Jesus Christ of (Mormons) (1830): 50 W. North Temple St., Salt Lake City, UT 84150; (801) 240-2640; www.lds.org; Pres., Russell M. Nelson

Lutheran Church—Missouri Synod (1847): 1333 S. Kirkwood Rd., St. Louis, MO 63122; (800) 248-1930; www.lcms.org; Pres., Rev. Dr. Matthew C. Harrison

Mennonite Church USA (2001): 718 N. Main St., Newton, KS 67114; (316) 283-5100; www.mennoniteusa.org; Exec. Dir., Glen Guyton

Moravian Church in North America (1735): www.moravian.org; *Northern Prov.*: 1021 Center St., P.O. Box 1245, Bethlehem, PA 18016; (610) 867-7566; Pres., Rev. Dr. Betsy Miller; *Southern Prov.*: 459 S. Church St., Winston-Salem, NC 27101; (336) 725-5811; Pres., Rev. Dr. Neil Routh

North American Shia Ithna-asheri Muslim Communities, Org. of (1986): 6120 Brooklyn Blvd., Suite B, P.O. Box 29691, Minneapolis, MN 55429; (905) 763-7512; nasimco.org; Pres., Br. Arif Jacksi

Orthodox Union (1898): 40 Rector St., 4th Fl., NY, NY 10006; (212) 563-4000; www.ou.org; Pres., Mitchel R. Aeder

Pentecostal Assemblies of the World, Inc. (1906): 3939 N. Meadows Dr., Indianapolis, IN 46205; (317) 547-9541; www.pawinc.org; Presiding Bishop, Theodore L. Brooks, Sr.

Presbyterian Church (U.S.A.) (1983): 100 Witherspoon St., Louisville, KY 40202; (800) 728-7228; www.pcusa.org; Pres., Kathy Lueckert

Progressive Natl. Baptist Convention, Inc. (1961): 601 50th St. NE, Washington, DC 20019; (202) 396-0558; www.pnbc.org; Pres., Rev. David Peoples

Rabbis, Central Conference of American (1889): 355 Lexington Ave., NY, NY 10017; (212) 972-3636; www.ccarnet.org; Pres., Rabbi Erica Asch

Reconstructing Judaism (fmr. Jewish Reconstructionist Communities) (2012): 1299 Church Rd., Wyncote, PA 19095; (215) 576-0800; www.reconstructingjudaism.org; Pres., Rabbi Deborah Waxman

Reform Judaism, Union for (1873): 633 3rd Ave., NY, NY 10017; (212) 650-4000; www.urj.org; Pres., Rabbi Rick Jacobs

Secular Humanism, Council for (1980): P.O. Box 664, Amherst, NY 14226; (716) 636-7571; www.secularhumanism.org; Pres., Robyn E. Blumner

Separation of Church and State, Americans United for (1947): 1310 L St. NW, Ste. 200, Washington, DC 20005; (202) 466-3234; www.au.org; Pres. and CEO, Rachel Laser

Seventh-day Adventist Church (1863): 12501 Old Columbia Pike, Silver Spring, MD 20904; (301) 680-6000; www.adventist.org; Pres., Ted N. C. Wilson

Seventh Day Baptist (1802): P.O. Box 1678, Janesville, WI 53547; (608) 752-5055; www.seventhdaybaptist.org; Exec. Dir., Rev. Carl P. Greene

Unitarian Universalist Assn. of Congregations (1961): 24 Farnsworth St., Boston, MA 02210; (617) 742-2100; www.uua.org; Pres., Rev. Susan Frederick-Gray

United Church of Christ (1957): 1300 E. 9th St., Ste. 1100, Cleveland, OH 44114; (216) 736-2100; www.ucc.org; Pres., Rev. John C. Dorhauer

United Methodist Church (1968): 100 Maryland Ave. NE, Washington, DC 20002; (202) 488-5600; www.umc.org; Council of Bishops Pres., Thomas J. Bickerton

United Pentecostal Church Intl. (1945): 36 Research Park Court, Weldon Spring, MO 63304; (636) 229-7900; www.upci.org; Gen. Supt., David K. Bernard

Wesleyan Church, The (1843): 13300 Olio Rd., Fishers, IN 46037; (317) 774-7900; www.wesleyan.org; Gen. Supt., Rev. Dr. Wayne Schmidt

Labor Unions and Professional Organizations

Source: Bureau of Labor Statistics, U.S. Dept. of Labor; AFL-CIO; World Almanac research

= Member of Strategic Organizing Center (fmr. Change to Win Federation), formed in 2005 by unions disaffiliated from AFL-CIO. * = Independent union or one not otherwise affiliated with Strategic Organizing Center or AFL-CIO. All other unions listed are affiliated with AFL-CIO as of 2024. Year established is in parentheses.

Labor Unions

Air Line Pilots Assn., Intl. (ALPA) (1931): 76,585 members, 41 U.S. and Canadian airlines; (703) 689-2270; www.alpa.org

American Federation of Labor and Congress of Industrial Organizations (AFL-CIO) (1955): federation of 60 unions, 12,996,375 members; (202) 637-5000; www.aflcio.org

Automobile, Aerospace & Agricultural Implement Workers of America, International Union, United (UAW) (1935): 370,239 members, 600+ locals; (313) 926-5000; www.uaw.org

Bakery, Confectionery, Tobacco Workers, and Grain Millers International Union (BCTGM) (1886): 62,323 members, 125 locals; (301) 933-8600; www.bctgm.org

Bricklayers and Allied Craftworkers, International Union of (BAC) (1865): 67,491 members, 39 locals; (202) 783-3788; www.bacweb.org

***Carpenters and Joiners of America, United Brotherhood of** (UBC) (1881): 442,363 members, 450+ locals; (202) 546-6206; www.carpenters.org

Communications Workers of America (CWA) (1938): 648,305 members, 1,200 locals; (202) 434-1100; www.cwa-union.org

***Education Assn., Natl.** (NEA) (1857): 2,857,703 members, 14,000+ affiliates; (202) 833-4000; www.nea.org

Electrical Workers, International Brotherhood of (IBEW) (1891): 699,886 members, 831 locals; (202) 833-7000; www.ibew.org

Engineers, International Union of Operating (IUOE) (1896): 405,517 members, 123 locals; (202) 429-9100; www.iuoe.org

#Farm Workers of America, United (UFW) (1962): 4,821 members; (661) 823-6151; www.ufw.org

Federal Employees, Natl. Federation of (NFFE; affiliated with IAM) (1917): about 110,000 members, about 200 locals; (202) 216-4420; www.nffe.org

Fire Fighters, International Assn. of (IAFF) (1918): 341,069 members, 3,500+ locals; (202) 737-8484; www.iaff.org

Flight Attendants, Assn. of (AFA-CWA) (1945): 45,500 members, 19 airlines; merged with Communications Workers of America in 2004; (202) 434-1300; www.afacwa.org

Food and Commercial Workers International Union, United (UFCW) (1979): 1,182,472 members, 1,000+ locals; (202) 223-3111; www.ufcw.org

Glass, Molders, Pottery, Plastics and Allied Workers Intl. Union (GMP) (1842): 25,000 members, 250+ locals; (610) 565-5051; www.gmpiu.org

Government Employees, American Federation of (AFGE) (1932): 313,108 members, 900 locals; (202) 737-8700; www.afge.org

Iron Workers, Intl. Assn. of Bridge, Structural, Ornamental, and Reinforcing (BSOIW) (1896): 127,933 members, 200+ locals; (202) 383-4800; www.ironworkers.org

Laborers' International Union of North America (LiUNA) (1903): 580,673 members, 400 locals; (202) 737-8320; www.liuna.org

Letter Carriers, Natl. Assn. of (NALC) (1889): 289,753 members, 2,000+ locals; (202) 393-4695; www.nalc.org

#Locomotive Engineers and Trainmen, Brotherhood of (BLET) (1863): 51,660 members, 500+ locals; (216) 241-2630; www.ble-t.org

Longshoremen's Assn., Intl. (ILA) (1892): 47,412 members, approx. 200 locals; (212) 425-1200; www.ilaunion.org

Machinists and Aerospace Workers, International Assn. of (IAM) (1888): 544,492 members; affiliated with TCU in 2005; (301) 967-4500; www.goiam.org

#Maintenance of Way Employes, Division of the Intl. Brotherhood of Teamsters; Brotherhood of (BMWED) (1887): 32,812 members (2024), 770 locals; merged with Teamsters in 2004; (248) 662-2660; www.bmwe.org (Note: In honor of tradition, the union maintains the variant spelling of "employes" in its logo.)

Mine Workers of America, United (UMWA) (1890): 45,124 members, 600 locals; (703) 291-2400; www.umwa.org

Musicians of the United States and Canada, American Federation of (AFM) (1896): 65,857 members, 240+ locals; (212) 869-1330; www.afm.org

National Nurses United (NNA) (2009): 201,992 members; (240) 235-2000; www.nationalnursesunited.org

NewsGuild—Communications Workers of America, The (TNG-CWA) (1933): 26,000 members, 63 locals; (202) 434-7177; www.newsguild.org

***Nurses Assn., American** (ANA) (1911): 195,884 members, 50+ constituent state and territorial assns.; (301) 628-5000; www.nursingworld.org

Office and Professional Employees Intl. Union (OPEIU) (1945): 63,290 members, 61 locals; (212) 675-3210; www.opeiu.org

Painters and Allied Trades, International Union of (IUPAT) (1887): 107,880 members, 425 locals; (410) 564-5900; www.iupat.org

Plumbing and Pipe Fitting Industry of the U.S. and Canada, United Assn. of Journeymen and Apprentices of the (UA) (1889): 366,230 members, 242 locals; (410) 269-2000; www.ua.org

***Police, Fraternal Order of** (FOP) (1915): 369,007 members, 2,200+ affiliates; (615) 399-0900; www.fop.net

Police Assns., International Union of (IUPA) (1979): 100,000+ members; (941) 487-2560; www.iupa.org

Postal Workers Union, American (APWU) (1971): 219,530 members, 900+ locals; (202) 842-4200; www.apwu.org

Printing, Packaging, & Production Workers Union of North America (PPPWU) (1983): 43,834 members; merged with Teamsters as Graphic Communications Conference, 2004-23; independent, July 2023; www.pppwu.org

Roofers, Waterproofers and Allied Workers, United Union of (RWAW) (1906): 22,598 members; (202) 463-7663; www.unionroofers.com

***Rural Letter Carriers' Assn., Natl.** (RLCA) (1903): 110,419 members, 50 state orgs.; (703) 684-5545; www.nrlca.org

***Security, Police, Fire Professionals of America, Intl. Union** (SPFPA) (1948): 16,088 members, 200 locals; (586) 772-7250; www.spfpa.org

#Service Employees International Union (SEIU) (1921): 1,845,500 members, 150+ locals; (202) 730-7000; www.seiu.org

Sheet Metal, Air, Rail, and Transportation Workers, Int. Assn. of (SMART) (2008, from merger of Sheet Metal Workers' Intl. Assn. and United Transportation Union): 201,830 members, 700 locals; (202) 662-0800; www.smart-union.org

State, County, and Municipal Employees, American Federation of (AFSCME) (1932): 1,248,681 members, 3,400 locals; (202) 429-1000; www.afscme.org

Steel, Paper and Forestry, Rubber, Manufacturing, Energy, Allied Industrial and Service Workers International Union, United (USW) (2005): 539,661 members, 1,800+ locals; formed from merger of United Steelworkers of America (USWA) (1936) and Paper, Allied-Industrial, Chemical and Energy Workers (PACE) (1999); (412) 562-2400; www.usw.org

#Strategic Organizing Center (SOC) (fmr. Change to Win Federation) (2005): 3 unions, ex-affiliates of AFL-CIO, 2,477,696 members; (202) 721-0660; www.thesoc.org

Teachers, American Federation of (AFT) (1916): 1,732,808 members, 3,000+ locals; (202) 879-4400; www.aft.org

#Teamsters, International Brotherhood of (IBT) (1903): 1,267,407 members, 380 locals, 1,900 affilates; (202) 624-6800; www.teamster.org

Theatrical Stage Employees, Moving Picture Technicians, Artists and Allied Crafts of the U.S., Its Territories, and Canada, Intl. Alliance of (IATSE) (1893): 168,296 members, 367 locals; (212) 730-1770; www.iatse.net

Transit Union, Amalgamated (ATU) (1892): 193,457 members, 270 locals; (301) 431-7100; www.atu.org

Transport Workers Union of America (TWU) (1934): 148,101 members, 89 locals; (202) 719-3900; www.twu.org

Transportation Communications Intl. Union (TCU) (1899): affiliated with IAM in 2005; see Machinists and Aerospace Workers.

***Treasury Employees Union, Natl.** (NTEU) (1938): 87,250 members, 200+ chapters; (202) 572-5500; www.nteu.org

UNITE HERE (UNITE, 1900; HERE, 1891; merged 2004): 264,334 members, 119 locals; (212) 265-7000; www.unitehere.org

#Workers United (affiliated with SEIU) (WU) (2009): 78,151 members; (646) 448-6414; www.workersunited.org

***Writers Guild of America, East** (WGAE) (1954): 7,618 (2024); (212) 767-7800; www.wgaeast.org

***Writers Guild of America, West** (WGAW) (1933): 14,388 members (2024); (323) 951-4000; www.wga.org

Professional Organizations and Societies

AASA, The School Superintendents Assn. (fmr. American Assn. of School Administrators) (1865): 10,000+ members; (703) 528-0700; www.aasa.org

Accountants, American Institute of Certified Public (1887): 597,000+ members; (888) 777-7077; www.aicpa.org

ACMP—Associated Chamber Music Players (1947): 3,000+ members; (212) 645-7424; www.acmp.net

Actuaries, Soc. of (1949): 33,500+ members; (847) 706-3500; www.soa.org

Administrative Professionals, Intl. Assn. of (1942): 40,000+ members; (816) 891-6600; www.iaap-hq.org

Agricultural and Biological Engineers, American Soc. of (1907): 7,000+ members; (269) 429-0300; www.asabe.org

AIGA (fmr. American Institute of Graphic Arts) (1914): 18,000+ members; (212) 807-1990; www.aiga.org

Air & Waste Management Assn. (1907): 5,000+ members; (412) 232-3444; www.awma.org

AMSUS—The Society of Federal Health Professionals (1891): nearly 8,000 members; (301) 897-8800; www.amsus.org

Architects, American Institute of (1857): 98,000+ members; (202) 626-7300; www.aia.org

ASCM—The Assn. for Supply Chain Management (1957): 70,000+ members; (773) 867-1777; www.ascm.org

ASHRAE (Heating, Refrigerating and Air-Conditioning Engineers, Inc., American Soc. of) (1894): 50,000+ members; (404) 636-8400; www.ashrae.org

ASIS Intl. (fmr. Amer. Soc. for Industrial Security) (1955): 34,000 members; (703) 519-6200; www.asisonline.org

Astrologers, Inc., American Federation of (1938): 4,000 members; (480) 838-1751; www.astrologers.com

Astronomical Society, American (1899): 8,850+ members; (202) 328-2010; www.aas.org

Authors Guild, The (1912): 14,000+ members; (212) 563-5904; www.authorsguild.org

Bankers of America, Independent Community (1930): over 3,000 banks; (202) 659-8111; www.icba.org

Bar Assn., American (1878): 400,000+ members; (312) 988-5000; www.american bar.org

Bar Assn., Federal (1920): 14,000+ members; (571) 481-9100; www.fedbar.org

Biochemistry and Molecular Biology, American Society for (1906): 11,000+ members; (240) 283-6600; www.asbmb.org

Broadcasters, Natl. Assn. of (1923): (202) 429-5300; www.nab.org

Business Women's Assn., American (1949): 40,000 members; (800) 228-0007; www.abwa.org

Cartoonists Society, Natl. (1946): 500+ members; (734) 239-8031; www.nationalcartoonists.com

Ceramic Society, American (1898): 10,000+ members; (614) 890-4700; www.ceramics.org

Chemical Society, American (1876): 200,000+ members; (202) 872-4600; www.acs.org

Chiefs of Police, Intl. Assn. of (1893): 34,000+ members; (703) 836-6767; www.theiacp.org

Chiropractic Assn., American (1963): 15,000+ members; (703) 276-8800; www.acatoday.org

Civil Engineers, American Soc. of (1852): 150,000+ members; (703) 295-6300; www.asce.org

College Admission Counseling, Natl. Assn. for (1937): 27,000+ members; (703) 836-2222; www.nacacnet.org

Communication Assn., Natl. (1914): 5,700+ members; (202) 464-4622; www.natcom.org

Composers, Authors & Publishers, American Soc. of (ASCAP) (1914): 990,000+ members; (212) 621-6000; www.ascap.com

Computing Machinery, Assn. for (1947): nearly 100,000 members; (212) 869-7440; www.acm.org

Computing Professionals, Institute for Certification of (1973): 75,000+ members; (847) 299-4227; www.iccp.org

Counseling Assn., American (1952): 58,000+ members; (800) 347-6647; www.counseling.org

Country Music Assn. (1958): 6,000+ members; (615) 244-2840; www.cmaworld.com

Dental Assn., American (1859): 161,000+ members; (312) 440-2500; www.ada.org

Directors Guild of America (1936): 19,500+ members; (310) 289-2000; www.dga.org

Electrical and Electronics Engineers, Institute of (1963): 400,000+ members; (732) 981-0060; www.ieee.org

Electronics Technicians, Intl. Soc. of Certified (1965): 50,000+ members; (817) 921-9061; www.iscet.org

Emergency Medical Technicians, Natl. Assn. of (1975): 92,000+ members; (601) 924-7744; www.naemt.org

Energy Engineers, Assn. of (1977): 17,000+ members; (770) 447-5083; www.aeecenter.org

Engineers, Natl. Society of Professional (1934): 35,000+ members; (888) 285-6773; www.nspe.org

Environmental Assessment Assn. (1972): 3,500 members; (877) 743-6806; www.eaa-assoc.org

Environmental Health Assn., Natl. (1937): 7,000+ members; (303) 756-9090; www.neha.org

Family Physicians, American Academy of (1947): 130,000 members; (800) 274-2237; www.aafp.org

Farm Bureau Federation, American (1919): nearly 6 mil member families; (202) 406-3600; www.fb.org

Farmers Union, Natl. (1902): nearly 220,000+ family farmers, fishers, ranchers; (202) 554-1600; www.nfu.org

Financial Professionals, Assn. for (1979): 16,000+ members; (301) 907-2862; www.afponline.org

Fire Chiefs, Intl. Assn. of (1873): nearly 12,000 members; (703) 273-0911; www.iafc.org

Fire Protection Engineers, Soc. of (1950): 5,000+ members; (301) 718-2910; www.sfpe.org

Food Technologists, Institute of (1939): 11,000+ members; (312) 782-8424; www.ift.org

Forensic Sciences, American Academy of (1948): 6,500+ members; (719) 636-1100; www.aafs.org

Funeral Directors Assn., Natl. (1882): 20,000 members; (262) 789-1880; www.nfda.org

General Contractors of America, Associated (1918): 27,000+ cos.; (703) 548-3118; www.agc.org

Geographers, American Assn. of (1904): 10,000 members; (202) 234-1450; www.aag.org

Ground Water Assn., Natl. (1948): nearly 15,000 members; (614) 898-7791; www.ngwa.org

Home Builders, Natl. Assn. of (1942): 140,000 members; (800) 368-5242; www.nahb.org

Human Resource Management, Soc. for (SHRM) (1948): 325,000+ members; (703) 548-3440; www.shrm.org

Illustrators, Society of (1901): 1,000 members; (212) 838-2560; www.societyillustrators.org

Industrial Designers Society of America (1965): 2,500 members; (703) 707-6000; www.idsa.org

Insurance and Financial Advisors, Natl. Assn. of (1890): 50,000+ members; (877) 866-2432; www.naifa.org

Intelligence Officers, Assn. of Former (1975): 19 chap., 3,400 members; (703) 790-0320; www.afio.com

Interior Designers, American Soc. of (1975): 25,000+ members; (202) 546-3480; www.asid.org

Jail Assn., American (1981): 3,200+ members; (301) 790-3930; www.americanjail.org

Journalists, Society of Professional (1909): 6,000 members; (317) 927-8000; www.spj.org

Landscape Architects, American Society of (1899): 18,000+ members; (202) 898-2444; www.asla.org

Legal Administrators, Assn. of (1971): 8,500+ members; (847) 267-1252; www.alanet.org

Legal Support Professionals, Natl. Assn. for (fmr. Natl. Assn. of Legal Secretaries) (1929): nearly 6,000 members; (918) 582-5188; www.nals.org

Library Assn., American (1876): 50,000+ members; (800) 545-2433; www.ala.org

Lifesaving Assn., U.S. (1964): 100+ chap., 12,600+ members; (866) 367-8752; www.usla.org

Logistics, Intl. Society of (SOLE) (1966): 100+ chap., 3,000+ members; (301) 459-8446; www.sole.org

Magicians, Intl. Brotherhood of (1922): nearly 11,000 members; (636) 724-2400; www.magician.org
Management Accountants, Inst. of (1919): about 140,000 members; (201) 573-9000; www.imanet.org
Management Assn., American (1923): 4,100 cos., 38,000 ind.; (877) 566-9441; www.amanet.org
Marketing Assn., American (1937): 30,000+ members; (800) 262-1150; www.ama.org
Master Brewers Assn. of the Americas (1887): 4,000+ members; (651) 454-7250; www.mbaa.com
Material and Process Engineering, Soc. for the Advancement of (1944): 5,000+ members; (626) 521-9460; www.sampe.org
Mechanical Engineers, American Soc. of (1880): 75,000+ members; (646) 616-3100; www.asme.org
Medical Assn., American (1847): 283,000 members; (800) 262-3211; www.ama-assn.org
Medical Library Assn. (1898): 3,000+ members, 400 institutions; (312) 419-9094; www.mlanet.org
Motion Picture Arts & Sciences, Academy of (1927): 10,500+ members; (310) 247-3000; www.oscars.org
Motion Picture and Television Engineers, Soc. of (1916): 5,000+ members; (914) 761-1100; www.smpte.org
Mystery Writers of America (1945): 3,000+ members; (212) 888-8171; www.mysterywriters.org
Notaries, American Society of (1965): 20,000+ members; (850) 671-5164; www.notaries.org
Nursing, Natl. League for (1893): nearly 45,000 members, 1,000+ institutions; (800) 669-1656; www.nln.org
Optometric Assn., American (1898): 45,000+ members; (800) 365-2219; www.aoa.org
Organists, American Guild of (1896): 12,000 members; (212) 870-2310; www.agohq.org
Pharmacists Assn., American (1852): 62,000+ members; (202) 628-4410; www.pharmacist.com
Physical Therapy Assn., American (1921): 100,000+ members; (703) 684-2782; www.apta.org
Plastics Engineers, Society of (1942): 60,000+ members; (203) 740-5400; www.4spe.org
Police Assn.—United States Section, Intl. (1962): 10,000 members; (855) 241-9998; www.ipa-usa.org
Population Assn. of America (1931): nearly 3,000 members; (301) 565-6710; www.populationassociation.org
Postmasters and Managers of America, United (2015): (703) 683-9027; www.unitedpma.org
Press Club, Natl. (1908): 3,000 members; (202) 662-7500; www.press.org
Professional Ball Players of America, Assn. of (1924): 101,500+ members; (602) 730-4528; www.apbpa.org
Professional Beauty Assn. (1904): 100,000+ members; (480) 281-0424; www.probeauty.org
Psychiatric Assn., American (1844): 38,900+ members; (202) 559-3900; www.psychiatry.org
Psychological Assn., American (1892): 157,000+ members; (202) 336-5500; www.apa.org
Public Administration, American Soc. for (1939): 10,000 members; (202) 393-7878; www.aspanet.org
Public Health Assn., American (1872): 25,000+ members; (202) 777-2742; www.apha.org
Public Relations Soc. of America Inc. (1947): nearly 32,000 members; (212) 460-1400; www.prsa.org
Range Management, Society for (1948): 4,000+ members; (303) 986-3309; www.rangelands.org
Real Estate Appraisers, Natl. Assn. of (1966): 10,000+ members; (877) 743-6806; www.narea-assoc.org
Rehabilitation Assn., Natl. (1923): 5,600 members; (703) 836-0850; www.nationalrehab.org
Road & Transportation Builders Assn., American (1902): 8,000+ members; (202) 289-4434; www.artba.org
Safety Professionals, American Soc. of (1911): 35,000 members; (847) 699-2929; www.assp.org
Science Teaching Assn., Natl. (1944): 35,000 members; (703) 524-3646; www.nsta.org
Screen Actors Guild—American Federation of Television and Radio Artists (2012): 160,000 members; (855) 724-2387; www.sagaftra.org
Songwriters Guild of America, Inc. (1931): 5,000+ members; (615) 742-9945; www.songwritersguild.com
Sportscasters Assn., American (1979): 500+ members; (212) 227-8080; www.americansportscastersonline.com
Supply Chain Management, Assn. for (fmr. Assn. for Operations Management) (1957): 45,000+ members; (773) 867-1777; www.ascm.org
Surgeons, American College of (1913): 90,000+ members; (312) 202-5000; www.facs.org
Tax Administrators, Federation of (1937): (202) 624-5890; www.taxadmin.org
Teachers of English, Natl. Council of (1911): 25,000+ members; (217) 328-3870; www.ncte.org
Teachers of French, American Assn. of (1927): nearly 6,000 members; (815) 310-0490; www.frenchteachers.org
Teachers of German, American Assn. of (1926): nearly 3,500 members; (856) 795-5553; www.aatg.org
Teachers of Mathematics, Natl. Council of (1920): 70,000 members; (703) 620-9840; www.nctm.org
Teachers of Spanish and Portuguese, American Assn. of (1917): nearly 10,000 members; (205) 506-0600; www.aatsp.org
Television Arts and Sciences, Natl. Academy of (1955): 24,000+ members; (212) 586-8424; www.theemmys.tv
TESOL International Assn. (fmr. Teachers of English to Speakers of Other Languages) (1966): 10,000+ members; (703) 518-2500; www.tesol.org
Theological Library Assn., American (1946): 800+ members; (872) 310-4200; www.atla.com
Transportation Engineers, Inst. of (1930): 18,000+ members; (202) 785-0060; www.ite.org
Travel Advisors, American Soc. of (fmr. Amer. Soc. of Travel Agents) (1931): nearly 8,000 members; (800) 275-2782; www.asta.org
University Women, American Assn. of (1881): 170,000+ members; (202) 785-7700; www.aauw.org
Veterinary Medical Assn., American (1863): 105,000+ members; (847) 925-8070; www.avma.org
Women Engineers, Society of (1950): 40,000+ members; (312) 596-5223; swe.org
Women in Media, Alliance for (1951): nearly 10,000 members; (202) 750-3664; www.allwomeninmedia.org

Professional Sports Organizations

Source: World Almanac research

Major League Baseball

Office of the Commissioner, 1271 Ave. of the Americas, NY, NY 10020; (212) 931-7800; www.mlb.com

American League

Baltimore Orioles (1953): 333 W. Camden St., Baltimore, MD 21201; (410) 685-9800; www.orioles.com
Boston Red Sox (1901): 4 Jersey St., Boston, MA 02215; (617) 267-9440; www.redsox.com
Chicago White Sox (1900, as Chicago White Stockings): 333 W. 35th St., Chicago, IL 60616; (312) 674-1000; www.whitesox.com
Cleveland Guardians (1901, as Cleveland Blues; name changed from Indians after 2021 season): 2401 Ontario St., Cleveland, OH 44115; (216) 420-4200; cleguardians.com
Detroit Tigers (1901): 2100 Woodward Ave., Detroit, MI 48201; (313) 471-2000; www.tigers.com
Houston Astros (1962, as Houston Colt 45s): 501 Crawford St., Houston, TX 77002; (713) 259-8000; www.astros.com (National League, 1962-2012; AL West, 2013-present)
Kansas City Royals (1969): One Royal Way, Kansas City, MO 64129; (816) 921-8000; www.royals.com
Los Angeles Angels (1961): 2000 Gene Autry Way, Anaheim, CA 92806; (714) 940-2000; www.angels.com
Minnesota Twins (1960): 1 Twins Way, Minneapolis, MN 55403; (612) 659-3400; www.twinsbaseball.com
New York Yankees (1903): One E. 161st St., Bronx, NY 10451; (718) 293-4300; www.yankees.com
Oakland Athletics (1901, as Philadelphia Athletics): 7000 Coliseum Way, Oakland, CA 94621; (510) 638-4900; www.athletics.com
Seattle Mariners (1977): 1250 First Ave. S., Seattle, WA 98134; (206) 346-4000; www.mariners.com
Tampa Bay Rays (1995, as Tampa Bay Devil Rays): 1 Tropicana Dr., St. Petersburg, FL 33705; (727) 825-3137; www.raysbaseball.com
Texas Rangers (1960, as Washington Senators): 734 Stadium Dr., Arlington, TX 76011; (817) 533-1972; www.texasrangers.com
Toronto Blue Jays (1976): One Blue Jays Way, Ste. 3200, Toronto, ON M5V 1J1, Canada; (416) 341-1000; www.bluejays.com

National League

Arizona Diamondbacks (1998): 401 E. Jefferson St., Phoenix, AZ 85004; (602) 462-6500; www.dbacks.com
Atlanta Braves (1876, as Boston Red Stockings): 755 Battery Ave., Atlanta, GA 30339; (404) 614-2300; www.braves.com
Chicago Cubs (1876, as Chicago White Stockings): 1060 W. Addison, Chicago, IL 60613; (773) 404-2827; www.cubs.com
Cincinnati Reds (1869, as Cincinnati Red Stockings): 100 Joe Nuxhall Way, Cincinnati, OH 45202; (513) 765-7000; www.reds.com
Colorado Rockies (1991): 2001 Blake St., Denver, CO 80205; (303) 292-0200; www.rockies.com
Los Angeles Dodgers (1890): 1000 Vin Scully Ave., Los Angeles, CA 90012; (323) 363-4377; www.dodgers.com
Miami Marlins (1991, as Florida Marlins): 501 Marlins Way, Miami, FL 33125; (305) 480-1300; www.marlins.com
Milwaukee Brewers (1970): One Brewers Way, Milwaukee, WI 53214; (414) 902-4400; www.brewers.com (American League, 1969-1997; NL Central, 1998-present)
New York Mets (1961): 41 Seaver Way, Queens, NY 11368; (718) 507-6387; www.mets.com
Philadelphia Phillies (1883): One Citizens Bank Way, Philadelphia, PA 19148; (215) 463-6000; www.phillies.com
Pittsburgh Pirates (1887, as Pittsburgh Alleghenies): 115 Federal St., Pittsburgh, PA 15212; (412) 323-5000; www.pirates.com
St. Louis Cardinals (1892, as St. Louis Browns): 700 Clark St., St. Louis, MO 63102; (314) 345-9600; www.cardinals.com
San Diego Padres (1969): 100 Park Blvd., San Diego, CA 92101; (619) 795-5000; www.padres.com
San Francisco Giants (1883, as New York Gothams): 24 Willie Mays Plz., San Francisco, CA 94107; (415) 972-2000; www.sfgiants.com
Washington Nationals (1969, as Montréal Expos): 1500 South Capitol St., SE, Washington, DC 20003; (202) 675-6287; www.nationals.com

National Basketball Association

League Office, 645 Fifth Ave., NY, NY 10022; (212) 407-8000; www.nba.com
Atlanta Hawks (1949, as Tri-Cities Blackhawks): 101 Marietta St. NW, Ste. 1900, Atlanta, GA 30303; (866) 715-1500; www.nba.com/hawks
Boston Celtics (1946): 100 Causeway St., Ste. 1210, Boston, MA 02114; (866) 423-5849; www.nba.com/celtics
Brooklyn Nets (1967, as New Jersey Americans): 168 39th St., 7th Fl., Brooklyn, NY 11232; (718) 933-3000; www.nba.com/nets

Charlotte Hornets (2004, as Charlotte Bobcats): 333 E. Trade St., Charlotte, NC 28202; (704) 688-8600; www.nba.com/hornets
Chicago Bulls (1966): 1901 W. Madison St., Chicago, IL 60612; (312) 455-4000; www.nba.com/bulls
Cleveland Cavaliers (1970): One Center Ct., Cleveland, OH 44115; (216) 420-2000; www.nba.com/cavaliers
Dallas Mavericks (1980): 2500 Victory Ave., Dallas, TX 75219; (214) 747-6287; www.nba.com/mavericks
Denver Nuggets (1967, as Denver Rockets): 1000 Chopper Cir., Denver, CO 80204; (303) 405-1100; www.nba.com/nuggets
Detroit Pistons (1948, as Fort Wayne Pistons): 6201 2nd Ave., Detroit, MI 48202; (313) 747-8667; www.nba.com/pistons
Golden State Warriors (1946, as Philadelphia Warriors): 1 Warriors Way, San Francisco, CA 94158; (888) 479-4667; www.nba.com/warriors
Houston Rockets (1967, as San Diego Rockets): 1510 Polk St., Houston, TX 77002; (713) 758-7200; www.nba.com/rockets
Indiana Pacers (1967): 125 S. Pennsylvania St., Indianapolis, IN 46204; (317) 917-2500; www.nba.com/pacers
Los Angeles Clippers (1970, as Buffalo Braves): 1212 S. Flower St., 5th Fl., Los Angeles, CA 90015; (213) 204-2950; www.nba.com/clippers
Los Angeles Lakers (1947, as Minneapolis Lakers): 1111 S. Figueroa St., Los Angeles, CA 90015; (310) 426-6000; www.nba.com/lakers
Memphis Grizzlies (1995, as Vancouver Grizzlies): 191 Beale St., Memphis, TN 38103; (901) 888-4667; www.nba.com/grizzlies
Miami Heat (1988): 601 Biscayne Blvd., Miami, FL 33132; (786) 777-1000; www.nba.com/heat
Milwaukee Bucks (1968): 1111 Vel R. Phillips Ave., Milwaukee, WI 53203; (414) 227-0599; www.nba.com/bucks
Minnesota Timberwolves (1989): 600 Hennepin Ave., Ste. 300, Minneapolis, MN 55403; (612) 673-1600; www.nba.com/timberwolves
New Orleans Pelicans (1988, as Charlotte Hornets): 5800 Airline Dr., Metairie, LA 70003; (504) 593-4700; www.nba.com/pelicans
New York Knickerbockers (1946): Two Pennsylvania Plz., NY, NY 10121; (212) 465-6471; www.nba.com/knicks
Oklahoma City Thunder (1967, as Seattle SuperSonics): 208 Thunder Dr., Oklahoma City, OK 73102; (405) 208-4800; www.nba.com/thunder
Orlando Magic (1989): 8701 Maitland Summit Blvd., Orlando, FL 32810; (407) 916-2400; www.nba.com/magic
Philadelphia 76ers (1949, as Syracuse Nationals): 3601 S. Broad St., Philadelphia, PA 19148; (215) 339-7676; www.nba.com/sixers
Phoenix Suns (1968): 201 E. Jefferson St., Phoenix, AZ 85004; (602) 379-7900; www.nba.com/suns
Portland Trail Blazers (1970): One Center Ct., Ste. 200, Portland, OR 97227; (503) 234-9291; www.nba.com/blazers
Sacramento Kings (1945, as Rochester Royals): 500 J St., 4th Fl., Sacramento, CA 95814; (888) 915-4647; www.nba.com/kings
San Antonio Spurs (1967, as Dallas Chaparrals): 1 Frost Bank Center Dr., San Antonio, TX 78219; (210) 444-5000; www.nba.com/spurs
Toronto Raptors (1995): 40 Bay St., Toronto, ON M5J 2X2, Canada; (416) 366-3865; www.nba.com/raptors
Utah Jazz (1974, as New Orleans Jazz): 301 W. South Temple, Salt Lake City, UT 84101; (801) 325-2500; www.nba.com/jazz
Washington Wizards (1961, as Chicago Packers): 601 F St. NW, Washington, DC 20004; (202) 661-5000; www.nba.com/wizards

National Hockey League

NHL Headquarters, 1 Manhattan West, 395 Ninth Ave., NY, NY 10001; (212) 789-2000; www.nhl.com
Anaheim Ducks (1993): 2695 E. Katella Ave., Anaheim, CA 92806; (877) 945-3946; ducks.nhl.com
Boston Bruins (1924): 100 Legends Way, Boston, MA 02114; (617) 614-2327; bruins.nhl.com
Buffalo Sabres (1970): One Seymour H. Knox III Plz., Buffalo, NY 14203; (716) 855-4100; sabres.nhl.com
Calgary Flames (1980): P.O. Box 1540, Station M, Calgary, AB T2P 3B9, Canada; (403) 777-2177; flames.nhl.com
Carolina Hurricanes (1972, as New England Whalers): 1400 Edwards Mill Rd., Raleigh, NC 27607; (919) 467-7825; hurricanes.nhl.com
Chicago Blackhawks (1926): 1901 W. Madison St., Chicago, IL 60612; (312) 455-7000; blackhawks.nhl.com
Colorado Avalanche (1972, as Quebec Nordiques): 1000 Chopper Cir., Denver, CO 80204; (303) 405-1100; avalanche.nhl.com
Columbus Blue Jackets (2000): 200 W. Nationwide Blvd., Suite Level, Columbus, OH 43215; (614) 246-4625; bluejackets.nhl.com
Dallas Stars (1967, as Minnesota North Stars): 2601 Ave. of the Stars, Frisco, TX 75034; (214) 387-5500; stars.nhl.com
Detroit Red Wings (1926, as Detroit Cougars): 2525 Woodward Ave., Detroit, MI 48201; (313) 471-7000; redwings.nhl.com
Edmonton Oilers (1972, as Alberta Oilers): 300, 10214 104 Ave. NW, Edmonton, AB T5J 0H6, Canada; (866) 414-4625; oilers.nhl.com
Florida Panthers (1993): One Panther Pkwy., Sunrise, FL 33323; (954) 835-7000; panthers.nhl.com
Los Angeles Kings (1967): 1111 S. Figueroa St., Los Angeles, CA 90015; (213) 742-7100; kings.nhl.com
Minnesota Wild (2000): 317 Washington St., St. Paul, MN 55102; (651) 602-6000; wild.nhl.com
Montréal Canadiens (1909): 1909 Avenue des Canadiens-de-Montréal, Montréal, QC H3B 5L2, Canada; (514) 932-2582; canadiens.nhl.com
Nashville Predators (1998): 501 Broadway, Nashville, TN 37203; (615) 770-2000; predators.nhl.com
New Jersey Devils (1974, as Kansas City Scouts): Prudential Center, 25 Lafayette St., Newark, NJ 07102; (973) 757-6100; devils.nhl.com
New York Islanders (1972): 200 Merrick Ave., East Meadow, NY 11554; (516) 501-6700; islanders.nhl.com
New York Rangers (1926): Two Pennsylvania Plz., NY, NY 10121; (212) 465-6000; rangers.nhl.com
Ottawa Senators (1992): 1000 Palladium Dr., Ottawa, ON K2V 1A5, Canada; (613) 599-0250; senators.nhl.com
Philadelphia Flyers (1967): 3601 S. Broad St., Philadelphia, PA 19148; (215) 465-4500; flyers.nhl.com
Pittsburgh Penguins (1967): 1001 5th Ave., Pittsburgh, PA 15219; (412) 642-1300; penguins.nhl.com
St. Louis Blues (1967): 1401 Clark Ave. at Brett Hull Way, St. Louis, MO 63103; (314) 622-2500; blues.nhl.com
San Jose Sharks (1991): 525 W. Santa Clara St., San Jose, CA 95113; (408) 287-7070; sharks.nhl.com
Seattle Kraken (2021): 334 1st Ave. N., Seattle, WA 98109; (206) 460-7825; nhl.com/kraken
Tampa Bay Lightning (1992): 401 Channelside Dr., Tampa, FL 33602; (813) 301-6500; lightning.nhl.com
Toronto Maple Leafs (1919, as Toronto St. Pats): 50 Bay St., Ste. 500, Toronto, ON M5J 2L2, Canada; (416) 815-5700; maple leafs.nhl.com
Utah Hockey Club (1979, as Winnipeg Jets): 301 W S Temple, Salt Lake City, UT 84101; 801-325-2208; nhl.com/utah
Vancouver Canucks (1945, joined NHL in 1970): 89 W. Georgia St., Vancouver, BC V6B 0N8, Canada; (604) 899-7400; canucks.nhl.com
Vegas Golden Knights (2017): 3780 S. Las Vegas Blvd., Las Vegas, NV 89158; (702) 692-1600; goldenknights.nhl.com
Washington Capitals (1974): 627 N. Glebe Rd., Ste. 850, Arlington, VA 22203; (202) 266-2200; capitals.nhl.com
Winnipeg Jets (1999, as Atlanta Thrashers): 600-223 Carlton St., Winnipeg, MB R3C 0V4, Canada; (204) 987-7825; jets.nhl.com

National Football League

League Office, 345 Park Ave., NY, NY 10154; (212) 450-2000; www.nfl.com
Arizona Cardinals (1898, as Morgan Athletic Club): P.O. Box 888, Phoenix, AZ 85001; (602) 379-0101; www.azcardinals.com
Atlanta Falcons (1966): 4400 Falcon Pkwy., Flowery Branch, GA 30542; (770) 965-3115; www.atlantafalcons.com
Baltimore Ravens (1996): 1101 Russell St., Baltimore, MD 21230; (410) 261-7283; www.baltimoreravens.com
Buffalo Bills (1960): One Bills Dr., Orchard Park, NY 14127; (716) 648-1800; www.buffalobills.com
Carolina Panthers (1995): 800 S. Mint St., Charlotte, NC 28202; (704) 358-7000; www.panthers.com
Chicago Bears (1920, as Decatur Staleys): 1920 Football Dr., Lake Forest, IL 60045; (847) 615-2327; www.chicagobears.com
Cincinnati Bengals (1968): 1 Paycor Stadium, Cincinnati, OH 45202; (513) 621-3550; www.bengals.com
Cleveland Browns (1946): 76 Lou Groza Blvd., Berea, OH 44017; (440) 891-5000; www.clevelandbrowns.com
Dallas Cowboys (1960): 1 Cowboys Way, Ste. 100, Frisco, TX 75034; (972) 497-4900; www.dallascowboys.com
Denver Broncos (1960): 13655 Broncos Pkwy., Englewood, CO 80112; (303) 649-9000; www.denverbroncos.com
Detroit Lions (1930, as Portsmouth Spartans): 222 Republic Dr., Allen Park, MI 48101; (313) 262-2000; www.detroitlions.com
Green Bay Packers (1919): 1265 Lombardi Ave., Green Bay, WI 54304; (920) 569-7500; www.packers.com
Houston Texans (2002): Two NRG Park, Houston, TX 77054; (832) 667-2000; www.houstontexans.com
Indianapolis Colts (1953, as Baltimore Colts): 7001 W. 56th St., Indianapolis, IN 46254; (317) 297-2658; www.colts.com
Jacksonville Jaguars (1995): 1 EverBank Stadium Dr., Jacksonville, FL 32202; (904) 633-2000; www.jaguars.com
Kansas City Chiefs (1960, as Dallas Texans): One Arrowhead Dr., Kansas City, MO 64129; (816) 920-9300; www.chiefs.com
Las Vegas Raiders (1960, as Oakland Raiders): 1475 Raiders Way, Henderson, NV 89052; (510) 864-5000; www.raiders.com
Los Angeles Chargers (1960): 3333 Susan St., Costa Mesa, CA 92626; (714) 540-7100; www.chargers.com
Los Angeles Rams (1937, as Cleveland Rams): 29899 Agoura Rd., Agoura Hills, CA 91301; (818) 540-2016; www.therams.com
Miami Dolphins (1966): 347 Don Shula Dr., Miami Gardens, FL 33056; (305) 943-8000; www.miamidolphins.com
Minnesota Vikings (1961): 2600 Vikings Cir., Eagan, MN 55121; (952) 828-6500; www.vikings.com
New England Patriots (1960): 1 Patriot Pl., Foxborough, MA 02035; (508) 543-8200; www.patriots.com
New Orleans Saints (1967): 5800 Airline Dr., Metairie, LA 70003; (504) 733-0255; www.neworleanssaints.com
New York Giants (1925): 1925 Giants Dr., E. Rutherford, NJ 07073; (201) 935-8111; www.giants.com
New York Jets (1960, as New York Titans): 1 Jets Dr., Florham Park, NJ 07932; (800) 469-5387; www.newyorkjets.com
Philadelphia Eagles (1933): One NovaCare Way, Philadelphia, PA 19145; (215) 463-2500; www.philadelphiaeagles.com
Pittsburgh Steelers (1933): 3400 S. Water St., Pittsburgh, PA 15203; (412) 432-7800; www.steelers.com
San Francisco 49ers (1946): 4949 Marie P. DeBartolo Way, Santa Clara, CA 95054; (408) 562-4949; www.49ers.com
Seattle Seahawks (1976): 12 Seahawks Way, Renton, WA 98056; (888) 635-4295; www.seahawks.com
Tampa Bay Buccaneers (1976): One Buccaneer Pl., Tampa, FL 33607; (813) 870-2700; www.buccaneers.com
Tennessee Titans (1960, as Houston Oilers): 460 Great Circle Rd., Nashville, TN 37228; (615) 565-4000; www.titansonline.com
Washington Commanders (1932, as Boston Braves): 1600 Fedex Way, Landover, MD 20785; (703) 726-7000; www.commanders.com

Health Organizations

Source: World Almanac research

Entries are roughly alphabetized by the basic condition addressed or organization name. Year established is in parentheses. Always check with a physician before any new health-related undertaking.

Al-Anon Family Groups (1951): (757) 563-1600; al-anon.org

Alcoholics Anonymous (1935): (212) 870-3400; www.aa.org

Aging, Natl. Institute on (1974): (800) 222-2225; www.nia.nih.gov

Aging's Eldercare Locator, Admin. on (1991): (800) 677-1116; www.eldercare.acl.gov

Allergy, Asthma and Immunology, American Academy of (1943): (414) 272-6071; www.aaaai.org

ALS Assn. [Lou Gehrig's disease] (1985): (800) 782-4747; www.als.org

Alzheimer's Assn. (1979): (800) 272-3900; www.alz.org

Anorexia Nervosa and Associated Disorders, Natl. Assn. of (1976): (888) 375-7767; www.anad.org

Arc, The [intellectual/developmental disabilities] (1950): (800) 433-5255; www.thearc.org

Arthritis Foundation (1948): (800) 283-7800; www.arthritis.org

Arthritis and Musculoskeletal and Skin Diseases, Natl. Institute of (1986): (877) 226-4267; www.niams.nih.gov

Asthma and Allergy Foundation of America (1953): (800) 727-8462; www.aafa.org

Autism Society (1965): (800) 328-8476; www.autismsociety.org

Blind, American Council of the (1961): (202) 467-5081; (800) 424-8666; www.acb.org

Blind, Natl. Federation of the (1940): (410) 659-9314; www.nfb.org

Blindness, Foundation Fighting (1971): (800) 683-5555; www.fightingblindness.org

Blindness, Prevent (1908): (800) 331-2020; www.preventblindness.org

Bone Health and Osteoporosis Foundation (1984): (800) 231-4222; www.bonehealthandosteoporosis.org

Brain Tumor Society, Natl. (2008): (617) 924-9997; www.braintumor.org

Breast Cancer Diagnosis, After (ABCD) (1999): (800) 977-4121; www.abcdbreastcancersupport.org

Cancer Institute's Cancer Information Service, Natl. (1975): (800) 422-6237; www.cancer.gov

Cancer Society, American (1913): (800) 227-2345; www.cancer.org

Cerebral Palsy, United (1949): (202) 776-0406; (800) 872-5827; www.ucp.org

Child Abuse and Family Violence, Natl. Council on (1984): (202) 429-6695; www.preventfamilyviolence.org

Childhelp Natl. Child Abuse Hotline (1959): (800) 422-4453; www.childhelp.org

Children, Natl. Center for Missing and Exploited (1984): (703) 224-2150; (800) 843-5678; www.missingkids.org

Children's Tumor Foundation (1978): (212) 344-6633; (800) 323-7938; www.ctf.org

Chronic Pain Assn., American (1980): (913) 991-4740; www.theacpa.org

Continence, Natl. Assn. for (1982): (843) 419-5307; (800) 252-3337; www.nafc.org

Cooley's Anemia Foundation (1954): (212) 279-8090; www.thalassemia.org

Long-COVID Alliance (2020): (704) 364-0016; longcovidalliance.org

Crohn's and Colitis Foundation (1967): (800) 932-2423; www.crohnscolitisfoundation.org

Cystic Fibrosis Foundation (1955): (800) 344-4823; (301) 951-4422; www.cff.org

Deaf, Natl. Assn. of the (1880): (301) 587-1788, TTY (301) 810-3182; www.nad.org

Depression and Bipolar Support Alliance (1985): (800) 826-3632; www.dbsalliance.org

Diabetes Assn., American (1940): (800) 342-2383; www.diabetes.org

Diabetes and Digestive and Kidney Diseases, Natl. Institute of (1950): (800) 860-8747; www.niddk.nih.gov

Disease Control and Prevention, Centers for (CDC) (1946): (800) 232-4636; www.cdc.gov

Domestic Violence Hotline, Natl. (1996): (800) 799-7233, TTY (800) 787-3224; www.thehotline.org

Down Syndrome Congress, Natl. (1973): (800) 232-6372; www.ndsccenter.org

Down Syndrome Society, Natl. (1979): (800) 221-4602; www.ndss.org

Dyslexia Assn., Intl. (1949): (410) 296-0232; dyslexiaida.org

Easterseals [special needs] (1919): (800) 221-6827; www.easterseals.com

Eating Disorders Assn., Natl. (2001): (800) 931-2237; www.nationaleatingdisorders.org

Endometriosis Assn. (1980): (414) 355-2200; www.endometriosisassn.org

Epilepsy Foundation (1968): (800) 332-1000; www.epilepsy.com

Fat Acceptance, Natl. Assn. to Advance (1969): (916) 558-6880; www.naafa.org

First Candle [sudden infant death syndrome] (1987): (800) 221-7437; www.firstcandle.org

FoodSafety.gov: Meat, poultry, eggs: (888) 674-6854; Food (non-meat): (888) 723-3366; Illness or food poisoning: (800) 232-4636 (CDC)

Gamblers Anonymous (1957): (909) 931-9056; www.gamblersanonymous.org

Geriatrics Society, American (1942): (212) 308-1414; www.americangeriatrics.org

Headache Foundation, Natl. (1970): (888) 643-5552; www.headaches.org

HealthyWomen (1988): (877) 986-9472; www.healthywomen.org

Hearing Society, Intl. (1951): (734) 522-7200; www.ihsinfo.org

Heart Assn., American (1924): (800) 242-8721; www.heart.org

Hearts, Inc., Mended (1951): (888) 432-7899; www.mendedhearts.org

HIVinfo: (800) 448-0440; hivinfo.nih.gov

Hospice Foundation of America (1982): (800) 854-3402; www.hospicefoundation.org

Hospice Intl., Children's (1983): (703) 684-0330; www.chionline.org

Hospital Assn., American (1898): (312) 422-3000; (800) 424-4301; www.aha.org

Huntington's Disease Society of America (1967): (800) 345-4372; www.hdsa.org

JDRF (fmr. Juvenile Diabetes Research Foundation) (1970): (800) 533-2873; www.jdrf.org

Kidney Foundation, Natl. (1950): (800) 622-9010; www.kidney.org

Kidney Fund, American (1971): (800) 638-8299; www.kidneyfund.org

La Leche League Intl. [breastfeeding] (1956): (800) 525-3243; www.llli.org

Leukemia and Lymphoma Society (1949): (800) 955-4572; www.lls.org

Lighthouse Guild [visual impairments] (1906): (800) 284-4422; www.lighthouseguild.org

Liver Foundation, American (1976): (800) 465-4837; www.liverfoundation.org

Living Bank [organ donation] (1968): (713) 961-9431; (800) 528-2971; www.livingbank.org

Lung Assn., American (1904): (800) 586-4872; www.lung.org

Lung Line (1983): (800) 222-5864

Lupus Foundation of America (1977): (202) 349-1155; www.lupus.org

March of Dimes [babies' health] (1938): (888) 663-4637; www.marchofdimes.org

Marfan Foundation (1981): (800) 8-MAR-FAN (862-7326); www.marfan.org

Mayo Clinic (1889): (507) 284-2511; www.mayoclinic.org

ME/CFS Initiative, Solve [myalgic encephalomyelitis/chronic fatigue syndrome] (1987): (704) 364-0016; solvecfs.org

Mental Health, Natl. Institute of (1949): (866) 615-6464; www.nimh.nih.gov

Mental Health America (1909): (703) 684-7722; (800) 969-6642; www.mhanational.org

Mental Illness, Natl. Alliance on (1979): (800) 950-6264; www.nami.org

Multiple Sclerosis Society, Natl. (1946): (800) 344-4867; www.nationalmssociety.org

Muscular Dystrophy Assn. (1950): (800) 572-1717; www.mda.org

Myeloma Foundation, Intl. (1990): (800) 452-2873; www.myeloma.org

Narcotics Anonymous (1953): (818) 773-9999; www.na.org

Natl. Health Council (1920): (202) 785-3910; www.nationalhealthcouncil.org

Natl. Institutes of Health (NIH) (1887): (301) 496-4000; www.nih.gov

Neurological Disorders and Stroke, Natl. Institute of (1950): (800) 352-9424; www.ninds.nih.gov

Organ Sharing, United Network for (1984): (804) 782-4800; (800) 292-9548; www.unos.org

Overeaters Anonymous (1960): (505) 891-2664; www.oa.org

Parkinson's Foundation (1957): (800) 473-4636; www.parkinson.org

Pediatrics, American Academy of (1930): (800) 433-9016; www.aap.org

Phoenix House [substance abuse] (1967): (888) 671-9392; www.phoenixhouse.org

Planned Parenthood Federation of America, Inc. (1916): (800) 230-7526; www.plannedparenthood.org

Plastic Surgeons, American Society of (1931): (847) 228-9900; www.plasticsurgery.org

Poison Control (1980): (800) 222-1222; www.poison.org

Post-Polio Health Intl. (1960): (314) 534-0475; post-polio.org

Psoriasis Foundation, Natl. (1967): (503) 244-7404; (800) 723-9166; www.psoriasis.org

RAINN (Rape, Abuse, & Incest Natl. Network) (1994): (800) 656-4673; www.rainn.org

Rare Disorders, Natl. Org. for (1983): (617) 249-7300; www.rarediseases.org

Rehabilitation Information Center, Natl. (1977): (800) 346-2742, TTY (301) 459-5984; www.naric.com

Reye's Syndrome Foundation, Natl. (1974): (800) 233-7393; www.reyessyndrome.org

Runaway Safeline, Natl. (1971): (800) 786-2929; www.1800runaway.org

Scleroderma Foundation, Natl. (1998): (978) 463-5843; (800) 722-4673; www.scleroderma.org

Sexual Health Assn., American (1914): (919) 361-8400; www.ashasexualhealth.org

Sickle Cell Disease Assn. of America (1971): (410) 528-1555; (800) 421-8453; www.sicklecelldisease.org

Sjögren's Foundation (1983): (301) 530-4420; www.sjogrens.org

Speech-Language-Hearing Assn., American (1925): (800) 638-8255; TTY (301) 296-5650; www.asha.org

Spinal Assn., United (1946): (718) 803-3782; www.unitedspinal.org

Stroke Assn., American (1998): (888) 478-7653; www.stroke.org

Stuttering Assn., Natl. (1977): (800) 937-8888; www.westutter.org

Stuttering Foundation of America (1947): (800) 992-9392; www.stutteringhelp.org

Substance Abuse and Mental Health Services Admin.: (877) 726-4727; www.samhsa.gov

Sudden Infant Death Syndrome Institute, Amer. (1983): (239) 431-5425; www.sids.org

988 Suicide and Crisis Lifeline (fmr. Natl. Suicide Prevention Lifeline) (2004): 988; (800) 273-TALK (8255); 988lifeline.org

Therapy Dogs Intl. (1976): (973) 252-9800; www.tdi-dog.org

Tourette Assn. of America (fmr. Tourette Syndrome Assn.) (1972): (888) 486-8738; www.tourette.org

TSC (Tuberous Sclerosis Complex) Alliance (1974): (301) 562-9890; (800) 225-6872; www.tsalliance.org

Urological Assn., American (1902): (866) 746-4282; www.auanet.org

Women's Health Network, Natl. (1975): (202) 682-2640; www.nwhn.org

UNITED STATES FACTS

Superlative U.S. Statistics

Source: U.S. Geological Survey, U.S. Dept. of the Interior; U.S. Census Bureau, U.S. Dept. of Commerce; World Almanac research

Superlative Statistics for the 50 States

Total area for 50 states and Washington, DC		3,809,525 sq mi
Land area for 50 states and Washington, DC		3,532,316 sq mi
Water area for 50 states and Washington, DC		277,209 sq mi
Largest state	Alaska	665,588 sq mi
Smallest state	Rhode Island	1,545 sq mi
Largest county (excluding Alaska)	San Bernardino County, CA	20,105 sq mi
Smallest county	Arlington County, VA[1]	26 sq mi
Largest incorporated city (by area, pop. 1,000+)	Sitka, AK	4,815 sq mi
Northernmost city	Utqiagvik (formerly Barrow), AK	71°15′ N
Northernmost point	Point Barrow, AK	71°23′ N
Southernmost city	Honolulu, HI	21°19′ N[2]
Southernmost settlement	Discovery Harbour, HI	19°02′ N
Southernmost point	Ka Lae (South Point), island of Hawaii	18°55′ N (155°41′ W)
Easternmost city	Eastport, ME	67°01′ W
Easternmost incorporated place	Lubec, ME	66°59′ W
Easternmost point[3]	Pochnoi Point, Semisopochnoi Island, AK	179°46′ E
Westernmost city	Adak (formerly Adak Station), AK	176°36′ W
Westernmost incorporated place	Adak (formerly Adak Station), AK	176°36′ W
Westernmost point	Amatignak Island, AK	179°07′ W
Highest incorporated city	Leadville, CO	10,158 ft
Lowest settlement	Bombay Beach, CA	–208 ft
Highest point on Atlantic coast	Cadillac Mountain, Mount Desert Island, ME	1,530 ft
Oldest national park	Yellowstone National Park (1872), WY-MT-ID	2,219,791 acres
Largest national park	Wrangell-St. Elias National Park, AK	8,323,146 acres
Longest river system	Mississippi-Missouri-Red Rock	3,710 mi
Highest mountain	Denali (formerly Mt. McKinley), AK	20,310 ft
Lowest point	Death Valley, CA	–282 ft
Deepest lake	Crater Lake, OR	1,949 ft
Rainiest spot	Mount Waialeale, Kauai, HI	annual avg. rainfall 460 in. (30-yr period)
Largest gorge	Grand Canyon, Colorado River, AZ	277 mi long, 600 ft to 18 mi wide, 1 mi deep
Deepest gorge	Hells Canyon, Snake River, OR-ID	7,913 ft
Largest dam	New Cornelia Tailings, Ten Mile Wash, AZ[4]	7.4 bil cu ft material used
Tallest building	One World Trade Center, New York, NY	1,782 ft
Largest building	Boeing Everett Production Facility, Everett, WA	472,000,000 cu ft; covers 98.3 acres
Largest office building	Pentagon, Arlington, VA	77,015,000 cu ft; covers 29 acres
Tallest supported structure	KRDK-TV Tower, Galesburg, ND	2,060 ft
Tallest freestanding tower	Stratosphere Tower, Las Vegas, NV	1,149 ft
Longest bridge span	Verrazzano-Narrows Bridge, New York, NY	4,260 ft
Highest bridge	Royal Gorge Bridge, Cañon City, CO	bridge deck 955 ft above water
Deepest well (onshore)	Bertha Rogers No. 1 (inactive gas well), Washita County, OK	31,441 ft

Superlative Statistics for the 48 Contiguous States

Total area for 48 states and Washington, DC		3,119,609 sq mi
Land area for 48 states and Washington, DC		2,954,822 sq mi
Water area for 48 states and Washington, DC		164,787 sq mi
Largest state	Texas	268,525 sq mi
Northernmost incorporated place	Sumas, WA	49°00′ N
Northernmost settlement	Angle Inlet, MN	49°21′ N
Northernmost point	Northwest Angle, MN	49°21′ N
Southernmost city	Key West, FL	24°34′ N
Southernmost mainland city	Florida City, FL	25°27′ N
Southernmost point	Ballast Key, FL	24°31′ N
Easternmost point[5]	West Quoddy Head, Lubec, ME	66°57′ W
Westernmost city	Port Orford, OR	124°30′ W
Westernmost point	Bodelteh Islands, WA	124°45′ W
Highest mountain	Mount Whitney, CA	14,505 ft

(1) Smallest total area. Smallest county by land area is Kalawao County, Hawaii, at 12 sq mi; its total area (including water) is 53 sq mi. (2) Latitude is for Urban Honolulu census designated place. (3) As measured if the prime meridian and 180° longitude are considered east-west boundaries. (4) Privately owned industrial dam composed of tailings, remnants of a mining process. (5) Some sources give Sail Rock (66°56′50″), off West Quoddy Head (66°57′01″), as the easternmost point.

Highest and Lowest Elevations in U.S. States and Territories

Source: U.S. Geological Survey, U.S. Dept. of the Interior
(negative sign indicates below sea level)

State/territory	Highest point Name	County	Elev. (ft)	Lowest point Name	County	Elev. (ft)
Alabama	Cheaha Mountain	Cleburne	2,413	Gulf of Mexico		Sea level
Alaska	Denali (fmr. Mt. McKinley)	Denali	20,310	Pacific Ocean		Sea level
American Samoa	Lata Mountain	Tau Island	3,160	Pacific Ocean		Sea level
Arizona	Humphreys Peak	Coconino	12,637	Colorado R.	Yuma	70
Arkansas	Magazine Mountain	Logan	2,753	Ouachita R.	Ashley-Union	55
California	Mount Whitney	Inyo-Tulare	14,505	Death Valley	Inyo	–282
Colorado	Mount Elbert	Lake	14,440	Arikaree R.	Yuma	3,315
Connecticut	S. slope of Mt. Frissell (peak in MA)	Litchfield	2,380	Long Island Sound		Sea level
Delaware	Nr. Ebright Azimuth	New Castle	450	Atlantic Ocean		Sea level
Dist. of Columbia	Fort Reno Park	NW quadrant	409	Potomac R.		1
Florida	Britton Hill	Walton	345	Atlantic Ocean		Sea level
Georgia	Brasstown Bald	Towns-Union	4,840	Atlantic Ocean		Sea level
Guam	Mount Lamlam	Agat District	1,332	Pacific Ocean		Sea level
Hawaii	Pu'u Wekiu, Mauna Kea	Hawaii	13,796	Pacific Ocean		Sea level
Idaho	Borah Peak	Custer	12,668	Snake R.	Nez Perce	710
Illinois	Charles Mound	Jo Daviess	1,235	Mississippi R.	Alexander	279
Indiana	Hoosier Hill	Wayne	1,257	Ohio R.	Posey	320
Iowa	Hawkeye Point	Osceola	1,670	Mississippi R.	Lee	480
Kansas	Mount Sunflower	Wallace	4,039	Verdigris R.	Montgomery	679
Kentucky	Black Mountain	Harlan	4,139	Mississippi R.	Fulton	257
Louisiana	Driskill Mountain	Bienville	535	New Orleans	Orleans	–8
Maine	Mount Katahdin	Piscataquis	5,269	Atlantic Ocean		Sea level
Maryland	Hoye Crest	Garrett	3,360	Bloody Point Hole, Chesapeake Bay	Queen Anne	–174
Massachusetts	Mount Greylock	Berkshire	3,491	Atlantic Ocean		Sea level
Michigan	Mount Arvon	Baraga	1,979	Lake Erie		571
Minnesota	Eagle Mountain	Cook	2,301	Lake Superior		601
Mississippi	Woodall Mountain	Tishomingo	806	Gulf of Mexico		Sea level
Missouri	Taum Sauk Mountain	Iron	1,772	St. Francis R.	Dunklin	230
Montana	Granite Peak	Park	12,807	Kootenai R.	Lincoln	1,800
Nebraska	Panorama Point	Kimball	5,424	Missouri R.	Richardson	840
Nevada	Boundary Peak	Esmeralda	13,146	Colorado R.	Clark	479
New Hampshire	Mount Washington	Coos	6,289	Atlantic Ocean		Sea level
New Jersey	High Point	Sussex	1,803	Atlantic Ocean		Sea level
New Mexico	Wheeler Peak	Taos	13,167	Red Bluff Reservoir	Eddy	2,842
New York	Mount Marcy	Essex	5,343	Atlantic Ocean		Sea level
North Carolina	Mount Mitchell	Yancey	6,683	Atlantic Ocean		Sea level
North Dakota	White Butte	Slope	3,506	Red R. of the North	Pembina	750
Northern Mariana Isls.	Mount Agrihan	Agrihan Island	3,166	Pacific Ocean		Sea level
Ohio	Campbell Hill	Logan	1,550	Ohio R.	Hamilton	455
Oklahoma	Black Mesa	Cimarron	4,973	Little R.	McCurtain	289
Oregon	Mount Hood	Clackamas-Hood R.	11,247	Pacific Ocean		Sea level
Pennsylvania	Mount Davis	Somerset	3,213	Delaware R.	Delaware	Sea level
Puerto Rico	Cerro de Punta	Ponce District	4,390	Atlantic Ocean		Sea level
Rhode Island	Jerimoth Hill	Providence	812	Atlantic Ocean		Sea level
South Carolina	Sassafras Mountain	Pickens	3,560	Atlantic Ocean		Sea level
South Dakota	Harney Peak	Pennington	7,244	Big Stone Lake	Roberts	966
Tennessee	Clingmans Dome	Sevier	6,644	Mississippi R.	Shelby	178
Texas	Guadalupe Peak	Culberson	8,751	Gulf of Mexico		Sea level
Utah	Kings Peak	Duchesne	13,518	Beaver Dam Wash	Washington	2,000
Vermont	Mount Mansfield	Chittenden	4,395	Lake Champlain		95
Virgin Islands	Crown Mountain	St. Thomas Island	1,556	Atlantic Ocean		Sea level
Virginia	Mount Rogers	Grayson-Smyth	5,729	Atlantic Ocean		Sea level
Washington	Mount Rainier	Pierce	14,410	Pacific Ocean		Sea level
West Virginia	Spruce Knob	Pendleton	4,863	Potomac R.	Jefferson	240
Wisconsin	Timms Hill	Price	1,951	Lake Michigan		579
Wyoming	Gannett Peak	Fremont	13,810	Belle Fourche R.	Crook	3,099

U.S. Coastline by State

Source: National Oceanic and Atmospheric Administration (NOAA), U.S. Dept. of Commerce
(in statute miles; only states with coastline or shoreline are shown)

	Coastline[1]	Shoreline[2]
Atlantic Coast	**2,069**	**28,673**
Connecticut	0	618
Delaware	28	381
Florida	580	3,331
Georgia	100	2,344
Maine	228	3,478
Maryland	31	3,190
Massachusetts	192	1,519
New Hampshire	13	131
New Jersey	130	1,792
New York	127	1,850
North Carolina	301	3,375
Pennsylvania	0	89
Rhode Island	40	384
South Carolina	187	2,876
Virginia	112	3,315

	Coastline[1]	Shoreline[2]
Gulf Coast	**1,631**	**17,141**
Alabama	53	607
Florida	770	5,095
Louisiana	397	7,721
Mississippi	44	359
Texas	367	3,359
Pacific Coast	**7,623**	**40,298**
Alaska	5,580	31,383
California	840	3,427
Hawaii	750	1,052
Oregon	296	1,410
Washington	157	3,026
Arctic Coast	**1,060**	**2,521**
United States	**12,383**	**88,633[3]**

(1) Length of general outline of seacoast. Measurements were made in 1948 with a unit measure of 30 minutes of latitude on charts as near the scale of 1:1,200,000 as possible. Includes coastlines of large sounds and bays. (2) Shoreline of outer coast, offshore islands, sounds, bays, rivers, and creeks to the head of tidewater or to a point where tidal waters narrow to a width of 100 ft. Figures obtained in 1939-40 with a recording instrument on the largest-scale charts and maps then available. (3) Total length of U.S. tidal shoreline is 95,471 statute miles, which incl. measurements of outlying U.S. territories and possessions.

States: Capitals, Key Dates, Geographic Data

Source: *Statistical Abstract of the United States*, U.S. Census Bureau, U.S. Dept. of Commerce

The 13 colonies that declared independence from Great Britain and fought the War of Independence (American Revolution) became the 13 original states. They were, in the order in which they ratified the Constitution: Delaware, Pennsylvania, New Jersey, Georgia, Connecticut, Massachusetts, Maryland, South Carolina, New Hampshire, Virginia, New York, North Carolina, and Rhode Island.

			Entered Union		Extent (mi)		Area (sq mi)			Rank
State	Settled[1]	Capital	Date	Order	Length (approx.	Width mean)	Land	Water	Total	by tot. area
AL	1702	Montgomery	Dec. 14, 1819	22	330	190	50,633	1,773	52,406	30
AK	1784	Juneau	Jan. 3, 1959	49	1,480[2]	810	570,866	94,722	665,588	1
AZ	1776	Phoenix	Feb. 14, 1912	48	400	310	113,623	332	113,955	6
AR	1686	Little Rock	June 15, 1836	25	260	240	52,024	1,141	53,165	29
CA	1769	Sacramento	Sept. 9, 1850	31	770	250	155,813	7,838	163,651	3
CO	1858	Denver	Aug. 1, 1876	38	380	280	103,610	457	104,067	8
CT	1634	Hartford	Jan. 9, 1788	5	110	70	4,841	701	5,542	48
DE	1638	Dover	Dec. 7, 1787	1	96	30	1,948	540	2,488	49
DC	NA	NA	NA	NA	NA	NA	61	7	68	51
FL	1565	Tallahassee	Mar. 3, 1845	27	447	361	53,634	12,106	65,740	22
GA	1733	Atlanta	Jan. 2, 1788	4	300	230	57,701	1,706	59,407	24
HI	1820	Honolulu	Aug. 21, 1959	50	NA	NA	6,421	4,546	10,967	43
ID	1842	Boise	July 3, 1890	43	479	305	82,623	923	83,547	14
IL	1720	Springfield	Dec. 3, 1818	21	390	210	55,499	2,399	57,898	25
IN	1733	Indianapolis	Dec. 11, 1816	19	270	140	35,817	593	36,410	38
IA	1788	Des Moines	Dec. 28, 1846	29	310	200	55,839	419	56,258	26
KS	1727	Topeka	Jan. 29, 1861	34	400	210	81,737	520	82,256	15
KY	1774	Frankfort	June 1, 1792	15	380	140	39,481	916	40,397	37
LA	1699	Baton Rouge	Apr. 30, 1812	18	380	130	43,193	9,168	52,361	31
ME	1624	Augusta	Mar. 15, 1820	23	320	190	30,837	4,534	35,370	39
MD	1634	Annapolis	Apr. 28, 1788	7	250	90	9,709	2,694	12,403	42
MA	1620	Boston	Feb. 6, 1788	6	190	50	7,799	2,752	10,551	44
MI	1668	Lansing	Jan. 26, 1837	26	490	240	56,591	40,097	96,688	11
MN	1805	St. Paul	May 11, 1858	32	400	250	79,605	7,312	86,917	12
MS	1699	Jackson	Dec. 10, 1817	20	340	170	46,913	1,515	48,428	32
MO	1735	Jefferson City	Aug. 10, 1821	24	300	240	68,727	961	69,688	21
MT	1809	Helena	Nov. 8, 1889	41	630	280	145,509	1,493	147,003	4
NE	1823	Lincoln	Mar. 1, 1867	37	430	210	76,796	531	77,327	16
NV	1849	Carson City	Oct. 31, 1864	36	490	320	109,831	710	110,541	7
NH	1623	Concord	June 21, 1788	9	190	70	8,951	396	9,347	46
NJ	1660	Trenton	Dec. 18, 1787	3	150	70	7,353	1,368	8,721	47
NM	1610	Santa Fe	Jan. 6, 1912	47	370	343	121,280	281	121,561	5
NY	1614	Albany	July 26, 1788	11	330	283	47,111	7,429	54,540	27
NC	1660	Raleigh	Nov. 21, 1789	12	500	150	48,607	5,197	53,804	28
ND	1812	Bismarck	Nov. 2, 1889	39	340	211	68,977	1,703	70,679	19
OH	1788	Columbus	Mar. 1, 1803	17	220	220	40,848	3,966	44,814	34
OK	1889	Oklahoma City	Nov. 16, 1907	46	400	220	68,578	1,303	69,881	20
OR	1811	Salem	Feb. 14, 1859	33	360	261	95,963	2,390	98,353	9
PA	1682	Harrisburg	Dec. 12, 1787	2	283	160	44,730	1,312	46,042	33
RI	1636	Providence	May 29, 1790	13	40	30	1,034	511	1,545	50
SC	1670	Columbia	May 23, 1788	8	260	200	30,056	1,959	32,015	40
SD	1859	Pierre	Nov. 2, 1889	40	370	210	75,790	1,306	77,096	17
TN	1769	Nashville	June 1, 1796	16	491	115	41,227	906	42,133	36
TX	1682	Austin	Dec. 29, 1845	28	790	660	261,194	7,331	268,525	2
UT	1847	Salt Lake City	Jan. 4, 1896	45	350	270	82,355	2,521	84,876	13
VT	1724	Montpelier	Mar. 4, 1791	14	160	80	9,215	398	9,613	45
VA	1607	Richmond	June 25, 1788	10	430	200	39,472	3,292	42,764	35
WA	1811	Olympia	Nov. 11, 1889	42	360	240	66,438	4,844	71,282	18
WV	1727	Charleston	June 20, 1863	35	240	130	24,035	189	24,224	41
WI	1766	Madison	May 29, 1848	30	310	260	54,153	11,327	65,480	23
WY	1834	Cheyenne	July 10, 1890	44	360	280	97,063	721	97,784	10

NA = Not applicable. **Note:** Land and water areas, which are as of Jan. 1, 2020, may not add up to totals because of rounding. (1) First permanent settlement by Europeans. (2) Does not include Aleutian Islands or Alexander Archipelago.

Continental Divide of the U.S.

The Continental Divide of the U.S., also known as the Great Divide, is located at the watershed created by the mountain ranges, or tablelands, of the Rocky Mountains. This watershed separates the waters that ultimately drain into the Atlantic Ocean and its marginal seas from those waters that drain into the Pacific Ocean. The majority of water flowing E in the U.S. drains into the Gulf of Mexico and then the Atlantic. The majority of water flowing W drains through the Columbia River or Colorado River, which flows into the Gulf of California before reaching the Pacific.

The location and route of the Continental Divide across the U.S. can be described as follows:

Beginning at the U.S.-Mexico border, near longitude 108°45´ W, the Divide, in a northerly direction, crosses New Mexico along the western edge of the Rio Grande drainage basin, entering Colorado near longitude 106°41´ W. From there by an irregular route N across Colorado along the western summits of the Rio Grande and Arkansas, South Platte, and North Platte river basins, and across Rocky Mountain National Park, entering Wyoming near longitude 106°52´ W.

From there in a northwesterly direction, forming the western rims of the North Platte, Big Horn, and Yellowstone river basins, crossing the SW portion of Yellowstone National Park. From there in a westerly and then northerly direction forming the boundary between Idaho and Montana, to a point on the boundary near longitude 114°00´ W. From there northeasterly and northwesterly through Montana and Glacier National Park, entering Canada near longitude 114°04´ W.

Depending on how a "divide" is defined, the U.S. can also be characterized as having a Northern (or Laurentian) Divide, Eastern Divide, and St. Lawrence Seaway Divide. Some of the waters at the Northern Divide drain into Hudson Bay and the Arctic Ocean. The Appalachian Mountains mark the Eastern Divide, with waters joining the Atlantic or Gulf of Mexico. The waters at the St. Lawrence Seaway Divide, near Chicago, flow into the Gulf of St. Lawrence or Gulf of Mexico.

Chronological List of Territories, With State Admissions to Union

Source: U.S. National Archives and Records Administration

Territory	Date of act creating territory	When act took effect	Date of admission as state	Years as terr.
Northwest Territory[1]	July 13, 1787	No fixed date	Mar. 1, 1803[2]	16
Territory South of Ohio River (Southwest Territory)	May 26, 1790	No fixed date	June 1, 1796[3]	6
Mississippi	Apr. 7, 1798	When president acted	Dec. 10, 1817	19
Indiana	May 7, 1800	July 4, 1800	Dec. 11, 1816	16
Orleans	Mar. 26, 1804	Oct. 1, 1804	Apr. 30, 1812[4]	7
Michigan	Jan. 11, 1805	June 30, 1805	Jan. 26, 1837	31
Louisiana-Missouri[5]	Mar. 3, 1805	July 4, 1805	Aug. 10, 1821	16
Illinois	Feb. 3, 1809	Mar. 1, 1809	Dec. 3, 1818	9
Alabama	Mar. 3, 1817	When MS formed state govt.	Dec. 14, 1819	2
Arkansas	Mar. 2, 1819	July 4, 1819	June 15, 1836	17
Florida	Mar. 30, 1822	No fixed date	Mar. 3, 1845	23
Wisconsin	Apr. 20, 1836	July 3, 1836	May 29, 1848	12
Iowa	June 12, 1838	July 3, 1838	Dec. 28, 1846	8
Oregon	Aug. 14, 1848	Date of act	Feb. 14, 1859	10
Minnesota	Mar. 3, 1849	Date of act	May 11, 1858	9
New Mexico	Sept. 9, 1850	On president's proclamation	Jan. 6, 1912	61
Utah	Sept. 9, 1850	Date of act	Jan. 4, 1896	46
Washington	Mar. 2, 1853	Date of act	Nov. 11, 1889	36
Kansas	May 30, 1854	Date of act	Jan. 29, 1861	6
Nebraska	May 30, 1854	Date of act	Mar. 1, 1867	12
Colorado	Feb. 28, 1861	Date of act	Aug. 1, 1876	15
Dakota	Mar. 2, 1861	Date of act	Nov. 2, 1889	28
Nevada	Mar. 2, 1861	Date of act	Oct. 31, 1864	3
Arizona	Feb. 24, 1863	Date of act	Feb. 14, 1912	49
Idaho	Mar. 3, 1863	Date of act	July 3, 1890	27
Montana	May 26, 1864	Date of act	Nov. 8, 1889	25
Wyoming	July 25, 1868	When officers were qualified	July 10, 1890	22
Alaska	May 17, 1884[6]	No fixed date	Jan. 3, 1959	75
Oklahoma	May 2, 1890	Date of act	Nov. 16, 1907	17
Hawaii	Apr. 30, 1900	June 14, 1900	Aug. 21, 1959	59

Note: California was never organized as a territory. It was administered by the military after its acquisition from Mexico (1848) until its admission as a state (1850). (1) Included what is now Ohio, Indiana, Illinois, Michigan, Wisconsin, and E Minnesota. (2) Date of admission for Ohio, the first state created out of territory, based on the date its General Assembly first met. Congress approved Ohio's entry into the Union on Feb. 19, 1803. (3) Admitted as the state of Tennessee. (4) Admitted as the state of Louisiana. (5) The act renaming Louisiana Territory as Missouri Territory (June 4, 1812) became effective Dec. 7, 1812. (6) Act constituted Alaska as a district, though it was often referred to and administered as a territory. The Territory of Alaska was formally organized by an act of Aug. 24, 1912.

U.S. Geographic Centers

Source: U.S. Geological Survey, U.S. Dept. of the Interior

There is no generally accepted definition of a geographic center and no uniform method for determining it. Geographic center is defined here as the center of gravity of the surface of an area, or that point on which an area would balance if it were a plane of uniform thickness.

No government agency has officially established any points marking the geographic center of the U.S., the conterminous U.S. (48 states), or the North American continent. In 1941, private citizens erected a monument in Lebanon, KS, marking it as the geographic center of the then U.S. (conterminous). Residents of Rugby, ND, installed a cairn after the U.S. Geologic Survey, in 1931, determined it to be the center of the North American continent. In 2017, a Univ. at Buffalo geography professor announced that Center, ND, was the continental center according to a mathematical method he developed. The geographic centers in the following list are approximate. They are indicated by county then city unless otherwise noted.

U.S. (50 states): W of Castle Rock, Butte County, South Dakota; 44°58´ N, 103°46´ W
Conterminous U.S. (48 states): nr. Lebanon, Smith County, Kansas; 39°50´ N, 98°35´ W
North American continent: 6 mi W of Balta, Pierce County, North Dakota; 48°10´ N, 100°10´ W
Alabama: Chilton, 12 mi SW of Clanton
Alaska: 63°50´ N, 152° W, approx. 60 mi NW of Denali
Arizona: Yavapai, 55 mi E-SE of Prescott
Arkansas: Pulaski, 12 mi NW of Little Rock
California: Madera, 38 mi E of Madera
Colorado: Park, 30 mi NW of Pikes Peak
Connecticut: Hartford, at East Berlin
Delaware: Kent, 11 mi S of Dover
District of Columbia: near 4th and L Sts. NW
Florida: Hernando, 12 mi N-NW of Brooksville
Georgia: Twiggs, 18 mi SE of Macon
Hawaii: Hawaii; 20°15´ N, 156°20´ W, off Maui Island
Idaho: Custer, SW of Challis
Illinois: Logan, 28 mi NE of Springfield
Indiana: Boone, 14 mi N-NW of Indianapolis
Iowa: Story, 5 mi NE of Ames
Kansas: Barton, 15 mi NE of Great Bend
Kentucky: Marion, 3 mi N-NW of Lebanon
Louisiana: Avoyelles, 3 mi SE of Marksville
Maine: Piscataquis, 18 mi N of Dover
Maryland: Prince George's, 4.5 mi NW of Davidsonville
Massachusetts: Worcester, N part of city of Worcester
Michigan: Wexford, 5 mi N-NW of Cadillac
Minnesota: Crow Wing, 10 mi SW of Brainerd
Mississippi: Leake, 9 mi W-NW of Carthage
Missouri: Miller, 20 mi SW of Jefferson City
Montana: Fergus, 11 mi W of Lewistown
Nebraska: Custer, 10 mi NW of Broken Bow
Nevada: Lander, 26 mi SE of Austin
New Hampshire: Belknap, 3 mi E of Ashland
New Jersey: Mercer, 5 mi SE of Trenton
New Mexico: Torrance, 12 mi S-SW of Willard
New York: Madison, 12 mi S of Oneida and 26 mi SW of Utica
North Carolina: Chatham, 10 mi NW of Sanford
North Dakota: Sheridan, 5 mi SW of McClusky
Ohio: Delaware, 25 mi N-NE of Columbus
Oklahoma: Oklahoma, 8 mi N of Oklahoma City
Oregon: Crook, 25 mi S-SE of Prineville
Pennsylvania: Centre, 2.5 mi SW of Bellefonte
Rhode Island: Kent, 1 mi S-SW of Crompton
South Carolina: Richland, 13 mi SE of Columbia
South Dakota: Hughes, 8 mi NE of Pierre
Tennessee: Rutherford, 5 mi NE of Murfreesboro
Texas: McCulloch, 15 mi NE of Brady
Utah: Sanpete, 3 mi N of Manti
Vermont: Washington, 3 mi E of Roxbury
Virginia: Buckingham, 5 mi SW of Buckingham
Washington: Chelan, 10 mi W-SW of Wenatchee
West Virginia: Braxton, 4 mi E of Sutton
Wisconsin: Wood, 9 mi SE of Marshfield
Wyoming: Fremont, 58 mi E-NE of Lander

Lengths of U.S. Boundaries

The length of the boundary between the U.S. and Canada is 5,525 mi—3,987 mi between the conterminous U.S. and Canada and 1,538 mi between Alaska and Canada. A 1925 treaty established a permanent International Boundary Commission to maintain the boundary. The U.S.-Mexican border was established by multiple treaties (1848, 1853, 1970) at 1,954-miles long. (The U.S. Census Bureau has put the border at 1,933-miles long.) It largely follows the Rio Grande and Colorado River, from the Gulf of Mexico to the Pacific Ocean. It is overseen by the International Boundary and Water Commission.

Origins of the Names of U.S. States and Territories

Source: State officials; Smithsonian Institution; Topographic Division, U.S. Geological Survey, U.S. Dept. of the Interior

Alabama: Choctaw word for a Chickasaw tribe. First noted in accounts of Hernando de Soto expedition.

Alaska: Russian version of Aleut word *alakshak* for "peninsula," "great lands," or "land that is not an island."

American Samoa: Etymology varies.

Arizona: Spanish version of Pima Indian word for "little spring place" or Aztec *arizuma*, meaning "silver-bearing."

Arkansas: Algonquin name for Quapaw Indians, meaning "south wind."

California: Bestowed by Spanish conquistadors (possibly Hernán Cortés). It was the name of an imaginary island in the 1510 Spanish novel *Las Sergas de Esplandián* (The Exploits of Esplandián), by Garci Rodríguez de Montalvo. The Spanish first visited *Baja* (Lower) *California* in 1533. The present-day U.S. state was called *Alta* (Upper) *California*.

Colorado: From Spanish for "red," first applied to Colorado River.

Connecticut: From Algonquin *quinnehtukqut*, meaning "long river place."

Delaware: Named for Lord De La Warr, early governor of Virginia; first applied to river, then to Indian tribe (Lenni-Lenape).

District of Columbia: For Christopher Columbus, 1791.

Florida: Named by Juan Ponce de León *Pascua Florida*, "Flowery Easter," on Easter Sunday, 1513.

Georgia: Named by colonial administrator James Oglethorpe for King George II of England in 1732.

Guam: From Chamorro name, *Guahan*, meaning "we have."

Hawaii: Possibly derived from *Hawaiki* or *Owhyhee*, Polynesian word for "homeland."

Idaho: George Willing claimed to have coined the name, with the invented meaning "gem of the mountains." He first suggested it for the Pikes Peak mining territory (Colorado) before the name was adopted for the new mining territory of the Pacific Northwest.

Illinois: French for *Illini* or "land of *Illini*," Algonquin word meaning "men" or "warriors."

Indiana: Means "land of the Indians."

Iowa: Indian word variously translated as "here I rest" or "beautiful land." Named for the Iowa River, which was named for the Iowa Indians.

Kansas: Sioux word for "south wind people."

Kentucky: Indian word variously translated as "dark and bloody ground," "meadowland," and "land of tomorrow."

Louisiana: Part of territory called Louisiana by René-Robert Cavelier Sieur de La Salle for French King Louis XIV.

Maine: From Maine, historic French province. Also descriptive, referring to the mainland as distinct from coastal islands.

Maryland: For Queen Henrietta Maria, wife of Charles I of England.

Massachusetts: From Indian tribe whose name meant "at or about the Great Hill" in Blue Hills region south of Boston.

Michigan: From Chippewa *mici gama*, meaning "great water," after lake of the same name.

Minnesota: From Dakota Sioux word meaning "cloudy water" or "sky-tinted water" of the Minnesota River.

Mississippi: Probably Chippewa *mici zibi*, meaning "great river" or "gathering-in of all the waters." Also Algonquin word *messipi*.

Missouri: Algonquin Indian term meaning "river of the big canoes."

Montana: Latin or Spanish for "mountainous."

Nebraska: From Omaha or Otos Indian word meaning "broad water" or "flat river," describing the Platte River.

Nevada: Spanish, meaning "snow-clad."

New Hampshire: Named by Capt. John Mason of Plymouth Council, in 1629, for his home county in England.

New Jersey: The Duke of York, in 1664, gave a patent to Lord John Berkeley and Sir George Carteret for *Nova Caesaria*, or New Jersey, after England's Isle of Jersey.

New Mexico: Spaniards in Mexico applied term to land north and west of Rio Grande in the 16th century.

New York: For James, Duke of York and Albany, who received patent for New Netherland from his brother Charles II and sent an expedition to capture it, 1664.

North Carolina: In 1619, Charles I gave patent to Sir Robert Heath for Province of Carolana, from *Carolus*, Latin name for Charles. Charles II granted a new patent to Earl of Clarendon and others. Divided into North and South Carolina, 1710.

North Dakota: Sioux word *Dakota*, meaning "friend" or "ally."

Northern Mariana Isls.: For Mariana of Austria, queen regent of Spain.

Ohio: Iroquois word for "fine or good river."

Oklahoma: Choctaw word meaning "red man," proposed by Rev. Allen Wright, Choctaw-speaking Indian.

Oregon: Origin unknown. One theory is that the name derives from Mohegan *wauregan*, meaning "beautiful," term used by Indians in Connecticut.

Pennsylvania: William Penn, Quaker who was made full proprietor of area by King Charles II in 1681, suggested "Sylvania," or "woodland," for his tract. The king's government owed 16,000 pounds to Penn's father, Adm. William Penn, and the land was granted as partial settlement. Charles II added "Penn" to "Sylvania," against the modest proprietor's desires, in honor of the admiral.

Puerto Rico: Spanish for "rich port."

Rhode Island: Origin unknown. One theory notes that Giovanni de Verrazzano recorded observing an island about the size of the Greek island of Rhodes in 1524. Another theory is that Dutch explorer Adriaen Block named the state *Roode Eylandt* for its red clay.

South Carolina: See North Carolina.

South Dakota: See North Dakota.

Tennessee: *Tanasi* was the name of Cherokee villages on the Little Tennessee River. From 1784 to 1788, this was the State of Franklin, or Frankland.

Texas: Variant of word used by Caddo and other Indians meaning "friends" or "allies" and applied to them by the Spanish in eastern Texas. Also written *Texias*, *Tejas*, *Teysas*.

Utah: From a Navajo word meaning "upper," or "higher up," as applied to Shoshone tribe called Ute. Proposed name *Deseret*, "land of honeybees," from Book of Mormon, was rejected by Congress.

Vermont: From French words *vert* (green) and *mont* (mountain). The Green Mountains were said to have been named by Samuel de Champlain. When the state was formed in 1777, Dr. Thomas Young suggested combining *vert* and *mont*.

Virgin Islands, U.S.: From Spanish name *Las Once Mil Virgenes* (11,000 Virgins), which Christopher Columbus gave to island group.

Virginia: Named by Sir Walter Raleigh, who outfitted an expedition in 1584, in honor of England's Queen Elizabeth, the Virgin Queen.

Washington: Named after George Washington. When the bill creating the Territory of Columbia was introduced in the 32nd Congress, its name was changed to Washington because of the existence of the District of Columbia.

West Virginia: So named when western counties of Virginia refused to secede from the U.S. in 1863.

Wisconsin: Indian name, spelled *Ouisconsin* or *Mesconsing* by early chroniclers, believed to mean "grassy place" in Chippewa. Congress made it *Wisconsin*.

Wyoming: From Algonquin words for "large prairie place," "at the big plains," or "on the great plain."

Territorial Sea of the U.S.

According to a Dec. 27, 1988, proclamation by Pres. Ronald Reagan, "The territorial sea of the United States henceforth extends to 12 nautical miles from the baselines of the United States determined in accordance with international law. In accordance with international law, as reflected in the applicable provisions of the 1982 United Nations Convention on the Law of the Sea, within the territorial sea of the United States, the ships of all countries enjoy the right of innocent passage and the ships and aircraft of all countries enjoy the right of transit passage through international straits."

Major Accessions of Territory by the U.S.

Source: U.S. Dept. of the Interior; U.S. Census Bureau, U.S. Dept. of Commerce

Not including territories such as the Panama Canal Zone and the Philippines, which are no longer under U.S. jurisdiction.

Accession	Date	Area (sq mi)	Accession	Date	Area (sq mi)	Accession	Date	Area (sq mi)
Territory in 1790[1]	NA	888,685	Mexican Cession	1848	529,017	Guam[3]	1899	212
Louisiana Purchase	1803	827,192	Gadsden Purchase	1853	29,640	American Samoa[4]	1900	76
Treaty of Florida	1819	72,003	Alaska	1867	586,412	U.S. Virgin Islands	1917	133
Texas	1845	390,143	Hawaii	1898	6,450	Northern Marianas[5]	1986	179
Oregon Territory	1846	285,680	Puerto Rico[2]	1899	3,435			

NA = Not applicable. (1) Includes that part of a drainage basin of Red River of the North, south of 49th parallel, sometimes considered part of Louisiana Purchase. (2) Ceded by Spain in 1898, ratified in 1899, and became the Commonwealth of Puerto Rico by Act of Congress on July 25, 1952. (3) Acquired in 1898; ratified 1899. (4) Acquired in 1899; ratified 1900. (5) Part of the UN Trust Territory of the Pacific Islands, which U.S. began administering in 1947; became U.S. commonwealth Nov. 3, 1986.

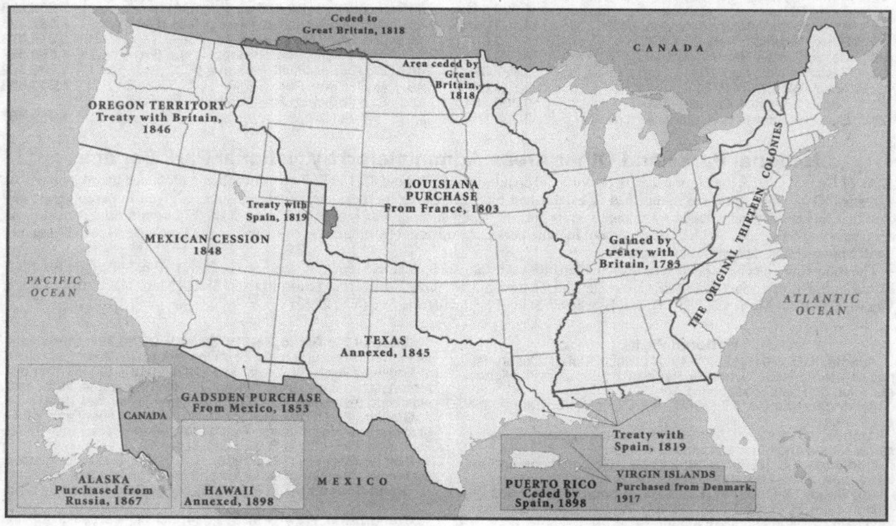

National Park System Recreation Visits, 1904-2023

Source: National Park Service (NPS), U.S. Dept. of the Interior

An NPS-administered site, regardless of its designation (as a park, monument, or preserve, etc.), is generally referred to as a unit. Not all units report public use statistics.

Year	Units reporting visits	Recreation visits	Year	Units reporting visits	Recreation visits	Year	Units reporting visits	Recreation visits
1904	6	120,690	1970	217	168,135,100	2010	363	281,303,769
1905	6	140,954	1975	251	188,085,700	2011	367	278,939,216
1910	9	173,416	1980	275	220,463,211	2012	367	282,765,682
1915	12	314,299	1985	303	263,441,808	2013	370	273,630,895
1920	26	1,022,091	1990	316	255,581,467	2014	370	292,800,082
1925	39	1,900,499	1995	328	269,564,307	2015	372	307,247,252
1930	45	3,038,935	2000	344	285,891,275	2016	376	330,971,689
1935	85	7,435,659	2002	349	277,299,880	2017	379	330,882,751
1940	113	16,410,148	2004	356	276,908,337	2018	379	318,211,833
1945	143	10,855,548	2005	356	273,488,751	2019	379	327,516,619
1950	139	32,706,172	2006	359	272,623,980	2020	383	237,064,332
1955	150	48,891,000	2007	360	275,581,547	2021	388	297,115,406
1960	166	71,586,000	2008	360	274,852,949	2022	389	311,985,998
1965	182	118,662,500	2009	360	285,579,941	2023	394	325,498,646

Most-Visited Sites in the National Park System, 2023

Source: National Park Service (NPS), U.S. Dept. of the Interior

Attendance at 394 of 428 NPS-administered sites totaled 325,498,646 recreation visits in 2023. (Not all units report public use statistics.)

Rank	Site (location)	Rec. visits
1.	Blue Ridge Parkway (NC-VA)	16,757,635
2.	Golden Gate Natl. Recreation Area (CA)	14,953,882
3.	Great Smoky Mountains Natl. Park (NC-TN)	13,297,647
4.	Gateway Natl. Recreation Area (NJ-NY)	8,705,329
5.	Gulf Islands Natl. Seashore (FL-MS)	8,277,857
6.	Lincoln Memorial (DC)	8,099,148
7.	George Washington Memorial Parkway (DC-MD-VA)	7,391,260
8.	Natchez Trace Parkway (AL-MS-TN)	6,784,853
9.	Lake Mead Natl. Recreation Area (AZ-NV)	5,798,541
10.	Glen Canyon Natl. Recreation Area (AZ-UT)	5,206,934
11.	World War II Memorial (DC)	5,119,541
12.	Vietnam Veterans Memorial (DC)	5,039,454
13.	Grand Canyon Natl. Park (AZ)	4,733,705
14.	Zion Natl. Park (UT)	4,623,238
15.	Yellowstone Natl. Park (ID-MT-WY)	4,501,382
16.	Chesapeake & Ohio Canal Natl. Historical Park (DC-MD-WV)	4,470,592
17.	Delaware Water Gap Natl. Recreation Area (NJ-PA)	4,207,541
18.	Korean War Veterans Memorial (DC)	4,132,456
19.	Rocky Mountain Natl. Park (CO)	4,115,837
20.	Castle Clinton Natl. Monument (NY)	3,929,749
21.	Yosemite Natl. Park (CA)	3,897,070
22.	Acadia Natl. Park (ME)	3,879,890
23.	Cape Cod Natl. Seashore (MA)	3,808,404
24.	Statue of Liberty Natl. Monument (NJ-NY)	3,739,607
25.	Grand Teton Natl. Park (WY)	3,417,106
26.	Martin Luther King Jr. Memorial (DC)	3,341,654
27.	Franklin Delano Roosevelt Memorial (DC)	3,298,788
28.	Joshua Tree Natl. Park (CA)	3,270,404
29.	Chattahoochee River Natl. Recreation Area (GA)	3,183,081
30.	Independence Natl. Historical Park (PA)	3,042,598
31.	Thomas Jefferson Memorial (DC)	2,984,919
32.	Olympic Natl. Park (WA)	2,947,503
33.	Glacier Natl. Park (MT)	2,933,616
34.	Cuyahoga Valley Natl. Park (OH)	2,860,059
35.	Cape Hatteras Natl. Seashore (NC)	2,826,169
36.	Indiana Dunes Natl. Park (IN)	2,765,892
37.	Colonial Natl. Historical Park (VA)	2,691,931
38.	Boston Natl. Historical Park (MA)	2,517,296
39.	Hot Springs Natl. Park (AR)	2,502,967
40.	Bryce Canyon Natl. Park (UT)	2,461,269
41.	Mount Rushmore Natl. Memorial (SD)	2,431,195
42.	Gateway Arch Natl. Park (MO)	2,422,836
43.	Assateague Island Natl. Seashore (MD-VA)	2,351,874
44.	Point Reyes Natl. Seashore (CA)	2,268,058
45.	Chickasaw Natl. Recreation Area (OK)	2,082,326
46.	Canaveral Natl. Seashore (FL)	2,019,073
47.	Valley Forge Natl. Historical Park (PA)	1,880,527
48.	Big Cypress Natl. Preserve (FL)	1,846,562
49.	Rock Creek Park (DC)	1,817,868
50.	San Francisco Maritime Natl. Historical Park (CA)	1,769,467

National Parks and Other Areas Administered by National Park Service

As of Dec. 31, 2023, the National Park Service (NPS) administered about 85,155,967 acres of federal and non-federal land across 428 sites. Date when area was authorized or established by Congress or by presidential proclamation is given in parentheses; any date that follows indicates when a site received its current designation or was transferred to the NPS. Figure after the date is gross area acres as of Dec. 31, 2023. Listings do not include parks administered by other agencies, such as the Forest Service or Bureau of Land Management. NA = Not available.

The following units have been authorized but are not yet established: Adams Mem. (DC, authorized 2001), Ronald Reagan Boyhood Home Natl. Historic Site (IL, 2002), Coltsville Natl. Historical Park (CT, 2014), Desert Storm/Desert Shield Mem. (DC, 2014), Global War on Terrorism Mem. (DC, 2017), and Blackwell School Natl. Historic Site (TX, 2022).

National Parks

Acadia, ME (1916/1919): 49,071. Incl. Mount Desert Isl., half of Isle au Haut, Schoodic Peninsula on mainland. Highest elevation on Eastern seaboard.

American Samoa, AS (1988): 8,257. Paleotropical rain forest, coral reef.

Arches, UT (1929/1971): 76,679. Contains giant red sandstone arches and other products of erosion.

Badlands, SD (1939/1978): 242,756. Reformations and native prairie; animal fossils 25-37 mil years old.

Big Bend, TX (1935): 801,163. Rio Grande, Chisos Mtns.

Biscayne, FL (1968/1980): 172,971. Aquatic park encompassing chain of islands south of Miami.

Black Canyon of the Gunnison, CO (1933/1999): 30,780. Has canyon 2,900 ft deep and 40 ft wide at narrowest part.

Bryce Canyon, UT (1923/1928): 35,835. Colorful display of erosion effects.

Canyonlands, UT (1964): 337,598. At junction of Colorado and Green Rivers; extensive evidence of prehistoric peoples.

Capitol Reef, UT (1937/1971): 241,905. Nearly 100-mi-long uplift of sandstone cliffs (Waterpocket Fold) dissected by gorges.

Carlsbad Caverns, NM (1923/1930): 46,766. More than 119 limestone caves, incl. Carlsbad Cavern; Chihuahuan Desert.

Channel Islands, CA (1938/1980): 249,561. Sea lion breeding place, nesting seabirds, unique plants.

Congaree, SC (1976/2003): 26,693. Largest intact tract of old-growth bottomland hardwood forest in U.S.

Crater Lake, OR (1902): 183,224. Deepest U.S. lake, in crater of Mt. Mazama, volcano that erupted about 7,700 years ago.

Cuyahoga Valley, OH (1974/2000): 32,597. Along Ohio and Erie Canal system between Akron and Cleveland.

Death Valley, CA-NV (1933/1994): 3,408,446. Large desert. Incl. lowest point in North America and Scotty's Castle (closed until further notice due to flood and fire damage).

Denali, AK (1917/1980): 4,740,911. Highest mountain in U.S.; formerly known as Mt. McKinley.

Dry Tortugas, FL (1935/1992): 64,701. Ft. Jefferson and seven coral reef and sand islands near Key West.

Everglades, FL (1934): 1,508,939. Largest remaining subtropical wilderness in continental U.S; incl. East Everglades Expansion Area acreage added in 1989.

Gates of the Arctic, AK (1978/1980): 7,523,897. Vast wilderness in north central region. Limited federal facilities.

Gateway Arch, St. Louis, MO (1935/2018): 193. Former Jefferson Natl. Expansion Memorial commemorates 19th cent. westward expansion; incl. Gateway Arch (authorized 1954).

Glacier, MT (1910): 1,013,126. Rocky Mt. scenery, numerous glaciers and glacial lakes. Part of Waterton-Glacier Intl. Peace Park established by U.S. and Canada in 1932.

Glacier Bay, AK (1925/1980): 3,223,383. Tidewater glaciers that move down mountainsides and break up into sea.

Grand Canyon, AZ (1919/1919): 1,201,647. Carved by Colorado River.

Grand Teton, WY (1929): 310,044. Incl. highest peaks of Teton Mtns.; summer feeding ground of largest American elk herd.

Great Basin, NV (1922/1986): 77,180. Incl. Wheeler Peak, Lexington Arch, Lehman Caves.

Great Sand Dunes, CO (1932/2004): 107,337. North America's tallest dunes.

Great Smoky Mountains, NC-TN (1926/1934): 522,427. Most biologically diverse NPS unit, with 19,000+ documented species.

Guadalupe Mountains, TX (1966): 86,367. Extensive Permian limestone fossil reef; tremendous earth fault.

Haleakalā, HI (1916/1960): 33,489. Dormant volcano on island of Maui with large craters.

Hawai'i Volcanoes, HI (1916/1961): 344,812. Contains Kilauea and Mauna Loa, active volcanoes.

Hot Springs, AR (1832/1921): 5,554. Waters from park's 47 hot springs used for bathing and drinking.

Indiana Dunes, IN (1966/2019): 15,508. Stretches 15 mi along Lake Michigan.

Isle Royale, MI (1931): 571,790. Largest island in Lake Superior.

Joshua Tree, CA (1936/1994): 795,156. Desert region incl. Joshua trees, other plant and animal life.

Katmai, AK (1918/1980): 3,674,529. "Valley of Ten Thousand Smokes," scene of 1912 volcanic eruption.

Kenai Fjords, AK (1978/1980): 669,650. Marine mammals, birdlife; over 30 glaciers flow from Harding Icefield.

Kings Canyon, CA (1890/1940): 461,901. Mountain wilderness, dominated by Kings River Canyons and High Sierra; giant sequoias.

Kobuk Valley, AK (1978/1980): 1,750,716. Geological and recreational sites. Limited federal facilities.

Lake Clark, AK (1978/1980): 2,619,816. Across Cook Inlet from Anchorage; scenic wilderness, fish and wildlife. Limited federal facilities.

Lassen Volcanic, CA (1907/1916): 106,589. Contains Lassen Peak, recently active volcano; other volcanic phenomena.

Mammoth Cave, KY (1926/1941): 72,042. Longest known cave system in world (more than 426 mi currently surveyed), river 300 ft below surface.

Mesa Verde, CO (1906): 52,485. Most notable and best preserved prehistoric cliff dwellings in U.S.

Mount Rainier, WA (1899): 236,382. Most glaciated peak in contiguous U.S.

New River Gorge (and Preserve), WV (1978/2020): 72,391. Appalachian Mountain forests along 53 mi of the New River.

North Cascades, WA (1968): 504,781. Mountainous region with many glaciers, lakes.

Olympic, WA (1909/1938): 922,649. Wilderness containing glacier-capped mountains, remnant of temperate rain forest, shoreline, endemic animal species.

Petrified Forest, AZ (1906/1962): 221,390. Extensive petrified wood and Indian artifacts. Contains part of Painted Desert.

Pinnacles, CA (1908/2013): 26,686. A release site for captive-bred California condors; talus caves.

Redwood, CA (1968): 139,091. 40 mi of Pacific coastline, groves of ancient redwoods, the world's tallest trees.

Rocky Mountain, CO (1915): 265,848. On Continental Divide; incl. peaks over 14,000 ft.

Saguaro, AZ (1933/1994): 92,800. Part of Sonoran Desert; incl. giant saguaro cacti, unique to region.

Sequoia, CA (1890): 404,063. Giant sequoia groves; world's largest tree (by volume). Mt. Whitney, highest mountain in conterminous U.S.

Shenandoah, VA (1926): 200,446. Portion of Blue Ridge Mtns. Overlooks Shenandoah Valley; Skyline Drive.

Theodore Roosevelt, ND (1947/1978): 70,447. Contains part of Roosevelt's ranch and scenic badlands.

Virgin Islands, VI (1956): 15,052. Covers more than half of St. John Isl. and nearly all of Hassel Isl.; beaches, Carib Indian petroglyphs, evidence of colonial Danes.

Voyageurs, MN (1971): 218,223. Abundant lakes, wildlife.

White Sands, NM (1933/2019): 146,344. World's largest gypsum dunefield.

Wind Cave, SD (1903): 33,971. Limestone caverns in Black Hills; extensive wildlife incl. bison herd.

Wrangell-St. Elias, AK (1978/1980): 8,323,146. Largest area in park system; most peaks over 16,000 ft.

Yellowstone, ID-MT-WY (1872): 2,219,791. World's first national park. More than 10,000 thermal features (geysers, hot springs); Yellowstone River falls and canyons; largest bison herd on U.S. public land.

Yosemite, CA (1890): 761,748. Yosemite Valley, country's highest waterfall, grove of sequoias, mountains.

Zion, UT (1909/1919): 147,243. Unusual shapes, landscapes resulting from erosion, faulting; evidence of past volcanic activity.

National Historical Parks

Abraham Lincoln Birthplace, Hodgenville, KY (1916/2009): 345. Memorial building, sinking spring.

Adams, Quincy, MA (1946/1998): 24. Home of Pres. John Adams, John Quincy Adams, and descendants.

Appomattox Court House, VA (1930/1954): 1,775. Where Confederate Gen. Lee surrendered to Gen. Grant, signaling Civil War's end.

Blackstone River Valley, MA-RI (2014): 1,489. Preserves the valley's industrial heritage.

Boston, MA (1974): 44. Incl. Faneuil Hall, Old North Church, Bunker Hill, Paul Revere House.

Brown v. Board of Education, KS (1992/2022): 3.15. Commemorates landmark 1954 U.S. Supreme Court decision, which ended legal segregation in schools.

Cane River Creole, LA (1994): 206. Preserves Creole culture as it developed along the Cane River.

Cedar Creek and Belle Grove, VA (2002): 3,708. Civil War battle site and an antebellum plantation in Shenandoah Valley.

Chaco Culture, NM (1907/1980): 33,960. Ruins of pueblos built by prehistoric peoples incl. Pueblo, Hopi, and Navajo.

Chesapeake & Ohio Canal, MD-DC-WV (1938/1971): 19,628. 184.5-mi historic canal; DC to Cumberland, MD.

Colonial, VA (1930/1936): 8,675. Incl. most of Jamestown Isl., site of first successful English colony; Yorktown, site of Cornwallis's surrender to George Washington.

Cumberland Gap, KY-TN-VA (1940): 24,547. Mountain pass of Wilderness Road, which carried first great migration of pioneers into America's interior.

Dayton Aviation Heritage, OH (1992): 111. Commemorates area's involvement in aviation.

First State, DE-PA (2013/2014): 1,409. Locations date from colonial past of DE, first state to ratify Constitution.

Fort Sumter and Fort Moultrie, SC (1948/2019): 233. Charleston Harbor sites, where Confederate forces fired the first shots of the Civil War.

George Rogers Clark, Vincennes, IN (1966): 26. Commemorates American defeat of British in West during Revolution.

Golden Spike, UT (1957/2019): 2,735. Commemorates completion of first transcontinental railroad in 1869.

Harpers Ferry, MD-VA-WV (1944/1963): 3,669. At confluence of Shenandoah and Potomac Rivers, the site of John Brown's 1859 raid on the Army arsenal.

Harriet Tubman, NY (2017): 32. Buildings incl. her home, a church, Tubman Home for the Aged.

Harriet Tubman Underground Railroad, MD (2013/2014): 480. Protects landscapes on the Eastern Shore, where Tubman was born and guided other slaves to freedom.

Homestead, NE (1936/2021): 210. Commemorates Homestead Act of 1862, which spurred U.S. westward expansion.

Hopewell Culture, OH (1923/1992): 1,776. Remains of ceremonial mounds built in the Ohio River Valley, 200 BCE-500 CE.

Independence, Philadelphia, PA (1948): 45. Several properties associated with American Revolution and founding of U.S., incl. Independence Hall, Liberty Bell Center.

Jean Lafitte (and Preserve), LA (1907/1978): 25,876. Incl. Chalmette, site of 1815 Battle of New Orleans; French Quarter.

Jimmy Carter, GA (1987/2021): 78. Birthplace and home of 39th president.

Kalaupapa, HI (1980): 10,779. Former colony on Molokai Isl. for those with Hansen's disease (leprosy).

Kaloko-Honokōhau, HI (1978): 1,163. Preserves native culture of Hawaii.

Keweenaw, MI (1992): 1,870. Site of first significant copper mine in U.S.

Klondike Gold Rush, AK-WA (1976): 12,996. Preserves Chilkoot Trail used in 1898 Gold Rush. Museum in Seattle.

Lewis and Clark, OR-WA (1958/2004): 3,409. Lewis and Clark encampment, 1805-06. Incorporates former Fort Clatsop Natl. Mem. Park.

Lowell, MA (1978): 143. Textile mills, canal, 19th-cent. structures; park shows planned city of Industrial Revolution.

Lyndon B. Johnson, TX (1969/1980): 1,572. 36th president's birthplace, boyhood home, ranch.

Manhattan Project, NM-TN-WA (2015): 114. Jointly operated with Dept. of Energy, consists of three sites (Los Alamos, NM; Oak Ridge, TN; Hanford, WA) where U.S. developed world's first atomic weapons.

Marsh-Billings-Rockefeller, VT (1992): 643. Boyhood home of conservationist George Perkins Marsh.

Martin Luther King Jr., Atlanta, GA (1980/2018): 39. Birthplace, grave, church of the civil rights leader.

Minute Man, MA (1959): 1,028. Where Minute Men battled British, Apr. 19, 1775. Also includes The Wayside, home to authors Louisa May Alcott and Nathaniel Hawthorne.

Morristown, NJ (1933): 1,711. Site of important military encampments during the American Revolution; Washington's headquarters, 1779-80.

Natchez, MS (1988): 121. Antebellum estate, other preserved properties related to history of Natchez as a Cotton Belt city.

New Bedford Whaling, MA (1996): 34. Preserves structures and relics associated with the city's 19th-cent. whaling industry.

New Orleans Jazz, LA (1994): 5. Preserves, educates, and interprets jazz as it has evolved in New Orleans.

Nez Perce, ID-MT-OR-WA (1965): 4,565. Illustrates history and culture of Nez Perce, or Nimiipuu, homeland (38 sites).

Ocmulgee Mounds, GA (1934/2019): 3,431. First inhabited by Paleo Indians by c. 15,000 BCE. Ancestral land of the Muscogee (Creek), who were forcibly moved to OK in 1830s.

Palo Alto Battlefield, TX (1978/2009): 3,427. Scene of first battle of the Mexican War.

Paterson Great Falls, NJ (2011): 51. Falls helped make city one of U.S.'s earliest industrial centers.

Pecos, NM (1965/1990): 6,886. Ruins of ancient Pueblo of Pecos, archaeological sites, and two associated Spanish colonial missions from 17th and 18th centuries.

Pullman, IL (2015/2022): 0.4. First planned model industrial community in U.S.; influenced American labor movement.

Pu'uhonua o Hōnaunau, HI (1955/1978): 420. Until 1819, a sanctuary for Hawaiians vanquished in battle and for those guilty of crimes or breaking taboos.

Reconstruction Era, SC (2017/2019): 16. Beaufort Co. sites that tell the story of how formerly enslaved people were integrated into free society.

Rosie the Riveter WWII Home Front, Richmond, CA (2000): 145. Site of shipyard that employed thousands of women during WWII; commemorates women who worked in wartime industries.

Saint-Gaudens, Cornish, NH (1964/2019): 191. Home, studio, and gardens of sculptor Augustus Saint-Gaudens.

Ste. Geneviève, MO (2020): 17. First permanent European settlement in state.

Salt River Bay (and Ecological Preserve), St. Croix, VI (1992): 989. Only known site where, in 1493, members of a Columbus party landed on what is now U.S. territory.

San Antonio Missions, TX (1978): 990. Four Spanish missions, 18th-cent. irrigation system.

San Francisco Maritime, CA (1988): 50. Artifacts, photographs, and historic vessels related to development of the Pacific Coast.

San Juan Island, WA (1966): 2,146. Commemorates peaceful relations between U.S., Canada, and Great Britain since the 1872 boundary disputes.

Saratoga, NY (1938): 3,608. Scene of a major 1777 battle that became a turning point in the American Revolution.

Sitka, AK (1910/1972): 116. Scene of Tlingit Indians' last major resistance to Russian colonizers, 1804.

Thomas Edison, West Orange, NJ (1955/2009): 21. Inventor's home and laboratory.

Tumacacori, AZ (1908/1990): 360. Historic Spanish mission building near site first visited by Father Kino in 1691.

Valley Forge, PA (1976): 3,469. Continental Army campsite in 1777-78 winter.

War in the Pacific, GU (1978): 2,030. Seven units illustrating the Pacific theater of WWII.

Weir Farm, CT (1990/2021): 74. Home and studio of American impressionist painter J. Alden Weir.

Women's Rights, NY (1980): 7. Where Lucretia Mott, Elizabeth Cady Stanton, and others organized movement in 1848.

National Battlefields/Parks/Sites

Antietam, MD (1890/1978): 3,288. Battle here ended first Confederate invasion of North, Sept. 17, 1862.

Big Hole, MT (1910/1963): 976. Site of major battle with Nez Perce Indians, Aug. 9-10, 1877.

Brices Cross Roads, Baldwyn, MS (1929): 1.00. Site of Confederate victory, June 10, 1864.

Cowpens, SC (1929/1972): 842. American Revolution battlefield, Jan. 17, 1781.

Fort Donelson, TN-KY (1928/1985): 1,319. Site of first major Union victory, Feb. 16, 1862.

Fort Necessity, PA (1931/1961): 903. Site of first battle of French and Indian War, July 3, 1754.

Kennesaw Mountain, GA (1917/1935): 2,914. Site of major battle of Atlanta campaign in Civil War.

Manassas, VA (1940): 5,073. Scene of two Civil War battles.

Monocacy, MD (1934/1976): 1,647. Civil War battle in defense of Washington, DC, fought here, July 9, 1864.

Moores Creek, Currie, NC (1926/1980): 88. Commemorates Feb. 27, 1776, battle between Patriots and Loyalists.

Petersburg, VA (1926/1962): 9,599. Scene of Union campaigns, 1864-65.

Richmond, VA (1936): 8,143. Site of battles defending Confederate capital.

River Raisin, Monroe, MI (2010): 42. Site of major battles of War of 1812.

Stones River, TN (1927/1960): 709. Scene of federal offensive to trisect Confederacy, Dec. 31, 1862-Jan. 2, 1863.

Tupelo, MS (1929/1961): 1. Site of crucial battle over Union Gen. Sherman's supply line, July 14-15, 1865.

Wilson's Creek, MO (1960/1970): 2,447. Site of second major Civil War battle, Aug. 10, 1861, for control of Missouri.

National Military Parks

Chickamauga and Chattanooga, GA-TN (1890): 9,523. Where Gen. Sherman and Union armies gained control of TN, 1863.

Fredericksburg and Spotsylvania, VA (1927/1933): 8,405. Sites of several major Civil War battles and campaigns.

Gettysburg, PA (1895/1933): 6,037. Site of decisive Confederate defeat in North, July 1863, and of Gettysburg Address.

Guilford Courthouse, NC (1917/1933): 255. American Revolution battle site.

Horseshoe Bend, AL (1956): 2,040. On Tallapoosa River, where Gen. Andrew Jackson broke power of Upper Creek Indian Confederacy on Mar. 27, 1814.

Kings Mountain, SC (1931/1933): 3,945. Site of American Revolution battle fought on Oct. 7, 1780.

Pea Ridge, AR (1956): 4,441. Civil War battle, Mar. 7-8, 1862.

Shiloh, TN-MS (1894/1933): 9,322. Major Civil War battle site, Apr. 6-7, 1862; incl. Shiloh Indian burial mounds.

Vicksburg, MS-LA (1899/1933): 3,049. Union victory gave North control of Mississippi and split Confederate forces.

National Memorials

Arkansas Post, AR (1960): 758. First permanent French settlement in lower Mississippi River valley.

Arlington House, The Robert E. Lee Memorial, VA (1925/1972): 17. Lee's home overlooking the Potomac River.

Chamizal, El Paso, TX (1966/1974): 55. Commemorates 1963 settlement of 99-year border dispute with Mexico.

Coronado, AZ (1941/1952): 4,830. Commemorates first European exploration of the Southwest.

De Soto, Bradenton, FL (1948): 30. Commemorates 16th-cent. Spanish explorations.

Dwight D. Eisenhower Memorial, Washington, DC (2020): 3.39. Honors his role as Supreme Commander of the Allied Expeditionary Force in WWII and as 34th pres.

Federal Hall, New York, NY (1939/1955): 0.45. First seat of U.S. government under the Constitution.

Flight 93, Shanksville, PA (2002): 2,263. Commemorates passengers and crew of Flight 93, who died thwarting an attack on Sept. 11, 2001.

Fort Caroline, Jacksonville, FL (1950): 138. On St. Johns River, site of first attempt by France, in 16th cent., at permanent North American settlement.

Franklin Delano Roosevelt Memorial, DC (1982): 8. Statues of Pres. Roosevelt and Eleanor Roosevelt; waterfalls and gardens.

General Grant, New York, NY (1958): 0.76. Tomb of Ulysses Grant and wife; largest mausoleum in U.S.

Hamilton Grange, New York, NY (1962): 1.75. Home of Alexander Hamilton.

Johnstown Flood, PA (1964): 178. Commemorates 1889 flood.

Korean War Veterans Memorial, DC (1986/1995): 1.56. Honors those who served in the Korean War.

Lincoln Boyhood, Lincoln City, IN (1962): 200. Site of Abraham Lincoln's boyhood home and grave site of his mother.

Lincoln Memorial, DC (1911/1933): 7. Marble statue of 16th president.

Lyndon Baines Johnson Memorial Grove on the Potomac, DC (1973): 17. Overlooks Potomac River; vista of the Capitol.

Martin Luther King Jr., DC (1996): 2.74. Granite statue of Dr. King close to where he delivered "I Have a Dream" speech.

Mount Rushmore, SD (1925): 1,278. Heads of presidents Washington, Jefferson, Lincoln, T. Roosevelt sculpted into mountain.

Pearl Harbor, HI (2019): 22. Site of Dec. 7, 1941, Japanese attack.

Perry's Victory and International Peace Memorial, Put-in-Bay, OH (1936/1972): 25. World's most massive Doric column promotes pursuit of peace through arbitration and disarmament.

Port Chicago Naval Magazine, Danville, CA (2009): 5. Where 1944 munitions ship explosion killed 320 men.

Roger Williams, Providence, RI (1965): 4.56. Memorial to founder of Rhode Island.

Thaddeus Kosciuszko, Philadelphia, PA (1972): 0.02. Memorial to Polish hero of American Revolution.

Theodore Roosevelt Island, DC (1932/1933): 89. Statue of Roosevelt in wooded island sanctuary.

Thomas Jefferson Memorial, DC (1934/1943): 18. Statue of Jefferson in an inscribed circular, colonnaded structure.

Vietnam Veterans Memorial, DC (1980): 2.18. Black granite wall with names of those missing or killed in action in Vietnam War.

Washington Monument, DC (1876/1933): 106. Obelisk honoring first U.S. president. Construction began in 1848 with private funding.

World War I Memorial, DC (1981/2014): 1.39. Formerly Pershing Park, dedicated to Gen. John J. Pershing.

World War II Memorial, DC (1993/2004): 8. Oval plaza with central pool commemorating those who fought and died.

Wright Brothers, Kill Devil Hills, NC (1927/1953): 428. Site of first powered flight, by Orville and Wilbur Wright.

National Historic Sites

Allegheny Portage Railroad, PA (1964): 1,284. Linked Pennsylvania Canal system and the West.

Amache, CO (2024): NA. WWII Japanese American internment camp.

Andersonville, GA (1970): 516. Civil War POW camp.

Andrew Johnson, Greeneville, TN (1935/1963): 17. Two homes, his tailor shop, and burial site of 17th U.S. pres.

Bent's Old Fort, CO (1960): 799. Replica of fort on Sante Fe Trail.

Boston African-American, MA (1980): 0.59. Pre-Civil War Black-owned structures.

Carl Sandburg Home, Flat Rock, NC (1968): 268. Home of Pulitzer Prize-winning poet and biographer.

Carter G. Woodson Home, DC (1976/2006): 0.15. Home of "Father of Black History."

Charles Pinckney, Mt. Pleasant, SC (1988): 28. Farm of a principal author and signer of the Constitution.

Christiansted, St. Croix, VI (1952/1961): 27. Preserves historic structures from time of Danish colony.

Clara Barton, Glen Echo, MD (1974): 9. Home of American Red Cross founder.

Edgar Allan Poe, Phila., PA (1978/1980): 0.52. Writer's home.

Eisenhower, Gettysburg, PA (1967): 690. Home of 34th pres.

Eleanor Roosevelt, Hyde Park, NY (1977): 181. Former first lady's personal retreat.

Eugene O'Neill, Danville, CA (1976): 13. Home where playwright wrote his final plays, incl. *The Iceman Cometh*.

First Ladies, Canton, OH (2000): 0.46. Home of first lady Ida Sexton McKinley. Library now devoted to U.S. first ladies.

Ford's Theatre, DC (1866/1970): 0.30. Incl. theater where Lincoln was assassinated, house where he died, and Lincoln Museum.

Fort Bowie, AZ (1964): 999. Focal point of operations against Geronimo and Apaches.

Fort Davis, TX (1961): 523. Frontier outpost in West Texas; established to guard the San Antonio-El Paso Road.

Fort Laramie, WY (1938/1960): 873. Military post on Oregon Trail.

Fort Larned, KS (1964/1966): 718. Military post on Santa Fe Trail.

Fort Point, CA (1970): 29. West Coast fortification; protected San Francisco during and after Civil War.

Fort Raleigh, NC (1941): 516. First attempted English settlement in North America.

Fort Scott, KS (1965/1978): 20. Commemorates U.S. frontier. Focal point of Black troop activity, training during Civil War.

Fort Smith, AR-OK (1961): 75. One of the earliest U.S. posts in Missouri Territory, active 1817-96.

Fort Union Trading Post, MT-ND (1966): 440. Principal fur-trading post on upper Missouri, 1829-67.

Fort Vancouver, WA-OR (1948/1961): 208. Headquarters for Hudson's Bay Company.

Frederick Douglass, DC (1962/1988): 9. Home of Black abolitionist, writer, orator.

Frederick Law Olmsted, Brookline, MA (1979): 7. Home of city planner, famous for designing Central Park in NYC.

Friendship Hill, PA (1978): 675. Home of Albert Gallatin, Jefferson's and Madison's secretary of treasury.

Grant-Kohrs Ranch, MT (1972): 1,618. Ranch house owned by John Grant, 19th-cent. range-cattle industry pioneer.

Hampton, Towson, MD (1948): 62. 18th-cent. Georgian mansion, which in 1790 was largest house in U.S.

Harry S Truman, Independence, MO (1982/1983): 14. House of 33rd pres. from 1919 on and farm where he worked as young man.

Herbert Hoover, West Branch, IA (1965): 187. Birthplace and boyhood home of 31st president.

Home of Franklin D. Roosevelt, Hyde Park, NY (1944): 838. FDR's birthplace, home, and "summer White House."

Honouliuli, HI (2015/2019): 154. Camp where POWs and civilians suspected of disloyalty—mostly Americans of Japanese ancestry—were imprisoned during WWII.

Hopewell Furnace, PA (1938/1985): 848. 19th-cent. iron-making village.

Hubbell Trading Post, AZ (1965): 160. Oldest continuously operating trading post in SW; founded in 1878 on Navajo Nation.

James A. Garfield, Mentor, OH (1980): 8. Home of 20th president; site of his front-porch campaign.

John Fitzgerald Kennedy, Brookline, MA (1967): 0.09. Birthplace and childhood home of 35th president.

John Muir, Martinez, CA (1964): 389. Home of Sierra Club co-founder and "Father of the National Park Service."

Knife River Indian Villages, ND (1974): 1,751. Remnants of villages last occupied by Hidatsa and Mandan Indians.

Lincoln Home, Springfield, IL (1971): 12. Lincoln's residence when he was elected 16th president, 1860.

Little Rock Central High School, AR (1998): 28. Commemorates 1957 desegregation during which federal troops were called in to protect nine Black students.

Longfellow House—Washington's Headquarters, Cambridge, MA (1972/2010): 1.98. Poet's home, 1837-82; Washington's headquarters during Boston siege, 1775-76.

Maggie L. Walker, Richmond, VA (1978): 1.29. Home of Black leader and first female bank president, daughter of former slave.

Manzanar, Lone Pine, CA (1992): 814. Manzanar War Relocation Ctr., a WWII Japanese American internment camp.

Martin Van Buren, Kinderhook, NY (1974): 285. Lindenwald, home of 8th president.

Mary McLeod Bethune Council House, DC (1982/1991): 0.07. HQ and home of Black women's movement leader.

Minidoka, ID (2001/2008): 396. WWII Japanese internment ctr.

Minuteman Missile, SD (1999): 44. Missile launch facilities dating to Cold War era.

New Philadelphia, IL (2022): 123. First known town planned, legally registered by an African American before the Civil War.

Nicodemus, KS (1996): 6. Only remaining Western town established by African Americans during Reconstruction.

Ninety Six, SC (1976): 1,022. Colonial trading village and site of Gen. Nathanael Greene's siege on Loyalist-held fort in 1781.

Pennsylvania Avenue, DC (1965/1996): 18. Incl. area between Capitol and White House, encompassing U.S. Navy Memorial, Freedom Plaza, Old Post Office Pavilion, other sites.

President William Jefferson Clinton Birthplace Home, Hope, AR (2010): 0.68. Birthplace and early home of 42nd pres.

Pu'ukoholā Heiau, Kawaihae, HI (1972): 86. Ruins of temple built by King Kamehameha, first king of united Hawaiian islands.

Sagamore Hill, Oyster Bay, NY (1962): 83. Home of Pres. Theodore Roosevelt from 1885 until his death in 1919.

Saint Paul's Church, Mount Vernon, NY (1943/1978): 6. One of the oldest parishes (1665-1980) in New York State.

Salem Maritime, MA (1938): 9. Major fishing and whaling port famous for 1692 witchcraft trials.

San Juan, PR (1949): 75. 16th-cent. Spanish fortifications.

Sand Creek Massacre, CO (2000): 12,583. Site where around 230 Cheyenne and Arapaho Indians—mostly women, children, and elderly—were killed by U.S. soldiers in 1864.

Saugus Iron Works, MA (1974): 9. Reconstructed 17th-cent. colonial ironworks.

Springfield Armory, MA (1974): 55. Small-arms manufacturing center for nearly 200 years.

Steamtown, Scranton, PA (1986): 62. Rail yard, roadhouse, repair shops of former Delaware, Lackawanna & Western Railroad.

Theodore Roosevelt Birthplace, New York, NY (1962): 0.11. Reconstructed brownstone where 26th president was born.

Theodore Roosevelt Inaugural, Buffalo, NY (1966): 1.18. Wilcox House, where 26th president took oath of office, 1901.

Thomas Stone, Port Tobacco, MD (1978): 328. Haberdeventure, home of signer of Declaration of Independence.

Tuskegee Airmen, AL (1998): 90. Airfield where pilots of all-Black WWII air corps unit received flight training.

Tuskegee Institute, AL (1974): 58. College founded by Booker T. Washington in 1881 for Black students.

Ulysses S. Grant, St. Louis, MO (1989): 10. Home of Grant during pre-Civil War years.

Vanderbilt Mansion, Hyde Park, NY (1940): 212. Mansion of 19th-cent. financier.

Washita Battlefield, OK (1996): 315. Scene of Nov. 27, 1868, battle between Plains tribes and U.S. army.

Whitman Mission, Walla Walla, WA (1936/1963): 139. Site of Protestant missionaries to Cayuse Indians beginning in 1830s.

William Howard Taft, Cincinnati, OH (1969): 3.64. Birthplace and early home of 27th president.

Name	Location	Year[1]	Acreage
National Lakeshores			
Apostle Islands	WI	1970	69,377
Pictured Rocks	MI	1966	73,236
Sleeping Bear Dunes	MI	1970	71,319
National Monuments			
African Burial Ground	NY	2006	0.35
Agate Fossil Beds	NE	1965	3,058
Alibates Flint Quarries	TX	1965	1,371
Aniakchak[2]	AK	1980	137,176
Aztec Ruins	NM	1923	318
Bandelier	NM	1916	33,677
Belmont-Paul Women's Equality	DC	2016	0.34
Birmingham Civil Rights	AL	2017	0.88
Booker T. Washington	VA	1956	239
Buck Island Reef	VI	1961	19,015
Cabrillo	CA	1913	160
Camp Nelson	KY	2018	465
Canyon de Chelly	AZ	1931	83,840
Cape Krusenstern	AK	1978	649,096
Capulin Volcano	NM	1916	793
Casa Grande Ruins	AZ	1918	473
Castillo de San Marcos	FL	1924	19
Castle Clinton	NY	1946	1.00
Castle Mountains	CA	2016	21,026
Cedar Breaks	UT	1933	6,155
César E. Chávez	CA	2012	117
Charles Young Buffalo Soldiers	OH	2013	60
Chiricahua	AZ	1924	12,025
Colorado	CO	1911	20,536
Craters of the Moon	ID	1924	53,438
Devils Postpile	CA	1911	800
Devils Tower	WY	1906	1,347
Dinosaur	CO-UT	1915	210,282
Effigy Mounds	IA	1949	2,526
El Malpais	NM	1987	114,347
El Morro	NM	1906	1,279
Emmett Till and Mamie Till-Mobley	IL, MS	2023	6
Florissant Fossil Beds	CO	1969	6,278
Fort Frederica	GA	1936	305
Fort Matanzas	FL	1924	300
Fort McHenry (and Historic Shrine)	MD	1939	43
Fort Monroe	VA	2011	367
Fort Pulaski	GA	1924	5,623
Fort Stanwix	NY	1935	16
Fort Union	NM	1954	721
Fossil Butte	WY	1972	8,198
Freedom Riders	AL	2017	6
George Washington Birthplace	VA	1930	654
George Washington Carver	MO	1943	240
Gila Cliff Dwellings	NM	1907	533
Governors Island	NY	2001	23
Grand Portage	MN	1958	710
Hagerman Fossil Beds	ID	1988	4,351
Hohokam Pima[3]	AZ	1972	1,690
Hovenweep	CO-UT	1923	785
Jewel Cave	SD	1908	1,274
John Day Fossil Beds	OR	1974	14,062
Katahdin Woods and Waters	ME	2016	87,564
Lava Beds	CA	1925	46,692
Little Bighorn Battlefield	MT	1946	765
Medgar and Myrlie Evers Home	MS	2020	0.74
Mill Springs Battlefield	KY	2020	1,457
Montezuma Castle	AZ	1906	1,016
Muir Woods	CA	1908	554
Natural Bridges	UT	1908	7,636
Navajo	AZ	1909	360
Oregon Caves (and Preserve)	OR	1909	4,554
Organ Pipe Cactus	AZ	1937	330,689
Petroglyph	NM	1990	7,204
Pipe Spring	AZ	1923	40
Pipestone	MN	1937	297
Poverty Point[2]	LA	1988	911
Rainbow Bridge	UT	1910	160

Name	Location	Year[1]	Acreage
Russell Cave	AL	1961	310
Salinas Pueblo Missions	NM	1909	1,071
Scotts Bluff	NE	1919	3,005
Statue of Liberty	NJ-NY	1924	58
Stonewall	NY	2016	8
Sunset Crater Volcano	AZ	1930	3,138
Timpanogos Cave	UT	1922	250
Tonto	AZ	1907	1,120
Tule Lake	CA	2019	37
Tule Springs Fossil Beds	NV	2014	22,650
Tuzigoot	AZ	1939	812
Virgin Islands Coral Reef	VI	2001	12,708
Waco Mammoth	TX	2015	107
Walnut Canyon	AZ	1915	3,201
Wupatki	AZ	1924	35,402
Yucca House[2]	CO	1919	34

National Parkways

Name	Location	Year[1]	Acreage
Blue Ridge	NC-VA	1933	101,076
George Washington Memorial	MD-DC-VA	1930	6,719
John D. Rockefeller Jr. Memorial	WY	1972	23,777
Natchez Trace	MS-TN-AL	1938	52,380

National Preserves

Name	Location	Year[1]	Acreage
Aniakchak[2]	AK	1980	464,118
Bering Land Bridge	AK	1980	2,697,391
Big Cypress[4]	FL	1974	720,564
Big Thicket	TX	1974	113,122
Craters of the Moon	ID	2002	698,940
Denali	AK	1980	1,334,118
Gates of the Arctic	AK	1980	948,608
Glacier Bay	AK	1980	58,406
Great Sand Dunes	CO	2004	41,686
Katmai	AK	1980	418,699
Lake Clark	AK	1980	1,410,294
Little River Canyon	AL	1992	15,292
Mojave	CA	1994	1,549,709
Noatak	AK	1980	6,587,071
Tallgrass Prairie	KS	1996	10,883
Timucuan Ecological and Historic	FL	1988	46,263
Valles Caldera	NM	2014	89,805
Wrangell-St. Elias	AK	1980	4,852,645
Yukon-Charley Rivers	AK	1980	2,526,512

National Recreation Areas

Name	Location	Year[1]	Acreage
Amistad	TX	1990	62,945
Bighorn Canyon	MT-WY	1966	120,296
Boston Harbor Islands	MA	1996	2,231
Chattahoochee River	GA	1978	12,417
Chickasaw	OK	1976	9,899
Curecanti	CO	1965	43,591
Delaware Water Gap	NJ-PA	1965	68,709
Gateway	NJ-NY	1972	26,607
Gauley River	WV	1988	11,483
Glen Canyon	AZ-UT	1972	1,254,117
Golden Gate	CA	1972	82,116
Lake Chelan	WA	1968	61,939
Lake Mead	AZ-NV	1964	1,495,856
Lake Meredith	TX	1990	44,978
Lake Roosevelt (fmr. Coulee Dam)	WA	1946	100,390
Ross Lake	WA	1968	117,575
Santa Monica Mountains	CA	1978	153,121
Whiskeytown-Shasta-Trinity[5]	CA	1972	42,503

National Reserves

Name	Location	Year[1]	Acreage
City of Rocks	ID	1988	14,512
Ebey's Landing Historical	WA	1978	19,334

National Rivers

Name	Location	Year[1]	Acreage
Big South Fork (and Rec. Area)	KY-TN	1991	123,699
Buffalo	AR	1972	94,301
Mississippi (and Rec. Area)	MN	1988	53,775
Ozark Scenic Riverways	MO	1972	80,784

National Seashores

Name	Location	Year[1]	Acreage
Assateague Island[6]	MD-VA	1965	41,281
Canaveral	FL	1975	57,662
Cape Cod	MA	1966	43,608
Cape Hatteras	NC	1953	30,351
Cape Lookout	NC	1966	28,243
Cumberland Island	GA	1972	36,347
Fire Island	NY	1964	19,581
Gulf Islands	FL-MS	1971	138,307
Padre Island	TX	1968	130,434
Point Reyes	CA	1972	71,053

International Historic Site

Name	Location	Year[1]	Acreage
Saint Croix Island	ME	1984	7

Other Designations

Name	Location	Year[1]	Acreage
Catoctin Mountain Park	MD	1954	5,891
Constitution Gardens	DC	1974	39
Fort Washington Park	MD	1940	345
Greenbelt Park	MD	1950	1,176
National Capital Parks-East	DC-MD	1933	8,704
National Mall/Memorial Parks	DC	1933	156
Piscataway Park	MD	1961	4,616
Prince William Forest Park	VA	1948	16,059
Rock Creek Park	DC	1933	1,755
White House	DC	1933	18
Wolf Trap National Park for the Performing Arts	VA	2002	130

National Wild and Scenic Rivers

Rivers in this system are designated by Congress or the Sec. of the Interior. As of June 2023, the system included 13,466.8 miles of 228 rivers in 41 states and Puerto Rico. Not all of the rivers that the NPS administers are official units of the park system. Only official NPS units are listed here.

Name	Location	Year[1]	Acreage
Alagnak Wild[2]	AK	1980	30,665
Bluestone Scenic	WV	1988	4,310
Delaware Scenic[7]	NJ-PA	1978	1,973
Great Egg Harbor Scenic and Rec.	NJ	1992	43,311
Missouri Recreational	NE-SD	1991	48,457
Niobrara Scenic	NE	1991	29,089
Obed	TN	1976	5,490
Rio Grande	TX	1978	13,123
Saint Croix Scenic Riverway[8]	MN-WI	1968	92,741
Upper Delaware Scenic and Rec.	NY-PA	1978	75,000

Affiliated Areas

Affiliated areas are administered in connection with the NPS but are not owned by that agency.

Name	Location	Year[1]	Acreage
Aleutian World War II Natl. Historic Area	AK	1996	135
American Memorial Park	MP	1978	133
Benjamin Franklin Natl. Memorial (NMEM)	PA	1972	NA
Chicago Portage Natl. Historic Site (NHS)	IL	1952	91
Chimney Rock NHS	NE	1956	83
Eutaw Springs Battlefield	SC	2021	NA
Fallen Timbers Battlefield and Fort Miamis NHS	OH	1999	185
Father Marquette NMEM	MI	1975	52
Gloria Dei (Old Swedes') Church NHS	PA	1942	3.71
Green Springs Natl. Historic Landmark District	VA	1974	15,645
Historic Camden Revolutionary War Site	SC	1982	107
Ice Age Natl. Scientific Reserve	WI	1964	32,500
International Peace Garden	ND-MB	1949	2,330
Iñupiat Heritage Center	AK	1999	0
Jamestown NHS	VA	1940	22
Kate Mullany NHS	NY	2004	0.06
Kettle Creek Battlefield	GA	2021	NA
Lower East Side Tenement NHS	NY	1998	1.2
Natural Bridge State Park	VA	2016	NA
Oklahoma City NMEM	OK	2004	6
Parkers Crossroads Battlefield	TN	2019	NA
Pinelands Natl. Reserve	NJ	1978	1,164,025
Red Hill Patrick Henry NMEM	VA	1986	NA
Roosevelt Campobello Intl. Park	NB	1964	2,722
Thomas Cole NHS	NY	1999	3.4
Touro Synagogue NHS	RI	1946	0.23
Wing Luke Museum of the Asian Pacific American Experience	WA	2013	NA

NA = Not available. (1) Year established or current designation received. (2) No federal facilities; state services may be available. (3) Located on Gila River Indian Reservation; not open to the public. (4) Incl. acreage added in 1988 expansion. (5) Shasta and Trinity units are administered by the Forest Service. Figure given is NPS acreage only. (6) Incl. acreage administered by U.S. Fish and Wildlife Service. (7) Comprises the Lower Delaware Wild and Scenic (2000) and Middle Delaware Scenic, whose year and acreage are given in table. (8) Incl. Lower Saint Croix acreage added in 1972.

National Trails System

Source: National Park Service and Bureau of Land Management, U.S. Dept. of the Interior; U.S. Forest Service, USDA

As of mid-2024, the National Trails System included 11 national scenic trails, 21 national historic trails, more than 1,300 national recreation trails, and 7 connecting and side trails. National scenic trails and national historic trails are established by Congress and administered by the NPS, Forest Service, or BLM. Official NPS units are indicated by an asterisk.

Name	Location	Year[1]	Length (mi)[2]
National Scenic Trails			
*Appalachian	ME to GA	1968	2,180+
Arizona	AZ	2009	807
Continental Divide	MT, ID, WY, CO, NM	1978	3,100
Florida	FL	1983	1,300
*Ice Age	WI	1980	1,200
*Natchez Trace	MS-AL-TN	1983	65
*New England	MA-CT	2009	215
*North Country	NY to ND	1980	4,600
Pacific Crest	CA-OR-WA	1968	2,650
Pacific Northwest	MT-ID-WA	2009	1,200
*Potomac Heritage	VA to PA	1983	924
National Historic Trails[3]			
Ala Kahakai	HI	2000	175
Butterfield Overland	MO, AR to CA	2023	3,292
California	MO, NE to CA, OR	1992	5,600
Capt. John Smith Chesapeake	NY to VA	2006	3,000
Chilkoot	AK	2022	17
El Camino Real de los Tejas	TX-LA	2004	2,580
El Camino Real de Tierra Adentro	NM-TX	2000	404
Iditarod	AK	1978	2,400
Juan Bautista de Anza	AZ-CA	1990	1,200
Lewis and Clark	PA to Pacific	1978	4,900
Mormon Pioneer	IL to UT	1978	1,300
Nez Perce (Nee-Me-Poo)	OR to MT	1986	1,170
Old Spanish	NM to CA	2002	2,700
Oregon	MO to OR	1978	2,170
Overmountain Victory	NC, SC, TN, VA	1980	330
Pony Express	MO to CA	1992	2,000
Santa Fe	MO, KS, OK, CO, NM	1987	1,203
Selma to Montgomery	AL	1996	54
Star-Spangled Banner	VA-DC-MD	2008	560
Trail of Tears	GA, NC to OK	1987	5,043
Washington-Rochambeau Revolutionary Route	MA to VA	2009	680+

(1) Year designation was received. (2) Authorized or currently completed length. (3) Trails may include both overland and water routes.

U.S. Forest Service Special Designated Areas

Source: U.S. Forest Service, U.S. Dept. of Agriculture; as of Sept. 30, 2023

These areas within the National Forest System have been specially designated by presidential proclamation or act of Congress. Size does not include acreage within National Forest boundaries not federally owned or administered by the Forest Service.

NGR = Natl. Game Refuge; NM = Natl. Monument; NRA = Natl. Recreation Area; NS(A) = Natl. Scenic (Area); NVM = Natl. Volcanic Monument; SMA = Special Management Area.

Area	Location	Estab.	Acreage
Admiralty Island NM	AK	1980	1,008,069
Allegheny NRA	PA	1984	23,789
Ancient Bristlecone Pine Forest	CA	2009	31,799
Apache Leap SMA	AZ	2014	714
Arapaho NRA	CO	1978	31,162
Ashley Karst NRA & Geologic Area	UT	2019	173,540
Barkshead (Ozark #2) NGR	AR	1926	5,851
Bear Creek NSA	VA	2009	5,122
Bears Ears NM	UT	2016	289,201
Beech Creek NSA & Botanical Area			
Beech Creek NSA	OK	1988	8,042
Beech Creek Natl. Botanical Area	OK	1988	538
Berryessa Snow Mountain NM	CA	2015	197,360
Big Levels NGR	VA	1935	12,147
Black Mountain (Ozark #5) NGR	AR	1926	18,929
Bowen Gulch Protection Area	CO	1993	10,862
Bridgeport Winter Recreation Area	CA	2009	7,250
Browns Canyon NM	CO	2015	11,822
Camp Hale-Continental Divide NM	CO	2022	53,628
Caney Creek (Ouachita #4) NGR	AR	1935	8,038
Cascade Head NS Research Area	OR	1974	7,156
Catahoula Wildlife Mgmt. Preserve	LA	1941	37,629
Cherokee Game Refuge #1	TN	1924	9,862
Chimney Rock NM	CO	2012	4,724
Columbia River Gorge NSA	OR-WA	1986	82,805
Burdoin Mountain SMA	WA	1986	7,294
Gates of Columbia R. Gorge SMA	OR-WA	1986	53,274
Rowena SMA	OR-WA	1986	3,537
Wind Mountain SMA	WA	1986	14,650
Coosa Bald NSA	GA	1991	7,044
Cradle of Forestry in America Natl. Historic Area	NC	1968	7,793
Crystal Springs Watershed	OR	2009	2,094
Cultus Creek	OR	2009	280
Ed Jenkins NRA	GA	1991	23,547
Flaming Gorge NRA	UT-WY	1968	188,665
Fossil Ridge Rec. Mgmt. Area	CO	1993	43,383
Frank and Jeanne Moore Wild Steelhead SMA	OR	2019	99,193
F. Marion Natl. Forest Wildlife Pres.	SC	1948	53,203
F. Church-River of No Return Spec. Mining Mgmt. Zone-Clear Creek	ID	1980	40,555
Giant Sequoia NM	CA	2000	328,568
Grand Canyon Natl. Game Preserve	AZ	1906	622,937
Grand Island NRA	MI	1990	13,302
Grey Towers Natl. Historic Site	PA	2004	95
Haw Creek (Ozark #4) NGR	AR	1926	3,783
Hells Canyon NRA	OR-ID	1975	635,244
Hermosa Creek SMA	CO	2014	70,396
Indian Nations Scenic Wildlife Area	OK	1988	44,519
James Peak Protection Area	CO	2002	17,510
Jemez NRA	NM	1993	48,872
Jewel Cave NM	SD	1908	2,540
Kelly Butte SMA	WA	1998	5,673
Kings River SMA	CA	1987	50,887
Land Between the Lakes NRA	KY-TN	1998	171,241
Livingston (Ozark #1) NGR	AR	1926	8,755
Misty Fiords NM	AK	1980	2,293,162
Moccasin (Ozark #3) NGR	AR	1926	4,048
Mono Basin NSA	CA	1984	51,394
Moosalamoo NRA	VT	2006	15,913
Mount Baker NRA	WA	1984	8,789
Mount Hood NRA	OR	2009	34,465
Mount Pleasant NSA	VA	1994	6,864
Mount Rogers NRA	VA	1966	114,998
Mount St. Helens NVM	WA	1989	112,867
Newberry NVM	OR	1990	56,596
Noontootly NGR	GA	1938	24,655
Norbeck Wildlife Preserve	SD	1920	32,079
North Cascades NSA	WA	1984	88,050
Oak Mountain (Ouachita #2) NGR	AR	1935	8,872
Ocala NGR	FL	1930	68,241
Opal Creek Scenic Recreation Area	OR	1996	13,666
Oregon Dunes NRA	OR	1972	30,227
Ouachita Wildlife Preserve	AR	1933	138,039
Quinault SMA	WA	1988	5,499
Piedra SMA	CO	1993	60,514
Pigeon Creek (Ouachita #1) NGR	AR	1935	8,107
Pine Ridge NRA	NE	1986	6,651
Pisgah Natl. Game Refuge	NC	1916	71,910
Rattlesnake NRA	MT	1980	60,092
Red Dirt Natl. Wildlife Mgmt. Pres.	LA	1941	40,213
Robert S. Kerr Botanical Area	OK	1988	7,971
Robert T. Stafford White Rocks NRA	VT	1984	36,442
Roubideau SMA	CO	1993	18,837
Saint Francis Dam NM	CA	2019	353
San Gabriel Mountains NM	CA	2014	336,926
Sand to Snow NM	CA	2016	70,942
Santa Rosa/San Jacinto Mtns. NM	CA	2000	70,056
Sawtooth NRA	ID	1972	732,192
Seng Mountain NSA	VA	2009	5,195
Sheep Mountain Game Refuge	WY	1924	21,569
Smith River NRA	CA	1990	323,051
Spring Mountains NRA	NV	1993	316,945
Spruce Knob-Seneca Rocks NRA	WV	1965	57,511
Tabeguache SMA	CO	1993	8,945
Tahquitz Natl. Game Preserve	CA	1926	18,813
Upper Big Bottom	OR	2009	1,581
Whiskeytown-Shasta-Trinity NRA	CA	1965	173,075
Winding Stair Mountain NRA	OK	1988	26,617

National Heritage Areas

Source: National Park Service (NPS), U.S. Dept. of the Interior; Alliance of National Heritage Areas

National Heritage Areas (NHAs) are designated by Congress for their national importance. NHAs are not units of the National Park system, though the NPS advises and provides limited financial assistance. NHC = Natl. Heritage Corridor. As of mid-2024.

Name	Location	Year[1]	Size (sq mi)
Abraham Lincoln	IL	2008	25,975
Alabama Black Belt	AL	2023	NA[2]
Appalachian Forest	MD-WV	2019	NA[3]
Arabia Mountain	GA	2006	64
Atchafalaya	LA	2006	10,400
Augusta Canal	GA	1996	3+
Baltimore	MD	2009	18
Blue Ridge	NC	2003	10,515
Bronzeville-Black Metropolis	IL	2023	NA
Cache La Poudre River*	CO	2009	45
Cane River	LA	1994	181
Champlain Valley Natl. Heritage Partnership	NY-VT	2006	NA[4]
Crossroads of the American Revolution	NJ	2006	2,155
Delaware & Lehigh NHC*	PA	1988	165
Downeast Maine	ME	2023	NA[5]
Erie Canalway NHC	NY	2000	4,834
Essex	MA	1996	550
Freedom's Frontier	KS-MO	2006	31,000
Freedom's Way	MA-NH	2009	994
Great Basin	NV-UT	2006	15,704
Gullah Geechee Cultural Heritage Corridor	NC, SC, GA, FL	2006	12,818
Illinois & Michigan Canal NHC	IL	1984	862
John H. Chafee Blackstone River Valley NHC	MA-RI	1986	720+
Journey Through Hallowed Ground*	PA, MD, WV, VA	2008	180
Kenai Mountains-Turnagain Arm	AK	2009	650
Lackawanna Heritage Valley	PA	2000	350
The Last Green Valley NHC	CT-MA	1994	1,105
Maritime Washington*	WA	2019	3,000
Maurice D. Hinchey Hudson River Valley	NY	1996	6,250
Mississippi Delta	MS	2009	10,976
Mississippi Gulf Coast	MS	2004	4,289
Mississippi Hills	MS	2009	NA[6]
Mormon Pioneer	UT	2006	16,070
MotorCities	MI	1998	10,000+
Mountains to Sound Greenway	WA	2019	2,344
Muscle Shoals	AL	2009	3,913
National Aviation Heritage Area	OH	2004	NA[7]
National Coal Heritage Area	WV	1996	5,300
Niagara Falls*	NY	2008	13
Northern Neck	VA	2023	1,070
Northern Plains	ND	2009	800
Northern Rio Grande	NM	2006	10,000
Ohio & Erie Canalway*	OH	1996	110
Oil Region	PA	2004	708
Rivers of Steel	PA	1996	5,000+
Sacramento-San Joaquin Delta	CA	2019	NA
Saint Croix	VI	2023	84
Sangre de Cristo	CO	2009	3,000+
Santa Cruz Valley	AZ	2019	3,325
Schuylkill River Greenways	PA	2000	1,700
Shenandoah Valley Battlefields Natl. Historic District	VA	1996	3,939
Silos & Smokestacks	IA	1996	20,000+
South Carolina NHC	SC	1996	NA[8]
South Park	CO	2009	1,800
Southern Campaign of the Revolution NHC	NC-SC	2023	NA
Southern Maryland	MD	2023	1,250
Southwestern Penn. Industrial Heritage Route (Path of Progress)*	PA	1988	500
Susquehanna	PA	2019	NA[5]
Tennessee Civil War[9]	TN	1996	42,144
Upper Housatonic Valley	MA-CT	2006	964
Wheeling	WV	2000	12
Yuma Crossing	AZ	2000	21

NA = Not available. * = Figure given is length of area. (1) Year designation was received. (2) Covers 19 counties. (3) 18 counties in both states. (4) 11 counties in both states. (5) 2 counties. (6) Parts of 30 counties. (7) 8 counties. (8) 17 counties. (9) Spans state of Tennessee.

Attractions in and Around Washington, DC

Most attractions are free. Hours are subject to change, especially on holidays, when some attractions may be closed. For a free official visitors guide and map, visit washington.org or call Destination DC at 1-800-422-8644. **Note:** Visit the listed websites for updated visitor information.

Arlington

Arlington National Cemetery, on the former Custis-Lee estate in Arlington, VA, was first used as a burial site during the Civil War. It is the final resting place of Pres. William Howard Taft and Pres. John F. Kennedy and his wife, Jacqueline Bouvier Kennedy Onassis. More than 400,000 U.S. military personnel from every major war are buried at Arlington. The **Tomb of the Unknown Soldier**, dedicated in 1921, is guarded by soldiers 24 hrs. a day. Unknowns from World War I, World War II, and Korea are interred in the plaza. (Vietnam Unknown was exhumed in 1998 and identified through DNA testing.)

A number of monuments and memorials are located throughout the 639-acre cemetery. They include the **Military Women's Memorial** (dedicated 1997), which honors the more than 3 mil women who have served or currently serve in the U.S. military.

Open daily 8 AM-5 PM. Arlington, VA; (877) 907-8585. **Website:** www.arlingtoncemetery.mil

The **U.S. Marine Corps War Memorial** stands north of Arlington National Cemetery. A bronze statue depicts the raising of the U.S. flag on Mt. Suribachi, Feb. 23, 1945, during the WWII battle of Iwo Jima. The memorial grounds are open daily 6 AM-midnight; (703) 235-1530. **Website:** www.nps.gov/gwmp/planyourvisit/usmc_memorial.htm

Bureau of Engraving and Printing

The Bureau of Engraving and Printing of the U.S. Treasury Dept. is the headquarters for the making of U.S. paper money. Open 8:30 AM-3:15 PM Mon.-Fri. (with extended summer hours). 14th and C Sts. SW; (866) 874-2330. **Website:** www.bep.gov

The Capitol

The United States Capitol was originally designed by Dr. William Thornton, an amateur architect, whose submission in 1793 won him $500 and a city lot. Three other architects designed or supervised construction of the Capitol before its completion.

The present cast-iron dome at its greatest exterior height measures 135 ft, 5 in. and is topped by the bronze Statue of Freedom, which stands 19½ ft and weighs 15,000 lbs. On its base are the words *E Pluribus Unum* (out of many, one).

The Capitol Visitor Center is open to the public Mon.-Sat., 8:30 AM-4:30 PM. Free guided tours are available by advance reservations. The Senate and House galleries are not part of the tour. To enter either gallery or to observe Congress in session, those living in the U.S. may obtain tickets from their U.S. representative or senators. Visitors from other countries may inquire at the House and Senate appointment desks. Between Constitution and Independence Aves., bounded by First St.; (202) 226-8000. **Website:** www.visitthecapitol.gov

Federal Bureau of Investigation

The Federal Bureau of Investigation discontinued tours of its headquarters following the Sept. 11, 2001, terrorist attacks. A self-guided tour called the FBI Experience, for U.S. citizens and permanent residents only, is available. Tours at 9 AM, 10 AM, 1 PM, and 2 PM Mon.-Fri.; visits must be arranged at least four weeks in advance through the office of one's congressional delegate. J. Edgar Hoover Bldg., Pennsylvania Ave., between 9th and 10th Sts. NW; (202) 324-3000. **Website:** www.fbi.gov

Folger Shakespeare Library

The Folger Shakespeare Library, on Capitol Hill, is a research institution with the world's largest collection of Shakespearean materials and other rare books and manuscripts of the Renaissance period. After a four-year renovation, the building reopened to visitors in June 2024. 201 E. Capitol St. SE; (202) 544-4600. **Website:** www.folger.edu

Holocaust Memorial Museum

The U.S. Holocaust Memorial Museum (opened 1993) documents the Holocaust through artifacts and interactive videos and educates the public on other genocides. The permanent exhibition is recommended for visitors age 11 and up.

The museum is open daily, 10 AM-5:30 PM. Entry into the permanent exhibition is timed. A limited number of same-day tickets are available online each day on a first-come, first-served basis; reserve advance tickets online for a fee. 100 Raoul Wallenberg Pl. SW; (202) 488-0400. **Website:** www.ushmm.org

Jefferson Memorial

Dedicated Apr. 13, 1943, the Thomas Jefferson Memorial stands on the south shore of the Tidal Basin in West Potomac Park. The circular stone structure combines architectural elements of the dome of the Pantheon in Rome and the rotunda designed by Jefferson for the Univ. of Virginia.

The memorial is open 24 hrs. a day and staffed 9:30 AM-10 PM. Ohio and E. Basin Drs. SW; (202) 426-6841. **Website:** www.nps.gov/thje/

Kennedy Center

The John F. Kennedy Center for the Performing Arts opened in 1971. Designed by Edward Durell Stone, it includes an opera house, concert hall, theaters, restaurants, and a library. Free tours available Mon.-Fri., 10 AM-4:30 PM, and Sat.-Sun., 10 AM-12:30 PM. 2700 F St. NW; (800) 444-1324. **Website:** www.kennedy-center.org

Martin Luther King Jr. Memorial

The MLK, Jr. Memorial (dedicated 2011) features a 30-ft figure of Dr. King, sculpted by artist Lei Yixin, emerging from a block of granite. The memorial is located on the Tidal Basin, between the Lincoln and Jefferson Memorials.

The memorial is open 24 hrs. a day and staffed 9:30 AM-10 PM. Independence Ave. SW and West Basin Dr. SW; (202) 426-6841. **Website:** www.nps.gov/mlkm/

Korean War Veterans Memorial

The Korean War Veterans Memorial, dedicated 1995 at the Mall's west end, features a multiservice formation of 19 combat-ready soldiers in ponchos. A granite wall, with images of service members, juts into the Pool of Remembrance.

The memorial is open 24 hrs. a day and staffed 9:30 AM-10 PM. Independence Ave. SW and French Dr. SW; (202) 426-6841. **Website:** www.nps.gov/kowa/

Library of Congress

Established by and for Congress in 1800, the Library of Congress extends its services to other government agencies and libraries, scholars, and the public. It contains more than 175 mil items in 470 languages, making it the world's largest library collection.

The Thomas Jefferson Building (Main Reading Room and exhibition galleries) is open to visitors with a free timed-entry pass, reservable online (a limited number of same-day passes are also available online), Tues.-Sat., 10 AM-5 PM (until 8 on Thursdays). First St. SE between Independence Ave. SE and East Capitol St.; (202) 707-8000. **Website:** www.loc.gov

Lincoln Memorial

Designed by Henry Bacon and dedicated in 1922, the Lincoln Memorial in West Potomac Park is a large marble hall enclosing a statue, designed by Daniel Chester French, of Abraham Lincoln seated in an armchair. The text of the Gettysburg Address is engraved in the south chamber, that of Lincoln's second inaugural speech in the north chamber.

The memorial is open 24 hrs. a day and staffed 9:30 AM-10 PM. Independence Ave. and French Dr. SW; (202) 426-6841. **Website:** www.nps.gov/linc/

Mount Vernon

Mount Vernon, George Washington's estate, is about 15 mi from Washington, DC, in northern Virginia. A one-and-a-half story house was first built on the site by Washington's father, Augustine Washington, in 1734. In 1754, George Washington began running and expanding the estate, named after Adm. Edward Vernon by Washington's half-brother Lawrence. The estate has been restored to its 18th-cent. appearance. Washington and his wife, Martha, are buried on the grounds.

Open all year; hours vary seasonally. Mount Vernon, VA; (703) 780-2000. General admission: adults $28, youth (6-11) $15, ages 5 and under free. **Website:** www.mountvernon.org

National Archives

Original copies of the Declaration of Independence, the Constitution, and the Bill of Rights are on display at the National Archives Museum. The National Archives also holds other U.S. government records, historic maps, photographs, and manuscripts.

Open daily 10 AM-5:30 PM. Constitution Ave. bet. 7th and 9th Sts. NW; (202) 357-5000. **Website:** www.archives.gov

National Gallery of Art

The National Gallery of Art, established by Congress, opened in 1941. The original West Building was designed by John Russell Pope. The East Building, opened in 1978, was designed by I. M. Pei. Galleries are open 10 AM-5 PM. Constitution Ave NW between 3rd and 9th Sts.; (202) 737-4215. **Website:** www.nga.gov

National World War II Memorial

The National WWII Memorial, opened in 2004, is dedicated to the approx. 16 mil veterans who served and the more than 400,000 who died in the war. The 8.25-acre site is at the east end of the Lincoln Memorial Reflecting Pool.

The 43-ft archways at the north and south entrances represent the Atlantic and Pacific theaters. A wall of 4,048 gold stars, each representing 100 American deaths, stands in an oval plaza surrounded by 56 pillars standing for the states, territories, and the Dist. of Columbia.

The memorial is open 24 hrs. a day and staffed 9:30 AM-10 PM. 17th St. and Independence Ave. SW; (202) 426-6841. **Website:** www.nps.gov/wwii/

The Pentagon

The Pentagon, headquarters of the Dept. of Defense, is the largest low-rise office building in the U.S. It houses some 26,000 employees in offices occupying 3,705,793 sq ft. The building was severely damaged when struck by a plane on Sept. 11, 2001.

The Pentagon offers one-hour public tours; all persons 18 and older on a tour must be U.S. citizens or permanent residents. Make reservations online 14-90 days in advance. Arlington, VA; (703) 697-1776. **Website:** www.defense.gov/Pentagon-Tours/

Franklin Delano Roosevelt Memorial

Opened in 1997, the FDR Memorial features four spaces with bronze statues and panels depicting FDR through his four terms in office. The 8.14-acre memorial is on the Tidal Basin.

Open daily with staff on grounds 9:30 AM-10 PM. Ohio and W. Basin Drs. SW; (202) 426-6841. **Website:** www.nps.gov/frde/

Smithsonian Institution

The Smithsonian Institution, established in 1846, is the world's largest museum and research complex. It holds some 157.3 mil artifacts and specimens in its trust. Seventeen of its 20 museums and the **National Zoo** are in the DC area. The **Smithsonian Institution Building** (or The Castle) houses the Smithsonian Visitor Center. Also on the National Mall are the **National Museum of African American History and Culture**, the **National Museum of African Art**, the **National Air and Space Museum**, **National Museum of American History**, the **National Museum of the American Indian**, the **Arts and Industries Building** (a special-events space), the **National Museum of Asian Art**, the **Hirshhorn Museum and Sculpture Garden**, and the **National Museum of Natural History**. Located nearby are the **National Postal Museum**, the **Smithsonian American Art Museum** and its **Renwick Gallery**, and the **National Portrait Gallery**. The **Anacostia Community Museum** is in SE DC. The Air and Space Museum's **Udvar-Hazy Center** is near Dulles Airport in Virginia.

Most museums are open daily, 10 AM-5:30 PM (later in summer); (202) 633-1000. **Website:** www.si.edu

Vietnam Veterans Memorial

Originally dedicated in 1982, the Vietnam Veterans Memorial recognizes those who served in the Vietnam War. The names of more than 58,000 Americans who lost their lives or remain missing are inscribed on polished black-granite walls arranged to form a V, designed by Maya Ying Lin.

Two additions have been made to Lin's design, the Frederick Hart sculpture *Three Servicemen* (1984), and the Vietnam Women's Memorial (1993), sculpted by Glenna Goodacre, honoring the approx. 11,000 women who served in Vietnam.

The memorial is open 24 hrs. a day and staffed 9:30 AM-10 PM. Constitution Ave. and Bacon Dr. NW; (202) 426-6841. **Website:** www.nps.gov/vive/

Washington Monument

The Washington Monument (dedicated 1885) is a tapering shaft, or obelisk, of white marble, 555 ft, 5⅛ in. in height and 55 ft, 1½ in. square at the base. Eight small windows, two on each side, are located on the observation deck at the 500-ft level.

The monument is open daily 9 AM-5 PM. 15th St. and Constitution Ave. NW; (202) 426-6841. **Website:** www.nps.gov/wamo/

White House

The White House, the president's residence, stands on 18 acres on the south side of Pennsylvania Ave., between the Treasury and the old Executive Office Building. The sandstone walls, quarried at Aquia Creek, VA, were first made white with lime-based whitewash in 1798, though the name did not become official until 1901.

Free tours of the residence's public areas are typically available Tues. through Sat., 9:30 AM-12:30 PM. Tour requests must be made 21-90 days in advance through one's member of Congress. Foreign visitors may make requests through their embassy. Tours are scheduled on a first-come, first-served basis. 1600 Pennsylvania Ave. NW; (202) 456-7041. **Website:** www.whitehouse.gov

The White House Visitor Center at 1450 Pennsylvania Ave. NW is open daily, 7:30 AM-4 PM; (202) 208-1631. **Website:** www.nps.gov/whho/

U.S. HISTORY: CHRONOLOGY OF EVENTS

1492 **Christopher Columbus** and crew sighted land Oct. 12 in what is now the Bahamas.

1513 **Juan Ponce de León** explored Florida coast.

1524 **Giovanni da Verrazzano** led French expedition along coast from Carolina north to Nova Scotia; entered New York Harbor.

1526 San Miguel de Guadalupe, **first European settlement** in what became U.S. territory, was established in the summer off South Carolina coast; abandoned in Oct.

1539 **Hernando de Soto** landed in Florida May 28; crossed Mississippi River, 1541.

1540 **Francisco Vásquez de Coronado** explored Southwest north of Rio Grande. **Hernando de Alarcón** reached Colorado River; **García López de Cárdenas** reached Grand Canyon. Others explored California coast.

1562 **First French colony** in what became U.S. territory founded on Parris Island off South Carolina coast; abandoned, 1564.

1565 **St. Augustine, FL**, oldest continuously occupied European settlement in U.S., founded Sept. 8 by Pedro Menéndez de Avilés. Spain ceded settlement to U.S. in 1821.

1579 **Sir Francis Drake** entered San Francisco Bay and claimed region for Britain.

1585 **First English colony** in America, sponsored by Sir Walter Raleigh, founded on **Roanoke Island**, off North Carolina coast; colony failed.

1587 Second colony attempted on Roanoke Island. Virginia Dare of colony became **first English infant born** in the New World. Settlers of second colony seemed to have vanished, 1590.

1607 Capt. **John Smith** and 105 cavaliers in three ships landed on Virginia coast and started Jamestown, **first permanent English settlement** in New World.

1609 **Henry Hudson**, English explorer of Northwest Passage, employed by Dutch, sailed into New York Harbor in Sept. and up Hudson to Albany. **Samuel de Champlain** explored Lake Champlain, to the north. Spaniards settled **Santa Fe, NM**.

1619 House of Burgesses, **first representative assembly** in New World, elected July 30 at Jamestown, VA. **Introduction of slavery:** first Black laborers in English North American colonies, brought to Jamestown in Aug. Chattel slavery laws passed in Massachusetts, 1641, and Virginia, 1661.

1620 **Pilgrims**, Puritan separatists, left Plymouth, England, Sept. 16 on *Mayflower*; reached Cape Cod Nov. 19; 103 passengers landed at Plymouth, Dec. 26. **Mayflower Compact**, signed Nov. 11, was agreement to form a self-government. Half of colony died during harsh winter.

1624 Dutch settled in Albany and along Hudson River, establishing the colony of **New Netherland** in May.

1626 Peter Minuit bought **Manhattan** for Dutch West India Co. from Manahatta Indians during summer for goods valued at $24; named island **New Amsterdam**.

1630 Settlement of **Boston** established by Massachusetts colonists led by John Winthrop; Winthrop began *The History of New England*. **William Bradford**, a governor of Plymouth Colony, began his chronicle *History of Plymouth Plantation (1620-1647)*, first published in entirety in 1856.

1634 **Maryland** founded as Catholic colony under charter to Lord Baltimore. Act of Toleration passed 1649 provided for religious tolerance.

1587: The first English baby, Virginia Dare, is born in the Americas in the Roanoke colony.

1635 Boston Latin School, **oldest public school** in continuous existence in U.S., founded Apr. 23.

1636 Roger Williams founded **Providence, RI**, in June, as a democratically ruled colony with separation of church and state. Charter granted, 1644. **Harvard College** founded; oldest institution of higher learning in U.S.

1640 **First book printed** in America, the so-called *Bay Psalm Book*.

1647 **Liberal constitution** drafted in Rhode Island. First law in America providing for **free compulsory basic education** enacted in Massachusetts.

1660 British Parliament passed first **Navigation Act** Dec. 1, regulating colonial commerce to suit English needs.

1661 Missionary John Eliot's translation of the New Testament into Algonquian became the **first Bible printed** in North America.

1664 British troops Sept. 8 seized New Netherland from Dutch. Charles II granted New Netherland and city of New Amsterdam to brother, Duke of York; both renamed **New York**. Dutch recaptured colony 1673 but ceded it to Britain Nov. 10, 1674.

1670 **Charles Town, SC**, founded by English colonists in Apr.

1673 **Regular mail service** on horseback instituted Jan. 1 between New York and Boston. **Jacques Marquette** and **Louis Jolliet** reached the upper Mississippi and traveled down it.

1674 Future **Salem witch trial** judge Samuel Sewall began renowned diary covering events through 1729.

1676 Bloody **Indian war** in New England ended Aug. 12. King Philip, Wampanoag chief, and Narragansett Indians killed. **Nathaniel Bacon** led planters against autocratic British Gov. Sir William Berkeley, burned Jamestown, VA, Sept. 19. Rebellion collapsed when Bacon died; 23 followers executed.

1678 A book of poetry by **Anne Bradstreet** (first published in Britain) revised and expanded for posthumous publication in Massachusetts. Considered first female poet in American colonies.

1679 Fire destroyed 150 houses in Boston. City imported **first fire engines** from England.

1681 John Bunyan's ***The Pilgrim's Progress*** published in America; became best seller.

1682 **René-Robert Cavelier, Sieur de La Salle**, claimed lower Mississippi River country for France and called it Louisiana Apr. 9. Had French outposts built in Illinois and Texas, 1684. Killed during mutiny, 1687. Spanish colonists became the **first Europeans to settle Texas**, at site of present-day El Paso.

1683 William Penn signed treaty with Delaware Indians Apr. 23 and made payment for **Pennsylvania** lands. The **first German colonists** in America settled near Philadelphia.

1689 New York's English colonial governor, **Sir Edmund Andros**, resigned after armed uprising in Boston on Apr. 18.

1690 **First colonial newspaper**, *Publick Occurrences*, published by Benjamin Harris but shut down after one issue for lack of official permission. Harris also published *New England Primer* for use as elementary school textbook. Large-scale **whaling** operations began in Nantucket, MA.

1692 Hysteria over **witchcraft** began in Salem Village (now Danvers), MA; 14 women and 6 men were executed by special court.

1697 *The Essays* of **Sir Francis Bacon**, first published in England in 1597, was published in America; it became a best seller.

1699 Former privateer Capt. **William Kidd** arrested and sent to England; hanged for piracy, 1701. French settlements made in Mississippi, Louisiana.

1702 Legislation enacted making **Church of England** the established church in Maryland.

1704 Indians and French allies attacked **Deerfield**, MA, Feb. 29; killed 40, captured and marched off 100. *Boston News Letter*, **first regular newspaper**, started by postmaster John Campbell.

1710 British-colonial troops captured French fort, Port Royal, Nova Scotia, in **Queen Anne's War**, 1702-13. France yielded Nova Scotia by treaty, 1713.

1712 **Enslaved Black laborers** rebelled against white colonists in New York City Apr. 6 and 9 whites were killed; 40 rebels put on trial and around 20 executed, with 6 committing suicide.

1716 **First theater** in colonies opened in Williamsburg, VA.

1726 **Great Awakening**, general revival of evangelical religion, began in colonies.

1776: Thomas Jefferson's final draft of the Declaration of Independence eliminates a phrase in an early draft that called slavery an "execrable commerce."

1731 America's **first subscription library** (paying members could freely borrow books) cofounded in Philadelphia by Benjamin Franklin.

1732 Benjamin Franklin published the **first *Poor Richard's Almanack***; published annually until 1757. Georgia, last of 13 colonies, chartered.

1733 **Influenza epidemic** swept through New York City and Philadelphia.

1735 Editor **John Peter Zenger** was acquitted of libel Aug. 5 in New York City after criticizing the British governor's conduct in office.

1739 A series of **slave uprisings** put down in South Carolina.

1741 Famous sermon "Sinners in the Hands of an Angry God," delivered July 8 at Enfield, MA, by Jonathan Edwards, one of the most important preachers in the **Great Awakening** religious revival. Danish navigator **Vitus Bering**, commanding Russian expedition, reached Alaska.

1744 **King George's War** pitted British and colonials versus French. Colonials captured Louisbourg, Cape Breton Isl., Nova Scotia, June 17, 1745. Returned to France 1748 by Treaty of Aix-la-Chapelle.

1752 According to legend, **Benjamin Franklin**, flying kite in thunderstorm, proved lightning is electricity, June 15; invented lightning rod. **Liberty Bell**, cast in England, was delivered to Pennsylvania.

1754 **French and Indian War** began with Ft. Necessity campaign in Pennsylvania. Skirmish May 28, battle at fort July 3-4. British moved Acadian French from Nova Scotia to Louisiana Oct. 8, 1755. British captured Québec Sept. 18, 1759, in battles in which French Gen. Joseph de Montcalm and British Gen. James Wolfe were killed. Peace pact signed Feb. 10, 1763. French lost Canada and Midwest. Delegates from seven colonies to New York for **Albany Congress**, July 19, approved plan of union by Benjamin Franklin; plan rejected by the colonies.

1757 **First streetlights** appeared in Philadelphia.

1764 **Sugar Act**, Apr. 5, placed duties on lumber, foodstuffs in colonies. First law passed by Parliament to specifically raise revenue from colonies, alleviate French and Indian War debts. British enforced this act, unlike with **Molasses Act** of 1733.

1765 **Stamp Act**, enacted by Parliament Mar. 22, required revenue stamps to help fund royal troops. Nine colonies, at Stamp Act Congress in New York Oct. 7-25, adopted Declaration of Rights. Stamp Act repealed Mar. 17, 1766. **Quartering Act**, requiring colonists to house British troops, went into effect Mar. 24.

1767 **Townshend Acts** levied taxes on glass, lead, paper, paint, and tea. In 1770 all duties except on tea were repealed.

1770 British troops fired Mar. 5 into Boston mob, killed five including **Crispus Attucks**, a Black man, reportedly leader of group; later called **Boston Massacre**.

1773 East India Co. tea ships turned back at Boston, New York, and Philadelphia in May. Cargo ship burned at Annapolis, Oct. 14; cargo thrown overboard at **Boston Tea Party**, Dec. 16, to protest the tea tax. **First museum** in the colonies was officially established in Charleston, SC; later named the Charleston Museum.

1774 **"Intolerable Acts"** of Parliament curtailed Massachusetts self-rule; barred use of Boston Harbor until dumped tea was paid for. **First Continental Congress** held in Philadelphia Sept. 5-Oct. 26; called for civil disobedience against British. Rhode Island **abolished slavery**.

1775 **Patrick Henry** addressed Virginia convention, Mar. 23, said, "Give me liberty, or give me death!" **Paul Revere**, **William Dawes**, and Dr. **Samuel Prescott**, Apr. 18, rode to alert patriots that British were on their way to Concord, MA, to destroy arms. At **Lexington**, MA, Apr. 19, Minutemen lost eight. On return from **Concord**, British suffered 273 casualties. Col. Ethan Allen (joined by Col. Benedict Arnold) captured **Ft. Ticonderoga** in New York, May 10, also Crown Point. Colonials headed for **Bunker Hill** and fortified nearby Breed's Hill, Charlestown, MA. Repulsed British under Gen. William Howe twice before retreating, June 17. Continental Congress June 15 named **George Washington** commander in chief; established a postal system, July 26. Benjamin Franklin became the **first postmaster general**.

1776 **Thomas Paine**'s *Common Sense*, famous pro-independence pamphlet, published Jan. 10; quickly sold some 100,000 copies. France and Spain agreed May 2 to provide arms to U.S. In Continental Congress June 7, Richard Henry Lee (VA) moved "that these United Colonies are, and of right ought to be, free and independent states." Resolution adopted July 2. **Declaration of Independence** approved July 4, signed Aug. 2. Col. William Moultrie's batteries at **Charleston, SC**, repulsed British sea attack June 28. Washington lost **Battle of Long Island** Aug. 27; evacuated New York. **Nathan Hale** executed as spy by British Sept. 22. Brig. Gen. Arnold's Lake Champlain fleet was defeated in **Battle of Valcour Island** Oct. 11, but British returned to Canada. Howe failed to destroy Washington's army at White Plains, NY, Oct. 28. Hessians captured Ft. Washington, Manhattan, and 3,000 men, Nov. 16; captured Ft. Lee, NJ, Nov. 20. Washington, in Pennsylvania, recrossed **Delaware River** Dec. 25-26, defeated Hessians at **Battle of Trenton**, NJ, Dec. 26.

1777 Washington defeated Lord Charles Cornwallis at **Princeton**, NJ, Jan. 3. Continental Congress, June 14, authorized an **American flag**, the Stars and Stripes. Maj. Gen. John Burgoyne's force of 8,000 from Canada captured **Ft. Ticonderoga**, NY, July 6. Americans beat back Burgoyne at Bemis Heights, Oct. 7, cut off British escape route. Burgoyne surrendered 5,000 men at Saratoga, NY, Oct. 17. **Articles of Confederation** adopted by Continental Congress, Nov. 15; took effect Mar. 1, 1781.

1778 **France signed treaty** of aid with U.S. Feb. 6; sent fleet. British evacuated Philadelphia, June 18.

1779 **George Rogers Clark** took Ft. Vincennes in what is now Indiana in Feb. **John Paul Jones** on the *Bonhomme Richard* defeated *Serapis* in British North Sea waters, Sept. 23.

1780 Charleston, SC, fell to the British May 12, but Loyalists were defeated in battle of **Kings Mountain**, NC, Oct. 7 in what Thomas Jefferson called "the turn of the tide of success." **Benedict Arnold** found to be a traitor Sept. 23. Arnold escaped, made brigadier general in British army.

1781 Bank of North America, **first commercial bank**, incorporated May 26. Cornwallis retired to **Yorktown, VA**. French fleet under Adm. François-Joseph-Paul, count de Grasse gained control of harbor; Washington's troops and French force led by Jean Baptiste de Rochambeau arrived near Yorktown, Sept. 28. After long siege, **Cornwallis surrendered** Oct. 19.

1782 New British cabinet agreed in Mar. to **recognize U.S. independence**. Preliminary agreement signed in Paris, Nov. 30. Use of **scarlet letter A**, sewn on clothing or branded on skin of adulterers, discontinued in New England.

1783 Massachusetts Supreme Court decision in final Quock Walker trial **declared slavery illegal**. Newspapers typically published weekly; **first regular daily newspaper**, *Pennsylvania Evening Post*, went on sale in Philadelphia, May 30. Britain, U.S. signed **Paris peace treaty**, Sept. 3, recognizing American independence; Congress ratified it Jan. 14, 1784. Washington ordered army disbanded Nov. 3, bade farewell to his officers at Fraunces Tavern, New York City, Dec. 4.

1784 Thomas Jefferson's proposal to **ban slavery in new territories** after 1802 was narrowly defeated, Mar. 1.

1785 Regular **stagecoach routes** established between Albany, NY; New York City; and Philadelphia.

1786 Delegates from five states at Annapolis, MD, Sept. 11-14 asked Congress to call a **constitutional convention**.

1787 **Shays's Rebellion** of debt-ridden farmers in Massachusetts failed, Jan. 25. **Constitutional convention** opened in

Philadelphia, May 25, with Washington presiding. Constitution accepted by delegates, Sept. 17. Delaware was first state to ratify it, Dec. 7; Pennsylvania and New Jersey followed. **Northwest Ordinance** adopted July 13 by Continental Congress for Northwest Territory, north of Ohio River, west of New York; made rules for statehood and guaranteed freedom of religion, support for schools, no slavery. ***Federalist Papers*** first appeared in *NY Independent Journal*.

1788 A large fire in **New Orleans**, then a Spanish territory, destroyed much of the city, Mar. 21. **Constitution adopted** June 21 after being ratified by the requisite ninth state (New Hampshire); also ratified by Georgia, Connecticut, Massachusetts, Maryland, South Carolina, Virginia, and New York throughout the year. **First U.S. senators elected** Sept. 30, from Pennsylvania.

1789 George Washington chosen president by all electors voting (73 eligible, 69 voting, 4 absent); **John Adams**, vice president, got 34 votes. **First Congress** met at Federal Hall, New York City, and declared Constitution in effect, Mar. 4; Washington inaugurated there Apr. 30; **first inaugural ball** held May 7. U.S. **State Dept.** established by Congress July 27. (Thomas Jefferson installed as first secretary of state Feb. 1790.) **War Dept.** created Aug. 7, with Henry Knox as secretary; **Treasury Dept.** created Sept. 2, with Alexander Hamilton to be secretary. **Supreme Court** created by Federal Judiciary Act, Sept. 24; **John Jay** confirmed by Congress as first Supreme Court chief justice, Sept. 26.

1790 First Supreme Court session held Feb. 2 in New York City. Congress, Mar. 1, authorized decennial **U.S. census**. Collection of data took 18 months. **Naturalization Act** (two-year residency) passed Mar. 26. John Carroll consecrated as **first American Catholic bishop**, Aug. 15. Congress met in **Philadelphia**, new temporary capital, Dec. 6.

1791 Bill of Rights, submitted to states, Sept. 25, 1789, went into effect Dec. 15. First Bank of the United States, **first bank chartered by federal government**, established in Philadelphia.

1792 Coinage Act established **U.S. Mint** in Philadelphia, Apr. 2. Gen. **"Mad" Anthony Wayne** made commander in Ohio-Indiana area, trained American Legion, established string of forts. Routed Indians at Fallen Timbers on Maumee River, Aug. 20, 1794; checked British at Fort Miami, OH, same year. **White House** cornerstone laid Oct. 13.

1793 Washington inaugurated for second term, Mar. 4, having received 132 electoral votes; **John Adams** again became vice president, having received second highest total, 77. Washington declared **U.S. neutrality**, Apr. 22, in war between Britain and France. Eli Whitney invented **cotton gin** (patented 1794), reviving Southern slavery.

1794 Whiskey Rebellion, western Pennsylvania farmers protesting liquor tax of 1791, suppressed by federal militia in Sept. **Jay's Treaty**, controversial treaty with Britain negotiated by John Jay, signed Nov. 19, ratified June 24, 1795. This treaty intended to settle long-standing differences between U.S. and Britain.

1795 U.S. bought peace from **Algerian pirates** by paying $1 mil ransom for 115 seamen Sept. 5, followed by annual tributes. Gen. Wayne signed **Treaty of Greenville** with Indians, opening Northwest Territory to settlers. Univ. of North Carolina became **first operating state university**.

1796 Washington's farewell address as president delivered Sept. 17. Warned against permanent alliances with foreign powers, big public debt, large military establishment, and devices of "small, artful, enterprising minority."

1797 John Adams inaugurated as second president Mar. 4, having received 71 electoral votes; **Thomas Jefferson** became vice president, having received 68. U.S. frigate *United States* launched at Philadelphia, May 10; ***Constellation*** at Baltimore, Sept. 7; ***Constitution*** (Old Ironsides) at Boston, Oct. 21.

1798 Alien and Sedition Acts passed by Federalists June-July; intended to silence political opposition. **War with France threatened** over French raids on U.S. shipping and rejection of U.S. diplomats. Navy (45 ships) and 365 privateers captured 84 French ships. USS *Constellation* took French warship *Insurgente*, 1799. Napoleon stopped French raids after becoming first consul.

1800 Federal government moved to **Washington, DC**.

1801 John Marshall named Supreme Court chief justice, Jan. 20. **Thomas Jefferson**, who had received same number of electoral votes as Aaron Burr in 1800 election, won out over Burr in House vote Feb. 17; Burr named vice president. **Tripoli declared war** June 10 against U.S., which refused added tribute to commerce-raiding Arab corsairs. Land and naval campaigns forced Tripoli to negotiate peace, June 4, 1805. **Oldest U.S. art institution**, Pennsylvania Academy of Fine Arts, founded in Philadelphia.

1804-06: Meriwether Lewis, William Clark, and the Corps of Discovery—including indispensable guide Sacagawea—explore the Missouri and Columbia Rivers from St. Louis to the Pacific Ocean and back.

1802 Congress established U.S. Military Academy at **West Point**, NY.

1803 Supreme Court, in ***Marbury v. Madison***, overturned U.S. law for first time, Feb. 24. Napoleon sold all of Louisiana, stretching to Canadian border, to U.S. for $11.25 mil in bonds, plus $3.75 mil indemnities to American citizens with claims against France. U.S. took title Dec. 20. **Louisiana Purchase** doubled U.S. area.

1804 Meriwether Lewis and **William Clark** expedition ordered by Pres. Thomas Jefferson to explore what is now Northwest U.S. Started from St. Louis May 14; ended Sept. 23, 1806, back in St. Louis. Vice Pres. **Aaron Burr** shot Alexander Hamilton in duel July 11 in Weehawken, NJ; Hamilton died next day.

1805 U.S. Marines aided by Arab mercenaries, Apr. 27, captured Tripolitan port of Derna. Major victory in war against **Barbary pirates**; inspiration for "to the shores of Tripoli" in Marines Corps hymn.

1807 Robert Fulton made **first practical steamboat trip**; left New York City Aug. 17 and reached Albany, NY, 150 mi away, in 32 hr. **Embargo Act** banned all trade with foreign countries, forbidding ships to set sail for foreign ports Dec. 22.

1808 Legislation **outlawing slave imports** goes into effect. Some 250,000 people were illegally imported as slaves, 1808-60.

1810 Third U.S. Census found population of 7,239,881. The enslaved population was put at 1,191,364 and the population of all other non-white free persons at 186,446.

1811 Indiana Territory governor William Henry Harrison defeated Indians led by Tenskwatawa, called the Prophet, in **Battle of Tippecanoe**, Nov. 7. Construction began on **Cumberland Road** in Cumberland, MD; road became important route to West. About 400 **slaves revolted** in Louisiana and marched on New Orleans. The insurrection was suppressed; two whites, some 75 slaves killed.

1812 War of 1812 had three main causes: Britain seized U.S. ships trading with France; Britain had seized 4,000 naturalized U.S. sailors by 1810; Britain armed Indians, who raided Western border. U.S. stopped trade with Europe 1807 and 1809. Trade with Britain only was stopped 1810. Unaware that Britain had raised blockade against France two days before, **Congress declared war** June 18. British took **Detroit** Aug. 16.

1813 Oliver H. Perry defeated British fleet at **Battle of Lake Erie**, Sept. 10. U.S. won **Battle of the Thames**, Ontario, Oct. 5, but failed in Canadian invasion attempts. York (Toronto) and Buffalo, NY, were burned.

1814 Troops under Andrew Jackson defeated Creek Indians led by Chief Weatherford at Battle of Horseshoe Bend in Alabama, Mar. 29, ending **Creek Indian War**, begun a year earlier. British landed in Maryland in Aug., defeated U.S.

force Aug. 24, **burned Capitol and White House**. Maryland militia stopped British advance, Sept. 12. British bombardment of Ft. McHenry, Baltimore, for 25 hr., Sept. 13-14, failed, inspiring **Francis Scott Key** to write the words to **"The Star-Spangled Banner."** U.S. won naval **Battle of Lake Champlain** Sept. 11. Peace treaty with Great Britain signed at Ghent, Belgium, Dec. 24.

1815 Some 5,300 British, unaware of peace treaty, attacked U.S. entrenchments near **New Orleans**, Jan. 8. British had more than 2,000 casualties; Americans lost 71. U.S. flotilla finally ended attacks by **pirates** from Ottoman states of Algiers, Tunis, Tripoli.

1816 Second Bank of the U.S. chartered Apr. 10. The **American Colonization Society**, which sought to address slavery issue by encouraging Black people to migrate to Africa, formed in Washington, DC, Dec. 1816-Jan. 1817.

1817 Thomas Hopkins Gallaudet established the **first free public school for the deaf** in Hartford, CT.

1818 Connecticut expanded **suffrage** among white male voters. Massachusetts followed suit in 1820, and New York in 1821, reducing or eliminating property qualifications.

1819 Spain ceded **Florida** to U.S. Feb. 22. American steamship *Savannah* made first part-steam-powered, part-sail-powered **crossing of Atlantic**, traveling from Savannah, GA, to Liverpool, England, in 29 days. **Washington Irving**'s *Sketch Book* became best seller.

1820 First organized immigration of Black people from **U.S. to Africa** began with a group of 86 sailing to Sierra Leone in Feb. Henry Clay's **Missouri Compromise** bill passed by Congress, Mar. 3. Slavery was allowed in Missouri but not west of the Mississippi River, north of 36° 30′ (the southern line of Missouri). Compromise repealed 1854.

1821 Emma Willard founded Troy Female Seminary, **first U.S. women's college**. Stephen Austin established **first American community in Texas**, San Felipe de Austin. **James Fenimore Cooper**'s *The Spy*, novel set during American Revolution, published and became a best seller.

1822 Tension between sports and academics surfaced when Yale College Pres. Timothy Dwight banned a **primitive form of football**, setting fines for violators.

1823 Monroe Doctrine, opposing European intervention in the Americas, enunciated by Pres. James Monroe Dec. 2. The **Hudson River School**, painters who focused on the beauties of nature, began to receive public attention.

1824 Pawtucket, RI, **weavers strike** is first organized factory strike in U.S. and one of earliest known involving women workers. **Slavery abolished** in state of Illinois Aug. 2.

1825 After a deadlocked election, **John Quincy Adams** was elected president by the House, Feb. 9. **Erie Canal** opened; first boat left Buffalo, NY, Oct. 26, reached New York City Nov. 4. John Stevens, of Hoboken, NJ, built and operated **first experimental steam locomotive** in U.S.

1826 Thomas Jefferson and **John Adams** both died July 4. **James Fenimore Cooper**'s *The Last of the Mohicans* published.

1827 Massachusetts became first state to pass a law providing for tax-supported **public high schools**.

1828 Baltimore & Ohio, the **first U.S. passenger railroad**, began operations July 4. South Carolina Dec. 19 declared right of **state nullification of federal laws**, opposing the "Tariff of Abominations." **Noah Webster** published his *American Dictionary of the English Language*.

1829 Andrew Jackson inaugurated as president, Mar. 4.

1830 Famous **debate** culminating Jan. 27 between Sen. **Daniel Webster** (MA) and Robert Hayne (SC), on state right to nullify federal law. **Mormon church** organized by Joseph Smith in Fayette, NY, Apr. 6. Pres. Jackson, May 28, signed **Indian Removal Act**, granting president authority to negotiate treaties whereby Indians living east of Mississippi R. give up lands in exchange for lands in West.

1831 William Lloyd Garrison began **abolitionist newspaper** *The Liberator* Jan. 1. **Nat Turner**, an enslaved man in Virginia, led local rebellion, starting Aug. 21; 57 whites killed. Troops called in, 100 rebellion participants killed. Turner captured, tried, and hanged Nov. 11.

1832 Black Hawk War in Illinois and Wisconsin Apr.-Sept. pushed Sauk and Fox Indians west across Mississippi.

1833 American Anti-Slavery Society founded in Philadelphia, Dec. 4. **Oberlin College** became first to adopt coeducation in U.S.

1835 According to tradition, the **Liberty Bell** cracked July 8 while tolling death of Chief Justice John Marshall. **Seminole Indians** in Florida under Osceola began attacks Nov. 1, protesting forced removal. The unpopular war ended Aug. 14, 1842; most of the Indians sent to Oklahoma. **Texas** proclaimed right to secede from Mexico; **Sam Houston** put in command of Texas army, Nov. 2-4. **Gold** discovered on Cherokee land in Georgia. Indians forced to cede lands, Dec. 20, and to cross Mississippi.

1836 Texans besieged at **Alamo** in San Antonio by Mexicans under Antonio López de Santa Anna, Feb. 23-Mar. 6; entire garrison killed. Texas independence had been declared, Mar. 2. At San Jacinto Apr. 21, Sam Houston and Texans defeated Mexicans. Ralph Waldo Emerson published his first work, *Nature*, espousing his philosophy of **transcendentalism**. Marcus Whitman, H. H. Spaulding, and wives reached Fort Walla Walla on Columbia River, OR, **first white women to cross the Continental Divide**, in the Rocky Mountains.

1838 Cherokee Indians forced to walk **"Trail of Tears"** from southeast U.S. to area in present-day Oklahoma. At least 4,000—nearly one-fifth of Cherokee population—are estimated to have died.

1841 First emigrant wagon train bound for California, 47 people, left Independence, MO, May 1; reached California Nov. 4. Edgar Allan Poe published one of the **first American detective stories**, *The Murders in the Rue Morgue*.

1842 Webster-Ashburton Treaty signed Aug. 9, fixing U.S.-Canada border in Maine and Minnesota. **First use of anesthetic** (sulfuric ether gas) in an operation performed by Georgia doctor Crawford Long.

1843 More than 1,000 settlers left Independence, MO, for Oregon May 22, arriving in Oct. via **Oregon Trail**.

1844 First message over first telegraph line sent May 24 by inventor Samuel F. B. Morse from Washington to Baltimore: "What hath God wrought?"

1845 Congress **overrode a presidential veto for the first time**, Mar. 3, after Pres. John Tyler vetoed a tariff bill. Congress of **Texas** voted for annexation by U.S., July 4; Texas admitted to Union, Dec. 29. **Edgar Allan Poe**'s poem "The Raven" published.

1846 Mexican War began after Pres. James K. Polk ordered Gen. Zachary Taylor to seize disputed Texan land settled by Mexicans. After border clash, U.S. declared war May 13; Mexico declared war May 23. About 12,000 U.S. troops took Vera Cruz Mar. 27, 1847, and Mexico City Sept. 14, 1847. Treaty signed Feb. 2, 1848, ended war, and Mexico ceded claims to Texas, California, and other territory. Bear flag of **Republic of California** raised by American settlers at Sonoma, June 14. Treaty with Britain June 15 set **Oregon territory** boundary at 49th parallel (extension of existing line). Expansionists had used slogan "54°40′ or fight." The term **"manifest destiny,"** coined by journalist in 1845, also came into play. **Mormons**, after violent clashes with settlers over polygamy, left Nauvoo, IL, for West under Brigham Young. They settled July 1847 at Salt Lake City, UT. Elias Howe invented **sewing machine**.

1847 First adhesive U.S. postage stamps—Benjamin Franklin 5¢, Washington 10¢—sold July 1. **Henry Wadsworth Longfellow**'s *Evangeline* published.

1838: Cherokee population is marched from their home in southeast U.S. to present-day Oklahoma on the "Trail of Tears."

1848 **Gold** discovered Jan. 24 in California; 80,000 prospectors emigrated in 1849. Lucretia Mott and Elizabeth Cady Stanton led Seneca Falls, NY, **Women's Rights Convention** July 19-20.

1850 Sen. Henry Clay's **Compromise of 1850** admitted California as 31st state Sept. 9, with slavery forbidden; made Utah and New Mexico territories; made **Fugitive Slave Law** harsher; and ended District of Columbia slave trade. **Nathaniel Hawthorne**'s *The Scarlet Letter* published.

1851 **Herman Melville**'s *Moby-Dick* published.

1852 **Harriet Beecher Stowe**'s *Uncle Tom's Cabin* published.

1853 Japan receives Comm. Matthew C. Perry, July 14. He negotiated treaty to **open Japan** to U.S. ships. New York City hosted **first World's Fair** in the U.S., beginning July 14. **Stephen Foster** published "My Old Kentucky Home."

1854 **Republican Party** formed at Ripon, WI, Feb. 28. Opposed Kansas-Nebraska Act, which left issue of slavery to vote of settlers. Act became law May 30. Treaty ratified with Mexico Apr. 25, providing for **Gadsden Purchase** of a strip of land. **Henry David Thoreau**'s *Walden* published.

1855 **First railroad train crossed Mississippi River** on river's first bridge, between Rock Island, IL, and Davenport, IA, Apr. 21. **Walt Whitman**'s *Leaves of Grass* published.

1856 Proslavery group sacked **Lawrence, KS**, May 21; abolitionist John Brown led antislavery contingent against Missourians at Osawatomie, KS, Aug. 30. Antislavery Republican Party's **first presidential nominee**, John C. Frémont, defeated by James Buchanan. Abraham Lincoln made 50 speeches for Frémont. **First U.S. kindergarten** opened in Watertown, WI.

1857 In **Dred Scott** case, which involved determination of constitutionality of already-repealed Missouri Compromise, Supreme Court decided Mar. 6 that enslaved individuals did not become free in a free state, and Black persons were not and could not be citizens. **Currier & Ives**, firm of American lithographers, issued their first print.

1858 **First Atlantic cable** completed by Cyrus W. Field Aug. 5. **Lincoln-Douglas debates** in Illinois, Aug. 21-Oct. 15.

1859 Edwin L. Drake drilled the **first commercially productive oil well** near Titusville, PA, Aug. 27. Abolitionist John Brown, with 21 men, seized U.S. armory at **Harpers Ferry**, WV, Oct. 16. U.S. Marines captured raiders, killing several. Brown was hanged for treason Dec. 2.

1860 Shoeworkers in Lynn, MA, went on strike Feb. 22. Within a week, strike spread to include 20,000 shoeworkers throughout New England in country's **largest strike to date**. **First Pony Express** between Sacramento, CA, and St. Joseph, MO, started Apr. 3. Republican **Abraham Lincoln** elected president Nov. 6 in four-way race.

1861 Seven southern states set up **Confederate States of America** Feb. 8, with **Jefferson Davis** as president. **Civil War** began as Confederates fired on **Ft. Sumter** in Charleston, SC, Apr. 12; they captured it Apr. 14. Pres. Lincoln called for 75,000 volunteers Apr. 15. Lincoln blockaded Southern ports Apr. 19, cutting off vital exports and aid. By May, 11 states had seceded. Confederates repelled Union forces at first **Battle of Bull Run**, July 21. **First transcontinental telegraph line** put in operation.

1862 Union forces were victorious in Western campaigns, took New Orleans May 1. Battles in East were largely inconclusive despite heavy casualties. The **Battle of Antietam**, in western Maryland Sept. 17, was bloodiest one-day battle of war; each side lost more than 2,000 men. **Homestead Act**, which granted free farms to settlers, approved May 20. **Land Grant Act**, which provided for public land sale to benefit agricultural education, approved July 7. It eventually led to establishment of state university systems.

1863 Pres. Lincoln issued **Emancipation Proclamation** Jan. 1, freeing "all slaves in areas still in rebellion." Union forces won major victory at Gettysburg, PA, July 1-3. Confederate forces under siege surrendered **Vicksburg, MS**, to Union forces under Gen. Ulysses S. Grant, July 4; control of Mississippi River in Union hands. About 1,000 were killed or wounded in **draft riots** in New York City; white mobs attacked and hanged Black individuals July 13-16. Pres. Lincoln gave his **Gettysburg Address** Nov. 19. Lincoln declared **Thanksgiving** a national holiday.

1863: President Abraham Lincoln's Emancipation Proclamation frees the enslaved population in seceding states.

1864 Gen. **William Tecumseh Sherman** marched through Georgia, taking Atlanta Sept. 1 and Savannah Dec. 22. **Sand Creek massacre** of Cheyenne and Arapaho Indians Nov. 29. Soldiers drove Indians out of village; about 150 killed.

1865 Gen. **Robert E. Lee surrendered** 27,800 Confederate troops to Gen. Grant at Appomattox Court House in VA, Apr. 9. J. E. Johnston surrendered 31,200 to Sherman at Durham Station, NC, Apr. 18. Last rebel troops surrendered May 26. Pres. Lincoln shot Apr. 14 by **John Wilkes Booth** in Ford's Theater, Washington, DC; died the following morning. Vice Pres. **Andrew Johnson** was sworn in as president. Booth was tracked down and fatally wounded, perhaps by his own hand, Apr. 26. Four co-conspirators were hanged July 7. **13th Amendment**, abolishing slavery except as a punishment for crime, ratified Dec. 6.

1866 Congress took control of Southern **Reconstruction**, backed freedmen's rights in legislation vetoed by Pres. Andrew Johnson; veto overridden by Congress, Apr. 9. **Ku Klux Klan** formed secretly in South to terrorize Black residents who voted. Disbanded 1869-71.

1867 **Alaska** sold to U.S. by Russia for $7.2 mil Mar. 30, through efforts of Sec. of State William H. Seward. Fraternal society the **Grange** was organized Dec. 4 to protect farmer interests. **Horatio Alger**'s *Ragged Dick* published.

1868 Pres. Andrew Johnson dismissed Sec. of War Edwin M. Stanton without Senate approval. **Johnson impeached** by the House Feb. 24 for violation of Tenure of Office Act, though charges were actually made in response to his opposition to congressional Reconstruction. He was acquitted by the Senate Mar.-May. **14th Amendment**, providing for citizenship of all persons born or naturalized in U.S. and subject to the jurisdiction thereof, ratified July 9. **Louisa May Alcott**'s *Little Women* published. ***The World Almanac***, a publication of the *New York World* newspaper, appeared for first time.

1869 First **Transcontinental railroad** completed; golden spike driven at Promontory Summit, UT, May 10, marking junction of Central Pacific and Union Pacific lines. Attempt to "corner" gold led to financial **"Black Friday"** in New York Sept. 24. **Woman suffrage law** passed in Wyoming Territory Dec. 10. **Knights of Labor** labor union formed in Philadelphia. By 1886, it had 700,000 members nationally.

1870 **15th Amendment**, making race no bar to voting rights, ratified Feb. 8. **First U.S. boardwalk** completed, in Atlantic City, NJ. **U.S. Weather Bureau** founded.

1871 **Great Chicago fire** destroyed city Oct. 8-11. **National Rifle Association (NRA)** founded.

1872 **Amnesty Act** May 22 restored civil rights to citizens of the South, except for 500 Confederate leaders. Congress established Yellowstone, **first national park**. James McNeill Whistler painted famous portrait known informally as **"Whistler's Mother."**

1873 **First U.S. postal card** issued May 1. **Jesse James** and his gang robbed their first passenger train July 21. Banks failed, panic began in Sept. **Depression** lasted five years. **"Boss" William Tweed** of New York City was convicted Nov. 19 of stealing public funds; he died in jail in 1878. New York's Bellevue Hospital started **first nursing school**.

1874 **Women's Christian Temperance Union** established in Cleveland. **First public zoo** in U.S. established in Philadelphia.

1875 Congress passed **Civil Rights Act** Mar. 1, giving equal rights to Black people in public accommodations and jury duty. Supreme Court invalidated act in 1883. First **Kentucky Derby** held May 17. First **Jim Crow segregation law** enacted, in Tennessee.

1876 **Alexander Graham Bell** patented the telephone Mar. 7. Col. **George A. Custer** and 264 soldiers of the 7th Cavalry were killed June 25 in "last stand," **Battle of the Little Bighorn**, MT, in Sioux Indian War. Democrat **Samuel J. Tilden** received majority of popular votes for president over Republican **Rutherford B. Hayes**, Nov. 7, but 22 electoral votes were in dispute. Congress agreed to certify Hayes as winner in Feb. 1877 after Republicans agreed to end federal Reconstruction of South.

1877 **Molly Maguires**—Irish terrorist society in mining areas of Scranton, PA—was broken up by hanging, June 21, of 11 leaders for murders of mine officials and police. Pres. Hayes sent federal troops to control violent national **railroad strike**, which began in July.

1878 **First commercial telephone exchange** opened, New Haven, CT, Jan. 28. **Thomas A. Edison** founded Edison Electric Light Co. on Oct. 15.

1879 **F. W. Woolworth** opened his first five-and-ten store, in Utica, NY, Feb. 22. French actress **Sarah Bernhardt** made her U.S. debut Nov. 8 at New York City's Booth Theater. Economist and social philosopher **Henry George** published *Progress & Poverty*, advocating single tax on land.

1881 **Clara Barton** founded **American Red Cross** May 21. Pres. **James A. Garfield** shot in Washington, DC, July 2, by mentally disturbed office seeker; died Sept. 19. Famous gun battle between the Earp brothers and outlaw rustlers Oct. 26 near the **OK Corral**, Tombstone, AZ. **Booker T. Washington** founded Tuskegee Institute for Black students. **Helen Hunt Jackson**'s *A Century of Dishonor*, about mistreatment of American Indians, published.

1882 **Chinese Exclusion Act**, barring immigration of Chinese laborers for 10 years, later made permanent, passed by Congress May 6; first significant law to restrict immigration to U.S.

1883 Civil Service Act, or **Pendleton Act**, passed Jan. 16, created foundations of American civil service system. The **Brooklyn Bridge** opened May 24 as world's longest suspension bridge. Transcontinental **Northern Pacific Railroad** was completed Sept. 8. **Buffalo Bill Cody**'s Wild West Show began its 30-year touring run.

1884 Switchback Railway—**first U.S. roller coaster** built as amusement park ride—opened at Coney Island in New York City. **Mark Twain**'s *The Adventures of Huckleberry Finn* published.

1885 **Washington Monument** dedicated Feb. 21.

1886 **Haymarket riot** and bombing, May 4, followed labor battles for 8-hr. work day in Chicago; seven police and four workers died. Eight anarchists found guilty Aug. 20; four hanged Nov. 11. **Coca-Cola** first sold, May 8, at Jacob's Pharmacy in Atlanta. Apache Indian **Geronimo** surrendered Sept. 4, ending last major Indian war. **Statue of Liberty** dedicated Oct. 28. **American Federation of Labor** (AFL) formed Dec. 8 by 25 craft unions.

1882: The Chinese Exclusion Act blocks immigration of new Chinese workers; workers from China played a key role in building the transformational railroads in the West.

1887 **Interstate Commerce Act** enacted Feb. 4, created Interstate Commerce Commission.

1888 **Great blizzard** struck Eastern U.S. Mar. 11-14, causing about 400 deaths. Ernest Thayer's poem **"Casey at the Bat"** recited for first time in public at New York City theater in May.

1889 U.S. opened 2-mil acre **Oklahoma District** to settlement Apr. 22, initiating land run; "sooner" settlers illegally entered the territory before that date to stake favorable claims. More than 2,200 lives lost in **Johnstown flood** (PA) May 31. **Electric lights** installed at White House.

1890 **Sherman Antitrust Act** passed July 2, began federal effort to curb monopolies. After decades of broken treaties and diminished reservations, U.S. Army massacre at **Wounded Knee**, SD, Dec. 29, kills about 250 Lakota Sioux men, women, and children; at least 25 soldiers were killed. **Jacob Riis**'s *How the Other Half Lives*, about city slums, published, instigating reform legislation in New York City. **Emily Dickinson**'s poems published, four years after her death.

1891 **Forest Reserve Act**, Mar. 3, let president close public forest land to settlement for establishment of national parks. **Carnegie Hall**, in New York City, opened May 5.

1892 **Ellis Island**, in New York Bay, opened Jan. 1 to receive immigrants; closed 1954. **Homestead strike** (PA) at Carnegie steel mills; 7 guards and 11 strikers and spectators shot to death July 6. James J. Corbett defeated John L. Sullivan Sept. 7 to become **first world heavyweight champion** under Marquess of Queensbury rules.

1893 **Columbian Exposition** world's fair held May-Oct. in Chicago. Financial panic led to four-year **depression**. **Mormon Temple** dedicated in Salt Lake City, UT.

1894 Thomas A. Edison's **kinetoscope**, for motion pictures (invented 1887), given first public showing Apr. 14. **Jacob S. Coxey** led army of unemployed from the Midwest, reaching Washington, DC, Apr. 30. Coxey arrested May 1 for trespassing on Capitol grounds; his army disbanded. **Pullman strike** began May 11 at railroad car plant in Chicago. Milton Hershey started **Hershey Chocolate Company**.

1895 **"America, the Beautiful"** appeared for first time, in church publication, July 4. **Stephen Crane**'s *The Red Badge of Courage* published.

1896 Supreme Court, in *Plessy v. Ferguson*, May 18, approved racial segregation under the **"separate but equal"** doctrine. **William Jennings Bryan** delivered "Cross of Gold" speech July 9; won Democratic Party nomination. **John Philip Sousa** composed "Stars and Stripes Forever" on Dec. 25.

1897 **Olney-Pauncefote Treaty** with Britain, Jan. 11, gave wide scope to arbitration in settling disputes; never ratified by U.S. John J. McDermott won **first Boston Marathon** Apr. 19. First Klondike gold arrived in San Francisco July 14, helping set off **Klondike gold rush**. **First subway service** in country opens to public in Boston, Sept. 1.

1898 U.S. battleship ***Maine*** exploded Feb. 15 in Havana, Cuba; 260 killed. U.S. blockaded Cuba Apr. 22 in aid of independence forces. U.S. declared **war on Spain** Apr. 24; destroyed Spanish fleet in Philippines May 1; took Guam June 20. U.S. took **Puerto Rico** July 25-Aug. 12. Spain agreed Dec. 10 to cede Philippines, Puerto Rico, and Guam, and approved independence for Cuba. Annexation of **Hawaii** signed by Pres. William McKinley, July 7.

1899 Filipino insurgents, unable to get recognition of independence from U.S., started guerrilla war Feb. 4. Their leader, Emilio Aguinaldo, captured May 23, 1901. **Philippine insurrection** ended 1902. Some 200,000 civilians and 20,000 Filipino troops died, mostly from disease and starvation. Pres. McKinley signed treaty officially ending **Spanish-American War**, Feb. 10. U.S. declared **Open Door Policy** Sept. 6, to make China an open international market. Philosopher **John Dewey**'s *School and Society*, advocating progressive education ("learn by doing"), published. Pianist Scott Joplin's "Maple Leaf Rag" published, popularizing **ragtime music**.

1900 **International Ladies' Garment Workers Union** founded in New York City June 3. Fought sweatshop working conditions. **Carry Nation**, Kansas temperance leader, began raiding saloons with a hatchet. U.S. helped suppress **Boxer Rebellion** in Beijing, China. Eastman Kodak Co. introduced the **Brownie camera**, popularizing picture-taking.

1901 Texas had first significant oil strike at **Spindletop** well near Beaumont, Jan. 10. U.S. withdrew troops from **Cuba** May 20, and Cuba became independent. Pres. **McKinley** shot Sept. 6 in Buffalo, NY, by anarchist Leon Czolgosz; died Sept. 14. Vice Pres. **Theodore Roosevelt** sworn in as youngest-ever president, at age 42 years, 11 months. **Booker T. Washington**'s *Up From Slavery* published.

1902 Permanent **Bureau of the Census** established Mar. 6. **Helen Keller** autobiography appeared in serial form.

1903 Treaty between U.S. and Colombia to have U.S. dig **Panama Canal** signed Jan. 22, but rejected by Colombia's Congress. Panama declared independence from Colombia with U.S. support Nov. 3; recognized by Pres. Roosevelt Nov. 6. U.S., Panama signed canal treaty Nov. 18. Wisconsin set first **direct primary voting system**, May 23. **Henry Ford** founded Ford Motor Co., June 16. Boston defeated Pittsburgh, 5 games to 3, Oct. 13 in **first modern World Series**. **First successful flight** in heavier-than-air mechanically propelled airplane by **Orville Wright** Dec. 17 near Kitty Hawk, NC, 120 ft in 12 sec. Later flight same day by **Wilbur Wright**, 852 ft in 59 sec. Improved plane patented, 1906. **Iroquois Theater fire** in Chicago killed about 600 out of 1,900 in audience, Dec. 30. Pioneering film ***Great Train Robbery*** produced.

1904 St. Louis hosted **first Olympics in U.S.**, July 1-Nov. 23. First section of **New York City subway** system opened, Oct. 27. **Ida Tarbell** published muckraking *The History of the Standard Oil Company*. **Henry James**'s last major novel, *The Golden Bowl*, published.

1905 Industrial Workers of the World, which advocated Marxian theory of class struggle between workers and capitalists, founded in Chicago, June 27. **Rotary**, oldest service club organization in U.S., founded in Chicago.

1906 San Francisco earthquake and fire, Apr. 18-19, caused more than 3,000 deaths and $400 mil in damages. **Upton Sinclair**'s *The Jungle*, which exposed working conditions in meat-packing industry, published. Helped spur passage of the **Pure Food and Drug Act** and **Meat Inspection Act** June 30.

1907 Financial panic and **depression** started Mar. 13. Pres. Roosevelt sent **"Great White Fleet"** of 16 U.S. battleships around the world in show of power.

1908 Springfield, IL, torn by **anti-Black rioting**, Aug. 14-15. Henry Ford introduced **Model T** car, priced at $850, Oct. 1.

1909 Adm. Robert E. Peary claimed to have reached **North Pole** Apr. 6 on sixth attempt, accompanied by Black explorer Matthew Henson and four Inuit men; may have fallen short. National Conference on the Negro convened May 30, leading to founding of **National Association for the Advancement of Colored People** (NAACP).

1910 Boy Scouts of America founded Feb. 8. Former Pres. Roosevelt called for **"new nationalism"** in famous speech in Kansas, Aug. 10.

1911 Building with New York City's **Triangle Shirtwaist Co.** factory caught fire Mar. 25; 146 died. Supreme Court ruled May 15 that **Standard Oil Co.** must be dissolved because it unreasonably restrained trade. **First transcontinental airplane flight** (with numerous stops) by C. P. Rodgers, from New York, NY, to Pasadena, CA, Sept. 17-Nov. 5; time in air 82 hr., 4 min.

1908: Ford's relatively affordable Model T is introduced, making car ownership more widely accessible.

1912 American Girl Guides founded Mar. 12; name changed in 1913 to **Girl Scouts**. U.S. Marines, Aug. 14, sent to **Nicaragua**, which was in default of loans to U.S. and Europe.

1913 16th Amendment, authorizing federal income tax, ratified Feb. 3. The **Armory Show** in New York City brought modern art to U.S. for first time, Feb. 17. **17th Amendment**, providing for direct popular election of U.S. senators (originally elected by state legislatures), ratified Apr. 8. **Federal Reserve System** authorized Dec. 23, in major reform of U.S. banking and finance.

1914 Ford Motor Co. raised basic wage rates from $2.40 for 9-hr. day to $5 for 8-hr. day, Jan. 5, increasing stability in labor force. When U.S. sailors were arrested in Tampico, Mexico, Apr. 9, Atlantic fleet was sent to **Veracruz**, occupied city. Pres. Woodrow Wilson proclaimed **U.S. neutrality** in the European war, Aug. 4. The **Panama Canal** officially opened Aug. 15. The **Clayton Antitrust Act** passed Oct. 15, strengthening federal antimonopoly powers.

1915 First transcontinental telephone call, New York to San Francisco, completed Jan. 25 by Alexander Graham Bell and Thomas A. Watson. British ship ***Lusitania*** sunk May 7 by German submarine; 1,198 passengers died, including 128 Americans. (In notice in morning newspapers the day *Lusitania* set sail, Germany had warned Americans against taking passage on British vessels.) As result of U.S. campaign, Germany issued apology and promise of payments, Oct. 5. U.S. troops landed in **Haiti**, July 28. Haiti became virtual U.S. protectorate under Sept. 16 treaty. Pres. Wilson asked for a military fund increase, Dec. 7. D. W. Griffith's film ***The Birth of a Nation*** released. William J. Simmons partly inspired by film to revive **Ku Klux Klan**, which peaks in 1920s.

1916 Gen. **John J. Pershing** entered Mexico in Mar. to pursue **Francisco (Pancho) Villa**, who had raided U.S. border areas. Forces withdrew Feb. 5, 1917. **Rural Credits Acts** passed July 17, followed by **Warehouse Act** Aug. 11; both provided financial aid to farmers. Bomb exploded during **San Francisco Preparedness Day parade** July 22, killed 10. Thomas J. Mooney, labor organizer, and Warren K. Billings, shoeworker, convicted 1917; both later pardoned. U.S. bought **Virgin Islands** from Denmark Aug. 4. U.S. established military government in the **Dominican Republic** Nov. 29. Jeannette Rankin (R, MT) elected to House of Representatives, **first woman to be a member of Congress**.

1917 Germany, suffering from British blockade, declared almost unrestricted **submarine warfare** Jan. 31. U.S. cut diplomatic ties with Germany Feb. 3 and formally **declared war** Apr. 6. Jones Act, passed Mar. 2, made **Puerto Rico** a U.S. territory, its inhabitants U.S. citizens. **Conscription law** passed May 18. First U.S. troops arrived in Europe June 26.

1918 Pres. Wilson set out his **14 Points** as basis for peace, Jan. 8. More than 1 mil American troops were in Europe by July. Allied counteroffensive launched at Château-Thierry July 18. War ended with signing of **armistice** Nov. 11. **Influenza pandemic** killed an estimated 50-100 mil worldwide, 675,000 in U.S.

1919 18th Amendment, providing for prohibition of manufacture, sale, or transportation of alcoholic beverages, ratified Jan. 16, to take effect on Jan. 16, 1920. **First transatlantic flight**, by U.S. Navy seaplane, left Rockaway, NY, May 8; stopped at Newfoundland, Azores, Lisbon May 27. **Boston police strike** Sept. 9, earliest strike conducted by government employees. About 250 **foreign-born radicals** deported Dec. 21 to Soviet Union.

1920 In national **Red Scare**, some 2,700 Communists, anarchists, and other radicals were arrested Jan.-May. **League of Women Voters** founded Feb. 14. Senate refused Mar. 19 to ratify **League of Nations Covenant**. **Nicola Sacco** and **Bartolomeo Vanzetti** accused of killing two men in Massachusetts payroll holdup Apr. 15; found guilty 1921. A seven-year campaign for their release failed; both executed Aug. 23, 1927. Verdict repudiated 1977 by proclamation of Massachusetts Gov. Michael Dukakis. **19th Amendment** ratified Aug. 18, giving women the vote. **First regular licensed radio broadcasting** began Aug. 20. **Wall St. bombing** in New York

1925: A Tennessee high school teacher, John T. Scopes, is tried and found guilty of violating the state's Butler Act, which banned the teaching of evolution in public schools.

City killed 39, injured 200-300, did $2 mil damage, Sept. 16. **Sinclair Lewis**'s *Main Street* published.

1921 Congress sharply curbed immigration, set **national quota system** May 19. **"Black Wall Street"** in Tulsa, OK, looted and burned by white rioters, May 31-June 1. Joint congressional resolution declaring **peace with Germany, Austria, and Hungary** signed July 2 by Pres. Warren G. Harding; treaties were signed in Aug. In so-called **Black Sox scandal**, eight Chicago White Sox players were banned from baseball Aug. 4 for conspiring with gamblers to throw the 1919 World Series. Limitation of Armaments Conference met in Washington, DC, Nov. 12-Feb. 6, 1922. Major powers agreed to curtail naval construction, outlaw poison gas, restrict submarine attacks on merchant vessels, and respect China's integrity.

1922 During nationwide coal strike, union miners killed some 21 strikebreakers at Herrin, IL, June 21-22, in incident referred to as the **Herrin Massacre**. **T. S. Eliot**'s *The Waste Land* published.

1923 **First sound-on-film motion picture**, *Phonofilm*, shown at Rivoli Theater, New York City, beginning in Apr. Pres. Calvin Coolidge addressed Congress, Dec. 6; **first radio broadcast of president's annual speech**.

1924 Law approved by Congress June 2 made all **Native Americans U.S. citizens. Immigration law** enacted May 24 excluded Asian immigrants and established permanent national quotas favoring N and W Europeans. **Nellie Tayloe Ross** and **Miriam (Ma) Ferguson** elected governor of Wyoming and Texas, respectively. Ross inaugurated as nation's **first woman governor** Jan. 5, 1925. **George Gershwin** wrote and premiered "Rhapsody in Blue."

1925 In so-called Monkey Trial, John T. Scopes found guilty of having taught **evolution** in Dayton, TN, high school and fined, July 24. **F. Scott Fitzgerald**'s *The Great Gatsby* published.

1926 Dr. Robert H. Goddard, Mar. 16, demonstrated **first liquid-fuel rocket**. Congress established **Army Air Corps** July 2. **Air Commerce Act** passed Nov. 2, established government agencies for development of airports, radio navigation, and other services. **Ernest Hemingway**'s *The Sun Also Rises* published.

1927 Capt. **Charles A. Lindbergh** left Roosevelt Field, NY, May 20 alone in ***Spirit of St. Louis*** on first New York-Paris nonstop flight. Reached Le Bourget airfield May 21, 3,610 mi in 33½ hr. *The Jazz Singer*, **first feature-length film** in which **spoken dialogue was part of narrative action**, released Oct. 6. The musical *Show Boat* opened in New York City Dec. 27.

1928 **Amelia Earhart** became first woman to fly across the Atlantic, June 17. **Herbert Hoover** elected president Nov. 6, defeating New York Gov. Alfred E. Smith, a Catholic.

1929 Gangsters killed seven rivals in Chicago **St. Valentine's Day massacre** Feb. 14, which won Al Capone control of Chicago's underworld. Stock market crash Oct. 29 marked end of past prosperity as stock prices plummeted. Stock losses for 1929-31 estimated at $50 bil; beginning of **Great Depression**. Albert B. Fall, former interior sec., was convicted of accepting $10,000 bribe in leasing of the **Elk Hills (Teapot Dome)** naval oil reserve; sentenced Nov. 1 to a year in prison and fined. **William Faulkner**'s *The Sound and the Fury* published.

1930 London **Naval Reduction Treaty** signed by U.S., Britain, Italy, France, and Japan Apr. 22; in effect Jan. 1, 1931; expired Dec. 31, 1936. **Hawley-Smoot Tariff** signed; rate hikes slash world trade. **Sinclair Lewis** became first American to win a Nobel Prize in literature. **Dashiell Hammett**'s *The Maltese Falcon* published.

1931 **Empire State Building** opened in New York City May 1, displacing NYC's Chrysler Building as world's tallest. **Al Capone** convicted of tax evasion Oct. 17. **Charlie Chaplin** film *City Lights* released.

1932 **Reconstruction Finance Corp.** established Jan. 22 to stimulate banking and business. Unemployment at 12 mil. Twenty-month-old **Charles Lindbergh Jr.** kidnapped Mar. 1; found dead May 12. Bruno Hauptmann found guilty Feb. 1935; executed Apr. 3, 1936. Unemployed World War I veterans demanding Congress pay promised bonus early launched **Bonus March** on Washington, DC, May 29. **Franklin D. Roosevelt** elected president for first time in Democratic landslide, Nov. 8. Chicago Bears won **first NFL title game** Dec. 18, defeating the Portsmouth (OH) Spartans, 9-0.

1933 Pres. Roosevelt named **Frances Perkins** U.S. sec. of labor; **first woman in U.S. cabinet**. Pres. Roosevelt ordered **all U.S. banks closed** Mar. 6. In a "100 days" special session, Mar. 9-June 16, Congress passed **New Deal**, including measures to regulate banks, distribute funds to the jobless, create jobs, raise agricultural prices, and set wage and production standards for industry. **Gold standard** dropped by U.S. in favor of "modified gold bullion standard"; announced by Pres. Roosevelt Apr. 19, ratified by Congress June 5. **Tennessee Valley Authority (TVA)** created by act of Congress, May 18. **Prohibition** ended in the U.S. as 36th state ratified **21st Amendment** Dec. 5. Pres. Roosevelt foreswore armed intervention in **Western Hemisphere** nations, Dec. 26.

1934 Pres. Roosevelt signed law creating **Securities and Exchange Commission**, June 6. U.S. troops pulled out of **Haiti**, Aug. 6.

1935 **Works Progress Administration (WPA)** instituted May 6. Rural Electrification Administration created May 11. National Industrial Recovery Act struck down by Supreme Court May 27. **Boulder Dam** (later renamed **Hoover Dam**) completed, May 29. **Social Security Act** passed by Congress Aug. 8-9. Comedian **Will Rogers** and aviator Wiley Post killed Aug. 15 in Alaska plane crash. Sen. **Huey Long**, former Louisiana governor, shot Sept. 8 by a political rival's son-in-law; died Sept. 10. George Gershwin's jazz opera ***Porgy and Bess*** opened Oct. 10 in New York. **Committee for Industrial Organization** (later Congress of Industrial Organizations) formed to expand industrial unionism Nov. 9.

1936 **Jesse Owens** won four gold medals at the **Berlin Olympics** in Aug. **Baseball Hall of Fame** founded in Cooperstown, NY. **Margaret Mitchell**'s *Gone With the Wind* published.

1937 Airship ***Hindenburg*** caught fire May 6 as it was landing in Lakehurst, NJ; 36 killed. **Golden Gate Bridge** in San Francisco opened May 27. **Joe Louis** knocked out James J. Braddock to become world heavyweight champ June 22. Aviator **Amelia Earhart** and copilot Fred Noonan disappeared July 2 near Howland Isl., in the Pacific. Pres. Roosevelt proposed judicial reforms that would allow him to appoint additional Supreme Court justices; his **"court-packing" plan** defeated. **Auto, steel labor unions** won first big contracts.

1938 **National minimum wage** enacted June 25. Orson Welles's radio dramatization of H. G. Wells's ***War of the Worlds***, Oct. 30, caused Martian invasion scare among some who had missed the introduction. **Seabiscuit** beat War Admiral in match race of the century, at Pimlico track, MD, Nov. 1. The work of folk artist Anna Mary Robertson Moses, **"Grandma Moses,"** discovered. **Thornton Wilder**'s *Our Town* produced on Broadway.

1939 Opera singer **Marian Anderson** performed for integrated crowd of 75,000 at Lincoln Memorial Apr. 9 after Daughters of the American Revolution refused to let Anderson sing in DC's Constitution Hall. **New York World's Fair**—theme: "The World of Tomorrow"—opened Apr. 30, closed Oct. 31. Reopened for second season May 11-Oct. 27, 1940. **Lou Gehrig**, seriously ill with disease that would come to bear his name, said farewell to fans at Yankee Stadium, July 4. Albert Einstein alerted Pres. Roosevelt to **A-bomb possibilities** in Aug. 2 letter. **U.S. declared its neutrality** in European war

1942: Pres. Franklin D. Roosevelt orders the relocation of 117,000 Japanese-Americans to detention camps for the duration of the war.

Sept. 5. Pres. Roosevelt proclaimed limited **national emergency** Sept. 8, unlimited emergency May 27, 1941. Both ended by Pres. Harry Truman, Apr. 28, 1952.

Pocket Books, **first paperback publisher** in U.S., established. **John Steinbeck**'s *The Grapes of Wrath* published. ***The Wizard of Oz*** and ***Gone With the Wind*** released, the latter to become highest-grossing film of all time (inflation-adjusted).

1940 U.S. OK'd sale of **surplus war material** to Britain June 3; announced transfer of 50 overaged destroyers Sept. 3. **First peacetime military draft** in U.S. history approved, Sept. 14. **Forty-hour work week** went into effect, Oct. 24. Pres. **Roosevelt** elected Nov. 5 to third presidential term. **Richard Wright**'s *Native Son* published.

1941 **Four Freedoms**—freedom of speech and religion, freedom from want and fear—termed essential by Pres. Roosevelt in speech to Congress Jan. 6. **Lend-Lease Act** signed Mar. 11 provided $7 bil in military credits for Britain. Lend-lease for USSR approved in Nov. Pres. Roosevelt signed executive order June 25 barring federal government and war contractors from **racial discrimination**. Order also established Fair Employment Practice Committee. The **Atlantic Charter**, 8-point declaration of principles, issued by Pres. Roosevelt and British Prime Min. Winston Churchill, Aug. 14. Japan attacked **Pearl Harbor**, Hawaii, 7:55 AM Hawaiian time, Dec. 7; 19 ships sunk or damaged, 2,403 dead. Pres. Roosevelt called it "a date which will live in infamy." U.S. declared war on Japan Dec. 8. Germany and Italy declared war on U.S. Dec. 11. U.S. responded with declaration of war later on same day. Japanese invaded **Philippines**, Dec. 22; Wake Island fell, Dec. 23. ***Citizen Kane***, directed by Orson Welles, released.

1942 Pres. Roosevelt issued executive order Feb. 19 authorizing relocation of Japanese-Americans. Federal government began forcibly moving 117,000 Japanese-Americans from West Coast to **detention camps**; exclusion lasted three years. Japanese troops took **Bataan** peninsula Apr. 8 and **Corregidor** May 6. **Battle of Midway** June 4-7 was Japan's first major defeat. Marines landed on **Guadalcanal** Aug. 7; last Japanese not expelled until Feb. 9, 1943. U.S., Britain invaded **North Africa** Nov. 8. **First nuclear chain reaction** (fission of uranium isotope U-235) produced at Univ. of Chicago under physicists Arthur Compton, Enrico Fermi, others, Dec. 2. The movie ***Casablanca***, starring Humphrey Bogart and Ingrid Bergman, released.

1943 ***Oklahoma!*** opened Mar. 31 on Broadway. Pres. Roosevelt signed June 10 pay-as-you-go income tax bill. Starting July 1, wage and salary earners were subject to **paycheck withholding tax**. **Detroit race riot** June 21 left 34 dead, 700 injured. Six killed in riot in New York City's **Harlem** section Aug. 2. U.S., Britain invaded **Sicily** July 9, Italian **mainland** Sept. 3. Marines in Nov. recaptured the **Gilbert Islands**, captured by Japan in 1941 and 1942.

1944 U.S., Allied forces invaded Europe at Normandy, France, on **"D-Day,"** June 6, in massive amphibious operation. **GI Bill of Rights**, providing benefits to veterans, signed by Pres. Roosevelt June 22. Representatives of the U.S. and other major powers met at **Dumbarton Oaks**, Washington, DC, Aug. 21-Oct. 7, to work out formation of postwar world organization that would become the **United Nations**. U.S. forces landed on **Leyte**, Philippines, Oct. 20. Pres. **Roosevelt** elected to fourth term as president Nov. 7. **Battle of the Bulge**, failed Nazi counteroffensive, waged Dec. 16 to Jan. 28, 1945.

1945 **Yalta Conference** met in the Crimea, USSR, Feb. 4-11. Pres. Roosevelt, Prime Min. Churchill, and Soviet leader Joseph Stalin agreed that their countries, plus France, would occupy Germany and that the Soviet Union would enter war against Japan. Marines landed on **Iwo Jima** Feb. 19, declared victory Mar. 26 after heavy casualties. U.S. forces invaded **Okinawa** Apr. 1, captured it June 21. Pres. **Roosevelt** died in Warm Springs, GA, Apr. 12; Vice Pres. **Harry S. Truman** became president. Germany surrendered May 7; May 8 proclaimed **V-E Day**. **First atomic bomb**, produced at Los Alamos, NM, exploded at Alamogordo, NM, July 16. Bomb dropped on **Hiroshima**, Japan, Aug. 6, killing about 75,000; bomb dropped on **Nagasaki**, Japan, Aug. 9, killing about 40,000. Japan agreed to surrender Aug. 14; formally surrendered Sept. 2. At **Potsdam Conference**, July 17-Aug. 2, leaders of U.S., USSR, and Britain agreed on disarmament of Germany, occupation zones, war crimes trials. **Empire State Building** struck accidentally by Army B-25 bomber, July 28, killing 14. U.S. forces entered **Korea** south of 38th parallel to displace Japanese Sept. 8. Gen. **Douglas MacArthur** took over supervision of Japan Sept. 9.

1946 **Steel strike** by 750,000 started Jan. 21, settled in four weeks. Strike by 400,000 **mine workers** began Apr. 1 (settled May 29); other industries (including rail, maritime) followed. Former Prime Min. Winston Churchill employed the phrase **"Iron Curtain"** in Mar. 5 speech at Westminster College in Fulton, MO. Atomic bomb tested off **Bikini Atoll** in Pacific, July 1. In all, U.S. conducted 23 nuclear tests between 1946 and 1958. **Philippines** given independence by U.S. July 4. Mother Frances Xavier Cabrini **first American to be canonized**, July 7. Dr. Benjamin Spock's *Baby and Child Care* published as **baby boom** began.

1947 Pres. Truman asked Congress for financial and military aid for Greece and Turkey to help combat Communist subversion, Mar. 12; **Truman Doctrine** approved May 15. UN Security Council voted Apr. 2 to place under U.S. trusteeship the **Pacific islands** formerly mandated to Japan. **Jackie Robinson** joined Brooklyn Dodgers Apr. 11, breaking color barrier in major league baseball. The **Marshall Plan** for U.S. aid to European countries proposed by Sec. of State George C. Marshall June 5. Congress authorized some $12 bil in next four years. **Taft-Hartley Labor Act** restricting labor union power vetoed by Pres. Truman June 20; Congress overrode veto. Air Force Capt. **Chuck Yeager** broke sound barrier, Oct. 14, in X-1 rocket plane. First families moved to new suburban Levittown, NY, development Oct. 1 (original construction ended 1951).

1948 **Organization of American States** (OAS) founded Apr. 30 by 21 countries. USSR halted all surface traffic into **West Berlin** June 24; in response, U.S. and British troops launched an **airlift**. Soviet blockade halted May 12, 1949; airlift ended Sept. 30. Pres. **Truman** elected Nov. 2, defeating NY Gov. Thomas E. Dewey in historic upset. Former State Dept. official **Alger Hiss** indicted Dec. 15 for perjury, after denying he had passed government documents to Whittaker Chambers to go to a Communist spy ring; convicted Jan. 21, 1950. **Kinsey Report** on sexuality in the human male published.

1949 North Atlantic Treaty Organization (**NATO**) established Aug. 24 by U.S., Canada, and 10 Western European nations, agreeing that an armed attack against one would be considered an attack against all. Eleven leaders of U.S. **Communist Party** convicted Oct. 14 of advocating violent overthrow of U.S. government; sentenced to prison. Supreme Court upheld convictions, 1951. Pres. Truman, Oct. 26, signed legislation raising **federal minimum wage** from 40¢ an hour to 75¢. **Arthur Miller**'s *Death of a Salesman* opened on Broadway.

1950 Masked bandits robbed **Brink's, Inc.**, Boston express office, Jan. 17, of $2.8 mil. Case solved 1956; eight sentenced to life. Pres. Truman authorized production of **H-bomb** Jan. 31. Special Senate committee to investigate organized crime established May 3, chaired by Sen. **Estes Kefauver** (D, TN).

North Korean forces **invaded South Korea** June 25. UN asked for troops to restore peace. Pres. Truman ordered Air Force and Navy to Korea June 27. Truman approved ground forces, airstrikes against North Korea June 30. U.S. sent 35 military advisers to **South Vietnam** June 27 and agreed to aid anti-Communist government. U.S. forces landed at **Inchon**, South Korea, Sept. 15. UN forces took Pyongyang Oct. 20, reached China border Nov. 20. China sent troops across border Nov. 26. U.S. banned shipments Dec. 8 to **Communist China** and to Asiatic ports trading with it.

Army **seized all U.S. railroads** Aug. 27 on Truman's order to prevent general strike; returned to owners in 1952. Two members of **Puerto Rican nationalist movement** tried to kill Pres. Truman Nov. 1.

Peanuts comic strip appeared in newspapers. Variety show ***Your Show of Shows*** debuted on TV. David Riesman's ***The Lonely Crowd*** published.

1951 **22nd Amendment**, limiting presidential term of office, ratified Feb. 27. **Julius Rosenberg**; his wife, **Ethel Rosenberg**; and **Morton Sobell** found guilty Mar. 29 of conspiracy to commit wartime espionage. Rosenbergs received death penalty. Sobell sentenced to 30 years; released 1969.

Pres. Truman removed Gen. **Douglas MacArthur** from Korea command Apr. 11 for unauthorized policy statements. **Korea cease-fire** talks began in July; lasted two years. Fighting ended July 27, 1953.

Transcontinental TV began Sept. 4 with Pres. Truman's address at Japanese Peace Treaty Conference in San Francisco. **Japanese peace treaty** signed in San Francisco Sept. 8 by U.S., Japan, and 47 other nations. **J. D. Salinger**'s *Catcher in the Rye* published. *I Love Lucy* sitcom premiered on TV.

1952 Pres. Truman ordered seizure of nation's **steel mills** Apr. 8 to avert strike; ruled illegal by Supreme Court June 2. **Peace contract** between West Germany, U.S., Great Britain, and France signed May 26. **Immigration** measure, passed over veto June 26-27, barred those deemed subversive and removed some barriers to Asian immigration, though quotas remained for nationalities and regions. **Puerto Rico** proclaimed commonwealth July 25, after referendum Mar. 3. Richard Nixon, as vice-pres. candidate, gave **"Checkers" speech**, so called because of sentimental reference to his dog Checkers, Sept. 23. **First hydrogen device explosion** Nov. 1 in Pacific. **Ralph Ellison**'s *Invisible Man* published.

1953 Federal jury in New York convicted 13 **Communist** leaders on conspiracy charges, Jan. 20. **Julius and Ethel Rosenberg** executed in electric chair, June 19, for relaying nuclear secrets to Soviet Union. **Korean War armistice** signed July 27. California Gov. **Earl Warren** sworn in Oct. 5 as 14th chief justice of U.S. Supreme Court.

1954 *Nautilus*, **first atomic-powered submarine**, launched at Groton, CT, Jan. 21. Five members of Congress were wounded in the House Mar. 1 by four **Puerto Rican independence supporters** who fired at random from a spectators' gallery.

At televised hearings, Apr. 22-June 17, before a Senate subcommittee, Army officials accused Sen. **Joseph McCarthy** (R, WI) of seeking preferential treatment for a draftee, and McCarthy accused Army of hindering probe of Communist infiltration. McCarthy was cleared in the hearings, but the Senate later voted to condemn him, 67-22, for abuse of the Senate during hearings and debates.

Supreme Court ruled unanimously May 17 that racial segregation in public schools was unconstitutional, in ***Brown v. Board of Education*** *of Topeka*. **Ernest Hemingway** won Nobel Prize in literature.

1955: The bus boycott beginning Dec. 5 in Montgomery, AL, led by Martin Luther King Jr., is a foundational event in the burgeoning civil rights movement.

1955 U.S. agreed Feb. 12 to help train **South Vietnamese army**. Supreme Court ordered "all deliberate speed" in **integration** of public schools, May 31. A summit meeting of leaders of **Big 4**—U.S., Britain, France, and USSR—took place July 18-23 in Geneva, Switzerland.

Rosa Parks refused Dec. 1 to give her seat to white man on bus in Montgomery, AL. Her arrest, detention, and conviction provided catalyst for Black community's planned boycott, fronted by Rev. **Martin Luther King Jr.**, of Montgomery's bus system, Dec. 5, 1955-Dec. 20, 1956. Bus segregation ordinance declared unconstitutional by federal court in 1956.

America's two largest labor organizations merged Dec. 5, creating **AFL-CIO**. Russian-born U.S. citizen **Vladimir Nabokov**'s *Lolita* published.

1956 Massive resistance to Supreme Court **desegregation rulings** was called for Mar. 12 by 101 Southern congressmen. U.S. Supreme Court, Apr. 23, unanimously ruled against **racial segregation** on intrastate buses.

Federal-Aid Highway Act signed June 29, creating **interstate highway system. First transatlantic telephone cable** activated Sept. 25. In Game 5, Oct. 8, Yankee right-hander Don Larsen pitched **only perfect World Series game. Eugene O'Neill**'s *Long Day's Journey Into Night* opened Nov. 7 on Broadway.

1957 Congress approved **Civil Rights Act of 1957**, Apr. 29, first such bill since Reconstruction to protect voting rights. Pres. Dwight D. Eisenhower signed act into law Sept. 9; provided for creation of Civil Rights Commission. The U.S. surgeon general July 12 said studies showed "direct link" between cigarette **smoking and lung cancer**.

Arkansas Gov. Orval Faubus (D) called National Guard Sept. 4 to bar nine Black students from entering all-white high school in **Little Rock**. Faubus complied Sept. 21 with federal court order to remove Guard, but local authorities ordered Black students to withdraw. Pres. Eisenhower sent troops Sept. 24 to enforce court order.

Jack Kerouac's *On the Road* published.

1958 Army launched **first U.S. Earth-orbiting satellite**, *Explorer I*, Jan. 31 from Cape Canaveral, FL; discovered Van Allen radiation belt. U.S. Marines sent to **Lebanon** to protect elected government from threatened overthrow July-Oct. Nuclear sub *Nautilus* made **first undersea crossing of North Pole** Aug. 5. Presidential aide **Sherman Adams** resigned Sept. 22 over scandal involving alleged improper gifts. **First domestic jet airline passenger service** in U.S. opened by National Airlines Dec. 10 between New York and Miami.

1959 **Alaska** admitted as 49th state, Jan. 3; **Hawaii** admitted as 50th, Aug. 21. **St. Lawrence Seaway** linking Atlantic Ocean and Great Lakes opened to traffic, Apr. 25.

Vice Pres. Richard Nixon, on tour of USSR, held **"kitchen debate,"** July 24, with Soviet Prem. Nikita Khrushchev at U.S. exhibit in Moscow. Prem. **Khrushchev** paid unprecedented visit to U.S. Sept. 15-27; made transcontinental tour.

Pres. Eisenhower issued injunction Oct. 12, upheld and made effective by Supreme Court Nov. 7, ending record **116-day steel strike.** In **quiz show scandal**, Columbia Univ. Prof. Charles Van Doren admitted to U.S. House subcommittee Nov. 2 that he had been coached before appearances on NBC-TV's *21* in 1956; he had won $129,000. William Wyler's ***Ben-Hur*** released; the movie won a record 11 Academy Awards the following year.

1960 **Sit-ins** began Feb. 1 when four Black college students in Greensboro, NC, refused to move from a Woolworth lunch counter after being denied service. By Sept. 1961, more than 70,000 students had participated in sit-ins. Pres. Eisenhower signed **Civil Rights Act** May 6.

A U.S. **U-2 reconnaissance plane** was shot down in the Soviet Union May 1; pilot Gary Powers captured. The incident led to cancellation of Paris summit conference; Powers traded for Soviet spy, 1962. A **birth control pill** approved as safe for first time by Food and Drug Administration May 9. Vice Pres. **Richard Nixon** and Sen. **John F. Kennedy** faced each other Sept. 26 in first in series of televised debates. Kennedy defeated Nixon to win presidency, Nov. 8. U.S. announced Dec. 15 its backing of rightist group in **Laos**, which took power the next day.

Alfred Hitchcock film ***Psycho*** released.

1961 U.S. severed diplomatic and consular relations with Cuba Jan. 3, after disputes over nationalizations of U.S. firms, U.S. military presence at Guantánamo base. U.S.-directed invasion of Cuba's **Bay of Pigs** Apr. 17 by Cuban exiles unsuccessfully attempted to overthrow the regime of Prem. Fidel Castro.

Peace Corps created by executive order, Mar. 1. **23rd Amendment**, giving DC citizens the right to vote in presidential elections, ratified Mar. 29. Alan B. Shepard Jr. rocketed from Cape Canaveral, FL, in a Mercury capsule May 5, in **first U.S.-crewed suborbital space flight**.

"Freedom Rides" from Washington, DC, across Deep South were launched May 20 to protest segregation in interstate transportation.

Joseph Heller's *Catch-22* published.

1962 Pres. Kennedy said Feb. 14 that U.S. military advisers in **Vietnam** would fire if fired upon. Lt. Col. John H. Glenn Jr. became **first American in orbit** Feb. 20 when he circled the Earth three times in the Mercury capsule *Friendship 7*.

In ***Baker v. Carr***, Mar. 26, U.S. Supreme Court ruled that constitutional challenges to unequal distribution of voters among legislative districts could be resolved by federal courts. **James Meredith** became first Black student at Univ. of Mississippi Oct. 1 after 3,000 federal troops put down riots.

A Soviet **offensive missile buildup** in Cuba was revealed Oct. 22 by Pres. Kennedy, who ordered naval and air quarantine on shipment of offensive military equipment to the island. He and Soviet Prem. Khrushchev agreed Oct. 28 on formula to end crisis. Kennedy announced Nov. 2 that missile bases in Cuba were being dismantled. **Rachel Carson**'s *Silent Spring* launched environmentalist movement.

1963 In ***Gideon v. Wainwright***, Mar. 18, Supreme Court ruled that all criminal defendants have a right to counsel.

March for civil rights began May 2 in Birmingham, AL; led to desegregation accord, which in turn sparked rioting and violence. Univ. of Alabama **desegregated** after Gov. George Wallace stepped aside when confronted by federally deployed National Guard troops June 11. Civil rights leader **Medgar Evers** assassinated June 12. On Aug. 28, 200,000 joined in **March on Washington** in support of Black demands for equal rights led by **Rev. Martin Luther King Jr.**; highlight was King's **"I Have a Dream" speech**.

Supreme Court ruled June 17 that laws requiring **recitation of Lord's Prayer or Bible verses** in public schools were unconstitutional. Pres. Kennedy, on Europe trip, addressed huge crowd in **West Berlin**, June 23. **Limited nuclear test-ban treaty** agreed upon July 25 by the U.S., the Soviet Union, and Britain. Four Black girls killed in bombing of **16th St. Baptist Church** in Birmingham, AL, Sept. 15.

South Vietnam Pres. **Ngo Dinh Diem** assassinated Nov. 2; U.S. had earlier withdrawn support. Pres. **Kennedy** shot and fatally wounded Nov. 22 as he rode in motorcade through downtown Dallas, TX. Vice Pres. **Lyndon B. Johnson** sworn in as president. **Lee Harvey Oswald** arrested and charged with murder but was himself shot and fatally wounded Nov. 24. Nightclub owner **Jack Ruby** convicted of Oswald's murder; Ruby died in 1967 while awaiting retrial following reversal of his conviction. **Betty Friedan**'s feminist work *The Feminine Mystique* published.

1964 **Panama** suspended relations with U.S. Jan. 9 after riots. U.S. offered Dec. 18 to negotiate new canal treaty. **The Beatles** appeared Feb. 9 on *The Ed Sullivan Show*. Supreme Court ruled Feb. 17 that **congressional districts** as near as practicable be equal in population. U.S. reported May 27 it was sending military planes to **Laos**.

Three **civil rights workers** reported missing in Mississippi June 22; bodies found Aug. 4. Eighteen white men tried. On Oct. 20, 1967, an all-white federal jury convicted seven of conspiracy in the slayings. Omnibus **civil rights bill** signed by Pres. Johnson July 2, banning discrimination in voting, jobs, public accommodations.

1964: The Beatles' appearance on *The Ed Sullivan Show* presages a pop cultural shift.

Congress Aug. 7 passed **Tonkin Gulf Resolution**, authorizing presidential action in Vietnam, after North Vietnamese boats reportedly attacked U.S. destroyers Aug. 2. (Resolution repealed, 1971.) Congress approved War on Poverty bill Aug. 11, providing for a domestic Peace Corps (**VISTA**), **Job Corps**, and antipoverty funding. The **Warren Commission** released a report Sept. 27 concluding that Lee Harvey Oswald was solely responsible for the Kennedy assassination. Pres. **Johnson** elected to full term, Nov. 3, defeating Sen. **Barry Goldwater** (R, AZ) in landslide. **Verrazzano-Narrows Bridge** opened in New York City, Nov. 21, with world's then-longest suspension span.

1965 In State of the Union address Jan. 4, Pres. Johnson outlined plans for **"Great Society,"** program of civil rights, antipoverty, and health-care legislation. Johnson in Feb. ordered continuous bombing of **North Vietnam** below 20th parallel.

Malcolm X assassinated by Nation of Islam members Feb. 21 at New York City rally. March from **Selma to Montgomery**, AL, Mar. 21-25, by Rev. Martin Luther King Jr. to demand federal protection of voting rights for Black citizens. Some 14,000 U.S. troops sent to **Dominican Republic** during civil war Apr. 28. All troops withdrawn by next year. Bill establishing **Medicare**, government health insurance program for elderly, signed by Pres. Johnson July 30.

New **Voting Rights Act**, which banned literacy tests and other voter qualification tests, signed Aug. 6. Arrest of Black motorist by white police officers precipitated **Watts riot** in predominantly Black Los Angeles neighborhood Aug. 11-16. Riots resulted in 34 deaths and $200 mil in property damage.

Major **immigration law**, signed Oct. 3, replaced national quota system with emphasis on immigrants' skills and family unification. **Electric power failure** blacked out most of northeastern U.S., parts of two Canadian provinces the night of Nov. 9-10.

1966 U.S. forces began firing into **Cambodia** May 1. Bombing of **Hanoi** area of North Vietnam by U.S. planes began June 29. By Dec. 31, 385,300 U.S. troops were stationed in South Vietnam, plus 60,000 offshore and 33,000 in Thailand.

Supreme Court ruled June 13, in ***Miranda v. Arizona***, that suspects must be read their rights before police questioning. **Medicare** began July 1. In **Univ. of Texas shooting** rampage, 25-year-old student Charles Whitman killed 15 and wounded 31 from tower observation deck on Austin campus, Aug. 1; shot dead by police.

Dept. of Transportation created, Oct. 15. Edward Brooke (R, MA) elected Nov. 8 as first Black U.S. senator in 85 years. Robert C. Weaver named secretary of newly created Dept. of Housing and Urban Development, becoming **first Black cabinet member**.

1967 Green Bay Packers beat Kansas City Chiefs, 35-10, in **first Super Bowl**, Jan. 15, in Los Angeles. Three astronauts died Jan. 27 in ***Apollo 1*** fire on ground at Cape Canaveral, FL. **25th Amendment**, providing for presidential succession, ratified Feb. 10. Pres. Johnson and Soviet Prem. **Aleksei Kosygin** met June 23 and 25 at Glassboro State College in New Jersey; agreed not to let any crisis push them into war.

Riots erupted among residents of predominantly Black **Newark**, NJ, July 12-17; 26 killed, 1,500 injured, more than 1,000 arrested. In **Detroit**, MI, July 23-30, 43 died, 2,000 injured; 5,000 left homeless by rioting, looting, and burning in city's Black neighborhoods. **Thurgood Marshall** sworn in Oct. 2 as first Black U.S. Supreme Court justice. **Antiwar march** on Washington, DC, Oct. 21-22, drew at least 70,000 participants. Carl B. Stokes (D, Cleveland) and Richard G. Hatcher (D, Gary, IN) elected **first Black mayors** of major U.S. cities Nov. 7.

1968 In **"Tet offensive,"** Communist troops attacked several provincial capitals and other major cities, including Saigon, Jan. 30, but suffered heavy casualties. Pres. Johnson **curbed bombing** of North Vietnam Mar. 31. Peace talks began in Paris May 10. All bombing of North halted Oct. 31.

Rev. **Martin Luther King Jr.** assassinated Apr. 4 in Memphis, TN. **James Earl Ray**, an escaped convict, pleaded guilty to slaying, was sentenced to 99 years. Students at **Columbia Univ.**, Apr. 23-24, seized school buildings in protest against school's involvement in military research, among other issues. Sen. **Robert F. Kennedy** (D, NY) shot June 5 in Los Angeles after celebrating presidential primary victories, died June 6. **Sirhan Sirhan** convicted of murder, 1969; death sentence commuted to life in prison, 1972.

Vice Pres. Hubert Humphrey nominated for president at **Democratic National Convention** in Chicago, marked by clash between police and antiwar protesters, Aug. 26-29. Republican nominee **Richard Nixon** won presidency, defeating Humphrey in close race Nov. 5.

Apollo 8 **orbited moon** in five-day mission, Dec. 21-27. North Korea released 82-man crew of the **USS *Pueblo*** Dec. 22, 11 months after seizing the ship in Sea of Japan; one crew member had been killed in battle.

1969 Expanded four-party **Vietnam peace talks** began Jan. 18. U.S. force peaked at 543,400 in Apr.; withdrawal started July 8. Pres. Nixon set Vietnamization policy of expanding role of South Vietnamese forces Nov. 3. Earl Warren retired upon swearing in **Warren Burger**, June 23, as Supreme Court chief justice. In incident that marked birth of **gay rights** movement, police clashed with patrons of gay bar, the **Stonewall Inn**, in New York City June 28.

U.S. astronaut **Neil Armstrong**, commander of the *Apollo 11* mission, became the **first person to set foot on the moon**, July 20, followed by astronaut **Edwin "Buzz" Aldrin**. Astronaut **Michael Collins** remained aboard command module.

Woodstock rock music festival near Bethel, NY, drew 400,000 people, Aug. 15-18. **Anti-Vietnam War demonstrations** held in cities across the U.S., marking Vietnam Moratorium day, Oct. 15; on Nov. 12, some 250,000 marched in Washington, DC. Massacre of hundreds of civilians by U.S. troops at **My Lai**, South Vietnam, in 1968 reported Nov. 16. **Kurt Vonnegut**'s *Slaughterhouse Five* published. ***Sesame Street*** launched on public TV.

1970 A federal jury Feb. 18 found the **"Chicago 7"** antiwar activists not guilty of conspiring to incite riots during 1968 Democratic National Convention. However, five were convicted of crossing state lines with intent to incite riots.

Three astronauts safely returned to Earth Apr. 17 after oxygen tank on ***Apollo 13*** ruptured. Lunar landing had been canceled. Millions of Americans participated in antipollution demonstrations Apr. 22 to mark **first Earth Day**.

U.S. and South Vietnamese forces crossed **Cambodian** borders Apr. 30 to get at enemy bases. Four students killed May 4 at **Kent State Univ.** in Ohio by National Guardsmen during war protest. In protest at **Jackson State Univ.** in Mississippi, two killed when police fired on protesters.

First female U.S. generals appointed June 11. **Postal reform** measure signed Aug. 12 created an independent U.S. Postal Service. Pres. Nixon, Dec. 31, signed **clean air bill** calling for development of cleaner auto engine and national air quality standards for 10 major pollutants. Garry Trudeau's ***Doonesbury*** comic strip launched in 30 papers.

1971 Charles Manson and three of his cult followers found guilty Jan. 25 of first-degree murder in 1969 slaying of actress Sharon Tate and six others. A court-martial jury Mar. 29 convicted Lt. **William Calley** in murder of 22 South Vietnamese at **My Lai** on Mar. 16, 1968. He was sentenced to life in prison Mar. 31, later reduced to 20 years.

Pres. Nixon, Apr. 14, relaxed 20-year **trade embargo with China**. *New York Times* began publishing June 13 classified **Pentagon Papers**, secret Pentagon study on U.S. involvement in Vietnam leaked by Daniel Ellsberg, military analyst consulting for government. Supreme Court June 30 upheld, 6-3, right to publish the documents. **26th Amendment**, lowering the minimum voting age to 18, ratified June 30. Pres. Nixon, Aug. 15, instituted 90-day **wage and price freeze**.

U.S. bombers initiated massive five-day strike Dec. 26 in North Vietnam in retaliation for alleged violations of agreements reached prior to 1968 bombing halt.

1972 Pres. Nixon arrived in **Beijing** Feb. 21 for eight-day visit to China, in "journey for peace." Joint communiqué released Feb. 27 called for increased Sino-U.S. contacts. Senate, Mar. 22, approved **Equal Rights Amendment** banning discrimination on basis of sex; sent measure to states for ratification.

North Vietnamese forces launched biggest attacks in four years across the demilitarized zone Mar. 30. The U.S. responded Apr. 15 with **resumption of bombing** of Hanoi and Haiphong. Pres. Nixon announced May 8 the mining of North Vietnam ports.

Gov. **George C. Wallace** (D, AL), campaigning for president at Laurel, MD, shopping center May 15, shot and seriously wounded. **Arthur Bremer** convicted Aug. 4, sentenced

1969: *Apollo 11* lands on the lunar surface; Neil Armstrong and Edwin "Buzz" Aldrin are first humans to walk on the moon.

to 63 years for shooting Wallace and three others. In **first visit of U.S. president to Moscow**, Pres. Nixon arrived May 22 for summit talks with Kremlin leaders that culminated in landmark strategic arms pact (**SALT I**). Five men arrested June 17 for breaking into Democratic National Committee offices in **Watergate** office complex in Washington, DC. U.S. Supreme Court in *Furman v. Georgia* June 29 ruled **capital punishment** as practiced was unconstitutional.

Mark Spitz won seven gold medals in world record times at the Munich Olympics in Aug.-Sept.

Pres. **Nixon** reelected Nov. 7 in landslide, carrying 49 states to defeat Sen. George McGovern (D, SD). Three astronauts, part of ***Apollo 17***, made 6th and last lunar landing on Dec. 11. Full-scale **bombing of North Vietnam** resumed after Paris peace negotiations reached impasse Dec. 18.

The Godfather, directed by Francis Ford Coppola, is released.

1973 In ***Roe v. Wade***, Supreme Court ruled, 7-2, Jan. 22, fetus not a person with constitutional rights and that right to privacy protected woman's decision to have abortion; states may not ban abortions during first three months of pregnancy but may regulate, not ban, abortions during second trimester.

Four-party **Vietnam peace pacts** signed in Paris Jan. 27. **End of military draft** announced on same day. Last U.S. troops left Vietnam Mar. 29. North Vietnam released some 590 U.S. prisoners by Apr. 1. Pres. Nixon announced, Apr. 30, resignation of top Nixon aides H. R. Haldeman and John Ehrlichman and firing of White House Counsel **John Dean** as a consequence of the widening **Watergate** scandal. Dean told Senate hearings June 25 that Nixon, his aides, and Justice Dept. had conspired to cover up Watergate facts. The U.S. officially ceased bombing in **Cambodia** at midnight Aug. 14 in accord with June congressional action.

Vice Pres. **Spiro Agnew**, Oct. 10, resigned and pleaded no contest to charge of tax evasion while Maryland governor. **Gerald R. Ford**, Oct. 12, became **first appointed vice president** under 25th Amendment; sworn in Dec. 6. The **"Saturday Night Massacre"** occurred Oct. 20, when Pres. Nixon ordered Atty. Gen. Elliot Richardson to fire Watergate special prosecutor **Archibald Cox**, who had sought handover of Nixon's subpoenaed **White House tapes**. Richardson refused to comply and resigned; Dep. Atty. Gen. William Ruckelshaus refused and was fired. Solicitor Gen. Robert Bork, as acting atty. gen., then fired Cox. Nixon administration named **Leon Jaworski**, Nov. 1, to succeed Cox.

Skylab, **first U.S. space station**, launched May 14. **Secretariat** became first Triple Crown winner since Citation in 1948 by winning Belmont Stakes June 9 in record time. **Billie Jean King** defeated Bobby Riggs in three straight sets in tennis's nationally televised "Battle of the Sexes," Sept. 20. Total **ban on oil exports** to U.S. imposed by Arab oil-producing nations Oct. 19-21 after outbreak of an Arab-Israeli war; lifted Mar. 1974. Congress overrode Nov. 7 Pres. Nixon's veto of **war powers bill** curbing president's power to commit forces to hostilities abroad without congressional approval.

1974 On Apr. 8, **Hank Aaron** of the Atlanta Braves hit his 715th career home run to break Babe Ruth's record.

House Judiciary Committee opened **impeachment** hearings May 9 against Pres. Nixon. John Ehrlichman and three **White House "plumbers"** found guilty July 12 of conspiring to violate the civil rights of the psychiatrist of **Pentagon Papers** leaker Daniel Ellsberg by breaking into psychiatrist's office. Supreme Court ruled, 8-0, July 24 that Pres. Nixon had to turn over 64 **audio tapes of White House conversations**. House Judiciary Committee, in televised hearings July 24-30, recommended **articles of impeachment** against Pres. Nixon, involving conspiracy to obstruct justice in Watergate cover-up, abuses of power, and defiance of committee subpoenas.

Pres. **Nixon** announced his **resignation**, Aug. 8, and stepped down the next day. His support in Congress had begun to collapse Aug. 5 after release of tapes appearing to implicate him in Watergate cover-up. Vice Pres. **Ford** sworn in Aug. 9 as 38th U.S. president. Pres. Ford, Aug. 20, nominated **Nelson Rockefeller** to be vice president; Rockefeller sworn in Dec. 10. Citing need to move on, Pres. Ford, Sept. 8, issued **pardon to Nixon** for any federal crimes he committed while president.

New York Times published article Dec. 22 on CIA engagement in illegal domestic surveillance. Reports of other apparently illegal CIA activities, recorded in **"family jewels"** file kept by the CIA, leaked out over the years.

1975 Former Atty. Gen. John Mitchell and ex-presidential advisers H. R. Haldeman and John Ehrlichman found guilty Jan. 1 of **Watergate cover-up** charges. Mitchell released 1979, last of 25 jailed over scandal to leave prison.

Bill Gates and Paul Allen founded Microsoft, Apr. 4. U.S. launched **evacuation from Saigon** of Americans and some South Vietnamese Apr. 29 as Communist forces completed takeover of South Vietnam; **South Vietnamese** government officially surrendered Apr. 30. U.S. merchant ship ***Mayaguez*** and its crew of 39 seized by Cambodian forces in Gulf of Siam May 12. In rescue operation, U.S. Marines attacked Koh Tang Island, recovered ship and crew but inadvertently left three Marines behind. Congress voted $405 mil for **South Vietnam refugees** May 16; 140,000 flown to U.S.

Publishing heiress **Patricia (Patty) Hearst**, kidnapped Feb. 5, 1974, by Symbionese Liberation Army (SLA), captured in San Francisco Sept. 18 with other militants. She was convicted Mar. 20, 1976, of bank robbery.

1976 In **right-to-die** case, New Jersey Supreme Court, Mar. 31, allowed comatose Karen Ann Quinlan to be removed from respirator; she survived until 1985. U.S. Supreme Court reinstated **death penalty**, July 2, subject to conditions.

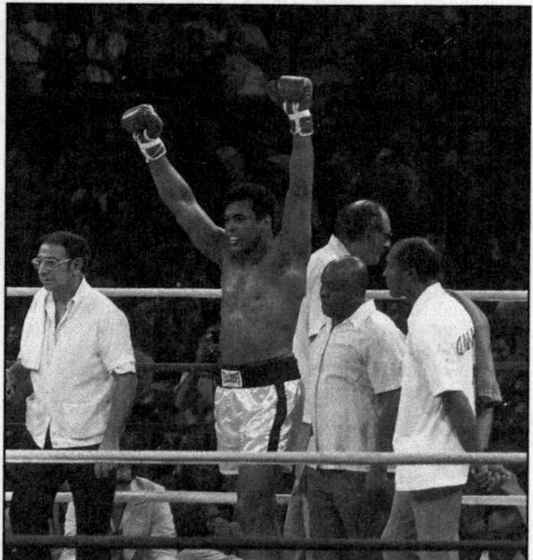

1975: Heavyweight champion Muhammad Ali defeats former champ Joe Frazier in their third and final match, dubbed the "Thrilla in Manila."

U.S. celebrated **200th anniversary of independence** July 4 with festivals, parades, and New York City's Operation Sail, gathering of tall ships from around the world. **"Legionnaire's disease"** killed 29 people who attended American Legion convention July 21-24 in Philadelphia.

Viking I made successful landing on Mars, July 20. Two U.S. officers on routine mission near DMZ slain by **North Korean soldiers** Aug. 18; North Korea stated "regret."

1977 Convicted murderer Gary Gilmore executed by Utah firing squad Jan. 17; **first use of capital punishment** in U.S. since 1967. Pres. Jimmy Carter Jan. 21 pardoned most Vietnam War **draft evaders**.

Natural gas shortage caused by severe winter weather led Congress Feb. 2 to approve emergency gas bill temporarily authorizing reallocation from surplus areas. Pres. Carter signed act Aug. 4 creating new cabinet-level **Energy Dept.** FBI Dec. 7 released 40,000 pages of previously secret files relating to **Kennedy assassination**.

George Lucas's first ***Star Wars*** film released.

1978 Senate voted Apr. 18 to turn over **Panama Canal** to Panama on Dec. 31, 1999; Mar. 16 vote had given approval to treaty guaranteeing area's neutrality after the year 2000. Californians, June 6, approved **Proposition 13**, state constitutional amendment slashing property taxes.

Supreme Court, June 28, ruled that while race could be a factor in admission to institutions of higher education, **numerical quotas** could not be used.

Egyptian Pres. **Anwar al-Sadat** and Israeli Prem. **Menachem Begin** reached accord on "framework for peace," Sept. 17, after Pres. Carter-mediated talks at **Camp David**. A mass murder-suicide, mostly by poisoning, kills more than 900 American members of the **Peoples Temple** cult led by Jim Jones in Guyana Nov. 18, 1978.

1979 Partial meltdown released radioactive material Mar. 28 at nuclear reactor on **Three Mile Island** near Middletown, PA. American Airlines DC-10 **jetliner crashed** May 25 after losing an engine following takeoff from Chicago, killing 275 people.

In speech July 15, Pres. Carter spoke of national "crisis of confidence" and outlined proposed 10-year, $140-bil program to reduce **dependence on foreign oil**. Militant followers of **Ayatollah Khomeini** took hostage some 90 people, including 66 Americans, Nov. 4 at **American embassy in Tehran**, Iran. Khomeini demanded return of ailing former Shah Muhammad Reza Pahlavi to stand trial.

1980 Pres. Carter announced, Jan. 4, economic **sanctions against USSR** in retaliation for Soviet invasion of Afghanistan. At his request, U.S. Olympic Committee voted, Apr. 12, against U.S. participation in **Moscow Summer Olympics**. At **Winter Olympics** in Lake Placid, NY, U.S. hockey team defeated Russian team Feb. 22, en route to gold medal in **"miracle on ice."**

Eight Americans were killed, Apr. 24, in **attempt to rescue hostages** held by Iranian militants. **Mt. St. Helens**, in Washington state, erupted May 18; the blast and later ones left 57 dead.

In sweeping victory, Nov. 4, **Ronald Reagan** (R) was elected president, defeating incumbent Pres. Carter. Former Beatle **John Lennon** was shot and killed by Mark David Chapman, Dec. 8, in New York City.

1981 Minutes after Reagan's inauguration Jan. 20, 52 **American hostages in Iran** were freed, after being held 444 days. Pres. **Reagan** was shot and seriously wounded, Mar. 30, in Washington, DC, along with a Secret Service agent, a police officer, and Press Sec. **James Brady**. John W. Hinckley Jr. was arrested, found not guilty by reason of insanity, and committed (released in 2016).

World's **first reusable spacecraft**, space shuttle ***Columbia***, sent into space, Apr. 12. U.S. Centers for Disease Control, June 5, reported first cases of what became known as **AIDS**. **Air controllers** went on strike Aug. 3; most were fired by Reagan after defying back-to-work order. Reagan, Aug. 13, signed **tax-cut legislation** expected to save taxpayers $750 bil over five years. The Senate, Sept. 21, confirmed **Sandra Day O'Connor**, 99-0, as **first female Supreme Court justice**.

1982 **Equal Rights Amendment** was defeated when ratification deadline passed June 30 with support from only 35 of the 38 states needed. The economy showed signs of recovery from a **recession** that began in mid-1981, as the Dow Jones industrial average, Oct. 13, hit highest level in 18 months.

NFL strike ended Nov. 16 after 57 days, with $1.6-bil pact. **Michael Jackson**'s album ***Thriller*** was released Nov. 30.

1987: Under pressure from activists, the FDA approves AZT, the first drug shown to be effective in treating HIV/AIDS.

Dr. Barney Clark became **first permanent artificial heart recipient**, Dec. 2.

1983 Pres. Reagan, Jan. 3, declared **Times Beach**, MO, a federal disaster area because of toxic **dioxin** in soil, prompting town's closure. **Harold Washington** (D) was elected Apr. 12 as **first Black mayor of Chicago**. On Apr. 20, Reagan signed bipartisan bill designed to save **Social Security** from bankruptcy.

Sally Ride became **first American woman to travel in space**, with launch June 18 of space shuttle *Challenger.* On Sept. 1, a **South Korean passenger jet** in Soviet air space was apparently misidentified and shot down; 269 people, including 61 Americans, killed. On Oct. 23, 241 U.S. service members were killed when a **suicide truck bomb** blew up Marine barracks in **Lebanon**. U.S. troops, with small force from six Caribbean nations, invaded **Grenada** Oct. 25; deposed Marxist regime.

1984 Seven regional companies took over local telephone service from **AT&T,** Jan. 1. On May 7, Vietnam War veterans reached $180-mil settlement with chemical companies in suit over the herbicide **Agent Orange**.

Former Vice Pres. **Walter Mondale** won Democratic presidential nomination, June 6. He chose Rep. **Geraldine Ferraro** (D, NY) as vice presidential candidate; first woman nominated to that post by a major party. Pres. Reagan signed bill July 17 cutting federal transportation aid to states that keep their **drinking age** under 21. **Reagan** was reelected Nov. 6 in Republican landslide, carrying 49 states for record 525 electoral votes.

1985 First international **AIDS conference** met in Atlanta, GA, Apr. 15-17. Philadelphia police bombed row house occupied by **MOVE radical group**, May 13; 11 killed, some 60 homes destroyed. On June 14, **terrorists seized TWA jet** after takeoff from Athens, Greece, with 153 aboard; 39 Americans held hostage for 17 days; one U.S. service member killed.

Reversing a highly unpopular decision, **Coca-Cola** said, July 10, it would resume marketing soda made under its original "Classic" formula. **Live Aid** rock concert, broadcast around the world July 13, raised $70 mil for **famine relief** in Ethiopia. On Oct. 7, four **Palestinian hijackers** seized Italian cruise ship ***Achille Lauro*** in the Mediterranean for two days; one American was killed. U.S. and Soviet leaders met at **summit in Geneva**, Nov. 19-20. **General Electric** agreed Dec. 11 to buy RCA Corp.

1986 U.S. officially observed **Martin Luther King Jr. Day** for first time, Jan. 20. Space shuttle ***Challenger*** exploded 73 seconds after liftoff, Jan. 28, killing six astronauts and teacher **Christa McAuliffe**. **Robert Penn Warren** named America's **first poet laureate**, Feb. 26.

The Senate, Sept. 17, confirmed **William Rehnquist** as Supreme Court chief justice (65-33) and **Antonin Scalia** as associate justice (98-0). Congress completed action Oct. 2 to override a Reagan veto and place economic sanctions on **South Africa**. On Nov. 3, news broke of the **Iran-Contra scandal**, involving secret U.S. sale of arms to Iran and diversion of proceeds to support anti-Communist "Contra" insurgents in Nicaragua.

Pres. Reagan, Nov. 7, signed measure giving legal status to some 2.7 mil **undocumented immigrants** who had applied for amnesty. In plea deal, financier **Ivan Boesky**, Nov. 14, agreed to pay $100 mil and serve time in prison for **insider trading**.

1987 Pres. Reagan produced nation's **first trillion-dollar budget**, Jan. 5. FDA, Mar. 20, approved AZT—first drug shown to be effective in fight against **AIDS**.

Senate and House committees held joint televised hearings, May 5-Aug. 3, investigating **Iran-Contra affair;** Pres. Reagan in speech to nation, Aug. 12, denied knowing of diversion of funds to Contras. An **Iraqi missile** killed 37 sailors on the **USS *Stark*** in the Persian Gulf, May 17; Iraq called it an accident.

Dow industrial average fell 508 points Oct. 19, ending bull market that began mid-1982. Pres. Reagan and Soviet leader **Mikhail Gorbachev**, Dec. 8, signed pact to dismantle all 1,752 U.S. and 859 Soviet intermediate- and shorter-range missiles.

1988 ***Phantom of the Opera*** opened Jan. 26; became longest-running Broadway show ever. In report issued May 16, Surgeon Gen. **C. Everett Koop** declared cigarettes addictive. U.S. missile fired from Navy warship *Vincennes* in the Persian Gulf mistakenly struck a commercial **Iranian airliner**, July 3, killing all 290 aboard.

George H. W. Bush (R) was elected president, Nov. 8, decisively defeating Massachusetts Gov. **Michael Dukakis** (D). **Pan Am Flight 103** exploded over **Lockerbie**, Scotland, due to terrorist bomb, Dec. 21; 270 killed, including 11 on the ground. Investment firm **Drexel Burnham Lambert** agreed, Dec. 21, to plead guilty to **insider trading** and other violations, and pay penalties of $650 mil.

U.S. suffered widespread **drought** conditions, the worst in over 50 years.

1989 ***Exxon Valdez*** struck Bligh Reef in Alaska's Prince William Sound, Mar. 24, spilling 10.8 mil gallons of oil. Former National Security Council staffer **Oliver North** was convicted, May 4, on charges related to **Iran-Contra scandal** (overturned in 1991). TV sitcom ***Seinfeld*** premiered July 5 on NBC.

Pres. George H. W. Bush signed $125 bil bailout measure, Aug. 9, to rescue **savings and loan industry.** Baseball legend **Pete Rose banned** from game for life, Aug. 24, for involvement with gamblers. **Hurricane Hugo** swept through the Caribbean and SE U.S. in Sept.; caused at least 86 deaths and billions in property damages. Army Gen. **Colin Powell**, Oct. 1, became first Black chairman of **Joint Chiefs of Staff.** An **earthquake** struck **San Francisco Bay** area just before a World Series game, Oct. 17, causing 63 deaths.

U.S. troops invaded **Panama**, Dec. 20, overthrowing government of **Manuel Noriega** Noriega surrendered to U.S. authorities; convicted and imprisoned for drug trafficking. **L. Douglas Wilder** (D) declared governor of Virginia Dec. 22, after recount; first elected Black governor in U.S.

1990 Junk bond financier **Michael Milken** pleaded guilty to fraud-related charges, Apr. 14; agreed to pay $500 mil in restitution and sentenced to 10 years in prison. U.S. fell into **recession** (July 1990-Mar. 1991). Pres. Bush signed **Americans With Disabilities Act** barring discrimination against and requiring accommodations for the disabled, July 26.

Operation Desert Shield forces left for Saudi Arabia Aug. 7, following invasion of **Kuwait** by Iraq. **David Souter** was confirmed Oct. 2 (90-9) to serve on **Supreme Court,** replacing retiring Justice **William Brennan**. Bush Nov. 15 signed new **Clean Air Act**, focused on limiting urban pollution, cancer-causing emissions from industrial sources.

1991 After **Iraq** rebuffed UN resolution to withdraw from **Kuwait**, U.S., with allies, launched massive air attacks against Iraq, Jan. 16, followed by ground war; with Kuwait liberated and Iraqi resistance collapsed, Bush declared cease-fire, Feb. 27.

U.S. Senate, voting 52-48 on Oct. 15, confirmed nomination of **Clarence Thomas** to replace retiring Justice **Thurgood Marshall**, after contentious hearings marked by allegations that Thomas had sexually harassed former aide **Anita Hill**.

1992 Trans World Airlines (**TWA**) filed for bankruptcy, Jan. 31. **Riots** swept South Central **Los Angeles** Apr. 29 after jury acquitted four white police officers on all but one count in the 1991 videotaped beating of Black motorist **Rodney King**. Death toll in L.A. violence was put at 53; two officers convicted Apr. 1993, in federal trial. **27th Amendment**, regarding congressional pay raises, ratified May 7.

Hurricane Andrew ravaged S Florida and Louisiana Aug. 24-26, causing 65 deaths. White supremacist and fugitive **Randall Weaver** surrendered Aug. 31 after 11-day FBI siege at his **Ruby Ridge**, ID, cabin, during which three others were killed.

Arkansas Gov. **Bill Clinton** (D) was elected president, Nov. 3, defeating Pres. **Bush** and independent **Ross Perot**. A UN-sanctioned military force, led by U.S. troops, arrived in **Somalia** Dec. 9. Presidents of U.S., Canada, and Mexico Dec. 17 signed North American Free Trade Agreement (**NAFTA**), which took effect Jan. 1, 1994.

1993 A bomb exploded in garage beneath the **World Trade Center** in New York City, Feb. 26, killing six; seven men found guilty of involvement by 1997. Four federal agents were killed, Feb. 28, during raid on **Branch Davidian** compound near **Waco**, TX; compound burned down Apr. 19, leaving over 70 cult members dead. Eleven members acquitted in deaths of federal agents.

Janet Reno became first female U.S. attorney general, Mar. 12. **"Motor-voter" bill** was signed by Pres. Clinton, May 20. **"Great Flood of 1993"** inundated parts of nine Midwestern states in summer, leaving about 50 dead and $15 bil in damages.

On July 19 Pres. Clinton announced **"don't ask, don't tell, don't pursue"** policy for homosexuals in the military (rescinded 2010). Senate, voting 96-3 on Aug. 3, confirmed nomination of **Ruth Bader Ginsburg** to Supreme Court, replacing retiring Justice **Byron White**. Clinton, Aug. 10, signed measure to reduce **federal budget deficits** by $496 bil over five years, through spending cuts and new taxes. **Brady Bill**, mandating background checks for gun buyers, was signed into law Nov. 30.

1994 Predawn **earthquake** in Los Angeles area, Jan. 17, claimed 61 lives. Pres. Clinton Feb. 3 lifted 19-year ban on U.S. trade with **Vietnam**. Byron De La Beckwith was convicted Feb. 5 of 1963 murder of civil rights leader **Medgar Evers**. Longtime CIA officer **Aldrich Ames** pleaded guilty, Apr. 28, to **spying** for Russians; received life in prison.

U.S. troops, Mar. 25, ended aid and peacekeeping mission in **Somalia**, begun in 1992. **Kenneth Starr** was named Aug. 5 as independent counsel to probe **Whitewater** affair. MLB players went on strike following Aug. 11 games. World Series canceled; strike ended Apr. 25, 1995.

Republicans gained control of Congress in Nov. 8 elections, after many years of Democratic control.

1995 Newt Gingrich (R, GA) elected U.S. House speaker. A bill to end Congress's exemption from federal labor laws, first in series of measures in Republicans' **"Contract With America,"** cleared Congress Jan. 17; signed into law Jan. 23. Pres. Clinton, Jan. 31, authorized $20-bil loan to **Mexico**. Peacekeeping responsibilities in **Haiti** transferred from U.S. to UN forces Mar. 31, with U.S. providing 2,400 soldiers.

Truck bomb exploded outside **Oklahoma City** federal office building Apr. 19, killing 168 people. Antigovernment extremist Timothy McVeigh was convicted as bomber; executed June 2011; a co-conspirator was sentenced to life. U.S. space shuttle ***Atlantis*** docked for first time with Russian space station *Mir*, June 29-July 4. The U.S. announced July 11 it was reestablishing **relations with Vietnam**.

Ten **Muslim militants** were convicted, Oct. 1, in failed plot to blow up **UN Headquarters** and assassinate political leaders. Former football star **O.J. Simpson** found not guilty Oct. 3 of June 1994 murders of his former wife and her friend. Hundreds of thousands of Black men participated in **Million Man March** in Washington, DC, Oct. 16, organized by **Louis Farrakhan**. Cumulative number of **AIDS** cases reported in the U.S. passed 500,000 by Oct. 31, with more than 310,000 deaths.

Five Americans were among seven killed, Nov. 13, in bombing of U.S. military post in **Riyadh, Saudi Arabia**. Budget impasse between Congress and Pres. Clinton led to partial **government shutdown** Nov. 14; operations resumed Nov. 20 under continuing resolutions. After U.S.-mediated talks outside Dayton, OH, warring parties in **Bosnia and Herzegovina** reached peace agreement Nov. 21.

A 1973 federal law imposing **55-mph speed limit** was repealed Nov. 28.

1996 U.S. Senate, Jan. 26, approved, 87-4, Second Strategic Arms Reduction Treaty (**START II**) with Russia. Congress, Mar. 28, approved **line-item veto**; struck down by Supreme Court, 1998.

Arkansas Gov. **Jim Guy Tucker** (D) and two other Clinton associates were convicted May 28 of fraud and conspiracy in **Whitewater** case. The antitax **Freemen** surrendered to federal authorities June 13 after 81-day standoff near Jordan, MT; four were convicted, July 1998, of conspiring to defraud banks. Bomb exploded at **Khobar Towers** military complex in Saudi Arabia, June 25, killing 19 U.S. service personnel. **Pipe bomb** exploded July 27 in **Atlanta**, GA, park during **Summer Olympics**; one person killed.

Major **welfare reform** bill signed into law, Aug. 22. Defense of Marriage Act (**DOMA**), passed by wide margins and signed Sept. 21, barred federal recognition of same-sex marriages (repealed by Congress, 2022). U.S. signed **Comprehensive Test Ban Treaty**, Sept. 24, which banned all nuclear weapons tests; Senate failed to ratify it.

Pres. **Clinton reelected**, Nov. 5, over Sen. **Bob Dole** (R, KS).

1997 Madeleine Albright sworn in as first woman sec. of state, Jan. 23. Former CIA official **Harold Nicholson** pleaded guilty, Mar. 3, to **spying for Russia**. Thirty-nine members of **Heaven's Gate** religious cult found dead in Rancho Santa Fe, CA, house Mar. 26, in apparent mass suicide.

The film ***Titanic*** was released Dec. 14; went on to win 11 Oscars, tying record set in 1960 by *Ben-Hur*.

1998 Media outlets in Jan. reported evidence of sexual relationship between Pres. Clinton and former White House intern **Monica Lewinsky**. Clinton initially denied affair, but in address to the nation, Aug. 17, acknowledged relationship that was "not appropriate." On Sept. 9, independent counsel **Kenneth Starr** sent findings to House, which, Dec. 19, approved two articles of **impeachment**.

"Unabomber" Theodore Kaczynski, arrested in Montana in 1993, pleaded guilty Jan. 22 to bombings that killed three people. **Bombs at U.S. embassies** in Kenya and Tanzania killed at least 257, Aug. 7. On Sept. 30, Pres. Clinton announced federal **budget surplus** of $79 bil for fiscal 1998, first since 1969.

Pres. Clinton, Nov. 13, agreed to pay $850,000 to **Paula Jones**, settling suit for an alleged unwanted sexual advance. **Matthew Shepard**, a gay Univ. of Wyoming student, died Oct. 12, after having been beaten and left for dead in what many deemed a hate crime. Biggest U.S. **tobacco companies**, Nov. 23, agreed to pay agreed to pay states and territories $206 bil over 25 years to cover public health costs.

1999 ***The Sopranos*** TV drama debuted, Jan. 10. Pres. Clinton was acquitted, Feb. 12, in **trial**. Perjury article drew 45 votes; obstruction of justice article drew 50-50 vote, short of the needed two-thirds majority.

Dr. **Jack Kevorkian** was convicted of second-degree murder Mar. 26 in death of **terminally ill man**.

Two teenagers killed 12 fellow students, a teacher, and themselves, Apr. 20 at **Columbine High School** in Littleton, CO. **John F. Kennedy Jr.** died, with his wife and sister-in-law, in crash of private plane July 16.

2000 Midnight celebrations marked changeover to year 2000; feared **Y2K** computer glitch fizzled. The first state law recognizing **same-sex civil unions** was enacted in **Vermont**, Apr. 26. U.S. and British scientists, June 26, announced they

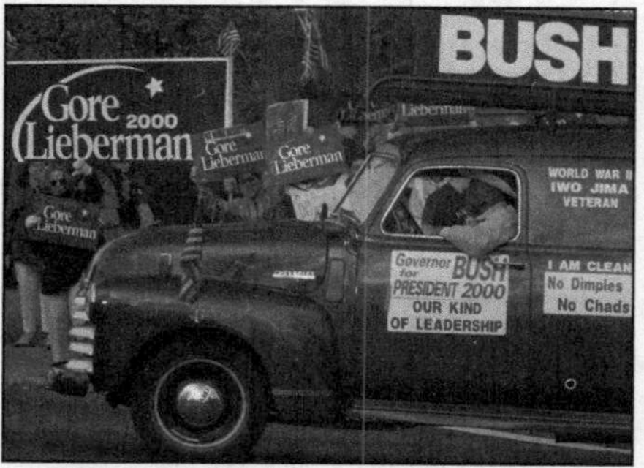

2000: The presidential election result remains disputed for over a month after Election Day amid manual recounts and legal jockeying by both the Bush and Gore campaigns.

2001: The attacks of Sept. 11, 2001, kill more than 2,750 people in New York City, including 343 firefighters.

had determined structure of the **human genome**. Six-year-old **Elián González** was returned to his father in **Cuba** June 28, after rescue from a refugee boat wreck in which his mother drowned.

Tiger Woods, at 24, became youngest player to win all four golf majors, July 23. FDA announced, Sept. 28, approval of **RU-486**, a pill that induces **abortion**. Seventeen U.S. sailors died Oct. 12 in terrorist bombing of **USS *Cole***, in Aden, Yemen.

With contested Nov. 7 **presidential election** result showing Texas Gov. **George W. Bush** (R) barely ahead of Vice Pres. **Al Gore** (D) in Florida, state's Supreme Court, Dec. 8, ordered partial manual recounts. U.S. Supreme Court reversed order, Dec. 12, leaving Bush as winner.

2001 **AOL-Time Warner megamerger** completed Jan. 11. **Colin Powell** sworn in Jan. 20 as first Black U.S. sec. of state. **U.S. Navy spy plane** collided with **Chinese fighter plane** over South China Sea Apr. 1, killing fighter pilot; 24 U.S. crew members detained in Hainan until U.S. apology, Apr. 12. Pres. Bush signed, June 7, $1.35-tril **tax-cut** package.

On **Sept. 11**, two hijacked airliners struck **World Trade Center twin towers** in New York City. A third plane destroyed part of the **Pentagon**; a fourth crashed in a field near **Shanksville**, PA. Some 3,000 people were killed, including about 2,750 at World Trade Center. U.S. and Britain, Oct. 7, launched airstrikes against Afghan-based terrorist organization **al-Qaeda** and Afghanistan's ruling **Taliban** militia. Bush Oct. 26 signed USA **Patriot Act**, with wide-ranging provisions aimed at preventing terrorism.

Taliban surrendered Kabul, Nov. 13, and fled from Kandahar, their stronghold, Dec. 7. U.S. government, Dec. 11, indicted al-Qaeda operative **Zacarias Moussaoui** as **Sept. 11 co-conspirator**; sentenced in 2006 to life. Five people died, Oct. 5-Nov. 21, from exposure to **anthrax** through letters in the U.S. mail; a suspect later died by suicide.

Energy-trading company **Enron** filed for bankruptcy, Dec. 2. Bush announced, Dec. 13, U.S. withdrawal from 1972 **Antiballistic Missile Treaty** with Russians. **"Shoe bomber"** prevented from in-flight attack on airliner, Dec. 22.

2002 **Taliban and al-Qaeda fighters** captured in **Afghanistan** sent to U.S. naval base at **Guantánamo Bay** in Cuba, starting Jan. 11. In State of the Union address, Jan. 29, Pres. Bush called Iran, Iraq, and North Korea part of **"axis of evil."** By early Mar., 200 U.S. troops were involved in **Operation Anaconda** against al-Qaeda and Taliban forces in **Afghanistan**.

Independent prosecutor's report, Mar. 20, found **insufficient evidence** that Pres. Clinton or Hillary Clinton committed a crime in connection with **Whitewater**. Pres. Bush, Mar. 27, signed McCain-Feingold **campaign-finance reform bill**, which restricted "soft money" donations and issue-advocacy ads (partly struck down by Supreme Court, 2007). On Oct. 10-11 the House, 296-133, and Senate, 77-23, gave Bush backing to use military force against **Iraq**. Bush administration revealed Oct. 16 that **North Korea** had acknowledged developing **nuclear arms** in violation of a 1994 agreement. Bush signed measure, Nov. 25, creating cabinet **Dept. of Homeland Security**.

U.S. **Catholic bishops**, Nov. 13, tightened policies for dealing with priests who **sexually abuse** minors.

2003 Space shuttle ***Columbia*** **broke apart** Feb. 1 during descent; all seven crew were killed. Senate, Mar. 6, approved **Strategic Offensive Reductions Treaty** (SORT) for reducing nuclear stockpiles. U.S.-led offensive aimed at ousting Iraqi dictator **Saddam Hussein** began Mar. 19, as cruise missiles hit Baghdad. Bush, May 1, declared **end of major combat operations**, though insurgent attacks continued.

Bush signed measure May 27 providing $15 bil to fight **AIDS** especially in **Africa**. He signed bill May 28 providing $330 bil in **tax cuts** over several years. A power failure caused **blackouts** affecting some 50 mil people, mostly in NE U.S. and Canada, Aug. 14.

The **archdiocese of Boston** agreed to pay up to $85 mil, in **sex abuse settlement** announced Sept. 9. Californians, Oct. 7, voted to recall Gov. **Gray Davis** (D) and replace him with actor-turned-politician **Arnold Schwarzenegger** (R). Virginia jury, Nov. 17, found **"Beltway sniper"** guilty in 2002 Washington, DC, area attacks that killed 10; he was executed, Nov. 2009; his teen accomplice was convicted and sentenced to life.

Pres. Bush signed bill Dec. 8 adding prescription drug benefit to **Medicare**. **Saddam Hussein captured** by U.S. forces Dec. 13; tried and executed (2006) by Iraqi authorities.

2004 Harvard undergrad **Mark Zuckerberg**, Feb. 4, launched the website that grew into the social media network **Facebook**. ***The Lord of the Rings**: The Return of the King* became third film to win a record 11 Oscars, Feb. 29.

Photos showing abuse of **Abu Ghraib** prison inmates in Iraq by American soldiers emerged Apr. 3; two soldiers found guilty (2005). U.S.-led coalition transferred power to interim Iraqi government, June 28. **9/11 Commission Report**, released July 22, called for restructuring U.S. intelligence operations.

On May 17, pursuant to a 2003 court decision, Massachusetts became first state to legalize **same-sex marriage**. **Boston Red Sox** won World Series Oct. 27, for first time since 1918.

Pres. **Bush reelected** Nov. 2, defeating Sen. **John Kerry** (D, MA). Bush signed **intelligence reform bill** Dec. 17, creating a director of national intelligence.

2005 **Condoleezza Rice** became first Black woman sec. of state, Jan. 26. **Terri Schiavo**, in vegetative state since 1990, died Mar. 31, after feeding tube was removed following legal battle.

Hurricane Katrina hit Gulf coast, Aug. 29, causing nearly 1,400 deaths and widespread devastation, especially in **New Orleans**. **John G. Roberts Jr.** was confirmed by Senate, Sept. 29, 78-22, to replace Chief Justice **William H. Rehnquist**, who died Sept. 3.

NY Times, Dec. 16, reported that Pres. Bush in 2002 had secretly authorized **NSA** to **eavesdrop without court warrant** on people in U.S. suspected of terrorist activities. Bush, Dec. 30, signed **anti-torture legislation**.

2006 **Samuel Alito Jr.** confirmed to Supreme Court, Jan. 31, 58-42, to replace retiring Justice **Sandra Day O'Connor**. The Court ruled June 29 that the system for trying terrorism detainees at **Guantánamo Bay** was unauthorized.

Pres. Bush, July 19, vetoed bill to end funding constraints on human embryonic **stem cell research**. On Sept. 6 he confirmed existence of **secret overseas prisons**, run by CIA, for terrorism suspects. Democrats won control of House and Senate in **midterm elections** Nov. 7.

2007 Rep. **Nancy Pelosi** (D, CA) chosen Jan. 4 as **first woman Speaker** of the House. On Jan. 10, Pres. Bush announced **troop "surge"** in Iraq. Reports of substandard conditions at **Walter Reed** Army Medical Center led to ousters of officials, Mar. 1-2. A **Virginia Tech** student fatally shot 32 people on campus, Apr. 16, before killing himself.

On Apr. 18, Supreme Court upheld, 5-4, a 2003 federal law banning so-called **partial-birth abortions**. Congress May 24 approved Iraq and Afghanistan war funding, with benchmarks for withdrawal of troops from Iraq; same bill raised federal hourly **minimum wage** from $5.15 to $7.25 over two years. Pres. Bush July 20 banned **"cruel, inhuman, or degrading"** treatment of imprisoned terror suspects.

***Harry Potter** and the Deathly Hallows*, final novel in blockbuster series, released July 21. Congress, Aug. 4, cleared bill allowing **NSA** to monitor communications without warrants if believed related to terrorism. **Barry Bonds** tied Hank Aaron's all-time career **home-run record** at 755 on Aug. 4 and hit No. 756 on Aug. 7. Report by former Sen. **George Mitchell** (D, ME), released Dec. 13, presented evidence of

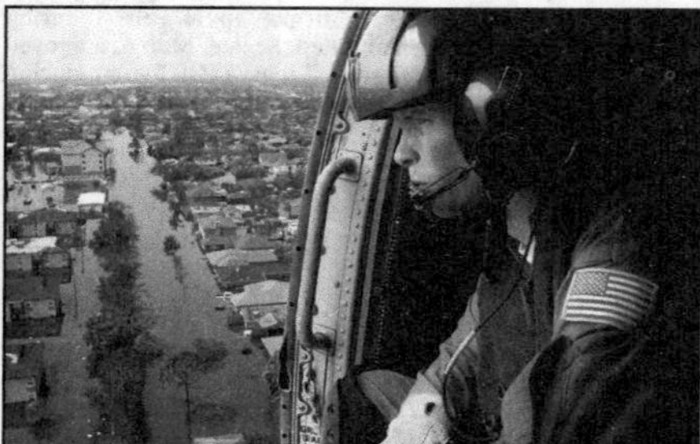

2005: Hurricane Katrina and subsequent failure of levees cause unprecedented destruction in New Orleans and along the Gulf Coast.

performance-enhancing drug use by 86 MLB players. Bush, Dec. 19, signed energy bill increasing automobile **fuel-economy** standards.

2008 Pres. Bush, Feb. 13, signed $168-bil **economic stimulus package** that provided significant tax rebates. With financial system in crisis, federal government Sept. 7 took control of mortgage finance companies **Fannie Mae** and **Freddie Mac**; **Lehman Brothers** declared bankruptcy Sept. 15. U.S., Sept. 16, took over insurance giant **AIG** in $85-bil bailout. A Treasury Dept. plan to purchase up to $700 bil of **"toxic" mortgage-backed securities**, Troubled Asset Relief Program (**TARP**), cleared Congress Oct. 3.

Sen. **Barack Obama** (D, IL) was elected, Nov. 4, as **first Black president** in U.S. history, defeating Sen. **John McCain** (R, AZ). Obama later named nomination campaign rival Sen. **Hillary Clinton** (NY) as sec. of state. California voters approved **Proposition 8**, banning same-sex marriage.

U.S. government Nov. 23 announced massive **bailout** to protect **Citigroup** from mortgage losses. Dow dropped 7.7% Dec. 1 after report that the economy was in **recession** that began Dec. 2007; Dow closed the year down 33.8%, its worst since 1931. Fed, Dec. 16, cut benchmark **interest rate** to near zero. Pres. Bush, Dec. 19, announced that $17 bil **TARP funds** would be used to help keep **General Motors** and **Chrysler** afloat.

2009 Pres. **Obama** issued executive orders Jan. 22 restricting CIA interrogation practices and calling for U.S. military prison at **Guantánamo Bay**, Cuba, to close (closing blocked by Congress). Illinois Gov. **Rod Blagojevich** (D) was convicted of corruption and removed from office, Jan. 29 (sentence commuted by Pres. Trump, 2020). Treasury Sec. **Timothy Geithner**, Feb. 10, outlined $2-tril program to stabilize banking and ease credit markets, with **stress tests** for banks. Obama signed **stimulus** bill Feb. 17, with $212 bil in tax cuts and $575 bil in new spending.

Swine flu outbreak declared a public health emergency Apr. 26. **Chrysler** filed for bankruptcy, Apr. 30. Obama, May 19, tightened vehicle **fuel efficiency** standards. **General Motors** filed for bankruptcy June 1, under plan providing new federal funds. On June 9, 10 financial firms received go-ahead from U.S. Treasury to return some $68 bil in **TARP funds**.

George Tiller, Kansas doctor and **abortion** provider, was murdered May 31 by anti-abortion extremist. Speaking June 4 in Egypt, Pres. Obama called for **"new beginning"** in relations with Muslim world. Financier **Bernard Madoff** sentenced to prison June 29, after pleading guilty in massive **Ponzi scheme**. **Sonia Sotomayor** confirmed Aug. 6, 68-31, as Supreme Court's **first Hispanic justice**, replacing retiring Justice **David Souter**.

Government reported Oct. 29 that GDP grew at 3.5% annual rate July-Sept., signaling technical **end of recession**. On Nov. 5, 13 were killed in **mass shooting** at **Ft. Hood**, TX; an Army major was convicted and sentenced to death.

Obama, Nov. 6, signed measure to extend unemployment benefits and give $8,000 tax credit to first-time homebuyers. A surge of 30,000 troops to **Afghanistan** was announced Dec. 1. Obama received **Nobel Peace Prize**, Dec. 10, and brokered multination **greenhouse-gas accord**, reached Dec. 18 in Copenhagen.

2010 In *Citizens United v. FEC*, U.S. Supreme Court Jan. 21 held that spending by corporations and unions on advertising to influence election outcomes could not be limited by law. Obama, Mar. 18, signed $18-bil **job-stimulus** measure. On Mar. 21, the House, with no GOP support, gave final approval to **"Obamacare"** health-care reform bill. Pres. Obama and Russian Pres. **Dmitri Medvedev**, Apr. 8, signed New Strategic Arms Reduction Treaty, or **New START**.

On Apr. 20, ***Deepwater Horizon*** drilling platform exploded in Gulf of Mexico, killing 11 and creating huge oil spill. Obama signed **financial reform** bill, July 21. Over 75,000 Afghanistan documents, many of them classified, were published July 25 on **WikiLeaks** website. **Elena Kagan** was confirmed as **Supreme Court** justice, 63-37, Aug. 5, to replace retiring Justice **John Paul Stevens**.

The Fed Nov. 3 announced plan to buy $600 bil in **Treasury securities** to stimulate economy. Bipartisan **Simpson-Bowles** commission, Dec. 1, called for deep spending cuts to stabilize national debt. Obama, Dec. 17, signed $858-bil compromise measure temporarily extending G. W. **Bush-era tax cuts** and unemployment insurance benefits.

2011 Gunman in **Tucson**, AZ, Jan. 8, killed 6 people and injured 13, including Rep. **Gabrielle Giffords** (D, AZ). On May 2, in Abbottabad, Pakistan, Navy **SEAL**s killed al-Qaeda leader **Osama bin Laden**. On May 26 Obama signed measure extending key provisions of **USA Patriot Act**.

Tornado hit **Joplin**, MO, May 22, claiming about 160 lives. NASA's **space shuttle** program ended with landing of *Atlantis*, July 21. **Budget control act**, Aug. 1-2, raised **debt ceiling** and cut some $900 bil in spending, with another $1.5 tril in cuts to be worked out by **supercommittee**. A left-wing protest movement that began Sept. 17 as **Occupy Wall Street** expanded across the U.S. and abroad.

Anwar al-Awlaki, a Muslim cleric linked to terrorist attacks in U.S., was killed Sept. 30 in U.S. drone attack in **Yemen**. U.S. military mission in **Iraq** formally ended Dec. 15; last troop convoy left Dec. 18.

2012 Pres. Obama Feb. 10 announced compromise **health insurance** mandate that exempted religiously affiliated employers from directly providing **contraceptive coverage**. On June 15 he announced Deferred Action for Childhood Arrivals (**DACA**) program, shielding from deportation certain **undocumented immigrants** who entered as minors.

Former Penn State assistant football coach **Jerry Sandusky** was convicted June 22 in **sexual abuse** of ten boys. Twelve people were killed July 20, in movie-theater shooting in Aurora, CO; shooter sentenced to life. A gunman opened fire Aug. 5 at a **Sikh temple** in Oak Creek, WI, leaving six dead, before killing himself. NASA rover ***Curiosity*** landed on **Mars** Aug. 6.

Islamist terrorists attacked U.S. facility in **Benghazi**, Libya, Sept. 11-12, killing U.S. **ambassador** and three other Americans. **Hurricane Sandy** made landfall in the U.S. Oct. 29, devastating mid-Atlantic coastal areas and leaving over 200 dead.

Pres. **Obama reelected** Nov. 6, defeating former Massachusetts Gov. **Mitt Romney** (R). Colorado and Washington became first states to vote to decriminalize recreational **marijuana**.

A gunman killed 20 young children and 6 adults before killing himself, Dec. 14, at **Sandy Hook** Elementary School in **Newtown**, CT.

2013 Averting **"fiscal cliff,"** Senate passed compromise Jan. 1, making **Bush-era tax** cuts permanent up to certain ceilings, while deferring automatic spending cuts (**sequestration**). Sequestration took effect Mar. 1, triggering $1.2 tril in spending cuts to both defense and domestic programs over ten years.

Bombs at the Boston Marathon, Apr. 15, killed three spectators and injured 264; two Chechen-born brothers were implicated.

The *Guardian*, June 5, disclosed details of classified **NSA electronic surveillance** program; NSA contractor **Edward Snowden** claimed responsibility for leaks, after having fled the country. Army Staff Sgt. **Robert Bales** pleaded guilty, June 5, to killing 16 Afghan civilians; sentenced to life. Supreme Court, June 25, overturned key provision of the 1965 **Voting Rights Act** and, June 26, struck down part of 1996 Defense of Marriage Act.

A jury, July 13, found George Zimmerman not guilty in Feb. 2012 shooting of **Trayvon Martin**, an unarmed Black teenager, in Sanford, FL. **Detroit** filed for **bankruptcy**, July 18. Army Pfc. **Chelsea Manning** was sentenced Aug. 21 to 35 years for releasing military and diplomatic documents to **WikiLeaks** (Obama commuted sentence, 2017). A gunman killed 12 people at the **Navy Yard** in Washington, DC, Sept. 16; he was killed by responding police.

Health insurance exchanges opened Oct. 1 in **Obamacare rollout** plagued by technical glitches. U.S. **government partially shut down** Oct. 1 over budget impasse; resolved by Congress Oct. 16. **JPMorgan Chase** agreed, Nov. 19, to $13-bil settlement on charges of deceptive mortgage-sale practices. Dow up 26.5% in 2013; biggest yearly gain since 1995.

2014 **Janet Yellen** was confirmed Jan. 6 as first woman **Fed** chair. **General Motors**, Feb. 7, began recall of vehicles with defect linked to deaths; fined $900 mil. **Toyota** agreed Mar. 19 to $1.2-bil fine on charges it concealed information about defective parts.

Gunman killed 6 people and injured 13 before killing himself, May 23, near **Univ. of California-Santa Barbara**. U.S. Army Sgt. **Bowe Bergdahl**, captured by Taliban in 2009, was freed May 31 in exchange for U.S. release of five Taliban captives. Veterans Affairs Sec. **Eric Shinseki** resigned May 30 after revelations that **VA hospitals** had hidden long waiting times.

The Sunni extremist Islamic State of Iraq and Syria (**ISIS**) declared a **"caliphate"** June 29. Pres. Obama announced June 19 that the U.S. would send **military advisers to Iraq**; he authorized airstrikes there, Aug. 7. ISIS released videos in Aug.-Nov. showing **beheadings** of three Americans.

A white police officer fatally shot unarmed Black 18-year-old **Michael Brown**, Aug. 9, in **Ferguson**, MO, precipitating sometimes violent **protests**; grand jury declined to indict. **Bank of America** agreed Aug. 21 to $16.65-bil settlement on charges it misled investors.

U.S. jury Oct. 22 convicted four former contract security guards in 2007 shootings that killed 17 **Iraqi civilians**. New York City's new **One World Trade Center** welcomed first tenants Nov. 3.

Tamir Rice, a Black 12-year-old holding a pellet gun, was fatally shot by a white police officer, Nov. 22, in **Cleveland**, OH; grand jury declined to indict. A grand jury decided Dec. 3 not to indict a **New York City** police officer for allegedly using a nonregulation **chokehold** to detain **Eric Garner**, a Black man who died July 17 in custody. A Black man shot and killed two **New York City police** officers in their patrol car, Dec. 20, then killed himself.

U.S.-led NATO mission in **Afghanistan** ended combat operations Dec. 28, after over 13 years; troops remained in support roles.

2015 **Standard & Poor's** agreed Feb. 3 to pay $1.4 bil, and **Morgan Stanley** agreed Feb. 15 to pay $2.6 bil, to resolve claims of financial deception. Justice Dept. Mar. 4 released report exposing widespread mistreatment of Black individuals by **Ferguson**, MO, police and court system.

A New York court Mar. 5 approved $8.5-bil settlement between **Bank of America** and investors in mortgage securities issued by **Countrywide Financial Corp.** Federal judge, Mar. 20, approved settlement in which **AIG** paid $970.5 mil to shareholders allegedly misled over high-risk mortgage loans. Facing continuing drought, California Gov. **Jerry Brown** (D) issued mandatory **water restrictions** Apr. 1. Pres. Obama met in Panama with Cuban Pres. **Raúl Castro**, Apr. 11; U.S. and Cuba reopened embassies in their countries July 20, reestablishing relations.

The Apr. 19 death of a Black man, **Freddie Gray**, from injury in a **Baltimore** police van, spurred riots and led to indictment of six officers; no convictions resulted. A **white supremacist** June 17 fatally shot nine people at historic Black church in **Charleston**, SC; shooter sentenced to death, 2017.

Obama June 2 signed a bill to end **NSA's bulk collection** of phone data, with telecom companies to hold custody of data instead. **American Pharoah**, June 6, became first in 37 years to take horse racing's **Triple Crown**. On June 26, the Supreme Court ruled that **same-sex couples** had constitutional right to marry.

Iran and six world powers led by the U.S. formally agreed July 14 on deal to limit **Iranian nuclear capability** in return for lifting economic sanctions (Pres. Trump announced U.S. withdrawal, 2018). Pres. Obama Aug. 3 unveiled EPA **Clean Power Plan** limiting carbon dioxide emissions from power plants (Supreme Court ruled it unconstitutional, 2022).

Pope Francis visited the U.S., Sept. 22-27, and addressed joint session of Congress. A student shooter at a community college, Oct. 1, in **Roseburg**, OR, killed nine people before killing himself. U.S. airstrike hit an **Afghanistan hospital** Oct. 3, killing more than 40; military report blamed human error.

U.S. and 11 other nations completed negotiations, Oct. 5, on **Trans-Pacific Partnership** trade agreement. An Oct. 22 U.S.-Iraqi mission freed about 70 hostages held by **ISIS** in Iraq; one U.S. soldier was killed. On Oct. 30, Obama announced he would deploy special operations forces to fight ISIS in **Syria**.

Three people were killed Nov. 27 at **Planned Parenthood** clinic in Colorado Springs, CO; alleged shooter found incompetent to stand trial. A married couple said by the FBI to be **Muslim extremists** fatally shot 14 people at a Dec. 2 office party in **San Bernardino**, CA; both died in shootout with police.

Defense Dept., Dec. 3, announced that all **military combat positions** would be **opened to women**. U.S. and 194 other parties reached agreement in Paris, Dec. 12, on plan to reduce greenhouse gases linked to **climate change**. The **Fed**, Dec. 16, **raised key interest rates** from near-zero levels. Obama signed $1.8-tril **spending and tax relief package** Dec. 18.

2016 Armed protesters, Jan. 2, began 41-day occupation of Oregon's **Malheur National Wildlife Refuge**, in land dispute; one fatally shot, Jan. 26, in confrontation with law enforcement. Obama declared federal state of emergency in **Flint, MI**, Jan. 16, because of **lead-contaminated drinking water**. Following the death in Feb. of conservative Supreme Court Justice **Antonin Scalia**, Obama Mar. 16 nominated appellate court judge **Merrick Garland**, but Senate Republicans declined to schedule confirmation hearings.

North Carolina Gov. **Pat McCrory** (R) Mar. 23 signed **"bathroom bill"** requiring that persons use state facilities corresponding to birth-certificate gender; boycotts followed. (Measure partly repealed, 2017.) Justice Dept. announced Apr. 11 that **Goldman Sachs** would pay $5.1 bil to settle charges of selling faulty mortgage-backed securities.

U.S. **drone strike** killed Afghan Taliban leader **Akhtar Muhammad Mansour** May 21. A gunman who declared allegiance to **ISIS** killed 49 mostly Hispanic people June 12 at **gay nightclub** in **Orlando**, FL; he was killed by responding police. The blockbuster musical ***Hamilton*** won 11 Tony Awards June 12.

In settlement announced June 28, **Volkswagen** agreed to pay some $15 bil for cheating in emissions tests. Defense Dept. announced, June 30, that **transgender individuals** could serve openly in the military. Protests followed **fatal police shootings** of a Black man in **Baton Rouge**, LA, July 5, and in a **St. Paul**, MN, suburb, July 6. Five police officers were killed by a sniper, July 7 in **Dallas**, TX, and three in an ambush, July 17 in **Baton Rouge**, LA.

After investigating Hillary Clinton's use of a **private email server** as sec. of state, FBI Dir. **James Comey**, July 5, said she was careless but did not show intent to violate the law. Justice Dept. report released Aug. 10 concluded that **Baltimore police** routinely used **excessive force** against Blacks.

2015: A Supreme Court decision effectively legalizes same-sex marriage nationwide.

WikiLeaks Oct. 7 began releasing apparently hacked emails from Clinton campaign chair **John Podesta**. **AT&T** agreed Oct. 22 to acquire **Time Warner** for about $85 bil. **Chicago Cubs** won World Series Nov. 2, for first time since 1908.

In Nov. 8 presidential election, **Donald Trump** (R) defeated former Sec. of State **Hillary Clinton** (D), with 304 electoral votes out of 538, though losing popular vote by about 3 mil. Tech pioneer **Yahoo** Dec. 14 revealed an Aug. 2013 hack, affecting some 3 bil user accounts. Following evidence of **Russian hacking**, Obama Dec. 29 expelled 35 Russian diplomats.

2017 Pres. **Trump inaugurated** Jan. 20. **Women's Marches**, Jan. 21, in Washington, DC, and other cities drew millions of protesters. Trump Jan. 23-27 withdrew U.S. from **Trans-Pacific Partnership** trade agreement, ordered building of a Mexican **border wall**, and issued executive order banning admission of travelers from certain **Muslim-majority nations** (expanded ban later upheld by Supreme Court).

After a suspected **chemical attack** in Syria, Apr. 4, Pres. Trump authorized **cruise-missile strike** against a government airfield. The U.S. military, Apr. 13, bombed a complex of caves and tunnels in **Afghanistan**; 94 militants reportedly killed.

After Republicans used the so-called **nuclear option** to end a Democratic filibuster, the Senate voted, 54-45, Apr. 7, to confirm nomination of **Neil Gorsuch** to Supreme Court. Pres. Trump fired FBI Dir. **James Comey** May 9; Justice Dept., May 17, appointed former FBI Dir. **Robert Mueller III** as special counsel to head investigation into Russian election meddling.

On June 1 the **Dakota Access oil pipeline**, protested by the **Standing Rock** tribe, became operational. A gunman targeting Republicans June 14 at a practice for the bipartisan **Congressional Baseball Game** critically injured Rep. **Steve Scalise** (R, LA) and wounded four others; perpetrator fatally wounded in shootout.

American student **Otto Warmbier** was returned to U.S., June 13, in a comatose state after imprisonment in **North Korea**; he soon died. Trump Aug. 2 signed bipartisan bill imposing certain economic sanctions against **Russia** as well as Iran and **North Korea**.

At a **white nationalist rally** in **Charlottesville**, VA, Aug. 12, one counterdemonstrator was killed and 19 were injured when a white nationalist drove into a crowd. On Aug. 21, millions viewed the first total **solar eclipse** visible coast to coast since 1918. **North Korea** Sept. 3 conducted its sixth nuclear weapons test; UN and U.S. imposed economic sanctions. Credit reporting firm **Equifax** revealed Sept. 7 that hackers had gained access to information on some 143 mil Americans; company agreed to pay up to $700 mil to resolve claims.

Hurricane Maria hit **Puerto Rico**, Sept. 20, causing widespread devastation and nearly 3,000 deaths. A gunman fatally shot 60 people and injured hundreds at a country music concert, Oct. 1, in **Las Vegas**. *NY Times* Oct. 5 reported multiple accusations of sexual assault or harassment against movie producer **Harvey Weinstein**, beginning a wave of **"Me Too"** allegations.

U.S.-backed militias in **Syria** reported, Oct. 20, capture of **Raqqa**, capital of ISIS's self-proclaimed caliphate. Former Trump adviser **Michael Flynn** pleaded guilty Nov. 30 to lying to the FBI about conversations with Russia's U.S. ambassador (pardoned by Trump in 2020).

2017: A gunman shooting from a high-rise hotel window in Las Vegas kills 58 people and injures hundreds more attending an outdoor country music festival Oct. 1.

A gunman killed 26 people, Nov. 5, at a **Baptist church** in **Sutherland Springs**, TX; shooter died by suicide. U.S. Navy report, Nov. 1, blamed personnel errors for collisions that killed 17 sailors. Pres. Trump, Dec. 6, recognized **Jerusalem** as Israel's capital. FCC voted 3-2, Dec. 14, to scrap **net neutrality** rules. On Dec. 22, Trump signed measure reducing tax rates, allowing oil drilling in Alaska's **Arctic National Wildlife Refuge**, and repealing Obamacare's individual mandate.

2018 Michigan State Univ. sports physician **Larry Nasser** sentenced to prison, Jan. 24, after pleading guilty to decades of **sexual abuse**. A shooting Feb. 14 at a **Parkland**, FL, high school left 17 dead; an expelled student was indicted for murder and pleaded guilty. Students protesting gun violence led **March for Our Lives** demonstrations, Mar. 24.

Uber suspended its self-driving cars from four North American test cities after pedestrian fatality Mar. 18. Facebook CEO **Mark Zuckerberg** apologized before Congress, Apr. 10-11, after revelations that British consulting firm **Cambridge Analytica** had gained access to data from Facebook users allegedly provided to political campaigns.

After a reported **chemical weapons attack** by Syria's **Assad regime**, U.S., UK, and France launched airstrikes against suspected weapons production sites, Apr. 14. Federal regulators announced $1 bil in fines Apr. 20 against **Wells Fargo** for financial improprieties.

U.S.-led coalition against **ISIS** Apr. 30 closed its land forces command headquarters in Iraq. Pres. Trump declared May 8 he was withdrawing U.S. from the **2015 Iran nuclear deal**. On May 18, eight students and two teachers were killed in shooting at a high school in **Santa Fe**, TX; a student was arrested and charged. **NFL** team owners May 23 announced players must either **stand during national anthem** or remain in locker room.

Following widespread criticism, Trump June 20 signed an executive order to end separation of **undocumented children** at the Mexican border. Cardinal **Theodore McCarrick** was removed from public ministry June 20, amid allegations of **sexual abuse**; later resigned as cardinal and was laicized. A gunman killed five employees and injured two at ***Capital Gazette*** offices in Annapolis, MD, June 28.

Justice Dept. charged 12 **Russian intelligence officers** July 13 with hacking the Clinton campaign and Democratic National Committee and leaking emails and data. Pres. Trump and Russian Pres. **Vladimir Putin** held summit in Helsinki, Finland, July 16.

Pennsylvania grand jury Aug. 14 released report detailing decades of **clerical sexual abuse** and cover-up in six Roman Catholic dioceses. Former Trump campaign chair **Paul Manafort** was found guilty Aug. 21 of **financial crimes** (pardoned by Trump, 2020). Former Trump attorney **Michael Cohen** pleaded guilty Aug. 21 to campaign finance violations for **hush money** he said he paid to cover up Trump extramarital affairs.

Saudi dissident journalist **Jamal Khashoggi**, a U.S. resident, was killed after entering the Saudi consulate in Istanbul, Oct. 2; U.S. intelligence implicated Saudi crown prince. A white Chicago police officer was convicted of second-degree murder, Oct. 5, in the 2014 shooting of Black teenager **Laquan McDonald**.

U.S. Senate, 50-48, Oct. 6 confirmed nomination of **Brett Kavanaugh** to Supreme Court, after hearings in which a psychology professor testified he had sexually assaulted her when both were teenagers.

Authorities intercepted **package bombs** addressed to prominent Democrats and CNN and arrested the suspected sender, Oct. 26. A gunman opened fire in **Tree of Life Congregation synagogue** in Pittsburgh, PA, Oct. 27, killing 11. Trump ordered 5,200 troops to the southern border, Oct. 29, to halt **Central American migrants**.

An ex-Marine fatally shot 12 people at a bar in **Thousand Oaks**, CA, Nov. 7, then killed himself. A **wildfire**, starting on Nov. 8, wiped out the town of **Paradise**, CA; 85 people died. Three U.S. service members were killed Nov. 27 in apparent Taliban bombing in Afghanistan; U.S. airstrike in response reportedly caused civilian deaths. Pres. Trump, Dec. 21, signed bipartisan **criminal justice reform** bill reducing or eliminating mandatory minimum sentences for many drug-related federal crimes. An impasse over border-wall funding

2018: Pres. Donald Trump continues to call for construction of a new wall on the southern U.S. border.

led to a partial federal government **shutdown**, Dec. 22, lasting a record 35 days.

2019 Trump administration, Jan. 25, initiated **"Remain in Mexico"** policy for asylum seekers. On Feb. 1 the administration announced it was suspending U.S. obligations under the 1987 Intermediate-Range Nuclear Forces **(INF) Treaty**. NASA announced the end of its **Mars *Opportunity*** rover mission Feb. 13, after 15 years.

Justice Dept. Mar. 12, charged some 50 people, including several celebrities, in **college admissions cheating** schemes. FAA Mar. 13 grounded **Boeing's 737 Max** aircraft after two fatal crashes abroad.

The U.S.-backed **Syrian Democratic Forces** declared victory over ISIS in Syria, Mar. 23. **OxyContin** maker **Purdue Pharma** and its owners, Mar. 26, agreed to pay $270 mil settling suits for allegedly minimizing the drug's addictive potential. **Apple** agreed Apr. 16 to pay wireless chipmaker **Qualcomm** at least $4.5 bil to settle dispute over technology used in iPhones.

Justice Dept. report released Apr. 18 found the **Russian government** had "worked to secure" Trump's election. Pres. Trump May 10 increased **tariffs** on Chinese products. On May 24 Trump declared tensions with **Iran** a national security emergency, allowing U.S. **arms sales** to Saudi Arabia, UAE, and Jordan.

On May 23 Justice Dept. announced charges against Australian **WikiLeaks** founder **Julian Assange**. Gunman killed 12 people in **Virginia Beach**, VA, May 31. The EPA, June 19, repealed Obama's **Clean Power Plan**, replacing it with weaker regulations.

Pres. Trump met June 30 with North Korean leader **Kim Jong Un** at the Demilitarized Zone (DMZ). Trump July 1 signed $4.6-bil package to help U.S. agencies deal with migrant surge at **U.S.-Mexican border**. Financier **Jeffrey Epstein** was indicted, July 8, on federal charges of **sexual abuse** involving dozens of girls; he died Aug. 10, in apparent suicide.

Citing signs of global economic cooling, the Fed July 31 began cutting **interest rates**. As U.S.-China **trade war** heated up, the Dow, Aug. 5, fell 767 points; recession fears contributed to 800-point drop Aug. 14.

On Aug. 3 a shooter reportedly targeting Mexicans fatally shot 23 people at an **El Paso, TX, Walmart**, before surrendering. On Aug. 4 a gunman killed nine people on a **Dayton**, OH, street, before being fatally shot by police.

U.S. unemployment rate for Sept. fell to 3.5%, lowest since 1969. White House, Oct. 6, announced withdrawal of some U.S. troops from **Syria** in the face of an imminent Turkish assault against **Kurdish** forces allied with the U.S. against ISIS. **ISIS leader** Abu Bakr al-**Baghdadi** was reported killed during U.S. military raid in Syria, Oct. 26. A **Saudi Arabian** military officer in flight training fatally shot three trainees Dec. 7 at U.S. naval base in **Pensacola**, FL; he was killed in gun battle.

On Nov. 15, Trump political adviser **Roger Stone** was convicted on charges stemming from the election-interference probe; Trump later commuted his sentence. A Justice Dept. **watchdog report**, released Dec. 6, found procedural errors in the probe but no evidence of bias against Trump.

House Judiciary Committee, Dec. 13, approved articles of **impeachment** against Pres. Trump for **abuse of power** and for **obstruction of Congress**. On Dec. 18 the full House, with no Republican support, passed the first article, 230-197, and the second, 229-198.

Dow closed the year up 22.3%. CDC reported 1,282 cases of **measles** for 2019, largest number since 1992.

2020 U.S. **drone strikes** in Iraq, Jan. 3, killed Iranian Islamic Revolutionary Guard Corps Major Gen. **Qassem Soleimani**; another drone attack, in **Yemen**, disclosed Feb. 6, killed **Qasim al-Raymi**, leader of al-Qaeda in the Arabian Peninsula. CDC, Jan. 21, announced **first confirmed COVID-19 case** in the U.S., in traveler from China; starting Feb. 2, Trump administration barred U.S. entry for most non-Americans recently in China. Former NBA star **Kobe Bryant** and his daughter Gianna were among nine people killed in helicopter crash in Calabasas, CA, Jan. 26.

After **impeachment trial**, senators on Feb. 5 voted, 52-48, to convict Pres. Trump for abuse of power, and 53-47 for obstruction of Congress, falling short of the needed two-thirds majority.

Wells Fargo, Feb. 21, agreed to pay $3 bil to end probe into unauthorized accounts under customers' names. **Boy Scouts**, facing sex-abuse suits and waning membership, filed for bankruptcy Feb. 18.

The fatal shooting of unarmed Black jogger **Ahmaud Arbery** (by white pursuers, Feb. 23 in Brunswick, GA) and Black woman **Breonna Taylor** (by police in botched raid on her apartment, Mar. 13, in Louisville, KY) fueled widespread protests in support of **Black Lives Matter** movement.

First U.S. **COVID-19 fatality** reported, Feb. 29. The administration declared a national emergency Mar. 13, banned most travel from Europe by non-Americans, and, Mar. 20, began invoking a legal provision (**"Title 42"**) to allow immediate expulsion of **asylum-seeking migrants** as threats to public health during the COVID emergency.

U.S. and **Taliban** militants approved pact Feb. 29 calling for all U.S. and coalition forces to leave **Afghanistan** within 14 months, with some 5,000 Taliban prisoners to be freed and a Taliban pledge to end attacks and engage in intra-Afghan talks; Taliban subsequently grew in strength.

Dow fell 2,352 points Mar. 12, a day after WHO declared the coronavirus a **global pandemic**, and 2,997 points Mar. 16, despite action by the Fed cutting its benchmark interest rate. Trump, Mar. 27, signed $2-tril economic aid and **stimulus bill**. Dow ended Apr. up 11.1%, but **unemployment** hit 14.7%, highest since the Great Depression. J. Crew, Neiman Marcus, J. C. Penney, and Hertz declared **bankruptcy** in May.

Idaho, Mar. 29, became the first state to bar **transgender** girls and women from participating in female sports. CDC, Apr. 3, urged Americans to wear **face masks** to prevent spread of COVID-19. Trump May 15 announced **Operation Warp Speed**, aimed at facilitating development, manufacture, and distribution of **COVID vaccines**.

On May 25 **Derek Chauvin**, a white **Minneapolis** police officer, kneeled on the neck of a prone Black man in custody, **George Floyd**, who died. Demonstrations followed, with instances of arson, looting, and vandalism; Chauvin later convicted of murder. The incident fueled widespread protests in support of **Black Lives Matter**.

2020: Spurred by the death of George Floyd and other Black men and women in dealings with police, protests call for an end to systemic racism.

The shooting of **Jacob Blake**, a Black man, in struggle with police in **Kenosha**, WI, Aug. 23, set off demonstrations in which two protesters were fatally shot by a vigilante claiming self-defense; he was acquitted.

SpaceX, May 30, became first private company to launch humans into orbit. **Bayer**, which acquired agricultural giant **Monsanto** in 2018, announced June 24 it would pay over $10 bil to resolve lawsuits over cancers allegedly caused by the **herbicide Roundup**.

Supreme Court ruled June 15, 6-3, that employers could not discriminate against workers for being **gay or transgender**. Ruling 7-2, July 8, the Court held that private employers could opt out of Affordable Care Act mandate requiring coverage of **contraceptives**, if on religious or moral grounds. On July 6, the Court ruled, 9-0, that states could compel **presidential electors** to vote for candidates they had pledged to support.

Executions of death row inmates for federal crimes resumed July 14, ending informal moratorium begun in 2003. Trump, in Aug.-Sept., announced agreements between **Israel** and **UAE** and **Bahrain** to normalize relations. Supreme Court Justice **Ruth Bader Ginsburg** died Sept. 18; **Amy Coney Barrett** was confirmed, Oct. 26, to replace her.

More than 3.9 mil acres burnt Aug.-Sept. in California's **wildfire** season; over 30 people died. **GDP** rose an estimated 33.4% in third quarter 2020, having fallen 31.4% in the second quarter. Federal officials Oct. 8 announced indictment of six people over failed right-wing extremist plot to kidnap Michigan Gov. **Gretchen Whitmer** (D). Justice Dept., Oct. 21, announced **OxyContin** maker **Purdue Pharma** would pay $8.3 bil to settle charges of illegal marketing and kickbacks to doctors.

Vote counting continued after **Election Day**, Nov. 3, with news organizations, Nov. 7, projecting **Biden** as winner of the presidential election. Republicans filed over 50 lawsuits challenging results or balloting procedures, to little effect. The Biden-Harris ticket won in Electoral College, 306-232, and came out ahead by 7 mil in popular vote. Trump refused to concede, claiming fraud.

The U.S., Nov. 4, formally withdrew from the 2015 **Paris climate agreement**. Massive **cyberattack** on U.S. government sites and other targets confirmed by U.S., Dec. 13; attributed to Russia. Congress easily passed a second **economic aid and stimulus** bill, signed Dec. 27 by Trump.

FDA approved **COVID-19 vaccines** from Pfizer, Dec. 11, and Moderna, Dec. 18, on emergency basis.

2021 On Jan. 6, after Pres. Trump told rally to "fight like hell" against accepting 2020 presidential results, a mob of supporters, some armed, broke into the **Capitol**, temporarily preventing Congress from certifying the election outcome. One woman was fatally shot by police, of whom over 100 were injured. By a 232-197 vote, the House, Jan. 13, voted to **impeach Trump** for a second time, this time for "incitement of insurrection." On Feb. 13, 7 Republican senators joined all 50 Democrats in a vote to convict, which fell short of the needed two-thirds majority.

Joe Biden was sworn in as president Jan. 20, at the Capitol. Beginning Jan. 20 he signed a series of **executive orders**, many aimed at revoking or modifying Trump policies. Pres. Biden announced, Feb. 4, that the U.S. would end its support for Saudi-led offensive against Iran-backed Houthi in devastating **Yemen civil war**. On Feb. 11 Biden halted diversion of Pentagon funding for construction of a **border wall**.

NASA's *Perseverance* rover landed on **Mars**, Feb. 18. U.S. officially reentered the **Paris climate accord** Feb. 19. Biden Mar. 11 signed $1.9-tril **COVID relief package**, which included direct payments to households.

Mass shootings occurred at **Atlanta** area spas (8 killed, mostly Asian women, Mar. 16), a **Boulder**, CO, supermarket (10 killed, Mar. 22), and an **Indianapolis** FedEx facility (8 workers killed, Apr. 15). A police officer, mistakenly firing her handgun instead of her **Taser**, killed a Black driver after a traffic stop in Minneapolis suburb Apr. 11.

GOP House members May 12 voted to remove Rep. **Liz Cheney** (R, WY), a Trump critic, as chair of the House Republican Conference. Biden administration June 1 suspended oil and gas leases in Alaska's **Arctic National Wildlife Refuge**. **Boy Scouts** July 1 agreed to pay $850 mil to settle sexual abuse claims.

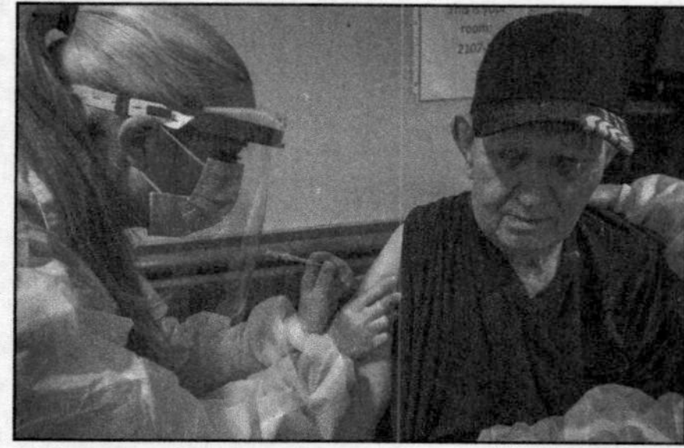

2021: Coronavirus vaccines are widely available by midyear, but virus variants and vaccine reluctance continue to pose challenges.

In Afghanistan, the U.S., July 2, handed over control of its largest military base, **Bagram Airfield**, to Afghan forces; Taliban continued expanding territorial control. A wildfire ignited July 13 in **California** burned nearly 1 mil acres. On July 20, **Jeff Bezos** launched Blue Origin's reusable and pilotless *New Shepard* rocket, with Bezos and three others aboard.

Taliban forces captured 26 provincial capitals and, Aug. 15, retook **Kabul**, while Afghan forces surrendered Bagram Airfield. Under a fixed Aug. 31 deadline, U.S. forces scrambled to evacuate Americans and Afghans who aided them, with many of the latter left behind. An airport bombing, Aug. 26, killed 13 U.S. soldiers and at least 169 Afghan civilians.

Hurricane Ian made landfall Aug. 29 in Louisiana, amid heat wave; close to 100 U.S. deaths reported.

A **Texas** law generally prohibiting **abortions** after a detectable fetal heartbeat took effect Sept. 1. Pres. Biden, Sept. 9, announced a COVID **vaccine mandate** for large companies (later struck down by Supreme Court).

Biden, Nov. 15, signed a major $1.5-tril **infrastructure package**.

Six people were run over and killed at **Waukesha**, WI, Christmas parade, Nov. 21, and four students were shot and killed, Nov. 30, at an **Oxford, MI**, high school; the shooter was sentenced to life imprisonment and his parents were convicted and imprisoned, for negligence.

2022 U.S. raid in NW Syria, Feb. 3, led to death of **ISIS** leader Abu Ibrahim al-Hashimi al-Qurayshi.

Gun manufacturer **Remington** agreed, Feb. 15, to pay $73 mil to families of nine victims of the 2012 **Newtown**, CT, school shooting. Jury Oct. 12 ordered Infowars host **Alex Jones** to pay $965 mil to families of eight victims, for having portrayed shootings as staged.

Puerto Rico exited **bankruptcy** Mar. 15. Florida Gov. **Ron DeSantis** (R) signed a bill, Mar. 28, barring public school "instruction on sexual orientation or gender identity" in primary grades. Pres. Biden signed bipartisan legislation Mar. 29 making **lynching** a federal crime.

Senate voted, 53-47, Apr. 7, to confirm federal appeals court judge **Ketanji Brown Jackson** to the Supreme Court. She replaced Justice **Stephen Breyer** upon his retirement, becoming the Court's first Black woman justice.

An 18-year-old armed with a semi-automatic rifle fatally shot 10 Black people at a **Buffalo supermarket** May 14. On May 24, an 18-year-old gunman killed 19 students and 2 teachers at Robb Elementary School in mostly Hispanic **Uvalde**, TX; after long delay, officers entered classrooms, and the shooter was killed. On June 25 Pres. Biden, signed a **gun control bill** which, though limited, was the most extensive passed by Congress in nearly three decades.

COVID-19 deaths in U.S. passed the 1 million mark, according to CDC data released May 16. A House select committee investigating the **Jan. 6, 2021, attack** on the Capitol began televised public hearings June 9.

Fifty-three **Hispanic migrants** were found dead or dying, June 27, in an abandoned tractor-trailer in San Antonio, TX.

On June 24, in ***Dobbs v. Jackson Women's Health Organization,*** U.S. Supreme Court voted, 6-3, to uphold Mississippi's 15-week **abortion ban** and, 5-4, to overturn the landmark 1973 ***Roe v. Wade*** decision that had asserted a constitutional right to abortion. Other 6-3 decisions, June 21-30, also highlighted the impact of Court conservatives.

A rooftop shooter opened fire July 4 into a parade in a Chicago suburb, killing seven. Inflation hit a new high in June, up 9.1% from a year earlier. U.S. House Speaker **Nancy Pelosi** (D, CA) met with Taiwan's president Aug. 3 in Taipei; China, in response, staged military drills around Taiwan and paused or ended cooperation with U.S. in eight policy areas.

On Aug. 8, the FBI searched former Pres. Trump's **Mar-a-Lago** residence, unearthing government documents, some classified. Florida Gov. **Ron DeSantis** (R) Sept. 14 sent some 50 **asylum seekers** aboard unannounced chartered flights to **Martha's Vineyard**, MA; the flights followed busing of thousands of migrants from Texas and Arizona to Democrat-led big cities.

Pres. Biden signed an executive order, Aug. 24, canceling up to $20,000 in **student loan debt** for millions of individual borrowers (struck down by Supreme Court, 2023). The Fed on Sept. 21 raised benchmark **interest rates** by 0.75% for the third time in three straight meetings, to fight persistent inflation.

Hurricane Ian made landfall in Florida on Sept. 28 and South Carolina on Sept. 30, causing over 150 deaths. In sale finalized Oct. 27, tech magnate **Elon Musk** took over **Twitter**, paying $44 bil; layoffs followed. **Paul Pelosi**, husband of House Speaker **Nancy Pelosi** (D, CA), was assaulted by a home intruder targeting his wife, Oct. 28.

In federal elections Nov. 8, Republicans won control of the **U.S. House** by an unexpectedly modest majority (ultimately 222-213); Democrats kept narrow control of the **Senate**.

Three students were fatally shot at **Univ. of Virginia**, and four fatally stabbed in off-campus housing at **Univ. of Idaho**, Nov. 13. An armor-clad shooter killed five people, Nov. 19, at an LGBTQ bar in **Colorado Springs**. Shooting at a Chesapeake, VA, **Walmart** left seven dead, including the killer, Nov. 22.

Pres. Biden met with Chinese Pres. **Xi Jinping**, Nov. 14, in Bali. On Nov. 29 **Oath Keepers** militia leader Stewart Rhodes and a codefendant were convicted of **seditious conspiracy** in Jan. 6 attack on the U.S. Capitol. **Trump Org.** Dec. 6 was found guilty of **tax fraud** and other crimes.

WNBA star Britney Griner, imprisoned in Russia (Feb. 2020) on a minor drug offense, was freed Dec. 8 in exchange for a notorious Russia arms dealer. On Dec. 13, Pres. Biden signed legislation protecting federal recognition of **same-sex marriages** that were legal under a state law.

Ukrainian Pres. **Volodymyr Zelenskyy** met with Pres. Biden and spoke before Congress, Dec. 21, seeking more financial support in fight against Russian invasion. On Dec. 29 Biden signed **$1.7 tril spending bill** passed by the outgoing Congress, avoiding a partial government shutdown.

2023 A gunman killed 11 people at a **Monterey Park, CA dance studio** popular among Asian Americans, Jan. 21. Footage released Jan. 27 showed five Black officers fatally assaulting **Tyre Nichols**, a 29-year-old Black man, after a traffic stop in **Memphis**, TN.

A Norfolk Southern freight train carrying industrial chemicals derailed Feb. 3 in **East Palestine**, OH, leading to evacuation of residents. A U.S. Air Force jet Feb. 4 shot down a **Chinese spy balloon** flying off the coast of South Carolina after traveling across the country.

On Mar. 13 the administration announced approval of the massive Willow **oil and gas drilling** project in Alaska's North Slope. The White House announced there would be new restrictions on future drilling in the Arctic Ocean.

A shooter, Mar. 27, killed six children and adults at the **Covenant School** in Nashville, TN. Students at schools across the nation held walkouts Apr. 5 calling for **gun reform**.

Former Pres. **Trump arraigned** Apr. 4 in a Manhattan court for allegedly falsifying business records to conceal a pre-election "hush-money" payment to cover up an affair with a porn star.

ProPublica reported Apr. 6 that a billionaire GOP donor paid for numerous luxury vacations for Associate Supreme Court Justice **Clarence Thomas** and his wife; these and other such disclosures led the Court to announce its first-ever **code of conduct**, Nov. 13.

The Phantom of the Opera closed Apr. 16, after 35 years, a record run for a Broadway musical.

Fox News agreed Apr. 18 to pay **Dominion Voting Systems** $787.5 mil, settling claims that Fox had promoted the fiction that Dominion manipulated its voting machines in the 2020 election.

U.S. Supreme Court, voting 7-2 Apr. 21, upheld access to **mifepristone,** a prescription drug commonly used for abortions. On July 13 the FDA announced its approval of first U.S. **over-the-counter birth control** pill.

A civil jury in New York City May 9 found that former Pres. Trump had sexually assaulted writer **E. Jean Carroll** in the mid-1990s and later defamed her; she was awarded $5 mil.

Pres. Biden Apr. 10 signed legislation ending the **COVID-19 national emergency** as of May 11, thus ending emergency use of **"Title 42"** to deport asylum seekers. On June 3, Biden signed a compromise bill suspending the federal $34.1 tril debt limit through Jan. 1, 2025.

A federal grand jury in Miami, FL, June 8, indicted former Pres. Trump for allegedly retaining **classified documents** unlawfully.

On June 29 the U.S. Supreme Court struck down **affirmative action**, or the direct use of race as a factor in college admissions.

The union representing TV and movie actors, **SAG-AFTRA**, went on strike July 13, joining screenwriters on strike since May 2. The combined **strike** crippled film and TV production. Both unions won concessions and writers returned to work Sept. 27; the actors' strike lasted until Nov. 8.

The Fed July 24 raised its key **interest rate** to the 5.25%-5.5% range, its highest in 22 years.

A federal grand jury indicted former Pres. Trump over alleged criminal acts aimed at **overturning 2020 presidential election** results on Aug. 1, and by a county grand jury in Georgia, with codefendants, on related charges Aug. 14. Eight presidential contenders joined in the first 2024 GOP debate, Aug. 23 in Milwaukee, WI; frontrunner Trump did not participate.

A wildfire Aug. 8 on the Hawaiian island of **Maui** left some 100 people dead.

Pres. Biden Sept. 30 signed into law a last-minute measure temporarily maintaining federal funding at current levels to avert **government shutdown**. House Speaker **Kevin McCarthy** (R, CA), who championed the bill, angered far-right Republicans, who had sought spending cuts. They engineered his removal, Oct. 3, and Rep. **Mike Johnson** (R, LA), was ultimately elected in his place, Oct. 25.

A shooter killed 18 people, Oct. 25, at two sites minutes apart in **Lewiston**, ME, prompting a citywide lockdown. A **six-week strike** by the autoworkers union (**UAW**) ended Oct. 30, after tentative agreements with automakers.

In off-year elections, Nov. 7, voters in strongly Republican Ohio easily approved a state constitutional amendment authorizing **access to abortion**.

The U.S. House, Dec. 1, expelled Rep. **George Santos** (R, NY) in a bipartisan 311-114 vote; the scandal-ridden freshman rep. was indicted in May on fraud-related charges. During a congressional committee hearing Dec. 5, presidents of Harvard, Univ. of Penn., and MIT drew criticism for seemingly hedging on answers to questions about **antisemitism**.

A Manhattan jury Dec. 5 found **Trump Org.** guilty of financial crimes, including falsifying records to conceal tax-free perks for employees. Federal regulators Dec. 13 announced that **Tesla** would recall over 2 mil vehicles in U.S. because of inadequate protections against driver misuse of its Autopilot system.

Colorado's Supreme Court Dec. 19 found former Pres. **Trump constitutionally ineligible** to run in the state's 2024 primary, because of his role in the Jan. 6, 2021, attack on the Capitol (insurrection); other states took similar actions. (Decision was unanimously overturned by U.S. Supreme Court, Mar. 2024.)

A House select committee investigating the 2021 **attack on the U.S. Capitol** Dec. 22 cited then-Pres. Trump as "central cause" of the attack and recommended criminal charges. U.S. Treasury Dept. Dec. 30 released Trump's 2015-20 federal **tax returns**, after the Supreme Court had rejected a last attempt by him to shield them from Congress. They showed little or no tax was paid in some years, due to declared business losses.

Pres. Biden Dec. 27 announced new defense **aid for Ukraine**, bringing the total since the war began to over $44 bil.

U.S. HISTORY: DOCUMENTS, SPEECHES, AND SYMBOLS

Patrick Henry's Speech to the Virginia Convention

The following is an excerpt from Patrick Henry's speech to the Virginia Convention, which met at St. John's Church in Richmond, on Mar. 23, 1775, to react to British oppression.

Gentlemen may cry, Peace, Peace—but there is no peace. The war is actually begun! The next gale that sweeps from the north will bring to our ears the clash of resounding arms! Our brethren are already in the field! Why stand we here idle? What is it that gentlemen wish? What would they have? Is life so dear, or peace so sweet, as to be purchased at the price of chains and slavery? Forbid it, Almighty God! I know not what course others may take; but as for me, give me liberty, or give me death!

Adoption of the Declaration of Independence

On June 7, 1776, Richard Henry Lee, who had issued the first call for a congress of the colonies, introduced in the Continental Congress at Philadelphia a resolution declaring "that these United Colonies are, and of right ought to be, free and independent states, that they are absolved from all allegiance to the British Crown, and that all political connection between them and the state of Great Britain is, and ought to be, totally dissolved."

The resolution, seconded by John Adams on behalf of the Massachusetts delegation, came up again June 11 when a committee of five chaired by Thomas Jefferson (VA) was appointed to express the purpose of the resolution in a declaration of independence. The other four were John Adams, Benjamin Franklin (PA), Robert R. Livingston (NY), and Roger Sherman (CT).

Drafting the Declaration was assigned to Jefferson, who worked on a portable desk of his own construction in a room at Market and 7th St. The committee reported the result on June 28, 1776. The members of the Congress suggested a number of changes, which Jefferson called "deplorable." They did not approve Jefferson's arraignment of the British people and King George III for encouraging and fostering the slave trade, which Jefferson called "an execrable commerce." They eliminated 630 words and added 146, leaving 1,322 words in the final draft. In its final form, capitalization was erratic. Jefferson had written that men were endowed with "inalienable" rights; in the final copy it came out as "unalienable."

The Lee-Adams resolution of independence was adopted by 12 yeas on July 2—the actual date of the act of independence. The Declaration, which explains the act, was adopted July 4.

After the Declaration was adopted, July 4, 1776, it was turned over to printer John Dunlap to be printed on broadsides. The original copy was lost and one of his broadsides was attached to a page in the journal of the Congress. It was read aloud July 8 in Philadelphia; Easton, PA; and Trenton, NJ. On July 9, it was read by order of Gen. George Washington to the troops assembled on the Common in New York City (now City Hall Park).

The Continental Congress of July 19, 1776, adopted the following resolution:

"Resolved, That the Declaration passed on the 4th, be fairly engrossed on parchment with the title and stile of 'The Unanimous Declaration of the thirteen United States of America' and that the same, when engrossed, be signed by every member of Congress." (Engrossing meant clearly writing out an official document.)

Not all delegates who signed the engrossed Declaration had been present on July 4. Among them were Robert Morris (PA), William Williams (CT), and Samuel Chase (MD), who signed on Aug. 2. Oliver Wolcott (CT), George Wythe (VA), Richard Henry Lee (VA), and Elbridge Gerry (MA) signed in Aug. and Sept.; Matthew Thornton (NH) joined the Congress Nov. 4 and signed later. Thomas McKean (DE) rejoined Washington's army before signing and said later that he signed in 1781.

Charles Carroll of Carrollton was appointed a delegate by Maryland on July 4, 1776, presented his credentials July 18, and signed the engrossed Declaration on Aug. 2. Born Sept. 19, 1737, he was 95 years old and the last surviving signer when he died Nov. 14, 1832.

Two Pennsylvania delegates who did not support the Declaration July 4, 1776, were replaced. The four New York delegates did not have authority from their state to vote on July 4. On July 9, the New York state convention authorized its delegates to approve the Declaration, and the Congress was so notified on July 15, 1776. The four signed the Declaration on Aug. 2.

Declaration of Independence

The Declaration of Independence was adopted by the Continental Congress in Philadelphia on July 4, 1776. John Hancock was president of the Congress, and Charles Thomson was secretary. A copy of the Declaration, engrossed (i.e., written in a clear hand) on parchment, was signed by members of Congress on and after Aug. 2, 1776. On Jan. 18, 1777, Congress ordered that "an authenticated copy, with the names of the members of Congress subscribing the same, be sent to each of the United States, and that they be desired to have the same put on record." Authenticated copies were printed in broadside form in Baltimore, where the Continental Congress was then in session. The following text is that of the original printed by John Dunlap in Philadelphia for the Continental Congress. The original is on display at the National Archives in Washington, DC.

In CONGRESS, July 4, 1776.
A DECLARATION
By the REPRESENTATIVES of the UNITED STATES OF AMERICA, In GENERAL CONGRESS assembled.

When in the Course of human Events, it becomes necessary for one People to dissolve the Political Bands which have connected them with another, and to assume among the Powers of the Earth, the separate and equal Station to which the Laws of Nature and of Nature's God entitle them, a decent Respect to the Opinions of Mankind requires that they should declare the causes which impel them to the Separation.

We hold these Truths to be self-evident, that all Men are created equal, that they are endowed by their Creator with certain unalienable Rights, that among these are Life, Liberty, and the Pursuit of Happiness—That to secure these Rights, Governments are instituted among Men, deriving their just Powers from the Consent of the Governed, that whenever any Form of Government becomes destructive of these Ends, it is the Right of the People to alter or to abolish it, and to institute new Government, laying its Foundation on such Principles, and organizing its Powers in such Form, as to them shall seem most likely to effect their Safety and Happiness. Prudence, indeed, will dictate that Governments long established should not be changed for light and transient Causes; and accordingly all Experience hath shewn, that Mankind are more disposed to suffer, while Evils are sufferable, than to right themselves by abolishing the Forms to which they are accustomed. But when a long Train of Abuses and Usurpations, pursuing invariably the same Object, evinces a Design to reduce them under absolute Despotism, it is their Right, it is their Duty, to throw off such Government, and to provide new Guards for their future Security. Such has been the patient Sufferance of these Colonies; and such is now the Necessity which constrains them to alter their former Systems of Government. The History of the present King of Great-Britain is a History of repeated Injuries and Usurpations, all having in direct Object the Establishment of an absolute Tyranny over these States. To prove this, let Facts be submitted to a candid World.

He has refused his Assent to Laws, the most wholesome and necessary for the public Good.

He has forbidden his Governors to pass Laws of immediate and pressing Importance, unless suspended in their Operation till his Assent should be obtained; and when so suspended, he has utterly neglected to attend to them.

He has refused to pass other Laws for the Accommodation of large Districts of People, unless those People would relinquish the Right of Representation in the Legislature, a Right inestimable to them, and formidable to Tyrants only.

He has called together Legislative Bodies at Places unusual, uncomfortable, and distant from the Depository of their Public Records, for the sole Purpose of fatiguing them into Compliance with his Measures.

He has dissolved Representative Houses repeatedly, for opposing with manly Firmness his Invasions on the Rights of the People.

He has refused for a long Time, after such Dissolutions, to cause others to be elected; whereby the Legislative Powers, incapable of Annihilation, have returned to the People at large for their exercise; the State remaining in the mean time exposed to all the Dangers of Invasion from without, and Convulsions within.

He has endeavoured to prevent the Population of these States; for that Purpose obstructing the Laws for Naturalization of Foreigners; refusing to pass others to encourage their Migrations hither, and raising the Conditions of new Appropriations of Lands.

He has obstructed the Administration of Justice, by refusing his Assent to Laws for establishing Judiciary Powers.

He has made Judges dependent on his Will alone, for the Tenure of their Offices, and the Amount and Payment of their Salaries.

He has erected a Multitude of new Offices, and sent hither Swarms of Officers to harrass our People, and eat out their Substance.

He has kept among us, in Times of Peace, Standing Armies, without the consent of our Legislatures.

He has affected to render the Military independent of and superior to the Civil Power.

He has combined with others to subject us to a Jurisdiction foreign to our Constitution, and unacknowledged by our Laws; giving his Assent to their Acts of pretended Legislation:

For quartering large Bodies of Armed Troops among us:

For protecting them, by a mock Trial, from Punishment for any Murders which they should commit on the Inhabitants of these States:

For cutting off our Trade with all Parts of the World:

For imposing Taxes on us without our Consent:

For depriving us, in many Cases, of the Benefits of Trial by Jury:

For transporting us beyond Seas to be tried for pretended Offences:

For abolishing the free System of English Laws in a neighbouring Province, establishing therein an arbitrary Government, and enlarging its Boundaries, so as to render it at once an Example and fit Instrument for introducing the same absolute Rule into these Colonies:

For taking away our Charters, abolishing our most valuable Laws, and altering fundamentally the Forms of our Governments:

For suspending our own Legislatures, and declaring themselves invested with Power to legislate for us in all Cases whatsoever.

He has abdicated Government here, by declaring us out of his Protection and waging War against us.

He has plundered our Seas, ravaged our Coasts, burnt our Towns, and destroyed the Lives of our People.

He is, at this Time, transporting large Armies of foreign Mercenaries to compleat the Works of Death, Desolation, and Tyranny, already begun with circumstances of Cruelty and Perfidy, scarcely paralleled in the most barbarous Ages, and totally unworthy the Head of a civilized Nation.

He has constrained our fellow Citizens taken Captive on the high Seas to bear Arms against their Country, to become the Executioners of their Friends and Brethren, or to fall themselves by their Hands.

He has excited domestic Insurrections amongst us, and has endeavoured to bring on the Inhabitants of our Frontiers, the merciless Indian Savages, whose known Rule of Warfare, is an undistinguished Destruction, of all Ages, Sexes and Conditions.

In every stage of these Oppressions we have Petitioned for Redress in the most humble Terms: Our repeated Petitions have been answered only by repeated Injury. A Prince, whose Character is thus marked by every act which may define a Tyrant, is unfit to be the Ruler of a free People.

Nor have we been wanting in Attentions to our British Brethren. We have warned them from Time to Time of Attempts by their Legislature to extend an unwarrantable Jurisdiction over us. We have reminded them of the Circumstances of our Emigration and Settlement here. We have appealed to their native Justice and Magnanimity, and we have conjured them by the Ties of our common Kindred to disavow these Usurpations, which, would inevitably interrupt our Connections and Correspondence. They too have been deaf to the Voice of Justice and of Consanguinity. We must, therefore, acquiesce in the Necessity, which denounces our Separation, and hold them, as we hold the rest of Mankind, Enemies in War, in Peace, Friends.

We, therefore, the Representatives of the UNITED STATES OF AMERICA, in General Congress, Assembled, appealing to the Supreme Judge of the World for the Rectitude of our Intentions, do, in the Name, and by Authority of the good People of these Colonies, solemnly Publish and Declare, That these United Colonies are, and of Right ought to be, Free and Independent States; that they are absolved from all Allegiance to the British Crown, and that all political Connection between them and the State of Great-Britain, is and ought to be totally dissolved; and that as Free and Independent States, they have full Power to levy War, conclude Peace, contract Alliances, establish Commerce, and to do all other Acts and Things which Independent States may of right do. And for the support of this Declaration, with a firm Reliance on the Protection of divine Providence, we mutually pledge to each other our Lives, our Fortunes, and our sacred Honor.

JOHN HANCOCK, President.

Attest.

CHARLES THOMSON, Secretary.

Signers of the Declaration of Independence

Delegate (state)	Occupation	Birthplace	Born	Died
Adams, John (MA)	Lawyer	Braintree (Quincy), MA	Oct. 30, 1735	July 4, 1826
Adams, Samuel (MA)	Merchant, brewer	Boston, MA	Sept. 27, 1722	Oct. 2, 1803
Bartlett, Josiah (NH)	Physician, judge	Amesbury, MA	Nov. 21, 1729	May 19, 1795
Braxton, Carter (VA)	Plantation owner	Newington Plantation, VA	Sept. 10, 1736	Oct. 10, 1797
Carroll, Charles, of Carrollton (MD)	Plantation owner	Annapolis, MD	Sept. 19, 1737	Nov. 14, 1832
Chase, Samuel (MD)	Lawyer, judge	Princess Anne, MD	Apr. 17, 1741	June 19, 1811
Clark, Abraham (NJ)	Surveyor	Elizabethtown, NJ	Feb. 15, 1726	Sept. 15, 1794
Clymer, George (PA)	Merchant	Philadelphia, PA	Mar. 16, 1739	Jan. 23, 1813
Ellery, William (RI)	Lawyer	Newport, RI	Dec. 22, 1727	Feb. 15, 1820
Floyd, William (NY)	Plantation owner, soldier	Brookhaven, NY	Dec. 17, 1734	Aug. 4, 1821
Franklin, Benjamin (PA)	Printer, inventor	Boston, MA	Jan. 17, 1706	Apr. 17, 1790
Gerry, Elbridge (MA)	Merchant	Marblehead, MA	July 17, 1744	Nov. 23, 1814
Gwinnett, Button (GA)	Merchant	Gloucester, England	c. 1735	May 19, 1777
Hall, Lyman (GA)	Physician	Wallingford, CT	Apr. 12, 1724	Oct. 19, 1790
Hancock, John (MA)	Merchant	Braintree (Quincy), MA	Jan. 12, 1737	Oct. 8, 1793
Harrison, Benjamin (VA)	Plantation owner	Charles City County, VA	Apr. 5, 1726	Apr. 24, 1791
Hart, John (NJ)	Plantation owner	Stonington, CT	c. 1713	May 11, 1779
Hewes, Joseph (NC)	Merchant	Kingston, NJ	Jan. 23, 1730	Nov. 10, 1779
Heyward, Thomas, Jr. (SC)	Lawyer, plantation owner	St. Luke's Parish, SC	July 28, 1746	Mar. 6, 1809
Hooper, William (NC)	Lawyer	Boston, MA	June 17, 1742	Oct. 14, 1790
Hopkins, Stephen (RI)	Judge, merchant	Providence, RI	Mar. 7, 1707	July 13, 1785
Hopkinson, Francis (NJ)	Composer, lawyer	Philadelphia, PA	Oct. 2, 1737	May 9, 1791
Huntington, Samuel (CT)	Lawyer, judge	Windham, CT	July 3, 1731	Jan. 5, 1796
Jefferson, Thomas (VA)	Lawyer, plantation owner	Shadwell, VA	Apr. 13, 1743	July 4, 1826
Lee, Francis Lightfoot (VA)	Plantation owner	Westmoreland County, VA	Oct. 14, 1734	Jan. 11, 1797
Lee, Richard Henry (VA)	Plantation owner	Westmoreland County, VA	Jan. 20, 1732	June 19, 1794
Lewis, Francis (NY)	Merchant	Llandaff, Wales	Mar. 21, 1713	Dec. 31, 1802
Livingston, Philip (NY)	Merchant	Albany, NY	Jan. 15, 1716	June 12, 1778
Lynch, Thomas, Jr. (SC)	Plantation owner	Winyah, SC	Aug. 5, 1749	(at sea) 1779
McKean, Thomas (DE)	Lawyer	New London, PA	Mar. 19, 1734	June 24, 1817
Middleton, Arthur (SC)	Plantation owner	Charleston, SC	June 26, 1742	Jan. 1, 1787
Morris, Lewis (NY)	Farmer, judge	Morrisania (Bronx County), NY	Apr. 8, 1726	Jan. 22, 1798
Morris, Robert (PA)	Merchant	Liverpool, England	Jan. 31, 1734	May 8, 1806
Morton, John (PA)	Surveyor	Ridley, PA	c. 1724	Apr. 1777
Nelson, Thomas, Jr. (VA)	Merchant	Yorktown, VA	Dec. 26, 1738	Jan. 4, 1789
Paca, William (MD)	Lawyer, judge	Abingdon, MD	Oct. 31, 1740	Oct. 23, 1799
Paine, Robert Treat (MA)	Lawyer, judge	Boston, MA	Mar. 11, 1731	May 11, 1814
Penn, John (NC)	Lawyer	Caroline County, VA	May 17, 1741	Sept. 14, 1788
Read, George (DE)	Lawyer, judge	Cecil County, MD	Sept. 18, 1733	Sept. 21, 1798
Rodney, Caesar (DE)	Farmer, judge	Dover, DE	Oct. 7, 1728	June 26, 1784
Ross, George (PA)	Lawyer, judge	New Castle, DE	May 10, 1730	July 14, 1779
Rush, Benjamin (PA)	Physician	Byberry Twp. (Philadelphia), PA	Jan. 4, 1746	Apr. 19, 1813
Rutledge, Edward (SC)	Lawyer, plantation owner	Charleston, SC	Nov. 23, 1749	Jan. 23, 1800
Sherman, Roger (CT)	Lawyer, judge	Newton, MA	Apr. 19, 1721	July 23, 1793
Smith, James (PA)	Lawyer	Ireland	c. 1719	July 11, 1806
Stockton, Richard (NJ)	Lawyer	Princeton, NJ	Oct. 1, 1730	Feb. 28, 1781
Stone, Thomas (MD)	Lawyer	Charles County, MD	c. 1743	Oct. 5, 1787
Taylor, George (PA)	Iron mfr., judge	Ireland	c. 1716	Feb. 23, 1781
Thornton, Matthew (NH)	Physician	Ireland	c. 1714	June 24, 1803
Walton, George (GA)	Lawyer, judge	Cumberland County, VA	c. 1749	Feb. 2, 1804
Whipple, William (NH)	Merchant, judge	Kittery, ME	Jan. 14, 1730	Nov. 28, 1785
Williams, William (CT)	Merchant	Lebanon, CT	c. 1731	Aug. 2, 1811
Wilson, James (PA)	Lawyer	Carskerdo, Scotland	Sept. 14, 1742	Aug. 21, 1798
Witherspoon, John (NJ)	Clergyman, educator	Gifford, Scotland	Feb. 5, 1723	Nov. 15, 1794
Wolcott, Oliver (CT)	Lawyer, judge	Windsor, CT	Nov. 20, 1726	Dec. 1, 1797
Wythe, George (VA)	Lawyer	Elizabeth City County, VA	c. 1726	June 8, 1806

Origin of the Constitution

The War of Independence was conducted by delegates from the original 13 states, who composed the Congress of the United States of America, known as the Continental Congress. In 1777 the Congress submitted to the legislatures of the states the Articles of Confederation and Perpetual Union, which were ratified by New Hampshire, Massachusetts, Rhode Island, Connecticut, New York, New Jersey, Pennsylvania, Delaware, Virginia, North Carolina, South Carolina, Georgia, and finally, in 1781, Maryland.

The first article read: "The stile of this confederacy shall be the United States of America." This did not signify a sovereign nation, because the states delegated only those powers they could not handle individually, such as to wage war, make treaties, and contract debts for general expenses (e.g., paying the army). Taxes for payment of such debts were levied by the individual states. The president signed himself "President of the United States in Congress assembled," but here the United States were considered in the plural, a cooperating group.

When the war was over, it became evident that a stronger federal union was needed. The Congress left the initiative to the legislatures. Virginia in Jan. 1786 appointed commissioners to meet with representatives of other states; delegates from Virginia, Delaware, New York, New Jersey, and Pennsylvania met at Annapolis. Alexander Hamilton prepared their call asking delegates from all states to meet in Philadelphia in May 1787 "to render the Constitution of the federal government adequate to the exigencies of the union." Congress endorsed the plan on Feb. 21, 1787. Delegates were appointed by all states except Rhode Island.

The convention was called for May 14, 1787, but a quorum was not present until May 25. George Washington was chosen president (presiding officer). The states certified 65 delegates, but 10 did not attend. The work was done by 55, not all of whom were present at all sessions. Of the 55 attending delegates, 39 signed Sept. 17, 1787, some with reservations, and 16 failed to sign. Some historians have said 74 delegates (nine more than the 65 actually certified) were named, and 19 failed to attend. These additional persons refused the appointment, were never delegates, and were never counted as absentees. Washington sent the Constitution to Congress, and that body, Sept. 28, 1787, ordered it sent to the legislatures, "in order to be submitted to a convention of delegates chosen in each state by the people thereof."

The Constitution was ratified by the votes of each state's convention as follows: Delaware, Dec. 7, 1787, unanimous; Pennsylvania, Dec. 12, 1787, 46 to 23; New Jersey, Dec. 18, 1787, unanimous; Georgia, Jan. 2, 1788, unanimous; Connecticut, Jan. 9, 1788, 128 to 40; Massachusetts, Feb. 6, 1788, 187 to 168; Maryland, Apr. 28, 1788, 63 to 11; South Carolina, May 23, 1788, 149 to 73; New Hampshire, June 21, 1788, 57 to 46; Virginia, June 25, 1788, 89 to 79; New York, July 26, 1788, 30 to 27. Nine states were needed to establish the operation of the Constitution "between the states so ratifying the same," and New Hampshire was the ninth state. The government did not declare the Constitution in effect until the first Wednesday in Mar. 1789, which was Mar. 4. After that, North Carolina ratified it on Nov. 21, 1789, 194 to 77; and Rhode Island, May 29, 1790, 34 to 32. Vermont in convention ratified it on Jan. 10, 1791, and by act of Congress approved on Feb. 18, 1791, was admitted into the Union as the 14th state, Mar. 4, 1791.

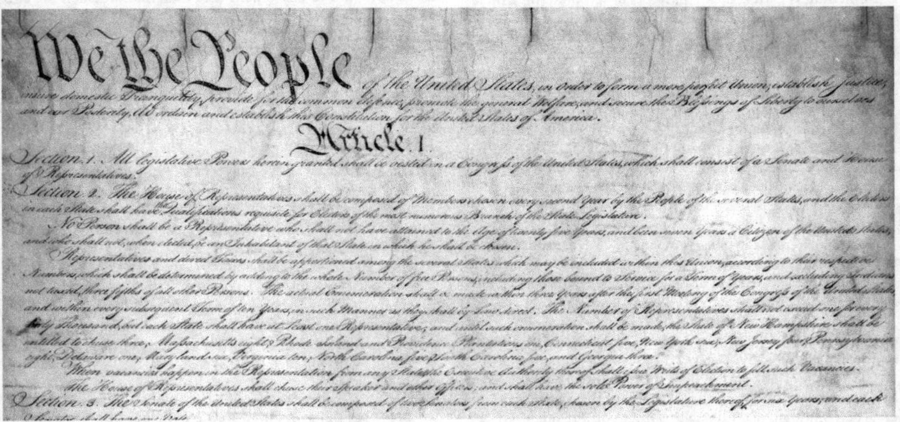
We the People of the United States, in Order to form a more perfect Union, establish Justice, insure domestic Tranquility, provide for the common defence, promote the general Welfare, and secure the Blessings of Liberty to ourselves and our Posterity, do ordain and establish this Constitution for the United States of America.

Article. I

Section. 1. All legislative Powers herein granted shall be vested in a Congress of the United States, which shall consist of a Senate and House of Representatives.

Section. 2. The House of Representatives shall be composed of Members chosen every second Year by the People of the several States, and the Electors in each State shall have Qualifications requisite for Electors of the most numerous Branch of the State Legislature.

No Person shall be a Representative who shall not have attained to the Age of twenty five Years, and been seven Years a Citizen of the United States, and who shall not, when elected, be an Inhabitant of that State in which he shall be chosen.

Representatives and direct Taxes shall be apportioned among the several States which may be included within this Union, according to their respective Numbers, which shall be determined by adding to the whole Number of free Persons, including those bound to Service for a Term of Years, and excluding Indians not taxed, three fifths of all other Persons. The actual Enumeration shall be made within three Years after the first Meeting of the Congress of the United States, and within every subsequent Term of ten Years, in such Manner as they shall by Law direct. The Number of Representatives shall not exceed one for every thirty Thousand, but each State shall have at Least one Representative; and until such enumeration shall be made, the State of New Hampshire shall be entitled to chuse three, Massachusetts eight, Rhode Island and Providence Plantations one, Connecticut five, New York six, New Jersey four, Pennsylvania eight, Delaware one, Maryland six, Virginia ten, North Carolina five, South Carolina five, and Georgia three.

When vacancies happen in the Representation from any State, the Executive Authority thereof shall issue Writs of Election to fill such Vacancies.

The House of Representatives shall chuse their Speaker and other Officers; and shall have the sole Power of Impeachment.

Section. 3. The Senate of the United States shall be composed of two Senators from each State, chosen by the Legislature thereof for six Years; and each

Constitution of the United States

The text of the Constitution given here is from the centennial edition of *The Constitution of the United States of America: Analysis and Interpretation*, prepared by the Library of Congress and issued by the U.S. Government Printing Office. Aug. 26, 2017. Text in brackets indicates that an item has been superseded or amended, or provides background information. **Boldface text** preceding an article, section, or amendment is a brief summary, added by *The World Almanac*.

The Original Seven Articles

PREAMBLE

We the People of the United States, in Order to form a more perfect Union, establish Justice, insure domestic Tranquility, provide for the common defence, promote the general Welfare, and secure the Blessings of Liberty to ourselves and our Posterity, do ordain and establish this Constitution for the United States of America.

ARTICLE I.

Section 1—Legislative powers, in whom vested.

All legislative Powers herein granted shall be vested in a Congress of the United States, which shall consist of a Senate and House of Representatives.

Section 2—House of Representatives, how and by whom chosen. Qualifications of a Representative. Representatives and direct taxes, how apportioned and enumerated. Vacancies to be filled. Choosing of officers and power of impeachment.

The House of Representatives shall be composed of Members chosen every second Year by the People of the several States, and the Electors in each State shall have the Qualifications requisite for Electors of the most numerous Branch of the State Legislature.

No Person shall be a Representative who shall not have attained to the Age of twenty five Years, and been seven Years a Citizen of the United States, and who shall not, when elected, be an Inhabitant of that State in which he shall be chosen.

[Representatives and direct Taxes shall be apportioned among the several States which may be included within this Union, according to their respective Numbers, which shall be determined by adding to the whole Number of free Persons, including those bound to Service for a Term of Years, and excluding Indians not taxed, three fifths of all other Persons.] *[The part of the previous sentence regarding apportionment of representatives among the states was changed by Amendment XIV, section 2, and apportionment of taxes by Amendment XVI.]* The actual Enumeration shall be made within three Years after the first Meeting of the Congress of the United States, and within every subsequent Term of ten Years, in such Manner as they shall by Law direct. The Number of Representatives shall not exceed one for every thirty Thousand, but each State shall have at Least one Representative; and until such enumeration shall be made, the State of New Hampshire shall be entitled to chuse three, Massachusetts eight, Rhode-Island and Providence Plantations one, Connecticut five, New York six, New Jersey four, Pennsylvania eight, Delaware one, Maryland six, Virginia ten, North Carolina five, South Carolina five, and Georgia three.

When vacancies happen in the Representation from any State, the Executive Authority thereof shall issue Writs of Election to fill such Vacancies.

The House of Representatives shall chuse their Speaker and other Officers; and shall have the sole Power of Impeachment.

Section 3—Senators, how and by whom chosen. How assembled. Qualifications of a Senator. President of the Senate. President pro tempore and other officers of the Senate, how chosen. Power to try impeachments. Judgment in cases of impeachment.

The Senate of the United States shall be composed of two Senators from each State, [chosen by the Legislature] *[The preceding words were superseded by Amendment XVII.]* thereof, for six Years; and each Senator shall have one Vote.

Immediately after they shall be assembled in Consequence of the first Election, they shall be divided as equally as may be into three Classes. The Seats of the Senators of the first Class shall be vacated at the Expiration of the second Year, of the second Class at the Expiration of the fourth Year, and of the third Class at the Expiration of the sixth Year, so that one third may be chosen every second Year; [and if Vacancies happen by Resignation, or otherwise, during the Recess of the Legislature of any State, the Executive thereof may make temporary Appointments until the next Meeting of the Legislature, which shall then fill such Vacancies.] *[The words in brackets were superseded by Amendment XVII.]*

No Person shall be a Senator who shall not have attained to the Age of thirty Years, and been nine Years a Citizen of the United States, and who shall not, when elected, be an Inhabitant of that State for which he shall be chosen.

The Vice President of the United States shall be President of the Senate, but shall have no Vote, unless they be equally divided.

The Senate shall chuse their other Officers, and also a President pro tempore, in the Absence of the Vice President, or when he shall exercise the Office of President of the United States.

The Senate shall have the sole Power to try all Impeachments. When sitting for that Purpose, they shall be on Oath or Affirmation. When the President of the United States is tried, the Chief Justice shall preside: And no Person shall be convicted without the Concurrence of two thirds of the Members present.

Judgment in Cases of Impeachment shall not extend further than to removal from Office, and disqualification to hold and enjoy any Office of honor, Trust or Profit under the United States: but the Party convicted shall nevertheless be liable and subject to Indictment, Trial, Judgment and Punishment, according to Law.

Section 4—Times, places, manner of elections. Time of assembly.

The Times, Places and Manner of holding Elections for Senators and Representatives, shall be prescribed in each State by the Legislature thereof; but the Congress may at any time by Law make or alter such Regulations, except as to the Places of chusing Senators.

The Congress shall assemble at least once in every Year, and such Meeting shall be [on the first Monday in December], *[The words in brackets were superseded by Amendment XX, section 2.]* unless they shall by Law appoint a different Day.

Section 5—Membership, quorums, adjournments. Rules of proceedings. Journal of proceedings. Time of adjournments.

Each House shall be the Judge of the Elections, Returns and Qualifications of its own Members, and a Majority of each shall constitute a Quorum to do Business; but a smaller Number may adjourn from day to day, and may be authorized to compel the Attendance of absent Members, in such Manner, and under such Penalties as each House may provide.

Each House may determine the Rules of its Proceedings, punish its Members for disorderly Behaviour, and, with the Concurrence of two thirds, expel a Member.

Each House shall keep a Journal of its Proceedings, and from time to time publish the same, excepting such Parts as may in their Judgment require Secrecy; and the Yeas and Nays of the Members of either House on any question shall, at the Desire of one fifth of those Present, be entered on the Journal.

Neither House, during the Session of Congress, shall, without the Consent of the other, adjourn for more than three days, nor to any other Place than that in which the two Houses shall be sitting.

Section 6—Compensation, privileges. Incompatible offices.

The Senators and Representatives shall receive a Compensation for their Services, to be ascertained by Law, and paid out of the Treasury of the United States. They shall in all Cases, except Treason, Felony and Breach of the Peace, be privileged from Arrest during their Attendance at the Session of their respective Houses, and in going to and returning from the same; and for any Speech or Debate in either House, they shall not be questioned in any other Place.

No Senator or Representative shall, during the Time for which he was elected, be appointed to any civil Office under the Authority of the United States, which shall have been created, or the Emoluments whereof shall have been encreased during such time; and no Person holding any Office under the United States, shall be a Member of either House during his Continuance in Office.

Section 7—House to originate revenue bills. Legislative process; bill presented to the President before becoming law. Passing of bill over objections of President, veto.

All Bills for raising Revenue shall originate in the House of Representatives; but the Senate may propose or concur with Amendments as on other Bills.

Every Bill which shall have passed the House of Representatives and the Senate, shall, before it become a Law, be presented to the President of the United States; If he approve he shall sign it, but if not he shall return it, with his Objections to that House in which it shall have originated, who shall enter the Objections at large on their Journal, and proceed to reconsider it. If after such Reconsideration two thirds of that House shall agree to pass the Bill, it shall be sent, together with the Objections, to the other House, by which it shall likewise be reconsidered, and if approved by two thirds of that House, it shall become a Law. But in all such Cases the Votes of both Houses shall be determined by Yeas and Nays, and the Names of the Persons voting for and against the Bill shall be entered on the Journal of each House respectively. If any Bill shall not be returned by the President within ten Days (Sundays excepted) after it shall have been presented to him, the Same shall be a Law, in like Manner as if he had signed it, unless the Congress by their Adjournment prevent its Return, in which Case it shall not be a Law.

Every Order, Resolution, or Vote to which the Concurrence of the Senate and House of Representatives may be necessary (except on a question of Adjournment) shall be presented to the President of the United States; and before the Same shall take Effect, shall be approved by him, or being disapproved by him, shall be repassed by two thirds of the Senate and House of Representatives, according to the Rules and Limitations prescribed in the Case of a Bill.

Section 8—Powers of Congress.

The Congress shall have Power To lay and collect Taxes, Duties, Imposts and Excises, to pay the Debts and provide for the common Defence and general Welfare of the United States; but all Duties, Imposts and Excises shall be uniform throughout the United States;

To borrow Money on the credit of the United States;

To regulate Commerce with foreign Nations, and among the several States, and with the Indian Tribes;

To establish an uniform Rule of Naturalization, and uniform Laws on the subject of Bankruptcies throughout the United States;

To coin Money, regulate the Value thereof, and of foreign Coin, and fix the Standard of Weights and Measures;

To provide for the Punishment of counterfeiting the Securities and current Coin of the United States;

To establish Post Offices and post Roads;

To promote the Progress of Science and useful Arts, by securing for limited Times to Authors and Inventors the exclusive Right to their respective Writings and Discoveries;

To constitute Tribunals inferior to the supreme Court;

To define and punish Piracies and Felonies committed on the high Seas, and Offences against the Law of Nations;

To declare War, grant Letters of Marque and Reprisal, and make Rules concerning Captures on Land and Water;

To raise and support Armies, but no Appropriation of Money to that Use shall be for a longer Term than two Years;

To provide and maintain a Navy;

To make Rules for the Government and Regulation of the land and naval Forces;

To provide for calling forth the Militia to execute the Laws of the Union, suppress Insurrections and repel Invasions;

To provide for organizing, arming, and disciplining, the Militia, and for governing such Part of them as may be employed in the Service of the United States, reserving to the States respectively, the Appointment of the Officers, and the Authority of training the Militia according to the discipline prescribed by Congress;

To exercise exclusive Legislation in all Cases whatsoever, over such District (not exceeding ten Miles square) as may, by Cession of particular States, and the Acceptance of Congress, become the Seat of the Government of the United States, and to exercise like Authority over all Places purchased by the Consent of the Legislature of the State in which the Same shall be, for the Erection of Forts, Magazines, Arsenals, dock-Yards, and other needful Buildings;—And

To make all Laws which shall be necessary and proper for carrying into Execution the foregoing Powers, and all other Powers vested by this Constitution in the Government of the United States, or in any Department or Officer thereof.

Section 9—Powers denied to Congress: Importation of slaves. Habeas corpus. Bills of attainder. Taxes, how apportioned. Export duty. Preference to ports. Money, how drawn from Treasury. Titles of nobility.

The Migration or Importation of such Persons as any of the States now existing shall think proper to admit, shall not be prohibited by the Congress prior to the Year one thousand eight hundred and eight, but a Tax or duty may be imposed on such Importation, not exceeding ten dollars for each Person.

The Privilege of the Writ of Habeas Corpus shall not be suspended, unless when in Cases of Rebellion or Invasion the public Safety may require it.

No Bill of Attainder or ex post facto Law shall be passed.

No Capitation, or other direct, Tax shall be laid, unless in Proportion to the Census or Enumeration herein before directed to be taken.

No Tax or Duty shall be laid on Articles exported from any State.

No Preference shall be given by any Regulation of Commerce or Revenue to the Ports of one State over those of another: nor shall Vessels bound to, or from, one State, be obliged to enter, clear, or pay Duties in another.

No Money shall be drawn from the Treasury, but in Consequence of Appropriations made by Law; and a regular Statement and Account of the Receipts and Expenditures of all public Money shall be published from time to time.

No Title of Nobility shall be granted by the United States: And no Person holding any Office of Profit or Trust under them, shall, without the Consent of the Congress, accept of any present, Emolument, Office, or Title, of any kind whatever, from any King, Prince, or foreign State.

Section 10—States prohibited from the exercise of certain powers.

No State shall enter into any Treaty, Alliance, or Confederation; grant Letters of Marque and Reprisal; coin Money; emit Bills of Credit; make any Thing but gold and silver Coin a Tender in Payment of Debts; pass any Bill of Attainder, ex post facto Law, or Law impairing the Obligation of Contracts, or grant any Title of Nobility.

No State shall, without the Consent of the Congress, lay any Imposts or Duties on Imports or Exports, except what may be absolutely necessary for executing it's inspection Laws: and the net Produce of all Duties and Imposts, laid by any State on Imports or Exports, shall be for the Use of the Treasury of the United States; and all such Laws shall be subject to the Revision and Controul of the Congress.

No State shall, without the Consent of Congress, lay any Duty of Tonnage, keep Troops, or Ships of War in time of Peace, enter into any Agreement or Compact with another State, or with a foreign Power, or engage in War, unless actually invaded, or in such imminent Danger as will not admit of delay.

ARTICLE II.

Section 1—President, powers and term of office. Electors, number and how appointed. Electors to vote for President. Qualifications of President. On whom duties devolve in case of removal, death, etc., of President. President's compensation. Oath of office.

The executive Power shall be vested in a President of the United States of America. He shall hold his Office during the Term of four Years, and, together with the Vice President, chosen for the same Term, be elected, as follows:

Each State shall appoint, in such Manner as the Legislature thereof may direct, a Number of Electors, equal to the whole Number of Senators and Representatives to which the State may be entitled in the Congress: but no Senator or Representative, or Person holding an Office of Trust or Profit under the United States, shall be appointed an Elector.

[The Electors shall meet in their respective States, and vote by Ballot for two Persons, of whom one at least shall not be an Inhabitant of the same State with themselves. And they shall make a List of all the Persons voted for, and of the Number of Votes for each; which List they shall sign and certify, and transmit sealed to the Seat of the Government of the United States, directed to the President of the Senate. The President of the Senate shall, in the Presence of the Senate and House of Representatives, open all the Certificates, and the Votes shall then be counted. The Person having the greatest Number of Votes shall be the President, if such Number be a Majority of the whole Number of Electors appointed; and if there be more than one who have such Majority, and have an equal Number of Votes, then the House of Representatives shall immediately chuse by Ballot one of them for President; and if no Person have a Majority, then from the five highest on the List the said House shall in like Manner chuse the President. But in chusing the President, the Votes shall be taken by States, the Representation from each State having one Vote; A quorum for this Purpose shall consist of a Member or Members from two thirds of the States, and a Majority of all the States shall be necessary to a Choice. In every Case, after the Choice of the President, the Person having the greatest Number of Votes of the Electors shall be the Vice President. But if there should remain two or more who have equal Votes, the Senate shall chuse from them by Ballot the Vice President.] *[This clause was superseded by Amendment XII.]*

The Congress may determine the Time of chusing the Electors, and the Day on which they shall give their Votes; which Day shall be the same throughout the United States.

No Person except a natural born Citizen, or a Citizen of the United States, at the time of the Adoption of this Constitution, shall be eligible to the Office of President; neither shall any Person be eligible to that Office who shall not have attained to the Age of thirty five Years, and been fourteen Years a Resident within the United States. *[For qualification of the Vice President, see Amendment XII.]*

[In Case of the Removal of the President from Office, or of his Death, Resignation, or Inability to discharge the Powers and Duties of the said Office, the Same shall devolve on the Vice President, and the Congress may by Law provide for the Case of Removal, Death, Resignation or Inability, both of the President and Vice President, declaring what Officer shall then act as President, and such Officer shall act accordingly, until the Disability be removed, or a President shall be elected.] *[This clause was superseded by Amendment XXV.]*

The President shall, at stated Times, receive for his Services, a Compensation, which shall neither be encreased nor diminished during the Period for which he shall have been elected, and he shall not receive within that Period any other Emolument from the United States, or any of them.

Before he enter on the Execution of his Office, he shall take the following Oath or Affirmation:—

"I do solemnly swear (or affirm) that I will faithfully execute the Office of President of the United States, and will to the best of my Ability, preserve, protect and defend the Constitution of the United States."

Section 2—President to be Commander in Chief. Power to make treaties; nominations for, appointments to certain offices. Power to fill vacancies during Senate recess.

The President shall be Commander in Chief of the Army and Navy of the United States, and of the Militia of the several States, when called into the actual Service of the United States; he may require the Opinion, in writing, of the principal Officer in each of the executive Departments, upon any Subject relating to the Duties of their respective Offices, and he shall have Power to Grant Reprieves and Pardons for Offences against the United States, except in Cases of Impeachment.

He shall have Power, by and with the Advice and Consent of the Senate, to make Treaties, provided two thirds of the Senators present concur; and he shall nominate, and by and with the Advice and Consent of the Senate, shall appoint Ambassadors, other public Ministers and Consuls, Judges of the supreme Court, and all other Officers of the United States, whose Appointments are not herein otherwise provided for, and which shall be established by Law: but the Congress may by Law vest the Appointment of such inferior Officers, as they think proper, in the President alone, in the Courts of Law, or in the Heads of Departments.

The President shall have Power to fill up all Vacancies that may happen during the Recess of the Senate, by granting Commissions which shall expire at the End of their next Session.

Section 3—President shall communicate to, may convene and adjourn Congress; shall receive ambassadors, execute laws, and commission officers.

He shall from time to time give to the Congress Information on the State of the Union, and recommend to their Consideration such Measures as he shall judge necessary and expedient; he may, on extraordinary Occasions, convene both Houses, or either of them, and in Case of Disagreement between them, with Respect to the Time of Adjournment, he may adjourn them to such Time as he shall think proper; he shall receive Ambassadors and other public Ministers; he shall take Care that the Laws be faithfully executed, and shall Commission all the Officers of the United States.

Section 4—All civil offices forfeited for certain crimes.

The President, Vice President and all civil Officers of the United States, shall be removed from Office on Impeachment for, and Conviction of, Treason, Bribery, or other high Crimes and Misdemeanors.

ARTICLE III.

Section 1—Judicial powers, tenure, compensation.

The judicial Power of the United States, shall be vested in one supreme Court, and in such inferior Courts as the Congress may from time to time ordain and establish. The Judges, both of the supreme and inferior Courts, shall hold their Offices during good Behaviour, and shall, at stated Times, receive for their Services, a Compensation, which shall not be diminished during their Continuance in Office.

Section 2—Judicial power, cases to which it extends. Jurisdiction of Supreme Court. Trial by jury; where held.

The judicial Power shall extend to all Cases, in Law and Equity, arising under this Constitution, the Laws of the United States, and Treaties made, or which shall be made, under their Authority;—to all Cases affecting Ambassadors, other public Ministers and Consuls;—to all Cases of admiralty and maritime Jurisdiction;—to Controversies to which the United States shall be a Party;—to Controversies between two or more States;—[between a State and Citizens of another State;]—between Citizens of different States;—between Citizens of the same State claiming Lands under Grants of different States, [and between a State, or the Citizens thereof, and foreign States, Citizens or Subjects.] *[This section was modified by Amendment XI.]*

In all Cases affecting Ambassadors, other public Ministers and Consuls, and those in which a State shall be Party, the supreme Court shall have original Jurisdiction. In all the other Cases before mentioned, the supreme Court shall have appellate Jurisdiction, both as to Law and Fact, with such Exceptions, and under such Regulations as the Congress shall make.

The Trial of all Crimes, except in Cases of Impeachment, shall be by Jury; and such Trial shall be held in the State where the said Crimes shall have been committed; but when not committed within any State, the Trial shall be at such Place or Places as the Congress may by Law have directed.

Section 3—Treason defined. Punishment of.

Treason against the United States, shall consist only in levying War against them, or in adhering to their Enemies, giving them Aid and Comfort. No Person shall be convicted of Treason unless on the Testimony of two Witnesses to the same overt Act, or on Confession in open Court.

The Congress shall have Power to declare the Punishment of Treason, but no Attainder of Treason shall work Corruption of Blood, or Forfeiture except during the Life of the Person attainted.

ARTICLE IV.

Section 1—Each State to give credit to the public acts, etc., of every other State.

Full Faith and Credit shall be given in each State to the public Acts, Records, and judicial Proceedings of every other State. And the Congress may by general Laws prescribe the Manner in which such Acts, Records and Proceedings shall be proved, and the Effect thereof.

Section 2—Privileges of citizens of each State. Fugitives from justice to be delivered up. Fugitives from service or labor, to be delivered up.

The Citizens of each State shall be entitled to all Privileges and Immunities of Citizens in the several States.

A Person charged in any State with Treason, Felony, or other Crime, who shall flee from Justice, and be found in another State, shall on Demand of the executive Authority of the State from which he fled, be delivered up, to be removed to the State having Jurisdiction of the Crime.

[No Person held to Service or Labour in one State, under the Laws thereof, escaping into another, shall, in Consequence of any Law or Regulation therein, be discharged from such Service or Labour, but shall be delivered up on Claim of the Party to whom such Service or Labour may be due.] *[This clause was superseded by Amendment XIII.]*

Section 3—Admission of new States. Power of Congress over territory and other property.

New States may be admitted by the Congress into this Union; but no new State shall be formed or erected within the Jurisdiction of any other State; nor any State be formed by the Junction of two or more States, or Parts of States, without the Consent of the Legislatures of the States concerned as well as of the Congress.

The Congress shall have Power to dispose of and make all needful Rules and Regulations respecting the Territory or other Property belonging to the United States; and nothing in this Constitution shall be so construed as to Prejudice any Claims of the United States, or of any particular State.

Section 4—Republican form of government guaranteed; each State to be protected.

The United States shall guarantee to every State in this Union a Republican Form of Government, and shall protect each of them against Invasion; and on Application of the Legislature, or of the Executive (when the Legislature cannot be convened) against domestic Violence.

ARTICLE V.

Constitution, how amended; proviso.

The Congress, whenever two thirds of both Houses shall deem it necessary, shall propose Amendments to this Constitution, or, on the Application of the Legislatures of two thirds of the several States, shall call a Convention for proposing Amendments, which, in either Case, shall be valid to all Intents and Purposes, as Part of this Constitution, when ratified by the Legislatures of three fourths of the several States, or by Conventions in three fourths thereof, as the one or the other Mode of Ratification may be proposed by the Congress; Provided that no Amendment which may be made prior to the Year One thousand eight hundred and eight shall in any Manner affect the first and fourth Clauses in the Ninth Section of the first Article; and that no State, without its Consent, shall be deprived of its equal Suffrage in the Senate.

ARTICLE VI.

Certain debts and engagements shall be valid. Constitution, laws and treaties made, shall be supreme law of the United States. Oath to support Constitution, by whom taken; no religious test shall be required.

All Debts contracted and Engagements entered into, before the Adoption of this Constitution, shall be as valid against the United States under this Constitution, as under the Confederation.

This Constitution, and the Laws of the United States which shall be made in Pursuance thereof; and all Treaties made, or which shall be made, under the Authority of the United States, shall be the supreme Law of the Land; and the Judges in every State shall be bound thereby, any Thing in the Constitution or Laws of any State to the Contrary notwithstanding.

The Senators and Representatives before mentioned, and the Members of the several State Legislatures, and all executive and judicial Officers, both of the United States and of the several States, shall be bound by Oath or Affirmation, to support this Constitution; but no religious Test shall ever be required as a Qualification to any Office or public Trust under the United States.

ARTICLE VII.

Ratification to establish the Constitution.

The Ratification of the Conventions of nine States, shall be sufficient for the Establishment of this Constitution between the States so ratifying the Same.

done in Convention by the Unanimous Consent of the States present the Seventeenth Day of September in the Year of our Lord one thousand seven hundred and Eighty seven and of the Independance of the United States of America the Twelfth. In witness whereof We have hereunto subscribed our Names,

G^{o}. Washington, Presid^{t}. and deputy from Virginia

New Hampshire—John Langdon, Nicholas Gilman

Massachusetts—Nathaniel Gorham, Rufus King

Connecticut—W^{m}. Saml. Johnson, Roger Sherman

New York—Alexander Hamilton

New Jersey—Wil: Livingston, David Brearley, W^{m}. Paterson, Jona: Dayton

Pennsylvania—B Franklin, Thomas Mifflin, Robt. Morris, Geo. Clymer, Thos. FitzSimons, Jared Ingersoll, James Wilson, Gouv Morris

Delaware—Geo: Read, Gunning Bedford jun, John Dickinson, Richard Bassett, Jaco: Broom

Maryland—James McHenry, Dan of St Thos. Jenifer, Danl Carroll

Virginia—John Blair, James Madison Jr.

North Carolina—W^{m}. Blount, Rich^{d}. Dobbs Spaight, Hu Williamson

South Carolina—J. Rutledge, Charles Cotesworth Pinckney, Charles Pinckney, Pierce Butler

Georgia—William Few, Abr Baldwin

[George Washington was first to sign the Constitution on Sept. 17, 1787, followed by state delegates in order of geography, from north to south. In total, 38 delegates signed the Constitution, although Delaware delegate George Reed signed for absent delegate John Dickinson, bringing the total signatures to 39. Three delegates abstained from signing in protest of the absent Bill of Rights.]

Origin of the Bill of Rights

Congress, at its first session in New York, NY, submitted to the states 12 amendments Sept. 25, 1789, to clarify certain individual and state rights not named in the Constitution. They are generally called the Bill of Rights.

Influential in framing these amendments was the Declaration of Rights of Virginia, written by George Mason (1725-92) in 1776. Mason, a Virginia delegate to the Constitutional Convention, did not sign the Constitution and opposed its ratification on the ground that it did not sufficiently oppose slavery or safeguard individual rights.

In the preamble to the resolution offering the proposed amendments, Congress said: "The Conventions of a number of the States, having at the time of their adopting the Constitution, expressed a desire, in order to prevent misconstruction or abuse of its powers, that further declaratory and restrictive clauses should be added: And as extending the ground of public confidence in the Government, will best insure the beneficent ends of its institution."

Ten of these amendments, originally three to 12 inclusive, were ratified by the states as follows: New Jersey, Nov. 20, 1789; Maryland, Dec. 19, 1789; North Carolina, Dec. 22, 1789; South Carolina, Jan. 19, 1790; New Hampshire, Jan. 25, 1790; Delaware, Jan. 28, 1790; New York, Feb. 27, 1790; Pennsylvania, Mar. 10, 1790; Rhode Island, June 7, 1790; Vermont, Nov. 3, 1791; Virginia, Dec. 15, 1791; Massachusetts, Mar. 2, 1939; Georgia, Mar. 18, 1939; Connecticut, Apr. 19, 1939. These original 10 ratified amendments follow as Amendments I to X inclusive.

Of the two original proposed amendments that were not ratified promptly by the necessary number of states, the first related to apportionment of Representatives; the second, relating to compensation of members of Congress, was ratified in 1992 and became Amendment XXVII.

The Bill of Rights

In force Dec. 15, 1791

AMENDMENT I.

Religious establishment prohibited. Freedom of speech and of press; right to assemble and to petition.

Congress shall make no law respecting an establishment of religion, or prohibiting the free exercise thereof; or abridging the freedom of speech, or of the press; or the right of the people peaceably to assemble, and to petition the Government for a redress of grievances.

AMENDMENT II.

Right to keep and bear arms.

A well regulated Militia, being necessary to the security of a free State, the right of the people to keep and bear Arms shall not be infringed.

AMENDMENT III.

Conditions for quartering of soldiers.

No Soldier shall, in time of peace be quartered in any house, without the consent of the Owner, nor in time of war, but in a manner to be prescribed by law.

AMENDMENT IV.

Protection from unreasonable search and seizure.

The right of the people to be secure in their persons, houses, papers, and effects, against unreasonable searches and seizures, shall not be violated, and no Warrants shall issue but upon probable cause, supported by Oath or affirmation, and particularly describing the place to be searched, and the persons or things to be seized.

AMENDMENT V.

Provisions concerning prosecution and due process of law. Compensation of private property taken for public use.

No person shall be held to answer for a capital, or otherwise infamous crime, unless on a presentment or indictment of a Grand Jury, except in cases arising in the land or naval forces, or in the Militia, when in actual service in time of War or public danger; nor shall any person be subject for the same offence to be twice put in jeopardy of life or limb; nor shall be compelled in any criminal case to be a witness against himself, nor be deprived of life, liberty, or property, without due process of law; nor shall private property be taken for public use, without just compensation.

AMENDMENT VI.

Rights of accused in criminal prosecutions.

In all criminal prosecutions, the accused shall enjoy the right to a speedy and public trial, by an impartial jury of the State and district wherein the crime shall have been committed, which district shall have been previously ascertained by law, and to be informed of the nature and cause of the accusation; to be confronted with the witnesses against him; to have compulsory process for obtaining witnesses in his favor, and to have the Assistance of Counsel for his defense.

AMENDMENT VII.

Right of trial by jury in civil cases.

In Suits at common law, where the value in controversy shall exceed twenty dollars, the right of trial by jury shall be preserved, and no fact tried by a jury, shall be otherwise reexamined in any Court of the United States, than according to the rules of the common law.

AMENDMENT VIII.

Excessive bail or fines; cruel and unusual punishment.

Excessive bail shall not be required, nor excessive fines imposed, nor cruel and unusual punishments inflicted.

AMENDMENT IX.

Unenumerated rights.

The enumeration in the Constitution, of certain rights, shall not be construed to deny or disparage others retained by the people.

AMENDMENT X.

Rights reserved to States.

The powers not delegated to the United States by the Constitution, nor prohibited by it to the States, are reserved to the States respectively, or to the people.

Amendments Since the Bill of Rights

AMENDMENT XI.

Judicial powers construed.

[Proposed by Congress Mar. 4, 1794. Ratification complete Feb. 7, 1795, though official announcement of ratification not made until Jan. 8, 1798.]

The Judicial power of the United States shall not be construed to extend to any suit in law or equity, commenced or prosecuted against one of the United States by Citizens of another State, or by Citizens or Subjects of any Foreign State.

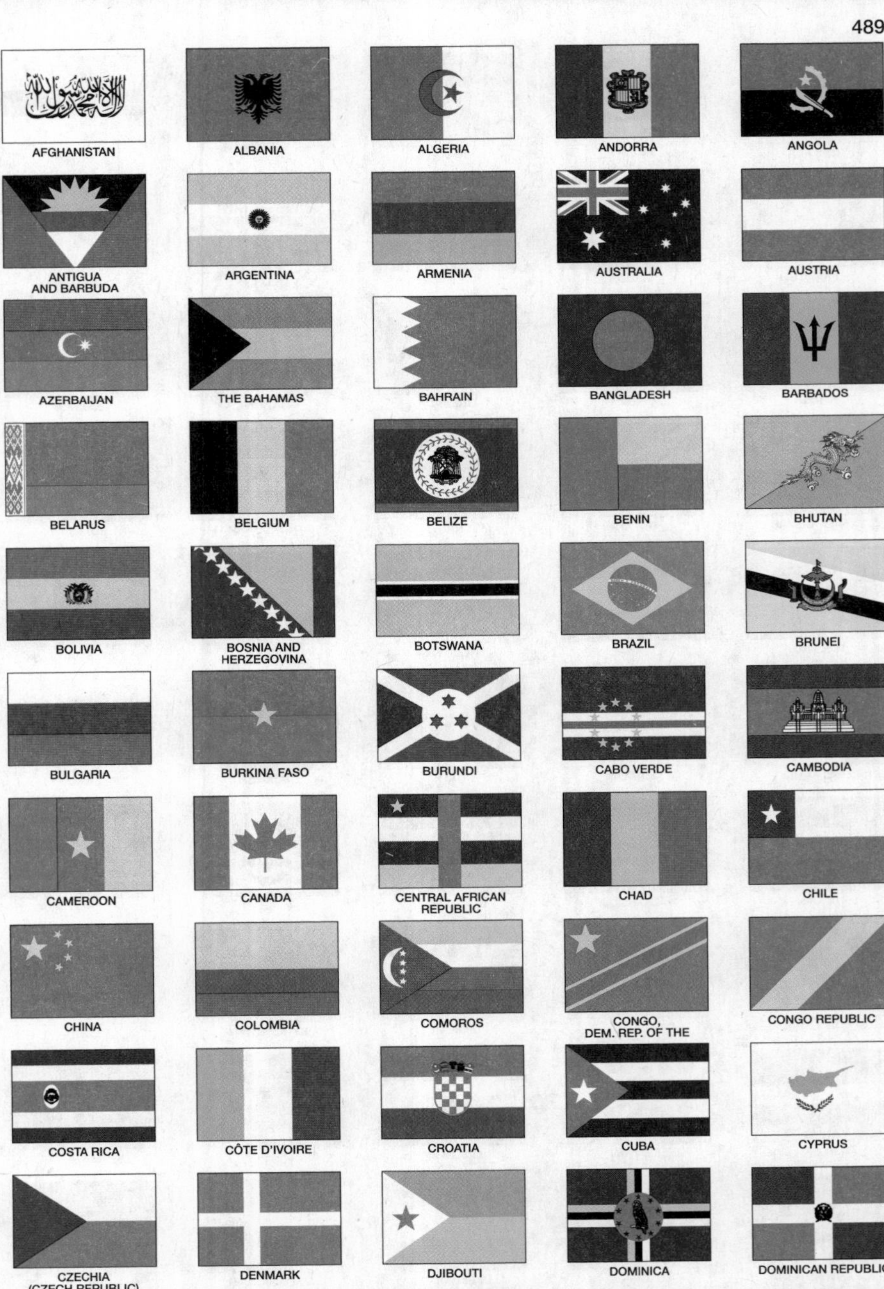
AFGHANISTAN
ALBANIA
ALGERIA
ANDORRA
ANGOLA
ANTIGUA AND BARBUDA
ARGENTINA
ARMENIA
AUSTRALIA
AUSTRIA
AZERBAIJAN
THE BAHAMAS
BAHRAIN
BANGLADESH
BARBADOS
BELARUS
BELGIUM
BELIZE
BENIN
BHUTAN
BOLIVIA
BOSNIA AND HERZEGOVINA
BOTSWANA
BRAZIL
BRUNEI
BULGARIA
BURKINA FASO
BURUNDI
CABO VERDE
CAMBODIA
CAMEROON
CANADA
CENTRAL AFRICAN REPUBLIC
CHAD
CHILE
CHINA
COLOMBIA
COMOROS
CONGO, DEM. REP. OF THE
CONGO REPUBLIC
COSTA RICA
CÔTE D'IVOIRE
CROATIA
CUBA
CYPRUS
CZECHIA (CZECH REPUBLIC)
DENMARK
DJIBOUTI
DOMINICA
DOMINICAN REPUBLIC
ECUADOR
EGYPT
EL SALVADOR
EQUATORIAL GUINEA
ERITREA

Note: Flag proportions have been standardized to fit page.

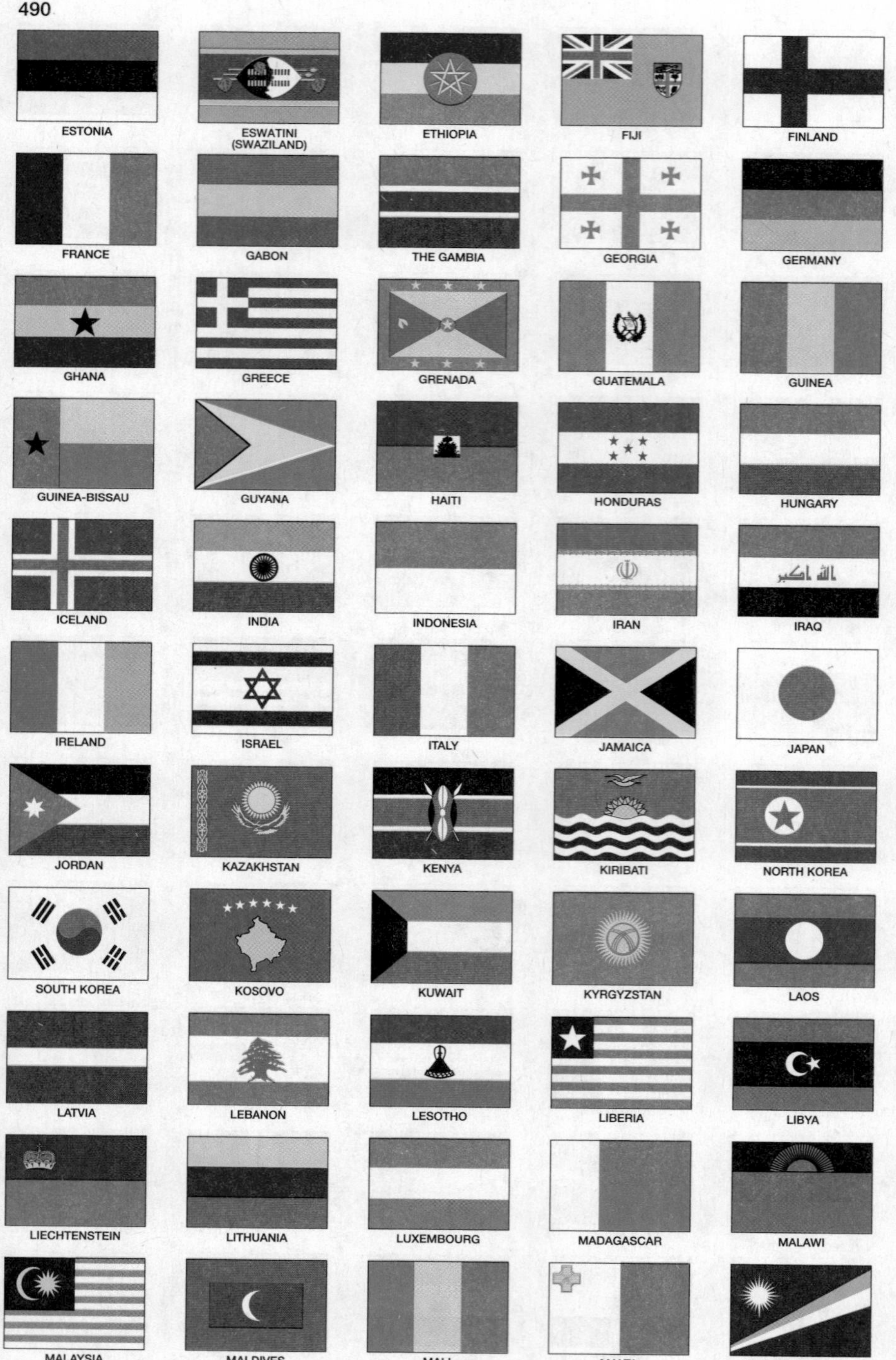

Note: Flag proportions have been standardized to fit page.

MAURITANIA
MAURITIUS
MEXICO
MICRONESIA
MOLDOVA
MONACO
MONGOLIA
MONTENEGRO
MOROCCO
MOZAMBIQUE
MYANMAR (BURMA)
NAMIBIA
NAURU
NEPAL
NETHERLANDS
NEW ZEALAND
NICARAGUA
NIGER
NIGERIA
NORTH MACEDONIA
NORWAY
OMAN
PAKISTAN
PALAU
PANAMA
PAPUA NEW GUINEA
PARAGUAY
PERU
PHILIPPINES
POLAND
PORTUGAL
QATAR
ROMANIA
RUSSIA
RWANDA
ST. KITTS AND NEVIS
ST. LUCIA
ST. VINCENT AND THE GRENADINES
SAMOA
SAN MARINO
SÃO TOMÉ AND PRÍNCIPE
SAUDI ARABIA
SENEGAL
SERBIA
SEYCHELLES
SIERRA LEONE
SINGAPORE
SLOVAKIA
SLOVENIA
SOLOMON ISLANDS
SOMALIA
SOUTH AFRICA
SOUTH SUDAN
SPAIN
SRI LANKA

Note: Flag proportions have been standardized to fit page.

SUDAN

SURINAME

SWEDEN

SWITZERLAND

SYRIA

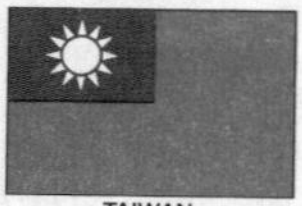

TAIWAN

TAJIKISTAN

TANZANIA

THAILAND

TIMOR-LESTE (EAST TIMOR)

TOGO

TONGA

TRINIDAD AND TOBAGO

TUNISIA

TURKEY

TURKMENISTAN

TUVALU

UGANDA

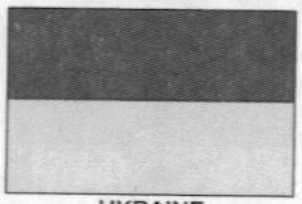

UKRAINE

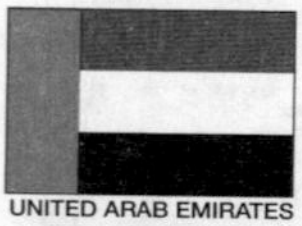

UNITED ARAB EMIRATES

UNITED KINGDOM

UNITED STATES

URUGUAY

UZBEKISTAN

VANUATU

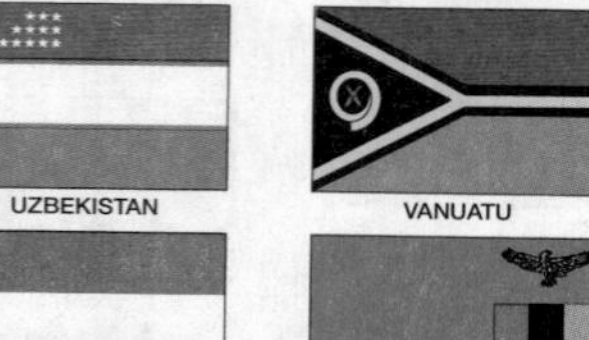

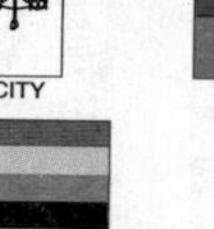

VATICAN CITY

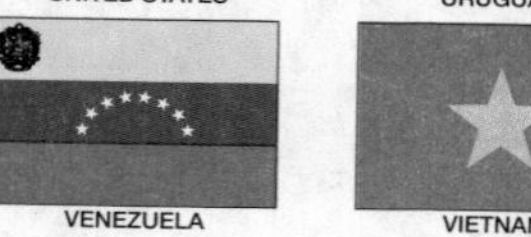

VENEZUELA

VIETNAM

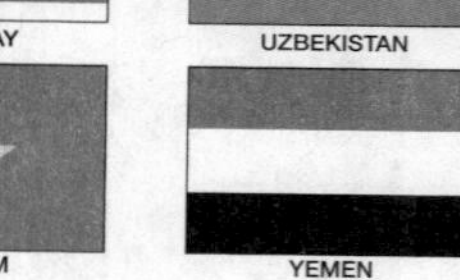

YEMEN

ZAMBIA

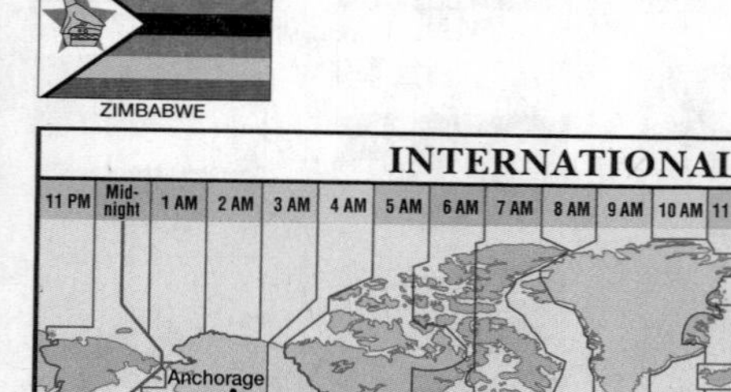

ZIMBABWE

INTERNATIONAL TIME ZONES

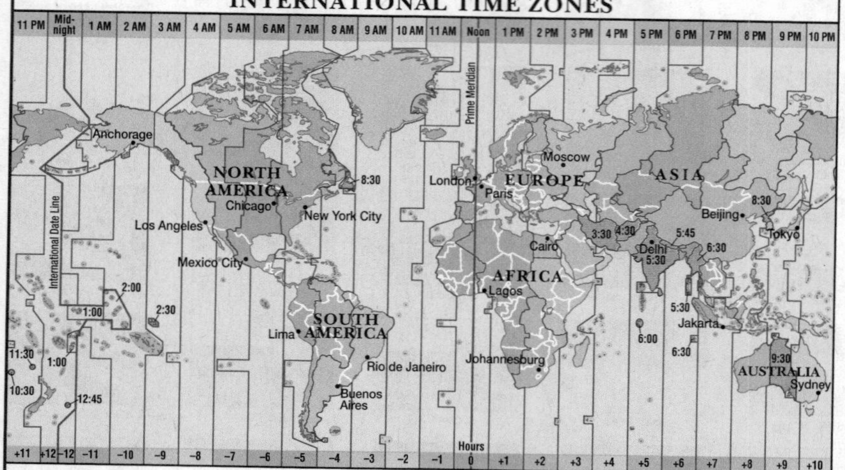

The world is divided into 24 time zones, each 15° longitude wide. The longitudinal meridian passing through Greenwich, England, is the starting point, and is called the *prime meridian*. The 12th zone is divided by the 180th meridian (International Date Line). When the line is crossed going west, the date is advanced one day; when crossed going east, the date becomes a day earlier.

Note: Flag proportions have been standardized to fit page.

UNITED STATES

ALASKA....See page 494

RUSSIA
ASIA
North Pole
ARCTIC OCEAN
Greenland Sea
Svalbard (Nor.)
NORWAY
Oslo
EUROPE
GREAT BRITAIN
Faroe Islands (Den.)
Jan Mayen (Nor.)
ICELAND
Reykjavík
Denmark Strait
Arctic Circle
Cape Morris Jesup
Nord
Cape Columbia
Alert
Ellesmere I.
Ittoqqortoormiit (Scoresbysund)
Qaanaaq (Thule)
GREENLAND (KALAALLIT NUNAAT) (Den.)
Tasiilaq
Nuuk
Cape Farewell
Davis Strait
Baffin Bay
Baffin Island
Pond Inlet
Arctic Bay
Grise Fiord
Devon I.
Queen Elizabeth Islands
Melville I.
Resolute
Banks I.
Sachs Harbour
Victoria I.
Cambridge Bay
Kugluktuk
Chukchi Sea
Bering Strait
Bering Sea
Point Hope
Point Barrow
Utqiagvik (Barrow)
Kotzebue
Nome
SEWARD PENINSULA
BROOKS RANGE
Beaufort Sea
Alaska
Highest point in North America
Denali (Mt. McKinley) 6190 m (20,310 ft)
ALASKA RANGE
Fort Yukon
Fairbanks
Yukon
Bethel
Mt. Katmai 2047 m (6,716 ft)
Kenai
Anchorage
Seward
Valdez
Kodiak
Kodiak I.
Mt. Logan 5959 m (19,551 ft)
Gulf of Alaska
Inuvik
Fort McPherson
Mackenzie
Great Bear Lake
Déline
Dawson
YUKON PLATEAU
Carmacks
Yukon
Whitehorse
Northwest Territories
Nunavut
Pangnirtung
Repulse Bay
Iqaluit
Southampton I.
Hudson Strait
Labrador Sea
Skagway
Juneau
Sitka
Alexander Archipelago
Watson Lake
Fort Simpson
Yellowknife
Great Slave Lake
Hay River
Fort Smith
Rankin Inlet
CANADA
Arviat
UNGAVA PENINSULA
Puvimituq
Hebron
COAST MOUNTAINS
British Columbia
Ketchikan
Prince Rupert
Queen Charlotte Is.
Kitimat
Alberta
Peace
Dawson Creek
Peace River
Grande Prairie
Ft. McMurray
Athabasca
Uranium City
Lake Athabasca
Saskatchewan
La Loche
Manitoba
Churchill
Hudson Bay
Belcher Is.
Labrador
Newfoundland and Labrador
Happy Valley-Goose Bay
St. Anthony
Newfoundland
St. John's
Corner Brook
Schefferville
Labrador City
Quebec
Prince George
Fraser
Williams Lake
Port Hardy
Vancouver I.
Mt. Waddington 3994 m (13,104 ft)
Jasper
Edmonton
ROCKY
GREAT
La Ronge
Thompson
Flin Flon
Saskatchewan
Prince Albert
Saskatoon
Lake Winnipeg
CANADIAN
SHIELD
James Bay
Moosonee
Sept-Îles
Anticosti I.
St. Pierre and Miquelon Is. (Fr.)
Vancouver
Victoria
Seattle
Mt. Rainier 4392 m (14,410 ft)
Tacoma
RANGE
Columbia
Spokane
Calgary
Regina
Brandon
Winnipeg
Ontario
Chibougamau
Chicoutimi
New Bruns.
Fredericton
P.E.I.
Charlottetown
Sydney
Cape Breton I.
160°
170°
180°
170°
160°
150°
140°
60°
70°
80°
50°
0°
10°
20°
30°
40°
50°
60°
70°
80°

NORTH AMERICA AND THE CARIBBEAN
UNITED STATES
MEXICO
PACIFIC OCEAN
ATLANTIC OCEAN
Gulf of Mexico
Caribbean Sea
Gulf of California
Bay of Campeche
SOUTH AMERICA
Wash.
Oregon
California
Idaho
Nevada
Utah
Arizona
Montana
Wyoming
Colorado
New Mexico
N. Dakota
S. Dakota
Nebraska
Kansas
Oklahoma
Texas
Minnesota
Iowa
Missouri
Arkansas
La.
Wisconsin
Ill.
Miss.
Michigan
Ind.
Kentucky
Tennessee
Alabama
Ohio
Georgia
Florida
Pa.
W. Va.
Virginia
N. Carolina
S. Carolina
N.Y.
Vt.
N.H.
Maine
Mass.
R.I.
Conn.
N.J.
Del.
Md.
Nova Scotia
CASCADE
COAST RANGES
SIERRA NEVADA
GREAT BASIN
COLORADO PLATEAU
ROCKY MOUNTAINS
GREAT PLAINS
APPALACHIAN MTS.
COASTAL PLAIN
BAJA CALIFORNIA
SIERRA MADRE OCCIDENTAL
SIERRA MADRE ORIENTAL
YUCATAN PENINSULA
Mt. Rainier 4392 m (14,410 ft)
Mt. Whitney 4421 m (14,505 ft)
Death Valley Lowest point in North America (–282 ft)
Mt. Mitchell 2037 m (6,683 ft)
Cerro Mohinora 3300 m (10,872 ft)
Pico de Orizaba 5675 m (18,619 ft)
Tajumulco 4220 m (13,845 ft)
Great Salt Lake
L. Superior
L. Michigan
L. Huron
L. Erie
L. Ontario
Lake Nicaragua
Missouri
Snake
Platte
Arkansas
Colorado
Ohio
Mississippi
Rio Grande
Cape Sable
Cape Hatteras
Point Conception
False Cape
Straits of Florida
Tropic of Cancer
Seattle
Portland
Eugene
Eureka
Sacramento
San Francisco
San Jose
Fresno
Reno
Santa Barbara
Los Angeles
San Diego
Tijuana
Mexicali
Las Vegas
Phoenix
Tucson
Nogales
Spokane
Missoula
Butte
Boise
Pocatello
Salt Lake City
Great Falls
Billings
Casper
Cheyenne
Denver
Colorado Springs
Albuquerque
El Paso
Ciudad Juárez
Williston
Bismarck
Fargo
Rapid City
Sioux Falls
Omaha
Kansas City
Wichita
Amarillo
Lubbock
Oklahoma City
Fort Worth
Dallas
Austin
San Antonio
Houston
Shreveport
Baton Rouge
New Orleans
Duluth
St. Paul
Minneapolis
Des Moines
Madison
Milwaukee
Chicago
St. Louis
Little Rock
Memphis
Jackson
Mobile
Nashville
Birmingham
Atlanta
Indianapolis
Cincinnati
Louisville
Detroit
Cleveland
Columbus
Pittsburgh
Toronto
Hamilton
Buffalo
Rochester
Ottawa
Montréal
Québec
Sherbrooke
Sudbury
Timmins
Val-d'Or
Thunder Bay
Brandon
Saint John
Halifax
Bangor
Portland
Boston
New York
Philadelphia
Baltimore
Washington, D.C.
Richmond
Norfolk
Raleigh
Charlotte
Charleston
Savannah
Jacksonville
Tampa
St. Petersburg
Sarasota
Miami
Bermuda (U.K.)
Hermosillo
Chihuahua
Ciudad Obregón
Culiacán
Durango
La Paz
Mazatlán
Torreón
Monterrey
Nuevo Laredo
Brownsville
Matamoros
Ciudad Victoria
Tampico
San Luis Potosí
Tepic
Guadalajara
León
Colima
Mexico City
Puebla
Veracruz
Acapulco
Oaxaca
Villahermosa
Tuxtla Gutiérrez
Mérida
Cancún
Campeche
BELIZE
Belmopan
GUATEMALA
Guatemala City
San Salvador
EL SALVADOR
HONDURAS
Tegucigalpa
NICARAGUA
Managua
COSTA RICA
San José
PANAMA
Panama City
THE BAHAMAS
Freeport
Nassau
CUBA
Havana
Santa Clara
Camagüey
Holguín
Guantánamo
Santiago de Cuba
Isla de la Juventud
Cayman Is. (U.K.)
JAMAICA
Montego Bay
Kingston
HAITI
Port-au-Prince
DOMINICAN REPUBLIC
Santiago
Santo Domingo
Turks and Caicos Is. (U.K.)
Puerto Rico (U.S.)
San Juan
Ponce
Virgin Is. (U.K.&U.S.)
Anguilla (U.K.)
ANTIGUA and BARBUDA
ST. KITTS and NEVIS
Guadeloupe (Fr.)
DOMINICA
Martinique (Fr.)
BARBADOS
ST. LUCIA
ST. VINCENT and THE GRENADINES
GRENADA
TRINIDAD and TOBAGO
Port of Spain
Greater Antilles
Lesser Antilles
Caracas
VENEZUELA
Bogotá
COLOMBIA
BRAZ
0 250 500 750 Miles
0 250 500 750 1,000 Kilometers
10° 20° 30° 40° 50° 60° 70° 80° 90° 100° 110° 120° 130°

ATLANTIC OCEAN
PACIFIC OCEAN
Caribbean Sea
CENTRAL AMERICA
HONDURAS
Tegucigalpa
EL SALVADOR
San Salvador
NICARAGUA
Managua
COSTA RICA
San José
PANAMA
Panama City
ST. VINCENT AND THE GRENADINES
BARBADOS
GRENADA
TRINIDAD AND TOBAGO
Port of Spain
Margarita I.
Aruba (Neth.)
Bonaire (Neth.)
Curaçao (Neth.)
VENEZUELA
Caracas
Maracaibo
Coro
Cabimas
Lake Maracaibo
Valencia
Maracay
Barquisimeto
Valera
Mérida
Barcelona
Cumaná
Maturín
El Tigre
Ciudad Guayana
Ciudad Bolívar
San Fernando de Apure
Puerto Ayacucho
Orinoco
LLANOS
COLOMBIA
Bogotá
Barranquilla
Santa Marta
Cartagena
Pico Cristóbal Colón 5775 m (18,947 ft)
Valledupar
Sincelejo
Montería
Cúcuta
San Cristóbal
Barrancabermeja
Bucaramanga
Medellín
Tunja
Manizales
Pereira
Armenia
Ibagué
Villavicencio
Buenaventura
Cali
Palmira
Neiva
Popayán
Nevada del Huila 5364 m (17,598 ft)
Tumaco
Pasto
Florencia
GUYANA
Georgetown
New Amsterdam
SURINAME
Paramaribo
French Guiana (Fr.)
Kourou
Cayenne
GUIANA HIGHLANDS
Boa Vista
Pico do Neblina 2994 m (9,823 ft)
ECUADOR
Esmeraldas
Quito
Equator
Cotopaxi 5911 m (19,393 ft)
Portoviejo
Ambato
Chimborazo 6268 m (20,564 ft)
Guayaquil
Riobamba
Cuenca
Machala
Tumbes
Loja
Galapagos Islands (Ecuador)
ANDES
AMAZON
SELVAS
BASIN
Negro
Amazon
Putumayo
Marañón
Juruá
Purus
Madeira
Tapajós
Xingu
Manaus
Santarém
Macapá
Marajó Island
Belém
Altamura
Itaituba
Iquitos
Leticia
Benjamin Constant
Cruzeiro do Sul
Rio Branco
Porto Velho
Guajará-Mirim
Ji-Paraná
PERU
Talara
Sullana
Piura
Aguja Point
Chiclayo
Cajamarca
Yurimaguas
Trujillo
Pucallpa
Nev. Huascarán 6768 m (22,205 ft)
Chimbote
Huánuco
Nev. Yerupajá 6634 m (21,765 ft)
Cerro de Pasco
Ucayali
LA MONTAÑA
Callao
Lima
Huancayo
Ayacucho
Cuzco
Puerto Maldonado
Ica
Arequipa
Juliaca
Puno
Lake Titicaca
BOLIVIA
Riberalta
Cobija
Guaporé
Beni
Mamoré
Trinidad
La Paz
Illimani 6462 m (21,201 ft)
Cochabamba
Santa Cruz
Oruro
Nev. Sajama 6542 m (21,463 ft)
Tacna
Arica
Lake Poopó
Sucre
Potosí
Camiri
ALTIPLANO
Iquique
ATACAMA DESERT
Tarija
Calama
Antofagasta
San Salvador de Jujuy
Salta
CHACO
Paraguay
Pilcomayo
PARAGUAY
Asunción
Concepción
Dourados
Corumbá
Campo Grande
MATO GROSSO
PLATEAU
Cuiabá
Rondonópolis
Jataí
BRAZIL
São Luís
Parnaíba
Fortaleza
Marabá
Imperatriz
Caxias
Teresina
Mossoró
Natal
Juàzeiro do Norte
João Pessoa
Araguaína
Floriano
Campina Grande
Recife
Petrolina
Juàzeiro
Maceió
Gurupi
Tocantins
Araguaia
São Francisco
Aracaju
Feira de Santana
Alagoinhas
Salvador
BRAZILIAN
HIGHLANDS
Vitória da Conquista
Jequié
Ilhéus
Itabuna
Brasília
Anápolis
Goiânia
Montes Claros
Teófilo Otoni
Uberlândia
Belo Horizonte
Governador Valadares
São José do Rio Preto
Grande
Pico da Bandeira 2890 m (9,482 ft)
Vitória
Presidente Prudente
CAMPOS
Bauru
Ribeirão Preto
Juiz de Fora
Paraná
Londrina
Campinas
Volta Redonda
Sorocaba
Jundiaí
Niterói
São Paulo
Santos
Rio de Janeiro

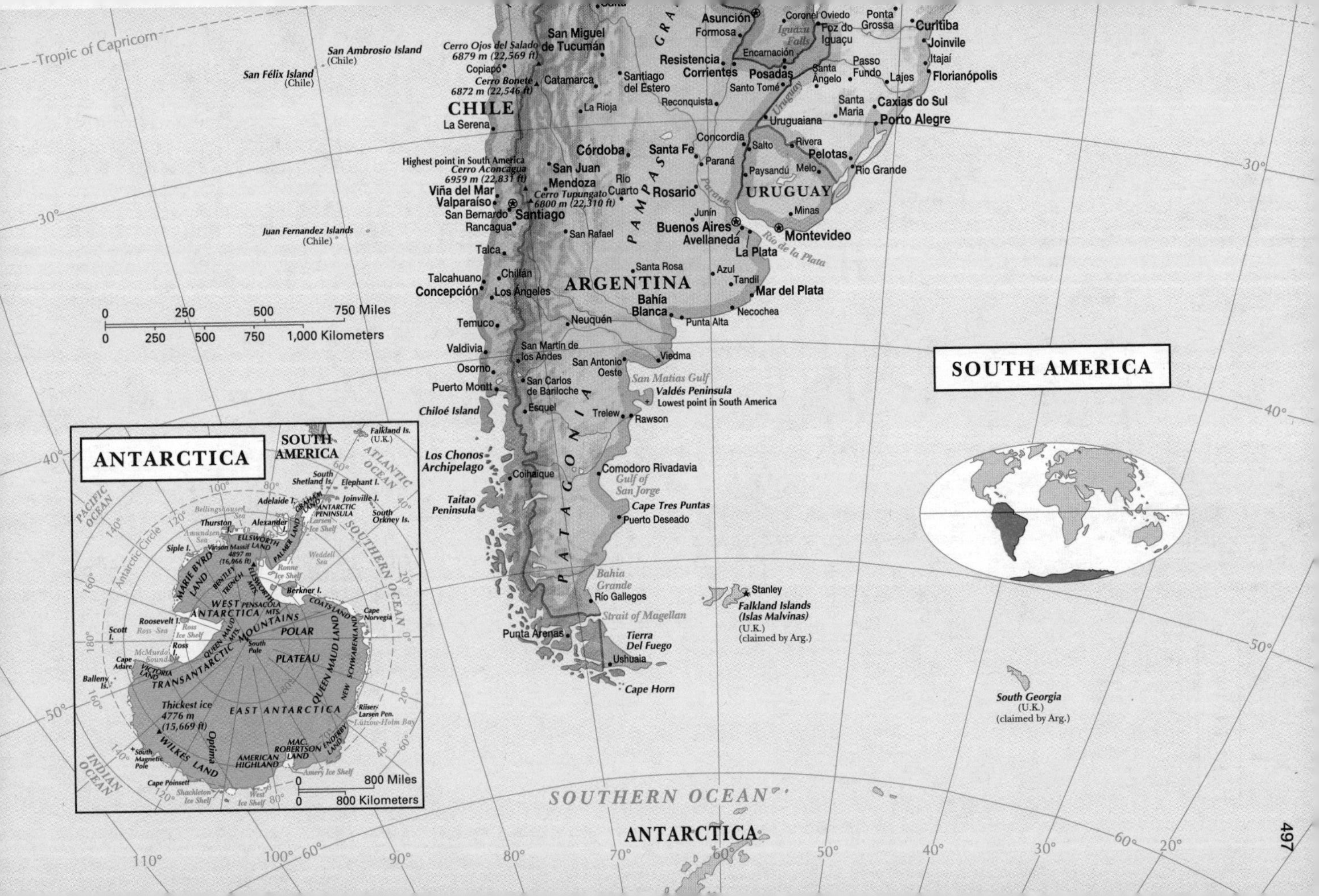
SOUTH AMERICA
ANTARCTICA
CHILE
ARGENTINA
URUGUAY
PAMPAS
PATAGONIA
SOUTHERN OCEAN
Tropic of Capricorn
Asunción
Formosa
Resistencia
Corrientes
Posadas
Encarnación
Santo Tomé
Reconquista
Santiago del Estero
San Miguel de Tucumán
Catamarca
La Rioja
Córdoba
Santa Fe
Paraná
Concordia
Salto
Paysandú
Rosario
Río Cuarto
San Juan
Mendoza
San Rafael
Buenos Aires
Avellaneda
La Plata
Junín
Santa Rosa
Azul
Tandil
Mar del Plata
Necochea
Bahía Blanca
Punta Alta
Viedma
San Antonio Oeste
Neuquén
San Carlos de Bariloche
San Martín de los Andes
Esquel
Trelew
Rawson
Comodoro Rivadavia
Puerto Deseado
Río Gallegos
Ushuaia
Punta Arenas
Coihaique
Montevideo
Minas
Melo
Rivera
Pelotas
Rio Grande
Porto Alegre
Caxias do Sul
Santa Maria
Passo Fundo
Lajes
Uruguaiana
Santo Ângelo
Foz do Iguaçu
Coronel Oviedo
Ponta Grossa
Curitiba
Joinvile
Itajaí
Florianópolis
Iguazu Falls
Uruguay
Paraná
Río de la Plata
Copiapó
La Serena
Viña del Mar
Valparaíso
Santiago
San Bernardo
Rancagua
Talca
Chillán
Los Ángeles
Talcahuano
Concepción
Temuco
Valdivia
Osorno
Puerto Montt
Chiloé Island
Los Chonos Archipelago
Taitao Peninsula
Cerro Ojos del Salado 6879 m (22,569 ft)
Cerro Bonete 6872 m (22,546 ft)
Highest point in South America Cerro Aconcagua 6959 m (22,831 ft)
Cerro Tupungato 6800 m (22,310 ft)
San Matías Gulf
Valdés Peninsula
Lowest point in South America
Gulf of San Jorge
Cape Tres Puntas
Bahía Grande
Strait of Magellan
Tierra Del Fuego
Cape Horn
Stanley
Falkland Islands (Islas Malvinas) (U.K.) (claimed by Arg.)
South Georgia (U.K.) (claimed by Arg.)
San Ambrosio Island (Chile)
San Félix Island (Chile)
Juan Fernandez Islands (Chile)
0 250 500 750 Miles
0 250 500 750 1,000 Kilometers
ANTARCTICA
SOUTH AMERICA
ATLANTIC OCEAN
PACIFIC OCEAN
INDIAN OCEAN
SOUTHERN OCEAN
Falkland Is. (U.K.)
South Orkney Is.
South Shetland Is.
Elephant I.
Joinville I.
ANTARCTIC PENINSULA
Larsen Ice Shelf
Weddell Sea
Ronne Ice Shelf
Berkner I.
COATS LAND
QUEEN MAUD LAND
NEW SCHWABENLAND
Cape Norvegia
Riiser-Larsen Pen.
Lützow-Holm Bay
POLAR PLATEAU
EAST ANTARCTICA
WEST ANTARCTICA
ELLSWORTH LAND
PALMER LAND
Alexander I.
Adelaide I.
Thurston I.
Bellingshausen Sea
Amundsen Sea
Vinson Massif 4897 m (16,066 ft)
MARIE BYRD LAND
BENTLEY TRENCH
ELLSWORTH MTS.
PENSACOLA MTS.
QUEEN MAUD MTS.
Siple I.
Roosevelt I.
Ross Sea
Ross Ice Shelf
Ross I.
McMurdo Sound
Scott I.
Cape Adare
VICTORIA LAND
Balleny Is.
TRANSANTARCTIC MOUNTAINS
South Pole
Thickest ice 4776 m (15,669 ft)
Optima
WILKES LAND
AMERICAN HIGHLAND
MAC. ROBERTSON LAND
ENDERBY LAND
Amery Ice Shelf
West Ice Shelf
Shackleton Ice Shelf
Cape Poinsett
South Magnetic Pole
Antarctic Circle
0 800 Miles
0 800 Kilometers

EUROPE
GREENLAND (KALAALLIT NUNAAT) (Denmark)
ICELAND
Ísafjörður
Akureyri
Keflavík
Reykjavík
Seydhisfjördhur
Arctic Circle
Norwegian Sea
Faroe Islands (Den.)
Torshavn
Shetland Islands (U.K.)
Orkney Islands
Hebrides
Thurso
Inverness
Scotland
Aberdeen
Dundee
Glasgow
Ayr
Edinburgh
ATLANTIC OCEAN
Londonderry
Northern Ireland
Belfast
UNITED KINGDOM
Newcastle
Galway
IRELAND
Dublin
Limerick
Cork
Waterford
Liverpool
Manchester
Leeds
Kingston upon Hull
Sheffield
Birmingham
Wales
Swansea
Coventry
Norwich
Cardiff
England
Bristol
Thames
London
Plymouth
Land's End
Portsmouth
Dover
English Channel
Channel Is. (U.K.)
North Sea
NORWAY
SWEDEN
Narvik
Bodø
Namsos
Trondheim
Molde
Ålesund
Östersund
Sundsvall
Bergen
Haugesund
Stavanger
Drammen
Oslo
Skien
Karlstad
Örebro
Uppsala
Borlänge
Stockholm
Vänern
Vättern
Norrköping
Linköping
Jönköping
Kristiansand
Göteborg
Ålborg
Jutland
Århus
Halmstad
Växjö
Öland
Esbjerg
Copenhagen
Helsingborg
Malmö
DENMARK
Odense
Baltic
Bornholm (Den.)
Kiel
Lubeck
Rostock
Gdańsk
Groningen
Hamburg
Szczecin
NETHERLANDS
Amsterdam
Bremen
Elbe
NORTHERN
The Hague
Rotterdam
Hannover
Berlin
Bydgoszcz
Antwerp
Bielefeld
Madgeburg
Poznań
Oder
Brussels
Essen
Lille
Cologne
GERMANY
POLAND
BELGIUM
Liege
Bonn
Kassel
Leipzig
Erfurt
Dresden
Wrocław
Le Havre
Brest
Caen
Rouen
LUXEMBOURG
Wiesbaden
Chemnitz
Liberec
Luxembourg
Frankfurt
Prague
Wałbrzych
Rennes
Paris
Seine
Mannheim
Plzen
CZECHIA (CZECH REP.)
Ostrava
Le Mans
Saarbrucken
Nantes
Orleans
Loire
Nancy
Nürnberg
Strasbourg
Tours
Stuttgart
Regensburg
Rhine
Brno
Dijon
Augsburg
Munich
Linz
Danube
Bratislava
Bay of Biscay
FRANCE
Basel
Zürich
Salzburg
Vienna
Bern
Innsbruck
LIECHTENSTEIN
AUSTRIA
Limoges
SWITZERLAND
Győr
HUNG
Clermont-Ferrand
Lyon
Geneva
ALPS
Klagenfurt
Graz
Bordeaux
Saint-Etienne
Mt. Blanc 4807 m (15,771 ft)
Matterhorn 4478 m (14,692 ft)
SLOVENIA
Garonne
Udine
Bergamo
Grenoble
Milan
Trieste
Ljubljana
Pécs
Zagreb
Torino
Verona
Venice
Rijeka
CROATIA
Toulouse
Rhone
Avignon
Genoa
Parma
Po
Bologna
Banja Luka
Montpellier
SAN MARINO
DINARIC ALPS
BOS. & HERZ.
Marseille
Nice
APENNINES
Ancona
Toulon
MONACO
Pisa
Florence
Split
Sarajevo
Perugia
Corsica (Fr.)
Ajaccio
Elba
Tiber
Adriatic Sea
Dubrovnik
VATICAN CITY
Rome
ITALY
Foggia
Sassari
Naples
Bari
Vesuvius 1277 m (4,190 ft)
Salerno
Taranto
Sardinia (It.)
Cagliari
Tyrrhenian Sea
Ionian Sea
Mediterranean Sea
Palermo
Messina
Etna 3369 m (11,053 ft)
Reggio di Calabria
Sicily (It.)
Catania
Tunis
TUNISIA
MALTA
Valletta
A Coruña
Gijón
Santander
Vigo
Bilbao
Donostia-San Sebastián
Leon
Vitoria-Gasteiz
Porto
Braga
Pamplona
PYRENEES
Duero
Valladolid
Pico de Aneto 3404 m (11,169 ft)
Coimbra
Ebro
IBERIAN
Salamanca
Zaragoza
ANDORRA
PORTUGAL
Lisbon
Madrid
Setubal
Tagus
Toledo
Barcelona
Badajoz
Tarragona
SPAIN
Castellon de la Plana
PENINSULA
Valencia
Majorca
Minorca
Palma de Mallorca
Balearic Is. (Sp.)
Cape St. Vincent
Cordoba
Seville
Alicante
Cádiz
Murcia
Málaga
Granada
Cartagena
Strait of Gibraltar
GIBRALTAR (U.K.)
Almería
Rabat
Algiers
AFRICA
MOROCCO
ALGERIA
0 250 500 Miles
0 250 500 750 Kilometers

Barents Sea
Novaya Zemlya
North Cape
Hammerfest
Vardø
Tromsø
Murmansk
Ivalo
LAPLAND
Apatity
KOLA PENINSULA
Kiruna
White Sea
Rovaniemi
Arkhangel'sk
Nar'yan-Mar
Pechora
ASIA
URAL MOUNTAINS
Ukhta
RUSSIA
Luleå
Oulu
Belomorsk
Syktyvkar
Skellefteå
Dvina
Berezniki
Umeå
FINLAND
Kotlas
Gulf of Bothnia
Vaasa
Kuopio
Lake Onega
Perm'
Jyvaskyla
Lake Ladoga
Petrozavodsk
Kirov
Pori
Tampere
Lahti
Izhevsk
Kama
Ufa
Kotka
Turku
Helsinki
St. Petersburg
Cherepovets
Vologda
Naberezhnye Chelny
Åland Is. (Fin.)
Gulf of Finland
Yoshkar Ola
Tallinn
Rybinsk
Kostroma
Kazan
ESTONIA
Velikiy Novgorod
Yaroslavl'
Nizhniy Novgorod
Cheboksary
Sterlitamak
Tartu
Ivanovo
Pskov
Ul'yanovsk
Orsk
Tver'
Vladimir
Tol'yatti
Orenburg
Gotland (Swe.)
Riga
Moscow
Saransk
Samara
Ural
LATVIA
Liepaja
Ryazan'
Penza
Daugavpils
Kaluga
Klaipeda
Vitsyebsk
Smolensk
Tula
LITHUANIA
Volga
Kaunas
Vilnius
Orsha
(RUSSIA)
Kaliningrad
PLAIN
Minsk
Mahilyow
Tambov
Saratov
Lipetsk
EUROPEAN
Bryansk
KAZAKHSTAN
Hrodna
Babruysk
Bialystok
BELARUS
Voronezh
Homyel'
Vistula
Warsaw
Brest
Pinsk
Chernihiv
Kursk
Sumy
Belgorod
Łódź
Kharkiv
Volgograd
Radom
Kyiv (Kiev)
Lublin
Poltava
Kielce
Zhytomyr
Cherkasy
Luhansk
Astrakhan'
Katowice
Dnieper
Horlivka
Kraków
L'viv
UKRAINE
Donetsk
Don
CARPATHIAN MOUNTAINS
Vinnytsia
Dnipro
Rostov-na-Donu
SLOVAKIA
Banska Bystrica
Kosice
Chernivtsi
Zaporizhzhia
Prut
Miskolc
MOLDOVA
Kryvyy Rih
Mariupol'
Budapest
Debrecen
Iasi
Chișinău
Mykolaiv
Sea of Azov
Caspian Sea
Stavropol
NGARY
Oradea
Cluj-Napoca
Odesa
CRIMEA PENINSULA (disputed territory)
Krasnodar
Mt. Elbrus 5642 m (18,510 ft) Highest point in Europe
Groznyy
Makhachkala
Kecskemét
Nal'chik
Vladikavkaz
Szeged
ROMANIA
Galati
Simferopol
CAUCASUS MTS.
Timișoara
Brasov
Sevastopol
Novi Sad
Ploiești
GEORGIA
Baku
Tbilisi
Bucharest
Constanța
Belgrade
Craiova
AZERBAIJAN
Black Sea
SERBIA
Danube
Ruse
ARMENIA
Pleven
Varna
Yerevan
Nis
BULGARIA
MONTENEGRO
KOSOVO
Pristina
Sofia
Stara Zagora
Burgas
AZER.
BALKAN
Podgorica
Skopje
Plovdiv
Shkoder
NORTH MACEDONIA
Istanbul
Durres
PENINSULA
Kavala
Tirana
Thessaloniki
Ankara
TURKEY
IRAN
ALBANIA
Vlore
Olympus 2917 m (9,570 ft)
Dardanelles
Larisa
Aegean Sea
Ioannina
Volos
Corfu
ASIA
GREECE
Patras
Athens
Corinth
SYRIA
Baghdad
Peloponnese
Cyclades
Kalamata
Sparta
IRAQ
Rhodes (Gr.)
Sea of Crete
Nicosia
Crete (Gr.)
CYPRUS
LEBANON
Hania
Iraklion
Beirut
Damascus

ATLANTIC OCEAN
ARCTIC OCEAN
IRELAND
UNITED KINGDOM
London
PORT.
Madrid
SPAIN
Paris
FRANCE
BEL.
NETH.
NORWAY
Oslo
SWEDEN
DEN.
Copenhagen
Stockholm
GERMANY
Berlin
SWITZ.
FINLAND
Helsinki
Baltic Sea
CZECHIA (CZECH REP.)
POLAND
Warsaw
EST.
LAT.
LITH.
AUS.
SLOV.
SLVK.
HUNG.
CRO.
BOS. & HERZ.
SERB.
MONT.
KOS.
ALB.
N. MAC.
ROMANIA
MOL.
Bucharest
BUL.
ITALY
Rome
BELARUS
EUROPE
Moscow
Kyiv (Kiev)
UKRAINE
GREECE
Athens
Mediterranean Sea
Black Sea
Izmir
Bursa
Ankara
Samsun
TURKEY
LIBYA
CAUCASUS MTS.
GEORGIA
Trabzon
Mt. Ararat 5137 m (16,854 ft)
Tbilisi
Erzurum
Yerevan
ARMENIA
Ganca
AZERBAIJAN
Baku
CYPRUS
Nicosia
Adana
Aleppo
Latakia
LEBANON
Beirut
Diyarbakir
SYRIA
Cairo
Tel Aviv-Yafo
Jerusalem
ISRAEL
Damascus
Amman
EGYPT
JORDAN
Al Aqabah
Mosul
Arbil
Kirkuk
Tabriz
Lake Urmia
IRAQ
Baghdad
Tabuk
AFRICA
INSET AREA
AN NAFUD
Hail
Al Hillah
Al Basrah
Kermanshah
Basht
Tehran
Qom
ELBURZ MTS.
ZAGROS MOUNTAINS
Esfahan
IRAN
Mt. Damavand 5610 m (18,406 ft)
Gorgan
DASHT-E KAVIR
DASHT-E LUT
Mashhad
Ashgabat
KARA KUM DESERT
Urganch
TURKMENISTAN
Turkmenbashy
Caspian Sea
Aktau
USTYURT PLATEAU
Aral Sea
Atyraū
Oral
KAZAKHSTAN
UZBEKISTAN
Nukus
KYZYL KUM DESERT
Bukhara
Syr Darya
Amu Darya
Qyzylorda
Zhezkazgan
Nur-Sultan
Qaraghandy (Karaganda)
Pavlodar
KAZAKH UPLAND
Balqash
Lake Balkhash
Taldykorgan
Ayagoz
Irtysh
Taraz
Almaty
Bishkek
KYRGYZSTAN
Tashkent
Dushanbe
TAJIKISTAN
Yining
Jengish Chokusu 7439 m (24,406 ft)
Ürümqi
Turpan Depression
TIEN SHAN
Kashi
Lenin Peak 7134 m (23,406 ft)
Ismail Samani Pk. 7495 m (24,590 ft)
PAMIRS
Tarim
Shache
TAKLIMAKAN DESERT
K2 8611 m (28,250 ft)
Herat
Mazar-e Sharif
AFGHANISTAN
HINDU KUSH
Kabul
Farah
Helmand
Kandahar
Peshawar
Islamabad
Rawalpindi
Srinagar
KUNLUN MTS.
PLATEAU OF TIBET
Buraydah
Kuwait City
KUWAIT
Shiraz
Yazd
Birjand
Kerman
Zahedan
Jeddah
Mecca
At Taif
Riyadh
Manama
BAHRAIN
QATAR
Doha
Persian Gulf
Bandar-e Abbas
SAUDI ARABIA
UNITED ARAB EMIRATES
Abu Dhabi
Quetta
Faisalabad
Lahore
Multan
Chandigarh
PAKISTAN
Mt. Everest 8849 m (29,032 ft)
Highest point in Asia
HIMALAYA
Brahmaputra
Lhasa
SUDAN
Khartoum
Red Sea
ERITIREA
Asmara
Abha
RU AL KHALI
Turbat
Gulf of Oman
Muscat
Sur
Ras al Hadd
Karachi
Sukkur
Indus
THAR DESERT
Hyderabad
Delhi
New Delhi
Agra
NEPAL
Lucknow
Kathmandu
BHUTAN
Thimphu
Jaipur
Jodhpur
Kanpur
Varanasi
Patna
Allahabad
Ganges
Imphal
Sanaa
YEMEN
Aden
Al Mukalla
Salalah
OMAN
Addis Ababa
ETHIOPIA
DJI.
Gulf of Aden
SOMALIA
Socotra (Yemen)
Arabian Sea
Ahmadabad
INDIA
Asansol
Ranchi
Khulna
BANGLADESH
Dhaka
DECCAN PLATEAU
Nagpur
Raipur
Kolkata (Calcutta)
Chittagong
Mumbai (Bombay)
WESTERN GHATS
Pune
Solapur
Hyderabad
Cuttack
Akyab
MYANMAR (BURMA)
Visakhapatnam
Pathein
Panaji
Hubballi (Hubli)
Vijayawada
Bay of Bengal
EASTERN GHATS
Bengaluru (Bangalore)
Laccadive Is. (India)
Mysuru (Mysore)
Chennai (Madras)
Andaman Is. (India)
Coimbatore
Kochi
Madurai
Thiruvananthapuram
Cape Comorin
Trincomalee
Colombo
SRI LANKA
Sri Jayewardenepura Kotte
Galle
Nicobar Is. (India)
Male
MALDIVES
Equator
INDIAN OCEAN
Arctic Circle
Severnaya Zemlya
Kara Sea
Dickson
Noril'sk
Vorkuta
Salekhard
Novyy Urengoy
Yenisey
Ob
URAL MOUNTAINS
RUSSIA
CEN
SIBE
Tura
Serov
Surgut
WEST SIBERIAN PLAIN
Nizhnevartovsk
Nizhniy Tagil
Yekaterinburg
Tobol'sk
Tyumen
Chelyabinsk
Kurgan
Magnitogorsk
Petropavlovsk
Tara
Kolpashevo
Lesosibirsk
Angara
Kansk
Tomsk
Achinsk
Krasnoyarsk
Omsk
Novosibirsk
Kemerovo
Novokuznetsk
Barnaul
Tashtagol
SAYAN MTS.
Semey (Semipalatinsk)
Öskemen (Ust' Kamenogorsk)
ALTAY MTS.
Dund-Us
PLA
TURKEY
Adana
Antalya
Mersin
Sanliurfa
Al Hasakah
Antakya
Aleppo
Ar Raqqah
Mosul
Latakia
CYPRUS
Nicosia
Limassol
Hamah
Homs
SYRIA
Abu Kamal
Euphrates
Bayji
LEBANON
Beirut
Tadmur
Damascus
Mediterranean Sea
Ar Ramadi
The West Bank currently occupied by Israel. Permanent status to be determined.
Haifa
WEST BANK
IRAQ
ISRAEL
Tel Aviv-Yafo
SYRIAN DESERT
Port Said
Jerusalem
Amman
Tanta
GAZA STRIP
Jericho
Cairo
Suez Canal
JORDAN
SAUDI ARABIA
Giza
Suez
Maan
AN NAFUD
EGYPT
Elat
Al Aqabah
SINAI
Nile
Gulf of Suez
Gulf of Aqaba
Tabuk
250 Miles
250 Kilometers

NORTH AMERICA
ASIA
Bering Strait
Chukchi Sea
Wrangel I.
East Siberian Sea
New Siberian Islands
Laptev Sea
Provideniya
Anadyr
Bering Sea
KOLYMA MOUNTAINS
Cherskiy
Kolyma
Indigirka
Zyryanka
Tiksi
Nordvik
VERKHOYANSK RA.
Verkhoyansk
Lena
Susuman
Magadan
Shelikhov Gulf
KAMCHATKA PEN.
Shiveluch 3283 m (10,771 ft)
Klyuchevskaya 4835 m (15,863 ft)
Karymsky 1536 m (5,039 ft)
Petropavlovsk-Kamchatskiy
Aldan
Okhotsk
Sea of Okhotsk
Alaid 2339 m (7,674 ft)
Sarycheva 1496 m (4,908 ft)
Kuril Is. (Russia)
Vilyuysk
Yakutsk
Okha
Sakhalin
Tatar Strait
Lensk
Aldan
STANOVOY RANGE
Berkakit
Tynda
Komsomol'sk-na-Amure
Bodaybo
Yuzhno-Sakhalinsk
Tiatia 1819 m (5,968 ft)
Ust'-Kut
Svobodnyy
Khabarovsk
Lake Baykal
Bratsk
Blagoveshchensk
Hokkaido
Sapporo
Tulun
YABLONOVYY RANGE
Chita
Amur
Ulan-Ude
Irkutsk
GREATER KHINGAN RANGE
Yichun
Hailar
Jixi
Qiqihar
Harbin
Ussuriysk
Vladivostok
Hakodate
Akita
Sendai
Darhan
Moron
Choybalsan
Jilin
Sea of Japan (East Sea)
Niigata
Honshu
Ulaanbaatar
Changchun
Chongjin
Tokyo
Yokohama
MONGOLIA
MONGOLIAN PLATEAU
Fushun
Shenyang
N. KOREA
JAPAN
Mt. Fuji 3776 m (12,388 ft)
Bayanhongor
GOBI DESERT
Anshan
Hamhung
Kyoto
Nagoya
Pyongyang
Kobe
Osaka
Dalian
Incheon
Seoul
Hiroshima
Beijing
Tianjin
Hohhot
Sejong City
Daegu
Busan
Shikoku
Baotou
Shijiazhuang
S. KOREA
Kitakyushu
Fukuoka
Yumen
Yinchuan
Taiyuan
Jinan
Qingdao
Nagasaki
Kagoshima
Kyushu
Huang
Handan
Grand Canal
Yellow Sea
Tropic of Cancer
Xining
Luoyang
Xuzhou
Zhengzhou
Nanjing
Lanzhou
Qinghai Lake
Xi'an
(Yellow)
Huainan
Hefei
Shanghai
Hangzhou
Ryukyu Is. (Japan)
PACIFIC OCEAN
CHINA
Wuhan
Jingdezhen
East China Sea
Okinawa
Naha
Chengdu
Nanchang
Wenzhou
Northern Mariana Islands (U.S.)
Chongqing
Changsha
Fuzhou
Zigong
Chang (Yangtze)
Shaoyang
Ganzhou
Taipei
TAIWAN
Xiamen
Gulyang
Guilin
Kaohsiung
0 500 1,000 Miles
0 500 1,000 1,500 Kilometers
Kunming
Xi
Liuzhou
Guangzhou
Myitkyina
Irrawaddy
Macau
Hong Kong
Nanning
Laoag
Luzon
Philippine Sea
Phongsali
Haiphong
Zhanjiang
Mandalay
LAOS
Hanoi
Haikou
Baguio
PHILIPPINES
Taunggyi
Louangphabang
Hainan (China)
Quezon City
Nay Pyi Taw
Vientiane
Vinh
Manila
Naga
Chiang Mai
Samar
PALAU
Pyay
Yangon (Rangoon)
THAILAND
Hue
Da Nang
South China Sea
Mindoro
Tacloban
Leyte
Equator 0°
Nakhon Ratchasima
Panay
Iloilo
Cebu
Mawlamyine
Butuan
Nakhon Sawan
VIETNAM
Puerto Princesa
Negros
Dawei
CAMBODIA
Nha Trang
Sulu Sea
Mindanao
Bangkok
Batdambang
Davao
Palawan
Phnom Penh
Ho Chi Minh City
Zamboanga
Kompong Som
Can Tho
Jayapura
Isthmus of Kra
Gulf of Thailand
Kota Kinabalu
Sandakan
Halmahera
PAPUA NEW GUINEA
Bandar Seri Begawan
Celebes Sea
Ternate
New Guinea
Phuket
Hat Yai
BRUNEI
Tarakan
Manado
Port Moresby
Andaman Sea
George Town
MALAYSIA
Gorontalo
Moluccas
Ceram
Banda Aceh
Kuala Lumpur
Natuna Is.
Kuching
Ambon
Medan
Kelang
Samainda
Sulawesi (Celebes)
Putrajaya
Singapore
Pontianak
Borneo
Balikpapan
Banda Sea
Arafura Sea
SINGAPORE
Sibolga
Pekanbaru
Sampit
Palopo
Jambi
Banjarmasin
Parepare
Baubau
Padang
Makassar
Sumatra
Palembang
Java Sea
Dili
TIMOR-LESTE
INDONESIA
Bengkulu
Ende
Timor
Timor Sea
AUSTRALIA
Bandar Lampung
Jakarta
Semarang
Surabaya
Mataram
Sumba
Kupang
Bandung
Yogyakarta
Java
Malang
Bali

ATLANTIC
OCEAN
Azores (Portugal)
Madeira Islands (Portugal)
Funchal
Canary Islands (Sp.)
Santa Cruz
Las Palmas
Jebel Toubkal 4165 m (13,665 ft)
Strait of Gibraltar
Tropic of Cancer
PORTUGAL
Lisbon
SPAIN
Madrid
FRANCE
Paris
E U R O P E
SWITZ.
ITALY
Rome
GER.
CZECH REP.
SLOVAKIA
AUSTRIA
HUNGARY
SLOVE.
CRO.
BOS. & HER.
MONT.
ALBANIA
SERB.
KOS.
N. MAC.
GREECE
Athens
BULGARIA
ROMANIA
Bucharest
MOLDOVA
UKRAINE
RUSSIA
GEORGIA
ARMENIA
AZERBAIJAN
KAZAKHSTAN
UZBEKISTAN
TURKMENISTAN
Aral Sea
Caspian Sea
Black Sea
TURKEY
Ankara
CYPRUS
MALTA
Mediterranean Sea
Gulf of Sidra
SYRIA
Damascus
LEBANON
ISRAEL
Jerusalem
JORDAN
IRAQ
Baghdad
IRAN
Tehran
KUWAIT
Persian Gulf
BAHRAIN
QATAR
A S I A
SAUDI ARABIA
Riyadh
YEMEN
Sanaa
Gulf of Aden
Cape Gwardafuy
Red Sea
Border in Dispute
SINAI
Suez Canal
Suez
Port Said
Cairo
Giza
Tanta
Alexandria
Al Fayyum
Asyut
Luxor
Aswan
Lake Nasser
Nile
EGYPT
Al Kharijah
Siwa
LIBYAN DESERT
NUBIAN DESERT
Port Sudan
Atbara
Marawi
Kassala
Al Qadarif
Omdurman
Khartoum
Wad Medani
Kusti
Blue Nile
Al Ubayyid
Al Fashir
Nyala
MARRA MTS.
SUDAN
SOUTH SUDAN
Malakal
Ramciel
Juba
Rumbek
Waw
ERITREA
Massawa
Asmara
Mekele
Assab
Ras Dashen 4533 m (14,872 ft)
Gonder
Lake Tana
Bahir Dar
Lowest point in Africa
Guna 4120 m (13,517 ft)
Dese
DJIBOUTI
Djibouti
Berbera
Hargeysa
Dire Dawa
Harer
ETHIOPIAN HIGHLANDS
Addis Ababa
Nazret
ETHIOPIA
Jima
Tullu Dimtu 4377 m (14,360 ft)
Batu 4307 m (14,131 ft)
RIFT VALLEY
SOMALI PENINSULA
Kelafo
Beledweyne
LIBYA
Tripoli
Misratah
Benghazi
Al Bayda
Tobruk
Waha
Al Jawf
Ghadamis
TUNISIA
Tunis
Cape Bon
Sfax
Tebessa
Annaba
Constantine
Skikda
Bejaia
Batna
Djebel Chelia 2326 m (7,631 ft)
Biskra
Touggourt
Algiers
Chlef
Oran
Sidi Bel Abbes
ATLAS MTS.
Ghardaïa
ALGERIA
I-n-Amenas
I-n-Salah
AHAGGAR
Mt. Tahat 2918 m (9,573 ft)
Tamanrasset
Béchar
Oujda
Melilla (Sp.)
Ceuta (Sp.)
Tetouan
Tangier
Kenitra
Rabat
Fès
Khouribga
Casablanca
Safi
Marrakech
Agadir
MOROCCO
Laayoune
Western Sahara (Occ. by Morocco)
Nouâdhibou
Atâr
MAURITANIA
Nouakchott
Kaédi
Ayoûn el Atroûs
S A H A R A
TIBESTI
Emi Koussi 3415 m (11,204 ft)
Faya-Largeau
CHAD
Abéché
N'Djamena
Lake Chad
Sarh
Moundou
Maroua
Garoua
CENTRAL AFRICAN REPUBLIC
Bambari
Bangui
Bouar
NIGER
AÏR
Mt. Greboun 1944 m (6,378 ft)
Agadez
Zinder
Maradi
Niamey
Niger
S A H E L
MALI
Tombouctou
Gao
Mopti
Ségou
Bamako
Sikasso
Kayes
BURKINA FASO
Ouagadougou
Bobo-Dioulasso
SENEGAL
Senegal
Saint-Louis
Dakar
Thies
Kaolack
THE GAMBIA
Banjul
Ziguinchor
GUINEA-BISSAU
Bissau
GUINEA
Labe
Kankan
Conakry
SIERRA LEONE
Freetown
LIBERIA
Monrovia
Cape Palmas
CÔTE D'IVOIRE
Korhogo
Bouaké
Yamoussoukro
Abidjan
GHANA
Tamale
Kumasi
Lake Volta
Accra
Takoradi
TOGO
Lomé
BENIN
Cotonou
Porto-Novo
NIGERIA
Sokoto
Katsina
Kano
Maiduguri
Kumo
Zaria
Abuja
Minna
Ilorin
Ogbomoso
Osogbo
Ibadan
Abeokuta
Lagos
Makurdi
Enugu
Onitsha
Aba
Port Harcourt
Benue
CAMEROON
Bafoussam
Douala

AFRICA

ATLANTIC OCEAN
INDIAN OCEAN
Gulf of Guinea
Equator
Tropic of Capricorn
Mozambique Channel
Ascension (U.K.)
Annobon (Eq. Guinea)
EQUATORIAL GUINEA
Bioko
Malabo
Douala
Yaounde
SÃO TOMÉ AND PRÍNCIPE
Príncipe
São Tomé
Libreville
Lambarene
Port-Gentil
GABON
Franceville
REPUBLIC OF THE CONGO
Brazzaville
Loubomo
Pointe-Noire
Cabinda (Angola)
Boma
Matadi
Mbanza-Ngungu
Kinshasa
Bandundu
Kikwit
Ilebo
Kananga
Tshikapa
Mbuji-Mayi
Kabinda
Mwene-Ditu
Kamina
KATANGA PLATEAU
Kolwezi
Likasi
Lubumbashi
CONGO BASIN
DEMOCRATIC REPUBLIC OF THE CONGO
Bumba
Buta
Isiro
Mbandaka
Kisangani
Boyoma Falls
Margherita Pk. 5110 m (16,765 ft)
Beni
Goma
Bukavu
Kindu
Bujumbura
Kabalo
Kalemie
Lake Albert
Lake Mweru
Lake Tanganyika
Lake Victoria
Lake Turkana
Lake Nyasa
Lake Kariba
Ubangi
Congo
Kasai
Zambezi
Cunene
Orange
Vaal
Limpopo
UGANDA
Kampala
Jinja
KENYA
Eldoret
Marsabit
Meru
Mt. Kenya 5199 m (17,057 ft)
Kisumu
Nakuru
Nairobi
Machakos
KENYA HIGHLANDS
SERENGETI PLAIN
Kilimanjaro 5895 m (19,341 ft) (Highest point in Africa)
Mt. Meru 4565 m (14,977 ft)
Arusha
Mombasa
SOMALIA
Baldea
Mogadishu
Marka
Kismaayo
RWANDA
Kigali
BURUNDI
Mwanza
Kigoma
Tabora
TANZANIA
Dodoma
Tanga
Pemba I.
Zanzibar
Zanzibar I.
Dar es Salaam
Morogoro
Iringa
Mbeya
Mbala
RIFT VALLEY
Songea
Mtwara
ANGOLA
Luanda
Malanje
Luena
Lobito
Benguela
Huambo
Lubango
Menongue
Namibe
ZAMBIA
Chingola
Kitwe
Ndola
Luanshya
Kabwe
Lusaka
Chipata
MALAWI
Lilongwe
Blantyre
Nampula
Nacala
Tete
MOZAMBIQUE
Quelimane
Chimoio
Beira
Inhambane
Xai-Xai
Maputo
Harare
ZIMBABWE
Mutare
Gweru
Bulawayo
Livingstone
Victoria Falls
Ruacana Falls
NAMIBIA
Tsumeb
Grootfontein
Windhoek
Walvis Bay
NAMIB DESERT
Lüderitz
Keetmanshoop
Augrabies Falls
BOTSWANA
Francistown
Serowe
Palapye
KALAHARI DESERT
Gaborone
Musina
Thohoyandou
Pretoria (Tshwane)
Mmabatho
Johannesburg
Klerksdorp
Vereeniging
Mbabane
Lobamba
ESWATINI (SWAZILAND)
Welkom
Newcastle
Upington
Kimberley
Bloemfontein
Maseru
LESOTHO
Pietermaritzburg
Durban
Springbok
SOUTH AFRICA
Middelburg
Umtata
Bisho
East London
Port Elizabeth
Cape Town
Worcester
Cape of Good Hope
Cape Agulhas
COMOROS
Moroni
Mayotte (Fr.)
SEYCHELLES
Antsiranana
Mahajanga
Toamasina
Antananarivo
Antsirabe
MADAGASCAR
Fianarantsoa
Toliara
Tolanaro

0 250 500 750 Miles
0 250 500 750 1,000 Kilometers

0° 10° 20° 30° 40° 50°

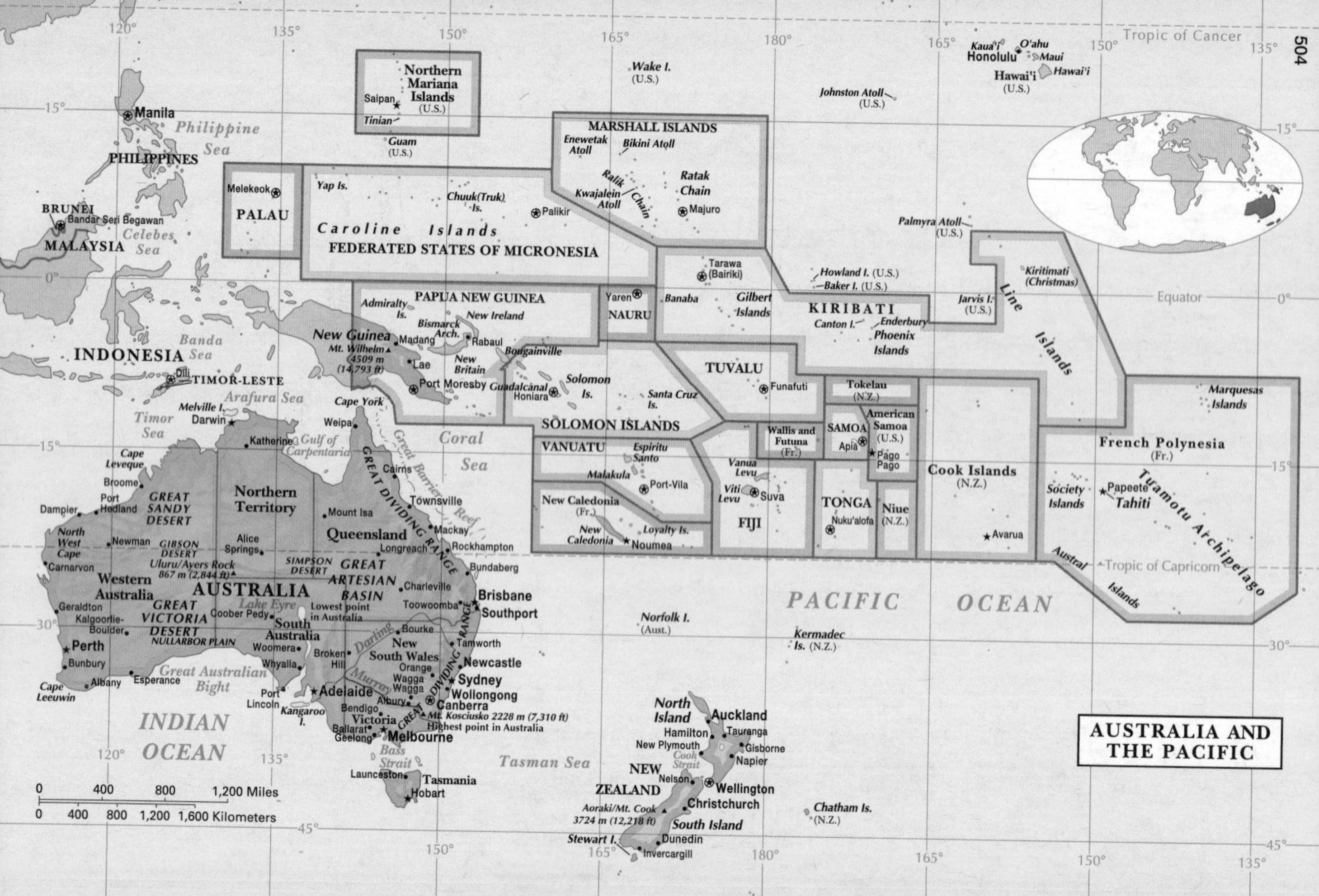
AUSTRALIA AND THE PACIFIC
Tropic of Cancer
Equator
Tropic of Capricorn
PACIFIC OCEAN
INDIAN OCEAN
Northern Mariana Islands (U.S.)
Saipan
Tinian
Guam (U.S.)
Wake I. (U.S.)
Johnston Atoll (U.S.)
Kaua'i
O'ahu
Honolulu
Maui
Hawai'i (U.S.)
Hawai'i
MARSHALL ISLANDS
Enewetak Atoll
Bikini Atoll
Ralik Chain
Ratak Chain
Kwajalein Atoll
Majuro
Palmyra Atoll (U.S.)
PHILIPPINES
Manila
Philippine Sea
BRUNEI
Bandar Seri Begawan
MALAYSIA
Celebes Sea
Melekeok
PALAU
Yap Is.
Chuuk(Truk) Is.
Palikir
Caroline Islands
FEDERATED STATES OF MICRONESIA
Tarawa (Bairiki)
Howland I. (U.S.)
Baker I. (U.S.)
Kiritimati (Christmas)
Jarvis I. (U.S.)
Line Islands
Yaren
NAURU
Banaba
Gilbert Islands
KIRIBATI
Canton I.
Enderbury
Phoenix Islands
PAPUA NEW GUINEA
Admiralty Is.
New Ireland
Bismarck Arch.
Rabaul
New Guinea
Mt. Wilhelm 4509 m (14,793 ft)
Madang
Lae
New Britain
Bougainville
Port Moresby
INDONESIA
Banda Sea
Dili
TIMOR-LESTE
Arafura Sea
Timor Sea
Melville I.
Darwin
Cape York
Weipa
Solomon Is.
Guadalcanal
Honiara
Santa Cruz Is.
SOLOMON ISLANDS
TUVALU
Funafuti
Tokelau (N.Z.)
American Samoa (U.S.)
SAMOA
Apia
Pago Pago
Wallis and Futuna (Fr.)
Marquesas Islands
French Polynesia (Fr.)
Coral Sea
VANUATU
Espiritu Santo
Malakula
Port-Vila
Vanua Levu
Viti Levu
Suva
FIJI
TONGA
Nuku'alofa
Niue (N.Z.)
Cook Islands (N.Z.)
Avarua
Society Islands
Papeete
Tahiti
Tuamotu Archipelago
Austral Islands
New Caledonia (Fr.)
New Caledonia
Loyalty Is.
Noumea
Katherine
Gulf of Carpentaria
Great Barrier Reef
Cairns
GREAT DIVIDING RANGE
Townsville
Mackay
Rockhampton
Bundaberg
Cape Leveque
Broome
Port Hedland
Dampier
GREAT SANDY DESERT
Northern Territory
Mount Isa
Queensland
Longreach
North West Cape
Newman
GIBSON DESERT
Alice Springs
Carnarvon
Uluru/Ayers Rock 867 m (2,844 ft)
SIMPSON DESERT
GREAT ARTESIAN BASIN
Charleville
Western Australia
AUSTRALIA
Brisbane
Southport
Geraldton
Kalgoorlie-Boulder
GREAT VICTORIA DESERT
Lake Eyre
Lowest point in Australia
Coober Pedy
South Australia
Toowoomba
NULLARBOR PLAIN
Perth
Bunbury
Woomera
Whyalla
Broken Hill
Bourke
Darling
New South Wales
Tamworth
Newcastle
Orange
Wagga Wagga
Murray
Sydney
Great Australian Bight
Albany
Esperance
Cape Leeuwin
Port Lincoln
Kangaroo I.
Adelaide
Albury
Canberra
Wollongong
Bendigo
Victoria
Mt. Kosciusko 2228 m (7,310 ft)
Highest point in Australia
Ballarat
Geelong
Melbourne
Bass Strait
Launceston
Tasmania
Hobart
Tasman Sea
Norfolk I. (Aust.)
Kermadec Is. (N.Z.)
North Island
Auckland
Hamilton
Tauranga
New Plymouth
Gisborne
Cook Strait
Napier
NEW ZEALAND
Nelson
Wellington
Aoraki/Mt. Cook 3724 m (12,218 ft)
Christchurch
South Island
Chatham Is. (N.Z.)
Stewart I.
Dunedin
Invercargill
0 400 800 1,200 Miles
0 400 800 1,200 1,600 Kilometers

AMENDMENT XII.

Election of President and Vice-President.

[Proposed by Congress Dec. 9, 1803; ratified June 15, 1804.]

The Electors shall meet in their respective states and vote by ballot for President and Vice-President, one of whom, at least, shall not be an inhabitant of the same state with themselves; they shall name in their ballots the person voted for as President, and in distinct ballots the person voted for as Vice-President, and they shall make distinct lists of all persons voted for as President, and of all persons voted for as Vice-President, and of the number of votes for each, which lists they shall sign and certify, and transmit sealed to the seat of the government of the United States, directed to the President of the Senate;—The President of the Senate shall, in the presence of the Senate and House of Representatives, open all the certificates and the votes shall then be counted;—The person having the greatest number of votes for President, shall be the President, if such number be a majority of the whole number of Electors appointed; and if no person have such majority, then from the persons having the highest numbers not exceeding three on the list of those voted for as President, the House of Representatives shall choose immediately, by ballot, the President. But in choosing the President, the votes shall be taken by states, the representation from each state having one vote; a quorum for this purpose shall consist of a member or members from two-thirds of the states, and a majority of all the states shall be necessary to a choice. [And if the House of Representatives shall not choose a President whenever the right of choice shall devolve upon them, before the fourth day of March next following, then the Vice-President shall act as President, as in the case of the death or other constitutional disability of the President.] *[The words in brackets were superseded by Amendment XX, section 3.]* The person having the greatest number of votes as Vice-President, shall be the Vice-President, if such number be a majority of the whole number of Electors appointed, and if no person have a majority, then from the two highest numbers on the list, the Senate shall choose the Vice-President; a quorum for the purpose shall consist of two-thirds of the whole number of Senators, and a majority of the whole number shall be necessary to a choice. But no person constitutionally ineligible to the office of President shall be eligible to that of Vice-President of the United States.

THE RECONSTRUCTION AMENDMENTS

[Amendments XIII, XIV, and XV are commonly known as the Reconstruction Amendments inasmuch as they followed the Civil War and were drafted by Republicans who wanted to impose their own policy of reconstruction on the South. Southern postbellum legislatures in states including Mississippi, South Carolina, and Georgia had set up laws that effectively perpetuated slavery under other names.]

AMENDMENT XIII.

Slavery abolished.

[Proposed by Congress Jan. 31, 1865; ratified Dec. 6, 1865.]

Section 1. Neither slavery nor involuntary servitude, except as a punishment for crime whereof the party shall have been duly convicted, shall exist within the United States, or any place subject to their jurisdiction.

Section 2. Congress shall have power to enforce this article by appropriate legislation.

AMENDMENT XIV.

Citizenship rights not to be abridged.

[Proposed by Congress June 13, 1866, ratified July 9, 1868, and declared to have been ratified in a proclamation by the Secretary of State, July 28, 1868.]

Section 1. All persons born or naturalized in the United States, and subject to the jurisdiction thereof, are citizens of the United States and of the State wherein they reside. No State shall make or enforce any law which shall abridge the privileges or immunities of citizens of the United States; nor shall any State deprive any person of life, liberty, or property, without due process of law; nor deny to any person within its jurisdiction the equal protection of the laws.

Section 2. Representatives shall be apportioned among the several States according to their respective numbers, counting the whole number of persons in each State, excluding Indians not taxed. But when the right to vote at any election for the choice of electors for President and Vice-President of the United States, Representatives in Congress, the Executive and Judicial officers of a State, or the members of the Legislature thereof, is denied to any of the male inhabitants of such State, being [twenty-one] *[The words in brackets were changed by Amendment XXVI.]* years of age, and citizens of the United States, or in any way abridged, except for participation in rebellion, or other crime, the basis of representation therein shall be reduced in the proportion which the number of such male citizens shall bear to the whole number of male citizens twenty-one years of age in such State.

Section 3. No person shall be a Senator or Representative in Congress, or elector of President and Vice-President, or hold any office, civil or military, under the United States, or under any State, who, having previously taken an oath, as a member of Congress, or as an officer of the United States, or as a member of any State legislature, or as an executive or judicial officer of any State, to support the Constitution of the United States, shall have engaged in insurrection or rebellion against the same, or given aid or comfort to the enemies thereof. But Congress may by a vote of two-thirds of each House, remove such disability.

Section 4. The validity of the public debt of the United States, authorized by law, including debts incurred for payment of pensions and bounties for services in suppressing insurrection or rebellion, shall not be questioned. But neither the United States nor any State shall assume or pay any debt or obligation incurred in aid of insurrection or rebellion against the United States, or any claim for the loss or emancipation of any slave; but all such debts, obligations and claims shall be held illegal and void.

Section 5. The Congress shall have power to enforce, by appropriate legislation, the provisions of this article.

AMENDMENT XV.

Race no bar to voting rights.

[Proposed by Congress Feb. 26, 1869; ratified Feb. 3, 1870.]

Section 1. The right of citizens of the United States to vote shall not be denied or abridged by the United States or by any State on account of race, color, or previous condition of servitude.

Section 2. The Congress shall have power to enforce this article by appropriate legislation.

AMENDMENT XVI.

Taxes on income.

[Proposed by Congress July 12, 1909; ratified Feb. 3, 1913.]

The Congress shall have power to lay and collect taxes on incomes, from whatever source derived, without apportionment among the several States, and without regard to any census or enumeration.

AMENDMENT XVII.

Popular election of Senators.

[Proposed by Congress May 13, 1912; ratified Apr. 8, 1913.]

The Senate of the United States shall be composed of two Senators from each State, elected by the people thereof, for six years; and each Senator shall have one vote. The electors in each State shall have the qualifications requisite for electors of the most numerous branch of the State legislatures.

When vacancies happen in the representation of any State in the Senate, the executive authority of such State shall issue writs of election to fill such vacancies: Provided, That the legislature of any State may empower the executive thereof to make temporary appointments until the people fill the vacancies by election as the legislature may direct.

This amendment shall not be so construed as to affect the election or term of any Senator chosen before it becomes valid as part of the Constitution.

AMENDMENT XVIII.

Liquor prohibition amendment.

[Proposed by Congress Dec. 18, 1917; ratified Jan. 16, 1919. Repealed by Amendment XXI, effective Dec. 5, 1933.]

Section 1. After one year from the ratification of this article the manufacture, sale, or transportation of intoxicating liquors within, the importation thereof into, or the exportation thereof from the United States and all territory subject to the jurisdiction thereof for beverage purposes is hereby prohibited.

Section 2. The Congress and the several States shall have concurrent power to enforce this article by appropriate legislation.

Section 3. This article shall be inoperative unless it shall have been ratified as an amendment to the Constitution by the legislatures of the several States, as provided in the Constitution, within seven years from the date of the submission hereof to the States by the Congress.

AMENDMENT XIX.

Nationwide suffrage to women.

[Proposed by Congress June 4, 1919; ratified Aug. 18, 1920.]

The right of citizens of the United States to vote shall not be denied or abridged by the United States or by any State on account of sex.

Congress shall have power to enforce this article by appropriate legislation.

AMENDMENT XX.

Commencement of terms of office.

[Proposed by Congress Mar. 2, 1932; ratified Jan. 23, 1933.]

Section 1. The terms of the President and Vice President shall end at noon on the 20th day of January, and the terms of Senators and Representatives at noon on the 3d day of January, of the years in which such terms would have ended if this article had not been ratified; and the terms of their successors shall then begin.

Section 2. The Congress shall assemble at least once in every year, and such meeting shall begin at noon on the 3d day of January, unless they shall by law appoint a different day.

Section 3. If, at the time fixed for the beginning of the term of the President, the President elect shall have died, the Vice President elect shall become President. If a President shall not have been chosen before the time fixed for the beginning of his term, or if the President elect shall have failed to qualify, then the Vice President elect shall act as President until a President shall have qualified; and the Congress may by law provide for the case wherein neither a President elect nor a Vice President elect shall have qualified, declaring who shall then act as President, or the manner in which one who is to act shall be selected, and such person shall act accordingly until a President or Vice President shall have qualified.

Section 4. The Congress may by law provide for the case of the death of any of the persons from whom the House of Representatives may choose a President whenever the right of choice shall have devolved upon them, and for the case of the death of any of the persons from whom the Senate may choose a Vice President whenever the right of choice shall have devolved upon them.

Section 5. Sections 1 and 2 shall take effect on the 15th day of October following the ratification of this article.

Section 6. This article shall be inoperative unless it shall have been ratified as an amendment to the Constitution by the legislatures of three-fourths of the several States within seven years from the date of its submission.

AMENDMENT XXI.

Repeal of Amendment XVIII.

[Proposed by Congress Feb. 20, 1933; ratified Dec. 5, 1933.]

Section 1. The eighteenth article of amendment to the Constitution of the United States is hereby repealed.

Section 2. The transportation or importation into any State, Territory, or possession of the United States for delivery or use therein of intoxicating liquors, in violation of the laws thereof, is hereby prohibited.

Section 3. This article shall be inoperative unless it shall have been ratified as an amendment to the Constitution by conventions in the several States, as provided in the Constitution, within seven years from the date of the submission hereof to the States by the Congress.

AMENDMENT XXII.

Limit on presidential terms of office.

[Proposed by Congress Mar. 24, 1947; ratified Feb. 27, 1951.]

Section 1. No person shall be elected to the office of the President more than twice, and no person who has held the office of President, or acted as President, for more than two years of a term to which some other person was elected President shall be elected to the office of the President more than once. But this Article shall not apply to any person holding the office of President when this Article was proposed by Congress, and shall not prevent any person who may be holding the office of President, or acting as President, during the term within which this Article becomes operative from holding the office of President or acting as President during the remainder of such term.

Section 2. This Article shall be inoperative unless it shall have been ratified as an amendment to the Constitution by the legislatures of three-fourths of the several States within seven years from the date of its submission to the States by the Congress.

AMENDMENT XXIII.

Presidential vote for District of Columbia.

[Proposed by Congress June 16, 1960; ratified Mar. 29, 1961.]

Section 1. The District constituting the seat of Government of the United States shall appoint in such manner as the Congress may direct:

A number of electors of President and Vice President equal to the whole number of Senators and Representatives in Congress to which the District would be entitled if it were a State, but in no event more than the least populous State; they shall be in addition to those appointed by the States, but they shall be considered, for the purposes of the election of President and Vice President, to be electors appointed by a State; and they shall meet in the District and perform such duties as provided by the twelfth article of amendment.

Section 2. The Congress shall have power to enforce this article by appropriate legislation.

AMENDMENT XXIV.

Poll tax barred in federal elections.

[Proposed by Congress Sept. 14, 1962; ratified Jan. 23, 1964.]

Section 1. The right of citizens of the United States to vote in any primary or other election for President or Vice President, for electors for President or Vice President, or for Senator or Representative in Congress, shall not be denied or abridged by the United States or any State by reason of failure to pay any poll tax or other tax.

Section 2. The Congress shall have power to enforce this article by appropriate legislation.

AMENDMENT XXV.

Presidential vacancy, inability, and succession.

[Proposed by Congress July 6, 1965; ratified Feb. 10, 1967.]

Section 1. In case of the removal of the President from office or of his death or resignation, the Vice President shall become President.

Section 2. Whenever there is a vacancy in the office of the Vice President, the President shall nominate a Vice President who shall take office upon confirmation by a majority vote of both Houses of Congress.

Section 3. Whenever the President transmits to the President pro tempore of the Senate and the Speaker of the House of Representatives his written declaration that he is unable to discharge the powers and duties of his office, and until he transmits to them a written declaration to the contrary, such powers and duties shall be discharged by the Vice President as Acting President.

Section 4. Whenever the Vice President and a majority of either the principal officers of the executive departments or of such other body as Congress may by law provide, transmit to the President pro tempore of the Senate and the Speaker of the House of Representatives their written declaration that the President is unable to discharge the powers and duties of his office, the Vice President shall immediately assume the powers and duties of the office as Acting President.

Thereafter, when the President transmits to the President pro tempore of the Senate and the Speaker of the House of Representatives his written declaration that no inability exists, he shall resume the powers and duties of his office unless the Vice President and a majority of either the principal officers of the executive department or of such other body as Congress may by law provide, transmit within four days to the President pro tempore of the Senate and the Speaker of the House of Representatives their written declaration that the President is unable to discharge the powers and duties of his office. Thereupon Congress shall decide the issue, assembling within forty-eight hours for that purpose if not in session. If the Congress, within twenty-one days after receipt of the latter written declaration, or, if Congress is not in session, within twenty-one days after Congress is required to assemble, determines by two-thirds vote of both Houses that the President is unable to discharge the powers and duties of his office, the Vice President shall continue to discharge the same as Acting President; otherwise, the President shall resume the powers and duties of his office.

AMENDMENT XXVI.

Voting age lowered to 18 years.

[Proposed by Congress Mar. 23, 1971; ratified July 1, 1971.]

Section 1. The right of citizens of the United States, who are eighteen years of age or older, to vote shall not be denied or abridged by the United States or by any State on account of age.

Section 2. The Congress shall have power to enforce this article by appropriate legislation.

AMENDMENT XXVII.

Congressional pay.

[Proposed by Congress Sept. 25, 1789; ratified May 7, 1992.]

No law, varying the compensation for the services of the Senators and Representatives, shall take effect, until an election of Representatives shall have intervened.

How a Bill Becomes a Law

A senator or representative introduces a bill in Congress by sending it to the clerk of the Senate or the House, who assigns it a number and title. This procedure is termed the first reading. The clerk then refers the bill to the appropriate committee of the Senate or House.

If the committee does not wish to consider the bill, it will table it. Otherwise, the committee holds hearings to gather information, such as by inviting experts and other members of the public to testify. The committee then debates the bill and may offer amendments. A vote is taken, and if favorable, the bill is sent back to the clerk of the Senate or House.

The clerk reads the bill to the house—the second reading. Members may then debate the bill and suggest amendments.

After debate and any amendments, the bill is given a third reading, simply of the title, and put to a voice or roll-call vote.

It should be noted that the Senate has additional rules that can further complicate the process of making laws. Most significantly, the Senate tradition of unlimited debate has allowed for the use of the filibuster, a tactic to prolong debate and thus delay or prevent a vote on measures, even as they may actually have majority support. In an early effort to limit the use of filibusters, the Senate in 1917 provided for "cloture," or a vote to end debate. Originally cloture required a two-thirds supermajority to succeed; in 1975 the Senate reduced the required supermajority to three-fifths of all senators duly chosen and sworn. If the bill passes, it goes to the other house, where it may be defeated or passed, with or without amendments. If defeated, the bill dies. If passed with amendments, a conference committee made up of members of both houses works out the differences between the two bills and arrives at a compromise.

After passage of the final version by both houses, the bill is sent to the president. If the president signs it, the bill becomes a law. The president may instead veto the bill by refusing to sign it and sending it back to the house where it originated, with reasons for the veto.

The president's objections are then read and debated, and a roll-call vote is taken. If the bill receives less than a two-thirds majority, it is defeated. If it receives at least two-thirds, it is sent to the other house. If that house also passes it by at least a two-thirds majority, the president's veto is overridden, and the bill becomes a law.

If the president neither signs nor vetoes the bill within 10 days—not including Sundays—it automatically becomes a law even without the president's signature. However, if Congress adjourns within those 10 days, the bill is automatically killed; this indirect rejection is termed a pocket veto.

Under the Line Item Veto Act, effective Jan. 1, 1997, the president was authorized, under certain circumstances, to veto a bill in part. The legislation was found unconstitutional by the Supreme Court, June 25, 1998.

Presidential Oath of Office

The Constitution (Article II, Section 1) directs that the president-elect shall take the following oath to be inaugurated: "I do solemnly swear [affirm] that I will faithfully execute the office of President of the United States, and will, to the best of my ability, preserve, protect, and defend the Constitution of the United States."

Custom decrees the addition of the words "So help me God" at the end of the oath when taken by the president-elect, with the left hand on the Bible for the duration of the oath, and the right hand slightly raised. However, the use of a Bible, or any other religious book, is not required.

Presidential Succession

If, by reason of death, resignation, removal from office, inability, or failure to qualify, there is neither a president nor vice president to discharge the powers and duties of the office of president, then the speaker of the House of Representatives shall, upon his resignation as speaker and as representative, act as president. The same rule shall apply in the case of the death, resignation, removal from office, or inability of an individual acting as president.

If, at the time when a speaker is to begin the discharge of the powers and duties of the office of president, there is no speaker, or the speaker fails to qualify as acting president, then the president pro tempore of the Senate, upon his resignation as president pro tempore and as senator, shall act as president.

An individual acting as president shall continue to act until the expiration of the then current presidential term, except that (1) if his discharge of the powers and duties of the office is founded in whole or in part in the failure of both the president-elect and the vice president-elect to qualify, then he shall act only until a president or vice president qualifies, and (2) if his discharge of the powers and duties of the office is founded in whole or in part on the inability of the president or vice president, then he shall act only until the removal of the disability of one of such individuals.

If, by reason of death, resignation, removal from office, or failure to qualify, there is no president pro tempore to act as president, then the officer of the United States who is highest on the following list, and who is not under any disability to discharge the powers and duties of president shall act as president: the secretaries of state, treasury, and defense; the attorney general; the secretaries of interior, agriculture, commerce, labor, health and human services, housing and urban development, transportation, energy, education, veterans affairs, and homeland security.

Legislation approved July 18, 1947; amended Sept. 9, 1965, Oct. 15, 1966, Aug. 4, 1977, Sept. 27, 1979, and Mar. 9, 2006. See also Constitutional Amendment XXV.

Confederate States: Secession and Government

The American Civil War (1861-65) grew out of sectional disputes over the continued existence of slavery in the South. Southern legislators contended that the states retained the right to enslave Black people and the right to secede.

The war was not fought by state against state but by one federal regime against another. A Confederate government in Richmond, VA, assumed control over the economic, political, and military life of the seceding states, under protest from Georgia and South Carolina.

South Carolina voted unanimously in convention to secede from the Union, repealing its 1788 ratification of the U.S. Constitution on Dec. 20, 1860, to take effect on Dec. 24. Other states seceded in 1861. Their votes in conventions were Mississippi, Jan. 9, 84-15; Florida, Jan. 10, 62-7; Alabama, Jan. 11, 61-39; Georgia, Jan. 19, 208-89; Louisiana, Jan. 26, 113-17; Texas, Feb. 1, 166-7, ratified by popular vote (34,794 to 11,325) Feb. 23; Virginia, Apr. 17, 88-55, ratified by popular vote (128,884 to 32,134) May 23; Arkansas, May 6, 69-1; Tennessee, May 7, ratified by popular vote (104,019 to 47,238) June 8; and North Carolina, unanimous, May 20.

Missouri Unionists stopped secession in conventions Feb. 28 and Mar. 9, 1861. Under the protection of Confederate troops, secessionist members of the legislature adopted a resolution of secession at Neosho, Oct. 31. The Confederate Congress seated the secessionists' representatives.

Kentucky did not secede, and its government remained Unionist. In a part of the state occupied by Confederate troops, Kentuckians approved secession, and the Confederate Congress admitted their representatives.

The Maryland legislature voted against secession Apr. 27, 1861, 53-13. Delaware did not secede. Pro-Union residents of western Virginia held conventions at Wheeling and, on June 17, 1861, formed the Restored Government of Virginia. It was admitted to the Union as West Virginia on June 20, 1863. Its constitution provided for gradual abolition of slavery.

Forty-two delegates from South Carolina, Georgia, Alabama, Mississippi, Louisiana, and Florida met in convention in Montgomery, AL, on Feb. 4, 1861. They adopted a provisional constitution of the Confederate States of America and elected Jefferson Davis (MS) as provisional president and Alexander H. Stephens (GA) as provisional vice president.

A permanent constitution was adopted Mar. 11. It banned the African slave trade but did not bar interstate commerce in slaves. On July 20 the Congress moved to Richmond. Davis was elected president in Nov. 1861 and was inaugurated Feb. 22, 1862.

The Confederate Congress adopted a flag ("The Stars and Bars") consisting of one white stripe and two red stripes and a blue canton with a circle of white stars. The Confederate battle flag, carried by the Army of Northern Virginia, was more popularly known. It has blue diagonal crossbars with 13 white stars, for the 11 states in the Confederacy plus Kentucky and Missouri, against a red field.

The Gettysburg Address

Delivered by Pres. Abraham Lincoln at the dedication of the Soldiers' National Cemetery in Gettysburg, PA, on Nov. 19, 1863. Five handwritten copies of the Gettysburg Address as made by Lincoln are known to exist. The text differs slightly between copies. The Bliss copy, made for Alexander Bliss, is shown here. The copy is kept on display in the White House.

Four score and seven years ago our fathers brought forth on this continent, a new nation, conceived in Liberty, and dedicated to the proposition that all men are created equal.

Now we are engaged in a great civil war, testing whether that nation, or any nation so conceived and so dedicated, can long endure. We are met on a great battle-field of that war. We have come to dedicate a portion of that field, as a final resting place for those who here gave their lives that that nation might live. It is altogether fitting and proper that we should do this.

But, in a larger sense, we can not dedicate—we can not consecrate—we can not hallow—this ground. The brave men, living and dead, who struggled here, have consecrated it, far above our poor power to add or detract. The world will little note, nor long remember what we say here, but it can never forget what they did here.

It is for us the living, rather, to be dedicated here to the unfinished work which they who fought here have thus far so nobly advanced. It is rather for us to be here dedicated to the great task remaining before us—that from these honored dead we take increased devotion to that cause for which they gave the last full measure of devotion—that we here highly resolve that these dead shall not have died in vain—that this nation, under God, shall have a new birth of freedom—and that government of the people, by the people, for the people, shall not perish from the earth.

Origin of the United States National Motto

In God We Trust, designated as the U.S. National Motto by Congress in 1956, originated during the Civil War as an inscription for U.S. coins. On Nov. 13, 1861, the Rev. M. R. Watkinson, of Ridleyville, PA, wrote to Treasury Sec. Salmon P. Chase requesting "recognition of the Almighty God in some form on our coins." Chase ordered designs prepared with the inscription *In God We Trust* and backed coinage legislation that authorized use of this slogan. The motto first appeared on some U.S. coins in 1864 and sporadically thereafter until 1938, after which all U.S. coins bear the inscription. A joint resolution passed by the 84th Congress and signed by Pres. Dwight D. Eisenhower July 30, 1956, declared *In God We Trust* the national motto of the United States.

Great Seal of the U.S.

On July 4, 1776, the Continental Congress appointed a committee consisting of Benjamin Franklin, John Adams, and Thomas Jefferson "to bring in a device for a seal of the United States of America." The designs submitted by this and a subsequent committee were considered unacceptable. After many delays, a third committee, appointed early in 1782, presented a design prepared by lawyer William Barton. Charles Thomson, the secretary of Congress, suggested certain changes, and Congress finally approved the design on June 20, 1782. The obverse of the seal shows a bald eagle. In the eagle's mouth is a ribbon bearing the motto *E Pluribus Unum* (out of many, one). In the eagle's talons are 13 arrows of war and an olive branch of peace. The reverse shows an unfinished pyramid with an eye (Eye of Providence) above it.

The Flag of the U.S.—The Stars and Stripes

The 50-star flag of the United States was raised for the first time officially at 12:01 AM on July 4, 1960, at Ft. McHenry National Monument in Baltimore, MD. The 50th star had been added for Hawaii; just a year earlier, the 49th star was added for Alaska.

There are so many myths and legends surrounding the history of the Stars and Stripes that the facts are difficult, and in some cases impossible, to establish. For example, it is not certain who designed the Stars and Stripes, who made the first such flag, or even whether it ever flew during any battle of the American Revolution.

Historians agree, however, that the Stars and Stripes originated as the result of a resolution offered by the Marine Committee of the Second Continental Congress at Philadelphia and adopted on June 14, 1777. It read:

"Resolved: that the flag of the United States be thirteen stripes, alternate red and white; that the union be thirteen stars, white in a blue field, representing a new constellation."

Congress gave no hint as to the designer of the flag, no instructions as to the arrangement of the stars, and no information on its appropriate uses.

The resolution establishing the flag was not published until Sept. 2, 1777. Despite repeated requests, George Washington did not get the flags until 1783, after the war was over. And there is no certainty that they were the Stars and Stripes.

Early Flags

Many historians consider the first flag of the U.S. to have been the Grand Union (sometimes called Great Union) flag, although the Continental Congress never officially adopted it. This flag was a modification of the British Meteor flag, which had the red cross of St. George and the white cross of St. Andrew combined in the blue canton. For the Grand Union flag, six horizontal stripes were imposed on the red field, dividing it into 13 alternating red and white stripes. On Jan. 1, 1776, when the Continental Army came into formal existence, this flag was unfurled on Prospect Hill, Somerville, MA. Washington wrote that "we hoisted the Union Flag in compliment to the United Colonies."

One of several flags about which controversy has raged is in Easton, PA. Containing the devices of the national flag in reversed order, this flag has been in the public library in Easton for more than 150 years. Some contend that this flag was actually the first Stars and Stripes, first displayed on July 8, 1776. This flag has 13 red and white stripes in the canton and 13 white stars centered in a blue field.

A flag was hastily improvised from garments by the defenders of Ft. Schuyler at Rome, NY, Aug. 3-22, 1777. Historians believe it was the Grand Union Flag.

The Sons of Liberty had a flag of nine red and white stripes, to signify nine colonies, when they met in New York in 1765 to oppose the Stamp Tax. By 1775, the flag had grown to 13 red and white stripes, with a rattlesnake on it.

At Concord, MA, Apr. 19, 1775, the minutemen from Bedford, MA, are said to have carried a flag having a silver arm with sword on a red field. At Cambridge, MA, the Sons of Liberty used a plain red flag with a green pine tree on it.

In June 1775, Washington went from Philadelphia to Boston to take command of the army. He was escorted to New York by the Philadelphia Light Horse Troop, which carried a yellow flag that had an elaborate coat of arms—the shield charged with 13 knots, the motto "For These We Strive"—and a canton of 13 blue and silver stripes.

In Feb. 1776, Col. Christopher Gadsden, a member of the Continental Congress, gave the South Carolina Provincial Congress a flag "such as is to be used by the commander-in-chief of the American Navy." It had a yellow field, with a rattlesnake about to strike and the words "Don't Tread on Me."

At the Battle of Bennington, Aug. 16, 1777, patriots used a flag of seven white and six red stripes with a blue canton extending down nine stripes. Eleven white stars arch over the figure 76 in the canton; a star appears in each of the canton's upper corners. The stars are seven-pointed. This flag is preserved in a museum in Bennington, VT.

At the Battle of Cowpens, Jan. 17, 1781, the 3rd Maryland Regiment is said to have carried a flag of 13 red and white stripes, with a blue canton containing 12 stars in a circle around one star.

Who Designed the Flag? No one knows for certain. Francis Hopkinson, designer of a naval flag, declared he had designed the flag and in 1781 asked Congress to reimburse him for his services. Congress did not do so.

Who Called the Flag "Old Glory"? The flag is said to have been named Old Glory by William Driver, a sea captain of Salem, MA. One legend has it that he did so when he raised the flag on his brig in 1824. But his daughter said he named it at his 21st birthday celebration on Mar. 17, 1824, when his mother presented the homemade flag to him.

The Betsy Ross Legend. The widely publicized legend that Betsy Ross made the first Stars and Stripes in June 1776, at the request of a committee composed of George Washington, Robert Morris, and George Ross, an uncle, was first made public in 1870, by a grandson of Ross. Historians have been unable to find a historical record of such a meeting or committee.

Adding New Stars

On the admission of Vermont and Kentucky to the Union, Congress designated that after May 1, 1795, the flag should have 15 stripes, alternating red and white, and 15 white stars on a blue field.

When more new states were admitted, it became evident that the flag would become burdened with stripes. Congress ordered that after July 4, 1818, the flag should have 13 stripes, symbolizing 13 original states; that the union have 20 stars; and that whenever a new state was admitted a new star should be added on the July 4 following admission.

No law designates the permanent arrangement of the stars. However, since 1912, when a new state has been admitted, the new design has been announced by executive order. No star is specifically identified with any state.

Pledge of Allegiance to the Flag

I pledge allegiance to the flag of the United States of America, and to the republic for which it stands, one nation under God, indivisible, with liberty and justice for all.

This, the current official version of the Pledge of Allegiance, developed from a pledge first published in the Sept. 8, 1892, issue of *Youth's Companion*, a weekly magazine. The original pledge contained the phrase "my flag," which was changed more than 30 years later to "flag of the United States of America." A 1954 act of Congress added the words "under God." (In 2002, the 9th Circuit U.S. Court of Appeals ruled that recitation of the pledge in public schools could not include that phrase. In 2004, however, the U.S. Supreme Court voted to decline to decide the case on a technicality. The lower court's decision was thus overturned.)

The authorship of the pledge was in dispute for many years. *Youth's Companion* stated in 1917 that the original draft was written by James B. Upham, an executive of the magazine who died in 1910. A leaflet circulated by the magazine later named Upham as the originator of the first draft.

Francis Bellamy, a former member of the *Youth's Companion* editorial staff, publicly claimed authorship of the pledge in 1923. In 1939, the United States Flag Association, acting on the advice of a committee named to study the controversy, upheld the claim by Bellamy, who had died eight years earlier. In 1957 the Library of Congress issued a report attributing the authorship to Bellamy.

According to the federal Flag Code, the pledge should be given while standing at attention facing the flag with the right hand over the heart. Those not in military uniform should remove any non-religious head coverings with their right hand and hold it at the left shoulder, the hand being over the heart. Those in uniform should remain silent, face the flag, and render a military salute. Members and veterans of the Armed Forces not in uniform may also render the military salute in the manner provided for persons in uniform.

History of the U.S. National Anthem

"The Star-Spangled Banner" was formally designated the national anthem by Act of Congress, Mar. 3, 1931. The words were written by Francis Scott Key, of Georgetown, in DC, marking the bombardment of Ft. McHenry in Baltimore, MD, Sept. 13-14, 1814. Key was a lawyer, a graduate of St. John's College in Annapolis, MD, and a volunteer in a light artillery company. When a friend, Dr. William Beanes, a Maryland physician, was arrested by the British for interfering with British deserters and straggling ground troops, Key and U.S. Col. John Skinner, with permission from Pres. Madison, went to the fleet under a flag of truce to ask for Beanes's release. The British consented, but as the fleet was about to sail up the Patapsco River to bombard Ft. McHenry, Key was detained for the duration of the battle.

The bombardment of Ft. McHenry began at 7 AM, Sept. 13, and lasted 25 hours. The British fired more than 1,500 shells. They were unable to approach closely because the U.S. had sunk 22 vessels to form a barrier. Only four Americans were killed and 24 wounded. A British bomb ship was disabled.

The morning after the shelling, Sept. 14, inspired by the flag still flying above the garrison, Key began to draft the poem. Released from British custody in Baltimore Sept. 16, Key revised the poem and gave it to his brother-in-law, Joseph Nicholson, who encouraged its printing on handbills. The first versions were titled "The Defence of Fort McHenry" and included a note suggesting use of the tune "Anacreon in Heaven" (attributed to British composer John Stafford Smith). The poem appeared in several newspapers within days and spread quickly.

The garrison flag that Key saw the morning after the bombardment is preserved at the Smithsonian Institution's National Museum of American History in Washington, DC. Major George Armistead, the commander of the militia unit stationed at Fort McHenry, had ordered a flag "so large that the British will have no difficulty seeing it from a distance." A government contract paid Baltimore flagmaker Mary Pickersgill $405.90 in 1813 for the garrison flag and $168.54 for a smaller storm flag (which was flown during the battle itself). The garrison flag originally measured 30 by 42 ft and had 15 alternating red and white stripes and 15 stars, for the original 13 states plus Kentucky and Vermont. The preserved flag measures 30 by 34 ft and is missing one star. Before the flag was placed in a museum, the family holding the flag would give clippings of it away as souvenirs.

The Star-Spangled Banner

I

Oh, say can you see by the dawn's early light
What so proudly we hailed at the twilight's last gleaming?
Whose broad stripes and bright stars through the perilous fight,
O'er the ramparts we watched were so gallantly streaming?
And the rockets' red glare, the bombs bursting in air,
Gave proof through the night that our flag was still there.
Oh, say does that star-spangled banner yet wave
O'er the land of the free and the home of the brave?

II

On the shore, dimly seen through the mists of the deep,
Where the foe's haughty host in dread silence reposes,
What is that which the breeze, o'er the towering steep,
As it fitfully blows, half conceals, half discloses?
Now it catches the gleam of the morning's first beam,
In full glory reflected now shines in the stream:
'Tis the star-spangled banner! Oh long may it wave
O'er the land of the free and the home of the brave!

III

And where is that band who so vauntingly swore
That the havoc of war and the battle's confusion,
A home and a country should leave us no more!
Their blood has washed out their foul footsteps' pollution.
No refuge could save the hireling and slave
From the terror of flight, or the gloom of the grave:
And the star-spangled banner in triumph doth wave
O'er the land of the free and the home of the brave!

IV

Oh! thus be it ever, when freemen shall stand
Between their loved home and the war's desolation!
Blest with victory and peace, may the heav'n rescued land
Praise the Power that hath made and preserved us a nation.
Then conquer we must, when our cause it is just,
And this be our motto: "In God is our trust."
And the star-spangled banner in triumph shall wave
O'er the land of the free and the home of the brave!

Statue of Liberty National Monument

Since 1886, the Statue of Liberty, formally known as "Liberty Enlightening the World," has stood as a symbol of freedom in New York Harbor. A gift from the people of France to the people of the U.S., it initially was conceived by legal philosopher Édouard de Laboulaye and intended to celebrate the U.S. centennial and commemorate the abolition of slavery. It was designed by French sculptor Frédéric Auguste Bartholdi (1834-1904).

On Feb. 22, 1877, Congress approved the use of a site on Bedloe's Island suggested by Bartholdi. This island of 12 acres had been owned in the 17th cent. by a colonist named Isaac Bedloe. (On Aug. 3, 1956, Pres. Dwight Eisenhower approved a measure changing the name to Liberty Island.)

The statue was finished on May 21, 1884, and presented to the U.S. minister to France, Levi Parsons Morton, July 4, 1884, by French diplomat Ferdinand de Lesseps.

On Aug. 5, 1884, the cornerstone for the granite pedestal—designed by architect Richard Morris Hunt—was laid on the foundations of Fort Wood, erected by the government in 1811. The American Committee for the Statue of Liberty had raised an inadequate $125,000, and *New York World* newspaper owner Joseph Pulitzer appealed Mar. 16, 1885, for general donations. By Aug. 11, 1885, he had raised $100,000. The statue itself arrived dismantled, in 214 packing cases, from Rouen, France, in June 1885. The last rivet of the statue was driven on Oct. 28, 1886, when Pres. Grover Cleveland dedicated the monument.

The Statue of Liberty National Monument was designated as such in 1924. It is administered by the National Park Service. A $2.5-mil building housing the American Museum of Immigration was opened by Pres. Richard Nixon on Sept. 26, 1972, at the base of the statue. It houses a permanent exhibition tracing the history of American immigration.

Four years of restoration work funded and led by the Statue of Liberty-Ellis Island Foundation were completed before the statue's 1986 centennial. The $87-mil project included the replacement of the 1,600 wrought iron bands that hold the statue's copper skin to its frame, replacement of the torch, and installation of an elevator. A four-day extravaganza of concerts, tall ships, cultural and heritage festivals, and fireworks, July 3-6, 1986, celebrated the 100th anniversary. U.S. Supreme Court Chief Justice Warren E. Burger swore in 5,000 new citizens on Ellis Island, while 20,000 others across the country were sworn in through a satellite telecast. Other ceremonies followed on Oct. 28, 1986, the statue's exact 100th birthday.

After the Sept. 11, 2001, terrorist attacks, Liberty Island was closed to visitors. The secretary of the interior reopened the island in Dec. 2001 after installing security screening facilities at passenger embarkation areas at Battery Park in Manhattan and Liberty State Park in New Jersey.

The federal government increased security throughout the park before reopening the statue. In addition to federally funded security upgrades, significant building safety improvements were made. Public access to the statue pedestal was restored in Aug. 2004, and the crown reopened July 4, 2009.

Following the 125th anniversary celebration Oct. 28, 2011, the statue was closed. A $30-mil renovation brought it up to contemporary safety standards and allowed for increased visitor access. Although the statue interior reopened Oct. 28, 2012, damages caused by Hurricane Sandy forced all of Liberty Island to close again within days. The island and the statue officially reopened to visitors July 4, 2013. A new, 26,000-sq-ft Statue of Liberty Museum opened in May 2019.

Ferry service to Liberty Island and to Ellis Island, from Battery Park in New York City and from Liberty State Park in New Jersey was suspended Mar. 16, 2020, in response to the COVID-19 outbreak, but resumed in July 2021, available only by specific time of departure.

Liberty Island can be reached by ferry only. There is public access to the Statue of Liberty Museum and theater, as well as (with reservations) to the statue pedestal and the crown. (The latter can be reached only by climbing a long, spiral staircase.) Tickets may sell out well beforehand. Reservations are available months in advance and can be made at www.statuecruises.com or 1-877-LADY-TIX. Prices were raised as of Mar. 2024. Before visiting, check www. nps.gov/stli for latest information on openings and guidelines, including age and height restrictions. Park rangers conduct English-language tours throughout the day. Standard self-guided audio tours and a family-friendly audio tour (aimed at children ages 6-10) are available in a number of languages.

Statue Statistics

The statue weighs 450,000 lbs, or 225 tons. The copper sheeting weighs 200,000 lbs. There are 377 steps from the main lobby to the crown platform. There are 146 steps from the top of the pedestal (the statue's feet) to the crown platform.

Statue feature	Measurement Ft	In.
Height from base to torch tip	151	1
Foundation of pedestal to torch tip	305	1
Heel to top of head	111	1
Hand, length	16	5
Index finger, length	8	0
Fingernail size		13x10
Head from chin to cranium	17	3
Head thickness, ear to ear	10	0
Nose, length	4	6
Right arm, length	42	0
Right arm, max. thickness	12	0
Waist, thickness	35	0
Mouth, width	3	0
Tablet, length	23	7
Tablet, width	13	7

Ellis Island

Ellis Island was the gateway to America for over 12 mil immigrants between 1892 and 1924. In the late 18th cent., Samuel Ellis, a New York City merchant, purchased the island. From Ellis, it passed to New York state before the U.S. government bought it in 1808. On Jan. 1, 1892, the government opened the first federal immigration center in the U.S. there. The 27.5-acre site eventually supported over 35 buildings, including the Main Building with its Great Hall, designed to process 5,000 people a day. In Ellis Island's peak year, 1907, it received 1,004,756 immigrants; on its peak day (Apr. 17, 1907), 11,747 immigrants were processed.

Closed as an immigration station in 1954, Ellis Island was proclaimed part of the Statue of Liberty National Monument in 1965 by Pres. Lyndon B. Johnson. After a six-year, $170-mil restoration project funded by the Statue of Liberty-Ellis Island Foundation, Ellis Island was reopened as a museum in 1990, now called the Ellis Island National Museum of Immigration. Artifacts, historic photographs and documents, oral histories, and ethnic music depicting 400 years of American immigration are housed in the museum.

In 1998, the U.S. Supreme Court ruled that nearly 90% of the island (the 24.2 acres that are landfill) lies in New Jersey, while the original 3.3 acres, on which the museum is located, are in New York. (The decision settled the issue of jurisdiction over potential development.)

The American Family Immigration History Center opened in Apr. 2001. Visitors can access arrival records on over 51 mil individuals who entered through the Port of New York and Ellis Island from 1892 to 1957. The searchable digitized archives include ships' images and manifests and passenger information such as age, ethnicity, and port of departure. **Website:** www.libertyellisfoundation.org

Damage caused by storm surges from Hurricane Sandy in late Oct. 2012 forced Ellis Island to close for repairs. It reopened Oct. 28, 2013, and new galleries focusing on post-Ellis Island-era immigration opened May 20, 2015. A project to repair the aging seawall was completed in fall 2023.

Ellis Island was closed Mar. 16, 2020, in response to the COVID-19 outbreak, but reopened in summer 2020, with limited capacity. Access is available by ferry only. For latest information see www.nps.gov/elis

PRESIDENTS OF THE UNITED STATES

U.S. Presidents

	Name	Politics	Born	Birthplace	Inaug.	Age at inaug.	Died	Age at death
1.	George Washington	Fed.	1732, Feb. 22	VA	1789	57	1799, Dec. 14	67
2.	John Adams	Fed.	1735, Oct. 30	MA	1797	61	1826, July 4	90
3.	Thomas Jefferson	Dem.-Rep.	1743, Apr. 13	VA	1801	57	1826, July 4	83
4.	James Madison	Dem.-Rep.	1751, Mar. 16	VA	1809	57	1836, June 28	85
5.	James Monroe	Dem.-Rep.	1758, Apr. 28	VA	1817	58	1831, July 4	73
6.	John Quincy Adams	Dem.-Rep.	1767, July 11	MA	1825	57	1848, Feb. 23	80
7.	Andrew Jackson	Dem.	1767, Mar. 15	SC	1829	61	1845, June 8	78
8.	Martin Van Buren	Dem.	1782, Dec. 5	NY	1837	54	1862, July 24	79
9.	William Henry Harrison	Whig	1773, Feb. 9	VA	1841	68	1841, Apr. 4	68
10.	John Tyler	Whig	1790, Mar. 29	VA	1841	51	1862, Jan. 18	71
11.	James Knox Polk	Dem.	1795, Nov. 2	NC	1845	49	1849, June 15	53
12.	Zachary Taylor	Whig	1784, Nov. 24	VA	1849	64	1850, July 9	65
13.	Millard Fillmore	Whig	1800, Jan. 7	NY	1850	50	1874, Mar. 8	74
14.	Franklin Pierce	Dem.	1804, Nov. 23	NH	1853	48	1869, Oct. 8	64
15.	James Buchanan	Dem.	1791, Apr. 23	PA	1857	65	1868, June 1	77
16.	Abraham Lincoln	Rep.	1809, Feb. 12	KY	1861	52	1865, Apr. 15	56
17.	Andrew Johnson	Dem.[1]	1808, Dec. 29	NC	1865	56	1875, July 31	66
18.	Ulysses S. Grant	Rep.	1822, Apr. 27	OH	1869	46	1885, July 23	63
19.	Rutherford Birchard Hayes	Rep.	1822, Oct. 4	OH	1877	54	1893, Jan. 17	70
20.	James Abram Garfield	Rep.	1831, Nov. 19	OH	1881	49	1881, Sept. 19	49
21.	Chester Alan Arthur	Rep.	1829, Oct. 5	VT	1881	51	1886, Nov. 18	57
22.	(Stephen) Grover Cleveland	Dem.	1837, Mar. 18	NJ	1885	47	1908, June 24	71
23.	Benjamin Harrison	Rep.	1833, Aug. 20	OH	1889	55	1901, Mar. 13	67
24.	(Stephen) Grover Cleveland	Dem.	1837, Mar. 18	NJ	1893	55	1908, June 24	71
25.	William McKinley	Rep.	1843, Jan. 29	OH	1897	54	1901, Sept. 14	58
26.	Theodore Roosevelt	Rep.	1858, Oct. 27	NY	1901	42	1919, Jan. 6	60
27.	William Howard Taft	Rep.	1857, Sept. 15	OH	1909	51	1930, Mar. 8	72
28.	(Thomas) Woodrow Wilson	Dem.	1856, Dec. 28	VA	1913	56	1924, Feb. 3	67
29.	Warren Gamaliel Harding	Rep.	1865, Nov. 2	OH	1921	55	1923, Aug. 2	57
30.	(John) Calvin Coolidge	Rep.	1872, July 4	VT	1923	51	1933, Jan. 5	60
31.	Herbert Clark Hoover	Rep.	1874, Aug. 10	IA	1929	54	1964, Oct. 20	90
32.	Franklin Delano Roosevelt	Dem.	1882, Jan. 30	NY	1933	51	1945, Apr. 12	63
33.	Harry S. Truman	Dem.	1884, May 8	MO	1945	60	1972, Dec. 26	88
34.	Dwight David Eisenhower	Rep.	1890, Oct. 14	TX	1953	62	1969, Mar. 28	78
35.	John Fitzgerald Kennedy	Dem.	1917, May 29	MA	1961	43	1963, Nov. 22	46
36.	Lyndon Baines Johnson	Dem.	1908, Aug. 27	TX	1963	55	1973, Jan. 22	64
37.	Richard Milhous Nixon	Rep.	1913, Jan. 9	CA	1969	56	1994, Apr. 22	81
38.	Gerald Rudolph Ford	Rep.	1913, July 14	NE	1974	61	2006, Dec. 26	93
39.	James Earl (Jimmy) Carter	Dem.	1924, Oct. 1	GA	1977	52		
40.	Ronald Wilson Reagan	Rep.	1911, Feb. 6	IL	1981	69	2004, June 5	93
41.	George Herbert Walker Bush	Rep.	1924, June 12	MA	1989	64	2018, Nov. 30	94
42.	Wm. Jefferson (Bill) Clinton	Dem.	1946, Aug. 19	AR	1993	46		
43.	George Walker Bush	Rep.	1946, July 6	CT	2001	54		
44.	Barack Hussein Obama	Dem.	1961, Aug. 4	HI	2009	47		
45.	Donald John Trump	Rep.	1946, June 14	NY	2017	70		
46.	Joseph Robinette Biden Jr.	Dem.	1942, Nov. 20	PA	2021	78		

(1) Johnson, a Democrat, was nominated vice president by Republicans and elected with Lincoln on National Union ticket.

U.S. Presidents, Vice Presidents, Congresses

President	Service	Vice President	Congresses
1. George Washington	Apr. 30, 1789-Mar. 3, 1797	1. John Adams	1, 2, 3, 4
2. John Adams	Mar. 4, 1797-Mar. 3, 1801	2. Thomas Jefferson	5, 6
3. Thomas Jefferson	Mar. 4, 1801-Mar. 3, 1805	3. Aaron Burr	7, 8
	Mar. 4, 1805-Mar. 3, 1809	4. George Clinton	9, 10
4. James Madison	Mar. 4, 1809-Mar. 3, 1813	George Clinton[1]	11, 12
	Mar. 4, 1813-Mar. 3, 1817	5. Elbridge Gerry[2]	13, 14
5. James Monroe	Mar. 4, 1817-Mar. 3, 1825	6. Daniel D. Tompkins	15, 16, 17, 18
6. John Quincy Adams	Mar. 4, 1825-Mar. 3, 1829	7. John C. Calhoun	19, 20
7. Andrew Jackson	Mar. 4, 1829-Mar. 3, 1833	John C. Calhoun[3]	21, 22
	Mar. 4, 1833-Mar. 3, 1837	8. Martin Van Buren	23, 24
8. Martin Van Buren	Mar. 4, 1837-Mar. 3, 1841	9. Richard M. Johnson	25, 26
9. William Henry Harrison[4]	Mar. 4, 1841-Apr. 4, 1841	10. John Tyler	27
10. John Tyler	Apr. 6, 1841-Mar. 3, 1845	(None)	27, 28
11. James K. Polk	Mar. 4, 1845-Mar. 3, 1849	11. George M. Dallas	29, 30
12. Zachary Taylor[4]	Mar. 5, 1849-July 9, 1850	12. Millard Fillmore	31
13. Millard Fillmore	July 10, 1850-Mar. 3, 1853	(None)	31, 32
14. Franklin Pierce	Mar. 4, 1853-Mar. 3, 1857	13. William R. King[5]	33, 34
15. James Buchanan	Mar. 4, 1857-Mar. 3, 1861	14. John C. Breckinridge	35, 36
16. Abraham Lincoln[4]	Mar. 4, 1861-Mar. 3, 1865	15. Hannibal Hamlin	37, 38
	Mar. 4, 1865-Apr. 15, 1865	16. Andrew Johnson	39
17. Andrew Johnson	Apr. 15, 1865-Mar. 3, 1869	(None)	39, 40
18. Ulysses S. Grant	Mar. 4, 1869-Mar. 3, 1873	17. Schuyler Colfax	41, 42
	Mar. 4, 1873-Mar. 3, 1877	18. Henry Wilson[6]	43, 44
19. Rutherford B. Hayes	Mar. 4, 1877-Mar. 3, 1881	19. William A. Wheeler	45, 46
20. James A. Garfield[4]	Mar. 4, 1881-Sept. 19, 1881	20. Chester A. Arthur	47
21. Chester A. Arthur	Sept. 20, 1881-Mar. 3, 1885	(None)	47, 48
22. Grover Cleveland[7]	Mar. 4, 1885-Mar. 3, 1889	21. Thomas A. Hendricks[8]	49, 50
23. Benjamin Harrison	Mar. 4, 1889-Mar. 3, 1893	22. Levi P. Morton	51, 52
24. Grover Cleveland[7]	Mar. 4, 1893-Mar. 3, 1897	23. Adlai E. Stevenson	53, 54
25. William McKinley[4]	Mar. 4, 1897-Mar. 3, 1901	24. Garret A. Hobart[9]	55, 56
	Mar. 4, 1901-Sept. 14, 1901	25. Theodore Roosevelt	57
26. Theodore Roosevelt	Sept. 14, 1901-Mar. 3, 1905	(None)	57, 58
	Mar. 4, 1905-Mar. 3, 1909	26. Charles W. Fairbanks	59, 60
27. William H. Taft	Mar. 4, 1909-Mar. 3, 1913	27. James S. Sherman[10]	61, 62
28. Woodrow Wilson	Mar. 4, 1913-Mar. 3, 1921	28. Thomas R. Marshall	63, 64, 65, 66

President	Service	Vice President	Congresses
29. Warren G. Harding[4]	Mar. 4, 1921-Aug. 2, 1923	29. Calvin Coolidge	67
30. Calvin Coolidge	Aug. 3, 1923-Mar. 3, 1925	(None)	68
	Mar. 4, 1925-Mar. 3, 1929	30. Charles G. Dawes	69, 70
31. Herbert C. Hoover	Mar. 4, 1929-Mar. 3, 1933	31. Charles Curtis	71, 72
32. Franklin D. Roosevelt[4,11]	Mar. 4, 1933-Jan. 20, 1941	32. John N. Garner	73, 74, 75, 76, 77
	Jan. 20, 1941-Jan. 20, 1945	33. Henry A. Wallace	77, 78, 79
	Jan. 20, 1945-Apr. 12, 1945	34. Harry S. Truman	79
33. Harry S. Truman	Apr. 12, 1945-Jan. 20, 1949	(None)	79, 80, 81
	Jan. 20, 1949-Jan. 20, 1953	35. Alben W. Barkley	81, 82, 83
34. Dwight D. Eisenhower	Jan. 20, 1953-Jan. 20, 1961	36. Richard M. Nixon	83, 84, 85, 86, 87
35. John F. Kennedy[4]	Jan. 20, 1961-Nov. 22, 1963	37. Lyndon B. Johnson	87, 88
36. Lyndon B. Johnson	Nov. 22, 1963-Jan. 20, 1965	(None)	88, 89
	Jan. 20, 1965-Jan. 20, 1969	38. Hubert H. Humphrey	89, 90, 91
37. Richard M. Nixon[13]	Jan. 20, 1969-Jan. 20, 1973	39. Spiro T. Agnew[12]	91, 92, 93
	Jan. 20, 1973-Aug. 9, 1974	40. Gerald R. Ford[14]	93
38. Gerald R. Ford[15]	Aug. 9, 1974-Jan. 20, 1977	41. Nelson A. Rockefeller[16]	93, 94, 95
39. Jimmy Carter	Jan. 20, 1977-Jan. 20, 1981	42. Walter F. Mondale	95, 96, 97
40. Ronald W. Reagan	Jan. 20, 1981-Jan. 20, 1989	43. George H. W. Bush	97, 98, 99, 100, 101
41. George H. W. Bush	Jan. 20, 1989-Jan. 20, 1993	44. Dan Quayle	101, 102, 103
42. Bill Clinton	Jan. 20, 1993-Jan. 20, 2001	45. Al Gore	103, 104, 105, 106, 107
43. George W. Bush	Jan. 20, 2001-Jan. 20, 2009	46. Dick Cheney	107, 108, 109, 110, 111
44. Barack H. Obama	Jan. 20, 2009-Jan. 20, 2017	47. Joe Biden	111, 112, 113, 114, 115
45. Donald J. Trump	Jan. 20, 2017-Jan. 20, 2021	48. Mike Pence	115, 116, 117
46. Joseph R. Biden	Jan. 20, 2021-	49. Kamala Harris	117, 118

(1) Died Apr. 20, 1812. (2) Died Nov. 23, 1814. (3) Resigned Dec. 28, 1832, to become U.S. senator. (4) Died in office. (5) Died Apr. 18, 1853. (6) Died Nov. 22, 1875. (7) Terms not consecutive. (8) Died Nov. 25, 1885. (9) Died Nov. 21, 1899. (10) Died Oct. 30, 1912. (11) First president to be inaugurated under 20th Amendment, Jan. 20, 1937. (12) Resigned Oct. 10, 1973, after pleading no contest to a charge of tax evasion. (13) Resigned Aug. 9, 1974. (14) First nonelected vice president, chosen under 25th Amendment procedure. (15) First president never elected president or vice president. (16) Second nonelected vice president, chosen under 25th Amendment. Confirmed Dec. 19, 1974.

Vice Presidents of the U.S.

The numerals given vice presidents do not coincide with those given presidents because some presidents (Tyler, Fillmore, A. Johnson, Arthur) had none, and some had more than one.

Name	Birthplace	Born	Home	Inaug.	Politics/ party	Place of death	Died	Age at death
1. John Adams	Quincy, MA	1735	MA	1789	Fed.	Quincy, MA	1826	90
2. Thomas Jefferson	Shadwell, VA	1743	VA	1797	Dem.-Rep.	Monticello, VA	1826	83
3. Aaron Burr	Newark, NJ	1756	NY	1801	Dem.-Rep.	Staten Island, NY	1836	80
4. George Clinton	Little Britain, NY	1739	NY	1805	Dem.-Rep.	Washington, DC	1812	73
5. Elbridge Gerry	Marblehead, MA	1744	MA	1813	Dem.-Rep.	Washington, DC	1814	70
6. Daniel D. Tompkins	Scarsdale, NY	1774	NY	1817	Dem.-Rep.	Staten Island, NY	1825	51
7. John C. Calhoun[1]	Abbeville, SC	1782	SC	1825	Dem.-Rep.	Washington, DC	1850	68
8. Martin Van Buren	Kinderhook, NY	1782	NY	1833	Dem.	Kinderhook, NY	1862	79
9. Richard M. Johnson[2]	Louisville, KY	1780	KY	1837	Dem.	Frankfort, KY	1850	70
10. John Tyler	Greenway, VA	1790	VA	1841	Whig	Richmond, VA	1862	71
11. George M. Dallas	Philadelphia, PA	1792	PA	1845	Dem.	Philadelphia, PA	1864	72
12. Millard Fillmore	Cayuga Co., NY	1800	NY	1849	Whig	Buffalo, NY	1874	74
13. William R. King	Sampson Co., NC	1786	AL	1853	Dem.	Cahaba, AL	1853	67
14. John C. Breckinridge	Lexington, KY	1821	KY	1857	Dem.	Lexington, KY	1875	54
15. Hannibal Hamlin	Paris, ME	1809	ME	1861	Rep.	Bangor, ME	1891	81
16. Andrew Johnson	Raleigh, NC	1808	TN	1865	Dem.[3]	Carter Co., TN	1875	66
17. Schuyler Colfax	New York, NY	1823	IN	1869	Rep.	Mankato, MN	1885	62
18. Henry Wilson	Farmington, NH	1812	MA	1873	Rep.	Washington, DC	1875	63
19. William A. Wheeler	Malone, NY	1819	NY	1877	Rep.	Malone, NY	1887	68
20. Chester A. Arthur	Fairfield, VT	1829	NY	1881	Rep.	New York, NY	1886	57
21. Thomas A. Hendricks	Zanesville, OH	1819	IN	1885	Dem.	Indianapolis, IN	1885	66
22. Levi P. Morton	Shoreham, VT	1824	NY	1889	Rep.	Rhinebeck, NY	1920	96
23. Adlai E. Stevenson[4]	Christian Co., KY	1835	IL	1893	Dem.	Chicago, IL	1914	78
24. Garret A. Hobart	Long Branch, NJ	1844	NJ	1897	Rep.	Paterson, NJ	1899	55
25. Theodore Roosevelt	New York, NY	1858	NY	1901	Rep.	Oyster Bay, NY	1919	60
26. Charles W. Fairbanks	Unionville Centre, OH	1852	IN	1905	Rep.	Indianapolis, IN	1918	66
27. James S. Sherman	Utica, NY	1855	NY	1909	Rep.	Utica, NY	1912	57
28. Thomas R. Marshall	N. Manchester, IN	1854	IN	1913	Dem.	Washington, DC	1925	71
29. Calvin Coolidge	Plymouth Notch, VT	1872	MA	1921	Rep.	Northampton, MA	1933	60
30. Charles G. Dawes	Marietta, OH	1865	IL	1925	Rep.	Evanston, IL	1951	85
31. Charles Curtis	Topeka, KS	1860	KS	1929	Rep.	Washington, DC	1936	76
32. John Nance Garner	Red River Co., TX	1868	TX	1933	Dem.	Uvalde, TX	1967	98
33. Henry A. Wallace	Adair County, IA	1888	IA	1941	Dem.	Danbury, CT	1965	77
34. Harry S. Truman	Lamar, MO	1884	MO	1945	Dem.	Kansas City, MO	1972	88
35. Alben W. Barkley	Graves Co., KY	1877	KY	1949	Dem.	Lexington, VA	1956	78
36. Richard M. Nixon	Yorba Linda, CA	1913	CA	1953	Rep.	New York, NY	1994	81
37. Lyndon B. Johnson	Stonewall, TX	1908	TX	1961	Dem.	San Antonio, TX	1973	64
38. Hubert H. Humphrey	Wallace, SD	1911	MN	1965	Dem.	Waverly, MN	1978	66
39. Spiro T. Agnew[5]	Baltimore, MD	1918	MD	1969	Rep.	Berlin, MD	1996	77
40. Gerald R. Ford[6]	Omaha, NE	1913	MI	1973	Rep.	Rancho Mirage, CA	2006	93
41. Nelson A. Rockefeller[7]	Bar Harbor, ME	1908	NY	1974	Rep.	New York, NY	1979	70
42. Walter F. Mondale	Ceylon, MN	1928	MN	1977	Dem.	Minneapolis, MN	2021	93
43. George H. W. Bush	Milton, MA	1924	TX	1981	Rep.	Houston, TX	2018	94
44. James Danforth (Dan) Quayle Jr.	Indianapolis, IN	1947	IN	1989	Rep.			
45. Albert A. Gore	Washington, DC	1948	TN	1993	Dem.			
46. Richard B. Cheney	Lincoln, NE	1941	WY	2001	Rep.			
47. Joseph R. Biden Jr.	Scranton, PA	1942	DE	2009	Dem.			
48. Michael R. Pence	Columbus, IN	1959	IN	2017	Rep.			
49. Kamala D. Harris	Oakland, CA	1964	CA	2021	Dem.			

(1) Resigned Dec. 28, 1832, having been elected to the Senate to fill a vacancy. (2) Richard M. Johnson was the only vice president to be chosen by the Senate because of a tied vote in the Electoral College. (3) Democrat Andrew Johnson was nominated vice president by Republicans and elected with Lincoln on the National Union ticket. (4) Grandfather of Democratic candidate for president in 1952 and 1956. (5) Resigned Oct. 10, 1973, after pleading no contest to a charge of tax evasion. (6) First nonelected vice president, chosen under 25th Amendment procedure. (7) Second nonelected vice president, chosen under 25th Amendment.

Biographies of the Presidents

George Washington (1789-97), first president, Federalist, was born on Feb. 22, 1732, in Wakefield on Pope's Creek, Westmoreland Co., VA, the son of Augustine and Mary Ball Washington. He spent his early childhood on a farm near Fredericksburg. His father died when Washington was 11. He studied mathematics and surveying, and at 16, he went to live with his elder half brother, Lawrence, who built and named Mount Vernon in Virginia. Washington surveyed the lands of Thomas Fairfax in the Shenandoah Valley. He accompanied Lawrence to Barbados, West Indies, where he contracted smallpox and was deeply scarred. Lawrence died in 1752, and Washington inherited his property. He valued land, and when he died, he was a slaveholder who owned 70,000 acres in Virginia and 40,000 acres in what is now West Virginia.

Washington's military service began in 1753, when Lt. Gov. Robert Dinwiddie of Virginia sent him on missions deep into Ohio country. He clashed with the French and had to surrender Fort Necessity on July 3, 1754. He was an aide to the British general Edward Braddock and was at his side when the army was ambushed and defeated (July 9, 1755) on a march to Fort Duquesne. He helped take Fort Duquesne from the French in 1758.

After Washington's marriage to Martha Dandridge Custis, a widow, in 1759, he managed his family estate at Mount Vernon. Although not in favor of independence initially, he opposed the repressive measures of the British crown and took charge of the Virginia troops before war broke out. He was made commander of the newly created Continental Army by the Continental Congress on June 15, 1775.

The American victory was due largely to Washington's leadership. He was resourceful, a disciplinarian, and a dependable force for unity. Washington favored a federal government. He became chairman of the Constitutional Convention of 1787 and helped get the Constitution ratified. Unanimously elected president by the Electoral College, he was inaugurated Apr. 30, 1789, on the balcony of New York's Federal Hall. He was reelected in 1792. Washington made an effort to avoid partisan politics as president.

Refusing to consider a third term, Washington retired to Mount Vernon in Mar. 1797. A ride in snow and rain around his estate led to what present-day doctors believe to have been an attack of acute epiglottitis. Doctors were unsuccessful in treating the inflammation in his throat, and Washington died Dec. 14, 1799.

John Adams (1797-1801), second president, Federalist, was born on Oct. 30, 1735, in Braintree (now Quincy), MA, the son of John and Susanna Boylston Adams. He was a great-grandson of Henry Adams, who came from England in 1636. He graduated from Harvard in 1755, then taught school and studied law. He married Abigail Smith in 1764. In 1770, he successfully defended in court the British soldiers who fired on civilians in the Boston Massacre. He was a delegate to the Continental Congress and a signer of the Declaration of Independence. In 1778, Congress sent Adams and John Jay to join Benjamin Franklin as diplomatic representatives in Europe. Because he ran second to Washington in Electoral College balloting in Feb. 1789, Adams became the nation's first vice president, a post he characterized as highly insignificant; he was reelected in 1792.

In 1796 Adams was chosen president by the electors. His administration was marked by growing conflict with fellow Federalist Alexander Hamilton and with those in his cabinet who shared Hamilton's anti-French position. Adams avoided a declared war with France but became unpopular, especially after securing passage of the Alien and Sedition Acts, which restricted speech critical of the government, in 1798. His foreign policy contributed significantly to the election of Thomas Jefferson in 1800.

Adams lived for a quarter century after he left office, during which time he wrote extensively. He died July 4, 1826, on the same day as his rival Thomas Jefferson (the 50th anniversary of the Declaration of Independence).

Thomas Jefferson (1801-09), third president, Democratic-Republican, was born on Apr. 13, 1743, in Shadwell in Goochland (now Albemarle) Co., VA, the son of Peter and Jane Randolph Jefferson. His father died when Jefferson was 14, leaving him 2,750 acres and his slaves. Jefferson attended (1760-62) the College of William and Mary, read Greek and Latin classics, and played the violin. In 1769 he was elected to the Virginia House of Burgesses. In 1770 he began building his home, Monticello, and in 1772 he married Martha Wayles Skelton, a wealthy widow. Jefferson helped establish the Virginia Committee of Correspondence. As a member of the Second Continental Congress he drafted the Declaration of Independence. He also was a member of the Virginia House of Delegates (1776-79) and was elected governor of Virginia in 1779. He resigned in 1781, after British troops invaded Virginia. During his term he wrote the Virginia Statute of Religious Freedom. After his wife's death in 1782, Jefferson again became a delegate to the Congress, and in 1784 he drafted the report that was the basis for the Ordinances of 1784, 1785, and 1787. He was minister to France from 1785 to 1789, when George Washington appointed him secretary of state.

Jefferson's strong faith in the consent of the governed conflicted with the emphasis on executive control, favored by Sec. of the Treasury Alexander Hamilton, and Jefferson resigned as secretary of state on Dec. 31, 1793. In the 1796 election Jefferson was the Democratic-Republican candidate for president; John Adams won the election, and Jefferson became vice president. In 1800, Jefferson and Aaron Burr received equal numbers of Electoral College votes; the House of Representatives elected Jefferson president. Jefferson was a strong advocate of westward expansion; major events of his first term were the Louisiana Purchase (1803) and the Lewis and Clark expedition. His second term saw the passage of the Embargo Act, barring U.S. ships from setting sail to foreign ports and forbidding foreign ships from loading cargo in U.S. ports. Jefferson established the Univ. of Virginia and designed its buildings. He died July 4, 1826, on the same day as John Adams (the 50th anniversary of the Declaration of Independence).

Jefferson called slavery a "moral depravity" and violation of natural rights, but he profited from it as a slaveholder. He advocated gradual emancipation through voting, in conjunction with deportation. Based partly on DNA taken from descendants of Jefferson and of Sally Hemings, an enslaved woman who lived at Monticello from a young age, many historians conclude that Jefferson fathered one or more of her six children.

James Madison (1809-17), fourth president, Democratic-Republican, was born on Mar. 16, 1751, in Port Conway, King George Co., VA, the son of James and Eleanor Rose Conway Madison. Madison graduated from the College of New Jersey in 1771. He served in the Virginia Constitutional Convention (1776), and, in 1780, became a delegate to the Second Continental Congress. He was chief recorder at the Constitutional Convention in 1787 and supported ratification in the *Federalist Papers*, written with Alexander Hamilton and John Jay. In 1789, Madison was elected to the House of Representatives, where he helped frame the Bill of Rights and fought against passage of the Alien and Sedition Acts. In the 1790s, he helped found the Democratic-Republican Party, which ultimately became the Democratic Party. He became Jefferson's secretary of state in 1801.

Madison was elected president in 1808. His first term was marked by tensions with Great Britain, and his conduct of foreign policy was criticized by the Federalists and by his own party. Nevertheless, he was reelected in 1812, the year war was declared on Great Britain. The war that many considered a second American revolution ended with a treaty that did not settle any of the issues. Madison's most important action after the war was demilitarizing the U.S.-Canadian border.

In 1817, Madison retired to his Virginia plantation, Montpelier, which made use of slave labor. He edited his famous papers on the Constitutional Convention and helped found the Univ. of Virginia, of which he became rector in 1826. He died June 28, 1836.

James Monroe (1817-25), fifth president, Democratic-Republican, was born on Apr. 28, 1758, in Westmoreland Co., VA, the son of Spence and Elizabeth Jones Monroe. He entered the College of William and Mary in 1774 but left to serve in the Third Virginia Regiment during the American Revolution. After the war, he studied law with Thomas Jefferson. In 1782 he was elected to the Virginia House of Delegates, and he served (1783-86) as a delegate to the Continental Congress. He opposed ratification of the Constitution because it lacked a bill of rights. Monroe was elected to the U.S. Senate in 1790. In 1794, Pres. Washington appointed Monroe minister to France. He was again minister to France (1803) under Pres. Jefferson as well as minister to Great Britain (1803-07). He served twice as governor of Virginia (1799-1802, 1811).

In 1816 Monroe was elected president; he was reelected in 1820 with all but one Electoral College vote. His administration became known as the Era of Good Feeling. He obtained Florida from Spain, settled boundary disputes with Britain over Canada, and eliminated border forts. Though a slaveholder himself, he supported the anti-slavery position that led to the Missouri Compromise. His most significant contribution was the Monroe Doctrine, which opposed European intervention in the Western Hemisphere and became a cornerstone of U.S. foreign policy.

Although Monroe retired to Oak Hill, VA, financial problems forced him to sell his property and move to New York City. He died there on July 4, 1831.

John Quincy Adams (1825-29), sixth president, independent Federalist, later Democratic-Republican, was born on July 11, 1767, in Braintree (now Quincy), MA, the son of John and Abigail Adams. His father was the second president. He studied abroad and at Harvard College, from which he graduated in 1787. In 1803, he was elected to the U.S. Senate. President Monroe chose him as his secretary of state in 1817. In this capacity he negotiated the cession of Florida from Spain, supported exclusion of slavery in the Missouri Compromise, and helped formulate the Monroe Doctrine.

After no candidate won an Electoral College majority in 1824, the presidential election was decided by the House of Representatives. Adams won with support from rival Henry Clay, whom he named secretary of state, fueling accusations of a "corrupt bargain." His expansion of executive powers was strongly opposed, and in the 1828 election he lost to Andrew Jackson. In 1831 he entered the House of Representatives and served 17 years. He opposed slavery, the annexation of Texas, and the Mexican War. He helped establish the Smithsonian Institution.

Adams suffered a stroke in the House and died in the Speaker's Room on Feb. 23, 1848.

Andrew Jackson (1829-37), seventh president, Democratic-Republican, later a Democrat, was born on Mar. 15, 1767, in the Waxhaw district, on the border of North and South Carolina, the son of Andrew and Elizabeth Hutchinson Jackson. At the age of 13, he joined the militia to fight in the American Revolution and was captured. Orphaned at age 14, Jackson was raised by an uncle. By age 20, he was practicing law, and he later served as prosecuting attorney in Nashville, TN. In 1796 he helped draft the constitution of Tennessee, and for a year he occupied its one seat in the House of Representatives. The next year he served in the U.S. Senate.

In the War of 1812, Jackson crushed the Creek Indians at Horseshoe Bend, AL (1814), and, with a greatly outnumbered army consisting chiefly of militia members, privateers, Choctaw Indians, and other volunteer fighters, defeated Gen. Edward Pakenham's British troops at the Battle of New Orleans (1815). Nicknamed "Old Hickory" for his toughness, he emerged a national hero.

In 1818 Jackson briefly invaded Spanish Florida to quell Seminoles and outlaws who harassed frontier settlements. He ran for president against John Quincy Adams in 1824, but did not achieve a majority despite winning the most popular and electoral votes. The House of Representatives decided the election and chose Adams. In the 1828 election, however, Jackson, a slaveholder, defeated Adams by carrying the West and the South.

As president, Jackson introduced what became known as the spoils system—rewarding party members with government posts. A self-professed champion of the common man, he also viewed the Second Bank of the U.S. as a bastion of privilege and made it a major issue in the election of 1832, the first where candidates were chosen at national conventions rather than in congressional caucuses. Defeating Henry Clay, Jackson increasingly diverted funds from the national bank into so-called pet banks run by members of his own party. When South Carolina refused to collect imports under a federal tariff, which it declared null and void, Jackson won passage of legislation confirming his right to use military force to obtain compliance; eventually the tariff rate was reduced and the nullifiers backed down. After leaving office in 1837, he retired to the Hermitage, his estate outside Nashville, where he died on June 8, 1845.

Martin Van Buren (1837-41), eighth president, Democrat, was born on Dec. 5, 1782, in Kinderhook, NY, the son of Abraham and Maria Hoes Van Buren. After attending local schools, he studied law and became a lawyer at the age of 20. A consummate politician, Van Buren began his career in the New York state senate and then served as state attorney general (1816-19). He was elected to the U.S. Senate in 1821. He helped swing Eastern support to Andrew Jackson in the 1828 election and served as Jackson's secretary of state from 1829 to 1831. In 1832 he was elected vice president. Known as the "Little Magician," Van Buren was extremely influential in Jackson's administration.

In 1836, Van Buren defeated William Henry Harrison for president and took office as the financial panic of 1837 initiated a nationwide depression. Although he instituted the independent treasury system, his refusal to spend land revenues led to his defeat by William Henry Harrison in 1840. In 1844 he lost the Democratic nomination to James K. Polk. In 1848 he again ran for president on the Free Soil ticket but lost. He died in Kinderhook on July 24, 1862.

William Henry Harrison (1841), ninth president, Whig, who served only 31 days, was born on Feb. 9, 1773, in Berkeley, Charles City Co., VA, the son of Benjamin Harrison—a signer of the Declaration of Independence—and of Elizabeth Bassett Harrison. He attended Hampden-Sydney College. Harrison served as secretary of the Northwest Territory in 1798 and was its delegate to the House of Representatives in 1799. He was the first governor of Indiana Territory and served as superintendent of Indian affairs. Leading some 950 troops, he repelled an attack by Shawnee Indians at Tippecanoe, IN, on Nov. 7, 1811. A generation later, in 1840, he waged a rousing presidential campaign using the slogan "Tippecanoe and Tyler Too." The Tyler of the slogan was his running mate, John Tyler.

Although born to one of the wealthiest, most prestigious, and most influential families in Virginia, Harrison also campaigned with the slogan "Log Cabin and Hard Cider." He died Apr. 4, 1841, after only one month in office, of what doctors now believe was typhoid fever.

John Tyler (1841-45), 10th president, independent Whig, was born on Mar. 29, 1790, in Greenway, Charles City Co., VA, the son of John and Mary Armistead Tyler. His father was governor of Virginia (1808-11). Tyler graduated from the College of William and Mary in 1807 and in 1811 was elected to the Virginia legislature. In 1816 he was chosen for the U.S. House of Representatives. He served in the Virginia legislature again from 1823 to 1825, when he was elected governor of Virginia. After a stint in the U.S. Senate (1827-36), he was elected vice president (1840).

When William Henry Harrison died only a month after taking office, Tyler succeeded him. Because he was the first person to occupy the presidency without having been elected to that office, he was referred to as "His Accidency." He gained passage of the Preemption Act of 1841, which gave squatters on government land the right to buy 160 acres at the minimum auction price. His last act as president was to sign a resolution annexing Texas. Tyler accepted renomination in 1844 from some Democrats but withdrew in favor of the official party candidate, James K. Polk. A slaveholder who consistently supported the expansion of slavery, he served briefly in the Confederate House of Representatives before he died in Richmond, VA, on Jan. 18, 1862.

James Knox Polk (1845-49), 11th president, Democrat, was born on Nov. 2, 1795, in Mecklenburg Co., NC, the son of Samuel and Jane Knox Polk. He graduated from the Univ. of North Carolina in 1818 and served in the Tennessee state legislature from 1823 to 1825. He served in the U.S. House of Representatives from 1825 to 1839, the last four years as Speaker. He was governor of Tennessee from 1839 to 1841. In 1844, after the Democratic National Convention became deadlocked, it nominated Polk, who became the first "dark horse" candidate for president. He was nominated primarily because he favored annexation of Texas and tolerated slavery.

As president, Polk reestablished the independent treasury system originated by Van Buren. He was so intent on acquiring California from Mexico that he sent troops to the Mexican border and declared a state of war after Mexicans attacked. The Mexican War ended with the annexation of California and much of the Southwest as part of America's "manifest destiny." Polk compromised on the Oregon boundary ("54-40 or fight!") by accepting the 49th parallel and yielding Vancouver Island to the British. Polk died in Nashville, TN, on June 15, 1849, a few months after leaving office.

Zachary Taylor (1849-50), 12th president, Whig, who served only 16 months, was born on Nov. 24, 1784, in Orange Co., VA, the son of Richard and Sarah Strother Taylor. He grew up on his father's plantation near Louisville, KY, where the work was done by enslaved persons and he was educated by private tutors. In 1808 Taylor joined the regular army and was commissioned first lieutenant. He fought in the War of 1812, the Black Hawk War (1832), and the second Seminole War (beginning in 1837). He was called "Old Rough and Ready" for his military prowess. In 1846 Pres. Polk sent him with an army to the Rio Grande. When the Mexicans attacked him, Polk declared war. Outnumbered four to one, Taylor defeated Antonio López de Santa Anna at Buena Vista (1847).

A national hero, Taylor received the Whig nomination in 1848 and was elected president, even though he had never bothered to vote. He resumed the spoils system and, though a slaveholder, worked to admit California as a free state. He fell ill, likely from a case of acute gastroenteritis, and died in office on July 9, 1850.

Millard Fillmore (1850-53), 13th president, Whig, was born on Jan. 7, 1800, in Cayuga Co., NY, the son of Nathaniel and Phoebe Millard Fillmore. Although he had little schooling, he became a law clerk at the age of 22 and was admitted to the bar a year later. He was elected to the New York state assembly in 1828 and served until 1831. From 1833 until 1835 and again from 1837 to 1843, he represented his district in the U.S. House of Representatives. He opposed the entrance of Texas as a slave state and voted for a protective tariff. In 1844 he was defeated for governor of New York.

In 1848, he was elected vice president; he became president after Taylor's death. Fillmore favored the Compromise of 1850 and signed the Fugitive Slave Law. His policies pleased neither expansionists nor slaveholders, and he was not renominated in 1852. In 1856 he was nominated by the American (Know-Nothing) Party, but despite the support of the Whigs, he was defeated by James Buchanan. He died in Buffalo, NY, on Mar. 8, 1874.

Franklin Pierce (1853-57), 14th president, Democrat, was born on Nov. 23, 1804, in Hillsboro, NH, the son of Benjamin Pierce, Revolutionary War general and governor of New Hampshire, and Anna Kendrick. He graduated from Bowdoin College in 1824 and was admitted to the bar in 1827. He was elected to the New Hampshire state legislature in 1829 and was chosen Speaker in 1831. He went to the U.S. House in 1833 and was elected a U.S. senator in 1837. He enlisted in the Mexican War and became brigadier general under Gen. Winfield Scott.

In 1852 Pierce was nominated as the Democratic presidential candidate on the 49th ballot. He decisively defeated Gen. Scott, his Whig opponent, in the election. Although he was against slavery, Pierce was influenced by proslavery Southerners. He supported the controversial Kansas-Nebraska Act, which left the question of slavery in the new territories of Kansas and Nebraska to popular vote. Pierce signed a reciprocity treaty with Canada and approved the Gadsden Purchase, from Mexico, of a border area on a proposed railroad route. Denied renomination, he spent most of his remaining years in Concord, NH, where he died on Oct. 8, 1869.

James Buchanan (1857-61), 15th president, Federalist, later Democrat, was born on Apr. 23, 1791, near Mercersburg, PA, the son of James and Elizabeth Speer Buchanan. He graduated from Dickinson College in 1809 and was admitted to the bar in 1812. He fought in the War of 1812 as a volunteer. He was twice elected to the Pennsylvania general assembly, and in 1821 he entered the U.S. House of Representatives. After briefly serving (1832-33) as minister to Russia, he was elected U.S. senator from Pennsylvania. As Polk's secretary of state (1845-49), he ended the Oregon dispute with Britain and supported the Mexican War and annexation of Texas. As minister to Great Britain, he signed the Ostend Manifesto (1854), declaring a U.S. right to take Cuba by force should efforts to purchase it fail.

Nominated by Democrats, Buchanan was elected president in 1856. On slavery he favored popular sovereignty and choice by state constitutions but did not consistently uphold this position. He denied the right of states to secede but opposed coercion and attempted to keep peace by not provoking secessionists. Buchanan left office having failed to deal decisively with the situation. He died at Wheatland, his estate, near Lancaster, PA, on June 1, 1868.

Abraham Lincoln (1861-65), 16th president, Whig, then Republican, was born on Feb. 12, 1809, in a log cabin on a farm in Hardin (now Larue) Co., KY, the son of Thomas and Nancy Hanks Lincoln. The Lincolns moved to Spencer Co., IN, near Gentryville, when Lincoln was 7. After Lincoln's mother died, his father married Mrs. Sarah Bush Johnston in 1819. In 1830 the family moved to Macon Co., IL.

Defeated in 1832 in a race for the state legislature, Lincoln was elected on the Whig ticket two years later and served in the lower house from 1834 to 1842. In 1837 Lincoln was admitted to the bar and became partner in a Springfield, IL, law office. In 1846, he was elected to Congress, where he attracted attention during a single term for his opposition to the Mexican War and his position on slavery. In 1856 he campaigned for the newly founded Republican Party, and in 1858 he became its senatorial candidate against Stephen A. Douglas. Although he lost the election, Lincoln gained national recognition from his debates with Douglas.

In 1860, Lincoln was nominated for president by the Republican Party on a platform of restricting slavery. He ran against Douglas, a northern Democrat; John C. Breckinridge, a Southern proslavery Democrat; and John Bell, of the Constitutional Union Party. In response to Lincoln's victory, South Carolina seceded from the Union on Dec. 20, 1860, soon followed by six other Southern states.

The Civil War erupted when South Carolina's Fort Sumter, which Lincoln decided to resupply, was attacked by Confederate forces on Apr. 12, 1861. Lincoln called for recruits from the North, and four more Southern states seceded. Hundreds of thousands of Union and Confederate soldiers were killed or wounded in four years of battle that followed. On Sept. 22, 1862, five days after the Battle of Antietam, Lincoln announced that those who were enslaved in territory then in rebellion would be free Jan. 1, 1863, under his Emancipation Proclamation. His speeches, including his Gettysburg and inaugural addresses, are remembered for their eloquence.

Lincoln was reelected, in 1864, over Gen. George B. McClellan, a Democrat. Confederate Gen. Robert E. Lee surrendered on Apr. 9, 1865. On Apr. 14, Lincoln was shot by actor John Wilkes Booth in Ford's Theatre, in Washington, DC. He died the next day.

Andrew Johnson (1865-69), 17th president, Democrat, was born on Dec. 29, 1808, in Raleigh, NC, the son of Jacob and Mary McDonough Johnson. He was apprenticed to a tailor as a youth but ran away after two years and eventually settled in Greeneville, TN, where he was elected councilman and later mayor. In 1835 he was sent to the state general assembly. In 1843 he was elected to the U.S. House of Representatives, where he served for 10 years. Johnson was also governor of Tennessee from 1853 to 1857, when he was elected to the U.S. Senate.

Although Johnson had himself exploited enslaved labor, he opposed secession and tried to prevent Tennessee from seceding. In Mar. 1862, Lincoln appointed him military governor of occupied Tennessee.

In 1864, in order to balance Lincoln's ticket with a Southern Democrat, the Republicans nominated Johnson for vice president. He was elected vice president with Lincoln and succeeded to the presidency upon Lincoln's death. Soon afterward, in conflict with Congress over the president's power over the South, he proclaimed an amnesty to all Confederates, except certain leaders, if they would ratify the 13th Amendment abolishing slavery. States doing so added anti-Negro provisions that enraged Congress, which restored military control over the South. When Johnson removed Sec. of War Edwin M. Stanton without notifying the Senate, the House impeached him in Feb. 1868 on the charge of violating the Tenure of Office Act. In reality, the House was responding to his opposition to harsh congressional Reconstruction, expressed in repeated vetoes. He was acquitted in the Senate by one-vote margins on each of two counts.

Johnson was denied renomination but remained politically active. He was reelected to the Senate in 1874. Johnson died July 31, 1875, at Carter Station, TN.

Ulysses S. Grant (1869-77), 18th president, Republican, was born on Apr. 27, 1822, in Point Pleasant, OH, the son of Jesse R. and Hannah Simpson Grant. The next year the family moved to Georgetown, OH. Grant was named Hiram Ulysses. Upon entering West Point in 1839, he found his name had been put down as Ulysses S. Grant, with his middle name first and his mother's maiden name as his middle name. He eventually adopted it as his true name but maintained the "S" did not stand for anything. Grant graduated in 1843.

During the Mexican War, Grant served under both Gen. Zachary Taylor and Gen. Winfield Scott. In 1854, he resigned his commission because of loneliness and drinking problems, and in the following years he engaged in generally unsuccessful farming and business ventures. With the start of the Civil War, he was named colonel and then brigadier general of the Illinois Volunteers. He took Forts Henry and Donelson and fought at Shiloh. His brilliant campaign against Vicksburg and his victory at Chattanooga made him so prominent that Lincoln placed him in command of all Union armies. Grant accepted Confederate Gen. Robert E. Lee's surrender at Appomattox Court House on Apr. 9, 1865.

Grant was nominated for president by the Republicans in 1868 and elected over Democrat Horatio Seymour. The 15th Amendment, the amnesty bill, and peaceful settlement of disputes with Great Britain were events of his administration. The Liberal Republicans and Democrats opposed him with Horace Greeley in the 1872 election, but Grant was reelected. His second administration was marked by scandals, including the Crédit Mobilier affair, the Whiskey Ring, in which high-ranked officials conspired to defraud the government of taxes, and the impeachment of his secretary of war. An attempt by the Stalwarts (Old Guard Republicans) to nominate him in 1880 failed. Left penniless by the 1884 collapse of an investment firm in which he was a partner, he wrote his well-regarded memoirs while suffering from cancer to provide income for his family. He died at Mt. McGregor, NY, on July 23, 1885.

Rutherford Birchard Hayes (1877-81), 19th president, Republican, was born on Oct. 4, 1822, in Delaware, OH, the son of Rutherford and Sophia Birchard Hayes. He was reared by his uncle, Sardis Birchard. Hayes graduated from Kenyon College in 1842 and from Harvard Law School in 1845. He practiced law in Lower Sandusky (now Fremont), OH, and was city solicitor of Cincinnati from 1858 to 1861. During the Civil War, he was major of the 23rd Ohio Volunteers. He was wounded several times, and by the end of the war he had risen to the rank of brevet major general. While serving (1865-67) in the U.S. House of Representatives, Hayes supported Reconstruction and Johnson's impeachment. He was twice elected governor of Ohio (1867, 1869). After losing a race for the U.S. House in 1872, he was reelected governor of Ohio in 1875.

In 1876, Hayes was nominated for president. He believed he had lost the election to Democrat Samuel J. Tilden. But a few Southern states submitted two sets of electoral votes, and the result was in dispute. An electoral commission, consisting of 8 Republicans and 7 Democrats, awarded all disputed votes to Hayes, allowing him to become president by one electoral vote. Hayes, keeping a promise to Southerners, withdrew troops from areas still occupied in the South, ending the era of Reconstruction. He proposed civil service reforms, alienating those favoring the spoils system, and advocated repeal of the Tenure of Office Act restricting presidential power to dismiss officials. He supported sound money and specie payments.

Hayes died in Fremont, OH, on Jan. 17, 1893.

James Abram Garfield (1881), 20th president, Republican, was born on Nov. 19, 1831, in Orange, Cuyahoga Co., OH, the son of Abram and Eliza Ballou Garfield. His father died in 1833, and he was reared in poverty by his mother. He worked as a canal bargeman, a farmer, and a carpenter. He attended Western Reserve Eclectic Institute and graduated from Williams College in 1856. He returned to Western Reserve to teach and in 1857, at age 25, he became the school's president. In 1859 he was elected to the Ohio legislature. Anti-slavery and anti-secession, he volunteered for military service in the Civil War, becoming colonel of the 42nd Ohio Infantry and brigadier in 1862. He fought at Shiloh, TN, was chief of staff for Gen. William Starke Rosecrans, and was made major general for gallantry at Chickamauga, GA. He entered Congress as a radical Republican in 1863, calling for execution or exile of Confederate leaders, but he moderated his views after the Civil War. On the electoral commission in 1877 he voted for Hayes against Tilden on strict party lines.

Garfield was a senator-elect in 1880 when he became the Republican nominee for president. He was chosen as a compromise over Gen. Grant, James G. Blaine, and John Sherman, and won election despite some bitterness among Grant's supporters. For much of his brief tenure as president, Garfield was concerned with a fight with New York Sen. Roscoe Conkling, who opposed two major appointments made by Garfield. On July 2, 1881, Garfield was shot and seriously wounded by a mentally disturbed office seeker, Charles J. Guiteau, while entering a railroad station in Washington, DC. He died on Sept. 19, 1881, in Elberon, NJ.

Chester Alan Arthur (1881-85), 21st president, Republican, was born on Oct. 5, 1829, in Fairfield, VT, to William and Malvina Stone Arthur. He graduated from Union College in 1848, taught school in Vermont, then studied law and practiced in New York City. In 1853, he argued that fugitives from enslaved labor transported through New York State were thereby freed. In 1871, he was appointed collector of the Port of New York. Pres. Hayes, an opponent of the spoils system, forced him to resign in 1878. This made the New York machine enemies of Hayes. Arthur and the Stalwarts (Old Guard Republicans) tried to nominate Grant for a third term as president in 1880. When Garfield was nominated, Arthur was nominated for vice president in the interests of harmony.

Upon Garfield's assassination, Arthur became president. Despite his past connections, he signed major civil service reform legislation. Arthur tried to dissuade Congress from enacting the high protective tariff of 1883. He was defeated for renomination in 1884 by James G. Blaine. He died in New York City on Nov. 18, 1886.

(Stephen) Grover Cleveland (1885-89; 1893-97) *(According to a State Dept. ruling, Grover Cleveland should be counted as both the 22nd and the 24th president because his two terms were not consecutive)*, Democrat, was born Stephen Grover Cleveland on Mar. 18, 1837, in Caldwell, NJ, the son of Richard F. and Ann Neal Cleveland. When he was a small boy, his family moved to New York. Prevented by his father's death from attending college, he studied on his own and was admitted to the bar in Buffalo, NY, in 1859. In succession he became assistant district attorney (1863), sheriff (1871), mayor (1881), and governor of New York (1882). He was an independent, honest administrator who hated corruption. Cleveland was nominated for president over opposition from New York City's Democratic party machine Tammany Hall in 1884 and defeated Republican James G. Blaine.

As president, he enlarged the civil service and vetoed many pension raids on the Treasury. In the 1888 election he was defeated by Benjamin Harrison, although his popular vote was larger. Reelected over Harrison in 1892, he faced a money crisis brought about by a lowered gold reserve, circulation of paper, and exorbitant silver purchases under the Sherman Silver Purchase Act. He obtained a repeal of the Sherman Act but was unable to secure effective tariff reform. A severe economic depression and labor troubles racked his administration, but he refused to interfere in business matters and rejected business owner Jacob Coxey's demand for unemployment relief. In 1894, he broke the Pullman railroad workers' strike. Cleveland was not renominated in 1896. He died in Princeton, NJ, on June 24, 1908.

Benjamin Harrison (1889-93), 23rd president, Republican, was born on Aug. 20, 1833, in North Bend, OH, the son of John Scott and Elizabeth Irwin Harrison. His great-grandfather, Benjamin Harrison, was a signer of the Declaration of Independence; his grandfather, William Henry Harrison, was the ninth president; his father was a member of Congress. He attended school on his father's farm and graduated from Miami Univ. in Oxford, OH, in 1852. He was admitted to the bar in 1854 and practiced in Indianapolis, IN. During the Civil War, he rose to the rank of brevet brigadier general and fought at Kennesaw Mountain, Peachtree Creek, Nashville, and in the Atlanta campaign. He lost the 1876 gubernatorial election in Indiana but succeeded in becoming a U.S. senator in 1881.

In 1888 he defeated Cleveland for president despite receiving fewer popular votes. As president, he expanded the pension list and signed the McKinley high tariff bill, the Sherman Antitrust Act, and the Sherman Silver Purchase Act. During his administration, six states were admitted to the Union. He was defeated for reelection in 1892. He died in Indianapolis, IN, on Mar. 13, 1901.

William McKinley (1897-1901), 25th president, Republican, was born on Jan. 29, 1843, in Niles, OH, the son of William and Nancy Allison McKinley. McKinley briefly attended Allegheny College in Pennsylvania. When the Civil War broke out in 1861, he enlisted and served for the duration. He rose to captain and in 1865 was made brevet major. After studying law in Albany, NY, he opened a law office in Canton, OH (1867). He served twice in the U.S. House (1877-83; 1885-91) and led the fight there for the McKinley Tariff, passed in 1890; he was not reelected to the House as a result. He served two terms (1892-96) as governor of Ohio.

In 1896 he was elected president as a proponent of a protective tariff and sound money (gold standard) over William Jennings Bryan, the Democrat and a proponent of free silver. McKinley was reluctant to intervene in Cuba, but the loss of the battleship *Maine* at Havana, blamed on Spain, crystallized opinion. He demanded Spain's withdrawal from Cuba; Spain made some concessions, but Congress announced a state of war as of Apr. 21, 1898. He was reelected in the 1900 campaign, defeating Bryan's anti-imperialist arguments with the promise of a "full dinner pail." He was known for a conservative stance on business issues. On Sept. 6, 1901, at the Pan-American Exposition, in Buffalo, NY, he was shot by Leon Czolgosz, an anarchist. He died Sept. 14.

Theodore Roosevelt (1901-09), 26th president, Republican, was born on Oct. 27, 1858, in New York City, the son of Theodore and Martha Bulloch Roosevelt. He was a fifth cousin of Franklin D. Roosevelt and an uncle of Eleanor Roosevelt. Roosevelt graduated from Harvard Univ. in 1880. He attended Columbia Law School briefly but abandoned law to enter politics. He was elected to the New York State Assembly in 1881 and served until 1884. He spent the next two years ranching and hunting in the Dakota Territory. In 1886, he ran unsuccessfully for mayor of New York City. He was civil service commissioner in Washington, DC, from 1889 to 1895. From 1895 to 1897, he served as New York City's police commissioner. He was assistant secretary of the Navy under McKinley. The Spanish-American War made him nationally known. He organized the First U.S. Volunteer Cavalry (Rough Riders) and, as lieutenant colonel, led the charge up Kettle Hill in San Juan, Cuba. Elected New York governor in 1898, he fought the spoils system and achieved taxation of corporation franchises.

Nominated for vice president in 1900, Roosevelt became the nation's youngest president at the age of 42 when McKinley was assassinated. He was reelected in 1904. As president he fought corruption of politics by big business, dissolved the Northern Securities Co. and others for violating antitrust laws, intervened in the 1902 coal strike on behalf of the public, obtained the Elkins Law (1903) forbidding rebates to favored corporations, and helped pass the Hepburn Railway Rate Act of 1906 (extending jurisdiction of the Interstate Commerce Commission). He helped obtain passage of the Pure Food and Drug Act (1906) and of employers' liability laws. Roosevelt vigorously organized conservation efforts. He mediated the peace between Japan and Russia in 1905, for which he won the Nobel Peace Prize. He abetted the 1903 revolution in Panama that led to U.S. acquisition of territory for the Panama Canal.

In 1908 Roosevelt obtained the nomination of William H. Taft, who was elected. Feeling that Taft had abandoned his policies, he unsuccessfully sought the nomination in 1912. He then ran on the Progressive "Bull Moose" ticket against Taft and Woodrow Wilson, splitting the Republicans and ensuring Wilson's election. During the campaign he was shot by a mentally deranged man but was not seriously wounded. In 1916, after unsuccessfully seeking the presidential nomination, he supported the Republican candidate, Charles E. Hughes. He strongly promoted U.S. intervention in World War I.

Roosevelt was a voracious reader and wrote some 40 books, including *The Winning of the West*. He died Jan. 6, 1919, at Sagamore Hill, his home in Oyster Bay, NY.

William Howard Taft (1909-13), 27th president, Republican, and 10th chief justice of the U.S., was born on Sept. 15, 1857, in Cincinnati, OH, the son of Alphonso and Louisa Maria Torrey Taft. His father was secretary of war and attorney general in Grant's cabinet and minister to Austria and Russia under Arthur. Taft graduated from Yale in 1878 and from Cincinnati Law School in 1880. After working as a law reporter for Cincinnati newspapers, he served as assistant prosecuting attorney (1881-82), assistant county solicitor (1885), superior court judge (1887), U.S. solicitor-general (1890), and federal circuit judge (1892). In 1900 he became head of the U.S. Philippines Commission and was the first civil governor of the Philippines (1901-04). In 1904 he served as secretary of war, and in 1906 he was sent to Cuba to help avert a threatened revolution.

Taft was groomed for the presidency by Theodore Roosevelt and elected over William Jennings Bryan in 1908. Taft vigorously continued Roosevelt's trust-busting, instituted the Dept. of Labor, and drafted amendments calling for direct election of senators and an income tax. However, his tariff and conservation policies angered progressives. Although renominated in 1912, he was opposed by Roosevelt, who ran on the Progressive Party ticket; the result was Wilson's election.

Taft, with reservations, supported the League of Nations. He became a professor of constitutional law at Yale (1913-21) and was appointed by Pres. Harding to serve as chief justice of the U.S. (1921-30). Taft was the only person to have been both president and chief justice. He died in Washington, DC, on Mar. 8, 1930.

(Thomas) Woodrow Wilson (1913-21), 28th president, Democrat, was born on Dec. 28, 1856, in Staunton, VA, the son of Joseph Ruggles and Janet (Jessie) Woodrow Wilson. He grew up in Georgia and South Carolina. He attended Davidson College in North Carolina before graduating from Princeton Univ. in 1879. He studied law at the Univ. of Virginia and political science at Johns Hopkins Univ., where he received his PhD in 1886. He taught at Bryn Mawr (1885-88) and at Wesleyan (1888-90) before joining the faculty at Princeton. He was president of Princeton from 1902 until 1910, when he was elected governor of New Jersey. In 1912 he was nominated for president with the aid of William Jennings Bryan, who sought to block James "Champ" Clark and New York City's Democratic party machine Tammany Hall. Wilson won because Theodore Roosevelt, running as a "Bull Moose" Progressive, siphoned votes away from Republican candidate Taft.

As president, Wilson protected American interests in revolutionary Mexico and fought for American rights on the high seas. He oversaw the creation of the Federal Reserve system, cut the tariff, and developed a reputation as a reformer. His sharp warnings to Germany led to the resignation of his secretary of state, Bryan, a pacifist. In 1916 he was reelected by a slim margin with the slogan "He kept us out of war," although his attempts to mediate in the war failed. After several American ships were sunk by the Germans, he secured a declaration of war against Germany on Apr. 6, 1917.

Wilson outlined his peace program on Jan. 8, 1918, in the Fourteen Points, a state paper that enunciated a doctrine of self-determination for the settlement of territorial disputes. The Germans accepted his terms and an armistice on Nov. 11, 1918. Wilson went to Paris to help negotiate the peace treaty, the crux of which he considered the League of Nations. The Senate demanded reservations that would not make the U.S. subordinate to the votes of other nations in case of war. Wilson refused and toured the country to get support. After he suffered a severe stroke in Oct. 1919, his wife, Edith Wilson, concealed the extent of his infirmity, controlled access to him, and in effect largely acted in his place.

Wilson was awarded the 1919 Nobel Peace Prize, but the treaty embodying the League of Nations was ultimately rejected by the Senate in 1920. He left the White House in Mar. 1921. He died in Washington, DC, on Feb. 3, 1924.

Warren Gamaliel Harding (1921-23), 29th president, Republican, was born on Nov. 2, 1865, near Corsica (now Blooming Grove), OH, the son of George Tyron and Phoebe Elizabeth Dickerson Harding. He attended Ohio Central College, studied law, and became editor and publisher of a county newspaper. He entered the political arena as state senator (1901-04) and then served as lieutenant governor (1904-06). In 1910 he ran unsuccessfully for governor of Ohio; in 1914 he was elected to the U.S. Senate. In the Senate he voted for anti-strike legislation, women's suffrage, and the Volstead Prohibition Enforcement Act over Pres. Wilson's veto. He opposed the League of Nations.

In 1920 he was nominated for president and defeated James M. Cox in the election. The Republicans capitalized on war weariness and fear that Wilson's League of Nations would curtail U.S. sovereignty. Harding stressed a return to "normalcy" and worked for tariff revision and the repeal of excess profits law and high income taxes. In the so-called Teapot Dome scandal, his secretary of the interior, Albert B. Fall, resigned and was later convicted of accepting bribes in the leasing of government-owned oil reserves to private companies.

As rumors began to circulate about the corruption in his administration, Harding fell ill after a trip to Alaska, and he died suddenly of a likely heart attack in San Francisco on Aug. 2, 1923. Harding's letters to a longtime mistress were made public by the Library of Congress in 2014, and DNA evidence in 2015 confirmed another mistress's claim that he had fathered her daughter.

(John) Calvin Coolidge (1923-29), 30th president, Republican, was born on July 4, 1872, in Plymouth Notch, VT, the son of John Calvin and Victoria J. Moor Coolidge. Coolidge graduated from Amherst College in 1895. He entered Republican state politics and served as mayor of Northampton, MA, as state senator, as lieutenant governor, and, in 1919, as governor. In Sept. 1919, Coolidge attained national prominence by calling out the state guard in the Boston police strike. He declared, "There is no right to strike against the public safety by anybody, anywhere, anytime." This brought his name before the Republican convention of 1920, where he was nominated for vice president.

Coolidge succeeded to the presidency on Harding's death. As president, he opposed the League of Nations and the soldiers' bonus bill, which was passed over his veto. In 1924 he was elected to the presidency by a huge majority. He substantially reduced the national debt. He twice vetoed legislation to aid financially hard-pressed farmers.

With Republicans eager to renominate him, Coolidge simply announced on Aug. 2, 1927, "I do not choose to run for president in 1928." He died in Northampton, MA, on Jan. 5, 1933.

Herbert Clark Hoover (1929-33), 31st president, Republican, was born on Aug. 10, 1874, in West Branch, IA, the son of Jesse Clark and Hulda Randall Minthorn Hoover. Hoover grew up in Indian Territory (now Oklahoma) and Oregon and graduated from Stanford Univ. with a degree in geology in 1895. He worked briefly with the U.S. Geological Survey and then managed mines in Australia, Asia, Europe, and Africa. While chief engineer of imperial mines in China, he directed food relief for victims of the Boxer Rebellion. He gained a reputation not only as an engineer but as a humanitarian as he directed the American Relief Committee, London (1914-15) and the U.S. Commission for Relief in Belgium (1915-19). He was U.S. Food Administrator (1917-19), American Relief Administrator (1918-23), and in charge of Russian Relief (1918-23). He served as secretary of commerce under both Harding and Coolidge.

In 1928 Hoover was elected president over Alfred E. Smith. In 1929 the stock market crashed, and the economy collapsed. During the Great Depression, Hoover inaugurated some government assistance programs, but he was opposed to administration of aid through a federal bureaucracy. As the effects of the Depression continued, he was defeated in the 1932 election by Franklin D. Roosevelt. Hoover remained active after leaving office. Pres. Truman named him coordinator of the European Food Program (1946) and chairman of the Commission on Organization of the Executive Branch (1947-49); he was later appointed by Pres. Eisenhower to serve in the same role (1953-55).

Hoover died in New York City on Oct. 20, 1964.

Franklin Delano Roosevelt (1933-45), 32nd president, Democrat, was born on Jan. 30, 1882, in Hyde Park, NY, the son of James and Sara Delano Roosevelt, and a fifth cousin of former Pres. Theodore Roosevelt. He graduated from Harvard Univ. in 1903. He attended Columbia University Law School without taking a degree and was admitted to the New York State bar in 1907. His political career began when he was elected to the New York State senate in 1910. In 1913 Pres. Wilson appointed him assistant secretary of the navy, a post he held during World War I.

In 1920 Roosevelt ran for vice president with James Cox and was defeated. From 1921 to 1928 he worked in his New York law office and was also vice president of a bank. In Aug. 1921, he was stricken with poliomyelitis, which left his legs paralyzed. As a result of therapy, he was able to stand and walk a few steps with the aid of leg braces.

Roosevelt served two terms as governor of New York (1929-33). In 1932, Democratic convention delegate W. G. McAdoo, pledged to nominee John N. Garner, threw his votes to Roosevelt, who was nominated for president. The Depression and the promise to repeal Prohibition ensured his election. He asked for emergency powers, proclaimed the New Deal, and put into effect a vast number of administrative changes. Foremost was the use of public funds for relief and public works, resulting in deficit financing. He greatly expanded the federal government's regulation of business and by an excess profits tax and progressive income taxes produced a redistribution of earnings on an unprecedented scale. He also promoted legislation establishing the Social Security system. He was the last president inaugurated on Mar. 4 (1933) and the first inaugurated on Jan. 20 (1937).

Roosevelt was the first president to use radio for "fireside chats." When the Supreme Court nullified some New Deal laws, he sought power to "pack" the Court with additional justices, but Congress refused to give him the authority. He was the first president to break the no-third-term tradition (1940) and was elected to a fourth term in 1944 despite failing health.

Roosevelt was openly hostile to fascist governments before World War II and launched a lend-lease program on behalf of the Allies. With British Prime Min. Winston Churchill he wrote a declaration of principles to be followed after Nazi defeat (the Atlantic Charter of Aug. 14, 1941) and urged the Four Freedoms (freedom of speech, of worship, from want, from fear) Jan. 6, 1941. After Japan attacked Pearl Harbor on Dec. 7, 1941, the U.S. entered the war. Roosevelt guided the nation through the war and conferred with allied heads of state but did not live to see the end of the war. He died of a cerebral hemorrhage in Warm Springs, GA, on Apr. 12, 1945.

Harry S. Truman (1945-53), 33rd president, Democrat, was born on May 8, 1884, in Lamar, MO, the son of John Anderson and Martha Ellen Young Truman. Because of a family disagreement over what his middle name should be, he used only the initial S. After graduating from high school (1901) in Independence, MO, he worked in clerical jobs. He ran his family's farm from 1906 to 1917, then fought in France during World War I. Following the war he opened a haberdashery, served as a judge on the Jackson Co. Court (1922-24), and attended Kansas City School of Law (1923-25).

Truman was elected to the U.S. Senate in 1934 and reelected in 1940. Running with Roosevelt, he was elected vice president in 1944 and became president after Roosevelt's death in Apr. 1945. In 1948, in a famous upset, he defeated Republican Gov. Thomas E. Dewey (NY) to win a new term.

Truman authorized the first uses of the atomic bomb (Hiroshima and Nagasaki, Aug. 1945), bringing World War II to a rapid end. Under his leadership the U.S. provided postwar military and economic aid to Greece and Turkey, threatened by Communist takeover (Truman Doctrine), financed economic recovery in Europe (Marshall Plan, 1948), and signed on to the NATO alliance against the Soviet Union in 1949. In 1948-49, he broke a Soviet blockade of West Berlin with a massive airlift. When Communist North Korea invaded South Korea (1950), he won UN approval to send in forces under Gen. Douglas MacArthur. When MacArthur opposed his policy of limited objectives, Truman removed him.

He died in Kansas City, MO, on Dec. 26, 1972.

Dwight David Eisenhower (1953-61), 34th president, Republican, was born on Oct. 14, 1890, in Denison, TX, the son of David Jacob and Ida Elizabeth Stover Eisenhower, as David Dwight Eisenhower. He grew up on a small farm in Abilene, KS, and graduated from West Point in 1915. He was on the staff of Gen. Douglas MacArthur in the Philippines from 1935 to 1939. In 1942, he was made commander of Allied forces landing in North Africa; the next year he became supreme Allied commander in Europe and led the Normandy invasion (June 6, 1944).

On May 7, 1945, Eisenhower received the surrender of Germany at Rheims, France. He returned to the U.S. to serve as chief of staff (1945-48). His memoir, *Crusade in Europe* (1948), was a best-seller. In 1948 he became president of Columbia Univ.; in 1950 he became commander of NATO forces.

Eisenhower won the Republican nomination for president in 1952 and defeated Illinois Gov. Adlai E. Stevenson (D) in the 1952 and 1956 elections. As president he opposed wage and price controls, kept government out of labor disputes, reorganized the defense establishment, and promoted missile development. He helped negotiate a cease-fire truce in the Korean War, endorsed Taiwan and SE Asia defense treaties, advocated the "open skies" policy of mutual inspection with the USSR, and backed the UN in condemning the Anglo-French raid on Egypt, even as the CIA advanced regime change in Iran and Guatemala. He sent U.S. troops into Little Rock, AR, in Sept. 1957, to enforce school integration.

Eisenhower died on Mar. 28, 1969, in Washington, DC.

John Fitzgerald Kennedy (1961-63), 35th president, Democrat, was born on May 29, 1917, in Brookline, MA, the son of Rose Fitzgerald Kennedy and Joseph P. Kennedy, a wealthy businessman, investor, and onetime U.S. ambassador to Britain. After graduating from Harvard (1940), Kennedy served in the Navy (1941-45), winning a medal for heroism as commander of a PT (patrol torpedo) boat in the Pacific. He served in the U.S. House, 1947-53, and was elected to the Senate in 1952 and 1958. In 1956, after spinal surgery, he published *Profiles in Courage*, which won a Pulitzer Prize.

In 1960, Kennedy narrowly defeated Vice Pres. Richard Nixon (R) for the presidency. He was the first Catholic and, at 43, the youngest person ever elected to that office. Despite his image of youth and vigor, Kennedy suffered from serious medical problems, including Addison's disease and severe back pain that required him to wear a back brace. The extent of these problems was concealed from the public, as were his frequent sexual liaisons.

In Apr. 1961, the new Kennedy administration was stung by the defeat of a CIA-directed invasion force of anti-Communist Cuban exiles, at Cuba's Bay of Pigs. But he successfully demanded, in Oct. 1962, that the Soviet Union dismantle its missile bases in Cuba. He also defied Soviet attempts to force the Allies out of Berlin. Kennedy established the Peace Corps and spurred on a program to land humans on the Moon, but Congress balked at some of his "New Frontier" initiatives, such as medical coverage for the aged. He eventually introduced major civil rights legislation but did not live to see it passed.

On Nov. 22, 1963, Kennedy was assassinated while riding in a motorcade in Dallas, TX. A commission chaired by Supreme Court Chief Justice Earl Warren concluded in Sept. 1964 that the sole assassin had been Lee Harvey Oswald, an ex-Marine and ardent Marxist. Oswald was captured shortly after the assassination but was shot dead by nightclub owner Jack Ruby while being moved to a county jail.

Lyndon Baines Johnson (1963-69), 36th president, Democrat, was born on Aug. 27, 1908, near Stonewall, TX, the son of Rebekah Baines Johnson and Sam Ealy Johnson, a state legislator. He graduated from Southwest Texas State Teachers College in 1930, with formative experience as a student teacher of underprivileged Mexican-American students in a segregated school, and briefly attended Georgetown Univ. Law School. He served as secretary to a congressman and in 1935 became director of the Texas branch of the New Deal National Youth Administration. In 1937 he won an election to fill a vacancy in Congress; he was subsequently elected to five full terms. During 1941-42 he also served in the Navy.

Johnson won a U.S. Senate seat after a close 1948 primary widely regarded as marred by fraud. After reelection in 1954, he served as a skillful Senate majority leader. Elected vice president in 1960 on the ticket headed by Sen. John Kennedy, he succeeded to the presidency when Kennedy was assassinated. He was elected to a full term in 1964, defeating Sen. Barry Goldwater (R, AZ) in a landslide.

As president Johnson won passage of landmark civil rights, anti-poverty, education (Head Start), and health care (Medicare, Medicaid) legislation—the "Great Society" program. However, in the face of objections to his escalation of the Vietnam war, he declined to seek another term. Johnson died on Jan. 22, 1973, at his ranch in Stonewall, TX.

Richard Milhous Nixon (1969-74), 37th president, Republican, was born on Jan. 9, 1913, in Yorba Linda, CA, the son of Francis Anthony and Hannah Milhous Nixon. He graduated from Whittier College in 1934 and from Duke Univ. Law School in 1937. After practicing law and working in the Office of Price Administration he joined the Navy, serving in the Pacific. Elected to the U.S. House in 1946 and 1948, he played a central role in spearheading the prosecution of suspected Communist spy Alger Hiss. Nixon was elected to the Senate in 1950 and served as vice president under Dwight Eisenhower (1953-61). He first ran for president in 1960, narrowly losing to John F. Kennedy, and ran unsuccessfully for governor of California in 1962. In 1968 he was elected president, defeating Vice Pres. Hubert Humphrey (D).

As president, Nixon appointed four Supreme Court justices, including the chief justice, moving the court to the right. He sought to shift greater responsibility to state and local governments, while also supporting broad federal initiatives such as creation of the Office of Management and Budget and the Environmental Protection Agency. The economy suffered periods of high unemployment and inflation, and he imposed wage and price controls in 1971.

In foreign affairs, Nixon dramatically altered relations with China, which he visited in 1972—the first U.S. president to do so. With adviser Henry Kissinger, he pursued détente with the Soviet Union, signing major arms limitation treaties and increasing trade. While beginning a gradual withdrawal from Vietnam, he ordered an incursion into Cambodia (1970) and the bombing of Hanoi and mining of Haiphong Harbor (1972). Reelected by a large majority in Nov. 1972, he secured a Vietnam cease-fire in Jan. 1973.

Nixon's second term was cut short by scandal, after disclosures relating to a June 1972 burglary of Democratic Party headquarters in the Watergate office complex. The courts and Congress sought tapes of Nixon's office conversations; Nixon claimed executive privilege, but the Supreme Court ruled against him. In July 1974, the House Judiciary Committee recommended adoption of impeachment articles charging obstruction of justice, abuse of power, and contempt of Congress. On Aug. 5, he released transcripts of conversations that linked him to cover-up activities. Nixon resigned on Aug. 9, becoming the first president ever to do so.

In later years, Nixon emerged as an elder statesman. He died Apr. 22, 1994, in New York City.

Gerald Rudolph Ford (1974-77), 38th president, Republican, was born on July 14, 1913, in Omaha, NE, the son of Leslie and Dorothy Gardner King, and was named Leslie Lynch King Jr. His parents divorced in Dec. 1913, and in 1917 his mother married Grand Rapids, MI, businessman Gerald R. Ford, whose name the future president ultimately took. He graduated from Univ. of Michigan in 1935 and Yale Law School in 1941. In 1942, he joined the Navy, serving in the Pacific. He won election in 1948 to the U.S. House, where he served for 25 years, eight of them as Republican leader.

On Oct. 12, 1973, after Vice Pres. Spiro Agnew resigned in a corruption scandal, Pres. Nixon nominated Ford to replace him, in the first use of procedures set out in the 25th Amendment (ratified 1967). When Nixon resigned, in Aug. 1974, Ford succeeded him; he was the only president never elected either to the presidency or to the vice presidency.

Ford was widely credited with helping rebuild morale after the Nixon presidency, though his pardoning of Nixon for any federal crimes in office was controversial. He vetoed 48 bills in his first 21 months in office, mostly in the interest of fighting high inflation; he was less successful in curbing high unemployment. Ford was narrowly defeated in the 1976 election. He died Dec. 26, 2006, at home in Rancho Mirage, CA.

James Earl (Jimmy) Carter (1977-81), 39th president, Democrat, was the first president from the Deep South since before the Civil War. He was born on Oct. 1, 1924, in Plains, GA, the son of James and Lillian Gordy Carter. Carter graduated from the U.S. Naval Academy in 1946 and in 1952 entered the Navy's nuclear submarine program as an aide to Capt. (later Adm.) Hyman Rickover. Carter left the Navy to take over the family peanut farming businesses after his father's death in 1953. He served in the Georgia state senate (1963-67) and as governor of Georgia (1971-75). In 1976, he won the Democratic presidential nomination and defeated Pres. Gerald Ford to win the presidency.

On taking office, Carter pardoned Vietnam draft evaders. He played a major role in negotiations leading to the 1979 peace treaty between Israel and Egypt and reached treaties with Panama ending U.S. control of the Panama Canal, effective in 2000. Carter was widely blamed, however, for the poor state of the economy and viewed by some as weak in handling foreign policy. In Nov. 1979, Iranian student militants attacked the U.S. embassy in Tehran and held 52 members of the embassy staff as hostages; efforts to obtain their release became a major preoccupation of the administration. He responded to the Soviet invasion of Afghanistan (Dec. 1979) by imposing a grain embargo and boycotting the 1980 Moscow Olympics.

Carter was defeated by Ronald Reagan in the 1980 election. The hostages in Iran were finally released on inauguration day, 1981, just after Reagan officially became president. After leaving office, Carter played an active role in diplomatic and humanitarian efforts around the world, especially through the Carter Center, which he founded with his wife, Rosalynn, in 1982. He was awarded the Nobel Peace Prize in 2002. In Feb. 2023 he began home hospice care.

Ronald Wilson Reagan (1981-89), 40th president, Republican, was born on Feb. 6, 1911, in Tampico, IL, the son of John Edward and Nellie Wilson Reagan. After graduating from Eureka College, he worked as a sports announcer in Des Moines, IA. In 1937 he began a career as a Hollywood movie actor. He served in the Army Air Force during World War II, making training films, and after the war became president of the Screen Actors Guild. Reagan served two terms as California governor (1967-75). He won a landslide victory in the 1980 presidential election and was reelected in 1984. He was shot and seriously wounded in an assassination attempt in 1981.

As president Reagan forged a bipartisan coalition in Congress, which led to enactment of large-scale tax cuts, cutbacks in government programs, and a major increase in defense spending. In 1982, the U.S. joined in maintaining a peacekeeping force in Beirut, Lebanon; the next year Reagan sent a task force to invade Grenada after two Marxist coups on the island. Reagan ordered airstrikes on Libyan military installations in 1986, after Libyan agents bombed a nightclub in West Berlin, Germany.

Reagan held four summit meetings with Soviet leader Mikhail Gorbachev and signed a major arms-reduction treaty with the Soviet Union in 1987. He also strongly supported anti-Communist governments and forces around the world. In 1986, it was revealed that the U.S. had secretly sold weapons to Iran in exchange for the release of U.S. hostages held in Lebanon and that some of the proceeds had been illegally diverted to anti-Communist contras in Nicaragua. The scandal led to the resignation of leading White House aides, but no proof was found that Reagan himself was involved. As Reagan left office the nation was experiencing its sixth consecutive year of GDP growth, though also piling up large budget deficits.

In 1994, Reagan revealed that he was suffering from Alzheimer's disease. He died on June 5, 2004, in Los Angeles, CA, from complications of the disease.

George Herbert Walker Bush (1989-93), 41st president, Republican, was born June 12, 1924, in Milton, MA, the son of U.S. Sen. Prescott Bush (R, CT, 1952-63) and Dorothy Walker Bush. He was shot down over the Pacific as a Navy pilot in World War II and was awarded the Distinguished Flying Cross. After graduating from Yale Univ. in 1948, he settled in Texas, where he helped found an oil company.

He lost a 1964 U.S. Senate race but was elected to two U.S. House terms, in 1966 and 1968. After losing a second Senate race, he served as U.S. ambassador to the UN, head of the U.S. Liaison Office in Beijing, and director of the CIA. Following an unsuccessful bid for the 1980 GOP presidential nomination, Bush became Ronald Reagan's running mate, and served two terms as vice president (1981-89).

In 1988, Bush defeated Gov. Michael Dukakis (D, MA) to win the presidency. He faced severe budget deficits, struggled with military cutbacks, and vetoed abortion-rights legislation. In 1990 he agreed to a deficit-reduction plan that included tax hikes, despite a campaign promise to the contrary. He successfully appointed two justices to the U.S. Supreme Court, David Souter and Clarence Thomas; the latter was confirmed after 1991 hearings in which he was accused of sexual harassment.

Abroad, Bush supported Soviet reforms, Eastern Europe democratization, and good relations with Beijing. In Dec. 1989, he sent troops to Panama, where they overthrew the government and captured dictator Manuel Noriega. Reacting to Iraq's Aug. 1990 invasion of Kuwait, Bush assembled a broad U.S.-led, UN-backed Allied force which retook Kuwait (Feb. 1991) after a month-long air war and four-day ground assault. But the coalition did not seek to drive Iraqi leader Saddam Hussein from power. The quick victory, with extremely light U.S. casualties, gave Bush then-record-high approval ratings, but his popularity plummeted as the economy slipped into recession. He was defeated by Bill Clinton in the 1992 election.

Bush saw his son George W. Bush inaugurated as the 43rd president in 2001. He died Nov. 30, 2018, at home in Houston, TX.

William Jefferson (Bill) Clinton (1993-2001), 42nd president, Democrat, was born Aug. 19, 1946, in Hope, AR, son of William Blythe and Virginia Cassidy Blythe, and was named William Jefferson Blythe IV. Blythe died in an auto accident before his son was born; his widow married Roger Clinton, whose last name Bill Clinton took. Clinton earned his undergraduate degree from Georgetown Univ. in 1968. While attending Oxford Univ. as a Rhodes scholar, he legally avoided the draft, according to some critics by misleading his draft board. Clinton worked on George McGovern's 1972 presidential campaign and earned a degree from Yale Law School in 1973. He taught at the Univ. of Arkansas law school until 1976, when he was elected state attorney general. In 1978 he was elected governor, becoming the nation's youngest at the time. Though defeated for reelection in 1980, he was returned to office several times thereafter. He married law school classmate Hillary Rodham in 1975; their daughter Chelsea was born in 1980.

Positioning himself as a centrist "New Democrat" in a crowded field, Clinton won the party's 1992 presidential nomination and was elected president, defeating Pres. George H. W. Bush and independent Ross Perot. In 1993, he won passage of a deficit reduction measure and congressional approval of the North American Free Trade Agreement. In 1994 he won passage of a stringent anti-crime bill, which became controversial over time. A plan for major health care reform legislation died in Congress. The administration did not intervene in 1994 as a massive genocide was committed in Rwanda. In 1995 Clinton sent troops to Bosnia to help implement a peace settlement there.

Buoyed by a strong economy, Clinton easily won reelection in 1996. He achieved federal budget surpluses in several years. Clinton was cleared of involvement in improprieties by associates in the Whitewater land-development venture, but investigation into the matter turned up evidence of a sexual relationship between Clinton and a White House intern. In 1998, he was impeached by the House, charged with perjury and obstruction of justice in an attempted cover-up of the affair. He was acquitted in a Senate trial, but in a separate proceeding agreed to certain penalties. In 1999 the U.S. joined other NATO nations in an aerial bombing campaign that induced Serbia to withdraw troops from Kosovo, where they had been terrorizing ethnic Albanians.

After leaving office, Clinton actively supported his wife's political career. He also founded what became the Bill, Hillary and Chelsea Clinton Foundation.

George Walker Bush (2001-09), 43rd president, Republican, was born on July 6, 1946, in New Haven, CT. He was the oldest of six children born to the 41st president, George Herbert Walker Bush, and the former Barbara Pierce. He became the first son of a former president to take office as president since John Quincy Adams in 1825.

Bush grew up in Midland and Houston, TX. He attended Phillips Academy in Andover, MA, and graduated from Yale Univ. in 1968. After serving with the Texas Air National Guard and earning an MBA from Harvard, he returned to Midland, where he went into the oil business. In 1977 he married Laura Welch, a librarian; they had twin daughters, Barbara and Jenna, in 1981. After aiding his father's winning 1988 presidential campaign, he became managing partner of the Texas Rangers baseball team. He was elected governor of Texas in 1994 and reelected in 1998. In 2000, Bush and running mate Dick Cheney defeated the Democratic ticket led by Vice Pres. Al Gore, in one of the closest-ever U.S. presidential elections. The result was not settled until a mid-Dec. Supreme Court ruling left Florida's crucial electoral votes in Bush's column.

Pres. Bush called his governing philosophy "compassionate conservatism." During his first term he won passage of two major tax cuts, the No Child Left Behind education bill, and a Medicare reform bill addressing prescription drug coverage, and he pioneered a major U.S. initiative to fight the AIDS epidemic, especially targeting Africa.

But Bush's first term was dominated by the Sept. 11, 2001, terrorist attack on the U.S. and the nation's response. In Oct. 2001, he signed the controversial USA Patriot Act, greatly expanding surveillance powers of the federal government, and created what became the U.S. Dept. of Homeland Security. Abroad, the U.S. military, aided by allies, deposed Afghanistan's Taliban regime, which was sheltering al-Qaeda terrorists. A new government that restored liberties but was condemned for corruption sought to hold off Taliban insurgents, with U.S. aid. Meanwhile, an operation to capture al-Qaeda leader Osama bin Laden, architect of the Sept. 11 attack, failed when he escaped to Pakistan. In 2003 the U.S., aided mainly by UK forces, launched an air and ground war against Iraq and deposed its autocratic leader, Saddam Hussein. However, no evidence was found that Hussein's regime had developed weapons of mass destruction, the key rationale for the war. A new Iraqi government was formed in June 2004, but insurgent violence and U.S. troop casualties continued.

Reelected in 2004, Bush pressed unsuccessfully for Social Security and immigration reforms, and his administration drew criticism for its response to Hurricane Katrina in 2005. He won Senate confirmation for John Roberts (2005) as Supreme Court chief justice and Samuel Alito (2006) as associate justice. After Democrats won majorities in 2006 midterm elections, Bush accepted the resignation of Defense Sec. Donald Rumsfeld, a target of widespread criticism over the Iraq war. Two months later, Bush announced a "surge" in U.S. troop strength in Iraq; a sharp drop in casualties ensued, aided by a shift in alliances. In 2008, the administration reached an agreement with Iraq allowing U.S. troops to remain there through 2011. But the Taliban was gaining strength in Afghanistan, and the Bush administration was damaged by revelations of prisoner abuse and extreme interrogation methods.

The U.S. economy fell into recession in Dec. 2007; Bush and congressional leaders responded with a $168-bil stimulus plan. Problems in home finance and credit markets triggered a deep economic crisis by Sept. 2008. The Treasury Dept. bailed out mortgage finance firms Fannie Mae and Freddie Mac, investment bank Lehman Bros. filed for bankruptcy, and the Federal Reserve rescued insurance giant AIG with a line of credit reaching $144 bil. An administration-backed plan to buy up to $700 bil in devalued mortgage-related assets cleared Congress in Oct., after a severe stock market plunge bolstered support.

In retirement Bush published a memoir, a biography of his father, and two books featuring his own paintings of U.S. war veterans and immigrants. He did not vote for GOP nominee Donald Trump in 2016 or 2020.

Barack Hussein Obama (2009-17), 44th president, Democrat, was born Aug. 4, 1961, in Honolulu, HI, son of Barack Obama Sr., a Black Kenyan, and Stanley Ann Dunham, a white American. They divorced, and after his mother remarried, he lived in Indonesia with his mother and stepfather; he also lived for a time with his maternal grandparents in Hawaii, where he attended high school. Obama graduated from Columbia Univ. (1983) and, after working as a community organizer in Chicago, earned a law degree from Harvard Univ. (1991). He practiced civil rights law in Chicago and taught at the Univ. of Chicago Law School. In 1992, he married attorney Michelle Robinson; they have two daughters, Malia (b. 1998) and Sasha (b. 2001).

Obama served eight years (1997-2004) in the Illinois state senate. He wrote a 1995 memoir, *Dreams From My Father*, and gave the keynote address at the 2004 Democratic National

Convention. Elected to the U.S. Senate that year, he won the Democratic nomination for president in 2008, stressing opposition to the Iraq war and a message of "hope and change," and was elected the nation's first Black president.

Awarded the 2009 Nobel Peace Prize, Pres. Obama gradually pulled U.S. troops from Iraq, though U.S. forces were reintroduced in noncombat roles as sectarian strife heightened. With Taliban gaining ground in Afghanistan, he authorized a surge in U.S. forces there, aimed at creating conditions for a handover to the Afghan government; he also stepped up drone strikes against Islamist militants abroad. In May 2011, al-Qaeda leader Osama bin Laden was killed in a U.S. raid on his hideout in Pakistan. Soon after, Obama began reducing U.S. forces in Afghanistan. The U.S. joined in NATO airstrikes leading to the overthrow of Libyan dictator Muammar al-Qaddafi, but rival militias refused to disarm and U.S. personnel were killed in a 2012 attack by Islamist radicals on a U.S. consulate in Benghazi.

The administration won passage of a $787-bil economic stimulus package early in 2009, and the U.S. pulled out of recession, though growth was modest. In Mar. 2010, Obama won passage of his signature health care reform bill ("Obamacare"). Democrats lost their House majority in Nov. 2010 elections, limiting Obama's legislative agenda. In 2012, he signed an executive order suspending deportations for most young undocumented immigrants ("dreamers") who came to the U.S. as children. Among other initiatives, his administration finalized regulations tightening fuel emission standards for motor vehicles. After Obama was reelected in Nov. 2012, a compromise in Congress averted a year-end "fiscal cliff" by making expiring G.W. Bush-era tax cuts permanent for most people. Battles over the federal budget, debt ceiling, and Obamacare funding continued.

Abroad, Russian forces annexed Crimea in 2014 and lent support to pro-Russian separatists in eastern Ukraine; Obama joined Europe in imposing economic sanctions. He called for an end to the repressive regime of Syria's Bashar al-Assad, but when Assad's forces apparently launched a chemical weapons attack on civilians, crossing what Obama had called a "red line," he agreed to a Russian-brokered disarmament pact with the regime. After the Sunni militant group Islamic State in Iraq and Syria (ISIS) took over large areas of both countries, proclaiming an Islamic "caliphate" in June 2014 and terrorizing dissenters and religious minorities, Obama sent military advisers. He also authorized U.S. airstrikes against ISIS and eventually provided arms to Syrian rebels.

After 2014 midterm elections, which left Republicans controlling both houses of Congress, Obama issued an executive order expanding protection of undocumented immigrants from deportation, but it was blocked in court. His administration introduced a plan to reduce carbon pollution from power plants and he signed onto the Paris Agreement aimed at global reductions in greenhouse gas emissions. The administration also restored relations with Cuba and entered a multination accord with Iran intended to curb Iranian nuclear weapons development for a time, in return for ending economic sanctions. In Dec. 2014, Obama declared an end to U.S. combat in Afghanistan, limiting U.S. forces to a support role, but he dropped plans for a full withdrawal.

Responding to a 2012 mass shooting at Sandy Hook Elementary School in Newtown, CT, Obama called unsuccessfully for federal gun control legislation. He also confronted racial violence (as in the 2015 massacre at a Black church in Charleston, SC) and racial tensions over the deaths of Black people in encounters with police (as in Ferguson, MO, 2014). After the death of Supreme Court Justice Antonin Scalia in early 2016, Senate Republicans refused to hold a confirmation hearing for Obama's nominee to replace him, contending it was too near the presidential election.

The first volume of Obama's two-part memoir was published in 2020. The Chicago-based Obama Foundation, founded in 2014, was overseeing creation of the Obama Presidential Center in Chicago.

Donald John Trump (2017-21), 45th president, Republican, was born June 14, 1946, in Queens, NY, the son of Frederick C. Trump, a wealthy real estate developer, and Mary Anne MacLeod Trump, a Scottish immigrant. From age 13 he attended a military boarding school. After earning a bachelor's degree from the Wharton School (1968), he joined the family real estate business. Trump spearheaded an expansion of New York City holdings and developed casinos in Atlantic City, NJ, though those eventually failed. He coauthored business-advice books, hosted two reality TV series (2008-15), and licensed his name to enterprises around the world. Trump's net worth in mid-2023 was estimated by *Forbes* at $2.5 bil, down from $3.2 bil in fall 2022, due mainly to his weak social media business.

After two marriages that ended in divorce, Trump married Melania Knauss in 2005. Their son, Barron, was born in 2006. He also had two sons, Donald Jr. (b. 1977) and Eric (b. 1984), and a daughter, Ivanka (b. 1981), from his first marriage, and a daughter, Tiffany (b. 1993), from his second. As president he surrendered control, but not ownership, of the Trump Organization to his elder sons.

In his 2015-16 campaign for the presidency, Trump portrayed himself as an outsider who would "make America great again." His provocative rhetoric at rallies and in tweets—which he continued in the White House and afterward—energized supporters, and he won nomination over a crowded field. Accusations of sexual misconduct and evidence of his crude remarks about women dogged but did not derail his fall campaign. He defeated former Sec. of State Hillary Clinton (D), though she received more of the popular vote.

Promptly after inauguration, Pres. Trump issued executive orders to ban immigration from seven Muslim-majority nations (upheld by the Supreme Court as later modified) and plan for a wall along the U.S.-Mexican border. His administration instituted a "remain in Mexico" policy for migrants awaiting U.S. asylum (ended under Pres. Biden after legal battle) and sought unsuccessfully to end the Obama-era DACA program, which temporarily protected many undocumented immigrants who had arrived in the U.S. as minors. Reports of inhumane conditions at migrant detention centers, and of children separated from parents, generated much criticism. In 2017, Trump controversially fired FBI director James Comey, who had led a probe into Russian interference in the 2016 presidential election; former FBI director Robert Mueller was appointed as special counsel to oversee the probe. The Mueller report, released Mar. 2019, found there had been Russian interference and possible obstruction of justice by Trump but did not take a position on charging him with a crime.

Abroad, Trump cultivated ties with Russian Pres. Vladimir Putin, met cordially with North Korean leader Kim Jong Un, and intensified U.S. support for Israel. In 2018 he announced U.S. withdrawal from a 2015 multination nuclear deal with Iran; as a counterweight to Iran, the U.S. aided Saudi Arabia in its intervention in the Yemen civil war. In Feb. 2020, the U.S. signed an accord with the Taliban, providing for a phased U.S. withdrawal from Afghanistan, to be completed by May 2021, along with separate intra-Afghan talks, which failed; release of imprisoned Taliban; and a Taliban pledge not to allow threats to security of the U.S. and its allies.

In Dec. 2017 Trump signed a measure lowering income tax rates; in early 2018 he reluctantly signed a federal budget bill, negotiated with Democrats, that set high spending levels and raised the debt ceiling. Support for Trump's impeachment grew after allegations that he had pressured Ukraine to investigate former Vice Pres. Joe Biden and his son, Hunter Biden, by withholding military aid. After congressional hearings at which officials alleged an illicit quid pro quo, the full House, with no Republican support, passed two articles of impeachment, which failed in the Senate.

During Trump's first three years in office the unemployment rate hit historically low levels, but the trend was reversed by the COVID-19 pandemic. Trump created a coronavirus task force and promoted successful efforts to develop vaccines, but he often downplayed the role of preventive measures and was accused of spreading misinformation.

The death in May 2020 of a Black man, George Floyd, caused by a white Minneapolis police officer, gave rise to widespread protests against systemic racism and police brutality. Trump disputed or downplayed protesters' grievances.

The Trump administration halted or reversed many environmental regulations and withdrew from the Paris Agreement on climate change. Trump also appointed many conservative-leaning judges to federal courts, including Neil Gorsuch (2017), Brett Kavanaugh (2018), and Amy Coney Barrett (2020) to the Supreme Court.

Former Vice Pres. Biden defeated Trump in Nov. 2020 by an Electoral College vote of 306-232, but Trump claimed victory, despite the dismissal of his suits challenging state vote counts.

On Jan. 6, 2021, energized by a Trump rally, a mob invaded the Capitol in an unsuccessful attempt to intimidate Vice Pres. Mike Pence and Congress into rejecting the presidential election certification. The House voted Jan. 13, 2021, to impeach Trump for "incitement to insurrection"; the Senate vote to convict a month later was 57-43, falling short of the needed two-thirds majority. A House select committee later charged that Trump had spurred the attack and pressured officials to put forward fake electors.

In 2023, Trump was indicted in four criminal cases; he was the first former president ever indicted. A New York case alleged criminal acts to cover up hush-money payments during the 2016 campaign; he was convicted on all 34 counts in May 2024. A federal indictment in Florida accused Trump of retaining classified documents after leaving office and obstructing government efforts to reclaim them; the judge in the case, a Trump appointee, dismissed it in July 2024, citing the unconstitutionality of the special prosecutor's appointment. Two other indictments arose directly from Trump's actions challenging the 2020 election: a federal case charged him with conspiracy to defraud the U.S. and obstruct an official proceeding, and a Georgia state prosecutor brought a racketeering case against Trump and 18 allies for an array of actions aimed at overturning election results.

All four criminal proceedings were expected to be affected by the July 1, 2024, Supreme Court ruling in *Trump v. U.S.* that the former president was partly immune from prosecution in the federal election interference case because he could not be prosecuted for his official acts—only for private or unofficial conduct—nor could any evidence stemming from his official acts be used to prosecute.

A federal jury in a civil case, Jan. 2024, ordered Trump to pay writer E. Jean Carroll $83.3 million in total damages for repeatedly defaming her on social media after she accused him publicly—in 2019, while he was president—of raping her in a Manhattan department store in the mid-1990s. In a separate case against Trump Org., a New York Supreme Court judge in Feb. 2024 ordered the former president to pay $354.9 mil in penalties related to allegations he and Trump Org. vastly inflated the values of real estate assets for years to secure more favorable loans.

After announcing his candidacy in Nov. 2022, Trump easily defeated a large field of Republican primary candidates, including his former UN ambassador Nikki Haley, to clinch the nomination in Mar. 2024, making him the first former U.S. president to win his party's nomination since Grover Cleveland in 1892. Trump and Pres. Biden met in a televised debate June 27, 2024, before either candidate had officially been nominated; most post-debate analysis called Trump the winner by a wide margin though some called attention to his many untruths.

At a campaign event in Butler, PA, July 13, 2024, a 20-year-old armed with an AR-style rifle on a nearby roof fired shots at Trump, who was wounded along with two other men; another attendee was killed. A sniper shot and killed the shooter, but multiple investigations were launched to investigate the security breach. In the wake of the attack, Pres. Biden condemned political violence and called for unity.

On July 15, 2024, the first day of the Republican National Convention in Milwaukee, Trump announced 39-year-old Sen. JD Vance (R, OH) as his vice presidential pick.

Joseph Robinette Biden Jr. (2021-), 46th president, Democrat, was born Nov. 20, 1942, in Scranton, PA, the oldest of four children in a middle-class Irish Catholic family. His parents were Joseph Robinette Biden Sr., a businessman, and Catherine Eugenia Finnegan. He graduated from the Univ. of Delaware (1965) and earned a law degree from Syracuse Univ. (1968). Biden worked as a public defender in Wilmington, DE, where he also served on the New Castle County Council, before winning a U.S. Senate seat from Delaware in Nov. 1972. In a car crash the next month, his wife, Neilia Hunter Biden (m. 1966), and infant daughter Naomi were killed, and their sons Beau (b. 1969) and Hunter (b. 1970) were seriously injured. In 1977 he married Jill Tracy Jacobs, an English teacher; they had a daughter, Ashley (b. 1981).

Biden won reelection to the Senate six times. He famously commuted regularly from Delaware to DC. As chair of the Judiciary Committee, he presided over contentious Supreme Court nomination hearings that ended in the defeat of Robert Bork's nomination (1987) and in Clarence Thomas's confirmation (1991). He was known for often working with Republicans on legislation. In 1987, Biden ran for the 1988 Democratic presidential nomination but withdrew, damaged by charges of plagiarism in a speech. He dropped out of the 2008 nomination battle after the Iowa caucus, but Barack Obama selected him as his running mate. As vice president, Biden worked closely with Obama, serving as his liaison to Congress. He decided against a 2016 run for president, citing bereavement over the recent death of his son Beau, but in 2020 he won the nomination over a wide field of rivals and defeated incumbent Pres. Trump in Nov.

In office, Biden signed executive orders that reversed Trump administration policies on immigration, the environment (recommitted to the 2016 Paris Agreement on climate change goals), and other issues. He gained passage of a $1.9-tril COVID relief bill, opposed by Republicans as inflationary, and a scaled-back bipartisan $1.2-tril infrastructure bill. In Aug. 2022, he signed a major health, tax, and clean energy bill, passed in a party line vote after long negotiations. The administration expanded COVID vaccine supply and access and stressed other preventative measures, but new variants and controversy contributed to persistence of the pandemic, which killed more than a million Americans by mid-2022, before starting to show declines.

In June 2022, after mass shootings in a Buffalo, NY, grocery store and an Uvalde, TX, elementary school, Pres. Biden signed a bipartisan federal gun control measure—the first in decades—though it fell short of his objectives. He condemned a series of Supreme Court rulings decided by a conservative majority, including the 2022 decision that ruled abortion was not a constitutional right and the 2024 decision in *Trump v. U.S.* that expanded presidential power. Biden's successful nomination of Ketanji Brown Jackson as the first Black female Supreme Court justice did not change the Court's ideological composition.

Abroad, Biden sought to revive a 2015 nuclear deal with Iran. He declared an end to U.S. support for a Saudi-led bombing campaign against Iranian-backed rebels in Yemen but sought to repair ties with Saudi Arabia, despite human rights concerns. Biden kept to a U.S. commitment to total U.S. troop withdrawal from the long war in Afghanistan, adopting Aug. 31, 2021, as a deferred but fixed deadline, despite rapid Taliban advances as the Afghan government collapsed. Amid chaos at the Kabul airport, over 120,000 people were evacuated, but many Afghans who had helped the U.S. were left behind. In Dec. 2021 the U.S. officially ended its combat role in Iraq.

After Russia launched a massive invasion of Ukraine in Feb. 2022, Biden had already vowed not to send troops, but he rallied NATO support for economic sanctions on Russia and sent financial aid and weaponry to assist in Ukraine's defense. U.S.-Russia prisoner swaps in 2022 and 2024—which freed Americans such as WNBA star Brittney Griner, reporter Evan Gershkovich, and former Marine Paul Whelan—required months of multinational negotiations by the Biden administration. U.S.-China relations grew more tense and in Feb. 2023, Biden ordered a Chinese high-altitude spy balloon shot down after it had transited the U.S.

After Hamas's attack on Israel in Oct. 2023, Biden voiced strong support for Israel and its counteroffensive, but relations with Israeli Prime Min. Benjamin Netanyahu suffered as the U.S. abstained from a UN Security Council vote calling for a ceasefire in Mar. 2024.

The administration saw strong job growth through mid-2024 and had to contend with historically high inflation and the high interest rates intended to combat it, along with the threat of recession.

In Apr. 2023 Biden announced he would be a candidate for reelection. He was the clear front runner for the nomination, though vulnerable because of his age and legal controversies related to the activities of his son Hunter Biden, who was convicted in June 2024 on three felony charges. Still, Biden easily clinched renomination in Mar. 2024. Concerns over Biden's age spiked following a special counsel's report in Feb. 2024 that found charges weren't warranted in the yearlong probe into classified documents found in Biden's home but noted "significant limitations" in the 81-year-old Biden's memory during interviews. After former Pres. Trump and Pres. Biden met in a televised debate June 27, 2024, most post-debate analysis focused on Biden's poor performance and subsequent days saw increasing calls from other Democrats and supporters to identify a new candidate. Biden tested positive for COVID-19 July 17. On July 21, 2024, in a letter posted to X and Instagram, he announced he would exit the presidential race and endorsed Vice Pres. Kamala Harris as his successor.

Presidential Rankings, 2021

Source: C-SPAN

As assessed by historians and other professional observers of the presidency, 142 of whom participated in the 2021 survey. Participants rated each president on 10 qualities of presidential leadership; rankings here reflect overall score.

2021 rank	President	2017 rank	2009 rank	2000 rank
1.	Abraham Lincoln	1	1	1
2.	George Washington	2	2	3
3.	Franklin D. Roosevelt	3	3	2
4.	Theodore Roosevelt	4	4	4
5.	Dwight D. Eisenhower	5	8	9
6.	Harry S. Truman	6	5	5
7.	Thomas Jefferson	7	7	7
8.	John F. Kennedy	8	6	8
9.	Ronald Reagan	9	10	11
10.	Barack Obama	12	NA	NA
11.	Lyndon B. Johnson	10	11	10
12.	James Monroe	13	15	14
13.	Woodrow Wilson	11	9	6
14.	William McKinley	16	16	15
15.	John Adams	19	17	16
16.	James Madison	17	20	18
17.	John Quincy Adams	21	19	19
18.	James K. Polk	14	12	12
19.	William J. Clinton	15	14	21
20.	Ulysses S. Grant	22	23	33
21.	George H. W. Bush	20	18	20
22.	Andrew Jackson	18	13	13
23.	William Howard Taft	24	24	24
24.	Calvin Coolidge	26	26	27
25.	Grover Cleveland	23	21	17
26.	Jimmy Carter	27	25	22
27.	James A. Garfield	29	28	29
28.	Gerald R. Ford	25	22	23
29.	George W. Bush	33	36	NA
30.	Chester A. Arthur	35	32	32
31.	Richard M. Nixon	28	27	26
32.	Benjamin Harrison	30	30	31
33.	Rutherford B. Hayes	31	33	25
34.	Martin Van Buren	34	31	30
35.	Zachary Taylor	32	29	28
36.	Herbert Hoover	36	34	34
37.	Warren G. Harding	40	38	38
38.	Millard Fillmore	37	37	35
39.	John Tyler	39	35	36
40.	William Henry Harrison	38	39	37
41.	Donald J. Trump	NA	NA	NA
42.	Franklin Pierce	41	40	39
43.	Andrew Johnson	42	41	40
44.	James Buchanan	43	42	41

NA = Not applicable.

Presidential Facts

Oldest president: Joe Biden, who was 78 when he took office

Longest-living president: Jimmy Carter, who on Mar. 22, 2019, reached the age of 94 years and 172 days old, surpassing George H. W. Bush, who died at the age of 94 years, 171 days

Youngest president: Theodore Roosevelt, who was 42 when sworn in after McKinley's death

Youngest person elected president: John F. Kennedy, who was 43 when elected in 1960

Tallest president: Abraham Lincoln, who was 6 feet, 4 inches

Shortest president: James Madison, who was 5 feet, 4 inches

Heaviest president: William Howard Taft, who was 332 pounds in 1911

First president to live in the White House: John Adams, who moved there in 1800

First president whose parents were immigrants: Andrew Jackson; his parents emigrated from Ireland in 1765

First president born a U.S. citizen: Martin Van Buren, in Kinderhook, NY, 1782

First president born outside the original colonies: Abraham Lincoln, in Kentucky, 1809

First president born west of the Mississippi: Herbert Hoover, in West Branch, IA, 1874

Most common presidential home state: Virginia, with 8 presidents

First president born in a hospital: Jimmy Carter, in Plains, GA, 1924

First president to have a telephone in the White House: Rutherford B. Hayes, in 1879

First president to travel outside U.S. while in office: Theodore Roosevelt visited Panama Canal site, 1906

First president to address the nation on radio: Warren G. Harding, in 1922

First president to appear on TV: Franklin D. Roosevelt, at opening ceremonies for the 1939 World's Fair

First president to give a live, televised news conference: John F. Kennedy, in 1961

First president to hold an internet chat: Bill Clinton, in 1999

Presidents who lost the popular vote while winning election: John Quincy Adams, in 1824 (elected by the House after general election failed to produce a majority); Rutherford B. Hayes, in 1876; Benjamin Harrison, in 1888; George W. Bush, in 2000; Donald J. Trump, in 2016. (Popular vote totals before 1824 are unknown.)

Only presidents chosen by the House of Representatives: Thomas Jefferson (1st term) and John Quincy Adams

Only president never elected either president or vice president: Gerald Ford; named vice president when Spiro Agnew resigned (1973), became president when Nixon resigned (1974)

Only president who never previously held government or military office: Donald J. Trump

Left-handed presidents: James Garfield, Herbert Hoover, Harry Truman, Gerald Ford, Ronald Reagan, George H. W. Bush, Bill Clinton, and Barack Obama

First Catholic president: John F. Kennedy; the most common religious affiliations have been Episcopalian (11) and Presbyterian (9)

Only bachelor presidents: James Buchanan, who never married, and Grover Cleveland, who married Frances Folsom in the White House in 1886

First divorced president: Ronald Reagan; divorced from Jane Wyman in 1948, married Nancy Davis in 1952

Only president convicted on criminal charges: Donald Trump, in 2024

Presidents who died on July 4: John Adams and Thomas Jefferson (both 1826) and James Monroe (1831)

First Lady Jill Biden

Jill Biden was born June 3, 1951, in Hammonton, NJ. She graduated from Univ. of Delaware (1975) and had a career as an educator, while earning advanced degrees that ultimately included a doctorate in educational leadership (2007). After an early marriage ended in divorce she married then-Sen. Joe Biden, a widower, in 1977, becoming stepmother to his two sons, Beau and Hunter. The Bidens' daughter, Ashley, was born in 1981. After Biden took office in 2021, she balanced her career as a professor of writing with her role as first lady, in which she promoted community college education, support for military families, cancer research, and COVID vaccination. In May 2022 she met with Ukrainian refugees and visited Ukraine itself, where she met with Ukraine's first lady.

Spouses and Children of the Presidents

Name (born-died; married)	Birth-place	Sons/ daughters
Martha Dandridge Custis Washington (1731-1802; 1759)	VA	None
Abigail Smith Adams (1744-1818; 1764)	MA	3/2
Martha Wayles Skelton Jefferson (1748-82; 1772)	VA	1/5
Dolley Payne Todd Madison (1768-1849; 1794)	NC	None
Elizabeth Kortright Monroe (1768-1830; 1786)	NY	1/2
Louisa Catherine Johnson Adams (1775-1852; 1797)	Eng.[1]	3/1
Rachel Donelson Robards Jackson (1767-1828; 1791)	VA	1/0[2]
Hannah Hoes Van Buren (1783-1819; 1807)	NY	4/0
Anna Tuthill Symmes Harrison (1775-1864; 1795)	NJ	6/4
Letitia Christian Tyler (1790-1842; 1813)	VA	3/5
Julia Gardiner Tyler (1820-89; 1844)	NY	5/2
Sarah Childress Polk (1803-91; 1824)	TN	None
Margaret (Peggy) Mackall Smith Taylor (1788-1852; 1810)	MD	1/5
Abigail Powers Fillmore (1798-1853; 1826)	NY	1/1
Caroline Carmichael McIntosh Fillmore (1813-81; 1858)	NJ	None
Jane Means Appleton Pierce (1806-63; 1834)	NH	3/0
Mary Todd Lincoln (1818-82; 1842)	KY	4/0
Eliza McCardle Johnson (1810-76; 1827)	TN	3/2
Julia Boggs Dent Grant (1826-1902; 1848)	MO	3/1
Lucy Ware Webb Hayes (1831-89; 1852)	OH	7/1
Lucretia Rudolph Garfield (1832-1918; 1858)	OH	5/2
Ellen Lewis Herndon Arthur (1837-80; 1859)	VA	2/1
Frances Folsom Cleveland (1864-1947; 1886)	NY	2/3
Caroline Lavinia Scott Harrison (1832-92; 1853)	OH	1/1
Mary Scott Lord Dimmick Harrison (1858-1948; 1896)	PA	0/1
Ida Saxton McKinley (1847-1907; 1871)	OH	0/2
Alice Hathaway Lee Roosevelt (1861-84; 1880)	MA	0/1
Edith Kermit Carow Roosevelt (1861-1948; 1886)	CT	4/1
Helen Herron Taft (1861-1943; 1886)	OH	2/1
Ellen Louise Axson Wilson (1860-1914; 1885)	GA	0/3
Edith Bolling Galt Wilson (1872-1961; 1915)	VA	None
Florence Kling De Wolfe Harding (1860-1924; 1891)	OH	None
Grace Anna Goodhue Coolidge (1879-1957; 1905)	VT	2/0
Lou Henry Hoover (1875-1944; 1899)	IA	2/0
Anna Eleanor Roosevelt (1884-1962; 1905)	NY	5/1
Elizabeth Virginia (Bess) Wallace Truman (1885-1982; 1919)	MO	0/1
Mamie Geneva Doud Eisenhower (1896-1979; 1916)	IA	2/0
Jacqueline Lee Bouvier Kennedy (1929-94; 1953)	NY	2/1
Claudia (Lady Bird) Alta Taylor Johnson (1912-2007; 1934)	TX	0/2
Thelma Catherine Patricia Ryan Nixon (1912-93; 1940)	NV	0/2
Elizabeth (Betty) Bloomer Warren Ford (1918-2011; 1948)	IL	3/1
Eleanor Rosalynn Smith Carter (1927-2023; 1946)	GA	3/1
Anne Frances (Nancy) Robbins Davis Reagan (1921-2016; 1952)	NY	1/1[3]
Barbara Pierce Bush (1925-2018; 1945)	NY	4/2
Hillary Diane Rodham Clinton (1947- ; 1975)	IL	0/1
Laura Lane Welch Bush (1946- ; 1977)	TX	0/2
Michelle LaVaughn Robinson Obama (1964- ; 1992)	IL	0/2
Melania Knauss Trump (1970- ; 2005)	Slovenia	1/0[4]
Jill Tracy Jacobs Biden (1951- ; 1977)	NJ	0/1[5]

Note: Pres. Buchanan was unmarried. Children not born to the marriages shown are not listed unless otherwise noted. (1) Born in London, father a MD citizen. (2) Adopted son. (3) Pres. Reagan's first wife, whom he later divorced, was Jane Wyman (m. 1940-48). They had two daughters, one of whom died in infancy, and an adopted son. (4) Pres. Trump had four children from two previous marriages: two sons (Donald Jr., Eric) and one daughter (Ivanka) with Ivana Marie Zelnícková Trump (m. 1977-92) and one daughter (Tiffany) with Marla Maples (m. 1993-99). (5) Pres. Biden also had two sons (Beau and Hunter) and a daughter (Naomi) with his first wife, Neilia Hunter Biden (m. 1966), who died along with Naomi in a car crash in 1972.

Presidential Impeachment in U.S. History

The U.S. Constitution provides for impeachment and removal from office of federal officials on grounds of "Treason, Bribery, or other high Crimes and Misdemeanors" (Article II, Sect. 4). Impeachment is the bringing of charges by the House of Representatives, whose members can adopt impeachment articles on a simple majority vote. It is followed by a Senate trial; a two-thirds majority vote of Senators present is needed for conviction and removal from office.

In 1868, **Andrew Johnson** became the first president impeached by the House, for his removal of Sec. of War Edwin M. Stanton without first notifying the Senate. He was tried but not convicted. In 1974, impeachment articles against Pres. **Richard Nixon**, in connection with the Watergate scandal, were adopted by the House Judiciary Committee. He resigned Aug. 9, and the House accepted the committee report without taking further action. In 1998, Pres. **Bill Clinton** was impeached by the House in connection with his cover-up of a sexual relationship with former White House intern Monica Lewinsky. He was tried in the Senate in 1999 and acquitted. Pres. **Donald Trump** was impeached in 2019 on charges related to allegations that he used his office to pressure the president of Ukraine to investigate a political rival; he was acquitted by the Senate in 2020. Trump was impeached again in Jan. 2021 for "incitement of insurrection" but again was not convicted.

Burial Places of the Presidents

President	Burial place	President	Burial place
Washington	Mt. Vernon, VA	Arthur	Albany, NY
J. Adams	Quincy, MA	Cleveland	Princeton, NJ
Jefferson	Charlottesville, VA	B. Harrison	Indianapolis, IN
Madison	Montpelier Station, VA	McKinley	Canton, OH
Monroe	Richmond, VA	T. Roosevelt	Oyster Bay, NY
J. Q. Adams	Quincy, MA	Taft	Arlington Natl. Cem., VA
Jackson	Nashville, TN	Wilson	Wash. Natl. Cathedral, DC
Van Buren	Kinderhook, NY	Harding	Marion, OH
W. H. Harrison	North Bend, OH	Coolidge	Plymouth Notch, VT
Tyler	Richmond, VA	Hoover	West Branch, IA
Polk	Nashville, TN	F. Roosevelt	Hyde Park, NY
Taylor	Louisville, KY	Truman	Independence, MO
Fillmore	Buffalo, NY	Eisenhower	Abilene, KS
Pierce	Concord, NH	Kennedy	Arlington Natl. Cem., VA
Buchanan	Lancaster, PA	L. B. Johnson	Stonewall, TX
Lincoln	Springfield, IL	Nixon	Yorba Linda, CA
A. Johnson	Greeneville, TN	Ford	Grand Rapids, MI
Grant	New York, NY	Reagan	Simi Valley, CA
Hayes	Fremont, OH	G. H. W. Bush	College Station, TX
Garfield	Cleveland, OH		

Presidential Libraries

Presidential libraries are coordinated by the National Archives and Records Administration (www.archives.gov/presidential-libraries/). Under the Presidential Records Act, material is available through Freedom of Information Act requests starting five years after a president has left office.

NARA's Barack Obama Presidential Library (www.obamalibrary.gov) will be a fully digital library. Ground was broken in Chicago, Sept. 2021, for the Obama Presidential Center (www.obama.org/the-center), a privately operated, non-governmental organization. Records of the Trump administration are housed at National Archives facilities in Washington, DC, and will be available through FOIA requests as of Jan. 2026. Plans to build a privately funded Trump presidential museum and library had not been announced as of mid-2024.

Herbert Hoover Library and Museum
210 Parkside Dr.
West Branch, IA 52358
Phone: (319) 643-5301
Email: hoover.library@nara.gov
Website: hoover.archives.gov

Franklin D. Roosevelt Library and Museum
4079 Albany Post Rd.
Hyde Park, NY 12538-1990
Phone: (800) FDR-VISIT
Email: roosevelt.library@nara.gov
Website: www.fdrlibrary.marist.edu

Harry S. Truman Library and Museum
500 West U.S. Hwy. 24
Independence, MO 64050-2481
Phone: (800) 833-1225
Email: truman.library@nara.gov
Website: www.trumanlibrary.org

Dwight D. Eisenhower Library
200 SE 4th St.
Abilene, KS 67410-2900
Phone: (877) RING-IKE
Email: eisenhower.library@nara.gov
Website: eisenhower.archives.gov

John F. Kennedy Library and Museum
Columbia Pt.
Boston, MA 02125-3312
Phone: (866) JFK-1960
Email: kennedy.library@nara.gov
Website: www.jfklibrary.org

Lyndon Baines Johnson Library and Museum
2313 Red River St.
Austin, TX 78705-5737
Phone: (512) 721-0200
Email: johnson.library@nara.gov
Website: www.lbjlibrary.org

Richard Nixon Library and Museum
18001 Yorba Linda Blvd.
Yorba Linda, CA 92886-3903
Phone: (714) 983-9120
Email: nixon@nara.gov
Website: www.nixonlibrary.gov

Gerald R. Ford Library and Museum
Library: 1000 Beal Ave.
Ann Arbor, MI 48109-2109
Phone: (734) 205-0555
Museum: 303 Pearl St. NW
Grand Rapids, MI 49504-5353
Phone: (616) 254-0400
Email: ford.library@nara.gov
Website: www.fordlibrarymuseum.gov

Jimmy Carter Library and Museum
441 Freedom Pkwy.
Atlanta, GA 30307-1498
Phone: (404) 865-7100
Email: carter.library@nara.gov
Website: www.jimmycarterlibrary.gov

Ronald Reagan Library and Museum
40 Presidential Dr.
Simi Valley, CA 93065-0600
Phone: (800) 410-8354
Email: reagan.library@nara.gov
Website: reaganlibrary.gov

George H. W. Bush Library and Museum
1000 George Bush Dr. West
College Station, TX 77845
Phone: (979) 691-4000
Email: library.bush@nara.gov
Website: www.bush41.org

William J. Clinton Library and Museum
1200 President Clinton Ave.
Little Rock, AR 72201
Phone: (501) 374-4242
Email: clinton.library@nara.gov
Website: www.clintonlibrary.gov

George W. Bush Library and Museum
2943 SMU Blvd.
Dallas, TX 75205
Phone: (214) 346-1650
Email: gwbush.library@nara.gov
Website: www.bushcenter.org

PRESIDENTIAL ELECTIONS

Note: Historical election statistics as of Sept. 2024. For information about the 2024 election, see pp. 6-40.

Popular and Electoral Vote for President, 1789-2020

(D) Democrat; (DR) Democratic Republican; (F) Federalist; (LB) Libertarian; (LR) Liberal Republican; (NR) National Republican; (P) People's/Populist; (PR) Progressive; (R) Republican; (W) Whig; * = See notes below table.

Year	President elected	Popular	Elec.	Major losing candidate(s)	Popular	Elec.
1789	George Washington	Unknown	69	No major opposition	—	—
1792	George Washington	Unknown	132	No major opposition	—	—
1796	John Adams (F)	Unknown	71	Thomas Jefferson (DR)	Unknown	68
1800*	Thomas Jefferson (DR)	Unknown	73	Aaron Burr (DR)	Unknown	73
				John Adams (F)	Unknown	65
1804	Thomas Jefferson (DR)	Unknown	162	Charles Pinckney (F)	Unknown	14
1808	James Madison (DR)	Unknown	122	Charles Pinckney (F)	Unknown	47
1812	James Madison (DR)	Unknown	128	DeWitt Clinton (F)	Unknown	89
1816	James Monroe (DR)	Unknown	183	Rufus King (F)	Unknown	34
1820	James Monroe (DR)	Unknown	231	John Quincy Adams (DR)	Unknown	1
1824*	John Quincy Adams (DR)	113,122	84	Andrew Jackson (DR)	151,271	99
				Henry Clay (DR)	46,587	37
				William H. Crawford (DR)	44,282	41
1828	Andrew Jackson (D)	642,553	178	John Quincy Adams (NR)	500,897	83
1832	Andrew Jackson (D)	701,780	219	Henry Clay (NR)	484,205	49
1836	Martin Van Buren (D)	764,176	170	William H. Harrison (W)	550,816	73
1840	William H. Harrison (W)	1,275,390	234	Martin Van Buren (D)	1,128,854	60
1844	James K. Polk (D)	1,339,494	170	Henry Clay (W)	1,300,004	105
1848	Zachary Taylor (W)	1,361,393	163	Lewis Cass (D)	1,223,460	127
				Martin Van Buren (Free Soil)	291,501	—
1852	Franklin Pierce (D)	1,607,510	254	Winfield Scott (W)	1,386,942	42
1856	James Buchanan (D)	1,836,072	174	John C. Frémont (R)	1,342,345	114
				Millard Fillmore (American/Know-Nothing)	873,053	8
1860	Abraham Lincoln (R)	1,865,908	180	Stephen A. Douglas (D)	848,019	12
				John C. Breckinridge (D)	845,763	72
				John Bell (Constitutional Union)	589,581	39
1864	Abraham Lincoln (R)	2,218,388	212	George McClellan (D)	1,812,807	21
1868	Ulysses S. Grant (R)	3,013,650	214	Horatio Seymour (D)	2,708,744	80
1872*	Ulysses S. Grant (R)	3,598,235	286	Horace Greeley (D-LR)	2,834,671	—
1876*	Rutherford B. Hayes (R)	4,034,311	185	Samuel J. Tilden (D)	4,288,546	184
1880	James A. Garfield (R)	4,446,158	214	Winfield S. Hancock (D)	4,444,260	155
1884	Grover Cleveland (D)	4,874,621	219	James G. Blaine (R)	4,848,936	182
1888	Benjamin Harrison (R)	5,443,892	233	Grover Cleveland (D)	5,534,488	168
1892	Grover Cleveland (D)	5,551,883	277	Benjamin Harrison (R)	5,179,244	145
				James Weaver (P)	1,027,329	22
1896	William McKinley (R)	7,108,480	271	William J. Bryan (D-P)	6,511,495	176
1900	William McKinley (R)	7,218,039	292	William J. Bryan (D)	6,358,345	155
1904	Theodore Roosevelt (R)	7,626,593	336	Alton B. Parker (D)	5,082,898	140
1908	William H. Taft (R)	7,676,258	321	William J. Bryan (D)	6,406,801	162
1912	Woodrow Wilson (D)	6,293,152	435	Theodore Roosevelt (PR)	4,119,207	88
				William H. Taft (R)	3,483,922	8
1916	Woodrow Wilson (D)	9,126,300	277	Charles E. Hughes (R)	8,546,789	254
1920	Warren G. Harding (R)	16,153,115	404	James M. Cox (D)	9,133,092	127
1924	Calvin Coolidge (R)	15,719,921	382	John W. Davis (D)	8,386,704	136
				Robert M. La Follette (PR)	4,822,856	13
1928	Herbert Hoover (R)	21,437,277	444	Alfred E. Smith (D)	15,007,698	87
1932	Franklin D. Roosevelt (D)	22,829,501	472	Herbert Hoover (R)	15,760,684	59
1936	Franklin D. Roosevelt (D)	27,757,333	523	Alfred Landon (R)	16,684,231	8
1940	Franklin D. Roosevelt (D)	27,313,041	449	Wendell Willkie (R)	22,348,480	82
1944	Franklin D. Roosevelt (D)	25,612,610	432	Thomas E. Dewey (R)	22,117,617	99
1948	Harry S. Truman (D)	24,179,345	303	Thomas E. Dewey (R)	21,991,291	189
				Strom Thurmond (States' Rights)	1,169,021	39
				Henry A. Wallace (PR)	1,157,172	—
1952	Dwight D. Eisenhower (R)	33,936,234	442	Adlai E. Stevenson (D)	27,314,992	89
1956*	Dwight D. Eisenhower (R)	35,590,472	457	Adlai E. Stevenson (D)	26,022,752	73
1960*	John F. Kennedy (D)	34,226,731	303	Richard M. Nixon (R)	34,108,157	219
1964	Lyndon B. Johnson (D)	43,129,566	486	Barry M. Goldwater (R)	27,178,188	52
1968	Richard M. Nixon (R)	31,785,480	301	Hubert H. Humphrey (D)	31,275,166	191
				George C. Wallace (Amer. Indep.)	9,906,473	46
1972*	Richard M. Nixon (R)	47,169,911	520	George S. McGovern (D)	29,170,383	17
1976*	Jimmy Carter (D)	40,830,763	297	Gerald R. Ford (R)	39,147,793	240
1980	Ronald Reagan (R)	43,904,153	489	Jimmy Carter (D)	35,483,883	49
				John B. Anderson (independent)	5,719,437	—
1984	Ronald Reagan (R)	54,455,075	525	Walter F. Mondale (D)	37,577,185	13
1988*	George H. W. Bush (R)	48,886,097	426	Michael S. Dukakis (D)	41,809,074	111
1992	Bill Clinton (D)	44,909,889	370	George H. W. Bush (R)	39,104,545	168
				H. Ross Perot (independent)	19,742,267	—
1996	Bill Clinton (D)	47,402,357	379	Bob Dole (R)	39,198,755	159
				H. Ross Perot (Reform)	8,085,402	—
2000*	George W. Bush (R)	50,456,002	271	Al Gore (D)	50,999,897	266
				Ralph Nader (Green)	2,882,955	—
2004*	George W. Bush (R)	62,040,610	286	John Kerry (D)	59,028,444	251
2008	Barack H. Obama (D)	69,498,516	365	John McCain (R)	59,948,283	173
2012	Barack H. Obama (D)	65,915,795	332	Mitt Romney (R)	60,933,504	206
2016*	Donald J. Trump (R)	62,984,828	304	Hillary Clinton (D)	65,853,514	227
2020	Joseph R. Biden (D)	81,283,501	306	Donald J. Trump (R)	74,223,975	232

Note: Not all candidates who received electoral votes are shown. ***1800**—Elected by House of Representatives because of tied electoral vote. **1824**—Elected by House of Representatives because no candidate polled a majority. By 1824, the Democratic Republicans had become a loose coalition of competing political groups. By 1828, Andrew Jackson supporters were known as Democrats and John Q. Adams and Henry Clay supporters as National Republicans. **1872**—Greeley died Nov. 29, 1872. His electoral votes were split among four individuals. **1876**—FL, LA, OR, and SC election returns were disputed. Congress in joint session (Mar. 2, 1877) declared Hayes and Wheeler elected president and vice president. **1956**—Democrats elected 74 electors, but one from AL refused to vote for Stevenson. **1960**—Sen. Harry F. Byrd (D, VA) received 15 electoral votes. **1972**—John Hospers of CA received a vote from an elector of VA. **1976**—Ronald Reagan of CA received a vote from an elector of WA. **1988**—Sen. Lloyd Bentsen (D, TX) received a vote from an elector of WV. **2000**—One Gore elector from Washington, DC, abstained. Nader was listed as "independent" on the ballot in some states; he was not on the ballot in all states. **2004**—One MN elector voted for VP candidate John Edwards for both president and vice president. **2016**—Seven electors from three states (HI, TX, WA) did not vote for the candidate to whom they were pledged (two Trump electors defected, as did five pledged to Clinton).

Voter Turnout in Presidential Elections, 1932-2020

Source: U.S. Census Bureau, U.S. Dept. of Commerce; Office of the Clerk, U.S. House of Representatives

Year	Candidates	Voter participation % of voting-age citizen pop.	Voter participation % of voting-age pop.
1932	F. D. Roosevelt-Hoover	NA	52.6%
1936	F. D. Roosevelt-Landon	NA	56.9
1940	F. D. Roosevelt-Willkie	NA	58.8
1944	F. D. Roosevelt-Dewey	NA	56.1
1948	Truman-Dewey	NA	51.1
1952	Eisenhower-Stevenson	NA	61.6
1956	Eisenhower-Stevenson	NA	59.3
1960	Kennedy-Nixon	NA	62.8
1964	L. B. Johnson-Goldwater	NA	69.3
1968	Nixon-Humphrey	NA	67.8
1972	Nixon-McGovern	NA	63.0
1976	Carter-Ford	NA	59.2
1980	Reagan-Carter	64.0%	59.3%
1984	Reagan-Mondale	64.9	59.9
1988	G. H. W. Bush-Dukakis	62.2	57.4
1992	Clinton-G. H. W. Bush-Perot	67.7	61.3
1996	Clinton-Dole-Perot	58.4	54.2
2000	G. W. Bush-Gore	59.5	54.7
2004	G. W. Bush-Kerry	63.8	58.3
2008	Obama-McCain	63.6	58.2
2012	Obama-Romney	61.8	56.5
2016	Trump-Clinton	61.0	55.7
2020	Biden-Trump	68.4	62.8

NA = Not available. **Note:** Data prior to 1964 is from a legacy source and may not be directly comparable to more recent data. The 1972 presidential election was the first for which eligible voters included 18- to 20-year-olds. The voting-age citizen pop. includes those who are ineligible to vote due to imprisonment or prior felony convictions. The voting-age pop. comprises the former group as well as residents who are ineligible to vote because they are not U.S. citizens.

Presidential Popular Vote, 2020

Source: Federal Election Commission

Candidate (party)	Vote total	Percent of vote
Joseph R. Biden (Democrat)	81,283,501	51.31%
Donald J. Trump (Republican)	74,223,975	46.85
Jo Jorgensen (Libertarian)	1,865,535	1.18
Howie Hawkins (Green)	407,068	0.26
Roque "Rocky" De La Fuente (American Independent)	88,241	0.06
Gloria Estela La Riva (Peace and Freedom/Socialism and Liberation)	85,685	0.05
Kanye West (Independent)	70,950	0.04
Don Blankenship (American Constitution)	60,080	0.04
Brock Pierce (American Shopping/ Freedom and Prosperity)	49,769	0.03
Brian Carroll (American Solidarity)	40,365	0.03
Jade Simmons (Independent)	7,211	<0.01
Alyson Kennedy (Socialist Workers)	6,791	<0.01
Bill Hammons (Unity Party)	6,647	<0.01
Jerome Segal (Bread and Roses)	5,949	<0.01
Dario Hunter (Progressive)	5,405	<0.01
Phil Collins (Prohibition)	4,857	<0.01
James G. "Jesse Ventura" Janos (Green)	3,284	<0.01
President Boddie (C.U.P.)	3,185	<0.01
Mark Charles (Unaffiliated)	3,141	<0.01
Joe McHugh (Unaffiliated)	2,843	<0.01%
Sheila "Samm" Tittle (Constitution)	1,806	<0.01
C. L. Gammon (Independent)	1,475	<0.01
John Richard Myers (Life and Liberty)	1,372	<0.01
Tom Hoefling (Life, Liberty, Constitution)	1,331	<0.01
H. Brooke Paige (Grumpy Old Patriots)	1,179	<0.01
Christopher LaFontaine (Independent)	856	<0.01
Kyle Kenley Kopitke (Independent American)	815	<0.01
Ricki Sue King (Geneology Know Your Family History)	546	<0.01
Princess Khadijah Maryam Jacob-Fambro (Unaffiliated)	505	<0.01
Blake Huber (Approval Voting)	409	<0.01
Joseph Kishore (Socialist Equality)	352	<0.01
Richard Duncan (Independent)	213	<0.01
Jordan "Cancer" Scott (Unaffiliated)	175	<0.01
Gary Swing (Boiling Frog)	141	<0.01
Keith McCormic (Bull Moose)	126	<0.01
Zachary Scalf (Independent)	29	<0.01
Write-in votes	179,740	0.11
None of these candidates (Nevada ballot option)	14,079	0.01
Total	**158,429,631**	

Note: Party designations vary from one state to another; party label listed may not necessarily represent a political party organization. Vote totals for the candidates listed above include any write-in votes.

The Electoral College

The president and the vice president are the only elective federal officials not chosen by direct vote of the people. They are elected by the members of the Electoral College, an institution provided for in the U.S. Constitution. Under the electoral college system, a candidate who fails to win the popular vote still may win a majority of electoral votes. This happened in the elections of 1876, 1888, 2000, and 2016.

Each state chooses as many electors as it has senators and representatives in Congress. With 100 senators and 435 representatives (plus, since 1964, three electors for Washington, DC), there are 538 members of the Electoral College, with a majority of 270 electoral votes needed to elect the president and vice president.

Each political party chooses its electors, by nomination at a state convention or by vote of the party central committee in each state. An elector cannot be a member of Congress or federal office holder. The electors of the party receiving the highest vote count are elected under a winner-take-all system. Two states, Maine and Nebraska, allow for proportional allocation.

The electors meet on the first Monday after the second Wednesday in Dec. Certified votes of the electors in each state are sent to the president of the U.S. Senate. He or she then opens them in a joint session of Congress held in early Jan. The electoral votes of all the states are then officially counted.

If no candidate for president has a majority, the House of Representatives chooses a president from the top three candidates, with all representatives from each state combining to cast one vote for that state. The House decided the outcomes of the 1800 and 1824 presidential elections. If no candidate for vice president has a majority, the Senate chooses from the top two, with the senators voting as individuals. The Senate chose the vice president following the 1836 election.

Major-Party Nominees for President and Vice President, 1856-2020

Asterisk (*) denotes winning ticket.

Democratic			Republican		
Year	President	Vice President	Year	President	Vice President
1856	James Buchanan*	John Breckinridge	1856	John Frémont	William Dayton
1860	Stephen A. Douglas[1]	Herschel V. Johnson	1860	Abraham Lincoln*	Hannibal Hamlin
1864	George McClellan	G. H. Pendleton	1864	Abraham Lincoln*	Andrew Johnson
1868	Horatio Seymour	Francis Blair	1868	Ulysses S. Grant*	Schuyler Colfax
1872	Horace Greeley	B. Gratz Brown	1872	Ulysses S. Grant*	Henry Wilson
1876	Samuel J. Tilden	Thomas Hendricks	1876	Rutherford B. Hayes*	William Wheeler
1880	Winfield Hancock	William English	1880	James A. Garfield*	Chester A. Arthur
1884	Grover Cleveland*	Thomas Hendricks	1884	James G. Blaine	John Logan
1888	Grover Cleveland	A. G. Thurman	1888	Benjamin Harrison*	Levi Morton
1892	Grover Cleveland*	Adlai Stevenson	1892	Benjamin Harrison	Whitelaw Reid
1896	William J. Bryan	Arthur Sewall	1896	William McKinley*	Garret Hobart
1900	William J. Bryan	Adlai Stevenson	1900	William McKinley*	Theodore Roosevelt
1904	Alton Parker	Henry Davis	1904	Theodore Roosevelt*	Charles Fairbanks
1908	William J. Bryan	John Kern	1908	William H. Taft*	James Sherman
1912	Woodrow Wilson*	Thomas Marshall	1912	William H. Taft	James Sherman[2]
1916	Woodrow Wilson*	Thomas Marshall	1916	Charles E. Hughes	Charles Fairbanks
1920	James M. Cox	Franklin D. Roosevelt	1920	Warren G. Harding*	Calvin Coolidge
1924	John W. Davis	Charles W. Bryan	1924	Calvin Coolidge*	Charles G. Dawes
1928	Alfred E. Smith	Joseph T. Robinson	1928	Herbert Hoover*	Charles Curtis
1932	Franklin D. Roosevelt*	John N. Garner	1932	Herbert Hoover	Charles Curtis
1936	Franklin D. Roosevelt*	John N. Garner	1936	Alfred M. Landon	Frank Knox
1940	Franklin D. Roosevelt*	Henry A. Wallace	1940	Wendell L. Willkie	Charles McNary
1944	Franklin D. Roosevelt*	Harry S. Truman	1944	Thomas E. Dewey	John W. Bricker
1948	Harry S. Truman*	Alben W. Barkley	1948	Thomas E. Dewey	Earl Warren
1952	Adlai E. Stevenson	John J. Sparkman	1952	Dwight D. Eisenhower*	Richard M. Nixon
1956	Adlai E. Stevenson	Estes Kefauver	1956	Dwight D. Eisenhower*	Richard M. Nixon
1960	John F. Kennedy*	Lyndon B. Johnson	1960	Richard M. Nixon	Henry Cabot Lodge
1964	Lyndon B. Johnson*	Hubert H. Humphrey	1964	Barry M. Goldwater	William E. Miller
1968	Hubert H. Humphrey	Edmund S. Muskie	1968	Richard M. Nixon*	Spiro T. Agnew
1972	George S. McGovern	R. Sargent Shriver Jr.[3]	1972	Richard M. Nixon*	Spiro T. Agnew
1976	Jimmy Carter*	Walter F. Mondale	1976	Gerald R. Ford	Bob Dole
1980	Jimmy Carter	Walter F. Mondale	1980	Ronald Reagan*	George H. W. Bush
1984	Walter F. Mondale	Geraldine Ferraro	1984	Ronald Reagan*	George H. W. Bush
1988	Michael S. Dukakis	Lloyd Bentsen	1988	George H. W. Bush*	Dan Quayle
1992	Bill Clinton*	Al Gore	1992	George H. W. Bush	Dan Quayle
1996	Bill Clinton*	Al Gore	1996	Bob Dole	Jack Kemp
2000	Al Gore	Joseph Lieberman	2000	George W. Bush*	Richard Cheney
2004	John Kerry	John Edwards	2004	George W. Bush*	Richard Cheney
2008	Barack Obama*	Joe Biden	2008	John McCain	Sarah Palin
2012	Barack Obama*	Joe Biden	2012	Mitt Romney	Paul Ryan
2016	Hillary Clinton	Tim Kaine	2016	Donald J. Trump*	Mike Pence
2020	Joe Biden*	Kamala Harris	2020	Donald J. Trump	Mike Pence

(1) Douglas and Johnson were nominated at the Baltimore convention. An earlier convention in Charleston, SC, failed to reach a consensus and resulted in a split in the party. The Southern faction of the Democrats nominated John Breckinridge for president and Joseph Lane for vice president. (2) Died Oct. 30; replaced on ballot by Nicholas Butler. (3) Chosen by Democratic National Committee after Thomas Eagleton withdrew because of controversy over past treatments for depression.

Third-Party and Independent Presidential Candidates

In most elections since 1860, fewer than one vote in 20 has been cast for a third-party candidate. Still, independent and third-party candidates often bring attention to prominent issues and can affect the outcome between major-party candidates.

Major vote-getters among third-party and independent candidates include James B. Weaver (People's Party), 1892; former Pres. Theodore Roosevelt (Progressive Party), 1912; Robert M. La Follette (Progressive Party), 1924; George C. Wallace (American Independent Party), 1968; and H. Ross Perot, as an independent in 1992 and with the Reform Party in 1996. In these six elections, non-major-party candidates combined polled at least 10% of the vote.

Roosevelt outpolled the Republican candidate, William Howard Taft, in 1912, capturing 28% of the popular vote and 88 electoral votes. In 1948, Strom Thurmond (States' Rights [Dixiecrat]) won 39 electoral votes from five Southern states; however, third-party candidates received only 5.75% of the popular vote. George Wallace's popularity in the same region in 1968 allowed him to get 46 electoral votes and 13.5% of the popular vote.

In 1992, Ross Perot captured 19% of the popular vote but failed to win a single electoral vote. In 1996, Perot won 8% of the popular vote; all third-party candidates combined won just over 10%. In 2000, Ralph Nader (Green, independent) won about 3% of the vote. Gary Johnson (Libertarian) won about 3% in 2016.

Notable Third-Party and Independent Campaigns by Year

Party	Presidential nominee	Year	Issues	Strength in
Free Soil	Martin Van Buren	1848	Anti-slavery	NY, OH
American (Know-Nothing)	Millard Fillmore	1856	Anti-immigrant	Northeast, South
Greenback	Peter Cooper	1876	For "cheap money," labor rights	National
Greenback	James B. Weaver	1880	For "cheap money," labor rights	National
Prohibition	John P. St. John	1884	Anti-liquor	National
People's (Populist)	James B. Weaver	1892	For "cheap money," end of national banks	South, West
Socialist	Eugene V. Debs	1900-12; 1920	For public ownership	National
Progressive (Bull Moose)	Theodore Roosevelt	1912	Against high tariffs	Midwest, West
Progressive	Robert M. La Follette	1924	For farmer and labor rights	Midwest, West
Socialist	Norman Thomas	1928-48	For liberal reforms	National
Union	William Lemke	1936	Anti-New Deal	National
States' Rights (Dixiecrat)	Strom Thurmond	1948	For states' rights	South
Progressive	Henry A. Wallace	1948	Anti-Cold War	NY, CA
American Independent	George C. Wallace	1968	For states' rights	South
American	John G. Schmitz	1972	For "law and order"	West, OH, LA
None (independent)	John B. Anderson	1980	A third choice	National
None (independent)	H. Ross Perot	1992	Federal budget deficit	National
Reform	H. Ross Perot	1996	Deficit, campaign finance	National
Green, independent	Ralph Nader	2000-08	Corporate power, domestic priorities	National
Libertarian	Gary Johnson	2012-16	Public debt, civil liberties	National

Presidential Election Results by State, 1960-2020

Source: Federal Election Commission (FEC); local secretaries of state and state elections offices. Some candidates who did not appear on ballots are omitted from historical results.

Alabama Vote Since 1960

2020: Trump, R, 1,441,170; Biden, D, 849,624; Jorgensen, LB, 25,176.

2016: Trump, R, 1,318,255; Clinton, D, 729,547; Johnson, Ind., 44,467; Stein, Ind., 9,391.

2012: Romney, R, 1,255,925; Obama, D, 795,696; Johnson, Ind., 12,328; Stein, Ind., 3,397; Goode, Ind., 2,981.

2008: McCain, R, 1,266,546; Obama, D, 813,479; Nader, Ind., 6,788; Barr, Ind., 4,991; Baldwin, Ind., 4,310.

2004: Bush, R, 1,176,394; Kerry, D, 693,933; Nader, Ind., 6,701; Badnarik, Ind., 3,529; Peroutka, Ind., 1,994.

2000: Bush, R, 941,173; Gore, D, 692,611; Nader, Ind., 18,323; Buchanan, Ind., 6,351; Browne LB, 5,893; Phillips, Ind., 775; Hagelin, Ind., 447.

1996: Dole, R, 769,044; Clinton, D, 662,165; Perot, RF, 92,149; Browne, LB, 5,290; Phillips, Ind., 2,365; Hagelin, Natural Law, 1,697; Harris, Ind., 516.

1992: Bush, R, 804,283; Clinton, D, 690,080; Perot, Ind., 183,109; Marrou, LB, 5,737; Fulani, New Alliance, 2,161.

1988: Bush, R, 815,576; Dukakis, D, 549,506; Paul, LB, 8,460; Fulani, Ind., 3,311.

1984: Reagan, R, 872,849; Mondale, D, 551,899; Bergland, LB, 9,504.

1980: Reagan, R, 654,192; Carter, D, 636,730; Anderson, Ind., 16,481; Rarick, Amer. Ind., 15,010; Clark, LB, 13,318; Bubar, Statesman, 1,743; Hall, Comm., 1,629; DeBerry, Soc. Workers, 1,303; McReynolds, Soc., 1,006; Commoner, Citizens, 517.

1976: Carter, D, 659,170; Ford, R, 504,070; Maddox, Amer. Ind., 9,198; Bubar, Prohib., 6,669; Hall, Comm., 1,954; MacBride, LB, 1,481.

1972: Nixon, R, 728,701; McGovern, D, 219,108 plus Natl. Dem. Party of AL, 37,815; Schmitz, Conservative, 11,918; Munn, Prohib., 8,551.

1968: Wallace, 3rd party, 691,425; Humphrey, D, 196,579; Nixon, R, 146,923; Munn, Prohib., 4,022.

1964: Goldwater, R, 479,085; D (electors unpledged), 209,848; scattered, 105.

1960: Kennedy, D, 324,050; Nixon, R, 237,981; Faubus, States' Rights, 4,367; Decker, Prohib., 2,106; King, Afro-Americans, 1,485; scattered, 236.

Alaska Vote Since 1960

2020: Trump, R, 189,951; Biden, D, 153,778; Jorgensen, LB, 8,897; Ventura, Green, 2,673; Blankenship, Const., 1,127; Pierce, petitioning cand., 825; De La Fuente, Alliance, 318.

2016: Trump, R, 163,387; Clinton, D, 116,454; Johnson, LB, 18,725; Stein, Green, 5,735; Castle, Const., 3,866; De La Fuente, unaff., 1,240.

2012: Romney, R, 164,676; Obama, D, 122,640; Johnson, LB, 7,392; Stein, Green, 2,917.

2008: McCain, R, 193,841; Obama, D, 123,594; Nader, Ind., 3,783; Baldwin, AK Ind., 1,660; Barr, LB, 1,589.

2004: Bush, R, 190,889; Kerry, D, 111,025; Nader, Populist, 5,069; Peroutka, AK Ind., 2,092; Badnarik, LB, 1,675; Cobb, Green, 1,058.

2000: Bush, R, 167,398; Gore, D, 79,004; Nader, Green, 28,747; Buchanan, RF, 5,192; Browne, LB, 2,636; Hagelin, Natural Law, 919; Phillips, Const., 596.

1996: Dole, R, 122,746; Clinton, D, 80,380; Perot, RF, 26,333; Nader, Green, 7,597; Browne, LB, 2,276; Phillips, U.S. Taxpayers, 925; Hagelin, Natural Law, 729.

1992: Bush, R, 102,000; Clinton, D, 78,294; Perot, Ind., 73,481; Gritz, Populist/America First, 1,379; Marrou, LB, 1,378.

1988: Bush, R, 119,251; Dukakis, D, 72,584; Paul, LB, 5,484; Fulani, New Alliance, 1,024.

1984: Reagan, R, 138,377; Mondale, D, 62,007; Bergland, LB, 6,378.

1980: Reagan, R, 86,112; Carter, D, 41,842; Clark, LB, 18,479; Anderson, Ind., 11,155; write-in, 857.

1976: Ford, R, 71,555; Carter, D, 44,058; MacBride, LB, 6,785.

1972: Nixon, R, 55,349; McGovern, D, 32,967; Schmitz, Amer., 6,903.

1968: Nixon, R, 37,600; Humphrey, D, 35,411; Wallace, 3rd party, 10,024.

1964: Johnson, D, 44,329; Goldwater, R, 22,930.

1960: Nixon, R, 30,953; Kennedy, D, 29,809.

Arizona Vote Since 1960

2020: Biden, D, 1,672,143; Trump, R, 1,661,686; Jorgensen, LB, 51,465.

2016: Trump, R, 1,252,401; Clinton, D, 1,161,167; Johnson, LB, 106,327; Stein, Green, 34,345; McMullin, Ind., 17,449; Castle, Const., 1,058.

2012: Romney, R, 1,233,654; Obama, D, 1,025,232; Johnson, LB, 32,100; Stein, Green, 7,816.

2008: McCain, R, 1,230,111; Obama, D, 1,034,707; Barr, LB, 12,555; Nader, New Prog., 11,301; McKinney, Green, 3,406.

2004: Bush, R, 1,104,294; Kerry, D, 893,524; Badnarik, LB, 11,856.

2000: Bush, R, 781,652; Gore, D, 685,341; Nader, Green, 45,645; Buchanan, RF, 12,373; Smith, LB, 5,775; Hagelin, Natural Law, 1,120.

1996: Clinton, D, 653,288; Dole, R, 622,073; Perot, RF, 112,072; Browne, LB, 14,358.

1992: Bush, R, 572,086; Clinton, D, 543,050; Perot, Ind., 353,741; Gritz, Populist/America First, 8,141; Marrou, LB, 6,759; Hagelin, Natural Law, 2,267.

1988: Bush, R, 702,541; Dukakis, D, 454,029; Paul, LB, 13,351; Fulani, New Alliance, 1,662.

1984: Reagan, R, 681,416; Mondale, D, 333,854; Bergland, LB, 10,585.

1980: Reagan, R, 529,688; Carter, D, 246,843; Anderson, Ind., 76,952; Clark, LB, 18,784; DeBerry, Soc. Workers, 1,100; Commoner, Citizens, 551; Hall, Comm., 25; Griswold, Workers World, 2.

1976: Ford, R, 418,642; Carter, D, 295,602; McCarthy, Ind., 19,229; MacBride, LB, 7,647; Camejo, Soc. Workers, 928; Anderson, Amer., 564; Maddox, Amer. Ind., 85.

1972: Nixon, R, 402,812; McGovern, D, 198,540; Jenness, Soc. Workers, 30,945; Schmitz, Amer. Ind., 21,208.

1968: Nixon, R, 266,721; Humphrey, D, 170,514; Wallace, 3rd party, 46,573; McCarthy, New Party, 2,751; Cleaver, Peace/Freedom, 217; Halstead, Soc. Workers, 85; Blomen, Soc. Labor, 75.

1964: Goldwater, R, 242,535; Johnson, D, 237,753; Hass, Soc. Labor, 482.

1960: Nixon, R, 221,241; Kennedy, D, 176,781; Hass, Soc. Labor, 469.

Arkansas Vote Since 1960

2020: Trump, R, 760,647; Biden, D, 423,932; Jorgensen, LB, 13,133; West, Ind., 4,099; Hawkins, Green, 2,980; Collins, Ind., 2,812; Pierce, Ind., 2,141; Blankenship, Const., 2,108; Carroll, Amer. Solidarity, 1,713; Gammon, Ind., 1,475; Myers, other, 1,372; La Riva, Socialism/Liberation, 1,336; De La Fuente, Ind., 1,321.

2016: Trump, R, 684,872; Clinton, D, 380,494; Johnson, LB, 29,949; McMullin, Better For America, 13,176; Stein, Green, 9,473; Hedges, Ind., 4,709; Castle, Const., 4,613; Kahn, Ind., 3,390.

2012: Romney, R, 647,744; Obama, D, 394,409; Johnson, LB, 16,276; Stein, Green, 9,305; Lindsay, Socialism/Liberation, 1,734.

2008: McCain, R, 638,017; Obama, D, 422,310; Nader, Ind., 12,882; Barr, LB, 4,776; Baldwin, Const., 4,023; McKinney, Green, 3,470; La Riva, Socialism/Liberation, 1,139.

2004: Bush, R, 572,898; Kerry, D, 469,953; Nader, Populist, 6,171; Badnarik, LB, 2,352; Peroutka, Const., 2,083; Cobb, Green, 1,488.

2000: Bush, R, 472,940; Gore, D, 422,768; Nader, Green, 13,421; Buchanan, RF, 7,358; Browne, LB, 2,781; Phillips, Const., 1,415; Hagelin, Natural Law, 1,098.

1996: Clinton, D, 475,171; Dole, R, 325,416; Perot, RF, 69,884; Nader, Ind., 3,649; Browne, Ind., 3,076; Phillips, Ind., 2,065;

Forbes, Ind., 932; Collins, Ind., 823; Masters, Ind., 749; Moorehead, Ind., 747; Hagelin, Ind., 729; Hollis, Ind., 538; Dodge, Ind., 483.

1992: Clinton, D, 505,823; Bush, R, 337,324; Perot, Ind., 99,132; Phillips, U.S. Taxpayers, 1,437; Marrou, LB, 1,261; Fulani, New Alliance, 1,022.

1988: Bush, R, 466,578; Dukakis, D, 349,237; Duke, Populist, 5,146; Paul, LB, 3,297.

1984: Reagan, R, 534,774; Mondale, D, 338,646; Bergland, LB, 2,220.

1980: Reagan, R, 403,164; Carter, D, 398,041; Anderson, Ind., 22,468; Clark, LB, 8,970; Commoner, Citizens, 2,345; Bubar, Statesman, 1,350; Hall, Comm., 1,244.

1976: Carter, D, 498,604; Ford, R, 267,903; McCarthy, Ind., 639; Anderson, Amer. Ind., 389.

1972: Nixon, R, 445,751; McGovern, D, 198,899; Schmitz, Amer. Ind., 3,016.

1968: Wallace, 3rd party, 235,627; Nixon, R, 189,062; Humphrey, D, 184,901.

1964: Johnson, D, 314,197; Goldwater, R, 243,264; Kasper, Natl. States' Rights, 2,965.

1960: Kennedy, D, 215,049; Nixon, R, 184,508; Faubus, Natl. States' Rights, 28,952.

California Vote Since 1960

2020: Biden, D, 11,110,639; Trump, R, 6,006,518; Jorgensen, LB, 187,910; Hawkins, Green, 81,032; De La Fuente, Amer. Ind., 60,162; La Riva, Peace/Freedom, 51,038.

2016: Clinton, D, 8,753,792; Trump, R, 4,483,814; Johnson, LB, 478,500; Stein, Green, 278,658; Sanders, Ind., 79,341; La Riva, Peace/Freedom, 66,101; McMullin, Ind., 39,596.

2012: Obama, D, 7,854,285; Romney, R, 4,839,958; Johnson, LB, 143,221; Stein, Green, 85,638; Barr, Peace/Freedom, 53,824; Hoefling, Amer. Ind., 38,372.

2008: Obama, D, 8,274,473; McCain, R, 5,011,781; Nader, Peace/Freedom, 108,381; Barr, LB, 67,582; Alan Keyes, Amer. Ind., 40,673; McKinney, Green, 38,774.

2004: Kerry, D, 6,745,485; Bush, R, 5,509,826; Badnarik, LB, 50,165; Cobb, Green, 40,771; Peltier, Peace/Freedom, 27,607; Peroutka, Amer. Ind., 26,645.

2000: Gore, D, 5,861,203; Bush, R, 4,567,429; Nader, Green, 418,707; Browne, LB, 45,520; Buchanan, RF, 44,987; Phillips, Amer. Ind., 17,042; Hagelin, Natural Law, 10,934.

1996: Clinton, D, 5,119,835; Dole, R, 3,828,380; Perot, RF, 697,847; Nader, Green, 237,016; Browne, LB, 73,600; Feinland, Peace/Freedom, 25,332; Phillips, Amer. Ind., 21,202; Hagelin, Natural Law, 15,403.

1992: Clinton, D, 5,121,325; Bush, R, 3,630,575; Perot, Ind., 2,296,006; Marrou, LB, 48,139; Daniels, Ind., 18,597; Phillips, U.S. Taxpayers, 12,711.

1988: Bush, R, 5,054,917; Dukakis, D, 4,702,233; Paul, LB, 70,105; Fulani, Ind., 31,181.

1984: Reagan, R, 5,305,410; Mondale, D, 3,815,947; Bergland, LB, 48,400.

1980: Reagan, R, 4,524,858; Carter, D, 3,083,661; Anderson, Ind., 739,833; Clark, LB, 148,434; Commoner, Ind., 61,063; Smith, Peace/Freedom, 18,116; Rarick, Amer. Ind., 9,856.

1976: Ford, R, 3,882,244; Carter, D, 3,742,284; McCarthy, write-in, 58,412; MacBride, LB, 56,388; Maddox, Amer. Ind., 51,098; Wright, People's, 41,731; Camejo, Soc. Workers, 17,259; Hall, Comm., 12,766; write-in, 4,935.

1972: Nixon, R, 4,602,096; McGovern, D, 3,475,847; Schmitz, Amer. Ind., 232,554; Spock, Peace/Freedom, 55,167; Hospers, LB, 980; Jenness, Soc. Workers, 574; Hall, Comm., 373; Fisher, Soc. Labor, 197; Munn, Prohib., 53; Green, Universal, 21.

1968: Nixon, R, 3,467,664; Humphrey, D, 3,244,318; Wallace, 3rd party, 487,270; Peace/Freedom, 27,707; McCarthy, Alternative, 20,721; Gregory, write-in, 3,230; Blomen, Soc. Labor, 341; Mitchell, Comm., 260; Munn, Prohib., 59; Soeters, Defense, 17.

1964: Johnson, D, 4,171,877; Goldwater, R, 2,879,108; Hass, Soc. Labor, 489; DeBerry, Soc. Workers, 378; Munn, Prohib., 305; Hensley, Universal, 19.

1960: Nixon, R, 3,259,722; Kennedy, D, 3,224,099; Decker, Prohib., 21,706; Hass, Soc. Labor, 1,051.

Colorado Vote Since 1960

2020: Biden, D, 1,804,352; Trump, R, 1,364,607; Jorgensen, LB, 52,460; Hawkins, Green, 8,986; West, unaff., 8,089; Blankenship, Amer. Const., 5,061; Hammons, Unity, 2,730; Carroll, Amer. Solidarity, 2,515; Charles, unaff., 2,011; La Riva, Socialism/Liberation, 1,035; Kopitke, Ind. Amer., 762; De La Fuente, Alliance, 636; McHugh, unaff., 614; Pierce, unaff., 572; Collins, Prohib., 568; Jacob-Fambro, unaff., 495; Hunter, Progressive, 379; Huber, Approval Voting, 355; Kennedy, Soc. Workers, 354; Kishore, Soc. Equal., 196; Scott, unaff., 175.

2016: Clinton, D, 1,338,870; Trump, R, 1,202,484; Johnson, LB, 144,121; Stein, Green, 38,437; McMullin, unaff., 28,917; Castle, Const., 11,699; Keniston, Veterans, 5,028; Smith, unaff., 1,819; De La Fuente, Amer. Delta, 1,255; Kopitke, Independent Amer., 1,096; Maldonado, Ind., 872; Maturen, Amer. Solidarity, 862; Silva, Nutrition, 751; Scott, unaff., 749; Hoefling, America's Party, 710; La Riva, Socialism/Liberation, 531; Kennedy, Soc. Workers, 452; Kotlikoff, Ind., 392; Lyttle, Nonviolent/Pacifist, 382; Atwood, Approval Voting, 337; Soltysik, Soc. USA, 271; Hedges, Prohib., 185.

2012: Obama, D, 1,323,102; Romney, R, 1,185,243; Johnson, LB, 35,545; Stein, Green, 7,508; Goode, Const., 6,234; Barr, Peace/Freedom, 5,059; Reed, unaff., 2,589; Anderson, Justice, 1,260; Tittle, We the People, 792; Hoefling, Amer. Ind., 679; La Riva, Socialism/Liberation, 317; Alexander, Soc. USA, 308; Miller, A3P, 266; Stevens, Objectivist, 235; Harris, Soc. Workers, 192; White, Soc. Equality, 189.

2008: Obama, D, 1,288,633; McCain, R, 1,073,629; Nader, unaff., 13,352; Barr, LB, 10,898; Baldwin, Const., 6,233; Alan Keyes, Amer. Ind., 3,051; McKinney, Green, 2,822; McEnulty, unaff., 829; Jay, Boston Tea, 598; Allen, HeartQuake '08, 348; Stevens, Objectivist, 336; Moore, Soc. USA, 226; La Riva, Socialism/Liberation, 158; Harris, Soc. Workers, 154; Lyttle, U.S. Pacifist, 110; Amondson, Prohib., 85.

2004: Bush, R, 1,101,255; Kerry, D, 1,001,732; Nader, RF, 12,718; Badnarik, LB, 7,664; Peroutka, Amer. Const., 2,562; Cobb, Green, 1,591; Andress, Ind., 804; Amondson, Concerns of People, 378; Van Auken, Soc. Equal., 329; Harris, Soc. Workers, 241; Brown, Soc., 216; Dodge, Prohib., 140.

2000: Bush, R, 883,748; Gore, D, 738,227; Nader, Green, 91,434; Browne, LB, 12,799; Buchanan, RF, 10,465; Hagelin, RF, 2,240; Phillips, Amer. Const., 1,319; McReynolds, Soc., 712; Harris, Soc. Workers, 216; Dodge, Prohib., 208.

1996: Dole, R, 691,848; Clinton, D, 671,152; Perot, RF, 99,629; Nader, Green, 25,070; Browne, LB, 12,392; Phillips, Amer. Const., 2,813; Collins, Ind., 2,809; Hagelin, Natural Law, 2,547; Hollis, Soc., 669; Moorehead, Workers World, 599; Templin, Amer., 557; Dodge, Prohib., 375; Harris, Soc. Workers, 244.

1992: Clinton, D, 629,681; Bush, R, 562,850; Perot, Ind., 366,010; Marrou, LB, 8,669; Fulani, New Alliance, 1,608.

1988: Bush, R, 728,177; Dukakis, D, 621,453; Paul, LB, 15,482; Dodge, Prohib., 4,604.

1984: Reagan, R, 821,817; Mondale, D, 454,975; Bergland, LB, 11,257.

1980: Reagan, R, 652,264; Carter, D, 367,973; Anderson, Ind., 130,633; Clark, LB, 25,744; Commoner, Citizens, 5,614; Bubar, Statesman, 1,180; Pulley, Soc., 520; Hall, Comm., 487.

1976: Ford, R, 584,367; Carter, D, 460,353; McCarthy, Ind., 26,107; MacBride, LB, 5,330; Bubar, Prohib., 2,882.

1972: Nixon, R, 597,189; McGovern, D, 329,980; Schmitz, Amer., 17,269; Fisher, Soc. Labor, 4,361; Spock, People's, 2,403; Hospers, LB, 1,111; Jenness, Soc. Workers, 555; Munn, Prohib., 467; Hall, Comm., 432.

1968: Nixon, R, 409,345; Humphrey, D, 335,174; Wallace, 3rd party, 60,813; Blomen, Soc. Labor, 3,016; Gregory, New Party, 1,393; Munn, Prohib., 275; Halstead, Soc. Workers, 235.

1964: Johnson, D, 476,024; Goldwater, R, 296,767; DeBerry, Soc. Workers, 2,537; Munn, Prohib., 1,356; Hass, Soc. Labor, 302.

1960: Nixon, R, 402,242; Kennedy, D, 330,629; Hass, Soc. Labor, 2,803; Dobbs, Soc. Workers, 572.

Connecticut Vote Since 1960

2020: Biden, D, 1,080,831; Trump, R, 714,717; Jorgensen, LB, 20,230; Hawkins, Green, 7,538.

2016: Clinton, D, 897,572; Trump, R, 673,215; Johnson, LB, 48,676; Stein, Green, 22,841; McMullin, Ind., 2,108.

2012: Obama, D, 905,083; Romney, R, 634,892; Johnson, LB, 12,580; Anderson, Ind., 5,487.

2008: Obama, D, 997,772; McCain, R, 629,428; Nader, Ind., 19,162.

2004: Kerry, D, 857,488; Bush, R, 693,826; Nader, petitioning cand., 12,969; Cobb, Green, 9,564; Badnarik, LB, 3,367; Peroutka, Concerned Citizens, 1,543.

2000: Gore, D, 816,015; Bush, R, 561,094; Nader, Green, 64,452; Phillips, Concerned Citizens, 9,695; Buchanan, RF, 4,731; Browne, LB, 3,484.

1996: Clinton, D, 735,740; Dole, R, 483,109; Perot, RF, 139,523; Nader, Green, 24,321; Browne, LB, 5,788; Phillips, Concerned Citizens, 2,425; Hagelin, Natural Law, 1,703.

1992: Clinton, D, 682,318; Bush, R, 578,313; Perot, Ind., 348,771; Marrou, LB, 5,391; Fulani, New Alliance, 1,363.

1988: Bush, R, 750,241; Dukakis, D, 676,584; Paul, LB, 14,071; Fulani, New Alliance, 2,491.

1984: Reagan, R, 890,877; Mondale, D, 569,597.

1980: Reagan, R, 677,210; Carter, D, 541,732; Anderson, Ind., 171,807; Clark, LB, 8,570; Commoner, Citizens, 6,130; scattered, 836.

1976: Ford, R, 719,261; Carter, D, 647,895; Maddox, George Wallace Party, 7,101; LaRouche, U.S. Labor, 1,789.

1972: Nixon, R, 810,763; McGovern, D, 555,498; Schmitz, Amer., 17,239; scattered, 777.

1968: Humphrey, D, 621,561; Nixon, R, 556,721; Wallace, 3rd party, 76,650; scattered, 1,300.

1964: Johnson, D, 826,269; Goldwater, R, 390,996; scattered, 1,313.

1960: Kennedy, D, 657,055; Nixon, R, 565,813.

Delaware Vote Since 1960

2020: Biden, D, 296,268; Trump, R, 200,603; Jorgensen, LB, 5,000; Hawkins, Green, 2,139.

2016: Clinton, D, 235,603; Trump, R, 185,127; Johnson, LB, 14,757; Stein, Green, 6,103; McMullin, Ind., 706.

2012: Obama, D, 242,584; Romney, R, 165,484; Johnson, LB, 3,882; Stein, Green, 1,940.

2008: Obama, D, 255,459; McCain, R, 152,374; Nader, Ind. (DE), 2,401; Barr, LB, 1,109; Baldwin, Const., 626; McKinney, Green, 385; Calero, Soc. Workers, 58.

2004: Kerry, D, 200,152; Bush, R, 171,660; Nader, Ind., 2,153; Badnarik, LB, 586; Peroutka, Const., 289; Cobb, Green, 250; Brown, Natural Law, 100.

2000: Gore, D, 180,068; Bush, R, 137,288; Nader, Green, 8,307; Buchanan, RF, 777; Browne, LB, 774; Phillips, Const., 208; Hagelin, Natural Law, 107.

1996: Clinton, D, 140,355; Dole, R, 99,062; Perot, RF, 28,719; Browne, LB, 2,052; Phillips, U.S. Taxpayers, 348; Hagelin, Natural Law, 274.

1992: Clinton, D, 126,054; Bush, R, 102,313; Perot, Ind., 59,213; Fulani, New Alliance, 1,105.

1988: Bush, R, 139,639; Dukakis, D, 108,647; Paul, LB, 1,162; Fulani, New Alliance, 443.

1984: Reagan, R, 152,190; Mondale, D, 101,656; Bergland, LB, 268.

1980: Reagan, R, 111,252; Carter, D, 105,754; Anderson, Ind., 16,288; Clark, LB, 1,974; Greaves, Amer., 400.

1976: Carter, D, 122,596; Ford, R, 109,831; McCarthy, nonpartisan, 2,437; Anderson, Amer., 645; LaRouche, U.S. Labor, 136; Bubar, Prohib., 103; Levin, Soc. Labor, 86.

1972: Nixon, R, 140,357; McGovern, D, 92,283; Schmitz, Amer., 2,638; Munn, Prohib., 238.

1968: Nixon, R, 96,714; Humphrey, D, 89,194; Wallace, 3rd party, 28,459.

1964: Johnson, D, 122,704; Goldwater, R, 78,078; Munn, Prohib., 425; Hass, Soc. Labor, 113.

1960: Kennedy, D, 99,590; Nixon, R, 96,373; Faubus, States' Rights, 354; Decker, Prohib., 284; Hass, Soc. Labor, 82.

District of Columbia Vote Since 1964

2020: Biden, D, 317,323; Trump, R, 18,586; Jorgensen, LB, 2,036; Hawkins, Green, 1,726; La Riva, Ind., 855; Pierce, Ind., 693.

2016: Clinton, D, 282,830; Trump, R, 12,723; Johnson, LB, 4,906; Stein, Green, 4,258.

2012: Obama, D, 267,070; Romney, R, 21,381; Stein, DC Statehood Green, 2,458; Johnson, LB, 2,083.

2008: Obama, D, 245,800; McCain, R, 17,367; Nader, Ind., 958; McKinney, Green, 590.

2004: Kerry, D, 202,970; Bush, R, 21,256; Nader, Ind., 1,485; Cobb, DC Statehood Green, 737; Badnarik, LB, 502; Harris, Soc. Workers, 130.

2000: Gore, D, 171,923; Bush, R, 18,073; Nader, Green, 10,576; Browne, LB, 669; Harris, Soc. Workers, 114.

1996: Clinton, D, 158,220; Dole, R, 17,339; Nader, Green, 4,780; Perot, RF, 3,611; Browne, LB, 588; Hagelin, Natural Law, 283; Harris, Soc. Workers, 257.

1992: Clinton, D, 192,619; Bush, R, 20,698; Perot, Ind., 9,681; Fulani, New Alliance, 1,459; Daniels, Ind., 1,186.

1988: Dukakis, D, 159,407; Bush, R, 27,590; Fulani, New Alliance, 2,901; Paul, LB, 554.

1984: Mondale, D, 180,408; Reagan, R, 29,009; Bergland, LB, 279.

1980: Carter, D, 130,231; Reagan, R, 23,313; Anderson, Ind., 16,131; Commoner, Citizens, 1,826; Clark, LB, 1,104; Hall, Comm., 369; DeBerry, Soc. Workers, 173; Griswold, Workers World, 52; write-in, 690.

1976: Carter, D, 137,818; Ford, R, 27,873; Camejo, Soc. Workers, 545; MacBride, LB, 274; Hall, Comm., 219; LaRouche, U.S. Labor, 157.

1972: McGovern, D, 127,627; Nixon, R, 35,226; Reed, Soc. Workers, 316; Hall, Comm., 252.

1968: Humphrey, D, 139, 566; Nixon, R, 31,012.

1964: Johnson, D, 169,796; Goldwater, R, 28,801.

Florida Vote Since 1960

2020: Trump, R, 5,668,731; Biden, D, 5,297,045; Jorgensen, LB, 70,324; Hawkins, Green, 14,721; De La Fuente, RF, 5,966; La Riva, Socialism/Liberation, 5,712; Blankenship, Const., 3,902.

2016: Trump, R, 4,617,886; Clinton, D, 4,504,975; Johnson, LB, 207,043; Stein, Green, 64,399; Castle, Const., 16,475; De La Fuente, RF, 9,108.

2012: Obama, D, 4,237,756; Romney, R, 4,163,447; Johnson, LB, 44,726; Stein, Green, 8,947; Barr, Peace/Freedom, 8,154; Stevens, Objectivist, 3,856; Goode, Const., 2,607; Anderson, Justice, 1,754; Hoefling, Amer. Ind., 946; Barnett, RF, 820; Alexander, Soc., 799; Lindsay, Socialism/Liberation, 322.

2008: Obama, D, 4,282,074; McCain, R, 4,045,624; Nader, Ecology (FL), 28,124; Barr, LB, 17,218; Baldwin, Const., 7,915; McKinney, Green, 2,887; Keyes, Amer. Ind., 2,550; La Riva, Socialism/Liberation, 1,516; Jay, Boston Tea, 795; Harris, Soc. Workers, 533; Stevens, Objectivist, 419; Moore, Soc. USA, 405; Amondson, Prohib., 293.

2004: Bush, R, 3,964,522; Kerry, D, 3,583,544; Nader, RF, 32,971; Badnarik, LB, 11,996; Peroutka, Const., 6,626; Cobb, Green, 3,917; Brown, Soc., 3,502; Harris, Soc. Workers, 2,732.

2000: Bush, R, 2,912,790; Gore, D, 2,912,253; Nader, Green, 97,488; Buchanan, RF, 17,484; Browne, LB, 16,415; Hagelin, Natural Law, 2,281; Moorehead, Workers World, 1,804; Phillips, Const., 1,371; McReynolds, Soc., 622; Harris, Soc. Workers, 562.

1996: Clinton, D, 2,545,968; Dole, R, 2,243,324; Perot, RF, 483,776; Browne, LB, 23,312.

1992: Bush, R, 2,171,781; Clinton, D, 2,071,651; Perot, Ind., 1,052,481; Marrou, LB, 15,068.

1988: Bush, R, 2,616,597; Dukakis, D, 1,655,851; Paul, LB, 19,796, Fulani, New Alliance, 6,655.

1984: Reagan, R, 2,728,775; Mondale, D, 1,448,344.

1980: Reagan, R, 2,046,951; Carter, D, 1,419,475; Anderson, Ind., 189,692; Clark, LB, 30,524; write-in, 285.

1976: Carter, D, 1,636,000; Ford, R, 1,469,531; McCarthy, Ind., 23,643; Anderson, Amer., 21,325.

1972: Nixon, R, 1,857,759; McGovern, D, 718,117; scattered, 7,407.

1968: Nixon, R, 886,804; Humphrey, D, 676,794; Wallace, 3rd party, 624,207.

1964: Johnson, D, 948,540; Goldwater, R, 905,941.

1960: Nixon, R, 795,476; Kennedy, D, 748,700.

Georgia Vote Since 1960

2020: Biden, D, 2,473,633; Trump, R, 2,461,854; Jorgensen, LB, 62,229.

2016: Trump, R, 2,089,104; Clinton, D, 1,877,963 Johnson, LB, 125,306; McMullin, Ind., 13,017; Stein, Ind., 7,674; Castle, Ind., 1,110.

2012: Romney, R, 2,078,688; Obama, D, 1,773,827; Johnson, LB, 45,324.

2008: McCain, R, 2,048,759; Obama, D, 1,844,123; Barr, LB, 28,731.

2004: Bush, R, 1,914,254; Kerry, D, 1,366,149; Badnarik, LB, 18,387.

2000: Bush, R, 1,419,720; Gore, D, 1,116,230; Browne, LB, 36,332; Buchanan, Ind., 10,926.

1996: Dole, R, 1,080,843; Clinton, D, 1,053,849; Perot, RF, 146,337; Browne, LB, 17,870.

1992: Clinton, D, 1,008,966; Bush, R, 995,252; Perot, Ind., 309,657; Marrou, LB, 7,110.

1988: Bush, R, 1,081,331; Dukakis, D, 714,792; Paul, LB, 8,435; Fulani, New Alliance, 5,099.

1984: Reagan, R, 1,068,722; Mondale, D, 706,628.

1980: Carter, D, 890,955; Reagan, R, 654,168; Anderson, Ind., 36,055; Clark, LB, 15,627.

1976: Carter, D, 979,409; Ford, R, 483,743; write-in, 4,306.

1972: Nixon, R, 881,496; McGovern, D, 289,529; Schmitz, Amer., 812; scattered, 2,935.

1968: Wallace, 3rd party, 535,550; Nixon, R, 380,111; Humphrey, D, 334,440; write-in, 162.

1964: Goldwater, R, 616,600; Johnson, D, 522,557.

1960: Kennedy, D, 458,638; Nixon, R, 274,472; write-in, 239.

Hawaii Vote Since 1960

2020: Biden, D, 366,130; Trump, R, 196,864; Jorgensen, LB, 5,539; Hawkins, Green, 3,822; Pierce, Amer. Shop., 1,183; Blankenship, Const., 931.

2016: Clinton, D, 266,891; Trump, R, 128,847; Johnson, LB, 15,594; Stein, Green, 12,737; Castle, Const., 4,508.

2012: Obama, D, 306,658; Romney, R, 121,015; Johnson, LB, 3,840; Stein, Green, 3,184.

2008: Obama, D, 325,871; McCain, R, 120,566; Nader, Ind. (HI), 3,825; Barr, LB, 1,314; Baldwin, Const., 1,013; McKinney, Green, 979.

2004: Kerry, D, 231,708; Bush, R, 194,191; Cobb, Green, 1,737; Badnarik, LB, 1,377.

2000: Gore, D, 205,286; Bush, R, 137,845; Nader, Green, 21,623; Browne, LB, 1,477; Buchanan, RF, 1,071; Phillips, Const., 343; Hagelin, Natural Law, 306.

1996: Clinton, D, 205,012; Dole, R, 113,943; Perot, RF, 27,358; Nader, Green, 10,386; Browne, LB, 2,493; Hagelin, Natural Law, 570; Phillips, Taxpayers, 358.

1992: Clinton, D, 179,310; Bush, R, 136,822; Perot, Ind., 53,003; Gritz, Populist/America First, 1,452; Marrou, LB, 1,119.

1988: Dukakis, D, 192,364; Bush, R, 158,625; Paul, LB, 1,999; Fulani, New Alliance, 1,003.

1984: Reagan, R, 184,934; Mondale, D, 147,098; Bergland, LB, 2,167.

1980: Carter, D, 135,879; Reagan, R, 130,112; Anderson, Ind., 32,021; Clark, LB, 3,269; Commoner, Citizens, 1,548; Hall, Comm., 458.

1976: Carter, D, 147,375; Ford, R, 140,003; MacBride, LB, 3,923.

1972: Nixon, R, 168,865; McGovern, D, 101,409.

1968: Humphrey, D, 141,324; Nixon, R, 91,425; Wallace, 3rd party, 3,469.

1964: Johnson, D, 163,249; Goldwater, R, 44,022.

1960: Kennedy, D, 92,410; Nixon, R, 92,295.

Idaho Vote Since 1960

2020: Trump, R, 554,119; Biden, D, 287,021; Jorgensen, LB, 16,404; West, Ind., 3,632; Pierce, Ind., 2,808; Blankenship, Const., 1,886; De La Fuente, Ind., 1,491.

2016: Trump, R, 409,055; Clinton, D, 189,765; McMullin, Ind., 46,476; Johnson, LB, 28,331; Stein, Ind., 8,496; Castle, Ind., 4,403; Copeland, Const., 2,356; De La Fuente, Ind., 1,373.

2012: Romney, R, 420,911; Obama, D, 212,787; Johnson, LB, 9,453; Stein, Ind., 4,402; Anderson, Ind., 2,499; Goode, Const., 2,222.

2008: McCain, R, 403,012; Obama, D, 236,440; Nader, Ind., 7,175; Baldwin, Const., 4,747; Barr, LB, 3,658.

2004: Bush, R, 409,235; Kerry, D, 181,098; Badnarik, LB, 3,844; Peroutka, Const., 3,084.

2000: Bush, R, 336,937; Gore, D, 138,637; Buchanan, RF, 7,615; Browne, LB, 3,488; Phillips, Const., 1,469; Hagelin, Natural Law, 1,177.

1996: Dole, R, 256,595; Clinton, D, 165,443; Perot, RF, 62,518; Browne, LB, 3,325; Phillips, U.S. Taxpayers, 2,230; Hagelin, Natural Law, 1,600.

1992: Bush, R, 202,645; Clinton, D, 137,013; Perot, Ind., 130,395; Gritz, Populist/America First, 10,281; Marrou, LB, 1,167.

1988: Bush, R, 253,881; Dukakis, D, 147,272; Paul, LB, 5,313; Fulani, Ind., 2,502.

1984: Reagan, R, 297,523; Mondale, D, 108,510; Bergland, LB, 2,823.

1980: Reagan, R, 290,699; Carter, D, 110,192; Anderson, Ind., 27,058; Clark, LB, 8,425; Rarick, Amer., 1,057.

1976: Ford, R, 204,151; Carter, D, 126,549; Maddox, Amer., 5,935; MacBride, LB, 3,558; LaRouche, U.S. Labor, 739.

1972: Nixon, R, 199,384; McGovern, D, 80,826; Schmitz, Amer., 28,869; Spock, People's, 903.

1968: Nixon, R, 165,369; Humphrey, D, 89,273; Wallace, 3rd party, 36,541.

1964: Johnson, D, 148,920; Goldwater, R, 143,557.

1960: Nixon, R, 161,597; Kennedy, D, 138,853.

Illinois Vote Since 1960

2020: Biden, D, 3,471,915; Trump, R, 2,446,891; Jorgensen, LB, 66,544; Hawkins, Green, 30,494; Carroll, Amer. Solidarity, 9,548; La Riva, Socialism/Liberation, 8,046.

2016: Clinton, D, 3,090,729; Trump, R, 2,146,015; Johnson, LB, 209,596; Stein, Green, 76,802; McMullin, Ind., 11,655; Castle, Const., 1,138.

2012: Obama, D, 3,019,512; Romney, R, 2,135,216; Johnson, LB, 56,229; Stein, Green, 30,222.

2008: Obama, D, 3,419,348; McCain, R, 2,031,179; Nader, Ind., 30,948; Barr, LB, 19,642; McKinney, Green, 11,838; Baldwin, Const., 8,256; Polachek, New Party, 1,149.

2004: Kerry, D, 2,891,550; Bush, R, 2,345,946; Badnarik, LB, 32,442.

2000: Gore, D, 2,589,026; Bush, R, 2,019,421; Nader, Green, 103,759; Buchanan, Ind., 16,106; Browne, LB, 11,623; Hagelin, RF, 2,127.

1996: Clinton, D, 2,341,744; Dole, R, 1,587,021; Perot, RF, 346,408; Browne, LB, 22,548; Phillips, U.S. Taxpayers, 7,606; Hagelin, Natural Law, 4,606.

1992: Clinton, D, 2,453,350; Bush, R, 1,734,096; Perot, Ind., 840,515; Marrou, LB, 9,218; Fulani, New Alliance, 5,267; Gritz, Populist/America First, 3,577; Hagelin, Natural Law, 2,751; Warren, Soc. Workers, 1,361.

1988: Bush, R, 2,310,939; Dukakis, D, 2,215,940; Paul, LB, 14,944; Fulani, Solidarity, 10,276.

1984: Reagan, R, 2,707,103; Mondale, D, 2,086,499; Bergland, LB, 10,086.

1980: Reagan, R, 2,358,049; Carter, D, 1,981,413; Anderson, Ind., 346,754; Clark, LB, 38,939; Commoner, Citizens, 10,692;

Hall, Comm., 9,711; Griswold, Workers World, 2,257; DeBerry, Soc. Workers, 1,302; write-in, 604.

1976: Ford, R, 2,364,269; Carter, D, 2,271,295; McCarthy, Ind., 55,939; Hall, Comm., 9,250; MacBride, LB, 8,057; Camejo, Soc. Workers, 3,615; Levin, Soc. Labor, 2,422; LaRouche, U.S. Labor, 2,018; write-in, 1,968.

1972: Nixon, R. 2,788,179; McGovern, D, 1,913,472; Fisher, Soc. Labor, 12,344; Hall, Comm., 4,541; Schmitz, Amer., 2,471; others, 2,229.

1968: Nixon, R, 2,174,774; Humphrey, D, 2,039,814; Wallace, 3rd party, 390,958; Blomen, Soc. Labor, 13,878; write-in, 325.

1964: Johnson, D, 2,796,833; Goldwater, R, 1,905,946; write-in, 62.

1960: Kennedy, D, 2,377,846; Nixon, R, 2,368,988; Hass, Soc. Labor, 10,560; write-in, 15.

Indiana Vote Since 1960

2020: Trump, R, 1,729,857; Biden, D, 1,242,498; Jorgensen, LB, 58,901.

2016: Trump, R, 1,557,286; Clinton, D, 1,033,126; Johnson, LB, 133,993; Stein, Green, 7,841; Castle, Const., 1,937.

2012: Romney, R, 1,420,543; Obama, D, 1,152,887; Johnson, LB, 50,111.

2008: Obama, D, 1,374,039; McCain, R, 1,345,648; Barr, LB, 29,257.

2004: Bush, R, 1,479,438; Kerry, D, 969,011; Badnarik, LB, 18,058.

2000: Bush, R, 1,245,836; Gore, D, 901,980; Buchanan, Ind., 16,959; Browne, LB, 15,530.

1996: Dole, R, 1,006,693; Clinton, D, 887,424; Perot, RF, 224,299; Browne, LB, 15,632.

1992: Bush, R, 989,375; Clinton, D, 848,420; Perot, Ind., 455,934; Marrou, LB, 7,936; Fulani, New Alliance, 2,583.

1988: Bush, R, 1,297,763; Dukakis, D, 860,643; Fulani, New Alliance, 10,215.

1984: Reagan, R, 1,377,230; Mondale, D, 841,481; Bergland, LB, 6,741.

1980: Reagan, R, 1,255,656; Carter, D, 844,197; Anderson, Ind., 111,639; Clark, LB, 19,627; Commoner, Citizens, 4,852; Greaves, Amer., 4,750; Hall, Comm., 702; DeBerry, Soc., 610.

1976: Ford, R, 1,185,958; Carter, D, 1,014,714; Anderson, Amer., 14,048; Camejo, Soc. Workers, 5,695; LaRouche, U.S. Labor, 1,947.

1972: Nixon, R, 1,405,154; McGovern, D, 708,568; Reed, Soc. Workers, 5,575; Spock, Peace/Freedom, 4,544; Fisher, Soc. Labor, 1,688.

1968: Nixon, R, 1,067,885; Humphrey, D, 806,659; Wallace, 3rd party, 243,108; Munn, Prohib., 4,616; Halstead, Soc. Workers, 1,293; Gregory, write-in, 36.

1964: Johnson, D, 1,170,848; Goldwater, R, 911,118; Munn, Prohib., 8,266; Hass, Soc. Labor, 1,374.

1960: Nixon, R, 1,175,120; Kennedy, D, 952,358; Decker, Prohib., 6,746; Hass, Soc. Labor, 1,136.

Iowa Vote Since 1960

2020: Trump, R, 897,672; Biden, D, 759,061; Jorgensen, LB, 19,637; West, no party, 3,210; Hawkins, Green, 3,075; Blankenship, Const., 1,707; De La Fuente, Alliance, 1,082; King, other, 546; Pierce, no party, 544.

2016: Trump, R, 800,983; Clinton, D, 653,669; Johnson, LB, 59,186; McMullin, petitioning cand., 12,366; Stein, Green, 11,479; Castle, Const., 5,335; Kahn, New Independent, 2,247; Vacek, Legal Marijuana, 2,246; De La Fuente, petitioning cand., 451; La Riva, Socialism/Liberation, 323.

2012: Obama, D, 822,544; Romney, R, 730,617; Johnson, LB, 12,926; Stein, Green, 3,769; Goode, Const., 3,038; Litzel, Ind., 1,027; Harris, Soc. Workers, 445; La Riva, Socialism/Liberation, 372.

2008: Obama, D, 828,940; McCain, R, 682,379; Nader, Peace/Freedom, 8,014; Barr, LB, 4,590; Baldwin, Const., 4,445; McKinney, Green, 1,423; Harris, Soc. Workers, 292; Moore, Soc. USA, 182; La Riva, Socialism/Liberation, 121.

2004: Bush, R, 751,957; Kerry, D, 741,898; Nader, petitioning cand., 5,973; Badnarik, LB, 2,992; Peroutka, Const., 1,304; Cobb, Green, 1,141; Harris, Soc. Workers, 373; Van Auken, petitioning cand., 176.

2000: Gore, D, 638,517; Bush, R, 634,373; Nader, Green, 29,374; Buchanan, RF, 5,731; Browne, LB, 3,209; Hagelin, Ind., 2,281; Phillips, Const., 613; Harris, Soc. Workers, 190; McReynolds, Soc., 107.

1996: Clinton, D, 620,258; Dole, R, 492,644; Perot, RF, 105,159; Nader, Green, 6,550; Hagelin, Natural Law, 3,349; Browne, LB, 2,315; Phillips, Taxpayers, 2,229; Harris, Soc. Workers, 331.

1992: Clinton, D, 586,353; Bush, R, 504,891; Perot, Ind., 253,468; Hagelin, Natural Law, 3,079; Gritz, Populist/America First, 1,177; Marrou, LB, 1,076.

1988: Dukakis, D, 670,557; Bush, R, 545,355; LaRouche, Ind., 3,526; Paul, LB, 2,494.

1984: Reagan, R, 703,088; Mondale, D, 605,620; Bergland, LB, 1,844.

1980: Reagan, R, 676,026; Carter, D, 508,672; Anderson, Ind., 115,633; Clark, LB, 13,123; Commoner, Citizens, 2,273; McReynolds, Soc., 534; Hall, Comm., 298; DeBerry, Soc. Workers, 244; Greaves, Amer., 189; Bubar, Statesman, 150; scattered, 519.

1976: Ford, R, 632,863; Carter, D, 619,931; McCarthy, Ind., 20,051; Anderson, Amer., 3,040; MacBride, LB, 1,452.

1972: Nixon, R, 706,207; McGovern, D, 496,206; Schmitz, Amer., 22,056; Jenness, Soc. Workers, 488; Hall, Comm., 272; Green, Universal, 199; Fisher, Soc. Labor, 195; scattered, 321.

1968: Nixon, R, 619,106; Humphrey, D, 476,699; Wallace, 3rd party, 66,422; Halstead, Soc. Workers, 3,377; Cleaver, Peace/Freedom, 1,332; Munn, Prohib., 362; Blomen, Soc. Labor, 241.

1964: Johnson, D, 733,030; Goldwater, R, 449,148; Munn, Prohib., 1,902; Hass, Soc. Labor, 182; DeBerry, Soc. Workers, 159.

1960: Nixon, R, 722,381; Kennedy, D, 550,565; Hass, Soc. Labor, 230; write-in, 634.

Kansas Vote Since 1960

2020: Trump, R, 771,406; Biden, D, 570,323; Jorgensen, LB, 30,574.

2016: Trump, R, 671,018; Clinton, D, 427,005; Johnson, LB, 55,406; Stein, Ind., 23,506; McMullin, Ind., 6,520.

2012: Romney, R, 692,634; Obama, D, 440,726; Johnson, LB, 20,456; Baldwin, RF, 5,017.

2008: McCain, R, 699,655; Obama, D, 514,765; Nader, Ind., 10,527; Barr, LB, 6,706; Baldwin, RF, 4,148.

2004: Bush, R, 736,456; Kerry, D, 434,993; Nader, RF, 9,348; Badnarik, LB, 4,013; Peroutka, Ind., 2,899.

2000: Bush, R, 622,332; Gore, D, 399,276; Nader, Ind., 36,086; Buchanan, RF, 7,370; Browne, LB, 4,525; Hagelin, Ind., 1,373; Phillips, Const., 1,254.

1996: Dole, R, 583,245; Clinton, D, 387,659; Perot, RF, 92,639; Browne, LB, 4,557; Phillips, Ind., 3,519; Hagelin, Ind., 1,655.

1992: Bush, R, 449,951; Clinton, D, 390,434; Perot, Ind., 312,358; Marrou, LB, 4,314.

1988: Bush, R, 554,049; Dukakis, D, 422,636; Paul, Ind., 12,553; Fulani, Ind., 3,806.

1984: Reagan, R, 674,646; Mondale, D, 332,471; Bergland, LB, 3,585.

1980: Reagan, R, 566,812; Carter, D, 326,150; Anderson, Ind., 68,231; Clark, LB, 14,470; Shelton, Amer., 1,555; Hall, Comm., 967; Bubar, Statesman, 821; Rarick, Conservative, 789.

1976: Ford, R, 502,752; Carter, D, 430,421; McCarthy, Ind., 13,185; Anderson, Amer., 4,724; MacBride, LB, 3,242; Maddox, Conservative, 2,118; Bubar, Prohib., 1,403.

1972: Nixon, R, 619,812; McGovern, D, 270,287; Schmitz, Conservative, 21,808; Munn, Prohib., 4,188.

1968: Nixon, R, 478,674; Humphrey, D, 302,996; Wallace, 3rd party, 88,921; Munn, Prohib., 2,192.

1964: Johnson, D, 464,028; Goldwater, R, 386,579; Munn, Prohib., 5,393; Hass, Soc. Labor, 1,901.

1960: Nixon, R, 561,474; Kennedy, D, 363,213; Decker, Prohib., 4,138.

Kentucky Vote Since 1960

2020: Trump, R, 1,326,646; Biden, D, 772,474; Jorgensen, LB, 26,234; West, Ind., 6,483; Pierce, Ind., 3,599.

2016: Trump, R, 1,202,971; Clinton, D, 628,854; Johnson, LB, 53,752; McMullin, Ind., 22,780; Stein, Green, 13,913; De La Fuente, Amer. Delta, 1,128.

2012: Romney, R, 1,087,190; Obama, D, 679,370; Johnson, LB, 17,063; Terry, Ind., 6,872; Stein, Green, 6,337.

2008: McCain, R, 1,048,462; Obama, D, 751,985; Nader, Ind., 15,378; Barr, LB, 5,989; Baldwin, Const., 4,694.

2004: Bush, R, 1,069,439; Kerry, D, 712,733; Nader, Ind., 8,856; Badnarik, LB, 2,619; Peroutka, Const., 2,213.

2000: Bush, R, 872,520; Gore, D, 638,923; Nader, Green, 23,118; Buchanan, RF, 4,152; Browne, LB, 2,885; Hagelin, Natural Law, 1,513; Phillips, Const., 915.

1996: Clinton, D, 636,614; Dole, R, 623,283; Perot, RF, 120,396; Browne, LB, 4,009; Phillips, U.S. Taxpayers, 2,204; Hagelin, Natural Law, 1,493.

1992: Clinton, D, 665,104; Bush, R, 617,178; Perot, Ind., 203,944; Marrou, LB, 4,513.

1988: Bush, R, 734,281; Dukakis, D, 580,368; Duke, Populist, 4,494; Paul, LB, 2,118.

1984: Reagan, R, 815,345; Mondale, D, 536,756.

1980: Reagan, R, 635,274; Carter, D, 616,417; Anderson, Ind., 31,127; Clark, LB, 5,531; McCormack, Respect for Life, 4,233; Commoner, Citizens, 1,304; Pulley, Soc., 393; Hall, Comm., 348.

1976: Carter, D, 615,717; Ford, R, 531,852; Anderson, Amer., 8,308; McCarthy, Ind., 6,837; Maddox, Amer. Ind., 2,328; MacBride, LB, 814.

1972: Nixon, R, 676,446; McGovern, D, 371,159; Schmitz, Amer., 17,627; Spock, People's, 1,118; Jenness, Soc. Workers, 685; Hall, Comm., 464.

1968: Nixon, R, 462,411; Humphrey, D, 397,547; Wallace, 3rd party, 193,098; Halstead, Soc. Workers, 2,843.

1964: Johnson, D, 669,659; Goldwater, R, 372,977; Kasper, Natl. States' Rights, 3,469.

1960: Nixon, R, 602,607; Kennedy, D, 521,855.

Louisiana Vote Since 1960

2020: Trump, R, 1,255,776; Biden, D, 856,034; Jorgensen, LB, 21,645; West, Birthday Party, 4,897; Carroll, Amer. Solidarity, 2,497; Simmons, Bec. One Nation, 1,626; Boddie, C.U.P., 1,125; La Riva, Socialism/Liberation, 987; Blankenship, Const., 860; Pierce, Freedom/Prosperity, 749; Hoefling, Life/Liberty/Const., 668; Hammons, Unity, 662; Kennedy, Soc. Workers, 536.

2016: Trump, R, 1,178,638; Clinton, D, 780,154; Johnson, LB, 37,978; Stein, Green, 14,031; McMullin, Courage/Char./Serv., 8,547; Castle, Const., 3,129; Keniston, Veterans, 1,881; Hoefling, Life/Fam./Const., 1,581; Kotlikoff, It's Our Children, 1,048; Jacob, Loyal/Trust., 749; Kennedy, Soc. Workers, 480; La Riva, Socialism/Liberation, 446; White, Soc./Eq./Anti-War, 370.

2012: Romney, R, 1,152,262; Obama, D, 809,141; Johnson, LB, 18,157; Stein, Green, 6,978; Goode, Const., 2,508; Tittle, We the People, 1,767; Anderson, Justice, 1,368; Lindsay, Socialism/Liberation, 622; Fellure, Prohib., 518; Harris, Soc. Workers, 389; White, Soc. Equality, 355.

2008: McCain, R, 1,148,275; Obama, D, 782,989; Paul, LA Taxpayers, 9,368; McKinney, Green, 9,187; Nader, Ind., 6,997; Baldwin, Const., 2,581; Harris, Soc. Workers, 735; La Riva, Socialism/Liberation, 354; Amondson, Prohib., 275.

2004: Bush, R, 1,102,169; Kerry, D, 820,299; Nader, Better Life, 7,032; Peroutka, Const., 5,203; Badnarik, LB, 2,781; Brown, Protect Working Families, 1,795; Amondson, Prohib., 1,566; Cobb, Green, 1,276; Harris, Soc. Workers, 985.

2000: Bush, R, 927,871; Gore, D, 792,344; Nader, Green, 20,473; Buchanan, RF, 14,356; Phillips, Const., 5,483; Browne, LB, 2,951; Harris, Soc. Workers, 1,103; Hagelin, Natural Law, 1,075.

1996: Clinton, D, 927,837; Dole, R, 712,586; Perot, RF, 123,293; Browne, LB, 7,499; Nader, Liberty, Ecology, Community, 4,719; Phillips, U.S. Taxpayers, 3,366; Hagelin, Natural Law, 2,981; Moorehead, Workers World, 1,678.

1992: Clinton, D, 815,971; Bush, R, 733,386; Perot, Ind., 211,478; Gritz, Populist/America First, 18,545; Marrou, LB, 3,155; Daniels, Ind., 1,663; Phillips, U.S. Taxpayers, 1,552; Fulani, New Alliance, 1,434; LaRouche, Ind., 1,136.

1988: Bush, R, 883,702; Dukakis, D, 717,460; Duke, Populist, 18,612; Paul, LB, 4,115.

1984: Reagan, R, 1,037,299; Mondale, D, 651,586; Bergland, LB, 1,876.

1980: Reagan, R, 792,853; Carter, D, 708,453; Anderson, Ind., 26,345; Rarick, Amer. Ind., 10,333; Clark, LB, 8,240; Commoner, Citizens, 1,584; DeBerry, Soc. Workers, 783.

1976: Carter, D, 661,365; Ford, R, 587,446; Maddox, Amer., 10,058; Hall, Comm., 7,417; McCarthy, Ind., 6,588; MacBride, LB, 3,325.

1972: Nixon, R, 686,852; McGovern, D, 298,142; Schmitz, Amer., 52,099; Jenness, Soc. Workers, 14,398.

1968: Wallace, 3rd party, 530,300; Humphrey, D, 309,615; Nixon, R, 257,535.

1964: Goldwater, R, 509,225; Johnson, D, 387,068.

1960: Kennedy, D, 407,339; Nixon, R, 230,890; States' Rights (unpledged), 169,572.

Maine Vote Since 1960

2020: Biden, D, 435,072; Trump, R, 360,737; Jorgensen, LB, 14,152; Hawkins, Green, 8,230; De La Fuente, Alliance, 1,183.

2016: Clinton, D, 357,735; Trump, R, 335,593; Johnson, LB, 38,105; Stein, Green, 14,251; McMullin, Ind., 1,887; Castle, Const., 333.

2012: Obama, D, 401,306; Romney, R, 292,276; Johnson, LB, 9,352; Stein, Green, 8,119.

2008: Obama, D, 421,923; McCain, R, 295,273; Nader, Ind., 10,636; McKinney, Green, 2,900.

2004: Kerry, D, 396,842; Bush, R, 330,201; Nader, Better Life, 8,069; Cobb, Green, 2,936; Badnarik, LB, 1,965; Peroutka, Const., 735.

2000: Gore, D, 319,951; Bush, R, 286,616; Nader, Green, 37,127; Buchanan, RF, 4,443; Browne, LB, 3,074; Phillips, Const., 579.

1996: Clinton, D, 312,788; Dole, R, 186,378; Perot, RF, 85,970; Nader, Green, 15,279; Browne, LB, 2,996; Phillips, Taxpayers, 1,517; Hagelin, Natural Law, 825.

1992: Clinton, D, 263,420; Perot, Ind., 206,820; Bush, R, 206,504; Marrou, LB, 1,681.

1988: Bush, R, 307,131; Dukakis, D, 243,569; Paul, LB, 2,700; Fulani, New Alliance, 1,405.

1984: Reagan, R, 336,500; Mondale, D, 214,515.

1980: Reagan, R, 238,522; Carter, D, 220,974; Anderson, Ind., 53,327; Clark, LB, 5,119; Commoner, Citizens, 4,394; Hall, Comm., 591; write-in, 84.

1976: Ford, R, 236,320; Carter, D, 232,279; McCarthy, Ind., 10,874; Bubar, Prohib., 3,495.

1972: Nixon, R, 256,458; McGovern, D, 160,584; scattered, 229.

1968: Humphrey, D, 217,312; Nixon, R, 169,254; Wallace, 3rd party, 6,370.

1964: Johnson, D, 262,264; Goldwater, R, 118,701.

1960: Nixon, R, 240,608; Kennedy, D, 181,159.

Maryland Vote Since 1960

2020: Biden, D, 1,985,023; Trump, R, 976,414; Jorgensen, LB, 33,488; Hawkins, Green, 15,799; Segal, Bread/Roses, 5,884.

2016: Clinton, D, 1,677,928; Trump, R, 943,169; Johnson, LB, 79,605; Stein, Green, 35,945; McMullin, Ind., 9,630; Castle, Const., 566; Maturen, Ind., 504.

2012: Obama, D, 1,677,844; Romney, R, 971,869; Johnson, LB, 30,195; Stein, Green, 17,110.

2008: Obama, D, 1,629,467; McCain, R, 959,862; Nader, MD Ind., 14,713; Barr, LB, 9,842; McKinney, Green, 4,747; Baldwin, RF, 3,760.

2004: Kerry, D, 1,334,493; Bush, R, 1,024,703; Nader, Populist, 11,854; Badnarik, LB, 6,094; Cobb, Green, 3,632; Peroutka, Const., 3,421.

2000: Gore, D, 1,144,008; Bush, R, 813,827; Nader, Green, 53,768; Browne, LB, 5,310; Buchanan, RF, 4,248; Phillips, Const., 918.

1996: Clinton, D, 966,207; Dole, R, 681,530; Perot, RF, 115,812; Browne, LB, 8,765; Phillips, Taxpayers, 3,402; Hagelin, Natural Law, 2,517.

1992: Clinton, D, 988,571; Bush, R, 707,094; Perot, Ind., 281,414; Marrou, LB, 4,715; Fulani, New Alliance, 2,786.

1988: Bush, R, 876,167; Dukakis, D, 826,304; Paul, LB, 6,748; Fulani, New Alliance, 5,115.

1984: Reagan, R, 879,918; Mondale, D, 787,935; Bergland, LB, 5,721.

1980: Carter, D, 726,161; Reagan, R, 680,606; Anderson, Ind., 119,537; Clark, LB, 14,192.

1976: Carter, D, 759,612; Ford, R, 672,661.

1972: Nixon, R, 829,305; McGovern, D, 505,781; Schmitz, Amer., 18,726.

1968: Humphrey, D, 538,310; Nixon, R, 517,995; Wallace, 3rd party, 178,734.

1964: Johnson, D, 730,912; Goldwater, R, 385,495; write-in, 50.

1960: Kennedy, D, 565,800; Nixon, R, 489,538.

Massachusetts Vote Since 1960

2020: Biden, D, 2,382,202; Trump, R, 1,167,202; Jorgensen, LB, 47,013; Hawkins, Green, 18,658.

2016: Clinton, D, 1,995,196; Trump, R, 1,090,893; Johnson, LB, 138,018; Stein, Green, 47,661; McMullin, Ind., 2,719.

2012: Obama, D, 1,921,290; Romney, R, 1,188,314; Johnson, LB, 30,920; Stein, Green, 20,691.

2008: Obama, D, 1,904,097; McCain, R, 1,108,854; Nader, Ind., 28,841; Barr, LB, 13,189; McKinney, Green, 6,550; Baldwin, RF, 4,971.

2004: Kerry, D, 1,803,800; Bush, R, 1,071,109; Badnarik, LB, 15,022; Cobb, Green, 10,623.

2000: Gore, D, 1,616,487; Bush, R, 878,502; Nader, Green, 173,564; Browne, LB, 16,366; Buchanan, RF, 11,149; Hagelin, Natural Law, 2,884.

1996: Clinton, D, 1,571,509; Dole, R, 718,058; Perot, RF, 227,206; Browne, LB, 20,424; Hagelin, Natural Law, 5,183; Moorehead, Workers World, 3,276.

1992: Clinton, D, 1,318,639; Bush, R, 805,039; Perot, Ind., 630,731; Marrou, LB, 9,021; Fulani, New Alliance, 3,172; Phillips, U.S. Taxpayers, 2,218; Hagelin, Natural Law, 1,812; LaRouche, Ind., 1,027.

1988: Dukakis, D, 1,401,415; Bush, R, 1,194,635; Paul, LB, 24,251; Fulani, New Alliance, 9,561.

1984: Reagan, R, 1,310,936; Mondale, D, 1,239,606.

1980: Reagan, R, 1,057,631; Carter, D, 1,053,802; Anderson, Ind., 382,539; Clark, LB, 22,038; DeBerry, Soc. Workers, 3,735; Commoner, Citizens, 2,056; McReynolds, Soc., 62; Bubar, Statesman, 34; Griswold, Workers World, 19; scattered, 2,382.

1976: Carter, D, 1,429,475; Ford, R, 1,030,276; McCarthy, Ind., 65,637; Camejo, Soc. Workers, 8,138; Anderson, Amer., 7,555; LaRouche, U.S. Labor, 4,922; MacBride, LB, 135.

1972: McGovern, D, 1,332,540; Nixon, R, 1,112,078; Jenness, Soc. Workers, 10,600; Schmitz, Amer., 2,877; Fisher, Soc. Labor, 129; Spock, People's, 101; Hall, Comm., 46; Hospers, LB, 43; scattered, 342.

1968: Humphrey, D, 1,469,218; Nixon, R, 766,844; Wallace, 3rd party, 87,088; Blomen, Soc. Labor, 6,180; Munn, Prohib., 2,369; scattered, 53; blank, 25,394.

1964: Johnson, D, 1,786,422; Goldwater, R, 549,727; Hass, Soc. Labor, 4,755; Munn, Prohib., 3,735; scattered, 159; blank, 48,104.

1960: Kennedy, D, 1,487,174; Nixon, R, 976,750; Hass, Soc. Labor, 3,892; Decker, Prohib., 1,633; others, 31; blank and void, 26,024.

Michigan Vote Since 1960

2020: Biden, D, 2,804,040; Trump, R, 2,649,852; Jorgensen, LB, 60,381; Hawkins, Green, 13,718; Blankenship, U.S. Taxpayers, 7,235; De La Fuente, Natural Law, 2,986.

2016: Trump, R, 2,279,543; Clinton, D, 2,268,839; Johnson, LB, 172,136; Stein, Green, 51,463; Castle, U.S. Taxpayers, 16,139; McMullin, Ind., 8,177; Soltysik, Natural Law, 2,209.

2012: Obama, D, 2,564,569; Romney, R, 2,115,256; Stein, Green, 21,897; Goode, U.S. Taxpayers, 16,119; Johnson, Ind., 7,774, Anderson, Natural Law, 5,147.

2008: Obama, D, 2,872,579; McCain, R, 2,048,639; Nader, Natural Law, 33,085; Barr, LB, 23,716; Baldwin, U.S. Taxpayers, 14,685; McKinney, Green, 8,892.

2004: Kerry, D, 2,479,183; Bush, R, 2,313,746; Nader, Ind., 24,035; Badnarik, LB, 10,552; Cobb, Green, 5,325; Peroutka, U.S. Taxpayers, 4,980; Brown, Natural Law, 1,431.

2000: Gore, D, 2,170,418; Bush, R, 1,953,139; Nader, Green, 84,165; Browne, LB, 16,711; Phillips, U.S. Taxpayers, 3,791; Hagelin, Natural Law, 2,426.

1996: Clinton, D, 1,989,653; Dole, R, 1,481,212; Perot, RF, 336,670; Browne, LB, 27,670; Hagelin, Natural Law, 4,254; Moorehead, Workers World, 3,153; White, Soc. Equality, 1,554.

1992: Clinton, D, 1,871,182; Bush, R, 1,554,940; Perot, Ind., 824,813; Marrou, LB, 10,175; Phillips, U.S. Taxpayers, 8,263; Hagelin, Natural Law, 2,954.

1988: Bush, R, 1,965,486; Dukakis, D, 1,675,783; Paul, LB, 18,336; Fulani, Ind., 2,513.

1984: Reagan, R, 2,251,571; Mondale, D, 1,529,638; Bergland, LB, 10,055.

1980: Reagan, R, 1,915,225; Carter, D, 1,661,532; Anderson, Ind., 275,223; Clark, LB, 41,597; Commoner, Citizens, 11,930; Hall, Comm., 3,262; Griswold, Workers World, 30; Greaves, Amer., 21; Bubar, Statesman, 9.

1976: Ford, R, 1,893,742; Carter, D, 1,696,714; McCarthy, Ind., 47,905; MacBride, LB, 5,406; Wright, People's, 3,504; Camejo, Soc. Workers, 1,804; LaRouche, U.S. Labor, 1,366; Levin, Soc. Labor, 1,148; scattered, 2,160.

1972: Nixon, R, 1,961,721; McGovern, D, 1,459,435; Schmitz, Amer., 63,321; Fisher, Soc. Labor, 2,437; Jenness, Soc. Workers, 1,603; Hall, Comm., 1,210.

1968: Humphrey, D, 1,593,082; Nixon, R, 1,370,665; Wallace, 3rd party, 331,968; Halstead, Soc. Workers, 4,099; Blomen, Soc. Labor, 1,762; Cleaver, New Politics, 4,585; Munn, Prohib., 60; scattered, 29.

1964: Johnson, D, 2,136,615; Goldwater, R, 1,060,152; DeBerry, Soc. Workers, 3,817; Hass, Soc. Labor, 1,704; Prohib. (no candidate listed), 699; scattered, 145.

1960: Kennedy, D, 1,687,269; Nixon, R, 1,620,428; Dobbs, Soc. Workers, 4,347; Decker, Prohib., 2,029; Daly, Tax Cut, 1,767; Hass, Soc. Labor, 1,718; Ind. Amer. (unpledged), 539.

Minnesota Vote Since 1960

2020: Biden, D, 1,717,077; Trump, R, 1,484,065; Jorgensen, LB, 34,976; Hawkins, Green, 10,033; West, Ind., 7,940; Pierce, Ind., 5,651; De La Fuente, Alliance, 5,611; La Riva, Socialism/Liberation, 1,210; Kennedy, Soc. Workers, 643.

2016: Clinton, D, 1,367,716; Trump, R, 1,322,951; Johnson, LB, 112,972; McMullin, Ind., 53,076; Stein, Green, 36,985; Vacek, Legal Marijuana, 11,291; Castle, Const., 9,456; Kennedy, Soc. Workers, 1,672; De La Fuente, Amer. Delta, 1,431.

2012: Obama, D, 1,546,167; Romney, R, 1,320,225; Johnson, LB, 35,098; Stein, Green, 13,023; Goode, Const., 3,722; Carlson, Grassroots, 3,149; Anderson, Justice, 1,996; Morstad, Constitutional, 1,092; Harris, Soc. Workers, 1,051; Lindsay, Socialism/Liberation, 397.

2008: Obama, D, 1,573,354; McCain, R, 1,275,409; Nader, Ind., 30,152; Barr, LB, 9,174; Baldwin, Const., 6,787; McKinney, Green, 5,174; Calero, Soc. Workers, 790.

2004: Kerry, D, 1,445,014; Bush, R, 1,346,695; Nader, Better Life, 18,683; Badnarik, LB, 4,639; Cobb, Green, 4,408; Peroutka, Const., 3,074; Harens, other, 2,387; Van Auken, Soc. Equal., 539; Calero, Soc. Workers, 416.

2000: Gore, D, 1,168,266; Bush, R, 1,109,659; Nader, Green, 126,696; Buchanan, RF MN, 22,166; Browne, LB, 5,282; Phillips, Const., 3,272; Hagelin, RF, 2,294; Harris, Soc. Workers, 1,022.

1996: Clinton, D, 1,120,438; Dole, R, 766,476; Perot, RF, 257,704; Nader, Green, 24,908; Browne, LB, 8,271; Peron, Grass Roots, 4,898; Phillips, U.S. Taxpayers, 3,416; Hagelin, Natural Law, 1,808; Birrenbach, Ind. Grass Roots, 787; Harris, Soc. Workers, 684; White, Soc. Equality, 347.

1992: Clinton, D, 1,020,997; Bush, R, 747,841; Perot, Ind., 562,506; Marrou, LB, 3,373; Gritz, Populist/America First, 3,363; Hagelin, Natural Law, 1,406.

1988: Dukakis, D, 1,109,471; Bush, R, 962,337; McCarthy, MN Prog., 5,403; Paul, LB, 5,109.

1984: Mondale, D, 1,036,364; Reagan, R, 1,032,603; Bergland, LB, 2,996.

1980: Carter, D, 954,173; Reagan, R, 873,268; Anderson, Ind., 174,997; Clark, LB, 31,593; Commoner, Citizens, 8,406; Hall, Comm., 1,117; DeBerry, Soc. Workers, 711; Griswold, Workers World, 698; McReynolds, Soc., 536; write-in, 281.

1976: Carter, D, 1,070,440; Ford, R, 819,395; McCarthy, Ind., 35,490; Anderson, Amer., 13,592; Camejo, Soc. Workers, 4,149; MacBride, LB, 3,529; Hall, Comm., 1,092.

1972: Nixon, R, 898,269; McGovern, D, 802,346; Schmitz, Amer., 31,407; Fisher, Soc. Labor, 4,261; Spock, People's, 2,805; Jenness, Soc. Workers, 940; Hall, Comm., 662; scattered, 962.

1968: Humphrey, D, 857,738; Nixon, R, 658,643; Wallace, 3rd party, 68,931; Cleaver, Peace/Freedom, 935; Halstead, Soc. Workers, 808; McCarthy, write-in, 585; Mitchell, Comm., 415; Blomen, Industrial Govt., 285; scattered, 2,613.

1964: Johnson, D, 991,117; Goldwater, R, 559,624; Hass, Industrial Govt., 2,544; DeBerry, Soc. Workers, 1,177.

1960: Kennedy, D, 779,933; Nixon, R, 757,915; Dobbs, Soc. Workers, 3,077; Hass, Industrial Govt., 962.

Mississippi Vote Since 1960

2020: Trump, R, 756,764; Biden, D, 539,398; Jorgensen, LB, 8,026; West, Ind., 3,657; Hawkins, Green, 1,498; Collins, Ind., 1,317; Blankenship, Amer. Const., 1,279; Carroll, Amer. Solidarity, 1,161; Pierce, Ind., 659.

2016: Trump, R, 700,714; Clinton, D, 485,131; Johnson, LB, 14,435; Castle, Const., 3,987; Stein, Green, 3,731; Hedges, Prohib., 715; De La Fuente, Amer. Delta, 644.

2012: Romney, R, 710,746; Obama, D, 562,949; Johnson, LB, 6,676; Goode, Const., 2,609; Stein, Green, 1,588; Washer, RF, 1,016.

2008: McCain, R, 724,597; Obama, D, 554,662; Nader, Ind., 4,011; Baldwin, Const., 2,551; Barr, LB, 2,529; McKinney, Green, 1,034; Weill, RF, 481.

2004: Bush, R, 684,981; Kerry, D, 458,094; Nader, RF, 3,177; Badnarik, LB, 1,793; Peroutka, Const., 1,759; Harris, Ind., 1,268; Cobb, Green, 1,073.

2000: Bush, R, 572,844; Gore, D, 404,614; Nader, Ind., 8,122; Phillips, Const., 3,267; Buchanan, RF, 2,265; Browne, LB, 2,009; Harris, Ind., 613; Hagelin, Natural Law, 450.

1996: Dole, R, 439,838; Clinton, D, 394,022; Perot, RF, 52,222; Browne, LB, 2,809; Phillips, U.S. Taxpayers, 2,314; Hagelin, Natural Law, 1,447; Collins, Ind., 1,205.

1992: Bush, R, 487,793; Clinton, D, 400,258; Perot, Ind., 85,626; Fulani, New Alliance, 2,625; Marrou, LB, 2,154; Phillips, U.S. Taxpayers, 1,652; Hagelin, Natural Law, 1,140.

1988: Bush, R, 557,890; Dukakis, D, 363,921; Duke, Ind., 4,232; Paul, LB, 3,329.

1984: Reagan, R, 582,377; Mondale, D, 352,192; Bergland, LB, 2,336.

1980: Reagan, R, 441,089; Carter, D, 429,281; Anderson, Ind., 12,036; Clark, LB, 5,465; Griswold, Workers World, 2,402; Pulley, Soc. Workers, 2,347.

1976: Carter, D, 381,309; Ford, R, 366,846; Anderson, Amer., 6,678; McCarthy, Ind., 4,074; Maddox, Ind., 4,049; Camejo, Soc. Workers, 2,805; MacBride, LB, 2,609.

1972: Nixon, R, 505,125; McGovern, D, 126,782; Schmitz, Amer., 11,598; Jenness, Soc. Workers, 2,458.

1968: Wallace, 3rd party, 415,349; Humphrey, D, 150,644; Nixon, R, 88,516.

1964: Goldwater, R, 356,528; Johnson, D, 52,618.

1960: D. (electors unpledged), 116,248; Kennedy, D, 108,362; Nixon, R, 73,561. Mississippi's victorious slate of 8 unpledged Dem. electors cast their votes for Sen. Harry F. Byrd (D, VA).

Missouri Vote Since 1960

2020: Trump, R, 1,718,736; Biden, D, 1,253,014; Jorgensen, LB, 41,205; Hawkins, Green, 8,283; Blankenship, Const., 3,919.

2016: Trump, R, 1,594,511; Clinton, D, 1,071,068; Johnson, LB, 97,359; Stein, Green, 25,419; Castle, Const., 13,092; McMullin, Ind., 7,071.

2012: Romney, R, 1,482,440; Obama, D, 1,223,796; Johnson, LB, 43,151; Goode, Const., 7,936.

2008: McCain, R, 1,445,814; Obama, D, 1,441,911; Nader, Ind., 17,813; Barr, LB, 11,386; Baldwin, Const., 8,201.

2004: Bush, R, 1,455,713; Kerry, D, 1,259,171; Badnarik, LB, 9,831; Peroutka, Const., 5,355.

2000: Bush, R, 1,189,924; Gore, D, 1,111,138; Nader, Green, 38,515; Buchanan, RF, 9,818; Browne, LB, 7,436; Phillips, Const., 1,957; Hagelin, Natural Law, 1,104.

1996: Clinton, D, 1,025,935; Dole, R, 890,016; Perot, RF, 217,188; Phillips, U.S. Taxpayers, 11,521; Browne, LB, 10,522; Hagelin, Natural Law, 2,287.

1992: Clinton, D, 1,053,873; Bush, R, 811,159; Perot, Ind., 518,741; Marrou, LB, 7,497.

1988: Bush, R, 1,084,953; Dukakis, D, 1,001,619; Fulani, New Alliance, 6,656; Paul, write-in, 434.

1984: Reagan, R, 1,274,188; Mondale, D, 848,583.

1980: Reagan, R, 1,074,181; Carter, D, 931,182; Anderson, Ind., 77,920; Clark, LB, 14,422; DeBerry, Soc. Workers, 1,515; Commoner, Citizens, 573; write-in, 31.

1976: Carter, D, 999,163; Ford, R, 928,808; McCarthy, Ind., 24,329.

1972: Nixon, R, 1,154,058; McGovern, D, 698,531.

1968: Nixon, R, 811,932; Humphrey, D, 791,444; Wallace, 3rd party, 206,126.

1964: Johnson, D, 1,164,344; Goldwater, R, 653,535.

1960: Kennedy, D, 972,201; Nixon, R, 962,221.

Montana Vote Since 1960

2020: Trump, R, 343,602; Biden, D, 244,786; Jorgensen, LB, 15,252.

2016: Trump, R, 279,240; Clinton, D, 177,709; Johnson, LB, 28,037; Stein, Green, 7,970; McMullin, Ind., 2,297; De La Fuente, Amer. Delta, 1,570.

2012: Romney, R, 267,928; Obama, D, 201,839; Johnson, LB, 14,165.

2008: McCain, R, 242,763; Obama, D, 231,667; Paul, Const., 10,638; Nader, Ind., 3,686; Barr, LB, 1,355.

2004: Bush, R, 266,063; Kerry, D, 173,710; Nader, Ind., 6,168; Peroutka, Const., 1,764; Badnarik, LB, 1,733; Cobb, Green, 996.

2000: Bush, R, 240,178; Gore, D, 137,126; Nader, Green, 24,437; Buchanan, RF, 5,697; Browne, LB, 1,718; Phillips, Const., 1,155; Hagelin, Natural Law, 675.

1996: Dole, R, 179,652; Clinton, D, 167,922; Perot, RF, 55,229; Browne, LB, 2,526; Hagelin, Natural Law, 1,754.

1992: Clinton, D, 154,507; Bush, R, 144,207; Perot, Ind., 107,225; Gritz, Populist/America First, 3,658.

1988: Bush, R, 190,412; Dukakis, D, 168,936; Paul, LB, 5,047; Fulani, New Alliance, 1,279.

1984: Reagan, R, 232,450; Mondale, D, 146,742; Bergland, LB, 5,185.

1980: Reagan, R, 206,814; Carter, D, 118,032; Anderson, Ind., 29,281; Clark, LB, 9,825.

1976: Ford, R, 173,703; Carter, D, 149,259; Anderson, Amer., 5,772.

1972: Nixon, R, 183,976; McGovern, D, 120,197; Schmitz, Amer., 13,430.

1968: Nixon, R, 138,835; Humphrey, D, 114,117; Wallace, 3rd party, 20,015; Munn, Prohib., 510; Caton, New RF, 470; Halstead, Soc. Workers, 457.

1964: Johnson, D, 164,246; Goldwater, R, 113,032; Kasper, Natl. States' Rights, 519; Munn, Prohib., 499; DeBerry, Soc. Workers, 332.

1960: Nixon, R, 141,841; Kennedy, D, 134,891; Decker, Prohib., 456; Dobbs, Soc. Workers, 391.

Nebraska Vote Since 1960

2020: Trump, R, 556,846; Biden, D, 374,583; Jorgensen, LB, 20,283.

2016: Trump, R, 495,961; Clinton, D, 284,494; Johnson, LB, 38,946; Stein, petitioning cand., 8,775.

2012: Romney, R, 475,064; Obama, D, 302,081; Johnson, LB, 11,109; Terry, petitioning cand., 2,408.

2008: McCain, R, 452,979; Obama, D, 333,319; Nader, petitioning cand., 5,406; Baldwin, Nebraska, 2,972; Barr, LB, 2,740; McKinney, Green, 1,028.

2004: Bush, R, 512,814; Kerry, D, 254,328; Nader, petitioning cand., 5,698; Badnarik, LB, 2,041; Peroutka, Nebraska, 1,314; Cobb, Green, 978; Calero, petitioning cand., 82.

2000: Bush, R, 433,862; Gore, D, 231,780; Nader, Green, 24,540; Buchanan, Ind., 3,646; Browne, LB, 2,245; Hagelin, Natural Law, 478; Phillips, Ind., 468.

1996: Dole, R, 363,467; Clinton, D, 236,761; Perot, RF, 71,278; Browne, LB, 2,792; Phillips, Ind., 1,928; Hagelin, Natural Law, 1,189.

1992: Bush, R, 343,678; Clinton, D, 216,864; Perot, Ind., 174,104; Marrou, LB, 1,340.

1988: Bush, R, 397,956; Dukakis, D, 259,235; Paul, LB, 2,534; Fulani, New Alliance, 1,740.

1984: Reagan, R, 459,135; Mondale, D, 187,475; Bergland, LB, 2,075.

1980: Reagan, R, 419,214; Carter, D, 166,424; Anderson, Ind., 44,854; Clark, LB, 9,041.

1976: Ford, R, 359,219; Carter, D, 233,287; McCarthy, Ind., 9,383; Maddox, Amer. Ind., 3,378; MacBride, LB, 1,476.

1972: Nixon, R, 406,298; McGovern, D, 169,991; scattered, 817.

1968: Nixon, R, 321,163; Humphrey, D, 170,784; Wallace, 3rd party, 44,904.

1964: Johnson, D, 307,307; Goldwater, R, 276,847.

1960: Nixon, R, 380,553; Kennedy, D, 232,542.

Nevada Vote Since 1960

2020: Biden, D, 703,486; Trump, R, 669,890; Jorgensen, LB, 14,783; None of These Candidates, 14,079; Blankenship, Ind. Amer., 3,138.

2016: Clinton, D, 539,260; Trump, R, 512,058; Johnson, LB, 37,384; None of These Candidates, 28,863; Castle, Ind. Amer., 5,268; De La Fuente, unaff., 2,552.

2012: Obama, D, 531,373; Romney, R, 463,567; Johnson, LB, 10,968; None of These Candidates, 5,770; Goode, Ind. Amer., 3,240.

2008: Obama, D, 533,736; McCain, R, 412,827; None of These Candidates, 6,267; Nader, Ind., 6,150; Barr, LB, 4,263; Baldwin, Const., 3,194; McKinney, Green, 1,411.

2004: Bush, R, 418,690; Kerry, D, 397,190; Nader, Ind., 4,838; None of These Candidates, 3,688; Badnarik, LB, 3,176; Peroutka, Ind. Amer., 1,152; Cobb, Green, 853.

2000: Bush, R, 301,575; Gore, D, 279,978; Nader, Green, 15,008; Buchanan, Citizens First, 4,747; None of These Candidates, 3,315; Browne, LB, 3,311; Phillips, Ind. Amer., 621; Hagelin, Natural Law, 415.

1996: Clinton, D, 203,974; Dole, R, 199,244; Perot, RF, 43,986; None of These Candidates, 5,608; Nader, Green, 4,730; Browne, LB, 4,460; Phillips, Ind. Amer., 1,732; Hagelin, Natural Law, 545.

1992: Clinton, D, 189,148; Bush, R, 175,828; Perot, Ind., 132,580; Gritz, Populist/America First, 2,892; Marrou, LB, 1,835.

1988: Bush, R, 206,040; Dukakis, D, 132,738; Paul, LB, 3,520; Fulani, New Alliance, 835.

1984: Reagan, R, 188,770; Mondale, D, 91,655; Bergland, LB, 2,292.

1980: Reagan, R, 155,017; Carter, D, 66,666; Anderson, Ind., 17,651; Clark, LB, 4,358.

1976: Ford, R, 101,273; Carter, D, 92,479; MacBride, LB, 1,519; Maddox, Amer. Ind., 1,497; scattered, 5,108.

1972: Nixon, R, 115,750; McGovern, D, 66,016.

1968: Nixon, R, 73,188; Humphrey, D, 60,598; Wallace, 3rd party, 20,432.

1964: Johnson, D, 79,339; Goldwater, R, 56,094.

1960: Kennedy, D, 54,880; Nixon, R, 52,387.

New Hampshire Vote Since 1960

2020: Biden, D, 424,937; Trump, R, 365,660; Jorgensen, LB, 13,236.

2016: Clinton, D, 348,526; Trump, R, 345,790; Johnson, LB, 30,777; Stein, Green, 6,496; De La Fuente, Amer. Delta, 678.

2012: Obama, D, 369,561; Romney, R, 329,918; Johnson, LB, 8,212; Goode, Const., 708.

2008: Obama, D, 384,826; McCain, R, 316,534; Nader, Ind., 3,503; Barr, LB, 2,217; Phillies, LB, 531.

2004: Kerry, D, 340,511; Bush, R, 331,237; Nader, Ind., 4,479.

2000: Bush, R, 273,559; Gore, D, 266,348; Nader, Green, 22,198; Browne, LB, 2,757; Buchanan, Independence, 2,615; Phillips, Const., 328.

1996: Clinton, D, 246,166; Dole, R, 196,486; Perot, RF, 48,387; Browne, LB, 4,214; Phillips, Taxpayers, 1,344.

1992: Clinton, D, 209,040; Bush, R, 202,484; Perot, Ind., 121,337; Marrou, LB, 3,548.

1988: Bush, R, 281,537; Dukakis, D, 163,696; Paul, LB, 4,502; Fulani, New Alliance, 790.

1984: Reagan, R, 267,051; Mondale, D, 120,377; Bergland, LB, 735.

1980: Reagan, R, 221,705; Carter, D, 108,864; Anderson, Ind., 49,693; Clark, LB, 2,067; Commoner, Citizens, 1,325; Hall, Comm., 129; Griswold, Workers World, 76; DeBerry, Soc. Workers, 72; scattered, 68.

1976: Ford, R, 185,935; Carter, D, 147,645; McCarthy, Ind., 4,095; MacBride, LB, 936; Reagan, write-in, 388; LaRouche, U.S. Labor, 186; Camejo, Soc. Workers, 161; Levin, Soc. Labor, 66; scattered, 215.

1972: Nixon, R, 213,724; McGovern, D, 116,435; Schmitz, Amer., 3,386; Jenness, Soc. Workers, 368; scattered, 142.

1968: Nixon, R, 154,903; Humphrey, D, 130,589; Wallace, 3rd party, 11,173; New Party, 421; Halstead, Soc. Workers, 104.

1964: Johnson, D, 182,065; Goldwater, R, 104,029.

1960: Nixon, R, 157,989; Kennedy, D, 137,772.

New Jersey Vote Since 1960

2020: Biden, D, 2,608,400; Trump, R, 1,883,313; Jorgensen, LB, 31,677; Hawkins, Green, 14,202; Hammons, Unity, 3,255; Blankenship, Const., 2,954; La Riva, Socialism/Liberation, 2,928; De La Fuente, Alliance, 2,728.

2016: Clinton, D, 2,148,278; Trump, R, 1,601,933; Johnson, LB, 72,477; Stein, Green, 37,772; Castle, Const., 6,161; Kennedy, Soc. Workers, 2,156; De La Fuente, Amer. Delta, 1,838; Moorehead, Workers World, 1,749; La Riva, Socialism/Liberation, 1,682.

2012: Obama, D, 2,125,101; Romney, R, 1,477,568; Johnson, LB, 21,045; Stein, Green, 9,888; Goode, Const., 2,064; Anderson, Justice, 1,724; Boss, Ind., 1,007; Harris, Soc. Workers, 710; Miller, A3P, 664; Lindsay, Socialism/Liberation, 521.

2008: Obama, D, 2,215,422; McCain, R, 1,613,207; Nader, Ind., 21,298; Barr, Ind., 8,441; Baldwin, Ind., 3,956; McKinney, Ind., 3,636; Moore, Ind., 699; Boss, Ind., 639; Calero, Ind., 523; La Riva, Ind., 416.

2004: Kerry, D, 1,911,430; Bush, R, 1,670,003; Nader, Ind., 19,418; Badnarik, Ind., 4,514; Peroutka, Ind., 2,750; Cobb, Ind., 1,807; Brown, Ind., 664; Van Auken, Ind., 575; Calero, Ind., 530.

2000: Gore, D, 1,788,850; Bush, R, 1,284,173; Nader, Ind., 94,554; Buchanan, Ind., 6,989; Browne, Ind., 6,312; Hagelin, Ind., 2,215; McReynolds, Ind., 1,880; Phillips, Ind., 1,409; Harris, Ind., 844.

1996: Clinton, D, 1,652,361; Dole, R, 1,103,099; Perot, RF, 262,134; Nader, Green, 32,465; Browne, LB, 14,763; Hagelin, Natural Law, 3,887; Phillips, U.S. Taxpayers, 3,440; Harris, Soc. Workers, 1,837; Moorehead, Workers World, 1,337; White, Soc. Equality, 537.

1992: Clinton, D, 1,436,206; Bush, R, 1,356,865; Perot, Ind., 521,829; Marrou, LB, 6,822; Fulani, New Alliance, 3,513; Phillips, U.S. Taxpayers, 2,670; LaRouche, Ind., 2,095; Warren, Soc. Workers, 2,011; Daniels, Ind., 1,996; Gritz, Populist/America First, 1,867; Hagelin, Natural Law, 1,353.

1988: Bush, R, 1,740,604; Dukakis, D, 1,317,541; Lewin, Peace/Freedom, 9,953; Paul, LB, 8,421.

1984: Reagan, R, 1,933,630; Mondale, D, 1,261,323; Bergland, LB, 6,416.

1980: Reagan, R, 1,546,557; Carter, D, 1,147,364; Anderson, Ind., 234,632; Clark, LB, 20,652; Commoner, Citizens, 8,203; McCormack, Right to Life, 3,927; Lynen, Middle Class, 3,694; Hall, Comm., 2,555; Pulley, Soc. Workers, 2,198; McReynolds, Soc., 1,973; Gahres, Down With Lawyers, 1,718; Griswold, Workers World, 1,288; Wendelken, Ind., 923.

1976: Ford, R, 1,509,688; Carter, D, 1,444,653; McCarthy, Ind., 32,717; MacBride, LB, 9,449; Maddox, Amer., 7,716; Levin, Soc. Labor, 3,686; Hall, Comm., 1,662; LaRouche, U.S. Labor, 1,650; Camejo, Soc. Workers, 1,184; Wright, People's, 1,044; Bubar, Prohib., 554; Zeidler, Soc., 469.

1972: Nixon, R, 1,845,502; McGovern, D, 1,102,211; Schmitz, Amer., 34,378; Spock, People's, 5,355; Fisher, Soc. Labor, 4,544; Jenness, Soc. Workers, 2,233; Mahalchik, America First, 1,743; Hall, Comm., 1,263.

1968: Nixon, R, 1,325,467; Humphrey, D, 1,264,206; Wallace, 3rd party, 262,187; Halstead, Soc. Workers, 8,667; Gregory, Peace/Freedom, 8,084; Blomen, Soc. Labor, 6,784.

1964: Johnson, D, 1,867,671; Goldwater, R, 963,843; DeBerry, Soc. Workers, 8,181; Hass, Soc. Labor, 7,075.

1960: Kennedy, D, 1,385,415; Nixon, R, 1,363,324; Dobbs, Soc. Workers, 11,402; Lee, Conservative, 8,708; Hass, Soc. Labor, 4,262.

New Mexico Vote Since 1960

2020: Biden, D, 501,614; Trump, R, 401,894; Jorgensen, LB, 12,585; Hawkins, Green, 4,426; Tittle, Const., 1,806; La Riva, Socialism/Liberation, 1,640.

2016: Clinton, D, 385,234; Trump, R, 319,667; Johnson, LB, 74,541; Stein, Green, 9,879; McMullin, Better for Amer., 5,825; Castle, Const., 1,514; La Riva, Socialism/Liberation, 1,184; De La Fuente, Amer. Delta, 475.

2012: Obama, D, 415,335; Romney, R, 335,788; Johnson, LB, 27,788; Stein, Green, 2,691; Anderson, Ind., 1,174; Goode, Const., 982.

2008: Obama, D, 472,422; McCain, R, 346,832; Nader, Ind., 5,327; Barr, LB, 2,428; Baldwin, Const., 1,597; McKinney, Green, 1,552.

2004: Bush, R, 376,930; Kerry, D, 370,942; Nader, Ind., 4,053; Badnarik, LB, 2,382; Cobb, Green, 1,226; Peroutka, Const., 771.

2000: Gore, D, 286,783; Bush, R, 286,417; Nader, Green, 21,251; Browne, LB, 2,058; Buchanan, RF, 1,392; Hagelin, Natural Law, 361; Phillips, Const., 343.

1996: Clinton, D, 273,495; Dole, R, 232,751; Perot, RF, 32,257; Nader, Green, 13,218; Browne, LB, 2,996; Phillips, Taxpayers, 713; Hagelin, Natural Law, 644.

1992: Clinton, D, 261,617; Bush, R, 212,824; Perot, Ind., 91,895; Marrou, LB, 1,615.

1988: Bush, R, 270,341; Dukakis, D, 244,497; Paul, LB, 3,268; Fulani, New Alliance, 2,237.

1984: Reagan, R, 307,101; Mondale, D, 201,769; Bergland, LB, 4,459.

1980: Reagan, R, 250,779; Carter, D, 167,826; Anderson, Ind., 29,459; Clark, LB, 4,365; Commoner, Citizens, 2,202; Bubar, Statesman, 1,281; Pulley, Soc. Workers, 325.

1976: Ford, R, 211,419; Carter, D, 201,148; Camejo, Soc. Workers, 2,462; MacBride, LB, 1,110; Zeidler, Soc., 240; Bubar, Prohib., 211.

1972: Nixon, R, 235,606; McGovern, D, 141,084; Schmitz, Amer., 8,767; Jenness, Soc. Workers, 474.

1968: Nixon, R, 169,692; Humphrey, D, 130,081; Wallace, 3rd party, 25,737; Chavez, 1,519; Halstead, Soc. Workers, 252.

1964: Johnson, D, 194,017; Goldwater, R, 131,838; Hass, Soc. Labor, 1,217; Munn, Prohib., 543.

1960: Kennedy, D, 156,027; Nixon, R, 153,733; Decker, Prohib., 777; Hass, Soc. Labor, 570.

New York Vote Since 1960

2020: Biden, D, 5,244,886; Trump, R, 3,251,997; Jorgensen, LB, 60,383; Hawkins, Green, 32,832; Pierce, Ind., 22,656.

2016: Clinton, D, 4,556,118; Trump, R, 2,819,533; Johnson, LB, 176,598; Stein, Green, 107,935; McMullin, Ind., 10,397.

2012: Obama, D, 4,485,741; Romney, R, 2,490,431; Johnson, LB, 47,256; Stein, Green, 39,982; Goode, Const., 6,274; Lindsay, Socialism/Liberation, 2,050.

2008: Obama, D, 4,804,945; McCain, R, 2,752,771; Nader, Populist, 41,249; Barr, LB, 19,596; McKinney, Green, 12,801; Calero, Soc. Workers, 3,615; La Riva, Socialism/Liberation, 1,639.

2004: Kerry, D, 4,314,280; Bush, R, 2,962,567; Nader, Ind., 99,873; Badnarik, LB, 11,607; Calero, Soc. Workers, 2,405.

2000: Gore, D, 4,112,965; Bush, R, 2,405,570; Nader, Green, 244,360; Buchanan, RF, 31,554; Hagelin, Independence, 24,369; Browne, LB, 7,664; Harris, Soc. Workers, 1,790; Phillips, Const., 1,503.

1996: Clinton, D, 3,756,177; Dole, R, 1,933,492; Perot, RF, 503,458; Nader, Green, 75,956; Phillips, Right to Life, 23,580; Browne, LB, 12,220; Hagelin, Natural Law, 5,011; Moorehead, Workers World, 3,473; Harris, Soc. Workers, 2,762.

1992: Clinton, D, 3,444,450; Bush, R, 2,346,649; Perot, Ind., 1,090,721; Warren, Soc. Workers, 15,472; Marrou, LB, 13,451; Fulani, New Alliance, 11,318; Hagelin, Natural Law, 4,420.

1988: Dukakis, D, 3,347,882; Bush, R, 3,081,871; Marra, Right to Life, 20,497; Fulani, New Alliance, 15,845.

1984: Reagan, R, 3,664,763; Mondale, D, 3,119,609; Bergland, LB, 11,949.

1980: Reagan, R, 2,893,831; Carter, D, 2,728,372; Anderson, Liberal, 467,801; Clark, LB, 52,648; McCormack, Right to Life, 24,159; Commoner, Citizens, 23,186; Hall, Comm., 7,414; DeBerry, Soc. Workers, 2,068; Griswold, Workers World, 1,416; scattered, 1,064.

1976: Carter, D, 3,389,558; Ford, R, 3,100,791; MacBride, LB, 12,197; Hall, Comm., 10,270; Camejo, Soc. Workers, 6,996; LaRouche, U.S. Labor, 5,413; blank, void, and scattered, 143,037.

1972: Nixon, R, 3,824,642; McGovern, D, 2,767,956 and Liberal, 183,128 (total, 2,951,084); Reed, Soc. Workers, 7,797; Fisher, Soc. Labor, 4,530; Hall, Comm., 5,641; blank, void, and scattered, 161,641.

1968: Humphrey, D, 3,378,470; Nixon, R, 3,007,932; Wallace, 3rd party, 358,864; Gregory, Peace/Freedom, 24,517; Halstead, Soc. Workers, 11,851; Blomen, Soc. Labor, 8,432; blank, void, and scattered, 171,624.

1964: Johnson, D, 4,913,156; Goldwater, R, 2,243,559; Hass, Soc. Labor, 6,085; DeBerry, Soc. Workers, 3,215; scattered, 188; blank and void, 151,383.

1960: Kennedy, D, 3,423,909 and Liberal, 406,176 (total, 3,830,085); Nixon, R, 3,446,419; Dobbs, Soc. Workers, 14,319; scattered, 256; blank and void, 88,896.

North Carolina Vote Since 1960

2020: Trump, R, 2,758,773; Biden, D, 2,684,292; Jorgensen, LB, 48,678; Hawkins, Green, 12,195; Blankenship, Const., 7,549.

2016: Trump, R, 2,362,631; Clinton, D, 2,189,316; Johnson, LB, 130,126; Stein, Ind., 12,105.

2012: Romney, R, 2,270,395; Obama, D, 2,178,391; Johnson, LB, 44,515.

2008: Obama, D, 2,142,651; McCain, R, 2,128,474; Barr, LB, 25,722.

2004: Bush, R, 1,961,166; Kerry, D, 1,525,849; Badnarik, LB, 11,731.

2000: Bush, R, 1,631,163; Gore, D, 1,257,692; Browne, LB, 13,891; Buchanan, RF, 8,874.

1996: Dole, R, 1,225,938; Clinton, D, 1,107,849; Perot, RF, 168,059; Browne, LB, 8,740; Hagelin, Natural Law, 2,771.

1992: Bush, R, 1,134,661; Clinton, D, 1,114,042; Perot, Ind., 357,864; Marrou, LB, 5,171.

1988: Bush, R, 1,237,258; Dukakis, D, 890,167; Fulani, New Alliance, 5,682; Paul, write-in, 1,263.

1984: Reagan, R, 1,346,481; Mondale, D, 824,287; Bergland, LB, 3,794.

1980: Reagan, R, 915,018; Carter, D, 875,635; Anderson, Ind., 52,800; Clark, LB, 9,677; Commoner, Citizens, 2,287; DeBerry, Soc. Workers, 416.

1976: Carter, D, 927,365; Ford, R, 741,960; Anderson, Amer., 5,607; MacBride, LB, 2,219; LaRouche, U.S. Labor, 755.

1972: Nixon, R, 1,054,889; McGovern, D, 438,705; Schmitz, Amer., 25,018.

1968: Nixon, R, 627,192; Wallace, 3rd party, 496,188; Humphrey, D, 464,113.

1964: Johnson, D, 800,139; Goldwater, R, 624,844.

1960: Kennedy, D, 713,136; Nixon, R, 655,420.

North Dakota Vote Since 1960

2020: Trump, R, 235,751; Biden, D, 115,042; Jorgensen, LB, 9,371.

2016: Trump, R, 216,794; Clinton, D, 93,758; Johnson, LB, 21,434; Stein, Green, 3,780; Castle, Const., 1,833; De La Fuente, Amer. Delta, 364.

2012: Romney, R, 188,163; Obama, D, 124,827; Johnson, LB, 5,231; Stein, Green, 1,361; Goode, Const., 1,185.

2008: McCain, R, 168,601; Obama, D, 141,278; Nader, Ind., 4,189; Barr, LB, 1,354; Baldwin, Const., 1,199.

2004: Bush, R, 196,651; Kerry, D, 111,052; Nader, Ind., 3,756; Badnarik, LB, 851; Peroutka, Const., 514.

2000: Bush, R, 174,852; Gore, D, 95,284; Nader, Ind., 9,486; Buchanan, RF, 7,288; Browne, Ind., 660; Phillips, Const., 373; Hagelin, Ind., 313.

1996: Dole, R, 125,050; Clinton, D, 106,905; Perot, RF, 32,515; Browne, LB, 847; Phillips, Ind., 745; Hagelin, Natural Law, 349.

1992: Bush, R, 136,244; Clinton, D, 99,168; Perot, Ind., 71,084.

1988: Bush, R, 166,559; Dukakis, D, 127,739; Paul, LB, 1,315; LaRouche, Natl. Econ. Recovery, 905.

1984: Reagan, R, 200,336; Mondale, D, 104,429; Bergland, LB, 703.

1980: Reagan, R, 193,695; Carter, D, 79,189; Anderson, Ind., 23,640; Clark, LB, 3,743; Commoner, LB, 429; McLain, Natl. People's League, 296; Greaves, Amer., 235; Hall, Comm., 93; DeBerry, Soc. Workers, 89; McReynolds, Soc., 82; Bubar, Statesman, 54.

1976: Ford, R, 153,470; Carter, D, 136,078; Anderson, Amer., 3,698; McCarthy, Ind., 2,952; Maddox, Amer. Ind., 269; MacBride, LB, 256; scattered, 371.

1972: Nixon, R, 174,109; McGovern, D, 100,384; Schmitz, Amer., 5,646; Jenness, Soc. Workers, 288; Hall, Comm., 87.

1968: Nixon, R, 138,669; Humphrey, D, 94,769; Wallace, 3rd party, 14,244; Halstead, Soc. Workers, 128; Munn, Prohib., 38; Troxell, Ind., 34.

1964: Johnson, D, 149,784; Goldwater, R, 108,207; DeBerry, Soc. Workers, 224; Munn, Prohib., 174.

1960: Nixon, R, 154,310; Kennedy, D, 123,963; Dobbs, Soc. Workers, 158.

Ohio Vote Since 1960

2020: Trump, R, 3,154,834; Biden, D, 2,679,165; Jorgensen, LB, 67,569; Hawkins, Ind., 18,812.

2016: Trump, R, 2,841,005; Clinton, D, 2,394,164; Johnson, LB, 174,498; Stein, Green, 46,271; Duncan, Ind., 24,235; McMullin, Ind., 12,574; Castle, Const., 1,887.

2012: Obama, D, 2,827,709; Romney, R, 2,661,437; Johnson, LB, 49,493; Stein, Green, 18,573; Duncan, Ind., 12,502; Goode, Const., 8,152; Alexander, Soc., 2,944.

2008: Obama, D, 2,940,044; McCain, R, 2,677,820; Nader, Ind., 42,337; Barr, LB, 19,917; Baldwin, Const., 12,565; McKinney, Green, 8,518; Duncan, Ind., 3,905; Moore, Soc., 2,735.

2004: Bush, R, 2,859,768; Kerry, D, 2,741,167; Badnarik, nonpartisan, 14,676; Peroutka, nonpartisan, 939.

2000: Bush, R, 2,351,209; Gore, D, 2,186,190; Nader, Ind., 117,857; Buchanan, Ind., 26,724; Browne, LB, 13,475; Hagelin, Natural Law, 6,169; Phillips, Ind., 3,823.

1996: Clinton, D, 2,148,222; Dole, R, 1,859,883; Perot, RF, 483,207; Browne, Ind., 12,851; Moorehead, Ind., 10,813; Hagelin, Natural Law, 9,120; Phillips, Ind., 7,361.

1992: Clinton, D, 1,984,942; Bush, R, 1,894,310; Perot, Ind., 1,036,426; Marrou, LB, 7,252; Fulani, New Alliance, 6,413; Gritz, Populist/America First, 4,699; Hagelin, Natural Law, 3,437; LaRouche, Ind., 2,446.

1988: Bush, R, 2,416,549; Dukakis, D, 1,939,629; Fulani, Ind., 12,017; Paul, Ind., 11,926.

1984: Reagan, R, 2,678,559; Mondale, D, 1,825,440; Bergland, LB, 5,886.

1980: Reagan, R, 2,206,545; Carter, D, 1,752,414; Anderson, Ind., 254,472; Clark, LB, 49,033; Commoner, Citizens, 8,564; Hall, Comm., 4,729; Congress, Ind., 4,029; Griswold, Workers World, 3,790; Bubar, Statesman, 27.

1976: Carter, D, 2,011,621; Ford, R, 2,000,505; McCarthy, Ind., 58,258; Maddox, Amer. Ind., 15,529; MacBride, LB, 8,961; Hall, Comm., 7,817; Camejo, Soc. Workers, 4,717; LaRouche, U.S. Labor, 4,335; scattered, 130.

1972: Nixon, R, 2,441,827; McGovern, D, 1,558,889; Schmitz, Amer., 80,067; Fisher, Soc. Labor, 7,107; Hall, Comm., 6,437; Wallace, Ind., 460.

1968: Nixon, R, 1,791,014; Humphrey, D, 1,700,586; Wallace, 3rd party, 467,495; Gregory, 372; Blomen, Soc. Labor, 120; Halstead, Soc. Workers, 69; Mitchell, Comm., 23; Munn, Prohib., 19.

1964: Johnson, D, 2,498,331; Goldwater, R, 1,470,865.

1960: Nixon, R, 2,217,611; Kennedy, D, 1,944,248.

Oklahoma Vote Since 1960

2020: Trump, R, 1,020,280; Biden, D, 503,890; Jorgensen, LB, 24,731; West, Ind., 5,597; Simmons, Ind., 3,654; Pierce, Ind., 2,547.

2016: Trump, R, 949,136; Clinton, D, 420,375; Johnson, LB, 83,481.

2012: Romney, R, 891,325; Obama, D, 443,547.

2008: McCain, R, 960,165; Obama, D, 502,496.

2004: Bush, R, 959,792; Kerry, D, 503,966.

2000: Bush, R, 744,337; Gore, D, 474,276; Buchanan, RF, 9,014; Browne, LB, 6,602.

1996: Dole, R, 582,315; Clinton, D, 488,105; Perot, RF, 130,788; Browne, LB, 5,505.

1992: Bush, R, 592,929; Clinton, D, 473,066; Perot, Ind., 319,878; Marrou, LB, 4,486.

1988: Bush, R, 678,367; Dukakis, D, 483,423; Paul, LB, 6,261; Fulani, New Alliance, 2,985.

1984: Reagan, R, 861,530; Mondale, D, 385,080; Bergland, LB, 9,066.

1980: Reagan, R, 695,570; Carter, D, 402,026; Anderson, Ind., 38,284; Clark, LB, 13,828.

1976: Ford, R, 545,708; Carter, D, 532,442; McCarthy, Ind., 14,101.

1972: Nixon, R, 759,025; McGovern, D, 247,147; Schmitz, Amer., 23,728.

1968: Nixon, R, 449,697; Humphrey, D, 301,658; Wallace, 3rd party, 191,731.

1964: Johnson, D, 519,834; Goldwater, R, 412,665.

1960: Nixon, R, 533,039; Kennedy, D, 370,111.

Oregon Vote Since 1960

2020: Biden, D, 1,340,383; Trump, R, 958,448; Jorgensen, LB, 41,582; Hawkins, Pacific Green, 11,831; Hunter, Progressive, 4,988.

2016: Clinton, D, 1,002,106; Trump, R, 782,403; Johnson, LB, 94,231; Stein, Pacific Green, 50,002.

2012: Obama, D, 970,488; Romney, R, 754,175; Johnson, LB, 24,089; Stein, Pacific Green, 19,427; Christensen, Const., 4,432; Anderson, OR Prog., 3,384.

2008: Obama, D, 1,037,291; McCain, R, 738,475; Nader, Peace Party of OR, 18,614; Baldwin, Const., 7,693; Barr, LB, 7,635; McKinney, Pacific Green, 4,543.

2004: Kerry, D, 943,163; Bush, R, 866,831; Badnarik, LB, 7,260; Cobb, Pacific Green, 5,315; Peroutka, Const., 5,257.

2000: Gore, D, 720,342; Bush, R, 713,577; Nader, Green, 77,357; Browne, LB, 7,447; Buchanan, Ind., 7,063; Hagelin, RF, 2,574; Phillips, Const., 2,189.

1996: Clinton, D, 649,641; Dole, R, 538,152; Perot, RF, 121,221; Nader, Pacific, 49,415; Browne, LB, 8,903; Phillips, Taxpayers, 3,379; Hagelin, Natural Law, 2,798; Hollis, Soc., 1,922.

1992: Clinton, D, 621,314; Bush, R, 475,757; Perot, Ind., 354,091; Marrou, LB, 4,277; Fulani, New Alliance, 3,030.

1988: Dukakis, D, 616,206; Bush, R, 560,126; Paul, LB, 14,811; Fulani, Ind., 6,487.

1984: Reagan, R, 658,700; Mondale, D, 536,479.

1980: Reagan, R, 571,044; Carter, D, 456,890; Anderson, Ind., 112,389; Clark, LB, 25,838; Commoner, Citizens, 13,642; scattered, 1,713.

1976: Ford, R, 492,120; Carter, D, 490,407; McCarthy, Ind., 40,207; write-in, 7,142.

1972: Nixon, R, 486,686; McGovern, D, 392,760; Schmitz, Amer., 46,211; write-in, 2,289.

1968: Nixon, R, 408,433; Humphrey, D, 358,866; Wallace, 3rd party, 49,683; write-ins: McCarthy, 1,496; N. Rockefeller, 69; others, 1,075.

1964: Johnson, D, 501,017; Goldwater, R, 282,779; write-in, 2,509.

1960: Nixon, R, 408,060; Kennedy, D, 367,402.

Pennsylvania Vote Since 1960

2020: Biden, D, 3,458,229; Trump, R, 3,377,674; Jorgensen, LB, 79,380.

2016: Trump, R, 2,970,733; Clinton, D, 2,926,441; Johnson, LB, 146,715; Stein, Green, 49,941; Castle, Const., 21,572.

2012: Obama, D, 2,990,274; Romney, R, 2,680,434; Johnson, LB, 49,991; Stein, Green, 21,341.

2008: Obama, D, 3,276,363; McCain, R, 2,655,885; Nader, Ind., 42,977; Barr, LB, 19,912.

2004: Kerry, D, 2,938,095; Bush, R, 2,793,847; Badnarik, LB, 21,185; Cobb, Green, 6,319; Peroutka, Const., 6,318.

2000: Gore, D, 2,485,967; Bush, R, 2,281,127; Nader, Green, 103,392; Buchanan, RF, 16,023; Phillips, Const., 14,428; Browne, LB, 11,248.

1996: Clinton, D, 2,215,819; Dole, R, 1,801,169; Perot, RF, 430,984; Browne, LB, 28,000; Phillips, Const., 19,552; Hagelin, Natural Law, 5,783.

1992: Clinton, D, 2,239,164; Bush, R, 1,791,841; Perot, Ind., 902,667; Marrou, LB, 21,477; Fulani, New Alliance, 4,661.

1988: Bush, R, 2,300,087; Dukakis, D, 2,194,944; McCarthy, Consumer, 19,158; Paul, LB, 12,051.

1984: Reagan, R, 2,584,323; Mondale, D, 2,228,131; Bergland, LB, 6,982.

1980: Reagan, R, 2,261,872; Carter, D, 1,937,540; Anderson, Ind., 292,921; Clark, LB, 33,263; DeBerry, Soc. Workers, 20,291; Commoner, Consumer, 10,430; Hall, Comm., 5,184.

1976: Carter, D, 2,328,677; Ford, R, 2,205,604; McCarthy, Ind., 50,584; Maddox, Const., 25,344; Camejo, Soc. Workers, 3,009; LaRouche, U.S. Labor, 2,744; Hall, Comm., 1,891; others, 2,934.

1972: Nixon, R, 2,714,521; McGovern, D, 1,796,951; Schmitz, Amer., 70,593; Jenness, Soc. Workers, 4,639; Hall, Comm., 2,686; others, 2,715.

1968: Humphrey, D, 2,259,405; Nixon, R, 2,090,017; Wallace, 3rd party, 378,582; Gregory, Peace/Freedom, 7,821; Blomen, Soc. Labor, 4,977; Halstead, Soc. Workers, 4,862; others, 2,264.

1964: Johnson, D, 3,130,954; Goldwater, R, 1,673,657; DeBerry, Soc. Workers, 10,456; Hass, Soc. Labor, 5,092; scattered, 2,531.

1960: Kennedy, D, 2,556,282; Nixon, R, 2,439,956; Hass, Soc. Labor, 7,185; Dobbs, Soc. Workers, 2,678; scattered, 440.

Rhode Island Vote Since 1960

2020: Biden, D, 307,486; Trump, R, 199,922; Jorgensen, LB, 5,053; De La Fuente, Alliance, 923; La Riva, Socialism/Liberation, 847; Carroll, Amer. Solidarity, 767.

2016: Clinton, D, 252,525; Trump, R, 180,543; Johnson, LB, 14,746; Stein, Green, 6,220; De La Fuente, Amer. Delta, 671.

2012: Obama, D, 279,677; Romney, R, 157,204; Johnson, LB, 4,388; Stein, Green, 2,421; Goode, Const., 430; Anderson, Justice, 416; Lindsay, Socialism/Liberation, 132.

2008: Obama, D, 296,571; McCain, R, 165,391; Nader, Ind., 4,829; Barr, LB, 1,382; McKinney, Green, 797; Baldwin, Const., 675; La Riva, Socialism/Liberation, 122.

2004: Kerry, D, 259,765; Bush, R, 169,046; Nader, RF, 4,651; Cobb, Green, 1,333; Badnarik, LB, 907; Peroutka, Const., 339; Parker, Workers World, 253.

2000: Gore, D, 249,508; Bush, R, 130,555; Nader, Ind., 25,052; Buchanan, RF, 2,273; Browne, Ind., 742; Hagelin, Ind., 271; Moorehead, Ind., 199; Phillips, Ind., 97; McReynolds, Ind., 52; Harris, Ind., 34.

1996: Clinton, D, 233,050; Dole, R, 104,683; Perot, RF, 43,723; Nader, Green, 6,040; Browne, LB, 1,109; Phillips, U.S. Taxpayers, 1,021; Hagelin, Natural Law, 435; Moorehead, Workers World, 186.

1992: Clinton, D, 213,299; Bush, R, 131,601; Perot, Ind., 105,045; Fulani, New Alliance, 1,878.

1988: Dukakis, D, 225,123; Bush, R, 177,761; Paul, LB, 825; Fulani, New Alliance, 280.

1984: Reagan, R, 212,080; Mondale, D, 197,106; Bergland, LB, 277.

1980: Carter, D, 198,342; Reagan, R, 154,793; Anderson, Ind., 59,819; Clark, LB, 2,458; Hall, Comm., 218; McReynolds, Soc., 170; DeBerry, Soc. Workers, 90; Griswold, Workers World, 77.

1976: Carter, D, 227,636; Ford, R, 181,249; MacBride, LB, 715; Camejo, Soc. Workers, 462; Hall, Comm., 334; Levin, Soc. Labor, 188.

1972: Nixon, R, 220,383; McGovern, D, 194,645; Jenness, Soc. Workers, 729.

1968: Humphrey, D, 246,518; Nixon, R, 122,359; Wallace, 3rd party, 15,678; Halstead, Soc. Workers, 383.

1964: Johnson, D, 315,463; Goldwater, R, 74,615.

1960: Kennedy, D, 258,032; Nixon, R, 147,502.

South Carolina Vote Since 1960

2020: Trump, R, 1,385,103; Biden, D, 1,091,541; Jorgensen, LB, 27,916; Hawkins, Green, 6,907; De La Fuente, Alliance, 1,862.

2016: Trump, R, 1,155,389; Clinton, D, 855,373; Johnson, LB, 49,204; McMullin, Ind., 21,016; Stein, Green, 13,034; Castle, Const., 5,765; Skewes, American, 3,246.

2012: Romney, R, 1,071,645; Obama, D, 865,941; Johnson, LB, 16,321; Stein, Green, 5,446; Goode, Const., 4,765.

2008: McCain, R, 1,034,896; Obama, D, 862,449; Barr, LB, 7,283; Baldwin, Const., 6,827; Nader, petitioning cand., 5,053; McKinney, Green, 4,461.

2004: Bush, R, 937,974; Kerry, D, 661,699; Nader, Ind., 5,520; Peroutka, Const., 5,317; Badnarik, LB, 3,608; Brown, United Citizens, 2,124; Cobb, Green, 1,488.

2000: Bush, R, 786,892; Gore, D, 566,039; Nader, United Citizens, 20,279; Browne, LB, 4,898; Buchanan, RF, 3,309; Phillips, Const., 1,682; Hagelin, Natural Law, 943.

1996: Dole, R, 573,458; Clinton, D, 506,283; Perot, RF/Patriot, 64,386; Browne, LB, 4,271; Phillips, U.S. Taxpayers, 2,043; Hagelin, Natural Law, 1,248.

1992: Bush, R, 577,507; Clinton, D, 479,514; Perot, Ind., 138,872; Marrou, LB, 2,719; Phillips, U.S. Taxpayers, 2,680; Fulani, New Alliance, 1,235.

1988: Bush, R, 606,443; Dukakis, D, 370,554; Paul, LB, 4,935; Fulani, United Citizens, 4,077.

1984: Reagan, R, 615,539; Mondale, D, 344,459; Bergland, LB, 4,359.

1980: Reagan, R, 439,277; Carter, D, 428,220; Anderson, Ind., 13,868; Clark, LB, 4,807; Rarick, Amer. Ind., 2,086.

1976: Carter, D, 450,807; Ford, R, 346,149; Anderson, Amer., 2,996; Maddox, Amer. Ind., 1,950; write-in, 681.

1972: Nixon, R, 477,044; McGovern, D, 184,559, and United Citizens, 2,265 (total, 186,824); Schmitz, Amer., 10,075; write-in, 17.

1968: Nixon, R, 254,062; Wallace, 3rd party, 215,430; Humphrey, D, 197,486.

1964: Goldwater, R, 309,048; Johnson, D, 215,700; write-ins: Wallace, 5; Nixon, 1; Powell, 1; Thurmond, 1.

1960: Kennedy, D, 198,129; Nixon, R, 188,558; write-in, 1.

South Dakota Vote Since 1960

2020: Trump, R, 261,043; Biden, D, 150,471; Jorgensen, LB, 11,095.

2016: Trump, R, 227,721; Clinton, D, 117,458; Johnson, LB, 20,850; Castle, Const., 4,064.

2012: Romney, R, 210,610; Obama, D, 145,039; Johnson, LB, 5,795; Goode, Const., 2,371.

2008: McCain, R, 203,054; Obama, D, 170,924; Nader, Ind., 4,267; Baldwin, Const., 1,895; Barr, Ind., 1,835.

2004: Bush, R, 232,584; Kerry, D, 149,244; Nader, Ind., 4,320; Peroutka, Const., 1,103; Badnarik, LB, 964.

2000: Bush, R, 190,700; Gore, D, 118,804; Buchanan, RF, 3,322; Phillips, Ind., 1,781; Browne, LB, 1,662.

1996: Dole, R, 150,543; Clinton, D, 139,333; Perot, RF, 31,250; Browne, LB, 1,472; Phillips, Taxpayers, 912; Hagelin, Natural Law, 316.

1992: Bush, R, 136,718; Clinton, D, 124,888; Perot, Ind., 73,295.

1988: Bush, R, 165,415; Dukakis, D, 145,560; Paul, LB, 1,060; Fulani, New Alliance, 730.

1984: Reagan, R, 200,267; Mondale, D, 116,113.

1980: Reagan, R, 198,343; Carter, D, 103,855; Anderson, Ind., 21,431; Clark, LB, 3,824; Pulley, Soc. Workers, 250.

1976: Ford, R, 151,505; Carter, D, 147,068; MacBride, LB, 1,619; Hall, Comm., 318; Camejo, Soc. Workers, 168.

1972: Nixon, R, 166,476; McGovern, D, 139,945; Jenness, Soc. Workers, 994.

1968: Nixon, R, 149,841; Humphrey, D, 118,023; Wallace, 3rd party, 13,400.

1964: Johnson, D, 163,010; Goldwater, R, 130,108.

1960: Nixon, R, 178,417; Kennedy, D, 128,070.

Tennessee Vote Since 1960

2020: Trump, R, 1,852,475; Biden, D, 1,143,711; Jorgensen, LB, 29,877; West, Ind., 10,279; Blankenship, Ind., 5,365; Hawkins, Ind., 4,545; Kennedy, Ind., 2,576; La Riva, Ind., 2,301; De La Fuente, Ind., 1,860.

2016: Trump, R, 1,522,925; Clinton, D, 870,695; Johnson, Ind., 70,397; Stein, Green, 15,993; McMullin, Ind., 11,991; Smith, Ind., 7,276; De La Fuente, Ind., 4,075; Kennedy, Ind., 2,877; Castle, Ind., 1,584.

2012: Romney, R, 1,462,330; Obama, D, 960,709; Johnson, Ind., 18,623; Stein, Green, 6,515; Goode, Const., 6,022; Anderson, Ind., 2,639, Miller, Ind., 1,739.

2008: McCain, R, 1,479,178; Obama, D, 1,087,437; Nader, Ind., 11,560; Barr, Ind., 8,547; Baldwin, Ind., 8,191; McKinney, Ind., 2,499; Moore, Ind., 1,326; Jay, Ind., 1,011.

2004: Bush, R, 1,384,375; Kerry, D, 1,036,477; Nader, Ind., 8,992; Badnarik, Ind., 4,866; Peroutka, Ind., 2,570.

2000: Bush, R, 1,061,949; Gore, D, 981,720; Nader, Green, 19,781; Browne, LB, 4,284; Buchanan, RF, 4,250; Brown, Ind., 1,606; Phillips, Ind., 1,015; Hagelin, RF, 613; Venson, Ind., 535.

1996: Clinton, D, 909,146; Dole, R, 863,530; Perot, RF, 105,918; Nader, Ind., 6,427; Browne, Ind., 5,020; Phillips, Ind., 1,818; Collins, Ind., 688; Hagelin, Ind., 636; Michael, Ind., 408; Dodge, Ind., 324.

1992: Clinton, D, 933,521; Bush, R, 841,300; Perot, Ind., 199,968; Marrou, LB, 1,847.

1988: Bush, R, 947,233; Dukakis, D, 679,794; Paul, Ind., 2,041; Duke, Ind., 1,807.

1984: Reagan, R, 990,212; Mondale, D, 711,714; Bergland, LB, 3,072.

1980: Reagan, R, 787,761; Carter, D, 783,051; Anderson, Ind., 35,991; Clark, LB, 7,116; Commoner, Citizens, 1,112; Bubar, Statesman, 521; McReynolds, Soc., 519; Hall, Comm., 503; DeBerry, Soc. Workers, 490; Griswold, Workers World, 400; write-in, 152.

1976: Carter, D, 825,879; Ford, R, 633,969; Anderson, Amer., 5,769; McCarthy, Ind., 5,004; Maddox, Amer. Ind., 2,303; MacBride, LB, 1,375; Hall, Comm., 547; LaRouche, U.S. Labor, 512; Bubar, Prohib., 442; Miller, Ind., 316; write-in, 230.

1972: Nixon, R, 813,147; McGovern, D, 357,293; Schmitz, Amer., 30,373; write-in, 369.

1968: Nixon, R, 472,592; Wallace, 3rd party, 424,792; Humphrey, D, 351,233.

1964: Johnson, D, 635,047; Goldwater, R, 508,965; write-in, 34.

1960: Nixon, R, 556,577; Kennedy, D, 481,453; Faubus, States' Rights, 11,304; Decker, Prohib., 2,458.

Texas Vote Since 1960

2020: Trump, R, 5,890,347; Biden, D, 5,259,126; Jorgensen, LB, 126,243; Hawkins, Green, 33,396.

2016: Trump, R, 4,685,047; Clinton, D, 3,877,868; Johnson, LB, 283,492; Stein, Green, 71,558; McMullin, Ind., 42,366.

2012: Romney, R, 4,569,843; Obama, D, 3,308,124; Johnson, LB, 88,580; Stein, Green, 24,657.

2008: McCain, R, 4,479,328; Obama, D, 3,528,633 Barr, LB, 56,116.

2004: Bush, R, 4,526,917; Kerry, D, 2,832,704; Badnarik, LB, 38,787.

2000: Bush, R, 3,799,639; Gore, D, 2,433,746; Nader, Green, 137,994; Browne, LB, 23,160; Buchanan, Ind., 12,394.

1996: Dole, R, 2,736,167; Clinton, D, 2,459,683; Perot, RF, 378,537; Browne, LB, 20,256; Phillips, U.S. Taxpayers, 7,472; Hagelin, Natural Law, 4,422.

1992: Bush, R, 2,496,071; Clinton, D, 2,281,815; Perot, Ind., 1,354,781; Marrou, LB, 19,699.

1988: Bush, R, 3,036,829; Dukakis, D, 2,352,748; Paul, LB, 30,355; Fulani, New Alliance, 7,208.

1984: Reagan, R, 3,433,428; Mondale, D, 1,949,276.

1980: Reagan, R, 2,510,705; Carter, D, 1,881,147; Anderson, Ind., 111,613; Clark, LB, 37,643; write-in, 528.

1976: Carter, D, 2,082,319; Ford, R, 1,953,300; McCarthy, Ind., 20,118; Anderson, Amer., 11,442; Camejo, Soc. Workers, 1,723; write-in, 2,982.

1972: Nixon, R, 2,298,896; McGovern, D, 1,154,289; Jenness, Soc. Workers, 8,664; Schmitz, Amer., 6,039; others, 3,393.

1968: Humphrey, D, 1,266,804; Nixon, R, 1,227,844; Wallace, 3rd party, 584,269; write-in, 489.

1964: Johnson, D, 1,663,185; Goldwater, R, 958,566; Lightburn, Const., 5,060.

1960: Kennedy, D, 1,167,932; Nixon, R, 1,121,699; Sullivan, Const., 18,169; Decker, Prohib., 3,870; write-in, 15.

Utah Vote Since 1960

2020: Trump, R, 865,140; Biden, D, 560,282; Jorgensen, LB, 38,447; West, unaff., 7,213; Blankenship, Const., 5,551; Hawkins, Green, 5,053; Pierce, unaff., 2,623; McHugh, unaff., 2,229; La Riva, unaff., 1,139.

2016: Trump, R, 515,231; Clinton, D, 310,676; McMullin, unaff., 243,690; Johnson, LB, 39,608; Stein, Green, 9,438; Castle, Const., 8,032; Giordani, Ind. Ameri., 2,752; De La Fuente, unaff., 883; Moorehead, unaff., 544; Kennedy, unaff., 521.

2012: Romney, R, 740,600; Obama, D, 251,813; Johnson, LB, 12,572; Anderson, Justice, 5,335; Stein, Green, 3,817; Goode, Const., 2,871; La Riva, unaff., 393.

2008: McCain, R, 596,030; Obama, D, 327,670; Baldwin, Const., 12,012; Nader, unaff., 8,416; Barr, LB, 6,966; McKinney, unaff., 982; La Riva, unaff., 262.

2004: Bush, R, 663,742; Kerry, D, 241,199; Nader, Ind., 11,305; Peroutka, Const., 6,841; Badnarik, LB, 3,375; Jay, Personal Choice, 946; Harris, Soc. Workers, 393.

2000: Bush, R, 515,096; Gore, D, 203,053; Nader, Green, 35,850; Buchanan, RF, 9,319; Browne, LB, 3,616; Phillips, Ind. American, 2,709; Hagelin, Natural Law, 763; Harris, Soc. Workers, 186; Youngkeit, Ind., 161.

1996: Dole, R, 361,911; Clinton, D, 221,633; Perot, RF, 66,461; Nader, Green, 4,615; Browne, LB, 4,129; Phillips, Taxpayers, 2,601; Templin, Ind. American, 1,290; Crane, Ind., 1,101; Hagelin, Natural Law, 1,085; Moorehead, Workers World, 298; Harris, Soc. Workers, 235; Dodge, Prohib., 111.

1992: Bush, R, 322,632; Perot, Ind., 203,400; Clinton, D, 183,429; Gritz, Populist/America First, 28,602; Marrou, LB, 1,900; Hagelin, Natural Law, 1,319; LaRouche, Ind., 1,089.

1988: Bush, R, 428,442; Dukakis, D, 207,352; Paul, LB, 7,473; Dennis, Amer., 2,158.

1984: Reagan, R, 469,105; Mondale, D, 155,369; Bergland, LB, 2,447.

1980: Reagan, R, 439,687; Carter, D, 124,266; Anderson, Ind., 30,284; Clark, LB, 7,226; Commoner, Citizens, 1,009; Greaves, Amer., 965; Rarick, Amer. Ind., 522; Hall, Comm., 139; DeBerry, Soc. Workers, 124.

1976: Ford, R, 337,908; Carter, D, 182,110; Anderson, Amer., 13,304; McCarthy, Ind., 3,907; MacBride, LB, 2,438; Maddox, Amer. Ind., 1,162; Camejo, Soc. Workers, 268; Hall, Comm., 121.

1972: Nixon, R, 323,643; McGovern, D, 126,284; Schmitz, Amer., 28,549.

1968: Nixon, R, 238,728; Humphrey, D, 156,665; Wallace, 3rd party, 26,906; Peace/Freedom, 180; Halstead, Soc. Workers, 89.

1964: Johnson, D, 219,628; Goldwater, R, 181,785.

1960: Nixon, R, 205,361; Kennedy, D, 169,248; Dobbs, Soc. Workers, 100.

Vermont Vote Since 1960

2020: Biden, D, 242,820; Trump, R, 112,704; Jorgensen, LB, 3,608; Hawkins, Green, 1,310; West, Ind., 1,269; Paige, Ind., 1,175; LaFontaine, Ind., 856; Duncan, Ind., 213; Carroll, Amer. Solidarity, 209; Blankenship, Const., 208; Kennedy, Soc. Workers, 195; La Riva, Liberty Union, 166; Swing, other, 141; Collins, Prohib., 137; McCormic, other, 126; Pierce, unaff., 100; Segal, Bread/Roses, 65; Huber, Approval Voting, 54; Kopitke, Ind., 53; De La Fuente, Alliance, 48; Scalf, Ind., 29.

2016: Clinton, D, 178,573; Trump, R, 95,369; Sanders, write-in, 18,218; Johnson, LB, 10,078; Stein, Green, 6,758; De La Fuente, Ind., 1,063; La Riva, Liberty Union, 327.

2012: Obama, D, 199,239; Romney, R, 92,698; Johnson, LB, 3,487; Anderson, Justice, 1,128; Lindsay, Socialism/Liberation, 695.

2008: Obama, D, 219,262; McCain, R, 98,974; Nader, Ind., 3,339; Barr, LB, 1,067; Baldwin, Const., 500; Calero, Soc. Workers, 150; La Riva, Socialism/Liberation, 149; Moore, Liberty Union, 141.

2004: Kerry, D, 184,067; Bush, R, 121,180; Nader, Ind., 4,494; Badnarik, LB, 1,102; Parker, Liberty Union, 265; Calero, Soc. Workers, 244.

2000: Gore, D, 149,022; Bush, R, 119,775; Nader, Green, 20,374; Buchanan, RF, 2,192; Lane, Grass Roots, 1,044; Browne, LB, 784; Hagelin, Natural Law, 219; McReynolds, Liberty Union, 161; Phillips, Const., 153; Harris, Soc. Workers, 70.

1996: Clinton, D, 137,894; Dole, R, 80,352; Perot, RF, 31,024; Nader, Green, 5,585; Browne, LB, 1,183; Hagelin, Natural Law, 498; Peron, Grass Roots, 480; Phillips, Taxpayers, 382; Hollis, Liberty Union, 292; Harris, Soc. Workers, 199.

1992: Clinton, D, 133,590; Bush, R, 88,122; Perot, Ind., 65,985.

1988: Bush, R, 124,331; Dukakis, D, 115,775; Paul, LB, 1,000; LaRouche, Ind., 275.

1984: Reagan, R, 135,865; Mondale, D, 95,730; Bergland, LB, 1,002.

1980: Reagan, R, 94,598; Carter, D, 81,891; Anderson, Ind., 31,760; Commoner, Citizens, 2,316; Clark, LB, 1,900; McReynolds, Liberty Union, 136; Hall, Comm., 118; DeBerry, Soc. Workers, 75; scattered, 413.

1976: Ford, R, 100,387; Carter, D, 77,798 and Ind. Vermonters, 991 (total, 79,789); McCarthy, Ind., 4,001; Camejo, Soc. Workers, 430; LaRouche, U.S. Labor, 196; scattered, 99.

1972: Nixon, R, 117,149; McGovern, D, 68,174; Spock, Liberty Union, 1,010; Jenness, Soc. Workers, 296; scattered, 318.

1968: Nixon, R, 85,142; Humphrey, D, 70,255; Wallace, 3rd party, 5,104; Gregory, New Party, 579; Halstead, Soc. Workers, 295.

1964: Johnson, D, 107,674; Goldwater, R, 54,868.

1960: Nixon, R, 98,131; Kennedy, D, 69,186.

Virginia Vote Since 1960

2020: Biden, D, 2,413,568; Trump, R, 1,962,430; Jorgensen, LB, 64,761.

2016: Clinton, D, 1,981,473; Trump, R, 1,769,443; Johnson, LB, 118,274; McMullin, Ind., 54,054; Stein, Green, 27,638.

2012: Obama, D, 1,971,820; Romney, R, 1,822,522; Johnson, LB, 31,216; Goode, Const., 13,058; Stein, Green, 8,627.

2008: Obama, D, 1,959,532; McCain, R, 1,725,005; Nader, Ind., 11,483; Barr, LB, 11,067; Baldwin, Ind. Green, 7,474; McKinney, Green, 2,344.

2004: Bush, R, 1,716,959; Kerry, D, 1,454,742; Badnarik, LB, 11,032; Peroutka, Const., 10,161.

2000: Bush, R, 1,437,490; Gore, D, 1,217,290; Nader, Green, 59,398; Browne, LB, 15,198; Buchanan, RF, 5,455; Phillips, Const., 1,809.

1996: Dole, R, 1,138,350; Clinton, D, 1,091,060; Perot, RF, 159,861; Phillips, Taxpayers, 13,687; Browne, LB, 9,174; Hagelin, Natural Law, 4,510.

1992: Bush, R, 1,150,517; Clinton, D, 1,038,650; Perot, Ind., 348,639; LaRouche, Ind., 11,937; Marrou, LB, 5,730; Fulani, New Alliance, 3,192.

1988: Bush, R, 1,309,162; Dukakis, D, 859,799; Fulani, Ind., 14,312; Paul, LB, 8,336.

1984: Reagan, R, 1,337,078; Mondale, D, 796,250.

1980: Reagan, R, 989,609; Carter, D, 752,174; Anderson, Ind., 95,418; Commoner, Citizens, 14,024; Clark, LB, 12,821; DeBerry, Soc. Workers, 1,986.

1976: Ford, R, 836,554; Carter, D, 813,896; Camejo, Soc. Workers, 17,802; Anderson, Amer., 16,686; LaRouche, U.S. Labor, 7,508; MacBride, LB, 4,648.

1972: Nixon, R, 988,493; McGovern, D, 438,887; Schmitz, Amer., 19,721; Fisher, Soc. Labor, 9,918.

1968: Nixon, R, 590,319; Humphrey, D, 442,387; Wallace, 3rd party, 320,272*; Blomen, Soc. Labor, 4,671; Gregory, Peace/Freedom, 1,680; Munn, Prohib., 601. *10,561 votes for Wallace were omitted in the count.

1964: Johnson, D, 558,038; Goldwater, R, 481,334; Hass, Soc. Labor, 2,895.

1960: Nixon, R, 404,521; Kennedy, D, 362,327; Coiner, Conservative, 4,204; Hass, Soc. Labor, 397.

Washington Vote Since 1960

2020: Biden, D, 2,369,612; Trump, R, 1,584,651; Jorgensen, LB, 80,500; Hawkins, Green, 18,289; La Riva, Socialism/Liberation, 4,840; Kennedy, Soc. Workers, 2,487.

2016: Clinton, D, 1,742,718; Trump, R, 1,221,747; Johnson, LB, 160,879; Stein, Green, 58,417; Castle, Const., 17,623; Kennedy, Soc. Workers, 4,307; La Riva, Socialism/Liberation, 3,523.

2012: Obama, D, 1,755,396; Romney, R, 1,290,670; Johnson, LB, 42,202; Stein, Green, 20,928; Goode, Const., 8,851; Anderson, Justice, 4,946; Lindsay, Socialism/Liberation, 1,318; Harris, Soc. Workers, 1,205.

2008: Obama, D, 1,750,848; McCain, R, 1,229,216; Nader, Ind., 29,489; Barr, LB, 12,728; Baldwin, Const., 9,432; McKinney, Green, 3,819; La Riva, Socialism/Liberation, 705; Harris, Soc. Workers, 641.

2004: Kerry, D, 1,510,201; Bush, R, 1,304,894; Nader, Ind., 23,283; Badnarik, LB, 11,955; Peroutka, Const., 3,922; Cobb, Green, 2,974; Parker, Workers World, 1,077; Harris, Soc. Workers, 547; Van Auken, Soc. Equality, 231.

2000: Gore, D, 1,247,652; Bush, R, 1,108,864; Nader, Green, 103,002; Browne, LB, 13,135; Buchanan, Freedom, 7,171; Hagelin, Natural Law, 2,927; Phillips, Const., 1,989; Moorehead, Workers World, 1,729; McReynolds, Soc., 660; Harris, Soc. Workers, 304.

1996: Clinton, D, 1,123,323; Dole, R, 840,712; Perot, RF, 201,003; Nader, Ind., 60,322; Browne, LB, 12,522; Hagelin, Natural Law, 6,076; Phillips, U.S. Taxpayers, 4,578; Collins, Ind., 2,374; Moorehead, Workers World, 2,189; Harris, Soc. Workers, 738.

1992: Clinton, D, 993,037; Bush, R, 731,234; Perot, Ind., 541,780; Marrou, LB, 7,533; Gritz, Populist/America First,

4,854; Hagelin, Natural Law, 2,456; Phillips, U.S. Taxpayers, 2,354; Fulani, New Alliance, 1,776; Daniels, Ind., 1,171.

1988: Dukakis, D, 933,516; Bush, R, 903,835; Paul, LB, 17,240; LaRouche, Ind., 4,412.

1984: Reagan, R, 1,051,670; Mondale, D, 798,352; Bergland, LB, 8,844.

1980: Reagan, R, 865,244; Carter, D, 650,193; Anderson, Ind., 185,073; Clark, LB, 29,213; Commoner, Citizens, 9,403; DeBerry, Soc. Workers, 1,137; McReynolds, Soc., 956; Hall, Comm., 834; Griswold, Workers World, 341.

1976: Ford, R, 777,732; Carter, D, 717,323; McCarthy, Ind., 36,986; Maddox, Amer. Ind., 8,585; Anderson, Amer., 5,046; MacBride, LB, 5,042; Wright, People's, 1,124; Camejo, Soc. Workers, 905; LaRouche, U.S. Labor, 903; Hall, Comm., 817; Levin, Soc. Labor, 713; Zeidler, Soc., 358.

1972: Nixon, R, 837,135; McGovern, D, 568,334; Schmitz, Amer., 58,906; Spock, Ind., 2,644; Hospers, LB, 1,537; Fisher, Soc. Labor, 1,102; Jenness, Soc. Workers, 623; Hall, Comm., 566.

1968: Humphrey, D, 616,037; Nixon, R, 588,510; Wallace, 3rd party, 96,990; Cleaver, Peace/Freedom, 1,609; Blomen, Soc. Labor, 488; Mitchell, Free Ballot, 377; Halstead, Soc. Workers, 270.

1964: Johnson, D, 779,699; Goldwater, R, 470,366; Hass, Soc. Labor, 7,772; DeBerry, Freedom Soc., 537.

1960: Nixon, R, 629,273; Kennedy, D, 599,298; Hass, Soc. Labor, 10,895; Curtis, Const., 1,401; Dobbs, Soc. Workers, 705.

West Virginia Vote Since 1960

2020: Trump, R, 545,382; Biden, D, 235,984; Jorgensen, LB, 10,687; Hawkins, Mountain, 2,599.

2016: Trump, R, 489,371; Clinton, D, 188,794; Johnson, LB, 23,004; Stein, Mountain, 8,075; Castle, Const., 3,807.

2012: Romney, R, 417,655; Obama, D, 238,269; Johnson, LB, 6,302; Stein, Mountain, 4,406; Terry, NPA, 3,806.

2008: McCain, R, 397,466; Obama, D, 303,857; Nader, unaff., 7,219; Baldwin, Const., 2,465; McKinney, Mountain, 2,355.

2004: Bush, R, 423,778; Kerry, D, 326,541; Nader, Ind., 4,063; Badnarik, LB, 1,405.

2000: Bush, R, 336,475; Gore, D, 295,497; Nader, Green, 10,680; Buchanan, RF, 3,169; Browne, LB, 1,912; Hagelin, Natural Law, 367.

1996: Clinton, D, 327,812; Dole, R, 233,946; Perot, RF, 71,639; Browne, LB, 3,062.

1992: Clinton, D, 331,001; Bush, R, 241,974; Perot, Ind., 108,829; Marrou, LB, 1,873.

1988: Dukakis, D, 341,016; Bush, R, 310,065; Fulani, New Alliance, 2,230.

1984: Reagan, R, 405,483; Mondale, D, 328,125.

1980: Carter, D, 367,462; Reagan, R, 334,206; Anderson, Ind., 31,691; Clark, LB, 4,356.

1976: Carter, D, 435,864; Ford, R, 314,726.

1972: Nixon, R, 484,964; McGovern, D, 277,435.

1968: Humphrey, D, 374,091; Nixon, R, 307,555; Wallace, 3rd party, 72,560.

1964: Johnson, D, 538,087; Goldwater, R, 253,953.

1960: Kennedy, D, 441,786; Nixon, R, 395,995.

Wisconsin Vote Since 1960

2020: Biden, D, 1,630,866; Trump, R, 1,610,184; Jorgensen, LB, 38,491; Carroll, Amer. Solidarity, 5,259; Blankenship, Const., 5,146.

2016: Trump, R, 1,405,284; Clinton, D, 1,382,536; Johnson, LB, 106,674; Stein, WI Green, 31,072; Castle, Const., 12,162; McMullin, Ind., 11,855; Moorehead, Ind., 1,770; De La Fuente, Ind., 1,502.

2012: Obama, D, 1,620,985; Romney, R, 1,407,966; Johnson, LB, 20,439; Stein, Green, 7,665; White, Soc. Equality, 553; La Riva, Socialism/Liberation, 526.

2008: Obama, D, 1,677,211; McCain, R, 1,262,393; Nader, Ind., 17,605; Barr, LB, 8,858; Baldwin, Ind., 5,072; McKinney, Green, 4,216; Wamboldt, Ind., 764; Moore, Ind., 540; La Riva, Ind., 237.

2004: Kerry, D, 1,489,504; Bush, R, 1,478,120; Nader, Ind., 16,390; Badnarik, LB, 6,464; Cobb, Green, 2,661; Brown, Ind., 471; Harris, Ind., 411.

2000: Gore, D, 1,242,987; Bush, R, 1,237,279; Nader, Green, 94,070; Buchanan, RF, 11,446; Browne, LB, 6,640; Phillips, Const., 2,042; Moorehead, Workers World, 1,063; Hagelin, RF, 878; Harris, Soc. Workers, 306.

1996: Clinton, D, 1,071,971; Dole, R, 845,029; Perot, RF, 227,339; Nader, Green, 28,723; Phillips, U.S. Taxpayers, 8,811; Browne, LB, 7,929; Hagelin, Natural Law, 1,379; Moorehead, Workers World, 1,333; Hollis, Soc., 848; Harris, Soc. Workers, 483.

1992: Clinton, D, 1,041,066; Bush, R, 930,855; Perot, Ind., 544,479; Marrou, LB, 2,877; Gritz, Populist/America First, 2,311; Daniels, Ind., 1,883; Phillips, U.S. Taxpayers, 1,772; Hagelin, Natural Law, 1,070.

1988: Dukakis, D, 1,126,794; Bush, R, 1,047,499; Paul, LB, 5,157; Duke, Populist, 3,056.

1984: Reagan, R, 1,198,584; Mondale, D, 995,740; Bergland, LB, 4,883.

1980: Reagan, R, 1,088,845; Carter, D, 981,584; Anderson, Ind., 160,657; Clark, LB, 29,135; Commoner, Citizens, 7,767; Rarick, Const., 1,519; McReynolds, Soc., 808; Hall, Comm., 772; Griswold, Workers World, 414; DeBerry, Soc. Workers, 383; scattered, 1,337.

1976: Carter, D, 1,040,232; Ford, R, 1,004,987; McCarthy, Ind., 34,943; Maddox, Amer. Ind., 8,552; Zeidler, Soc., 4,298; MacBride, LB, 3,814; Camejo, Soc. Workers, 1,691; Wright, People's, 943; Hall, Comm., 749; LaRouche, U.S. Labor, 738; Levin, Soc. Labor, 389; scattered, 2,839.

1972: Nixon, R, 989,430; McGovern, D, 810,174; Schmitz, Amer., 47,525; Spock, Ind., 2,701; Fisher, Soc. Labor, 998; Hall, Comm., 663; Reed, Ind., 506; scattered, 893.

1968: Nixon, R, 809,997; Humphrey, D, 748,804; Wallace, 3rd party, 127,835; Blomen, Soc. Labor, 1,338; Halstead, Soc. Workers, 1,222; scattered, 2,342.

1964: Johnson, D, 1,050,424; Goldwater, R, 638,495; DeBerry, Soc. Workers, 1,692; Hass, Soc. Labor, 1,204.

1960: Nixon, R, 895,175; Kennedy, D, 830,805; Dobbs, Soc. Workers, 1,792; Hass, Soc. Labor, 1,310.

Wyoming Vote Since 1960

2020: Trump, R, 193,559; Biden, D, 73,491; Jorgensen, LB, 5,768; Pierce, Ind., 2,208.

2016: Trump, R, 174,419; Clinton, D, 55,973; Johnson, LB, 13,287; Stein, Ind., 2,515; Castle, Const., 2,042; De La Fuente, Ind., 709.

2012: Romney, R, 170,962; Obama, D, 69,286; Johnson, LB, 5,326; Goode, Const., 1,452.

2008: McCain, R, 164,958; Obama, D, 82,868; Nader, Ind., 2,525; Barr, LB, 1,594; Baldwin, Ind., 1,192.

2004: Bush, R, 167,629; Kerry, D, 70,776; Nader, Ind., 2,741; Badnarik, LB, 1,171; Peroutka, Ind., 631.

2000: Bush, R, 147,947; Gore, D, 60,481; Buchanan, RF, 2,724; Browne, LB, 1,443; Phillips, Ind., 720; Hagelin, Natural Law, 411.

1996: Dole, R, 105,388; Clinton, D, 77,934; Perot, RF, 25,928; Browne, LB, 1,739; Hagelin, Natural Law, 582.

1992: Bush, R, 79,347; Clinton, D, 68,160; Perot, Ind., 51,263.

1988: Bush, R, 106,867; Dukakis, D, 67,113; Paul, LB, 2,026; Fulani, New Alliance, 545.

1984: Reagan, R, 133,241; Mondale, D, 53,370; Bergland, LB, 2,357.

1980: Reagan, R, 110,700; Carter, D, 49,427; Anderson, Ind., 12,072; Clark, LB, 4,514.

1976: Ford, R, 92,717; Carter, D, 62,239; McCarthy, Ind., 624; Reagan, Ind., 307; Anderson, Amer., 290; MacBride, LB, 89; Brown, Ind., 47; Maddox, Amer. Ind., 30.

1972: Nixon, R, 100,464; McGovern, D, 44,358; Schmitz, Amer., 748.

1968: Nixon, R, 70,927; Humphrey, D, 45,173; Wallace, 3rd party, 11,105.

1964: Johnson, D, 80,718; Goldwater, R, 61,998.

1960: Nixon, R, 77,451; Kennedy, D, 63,331.

UNITED STATES GOVERNMENT

EXECUTIVE BRANCH	LEGISLATIVE BRANCH	JUDICIAL BRANCH
President **Vice President** **Executive Office of the President** Council of Economic Advisers Council on Environmental Quality National Security Council Office of Administration Office of Management and Budget Office of National Drug Control Policy Office of Science and Technology Policy Office of the U.S. Trade Representative Office of the Vice President White House Office	**CONGRESS** **Senate/House of Representatives** Architect of the Capitol Congressional Budget Office Government Accountability Office Government Publishing Office Library of Congress U.S. Botanic Garden	**Supreme Court of the United States** Administrative Office of the U.S. Courts Federal Judicial Center Territorial Courts Courts of Appeals Court of Appeals for the Armed Forces Court of Appeals for Veterans Claims District Courts Court of Federal Claims Court of International Trade Sentencing Commission Tax Court

Biden Administration

1600 Pennsylvania Ave. NW, 20500; www.whitehouse.gov
As of Sept. 2024. Mailing addresses are for Washington, DC, except where otherwise noted.
Terms of office of the president and vice president: Jan. 20, 2021, to Jan. 20, 2025.

White House Staff

Assistants to the President:
- **Chief of Staff:** Jeff Zients
- **Deputy Chiefs of Staff:** Annie Tomasini, Natalie Quillian, Bruce Reed
- **Senior Advisers:** Anita Dunn, John Podesta
- **Counselor to the President:** Steven J. Ricchetti
- **White House Counsel:** Edward Siskel
- **National Security Adviser:** Jake Sullivan
- **Principal Deputy National Security Adviser:** Jonathan Finer
- **Deputy National Security Adviser:** Elizabeth Sherwood-Randall
- **Director of Communications:** Ben LaBolt
- **Press Secretary:** Karine Jean-Pierre
- **Cabinet Secretary:** Evan M. Ryan
- **Director of Digital Strategy:** Christian Tom
- **Director of Legislative Affairs:** Shuwanza Goff
- **Director of Management and Administration:** David Noble
- **Director of Oval Office Operations:** Richard Ruffner
- **Director of Political Strategy and Outreach:** Emma Ruiz
- **Director of Presidential Personnel:** Gautam Raghavan
- **Director of Scheduling and Advance:** Ryan Montoya
- **Director of Speechwriting:** Vinay Reddy
- **Staff Secretary:** Stefanie Feldman
- **Chief of Staff to the First Lady:** Vacant
- **Senior Adviser to the First Lady:** Anthony Bernal

Executive Offices

Climate Policy Office: Ali Zaidi, dir.; www.whitehouse.gov/cpo/
Council of Economic Advisers: Jared Bernstein, chair; www.whitehouse.gov/cea/
Council on Environmental Quality: Brenda Mallory, chair; www.whitehouse.gov/ceq/
Domestic Policy Council: Neera Tanden, chair; www.whitehouse.gov/dpc/
Gender Policy Council: Jennifer Klein, chair; www.whitehouse.gov/gpc
National Economic Council: Lael Brainard, dir.; www.whitehouse.gov/nec/
Office of Intergovernmental Affairs: Tom Perez, dir.; www.whitehouse.gov/iga/
Office of Management and Budget: Shalanda Young, dir.; www.whitehouse.gov/omb/
Office of National Drug Control Policy: Rahul Gupta, dir.; www.whitehouse.gov/ondcp/
Office of Pandemic Preparedness and Response Policy: Paul Friedrichs, dir.; www.whitehouse.gov/oppr
Office of Public Engagement: Stephen Benjamin, dir.; www.whitehouse.gov/ope/
Office of Science and Technology Policy: Arati Prabhakar, dir.; www.whitehouse.gov/ostp/
Office of the National Cyber Director: Harry Coker Jr., dir.; www.whitehouse.gov/oncd
Office of the U.S. Trade Representative: Katherine Tai, amb.; www.ustr.gov
Office of the Director of National Intelligence (not formally an executive office): Avril Haines, dir.; www.dni.gov

The Cabinet

The heads of major executive departments of the federal government constitute the Cabinet. This institution, not provided for in the U.S. Constitution, developed as an advisory body out of the desire of presidents to consult on policy matters. Aside from its advisory role, the Cabinet as a body has no formal function and wields no executive authority. Individual members exercise authority as heads of their departments, reporting to the president. The Cabinet meets at times set by the president. In addition, the Cabinet commonly includes other officials designated by the president as being of Cabinet rank.

The officials so designated by Pres. Joe Biden include the Vice President, White House Chief of Staff, U.S. Ambassador to the United Nations, Director of National Intelligence, and U.S. Trade Representative, as well as the heads of the Central Intelligence Agency, Environmental Protection Agency, Office of Management and Budget, Council of Economic Advisers, Office of Science and Technology Policy, and Small Business Administration.

Cabinet Department Heads

Secretary of State: Antony Blinken
Secretary of the Treasury: Janet Yellen
Secretary of Defense: Lloyd Austin
Attorney General (Dept. of Justice head): Merrick Garland
Secretary of the Interior: Deb Haaland
Secretary of Agriculture: Tom Vilsack
Secretary of Commerce: Gina Raimondo
Secretary of Labor (acting): Julie Su
Secretary of Health and Human Services: Xavier Becerra
Secretary of Housing and Urban Development (acting): Adrianne Todman
Secretary of Transportation: Pete Buttigieg
Secretary of Energy: Jennifer Granholm
Secretary of Education: Miguel Cardona
Secretary of Veterans Affairs: Denis McDonough
Secretary of Homeland Security: Alejandro Mayorkas

Other Cabinet Rank Officials

Environmental Protection Agency Administrator: Michael Regan
Director of National Intelligence: Avril Haines
U.S. Trade Representative: Katherine Tai
U.S. Ambassador to the United Nations: Linda Thomas-Greenfield
Chair of the Council of Economic Advisers: Jared Bernstein
Small Business Administration Administrator: Isabel Casillas Guzman
Director of the Office of Management and Budget: Shalanda Young
White House Chief of Staff: Jeff Zients
Director of the Central Intelligence Agency: William J. Burns

Cabinet-Level Departments

Department mailing address applies to subordinate bureaus/agencies unless otherwise noted. Mailing addresses are for Washington, DC, except where otherwise noted.

Department of State

2201 C St. NW, 20520; www.state.gov

The Dept. of Foreign Affairs was created by act of Congress on July 27, 1789, and the name changed to Dept. of State on Sept. 15, 1789. Conducts U.S. foreign policy. The Foreign Service protects American citizens and interests through embassies in some 180 countries. Maintains contact with foreign governments, negotiates agreements and treaties, and supports U.S. foreign trade. Promotes democracy, international security, human rights—including issues related to AIDS, human trafficking, war crimes, and migration—and arms and narcotics control. Represents the nation in international organizations. Issues passports to U.S. citizens and visas to foreigners. **Budget:** $35.8 bil (2021); $33.2 bil (2022); $33.0 bil (2023); $37.3 bil (2024 est.); $35.4 bil (2025 est.). Budget for other intl. programs: $20.1 bil (2021); $36.0 bil (2022); $36.1 bil (2023); $46.5 bil (2024 est.); $38.4 bil (2025 est.).

Secretaries of State

President	Secretary	Home	Sworn in
Washington	Thomas Jefferson	VA	1789
	Edmund J. Randolph	VA	1794
	Timothy Pickering	PA	1795
Adams, J.	Timothy Pickering	PA	1797
	John Marshall	VA	1800
Jefferson	James Madison	VA	1801
Madison	Robert Smith	MD	1809
	James Monroe	VA	1811
Monroe	John Quincy Adams	MA	1817
Adams, J. Q.	Henry Clay	KY	1825
Jackson	Martin Van Buren	NY	1829
	Edward Livingston	LA	1831
	Louis McLane	DE	1833
	John Forsyth	GA	1834
Van Buren	John Forsyth	GA	1837
Harrison, W. H.	Daniel Webster	MA	1841
Tyler	Daniel Webster	MA	1841
	Abel P. Upshur	VA	1843
	John C. Calhoun	SC	1844
Polk	John C. Calhoun	SC	1845
	James Buchanan	PA	1845
Taylor	James Buchanan	PA	1849
	John M. Clayton	DE	1849
Fillmore	John M. Clayton	DE	1850
	Daniel Webster	MA	1850
	Edward Everett	MA	1852
Pierce	William L. Marcy	NY	1853
Buchanan	William L. Marcy	NY	1857
	Lewis Cass	MI	1857
	Jeremiah S. Black	PA	1860
Lincoln	Jeremiah S. Black	PA	1861
	William H. Seward	NY	1861
Johnson, A.	William H. Seward	NY	1865
Grant	Elihu B. Washburne	IL	1869
	Hamilton Fish	NY	1869
Hayes	Hamilton Fish	NY	1877
	William M. Evarts	NY	1877
Garfield	William M. Evarts	NY	1881
	James G. Blaine	ME	1881
Arthur	James G. Blaine	ME	1881
	F. T. Frelinghuysen	NJ	1881
Cleveland	F. T. Frelinghuysen	NJ	1885
	Thomas F. Bayard	DE	1885
Harrison, B.	Thomas F. Bayard	DE	1889
	James G. Blaine	ME	1889
	John W. Foster	IN	1892
Cleveland	Walter Q. Gresham	IN	1893
	Richard Olney	MA	1895
McKinley	Richard Olney	MA	1897
	John Sherman	OH	1897
	William R. Day	OH	1898
	John M. Hay	DC	1898
Roosevelt, T.	John M. Hay	DC	1901
	Elihu Root	NY	1905
	Robert Bacon	NY	1909
Taft	Robert Bacon	NY	1909
	Philander C. Knox	PA	1909
Wilson	Philander C. Knox	PA	1913
	William J. Bryan	NE	1913
	Robert Lansing	NY	1915
	Bainbridge Colby	NY	1920
Harding	Charles E. Hughes	NY	1921
Coolidge	Charles E. Hughes	NY	1923
	Frank B. Kellogg	MN	1925
Hoover	Frank B. Kellogg	MN	1929
	Henry L. Stimson	NY	1929
Roosevelt, F. D.	Cordell Hull	TN	1933
	Edward R. Stettinius Jr.	VA	1944
Truman	Edward R. Stettinius Jr.	VA	1945
	James F. Byrnes	SC	1945
	George C. Marshall	PA	1947
	Dean G. Acheson	CT	1949
Eisenhower	John Foster Dulles	NY	1953
	Christian A. Herter	MA	1959
Kennedy	D. Dean Rusk	GA	1961
Johnson, L. B.	D. Dean Rusk	GA	1963
Nixon	William P. Rogers	NY	1969
	Henry A. Kissinger	DC	1973
Ford	Henry A. Kissinger	DC	1974
Carter	Cyrus R. Vance	NY	1977
	Edmund S. Muskie	ME	1980
Reagan	Alexander M. Haig Jr.	CT	1981
	George P. Shultz	CA	1982
Bush, G. H. W.	James A. Baker III	TX	1989
	Lawrence S. Eagleburger	MI	1992
Clinton	Warren M. Christopher	CA	1993
	Madeleine K. Albright	DC	1997
Bush, G. W.	Colin L. Powell	NY	2001
	Condoleezza Rice	AL	2005
Obama	Hillary Rodham Clinton	NY	2009
	John Kerry	MA	2013
Trump	Rex W. Tillerson	TX	2017
	Mike Pompeo	KS	2018
Biden	Antony Blinken	NY	2021

Department of the Treasury

1500 Pennsylvania Ave. NW, 20220; www.treasury.gov

Organized by act of Congress on Sept. 2, 1789. Responsible for the fiscal affairs of the U.S. Serves as the government's financial agent; collects, borrows, and disburses funds for the federal government. Monitors the nation's financial infrastructure and economic development; recommends domestic and international financial, monetary, economic, trade, and tax policies. Manufactures currency and coins. Carries out monetary and tax law enforcement activities, sanctions, embargoes, and fights illicit finance—counterfeiting, money laundering, narcotics trafficking, terrorist financing. **Budget** (including interest on the public debt): $1.63 tril (2021); $1.16 tril (2022); $1.11 tril (2023); $1.35 tril (2024 est.); $1.60 tril (2025 est.).

- Alcohol and Tobacco Tax and Trade Bureau (1310 G St. NW, Box 12, 20005); www.ttb.gov
- Bureau of Engraving and Printing (14th and C Sts. SW, 20228); www.moneyfactory.gov
- Bureau of the Fiscal Service (3201 Pennsy Dr., Bldg. E, Landover, MD 20785); www.fiscal.treasury.gov
- Internal Revenue Service (1111 Constitution Ave. NW, 20224); www.irs.gov
- Office of the Comptroller of the Currency (400 7th St. SW, 20219); www.occ.gov
- U.S. Mint (801 9th St. NW, 20220); www.usmint.gov

Secretaries of the Treasury

President	Secretary	Home	Sworn in
Washington	Alexander Hamilton	NY	1789
	Oliver Wolcott Jr.	CT	1795
Adams, J.	Oliver Wolcott Jr.	CT	1797
	Samuel Dexter	MA	1801
Jefferson	Samuel Dexter	MA	1801
	Albert Gallatin	PA	1801
Madison	Albert Gallatin	PA	1809
	George W. Campbell	TN	1814
	Alexander J. Dallas	PA	1814
	William H. Crawford	GA	1816
Monroe	William H. Crawford	GA	1817
Adams, J. Q.	Richard Rush	PA	1825

President	Secretary	Home	Sworn in
Jackson	Samuel D. Ingham	PA	1829
	Louis McLane	DE	1831
	William J. Duane	PA	1833
	Roger B. Taney	MD	1833
	Levi Woodbury	NH	1834
Van Buren	Levi Woodbury	NH	1837
Harrison, W. H.	Thomas Ewing	OH	1841
Tyler	Thomas Ewing	OH	1841
	Walter Forward	PA	1841
	John C. Spencer	NY	1843
	George M. Bibb	KY	1844
Polk	Robert J. Walker	MS	1845
Taylor	William M. Meredith	PA	1849
Fillmore	Thomas Corwin	OH	1850
Pierce	James Guthrie	KY	1853
Buchanan	Howell Cobb	GA	1857
	Phillip F. Thomas	MD	1860
	John A. Dix	NY	1861
Lincoln	Salmon P. Chase	OH	1861
	William P. Fessenden	ME	1864
	Hugh McCulloch	IN	1865
Johnson, A.	Hugh McCulloch	IN	1865
Grant	George S. Boutwell	MA	1869
	William A. Richardson	MA	1873
	Benjamin H. Bristow	KY	1874
	Lot M. Morrill	ME	1876
Hayes	John Sherman	OH	1877
Garfield	William Windom	MN	1881
Arthur	Charles J. Folger	NY	1881
	Walter Q. Gresham	IN	1884
	Hugh McCulloch	IN	1884
Cleveland	Daniel Manning	NY	1885
	Charles S. Fairchild	NY	1887
Harrison, B.	William Windom	MN	1889
	Charles Foster	OH	1891
Cleveland	John G. Carlisle	KY	1893
McKinley	Lyman J. Gage	IL	1897
Roosevelt, T.	Lyman J. Gage	IL	1901
	Leslie M. Shaw	IA	1902
	George B. Cortelyou	NY	1907
Taft	Franklin MacVeagh	IL	1909
Wilson	William G. McAdoo	NY	1913
	Carter Glass	VA	1918
	David F. Houston	MO	1920
Harding	Andrew W. Mellon	PA	1921
Coolidge	Andrew W. Mellon	PA	1923
Hoover	Andrew W. Mellon	PA	1929
	Ogden L. Mills	NY	1932
Roosevelt, F. D.	William H. Woodin	NY	1933
	Henry Morgenthau Jr.	NY	1934
Truman	Fred M. Vinson	KY	1945
	John W. Snyder	MO	1946
Eisenhower	George M. Humphrey	OH	1953
	Robert B. Anderson	CT	1957
Kennedy	C. Douglas Dillon	NJ	1961
Johnson, L. B.	C. Douglas Dillon	NJ	1963
	Henry H. Fowler	VA	1965
	Joseph W. Barr	IN	1968
Nixon	David M. Kennedy	IL	1969
	John B. Connally	TX	1971
	George P. Shultz	IL	1972
	William E. Simon	NJ	1974
Ford	William E. Simon	NJ	1974
Carter	W. Michael Blumenthal	MI	1977
	G. William Miller	RI	1979
Reagan	Donald T. Regan	NY	1981
	James A. Baker III	TX	1985
	Nicholas F. Brady	NJ	1988
Bush, G. H. W.	Nicholas F. Brady	NJ	1989
Clinton	Lloyd M. Bentsen	TX	1993
	Robert E. Rubin	NY	1995
	Lawrence H. Summers	CT	1999
Bush, G. W.	Paul H. O'Neill	MO	2001
	John W. Snow	OH	2003
	Henry M. Paulson Jr.	FL	2006
Obama	Timothy F. Geithner	NY	2009
	Jack Lew	NY	2013
Trump	Steven T. Mnuchin	NY	2017
Biden	Janet Yellin	NY	2021

Department of Defense

1400 Defense Pentagon, 20301; www.defense.gov

The Dept. of Defense, originally designated the National Military Establishment, was created on Sept. 18, 1947. Directs and controls the armed forces and assists the president in protecting the nation's security. Military departments of the Army, Navy, and Air Force are each separately organized under its own secretary but all function under the command of the secretary of defense. They conduct military operations as unified commands. The chairman of the Joint Chiefs of Staff is the principal military adviser to the president. Undersecretaries supervise acquisition, technology, and logistics; intelligence; personnel and readiness; and policy. **Budget** for military programs: $717.6 bil (2021); $726.5 bil (2022); $775.9 bil (2023); $844.9 bil (2024 est.); $871.6 bil (2025 est.). **Budget** for civil programs: $66.0 bil (2021); $65.0 bil (2022); $76.7 bil (2023); $75.2 bil (2024 est.); $90.7 bil (2025 est.).

- Def. Advanced Research Projects Agency (675 N. Randolph St., Arlington, VA 22203); www.darpa.mil
- Def. Intelligence Agency (7400 Pentagon, 20301); www.dia.mil
- Def. Security Cooperation Agency (2800 Defense Pentagon, 20301); www.dsca.mil
- Missile Def. Agency (5700 18th St., Bldg. 245, Fort Belvoir, VA 22060); www.mda.mil
- Natl. Geospatial-Intelligence Agency (7500 GEOINT Dr., MS N73, Springfield, VA 22150); www.nga.mil
- Natl. Security Agency (9800 Savage Rd., Ste. 6272, Ft. Meade, MD 20755); www.nsa.gov

Secretaries of Defense

President	Secretary	Home	Sworn in
Truman	James V. Forrestal	NY	1947
	Louis A. Johnson	WV	1949
	George C. Marshall	PA	1950
	Robert A. Lovett	NY	1951
Eisenhower	Charles E. Wilson	MI	1953
	Neil H. McElroy	OH	1957
	Thomas S. Gates Jr.	PA	1959
Kennedy	Robert S. McNamara	MI	1961
Johnson, L. B.	Robert S. McNamara	MI	1963
	Clark M. Clifford	MD	1968
Nixon	Melvin R. Laird	WI	1969
	Elliot L. Richardson	MA	1973
	James R. Schlesinger	VA	1973
Ford	James R. Schlesinger	VA	1974
	Donald H. Rumsfeld	IL	1975
Carter	Harold Brown	CA	1977
Reagan	Caspar W. Weinberger	CA	1981
	Frank C. Carlucci	PA	1987
Bush, G. H. W.	Richard B. Cheney	WY	1989
Clinton	Les Aspin	WI	1993
	William J. Perry	CA	1994
	William S. Cohen	ME	1997
Bush, G. W.	Donald H. Rumsfeld	IL	2001
	Robert M. Gates	TX	2006
Obama	Robert M. Gates	TX	2009
	Leon E. Panetta	CA	2011
	Chuck Hagel	NE	2013
	Ashton Carter	PA	2015
Trump	James Mattis	WA	2017
	Mark T. Esper	PA	2019
Biden	Lloyd Austin	GA	2021

Secretaries of War

The War Dept. (which included jurisdiction over the Navy until 1798) was created by act of Congress on Aug. 7, 1789.

President	Secretary	Home	Sworn in
Washington	Henry Knox	MA	1789
	Timothy Pickering	PA	1795
	James McHenry	MD	1796
Adams, J.	James McHenry	MD	1797
	Samuel Dexter	MA	1800
Jefferson	Henry Dearborn	MA	1801
Madison	William Eustis	MA	1809
	John Armstrong	NY	1813
	James Monroe	VA	1814
	William H. Crawford	GA	1815
Monroe	John C. Calhoun	SC	1817
Adams, J. Q.	James Barbour	VA	1825
	Peter B. Porter	NY	1828
Jackson	John H. Eaton	TN	1829
	Lewis Cass	MI	1831
	Benjamin F. Butler	NY	1837
Van Buren	Joel R. Poinsett	SC	1837
Harrison, W. H.	John Bell	TN	1841
Tyler	John Bell	TN	1841
	John C. Spencer	NY	1841
	James M. Porter	PA	1843
	William Wilkins	PA	1844
Polk	William L. Marcy	NY	1845
Taylor	George W. Crawford	GA	1849
Fillmore	Charles M. Conrad	LA	1850

President	Secretary	Home	Sworn in
Pierce	Jefferson Davis	MS	1853
Buchanan	John B. Floyd	VA	1857
	Joseph Holt	KY	1861
Lincoln	Simon Cameron	PA	1861
	Edwin M. Stanton	PA	1862
Johnson, A.	Edwin M. Stanton	PA	1865
	John M. Schofield	IL	1868
Grant	John A. Rawlins	IL	1869
	William T. Sherman	OH	1869
	William W. Belknap	IA	1869
	Alphonso Taft	OH	1876
	James D. Cameron	PA	1876
Hayes	George W. McCrary	IA	1877
	Alexander Ramsey	MN	1879
Garfield	Robert T. Lincoln	IL	1881
Arthur	Robert T. Lincoln	IL	1881
Cleveland	William C. Endicott	MA	1885
Harrison, B.	Redfield Proctor	VT	1889
	Stephen B. Elkins	WV	1891
Cleveland	Daniel S. Lamont	NY	1893
McKinley	Russell A. Alger	MI	1897
	Elihu Root	NY	1899
Roosevelt, T.	Elihu Root	NY	1901
	William H. Taft	OH	1904
	Luke E. Wright	TN	1908
Taft	Jacob M. Dickinson	TN	1909
	Henry L. Stimson	NY	1911
Wilson	Lindley M. Garrison	NJ	1913
	Newton D. Baker	OH	1916
Harding	John W. Weeks	MA	1921
Coolidge	John W. Weeks	MA	1923
	Dwight F. Davis	MO	1925
Hoover	James W. Good	IL	1929
	Patrick J. Hurley	OK	1929
Roosevelt, F. D.	George H. Dern	UT	1933
	Harry H. Woodring	KS	1937
	Henry L. Stimson	NY	1940
Truman	Robert P. Patterson	NY	1945
	Kenneth C. Royall[1]	NC	1947

(1) Last member of Cabinet with this title. The War Dept. became the Dept. of the Army with the creation of the Defense Dept. in 1947, though the Army secretary maintained Cabinet-level status until 1949.

Secretaries of the Navy

The Navy Dept. was created by act of Congress on Apr. 30, 1798. The Marine Corps is part of this department.

President	Secretary	Home	Sworn in
Adams, J.	Benjamin Stoddert	MD	1798
Jefferson	Benjamin Stoddert	MD	1801
	Robert Smith	MD	1801
Madison	Paul Hamilton	SC	1809
	William Jones	PA	1813
	Benjamin W. Crowninshield	MA	1814
Monroe	Benjamin W. Crowninshield	MA	1817
	Smith Thompson	NY	1818
	Samuel L. Southard	NJ	1823
Adams, J. Q.	Samuel L. Southard	NJ	1825
Jackson	John Branch	NC	1829
	Levi Woodbury	NH	1831
	Mahlon Dickerson	NJ	1834
Van Buren	Mahlon Dickerson	NJ	1837
	James K. Paulding	NY	1838
Harrison, W. H.	George E. Badger	NC	1841
Tyler	George E. Badger	NC	1841
	Abel P. Upshur	VA	1841
	David Henshaw	MA	1843
	Thomas W. Gilmer	VA	1844
	John Y. Mason	VA	1844
Polk	George Bancroft	MA	1845
	John Y. Mason	VA	1846
Taylor	William B. Preston	VA	1849
Fillmore	William A. Graham	NC	1850
	John P. Kennedy	MD	1852
Pierce	James C. Dobbin	NC	1853
Buchanan	Isaac Toucey	CT	1857
Lincoln	Gideon Welles	CT	1861
Johnson, A.	Gideon Welles	CT	1865
Grant	Adolph E. Borie	PA	1869
	George M. Robeson	NJ	1869
Hayes	Richard W. Thompson	IN	1877
	Nathan Goff Jr.	WV	1881
Garfield	William H. Hunt	LA	1881
Arthur	William E. Chandler	NH	1882
Cleveland	William C. Whitney	NY	1885
Harrison, B.	Benjamin F. Tracy	NY	1889
Cleveland	Hilary A. Herbert	AL	1893
McKinley	John D. Long	MA	1897
Roosevelt, T.	John D. Long	MA	1901
	William H. Moody	MA	1902
	Paul Morton	IL	1904
	Charles J. Bonaparte	MD	1905
	Victor H. Metcalf	CA	1906
	Truman H. Newberry	MI	1908
Taft	George von L. Meyer	MA	1909
Wilson	Josephus Daniels	NC	1913
Harding	Edwin Denby	MI	1921
Coolidge	Edwin Denby	MI	1923
	Curtis D. Wilbur	CA	1924
Hoover	Charles Francis Adams	MA	1929
Roosevelt, F. D.	Claude A. Swanson	VA	1933
	Charles Edison	NJ	1940
	Frank Knox	IL	1940
	James V. Forrestal	NY	1944
Truman	James V. Forrestal[1]	NY	1945

(1) Last member of Cabinet with this title. The Navy Dept. became a branch of the Dept. of Defense when the latter was created in 1947, though the Navy secretary maintained Cabinet-level status until 1949.

Department of Justice

950 Pennsylvania Ave. NW, 20530; www.justice.gov

The Office of Attorney General was established by act of Congress on Sept. 24, 1789. It officially reached Cabinet rank in Mar. 1792, when the first attorney general, Edmund Randolph, attended his initial Cabinet meeting. The Dept. of Justice, headed by the attorney general, was created June 22, 1870. Provides for the enforcement of federal laws and investigation of violations; furnishes legal counsel in cases involving the federal government and interprets laws relating to the activities of other federal departments; supervises federal penal institutions. The attorney general and Office of Legal Counsel render legal advice, upon request, to the president and department heads. The solicitor general conducts all suits brought before the U.S. Supreme Court in which the federal government is concerned. The Civil Division represents the U.S. government in many civil or criminal matters. The 93 U.S. attorneys (for 94 federal districts) are the principal litigators in the U.S. and its territories. **Budget:** $39.3 bil (2021); $39.6 bil (2022); $44.3 bil (2023); $51.6 bil (2024 est.); $46.9 bil (2025 est.).

- Bureau of Alcohol, Tobacco, Firearms and Explosives (99 New York Ave. NE, 20226); www.atf.gov
- Drug Enforcement Admin. (8701 Morrissette Dr., Springfield, VA 22152); www.dea.gov
- Executive Office for Immigration Review (5107 Leesburg Pike, Ste. 1902, Falls Church, VA 22041); www.usdoj.gov/eoir
- Federal Bureau of Investigation (935 Pennsylvania Ave. NW, 20535); www.fbi.gov
- Federal Bureau of Prisons (320 First St. NW, 20534); www.bop.gov
- Foreign Claims Settlement Commission (441 G St. NW, Ste. 6330, 20579); www.justice.gov/fcsc
- INTERPOL Washington (U.S. Natl. Central Bureau) (20530); www.justice.gov/interpol-washington
- Office of Community Oriented Policing Services (145 N St. NE, 20530); www.cops.usdoj.gov
- Office of Justice Programs (810 Seventh St. NW, 20531); www.ojp.gov
- Office on Violence Against Women (145 N St. NE, 20530); www.justice.gov/ovw
- U.S. Marshals Service (1215 S. Clark St., Arlington, VA 22202); www.usmarshals.gov
- U.S. Parole Commission (90 K St. NE, 20530); www.justice.gov/uspc

Attorneys General

President	Attorney General	Home	Sworn in
Washington	Edmund J. Randolph	VA	1789
	William Bradford	PA	1794
	Charles Lee	VA	1795
Adams, J.	Charles Lee	VA	1797
Jefferson	Levi Lincoln	MA	1801
	John Breckenridge	KY	1805
	Caesar A. Rodney	DE	1807
Madison	Caesar A. Rodney	DE	1807
	William Pinkney	MD	1811
	Richard Rush	PA	1814

President	Attorney General	Home	Sworn in
Monroe	Richard Rush	PA	1817
	William Wirt	VA	1817
Adams, J. Q.	William Wirt	VA	1825
Jackson	John M. Berrien	GA	1829
	Roger B. Taney	MD	1831
	Benjamin F. Butler	NY	1833
Van Buren	Benjamin F. Butler	NY	1837
	Felix Grundy	TN	1838
	Henry D. Gilpin	PA	1840
Harrison, W. H.	John J. Crittenden	KY	1841
Tyler	John J. Crittenden	KY	1841
	Hugh S. Legaré	SC	1841
	John Nelson	MD	1843
Polk	John Y. Mason	VA	1845
	Nathan Clifford	ME	1846
	Isaac Toucey	CT	1848
Taylor	Reverdy Johnson	MD	1849
Fillmore	John J. Crittenden	KY	1850
Pierce	Caleb Cushing	MA	1853
Buchanan	Jeremiah S. Black	PA	1857
	Edwin M. Stanton	PA	1860
Lincoln	Edward Bates	MO	1861
	James Speed	KY	1864
Johnson, A.	James Speed	KY	1865
	Henry Stanbery	OH	1866
	William M. Evarts	NY	1868
Grant	Ebenezer R. Hoar	MA	1869
	Amos T. Akerman	GA	1870
	George H. Williams	OR	1871
	Edwards Pierrepont	NY	1875
	Alphonso Taft	OH	1876
Hayes	Charles Devens	MA	1877
Garfield	I. Wayne MacVeagh	PA	1881
Arthur	Benjamin H. Brewster	PA	1882
Cleveland	Augustus H. Garland	AR	1885
Harrison, B.	William H. H. Miller	IN	1889
Cleveland	Richard Olney	MA	1893
	Judson Harmon	OH	1895
McKinley	Joseph McKenna	CA	1897
	John W. Griggs	NJ	1898
	Philander C. Knox	PA	1901
Roosevelt, T.	Philander C. Knox	PA	1901
	William H. Moody	MA	1904
	Charles J. Bonaparte	MD	1906
Taft	George W. Wickersham	NY	1909
Wilson	James C. McReynolds	TN	1913
	Thomas W. Gregory	TX	1914
	A. Mitchell Palmer	PA	1919
Harding	Harry M. Daugherty	OH	1921
Coolidge	Harry M. Daugherty	OH	1923
	Harlan F. Stone	NY	1924
	John G. Sargent	VT	1925
Hoover	William D. Mitchell	MN	1929
Roosevelt, F. D.	Homer S. Cummings	CT	1933
	Frank Murphy	MI	1939
	Robert H. Jackson	NY	1940
	Francis Biddle	PA	1941
Truman	Thomas C. Clark	TX	1945
	J. Howard McGrath	RI	1949
	James P. McGranery	PA	1952
Eisenhower	Herbert Brownell Jr.	NY	1953
	William P. Rogers	MD	1957
Kennedy	Robert F. Kennedy	MA	1961
Johnson, L. B.	Robert F. Kennedy	MA	1963
	Nicholas Katzenbach	IL	1964
	W. Ramsey Clark	TX	1967
Nixon	John N. Mitchell	NY	1969
	Richard G. Kleindienst	AZ	1972
	Elliot L. Richardson	MA	1973
	William B. Saxbe	OH	1974
Ford	William B. Saxbe	OH	1974
	Edward H. Levi	IL	1975
Carter	Griffin B. Bell	GA	1977
	Benjamin R. Civiletti	MD	1979
Reagan	William French Smith	CA	1981
	Edwin Meese III	CA	1985
	Richard L. Thornburgh	PA	1988
Bush, G. H. W.	Richard L. Thornburgh	PA	1989
	William P. Barr	NY	1991
Clinton	Janet Reno	FL	1993
Bush, G. W.	John Ashcroft	MO	2001
	Alberto R. Gonzales	TX	2005
	Michael B. Mukasey	NY	2007
Obama	Eric H. Holder Jr.	DC	2009
	Loretta E. Lynch	NY	2015
Trump	Jeff Sessions	AL	2017
	William P. Barr	NY	2019
Biden	Merrick Garland	IL	2021

Department of the Interior

1849 C St. NW, 20240; www.doi.gov

Created by act of Congress on Mar. 3, 1849. Custodian of natural resources. Has the responsibility of protecting and conserving the country's land, water, minerals, fish, and wildlife; of promoting the wise use of all these natural resources; of maintaining national parks and recreation areas; and of preserving historic places. It also provides for the welfare of American Indian reservation communities and of inhabitants of island territories under U.S. administration. **Budget:** $15.8 bil (2021); $13.9 bil (2022); $15.9 bil (2023); $23.1 bil (2024 est.); $24.5 bil (2025 est.).

- Bureau of Indian Affairs; www.bia.gov
- Bureau of Indian Education; www.bie.edu
- Bureau of Land Management; www.blm.gov
- Bureau of Ocean Energy Management; www.boem.gov
- Bureau of Reclamation; www.usbr.gov
- Bureau of Safety and Environmental Enforcement; www.bsee.gov
- National Park Service; www.nps.gov
- Office of Surface Mining Reclamation and Enforcement; www.osmre.gov
- U.S. Fish and Wildlife Service; www.fws.gov
- U.S. Geological Survey (12201 Sunrise Valley Dr., Reston, VA 20192); www.usgs.gov

Secretaries of the Interior

President	Secretary	Home	Sworn in
Taylor	Thomas Ewing	OH	1849
Fillmore	Thomas M. T. McKennan	PA	1850
	Alex H. H. Stuart	VA	1850
Pierce	Robert McClelland	MI	1853
Buchanan	Jacob Thompson	MS	1857
Lincoln	Caleb B. Smith	IN	1861
	John P. Usher	IN	1863
Johnson, A.	John P. Usher	IN	1865
	James Harlan	IA	1865
	Orville H. Browning	IL	1866
Grant	Jacob D. Cox	OH	1869
	Columbus Delano	OH	1870
	Zachariah Chandler	MI	1875
Hayes	Carl Schurz	MO	1877
Garfield	Samuel J. Kirkwood	IA	1881
Arthur	Henry M. Teller	CO	1882
Cleveland	Lucius Q. C. Lamar	MS	1885
	William F. Vilas	WI	1888
Harrison, B.	John W. Noble	MO	1889
Cleveland	M. Hoke Smith	GA	1893
	David R. Francis	MO	1896
McKinley	Cornelius N. Bliss	NY	1897
	Ethan A. Hitchcock	MO	1898
Roosevelt, T.	Ethan A. Hitchcock	MO	1901
	James R. Garfield	OH	1907
Taft	Richard A. Ballinger	WA	1909
	Walter L. Fisher	IL	1911
Wilson	Franklin K. Lane	CA	1913
	John B. Payne	IL	1920
Harding	Albert B. Fall	NM	1921
	Hubert Work	CO	1923
Coolidge	Hubert Work	CO	1923
	Roy O. West	IL	1929
Hoover	Ray Lyman Wilbur	CA	1929
Roosevelt, F. D.	Harold L. Ickes	IL	1933
Truman	Harold L. Ickes	IL	1945
	Julius A. Krug	WI	1946
	Oscar L. Chapman	CO	1949
Eisenhower	Douglas McKay	OR	1953
	Fred A. Seaton	NE	1956
Kennedy	Stewart L. Udall	AZ	1961
Johnson, L. B.	Stewart L. Udall	AZ	1963
Nixon	Walter J. Hickel	AK	1969
	Rogers C. B. Morton	MD	1971
Ford	Rogers C. B. Morton	MD	1971
	Stanley K. Hathaway	WY	1975
	Thomas S. Kleppe	ND	1975
Carter	Cecil D. Andrus	ID	1977
Reagan	James G. Watt	CO	1981
	William P. Clark	CA	1983
	Donald P. Hodel	OR	1985
Bush, G. H. W.	Manuel Lujan	NM	1989
Clinton	Bruce Babbitt	AZ	1993
Bush, G. W.	Gale Norton	CO	2001
	Dirk Kempthorne	ID	2006
Obama	Kenneth L. Salazar	CO	2009
	Sally Jewell	WA	2013
Trump	Ryan Zinke	MT	2017
	David Bernhardt	CO	2019
Biden	Deb Haaland	NM	2021

Department of Agriculture

1400 Independence Ave. SW, 20250; www.usda.gov

Created by act of Congress on May 15, 1862. On Feb. 8, 1889, its commissioner was renamed secretary of agriculture and became a member of the Cabinet. Provides leadership on food, agriculture, and natural resources; supports scientific research and education for agriculture, nutrition, and food safety. Develops nutrition assistance programs, promotes healthy eating, supplies food stamps, grades and inspects the commercial supply of food. Responsible for the health of the land through sustainable management and conservation, manages public lands in national forests and grasslands; safeguards against invasive pests and diseases; ensures the health and care of animals and plants. Oversees assistance and conservation programs for farmers and ranchers and programs to improve the rural economy and quality of life. Facilitates domestic and international marketing of U.S. agricultural products. **Budget:** $235.2 bil (2021); $245.2 bil (2022); $228.9 bil (2023); $254.8 bil (2024 est.); $233.2 bil (2025 est.).

- Agricultural Research Service; www.ars.usda.gov
- Economic Research Service; www.ers.usda.gov
- Food and Nutrition Service (1320 Braddock Pl., Alexandria, VA 22314); www.fns.usda.gov
- Food Safety and Inspection Service; www.fsis.usda.gov
- Foreign Agricultural Service; www.fas.usda.gov
- Natl. Agricultural Statistics Service; www.nass.usda.gov
- Natural Resources Conservation Service; www.nrcs.usda.gov
- U.S. Forest Service; www.fs.usda.gov

Secretaries of Agriculture

President	Secretary	Home	Sworn in
Cleveland	Norman J. Colman	MO	1889
Harrison, B.	Jeremiah M. Rusk	WI	1889
Cleveland	J. Sterling Morton	NE	1893
McKinley	James Wilson	IA	1897
Roosevelt, T.	James Wilson	IA	1901
Taft	James Wilson	IA	1909
Wilson	David F. Houston	MO	1913
	Edwin T. Meredith	IA	1920
Harding	Henry C. Wallace	IA	1921
Coolidge	Henry C. Wallace	IA	1923
	Howard M. Gore	WV	1924
	William M. Jardine	KS	1925
Hoover	Arthur M. Hyde	MO	1929
Roosevelt, F. D.	Henry A. Wallace	IA	1933
	Claude R. Wickard	IN	1940
Truman	Clinton P. Anderson	NM	1945
	Charles F. Brannan	CO	1948
Eisenhower	Ezra Taft Benson	UT	1953
Kennedy	Orville L. Freeman	MN	1961
Johnson, L. B.	Orville L. Freeman	MN	1963
Nixon	Clifford M. Hardin	IN	1969
	Earl L. Butz	IN	1971
Ford	Earl L. Butz	IN	1974
	John A. Knebel	VA	1976
Carter	Bob Bergland	MN	1977
Reagan	John R. Block	IL	1981
	Richard E. Lyng	CA	1986
Bush, G. H. W.	Clayton K. Yeutter	NE	1989
	Edward Madigan	IL	1991
Clinton	Mike Espy	MS	1993
	Dan Glickman	KS	1995
Bush, G. W.	Ann M. Veneman	CA	2001
	Mike Johanns	NE	2005
	Ed Schafer	ND	2008
Obama	Tom Vilsack	IA	2009
Trump	Sonny Perdue	GA	2017
Biden	Tom Vilsack	IA	2021

Department of Commerce

1401 Constitution Ave. NW, 20230; www.commerce.gov

The Dept. of Commerce was formed by Congress Mar. 4, 1913, when it divided the Dept. of Commerce and Labor into two departments. Fosters, serves, and promotes the nation's economic development and technological advancement; supports the comprehension and use of the environment and its oceanic life; assists states, communities, and individuals with economic progress; promotes trade abroad and ensures an effective export control and treaty compliance system. Issues trademarks and patents, maintains measurement standards, and manages the federal telecommunications spectrum. Collects, analyzes, and distributes statistics regarding the nation and the economy through the Bureaus of the Census and of Economic Analysis. NOAA explores, monitors, and conserves oceans and coasts, tracks weather and other environmental data. **Budget:** $13.1 bil (2021); $11.7 bil (2022); $12.0 bil (2023); $20.5 bil (2024 est.); $33.7 bil (2025 est.).

- Bureau of Economic Analysis (4600 Silver Hill Rd., Suitland, MD 20746); www.bea.gov
- Minority Business Development Agency; www.mbda.gov
- Natl. Institute of Standards and Technology (100 Bureau Dr., Gaithersburg, MD 20899); www.nist.gov
- Natl. Oceanic and Atmospheric Admin.; www.noaa.gov
- Natl. Technical Information Service (5301 Shawnee Rd., Alexandria, VA 22312); www.ntis.gov
- Natl. Telecommunications and Information Admin.; www.ntia.doc.gov
- U.S. Census Bureau (4600 Silver Hill Rd., 20233); www.census.gov
- U.S. Patent and Trademark Office (600 Dulany St., Alexandria, VA 22314); www.uspto.gov

Secretaries of Commerce

President	Secretary	Home	Sworn in
Wilson	William C. Redfield	NY	1913
	Joshua W. Alexander	MO	1919
Harding	Herbert C. Hoover	CA	1921
Coolidge	Herbert C. Hoover	CA	1923
	William F. Whiting	MA	1928
Hoover	Robert P. Lamont	IL	1929
	Roy D. Chapin	MI	1932
Roosevelt, F. D.	Daniel C. Roper	SC	1933
	Harry L. Hopkins	NY	1939
	Jesse H. Jones	TX	1940
	Henry A. Wallace	IA	1945
Truman	Henry A. Wallace	IA	1945
	W. Averell Harriman	NY	1947
	Charles W. Sawyer	OH	1948
Eisenhower	Sinclair Weeks	MA	1953
	Lewis L. Strauss	NY	1958
	Frederick H. Mueller	MI	1959
Kennedy	Luther H. Hodges	NC	1961
Johnson, L. B.	Luther H. Hodges	NC	1963
	John T. Connor	NJ	1965
	Alex B. Trowbridge	NJ	1967
	Cyrus R. Smith	NY	1968
Nixon	Maurice H. Stans	MN	1969
	Peter G. Peterson	IL	1972
	Frederick B. Dent	SC	1973
Ford	Frederick B. Dent	SC	1974
	Rogers C. B. Morton	MD	1975
	Elliot L. Richardson	MA	1975
Carter	Juanita M. Kreps	NC	1977
	Philip M. Klutznick	IL	1979
Reagan	Malcolm Baldrige	CT	1981
	C. William Verity Jr.	OH	1987
Bush, G. H. W.	Robert A. Mosbacher	TX	1989
	Barbara H. Franklin	PA	1992
Clinton	Ronald H. Brown	DC	1993
	Mickey Kantor	CA	1996
	William M. Daley	IL	1997
	Norman Y. Mineta	CA	2000
Bush, G. W.	Donald L. Evans	TX	2001
	Carlos M. Gutierrez	MI	2005
Obama	Gary F. Locke	WA	2009
	John Bryson	CA	2011
	Penny Pritzker	IL	2013
Trump	Wilbur L. Ross Jr.	NJ	2017
Biden	Gina Raimondo	RI	2021

Secretaries of Commerce and Labor

The Dept. of Commerce and Labor was created by Congress on Feb. 14, 1903.

President	Secretary	Home	Sworn in
Roosevelt, T.	George B. Cortelyou	NY	1903
	Victor H. Metcalf	CA	1904
	Oscar S. Straus	NY	1906
Taft	Charles Nagel	MO	1909

Department of Labor

200 Constitution Ave. NW, 20210; www.dol.gov

The Dept. of Labor was formed by Congress Mar. 4, 1913, when it divided the Dept. of Commerce and Labor into two departments. Administers federal labor laws to foster, promote, and develop the welfare of job seekers, wage earners, and retirees of the U.S.; to improve working conditions; and to advance opportunities for profitable employment. Administers standards for wages and overtime pay, safety and health conditions, workers' compensation. Tracks changes in employment, prices, and other national economic measurements. Regulates pension and welfare benefit plans, the hiring and employment of migrant and seasonal workers, and requirements pertaining to the mining, construction, and transportation industries. Monitors labor unions and their funds. **Budget:** $404.8 bil (2021); $51.7 bil (2022); $87.5 bil (2023); $84.4 bil (2024 est.); $63.8 bil (2025 est.).

- Bureau of Labor Statistics (2 Massachusetts Ave. NE, 20212); www.bls.gov
- Employment and Training Admin.; www.doleta.gov
- Mine Safety and Health Admin. (201 12th St. S, Ste. 401, Arlington, VA 22202); www.msha.gov
- Occupational Safety and Health Admin.; www.osha.gov
- Wage and Hour Div.; www.dol.gov/whd

Secretaries of Labor

President	Secretary	Home	Sworn in
Wilson	William B. Wilson	PA	1913
Harding	James J. Davis	PA	1921
Coolidge	James J. Davis	PA	1923
Hoover	James J. Davis	PA	1929
	William N. Doak	VA	1930
Roosevelt, F. D.	Frances Perkins	NY	1933
Truman	L. B. Schwellenbach	WA	1945
	Maurice J. Tobin	MA	1949
Eisenhower	Martin P. Durkin	IL	1953
	James P. Mitchell	NJ	1953
Kennedy	Arthur J. Goldberg	IL	1961
	W. Willard Wirtz	IL	1962
Johnson, L. B.	W. Willard Wirtz	IL	1963
Nixon	George P. Shultz	IL	1969
	James D. Hodgson	CA	1970
	Peter J. Brennan	NY	1973
Ford	Peter J. Brennan	NY	1974
	John T. Dunlop	CA	1975
	W. J. Usery Jr.	GA	1976
Carter	F. Ray Marshall	TX	1977
Reagan	Raymond J. Donovan	NJ	1981
	William E. Brock	TN	1985
	Ann D. McLaughlin	DC	1987
Bush, G. H. W.	Elizabeth H. Dole	NC	1989
	Lynn Martin	IL	1991
Clinton	Robert B. Reich	MA	1993
	Alexis M. Herman	AL	1997
Bush, G. W.	Elaine L. Chao	KY	2001
Obama	Hilda L. Solis	CA	2009
	Thomas E. Perez	MD	2013
Trump	R. Alexander Acosta	FL	2017
	Eugene Scalia	DC	2019
Biden	Marty Walsh	MA	2021

Department of Housing and Urban Development

451 7th St. SW, 20410; www.hud.gov

Created by act of Congress on Sept. 9, 1965. Responsible for housing needs and the improvement and development of urban areas. Supports affordable housing, provides grants for community development and redevelopment. Enforces fair and safe housing standards. Provides funds to assist homeless individuals and families with emergency and transitional shelters. The Federal Housing Administration provides mortgage insurance on loans made by approved lenders. **Budget:** $35.1 bil (2021); $29.3 bil (2022); $55.2 bil (2023); $56.3 bil (2024 est.); $76.1 bil (2025 est.).

- Fannie Mae (Federal Natl. Mortgage Association) (1100 15th St. NW, 20005); www.fanniemae.com
- Federal Housing Admin.; www.hud.gov/federal_housing_administration
- Freddie Mac (Federal Home Loan Mortgage Corporation) (8200 Jones Branch Dr., McLean, VA 22102); www.freddiemac.com
- Ginnie Mae (Government Natl. Mortgage Association) (425 3rd St. SW, Ste. 500, 20024); www.ginniemae.gov

Note: Fannie Mae and Freddie Mac are government-sponsored enterprises (GSEs).

Secretaries of Housing and Urban Development

President	Secretary	Home	Sworn in
Johnson, L. B.	Robert C. Weaver	WA	1966
	Robert C. Wood	MA	1969
Nixon	George W. Romney	MI	1969
	James T. Lynn	OH	1973
Ford	James T. Lynn	OH	1974
	Carla Anderson Hills	CA	1975
Carter	Patricia Roberts Harris	DC	1977
	Moon Landrieu	LA	1979
Reagan	Samuel R. Pierce Jr.	NY	1981
Bush, G. H. W.	Jack F. Kemp	NY	1989
Clinton	Henry G. Cisneros	TX	1993
	Andrew M. Cuomo	NY	1997
Bush, G. W.	Mel Martinez	FL	2001
	Alphonso Jackson	TX	2004
	Steve Preston	VA	2008
Obama	Shaun L. S. Donovan	NY	2009
	Julián Castro	TX	2014
Trump	Ben Carson	MD	2017
Biden	Marcia Fudge	OH	2021

Department of Transportation

1200 New Jersey Ave. SE, 20590; www.transportation.gov

Created by act of Congress on Oct. 15, 1966. Promotes and develops rapid, safe, efficient, and convenient transportation in the U.S.; monitors and administers assistance to transportation industries; negotiates and implements international transportation agreements. Manages airspace, commercial space transportation, and the movement of hazardous materials. Resolves railroad rate and service disputes and reviews proposed railroad mergers. Analyzes and shares research and statistics to develop and improve transportation. Develops and enforces regulations on the nation's pipeline transportation system. The Maritime Administration maintains a fleet of cargo ships in reserve for war or national emergencies and commissions officers of the Merchant Marine. Operates the U.S. portion of the St. Lawrence Seaway between Montréal and Lake Erie. **Budget:** $104.9 bil (2021); $113.7 bil (2022); $109.5 bil (2023); $121.1 bil (2024 est.); $131.7 bil (2025 est.).

- Federal Aviation Admin. (800 Independence Ave. SW, 20591); www.faa.gov
- Federal Highway Admin.; www.fhwa.dot.gov
- Federal Motor Carrier Safety Admin.; www.fmcsa.dot.gov
- Federal Railroad Admin.; www.fra.dot.gov
- Federal Transit Admin.; www.transit.dot.gov
- Maritime Admin.; www.maritime.dot.gov
- Natl. Highway Traffic Safety Admin.; www.nhtsa.gov
- Pipeline and Hazardous Materials Safety Admin.; www.phmsa.dot.gov
- St. Lawrence Seaway Development Corp.; www.seaway.dot.gov

Secretaries of Transportation

President	Secretary	Home	Sworn in
Johnson, L. B.	Alan S. Boyd	FL	1966
Nixon	John A. Volpe	MA	1969
	Claude S. Brinegar	CA	1973
Ford	Claude S. Brinegar	CA	1974
	William T. Coleman Jr.	PA	1975
Carter	Brock Adams	WA	1977
	Neil E. Goldschmidt	OR	1979
Reagan	Andrew L. Lewis Jr.	PA	1981
	Elizabeth H. Dole	NC	1983
	James H. Burnley	NC	1987
Bush, G. H. W.	Samuel K. Skinner	IL	1989
	Andrew H. Card Jr.	MA	1992
Clinton	Federico F. Peña	CO	1993
	Rodney E. Slater	AR	1997
Bush, G. W.	Norman Y. Mineta	CA	2001
	Mary E. Peters	AZ	2006
Obama	Raymond L. LaHood	IL	2009
	Anthony Foxx	NC	2013
Trump	Elaine L. Chao	KY	2017
Biden	Pete Buttigieg	IN	2021

Department of Energy

1000 Independence Ave. SW, 20585; www.energy.gov

Created by federal law on Aug. 4, 1977. Secures the nation's energy and promotes scientific and technological innovation. Oversees the national energy supply and electric grid. Investigates and promotes clean and reliable energy. Manages and cleans up nuclear and other radioactive material, including nuclear weapons. The Office of Scientific and Technical Information supports much of America's scientific research through program offices, education initiatives, national laboratories, and technology centers. Four power marketing administrations sell power from federal hydroelectric projects across the West and Southeast. **Budget:** $33.7 bil (2021); $22.4 bil (2022); $34.4 bil (2023); $58.3 bil (2024 est.); $61.6 bil (2025 est.).

- Federal Energy Regulatory Commission (independent regulatory agency) (888 1st St. NE, 20426); www.ferc.gov
- Natl. Nuclear Security Admin.; www.energy.gov/nnsa/national-nuclear-security-administration
- Science Office; www.energy.gov/science/office-science
- U.S. Energy Information Admin.; www.eia.gov

Secretaries of Energy

President	Secretary	Home	Sworn in
Carter	James R. Schlesinger	VA	1977
	Charles W. Duncan Jr.	WY	1979
Reagan	James B. Edwards	SC	1981
	Donald P. Hodel	OR	1982
	John S. Herrington	CA	1985
Bush, G. H. W.	James D. Watkins	CA	1989
Clinton	Hazel R. O'Leary	MN	1993
	Federico F. Peña	CO	1997
	Bill Richardson	NM	1998
Bush, G. W.	Spencer Abraham	MI	2001
	Samuel W. Bodman	MA	2005
Obama	Steven Chu	CA	2009
	Ernest Moniz	MA	2013
Trump	Rick Perry	TX	2017
	Dan Brouillette	TX	2019
Biden	Jennifer Granholm	MI	2021

Department of Health and Human Services

200 Independence Ave. SW, 20201; www.hhs.gov

The Dept. of Health, Education, and Welfare was created by Congress on Apr. 11, 1953. On Sept. 27, 1979, Congress approved creation of a separate Dept. of Education. The existing department was renamed the Dept. of Health and Human Services. Administers a wide range of programs in the fields of health care and social services that affect nearly all Americans. Medicare and Medicaid provide health care insurance for one in four Americans. The HRSA improves health care services for people who are uninsured, isolated, or medically vulnerable; oversees organ, tissue, and blood cell donations. The FDA assures the safety of food, drugs, cosmetics, biological products, and medical devices. The CDC monitors and safeguards against disease outbreaks. The NIH supports research projects nationwide and 27 health institutes and centers. The surgeon general is the nation's chief health educator and leads the U.S. Public Health Service Commissioned Corps. **Budget:** $1.47 tril (2021); $1.64 tril (2022); $1.71 tril (2023); $1.67 tril (2024 est.); $1.80 tril (2025 est.).

- Admin. for Children and Families (330 C St. SW, 20201); www.acf.hhs.gov
- Admin. for Community Living (330 C St. SW, 20201); www.acl.gov
- Agency for Healthcare Research and Quality (5600 Fishers Ln., Rockville, MD 20857); www.ahrq.gov
- Centers for Disease Control and Prevention (1600 Clifton Rd., Atlanta, GA 30333); www.cdc.gov
- Centers for Medicare and Medicaid Services (7500 Security Blvd., Baltimore, MD 21244); www.cms.gov
- Food and Drug Admin. (10903 New Hampshire Ave., Silver Spring, MD 20993); www.fda.gov
- Health Resources and Services Admin. (5600 Fishers Ln., Rockville, MD 20857); www.hrsa.gov
- Indian Health Service (5600 Fishers Ln., Rockville, MD 20857); www.ihs.gov
- Natl. Institutes of Health (9000 Rockville Pike, Bethesda, MD 20892); www.nih.gov
- Substance Abuse and Mental Health Services Admin. (5600 Fishers Ln., Rockville, MD 20857); www.samhsa.gov

Secretaries of Health and Human Services

President	Secretary	Home	Sworn in
Carter	Patricia Roberts Harris	DC	1979
Reagan	Richard S. Schweiker	PA	1981
	Margaret M. Heckler	MA	1983
Reagan	Otis R. Bowen	IN	1985
Bush, G. H. W.	Louis W. Sullivan	GA	1989
Clinton	Donna E. Shalala	WI	1993
Bush, G. W.	Tommy Thompson	WI	2001
	Michael O. Leavitt	UT	2005
Obama	Kathleen Sebelius	KS	2009
	Sylvia Mathews Burwell	WV	2014
Trump	Thomas E. Price	GA	2017
	Alex Azar	IN	2018
Biden	Xavier Becerra	CA	2021

Secretaries of Health, Education, and Welfare

President	Secretary	Home	Sworn in
Eisenhower	Oveta Culp Hobby	TX	1953
	Marion B. Folsom	NY	1955
	Arthur S. Flemming	OH	1958
Kennedy	Abraham A. Ribicoff	CT	1961
	Anthony J. Celebrezze	OH	1962
Johnson, L. B.	Anthony J. Celebrezze	OH	1963
	John W. Gardner	NY	1965
	Wilbur J. Cohen	MI	1968
Nixon	Robert H. Finch	CA	1969
	Elliot L. Richardson	MA	1970
	Caspar W. Weinberger	CA	1973
Ford	Caspar W. Weinberger	CA	1974
	Forrest D. Mathews	AL	1975
Carter	Joseph A. Califano Jr.	DC	1977
	Patricia Roberts Harris	DC	1979

Department of Education

400 Maryland Ave. SW, 20202; www.ed.gov

The Dept. of Health, Education, and Welfare was created by Congress on Apr. 11, 1953. On Sept. 27, 1979, Congress approved creation of a separate Dept. of Education. Works with state agencies and local systems to ensure equal access to all levels of education and seeks to improve the quality of that education through federal support, research programs, and information sharing. Oversees a variety of financial aid distributed through competition, need-based requests, or a set formula. Sets policy goals and initiatives. Conducts research and gathers educational information to disseminate to educators and the general public. **Budget:** $260.4 bil (2021); $639.4 bil (2022); –$41.1 bil (2023); $250.7 bil (2024 est.); $141.9 bil (2025 est.).

Secretaries of Education

President	Secretary	Home	Sworn in
Carter	Shirley Hufstedler	CA	1979
Reagan	Terrel H. Bell	UT	1981
	William J. Bennett	NY	1985
	Lauro F. Cavazos	TX	1988
Bush, G. H. W.	Lauro F. Cavazos	TX	1989
	Lamar Alexander	TN	1991
Clinton	Richard W. Riley	SC	1993
Bush, G. W.	Roderick R. Paige	TX	2001
	Margaret Spellings	TX	2005
Obama	Arne Duncan	IL	2009
	John King	NY	2016
Trump	Betsy DeVos	MI	2017
Biden	Miguel Cardona	CT	2021

Department of Veterans Affairs

810 Vermont Ave. NW, 20420; www.va.gov

Pres. Ronald Reagan signed a bill in 1988 granting Cabinet-level status to the Veterans Administration. The agency became the Dept. of Veterans Affairs on Mar. 15, 1989. Supports veterans and their families with nationwide programs for health care, financial assistance, and burial benefits. Compensates for disabilities incurred during wartime. Provides pensions for veterans with low incomes, education assistance, loan guaranty, and life insurance. Manages America's largest medical education and health professions training program, which includes hospitals, clinics, nursing homes, veterans centers, rehabilitation treatment, readjustment counseling, and home-care programs. Also funds medical research pertaining to veterans issues. Manages 143 national cemeteries; provides headstones and markers. **Budget:** $233.8 bil (2021); $273.9 bil (2022); $301.0 bil (2023); $346.0 bil (2024 est.); $369.7 bil (2025 est.).

Secretaries of Veterans Affairs

President	Secretary	Home	Sworn in
Bush, G. H. W.	Edward J. Derwinski	IL	1989
Clinton	Jesse Brown	IL	1993
	Togo D. West Jr.	NC	1998
Bush, G. W.	Anthony J. Principi	CA	2001
	R. James Nicholson	CO	2005
	James B. Peake	MO	2007
Obama	Eric K. Shinseki	VA	2009
	Robert A. McDonald	OH	2014
Trump	David J. Shulkin	PA	2017
	Robert Wilkie	NC	2018
Biden	Denis McDonough	MD	2021

Department of Homeland Security

245 Murray Ln. SW, 20528; www.dhs.gov

Created by act of Congress on Nov. 25, 2002. Provides a unified core for the national network of organizations and institutions involved in efforts to secure the U.S., its borders, infrastructure, and major events. Provides funding, intelligence, and training for law enforcement and disaster relief. Leads and coordinates response teams to natural and manmade emergencies. Identifies threats, administers the Natl. Terrorism Advisory

System. **Budget:** $91.1 bil (2021); $80.9 bil (2022); $89.0 bil (2023); $134.2 bil (2024 est.); $90.6 bil (2025 est.).

- Cybersecurity and Infrastructure Security Agency (1110 N. Glebe Road, Arlington, VA 20598-0630); www.cisa.gov
- Fed. Emergency Management Agency (500 C St. SW, 20472); www.fema.gov
- Transportation Security Admin. (6595 Springfield Center Dr, Springfield, VA 22150); www.tsa.gov
- U.S. Citizenship and Immigration Services (5900 Capital Gateway Dr., Camp Springs, MD 20588); www.uscis.gov
- U.S. Coast Guard (2703 Martin Luther King Jr. Ave. SE, 20593); www.uscg.mil
- U.S. Customs and Border Protection (1300 Pennsylvania Ave. NW, 20229); www.cbp.gov
- U.S. Immigration and Customs Enforcement (500 12th St. SW, 20536); www.ice.gov
- U.S. Secret Service; www.secretservice.gov

Secretaries of Homeland Security

President	Secretary	Home	Sworn in
Bush, G. W.	Thomas Ridge	PA	2003
	Michael Chertoff	NJ	2005
Obama	Janet A. Napolitano	AZ	2009
	Jeh Johnson	NY	2014
Trump	John F. Kelly	MA	2017
	Kirstjen M. Nielsen	FL	2017
Biden	Alejandro Mayorkas	CA	2021

Other Notable U.S. Government Agencies

Source: *The U.S. Government Manual*; National Archives and Records Administration; World Almanac research
All addresses are for Washington, DC, unless otherwise noted; as of Aug. 2024.

Administrative Conference of the U.S.: Andrew Fois, chair (1120 20th St. NW, Ste. 706S, 20036); www.acus.gov
African Development Foundation: Travis Adkins, pres. and CEO (1400 I St. NW, 20005); www.usadf.gov
AmeriCorps (fmr. Corp. for Natl. and Community Service): Michael D. Smith, CEO (250 E St. SW, 20525); www.americorps.gov
Amtrak: Stephen J. Gardner, CEO (1 Massachusetts Ave. NW, 20001); www.amtrak.com
Central Intelligence Agency: William J. Burns, dir. (Cabinet rank) (20505); www.cia.gov
Commodity Futures Trading Commission: Rostin Behnam, chair (1155 21st St. NW, 20581); www.cftc.gov
Consumer Financial Protection Bureau: Rohit Chopra, dir. (1700 G St. NW, 20552); www.consumerfinance.gov
Consumer Product Safety Commission: Alexander Hoehn-Saric, chair (4330 East-West Hwy., Bethesda, MD 20814); www.cpsc.gov
Defense Nuclear Facilities Safety Board: Joyce L. Connery, chair (625 Indiana Ave. NW, Ste. 700, 20004); www.dnfsb.gov
Election Assistance Commission: Benjamin W. Hovland, chair (633 3rd Street NW, Ste. 200, 20001); www.eac.gov
Environmental Protection Agency: Michael S. Regan, admin. (Cabinet rank) (1200 Pennsylvania Ave. NW, 20460); www.epa.gov
Equal Employment Opportunity Commission: Charlotte A. Burrows, chair (131 M St. NE, 20507); www.eeoc.gov
Export-Import Bank of the U.S.: Reta Jo Lewis, chair (811 Vermont Ave. NW, 20571); www.exim.gov
Farm Credit Admin.: Vincent G. Logan, chair and CEO (1501 Farm Credit Dr., McLean, VA 22102); www.fca.gov
Federal Communications Commission: Jessica Rosenworcel, chair (45 L St. NE, 20554); www.fcc.gov
Federal Deposit Insurance Corp.: Martin J. Gruenberg, chair (550 17th St. NW, 20429); www.fdic.gov
Federal Election Commission: Sean J. Cooksey, chair (1050 1st St. NE, 20463); www.fec.gov
Federal Housing Finance Agency: Sandra L. Thompson, dir. (400 7th St. SW, 20219); www.fhfa.gov
Federal Labor Relations Authority: Susan Tsui Grundmann, chair (1400 K St. NW, 20424); www.flra.gov
Federal Maritime Commission: Daniel B. Maffei, chair (800 N. Capitol St. NW, 20573); www.fmc.gov
Federal Mediation and Conciliation Service: Gregory Goldstein, acting dir. (250 E St. SW, 20427); www.fmcs.gov
Federal Mine Safety and Health Review Commission: Mary Lu Jordan, chair (1331 Pennsylvania Ave. NW, Ste. 520N, 20004); www.fmshrc.gov
Federal Reserve System: Jerome H. Powell, chair (20th St. and Constitution Ave. NW, 20551); www.federalreserve.gov
Federal Retirement Thrift Investment Board: Mike Gerber, chair (77 K St. NE, Ste. 1000, 20002); www.frtib.gov
Federal Trade Commission: Lina Khan, chair (600 Pennsylvania Ave. NW, 20580); www.ftc.gov
General Services Admin.: Robin Carnahan, admin. (1800 F St. NW, 20405); www.gsa.gov
Institute of Museum and Library Services: Cyndee Landrum, acting dir. (955 L'Enfant Plaza North SW, Ste. 4000, 20024); www.imls.gov
Inter-American Foundation: Eddy Arriola, chair (1331 Pennsylvania Ave. NW, Ste. 1200N, 20004); www.iaf.gov
Merit Systems Protection Board: Cathy A. Harris, chair (1615 M St. NW, 5th Fl., 20419); www.mspb.gov
Natl. Aeronautics and Space Admin.: Bill Nelson, admin. (300 E St. SW, Ste. 5R30, 20546); www.nasa.gov
Natl. Archives and Records Admin.: Colleen Shogan, archivist (8601 Adelphi Rd., College Park, MD 20740); www.archives.gov
Natl. Capital Planning Commission: Teri Hawks Goodmann, chair (401 9th St. NW, Ste. 500N, 20004); www.ncpc.gov
Natl. Council on Disability: Claudia L. Gordon, chair (1331 F St. NW, Ste. 850, 20004); www.ncd.gov
Natl. Credit Union Admin.: Todd M. Harper, chair (1775 Duke St., Alexandria, VA 22314); www.ncua.gov
Natl. Endowment for the Arts: Maria Rosario Jackson, chair (400 7th St. SW, 20506); www.arts.gov
Natl. Endowment for the Humanities: Shelly C. Lowe, chair (400 7th St. SW, 20506); www.neh.gov
Natl. Indian Gaming Commission: Sharon M. Avery, acting chair (1849 C St. NW, Mail Stop 1621, 20240); www.nigc.gov
Natl. Labor Relations Board: Lauren McFerran, chair (1015 Half St. SE, 20570); www.nlrb.gov
Natl. Mediation Board: Deirdre Hamilton, chair (1301 K St. NW, Ste. 250E, 20005); www.nmb.gov
Natl. Science Foundation: Sethuraman Panchanathan, dir. (2415 Eisenhower Ave., Arlington, VA 22314); www.nsf.gov
Natl. Transportation Safety Board: Jennifer L. Homendy, chair (490 L'Enfant Plaza SW, 20594); www.ntsb.gov
Nuclear Regulatory Commission: Christopher T. Hanson, chair (20555); www.nrc.gov
Nuclear Waste Technical Review Board: Nathan Siu, chair (2300 Clarendon Blvd., Ste. 1300, Arlington, VA 22201); www.nwtrb.gov
Occupational Safety and Health Review Commission: Cynthia L. Attwood, chair (1120 20th St. NW, 9th Fl., 20036); www.oshrc.gov
Office of the Dir. of Natl. Intelligence: Avril Haines, dir. (Cabinet rank) (20511); www.dni.gov
Office of Government Ethics: Shelley K. Finlayson, acting dir. (1201 New York Ave. NW, Ste. 500, 20005); www.oge.gov
Office of Personnel Management: Rob Shriver, acting dir. (1900 E St. NW, 20415); www.opm.gov
Office of Special Counsel: Hampton Dellinger, spec. counsel (1730 M St. NW, Ste. 218, 20036); www.osc.gov
Peace Corps: Carol Spahn, dir. (1275 1st St. NE, 20526); www.peacecorps.gov
Pension Benefit Guaranty Corp.: Ann Orr, acting dir. (1200 K St. NW, 20005); www.pbgc.gov
Postal Regulatory Commission: Michael M. Kubayanda, chair (901 New York Ave. NW, Ste. 200, 20268); www.prc.gov
Railroad Retirement Board: Erhard R. Chorlé, chair (844 N. Rush St., Chicago, IL 60611); www.rrb.gov
Securities and Exchange Commission: Gary Gensler, chair (100 F St. NE, 20549); www.sec.gov
Selective Service System: Joel C. Spangenberg, acting dir. (Natl. Headquarters, Arlington, VA 22209); www.sss.gov
Small Business Admin.: Isabella Casillas Guzman, admin. (Cabinet rank) (409 3rd St. SW, 20416); www.sba.gov
Social Security Admin.: Martin O'Malley, comm. (1100 West High Rise, 6401 Security Blvd., Baltimore, MD 21235); www.ssa.gov
Tennessee Valley Authority: Joe Ritch, chair (400 W. Summit Hill Dr., Knoxville, TN 37902); www.tva.gov
U.S. Agency for Global Media (fmr. Broadcasting Board of Governors): Amanda Bennett, CEO (330 Independence Ave. SW, 20037); www.usagm.gov
U.S. Agency for Intl. Development: Samantha Power, admin. (Ronald Reagan Bldg., 20523); www.usaid.gov
U.S. Commission on Civil Rights: Rochelle Garza, chair (1331 Pennsylvania Ave. NW, Ste. 1150, 20425); www.usccr.gov
U.S. Intl. Development Finance Corp. (fmr. Overseas Private Investment Corp.): Scott A. Nathan, CEO (1100 New York Ave. NW, 20527); www.dfc.gov
U.S. Intl. Trade Commission: David S. Johanson, chair (500 E St. SW, 20436); www.usitc.gov
U.S. Postal Service: Louis DeJoy, postmaster general and CEO (475 L'Enfant Plaza SW, 20260); www.usps.com
U.S. Trade and Development Agency: Enoh T. Ebong, dir. (1101 Wilson Blvd., Ste. 1100, Arlington, VA 22209); www.ustda.gov

CONGRESS

Floor Leaders in the U.S. Senate, 1920-2024

MAJORITY LEADERS

Name	Party	State	Tenure
Charles Curtis[1]	Rep.	KS	1925-1929
James E. Watson	Rep.	IN	1929-1933
Joseph T. Robinson	Dem.	AR	1933-1937
Alben W. Barkley	Dem.	KY	1937-1947
Wallace H. White	Rep.	ME	1947-1949
Scott W. Lucas	Dem.	IL	1949-1951
Ernest W. McFarland	Dem.	AZ	1951-1953
Robert A. Taft	Rep.	OH	1953
William F. Knowland	Rep.	CA	1953-1955
Lyndon B. Johnson	Dem.	TX	1955-1961
Mike Mansfield	Dem.	MT	1961-1977
Robert C. Byrd	Dem.	WV	1977-1981
Howard H. Baker Jr.	Rep.	TN	1981-1985
Robert J. Dole	Rep.	KS	1985-1987
Robert C. Byrd	Dem.	WV	1987-1989
George J. Mitchell	Dem.	ME	1989-1995
Robert J. Dole	Rep.	KS	1995-1996
Trent Lott	Rep.	MS	1996-2001[3]
Thomas A. Daschle	Dem.	SD	2001-2003[3]
William Frist	Rep.	TN	2003-2007[4]
Harry M. Reid	Dem.	NV	2007-2015
Mitch McConnell	Rep.	KY	2015-2021
Charles E. Schumer	Dem.	NY	2021-

MINORITY LEADERS

Name	Party	State	Tenure
Oscar W. Underwood[2]	Dem.	AL	1920-1923
Joseph T. Robinson	Dem.	AR	1923-1933
Charles L. McNary	Rep.	OR	1933-1944
Wallace H. White	Rep.	ME	1944-1947
Alben W. Barkley	Dem.	KY	1947-1949
Kenneth S. Wherry	Rep.	NE	1949-1951
Henry Styles Bridges	Rep.	NH	1952-1953
Lyndon B. Johnson	Dem.	TX	1953-1955
William F. Knowland	Rep.	CA	1955-1959
Everett M. Dirksen	Rep.	IL	1959-1969
Hugh D. Scott	Rep.	PA	1969-1977
Howard H. Baker Jr.	Rep.	TN	1977-1981
Robert C. Byrd	Dem.	WV	1981-1987
Robert J. Dole	Rep.	KS	1987-1995
Thomas A. Daschle	Dem.	SD	1995-2001[3]
Trent Lott	Rep.	MS	2001-2002[3,4]
Thomas A. Daschle	Dem.	SD	2003-2005
Harry M. Reid	Dem.	NV	2005-2007
Mitch McConnell	Rep.	KY	2007-2015
Harry M. Reid	Dem.	NV	2015-2017
Charles E. Schumer	Dem.	NY	2017-2021
Mitch McConnell	Rep.	KY	2021-

Note: The offices of party (majority and minority) leaders in the Senate did not evolve until the 20th century. (1) First Republican to be formally designated floor leader. Henry Cabot Lodge (MA) served as unofficial party leader prior to Curtis's election. (2) First Democrat to be designated floor leader. (3) Democrats held the majority Jan. 3, 2001, until Dick Cheney (R) was installed as vice pres., Jan. 20. Republicans subsequently lost the majority when Jim Jeffords (VT) switched his affiliation from Republican to Independent, June 6, 2001. (4) Trent Lott resigned from Republican leadership Dec. 20, 2002. William Frist was elected Republican leader Dec. 23, 2002, and began service Jan. 7, 2003, as majority leader.

Speakers of the U.S. House of Representatives, 1789-2024

Name	Party	State	Tenure
Frederick A. C. Muhlenberg	Federalist	PA	1789-1791
Jonathan Trumbull	Federalist	CT	1791-1793
Frederick A. C. Muhlenberg	Federalist	PA	1793-1795
Jonathan Dayton	Federalist	NJ	1795-1799
Theodore Sedgwick	Federalist	MA	1799-1801
Nathaniel Macon	Dem.-Rep.	NC	1801-1807
Joseph B. Varnum	Dem.-Rep.	MA	1807-1811
Henry Clay	Dem.-Rep.	KY	1811-1814
Langdon Cheves	Dem.-Rep.	SC	1814-1815
Henry Clay	Dem.-Rep.	KY	1815-1820
John W. Taylor	Dem.-Rep.	NY	1820-1821
Philip P. Barbour	Dem.-Rep.	VA	1821-1823
Henry Clay	Dem.-Rep.	KY	1823-1825
John W. Taylor	Dem.	NY	1825-1827
Andrew Stevenson	Dem.	VA	1827-1834
John Bell	Dem.	TN	1834-1835
James K. Polk	Dem.	TN	1835-1839
Robert M. T. Hunter	Dem.	VA	1839-1841
John White	Whig	KY	1841-1843
John W. Jones	Dem.	VA	1843-1845
John W. Davis	Dem.	IN	1845-1847
Robert C. Winthrop	Whig	MA	1847-1849
Howell Cobb	Dem.	GA	1849-1851
Linn Boyd	Dem.	KY	1851-1855
Nathaniel P. Banks	American	MA	1856-1857
James L. Orr	Dem.	SC	1857-1859
William Pennington	Rep.	NJ	1860-1861
Galusha A. Grow	Rep.	PA	1861-1863
Schuyler Colfax	Rep.	IN	1863-1869
Theodore M. Pomeroy	Rep.	NY	1869
James G. Blaine	Rep.	ME	1869-1875
Michael C. Kerr	Dem.	IN	1875-1876
Samuel J. Randall	Dem.	PA	1876-1881
J. Warren Keifer	Rep.	OH	1881-1883
John G. Carlisle	Dem.	KY	1883-1889
Thomas B. Reed	Rep.	ME	1889-1891
Charles F. Crisp	Dem.	GA	1891-1895
Thomas B. Reed	Rep.	ME	1895-1899
David B. Henderson	Rep.	IA	1899-1903
Joseph G. Cannon	Rep.	IL	1903-1911
Champ Clark	Dem.	MO	1911-1919
Frederick H. Gillett	Rep.	MA	1919-1925
Nicholas Longworth	Rep.	OH	1925-1931
John N. Garner	Dem.	TX	1931-1933
Henry T. Rainey	Dem.	IL	1933-1934
Joseph W. Byrns	Dem.	TN	1935-1936
William B. Bankhead	Dem.	AL	1936-1940
Sam Rayburn	Dem.	TX	1940-1947
Joseph W. Martin Jr.	Rep.	MA	1947-1949
Sam Rayburn	Dem.	TX	1949-1953
Joseph W. Martin Jr.	Rep.	MA	1953-1955
Sam Rayburn	Dem.	TX	1955-1961
John W. McCormack	Dem.	MA	1962-1971
Carl B. Albert	Dem.	OK	1971-1977
Thomas P. O'Neill Jr.	Dem.	MA	1977-1987
James C. Wright Jr.	Dem.	TX	1987-1989
Thomas S. Foley	Dem.	WA	1989-1995
Newt Gingrich	Rep.	GA	1995-1999
J. Dennis Hastert	Rep.	IL	1999-2007
Nancy Pelosi	Dem.	CA	2007-2011
John Boehner	Rep.	OH	2011-2015
Paul Ryan	Rep.	WI	2015-2019
Nancy Pelosi	Dem.	CA	2019-2023
Kevin McCarthy	Rep.	CA	2023
Mike Johnson	Rep.	LA	2023-

Political Divisions of Congress, 1901-2024

Source: Office of the Clerk, U.S. House of Representatives; Congressional Research Service, Library of Congress

All figures reflect post-election party breakdown except where noted; **boldface** denotes party in majority after election.

		SENATE					HOUSE OF REPRESENTATIVES				
Congress	Years	Total members	Dem.	Rep.	Other parties	Vacant	Total members	Dem.	Rep.	Other parties	Vacant
57th	1901-1903	90	29	**56**	3	2	357	153	**198**	5	1
58th	1903-1905	90	32	**58**			386	178	**207**		1
59th	1905-1907	90	32	**58**			386	136	**250**		
60th	1907-1909	92	29	**61**		2	386	164	**222**		
61st	1909-1911	92	32	**59**		1	391	172	**219**		
62nd	1911-1913	92	42	**49**		1	391	**228**	162	1	
63rd	1913-1915	96	**51**	44	1		435	**290**	127	18	
64th	1915-1917	96	**56**	39	1		435	**231**	193	8	3
65th	1917-1919	96	**53**	42	1		435	210[1]	216	9	
66th	1919-1921	96	47	**48**	1		435	191	**237**	7	
67th	1921-1923	96	37	**59**			435	132	**300**	1	2
68th	1923-1925	96	43	**51**	2		435	207	**225**	3	

Congress	Years	SENATE Total members	Dem.	Rep.	Other parties	Vacant	HOUSE OF REPRESENTATIVES Total members	Dem.	Rep.	Other parties	Vacant
69th	1925-1927	96	40	**54**	1	1	435	183	**247**	5	
70th	1927-1929	96	47	**48**	1		435	195	**237**	3	
71st	1929-1931	96	39	**56**	1		435	163	**267**	1	4
72nd	1931-1933	96	47	**48**	1		435	216[2]	**218**	1	
73rd	1933-1935	96	**59**	36	1		435	**313**	117	5	
74th	1935-1937	96	**69**	25	2		435	**322**	103	10	
75th	1937-1939	96	**75**	17	4		435	**333**	89	13	
76th	1939-1941	96	**69**	23	4		435	**262**	169	4	
77th	1941-1943	96	**66**	28	2		435	**267**	162	6	
78th	1943-1945	96	**57**	38	1		435	**222**	209	4	
79th	1945-1947	96	**57**	38	1		435	**243**	190	2	
80th	1947-1949	96	45	**51**			435	188	**246**	1	
81st	1949-1951	96	**54**	42			435	**263**	171	1	
82nd	1951-1953	96	**48**	47	1		435	**234**	199	2	
83rd	1953-1955	96	46	**48**	2		435	213	**221**	1	
84th	1955-1957	96	**48**	47	1		435	**232**	203		
85th	1957-1959	96	**49**	47			435	**234**	201		
86th	1959-1961	98	**64**	34			436[3]	**283**	153		
87th	1961-1963	100	**64**	36			437[3]	**262**	175		
88th	1963-1965	100	**67**	33			435	**258**	176		1
89th	1965-1967	100	**68**	32			435	**295**	140		
90th	1967-1969	100	**64**	36			435	**248**	187		
91st	1969-1971	100	**58**	42			435	**243**	192		
92nd	1971-1973	100	**54**	44	2		435	**255**	180		
93rd	1973-1975	100	**56**	42	2		435	**242**	192	1	
94th	1975-1977	100	**61**	37	2		435	**291**	144		
95th	1977-1979	100	**61**	38	1		435	**292**	143		
96th	1979-1981	100	**58**	41	1		435	**277**	158		
97th	1981-1983	100	46	**53**	1		435	**242**	192	1	
98th	1983-1985	100	46	**54**			435	**269**	166		
99th	1985-1987	100	47	**53**			435	**253**	182		
100th	1987-1989	100	**55**	45			435	**258**	177		
101st	1989-1991	100	**55**	45			435	**260**	175		
102nd	1991-1993	100	**56**	44			435	**267**	167	1	
103rd	1993-1995	100	**57**	43			435	**258**	176	1	
104th	1995-1997	100	48	**52**			435	204	**230**	1	
105th	1997-1999	100	45	**55**			435	207	**226**	2	
106th	1999-2001	100	45	**55**			435	211	**223**	1	
107th	2001-2003	100	50	50[4]			435	212	**221**	2	
108th	2003-2005	100	48	**51**	1		435	204	**229**	1	1
109th	2005-2007	100	44	**55**	1		435	202	**232**	1	
110th	2007-2009	100	49	49	2[5]		435	**233**	202		
111th	2009-2011	100	**55**	41	2[5]	2	435	**256**	178		1
112th	2011-2013	100	**51**	47	2[5]		435	193	**242**		
113th	2013-2015	100	**53**	45	2[5]		435	200	**234**		1
114th	2015-2017	100	44	**54**	2[5]		435	188	**247**		
115th	2017-2019	100	46	**52**	2[5]		435	194	**241**		
116th	2019-2021	100	45	**53**	2[5]		435	**235**	199		1
117th	2021-2023	100	**48**	50	2[5]		435	**222**	212		1
118th	2023-	100	**48**	49	3[5]		435	212	**222**		1

(1) Democrats organized the House with help of other parties. (2) Democrats organized the House because of Republican deaths. (3) Number of House seats was increased temporarily when proclamations were issued declaring Alaska (Jan. 3, 1959) and Hawaii (Aug. 21, 1959) new states. (4) While the Senate was split 50-50, control was held by whichever party had an incumbent vice president. Republican Sen. Jim Jeffords (VT) changed his party designation to Independent on June 6, 2001, switching control of the Senate to Democrats. (5) Independent senators chose to caucus with the Democrats.

Congressional Bills Vetoed, 1789-2024

Source: Virtual Reference Desk, U.S. Senate; as of Sept. 2024

The president has 10 days (excluding Sundays) to consider a bill or joint resolution passed by Congress. The president can sign it into law or exercise a veto. Only a two-thirds vote in both the Senate and the House can override a regular veto. (A pocket veto cannot be overridden as it takes effect when Congress is adjourned.)

President	Regular vetoes	Pocket vetoes	Total vetoes	Vetoes overridden
Washington	2	—	2	—
J. Adams	—	—	—	—
Jefferson	—	—	—	—
Madison	5	2	7	—
Monroe	1	—	1	—
J. Q. Adams	—	—	—	—
Jackson	5	7	12	—
Van Buren	—	1	1	—
W. H. Harrison	—	—	—	—
Tyler	6	4	10	1
Polk	2	1	3	—
Taylor	—	—	—	—
Fillmore	—	—	—	—
Pierce	9	—	9	5
Buchanan	4	3	7	—
Lincoln	2	5	7	—
A. Johnson	21	8	29	15
Grant	45	48	93	4
Hayes	12	1	13	1
Garfield	—	—	—	—
Arthur	4	8	12	1
Cleveland[1]	304	110	414	2
B. Harrison	19	25	44	1
Cleveland[2]	42	128	170	5
McKinley	6	36	42	—
T. Roosevelt	42	40	82	1
Taft	30	9	39	1
Wilson	33	11	44	6
Harding	5	1	6	—
Coolidge	20	30	50	4
Hoover	21	16	37	3
F. D. Roosevelt	372	263	635	9
Truman	180	70	250	12
Eisenhower	73	108	181	2
Kennedy	12	9	21	—
L. Johnson	16	14	30	—
Nixon	26	17	43	7
Ford	48	18	66	12
Carter	13	18	31	2
Reagan	39	39	78	9
G. H. W. Bush[3]	29	15	44	1
Clinton[4]	36	1	37	2
G. W. Bush	12	—	12	4
Obama	12	—	12	1
Trump	10	—	10	1
Biden	12	—	12	—
Total[3,4]	**1,530**	**1,066**	**2,596**	**112**

— = 0. (1) First term only. (2) Second term only. (3) Excluded from the figures are two bills that Pres. George H. W. Bush claimed were pocket vetoed but which Congress considered to be enacted because the president had failed to return them during a Congressional recess. (4) Does not include line-item vetoes, which were ruled unconstitutional by the U.S. Supreme Court on June 25, 1998.

Congressional Firsts and Milestones

House of Representatives

First House meeting: Mar. 4, 1789, at Federal Hall in New York, NY. A quorum of 30 representatives was not reached until Apr. 1, 1789.

First House meeting in its current Capitol Building chamber: Dec. 16, 1857.

First former president to serve as representative: John Quincy Adams (MA, 1831-48); president, 1825-29.

First woman representative: Jeannette Rankin (R, MT, 1917-19, 1941-43).

First woman House speaker: Nancy Pelosi (D, CA), on Jan. 4, 2007.

First Black representative: Joseph Rainey (R, SC, 1870-79).

First Black woman representative: Shirley Chisholm (D, NY, 1969-83).

First American Indian women representatives: Deb Haaland (Laguna Pueblo) (D, NM, 2019-21) and Sharice Davids (Ho-Chunk) (D, KS, 2019-).

First Asian-Pacific American representative: India-born Dalip Saund (D, CA, 1957-63).

First elected Hispanic-American representative: Romualdo Pacheco (R, CA, 1877-83); Pacheco was born in California when it was Mexican territory.

First Jewish representative: Lewis Charles Levin (PA, 1845-51).

First Muslim representative: Keith Ellison (D, MN, 2007-19).

First Muslim women representatives: Ilhan Omar (D, MN, 2019-) and Rashida Tlaib (D, MI, 2019-). Omar was also the first Somali-American member of Congress and the first member to wear a hijab, or headscarf.

First representative to give birth in office: Yvonne Brathwaite Burke (D, CA, 1973-79), on Nov. 23, 1973.

Longest-serving representative: John Dingell Jr. (D, MI, 1955-2015), with more than 59 years of service.

Longest-serving House speaker: Sam Rayburn (D, TX, 1913-61), speaker for 17 years, 2 months, 2 days (non-consecutive).

Oldest representative: Ralph Hall (D-R, TX, 1981-2015); retired at age 91.

Youngest representative: William Charles Cole Claiborne (TN), who was elected at 22 years of age and began service Nov. 23, 1797.

First live-TV broadcast of House proceedings: Mar. 19, 1979, by public television and C-SPAN. Al Gore Jr. (D, TN) was the first representative to give a speech before cameras that day.

First declaration of war made by the House: June 4, 1812, against Great Britain and Ireland.

Senate

First Senate meeting: Mar. 4, 1789, at Federal Hall in New York, NY. A quorum of senators (12) was not reached until Apr. 6, 1789.

First Senate meeting in its current chamber in the Capitol Building: Jan. 4, 1859.

First woman senator: Rebecca Felton (D, GA, 1922). Appointed to a seat left vacant by a death, 87-year-old Felton served only 24 hours after being sworn in Nov. 21. (Felton was also the oldest freshman senator and the last senator to have been a slave owner.)

First elected woman senator: Hattie Caraway (D, AR, 1931-45). Appointed in 1931 to fill the vacancy left by the death of her husband, Thaddeus H. Caraway, she was elected in 1932.

First Black senator: Hiram R. Revels (R, MS, 1870-71).

First Black woman senator: Carol Moseley-Braun (D, IL, 1993-99).

First American Indian senators: Charles Curtis (Kaw) (R, KS, 1907-13, 1915-29) and Robert Owen (Cherokee) (D, OK, 1907-25).

First Hispanic American senator: Mexico-born Octaviano Larrazolo (R, NM, 1928-29).

First Asian American senator: Hiram L. Fong (R, HI, 1959-77).

First Jewish senator: David Levy Yulee (D, FL, 1845-51, 1855-61).

First senator to give birth in office: Tammy Duckworth (D, IL, 2017-), on Apr. 9, 2018.

Longest-serving senator: Robert C. Byrd (D, WV, 1959-2010) died while in office, having served 51 years, 5 months, and 26 days.

Oldest senator: Strom Thurmond (R, SC), who turned 100 years of age on Dec. 5, 2002, one month before he retired from office.

Youngest senator: John H. Eaton (TN), who was 28 years, 5 months old when he was sworn in Nov. 16, 1818.

Longest speech by a senator (since 1900): 24 hours, 18 minutes, by Strom Thurmond (D, SC) in his filibuster against the 1957 Civil Rights Act, Aug. 28-29, 1957.

Number of Senate impeachment trials: 20, resulting in 8 acquittals, 8 convictions, 3 dismissals, and 1 resignation with no further action.

First regular live-TV broadcast from the Senate chamber: June 2, 1986, by the C-SPAN network.

Number of senators who have received the Nobel Peace Prize: 5 (Elihu Root, Frank Kellogg, Cordell Hull, Al Gore, Barack Obama). Root is the only one of the five to receive the award while serving as senator.

Number of senators who have changed party affiliation during their Senate service (since 1890): 23.

Congressional Activity, 1947-2022

Source: *Congressional Record*, U.S. Govt. Publishing Office; Library of Congress

Congress in recent years has been widely perceived as being less productive than in previous sessions. The data below shows the number of public laws and measures passed in every complete session of Congress since 1947.

Congress (years)	Public laws passed	Measures passed	Congress (years)	Public laws passed	Measures passed
80th (1947-48)	906	4,132	99th (1985-86)	664	2,698
81st (1949-50)	921	5,764	100th (1987-88)	713	2,932
82nd (1951-52)	594	4,593	101st (1989-90)	650	2,691
83rd (1953-54)	781	5,201	102nd (1991-92)	590	2,615
84th (1955-56)	1,028	5,713	103rd (1993-94)	465	2,054
85th (1957-58)	936	5,126	104th (1995-96)	333	1,834
86th (1959-60)	800	4,165	105th (1997-98)	394	2,077
87th (1961-62)	885	4,769	106th (1999-2000)	580	2,779
88th (1963-64)	666	3,425	107th (2001-02)	377	2,163
89th (1965-66)	810	4,116	108th (2003-04)	498	2,674
90th (1967-68)	640	3,390	109th (2005-06)	482	2,684
91st (1969-70)	695	3,318	110th (2007-08)	460	3,336
92nd (1971-72)	607	2,840	111th (2009-10)	383	2,939
93rd (1973-74)	649	3,088	112th (2011-12)	283	1,744
94th (1975-76)	588	3,176	113th (2013-14)	297	1,788
95th (1977-78)	633	3,211	114th (2015-16)	328	2,110
96th (1979-80)	613	2,960	115th (2017-18)	338	2,563
97th (1981-82)	473	2,267	116th (2019-20)	284	2,207
98th (1983-84)	623	2,670	117th (2021-22)	242	2,179

Note: Public laws are bills or joint resolutions that have been enacted. Measures passed refers to bills, joint resolutions, concurrent resolutions, or simple resolutions approved by the House or Senate.

U.S. SUPREME COURT

Justices of the U.S. Supreme Court

The Supreme Court comprises the chief justice of the U.S. and eight associate justices, all appointed for life by the president with advice and consent of the U.S. Senate. Names of chief justices are in **boldface**. Terms of service begin with the year each justice took the judicial oath. Years served is a total of complete years served by a past justice. 2024 salaries: chief justice, $312,200; associate justices, $298,500. The U.S. Supreme Court Building is at 1 First St. NE, Washington, DC 20543.

Website: www.supremecourt.gov

Name, appointed from	Service Term	Service Yrs.	Born	Died
John Jay, NY	1789-1795	5	1745	1829
John Rutledge, SC[1]	1790-1791	1	1739	1800
William Cushing, MA	1790-1810*	20	1732	1810
James Wilson, PA	1789-1798	8	1742	1798
John Blair, VA	1790-1795*	5	1732	1800
James Iredell, NC	1790-1799	9	1751	1799
Thomas Johnson, MD	1792-1793	<1	1732	1819
William Paterson, NJ	1793-1806	13	1745	1806
John Rutledge, SC[2,3]	1795	<1	1739	1800
Samuel Chase, MD	1796-1811	15	1741	1811
Oliver Ellsworth, CT	1796-1800	4	1745	1807
Bushrod Washington, VA	1799-1829*	30	1762	1829
Alfred Moore, NC	1800-1804	3	1755	1810
John Marshall, VA	1801-1835	34	1755	1835
William Johnson, SC	1804-1834	30	1771	1834
Henry B. Livingston, NY	1807-1823	16	1757	1823
Thomas Todd, KY	1807-1826	18	1765	1826
Gabriel Duvall, MD	1811-1835	23	1752	1844
Joseph Story, MA	1812-1845*	33	1779	1845
Smith Thompson, NY	1823-1843	20	1768	1843
Robert Trimble, KY	1826-1828	2	1777	1828
John McLean, OH	1830-1861*	31	1785	1861
Henry Baldwin, PA	1830-1844	14	1780	1844
James M. Wayne, GA	1835-1867	32	1790	1867
Roger B. Taney, MD	1836-1864	28	1777	1864
Philip P. Barbour, VA	1836-1841	4	1783	1841
John Catron, TN	1837-1865	28	1786	1865
John McKinley, AL	1838-1852*	14	1780	1852
Peter V. Daniel, VA	1842-1860*	18	1784	1860
Samuel Nelson, NY	1845-1872	27	1792	1873
Levi Woodbury, NH	1845-1851	5	1789	1851
Robert C. Grier, PA	1846-1870	23	1794	1870
Benjamin R. Curtis, MA	1851-1857	5	1809	1874
John A. Campbell, AL	1853-1861*	8	1811	1889
Nathan Clifford, ME	1858-1881	23	1803	1881
Noah H. Swayne, OH	1862-1881	18	1804	1884
Samuel F. Miller, IA	1862-1890	28	1816	1890
David Davis, IL	1862-1877	14	1815	1886
Stephen J. Field, CA	1863-1897	33	1816	1899
Salmon P. Chase, OH	1864-1873	8	1808	1873
William Strong, PA	1870-1880	10	1808	1895
Joseph P. Bradley, NJ	1870-1892	21	1813	1892
Ward Hunt, NY	1873-1882	9	1810	1886
Morrison R. Waite, OH	1874-1888	14	1816	1888
John M. Harlan, KY	1877-1911	33	1833	1911
William B. Woods, GA	1881-1887	6	1824	1887
Stanley Matthews, OH	1881-1889	7	1824	1889
Horace Gray, MA	1882-1902	20	1828	1902
Samuel Blatchford, NY	1882-1893	11	1820	1893
Lucius Q. C. Lamar, MS	1888-1893	5	1825	1893
Melville W. Fuller, IL	1888-1910	21	1833	1910
David J. Brewer, KS	1890-1910	20	1837	1910
Henry B. Brown, MI	1891-1906	15	1836	1913
George Shiras Jr., PA	1892-1903	10	1832	1924
Howell E. Jackson, TN	1893-1895	2	1832	1895
Edward D. White, LA[1]	1894-1910	16	1845	1921
Rufus W. Peckham, NY	1896-1909	13	1838	1909
Joseph McKenna, CA	1898-1925	26	1843	1926
Oliver W. Holmes, MA	1902-1932	29	1841	1935
William R. Day, OH	1903-1922	19	1849	1923
William H. Moody, MA	1906-1910	3	1853	1917
Horace H. Lurton, TN	1910-1914	4	1844	1914
Charles E. Hughes, NY[1]	1910-1916	5	1862	1948
Willis Van Devanter, WY	1911-1937	26	1859	1941
Joseph R. Lamar, GA	1911-1916	5	1857	1916
Edward D. White, LA[2]	1910-1921	10	1845	1921
Mahlon Pitney, NJ	1912-1922	10	1858	1924
James C. McReynolds, TN	1914-1941	26	1862	1946
Louis D. Brandeis, MA	1916-1939	22	1856	1941
John H. Clarke, OH	1916-1922	5	1857	1945
William H. Taft, CT	1921-1930	8	1857	1930
George Sutherland, UT	1922-1938	15	1862	1942
Pierce Butler, MN	1923-1939	16	1866	1939
Edward T. Sanford, TN	1923-1930	7	1865	1930
Harlan F. Stone, NY[1]	1925-1941	16	1872	1946
Charles E. Hughes, NY[2]	1930-1941	11	1862	1948
Owen J. Roberts, PA	1930-1945	15	1875	1955
Benjamin N. Cardozo, NY	1932-1938	6	1870	1938
Hugo L. Black, AL	1937-1971	34	1886	1971
Stanley F. Reed, KY	1938-1957	19	1884	1980
Felix Frankfurter, MA	1939-1962	23	1882	1965
William O. Douglas, CT	1939-1975	36[4]	1898	1980
Frank Murphy, MI	1940-1949	9	1890	1949
Harlan F. Stone, NY[2]	1941-1946	4	1872	1946
James F. Byrnes, SC	1941-1942	1	1879	1972
Robert H. Jackson, NY	1941-1954	13	1892	1954
Wiley B. Rutledge, IA	1943-1949	6	1894	1949
Harold H. Burton, OH	1945-1958	13	1888	1964
Fred M. Vinson, KY	1946-1953	7	1890	1953
Tom C. Clark, TX	1949-1967	17	1899	1977
Sherman Minton, IN	1949-1956	7	1890	1965
Earl Warren, CA	1953-1969	15	1891	1974
John Marshall Harlan, NY	1955-1971	16	1899	1971
William J. Brennan Jr., NJ	1956-1990	33	1906	1997
Charles E. Whittaker, MO	1957-1962	5	1901	1973
Potter Stewart, OH	1958-1981	22	1915	1985
Byron R. White, CO	1962-1993	31	1917	2002
Arthur J. Goldberg, IL	1962-1965	2	1908	1990
Abe Fortas, TN	1965-1969	3	1910	1982
Thurgood Marshall, NY	1967-1991	24	1908	1993
Warren E. Burger, VA	1969-1986	17	1907	1995
Harry A. Blackmun, MN	1970-1994	24	1908	1999
Lewis F. Powell Jr., VA	1972-1987	15	1907	1998
William H. Rehnquist, AZ[1]	1972-1986	14	1924	2005
John Paul Stevens, IL	1975-2010	34	1920	2019
Sandra Day O'Connor, AZ	1981-2006	24	1930	
William H. Rehnquist, VA[2]	1986-2005	18	1924	2005
Antonin Scalia, VA	1986-2016	29	1936	2016
Anthony M. Kennedy, CA	1988-2018	30	1936	
David H. Souter, NH	1990-2009	18	1939	
Clarence Thomas, GA	1991-		1948	
Ruth Bader Ginsburg, NY	1993-2020	27	1933	2020
Stephen G. Breyer, MA	1994-2022	28	1938	
John G. Roberts Jr., MD	2005-		1955	
Samuel A. Alito Jr., NJ	2006-		1950	
Sonia Sotomayor, NY	2009-		1954	
Elena Kagan, MA	2010-		1960	
Neil M. Gorsuch, CO	2017-		1967	
Brett Kavanaugh, MD	2018-		1965	
Amy Coney Barrett, IN	2020-		1972	
Ketanji Brown Jackson, DC	2022-		1970	

* = Because of inadequate government record keeping, date of oath is estimated. (1) Later, chief justice, as listed. (2) Formerly associate justice. (3) Named acting chief justice; confirmation rejected by the Senate. (4) Longest term of service.

Supreme Court History and Notable Firsts

The U.S. Supreme Court first convened Feb. 1, 1790, in New York, NY. Acting on the authority of Congress as outlined in the Judiciary Act of 1789, the court consisted of Chief Justice John Jay and five associate justices who held sessions for a few weeks in Feb. and Aug. The justices also served twice a year in each of the nation's then-13 judicial districts, a requirement known as riding circuit. The number of Justices on the Court changed six times before settling at a total of nine in 1869. Through the 2022-23 term, 116 justices have served on the Court.

The Court's first major legal decision, *Chisholm v. Georgia* (1793), ruled that federal courts held jurisdiction over disputes between individual states and citizens of other states. (The 11th Amendment, which the states ratified in 1795, removed that jurisdiction.) The Court over time has expanded its impact on the nation's affairs. Since 1803 it has declared unconstitutional more than 180 acts of Congress and over 1,000 state, territorial, and municipal laws and statutes. The Court usually hears oral arguments in about 70-80 cases per term. In May 2020 the Court began holding oral arguments by telephone and offering a livestream audio broadcast of the session, both for the first time. Oral arguments in person resumed Oct. 4, 2021.

Of 164 nominations to the Court (including chief justice nominations), the Senate has voted to reject just 12, most recently Robert Bork in 1987. George W. Bush-nominee Harriet Miers withdrew her nomination before the Senate considered it, in 2005. The Senate did not hold hearings on Obama nominee Merrick Garland in 2016, citing the impending presidential election.

Justices may be removed from the Court by impeachment. In 1804, the House of Representatives, in the control of Jeffersonian Republicans, impeached Samuel Chase, a Federalist; he was acquitted by the Senate in 1805.

First fully vested justice: James Wilson, who took the Constitutional Oath of the Court Oct. 5, 1789
First Catholic justice: Roger B.Taney (1836-64)
First Jewish justice: Louis D. Brandeis (1916-39)
Only person to serve as both U.S. president and chief justice: William Howard Taft (pres., 1909-13; chief justice, 1921-30)
First justice to take an oath at the White House: Frank Murphy, Jan. 18, 1940
First Black justice: Thurgood Marshall (1967-91)
First woman justice: Sandra Day O'Connor (1981-2006)
First Hispanic justice: Sonia Sotomayor (2009-)
First Black woman justice: Ketanji Brown Jackson (2022-)

Selected Landmark Decisions of the U.S. Supreme Court

1803: *Marbury v. Madison*. The Court ruled that Congress exceeded its power in the Judiciary Act of 1789. The Court thus established its power to review acts of Congress and to declare invalid those it found to be in conflict with the Constitution.

1819: *Trustees of Dartmouth College v. Woodward*. The Court ruled that a state could not arbitrarily alter the terms of a college's contract. The Court later used a similar principle to limit the states' ability to interfere with business contracts.

1819: *McCulloch v. Maryland*. The Court ruled that Congress had the authority to charter a national bank, under the Constitution's granting of power to enact all laws "necessary and proper" to responsibilities of government.

1824: *Gibbons v. Ogden*. The Court ruled that New York state had overstepped its authority in granting a monopoly to two steamboat operators. According to the ruling, Congress's power to regulate interstate commerce included transportation.

1857: *Dred Scott v. Sandford*. The Court declared unconstitutional the already-repealed Missouri Compromise of 1820 because it deprived a person of "property"—an enslaved person—without due process of law. The Court also ruled that enslaved individuals were not citizens of any state nor of the U.S. The latter part of the decision was overturned by ratification of the 14th Amendment in 1868.

1880: *Strauder v. West Virginia*. The Court struck down a state law mandating that jurors must be white, ruling it a violation of the right to equal protection under the 14th Amendment.

1896: *Plessy v. Ferguson*. The Court ruled that a state law requiring federal railroad trains to provide "equal but separate" facilities for Black and white passengers neither infringed upon federal authority to regulate interstate commerce nor violated the 13th and 14th Amendments. What became known as the "separate but equal" doctrine remained in effect until the 1954 ***Brown v. Board of Education*** decision.

1904: *Northern Securities Co. v. U.S.* The Court ruled that a holding company formed solely to eliminate competition between two railroad lines was a combination in restraint of trade, violating the 1890 federal Sherman Antitrust Act.

1908: *Muller v. Oregon*. The Court upheld a state law limiting the working hours of women. (Louis D. Brandeis, counsel for the state, in what is known as the "Brandeis brief," cited evidence from social workers, physicians, and factory inspectors that long work hours were harmful to women.)

1911: *Standard Oil Co. of New Jersey v. U.S.* The Court ruled that the Standard Oil Trust must be dissolved because of its unreasonable restraint of trade.

1919: *Schenck v. U.S.* The Court sustained the Espionage Act of 1917, maintaining that freedom of speech and press could be constrained if "the words used ... create a clear and present danger."

1925: *Gitlow v. New York*. The Court ruled that the 1st Amendment free-speech guarantee applied to the states as well as to the federal government. The decision was the first of a number of rulings holding that the 14th Amendment extended the guarantees of the Bill of Rights to state action.

1926: *Myers v. U.S.* The Court held that the president has the power to remove appointed executive-branch officials, without congressional approval. In ***Seila Law v. CFPB*** (2020) the Court further found that Congress could not make the head of a federal agency, the Consumer Financial Protection Bureau, immune by law from being fired by a president.

1935: *Schechter Poultry Corp. v. U.S.* The Court ruled that Congress exceeded its authority to delegate legislative powers and to regulate interstate commerce when it enacted the National Industrial Recovery Act (1933), which afforded the U.S. president too much discretionary power.

1944: *Korematsu v. U.S.* The Court upheld the constitutionality of an order barring all persons of Japanese ancestry, including U.S. citizens, from much of the West Coast, forcing them into internment camps, ruling that the need to prevent espionage outweighed the petitioner's civil rights. The ruling, never officially overturned, followed ***Hirabayashi v. U.S.*** (1943), in which the Court upheld the imposition of curfews on minority populations perceived to be a potential wartime threat.

1951: *Dennis v. U.S.* The Court upheld convictions under the Smith Act of 1940 for invoking Communist theory advocating the forcible overthrow of the government. In ***Yates v. U.S.*** (1957), the Court moderated this ruling by allowing such advocacy in the abstract, if not connected to action to achieve the goal.

1952: *Youngstown Sheet & Tube Co. v. Sawyer*. The Court ruled that the president had exceeded his wartime power in ordering the seizure of private steel mills during a nationwide steelworkers' strike.

1954: *Brown v. Board of Education of Topeka*. The Court ruled that separate public schools for Black and white students were inherently unequal, so state-sanctioned segregation in public schools violated the equal protection guarantee of the 14th Amendment. The Court decided ***Bolling v. Sharpe*** the same year, ruling that the congressionally mandated segregated public school system in the District of Columbia violated the 5th Amendment's due process guarantee of personal liberty. In **Brown II** (1955), the Court ordered the integration of schools with "all deliberate speed." The Brown rulings also led to abolition of state-sponsored segregation in other public facilities.

1957: *Roth v. U.S.; Alberts v. California*. The Court ruled obscene material—defined as appealing primarily to "prurient interest" in the view of "the average person, applying contemporary community standards"—was not protected by 1st Amendment guarantees of freedom of speech and press, being "utterly without redeeming social importance." This definition was modified in later decisions, including ***Miller v. California*** (1973).

1958: *Cooper v. Aaron*. The Court held that Arkansas could not nullify ***Brown v. Board of Education*** (1954) through the passage of legislation or constitutional amendments barring integration. The opinion of the Court affirmed its reading of the Constitution as the "supreme law of the land."

1961: *Mapp v. Ohio*. The Court ruled that evidence obtained in violation of the 4th Amendment guarantee against unreasonable search and seizure must be excluded from use in state as well as federal trials.

1962: *Baker v. Carr*. The Court held that constitutional challenges to the unequal distribution of voters among legislative districts could be resolved by federal courts.

1962: *Engel v. Vitale*. The Court held that government bodies could not encourage the recitation of a state-composed prayer in public schools, even if nondenominational, because that would be an unconstitutional attempt to establish religion.

1963: *Gideon v. Wainwright*. The Court ruled that indigent defendants, even in state cases, have a right to legal counsel as guaranteed by the 6th Amendment.

1964: *New York Times Co. v. Sullivan*. The Court ruled that the 1st Amendment protected the press from libel suits for defamatory reports about public officials unless an injured party could prove "malice," with "reckless disregard" for truth.

1964: *Heart of Atlanta Motel v. U.S.* The Court upheld Title II of the 1964 Civil Rights Act banning racial discrimination in motels/hotels engaged in interstate commerce (by accommodating travelers from other states). The Court in ***Katzenbach v. McClung*** (1964) held that Title II also applied to many restaurants and businesses.

1965: *Griswold v. Connecticut*. The Court ruled that a state unconstitutionally interfered with privacy in a marriage when it prohibited the use of contraceptives.

1966: *Miranda v. Arizona*. The Court ruled that, under the guarantee of due process, suspects in custody, before being questioned, must be informed that they have the right to remain silent, that anything they say may be used against them, and that they have the right to counsel.

1967: *Loving v. Virginia*. The Court unanimously struck down all state laws banning interracial marriage.

1968: *Terry v. Ohio*. The Court ruled that a "stop and frisk" performed without a warrant or probable cause was not a violation of 4th Amendment rights, provided that the officer had a reasonable suspicion that the subject was armed and dangerous, or had committed or was about to commit a crime.

1969: *Brandenburg v. Ohio*. The Court held that government cannot restrict inflammatory speech unless it is "directed to inciting or producing imminent lawless action AND is likely to incite or produce such action." The so-called Brandenburg test refined the "clear and present danger" test outlined in ***Schenck v. U.S.*** (1927).

1969: *Tinker v. Des Moines Community School District*. The majority held that students' wearing of armbands in a symbolic political statement did not disrupt school operations and thus was protected under the 1st Amendment.

1973: *Roe v. Wade*. The Court ruled that the fetus was not a "person" with constitutional rights and that a right to privacy inherent in the 14th Amendment's due process guarantee of personal liberty protected a woman's decision to have an abortion. Some regulation of abortion procedures was allowed in the second trimester and some restriction of abortion in the third. In ***Planned Parenthood v. Casey*** (1992) the Court affirmed the basic right to abortion prior to fetal viability; it allowed states to impose regulations only if they did not impose an "undue burden" on access.

1974: *U.S. v. Nixon*. The Court ruled that neither the separation of powers nor the need to preserve the confidentiality of presidential communications could alone justify an absolute executive privilege of immunity from judicial demands for evidence to be used in a criminal trial.

1976: *Gregg v. Georgia*; *Proffitt v. Florida*; *Jurek v. Texas*. The Court held that death, as a punishment for persons convicted of first-degree murder, was not in and of itself cruel and unusual punishment in violation of the 8th Amendment. But the Court ruled that the sentencing judge and jury must consider the character of the offender and the circumstances.

1978: *Regents of the Univ. of Calif. v. Bakke*. The Court ruled that an admissions program for a state medical school that set specific quotas for minorities violated the 1964 Civil Rights Act, which forbids the exclusion of anyone from a federally funded program based on race. But the Court ruled that race could be considered as one of a complex of factors.

1985: *New Jersey v. T.L.O.* The Court ruled that searches on school grounds do not necessarily violate students' 4th Amendment rights because they may be outweighed by schools' need to maintain learning environments.

1986: *Batson v. Kentucky*. The Court ruled that a peremptory challenge cannot be used in a criminal case to exclude a juror solely because of race.

1986: *Bowers v. Hardwick*. The Court refused to extend any right of privacy to homosexual activity, upholding a Georgia antisodomy law that in effect made it a crime. But in ***Lawrence v. Texas*** (2003), the Court struck down all state antisodomy laws as violating the 14th Amendment's due process clause. In ***Romer v. Evans*** (1996), the Court struck down a Colorado constitutional provision that barred homosexuals from recognition as a protected class.

1989: *Texas v. Johnson*. The Court held the actions of a political activist who burned an American flag were expressive and thus protected by the 1st Amendment. The ruling invalidated laws in 48 states barring flag desecration.

1990: *Cruzan v. Missouri*. The Court ruled that while a person had the right to refuse life-sustaining medical treatment, a state could require evidence that a comatose patient would not have wanted to live before withholding treatment. In two 1997 rulings, ***Washington v. Glucksberg*** and ***Vacco v. Quill***, the Court ruled that states could ban doctor-assisted suicide.

1995: *U.S. Term Limits, Inc. v. Thornton*. The Court ruled that neither states nor Congress could limit terms of members of Congress because the Constitution reserves to the people the right to choose federal lawmakers.

1995: *Adarand Constructors, Inc. v. Peña*. The Court held that federal programs that classify people by race, unless "narrowly tailored" to further a "compelling governmental interest," are subject to strict scrutiny.

1997: *Clinton v. Jones*. Rejecting an appeal by Pres. Clinton in a sexual harassment suit, the Court ruled that a sitting president did not have temporary immunity from a lawsuit for actions outside the realm of official duties.

1997: *City of Boerne v. Flores*. The Court overturned the portion of a 1993 law banning enforcement of state laws that "substantially burden" religious practice unless there is a "compelling governmental interest" to do so. The Court held that the act was an unwarranted intrusion by Congress on states' prerogatives and an infringement of the judiciary's role.

1997: *Reno v. ACLU*. Citing the right to free expression, the Court overturned a provision making it a crime to display or distribute "obscene or indecent" or "patently offensive" material on the Internet. The Court ruled, however, in ***NEA v. Finley*** (1998) that "general standards of decency" may be used as a criterion in federal arts funding.

1998: *Clinton v. City of New York*. The Court struck down the Line-Item Veto Act (1996), holding that it gave presidents "unilateral power to change the text of duly enacted statutes."

1998: *Faragher v. City of Boca Raton*; *Burlington Industries, Inc. v. Ellerth*. The Court issued new guidelines for workplace sexual harassment suits, holding employers responsible for misconduct by supervisory employees. And in ***Oncale v. Sundowner Offshore Services, Inc.*** the same year, the Court ruled that the law against discrimination based on sex applies even if the harasser and harassed are the same sex.

1999: *Dept. of Commerce v. U.S. House of Representatives*. Upholding a challenge to plans for the 2000 census, the Court prohibited statistical sampling, favored by Democrats, in apportioning seats in the U.S. House.

1999: *Alden v. Maine*; *Florida Prepaid v. College Savings Bank*; *College Savings Bank v. Florida Prepaid*. In a series of rulings, the Court applied the principle of sovereign immunity to shield states in large part from being sued under federal law.

2000: *Boy Scouts of America v. Dale*. The Court ruled that the Boy Scouts could dismiss a troop leader after learning he was gay, holding that the right to freedom of association outweighed a New Jersey antidiscrimination statute.

2000: *Bush v. Gore*. The Court ruled that manual recounts in Florida of ballots cast in the 2000 presidential election could not proceed because inconsistent evaluation standards violated the equal protection clause. In effect, the ruling let the official results stand, making George W. Bush the winner.

2001: *Good News Club v. Milford Central School*. The justices found that a private religious organization could not be denied equal access to a public school facility for after-school meetings because that would violate free speech rights.

2002: *Federal Maritime Commission v. South Carolina State Ports Authority*. The Court ruled that the 11th Amendment gave states immunity from private lawsuits involving federal agencies.

2002: *Atkins v. Virginia*. The Court ruled that executing a person with intellectual disabilities violated the 8th Amendment ban on cruel and unusual punishment.

2002: *Zelman v. Simmons-Harris*. The Court ruled that publicly funded tuition vouchers could be used at religious schools without violating the separation of church and state.

2003: *Grutter v. Bollinger*; *Gratz v. Bollinger*. The Court upheld the use of race as a factor in the Univ. of Michigan Law School's admissions policies because of the school's interest in a diverse student body. But the Court ruled against a strict point system based on racial and ethnic backgrounds as used in the university's undergraduate admissions process.

2004: *Tennessee v. Lane*. The Court ruled that disabled individuals could sue states under the Americans With Disabilities Act (1990) for failing to provide adequate access to state courthouses, despite states' usual immunity from private lawsuits in federal court under the 11th Amendment.

2004: *Locke v. Davey*. The justices decided that a scholarship program provided by the state of Washington did not violate the right to free exercise of religion in denying aid to students preparing for the clergy.

2004: *Ashcroft v. ACLU*. The Court struck down federal legislation passed in 1998 to restrict online access to pornography by minors, as violating the right of free speech.

2005: *Roper v. Simmons*. The Court barred execution for crimes committed before age 18, as violating the 8th Amendment ban on "cruel and unusual" punishment.

2005: *Kelo v. City of New London*. The Court ruled that local governments could force property owners to sell their land in order to facilitate private development projects deemed to be economically beneficial to the community.

2006: *Garcetti v. Ceballos*. The Court ruled that the 1st Amendment guarantee of free speech did not protect statements made by public employees in the course of their official duties.

2006: *Hamdan v. Rumsfeld*. The Court ruled that Pres. George W. Bush's system for trying terrorism detainees at the U.S. military base in Guantánamo Bay, Cuba, was unauthorized under federal law and the international Geneva Conventions. The Court furthermore ruled in ***Boumediene v. Bush*** (2008) that detainees had a right to challenge their detention in federal court by applying for a writ of habeas corpus.

2007: *Gonzales v. Carhart*; *Gonzales v. Planned Parenthood Federation of America*. The Court upheld a 2003 federal law prohibiting the abortion procedure known as intact dilation and extraction, or "partial-birth" abortion.

2007: *Parents Involved in Community Schools v. Seattle School District No. 1*; *Meredith v. Jefferson County Board of Education*. The Court ruled that two school districts could not, to encourage diversity, use "racial classifications in making school assignments."

2008: *Crawford v. Marion County Election Board*. The Court upheld the constitutionality of an Indiana law requiring in-person voters to present valid government photo identification.

2008: *District of Columbia v. Heller*. The Court overturned DC's handgun ban, ruling that the 2nd Amendment protected an individual's right to own guns for personal use.

2010: *Citizens United v. Federal Election Commission*. The Court ruled that a federal law barring corporations from using general funds to finance campaign advertisements was unconstitutional. The decision cast doubt on many laws restricting political spending by corporations and unions.

2011: *Snyder v. Phelps*. The justices found that an antigay church whose members protested at the funeral of a Marine could not be held liable for intrusion or emotional distress because the protests were protected by the 1st Amendment.

2012: *U.S. v. Jones*. The Court ruled that attaching a GPS tracking device to a suspect's car and monitoring its movements requires a search warrant, as the 4th Amendment prohibition against unreasonable search and seizure applies.

2012: *Miller v. Alabama*. The Court ruled that mandatory life sentences of juveniles without the possibility of parole constitute cruel and unusual punishment, barred by the 8th Amendment. The decision extended ***Graham v. Florida*** (2010), which barred life sentences for juveniles for nonhomicide crimes. But in ***Jones v. Mississippi*** (2021) the Court ruled that juvenile offenders need not be deemed permanently incorrigible before they can be so sentenced.

2012: *Natl. Federation of Independent Business v. Sebelius*. The Court ruled Congress acted within its powers of taxation in enacting the individual-mandate provision of the Patient Protection and Affordable Care Act (ACA). But the Court ruled unconstitutional the provision of the act's Medicaid expansion that threatened non-compliant states with loss of funding.

2013: *Shelby County v. Holder*. The justices struck down a key provision of the 1965 Voting Rights Act, meant to prevent discriminatory voting regulations, because it relied on outdated information to identify jurisdictions for additional scrutiny.

2013: *U.S. v. Windsor*. The Court struck down the central provision of the 1996 federal Defense of Marriage Act (DOMA), which prohibited federal recognition of same-sex marriages. A separate decision the same year, in ***Hollingsworth v. Perry***, had the effect of legalizing same-sex marriage in California.

2014: *Riley v. California*; *U.S. v. Wurie*. The Court decided that police generally could not search the mobile telephones of arrested individuals without a search warrant.

2014: *Burwell v. Hobby Lobby Stores*; *Conestoga Wood Specialties Corp. v. Burwell*. The justices ruled that some closely held corporations could claim an exemption on religious grounds from a 2010 ACA mandate requiring many businesses to provide health insurance that covers contraception.

2015: *Obergefell v. Hodges*. The Court ruled that state bans on same-sex marriage violated couples' rights under the due process and equal protection clauses of the 14th Amendment.

2016: *Whole Woman's Health v. Hellerstedt*. The justices ruled that a Texas law that included stringent regulations on abortion providers did not pass the "undue burden" standard the Court established in 1992's ***Planned Parenthood v. Casey***.

2018: *Janus v. American Federation of State, County and Municipal Employees (AFSCME)*. The Court struck down rules compelling public employees who opted not to join a union to pay fees in support of its collective-bargaining efforts.

2019: *Rucho v. Common Cause; Lamone v. Benisek*. The Court found that federal courts have no constitutional basis for intervening to block partisan gerrymandering.

2020: *Chiafalo v. Washington*. The Court ruled that a state could require presidential electors to vote for the candidate who won the most popular votes in the state.

2020: *Bostock v. Clayton County*. The Court found that gay and transgender employees were protected from workplace discrimination under 1964 civil rights legislation.

2021: *Edwards v. Vannoy*. The Court ruled that when it issues new rules for criminal procedure that benefit defendants they do not apply retroactively to past final convictions.

2021: *Americans for Prosperity v. Bonta*. The Court found that California violated free speech rights of donors in requiring tax-exempt charities to file federal forms with state regulators that identify major contributors.

2021: *Cedar Point Nursery v. Hassid*. The Court struck down a California regulation giving union organizers a right to visit workers on farms, as a violation of property rights.

2021: *Brnovich v. Democratic National Committee*. The Court ruled that Arizona could enforce measures that restrict collection of mail-in ballots by third parties and disallow votes cast in the wrong precinct, rejecting claims of substantial disproportionate burden on minorities in violation of the 1965 federal Voting Rights Act.

2022: *NY State Rifle & Pistol Assn. v. Bruen*. The Court struck down a New York state law that required "special need" for a license to carry guns outside the home, finding that the 2nd Amendment gives a broad right to carry firearms in public.

2022: *Dobbs v. Jackson Women's Health Organization*. The Court ruled that a Mississippi law banning most abortions after 15 weeks of gestation was constitutional and overturned the decision in *Roe v. Wade* (1973).

2023: *Students for Fair Admissions v. Harvard; Students for Fair Admissions v. University of North Carolina*. The Court ruled that race-conscious admissions policies at colleges and universities were unlawful, effectively rejecting 20-year precedent set in *Grutter v. Bollinger* (2003).

2023: *303 Creative LLC v. Elenis*. The justices held that First Amendment protections prevented a Colorado antidiscrimination law from requiring a designer to create wedding websites for same-sex couples.

See Year in Review: Notable Supreme Court Decisions for major 2023-24 decisions in detail.

STATES AND OTHER AREAS OF THE U.S.

Sources: Population: Decennial Censuses and Population Estimates Program, U.S. Census Bureau, U.S. Dept. of Commerce; population as of July 1, 2023, unless otherwise noted. Pop. density is for land area only. **Racial distribution** categories, as of July 1, 2023, are abbreviated; their full forms are white, Black or African American, Asian, American Indian and Alaska Native, Native Hawaiian and Pacific Islander, two or more races. Categories do not add up to 100% due to rounding. **Hispanic** or Latino persons, as of July 1, 2023, may be of any race. **Area:** Geography Division, U.S. Census Bureau, U.S. Dept. of Commerce. **Acres forested:** U.S. Forest Service, U.S. Dept. of Agriculture; source year may vary. **Chief airports:** Federal Aviation Admin., U.S. Dept. of Transportation preliminary data. Chief airports had 500,000+ boardings in 2023; not all states had airports meeting this threshold. All **Economy** data as of 2023 unless otherwise noted. **Chief manuf. goods:** Manufacturing and Construction Division, U.S. Census Bureau, U.S. Dept. of Commerce. **Chief crops:** Natl. Agricultural Statistics Service, U.S. Dept. of Agriculture. **Farm income:** Economic Research Service, U.S. Dept. of Agriculture; 2022 cash receipts. **Nonfuel minerals:** Office of Mineral Information, U.S. Dept. of Interior; estimated 2023 data. Some states exclude small amounts to avoid disclosing proprietary data. **Commercial fishing:** Natl. Marine Fisheries Service, U.S. Dept. of Commerce; 2022 value. **Gross state product** and **Per cap. pers. income:** Bureau of Economic Analysis, U.S. Dept. of Commerce; as of Dec. 2023. **Sales tax:** Federation of Tax Administrators; as of Feb. 6, 2024. **Gasoline tax:** Energy Information Admin., U.S. Dept. of Energy; as of Jan. 1, 2024; incl. state excise tax, federal excise tax (18.4 cents per gallon), and other state fees. **Employment distrib.** and **Unemployment:** Bureau of Labor Statistics, U.S. Dept. of Labor; distribution is for non-farm jobs as of Apr. 2024; annual unemployment rate for 2023. **Min. wage/hr.:** U.S. Dept. of Labor; as of July 1, 2024. If a state has no minimum wage, or the state minimum wage is lower than the federal minimum wage, the federal rate of $7.25 applies. Small businesses may have lower minimum wages. Some municipalities may have different minimum wages. **New private housing:** Manufacturing and Construction Division, U.S. Census Bureau, U.S. Dept. of Commerce. Figures are building permits issued and est. value of the construction, as of 2023. **Broadband internet:** Industry Analysis and Tech. Division, Fed. Communications Commission; Natl. Telecommunications and Information Administration, U.S. Dept. of Commerce. Broadband connections have minimum speeds of at least 10 megabits per second (Mbps) downstream and 200 kilobits per second (kbps) upstream as of June 2022; figure given is broadband as a percentage of total internet connections. **Commercial banks** and **Savings institutions:** Federal Deposit Insurance Corp., as of June 30, 2023; FDIC-insured institutions only. **Lottery:** North American Assn. of State and Provincial Lotteries, FY 2023. Data may be unaudited and in some cases were gathered by third party; profit is amount of total funds transferred to public beneficiaries, after prizes to players/retailers and administrative costs. **Fed. civ. employees:** Office of Personnel Mgmt., U.S. Dept. of Labor; as of Jan. 2024. **Education:** Natl. Ctr. for Education Statistics; high school graduation rates as of 2021-22 school year unless otherwise noted; number of colleges/univ. as of 2022-23. Data for 4-yr. private institutions does not include for-profit colleges/universities. **Energy:** Energy Information Admin., U.S. Dept. of Energy; average per capita monthly electricity consumption and cost for residential customers in 2022. **Tourism:** U.S. Travel Assn. 2022. Other information from sources in individual states. NA = Not available; AFB = Air Force base; JRB = joint reserve base; NAS = naval air station.

Famous persons lists may include non-natives associated with the state as well as persons born there. **Websites** are subject to change and are not endorsed by *The World Almanac*.

Alabama (AL)

Heart of Dixie (unofficial)

People. Population: 5,108,468; rank: 24. **Pop. change** (2020-23): 1.7%. **Pop. density:** 101 per sq mi. **Racial distribution:** 68.9% white; 26.6% Black; 1.6% Asian; 0.7% Amer. Ind.; 0.1% Hawaiian/Pacific Islander; 2 or more races, 2.0%. **Hispanic pop.:** 5.7%.

Geography. Total area: 52,406 sq mi; rank: 30. **Land area:** 50,633 sq mi; rank: 28. **Acres forested:** 23.0 mil. **Location:** East South Central state extending N-S from Tennessee to the Gulf of Mexico; E of the Mississippi R. **Climate:** long, hot summers; mild winters; generally abundant rain. **Topography:** coastal plains, including Prairie Black Belt, give way to hills, broken terrain; highest elevation 2,413 ft. **Capital:** Montgomery. **Chief airports:** Birmingham, Huntsville.

Economy. Chief industries: chemicals, electronics, apparel, primary metals, lumber and wood products, food processing, fabricated metals, automotive tires, oil and gas exploration. **Chief manuf. goods:** poultry processing, paper and paperboard, iron and steel, petroleum, automotive tires, aerospace, aluminum, auto body and parts. **Chief crops:** cotton, greenhouse and nursery, hay, peanuts, corn, soybeans. **Farm income:** Crops: $1.53 bil. Livestock: $6.98 bil. **Nonfuel minerals:** $2.0 bil; cement, lime, sand and gravel (construction), sand and gravel (industrial), stone (crushed). **Commercial fishing:** $62.7 mil. **Chief port:** Mobile. **Gross state product:** $300.2 bil. **Sales tax:** 4.0%. **Gasoline tax:** 48.60 cents/gal. **Employment distrib.:** 18.6% govt.; 18.6% trade/trans./util.; 13.0% mfg.; 12.3% ed./health; 12.3% prof./bus. serv.; 9.4% leisure/hosp.; 4.7% finance; 5.2% constr./mining/log.; 1.1% info.; 4.8% other serv. **Unemployment:** 2.5%. **Min. wage/hr.:** none. **Per cap. pers. income:** $53,175. **New private housing:** 20,337 units/$5.1 bil. **Broadband internet:** 93.7%. **Commercial banks:** 131; deposits: $134.7 bil. **Savings institutions:** 3; deposits: $428.0 mil.

Federal govt. Fed. civ. employees: 40,501; **avg. salary:** $104,993. **Notable fed. facilities:** Redstone Arsenal; Ft. Novosel (fmr. Rucker); Marshall Space Flight Ctr., Huntsville; Anniston Army Depot; Maxwell AFB and Gunter Annex; Army Corps of Engineers, Mobile District.

Education. High school grad. rate: 88.2%. **4-yr. public coll./univ.:** 14; **2-yr. public:** 23; **4-yr. private:** 17.

Energy. Electricity use/cost: 1,178 kWh, $167.80.

State data. Motto: Audemus Jura Nostra Defendere (We dare defend our rights). **Flower:** Camellia. **Bird:** Northern flicker (yellowhammer is local nickname). **Tree:** Southern longleaf pine. **Song:** "Alabama." **Entered union:** Dec. 14, 1819; rank: 22nd.

Tourism. Tourist spending: $11.6 bil (2022); change, 2019-22: 0.5%. **Attractions:** First White House of the Confederacy, Civil Rights Memorial, Alabama Shakespeare Festival, Legacy Museum, National Memorial for Peace and Justice, in Montgomery; Ivy Green (Helen Keller birthplace), Tuscumbia; Barber Vintage Motorsports Museum, Civil Rights Institute, Vulcan Park and Museum (world's largest cast iron statue), in Birmingham; G. W. Carver Interpretive Museum, Tuskegee; W. C. Handy Home, Museum, and Library, Frank Lloyd Wright's Rosenbaum House, in Florence; U.S. Space & Rocket Ctr., Huntsville; Moundville Archaeological Park; USS *Alabama* Memorial Park, Mobile; Gulf State Park, Gulf Shores. **Information:** Alabama Tourism Dept., 401 Adams Ave., P.O. Box 4927, Montgomery, AL 36104; 1-800-ALABAMA, (334) 242-4169; alabama.travel

History. Alabama was inhabited by the Creek, Cherokee, Chickasaw, Alabama, and Choctaw peoples when Spanish explorers arrived in the early 1500s. The French made the first permanent settlement at Ft. Louis, 1702, and founded Mobile, 1711. France later gave up the entire region to England under the Treaty of Paris, 1763. Spanish forces took control of the Mobile Bay area, 1780, and it remained under Spanish control until seized by U.S. troops, 1813. Most of present-day Alabama was held by the Creeks until Gen. Andrew Jackson broke their power, 1814. When Alabama became a state, 1819, enslaved Black people made up about one-third of the population. The Indian Removal Act of 1830 forced most remaining Creeks west. The state seceded, 1861, and the Confederate states were organized Feb. 4, at Montgomery, the first capital. The state was readmitted, 1868. Birmingham, founded 1871, became a center for iron- and steelmaking. The Montgomery bus boycott, 1955, sparked by Rosa Parks, helped launch the civil rights movement. Other confrontations occurred at Birmingham, 1963, and Selma, 1965. The leading political figure from the 1960s through the '80s, four-term Gov. George Wallace, started as a segregationist but later won with Black support. Growth in the auto industry boosted the economy as the 21st cent. began. A string of tornadoes in 2011 killed at least 248. Jefferson County, which includes Birmingham, filed the then-most expensive municipal bankruptcy in 2011. Gov. Robert Bentley pleaded guilty to misdemeanor charges connected with a sex scandal and resigned, 2017. Roy Moore, a former state chief justice, was upset by Doug Jones (D) in a special election for the U.S. Senate in 2017 after several women alleged Moore had a history of sexual misconduct. The state in May 2019 passed a law outlawing abortion in nearly all cases, which went into effect after *Roe v. Wade* was overturned in June 2022. Alabama's supreme court Feb. 16, 2024, said that frozen embryos are legally children, a ruling with wide-ranging potential impact; on Mar. 6, Gov. Kay Ivey signed a bill that provided fertility clinics with civil and criminal immunity for operations including discarding embryos.

Famous Alabamians. Hank Aaron, Tallulah Bankhead, Charles Barkley, Hugo L. Black, Paul "Bear" Bryant, George Washington Carver, Nat King Cole, Courteney Cox, William Christopher "W. C." Handy, Polly Holliday, Bo Jackson, Helen Keller, Coretta Scott King, Harper Lee, Joe Louis, Willie Mays, Jim Nabors, Jesse Owens, Terrell Owens, Rosa Parks, Condoleezza Rice, Lionel Richie, Robin Roberts, Octavia Spencer, Channing Tatum, George C. Wallace, Booker T. Washington, Hank Williams.

Website. www.alabama.gov

Alaska (AK)

The Last Frontier (unofficial)

People. Population: 733,406; rank: 48. **Pop. change** (2020-23): 0.0%. **Pop. density:** 1 per sq mi. **Racial distribution:** 64.2% white; 3.7% Black; 6.8% Asian; 15.6% Amer. Ind.; 1.7% Hawaiian/Pacific Islander; 2 or more races, 8.1%. **Hispanic pop.:** 7.5%.

Geography. Total area: 665,588 sq mi; rank: 1. **Land area:** 570,866 sq mi; rank: 1. **Acres forested:** 12.1 mil. **Location:** NW corner of North America, bordered on E by Canada. **Climate:** SE, SW, and central regions, moist and mild; far N extremely dry. Extended summer days, winter nights throughout. **Topography:** includes Pacific and Arctic mountain systems, central plateau, and Arctic slope. Denali, formerly Mt. McKinley, 20,310 ft, is the highest point in N. America. **Capital:** Juneau. **Chief airports:** Anchorage, Fairbanks.

Economy. Chief industries: petroleum, tourism, fishing, mining, forestry, transportation, aerospace. **Chief manuf. goods:** petroleum, seafood. **Chief crops:** greenhouse products, barley, oats, hay, potatoes, carrots. **Farm income:** Crops: $36.29 mil. Livestock: $9.30 mil. **Nonfuel minerals:** $4.1 bil; gold, lead, sand and gravel (construction), silver, zinc. **Commercial fishing:** $2.1 bil. **Chief ports:** Anchorage, Dutch Harbor, Kodiak, Juneau, Sitka, Valdez. **Gross state product:** $67.3 bil. **Sales tax:** none. **Gasoline tax:** 27.35 cents/gal. **Employment distrib.:** 24.6% govt.; 19.7% trade/trans./util.; 3.7% mfg.; 16.0% ed./health; 8.5% prof./bus. serv.; 10.0% leisure/hosp.; 3.3% finance; 9.4% constr./mining/log.; 1.3% info.; 3.6% other serv. **Unemployment:** 4.2%. **Min. wage/hr.:** $11.73. **Per cap. pers. income:** $71,616. **New private housing:** 937 units/$261.9 mil. **Broadband internet:** 92.8%. **Commercial banks:** 6; deposits: $15.0 bil. **Savings institutions:** 1; deposits: $521.0 mil.

Federal govt. Fed. civ. employees: 10,814; **avg. salary:** $102,020. **Notable fed. facilities:** Joint Base Elmendorf-Richardson; Ft. Wainwright; Eielson AFB; Ft. Greely.

Education. High school grad. rate: 77.8%. **4-yr. public coll./univ.:** 4; **2-yr. public:** 0; **4-yr. private:** 2.

Energy. Electricity use/cost: 580 kWh, $134.11.

State data. Motto: North to the future. **Flower:** Forget-me-not. **Bird:** Willow ptarmigan. **Tree:** Sitka spruce. **Song:** "Alaska's Flag." **Entered union:** Jan. 3, 1959; rank: 49th.

Tourism. Tourist spending: $3.0 bil (2022); change, 2019-22: –7.4%. **Attractions:** Portage Glacier, in Chugach Natl. Forest; Mendenhall Glacier, in Tongass Natl. Forest; Totem Heritage Ctr., Ketchikan; Glacier Bay Natl. Park and Preserve; Denali (formerly Mt. McKinley, N. America's highest peak), in Denali Natl. Park and Preserve; Mt. Roberts Tramway, Juneau; Alaska Maritime Natl. Wildlife Refuge; St. Michael's Cathedral, Alaska Raptor Ctr., in Sitka; White Pass & Yukon Route railroad, Skagway; Katmai Natl. Park and Preserve; Univ. of Alaska Museum of the North, Fairbanks. **Information:** Alaska Travel Industry Association, 610 E. 5th Ave., Ste. 200, Anchorage, AK 99501; 1-800-327-9372; www.travelalaska.com

History. Early inhabitants included the Tlingit-Haida and Athabascan peoples. Ancestors of the Aleut and Inuit (Eskimo) probably arrived from Siberia between 10,000 and 6,000 years ago. Vitus Bering, a Dane sailing for Russia, was the first European to land in Alaska, 1741. Russians, pursuing the fur trade, established a permanent settlement on Kodiak Island, 1784. Sec. of State William H. Seward bought Alaska from Russia for $7.2 mil in 1867, a deal some called "Seward's Folly." Discovery of gold in the Klondike region of Canada's Yukon Territory, 1896, triggered an Alaskan gold rush. Alaska became a territory, 1912, and a state, 1959. A huge oil find at Prudhoe Bay, 1968, led to construction of the Trans-Alaska Pipeline, 1974-77. The *Exxon Valdez* supertanker ran aground, 1989, spilling about 11 mil gallons of crude oil; the cleanup cost more than $2.2 bil. Congress included a measure permitting oil and gas drilling in the Arctic National Wildlife Refuge in the tax bill passed in Dec. 2017, ending a four-decade battle. A magnitude 7.0 earthquake centered near Anchorage struck Nov. 30, 2018, causing at least $75 mil in damage.

Famous Alaskans. Tom Bodett, Susan Butcher, Ernest Gruening, Jewel (Kilcher), Tony Knowles, Sydney Laurence, Sarah Palin, Libby Riddles, Curt Schilling, Jefferson "Soapy" Smith.

Website. www.alaska.gov

Arizona (AZ)

Grand Canyon State

People. Population: 7,431,344; rank: 14. **Pop. change** (2020-23): 3.8%. **Pop. density:** 65 per sq mi. **Racial distribution:** 81.5% white; 5.7% Black; 4.1% Asian; 5.2% Amer. Ind.; 0.3% Hawaiian/Pacific Islander; 2 or more races, 3.3%. **Hispanic pop.:** 31.6%.

Geography. Total area: 113,955 sq mi; rank: 6. **Land area:** 113,623 sq mi; rank: 6. **Acres forested:** 19.1 mil. **Location:** southwestern U.S. **Climate:** clear and dry in southern regions and northern plateau; high central areas have heavy winter snows. **Topography:** Colorado Plateau in the N, containing the Grand Canyon; Mexican Highlands run NW to SE; Sonoran Desert in the SW. **Capital:** Phoenix. **Chief airports:** Phoenix, Tucson, Mesa.

Economy. Chief industries: manufacturing, construction, tourism, mining, agriculture. **Chief manuf. goods:** aerospace, semiconductors, navigational instruments, cement, plastics, structural metals, dairy, printing, furniture. **Chief crops:** cotton, grapes, apples, lettuce, hay, potatoes, sorghum, barley, corn, wheat. **Farm income:** Crops: $3.00 bil. Livestock: $2.24 bil. **Nonfuel minerals:** $9.5 bil; cement, copper, molybdenum mineral concentrates, sand and gravel (construction), stone (crushed). **Gross state product:** $508.3 bil. **Sales tax:** 5.6%. **Gasoline tax:** 37.40 cents/gal. **Employment distrib.:** 13.6% govt.; 19.2% trade/trans./util.; 5.9% mfg.; 16.7% ed./health; 14.6% prof./bus. serv.; 10.9% leisure/hosp.; 7.4% finance; 7.1% constr./mining/log.; 1.5% info.; 3.2% other serv. **Unemployment:** 3.9%. **Min. wage/hr.:** $14.35. **Per cap. pers. income:** $61,652. **New private housing:** 58,433 units/$13.6 bil. **Broadband internet:** 95.4%. **Commercial banks:** 59; deposits: $204.1 bil. **Savings institutions:** 4; deposits: $4.8 bil. **Lottery:** total sales: $1.5 bil; profit: $318.4 mil.

Federal govt. Fed. civ. employees: 33,955; **avg. salary:** $95,085. **Notable fed. facilities:** Luke AFB; Davis-Monthan AFB; Ft. Huachuca; Yuma Proving Ground.

Education. High school grad. rate: 77.3%. **4-yr. public coll./univ.:** 5; **2-yr. public:** 20; **4-yr. private:** 9.

Energy. Electricity use/cost: 1,061 kWh, $138.13.

State data. Motto: Ditat Deus (God enriches). **Flower:** Blossom of the saguaro cactus. **Bird:** Cactus wren. **Tree:** Palo verde. **Song:** "Arizona." **Entered union:** Feb. 14, 1912; rank: 48th.

Tourism. Tourist spending: $22.3 bil (2022); change, 2019-22: –5.2%. **Attractions:** Grand Canyon; Painted Desert, in Grand Canyon and Petrified Forest Natl. Parks; Glen Canyon Natl. Recreation Area; Canyon de Chelly Natl. Monument; Meteor Crater, near Winslow; London Bridge, Lake Havasu City; Biosphere 2, Oracle; Navajo Natl. Monument; Tombstone historic mining town; Tempe Town Lake. **Information:** Arizona Office of Tourism, 100 N. 7th Ave., Ste. 400, Phoenix, AZ 85007; 1-866-275-5816; www.visitarizona.com

History. Paleo-Indians hunted large game in the area at least 12,000 years ago. Anasazi, Mogollon, and Hohokam civilizations lived there c. 300 BCE-1300 CE; Navajo and Apache came c. 15th cent. Marcos de Niza, a Spanish Franciscan, and Estevanico, a Moroccan-born enslaved Black man, explored, 1539; explorer Francisco Vásquez de Coronado visited, 1540. Eusebio Francisco Kino, a Jesuit missionary, taught Indians, 1692-1711, and left missions. Tubac, a Spanish fort, became the first European settlement, 1752. Spain ceded Arizona to Mexico, 1821. The U.S. took over, 1848, after the Mexican War. The area below the Gila R. came from Mexico in the Gadsden Purchase, 1853. Arizona became a territory, 1863. Apache wars ended with Geronimo's surrender, 1886. Arizona became a state, 1912, and grew rapidly after 1960 with a fourfold rise in population over the next four decades. The border with Mexico is a major gateway for illegal immigration to the U.S. In 2012, the U.S. Supreme Court struck down most provisions of a 2010 state immigration law that allowed police to make warrantless arrests of those reasonably suspected of having immigrated illegally. On July 31, 2023, Phoenix ended a record-breaking heat streak of 31 days at or above 110 °F. Superseding Arizona's 15-week abortion ban, the state's supreme court on Apr. 9, 2024, upheld a 160-year-old ban on all abortions except to save a mother's life. Gov. Katie Hobbs (D) signed a repeal of the more stringent law May 2. On Apr. 24, 2024, an Arizona grand jury charged 18 people with 2020 election interference, including former Trump chief of staff Mark Meadows and attorney Rudy Giuliani.

Famous Arizonans. Bruce Babbitt, Cochise, Alice Cooper, Geronimo, Gabrielle Giffords, Barry Goldwater, Zane Grey, Carl Hayden, George W. P. Hunt, Helen Hull Jacobs, Bil Keane, Percival Lowell, John McCain, John J. Rhodes, Linda Ronstadt, Emma Stone, Morris K. Udall, Stewart L. Udall, Frank Lloyd Wright.

Website. www.az.gov

Arkansas (AR)

Natural State, Razorback State

People. Population: 3,067,732; rank: 33. **Pop. change** (2020-23): 1.9%. **Pop. density:** 59 per sq mi. **Racial distribution:** 78.4% white; 15.6% Black; 1.9% Asian; 1.1% Amer. Ind.; 0.5% Hawaiian/Pacific Islander; 2 or more races, 2.5%. **Hispanic pop.:** 9.2%.

Geography. Total area: 53,165 sq mi; rank: 29. **Land area:** 52,024 sq mi; rank: 27. **Acres forested:** 18.8 mil. **Location:**

West South Central state. **Climate:** long, hot summers, mild winters; generally abundant rainfall. **Topography:** eastern delta and prairie, southern lowland forests, and the northwestern highlands, which include the Ozark Plateaus. **Capital:** Little Rock. **Chief airports:** Little Rock, Bentonville.

Economy. Chief industries: manufacturing, agriculture, tourism, forestry. **Chief manuf. goods:** poultry processing, motor vehicles and parts, iron and steel, paper and paperboard, plastics, preserved fruits and vegetables, aerospace, rubber. **Chief crops:** rice, soybeans, cotton, hay, wheat, corn, sorghum, tomatoes, peaches, watermelons, pecans, blueberries, grapes. **Farm income:** Crops: $5.43 bil. Livestock: $8.56 bil. **Nonfuel minerals:** $1.2 bil; bromine, cement, sand and gravel (construction), sand and gravel (industrial), stone (crushed). **Chief port:** Helena. **Gross state product:** $176.2 bil. **Sales tax:** 6.5%. **Gasoline tax:** 43.40 cents/gal. **Employment distrib.:** 15.8% govt.; 19.6% trade/trans./util.; 11.7% mfg.; 15.6% ed./health; 11.6% prof./bus. serv.; 9.6% leisure/hosp.; 5.1% finance; 5.3% constr./mining/log.; 0.9% info.; 4.9% other serv. **Unemployment:** 3.3%. **Min. wage/hr.:** $11.00. **Per cap. pers. income:** $54,347. **New private housing:** 12,842 units/$2.8 bil. **Broadband internet:** 91.5%. **Commercial banks:** 110; deposits: $96.8 bil. **Savings institutions:** 2; deposits: $231.0 mil. **Lottery:** total sales: $607.6 mil; profit: $113.1 mil.

Federal govt. Fed. civ. employees: 14,298; **avg. salary:** $90,845. **Notable fed. facilities:** Little Rock AFB; Pine Bluff Arsenal; Natl. Ctr. for Toxicological Research, Jefferson.

Education. High school grad. rate: 88.2%. **4-yr. public coll./univ.:** 12; **2-yr. public:** 22; **4-yr. private:** 14.

Energy. Electricity use/cost: 1,110 kWh, $133.78.

State data. Motto: Regnat Populus (The people rule). **Flower:** Apple blossom. **Bird:** Northern mockingbird. **Tree:** Pine. **Song:** "Arkansas." **Entered union:** June 15, 1836; rank: 25th.

Tourism. Tourist spending: $9.2 bil (2022); change, 2019-22: 14.8%. **Attractions:** Eureka Springs; Ozark Folk Ctr. State Park, Mountain View; Blanchard Springs Caverns, in Ozark Natl. Forest; Crater of Diamonds State Park, Murfreesboro; Toltec Mounds Archeological State Park, Scott; Buffalo Natl. River; Hot Springs Natl. Park; Pea Ridge Natl. Military Park; William J. Clinton Presidential Library and Museum, Little Rock Central High School Natl. Historic Site, in Little Rock; Crystal Bridges Museum of American Art, Bentonville. **Information:** Arkansas Dept. of Parks & Tourism, 1 Capitol Mall, Little Rock, AR 72201; 1-800-NATURAL; www.arkansas.com

History. Quapaw, Caddo, Osage, Cherokee, and Choctaw peoples lived in the area at the time of European contact. The first European explorers were Hernando de Soto, 1541; Jacques Marquette and Louis Jolliet, 1673; and René-Robert Cavelier, sieur de La Salle, 1682. French fur trader Henri de Tonty founded the first settlement, 1686, at Arkansas Post. In 1762, the area was ceded by France to Spain, then given back, 1800, and was part of the Louisiana Purchase, 1803. It was made a territory, 1819, and entered the Union as a slave state, 1836. Arkansas seceded in 1861, after the Civil War began; it was readmitted, 1868. Pres. Eisenhower sent federal troops, 1957, to keep Gov. Orval Faubus from blocking racial integration at Central High School in Little Rock. Walmart, now the world's leading retailer, opened its first store in Rogers, 1962. Elected five times as governor, Bill Clinton later served two terms as president (1993-2001). His presidential library opened, 2004, in Little Rock. After 12 years without an execution, the state put to death four inmates in eight days in 2017. The state's legislature in Apr. 2021 overrode Gov. Asa Hutchinson's (R) veto of a bill prohibiting doctors from providing gender-affirming care to transgender youth, making it the first state to ban such medical treatment; a federal judge blocked the ban from going into effect.

Famous Arkansans. Daisy Bates, Dee Brown, Paul "Bear" Bryant, Glen Campbell, Hattie Wyatt Caraway, Johnny Cash, Wesley Clark, Bill Clinton, Jay Hanna "Dizzy" Dean, Orval Faubus, James William Fulbright, Al Green, John Grisham, Levon Helm, John H. Johnson, Douglas MacArthur, John Little McClellan, James S. McDonnell, Scottie Pippen, Dick Powell, Brooks Robinson, Winthrop Rockefeller, Mary Steenburgen, Edward Durell Stone, Billy Bob Thornton, Sam Walton, Archibald Yell.

Website. www.arkansas.gov

California (CA)

Golden State

People. Population: 38,965,193; rank: 1. **Pop. change** (2020-23): –1.4%. **Pop. density:** 250 per sq mi. **Racial distribution:** 70.4% white; 6.5% Black; 16.5% Asian; 1.7% Amer. Ind.; 0.5% Hawaiian/Pacific Islander; 2 or more races, 4.3%. **Hispanic pop.:** 40.4%.

Geography. Total area: 163,651 sq mi; rank: 3. **Land area:** 155,813 sq mi; rank: 3. **Acres forested:** 31.6 mil. **Location:** western coast of U.S. **Climate:** moderate temperatures and rainfall along the coast; extremes in the interior. **Topography:** long mountainous coastline; central valley; Sierra Nevada on the E; desert basins in southern interior; rugged mountains in N. **Capital:** Sacramento. **Chief airports:** Los Angeles, San Francisco, San Diego, Sacramento, San Jose, Santa Ana, Oakland, Ontario, Burbank, Long Beach, Palm Springs, Fresno, Santa Barbara.

Economy. Chief industries: agriculture, tourism, apparel, electronics, telecommunications, entertainment. **Chief manuf. goods:** petroleum, aerospace, precision instruments, semiconductors, telecom and broadcasting equip., pharmaceutical, wineries, plastics, medical equip., preserved fruits and vegetables, printing, dairy, cut and sew apparel, motor vehicles. **Chief crops:** grapes, nursery products, almonds, lettuce, hay, strawberries, floriculture, tomatoes, cotton, oranges, pistachios, walnuts, broccoli, carrots, rice, peaches, lemons. **Farm income:** Crops: $41.01 bil. Livestock: $17.40 bil. **Nonfuel minerals:** $5.1 bil; boron minerals, cement, rare earths, sand and gravel (construction), stone (crushed). **Commercial fishing:** $207.9 mil. **Chief ports:** Long Beach, Los Angeles, San Diego, Port Hueneme, Richmond, Oakland, San Francisco, Stockton. **Gross state product:** $3.9 tril. **Sales tax:** 7.25%. **Gasoline tax:** 86.50 cents/gal. **Employment distrib.:** 15.0% govt.; 17.1% trade/trans./util.; 7.3% mfg.; 18.1% ed./health; 15.4% prof./bus. serv.; 11.3% leisure/hosp.; 4.4% finance; 5.2% constr./mining/log.; 2.9% info.; 3.3% other serv. **Unemployment:** 4.8%. **Min. wage/hr.:** $16.00. **Per cap. pers. income:** $80,423. **New private housing:** 111,760 units/$27.9 bil. **Broadband internet:** 96.8%. **Commercial banks:** 168; deposits: $1.8 tril. **Savings institutions:** 12; deposits: $29.1 bil. **Lottery:** total sales: $9.2 bil; profit: $2.3 bil.

Federal govt. Fed. civ. employees: 146,810; **avg. salary:** $113,010. **Notable fed. facilities:** USMC Camp Pendleton; Naval Base Coronado; Marine Corps Air Ground Combat Ctr., 29 Palms; Marine Corps Air Station Miramar; Travis AFB; Naval Research Lab, Monterey; Lawrence Livermore Natl. Lab; Lawrence Berkeley Natl. Lab; NASA Jet Propulsion Lab, Pasadena; Edwards AFB (NASA Armstrong Flight Research Ctr., AF Test Ctr.); San Francisco Mint.

Education. High school grad. rate: 87.0%. **4-yr. public coll./univ.:** 50; **2-yr. public:** 101; **4-yr. private:** 133.

Energy. Electricity use/cost: 535 kWh, $138.29.

State data. Motto: Eureka (I have found it). **Flower:** California poppy. **Bird:** California valley quail. **Tree:** California redwood. **Song:** "I Love You, California." **Entered union:** Sept. 9, 1850; rank: 31st.

Tourism. Tourist spending: $145.5 bil (2022); change, 2019-22: –8.7%. **Attractions:** *Queen Mary*, Aquarium of the Pacific, in Long Beach; Palomar Observatory, Palomar Mountain; Disneyland Resort, Anaheim; Getty Center, Universal Studios Hollywood, Griffith Observatory, in Los Angeles; Tournament of Roses and Rose Bowl, Pasadena; The California Museum, California State Railroad Museum, in Sacramento; San Diego Zoo, USS *Midway* Museum, in San Diego; Yosemite Valley; Lassen Volcanic, Sequoia, and Kings Canyon Natl. Parks; Mojave and Sonoran Deserts; Death Valley; Golden Gate Park, Alcatraz Island, in San Francisco; Napa Valley wine region; Monterey Bay Aquarium, Monterey Peninsula; Ancient Bristlecone Pine Forest (oldest known living trees on Earth), in Inyo Natl. Forest; Redwood Natl. and State Parks; Muir Woods Natl. Monument, Mill Valley. **Information:** California Office of Tourism, 555 Capitol Mall, Ste. 1100, Sacramento, CA 95814; 1-800-621-0021; www.visitcalifornia.com

History. Early inhabitants included more than 100 different Native American tribes with multiple dialects. The first European explorers were Juan Rodríguez Cabrillo, 1542, and Sir Francis Drake, 1579. The first settlement was the Spanish Alta California mission at San Diego, 1769, first in a string founded by Franciscan Father Junípero Serra. California became a province of independent Mexico, 1821. U.S. traders and settlers arrived in the 19th cent. and staged the Bear Flag revolt, 1846, in protest against Mexican rule; later that year U.S. forces occupied California. At the end of the Mexican War, Mexico ceded the territory to the U.S., 1848; that same year gold was discovered, and the famed gold rush began. California became a state, 1850. An economic downturn in the 1870s spurred riots against Chinese immigrants, who had come as laborers in the boom years. An earthquake and related fires devastated San Francisco, 1906. During World War II, Japanese Americans, many of them U.S. citizens, were held in detention camps, 1942-45. Ronald Reagan, a former movie actor, became state governor (1967-75) and U.S. president (1981-89). A budget crisis, 2003, resulted in the recall of Gov. Gray Davis and the election of another actor, Arnold Schwarzenegger. A 6-year-old drought mostly ended in 2017. Wildfires caused 54 deaths in 2017 and destroyed thousands of homes and other structures. The 2018 fire season was the deadliest—at least 85 killed in Nov. 2018 Camp fire alone—

in state history. Gov. Gavin Newsom (D) in 2019 issued a moratorium on the death penalty. More than 4.2 mil acres burned during the 2020 fire season, the most on record and twice the previous high. Beginning June 1, 2022, some 6 mil residents faced unprecedented water restrictions due to continuing drought conditions. Severe "atmospheric river" storms from Dec. 2022 through late Mar. 2023 triggered flooding and landslides causing more than 25 deaths and at least $3.5 bil in damages. Ending a historic 118-day strike, the Hollywood actors' union SAG-AFTRA in Nov. 2023 reached a tentative agreement with major studios and streaming companies; the deal was formally approved Dec. 5, 2023.

Famous Californians. Tom Brady, Edmund G. (Pat) Brown, Jerry Brown, Luther Burbank, Julia Child, Ted Danson, Cameron Diaz, Leonardo DiCaprio, Joe DiMaggio, Landon Donovan, Clint Eastwood, Billie Eilish, Dianne Feinstein, John C. Fremont, Tom Hanks, Kamala Harris, William Randolph Hearst, Helen Hunt, Steve Jobs, Jimmie Johnson, Angelina Jolie, Jack Kemp, Jason Kidd, Brie Larson, Lisa Leslie, Monica Lewinsky, Jack London, George Lucas, Phil Mickelson, Marilyn Monroe, John Muir, Richard M. Nixon, Gwyneth Paltrow, George S. Patton Jr., Gregory Peck, Nancy Pelosi, Ronald Reagan, Sally K. Ride, William Saroyan, Arnold Schwarzenegger, Junípero Serra, O. J. Simpson, Kevin Spacey, Leland Stanford, Gwen Stefani, John Steinbeck, Shirley Temple, Earl Warren, Serena Williams, Ted Williams, Venus Williams, Tiger Woods.

Website. www.ca.gov

Colorado (CO)

Centennial State

People. Population: 5,877,610; rank: 21. **Pop. change** (2020-23): 1.8%. **Pop. density:** 57 per sq mi. **Racial distribution:** 86.0% white; 4.8% Black; 3.8% Asian; 1.7% Amer. Ind.; 0.2% Hawaiian/Pacific Islander; 2 or more races, 3.5%. **Hispanic pop.:** 22.7%.

Geography. Total area: 104,067 sq mi; rank: 8. **Land area:** 103,610 sq mi; rank: 8. **Acres forested:** 22.8 mil. **Location:** W central U.S. **Climate:** low relative humidity, abundant sun, wide daily/seasonal temperature ranges; alpine conditions in the high mountains. **Topography:** eastern dry high plains; hilly to mountainous central plateau; western Rocky Mts. of high ranges with broad valleys, deep, narrow canyons. **Capital:** Denver. **Chief airports:** Denver, Colorado Springs.

Economy. Chief industries: manufacturing, construction, government, tourism, agriculture, aerospace, electronics equip. **Chief manuf. goods:** animal slaughtering, beer, petroleum, pharmaceuticals, aerospace, medical equip., precision instruments, printing, semiconductors. **Chief crops:** hay, corn, potatoes, wheat, onions, dry edible beans, sunflowers, sugar beets, barley, proso millet, cabbage, peaches, lettuce, apples, cantaloupes. **Farm income:** Crops: $2.58 bil. Livestock: $6.38 bil. **Nonfuel minerals:** $2.2 bil; cement, gold, molybdenum mineral concentrates, sand and gravel (construction), stone (crushed). **Gross state product:** $520.4 bil. **Sales tax:** 2.9%. **Gasoline tax:** 47.64 cents/gal. **Employment distrib.:** 16.7% govt.; 16.8% trade/trans./util.; 5.1% mfg.; 12.9% ed./health; 16.9% prof./bus. serv.; 11.9% leisure/hosp.; 6.1% finance; 6.8% constr./mining/log.; 2.5% info.; 4.3% other serv. **Unemployment:** 3.2%. **Min. wage/hr.:** $14.42. **Per cap. pers. income:** $78,918. **New private housing:** 39,404 units/$11.0 bil. **Broadband internet:** 96.9%. **Commercial banks:** 114; deposits: $182.9 bil. **Savings institutions:** 12; deposits: $4.4 bil. **Lottery:** total sales: $889.8 mil; profit: $195.3 mil.

Federal govt. Fed. civ. employees: 39,709; **avg. salary:** $109,929. **Notable fed. facilities:** U.S. Air Force Academy; Peterson SFB; Denver Mint; Ft. Carson; Natl. Renewable Energy Lab, Golden; Transportation Tech. Ctr., Pueblo; NORAD and USNORTHCOM Alt. Command Ctr., Cheyenne Mtn. Complex; Denver Fed. Ctr.; Natl. Ctr. for Atmospheric Research, Natl. Inst. of Standards & Technology, NOAA Earth System Research Lab, Boulder; Natl. Wildlife Research Ctr., Fort Collins.

Education. High school grad. rate: 82.3%. **4-yr. public coll./univ.:** 18; **2-yr. public:** 10; **4-yr. private:** 9.

Energy. Electricity use/cost: 692 kWh, $98.18.

State data. Motto: Nil Sine Numine (Nothing without Providence). **Flower:** Rocky Mountain columbine. **Bird:** Lark bunting. **Tree:** Colorado blue spruce. **Songs:** "Where the Columbines Grow"; "Rocky Mountain High." **Entered union:** Aug. 1, 1876; rank: 38th.

Tourism. Tourist spending: $25.0 bil (2022); change, 2019-22: 2.8%. **Attractions:** Denver Museum of Nature & Science, Denver Botanic Gardens, Denver Zoo; Red Rocks Park and Amphitheatre, Morrison; Natl. Ctr. for Atmospheric Research, Boulder; Rocky Mountain, Black Canyon of the Gunnison, and Mesa Verde (Anasazi cliff dwellings) Natl. Parks; Aspen, Breckenridge, Steamboat, and Vail ski resorts; Garden of the Gods, Colorado Springs; Great Sand Dunes Natl. Park and Preserve; Dinosaur and Colorado Natl. Monuments; Pikes Peak and Mount Evans; Grand Mesa Natl. Forest; historic mining towns of Central City, Silverton, Cripple Creek; Bent's Old Fort Natl. Historic Site, near La Junta; Georgetown Loop Historic Mining and Railroad Park; Durango & Silverton Narrow Gauge Railroad Museum, Durango; Cumbres & Toltec Scenic Railroad, Antonito; gambling in Black Hawk, Central City, Cripple Creek and on tribal land in Ignacio and Towaoc. **Information:** Colorado Tourism Office, 1600 Broadway, Ste. 2500, Denver, CO 80202; 1-800-265-6723; www.colorado.com

History. Paleo-Indians hunted big game in the area at least 11,000 years ago. Anasazi cliff dwellers flourished around Mesa Verde until about 1300 CE; other Native Americans were the Ute, Pueblo, Cheyenne, and Arapaho. The region was claimed by Spain but passed to France, 1800. The U.S. acquired eastern Colorado in the Louisiana Purchase, 1803. Lt. Zebulon M. Pike explored the area, 1806, sighting the peak that bears his name. After the Mexican War, 1846-48, U.S. immigrants settled in the east, former Mexicans in the south. Gold was discovered in 1858, causing a population boom. Congress created Colorado Territory, 1861. Conflict between newcomers and displaced Native Americans led to the Sand Creek Massacre, 1864, in which U.S. soldiers and settlers killed some 150 Cheyenne and Arapaho. U.S. Army troops forced the removal to reservations (mostly in present-day Oklahoma) of most Native Americans in the state, 1867. The 1870s brought statehood, 1876, and rich silver finds that turned Leadville into a boomtown. Federal military and civilian employment in Colorado surged in the 1940s and '50s; since then, tourism and technology have fueled the economy. The state's Hispanic population grew from 5.8% in 1980 to 21.9% in 2020. Colorado became the first state in the U.S. to legalize selling recreational marijuana in 2014. Colorado's Supreme Court in Dec. 2023 ruled former Pres. Donald Trump ineligible to run in the state's primary, citing his alleged role in the Jan. 6, 2021, attack on the U.S. Capitol; the U.S. Supreme Court in Mar. 2024 overturned the ruling.

Famous Coloradans. Tim Allen, Chauncey Billups, Frederick Bonfils, Molly Brown, William N. Byers, M. Scott Carpenter, Lon Chaney, Jack Dempsey, Mamie Eisenhower, Douglas Fairbanks, Barney Ford, Neil Gorsuch, Roy Halladay, Ouray, Trey Parker, "Baby Doe" Tabor, Lowell Thomas, Byron R. White, Paul Whiteman.

Website. www.colorado.gov

Connecticut (CT)

Constitution State, Nutmeg State

People. Population: 3,617,176; rank: 29. **Pop. change** (2020-23): 0.3%. **Pop. density:** 747 per sq mi. **Racial distribution:** 78.0% white; 13.1% Black; 5.2% Asian; 0.8% Amer. Ind.; 0.1% Hawaiian/Pacific Islander; 2 or more races, 2.8%. **Hispanic pop.:** 18.6%.

Geography. Total area: 5,542 sq mi; rank: 48. **Land area:** 4,841 sq mi; rank: 48. **Acres forested:** 1.8 mil. **Location:** New England state in NE corner of U.S. **Climate:** moderate; winters avg. slightly below freezing; warm, humid summers. **Topography:** western upland, the Berkshires, in the NW, highest elevations; narrow central lowland N-S; hilly eastern upland drained by rivers. **Capital:** Hartford. **Chief airport:** Windsor Locks.

Economy. Chief industries: manufacturing, retail trade, government, services, finances, insurance, real estate. **Chief manuf. goods:** aerospace, chemicals, fabricated metals, precision instruments, toiletries, medical equip., printing, plastics. **Chief crops:** nursery stock, Christmas trees, mushrooms, sweet corn, apples, tobacco, hay. **Farm income:** Crops: $437.32 mil. Livestock: $248.71 mil. **Nonfuel minerals:** $264 mil; sand and gravel (construction), stone (crushed), stone (dimension). **Commercial fishing:** $15.8 mil. **Chief ports:** New Haven, Bridgeport, New London. **Gross state product:** $340.2 bil. **Sales tax:** 6.35%. **Gasoline tax:** 43.40 cents/gal. **Employment distrib.:** 14.0% govt.; 17.2% trade/trans./util.; 9.3% mfg.; 21.5% ed./health; 12.9% prof./bus. serv.; 8.8% leisure/hosp.; 7.0% finance; 3.7% constr./mining/log.; 1.8% info.; 3.8% other serv. **Unemployment:** 3.8%. **Min. wage/hr.:** $15.69. **Per cap. pers. income:** $87,447. **New private housing:** 6,272 units/$1.5 bil. **Broadband internet:** 97.4%. **Commercial banks:** 28; deposits: $141.4 bil. **Savings institutions:** 24; deposits: $25.3 bil. **Lottery:** total sales: $1.5 bil; profit: $412.9 mil.

Federal govt. Fed. civ. employees: 4,682; **avg. salary:** $115,998. **Notable fed. facilities:** U.S. Coast Guard Academy; Naval Sub Base New London.

Education. High school grad. rate: 88.9%. **4-yr. public coll./univ.:** 6; **2-yr. public:** 12; **4-yr. private:** 17.

Energy. Electricity use/cost: 716 kWh, $176.10.

State data. Motto: Qui Transtulit Sustinet (He who transplanted still sustains). **Flower:** Mountain laurel. **Bird:** American robin. **Tree:** White oak. **Song:** "Yankee Doodle." **Fifth** of the 13 original states to ratify the Constitution, Jan. 9, 1788.

Tourism. Tourist spending: $11.8 bil (2022); change, 2019-22: –11.6%. **Attractions:** Mark Twain House and Museum, Hartford; Yale Univ. Art Gallery, Peabody Museum of Natural History, in New Haven; Mystic Seaport, Mystic Aquarium; Barnum Museum, Bridgeport; Gillette Castle State Park, East Haddam; USS *Nautilus* (1st nuclear-powered submarine) at Submarine Force Library and Museum, Groton; Mashantucket Pequot Museum and Research Ctr.; Foxwoods Resort Casino, Ledyard; Mohegan Sun, Uncasville; Lake Compounce (est. 1846; oldest continuously operating amusement park in U.S.), Bristol; Philip Johnson Glass House, New Canaan. **Information:** Connecticut Office of Tourism, 450 Columbus Blvd., Ste. 5, Hartford, CT 06103; 1-888-CTVISIT, (860) 256-2800; www.ctvisit.com

History. At the time of European contact, inhabitants of the area were Algonquian peoples, including the Mohegan and Pequot. Dutch explorer Adriaen Block was the first European visitor, 1614. By 1634, English settlers from Plymouth had started colonies along the Connecticut R.; in 1637 they defeated the Pequots. The Colony of Connecticut was chartered by England, 1662; New Haven colony was added, 1665. A Patriot stronghold in the American Revolution, the state actively supported the antislavery movement and the Union cause in the Civil War. The state economy prospered in the 20th cent. from insurance- and defense-related industries. *Nautilus*, the first nuclear-powered submarine, was launched at Groton, 1954. Connecticut Sen. Joseph Lieberman was the Democratic nominee for vice president in 2000. American Indian casinos, starting with Foxwoods in 1992, were an economic boon to the state, but tourism revenues declined sharply with the recession that began in late 2007. Twenty children and six staff members were killed in a mass shooting at Sandy Hook Elementary School in Newtown, Dec. 14, 2012. In Oct. 2022, Infowars host Alex Jones was ordered to pay $965 mil to families of some of the victims, over conspiracy theories he spread about the shooting.

Famous "Nutmeggers." Ethan Allen, P. T. Barnum, Michael Bolton, Glenn Close, Samuel Colt, Ann Coulter, Jonathan Edwards, Nathan Hale, Katharine Hepburn, Isaac Hull, Norman Lear, Seth MacFarlane, John Mayer, Robert Mitchum, J. P. Morgan, Ralph Nader, Israel Putnam, Wallace Stevens, Harriet Beecher Stowe, Mark Twain, Noah Webster, Eli Whitney.

Website. www.ct.gov

Delaware (DE)

First State, Diamond State

People. Population: 1,031,890; rank: 45. **Pop. change** (2020-23): 4.2%. **Pop. density:** 530 per sq mi. **Racial distribution:** 67.6% white; 24.1% Black; 4.4% Asian; 0.7% Amer. Ind.; 0.1% Hawaiian/Pacific Islander; 2 or more races, 3.1%. **Hispanic pop.:** 11.1%.

Geography. Total area: 2,488 sq mi; rank: 49. **Land area:** 1,948 sq mi; rank: 49. **Acres forested:** 0.4 mil. **Location:** Delmarva Peninsula on the Atlantic coastal plain. **Climate:** moderate. **Topography:** Piedmont Plateau to the N, sloping to a near sea-level plain. **Capital:** Dover.

Economy. Chief industries: chemicals, agriculture, finance, poultry, shellfish, tourism, auto assembly, food processing, transportation equip. **Chief manuf. goods:** pharmaceuticals, poultry processing, soap and cleaning compounds, precision instruments, basic chemicals, plastics. **Chief crops:** soybeans, corn, greenhouse and nursery, wheat, potatoes, barley, hay, watermelons, lima beans, green peas, pumpkins, mushrooms, cabbage. **Farm income:** Crops: $397.33 mil. Livestock: $1.62 bil. **Nonfuel minerals:** $17 mil; magnesium compounds, sand and gravel (construction), stone (crushed). **Commercial fishing:** $15.7 mil. **Chief port:** Wilmington. **Gross state product:** $93.6 bil. **Sales tax:** none. **Gasoline tax:** 41.40 cents/gal. **Employment distrib.:** 14.9% govt.; 18.1% trade/trans./util.; 5.7% mfg.; 17.5% ed./health; 13.1% prof./bus. serv.; 10.6% leisure/hosp.; 10.4% finance; 5.0% constr./mining/log.; 0.7% info.; 3.9% other serv. **Unemployment:** 4.0%. **Min. wage/hr.:** $13.25. **Per cap. pers. income:** $65,392. **New private housing:** 5,765 units/$827.7 mil. **Broadband internet:** 98.1%. **Commercial banks:** 33; deposits: $493.1 bil. **Savings institutions:** 4; deposits: $8.2 bil. **Lottery:** total sales: $758.6 mil; profit: $244.2 mil.

Federal govt. Fed. civ. employees: 3,843; **avg. salary:** $102,210. **Notable fed. facilities:** Dover AFB; Bombay Hook Natl. Wildlife Refuge.

Education. High school grad. rate: 87.8%. **4-yr. public coll./univ.:** 3; **2-yr. public:** 0; **4-yr. private:** 2.

Energy. Electricity use/cost: 941 kWh, $128.99.

State data. Motto: Liberty and independence. **Flower:** Peach blossom. **Bird:** Blue hen chicken. **Tree:** American holly. **Song:** "Our Delaware." **First** of original 13 states to ratify the Constitution, Dec. 7, 1787.

Tourism. Tourist spending: $2.3 bil (2022); change, 2019-22: –9.5%. **Attractions:** Fort Christina (site of founding of colony of New Sweden), Holy Trinity (Old Swedes) Church (erected 1698, oldest church in U.S. still standing as built and in use), Hagley Museum and Library, Nemours Mansion and Gardens, in Wilmington; Winterthur Museum, Garden, and Library, near Wilmington; New Castle Historic District; John Dickinson "Penman of the Revolution" Plantation, First State Heritage Park, Dover Intl. Speedway, in Dover; Rehoboth Beach. **Information:** Delaware Tourism Office, 99 Kings Hwy., Dover, DE 19901; 1-866-2VISITDE; www.visitdelaware.com

History. The Lenni Lenape (Delaware) people lived in the region at the time of European contact. Henry Hudson located the Delaware R., 1609. In 1610, English explorer Samuel Argall entered Delaware Bay and named the area after Virginia's governor, Lord De La Warr. Dutch, Swedish, and Finnish settlers were followed by the British, who took control in 1664. After 1682, Delaware became part of Pennsylvania, and in 1704 it was granted its own assembly. It adopted a constitution as the state of Delaware, 1776, and was the first state to ratify the federal Constitution, 1787. Although it remained in the Union during the Civil War, Delaware retained slavery until the 13th Amendment abolished it in 1865. The DuPont company, founded as a gunpowder mill in 1802, became an industrial giant in the 20th cent. making nylon, Teflon, and other synthetics. Pro-business laws drew many out-of-state firms to incorporate in Delaware. In 2000, Ruth Ann Minner was elected Delaware's first woman governor. Joe Biden, the state's former U.S. senator, served as U.S. vice president, 2009-17, and began serving as president in Jan. 2021.

Famous Delawareans. Thomas F. Bayard, Joe Biden, Henry Seidel Canby, E. I. du Pont, John P. Marquand, Aubrey Plaza, Howard Pyle, Caesar Rodney, Susan Stroman.

Website. www.delaware.gov

Florida (FL)

Sunshine State

People. Population: 22,610,726; rank: 3. **Pop. change** (2020-23): 5.0%. **Pop. density:** 422 per sq mi. **Racial distribution:** 76.7% white; 16.9% Black; 3.2% Asian; 0.6% Amer. Ind.; 0.1% Hawaiian/Pacific Islander; 2 or more races, 2.5%. **Hispanic pop.:** 27.4%.

Geography. Total area: 65,740 sq mi; rank: 22. **Land area:** 53,634 sq mi; rank: 26. **Acres forested:** 16.9 mil. **Location:** peninsula jutting southward 500 mi between the Atlantic and Gulf of Mexico. **Climate:** subtropical N of Bradenton-Lake Okeechobee-Vero Beach line; tropical S of line. **Topography:** land is flat or rolling; highest point is 345 ft in the NW. **Capital:** Tallahassee. **Chief airports:** Orlando, Miami, Fort Lauderdale, Tampa, Fort Myers, West Palm Beach, Jacksonville, Sarasota, Sanford, Pensacola, Clearwater, Valparaiso, Punta Gorda, Panama City, Key West.

Economy. Chief industries: tourism, agriculture, manufacturing, construction, services, international trade. **Chief manuf. goods:** navigational instruments, medical equip., cement, broadcasting equip., beverages, phosphatic fertilizer, preserved fruits and vegetables, structural metal, printing. **Chief crops:** greenhouse and nursery, oranges, sugarcane, tomatoes, green peppers, grapefruit, strawberries, snap beans, sweet corn, potatoes, cucumbers, tangerines. **Farm income:** Crops: $6.87 bil. Livestock: $2.01 bil. **Nonfuel minerals:** $2.9 bil; cement, clay (attapulgite and kaolin), phosphate rock, sand and gravel (construction), stone (crushed). **Commercial fishing:** $270.7 mil. **Chief ports:** Pensacola, Tampa, Port Manatee, Miami, Port Everglades, Jacksonville, Canaveral. **Gross state product:** $1.6 tril. **Sales tax:** 6.0%. **Gasoline tax:** 57.00 cents/gal. **Employment distrib.:** 11.7% govt.; 20.1% trade/trans./util.; 4.3% mfg.; 15.2% ed./health; 16.3% prof./bus. serv.; 13.5% leisure/hosp.; 6.8% finance; 6.5% constr./mining/log.; 1.6% info.; 3.8% other serv. **Unemployment:** 2.9%. **Min. wage/hr.:** $12.00. **Per cap. pers. income:** $68,248. **New private housing:** 193,788 units/$50.7 bil. **Broadband internet:** 96.7%. **Commercial banks:** 176; deposits: $799.6 bil. **Savings institutions:** 12; deposits: $34.0 bil. **Lottery:** total sales: $9.8 bil; profit: $2.5 bil.

Federal govt. Fed. civ. employees: 93,531; **avg. salary:** $100,583. **Notable fed. facilities:** John F. Kennedy Space Ctr.; Eglin AFB; MacDill AFB; Hurlburt Field; NAS Pensacola; NAS Jacksonville; Naval Sta. Mayport.

Education. High school grad. rate: 87.3%. **4-yr. public coll./univ.:** 40; **2-yr. public:** 1; **4-yr. private:** 53.

Energy. Electricity use/cost: 1,111 kWh, $154.51.

State data. Motto: In God we trust. **Flower:** Orange blossom. **Bird:** Northern mockingbird. **Tree:** Sabal palmetto palm. **Song:** "Old Folks at Home." **Entered union:** Mar. 3, 1845; rank: 27th.

Tourism. Tourist spending: $136.4 bil (2022); change, 2019-22: 21.2%. **Attractions:** Miami Beach; Castillo de San Marcos Natl. Monument, St. Augustine Lighthouse & Museum, Lightner Museum, in St. Augustine (oldest permanent European settlement in U.S.); Walt Disney World Resort, SeaWorld Orlando, Universal Studios, Discovery Cove, in Orlando; Kennedy Space Ctr., U.S. Astronaut Hall of Fame; Everglades Natl. Park; Ringling Museum of Art, Ringling Circus Museum, in Sarasota; Cypress Gardens at Legoland Florida, Winter Haven; Busch Gardens, Big Cat Rescue, in Tampa; Florida Caverns State Park, Marianna; Key West. **Information:** Visit Florida, 2540 W. Executive Center Cir., Ste. 200, Tallahassee, FL 32301; 1-888-7FLA-USA; www.visitflorida.com

History. Florida has been inhabited for at least 12,000 years. Timucua, Apalachee, and Calusa peoples were living in the region when the earliest Europeans came; later the Seminole migrated from Georgia to Florida, becoming dominant there in the early 18th cent. The first European to see Florida was Spain's Ponce de León, 1513. France established a colony, Ft. Caroline, on the St. Johns R., 1564. Spain settled St. Augustine, 1565, and Spanish troops massacred most of the French. Britain's Sir Francis Drake burned St. Augustine, 1586. In 1763, Spain ceded Florida to Great Britain, which held the area 20 years before returning it to Spain. Florida was ceded to the U.S. in the Adams-Onís Treaty, 1819. The Seminole War, 1835-42, resulted in the removal of most Native Americans to Indian Territory. Florida joined the Union in 1845, seceded in 1861, and was readmitted in 1868. In the late 19th cent., hotel and railroad builder Henry M. Flagler laid the foundations of the tourism industry. The state experienced phenomenal population growth in the 20th cent., especially after 1950. The first U.S. astronaut was launched into space from Cape Canaveral, 1961. Walt Disney World opened near Orlando, 1971. Hurricane Andrew slammed Florida, 1992, causing at least $25 bil in property damage. A dispute over Florida's presidential vote in 2000 was decided by the U.S. Supreme Court. In June 2016, a gunman carried out the then-deadliest mass shooting in modern U.S. history when he killed 49 people at a gay nightclub in Orlando. The CDC in 2016 issued its first-ever travel warning for part of the continental U.S. amid reports of the Zika virus in a Miami neighborhood. A Feb. 2018 mass shooting at a Parkland high school killed 17 and galvanized a wave of youth-led activism against gun violence. In June 2021, the sudden collapse of a section of a 12-story beachfront condo in the Miami suburb of Surfside killed nearly 100 people. On Mar. 28, 2022, Gov. Ron DeSantis (R) signed a bill that bans classroom instruction related to sexual orientation/gender identity in early grades. On Sept. 28, 2022, Hurricane Ian made landfall in SW Florida, killing more than 100 people and causing an estimated $109 bil in damages. On Apr. 1, 2024, the Florida Supreme Court upheld a state ban on abortions after 15 weeks of pregnancy and permitted a six-week ban to go into effect May 1.

Famous Floridians. Edna Buchanan, Jeb Bush, Marjory Stoneman Douglas, Gloria Estefan, Henry Morrison Flagler, Ariana Grande, Carl Hiaasen, Zora Neale Hurston, James Weldon Johnson, Deacon Jones, MacKinlay Kantor, Osceola, Claude Pepper, Tom Petty, Henry B. Plant, A. Philip Randolph, Marjorie Kinnan Rawlings, Janet Reno, Marco Rubio, Deion Sanders, Emmitt Smith, Joseph W. Stilwell, Amar'e Stoudemire, Charles P. Summerall.

Website. www.myflorida.com

Georgia (GA)

Empire State of the South, Peach State

People. Population: 11,029,227; rank: 8. **Pop. change** (2020-23): 2.9%. **Pop. density:** 191 per sq mi. **Racial distribution:** 58.7% white; 33.2% Black; 4.9% Asian; 0.6% Amer. Ind.; 0.1% Hawaiian/Pacific Islander; 2 or more races, 2.5%. **Hispanic pop.:** 11.1%.

Geography. Total area: 59,407 sq mi; rank: 24. **Land area:** 57,701 sq mi; rank: 21. **Acres forested:** 24.2 mil. **Location:** South Atlantic state. **Climate:** maritime tropical air masses dominate in summer; polar air masses in winter; E central area drier. **Topography:** most southerly of the Blue Ridge Mts. cover NE and N central; central Piedmont extends to the fall line of rivers; coastal plain levels to the coast flatlands. **Capital:** Atlanta. **Chief airports:** Atlanta, Savannah.

Economy. Chief industries: services, manufacturing, retail trade. **Chief manuf. goods:** carpet and rugs, animal slaughtering and processing, motor vehicles and parts, plastics, aircrafts, paper, chemicals, food. **Chief crops:** cotton, greenhouse and nursery, peanuts, pecans, corn, tomatoes, cucumbers, onions, watermelons, tobacco, squash, blueberries, hay, cabbage, soybeans, peaches, snap beans, wheat. **Farm income:** Crops: $4.24 bil. Livestock: $8.84 bil. **Nonfuel minerals:** $2.6 bil; cement, clay (common clay, kaolin, montmorillonite), sand and gravel (construction), sand and gravel (industrial), stone (crushed). **Commercial fishing:** $19.7 mil. **Chief ports:** Savannah, Brunswick. **Gross state product:** $805.4 bil. **Sales tax:** 4.0%. **Gasoline tax:** 51.45 cents/gal. **Employment distrib.:** 14.4% govt.; 20.7% trade/trans./util.; 8.8% mfg.; 13.7% ed./health; 15.7% prof./bus. serv.; 10.7% leisure/hosp.; 5.8% finance; 4.7% constr./mining/log.; 2.2% info.; 3.4% other serv. **Unemployment:** 3.2%. **Min. wage/hr.:** none. **Per cap. pers. income:** $58,581. **New private housing:** 63,621 units/$14.7 bil. **Broadband internet:** 94.8%. **Commercial banks:** 184; deposits: $338.5 bil. **Savings institutions:** 10; deposits: $3.0 bil. **Lottery:** total sales: $5.7 bil; profit: $1.5 bil.

Federal govt. Fed. civ. employees: 79,474; **avg. salary:** $97,430. **Notable fed. facilities:** Ft. Moore (fmr. Benning); Ft. Stewart; Fed. Law Enforcement Training Ctr. HQ, Brunswick; Robins AFB; Ft. Eisenhower (fmr. Gordon); Naval Sub Base Kings Bay; Moody AFB; Centers for Disease Control, Atlanta; Marine Corps Logistics Base Albany.

Education. High school grad. rate: 84.1%. **4-yr. public coll./univ.:** 27; **2-yr. public:** 23; **4-yr. private:** 33.

Energy. Electricity use/cost: 1,096 kWh, $151.25.

State data. Motto: Wisdom, justice, and moderation. **Flower:** Cherokee rose. **Bird:** Brown thrasher. **Tree:** Southern live oak. **Song:** "Georgia on My Mind." **Fourth** of the 13 original states to ratify the Constitution, Jan. 2, 1788.

Tourism. Tourist spending: $37.4 bil (2022); change, 2019-22: 7.1%. **Attractions:** Georgia State Capitol, Stone Mountain, Centennial Olympic Park, Six Flags Over Georgia, Martin Luther King Jr. Natl. Historical Park, Jimmy Carter Library and Museum, Atlanta Botanical Garden, Georgia Aquarium (largest in Western Hemisphere), College Football Hall of Fame, in Atlanta; Kennesaw Mountain Natl. Battlefield Park; Chickamauga and Chattanooga Natl. Military Park; Chattahoochee-Oconee Natl. Forest; Dahlonega, site of earliest U.S. gold rush; Brasstown Bald (highest mtn. in state); Franklin D. Roosevelt's Little White House Historic Site, Warm Springs; Callaway Gardens, Pine Mountain; Andersonville Natl. Historic Site; Okefenokee Natl. Wildlife Refuge; Jekyll, St. Simons, and Cumberland barrier islands; Savannah Historic District. **Information:** Dept. of Economic Development, 75 Fifth St., NW, Ste. 1200, Atlanta, GA 30308; 1-800-VISITGA; www.exploregeorgia.org

History. Creek and Cherokee peoples were living in the region when Spaniards founded Santa Catalina mission, 1566, on Saint Catherines Island. Gen. James Oglethorpe established a colony at Savannah, 1733, for the poor and religiously persecuted. Oglethorpe defeated a Spanish army from Florida at Bloody Marsh, 1742. Georgia was a battleground in the American Revolution, with the British finally evacuating Savannah in 1782. When Georgia entered the Union, 1788, its plantation economy relied on enslaving Black workers for rice and cotton growing. The Cherokee were removed to Indian Territory, 1838-39, and thousands died on the long march, known as the Trail of Tears. By 1860 the enslaved population exceeded 462,000 (nearly 44% of the total population). Georgia seceded from the Union, 1861, and was invaded by Union forces, 1864, under Gen. William T. Sherman, who took Atlanta, Sept. 2, and proceeded on his famous "march to the sea," ending in Savannah in Dec. Georgia was readmitted, 1870. Born 1929 in Atlanta, Martin Luther King Jr. made the city his base during the civil rights struggles of the 1960s. Atlanta became the leading city of the "New South," world headquarters of Coca-Cola and CNN, and host of the 1996 Summer Olympic Games. With the state offering significant tax breaks and other economic incentives, film and TV production was a $2.9-bil industry in 2019. Amid groundless claims of voter fraud in the 2020 election, Georgia became the first state to enact new voter restrictions. Three white men were convicted in Nov. 2021 of murdering 25-year-old Black jogger Ahmaud Arbery near Brunswick, in Feb. 2020. The state increasingly found itself in the national political spotlight with Dec. runoff elections to determine its Senate seats extending the biannual federal election cycle. A federal judge Dec. 20, 2023, ordered Rudy Giuliani to pay $146 mil to two Fulton County poll workers he publicly accused of manipulating ballots during the 2020 presidential election.

Famous Georgians. Kim Basinger, Griffin Bell, James Brown, Erskine Caldwell, Jimmy Carter, Ray Charles, Ty Cobb, James Dickey, Walt Frazier, John C. Fremont, Newt Gingrich, Nancy Grace, Joel Chandler Harris, "Doc" Holliday, Larry Holmes, Holly Hunter, Alan Jackson, Martin Luther King Jr., Gladys Knight, Sidney Lanier, Little Richard, Juliette Gordon Low, Margaret Mitchell, Jessye Norman, Sam Nunn, Flannery O'Connor, Otis Redding, Burt Reynolds, Julia Roberts, Jackie Robinson, Ryan Seacrest, Clarence Thomas, Travis Tritt, Ted Turner, Carl Vinson, Alice Walker, Herschel Walker, Joanne Woodward, Trisha Yearwood, Andrew Young.

Website. www.georgia.gov

Hawai'i (HI)

Aloha State

People. Population: 1,435,138; rank: 40. **Pop. change** (2020-23): –1.4%. **Pop. density:** 224 per sq mi. **Racial**

distribution: 25.2% white; 2.2% Black; 37.3% Asian; 0.4% Amer. Ind.; 10.3% Hawaiian/Pacific Islander; 2 or more races, 24.6%. **Hispanic pop.:** 10.1%.

Geography. Total area: 10,967 sq mi; rank: 43. **Land area:** 6,421 sq mi; rank: 47. **Acres forested:** 1.8 mil. **Location:** Pacific archipelago of about 132 islands 2,100 mi SW of U.S. mainland. **Climate:** subtropical, with wide variations in rainfall; Mt. Waialeale, on Kaua'i, wettest spot in U.S. (annual avg. rainfall 422 in., 1912-2015). **Topography:** islands are tops of a chain of submerged volcanic mountains; Mauna Loa, Kilauea are active volcanoes. **Capital:** Honolulu. **Chief airports:** Honolulu, Kahului, Kailua Kona, Lihue, Hilo.

Economy. Chief industries: tourism, defense, sugar, pineapples. **Chief manuf. goods:** concrete, printing, baked goods, sugar, preserved fruits and vegetables, apparel. **Chief crops:** flowers and nursery, pineapples, seed crops, sugarcane, macadamia nuts, coffee, algae, papayas, tomatoes, bananas, basil, ginger. **Farm income:** Crops: $458.39 mil. Livestock: $180.83 mil. **Nonfuel minerals:** $154 mil; sand and gravel (construction), stone (crushed). **Commercial fishing:** $135.2 mil. **Chief ports:** Honolulu, Hilo, Barbers Point, Kahului. **Gross state product:** $108.0 bil. **Sales tax:** 4.0%. **Gasoline tax:** 36.90 cents/gal. **Employment distrib.:** 19.9% govt.; 18.0% trade/trans./util.; 2.0% mfg.; 14.3% ed./health; 11.2% prof./bus. serv.; 18.8% leisure/hosp.; 4.2% finance; 6.5% constr./mining/log.; 1.0% info.; 4.1% other serv. **Unemployment:** 3.0%. **Min. wage/hr.:** $14.00. **Per cap. pers. income:** $65,151. **New private housing:** 3,791 units/$1.6 bil. **Broadband internet:** 97.0%. **Commercial banks:** 10; deposits: $47.9 bil. **Savings institutions:** 3; deposits: $9.9 bil.

Federal govt. Fed. civ. employees: 24,473; **avg. salary:** $97,877. **Notable fed. facilities:** Joint Base Pearl Harbor-Hickam; Schofield Barracks; Marine Corps Base Hawaii, Kaneohe Bay; Tripler Army Med. Ctr.; Ft. Shafter; Wheeler Army Airfield; Prince Kuhio Federal Bldg., Honolulu.

Education. High school grad. rate: 86.0%. **4-yr. public coll./univ.:** 4; **2-yr. public:** 6; **4-yr. private:** 4.

Energy. Electricity use/cost: 515 kWh, $221.53.

State data. Motto: Ua mau ke ea o ka aina i ka pono (The life of the land is perpetuated in righteousness). **Flower:** Yellow hibiscus. **Bird:** Nene (Hawaiian goose). **Tree:** Kukui (candlenut). **Song:** "Hawai'i Pono'i" (Hawai'i's Own). **Entered union:** Aug. 21, 1959; rank: 50th.

Tourism. Tourist spending: $27.3 bil (2022); change, 2019-22: –5.8%. **Attractions:** Oahu Isl.: Natl. Memorial Cemetery of the Pacific, Waikiki Beach, Diamond Head, in Honolulu; USS *Arizona* Memorial, Pearl Harbor; Polynesian Cultural Ctr., Laie; Hanauma Bay; Nu'uanu Pali. Kaua'i Isl.: Waimea Canyon. Maui Isl.: Haleakala Natl. Park. Hawai'i Isl.: Hawaii Volcanoes Natl. Park, Wailoa and Wailuku River State Parks. **Information:** Hawaii Visitors and Conventions Bureau, 2270 Kalakaua Ave., Ste. 801, Honolulu, HI 96815; 1-800-GOHAWAII; www.gohawaii.com

History. Polynesians from islands 2,000 mi to the S settled the Hawaiian Islands, probably 300-600 CE. The first European visitor was British captain James Cook, 1778. King Kamehameha I united the islands by 1810. Christian missionaries arrived, 1819, bringing Western culture. Under the reign, 1825-54, of King Kamehameha III, a constitution, legislature, and public school system were instituted. Sugar production began, 1835, and it became the dominant industry. Queen Liliuokalani was deposed, 1893, and a republic was established, 1894, headed by Sanford B. Dole. Annexation by the U.S. came in 1898. The Japanese attack on Pearl Harbor, Dec. 7, 1941, brought the U.S. into World War II. Hawai'i attained statehood, 1959. Hurricane Iniki pounded Kaua'i, 1992, causing about $1 bil in damage. In 2006, Pres. George W. Bush designated the Northwestern Hawaiian Islands Natl. Monument, a marine area of 140,000 sq mi. The Kilauea volcano on Hawaii's Big Island started to erupt, May 2018, forcing a series of evacuations. Mauna Loa, the world's largest active volcano, erupted in Nov. 2022 for the first time since 1984. Devastating Maui wildfires killed at least 115, Aug. 2023.

Famous Islanders. Bernice Pauahi Bishop, Tia Carrere, Alexander Cartwright, St. Damien de Veuster, Tulsi Gabbard, Don Ho, Daniel K. Inouye, Duke Kahanamoku, King Kamehameha, Nicole Kidman, Brook Mahealani Lee, Jason Scott Lee, Queen Liliuokalani, Bruno Mars, Bette Midler, Barack Obama, Ellison S. Onizuka, Michelle Wie.

Website. www.hawaii.gov

Idaho (ID)

Gem State

People. Population: 1,964,726; rank: 38. **Pop. change** (2020-23): 6.8%. **Pop. density:** 24 per sq mi. **Racial distribution:** 92.5% white; 1.0% Black; 1.7% Asian; 1.7% Amer. Ind.; 0.2% Hawaiian/Pacific Islander; 2 or more races, 2.8%. **Hispanic pop.:** 13.8%.

Geography. Total area: 83,547 sq mi; rank: 14. **Land area:** 82,623 sq mi; rank: 11. **Acres forested:** 21.9 mil. **Location:** northwestern Mountain state bordering British Columbia, Canada. **Climate:** tempered by Pacific westerly winds; drier, colder, continental climate in SE; altitude an important factor. **Topography:** Snake R. plains in the S; central region of mountains, canyons, gorges (Hells Canyon, 7,900 ft, deepest in N. America); subalpine northern region. **Capital:** Boise. **Chief airport:** Boise.

Economy. Chief industries: manufacturing, agriculture, tourism, lumber, mining, electronics. **Chief manuf. goods:** computers and electronics, preserved fruits and vegetables, cheese, lumber. **Chief crops:** potatoes, wheat, hay, sugar beets, barley, greenhouse and nursery, onions, dry beans, corn, mint, apples, hops, peaches, lentils, peas, cherries, plums and prunes, oats. **Farm income:** Crops: $4.43 bil. Livestock: $6.86 bil. **Nonfuel minerals:** $482 mil; lead, phosphate rock, sand and gravel (construction), silver, stone (crushed). **Chief port:** Lewiston. **Gross state product:** $118.8 bil. **Sales tax:** 6.0%. **Gasoline tax:** 51.40 cents/gal. **Employment distrib.:** 15.9% govt.; 18.8% trade/trans./util.; 9.0% mfg.; 15.3% ed./health; 12.8% prof./bus. serv.; 10.6% leisure/hosp.; 4.8% finance; 8.7% constr./mining/log.; 1.1% info.; 3.1% other serv. **Unemployment:** 3.1%. **Min. wage/hr.:** $7.25. **Per cap. pers. income:** $59,035. **New private housing:** 17,919 units/$4.4 bil. **Broadband internet:** 92.0%. **Commercial banks:** 28; deposits: $37.9 bil. **Savings institutions:** 2; deposits: $1.1 bil. **Lottery:** total sales: $422.5 mil; profit: $82.0 mil.

Federal govt. Fed. civ. employees: 9,599; **avg. salary:** $88,644. **Notable fed. facilities:** Idaho Natl. Lab, Idaho Falls; Mountain Home AFB.

Education. High school grad. rate: 79.9%. **4-yr. public coll./univ.:** 4; **2-yr. public:** 4; **4-yr. private:** 4.

Energy. Electricity use/cost: 1,005 kWh, $104.23.

State data. Motto: Esto Perpetua (It is perpetual). **Flower:** Syringa. **Bird:** Mountain bluebird. **Tree:** White pine. **Song:** "Here We Have Idaho." **Entered union:** July 3, 1890; rank: 43rd.

Tourism. Tourist spending: $5.8 bil (2022); change, 2019-22: 1.6%. **Attractions:** Hells Canyon (deepest river gorge in N. America); World Ctr. for Birds of Prey, Boise Art Museum, in Boise; Craters of the Moon Natl. Monument and Preserve; Sun Valley; Shoshone Falls, near Twin Falls; Lava Hot Springs; Lake Coeur d'Alene; Sawtooth Natl. Recreation Area; Frank Church-River of No Return Wilderness Area; Nez Perce Natl. Historical Park. **Information:** Idaho Dept. of Commerce-Tourism Development, 700 W. State St., P.O. Box 83720, Boise, ID 83720; 1-800-VISITID; www.visitidaho.org

History. Paleo-Indian hunters roamed the land over 13,000 years ago; later inhabitants included Shoshone, Northern Paiute, Bannock, and Nez Percé peoples. The Meriwether Lewis and William Clark Expedition took place 1804-06. Next came fur traders, 1809-34, and missionaries, 1830s-50s. Mormons made their first permanent settlement at Franklin, 1860. Idaho's gold rush began the same year and brought thousands of permanent settlers. A series of wars with the territory's Indigenous residents followed, including a campaign by Chief Joseph and the Nez Percé that ended with his surrender in Montana, 1877. Idaho became a territory, 1863, and a state, 1890. In the 20th cent., it emerged as a leader in potato, lumber, and silver output. The Sun Valley ski resort opened in 1936, boosting tourism. Startup of Lewiston's river port, 1975, opened Idaho to ocean-going trade. Fueled by technology job growth, the state's population jumped 21.2%, 2000-10, and 21.3%, 2010-21. In 2020, Idaho became the first state to ban transgender girls and women from sports participation at public schools and colleges/universities, as well as the first, in Apr. 2023, to criminalize helping minors leave the state to receive an abortion without parental consent. Four university students were stabbed to death in Moscow, ID, in Nov. 2022; after a lengthy manhunt, a suspect was arrested in Pennsylvania. In a limited ruling, the U.S. Supreme Court on June 27, 2024, allowed emergency abortions to take place in Idaho in spite of the state's near-total ban.

Famous Idahoans. William Borah, Frank Church, Lou Dobbs, Fred Dubois, W. Mark Felt, Chief Joseph, Harmon Killebrew, Aaron Paul, Ezra Pound, Marilynne Robinson, Sacagawea, Picabo Street, Lana Turner.

Website. www.idaho.gov

Illinois (IL)

Prairie State

People. Population: 12,549,689; rank: 6. **Pop. change** (2020-23): –2.1%. **Pop. density:** 226 per sq mi. **Racial distribution:** 76.0% white; 14.6% Black; 6.3% Asian; 0.6% Amer. Ind.; 0.1% Hawaiian/Pacific Islander; 2 or more races, 2.3%. **Hispanic pop.:** 19.0%.

Geography. Total area: 57,898 sq mi; rank: 25. **Land area:** 55,499 sq mi; rank: 24. **Acres forested:** 4.9 mil. **Location:**

East North Central state; western, southern, and eastern boundaries formed by Mississippi, Ohio, and Wabash Rivers, respectively. **Climate:** temperate; typically cold, snowy winters, hot summers. **Topography:** prairie and fertile plains throughout; open hills in the southern region. **Capital:** Springfield. **Chief airports:** Chicago (2).

Economy. Chief industries: services, manufacturing, travel, wholesale and retail trade, finance, insurance, real estate, construction, health care, agriculture. **Chief manuf. goods:** food, petroleum, plastics, chemicals, agricultural machinery, pharmaceuticals, motor vehicles, printing. **Chief crops:** corn, soybeans, hay, wheat, greenhouse and nursery, apples, peaches, sorghum. **Farm income:** Crops: $24.35 bil. Livestock: $3.60 bil. **Nonfuel minerals:** $1.8 bil; cement (portland), magnesium compounds, sand and gravel (construction), sand and gravel (industrial), stone (crushed). **Chief port:** Chicago. **Gross state product:** $1.1 tril. **Sales tax:** 6.25%. **Gasoline tax:** 84.90 cents/gal. **Employment distrib.:** 13.8% govt.; 19.8% trade/trans./util.; 9.5% mfg.; 16.3% ed./health; 15.0% prof./bus. serv.; 9.8% leisure/hosp.; 6.4% finance; 3.9% constr./mining/log.; 1.5% info.; 4.2% other serv. **Unemployment:** 4.5%. **Min. wage/hr.:** $14.00. **Per cap. pers. income:** $70,953. **New private housing:** 16,863 units/$4.5 bil. **Broadband internet:** 95.5%. **Commercial banks:** 376; deposits: $655.4 bil. **Savings institutions:** 45; deposits: $9.5 bil. **Lottery:** total sales: $3.6 bil; profit: $970.7 mil.

Federal govt. Fed. civ. employees: 44,474; **avg. salary:** $106,978. **Notable fed. facilities:** Naval Station Great Lakes; Fermi Natl. Accelerator Lab, Batavia; Argonne Natl. Lab, Lemont; Scott AFB; Rock Island Arsenal.

Education. High school grad. rate: 87.3%. **4-yr. public coll./univ.:** 12; **2-yr. public:** 48; **4-yr. private:** 72.

Energy. Electricity use/cost: 720 kWh, $112.74.

State data. Motto: State sovereignty, national union. **Flower:** Native violet. **Bird:** Northern cardinal. **Tree:** White oak. **Song:** "Illinois." **Entered union:** Dec. 3, 1818; rank: 21st.

Tourism. Tourist spending: $44.3 bil (2022); change, 2019-22: –2.7%. **Attractions:** Art Institute of Chicago, Field Museum of Natural History, Shedd Aquarium, Millennium Park, Navy Pier, in Chicago; Illinois State Museum, Abraham Lincoln Presidential Library and Museum, in Springfield; Cahokia Mounds State Historic Site, Collinsville; Starved Rock State Park; Crab Orchard Natl. Wildlife Refuge; Forts Kaskaskia, de Chartres, Massac; Shawnee Natl. Forest; Dickson Mounds Museum, Lewistown. **Information:** Illinois Office of Tourism, 555 W. Monroe, Suite 1200, Chicago, IL 60661; 1-800-226-6632; www.enjoyillinois.com

History. The region has been inhabited for at least 10,000 years; seminomadic Algonquian peoples, including the Peoria, Illinois, Kaskaskia, and Tamaroa, lived there at the time of European contact. Fur traders were the first Europeans in Illinois, followed shortly by Louis Jolliet and Jacques Marquette, 1673, and René-Robert Cavelier, sieur de La Salle, 1680, who built a fort near present-day Peoria. French priests established the first permanent settlements at Cahokia, near present-day St. Louis, 1699, and Kaskaskia, 1703. France ceded the area to Britain, 1763, and in 1778, American Gen. George Rogers Clark took Kaskaskia from the British without a shot. Illinois became a separate territory, 1809, and a state, 1818. Defeat of Native American tribes in the Black Hawk War, 1832, and canal, rail, and road construction brought rapid change. Mormon settlers at Nauvoo, 1839, met with hostility, and a Carthage mob killed Mormon leader Joseph Smith and his brother, 1844. The Great Chicago Fire, 1871, destroyed the city's downtown. Illinois became a center for the labor movement, leading to bitter conflicts such as the Haymarket riot, 1886, and Pullman strike, 1894. Social reformer Jane Addams founded Hull House, 1889, to aid immigrants and the poor. The expansion of manufacturing, 1900-70, drew African Americans from the South in the Great Migration. Chicago police violently suppressed antiwar protests at the 1968 Democratic National Convention. Barack Obama, elected in 2004 to serve in the U.S. Senate, became the 44th U.S. president in 2009. Political corruption and criminality have plagued the state; since 1960, five former governors have been charged with criminal offenses. A U.S. Justice Dept. investigation of the Chicago Police Dept., launched after a 2014 video of a white officer fatally shooting a Black teen sparked protests, found in 2017 that officers used excessive force too often and without repercussions. The officer was found guilty of 2nd-degree murder and sentenced in Jan. 2019 to 6.75 years in prison. A Chicago public school teachers' strike shut down schools for 11 days in Oct. 2019. On July 4, 2022, a rooftop shooter in the Chicago suburb of Highland Park killed seven people at a parade.

Famous Illinoisans. Jane Addams, Saul Bellow, John Belushi, Jack Benny, Ray Bradbury, Gwendolyn Brooks, St. Frances Xavier Cabrini, Al Capone, Hillary Rodham Clinton, Clarence Darrow, John Deere, Stephen A. Douglas, Katherine Dunham, Wyatt Earp, Roger Ebert, James T. Farrell, Marshall Field, Harrison Ford, Betty Friedan, Benny Goodman, Ulysses S. Grant, Dennis Hastert, Hugh Hefner, Ernest Hemingway, Charlton Heston, Jennifer Hudson, Henry J. Hyde, Abraham Lincoln, Vachel Lindsay, David Mamet, Edgar Lee Masters, Oscar Mayer, Cyrus McCormick, Eliot Ness, Bob Newhart, Michelle Obama, Ronald Reagan, Shonda Rhimes, Donald Rumsfeld, Carl Sandburg, Shel Silverstein, Adlai E. Stevenson, James Watson, Frank Lloyd Wright, Philip K. Wrigley.

Website. www.illinois.gov

Indiana (IN)

Hoosier State

People. Population: 6,862,199; rank: 17. **Pop. change** (2020-23): 1.1%. **Pop. density:** 192 per sq mi. **Racial distribution:** 83.7% white; 10.4% Black; 2.9% Asian; 0.5% Amer. Ind.; 0.1% Hawaiian/Pacific Islander; 2 or more races, 2.5%. **Hispanic pop.:** 8.8%.

Geography. Total area: 36,410 sq mi; rank: 38. **Land area:** 35,817 sq mi; rank: 38. **Acres forested:** 4.8 mil. **Location:** East North Central state; Lake Michigan on N border. **Climate:** four distinct seasons with temperate climate. **Topography:** hilly southern region; fertile rolling plains of central region; flat, heavily glaciated N; dunes along Lake Michigan shore. **Capital:** Indianapolis. **Chief airport:** Indianapolis.

Economy. Chief industries: manufacturing, services, agriculture, government, wholesale and retail trade, transportation, public utilities. **Chief manuf. goods:** motor vehicles and parts, iron and steel mills, pharmaceuticals, petroleum, plastics, medical equip., printing. **Chief crops:** corn, soybeans, greenhouse and nursery, wheat, hay, tomatoes, watermelons, apples. **Farm income:** Crops: $12.00 bil. Livestock: $6.35 bil. **Nonfuel minerals:** $1.4 bil; cement, lime, sand and gravel (construction), stone (crushed), stone (dimension). **Chief ports:** Burns Harbor-Portage, Mt. Vernon, Jeffersonville. **Gross state product:** $497 bil. **Sales tax:** 7.0%. **Gasoline tax:** 70.10 cents/gal. **Employment distrib.:** 13.4% govt.; 19.3% trade/trans./util.; 16.2% mfg.; 15.7% ed./health; 11.2% prof./bus. serv.; 9.6% leisure/hosp.; 4.5% finance; 5.3% constr./mining/log.; 0.8% info.; 4.0% other serv. **Unemployment:** 3.3%. **Min. wage/hr.:** $7.25. **Per cap. pers. income:** $60,038. **New private housing:** 27,055 units/$7.7 bil. **Broadband internet:** 94.5%. **Commercial banks:** 110; deposits: $191.5 bil. **Savings institutions:** 22; deposits: $8.7 bil. **Lottery:** total sales: $1.7 bil; profit: $370.2 mil.

Federal govt. Fed. civ. employees: 24,566; **avg. salary:** $94,494. **Notable fed. facilities:** Naval Surface Warfare Ctr., Crane Div.; Grissom Air Reserve Base.

Education. High school grad. rate: 87.7%. **4-yr. public coll./univ.:** 15; **2-yr. public:** 1; **4-yr. private:** 41.

Energy. Electricity use/cost: 950 kWh, $138.61.

State data. Motto: Crossroads of America. **Flower:** Peony. **Bird:** Northern cardinal. **Tree:** Tulip poplar. **Song:** "On the Banks of the Wabash, Far Away." **Entered union:** Dec. 11, 1816; rank: 19th.

Tourism. Tourist spending: $12.7 bil (2022); change, 2019-22: –4.6%. **Attractions:** Lincoln Boyhood Natl. Memorial, Lincoln City; George Rogers Clark Natl. Historical Park, Vincennes; Tippecanoe Battlefield Museum and Park, Battle Ground; Benjamin Harrison Presidential Site, Indianapolis Motor Speedway and Hall of Fame Museum, Indianapolis Museum of Art, in Indianapolis; Indiana Dunes Natl. Park, Chesterton; Studebaker Natl. Museum, in South Bend; Hoosier Natl. Forest. **Information:** Indiana Destination Development Corp., 143 W. Market Street, Suite 700, Indianapolis, IN 46204; 1-800-677-9800; www.visitindiana.com

History. When the Europeans arrived, Miami, Potawatomi, Kickapoo, Piankashaw, Wea, and Shawnee peoples inhabited the region. René-Robert Cavelier, sieur de La Salle, visited the present South Bend area, 1679 and 1681. The first French fort was built near present-day Lafayette, 1717. A French trading post was established, 1731-32, at Vincennes. France ceded the area to Britain, 1763. During the American Revolution, American Gen. George Rogers Clark captured Vincennes, 1778, and defeated British forces, 1779. Indiana became a territory, 1800, and a state, 1816. The Miami were beaten, 1794, at Fallen Timbers, and Gen. William H. Harrison defeated Tecumseh's Indian confederation, 1811, at Tippecanoe. Manufacturing grew rapidly after the Civil War. U.S. Steel founded Gary, 1906. An automotive test track was the site of the first Indianapolis 500 race, 1911. The auto industry remains key to the state economy; in 2008, Honda opened a $550-mil plant near Greensburg. Heavy rain in June 2008 flooded southwest and central Indiana. Some rights groups and businesses criticized the state's 2015 Religious Freedom Restoration Act as discriminatory to LGBT individuals. Mike Pence, the state's governor, 2013-17, served as U.S. vice president, 2017-21. A former employee in Apr. 2021 fatally shot eight workers at a FedEx facility in Indianapolis.

Famous "Hoosiers." Larry Bird, Ambrose Burnside, Meg Cabot, Hoagy Carmichael, Jim Davis, James Dean, Eugene V. Debs, John Dillinger, Theodore Dreiser, Paul Dresser, Jeff Gordon, Benjamin Harrison, Gil Hodges, Michael Jackson, David Letterman, Carole Lombard, Marjorie Main, John Mellencamp, Jane Pauley, Cole Porter, Gene Stratton Porter, Ernie Pyle, Dan Quayle, James Whitcomb Riley, Oscar Robertson, Red Skelton, Tony Stewart, Booth Tarkington, Kurt Vonnegut, Lew Wallace, Ryan White, Wendell L. Willkie, Wilbur Wright.

Website. www.in.gov

Iowa (IA)

Hawkeye State

People. Population: 3,207,004; rank: 31. **Pop. change** (2020-23): 0.5%. **Pop. density:** 57 per sq mi. **Racial distribution:** 89.6% white; 4.5% Black; 2.7% Asian; 0.6% Amer. Ind.; 0.3% Hawaiian/Pacific Islander; 2 or more races, 2.2%. **Hispanic pop.:** 7.4%.

Geography. Total area: 56,258 sq mi; rank: 26. **Land area:** 55,839 sq mi; rank: 23. **Acres forested:** 2.9 mil. **Location:** West North Central state bordered by Mississippi R. on the E, Missouri R. on the W. **Climate:** humid, continental. **Topography:** watershed from NW to SE; soil especially rich and land level in the N central counties. **Capital:** Des Moines. **Chief airports:** Des Moines, Cedar Rapids.

Economy. Chief industries: agriculture, communications, construction, finance, insurance, trade, services, manufacturing. **Chief manuf. goods:** machinery, vegetable oils, animal slaughtering and processing, laundry equip., plastics, motor vehicles and parts. **Chief crops:** corn, soybeans, hay, greenhouse and nursery, oats. **Farm income:** Crops: $24.48 bil. Livestock: $20.30 bil. **Nonfuel minerals:** $879 mil; cement (portland), lime, sand and gravel (construction), sand and gravel (industrial), stone (crushed). **Gross state product:** $248.9 bil. **Sales tax:** 6.0%. **Gasoline tax:** 48.40 cents/gal. **Employment distrib.:** 16.9% govt.; 19.2% trade/trans./util.; 14.1% mfg.; 14.9% ed./health; 9.3% prof./bus. serv.; 8.9% leisure/hosp.; 6.7% finance; 5.4% constr./mining/log.; 1.1% info.; 3.5% other serv. **Unemployment:** 2.9%. **Min. wage/hr.:** $7.25. **Per cap. pers. income:** $62,351. **New private housing:** 11,230 units/$3.1 bil. **Broadband internet:** 93.9%. **Commercial banks:** 272; deposits: $112.4 bil. **Savings institutions:** 7; deposits: $8.5 bil. **Lottery:** total sales: $481.5 mil; profit: $108.4 mil.

Federal govt. Fed. civ. employees: 9,752; **avg. salary:** $93,759. **Notable fed. facilities:** Ames Lab; Natl. Animal Disease Ctr.

Education. High school grad. rate: 84.1%. **4-yr. public coll./univ.:** 3; **2-yr. public:** 16; **4-yr. private:** 33.

Energy. Electricity use/cost: 888 kWh, $116.70.

State data. Motto: Our liberties we prize, and our rights we will maintain. **Flower:** Wild rose. **Bird:** Eastern goldfinch. **Tree:** Oak. **Song:** "The Song of Iowa." **Entered union:** Dec. 28, 1846; rank: 29th.

Tourism. Tourist spending: $10.6 bil (2022); change, 2019-22: 7.5%. **Attractions:** Des Moines Art Ctr., Iowa State Fairgrounds, Iowa State Capitol, in Des Moines; Natl. Czech & Slovak Museum & Library, Cedar Rapids; Herbert Hoover Natl. Historic Site, Presidential Library and Museum, in West Branch; Effigy Mounds Natl. Monument, Marquette; Amana Colonies (former communal society); Figge Art Museum, Davenport; Living History Farms, Urbandale; Adventureland, Altoona; Boone & Scenic Valley Railroad and Museum; riverboat cruises and casino gambling, Mississippi and Missouri Rivers; Iowa Great Lakes, Okoboji; American Gothic House, Eldon; *Field of Dreams* movie site, Dyersville; Natl. Mississippi River Museum & Aquarium, Dubuque. **Information:** Iowa Tourism Office, Iowa Economic Development Authority, 1963 Bell Ave., Ste. 200, Des Moines, IA 50309; 1-800-345-IOWA; www.traveliowa.com

History. Early inhabitants were Mound Builders who dwelt on Iowa's fertile plains. Later, Iowa and Yankton Sioux lived in the area. The first Europeans, Jacques Marquette and Louis Jolliet, gave France its claim to the area, 1673. In 1762, France ceded the region to Spain, but Napoleon took it back, 1800. It became part of the U.S. through the Louisiana Purchase, 1803. Native American Sauk and Fox tribes moved into the area but relinquished their land in defeat after the 1832 uprising led by Sauk chieftain Black Hawk. Iowa became a territory in 1838 and a free state in 1846, strongly supporting the Union. Fertile land lured farmers from eastern states, 1850-1900, and the population rose rapidly. Growth slowed in the 20th cent., as farming became mechanized. Severe flooding in eastern Iowa in June 2008 caused billions of dollars in damages and forced the evacuation of thousands of residents. The Iowa caucuses have been the first statewide electoral event in the presidential nomination process since 1972. A wind and thunderstorm complex known as a "derecho" severely affected Iowa in Aug. 2020, with regional damage estimates exceeding $11 bil. An apartment building collapsed in Davenport in May 2023, killing three people.

Famous Iowans. Tom Arnold, Johnny Carson, William F. "Buffalo Bill" Cody, Mamie Dowd Eisenhower, Michael Emerson, Bob Feller, George Gallup, Susan Glaspell, James Norman Hall, Herbert Hoover, Shawn Johnson, Ashton Kutcher, Ann Landers, Cloris Leachman, Glenn Miller, Lillian Russell, Billy Sunday, James A. Van Allen, Abigail Van Buren, Carl Van Vechten, Henry Wallace, Kurt Warner, John Wayne, Meredith Willson, Elijah Wood, Grant Wood.

Website. www.iowa.gov

Kansas (KS)

Sunflower State

People. Population: 2,940,546; rank: 34. **Pop. change** (2020-23): 0.1%. **Pop. density:** 36 per sq mi. **Racial distribution:** 85.9% white; 6.2% Black; 3.2% Asian; 1.3% Amer. Ind.; 0.2% Hawaiian/Pacific Islander; 2 or more races, 3.3%. **Hispanic pop.:** 13.7%.

Geography. Total area: 82,256 sq mi; rank: 15. **Land area:** 81,737 sq mi; rank: 13. **Acres forested:** 2.5 mil. **Location:** West North Central state with Missouri R. on E. **Climate:** temperate but continental, with great extremes between summer and winter. **Topography:** hilly Osage Plains in the E; central region level prairie and hills; high plains in the W. **Capital:** Topeka. **Chief airport:** Wichita.

Economy. Chief industries: manufacturing, finance, insurance, real estate, services. **Chief manuf. goods:** animal slaughtering, aerospace, petroleum, plastics, machinery, navigational instruments, printing. **Chief crops:** wheat, corn, soybeans, hay, sorghum, sunflowers, cotton, potatoes. **Farm income:** Crops: $9.92 bil. Livestock: $13.61 bil. **Nonfuel minerals:** $915 mil; cement, helium, salt, sand and gravel (construction), stone (crushed). **Chief port:** Kansas City. **Gross state product:** $226.0 bil. **Sales tax:** 6.5%. **Gasoline tax:** 43.43 cents/gal. **Employment distrib.:** 17.9% govt.; 18.9% trade/trans./util.; 11.8% mfg.; 14.6% ed./health; 12.2% prof./bus. serv.; 9.2% leisure/hosp.; 5.2% finance; 5.2% constr./mining/log.; 1.2% info.; 3.7% other serv. **Unemployment:** 2.7%. **Min. wage/hr.:** $7.25. **Per cap. pers. income:** $63,732. **New private housing:** 9,504 units/$2.5 bil. **Broadband internet:** 95.3%. **Commercial banks:** 241; deposits: $91.7 bil. **Savings institutions:** 11; deposits: $7.1 bil. **Lottery:** total sales: $338.2 mil; profit: $87.1 mil.

Federal govt. Fed. civ. employees: 17,806; **avg. salary:** $92,818. **Notable fed. facilities:** Ft. Riley; Leavenworth Fed. Penitentiary, Dwight D. Eisenhower VA Medical Ctr., Leavenworth; McConnell AFB; Colmery-O'Neil VA Medical Ctr., Topeka.

Education. High school grad. rate: 86.0%. **4-yr. public coll./univ.:** 8; **2-yr. public:** 25; **4-yr. private:** 24.

Energy. Electricity use/cost: 928 kWh, $129.80.

State data. Motto: Ad Astra per Aspera (To the stars through difficulties). **Flower:** Native sunflower. **Bird:** Western meadowlark. **Tree:** Cottonwood. **Song:** "Home on the Range." **Entered union:** Jan. 29, 1861; rank: 34th.

Tourism. Tourist spending: $9.0 bil (2022); change, 2019-22: 4.7%. **Attractions:** Eisenhower Presidential Library and Museum, Abilene; Natl. Agricultural Ctr. and Hall of Fame, Bonner Springs; Boot Hill Museum, Dodge City; Old Cowtown Museum, Wichita; Ft. Scott and Ft. Larned Natl. Historic Sites; Kansas Cosmosphere and Space Ctr., Hutchinson; U.S. Cavalry Museum, Ft. Riley; Tallgrass Prairie Natl. Preserve, Strong City; Kansas Speedway, Kansas City. **Information:** Kansas Dept. of Commerce, Travel and Tourism Div., 1000 SW Jackson St., Ste. 100, Topeka, KS 66612; (785) 296-2009; www.travelks.com

History. Wichita, Pawnee, Kansa, and Osage peoples lived in the area when Spain's Francisco de Coronado explored it in 1541. These Native Americans—hunters who also farmed—were joined on the Plains by the nomadic Cheyenne, Arapaho, Comanche, and Kiowa about 1800. France claimed the region, 1682, ceded its claim to Spain, 1762, then regained control, 1800, before selling it to the U.S. in the Louisiana Purchase, 1803. After 1830, thousands of Native Americans were removed from more eastern states to Kansas. Organized as a territory, 1854, the area witnessed violent clashes between pro- and antislavery settlers and became known as "Bleeding Kansas." It entered the Union as a free state, 1861. After the Civil War, rail construction and huge cattle drives from Texas turned Abilene and Dodge City into cowboy capitals. Russian Mennonite immigrants brought a new strain of winter wheat, 1874, transforming Kansas agriculture. Carry Nation launched her anti-saloon crusade in the 1890s. Part of the Dust Bowl, the state experienced drought and depression in the 1930s. Topeka was the focus of the famous *Brown v. Board of Education* decision, 1954, that led to desegregation of U.S. public schools. Bob Dole represented Kansas in the U.S. Senate (1969-96) but failed in several efforts to win higher office.

Famous Kansans. Kirstie Alley, Roscoe "Fatty" Arbuckle, Ed Asner, John Brown, Walter P. Chrysler, Glenn Cunningham, John Steuart Curry, Robert Joseph "Bob" Dole, Amelia Earhart, Dwight D. Eisenhower, Melissa Etheridge, Ron Evans, Georgia Neese Clark Gray, Maurice Greene, James Butler "Wild Bill" Hickok, Cyrus K. Holliday, Dennis Hopper, William Inge, Don Johnson, Walter Johnson, Nancy Landon Kassebaum, Buster Keaton, Emmett Kelly, Alfred M. "Alf" Landon, Hattie McDaniel, Oscar Micheaux, Carry Nation, Charlie Parker, Gordon Parks, Jim Ryun, Barry Sanders, Vivian Vance, William Allen White, Jess Willard.

Website. www.kansas.gov

Kentucky (KY)

Bluegrass State

People. Population: 4,526,154; rank: 26. **Pop. change** (2020-23): 0.4%. **Pop. density:** 115 per sq mi. **Racial distribution:** 86.7% white; 8.8% Black; 1.8% Asian; 0.3% Amer. Ind.; 0.1% Hawaiian/Pacific Islander; 2 or more races, 2.3%. **Hispanic pop.:** 5.0%.

Geography. Total area: 40,397 sq mi; rank: 37. **Land area:** 39,481 sq mi; rank: 36. **Acres forested:** 12.4 mil. **Location:** East South Central state bordered on N by Illinois, Indiana, Ohio; on E by West Virginia and Virginia; on S by Tennessee; on W by Missouri. **Climate:** moderate, with plentiful rainfall. **Topography:** mountainous in E; rounded hills of the Knobs region in the N; Bluegrass region in heart of state; wooded rocky hillsides of the Pennyroyal Plateau; Western Coal Field; the fertile Jackson Purchase region in the SW. **Capital:** Frankfort. **Chief airports:** Hebron (Cincinnati metro area), Louisville, Lexington.

Economy. Chief industries: manufacturing, services, finance, insurance and real estate, retail trade, public utilities. **Chief manuf. goods:** motor vehicles and parts, aluminum, basic chemicals, plastics, iron and steel, rubber, printing. **Chief crops:** hay, corn, soybeans, tobacco, wheat. **Farm income:** Crops: $3.73 bil. Livestock: $4.47 bil. **Nonfuel minerals:** $919 mil; cement, clay (common clay), lime, sand and gravel (construction), stone (crushed). **Chief ports:** Louisville, Hickman-Fulton County. **Gross state product:** $277.7 bil. **Sales tax:** 6.0%. **Gasoline tax:** 48.50 cents/gal. **Employment distrib.:** 15.5% govt.; 20.7% trade/trans./util.; 12.5% mfg.; 15.5% ed./health; 11.3% prof./bus. serv.; 10.2% leisure/hosp.; 4.7% finance; 4.9% constr./mining/log.; 1.1% info.; 3.6% other serv. **Unemployment:** 4.2%. **Min. wage/hr.:** $7.25. **Per cap. pers. income:** $54,326. **New private housing:** 15,415 units/$3.0 bil. **Broadband internet:** 92.9%. **Commercial banks:** 148; deposits: $113.0 bil. **Savings institutions:** 10; deposits: $1.2 bil. **Lottery:** total sales: $1.5 bil; profit: $384.3 mil.

Federal govt. Fed. civ. employees: 23,040; **avg. salary:** $86,519. **Notable fed. facilities:** U.S. Bullion Depository, Ft. Knox; Ft. Campbell; Fed. Medical Ctr., Lexington; Army Corps of Engineers, Louisville District.

Education. High school grad. rate: 79.9%. **4-yr. public coll./univ.:** 8; **2-yr. public:** 16; **4-yr. private:** 25.

Energy. Electricity use/cost: 1,094 kWh, $141.23.

State data. Motto: United we stand, divided we fall. **Flower:** Goldenrod. **Bird:** Northern cardinal. **Tree:** Tulip poplar. **Song:** "My Old Kentucky Home." **Entered union:** June 1, 1792; rank: 15th.

Tourism. Tourist spending: $12.5 bil (2022); change, 2019-22: 11.7%. **Attractions:** Churchill Downs (Kentucky Derby), Louisville Slugger Museum and Factory, in Louisville; Land Between the Lakes Natl. Recreation Area (Kentucky and Barkley Lakes); Mammoth Cave Natl. Park (world's longest known cave system); Abraham Lincoln Birthplace Natl. Historical Park, Hodgenville; My Old Kentucky Home State Park, Bardstown; Cumberland Gap Natl. Historical Park, Middlesboro; Creation Museum, Petersburg; Kentucky Horse Park, Lexington; Shaker Village of Pleasant Hill, Harrodsburg; Natl. Corvette Museum, Bowling Green. **Information:** Kentucky Dept. of Tourism, 500 Mero St., 5th Fl., Frankfort, KY 40601; 1-800-225-8747; www.kentuckytourism.com

History. Paleo-Indians first arrived about 14,000 years ago. Much later, Shawnee, Wyandot, Delaware, and Cherokee peoples used the area mostly for hunting. Explored by Thomas Walker and Christopher Gist, 1750-51, Kentucky was the first area W of the Alleghenies settled by American pioneers. The first permanent settlement was Harrodsburg, 1774. Daniel Boone blazed the Wilderness Trail through the Cumberland Gap and founded Ft. Boonesborough, 1775. Clashes with Native Americans were frequent, 1774-94. Virginia dropped its claims to the region, and Kentucky became a state, 1792. Tobacco growing, horse breeding, coal mining, and bourbon whiskey making were major industries in the 19th cent. A slave state, Kentucky tried to stay neutral in the Civil War, but then opted for the Union; many Kentuckians sided with the Confederacy. The U.S. gold depository at Ft. Knox opened, 1937. Prior to the 2008 economic downturn, auto manufacturing had grown in recent decades. A statewide teacher walkout in Mar.-Apr. 2018 demanded increased pay and school funding. Tornadoes killed 77 people in western Kentucky Dec. 10-11, 2021, including 17 in Bowling Green and 9 at a candle factory in Mayfield. Record flooding from torrential rains in July 2022 killed nearly 40 people in the state's Appalachian foothills.

Famous Kentuckians. Muhammad Ali, Alben W. Barkley, Ned Beatty, Louis D. Brandeis, John C. Breckinridge, Kit Carson, Albert B. "Happy" Chandler, Henry Clay, George Clooney, Rosemary Clooney, Jefferson Davis, D. W. Griffith, "Casey" Jones, Jennifer Lawrence, Abraham Lincoln, Mary Todd Lincoln, Thomas Hunt Morgan, Carry Nation, Colonel Harland Sanders, Diane Sawyer, Chris Stapleton, Jesse Stuart, Zachary Taylor, Hunter S. Thompson, Robert Penn Warren, Whitney M. Young Jr.

Website. www.kentucky.gov

Louisiana (LA)

Pelican State

People. Population: 4,573,749; rank: 25. **Pop. change** (2020-23): –1.8%. **Pop. density:** 106 per sq mi. **Racial distribution:** 62.6% white; 32.6% Black; 1.9% Asian; 0.9% Amer. Ind.; 0.1% Hawaiian/Pacific Islander; 2 or more races, 2.0%. **Hispanic pop.:** 7.3%.

Geography. Total area: 52,361 sq mi; rank: 31. **Land area:** 43,193 sq mi; rank: 33. **Acres forested:** 15.0 mil. **Location:** West South Central state on the Gulf Coast. **Climate:** subtropical, affected by continental weather patterns. **Topography:** lowlands of marshes and Mississippi R. floodplain; Red R. Valley lowlands; upland hills in the Florida Parishes; avg. elevation, 100 ft. **Capital:** Baton Rouge. **Chief airport:** New Orleans (Kenner).

Economy. Chief industries: wholesale and retail trade, tourism, manufacturing, construction, transportation, communication, public utilities, finance, insurance, real estate, mining. **Chief manuf. goods:** petroleum, chemicals, plastics material and resin, pesticides and fertilizers, cleaning prods., paper and paperboard, ships, structural metals. **Chief crops:** sugarcane, cotton, rice, soybeans, corn, sweet potatoes. **Farm income:** Crops: $2.74 bil. Livestock: $1.51 bil. **Nonfuel minerals:** $1.1 bil; clay (common clay), lime, salt, sand and gravel (construction), sand and gravel (industrial), stone (crushed). **Commercial fishing:** $416.7 mil. **Chief ports:** New Orleans, Baton Rouge, Lake Charles, Port of S. Louisiana (La Place), Shreveport, Plaquemine, St. Bernard, Alexandria. **Gross state product:** $309.6 bil. **Sales tax:** 4.45%. **Gasoline tax:** 39.33 cents/gal. **Employment distrib.:** 16.4% govt.; 18.8% trade/trans./util.; 7.0% mfg.; 17.2% ed./health; 11.2% prof./bus. serv.; 11.3% leisure/hosp.; 4.7% finance; 8.5% constr./mining/log.; 0.9% info.; 3.8% other serv. **Unemployment:** 3.7%. **Min. wage/hr.:** none. **Per cap. pers. income:** $57,100. **New private housing:** 14,247 units/$3.2 bil. **Broadband internet:** 93.7%. **Commercial banks:** 105; deposits: $131.3 bil. **Savings institutions:** 17; deposits: $4.8 bil. **Lottery:** total sales: $652.4 mil; profit: $212.1 mil.

Federal govt. Fed. civ. employees: 19,408; **avg. salary:** $93,001. **Notable federal facilities:** Ft. Johnson (fmr. Polk) (Joint Readiness Training Ctr.); Barksdale AFB; Strategic Petroleum Reserve; Michoud Assembly Facility; USDA Southern Regional Research Ctr.; NAS JRB New Orleans.

Education. High school grad. rate: 87.3%. **4-yr. public coll./univ.:** 17; **2-yr. public:** 14; **4-yr. private:** 11.

Energy. Electricity use/cost: 1,231 kWh, $159.24.

State data. Motto: Union, justice, and confidence. **Flower:** Magnolia blossom. **Bird:** Eastern brown pelican. **Tree:** Bald cypress. **Song:** "Give Me Louisiana." **Entered union:** Apr. 30, 1812; rank: 18th.

Tourism. Tourist spending: $14.0 bil (2022); change, 2019-22: 0.7%. **Attractions:** Mardi Gras, French Quarter, Bourbon Street, in New Orleans; Jean Lafitte Natl. Historical Park and Preserve; Longfellow-Evangeline State Historic Site, St. Martinville; Kent Plantation House, Alexandria; Oak Alley Plantation, Vacherie; Whitney Plantation, Wallace; Hodges Gardens State Park, Florien; USS *Kidd* Veterans Memorial, Baton Rouge. **Information:** Louisiana Office of Tourism, P.O. Box 94291, Baton Rouge, LA 70804-9291; (225) 342-8100; www.explorelouisiana.com

History. Caddo, Tunica, Choctaw, Chitimacha, and Chawash peoples lived in the region at the time of European contact. Spanish explorers in the early 16th cent. reached the mouth of the Mississippi. René-Robert Cavelier, sieur de La Salle, 1682, claimed the region for France. Early French and Spanish settlers were the ancestors of Louisiana Creoles.

Cajuns descended from the Acadians, French settlers expelled by the British from Nova Scotia, Canada, in 1755. France ceded the Louisiana region to Spain, 1762, took it back, 1800, and sold it to the U.S., 1803, in the Louisiana Purchase. Admitted as a state in 1812, Louisiana witnessed the Battle of New Orleans, 1815. Cotton and sugar plantations relied on the enslaved labor of Black workers, who made up close to 47% of the population in 1860, on the eve of the Civil War. Louisiana seceded, 1861, and was readmitted, 1868. Jazz was born in New Orleans in the early 20th cent. As governor (1928-32), Huey Long pushed populist programs. Many tropical storms and floods have battered Louisiana, including Hurricane Katrina and subsequent flooding, 2005, which devastated New Orleans. The offshore oil and gas industry developed after World War II. An oil rig explosion off the state's Gulf coast spilled millions of barrels of oil, damaging coastal wetlands and many of the state's marine-dependent industries in 2010. In May 2017, New Orleans removed several monuments honoring the Confederacy and a racially motivated Reconstruction-era attack. Category 4 hurricanes Laura (2020) and Ida (2021) severely impacted parts of the state and killed dozens. A U.S. Supreme Court ruling May 15, 2024, approved a voting map with a second largely Black congressional district.

Famous Louisianans. Louis Armstrong, Pierre Beauregard, Judah P. Benjamin, Braxton Bragg, Kate Chopin, Harry Connick Jr., Ellen DeGeneres, Fats Domino, George "Buddy" Guy, Lillian Hellman, Grace King, Jerry Lee Lewis, Bob Livingston, Huey Long, Eli Manning, Peyton Manning, Wynton Marsalis, Tim McGraw, Leonidas K. Polk, Anne Rice, Bill Russell, Henry Miller Shreve, Britney Spears, Madam C. J. Walker (Sarah Breedlove), Edward Douglass White Jr.

Website. www.louisiana.gov

Maine (ME)

Pine Tree State

People. Population: 1,395,722; rank: 42. **Pop. change** (2020-23): 2.4%. **Pop. density:** 45 per sq mi. **Racial distribution:** 93.7% white; 2.1% Black; 1.4% Asian; 0.7% Amer. Ind.; <0.05% Hawaiian/Pacific Islander; 2 or more races, 2.0%. **Hispanic pop.:** 2.3%.

Geography. Total area: 35,370 sq mi; rank: 39. **Land area:** 30,837 sq mi; rank: 39. **Acres forested:** 17.5 mil. **Location:** New England state at northeastern tip of U.S. **Climate:** southern interior and coast influenced by air masses from the S and W; northern clime harsher, avg. over 100 in. snow in winter. **Topography:** Appalachian Mts. extend through state; western borders have rugged terrain; long sand beaches on southern coast; northern coast mainly rocky promontories, peninsulas, fjords. **Capital:** Augusta. **Chief airport:** Portland.

Economy. Chief industries: manufacturing, agriculture, fishing, services, trade, government, finance, insurance, real estate, construction. **Chief manuf. goods:** paper, ships and boats, cardboard, frozen/canned fruits and vegetables, plastics, baked goods. **Chief crops:** potatoes, greenhouse and nursery, wild blueberries, apples, hay, maple syrup. **Farm income:** Crops: $543.15 mil. Livestock: $396.71 mil. **Nonfuel minerals:** $116 mil; cement, peat, sand and gravel (construction), stone (crushed), stone (dimension). **Commercial fishing:** $584.9 mil. **Chief ports:** Searsport, Portland, Eastport. **Gross state product:** $91.1 bil. **Sales tax:** 5.5%. **Gasoline tax:** 49.80 cents/gal. **Employment distrib.:** 15.9% govt.; 18.5% trade/trans./util.; 8.3% mfg.; 21.1% ed./health; 11.8% prof./bus. serv.; 9.4% leisure/hosp.; 5.2% finance; 5.3% constr./mining/log.; 1.3% info.; 3.4% other serv. **Unemployment:** 2.9%. **Min. wage/hr.:** $14.15. **Per cap. pers. income:** $63,117. **New private housing:** 6,183 units/$1.6 bil. **Broadband internet:** 92.6%. **Commercial banks:** 11; deposits: $23.7 bil. **Savings institutions:** 18; deposits: $19.0 bil. **Lottery:** total sales: $410.3 mil; profit: $73.2 mil.

Federal govt. Fed. civ. employees: 12,105; **avg. salary:** $91,713. **Notable fed. facilities:** Portsmouth Naval Shipyard; NOAA Fisheries, Maine Field Station.

Education. High school grad. rate: 87.7%. **4-yr. public coll./univ.:** 7; **2-yr. public:** 7; **4-yr. private:** 13.

Energy. Electricity use/cost: 583 kWh, $130.78.

State data. Motto: Dirigo (I direct). **Flower:** White pine cone and tassel. **Bird:** Black-capped chickadee. **Tree:** Eastern white pine. **Song:** "State of Maine Song." **Entered union:** Mar. 15, 1820; rank: 23rd.

Tourism. Tourist spending: $5.5 bil (2022); change, 2019-22: 11.6%. **Attractions:** Acadia Natl. Park, Bar Harbor, on Mt. Desert Island; Old Orchard Beach; Old Port historic waterfront, Victoria Mansion, Portland; Portland Head Light, Cape Elizabeth; Maine Maritime Museum, Bath; Baxter State Park; L.L. Bean flagship store and outlet shopping, Freeport. **Information:** Maine Office of Tourism, 59 State House Station, Augusta, ME 04330; 1-888-624-6345; www.visitmaine.com

History. Paleo-Indians arrived about 11,500 years ago. Maine was inhabited by Algonquian peoples including the Abnaki, Penobscot, and Passamaquoddy at the time of European contact. French settled, 1604, at the St. Croix R., the English, c. 1607, on the Kennebec; both settlements failed. A royal charter, 1691, made Maine part of Massachusetts. Maine broke off, 1819, and became a separate state, 1820. Drawing on vast forest resources, the pulp and paper industry developed after the Civil War. Bath Iron Works began building U.S. Navy vessels and other ships in the 1890s. Mail-order and retail giant L.L. Bean was founded, 1912. Women have fared well in state politics: Margaret Chase Smith became the first woman to serve in both houses of Congress (House, 1940-49; Senate, 1949-73), and Olympia Snowe (1995-2013) and Susan Collins (1997-present) represented Maine in the Senate. An army reservist Oct. 25, 2023, fatally shot 18 people in two separate attacks in Lewiston; he was found dead two days later.

Famous "Down Easters." Leon Leonwood (L. L.) Bean, James G. Blaine, Patrick Dempsey, Hannibal Hamlin, Sarah Orne Jewett, Anna Kendrick, Stephen King, Henry Wadsworth Longfellow, Sir Hiram and Hudson Maxim, Edna St. Vincent Millay, George J. Mitchell, Edmund Muskie, Judd Nelson, Edwin Arlington Robinson, Joan Benoit Samuelson, Liv Tyler, Kate Douglas Wiggin, Ben Ames Williams.

Website. www.maine.gov

Maryland (MD)

Old Line State, Free State

People. Population: 6,180,253; rank: 19. **Pop. change** (2020-23): 0.0%. **Pop. density:** 637 per sq mi. **Racial distribution:** 57.2% white; 31.6% Black; 7.1% Asian; 0.8% Amer. Ind.; 0.1% Hawaiian/Pacific Islander; 2 or more races, 3.3%. **Hispanic pop.:** 12.6%.

Geography. Total area: 12,403 sq mi; rank: 42. **Land area:** 9,709 sq mi; rank: 42. **Acres forested:** 2.4 mil. **Location:** South Atlantic state stretching from the ocean to the Allegheny Mts. **Climate:** continental in the W; humid subtropical in the E. **Topography:** coastal plain on Eastern Shore separated by Chesapeake Bay from coastal plain, Piedmont Plateau, and the Blue Ridge. **Capital:** Annapolis. **Chief airport:** Glen Burnie (Baltimore/Washington, DC).

Economy. Chief industries: manufacturing, biotechnology and information technology, services, tourism. **Chief manuf. goods:** navigational instruments, pharmaceutical and medicine, broadcasting equip., plastics, printing, milk and ice cream. **Chief crops:** greenhouse and nursery, corn, soybeans, wheat, hay, tomatoes, watermelons, barley, potatoes, apples. **Farm income:** Crops: $1.25 bil. Livestock: $2.02 bil. **Nonfuel minerals:** $431 mil; cement, sand and gravel (construction), stone (crushed), stone (dimension). **Commercial fishing:** $78.6 mil. **Chief port:** Baltimore. **Gross state product:** $512.3 bil. **Sales tax:** 6.0%. **Gasoline tax:** 65.59 cents/gal. **Employment distrib.:** 19.8% govt.; 16.6% trade/trans./util.; 4.0% mfg.; 17.3% ed./health; 17.2% prof./bus. serv.; 9.4% leisure/hosp.; 5.0% finance; 5.6% constr./mining/log.; 1.2% info.; 3.9% other serv. **Unemployment:** 2.1%. **Min. wage/hr.:** $15.00. **Per cap. pers. income:** $73,849. **New private housing:** 18,453 units/$4.3 bil. **Broadband internet:** 97.8%. **Commercial banks:** 66; deposits: $191.1 bil. **Savings institutions:** 11; deposits: $3.4 bil. **Lottery:** total sales: $5.2 bil; profit: $1.5 bil.

Federal govt. Fed. civ. employees: 142,730; **avg. salary:** $135,156. **Notable fed. facilities:** U.S. Naval Academy; Beltsville Agriculture Res. Ctr.; Ft. Meade; Aberdeen Proving Ground; Joint Base Andrews; Naval Air Sys. Command; Goddard Space Flight Ctr.; Natl. Inst. of Standards & Technology, Gaithersburg; Food & Drug Admin., Natl. Marine Fisheries Serv., Natl. Oceanic and Atmospheric Admin., Silver Spring; Bureau of the Census, Suitland; Natl. Inst. of Health, Walter Reed Natl. Military Med. Ctr., Bethesda.

Education. High school grad. rate: 86.3%. **4-yr. public coll./univ.:** 13; **2-yr. public:** 16; **4-yr. private:** 18.

Energy. Electricity use/cost: 968 kWh, $139.99.

State data. Motto: Fatti Maschii, Parole Femine (Manly deeds, womanly words). **Flower:** Black-eyed Susan. **Bird:** Baltimore oriole. **Tree:** White oak. **Song:** None. "Maryland, My Maryland" repealed in 2021 over pro-Confederacy lyrics. Seventh of original 13 states to ratify the Constitution, Apr. 28, 1788.

Tourism. Tourist spending: $20.4 bil (2022); change, 2019-22: 3.8%. **Attractions:** Ocean City; Ft. McHenry (the defense of which inspired Francis Scott Key to write "The Star-Spangled Banner"), Pimlico Race Course (Preakness Stakes), Edgar Allan Poe House and Museum, Oriole Park at Camden Yards, Natl. Aquarium, Inner Harbor, in Baltimore; Antietam Natl. Battlefield, Sharpsburg; South Mountain State Battlefield, Middletown; U.S. Naval Academy, Maryland

State House (oldest in continuous legislative use in U.S.), in Annapolis; Natl. Cryptologic Museum, Ft. Meade. **Information:** Maryland Office of Tourism Development, 401 E. Pratt St., 14th Fl., Baltimore, MD 21202; 1-866-639-3526; www.visitmaryland.org

History. Europeans encountered Algonquian-speaking Nanticoke and Piscataway and Iroquois-speaking Susquehannock when they first visited the area. Italian navigator Giovanni da Verrazzano reached the Chesapeake region in the early 16th cent. English Capt. John Smith explored and mapped the area, 1608. William Claiborne set up a trading post on Kent Island in Chesapeake Bay, 1631. King Charles I granted land to Cecilius Calvert, Lord Baltimore, 1632; Calvert's brother Leonard, with about 200 settlers, founded St. Mary's, 1634. During the Revolutionary War, Baltimore (1776-77) and Annapolis (1783-84) served as temporary capitals of the U.S. When a British fleet tried to take Ft. McHenry in the War of 1812, Marylander Francis Scott Key wrote "The Star-Spangled Banner," 1814. Born into slavery at Tuckahoe in 1818, Frederick Douglass became a leading abolitionist. Although a slaveholding state, Maryland stayed in the Union during the Civil War and was the site of the battle of Antietam, 1862. Gov. Spiro Agnew, elected U.S. vice pres., 1968 and 1972, pleaded no contest to tax evasion and resigned, 1973. Israeli and Egyptian leaders reached a historic peace accord at the Camp David presidential retreat, 1978. The death of a young Black man in police custody touched off sometimes violent protests in Baltimore in 2015. According to a 2016 Justice Dept. report, Baltimore's police dept. regularly violated the constitutional rights of Black residents. A gunman in June 2018 fatally shot five employees at the office of Annapolis's *Capital Gazette*. In Nov. 2022, the state elected its first Black governor, Wes Moore; Moore issued more than 175,000 pardons for low-level marijuana convictions in June 2024. A container ship struck Baltimore's 1.6-mile Francis Scott Key Bridge on Mar. 26, 2024, killing six construction workers and partially collapsing it.

Famous Marylanders. John Astin, Benjamin Banneker, Tom Clancy, Frederick Douglass, Matthew Henson, Francis Scott Key, Thurgood Marshall, H. L. Mencken, Kweisi Mfume, Ogden Nash, Charles Willson Peale, Michael Phelps, William Pinkney, Edgar Allan Poe, Cal Ripken Jr., Babe Ruth, Upton Sinclair, Roger B. Taney, Harriet Tubman, John Waters, Montel Williams.

Website. www.maryland.gov

Massachusetts (MA)

Bay State, Old Colony

People. Population: 7,001,399; rank: 16. **Pop. change** (2020-23): –0.4%. **Pop. density:** 898 per sq mi. **Racial distribution:** 79.0% white; 9.6% Black; 7.9% Asian; 0.6% Amer. Ind.; 0.1% Hawaiian/Pacific Islander; 2 or more races, 2.8%. **Hispanic pop.:** 13.5%.

Geography. Total area: 10,551 sq mi; rank: 44. **Land area:** 7,799 sq mi; rank: 45. **Acres forested:** 3.0 mil. **Location:** New England state on Atlantic seaboard. **Climate:** temperate, with colder, drier clime in western region. **Topography:** jagged indented coast from Rhode Island around Cape Cod; flat land yields to stony upland pastures near central region and gentle hilly country in W; except in W, land is rocky, sandy, and not fertile. **Capital:** Boston. **Chief airport:** Boston.

Economy. Chief industries: services, trade, manufacturing. **Chief manuf. goods:** electronics and instruments, pharmaceuticals, telecom and broadcasting equip., plastics, medical equip., printing. **Chief crops:** greenhouse and nursery, cranberries, tomatoes, sweet corn, apples, hay, tobacco. **Farm income:** Crops: $365.35 mil. Livestock: $137.95 mil. **Nonfuel minerals:** $329 mil; clay (common clay), lime, sand and gravel (construction), stone (crushed), stone (dimension). **Commercial fishing:** $689.0 mil. **Chief ports:** Boston, Fall River. **Gross state product:** $733.9 bil. **Sales tax:** 6.25%. **Gasoline tax:** 45.77 cents/gal. **Employment distrib.:** 12.6% govt.; 14.9% trade/trans./util.; 6.3% mfg.; 22.8% ed./health; 16.9% prof./bus. serv.; 9.4% leisure/hosp.; 6.1% finance; 4.7% constr./mining/log.; 2.5% info.; 3.7% other serv. **Unemployment:** 3.4%. **Min. wage/hr.:** $15.00. **Per cap. pers. income:** $87,812. **New private housing:** 13,214 units/$4.4 bil. **Broadband internet:** 97.9%. **Commercial banks:** 42; deposits: $480.1 bil. **Savings institutions:** 85; deposits: $76.0 bil. **Lottery:** total sales: $6.1 bil; profit: $1.2 bil.

Federal govt. Fed. civ. employees: 25,415; **avg. salary:** $113,106. **Notable fed. facilities:** Thomas P. O'Neill Jr. Fed. Bldg., J.W. McCormack Bldg., JFK Fed. Bldg., Boston; Hanscom AFB; Army Natick Soldier Systems Ctr.

Education. High school grad. rate: 90.1%. **4-yr. public coll./univ.:** 14; **2-yr. public:** 16; **4-yr. private:** 70.

Energy. Electricity use/cost: 577 kWh, $149.91.

State data. Motto: Ense Petit Placidam Sub Libertate Quietem (By the sword we seek peace, but peace only under liberty). **Flower:** Mayflower. **Bird:** Black-capped chickadee. **Tree:** American elm. **Song:** "All Hail to Massachusetts." **Sixth** of original 13 states to ratify the Constitution, Feb. 6, 1788.

Tourism. Tourist spending: $25.5 bil (2022); change, 2019-22: –3.8%. **Attractions:** Provincetown art colony; Cape Cod; Plymouth Rock, Plimoth Plantation, Mayflower II, in Plymouth; Freedom Trail, Museum of Fine Arts, New England Aquarium, Faneuil Hall, Boston Harbor Isls. Natl. Recreation Area, Boston Public Garden, in Boston; Tanglewood, Hancock Shaker Village, Berkshire Scenic Railway Museum, Norman Rockwell Museum, in the Berkshires region; Peabody Essex Museum, House of the Seven Gables, in Salem; Old Sturbridge Village; Historic Deerfield; Walden Pond, Louisa May Alcott's Orchard House, in Concord; Naismith Memorial Basketball Hall of Fame, Springfield. **Information:** Massachusetts Office of Travel & Tourism, McCormack Building, One Ashburton Place, Room 2101, Boston, MA 02108; 1-800-227-MASS; www.visitma.com

History. Early inhabitants were Algonquian peoples: Nauset, Wampanoag, Massachuset, Pennacook, Nipmuc, and Pocumtuc. Pilgrims settled in Plymouth, 1620, giving thanks for their survival with a Thanksgiving feast alongside Wampanoag living there, 1621. About 20,000 new settlers arrived, 1630-40. Colonist-Native American relations deteriorated, leading to King Philip's War, 1675-76, which the colonists won. Witch trials at Salem, 1692, led to the execution of 20 people. Demonstrations against British restrictions set off the Boston Massacre, 1770, and the Boston Tea Party, 1773. The first bloodshed of the American Revolution was at Lexington, 1775. After statehood, Massachusetts prospered from shipbuilding, seafaring, and the making of textiles, shoes, and metal goods, while artists, writers, and social reformers flourished. The controversial Sacco-Vanzetti case, 1920-27, ended with the execution of two Italian immigrants on murder and robbery charges. After World War II, old industries declined, knowledge-intensive enterprises thrived, and the Kennedys became a dominant political family. The state's highest court ruled, 2003, that same-sex couples could legally marry. Two bombs exploded Apr. 15, 2013, near the finish line of the Boston Marathon, killing three and injuring more than 250. The surviving of two brothers believed to have planted the bombs was convicted on multiple charges in Apr. 2015 and sentenced to death. U.S. Supreme Court in Mar. 2022 upheld the death sentence.

Famous "Bay Staters." John Adams, John Quincy Adams, Samuel Adams, Louisa May Alcott, Horatio Alger, Susan B. Anthony, Crispus Attucks, Clara Barton, Michael Bloomberg, George H. W. Bush, Steve Carell, John Cheever, E. E. Cummings, Bette Davis, Emily Dickinson, Charles Eliot, Ralph Waldo Emerson, William Lloyd Garrison, Edward Everett Hale, John Hancock, Nathaniel Hawthorne, Oliver Wendell Holmes Jr., Winslow Homer, Elias Howe, John F. Kennedy, Jack Kerouac, John Kerry, Emeril Lagasse, Jack Lemmon, James Russell Lowell, Cotton Mather, Maria Mitchell, Samuel F. B. Morse, Conan O'Brien, Paul Revere, Norman Rockwell, Dr. Seuss (Theodor Seuss Geisel), Henry David Thoreau, Barbara Walters, James Abbott McNeil Whistler, John Greenleaf Whittier.

Website. www.mass.gov

Michigan (MI)

Great Lakes State, Wolverine State

People. Population: 10,037,261; rank: 10. **Pop. change** (2020-23): –0.4%. **Pop. density:** 177 per sq mi. **Racial distribution:** 78.7% white; 14.1% Black; 3.6% Asian; 0.8% Amer. Ind.; <0.05% Hawaiian/Pacific Islander; 2 or more races, 2.8%. **Hispanic pop.:** 6.0%.

Geography. Total area: 96,688 sq mi; rank: 11. **Land area:** 56,591 sq mi; rank: 22. **Acres forested:** 20.1 mil. **Location:** East North Central state bordering four of the Great Lakes, divided into an Upper and Lower Peninsula by the Straits of Mackinac, which link Lakes Michigan and Huron. **Climate:** well-defined seasons tempered by the Great Lakes. **Topography:** low rolling hills give way to northern tableland of hilly belts in Lower Peninsula; Upper Peninsula is level in the E with swampy areas; western region is higher and more rugged. **Capital:** Lansing. **Chief airports:** Detroit, Grand Rapids.

Economy. Chief industries: manufacturing, services, tourism, agriculture, forestry/lumber. **Chief manuf. goods:** motor vehicles and parts, plastics, metalworking machinery, non-wood office furniture, fabricated metals. **Chief crops:** greenhouse and nursery, soybeans, corn, wheat, sugar beets, apples, blueberries, potatoes, dry beans, cherries, hay, cucumbers, tomatoes, grapes. **Farm income:** Crops: $6.86 bil. Livestock: $5.22 bil. **Nonfuel minerals:** $4.1 bil; cement, iron ore, nickel sulfide concentrates, sand and gravel (construction), stone (crushed). **Commercial fishing** (2018): $8.0 mil. **Chief ports:** Detroit, Escanaba,

Calcite, Port Inland, Muskegon, Port Huron. **Gross state product:** $659.0 bil. **Sales tax:** 6.0%. **Gasoline tax:** 66.40 cents/gal. **Employment distrib.:** 14.2% govt.; 18.2% trade/trans./util.; 13.6% mfg.; 15.8% ed./health; 14.5% prof./bus. serv.; 9.2% leisure/hosp.; 5.0% finance; 4.6% constr./mining/log.; 1.3% info.; 3.8% other serv. **Unemployment:** 3.9%. **Min. wage/hr.:** $10.33. **Per cap. pers. income:** $59,714. **New private housing:** 20,592 units/$5.7 bil. **Broadband internet:** 95.3%. **Commercial banks:** 98; deposits: $292.0 bil. **Savings institutions:** 5; deposits: $1.1 bil. **Lottery:** total sales: $4.9 bil; profit: $1.4 bil.

Federal govt. Fed. civ. employees: 29,460; **avg. salary:** $105,357. **Notable fed. facilities:** Army TACOM Life Cycle Mgmt., Detroit Arsenal; DLA Logistics Info. Service; Selfridge Air Natl. Guard Base; Hart-Dole-Inouye Fed. Ctr., Battle Creek.

Education. High school grad. rate: 81.0%. **4-yr. public coll./univ.:** 22; **2-yr. public:** 24; **4-yr. private:** 38.

Energy. Electricity use/cost: 652 kWh, $116.49.

State data. Motto: Si Quaeris Peninsulam Amoenam, Circumspice (If you seek a pleasant peninsula, look about you). **Flower:** Apple blossom. **Bird:** American robin. **Tree:** White pine. **Song:** "Michigan, My Michigan." **Entered union:** Jan. 26, 1837; rank: 26th.

Tourism. Tourist spending: $25.8 bil (2022); change, 2019-22: 3.7%. **Attractions:** Henry Ford Museum and Greenfield Village, Dearborn; Frederik Meijer Gardens and Sculpture Park, Grand Rapids; Tahquamenon Falls (of Longfellow's poem *Song of Hiawatha*); De Zwaan windmill, Tulip Time Festival, in Holland; Soo Locks (bet. Lakes Superior and Huron), Sault Ste. Marie; Air Zoo, Portage; Mackinac Island; Belle Isle Park, Detroit Institute of Arts, Charles H. Wright Museum of African-American History, Motown Museum, in Detroit. **Information:** Michigan Economic Development Corp., 300 N. Washington Sq., Lansing, MI 48913; 1-888-784-7328; www.michigan.org

History. Hunting and fishing peoples lived in the region as early as 11,000 years ago. Ojibwa, Ottawa, Miami, Potawatomi, and Huron inhabited the area at the time of European contact. French fur traders and missionaries arrived in the 17th cent. and established a settlement at Sault Ste. Marie, 1668. British took over, 1763, and crushed a Native American uprising led by Ottawa chieftain Pontiac. The area was ceded to the U.S. by the Treaty of Paris, 1783, but the British remained until 1796. Michigan was organized as a territory, 1805. The British seized Ft. Mackinac and Detroit, 1812, but the U.S. regained control, 1814. The opening of the Erie Canal, 1825, and new land laws and Native American cessions led the way for a flood of settlers. Strongly antislavery, Michigan became a state, 1837, and supplied 90,000 soldiers to the Union army in the Civil War. Henry Ford launched the Model T car, 1908; the United Auto Workers union was founded, 1935. Motown music flourished in Detroit in the 1960s, but riots in 1967 dealt the city a heavy blow. As the auto industry faltered, Michigan lost more than 20% of its automotive-related jobs in 2002-07. In 2009, the federal government loaned billions of dollars to GM and Chrysler to keep them solvent. Detroit formally emerged from a 17-month bankruptcy process—the largest in U.S. municipal history—in Dec. 2014. In Aug. 2020, the state announced a $600 mil settlement with children/families affected by the lead-contamination crisis that began in 2014 in Flint's municipal water supply system. Michigan State Univ. in May 2018 agreed to pay $500 mil to settle sexual abuse lawsuits related to claims against former MSU doctor Larry Nassar. In Jan. 2022, the Univ. of Michigan agreed to pay $490 mil to settle claims from more than 1,000 people, mostly men, of sexual assault by former Univ. of Michigan sports doctor Robert Anderson. In Dec. 2022, two co-leaders of a foiled right-wing plot to kidnap Gov. Gretchen Whitmer (D) ahead of the 2020 election were sentenced to 16 and 19 years, respectively, in federal prison. In 2024, James and Jennifer Crumbley were convicted of involuntary manslaughter and sentenced to 10-15 years in connection with a 2021 school shooting committed by their son.

Famous Michiganders. Ralph Bunche, Paul de Kruif, Thomas Edison, Eminem (Marshall Mathers), Edna Ferber, Gerald R. Ford, Henry Ford, Aretha Franklin, Edgar Guest, Lee Iacocca, Magic Johnson, Casey Kasem, Will Kellogg, Ring Lardner, Elmore Leonard, Charles Lindbergh, Joe Louis, Madonna, Malcolm X, Terry McMillan, Michael Moore, Larry Page, Pontiac, Gilda Radner, Smokey Robinson, Mitt Romney, Diana Ross, Tom Selleck, Sinbad (David Adkins), John Smoltz, Lily Tomlin, Serena Williams, Stevie Wonder.

Website. www.michigan.gov

Minnesota (MN)

North Star State, Gopher State

People. Population: 5,737,915; rank: 22. **Pop. change** (2020-23): 0.5%. **Pop. density:** 72 per sq mi. **Racial distribution:** 82.3% white; 7.9% Black; 5.5% Asian; 1.4% Amer. Ind.; 0.1% Hawaiian/Pacific Islander; 2 or more races, 2.9%. **Hispanic pop.:** 6.5%.

Geography. Total area: 86,917 sq mi; rank: 12. **Land area:** 79,605 sq mi; rank: 14. **Acres forested:** 17.7 mil. **Location:** West North Central state bounded on the E by Wisconsin and Lake Superior, on the N by Canada, on the W by the Dakotas, and on the S by Iowa. **Climate:** northern part of state lies in the moist Great Lakes storm belt; the western border lies at the edge of the semiarid Great Plains. **Topography:** central hill and lake region covers approx. half the state; to the NE, rocky ridges and deep lakes; to the NW, flat plain; to the S, rolling plains and deep river valleys. **Capital:** St. Paul. **Chief airport:** Minneapolis.

Economy. Chief industries: agribusiness, forest prods., mining, manufacturing, tourism. **Chief manuf. goods:** petroleum and asphalt, computers and electronics, milk and cheese, printing, animal slaughtering, paper and paper prods., medical equip. **Chief crops:** corn, soybeans, hay, sugar beets, wheat, potatoes, greenhouse and nursery, dry edible beans, green peas, sunflowers. **Farm income:** Crops: $15.83 bil. Livestock: $10.19 bil. **Nonfuel minerals:** $6.8 bil; iron ore, lime, sand and gravel (construction), sand and gravel (industrial), stone (crushed). **Commercial fishing** (2018): $0.2 mil. **Chief ports:** Two Harbors, Silver Bay, Duluth, St. Paul. **Gross state product:** $471.8 bil. **Sales tax:** 6.875%. **Gasoline tax:** 47.00 cents/gal. **Employment distrib.:** 14.7% govt.; 17.7% trade/trans./util.; 10.8% mfg.; 19.7% ed./health; 12.5% prof./bus. serv.; 8.9% leisure/hosp.; 6.2% finance; 4.4% constr./mining/log.; 1.4% info.; 3.8% other serv. **Unemployment:** 2.8%. **Min. wage/hr.:** $10.85. **Per cap. pers. income:** $71,866. **New private housing:** 25,667 units/$6.7 bil. **Broadband internet:** 96.0%. **Commercial banks:** 295; deposits: $273.0 bil. **Savings institutions:** 14; deposits: $26.1 bil. **Lottery:** total sales: $787.2 mil; profit: $196.1 mil.

Federal govt. Fed. civ. employees: 17,916; **avg. salary:** $102,832. **Notable fed. facilities:** Bishop Henry Whipple Fed. Bldg.; Minneapolis-St. Paul Air Reserve Station.

Education. High school grad. rate: 83.6%. **4-yr. public coll./univ.:** 13; **2-yr. public:** 27; **4-yr. private:** 32.

Energy. Electricity use/cost: 773 kWh, $110.19.

State data. Motto: L'Etoile du Nord (The star of the north). **Flower:** Pink and white lady's-slipper. **Bird:** Common loon. **Tree:** Red pine. **Song:** "Hail! Minnesota." **Entered union:** May 11, 1858; rank: 32nd.

Tourism. Tourist spending: $13.0 bil (2022); change, 2019-22: –21.6%. **Attractions:** Minneapolis Institute of Arts, Walker Art Center, Minneapolis Sculpture Garden, Minnehaha Falls (in Longfellow's poem *Song of Hiawatha*), Guthrie Theater, in Minneapolis; Mall of America, Bloomington; Ordway Ctr. for the Performing Arts, Science Museum of Minnesota, in St. Paul; Voyageurs Natl. Park; Mayo Clinic, Rochester; North Shore (Lake Superior); Lake Minnetonka; Boundary Waters Canoe Area Wilderness; Superior Natl. Forest; Aerial Lift Bridge, Duluth. **Information:** Explore Minnesota Tourism, Metro Square, 121 7th Pl. E., Ste. 360, St. Paul, MN 55101; 1-888-VISITMN; www.exploreminnesota.com

History. Inhabited for at least 10,000 years, the region was home to Dakota Sioux when Europeans arrived. French fur traders Pierre Esprit Radisson and Médard Chouart, sieur des Groseilliers, explored in the mid-17th cent. In 1679, Daniel Greysolon, sieur Duluth, claimed the entire region for France. Ojibwa arrived in the 18th cent. and warred with the Sioux for over 100 years. Britain took the area east of the Mississippi, 1763. The U.S. took over that portion after the American Revolution and gained the western area, 1803, in the Louisiana Purchase. The U.S. built Ft. St. Anthony (now Ft. Snelling), 1819, and bought Native American lands, 1837, spurring an influx of settlers from the east. Minnesota became a territory, 1849, and a state, 1858. The Sioux staged a bloody uprising, the Battle of Wood Lake, 1862, and were driven from the state. Railroad construction after the Civil War spurred the growth of the grain, timber, and iron mining industries. The opening of the St. Lawrence Seaway, 1959, aided the port of Duluth. Elected as a reformer, former pro wrestler Jesse Ventura served as governor, 1999-2003. Sen. Paul Wellstone (D) died when his campaign plane crashed, 2002. The I-35W Mississippi River Bridge in Minneapolis collapsed in 2007, killing 13. After George Floyd, a Black man, was killed in Minneapolis police custody May 25, 2020, several days of protests/riots damaged about 1,500 businesses in the Twin Cities. The protest movement spread to hundreds of cities, calling for an end to police brutality and other forms of systemic racism. In June 2021, former Minneapolis police officer Derek Chauvin was sentenced to 22.5 years in prison after his conviction on murder and manslaughter charges for his role in Floyd's death; in July 2022, he received a concurrent 21-year federal sentence. Three other officers involved were convicted in Feb. 2022 on lesser federal charges.

Famous Minnesotans. Andrews Sisters, Warren E. Burger, Ethan and Joel Coen, Bob Dylan, F. Scott Fitzgerald, Al Franken, Judy Garland, Cass Gilbert, Hubert H. Humphrey, Garrison

Keillor, Sister Elizabeth Kenny, Jessica Lange, Sinclair Lewis, Paul Manship, E. G. Marshall, William J. and Charles H. Mayo, Eugene McCarthy, Walter F. Mondale, Prince (Prince Rogers Nelson), Charles M. Schulz, Ann Sothern, Harold Stassen, Thorstein Veblen, Jesse Ventura, Lindsey Vonn, Paul Wellstone.

Website. www.mn.gov

Mississippi (MS)

Magnolia State

People. Population: 2,939,690; rank: 35. **Pop. change** (2020-23): –0.7%. **Pop. density:** 63 per sq mi. **Racial distribution:** 58.7% white; 37.8% Black; 1.2% Asian; 0.7% Amer. Ind.; 0.1% Hawaiian/Pacific Islander; 2 or more races, 1.5%. **Hispanic pop.:** 3.9%.

Geography. Total area: 48,428 sq mi; rank: 32. **Land area:** 46,913 sq mi; rank: 31. **Acres forested:** 19.2 mil. **Location:** East South Central state bordered on the W by the Mississippi R., on the S by the Gulf of Mexico. **Climate:** semitropical, with abundant rainfall and long growing season. **Topography:** low, fertile delta between the Yazoo and Mississippi Rivers; loess bluffs stretch around delta border; sandy gulf coastal terraces followed by piney woods and prairie; rugged, high sandy hills in extreme NE followed by Prairie Black Belt, Pontotoc Ridge, and flatwoods into the N central highlands. **Capital:** Jackson. **Chief airport:** Jackson.

Economy. Chief industries: warehousing and distribution, services, manufacturing, government, wholesale and retail trade. **Chief manuf. goods:** petroleum, upholstered furniture, poultry processing, motor vehicle parts, plastics, ships and boats, chemicals. **Chief crops:** cotton, soybeans, rice, hay, corn, sweet potatoes. **Farm income:** Crops: $3.19 bil. Livestock: $4.64 bil. **Nonfuel minerals:** $338 mil; clay (ball clay, bentonite, common clay, montmorillonite), sand and gravel (construction), sand and gravel (industrial), stone (crushed). **Commercial fishing:** $55.2 mil. **Chief ports:** Pascagoula, Vicksburg, Gulfport, Biloxi, Greenville. **Gross state product:** $146.4 bil. **Sales tax:** 7.0%. **Gasoline tax:** 36.80 cents/gal. **Employment distrib.:** 20.2% govt.; 20.7% trade/trans./util.; 12.2% mfg.; 13.1% ed./health; 9.8% prof./bus. serv.; 11.5% leisure/hosp.; 3.8% finance; 4.7% constr./mining/log.; 0.8% info.; 3.3% other serv. **Unemployment:** 3.2%. **Min. wage/hr.:** none. **Per cap. pers. income:** $48,110. **New private housing:** 7,700 units/$1.5 bil. **Broadband internet:** 90.2%. **Commercial banks:** 82; deposits: $76.1 bil. **Savings institutions:** 4; deposits: $443.0 mil. **Lottery:** total sales: $467.7 mil; profit: $122.4 mil.

Federal govt. Fed. civ. employees: 19,459; **avg. salary:** $88,126. **Notable fed. facilities:** Keesler AFB; NAS Meridian; Columbus AFB; NASA Stennis Space Ctr.; Army Corps of Eng. Waterways Experiment Sta., Vicksburg; Naval Constr. Battalion Ctr., Gulfport.

Education. High school grad. rate: 88.9%. **4-yr. public coll./univ.:** 8; **2-yr. public:** 15; **4-yr. private:** 9.

Energy. Electricity use/cost: 1,186 kWh, $147.25.

State data. Motto: Virtute et Armis (By valor and arms). **Flower:** Magnolia. **Bird:** Northern mockingbird. **Tree:** Magnolia. **Song:** "Go, Mississippi!" **Entered union:** Dec. 10, 1817; rank: 20th.

Tourism. Tourist spending: $6.3 bil (2022); change, 2019-22: –11.4%. **Attractions:** Vicksburg Natl. Military Park and Cemetery; Natchez Trace Parkway; antebellum home tours in Natchez and other cities; Tupelo Natl. Battlefield, Elvis Presley Birthplace, in Tupelo; Smith Robertson Museum and Cultural Ctr., Mynelle Gardens, Eudora Welty House, in Jackson; Mardi Gras parades on Gulf Coast; Beauvoir (Jefferson Davis Home and Presidential Library), Biloxi; Gulf Islands Natl. Seashore; Delta Blues Museum, Clarksdale. **Information:** Mississippi Division of Tourism, P.O. Box 849, Jackson, MS 39205; 1-866-SEE-MISS; www.visitmississippi.org

History. Choctaw, Chickasaw, and Natchez peoples were living in the region at the time of European contact. The Spaniard Hernando de Soto explored the area, 1540-41. René-Robert Cavelier, sieur de La Salle, claimed the entire Mississippi R. Valley for France, 1682. The first settlement was the French Ft. Maurepas, 1699, on Biloxi Bay. The region was ceded to Britain, 1763, and claimed by Spain, 1779-98, then became a U.S. territory, 1798, and a state, 1817. Slavery spread along with cotton plantations dependent on forced Black labor. By 1860, enslaved Black laborers made up 55% of the population. Mississippi seceded, 1861. In the Civil War, Union forces captured Vicksburg, 1863, and caused extensive damage elsewhere. Mississippi reentered the Union, 1870. For the next 100 years, resistance to desegregation and violence against the Black population made the state a battleground for the civil rights movement. Hurricanes Camille, 1969, and Katrina, 2005, caused substantial damage to the Gulf Coast. Since the early 1990s, casino gambling has boosted the economy, but the state's poverty rate remained the highest in the nation. Legislation retiring the state flag, which featured a Confederate battle flag emblem, was signed into law June 30, 2020. In its consideration of a Mississippi law banning abortion after 15 weeks, the U.S. Supreme Court on June 24, 2022, more broadly overturned the landmark 1973 decision in Roe v. Wade that established a constitutional right to an abortion. Floods shut down water treatment plants in Jackson, Aug. 2022, causing a major crisis. Six white officers were sentenced Apr. 10, 2024, to 15-45 years in prison for torturing two Black men outside of Jackson.

Famous Mississippians. Margaret Walker Alexander, Dana Andrews, Jimmy Buffett, Bo Diddley, Medgar Evers, William Faulkner, Brett Favre, Shelby Foote, Morgan Freeman, John Grisham, Fannie Lou Hamer, Jim Henson, Faith Hill, John Lee Hooker, Robert Johnson, James Earl Jones, B. B. King, L. Q. C. Lamar, Trent Lott, Gerald McRaney, Willie Morris, Walter Payton, Elvis Presley, Leontyne Price, Charley Pride, LeAnn Rimes, Robin Roberts, Muddy Waters, Eudora Welty, Tennessee Williams, Oprah Winfrey, Johnny Winter, Richard Wright, Tammy Wynette.

Website. www.ms.gov

Missouri (MO)

Show Me State

People. Population: 6,196,156; rank: 18. **Pop. change** (2020-23): 0.7%. **Pop. density:** 90 per sq mi. **Racial distribution:** 82.4% white; 11.7% Black; 2.3% Asian; 0.6% Amer. Ind.; 0.2% Hawaiian/Pacific Islander; 2 or more races, 2.7%. **Hispanic pop.:** 5.3%.

Geography. Total area: 69,688 sq mi; rank: 21. **Land area:** 68,727 sq mi; rank: 18. **Acres forested:** 15.4 mil. **Location:** West North Central state near the geographic center of the conterminous U.S.; bordered on the E by Mississippi R., on the NW by Missouri R. **Climate:** continental, susceptible to cold Canadian air; moist, warm Gulf air; and drier SW air. **Topography:** rolling hills, open, fertile plains, and well-watered prairie N of the Missouri R.; S of the river, land is rough and hilly with deep, narrow valleys; alluvial plain in the SE; low elevation in the W. **Capital:** Jefferson City. **Chief airports:** St. Louis, Kansas City, Springfield.

Economy. Chief industries: agriculture, manufacturing, aerospace, tourism. **Chief manuf. goods:** motor vehicles and parts, aerospace, pharmaceuticals, plastics, soap, animal slaughtering and processing, printing. **Chief crops:** soybeans, corn, hay, cotton and cottonseed, wheat, rice, sorghum. **Farm income:** Crops: $8.76 bil. Livestock: $6.15 bil. **Nonfuel minerals:** $3.2 bil; cement, lead, lime, sand and gravel (industrial), stone (crushed). **Gross state product:** $422.3 bil. **Sales tax:** 4.225%. **Gasoline tax:** 43.37 cents/gal. **Employment distrib.:** 14.7% govt.; 18.5% trade/trans./util.; 9.5% mfg.; 17.4% ed./health; 12.5% prof./bus. serv.; 10.6% leisure/hosp.; 6.1% finance; 5.1% constr./mining/log.; 1.6% info.; 3.9% other serv. **Unemployment:** 3.0%. **Min. wage/hr.:** $12.30. **Per cap. pers. income:** $61,302. **New private housing:** 16,781 units/$4.3 bil. **Broadband internet:** 94.1%. **Commercial banks:** 257; deposits: $247.2 bil. **Savings institutions:** 8; deposits: $2.7 bil. **Lottery:** total sales: $1.8 bil; profit: $396.9 mil.

Federal govt. Fed. civ. employees: 37,260; **avg. salary:** $89,173. **Notable fed. facilities:** Federal Reserve Bank of St. Louis; Ft. Leonard Wood; Jefferson Barracks Natl. Cemetery; Natl. Personnel Records Ctr., St. Louis; Whiteman AFB.

Education. High school grad. rate: 89.8%. **4-yr. public coll./univ.:** 13; **2-yr. public:** 14; **4-yr. private:** 49.

Energy. Electricity use/cost: 1,077 kWh, $126.46.

State data. Motto: Salus Populi Suprema Lex Esto (Let the welfare of the people be the supreme law). **Flower:** Hawthorn. **Bird:** Eastern bluebird. **Tree:** Flowering dogwood. **Song:** "Missouri Waltz." **Entered union:** Aug. 10, 1821; rank: 24th.

Tourism. Tourist spending: $14.6 bil (2022); change, 2019-22: –11.2%. **Attractions:** Silver Dollar City, Branson; Mark Twain Boyhood Home and Museum, Hannibal; Pony Express Natl. Museum, St. Joseph; Harry S. Truman Library and Museum, Independence; Gateway Arch Natl. Park, Ulysses S. Grant Natl. Historic Site, St. Louis Zoo, in St. Louis; Worlds of Fun amusement park, Kansas City; Lake of the Ozarks; Ozark Natl. Scenic Riverways; Natl. Churchill Museum, Fulton; State Capitol, Jefferson City; Wilson's Creek Natl. Battlefield; George Washington Carver Natl. Monument, Diamond; Bass Pro Shops Outdoor World, Springfield. **Information:** Missouri Division of Tourism, P.O. Box 1055, Jefferson City, MO 65102; 1-800-519-2100; www.visitmo.com

History. In the 17th cent., when French explorers arrived, Algonquian-speaking Sauk, Fox, and Illinois, as well as Siouan-speaking Osage, Missouri, Iowa, and Kansa peoples, were living in the region; few remained by the 1830s. French hunters and lead miners made the first settlement, c. 1735, at Ste. Genevieve. The territory was ceded to Spain by the French, 1762, then returned to France, 1800, and acquired by the U.S. in the Louisiana Purchase, 1803. Powerful earthquakes rocked New Madrid, 1811-12. Missouri became a territory, 1812, and entered the Union as a slave state, 1821. St. Louis became the gateway for pioneers heading west. Though Missouri stayed with the Union, pro- and antislavery forces battled there during the Civil War. In the late 19th cent., railroad building and the cattle trade made Kansas City a boomtown. The most notable Missourian of the 20th cent., Harry S. Truman, was U.S. president, 1945-53. The state, a political bellwether, voted for the winner in every presidential election from 1960 to 2004. In May 2011, a tornado in Joplin killed about 162. The police-shooting death of Michael Brown in Ferguson in Aug. 2014 touched off major protests that spread nationwide and revived debate over the relationship between law enforcement officers and the communities they serve. With the state legislature considering impeachment, Gov. Eric Greitens resigned his office June 1, 2018, four months after he was indicted on felony charges related to an extramarital affair. More than 200 flood incidents occurred in Mar. 2019; additional flooding affected the NE that June and the NW in July.

Famous Missourians. Maya Angelou, Robert Altman, John Ashcroft, Burt Bacharach, Josephine Baker, Scott Bakula, Thomas Hart Benton, Yogi Berra, Chuck Berry, George Caleb Bingham, Daniel Boone, Omar Bradley, William S. Burroughs, Kate Capshaw, Dale Carnegie, George Washington Carver, Bob Costas, Walter Cronkite, Sheryl Crow, Walt Disney, T. S. Eliot, Richard "Dick" Gephardt, John Goodman, Betty Grable, Jon Hamm, Edwin Hubble, Jesse James, Rush Limbaugh, Marianne Moore, Reinhold Niebuhr, J. C. Penney, John J. Pershing, Brad Pitt, Joseph Pulitzer, Ginger Rogers, Bess Truman, Harry S. Truman, Kathleen Turner, Tina Turner, Mark Twain, Dick Van Dyke, Tennessee Williams, Lanford Wilson, Shelley Winters, Jane Wyman.

Website. www.mo.gov

Montana (MT)

Treasure State

People. Population: 1,132,812; rank: 43. **Pop. change** (2020-23): 4.5%. **Pop. density:** 8 per sq mi. **Racial distribution:** 88.7% white; 0.6% Black; 1.1% Asian; 6.4% Amer. Ind.; 0.1% Hawaiian/Pacific Islander; 2 or more races, 3.1%. **Hispanic pop.:** 4.7%.

Geography. Total area: 147,003 sq mi; rank: 4. **Land area:** 145,509 sq mi; rank: 4. **Acres forested:** 26.3 mil. **Location:** Mountain state bounded on the E by the Dakotas, on the S by Wyoming, on the W and SW by Idaho, on the N by Canada. **Climate:** colder, continental with low humidity. **Topography:** Rocky Mts. in western third of state; eastern two-thirds gently rolling northern Great Plains. **Capital:** Helena. **Chief airport:** Bozeman.

Economy. Chief industries: agriculture, timber, mining, tourism, oil and gas. **Chief manuf. goods:** sawmills, softwood veneer and plywood, petroleum. **Chief crops:** wheat, barley, hay, sugar beets, potatoes, dry beans, flaxseed, cherries, corn, oats. **Farm income:** Crops: $2.61 bil. Livestock: $1.97 bil. **Nonfuel minerals:** $1.3 bil; copper, molybdenum mineral concentrates, palladium, platinum, sand and gravel (construction). **Gross state product:** $70.6 bil. **Sales tax:** none. **Gasoline tax:** 52.15 cents/gal. **Employment distrib.:** 18.1% govt.; 19.2% trade/trans./util.; 4.1% mfg.; 16.3% ed./health; 9.8% prof./bus. serv.; 13.6% leisure/hosp.; 5.3% finance; 8.6% constr./mining/log.; 1.0% info.; 3.8% other serv. **Unemployment:** 2.9%. **Min. wage/hr.:** $10.30. **Per cap. pers. income:** $63,918. **New private housing:** 4,307 units/$1.0 bil. **Broadband internet:** 93.7%. **Commercial banks:** 46; deposits: $35.5 bil. **Savings institutions:** 3; deposits: $116.0 mil. **Lottery:** total sales: $96.9 mil; profit: $24.7 mil.

Federal govt. Fed. civ. employees: 9,852; **avg. salary:** $88,819. **Notable fed. facilities:** Malmstrom AFB and missile silos; Ft. Peck, Hungry Horse, Libby, Yellowtail, and other dams.

Education. High school grad. rate: 85.8%. **4-yr. public coll./univ.:** 9; **2-yr. public:** 9; **4-yr. private:** 4.

Energy. Electricity use/cost: 908 kWh, $102.94.

State data. Motto: Oro y Plata (Gold and silver). **Flower:** Bitterroot. **Bird:** Western meadowlark. **Tree:** Ponderosa pine. **Song:** "Montana." **Entered union:** Nov. 8, 1889; rank: 41st.

Tourism. Tourist spending: $5.9 bil (2022); change, 2019-22: 11.5%. **Attractions:** Glacier and Yellowstone Natl. Parks; Museum of the Rockies, Bozeman; Museum of the Plains Indian, Blackfeet Reservation, in Browning; Custer Natl. Cemetery at Little Bighorn Battlefield Natl. Monument; Lewis and Clark Caverns State Park, Whitehall; Lewis and Clark Natl. Historic Trail Interpretive Ctr., Great Falls. **Information:** Montana Office of Tourism, Dept. of Commerce, 301 S. Park Ave., P.O. Box 200533, Helena, MT 59620; 1-800-VISITMT; www.visitmt.com

History. Paleo-Indian hunters reached the area over 12,000 years ago. Cheyenne, Blackfoot, Crow, Assiniboin, Salish (Flatheads), Kootenai, and Kalispel peoples lived in the region before Europeans arrived. French explorers visited the region, 1742. The U.S. acquired the area partly through the Louisiana Purchase, 1803, partly through the Lewis and Clark Expedition, 1804-06. Fur traders and missionaries established posts in the early 19th cent. Gold was discovered on Grasshopper Creek, 1862, and Montana Territory was established, 1864. Indian uprisings reached their peak with the defeat of Gen. George Custer at the Battle of Little Bighorn, 1876. Chief Joseph and the Nez Percé tribe surrendered in Montana, 1877, after being driven from their lands in Oregon. Mining activity and the coming of the Northern Pacific Railway, 1883, brought population growth. Montana became a state, 1889. Copper wealth from the Butte pits resulted in the turn of the century "War of Copper Kings" as feuding factions contended for "the richest hill on earth." During the first half of the 20th cent., the Anaconda Copper firm wielded enormous political influence. Jeannette Rankin, a suffragist and pacifist, was the first woman elected to Congress, 1916. Mike Mansfield served 34 years in Congress and was Senate Democratic leader, 1961-77. An 18-year hunt for notorious "Unabomber" Theodore Kaczynski ended with his arrest, 1996, at his cabin near Lincoln. Ryan Zinke became the first Montanan in the president's cabinet since statehood when he served as interior secretary, 2017-18. Gov. Greg Gianforte (R) signed a bill May 17, 2023, banning Chinese-owned app TikTok over privacy concerns (judge blocked law from taking effect, Nov. 2023).

Famous Montanans. Dana Carvey, Gary Cooper, Marcus Daly, Chet Huntley, Phil Jackson, Will James, Myrna Loy, David Lynch, Mike Mansfield, Brent Musburger, Jeannette Rankin, Charles M. Russell, Lester Thurow.

Website. www.mt.gov

Nebraska (NE)

Cornhusker State

People. Population: 1,978,379; rank: 37. **Pop. change** (2020-23): 0.8%. **Pop. density:** 26 per sq mi. **Racial distribution:** 87.3% white; 5.5% Black; 2.8% Asian; 1.7% Amer. Ind.; 0.1% Hawaiian/Pacific Islander; 2 or more races, 2.6%. **Hispanic pop.:** 12.9%.

Geography. Total area: 77,327 sq mi; rank: 16. **Land area:** 76,796 sq mi; rank: 15. **Acres forested:** 1.5 mil. **Location:** West North Central state with the Missouri R. for a border on NE and E. **Climate:** continental semiarid. **Topography:** till plains of the central lowland in the eastern third rises to the Great Plains and hill country of the N central and NW. **Capital:** Lincoln. **Chief airport:** Omaha.

Economy. Chief industries: agriculture, manufacturing. **Chief manuf. goods:** animal slaughtering, grain and oilseed, farm machinery, medical equip., motor vehicle parts, printing, structural metals. **Chief crops:** corn, sorghum, soybeans, hay, wheat, dry beans, oats, potatoes, sugar beets. **Farm income:** Crops: $16.06 bil. Livestock: $15.56 bil. **Nonfuel minerals:** $260 mil; cement (portland), lime, sand and gravel (construction), sand and gravel (industrial), stone (crushed). **Gross state product:** $178.4 bil. **Sales tax:** 5.5%. **Gasoline tax:** 48.40 cents/gal. **Employment distrib.:** 16.7% govt.; 18.9% trade/trans./util.; 10.1% mfg.; 15.7% ed./health; 11.9% prof./bus. serv.; 9.2% leisure/hosp.; 6.5% finance; 5.8% constr./mining/log.; 1.7% info.; 3.5% other serv. **Unemployment:** 2.3%. **Min. wage/hr.:** $12.00. **Per cap. pers. income:** $67,800. **New private housing:** 8,877 units/$1.7 bil. **Broadband internet:** 95.8%. **Commercial banks:** 162; deposits: $86.1 bil. **Savings institutions:** 7; deposits: $764.0 mil. **Lottery:** total sales: $220.1 mil; profit: $55.8 mil.

Federal govt. Fed. civ. employees: 10,269; **avg. salary:** $95,076. **Notable fed. facilities:** Offutt AFB.

Education. High school grad. rate: 87.1%. **4-yr. public coll./univ.:** 7; **2-yr. public:** 9; **4-yr. private:** 14.

Energy. Electricity use/cost: 1,043 kWh, $112.57.

State data. Motto: Equality before the law. **Flower:** Giant goldenrod. **Bird:** Western meadowlark. **Tree:** Cottonwood. **Song:** "Beautiful Nebraska." **Entered union:** Mar. 1, 1867; rank: 37th.

Tourism. Tourist spending: $6.1 bil (2022); change, 2019-22: 3.5%. **Attractions:** Univ. of Nebraska State Museum at Morrill Hall, Nebraska State Capitol, in Lincoln; Stuhr Museum of the Prairie Pioneer, Grand Island; Boys Town; Omaha's Henry Doorly Zoo and Aquarium, Joslyn Art Museum, The Durham Museum, in Omaha; Ashfall Fossil Beds State Hist. Park, near Royal; Strategic Air and Space Museum, Ashland; Arbor Lodge State Historical Park, Nebraska City; Buffalo Bill Ranch State Historical Park, North Platte; Pioneer Village, Minden; Oregon Trail landmarks, incl. at Scotts Bluff Natl. Monument and Chimney Rock Natl. Historic Site; Great Platte River Road Archway, Museum of Nebraska Art, in Kearney. **Information:** Nebraska Tourism Commission, 301 Centennial Mall S., P.O. Box 98907, Lincoln, NE 68509-8907; 1-888-444-1867; www.visitnebraska.com

History. When Europeans arrived, Pawnee, Ponca, Omaha, and Oto peoples lived in the region. Spanish and French explorers and fur traders visited the area prior to its acquisition in the Louisiana Purchase, 1803. Meriwether Lewis and William Clark passed through, 1804-06. The first permanent settlement was Bellevue, near Omaha, 1823. The 1834 Indian Intercourse Act declared Nebraska Indian country and excluded white settlement, but conflicts with settlers eventually forced Native Americans to move to reservations. Nebraska became a territory, 1854, and a state, 1867. Many Civil War veterans settled under free land terms of the 1862 Homestead Act; as agriculture grew, struggles followed between homesteaders and ranchers. Since the mid-1930s, Nebraska has been the only state with a unicameral legislature. A leader in agribusiness, Nebraska has also become a major telemarketing center. Investor Warren Buffett, one of the world's wealthiest men, said in 2006 he would give most of his then-$44-bil fortune to charity. Historic flooding from a so-called "bomb cyclone" Mar. 13-15, 2019, caused nearly $1.4 bil in damage.

Famous Nebraskans. Grover Cleveland Alexander, Fred Astaire, Marlon Brando, Charles W. Bryan, William Jennings Bryan, Warren Buffett, Johnny Carson, Willa Cather, Dick Cavett, Dick Cheney, Loren Eiseley, Father Edward J. Flanagan, Henry Fonda, Bob Gibson, Rollin Kirby, Harold Lloyd, Malcolm X, J. Sterling Morton, John G. Neihardt, Nick Nolte, George W. Norris, Tom Osborne, Roscoe Pound, Red Cloud, Mari Sandoz, Robert Taylor, Darryl F. Zanuck.

Website. www.nebraska.gov

Nevada (NV)

Sagebrush State, Battle Born State, Silver State

People. Population: 3,194,176; rank: 32. **Pop. change** (2020-23): 2.9%. **Pop. density:** 29 per sq mi. **Racial distribution:** 71.5% white; 11.0% Black; 9.7% Asian; 1.7% Amer. Ind.; 0.9% Hawaiian/Pacific Islander; 2 or more races, 5.2%. **Hispanic pop.:** 29.9%.

Geography. Total area: 110,541 sq mi; rank: 7. **Land area:** 109,831 sq mi; rank: 7. **Acres forested:** 10.6 mil. **Location:** Mountain state bordered on N by Oregon and Idaho, on E by Utah, on SE by Arizona, and on SW and W by California. **Climate:** semiarid and arid. **Topography:** rugged N-S mountain ranges; highest elevation, Boundary Peak, 13,146 ft; southern area is within the Mojave Desert; lowest elevation, Colorado R., at southern tip of state, 479 ft. **Capital:** Carson City. **Chief airports:** Las Vegas, Reno.

Economy. Chief industries: gaming, tourism, mining, manufacturing, government, retailing, warehousing, trucking. **Chief manuf. goods:** gaming machines, cement and concrete, plastics, printing, architectural and structural metals, electricity instruments. **Chief crops:** hay, onions, potatoes, alfalfa, wheat, garlic, mint, barley. **Farm income:** Crops: $322.29 mil. Livestock: $636.40 mil. **Nonfuel minerals:** $8.9 bil; copper, gold, lime, sand and gravel (construction), stone (crushed). **Gross state product:** $239.4 bil. **Sales tax:** 6.85%. **Gasoline tax:** 42.21 cents/gal. **Employment distrib.:** 11.8% govt.; 19.0% trade/trans./util.; 4.4% mfg.; 10.7% ed./health; 13.7% prof./bus. serv.; 22.8% leisure/hosp.; 4.9% finance; 8.8% constr./mining/log.; 1.2% info.; 2.8% other serv. **Unemployment:** 5.1%. **Min. wage/hr.:** $12.00. **Per cap. pers. income:** $65,168. **New private housing:** 18,451 units/$4.7 bil. **Broadband internet:** 97.0%. **Commercial banks:** 42; deposits: $114.9 bil. **Savings institutions:** 7; deposits: $2.6 bil.

Federal govt. Fed. civ. employees: 13,629; **avg. salary:** $98,105. **Notable fed. facilities:** Nevada Natl. Security Site; Hawthorne Army Depot; Creech AFB; Nellis AFB; NAS Fallon; Natl. Wild Horse & Burro Ctr. at Palomino Valley.

Education. High school grad. rate: 81.7%. **4-yr. public coll./univ.:** 7; **2-yr. public:** 0; **4-yr. private:** 3.

Energy. Electricity use/cost: 939 kWh, $129.35.

State data. Motto: All for our country. **Flower:** Sagebrush. **Bird:** Mountain bluebird. **Trees:** Single-leaf piñon and bristlecone pine. **Song:** "Home Means Nevada." **Entered union:** Oct. 31, 1864; rank: 36th.

Tourism. Tourist spending: $53.1 bil (2022); change, 2019-22: 15.9%. **Attractions:** Legalized gambling, incl. at Lake Tahoe, Reno, Las Vegas, Laughlin, and Elko; Hoover Dam, Lake Mead Natl. Recreation Area, near Boulder City; Great Basin Natl. Park; Valley of Fire State Park; Red Rock Canyon Natl. Conservation Area; Las Vegas Strip, Fremont St., Natl. Atomic Testing Museum, Pinball Hall of Fame, Las Vegas Motor Speedway, in Las Vegas; Natl. Automobile Museum, Reno. **Information:** Travel Nevada, 401 N. Carson St., Carson City, NV 89701; 1-800-NEVADA-8; www.travelnevada.com

History. Shoshone, Paiute, Bannock, and Washoe peoples lived in the area at the time of European contact. Nevada was first explored by Spaniards, 1776. In the 1820s, fur traders Peter Skene Ogden, a Canadian, and Jedediah Smith separately explored the area. It was acquired by the U.S., 1848, at the end of the Mexican War. A trading post at Mormon Station, now Genoa, was established, 1850. Discovery of the Comstock Lode, rich in gold and silver, 1859, spurred a population boom. Nevada became a territory, 1861, and a state, 1864. Hoover Dam was built, 1931-36. With gambling legal since 1931, a surge in resort casino construction after World War II turned Las Vegas into one of the nation's most popular tourist destinations. An influx of both native and foreign-born Hispanics and Asians, attracted by the thriving service and construction industries, helped make Nevada the fastest-growing state in the U.S. in 1990-2005. The 2007-09 recession had an equally powerful effect, with high unemployment and foreclosures. In the deadliest mass shooting in modern U.S. history, a gunman killed 58 when he fired indiscriminately from his 32nd floor Las Vegas hotel suite on an outdoor country music festival in Oct. 2017.

Famous Nevadans. Andre Agassi, Kurt Busch, Kyle Busch, Walter Van Tilburg Clark, George W. G. Ferris, Sarah Winnemucca Hopkins, Paul Laxalt, Dat So La Lee, John William Mackay, Anne Henrietta Martin, Pat McCarran, Key Pittman, William Morris Stewart.

Website. www.nv.gov

New Hampshire (NH)

Granite State

People. Population: 1,402,054; rank: 41. **Pop. change** (2020-23): 1.8%. **Pop. density:** 157 per sq mi. **Racial distribution:** 92.5% white; 2.1% Black; 3.1% Asian; 0.3% Amer. Ind.; 0.1% Hawaiian/Pacific Islander; 2 or more races, 1.9%. **Hispanic pop.:** 4.8%.

Geography. Total area: 9,347 sq mi; rank: 46. **Land area:** 8,951 sq mi; rank: 44. **Acres forested:** 4.7 mil. **Location:** New England state bounded on S by Massachusetts, on W by Vermont, on N by Canada, on E by Maine and the Atlantic Ocean. **Climate:** highly varied, due to its nearness to high mountains and ocean. **Topography:** low, rolling coast followed by countless hills and mountains rising out of a central plateau. **Capital:** Concord. **Chief airport:** Manchester.

Economy. Chief industries: tourism, manufacturing, agriculture, trade, mining. **Chief manuf. goods:** navigational instruments, circuit boards, electrical equip., fabricated metal, machinery, medical equip., plastics. **Chief crops:** greenhouse and nursery, apples, sweet corn, hay, Christmas trees, berries, maple syrup. **Farm income:** Crops: $103.06 mil. Livestock: $163.46 mil. **Nonfuel minerals:** $203 mil; sand and gravel (construction), stone (crushed), stone (dimension). **Commercial fishing:** $37.3 mil. **Chief port:** Portsmouth. **Gross state product:** $111.1 bil. **Sales tax:** none. **Gasoline tax:** 42.23 cents/gal. **Employment distrib.:** 12.9% govt.; 19.7% trade/trans./util.; 9.9% mfg.; 19.1% ed./health; 14.2% prof./bus. serv.; 9.7% leisure/hosp.; 4.8% finance; 4.6% constr./mining/log.; 1.6% info.; 3.5% other serv. **Unemployment:** 2.2%. **Min. wage/hr.:** $7.25. **Per cap. pers. income:** $77,260. **New private housing:** 4,555 units/$1.4 bil. **Broadband internet:** 94.8%. **Commercial banks:** 18; deposits: $36.0 bil. **Savings institutions:** 25; deposits: $11.9 bil. **Lottery:** total sales: $628.9 mil; profit: $189.5 mil.

Federal govt. Fed. civ. employees: 4,972; **avg. salary:** $113,179. **Notable fed. facilities:** Army Cold Regions Res. and Engineering Lab, Hanover.

Education. High school grad. rate: 87.7%. **4-yr. public coll./univ.:** 6; **2-yr. public:** 7; **4-yr. private:** 10.

Energy. Electricity use/cost: 623 kWh, $158.67.

State data. Motto: Live free or die. **Flower:** Purple lilac. **Bird:** Purple finch. **Tree:** White birch. **Song:** "Old New Hampshire." **Ninth** of original 13 states to ratify the Constitution, June 21, 1788.

Tourism. Tourist spending: $4.0 bil (2022); change, 2019-22: –14.0%. **Attractions:** Mt. Washington Cog Railway, Mt. Washington (highest peak in Northeast); Lake Winnipesaukee; Crawford, Franconia, Pinkham Notches (mountain passes), Flume Gorge, Cannon Mountain Aerial Tramway, in White Mountains region; Strawbery Banke Museum, Portsmouth; Canterbury Shaker Village; Saint-Gaudens Natl. Historical Park, Cornish; Mt. Monadnock; Santa's Village, Jefferson. **Information:** Dept. of Business and Econ. Affairs, Division of Travel & Tourism Development, 100 N. Main St., Ste. 100, Concord, NH 03301; 1-800-FUN-IN-NH; www.visitnh.gov

History. The area has been inhabited for about 10,000 years. Algonquian-speaking peoples, including the Pennacook, lived in the region when the Europeans arrived. The first explorers to visit the area were England's Martin Pring, 1603, and France's Samuel de Champlain, 1605. The first settlement was Odiorne's Point (now port of Rye), 1623. Before the American Revolution, New Hampshire residents raided a

British fort at Portsmouth, 1774, and drove the royal governor out, 1775. New Hampshire became the first colony to adopt its own constitution, 1776. After statehood, 1788, New Hampshire became a textile manufacturing center. The mill towns declined in the first half of the 20th cent., but tourism and technology industries, lured by low taxes, have revived the economy since the 1960s. A state law requires it to hold the first primary of the presidential campaign season.

Famous New Hampshirites. Dan Brown, Salmon P. Chase, Ralph Adams Cram, Mary Baker Eddy, Daniel Chester French, Robert Frost, Horace Greeley, Sarah Josepha Buell Hale, John Irving, Seth Meyers, Bode Miller, Franklin Pierce, Augustus Saint-Gaudens, Adam Sandler, Alan B. Shepard Jr., Sarah Silverman, David H. Souter, Daniel Webster.

Website. www.nh.gov

New Jersey (NJ)

Garden State

People. Population: 9,290,841; rank: 11. **Pop. change** (2020-23): 0.0%. **Pop. density:** 1,264 per sq mi. **Racial distribution:** 70.4% white; 15.5% Black; 10.6% Asian; 0.8% Amer. Ind.; 0.1% Hawaiian/Pacific Islander; 2 or more races, 2.5%. **Hispanic pop.:** 22.7%.

Geography. Total area: 8,721 sq mi; rank: 47. **Land area:** 7,353 sq mi; rank: 46. **Acres forested:** 2.0 mil. **Location:** Middle Atlantic state bounded on N and E by New York and Atlantic Ocean, on S and W by Delaware and Pennsylvania. **Climate:** moderate, with marked difference between NW and SE extremities. **Topography:** Appalachian Valley in NW also has highest elevation, High Pt., 1,803 ft; Appalachian Highlands, flat-topped NE-SW mountain ranges; Piedmont Plateau, low plains broken by high ridges (Palisades) rising 400-500 ft; Coastal Plain, covering three-fifths of state in SE, rises from sea level to gentle slopes. **Capital:** Trenton. **Chief airport:** Newark.

Economy. Chief industries: pharmaceuticals, telecommunications, biotechnology, printing and publishing. **Chief manuf. goods:** petroleum, pharmaceuticals, toiletries, chemicals, plastics, printing, navigational instruments, medical equip., paper prods. **Chief crops:** greenhouse and nursery, blueberries, peaches, corn, hay, tomatoes, bell peppers, cranberries, soybeans, apples. **Farm income:** Crops: $1.28 bil. Livestock: $201.00 mil. **Nonfuel minerals:** $515 mil; sand and gravel (construction), sand and gravel (industrial), stone (crushed). **Commercial fishing:** $141.9 mil. **Chief ports:** Newark-Elizabeth, Camden. **Gross state product:** $799.3 bil. **Sales tax:** 6.625%. **Gasoline tax:** 60.75 cents/gal. **Employment distrib.:** 14.1% govt.; 20.8% trade/trans./util.; 5.8% mfg.; 18.0% ed./health; 16.5% prof./bus. serv.; 8.9% leisure/hosp.; 6.1% finance; 3.9% constr./mining/log.; 1.7% info.; 4.0% other serv. **Unemployment:** 4.4%. **Min. wage/hr.:** $15.13. **Per cap. pers. income:** $80,724. **New private housing:** 32,840 units/$5.2 bil. **Broadband internet:** 98.4%. **Commercial banks:** 75; deposits: $401.9 bil. **Savings institutions:** 36; deposits: $43.2 bil. **Lottery:** total sales: $3.7 bil; profit: $1.2 bil.

Federal govt. Fed. civ. employees: 22,353; **avg. salary:** $119,158. **Notable fed. facilities:** Joint Base McGuire-Dix-Lakehurst; Picatinny Arsenal; FAA William J. Hughes Technical Ctr.

Education. High school grad. rate: 85.2%. **4-yr. public coll./univ.:** 13; **2-yr. public:** 19; **4-yr. private:** 36.

Energy. Electricity use/cost: 682 kWh, $114.08.

State data. Motto: Liberty and prosperity. **Flower:** Purple violet. **Bird:** Eastern goldfinch. **Tree:** Red oak. **Third** of the original 13 states to ratify the Constitution, Dec. 18, 1787.

Tourism. Tourist spending: $25.9 bil (2022); change, 2019-22: –2.4%. **Attractions:** 130 mi of beaches, boardwalks on the Jersey Shore at Atlantic City (with gambling), Seaside Heights, Ocean City, Wildwood; Grover Cleveland Birthplace, Caldwell; Cape May Historic District; Thomas Edison Natl. Historical Park, West Orange; Six Flags Great Adventure, Jackson; Liberty State Park, Liberty Science Ctr., in Jersey City; Pine Barrens wilderness; Princeton Univ., Princeton Battlefield State Park, in Princeton; Morristown Natl. Historical Park; Adventure Aquarium, Battleship *New Jersey*, Walt Whitman House, in Camden. **Information:** Dept. of State, Division of Travel and Tourism, P.O. Box 460, Trenton, NJ 08625; 1-800-VISITNJ; www.visitnj.org

History. The Lenni Lenape (Delaware) peoples lived in the region and had mostly peaceful relations with European colonists, who arrived after the explorers Giovanni da Verrazzano, 1524, and Henry Hudson, 1609. The first permanent European settlement was Dutch, at Bergen (now Jersey City), 1660. When the British took New Netherland, 1664, the area between the Delaware and Hudson Rivers was given to Lord John Berkeley and Sir George Carteret. During the American Revolution, New Jersey was the scene of many major battles, including Trenton, 1776; Princeton, 1777; and Monmouth, 1778. New Jersey was the third state to ratify the Constitution, 1787, and the first to approve the Bill of Rights, 1789. In a duel at Weehawken, 1804, Vice Pres. Aaron Burr fatally shot former Treasury Sec. Alexander Hamilton. Canal and railroad building stimulated the growth of cities and industries in the 19th cent. The 20th-cent. arrival of large numbers of African Americans, Italians, Irish, European Jews, Puerto Ricans, South Asians, and other groups made New Jersey one of the most diverse states in the U.S. Construction of resort casinos in Atlantic City from the late 1970s revitalized tourism. Gov. James McGreevey resigned, 2004, after acknowledging an extramarital affair with a man identified as his former homeland security adviser. An estimated 37 people in New Jersey were killed when Hurricane Sandy (by then downgraded to a tropical storm) made landfall in 2012. Two members of Gov. Chris Christie's administration were convicted in 2016 on federal charges related to allegations that officials had created traffic jams to punish a political opponent. Three-term U.S. Sen. Bob Menendez (D) was found guilty July 16, 2024, of 16 criminal charges stemming from a bribery scheme.

Famous New Jerseyans. Buzz Aldrin, Jason Alexander, Samuel Alito, Count Basie, Judy Blume, Jon Bon Jovi, Bill Bradley, Aaron Burr, Grover Cleveland, Stephen Crane, Danny DeVito, Thomas Edison, Albert Einstein, James Gandolfini, Allen Ginsberg, Alexander Hamilton, Ed Harris, Whitney Houston, Joyce Kilmer, Jack Nicholson, Shaquille O'Neal, Thomas Paine, Bill Parcells, Dorothy Parker, Joe Pesci, Molly Pitcher, Paul Robeson, Philip Roth, Antonin Scalia, Wally Schirra, H. Norman Schwarzkopf, Frank Sinatra, Bruce Springsteen, Martha Stewart, Meryl Streep, Dave Thomas, John Travolta, Walt Whitman, William Carlos Williams, Woodrow Wilson.

Website. www.nj.gov

New Mexico (NM)

Land of Enchantment

People. Population: 2,114,371; rank: 36. **Pop. change** (2020-23): –0.1%. **Pop. density:** 17 per sq mi. **Racial distribution:** 80.7% white; 2.8% Black; 2.0% Asian; 11.4% Amer. Ind.; 0.2% Hawaiian/Pacific Islander; 2 or more races, 2.8%. **Hispanic pop.:** 48.6%.

Geography. Total area: 121,561 sq mi; rank: 5. **Land area:** 121,280 sq mi; rank: 5. **Acres forested:** 24.6 mil. **Location:** southwestern state bounded by Colorado on the N; Oklahoma on NE; Texas on E and S; Mexico on S; Arizona on the W. **Climate:** dry, with temperatures rising or falling 5°F with every 1,000 ft elevation. **Topography:** eastern third, Great Plains; central third, Rocky Mts. (85% of the state is over 4,000-ft elevation); western third, high plateau. **Capital:** Santa Fe. **Chief airport:** Albuquerque.

Economy. Chief industries: government, services, trade. **Chief manuf. goods:** semiconductors, medical equip., navigational/measuring/medical/control instruments, aircraft, chemicals, jewelry. **Chief crops:** hay, pecans, corn, greenhouse and nursery, chiles, onions, cotton, wheat, peanuts. **Farm income:** Crops: $756.08 mil. Livestock: $2.97 bil. **Nonfuel minerals:** $1.5 bil; cement, copper, potash, sand and gravel (construction), stone (crushed). **Gross state product:** $130.2 bil. **Sales tax:** 4.875%%. **Gasoline tax:** 37.28 cents/gal. **Employment distrib.:** 21.8% govt.; 16.3% trade/trans./util.; 3.3% mfg.; 16.6% ed./health; 13.9% prof./bus. serv.; 11.2% leisure/hosp.; 4.1% finance; 8.5% constr./mining/log.; 1.0% info.; 3.2% other serv. **Unemployment:** 3.8%. **Min. wage/hr.:** $12.00. **Per cap. pers. income:** $54,428. **New private housing:** 8,511 units/$2.5 bil. **Broadband internet:** 93.0%. **Commercial banks:** 49; deposits: $42.3 bil. **Savings institutions:** 6; deposits: $1.5 bil. **Lottery:** total sales: $168.5 mil; profit: $50.6 mil.

Federal govt. Fed. civ. employees: 22,343; **avg. salary:** $93,794. **Notable fed. facilities:** Kirtland, Cannon, Holloman AF Bases; Los Alamos Natl. Lab; White Sands Missile Range; Natl. Solar Observatory, Sunspot; Natl. Radio Astronomy Observatory (Very Large Array), Socorro; Sandia Natl. Labs, Albuquerque.

Education. High school grad. rate (2020-21): 76.6%. **4-yr. public coll./univ.:** 9; **2-yr. public:** 19; **4-yr. private:** 3.

Energy. Electricity use/cost: 659 kWh, $91.21.

State data. Motto: Crescit Eundo (It grows as it goes). **Flower:** Yucca. **Bird:** Roadrunner. **Tree:** Piñon. **Songs:** "O, Fair New Mexico"; "Asi Es Nuevo Mexico." **Entered union:** Jan. 6, 1912; rank: 47th.

Tourism. Tourist spending: $9.2 bil (2022); change, 2019-22: 11.0%. **Attractions:** Carlsbad Caverns Natl. Park (with Lechuguilla Cave, among world's longest caves); Petroglyph Natl. Monument, Sandia Peak Tramway, in Albuquerque; New Mexico History Museum, Museum of Intl. Folk Art, in Santa Fe (oldest U.S. capital); White Sands Natl. Monument (world's largest gypsum dune field); Chaco Culture Natl. Historical Park; Acoma Pueblo, or Sky City, built atop a 367-ft mesa; Taos Art Colony, Taos Ski Valley; Elephant Butte Lake State Park; Shiprock volcanic remnant; Intl. UFO Museum and Research Ctr., Roswell.

Information: New Mexico Tourism Dept., 491 Old Santa Fe Trl., Santa Fe, NM 87501; (505) 795-0343; www.newmexico.org

History. Inhabited for more than 10,000 years, the region was home to Sandia, Clovis, Folsom, Mogollon, and Anasazi cultures, followed by the Pueblo people, Anasazi descendants; later, nomadic Navajo and Apache came. Spanish Franciscan Marcos de Niza and Estevanico, a Moroccan-born enslaved Black man, explored the area, 1539, seeking gold; Coronado followed, 1540. First settlements were near San Juan Pueblo, 1598, and at Santa Fe, 1610. Settlers alternately traded and fought with the Apache, Comanche, and Navajo. Trade on the Santa Fe Trail to Missouri started, 1821. After the Mexican War began, 1846, Gen. Stephen Kearny took Santa Fe without firing a shot, and declared New Mexico part of the U.S. All Hispanic New Mexicans and Pueblo became U.S. citizens by terms of the 1848 treaty ending the war. New Mexico became a territory, 1850, but did not attain statehood until 1912. Mexican revolutionary leader Pancho Villa raided Columbus, 1916, and U.S. troops were sent to the area. The world's first atomic bomb was exploded at a test site near Alamogordo, 1945. An underground nuclear waste depository opened near Carlsbad, 1999. Spaceport America, a state-owned commercial spaceport, hosted Virgin Galactic's first space launches with people aboard in 2021. In Oct. 2021, a fatal shooting of a cinematographer by actor Alec Baldwin on a movie set near Santa Fe drew scrutiny to gun safety practices in the film industry. The combined Calf Canyon/Hermits Peak forest fire burned nearly 350,000 acres by July 2022, becoming the state's largest forest fire.

Famous New Mexicans. Ben Abruzzo, Maxie Anderson, Jeff Bezos, William Bonney (Billy the Kid), Kit Carson, Bob Foster, Neil Patrick Harris, Tony Hillerman, Peter Hurd, Jean Baptiste Lamy, Nancy Lopez, Demi Lovato, Bill Mauldin, Georgia O'Keeffe, Bill Richardson, Kim Stanley, Al Unser, Bobby Unser.

Website. www.nm.gov

New York (NY)

Empire State

People. Population: 19,571,216; rank: 4. **Pop. change** (2020-23): –3.1%. **Pop. density:** 415 per sq mi. **Racial distribution:** 68.5% white; 17.7% Black; 9.7% Asian; 1.1% Amer. Ind.; 0.1% Hawaiian/Pacific Islander; 2 or more races, 2.9%. **Hispanic pop.:** 19.8%.

Geography. Total area: 54,540 sq mi; rank: 27. **Land area:** 47,111 sq mi; rank: 30. **Acres forested:** 18.6 mil. **Location:** Middle Atlantic state bordered by the New England states, Atlantic Ocean on E; New Jersey and Pennsylvania on S; Lakes Ontario and Erie on W; Canada on N. **Climate:** variable; the SE region moderated by the ocean. **Topography:** highest and most rugged mountains in the NE Adirondack upland; St. Lawrence-Champlain lowlands extend from Lake Ontario NE along the Canadian border; Hudson-Mohawk lowland follows rivers N and W, 10-30 mi wide; Atlantic coastal plain in the SE; Appalachian Highlands, covering half the state westward from the Hudson Valley, include the Catskill Mts., Finger Lakes; plateau of Erie-Ontario lowlands. **Capital:** Albany. **Chief airports:** New York (2), Buffalo, Syracuse, Albany, Rochester, White Plains, Islip.

Economy. Chief industries: manufacturing, finance, communications, tourism, transportation, services. **Chief manuf. goods:** pharmaceuticals, photographic chemicals, electronics, automotive parts, toiletries, printing, plastics, apparel. **Chief crops:** greenhouse and nursery, apples, corn, hay, cabbage, onions, soybeans, potatoes, snap beans, grapes, squash, pumpkins, tomatoes, wheat, cucumbers, green peas. **Farm income:** Crops: $2.62 bil. Livestock: $4.94 bil. **Nonfuel minerals:** $1.8 bil; cement, salt, sand and gravel (construction), stone (crushed), zinc. **Commercial fishing:** $38.9 mil. **Chief ports:** New York, Buffalo, Albany. **Gross state product:** $2.2 tril. **Sales tax:** 4.0%. **Gasoline tax:** 44.08 cents/gal. **Employment distrib.:** 15.2% govt.; 14.9% trade/trans./util.; 4.2% mfg.; 23.9% ed./health; 14.2% prof./bus. serv.; 9.4% leisure/hosp.; 7.6% finance; 3.9% constr./mining/log.; 2.8% info.; 4.0% other serv. **Unemployment:** 4.2%. **Min. wage/hr.:** $15.00. **Per cap. pers. income:** $79,581. **New private housing:** 48,807 units/$10.2 bil. **Broadband internet:** 98.4%. **Commercial banks:** 145; deposits: $2.3 tril. **Savings institutions:** 39; deposits: $54.1 bil. **Lottery:** total sales: $10.5 bil; profit: $3.7 bil.

Federal govt. Fed. civ. employees: 53,379; **avg. salary:** $103,572. **Notable fed. facilities:** Ft. Drum; West Point Military Academy; Merchant Marine Academy, Kings Point; NY Fed. Reserve; U.S. Army Watervliet Arsenal; Brookhaven Natl. Lab; U.S. Mission to the United Nations.

Education. High school grad. rate: 86.7%. **4-yr. public coll./univ.:** 43; **2-yr. public:** 36; **4-yr. private:** 167.

Energy. Electricity use/cost: 592 kWh, $130.81.

State data. Motto: Excelsior (Ever upward). **Flower:** Rose. **Bird:** Eastern bluebird. **Tree:** Sugar maple. **Song:** "I Love New York." **Eleventh** of original 13 states to ratify the Constitution, July 26, 1788.

Tourism. Tourist spending: $95.7 bil (2022); change, 2019-22: 6.8%. **Attractions:** New York City; Adirondack and Catskill Mountains; Watkins Glen State Park; Thousand Islands region; Niagara Falls; Saratoga Race Course, Saratoga Springs; Philipsburg Manor, Old Dutch Church of Sleepy Hollow, in Sleepy Hollow; Washington Irving's Sunnyside, Tarrytown; Corning Museum of Glass; Fenimore Art Museum, Natl. Baseball Hall of Fame and Museum, in Cooperstown; Ft. Ticonderoga; New York State Capitol, Albany; LEGOLAND New York Resort, Goshen; Home of Franklin D. Roosevelt Natl. Historic Site, Hyde Park; Long Island beaches; Sagamore Hill (Theodore Roosevelt's "Summer White House"), Oyster Bay. **Information:** Empire State Development, Travel Information Center, 30 South Pearl St., Albany, NY 12245; 1-800-CALLNYS; www.iloveny.com

History. When Europeans arrived, Algonquians including the Mahican, Wappinger, and Lenni Lenape inhabited the region, as did the Iroquoian Mohawk, Oneida, Onondaga, Cayuga, and Seneca tribes, who established the League of the Five Nations. Italian Giovanni da Verrazzano entered New York harbor, 1524. In 1609, England's Henry Hudson visited the river later named for him, and France's Samuel de Champlain explored the lake that now bears his name. The first permanent settlement was Dutch, near present-day Albany, 1624. New Amsterdam was settled, 1626, at the southern tip of Manhattan island. A British fleet seized New Netherland, 1664. Key battles of the American Revolution included Saratoga, 1777. In the 19th cent., New York City emerged as one of the world's great metropolitan areas, a center for trade, finance, and arts, and a haven for millions of immigrants. Completion of the Erie Canal, 1825, established the state as a gateway to the West. The first women's rights convention was held in Seneca Falls, 1848. Although the state backed the Union in the Civil War, an 1863 military draft triggered three days of riots in New York City. Industry declined in the 20th cent., and California and Texas passed New York in population. Attica was the scene of a bloody prison revolt, 1971. Two jet aircraft hijacked by terrorists on Sept. 11, 2001, destroyed the World Trade Center in lower Manhattan and killed thousands. An estimated 65 people in New York state were killed when Hurricane Sandy (by then downgraded to a tropical storm) made landfall in Oct. 2012. Citing concerns over health risks, Gov. Andrew Cuomo in 2014 announced a statewide ban on hydraulic fracturing (or "fracking"). New York City became an early U.S. epicenter of the coronavirus pandemic beginning in Mar. 2020. Cuomo, accused by multiple women of sexual misconduct, resigned in Aug. 2021. Amazon warehouse workers in Staten Island voted in late Mar. 2022 in favor of unionizing. A white supremacist fatally shot 10 Black people and injured three others at a Buffalo supermarket in May 2022; he was charged with domestic terrorism. Freshman U.S. Rep. George Santos (R), who admitted to lying about his education and work history, was charged in May 2023 on 13 federal counts including fraud and money laundering; the House expelled him Dec. 1. On May 30, 2024, a New York jury found former Pres. Donald Trump guilty on all 34 state criminal charges in connection with a "hush money" payment over an alleged affair.

Famous New Yorkers. Woody Allen, Susan B. Anthony, James Baldwin, Lucille Ball, Ann Bancroft, L. Frank Baum, Tony Bennett, Milton Berle, Humphrey Bogart, Barbara Boxer, Mel Brooks, Benjamin Cardozo, De Witt Clinton, James Fenimore Cooper, Peter Cooper, Aaron Copland, Francis Ford Coppola, Tom Cruise, Robert De Niro, George Eastman, Jimmy Fallon, Millard Fillmore, Lou Gehrig, George and Ira Gershwin, Ruth Bader Ginsburg, Rudolph Giuliani, Jackie Gleason, Stephen Jay Gould, Julia Ward Howe, Charles Evans Hughes, Washington Irving, Henry and William James, John Jay, Carole King, Edward Koch, Lady Gaga, Fiorello LaGuardia, Herman Melville, Arthur Miller, Lin-Manuel Miranda, J. Pierpont Morgan Jr., Eddie Murphy, Joyce Carol Oates, Carroll O'Connor, Rosie O'Donnell, Eugene O'Neill, Jerry Orbach, George Pataki, Colin Powell, Nancy Reagan, John Roberts, John D. Rockefeller, Nelson Rockefeller, Richard Rodgers, Ray Romano, Eleanor Roosevelt, Franklin D. Roosevelt, Theodore Roosevelt, J. D. Salinger, Caroline Kennedy Schlossberg, Jerry Seinfeld, Al Sharpton, Paul Simon, Alfred E. Smith, Elizabeth Cady Stanton, Barbra Streisand, Donald Trump, William (Boss) Tweed, Martin Van Buren, Luther Vandross, Gore Vidal, Denzel Washington, Edith Wharton, Walt Whitman, Mark Zuckerberg.

Website. www.ny.gov

North Carolina (NC)

Tar Heel State, Old North State

People. Population: 10,835,491; rank: 9. **Pop. change** (2020-23): 3.8%. **Pop. density:** 223 per sq mi. **Racial distribution:** 69.8% white; 22.1% Black; 3.7% Asian; 1.6% Amer.

Ind.; 0.2% Hawaiian/Pacific Islander; 2 or more races, 2.7%. **Hispanic pop.:** 11.4%.

Geography. Total area: 53,804 sq mi; rank: 28. **Land area:** 48,607 sq mi; rank: 29. **Acres forested:** 18.7 mil. **Location:** South Atlantic state bounded on N by Virginia, on S by South Carolina, on SW by Georgia, on W by Tennessee, and on E by Atlantic. **Climate:** subtropical in SE, medium-continental in mountain region; tempered by the Gulf Stream and mountains in W. **Topography:** coastal plain and tidewater in two-fifths of state, extending to the fall line of the rivers; Piedmont Plateau in another two-fifths has gentle to rugged hills; southern Appalachian Mts. contain the Blue Ridge and Great Smoky Mts. **Capital:** Raleigh. **Chief airports:** Charlotte, Raleigh, Asheville, Greensboro, Wilmington.

Economy. Chief industries: manufacturing, agriculture, tourism. **Chief manuf. goods:** transportation, tobacco, pharmaceuticals, toiletries, plastics, animal slaughtering and processing, household furniture, fabric and apparel. **Chief crops:** greenhouse and nursery, tobacco, cotton, soybeans, corn, Christmas trees, sweet potatoes, wheat, peanuts, blueberries, cucumbers, tomatoes, hay, potatoes. **Farm income:** Crops: $4.34 bil. Livestock: $12.52 bil. **Nonfuel minerals:** $2.5 bil; phosphate rock, quartz (high-purity), sand and gravel (construction), sand and gravel (industrial), stone (crushed). **Commercial fishing:** $68.4 mil. **Chief ports:** Morehead City, Wilmington. **Gross state product:** $766.9 bil. **Sales tax:** 4.75%. **Gasoline tax:** 59.05 cents/gal. **Employment distrib.:** 15.5% govt.; 18.5% trade/trans./util.; 9.3% mfg.; 13.8% ed./health; 14.9% prof./bus. serv.; 10.7% leisure/hosp.; 6.2% finance; 5.4% constr./mining/log.; 1.6% info.; 4.0% other serv. **Unemployment:** 3.5%. **Min. wage/hr.:** $7.25. **Per cap. pers. income:** $60,484. **New private housing:** 98,853 units/$22.7 bil. **Broadband internet:** 95.0%. **Commercial banks:** 72; deposits: $603.2 bil. **Savings institutions:** 16; deposits: $2.8 bil. **Lottery:** total sales: $4.3 bil; profit: $1.0 bil.

Federal govt. Fed. civ. employees: 50,507; **avg. salary:** $96,932. **Notable fed. facilities:** Ft. Liberty (fmr. Bragg); Camp Lejeune Marine Base, Marine Corps Air Station Cherry Point; NOAA Natl. Centers for Environmental Information, Asheville; Natl. Inst. of Environmental Health Sciences, EPA Research and Dev. Labs, all in Research Triangle Park.

Education. High school grad. rate: 86.4%. **4-yr. public coll./univ.:** 17; **2-yr. public:** 58; **4-yr. private:** 48.

Energy. Electricity use/cost: 1,072 kWh, $124.48.

State data. Motto: Esse Quam Videri (To be rather than to seem). **Flower:** Dogwood. **Bird:** Cardinal. **Tree:** Pine. **Song:** "The Old North State." **Twelfth** of the original 13 states to ratify the Constitution, Nov. 21, 1789.

Tourism. Tourist spending: $32.4 bil (2022); change, 2019-22: 10.9%. **Attractions:** Cape Hatteras and Cape Lookout Natl. Seashores; Great Smoky Mountains Natl. Park; Guilford Courthouse Natl. Military Park; Moore's Creek Natl. Battlefield (1776 victory ended British rule in colony); Bennett Place (site of largest troop surrender of Civil War), Durham; Ft. Raleigh Natl. Historic Site, North Carolina Aquarium, on Roanoke Island; Wright Brothers Natl. Mem., Kill Devil Hills; USS *North Carolina*, Wilmington; North Carolina Zoo, Asheboro; North Carolina Symphony, Marbles Kids Museum, North Carolina Museum of Art, North Carolina Museum of Natural Sciences, in Raleigh; Carl Sandburg Home, Flat Rock; Biltmore House and Gardens, North Carolina Arboretum, in Asheville; U.S. Natl. Whitewater Ctr., Discovery Place, in Charlotte; Fort Macon State Park, Atlantic Beach. **Information:** North Carolina Dept. of Commerce, Tourism Div., 301 N. Wilmington St., Raleigh, NC 27601-1058; 1-800-VISIT-NC, (919) 814-4600; www.visitnc.com

History. Algonquian, Siouan, and Iroquoian peoples lived in the region at the time of European contact. Sir Walter Raleigh tried to found a colony, 1584-87; the "Lost Colony" on Roanoke Island, 1587, seemingly disappeared. Permanent settlers came from Virginia in the mid-17th cent. The province's congress was the first to vote for independence, 1776. In the Revolutionary War, Gen. Charles Cornwallis's forces were defeated at Kings Mountain, 1780, and forced out after Guilford Courthouse, 1781. The state ratified the Constitution, 1789, only after Congress passed the Bill of Rights. North Carolina, where one-third of the population was enslaved, seceded from the Union, 1861, and provided more troops to the Confederacy than any other state; it was readmitted, 1868. The Wright brothers made the first powered airplane flight at Kitty Hawk, 1903. Sit-ins at segregated Greensboro lunch counters, 1960, drew national attention to the civil rights movement. Long reliant on tobacco, textiles, and wood products, North Carolina has prospered since the 1960s from advanced technologies in the Raleigh-Durham-Chapel Hill area and banking in Charlotte. The hurricane-prone state was hit hard by Hazel, 1954, Fran, 1996, and Floyd, 1999. The state drew immediate backlash in 2016 after passing a "bathroom bill" requiring people to use public facilities that correspond with the sex assigned on their birth certificate; a revised bill was passed in 2017. The state's election board Feb. 21, 2019, ordered the 9th U.S. Congressional District to redo its 2018 general election, citing ballot fraud allegedly committed by GOP nominee Mark Harris's campaign.

Famous North Carolinians. David Brinkley, Shirley Caesar, John Coltrane, Stephen Curry, Rick Dees, Elizabeth Hanford Dole, Dale Earnhardt Sr., John Edwards, Ava Gardner, Richard Jordan Gatling, Billy Graham, Andy Griffith, O. Henry, Andrew Jackson, Andrew Johnson, Michael Jordan, William Rufus King, Charles Kuralt, Meadowlark Lemon, Dolley Madison, Thelonious Monk, Edward R. Murrow, Richard Petty, James K. Polk, Charlie Rose, Carl Sandburg, Enos Slaughter, Dean Smith, James Taylor, Thomas Wolfe.

Website. www.nc.gov

North Dakota (ND)

Peace Garden State

People. Population: 783,926; rank: 47. **Pop. change** (2020-23): 0.6%. **Pop. density:** 11 per sq mi. **Racial distribution:** 86.4% white; 3.8% Black; 1.7% Asian; 5.3% Amer. Ind.; 0.2% Hawaiian/Pacific Islander; 2 or more races, 2.6%. **Hispanic pop.:** 4.9%.

Geography. Total area: 70,679 sq mi; rank: 19. **Land area:** 68,977 sq mi; rank: 17. **Acres forested:** 0.8 mil. **Location:** West North Central state situated exactly in the middle of North America, bounded on the N by Canada, on the E by Minnesota, on the S by South Dakota, on the W by Montana. **Climate:** continental, with a wide range of temperatures and moderate rainfall. **Topography:** Central Lowland in the E comprises the flat Red R. Valley and the Rolling Drift Prairie; Missouri Plateau of the Great Plains on the W. **Capital:** Bismarck. **Chief airport:** Fargo.

Economy. Chief industries: agriculture, mining, tourism, manufacturing, telecommunications, energy, food processing. **Chief manuf. goods:** machinery, wood prods., motor vehicles and parts, furniture, processed foods. **Chief crops:** wheat, soybeans, corn, sugar beets, barley, dry beans, sunflowers, canola, potatoes, flaxseed, hay, dry peas, lentils, oats. **Farm income:** Crops: $9.78 bil. Livestock: $1.57 bil. **Nonfuel minerals:** $78 mil; lime, sand and gravel (construction), sand and gravel (industrial), stone (crushed). **Gross state product:** $74.1 bil. **Sales tax:** 5.0%. **Gasoline tax:** 41.43 cents/gal. **Employment distrib.:** 19.4% govt.; 21.2% trade/trans./util.; 6.5% mfg.; 16.0% ed./health; 7.6% prof./bus. serv.; 8.6% leisure/hosp.; 5.7% finance; 10.2% constr./mining/log.; 1.2% info.; 3.5% other serv. **Unemployment:** 1.9%. **Min. wage/hr.:** $7.25. **Per cap. pers. income:** $73,341. **New private housing:** 2,618 units/$689.4 mil. **Broadband internet:** 98.1%. **Commercial banks:** 72; deposits: $36.9 bil. **Savings institutions:** 2; deposits: $2.9 bil. **Lottery:** total sales: $39.3 mil; profit: $11.3 mil.

Federal govt. Fed. civ. employees: 5,616; **avg. salary:** $87,659. **Notable fed. facilities:** Minot AFB; Grand Forks AFB; Northern Prairie Wildlife Res. Ctr., Jamestown; Garrison Dam Natl. Fish Hatchery; Grand Forks Human Nutrition Res. Ctr.

Education. High school grad. rate: 85.1%. **4-yr. public coll./univ.:** 9; **2-yr. public:** 5; **4-yr. private:** 5.

Energy. Electricity use/cost: 1,119 kWh, $122.20.

State data. Motto: Liberty and union, now and forever, one and inseparable. **Flower:** Wild prairie rose. **Bird:** Western meadowlark. **Tree:** American elm. **Song:** "North Dakota Hymn." **Entered union:** Nov. 2, 1889; rank: 39th.

Tourism. Tourist spending: $3.3 bil (2022); change, 2019-22: 2.0%. **Attractions:** North Dakota Heritage Ctr., North Dakota State Capitol, in Bismarck; Bonanzaville, West Fargo; Ft. Union Trading Post Natl. Historic Site; Intl. Peace Garden, Dunseith; Elkhorn Ranch site, in Theodore Roosevelt Natl. Park; Ft. Abraham Lincoln State Park and Museum, Mandan; Dakota Dinosaur Museum, Dickinson; Knife River Indian Villages Natl. Historic Site; Scandinavian Heritage Park, Minden. **Information:** North Dakota Tourism Division, Century Center, 1600 E. Century Ave., Ste. 2, P.O. Box 2057, Bismarck, ND 58502-2057; 1-800-435-5663; www.ndtourism.com

History. Paleo-Indian peoples hunted in the area at least 11,000 years ago. At the time of European contact, the Ojibwa, Yanktonai and Teton Sioux, Mandan, Arikara, and Hidatsa peoples lived in the region. Pierre de Varennes, sieur de La Vérendrye, was the first French fur trader in the area, 1738, followed by the English at the end of the 18th cent. Lewis and Clark built Ft. Mandan, near present-day Washburn, 1804-05, and wintered there. The first permanent settlement was at Pembina, 1812. Missouri River steamboats reached the area, 1832. Dakota Territory was organized, 1861. The first railroad arrived, 1872. The "bonanza farm" craze of the 1870s-80s led to statehood, 1889. The Nonpartisan League, a farmers' group favoring state ownership of industries, helped elect Lynn Frazier as governor, 1916, but he and others were ousted in a recall vote, 1921. The predominantly agricultural state has one of the nation's lowest unemployment rates, mostly due to increased oil production since late 2008 in the state's Bakken Formation. Construction of the Dakota Access Pipeline drew international attention and vigorous protests in 2016-17, in particular from the Standing Rock Sioux tribe.

Famous North Dakotans. Maxwell Anderson, Angie Dickinson, Josh Duhamel, John Bernard Flannagan, Phil Jackson, Louis L'Amour, Peggy Lee, Roger Maris, Eric Sevareid, Vilhjalmur Stefansson, Lawrence Welk.

Website. www.nd.gov

Ohio (OH)

Buckeye State

People. Population: 11,785,935; rank: 7. **Pop. change** (2020-23): –0.1%. **Pop. density:** 289 per sq mi. **Racial distribution:** 80.6% white; 13.4% Black; 2.8% Asian; 0.3% Amer. Ind.; 0.1% Hawaiian/Pacific Islander; 2 or more races, 2.7%. **Hispanic pop.:** 4.8%.

Geography. Total area: 44,814 sq mi; rank: 34. **Land area:** 40,848 sq mi; rank: 35. **Acres forested:** 7.8 mil. **Location:** East North Central state bounded on the N by Michigan and Lake Erie; on the E by Pennsylvania; on the E and S by West Virginia; on the S by Kentucky; on the W by Indiana. **Climate:** temperate but variable; weather subject to much precipitation. **Topography:** generally rolling plain; Allegheny Plateau in E; Lake Erie Plains extend southward; central plains in the W. **Capital:** Columbus. **Chief airports:** Cleveland, Columbus, Dayton.

Economy. Chief industries: manufacturing, trade, services. **Chief manuf. goods:** motor vehicles and parts, petroleum, plastics and rubber, iron and steel, aircraft, machinery, fabricated metal, printing. **Chief crops:** corn, soybeans, hay, wheat, grapes, potatoes, tomatoes, apples, strawberries, tobacco. **Farm income:** Crops: $9.24 bil. Livestock: $6.19 bil. **Nonfuel minerals:** $1.6 bil; cement, lime, salt, sand and gravel (construction), stone (crushed). **Commercial fishing** (2018): $3.8 mil. **Chief ports:** Cincinnati, Toledo, Conneaut, Cleveland, Ashtabula. **Gross state product:** $872.7 bil. **Sales tax:** 5.75%. **Gasoline tax:** 56.90 cents/gal. **Employment distrib.:** 14.1% govt.; 18.6% trade/trans./util.; 12.2% mfg.; 17.2% ed./health; 13.2% prof./bus. serv.; 9.9% leisure/hosp.; 5.6% finance; 4.2% constr./mining/log.; 1.2% info.; 3.8% other serv. **Unemployment:** 3.5%. **Min. wage/hr.:** $10.45. **Per cap. pers. income:** $60,402. **New private housing:** 27,318 units/$7.0 bil. **Broadband internet:** 95.7%. **Commercial banks:** 157; deposits: $527.0 bil. **Savings institutions:** 42; deposits: $20.7 bil. **Lottery:** total sales: $5.8 bil; profit: $1.5 bil.

Federal govt. Fed. civ. employees: 55,199; **avg. salary:** $104,454. **Notable fed. facilities:** Wright-Patterson AFB; Defense Supply Ctr. Columbus; NASA Glenn Research Ctr., Cleveland; Joint Systems Manufacturing Ctr., Lima.

Education. High school grad. rate: 86.2%. **4-yr. public coll./univ.:** 30; **2-yr. public:** 29; **4-yr. private:** 65.

Energy. Electricity use/cost: 874 kWh, $121.07.

State data. Motto: With God, all things are possible. **Flower:** Scarlet carnation. **Bird:** Northern cardinal. **Tree:** Ohio buckeye. **Song:** "Beautiful Ohio." **Entered union:** Mar. 1, 1803; rank: 17th.

Tourism. Tourist spending: $24.4 bil (2022); change, 2019-22: 5.9%. **Attractions:** Hopewell Culture Natl. Historical Park, Chillicothe; Cuyahoga Valley Natl. Park; Armstrong Air and Space Museum, Wapakoneta; Natl. Museum of the U.S. Air Force, near Dayton; Pro Football Hall of Fame, First Ladies Natl. Historic Site, in Canton; Kings Island amusement park, Mason; Lake Erie Islands, Cedar Point amusement park, in Sandusky; birthplaces, homes of, and memorials to presidents W. H. Harrison, Grant, Hayes, Garfield, B. Harrison, McKinley, Taft, and Harding; Amish Country, particularly in Holmes County; German Village historic neighborhood, Franklin Park Conservatory and Botanical Gardens, in Columbus; Rock and Roll Hall of Fame and Museum, West Side Market, Cleveland Metroparks Zoo, in Cleveland; Cincinnati Museum Center at Union Terminal; Toledo Zoo. **Information:** TourismOhio, 77 South High Street, Fl. #29, Columbus, OH 43215; 1-800-BUCKEYE; www.ohio.org

History. Paleo-Indians hunted in the area about 11,000 years ago; the Adena and Hopewell cultures followed. Wyandot, Delaware, Miami, and Shawnee peoples sparsely occupied the area when the first Europeans arrived. René-Robert Cavelier, sieur de La Salle, visited the region, 1669. France claimed it, 1682, but ceded it to Britain, 1763. After the American Revolution, Ohio became part of the Northwest Territory, 1787. The first permanent settlement was at Marietta, 1788. Cincinnati was also founded, 1788; Cleveland, 1796. Indian warfare abated with the Treaty of Greenville, 1795. Ohio became a state, 1803. In the War of 1812, Oliver Hazard Perry's victory on Lake Erie and William Henry Harrison's invasion of Canada, 1813, ended British incursions. Columbus, founded 1812, became the state capital, 1816. Before the Civil War, some Ohioans aided the Underground Railroad. Agricultural for much of the 19th cent., the state became an industrial powerhouse in the 20th cent. but struggled to replace well-paying manufacturing jobs that began disappearing even before the 2007-09 recession. Cleveland hosted the Republican Natl. Convention in July 2016; no Republican has ever won the presidency without winning Ohio's electoral votes. A mass shooting in Aug. 2019 killed 10 in a Dayton nightlife district. In Feb. 2023, a Norfolk Southern freight train derailed in East Palestine, spilling highly toxic chemicals that forced the evacuation of thousands and necessitated intensive environmental remediation. On Apr. 9, 2024, the company agreed to pay $600 mil to settle a class-action lawsuit after spending more than $800 mil in cleanup costs.

Famous Ohioans. Berenice Abbott, Sherwood Anderson, Neil Armstrong, George Bellows, Halle Berry, Ambrose Bierce, Erma Bombeck, Drew Carey, Hart Crane, George Custer, Clarence Darrow, Paul Laurence Dunbar, Thomas Edison, Clark Gable, John Glenn, Zane Grey, Bob Hope, William Dean Howells, LeBron James, John Legend, Maya Lin, Toni Morrison, Paul Newman, Jack Nicklaus, Annie Oakley, Jesse Owens, Jack Paar, Pontiac, Eddie Rickenbacker, John D. Rockefeller Sr. and Jr., Roy Rogers, Pete Rose, Arthur Schlesinger Jr., Gen. William Sherman, Steven Spielberg, Gloria Steinem, Harriet Beecher Stowe, Robert A. Taft, William H. Taft, Tecumseh, James Thurber, Orville and Wilbur Wright.

Website. www.ohio.gov

Oklahoma (OK)

Sooner State

People. Population: 4,053,824; rank: 28. **Pop. change** (2020-23): 2.4%. **Pop. density:** 59 per sq mi. **Racial distribution:** 72.9% white; 7.9% Black; 2.6% Asian; 9.5% Amer. Ind.; 0.3% Hawaiian/Pacific Islander; 2 or more races, 6.8%. **Hispanic pop.:** 12.9%.

Geography. Total area: 69,881 sq mi; rank: 20. **Land area:** 68,578 sq mi; rank: 19. **Acres forested:** 11.4 mil. **Location:** West South Central state bounded on the N by Colorado and Kansas, on the E by Missouri and Arkansas, on the S and W by Texas, on the W by New Mexico. **Climate:** temperate; southern humid belt merging with colder northern continental; humid eastern and dry western zones. **Topography:** high plains predominate in the W, hills and small mountains in the E; the E central region is dominated by the Arkansas R. Basin, and the S by the Red R. Plains. **Capital:** Oklahoma City. **Chief airports:** Oklahoma City, Tulsa.

Economy. Chief industries: manufacturing, mineral and energy exploration and production, agriculture, services. **Chief manuf. goods:** animal slaughtering and processing, petroleum, plastics and rubber, fabricated metals, machinery, motor vehicles and parts. **Chief crops:** wheat, greenhouse and nursery, hay, cotton, corn, soybeans, pecans, sorghum, peanuts. **Farm income:** Crops: $1.76 bil. Livestock: $7.77 bil. **Nonfuel minerals:** $1.2 bil; cement, iodine, sand and gravel (construction), sand and gravel (industrial), stone (crushed). **Chief port:** Catoosa. **Gross state product:** $254.1 bil. **Sales tax:** 4.5%. **Gasoline tax:** 38.40 cents/gal. **Employment distrib.:** 20.8% govt.; 18.0% trade/trans./util.; 7.8% mfg.; 15.1% ed./health; 11.5% prof./bus. serv.; 10.5% leisure/hosp.; 4.7% finance; 6.7% constr./mining/log.; 0.9% info.; 3.9% other serv. **Unemployment:** 3.2%. **Min. wage/hr.:** $7.25. **Per cap. pers. income:** $58,499. **New private housing:** 13,405 units/$3.2 bil. **Broadband internet:** 93.1%. **Commercial banks:** 200; deposits: $117.0 bil. **Savings institutions:** 2; deposits: $14.7 bil. **Lottery:** total sales: $379.8 mil; profit: $88.3 mil.

Federal govt. Fed. civ. employees: 41,781; **avg. salary:** $88,458. **Notable fed. facilities:** Tinker AFB; FAA Mike Monroney Aeronautical Ctr., Oklahoma City; Ft. Sill; Altus AFB; McAlester Army Ammunition Plant; Vance AFB; NOAA Natl. Severe Storms Lab, Norman.

Education. High school grad. rate (2020-21): 80.0%. **4-yr. public coll./univ.:** 17; **2-yr. public:** 13; **4-yr. private:** 13.

Energy. Electricity use/cost: 1,155 kWh, $143.65.

State data. Motto: Labor Omnia Vincit (Labor conquers all things). **Flower:** Oklahoma rose. **Bird:** Scissor-tailed flycatcher. **Tree:** Redbud. **Song:** "Oklahoma!" **Entered union:** Nov. 16, 1907; rank: 46th.

Tourism. Tourist spending: $7.8 bil (2022); change, 2019-22: –16.1%. **Attractions:** Cherokee Heritage Ctr., Tahlequah; Oklahoma City Natl. Memorial and Museum, Natl. Cowboy and Western Heritage Museum, White Water Bay and Frontier City amusement parks, Museum of Osteology, Bricktown neighborhood, in Oklahoma City; Will Rogers Memorial Museum and Birthplace Ranch, Claremore and Oologah; Gathering Place, Philbrook Museum of Art, Gilcrease Museum, in Tulsa; Wichita Mountains Wildlife Refuge; Woolaroc Museum and Wildlife Preserve, Price Tower Arts Center, in Bartlesville; Sequoyah's Cabin, Sallisaw; Sam Noble Museum of Natural

History, Norman. **Information:** Oklahoma Tourism Dept., Travel Promotion Division, 123 Robert S. Kerr Ave., Oklahoma City, OK 73102-6406; 1-800-652-6552; www.travelok.com

History. Few Native Americans inhabited the region when Spanish explorer Coronado arrived, 1541; in the 16th and 17th cent., French traders visited. Part of the Louisiana Purchase, 1803, Oklahoma was known as Indian Country and, from 1834, Indian Territory. It became home to the "Five Civilized Tribes"—Cherokee, Choctaw, Chickasaw, Creek, and Seminole—after the forced removal of Indians from the eastern U.S., 1828-46. The land was also used by Comanche, Osage, and other Plains Indians. As white settlers pressed west, land was opened for homesteading by "runs" and lottery. The first run was in 1889; the most famous run, 1893, was to the Cherokee Outlet. Oklahoma became a state, 1907. In the early 20th cent., oil finds brought wealth to the Tulsa area; Tulsa's Greenwood section, then known as the "Negro Wall Street," was looted and destroyed by a white mob, 1921. Depression and drought drove many "Okies" from the Dust Bowl to California in the 1930s. A truck bomb in Oklahoma City, 1995, destroyed a federal office building, killing 168 people; an anti-government extremist was executed for the crime, 2001. A tornado in Moore killed 23 people, May 20, 2013; the widest tornado on record touched down in El Reno, May 31, 2013, killing 10 people. Since 2010, Oklahoma has experienced thousands of earthquakes (more than 1,400 greater than 3 magnitude in 2015-16 alone) believed to be connected with the use of disposal wells for wastewater from oil and gas operations. Oklahoma's top education official in late June 2024 mandated public schools incorporate the Bible in instruction.

Famous Oklahomans. Troy Aikman, Carl Albert, Gene Autry, Johnny Bench, William Boyd (Hopalong Cassidy), Garth Brooks, Lon Chaney, Gordon Cooper, Ralph Ellison, John Hope Franklin, James Garner, Vince Gill, Woody Guthrie, Paul Harvey, Ron Howard, Patrick J. Hurley, Ben Johnson, Jeane Kirkpatrick, Louis L'Amour, Shannon Lucid, Wilma Mankiller, Mickey Mantle, Reba McEntire, Wiley Post, Tony Randall, Oral Roberts, Will Rogers, Blake Shelton, Barry Switzer, Maria Tallchief, Jim Thorpe, Carrie Underwood, J. C. Watts Jr.

Website. www.oklahoma.gov

Oregon (OR)

Beaver State

People. Population: 4,233,358; rank: 27. **Pop. change** (2020-23): –0.1%. **Pop. density:** 44 per sq mi. **Racial distribution:** 85.6% white; 2.4% Black; 5.2% Asian; 1.9% Amer. Ind.; 0.5% Hawaiian/Pacific Islander; 2 or more races, 4.4%. **Hispanic pop.:** 14.9%.

Geography. Total area: 98,353 sq mi; rank: 9. **Land area:** 95,963 sq mi; rank: 10. **Acres forested:** 29.7 mil. **Location:** Pacific state bounded on N by Washington, on E by Idaho, on S by Nevada and California, on W by the Pacific. **Climate:** mild and humid on coast; continental dryness and extreme temperatures in the interior. **Topography:** Coast Range of rugged mountains; fertile Willamette R. Valley to E and S; Cascade Mt. Range of volcanic peaks E of the valley; plateau E of Cascades, remaining two-thirds of state. **Capital:** Salem. **Chief airports:** Portland, Eugene, Redmond.

Economy. Chief industries: manufacturing, services, trade, finance, insurance, real estate, government, construction. **Chief manuf. goods:** wood prods., frozen produce, printing, computers and electronics, transportation equip., industrial machinery. **Chief crops:** greenhouse and nursery, grass seed, hay, wheat, potatoes, Christmas trees, onions, pears, hazelnuts, corn, grapes, cherries, blackberries, blueberries, peppermint, snap beans, apples, hops. **Farm income:** Crops: $4.14 bil. Livestock: $2.11 bil. **Nonfuel minerals:** $527 mil; cement (portland), diatomite, perlite, sand and gravel (construction), stone (crushed). **Commercial fishing:** $132.6 mil. **Chief ports:** Portland, Coos Bay. **Gross state product:** $316.5 bil. **Sales tax:** none. **Gasoline tax:** 58.40 cents/gal. **Employment distrib.:** 16.2% govt.; 18.1% trade/trans./util.; 9.4% mfg.; 16.9% ed./health; 13.1% prof./bus. serv.; 10.2% leisure/hosp.; 5.1% finance; 6.1% constr./mining/log.; 1.7% info.; 3.2% other serv. **Unemployment:** 3.7%. **Min. wage/hr.:** $14.70. **Per cap. pers. income:** $65,426. **New private housing:** 17,697 units/$4.6 bil. **Broadband internet:** 95.9%. **Commercial banks:** 33; deposits: $103.3 bil. **Savings institutions:** 4; deposits: $1.4 bil. **Lottery:** total sales: $1.7 bil; profit: $901.8 mil.

Federal govt. Fed. civ. employees: 19,244; **avg. salary:** $99,616. **Notable fed. facilities:** Bonneville Power Admin; Detroit Dam; Air Natl. Guard bases, Klamath Falls, Portland, Warrenton.

Education. High school grad. rate: 81.3%. **4-yr. public coll./univ.:** 8; **2-yr. public:** 17; **4-yr. private:** 18.

Energy. Electricity use/cost: 946 kWh, $108.03.

State data. Motto: She flies with her own wings. **Flower:** Oregon grape. **Bird:** Western meadowlark. **Tree:** Douglas fir. **Song:** "Oregon, My Oregon." **Entered union:** Feb. 14, 1859; rank: 33rd.

Tourism. Tourist spending: $12.5 bil (2022); change, 2019-22: –11.5%. **Attractions:** John Day Fossil Beds Natl. Monument; Multnomah Falls, Columbia River Gorge; Timberline Lodge, Mount Hood Natl. Forest; Crater Lake Natl. Park; Oregon Dunes Natl. Rec. Area; Ft. Clatsop (Lewis and Clark Natl. Historical Park), Astoria Column, in Astoria; Oregon Caves Natl. Monument and Preserve; Intl. Rose Test Garden, Lan Su Chinese Garden, Pittock Mansion, Oregon Museum of Science and Industry, in Portland; Oregon Shakespeare Festival, Ashland; High Desert Museum, Bend; "Spruce Goose" (largest aircraft ever built), Evergreen Aviation and Space Museum, McMinnville; Yaquina Head Outstanding Natural Area, Oregon Coast Aquarium, in Newport. **Information:** Travel Oregon, 530 Center St. NE, Ste. 200, Salem, OR 97301; 1-800-547-7842; www.traveloregon.com

History. More than 100 Native American tribes inhabited the area at the time of European contact, including the Chinook, Yakima, Cayuse, Modoc, and Nez Percé. Capt. Robert Gray sighted and sailed into the Columbia R., 1792. Lewis and Clark, traveling overland, wintered at its mouth, 1805-06. Fur traders sent by John Jacob Astor established the Astoria trading post in the Columbia River region, 1811. Settlers arrived in the Willamette Valley, 1834. In 1843, the first large wave of settlers arrived via the Oregon Trail. Oregon became a territory, 1848, and a state, 1859. Early in the 20th cent., the "Oregon System"—political reforms that included initiative, referendum, recall, direct primary, and woman suffrage—was adopted. Originally dominated by forest products, the economy diversified after World War II, with technology firms clustering in the "Silicon Forest" area around Portland. Oregonians were the first in the U.S. to pass measures allowing physician-assisted suicide for terminally ill patients, 1994, and establishing an all-mail voting system, 1998. Gov. John Kitzhaber resigned in 2015, amidst an ethics scandal. A 41-day armed occupation of Malheur Natl. Wildlife Refuge ended in Feb. 2016. In July 2020, federal Dept. of Homeland Security agents reportedly detained anti-racism protesters in Portland. Oregon voters in Nov. 2020 voted to legalize possession of small amounts of "hard" drugs such as cocaine and heroin, making it the first state to do so.

Famous Oregonians. Ernest Bloch, Bill Bowerman, Ty Burrell, Beverly Cleary, Matt Groening, Ernest Haycox, Chief Joseph, Ken Kesey, Phil Knight, Ursula K. Le Guin, Edwin Markham, Tom McCall, John McLoughlin, Joaquin Miller, Bob Packwood, Linus Pauling, Steve Prefontaine, John "Jack" Reed, Alberto Salazar, Mary Decker Slaney, William Simon U'Ren.

Website. www.oregon.gov

Pennsylvania (PA)

Keystone State

People. Population: 12,961,683; rank: 5. **Pop. change** (2020-23): –0.3%. **Pop. density:** 290 per sq mi. **Racial distribution:** 80.6% white; 12.3% Black; 4.2% Asian; 0.5% Amer. Ind.; 0.1% Hawaiian/Pacific Islander; 2 or more races, 2.4%. **Hispanic pop.:** 8.9%.

Geography. Total area: 46,042 sq mi; rank: 33. **Land area:** 44,730 sq mi; rank: 32. **Acres forested:** 16.6 mil. **Location:** Middle Atlantic state bordered on the N and NE by New York, E by New Jersey, SE by Delaware, S by Maryland, S and SW by West Virginia, and W by Ohio. **Climate:** continental with wide fluctuations in seasonal temperatures. **Topography:** Allegheny Mts. run SW-NE, with Piedmont and Coast Plain in the SE triangle; Allegheny Front a diagonal spine across the state's center; N and W rugged plateau falls to Lake Erie Lowland. **Capital:** Harrisburg. **Chief airports:** Philadelphia, Pittsburgh, Harrisburg.

Economy. Chief industries: agribusiness, advanced manufacturing, health care, travel and tourism, depository institutions, biotechnology, printing and publishing, research and consulting, trucking and warehousing, transportation by air, engineering and management, legal services. **Chief manuf. goods:** petroleum, pharmaceuticals, plastics, iron and steel, printing, paper and paperboard, confectionery and snacks, animal slaughtering and processing. **Chief crops:** greenhouse and nursery, mushrooms, corn, hay, soybeans, apples, tomatoes, wheat, grapes, peaches, potatoes, strawberries, tobacco. **Farm income:** Crops: $3.17 bil. Livestock: $6.49 bil. **Nonfuel minerals:** $2.2 bil; cement, lime, sand and gravel (construction), sand and gravel (industrial), stone (crushed). **Commercial fishing** (2018): $0.3 mil. **Chief ports:** Philadelphia, Pittsburgh. **Gross state product:** $965.1 bil. **Sales tax:** 6.0%. **Gasoline tax:** 77.10 cents/gal. **Employment distrib.:** 11.5% govt.; 18.4% trade/trans./util.; 9.2% mfg.; 22.3% ed./health; 13.6% prof./bus. serv.; 9.2% leisure/hosp.; 5.5%

finance; 4.5% constr./mining/log.; 1.5% info.; 4.2% other serv. **Unemployment:** 3.4%. **Min. wage/hr.:** $7.25. **Per cap. pers. income:** $67,839. **New private housing:** 25,320 units/$6.0 bil. **Broadband internet:** 95.7%. **Commercial banks:** 118; deposits: $521.7 bil. **Savings institutions:** 48; deposits: $41.6 bil. **Lottery:** total sales: $5.1 bil; profit: $1.1 bil.

Federal govt. Fed. civ. employees: 65,895; **avg. salary:** $97,754. **Notable fed. facilities:** Army War College, Carlisle Barracks; Naval Supply Systems Command (NAVSUP), Mechanicsburg; Philadelphia Mint, Defense Supply Ctr., Naval Surface Warfare Ctr., all in Phila.; DLA Distribution Ctr. Susquehanna, New Cumberland, Mechanicsburg; Tobyhanna Army Depot; Letterkenny Army Depot.

Education. High school grad. rate: 87.0%. **4-yr. public coll./univ.:** 17; **2-yr. public:** 18; **4-yr. private:** 101.

Energy. Electricity use/cost: 854 kWh, $136.17.

State data. Motto: Virtue, liberty, and independence. **Flower:** Mountain laurel. **Bird:** Ruffed grouse. **Tree:** Eastern hemlock. **Song:** "Pennsylvania." **Second** of the original 13 states to ratify the Constitution, Dec. 12, 1787.

Tourism. Tourist spending: $29.9 bil (2022); change, 2019-22: –1.3%. **Attractions:** Liberty Bell Ctr. at Independence Natl. Historical Park, Franklin Institute, Philadelphia Museum of Art, in Philadelphia; Valley Forge Natl. Historical Park, King of Prussia; Gettysburg Natl. Military Park; Pennsylvania Dutch Country, Lancaster County; Hersheypark, Hershey; Duquesne Incline, Carnegie Museums of Pittsburgh, Heinz Hall for the Performing Arts, in Pittsburgh; Pocono Mountains; Pine Creek Gorge (Pennsylvania Grand Canyon), Allegheny Natl. Forest; Fallingwater (house designed by Frank Lloyd Wright), Mill Run; Johnstown Flood Natl. Memorial; Steamtown Natl. Historic Site, Scranton; U.S. Brig *Niagara*, Erie Maritime Museum, Presque Isle State Park, in Erie; Oil Region Natl. Heritage Area; Longwood Gardens, Kennett Square. **Information:** Pennsylvania Tourism Office, Dept. of Community and Economic Development, Commonwealth Keystone Building, 4th Fl., 400 North St., Harrisburg, PA 17120-0225; 1-800-VISITPA; www.visitpa.com

History. When Europeans came, Algonquian-speaking Lenni Lenape (Delaware) and Shawnee and the Iroquoian Susquehannocks, Erie, and Seneca occupied the region. Swedish explorers made the first permanent settlement, 1643, on Tinicum Island. The Dutch seized the settlement, 1655, but lost it to the British, 1664. The region was given by Charles II to William Penn, 1681. Philadelphia ("brotherly love") was the capital of the colonies during most of the American Revolution and of the U.S., 1790-1800; the Declaration of Independence, 1776, and Constitution, 1787, were signed here. Philadelphia was taken by the British, 1777. George Washington's troops encamped at Valley Forge in the bitter winter of 1777-78. Slavery was abolished, 1780. Union victory at the Battle of Gettysburg, July 1-3, 1863, marked a turning point in the Civil War. A dam collapse at Johnstown, 1889, killed at least 2,200 people. From the late 19th to the mid-20th cent., Pittsburgh prospered from coal and steel; later, heavy industry declined, but the city revived as a hub of finance, health care, and research. The Three Mile Island nuclear plant near Harrisburg had a near-meltdown, 1979. One of four hijacked planes on Sept. 11, 2001, crashed near Shanksville; the Flight 93 national memorial was officially dedicated on the site in 2011. A shooting at Pittsburgh's Tree of Life synagogue, Oct. 2018, killed 11; the shooter was sentenced to death, Aug. 2023. In Oct. 2020, the police shooting of a Black man, Walter Wallace Jr., in Philadelphia, captured on video, triggered multiple days of protests.

Famous Pennsylvanians. Marian Anderson, Maxwell Anderson, George Blanda, Kobe Bryant, James Buchanan, Andrew Carnegie, Rachel Carson, Wilt Chamberlain, Noam Chomsky, Perry Como, Bill Cosby, Cyrus H. K. Curtis, Thomas Eakins, Tina Fey, Stephen Foster, Benjamin Franklin, Robert Fulton, Martha Graham, Milton Hershey, Gene Kelly, Grace Kelly (Princess Grace of Monaco), Dan Marino, George C. Marshall, Chris Matthews, John J. McCloy, Margaret Mead, Andrew W. Mellon, Joe Montana, Stan Musial, Joe Namath, John O'Hara, Arnold Palmer, Robert E. Peary, Mike Piazza, Pink (Alecia Beth Moore), Mary Roberts Rinehart, Fred Rogers, Betsy Ross, Will Smith, Jimmy Stewart, Taylor Swift, Jim Thorpe, Johnny Unitas, John Updike, Honus Wagner, Andy Warhol, Benjamin West.

Website. www.pa.gov

Rhode Island (RI)

Little Rhody, Ocean State

People. Population: 1,095,962; rank: 44. **Pop. change** (2020-23): –0.1%. **Pop. density:** 1,060 per sq mi. **Racial distribution:** 82.4% white; 9.3% Black; 3.7% Asian; 1.3% Amer. Ind.; 0.2% Hawaiian/Pacific Islander; 2 or more races, 3.1%. **Hispanic pop.:** 18.0%.

Geography. Total area: 1,545 sq mi; rank: 50. **Land area:** 1,034 sq mi; rank: 50. **Acres forested:** 0.4 mil. **Location:** New England state. **Climate:** invigorating and changeable. **Topography:** eastern lowlands of Narragansett Basin; western uplands of flat and rolling hills. **Capital:** Providence. **Chief airport:** Warwick.

Economy. Chief industries: services, manufacturing. **Chief manuf. goods:** plastics, fabricated metals, electrical equip., jewelry. **Chief crops:** greenhouse and nursery, sweet corn, berries, potatoes, apples, hay. **Farm income:** Crops: $43.99 mil. Livestock: $32.78 mil. **Nonfuel minerals:** $109 mil; sand and gravel (construction), sand and gravel (industrial), stone (crushed). **Commercial fishing:** $107.3 mil. **Chief ports:** Providence, Davisville, Newport. **Gross state product:** $77.3 bil. **Sales tax:** 7.0%. **Gasoline tax:** 56.52 cents/gal. **Employment distrib.:** 13.1% govt.; 15.0% trade/trans./util.; 8.0% mfg.; 22.3% ed./health; 14.1% prof./bus. serv.; 11.2% leisure/hosp.; 6.8% finance; 4.2% constr./mining/log.; 1.1% info.; 4.2% other serv. **Unemployment:** 3.0%. **Min. wage/hr.:** $14.00. **Per cap. pers. income:** $66,480. **New private housing:** 1,169 units/$282.5 mil. **Broadband internet:** 99.0%. **Commercial banks:** 11; deposits: $38.2 bil. **Savings institutions:** 8; deposits: $4.3 bil. **Lottery:** total sales: $1.0 bil; profit: $434.7 mil.

Federal govt. Fed. civ. employees: 8,363; **avg. salary:** $113,318. **Notable fed. facilities:** Naval War College, Naval Undersea Warfare Ctr., Newport; EPA Atlantic Ecology Div. Lab, Narragansett.

Education. High school grad. rate: 83.3%. **4-yr. public coll./univ.:** 2; **2-yr. public:** 1; **4-yr. private:** 11.

Energy. Electricity use/cost: 589 kWh, $136.74.

State data. Motto: Hope. **Flower:** Common blue violet. **Bird:** Rhode Island red chicken. **Tree:** Red maple. **Song:** "Rhode Island." **Thirteenth** of original 13 states to ratify the Constitution, May 29, 1790.

Tourism. Tourist spending: $2.6 bil (2022); change, 2019-22: 2.5%. **Attractions:** Block Island; mansions (The Breakers, The Elms, others), Cliff Walk, Intl. Tennis Hall of Fame and Museum, Touro Synagogue (completed 1763, oldest in U.S.), in Newport; First Baptist Church in America, Rhode Island School of Design Museum of Art, WaterFire art installation, in Providence; Slater Mill Historic Site, Pawtucket; Gilbert Stuart Birthplace and Museum, Saunderstown. **Information:** Rhode Island Tourism Division, 315 Iron Horse Way, Ste. 101, Providence, RI 02908; 1-800-556-2484; www.visitrhodeisland.com

History. When Europeans arrived, Narragansett, Niantic, Nipmuc, and Wampanoag peoples lived in the region. Italian Giovanni da Verrazzano visited the area, 1524. The first permanent settlement was founded at Providence, 1636, by Roger Williams, who was exiled from the Massachusetts Bay Colony. Anne Hutchinson, also exiled, settled Portsmouth, 1638. Quaker and Jewish immigrants seeking freedom of worship began arriving, 1650s-60s. The colonists broke the power of the Narragansett in the Great Swamp Fight, 1675, the decisive battle in King Philip's War. The colony was the first to formally renounce all allegiance to King George III, May 4, 1776. Initially opposed to joining the Union, Rhode Island was the last of the 13 colonies to ratify the Constitution, 1790. Trade, textiles, and metal goods dominated the economy in the 19th cent., and Newport became a fashionable resort after the Civil War. The U.S. Navy was the state's largest civilian employer, 1945-73, until the destroyer force was relocated from Newport. A nightclub fire in West Warwick killed 100 people in 2003.

Famous Rhode Islanders. Ambrose Burnside, George M. Cohan, Viola Davis, Nelson Eddy, Jabez Gorham, Nathanael Greene, Elisabeth Hasselbeck, Christopher and Oliver La Farge, Cormac McCarthy, John McLaughlin, Matthew C. and Oliver Hazard Perry, Gilbert Stuart, Meredith Vieira.

Website. www.ri.gov

South Carolina (SC)

Palmetto State

People. Population: 5,373,555; rank: 23. **Pop. change** (2020-23): 5.0%. **Pop. density:** 179 per sq mi. **Racial distribution:** 69.0% white; 26.0% Black; 2.0% Asian; 0.6% Amer. Ind.; 0.1% Hawaiian/Pacific Islander; 2 or more races, 2.3%. **Hispanic pop.:** 7.5%.

Geography. Total area: 32,015 sq mi; rank: 40. **Land area:** 30,056 sq mi; rank: 40. **Acres forested:** 12.8 mil. **Location:** South Atlantic state bordered by North Carolina on the N; Georgia on the SW and W; the Atlantic Ocean on the E, SE, and S. **Climate:** humid subtropical. **Topography:** Blue Ridge province in NW has highest peaks; piedmont lies between the mountains and the fall line; coastal plain covers two-thirds of state. **Capital:** Columbia. **Chief airports:** Charleston, Myrtle Beach, Greer (Greenville), Columbia.

Economy. Chief industries: tourism, agriculture, manufacturing. **Chief manuf. goods:** chemicals and synthetics, motor vehicles and parts, plastics, paper and paper prods., turbines, rubber, textiles. **Chief crops:** greenhouse and nursery, tobacco, soybeans, cotton, corn, peaches, wheat, tomatoes, peanuts. **Farm income:** Crops: $1.51 bil. Livestock: $2.04 bil. **Nonfuel minerals:** $1.7 bil; cement, gold, sand and gravel (construction), sand and gravel (industrial), stone (crushed). **Commercial fishing:** $24.6 mil. **Chief ports:** Charleston, Georgetown. **Gross state product:** $322.3 bil. **Sales tax:** 6.0%. **Gasoline tax:** 47.15 cents/gal. **Employment distrib.:** 16.1% govt.; 18.9% trade/trans./util.; 11.3% mfg.; 12.5% ed./health; 13.5% prof./bus. serv.; 12.4% leisure/hosp.; 5.2% finance; 5.0% constr./mining/log.; 1.2% info.; 3.8% other serv. **Unemployment:** 3.0%. **Min. wage/hr.:** none. **Per cap. pers. income:** $56,123. **New private housing:** 42,474 units/$11.3 bil. **Broadband internet:** 96.1%. **Commercial banks:** 63; deposits: $123.0 bil. **Savings institutions:** 13; deposits: $1.7 bil. **Lottery:** total sales: $2.4 bil; profit: $605.3 mil.

Federal govt. Fed. civ. employees: 24,296; **avg. salary:** $95,502. **Notable fed. facilities:** Ft. Jackson; Joint Base Charleston; Marine Corps Recruit Depot Parris Island; Shaw AFB; USMC Air Station Beaufort; Savannah River Site.

Education. High school grad. rate: 83.8%. **4-yr. public coll./univ.:** 13; **2-yr. public:** 20; **4-yr. private:** 23.

Energy. Electricity use/cost: 1,088 kWh, $147.87.

State data. Motto: Dum Spiro Spero (While I breathe, I hope). **Flower:** Yellow jessamine. **Bird:** Carolina wren. **Tree:** Palmetto. **Song:** "Carolina." **Eighth** of the original 13 states to ratify the Constitution, May 23, 1788.

Tourism. Tourist spending: $17.2 bil (2022); change, 2019-22: 2.2%. **Attractions:** Historic Charleston, Waterfront Park, Charleston Museum (est. 1773, oldest in U.S.), Middleton Place, Magnolia Plantation and Gardens, Drayton Hall, in Charleston; Ft. Sumter Natl. Monument (where first shots of Civil War were fired), in Charleston Harbor; Cypress Gardens, Moncks Corner; Boone Hall Plantation and Gardens, Mt. Pleasant; Brookgreen Gardens, Murrells Inlet; Myrtle Beach; Hilton Head Island; Andrew Jackson State Park, Lancaster; South Carolina State Museum, Riverbanks Zoo, in Columbia. **Information:** SC Dept. of Parks, Recreation, and Tourism, 1205 Pendleton St., Columbia, SC 29201; (803) 734-0124; discoversouthcarolina.com

History. When Europeans arrived, Cherokee, Catawba, and Muskogean peoples lived in the area. Spanish and French came in the 16th cent. The first English colonists settled near the Ashley R., 1670, and moved to the site of present-day Charleston, 1680. The colonists seized the government, 1775, and the royal governor fled. The British took Charleston, 1780, but were defeated at Kings Mountain that same year and at Cowpens, 1781. In the 1830s, South Carolinians, angered by federal protective tariffs, adopted the Nullification Doctrine, holding that a state can void an act of Congress. Plantation agriculture relied on the enslaved labor of Black workers to cultivate rice and cotton. Enslaved Black people made up 57% of the population in 1860, when South Carolina was the first state to secede from the Union. Confederate troops fired on and forced the surrender of U.S. troops at Ft. Sumter, in Charleston Harbor, 1861, launching the Civil War. The state was readmitted to the Union, 1868. Strom Thurmond, who ran for president as a segregationist in 1948, later served 48 years in the U.S. Senate (1955-2003). Formerly dependent on textiles, the state has attracted new industries by courting foreign investment. The state removed the Confederate flag from its capitol grounds in July 2015 after an alleged white supremacist shot and killed nine Black parishioners at a Charleston church the previous month; the shooter was sentenced to death in 2017.

Famous South Carolinians. Aziz Ansari, Charles F. Bolden Jr., Chadwick Boseman, James F. Byrnes, John C. Calhoun, Stephen Colbert, Marian Wright Edelman, Joe Frazier, DuBose Heyward, Ernest F. Hollings, Andrew Jackson, Jesse Jackson, "Shoeless" Joe Jackson, Jasper Johns, Andie MacDowell, Francis Marion, Ronald E. McNair, Charles Pinckney, John Rutledge, Thomas Sumter, Strom Thurmond, John B. Watson.

Website. www.sc.gov

South Dakota (SD)

Coyote State, Mount Rushmore State

People. Population: 919,318; rank: 46. **Pop. change** (2020-23): 3.7%. **Pop. density:** 12 per sq mi. **Racial distribution:** 84.2% white; 2.6% Black; 1.8% Asian; 8.5% Amer. Ind.; 0.1% Hawaiian/Pacific Islander; 2 or more races, 2.8%. **Hispanic pop.:** 5.1%.

Geography. Total area: 77,096 sq mi; rank: 17. **Land area:** 75,790 sq mi; rank: 16. **Acres forested:** 1.9 mil. **Location:** West North Central state bounded on the N by North Dakota, on the E by Minnesota and Iowa, on the S by Nebraska, on the W by Wyoming and Montana. **Climate:** characterized by extremes of temperature, persistent winds, low precipitation and humidity. **Topography:** Prairie Plains in the E; rolling hills of the Great Plains in the W; the Black Hills, rising 3,500 ft, in the SW corner. **Capital:** Pierre. **Chief airport:** Sioux Falls.

Economy. Chief industries: agriculture, services, manufacturing. **Chief manuf. goods:** animal slaughtering, machinery, semiconductors, surgical appliances. **Chief crops:** corn, soybeans, wheat, hay, sunflowers, sorghum, oats, barley. **Farm income:** Crops: $8.30 bil. Livestock: $5.84 bil. **Nonfuel minerals:** $549 mil; cement (portland), gold, lime, sand and gravel (construction), stone (crushed). **Gross state product:** $72.4 bil. **Sales tax:** 4.2%. **Gasoline tax:** 48.40 cents/gal. **Employment distrib.:** 18.0% govt.; 19.6% trade/trans./util.; 9.7% mfg.; 16.8% ed./health; 8.2% prof./bus. serv.; 10.3% leisure/hosp.; 5.9% finance; 6.5% constr./mining/log.; 1.1% info.; 4.0% other serv. **Unemployment:** 2.0%. **Min. wage/hr.:** $11.20. **Per cap. pers. income:** $70,353. **New private housing:** 7,072 units/$1.5 bil. **Broadband internet:** 98.2%. **Commercial banks:** 79; deposits: $796.0 bil. **Savings institutions:** 3; deposits: $533.0 mil. **Lottery:** total sales: $414.6 mil; profit: $181.9 mil.

Federal govt. Fed. civ. employees: 8,692; **avg. salary:** $84,940. **Notable fed. facilities:** Ellsworth AFB.

Education. High school grad. rate: 82.1%. **4-yr. public coll./univ.:** 9; **2-yr. public:** 4; **4-yr. private:** 6.

Energy. Electricity use/cost: 1,058 kWh, $127.92.

State data. Motto: Under God, the people rule. **Flower:** Pasqueflower. **Bird:** Chinese ring-necked pheasant. **Tree:** Black Hills spruce. **Song:** "Hail, South Dakota." **Entered union:** Nov. 2, 1889; rank: 40th.

Tourism. Tourist spending: $3.6 bil (2022); change, 2019-22: 15.9%. **Attractions:** Mt. Rushmore Natl. Memorial, Keystone; Harney Peak (tallest E of Rockies); Custer State Park; Crazy Horse Memorial (mtn. carving in progress); Wind Cave Natl. Park, near Hot Springs; Black Hills Natl. Forest; Needles Hwy., part of Peter Norbeck Natl. Scenic Byway; Minuteman Missile Natl. Historic Site; Deadwood (1876 gold rush town); Jewel Cave Natl. Monument, near Custer; Badlands Natl. Park; Great Lakes of South Dakota; Great Plains Zoo and Delbridge Museum of Natural History, Sioux Falls; Corn Palace, Mitchell; Reptile Gardens, Chapel in the Hills, Bear Country USA, in Rapid City. **Information:** Dept. of Tourism, Dolly Reed Plaza, 711 E. Wells Ave., c/o 500 E. Capitol Ave., Pierre, SD 57501-5070; 1-800-SDAKOTA; www.travelsd.com

History. Paleo-Indians hunted in the region at least 11,500 years ago. At the time of first European contact, Mandan, Hidatsa, Arikara, and Sioux lived in the area. The French Vérendrye brothers explored the region, 1742-43. The U.S. acquired the territory in the Louisiana Purchase, 1803, and Meriwether Lewis and William Clark passed through, 1804-06. In 1817, a trading post opened at what would become Ft. Pierre. Dakota Territory was established, 1861. Gold was discovered, 1874, in the Black Hills on Lakota Sioux land; the "Great Dakota Boom" began in 1879. South Dakota became a state, 1889. The massacre of more than 200 Native American men, women, and children at Wounded Knee, 1890, ended Sioux resistance. Armed supporters of the American Indian Movement, a Native American rights group, occupied the area, leading to a 70-day standoff, 1973. Major economic activities include agribusiness and, since the 1980s, credit card services. Republicans scored a key election victory, 2004, with the defeat of three-term U.S. Sen. Tom Daschle, a national Democratic leader. A Smithfield Foods pork processing facility in Sioux Falls in Apr. 2020 became the site of the U.S.'s largest known single-source coronavirus cluster.

Famous South Dakotans. Sparky Anderson, Bob Barker, Black Elk, Tom Brokaw, Crazy Horse, Tom Daschle, Myron Floren, Mary Hart, Cheryl Ladd, Ernest O. Lawrence, George McGovern, Russell Means, Billy Mills, Allen H. Neuharth, Pat O'Brien, Sitting Bull.

Website. www.sd.gov

Tennessee (TN)

Volunteer State

People. Population: 7,126,489; rank: 15. **Pop. change** (2020-23): 3.1%. **Pop. density:** 173 per sq mi. **Racial distribution:** 78.4% white; 16.5% Black; 2.1% Asian; 0.6% Amer. Ind.; 0.1% Hawaiian/Pacific Islander; 2 or more races, 2.3%. **Hispanic pop.:** 7.5%.

Geography. Total area: 42,133 sq mi; rank: 36. **Land area:** 41,227 sq mi; rank: 34. **Acres forested:** 13.8 mil. **Location:** East South Central state bounded on the N by Kentucky and Virginia; on the E by North Carolina; on the S by Georgia, Alabama, and Mississippi; on the W by Arkansas and Missouri.

Climate: humid continental to the N; humid subtropical to the S. **Topography:** rugged country in E; Great Smoky Mts. of the Unaka Range; low ridges of the Appalachian Valley; flat Cumberland Plateau; slightly rolling terrain and knobs of the Interior Low Plateau, the largest region; Eastern Gulf Coastal Plain to the W, laced with streams; Mississippi Alluvial Plain, a narrow strip of swamp and floodplain in extreme W. **Capital:** Nashville. **Chief airports:** Nashville, Memphis, Alcoa (Knoxville).

Economy. Chief industries: manufacturing, trade, services, tourism, finance, insurance, real estate. **Chief manuf. goods:** motor vehicles and parts, computers and electronics, food, chemicals, plastics, printing, appliances, aluminum. **Chief crops:** greenhouse and nursery, soybeans, cotton, corn, tobacco, hay, tomatoes, wheat. **Farm income:** Crops: $3.03 bil. Livestock: $2.10 bil. **Nonfuel minerals:** $2.0 bil; cement, sand and gravel (construction), sand and gravel (industrial), stone (crushed), zinc. **Chief ports:** Memphis, Nashville, Chattanooga. **Gross state product:** $523.2 bil. **Sales tax:** 7.0%. **Gasoline tax:** 45.80 cents/gal. **Employment distrib.:** 13.7% govt.; 20.5% trade/trans./util.; 10.9% mfg.; 14.9% ed./health; 13.4% prof./bus. serv.; 11.0% leisure/hosp.; 5.4% finance; 4.8% constr./mining/log.; 1.6% info.; 3.9% other serv. **Unemployment:** 3.3%. **Min. wage/hr.:** none. **Per cap. pers. income:** $61,049. **New private housing:** 47,463 units/$11.5 bil. **Broadband internet:** 95.9%. **Commercial banks:** 164; deposits: $218.1 bil. **Savings institutions:** 8; deposits: $3.9 bil. **Lottery:** total sales: $2.1 bil; profit: $515.4 mil.

Federal govt. Fed. civ. employees: 32,377; **avg. salary:** $89,743. **Notable fed. facilities:** Tennessee Valley Authority, Knoxville; Oak Ridge Natl. Lab; Arnold Engineering Development Complex; Ft. Campbell; NSA Mid-South, Millington.

Education. High school grad. rate: 90.4%. **4-yr. public coll./univ.:** 11; **2-yr. public:** 13; **4-yr. private:** 39.

Energy. Electricity use/cost: 1,188 kWh, $145.49.

State data. Motto: Agriculture and commerce. **Flower:** (cultivated) iris; (wildflower) passion flower, Tennessee coneflower. **Bird:** Northern mockingbird. **Tree:** Tulip poplar. **Songs:** "My Homeland, Tennessee"; "When It's Iris Time in Tennessee"; "My Tennessee"; "Tennessee Waltz"; "Rocky Top"; "Smoky Mountain Rain." **Entered union:** June 1, 1796; rank: 16th.

Tourism. Tourist spending: $28.9 bil (2022); change, 2019-22: 17.7%. **Attractions:** Lookout Mountain, Tennessee Aquarium, Ruby Falls, in Chattanooga; Great Smoky Mountains Natl. Park; Lost Sea (largest underground lake in U.S.), Sweetwater; Cherokee Natl. Forest; Cumberland Gap Natl. Historical Park; James K. Polk Ancestral Home, Columbia; American Museum of Science and Energy, Oak Ridge; The Hermitage (home of Pres. Andrew Jackson), Country Music Hall of Fame and Museum, Ryman Auditorium, Belle Meade Plantation, Parthenon replica, Grand Ole Opry, in Nashville; Dollywood theme park, Pigeon Forge; Graceland (home of Elvis Presley), Sun Studio, in Memphis; Alex Haley Museum and Interpretive Ctr., Henning; Casey Jones Village, Jackson; Bristol Motor Speedway. **Information:** Dept. of Tourist Development, Wm. Snodgrass/Tennessee Tower, 312 Rosa L. Parks Ave., 13th Fl., Nashville, TN 37243; (615) 741-2159; www.tnvacation.com

History. Inhabited for at least 20,000 years, the region was home to Creek and Yuchi peoples when the first Europeans arrived; the Cherokee moved into the region in the early 18th cent. Spanish explorers visited the area, 1540. English traders crossed the Great Smoky Mtns. from the east, while France's Jacques Marquette and Louis Jolliet sailed down the Mississippi on the west, 1673. The first permanent settlement was of Virginians on the Watauga R., 1769. After the American Revolution, in which Tennesseans fought in eastern campaigns, the region became a territory, 1790, and a state, 1796. Slavery was widespread in western Tennessee, where cotton was the main crop, but much less common in the east. The state seceded, 1861, and saw many Civil War engagements; some 187,000 Tennesseans fought for the Confederacy and 51,000 for the Union. Tennessee was readmitted in 1866, the only former Confederate state not to have a postwar military government. The famous Scopes trial, 1925, questioned the teaching of evolution in public schools. In the 1930s, the Tennessee Valley Authority, a federal program, brought electric power to rural areas. Nashville became the capital of country music while Memphis fostered the blues and, with Elvis Presley in the 1950s, rock 'n' roll. Martin Luther King Jr. was assassinated in Memphis, 1968. Since the 1970s, auto plants have become major employers, as has Federal Express. Al Gore Jr., U.S. vice pres. (1993-2001), lost his 2000 presidential bid partly because he failed to carry his home state of Tennessee. Record amounts of rainfall flooded Nashville in 2010. Wildfires killed 14 in East Tennessee in Nov. 2016. On Mar. 2-3, 2020, tornadoes in central TN killed at least 25 people. In Aug. 2021, flash flooding killed at least 22 people in Humphreys County. Memphis police in Jan. 2023 released video showing the beating death by officers of 29-year-old Black man Tyre Nichols, sparking protests. Legislation in Mar. 2023 outlawed certain drag shows; a federal judge blocked it, citing First Amendment concerns. State officials attributed at least 36 deaths to winter storms in mid-Jan. 2024.

Famous Tennesseans. Roy Acuff, Kenny Chesney, Davy Crockett, Miley Cyrus, David Farragut, Ernie Ford, Aretha Franklin, Bill Frist, Al Gore Jr., Alex Haley, William C. Handy, Sam Houston, Cordell Hull, Andrew Jackson, Andrew Johnson, Casey Jones, Estes Kefauver, Grace Moore, Dolly Parton, Minnie Pearl, James Polk, Elvis Presley, Wilma Rudolph, Dinah Shore, Bessie Smith, Fred Thompson, Justin Timberlake, Tina Turner, Hank Williams Jr., Alvin York.

Website. www.tn.gov

Texas (TX)

Lone Star State

People. Population: 30,503,301; rank: 2. **Pop. change** (2020-23): 4.7%. **Pop. density:** 117 per sq mi. **Racial distribution:** 76.8% white; 13.6% Black; 6.0% Asian; 1.1% Amer. Ind.; 0.2% Hawaiian/Pacific Islander; 2 or more races, 2.3%. **Hispanic pop.:** 39.8%.

Geography. Total area: 268,525 sq mi; rank: 2. **Land area:** 261,194 sq mi; rank: 2. **Acres forested:** 59.0 mil. **Location:** southwestern state bounded on the SE by the Gulf of Mexico; on the SW by Mexico, separated by the Rio Grande; surrounding states are Louisiana, Arkansas, Oklahoma, New Mexico. **Climate:** extremely varied; driest region is the Trans-Pecos; wettest is the NE. **Topography:** Gulf Coast Plain in the S and SE; North Central Plains slope upward with some hills; the Great Plains extend over the Panhandle, are broken by low mountains; the Trans-Pecos is the southern extension of the Rockies. **Capital:** Austin. **Chief airports:** Fort Worth, Houston (2), Austin, Dallas, San Antonio, El Paso, Midland, Lubbock, Harlingen, McAllen.

Economy. Chief industries: manufacturing, trade, oil and gas extraction, services. **Chief manuf. goods:** petroleum, chemicals and resins, computers and electronics, animal slaughtering and processing, plastics, aerospace. **Chief crops:** cotton, greenhouse and nursery, corn, wheat, sorghum, hay, peanuts, onions, rice, pecans, grapefruit. **Farm income:** Crops: $7.72 bil. Livestock: $22.06 bil. **Nonfuel minerals:** $9.8 bil; cement, lime, sand and gravel (construction), sand and gravel (industrial), stone (crushed). **Commercial fishing:** $169.7 mil. **Chief ports:** Houston, Galveston, Brownsville, Beaumont, Port Arthur, Corpus Christi, Texas City, Freeport. **Gross state product:** $2.6 tril. **Sales tax:** 6.25%. **Gasoline tax:** 38.40 cents/gal. **Employment distrib.:** 15.0% govt.; 19.5% trade/trans./util.; 6.8% mfg.; 13.7% ed./health; 15.1% prof./bus. serv.; 10.8% leisure/hosp.; 6.5% finance; 7.4% constr./mining/log.; 1.6% info.; 3.5% other serv. **Unemployment:** 3.9%. **Min. wage/hr.:** $7.25. **Per cap. pers. income:** $65,422. **New private housing:** 232,373 units/$50.8 bil. **Broadband internet:** 96.8%. **Commercial banks:** 444; deposits: $1.1 tril. **Savings institutions:** 31; deposits: $420.3 bil. **Lottery:** total sales: $8.7 bil; profit: $2.2 bil.

Federal govt. Fed. civ. employees: 128,581; **avg. salary:** $98,731. **Notable fed. facilities:** Ft. Cavazos (fmr. Hood); Ft. Bliss; Sheppard, Dyess, Goodfellow AF Bases; Joint Base San Antonio; NASA Johnson Space Ctr., Houston; Naval Air Training Command, NAS Corpus Christi; Red River Army Depot; Western Currency Facility, Ft. Worth.

Education. High school grad. rate: 89.7%. **4-yr. public coll./univ.:** 50; **2-yr. public:** 52; **4-yr. private:** 64.

Energy. Electricity use/cost: 1,178 kWh, $162.17.

State data. Motto: Friendship. **Flower:** Bluebonnet. **Bird:** Northern mockingbird. **Tree:** Pecan. **Song:** "Texas, Our Texas." **Entered union:** Dec. 29, 1845; rank: 28th.

Tourism. Tourist spending: $81.9 bil (2022); change, 2019-22: –0.2%. **Attractions:** Big Bend and Guadalupe Mountains Natl. Parks; Fort Davis Natl. Historic Site; Six Flags Over Texas, Arlington; SeaWorld San Antonio, Six Flags Fiesta Texas, The Alamo, San Antonio Missions Natl. Historical Park, San Antonio River Walk, in San Antonio; Natl. Cowgirl Museum and Hall of Fame, Kimbell Art Museum, Ft. Worth Zoo, Bureau of Engraving and Printing, in Ft. Worth; Lyndon B. Johnson Natl. Historical Park, Johnson City; LBJ Presidential Library and Museum, Bullock Texas State History Museum, Austin; George H. W. Bush Presidential Library and Museum, College Station; Dallas Arboretum and Botanical Garden, Sixth Floor Museum at Dealey Plaza, George W. Bush Presidential Library and Museum, in Dallas; USS *Lexington*, Texas State Aquarium, Padre Island Natl. Seashore, in Corpus Christi. **Information:** Office of the Governor, Econ. Dev. & Tourism, 1100 San Jacinto Blvd., Austin, TX 78701; 1-800-452-9292, (512) 463-2000; www.traveltexas.com

History. Humans have lived in the region for at least 12,000 years. Coahuiltecan, Karankawa, Caddo, Jumano, and Tonkawa peoples were in the area when the first Europeans came; later, Apache, Comanche, Cherokee, and Wichita arrived. Early Spanish explorers included Alonso Alvarez de Pineda, who sailed along the Texas coast, 1519; Cabeza de Vaca, shipwrecked near Galveston along with Estevanico, a Moroccan-born enslaved black man, 1528; and Coronado, who crossed the Panhandle, 1541. Spaniards made the first settlement at Ysleta, near El Paso, 1682. Americans moved into the land early in the 19th cent. Mexico, of which Texas was a part, won independence from Spain, 1821. Texans rebelled, 1836, losing to Mexican Gen. Santa Anna at the Alamo but winning decisively under Sam Houston at San Jacinto. With Houston as president, 1836-38 and 1841-44, the Republic of Texas functioned as a nation until admitted to the Union. With an enslaved population of 30%, Texas seceded, 1861; mostly unscathed by the Civil War, it was readmitted, 1870. In 1900, a powerful hurricane lashed Galveston, killing at least 8,000. Cotton and cattle were dominant until 1901, when the Spindletop gusher, near Beaumont, launched the petroleum and petrochemical industries. With wealth and population came political power, notably in the presidencies of Lyndon B. Johnson (1963-69), George H. W. Bush (1989-93), and George W. Bush (2001-09). Hurricane Harvey brought historic rainfall and flooding to Houston and surrounding areas in Aug. 2017, displacing thousands. A shooter killed 26 at a Baptist church in Sutherland Springs in Nov. 2017. A shooter at a Santa Fe (TX) high school killed 10 in May 2018. Mass shootings in El Paso, Aug. 2019, and Odessa, Sept. 2019, killed dozens. In Feb. 2021, severe winter weather killed 246 people in the state, mainly through hypothermia brought on by utility outages. Gov. Greg Abbott (R) in Feb. 2022 directed state agencies to investigate gender-affirming medical care for transgender youth as child abuse. On May 24, 2022, a gunman killed 19 students and two teachers at an elementary school in Uvalde. Texas's GOP-led state House voted May 27, 2023, to impeach the state's Republican attorney gen., Ken Paxton, over bribery and abuse-of-office allegations; he was acquitted by the Texas Senate. Igniting in late Feb. 2024, the panhandle's Smokehouse Creek fire grew into the state's largest on record, burning more than 1 mil acres. A divided U.S. appeals court in Mar. 2024 blocked enforcement of a new state law allowing local and state police to arrest and deport migrants. Hurricane Beryl made landfall near Houston July 8 as a Category 1 storm, knocking out power to almost 3 mil people and killing at least 18, some as a result of heat exposure.

Famous Texans. Lance Armstrong, Stephen F. Austin, Lloyd Bentsen, James Bowie, Drew Brees, Carol Burnett, George H. W. Bush, George W. Bush, Earl Campbell, Kelly Clarkson, Joan Crawford, Dwight D. Eisenhower, Morgan Fairchild, Farrah Fawcett, George Foreman, Sam Houston, Howard Hughes, Molly Ivins, Lyndon B. Johnson, Tommy Lee Jones, Janis Joplin, Barbara Jordan, Beyoncé Knowles, Mary Martin, Matthew McConaughey, Chester Nimitz, Sandra Day O'Connor, H. Ross Perot, Katherine Anne Porter, Dan Rather, Sam Rayburn, Ann Richards, Michael Strahan, George Strait, Bob Wills, Babe Didrikson Zaharias.

Website. www.texas.gov

Utah (UT)

Beehive State

People. Population: 3,417,734; rank: 30. **Pop. change** (2020-23): 4.5%. **Pop. density:** 42 per sq mi. **Racial distribution:** 89.8% white; 1.6% Black; 2.9% Asian; 1.6% Amer. Ind.; 1.2% Hawaiian/Pacific Islander; 2 or more races, 3.0%. **Hispanic pop.:** 16.0%.

Geography. Total area: 84,876 sq mi; rank: 13. **Land area:** 82,355 sq mi; rank: 12. **Acres forested:** 18.1 mil. **Location:** middle Rocky Mountain state; its SE corner touches Colorado, New Mexico, and Arizona and is the only spot in the U.S. where four states join. **Climate:** arid; ranges from warm desert in SW to alpine in NE. **Topography:** high Colorado Plateau is cut by brilliantly colored canyons of the SE; broad, flat, desertlike Great Basin of the W; the Great Salt Lake and Bonneville Salt Flats to the NW; Middle Rockies in the NE run E-W; valleys and plateaus of the Wasatch Front. **Capital:** Salt Lake City. **Chief airport:** Salt Lake City.

Economy. Chief industries: services, trade, manufacturing, government, transportation, utilities. **Chief manuf. goods:** food, petroleum, nonferrous metal, motor vehicles and parts, aerospace, sporting goods, fabricated metal, computers and electronics. **Chief crops:** hay, greenhouse and nursery, wheat, cherries, onions, apples, barley, peaches, corn. **Farm income:** Crops: $715.61 mil. Livestock: $2.00 bil. **Nonfuel minerals:** $3.1 bil; cement (portland), copper, gold, potash, salt. **Gross state product:** $272.6 bil. **Sales tax:** 6.1%. **Gasoline tax:** 55.55 cents/gal. **Employment distrib.:** 15.8% govt.; 18.0% trade/trans./util.; 8.8% mfg.; 14.2% ed./health; 14.3% prof./bus. serv.; 9.8% leisure/hosp.; 5.5% finance; 8.5% constr./mining/log.; 2.4% info.; 2.7% other serv. **Unemployment:** 2.6%. **Min. wage/hr.:** $7.25. **Per cap. pers. income:** $62,823. **New private housing:** 25,361 units/$7.0 bil. **Broadband internet:** 97.2%. **Commercial banks:** 55; deposits: $865.8 bil. **Savings institutions:** 2; deposits: $78.0 bil.

Federal govt. Fed. civ. employees: 32,797; **avg. salary:** $85,984. **Notable fed. facilities:** Hill AFB; Tooele Army Depot; Army Dugway Proving Ground; NSA Utah Data Ctr.

Education. High school grad. rate: 88.2%. **4-yr. public coll./univ.:** 7; **2-yr. public:** 1; **4-yr. private:** 4.

Energy. Electricity use/cost: 783 kWh, $84.87.

State data. Motto: Industry. **Flower:** Sego lily. **Bird:** (California) sea gull. **Tree:** Blue spruce. **Song:** "Utah, This Is the Place." **Entered union:** Jan. 4, 1896; rank: 45th.

Tourism. Tourist spending: $12.4 bil (2022); change, 2019-22: 18.3%. **Attractions:** Temple Square (site of Mormon Church headquarters), Salt Lake City; Great Salt Lake; Zion, Canyonlands, Bryce Canyon, Arches, and Capitol Reef Natl. Parks; Dinosaur, Rainbow Bridge, Timpanogos Cave, and Natural Bridges Natl. Monuments; Lake Powell; Flaming Gorge Natl. Recreation Area; Utah Olympic Park, Sundance Film Festival, in Park City. **Information:** Utah Office of Tourism, Council Hall/Capitol Hill, 300 N. State St., Salt Lake City, UT 84114; 1-800-200-1160; visit www.visitutah.com

History. Ute, Gosiute, Southern Paiute, and Navajo peoples lived in the region at the time of European contact. Spanish Franciscans visited the area, 1776; American fur traders followed. Permanent settlement began with the arrival of the Latter-day Saints, or Mormons, 1847, who created a prosperous economy. Organized in 1849, the State of Deseret asked admission to the Union; instead, Congress established Utah Territory, 1850, and appointed Brigham Young governor. The Union Pacific and Central Pacific railroads met near Promontory Point, May 10, 1869, creating the first transcontinental railroad. Statehood was not achieved until 1896, after a long controversy over the Mormon practices of economic isolationism and polygamy (the church renounced the latter in 1890). The 20th cent. brought expansion in mining, defense-related industries, and, more recently, information technologies. More than two-thirds of Utahans are Mormons; the church has its world headquarters in Salt Lake City. Utah experienced 60% population growth, 1990-2010. Environmentalists and tribal groups said they would challenge a Trump administration decision in Dec. 2017 to drastically cut the land area covered by Bears Ears and Grand Staircase-Escalante National Monuments. Pres. Biden ordered a review of the monuments' boundaries, Jan. 2021.

Famous Utahans. Maude Adams, Roseanne Barr, Ezra Taft Benson, John Moses Browning, Butch Cassidy, Marriner S. Eccles, Philo T. Farnsworth, David M. Kennedy, J. Willard Marriott, Merlin Olsen, the Osmonds, Ivy Baker Priest, George W. Romney, Wallace Stegner, Brigham Young, Loretta Young.

Website. www.utah.gov

Vermont (VT)

Green Mountain State

People. Population: 647,464; rank: 50. **Pop. change** (2020-23): 0.7%. **Pop. density:** 70 per sq mi. **Racial distribution:** 93.6% white; 1.6% Black; 2.1% Asian; 0.4% Amer. Ind.; <0.05% Hawaiian/Pacific Islander; 2 or more races, 2.2%. **Hispanic pop.:** 2.6%.

Geography. Total area: 9,613 sq mi; rank: 45. **Land area:** 9,215 sq mi; rank: 43. **Acres forested:** 4.5 mil. **Location:** northern New England state. **Climate:** temperate, with considerable temperature extremes; heavy snowfall in mountains. **Topography:** Green Mts. N-S backbone 20-36 mi wide; avg. altitude 1,000 ft. **Capital:** Montpelier. **Chief airport:** Burlington.

Economy. Chief industries: manufacturing, tourism, agriculture, trade, finance, insurance, real estate, government. **Chief manuf. goods:** dairy, plastics, printing, wood furniture, sporting goods, metalworking machinery. **Chief crops:** greenhouse and nursery, hay, maple syrup, apples, berries, sweet corn. **Farm income:** Crops: $237.44 mil. Livestock: $801.72 mil. **Nonfuel minerals:** $160 mil; sand and gravel (construction), stone (crushed), stone (dimension), talc (crude). **Gross state product:** $43.1 bil. **Sales tax:** 6.0%. **Gasoline tax:** 51.01 cents/gal. **Employment distrib.:** 18.3% govt.; 16.7% trade/trans./util.; 8.9% mfg.; 20.8% ed./health; 10.9% prof./bus. serv.; 10.7% leisure/hosp.; 3.9% finance; 5.0% constr./mining/log.; 1.4% info.; 3.3% other serv. **Unemployment:** 2.0%. **Min. wage/hr.:** $13.67. **Per cap. pers. income:** $66,463. **New private housing:** 2,456 units/$573.2 mil. **Broadband internet:** 90.3%. **Commercial banks:** 17; deposits: $14.7 bil. **Savings institutions:** 8; deposits: $3.4 bil. **Lottery:** total sales: $159.0 mil; profit: $33.6 mil.

Federal govt. Fed. civ. employees: 3,262; **avg. salary:** $105,080. **Notable fed. facilities:** Law Enforcement Support Ctr., Williston.

Education. High school grad. rate: 82.8%. **4-yr. public coll./univ.:** 4; **2-yr. public:** 1; **4-yr. private:** 11.

Energy. Electricity use/cost: 568 kWh, $113.21.

State data. Motto: Freedom and unity. **Flower:** Red clover. **Bird:** Hermit thrush. **Tree:** Sugar maple. **Song:** "These Green Mountains." **Entered union:** Mar. 4, 1791; rank: 14th.

Tourism. Tourist spending: $2.9 bil (2022); change, 2019-22: 2.2%. **Attractions:** Shelburne Museum; Shelburne Farms; Vermont Marble Museum, Proctor; Bennington Battle Monument; Pres. Calvin Coolidge Homestead, Plymouth; Ben & Jerry's Factory, Waterbury; Stowe, Killington, and Burke ski resorts: Hildene (Robert Todd Lincoln home), Manchester; Marsh-Billings-Rockefeller Natl. Historical Park, Woodstock. **Information:** Vermont Dept. of Tourism and Marketing, Natl. Life Drive, Deane C. Davis Building, 6th Fl., Montpelier, VT 05620; 1-800-VERMONT, (802) 828-3237; www.vermontvacation.com

History. Inhabited for 10,000 years or more, the region attracted Abenaki and Mahican peoples before Europeans arrived. France's Champlain explored the lake that now bears his name, 1609. The first European settlement was on Isle la Motte in Lake Champlain, 1666. During the American Revolution, Ethan Allen and the Green Mountain Boys captured Ft. Ticonderoga (NY), 1775. Under a constitution that provided for public schools and abolished slavery, settlers declared a republic, 1777. Vermont joined the Union, 1791. Agriculture dominated in the 19th cent. Still mainly rural, the state expanded tourism and manufacturing after World War II, and IBM became the largest private employer. Vermont was the first state to recognize same-sex civil unions (2000) and to enact equal same-sex marriage rights via legislation (2009). Legislation to legalize recreational marijuana went into effect in July 2018. Pres. Joe Biden on July 9, 2023, declared a state of emergency in all of the state's 14 counties amid catastrophic flooding.

Famous Vermonters. Ethan Allen, Chester A. Arthur, Calvin Coolidge, Howard Dean, John Deere, George Dewey, John Dewey, Stephen A. Douglas, Dorothy Canfield Fisher, James Fisk, James "Jim" Jeffords, Bernie Sanders, Jody Williams.

Website. www.vermont.gov

Virginia (VA)

Old Dominion

People. Population: 8,715,698; rank: 12. **Pop. change** (2020-23): 1.0%. **Pop. density:** 221 per sq mi. **Racial distribution:** 68.3% white; 20.0% Black; 7.4% Asian; 0.6% Amer. Ind.; 0.1% Hawaiian/Pacific Islander; 2 or more races, 3.5%. **Hispanic pop.:** 11.2%.

Geography. Total area: 42,764 sq mi; rank: 35. **Land area:** 39,472 sq mi; rank: 37. **Acres forested:** 16.0 mil. **Location:** South Atlantic state bounded by the Atlantic Ocean on the E and surrounded by North Carolina, Tennessee, Kentucky, West Virginia, and Maryland. **Climate:** mild and equable. **Topography:** mountain and valley region in the W, including the Blue Ridge Mts.; rolling Piedmont Plateau; tidewater, or coastal plain, including the Eastern Shore. **Capital:** Richmond. **Chief airports:** Arlington, Dulles (Washington, DC), Highland Springs (Richmond), Norfolk.

Economy. Chief industries: services, trade, government, manufacturing, tourism, agriculture. **Chief manuf. goods:** beverages and tobacco, transportation equip., animal slaughtering and processing, plastics, textiles, paper and paper prods., printing, pharmaceuticals, furniture, chemicals. **Chief crops:** greenhouse and nursery, soybeans, tomatoes, corn, tobacco, hay, cotton, apples, wheat, peanuts, potatoes. **Farm income:** Crops: $1.65 bil. Livestock: $3.41 bil. **Nonfuel minerals:** $1.6 mil; cement, lime, sand and gravel (construction), sand and gravel (industrial), stone (crushed). **Commercial fishing:** $169.0 mil. **Chief ports:** Norfolk Harbor, Newport News, Richmond, Hopewell. **Gross state product:** $707.1 bil. **Sales tax:** 5.3%. **Gasoline tax:** 57.50 cents/gal. **Employment distrib.:** 17.8% govt.; 15.9% trade/trans./util.; 5.9% mfg.; 14.3% ed./health; 19.3% prof./bus. serv.; 9.8% leisure/hosp.; 5.2% finance; 5.4% constr./mining/log.; 1.6% info.; 4.8% other serv. **Unemployment:** 2.9%. **Min. wage/hr.:** $12.00. **Per cap. pers. income:** $72,855. **New private housing:** 36,096 units/$7.4 bil. **Broadband internet:** 96.0%. **Commercial banks:** 109; deposits: $302.9 bil. **Savings institutions:** 4; deposits: $376.0 mil. **Lottery:** total sales: $3.6 bil; profit: $991.7 mil.

Federal govt. Fed. civ. employees: 143,775; **avg. salary:** $119,366. **Notable fed. facilities:** Pentagon; Norfolk Naval Sta., Shipyard; Ft. Belvoir; Joint Base Langley-Eustis; NASA Langley Res. Ctr.; CIA George Bush Ctr. for Intelligence, Langley; FBI Academy, Quantico USMC Base; Nav. Surface Warfare Ctr. Dahlgren Div.; USDA Food and Nutrition Serv., Alexandria; U.S. Geological Survey Natl. Ctr., Reston.

Education. High school grad. rate: 89.1%. **4-yr. public coll./univ.:** 16; **2-yr. public:** 24; **4-yr. private:** 38.

Energy. Electricity use/cost: 1,086 kWh, $144.96.

State data. Motto: Sic Semper Tyrannis (Thus always to tyrants). **Flower:** American dogwood. **Bird:** Northern cardinal. **Tree:** American dogwood. **Song emeritus:** "Carry Me Back to Old Virginia." **Tenth** of original 13 states to ratify the Constitution, June 25, 1788.

Tourism. Tourist spending: $30.3 bil (2022); change, 2019-22: 4.4%. **Attractions:** Colonial Williamsburg, Busch Gardens Williamsburg, Jamestown Settlement, in Williamsburg; Yorktown Victory Ctr.; Wolf Trap Natl. Park for the Performing Arts, near Vienna; Arlington Natl. Cemetery; George Washington's Mount Vernon; Thomas Jefferson's Monticello, Charlottesville; Stratford Hall (Robert E. Lee birthplace); Appomattox Court House Natl. Historical Park; Shenandoah Natl. Park; Blue Ridge Natl. Parkway; Virginia Beach; Kings Dominion amusement park, Doswell. **Information:** Virginia Tourism Corp., 901 E. Cary St., Ste. 900, Richmond, VA 23219; 1-800-VISITVA; www.virginia.org

History. Cherokee and Susquehanna peoples and the Algonquians of the Powhatan Confederacy were in the region when Europeans arrived. English settlers founded Jamestown, 1607. Four of the first five U.S. presidents—Washington, Jefferson, Madison, and Monroe—came from Virginia. The conclusive battle of the American Revolution took place at Yorktown, 1781. The state profited from tobacco, cotton, and the slave trade; in 1860, nearly one-third of the population was enslaved. Virginia seceded from the Union, 1861, and Richmond became the capital of the Confederacy. Western counties, loyal to the Union, split off to become West Virginia, 1863. The war ended with Robert E. Lee's surrender to Ulysses S. Grant at Appomattox, 1865; Virginia was readmitted to the Union, 1870. In the 20th cent., expansion of federal civilian jobs and military facilities transformed the economy. State officials pledged "massive resistance" to racial integration in the mid-1950s. In 1989, L. Douglas Wilder became the first elected Black governor in U.S. history. On Sept. 11, 2001, terrorist hijackers crashed a jet into U.S. defense headquarters at the Pentagon, in Arlington. A driver who steered his car into a crowd of counterprotesters at a 2017 white nationalist rally in Charlottesville was convicted of murder in state court, 2018, and pleaded guilty to federal hate crimes charges in 2019. In 2019, Virginia's top three state officeholders faced calls to resign, over separate blackface and sexual assault scandals.

Famous Virginians. Arthur Ashe, Sandra Bullock, Richard E. Byrd, James B. Cabell, Henry Clay, Katie Couric, Gabby Douglas, Jubal Early, Jerry Falwell, William Henry Harrison, Patrick Henry, A. P. Hill, Thomas Jefferson, Joseph E. Johnston, Robert E. Lee, Meriwether Lewis and William Clark, James Madison, John Marshall, George Mason, James Monroe, Sean Parker, George Pickett, Pocahontas, Edgar Allan Poe, John Randolph, Walter Reed, Rev. Pat Robertson, John Smith, J. E. B. Stuart, William Styron, Zachary Taylor, John Tyler, Maggie Walker, Booker T. Washington, George Washington, L. Douglas Wilder, Woodrow Wilson.

Website. www.virginia.gov

Washington (WA)

Evergreen State

People. Population: 7,812,880; rank: 13. **Pop. change** (2020-23): 1.4%. **Pop. density:** 118 per sq mi. **Racial distribution:** 76.3% white; 4.7% Black; 10.8% Asian; 2.0% Amer. Ind.; 0.9% Hawaiian/Pacific Islander; 2 or more races, 5.4%. **Hispanic pop.:** 14.6%.

Geography. Total area: 71,282 sq mi; rank: 18. **Land area:** 66,438 sq mi; rank: 20. **Acres forested:** 22.1 mil. **Location:** Pacific state bordered by Canada on the N, Idaho on the E, Oregon on the S, the Pacific Ocean on the W. **Climate:** mild, dominated by the Pacific Ocean and protected by the Cascades. **Topography:** Olympic Mts. on NW peninsula; open land along coast to Columbia R.; flat terrain of Puget Sound Lowland; high peaks of Cascade Mts. to the E; Columbia Basin in central portion; highlands to the NE; mountains to the SE. **Capital:** Olympia. **Chief airports:** Seattle, Spokane.

Economy. Chief industries: advanced technology, aerospace, biotechnology, intl. trade, forestry, tourism, recycling, agriculture and food processing. **Chief manuf. goods:** aerospace, petroleum, food, paper, milled lumber, plastics, structural metals, computers and electronics. **Chief crops:** apples, potatoes, wheat, hay, cherries, greenhouse and nursery, forest products, pears, grapes, onions, hops, sweet corn, Christmas trees, mint, raspberries. **Farm income:** Crops: $8.01 bil. Livestock: $4.13 bil. **Nonfuel minerals:** $796 mil; cement, diatomite, lime, sand and gravel (construction), stone (crushed). **Commercial fishing:** $325.6 mil. **Chief ports:** Seattle, Tacoma, Vancouver, Kelso-Longview, Anacortes. **Gross state product:** $801.5 bil. **Sales tax:** 6.5%. **Gasoline tax:** 71.22 cents/gal. **Employment distrib.:** 16.7% govt.; 16.9% trade/trans./util.; 7.6% mfg.; 15.3% ed./health; 14.9% prof./bus. serv.; 9.6% leisure/hosp.; 4.6% finance; 6.5% constr./mining/log.; 4.5% info.; 3.5% other serv.

Unemployment: 4.1%. **Min. wage/hr.:** $16.28. **Per cap. pers. income:** $79,659. **New private housing:** 37,097 units/$9.5 bil. **Broadband internet:** 95.5%. **Commercial banks:** 65; deposits: $207.6 bil. **Savings institutions:** 8; deposits: $6.8 bil. **Lottery:** total sales: $1.0 bil; profit: $253.1 mil.

Federal govt. Fed. civ. employees: 56,264; **avg. salary:** $101,324. **Notable fed. facilities:** Bonneville Power Admin.; Lewis-McChord Joint Base; Fairchild AFB; Hanford Site (fmr. nuclear weapons production facility); Naval Base Kitsap (Bremerton and Bangor); NAS Whidbey Island; Pacific Northwest Natl. Lab, Richland.

Education. High school grad. rate: 83.6%. **4-yr. public coll./univ.:** 36; **2-yr. public:** 6; **4-yr. private:** 21.

Energy. Electricity use/cost: 1,013 kWh, $103.84.

State data. Motto: Alki (By and by). **Flower:** Western rhododendron. **Bird:** Willow goldfinch. **Tree:** Western hemlock. **Song:** "Washington, My Home." **Entered union:** Nov. 11, 1889; rank: 42nd.

Tourism. Tourist spending: $22.6 bil (2022); change, 2019-22: 0.9%. **Attractions:** Seattle Center, Space Needle, EMP Museum, Museum of Flight, Pike Place Market, Underground Tour, in Seattle; Mount Rainier, Olympic, and North Cascades Natl. Parks; Mount St. Helens Natl. Volcanic Monument; Puget Sound; San Juan Islands; Grand Coulee Dam; Columbia R. Gorge Natl. Scenic Area; Riverfront Park, Spokane; Snoqualmie Falls. **Information:** State of Washington Tourism, P.O. Box 16612, Seattle, WA 98116; 1-800-544-1800; www.stateofwatourism.com

History. People of the Clovis culture lived in the region 11,000 years ago. At the time of European contact, Native Americans in the area included Nez Percé, Spokane, Yakima, Cayuse, Okanogan, Walla Walla, and Colville peoples in the interior, and Nooksak, Chinook, Nisqually, Clallam, Makah, Quinault, and Puyallup peoples along the coast. Spain's Bruno de Heceta sailed the coast, 1775. In 1792, British naval officer George Vancouver mapped the Puget Sound area, and American Capt. Robert Gray sailed up the Columbia R. Fur traders and missionaries arrived in the first half of the 19th cent. Final agreement on the border of Washington and Canada was made with Britain, 1846. Completion in 1883 of a transcontinental rail link between Puget Sound and the eastern U.S. aided immigration, and Washington became a state in 1889. In the 20th cent., cheap hydroelectric power spurred growth in the aluminum and aircraft industries. Founded in 1975, Microsoft became a computer software giant. Mount St. Helens erupted, 1980. With Starbucks coffee and Amazon.com, Seattle became a national trendsetter in the 1990s. Violent street protests disrupted a World Trade Organization meeting there in 1999. Gary Locke, in office 1997-2005, was the first U.S. governor of Chinese ancestry. A mudslide in Mar. 2014 killed 43 people in a rural area north of Seattle.

Famous Washingtonians. Paul Allen, Glenn Beck, Raymond Carver, Kurt Cobain, Bing Crosby, William O. Douglas, Bill Gates, Jimi Hendrix, Henry M. Jackson, Gary Larson, Mary McCarthy, Robert Motherwell, Edward R. Murrow, Apolo Ohno, Chris Pratt, Theodore Roethke, Ann Rule, Hope Solo, Hilary Swank, Julia Sweeney, Adam West, Marcus Whitman, Minoru Yamasaki.

Website. access.wa.gov

West Virginia (WV)

Mountain State

People. Population: 1,770,071; rank: 39. **Pop. change** (2020-23): –1.3%. **Pop. density:** 74 per sq mi. **Racial distribution:** 92.8% white; 3.8% Black; 0.9% Asian; 0.3% Amer. Ind.; <0.05% Hawaiian/Pacific Islander; 2 or more races, 2.1%. **Hispanic pop.:** 2.2%.

Geography. Total area: 24,224 sq mi; rank: 41. **Land area:** 24,035 sq mi; rank: 41. **Acres forested:** 12.0 mil. **Location:** South Atlantic state bounded on the N by Pennsylvania, Maryland; on the S, W, and NW by Virginia, Kentucky, Ohio; on the E by Maryland and Virginia. **Climate:** humid continental except for marine modification in the lower panhandle. **Topography:** hilly to mountainous; Allegheny Plateau in the W covers two-thirds of state; mountains here are the highest in the state, over 4,000 ft. **Capital:** Charleston.

Economy. Chief industries: manufacturing, services, mining, tourism. **Chief manuf. goods:** chemicals, aluminum, motor vehicle parts, lumber and plywood, primary and fabricated metals. **Chief crops:** hay, apples, corn, peaches, soybeans, tobacco, wheat. **Farm income:** Crops: $185.16 mil. Livestock: $714.29 mil. **Nonfuel minerals:** $231 mil; cement, lime, sand and gravel (construction), sand and gravel (industrial), stone (crushed). **Chief port:** Huntington. **Gross state product:** $99.5 bil. **Sales tax:** 6.0%. **Gasoline tax:** 54.10 cents/gal. **Employment distrib.:** 21.9% govt.; 16.9% trade/trans./util.; 6.3% mfg.; 19.2% ed./health; 10.3% prof./bus. serv.; 9.9% leisure/hosp.; 3.6% finance; 7.6% constr./mining/log.; 1.1% info.; 3.3% other serv. **Unemployment:** 3.9%. **Min. wage/hr.:** $8.75. **Per cap. pers. income:** $52,585. **New private housing:** 4,014 units/$760.5 mil. **Broadband internet:** 89.3%. **Commercial banks:** 63; deposits: $44.4 bil. **Savings institutions:** 4; deposits: $891.0 mil. **Lottery:** total sales: $1.4 bil; profit: $576.5 mil.

Federal govt. Fed. civ. employees: 17,187; **avg. salary:** $98,471. **Notable fed. facilities:** Natl. Radio Astronomy Observatory, Green Bank; Bureau of the Fiscal Service Bldg.; Alderson Fed. Prison Camp; FBI Criminal Justice Information Services.

Education. High school grad. rate: 91.2%. **4-yr. public coll./univ.:** 13; **2-yr. public:** 9; **4-yr. private:** 9.

Energy. Electricity use/cost: 1,074 kWh, $142.13.

State data. Motto: Montani Semper Liberi (Mountaineers are always free). **Flower:** Big rhododendron. **Bird:** Cardinal. **Tree:** Sugar maple. **Songs:** "The West Virginia Hills"; "This Is My West Virginia"; "West Virginia, My Home, Sweet Home." **Entered union:** June 20, 1863; rank: 35th.

Tourism. Tourist spending: $5.3 bil (2022); change, 2019-22: 17.3%. **Attractions:** Harpers Ferry Natl. Historical Park, Appalachian Trail Conservancy and Visitor Ctr., in Harpers Ferry; Clay Center for the Arts and Sciences and Avampato Discovery Museum, Charleston; The Greenbrier resort, White Sulphur Springs; Berkeley Springs State Park; Seneca Rocks State Park; New River Gorge Natl. River; Beckley Exhibition Coal Mine; Monongahela Natl. Forest; Fenton Art Glass Company, Williamstown; Mountain State Forest Festival, Elkins; Mountain State Art & Craft Fair, Ripley; Green Bank Telescope (world's largest fully steerable radio telescope); Cass Scenic Railroad State Park. **Information:** West Virginia Tourism Office, Bldg. 3, Ste. 100, State Capitol Complex, 1900 Kanawha Blvd. East, Charleston, WV 25305; 1-800-CALLWVA; wvtourism.com

History. Sparsely inhabited at the time of European contact, the area was primarily Native American hunting grounds. British explorers Thomas Batts and Robert Fallam reached the New R., 1671. Coal, discovered in 1742, was mined extensively by the mid-19th cent. White settlement led to conflicts with Native Americans, including a major battle in which settlers defeated an Indian confederacy at Point Pleasant, 1774. The region joined the Union as part of Virginia, 1788. Long-standing tensions between the E and W parts of the state came to a head in 1861, when Virginia seceded. Delegates of western counties, meeting at Wheeling, repudiated the act and created a new state, Kanawha, later renamed West Virginia, which was admitted to the Union in 1863. Poverty has been a problem for much of the state's subsequent history. It continued to rank low in per capita personal income, despite billions of dollars in federal contracts brought to the state by nine-term U.S. Sen. Robert Byrd, who passed away in 2010. Coal mining, though dangerous and challenged by environmental concerns, continues to be a major industry; nearly 30 miners were killed in a mine explosion in 2010. Flash flooding across the state killed at least 23 people in late June 2016. A statewide teacher walkout in Apr. 2018 demanded increased pay and school funding.

Famous West Virginians. George Brett, Pearl S. Buck, Robert C. Byrd, Henry Louis Gates Jr., Stonewall Jackson, Don Knotts, Michael Joseph Owens, Brad Paisley, Mary Lou Retton, Walter Reuther, Cyrus Vance, Jerry West, Charles "Chuck" Yeager.

Website. www.wv.gov

Wisconsin (WI)

Badger State

People. Population: 5,910,955; rank: 20. **Pop. change** (2020-23): 0.3%. **Pop. density:** 109 per sq mi. **Racial distribution:** 86.4% white; 6.6% Black; 3.3% Asian; 1.2% Amer. Ind.; 0.1% Hawaiian/Pacific Islander; 2 or more races, 2.3%. **Hispanic pop.:** 8.1%.

Geography. Total area: 65,480 sq mi; rank: 23. **Land area:** 54,153 sq mi; rank: 25. **Acres forested:** 16.9 mil. **Location:** East North Central state bounded on the N by Lake Superior and Upper Michigan, on the E by Lake Michigan, on the S by Illinois, on the W by Minnesota and Iowa. **Climate:** long, cold winters and short, warm summers tempered by the Great Lakes. **Topography:** narrow Lake Superior Lowland plain met by Northern Highland, which slopes gently to the sandy crescent Central Plain; Western Upland in the SW; three broad parallel limestone ridges running N-S are separated by wide and shallow lowlands in the SE. **Capital:** Madison. **Chief airports:** Milwaukee, Madison.

Economy. Chief industries: services, manufacturing, trade, government, agriculture, tourism. **Chief manuf. goods:** transportation, dairy, animal slaughtering and processing, paper, printing, plastics, computers and electronics. **Chief crops:** corn, greenhouse and nursery, soybeans, potatoes, cranberries, hay, wheat, snap beans, apples, peas. **Farm income:**

Crops: $5.71 bil. Livestock: $10.90 bil. **Nonfuel minerals:** $1.5 bil; lime, sand and gravel (construction), sand and gravel (industrial), stone (crushed), stone (dimension). **Commercial fishing** (2018): $2.9 mil. **Chief ports:** Superior, Milwaukee, Green Bay. **Gross state product:** $414.0 bil. **Sales tax:** 5.0%. **Gasoline tax:** 51.30 cents/gal. **Employment distrib.:** 14.0% govt.; 18.2% trade/trans./util.; 15.8% mfg.; 15.9% ed./health; 10.8% prof./bus. serv.; 9.1% leisure/hosp.; 5.3% finance; 4.7% constr./mining/log.; 1.6% info.; 4.8% other serv. **Unemployment:** 3.0%. **Min. wage/hr.:** $7.25. **Per cap. pers. income:** $63,963. **New private housing:** 21,494 units/$6.0 bil. **Broadband internet:** 94.8%. **Commercial banks:** 173; deposits: $186.3 bil. **Savings institutions:** 24; deposits: $9.4 bil. **Lottery:** total sales: $981.7 mil; profit: $324.6 mil.

Federal govt. Fed. civ. employees: 17,868; **avg. salary:** $94,949. **Notable fed. facilities:** Ft. McCoy; USDA Forest Products Lab, Madison.

Education. High school grad. rate: 90.3%. **4-yr. public coll./univ.:** 16; **2-yr. public:** 16; **4-yr. private:** 31.

Energy. Electricity use/cost: 684 kWh, $106.94.

State data. Motto: Forward. **Flower:** Wood violet. **Bird:** American robin. **Tree:** Sugar maple. **Song:** "On, Wisconsin!" **Entered union:** May 29, 1848; rank: 30th.

Tourism. Tourist spending: $14.5 bil (2022); change, 2019-22: 8.8%. **Attractions:** Wade House, Greenbush; Villa Louis, Prairie du Chien; Circus World Museum, Baraboo; Wisconsin Dells; Old World Wisconsin, Eagle; shoreline and state parks of Door County; Chequamegon-Nicolet Natl. Forest; House on the Rock, Taliesin, in Spring Green; Monona Terrace Community and Convention Ctr., Madison; Milwaukee Art Museum, Pabst Mansion, in Milwaukee. **Information:** Wisconsin Dept. of Tourism, 3319 West Beltline Hwy., P.O. Box 8690, Madison, WI 53708-8690; 1-800-432-TRIP; www.travelwisconsin.com

History. At the time of European contact, Ojibwa, Menominee, Winnebago, Kickapoo, Sauk, Fox, and Potawatomi peoples inhabited the area. French explorer Jean Nicolet reached Green Bay, 1634; French missionaries and fur traders followed. The British took over, 1763. The U.S. won the land after the American Revolution but did not wield control until forts were established at Green Bay and Prairie du Chien, 1816. Native Americans rebelled against the seizure of tribal lands in the Black Hawk War, 1832, but were defeated and relocated to reservations. Wisconsin became a territory, 1836, and a state, 1848. Some 96,000 soldiers served the Union cause during the Civil War. Many immigrants arrived from Germany, Poland, and Scandinavia. Wisconsin agriculture focused on dairy; Milwaukee became a manufacturing center. As governor, 1901-06, Robert La Follette pushed Progressive reforms such as direct primary voting and consumer protection laws. The era of McCarthyism ended when anti-Communist crusader U.S. Sen. Joseph McCarthy of Wisconsin was censured by the Senate, 1954. The state legislature passed controversial measures in 2011 to restrict collective bargaining by some 170,000 public-sector employees, and in 2014 became the 25th state to pass a "right-to-work" law. A Kenosha police officer in Aug. 2020 shot Black man Jacob Blake, sparking multiple nights of unrest quelled by Natl. Guard troops; a pro-police 17-year-old, claiming self-defense, fatally shot two protesters. In Dec. 2021, a driver plowed into a Christmas parade in Waukesha, killing six people.

Famous Wisconsinites. Don Ameche, Carrie Chapman Catt, Willem Dafoe, Edna Ferber, Hamlin Garland, King Camp Gillette, Harry Houdini, Robert La Follette, (Vladzio Valentino) Liberace, Alfred Lunt, Pat O'Brien, Georgia O'Keeffe, Danica Patrick, Les Paul, William H. Rehnquist, John Ringling, Donald K. "Deke" Slayton, Spencer Tracy, Orson Welles, Laura Ingalls Wilder, Thornton Wilder, Frank Lloyd Wright.

Website. www.wisconsin.gov

Wyoming (WY)

Equality State, Cowboy State

People. Population: 584,057; rank: 51. **Pop. change** (2020-23): 1.2%. **Pop. density:** 6 per sq mi. **Racial distribution:** 92.3% white; 1.2% Black; 1.2% Asian; 2.8% Amer. Ind.; 0.1% Hawaiian/Pacific Islander; 2 or more races, 2.4%. **Hispanic pop.:** 10.8%.

Geography. Total area: 97,784 sq mi; rank: 10. **Land area:** 97,063 sq mi; rank: 9. **Acres forested:** 10.8 mil. **Location:** Mountain state in the high western plateaus of the Great Plains. **Climate:** semidesert conditions throughout; true desert in the Bighorn and Great Divide Basins. **Topography:** eastern Great Plains rise to the foothills of the Rocky Mts.; the Continental Divide crosses the state from the NW to the SE. **Capital:** Cheyenne.

Economy. Chief industries: mineral extraction, oil, natural gas, tourism and recreation, agriculture. **Chief manuf. goods:** petroleum, chemicals, fabricated metal, beet sugar, lumber. **Chief crops:** hay, sugar beets, barley, dry beans, wheat, corn, greenhouse and nursery, oats. **Farm income:** Crops: $489.75 mil. Livestock: $1.42 bil. **Nonfuel minerals:** $3.2 bil; clay (bentonite and common clay), helium, sand and gravel (construction), soda ash, stone (crushed). **Gross state product:** $50.2 bil. **Sales tax:** 4.0%. **Gasoline tax:** 42.40 cents/gal. **Employment distrib.:** 24.7% govt.; 17.9% trade/trans./util.; 3.6% mfg.; 10.2% ed./health; 7.3% prof./bus. serv.; 12.6% leisure/hosp.; 4.0% finance; 13.4% constr./mining/log.; 1.1% info.; 5.3% other serv. **Unemployment:** 2.9%. **Min. wage/hr.:** $7.25. **Per cap. pers. income:** $77,837. **New private housing:** 1,681 units/$575.3 mil. **Broadband internet:** 94.2%. **Commercial banks:** 43; deposits: $20.4 bil. **Savings institutions:** 2; deposits: $791.0 mil. **Lottery:** total sales: $44.2 mil; profit: $6.5 mil.

Federal govt. Fed. civ. employees: 6,067; **avg. salary:** $87,548. **Notable fed. facilities:** Warren AFB.

Education. High school grad. rate: 81.8%. **4-yr. public coll./univ.:** 1; **2-yr. public:** 7; **4-yr. private:** 0.

Energy. Electricity use/cost: 891 kWh, $98.78.

State data. Motto: Equal rights. **Flower:** Indian paintbrush. **Bird:** Western meadowlark. **Tree:** Plains cottonwood. **Song:** "Wyoming." **Entered union:** July 10, 1890; rank: 44th.

Tourism. Tourist spending: $3.9 bil (2022); change, 2019-22: –1.5%. **Attractions:** Yellowstone Natl. Park (est. 1872, first U.S. national park); Grand Teton Natl. Park; Natl. Elk Refuge, Jackson; Devils Tower Natl. Monument; Ft. Laramie Natl. Historic Site; Oregon Trail ruts, Guernsey; Buffalo Bill Historical Ctr., Cody; Cheyenne Frontier Days. **Information:** Wyoming Office of Tourism, 5611 High Plains Rd., Cheyenne, WY 82007; 1-800-225-5996; www.travelwyoming.com

History. Inhabited for at least 12,000 years, the region supported Shoshone, Crow, Cheyenne, Oglala Sioux, and Arapaho peoples when Europeans arrived. France's Vérendrye brothers were the first Europeans to see the region, 1742-43. John Colter, an American, traversed the Yellowstone area, 1807-08. Trappers and fur traders followed in the 1820s. Forts Laramie and Bridger became important stops on trails to the West Coast. Population grew after the Union Pacific railroad crossed the state, 1867-68. Wyoming became a territory, 1868, and the first to extend full voting rights to women, 1869. Statehood was attained, 1890. Disputes between large landowners and small ranchers culminated in the Johnson County Cattle War, 1892; federal troops were called in to restore order. Nellie Tayloe Ross was the first woman governor to take office in the U.S., 1925. Wyoming, the least populous state, has relied on the energy, tourism, and ranching industries in recent decades. Dick Cheney, Wyoming's representative in the U.S. House, 1979-89, served as U.S. vice pres., 2001-09. Cheney's daughter, three-term U.S. Rep. Liz Cheney, was stripped of her U.S. House leadership position in May 2021 after refusing to back former Pres. Trump's groundless assertions of election fraud.

Famous Wyomingites. James Bridger, Dick Cheney, William F. "Buffalo Bill" Cody, Curt Gowdy, Esther Hobart Morris, Nellie Tayloe Ross.

Website. www.wyo.gov

District of Columbia (DC)

People. Population: 678,972; rank: 49. **Pop. change** (2020-23): –1.5%. **Pop. density:** 11,112 per sq mi. **Racial distribution:** 46.6% white; 44.4% Black; 4.9% Asian; 0.7% Amer. Ind.; 0.2% Hawaiian/Pacific Islander; 2 or more races, 3.3%. **Hispanic pop.:** 12.0%.

Geography. Total area: 68 sq mi; rank: 51. **Land area:** 61 sq mi; rank: 51. **Acres forested:** NA. **Location:** at the confluence of the Potomac and Anacostia Rivers, flanked by Maryland on the N, E, and SE and by Virginia on the SW. **Climate:** hot humid summers, mild winters. **Topography:** low hills rise toward the N away from the Potomac R. and slope to the S; highest elevation, 409 ft; lowest on Potomac R., 1 ft.

Economy. Chief industries: government, legal, publishing, medical, service, tourism. **Farm income:** NA. **Nonfuel minerals:** NA. **Gross state product:** $174.8 bil. **Sales tax:** 6.0%. **Gasoline tax:** 53.30 cents/gal. **Employment distrib.:** 30.4% govt.; 3.9% trade/trans./util.; 0.1% mfg.; 16.1% ed./health; 22.6% prof./bus. serv.; 10.1% leisure/hosp.; 3.3% finance; 1.9% constr./mining/log.; 2.5% info.; 9.0% other serv. **Unemployment:** 4.9%. **Min. wage/hr.:** $17.50. **Per cap. pers. income:** $100,909. **New private housing:** 3,020 units/$427.9 mil. **Broadband internet:** 97.1%. **Commercial banks:** 32; deposits: $61.8 bil. **Savings institutions:** 2; deposits: $115.0 mil. **Lottery:** total sales: $203.5 mil; profit: $33.5 mil.

Federal govt. Fed. civ. employees: 161,788; **avg. salary:** $137,451.

Education. High school grad. rate: 76.4%. **4-yr. public coll./univ.:** 1; **2-yr. public:** 0; **4-yr. private:** 12.

Energy. Electricity use/cost: 685 kWh, $97.15.

District data. Motto: Justitia omnibus (Justice for all). **Flower:** American beauty rose. **Bird:** Wood thrush. **Tree:** Scarlet oak.

Tourism. Tourist spending: $12.9 bil (2022); change, 2019-22: –14.7%. **Attractions:** See Attractions in and Around Washington, DC, pp. 456-57. **Information:** Destination DC, 901 7th St. NW, 4th Fl., Washington, DC, 20001-3719; 1-800-422-8644; www.washington.org

History. The District of Columbia, coextensive with the city of Washington, is the seat of the U.S. federal government. It lies on the west central edge of Maryland on the Potomac R., opposite Virginia. The Piscataway, an Algonquian-speaking people, were living in the region when Europeans arrived in the 17th cent. Proposals for a "federal town" for the deliberations of the Continental Congress were made in 1783. Authorized by Congress, 1790, Pres. George Washington chose the Potomac site and persuaded landowners to sell their holdings to the government. Its area was originally 100 sq mi taken from the sovereignty of Maryland and Virginia. Virginia's portion south of the Potomac was given back to that state in 1846.

Pres. Washington chose Pierre Charles L'Enfant, a Frenchman, to plan the capital. Surveyor Andrew Ellicott finished the official map and design of the city, assisted by Benjamin Banneker, a Black architect and astronomer. Washington laid the cornerstone of the north wing of the Capitol building, 1793, and Pres. John Adams moved to the new national capital, 1800. The City of Washington was incorporated, 1802. British troops invaded, 1814, setting fire to the Capitol, the President's House (as the White House was then called), and other buildings. Pres. Abraham Lincoln ended slavery in the district, 1862. Many African Americans arrived after the Civil War, but racial segregation remained legal until the mid-20th cent. After federal government expansion spurred population growth, 1930-50, an exodus to the suburbs shrank the city's population, 1950-2005.

The 23rd Amendment (1961) granted residents the right to vote for president and vice president. Congress, which has legislative authority over the District under the Constitution, approved legislation in 1970 giving the District one delegate to the House of Representatives, who could vote in committee but not on the floor. Voters approved, 1974, a congressionally drafted charter giving them the right to elect their own mayor and city council. The district won the right to levy taxes, but Congress retained power to veto council actions and approve the city budget. Security measures were dramatically increased after terrorists attacked the U.S. on Sept. 11, 2001. After a 34-year absence, major league baseball returned to the city in 2005. On Jan. 6, 2021, a mob of supporters of outgoing Pres. Donald Trump stormed the Capitol in an apparent attempt to disrupt the joint session of Congress's certification of Pres.-elect Joe Biden's victory. Five deaths resulted, including that of a Capitol police officer and a woman shot by police; as of Aug. 2023, more than 1,000 people had been charged in the insurrection, and more than 560 had been sentenced.

Famous Washingtonians. Edward Albee, Michael Chabon, Frederick Douglass, John Foster Dulles, Kevin Durant, Edward Kennedy, Duke Ellington, Marvin Gaye, Katharine Graham, Goldie Hawn, Taraji P. Henson, J. Edgar Hoover, Bill Nye, Pete Sampras, John Philip Sousa.

Website. www.dc.gov

OUTLYING U.S. AREAS

American Samoa (AS)

People. Population (2024 est.): 43,895. **Pop. change** (2010-20): –10.5%. **Pop. density:** 575 per sq mi. **Racial distribution** (2020 est.): 88.7% Hawaiian/Pacific Islander 88.7% (includes Samoan 83.2%, Tongan 2.2%, other 3.3%), Asian 5.8% (includes Filipino 3.4%, other 2.4%), mixed 4.4%, other 1.1%. **Languages:** Samoan 87.9% (closely related to Hawaiian and other Polynesian languages), English 3.3%, Tongan 2.1%, other Pacific Islander 4.1%, Asian languages 2.1%, other 0.5% (2020 est.).

Geography. Total area: 581 sq mi. **Land area:** 76 sq mi. **Acres forested:** 39,535. **Location:** most southerly of all lands under U.S. sovereignty, about 2,300 mi SW of Honolulu. It is an unincorporated territory consisting of seven islands: Samoan group: **Tutuila** (52.59 sq mi), **Aunu'u** (0.59 sq mi); Manu'a group: **Ta'u** (17.57 sq mi), **Olosega** (2.03 sq mi), **Ofu** (2.83 sq mi); and the atolls **Rose** (0.03 sq mi) and **Swains** (1.38 sq mi). **Climate:** marine tropical, avg. temp 82°F with little seasonal variation; avg. annual rainfall about 36 in. **Topography:** volcanic islands, rugged peaks, and limited coastal plains. About 70% of the land is bush and mountains. **Capital:** Pago Pago, on Tutuila. **Chief airport:** Pago Pago.

Economy. Chief industries: tuna fishing and processing, trade, services, tourism. **Chief crops:** giant taro, taro, yams, coconuts, breadfruits, bananas, papayas. **Livestock** (2008): 35,709 chickens, 16,904 hogs/pigs. **Nonfuel minerals:** crushed stone, trap rock. **Commercial fishing** (2008): $9.7 mil. **Unemployment** (2010): 9.2%. **Min. wage/hr.:** $5.38-$6.79. **Gross domestic product** (2022 est.): $871.0 mil. **Broadband internet** (Dec. 2013): 96.8%. **Commercial banks:** 1; deposits: $2.0 mil.

Fed. govt. Fed. civ. employees: 113; **avg. salary:** $82,210.

Education. 4-yr. public coll./univ.: 1; **2-yr. public:** 0; **4-yr. private:** 0.

Energy. Total electricity consumption (2022 est.): 157.3 mil kWh.

Misc. data. Motto: Samoa Muamua le Atua (In Samoa, God is first). **Flower:** Paogo (Ula-fala). **Plant:** Ava. **Song:** "Amerika Samoa."

Tourism. Attractions: Natl. Park of American Samoa; Natl. Marine Sanctuary of American Samoa; Jean P. Haydon Museum. **Information:** American Samoa Visitors Bureau, Ground Fl., Fagatogo Sq., Route 001, Fagatogo, AS 96799; (684) 633-9805; www.americansamoa.travel

History. A tripartite agreement between Great Britain, Germany, and the U.S. in 1899 gave the U.S. sovereignty over the eastern islands of the Samoan group; these islands became American Samoa. Local chiefs ceded Tutuila and Aunu'u to the U.S. in 1900 and the Manu'a group and Rose Island in 1904; Swains Island was annexed in 1925. Samoa (Western), comprising the larger islands of the Samoan group, was a New Zealand mandate and UN Trusteeship until it became independent Jan. 1, 1962 (now called Samoa).

From 1900 to 1951, American Samoa was under the jurisdiction of the U.S. Navy. Since 1951, it has been under the Interior Dept. On Jan. 3, 1978, the first popularly elected Samoan governor and lieutenant governor were inaugurated. Previously, the governor was appointed by the Sec. of the Interior. American Samoa has a bicameral legislature and elects a delegate to the U.S. House of Representatives who has a voice but no vote, except in committees.

Five of the seven islands are volcanoes. Scientists discovered a rapidly growing volcano, Vailulu'u, between Ta'u and Rose in 1975.

The tuna canning industry has been the backbone of the economy since the 1950s, but one of two canneries closed in 2009, and a third cannery closed in 2016 after opening the year before. An 8.1 magnitude earthquake in Sept. 2009 triggered a tsunami that severely damaged Tutuila.

American Samoans are of Polynesian origin. They are nationals of the U.S. As of 2010, 109,637 lived in the U.S., including 18,287 in Hawaii and 40,100 in California.

Website. www.americansamoa.gov

Guam (GU)

People. Population (2024 est.): 169,532. **Pop change** (2010-20): –3.5%. **Pop. density:** 808 per sq mi. **Racial/ethnic distribution** (2020 est.): 46.1% Native Hawaiian and other Pacific Islander (32.8% Chamorro, 6.7% Chuukese, 1.4% Palauan, 1.4% Pohnpeian. 1.0% Yapese, 2.8% other Native Hawaiian and other Pacific Islander), 35.5% Asian (29.1% Filipino, 2.2% Korean, 1.4% Japanese, 1.3% Chinese [except Taiwanese], 1.5% other Asian), 6.8% white, 0.9% African descent or African-American, 0.1% Indigenous, 0.6% other, 10.0% mixed. **Languages:** English 43.3%, Filipino 24.9%, Chamorro 16.0%, other Pacific Island languages 9.4%, Asian languages 6.5% (2020 est.).

Geography. Total area: 571 sq mi. **Land area:** 210 sq mi. Land use (2018 est.): agricultural land, 33.4%; arable land, 1.9%; permanent crops, 16.7%; permanent pasture, 14.8%; forest, 47.9%; other, 18.7%. **Acres forested:** 69,703. **Location:** largest and southernmost of the Mariana Islands in the West Pacific, 3,700 mi W of Hawaii. **Climate:** tropical, with temperatures from 70° to 90°F; rainy July to Nov., avg. annual rainfall about 80-100 in. **Topography:** coralline limestone plateau in the N; southern chain of low volcanic mountains slopes gently to the W, more steeply to coastal cliffs on the E; general elevation, 500 ft; highest point, Mt. Lamlam, 1,332 ft. **Capital:** Hagåtña. **Chief airport:** Tamuning.

Economy. Chief industries: U.S. military, tourism, construction, shipping, concrete prods., printing and publishing. **Chief manuf. goods:** textiles, foods. **Chief crops:** watermelons, cucumbers, eggplant, long beans, bananas, corn. **Livestock** (2007): 533 chickens, 112 cattle, 635 hogs/pigs, 124 goats. **Nonfuel minerals** (2008): $3.8 mil; crushed stone. **Commercial fishing** (2008): $499,095. **Chief port:** Apra Harbor. **Gross domestic product** (2022 est.): $6.9 bil. **Employment distrib.** (Dec. 2023): 23.9% govt.; 24.4% serv.; 21.6% trade; 18.5% constr.; 5.5% pub. util./trans.; 3.5% insur./real estate/finance; 2.3% mfg.; 0.4% agric. **Unemployment** (2023): 5.4%. **Min. wage/hr.:** $9.25. **Per capita income** (2016): $31,961. **Broadband internet** : 87.2%. **Commercial banks:** 4; deposits: $3.6 bil. **Savings institutions:** 1; deposits: $130.0 mil.

Federal govt. Fed. civ. employees: 3,140; **avg. salary:** $80,088. **Notable fed. facilities:** Andersen AFB.

Education. 4-yr. public coll./univ.: 1; **2-yr. public:** 1; **4-yr. private:** 1.

Energy. Total electricity consumption (2022 est.): 1.7 bil kWh.

Misc. data. Motto: Where America's day begins. **Flower:** Puti Tai Nobio (Bougainvillea). **Bird:** Ko'ko (Guam rail). **Tree:** Ifit (Intsia bijuga). **Song:** "Stand Ye Guamanians."

Tourism. Attractions: Ritidian Point, Guam Natl. Wildlife Refuge; War in the Pacific Natl. Historical Park; Chamorro Village; Two Lovers Point. **Information:** Guam Visitors Bureau, 401 Pale San Vitores Rd., Tumon, Guam 96913; (671) 646-5278; www.visitguam.com

History. Guam was probably settled by voyagers from the Indonesian-Philippine archipelago by 3rd cent. BCE. Pottery, rice cultivation, and megalithic technology show strong East Asian cultural influence. Centralized, village clan-based communities engaged in agriculture and offshore fishing. The estimated population by the early 16th cent. was 50,000-75,000. Portuguese explorer Ferdinand Magellan, sailing for Spain, arrived in the Marianas, Mar. 6, 1521. They were colonized in 1668 by Spanish missionaries, who named them the Mariana Islands in honor of Maria Anna, queen of Spain. When Spain ceded Guam to the U.S., it sold the other Marianas to Germany. Japan obtained a League of Nations mandate over the German islands in 1919; in Dec. 1941, it seized Guam, which was retaken by the U.S. in July-Aug. 1944.

Guam is a self-governing organized unincorporated U.S. territory. The Organic Act of 1950 provided for a governor, elected to a four-year term, and a 21-member unicameral legislature, elected biennially by the residents, who are American citizens. In 1970, the first governor was elected. In 1972, a U.S. law gave Guam one U.S. House delegate, who has a voice but no vote, except in committees.

Guam's quest to change its status to a U.S. commonwealth began in the late 1970s. The Guam Commission on Self-Determination, created in 1984, developed a draft Commonwealth Act. In 1993, legislation proposing a change of status was submitted to the U.S. Congress. In 1994, the U.S. Congress passed legislation transferring 3,200 acres of land on Guam from federal to local control. The Navy approved in 2015 a plan to move 5,000 Marines stationed in Okinawa, Japan, to Guam by 2021. North Korea in Aug. 2017 threatened to target Guam in the wake of new UN sanctions and increasingly heated rhetoric from Pres. Trump.

Website. www.guam.gov

Commonwealth of the Northern Mariana Islands (MP)

People. Population (2024 est.): 51,118. **Pop. change** (2010-20): –12.2%. **Pop. density:** 280 per sq mi. **Racial/ethnic distribution** (2010 est.): 50.0% Asian (includes 35.3% Filipino, 6.8% Chinese, 4.2% Korean, and 3.7% other Asian); 34.9% Native Hawaiian/Pacific Islander (includes 23.9% Chamorro, 4.6% Carolinian, and 6.4% other Native Hawaiian or Pacific Islander); 2.5% other; 2 or more races/ethnicities, 12.7%. **Languages:** Philippine languages 32.8%, Chamorro (official) 24.1%, English (official) 17.0%, other Pacific Island languages 10.1% (includes Carolinian (official), Chinese 6.8%, other Asian languages 7.3%, other 1.9% (2010 est.).

Geography. Total area: 1,975 sq mi. **Land area:** 182 sq mi. **Acres forested:** 60,207. **Location:** between Guam and the Tropic of Cancer, the 14 islands of the Northern Marianas form a 300-mi-long archipelago. Indigenous population is concentrated on the three largest of the six inhabited islands: **Saipan**, the seat of government and commerce, **Rota**, and **Tinian**. **Climate:** tropical, with avg. temperature around 82°F, moderated by NE trade winds; avg. annual rainfall 80-100 in. **Topography:** limestone southern islands with even terraces, coral reefs; volcanic northern isles. **Capital:** Saipan. **Chief airport:** Saipan.

Economy. Chief industries: banking, construction, fishing, mining, tourism, apparel manufacturing, retail. **Chief manuf. goods:** apparel, stone, clay and glass prods. **Chief crops:** bananas, cucumbers, sweet potatoes, taro, watermelons. **Livestock** (2007): 9,700 chickens, 1,395 cattle, 1,483 hogs/pigs. **Commercial fishing** (2010 est.): $608,971. **Chief port:** Saipan. **Gross domestic product** (2020 est.): $661 mil. **Employment distrib.:** 1.9% agriculture; 10.0% industry; 88.1% serv. **Unemployment** (2016): 13.8%. **Min. wage/hr.:** $7.25. **Broadband internet** (Dec. 2013): 80.9%. **Commercial banks:** 3; deposits: $978.0 mil. **Savings institutions:** 1; deposits: $10.0 mil.

Federal govt. Fed. civ. employees: 86; **avg. salary:** $77,344.

Education. 4-yr. public coll./univ.: 1; **2-yr. public:** 0; **4-yr. private:** 0.

Misc. data. Flower: Plumeria. **Bird:** Mariana fruit-dove. **Tree:** Flame tree. **Song:** "Gi Talo Gi Halom Tasi" (In the Middle of the Sea).

Tourism. Attractions: House of Taga; American Memorial Park; Banzai Cliff. **Information:** Marianas Visitors Authority, P.O. Box 500861, Saipan, MP 96950; (670) 664-3200; www.mymarianas.com

History. The people of the Northern Marianas are predominantly of Chamorro cultural extraction, although Carolinians and immigrants from other areas of E. Asia and Micronesia have also settled in the islands. English is among the several languages commonly spoken.

The German-controlled Northern Marianas were placed under Japanese control by a League of Nations mandate after World War I. The U.S. captured the islands during World War II. From July 18, 1947, the U.S. administered the Northern Marianas under a trusteeship agreement with the UN Security Council. In 1975, the residents voted to become a U.S. commonwealth.

The Northern Mariana Islands has been self-governing since 1978, when a constitution drafted and adopted by the people became effective and a popularly elected bicameral legislature (two-year term), with offices of governor (four-year term) and lieut. governor, was inaugurated. Pres. Ronald Reagan proclaimed the Northern Marianas a commonwealth, 1986, and the UN formally ended its trusteeship, 1990. In 2008, U.S. law gave the islands one delegate to the U.S. House of Representatives who has a voice but no vote, except in committees.

Under the 1976 Commonwealth Covenant with the U.S., the islands are exempt from federal immigration and import laws, and minimum wage was lower than on the mainland. The garment-making industry, which has since boomed, has drawn accusations of sweatshop conditions from some critics. As mandated by legislation passed in 2007, the minimum wage finally reached the federal rate in Sept. 2018.

Website. governor.gov.mp

Commonwealth of Puerto Rico (PR)

Estado Libre Asociado de Puerto Rico

People. Population: 3,205,691 (about 5.8 mil additional Puerto Ricans reside in mainland U.S.). **Pop. change** (2020-23): –2.4%. **Pop. density:** 936 per sq mi. **Racial distribution** (2022): 43.6% white; 8.8% Black; 0.2% Asian; 0.2% Amer. Ind.; <0.05% Hawaiian/Pacific Islander; 2 or more races, 23.3%. **Hispanic pop.** (2022): 98.7%. **Languages:** Spanish and English are joint official languages.

Geography. Total area: 5,323 sq mi. **Land area:** 3,423 sq mi. **Acres forested:** 1.1 mil. **Location:** island between the Atlantic to the N and the Caribbean to the S; it is easternmost of the West Indies group called the Greater Antilles, of which Cuba, Hispaniola, and Jamaica are the larger islands. **Climate:** mild, with a mean temperature of 77°F. **Topography:** mountainous throughout three-fourths of its rectangular area, surrounded by a broken coastal plain; highest peak, Cerro de Punto, 4,390 ft. **Capital:** San Juan. **Chief airport:** San Juan.

Economy. Chief industries: manufacturing, service, tourism. **Chief manuf. goods:** pharmaceuticals, medical equip., electronics, apparel, food products. **Chief crops:** pumpkins, coffee, watermelons, plantains, yams, oranges, pineapples, sugarcane, bananas. **Livestock** (2012): 10.9 mil chickens, 257,285 cattle, 12,539 sheep, 48,262 hogs/pigs. **Nonfuel minerals** (2013): $66.3 mil; crushed stone, lime, salt, cement (portland), clays (common), cement (masonry). **Commercial fishing** (2008): $3.8 mil. **Chief ports:** San Juan, Ponce, Mayagüez. **Gross domestic product** (2022 est.): $113.2 bil. **Sales tax:** 11.5%. **Employment distrib.:** 21.2% govt.; 19.6% trade/trans./util.; 8.9% mfg.; 13.4% ed./health; 14.6% prof./bus. serv.; 10.1% leisure/hosp.; 5.0% finance; 3.8% constr./mining/log.; 1.5% info.; 2.0% other serv. **Unemployment** (2023): 6.0%. **Min. wage/hr.:** $10.50. **Per capita income** (2022): $15,637. **Broadband internet:** 89.8%. **Commercial banks:** 5; deposits: $90.0 bil. **Lottery** (2009): total sales: $421.2 mil; profit: $146.9 mil.

Federal govt. Fed. civ. employees: 14,350; **avg. salary:** $78,046. **Notable fed. facilities:** PR Natl. Guard Training Area at Camp Santiago; Ft. Buchanan; Intl. Inst. of Tropical Forestry, San Juan; Vieques Natl. Wildlife Refuge; USGS Caribbean Water Science Ctr., Guaynabo.

Education. High school grad. rate: 73.8%. **4-yr. public coll./univ.:** 14; **2-yr. public:** 3; **4-yr. private:** 45.

Energy. Total electricity consumption (2022 est.): 18.1 bil kWh.

Misc. data. Motto: Joannes Est Nomen Eius (John is his name). **Flower:** Maga. **Bird:** Reinita. **Tree:** Ceiba. **Anthem:** "La Borinqueña."

Tourism. Tourist spending: $8.7 bil (2022); change, 2019-22: 33.5%. **Tourism. Attractions:** Museo de Arte de Ponce; San Felipe del Morro and San Cristóbal forts, San Juan Natl. Historic Site, Walled City of Old San Juan, Casa Blanca, in San Juan; Arecibo Observatory; Cordillera Central mtn. range; El Yunque Natl. Forest (only tropical rain forest in Natl. Forest system); Cathedral of San Juan Bautista; Porta Coeli (Doorway to Heaven) Church and Religious Art Museum, San Germán; Rio Camuy Cave Park, Camuy; Mosquito Bay. **Information:** The Puerto Rico Tourism Company, La Princesa Bldg. #2, Paseo La Princesa, Old San Juan, PR 00902; (800) 981-7575; www.prtourism.com

History. Puerto Rico (or Borinquen, after the original Arawak Indian name, Boriquen) was visited by Christopher Columbus on his second voyage, Nov. 19, 1493. In 1508, the Spanish arrived.

Sugarcane was introduced, 1515, and enslaved Black laborers arrived three years later. Gold mining petered out, 1570. Spaniards fought off a series of British and Dutch attacks; slavery was abolished, 1873. Under the Treaty of Paris, Puerto Rico was ceded to the U.S. after the Spanish-American War, 1898. In 1952 the people voted in favor of commonwealth status.

The Commonwealth of Puerto Rico is a self-governing part of the U.S. with a primarily Hispanic culture. The island's citizens have virtually the same control over their internal affairs as do the 50 states of the U.S. However, they do not vote in national general elections, only in national primaries.

Puerto Rico is represented in the U.S. House of Representatives by a Resident Commissioner who has a voice but no vote, except in committees.

No federal income tax is collected from residents on income earned from local sources in Puerto Rico. Nevertheless, as part of the U.S. legal system, Puerto Rico is subject to the provisions of the U.S. Constitution; most federal laws apply as they do in the 50 states.

Puerto Rico's "Operation Bootstrap," begun in the late 1940s, succeeded in changing the island from the "Poorhouse of the Caribbean" to an area with the highest per capita income in Latin America. This program encouraged manufacturing and development of the tourist trade by selective tax exemptions, low-interest loans, and other incentives. Despite the marked success of Puerto Rico's development efforts over an extended period of time, per capita income in Puerto Rico is low in comparison to that of the 50 states.

In plebiscites held in 1967, 1993, and 1998, voters chose to retain commonwealth status. In 2012, a half-million ballots were left blank, with 61.1% of those casting votes favoring statehood over free association (33.3%) or independence (5.6%). In a June 2017 referendum, 97% favored statehood, but only 23% of eligible voters participated, rendering the result indecisive. Protests mounted in the late 1990s over the U.S. Navy's use of Vieques Island for live ammunition training; official military exercises there were terminated, 2003. Puerto Rico went into default for the first time in its history in Aug. 2015 after it missed a bond payment. Pres. Barack Obama signed contentious debt-relief legislation in 2016. Hurricane Maria in Sept. 2017 caused some $90 bil in damages, including widespread devastation of infrastructure. A Harvard study published May 2018 in the *New England Journal of Medicine* estimated at least 4,645 deaths were linked with the hurricane and its aftermath, far greater than the government estimate of 64. A separate analysis, commissioned and accepted by the government, raised the official death toll to 2,975 in Aug. 2018. Gov. Ricardo Rosselló resigned effective Aug. 2, 2019, following weeks of mass protests over corruption allegations and the public leak of offensive private chat messages. In Dec. 2020, the nearly 60-year-old Arecibo Observatory radio telescope, one of the world's largest, collapsed. On Mar. 15, 2022, the territory's govt. formally exited bankruptcy proceedings, capping the largest public debt restructuring in U.S. history, of more than $70 bil it was not able to pay back, initiated in 2017.

Cultural facilities and events. Festival Casals classical music concerts, mid-June; Puerto Rico Symphony Orchestra at Music Conservatory; Botanical Garden and Museum of Anthropology, Art, and History at the Univ. of Puerto Rico; Institute of Puerto Rican Culture, at the Dominican Convent.

Famous Puerto Ricans. Julia de Burgos, Marta Casals Istomin, Pablo Casals, José Celso Barbosa, Orlando Cepeda, Roberto Clemente, José de Diego, José Feliciano, Doña Felisa Rincón de Gautier, Luis A. Ferré, José Ferrer, Commodore Diégo E. Hernández, Miguel Hernández Agosto, Rafael Hernández (El Jibarito), Rafael Hernández Colón, Raúl Juliá, René Marqués, Ricky Martin, Concha Meléndez, Rita Moreno, Luis Muñoz Marín, Luis Palés Matos, Joaquin Phoenix, Adm. Horacio Rivero.

Website. www.pr.gov (in Spanish)

Virgin Islands (VI)

St. John, St. Croix, St. Thomas

People. Population (2024 est.): 104,377. **Pop. change** (2010-20): –18.1%. **Pop. density:** 777 per sq mi. **Racial distribution** (2020): 71.4% African-American or African descent; 13.3% white; 0.4% indigenous,; 0.1% Native Hawaiian and other Pacific Islander; 6.3% other; 7.5% mixed. **Languages:** English 71.6%, Spanish or Spanish Creole 17.2%, French or French Creole 8.6%, other 2.5% (2010 est.).

Geography. Total area: 733 sq mi. **Land area:** 134 sq mi. **Acres forested:** 46,967. **Location:** 3 larger and 50 smaller islands and cays in the S and W of the V.I. group (British V.I. colony to the N and E), which is situated 70 mi E of Puerto Rico; W of Anegada Passage, a major channel connecting the Atlantic Ocean and Caribbean Sea. **Climate:** subtropical; sun tempered by gentle trade winds; humidity is low; avg. temperature 78°F. **Topography:** St. Thomas is mainly a ridge of hills running E-W and has little tillable land; St. Croix rises abruptly in the N, slopes to flatlands and lagoons in the S; St. John has steep, lofty hills and valleys with little level tillable land. **Capital:** Charlotte Amalie, on St. Thomas. **Chief airport:** Charlotte Amalie.

Economy. Chief industries: retail, petroleum, tourism, prof. consulting. **Chief manuf. goods:** rum, stone, glass and clay products, electronics, textiles. **Chief crops:** cucumbers, coconuts, mangoes, tomatoes, bananas. **Livestock** (2007): 699 chickens, 776 cattle, 2,981 sheep, 1,125 hogs/pigs, 2,331 goats. **Nonfuel minerals:** crushed stone, limestone, trap rock. **Commercial fishing** (2011): $7.1 mil. **Chief port:** Charlotte Amalie. **Gross domestic product** (2022 est.): $4.7 bil. **Employment distrib.:** 30.9% govt.; 19.4% trade/trans./util.; 1.4% mfg.; 7.0% ed./health; 8.1% prof./bus. serv.; 18.5% leisure/hosp.; 4.8% finance; 5.9% constr./mining/log.; 1.4% info.; 2.5% other serv. **Unemployment** (2023): 12.1%. **Min. wage/hr.:** $10.50. **Per capita income** (2012): $19,982. **Broadband internet:** 99.8%. **Commercial banks:** 4; deposits: $3.5 bil. **Savings institutions:** 1; deposits: $328.0 mil.

Federal govt. Fed. civ. employees: 427; **avg. salary:** $81,959.

Education. 4-yr. public coll./univ.: 1; **2-yr. public:** 0; **4-yr. private:** 0.

Energy. Total electricity consumption (2022 est.): 625.1 mil kWh.

Misc. data. Motto: United in pride and hope. **Flower:** Yellow cedar. **Bird:** Bananaquit (yellow breast). **Song:** "Virgin Islands March."

Tourism. Attractions: St. Croix Isl.: Salt River Bay Natl. Historic Park and Ecological Preserve, Christiansted Natl. Historic Site. St. John and Hassel Isls.: Virgin Islands Natl. Park. St. Thomas Isl.: Blackbeard's Castle, Coral World Ocean Park, Magens Bay, 99 Steps. **Information:** USVI Division of Tourism, P.O. Box 6400, St. Thomas, VI 00804; 1-800-372-USVI; www.visitusvi.com

History. The islands were visited by Columbus in 1493. Spanish forces, 1555, defeated the Caribes and claimed the territory; by 1596 the native population was annihilated. The first permanent settlement in the U.S. territory, 1672, was by the Danes; U.S. purchased the islands, 1917, for defense purposes.

The Virgin Islands has a republican form of government, headed by a governor and lieut. governor elected, since 1970, by popular vote for four-year terms. There is a 15-member unicameral legislature, elected by popular vote for a two-year term. Residents of the V.I. have been U.S. citizens since 1927. Since 1973 they have elected a U.S. House delegate, who has a voice but no vote except in committees. Hurricanes Maria and Irma in Sept. 2017 caused some $5.5 bil in damages, according to Gov. Kenneth Mapp.

Website. www.vi.gov

Other Islands

Navassa lies between Haiti and Jamaica, 100 mi S of Guantánamo Bay, Cuba, in the Caribbean. It covers 1,147 acres and is uninhabited. Claimed 1857, a Coast Guard lighthouse was built 1917, now inoperative. Natl. Wildlife Refuge since 1999. Administered by the Dept. of Interior.

The three coral islands of **Wake Atoll—Wake, Wilkes**, and **Peale**—lie in the Pacific Ocean on a direct route from Hawaii to Hong Kong, about 2,300 mi W of Honolulu and 1,500 mi NE of Guam. The group is 4.5 mi long, 1.5 mi wide. Land area totals 2.5 sq mi. The U.S. annexed Wake Atoll Jan. 17, 1899. Japan occupied Wake 1941-45. Designated a National Historic Landmark in 1985. Wake is owned by the U.S. Air Force, administered by the Dept. of Interior, and used by the Army as a missile launch facility. The population consists of military personnel and contractors. Most infrastructure was damaged by super typhoon Ioke in 2006.

The following mostly uninhabited islands are part of the **Pacific/Remote Islands National Wildlife Refuge Complex**, which along with Wake Atoll are administered by the Dept. of Interior: **Midway Atoll**, acquired in 1867, has three main islands—Sand, Spit, and Eastern—1,250 mi WNW of Honolulu, with an area of about 1,500 acres. Naval activity ended in 1997. Has the world's largest albatross colony (Laysan and black-footed). **Johnston Atoll**, 800 mi WSW of Honolulu, is two natural and two artificial islands across 107 sq mi administered by the Navy. Johnston was a nuclear test site in 1958, 1962; the Army disposed of chemical weapons 1990-2000. Cleanup ended in 2005. **Kingman Reef** is a barren coral atoll 932 mi S of Hawaii, annexed 1922. **Palmyra Atoll** is about 54 islets over 753 sq mi, 1,052 mi S of Hawaii; annexed with Hawaii in 1898. Part privately owned by the Nature Conservancy. **Jarvis Island** covers 1,086 acres, 1,300 mi S of Honolulu near the equator. West of Jarvis are **Howland and Baker Islands**, 36 mi apart and about 1,600 mi SW of Honolulu.

100 MOST POPULOUS U.S. CITIES

Sources: Population: Decennial Census and Population Estimates Program, U.S. Census Bureau, U.S. Dept. of Commerce. Population is as of July 1, 2023; population rank is indicated within parentheses. **Pop. density** specifies the number of persons per square mile (sq mi) of land area. Unless otherwise noted, **all other figures** are estimates for 2018-22 by American Community Survey, U.S. Census Bureau. **Racial distribution** categories are abbreviated; their full forms are white, Black or African American, Asian, American Indian and Alaska Native, Native Hawaiian and Other Pacific Islander, some other race, two or more races. **Hispanic** or Latino persons may be of any race. **Language** is what is spoken at home. **Employment:** Bureau of Labor Statistics, U.S. Dept. of Labor for 2023. **Per capita income:** in 2022 inflation-adjusted dollars. Uninsured is the percentage of people aged 19-64 without health insurance. **Educational attainment** is the percentage of persons age 25 and up who have graduated high school (HS) and who have a bachelor's degree or higher. **Avg. commute** is the time it takes for workers 16 years and over to travel from home to work. "Drive" includes only those who drive to work alone. Forms of transport and work-from-home figures that do not surpass 10% are omitted. **Avg. home:** National Association of Realtors®. Figures represent median 2023 sales price of existing single-family homes in the metropolitan area; data not available for all cities. **Avg. rent** is the median gross rent (rent asked plus est. avg. cost of utilities) per month. **Crime rates:** *Crime in the United States, 2022*, Federal Bureau of Investigation, U.S. Dept. of Justice. Rates are per 100,000 in population; data as of 2022 unless otherwise noted. Violent crimes include murder, nonnegligent manslaughter, rape, robbery, aggravated assault; property crimes include burglary, larceny-theft, motor vehicle theft. **Mayor** (or other city leader) and **website:** World Almanac research as of mid-2024; subject to change. A nonpartisan mayor is one whose party affiliation was not indicated on the ballot.

Included here are the 100 most populous U.S. cities, according to U.S. Census Bureau estimates released in May 2024. Most data are for the city proper; some, where noted, apply to the Metropolitan Statistical Area (MSA). Inc. = incorporated; est. = established; NA = Not available.

Albuquerque, New Mexico

Population: 560,274 (32). **Pop. density:** 2,992. **Pop. change (2020-23):** –0.8%. **Area:** 187.3 sq mi. **Racial distribution:** 60.6% white; 3.2% Black; 3.1% Asian; 4.8% Amer. Ind.; 0.1% Pac. Isl.; 10.0% other; 2+ races, 18.1%. **Hispanic pop.:** 49.8%. **Foreign born:** 10.2%. **U.S. citizens:** 94.8%. **Language:** 73.6% English only; 20.6% Spanish.

Employment: 280,226 employed; 3.4% unemployment. **Per capita income:** $36,879. **Below poverty:** 15.1%; 11.9% of families. **Uninsured:** 11.4%. **Educational attainment:** 90.7% HS; 37.8% bachelor's. **Avg. commute:** 22.1 min. 74.9% drive, 11.0% work from home. **Housing units:** 255,178; 94.0% occupied. **Home ownership:** 60.7%. **Avg. home:** $353,300; change (2021-23): 20.8%. **Avg. rent:** $1,014. **Crime rates:** violent: 1,380; property: 4,796.

Mayor: Tim Keller, nonpartisan

History: Founded 1706 by the Spanish; inc. 1891.

Website: www.cabq.gov

Anaheim, California

Population: 340,512 (56). **Pop. density:** 6,772. **Pop. change (2020-23):** –1.8%. **Area:** 50.3 sq mi. **Racial distribution:** 48.1% white; 2.6% Black; 17.6% Asian; 0.9% Amer. Ind.; 0.4% Pac. Isl.; 14.5% other; 2+ races, 15.9%. **Hispanic pop.:** 53.3%. **Foreign born:** 34.6%. **U.S. citizens:** 82.5%. **Language:** 40.4% English only; 41.9% Spanish.

Employment: 163,734 employed; 3.7% unemployment. **Per capita income:** $35,331. **Below poverty:** 11.3%; 9.4% of families. **Uninsured:** 15.1%. **Educational attainment:** 77.8% HS; 28.1% bachelor's. **Avg. commute:** 28.4 min. 75.5% drive, 11.4% carpool. **Housing units:** 109,685; 95.4% occupied. **Home ownership:** 46.6%. **Avg. home:** $1,260,000; change (2021-23): 14.6%. **Avg. rent:** $1,958. **Crime rates:** violent: 766; property: 2,769.

Mayor: Ashleigh Aitken, nonpartisan

History: Founded 1857; inc. 1876. Home of Disneyland, the Anaheim Ducks, and the Los Angeles Angels.

Website: www.anaheim.net

Anchorage, Alaska

Population: 286,075 (74). **Pop. density:** 168. **Pop. change (2020-23):** –1.7%. **Area:** 1,707.0 sq mi. **Racial distribution:** 59.2% white; 5.3% Black; 9.8% Asian; 7.4% Amer. Ind.; 2.9% Pac. Isl.; 2.7% other; 2+ races, 12.7%. **Hispanic pop.:** 9.7%. **Foreign born:** 10.8%. **U.S. citizens:** 96.2%. **Language:** 82.5% English only; 4.7% Spanish.

Employment: 145,654 employed; 3.4% unemployment. **Per capita income:** $46,554. **Below poverty:** 9.0%; 6.3% of families. **Uninsured:** 13.6%. **Educational attainment:** 94.2% HS; 37.0% bachelor's. **Avg. commute:** 19.1 min. 71.8% drive, 12.7% carpool. **Housing units:** 118,938; 90.1% occupied. **Home ownership:** 63.8%. **Avg. home:** $423,900; change (2021-23): 11.4%. **Avg. rent:** $1,405. **Crime rates:** violent: 1,151; property: 2,764.

Mayor: Dave Bronson, nonpartisan

History: Founded 1914 as a railroad construction port; HQ of Alaska Defense Command, WWII. Severely damaged in earthquake, 1964.

Website: www.muni.org

Arlington, Texas

Population: 398,431 (50). **Pop. density:** 4,157. **Pop. change (2020-23):** 1.1%. **Area:** 95.8 sq mi. **Racial distribution:** 46.9% white; 22.8% Black; 7.3% Asian; 0.5% Amer. Ind.; 0.4% Pac. Isl.; 8.5% other; 2+ races, 13.7%. **Hispanic pop.:** 30.0%. **Foreign born:** 20.8%. **U.S. citizens:** 88.1%. **Language:** 65.0% English only; 22.6% Spanish.

Employment: 219,125 employed; 3.7% unemployment. **Per capita income:** $33,477. **Below poverty:** 11.2%; 9.9% of families. **Uninsured:** 25.4%. **Educational attainment:** 85.9% HS; 32.4% bachelor's. **Avg. commute:** 26.9 min. 77.2% drive. **Housing units:** 147,492; 93.2% occupied. **Home ownership:** 54.9%. **Avg. home:** $381,900; change (2021-23): 13.4%. **Avg. rent:** $1,297. **Crime rates:** violent: 580; property: 2,525.

Mayor: Jim Ross, nonpartisan

History: Anglo-Americans began to settle in 1840s; inc. 1884.

Website: www.arlingtontx.gov

Atlanta, Georgia

Population: 510,823 (37). **Pop. density:** 3,777. **Pop. change (2020-23):** 2.2%. **Area:** 135.3 sq mi. **Racial distribution:** 40.8% white; 47.6% Black; 4.9% Asian; 0.3% Amer. Ind.; < 0.05% Pac. Isl.; 1.8% other; 2+ races, 4.7%. **Hispanic pop.:** 5.4%. **Foreign born:** 8.2%. **U.S. citizens:** 95.6%. **Language:** 89.0% English only; 4.1% Spanish.

Employment: 265,779 employed; 3.8% unemployment. **Per capita income:** $60,778. **Below poverty:** 16.1%; 12.8% of families. **Uninsured:** 13.5%. **Educational attainment:** 92.9% HS; 57.3% bachelor's. **Avg. commute:** 27.5 min. 57.4% drive, 23.2% work from home. **Housing units:** 255,220; 89.1% occupied. **Home ownership:** 45.7%. **Avg. home:** $370,000; change (2021-23): 16.6%. **Avg. rent:** $1,512. **Crime rates:** violent: 841; property: 3,748.

Mayor: Andre Dickens, nonpartisan

History: Founded as Terminus, 1837; renamed Atlanta, 1845; inc. 1847. Played major role in Civil War; became state capital, 1868. Birthplace of civil rights movement; host to 1996 Olympic Games.

Website: www.atlantaga.gov

Aurora, Colorado

Population: 395,052 (52). **Pop. density:** 2,423. **Pop. change (2020-23):** 2.1%. **Area:** 163.0 sq mi. **Racial distribution:** 52.2% white; 16.6% Black; 6.0% Asian; 1.1% Amer. Ind.; 0.3% Pac. Isl.; 10.5% other; 2+ races, 13.3%. **Hispanic pop.:** 29.7%. **Foreign born:** 21.0%. **U.S. citizens:** 87.8%. **Language:** 67.6% English only; 20.3% Spanish.

Employment: 204,765 employed; 3.4% unemployment. **Per capita income:** $38,047. **Below poverty:** 9.0%; 7.7% of families. **Uninsured:** 16.3%. **Educational attainment:** 86.9% HS; 31.8% bachelor's. **Avg. commute:** 29.4 min. 69.8% drive, 10.6% carpool, 13.0% work from home. **Housing units:** 147,725; 95.5% occupied. **Home ownership:** 62.5%. **Avg. home:** $661,000; change (2021-23): 8.9%. **Avg. rent:** $1,651. **Crime rates:** violent: 1,077; property: 4,229.

Mayor: Mike Coffman, nonpartisan

History: Founded as Fletcher, 1891; renamed Aurora, 1907; inc. 1928. Early growth stimulated by military bases; fast-growing trade, technology, and med. science center.

Website: www.auroragov.org

Austin, Texas

Population: 979,882 (11). **Pop. density:** 3,002. **Pop. change (2020-23):** 1.5%. **Area:** 326.4 sq mi. **Racial distribution:** 63.2% white; 7.9% Black; 8.4% Asian; 0.8% Amer. Ind.; < 0.05% Pac. Isl.; 8.2% other; 2+ races, 11.5%. **Hispanic pop.:** 32.5%. **Foreign born:** 18.3%. **U.S. citizens:** 88.5%. **Language:** 70.0% English only; 20.5% Spanish.

Employment: 658,464 employed; 3.2% unemployment. **Per capita income:** $54,673. **Below poverty:** 11.6%; 8.2% of families. **Uninsured:** 15.4%. **Educational attainment:** 91.1% HS; 56.5% bachelor's. **Avg. commute:** 24.1 min. 62.6% drive, 22.9% work from home. **Housing units:** 449,452; 94.1% occupied. **Home ownership:** 44.4%. **Avg. home:** $481,200; change (2021-23): –1.5%. **Avg. rent:** $1,549. **Crime rates:** violent: 540; property: 3,590.

Mayor: Kirk Watson, nonpartisan

History: First permanent Anglo-American settlement, 1830s; capital of Rep. of Texas, 1839; named after Stephen Austin.

Website: www.austintexas.gov

Bakersfield, California

Population: 413,381 (47). **Pop. density:** 2,751. **Pop. change (2020-23):** 2.0%. **Area:** 150.3 sq mi. **Racial distribution:** 52.8% white; 6.4% Black; 7.5% Asian; 1.0% Amer. Ind.; 0.3% Pac. Isl.; 15.2% other; 2+ races, 16.7%. **Hispanic pop.:** 52.9%. **Foreign born:** 19.6%. **U.S. citizens:** 89.7%. **Language:** 57.3% English only; 34.3% Spanish.

Employment: 169,678 employed; 6.0% unemployment. **Per capita income:** $31,892. **Below poverty:** 14.0%; 13.0% of families. **Uninsured:** 10.8%. **Educational attainment:** 81.6% HS; 23.3% bachelor's. **Avg. commute:** 23.6 min. 80.3% drive. **Housing units:** 131,310; 95.0% occupied. **Home ownership:** 60.2%. **Avg. home:** $370,400; change (2021-23): 14.6%. **Avg. rent:** $1,283. **Crime rates:** violent: 546; property: 3,972.

Mayor: Karen Goh, nonpartisan

History: Named after Col. Thomas Baker, an early settler; inc. 1898.

Website: www.bakersfieldcity.us

Baltimore, Maryland

Population: 565,239 (30). **Pop. density:** 6,983. **Pop. change (2020-23):** –3.1%. **Area:** 80.9 sq mi. **Racial distribution:** 28.4% white; 61.2% Black; 2.6% Asian; 0.3% Amer. Ind.; < 0.05% Pac. Isl.; 3.0% other; 2+ races, 4.4%. **Hispanic pop.:** 5.9%. **Foreign born:** 8.1%. **U.S. citizens:** 95.7%. **Language:** 89.7% English only; 4.4% Spanish.

Employment: 266,276 employed; 2.9% unemployment. **Per capita income:** $37,845. **Below poverty:** 17.9%; 14.5% of families. **Uninsured:** 7.4%. **Educational attainment:** 87.1% HS; 34.9% bachelor's. **Avg. commute:** 30.1 min. 57.5% drive, 12.8% public trans., 13.4% work from home. **Housing units:** 293,555; 84.2% occupied. **Home ownership:** 47.8%. **Avg. home:** $388,600; change (2021-23): 8.5%. **Avg. rent:** $1,235. **Crime rates** violent: 1,553; property: 3,277.

Mayor: Brandon M. Scott, Democrat

History: Founded by Maryland legislature, 1729; inc. 1797. British artillery barrage of Ft. McHenry (1814) inspired "Star-Spangled Banner." Birthplace of America's railroads, 1828; rebuilt after fire, 1904. Site of National Aquarium.

Website: www.baltimorecity.gov

Boise City, Idaho

Population: 235,421 (95). **Pop. density:** 2,784. **Pop. change (2020-23):** –0.3%. **Area:** 84.6 sq mi. **Racial distribution:** 85.0% white; 1.5% Black; 3.4% Asian; 0.6% Amer. Ind.; 0.3% Pac. Isl.; 2.4% other; 2+ races, 6.8%. **Hispanic pop.:** 9.1%. **Foreign born:** 6.7%. **U.S. citizens:** 96.9%. **Language:** 90.0% English only; 4.6% Spanish.

Employment: 138,421 employed; 2.7% unemployment. **Per capita income:** $44,728. **Below poverty:** 10.6%; 6.4% of families. **Uninsured:** 10.2%. **Educational attainment:** 95.2% HS; 45.8% bachelor's. **Avg. commute:** 19.2 min. 70.4% drive, 14.4% work from home. **Housing units:** 102,878; 95.1% occupied. **Home ownership:** 62.9%. **Avg. home:** $474,000; change (2021-23): 1.2%. **Avg. rent:** $1,223. **Crime rates:** violent: 247; property: 1,204.

Mayor: Lauren McLean, nonpartisan

History: Gold discovered in area, 1862; proclaimed capital of Idaho Terr., 1864; inc. 1866; on Oregon Trail.

Website: www.cityofboise.org

Boston, Massachusetts

Population: 653,833 (25). **Pop. density:** 13,526. **Pop. change (2020-23):** –3.2%. **Area:** 48.3 sq mi. **Racial distribution:** 48.6% white; 22.5% Black; 9.7% Asian; 0.3% Amer. Ind.; 0.1% Pac. Isl.; 6.8% other; 2+ races, 12.0%. **Hispanic pop.:** 19.6%. **Foreign born:** 28.1%. **U.S. citizens:** 86.8%. **Language:** 64.0% English only; 16.1% Spanish.

Employment: 382,479 employed; 3.2% unemployment. **Per capita income:** $55,949. **Below poverty:** 16.5%; 12.2% of families. **Uninsured:** 4.0%. **Educational attainment:** 88.4% HS; 53.4% bachelor's. **Avg. commute:** 30.6 min. 35.1% drive, 25.7% public trans., 14.0% walk, 16.1% work from home. **Housing units:** 304,079; 90.8% occupied. **Home ownership:** 34.8%. **Avg. home:** $714,000; change (2021-23): 11.2%. **Avg. rent:** $1,981. **Crime rates:** violent: 619; property: 1,802.

Mayor: Michelle Wu, nonpartisan

History: Settled 1630 by John Winthrop; capital of Mass. Bay Colony; figured strongly in American Revolution; inc. 1822.

Website: www.boston.gov

Buffalo, New York

Population: 274,678 (81). **Pop. density:** 6,802. **Pop. change (2020-23):** –1.0%. **Area:** 40.4 sq mi. **Racial distribution:** 46.5% white; 33.2% Black; 7.6% Asian; 0.4% Amer. Ind.; < 0.05% Pac. Isl.; 5.6% other; 2+ races, 6.5%. **Hispanic pop.:** 12.3%. **Foreign born:** 10.8%. **U.S. citizens:** 94.8%. **Language:** 80.9% English only; 7.6% Spanish.

Employment: 104,357 employed; 5.1% unemployment. **Per capita income:** $29,558. **Below poverty:** 23.5%; 21.8% of families. **Uninsured:** 5.7%. **Educational attainment:** 86.2% HS; 30.0% bachelor's. **Avg. commute:** 19.6 min. 66.4% drive. **Housing units:** 136,421; 87.2% occupied. **Home ownership:** 42.6%. **Avg. home:** $240,500; change (2021-23): 14.6%. **Avg. rent:** $942. **Crime rates:** violent: 736; property: 3,211.

Mayor: Byron W. Brown, Democrat

History: Settled 1780 by Seneca Indians; raided by British in War of 1812; inc. 1832. Served as western terminus for Erie Canal and a center for trade and manufacturing.

Website: www.buffalony.gov

Chandler, Arizona

Population: 280,167 (78). **Pop. density:** 4,268. **Pop. change (2020-23):** 1.0%. **Area:** 65.6 sq mi. **Racial distribution:** 64.1% white; 5.8% Black; 11.8% Asian; 1.9% Amer. Ind.; 0.2% Pac. Isl.; 4.6% other; 2+ races, 11.6%. **Hispanic pop.:** 21.2%. **Foreign born:** 15.9%. **U.S. citizens:** 92.5%. **Language:** 76.3% English only; 11.3% Spanish.

Employment: 156,501 employed; 3.1% unemployment. **Per capita income:** $48,987. **Below poverty:** 7.0%; 5.9% of families. **Uninsured:** 9.0%. **Educational attainment:** 94.2% HS; 46.2% bachelor's. **Avg. commute:** 24.2 min. 68.0% drive, 19.6% work from home. **Housing units:** 110,002; 94.9% occupied. **Home ownership:** 64.6%. **Avg. home:** $459,600; change (2021-23): 10.6%. **Avg. rent:** $1,675. **Crime rates:** violent: 182; property: 1,808.

Mayor: Kevin Hartke, nonpartisan

History: Formed 1912; population doubled in 1990s when marketed as "the high-tech oasis of the Silicon Desert."

Website: www.chandleraz.gov

Charlotte, North Carolina

Population: 911,311 (15). **Pop. density:** 2,933. **Pop. change (2020-23):** 4.1%. **Area:** 310.8 sq mi. **Racial distribution:** 43.1% white; 35.2% Black; 6.6% Asian; 0.4% Amer. Ind.; < 0.05% Pac. Isl.; 7.6% other; 2+ races, 7.1%. **Hispanic pop.:** 15.3%. **Foreign born:** 17.4%. **U.S. citizens:** 89.2%. **Language:** 77.7% English only; 13.1% Spanish.

Employment: 511,641 employed; 3.4% unemployment. **Per capita income:** $47,476. **Below poverty:** 10.0%; 8.4% of families. **Uninsured:** 16.2%. **Educational attainment:** 89.7% HS; 46.6% bachelor's. **Avg. commute:** 25.2 min. 64.9% drive, 21.3% work from home. **Housing units:** 383,380; 92.5% occupied. **Home ownership:** 52.1%. **Avg. home:** $398,000; change (2021-23): 12.4%. **Avg. rent:** $1,399. **Crime rates:** violent: 746; property: 3,375.

Mayor: Vi Lyles, Democrat

History: Scotch-Irish immigrants arrived, c. 1750; inc. 1768 and named after Queen Charlotte, wife of King George III. Site of first major U.S. gold discovery, 1799.

Website: www.charlottenc.gov

Chesapeake, Virginia

Population: 253,886 (89). **Pop. density:** 750. **Pop. change (2020-23):** 1.6%. **Area:** 338.5 sq mi. **Racial distribution:** 57.3% white; 29.3% Black; 3.7% Asian; 0.2% Amer. Ind.; 0.1% Pac. Isl.; 2.4% other; 2+ races, 7.1%. **Hispanic pop.:** 7.0%. **Foreign born:** 6.0%. **U.S. citizens:** 97.8%. **Language:** 91.6% English only; 3.7% Spanish.

Employment: 123,987 employed; 2.9% unemployment. **Per capita income:** $42,753. **Below poverty:** 6.8%; 5.5% of families. **Uninsured:** 9.4%. **Educational attainment:** 93.3% HS; 35.8% bachelor's. **Avg. commute:** 26.0 min. 79.2% drive. **Housing units:** 95,076; 96.1% occupied. **Home ownership:** 73.3%. **Avg. home:** $334,400; change (2021-23): 17.3%. **Avg. rent:** $1,446. **Crime rates:** violent: 417; property: 2,011.

Mayor: Richard W. "Rick" West, Republican

History: First English colonies on banks of Elizabeth River, 1620s; home to Dismal Swamp Canal, first envisioned by George Washington in 1763. Battle of Great Bridge, Dec. 1775; inc. 1963.

Website: www.cityofchesapeake.net

Chicago, Illinois

Population: 2,664,452 (3). **Pop. density:** 11,699. **Pop. change (2020-23):** –2.9%. **Area:** 227.7 sq mi. **Racial distribution:** 42.4% white; 28.8% Black; 7.0% Asian; 0.7% Amer. Ind.; 0.1% Pac. Isl.; 11.3% other; 2+ races, 9.7%. **Hispanic pop.:** 29.0%. **Foreign born:** 20.2%. **U.S. citizens:** 89.6%. **Language:** 64.8% English only; 23.5% Spanish.

Employment: 1,310,713 employed; 4.7% unemployment. **Per capita income:** $45,840. **Below poverty:** 15.1%; 13.0% of families. **Uninsured:** 13.3%. **Educational attainment:** 86.6% HS; 42.4% bachelor's. **Avg. commute:** 34.1 min. 46.7% drive, 21.2% public trans., 15.6% work from home. **Housing units:** 1,258,704; 89.8% occupied. **Home ownership:** 45.6%. **Avg. home:** $351,200; change (2021-23): 6.3%. **Avg. rent:** $1,314. **Crime rates:** violent: 540; property: 3,133.

Mayor: Brandon Johnson, nonpartisan

History: First nonnative residence established by Point Du Sable, 1780s; Fort Dearborn built, 1803; significant white settlement began with completion of Erie Canal, 1825; inc. 1837. Boomed with arrival of railroads and canal to Mississippi R.; one-third of city destroyed by fire, 1871. Major Great Migration destination, 1910-30.

Website: www.chicago.gov

Chula Vista, California

Population: 274,333 (82). **Pop. density:** 5,527. **Pop. change (2020-23):** –0.5%. **Area:** 49.6 sq mi. **Racial distribution:** 40.9% white; 5.2% Black; 15.5% Asian; 0.8% Amer. Ind.; 0.4% Pac. Isl.; 14.1% other; 2+ races, 23.2%. **Hispanic pop.:** 60.2%. **Foreign born:** 29.3%. **U.S. citizens:** 88.6%. **Language:** 43.9% English only; 45.6% Spanish.

Employment: 119,864 employed; 4.2% unemployment. **Per capita income:** $37,618. **Below poverty:** 8.2%; 7.1% of families. **Uninsured:** 10.0%. **Educational attainment:** 85.3% HS; 31.2% bachelor's. **Avg. commute:** 29.1 min. 74.4% drive, 10.1% carpool, 10.2% work from home. **Housing units:** 88,526; 93.8% occupied. **Home ownership:** 59.9%. **Avg. home:** $931,200; change (2021-23): 12.2%. **Avg. rent:** $2,035. **Crime rates:** violent: 351; property: 1,277.

Mayor: John McCann, nonpartisan

History: Visited by Spanish, 1542; became part of Spanish land grant, 1795; claimed by U.S. in Mexican-American War, 1847; inc. 1911. WWII brought aircraft industry and growth.

Website: www.chulavistaca.gov

Cincinnati, Ohio

Population: 311,097 (64). **Pop. density:** 3,993. **Pop. change (2020-23):** 0.5%. **Area:** 77.9 sq mi. **Racial distribution:** 50.4% white; 39.6% Black; 2.6% Asian; 0.1% Amer. Ind.; < 0.05% Pac. Isl.; 1.6% other; 2+ races, 5.6%. **Hispanic pop.:** 4.6%. **Foreign born:** 6.8%. **U.S. citizens:** 95.9%. **Language:** 91.2% English only; 3.1% Spanish.

Employment: 144,689 employed; 3.6% unemployment. **Per capita income:** $37,280. **Below poverty:** 21.9%; 18.9% of families. **Uninsured:** 9.5%. **Educational attainment:** 89.1% HS; 40.5% bachelor's. **Avg. commute:** 23.4 min. 67.3% drive, 11.5% work from home. **Housing units:** 159,732; 88.3% occupied. **Home ownership:** 39.3%. **Avg. home:** $282,000; change (2021-23): 15.9%. **Avg. rent:** $893. **Crime rates:** violent: 842; property: 3,751.

Mayor: Aftab Pureval, nonpartisan

History: Founded 1788; named after Society of the Cincinnati, an organization of Revolutionary War officers; chartered as town, 1802; inc. 1819.

Website: www.cincinnati-oh.gov

Cleveland, Ohio

Population: 362,656 (54). **Pop. density:** 4,665. **Pop. change (2020-23):** –2.5%. **Area:** 77.7 sq mi. **Racial distribution:** 38.3% white; 46.6% Black; 2.5% Asian; 0.4% Amer. Ind.; < 0.05% Pac. Isl.; 4.0% other; 2+ races, 8.2%. **Hispanic pop.:** 12.5%. **Foreign born:** 6.0%. **U.S. citizens:** 97.0%. **Language:** 85.3% English only; 9.1% Spanish.

Employment: 149,179 employed; 4.7% unemployment. **Per capita income:** $26,040. **Below poverty:** 27.1%; 25.6% of families. **Uninsured:** 10.3%. **Educational attainment:** 82.9% HS; 20.3% bachelor's. **Avg. commute:** 23.3 min. 66.8% drive. **Housing units:** 200,730; 83.6% occupied. **Home ownership:** 40.9%. **Avg. home:** $214,300; change (2021-23): 7.8%. **Avg. rent:** $851. **Crime rates:** violent: 1,614; property: 4,317.

Mayor: Justin M. Bibb, nonpartisan

History: Surveyed in 1796; inc. as village, 1814; inc. as city, 1836; annexed Ohio City 1854. Major Great Lakes port and early hub for steel, oil industries.

Website: www.clevelandohio.gov

Colorado Springs, Colorado

Population: 488,664 (39). **Pop. density:** 2,421. **Pop. change (2020-23):** 1.7%. **Area:** 201.9 sq mi. **Racial distribution:** 73.4% white; 6.0% Black; 3.1% Asian; 1.1% Amer. Ind.; 0.3% Pac. Isl.; 4.6% other; 2+ races, 11.5%. **Hispanic pop.:** 18.5%. **Foreign born:** 7.5%. **U.S. citizens:** 96.6%. **Language:** 87.9% English only; 7.7% Spanish.

Employment: 245,077 employed; 3.2% unemployment. **Per capita income:** $41,849. **Below poverty:** 9.8%; 6.6% of families. **Uninsured:** 11.2%. **Educational attainment:** 94.3% HS; 41.1% bachelor's. **Avg. commute:** 22.9 min. 72.7% drive, 13.8% work from home. **Housing units:** 201,936; 95.6% occupied. **Home ownership:** 61.1%. **Avg. home:** $460,400; change (2021-23): 6.4%. **Avg. rent:** $1,464. **Crime rates:** violent: 643; property: 3,400.

Mayor: Yemi Mobolade, nonpartisan

History: Founded 1871 at the foot of Pikes Peak; inc. 1886.

Website: coloradosprings.gov

Columbus, Ohio

Population: 913,175 (14). **Pop. density:** 4,137. **Pop. change (2020-23):** 0.7%. **Area:** 220.7 sq mi. **Racial distribution:** 54.9% white; 29.1% Black; 5.8% Asian; 0.2% Amer. Ind.; < 0.05% Pac. Isl.; 2.8% other; 2+ races, 7.1%. **Hispanic pop.:** 6.7%. **Foreign born:** 14.0%. **U.S. citizens:** 92.6%. **Language:** 82.9% English only; 4.7% Spanish.

Employment: 472,076 employed; 3.3% unemployment. **Per capita income:** $35,640. **Below poverty:** 15.7%; 13.7% of families. **Uninsured:** 12.1%. **Educational attainment:** 90.3% HS; 38.3% bachelor's. **Avg. commute:** 22.0 min. 71.9% drive, 13.8% work from home. **Housing units:** 414,823; 92.1% occupied. **Home ownership:** 44.7%. **Avg. home:** $312,700; change (2021-23): 14.1%. **Avg. rent:** $1,161. **Crime rates:** violent: 450; property: 3,484.

Mayor: Andrew J. Ginther, nonpartisan

History: Laid out as state capital, 1812; inc. 1834.

Website: www.columbus.gov

Corpus Christi, Texas

Population: 316,595 (62). **Pop. density:** 1,951. **Pop. change (2020-23):** –0.5%. **Area:** 162.3 sq mi. **Racial distribution:** 63.3% white; 4.0% Black; 2.4% Asian; 0.3% Amer. Ind.; 0.1% Pac. Isl.; 4.4% other; 2+ races, 25.6%. **Hispanic pop.:** 64.3%. **Foreign born:** 9.2%. **U.S. citizens:** 94.4%. **Language:** 66.7% English only; 30.7% Spanish.

Employment: 146,581 employed; 4.2% unemployment. **Per capita income:** $32,395. **Below poverty:** 14.7%; 13.3% of families. **Uninsured:** 26.9%. **Educational attainment:** 85.0% HS; 23.1% bachelor's. **Avg. commute:** 19.5 min. 82.2% drive. **Housing units:** 134,044; 87.7% occupied. **Home ownership:** 57.3%. **Avg. home:** $273,700; change (2021-23): 9.5%. **Avg. rent:** $1,178. **Crime rates:** violent: 791; property: 3,121.

Mayor: Paulette M. Guajardo, nonpartisan

History: Anglo-Americans settled, 1838-39; inc. 1852. One of the largest U.S. ports.

Website: www.cctexas.com

Dallas, Texas

Population: 1,302,868 (9). **Pop. density:** 3,836. **Pop. change (2020-23):** –0.03%. **Area:** 339.7 sq mi. **Racial distribution:** 48.1% white; 23.6% Black; 3.7% Asian; 0.6% Amer. Ind.; < 0.05% Pac. Isl.; 10.9% other; 2+ races, 13.1%. **Hispanic pop.:** 42.4%. **Foreign born:** 23.8%. **U.S. citizens:** 82.9%. **Language:** 57.6% English only; 36.4% Spanish.

Employment: 712,682 employed; 3.9% unemployment. **Per capita income:** $41,761. **Below poverty:** 14.8%; 13.9% of families. **Uninsured:** 30.1%. **Educational attainment:** 80.2% HS; 36.5% bachelor's. **Avg. commute:** 26.4 min. 70.6% drive, 11.0% carpool, 11.9% work from home. **Housing units:** 578,996; 90.0% occupied. **Home ownership:** 41.9%. **Avg. home:** $381,900; change (2021-23): 13.4%. **Avg. rent:** $1,305. **Crime rates:** violent: 778; property: 3,813.

Mayor: Eric Johnson, nonpartisan

History: First nonnatives settled, 1841; inc. 1871. Developed as financial and commercial hub; center of TX oil boom from 1930s.

Website: dallascityhall.com

Denver, Colorado

Population: 716,577 (19). **Pop. density:** 4,681. **Pop. change (2020-23):** –0.1%. **Area:** 153.1 sq mi. **Racial distribution:** 65.7% white; 8.9% Black; 3.6% Asian; 0.8% Amer. Ind.; 0.1% Pac. Isl.; 8.2% other; 2+ races, 12.7%. **Hispanic pop.:** 29.2%. **Foreign born:** 13.9%. **U.S. citizens:** 92.5%. **Language:** 75.6% English only; 17.5% Spanish.

Employment: 426,428 employed; 3.3% unemployment. **Per capita income:** $56,381. **Below poverty:** 10.7%; 8.2% of families. **Uninsured:** 11.6%. **Educational attainment:** 90.5% HS; 54.2% bachelor's. **Avg. commute:** 25.3 min. 60.1% drive, 20.9% work from home. **Housing units:** 344,760; 93.7% occupied. **Home ownership:** 49.4%. **Avg. home:** $661,000; change (2021-23): 8.9%. **Avg. rent:** $1,665. **Crime rates:** violent: 1,070; property: 6,428.

Mayor: Mike Johnston, nonpartisan

History: Miners arrived, 1858; inc. 1861; became territorial capital, 1867. Growth spurred by gold and silver boom; became financial, industrial, cultural center of Rocky Mtn. region.

Website: www.denvergov.org

Detroit, Michigan

Population: 633,218 (26). **Pop. density:** 4,564. **Pop. change (2020-23):** –0.8%. **Area:** 138.7 sq mi. **Racial distribution:** 12.2% white; 77.8% Black; 1.6% Asian; 0.4% Amer. Ind.; < 0.05% Pac. Isl.; 4.2% other; 2+ races, 3.8%. **Hispanic pop.:** 7.5%. **Foreign born:** 5.6%. **U.S. citizens:** 96.6%. **Language:** 89.2% English only; 6.3% Spanish.

Employment: 233,224 employed; 7.6% unemployment. **Per capita income:** $22,861. **Below poverty:** 27.3%; 26.8% of families. **Uninsured:** 11.3%. **Educational attainment:** 82.8% HS; 16.9% bachelor's. **Avg. commute:** 25.7 min. 66.4% drive, 11.9% carpool. **Housing units:** 323,368; 77.2% occupied. **Home ownership:** 48.8%. **Avg. home:** $251,100; change (2021-23): 2.2%. **Avg. rent:** $989. **Crime rates:** violent: 2,028; property: 4,478.

Mayor: Mike Duggan, nonpartisan

History: Founded by French, 1701; controlled by British, 1760; acquired by U.S., 1796; inc. 1815; capital of state 1837-47. First automobile factory opened, 1899. Major Great Migration destination, 1910-30.

Website: detroitmi.gov

Durham, North Carolina

Population: 296,186 (70). **Pop. density:** 2,537. **Pop. change (2020-23):** 4.1%. **Area:** 116.8 sq mi. **Racial distribution:** 45.7% white; 36.1% Black; 5.7% Asian; 0.4% Amer. Ind.; < 0.05% Pac. Isl.; 5.0% other; 2+ races, 7.0%. **Hispanic pop.:** 13.3%. **Foreign

born: 14.8%. **U.S. citizens:** 90.7%. **Language:** 81.1% English only; 11.4% Spanish.

Employment: 156,269 employed; 3.1% unemployment. **Per capita income:** $44,012. **Below poverty:** 11.3%; 8.1% of families. **Uninsured:** 15.0%. **Educational attainment:** 91.3% HS; 53.8% bachelor's. **Avg. commute:** 22.3 min. 67.2% drive, 17.9% work from home. **Housing units:** 129,155; 93.2% occupied. **Home ownership:** 52.0%. **Avg. home:** $468,300; change (2021-23): 17.7%. **Avg. rent:** $1,296. **Crime rates:** violent: 687; property: 3,317.

Mayor: Leonardo "Leo" Williams, nonpartisan

History: Inc. 1869. Trinity College moved to Durham, 1892, renamed Duke Univ.,1924.

Website: www.durhamnc.gov

El Paso, Texas

Population: 678,958 (23). **Pop. density:** 2,624. **Pop. change (2020-23):** –0.04%. **Area:** 258.8 sq mi. **Racial distribution:** 49.4% white; 3.6% Black; 1.4% Asian; 0.7% Amer. Ind.; 0.2% Pac. Isl.; 14.8% other; 2+ races, 29.9%. **Hispanic pop.:** 81.6%. **Foreign born:** 22.6%. **U.S. citizens:** 89.7%. **Language:** 33.0% English only; 64.8% Spanish.

Employment: 302,323 employed; 4.2% unemployment. **Per capita income:** $27,434. **Below poverty:** 16.4%; 16.1% of families. **Uninsured:** 29.7%. **Educational attainment:** 81.5% HS; 27.1% bachelor's. **Avg. commute:** 23.7 min. 78.2% drive, 10.5% carpool. **Housing units:** 260,240; 92.1% occupied. **Home ownership:** 59.5%. **Avg. home:** $240,600; change (2021-23): 19.8%. **Avg. rent:** $976. **Crime rates:** violent: 313; property: 1,379.

Mayor: Oscar Leeser, nonpartisan

History: First nonnatives settled, 1598; inc. 1873; arrival of railroad, 1881, boosted population and industries.

Website: www.elpasotexas.gov

Fort Wayne, Indiana

Population: 269,994 (83). **Pop. density:** 2,441. **Pop. change (2020-23):** 2.1%. **Area:** 110.6 sq mi. **Racial distribution:** 68.1% white; 15.2% Black; 5.6% Asian; 0.3% Amer. Ind.; < 0.05% Pac. Isl.; 3.8% other; 2+ races, 7.0%. **Hispanic pop.:** 9.7%. **Foreign born:** 8.7%. **U.S. citizens:** 95.3%. **Language:** 86.8% English only; 6.5% Spanish.

Employment: 127,282 employed; 3.3% unemployment. **Per capita income:** $31,910. **Below poverty:** 12.9%; 11.3% of families. **Uninsured:** 12.4%. **Educational attainment:** 88.8% HS; 28.1% bachelor's. **Avg. commute:** 21.1 min. 79.7% drive. **Housing units:** 116,467; 92.5% occupied. **Home ownership:** 62.6%. **Avg. home:** $228,300; change (2021-23): 20.2%. **Avg. rent:** $904. **Crime rates:** violent: 262; property: 2,387.

Mayor: Sharon Tucker, Democrat

History: U.S. fort founded, 1794; inc. 1840 prior to Wabash-Erie Canal completion, 1843.

Website: www.cityoffortwayne.org

Fort Worth, Texas

Population: 978,468 (12). **Pop. density:** 2,793. **Pop. change (2020-23):** 5.9%. **Area:** 350.3 sq mi. **Racial distribution:** 51.8% white; 19.2% Black; 4.9% Asian; 0.6% Amer. Ind.; 0.1% Pac. Isl.; 10.9% other; 2+ races, 12.4%. **Hispanic pop.:** 35.2%. **Foreign born:** 16.6%. **U.S. citizens:** 89.8%. **Language:** 67.8% English only; 25.2% Spanish.

Employment: 465,371 employed; 3.9% unemployment. **Per capita income:** $35,428. **Below poverty:** 11.3%; 10.0% of families. **Uninsured:** 24.8%. **Educational attainment:** 84.1% HS; 31.2% bachelor's. **Avg. commute:** 27.0 min. 75.5% drive, 10.5% carpool, 10.9% work from home. **Housing units:** 356,210; 91.7% occupied. **Home ownership:** 56.7%. **Avg. home:** $381,900; change (2021-23): 13.4%. **Avg. rent:** $1,313. **Crime rates:** violent: 502; property: 2,740.

Mayor: Mattie Parker, nonpartisan

History: Established as military post, 1849; inc. 1873; oil discovered, 1917.

Website: www.fortworthtexas.gov

Fremont, California

Population: 226,208 (99). **Pop. density:** 2,896. **Pop. change (2020-23):** –1.8%. **Area:** 78.1 sq mi. **Racial distribution:** 20.6% white; 3.2% Black; 61.8% Asian; 0.5% Amer. Ind.; 0.7% Pac. Isl.; 6.9% other; 2+ races, 6.4%. **Hispanic pop.:** 12.0%. **Foreign born:** 48.8%. **U.S. citizens:** 78.2%. **Language:** 37.3% English only; 7.7% Spanish.

Employment: 112,505 employed; 3.8% unemployment. **Per capita income:** $68,357. **Below poverty:** 5.5%; 3.4% of families. **Uninsured:** 3.4%. **Educational attainment:** 93.1% HS; 61.9% bachelor's. **Avg. commute:** 33.1 min. 56.2% drive, 28.1% work from home. **Housing units:** 78,667; 95.3% occupied. **Home ownership:** 60.7%. **Avg. home:** $1,272,500; change (2021-23): –3.6%. **Avg. rent:** $2,824. **Crime rates:** violent: 209; property: 2,872.

Mayor: Lily Mei, nonpartisan

History: Spanish mission founded, 1797; inc. 1956 as consolidation of five communities.

Website: www.fremont.gov

Fresno, California

Population: 545,716 (34). **Pop. density:** 4,712. **Pop. change (2020-23):** 0.6%. **Area:** 115.8 sq mi. **Racial distribution:** 44.3% white; 6.6% Black; 14.1% Asian; 1.3% Amer. Ind.; 0.2% Pac. Isl.; 15.1% other; 2+ races, 18.5%. **Hispanic pop.:** 50.5%. **Foreign born:** 19.0%. **U.S. citizens:** 91.1%. **Language:** 56.8% English only; 29.7% Spanish.

Employment: 224,343 employed; 6.1% unemployment. **Per capita income:** $29,293. **Below poverty:** 18.9%; 17.4% of families. **Uninsured:** 10.2%. **Educational attainment:** 79.7% HS; 24.4% bachelor's. **Avg. commute:** 22.3 min. 75.3% drive, 11.2% carpool. **Housing units:** 186,461; 95.3% occupied. **Home ownership:** 48.1%. **Avg. home:** $410,000; change (2021-23): 10.8%. **Avg. rent:** $1,227. **Crime rates:** violent: 865; property: 3,449.

Mayor: Jerry P. Dyer, nonpartisan

History: Founded by railroad company, 1872; inc. 1885.

Website: www.fresno.gov

Garland, Texas

Population: 243,470 (94). **Pop. density:** 4,282. **Pop. change (2020-23):** –1.2%. **Area:** 56.9 sq mi. **Racial distribution:** 44.0% white; 15.6% Black; 10.9% Asian; 0.7% Amer. Ind.; < 0.05% Pac. Isl.; 8.1% other; 2+ races, 20.7%. **Hispanic pop.:** 44.5%. **Foreign born:** 30.8%. **U.S. citizens:** 81.5%. **Language:** 48.1% English only; 37.5% Spanish.

Employment: 128,914 employed; 3.6% unemployment. **Per capita income:** $30,132. **Below poverty:** 9.2%; 9.2% of families. **Uninsured:** 32.8%. **Educational attainment:** 78.6% HS; 24.1% bachelor's. **Avg. commute:** 29.7 min. 75.4% drive, 11.2% carpool. **Housing units:** 83,657; 95.4% occupied. **Home ownership:** 62.0%. **Avg. home:** $381,900; change (2021-23): 13.4%. **Avg. rent:** $1,421. **Crime rates:** violent: 246; property: 2,562.

Mayor: Scott LeMay, nonpartisan

History: Settled 1850s; inc. 1891.

Website: www.garlandtx.gov

Gilbert, Arizona

Population: 275,411 (79). **Pop. density:** 4,011. **Pop. change (2020-23):** 2.3%. **Area:** 68.7 sq mi. **Racial distribution:** 75.6% white; 4.1% Black; 6.1% Asian; 0.8% Amer. Ind.; 0.1% Pac. Isl.; 3.5% other; 2+ races, 10.0%. **Hispanic pop.:** 17.6%. **Foreign born:** 9.7%. **U.S. citizens:** 97.0%. **Language:** 85.4% English only; 7.2% Spanish.

Employment: 147,212 employed; 2.9% unemployment. **Per capita income:** $46,964. **Below poverty:** 5.3%; 3.8% of families. **Uninsured:** 6.9%. **Educational attainment:** 96.3% HS; 47.1% bachelor's. **Avg. commute:** 26.7 min. 68.6% drive, 20.5% work from home. **Housing units:** 93,761; 96.3% occupied. **Home ownership:** 74.7%. **Avg. home:** $459,600; change (2021-23): 10.6%. **Avg. rent:** $1,839. **Crime rates:** violent: 117; property: 1,017.

Mayor: Brigette Peterson, nonpartisan

History: Est. 1902; inc. 1920.

Website: www.gilbertaz.gov

Glendale, Arizona

Population: 253,855 (90). **Pop. density:** 3,782. **Pop. change (2020-23):** 2.0%. **Area:** 67.1 sq mi. **Racial distribution:** 58.5% white; 6.9% Black; 4.3% Asian; 1.8% Amer. Ind.; 0.1% Pac. Isl.; 9.1% other; 2+ races, 19.3%. **Hispanic pop.:** 40.4%. **Foreign born:** 16.8%. **U.S. citizens:** 90.7%. **Language:** 66.0% English only; 26.5% Spanish.

Employment: 128,358 employed; 3.6% unemployment. **Per capita income:** $30,316. **Below poverty:** 14.8%; 13.2% of families. **Uninsured:** 17.4%. **Educational attainment:** 84.1% HS; 22.6% bachelor's. **Avg. commute:** 28.3 min. 71.2% drive, 11.8% carpool, 11.3% work from home. **Housing units:** 90,711; 94.1% occupied. **Home ownership:** 57.2%. **Avg. home:** $459,600; change (2021-23): 10.6%. **Avg. rent:** $1,268. **Crime rates:** violent: 545; property: 3,240.

Mayor: Jerry P. Weiers, nonpartisan

History: Est. 1892; inc. 1910.

Website: www.glendaleaz.com

Greensboro, North Carolina

Population: 302,296 (69). **Pop. density:** 2,258. **Pop. change (2020-23):** 2.0%. **Area:** 133.9 sq mi. **Racial distribution:** 41.8% white; 43.1% Black; 5.3% Asian; 0.4% Amer. Ind.; < 0.05% Pac. Isl.; 3.6% other; 2+ races, 5.8%. **Hispanic pop.:** 9.0%. **Foreign born:** 12.3%. **U.S. citizens:** 93.4%. **Language:** 84.4% English only; 6.5% Spanish.

Employment: 138,608 employed; 4.1% unemployment. **Per capita income:** $34,209. **Below poverty:** 16.0%; 13.4% of families. **Uninsured:** 13.2%. **Educational attainment:** 90.1% HS; 39.9% bachelor's. **Avg. commute:** 21.4 min. 76.0% drive. **Housing units:** 133,029; 90.3% occupied. **Home ownership:** 49.6%. **Avg. home:** $282,400; change (2021-23): 23.5%. **Avg. rent:** $1,048. **Crime rates:** violent: 819; property: 3,785.

Mayor: Nancy Vaughan, nonpartisan

History: Est. c. 1740; site of Revolutionary War conflict, 1781, between namesake Gen. Nathanael Greene and Gen. Cornwallis; inc. 1807. Origin of civil rights sit-in movement.

Website: www.greensboro-nc.gov

Henderson, Nevada

Population: 337,305 (57). **Pop. density:** 2,799. **Pop. change (2020-23):** 5.7%. **Area:** 120.5 sq mi. **Racial distribution:** 66.4% white; 6.0% Black; 9.3% Asian; 0.8% Amer. Ind.; 0.7% Pac. Isl.; 5.9% other; 2+ races, 10.9%. **Hispanic pop.:** 19.1%. **Foreign born:** 14.1%. **U.S. citizens:** 95.5%. **Language:** 80.3% English only; 10.4% Spanish.

Employment: 165,995 employed; 5.0% unemployment. **Per capita income:** $46,882. **Below poverty:** 7.7%; 5.5% of families. **Uninsured:** 8.9%. **Educational attainment:** 93.6% HS; 35.3% bachelor's. **Avg. commute:** 23.8 min. 75.2% drive, 13.8% work from home. **Housing units:** 134,170; 92.9% occupied. **Home ownership:** 65.2%. **Avg. home:** $450,400; change (2021-23): 13.5%. **Avg. rent:** $1,641. **Crime rates:** violent: 303; property: 1,919.

Mayor: Michelle Romero, nonpartisan

History: Early growth spurred by WWII magnesium mining; inc. 1953.

Website: www.cityofhenderson.com

Honolulu, Hawaii

Population: 341,778 (55). **Pop. density:** 5,638. **Pop. change (2020-23):** –1.9%. **Area:** 60.6 sq mi. **Racial distribution:** 17.2% white; 1.8% Black; 52.3% Asian; 0.2% Amer. Ind.; 8.5% Pac. Isl.; 1.3% other; 2+ races, 18.7%. **Hispanic pop.:** 7.3%. **Foreign born:** 27.5%. **U.S. citizens:** 88.5%. **Language:** 64.6% English only; 1.6% Spanish.

Employment: 445,151 employed; 2.7% unemployment. **Per capita income:** $45,784. **Below poverty:** 10.7%; 7.3% of families. **Uninsured:** 5.7%. **Educational attainment:** 90.5% HS; 39.2% bachelor's. **Avg. commute:** 22.5 min. 56.8% drive, 13.9% carpool. **Housing units:** 155,489; 86.3% occupied. **Home ownership:** 48.0%. **Avg. home:** $1,055,900; change (2021-23): 6.0%. **Avg. rent:** $1,734. **Crime rates:** violent: 253; property: 2,578.

Mayor: Rick Blangiardi, nonpartisan

History: Europeans entered harbor, 1794; declared capital of the Hawaii Kingdom by King Kamehameha III, 1850. Pearl Harbor naval base attacked by Japanese, Dec. 7, 1941.

Website: www.honolulu.gov

Houston, Texas

Population: 2,314,157 (4). **Pop. density:** 3,612. **Pop. change (2020-23):** 0.6%. **Area:** 640.6 sq mi. **Racial distribution:** 40.8% white; 22.4% Black; 6.9% Asian; 0.7% Amer. Ind.; 0.1% Pac. Isl.; 14.3% other; 2+ races, 14.9%. **Hispanic pop.:** 44.8%. **Foreign born:** 28.9%. **U.S. citizens:** 80.7%. **Language:** 51.9% English only; 38.2% Spanish.

Employment: 1,142,836 employed; 4.6% unemployment. **Per capita income:** $38,834. **Below poverty:** 16.3%; 16.3% of families. **Uninsured:** 31.5%. **Educational attainment:** 79.6% HS; 35.2% bachelor's. **Avg. commute:** 27.4 min. 71.8% drive. **Housing units:** 1,006,392; 89.2% occupied. **Home ownership:** 42.0%. **Avg. home:** $340,300; change (2021-23): 11.9%. **Avg. rent:** $1,235. **Crime rates:** violent: 1,142; property: 4,582.

Mayor: John Whitmire, nonpartisan

History: Founded 1836; inc. 1837; capital of Rep. of Texas, 1837-39; developed rapidly after completion of channel to Gulf of Mexico, 1914. World center of oil, natural gas technology.

Website: www.houstontx.gov

Huntsville, Alabama

Population: 225,564 (100). **Pop. density:** 1,009. **Pop. change (2020-23):** 4.2%. **Area:** 223.6 sq mi. **Racial distribution:** 59.0% white; 30.4% Black; 2.1% Asian; 0.5% Amer. Ind.; 0.1% Pac. Isl.; 2.7% other; 2+ races, 5.2%. **Hispanic pop.:** 6.4%. **Foreign born:** 6.2%. **U.S. citizens:** 96.8%. **Language:** 92.1% English only; 4.5% Spanish.

Employment: 107,079 employed; 2.2% unemployment. **Per capita income:** $43,202. **Below poverty:** 12.6%; 10.8% of families. **Uninsured:** 13.8%. **Educational attainment:** 91.5% HS; 45.8% bachelor's. **Avg. commute:** 19.2 min. 79.4% drive, 11.4% work from home. **Housing units:** 100,345; 92.0% occupied. **Home ownership:** 57.5%. **Avg. home:** $324,200; change (2021-23): 15.6%. **Avg. rent:** $1,020. **Crime rates:** violent: 299; property: 1,506.

Mayor: Tommy Battle, nonpartisan

History: Settled by John Hunt 1805; founded as Twickenham 1809; inc. as Huntsville 1811; temporary state capital 1819-20.

Website: www.huntsvilleal.gov

Indianapolis, Indiana

Population: 879,293 (16). **Pop. density:** 2,436. **Pop. change (2020-23):** –0.9%. **Area:** 361.0 sq mi. **Racial distribution:** 55.7% white; 28.8% Black; 4.2% Asian; 0.3% Amer. Ind.; < 0.05% Pac. Isl.; 4.7% other; 2+ races, 6.3%. **Hispanic pop.:** 10.9%. **Foreign born:** 10.3%. **U.S. citizens:** 93.1%. **Language:** 85.2% English only; 8.3% Spanish.

Employment: 448,404 employed; 3.3% unemployment. **Per capita income:** $34,592. **Below poverty:** 13.9%; 11.5% of families. **Uninsured:** 12.6%. **Educational attainment:** 87.2% HS; 33.4% bachelor's. **Avg. commute:** 24.0 min. 75.6% drive, 10.3% work from home. **Housing units:** 397,597; 89.6% occupied. **Home ownership:** 54.9%. **Avg. home:** $305,200; change (2021-23): 17.2%. **Avg. rent:** $1,046. **Crime rates:** violent: 1,028; property: 3,377.

Mayor: Joe Hogsett, Democrat

History: Founded 1821; became planned state capital, 1825.

Website: www.indy.gov

Irvine, California

Population: 314,621 (63). **Pop. density:** 4,795. **Pop. change (2020-23):** 2.0%. **Area:** 65.6 sq mi. **Racial distribution:** 40.1% white; 2.0% Black; 44.3% Asian; 0.2% Amer. Ind.; 0.4% Pac. Isl.; 2.8% other; 2+ races, 10.3%. **Hispanic pop.:** 11.2%. **Foreign born:** 39.6%. **U.S. citizens:** 80.6%. **Language:** 49.6% English only; 6.4% Spanish.

Employment: 141,654 employed; 3.7% unemployment. **Per capita income:** $59,354. **Below poverty:** 13.5%; 8.5% of families. **Uninsured:** 5.6%. **Educational attainment:** 96.3% HS; 70.0% bachelor's. **Avg. commute:** 24.3 min. 63.7% drive, 23.1% work from home. **Housing units:** 119,149; 92.7% occupied. **Home ownership:** 43.9%. **Avg. home:** $1,260,000; change (2021-23): 14.6%. **Avg. rent:** $2,749. **Crime rates:** violent: 75; property: 1,479.

Mayor: Farrah N. Khan, nonpartisan

History: Univ. of CA–Irvine campus announced, 1959; planned city developed around campus; inc. 1971.

Website: www.cityofirvine.org

Irving, Texas

Population: 254,373 (88). **Pop. density:** 3,798. **Pop. change (2020-23):** –0.9%. **Area:** 67.0 sq mi. **Racial distribution:** 37.5% white; 13.2% Black; 22.3% Asian; 0.5% Amer. Ind.; 0.1% Pac. Isl.; 15.2% other; 2+ races, 11.2%. **Hispanic pop.:** 43.2%. **Foreign born:** 41.1%. **U.S. citizens:** 70.9%. **Language:** 39.4% English only; 37.2% Spanish.

Employment: 137,362 employed; 3.4% unemployment. **Per capita income:** $37,211. **Below poverty:** 9.1%; 8.1% of families. **Uninsured:** 26.2%. **Educational attainment:** 79.7% HS; 40.5% bachelor's. **Avg. commute:** 23.8 min. 71.5% drive, 10.5% carpool, 14.0% work from home. **Housing units:** 99,505; 93.3% occupied. **Home ownership:** 37.2%. **Avg. home:** $381,900; change (2021-23): 13.4%. **Avg. rent:** $1,423. **Crime rates:** violent: 336; property: 2,531.

Mayor: Rick Stopfer, nonpartisan

History: Founded 1903; inc. 1914; remained small until 1950s.

Website: www.cityofirving.org

Jacksonville, Florida

Population: 985,843 (10). **Pop. density:** 1,319. **Pop. change (2020-23):** 3.6%. **Area:** 747.3 sq mi. **Racial distribution:** 53.1% white; 30.4% Black; 4.9% Asian; 0.2% Amer. Ind.; 0.1% Pac. Isl.; 3.4% other; 2+ races, 7.9%. **Hispanic pop.:** 11.3%. **Foreign born:** 12.0%. **U.S. citizens:** 94.8%. **Language:** 83.9% English only; 7.7% Spanish.

Employment: 475,896 employed; 3.2% unemployment. **Per capita income:** $35,870. **Below poverty:** 12.9%; 11.0% of families. **Uninsured:** 16.4%. **Educational attainment:** 90.5% HS; 31.0% bachelor's. **Avg. commute:** 24.4 min. 74.9% drive, 11.1% work from home. **Housing units:** 414,089; 90.8% occupied. **Home ownership:** 57.0%. **Avg. home:** $389,400; change (2021-23): 19.8%. **Avg. rent:** $1,281. **Crime rates (MSA):** violent: 420; property: 1,758.

Mayor: Donna Deegan, Democrat

History: Settled as Cow Ford; renamed after Andrew Jackson, 1822; inc. 1832; scene of Civil War conflict, 1864.

Website: www.coj.net

Jersey City, New Jersey

Population: 291,657 (72). **Pop. density:** 19,776. **Pop. change (2020-23):** –0.1%. **Area:** 14.7 sq mi. **Racial distribution:** 30.5% white; 21.5% Black; 25.8% Asian; 0.6% Amer. Ind.; < 0.05% Pac. Isl.; 9.4% other; 2+ races, 12.2%. **Hispanic pop.:** 27.2%. **Foreign born:** 41.2%. **U.S. citizens:** 78.5%. **Language:** 48.6% English only; 20.5% Spanish.

Employment: 142,870 employed; 4.7% unemployment. **Per capita income:** $54,582. **Below poverty:** 13.4%; 12.0% of families. **Uninsured:** 11.3%. **Educational attainment:** 90.0% HS; 51.9% bachelor's. **Avg. commute:** 37.0 min. 28.5% drive, 38.9% public trans., 18.7% work from home. **Housing units:** 129,084; 92.4% occupied. **Home ownership:** 29.2%. **Avg. home:** $623,900; change (2021-23): 16.4%. **Avg. rent:** $1,799. **Crime rates:** violent: 220; property: 1,384.

Mayor: Steven M. Fulop, nonpartisan

History: Chartered as town by British 1668; scene of Revolutionary War conflict, 1779. Important station on Underground Railroad.

Website: www.jerseycitynj.gov

Kansas City, Missouri

Population: 510,704 (38). **Pop. density:** 1,623. **Pop. change (2020-23):** 0.5%. **Area:** 314.7 sq mi. **Racial distribution:** 59.0% white; 26.2% Black; 2.7% Asian; 0.4% Amer. Ind.; 0.2% Pac. Isl.; 4.0% other; 2+ races, 7.4%. **Hispanic pop.:** 11.1%. **Foreign born:**

8.2%. **U.S. citizens:** 95.7%. **Language:** 87.9% English only; 6.9% Spanish.

Employment: 253,982 employed; 3.3% unemployment. **Per capita income:** $38,146. **Below poverty:** 13.0%; 10.4% of families. **Uninsured:** 15.5%. **Educational attainment:** 91.5% HS; 37.1% bachelor's. **Avg. commute:** 22.0 min. 74.8% drive, 12.2% work from home. **Housing units:** 241,827; 89.5% occupied. **Home ownership:** 54.0%. **Avg. home:** $320,100; change (2021-23): 14.6%. **Avg. rent:** $1,131. **Crime rates:** violent: 1,481; property: 4,715.

Mayor: Quinton Lucas, nonpartisan

History: Est. by 1838 at confluence of Missouri and Kansas Rivers; inc. 1850.

Website: www.kcmo.gov

Laredo, Texas

Population: 257,602 (87). **Pop. density:** 2,411. **Pop. change (2020-23):** 0.8%. **Area:** 106.8 sq mi. **Racial distribution:** 53.4% white; 0.5% Black; 0.5% Asian; 0.3% Amer. Ind.; < 0.05% Pac. Isl.; 5.8% other; 2+ races, 39.5%. **Hispanic pop.:** 95.5%. **Foreign born:** 25.1%. **U.S. citizens:** 83.2%. **Language:** 11.5% English only; 87.7% Spanish.

Employment: 111,134 employed; 4.0% unemployment. **Per capita income:** $23,669. **Below poverty:** 17.7%; 18.9% of families. **Uninsured:** 40.0%. **Educational attainment:** 69.7% HS; 21.1% bachelor's. **Avg. commute:** 21.3 min. 79.3% drive, 11.2% carpool. **Housing units:** 80,644; 92.2% occupied. **Home ownership:** 62.7%. **Avg. rent:** $968. **Crime rates:** violent: 317; property: 1,285.

Mayor: Victor D. Treviño, nonpartisan

History: Founded by Spanish colonists, 1755; part of U.S. from 1848. Fast growth fueled by immigration; principal port of entry into Mexico.

Website: www.cityoflaredo.com

Las Vegas, Nevada

Population: 660,929 (24). **Pop. density:** 4,659. **Pop. change (2020-23):** 2.2%. **Area:** 141.9 sq mi. **Racial distribution:** 52.0% white; 11.8% Black; 6.9% Asian; 1.1% Amer. Ind.; 0.8% Pac. Isl.; 13.5% other; 2+ races, 13.9%. **Hispanic pop.:** 34.3%. **Foreign born:** 20.8%. **U.S. citizens:** 89.3%. **Language:** 66.9% English only; 25.1% Spanish.

Employment: 308,984 employed; 5.6% unemployment. **Per capita income:** $36,275. **Below poverty:** 13.1%; 10.7% of families. **Uninsured:** 17.9%. **Educational attainment:** 85.6% HS; 26.3% bachelor's. **Avg. commute:** 25.9 min. 73.5% drive, 10.0% carpool. **Housing units:** 260,767; 92.2% occupied. **Home ownership:** 54.8%. **Avg. home:** $450,400; change (2021-23): 13.5%. **Avg. rent:** $1,356. **Crime rates:** violent: 516; property: 2,918.

Mayor: Carolyn G. Goodman, nonpartisan

History: Occupied by Mormons 1855-57; bought by railroad 1903; city of Las Vegas inc. 1911; gambling legalized 1931.

Website: www.lasvegasnevada.gov

Lexington-Fayette, Kentucky

Population: 320,154 (59). **Pop. density:** 1,128. **Pop. change (2020-23):** –0.8%. **Area:** 283.9 sq mi. **Racial distribution:** 71.8% white; 14.7% Black; 4.1% Asian; 0.2% Amer. Ind.; < 0.05% Pac. Isl.; 2.8% other; 2+ races, 6.4%. **Hispanic pop.:** 7.4%. **Foreign born:** 10.2%. **U.S. citizens:** 93.5%. **Language:** 86.4% English only; 6.1% Spanish.

Employment: 169,623 employed; 3.4% unemployment. **Per capita income:** $40,953. **Below poverty:** 14.2%; 8.7% of families. **Uninsured:** 9.7%. **Educational attainment:** 92.2% HS; 46.5% bachelor's. **Avg. commute:** 20.8 min. 75.8% drive. **Housing units:** 146,345; 93.0% occupied. **Home ownership:** 54.3%. **Avg. home:** $257,800; change (2021-23): 15.0%. **Avg. rent:** $1,065. **Crime rates:** violent: 270; property: 2,716.

Mayor: Linda Gorton, nonpartisan

History: Site founded and named in 1775 after site of the Revolutionary War's opening battle at Lexington, MA; chartered 1782. Merged with Fayette County, 1974.

Website: www.lexingtonky.gov

Lincoln, Nebraska

Population: 294,757 (71). **Pop. density:** 2,948. **Pop. change (2020-23):** 1.1%. **Area:** 100.0 sq mi. **Racial distribution:** 82.0% white; 4.1% Black; 4.5% Asian; 0.7% Amer. Ind.; 0.1% Pac. Isl.; 2.0% other; 2+ races, 6.6%. **Hispanic pop.:** 8.3%. **Foreign born:** 9.1%. **U.S. citizens:** 95.4%. **Language:** 87.2% English only; 4.7% Spanish.

Employment: 160,556 employed; 2.1% unemployment. **Per capita income:** $37,210. **Below poverty:** 12.6%; 7.3% of families. **Uninsured:** 9.6%. **Educational attainment:** 92.9% HS; 40.9% bachelor's. **Avg. commute:** 18.6 min. 76.8% drive. **Housing units:** 124,294; 95.2% occupied. **Home ownership:** 56.3%. **Avg. home:** $288,600; change (2021-23): 17.7%. **Avg. rent:** $998. **Crime rates:** violent: 382; property: 2,842.

Mayor: Leirion Gaylor Baird, nonpartisan

History: Originally called Lancaster; chosen state capital, 1867, renamed after Abraham Lincoln; inc. 1871.

Website: www.lincoln.ne.gov

Long Beach, California

Population: 449,468 (44). **Pop. density:** 8,870. **Pop. change (2020-23):** –3.5%. **Area:** 50.7 sq mi. **Racial distribution:** 43.9% white; 12.0% Black; 12.7% Asian; 1.3% Amer. Ind.; 0.6% Pac. Isl.; 18.2% other; 2+ races, 11.3%. **Hispanic pop.:** 44.1%. **Foreign born:** 24.6%. **U.S. citizens:** 88.0%. **Language:** 54.8% English only; 33.8% Spanish.

Employment: 220,261 employed; 4.9% unemployment. **Per capita income:** $39,589. **Below poverty:** 13.6%; 10.5% of families. **Uninsured:** 12.2%. **Educational attainment:** 81.2% HS; 33.7% bachelor's. **Avg. commute:** 30.4 min. 69.7% drive, 12.5% work from home. **Housing units:** 180,015; 94.5% occupied. **Home ownership:** 40.6%. **Avg. home:** $833,400; change (2021-23): 4.0%. **Avg. rent:** $1,698. **Crime rates:** violent: 549; property: 2,599.

Mayor: Rex Richardson, nonpartisan

History: Settled c. 1784 by Spanish; by 1884, developed as harbor; inc. 1888; oil discovered 1921.

Website: www.longbeach.gov

Los Angeles, California

Population: 3,820,914 (2). **Pop. density:** 8,121. **Pop. change (2020-23):** –1.9%. **Area:** 470.5 sq mi. **Racial distribution:** 41.2% white; 8.6% Black; 11.8% Asian; 1.0% Amer. Ind.; 0.1% Pac. Isl.; 24.5% other; 2+ races, 12.7%. **Hispanic pop.:** 48.1%. **Foreign born:** 36.0%. **U.S. citizens:** 81.9%. **Language:** 42.6% English only; 40.8% Spanish.

Employment: 1,957,001 employed; 5.3% unemployment. **Per capita income:** $43,527. **Below poverty:** 15.2%; 12.0% of families. **Uninsured:** 14.5%. **Educational attainment:** 78.7% HS; 36.7% bachelor's. **Avg. commute:** 31.3 min. 63.1% drive, 15.1% work from home. **Housing units:** 1,518,992; 92.1% occupied. **Home ownership:** 36.6%. **Avg. home:** $833,400; change (2021-23): 4.0%. **Avg. rent:** $1,791. **Crime rates:** violent: 834; property: 2,708.

Mayor: Karen Bass, nonpartisan

History: Est. by Mexicans near Spanish mission, 1781; ceded to U.S., 1848; inc. 1850; grew rapidly after coming of railroads, 1876 and 1885. Film and defense industries drove 20th-century growth.

Website: lacity.gov

Louisville/Jefferson County, Kentucky

Population: 622,981 (28). **Pop. density:** 2,368. **Pop. change (2020-23):** –1.4%. **Area:** 263.1 sq mi. **Racial distribution:** 65.4% white; 23.9% Black; 2.7% Asian; 0.1% Amer. Ind.; 0.1% Pac. Isl.; 1.7% other; 2+ races, 6.1%. **Hispanic pop.:** 6.8%. **Foreign born:** 8.8%. **U.S. citizens:** 95.2%. **Language:** 88.9% English only; 5.4% Spanish.

Employment: 374,287 employed; 3.9% unemployment. **Per capita income:** $37,588. **Below poverty:** 13.5%; 11.3% of families. **Uninsured:** 7.9%. **Educational attainment:** 90.3% HS; 32.9% bachelor's. **Avg. commute:** 22.6 min. 75.6% drive, 10.1% work from home. **Housing units:** 286,976; 91.0% occupied. **Home ownership:** 60.4%. **Avg. home:** $263,800; change (2021-23): 12.0%. **Avg. rent:** $1,014. **Crime rates (2021):** violent: 981; property: 3,310.

Mayor: Craig Greenberg, Democrat

History: Est. 1778; named for Louis XVI of France; inc. 1828; base for Union forces in Civil War.

Website: louisvilleky.gov

Lubbock, Texas

Population: 266,878 (84). **Pop. density:** 1,880. **Pop. change (2020-23):** 3.4%. **Area:** 142.0 sq mi. **Racial distribution:** 67.5% white; 8.0% Black; 2.8% Asian; 0.6% Amer. Ind.; 0.1% Pac. Isl.; 7.2% other; 2+ races, 13.8%. **Hispanic pop.:** 37.6%. **Foreign born:** 6.5%. **U.S. citizens:** 96.0%. **Language:** 78.9% English only; 17.4% Spanish.

Employment: 135,172 employed; 3.4% unemployment. **Per capita income:** $33,259. **Below poverty:** 19.0%; 12.7% of families. **Uninsured:** 17.8%. **Educational attainment:** 88.6% HS; 34.2% bachelor's. **Avg. commute:** 16.1 min. 78.0% drive, 11.8% carpool. **Housing units:** 112,981; 91.1% occupied. **Home ownership:** 51.0%. **Avg. home:** $229,100; change (2021-23): 10.7%. **Avg. rent:** $1,093. **Crime rates:** violent: 1,063; property: 4,135.

Mayor: Tray Payne, nonpartisan

History: Became county seat, 1891; inc. 1909.

Website: ci.lubbock.tx.us

Madison, Wisconsin

Population: 280,305 (77). **Pop. density:** 3,374. **Pop. change (2020-23):** 1.9%. **Area:** 83.1 sq mi. **Racial distribution:** 74.6% white; 7.3% Black; 8.4% Asian; 0.3% Amer. Ind.; < 0.05% Pac. Isl.; 1.6% other; 2+ races, 7.8%. **Hispanic pop.:** 7.8%. **Foreign born:** 11.3%. **U.S. citizens:** 93.2%. **Language:** 86.6% English only; 4.9% Spanish.

Employment: 162,004 employed; 2.3% unemployment. **Per capita income:** $46,652. **Below poverty:** 17.6%; 6.0% of families. **Uninsured:** 5.0%. **Educational attainment:** 95.5% HS; 58.9% bachelor's. **Avg. commute:** 19.5 min. 58.9% drive, 15.3%

work from home. **Housing units:** 125,713; 95.9% occupied. **Home ownership:** 47.0%. **Avg. home:** $417,900; change (2021-23): 15.6%. **Avg. rent:** $1,291. **Crime rates:** violent: 301; property: 2,396.

Mayor: Satya Rhodes-Conway, nonpartisan

History: Selected as site for state capital, named for James Madison, 1836; chartered 1856.

Website: www.cityofmadison.com

Memphis, Tennessee

Population: 618,639 (29). **Pop. density:** 2,089. **Pop. change (2020-23):** –2.6%. **Area:** 296.2 sq mi. **Racial distribution:** 26.5% white; 64.4% Black; 1.6% Asian; 0.3% Amer. Ind.; < 0.05% Pac. Isl.; 3.9% other; 2+ races, 3.3%. **Hispanic pop.:** 8.0%. **Foreign born:** 6.3%. **U.S. citizens:** 95.8%. **Language:** 90.4% English only; 6.6% Spanish.

Employment: 272,412 employed; 4.9% unemployment. **Per capita income:** $31,060. **Below poverty:** 19.2%; 18.5% of families. **Uninsured:** 20.4%. **Educational attainment:** 87.2% HS; 27.9% bachelor's. **Avg. commute:** 21.6 min. 79.1% drive, 10.3% carpool. **Housing units:** 290,047; 86.7% occupied. **Home ownership:** 46.6%. **Avg. home:** $274,500; change (2021-23): 10.4%. **Avg. rent:** $1,050. **Crime rates:** violent: 2,421; property: 7,166.

Mayor: Paul Young, nonpartisan

History: French, Spanish, and U.S. forts by 1797; settled by 1819; inc. 1826; surrendered charter to state 1879 after yellow fever epidemics; rechartered as city 1893.

Website: www.memphistn.gov

Mesa, Arizona

Population: 511,648 (36). **Pop. density:** 3,619. **Pop. change (2020-23):** 1.1%. **Area:** 141.4 sq mi. **Racial distribution:** 72.1% white; 4.6% Black; 2.3% Asian; 2.1% Amer. Ind.; 0.2% Pac. Isl.; 6.8% other; 2+ races, 11.8%. **Hispanic pop.:** 27.3%. **Foreign born:** 11.6%. **U.S. citizens:** 92.8%. **Language:** 79.6% English only; 16.9% Spanish.

Employment: 267,349 employed; 3.5% unemployment. **Per capita income:** $37,197. **Below poverty:** 9.7%; 8.0% of families. **Uninsured:** 15.7%. **Educational attainment:** 90.7% HS; 30.0% bachelor's. **Avg. commute:** 24.8 min. 69.3% drive, 11.6% carpool, 14.6% work from home. **Housing units:** 219,909; 87.9% occupied. **Home ownership:** 63.2%. **Avg. home:** $459,600; change (2021-23): 10.6%. **Avg. rent:** $1,352. **Crime rates:** violent: 427; property: 1,770.

Mayor: John Giles, nonpartisan

History: Founded by Mormons from Utah and Idaho, 1878; inc. 1883.

Website: www.mesaaz.gov

Miami, Florida

Population: 455,924 (42). **Pop. density:** 12,666. **Pop. change (2020-23):** 3.0%. **Area:** 36.0 sq mi. **Racial distribution:** 45.4% white; 14.1% Black; 1.5% Asian; 0.3% Amer. Ind.; < 0.05% Pac. Isl.; 6.4% other; 2+ races, 32.3%. **Hispanic pop.:** 72.3%. **Foreign born:** 57.9%. **U.S. citizens:** 71.7%. **Language:** 22.2% English only; 70.0% Spanish.

Employment: 233,262 employed; 1.8% unemployment. **Per capita income:** $39,055. **Below poverty:** 18.9%; 15.8% of families. **Uninsured:** 25.5%. **Educational attainment:** 78.8% HS; 34.2% bachelor's. **Avg. commute:** 28.2 min. 63.5% drive, 11.9% work from home. **Housing units:** 214,820; 86.6% occupied. **Home ownership:** 30.1%. **Avg. home:** $593,000; change (2021-23): 23.5%. **Avg. rent:** $1,494.

Mayor: Francis Suarez, nonpartisan

History: Site of fort, 1836; inc. 1896. Modern city developed into financial and tourism center. Land speculation in 1920s added to city's growth.

Website: www.miami.gov

Milwaukee, Wisconsin

Population: 561,385 (31). **Pop. density:** 5,837. **Pop. change (2020-23):** –2.7%. **Area:** 96.2 sq mi. **Racial distribution:** 38.8% white; 38.6% Black; 4.7% Asian; 0.6% Amer. Ind.; < 0.05% Pac. Isl.; 7.3% other; 2+ races, 9.9%. **Hispanic pop.:** 20.2%. **Foreign born:** 10.3%. **U.S. citizens:** 93.7%. **Language:** 78.4% English only; 15.5% Spanish.

Employment: 261,588 employed; 4.3% unemployment. **Per capita income:** $28,079. **Below poverty:** 20.5%; 19.1% of families. **Uninsured:** 13.6%. **Educational attainment:** 85.4% HS; 26.1% bachelor's. **Avg. commute:** 22.2 min. 69.8% drive. **Housing units:** 257,441; 89.6% occupied. **Home ownership:** 41.2%. **Avg. home:** $372,400; change (2021-23): 16.7%. **Avg. rent:** $982. **Crime rates:** violent: 1,509; property: 3,507.

Mayor: Cavalier Johnson, nonpartisan

History: Indian trading post by 1674; inc. 1846. Famous beer industry.

Website: city.milwaukee.gov

Minneapolis, Minnesota

Population: 425,115 (46). **Pop. density:** 7,873. **Pop. change (2020-23):** –1.3%. **Area:** 54.0 sq mi. **Racial distribution:** 62.7% white; 18.5% Black; 5.2% Asian; 1.2% Amer. Ind.; < 0.05% Pac. Isl.; 4.5% other; 2+ races, 7.8%. **Hispanic pop.:** 9.9%. **Foreign born:** 14.5%. **U.S. citizens:** 93.4%. **Language:** 79.0% English only; 7.1% Spanish.

Employment: 239,559 employed; 2.6% unemployment. **Per capita income:** $48,373. **Below poverty:** 16.1%; 9.6% of families. **Uninsured:** 7.8%. **Educational attainment:** 90.8% HS; 53.5% bachelor's. **Avg. commute:** 22.9 min. 54.7% drive, 19.6% work from home. **Housing units:** 198,971; 93.3% occupied. **Home ownership:** 48.1%. **Avg. home:** $379,900; change (2021-23): 7.1%. **Avg. rent:** $1,267. **Crime rates:** violent: 1,226; property: 5,262.

Mayor: Jacob Frey, Democrat (DFL)

History: Visited by French missionary Louis Hennepin, 1680; included in area of military reservations, 1819; inc. 1867.

Website: www.minneapolismn.gov

Nashville-Davidson, Tennessee

Population: 687,788 (21). **Pop. density:** 1,446. **Pop. change (2020-23):** –0.3%. **Area:** 475.6 sq mi. **Racial distribution:** 59.1% white; 26.8% Black; 3.6% Asian; 0.1% Amer. Ind.; 0.1% Pac. Isl.; 3.8% other; 2+ races, 6.4%. **Hispanic pop.:** 10.8%. **Foreign born:** 13.7%. **U.S. citizens:** 91.6%. **Language:** 82.5% English only; 8.7% Spanish.

Employment: 408,625 employed; 2.7% unemployment. **Per capita income:** $44,433. **Below poverty:** 12.3%; 10.7% of families. **Uninsured:** 15.8%. **Educational attainment:** 90.2% HS; 45.5% bachelor's. **Avg. commute:** 24.8 min. 70.5% drive, 15.5% work from home. **Housing units:** 322,179; 90.6% occupied. **Home ownership:** 53.8%. **Avg. home:** $401,500; change (2021-23): 14.9%. **Avg. rent:** $1,392. **Crime rates:** violent: 1,102; property: 3,825.

Mayor: Freddie O'Connell, nonpartisan

History: Est. 1779; first chartered, 1806; became permanent state capital 1843. Home of Grand Ole Opry.

Website: www.nashville.gov

New Orleans, Louisiana

Population: 364,136 (53). **Pop. density:** 2,148. **Pop. change (2020-23):** –5.0%. **Area:** 169.5 sq mi. **Racial distribution:** 32.4% white; 57.0% Black; 2.8% Asian; 0.2% Amer. Ind.; < 0.05% Pac. Isl.; 2.2% other; 2+ races, 5.3%. **Hispanic pop.:** 5.7%. **Foreign born:** 5.6%. **U.S. citizens:** 97.2%. **Language:** 91.6% English only; 4.0% Spanish.

Employment: 167,786 employed; 4.5% unemployment. **Per capita income:** $37,013. **Below poverty:** 20.5%; 16.5% of families. **Uninsured:** 11.5%. **Educational attainment:** 88.7% HS; 40.7% bachelor's. **Avg. commute:** 23.4 min. 64.5% drive, 11.3% work from home. **Housing units:** 193,999; 80.2% occupied. **Home ownership:** 49.3%. **Avg. home:** $275,900; change (2021-23): 2.9%. **Avg. rent:** $1,162. **Crime rates:** violent: 1,444; property: 4,641.

Mayor: LaToya Cantrell, Democrat

History: Founded by French colonists, 1718; became major seaport on Mississippi R.; acquired by U.S. in Louisiana Purchase, 1803; inc. 1805. Hurricane Katrina, 2005, inflicted major damage and killed 1,450+.

Website: nola.gov

New York, New York

Population: 8,258,035 (1). **Pop. density:** 27,485. **Pop. change (2020-23):** –5.5%. **Area:** 300.5 sq mi. **Racial distribution:** 37.5% white; 23.1% Black; 14.5% Asian; 0.6% Amer. Ind.; 0.1% Pac. Isl.; 15.4% other; 2+ races, 8.9%. **Hispanic pop.:** 29.0%. **Foreign born:** 36.3%. **U.S. citizens:** 85.0%. **Language:** 52.2% English only; 23.3% Spanish.

Employment: 3,935,382 employed; 5.2% unemployment. **Per capita income:** $48,066. **Below poverty:** 15.7%; 13.6% of families. **Uninsured:** 9.5%. **Educational attainment:** 83.3% HS; 40.2% bachelor's. **Avg. commute:** 41.1 min. 22.2% drive, 47.3% public trans., 13.0% work from home. **Housing units:** 3,620,774; 90.7% occupied. **Home ownership:** 32.9%. **Avg. home:** $623,900; change (2021-23): 16.4%. **Avg. rent:** $1,714. **Crime rates:** violent: 744; property: 2,141.

Mayor: Eric Adams, Democrat

History: Trading post est., 1624; British took control from Dutch, 1664, named city New York; U.S. capital, 1785-90. Under new charter, 1898, city expanded to include five boroughs: Bronx, Brooklyn, Queens, and Staten Island, as well as Manhattan. Sept. 11, 2001, terrorist attacks destroyed World Trade Center, killed more than 2,750.

Website: www.nyc.gov

Newark, New Jersey

Population: 304,960 (66). **Pop. density:** 12,631. **Pop. change (2020-23):** –1.8%. **Area:** 24.1 sq mi. **Racial distribution:** 19.6% white; 47.0% Black; 2.0% Asian; 0.4% Amer. Ind.; < 0.05% Pac. Isl.; 19.8% other; 2+ races, 11.1%. **Hispanic pop.:** 37.2%. **Foreign born:** 34.7%. **U.S. citizens:** 79.6%. **Language:** 49.5% English only; 32.8% Spanish.

Employment: 115,801 employed; 7.1% unemployment. **Per capita income:** $24,716. **Below poverty:** 21.1%; 21.4% of families. **Uninsured:** 24.2%. **Educational attainment:** 77.7% HS; 17.0%

bachelor's. **Avg. commute:** 33.0 min. 52.1% drive, 20.2% public trans.. **Housing units:** 121,773; 92.5% occupied. **Home ownership:** 23.9%. **Avg. home:** $621,700; change (2021-23): 21.4%. **Avg. rent:** $1,273. **Crime rates:** violent: 520; property: 1,820.

Mayor: Ras J. Baraka, nonpartisan

History: Est. by Puritans, 1666; inc. as city, 1836. Major industry and shipping hub from mid-19th century.

Website: www.newarknj.gov

Norfolk, Virginia

Population: 230,930 (96). **Pop. density:** 4,335. **Pop. change (2020-23):** –2.9%. **Area:** 53.3 sq mi. **Racial distribution:** 44.8% white; 40.7% Black; 3.8% Asian; 0.4% Amer. Ind.; 0.2% Pac. Isl.; 3.3% other; 2+ races, 6.7%. **Hispanic pop.:** 8.7%. **Foreign born:** 7.4%. **U.S. citizens:** 96.5%. **Language:** 89.3% English only; 5.1% Spanish.

Employment: 109,605 employed; 3.4% unemployment. **Per capita income:** $35,761. **Below poverty:** 14.6%; 12.3% of families. **Uninsured:** 14.0%. **Educational attainment:** 89.3% HS; 32.2% bachelor's. **Avg. commute:** 22.7 min. 72.7% drive. **Housing units:** 101,710; 92.2% occupied. **Home ownership:** 44.8%. **Avg. home:** $334,400; change (2021-23): 17.3%. **Avg. rent:** $1,188. **Crime rates:** violent: 703; property: 4,872.

Mayor: Kenneth Cooper Alexander, nonpartisan

History: Founded 1682; burned by colonists to prevent capture by British during Revolutionary War. Inc. as city, 1845. Site of world's largest naval base; major commercial port.

Website: www.norfolk.gov

North Las Vegas, Nevada

Population: 284,771 (75). **Pop. density:** 2,704. **Pop. change (2020-23):** 9.0%. **Area:** 105.3 sq mi. **Racial distribution:** 38.1% white; 22.1% Black; 6.7% Asian; 0.9% Amer. Ind.; 0.8% Pac. Isl.; 14.4% other; 2+ races, 17.1%. **Hispanic pop.:** 42.2%. **Foreign born:** 21.1%. **U.S. citizens:** 89.2%. **Language:** 61.5% English only; 31.8% Spanish.

Employment: 115,857 employed; 6.3% unemployment. **Per capita income:** $29,460. **Below poverty:** 10.5%; 9.9% of families. **Uninsured:** 18.2%. **Educational attainment:** 81.9% HS; 17.8% bachelor's. **Avg. commute:** 27.6 min. 77.1% drive, 11.2% carpool. **Housing units:** 88,787; 93.7% occupied. **Home ownership:** 61.2%. **Avg. home:** $450,400; change (2021-23): 13.5%. **Avg. rent:** $1,479. **Crime rates:** violent: 422; property: 1,774.

Mayor: Pamela Goynes-Brown, nonpartisan

History: Inc. 1946.

Website: www.cityofnorthlasvegas.com

Oakland, California

Population: 436,504 (45). **Pop. density:** 7,800. **Pop. change (2020-23):** –1.0%. **Area:** 56.0 sq mi. **Racial distribution:** 32.3% white; 21.8% Black; 15.9% Asian; 1.2% Amer. Ind.; 0.5% Pac. Isl.; 18.2% other; 2+ races, 10.0%. **Hispanic pop.:** 26.6%. **Foreign born:** 26.3%. **U.S. citizens:** 86.7%. **Language:** 61.2% English only; 21.0% Spanish.

Employment: 199,424 employed; 4.6% unemployment. **Per capita income:** $56,628. **Below poverty:** 12.2%; 9.5% of families. **Uninsured:** 7.8%. **Educational attainment:** 85.6% HS; 48.4% bachelor's. **Avg. commute:** 31.5 min. 48.1% drive, 16.5% public trans., 20.3% work from home. **Housing units:** 184,530; 92.3% occupied. **Home ownership:** 42.1%. **Avg. home:** $1,272,500; change (2021-23): –3.6%. **Avg. rent:** $1,849. **Crime rates:** violent: 1,521; property: 6,475.

Mayor: Sheng Thao, nonpartisan

History: Area settled by Spanish, 1820; inc. 1854.

Website: www.oaklandca.gov

Oklahoma City, Oklahoma

Population: 702,767 (20). **Pop. density:** 1,159. **Pop. change (2020-23):** 2.9%. **Area:** 606.5 sq mi. **Racial distribution:** 61.4% white; 13.7% Black; 4.5% Asian; 3.4% Amer. Ind.; 0.1% Pac. Isl.; 5.1% other; 2+ races, 11.8%. **Hispanic pop.:** 20.1%. **Foreign born:** 11.9%. **U.S. citizens:** 92.8%. **Language:** 79.8% English only; 14.9% Spanish.

Employment: 339,919 employed; 3.1% unemployment. **Per capita income:** $35,954. **Below poverty:** 13.0%; 11.3% of families. **Uninsured:** 19.9%. **Educational attainment:** 87.7% HS; 33.2% bachelor's. **Avg. commute:** 22.0 min. 78.4% drive. **Housing units:** 298,877; 90.4% occupied. **Home ownership:** 59.5%. **Avg. home:** $243,800; change (2021-23): 25.5%. **Avg. rent:** $1,012. **Crime rates:** violent: 642; property: 3,059.

Mayor: David Holt, nonpartisan

History: Settled during land rush, 1889; inc. 1890; became capital, 1910; oil discovered, 1928. Bomb in 1995 destroyed federal office bldg., killed 168 people.

Website: www.okc.gov

Omaha, Nebraska

Population: 483,335 (40). **Pop. density:** 3,380. **Pop. change (2020-23):** –1.9%. **Area:** 143.0 sq mi. **Racial distribution:** 71.5% white; 11.9% Black; 4.1% Asian; 0.6% Amer. Ind.; < 0.05% Pac. Isl.; 3.9% other; 2+ races, 8.0%. **Hispanic pop.:** 14.8%. **Foreign born:** 10.7%. **U.S. citizens:** 93.2%. **Language:** 83.5% English only; 10.4% Spanish.

Employment: 244,870 employed; 2.6% unemployment. **Per capita income:** $40,081. **Below poverty:** 11.5%; 8.3% of families. **Uninsured:** 13.5%. **Educational attainment:** 90.4% HS; 39.2% bachelor's. **Avg. commute:** 19.3 min. 75.0% drive, 11.5% work from home. **Housing units:** 210,493; 94.0% occupied. **Home ownership:** 57.9%. **Avg. home:** $290,000; change (2021-23): 19.8%. **Avg. rent:** $1,099. **Crime rates:** violent: 561; property: 3,468.

Mayor: Jean Stothert, nonpartisan

History: Founded 1854; inc. 1857. Large food-processing, telecommunications, information-processing center.

Website: www.cityofomaha.org

Orlando, Florida

Population: 320,742 (58). **Pop. density:** 2,883. **Pop. change (2020-23):** 4.2%. **Area:** 111.2 sq mi. **Racial distribution:** 48.5% white; 23.3% Black; 4.0% Asian; 0.1% Amer. Ind.; 0.1% Pac. Isl.; 7.6% other; 2+ races, 16.4%. **Hispanic pop.:** 34.8%. **Foreign born:** 22.5%. **U.S. citizens:** 87.1%. **Language:** 59.4% English only; 28.8% Spanish.

Employment: 176,289 employed; 2.8% unemployment. **Per capita income:** $40,253. **Below poverty:** 13.3%; 12.4% of families. **Uninsured:** 17.7%. **Educational attainment:** 91.4% HS; 41.7% bachelor's. **Avg. commute:** 26.9 min. 72.7% drive, 12.1% work from home. **Housing units:** 144,377; 84.9% occupied. **Home ownership:** 39.2%. **Avg. home:** $434,000; change (2021-23): 21.6%. **Avg. rent:** $1,509. **Crime rates:** violent: 836; property: 4,028.

Mayor: Buddy Dyer, nonpartisan

History: Ft. Gatlin built just south of present-day Orlando, 1838; name changed from Jernigan, 1856; inc. 1875. Walt Disney World opened, 1971.

Website: www.orlando.gov

Philadelphia, Pennsylvania

Population: 1,550,542 (6). **Pop. density:** 11,541. **Pop. change (2020-23):** –3.1%. **Area:** 134.4 sq mi. **Racial distribution:** 37.1% white; 40.1% Black; 7.6% Asian; 0.3% Amer. Ind.; 0.1% Pac. Isl.; 8.5% other; 2+ races, 6.3%. **Hispanic pop.:** 15.7%. **Foreign born:** 14.6%. **U.S. citizens:** 93.0%. **Language:** 76.0% English only; 11.2% Spanish.

Employment: 711,377 employed; 4.2% unemployment. **Per capita income:** $35,553. **Below poverty:** 20.3%; 18.0% of families. **Uninsured:** 10.0%. **Educational attainment:** 86.9% HS; 33.6% bachelor's. **Avg. commute:** 32.8 min. 47.5% drive, 19.8% public trans., 13.8% work from home. **Housing units:** 730,630; 90.2% occupied. **Home ownership:** 52.2%. **Avg. home:** $349,800; change (2021-23): 14.7%. **Avg. rent:** $1,250. **Crime rates:** violent: 1,041; property: 4,321.

Mayor: Cherelle Parker, Democrat

History: Named Philadelphia, 1682; chartered 1701. Continental Congresses convened 1774, 1775; Declaration of Independence signed, 1776; U.S. capital, 1790-1800.

Website: www.phila.gov

Phoenix, Arizona

Population: 1,650,070 (5). **Pop. density:** 3,183. **Pop. change (2020-23):** 2.3%. **Area:** 518.3 sq mi. **Racial distribution:** 59.4% white; 7.4% Black; 3.7% Asian; 2.1% Amer. Ind.; 0.2% Pac. Isl.; 10.3% other; 2+ races, 16.9%. **Hispanic pop.:** 42.9%. **Foreign born:** 19.3%. **U.S. citizens:** 88.3%. **Language:** 63.1% English only; 30.4% Spanish.

Employment: 877,054 employed; 3.5% unemployment. **Per capita income:** $37,499. **Below poverty:** 12.5%; 10.9% of families. **Uninsured:** 19.1%. **Educational attainment:** 83.9% HS; 31.2% bachelor's. **Avg. commute:** 25.7 min. 68.5% drive, 11.0% carpool, 14.4% work from home. **Housing units:** 633,863; 93.3% occupied. **Home ownership:** 56.4%. **Avg. home:** $459,600; change (2021-23): 10.6%. **Avg. rent:** $1,322. **Crime rates:** violent: 825; property: 2,902.

Mayor: Kate Gallego, nonpartisan

History: Founded 1867; inc. 1881; became territorial capital, 1889.

Website: www.phoenix.gov

Pittsburgh, Pennsylvania

Population: 303,255 (68). **Pop. density:** 5,476. **Pop. change (2020-23):** 0.2%. **Area:** 55.4 sq mi. **Racial distribution:** 64.5% white; 23.2% Black; 5.6% Asian; 0.2% Amer. Ind.; < 0.05% Pac. Isl.; 1.2% other; 2+ races, 5.3%. **Hispanic pop.:** 3.6%. **Foreign born:** 9.0%. **U.S. citizens:** 94.5%. **Language:** 88.8% English only; 2.5% Spanish.

Employment: 147,925 employed; 3.2% unemployment. **Per capita income:** $41,146. **Below poverty:** 18.0%; 11.8% of families. **Uninsured:** 6.9%. **Educational attainment:** 93.9% HS; 46.7% bachelor's. **Avg. commute:** 23.4 min. 49.7% drive, 13.4% public trans., 10.4% walk, 17.5% work from home. **Housing units:** 157,943; 86.9% occupied. **Home ownership:** 47.4%. **Avg. home:** $216,300; change (2021-23): 5.3%. **Avg. rent:** $1,153.

Mayor: Ed Gainey, Democrat

History: Settled around Ft. Pitt, 1758; inc. 1816; became an inland port; a center for iron production by Civil War.

Website: pittsburghpa.gov

Plano, Texas

Population: 290,190 (73). **Pop. density:** 4,047. **Pop. change (2020-23):** 1.3%. **Area:** 71.7 sq mi. **Racial distribution:** 55.6% white; 9.0% Black; 22.7% Asian; 0.3% Amer. Ind.; < 0.05% Pac. Isl.; 3.3% other; 2+ races, 9.2%. **Hispanic pop.:** 15.6%. **Foreign born:** 28.5%. **U.S. citizens:** 84.2%. **Language:** 63.3% English only; 11.6% Spanish.

Employment: 171,663 employed; 3.4% unemployment. **Per capita income:** $55,938. **Below poverty:** 6.5%; 5.0% of families. **Uninsured:** 15.0%. **Educational attainment:** 93.6% HS; 58.4% bachelor's. **Avg. commute:** 25.8 min. 66.5% drive, 22.3% work from home. **Housing units:** 113,626; 94.6% occupied. **Home ownership:** 56.7%. **Avg. home:** $381,900; change (2021-23): 13.4%. **Avg. rent:** $1,699. **Crime rates:** violent: 158; property: 1,896.

Mayor: John B. Muns, nonpartisan

History: Settled 1846; inc. 1873.

Website: www.plano.gov

Port St. Lucie, Florida

Population: 245,021 (92). **Pop. density:** 2,055. **Pop. change (2020-23):** 18.5%. **Area:** 119.2 sq mi. **Racial distribution:** 63.3% white; 18.3% Black; 2.2% Asian; 0.2% Amer. Ind.; 0.1% Pac. Isl.; 4.7% other; 2+ races, 11.3%. **Hispanic pop.:** 22.9%. **Foreign born:** 19.5%. **U.S. citizens:** 95.0%. **Language:** 74.0% English only; 16.7% Spanish.

Employment: 102,666 employed; 3.2% unemployment. **Per capita income:** $35,301. **Below poverty:** 7.6%; 5.7% of families. **Uninsured:** 16.3%. **Educational attainment:** 90.7% HS; 26.2% bachelor's. **Avg. commute:** 29.2 min. 81.0% drive. **Housing units:** 82,293; 91.1% occupied. **Home ownership:** 82.8%. **Avg. home:** $409,900; change (2021-23): 23.5%. **Avg. rent:** $1,684. **Crime rates:** violent: 117; property: 762.

Mayor: Shannon M. Martin, nonpartisan

History: Inc. 1961.

Website: www.cityofpsl.com

Portland, Oregon

Population: 630,498 (27). **Pop. density:** 4,723. **Pop. change (2020-23):** –3.5%. **Area:** 133.5 sq mi. **Racial distribution:** 72.1% white; 5.9% Black; 8.4% Asian; 1.0% Amer. Ind.; 0.6% Pac. Isl.; 2.8% other; 2+ races, 9.2%. **Hispanic pop.:** 10.3%. **Foreign born:** 12.6%. **U.S. citizens:** 94.7%. **Language:** 82.1% English only; 6.2% Spanish.

Employment: 370,993 employed; 3.6% unemployment. **Per capita income:** $52,577. **Below poverty:** 12.0%; 6.4% of families. **Uninsured:** 7.5%. **Educational attainment:** 93.4% HS; 52.5% bachelor's. **Avg. commute:** 24.8 min. 51.9% drive, 22.0% work from home. **Housing units:** 301,084; 94.3% occupied. **Home ownership:** 53.3%. **Avg. home:** $584,800; change (2021-23): 9.0%. **Avg. rent:** $1,530. **Crime rates:** violent: 751; property: 6,324.

Mayor: Ted Wheeler, nonpartisan

History: Est. 1843; developed as trading center, aided by California Gold Rush, 1849; city chartered, 1851.

Website: www.portland.gov

Raleigh, North Carolina

Population: 482,295 (41). **Pop. density:** 3,227. **Pop. change (2020-23):** 3.6%. **Area:** 149.4 sq mi. **Racial distribution:** 55.5% white; 28.1% Black; 4.5% Asian; 0.3% Amer. Ind.; < 0.05% Pac. Isl.; 4.7% other; 2+ races, 6.9%. **Hispanic pop.:** 11.6%. **Foreign born:** 13.0%. **U.S. citizens:** 92.5%. **Language:** 82.3% English only; 9.3% Spanish.

Employment: 265,885 employed; 3.2% unemployment. **Per capita income:** $47,257. **Below poverty:** 11.0%; 7.1% of families. **Uninsured:** 13.1%. **Educational attainment:** 92.4% HS; 52.7% bachelor's. **Avg. commute:** 23.7 min. 68.0% drive, 20.1% work from home. **Housing units:** 211,412; 89.8% occupied. **Home ownership:** 51.1%. **Avg. home:** $459,900; change (2021-23): 17.1%. **Avg. rent:** $1,371. **Crime rates:** violent: 500; property: 2,335.

Mayor: Mary-Ann Baldwin, nonpartisan

History: Named after Sir Walter Raleigh; chosen state capital, 1788; inc. 1795; occupied by Union Gen. Sherman, 1865.

Website: raleighnc.gov

Reno, Nevada

Population: 274,915 (80). **Pop. density:** 2,522. **Pop. change (2020-23):** 3.7%. **Area:** 109.0 sq mi. **Racial distribution:** 66.1% white; 3.4% Black; 6.9% Asian; 0.9% Amer. Ind.; 0.8% Pac. Isl.; 11.2% other; 2+ races, 10.6%. **Hispanic pop.:** 23.6%. **Foreign born:** 15.9%. **U.S. citizens:** 91.5%. **Language:** 76.7% English only; 15.0% Spanish.

Employment: 137,478 employed; 4.1% unemployment. **Per capita income:** $43,245. **Below poverty:** 12.3%; 7.3% of families. **Uninsured:** 13.8%. **Educational attainment:** 89.6% HS; 35.3% bachelor's. **Avg. commute:** 20.5 min. 69.5% drive, 12.2% carpool. **Housing units:** 117,569; 94.0% occupied. **Home ownership:** 48.3%. **Avg. home:** $585,800; change (2021-23): 10.2%. **Avg. rent:** $1,360. **Crime rates:** violent: 572; property: 2,556.

Mayor: Hillary Schieve, nonpartisan

History: Originally named Lake's Crossing; name changed to Reno, after a Union Civil War general, 1868, with arrival of transcontinental railroad.

Website: www.reno.gov

Richmond, Virginia

Population: 229,247 (98). **Pop. density:** 3,826. **Pop. change (2020-23):** 1.0%. **Area:** 59.9 sq mi. **Racial distribution:** 44.6% white; 44.0% Black; 2.3% Asian; 0.2% Amer. Ind.; < 0.05% Pac. Isl.; 3.3% other; 2+ races, 5.7%. **Hispanic pop.:** 7.6%. **Foreign born:** 7.4%. **U.S. citizens:** 95.0%. **Language:** 89.9% English only; 6.4% Spanish.

Employment: 120,442 employed; 3.5% unemployment. **Per capita income:** $42,132. **Below poverty:** 17.2%; 12.4% of families. **Uninsured:** 12.3%. **Educational attainment:** 88.8% HS; 44.1% bachelor's. **Avg. commute:** 22.0 min. 66.1% drive, 14.3% work from home. **Housing units:** 111,524; 90.7% occupied. **Home ownership:** 43.2%. **Avg. home:** $393,000; change (2021-23): 14.6%. **Avg. rent:** $1,227. **Crime rates:** violent: 360; property: 3,433.

Mayor: Levar M. Stoney, nonpartisan

History: First explored, 1607; became capital of Virginia, 1779; attacked by British, 1781; inc. as city, 1782; capital of Confederate States of America, 1861-65.

Website: www.rva.gov

Riverside, California

Population: 318,858 (61). **Pop. density:** 3,929. **Pop. change (2020-23):** 1.2%. **Area:** 81.1 sq mi. **Racial distribution:** 45.2% white; 5.8% Black; 8.5% Asian; 0.8% Amer. Ind.; 0.4% Pac. Isl.; 26.6% other; 2+ races, 12.7%. **Hispanic pop.:** 55.4%. **Foreign born:** 22.2%. **U.S. citizens:** 90.0%. **Language:** 53.6% English only; 37.3% Spanish.

Employment: 153,563 employed; 4.4% unemployment. **Per capita income:** $31,632. **Below poverty:** 11.9%; 9.0% of families. **Uninsured:** 12.9%. **Educational attainment:** 82.6% HS; 24.4% bachelor's. **Avg. commute:** 31.3 min. 74.9% drive, 11.0% carpool. **Housing units:** 95,517; 94.8% occupied. **Home ownership:** 55.5%. **Avg. home:** $565,000; change (2021-23): 10.8%. **Avg. rent:** $1,711. **Crime rates:** violent: 516; property: 3,240.

Mayor: Patricia Lock Dawson, nonpartisan

History: Founded 1870; inc. 1883. Known for citrus industry; home of the parent navel orange tree.

Website: riversideca.gov

Sacramento, California

Population: 526,384 (35). **Pop. density:** 5,336. **Pop. change (2020-23):** 0.2%. **Area:** 98.6 sq mi. **Racial distribution:** 39.3% white; 12.6% Black; 19.5% Asian; 0.8% Amer. Ind.; 1.8% Pac. Isl.; 12.8% other; 2+ races, 13.1%. **Hispanic pop.:** 29.4%. **Foreign born:** 21.3%. **U.S. citizens:** 91.3%. **Language:** 64.0% English only; 16.9% Spanish.

Employment: 231,613 employed; 4.7% unemployment. **Per capita income:** $39,336. **Below poverty:** 13.7%; 10.0% of families. **Uninsured:** 7.6%. **Educational attainment:** 86.4% HS; 35.8% bachelor's. **Avg. commute:** 25.4 min. 67.6% drive, 15.1% work from home. **Housing units:** 206,808; 95.0% occupied. **Home ownership:** 50.7%. **Avg. home:** $527,100; change (2021-23): 5.4%. **Avg. rent:** $1,592. **Crime rates:** violent: 902; property: 3,167.

Mayor: Darrell Steinberg, nonpartisan

History: Est. 1839; important trading center during Gold Rush; became state capital, 1854.

Website: www.cityofsacramento.gov

St. Louis, Missouri

Population: 281,754 (76). **Pop. density:** 4,565. **Pop. change (2020-23):** –6.2%. **Area:** 61.7 sq mi. **Racial distribution:** 46.3% white; 43.9% Black; 3.5% Asian; 0.2% Amer. Ind.; 0.1% Pac. Isl.; 1.4% other; 2+ races, 4.7%. **Hispanic pop.:** 4.3%. **Foreign born:** 6.3%. **U.S. citizens:** 96.5%. **Language:** 90.8% English only; 2.7% Spanish.

Employment: 145,099 employed; 3.7% unemployment. **Per capita income:** $36,722. **Below poverty:** 18.1%; 14.3% of families. **Uninsured:** 14.0%. **Educational attainment:** 90.0% HS; 38.6% bachelor's. **Avg. commute:** 23.0 min. 68.2% drive, 12.5% work from home. **Housing units:** 173,792; 82.3% occupied. **Home ownership:** 44.9%. **Avg. home:** $254,400; change (2021-23): 12.5%. **Avg. rent:** $938. **Crime rates:** violent: 1,472; property: 7,254.

Mayor: Tishaura O. Jones, nonpartisan

History: Founded 1764 as French fur trading post on Mississippi R., near confluence with Missouri R.; acquired by U.S., 1803; chartered as city, 1823.

Website: www.stlouis-mo.gov

St. Paul, Minnesota

Population: 303,820 (67). **Pop. density:** 5,846. **Pop. change (2020-23):** –2.4%. **Area:** 52.0 sq mi. **Racial distribution:** 54.3% white; 15.6% Black; 18.4% Asian; 0.7% Amer. Ind.; < 0.05% Pac. Isl.; 3.2% other; 2+ races, 7.8%. **Hispanic pop.:** 8.6%. **Foreign

born: 18.8%. **U.S. citizens:** 92.5%. **Language:** 71.7% English only; 6.3% Spanish.

Employment: 153,004 employed; 2.8% unemployment. **Per capita income:** $39,726. **Below poverty:** 14.2%; 11.8% of families. **Uninsured:** 8.4%. **Educational attainment:** 88.2% HS; 42.8% bachelor's. **Avg. commute:** 23.1 min. 60.9% drive, 10.5% carpool, 15.4% work from home. **Housing units:** 129,525; 93.6% occupied. **Home ownership:** 53.0%. **Avg. home:** $379,900; change (2021-23): 7.1%. **Avg. rent:** $1,174. **Crime rates:** violent: 766; property: 4,648.

Mayor: Melvin Carter, nonpartisan

History: Est. c. 1840 as Pig's Eye Landing; became capital of Minnesota territory, 1849; chartered as St. Paul, 1854.

Website: www.stpaul.gov

St. Petersburg, Florida

Population: 263,553 (86). **Pop. density:** 4,264. **Pop. change (2020-23):** 1.7%. **Area:** 61.8 sq mi. **Racial distribution:** 67.0% white; 20.1% Black; 3.5% Asian; 0.2% Amer. Ind.; < 0.05% Pac. Isl.; 1.7% other; 2+ races, 7.5%. **Hispanic pop.:** 8.8%. **Foreign born:** 9.8%. **U.S. citizens:** 96.9%. **Language:** 87.5% English only; 5.8% Spanish.

Employment: 147,501 employed; 2.8% unemployment. **Per capita income:** $46,755. **Below poverty:** 10.8%; 7.9% of families. **Uninsured:** 14.8%. **Educational attainment:** 93.8% HS; 40.6% bachelor's. **Avg. commute:** 24.0 min. 70.3% drive, 15.7% work from home. **Housing units:** 139,752; 81.4% occupied. **Home ownership:** 62.6%. **Avg. home:** $405,000; change (2021-23): 22.7%. **Avg. rent:** $1,410. **Crime rates:** violent: 629; property: 2,663.

Mayor: Kenneth T. "Ken" Welch, nonpartisan

History: Founded 1888; inc. 1903. Site of Salvador Dali Museum.

Website: www.stpete.org

San Antonio, Texas

Population: 1,495,295 (7). **Pop. density:** 2,997. **Pop. change (2020-23):** 3.9%. **Area:** 498.9 sq mi. **Racial distribution:** 56.6% white; 6.6% Black; 3.0% Asian; 0.9% Amer. Ind.; 0.1% Pac. Isl.; 9.4% other; 2+ races, 23.3%. **Hispanic pop.:** 65.8%. **Foreign born:** 14.3%. **U.S. citizens:** 91.6%. **Language:** 58.6% English only; 37.5% Spanish.

Employment: 747,533 employed; 3.7% unemployment. **Per capita income:** $31,148. **Below poverty:** 15.1%; 13.7% of families. **Uninsured:** 24.5%. **Educational attainment:** 83.8% HS; 27.7% bachelor's. **Avg. commute:** 24.5 min. 72.2% drive, 12.2% carpool. **Housing units:** 594,026; 91.4% occupied. **Home ownership:** 51.9%. **Avg. home:** $326,800; change (2021-23): 12.2%. **Avg. rent:** $1,189. **Crime rates:** violent: 883; property: 5,069.

Mayor: Ron Nirenberg, nonpartisan

History: First Spanish mission est., 1718; Battle of the Alamo, 1836; city subsequently captured by Texans; inc. 1837.

Website: www.sanantonio.gov

San Diego, California

Population: 1,388,320 (8). **Pop. density:** 4,258. **Pop. change (2020-23):** 0.1%. **Area:** 326.1 sq mi. **Racial distribution:** 54.5% white; 5.9% Black; 17.4% Asian; 0.6% Amer. Ind.; 0.4% Pac. Isl.; 8.5% other; 2+ races, 12.8%. **Hispanic pop.:** 30.1%. **Foreign born:** 24.9%. **U.S. citizens:** 89.6%. **Language:** 61.4% English only; 21.4% Spanish.

Employment: 697,124 employed; 3.8% unemployment. **Per capita income:** $51,368. **Below poverty:** 11.0%; 7.1% of families. **Uninsured:** 9.2%. **Educational attainment:** 89.7% HS; 48.7% bachelor's. **Avg. commute:** 24.0 min. 66.2% drive, 16.9% work from home. **Housing units:** 552,285; 93.3% occupied. **Home ownership:** 47.6%. **Avg. home:** $931,200; change (2021-23): 12.2%. **Avg. rent:** $2,080. **Crime rates:** violent: 431; property: 1,818.

Mayor: Todd Gloria, nonpartisan

History: Claimed by Spanish, 1542; first mission est., 1769; scene of conflict during Mexican-American War, 1846; inc. 1850.

Website: www.sandiego.gov

San Francisco, California

Population: 808,988 (17). **Pop. density:** 17,323. **Pop. change (2020-23):** –7.1%. **Area:** 46.7 sq mi. **Racial distribution:** 41.9% white; 5.2% Black; 34.8% Asian; 0.6% Amer. Ind.; 0.4% Pac. Isl.; 7.7% other; 2+ races, 9.5%. **Hispanic pop.:** 15.5%. **Foreign born:** 33.9%. **U.S. citizens:** 87.4%. **Language:** 57.1% English only; 10.8% Spanish.

Employment: 544,928 employed; 3.3% unemployment. **Per capita income:** $86,186. **Below poverty:** 10.7%; 5.5% of families. **Uninsured:** 4.6%. **Educational attainment:** 88.8% HS; 59.8% bachelor's. **Avg. commute:** 31.8 min. 28.7% drive, 23.9% public trans., 10.5% walk, 23.4% work from home. **Housing units:** 408,198; 88.4% occupied. **Home ownership:** 38.6%. **Avg. home:** $1,272,500; change (2021-23): –3.6%. **Avg. rent:** $2,316. **Crime rates:** violent: 696; property: 6,246.

Mayor: London N. Breed, nonpartisan

History: Est. by 1776; claimed by U.S., 1846; became major city during Gold Rush, 1849; inc. 1850. Devastated by earthquake, 1906.

Website: sf.gov

San Jose, California

Population: 969,655 (13). **Pop. density:** 5,449. **Pop. change (2020-23):** –3.9%. **Area:** 177.9 sq mi. **Racial distribution:** 32.0% white; 2.9% Black; 38.1% Asian; 0.8% Amer. Ind.; 0.5% Pac. Isl.; 13.2% other; 2+ races, 12.4%. **Hispanic pop.:** 30.8%. **Foreign born:** 41.0%. **U.S. citizens:** 82.2%. **Language:** 41.9% English only; 21.9% Spanish.

Employment: 527,658 employed; 3.7% unemployment. **Per capita income:** $59,913. **Below poverty:** 7.9%; 4.8% of families. **Uninsured:** 6.8%. **Educational attainment:** 85.5% HS; 46.0% bachelor's. **Avg. commute:** 28.8 min. 66.4% drive, 10.3% carpool, 16.3% work from home. **Housing units:** 340,392; 95.4% occupied. **Home ownership:** 55.8%. **Avg. home:** $1,765,000; change (2021-23): 7.6%. **Avg. rent:** $2,526. **Crime rates:** violent: 527; property: 2,651.

Mayor: Matt Mahan, nonpartisan

History: Founded by Spanish, 1777, between San Francisco and Monterey; state capital, 1849-51; inc. 1850.

Website: www.sanjoseca.gov

Santa Ana, California

Population: 310,539 (65). **Pop. density:** 11,343. **Pop. change (2020-23):** –0.2%. **Area:** 27.4 sq mi. **Racial distribution:** 25.3% white; 1.1% Black; 11.8% Asian; 1.1% Amer. Ind.; 0.2% Pac. Isl.; 47.5% other; 2+ races, 13.0%. **Hispanic pop.:** 77.0%. **Foreign born:** 40.9%. **U.S. citizens:** 77.4%. **Language:** 21.7% English only; 67.6% Spanish.

Employment: 149,617 employed; 3.5% unemployment. **Per capita income:** $27,328. **Below poverty:** 10.1%; 9.4% of families. **Uninsured:** 18.5%. **Educational attainment:** 65.2% HS; 17.9% bachelor's. **Avg. commute:** 25.0 min. 71.7% drive, 13.2% carpool. **Housing units:** 80,240; 96.7% occupied. **Home ownership:** 44.8%. **Avg. home:** $1,260,000; change (2021-23): 14.6%. **Avg. rent:** $1,885.

Mayor: Valerie Amezcua, nonpartisan

History: Founded by Spanish, 1769; inc. 1886.

Website: www.santa-ana.org

Scottsdale, Arizona

Population: 244,394 (93). **Pop. density:** 1,328. **Pop. change (2020-23):** 1.0%. **Area:** 184.0 sq mi. **Racial distribution:** 83.0% white; 2.1% Black; 5.2% Asian; 0.7% Amer. Ind.; 0.2% Pac. Isl.; 2.0% other; 2+ races, 6.8%. **Hispanic pop.:** 10.4%. **Foreign born:** 11.8%. **U.S. citizens:** 95.3%. **Language:** 86.8% English only; 5.9% Spanish.

Employment: 153,461 employed; 3.0% unemployment. **Per capita income:** $77,594. **Below poverty:** 6.5%; 4.2% of families. **Uninsured:** 7.5%. **Educational attainment:** 97.3% HS; 61.3% bachelor's. **Avg. commute:** 21.4 min. 64.2% drive, 26.5% work from home. **Housing units:** 136,665; 84.8% occupied. **Home ownership:** 67.0%. **Avg. home:** $459,600; change (2021-23): 10.6%. **Avg. rent:** $1,768. **Crime rates (2021):** violent: 214; property: 2,356.

Mayor: David D. Ortega, nonpartisan

History: Founded 1888 by namesake Army Chaplain Winfield Scott; inc. 1951.

Website: www.scottsdaleaz.gov

Seattle, Washington

Population: 755,078 (18). **Pop. density:** 8,989. **Pop. change (2020-23):** 2.0%. **Area:** 84.0 sq mi. **Racial distribution:** 63.6% white; 6.7% Black; 16.8% Asian; 0.6% Amer. Ind.; 0.2% Pac. Isl.; 2.6% other; 2+ races, 9.4%. **Hispanic pop.:** 7.5%. **Foreign born:** 19.8%. **U.S. citizens:** 89.3%. **Language:** 77.1% English only; 4.3% Spanish.

Employment: 489,254 employed; 3.2% unemployment. **Per capita income:** $77,616. **Below poverty:** 10.3%; 5.0% of families. **Uninsured:** 5.7%. **Educational attainment:** 95.6% HS; 66.7% bachelor's. **Avg. commute:** 27.2 min. 38.6% drive, 15.6% public trans., 27.0% work from home. **Housing units:** 372,436; 92.7% occupied. **Home ownership:** 44.5%. **Avg. home:** $735,000; change (2021-23): 5.2%. **Avg. rent:** $1,945. **Crime rates:** violent: 838; property: 5,721.

Mayor: Bruce Harrell, nonpartisan

History: Settled 1851; inc. 1869. Suffered severe fire, 1889; played prominent role in Alaska Gold Rush, 1897; growth followed opening of Panama Canal 1914. Center of aircraft industry during WWII.

Website: www.seattle.gov

Spokane, Washington

Population: 229,447 (97). **Pop. density:** 3,337. **Pop. change (2020-23):** 0.1%. **Area:** 68.8 sq mi. **Racial distribution:** 82.0% white; 2.6% Black; 2.6% Asian; 1.3% Amer. Ind.; 0.9% Pac. Isl.; 1.9% other; 2+ races, 8.7%. **Hispanic pop.:** 7.2%. **Foreign born:** 5.8%. **U.S. citizens:** 97.2%. **Language:** 91.9% English only; 2.7% Spanish.

Employment: 106,344 employed; 4.3% unemployment. **Per capita income:** $36,513. **Below poverty:** 14.5%; 8.4% of families. **Uninsured:** 7.8%. **Educational attainment:** 93.2% HS; 32.7% bachelor's. **Avg. commute:** 20.7 min. 70.0% drive, 12.0% work from home. **Housing units:** 101,157; 94.9% occupied. **Home ownership:** 57.5%. **Avg. home:** $412,700; change (2021-23): 8.0%. **Avg. rent:** $1,060. **Crime rates:** violent: 672; property: 5,736.

Mayor: Lisa Brown, nonpartisan

History: Founded 1872; inc. as village of Spokane Falls 1881; destroyed in fire 1889; re-inc. as city of Spokane, 1891.

Website: my.spokanecity.org

Stockton, California

Population: 319,543 (60). **Pop. density:** 5,064. **Pop. change (2020-23):** –0.4%. **Area:** 63.1 sq mi. **Racial distribution:** 31.3% white; 11.6% Black; 20.9% Asian; 1.2% Amer. Ind.; 0.6% Pac. Isl.; 15.5% other; 2+ races, 18.8%. **Hispanic pop.:** 45.2%. **Foreign born:** 25.1%. **U.S. citizens:** 88.2%. **Language:** 54.4% English only; 29.0% Spanish.

Employment: 126,608 employed; 7.0% unemployment. **Per capita income:** $29,095. **Below poverty:** 13.7%; 12.9% of families. **Uninsured:** 10.0%. **Educational attainment:** 77.8% HS; 18.3% bachelor's. **Avg. commute:** 32.8 min. 77.8% drive, 13.1% carpool. **Housing units:** 103,378; 93.8% occupied. **Home ownership:** 51.7%. **Avg. rent:** $1,417. **Crime rates:** violent: 1,157; property: 2,744.

Mayor: Kevin J. Lincoln II, nonpartisan

History: Est. 1849 to serve gold miners; inc. 1850.

Website: www.stocktonca.gov

Tampa, Florida

Population: 403,364 (49). **Pop. density:** 3,550. **Pop. change (2020-23):** 4.0%. **Area:** 113.6 sq mi. **Racial distribution:** 54.9% white; 21.8% Black; 4.6% Asian; 0.3% Amer. Ind.; 0.1% Pac. Isl.; 4.5% other; 2+ races, 13.7%. **Hispanic pop.:** 26.7%. **Foreign born:** 18.4%. **U.S. citizens:** 91.4%. **Language:** 71.8% English only; 20.6% Spanish.

Employment: 216,007 employed; 3.1% unemployment. **Per capita income:** $45,586. **Below poverty:** 15.3%; 12.7% of families. **Uninsured:** 15.3%. **Educational attainment:** 89.0% HS; 43.3% bachelor's. **Avg. commute:** 24.8 min. 69.1% drive, 16.0% work from home. **Housing units:** 172,995; 90.8% occupied. **Home ownership:** 50.5%. **Avg. home:** $405,000; change (2021-23): 22.7%. **Avg. rent:** $1,422. **Crime rates:** violent: 497; property: 1,674.

Mayor: Jane Castor, nonpartisan

History: U.S. army fort on site, 1824; inc. 1855.

Website: www.tampa.gov

Toledo, Ohio

Population: 265,304 (85). **Pop. density:** 3,296. **Pop. change (2020-23):** –1.8%. **Area:** 80.5 sq mi. **Racial distribution:** 59.6% white; 28.1% Black; 1.3% Asian; 0.2% Amer. Ind.; 0.1% Pac. Isl.; 3.1% other; 2+ races, 7.7%. **Hispanic pop.:** 8.9%. **Foreign born:** 3.3%. **U.S. citizens:** 98.5%. **Language:** 93.8% English only; 3.0% Spanish.

Employment: 118,163 employed; 4.7% unemployment. **Per capita income:** $25,860. **Below poverty:** 21.1%; 18.6% of families. **Uninsured:** 9.8%. **Educational attainment:** 88.1% HS; 20.2% bachelor's. **Avg. commute:** 19.9 min. 78.9% drive, 11.2% carpool. **Housing units:** 133,113; 88.4% occupied. **Home ownership:** 52.4%. **Avg. home:** $174,100; change (2021-23): 9.8%. **Avg. rent:** $854. **Crime rates:** violent: 1,163; property: 3,081.

Mayor: Wade Kapszukiewicz, nonpartisan

History: Site of Ft. Industry, 1800; figured in Toledo War between OH and MI over borders, 1835-36; inc. 1837.

Website: toledo.oh.gov

Tucson, Arizona

Population: 547,239 (33). **Pop. density:** 2,260. **Pop. change (2020-23):** 0.8%. **Area:** 242.2 sq mi. **Racial distribution:** 60.9% white; 4.8% Black; 3.2% Asian; 3.2% Amer. Ind.; 0.2% Pac. Isl.; 11.9% other; 2+ races, 15.8%. **Hispanic pop.:** 44.8%. **Foreign born:** 14.2%. **U.S. citizens:** 92.5%. **Language:** 67.9% English only; 26.9% Spanish.

Employment: 253,220 employed; 4.0% unemployment. **Per capita income:** $29,009. **Below poverty:** 18.1%; 14.0% of families. **Uninsured:** 15.5%. **Educational attainment:** 86.6% HS; 29.4% bachelor's. **Avg. commute:** 22.3 min. 70.4% drive, 10.3% carpool, 10.7% work from home. **Housing units:** 243,749; 90.6% occupied. **Home ownership:** 50.9%. **Avg. home:** $377,100; change (2021-23): 13.9%. **Avg. rent:** $991.

Mayor: Regina Romero, Democrat

History: Est. 1775 by Spanish as a presidio; acquired by U.S. in Gadsden Purchase, 1854; inc. 1877.

Website: www.tucsonaz.gov

Tulsa, Oklahoma

Population: 411,894 (48). **Pop. density:** 2,083. **Pop. change (2020-23):** –0.4%. **Area:** 197.8 sq mi. **Racial distribution:** 60.1% white; 14.6% Black; 3.4% Asian; 4.4% Amer. Ind.; 0.2% Pac. Isl.; 4.8% other; 2+ races, 12.5%. **Hispanic pop.:** 17.3%. **Foreign born:** 11.2%. **U.S. citizens:** 92.5%. **Language:** 81.0% English only; 14.2% Spanish.

Employment: 198,879 employed; 3.4% unemployment. **Per capita income:** $36,490. **Below poverty:** 15.4%; 13.8% of families. **Uninsured:** 23.7%. **Educational attainment:** 88.0% HS; 32.9% bachelor's. **Avg. commute:** 18.6 min. 77.0% drive, 10.1% carpool. **Housing units:** 192,244; 88.3% occupied. **Home ownership:** 52.3%. **Avg. home:** $254,300; change (2021-23): 14.8%. **Avg. rent:** $958. **Crime rates:** violent: 929; property: 4,272.

Mayor: G.T. Bynum, nonpartisan

History: Settled in 1836 by Creek Indians; modern town founded 1882; inc. 1898; oil discovered early 20th century.

Website: www.cityoftulsa.org

Virginia Beach, Virginia

Population: 453,649 (43). **Pop. density:** 1,854. **Pop. change (2020-23):** –1.3%. **Area:** 244.7 sq mi. **Racial distribution:** 62.8% white; 18.9% Black; 7.1% Asian; 0.2% Amer. Ind.; 0.1% Pac. Isl.; 2.3% other; 2+ races, 8.5%. **Hispanic pop.:** 8.8%. **Foreign born:** 9.3%. **U.S. citizens:** 96.6%. **Language:** 87.8% English only; 4.6% Spanish.

Employment: 232,278 employed; 2.8% unemployment. **Per capita income:** $45,320. **Below poverty:** 7.3%; 6.4% of families. **Uninsured:** 9.6%. **Educational attainment:** 94.5% HS; 39.8% bachelor's. **Avg. commute:** 23.5 min. 77.1% drive, 10.7% work from home. **Housing units:** 189,951; 94.2% occupied. **Home ownership:** 64.6%. **Avg. home:** $334,400; change (2021-23): 17.3%. **Avg. rent:** $1,568. **Crime rates:** violent: 87; property: 1,611.

Mayor: Robert M. "Bobby" Dyer, nonpartisan

History: Settlement by Capt. John Smith, 1607; formed by merger with Princess Anne Co., 1963.

Website: virginiabeach.gov

Washington, District of Columbia

Population: 678,972 (22). **Pop. density:** 11,108. **Pop. change (2020-23):** 1.2%. **Area:** 61.1 sq mi. **Racial distribution:** 39.6% white; 44.3% Black; 4.0% Asian; 0.3% Amer. Ind.; 0.1% Pac. Isl.; 4.6% other; 2+ races, 7.1%. **Hispanic pop.:** 11.5%. **Foreign born:** 13.4%. **U.S. citizens:** 93.1%. **Language:** 82.5% English only; 9.2% Spanish.

Employment: 378,714 employed; 4.9% unemployment. **Per capita income:** $71,297. **Below poverty:** 13.6%; 10.8% of families. **Uninsured:** 4.2%. **Educational attainment:** 92.7% HS; 62.6% bachelor's. **Avg. commute:** 30.5 min. 29.7% drive, 24.7% public trans., 10.3% walk, 25.0% work from home. **Housing units:** 350,372; 90.1% occupied. **Home ownership:** 41.4%. **Avg. home:** $602,700; change (2021-23): 10.7%. **Avg. rent:** $1,817. **Crime rates:** violent: 745; property: 3,484.

Mayor: Muriel Bowser, Democrat

History: U.S. capital; planned site on Potomac R. chosen by George Washington, 1790, on land ceded from VA and MD (portion S of Potomac returned to VA, 1846). Congress first met there, 1800; inc. 1802; sacked by British, War of 1812.

Website: dc.gov

Wichita, Kansas

Population: 396,119 (51). **Pop. density:** 2,431. **Pop. change (2020-23):** –0.5%. **Area:** 162.9 sq mi. **Racial distribution:** 69.0% white; 9.9% Black; 4.8% Asian; 1.1% Amer. Ind.; < 0.05% Pac. Isl.; 5.1% other; 2+ races, 10.0%. **Hispanic pop.:** 17.6%. **Foreign born:** 9.9%. **U.S. citizens:** 94.6%. **Language:** 82.4% English only; 12.0% Spanish.

Employment: 187,874 employed; 3.1% unemployment. **Per capita income:** $34,393. **Below poverty:** 13.9%; 10.7% of families. **Uninsured:** 17.9%. **Educational attainment:** 88.0% HS; 31.0% bachelor's. **Avg. commute:** 18.8 min. 80.0% drive, 10.3% carpool. **Housing units:** 174,713; 89.3% occupied. **Home ownership:** 58.5%. **Avg. home:** $216,200; change (2021-23): 13.1%. **Avg. rent:** $915. **Crime rates:** violent: 931; property: 3,524.

Mayor: Lily Wu, nonpartisan

History: Founded 1864; inc. 1871.

Website: www.wichita.gov

Winston-Salem, North Carolina

Population: 252,975 (91). **Pop. density:** 1,894. **Pop. change (2020-23):** 1.3%. **Area:** 133.6 sq mi. **Racial distribution:** 51.0% white; 33.2% Black; 2.5% Asian; 0.3% Amer. Ind.; 0.1% Pac. Isl.; 5.4% other; 2+ races, 7.4%. **Hispanic pop.:** 16.6%. **Foreign born:** 10.4%. **U.S. citizens:** 92.9%. **Language:** 81.8% English only; 13.9% Spanish.

Employment: 114,135 employed; 3.8% unemployment. **Per capita income:** $33,279. **Below poverty:** 15.2%; 13.3% of families. **Uninsured:** 18.0%. **Educational attainment:** 87.9% HS; 35.5% bachelor's. **Avg. commute:** 21.6 min. 74.6% drive, 10.4% carpool, 10.5% work from home. **Housing units:** 112,191; 88.0% occupied. **Home ownership:** 53.9%. **Avg. home:** $289,900; change (2021-23): 23.0%. **Avg. rent:** $956. **Crime rates:** violent: 1,176; property: 3,894.

Mayor: J. Allen Joines, Democrat

History: Salem founded, 1766; Winston founded, 1849; became Winston-Salem, 1913. Reynolds Building, completed 1929, used as model for Empire State Building (designed by same architects).

Website: www.cityofws.org

UNITED STATES POPULATION

Census Origins and Methods

A census is conducted in the U.S. every 10 years. The primary purpose is to apportion seats in the House of Representatives. Census data is also used to determine the boundaries of state legislative districts and the distribution of federal funds to local, state, and tribal governments.

The first U.S. census, mandated by the Constitution, was conducted in 1790, a little more than a year after George Washington became president. It counted the numbers of free white males ages 16 and over (as a measure of available workers and military personnel), free white males under 16, free white females, all other free persons, and enslaved persons. The data was collected over 18 months, at a cost of about $44,000, or $1.2 million in current dollars. (The U.S. Government Accountability Office estimated the cost of the 2020 census would be $13.7 billion by the time work ends in 2024.) The 1790 census counted 3.9 million people, resulting in an increase from 65 to 105 U.S. House seats.

As the nation grew, so did the scope of the census. The first inquiries on manufacturing were made in 1810. Questions on "the pursuits, industry, education, and resources of the country" were added to the 1840 census. Because it took a full 10 years to publish the 1880 and 1890 census results, Congress limited the 1900 census to questions on population, mortality, agriculture, and manufacturing.

Today, the secretary of commerce and the Census Bureau are directed by law to collect data on population, housing, employment, trade, and transportation, among other things, at stated intervals. They also conduct smaller-scale surveys on behalf of other federal agencies. The Census Bureau launched the experimental Household Pulse Survey in 2020 to measure the COVID-19 pandemic's social and economic impact.

U.S. marshals administered the earliest decennial censuses by visiting each household and reporting to the president (1790), to the secretary of state (1800-40), or to the secretary of the interior (1850-70). Trained census-takers were hired for the 1880 census and on. In 1902, Congress authorized a permanent Census Office within the Interior Department. In 1903, the agency was transferred to the new Department of Commerce and Labor and remained with Commerce when a separate labor department was created in 1913.

The 1790 through 1820 decennial censuses were officially enumerated the first Monday in Aug. The 1830-1900 censuses were as of June 1, though the 1890 census was not started until June 2 (June 1 being a Sunday). The 1910 census was as of Apr. 15, the 1920 census as of Jan. 1, and every census since 1930 has been for Apr. 1.

The Census Bureau began using statistical sampling techniques in the 1940s, the first modern computer in the 1950s, and enumeration by mail in the 1960s. Any personally identifiable information gathered is withheld from the public for 72 years, after which records are made available through the National Archives. The 1940 census records, the first to be digitized and released online, can be accessed at 1940census.archives.gov. The 1950 records are found at 1950census.archives.gov.

In 1970 through 2000, about five in six households responded to a short-form census while one in six households answered a long-form questionnaire, which asked about details such as ancestry, marital status, and citizenship status. The annual American Community Survey (ACS) was implemented in 2005 to replace the long-form questionnaire.

The first 2020 census counts of the U.S. resident population were released Apr. 26, 2021. The Census Bureau also delivered the population counts for apportioning Congressional House seats to the president on the same day. States were provided census results for the redrawing of legislative districts in Sept. 2021. The agency released its final 2020 census data products in 2024.

U.S. Population by State and Region, 2010-23

Source: Population Estimates Program and Decennial Census, U.S. Census Bureau, U.S. Dept. of Commerce (ranked by 2023 resident population, estimated as of July 1; 2010 decennial census figures are for Apr. 1)

Rank	State	2023	2010	% change, 2010-23
1.	California	38,965,193	37,253,956	4.6%
2.	Texas	30,503,301	25,145,561	21.3
3.	Florida	22,610,726	18,801,310	20.3
4.	New York	19,571,216	19,378,102	1.0
5.	Pennsylvania	12,961,683	12,702,379	2.0
6.	Illinois	12,549,689	12,830,632	−2.2
7.	Ohio	11,785,935	11,536,504	2.2
8.	Georgia	11,029,227	9,687,653	13.8
9.	North Carolina	10,835,491	9,535,483	13.6
10.	Michigan	10,037,261	9,883,640	1.6
11.	New Jersey	9,290,841	8,791,894	5.7
12.	Virginia	8,715,698	8,001,024	8.9
13.	Washington	7,812,880	6,724,540	16.2
14.	Arizona	7,431,344	6,392,017	16.3
15.	Tennessee	7,126,489	6,346,105	12.3
16.	Massachusetts	7,001,399	6,547,629	6.9
17.	Indiana	6,862,199	6,483,802	5.8
18.	Missouri	6,196,156	5,988,927	3.5
19.	Maryland	6,180,253	5,773,552	7.0
20.	Wisconsin	5,910,955	5,686,986	3.9
21.	Colorado	5,877,610	5,029,196	16.9
22.	Minnesota	5,737,915	5,303,925	8.2
23.	South Carolina	5,373,555	4,625,364	16.2
24.	Alabama	5,108,468	4,779,736	6.9
25.	Louisiana	4,573,749	4,533,372	0.9
26.	Kentucky	4,526,154	4,339,367	4.3
27.	Oregon	4,233,358	3,831,074	10.5
28.	Oklahoma	4,053,824	3,751,351	8.1
29.	Connecticut	3,617,176	3,574,097	1.2%
30.	Utah	3,417,734	2,763,885	23.7
31.	Iowa	3,207,004	3,046,355	5.3
32.	Nevada	3,194,176	2,700,551	18.3
33.	Arkansas	3,067,732	2,915,918	5.2
34.	Kansas	2,940,546	2,853,118	3.1
35.	Mississippi	2,939,690	2,967,297	−0.9
36.	New Mexico	2,114,371	2,059,179	2.7
37.	Nebraska	1,978,379	1,826,341	8.3
38.	Idaho	1,964,726	1,567,582	25.3
39.	West Virginia	1,770,071	1,852,994	−4.5
40.	Hawaii	1,435,138	1,360,301	5.5
41.	New Hampshire	1,402,054	1,316,470	6.5
42.	Maine	1,395,722	1,328,361	5.1
43.	Montana	1,132,812	989,415	14.5
44.	Rhode Island	1,095,962	1,052,567	4.1
45.	Delaware	1,031,890	897,934	14.9
46.	South Dakota	919,318	814,180	12.9
47.	North Dakota	783,926	672,591	16.6
48.	Alaska	733,406	710,231	3.3
49.	Dist. of Columbia	678,972	601,723	12.8
50.	Vermont	647,464	625,741	3.5
51.	Wyoming	584,057	563,626	3.6
	United States	**334,914,895**	**308,745,538**	**8.5**
	Northeast[1]	56,983,517	55,317,240	3.0
	Midwest[2]	68,909,283	66,927,001	3.0
	South[3]	130,125,290	114,555,744	13.6
	West[4]	78,896,805	71,945,553	9.7
	Puerto Rico	3,205,691	3,725,789	−14.0

Note: The U.S. resident population consists of individuals whose usual residence, or where they live and sleep most of the time, is in one of the 50 states or DC. It excludes U.S. military personnel stationed or assigned overseas and civilian U.S. citizens living abroad. Population estimates are as of July 1; decennial census results are for Apr. 1 and may reflect revisions/corrections to initial tabulated counts. (1) Incl. the states of the New England (Connecticut, Maine, Massachusetts, New Hampshire, Rhode Island, Vermont) and Middle Atlantic (New Jersey, New York, Pennsylvania) divisions. (2) Incl. the states of the East North Central (Illinois, Indiana, Michigan, Ohio, Wisconsin) and West North Central (Iowa, Kansas, Minnesota, Missouri, Nebraska, North Dakota, South Dakota) divisions. (3) Incl. the states of the South Atlantic (Delaware, DC, Florida, Georgia, Maryland, North Carolina, South Carolina, Virginia, West Virginia), East South Central (Alabama, Kentucky, Mississippi, Tennessee), and West South Central (Arkansas, Louisiana, Oklahoma, Texas) divisions. (4) Incl. the states of the Mountain (Arizona, Colorado, Idaho, Montana, Nevada, New Mexico, Utah, Wyoming) and Pacific (Alaska, California, Hawaii, Oregon, Washington) divisions.

Density of U.S. Population by State, 1930-2020

Source: Decennial Censuses, U.S. Census Bureau, U.S. Dept. of Commerce

(per square mile of land area)

State	1930	1950	1970	1990	2020	State	1930	1950	1970	1990	2020
AL	52.3	60.5	68.0	79.8	99.2	MT	3.7	4.1	4.8	5.5	7.4
AK	0.1	0.2	0.5	1.0	1.3	NE	17.9	17.3	19.3	20.5	25.5
AZ	3.8	6.6	15.6	32.3	62.9	NV	0.8	1.5	4.5	10.9	28.3
AR	35.6	36.7	37.0	45.2	57.9	NH	52.0	59.6	82.4	123.9	153.8
CA	36.4	68.0	128.1	191.0	253.7	NJ	549.5	657.5	974.7	1,051.1	1,263.0
CO	10.0	12.8	21.3	31.8	55.7	NM	3.5	5.6	8.4	12.5	17.5
CT	331.8	414.5	626.1	678.8	744.7	NY	267.1	314.7	387.0	381.7	428.7
DE	122.3	163.2	281.3	341.9	508.0	NC	65.2	83.5	104.5	136.3	214.7
DC	7,975.1	13,140.0	12,392.0	9,941.3	11,280.0	ND	9.9	9.0	9.0	9.3	11.3
FL	27.4	51.7	126.6	241.3	401.4	OH	162.7	194.5	260.7	265.5	288.8
GA	50.6	59.9	79.8	112.6	185.6	OK	34.9	32.6	37.3	45.9	57.7
HI	57.3	77.8	119.7	172.6	226.6	OR	9.9	15.8	21.8	29.6	44.1
ID	5.4	7.1	8.6	12.2	22.3	PA	215.3	234.6	263.6	265.6	290.6
IL	137.4	156.9	200.2	205.9	230.8	RI	665.0	766.0	915.8	970.6	1,061.4
IN	90.4	109.8	145.0	154.8	189.4	SC	57.8	70.4	86.2	116.0	170.2
IA	44.2	46.9	50.6	49.7	57.1	SD	9.1	8.6	8.8	9.2	11.7
KS	23.0	23.3	27.5	30.3	35.9	TN	63.5	79.8	95.2	118.3	167.6
KY	66.2	74.6	81.5	93.3	114.1	TX	22.3	29.5	42.9	65.0	111.6
LA	48.6	62.1	84.3	97.7	107.8	UT	6.2	8.4	12.9	21.0	39.7
ME	25.9	29.6	32.2	39.8	44.2	VT	39.0	41.0	48.2	61.1	69.8
MD	168.1	241.4	404.1	492.6	636.1	VA	61.3	84.0	117.7	156.7	218.6
MA	544.8	601.3	729.4	771.3	901.2	WA	23.5	35.8	51.3	73.2	115.9
MI	85.6	112.7	157.0	164.4	178.0	WV	71.9	83.4	72.6	74.6	74.6
MN	32.2	37.5	47.8	54.9	71.7	WI	54.3	63.4	81.6	90.3	108.8
MS	42.8	46.4	47.2	54.8	63.1	WY	2.3	3.0	3.4	4.7	5.9
MO	52.8	57.5	68.0	74.4	89.5	**U.S.**	**34.7**	**42.6**	**57.5**	**70.4**	**93.8**

Note: For the sake of comparison, the densities of Alaska and Hawaii in 1930 and 1950 are included though they were not yet states.

U.S. Area and Population, 1790-2020

Source: Decennial Censuses, U.S. Census Bureau, U.S. Dept. of Commerce

Census date	AREA (square miles)			RESIDENT POPULATION			
						Increase over preceding census	
	Total area[1]	Land area	Water area[1]	Number	Per sq mi of land	Number	%
1790 (Aug. 2)	891,364	864,746	24,065	3,929,214	4.5	—	—
1800 (Aug. 4)	891,364	864,746	24,065	5,308,483	6.1	1,379,269	35.1%
1810 (Aug. 6)	1,722,685	1,681,828	34,175	7,239,881	4.3	1,931,398	36.4
1820 (Aug. 7)	1,792,552	1,749,462	38,544	9,638,453	5.5	2,398,572	33.1
1830 (June 1)	1,792,552	1,749,462	38,544	12,860,702	7.4	3,222,249	33.4
1840 (June 1)	1,792,552	1,749,462	38,544	17,063,453	9.8	4,203,751	32.7
1850 (June 1)	2,991,655	2,940,042	52,705	23,191,876	7.9	6,128,423	35.9
1860 (June 1)	3,021,295	2,969,640	52,747	31,443,321	10.6	8,251,445	35.6
1870 (June 1)	3,612,299	3,540,705	68,082	38,558,371	10.9	7,115,050	22.6
1880 (June 1)	3,612,299	3,540,705	68,082	50,189,209	14.2	11,630,838	30.2
1890 (June 1)	3,612,299	3,540,705	68,082	62,979,766	17.8	12,790,557	25.5
1900 (June 1)	3,618,770	3,547,314	67,901	76,212,168	21.5	13,232,402	21.0
1910 (Apr. 15)	3,618,770	3,547,045	68,170	92,228,496	26.0	16,016,328	21.0
1920 (Jan. 1)	3,618,770	3,546,931	68,284	106,021,537	29.9	13,793,041	15.0
1930 (Apr. 1)	3,618,770	3,554,608	60,607	123,202,624	34.7	17,181,087	16.2
1940 (Apr. 1)	3,618,770	3,554,608	60,607	132,164,569	37.2	8,961,945	7.3
1950 (Apr. 1)	3,618,770	3,552,206	63,005	151,325,798	42.6	19,161,229	14.5
1960 (Apr. 1)	3,618,770	3,540,911	74,212	179,323,175	50.6	27,997,377	18.5
1970 (Apr. 1)	3,618,770	3,536,855	78,444	203,302,031	57.5	23,978,856	13.4
1980 (Apr. 1)	3,618,770	3,539,289	79,481	226,542,199	64.0	23,240,168	11.4
1990 (Apr. 1)	3,717,796	3,536,278	181,518	248,718,302	70.3	22,176,103	9.8
2000 (Apr. 1)	3,794,083	3,537,438	256,645	281,424,603	79.6	32,706,301	13.1
2010 (Apr. 1)	3,796,742	3,531,905	264,837	308,746,065	87.4	27,321,462	9.7
2020 (Apr. 1)	3,802,820	3,533,038	269,782	331,449,281	93.8	22,703,216	7.4

Note: Area and population density figures represent the area within the boundaries of the U.S. under its jurisdiction on the date in question including, in some cases, considerable areas not organized or settled and not covered by the census. Beginning in 1870, area data include Alaska; from 1900 on, data include Hawaii. Population figures may reflect revisions/corrections to initial tabulated census counts. (1) Figures for 1790-1980 cover inland water only. Figures for 1990 include inland, coastal, and Great Lakes water. Figures for 2000-20 include additional territorial water.

U.S. Population by Official

Source: Decennial Censuses, U.S. Census Bureau,
(population figures for 1790-1870

State	1790	1800	1810	1820	1830	1840	1850	1860	1870	1880	1890	1900	1910	1920
AL	—	1	9	128	310	591	772	964	997	1,262,505	1,513,401	1,828,697	2,138,093	2,348,174
AK	—	—	—	—	—	—	—	—	—	33,426	32,052	63,592	64,356	55,036
AZ	—	—	—	—	—	—	—	—	10	40,440	88,243	122,931	204,354	334,162
AR	—	—	1	14	30	98	210	435	484	802,525	1,128,211	1,311,564	1,574,449	1,752,204
CA	—	—	—	—	—	—	93	380	560	864,694	1,213,398	1,485,053	2,377,549	3,426,861
CO	—	—	—	—	—	—	—	34	40	194,327	413,249	539,700	799,024	939,629
CT	238	251	262	275	298	310	371	460	537	622,700	746,258	908,420	1,114,756	1,380,631
DE	59	64	73	73	77	78	92	112	125	146,608	168,493	184,735	202,322	223,003
DC[1]	—	8	15	23	30	34	52	75	132	177,624	230,392	278,718	331,069	437,571
FL	—	—	—	—	35	54	87	140	188	269,493	391,422	528,542	752,619	968,470
GA	83	163	251	341	517	691	906	1,057	1,184	1,542,180	1,837,353	2,216,331	2,609,121	2,895,832
HI	—	—	—	—	—	—	—	—	—	—	—	154,001	191,874	255,881
ID	—	—	—	—	—	—	—	—	15	32,610	88,548	161,772	325,594	431,866
IL	—	—	12	55	157	476	851	1,712	2,540	3,077,871	3,826,352	4,821,550	5,638,591	6,485,280
IN	—	6	25	147	343	686	988	1,350	1,681	1,978,301	2,192,404	2,516,462	2,700,876	2,930,390
IA	—	—	—	—	—	43	192	675	1,194	1,624,615	1,912,297	2,231,853	2,224,771	2,404,021
KS	—	—	—	—	—	—	—	107	364	996,096	1,428,108	1,470,495	1,690,949	1,769,257
KY[1]	74	221	407	564	688	780	982	1,156	1,321	1,648,690	1,858,635	2,147,174	2,289,905	2,416,630
LA	—	—	77	153	216	352	518	708	727	939,946	1,118,588	1,381,625	1,656,388	1,798,509
ME[2]	97	152	229	298	399	502	583	628	627	648,936	661,086	694,466	742,371	768,014
MD	320	342	381	407	447	470	583	687	781	934,943	1,042,390	1,188,044	1,295,346	1,449,661
MA[2]	379	423	472	523	610	738	995	1,231	1,457	1,783,085	2,238,947	2,805,346	3,366,416	3,852,356
MI	—	—	5	7	28	212	398	749	1,184	1,636,937	2,093,890	2,420,982	2,810,173	3,668,412
MN	—	—	—	—	—	—	6	172	440	780,773	1,310,283	1,751,394	2,075,708	2,387,125
MS	—	8	31	75	137	376	607	791	828	1,131,597	1,289,600	1,551,270	1,797,114	1,790,618
MO	—	—	20	67	140	384	682	1,182	1,721	2,168,380	2,679,185	3,106,665	3,293,335	3,404,055
MT	—	—	—	—	—	—	—	—	21	39,159	142,924	243,329	376,053	548,889
NE	—	—	—	—	—	—	—	29	123	452,402	1,062,656	1,066,300	1,192,214	1,296,372
NV	—	—	—	—	—	—	—	7	42	62,266	47,355	42,335	81,875	77,407
NH	142	184	214	244	269	285	318	326	318	346,991	376,530	411,588	430,572	443,083
NJ	184	211	246	278	321	373	490	672	906	1,131,116	1,444,933	1,883,669	2,537,167	3,155,900
NM	—	—	—	—	—	—	62	94	92	119,565	160,282	195,310	327,301	360,350
NY	340	589	959	1,373	1,919	2,429	3,097	3,881	4,383	5,082,871	6,003,174	7,268,894	9,113,614	10,385,227
NC	394	478	557	639	738	753	869	993	1,071	1,399,750	1,617,949	1,893,810	2,206,287	2,559,123
ND[3]	—	—	—	—	—	—	—	—	2	36,909	190,983	319,146	577,056	646,872
OH	—	42	231	581	938	1,519	1,980	2,340	2,665	3,198,062	3,672,329	4,157,545	4,767,121	5,759,394
OK[4]	—	—	—	—	—	—	—	—	—	—	258,657	790,391	1,657,155	2,028,283
OR	—	—	—	—	—	—	12	52	91	174,768	317,704	413,536	672,765	783,389
PA	434	602	810	1,049	1,348	1,724	2,312	2,906	3,522	4,282,891	5,258,113	6,302,115	7,665,111	8,720,017
RI	69	69	77	83	97	109	148	175	217	276,531	345,506	428,556	542,610	604,397
SC	249	346	415	503	581	594	669	704	706	995,577	1,151,149	1,340,316	1,515,400	1,683,724
SD[3]	—	—	—	—	—	—	—	5	12	98,268	348,600	401,570	583,888	636,547
TN	36	106	262	423	682	829	1,003	1,110	1,259	1,542,359	1,767,518	2,020,616	2,184,789	2,337,885
TX	—	—	—	—	—	—	213	604	819	1,591,749	2,235,527	3,048,710	3,896,542	4,663,228
UT	—	—	—	—	—	—	11	40	86	143,963	210,779	276,749	373,351	449,396
VT	85	154	218	236	281	292	314	315	331	332,286	332,422	343,641	355,956	352,428
VA[1]	692	808	878	938	1,044	1,025	1,119	1,220	1,225	1,512,565	1,655,980	1,854,184	2,061,612	2,309,187
WA	—	—	—	—	—	—	1	12	24	75,116	357,232	518,103	1,141,990	1,356,621
WV[1]	56	79	105	137	177	225	302	377	442	618,457	762,794	958,800	1,221,119	1,463,701
WI	—	—	—	—	—	31	305	776	1,055	1,315,497	1,693,330	2,069,042	2,333,860	2,632,067
WY	—	—	—	—	—	—	—	—	9	20,789	62,555	92,531	145,965	194,402
U.S.[5]	**3,929**	**5,308**	**7,240**	**9,638**	**12,861**	**17,063**	**23,192**	**31,443**	**38,558**	**50,189,209**	**62,979,766**	**76,212,168**	**92,228,496**	**106,021,537**

Note: With some exceptions, pop. shown is number of residents in a state (or territory of the same name) at the time of each census. Figures may differ from originally published census data because of corrections through the bureau's Count Question Resolution operation. Excl. U.S. military personnel stationed/assigned overseas and civilian U.S. citizens living abroad. (1) 1790-1860 VA figures are for present-day boundaries: they incl. pop. in areas then part of DC (1800-40) and excl. pop. of areas that went to KY (1790) and WV (1790-1860). (2) 1790-1810 figures for MA do not incl. district taken to form state of ME in 1820. (3) 1860 SD figure is for "unorganized Dakota"; 1870-80 figures are for present-day ND and SD. (4) 1890-1900 figures incl. Indian Terr. pop. (5) 1830-40 totals excl. persons (5,318 in 1830; 6,100 in 1840) on public ships in service of the U.S. not credited to any state. 1890 total incl. Indian Terr. and Indian Reservations pop. (325,464) specially enumerated.

Estimated Population of American Colonies, 1630-1780

Source: U.S. Census Bureau, U.S. Dept. of Commerce
(numbers in thousands)

Colony	1630	1650	1670	1690	1700	1720	1740	1750	1760	1770	1780
Total	**4.6**	**50.4**	**111.9**	**210.4**	**250.9**	**466.2**	**905.6**	**1,170.8**	**1,593.6**	**2,148.1**	**2,780.4**
Connecticut	—	4.1	12.6	21.6	26.0	58.8	89.6	111.3	142.5	183.9	206.7
Delaware	—	0.2	0.7	1.5	2.5	5.4	19.9	28.7	33.3	35.5	45.4
Georgia	—	—	—	—	—	—	2.0	5.2	9.6	23.4	56.1
Kentucky[1]	—	—	—	—	—	—	—	—	—	15.7	45.0
Maine (counties)[2]	0.4	1.0	—	—	—	—	—	—	20.0	31.3	49.1
Maryland	—	4.5	13.2	24.0	29.6	66.1	116.1	141.1	162.3	202.6	245.5
Massachusetts and Plymouth[2,3]	0.9	15.6	35.3	56.9	55.9	91.0	151.6	188.0	202.6	235.3	268.6
New Hampshire	0.5	1.3	1.8	4.2	5.0	9.4	23.3	27.5	39.1	62.4	87.8
New Jersey	—	—	1.0	8.0	14.0	29.8	51.4	71.4	93.8	117.4	139.6
New York	0.4	4.1	5.8	13.9	19.1	36.9	63.7	76.7	117.1	162.9	210.5
North Carolina	—	—	3.9	7.6	10.7	21.3	51.8	73.0	110.4	197.2	270.1
Pennsylvania	—	—	—	11.4	18.0	31.0	85.6	119.7	183.7	240.1	327.3
Rhode Island	—	0.8	2.2	4.2	5.9	11.7	25.3	33.2	45.5	58.2	52.9
South Carolina	—	—	0.2	3.9	5.7	17.0	45.0	64.0	94.1	124.2	180.0
Tennessee[4]	—	—	—	—	—	—	—	—	—	1.0	10.0
Vermont[5]	—	—	—	—	—	—	—	—	—	10.0	47.6
Virginia	2.5	18.7	35.3	53.0	58.6	87.8	180.4	231.0	339.7	447.0	538.0

Note: With the exception of KY, ME, Plymouth, TN, and VT, colonies shown are the original 13 states (ratified the Constitution 1787-90). (1) Admitted as state 1792. (2) For 1660-1750, the pop. of ME counties are included with MA. ME was annexed by MA in the 1650s but became a separate state in 1820. (3) Plymouth became part of Prov. of Massachusetts in 1691. (4) Admitted as state 1796. (5) Admitted as state 1791.

Census, 1790-2020

U.S. Dept. of Commerce
only are in thousands)

1930	1940	1950	1960	1970	1980	1990	2000	2010	2020	State
2,646,248	2,832,961	3,061,743	3,266,740	3,444,354	3,894,025	4,040,389	4,447,351	4,779,753	5,024,279	AL
59,278	72,524	128,643	226,167	302,583	401,851	550,043	626,931	710,235	733,391	AK
435,573	499,261	749,587	1,302,161	1,775,399	2,716,546	3,665,339	5,130,632	6,392,017	7,151,502	AZ
1,854,482	1,949,387	1,909,511	1,786,272	1,923,322	2,286,357	2,350,624	2,673,400	2,915,919	3,011,524	AR
5,677,251	6,907,387	10,586,223	15,717,204	19,971,069	23,667,764	29,758,213	33,871,653	37,253,956	39,538,223	CA
1,035,791	1,123,296	1,325,089	1,753,947	2,209,596	2,889,735	3,294,473	4,302,015	5,029,196	5,773,714	CO
1,606,903	1,709,242	2,007,280	2,535,234	3,032,217	3,107,564	3,287,116	3,405,602	3,574,097	3,605,944	CT
238,380	266,505	318,085	446,292	548,104	594,338	666,168	783,600	897,934	989,948	DE
486,869	663,091	802,178	763,956	756,668	638,432	606,900	572,059	601,767	689,545	DC
1,468,211	1,897,414	2,771,305	4,951,560	6,791,418	9,746,961	12,938,071	15,982,824	18,801,332	21,538,187	FL
2,908,506	3,123,723	3,444,578	3,943,116	4,587,930	5,462,982	6,478,149	8,186,816	9,687,850	10,711,908	GA
368,300	422,770	499,794	632,772	769,913	964,691	1,108,229	1,211,537	1,360,301	1,455,271	HI
445,032	524,873	588,637	667,191	713,015	944,127	1,006,734	1,293,956	1,567,652	1,839,106	ID
7,630,654	7,897,241	8,712,176	10,081,158	11,110,285	11,427,409	11,430,602	12,419,647	12,830,632	12,812,508	IL
3,238,503	3,427,796	3,934,224	4,662,498	5,195,392	5,490,210	5,544,156	6,080,517	6,483,802	6,785,528	IN
2,470,939	2,538,268	2,621,073	2,757,537	2,825,368	2,913,808	2,776,831	2,926,382	3,046,355	3,190,369	IA
1,880,999	1,801,028	1,905,299	2,178,611	2,249,071	2,364,236	2,477,588	2,688,824	2,853,118	2,937,880	KS
2,614,589	2,845,627	2,944,806	3,038,156	3,220,711	3,660,324	3,686,892	4,042,285	4,339,367	4,505,836	KY
2,101,593	2,363,880	2,683,516	3,257,022	3,644,637	4,206,116	4,220,164	4,468,958	4,533,372	4,657,757	LA
797,423	847,226	913,774	969,265	993,722	1,125,043	1,227,928	1,274,923	1,328,361	1,362,359	ME
1,631,526	1,821,244	2,343,001	3,100,689	3,923,897	4,216,933	4,780,753	5,296,507	5,773,626	6,177,224	MD
4,249,614	4,316,721	4,690,514	5,148,578	5,689,170	5,737,093	6,016,425	6,349,105	6,547,629	7,029,917	MA
4,842,325	5,256,106	6,371,766	7,823,194	8,881,826	9,262,044	9,295,287	9,938,480	9,883,706	10,077,331	MI
2,563,953	2,792,300	2,982,483	3,413,864	3,806,103	4,075,970	4,375,665	4,919,492	5,303,925	5,706,494	MN
2,009,821	2,183,796	2,178,914	2,178,141	2,216,994	2,520,770	2,575,475	2,844,656	2,967,297	2,961,279	MS
3,629,367	3,784,664	3,954,653	4,319,813	4,677,623	4,916,766	5,116,901	5,596,683	5,988,927	6,154,913	MO
537,606	559,456	591,024	674,767	694,409	786,690	799,065	902,195	989,415	1,084,225	MT
1,377,963	1,315,834	1,325,510	1,411,330	1,485,333	1,569,825	1,578,417	1,711,265	1,826,341	1,961,504	NE
91,058	110,247	160,083	285,278	488,738	800,508	1,201,675	1,998,257	2,700,551	3,104,614	NV
465,293	491,524	533,242	606,921	737,681	920,610	1,109,252	1,235,786	1,316,470	1,377,529	NH
4,041,334	4,160,165	4,835,329	6,066,782	7,171,112	7,365,011	7,730,188	8,414,347	8,791,909	9,288,994	NJ
423,317	531,818	681,187	951,023	1,017,055	1,303,302	1,515,069	1,819,046	2,059,181	2,117,522	NM
12,588,066	13,479,142	14,830,192	16,782,304	18,241,391	17,558,165	17,990,778	18,976,821	19,378,102	20,201,249	NY
3,170,276	3,571,623	4,061,929	4,556,155	5,084,411	5,880,095	6,632,448	8,046,485	9,535,483	10,439,388	NC
680,845	641,935	619,636	632,446	617,792	652,717	638,800	642,200	672,591	779,094	ND
6,646,697	6,907,612	7,946,627	9,706,397	10,657,423	10,797,603	10,847,115	11,353,145	11,536,504	11,799,448	OH
2,396,040	2,336,434	2,233,351	2,328,284	2,559,463	3,025,487	3,145,576	3,450,652	3,751,351	3,959,353	OK
953,786	1,089,684	1,521,341	1,768,687	2,091,533	2,633,156	2,842,337	3,421,436	3,831,074	4,237,256	OR
9,631,350	9,900,180	10,498,012	11,319,366	11,800,766	11,864,720	11,882,842	12,281,054	12,702,379	13,002,700	PA
687,497	713,346	791,896	859,488	949,723	947,154	1,003,464	1,048,319	1,052,567	1,097,379	RI
1,738,765	1,899,804	2,117,027	2,382,594	2,590,713	3,120,729	3,486,310	4,011,816	4,625,364	5,118,425	SC
692,849	642,961	652,740	680,514	666,257	690,768	696,004	754,844	814,191	886,667	SD
2,616,556	2,915,841	3,291,718	3,567,089	3,926,018	4,591,023	4,877,203	5,689,267	6,346,105	6,910,840	TN
5,824,715	6,414,824	7,711,194	9,579,677	11,198,655	14,225,513	16,986,335	20,851,790	25,145,565	29,145,505	TX
507,847	550,310	688,862	890,627	1,059,273	1,461,037	1,722,850	2,233,198	2,763,885	3,271,616	UT
359,611	359,231	377,747	389,881	444,732	511,456	562,758	608,827	625,741	643,077	VT
2,421,851	2,677,773	3,318,680	3,966,949	4,651,448	5,346,797	6,189,197	7,079,030	8,001,024	8,631,393	VA
1,563,396	1,736,191	2,378,963	2,853,214	3,413,244	4,132,353	4,866,669	5,894,141	6,724,540	7,705,281	WA
1,729,205	1,901,974	2,005,552	1,860,421	1,744,237	1,950,186	1,793,477	1,808,350	1,852,994	1,793,716	WV
2,939,006	3,137,587	3,434,575	3,951,777	4,417,821	4,705,642	4,891,769	5,363,715	5,686,986	5,893,718	WI
225,565	250,742	290,529	330,066	332,416	469,557	453,589	493,782	563,626	576,851	WY
123,202,624	**132,164,569**	**151,325,798**	**179,323,175**	**203,302,031**	**226,542,199**	**248,718,302**	**281,424,603**	**308,746,065**	**331,449,281**	**U.S.**

U.S. Center of Population, 1790-2020

Source: Decennial Censuses, Geography Division, U.S. Census Bureau, U.S. Dept. of Commerce

The country's **(mean) center of population** is the center of population gravity. In other words, it is the point upon which the U.S. would balance if the country were a rigid, weightless plane and its population was distributed thereon, with each individual assuming an equal weight.

	N Latitude			W Longitude			
Census year	°	′	″	°	′	″	**Approximate location**
1790	39	16	30	76	11	12	Kent Co., MD, 23 miles east of Baltimore
1800	39	16	6	76	56	30	Howard Co., MD, 18 miles west of Baltimore
1810	39	11	30	77	37	12	Loudoun Co., VA, 40 miles northwest by west of Washington, DC
1820	39	5	42	78	33	0	Hardy Co., WV[1], 16 miles east of Moorefield
1830	38	57	54	79	16	54	Grant Co., WV[1], 19 miles west-southwest of Moorefield
1840	39	2	0	80	18	0	Upshur Co., WV[1], 16 miles south of Clarksburg
1850	38	59	0	81	19	0	Wirt Co., WV[1], 23 miles southeast of Parkersburg
1860	39	0	24	82	48	48	Pike Co., OH, 20 miles south by east of Chillicothe
1870	39	12	0	83	35	42	Highland Co., OH, 48 miles east by north of Cincinnati
1880	39	4	8	84	39	40	Boone Co., KY, 8 miles west by south of Cincinnati, OH
1890	39	11	56	85	32	53	Decatur Co., IN, 20 miles east of Columbus
1900	39	9	36	85	48	54	Bartholomew Co., IN, 6 miles southeast of Columbus
1910	39	10	12	86	32	20	Monroe Co., IN, in the city of Bloomington
1920	39	10	21	86	43	15	Owen Co., IN, 8 miles south-southeast of Spencer
1930	39	3	45	87	8	6	Greene Co., IN, 3 miles northeast of Linton
1940	38	56	54	87	22	35	Sullivan Co., IN, 2 miles southeast by east of Carlisle
1950	38	50	21	88	9	33	Richland Co., IL, 8 miles north-northwest of Olney
1950[2]	38	48	15	88	22	8	Clay Co., IL, 3 miles northeast of Louisville
1960[2]	38	35	58	89	12	35	Clinton Co., IL, 6.5 miles northwest of Centralia
1970[2]	38	27	47	89	42	22	St. Clair Co., IL, 5 miles east-southeast of Mascoutah
1980[2]	38	8	13	90	34	26	Jefferson Co., MO, 0.25 mile west of DeSoto
1990[2]	37	52	20	91	12	55	Crawford Co., MO, 9.7 miles southeast of Steelville
2000[2]	37	41	49	91	48	34	Phelps Co., MO, 2.8 miles east of Edgar Springs
2010[2]	37	31	3	92	10	23	Texas Co., MO, 2.7 miles northeast of Plato
2020[2]	37	24	57	92	20	47	Wright Co., MO, 14.6 miles northeast of Hartville

(1) Pres. Lincoln signed a bill Dec. 31, 1862, approving statehood for West Virginia (made up of former Virginia counties). It was admitted to the Union June 20, 1863. (2) Incl. Alaska and Hawaii.

U.S. Congressional Apportionment by Census Year, 1850-2020

Source: Decennial Censuses, U.S. Census Bureau, U.S. Dept. of Commerce

The U.S. Constitution, in Article 1, Section 2, mandates that the population be counted every 10 years so that the number of U.S. representatives can be apportioned among the states. Every state is entitled to at least one House seat, with the size of a state's resident population (citizens and noncitizens) determining any additional representation. Apportionment has been made after every decennial census except for that of 1920. Prior to 1870, an enslaved person was counted as three-fifths of a person in the apportionment population. Since the 1970 census (excluding 1980), U.S. military personnel and federal civilian employees stationed or assigned overseas as well as their dependents have been allocated to a home state for apportionment. Dist. of Columbia, Puerto Rico, and U.S. island area residents are not included in the apportionment population because they lack voting seats in the U.S. House. House seats are allocated using the Huntington-Hill, or equal proportions, method for the least possible variation in the average number of people each House member represents.

The first House of Representatives, in 1789, had 65 members as provided by the Constitution. The number of representatives grew with the nation. A 1911 act fixed the total House membership at 433 (allowing for the addition of one seat each for Arizona and New Mexico upon statehood). Alaska and Hawaii each gained one House seat when they became states, temporarily raising the total to 437 representatives until after the 1960 census.

State	2020	2010	1990	1970	1950	1900	1850
AL	7	7	7	7	9	9	7
AK	1	1	1	1	1	NA	NA
AZ	9	9	6	4	2	NA	NA
AR	4	4	4	4	6	7	2
CA	52	53	52	43	30	8	2
CO	8	7	6	5	4	3	NA
CT	5	5	6	6	6	5	4
DE	1	1	1	1	1	1	1
FL	28	27	23	15	8	3	1
GA	14	14	11	10	10	11	8
HI	2	2	2	2	1	NA	NA
ID	2	2	2	2	2	1	NA
IL	17	18	20	24	25	25	9
IN	9	9	10	11	11	13	11
IA	4	4	5	6	8	11	2
KS	4	4	4	5	6	8	NA
KY	6	6	6	7	8	11	10
LA	6	6	7	8	8	7	4
ME	2	2	2	2	3	4	6
MD	8	8	8	8	7	6	6
MA	9	9	10	12	14	14	11
MI	13	14	16	19	18	12	4
MN	8	8	8	8	9	9	2
MS	4	4	5	5	6	8	5
MO	8	8	9	10	11	16	7
MT	2	1	1	2	2	1	NA
NE	3	3	3	3	4	6	NA
NV	4	4	2	1	1	1	NA
NH	2	2	2	2	2	2	3
NJ	12	12	13	15	14	10	5
NM	3	3	3	2	2	NA	NA
NY	26	27	31	39	43	37	33
NC	14	13	12	11	12	10	8
ND	1	1	1	1	2	2	NA
OH	15	16	19	23	23	21	21
OK	5	5	6	6	6	5	NA
OR	6	5	5	4	4	2	1
PA	17	18	21	25	30	32	25
RI	2	2	2	2	2	2	2
SC	7	7	6	6	6	7	6
SD	1	1	1	2	2	2	NA
TN	9	9	9	8	9	10	10
TX	38	36	30	24	22	16	2
UT	4	4	3	2	2	1	NA
VT	1	1	1	1	1	2	3
VA	11	11	11	10	10	10	13
WA	10	10	9	7	7	3	NA
WV	2	3	3	4	6	5	NA
WI	8	8	9	9	10	11	3
WY	1	1	1	1	1	1	NA
Total	**435**	**435**	**435**	**435**	**437**	**391**	**237**

NA = Not applicable.

U.S. Enslaved and "Free Colored" Population, 1790, 1820, 1860

Source: Decennial Censuses, U.S. Census Bureau, U.S. Dept. of Commerce

	1790			1820			1860		
	Enslaved	% enslaved[1]	Free colored	Enslaved	% enslaved[1]	Free colored	Enslaved	% enslaved[1]	Free colored
Northern states[2]	**40,354**	**2.1%**	**27,070**	**19,108**	**0.4%**	**99,307**	**18**	**0.0%**	**225,224**
Connecticut	2,764	1.2	2,808	97	0.0	7,870	0	0.0	8,627
New Jersey	11,423	6.2	2,762	7,557	2.7	12,460	18	0.0	25,318
New York	21,324	6.3	4,654	10,088	0.7	29,279	0	0.0	49,005
Pennsylvania	3,737	0.9	6,537	211	0.0	30,202	0	0.0	56,949
Border/disputed states	**124,353**	**27.5**	**12,056**	**248,860**	**22.4**	**55,794**	**429,403**	**13.2**	**118,652**
Delaware	8,887	15.0	3,899	4,509	6.2	12,958	1,798	1.6	19,829
Kansas	—	—	—	—	—	—	2	0.0	625
Kentucky	12,430	16.9	114	126,732	22.5	2,759	225,483	19.5	10,684
Maryland	103,036	32.2	8,043	107,397	26.4	39,730	87,189	12.7	83,942
Missouri	—	—	—	10,222	15.4	347	114,931	9.7	3,572
Southern states	**532,974**	**35.3**	**20,401**	**1,265,534**	**37.8**	**75,775**	**3,521,110**	**38.7**	**132,760**
Alabama	—	—	—	41,879	32.7	571	435,080	45.1	2,690
Arkansas	—	—	—	1,617	11.3	59	111,115	25.5	144
Florida	—	—	—	—	—	—	61,745	44.0	932
Georgia	29,264	35.5	398	149,656	43.9	1,763	462,198	43.7	3,500
Louisiana	—	—	—	69,064	45.0	10,476	331,726	46.9	18,647
Mississippi	—	—	—	32,814	43.5	458	436,631	55.2	773
North Carolina	100,572	25.5	4,975	204,917	32.1	14,712	331,059	33.4	30,463
South Carolina	107,094	43.0	1,801	258,475	51.4	6,826	402,406	57.2	9,914
Tennessee	3,417	9.6	361	80,107	18.9	2,737	275,719	24.8	7,300
Texas	—	—	—	—	—	—	182,566	30.2	355
Virginia	292,627	39.1	12,866	427,005	39.7	38,173	490,865	30.7	58,042
Total territories[3]	—	—	—	**4,520**	**19.4**	**2,758**	**3,229**	**1.1**	**11,434**
Total states and territories	**697,681**	**17.8**	**59,527**	**1,538,022**	**16.0**	**233,634**	**3,953,760**	**12.6**	**488,070**

Note: "Free colored" was an official Census Bureau designation in these decades. States are grouped roughly by allegiance in the Civil War. (1) Percentage of total pop., all races. (2) The following states are not listed separately but are included in totals for Northern states (relevant census years in parentheses): CA (1860), IL (1820, 1860), IN (1820, 1860), IA (1860), ME (1790, 1820, 1860), MA (1790, 1820, 1860), MI (1820, 1860), MN (1860), NH (1790, 1820, 1860), OH (1820, 1860), OR (1860), RI (1790, 1820, 1860), VT (1790, 1820, 1860), WI (1820, 1860). (3) Incl. AZ (1860), CO (1860), Dakota (1860), DC (1820, 1860), NE (1860), NV (1860), NM (1860), UT (1860), WA (1860).

U.S. Population by Sex, Race, Residence, and Median Age, 1790-2020

Source: Decennial Censuses, U.S. Census Bureau, U.S. Dept. of Commerce

(numbers in thousands, unless otherwise noted)

	SEX		RACE[2, 3]				RESIDENCE		MEDIAN AGE (years)		
				Black							
Census date	Male	Female	White	Number	% tot. pop.	Other	Urban[4]	Rural	All races	White[2,3]	Black[2]
Conterminous U.S.[1]											
1790 (Aug. 2)	NA	NA	3,172	757	19.3%	NA	202	3,728	NA	NA	NA
1800 (Aug. 4)	NA	NA	4,306	1,002	18.9	NA	322	4,986	NA	NA	NA
1810 (Aug. 6)	NA	NA	5,862	1,378	19.0	NA	525	6,714	NA	16.0	NA
1820 (Aug. 7)	4,897	4,742	7,867	1,772	18.4	NA	693	8,945	16.7	16.6	17.2
1830 (June 1)	6,532	6,334	10,537	2,329	18.1	NA	1,127	11,733	17.2	17.3	17.2
1840 (June 1)	8,689	8,381	14,196	2,874	16.8	NA	1,845	15,218	17.8	17.9	17.6
1850 (June 1)	11,838	11,354	19,553	3,639	15.7	NA	3,574	19,617	18.9	19.2	17.4
1860 (June 1)	16,085	15,358	26,923	4,442	14.1	79	6,217	25,227	19.4	19.7	17.5
1870 (June 1)	19,494	19,065	33,589	4,880	12.7	89	9,902	28,656	20.2	20.4	18.5
1880 (June 1)	25,519	24,637	43,403	6,581	13.1	172	14,130	36,059	20.9	21.4	18.0
1890 (June 1)	32,237	30,711	55,101	7,489	11.9	358	22,106	40,874	22.0	22.5	17.8
1900 (June 1)	38,816	37,178	66,809	8,834	11.6	351	30,215	45,997	22.9	23.4	19.4
1910 (Apr. 15)	47,332	44,640	81,732	9,828	10.7	413	42,064	50,164	24.1	24.5	20.8
1920 (Jan. 1)	53,900	51,810	94,821	10,463	9.9	427	54,253	51,768	25.3	25.5	22.3
1930 (Apr. 1)	62,137	60,638	110,287	11,891	9.7	597	69,161	54,042	26.5	26.9	23.5
1940 (Apr. 1)	66,062	65,608	118,215	12,866	9.8	589	74,705	57,459	29.0	29.5	25.3
United States											
1950 (Apr. 1)	74,833	75,864	135,150	15,045	10.0	713	96,847	54,479	30.2	30.8	26.1
1960 (Apr. 1)	88,331	90,992	158,832	18,872	10.5	1,620	125,269	54,054	29.5	30.3	23.5
1970 (Apr. 1)	98,926	104,309	178,098	22,581	11.1	2,557	149,647	53,565	28.1	28.9	22.4
1980 (Apr. 1)	110,053	116,493	194,713	26,683	11.8	5,150	167,051	59,495	30.0	30.9	24.9
1990 (Apr. 1)	121,284	127,507	208,741	30,517	12.3	9,533	187,053	61,656	32.9	33.7	27.9
2000 (Apr. 1)	138,054	143,368	194,553	33,948	12.1	13,013	222,361	59,061	35.3	38.6	30.2
2010 (Apr. 1)	151,781	156,964	196,818	37,686	12.2	17,798	249,253	59,492	37.2	42.0	32.4
2020 (Apr. 1)	162,686	168,763	191,698	39,940	12.1	24,182	265,149	66,300	38.8	44.5	35.1

NA = Not available. **Note:** Population figures may reflect revisions/corrections to initial tabulated census counts. (1) Excludes Alaska and Hawaii. (2) New race categories were introduced in the 2000 census. Race data for 2000 and on are for persons who reported being of one race alone. "Other" comprises Asians, Native Hawaiians and other Pacific Islanders, American Indians and Alaska Natives. Because of these changes, race data from 2000 on are not comparable to figures from previous years. (3) Does not include persons who reported being of Hispanic or Latino origin. (4) The Census Bureau's definition of "urban" has changed over time. Figures for 2000 and 2010 include residents of urbanized areas (50,000 or more inhabitants) and urban clusters (at least 2,500 but fewer than 50,000 inhabitants).

U.S. Population by Race and Hispanic Origin, 2010-20

Source: Decennial Censuses, U.S. Census Bureau, U.S. Dept. of Commerce

	2020		2010		% change, 2010-20	
	One race alone	One or more races[1]	One race alone	One or more races[1]	One race alone	One or more races[1]
Total population	**297,600,338**	**331,449,281**	**299,736,465**	**308,746,065**	**–0.7%**	**7.4%**
Race						
White	204,277,273	235,411,507	223,553,265	231,040,398	–8.6	1.9
Black or African American	41,104,200	46,936,733	38,929,319	42,020,743	5.6	11.7
Asian	19,886,049	24,000,998	14,674,252	17,320,856	35.5	38.6
American Indian and Alaska Native	3,727,135	9,666,058	2,932,248	5,220,579	27.1	85.2
Native Hawaiian and Other Pac. Isl.	689,966	1,586,463	540,013	1,225,195	27.8	29.5
Some other race	27,915,715	49,902,536	19,107,368	21,748,084	46.1	129.5
Hispanic origin and race						
Hispanic or Latino, any race	41,780,084	62,080,044	47,435,002	50,477,594	–11.9	23.0
Not Hispanic or Latino	255,820,254	269,369,237	252,301,463	258,267,944	1.4	4.3
White	191,697,647	203,890,286	196,817,552	201,856,108	–2.6	1.0
Black or African American	39,940,338	44,277,916	37,685,848	40,123,525	6.0	10.4
Asian	19,618,719	23,142,519	14,465,124	16,722,710	35.6	38.4
American Indian and Alaska Native	2,251,699	6,691,567	2,247,098	4,029,675	0.2	66.1
Native Hawaiian and Other Pac. Isl.	622,018	1,336,035	481,576	1,014,888	29.2	31.6
Some other race	1,689,833	4,584,438	604,265	1,033,866	179.7	343.4

Note: Population figures may reflect revisions/corrections to initial tabulated census counts. (1) Alone or in combination with one or more of the other races listed. Numbers do not add up to totals because of individuals reporting more than one race.

U.S. Population Growth by Race and Hispanic Origin, 1970-2030

Source: Decennial Censuses and Population Projections Program, U.S. Census Bureau, U.S. Dept. of Commerce

(numbers in millions)

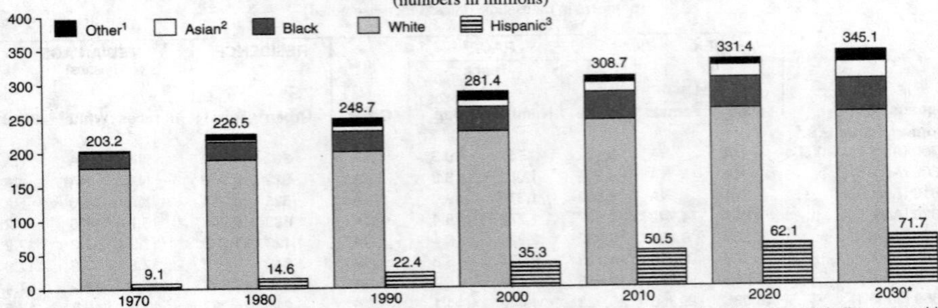

*Projected. **Note:** Because of changes in census questions and methods, data on race and Hispanic origin are not wholly comparable over time. Population figures may reflect revisions/corrections to initial tabulated census counts. (1) Includes American Indians and Alaska Natives as well as other races not shown. For 2000 and on, this category also includes Native Hawaiians and Other Pacific Islanders along with persons reporting two or more races. (2) Figures for 1970-90 include Pacific Islanders. (3) May be of any race. 1970 figure is based on sample of households.

State Population by Race and Hispanic Origin, 2020

Source: Decennial Census, U.S. Census Bureau, U.S. Dept. of Commerce

(percentage of state or country's total population)

	One race alone[1]							
State	**White**	**Black or African American**	**Asian**	**American Indian and Alaska Native**	**Native Hawaiian and Other Pacific Islander**	**Some other race**	**Two or more races[1]**	**Hispanic or Latino, any race**
Alabama	63.1%	25.6%	1.5%	0.5%	0.05%	0.29%	3.7%	5.3%
Alaska	57.5	2.8	5.9	14.8	1.70	0.62	9.8	6.8
Arizona	53.4	4.4	3.5	3.7	0.20	0.44	3.7	30.7
Arkansas	68.5	14.9	1.7	0.7	0.47	0.27	4.9	8.5
California	34.7	5.4	15.1	0.4	0.35	0.57	4.1	39.4
Colorado	65.1	3.8	3.4	0.6	0.16	0.51	4.5	21.9
Connecticut	63.2	10.0	4.7	0.2	0.03	0.75	3.8	17.3
Delaware	58.6	21.5	4.3	0.3	0.03	0.46	4.3	10.5
Dist. of Columbia	38.0	40.9	4.8	0.2	0.05	0.54	4.3	11.3
Florida	51.5	14.5	2.9	0.2	0.05	0.64	3.7	26.5
Georgia	50.1	30.6	4.4	0.2	0.06	0.52	3.6	10.5
Hawaii	21.6	1.5	36.5	0.2	10.24	0.36	20.1	9.5
Idaho	78.9	0.8	1.4	1.0	0.18	0.45	4.2	13.0
Illinois	58.3	13.9	5.8	0.1	0.02	0.35	3.2	18.2
Indiana	75.5	9.4	2.5	0.2	0.04	0.37	3.9	8.2
Iowa	82.7	4.1	2.4	0.3	0.18	0.27	3.4	6.8
Kansas	72.2	5.6	2.9	0.7	0.11	0.34	5.1	13.0
Kentucky	81.3	7.9	1.6	0.2	0.08	0.33	3.9	4.6
Louisiana	55.8	31.2	1.8	0.6	0.04	0.36	3.4	6.9
Maine	90.2	1.8	1.2	0.5	0.03	0.33	3.9	2.0
Maryland	47.2	29.1	6.8	0.2	0.04	0.57	4.4	11.8
Massachusetts	67.6	6.5	7.2	0.1	0.02	1.31	4.7	12.6
Michigan	72.4	13.5	3.3	0.5	0.03	0.37	4.4	5.6
Minnesota	76.3	6.9	5.2	1.0	0.05	0.37	4.1	6.1
Mississippi	55.4	36.4	1.1	0.5	0.04	0.24	2.8	3.6
Missouri	75.8	11.3	2.1	0.4	0.15	0.36	5.0	4.9
Montana	83.1	0.5	0.7	6.0	0.08	0.40	5.0	4.2
Nebraska	75.7	4.8	2.7	0.8	0.07	0.32	3.7	12.0
Nevada	45.9	9.4	8.6	0.8	0.74	0.55	5.4	28.7
New Hampshire	87.2	1.4	2.6	0.2	0.03	0.43	4.0	4.3
New Jersey	51.9	12.4	10.2	0.1	0.02	0.76	3.1	21.6
New Mexico	36.5	1.8	1.7	8.9	0.07	0.49	2.8	47.7
New York	52.5	13.7	9.5	0.3	0.03	0.98	3.6	19.5
North Carolina	60.5	20.2	3.3	1.0	0.07	0.44	3.9	10.7
North Dakota	81.7	3.4	1.7	4.8	0.11	0.24	3.9	4.3
Ohio	75.9	12.3	2.5	0.2	0.04	0.38	4.3	4.4
Oklahoma	60.8	7.2	2.3	7.9	0.21	0.34	9.4	11.9
Oregon	71.7	1.9	4.5	1.0	0.43	0.54	6.1	13.9
Pennsylvania	73.5	10.5	3.9	0.1	0.02	0.42	3.5	8.1
Rhode Island	68.7	5.0	3.5	0.3	0.03	1.04	4.8	16.6
South Carolina	62.1	24.8	1.7	0.3	0.06	0.38	3.7	6.9
South Dakota	79.6	2.0	1.5	8.4	0.06	0.23	3.9	4.4
Tennessee	70.9	15.7	1.9	0.2	0.05	0.35	3.9	6.9
Texas	39.7	11.8	5.4	0.3	0.10	0.39	3.0	39.3
Utah	75.4	1.1	2.4	0.9	1.10	0.38	3.7	15.1
Vermont	89.1	1.3	1.8	0.3	0.03	0.40	4.6	2.4
Virginia	58.6	18.3	7.1	0.2	0.07	0.53	4.7	10.5
Washington	63.8	3.8	9.4	1.2	0.81	0.56	6.6	13.7
West Virginia	89.1	3.6	0.8	0.2	0.02	0.26	4.0	1.9
Wisconsin	78.6	6.2	3.0	0.8	0.03	0.30	3.5	7.6
Wyoming	81.4	0.8	0.9	2.0	0.08	0.42	4.1	10.2
United States	**57.8**	**12.1**	**5.9**	**0.7**	**0.19**	**0.51**	**4.1**	**18.7**

(1) Not Hispanic or Latino.

American Indian and Alaska Native Population by State, 2021

Source: American Community Survey (ACS), U.S. Census Bureau, U.S. Dept. of Commerce
(ranked by American Indian and Alaska Native [AIAN] alone)

Rank	State	AIAN alone	AIAN alone or in combination[1]
1.	California	360,607	920,261
2.	Oklahoma	303,792	545,381
3.	Arizona	300,862	413,837
4.	New Mexico	197,712	239,040
5.	Texas	147,892	428,337
6.	North Carolina	113,719	217,203
7.	Alaska	107,531	148,918
8.	Washington	90,789	237,274
9.	New York	83,734	234,614
10.	South Dakota	73,296	91,514
11.	Montana	65,452	88,093
12.	Florida	54,466	206,539
13.	Colorado	53,143	143,399
14.	Minnesota	52,695	114,778
15.	Michigan	48,361	152,454
16.	Oregon	46,075	139,496
17.	Wisconsin	45,831	97,998
18.	Illinois	42,714	130,460
19.	North Dakota	39,103	52,961
20.	Nevada	37,850	75,179
21.	Georgia	34,928	127,492
22.	Utah	33,242	64,425
23.	Louisiana	25,550	66,958
24.	New Jersey	24,719	77,404
25.	Virginia	24,007	101,008
26.	Idaho	22,799	47,870
27.	Alabama	21,661	68,630
28.	Kansas	21,657	67,761
29.	Pennsylvania	20,511	99,345
30.	Missouri	19,904	88,968
31.	Ohio	18,416	108,909
32.	Nebraska	17,937	36,992
33.	Arkansas	17,459	64,805
34.	Maryland	17,266	73,341
35.	South Carolina	15,595	54,549
36.	Tennessee	15,219	70,338
37.	Massachusetts	14,939	59,748
38.	Mississippi	13,357	29,230
39.	Wyoming	12,987	21,142
40.	Indiana	11,399	59,943
41.	Iowa	10,889	32,815
42.	Connecticut	8,714	38,241
43.	Maine	7,578	23,381
44.	Kentucky	7,114	38,815
45.	Rhode Island	4,437	14,451
46.	Hawaii	4,286	34,910
47.	Delaware	3,064	10,981
48.	New Hampshire	1,988	11,567
49.	District of Columbia	1,984	8,712
50.	West Virginia	1,911	15,656
51.	Vermont	1,520	8,470
	United States	**2,722,661**	**6,304,593**
	Puerto Rico	5,407	42,626

Note: Data based on sample and subject to sampling variability. Figures are five-year estimates representing data collected over 60 months (Jan. 2017-Dec. 2021). (1) Respondents who self-identified as AIAN alone or in combination with one or more other races.

American Indian and Alaska Native Population by Selected Groups, 2020

Source: Decennial Census, U.S. Census Bureau, U.S. Dept. of Commerce

(for each regional group, selected tribes and villages ranked by size of detailed race alone counts)

Population group	Alone[1]		Alone or in any combination[2]	
	Count	Percent	Count	Percent
Alaska Native	**133,311**	**100.0%**	**241,797**	**100.0%**
Yup'ik (Yup'ik Eskimo)	9,026	6.8	13,706	5.7
Tlingit	7,792	5.8	22,601	9.3
Inupiat (Inupiaq)	5,674	4.3	10,501	4.3
Alaskan Athabascan	4,893	3.7	11,514	4.8
Aleut	4,878	3.7	13,805	5.7
Eskimo	3,337	2.5	9,737	4.0
Native Village of Barrow Inupiat Traditional Government[3]	2,565	1.9	3,824	1.6
Nome Eskimo Community[3]	1,914	1.4	3,786	1.6
Central Council of the Tlingit and Haida Indian Tribes[3]	1,424	1.1	3,003	1.2
Native Village of Hooper Bay (Naparyarmiut)[3]	1,384	1.0	1,476	0.6
American Indian	**2,159,802**	**100.0**	**6,363,796**	**100.0**
Navajo Nation[3]	315,086	14.6	423,412	6.7
Cherokee	214,940	10.0	1,513,326	23.8
Choctaw	69,454	3.2	255,557	4.0
Lumbee Tribe of North Carolina[4]	54,293	2.5	79,424	1.2
The Muscogee (Creek) Nation[3]	40,677	1.9	121,581	1.9
Chippewa	39,057	1.8	130,048	2.0
Apache	36,492	1.7	129,589	2.0
Blackfeet Tribe of the Blackfeet Indian Reservation of Montana[3]	34,810	1.6	297,899	4.7
Cherokee Nation[3]	31,432	1.5	77,232	1.2
Sioux	30,408	1.4	126,571	2.0
Canadian Indian	**7,723**	**100.0**	**72,701**	**100.0**
Chippewa/Ojibwe Canadian	1,149	14.9	2,576	3.5
Metis	855	11.1	3,936	5.4
French Canadian/French American Indian	610	7.9	38,034	52.3
Canadian Indian	564	7.3	7,126	9.8
Six Nations Canada	229	3.0	809	1.1
Latin American Indian	**766,112**	**100.0**	**1,319,523**	**100.0**
Aztec	387,122	50.5	583,981	44.3
Maya	180,359	23.5	300,519	22.8
Taino	28,346	3.7	112,682	8.5
Maya Central American	18,942	2.5	21,542	1.6
Mexican Indian	15,235	2.0	34,005	2.6

(1) Incl. respondents who reported only one response (e.g., Native Village of Barrow Inupiat Traditional Government). (2) Incl. respondents as in footnote 1 and respondents who reported multiple responses (e.g., Native Village of Barrow Inupiat Traditional Government and Arctic Slope Corporation, or the former and Black or African American). (3) Federally recognized tribe or village. (4) State recognized tribe.

Largest U.S. Cities by Population, 1850-2023

Source: Population Estimates Program and Decennial Censuses, U.S. Census Bureau, U.S. Dept. of Commerce
(ranked by 2023 resident population)

Rank	City	2023	2020	2010	2000	1980	1950	1900	1850
1.	New York, NY	8,258,035	8,804,190	8,175,133	8,008,654	7,071,639	7,891,957	3,437,202	515,547
2.	Los Angeles, CA	3,820,914	3,898,747	3,792,621	3,694,742	2,968,528	1,970,358	102,479	1,610
3.	Chicago, IL	2,664,452	2,746,388	2,695,598	2,896,016	3,005,072	3,620,962	1,698,575	29,963
4.	Houston, TX	2,314,157	2,304,580	2,099,451	1,953,631	1,595,138	596,163	44,633	2,396
5.	Phoenix, AZ	1,650,070	1,608,139	1,445,632	1,321,045	789,704	106,818	5,544	—
6.	Philadelphia, PA	1,550,542	1,603,797	1,526,006	1,517,550	1,688,210	2,071,605	1,293,697	121,376
7.	San Antonio, TX	1,495,295	1,434,625	1,327,407	1,144,646	785,940	408,442	53,321	3,488
8.	San Diego, CA	1,388,320	1,386,932	1,307,402	1,223,400	875,538	334,387	17,700	—
9.	Dallas, TX	1,302,868	1,304,379	1,197,816	1,188,580	904,599	434,462	42,638	—
10.	Jacksonville, FL[1]	985,843	949,611	821,784	735,617	540,920	204,517	28,429	1,045
11.	Austin, TX	979,882	961,855	790,390	656,562	345,890	132,459	22,258	629
12.	Fort Worth, TX	978,468	918,915	741,206	534,694	385,164	278,778	26,688	—
13.	San Jose, CA	969,655	1,013,240	945,942	894,943	629,400	95,280	21,500	—
14.	Columbus, OH	913,175	905,748	787,033	711,470	565,021	375,901	125,560	17,882
15.	Charlotte, NC	911,311	874,579	731,424	540,167	315,474	134,042	18,091	1,065
16.	Indianapolis, IN[1]	879,293	887,642	820,445	791,926	710,868	427,173	169,164	8,091
17.	San Francisco, CA[2]	808,988	873,965	805,235	776,733	678,974	775,357	342,782	34,776
18.	Seattle, WA	755,078	737,015	608,660	563,376	493,846	467,591	80,671	—
19.	Denver, CO	716,577	715,522	600,158	553,693	492,686	415,786	133,859	—
20.	Oklahoma City, OK	702,767	681,054	579,999	506,132	404,014	243,504	10,037	—
21.	Nashville-Davidson, TN[1]	687,788	689,447	601,222	569,892	477,811	174,307	80,865	10,165
22.	Washington, DC	678,972	689,545	601,723	572,059	638,432	802,178	278,718	40,001
23.	El Paso, TX	678,958	678,815	649,121	563,662	425,259	130,485	15,906	—
24.	Las Vegas, NV	660,929	641,903	583,756	479,137	164,674	24,624	—	—
25.	Boston, MA	653,833	675,647	617,594	589,141	562,994	801,444	560,892	136,881
26.	Detroit, MI	633,218	639,111	713,777	951,270	1,203,368	1,849,568	285,704	21,019
27.	Portland, OR	630,498	652,503	583,776	529,121	368,148	373,628	90,426	—
28.	Louisville/Jefferson Co., KY[1]	622,981	386,884	597,337	256,231	298,694	369,129	204,731	43,194
29.	Memphis, TN	618,639	633,104	646,889	650,100	646,174	396,000	102,320	8,841
30.	Baltimore, MD	565,239	585,708	620,961	651,154	786,741	949,708	508,957	169,054
31.	Milwaukee, WI	561,385	577,222	594,833	596,974	636,297	637,392	285,315	20,061
32.	Albuquerque, NM	560,274	564,559	545,852	448,607	332,619	96,815	6,238	—
33.	Tucson, AZ	547,239	542,629	520,116	486,699	330,537	45,454	7,531	—
34.	Fresno, CA	545,716	542,107	494,665	427,652	217,491	91,669	12,470	—
35.	Sacramento, CA	526,384	524,943	466,488	407,018	275,741	137,572	29,282	6,820
36.	Mesa, AZ	511,648	504,258	439,041	396,375	152,404	16,790	722	—
37.	Atlanta, GA	510,823	498,715	420,003	416,267	425,022	331,314	89,872	2,572
38.	Kansas City, MO	510,704	508,090	459,787	441,545	448,028	456,622	163,752	—
39.	Colorado Springs, CO	488,664	478,961	416,427	360,890	215,105	45,472	21,085	—
40.	Omaha, NE	483,335	486,051	408,958	390,007	313,939	251,117	102,555	—
41.	Raleigh, NC	482,295	467,665	403,892	276,094	150,255	65,679	13,643	4,518
42.	Miami, FL	455,924	442,241	399,457	362,470	346,681	249,276	1,681	—
43.	Virginia Beach, VA	453,649	459,470	437,994	425,257	262,199	5,390	—	—
44.	Long Beach, CA	449,468	466,742	462,257	461,522	361,498	250,767	2,252	—
45.	Oakland, CA	436,504	440,646	390,724	399,484	339,337	384,575	66,960	—
46.	Minneapolis, MN	425,115	429,954	382,578	382,747	370,951	521,718	202,718	—
47.	Bakersfield, CA	413,381	403,455	347,483	246,889	105,611	34,784	4,836	—
48.	Tulsa, OK	411,894	413,066	391,906	393,049	360,919	182,740	1,390	—
49.	Tampa, FL	403,364	384,959	335,709	303,447	271,577	124,681	15,839	—
50.	Arlington, TX	398,431	394,266	365,438	332,969	160,113	7,692	1,079	—
51.	Wichita, KS	396,119	397,532	382,368	346,753	279,838	168,279	24,671	—
52.	Aurora, CO	395,052	386,261	325,078	275,921	158,588	11,421	202	—
53.	New Orleans, LA	364,136	383,997	343,829	484,674	557,927	570,445	287,104	116,375
54.	Cleveland, OH	362,656	372,624	396,815	477,459	573,822	914,808	381,768	17,034
55.	Urban Honolulu, HI[3]	341,778	350,964	337,256	371,657	365,048	248,034	39,306	—
56.	Anaheim, CA	340,512	346,824	336,265	328,014	219,494	14,556	1,456	—
57.	Henderson, NV	337,305	317,610	257,729	175,381	24,363	—	—	—
58.	Orlando, FL	320,742	307,573	238,300	185,951	128,291	52,367	2,481	—
59.	Lexington-Fayette, KY[1]	320,154	322,570	295,803	260,512	204,165	55,534	26,369	8,159
60.	Stockton, CA	319,543	320,804	291,707	243,771	148,283	70,853	17,506	—
61.	Riverside, CA	318,858	314,998	303,871	255,166	170,591	46,764	7,973	—
62.	Corpus Christi, TX	316,595	317,863	305,215	277,454	232,134	108,287	4,703	—
63.	Irvine, CA	314,621	307,670	212,375	143,072	62,134	—	—	—
64.	Cincinnati, OH	311,097	309,317	296,943	331,285	385,409	503,998	325,902	115,435
65.	Santa Ana, CA	310,539	310,227	324,528	337,977	204,023	45,533	4,933	—
66.	Newark, NJ	304,960	311,549	277,140	272,537	329,248	438,776	246,070	38,894
67.	St. Paul, MN	303,820	311,527	285,068	286,840	270,230	311,349	163,065	1,112
68.	Pittsburgh, PA	303,255	302,971	305,704	334,563	423,959	676,806	321,616	46,601
69.	Greensboro, NC	302,296	299,035	269,666	223,891	155,642	74,389	10,035	—
70.	Durham, NC	296,186	283,506	228,330	187,035	101,149	71,311	6,679	—
71.	Lincoln, NE	294,757	291,082	258,379	225,581	171,932	98,884	40,169	—
72.	Jersey City, NJ	291,657	292,449	247,597	240,055	223,532	299,017	206,433	6,856
73.	Plano, TX	290,190	285,494	259,841	222,030	72,331	2,126	1,304	—
74.	Anchorage, AK	286,075	291,247	291,826	260,283	174,431	11,254	—	—
75.	North Las Vegas, NV	284,771	262,527	216,961	115,488	42,739	—	—	—
76.	St. Louis, MO	281,754	301,578	319,294	348,189	452,801	856,796	575,238	77,860
77.	Madison, WI	280,305	269,840	233,209	208,054	170,616	96,056	19,164	1,525
78.	Chandler, AZ	280,167	275,987	236,123	176,581	29,673	3,799	—	—
79.	Gilbert, AZ	275,411	267,918	208,453	109,697	5,717	1,114	—	—
80.	Reno, NV	274,915	264,165	225,221	180,480	100,756	32,497	4,500	—
81.	Buffalo, NY	274,678	278,349	261,310	292,648	357,870	580,132	352,387	42,261
82.	Chula Vista, CA	274,333	275,487	243,916	173,556	83,927	15,927	—	—
83.	Fort Wayne, IN	269,994	263,886	253,691	205,727	172,391	133,607	45,115	4,282
84.	Lubbock, TX	266,878	257,141	229,573	199,564	174,361	71,747	—	—
85.	Toledo, OH	265,304	270,871	287,208	313,782	354,635	303,616	131,822	3,829
86.	St. Petersburg, FL	263,553	258,308	244,769	248,232	238,647	96,738	1,575	—

Rank	City	2023	2020	2010	2000	1980	1950	1900	1850
87.	Laredo, TX	257,602	255,205	236,091	176,576	91,449	51,910	13,429	—
88.	Irving, TX	254,373	256,684	216,290	191,615	109,943	2,621	—	—
89.	Chesapeake, VA	253,886	249,422	222,209	199,184	114,486	—	—	—
90.	Glendale, AZ	253,855	248,325	226,721	218,812	97,172	8,179	—	—
91.	Winston-Salem, NC	252,975	249,545	229,617	185,776	131,885	87,811	13,650	—
92.	Port St. Lucie, FL	245,021	204,851	164,603	88,769	14,690	—	—	—
93.	Scottsdale, AZ	244,394	241,361	217,385	202,705	88,412	2,032	—	—
94.	Garland, TX	243,470	246,018	226,876	215,768	138,857	10,571	819	—
95.	Boise City, ID	235,421	235,684	205,671	185,787	102,249	34,393	5,957	—
96.	Norfolk, VA	230,930	238,005	242,803	234,403	266,979	213,513	46,624	14,326
97.	Spokane, WA	229,447	228,989	208,916	195,629	171,300	161,721	36,848	—
98.	Richmond, VA	229,247	226,610	204,214	197,790	219,214	230,310	85,050	27,570
99.	Fremont, CA	226,208	230,504	214,089	203,413	131,945	—	—	—
100.	Huntsville, AL	225,564	215,006	180,105	158,635	142,513	16,437	8,068	2,863

— = Not available. **Note:** Population estimates are as of July 1. Decennial census figures for 1950-2020 are for Apr. 1; 1850 and 1900 are for June 1. Figures may reflect revisions/corrections to initial tabulated census counts. Cities are incorporated places unless otherwise noted. (1) Consolidated city-county government. For years predating consolidation, city population figures are shown. (2) 1850 figure is for 1852, from state census. 1850 census results were destroyed by fire. (3) Census designated place (CDP). Figures for years prior to 2010 are for Honolulu CDP and are not directly comparable.

Population Change in Largest U.S. Cities, 2010-23

Source: Population Estimates Program and Decennial Census, U.S. Census Bureau, U.S. Dept. of Commerce

(ranked by % change, 2010-23; 2023 estimates are as of July 1; 2010 decennial census figures are for Apr. 1)

Cities With Most Growth

Rank	City	Population 2023	Population 2010	% change, 2010-23
1.	Port St. Lucie, FL	245,021	164,603	48.9%
2.	Irvine, CA	314,621	212,375	48.1
3.	Orlando, FL	320,742	238,300	34.6
4.	Gilbert, AZ	275,411	208,453	32.1
5.	Fort Worth, TX	978,468	741,206	32.0
6.	North Las Vegas, NV	284,771	216,961	31.3
7.	Henderson, NV	337,305	257,729	30.9
8.	Durham, NC	296,186	228,330	29.7
9.	Huntsville, AL	225,564	180,105	25.2
10.	Charlotte, NC	911,311	731,424	24.6
11.	Seattle, WA	755,078	608,660	24.1
12.	Austin, TX	979,882	790,390	24.0
13.	Reno, NV	274,915	225,221	22.1
14.	Atlanta, GA	510,823	420,003	21.6
15.	Aurora, CO	395,052	325,078	21.5
16.	Oklahoma City, OK	702,767	579,999	21.2
17.	Madison, WI	280,305	233,209	20.2
18.	Tampa, FL	403,364	335,709	20.2
19.	Jacksonville, FL	985,843	821,784	20.0
20.	Raleigh, NC	482,295	403,892	19.4

Cities With Least Growth

Rank	City	Population 2023	Population 2010	% change, 2010-23
1.	St. Louis, MO	281,754	319,294	–11.8%
2.	Detroit, MI	633,218	713,777	–11.3
3.	Baltimore, MD	565,239	620,961	–9.0
4.	Cleveland, OH	362,656	396,815	–8.6
5.	Toledo, OH	265,304	287,208	–7.6
6.	Milwaukee, WI	561,385	594,833	–5.6
7.	Norfolk, VA	230,930	242,803	–4.9
8.	Memphis, TN	618,639	646,889	–4.4
9.	Santa Ana, CA	310,539	324,528	–4.3
10.	Long Beach, CA	449,468	462,257	–2.8
11.	Anchorage, AK	286,075	291,826	–2.0
12.	Chicago, IL	2,664,452	2,695,598	–1.2
13.	Pittsburgh, PA	303,255	305,704	–0.8
14.	San Francisco, CA	808,988	805,235	0.5
15.	Los Angeles, CA	3,820,914	3,792,621	0.7
16.	New York, NY	8,258,035	8,175,133	1.0
17.	Anaheim, CA	340,512	336,265	1.3
18.	Urban Honolulu, HI	341,778	337,256	1.3
19.	Philadelphia, PA	1,550,542	1,526,006	1.6
20.	San Jose, CA	969,655	945,942	2.5

Note: This table shows which of the 100 largest U.S. cities by 2023 population size experienced the most and least population growth since 2010. Figures may reflect revisions/corrections to initial tabulated census counts. Cities are typically incorporated places.

Largest U.S. Counties by Population, 2010-23

Source: Population Estimates Program and Decennial Census, U.S. Census Bureau, U.S. Dept. of Commerce

(ranked by 2023 resident population, estimated as of July 1; 2010 decennial census figures are for Apr. 1)

Rank	County	2023	2010	% change, 2010-23
1.	Los Angeles Co., CA	9,663,345	9,818,605	–1.6%
2.	Cook Co., IL	5,087,072	5,194,675	–2.1
3.	Harris Co., TX	4,835,125	4,092,459	18.1
4.	Maricopa Co., AZ	4,585,871	3,817,117	20.1
5.	San Diego Co., CA	3,269,973	3,095,313	5.6
6.	Orange Co., CA	3,135,755	3,010,232	4.2
7.	Miami-Dade Co., FL	2,686,867	2,496,435	7.6
8.	Dallas Co., TX	2,606,358	2,368,139	10.1
9.	Kings Co., NY	2,561,225	2,504,700	2.3
10.	Riverside Co., CA	2,492,442	2,189,641	13.8
11.	Clark Co., NV	2,336,573	1,951,269	19.7
12.	King Co., WA	2,271,380	1,931,249	17.6
13.	Queens Co., NY	2,252,196	2,230,722	1.0
14.	San Bernardino Co., CA	2,195,611	2,035,210	7.9
15.	Tarrant Co., TX	2,182,947	1,809,034	20.7
16.	Bexar Co., TX	2,087,679	1,714,773	21.7
17.	Broward Co., FL	1,962,531	1,748,066	12.3
18.	Santa Clara Co., CA	1,877,592	1,781,642	5.4
19.	Wayne Co., MI	1,751,169	1,820,584	–3.8
20.	Middlesex Co., MA	1,623,952	1,503,085	8.0
21.	Alameda Co., CA	1,622,188	1,510,271	7.4
22.	New York Co., NY	1,597,451	1,585,873	0.7
23.	Sacramento Co., CA	1,584,288	1,418,788	11.7
24.	Philadelphia Co., PA	1,550,542	1,526,006	1.6

Rank	County	2023	2010	% change, 2010-23
25.	Hillsborough Co., FL	1,535,564	1,229,226	24.9%
26.	Palm Beach Co., FL	1,533,801	1,320,134	16.2
27.	Suffolk Co., NY	1,523,170	1,493,350	2.0
28.	Orange Co., FL	1,471,416	1,145,956	28.4
29.	Nassau Co., NY	1,381,715	1,339,532	3.1
30.	Bronx Co., NY	1,356,476	1,385,108	–2.1
31.	Travis Co., TX	1,334,961	1,024,266	30.3
32.	Franklin Co., OH	1,326,063	1,163,414	14.0
33.	Oakland Co., MI	1,270,426	1,202,362	5.7
34.	Hennepin Co., MN	1,258,713	1,152,425	9.2
35.	Cuyahoga Co., OH	1,233,088	1,280,122	–3.7
36.	Allegheny Co., PA	1,224,825	1,223,348	0.1
37.	Collin Co., TX	1,195,359	782,341	52.8
38.	Wake Co., NC	1,190,275	900,993	32.1
39.	Salt Lake Co., UT	1,185,813	1,029,655	15.2
40.	Mecklenburg Co., NC	1,163,701	919,628	26.5
41.	Contra Costa Co., CA	1,155,025	1,049,025	10.1
42.	Fairfax Co., VA	1,141,878	1,081,726	5.6
43.	Fulton Co., GA	1,079,105	920,581	17.2
44.	Pima Co., AZ	1,063,162	980,263	8.5
45.	Montgomery Co., MD	1,058,474	971,777	8.9
46.	Duval Co., FL	1,030,822	864,263	19.3
47.	Fresno Co., CA	1,017,162	930,450	9.3
48.	Denton Co., TX	1,007,703	662,614	52.1
49.	Westchester Co., NY	990,817	949,113	4.4
50.	Honolulu Co., HI	989,408	953,207	3.8

Note: Decennial pop. figures may reflect revisions/corrections to initial tabulated census counts. The 10 smallest counties or county equivalents by estimated 2023 population: (1) Loving Co., TX (pop. 43); (2) Kalawao Co., HI (81); (3) King Co., TX (217); (4) Kenedy Co., TX (343); (5) McPherson Co., NE (383); (6) Arthur Co., NE (412); (7) Blaine Co., NE (436); (8) Petroleum Co., MT (554); (9) Grant Co., NE (565); and (10) McMullen Co., TX (568).

Largest U.S. Metropolitan Areas by Population, 2000-23

Source: Population Estimates Program and Decennial Censuses, U.S. Census Bureau, U.S. Dept. of Commerce

Metropolitan Statistical Areas (MSAs) are defined, or delineated geographically, for federal statistical use by the Office of Management and Budget (OMB) with technical assistance from the Census Bureau. An MSA consists of at least one urbanized area of 50,000 or more inhabitants, plus adjacent territory closely integrated socially and economically with the core as measured by commuting ties. The Census Bureau's 2023 population estimates are for delineations issued by the OMB in July 2021, which designated 387 MSAs in the U.S. (Because of changes in delineations over time, the Census Bureau advises caution in comparing data for MSAs from different dates.) About 86.3% of the resident population lived in an MSA in 2023.

(ranked by 2023 resident population, estimated as of July 1; 2000 and 2010 decennial census figures are for Apr. 1)

Rank	Metropolitan Statistical Area	Population 2023	2010	2000	Percent change 2010-23	2000-23
1.	New York-Newark-Jersey City, NY-NJ	19,498,249	18,897,109	18,944,519	3.2%	2.9%
2.	Los Angeles-Long Beach-Anaheim, CA	12,799,100	12,828,837	12,365,627	–0.2	3.5
3.	Chicago-Naperville-Elgin, IL-IN	9,262,825	9,461,105	9,098,316	–2.1	1.8
4.	Dallas-Fort Worth-Arlington, TX	8,100,037	6,366,542	5,204,126	27.2	55.6
5.	Houston-Pasadena-The Woodlands, TX	7,510,253	5,920,416	4,693,161	26.9	60.0
6.	Atlanta-Sandy Springs-Roswell, GA	6,307,261	5,286,728	4,263,438	19.3	47.9
7.	Washington-Arlington-Alexandria, DC-VA-MD-WV	6,304,975	5,649,540	4,837,428	11.6	30.3
8.	Philadelphia-Camden-Wilmington, PA-NJ-DE-MD	6,246,160	5,965,343	5,687,147	4.7	9.8
9.	Miami-Fort Lauderdale-West Palm Beach, FL	6,183,199	5,564,635	5,007,564	11.1	23.5
10.	Phoenix-Mesa-Chandler, AZ	5,070,110	4,192,887	3,251,876	20.9	55.9
11.	Boston-Cambridge-Newton, MA-NH	4,919,179	4,552,402	4,391,344	8.1	12.0
12.	Riverside-San Bernardino-Ontario, CA	4,688,053	4,224,851	3,254,821	11.0	44.0
13.	San Francisco-Oakland-Fremont, CA	4,566,961	4,335,391	4,123,740	5.3	10.7
14.	Detroit-Warren-Dearborn, MI	4,342,304	4,296,250	4,452,557	1.1	–2.5
15.	Seattle-Tacoma-Bellevue, WA	4,044,837	3,439,809	3,043,878	17.6	32.9
16.	Minneapolis-St. Paul-Bloomington, MN-WI	3,712,020	3,333,633	3,031,918	11.4	22.4
17.	Tampa-St. Petersburg-Clearwater, FL	3,342,963	2,783,243	2,395,997	20.1	39.5
18.	San Diego-Chula Vista-Carlsbad, CA	3,269,973	3,095,313	2,813,833	5.6	16.2
19.	Denver-Aurora-Centennial, CO	3,005,131	2,543,482	2,179,240	18.2	37.9
20.	Baltimore-Columbia-Towson, MD	2,834,316	2,710,489	2,552,994	4.6	11.0
21.	Orlando-Kissimmee-Sanford, FL	2,817,933	2,134,411	1,644,561	32.0	71.3
22.	Charlotte-Concord-Gastonia, NC-SC	2,805,115	2,243,960	1,717,372	25.0	63.3
23.	St. Louis, MO-IL	2,796,999	2,787,701	2,675,343	0.3	4.5
24.	San Antonio-New Braunfels, TX	2,703,999	2,142,508	1,711,703	26.2	58.0
25.	Portland-Vancouver-Hillsboro, OR-WA	2,508,050	2,226,009	1,927,881	12.7	30.1
26.	Austin-Round Rock-San Marcos, TX	2,473,275	1,716,289	1,249,763	44.1	97.9
27.	Pittsburgh, PA	2,422,725	2,356,285	2,431,087	2.8	–0.3
28.	Sacramento-Roseville-Folsom, CA	2,420,608	2,149,127	1,796,857	12.6	34.7
29.	Las Vegas-Henderson-North Las Vegas, NV	2,336,573	1,951,269	1,375,765	19.7	69.8
30.	Cincinnati, OH-KY-IN	2,271,479	2,137,667	1,994,830	6.3	13.9
31.	Kansas City, MO-KS	2,221,343	2,009,342	1,811,254	10.6	22.6
32.	Columbus, OH	2,180,271	1,901,974	1,675,013	14.6	30.2
33.	Cleveland, OH	2,158,932	2,077,240	2,148,143	3.9	0.5
34.	Indianapolis-Carmel-Greenwood, IN	2,138,468	1,887,877	1,658,462	13.3	28.9
35.	Nashville-Davidson—Murfreesboro—Franklin, TN	2,102,573	1,646,200	1,381,287	27.7	52.2
36.	San Jose-Sunnyvale-Santa Clara, CA	1,945,767	1,836,911	1,735,819	5.9	12.1
37.	Virginia Beach-Chesapeake-Norfolk, VA-NC	1,787,169	1,713,954	1,580,057	4.3	13.1
38.	Jacksonville, FL	1,713,240	1,345,596	1,122,750	27.3	52.6
39.	Providence-Warwick, RI-MA	1,677,803	1,600,852	1,582,997	4.8	6.0
40.	Milwaukee-Waukesha, WI	1,560,424	1,555,908	1,500,741	0.3	4.0
41.	Raleigh-Cary, NC	1,509,231	1,130,490	797,071	33.5	89.3
42.	Oklahoma City, OK	1,477,926	1,252,987	1,095,421	18.0	34.9
43.	Louisville/Jefferson County, KY-IN	1,365,557	1,202,718	1,121,109	13.5	21.8
44.	Richmond, VA	1,349,732	1,186,501	1,055,683	13.8	27.9
45.	Memphis, TN-MS-AR	1,335,674	1,316,100	1,213,230	1.5	10.1
46.	Salt Lake City-Murray, UT	1,267,864	1,087,873	939,122	16.5	35.0
47.	Birmingham, AL	1,184,290	1,061,024	1,052,238	11.6	12.5
48.	Fresno, CA	1,180,020	930,450	799,407	26.8	47.6
49.	Grand Rapids-Wyoming-Kentwood, MI	1,162,950	993,670	930,670	17.0	25.0
50.	Buffalo-Cheektowaga, NY	1,155,604	1,135,509	1,170,111	1.8	–1.2
51.	Hartford-West Hartford-East Hartford, CT	1,151,543	1,212,381	1,148,618	–5.0	0.3
52.	Tucson, AZ	1,063,162	980,263	843,746	8.5	26.0
53.	Rochester, NY	1,052,087	1,079,671	1,062,452	–2.6	–1.0
54.	Tulsa, OK	1,044,757	937,478	859,532	11.4	21.5

Population by Urban and Rural Residency, 1790-2020

Source: Decennial Censuses, U.S. Census Bureau, U.S. Dept. of Commerce

For the 2020 decennial census, the Census Bureau defined an area as urban if it had 5,000 or more people or at least 2,000 housing units. For the 1990-2010 decennial censuses, an area was considered urban if it had 2,500 or more people, at least 1,500 of whom did not reside in institutional group quarters (e.g., a correctional facility). All other areas were rural. Prior to 1950, the definition of urban was limited to incorporated places and other areas meeting certain criteria.

Year	Total U.S. pop.	No. of places of 2,500 or more	% of total pop. Urban	Rural
Pre-1950 urban definition				
1790	3,929,214	24	5.1%	94.9%
1800	5,308,483	33	6.1	93.9
1810	7,239,881	46	7.3	92.7
1820	9,638,453	61	7.2	92.8
1830	12,860,702	90	8.8	91.2
1840	17,063,353	131	10.8	89.2
1850	23,191,876	237	15.4	84.6
1860	31,443,321	392	19.8	80.2
1870	38,558,371	663	25.7	74.3
1880	50,189,209	939	28.2	71.8
1890	62,979,766	1,348	35.1	64.9
1900	76,212,168	1,740	39.6	60.4
1910	92,228,496	2,266	45.6	54.4
1920	106,021,537	2,725	51.2	48.8
1930	123,202,624	3,183	56.1	43.9
1940	132,164,569	3,485	56.5%	43.5%
1950	151,325,798	4,077	59.6	40.4
1960	179,323,175	5,023	63.1	36.9
1950-90 urban definition				
1950	151,325,798	4,307	64.0	36.0
1960	179,323,175	5,445	69.9	30.1
1970	203,302,031	6,433	73.6	26.3
1980	226,542,199	7,749	73.7	26.3
1990	248,718,302	8,510	75.2	24.8
1990-2010 urban definition				
1990	248,718,302	8,510	78.0	22.0
2000	281,424,603	9,063	79.0	21.0
2010	308,746,065	9,644	80.7	19.3
2020 urban definition				
2020	331,449,281	2,611[1]	80.0	20.0

Note: Figures may not add up to 100 due to rounding. (1) No. of places of 5,000 or more.

Mobility of U.S. Population by Selected Characteristics, 2021-22

Source: Annual Social and Economic Supplement, Current Population Survey (CPS), U.S. Census Bureau, U.S. Dept. of Commerce (numbers in thousands)

	Total movers	Previous residence: Same county	Diff. county, same state	Diff. state	Abroad
Total movers	**28,179**	**15,068**	**6,857**	**4,884**	**1,369**
Age					
1 to 14 years	5,281	2,912	1,268	859	241
1 to 24 years	10,675	5,884	2,568	1,690	532
15 years and older	22,899	12,156	5,589	4,025	1,129
25 years and older	17,506	9,184	4,289	3,196	838
65 years and older	1,848	979	455	374	41
75 years and older	718	386	196	125	11
Marital status[1]					
Married, spouse present	8,346	4,069	2,088	1,742	448
Married, spouse absent, or separated	952	528	216	122	86
Widowed	687	421	161	93	12
Divorced	2,117	1,238	467	351	61
Never married	10,796	5,901	2,656	1,718	521
Educational attainment[2]					
Not a HS graduate	1,316	727	292	209	88
High school graduate	4,394	2,353	1,079	772	190
Some college/ associate's degree	4,359	2,391	1,085	717	167
Bachelor's degree	4,742	2,411	1,245	851	235
Advanced degree	2,693	1,303	587	646	157
Income[1]					
Without income	2,819	1,403	519	496	400
Under $10,000 or loss	2,634	1,261	661	485	227
$10,000-$19,999	2,579	1,465	619	400	95
$20,000-$29,999	2,687	1,573	672	381	61
$30,000-$39,999	2,453	1,356	650	370	77
$40,000-$49,999	1,949	1,056	463	385	46
$50,000-$59,999	1,711	932	468	274	37
$60,000-$74,999	1,780	915	455	382	28
$75,000-$99,999	1,646	905	399	295	47
$100,000 and over	2,641	1,290	683	558	111
Tenure					
In owner-occupied unit	11,601	5,805	3,301	2,128	367
In renter-occupied unit	16,578	9,263	3,557	2,756	1,002

Note: Total movers consist of noninstitutionalized persons ages 1 and older whose place of residence one year prior to completing the survey was different. Figures may not add up to totals due to rounding. (1) Ages 15 and older. (2) Ages 25 and older.

Mobility of U.S. Population, 1947-2022

Source: Annual Social and Economic Supplement, Current Population Survey (CPS), U.S. Census Bureau, U.S. Dept. of Commerce (numbers in thousands unless otherwise noted)

Mobility period	Total movers No.	Total movers % of pop.	Same county No.	Same county % distrib.	Diff. county, same state No.	Diff. county, same state % distrib.	Diff. state No.	Diff. state % distrib.	Abroad No.	Abroad % distrib.
1947-48	28,672	20.2%	19,202	67.0%	4,638	16.2%	4,370	15.2%	462	1.6%
1950-51	31,464	21.2	20,694	65.8	5,276	16.8	5,188	16.5	306	1.0
1955-56	34,040	21.1	22,186	65.2	5,859	17.2	5,053	14.8	942	2.8
1960-61	36,533	20.6	24,289	66.5	5,493	15.0	5,753	15.7	998	2.7
1965-66	37,586	19.8	24,165	64.3	6,275	16.7	6,263	16.7	883	2.3
1970-71	37,705	18.7	23,018	61.0	6,197	16.4	6,946	18.4	1,544	4.1
1975-76	36,793	17.7	22,399	60.9	7,106	19.3	6,140	16.7	1,148	3.1
1980-81	38,200	17.2	23,097	60.5	7,614	19.9	6,175	16.2	1,313	3.4
1985-86	43,237	18.6	26,401	61.1	8,665	20.0	6,971	16.1	1,200	2.8
1990-91	41,539	17.0	25,151	60.5	7,881	19.0	7,122	17.1	1,385	3.3
1995-96	42,537	16.3	26,696	62.8	8,009	18.8	6,471	15.2	1,361	3.2
2000-01	39,007	14.2	21,918	56.2	7,550	19.4	7,783	20.0	1,756	4.5
2005-06	39,837	13.7	24,851	62.4	8,010	20.1	5,679	14.3	1,296	3.3
2010-11	35,038	11.6	23,330	66.6	5,868	16.7	4,756	13.6	1,084	3.1
2015-16	35,138	11.2	21,588	61.4	7,501	21.3	4,768	13.6	1,281	3.6
2021-22	28,179	8.7	15,068	53.5	6,857	24.3	4,884	17.3	1,369	4.9

Note: Total movers consist of noninstitutionalized persons ages 1 and older whose place of residence one year prior to completing the survey was different. Figures may not add up to totals due to rounding. Because of changes in survey processing, numbers may not be comparable over time.

U.S. Households by Size, 1900-2020

Source: Decennial Censuses, U.S. Census Bureau, U.S. Dept. of Commerce

The household population does not include those living in group quarters (either institutionalized like a correctional facility or noninstitutionalized like a college dormitory). Data on households by size not available for 1910, 1920, or 1930; 1960 figures are based on a sample of the population. Average household size is shown above each bar.

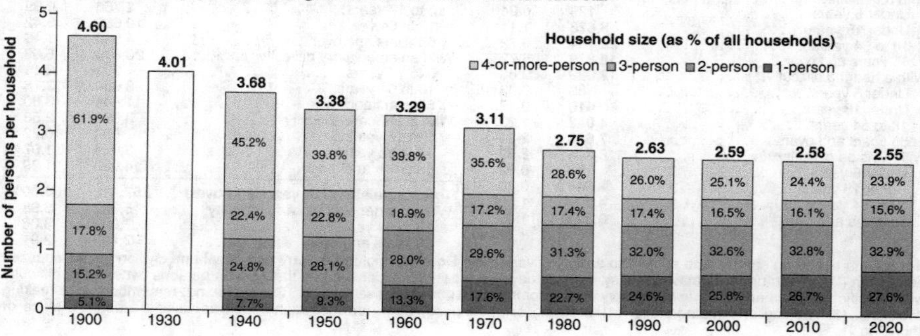

U.S. Population by Age, Sex, and Household, 2023

Source: American Community Survey (ACS), U.S. Census Bureau, U.S. Dept. of Commerce

	Number	% of tot.
Total population[1]	**334,914,896**	**100.0%**
Age		
Under 5 years	18,333,697	5.5
5 to 14 years	41,003,309	12.2
15 to 17 years	13,311,430	4.0
18 years and over	262,266,460	78.3
Male	128,493,039	38.4
Female	133,773,421	39.9
18 to 24 years	30,475,343	9.1
25 to 34 years	45,311,762	13.5
35 to 44 years	44,776,584	13.4
45 to 54 years	40,521,171	12.1
55 to 64 years	41,874,544	12.5
65 years and over	59,307,056	17.7
75 years and over	24,482,238	7.3
85 years and over	6,122,068	1.8
Median age (years)	39.2	NA

	Number	% of tot.
Sex		
Male	165,729,373	49.5%
Female	169,185,523	50.5
Total households[2]	**131,332,360**	**100.0%**
Family households	84,045,684	64.0
2-person household	37,126,085	28.3
3-person household	18,946,383	14.4
4-person household	15,705,195	12.0
5-or-more-person household	12,268,021	9.3
Married-couple family household	61,421,188	46.8
Male HH, no spouse present	6,750,842	5.1
Female HH, no spouse present	15,873,654	12.1
Average family size	3.09	NA
Nonfamily households	47,286,676	36.0
1-person household, or HH living alone	37,840,069	28.8
HH 65 years and over	15,255,393	11.6
2-person household	7,857,213	6.0
3-or-more-person household	1,589,394	1.2
Average household size	2.49	NA

NA = Not applicable. HH = Householder, or person in whose name a home is owned or rented. **Note:** Data based on sample and subject to sampling variability. (1) Includes population living in group quarters (institutional and noninstitutional, e.g., correctional facilities, university housing). (2) Number of occupied housing units, not household members. Group quarters are not considered households.

Elderly U.S. Population, 1900-2060

Source: Decennial Censuses and Population Projections Program, U.S. Census Bureau, U.S. Dept. of Commerce
(numbers of resident population in thousands)

Year	65 and over Number	65 and over % tot. pop.	85 and over Number	85 and over % tot. pop.
1900[1]	3,080	4.1%	122	0.2%
1920[1]	4,933	4.7	210	0.2
1940[1]	9,019	6.8	365	0.3
1960	16,560	9.2	929	0.5
1980	25,549	11.3	2,240	1.0
2000	34,992	12.4	4,240	1.5
2010	40,268	13.0%	5,493	1.8%
2020	55,793	16.8	6,336	1.9
2030	71,183	20.6	8,560	2.5
2040	78,294	22.0	13,676	3.8
2050	82,130	22.8	17,375	4.8
2060	88,788	24.4	17,526	4.8

Note: 1900 figures are for June 1; 1920 figures are for Jan. 1; and 1940-2020 figures are for Apr. 1. 2030-60 projections are as of July 1. (1) Excludes Alaska and Hawaii.

U.S. Population Projections by Age, 2030-70

Source: Population Projections Program, U.S. Census Bureau, U.S. Dept. of Commerce
(numbers of resident population in thousands)

Age	2030 No.	2030 % distrib.	2040 No.	2040 % distrib.	2050 No.	2050 % distrib.	2060 No.	2060 % distrib.	2070 No.	2070 % distrib.
Total	**345,074**	**100.0%**	**355,309**	**100.0%**	**360,639**	**100.0%**	**364,287**	**100.0%**	**367,913**	**100.0%**
Under 5 years	18,422	5.3	18,299	5.2	17,535	4.9	17,132	4.7	16,992	4.6
5 to 13 years	34,178	9.9	34,061	9.6	33,457	9.3	32,183	8.8	31,760	8.6
14 to 17 years	16,487	4.8	15,386	4.3	15,498	4.3	15,021	4.1	14,551	4.0
18 to 24 years	30,710	8.9	28,499	8.0	28,133	7.8	27,956	7.7	26,975	7.3
25 to 44 years	93,057	27.0	94,068	26.5	91,169	25.3	88,502	24.3	88,168	24.0
45 to 64 years	81,036	23.5	86,702	24.4	92,716	25.7	94,705	26.0	92,555	25.2
65 years and over	71,183	20.6	78,294	22.0	82,130	22.8	88,788	24.4	96,910	26.3
85 years and over	8,560	2.5	13,676	3.8	17,375	4.8	17,526	4.8	19,403	5.3
100 years and over	134	0.04	189	0.05	357	0.10	519	0.14	573	0.16

Note: Projections are as of July 1 of given year. They are based on assumptions about future births, deaths, and net international migration.

Disability Status of U.S. Population by Age, 2023

Source: American Community Survey (ACS), U.S. Census Bureau, U.S. Dept. of Commerce
(numbers in thousands, by difficulty type)

Characteristic	Number	% of pop.
Total population (all ages)	**329,988**	**100.00%**
With a disability[1]	44,741	13.56
Under 5 years	129	0.04
Under 18 years	3,678	1.11
18 to 64 years	22,184	6.72
65 years and over	18,879	5.72
With a hearing difficulty	12,089	3.66
Under 5 years	89	0.03
Under 18 years	410	0.12
18 to 64 years	4,043	1.23
65 years and over	7,636	2.31
With a vision difficulty	8,314	2.52
Under 5 years	72	0.02
Under 18 years	644	0.20
18 to 64 years	4,279	1.30
65 years and over	3,392	1.03

Characteristic	Number	% of pop.
Total population (5 years and over)	**311,655**	**100.00%**
With a cognitive difficulty[2]	17,978	5.77
5 to 17 years	2,766	0.89
18 to 64 years	10,663	3.42
65 years and over	4,548	1.46
With an ambulatory difficulty[3]	20,840	6.69
5 to 17 years	331	0.11
18 to 64 years	8,664	2.78
65 years and over	11,846	3.80
With a self-care difficulty[4]	8,028	2.58
5 to 17 years	683	0.22
18 to 64 years	3,324	1.07
65 years and over	4,020	1.29
Total population (18 years and over)	**257,416**	**100.00%**
With an independent living difficulty[5]	15,388	5.98
18 to 64 years	7,889	3.06
65 years and over	7,499	2.91

Note: Data based on sample and subject to sampling variability. Does not include military personnel and civilian institutionalized population (i.e., those under formal supervision or custody in a facility). (1) Identified by the ACS as persons "who report difficulty with specific functions and may, in the absence of accommodation, have a disability." (2) Concentrating, remembering, or making decisions. (3) Walking or climbing stairs. (4) Dressing or bathing. (5) Doing errands alone such as visiting a doctor's office or shopping.

Marital Status of the U.S. Population, 1960-2023

Source: Annual Social and Economic Supplements, Current Population Surveys (CPS), U.S. Census Bureau, U.S. Dept. of Commerce
(numbers in millions; data based on sample of occupied households in civilian noninstitutional pop.)

Marital status	Both sexes				Male				Female			
	2023	2000	1980	1960	2023	2000	1980	1960	2023	2000	1980	1960
Total	**271.3**	**213.8**	**171.9**	**124.9**	**133.1**	**103.1**	**81.9**	**60.3**	**138.2**	**110.7**	**89.9**	**64.6**
Married[1]	137.8	120.2	104.8	84.4	68.7	59.7	51.8	41.8	69.0	60.5	53.0	42.6
Never married	92.4	60.0	44.5	27.5	49.5	32.3	24.2	15.3	43.0	27.8	20.2	12.3
Divorced	26.0	19.9	9.9	2.8	11.1	8.6	3.9	1.1	14.9	11.3	6.0	1.7
Widowed	15.1	13.7	12.7	10.2	3.8	2.6	2.0	2.1	11.3	11.1	10.8	8.1
% of total or subset pops.												
Married[1]	50.8%	56.2%	61.0%	67.6%	51.6%	57.9%	63.2%	69.3%	50.0%	54.7%	58.9%	65.9%
Never married	34.1	28.1	25.9	22.0	37.2	31.3	29.6	25.3	31.1	25.1	22.5	19.0
Divorced	9.6	9.3	5.8	2.3	8.3	8.3	4.8	1.8	10.8	10.2	6.6	2.6
Widowed	5.6	6.4	7.4	8.1	2.8	2.5	2.4	3.5	8.2	10.0	12.0	12.5

Note: Total pop. for 1980 and on is persons ages 15 and older and for 1960, persons ages 14 and older. Figures may not add up to totals due to rounding. (1) Comprises subcategories Married, spouse present; Married, spouse absent; and Separated.

Household Characteristics of Couples in the U.S., 2022

Source: American Community Survey (ACS), U.S. Census Bureau, U.S. Dept. of Commerce
(as percent of all households with same relationship type, unless otherwise specified)

Household characteristics	Opposite-sex couples		Same-sex couples					
			Married			Unmarried		
	Married	Unmarried	Total couples	Male-male	Female-female	Total couples	Male-male	Female-female
Total number of households (thous.)	**60,180.0**	**8,985.0**	**740.5**	**348.3**	**392.3**	**536.7**	**259.8**	**276.9**
Age of householder								
15 to 24 years	1.2%	11.9%	2.3%	2.2%	2.4%	11.4%	7.3%	15.2%
25 to 34 years	12.3	35.0	19.1	14.9	22.8	34.1	32.2	35.9
35 to 44 years	20.3	21.0	22.9	21.0	24.5	19.7	21.8	17.8
45 to 54 years	20.1	13.7	19.2	21.1	17.5	12.4	13.6	11.3
55 to 64 years	20.5	10.4	20.7	23.5	18.1	12.7	14.9	10.6
65 years and over	25.6	7.9	15.9	17.4	14.7	9.7	10.2	9.2
Average age of householder (years)	52.9	39.8	48.6	50.3	47.1	40.9	42.7	39.3
Household income								
Less than $35,000	8.7%	13.6%	7.4%	6.1%	8.6%	11.7%	7.9%	15.2%
$35,000 to $49,999	7.2	10.2	5.1	4.3	5.9	8.8	7.6	9.9
$50,000 to $74,999	14.3	19.1	12.3	10.6	13.8	16.5	13.0	19.7
$75,000 to $99,999	14.4	16.7	13.3	11.7	14.8	16.0	14.6	17.2
$100,000 or more	55.4	40.3	61.9	67.3	57.0	47.1	56.9	37.9
Median household income (dollars)	$109,700	$84,740	$123,500	$138,700	$111,100	$94,650	$113,800	$81,050
Children in household[2]	38.1%	34.5%	18.2%	8.1%	27.1%	9.6%	2.6%	16.2%

Note: Data based on sample and subject to sampling variability. Householder is person in whose name a home is owned or rented. (1) Includes biological, step-, and adopted children and nonrelatives of the householder under 18 years.

Same-Sex Couple Households in the U.S., 2008-22

Source: American Community Survey (ACS), U.S. Census Bureau, U.S. Dept. of Commerce
(in thousands; data based on sample and subject to sampling variability)

Year	Total same-sex couples			Same-sex married couples			Same-sex unmarried partner couples		
	Total	Male-male	Female-female	Total	Male-male	Female-female	Total	Male-male	Female-female
2008	539.2	257.9	281.3	142.5	62.2	80.3	396.7	195.8	201.0
2010	593.3	287.7	305.6	152.3	68.5	83.8	441.0	219.2	221.8
2011	605.5	284.3	321.2	168.1	69.5	98.6	437.4	214.8	222.6
2012	639.4	305.8	333.6	181.9	80.7	101.2	457.5	225.1	232.5
2013	726.6	352.6	374.0	251.7	117.5	134.2	474.9	235.1	239.8
2014	783.1	377.9	405.2	334.8	163.2	171.6	448.3	214.7	233.6
2015	858.9	412.0	446.9	425.4	201.8	223.6	433.5	210.2	223.3
2016	887.5	435.9	451.6	487.0	235.2	251.8	400.5	200.7	199.8
2017	935.2	451.5	483.7	555.5	262.3	293.2	379.7	189.2	190.6
2018	995.4	485.1	510.4	592.6	285.0	307.6	402.9	200.1	202.8
2019	980.3	462.2	518.1	568.1	264.7	303.4	412.2	197.5	214.6
2021	1,209.5	577.6	631.9	711.1	336.9	374.2	498.3	240.7	257.7
2022	1,277.2	608.0	669.2	740.5	348.3	392.3	536.7	259.8	276.9

Note: 2020 estimates were not available because of the COVID-19 pandemic.

Children in the U.S. by Selected Characteristics, 2023

Source: Annual Social and Economic Supplement, Current Population Survey (CPS), U.S. Census Bureau, U.S. Dept. of Commerce
(numbers in thousands; data based on sample of occupied households in civilian noninstitutional pop.)

Characteristic	Number	% of tot.
All children	**72,296**	**100.0%**
Age of child		
Under 3 years	10,923	15.1
3-5 years	11,402	15.8
6-8 years	12,014	16.6
9-11 years	12,142	16.8
12-14 years	12,612	17.4
15-17 years	13,202	18.3
Presence of siblings		
None	15,258	21.1
One or more siblings	57,038	78.9
Race and Hispanic origin of child		
White alone	50,921	70.4

Characteristic	Number	% of tot.
White alone, non-Hispanic	35,141	48.6%
Black alone	11,227	15.5
Asian alone	4,256	5.9
Hispanic (any race)	18,781	26.0
Parents' labor force status		
Mother and father in labor force	33,233	46.0
Father in labor force, mother not in labor force	14,086	19.5
Mother in labor force, father not present	11,637	16.1
Mother not in labor force, father not present	3,450	4.8
All other combinations[1]	9,888	13.7

Note: Children are defined as all persons under 18 years of age excluding those who are a family reference person or spouse. Details may not sum to total due to rounding. (1) Incl. Father in labor force, mother not present, and No parent present or parents are same-sex, among others.

Persons Granted Lawful Permanent Resident Status by State, 2022

Source: Office of Immigration Statistics, U.S. Dept. of Homeland Security

(ranked by fiscal year 2022 number)

State/territory	Number	State/territory	Number	State/territory	Number	State/territory	Number
Total	**1,018,349**	Ohio	18,057	South Carolina	5,854	Idaho	2,050
California	182,921	Arizona	16,984	Louisiana	4,819	Puerto Rico	1,958
Florida	113,653	Michigan	16,881	Iowa	4,737	Mississippi	1,721
New York	111,309	Colorado	11,410	Oklahoma	4,631	Maine	1,363
Texas	109,720	Connecticut	11,219	Kansas	4,449	North Dakota	1,164
New Jersey	54,958	Tennessee	10,821	Nebraska	3,755	West Virginia	814
Illinois	34,551	Minnesota	9,762	Alabama	3,747	South Dakota	683
Massachusetts	32,885	Indiana	8,681	Arkansas	3,391	Alaska	673
Washington	31,835	Nevada	8,587	Rhode Island	3,381	Guam	566
Virginia	28,902	Oregon	8,143	New Mexico	3,327	Vermont	523
Pennsylvania	28,381	Missouri	7,178	Hawaii	2,706	Montana	486
Georgia	26,312	Kentucky	6,476	Dist. of Columbia	2,595	Wyoming	357
Maryland	24,233	Wisconsin	6,109	Delaware	2,385	Other[1]	1,041
North Carolina	21,868	Utah	6,053	New Hampshire	2,086	Unknown	5,198

Note: Applicants for lawful permanent resident (LPR) status, or "green cards," may already live in the U.S. They include refugees and asylees, temp. workers, foreign students, family members of U.S. citizens, and unauthorized immigrants. Applicants from outside the U.S. are granted LPR status upon entry with a visa. (1) Incl. Amer. Samoa, Northern Mariana Isls., U.S. Virgin Isls., and armed forces posts.

Persons Granted Lawful Permanent Resident Status by Top Areas of Residence, 2022

Source: Office of Immigration Statistics, U.S. Dept. of Homeland Security

(ranked by fiscal year 2022 number)

Area of residence[1]	Number	% of total	Area of residence[1]	Number	% of total
Total	**1,018,349**	**100.0%**	San Diego-Chula Vista-Carlsbad, CA	13,314	1.3%
New York-Newark-Jersey City, NY-NJ-PA	148,559	14.6	Phoenix-Mesa-Chandler, AZ	12,396	1.2
Los Angeles-Long Beach-Anaheim, CA	63,584	6.2	Tampa-Saint Petersburg-Clearwater, FL	12,271	1.2
Miami-Fort Lauderdale-Pompano Beach, FL	62,475	6.1	Detroit-Warren-Dearborn, MI	11,930	1.2
Washington-Arlington-Alexandria, DC-VA-MD-WV	39,450	3.9	Austin-Round Rock-Georgetown, TX	10,907	1.1
Houston-The Woodlands-Sugar Land, TX	38,186	3.7	Charlotte-Concord-Gastonia, NC-SC	9,500	0.9
San Francisco-Oakland-Berkeley, CA	35,369	3.5	Sacramento-Roseville-Folsom, CA	9,298	0.9
Dallas-Fort Worth-Arlington, TX	35,330	3.5	Minneapolis-Saint Paul-Bloomington, MN-WI	8,203	0.8
Chicago-Naperville-Elgin, IL-IN-WI	31,564	3.1	Baltimore-Columbia-Towson, MD	7,925	0.8
Seattle-Tacoma-Bellevue, WA	26,452	2.6	Denver-Aurora-Lakewood, CO	7,716	0.8
Boston-Cambridge-Newton, MA-NH	26,370	2.6	Las Vegas-Henderson-Paradise, NV	7,101	0.7
San Jose-Sunnyvale-Santa Clara, CA	23,062	2.3	Portland-Vancouver-Hillsboro, OR-WA	6,756	0.7
Atlanta-Sandy Springs-Alpharetta, GA	21,044	2.1	San Antonio-New Braunfels, TX	6,388	0.6
Philadelphia-Camden-Wilmington, PA-NJ-DE-MD	20,234	2.0	Columbus, OH	6,240	0.6
Orlando-Kissimmee-Sanford, FL	17,257	1.7	Nashville-Davidson–Murfreesboro–Franklin, TN	5,874	0.6
Riverside-San Bernardino-Ontario, CA	13,980	1.4	Other CBSAs	76,583	7.5
			Non-CBSA, other, and unknown	203,031	19.9

Note: Applicants for lawful permanent resident (LPR) status, or "green cards," may already live in the U.S. They include refugees and asylees, temporary workers, foreign students, family members of U.S. citizens, and unauthorized immigrants. Applicants from outside the U.S. are granted LPR status upon entry with a visa. (1) Residence by Core Based Statistical Areas, or CBSAs, which refer collectively to metropolitan and micropolitan statistical areas. These areas are defined for federal statistical use by the Office of Management and Budget with Census Bureau assistance.

Unauthorized Immigrant Population in the U.S., 1990-2021

Source: Pew Research Center

The unauthorized immigrant population had been increasing steadily since 1990 before it peaked in 2007 with the beginning of the Great Recession. Pew's 2021 estimate of the unauthorized immigrant population includes 2 mil people with temporary permission to be in the U.S. but who may be deported based on policy changes. Among that number, about 500,000 were covered by the Temporary Protected Status (TPS) program for people from countries where return would be dangerous, and more than 600,000 at year-end 2021 were Deferred Action for Childhood Arrivals (DACA) beneficiaries. Asylum applicants are also included. Estimates for 2021 do not take into account increased apprehensions and expulsions beginning that Mar.

(ranked by 2021 est. population; numbers in thousands)

Country of Birth

Country	Est. population 2021	2007	1990	% change, 2007-21
Total	**10,500**	**12,200**	**3,500**	**–13.9%**
Mexico	4,050	6,950	2,050	–41.7
El Salvador	800	600	300	33.3
India	725	325	30	123.1
Guatemala	700	400	120	75.0
Honduras	525	300	40	75.0
China	375	325	80	15.4
Dominican Republic	230	200	50	15.0
Brazil	200	180	20	11.1
Venezuela	190	55	10	245.5
Colombia	140	180	50	–22.2
All other countries	2,565	2,685	750	–4.5

State of Residence

State	Est. population 2021	2007	1990	% change, 2007-21
Total	**10,500**	**12,200**	**3,500**	**–13.9%**
California	1,850	2,800	1,450	–33.9
Texas	1,600	1,550	450	3.2
Florida	900	1,050	240	–14.3
New York	600	1,000	350	–40.0
New Jersey	450	550	95	–18.2
Illinois	400	550	200	–27.3
Georgia	350	425	35	–17.6
North Carolina	325	325	25	0.0
Massachusetts	300	220	55	36.4
Washington	300	250	40	20.0
All other states	3,425	3,480	560	–1.6

Note: Unauthorized immigrant pop. ests. are made using the residual method. The estimated number of immigrants residing legally in the U.S. is subtracted from the total immigrant pop. Details may not sum to totals because of rounding. Because of changes in methodology and source, ests. for 1990 may not be directly comparable over time.

Active U.S. DACA Population by Birth Country, 2024

Source: U.S. Citizenship and Immigration Services, U.S. Dept. of Homeland Security

The Deferred Action for Childhood Arrivals (DACA) program grants (1) temporary protection from deportation and (2) permission to legally work to undocumented individuals living in the U.S. who were brought to the country as children. While a 2021 federal injunction prevents DHS from processing first-time DACA applications, active DACA recipients can apply for renewal of their status.

(number of active DACA recipients as of Mar. 31, 2024, ranked by country of birth)

Country of birth	Number	Country of birth	Number	Country of birth	Number
Total	**528,300**	Brazil	3,900	Venezuela	1,610
Mexico	428,340	Ecuador	3,630	Dominican Republic	1,440
El Salvador	20,770	Colombia	3,080	Uruguay	1,320
Guatemala	13,970	Argentina	2,560	Bolivia	1,110
Honduras	12,680	Philippines	2,540	Trinidad and Tobago	1,110
Peru	4,850	Jamaica	1,730	Nicaragua	1,030
South Korea	4,730	India	1,660	Costa Rica	1,010

Note: Numbers are approximate and rounded and may not add up to total. Countries with fewer than 1,000 active DACA recipients are not shown here. Does not include individuals who have obtained lawful permanent resident status or U.S. citizenship.

Refugee Arrivals in the U.S. by Region and Nationality, 2001-23

Source: Refugee Processing Center, Bureau of Population, Refugees, and Migration, U.S. Dept. of State

Under the Refugee Act of 1980, the president in consultation with Congress establishes a refugee admissions ceiling and regional allocations before each fiscal year (Oct. 1-Sept. 30). Applicants for refugee status are outside of the U.S. whereas applicants seeking asylum are in the U.S. or at a U.S. port of entry.

(countries ranked by nationality of most refugee arrivals in fiscal year 2023)

Region/country of nationality	2023	2021	2019	2017	2015	2013	2010	2007	2004	2001
Total ceiling	**125,000**	**62,500**	**30,000**	**110,000**	**70,000**	**70,000**	**80,000**	**70,000**	**70,000**	**80,000**
Total refugee arrivals	**60,014**	**11,411**	**30,000**	**53,716**	**69,933**	**69,926**	**73,311**	**48,282**	**52,873**	**69,886**
COUNTRY										
Congo, Dem. Rep. of the	18,145	4,891	12,958	9,377	7,876	2,563	3,174	848	569	264
Syria	10,781	1,246	563	6,557	1,682	36	25	17	0	8
Afghanistan	6,594	872	1,198	1,311	910	661	515	441	959	2,930
Myanmar (Burma)	6,185	772	4,932	5,078	18,386	16,299	16,693	13,896	1,056	544
Guatemala	1,748	64	118	50	0	0	0	0	0	0
Sudan	1,635	513	382	980	1,578	2,160	558	705	3,500	5,944
Venezuela	1,442	3	0	0	0	3	3	0	0	0
Somalia	1,385	174	231	6,130	8,858	7,608	4,884	6,969	13,331	4,946
Ukraine	1,337	803	4,451	4,264	1,451	227	449	1,605	3,482	7,313
Iraq	1,235	497	465	6,886	12,676	19,488	18,016	1,608	66	2,465
Colombia	1,165	48	298	233	521	230	123	54	577	0
El Salvador	1,056	200	311	1,124	0	0	0	0	0	0
Eritrea	973	184	1,757	1,917	1,596	1,824	2,570	963	128	114
Iran	743	184	199	2,577	3,109	2,578	3,543	5,482	1,786	6,461
Central African Republic	634	22	244	275	270	318	45	15	24	1
Honduras	598	83	74	104	0	0	20	0	0	0
South Sudan	592	93	42	176	79	17	—	—	—	—
Pakistan	492	131	264	346	159	158	59	30	11	3
Moldova	489	78	120	301	333	119	356	565	1,711	1,199
Ethiopia	441	72	247	766	626	765	668	1,028	2,689	1,457
All other countries	2,344	481	1,146	5,264	9,823	14,872	21,610	14,056	22,984	36,237
REGION										
Africa	24,481	6,219	16,366	20,232	22,472	15,980	13,305	17,483	29,104	19,020
East Asia	6,262	776	5,030	5,173	18,469	16,537	17,716	15,643	8,084	4,163
Europe/Central Asia[1]	2,765	983	4,994	5,205	2,363	580	1,526	4,560	9,254	15,794
Latin America/Caribbean	6,312	400	809	1,688	2,050	4,439	4,982	2,976	3,577	2,975
Near East/South Asia	20,194	3,033	2,801	21,418	24,579	32,390	35,782	7,620	2,854	11,956

— = Not applicable. **Note:** Includes Amerasian immigrants (children born in Cambodia, Korea, Laos, Thailand, or Vietnam in 1950-82 and fathered by a U.S. citizen). (1) 2001 total includes 15,978 refugee arrivals from former Soviet Union countries.

Persons Granted Asylum and Refugee Arrivals in the U.S., 1980-2022

Source: U.S. Dept. of Homeland Security; U.S. Dept. of Justice; Refugee Processing Ctr., Bureau of Population, Refugees, and Migration, U.S. Dept. of State

Individuals apply for asylum from within the U.S. or at a U.S. port of entry. Applicants for refugee status are outside of the U.S.

Year	Number granted asylum	Number of refugee arrivals[1]	Year	Number granted asylum	Number of refugee arrivals[1]	Year	Number granted asylum	Number of refugee arrivals[1]
1980	—	207,116	1995	20,703	98,973	2009	22,303	74,602
1981	—	159,252	1996	23,532	75,421	2010	19,777	73,293
1982	—	98,096	1997	22,939	69,653	2011	23,631	56,384
1984	—	70,393	1998	20,507	76,712	2012	27,446	58,179
1985	—	67,704	1999	26,571	85,285	2013	24,657	69,909
1986	—	62,146	2000	32,514	72,165	2014	23,061	69,975
1987	—	64,528	2001	39,148	68,920	2015	25,947	69,920
1988	—	76,483	2002	36,937	26,785	2016	20,313	84,989
1989	—	107,070	2003	28,743	28,286	2017	26,380	53,691
1990	8,472	122,066	2004	27,376	52,840	2018	37,740	22,405
1991	5,035	113,389	2005	25,304	53,738	2019	45,888	29,916
1992	6,307	115,548	2006	26,352	41,094	2020	30,964	11,840
1993	9,543	114,181	2007	25,318	48,218	2021	17,692	11,454
1994	13,828	111,680	2008	23,022	60,107	2022	—	25,465

— = Not available. Fiscal year (Oct. 1-Sept. 30) data. (1) Excludes Amerasians (children born in Cambodia, Korea, Laos, Thailand, or Vietnam after Dec. 31, 1950, and before Oct. 22, 1982, and fathered by a U.S. citizen) except in FY 1989-91. Figures based on refugee arrival date.

U.S. Foreign-Born Population

Source: Decennial Censuses and Annual Social and Economic Supplements, Current Population Surveys (CPS), U.S. Census Bureau, U.S. Dept. of Commerce

Foreign-Born as a Percentage of U.S. Population, 1900-2023

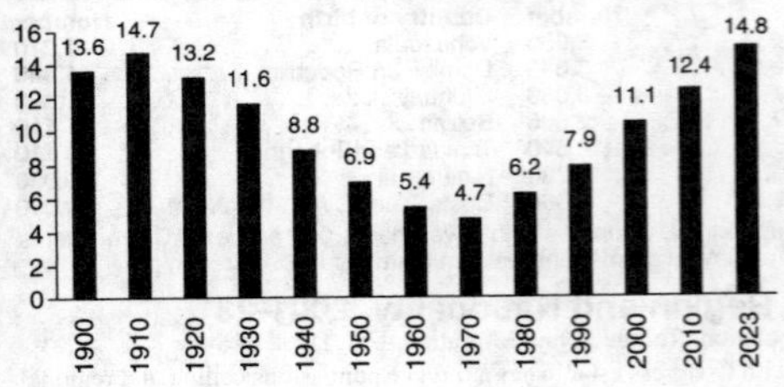

Foreign-Born Population by Region of Birth, 1995-2023

(numbers in thousands)

Region	2023[1] No.	2023[1] %	2000	1995
Asia	14,734	30.2%	7,916	6,121
Under 18	807	28.6	696	767
Europe	4,374	9.0	4,382	3,937
Under 18	208	7.4	247	232
Latin America	25,746	52.8	15,323	11,777
Under 18	1,461	51.8	1,786	1,451
Other[2]	3,924	8.0	2,364	2,658
Under 18	344	12.2	249	275
All regions	**48,778**	**100.0**	**29,985**	**24,493**
Under 18	**2,819**	**100.0**	**2,977**	**2,726**

(1) Percentages are of total foreign-born pop. or total foreign-born pop. under age 18. (2) Incl. those born at sea.

U.S. Foreign-Born Population: Top Countries of Origin, 1880-2023

Source: Decennial Censuses and American Community Survey (ACS), U.S. Census Bureau, U.S. Dept. of Commerce

(numbers in thousands; percentage is of all foreign-born excluding population born at sea)

1880 Country	No.	%	1920 Country	No.	%	1960 Country	No.	%	2000 Country	No.	%	2023[1] Country	No.	%
Germany	1,967	29.4	Germany	1,686	12.1	Italy	1,257	12.9	Mexico	9,177	29.5	Mexico	10,918	22.8
Ireland	1,855	27.8	Italy	1,610	11.6	Germany	990	10.2	China[3]	1,519	4.9	India	2,910	6.1
UK	918	13.7	USSR	1,400	10.1	Canada	953	9.8	Philippines	1,369	4.4	China[5]	2,436	5.1
Canada	717	10.7	Poland	1,140	8.2	UK	765	7.9	India	1,023	3.3	Philippines	2,052	4.3
Sweden	194	2.9	Canada	1,138	8.2	Poland	748	7.7	Vietnam	988	3.2	El Salvador	1,495	3.1
Norway	182	2.7	UK	1,135	8.2	USSR	691	7.1	Cuba	873	2.8	Cuba	1,451	3.0
France	107	1.6	Ireland	1,037	7.5	Mexico	576	5.9	Korea[4]	864	2.8	Vietnam	1,366	2.9
China[2]	104	1.6	Sweden	626	4.5	Ireland	339	3.5	Canada	821	2.6	Dominican Republic	1,265	2.6
Switzerland	89	1.3	Austria	576	4.1	Austria	305	3.1	El Salvador	817	2.6	Guatemala	1,250	2.6
Czech.	85	1.3	Mexico	486	3.5	Hungary	245	2.5	Germany	707	2.3	Colombia	1,050	2.2
Total	**6,680**	**100.0**	**Total**	**13,921**	**100.0**	**Total**	**9,738**	**100.0**	**Total**	**31,108**	**100.0**	**Total**	**47,831**	**100.0**

(1) Data based on sample and subject to sampling variability. The Census Bureau collects data from residents regardless of immigration status, so the foreign-born population implicitly includes unauthorized migrants. (2) Incl. Taiwan. (3) Incl. Hong Kong and Taiwan. (4) North and South Korea. (5) Incl. Hong Kong

Language Spoken at Home by the U.S. Population, 2023

Source: American Community Survey (ACS), U.S. Census Bureau, U.S. Dept. of Commerce

(number of speakers 5 years of age and over by language or language group most often used)

Language	Number (thous.)	% of tot. pop.	% English inability[1]
Total population	**316,581**	**100.00%**	**8.7%**
Speak only English	**245,472**	**77.54**	**NA**
Speak another language	**71,109**	**22.46**	**38.8**
Spanish	43,370	13.70	40.6
Other Indo-European languages			
Armenian	245	0.08	41.5
Bengali	453	0.14	41.1
French (incl. Cajun)	1,195	0.38	21.1
German	859	0.27	14.4
Greek	252	0.08	20.9
Gujarati	473	0.15	32.6
Haitian	973	0.31	41.7
Hindi	948	0.30	16.6
Italian	505	0.16	24.5
Malayalam, Kannada, other Dravidian langs.	314	0.10	21.2
Nepali, Marathi, other Indic langs.	476	0.15	32.7
Persian (incl. Farsi, Dari)	563	0.18	37.2
Polish	499	0.16	35.6
Portuguese	1,091	0.34	36.2
Punjabi	337	0.11	35.9
Russian	998	0.32	43.7
Serbo-Croatian	249	0.08	31.8
Tamil	357	0.11	15.8
Telugu	515	0.16	17.9
Ukrainian, other Slavic langs.	485	0.15	42.9
Urdu	564	0.18	27.5
Yiddish, Penn. Dutch, other West Germanic langs.	614	0.19	31.9%
Other Indo-European langs.	633	0.20	29.7
Asian and Pacific Island languages			
Chinese (incl. Mandarin, Cantonese)	3,531	1.12	51.5
Hmong	228	0.07	42.3
Ilocano, Samoan, Hawaiian, other Austronesian langs.	500	0.16	34.6
Japanese	459	0.15	38.1
Khmer	195	0.06	52.5
Korean	1,079	0.34	51.6
Tagalog (incl. Filipino)	1,803	0.57	30.2
Thai, Lao, other Tai-Kadai langs.	294	0.09	50.5
Vietnamese	1,571	0.50	57.3
Other langs. of Asia	499	0.16	47.5
All other languages			
Amharic, Somali, other Afro-Asiatic	612	0.19	38.7
Arabic	1,423	0.45	34.0
Hebrew	236	0.07	12.7
Navajo	139	0.04	27.4
Swahili, other langs. of Central/Eastern/Southern Africa	360	0.11	31.3
Yoruba, Twi, Igbo, other langs. of Western Africa	722	0.23	19.4
Other Native langs. of North America	162	0.05	14.6
Other and unspecified	328	0.10	30.0

NA = Not applicable. **Note:** Data based on sample and subject to sampling variability. (1) Percent of respondents who speak the language at left who indicated that they spoke English less than "very well." For example, 41.5% of respondents who use Armenian at home do not speak English very well.

U.S. Population by Ancestry Reported, 2023

Source: American Community Survey (ACS), U.S. Census Bureau, U.S. Dept. of Commerce
(numbers in thousands; ranked by number)

Ancestry	Number	% of total	Ancestry	Number	% of total	Ancestry	Number	% of total
Total population	**334,915**	**100.0%**	Subsaharan African[1]	4,179	1.2%	Welsh	1,530	0.5%
German	40,502	12.1	Norwegian	3,888	1.2	Portuguese	1,360	0.4
English	30,895	9.2	Swedish	3,254	1.0	Ukrainian	1,259	0.4
Irish	30,467	9.1	West Indian (excl. Hispanic groups)[2]	3,217	1.0	British	1,247	0.4
American	18,027	5.4	Dutch	3,030	0.9	Hungarian	1,220	0.4
Italian	16,110	4.8	Scotch-Irish	2,489	0.7	Greek	1,208	0.4
Polish	8,244	2.5	Arab[3]	2,224	0.7	Other ancestry not shown here	125,861	37.6
French (excl. Basque)	6,166	1.8	Russian	2,052	0.6	Unclassified or not reported	83,150	24.8
Scottish	5,454	1.6	French Canadian	1,590	0.5			
European	4,974	1.5						

Note: Data based on sample and subject to sampling variability. Because respondents could self-identify with more than one ancestry, numbers do not add up to total. (1) Incl. Cabo Verdean, Ethiopian, Ghanian, Kenyan, Liberian, Nigerian, Senegalese, Sierra Leonean, Somali, South African, Sudanese, Ugandan, Zimbabwean, African, and other Subsaharan African. (2) Incl. Bahamian, Barbadian, Belizean, Bermudan, British or Dutch West Indian, Haitian, Jamaican, Trinidadian and Tobagonian, U.S. Virgin Islander, West Indian, and other West Indian. (3) Incl. Egyptian, Iraqi, Jordanian, Lebanese, Moroccan, Palestinian, Syrian, Arab, and other Arab.

U.S. Population by Race, Hispanic Origin, and Age, 2023

Source: American Community Survey (ACS), U.S. Census Bureau, U.S. Dept. of Commerce

Race and origin/age	Number	% of group	Race and origin/age	Number	% of group
White (not Hispanic or Latino)	**191,347,640**	**100.0%**	**Native Hawaiian and other Pacific Islander**	**662,417**	**100.0%**
Under 5 years	8,407,297	4.4	Under 5 years	42,933	6.5
Under 18 years	34,125,799	17.8	Under 18 years	163,205	24.6
18 to 64 years	113,700,098	59.4	18 to 64 years	433,551	65.4
65 years and over	43,521,743	22.7	65 years and over	65,661	9.9
85 years and over	4,688,711	2.5	85 years and over	5,997	0.9
Black or African American	**40,619,972**	**100.0**	**Some other race**	**24,848,381**	**100.0**
Under 5 years	2,406,415	5.9	Under 5 years	1,638,124	6.6
Under 18 years	9,592,699	23.6	Under 18 years	6,721,647	27.1
18 to 64 years	25,463,590	62.7	18 to 64 years	16,098,831	64.8
65 years and over	5,563,683	13.7	65 years and over	2,027,903	8.2
85 years and over	475,504	1.2	85 years and over	170,621	0.7
American Indian and Alaska Native	**3,341,333**	**100.0**	**Two or more races**	**42,738,818**	**100.0**
Under 5 years	195,267	5.8	Under 5 years	3,735,779	8.7
Under 18 years	847,765	25.4	Under 18 years	13,839,266	32.4
18 to 64 years	2,162,805	64.7	18 to 64 years	24,938,830	58.4
65 years and over	330,763	9.9	65 years and over	3,960,722	9.3
85 years and over	25,521	0.8	85 years and over	363,186	0.8
Asian	**20,052,323**	**100.0**	**Hispanic or Latino (any race)**	**65,140,277**	**100.0**
Under 5 years	906,172	4.5	Under 5 years	4,943,402	7.6
Under 18 years	3,750,949	18.7	Under 18 years	19,095,194	29.3
18 to 64 years	13,371,633	66.7	18 to 64 years	40,451,307	62.1
65 years and over	2,929,741	14.6	65 years and over	5,593,776	8.6
85 years and over	292,287	1.5	85 years and over	530,458	0.8

Note: Data based on sample and subject to sampling variability. Categories are for one race alone, not in combination with any other race, unless otherwise noted.

Educational Attainment of the U.S. Population, 2023

Source: American Community Survey (ACS), U.S. Census Bureau, U.S. Dept. of Commerce
(numbers in thousands; population 25 years of age and over)

Race and origin/highest ed. completed	Number	% of group	Race and origin/highest ed. completed	Number	% of group
White (not Hispanic or Latino)	**141,784**	**100.0%**	**Native Hawaiian and other Pacific Islander**	**424**	**100.0%**
Less than HS diploma	7,909	5.6	Less than HS diploma	50	11.8
HS diploma or equiv. credential	36,453	25.7	HS diploma or equiv. credential	153	36.1
Some college or associate's degree	40,644	28.7	Some college or associate's degree	140	33.0
Bachelor's degree or higher	56,779	40.0	Bachelor's degree or higher	81	19.1
Black or African American	**27,004**	**100.0**	**Some other race**	**15,329**	**100.0**
Less than HS diploma	3,047	11.3	Less than HS diploma	4,843	31.6
HS diploma or equiv. credential	8,332	30.9	HS diploma or equiv. credential	4,566	29.8
Some college or associate's degree	8,536	31.6	Some college or associate's degree	3,373	22.0
Bachelor's degree or higher	7,088	26.2	Bachelor's degree or higher	2,548	16.6
American Indian and Alaska Native	**2,113**	**100.0**	**Two or more races**	**24,343**	**100.0**
Less than HS diploma	465	22.0	Less than HS diploma	4,524	18.6
HS diploma or equiv. credential	656	31.0	HS diploma or equiv. credential	6,241	25.6
Some college or associate's degree	636	30.1	Some college or associate's degree	6,610	27.2
Bachelor's degree or higher	356	16.8	Bachelor's degree or higher	6,968	28.6
Asian	**14,558**	**100.0**	**Hispanic or Latino (any race)**	**38,596**	**100.0**
Less than HS diploma	1,683	11.6	Less than HS diploma	10,255	26.6
HS diploma or equiv. credential	2,006	13.8	HS diploma or equiv. credential	10,867	28.2
Some college or associate's degree	2,452	16.8	Some college or associate's degree	9,450	24.5
Bachelor's degree or higher	8,417	57.8	Bachelor's degree or higher	8,024	20.8

HS = High school. **Note:** Data based on sample and subject to sampling variability. Categories are for one race alone, not in combination with any other race, unless otherwise noted.

Populations for U.S. Places of 10,000 or More Residents

Source: Decennial Census and Pop. Ests. Program, U.S. Census Bureau, U.S. Dept. of Commerce; NANPA—Somos; www.usps.com

The following is a list of places of 10,000 or more residents according to the Census Bureau's 2023 population estimates, along with each place's 2010 and 2020 census results. Included are **places incorporated** under state law as cities, towns, villages, or boroughs, and **Census designated places (CDPs)**, marked with a (c). The Census Bureau delineates CDPs as statistical counterparts to incorporated places but does not typically include CDPs in its estimates program. This list also includes, in italics, **minor civil divisions (MCDs)** in Connecticut, Maine, Massachusetts, New Hampshire, Rhode Island, and Vermont. MCDs, which are also not incorporated, are often the primary political or administrative divisions of a county. (Balance) indicates the given population is for a consolidated area minus the residents of any separately incorporated places within its boundaries. **Townships are not included.**

An asterisk (*) denotes a **ZIP code** for general delivery; mail routes and/or P.O. boxes within the place may use a different one. More than one area code can serve a geographic area; overlay area codes are separated by slashes. A date within parentheses indicates when a new area code is expected to be in service. Area codes based on latest information as of mid-2024. — = Not available.

Alabama

Area codes: 205/659, 251, 256/938, 334

ZIP	Place	2010 population	2020 population	2023 estimate
*35007	Alabaster	30,352	33,284	34,107
*35950	Albertville	21,160	22,386	23,031
*35010	Alexander City	14,875	14,843	14,470
*36201	Anniston	23,106	21,564	21,167
*35611	Athens	21,897	25,406	30,904
*36830	Auburn	53,380	76,143	82,025
*35020	Bessemer	27,456	26,019	25,037
*35203	Birmingham	212,237	200,733	196,644
*35956	Boaz	9,551	10,107	10,369
35040	Calera	11,620	16,494	18,189
*35215	Center Point	16,921	16,406	15,705
35043	Chelsea	10,183	14,982	16,771
*35215	Clay	9,708	10,291	10,221
*35055	Cullman	14,775	18,213	19,913
*36526	Daphne	21,570	27,462	30,321
*35601	Decatur	55,683	57,938	58,321
*36303	Dothan	65,496	71,072	71,258
*36330	Enterprise	26,562	28,711	30,271
*36027	Eufaula	13,137	12,882	12,451
*36532	Fairhope	15,326	22,477	24,974
*35630	Florence	39,319	40,184	42,437
*36535	Foley	14,618	20,335	24,873
35214	Forestdale (c)	10,162	10,409	—
*35967	Fort Payne	14,012	14,877	14,957
*35901	Gadsden	36,856	33,945	33,229
35071	Gardendale	13,893	16,044	16,096
36542	Gulf Shores	9,741	15,014	16,850
35640	Hartselle	14,255	15,455	15,875
*35080	Helena	16,793	20,914	22,117
*35209	Homewood	25,167	26,414	27,758
*35216	Hoover	81,619	92,606	92,448
*35023	Hueytown	16,105	16,776	16,202
*35801	Huntsville	180,105	215,006	225,564
35210	Irondale	12,349	13,497	13,526
36265	Jacksonville	12,548	14,385	14,682
*35501	Jasper	14,352	14,572	14,448
35094	Leeds	11,773	12,324	12,416
*35758	Madison	42,938	56,933	60,854
35111	McCalla (c)	—	12,965	—
36054	Millbrook	14,640	16,564	17,367
*36602	Mobile	195,111	187,041	182,595
*36104	Montgomery	205,764	200,603	195,287
35004	Moody	11,726	13,170	13,595
*35223	Mountain Brook	20,413	22,461	21,737
*35661	Muscle Shoals	13,146	16,275	17,210
*35476	Northport	23,330	31,125	31,111
*36801	Opelika	26,477	30,995	33,572
36203	Oxford	21,348	22,069	22,078
*36360	Ozark	14,907	14,368	14,346
35124	Pelham	21,352	24,318	25,121
*35125	Pell City	12,695	12,939	13,924
*36867	Phenix City	32,822	38,816	38,441
36064	Pike Road	5,406	9,439	11,117
*36066	Prattville	33,960	37,781	39,318
*36610	Prichard	22,659	19,322	18,816
35906	Rainbow City	9,602	10,191	10,322
*35653	Russellville	9,830	10,855	10,722
36571	Saraland	13,405	16,171	16,435
*35768	Scottsboro	14,770	15,578	15,863
*36701	Selma	20,756	17,971	16,666
*36527	Spanish Fort	6,798	10,049	10,923
*35150	Sylacauga	12,749	12,578	12,216
*35160	Talladega	15,676	15,861	14,768
36619	Tillman's Corner (c)	17,398	17,731	—
*36081	Troy	18,033	17,727	17,836
35173	Trussville	19,933	26,123	26,770
*35401	Tuscaloosa	90,468	99,600	111,338
*36854	Valley	9,524	10,529	10,308
*35216	Vestavia Hills	34,033	39,102	38,020

Alaska

Area code: 907 applies to the entire state

ZIP	Place	2010 population	2020 population	2023 estimate
*99501	Anchorage	291,826	291,247	286,075
99711	Badger (c)	19,482	19,031	—
*99708	College (c)	12,964	11,332	—
*99701	Fairbanks	31,535	32,515	31,856
*99801	Juneau	31,275	32,255	31,555
99654	Knik-Fairview (c)	14,923	19,297	—

Arizona

Area codes: 480, 520, 602, 623, 928

ZIP	Place	2010 population	2020 population	2023 estimate
85086	Anthem (c)	21,700	23,190	—
*85119	Apache Junction	35,840	38,499	41,153
*85323	Avondale	76,238	89,334	93,545
*85326	Buckeye	50,876	91,502	108,909
*86442	Bullhead City	39,540	41,348	43,302
86322	Camp Verde	10,873	12,147	12,489
*85122	Casa Grande	48,571	53,658	63,743
85740	Casas Adobes (c)	66,795	70,973	—
85718	Catalina Foothills (c)	50,796	52,401	—
*85225	Chandler	236,123	275,987	280,167
86323	Chino Valley	10,817	13,020	13,815
85128	Coolidge	11,825	13,218	18,293
86326	Cottonwood	11,265	12,029	13,124
*85607	Douglas	17,378	16,534	15,638
*85746	Drexel Heights (c)	27,749	27,523	—
85335	El Mirage	31,797	35,805	35,850
85131	Eloy	16,631	15,635	18,528
*86001	Flagstaff	65,870	76,831	76,586
85132	Florence	25,536	26,785	24,291
85705	Flowing Wells (c)	16,419	15,657	—
*86426	Fort Mohave (c)	14,364	16,190	—
85367	Fortuna Foothills (c)	26,265	27,776	—
*85268	Fountain Hills	22,489	23,820	23,611
*85234	Gilbert	208,453	267,918	275,411
*85301	Glendale	226,721	248,325	253,855
85118	Gold Canyon (c)	10,159	11,404	—
*85338	Goodyear	65,275	95,294	111,805
*85622	Green Valley (c)	21,391	22,616	—
*86401	Kingman	28,068	32,689	35,334
*86403	Lake Havasu City	52,527	57,144	59,257
*85653	Marana	34,961	51,908	58,430
*85138	Maricopa	43,482	58,125	71,022
*85201	Mesa	439,041	504,258	511,648
86401	New Kingman-Butler (c)	12,134	12,907	—
85087	New River (c)	14,952	17,290	—
*85621	Nogales	20,837	19,770	19,702
*85737	Oro Valley	41,011	47,070	48,311
85253	Paradise Valley	12,820	12,658	12,502
*85541	Payson	15,301	16,351	16,731
*85345	Peoria	154,065	190,985	198,750
*85003	Phoenix	1,445,632	1,608,139	1,650,070
*86301	Prescott	39,843	45,827	47,757
*86314	Prescott Valley	38,822	46,785	50,045
*85142	Queen Creek	26,361	59,519	76,570
85648	Rio Rico (c)	18,962	20,549	—
85739	Saddlebrooke (c)	9,614	12,574	—
*85546	Safford	9,566	10,129	10,270
85629	Sahuarita	25,259	34,134	36,356
85349	San Luis	25,505	35,257	37,966
*85142	San Tan Valley (c)	81,321	99,894	—
*85251	Scottsdale	217,385	241,361	244,394
*85901	Show Low	10,660	11,732	12,192
*85635	Sierra Vista	43,888	45,308	44,431
*85615	Sierra Vista Southeast (c)	14,797	14,428	—
85350	Somerton	14,287	14,197	14,594
*85351	Sun City (c)	37,499	39,931	—
*85375	Sun City West (c)	24,535	25,806	—

ZIP	Place	2010 population	2020 population	2023 estimate
85248	Sun Lakes (c)	13,975	14,868	—
*85374	Surprise	117,517	143,148	158,285
85749	Tanque Verde (c)	16,901	16,250	—
*85281	Tempe	161,719	180,587	189,834
*85701	Tucson	520,116	542,629	547,239
85735	Tucson Estates (c)	12,192	12,069	—
*85743	Tucson Mountains (c)	—	10,862	—
85641	Vail (c)	10,208	13,604	—
85757	Valencia West (c)	9,355	14,101	—
86326	Verde Village (c)	11,605	12,019	—
*85364	Yuma	93,064	95,548	100,858

Arkansas

Area codes: 327/870, 479, 501

ZIP	Place	2010 population	2020 population	2023 estimate
*71923	Arkadelphia	10,714	10,380	10,255
*72501	Batesville	10,248	11,191	11,515
*72714	Bella Vista	26,461	30,104	32,368
*72015	Benton	30,681	35,014	37,558
*72712	Bentonville	35,301	54,164	59,471
*72315	Blytheville	15,620	13,406	12,594
*72022	Bryant	16,688	20,663	21,877
72023	Cabot	23,776	26,569	27,190
*71701	Camden	12,183	10,612	10,165
72719	Centerton	9,515	17,792	23,953
*72032	Conway	58,908	64,134	69,580
*71730	El Dorado	18,884	17,756	16,869
*72701	Fayetteville	73,580	93,949	101,680
*72335	Forrest City	15,371	13,015	12,490
*72901	Fort Smith	86,209	89,142	89,770
*72601	Harrison	12,943	13,069	13,409
*71901	Hot Springs	35,193	37,930	37,994
*71909	Hot Springs Village (c)	12,807	15,861	—
*72076	Jacksonville	28,364	29,477	29,094
*72401	Jonesboro	67,263	78,576	80,650
*72201	Little Rock	193,524	202,591	203,842
72745	Lowell	7,327	9,839	11,466
*71753	Magnolia	11,577	11,162	10,769
72104	Malvern	10,318	10,867	11,080
72364	Marion	12,345	13,752	13,654
72113	Maumelle	17,163	19,251	19,452
*72653	Mountain Home	12,448	12,825	13,278
*72113	North Little Rock	62,304	64,591	64,531
*72450	Paragould	26,113	29,537	30,520
*71601	Pine Bluff	49,083	41,253	39,123
*72756	Rogers	55,964	69,908	74,035
*72801	Russellville	27,920	28,940	29,338
*72143	Searcy	22,858	22,937	23,813
*72120	Sherwood	29,523	32,731	33,118
72761	Siloam Springs	15,039	17,287	19,336
*72764	Springdale	69,797	84,161	88,224
71854	Texarkana	29,919	29,387	29,223
*72956	Van Buren	22,791	23,218	24,138
*72301	West Memphis	26,245	24,520	23,825

California

Area codes: 209/350, 213/323/738, 279/916, 310/424, 341/510, 369/707, 408/669, 415/628, 442/760, 530/837 (Jan. 31, 2025), 357 (Mar. 26, 2025)/559, 562, 619, 626, 650, 657/714, 661, 747/818, 805/820, 831, 840/909, 858, 949, 951

ZIP	Place	2010 population	2020 population	2023 estimate
92301	Adelanto	31,765	38,046	38,187
*91301	Agoura Hills	20,330	20,299	19,474
*94501	Alameda	73,812	78,280	75,353
94507	Alamo (c)	14,570	15,314	—
*94706	Albany	18,539	20,271	19,097
*91801	Alhambra	83,089	82,868	79,776
*92656	Aliso Viejo	47,823	52,176	50,263
*91901	Alpine (c)	14,236	14,696	—
*91001	Altadena (c)	42,777	42,846	—
95127	Alum Rock (c)	15,536	12,042	—
*94503	American Canyon	19,454	21,837	21,347
*92805	Anaheim	336,265	346,824	340,512
96007	Anderson	9,932	11,323	11,210
95843	Antelope (c)	45,770	48,733	—
*94509	Antioch	102,372	115,291	117,096
*92307	Apple Valley	69,135	75,791	75,036
*91006	Arcadia	56,364	56,681	54,157
*95521	Arcata	17,231	18,857	19,012
*95825	Arden-Arcade (c)	92,186	94,659	—
*93420	Arroyo Grande	17,252	18,441	18,243
*90701	Artesia	16,522	16,395	15,597
93203	Arvin	19,304	19,495	19,364
94541	Ashland (c)	21,925	23,823	—
*93422	Atascadero	28,310	29,773	29,700
95301	Atwater	28,168	31,970	32,052
*95603	Auburn	13,330	13,776	13,658
93204	Avenal	15,505	13,696	14,075
*90601	Avocado Heights (c)	15,411	13,317	—
91702	Azusa	46,361	50,000	48,272
*93301	Bakersfield	347,483	403,455	413,381
91706	Baldwin Park	75,390	72,176	68,806
92220	Banning	29,603	29,505	31,680
*92310	Barstow	22,639	25,415	24,964
94565	Bay Point (c)	21,349	23,896	—
92223	Beaumont	36,877	53,036	58,463
*90201	Bell	35,477	33,559	31,864
*90201	Bell Gardens	42,072	39,501	37,467
*90706	Bellflower	76,616	79,190	75,122
94002	Belmont	25,835	28,335	26,622
94510	Benicia	26,997	27,131	26,429
*94704	Berkeley	112,580	124,321	118,962
*90210	Beverly Hills	34,109	32,701	30,974
*92314	Big Bear City (c)	12,304	12,738	—
92316	Bloomington (c)	23,851	24,339	—
*92225	Blythe	20,817	18,317	18,045
*91902	Bonita (c)	12,538	12,917	—
92021	Bostonia (c)	15,379	16,882	—
92227	Brawley	24,953	26,416	27,849
*92821	Brea	39,282	47,325	48,479
94513	Brentwood	51,481	64,292	65,126
*90620	Buena Park	80,530	84,034	81,958
*91502	Burbank	103,340	107,337	102,755
*94010	Burlingame	28,806	31,386	29,910
*91301	Calabasas	23,058	23,241	22,227
*92231	Calexico	38,572	38,633	38,224
*93505	California City	14,120	14,973	13,802
92320	Calimesa	7,879	10,026	11,165
*93010	Camarillo	65,201	70,741	69,514
95682	Cameron Park (c)	18,228	18,881	—
*92058	Camp Pendleton South (c)	10,616	12,468	—
*95008	Campbell	39,349	43,959	41,700
92587	Canyon Lake	10,561	11,082	11,096
*92008	Carlsbad	105,328	114,746	113,495
*95608	Carmichael (c)	61,762	79,793	—
*93013	Carpinteria	13,040	13,264	12,828
*90745	Carson	91,714	95,558	91,139
*91941	Casa de Oro-Mt. Helix (c)	18,762	19,576	—
*91384	Castaic (c)	19,015	18,937	—
*94546	Castro Valley (c)	61,388	66,441	—
*92234	Cathedral City	51,200	51,493	52,356
95307	Ceres	45,417	49,302	48,397
90703	Cerritos	49,041	49,578	46,797
*94541	Cherryland (c)	14,728	15,808	—
*95926	Chico	86,187	101,475	101,301
*91708	Chino	77,983	91,403	93,114
91709	Chino Hills	74,799	78,411	77,212
93610	Chowchilla	18,720	19,039	19,328
*91910	Chula Vista	243,916	275,487	274,333
91702	Citrus (c)	10,866	10,243	—
*95610	Citrus Heights	83,301	87,583	86,239
91711	Claremont	34,926	37,266	35,640
94517	Clayton	10,897	11,070	10,754
95422	Clearlake	15,250	16,685	16,481
*93612	Clovis	95,631	120,124	125,826
92236	Coachella	40,704	41,941	43,590
93210	Coalinga	13,380	17,590	17,369
92324	Colton	52,154	53,909	53,357
*90040	Commerce	12,823	12,378	11,672
*90220	Compton	96,455	95,740	90,986
*94520	Concord	122,067	125,410	122,315
*93212	Corcoran	24,813	22,339	22,044
*92882	Corona	152,374	157,136	160,238
*92118	Coronado	18,912	20,192	18,437
*92626	Costa Mesa	109,960	111,918	108,354
92679	Coto de Caza (c)	14,866	14,710	—
95204	Country Club (c)	9,379	10,777	—
*91722	Covina	47,796	51,268	48,728
92325	Crestline (c)	10,770	11,650	—
90201	Cudahy	23,805	22,811	21,723
*90230	Culver City	38,883	40,779	39,041
*95014	Cupertino	58,302	60,381	57,285
*90630	Cypress	47,802	50,151	48,782
*94015	Daly City	101,123	104,901	99,833
*92629	Dana Point	33,351	33,107	32,567
*94526	Danville	42,039	43,582	42,999
*95616	Davis	65,622	66,850	65,832
90250	Del Aire (c)	10,001	10,338	—
*93215	Delano	53,041	51,428	51,500

ZIP	Place	2010 population	2020 population	2023 estimate
95315	Delhi (c)	10,755	10,656	—
*92240	Desert Hot Springs	25,938	32,512	33,438
*91765	Diamond Bar	55,544	55,072	52,041
95619	Diamond Springs (c)	11,037	11,345	—
93618	Dinuba	21,453	24,563	25,863
*94514	Discovery Bay (c)	13,352	15,358	—
95620	Dixon	18,351	18,988	19,309
*90240	Downey	111,772	114,355	108,816
*91008	Duarte	21,321	21,727	23,131
94568	Dublin	46,036	72,589	69,128
92544	East Hemet (c)	17,418	19,432	—
90022	East Los Angeles (c)	126,496	118,786	—
*93306	East Niles (c)	—	28,390	—
94303	East Palo Alto	28,155	30,034	28,216
90221	East Rancho Dominguez (c)	15,135	15,114	—
91775	East San Gabriel (c)	14,874	22,769	—
90604	East Whittier (c)	—	10,394	—
93117	Eastern Goleta Valley (c)	—	28,656	—
*91752	Eastvale	53,668	69,757	70,510
*92020	El Cajon	99,478	106,215	102,991
*92243	El Centro	42,598	44,322	43,772
94530	El Cerrito	23,549	25,962	25,552
95762	El Dorado Hills (c)	42,108	50,547	—
*91731	El Monte	113,475	109,450	103,794
*93446	El Paso de Robles (Paso Robles)	29,793	31,490	31,134
90245	El Segundo	16,654	17,272	16,445
*94803	El Sobrante (c) (Contra Costa Co.)	12,669	15,524	—
92503	El Sobrante (c) (Riverside Co.)	12,723	14,039	—
*95624	Elk Grove	153,015	176,124	178,444
*94608	Emeryville	10,080	12,905	12,732
*92024	Encinitas	59,518	62,007	60,841
*92025	Escondido	143,911	151,038	148,122
*95501	Eureka	27,191	26,512	25,734
93221	Exeter	10,334	10,321	10,206
95628	Fair Oaks (c)	30,912	32,514	—
*94533	Fairfield	105,321	119,881	120,768
*94541	Fairview (c)	10,003	11,341	—
*92028	Fallbrook (c)	30,534	32,267	—
93223	Farmersville	10,588	10,397	10,243
*93015	Fillmore	15,002	16,419	17,190
*90001	Florence-Graham (c)	63,387	61,983	—
95828	Florin (c)	47,513	52,388	—
*95630	Folsom	72,203	80,454	84,782
*92335	Fontana	196,069	208,393	215,465
95841	Foothill Farms (c)	33,121	35,834	—
95540	Fortuna	11,926	12,516	12,285
94404	Foster City	30,567	33,805	32,180
*92704	Fountain Valley	55,313	57,047	55,468
*94538	Fremont	214,089	230,504	226,208
92596	French Valley (c)	23,067	35,280	—
*93721	Fresno	494,665	542,107	545,716
*92831	Fullerton	135,161	143,617	139,250
95632	Galt	23,647	25,383	25,767
95215	Garden Acres (c)	10,648	11,398	—
*92840	Garden Grove	170,883	171,949	168,234
*90247	Gardena	58,829	61,027	58,377
*95020	Gilroy	48,821	59,520	58,250
*91201	Glendale	191,719	196,543	187,050
*91741	Glendora	50,073	52,558	49,934
*93117	Goleta	29,888	32,690	32,665
*92313	Grand Terrace	12,040	13,150	12,939
*95746	Granite Bay (c)	20,402	21,247	—
*95945	Grass Valley	12,860	14,016	14,074
93927	Greenfield	16,330	18,937	20,634
*93433	Grover Beach	13,156	12,701	12,547
91745	Hacienda Heights (c)	54,038	54,191	—
94019	Half Moon Bay	11,324	11,795	11,105
*93230	Hanford	53,967	57,990	59,938
90716	Hawaiian Gardens	14,254	14,149	13,396
*90250	Hawthorne	84,293	88,083	83,364
*94541	Hayward	144,186	162,954	155,675
95448	Healdsburg	11,254	11,340	11,137
*92543	Hemet	78,657	89,833	92,368
94547	Hercules	24,060	26,016	26,582
90254	Hermosa Beach	19,506	19,728	18,641
*92344	Hesperia	90,173	99,818	100,633
92346	Highland	53,104	56,999	56,202
92103	Hillcrest (c)	—	10,528	—
94010	Hillsborough	10,825	11,387	10,883
*95023	Hollister	34,928	41,678	44,658
*92503	Home Gardens (c)	11,570	11,203	—
*92648	Huntington Beach	189,992	198,711	192,129
90255	Huntington Park	58,114	54,883	51,942
92251	Imperial	14,758	20,263	21,591
*91932	Imperial Beach	26,324	26,137	25,458
*92201	Indio	76,036	89,137	93,057
*90301	Inglewood	109,673	107,762	102,865
*92602	Irvine	212,375	307,670	314,621
93117	Isla Vista (c)	23,096	15,500	—
*91752	Jurupa Valley[1]	—	105,053	107,321
93630	Kerman	13,544	16,016	17,238
93930	King City	12,874	13,332	13,917
93631	Kingsburg	11,382	12,380	13,013
*91011	La Cañada Flintridge	20,246	20,573	19,538
*91214	La Crescenta-Montrose (c)	19,653	19,997	—
*90631	La Habra	60,239	63,097	60,991
*91941	La Mesa	57,065	61,121	60,537
*90638	La Mirada	48,527	48,008	45,505
90623	La Palma	15,568	15,581	15,029
91977	La Presa (c)	34,169	35,033	—
*91744	La Puente	39,816	38,062	36,516
*92253	La Quinta	37,467	37,558	39,081
*95826	La Riviera (c)	10,802	11,252	—
91750	La Verne	31,063	31,334	29,898
92694	Ladera Ranch (c)	22,980	26,170	—
94549	Lafayette	23,893	25,391	25,048
*92651	Laguna Beach	22,723	23,032	22,332
*92653	Laguna Hills	30,344	31,374	30,243
*92677	Laguna Niguel	62,979	64,355	62,899
*92637	Laguna Woods	16,192	17,644	16,998
92352	Lake Arrowhead (c)	12,424	12,401	—
*92530	Lake Elsinore	51,821	70,265	73,028
*92630	Lake Forest	77,264	85,858	85,840
*93535	Lake Los Angeles (c)	12,328	13,187	—
92530	Lakeland Village (c)	11,541	12,364	—
92040	Lakeside (c)	20,648	21,152	—
*90712	Lakewood	80,048	82,496	78,135
93241	Lamont (c)	15,120	14,049	—
*93534	Lancaster	156,633	173,516	166,236
*94939	Larkspur	11,926	13,064	12,589
95330	Lathrop	18,023	28,701	39,857
*90260	Lawndale	32,769	31,807	30,155
*91945	Lemon Grove	25,320	27,627	27,569
95824	Lemon Hill (c)	13,729	14,496	—
*93245	Lemoore	24,531	27,038	26,809
90304	Lennox (c)	22,753	20,323	—
95648	Lincoln	42,819	49,757	54,538
95901	Linda (c)	17,773	21,654	—
93247	Lindsay	11,768	12,659	12,496
95953	Live Oak (c)	17,158	17,038	—
*94550	Livermore	80,968	87,955	82,908
95334	Livingston	13,058	14,172	14,643
*95240	Lodi	62,134	66,348	67,679
*92354	Loma Linda	23,261	24,791	25,111
90717	Lomita	20,256	20,921	19,782
*93436	Lompoc	42,434	44,444	43,045
*90802	Long Beach	462,257	466,742	449,468
*90720	Los Alamitos	11,449	11,780	11,901
*94022	Los Altos	28,976	31,625	29,990
*90012	Los Angeles	3,792,621	3,898,747	3,820,914
93635	Los Banos	35,972	45,532	48,553
*95030	Los Gatos	29,413	33,529	32,216
*93402	Los Osos (c)	14,276	14,465	—
90262	Lynwood	69,772	67,265	63,234
*93638	Madera	61,416	66,224	68,079
*90265	Malibu	12,645	10,654	10,277
*90266	Manhattan Beach	35,135	35,506	33,369
*95336	Manteca	67,096	83,498	91,059
93933	Marina	19,718	22,359	22,833
*90292	Marina del Rey (c)	8,866	11,373	—
94553	Martinez	35,824	37,287	36,395
95901	Marysville	12,072	12,844	12,674
90270	Maywood	27,395	25,138	23,824
93250	McFarland	12,707	14,161	14,049
*95521	McKinleyville (c)	15,177	16,262	—
92570	Mead Valley (c)	18,510	19,819	—
93640	Mendota	11,014	12,595	12,530
*92586	Menifee	77,519	102,527	113,433
*94025	Menlo Park	32,026	33,780	31,690
*95340	Merced	78,958	86,333	93,692
*94941	Mill Valley	13,903	14,231	13,792
94030	Millbrae	21,532	23,216	22,087
*95035	Milpitas	66,790	80,273	77,321
*92691	Mission Viejo	93,305	93,653	90,624
*95354	Modesto	201,165	218,464	218,915
*91016	Monrovia	36,590	37,931	36,768
*91763	Montclair	36,664	37,865	37,545
90640	Montebello	62,500	62,640	60,015

ZIP	Place	2010 population	2020 population	2023 estimate
*93940	Monterey	27,810	30,218	29,116
*91754	Monterey Park	60,269	61,096	57,877
*93021	Moorpark	34,421	36,284	35,543
*94556	Moraga	16,016	16,870	16,547
*92551	Moreno Valley	193,365	208,634	212,392
*95037	Morgan Hill	37,882	45,483	44,478
*93442	Morro Bay	10,234	10,757	10,589
95391	Mountain House (c)	9,675	24,499	—
*94041	Mountain View	74,066	82,376	81,785
*92562	Murrieta	103,466	110,949	111,878
92407	Muscoy (c)	10,644	10,719	—
*94558	Napa	76,915	79,246	77,492
*91950	National City	58,582	56,173	55,236
94560	Newark	42,573	47,529	46,929
95360	Newman	10,224	12,351	12,207
*92657	Newport Beach	85,186	85,239	82,637
93444	Nipomo (c)	16,714	18,176	—
92860	Norco	27,063	26,316	25,398
*95602	North Auburn (c)	13,022	13,452	—
*94025	North Fair Oaks (c)	14,687	14,027	—
95660	North Highlands (c)	42,694	49,327	—
92705	North Tustin (c)	24,917	25,718	—
*90650	Norwalk	105,549	102,773	98,078
*94947	Novato	51,904	53,225	51,722
*91377	Oak Park (c)	13,811	13,898	—
95361	Oakdale	20,675	23,181	23,045
*94601	Oakland	390,724	440,646	436,504
94561	Oakley	35,432	43,357	45,761
*92054	Oceanside	167,086	174,068	170,020
93308	Oildale (c)	32,684	36,135	—
95961	Olivehurst (c)	13,656	16,595	—
*91761	Ontario	163,924	175,265	182,457
*92866	Orange	136,416	139,911	138,337
95662	Orangevale (c)	33,960	35,569	—
*93455	Orcutt (c)	28,905	32,034	—
94563	Orinda	17,643	19,514	19,364
*95965	Oroville	15,546	20,042	19,449
*93030	Oxnard	197,899	202,063	198,488
93950	Pacific Grove	15,041	15,090	14,757
94044	Pacifica	37,234	38,640	36,426
*92260	Palm Desert	48,445	51,163	51,951
*92262	Palm Springs	44,552	44,575	45,218
*93550	Palmdale	152,750	169,450	161,404
*94303	Palo Alto	64,403	68,572	65,882
*90274	Palos Verdes Estates	13,438	13,347	12,646
90723	Paramount	54,098	53,733	51,072
95823	Parkway (c)	14,670	15,962	—
93648	Parlier	14,494	14,576	14,426
*91101	Pasadena	137,122	138,699	133,560
	Paso Robles. *See* El Paso de Robles			
95363	Patterson	20,413	23,781	25,063
*92570	Perris	68,386	78,700	80,603
*94952	Petaluma	57,941	59,776	58,800
*92371	Phelan (c)	14,304	13,859	—
*90660	Pico Rivera	62,942	62,088	59,189
*94611	Piedmont	10,667	11,270	10,635
94564	Pinole	18,390	19,022	18,481
94565	Pittsburg	63,264	76,416	75,803
*92870	Placentia	50,533	51,824	52,192
95667	Placerville	10,389	10,747	10,656
94523	Pleasant Hill	33,152	34,613	33,802
*94566	Pleasanton	70,285	79,871	74,653
*91765	Pomona	149,058	151,713	145,502
*93041	Port Hueneme	21,723	21,954	21,217
*93257	Porterville	54,165	62,623	62,876
*92064	Poway	47,811	48,841	48,051
93907	Prunedale (c)	17,560	18,885	—
*93536	Quartz Hill (c)	10,912	11,447	—
92065	Ramona (c)	20,292	21,468	—
*95670	Rancho Cordova	64,776	79,332	82,605
*91730	Rancho Cucamonga	165,269	174,453	174,405
92270	Rancho Mirage	17,218	16,999	17,795
92694	Rancho Mission Viejo (c)	—	10,378	—
90275	Rancho Palos Verdes	41,643	42,287	39,980
*92019	Rancho San Diego (c)	21,208	21,858	—
92688	Rancho Santa Margarita	47,853	47,949	46,182
96080	Red Bluff	14,076	14,710	14,413
*96001	Redding	89,861	93,611	92,727
*92373	Redlands	68,747	73,168	72,556
*90277	Redondo Beach	66,748	71,576	67,749
*94063	Redwood City	76,815	84,292	80,996
93654	Reedley	24,194	25,227	25,958
*92376	Rialto	99,171	104,026	103,391
*94801	Richmond	103,701	116,448	114,106
*93555	Ridgecrest	27,616	27,959	28,088
95673	Rio Linda (c)	15,106	15,944	—
94571	Rio Vista	7,360	10,005	10,145
95366	Ripon	14,297	16,013	16,068
95367	Riverbank	22,678	24,865	25,001
*92501	Riverside	303,871	314,998	318,858
*95677	Rocklin	56,974	71,601	73,472
*94928	Rohnert Park	40,971	44,390	44,546
93560	Rosamond (c)	18,150	20,961	—
93314	Rosedale (c)	14,058	18,639	—
*91770	Rosemead	53,764	51,185	49,305
*95826	Rosemont (c)	22,681	23,510	—
*95678	Roseville	118,788	147,773	159,135
90720	Rossmoor (c)	10,244	10,625	—
91748	Rowland Heights (c)	48,993	48,231	—
*95814	Sacramento	466,488	524,943	526,384
95368	Salida (c)	13,722	13,886	—
*93901	Salinas	150,441	163,542	159,506
*94960	San Anselmo	12,336	12,830	12,498
*92401	San Bernardino	209,924	222,101	223,728
94066	San Bruno	41,114	43,908	41,327
*93001	San Buenaventura (Ventura)	106,433	110,763	109,058
94070	San Carlos	28,406	30,722	28,862
*92672	San Clemente	63,522	64,293	62,313
*92101	San Diego	1,307,402	1,386,932	1,388,320
92065	San Diego Country Estates (c)	10,109	10,395	—
91773	San Dimas	33,371	34,924	33,105
*91340	San Fernando	23,645	23,946	23,364
*94102	San Francisco	805,235	873,965	808,988
91775	San Gabriel	39,718	39,568	37,732
*92582	San Jacinto	44,199	53,898	55,440
*95113	San Jose	945,942	1,013,240	969,655
*92675	San Juan Capistrano	34,593	35,196	34,754
*94577	San Leandro	84,950	91,008	85,784
94580	San Lorenzo (c)	23,452	29,581	—
*93401	San Luis Obispo	45,119	47,063	49,244
*92069	San Marcos	83,781	94,833	94,188
*91108	San Marino	13,147	12,513	11,977
*94403	San Mateo	97,207	105,661	101,327
*94806	San Pablo	29,139	32,127	31,249
*94901	San Rafael	57,713	61,271	59,555
*94583	San Ramon	72,148	84,605	84,929
93657	Sanger	24,270	26,617	26,343
*92701	Santa Ana	324,528	310,227	310,539
*93101	Santa Barbara	88,410	88,665	86,499
*95050	Santa Clara	116,468	127,647	131,062
*91355	Santa Clarita	176,320	228,673	224,028
*95060	Santa Cruz	59,946	62,956	61,501
90670	Santa Fe Springs	16,223	19,219	20,174
*93454	Santa Maria	99,553	109,707	109,987
*90401	Santa Monica	89,736	93,076	89,922
*93060	Santa Paula	29,321	30,657	31,792
*95401	Santa Rosa	167,815	178,127	175,845
*92071	Santee	53,413	60,037	59,478
*95070	Saratoga	29,926	31,051	29,607
*95066	Scotts Valley	11,580	12,224	11,879
90740	Seal Beach	24,168	25,242	24,352
93955	Seaside	33,025	32,366	31,317
93662	Selma	23,219	24,674	24,467
93263	Shafter	16,988	19,953	21,915
*96019	Shasta Lake	10,164	10,371	10,262
*91024	Sierra Madre	10,917	11,268	10,713
*90755	Signal Hill	11,016	11,848	11,249
*93065	Simi Valley	124,237	126,356	125,113
92075	Solana Beach	12,867	12,941	12,675
93960	Soledad	25,738	24,925	23,947
95476	Sonoma	10,648	10,739	10,619
91733	South El Monte	20,116	19,567	19,032
90280	South Gate	94,396	92,726	90,070
*96150	South Lake Tahoe	21,403	21,330	21,079
*91030	South Pasadena	25,619	26,943	25,623
*94080	South San Francisco	63,632	66,105	63,123
91744	South San Jose Hills (c)	20,551	19,855	—
90605	South Whittier (c)	57,156	56,415	—
*91977	Spring Valley (c) (San Diego Co.)	28,205	30,998	—
*94305	Stanford (c)	13,809	21,150	—
90680	Stanton	38,186	37,962	38,815
91381	Stevenson Ranch (c)	17,557	20,178	—
*95202	Stockton	291,707	320,804	319,543
*94585	Suisun City	28,111	29,518	28,743
93543	Sun Village (c)	11,565	12,345	—
*94086	Sunnyvale	140,081	155,805	151,967
*96130	Susanville	17,947	16,728	12,689

ZIP	Place	2010 population	2020 population	2023 estimate
94941	Tamalpais-Homestead Valley (c)	10,735	11,492	—
*93561	Tehachapi	14,414	12,939	10,881
*92590	Temecula	100,097	110,003	110,682
92883	Temescal Valley (c)	22,535	26,232	—
91780	Temple City	35,558	36,494	34,854
*91360	Thousand Oaks	126,683	126,966	123,463
*90503	Torrance	145,438	147,067	139,224
*95376	Tracy	82,922	93,000	98,010
*96161	Truckee	16,180	16,729	17,039
*93274	Tulare	59,278	68,875	71,092
*95380	Turlock	68,549	72,740	72,100
*92780	Tustin	75,540	80,276	77,704
*92277	Twentynine Palms	25,048	28,065	28,734
*95482	Ukiah	16,075	16,607	16,072
94587	Union City	69,516	70,143	65,414
*91784	Upland	73,732	79,040	78,699
*95687	Vacaville	92,428	102,386	102,526
91744	Valinda (c)	22,822	22,437	—
92544	Valle Vista (c)	14,578	16,194	—
*94590	Vallejo	115,942	126,090	122,807
92082	Valley Center (c)	9,277	10,087	—
	Ventura. *See* San Buenaventura			
*92392	Victorville	115,903	134,810	138,869
*90043	View Park-Windsor Hills (c)	11,075	11,419	—
*91702	Vincent (c)	15,922	15,714	—
95829	Vineyard (c)	24,836	43,935	—
*93277	Visalia	124,442	141,384	144,998
*92084	Vista	93,834	98,381	98,344
*91789	Walnut	29,172	28,430	27,104
*94596	Walnut Creek	64,173	70,127	69,152
90255	Walnut Park (c)	15,966	15,214	—
93280	Wasco	25,545	27,047	26,917
*95076	Watsonville	51,199	52,590	50,867
90502	West Carson (c)	21,699	22,870	—
*91790	West Covina	106,098	109,501	105,617
*90069	West Hollywood	34,399	35,757	34,349
91746	West Puente Valley (c)	22,636	22,959	—
*90220	West Rancho Dominguez (c)	5,669	24,347	—
*95691	West Sacramento	48,744	53,915	55,842
*90606	West Whittier-Los Nietos (c)	25,540	25,325	—
*92683	Westminster	89,701	90,911	88,729
*90047	Westmont (c)	31,853	33,913	—
*90602	Whittier	85,331	87,306	84,143
92595	Wildomar	32,176	36,875	37,087
*90222	Willowbrook (c)	35,983	24,295	—
95492	Windsor	26,801	26,344	25,828
92040	Winter Gardens (c)	20,631	22,380	—
95388	Winton (c)	10,613	11,709	—
92504	Woodcrest (c)	14,347	15,378	—
*95695	Woodland	55,468	61,032	61,123
*92886	Yorba Linda	64,234	68,336	66,147
*95991	Yuba City	64,925	70,117	68,666
92399	Yucaipa	51,367	54,542	53,947
*92284	Yucca Valley	20,700	21,738	21,664

(1) Incorporated after 2010 Census.

Colorado

Area codes: 303/720/983, 719, 748 (July 7, 2025)/970

ZIP	Place	2010 population	2020 population	2023 estimate
*80004	Arvada	106,433	124,402	121,414
*80010	Aurora	325,078	386,261	395,052
*80211	Berkley (c)	11,207	12,536	—
80513	Berthoud	5,105	10,332	13,238
*80908	Black Forest (c)	13,116	15,097	—
*80302	Boulder	97,385	108,250	105,898
*80601	Brighton	33,352	40,083	42,477
*80020	Broomfield	55,889	74,112	76,860
*81212	Cañon City	16,400	17,141	17,241
80108	Castle Pines	3,614	11,036	14,747
*80104	Castle Rock	48,231	73,158	81,415
*80015	Centennial	100,377	108,418	106,883
80206	Cherry Creek (c)	11,120	11,488	—
80915	Cimarron Hills (c)	16,161	19,311	—
81520	Clifton (c)	19,889	20,413	—
*80903	Colorado Springs	416,427	478,961	488,664
*80123	Columbine (c)	24,280	25,229	—
*80022	Commerce City	45,913	62,418	68,245
80127	Dakota Ridge (c)	32,005	33,892	—
*80202	Denver	600,158	715,522	716,577
*81301	Durango	16,887	19,071	19,534
81632	Edwards (c)	10,266	11,246	—
*80110	Englewood	30,255	33,659	34,275
*80516	Erie	18,135	30,038	35,269
*80620	Evans	18,537	22,165	22,326
*80260	Federal Heights	11,467	14,382	13,943
*80504	Firestone	10,147	16,381	18,589
*80913	Fort Carson (c)	13,813	17,693	—
*80521	Fort Collins	143,986	169,810	170,376
*80701	Fort Morgan	11,315	11,597	11,564
80817	Fountain	25,846	29,802	28,489
*80231	Four Square Mile (c)	—	22,872	—
*80530	Frederick	8,679	14,513	17,676
81521	Fruita	12,646	13,395	13,816
*81601	Glenwood Springs	9,614	9,963	10,250
*80401	Golden	18,867	20,399	20,242
*81501	Grand Junction	58,566	65,560	69,412
*80631	Greeley	92,889	108,795	112,609
*80111	Greenwood Village	13,925	15,691	15,205
*80126	Highlands Ranch (c)	96,713	103,444	—
80534	Johnstown	9,887	17,303	19,511
*80127	Ken Caryl (c)	32,438	33,811	—
80026	Lafayette	24,453	30,411	30,439
*80226	Lakewood	142,980	155,984	155,961
*80120	Littleton	41,737	45,652	44,451
*80124	Lone Tree	10,218	14,253	14,063
*80501	Longmont	86,270	98,885	98,630
80027	Louisville	18,376	21,226	20,390
*80537	Loveland	66,859	76,378	79,352
*81401	Montrose	19,132	20,291	21,333
80132	Monument	5,530	10,399	12,088
*80233	Northglenn	35,789	38,131	38,164
*80134	Parker	45,297	58,512	62,743
*81003	Pueblo	106,595	111,876	111,077
81007	Pueblo West (c)	29,637	33,086	—
81650	Rifle	9,172	10,437	10,563
80911	Security-Widefield (c)	32,882	38,639	—
80524	Severance	3,165	7,683	10,820
80221	Sherrelwood (c)	18,287	19,228	—
*80487	Steamboat Springs	12,088	13,224	13,508
80751	Sterling	14,777	13,735	12,954
80027	Superior	12,483	13,094	13,361
80134	The Pinery (c)	10,517	11,311	—
*80229	Thornton	118,772	141,867	144,922
80229	Welby (c)	14,846	15,553	—
80549	Wellington	6,289	11,047	12,078
*80031	Westminster	106,114	116,317	114,875
*80033	Wheat Ridge	30,166	32,398	31,804
*80550	Windsor	18,644	32,716	40,349

Connecticut

Area codes: 203/475, 860/959. See introductory note.

ZIP	Place	2010 population	2020 population	2023 estimate
06401	Ansonia	19,249	18,918	19,008
06001	*Avon*	18,098	18,932	18,883
06037	*Berlin*	19,866	20,175	20,429
06801	*Bethel*	18,584	20,358	20,678
06801	Bethel (c)	9,549	11,582	—
06002	*Bloomfield*	20,486	21,535	21,884
06405	*Branford*	28,026	28,273	28,031
*06604	Bridgeport	144,229	148,654	148,028
*06010	Bristol	60,477	60,833	61,601
06804	*Brookfield*	16,452	17,528	17,489
06019	*Canton*	10,292	10,124	10,146
*06410	*Cheshire*	29,261	28,733	29,200
06413	*Clinton*	13,260	13,185	13,402
*06415	*Colchester*	16,068	15,555	15,504
06238	*Coventry*	12,435	12,235	12,308
06416	*Cromwell*	14,005	14,225	14,363
*06810	Danbury	80,893	86,518	86,124
06820	*Darien*	20,732	21,499	22,020
06418	Derby	12,902	12,325	12,406
*06424	*East Hampton*	12,959	12,717	12,989
*06108	*East Hartford*	51,252	51,045	50,654
*06512	*East Haven*	29,257	27,923	27,533
06333	*East Lyme*	19,159	18,693	18,929
06088	*East Windsor*	11,162	11,190	11,170
06029	*Ellington*	15,602	16,426	16,994
*06082	*Enfield*	44,654	42,141	40,792
*06824	*Fairfield*	59,404	61,512	63,433
*06032	*Farmington*	25,340	26,712	26,798
06033	*Glastonbury*	34,427	35,159	35,204
06035	*Granby*	11,282	10,903	11,249
*06830	*Greenwich*	61,171	63,518	63,574
*06830	Greenwich (c)	12,942	13,836	—
06351	*Griswold*	11,951	11,402	11,624
*06340	*Groton*	40,115	38,411	37,878

ZIP	Place	2010 population	2020 population	2023 estimate
06437	*Guilford*	22,375	22,073	22,020
*06514	*Hamden*	60,960	61,169	60,014
*06103	Hartford	124,775	121,054	119,669
*06239	*Killingly*	17,370	17,752	17,945
*06339	*Ledyard*	15,051	15,413	15,459
06443	*Madison*	18,269	17,691	17,498
*06040	*Manchester*	58,241	59,713	59,408
*06040	Manchester (c)	30,577	36,379	—
*06250	*Mansfield*	26,543	25,892	25,401
*06450	Meriden	60,868	60,850	60,111
*06457	Middletown	47,648	47,717	47,984
*06460	Milford (balance)	51,271	50,558	50,421
*06460	*Milford*	52,759	52,044	52,793
06468	*Monroe*	19,479	18,825	18,831
06353	*Montville*	19,571	18,387	17,814
06770	Naugatuck	31,862	31,519	31,820
*06051	New Britain	73,206	74,135	74,080
06840	*New Canaan*	19,738	20,622	20,862
06812	*New Fairfield*	13,881	13,579	13,487
*06511	New Haven	129,779	134,023	135,319
06320	New London	27,620	27,367	27,560
06776	*New Milford*	28,142	28,115	28,276
*06111	*Newington*	30,562	30,536	31,227
06470	*Newtown*	27,560	27,173	27,673
06471	*North Branford*	14,407	13,544	13,415
06473	*North Haven*	24,093	24,253	24,295
*06850	Norwalk	85,603	91,184	92,458
*06360	Norwich	40,493	40,125	39,881
06475	*Old Saybrook*	10,242	10,481	10,571
06477	*Orange*	13,956	14,280	14,322
06478	*Oxford*	12,683	12,706	13,125
06374	*Plainfield*	15,405	14,973	15,193
06062	*Plainville*	17,716	17,525	17,491
06782	*Plymouth*	12,243	11,671	11,766
*06877	*Ridgefield*	24,638	25,033	24,931
06067	*Rocky Hill*	19,709	20,845	20,708
*06483	*Seymour*	16,540	16,748	16,953
06484	Shelton	39,559	40,869	42,144
06070	*Simsbury*	23,511	24,517	24,953
06071	*Somers*	11,444	10,255	10,725
06074	*South Windsor*	25,709	26,918	26,773
06488	*Southbury*	19,904	19,879	20,127
06489	*Southington*	43,069	43,501	43,743
*06075	*Stafford*	12,087	11,472	11,567
*06901	Stamford	122,643	135,470	136,226
06378	*Stonington*	18,545	18,335	18,431
*06268	Storrs (c)	15,344	15,979	—
*06614	*Stratford*	51,384	52,355	52,454
*06078	*Suffield*	15,735	15,752	15,650
06084	*Tolland*	15,052	14,563	14,574
*06790	Torrington	36,383	35,515	35,550
06611	*Trumbull*	36,018	36,827	37,269
06066	*Vernon*	29,179	30,215	30,596
*06492	*Wallingford*	45,135	44,396	43,725
06492	Wallingford Center (c)	18,209	18,278	—
*06702	Waterbury	110,366	114,403	114,990
06385	*Waterford*	19,517	19,571	19,829
*06795	*Watertown*	22,514	22,105	22,274
*06105	*West Hartford*	63,268	64,083	63,969
06516	West Haven	55,564	55,584	54,790
06883	*Weston*	10,179	10,354	10,344
*06880	*Westport*	26,391	27,141	27,470
*06109	*Wethersfield*	26,668	27,298	27,114
06226	Willimantic (c)	17,737	18,149	—
06897	*Wilton*	18,062	18,503	18,400
*06098	*Winchester*	11,242	10,224	10,236
06280	*Windham*	25,268	24,425	23,833
*06095	*Windsor*	29,044	29,492	29,372
06096	*Windsor Locks*	12,498	12,613	12,529
*06716	*Wolcott*	16,680	16,142	16,309

Delaware

Area code: 302 applies to the entire state

ZIP	Place	2010 population	2020 population	2023 estimate
19701	Bear (c)	19,371	23,060	—
19713	Brookside (c)	14,353	14,974	—
*19901	Dover	36,047	39,403	39,894
19702	Glasgow (c)	14,303	15,288	—
19707	Hockessin (c)	13,527	13,478	—
19709	Middletown	18,871	23,192	25,022
19963	Milford	9,559	11,190	13,289
*19711	Newark	31,454	30,601	30,169
19808	Pike Creek Valley (c)	11,217	11,692	—
19977	Smyrna	10,023	12,883	13,277
*19801	Wilmington	70,851	70,898	71,675

District of Columbia

Area codes: 202/771 apply to the entire district

ZIP	Place	2010 population	2020 population	2023 estimate
*20001	Washington	601,723	689,545	678,972

Florida

Area codes: 239, 305/645/786, 321 (part)/407, 324/904, 352, 386, 407/689, 448/850, 561/728, 656/813, 727, 754/954, 772, 863, 941

ZIP	Place	2010 population	2020 population	2023 estimate
*32615	Alachua	9,059	10,574	10,770
*32820	Alafaya (c)	78,113	92,452	—
*32701	Altamonte Springs	41,496	46,231	45,257
33572	Apollo Beach (c)	14,055	26,002	—
*32712	Apopka	41,542	54,873	59,113
32043	Asbury Lake (c)	8,700	11,036	—
32233	Atlantic Beach	12,655	13,513	13,182
33823	Auburndale	13,507	15,616	20,011
*33180	Aventura	35,762	40,242	38,741
*33825	Avon Park	8,836	9,658	10,219
32807	Azalea Park (c)	12,556	14,141	—
*33830	Bartow	17,298	19,309	20,584
34667	Bayonet Point (c)	23,467	26,713	—
34207	Bayshore Gardens (c)	16,323	19,904	—
32073	Bellair-Meadowbrook Terrace (c)	13,343	14,482	—
33430	Belle Glade	17,467	16,698	16,840
32526	Bellview (c)	23,355	25,541	—
*33596	Bloomingdale (c)	22,711	22,947	—
*33431	Boca Raton	84,392	97,422	99,974
*34135	Bonita Springs	43,914	53,644	56,229
*33436	Boynton Beach	68,217	80,380	81,267
*34201	Bradenton	49,546	55,698	57,076
32312	Bradfordville (c)	—	19,183	—
*33510	Brandon (c)	103,483	114,626	—
32503	Brent (c)	21,804	23,447	—
33142	Brownsville (c)	15,313	16,583	—
34743	Buenaventura Lakes (c)	26,079	30,251	—
32404	Callaway	14,405	13,045	13,661
32920	Cape Canaveral	9,912	9,972	10,014
*33990	Cape Coral	154,305	194,016	224,455
*33618	Carrollwood (c)	33,365	34,352	—
*32707	Casselberry	26,241	28,794	30,595
34747	Celebration (c)	7,427	11,178	—
33558	Cheval (c)	10,702	12,522	—
33625	Citrus Park (c)	24,252	28,178	—
*34433	Citrus Springs (c)	8,622	10,246	—
*33755	Clearwater	107,685	117,292	116,850
*34711	Clermont	28,742	43,021	48,621
*32922	Cocoa	17,140	19,041	19,930
*32931	Cocoa Beach	11,231	11,354	11,389
*33063	Coconut Creek	52,909	57,833	57,694
*32806	Conway (c)	13,467	13,596	—
*33328	Cooper City	28,547	34,401	34,321
*33134	Coral Gables	46,780	49,248	48,353
*33065	Coral Springs	121,096	134,394	134,906
33155	Coral Terrace (c)	24,376	23,142	—
33015	Country Club (c)	47,105	49,967	—
*33186	Country Walk (c)	15,997	16,951	—
*32536	Crestview	20,978	27,134	29,300
*33189	Cutler Bay	40,286	45,425	43,762
33884	Cypress Gardens (c)	8,917	10,169	—
33919	Cypress Lake (c)	11,846	13,727	—
*33004	Dania Beach	29,639	31,723	31,915
*33837	Davenport	2,888	9,043	15,068
*33314	Davie	91,992	105,691	107,799
*32114	Daytona Beach	61,005	72,647	82,485
*32713	DeBary	19,320	22,260	23,209
*33441	Deerfield Beach	75,018	86,859	87,325
*32720	DeLand	27,031	37,351	43,009
*33444	Delray Beach	60,522	66,846	67,536
*32738	Deltona	85,182	93,692	98,739
*32541	Destin	12,305	13,931	14,188
*32819	Doctor Phillips (c)	10,981	12,328	—
*33166	Doral	45,704	75,874	79,359
*34698	Dunedin	35,321	36,068	35,930
*34685	East Lake (c)	30,962	32,344	—
*33610	East Lake-Orient Park (c)	22,753	28,050	—
32583	East Milton (c)	11,074	14,309	—
*32132	Edgewater	20,750	23,097	23,636
33614	Egypt Lake-Leto (c)	35,282	36,644	—
*34680	Elfers (c)	13,986	14,573	—
*34223	Englewood (c)	14,863	20,800	—
*32514	Ensley (c)	20,602	23,817	—
*33928	Estero	22,612	36,939	37,908
*32726	Eustis	18,558	23,189	24,457

ZIP	Place	2010 population	2020 population	2023 estimate
*32789	Fairview Shores (c)	10,239	10,722	—
*32034	Fernandina Beach	11,487	13,052	13,647
32514	Ferry Pass (c)	28,921	29,921	—
33547	Fish Hawk (c)	14,087	24,625	—
*32003	Fleming Island (c)	27,126	29,142	—
33034	Florida City	11,245	13,085	12,582
*32962	Florida Ridge (c)	18,164	21,302	—
*32703	Forest City (c)	13,854	14,623	—
*33301	Fort Lauderdale	165,521	182,760	184,255
*33901	Fort Myers	62,298	86,395	97,372
*34950	Fort Pierce	41,590	47,297	49,374
*32548	Fort Walton Beach	19,507	20,922	20,925
*33144	Fountainebleau (c)	59,764	59,870	—
*33896	Four Corners (c)	26,116	56,381	—
32259	Fruit Cove (c)	29,362	32,143	—
*34232	Fruitville (c)	13,224	15,484	—
33860	Fuller Heights (c)	8,758	10,467	—
*32601	Gainesville	124,354	141,085	145,812
33913	Gateway (c)	8,401	10,376	—
33534	Gibsonton (c)	14,234	18,566	—
*33147	Gladeview (c)	11,535	14,927	—
*33143	Glenvar Heights (c)	16,898	20,786	—
34116	Golden Gate (c)	23,961	25,321	—
*33161	Golden Glades (c)	33,145	32,499	—
32733	Goldenrod (c)	12,039	13,431	—
*32533	Gonzalez (c)	13,273	14,586	—
33170	Goulds (c)	10,103	11,446	—
32043	Green Cove Springs	6,908	9,786	10,130
*33463	Greenacres	37,573	43,990	44,103
*34736	Groveland	8,729	18,505	23,628
*33707	Gulfport	12,029	11,783	11,655
*33844	Haines City	20,535	26,669	37,272
*33009	Hallandale Beach	37,113	41,217	41,547
*33010	Hialeah	224,669	223,109	221,300
*33016	Hialeah Gardens	21,744	23,068	22,286
*33813	Highland City (c)	10,834	12,355	—
*33455	Hobe Sound (c)	11,521	13,163	—
*34690	Holiday (c)	22,403	24,939	—
*32117	Holly Hill	11,659	12,958	13,075
*33019	Hollywood	140,768	153,067	153,859
*33030	Homestead	60,512	80,737	81,659
*34446	Homosassa Springs (c)	13,791	14,283	—
*34786	Horizon West (c)	14,000	58,101	—
*34667	Hudson (c)	12,158	12,944	—
32837	Hunters Creek (c)	14,321	24,433	—
*34142	Immokalee (c)	24,154	24,557	—
33908	Iona (c)	15,369	16,908	—
33179	Ives Estates (c)	19,525	25,005	—
*32202	Jacksonville	821,784	949,611	985,843
*32250	Jacksonville Beach	21,362	23,830	23,447
*34668	Jasmine Estates (c)	18,989	21,525	—
*34957	Jensen Beach (c)	11,707	12,652	—
*33458	Jupiter	55,156	61,047	61,291
33478	Jupiter Farms (c)	11,994	12,572	—
*33183	Kendale Lakes (c)	56,148	55,646	—
*33156	Kendall (c)	75,371	80,241	—
*33185	Kendall West (c)	36,154	36,536	—
33149	Key Biscayne	12,344	14,809	14,414
33037	Key Largo (c)	10,433	12,447	—
*33040	Key West	24,649	26,444	25,103
*33556	Keystone (c)	24,039	25,211	—
*34741	Kissimmee	59,682	79,226	81,269
*32159	Lady Lake	13,926	15,970	16,967
32054	Lake Butler (c)	15,400	18,851	—
*32055	Lake City	12,046	12,329	12,602
*33612	Lake Magdalene (c)	28,509	30,742	—
*32746	Lake Mary	13,822	16,798	16,709
*33853	Lake Wales	14,225	16,361	16,681
*33460	Lake Worth Beach	34,910	42,219	43,346
*33801	Lakeland	97,422	112,641	122,264
33813	Lakeland Highlands (c)	11,056	12,187	—
*32065	Lakeside (c)	30,943	31,275	—
*34951	Lakewood Park (c)	11,323	12,510	—
*34202	Lakewood Ranch (c)	—	34,877	—
*34639	Land O' Lakes (c)	31,996	35,929	—
*33462	Lantana	10,423	11,504	12,086
*33770	Largo	77,648	82,485	82,248
*33319	Lauderdale Lakes	32,593	35,954	36,035
*33313	Lauderhill	66,887	74,482	73,974
34272	Laurel (c)	8,171	12,186	—
*33702	Lealman (c)	19,879	21,189	—
*34748	Leesburg	20,117	27,000	31,721
*33936	Lehigh Acres (c)	86,784	114,287	—
*33030	Leisure City (c)	22,655	26,324	—
34476	Liberty Triangle (c)	—	23,759	—
*33064	Lighthouse Point	10,344	10,486	10,501
32810	Lockhart (c)	13,060	14,058	—

ZIP	Place	2010 population	2020 population	2023 estimate
*32750	Longwood	13,657	15,087	16,794
*33548	Lutz (c)	19,344	23,707	—
32444	Lynn Haven	18,493	18,695	20,501
*32751	Maitland	15,751	19,543	19,215
*33550	Mango (c)	11,313	12,699	—
*34145	Marco Island	16,413	15,760	16,210
*33063	Margate	53,284	58,712	58,593
34473	Marion Oaks (c)	—	19,034	—
32824	Meadow Woods (c)	25,558	43,790	—
*33811	Medulla (c)	8,892	10,871	—
*32901	Melbourne	76,068	84,678	86,960
*32953	Merritt Island (c)	34,743	34,518	—
*33125	Miami	399,457	442,241	455,924
*33140	Miami Beach	87,779	82,890	79,607
*33014	Miami Gardens	107,167	111,640	110,717
*33014	Miami Lakes	29,361	30,467	31,238
*33138	Miami Shores	10,493	11,567	11,530
*33166	Miami Springs	13,809	13,859	13,325
*32068	Middleburg (c)	13,008	12,881	—
32563	Midway (c) (Santa Rosa Co.)	16,115	19,567	—
*32570	Milton	8,826	10,197	10,957
34715	Minneola	9,403	13,843	18,001
*33023	Miramar	122,041	134,721	138,319
*32757	Mount Dora	12,370	16,341	17,756
32526	Myrtle Grove (c)	15,870	17,224	—
*34102	Naples	19,537	19,115	19,704
*33032	Naranja (c)	8,303	13,509	—
32566	Navarre (c)	31,378	40,817	—
*34652	New Port Richey	14,911	16,728	17,708
34653	New Port Richey East (c)	10,036	11,015	—
*32168	New Smyrna Beach	22,464	30,142	32,655
*32578	Niceville	12,749	15,772	16,490
34268	Nocatee (c)	4,524	22,503	—
*33917	North Fort Myers (c)	39,407	42,719	—
*33068	North Lauderdale	41,023	44,794	44,784
*33161	North Miami	58,786	60,191	59,008
*33160	North Miami Beach	41,523	43,676	42,789
*33408	North Palm Beach	12,015	13,162	13,095
*34286	North Port	57,357	74,793	88,934
*33624	Northdale (c)	22,079	23,033	—
*32809	Oak Ridge (c)	22,685	25,062	—
*33334	Oakland Park	41,363	44,229	44,105
32065	Oakleaf Plantation (c)	20,315	31,034	—
*34470	Ocala	56,315	63,591	68,426
34761	Ocoee	35,579	47,295	49,261
33163	Ojus (c)	18,036	19,673	—
34677	Oldsmar	13,591	14,898	14,831
*33165	Olympia Heights (c)	13,488	12,873	—
34481	On Top of the World (c)	—	12,668	—
*33054	Opa-locka	15,219	16,463	15,794
*32763	Orange City	10,599	12,632	14,928
*32801	Orlando	238,300	307,573	320,742
*32174	Ormond Beach	38,137	43,080	44,277
*32765	Oviedo	33,342	40,059	41,231
32571	Pace (c)	20,039	24,684	—
*32177	Palatka	10,558	10,446	10,730
*32905	Palm Bay	103,190	119,760	135,566
*33410	Palm Beach Gardens	48,452	59,182	61,146
*34990	Palm City (c)	23,120	25,883	—
*32137	Palm Coast	75,180	89,258	102,113
*34683	Palm Harbor (c)	57,439	61,366	—
*33619	Palm River-Clair Mel (c)	21,024	26,142	—
*33406	Palm Springs	18,928	26,890	27,132
32082	Palm Valley (c)	20,019	21,827	—
34238	Palmer Ranch (c)	—	14,966	—
*34221	Palmetto	12,606	13,323	13,577
*33157	Palmetto Bay	23,410	24,439	24,264
33157	Palmetto Estates (c)	13,535	13,498	—
*32401	Panama City	36,484	32,939	35,660
*32413	Panama City Beach	12,018	18,094	19,393
*33067	Parkland	23,962	34,670	37,911
35541	Pasadena Hills (c)	7,570	11,120	—
*33025	Pembroke Pines	154,750	171,178	171,119
*32502	Pensacola	51,923	54,312	53,724
*32809	Pine Castle (c)	10,805	11,122	—
*32808	Pine Hills (c)	60,076	66,111	—
34465	Pine Ridge (c) (Citrus Co.)	9,598	11,042	—
*33156	Pinecrest	18,223	18,388	18,051
*33781	Pinellas Park	49,079	53,093	53,456
*33147	Pinewood (c)	16,520	17,246	—
*33566	Plant City	34,721	39,764	40,571
*33311	Plantation	84,955	91,750	96,548
*34758	Poinciana (c)	53,193	69,309	—
*33060	Pompano Beach	99,845	112,046	113,619

ZIP	Place	2010 population	2020 population	2023 estimate
*33952	Port Charlotte (c)	54,392	60,625	—
*32129	Port Orange	56,048	62,596	65,966
32927	Port St. John (c)	12,267	23,474	—
*34953	Port St. Lucie	164,603	204,851	245,021
*34997	Port Salerno (c)	10,091	10,401	—
*33032	Princeton (c)	22,038	39,308	—
*33578	Progress Village (c)	5,392	11,188	—
*33950	Punta Gorda	16,641	19,471	20,227
*33177	Richmond West (c)	31,973	35,884	—
*33569	Riverview (c)	71,050	107,396	—
*33404	Riviera Beach	32,488	37,604	38,663
*32955	Rockledge	24,926	27,678	29,452
33947	Rotonda (c)	8,759	10,114	—
*33411	Royal Palm Beach	34,140	38,932	39,489
*33570	Ruskin (c)	17,208	28,620	—
34695	Safety Harbor	16,884	17,072	16,955
*32084	Saint Augustine	12,975	14,329	15,596
*34769	Saint Cloud	35,183	58,964	66,448
*33701	Saint Petersburg	244,769	258,308	263,553
*33912	San Carlos Park (c)	16,824	18,563	—
*32771	Sanford	53,570	61,051	65,394
*34231	Sarasota	51,917	54,842	57,602
*34232	Sarasota Springs (c)	14,395	12,521	—
32937	Satellite Beach	10,109	11,226	11,343
*32958	Sebastian	21,929	25,054	26,846
*33870	Sebring	10,491	10,729	11,563
*33772	Seminole	17,233	19,364	19,252
34610	Shady Hills (c)	11,523	11,690	—
34472	Silver Springs Shores (c)	6,539	24,846	—
*34207	South Bradenton (c)	22,178	26,858	—
*32119	South Daytona	12,252	12,865	13,781
*33143	South Miami	11,657	12,026	12,073
33157	South Miami Heights (c)	35,696	36,770	—
34293	South Venice (c)	13,949	15,619	—
32824	Southchase (c)	15,921	16,276	—
*34604	Spring Hill (c)	98,621	113,568	—
*34994	Stuart	15,593	17,425	19,430
34446	Sugarmill Woods (c)	8,287	11,204	—
*33573	Sun City Center (c)	19,258	30,952	—
33160	Sunny Isles Beach	20,832	22,342	21,885
*33325	Sunrise	84,439	97,335	96,808
*33165	Sunset (c)	16,389	15,912	—
*33144	Sweetwater	13,499	19,363	20,352
*32301	Tallahassee	181,376	196,169	202,221
*33321	Tamarac	60,427	71,897	72,372
*33184	Tamiami (c)	55,271	54,212	—
*33602	Tampa	335,709	384,959	403,364
*34689	Tarpon Springs	23,484	25,117	25,872
32778	Tavares	13,951	19,003	21,061
*33617	Temple Terrace	24,541	26,690	26,972
*33412	The Acreage (c)	38,704	41,654	—
33186	The Crossings (c)	22,758	23,276	—
33196	The Hammocks (c)	51,003	59,480	—
*32162	The Villages (c)	51,442	79,077	—
33592	Thonotosassa (c)	13,014	15,238	—
33186	Three Lakes (c)	15,047	16,540	—
*32780	Titusville	43,761	48,789	49,680
33615	Town 'n' Country (c)	78,442	85,951	—
34655	Trinity (c)	10,907	11,924	—
32817	Union Park (c)	9,765	10,452	—
*33612	University (c) (Hillsborough Co.)	41,163	50,893	—
32826	University (c) (Orange Co.)	31,084	45,284	—
*32407	Upper Grand Lagoon (c)	13,963	15,778	—
*33594	Valrico (c)	35,545	37,895	—
*34285	Venice	20,748	25,463	28,150
*32960	Vero Beach	15,220	16,354	17,317
*32960	Vero Beach South (c)	23,092	28,020	—
32955	Viera East (c)	10,757	11,687	—
32940	Viera West (c)	6,641	16,688	—
*33907	Villas (c)	11,569	12,687	—
32507	Warrington (c)	14,531	15,218	—
32779	Wekiwa Springs (c)	21,998	23,428	—
*33414	Wellington	56,508	61,637	61,634
*33544	Wesley Chapel (c)	44,092	64,866	—
*33709	West Lealman (c)	15,651	16,438	—
33147	West Little River (c)	34,699	34,128	—
*32904	West Melbourne	18,355	25,924	29,144
*33401	West Palm Beach	99,919	117,415	124,130
33023	West Park	14,156	15,130	15,109
*32505	West Pensacola (c)	21,339	21,019	—
33157	West Perrine (c)	9,460	10,602	—
32966	West Vero Corridor (c)	7,138	10,039	—
33626	Westchase (c)	21,747	25,952	—
33165	Westchester (c)	29,862	56,384	—
*33326	Weston	65,333	68,107	68,181
33165	Westwood Lakes (c)	11,838	11,373	—
34785	Wildwood	6,709	15,730	18,636
*33305	Wilton Manors	11,632	11,426	11,403
*34787	Winter Garden	34,568	46,964	47,294
*33880	Winter Haven	33,874	49,219	57,109
*32789	Winter Park	27,852	29,795	29,894
*32708	Winter Springs	33,282	38,342	38,941
32092	World Golf Village (c)	12,310	22,117	—
32547	Wright (c)	23,127	26,277	—
*32097	Yulee (c)	11,491	14,195	—
*33540	Zephyrhills	13,288	17,194	20,883

Georgia

Area codes: 229, 404/470/678/770/943, 478, 706/762, 912

ZIP	Place	2010 population	2020 population	2023 estimate
*30101	Acworth	20,425	22,440	22,379
*31701	Albany	77,434	69,647	66,877
*30004	Alpharetta	57,551	65,818	67,056
*31709	Americus	17,041	16,230	15,703
*30601	Athens-Clarke Co. (balance)	115,452	127,315	128,628
*30303	Atlanta	420,003	498,715	510,823
*30901	Augusta-Richmond Co. (balance)	195,844	202,081	200,884
*39817	Bainbridge	12,697	14,468	14,423
30032	Belvedere Park (c)	15,152	15,113	—
30517	Braselton	7,511	13,403	15,538
*30319	Brookhaven[1]	—	55,161	57,945
*31520	Brunswick	15,383	15,210	15,404
*30518	Buford	12,225	17,144	18,273
*39827	Cairo	9,607	10,179	10,007
*30701	Calhoun	15,650	16,949	18,900
30032	Candler-McAfee (c)	23,025	22,468	—
*30114	Canton	22,958	32,973	36,857
*30116	Carrollton	24,388	26,738	27,793
*30120	Cartersville	19,731	23,187	24,937
30125	Cedartown	9,750	10,190	10,300
*30341	Chamblee	9,892	30,164	31,841
30021	Clarkston	7,554	14,756	14,396
*30337	College Park	13,942	13,930	13,867
*31901	Columbus	189,885	206,922	201,877
*30013	Conyers	15,195	17,305	19,505
*30014	Covington	13,118	14,192	14,677
*30132	Dallas	11,544	14,042	14,985
*30720	Dalton	33,128	34,417	34,508
*30030	Decatur	19,335	24,928	24,307
*30340	Doraville	8,330	10,623	10,780
*31533	Douglas	11,589	11,722	11,769
*30134	Douglasville	30,961	34,650	39,049
*31021	Dublin	16,201	16,074	16,008
*30096	Duluth	26,600	31,873	32,350
*30338	Dunwoody	46,267	51,683	51,713
*30344	East Point	33,712	38,358	38,115
30809	Evans (c)	29,011	34,536	—
30213	Fairburn	12,950	16,483	16,661
*30214	Fayetteville	15,945	18,957	20,083
30542	Flowery Branch	5,679	9,391	11,607
*30297	Forest Park	18,468	19,932	19,368
30742	Fort Oglethorpe	9,263	10,423	10,598
*30501	Gainesville	33,804	42,296	47,265
*31405	Garden City	8,778	10,289	10,373
39854	Georgetown (c)	11,823	11,916	—
*30223	Griffin	23,643	23,478	24,044
30813	Grovetown	11,216	15,577	17,580
*31313	Hinesville	33,437	34,891	36,181
*30114	Holly Springs	9,189	16,213	19,540
30549	Jefferson	9,432	13,233	15,756
*31545	Jesup	10,214	9,809	10,065
*30097	Johns Creek	76,728	82,453	81,108
*30144	Kennesaw	29,783	33,036	34,683
31548	Kingsland	15,946	18,337	20,343
*30240	LaGrange	29,588	30,858	32,343
*30045	Lawrenceville	28,546	30,629	31,015
*30047	Lilburn	11,596	14,502	15,862
30122	Lithia Springs (c)	15,491	16,644	—
30248	Locust Grove	5,402	8,947	11,199
30052	Loganville	10,458	14,127	16,516
30250	Lovejoy	6,422	10,122	12,080
30126	Mableton (c)	37,115	40,834	—
*31201	Macon-Bibb Co.	91,351	157,346	156,512
*30060	Marietta	56,579	60,972	62,769
30907	Martinez (c)	35,795	34,535	—
*30253	McDonough	22,084	29,051	32,138
*31061	Milledgeville	17,715	17,070	16,486

ZIP	Place	2010 population	2020 population	2023 estimate
*30004	Milton	32,661	41,296	41,383
*30655	Monroe	13,234	14,928	15,929
*31768	Moultrie	14,268	14,638	14,565
30075	Mountain Park (c)	11,554	13,089	—
*30263	Newnan	33,039	42,549	44,940
*30071	Norcross	9,116	17,209	18,043
30033	North Decatur (c)	16,698	18,511	—
*30329	North Druid Hills (c)	18,947	20,385	—
30034	Panthersville (c)	9,749	11,237	—
*30269	Peachtree City	34,364	38,244	40,193
*30092	Peachtree Corners[1]	—	42,243	42,136
31069	Perry	13,839	20,624	24,029
31322	Pooler	19,140	25,711	29,544
31407	Port Wentworth	5,359	10,878	14,468
30127	Powder Springs	13,940	16,887	18,950
30074	Redan (c)	33,015	31,749	—
31324	Richmond Hill	9,281	16,633	18,459
31326	Rincon	8,836	10,934	11,624
*30274	Riverdale	15,134	15,129	14,672
*30161	Rome	36,303	37,713	38,111
*30075	Roswell	88,346	92,833	91,706
31558	Saint Marys	17,121	18,256	19,537
31522	Saint Simons (c)	12,743	14,982	—
*30350	Sandy Springs	93,853	108,080	105,793
*31401	Savannah	136,286	147,780	147,748
30079	Scottdale (c)	10,631	10,698	—
*30080	Smyrna	51,271	55,663	56,566
*30078	Snellville	18,242	20,573	22,067
*30336	South Fulton[1]	—	107,436	110,920
*30458	Statesboro	28,422	33,438	34,452
30281	Stockbridge	25,636	28,973	35,452
*30038	Stonecrest[1]	—	59,194	60,677
30518	Sugar Hill	18,522	25,076	25,889
30024	Suwanee	15,355	20,786	22,913
*31792	Thomasville	18,413	18,881	18,558
*31794	Tifton	16,350	17,045	17,357
*30084	Tucker	27,581	37,005	36,975
30291	Union City	19,456	26,830	27,832
*31601	Valdosta	54,518	55,378	55,025
*30474	Vidalia	10,473	10,785	10,741
30180	Villa Rica	13,956	16,970	18,703
30339	Vinings (c)	9,734	12,581	—
*31088	Warner Robins	66,588	80,308	84,537
*31501	Waycross	14,649	13,942	13,714
31410	Wilmington Island (c)	15,138	15,129	—
30680	Winder	14,099	18,338	19,669
*30188	Woodstock	23,896	35,065	38,473

(1) Incorporated after 2010 Census.

Hawaii

Area code: 808 applies to the entire state

ZIP	Place	2010 population	2020 population	2023 estimate
96701	Aiea (c)	9,338	10,408	—
*96821	East Honolulu (c)	49,914	50,922	—
96706	Ewa Beach (c)	14,955	16,415	—
96706	Ewa Gentry (c)	22,690	25,707	—
96701	Halawa (c)	14,014	15,016	—
96749	Hawaiian Paradise Park (c)	11,404	14,957	—
*96720	Hilo (c)	43,263	44,186	—
*96813	Honolulu, urban (c)	337,256	350,964	341,778
*96732	Kahului (c)	26,337	28,219	—
*96740	Kailua (c) (Hawaii Co.)	11,975	19,713	—
96734	Kailua (c) (Honolulu Co.)	38,635	40,514	—
*96725	Kaiminani (c)	—	12,590	—
96744	Kaneohe (c)	34,597	37,430	—
96746	Kapaa (c)	10,699	11,652	—
*96707	Kapolei (c)	15,186	21,411	—
96753	Kihei (c)	20,881	21,423	—
*96761	Lahaina (c)	11,704	12,702	—
96792	Maili (c)	9,488	11,535	—
96707	Makakilo (c)	18,248	19,877	—
96789	Mililani (c)	27,629	28,121	—
96789	Mililani Mauka (c)	21,039	21,075	—
96792	Nanakuli (c)	12,666	12,195	—
96706	Ocean Pointe (c)	8,361	14,965	—
96782	Pearl City (c)	47,698	45,295	—
96797	Royal Kunia (c)	14,525	14,896	—
96857	Schofield Barracks (c)	16,370	14,904	—
96786	Wahiawa (c)	17,821	18,658	—
96792	Waianae (c)	13,177	13,614	—
96793	Wailuku (c)	15,313	17,697	—
96701	Waimalu (c)	13,730	13,817	—
96797	Waipahu (c)	38,216	43,485	—
*96797	Waipio (c)	11,674	12,082	—

Idaho

Area codes: 208/986 apply to the entire state

ZIP	Place	2010 population	2020 population	2023 estimate
*83401	Ammon	13,816	17,694	19,617
83221	Blackfoot	11,899	12,346	12,999
*83702	Boise	205,671	235,684	235,421
83318	Burley	10,345	11,704	12,146
*83605	Caldwell	46,237	59,996	68,336
83202	Chubbuck	13,922	15,570	16,362
*83814	Coeur d'Alene	44,137	54,628	56,894
*83616	Eagle	19,908	30,346	32,319
*83714	Garden City	10,972	12,316	12,784
83835	Hayden	13,294	15,570	16,422
*83402	Idaho Falls	56,813	64,818	68,001
83338	Jerome	10,890	12,349	13,135
*83634	Kuna	15,210	24,011	28,050
83501	Lewiston	31,894	34,203	34,836
*83642	Meridian	75,092	117,635	134,801
83644	Middleton	5,524	9,425	11,016
*83843	Moscow	23,800	25,435	26,387
83647	Mountain Home	14,206	15,979	16,703
*83651	Nampa	81,557	100,200	114,268
*83201	Pocatello	54,255	56,320	58,064
*83854	Post Falls	27,574	38,485	44,798
83858	Rathdrum	6,826	9,211	11,580
*83440	Rexburg	25,484	39,409	39,975
83864	Sandpoint	7,365	8,639	10,024
83669	Star	5,793	11,117	16,333
*83301	Twin Falls	44,125	51,807	54,943

Illinois

Area codes: 217/447, 224/847, 309/861, 312/773/872, 331/630, 464/708, 618/730, 779/815

ZIP	Place	2010 population	2020 population	2023 estimate
60101	Addison	36,942	35,702	35,167
*60102	Algonquin	30,046	29,700	30,134
60803	Alsip	19,277	19,063	18,198
62002	Alton	27,865	25,676	25,006
60002	Antioch	14,430	14,622	14,833
*60005	Arlington Heights	75,101	77,676	74,495
*60505	Aurora	197,899	180,542	177,563
*60010	Barrington	10,327	10,722	10,476
*60103	Bartlett	41,208	41,105	39,992
*60510	Batavia	26,045	26,098	26,235
*60099	Beach Park	13,638	14,249	14,057
*62220	Belleville	44,478	42,404	40,726
60104	Bellwood	19,071	18,789	17,890
61008	Belvidere	25,585	25,339	25,297
*60106	Bensenville	18,352	18,813	18,352
60402	Berwyn	56,657	57,250	54,414
*60108	Bloomingdale	22,018	22,382	22,298
*61701	Bloomington	76,610	78,680	78,587
60406	Blue Island	23,706	22,558	21,494
*60440	Bolingbrook	73,366	73,922	74,088
60914	Bourbonnais	18,631	18,164	18,042
60915	Bradley	15,895	15,419	15,263
60455	Bridgeview	16,446	17,027	16,324
60513	Brookfield	18,978	19,476	18,591
60089	Buffalo Grove	41,496	43,212	42,482
60459	Burbank	28,925	29,439	28,164
60527	Burr Ridge	10,559	11,192	11,023
*62203	Cahokia Heights[1]	—	—	17,114
60409	Calumet City	37,042	36,033	34,358
*60175	Campton Hills	11,131	10,885	10,795
61520	Canton	14,704	13,242	12,875
*62901	Carbondale	25,902	21,857	21,592
*60188	Carol Stream	39,711	39,854	38,966
60110	Carpentersville	37,691	37,983	37,099
60013	Cary	18,271	17,826	17,977
62801	Centralia	13,032	12,182	11,848
*61820	Champaign	81,055	88,302	89,189
60410	Channahon	12,560	13,383	14,138
61920	Charleston	21,838	17,286	17,028
62629	Chatham	11,500	14,377	14,525
*60602	Chicago	2,695,598	2,746,388	2,664,452
*60411	Chicago Heights	30,276	27,480	26,184
60415	Chicago Ridge	14,305	14,433	13,834
60804	Cicero	83,891	85,268	81,004
62234	Collinsville	25,579	24,366	23,779
62236	Columbia	9,707	10,999	10,933
60478	Country Club Hills	16,541	16,775	16,013
*60403	Crest Hill	20,837	20,459	20,118
*60418	Crestwood	10,950	10,826	10,387
*60014	Crystal Lake	40,743	40,269	40,861
*61832	Danville	33,027	29,204	28,206
60561	Darien	22,086	22,011	21,698

ZIP	Place	2010 population	2020 population	2023 estimate
*62521	Decatur	76,122	70,522	68,670
60015	Deerfield	18,225	19,196	18,884
60115	DeKalb	43,862	40,290	40,211
*60016	Des Plaines	58,364	60,675	58,010
61021	Dixon	15,733	15,274	15,096
60419	Dolton	23,153	21,426	20,410
*60515	Downers Grove	47,833	50,247	49,706
61244	East Moline	21,302	21,374	20,806
*61611	East Peoria	23,402	22,484	22,012
*62201	East St. Louis	27,006	18,469	17,642
*62025	Edwardsville	24,293	26,808	26,698
62401	Effingham	12,328	12,252	12,258
*60120	Elgin	108,188	114,797	113,310
*60007	Elk Grove Village	33,127	32,812	31,350
60126	Elmhurst	44,121	45,786	45,336
60707	Elmwood Park	24,883	24,521	23,369
*60201	Evanston	74,486	78,110	75,070
60805	Evergreen Park	19,852	19,943	19,010
62208	Fairview Heights	17,078	16,706	16,125
60130	Forest Park	14,167	14,339	13,660
60020	Fox Lake	10,579	10,978	10,805
60423	Frankfort	17,782	20,296	20,907
60131	Franklin Park	18,333	18,467	17,871
61032	Freeport	25,638	23,973	23,136
60030	Gages Lake (c)	10,198	10,637	—
*61401	Galesburg	32,195	30,052	29,130
60134	Geneva	21,495	21,393	21,129
62034	Glen Carbon	12,934	13,842	13,868
*60137	Glen Ellyn	27,450	28,846	28,347
*60139	Glendale Heights	34,208	33,176	32,409
*60025	Glenview	44,692	48,705	46,904
62035	Godfrey	17,982	17,825	17,597
62040	Granite City	29,849	27,549	26,908
60030	Grayslake	20,957	21,248	20,954
60031	Gurnee	31,295	30,706	30,193
60133	Hanover Park	37,973	37,470	36,165
*60426	Harvey	25,282	20,324	19,397
60429	Hazel Crest	14,100	13,382	12,771
62948	Herrin	12,501	12,352	12,178
60457	Hickory Hills	14,049	14,505	13,884
*60035	Highland Park	29,763	30,176	30,272
*60521	Hinsdale	16,816	17,395	17,297
*60195	Hoffman Estates	51,895	52,530	50,179
*60491	Homer Glen	24,220	24,543	24,546
*60430	Homewood	19,323	19,463	18,540
60142	Huntley	24,291	27,740	28,269
*62650	Jacksonville	19,446	17,616	17,237
*60432	Joliet	147,433	150,362	150,489
60458	Justice	12,926	12,600	12,081
60901	Kankakee	27,537	24,052	23,503
61443	Kewanee	12,916	12,509	12,222
*60525	La Grange	15,550	16,321	15,667
60526	La Grange Park	13,579	13,475	13,011
60045	Lake Forest	19,375	19,367	19,354
*60102	Lake in the Hills	28,965	28,982	28,661
60047	Lake Zurich	19,631	19,759	19,676
60438	Lansing	28,331	29,076	27,713
60439	Lemont	16,000	17,629	17,575
60048	Libertyville	20,315	20,579	20,332
62656	Lincoln	14,504	13,288	13,072
*60712	Lincolnwood	12,590	13,463	12,872
60046	Lindenhurst	14,462	14,406	14,339
60532	Lisle	22,390	24,223	23,222
*60441	Lockport	24,839	26,094	26,537
60148	Lombard	43,165	44,476	43,779
*61111	Loves Park	23,996	23,397	23,335
60534	Lyons	10,729	10,817	10,304
*61115	Machesney Park	23,499	22,950	22,630
61455	Macomb	19,288	15,051	14,849
61853	Mahomet	7,258	9,434	10,273
60442	Manhattan	7,051	9,385	10,547
62959	Marion	17,193	16,855	16,852
*60428	Markham	12,508	11,661	11,129
60443	Matteson	19,009	19,073	18,293
61938	Mattoon	18,555	16,870	16,560
*60153	Maywood	24,090	23,512	22,880
*60050	McHenry	26,992	27,135	28,251
*60160	Melrose Park	25,411	24,796	23,666
60445	Midlothian	14,819	14,325	13,675
60447	Minooka	10,924	12,758	12,879
60448	Mokena	18,740	19,887	19,759
*61265	Moline	43,483	42,985	41,965
60538	Montgomery	18,438	20,262	21,955
60450	Morris	13,636	14,163	14,508
61550	Morton	16,267	17,117	17,469
60053	Morton Grove	23,270	25,297	24,131
60056	Mount Prospect	54,167	56,852	54,298
62864	Mount Vernon	15,277	14,600	14,247
60060	Mundelein	31,064	31,560	31,790
*60540	Naperville	141,853	149,540	150,245
60451	New Lenox	24,394	27,214	28,047
60714	Niles	29,803	30,912	29,513
*61761	Normal	52,497	52,736	52,618
*60706	Norridge	14,572	15,251	14,620
60542	North Aurora	16,760	18,261	19,022
*60064	North Chicago	32,574	30,759	30,416
*60062	Northbrook	33,170	35,222	33,977
60164	Northlake	12,323	12,840	12,270
60452	Oak Forest	27,962	27,478	26,199
*60453	Oak Lawn	56,690	58,362	55,734
*60301	Oak Park	51,878	54,583	52,055
62269	O'Fallon	28,281	32,289	31,968
*60462	Orland Park	56,767	58,703	57,074
60543	Oswego	30,355	34,585	37,074
61350	Ottawa	18,768	18,840	18,752
*60067	Palatine	68,557	67,908	64,869
60463	Palos Heights	12,515	12,068	11,515
60465	Palos Hills	17,484	18,530	17,759
*60466	Park Forest	21,975	21,687	20,763
60068	Park Ridge	37,480	39,656	37,897
*61554	Pekin	34,094	31,731	31,126
*61602	Peoria	115,007	113,150	110,460
60140	Pingree Grove	4,532	10,365	11,137
*60544	Plainfield	39,581	44,762	47,448
60545	Plano	10,856	11,847	12,676
61764	Pontiac	11,931	11,150	11,010
60070	Prospect Heights	16,256	16,058	15,334
*62301	Quincy	40,633	39,463	38,803
61866	Rantoul	12,941	12,371	11,956
60471	Richton Park	13,646	12,775	12,322
60305	River Forest	11,172	11,717	11,227
60171	River Grove	10,227	10,612	10,282
60827	Riverdale	13,549	10,663	10,159
*61201	Rock Island	39,018	37,108	36,132
*61101	Rockford	152,871	148,655	146,120
60008	Rolling Meadows	24,099	24,200	23,329
60446	Romeoville	39,680	39,863	40,955
61073	Roscoe	10,785	10,983	10,843
60172	Roselle	22,763	22,897	22,508
60073	Round Lake	18,289	18,721	18,430
60073	Round Lake Beach	28,175	27,252	26,783
*60174	Saint Charles	32,974	33,081	32,654
*60193	Schaumburg	74,227	78,723	75,750
*60176	Schiller Park	11,793	11,709	11,164
*62269	Shiloh	12,651	14,098	14,736
*60404	Shorewood	15,615	18,186	18,369
*60077	Skokie	64,784	67,824	64,937
60177	South Elgin	21,985	23,865	24,277
60473	South Holland	22,030	21,465	20,483
*62701	Springfield	116,250	114,394	112,544
61081	Sterling	15,370	14,764	14,508
60107	Streamwood	39,858	39,577	37,780
*61364	Streator	13,710	12,500	12,269
60501	Summit	11,054	11,161	10,616
*62226	Swansea	13,430	14,386	14,472
60178	Sycamore	17,519	18,577	18,682
62568	Taylorville	11,246	10,506	10,247
*60477	Tinley Park	56,703	55,971	53,886
62294	Troy	9,888	10,960	11,209
*61801	Urbana	41,250	38,336	38,209
60061	Vernon Hills	25,113	26,850	26,677
60181	Villa Park	21,904	22,263	21,727
60555	Warrenville	13,140	13,553	15,027
61571	Washington	15,134	16,071	15,833
62298	Waterloo	9,811	11,013	11,144
60084	Wauconda	13,603	14,084	13,891
*60085	Waukegan	89,078	89,321	87,642
*60185	West Chicago	27,086	25,614	25,116
60154	Westchester	16,718	16,892	16,094
60558	Western Springs	12,975	13,629	13,290
60559	Westmont	24,685	24,429	23,933
*60187	Wheaton	52,894	53,970	52,938
60090	Wheeling	37,648	39,137	37,725
60091	Wilmette	27,087	28,170	27,026
60190	Winfield	9,080	9,835	10,054
60093	Winnetka	12,187	12,744	12,292
*60191	Wood Dale	13,770	14,012	13,774
62095	Wood River	10,657	10,464	10,270
60517	Woodridge	32,971	34,158	33,566
60098	Woodstock	24,770	25,630	25,699
60482	Worth	10,789	10,970	10,494
60560	Yorkville	16,921	21,533	24,693
60099	Zion	24,413	24,655	24,206

(1) Incorporated after 2020 Census.

Indiana

Area codes: 219, 260, 317/463, 574, 765, 812/930

ZIP	Place	2010 population	2020 population	2023 estimate
*46011	Anderson	56,129	54,788	55,199
46706	Auburn	12,731	13,412	13,888
46123	Avon	12,446	21,474	24,231
46106	Bargersville	4,013	9,560	11,075
47421	Bedford	13,413	13,792	13,855
46107	Beech Grove	14,192	14,717	14,422
*47408	Bloomington	80,405	79,168	78,840
46714	Bluffton	9,897	10,308	10,467
46112	Brownsburg	21,285	28,973	32,250
*46032	Carmel	79,191	99,757	102,296
46303	Cedar Lake	11,560	14,106	16,068
46304	Chesterton	13,068	14,241	14,657
*47129	Clarksville	21,724	22,333	22,208
46725	Columbia City	8,750	9,892	10,126
*47201	Columbus	44,061	50,474	51,522
47331	Connersville	13,481	13,324	13,298
47933	Crawfordsville	15,915	16,306	16,577
*46307	Crown Point	27,317	33,899	34,884
46122	Danville	9,001	10,559	11,525
46733	Decatur	9,405	9,913	10,020
*46311	Dyer	16,390	16,517	16,333
46312	East Chicago	29,698	26,370	25,830
*46514	Elkhart	50,949	53,923	53,484
*47708	Evansville	117,429	117,298	115,332
*46038	Fishers	76,794	98,977	104,094
*46802	Fort Wayne	253,691	263,886	269,994
*46041	Frankfort	16,422	16,715	16,409
46131	Franklin	23,712	25,313	25,908
*46402	Gary	80,294	69,093	67,652
*46526	Goshen	31,719	34,517	34,355
46530	Granger (c)	30,465	30,337	—
46140	Greenfield	20,602	23,488	25,920
47240	Greensburg	11,492	12,312	12,363
*46142	Greenwood	49,791	63,830	66,296
46319	Griffith	16,893	16,528	16,222
*46320	Hammond	80,830	77,879	76,193
*46322	Highland	23,727	23,984	23,525
46342	Hobart	29,059	29,752	29,408
46748	Huntertown	4,810	9,141	11,316
46750	Huntington	17,391	17,022	16,992
*46201	Indianapolis (balance)	820,445	887,642	879,293
*47546	Jasper	15,038	16,703	16,781
*47130	Jeffersonville	44,953	49,447	51,235
46755	Kendallville	9,862	10,271	10,239
*46902	Kokomo	45,468	59,604	59,890
*46350	La Porte	22,053	22,471	22,486
*47901	Lafayette	67,140	70,783	71,216
46405	Lake Station	12,572	13,235	13,047
46226	Lawrence	46,001	49,370	49,235
46052	Lebanon	15,792	16,662	17,252
46947	Logansport	18,396	18,366	18,233
46356	Lowell	9,276	10,680	11,239
47250	Madison	11,967	12,357	12,208
*46952	Marion	29,948	28,310	28,105
46151	Martinsville	11,828	11,932	11,946
46055	McCordsville	4,797	8,503	11,273
*46410	Merrillville	35,246	36,444	36,347
*46360	Michigan City	31,479	32,075	31,659
*46544	Mishawaka	48,252	51,063	50,842
*47302	Muncie	70,085	65,194	65,081
46321	Munster	23,603	23,894	23,614
*47150	New Albany	36,372	37,841	37,329
47362	New Castle	18,114	17,396	17,329
46774	New Haven	14,794	15,583	15,974
*46060	Noblesville	51,969	69,604	73,916
*46970	Peru	11,417	11,073	10,953
*46168	Plainfield	27,631	34,625	37,047
46563	Plymouth	10,033	10,214	10,989
46368	Portage	36,828	37,926	38,513
*47374	Richmond	36,812	35,720	35,425
46373	Saint John	14,850	20,303	23,644
46375	Schererville	29,243	29,646	29,657
47172	Sellersburg	6,128	9,310	10,058
47274	Seymour	17,503	21,569	21,666
46176	Shelbyville	19,191	20,067	20,609
*46601	South Bend	101,168	103,453	103,395
46224	Speedway	11,812	13,952	14,157
*47802	Terre Haute	60,785	58,389	58,502
*46383	Valparaiso	31,730	34,151	34,627
47591	Vincennes	18,423	16,759	16,588
46992	Wabash	10,666	10,440	10,269
*46580	Warsaw	13,559	15,804	16,097
47501	Washington	11,509	12,017	12,513
*47906	West Lafayette	29,596	44,595	44,829
*46074	Westfield	30,068	46,410	57,746
46075	Whitestown	2,867	10,178	13,049
47396	Yorktown	9,405	11,548	11,740
46077	Zionsville	14,160	30,603	32,534

Iowa

Area codes: 319, 515, 563, 641, 712

ZIP	Place	2010 population	2020 population	2023 estimate
50009	Altoona	14,541	19,565	21,698
*50010	Ames	58,965	66,427	65,686
*50023	Ankeny	45,582	67,887	74,458
52722	Bettendorf	33,217	39,102	39,858
*50036	Boone	12,661	12,460	12,416
52601	Burlington	25,663	23,982	23,565
51401	Carroll	10,103	10,321	10,163
*50613	Cedar Falls	39,260	40,713	40,737
*52401	Cedar Rapids	126,326	137,710	135,958
*52732	Clinton	26,885	24,469	24,239
*50325	Clive	15,447	18,601	19,005
52241	Coralville	18,907	22,318	23,596
*51501	Council Bluffs	62,230	62,799	62,399
*52801	Davenport	99,685	101,724	100,354
*50309	Des Moines	203,433	214,133	210,381
*52001	Dubuque	57,637	59,667	58,877
50501	Fort Dodge	25,206	24,871	24,591
52627	Fort Madison	11,051	10,270	10,053
50111	Grimes	8,246	15,392	16,362
50125	Indianola	14,782	15,833	16,043
*52240	Iowa City	67,862	74,828	75,678
50131	Johnston	17,278	24,064	24,640
51031	Le Mars	9,826	10,571	10,618
52302	Marion	34,768	41,535	42,213
50158	Marshalltown	27,552	27,591	27,574
*50401	Mason City	28,079	27,338	26,906
52761	Muscatine	22,886	23,797	23,341
50208	Newton	15,254	15,760	15,645
52317	North Liberty	13,374	20,479	21,345
50211	Norwalk	8,945	12,799	14,873
52577	Oskaloosa	11,463	11,558	11,448
52501	Ottumwa	25,023	25,529	25,252
50219	Pella	10,352	10,464	10,820
*50327	Pleasant Hill	8,785	10,147	11,617
*51101	Sioux City	82,684	85,797	85,727
51301	Spencer	11,233	11,325	11,451
50588	Storm Lake	10,600	11,269	11,434
*50322	Urbandale	39,463	45,580	46,729
*50701	Waterloo	68,406	67,314	66,606
50263	Waukee	13,790	23,940	31,645
50677	Waverly	9,874	10,394	10,561
*50265	West Des Moines	56,609	68,723	72,205

Kansas

Area codes: 316, 620, 785, 913

ZIP	Place	2010 population	2020 population	2023 estimate
67002	Andover	11,791	14,892	15,814
67005	Arkansas City	12,415	11,974	11,765
66002	Atchison	11,021	10,885	10,670
67037	Derby	22,158	25,625	26,233
*67801	Dodge City	27,340	27,788	27,514
67042	El Dorado	13,021	12,870	12,919
66801	Emporia	24,916	24,139	24,105
*67846	Garden City	26,658	28,151	27,371
66030	Gardner	19,123	23,287	25,378
67530	Great Bend	15,995	14,733	14,372
*67601	Hays	20,510	21,116	21,040
67060	Haysville	10,826	11,262	11,268
*67501	Hutchinson	42,080	40,006	39,662
*66441	Junction City	23,353	22,932	21,856
*66101	Kansas City	145,786	156,607	152,933
66043	Lansing	11,265	11,239	11,221
*66044	Lawrence	87,643	94,934	96,207
*66048	Leavenworth	35,251	37,351	37,034
*66211	Leawood	31,867	33,902	33,980
*66215	Lenexa	48,190	57,434	58,536
*67901	Liberal	20,525	19,825	18,999
*66502	Manhattan	52,281	54,100	53,682
67460	McPherson	13,155	14,082	13,906
*66202	Merriam	11,003	11,098	10,875
*66202	Mission	9,323	9,954	10,014
*67114	Newton	19,132	18,602	18,251
*66061	Olathe	125,872	141,290	147,461
66067	Ottawa	12,649	12,625	12,686
*66212	Overland Park	173,372	197,238	197,089
*66762	Pittsburg	20,233	20,646	20,504
*66208	Prairie Village	21,447	22,957	22,900
*67401	Salina	47,707	46,889	45,792
*66203	Shawnee	62,209	67,311	69,417
*66603	Topeka	127,473	126,587	125,475
*67202	Wichita	382,368	397,532	396,119
67156	Winfield	12,301	11,777	11,669

Kentucky

Area codes: 270/364, 502, 606, 859

ZIP	Place	2010 population	2020 population	2023 estimate
41001	Alexandria	8,477	10,341	10,673
*41101	Ashland	21,684	21,625	21,154
40004	Bardstown	11,700	13,567	13,832
*40403	Berea	13,561	15,539	15,998
*42101	Bowling Green	58,067	72,294	76,212
41005	Burlington (c)	15,926	17,318	—
*42718	Campbellsville	9,108	11,426	11,653
*41011	Covington	40,640	40,961	40,972
*40422	Danville	16,218	17,234	17,383
*42701	Elizabethtown	28,531	31,394	32,978
*41018	Erlanger	18,082	19,611	19,777
*41042	Florence	29,951	31,946	32,917
42223	Fort Campbell North (c)	13,685	12,825	—
41075	Fort Thomas	16,325	17,438	16,973
*40601	Frankfort	25,527	28,602	28,285
*42134	Franklin	8,408	10,176	10,468
40324	Georgetown	29,098	37,086	39,462
*42141	Glasgow	14,028	15,014	15,313
*42420	Henderson	28,757	27,981	27,734
*42240	Hopkinsville	31,577	31,180	30,813
41051	Independence	24,757	28,676	29,503
*40299	Jeffersontown	26,595	28,474	28,716
*40031	La Grange	8,082	10,067	10,417
40342	Lawrenceburg	10,505	11,728	12,112
*40507	Lexington-Fayette	295,803	322,570	320,154
*40202	Louisville-Jefferson Co. (balance)	597,337	386,884	622,981
*40222	Lyndon	11,002	11,008	10,909
42431	Madisonville	19,591	19,542	19,355
40047	Mount Washington	9,117	18,090	18,637
42071	Murray	17,741	17,307	18,086
*41071	Newport	15,273	14,150	13,812
*40356	Nicholasville	28,015	31,093	32,425
*42303	Owensboro	57,265	60,183	60,140
*42003	Paducah	25,024	27,137	26,749
*40361	Paris	8,553	10,171	10,089
*40160	Radcliff	21,688	23,042	22,749
*40475	Richmond	31,364	34,585	37,206
*40207	Saint Matthews	17,472	17,534	17,356
*40066	Shelbyville	14,045	17,282	17,804
40165	Shepherdsville	11,222	14,201	14,691
*40216	Shively	15,264	15,636	15,455
*42501	Somerset	11,196	11,924	12,267
*40383	Versailles	8,568	10,347	10,491
*40391	Winchester	18,368	19,134	19,254

Louisiana

Area codes: 225, 318, 337, 504, 985

ZIP	Place	2010 population	2020 population	2023 estimate
*70510	Abbeville	12,257	11,186	10,890
*71301	Alexandria	47,723	45,275	43,466
70714	Baker	13,895	12,455	12,057
*70801	Baton Rouge	229,493	227,470	219,573
70360	Bayou Blue (c)	12,352	13,352	—
*70360	Bayou Cane (c)	19,355	19,770	—
*70037	Belle Chasse (c)	12,679	10,579	—
*70427	Bogalusa	12,232	10,659	10,343
*71111	Bossier City	61,315	62,701	62,738
70518	Broussard	8,197	13,417	14,543
70520	Carencro	7,526	9,272	12,639
*70818	Central	26,864	29,565	29,781
*70043	Chalmette (c)	16,751	21,562	—
70433	Claiborne (c)	11,507	12,631	—
*70433	Covington	8,765	11,564	11,618
*70526	Crowley	13,265	11,710	11,272
70047	Destrehan (c)	11,535	11,340	—
70072	Estelle (c)	16,377	17,952	—
*70810	Gardere (c)	10,580	13,203	—
*70737	Gonzales	9,781	12,231	13,737
*70053	Gretna	17,736	17,814	17,026
*70401	Hammond	20,019	19,584	22,527
*70058	Harvey (c)	20,348	22,236	—
*70360	Houma	33,727	33,406	31,733
70121	Jefferson (c)	11,193	10,633	—
*70062	Kenner	66,702	66,448	63,333
*70506	Lafayette	120,623	121,374	121,467
*70601	Lake Charles	71,993	84,872	79,633
*70068	LaPlace (c)	29,872	28,841	—
70070	Luling (c)	12,119	13,716	—
*70448	Mandeville	11,560	13,192	12,999
*70072	Marrero (c)	33,141	32,382	—
*70001	Metairie (c)	138,481	143,507	—
*71055	Minden	13,082	11,928	11,248
*71201	Monroe	48,815	47,702	46,616
*70380	Morgan City	12,404	11,472	10,873
70611	Moss Bluff (c)	11,557	12,522	—
*71457	Natchitoches	18,323	18,039	17,195
*70560	New Iberia	30,617	28,555	27,080
*70112	New Orleans	343,829	383,997	364,136
*70570	Opelousas	16,634	15,786	15,390
*71360	Pineville	14,555	14,384	14,034
70769	Prairieville (c)	26,895	33,197	—
70123	River Ridge (c)	13,494	13,591	—
*71270	Ruston	21,859	22,166	22,233
70817	Shenandoah (c)	18,399	19,292	—
*71101	Shreveport	199,311	187,593	177,959
*70458	Slidell	27,068	28,781	28,510
*70663	Sulphur	20,410	21,809	20,400
70056	Terrytown (c)	23,319	25,278	—
*70301	Thibodaux	14,566	15,948	15,646
70056	Timberlane (c)	10,243	10,364	—
*71291	West Monroe	13,065	13,103	12,535
70058	Woodmere (c)	12,080	11,238	—
70592	Youngsville	8,105	15,929	18,002
70791	Zachary	14,960	19,316	19,968

Maine

Area code: 207 applies to the entire state. See introductory note.

ZIP	Place	2010 population	2020 population	2023 estimate
*04210	Auburn	23,055	24,061	24,793
*04330	Augusta	19,136	18,899	19,102
*04401	Bangor	33,039	31,753	31,628
*04005	Biddeford	21,277	22,552	22,367
04011	*Brunswick*	20,278	21,756	22,434
04011	Brunswick (c)	15,175	17,033	—
04105	*Falmouth*	11,185	12,444	12,868
04038	*Gorham*	16,381	18,336	18,346
04043	*Kennebunk*	10,798	11,536	11,915
03904	*Kittery*	9,490	10,070	10,784
*04240	Lewiston	36,592	37,121	38,404
*04473	*Orono*	10,362	11,183	12,253
*04473	Orono (c)	9,474	10,185	—
*04101	Portland	66,194	68,408	69,104
04072	Saco	18,482	20,381	20,960
04073	Sanford	9,761	21,982	22,251
*04074	*Scarborough*	18,919	22,135	23,656
*04106	South Portland	25,002	26,498	26,840
04084	*Standish*	9,874	10,244	10,820
*04901	Waterville	15,722	15,828	16,823
04090	*Wells*	9,589	11,314	11,855
*04092	Westbrook	17,494	20,400	20,564
*04062	*Windham*	17,001	18,434	19,658
03909	*York*	12,529	13,723	14,118

Maryland

Area codes: 227/240/301, 410/443/667

ZIP	Place	2010 population	2020 population	2023 estimate
21001	Aberdeen	14,959	16,254	18,006
20607	Accokeek (c)	10,573	13,927	—
20783	Adelphi (c)	15,086	16,823	—
*21401	Annapolis	38,394	40,812	40,552
21403	Annapolis Neck (c)	10,950	10,973	—
21227	Arbutus (c)	20,483	21,655	—
21012	Arnold (c)	23,106	24,064	—
*20906	Aspen Hill (c)	48,759	51,063	—
21220	Ballenger Creek (c)	18,274	24,999	—
*21202	Baltimore	620,961	585,708	565,239
*21014	Bel Air	10,120	10,661	10,490
21050	Bel Air North (c)	30,568	31,841	—
*21015	Bel Air South (c)	47,709	57,648	—
*20705	Beltsville (c)	16,772	20,133	—
20603	Bensville (c)	11,923	15,288	—
*20814	Bethesda (c)	60,858	68,056	—
*20715	Bowie	54,727	58,329	57,254
20613	Brandywine (c)	6,719	10,550	—
20772	Brock Hall (c)	9,552	13,181	—
21225	Brooklyn Park (c)	14,373	16,112	—
20619	California (c)	11,857	12,947	—
20705	Calverton (c)	17,724	17,316	—
21613	Cambridge	12,326	13,096	13,176
*20748	Camp Springs (c)	19,096	22,734	—
21234	Carney (c)	29,941	29,363	—
21228	Catonsville (c)	41,567	44,701	—
20657	Chesapeake Ranch Estates (c)	10,519	10,308	—
*20815	Chevy Chase (c)	9,545	10,176	—
20782	Chillum (c)	33,513	36,039	—
20871	Clarksburg (c)	13,766	29,051	—

ZIP	Place	2010 population	2020 population	2023 estimate
20735	Clinton (c)	35,970	38,760	—
20904	Cloverly (c)	15,126	15,285	—
21030	Cockeysville (c)	20,776	24,184	—
*20904	Colesville (c)	14,647	15,421	—
*20740	College Park	30,413	34,740	34,187
*21044	Columbia (c)	99,615	104,681	—
21114	Crofton (c)	27,348	29,641	—
*21502	Cumberland	20,859	19,076	18,751
20872	Damascus (c)	15,257	17,224	—
21222	Dundalk (c)	63,597	67,796	—
20737	East Riverdale (c)	15,509	18,459	—
21601	Easton	15,945	17,101	17,225
21040	Edgewood (c)	25,562	25,713	—
21784	Eldersburg (c)	30,531	32,582	—
21075	Elkridge (c)	15,593	25,171	—
*21921	Elkton	15,443	15,807	15,968
*21042	Ellicott City (c)	65,834	75,947	—
21221	Essex (c)	39,262	40,505	—
20904	Fairland (c)	23,681	25,396	—
21061	Ferndale (c)	16,746	17,091	—
20879	Flower Hill (c)	—	14,108	—
*20747	Forestville (c)	12,353	12,831	—
*20744	Fort Washington (c)	23,717	24,261	—
*21701	Frederick	65,239	78,171	85,793
*20877	Gaithersburg	59,933	69,657	69,563
*20874	Germantown (c)	86,395	91,249	—
20745	Glassmanor (c)	17,295	18,430	—
*21061	Glen Burnie (c)	67,639	72,891	—
20906	Glenmont (c)	13,529	16,710	—
20769	Glenn Dale (c)	13,466	14,698	—
21770	Green Valley (c)	—	12,643	—
*20770	Greenbelt	23,068	24,921	24,360
*21740	Hagerstown	39,662	43,527	43,553
21740	Halfway (c)	10,701	11,896	—
21078	Havre de Grace	12,952	14,807	15,032
20748	Hillcrest Heights (c)	16,469	15,793	—
21128	Honeygo (c)	—	12,927	—
*20781	Hyattsville	17,557	21,187	20,662
21043	Ilchester (c)	23,476	26,824	—
20794	Jessup (c)	7,137	10,535	—
21085	Joppatowne (c)	12,616	13,425	—
20902	Kemp Mill (c)	12,564	13,378	—
*20774	Kettering (c)	12,790	14,424	—
20646	La Plata	8,753	10,159	10,878
*20774	Lake Arbor (c)	9,776	14,541	—
*21122	Lake Shore (c)	19,477	19,551	—
20785	Landover (c)	23,078	25,998	—
*20787	Langley Park (c)	18,755	20,126	—
*20706	Lanham (c)	10,157	11,282	—
*20774	Largo (c)	10,709	11,605	—
*20707	Laurel	25,115	30,060	29,400
20653	Lexington Park (c)	11,626	13,317	—
21771	Linganore (c)	8,543	12,351	—
21090	Linthicum (c)	10,324	11,190	—
21207	Lochearn (c)	25,333	25,511	—
20724	Maryland City (c)	16,093	19,153	—
21093	Mays Chapel (c)	11,420	12,224	—
21220	Middle River (c)	25,191	33,203	—
*21244	Milford Mill (c)	29,042	30,622	—
*20716	Mitchellville (c)	10,967	11,136	—
*20886	Montgomery Village (c)	32,032	34,893	—
20784	New Carrollton	12,135	13,715	13,405
*20852	North Bethesda (c)	43,828	50,094	—
20723	North Laurel (c)	4,474	25,379	—
20878	North Potomac (c)	24,410	23,790	—
21811	Ocean Pines (c)	11,710	12,145	—
21113	Odenton (c)	37,132	42,947	—
*20832	Olney (c)	33,844	35,820	—
21236	Overlea (c)	12,275	12,832	—
21117	Owings Mills (c)	30,622	35,674	—
*20745	Oxon Hill (c)	17,722	18,791	—
21234	Parkville (c)	30,734	31,812	—
21401	Parole (c)	15,922	17,877	—
*21122	Pasadena (c)	24,287	32,979	—
21128	Perry Hall (c)	28,474	29,409	—
*21207	Pikesville (c)	30,764	34,168	—
*20850	Potomac (c)	44,965	47,018	—
21133	Randallstown (c)	32,430	33,655	—
20855	Redland (c)	17,242	18,592	—
*21136	Reisterstown (c)	25,968	26,822	—
*21122	Riviera Beach (c)	12,677	12,384	—
*20850	Rockville	61,209	67,117	67,297
20772	Rosaryville (c)	10,697	11,548	—
21237	Rosedale (c)	19,257	19,961	—
21221	Rossville (c)	15,147	16,029	—
*21801	Salisbury	30,343	33,050	33,159
*20706	Seabrook (c)	17,287	19,627	—
21144	Severn (c)	44,231	57,118	—
21146	Severna Park (c)	37,634	39,933	—
*20901	Silver Spring (c)	71,452	81,015	—
20707	South Laurel (c)	26,112	29,602	—
*20746	Suitland (c)	25,825	25,839	—
21842	Summerfield (c)	10,898	14,758	—
*20912	Takoma Park	16,715	17,629	17,464
*21093	Timonium (c)	9,925	10,458	—
*21204	Towson (c)	55,197	59,553	—
20854	Travilah (c)	12,159	11,985	—
21704	Urbana (c)	9,175	13,304	—
*20602	Waldorf (c)	67,752	81,410	—
20743	Walker Mill (c)	11,302	12,187	—
*21157	Westminster	18,590	20,126	20,536
20774	Westphalia (c)	7,266	11,770	—
*20902	Wheaton (c)	48,284	52,150	—
21162	White Marsh (c)	9,513	10,287	—
20904	White Oak (c)	17,403	16,347	—
21207	Woodlawn (c) (Balt. Co.)	37,879	39,986	—

Massachusetts

Area codes: 339/781, 351/978, 413, 508/774, 617/857. See introductory note.

ZIP	Place	2010 population	2020 population	2023 estimate
02351	*Abington*	15,985	17,062	16,970
*01720	*Acton*	21,924	24,021	24,029
*02743	*Acushnet*	10,303	10,559	10,602
01001	Agawam	28,438	28,692	28,406
01913	Amesbury	16,283	17,366	17,303
*01002	Amherst	37,819	39,263	40,277
*01810	*Andover*	33,201	36,569	36,485
*02476	*Arlington*	42,844	46,308	46,111
01721	*Ashland*	16,593	18,832	18,591
01331	*Athol*	11,584	11,945	11,937
02703	Attleboro	43,593	46,461	46,654
01501	*Auburn*	16,188	16,889	16,820
02630	Barnstable	45,193	48,916	49,709
*01730	*Bedford*	13,320	14,383	14,394
01007	*Belchertown*	14,649	15,350	15,339
02019	*Bellingham*	16,332	16,945	17,556
02478	*Belmont*	24,729	27,295	26,886
01915	Beverly	39,502	42,670	42,318
*01821	*Billerica*	40,243	42,119	41,619
*02108	Boston	617,594	675,647	653,833
02532	*Bourne*	19,754	20,452	20,422
*02184	Braintree	35,744	39,143	38,490
02631	*Brewster*	9,820	10,318	10,381
*02324	Bridgewater	26,563	28,633	28,818
*02301	Brockton	93,810	105,643	104,890
*02446	*Brookline*	58,732	63,191	62,962
*01803	*Burlington*	24,498	26,377	26,527
*02139	Cambridge	105,162	118,403	118,214
02021	*Canton*	21,561	24,370	24,635
02330	*Carver*	11,509	11,645	11,675
01507	*Charlton*	12,981	13,315	13,391
01824	*Chelmsford*	33,802	36,392	36,180
02150	Chelsea	35,177	40,787	38,319
*01020	Chicopee	55,298	55,560	54,838
01510	*Clinton*	13,606	15,428	15,530
01742	*Concord*	17,668	18,491	18,086
01923	*Danvers*	26,493	28,087	27,896
*02747	*Dartmouth*	34,032	33,783	33,419
*02026	*Dedham*	24,729	25,364	24,968
02638	*Dennis*	14,207	14,674	14,903
01826	*Dracut*	29,457	32,617	32,291
01571	*Dudley*	11,390	11,921	11,849
*02332	*Duxbury*	15,059	16,090	16,185
02333	*East Bridgewater*	13,794	14,440	14,408
*01028	*East Longmeadow*	15,720	16,430	16,378
01027	Easthampton	16,053	16,211	16,031
*02356	*Easton*	23,112	25,058	25,364
02149	Everett	41,667	49,075	50,318
02719	*Fairhaven*	15,873	15,924	15,878
*02720	Fall River	88,857	94,000	93,840
*02540	*Falmouth*	31,531	32,517	33,069
01420	Fitchburg	40,318	41,946	41,579
02035	*Foxborough*	16,865	18,618	18,484
*01701	Framingham	68,318	72,362	71,875
02038	Franklin	31,635	33,261	33,125
01440	Gardner	20,228	21,287	20,974
*01930	Gloucester	28,789	29,729	29,959
01519	*Grafton*	17,765	19,664	19,975
*01301	Greenfield	17,456	17,768	17,628
01450	*Groton*	10,646	11,315	11,277
02339	*Hanover*	13,879	14,833	14,753
02341	*Hanson*	10,209	10,639	10,586
02645	*Harwich*	12,243	13,440	13,595
*01830	Haverhill	60,879	67,787	67,415

ZIP	Place	2010 population	2020 population	2023 estimate
*02043	*Hingham*	22,157	24,284	24,189
02343	*Holbrook*	10,791	11,405	11,284
01520	*Holden*	17,346	19,905	19,934
01746	*Holliston*	13,547	14,996	15,015
*01040	Holyoke	39,880	38,238	37,628
01748	*Hopkinton*	14,925	18,758	19,540
01749	*Hudson*	19,063	20,092	19,904
01749	Hudson (c)	14,907	15,749	—
02045	*Hull*	10,293	10,072	10,108
01938	*Ipswich*	13,175	13,785	13,903
02364	*Kingston*	12,629	13,708	13,948
*02347	*Lakeville*	10,602	11,523	11,968
*01840	Lawrence	76,377	89,143	88,172
01524	*Leicester*	10,970	11,087	11,066
01453	Leominster	40,759	43,782	43,627
*02420	*Lexington*	31,394	34,454	33,882
01460	*Littleton*	8,924	10,141	10,251
*01106	*Longmeadow*	15,784	15,853	15,621
*01850	Lowell	106,519	115,554	114,296
01056	*Ludlow*	21,103	21,002	20,845
01462	*Lunenburg*	10,086	11,782	11,851
*01901	Lynn	90,329	101,253	101,241
01940	*Lynnfield*	11,596	13,000	13,034
02148	Malden	59,450	66,263	65,133
02048	*Mansfield*	23,184	23,860	23,862
01945	*Marblehead*	19,808	20,441	20,296
01752	Marlborough	38,499	41,793	41,179
*02050	*Marshfield*	25,132	25,825	25,765
02649	*Mashpee*	14,006	15,060	15,396
01754	*Maynard*	10,106	10,746	10,604
02052	*Medfield*	12,024	12,799	13,088
*02155	Medford	56,173	59,659	58,744
02053	*Medway*	12,752	13,115	13,560
02176	Melrose	26,983	29,817	29,357
01844	Methuen	47,255	53,059	53,455
*02346	*Middleborough*	23,116	24,245	24,504
01757	*Milford*	27,999	30,379	30,257
01757	Milford (c)	25,055	26,971	—
*01527	*Millbury*	13,261	13,831	14,002
02186	*Milton*	27,003	28,630	28,374
*02554	*Nantucket*	10,172	14,255	14,444
*02554	Nantucket (c)	7,446	10,166	—
01760	*Natick*	33,006	37,006	36,518
*02494	*Needham*	28,886	32,091	32,157
*02740	New Bedford	95,072	101,079	100,695
*01950	Newburyport	17,416	18,289	18,731
*02456	Newton	85,146	88,923	88,415
02056	*Norfolk*	11,227	11,662	11,594
01247	North Adams	13,708	12,961	12,483
01845	*North Andover*	28,352	30,915	31,615
*02760	North Attleborough	28,712	30,834	30,943
*01864	*North Reading*	14,892	15,554	16,054
*01060	Northampton	28,549	29,571	29,370
01532	*Northborough*	14,155	15,741	15,689
01534	*Northbridge*	15,707	16,335	16,455
02766	*Norton*	19,031	19,202	19,146
02061	*Norwell*	10,506	11,351	11,299
02062	*Norwood*	28,602	31,599	31,230
01540	*Oxford*	13,709	13,347	13,306
01069	Palmer	12,140	12,448	12,315
*01960	Peabody	51,251	54,481	54,056
02359	*Pembroke*	17,837	18,361	18,286
01463	*Pepperell*	11,497	11,604	11,710
*01201	Pittsfield	44,737	43,927	43,076
*02360	*Plymouth*	56,468	61,217	65,405
*02169	Quincy	92,271	101,636	101,597
02368	Randolph	32,112	34,984	34,487
02767	*Raynham*	13,383	15,142	15,649
01867	*Reading*	24,747	25,518	25,428
02769	*Rehoboth*	11,608	12,502	13,313
02151	Revere	51,755	62,186	57,954
02370	*Rockland*	17,489	17,803	17,594
*01970	Salem	41,340	44,480	44,744
02563	*Sandwich*	20,675	20,259	20,469
01906	*Saugus*	26,628	28,619	28,630
*02066	*Scituate*	18,133	19,063	19,297
02771	*Seekonk*	13,722	15,531	15,725
02067	*Sharon*	17,612	18,575	18,442
*01545	*Shrewsbury*	35,608	38,325	38,889
*02725	*Somerset*	18,165	18,303	18,209
*02143	Somerville	75,754	81,045	80,407
01075	*South Hadley*	17,514	18,150	17,992
02664	South Yarmouth (c)	11,092	11,703	—
*01745	*Southborough*	9,767	10,450	10,429
01550	Southbridge	16,719	17,740	17,880
01562	*Spencer*	11,688	11,992	11,920
*01103	Springfield	153,060	155,929	153,672
02180	*Stoneham*	21,437	23,244	22,854
02072	*Stoughton*	26,962	29,281	28,962
01776	*Sudbury*	17,659	18,934	19,394
01907	*Swampscott*	13,787	15,111	15,487
02777	*Swansea*	15,865	17,144	17,375
*02780	Taunton	55,874	59,408	60,412
01876	*Tewksbury*	28,961	31,342	31,243
01879	*Tyngsborough*	11,292	12,380	12,475
01569	*Uxbridge*	13,457	14,162	14,526
01880	*Wakefield*	24,932	27,090	27,810
02081	*Walpole*	24,070	26,383	25,964
*02451	Waltham	60,632	65,218	64,477
01082	*Ware*	9,872	10,066	10,067
02571	*Wareham*	21,822	23,303	23,198
*02742	Watertown	31,915	35,329	35,256
01778	*Wayland*	12,994	13,943	13,752
01570	*Webster*	16,767	17,776	17,593
01570	Webster (c)	11,412	12,194	—
*02457	*Wellesley*	27,982	29,550	30,733
*01089	West Springfield	28,391	28,835	28,424
01581	*Westborough*	18,272	21,567	22,012
*01085	Westfield	41,094	40,834	40,509
01886	*Westford*	21,951	24,643	24,543
02493	*Weston*	11,261	11,851	11,645
02790	*Westport*	15,532	16,339	16,461
02090	*Westwood*	14,618	16,266	16,244
*02188	Weymouth	53,743	57,437	59,114
02382	*Whitman*	14,489	15,121	15,316
01095	*Wilbraham*	14,219	14,613	14,518
01887	*Wilmington*	22,325	23,349	23,148
01475	*Winchendon*	10,300	10,364	10,441
01890	*Winchester*	21,374	22,970	22,837
02152	Winthrop	17,497	19,316	18,319
*01801	Woburn	38,120	40,876	41,647
*01608	Worcester	181,045	206,518	207,621
*02093	*Wrentham*	10,955	12,178	12,543
*02664	*Yarmouth*	23,793	25,023	25,103

Michigan

Area codes: 231, 248/947, 269, 313, 517, 586, 616, 734, 810, 906, 989

ZIP	Place	2010 population	2020 population	2023 estimate
49221	Adrian	21,133	20,645	20,238
48101	Allen Park	28,210	28,638	27,528
49401	Allendale (c)	17,579	27,073	—
49707	Alpena	10,483	10,197	10,130
*48103	Ann Arbor	113,934	123,851	119,381
*48326	Auburn Hills	21,412	24,360	25,597
*49014	Battle Creek	52,347	52,721	52,175
*48708	Bay City	34,932	32,661	32,082
48072	Berkley	14,970	15,194	14,934
48025	Beverly Hills	10,267	10,584	10,390
*48009	Birmingham	20,103	21,813	21,434
*48509	Burton	29,999	29,715	29,376
49601	Cadillac	10,355	10,371	10,430
48017	Clawson	11,825	11,389	11,176
49036	Coldwater	10,945	13,822	14,439
49321	Comstock Park (c)	10,088	10,500	—
*49508	Cutlerville (c)	14,370	17,849	—
*48120	Dearborn	98,153	109,976	105,811
*48127	Dearborn Heights	57,774	63,292	60,872
*48201	Detroit	713,777	639,111	633,218
*49506	East Grand Rapids	10,694	11,371	11,429
*48823	East Lansing	48,579	47,741	48,528
48021	Eastpointe	32,442	34,318	33,676
49829	Escanaba	12,616	12,450	12,343
*48335	Farmington	10,372	11,597	11,391
*48331	Farmington Hills	79,740	83,986	82,528
48430	Fenton	11,756	12,050	11,863
48220	Ferndale	19,900	19,190	19,083
48134	Flat Rock	9,878	10,541	10,289
*48502	Flint	102,434	81,252	79,661
49506	Forest Hills (c)	25,867	28,573	—
48026	Fraser	14,480	14,726	14,434
*48135	Garden City	27,692	27,380	26,325
49417	Grand Haven	10,412	11,011	11,002
*49503	Grand Rapids	188,040	198,917	196,608
*49418	Grandville	15,378	16,083	16,682
*48230	Grosse Pointe Park	11,555	11,595	11,124
*48236	Grosse Pointe Woods	16,135	16,487	15,854
*48212	Hamtramck	22,423	28,433	27,339
48225	Harper Woods	14,236	15,492	14,895
48840	Haslett (c)	19,220	19,670	—
48030	Hazel Park	16,422	14,983	14,808
*49423	Holland	33,051	34,378	34,540
48842	Holt (c)	23,973	25,625	—
*48843	Howell	9,489	10,068	10,008
48141	Inkster	25,369	26,088	25,056
48846	Ionia	11,394	13,378	12,249
*49201	Jackson	33,534	31,309	30,854
*49428	Jenison (c)	16,538	16,640	—
*49001	Kalamazoo	74,262	73,598	73,126
*49508	Kentwood	48,707	54,304	53,987

ZIP	Place	2010 population	2020 population	2023 estimate
48144	Lambertville (c)	9,953	10,433	—
*48933	Lansing	114,297	112,644	112,115
48146	Lincoln Park	38,144	40,245	38,646
*48150	Livonia	96,942	95,535	92,185
48071	Madison Heights	29,694	28,468	28,238
49855	Marquette	21,355	20,629	21,079
48122	Melvindale	10,715	12,851	12,402
*48640	Midland	41,863	42,547	42,663
*48161	Monroe	20,733	20,462	20,089
*48043	Mount Clemens	16,314	15,697	15,378
*48858	Mount Pleasant	26,016	21,688	20,859
*49440	Muskegon	38,401	38,318	37,183
*48047	New Baltimore	12,084	12,117	11,992
49120	Niles	11,600	11,988	11,665
49525	Northview (c)	14,541	15,301	—
*49441	Norton Shores	23,994	25,030	25,005
*48374	Novi	55,224	66,243	66,314
48237	Oak Park	29,319	29,560	29,023
*48864	Okemos (c)	21,369	25,121	—
*48867	Owosso	15,194	14,714	14,581
*48340	Pontiac	59,515	61,606	61,689
*48060	Port Huron	30,184	28,983	28,383
*49024	Portage	46,292	48,891	49,302
*48193	Riverview	12,486	12,490	11,976
*48307	Rochester	12,711	13,035	12,779
*48306	Rochester Hills	70,995	76,300	76,002
48174	Romulus	23,989	25,178	24,702
48066	Roseville	47,299	47,710	46,666
*48067	Royal Oak	57,236	58,211	57,452
*48601	Saginaw	51,508	44,202	43,185
*48080	Saint Clair Shores	59,715	58,874	57,548
*49783	Sault Ste. Marie	14,144	13,337	13,320
48178	South Lyon	11,327	11,746	11,941
*48033	Southfield	71,739	76,618	75,687
48195	Southgate	30,047	30,014	29,002
*48310	Sterling Heights	129,699	134,346	133,306
49091	Sturgis	10,994	11,082	11,012
48180	Taylor	63,131	63,409	61,241
*49684	Traverse City	14,674	15,678	15,707
48183	Trenton	18,853	18,544	17,891
*48083	Troy	80,980	87,294	87,339
*49534	Walker	23,537	25,132	25,289
*48088	Warren	134,056	139,387	136,655
48917	Waverly (c)	23,925	23,812	—
48184	Wayne	17,593	17,713	17,078
*48185	Westland	84,094	85,420	82,574
48393	Wixom	13,498	17,193	17,134
48183	Woodhaven	12,875	12,941	12,559
*48192	Wyandotte	25,883	25,058	24,057
*49509	Wyoming	72,125	76,501	77,451
*48197	Ypsilanti	19,435	20,648	19,393

Minnesota

Area codes: 218, 320, 507/924, 612, 651, 763, 952

ZIP	Place	2010 population	2020 population	2023 estimate
56007	Albert Lea	18,016	18,492	18,269
56308	Alexandria	11,070	14,335	14,943
*55304	Andover	30,598	32,601	33,089
*55303	Anoka	17,142	17,921	17,996
55124	Apple Valley	49,084	56,374	55,336
55912	Austin	24,718	26,174	26,171
*56601	Bemidji	13,431	14,574	15,743
55309	Big Lake	10,060	11,686	12,610
*55014	Blaine	57,186	70,222	73,774
*55420	Bloomington	82,893	89,987	87,398
*56401	Brainerd	13,590	14,395	14,563
*55430	Brooklyn Center	30,104	33,782	31,688
*55443	Brooklyn Park	75,781	86,478	82,017
55313	Buffalo	15,453	16,168	16,541
*55337	Burnsville	60,306	64,317	64,772
55008	Cambridge	8,111	9,611	10,509
55316	Champlin	23,089	23,919	22,856
55317	Chanhassen	22,952	25,947	25,937
55318	Chaska	23,770	27,810	29,034
55720	Cloquet	12,124	12,568	12,570
55421	Columbia Heights	19,496	21,973	22,278
*55433	Coon Rapids	61,476	63,599	63,377
55016	Cottage Grove	34,589	38,839	42,056
*55422	Crystal	22,151	23,330	21,906
55327	Dayton	4,671	7,262	10,157
*55802	Duluth	86,265	86,697	87,680
*55121	Eagan	64,206	68,855	67,396
*55011	East Bethel	11,626	11,786	12,189
*55344	Eden Prairie	60,797	64,198	62,166
*55424	Edina	47,941	53,494	53,348
55330	Elk River	22,974	25,835	27,342
*56031	Fairmont	10,666	10,487	10,240
55021	Faribault	23,352	24,453	24,642
55024	Farmington	21,086	23,632	23,909
*56537	Fergus Falls	13,138	14,119	14,214
55025	Forest Lake	18,375	20,611	20,685
*55432	Fridley	27,208	29,590	30,156
*55427	Golden Valley	20,371	22,552	21,211
*55744	Grand Rapids	10,869	11,126	11,271
55304	Ham Lake	15,296	16,464	16,726
55033	Hastings	22,172	22,154	22,121
*55810	Hermantown	9,414	10,221	10,202
55746	Hibbing	16,361	16,214	15,979
*55343	Hopkins	17,591	19,079	18,589
55038	Hugo	13,332	15,766	16,501
55350	Hutchinson	14,178	14,599	14,701
*55077	Inver Grove Heights	33,880	35,801	36,114
55042	Lake Elmo	8,069	11,335	13,756
55044	Lakeville	55,954	69,490	76,243
*55014	Lino Lakes	20,216	21,399	22,376
*55117	Little Canada	9,773	10,819	10,297
*56001	Mankato	39,309	44,488	45,742
*55311	Maple Grove	61,567	70,253	71,288
*55109	Maplewood	38,018	42,088	39,958
56258	Marshall	13,680	13,628	13,906
*55118	Mendota Heights	11,071	11,744	11,564
*55401	Minneapolis	382,578	429,954	425,115
*55345	Minnetonka	49,734	53,781	52,463
55362	Monticello	12,759	14,455	14,831
*56560	Moorhead	38,065	44,505	45,202
55112	Mounds View	12,155	13,249	12,782
55112	New Brighton	21,456	23,454	22,228
*54427	New Hope	20,339	21,986	20,705
56073	New Ulm	13,522	14,120	13,925
55056	North Branch	10,125	10,787	11,791
*56002	North Mankato	13,394	14,275	14,091
55109	North St. Paul	11,460	12,364	12,574
55057	Northfield	20,007	20,790	21,020
*55128	Oakdale	27,378	28,303	28,226
*55330	Otsego	13,571	19,966	23,241
55060	Owatonna	25,599	26,420	26,534
*55446	Plymouth	70,576	81,026	77,648
*55372	Prior Lake	22,796	27,617	28,027
*55303	Ramsey	23,668	27,646	28,560
55066	Red Wing	16,459	16,547	16,756
55423	Richfield	35,228	36,994	36,445
55422	Robbinsdale	13,953	14,646	13,968
*55904	Rochester	106,769	121,395	122,413
55374	Rogers	8,597	13,295	13,617
55068	Rosemount	21,874	25,650	27,590
*55113	Roseville	33,660	36,254	35,451
*56301	Saint Cloud	65,842	68,881	71,013
*55416	Saint Louis Park	45,250	50,010	49,697
55376	Saint Michael	16,399	18,235	21,034
*55101	Saint Paul	285,068	311,527	303,820
56082	Saint Peter	11,196	12,066	12,291
*56377	Sartell	15,876	19,351	19,726
56379	Sauk Rapids	12,773	13,862	13,775
55378	Savage	26,911	32,465	32,999
*55379	Shakopee	37,076	43,698	47,158
55126	Shoreview	25,043	26,921	26,374
*55075	South St. Paul	20,160	20,759	20,664
*55082	Stillwater	18,225	19,394	19,240
*55127	Vadnais Heights	12,302	12,912	12,632
*55318	Victoria	7,345	10,546	11,493
55387	Waconia	10,697	13,033	13,742
*55118	West St. Paul	19,540	20,615	21,722
*55110	White Bear Lake	23,797	24,883	23,363
56201	Willmar	19,610	21,015	21,335
55987	Winona	27,592	25,948	26,029
*55125	Woodbury	61,961	75,102	79,538
56187	Worthington	12,764	13,947	13,614

Mississippi

Area codes: 228, 601/769, 662

ZIP	Place	2010 population	2020 population	2023 estimate
*39520	Bay St. Louis	9,260	9,284	10,511
*39530	Biloxi	44,054	49,449	48,235
*39042	Brandon	21,705	25,138	25,719
*39601	Brookhaven	12,513	11,674	11,571
*39272	Byram	11,489	12,666	12,651
39046	Canton	13,189	10,948	10,742
*38614	Clarksdale	17,962	14,903	13,850
*38732	Cleveland	12,334	11,199	10,401
*39056	Clinton	25,216	28,100	26,698
*39701	Columbus	23,640	24,084	23,035
*38834	Corinth	14,573	14,622	14,259
39540	D'Iberville	9,486	12,721	13,286
*39232	Flowood	7,823	10,202	10,675
39553	Gautier	18,572	19,024	19,021

ZIP	Place	2010 population	2020 population	2023 estimate
*38701	Greenville	34,400	29,670	27,644
*38930	Greenwood	15,205	14,490	13,421
*38901	Grenada	13,092	12,700	12,267
*39501	Gulfport	67,793	72,926	72,823
*39401	Hattiesburg	45,989	48,730	48,414
38632	Hernando	14,090	17,138	18,239
38637	Horn Lake	26,066	26,736	26,468
*39201	Jackson	173,514	153,701	143,709
*39440	Laurel	18,540	17,161	16,979
39560	Long Beach	14,792	16,780	16,991
*39110	Madison	24,149	27,747	27,987
*39648	McComb	12,790	12,413	11,914
*39301	Meridian	41,148	35,052	33,551
*39563	Moss Point	13,704	12,147	11,890
*39120	Natchez	15,792	14,520	13,933
*39564	Ocean Springs	17,442	18,429	18,997
38654	Olive Branch	33,484	39,711	47,029
*38655	Oxford	18,916	25,416	27,008
*39567	Pascagoula	22,392	22,010	21,582
*39208	Pearl	25,092	27,115	28,117
39465	Petal	10,454	11,010	11,403
39466	Picayune	10,878	11,885	11,862
*39157	Ridgeland	24,047	24,340	24,459
*38671	Southaven	48,982	54,648	56,851
*39759	Starkville	23,888	24,360	25,444
*38804	Tupelo	34,546	37,923	37,675
*39180	Vicksburg	23,856	21,573	20,192

Missouri

Area codes: 235/573, 314/557, 417, 636, 660, 816/975

ZIP	Place	2010 population	2020 population	2023 estimate
63123	Affton (c)	20,307	20,417	—
63010	Arnold	20,808	20,858	21,059
*63011	Ballwin	30,404	31,103	30,410
63137	Bellefontaine Neighbors	10,860	10,740	10,370
64012	Belton	23,116	23,953	25,534
*64015	Blue Springs	52,575	58,603	60,539
*65613	Bolivar	10,325	10,679	11,338
*65616	Branson	10,520	12,638	12,897
63044	Bridgeton	11,550	11,445	11,261
*63701	Cape Girardeau	37,941	39,540	40,508
64836	Carthage	14,378	15,522	15,556
*63017	Chesterfield	47,484	49,999	49,166
*63105	Clayton	15,939	17,355	17,461
*65201	Columbia	108,500	126,254	129,330
*63128	Concord (c)	16,421	17,668	—
63126	Crestwood	11,912	12,404	12,175
63141	Creve Coeur	17,833	18,834	18,457
*63366	Dardenne Prairie	11,494	12,743	13,803
63025	Eureka	10,189	11,646	13,092
64024	Excelsior Springs	11,084	10,553	10,612
63640	Farmington	16,240	18,217	18,362
63135	Ferguson	21,203	18,527	17,996
63028	Festus	11,602	12,706	13,443
*63031	Florissant	52,158	52,533	51,128
65473	Fort Leonard Wood (c)	15,061	15,959	—
65251	Fulton	12,790	12,600	12,473
*64118	Gladstone	25,410	27,063	27,329
64029	Grain Valley	12,854	15,627	16,609
64030	Grandview	24,475	26,209	25,436
63401	Hannibal	17,916	17,108	16,838
*63042	Hazelwood	25,703	25,458	24,863
*64050	Independence	116,830	123,011	120,922
63755	Jackson	13,758	15,481	15,742
*65101	Jefferson City	43,079	43,228	42,552
63136	Jennings	14,712	12,895	12,836
*64801	Joplin	50,150	51,762	53,095
*64106	Kansas City	459,787	508,090	510,704
64060	Kearney	8,381	10,404	11,060
63857	Kennett	10,932	10,515	10,117
63501	Kirksville	17,505	17,530	17,483
63122	Kirkwood	27,540	29,461	29,174
63367	Lake St. Louis	14,545	16,707	18,661
65536	Lebanon	14,474	15,013	15,429
*64063	Lee's Summit	91,364	101,108	104,184
63125	Lemay (c)	16,645	17,117	—
*64068	Liberty	29,149	30,167	30,794
*63011	Manchester	18,094	18,333	18,012
65340	Marshall	13,065	13,806	13,642
63043	Maryland Heights	27,472	28,284	27,575
64468	Maryville	11,972	10,633	10,309
63129	Mehlville (c)	28,380	28,955	—
65265	Mexico	11,543	11,469	11,507
65270	Moberly	13,974	13,783	13,296
65708	Monett	8,873	9,576	10,000
*64850	Neosho	11,835	12,590	13,328
65714	Nixa	19,022	23,257	25,405
63129	Oakville (c)	36,143	36,301	—
*63366	O'Fallon	79,329	91,316	94,074
63034	Old Jamestown (c)	19,184	19,790	—
63114	Overland	16,062	15,955	15,496
65721	Ozark	17,820	21,284	22,907
*63901	Poplar Bluff	17,023	16,225	16,132
*64083	Raymore	19,206	22,941	25,306
*64133	Raytown	29,526	30,012	29,097
65738	Republic	14,751	18,750	20,144
*65401	Rolla	19,559	19,943	20,423
63074	Saint Ann	13,020	13,019	12,658
*63301	Saint Charles	65,794	70,493	71,800
*64501	Saint Joseph	76,780	72,473	70,634
*63103	Saint Louis	319,294	301,578	281,754
*63376	Saint Peters	52,575	57,732	59,413
*65301	Sedalia	21,387	21,725	22,086
63801	Sikeston	16,318	16,291	16,085
64089	Smithville	8,425	10,406	10,785
63138	Spanish Lake (c)	19,650	18,413	—
*65802	Springfield	159,498	169,176	170,188
63017	Town and Country	10,815	11,640	11,553
63379	Troy	10,540	12,686	14,591
63084	Union	10,204	12,348	13,000
63130	University City	35,371	35,065	34,096
64093	Warrensburg	18,838	19,337	19,673
63090	Washington	13,982	14,500	15,450
64870	Webb City	10,996	13,031	13,325
63119	Webster Groves	22,995	24,010	23,449
63385	Wentzville	29,070	44,372	47,497
65775	West Plains	11,986	12,184	12,598
*63040	Wildwood	35,517	35,417	34,851

Montana

Area code: 406 applies to the entire state

ZIP	Place	2010 population	2020 population	2023 estimate
59714	Belgrade	7,389	10,460	12,509
*59101	Billings	104,170	117,116	120,864
*59715	Bozeman	37,280	53,293	57,305
*59701	Butte-Silver Bow (balance)	33,525	34,494	35,701
*59401	Great Falls	58,505	60,442	60,422
*59601	Helena	28,190	32,091	34,464
*59901	Kalispell	19,927	24,558	29,886
*59801	Missoula	66,788	73,489	77,757

Nebraska

Area codes: 308, 402/531

ZIP	Place	2010 population	2020 population	2023 estimate
68310	Beatrice	12,459	12,261	12,262
*68005	Bellevue	50,137	64,176	63,922
68138	Chalco (c)	10,994	11,064	—
*68601	Columbus	22,111	24,028	24,464
*68025	Fremont	26,397	27,141	27,602
*68801	Grand Island	48,520	53,131	52,622
*68901	Hastings	24,907	25,152	24,896
*68847	Kearney	30,787	33,790	34,362
*68128	La Vista	15,758	16,746	16,346
68850	Lexington	10,230	10,348	10,816
*68502	Lincoln	258,379	291,082	294,757
*68701	Norfolk	24,210	24,955	26,147
*69101	North Platte	24,733	23,390	22,523
*68102	Omaha	408,958	486,051	483,335
*68046	Papillion	18,894	24,159	23,791
*69361	Scottsbluff	15,039	14,436	14,305
68776	South Sioux City	13,353	14,043	13,856

Nevada

Area codes: 702/725, 775

ZIP	Place	2010 population	2020 population	2023 estimate
*89005	Boulder City	15,023	14,885	14,828
*89701	Carson City	55,274	58,639	58,036
89508	Cold Springs (c)	8,544	10,153	—
89403	Dayton (c)	8,964	15,153	—
*89801	Elko	18,297	20,564	20,785
89124	Enterprise (c)	108,481	221,831	—
89408	Fernley	19,368	22,895	24,744
*89410	Gardnerville Ranchos (c)	11,312	11,318	—
*89015	Henderson	257,729	317,610	337,305
*89101	Las Vegas	583,756	641,903	660,929
*89027	Mesquite	15,276	20,471	22,786
*89030	North Las Vegas	216,961	262,527	284,771
*89048	Pahrump (c)	36,441	44,738	—
*89121	Paradise (c)	223,167	191,238	—
*89501	Reno	225,221	264,165	274,915
*89436	Spanish Springs (c)	15,064	17,314	—

ZIP	Place	2010 population	2020 population	2023 estimate
*89431	Sparks	90,264	108,445	110,323
89815	Spring Creek (c)	12,361	14,967	—
*89117	Spring Valley (c)	178,395	215,597	—
89135	Summerlin South (c)	24,085	30,744	—
89433	Sun Valley (c)	19,299	21,178	—
*89110	Sunrise Manor (c)	189,372	205,618	—
89122	Whitney (c)	38,585	49,061	—
*89109	Winchester (c)	27,978	36,403	—

New Hampshire

Area code: 603 applies to the entire state. See introductory note.

ZIP	Place	2010 population	2020 population	2023 estimate
03031	*Amherst*	11,201	11,753	11,879
03110	*Bedford*	21,203	23,322	23,764
03743	Claremont	13,355	12,949	13,111
*03301	Concord	42,695	43,976	44,629
03818	*Conway*	10,115	9,822	10,289
03038	*Derry*	33,109	34,317	34,248
03038	Derry (c)	22,015	22,879	—
*03820	Dover	29,987	32,741	33,485
03824	*Durham*	14,638	15,490	14,921
03824	Durham (c)	10,345	11,147	—
03833	*Exeter*	14,306	16,049	16,172
03833	Exeter (c)	9,242	10,109	—
03045	*Goffstown*	17,651	18,577	18,529
*03842	*Hampton*	15,430	16,214	16,424
03755	*Hanover*	11,260	11,870	12,209
03106	*Hooksett*	13,451	14,871	15,312
03051	*Hudson*	24,467	25,394	25,595
*03431	Keene	23,409	23,047	22,917
*03246	Laconia	15,951	16,871	17,142
*03766	Lebanon	13,151	14,282	15,342
*03053	*Londonderry*	24,129	25,826	26,708
*03053	Londonderry (c)	11,037	11,645	—
*03101	Manchester	109,565	115,644	115,474
03054	*Merrimack*	25,494	26,632	28,916
03055	*Milford*	15,115	16,131	16,420
*03060	Nashua	86,494	91,322	91,003
03076	*Pelham*	12,897	14,222	14,513
*03801	Portsmouth	20,779	21,956	22,733
03077	*Raymond*	10,138	10,684	10,972
*03867	Rochester	29,752	32,492	33,519
03079	*Salem*	28,776	30,089	31,549
03878	Somersworth	11,766	11,855	12,192
03087	*Windham*	13,592	15,817	16,086

New Jersey

Area codes: 201/551, 609/640, 732/848, 856, 862/973, 908

ZIP	Place	2010 population	2020 population	2023 estimate
07712	Asbury Park	16,116	15,188	15,391
*08401	Atlantic City	39,558	38,497	38,464
07001	Avenel (c)	17,011	16,920	—
07002	Bayonne	63,024	71,686	70,300
08722	Beachwood	11,045	10,859	11,153
*08031	Bellmawr	11,583	11,707	11,724
07621	Bergenfield	26,764	28,321	28,274
08805	Bound Brook	10,402	11,988	12,371
08807	Bradley Gardens (c)	14,206	14,077	—
08302	Bridgeton	25,349	27,263	26,763
08015	Browns Mills (c)	11,223	10,734	—
08016	Burlington	9,920	9,743	10,024
*08101	Camden	77,344	71,791	71,100
07008	Carteret	22,844	25,326	25,281
08002	Cherry Hill Mall (c)	14,171	14,805	—
07010	Cliffside Park	23,594	25,693	25,570
*07013	Clifton	84,136	90,296	88,461
*08108	Collingswood	13,926	14,186	14,204
07067	Colonia (c)	17,795	18,609	—
*07801	Dover	18,157	18,460	18,435
07628	Dumont	17,479	17,863	18,234
*07018	East Orange	64,270	69,612	69,556
07073	East Rutherford	8,913	10,022	10,421
*07724	Eatontown	12,709	13,597	13,496
08043	Echelon (c)	10,743	11,896	—
07020	Edgewater	11,513	14,336	14,678
*07201	Elizabeth	124,969	137,298	135,829
07407	Elmwood Park	19,403	21,422	21,256
*07631	Englewood	27,147	29,308	29,624
07410	Fair Lawn	32,457	34,927	35,564
07022	Fairview	13,835	15,025	14,927
07932	Florham Park	11,696	12,585	14,092
08863	Fords (c)	15,187	12,941	—
07024	Fort Lee	35,345	40,191	39,700
07417	Franklin Lakes	10,590	11,079	11,021
08823	Franklin Park (c)	13,295	13,430	—
07728	Freehold	12,052	12,538	12,430
07026	Garfield	30,487	32,655	32,456
08028	Glassboro	18,579	23,149	23,987
07452	Glen Rock	11,601	12,133	12,076
08030	Gloucester City	11,456	11,484	11,507
*08053	Greentree (c)	11,367	12,012	—
07093	Guttenberg	11,176	12,017	11,365
*07601	Hackensack	43,010	46,030	45,736
07840	Hackettstown	9,724	10,248	10,125
08033	Haddonfield	11,593	12,550	12,571
08690	Hamilton Square (c)	12,784	12,679	—
08037	Hammonton	14,791	14,711	14,797
07029	Harrison	13,620	19,450	20,520
07604	Hasbrouck Heights	11,842	12,125	12,030
*07506	Hawthorne	18,791	19,637	19,496
08904	Highland Park	13,982	15,072	14,959
08844	Hillsborough (c)	—	22,214	—
07642	Hillsdale	10,219	10,143	10,062
07030	Hoboken	50,005	60,419	57,010
08757	Holiday City-Berkeley (c)	12,831	12,943	—
07843	Hopatcong	15,147	14,362	14,622
08830	Iselin (c)	18,695	20,088	—
*07302	Jersey City	247,597	292,449	291,657
*07032	Kearny	40,684	41,999	39,370
07405	Kinnelon	10,248	9,966	10,009
07034	Lake Hiawatha (c)	—	10,194	—
07849	Lake Hopatcong (c)	—	10,232	—
08701	Lakewood (c)	53,805	69,398	—
07035	Lincoln Park	10,521	10,915	10,951
07036	Linden	40,499	43,738	43,950
08021	Lindenwold	17,613	21,641	21,685
07643	Little Ferry	10,626	10,987	10,914
07644	Lodi	24,136	26,206	25,832
07740	Long Branch	30,719	31,667	32,745
07940	Madison	15,845	16,937	16,432
08835	Manville	10,344	10,953	10,779
08053	Marlton (c)	10,133	10,594	—
08836	Martinsville (c)	11,980	12,147	—
07607	Maywood	9,555	10,080	10,023
08619	Mercerville (c)	13,230	13,447	—
08840	Metuchen	13,574	15,049	14,977
08846	Middlesex	13,635	14,636	14,461
08332	Millville	28,400	27,491	27,358
08057	Moorestown-Lenola (c)	14,217	14,240	—
*07960	Morristown	18,411	20,180	20,571
*08901	New Brunswick	55,181	55,266	55,846
07646	New Milford	16,341	16,923	16,889
07974	New Providence	12,171	13,650	13,488
*07102	Newark	277,140	311,549	304,960
07031	North Arlington	15,392	16,457	16,370
*07060	North Plainfield	21,936	22,808	22,566
07438	Oak Ridge (c)	—	10,996	—
07436	Oakland	12,754	12,748	12,680
*08050	Ocean Acres (c)	16,142	18,185	—
08226	Ocean City	11,701	11,229	11,242
08857	Old Bridge (c)	23,753	27,210	—
07650	Palisades Park	19,622	20,292	20,102
*07652	Paramus	26,342	26,698	26,282
07054	Parsippany (c)	—	22,778	—
07055	Passaic	69,781	70,537	68,903
*07505	Paterson	146,199	159,732	156,452
08070	Pennsville (c)	11,888	12,043	—
*08861	Perth Amboy	50,814	55,436	55,249
08865	Phillipsburg	14,950	15,249	15,328
08021	Pine Hill	10,233	10,743	10,783
*07060	Plainfield	49,808	54,586	54,670
08232	Pleasantville	20,249	20,629	20,613
08742	Point Pleasant	18,392	18,941	19,429
07442	Pompton Lakes	11,097	11,127	10,874
07444	Pompton Plains (c)	—	11,144	—
07470	Preakness (c)	—	18,487	—
*08540	Princeton	12,307	30,681	30,289
08536	Princeton Meadows (c)	13,834	14,776	—
07065	Rahway	27,346	29,556	29,813
07446	Ramsey	14,473	14,798	14,706
*07701	Red Bank	12,206	12,936	12,779
07657	Ridgefield	11,032	11,501	11,417
07660	Ridgefield Park	12,729	13,224	13,135
*07450	Ridgewood	24,958	25,979	26,194
07456	Ringwood	12,228	11,735	11,451
07661	River Edge	11,340	12,049	11,995
07751	Robertsville (c)	11,297	11,399	—
07203	Roselle	21,085	22,695	22,342
07204	Roselle Park	13,297	13,967	13,932
07070	Rutherford	18,061	18,834	18,852
*08872	Sayreville	42,704	45,345	45,496
*07094	Secaucus	16,264	22,181	21,005
07078	Short Hills (c)	13,165	14,422	—

ZIP	Place	2010 population	2020 population	2023 estimate
08081	Sicklerville (c)	—	45,084	—
08244	Somers Point	10,795	10,469	10,465
*08873	Somerset (c)	22,083	22,968	—
08876	Somerville	12,098	12,346	14,112
08879	South Amboy	8,631	9,411	10,237
07080	South Plainfield	23,385	24,338	24,131
08882	South River	16,008	16,118	15,931
08003	Springdale (c)	14,518	14,811	—
07876	Succasunna (c)	9,152	10,338	—
*07901	Summit	21,457	22,719	22,344
07670	Tenafly	14,488	15,409	15,178
07920	The Hills (c)	—	11,410	—
*07724	Tinton Falls	17,892	19,181	19,354
08753	Toms River (c)	88,791	92,830	—
*07512	Totowa	10,804	11,065	10,785
*08608	Trenton	84,913	90,871	89,620
07087	Union City	66,455	68,589	64,462
07043	Upper Montclair (c)	11,565	13,146	—
*08360	Vineland	60,724	60,780	60,797
07463	Waldwick	9,625	10,058	10,105
07057	Wallington	11,335	11,868	11,825
07465	Wanaque	11,116	11,317	11,048
07728	West Freehold (c)	13,613	13,596	—
07093	West New York	49,708	52,912	50,754
*07090	Westfield	30,316	31,032	30,559
08108	Westmont (c)	—	13,726	—
*07675	Westwood	10,908	11,282	11,210
08094	Williamstown (c)	15,567	15,082	—
07075	Wood-Ridge	7,626	10,137	10,197
07095	Woodbridge (c)	19,265	19,839	—
*08096	Woodbury	10,174	9,963	10,063
07424	Woodland Park	11,819	13,484	13,138

New Mexico

Area codes: 505, 575

ZIP	Place	2010 population	2020 population	2023 estimate
*88310	Alamogordo	30,403	30,898	31,284
*87102	Albuquerque	545,852	564,559	560,274
*88210	Artesia	11,301	12,875	12,326
*88220	Carlsbad	26,138	32,238	31,499
*88021	Chaparral (c)	14,631	16,551	—
*88101	Clovis	37,775	38,567	37,612
*88030	Deming	14,855	14,758	14,603
*87532	Española	10,224	10,526	10,431
*87401	Farmington	45,877	46,624	46,237
*87301	Gallup	21,678	21,899	20,451
*88240	Hobbs	34,122	40,508	39,386
*88001	Las Cruces	97,618	111,385	114,892
*87701	Las Vegas	13,753	13,166	12,905
*87544	Los Alamos (c)	12,019	13,179	—
87031	Los Lunas	14,835	17,242	19,079
88260	Lovington	11,009	11,668	11,237
87107	North Valley (c)	11,333	11,149	—
*88130	Portales	12,280	12,137	11,859
*87124	Rio Rancho	87,521	104,046	110,660
*88201	Roswell	48,366	48,422	47,109
*87501	Santa Fe	67,947	87,505	89,167
87105	South Valley (c)	40,976	38,338	—
*88063	Sunland Park	14,106	16,702	17,689

New York

Area codes: 212/332/646/917, 315/680, 329/845, 347/718/917/929, 363/516, 518/838, 585, 607, 624/716, 631/934, 914

ZIP	Place	2010 population	2020 population	2023 estimate
*10901	Airmont	8,628	10,166	10,163
*12202	Albany	97,856	99,224	101,228
12010	Amsterdam	18,620	18,219	18,093
*13021	Auburn	27,687	26,866	25,983
*11702	Babylon	12,166	12,188	12,106
11510	Baldwin (c)	24,033	33,919	—
*14020	Batavia	15,465	15,600	15,437
11706	Bay Shore (c)	26,337	29,244	—
12508	Beacon	15,541	13,769	15,025
11710	Bellmore (c)	16,218	16,297	—
11714	Bethpage (c)	16,429	16,658	—
*13901	Binghamton	47,376	47,969	46,727
11717	Brentwood (c)	60,664	62,387	—
*14610	Brighton (c)	36,609	37,137	—
*14202	Buffalo	261,310	278,349	274,678
*14424	Canandaigua	10,545	10,576	10,480
11720	Centereach (c)	31,578	30,980	—
*11722	Central Islip (c)	34,450	36,714	—
*14227	Cheektowaga (c)	75,178	76,829	—
*10952	Chestnut Ridge	7,916	10,505	10,526
12047	Cohoes	16,168	18,147	18,206
11725	Commack (c)	36,124	36,536	—
11726	Copiague (c)	22,993	23,429	—
11727	Coram (c)	39,113	40,220	—
*14830	Corning	11,183	10,551	10,612
13045	Cortland	19,204	17,556	17,276
13214	De Witt (c)	—	11,247	—
11729	Deer Park (c)	27,745	28,837	—
14043	Depew	15,303	15,178	14,891
*11746	Dix Hills (c)	26,892	26,180	—
10522	Dobbs Ferry	10,875	11,541	11,309
*14048	Dunkirk	12,563	12,743	12,442
12302	East Glenville (c)	6,616	11,896	—
11730	East Islip (c)	14,475	13,931	—
11758	East Massapequa (c)	19,069	19,854	—
11554	East Meadow (c)	38,132	37,796	—
11731	East Northport (c)	20,217	20,048	—
11772	East Patchogue (c)	22,469	21,580	—
11518	East Rockaway	9,818	10,159	10,010
11733	East Setauket (c)	—	10,998	—
*10709	Eastchester (c)	19,554	20,901	—
14226	Eggertsville (c)	15,019	15,561	—
*14901	Elmira	29,200	26,523	26,176
11003	Elmont (c)	33,198	35,265	—
11731	Elwood (c)	11,177	11,426	—
*13760	Endicott	13,392	13,667	13,211
*13760	Endwell (c)	11,446	11,762	—
*13219	Fairmount (c)	10,224	10,248	—
11738	Farmingville (c)	15,481	14,983	—
*11001	Floral Park	15,863	16,172	15,879
*13602	Fort Drum (c)	12,955	15,896	—
11010	Franklin Square (c)	29,320	30,903	—
11520	Freeport	42,860	44,472	43,756
13069	Fulton	11,896	11,389	11,248
*11530	Garden City	22,371	23,272	22,835
14456	Geneva	13,261	12,812	12,391
11542	Glen Cove	26,964	28,365	27,879
*12801	Glens Falls	14,700	14,830	14,507
12078	Gloversville	15,665	15,131	14,843
*11023	Great Neck	9,989	11,145	11,007
*14612	Greece (c)	14,519	14,429	—
11740	Greenlawn (c)	13,742	13,661	—
11946	Hampton Bays (c)	13,603	15,228	—
10528	Harrison	27,472	28,218	30,780
*11788	Hauppauge (c)	20,882	20,083	—
10927	Haverstraw	11,910	12,323	12,226
*11550	Hempstead	53,891	59,169	58,225
*11801	Hicksville (c)	41,547	43,869	—
11741	Holbrook (c)	27,195	26,487	—
*11742	Holtsville (c)	19,714	18,937	—
11743	Huntington (c)	18,046	19,645	—
*11746	Huntington Station (c)	33,029	34,878	—
11096	Inwood (c)	9,792	11,340	—
*14617	Irondequoit (c)	51,692	51,043	—
11751	Islip (c)	18,689	18,418	—
*14850	Ithaca	30,014	32,108	32,724
*14701	Jamestown	31,146	28,712	27,965
*10535	Jefferson Valley-Yorktown (c)	14,142	14,444	—
*11753	Jericho (c)	13,567	14,808	—
13790	Johnson City	15,174	15,343	14,874
*14217	Kenmore	15,423	15,205	14,916
11754	Kings Park (c)	17,282	17,085	—
*12401	Kingston	23,893	24,069	23,777
10950	Kiryas Joel	20,175	32,954	41,857
14218	Lackawanna	18,141	19,949	19,593
11755	Lake Grove	11,163	11,072	11,021
11779	Lake Ronkonkoma (c)	20,155	18,619	—
14086	Lancaster	10,352	10,027	10,047
*12110	Latham (c)	—	13,680	—
11756	Levittown (c)	51,881	51,758	—
11757	Lindenhurst	27,253	27,148	26,972
*14094	Lockport	21,165	20,876	20,436
11561	Long Beach	33,275	35,029	34,595
12211	Loudonville (c)	—	10,296	—
11563	Lynbrook	19,427	20,438	20,071
10543	Mamaroneck	18,929	20,151	19,533
11949	Manorville (c)	14,314	14,317	—
11758	Massapequa (c)	21,685	21,355	—
11762	Massapequa Park	17,008	17,109	16,826
13662	Massena	10,936	10,151	10,082
11950	Mastic (c)	15,481	15,404	—
11951	Mastic Beach (c)	12,930	14,199	—
11763	Medford (c)	24,142	24,247	—
*11747	Melville (c)	18,985	19,284	—
11566	Merrick (c)	22,097	22,040	—
11953	Middle Island (c)	10,483	10,546	—
*10940	Middletown	28,086	30,345	30,152
11764	Miller Place (c)	12,339	11,723	—

ZIP	Place	2010 population	2020 population	2023 estimate
11501	Mineola	18,799	20,800	21,169
10952	Monsey (c)	18,412	26,954	—
10549	Mount Kisco	10,877	10,959	10,567
11766	Mount Sinai (c)	12,118	11,623	—
*10550	Mount Vernon	67,292	73,893	71,168
12590	Myers Corner (c)	6,790	10,598	—
10954	Nanuet (c)	17,882	18,886	—
11767	Nesconset (c)	13,387	13,207	—
11590	New Cassel (c)	14,059	14,199	—
10956	New City (c)	33,559	34,135	—
*11040	New Hyde Park	9,712	10,257	10,129
*10801	New Rochelle	77,062	79,726	83,742
*10001	New York	8,175,133	8,804,190	8,258,035
*12550	Newburgh	28,866	28,856	28,237
*14301	Niagara Falls	50,193	48,671	47,599
12309	Niskayuna (c)	—	20,787	—
11701	North Amityville (c)	17,862	18,643	—
11703	North Babylon (c)	17,509	17,927	—
11706	North Bay Shore (c)	18,944	19,619	—
11710	North Bellmore (c)	19,941	20,583	—
11713	North Bellport (c)	11,545	11,900	—
11757	North Lindenhurst (c)	11,652	12,000	—
11758	North Massapequa (c)	17,886	17,829	—
11566	North Merrick (c)	12,272	12,238	—
*11040	North New Hyde Park (c)	14,899	15,657	—
14120	North Tonawanda	31,568	30,496	30,031
11580	North Valley Stream (c)	16,628	18,197	—
11793	North Wantagh (c)	11,960	11,931	—
11572	Oceanside (c)	32,109	32,637	—
14760	Olean	14,452	13,937	13,650
13421	Oneida	11,393	10,329	10,094
13820	Oneonta	13,901	13,079	15,331
10562	Ossining	25,060	27,551	26,542
13126	Oswego	18,142	16,921	17,022
11772	Patchogue	11,798	12,408	12,337
10965	Pearl River (c)	15,876	16,567	—
10566	Peekskill	23,583	25,431	25,442
11803	Plainview (c)	26,217	27,100	—
*12901	Plattsburgh	19,989	19,841	19,867
*10573	Port Chester	28,967	31,693	30,584
*11050	Port Washington (c)	15,846	16,753	—
*12601	Poughkeepsie	32,736	31,577	31,772
11961	Ridge (c)	13,336	13,271	—
11901	Riverhead (c)	13,299	14,993	—
*14604	Rochester	210,565	211,328	207,274
*11570	Rockville Centre	24,023	26,016	25,578
11778	Rocky Point (c)	14,014	13,633	—
12205	Roessleville (c)	—	11,518	—
*13440	Rome	33,725	32,127	31,652
*11779	Ronkonkoma (c)	19,082	18,955	—
11575	Roosevelt (c)	16,258	18,066	—
12306	Rotterdam (c)	20,652	22,968	—
10580	Rye	15,720	16,592	16,202
11780	Saint James (c)	13,338	13,487	—
11590	Salisbury (c)	12,093	12,618	—
12866	Saratoga Springs	26,586	28,491	28,544
11782	Sayville (c)	16,853	16,569	—
*10583	Scarsdale	17,166	18,253	17,747
*12305	Schenectady	66,135	67,047	68,544
*10940	Scotchtown (c)	9,212	10,578	—
11783	Seaford (c)	15,294	15,251	—
11784	Selden (c)	19,851	21,262	—
11967	Shirley (c)	27,854	26,360	—
10591	Sleepy Hollow	9,870	9,986	10,962
*11787	Smithtown (c)	26,470	25,629	—
11735	South Farmingdale (c)	14,486	14,345	—
10977	Spring Valley	31,347	33,066	32,969
*11790	Stony Brook (c)	13,740	13,467	—
11794	Stony Brook University (c)	9,216	10,409	—
10980	Stony Point (c)	12,147	12,126	—
10901	Suffern	10,723	11,441	11,341
*11791	Syosset (c)	18,829	19,259	—
*13202	Syracuse	145,170	148,620	145,560
10591	Tarrytown	11,277	11,860	11,691
11776	Terryville (c)	11,849	11,472	—
*14150	Tonawanda	15,130	15,129	14,899
*14150	Tonawanda (c)	58,144	57,431	—
*12180	Troy	50,129	51,401	50,607
*11553	Uniondale (c)	24,759	32,473	—
*13501	Utica	62,235	65,283	63,607
*11580	Valley Stream	37,511	40,634	40,007
11793	Wantagh (c)	18,871	18,613	—
*13601	Watertown	27,023	24,685	24,157
12189	Watervliet	10,254	10,375	10,170
*11704	West Babylon (c)	43,213	43,213	—
10993	West Haverstraw	10,165	10,678	10,622
11552	West Hempstead (c)	18,862	19,835	—
11795	West Islip (c)	28,335	27,048	—
*14224	West Seneca (c)	44,711	45,500	—
*11590	Westbury	15,146	15,864	15,739
*10601	White Plains	56,853	59,559	61,288
11797	Woodbury	10,686	11,526	11,512
11598	Woodmere (c)	17,121	18,669	—
11798	Wyandanch (c)	11,647	12,990	—
*10701	Yonkers	195,976	211,569	207,657

North Carolina

Area codes: 252, 336/743, 472/910, 704/980, 828, 919/984

ZIP	Place	2010 population	2020 population	2023 estimate
*28001	Albemarle	15,903	16,432	16,936
28390	Anderson Creek (c)	—	13,636	—
*27502	Apex	37,476	58,780	72,225
27263	Archdale	11,415	11,907	12,084
*27203	Asheboro	25,012	27,156	27,726
*28801	Asheville	83,393	94,589	95,056
28012	Belmont	10,076	15,010	15,515
*28607	Boone	17,122	19,092	19,811
*27215	Burlington	49,963	57,303	60,032
27510	Carrboro	19,582	21,295	21,103
*27511	Cary	135,234	174,721	180,010
*27514	Chapel Hill	57,233	61,960	62,043
*28202	Charlotte	731,424	874,579	911,311
*27520	Clayton	16,116	26,307	30,216
27012	Clemmons	18,627	21,163	22,159
*28025	Concord	79,066	105,240	110,119
28031	Cornelius	24,866	31,412	33,139
*28036	Davidson	10,944	15,106	14,521
*27701	Durham	228,330	283,506	296,186
*27288	Eden	15,527	15,421	15,332
*27909	Elizabeth City	18,683	18,631	18,948
27244	Elon	9,419	11,336	11,520
*28301	Fayetteville	200,564	208,501	209,749
27526	Fuquay-Varina	17,937	34,152	43,817
27529	Garner	25,745	31,159	35,265
*28052	Gastonia	71,741	80,411	83,942
*27530	Goldsboro	36,437	33,657	33,469
27253	Graham	14,153	17,157	18,354
*27401	Greensboro	269,666	299,035	302,296
*27834	Greenville	84,554	87,521	90,053
28075	Harrisburg	11,526	18,967	19,883
*28532	Havelock	20,735	16,621	16,500
*27536	Henderson	15,368	15,060	14,857
*28792	Hendersonville	13,137	15,137	15,466
*28601	Hickory	40,010	43,490	44,415
*27260	High Point	104,371	114,059	116,926
27540	Holly Springs	24,661	41,239	46,271
28348	Hope Mills	15,176	17,808	17,973
*28078	Huntersville	46,773	61,376	64,688
28079	Indian Trail	33,518	39,997	42,854
*28540	Jacksonville	70,145	72,723	72,879
*28081	Kannapolis	42,625	53,114	59,321
*27284	Kernersville	23,123	26,449	28,016
28086	Kings Mountain	10,296	11,142	11,823
*28501	Kinston	21,677	19,900	19,411
27545	Knightdale	11,401	19,435	20,275
28117	Lake Norman of Iredell (c)	7,411	11,395	—
*28352	Laurinburg	15,962	14,978	15,021
28451	Leland	13,527	22,908	30,542
*28645	Lenoir	18,228	18,352	18,238
27023	Lewisville	12,639	13,381	14,002
*27292	Lexington	18,931	19,632	19,840
*28092	Lincolnton	10,486	11,091	12,128
*28358	Lumberton	21,542	19,025	19,121
*28105	Matthews	27,198	29,435	30,934
27302	Mebane	11,393	17,797	20,212
28227	Mint Hill	22,722	26,450	27,815
*28110	Monroe	32,797	34,562	37,797
*28115	Mooresville	32,711	50,193	53,721
*28655	Morganton	16,918	17,474	17,708
27560	Morrisville	18,576	29,630	31,703
*27030	Mount Airy	10,388	10,676	10,610
28120	Mount Holly	13,656	17,703	18,373
28411	Murraysville (c)	14,215	16,582	—
28409	Myrtle Grove (c)	8,875	11,476	—
*28560	New Bern	29,524	31,291	32,226
28658	Newton	12,968	13,148	13,399
*28374	Pinehurst	13,124	17,581	18,449
28134	Pineville	7,479	10,602	11,153
*28544	Piney Green (c)	13,293	14,386	—
*27601	Raleigh	403,892	467,665	482,295
*27320	Reidsville	14,520	14,583	14,585

ZIP	Place	2010 population	2020 population	2023 estimate
27870	Roanoke Rapids	15,754	15,229	14,669
*27801	Rocky Mount	57,477	54,341	54,245
27571	Rolesville	3,786	9,475	11,297
*28144	Salisbury	33,662	35,540	36,319
*27330	Sanford	28,094	30,261	32,064
*28150	Shelby	20,323	21,918	22,010
27577	Smithfield	10,966	11,292	12,468
*28387	Southern Pines	12,334	15,545	16,728
28326	Spout Springs (c)	—	11,040	—
28390	Spring Lake	11,964	11,660	11,507
28104	Stallings	13,831	16,112	17,212
*28677	Statesville	24,532	28,419	30,220
27358	Summerfield	10,232	10,951	11,150
27886	Tarboro	11,415	10,721	10,859
*27360	Thomasville	26,757	27,183	27,435
*27587	Wake Forest	30,117	47,601	54,337
28173	Waxhaw	9,859	20,534	23,073
*28785	Waynesville	9,869	10,140	10,667
28104	Weddington	9,459	13,181	14,080
27591	Wendell	5,845	9,793	14,400
*28401	Wilmington	106,476	115,451	122,698
*27893	Wilson	49,167	47,851	47,833
*27101	Winston-Salem	229,617	249,545	252,975
28590	Winterville	9,269	10,462	10,821

North Dakota

Area code: 701 applies to the entire state

ZIP	Place	2010 population	2020 population	2023 estimate
*58501	Bismarck	61,272	73,622	75,092
*58601	Dickinson	17,787	25,679	25,130
*58102	Fargo	105,549	125,990	133,188
*58201	Grand Forks	52,838	59,166	58,921
*58401	Jamestown	15,427	15,849	15,691
58554	Mandan	18,331	24,206	24,586
*58701	Minot	40,888	48,377	47,373
58078	West Fargo	25,830	38,626	40,400
*58801	Williston	14,716	29,160	27,706

Ohio

Area codes: 216, 220/740, 234/330, 283/513, 326/937, 380/614, 419/567, 436/440

ZIP	Place	2010 population	2020 population	2023 estimate
*44308	Akron	199,110	190,469	188,701
44601	Alliance	22,322	21,672	21,525
45102	Amelia (c)	4,801	12,575	—
44001	Amherst	12,021	12,681	12,928
44805	Ashland	20,362	19,225	18,718
*44004	Ashtabula	19,124	17,975	17,785
45701	Athens	23,832	23,849	24,673
44202	Aurora	15,548	17,239	17,717
44515	Austintown (c)	29,677	29,594	—
44011	Avon	21,193	24,847	25,403
44012	Avon Lake	22,581	25,206	25,942
44203	Barberton	26,550	25,191	24,563
44140	Bay Village	15,651	16,163	15,810
44122	Beachwood	11,953	14,040	13,734
*45432	Beavercreek	45,193	46,549	47,193
44146	Bedford	13,074	13,149	12,767
*44146	Bedford Heights	10,751	11,020	10,721
43311	Bellefontaine	13,370	14,115	14,073
44017	Berea	19,093	18,545	17,922
43209	Bexley	13,057	13,928	12,785
*45242	Blue Ash	12,114	13,394	13,408
*43402	Bowling Green	30,028	30,808	30,384
44141	Brecksville	13,656	13,635	13,850
45211	Bridgetown (c)	14,407	14,731	—
44147	Broadview Heights	19,400	19,936	19,634
44142	Brook Park	19,212	18,595	18,063
44144	Brooklyn	11,169	11,359	11,022
44212	Brunswick	34,255	35,426	35,072
44820	Bucyrus	12,362	11,684	11,542
*44702	Canton	73,007	70,872	69,197
*45822	Celina	10,400	10,935	10,885
*45458	Centerville	23,999	24,240	25,754
45601	Chillicothe	21,901	22,059	21,895
*45202	Cincinnati	296,943	309,317	311,097
43113	Circleville	13,314	13,927	14,452
45315	Clayton	13,209	13,310	13,222
*44102	Cleveland	396,815	372,624	362,656
*44118	Cleveland Heights	46,121	45,312	43,908
*43201	Columbus	787,033	905,748	913,175
44030	Conneaut	12,841	12,318	12,360
43812	Coshocton	11,216	11,050	11,091
*44221	Cuyahoga Falls	49,652	51,114	50,742
*45402	Dayton	141,527	137,644	135,512
43512	Defiance	16,494	17,066	17,043
43015	Delaware	34,753	41,302	45,158
*45247	Dent (c)	10,497	12,301	—
44622	Dover	12,826	13,112	12,985
*43016	Dublin	41,751	49,328	48,923
*44112	East Cleveland	17,843	13,792	13,352
*44095	Eastlake	18,577	17,670	17,363
*44035	Elyria	54,533	52,656	53,117
45322	Englewood	13,465	13,463	13,249
*44117	Euclid	48,920	49,692	48,212
45324	Fairborn	32,352	34,510	34,729
*45011	Fairfield	42,510	44,907	44,447
44126	Fairview Park	16,826	17,291	16,785
*45840	Findlay	41,202	40,313	40,139
*45224	Finneytown (c)	12,741	12,399	—
45240	Forest Park	18,720	20,189	19,839
45255	Forestville (c)	10,532	10,615	—
44830	Fostoria	13,441	13,046	13,039
45005	Franklin	11,771	11,690	11,653
43420	Fremont	16,734	15,930	15,812
43230	Gahanna	33,248	35,726	35,159
44833	Galion	10,512	10,453	10,293
*44125	Garfield Heights	28,849	29,781	28,900
44232	Green	25,699	27,475	27,338
45331	Greenville	13,227	12,786	12,696
43123	Grove City	35,575	41,252	42,782
*45011	Hamilton	62,477	63,399	62,997
45030	Harrison	9,897	12,563	13,320
43056	Heath	10,310	10,412	10,693
43026	Hilliard	28,435	37,114	37,262
45424	Huber Heights	38,101	43,439	43,313
*44236	Hudson	22,262	23,110	22,968
45638	Ironton	11,129	10,571	10,187
*44240	Kent	28,904	28,215	27,601
*45429	Kettering	56,163	57,862	56,876
44107	Lakewood	52,131	50,942	49,337
43130	Lancaster	38,780	40,552	41,422
45036	Lebanon	20,033	20,841	21,699
*45801	Lima	38,771	35,579	34,794
43140	London	9,904	10,279	10,533
*44052	Lorain	64,097	65,211	65,337
*45140	Loveland	12,081	13,307	13,156
44124	Lyndhurst	14,001	14,050	13,641
*44056	Macedonia	11,188	12,168	12,025
*45211	Mack (c)	11,585	11,088	—
*44902	Mansfield	47,821	47,534	47,711
44137	Maple Heights	23,138	23,701	22,984
45750	Marietta	14,085	13,385	13,090
*43302	Marion	36,837	35,999	35,531
*43040	Marysville	22,094	25,571	28,423
*45036	Mason	30,712	34,792	35,660
*44646	Massillon	32,149	32,146	32,439
43537	Maumee	14,286	13,896	13,633
44124	Mayfield Heights	19,155	20,351	19,793
*44256	Medina	26,678	26,094	25,889
*44060	Mentor	47,159	47,450	46,929
*45343	Miamisburg	20,181	19,923	19,814
44130	Middleburg Heights	15,946	16,004	15,597
*45042	Middletown	48,694	50,987	51,478
*45247	Monfort Heights (c)	11,948	12,070	—
*45050	Monroe	12,442	15,412	15,600
45242	Montgomery	10,251	10,853	10,801
43050	Mount Vernon	16,990	16,956	16,551
43054	New Albany	7,724	10,825	11,335
*44216	New Franklin	14,227	13,877	13,788
44663	New Philadelphia	17,288	17,677	17,440
*43055	Newark	47,573	49,934	51,046
44446	Niles	19,266	18,443	18,256
*44720	North Canton	17,488	17,842	17,637
44070	North Olmsted	32,718	32,442	31,538
*44039	North Ridgeville	29,465	35,280	37,058
44133	North Royalton	30,444	31,322	30,687
*45251	Northbrook (c)	10,668	10,912	—
44203	Norton	12,085	11,673	11,398
44857	Norwalk	17,012	17,068	17,130
45212	Norwood	19,207	19,043	19,046
*43616	Oregon	20,291	19,950	19,711
45056	Oxford	21,371	23,035	22,340
44077	Painesville	19,563	20,312	20,605
*44129	Parma	81,601	81,146	78,951
44130	Parma Heights	20,718	20,863	20,431
*43062	Pataskala	14,962	17,886	18,346
*43551	Perrysburg	20,623	25,041	25,236
43147	Pickerington	18,291	23,094	25,256
45356	Piqua	20,522	20,354	20,747
*45662	Portsmouth	20,226	18,252	17,555
43065	Powell	11,500	14,163	14,491
44266	Ravenna	11,724	11,323	11,215

ZIP	Place	2010 population	2020 population	2023 estimate
*45215	Reading	10,385	10,600	10,380
*43068	Reynoldsburg	35,893	41,076	41,220
44143	Richmond Heights	10,546	10,801	10,509
45431	Riverside	25,201	24,474	24,340
44116	Rocky River	20,213	21,755	21,236
44460	Salem	12,303	11,915	11,715
*44870	Sandusky	25,793	25,095	24,241
44131	Seven Hills	11,804	11,720	11,499
*44120	Shaker Heights	28,448	29,439	28,541
45241	Sharonville	13,560	14,117	13,882
44878	Shiloh (c)	—	10,952	—
*45365	Sidney	21,229	20,589	20,309
44139	Solon	23,348	24,262	23,702
*44121	South Euclid	22,295	21,883	21,264
45066	Springboro	17,409	19,062	19,475
45246	Springdale	11,223	11,007	11,073
*45502	Springfield	60,608	58,662	58,082
*43952	Steubenville	18,659	18,161	18,064
44224	Stow	34,837	34,483	33,957
44241	Streetsboro	16,028	17,260	17,796
*44136	Strongsville	44,750	46,491	45,511
43560	Sylvania	18,965	19,011	19,035
44278	Tallmadge	17,537	18,394	18,317
44883	Tiffin	17,963	17,953	17,603
45371	Tipp City	9,689	10,274	10,484
*43604	Toledo	287,208	270,871	265,304
45067	Trenton	11,869	13,021	13,758
*45426	Trotwood	24,431	23,070	22,940
*45373	Troy	25,058	26,305	26,848
44087	Twinsburg	18,795	19,248	19,439
*44122	University Heights	13,539	13,914	13,203
*43221	Upper Arlington	33,771	36,800	35,743
43078	Urbana	11,793	11,115	11,161
45891	Van Wert	10,846	11,092	11,040
45377	Vandalia	15,246	15,209	14,938
*44089	Vermilion	10,594	10,659	10,704
*44281	Wadsworth	21,567	24,007	24,709
*44481	Warren	41,557	39,201	38,751
*44122	Warrensville Heights	13,542	13,789	13,388
43160	Washington Court House	14,192	14,401	14,412
*45449	West Carrollton	13,143	13,129	12,874
*43081	Westerville	36,120	39,190	37,958
44145	Westlake	32,729	34,228	33,972
*45239	White Oak (c)	19,167	19,541	—
43213	Whitehall	18,062	20,127	19,727
44092	Wickliffe	12,750	12,652	12,616
*44094	Willoughby	22,268	23,959	24,163
44095	Willowick	14,171	14,204	14,123
45177	Wilmington	12,520	12,664	12,600
44691	Wooster	26,119	27,232	27,030
43085	Worthington	13,575	14,786	14,497
45385	Xenia	25,719	25,441	25,725
*44503	Youngstown	66,982	60,068	59,108
*43701	Zanesville	25,487	24,765	24,651

Oklahoma

Area codes: 405/572, 539/918, 580

ZIP	Place	2010 population	2020 population	2023 estimate
*74820	Ada	16,810	16,481	16,611
*73521	Altus	19,813	18,729	18,635
*73401	Ardmore	24,283	24,725	24,847
*74003	Bartlesville	35,750	37,290	38,114
73008	Bethany	19,051	20,831	20,369
74008	Bixby	20,884	28,609	30,698
*74012	Broken Arrow	98,850	113,540	119,194
*73018	Chickasha	16,036	16,051	16,745
73020	Choctaw	11,146	12,182	12,240
*74017	Claremore	18,581	19,580	20,385
74429	Coweta	9,943	9,654	10,786
*73115	Del City	21,332	21,822	21,312
*73533	Duncan	23,431	22,692	23,170
*74701	Durant	15,856	18,589	20,296
*73034	Edmond	81,405	94,428	98,103
73036	El Reno	16,749	16,989	19,216
*73644	Elk City	11,693	11,561	11,279
*73701	Enid	49,379	51,308	50,577
74033	Glenpool	10,808	13,691	14,349
73044	Guthrie	10,191	10,749	11,398
73942	Guymon	11,442	12,965	12,287
74037	Jenks	16,924	25,949	27,553
*73501	Lawton	96,867	90,381	90,245
*74501	McAlester	18,383	18,171	18,140
*74354	Miami	13,570	12,969	12,866
*73110	Midwest City	54,371	58,409	58,086
*73160	Moore	55,081	62,793	63,470
*74401	Muskogee	39,223	36,878	36,873
73064	Mustang	17,395	19,879	23,270
73065	Newcastle	7,685	10,984	14,001
*73069	Norman	110,925	128,026	130,046
*73102	Oklahoma City	579,999	681,054	702,767
74447	Okmulgee	12,321	11,322	11,376
74055	Owasso	28,915	38,240	41,162
*74601	Ponca City	25,387	24,424	24,306
74063	Sand Springs	18,906	19,874	20,075
*74066	Sapulpa	20,544	21,929	22,981
*74801	Shawnee	29,857	31,377	31,803
*74074	Stillwater	45,688	48,394	49,525
*74464	Tahlequah	15,753	16,209	16,833
*74103	Tulsa	391,906	413,066	411,894
*73122	Warr Acres	10,043	10,452	10,472
73096	Weatherford	10,833	12,076	12,023
*73801	Woodward	12,051	12,133	11,753
*73099	Yukon	22,709	23,630	26,388

Oregon

Area codes: 458/541, 503/971

ZIP	Place	2010 population	2020 population	2023 estimate
*97321	Albany	50,158	56,472	57,053
*97003	Aloha (c)	49,425	53,828	—
97603	Altamont (c)	19,257	20,233	—
97520	Ashland	20,078	21,360	21,061
97814	Baker City	9,828	10,099	10,225
*97005	Beaverton	89,803	97,494	96,945
*97701	Bend	76,639	99,178	104,557
97229	Bethany (c)	20,646	31,350	—
97013	Canby	15,829	18,171	17,944
*97229	Cedar Mill (c)	14,546	17,259	—
97502	Central Point	17,169	18,997	19,171
97420	Coos Bay	15,967	15,985	15,595
*97113	Cornelius	11,869	12,694	14,981
*97330	Corvallis	54,462	59,922	61,087
97424	Cottage Grove	9,686	10,574	10,623
97338	Dallas	14,583	16,854	17,644
*97009	Damascus (c)	10,539	11,050	—
*97401	Eugene	156,185	176,654	177,899
97024	Fairview	8,920	10,424	10,782
97116	Forest Grove	21,083	26,225	26,799
*97301	Four Corners (c)	15,947	16,740	—
97027	Gladstone	11,497	12,017	11,865
*97526	Grants Pass	34,533	39,189	39,149
*97030	Gresham	105,594	114,247	110,685
*97015	Happy Valley	13,903	23,733	28,409
97305	Hayesville (c)	19,936	21,891	—
97838	Hermiston	16,745	19,354	19,489
*97123	Hillsboro	91,611	106,447	107,730
97351	Independence	8,590	9,828	10,247
*97303	Keizer	36,478	39,376	38,564
*97601	Klamath Falls	20,840	21,813	21,888
97850	La Grande	13,082	13,026	12,973
*97034	Lake Oswego	36,619	40,731	39,924
97355	Lebanon	15,518	18,447	19,726
97367	Lincoln City	7,930	9,815	10,007
97128	McMinnville	32,187	34,319	34,450
*97501	Medford	74,907	85,824	85,098
*97222	Milwaukie	20,291	21,119	21,594
97038	Molalla	8,108	10,228	10,103
97361	Monmouth	9,534	11,110	11,270
97132	Newberg	22,068	25,138	26,095
*97365	Newport	9,989	10,256	10,489
97459	North Bend	9,695	10,317	10,054
*97222	Oak Grove (c)	16,629	17,290	—
97006	Oak Hills (c)	11,333	11,903	—
97267	Oatfield (c)	13,415	13,977	—
97914	Ontario	11,366	11,645	11,866
97045	Oregon City	31,859	37,572	37,351
97801	Pendleton	16,612	17,107	17,289
*97204	Portland	583,776	652,503	630,498
97754	Prineville	9,253	10,736	11,745
97756	Redmond	26,215	33,274	37,009
*97470	Roseburg	21,181	23,683	23,861
97051	Saint Helens	12,883	13,817	14,437
*97301	Salem	154,637	175,535	177,432
97055	Sandy	9,570	12,612	12,946
97404	Santa Clara (c)	—	11,239	—
97140	Sherwood	18,194	20,450	19,957
97381	Silverton	9,222	10,484	10,341
*97477	Springfield	59,403	61,851	61,085
97386	Sweet Home	8,925	9,828	10,206
97058	The Dalles	13,620	16,010	15,786
*97223	Tigard	48,035	54,539	55,590
97060	Troutdale	15,962	16,300	15,717
97062	Tualatin	26,054	27,942	27,383
97068	West Linn	25,109	27,373	26,629

ZIP	Place	2010 population	2020 population	2023 estimate
97070	Wilsonville	19,509	26,664	26,345
97071	Woodburn	24,080	26,013	29,033

Pennsylvania

Area codes: 215/267/445, 223/717, 272/570, 412/724/878, 484/610/835, 582/814

ZIP	Place	2010 population	2020 population	2023 estimate
*18101	Allentown	118,032	125,845	124,880
15101	Allison Park (c)	21,552	21,864	—
*16601	Altoona	46,320	43,963	42,788
19003	Ardmore (c)	12,455	13,566	—
15234	Baldwin	19,767	21,510	20,708
18603	Berwick	10,477	10,327	10,261
15102	Bethel Park	32,313	33,577	32,398
*18016	Bethlehem	74,982	75,781	78,300
17815	Bloomsburg	14,855	12,711	13,112
19008	Broomall (c)	10,789	11,718	—
*16001	Butler	13,757	13,502	13,099
*17013	Carlisle	18,682	20,118	22,341
15108	Carnot-Moon (c)	11,372	13,151	—
*17201	Chambersburg	20,268	21,903	22,245
*19013	Chester	33,972	32,605	33,595
19320	Coatesville	13,100	13,350	13,275
*17109	Colonial Park (c)	13,229	16,243	—
17512	Columbia	10,400	10,207	10,380
19021	Croydon (c)	9,950	10,014	—
19023	Darby	10,687	10,715	10,614
19026	Drexel Hill (c)	28,043	29,181	—
*18512	Dunmore	14,057	14,042	14,186
*18042	Easton	26,800	28,127	29,538
17022	Elizabethtown	11,545	11,639	12,000
*18049	Emmaus	11,211	11,652	12,017
17522	Ephrata	13,394	13,794	13,660
*16501	Erie	101,786	94,831	92,957
15237	Franklin Park	13,470	15,479	15,024
18052	Fullerton (c)	14,925	16,588	—
*15601	Greensburg	14,892	14,976	14,603
*17331	Hanover	15,289	16,429	16,573
*17101	Harrisburg	49,528	50,099	50,012
*18201	Hazleton	25,340	29,963	30,037
16148	Hermitage	16,220	16,230	15,923
17033	Hershey (c)	14,257	13,858	—
19044	Horsham (c)	14,842	15,193	—
*15701	Indiana	13,975	14,044	14,289
15025	Jefferson Hills	10,619	12,424	12,178
*15901	Johnstown	20,978	18,411	17,950
*19406	King of Prussia (c)	19,936	24,695	—
18704	Kingston	13,182	13,349	13,331
*17601	Lancaster	59,322	58,039	57,153
19446	Lansdale	16,269	18,773	18,978
19050	Lansdowne	10,620	11,107	11,077
*17042	Lebanon	25,477	26,814	26,378
*19055	Levittown (c)	52,983	52,699	—
15068	Lower Burrell	11,761	11,758	11,561
*15132	McKeesport	19,731	17,727	17,132
*16335	Meadville	13,388	13,050	12,361
*15146	Monroeville	28,386	28,640	27,974
18936	Montgomeryville (c)	12,624	12,998	—
18707	Mountain Top (c)	10,982	11,489	—
15120	Munhall	11,406	10,774	10,380
*15668	Murrysville	20,079	21,006	20,745
18634	Nanticoke	10,465	10,628	10,615
*16101	New Castle	23,273	21,926	21,413
*15068	New Kensington	13,116	12,170	11,911
*19401	Norristown	34,324	35,748	35,769
18067	Northampton	9,926	10,395	10,404
*19107	Philadelphia	1,526,006	1,603,797	1,550,542
*19460	Phoenixville	16,440	18,602	19,871
*15201	Pittsburgh	305,704	302,971	303,255
15239	Plum	27,126	27,144	26,391
*19464	Pottstown	22,377	23,433	23,349
17901	Pottsville	14,324	13,346	13,355
17109	Progress (c)	9,765	11,168	—
*19601	Reading	88,082	95,112	94,903
15857	Saint Marys	13,070	12,738	12,399
*18503	Scranton	76,089	76,328	75,805
*16146	Sharon	14,038	13,147	12,813
17404	Shiloh (c)	11,218	11,524	—
*16801	State College	42,034	40,501	40,687
15301	Washington	13,663	13,176	13,429
17268	Waynesboro	10,568	10,951	11,067
17315	Weigelstown (c)	12,875	15,136	—
*19380	West Chester	18,461	18,671	19,658
*15122	West Mifflin	20,313	19,589	18,916
18052	Whitehall	13,944	15,064	14,615
*18701	Wilkes-Barre	41,498	44,328	44,254
15221	Wilkinsburg	15,930	14,349	13,813
*17701	Williamsport	29,381	27,754	27,470
19090	Willow Grove (c)	15,726	13,730	—
19610	Wyomissing	10,461	11,114	11,132
19050	Yeadon	11,443	12,054	12,247
*17401	York	43,718	44,800	44,867

Rhode Island

Area code: 401 applies to the entire state. See introductory note.

ZIP	Place	2010 population	2020 population	2023 estimate
02806	*Barrington*	16,310	17,153	17,061
02809	*Bristol*	22,954	22,493	22,069
*02830	*Burrillville*	15,955	16,158	16,393
02863	Central Falls	19,376	22,583	22,543
*02816	*Coventry*	35,014	35,688	35,819
*02910	Cranston	80,387	82,934	82,635
02864	*Cumberland*	33,506	36,405	36,591
02818	*East Greenwich*	13,146	14,312	14,626
02914	East Providence	47,037	47,139	46,900
*02814	*Glocester*	9,746	9,974	10,200
02919	*Johnston*	28,769	29,568	29,679
*02865	*Lincoln*	21,105	22,529	22,846
02842	*Middletown*	16,150	17,075	16,588
*02882	*Narragansett*	15,868	14,532	14,409
*02840	Newport	24,672	25,163	24,717
02842	Newport East (c)	11,769	12,337	—
02852	*North Kingstown*	26,486	27,732	27,771
*02904	*North Providence*	32,078	34,114	33,902
02896	*North Smithfield*	11,967	12,588	12,601
*02860	Pawtucket	71,148	75,604	75,321
02871	*Portsmouth*	17,389	17,871	17,447
*02903	Providence	178,042	190,934	190,792
*02857	*Scituate*	10,329	10,384	10,494
*02917	*Smithfield*	21,430	22,118	22,090
*02879	*South Kingstown*	30,639	31,931	32,025
02878	*Tiverton*	15,780	16,359	16,035
02864	Valley Falls (c)	11,547	12,094	—
02885	*Warren*	10,611	11,147	11,125
*02886	Warwick	82,672	82,823	82,999
02893	*West Warwick*	29,191	31,012	31,151
02891	*Westerly*	22,787	23,359	23,223
02891	Westerly (c)	17,936	18,423	—
02895	Woonsocket	41,186	43,240	43,135

South Carolina

Area codes: 605, 803/839, 821/864, 843/854

ZIP	Place	2010 population	2020 population	2023 estimate
*29801	Aiken	29,524	32,025	32,947
*29621	Anderson	26,686	28,106	29,980
*29902	Beaufort	12,361	13,607	13,850
29611	Berea (c)	14,295	15,578	—
*29910	Bluffton	12,530	27,716	35,243
29316	Boiling Springs (c)	8,219	10,405	—
29579	Carolina Forest (c)	—	23,342	—
*29033	Cayce	12,528	13,781	13,660
*29401	Charleston	120,083	150,227	155,369
*29631	Clemson	13,905	17,681	17,838
*29201	Columbia	129,272	136,632	142,416
*29526	Conway	17,103	24,849	27,985
29223	Dentsville (c)	14,062	14,431	—
*29640	Easley	19,993	22,921	26,386
29681	Five Forks (c)	14,140	17,737	—
*29501	Florence	37,056	39,899	40,609
29206	Forest Acres	10,361	10,617	10,376
*29715	Fort Mill	10,811	24,521	33,626
29644	Fountain Inn	7,799	10,416	13,027
*29341	Gaffney	12,414	12,764	12,484
29605	Gantt (c)	14,229	15,006	—
29576	Garden City (c)	9,209	10,235	—
29445	Goose Creek	35,938	45,946	49,249
*29601	Greenville	58,409	70,720	72,824
*29646	Greenwood	23,222	22,545	22,498
*29650	Greer	25,515	35,308	44,387
29410	Hanahan	17,997	20,325	21,796
29927	Hardeeville	2,952	7,473	11,897
*29928	Hilton Head Island	37,099	37,661	38,097
29063	Irmo	11,097	11,569	12,033
29412	James Island[1]	—	11,621	11,903
*29456	Ladson (c)	13,790	15,550	—
29710	Lake Wylie (c)	8,841	13,655	—
*29072	Lexington	17,870	23,568	24,921
29566	Little River (c)	8,960	11,711	—
29662	Mauldin	22,889	24,724	28,010
29461	Moncks Corner	7,885	13,297	16,621
*29464	Mount Pleasant	67,843	90,801	95,232
*29572	Myrtle Beach	27,109	35,682	39,697
29108	Newberry	10,277	10,691	10,866

ZIP	Place	2010 population	2020 population	2023 estimate
*29841	North Augusta	21,348	24,379	25,891
*29410	North Charleston	97,471	114,852	121,469
*29582	North Myrtle Beach	13,752	18,790	20,303
29073	Oak Grove (c)	10,291	12,899	—
*29115	Orangeburg	13,964	13,240	13,280
29611	Parker (c)	11,431	13,407	—
29935	Port Royal	10,678	14,220	16,287
*29611	Powdersville (c)	7,618	10,025	—
29072	Red Bank (c)	9,617	10,924	—
*29020	Red Hill (c)	13,223	15,906	—
*29730	Rock Hill	66,154	74,372	75,654
29407	Saint Andrews (c)	20,493	20,675	—
29210	Seven Oaks (c)	15,144	14,652	—
*29681	Simpsonville	18,238	23,354	27,506
29588	Socastee (c)	19,952	22,213	—
*29306	Spartanburg	37,013	38,732	39,040
*29483	Summerville	43,392	50,915	51,884
*29150	Sumter	40,524	43,463	42,766
29687	Taylors (c)	21,617	23,222	—
29708	Tega Cay	7,620	12,832	14,057
*29607	Wade Hampton (c)	20,622	21,482	—
*29169	West Columbia	14,988	17,416	18,316

(1) Incorporated after 2010 Census.

South Dakota

Area code: 605 applies to the entire state

ZIP	Place	2010 population	2020 population	2023 estimate
*57401	Aberdeen	26,091	28,495	28,110
57719	Box Elder	7,800	11,746	13,868
57005	Brandon	8,785	11,048	10,958
*57006	Brookings	22,056	23,377	24,312
*57350	Huron	12,592	14,263	14,618
57301	Mitchell	15,254	15,660	15,621
57501	Pierre	13,646	14,091	13,880
*57701	Rapid City	67,956	74,703	79,404
*57103	Sioux Falls	153,888	192,517	206,410
*57783	Spearfish	10,494	12,193	13,282
57069	Vermillion	10,571	11,695	12,011
57201	Watertown	21,482	22,655	23,230
57078	Yankton	14,454	15,411	15,630

Tennessee

Area codes: 423/729 (Mar. 5, 2025), 615/629, 731, 865, 901, 931

ZIP	Place	2010 population	2020 population	2023 estimate
37701	Alcoa	8,449	10,978	13,349
38002	Arlington	11,517	14,549	15,305
*37303	Athens	13,458	14,084	14,731
38004	Atoka	8,387	10,008	10,593
*38133	Bartlett	54,613	57,786	56,030
*37027	Brentwood	37,060	45,373	45,265
*37620	Bristol	26,702	27,147	27,854
*37402	Chattanooga	167,674	181,099	187,030
*37040	Clarksville	132,929	166,722	180,716
*37311	Cleveland	41,285	47,356	49,086
*37716	Clinton	9,841	10,056	10,337
37315	Collegedale	8,282	11,109	11,476
*38017	Collierville	43,965	51,324	51,317
*38401	Columbia	34,681	41,690	47,445
*38501	Cookeville	30,435	34,842	36,657
*38555	Crossville	10,795	12,071	12,652
*37055	Dickson	14,538	16,058	16,744
*38024	Dyersburg	17,145	16,164	15,968
37412	East Ridge	20,979	22,167	21,961
*37643	Elizabethton	14,176	14,546	14,302
37062	Fairview	7,720	9,357	10,240
*37922	Farragut	20,676	23,506	25,579
*37064	Franklin	62,487	83,454	88,558
37066	Gallatin	30,278	44,431	50,355
*38138	Germantown	38,844	41,333	40,267
*37072	Goodlettsville	15,921	17,789	17,429
*37743	Greeneville	15,062	15,479	15,776
38040	Halls (c)	—	10,341	—
37074	Hartsville/Trousdale Co.	7,870	11,615	12,271
*37075	Hendersonville	51,372	61,753	63,618
*38301	Jackson	65,211	68,205	68,264
*37601	Johnson City	63,152	71,046	73,337
*37660	Kingsport	48,205	55,442	56,704
*37902	Knoxville	178,874	190,740	198,162
*37086	La Vergne	32,588	38,719	39,597
38002	Lakeland	12,430	13,904	14,147
38464	Lawrenceburg	10,428	11,633	11,990
*37087	Lebanon	26,190	38,431	48,112
*37771	Lenoir City	8,642	10,117	11,754
37091	Lewisburg	11,100	12,288	13,135
*37355	Manchester	10,102	12,212	13,272
*38237	Martin	11,473	10,825	11,000
*37801	Maryville	27,465	31,907	32,436
*37110	McMinnville	13,605	13,788	13,790
*38103	Memphis	646,889	633,104	618,639
37343	Middle Valley (c)	12,684	11,695	—
*38053	Millington	10,176	10,582	11,467
*37813	Morristown	29,137	30,431	32,099
*37122	Mount Juliet	23,671	39,289	42,912
*37130	Murfreesboro	108,755	152,769	165,430
*37201	Nashville-Davidson (bal.)	601,222	689,447	687,788
37135	Nolensville	5,861	13,829	15,437
*37830	Oak Ridge	29,330	31,402	33,397
*38060	Oakland	6,623	8,936	10,488
38242	Paris	10,156	10,316	10,343
37148	Portland	11,480	13,156	13,578
37849	Powell (c)	—	13,802	—
37415	Red Bank	11,651	11,899	12,065
*37862	Sevierville	14,807	17,889	18,102
37865	Seymour (c)	10,919	14,705	—
*37160	Shelbyville	20,335	23,557	25,132
37167	Smyrna	39,974	53,070	57,418
*37379	Soddy-Daisy	12,714	13,070	13,234
37174	Spring Hill	29,036	50,005	57,637
37172	Springfield	16,440	18,782	19,494
*37388	Tullahoma	18,655	20,339	21,001
*38261	Union City	10,895	11,170	10,954
37188	White House	10,255	12,982	15,340

Texas

Area codes: 210/726, 214/469/945/972, 254, 281/346/621 (Jan. 23, 2025)/713/832, 325, 361, 409, 430/903, 432, 512/737, 682/817, 806, 830, 915, 936, 940, 956, 979

ZIP	Place	2010 population	2020 population	2023 estimate
*79601	Abilene	117,063	125,182	129,043
75001	Addison	13,056	16,661	17,100
78516	Alamo	18,353	19,493	20,460
77039	Aldine (c)	15,869	15,999	—
*78332	Alice	19,104	17,891	17,579
*75002	Allen	84,246	104,627	111,620
78573	Alton	12,341	18,198	21,130
*77511	Alvin	24,236	27,098	28,633
*79101	Amarillo	190,695	200,393	202,408
79714	Andrews	11,088	13,487	13,502
*77515	Angleton	18,862	19,429	20,206
75409	Anna	8,249	16,896	27,501
*76001	Arlington	365,438	394,266	398,431
77346	Atascocita (c)	65,844	88,174	—
*75751	Athens	12,710	12,857	13,503
*78701	Austin	790,390	961,855	979,882
*76020	Azle	10,947	13,369	14,562
*75180	Balch Springs	23,728	27,685	26,711
78602	Bastrop	7,218	9,688	11,679
*77414	Bay City	17,614	18,061	17,561
*77520	Baytown	71,802	83,701	84,067
*77701	Beaumont	118,296	115,282	112,193
*76021	Bedford	46,979	49,928	48,370
*78102	Beeville	12,863	13,669	13,211
*77401	Bellaire	16,855	17,202	17,016
*76704	Bellmead	9,901	10,494	10,620
76513	Belton	18,216	23,054	25,171
*76126	Benbrook	21,234	24,520	24,336
*79720	Big Spring	27,282	26,144	22,373
*78006	Boerne	10,471	17,850	21,774
75418	Bonham	10,127	10,408	10,879
*79007	Borger	13,251	12,551	12,115
*77833	Brenham	15,716	17,369	19,142
*78520	Brownsville	175,023	186,738	190,158
*76801	Brownwood	19,288	18,862	18,790
78717	Brushy Creek (c)	21,764	22,519	—
*77801	Bryan	76,201	83,980	89,615
78610	Buda	7,295	15,108	16,030
76354	Burkburnett	10,811	10,939	11,089
*76028	Burleson	36,690	47,641	55,220
*79015	Canyon	13,303	14,836	16,171
*78130	Canyon Lake (c)	21,262	31,124	—
*75006	Carrollton	119,097	133,434	132,918
*75104	Cedar Hill	45,028	49,148	48,411
*78613	Cedar Park	48,937	77,595	77,516
75009	Celina	6,028	16,739	43,317
77530	Channelview (c)	38,289	45,688	—
78108	Cibolo	15,349	32,276	36,374
*77494	Cinco Ranch (c)	18,274	16,899	—
*76031	Cleburne	29,337	31,352	36,209
77015	Cloverleaf (c)	22,942	24,100	—
77531	Clute	11,211	10,604	10,704
*77840	College Station	93,857	120,511	125,192
76034	Colleyville	22,807	26,057	25,736
*77301	Conroe	56,207	89,956	108,248
78109	Converse	18,198	27,466	30,321
*75019	Coppell	38,659	42,983	41,404
76522	Copperas Cove	32,032	36,670	38,696

ZIP	Place	2010 population	2020 population	2023 estimate
*76208	Corinth	19,935	22,634	23,707
*78401	Corpus Christi	305,215	317,863	316,595
*75110	Corsicana	23,770	25,109	25,671
76036	Crowley	12,838	18,070	19,932
*75201	Dallas	1,197,816	1,304,379	1,302,868
77536	Deer Park	32,010	34,495	33,176
*78840	Del Rio	35,591	34,673	34,574
*75020	Denison	22,682	24,479	26,343
*76205	Denton	113,383	139,869	158,349
*75115	DeSoto	49,047	56,145	55,740
77539	Dickinson	18,680	20,847	21,834
78537	Donna	15,798	16,797	16,782
79029	Dumas	14,691	14,501	14,291
*75116	Duncanville	38,524	40,706	38,883
*78852	Eagle Pass	26,248	28,130	28,282
*78539	Edinburg	77,100	100,243	105,799
77437	El Campo	11,602	12,350	12,062
*79901	El Paso	649,121	678,815	678,958
78621	Elgin	8,135	9,784	12,304
*75119	Ennis	18,513	20,159	23,686
*76039	Euless	51,277	61,032	59,686
*78015	Fair Oaks Ranch	5,986	9,833	11,406
75069	Fairview	7,248	10,372	10,790
*75234	Farmers Branch	28,616	35,991	36,917
*75087	Fate	6,357	17,958	24,626
*75022	Flower Mound	64,669	75,956	79,445
*76119	Forest Hill	12,355	13,955	14,157
75126	Forney	14,661	23,455	35,470
*79906	Fort Bliss (c)	8,591	11,260	—
76544	Fort Hood (c)	29,589	28,295	—
*76102	Fort Worth	741,206	918,915	978,468
*77498	Four Corners (c)	12,382	12,103	—
78624	Fredericksburg	10,530	10,875	11,542
*77541	Freeport	12,049	10,696	10,550
77545	Fresno (c)	19,069	24,486	—
*77546	Friendswood	35,805	41,213	40,826
*75034	Frisco	116,989	200,509	225,007
*77441	Fulshear	1,134	16,856	42,616
*76240	Gainesville	16,002	17,394	18,107
77547	Galena Park	10,887	10,740	10,271
*77550	Galveston	47,743	53,695	53,237
*75040	Garland	226,876	246,018	243,470
*76528	Gatesville	15,751	16,135	16,148
*78626	Georgetown	47,400	67,176	96,312
75154	Glenn Heights	11,278	15,819	18,793
*76048	Granbury	7,978	10,958	12,622
*75051	Grand Prairie	175,396	196,100	202,134
*76051	Grapevine	46,334	50,631	50,928
*75401	Greenville	25,557	28,164	32,717
77619	Groves	16,144	17,335	16,764
*76117	Haltom City	42,409	46,073	45,290
76548	Harker Heights	26,700	33,097	34,447
*78550	Harlingen	64,849	71,829	71,510
*75032	Heath	6,921	9,769	11,238
*75652	Henderson	13,712	13,271	13,464
79045	Hereford	15,370	14,972	14,752
76643	Hewitt	13,549	16,026	16,691
78557	Hidalgo	11,198	13,964	14,678
75077	Highland Village	15,056	15,899	16,100
*79927	Horizon City	16,735	22,489	24,168
78725	Hornsby Bend (c)	6,791	12,168	—
*77002	Houston	2,099,451	2,304,580	2,314,157
*77338	Humble	15,133	16,795	16,237
*77340	Huntsville	38,548	45,941	48,552
*76053	Hurst	37,337	40,413	39,304
78634	Hutto	14,698	27,577	38,765
78362	Ingleside	9,387	9,519	10,147
77583	Iowa Colony	1,170	8,154	14,823
*75060	Irving	216,290	256,684	254,373
75766	Jacksonville	14,544	13,997	14,420
*77449	Katy	14,102	21,894	26,360
*76248	Keller	39,627	45,776	46,316
76060	Kennedale	6,763	8,517	10,052
*78028	Kerrville	22,347	24,278	24,930
*75662	Kilgore	12,975	13,376	13,523
*76541	Killeen	127,921	153,095	159,643
*78363	Kingsville	26,213	25,402	24,586
78640	Kyle	28,016	45,697	62,548
*78572	La Homa (c)	11,985	11,267	—
77568	La Marque	14,509	18,030	19,605
*77571	La Porte	33,800	35,124	36,991
78645	Lago Vista	6,041	8,896	10,009
77566	Lake Jackson	26,849	28,177	27,768
*78734	Lakeway	11,391	19,189	19,189
*75146	Lancaster	36,361	41,275	40,215
76226	Lantana (c)	6,874	10,785	—
*78040	Laredo	236,091	255,205	257,602
*77573	League City	83,560	114,392	116,320
*78641	Leander	26,521	59,202	80,067
*78238	Leon Valley	10,151	11,542	11,337

ZIP	Place	2010 population	2020 population	2023 estimate
*79336	Levelland	13,542	12,652	12,530
*75057	Lewisville	95,290	111,822	133,553
78642	Liberty Hill	967	3,646	10,428
75068	Little Elm	25,898	46,453	58,496
*78233	Live Oak	13,131	15,781	15,988
78644	Lockhart	12,698	14,379	15,318
*75601	Longview	80,455	81,638	83,236
*79401	Lubbock	229,573	257,141	266,878
*75901	Lufkin	35,067	34,143	34,181
77657	Lumberton	11,943	13,554	14,129
78653	Manor	5,037	13,652	20,209
76063	Mansfield	56,368	72,602	78,542
77578	Manvel	5,179	9,992	17,261
*75670	Marshall	23,523	23,392	24,118
*78501	McAllen	129,877	142,210	146,593
*75070	McKinney	131,117	195,308	213,509
75454	Melissa	4,695	13,901	23,571
78570	Mercedes	15,570	16,258	16,732
*75149	Mesquite	139,824	150,108	147,317
*79701	Midland	111,147	132,524	138,397
76065	Midlothian	18,037	35,125	41,352
*76067	Mineral Wells	16,788	14,820	15,454
*78572	Mission	77,058	85,778	87,292
*77083	Mission Bend (c)	36,501	36,914	—
*77489	Missouri City	67,358	74,259	76,773
*75455	Mount Pleasant	15,564	16,047	16,055
*75094	Murphy	17,708	21,013	20,920
*75961	Nacogdoches	32,996	32,147	32,156
77627	Nederland	17,547	18,856	18,118
*78130	New Braunfels	57,740	90,403	110,958
*76117	North Richland Hills	63,343	69,917	70,658
*79761	Odessa	99,940	114,428	115,743
*77630	Orange	18,595	19,324	19,108
*75801	Palestine	18,712	18,544	19,372
*78572	Palmview	5,460	15,830	15,874
*79065	Pampa	17,994	16,867	16,543
*75460	Paris	25,171	24,476	24,969
*77502	Pasadena	149,043	151,950	146,716
*77581	Pearland	91,252	125,828	127,736
*77406	Pecan Grove (c)	15,963	22,782	—
*78660	Pflugerville	46,936	65,191	65,301
78577	Pharr	70,400	79,715	80,410
*79072	Plainview	22,194	20,187	19,420
*75074	Plano	259,841	285,494	290,190
78064	Pleasanton	8,934	10,648	11,195
*77640	Port Arthur	53,818	56,039	55,547
77979	Port Lavaca	12,248	11,557	11,212
77651	Port Neches	13,040	13,692	13,591
78374	Portland	15,099	20,383	20,481
75407	Princeton	6,807	17,027	28,027
75078	Prosper	9,423	30,174	41,660
*78580	Raymondville	11,284	10,236	10,135
75154	Red Oak	10,769	14,222	18,624
*76028	Rendon (c)	12,552	13,533	—
*75080	Richardson	99,223	119,469	117,435
*77469	Richmond	11,679	11,627	12,816
78582	Rio Grande City	13,834	15,317	15,311
76262	Roanoke	5,962	9,665	10,798
76706	Robinson	10,509	12,443	12,987
78380	Robstown	11,487	10,143	10,335
*78382	Rockport	8,766	10,070	10,929
*75087	Rockwall	37,490	47,251	52,918
78584	Roma	9,765	11,561	11,554
*77471	Rosenberg	30,618	38,282	41,104
*78664	Round Rock	99,887	119,468	130,406
*75088	Rowlett	56,199	62,535	66,813
75189	Royse City	9,349	13,508	24,138
75048	Sachse	20,329	27,103	32,294
*76179	Saginaw	19,806	23,890	25,139
*76901	San Angelo	93,200	99,893	99,262
*78201	San Antonio	1,327,407	1,434,625	1,495,295
78586	San Benito	24,250	24,861	24,493
79849	San Elizario	13,603	10,116	10,164
78589	San Juan	33,856	35,294	36,448
*78666	San Marcos	44,894	67,553	71,569
*77510	Santa Fe	12,222	12,735	12,980
78006	Scenic Oaks (c)	4,957	10,458	—
*78154	Schertz	31,465	42,002	43,239
77586	Seabrook	11,952	13,618	13,662
75159	Seagoville	14,835	18,446	19,643
*78155	Seguin	25,175	29,433	36,013
78154	Selma	5,540	10,952	11,748
*75090	Sherman	38,521	43,645	47,473
77459	Sienna (c)	—	20,204	—
*79549	Snyder	11,202	11,438	11,187
*79927	Socorro	32,013	34,306	38,238
77587	South Houston	16,983	16,153	15,808
76092	Southlake	26,575	31,265	31,137
*77373	Spring (c)	54,298	62,559	—
*77477	Stafford	17,693	17,666	17,338

ZIP	Place	2010 population	2020 population	2023 estimate
78732	Steiner Ranch (c)	—	16,713	—
*76401	Stephenville	17,123	20,897	21,946
*77478	Sugar Land	78,817	111,026	108,515
*75482	Sulphur Springs	15,449	15,941	16,564
79556	Sweetwater	10,906	10,622	10,285
76574	Taylor	15,191	16,267	17,337
*76501	Temple	66,102	82,073	93,095
*75160	Terrell	15,816	17,465	21,480
*75501	Texarkana	36,411	36,193	35,741
*77510	Texas City	45,099	51,898	56,609
75056	The Colony	36,328	44,534	45,471
*77381	The Woodlands (c)	93,847	114,436	—
78260	Timberwood Park (c)	13,447	35,217	—
*77375	Tomball	10,753	12,341	14,201
76262	Trophy Club	8,024	13,688	13,666
*75702	Tyler	96,900	105,995	110,327
*78148	Universal City	18,530	19,720	20,028
75205	University Park	23,068	25,278	24,954
*78801	Uvalde	15,751	15,217	15,436
*77901	Victoria	62,592	65,534	65,800
*76701	Waco	124,805	138,486	144,816
*76148	Watauga	23,497	23,650	22,934
*75165	Waxahachie	29,621	41,140	47,201
*76086	Weatherford	25,250	30,854	38,109
77598	Webster	10,400	12,499	12,182
78728	Wells Branch (c)	12,120	14,000	—
*78596	Weslaco	35,670	40,160	43,053
79764	West Odessa (c)	22,707	33,340	—
77005	West University Place	14,787	14,955	14,791
76108	White Settlement	16,116	18,269	18,005
*76301	Wichita Falls	104,553	102,316	102,691
75098	Wylie	41,427	57,526	61,078

Utah

Area codes: 385/801 apply to the entire state

ZIP	Place	2010 population	2020 population	2023 estimate
84004	Alpine	9,555	10,251	10,298
84003	American Fork	26,263	33,337	38,549
84065	Bluffdale	7,598	17,014	19,090
*84010	Bountiful	42,552	45,762	44,144
84302	Brigham City	17,899	19,650	19,970
*84720	Cedar City	28,857	35,235	39,942
84014	Centerville	15,335	16,884	16,517
*84015	Clearfield	30,112	31,909	34,470
84015	Clinton	20,426	23,386	23,588
*84047	Cottonwood Heights	33,433	33,617	32,204
84020	Draper	42,274	51,017	49,602
*84005	Eagle Mountain	21,415	43,623	56,932
84025	Farmington	18,275	24,531	25,771
*84029	Grantsville	8,893	12,617	15,267
*84032	Heber	11,362	16,856	18,533
*84096	Herriman	21,785	55,144	60,049
84003	Highland	15,523	19,348	20,217
*84117	Holladay	26,472	31,965	30,298
84737	Hurricane	13,748	20,036	23,959
84319	Hyrum	7,609	9,362	10,849
84738	Ivins	6,753	8,978	10,164
84037	Kaysville	27,300	32,945	32,941
84118	Kearns	35,731	36,723	37,767
*84041	Layton	67,311	81,773	83,516
*84043	Lehi	47,407	75,907	90,227
84042	Lindon	10,070	11,397	11,734
*84321	Logan	48,174	52,778	55,250
84044	Magna	26,505	29,251	30,087
84664	Mapleton	7,979	11,365	13,732
84047	Midvale	27,964	36,028	35,561
*84106	Millcreek	62,139	63,380	62,205
*84107	Murray	46,746	50,637	49,553
84341	North Logan	8,269	10,986	11,711
*84404	North Ogden	17,357	20,916	22,233
84054	North Salt Lake	16,322	21,907	23,560
*84401	Ogden	82,825	87,321	87,267
*84057	Orem	88,328	98,129	95,519
84651	Payson	18,294	21,101	24,054
84062	Pleasant Grove	33,509	37,726	37,294
*84414	Pleasant View	7,979	11,083	11,265
*84601	Provo	112,488	115,162	113,343
*84065	Riverton	38,753	45,285	44,854
*84067	Roy	36,884	39,306	38,592
*84770	Saint George	72,897	95,342	104,578
84653	Salem	6,423	9,298	10,725
*84101	Salt Lake City	186,440	199,723	209,593
*84070	Sandy	87,461	96,904	91,943
84655	Santaquin	9,128	13,725	17,532
*84043	Saratoga Springs	17,781	37,696	52,532
84335	Smithfield	9,495	13,571	14,726
*84095	South Jordan	50,418	77,487	84,528
*84403	South Ogden	16,532	17,488	17,678
*84115	South Salt Lake	23,617	26,777	26,122
84660	Spanish Fork	34,691	42,602	45,557
*84663	Springville	29,466	35,268	35,471
84075	Syracuse	24,331	32,141	37,022
*84118	Taylorsville	58,652	60,448	57,098
84074	Tooele	31,605	35,742	39,263
84337	Tremonton	7,647	9,894	12,411
*84078	Vernal	9,089	10,079	10,557
*84058	Vineyard	139	12,543	14,500
84780	Washington	18,761	27,993	33,877
84401	West Haven	10,272	16,739	24,014
*84084	West Jordan	103,712	116,961	114,908
84015	West Point	9,511	10,963	12,479
*84119	West Valley City	129,480	140,230	134,470
*84087	Woods Cross	9,761	11,410	11,480

Vermont

Area code: 802 applies to the entire state. See introductory note.

ZIP	Place	2010 population	2020 population	2023 estimate
05201	*Bennington*	15,764	15,333	15,200
*05301	*Brattleboro*	12,046	12,184	12,110
*05401	Burlington	42,417	44,743	44,528
*05446	*Colchester*	17,067	17,524	17,588
*05452	*Essex*	19,587	22,094	11,462
*05452	Essex Junction	9,271	10,590	10,817
05047	*Hartford*	9,952	10,686	10,743
05468	*Milton*	10,352	10,723	10,735
*05701	Rutland	16,495	15,807	15,630
*05403	South Burlington	17,904	20,292	21,043
05495	*Williston*	8,698	10,103	10,092

Virginia

Area codes: 276, 434, 540/826, 571/703, 686/804, 757/948

ZIP	Place	2010 population	2020 population	2023 estimate
*22314	Alexandria	139,966	159,467	155,230
22003	Annandale (c)	41,008	43,363	—
*22201	Arlington (c)	207,627	238,643	—
*20147	Ashburn (c)	43,511	46,349	—
22041	Bailey's Crossroads (c)	23,643	24,749	—
20147	Belmont (c)	5,966	10,268	—
*24060	Blacksburg	42,620	44,826	45,485
23235	Bon Air (c)	16,366	18,022	—
20148	Brambleton (c)	9,845	23,486	—
23112	Brandermill (c)	13,173	13,730	—
*24201	Bristol	17,835	17,219	16,807
20148	Broadlands (c)	12,313	14,021	—
20111	Buckhall (c)	16,293	20,420	—
20109	Bull Run (c) (Prince William Co.)	14,983	16,794	—
*22015	Burke (c)	41,055	42,312	—
22015	Burke Centre (c)	17,326	17,518	—
24069	Cascades (c)	11,912	12,366	—
24018	Cave Spring (c)	24,922	26,755	—
*20120	Centreville (c)	71,135	73,518	—
*20151	Chantilly (c)	23,039	24,301	—
*22901	Charlottesville	43,475	46,553	44,983
22026	Cherry Hill (c)	16,000	23,683	—
*23320	Chesapeake	222,209	249,422	253,886
*23831	Chester (c)	20,987	23,414	—
*24073	Christiansburg	21,041	23,348	22,542
23834	Colonial Heights	17,411	18,170	18,393
20165	Countryside (c)	10,072	10,418	—
22701	Culpeper	16,379	20,062	21,012
22193	Dale City (c)	65,969	72,088	—
*24541	Danville	43,055	42,590	41,837
20191	Difficult Run (c)	—	10,600	—
20170	Dranesville (c)	11,921	11,785	—
*23222	East Highland Park (c)	14,796	15,131	—
22033	Fair Oaks (c)	30,223	34,052	—
*22030	Fairfax	22,565	24,146	25,144
22039	Fairfax Station (c)	12,030	12,420	—
*22046	Falls Church	12,332	14,658	14,685
24551	Forest (c)	9,106	11,709	—
22308	Fort Hunt (c)	16,045	17,231	—
22310	Franconia (c)	18,245	18,943	—
20171	Franklin Farm (c)	19,288	19,189	—
*22401	Fredericksburg	24,286	27,982	28,928
22630	Front Royal	14,440	15,011	15,400
*20155	Gainesville (c)	11,481	18,112	—
22030	George Mason (c)	9,496	11,162	—
*23059	Glen Allen (c)	14,774	16,187	—
23062	Gloucester Point (c)	9,402	10,587	—
22066	Great Falls (c)	15,427	15,953	—
22306	Groveton (c)	14,598	15,725	—
*23669	Hampton	137,436	137,148	137,098
*22801	Harrisonburg	48,914	51,814	51,082
*20170	Herndon	23,292	24,655	24,935
23075	Highland Springs (c)	15,711	16,604	—
24019	Hollins (c)	14,673	15,574	—

ZIP	Place	2010 population	2020 population	2023 estimate
23860	Hopewell	22,591	23,033	22,752
22303	Huntington (c)	11,267	13,749	—
22306	Hybla Valley (c)	15,801	16,319	—
22043	Idylwood (c)	17,288	17,954	—
20112	Independent Hill (c)	7,419	10,165	—
22032	Kings Park West (c)	13,390	13,465	—
22315	Kingstowne (c)	15,556	16,825	—
22963	Lake Monticello (c)	9,920	10,126	—
22192	Lake Ridge (c)	41,058	46,162	—
23228	Lakeside (c)	11,849	12,203	—
20176	Lansdowne (c)	11,253	12,427	—
23228	Laurel (c)	16,713	17,769	—
*20175	Leesburg	42,616	48,250	49,312
22191	Leesylvania (c)	—	21,193	—
22312	Lincolnia (c)	22,855	22,922	—
20136	Linton Hall (c)	35,725	41,754	—
*22079	Lorton (c)	18,610	20,072	—
20148	Loudoun Valley Estates (c)	3,656	11,436	—
20165	Lowes Island (c)	10,756	11,023	—
*24501	Lynchburg	75,568	79,009	79,535
24572	Madison Heights (c)	11,285	10,893	—
*20110	Manassas	37,821	42,772	42,696
*20111	Manassas Park	14,273	17,219	16,361
23224	Manchester (c)	10,804	12,129	—
*24112	Martinsville	13,821	13,485	13,763
*22101	McLean (c)	48,115	50,773	—
20171	McNair (c)	17,513	21,598	—
23234	Meadowbrook (c)	18,312	20,898	—
*23111	Mechanicsville (c)	36,348	39,482	—
*22081	Merrifield (c)	15,212	20,488	—
*23112	Midlothian (c)	—	18,320	—
22025	Montclair (c)	19,570	22,279	—
22121	Mount Vernon (c)	12,416	12,914	—
20187	New Baltimore (c)	8,119	11,251	—
22122	Newington (c)	12,943	13,223	—
22153	Newington Forest (c)	12,442	12,957	—
*23607	Newport News	180,719	186,247	183,118
*23502	Norfolk	242,803	238,005	230,930
*22124	Oakton (c)	34,166	36,732	—
*23704	Petersburg	32,420	33,458	33,309
23662	Poquoson	12,150	12,460	12,635
*23704	Portsmouth	95,535	97,915	96,793
*24141	Radford	16,408	16,070	16,971
*20190	Reston (c)	58,404	63,226	—
*23219	Richmond	204,214	226,610	229,247
*24011	Roanoke	97,032	100,011	97,171
24281	Rose Hill (c) (Fairfax Co.)	20,226	21,045	—
24153	Salem	24,802	25,346	25,600
23233	Short Pump (c)	24,729	30,626	—
20152	South Riding (c)	24,256	33,877	—
*22150	Springfield (c)	30,484	31,339	—
*24401	Staunton	23,746	25,750	25,915
*20164	Sterling (c)	27,822	30,337	—
20105	Stone Ridge (c)	7,214	15,039	—
24477	Stuarts Draft (c)	9,235	12,142	—
20109	Sudley (c)	16,203	19,008	—
*23434	Suffolk	84,585	94,324	100,659
20164	Sugarland Run (c)	11,799	12,345	—
24502	Timberlake (c)	12,183	13,267	—
23229	Tuckahoe (c)	44,990	48,051	—
*22102	Tysons (c)	19,627	26,374	—
*22180	Vienna	15,687	16,473	16,306
*23451	Virginia Beach	437,994	459,470	453,649
23888	Wakefield (c)	11,275	11,805	—
*20186	Warrenton	9,611	10,057	10,210
22980	Waynesboro	21,006	22,196	23,182
22042	West Falls Church (c)	29,207	30,243	—
22152	West Springfield (c)	22,460	23,369	—
*23185	Williamsburg	14,068	15,425	15,847
*22601	Winchester	26,203	28,120	27,617
*22182	Wolf Trap (c)	16,131	16,496	—
*22191	Woodbridge (c)	4,055	44,668	—
24381	Woodlawn (c) (Fairfax Co.)	20,804	20,859	—
23059	Wyndham (c)	9,785	11,087	—
20111	Yorkshire (c)	7,541	10,992	—

Washington

Area codes: 206, 253, 360/564, 425, 509

ZIP	Place	2010 population	2020 population	2023 estimate
98520	Aberdeen	16,896	17,013	17,014
99001	Airway Heights	6,114	10,757	10,973
*98021	Alderwood Manor (c)	8,442	10,198	—
*98221	Anacortes	15,778	17,637	18,012
98223	Arlington	17,926	19,868	21,206
98335	Artondale (c)	12,653	13,641	—
*98001	Auburn	70,180	87,256	83,870
98110	Bainbridge Island	23,025	24,825	24,254
98604	Battle Ground	17,571	20,743	22,285
*98004	Bellevue	122,363	151,854	151,574
*98225	Bellingham	80,885	91,482	94,720
98230	Birch Bay (c)	8,413	10,115	—
98391	Bonney Lake	17,374	22,487	22,835
*98011	Bothell	33,505	48,161	50,213
*98021	Bothell East (c)	8,018	13,970	—
*98021	Bothell West (c)	16,607	22,015	—
*98337	Bremerton	37,729	43,505	45,450
98178	Bryn Mawr-Skyway (c)	15,645	17,397	—
*98166	Burien	33,313	52,066	50,730
98233	Burlington	8,388	9,152	10,358
98282	Camano (c)	—	17,356	—
98607	Camas	19,355	26,065	27,254
98531	Centralia	16,336	18,183	18,754
99004	Cheney	10,590	13,255	12,620
98072	Cottage Lake (c)	22,494	22,857	—
98042	Covington	17,575	20,777	21,125
*98198	Des Moines	29,673	32,888	31,988
98059	East Renton Highlands (c)	11,140	11,937	—
98802	East Wenatchee	13,190	14,158	14,102
98204	Eastmont (c)	20,101	24,059	—
*98372	Edgewood	9,387	12,327	13,257
*98020	Edmonds	39,709	42,853	42,701
98387	Elk Plain (c)	14,205	14,534	—
*98926	Ellensburg	18,174	18,666	18,694
98022	Enumclaw	10,669	12,543	12,697
*98201	Everett	103,019	110,629	111,180
98058	Fairwood (c) (King Co.)	19,102	19,396	—
99218	Fairwood (c) (Spokane Co.)	7,905	10,541	—
*98003	Federal Way	89,306	101,030	97,701
98248	Ferndale	11,415	15,048	15,992
98424	Fife	9,173	10,999	10,723
98662	Five Corners (c)	18,159	20,973	—
98433	Fort Lewis (c)	11,046	14,052	—
98375	Frederickson (c)	18,719	24,906	—
*98329	Gig Harbor	7,126	12,029	12,604
98338	Graham (c)	23,491	32,658	—
98930	Grandview	10,862	10,907	11,149
98665	Hazel Dell (c)	19,435	23,569	—
*98027	Issaquah	30,434	40,051	38,977
98626	Kelso	11,925	12,720	12,648
98028	Kenmore	20,460	23,914	23,391
*99336	Kennewick	73,917	83,921	85,158
*98031	Kent	92,411	136,588	133,378
*98033	Kirkland	48,787	92,175	91,194
*98503	Lacey	42,393	53,526	58,326
98155	Lake Forest Park	12,598	13,630	13,006
98042	Lake Morton-Berrydale (c)	10,160	10,474	—
98258	Lake Stevens	28,069	35,630	40,521
*98087	Lake Stickney (c)	7,777	15,413	—
98391	Lake Tapps (c)	11,859	12,962	—
98001	Lakeland North (c)	12,942	13,663	—
98001	Lakeland South (c)	11,574	13,169	—
*98499	Lakewood	58,163	63,612	62,303
*99016	Liberty Lake	7,591	12,003	13,188
98632	Longview	36,648	37,818	37,925
98264	Lynden	11,951	15,749	16,551
*98036	Lynnwood	35,836	38,568	43,867
98296	Maltby (c)	10,830	11,277	—
98038	Maple Valley	22,684	28,013	28,434
*98037	Martha Lake (c)	15,473	21,660	—
*98270	Marysville	60,020	70,714	72,916
98040	Mercer Island	22,699	25,748	24,742
*98012	Mill Creek	18,244	20,926	20,742
98012	Mill Creek East (c)	15,709	24,912	—
98661	Minnehaha (c)	9,771	11,871	—
98272	Monroe	17,304	19,699	19,447
98837	Moses Lake	20,366	25,146	26,299
*98273	Mount Vernon	31,743	35,219	35,259
*98686	Mount Vista (c)	7,850	10,051	—
98043	Mountlake Terrace	19,909	21,286	21,516
98275	Mukilteo	20,254	21,538	21,011
*98056	Newcastle	10,380	13,017	12,761
98037	North Lynnwood (c)	16,574	22,802	—
*98277	Oak Harbor	22,075	24,622	24,016
*98501	Olympia	46,478	55,605	55,733
98662	Orchards (c)	19,556	27,729	—
*98444	Parkland (c)	35,803	38,623	—
*99301	Pasco	59,781	77,108	80,038
*98362	Port Angeles	19,038	19,960	20,101
*98366	Port Orchard	11,144	15,587	17,950
98368	Port Townsend	9,113	10,148	10,502
98370	Poulsbo	9,200	11,975	12,171
98391	Prairie Ridge (c)	11,464	12,288	—
*99163	Pullman	29,799	32,901	32,863

ZIP	Place	2010 population	2020 population	2023 estimate
*98371	Puyallup	37,022	42,973	42,179
*98052	Redmond	54,144	73,256	80,280
*98057	Renton	90,927	106,785	104,491
*99352	Richland	48,058	60,560	63,757
98642	Ridgefield	4,763	10,319	15,027
*98685	Salmon Creek (c)	19,686	21,293	—
*98074	Sammamish	45,780	67,455	65,116
*98148	SeaTac	26,909	31,454	31,799
*98101	Seattle	608,660	737,015	755,078
98284	Sedro-Woolley	10,540	12,421	12,940
98584	Shelton	9,834	10,371	10,806
*98133	Shoreline	53,007	58,608	61,353
98208	Silver Firs (c)	20,891	22,174	—
*98315	Silverdale (c)	19,204	20,733	—
*98290	Snohomish	9,098	10,126	10,243
98065	Snoqualmie	10,670	14,121	13,465
*98373	South Hill (c)	52,431	64,708	—
98387	Spanaway (c)	27,227	35,476	—
*99201	Spokane	208,916	228,989	229,447
*99206	Spokane Valley	89,755	102,976	108,235
*98390	Sumner	9,451	10,621	10,853
98944	Sunnyside	15,858	16,375	16,264
*98402	Tacoma	198,397	219,346	222,906
*98188	Tukwila	19,107	21,798	21,135
*98501	Tumwater	17,371	25,350	27,239
98053	Union Hill-Novelty Hill (c)	18,805	22,683	—
*98466	University Place	31,144	34,866	35,049
*98660	Vancouver	161,791	190,915	196,442
*98070	Vashon (c)	10,624	11,055	—
99362	Walla Walla	31,731	34,060	33,339
98671	Washougal	14,095	17,039	16,985
*98801	Wenatchee	31,925	35,508	35,526
*99353	West Richland	11,811	16,295	18,456
*98106	White Center (c)	13,495	16,631	—
*98072	Woodinville	10,938	13,069	13,718
*98901	Yakima	91,067	96,968	96,750
98597	Yelm	6,848	10,617	10,780

West Virginia

Area codes: 304/681 apply to the entire state

ZIP	Place	2010 population	2020 population	2023 estimate
*25801	Beckley	17,614	17,286	16,576
*25301	Charleston	51,400	48,864	46,838
*26301	Clarksburg	16,578	16,061	15,489
*26554	Fairmont	18,704	18,416	18,155
*25701	Huntington	49,138	46,842	45,325
*25401	Martinsburg	17,227	18,777	18,935
*26505	Morgantown	29,660	30,347	30,429
*26101	Parkersburg	31,492	29,738	29,025
25177	Saint Albans	11,044	10,861	10,387
*25303	South Charleston	13,450	13,647	13,281
*25526	Teays Valley (c)	13,175	14,350	—
26105	Vienna	10,749	10,652	10,457
26062	Weirton	19,746	19,163	18,386
26003	Wheeling	28,486	27,052	26,208

Wisconsin

Area codes: 274/920, 353/608, 414, 534/715

ZIP	Place	2010 population	2020 population	2023 estimate
54301	Allouez	13,975	14,156	13,839
*54911	Appleton	72,623	75,644	74,719
*54304	Ashwaubenon	16,963	16,991	16,986
53913	Baraboo	12,048	12,556	12,554
53916	Beaver Dam	16,214	16,708	16,531
54311	Bellevue	14,570	15,935	16,730
*53511	Beloit	36,966	36,657	36,342
*53045	Brookfield	37,920	41,464	41,884
*53223	Brown Deer	11,999	12,507	12,553
53105	Burlington	10,464	11,047	11,040
53108	Caledonia	24,705	25,361	25,326
53012	Cedarburg	11,412	12,121	12,527
*54729	Chippewa Falls	13,661	14,731	14,656
53110	Cudahy	18,267	18,204	17,706
54115	De Pere	23,800	25,410	25,348
53532	DeForest	8,936	10,811	11,107
*54701	Eau Claire	65,883	69,421	70,542
53121	Elkhorn	10,084	10,247	10,230
*53711	Fitchburg	25,260	29,609	32,284
*54935	Fond du Lac	43,021	44,678	44,300
53538	Fort Atkinson	12,368	12,579	12,350
*54956	Fox Crossing[1]	—	18,974	18,947
53132	Franklin	35,451	36,816	35,485
53022	Germantown	19,749	20,917	21,020
*53209	Glendale	12,872	13,357	12,919
53024	Grafton	11,459	12,094	12,608
*54301	Green Bay	104,057	107,395	105,744
53129	Greendale	14,046	14,854	14,472
*53220	Greenfield	36,720	37,803	36,916
54942	Greenville[2]	—	—	13,286
54952	Harrison[1]	—	12,418	14,524
53027	Hartford	14,223	15,626	15,894
53029	Hartland	9,110	9,501	10,065
*54155	Hobart	6,182	10,211	10,960
54636	Holmen	9,005	10,661	11,581
*54303	Howard	17,399	19,950	20,775
54016	Hudson	12,719	14,755	15,473
*53545	Janesville	63,575	65,615	66,102
*54130	Kaukauna	15,462	17,089	17,493
*53140	Kenosha	99,218	99,986	98,211
*54601	La Crosse	51,320	52,680	51,327
*54140	Little Chute	10,449	11,619	12,178
*53703	Madison	233,209	269,840	280,305
*54220	Manitowoc	33,736	34,626	34,568
54143	Marinette	10,968	11,119	11,045
*54449	Marshfield	19,118	18,929	18,736
54952	Menasha	17,353	18,268	18,069
*53051	Menomonee Falls	35,626	38,527	39,700
54751	Menomonie	16,264	16,843	16,642
*53092	Mequon	23,132	25,142	25,489
*53562	Middleton	17,442	21,827	22,967
*53202	Milwaukee	594,833	577,222	561,385
53566	Monroe	10,827	10,661	10,439
*53406	Mount Pleasant	26,197	27,732	27,727
53150	Muskego	24,135	25,032	25,312
*54956	Neenah	25,501	27,319	27,453
*53151	New Berlin	39,584	40,451	40,260
54017	New Richmond	8,375	10,079	10,705
53154	Oak Creek	34,451	36,497	37,156
53066	Oconomowoc	15,759	18,203	18,682
54650	Onalaska	17,736	18,803	19,018
53575	Oregon	9,231	11,179	11,676
*54901	Oshkosh	66,083	66,816	66,184
53072	Pewaukee	13,195	15,914	16,293
53818	Platteville	11,224	11,836	11,128
53158	Pleasant Prairie	19,719	21,250	21,818
54467	Plover	12,123	13,519	14,110
53074	Port Washington	11,250	12,353	12,763
53901	Portage	10,324	10,581	10,126
*53402	Racine	78,860	77,816	76,602
*53939	Reedsburg	9,200	9,984	10,190
*53076	Richfield	11,300	11,739	11,841
54022	River Falls	15,000	16,182	16,935
53168	Salem Lakes[1]	—	14,601	14,367
*53081	Sheboygan	49,288	49,929	49,686
53211	Shorewood	13,162	13,859	13,603
53172	South Milwaukee	21,156	20,795	20,211
*54481	Stevens Point	26,717	25,666	25,752
53589	Stoughton	12,611	13,173	13,044
*54313	Suamico	11,346	12,820	13,225
*53590	Sun Prairie	29,364	35,967	37,890
54880	Superior	27,244	26,751	26,423
53089	Sussex	10,518	11,487	12,162
54241	Two Rivers	11,712	11,271	11,169
53593	Verona	10,619	14,030	15,815
*53094	Watertown	23,861	22,926	22,692
*53186	Waukesha	70,718	71,158	70,446
53597	Waunakee	12,097	14,879	15,152
53963	Waupun	11,340	11,344	11,039
*54403	Wausau	39,106	39,994	39,968
*53213	Wauwatosa	46,396	48,387	47,038
*53214	West Allis	60,411	60,325	58,874
*53095	West Bend	31,078	31,752	31,886
*54476	Weston	14,868	15,723	15,969
*53217	Whitefish Bay	14,110	14,954	14,553
53190	Whitewater	14,390	14,889	15,627
*54494	Wisconsin Rapids	18,367	18,877	18,670

(1) Incorporated after 2010 Census. (2) Incorporated after 2020 Census.

Wyoming

Area code: 307 applies to the entire state

ZIP	Place	2010 population	2020 population	2023 estimate
*82601	Casper	55,316	59,038	58,720
*82001	Cheyenne	59,466	65,132	65,168
82414	Cody	9,520	10,028	10,240
*82930	Evanston	12,359	11,747	11,807
*82716	Gillette	29,087	33,403	33,496
*82935	Green River	12,515	11,825	11,496
*83001	Jackson	9,577	10,760	10,639
*82070	Laramie	30,816	31,407	32,152
82501	Riverton	10,615	10,682	10,923
*82901	Rock Springs	23,036	23,526	22,954
82801	Sheridan	17,444	18,737	19,543

Chronology of World History

Note: In this section, the notation BCE (before the common era) is applied to years dating to the traditional BC (before Christ) era, and CE (common era) is applied to AD (anno domini) dates. This notation is now preferred in many scientific and academic publications. The traditional Gregorian calendar system and its dates and years are unaltered except by these labels.

Other abbreviations used in this chapter include the following: KYA = thousand years ago, MYA = million years ago, c. = circa, fl. = flourished, r. = ruled, b. = born, d. = died.

Prehistory: Our Ancestors Emerge

Reviewed by Marc Kissel, Ph.D., Univ. of Notre Dame, 2016; other updates per World Almanac research.

Evidence of the origins of *Homo sapiens*, the genus and species to which all living humans belong, comes from an ever increasing number of fossils and DNA studies, and from the archaeological record. Put together, the latest evidence suggests that humans evolved from an ape-like ancestor that lived in eastern and central Africa 8 to 5 million years ago.

Current theories trace the first hominin[1] (primates more closely related to humans than to any other living primate) to Africa, where several distinct genera appear in the fossil record 6-4 MYA. Skeletally, hominins are defined by signs of bipedalism (walking on two legs). They lived in a variety of environments, including swampy forest margins, woodlands, and open savannas (usually near lakes or springs).

Claims of the earliest hominin are inherently controversial. The earliest currently proposed species are *Sahelanthropus tchadensis* (c. 7 MYA, Chad) and *Orrorin tugenensis* (c. 6 MYA, Kenya). The recently described species *Ardipithecus ramidus* (4.4 MYA, Ethiopia) had a chimp-sized brain and a fairly primitive body plan but was bipedal.

Although all humans living today are members of a single species, the fossil record confirms that our ancestors coexisted with a number of similar species throughout our evolutionary history. Starting around 4 MYA one of these earliest hominins gave rise to the australopithecines, a genus of early hominins referred to as "bipedal apes." Scientists divided these into two groups, "gracile" and "robust," each containing a number of species.

The robust australopithecines were characterized by larger molar and premolar teeth; they probably went extinct around 1 MYA. Members of this species adapted a new dietary niche of eating hard foods such as nuts and tubers and have been found in both E and S Africa.

The gracile lineage most likely led to modern humans. *Australopithecus sediba* (2 MYA, South Africa) shows a mosaic of both Australopithecus and early *Homo* traits, leading some to suggest that this is the predecessor to our genus; the morphology of its hand is very suggestive of tool-use. However, while originally believed to arise solely within the genus *Homo*, recent work at the sites of Dikika (3.3 MYA, Ethiopia) and Lomekwi (3.3 MYA, Kenya) suggest that earlier hominins were making stone tools.

Our genus, *Homo*, arose 3-2 MYA, with fossils showing early members of our genus being fully bipedal, having larger brains, and hands well-adapted to tool use. The Oldowan tools first appear 2.6 MYA and were used to cut and scrape meat. It is not known whether these early hominins had the ability to speak, but they were social primates, had campsites, and subsisted by gathering plants and small animals and by scavenging other kills, as well as perhaps hunting.

Homo ergaster appeared in E Africa around 1.9 MYA and was the first to leave the continent, spreading throughout Eurasia by c. 1.8 MYA. *H. ergaster* is sometimes grouped with *H. erectus*, a species first identified on the Indonesian island of Java. It was capable of hunting large and medium-sized animals, such as antelopes and horses, learned to make and control fire, and produced bifacially-flaked tools (sharpened on both sides).

The ability to control fire enormously expanded the human food niche as well as creating new opportunities in the social world. Fire-making possibly began as early as 1 MYA in Africa and is clearly documented throughout Eurasia after c. 500 KYA. Hearths were found in northern Israel by c. 750 KYA, and by 465 KYA in southwestern France.

Cave paintings in Lascaux, France, discovered in 1940, have been carbon-dated to 11,000 to 30,000 years before the present.

After about 800 KYA, Europe provides a particularly rich set of fossil evidence usually assigned to *H. erectus*, *H. antecessor*, or *H. heidelbergensis*. This population gave rise to the Neanderthals, who appeared c. 350 KYA. While originally portrayed as savage and unhuman-like, recent research suggests they could probably speak, were proficient hunters of large game, had sophisticated tools and weapons, had ornamentation and other forms of symbolic expression, and a well-developed social organization. On the island of Flores, Indonesia, remains of a species known as *Homo floresiensis*, a 1.1-m (3.5-ft) tall hominin, date from c. 100-60 KYA. Its small stature may be due to limited food and few predators on the small island.

The remains of *Homo naledi*, dating to c. 335-236 KYA, raised questions about a possible overlap in existence and behaviors with early humans. It has a human-like foot and lower limbs, but other aspects of the skeleton, such as the pelvis and shoulder, are more primitive looking. They seem to have been deliberately deposited into a cave system, suggesting an early form of burial.

Improved dating techniques call into question the age of modern humans. The oldest modern human fossils (*Homo sapiens*) were dated to c. 300 KYA and were found at the Jebel Irhoud site in Morocco. Until that 2017 analysis, the oldest, found in Omo Kibish, Ethiopia, were believed to date to c. 195 KYA. Fossils considered some of the oldest modern humans were also found at the Herto site in Ethiopia's Middle Awash Valley. The species spread out of Africa, reaching Israel by c. 100 KYA, and parts of Europe perhaps as early as 54 KYA. Migration from Asia to Australia took place as early as 60 KYA. What happened when they met other hominins is a subject of intense research. Genetic evidence in the form of ancient DNA suggests that Neanderthals interbred with modern humans. Genetic data also provide information about the Denisovans, a population of early humans dated to perhaps c. 200 KYA, fossils of which were found in caves in Siberia and Tibet. Some contemporary human populations retain Denisovan DNA, suggesting a complex web of interactions between these populations. Researchers studying (2021) fossilized skull found in NE China contended it represents another separate species (dated to c. 150 KYA or earlier), which they named *Homo longi*.

Most evidence for the crossing from Asia to the Americas by the Bering land bridge dates to the end of the last Ice Age, at c. 14 KYA, but recent evidence suggests some arrived sooner, especially the 2021 reported discovery of fossilized human footprints in New Mexico dated at earlier than 20 KYA. The arrival of humans was followed by the extinction of the indigenous Pleistocene megafauna (e.g., mammoths, mastodons) due either to overexploitation by humans, climate change, or a combination of both.

Wooden throwing spears about 3 m (10 ft) long were fashioned by big-game hunters 300 KYA at Schöningen, Germany. Scraping tools, dated after 750 KYA in Europe, N Africa, the Middle East, and Central Asia, suggest the preparation of hides for clothing. Some of the oldest evidence of personal adornment date to around 300 KYA in the form of ochre, while various sites around 100 KYA from South Africa, Morocco, and Israel show the use of perforated shell beads, suggestive of symbolic expression. Although they were probably invented much earlier, impressions in burnt clay from the Czech Republic document the ability to weave cloth baskets and nets by 28 KYA.

Some of the earliest well-dated cave paintings come from the island of Sulawesi, Indonesia, where they date to around the same time as the earliest cave paintings in Europe. The painted caves of Cosquer and Chauvet in southern France have (contested) radiocarbon dates of c. 32 KYA. Painting, engraving, and bodily decoration flourished in Europe 15 KYA, along with stone and ivory sculpture. More than 200 western European caves show remarkable examples of naturalistic wall painting. A few musical instruments—bone flutes with precisely bored holes—have been found in sites dated after 40 KYA.

Skeletal data suggests that after 60-30 KYA the number of people who survived to become grandparents increased. With more adults available to provide child care, humans began to develop more complex, multigenerational social systems. In general, as human cognitive capacities slowly expanded over the Pleistocene, a variety of behavioral modes—in toolmaking, diet, shelter, social arrangements, and spiritual expression—arose as humans adapted to different geographic and climatic zones. By about 13,000 years ago, sites from all over the world show seasonal migration patterns and efficient exploitation of a wide range of plant and animal foods, some of which were eventually domesticated.

Shortly after 12 KYA, among widely separated foraging communities in both hemispheres, a series of dramatic technological and social changes occurred, marking the Neolithic, or New Stone Age. As the world climate became drier and warmer, population/resource imbalances ensued, creating the conditions that allowed for increased human interference in the life cycles of certain plants and animals. This interference ultimately resulted in the appearance of domestication, initially in the northern Middle East.

Domesticated plants and animals encouraged population growth and the appearance of permanent settlements. Agricultural economies increasingly replaced or assimilated hunting and gathering. Reliance upon domesticated plants and animals, coupled with technological advances like pottery-making, precipitated a dramatic increase in world population and social complexity. Genetic research suggests that mutations related to traits currently found in some human populations, such as Europeans' ability to process lactose, arose after this time.

Sites in the Americas, SE Europe, and the Middle East show roughly contemporaneous (12-6 KYA) evidence of Neolithic domestication economies; similar evidence of E and S Asian, W European, and sub-Saharan African Neolithic adaptations dates to 10-7 KYA. From W Asian sources, farming and the herding of sheep and goats spread rapidly throughout the Mediterranean Basin, perhaps in as short a time interval as 100-200 years. The variety of crops—wheat, barley, rice, maize, squash, beans, and tubers—and a mix of other characteristics suggest that this adaptation occurred independently in as many as 12 or 13 places in both hemispheres.

Evidence for fermented beverages likewise coincides with the early Neolithic settled farming lifestyle. Northern Chinese farmers concocted a wine-like drink from rice, honey, and fruit between 9 and 8 KYA. In highland W Asia, in what is today Iran, vintners were fermenting grapes and making wine by c. 7.4 KYA. The plants and animals associated with the Neolithic Revolution provided the basis for all subsequent social and cultural evolution worldwide.

(1) Although "hominid" was standard usage several decades ago, "hominin" is now more commonly used in reference to human ancestors because of developments in the interpretation of primate evolution.

Earliest Civilizations: 4000-1000 BCE

Mesopotamia. Recorded history began with writing in Mesopotamia in the Tigris-Euphrates river valley. The Sumerians used clay tablets with pictographs to keep records after 4000 BCE. A **cuneiform** (wedge-shaped) script, evolved by 3000 BCE as a full syllabic alphabet. Neighboring peoples adapted the script for their own use.

Sumerian life centered, from 4000 BCE, on large cities (Eridu, Ur, Uruk, Nippur, Kish, and Lagash) organized around temples and priestly bureaucracies, with surrounding plains watered by vast irrigation works and worked with traction plows. Sailboats, wheeled vehicles, potter's wheels, and kilns were used. Copper was smelted and tempered from c. 4000 BCE; bronze was produced not long after. Ores, as well as precious stones and metals, were obtained through long-distance ship and caravan trade. Iron was used from c. 2000 BCE. Improved ironworking, developed partly by the Hittites, became widespread by 1200 BCE.

Sumerian political primacy passed among cities and their kingly dynasties. Semitic-speaking peoples, with cultures derived from the Sumerian, founded a succession of dynasties that ruled in Mesopotamia and neighboring areas for most of 1,800 years. Among them were the **Akkadians** (first under Sargon I, c. 2350 BCE), the Amorites (whose laws, codified by **Hammurabi**, c. 1792-1750 BCE, have biblical parallels), and the Assyrians, with interludes of rule by the Hittites, Kassites, and Mitanni.

Mesopotamian learning, preserved in vast libraries, was practically oriented. Scribes maintained lists of astronomical phenomena, plants, animals, and stones. Medical texts listed ailments and herbal cures. The Sumerians worshipped anthropomorphic gods representing natural forces. Sacrifices were made at **ziggurats**, or huge stepped temples.

The Syria-Palestine area, site of some of the earliest urban remains (Jericho, 7000 BCE) and of the **Ebla** civilization (fl. 2500 BCE), experienced Egyptian cultural and political influence along with Mesopotamian. The **Phoenician** coast was an active commercial center. A phonetic alphabet was invented here before 1600 BCE. It became the ancestor of many other alphabets.

Egypt. Agricultural villages along the Nile R. were united by around 3300 BCE into two kingdoms, Upper and Lower Egypt. They were unified (c. 3100 BCE) under the pharaoh Menes, as detailed on the Narmer Palate. A bureaucracy supervised construction of canals and monuments (**pyramids** starting 2700 BCE). Control over Nubia to the S was asserted from 2600 BCE.

Brilliant **Old Kingdom** period achievements in architecture, sculpture, and painting reached their height during the 3rd and 4th dynasties. **Hieroglyphic writing** appeared by 3200 BCE, recording a sophisticated literature that included religious writings, philosophy, history, and science. An ordered hierarchy of gods, including totemistic animal elements, was served by a powerful priesthood in Memphis. The pharaoh was identified with the falcon god Horus. Other trends included belief in an afterlife and short-lived quasi-monotheistic reforms introduced by the pharaoh **Akhenaton** (c. 1379-1362 BCE), who was married to Nefertiti.

After a period of dominance by Semitic Hyksos from Asia (c. 1700-1550 BCE), the **New Kingdom** established an empire in Syria. Egypt became increasingly embroiled in Asiatic wars and diplomacy. Conquered by Persia in 525 BCE, it eventually faded away as an independent culture.

South Asia. The Bronze Age Indus Civilization spanned more than a million square kilometers in Pakistan and Northwestern India with many sites that expanded beyond the fertile core area of the Indus river system. The civilization independently grew out of local traditions developing complex trade networks and technologies during the Regionalization Era (5500-2600 BCE). The fully urban Harappan 2600-1900 BCE phase featured a standardized system of weights, uniform bricks, stamp seals featuring animals and unicorns, well laid out streets, and water management systems. Long distance trade with Mesopotamia and complex technologies were important. The writing system is one of the last to not be fully deciphered.

The major urban centers such as Dholavira, Harappa, and **Mohenjo-daro** were independent states. The civilization gradually changed due to environmental and cultural changes during the Localization Era (1900-1300 BCE). Post-Indus cultural complexes include the Gandara Grave culture (Swat, c. 1500-500 BCE) and the Painted Grey Ware (1200-800 BCE) culture, which some have associated with Vedic chiefdoms of the **Rig Veda**.

Europe. On Crete, the Bronze Age **Minoan civilization** emerged c. 2500 BCE. A prosperous economy and richly decorative art was supported by seaborne commerce. Mycenae and other cities in mainland Greece and Asia Minor (e.g., **Troy**) preserved elements of the culture until c. 1200 BCE. Cretan Linear A script (c. 2000-1700 BCE) remains undeciphered; Linear B script (c. 1300-1200 BCE) records an early Greek dialect. The possible connection between Mycenaean monumental stonework and the megalithic monuments of Western Europe, Iberia, and Malta (c. 4000-1500 BCE) is unclear.

Under the Shang dynasty (c. 1523 BCE), an early writing system was developed.

China. Proto-Chinese Neolithic cultures had long covered N and SE China when the first large political state was organized in the N by the **Shang dynasty** (c. 1523 BCE). Shang kings called themselves Sons of Heaven, and they presided over a cult of human and animal sacrifice to ancestors and nature gods. The Zhou dynasty, starting c. 1027 BCE, expanded the area of the Sons of Heaven's dominion, but feudal states exercised most temporal power.

A writing system with 2,000 characters was already in use under the Shang, with **pictographs** later supplemented by phonetic characters. Many of its principles and symbols, despite changes in spoken Chinese, were preserved in later writing systems. Technical advances allowed urban specialists to create fine ceramic and jade products, and bronze casting after 1500 BCE was the most advanced in the world. Bronze artifacts discovered in northern Thailand date from 3600 BCE, hundreds of years before similar Middle Eastern finds.

Americas. Olmecs settled (1500 BCE) on the Gulf coast of Mexico and developed the first known civilization in the Western Hemisphere. Temple cities and huge stone sculptures date from 1200 BCE. A rudimentary calendar and writing system existed. Olmec religion—centered on a jaguar god—and art forms influenced later Mesoamerican cultures.

Formation of Classical Societies: 1000-400 BCE

Greece. After a period of decline during the Dorian Greek invasions (1200-1000 BCE), the Aegean area developed a unique civilization. Drawing on Mycenaean traditions, Mesopotamian learning (weights and measures, lunisolar calendar, astronomy, musical scales), the Phoenician alphabet (modified for Greek), and Egyptian art, **Greek city-states** saw a rich elaboration of intellectual life. The two great epic poems attributed to **Homer**, the *Iliad* and the *Odyssey*, were probably composed around the 8th cent. BCE. Long-range commerce was aided by metal coinage (introduced by the Lydians in Asia Minor before 700 BCE). Colonies were founded around the Mediterranean (Cumae in Italy in 760 BCE; Massalia in France c. 600 BCE) and Black Sea shores.

Philosophy, starting with Ionian speculation on the nature of matter (Thales, c. 634-546 BCE), continued by other "Pre-Socratics" (e.g., Heraclitus, c. 540-480 BCE; Parmenides, b. c. 515 BCE), reached a high point in Athens in the rationalist idealism of **Plato** (c. 428-347 BCE), a disciple of **Socrates** (c. 469-399 BCE; executed for alleged impiety), and in **Aristotle** (384-322 BCE), a pioneer in many fields, from natural sciences to logic, ethics, and metaphysics. The arts were highly valued. Architecture culminated in the **Parthenon** (438 BCE) by Phidias (fl. 490-430 BCE). Poetry (Sappho, c. 610-580 BCE; Pindar, c. 518-438 BCE) and drama (Aeschylus, 525-456 BCE; Sophocles, c. 496-406 BCE; Euripides, c. 484-406 BCE) thrived. Male beauty and strength, a chief artistic theme, were celebrated at the national games at Olympia.

Ruled by local tyrants or **oligarchies**, the Greeks were not politically united but managed to resist inclusion in the Persian Empire. Persian king Darius was defeated at Marathon (490 BCE), his son Xerxes at Salamis (480 BCE), and the Persian army at Plataea (479 BCE). Democracy sprouted in Athens as statesman Pericles (495-429 BCE) sought participation in government from all citizens. Local warfare was common; the **Peloponnesian Wars** (431-404 BCE) ended in Sparta's victory over Athens. Greek political power subsequently waned, but Greek cultural forms spread far and wide.

Hebrews. Nomadic Hebrew tribes entered Canaan before 1200 BCE, settling among other Semitic peoples speaking the same language. They brought from the desert a **monotheistic** faith said to have been revealed to Abraham in Canaan c. 1800 BCE and Moses at Mt. Sinai c. 1250 BCE, after the Hebrews' escape from bondage in Egypt. David (r. 1000-961 BCE) and Solomon (r. 961-922 BCE) united them in a kingdom that briefly dominated the area. **Phoenicians** to the N founded Mediterranean colonies (Carthage, c. 814 BCE) and sailed into the Atlantic.

The Parthenon, a Doric temple, is part of the Acropolis in Athens, which took shape in Greece in the 5th century BCE.

A temple in Jerusalem became the national religious center, with sacrifices performed by a hereditary priesthood. Polytheistic influences, especially of the fertility cult of Baal, were opposed by **prophets** (Elijah, Amos, Isaiah).

Divided into **two kingdoms** after Solomon, the Hebrews were unable to resist the revived Assyrian empire, which conquered **Israel**, the northern kingdom, in 722 BCE. **Judah**, the southern kingdom, was conquered in 586 BCE by the Babylonians under Nebuchadnezzar II. With the fixing of most of the biblical canon by the mid-4th cent. BCE and the emergence of rabbis, Judaism successfully survived the loss of Hebrew autonomy. A Jewish kingdom was revived under the Hasmoneans (168-42 BCE).

China. During the **Eastern Zhou** dynasty (770-256 BCE), Chinese culture spread E to the sea and S to the Yangtze R. Large feudal states on the periphery of the empire contended for preeminence but continued to recognize the Son of Heaven (king), who retained a purely ritual role enriched with courtly music and dance. In the Age of Warring States (403-221 BCE), when the first sections of the **Great Wall** were built, the Qin state in the W gained supremacy and finally united all of China.

Iron tools entered China c. 500 BCE. Casting techniques were advanced, aiding agriculture. Peasants owned their land and owed civil and military service to nobles. China's cities grew in number and size; barter remained the chief trade medium.

Intellectual ferment among noble scribes and officials produced a classical age of Chinese literature and philosophy. **Confucius** (551-479 BCE) urged a restoration of a supposedly harmonious social order of the past through proper conduct in accordance with one's station and through filial and ceremonial piety. The *Analects* attributed to him are revered throughout E Asia.

Among other thinkers, **Mencius** (d. 289 BCE) added the view that the Mandate of Heaven can be removed from an unjust dynasty. The Legalists sought to curb the supposed natural wickedness of people through new institutions and harsh laws. The Naturalists emphasized the balance of opposites—yin, yang—in the world. **Daoists** sought mystical knowledge through meditation and disengagement.

India. The political and cultural center of India shifted from the Indus to the Ganges River Valley. Buddhism, Jainism, and mystical revisions of orthodox Vedism all developed c. 500-300 BCE. The *Upanishads*, last part of the *Veda*, urged escape from the cycle of rebirth into the physical world. Vedism remained the preserve of the Brahman caste.

In contrast, **Buddhism**, founded by Siddhartha Gautama (c. 563-c. 483 BCE)—Buddha ("Enlightened One")—appealed to merchants in the urban centers and took hold at first (and most lastingly) on the geographic fringes of Indian civilization. The classic Indian epics were composed in this era: the ***Ramayana*** perhaps c. 300 BCE, the ***Mahabharata*** over a period starting around 400 BCE.

Northern India was divided into a large number of monarchies and aristocratic republics, probably derived from tribal groupings, when the Magadha kingdom was formed in Bihar c. 542 BCE. It soon became the dominant power. The **Maurya** dynasty, founded by Chandragupta c. 321 BCE, expanded the kingdom, uniting most of Northern India in a centralized bureaucratic empire. The third Mauryan king, **Asoka** (r. c. 274-236 BCE), conquered most of the subcontinent. He converted to Buddhism, inscribed its tenets on pillars throughout India, and downplayed the caste system.

Before its final decline in India, Buddhism developed into a popular worship of heavenly Bodhisattvas ("enlightened beings"), and it produced a refined architecture (the Great Stupa [shrine] at Sanchi, 100 CE) and sculpture (Gandhara reliefs, 1-400 CE).

Persia. Aryan peoples (Persians, Medes) dominated the area of present Iran by the beginning of the 1st millennium BCE.

The prophet **Zoroaster** (b. c. 628 BCE) introduced a dualistic religion in which the forces of good (Ahura Mazda, "Lord of Wisdom") and evil (Ahriman) battle for dominance; individuals are judged by their actions and earn damnation or salvation. Zoroaster's hymns (*Gathas*) are included in the *Avesta*, the Zoroastrian scriptures. A version of this faith became the established religion of the Persian Empire.

Africa. Nubia, periodically occupied by Egypt since about 2600 BCE, ruled Egypt c. 750-661 BCE and survived as an independent Egyptianized kingdom (**Kush**; capital Meroe) for 1,000 years. The Iron Age Nok culture flourished c. 500 BCE-200 CE on the Benue Plateau of **Nigeria**.

Americas. The Chavin culture controlled Northern Peru c. 900 BCE to 200 BCE. Its ceremonial centers, featuring the jaguar god, survived long after. Its architecture, ceramics, and textiles had influenced other Peruvian cultures. **Mayan civilization** began to develop in Central America as early as 1500 BCE.

Great Empires Unite the Classical World: 400 BCE-400 CE

Persia and the Mediterranean. **Cyrus**, ruler of a small kingdom in Persia from 559 BCE, united the Persians and Medes within 10 years and conquered Asia Minor and Babylonia in another 10. His son Cambyses, followed by **Darius** (r. 522-486 BCE), added vast lands to the E and N as far as the Indus Valley and Central Asia, as well as Egypt and Thrace. The whole empire was ruled by an international bureaucracy and army, with Persians holding the chief positions. The resources and styles of all the subject civilizations were exploited to create a rich syncretic art.

The kingdom of Macedon, which under Philip II dominated the Greek world and Egypt, was passed on to Philip's son **Alexander** in 336 BCE. Within 13 years, Alexander had conquered all the Persian dominions. Imbued by his tutor Aristotle with Greek ideals, Alexander encouraged colonization, and Greek-style cities were founded. After his death in 323 BCE, wars of succession divided the empire into three significant dynasties—the **Antigonids** in Asia Minor and Macedon, the **Ptolemies** in Egypt, and the **Seleucids** in Mesopotamia. In the ensuing 300 years (the **Hellenistic Era**), a cosmopolitan Greek-oriented culture permeated the ancient world from Western Europe to the borders of India, absorbing native elites everywhere.

Hellenistic philosophy stressed the private individual's search for happiness. The Cynics followed Diogenes (c. 400-c. 325 BCE), who stressed self-sufficiency and restriction of desires and expressed contempt for luxury and social convention. Zeno (c. 335-c. 263 BCE) and the **Stoics** exalted reason, identified it with virtue, and counseled an ascetic disregard for misfortune. The **Epicureans** tried to build lives of moderate pleasure without political or emotional involvement. Hellenistic arts imitated life realistically, especially in sculpture and literature (comedies of Menander, 342-292 BCE).

The sciences thrived, especially at Alexandria, where the Ptolemies financed a great library and museum. Fields of study included mathematics (**Euclid**'s geometry, c. 300 BCE); astronomy (heliocentric theory of Aristarchus, 310-230 BCE; Julian calendar, 45 BCE; **Ptolemy**'s *Almagest*, c. 150 CE); geography (world map of Eratosthenes, 276-194 BCE); hydraulics (**Archimedes**, 287-212 BCE); medicine (Galen, 130-200 CE); and chemistry. Inventors refined uses for siphons, valves, gears, springs, screws, levers, cams, and pulleys.

A restored Persian empire under the **Parthians** (northern Iranian tribespeople) controlled the eastern Hellenistic world from 250 BCE to 229 CE. The Parthians and the succeeding **Sassanian dynasty** (c. 224-651 CE) fought with Rome periodically. The Sassanians revived Zoroastrianism as a state religion and patronized a nationalistic artistic and scholarly renaissance.

Rome. The city of Rome was founded, according to legend, by Romulus in 753 BCE. Through military expansion and colonization, and by granting citizenship to leading members of conquered tribes, the city annexed all of Italy S of the Po R. in the 100-year period before 268 BCE. The Latin and other Italic tribes were annexed first, followed by the **Etruscans** (founders of a great civilization N of Rome) and Greek colonies in the S. With a large standing army and reserve forces of several hundred thousand, Rome was able to defeat **Carthage** in the three **Punic Wars** (264-241 BCE, 218-201 BCE, 149-146 BCE), despite the invasion of Italy by **Hannibal** (218 BCE), thus gaining Sicily and territory in Spain and N Africa.

Rome exploited local disputes to conquer Greece and Asia Minor in the 2nd cent. BCE and Egypt in the 1st (after the defeat and suicide of **Antony and Cleopatra**, 30 BCE). The Mediterranean civilized world, up to the disputed Parthian border, was now Roman and remained so for 500 years. Less civilized regions were added to the Empire: Gaul (conquered by **Julius Caesar**, 58-51 BCE), Britain (43 CE), and Dacia NE of the Danube (107 CE).

The original aristocratic republican government, with democratic features added in the 5th and 4th cent. BCE, deteriorated under the pressures of empire and class conflict (**Gracchus** brothers, social reformers, murdered in 133 BCE and 121 BCE; slave revolts in 135 BCE and 73 BCE). After a series of civil wars (Marius vs. Sulla, 88-82 BCE; Caesar vs. **Pompey**, 49-45 BCE; triumvirate vs. Caesar's assassins, 44-43 BCE; Antony vs. Octavian, 32-30 BCE), the empire came under the rule of a deified monarch (first emperor, **Augustus**, 27 BCE-14 CE).

Provincials (nearly all granted citizenship by Caracalla, 212 CE) came to dominate the army and civil service. Traditional **Roman law**, systematized and interpreted by independent jurists, and local self-rule in provincial cities were supplanted by a vast tax-collecting bureaucracy in the 3rd and 4th cent. The legal rights of women, children, and slaves were strengthened.

Roman innovations in **civil engineering** included water mills, windmills, and rotary mills and the use of cement that hardened under water. Monumental architecture (baths, theaters, temples) relied on the arch and the dome. A network of roads (some still standing) stretched 53,000 mi, passing through mountain tunnels as long as 3.5 mi. Aqueducts brought water to cities; underground sewers removed waste.

Roman art and literature were derivative of Greek models. Innovations were made in sculpture (naturalistic busts, equestrian statues), decorative wall painting (as at Pompeii), satire (**Juvenal**, 60-127 CE), history (**Tacitus**, 56-120 CE), and prose romance (**Petronius**, d. 66 CE). Gladiatorial contests dominated public amusements, which were supported by the state.

India. The **Gupta** monarchs reunited Northern India c. 320 CE. Their peaceful and prosperous reign saw a revival of Hindu religious thought and Brahman power. The old Vedic traditions were combined with devotion to many indigenous deities (who were seen as manifestations of Vedic gods). Caste lines were reinforced, and Buddhist practices gradually disappeared or were integrated with **Hindu** traditions. The art (often erotic), architecture, and literature of the period, patronized by the Gupta court, are considered among India's finest achievements (Kalidasa, poet and dramatist, fl. c. 400 CE). Mathematical innovations included the use of zero and decimal numbers. Invasions by White Huns from the NW led to the empire's destruction c. 550 CE. Rich cultures also developed in Southern India during this period. Emotional Tamil religious poetry contributed to the Hindu revival. The Pallava kingdom controlled much of Southern India c. 350-880 CE and helped to spread Indian civilization to SE Asia.

China. The Qin ruler Shi Huang (r. 221-210 BCE), known as the First Emperor, centralized political authority; standardized the written language, laws, weights, measures, and coinage; and conducted a census. But he tried to destroy most philosophical texts. The **Han** dynasty (202 BCE-220 CE) instituted the Mandarin bureaucracy, which lasted 2,000 years. Local officials were selected by examination in Confucian classics and trained at the imperial university and provincial schools.

The invention of **paper** facilitated this bureaucratic system. Agriculture was promoted, but peasants bore most of the tax burden. Irrigation was improved, water clocks and sundials were used, astronomy and mathematics thrived, and landscape painting was perfected.

With the expansion S and W (to nearly the present borders of today's China), trade was opened with India, SE Asia, and the Middle East over sea and caravan routes. Indian missionaries brought Mahayana Buddhism to China by the 1st cent. CE and spawned a variety of sects. Daoism was revived and merged with popular superstitions. **Daoist and Buddhist monasteries** and convents multiplied in the turbulent centuries after the collapse of the Han dynasty in 220 CE.

Monotheism Spreads: 1-750 CE

Roman Empire. Polytheism was practiced in the Roman Empire, and religions indigenous to particular Middle Eastern nations became international. Roman citizens worshiped **Isis** of Egypt, **Mithras** of Persia, **Demeter** of Greece, and the great mother **Cybele** of Phrygia. Their cults centered on mysteries (secret ceremonies) and the promise of an afterlife, symbolized by the death and rebirth of the god. The Jews of the empire preserved their monotheistic religion, Judaism, the world's oldest (c. 1300 BCE) continuous religion. Its teachings are contained in the Bible (the Old Testament). 1st-cent. CE Judaism embraced several sects, including the **Sadducees**, mostly drawn from the Temple priesthood, who were culturally Hellenized; the **Pharisees**, who upheld the full range of traditional customs and practices as of equal weight to literal scriptural law and elaborated synagogue worship; and the **Essenes**, an ascetic, millenarian sect. Messianic fervor led to repeated, unsuccessful rebellions against Rome (66-70, 135 CE). As a result, the Temple in Jerusalem was destroyed and the population decimated; this event marked the beginning of the Diaspora (living in exile). To preserve the faith, codification of law was begun at the academy of Yavneh. The work continued for some 500 years in Palestine and in Babylonia, ending in the final redaction (c. 600) of the **Talmud**, a huge collection of legal and moral debates, rulings, liturgy, biblical exegesis, and legendary materials.

Christianity. Emerging as a distinct sect by the second half of the 1st cent. CE, Christianity is based on the teachings of **Jesus**, whom believers considered the Savior (Messiah or Christ) and son of God. Missionary activities of the Apostles and such early leaders as **Paul of Tarsus** spread the faith. Intermittent persecution, as in Rome under Nero in 64 CE, on grounds of suspected disloyalty, failed to disrupt Christian communities. Each congregation, generally urban and of plebeian character, was tightly organized under a leader (bishop), elders (presbyters or priests), and assistants (deacons). The four **Gospels** (accounts of the life and teachings of Jesus) and the Acts of the Apostles were written down in the late 1st and early 2nd cent. and circulated along with letters of Paul and other Christian leaders. An authoritative canon of these writings was not fixed until the 4th cent.

A school for priests was established at Alexandria in the 2nd cent. Its teachers (**Origen**, c. 182-251) helped define doctrine and promote the faith in Greek-style philosophical works. Neoplatonism underwent Christian coloration in the writings of Church Fathers such as **Augustine** (354-430). Christian hermits began to associate in monasteries, first in Egypt (St. Pachomius, c. 290-345), then in other eastern lands, then in the W (**St. Benedict's rule**, 529). Devotion to saints, especially Mary, mother of Jesus, spread. Under **Constantine** (r. 306-37), Christianity became in effect the established religion of the Empire. Pagan temples were expropriated, state funds were used to build churches and support the hierarchy, and laws were adjusted in accordance with Christian ideas. Pagan worship was banned by the end of the 4th cent., and severe restrictions were placed on Judaism.

The newly established church was rocked by doctrinal disputes, often exacerbated by regional rivalries. Chief heresies (as defined by church councils, backed by imperial authority) were **Arianism**, which denied the divinity of Jesus; **Monophysitism**, denying the human nature of Christ; **Donatism**, which regarded as invalid any sacraments administered by sinful clergy; and **Pelagianism**, which denied the necessity of unmerited divine aid (grace) for salvation.

Islam. The earliest Arab civilization emerged by the end of the 2nd millennium BCE in the watered highlands of Yemen. Seaborne and caravan trade in frankincense and myrrh connected the area with the Nile and Fertile Crescent. The Minaean, Sabean (Sheba), and Himyarite states successively held sway. By Muhammad's time (7th cent. CE), the region was a province of Sassanian Persia. In the N, the Nabataean kingdom at Petra and the kingdom of Palmyra were Aramaicized, Romanized, and finally absorbed, as neighboring Judea had been, into the Roman Empire. Nomads shared the central region with a few trading towns and oases. Wars between tribes and raids on communities were common and were celebrated in a poetic tradition that by the 6th cent. helped establish a classic literary Arabic.

About 610, **Muhammad**, a 40-year-old Arab man of Mecca, emerged as a prophet. He proclaimed a revelation from the one true God, calling on contemporaries to abandon idolatry and restore the faith of Abraham. He introduced his religion as **Islam**, meaning "submission" to the one God, Allah, as a continuation of the biblical faith of Abraham, Moses, and Jesus, all respected as prophets in this system. His teachings, recorded in the Quran, in many ways were inclusive of Abrahamic monotheistic ideas known to the Jews and Christians in Arabia. A key aspect of the Abrahamic connection was insistence on justice in society, which led to severe opposition among the aristocrats in Mecca. As conditions worsened for Muhammad and his followers, he decided in 622 to make a ***hegira*** (flight) to Medina, 200 mi to the N. This event marks the beginning of the Muslim lunar calendar. Hostilities between Mecca and Medina increased, and in 629 Muhammad conquered Mecca. By the time he died in 632, nearly all the Arabian peninsula accepted his political and religious leadership.

After his death the majority of Muslims (later known as **Sunni** Muslims) recognized the leadership of the **caliph** (successor) Abu Bakr (632-34), followed by Umar (634-44), Uthman (644-56), and Ali (656-60). A minority, the **Shiites**, insisted instead on the leadership of Ali, Muhammad's cousin and son-in-law. By 644, **Muslim rule** over Arabia was confirmed. Muslim armies had threatened the Byzantine and Persian empires, which were weakened by wars and disaffection among subject peoples (including Coptic and Syriac Christians opposed to the Byzantine Orthodox establishment). Syria, Palestine, Egypt, Iraq, and Persia fell to Muslim armies. The new administration assimilated existing systems in the region; hence the conquered peoples participated in running the empire. The Quran recognized the so-called Peoples of the Book, i.e., Christians, Jews, and Zoroastrians, as tolerated monotheists, and Muslim policy was relatively tolerant to minorities living as "protected" peoples. An expanded tax system, based on conquests of the Persian and Byzantine empires, provided revenue to organize campaigns against neighboring non-Muslim regions.

Under the **Umayyads** (661-750) and **Abbasids** (750-1256), territorial expansion led Muslim armies across N Africa and into Spain (711). Muslim armies in the W were stopped at Tours, France, in 732 by the Frankish ruler **Charles Martel**. Asia Minor, the Indus Valley, and Transoxiana were conquered in the E. The conversion of conquered peoples to Islam was gradual. In many places the official Arabic language supplanted the local tongues. But in the eastern regions the Arab rulers and their armies adopted Persian cultures and language as part of their Muslim identity.

Disputes over succession and pious opposition to injustices in society led to a number of oppositional movements, which led to the factionalization of Muslim community. The **Shiites** supported leadership candidates descended from Muhammad, believing them to be carriers of some kind of divine authority. The **Kharijites** supported an egalitarian system derived from the Quran, opposing and even engaging in battle against those who did not agree with them.

Islam's primary religious text, the Quran, contains 114 chapters known as *sura*.

New Peoples Enter World History: 400-900 CE

Barbarian invasions and fall of Rome. Germanic tribes infiltrated S and E from their Baltic homeland during the 1st millennium BCE, reaching southern Germany by 100 BCE and the Black Sea by 214 CE. Organized into large federated tribes under elected kings, most resisted Roman domination and raided the empire in times of civil war (Goths took Dacia in 214, raided Thrace in 251-69). Germanic troops and commanders dominated the Roman armies by the end of the 4th cent. **Huns**, invaders from Asia, entered Europe in 372, driving more Germans into the empire. Emperor Valens allowed Visigoths to cross the Danube in 376. Huns under Attila (d. 453) raided Gaul, Italy, and the Balkans.

The western empire, weakened by overtaxation and social stagnation, was overrun in the 5th cent. Gaul was effectively lost in 406-07, Spain in 409, Britain in 410, and Africa in 429-39. Rome was sacked in 410 by Visigoths under Alaric and in 455 by Vandals. The **last western emperor**, Romulus Augustulus, was deposed in 476 by the Germanic chief Odoacer.

Celts. Celtic cultures, which in pre-Roman times covered most of W Europe, were confined almost entirely to the British Isles after the Germanic invasions. **St. Patrick** completed (c. 457-92) the conversion of Ireland and a strong monastic tradition took hold. Irish monastic missionaries in Scotland, England, and on the continent (Columba, c. 521-97; Columbanus, c. 543-615) helped restore Christianity after the Germanic invasions. **Monasteries** became centers of classic and Christian learning and presided over the recording of a Christianized Celtic mythology, elaborated by secular writers and bards. An intricate decorative art style developed, especially in book illumination (Lindisfarne Gospels, c. 700; Book of Kells, 8th cent.).

Successor states. The Visigothic kingdom in Spain (from 419) and much of France (to 507) saw continuation of Roman administration, language, and law (Breviary of Alaric, 506) until its destruction by Muslim forces from North Africa (711). The Vandal kingdom in Africa (from 429) was conquered by the Byzantines in 533. Italy was ruled successively by an Ostrogothic kingdom under Byzantine suzerainty (489-554), direct Byzantine government, and German Lombards (568-774). The Lombards divided the peninsula with the Byzantines and papacy under the dynamic reformer **Pope Gregory the Great** (590-604) and successors.

King Clovis (r. 481-511) united the Franks on both sides of the Rhine and, after his conversion to Christianity, defeated the Arian heretics, Burgundians (after 500), and Visigoths (507) with the support of native clergy and the papacy. Under the **Merovingian** kings, a feudal system emerged: power was fragmented among hierarchies of military landowners. Social stratification, which in late Roman times had acquired legal, hereditary sanction, was reinforced.

The Carolingians (747-987) expanded the kingdom and restored central power. **Charlemagne** (r. 768-814) conquered nearly all the Germanic lands, including Lombard Italy. He was crowned emperor by Pope Leo III in Rome in 800. A centuries-long decline in commerce and arts was reversed under Charlemagne's patronage. He welcomed Jews to his kingdom, which became a center of Jewish learning (Rashi, 1040-1105). He sponsored the Carolingian Renaissance of learning under the Anglo-Latin scholar Alcuin (c. 732-804), who reformed church liturgy.

The pyramid of Kukulkan (El Castillo) at Chichen Itza is one of the existing examples of Mayan architecture in present-day Mexico.

Byzantine Empire. Under **Diocletian** (r. 284-305) the Roman empire had been divided into two parts to facilitate administration and defense. **Constantine** founded (330) **Constantinople** (at old Byzantium) as a fully Christian city. Commerce and taxation financed a sumptuous, orientalized court, a class of hereditary bureaucratic families, and magnificent urban construction (Hagia Sophia, 532-37). The city's fortifications and naval innovations repelled assaults by Goths, Huns, Slavs, Bulgars, Avars, Arabs, and Scandinavians. Greek replaced Latin as the official language by c. 700. **Byzantine art**, a solemn, sacral, and stylized variation of late classical styles (mosaics at the Church of San Vitale, Ravenna, Italy, 526-48), was a starting point for medieval art in Eastern and Western Europe.

Justinian (r. 527-65) briefly reconquered parts of Spain, N Africa, and Italy, codified **Roman law** (Codex Justinianus [529] was medieval Europe's chief legal text), closed the Platonic Academy at Athens, and ordered all pagans to convert. Lombards in Italy and Arabs in Africa retook most of his conquests. The Isaurian dynasty from Anatolia (from 717) and the Macedonian dynasty (867-1054) restored military and commercial power. The Iconoclast controversy (726-843) over the permissibility of images helped alienate the Eastern Church from the papacy.

Abbasid Empire. Baghdad (established 762) became seat of the **Abbasid dynasty** (established 750), while Umayyads continued to rule in Spain. A brilliant cosmopolitan civilization emerged, inaugurating a Muslim-Arab golden age. Arabic was the lingua franca of the empire; intellectual sources from Persian, Sanskrit, Greek, and Syriac were rendered into Arabic. Christians and Jews equally participated in this translation movement, which also involved interaction between Jewish legal thought and Islamic law, as much as between Christian theology and Muslim scholasticism. Persian-style court life, with art and music, flourished at the court of **Harun al-Rashid** (786-809), celebrated in the masterpiece known to English readers as *The Arabian Nights*. The sciences, medicine, and mathematics were pursued at Baghdad, Cordova, and Cairo (c. 969). The culmination of this intellectual synthesis in Islamic civilization came with the scientific and philosophical works of **Avicenna** (Ibn Sina, 980-1037), **Averroes** (Ibn Rushd, 1126-98), and **Maimonides** (1135-1204), a Jew who wrote in Arabic. This intellectual tradition was translated into Latin and opened a new period in Christian thought.

The decentralization of the Abbasid empire, from 874, led to the establishment of various Muslim dynasties under different ethnic groups. Persians, Berbers, and Turks ruled different regions, retaining connection with the Abbasid caliph at the religious level. The Abbasid period also saw various religious movements against the orthodox position held by governing authorities. This situation in Islam led to the establishment of different legal, theological, and mystical schools of thought. The most influential mass movement was **Sufism**, which aimed at the reaching out of the average individual in quest of a spiritual path. Al-Ghazali (1058-1111) is credited with reconciling personal Sufism with orthodox Sunni tradition.

Africa. Immigrants from Saba in S Arabia helped set up the **Axum** kingdom in Ethiopia in the 1st cent. (their language, Ge'ez, is preserved by the Ethiopian Church). In the 3rd cent., when the kingdom became Christianized, it defeated Kushite Meroe and expanded its influence into Yemen. Axum was the center of a vast ivory trade and controlled the Red Sea coast until c. 1100. Arab conquest in Egypt cut Axum's political and economic ties with Byzantium.

The Iron Age entered W Africa by the end of the 1st millennium BCE. **Ghana**, the first known sub-Saharan state, ruled in the upper Senegal-Niger region c. 400-1240, controlling the trade of gold from mines in the S to trans-Sahara caravan routes to the N. The **Bantu** peoples, probably of W African origin, began to spread E and S perhaps 2,000 years ago, displacing the Pygmies and Bushmen of central and southern Africa during a 1,500-year period.

Japan. The advanced Neolithic Yayoi period, when irrigation, rice farming, and iron and bronze casting techniques were introduced from China or Korea, persisted to c. 400 CE. The myriad Japanese states were then united by the **Yamato** clan, under an emperor who acted as chief priest of the animistic Shinto cult. Japanese political and military intervention by the 6th cent. in Korea, then under strong Chinese influence, quickened a Chinese cultural invasion of Japan, bringing Buddhism, the Chinese language (which long remained a literary and governmental medium), Chinese ideographs, and Buddhist styles in painting, sculpture, literature, and architecture (7th cent., Horyuji temple at Nara). The Taika Reforms (646) tried unsuccessfully to centralize Japan according to Chinese bureaucratic and Buddhist philosophical values.

A nativist reaction against the Buddhist **Nara** period (710-94) ushered in the **Heian** period (794-1185) centered at the new capital, Kyoto. Japanese elegance and simplicity modified Chinese styles in architecture, scroll painting, and literature; the writing system was also simplified. The courtly novel *Tale of Genji* (1010-20) testifies to the enhanced role of women in medieval Japanese literature and culture.

Southeast Asia. The historic peoples of SE Asia began arriving some 2,500 years ago from China and Tibet, displacing scattered aborigines. Their agriculture relied on rice and yams. Indian cultural influences were strongest; literacy and Hindu and Buddhist ideas followed the S India-China trade route. From the southern tip of Indochina, the kingdom of **Funan** (1st-7th cent.) traded as far W as Persia. It was absorbed by Chenla, itself conquered by the **Khmer** empire (800-1300). The Khmers, under Hindu god-kings (Suryavarman II, 1113-c. 1150), built the monumental Angkor Wat temple center for the royal phallic cult. The **Nam-Viet** kingdom in Annam, dominated by China and Chinese culture for 1,000 years, emerged in the 10th cent., growing at the expense of the Khmers, who also lost ground in the NW to the new, highly organized **Thai** kingdom. On Sumatra, the **Srivijaya** empire controlled vital sea lanes (7th-10th cent.). A Buddhist dynasty, the Sailendras, ruled central **Java** (8th-9th cent.), building at Borobudur one of the largest stupas (dome-shaped Buddhist shrines) in the world.

China. The Sui dynasty (581-618) ushered in a period of commercial, artistic, and scientific achievement in China, which continued under the **Tang** dynasty (618-906). Inventions like the magnetic compass, gunpowder, the abacus, and printing were introduced or perfected. Medical innovations included cataract surgery. The state, from its cosmopolitan capital, Chang-an, supervised foreign trade, which exchanged Chinese silks, porcelains, and art for spices and ivory over Central Asian caravan routes and sea routes reaching Africa. A golden age of poetry bequeathed valuable works to later generations (Tu Fu, 712-70; Li Po, 701-62). Landscape painting flourished.

Commercial and industrial expansion continued under the **Northern Song** (960-1126), facilitated by paper money and credit notes. But commerce never achieved full respectability; government monopolies expropriated successful merchants. The population, long stable at 50 million, doubled in 200 years with the introduction of early-ripening rice and the double harvest. In art, native Chinese styles were revived.

Americas. From 300 to 600, a Native American empire stretched from the Valley of Mexico to Guatemala, centering on the huge city **Teotihuacán** (founded 100 BCE). To the S, in Guatemala, a high **Mayan** civilization developed (150-900) around hundreds of rural ceremonial centers. The Mayans improved on Olmec writing and the calendar and pursued astronomy and mathematics. In South America, a widespread pre-Inca culture grew from **Tiahuanacu**, Bolivia, near Lake Titicaca (Gateway of the Sun doorway, c. 700).

Christian Europe Regroups and Expands: 900-1300

Scandinavia. Pagan Danish and Norse (Viking) adventurers, traders, and pirates raided the coasts of the British Isles (Dublin, c. 831), France, and even the Mediterranean for over 200 years beginning in the late 8th cent. Inland settlement in the W was limited to Great Britain (King Canute, 994-1035) and Normandy, settled (911) under Rollo, as a fief of France. Vikings also reached Iceland (874), Greenland (c. 986), and North America (**Leif Ericson** and others, c. 1000). Norse traders (**Varangians**) developed Russian river commerce from the 8th to the 11th cent. and helped set up a state at Kiev in the late 9th cent. Conversion to Christianity occurred in the 10th cent., reaching Sweden 100 years later. In the 11th cent. Norman bands conquered Southern Italy and Sicily, and Duke **William of Normandy** conquered (1066) England, bringing feudal government and the French language, essential elements in later English civilization.

Central and East Europe. Slavs began to expand from about 150 CE in all directions in Europe. By the 7th cent. they reached as far S as the Adriatic and Aegean seas. In the Balkan Peninsula they dislocated Romanized local populations or assimilated newcomers (Bulgarians, a Turkic people). The first **Slavic states** were Moravia (628) in Central Europe and the Bulgarian state (680) in the Balkans. Byzantine missions of St. Methodius and Cyril (whose Greek-based cyrillic alphabet is still used by some Southern and Eastern Slavs) converted (863) Moravia.

The Eastern Slavs, part-civilized under the overlordship of the Turkish-Jewish **Khazar** trading empire (7th-10th cent.), gravitated toward Constantinople by the 9th cent. The **Kievan** state adopted (989) Eastern Christianity under Prince Vladimir. King Boleslav I (992-1025) began **Poland**'s long history of conquest. The Magyars (**Hungarians**), in present-day Hungary since 896, accepted (1001) Latin Christianity.

Germany. The German kingdom that emerged after the breakup of Charlemagne's Western Empire remained a confederation of largely autonomous states. Otto I, a Saxon who was king from 936, established the **Holy Roman Empire**—a union of Germany and Northern Italy—in alliance with Pope John XII, who crowned (962) him emperor; he defeated (955) the Magyars. Imperial power was greatest under the **Hohenstaufens** (1138-1254), despite the growing opposition of the papacy, which ruled central Italy, and the Lombard League cities. Frederick II (1194-1250) improved administration and patronized the arts. After his death, German influence was removed from Italy.

Christian Spain. From its northern mountain redoubts, Christian rule slowly migrated S through the 11th cent., when Muslim unity collapsed. After the capture (1085) of **Toledo**, the kingdoms of Portugal, Castile, and Aragon undertook repeated crusades of reconquest, finally completed in 1492. Elements of Islamic civilization persisted in recaptured areas, influencing all Western Europe.

Crusades. **Pope Urban II** called for a crusade (1095) to restore Asia Minor to Byzantium and the Holy Land to Christendom. This first crusade captured Jerusalem and led to the foundation of four Frankish states in the Levant. The defeat inflicted upon crusaders at the Battle of Hattin (1187) by **Saladin** (c. 1137-93), the Kurdish ruler of Egypt and Syria, effectively negated territorial gains. Many crusades followed until 1291. The 4th crusade sacked Constantinople (1204). Other crusades were launched against Christian heretics (Albigensian Crusade, 1229), pagans, and enemies of the papacy.

Economy. The agricultural base of European life benefited from improvements in **plow design** (c. 1000) and by the draining of lowlands and clearing of forests, leading to a rural population increase. Towns grew in Northern Italy, Flanders, and Northern Germany (Hanseatic League). Improvements in **loom design** permitted factory textile production. **Guilds** dominated urban trades from the 12th cent. Banking (centered in Italy, 12th-15th cent.) facilitated long-distance trade.

Christianity. The split between the Eastern and Western churches was formalized in 1054. Western and Central Europe was divided into 500 bishoprics under one united hierarchy, but conflicts between secular and church authorities were frequent (German **Investiture Controversy**, 1075-1122). Clerical power was first strengthened through the international monastic reform begun at Cluny in 910. Popular religious enthusiasm often expressed itself in heretical movements (Waldensians from 1173), but was channeled by the **Dominican** (1215) and **Franciscan** (1223) friars into the religious mainstream.

Arts. **Romanesque** architecture (9th to mid-12th cent.) expanded on late Roman models, using the rounded arch and massed stone to support enlarged basilicas. Painting and sculpture followed Byzantine models. The literature of **chivalry** was exemplified by the epic (*Chanson de Roland*, c. 1100) and by courtly love poems of the troubadours of Provence and minnesingers of Germany. **Gothic** architecture emerged in France (choir of St. Denis, c. 1140) and spread along with French cultural influence. Rib vaulting and pointed arches were used to combine soaring heights with delicacy, and they freed walls for display of stained glass. Exteriors were covered with painted relief sculpture and embellished with elaborate architectural detail.

Learning. Law, medicine, and philosophy were advanced at independent **universities** (Bologna, Paris, 12th cent.), originally corporations of students and masters. Twelfth-cent. translations of Greek classics, especially by Aristotle, encouraged an analytic approach. Scholastic philosophy, from Anselm (1033-1109) to **Aquinas** (1225-74), attempted to understand revelation through reason.

Apogee of Central Asian Power and the Spread of Islam: 1250-1500

Turks. Turkic peoples, of Central Asian ancestry, were a military threat to the Byzantine and Persian Empires from the 6th cent. After several waves of invasions, during which most of the Turks adopted Islam, the **Seljuk Turks** took (1055) Baghdad. They ruled Persia, Iraq, and, after 1071, Asia Minor, where massive numbers of Turks settled. The empire was divided in the 12th cent. into smaller states ruled by Seljuks, Kurds, and Mamluks (a military caste of former Turk, Kurd, and Circassian slaves), which governed Egypt and the Middle East until the Ottoman era (c. 1290-1922).

Osman I (r. c. 1290-1326) and succeeding sultans united Anatolian Turkish warriors in a militaristic state that waged holy war against Byzantium and Balkan Christians. Most of the Balkans had been subdued and Anatolia united when Constantinople fell (1453). By the mid-16th cent., Hungary, the Middle East, and N Africa had been conquered. The Turkish advance was stopped at Vienna (1529) and at the naval battle of Lepanto (1571) by Spain, Venice, and the papacy.

The **Ottoman state** was governed in accordance with orthodox Muslim law. Greek, Armenian, and Jewish communities were segregated and were ruled by religious leaders responsible for taxation; they dominated trade. Many state offices and most army ranks were filled by slaves, in part through a system of child conscription among Christians.

India. Mahmud of Ghazni (971-1030) led repeated Turkish raids into N India. Turkish power was consolidated in 1206 with the start of the **Sultanate at Delhi**. Centralization of state power under the early Delhi sultans went far beyond traditional Indian practice. Muslim rule of much of the subcontinent lasted until the British conquest 600 years later, though Hinduism remained the majority religion.

Mongols. **Genghis Khan** (c. 1167-1227) first united the feuding Mongol tribes and built their armies into an effective offensive force around a core of highly mobile cavalry. He and his immediate successors created the largest land empire in history; by 1279 it stretched from the E coast of Asia to the Danube and from the Siberian steppes to the Arabian Sea. East-West trade and contacts were facilitated (Marco Polo, c. 1254-1324). The western Mongols were Islamized by 1295; successor states soon lost their Mongol character by assimilation. They were briefly reunited under the Turk Tamerlane (1336-1405).

Kublai Khan ruled China from his new capital Beijing (established c. 1264). Naval campaigns against Japan (1274, 1281) and Java (1293) were defeated, the latter by the Hindu-Buddhist maritime kingdom of Majapahit. The **Yuan** dynasty used Mongols and other foreigners (including Europeans) in official posts and tolerated the return of Nestorian Christianity (suppressed 841-45) and the spread of Islam in the S and W. A native reaction expelled the Mongols in 1367-68.

Russia. The Kievan state in Russia, weakened by the decline of Byzantium and the rise of the Catholic Polish-Lithuanian state, was overrun (1238-40) by the Mongols. Only the northern trading republic of Novgorod remained independent. The grand dukes of Moscow emerged as leaders of a coalition of princes that eventually (by 1481) defeated the Mongols. After the fall of Constantinople in 1453, the **Tsars** (Caesars) at Moscow (from Ivan III, r. 1462-1505) set up an independent Russian Orthodox Church. Commerce failed to revive. The isolated Russian state remained agrarian with the peasant class falling into serfdom.

Persia. A revival of Persian literature, making use of the Arab alphabet and literary forms, began in the 10th cent. (epic of Firdausi, 935-1020). An art revival, influenced by Chinese styles introduced after the Mongols came to power in Iran, began in the 13th cent. Persian cultural and political forms, and often the Persian language, were used for centuries by Turkish and Mongol elites from the Balkans to India. Persian mystics from Rumi (1207-73) to Jami (1414-92) promoted **Sufism** in their poetry.

Africa. Two militant Islamic Berber dynasties emerged from the Sahara to carve out empires from the Sahel to central Spain—the **Almoravids** (c. 1050-1140) and the fanatical **Almohads** (c. 1125-1269). The Ghanaian empire was replaced in the upper Niger by Mali (c. 1230-1340), whose Muslim rulers imported Egyptians to help make **Timbuktu** a center of commerce (in gold, leather, and slaves) and learning. The Songhay empire (to 1590) replaced Mali. To the S, forest kingdoms produced refined artworks (Ife terra cotta, **Benin** bronzes).

Other **Muslim states** in Nigeria (Hausas) and Chad originated in the 11th cent. and continued in some form until the 19th-cent. European conquest. Less-developed Bantu kingdoms existed across central Africa.

Some 40 Muslim Arab-Persian trading colonies and city-states were established all along the E African coast from the 10th cent. (Kilwa, Mogadishu). The interchange with Bantu peoples produced the **Swahili** language and culture. Gold, palm oil, and people to enslave were brought from the interior, stimulating the growth of the Monamatapa kingdom of the Zambezi (15th cent.). The Christian Ethiopian empire (from 13th cent.) continued the traditions of Axum.

Southeast Asia. Islam was introduced into Malaya and the Indonesian islands by Arab, Persian, and Indian traders. Coastal Muslim cities and states (starting before 1300) soon dominated the interior. Chief among these was the **Malacca** state (c. 1400-1511), on the Malay peninsula.

Arts and Statecraft Thrive in Europe; New Asian Empires Rise: 1350-1600

Italy. Distinctive Italian achievements in literature and fine arts during the late Middle Ages (**Dante**, 1265-1321; Giotto, 1276-1337) led to the vigorous new styles of the Renaissance (14th-16th cent.). Patronized by the rulers of the quarreling petty states of Italy (**Medicis** in Florence and the papacy, c. 1400-1737), the plastic arts perfected realistic techniques, including **perspective** (Masaccio, 1401-28; Leonardo **da Vinci**, 1452-1519). Classical motifs were used in architecture, and increased talent and expense were put into secular buildings. The Florentine dialect was refined as a national literary language (**Petrarch**, 1304-74). Greek refugees from the E strengthened the respect of humanist scholars for the classic sources. Soon an international movement aided by the spread of **printing** (Gutenberg, c. 1397-1468), **humanism** was optimistic about the power of human reason (Erasmus of Rotterdam, 1466-1536, **More**'s *Utopia*, 1516) and valued individual effort in the arts and in politics (**Machiavelli**, 1469-1527).

France. The French monarchy, strengthened in its repeated struggles with powerful nobles (Burgundy, Flanders, Aquitaine) by alliances with the growing commercial towns, consolidated bureaucratic control under Philip IV (r. 1285-1314) and extended French influence into Germany and Italy (popes at Avignon, France, 1309-1417). The **Hundred Years War** (1337-1453) ended English dynastic claims in France (battles of Crécy, 1346, and Poitiers, 1356; Joan of Arc executed, 1431). A French Renaissance, dating from royal invasions (1494, 1499) of Italy, was encouraged at the court of Francis I (r. 1515-47), who centralized taxation and law. French vernacular literature consciously asserted its independence (La Pléiade, 1549).

England. The evolution of England's political institutions began with the **Magna Carta** (1215), by which King John guaranteed the privileges of nobles and church against the monarchy and assured jury trial. After the **Wars of the Roses** (1455-85), the **Tudor** dynasty reasserted royal prerogatives (Henry VIII, r. 1509-47), but the trend toward independent departments and ministerial government also continued. English trade (wool exports from c. 1340) was protected by the nation's growing maritime power (**Spanish Armada** destroyed, 1588).

English replaced French and Latin in the late 14th cent. in law and literature (**Chaucer**, c. 1340-1400), and English translation of the Bible began (Wycliffe, 1380s). **Elizabeth I** (r. 1558-1603) presided over the development of poetry (Spenser, 1552-99), drama (**Shakespeare**, 1564-1616), and music.

German Empire. From among a welter of minor feudal states, church lands, and independent cities, the **Habsburgs** assembled a far-flung territorial domain, based in Austria from 1276. Family members held the title of Holy Roman Emperor from 1438 to the Empire's dissolution in 1806 but failed to centralize its domains, leaving Germany disunited for centuries. Resistance to Turkish expansion brought Hungary under Austrian control from the 16th cent. The Netherlands, Luxembourg, and Burgundy were added in 1477, curbing French expansion.

The Flemish painting tradition of naturalism, technical proficiency, and bourgeois subject matter began in the 15th cent. (Jan **van Eyck**, c. 1390-1441), the earliest northern manifestation of the Renaissance. Albrecht **Dürer** (1471-1528) typified the merging of late Gothic and Italian trends in 16th-cent. German art. Imposing civic architecture flourished in the prosperous commercial cities.

Black Death. The bubonic plague reached Europe from the E in 1348, killing up to half the population by 1350 (and recurring periodically in most areas until the early 18th cent.). Labor scarcity forced wages to rise and brought greater freedom to the peasantry, making possible **peasant uprisings** (Jacquerie in France, 1358; Wat Tyler's rebellion in England, 1381).

Spain. Despite the unification of Castile and Aragon in 1479, the two countries retained separate governments, and the nobility, especially in Aragon and Catalonia, retained many privileges. Spanish lands in Italy (Naples, Sicily) and the Netherlands entangled the country in European wars through the mid-17th cent., while explorers, traders, and conquerors built up a Spanish empire in the Americas and the Philippines.

From the late 15th cent., a **golden age** of literature and art produced works of social satire (plays of Lope de Vega, 1562-1635; **Cervantes**, 1547-1616), as well as spiritual intensity (**El Greco**, 1541-1614; **Velázquez**, 1599-1660).

Explorations. Organized European maritime exploration began, seeking to evade the Venice-Ottoman monopoly of eastern trade and to promote Christianity. A key goal was to satisfy a growing taste for Asian goods. Beginning in 1418, expeditions from Portugal explored the W coast of Africa, until Vasco da Gama rounded the Cape of Good Hope in 1497 and reached India. A Portuguese trading empire was consolidated by the seizure of Goa (1510) and Malacca (1551). Japan was reached in 1542. The voyages of Christopher **Columbus** (1492-1504) uncovered a world new to Europeans, which Spain hastened to subdue. Navigation schools in Spain and Portugal, the development of large sailing ships (carracks) mounted with cannons, and the invention (c. 1475) of the rifle aided European penetration.

Mughals and Safavids. E of the Ottoman Empire, two Muslim dynasties ruled unchallenged in the 16th and 17th cent. The Mughal dynasty of India, founded by Persianized Turkish invaders from the NW under Babur, dates from their 1526 conquest of the Delhi Sultanate. The dynasty ruled most of India for more than 200 years, surviving nominally until 1857. **Akbar** (r. 1556-1605) consolidated administration at his glorious court, where the Urdu language (Persian-influenced Hindi) developed. Trade relations with Europe increased. Under Shah Jahan (1629-58), a secularized art fusing Hindu and Muslim elements flourished in miniature painting and in architecture (**Taj Mahal**). **Sikhism** (founded late 15th cent.) combined elements of both faiths. Suppression of Hindus and Shiite Muslims in S India in the late 17th cent. weakened the empire.

Intense devotion to the Shiite sect characterized the Safavids (1502-1736) of Persia and led to hostilities with the Sunni Ottomans for more than a century. The prosperity and the strength of the empire are evidenced by the mosques at its

The population of Western Europe was so reduced by the bubonic plague, or "Black Death," that it would not reach pre-plague levels again until the early 16th century.

capital city, **Isfahan**. The Safavids enhanced Iranian national consciousness.

China. The **Ming** emperors (1368-1644), the last native dynasty in China, wielded strong personal power. European trade (Portuguese monopoly through **Macau** from 1557) was strictly controlled. Jesuit scholars and scientists (Matteo Ricci, 1552-1610) introduced some Western science; their writings familiarized the West with China. The arts thrived, especially in the areas of painting and ceramics. Chinese manufacturing boomed, bringing in new profits from world trade.

Japan. After the decline of the first hereditary *shogunate* (chief generalship) at **Kamakura** (1185-1333), fragmentation of power accelerated, as did the consequent social mobility. Under Kamakura and the Ashikaga shogunate (1338-1573), the *daimyos* (lords) and *samurai* (warriors) grew more powerful and promoted a martial ideology. Japanese pirates and traders plied the China coast. Popular Buddhist movements included the nationalist Nichiren sect (from c. 1250) and **Zen** (brought from China, 1191), which stressed meditation and a disciplined aesthetic (tea ceremony, gardening, martial arts, *No* drama).

Change and Development in Europe: 1500-1700

Reformation. Theological debate and protests against real and perceived clerical corruption existed in the medieval Christian world, expressed by such dissenters as John **Wycliffe** (c. 1320-84) and his followers (the Lollards) in England, and **Huss** (burned as a heretic, 1415) in Bohemia.

Martin **Luther** (1483-1546) preached that faith alone, without the mediation of clergy or good works, leads to salvation. He attacked the authority of the pope, rejected priestly celibacy, and recommended individual study of the Bible (which he translated into German c. 1525). His 95 Theses (1517) led to his excommunication (1521). John **Calvin** (1509-64) said that God's elect were predestined for salvation and all others for damnation; good conduct and success were signs of election. Calvin in Geneva and John **Knox** (1505-72) in Scotland established theocratic states.

Henry VIII asserted English national authority and secular power by breaking away (1534) from the Catholic Church, creating what would become the Anglican Church. Monastic property was confiscated, and some Protestant doctrines given official sanction.

Religious wars. A century and a half of religious wars began with a southern German peasant uprising (1524), repressed with Luther's support. Radical sects—democratic, pacifist, millenarian—arose (Anabaptists ruled Münster, 1534-35) and were suppressed violently. Civil war in France from 1562 between **Huguenots** (Protestant nobles and merchants) and Catholics ended with the 1598 **Edict of Nantes**, tolerating Protestants (revoked 1685). Habsburg attempts to restore Catholicism in Germany were resisted in 25 years of fighting. The 1555 Peace of Augsburg guarantee of religious independence to local princes and cities was confirmed only after the **Thirty Years' War** (1618-48), when much of Germany was devastated by local and foreign armies (Sweden, France).

A Catholic Reformation, or **Counter-Reformation**, met the Protestant challenge, defining an official theology at the Council of Trent (1545-63). The **Jesuit** order (Society of Jesus), founded in 1534 by Ignatius Loyola (1491-1556), helped reconvert large areas of Poland, Hungary, and S Germany and sent missionaries to the New World, India, and China. The **Inquisition** suppressed heresy in Catholic countries. A revival of religious fervor appeared in devotional literature (Teresa of Avila, 1515-82) and in grandiose **Baroque** art (Bernini, 1598-1680).

Scientific Revolution. The late nominalist thinkers (Ockham, c. 1300-49) of Paris and Oxford challenged Aristotelian orthodoxy, allowing for a freer scientific approach. At the same time, metaphysical values, such as the Neoplatonic faith in an orderly, mathematical cosmos, still motivated and directed inquiry. Nicolaus **Copernicus** (1473-1543) promoted the heliocentric theory, which was confirmed when Johannes **Kepler** (1571-1630) discovered the mathematical laws describing the elliptical orbits of the planets. The traditional Christian-Aristotelian belief that the heavens and the Earth were fundamentally different collapsed when **Galileo Galilei** (1564-1642) discovered moving sunspots, irregular moon topography, and moons around Jupiter, but he faced religious opposition (Galileo's retraction, 1633). He and Sir Isaac **Newton** (1642-1727) developed a mechanics that unified cosmic and earthly phenomena. Newton and Gottfried von **Leibniz** (1646-1716) invented calculus. René **Descartes** (1596-1650), best known for his influential philosophy, also invented analytic geometry.

An explosion of **observational science** included the discovery of blood circulation (Harvey, 1578-1657) and microscopic life (Leeuwenhoek, 1632-1723) and advances in anatomy (Vesalius, 1514-64, dissected corpses) and chemistry (Boyle, 1627-91). Scientific research institutes were founded in Florence (1657), London (**Royal Society**, 1660), and Paris (1666). Inventions proliferated (Savery's steam engine, 1698).

Arts. Mannerist trends of the High Renaissance (**Michelangelo**, 1475-1564) exploited virtuosity, grace, novelty, and exotic subjects and poses. The notion of artistic genius was promoted. Private connoisseurs entered the art market. These trends were elaborated in the 17th cent. **Baroque** era on a grander scale. Dynamic movement in painting and sculpture was emphasized by sharp lighting effects, rich materials (colored marble, gilt), and realistic details. Curved facades, broken lines, rich detail, and ceiling decoration characterized Baroque architecture. Monarchs, princes, and prelates, usually Catholic, used Baroque art to enhance and embellish their authority, as in royal portraits (Velázquez, 1599-1660; Van Dyck, 1599-1641).

National styles emerged. In France, a taste for rectilinear order and serenity (Poussin, 1594-1665), linked to the new rational philosophy, was expressed in classical forms. The influence of **classical values** in French literature (tragedies of **Racine**, 1639-99) gave rise to the "battle of the Ancients and Moderns." New forms included the essay (**Montaigne**, 1533-92) and novel (*Princesse de Clèves*, La Fayette, 1678).

Dutch painting of the 17th cent. was unique in its wide social distribution. The Flemish tradition of undemonstrative realism reached its peak in **Rembrandt** (1606-69) and Jan Vermeer (1632-75).

Economy. European economic expansion, known as the **commercial revolution**, was stimulated by new trade with the East, by New World gold and silver, and by a doubling of population (50 million in 1450, 100 million in 1600). **New business and financial techniques** were developed and refined, such as joint-stock companies, insurance, and letters of credit and exchange. The Bank of Amsterdam (1609) and the Bank of England (1694) broke the old monopoly of private banking families. The rise of a business mentality was typified by the spread of clock towers in cities in the 14th cent. By the mid-15th cent., portable clocks were available; the first watch was invented in 1502.

By 1650, most governments had adopted the **mercantile system**, in which they sought to amass metallic wealth by protecting merchants' foreign and colonial trade monopolies. The rise in prices and the new coin-based economy undermined craft guild and feudal manorial systems. Expanding industries (clothweaving, mining) benefited from technical advances. Coal began to replace wood as the chief fuel; it was used to fuel new 16th-cent. blast furnaces making cast iron.

New World. The **Aztecs** united much of the Mesoamerican area in a militarist empire by 1519 from their capital, Tenochtitlán (pop. 300,000), which was the center of a cult requiring ritual human sacrifice. Most of the civilized areas of South America were ruled by the centralized Inca Empire (1476-1534), stretching 2,000 mi from Ecuador to NW Argentina. Lavish and sophisticated traditions in pottery, weaving, sculpture, and architecture were maintained in both regions.

These empires, beset by revolts, fell in two short campaigns to gold-seeking Spanish forces based in the Antilles and Panama. Hernán **Cortés** took Mexico (1519-21); Francisco **Pizarro**, Peru (1532-35). From these centers, land and sea expeditions claimed most of North and South America for Spain. The indigenous high cultures did not survive the impact of **Christian missionaries** and the new upper class of whites. Although the Spanish administration intermittently concerned itself with their welfare, the population was devastated by European diseases and remained impoverished at most levels. New World silver and such native products as potatoes, tobacco, corn, peanuts, chocolate, and rubber exercised a major economic influence on Europe.

The exact purpose of the Incan city of Machu Picchu, built in the 15th century and abandoned less than 150 years later, is unknown; one theory is that it served as a royal retreat.

Brazil, which the Portuguese reached in 1500 and settled after 1530, and the Caribbean colonies of several European nations developed a plantation economy where sugarcane, tobacco, cotton, coffee, rice, indigo, and lumber were grown by enslaved people. From the early 16th to late 19th cent., 10 million Africans were transported to **slavery** in the Americas and Caribbean islands.

Netherlands. The urban, Calvinist northern provinces of the Netherlands rebelled (1568) against Habsburg Spain and founded an oligarchic mercantile republic. Their control of the Baltic grain market enabled them to exploit Mediterranean food shortages. Religious refugees—French and Belgian Protestants, Iberian Jews—added to the commercial talent pool. After Spain absorbed Portugal (1580), the Dutch seized Portuguese possessions and created a vast commercial empire ultimately centered in parts of the Caribbean and in Indonesia. The Dutch also challenged or supplanted Portuguese traders in China and Japan. Revolution in 1640 restored Portuguese independence.

England. Anglicanism became firmly established under **Elizabeth I** after a brief Catholic interlude under "Bloody" Mary I (1553-58). But religious and political conflicts led to a rebellion (1642) by Parliament. Forces of the Roundheads (Puritans) defeated the Cavaliers (Royalists); Charles I was beheaded (1649). The new Commonwealth was ruled as a military dictatorship by Oliver **Cromwell**, who also brutally crushed (1649-51) an Irish rebellion. Conflicts within the Puritan camp (democratic Levelers defeated, 1649) aided the Stuart restoration (1660), but Parliament was strengthened and the peaceful **"Glorious Revolution"** (1688) advanced political and religious liberties (writings of **Locke**, 1632-1704). British privateers (Drake, 1540-96) challenged Spanish control of the New World and penetrated Asian trade routes (Madras taken, 1639). North American colonies (Jamestown, 1607; Plymouth, 1620) provided an outlet for private enterprise and religious dissenters from Europe. The British East India Co. gained growing sway in 18th-cent. India, as Mughal power declined.

France. Emerging from the religious civil wars in 1628, France regained military and commercial great power status (under the ministries of **Richelieu**, Mazarin, and Colbert). Under **Louis XIV** (r. 1643-1715), royal absolutism triumphed over nobles and local *parlements* (defeat of Fronde, 1648-53). Durable colonies were founded in Canada (1608), the Caribbean (1626), and India (1674).

Sweden. Sweden seceded from the Scandinavian Union in 1523. The thinly populated agrarian state (with copper, iron, and timber exports) was united by the Vasa kings, whose conquests by the mid-17th cent. made Sweden the dominant Baltic power. The empire collapsed in the Great Northern War (1700-21).

Poland. After the union with Lithuania in 1447, Poland ruled vast territories from the Baltic to the Black Sea, resisting German and Turkish incursions. Catholic nobles failed to gain the loyalty of their Orthodox Christian subjects in the E; commerce and trades were practiced by German and Jewish immigrants. The bloody 1648-49 Cossack uprising began the kingdom's dismemberment.

Russia. Growing authority of the tsars continued with advancing serfdom. Around 1700, **Peter the Great** imported new Western styles and technologies. Steady territorial expansion created a vast territory touching China, the Ottoman Empire, and east-central Europe.

China. A new dynasty, the **Manchus**, invaded from the NE, seized power in 1644, and expanded Chinese control to its greatest extent in Central and SE Asia. Trade and diplomatic contact with Europe grew, carefully controlled by China. New crops (sweet potato, maize, peanut) allowed economic and population growth (pop. 300 million, in 1800). Traditional arts and literature were pursued with increased sophistication (*Dream of the Red Chamber*, novel, mid-18th cent.).

Japan. Tokugawa Ieyasu, shogun from 1603, finally unified and pacified feudal Japan. Hereditary nobles (daimyos and samurai) monopolized government office and the professions. An urban merchant class grew, literacy spread, and a cultural renaissance occurred (**haiku**, a verse innovation of the poet Basho, 1644-94). Fear of European domination led to persecution of Christian converts from 1597 and to substantial isolation from outside contact from 1640.

Philosophy, Industry, and Revolution: 1700-1800

Science and reason. Greater faith in reason and empirical observation, instead of tradition and religious beliefs, espoused since the Renaissance (Francis Bacon, 1561-1626), was bolstered by scientific discoveries. René **Descartes** (1596-1650) used a rationalistic approach modeled on geometry and introspection to discover "self-evident" truths as a foundation of knowledge. Sir Isaac **Newton** emphasized induction from experimental observation. Baruch de **Spinoza** (1632-77), who called for political and intellectual freedom, developed a systematic rationalistic philosophy in his classic work *Ethics*.

French philosophers assumed leadership of the **Enlightenment** in the 18th cent. Montesquieu (1689-1755) used British history to support his notions of limited government. **Voltaire**'s (1694-1778) diaries and novels of exotic travel illustrated the intellectual trends toward secular ethics and relativism. Jean-Jacques **Rousseau**'s (1712-78) radical concepts of the **social contract** and of the inherent goodness of the common man gave impetus to antimonarchical republicanism. The *Encyclopedia* (1751-72, edited by Diderot and d'Alembert), designed as a monument to reason, was largely devoted to practical technology.

In England, ideals of liberty were connected with empiricist philosophy and science in the followers of John **Locke**. But British empiricism, especially as developed by the skeptical David **Hume** (1711-76), radically reduced the role of reason in philosophy, as did the evolutionary approach to law and politics of Edmund Burke (1729-97) and the utilitarian ethics of Jeremy Bentham (1748-1832). Adam Smith (1723-90) and other economists called for a rationalization of economic activity by removing artificial barriers to a supposedly natural free exchange of goods known as **laissez-faire**.

German writers participated in the new philosophical trends popularized by Christian von Wolff (1679-1754). Immanuel **Kant**'s (1724-1804) transcendental idealism, unifying an empirical epistemology with a priori moral and logical concepts, directed German thought away from skepticism. Italian contributions included work on electricity (Galvani, 1737-98; Volta, 1745-1827), the pioneer historiography of Vico (1668-1744), and writings on penal reform (Beccaria, 1738-94).

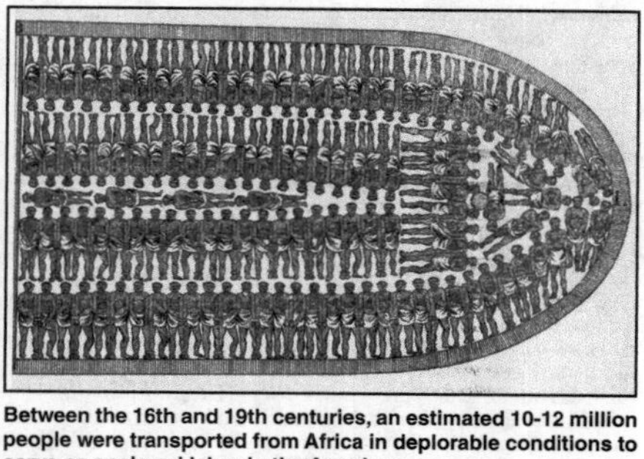

Between the 16th and 19th centuries, an estimated 10-12 million people were transported from Africa in deplorable conditions to serve as enslaved labor in the Americas.

Benjamin Franklin (1706-90) was celebrated in Europe for his varied achievements.

The growth of the **press** (*Spectator*, 1711-12) and the wide distribution of sentimental **novels** attested to the increase of a large bourgeois public.

Arts. Rococo art, characterized by extravagant decorative effects, asymmetries copied from organic models, and artificial pastoral subjects, was favored by the continental aristocracy for most of the century (Watteau, 1684-1721) and had musical analogies in the ornamentalized polyphony of late Baroque. The **Neoclassical** art after 1750, associated with the new scientific archaeology, was more streamlined and was infused with the supposed moral and geometric rectitude of the Roman Republic (David, 1748-1825). In England, **town planning** on a grand scale began.

Industrial Revolution in England. Agricultural improvements, such as the sowing drill (1701) and livestock breeding, were implemented on the large fields provided by enclosure of common lands by private owners. Profits from agriculture and from colonial and foreign trade (1800 volume, £54 million) were channeled through hundreds of banks and the **Stock Exchange** (est. 1773) into new industrial processes.

The Newcomen steam pump (1712) aided coal mining. Coal fueled the new efficient steam engines patented by James Watt in 1769, and coke-smelting produced cheap, sturdy iron for machinery by the 1730s. The **flying shuttle** (1733) and **spinning jenny** (c. 1764) were used in the large new cotton textile factories, where women and children were much of the workforce. Goods were transported cheaply over **canals** (2,000 mi; built 1760-1800). By the early 19th cent., industrialization spread in Western Europe and North America.

American Revolution. The British colonies in North America attracted a mass immigration of religious dissenters and poor people throughout the 17th and 18th cent., coming from the British Isles, Germany, the Netherlands, and other countries, along with Africans to serve as enslaved labor. The population reached 3 million non-natives by the 1770s. The Indigenous population was greatly reduced by European diseases and by wars with the various colonies. British attempts to control colonial trade and to tax the colonists to pay for the costs of colonial administration and defense clashed with local self-government and eventually provoked the colonies to a successful rebellion.

Central and East Europe. The monarchs of the three states that dominated E Europe—Austria, Prussia, and Russia—expanded royal power and centralized institutions in their kingdoms, which were enlarged by the division (1772-95) of Poland.

Under **Frederick II** (the Great) (r. 1740-86), Prussia, with its efficient modern army, doubled in size. State monopolies and tariff protection fostered industry, and some legal reforms were introduced. Austria's heterogeneous realms were unified under **Maria Theresa** (r. 1740-80) and **Joseph II** (r. 1765-90). Reforms in education, law, and religion were enacted, and the Austrian serfs were freed (1781). With its defeat in the Seven Years' War in 1763, Austria failed to regain Silesia, which had been seized by Prussia, but it was compensated by expansion to the E and S (Hungary, Slavonia, 1699; Galicia, 1772).

Russia, whose borders continued to expand, adopted some Western bureaucratic and economic policies under **Peter I** (r. 1682-1725) and **Catherine II** (r. 1762-96). Trade and cultural contacts with the West multiplied from the new Baltic Sea capital, **St. Petersburg** (est. 1703).

French Revolution. The growing French middle class lacked political power and resented aristocratic tax privileges, especially in light of the successful American Revolution. Peasants lacked adequate land and were burdened with feudal obligations to nobles. War with Britain led to the loss of French Canada and drained the treasury, finally forcing the king to call the **Estates-General** in 1789 for the first time since 1614, in an atmosphere of food riots (poor crop in 1788).

Aristocratic resistance to absolutism was soon overshadowed by the reformist Third Estate (middle class), which proclaimed itself the **National Constituent Assembly** June 17 and took the "Tennis Court Oath" on June 20 to secure a constitution. The storming of the **Bastille** fortress/prison on July 14, 1789, by Parisian artisans was followed by looting and the seizure of aristocratic property throughout France. Assembly reforms included abolition of class and regional privileges, a Declaration of Rights, suffrage by taxpayers (75% of male population), and the **Civil Constitution of the Clergy** providing for election and loyalty oaths for priests. A republic was declared Sept. 22, 1792, in spite of royalist pressure from Austria and Prussia, which had declared war in Apr. (joined by Britain the next year). Louis XVI was beheaded Jan. 21, 1793, and Queen Marie Antoinette was beheaded Oct. 16, 1793.

Royalist uprisings in La Vendée and military reverses led to institution of a **reign of terror** in which tens of thousands of opponents of the Revolution and criminals were executed. Radical reforms in the **Convention** period (Sept. 1793-Oct. 1795) included the abolition of colonial slavery, economic measures to aid the poor, support of public education, and a short-lived de-Christianization.

Division among radicals (execution of Hebert, Danton, and Robespierre, 1794) aided the ascendancy of a moderate **Directory**, which consolidated military victories. **Napoleon Bonaparte** (1769-1821), a popular young general, exploited political divisions and participated in a coup Nov. 9, 1799, making himself first consul (dictator).

India. Sikh and Hindu rebels (Rajputs, Marathas) and Afghans destroyed the power of the Mughals during the 18th cent. After France's defeat (1763) in the Seven Years' War, Britain was the primary European trade power in India. Its control of inland **Bengal** and **Bihar** was recognized (1765) by the Mughal shah, who granted the **British East India Co.** (under Clive, 1725-74) the right to collect land revenue there. Despite objections from Parliament (1784 India Act), the company's involvement in local wars and politics led to repeated acquisitions of new territory. The company exported Indian textiles, sugar, and indigo, but industry was discouraged to promote British imports.

Nationalism Gathers Momentum: 1800-40

French ideals and empire spread. Inspired by the ideals of the French Revolution, and supported by the expanding French armies, new republican regimes arose near France: the **Batavian** Republic in the Netherlands (1795-1806), the **Helvetic** Republic in Switzerland (1798-1803), the **Cisalpine** Republic in Northern Italy (1797-1805), the **Ligurian** Republic in Genoa (1797-1805), and the **Parthenopean** Republic in Southern Italy (1799). A Roman Republic existed briefly in 1798 after Pope Pius VI was arrested by French troops. In Italy and Germany, new nationalist sentiments were stimulated both in imitation of and in reaction to developments in France (anti-French and anti-Jacobin peasant uprisings in Italy, 1796-99).

From 1804, when Napoleon declared himself emperor, to 1812, a succession of military victories (Austerlitz, 1805; Jena, 1806) extended his control over most of Europe through puppet states (**Confederation of the Rhine** united W German states for the first time and **Grand Duchy of Warsaw** revived Polish national hopes), expansion of the empire, and alliances.

Among the lasting reforms initiated under Napoleon's absolutist reign were establishment of the Bank of France, centralization of tax collection, codification of law along Roman models (Code Napoléon), and reform and extension of secondary and university education. In an 1801 concordat, the papacy recognized the effective autonomy of the French Catholic Church.

Napoleon's continental successes were offset by a British victory under Adm. Horatio Nelson in the **Battle of Trafalgar** (1805). Some 400,000 French soldiers were killed in the Napoleonic Wars, along with about 600,000 foreign troops.

Louis Daguerre's 10-minute exposure of Boulevard du Temple in Paris (1838) omits moving traffic but includes the earliest candid image of a person: a man having his shoes polished.

Last gasp of old regimes. The disastrous 1812 invasion of Russia exposed Napoleon's overextension. After Napoleon's 1814 exile to Elba, his armies were defeated (1815) at **Waterloo** by British and Prussian troops.

At the **Congress of Vienna**, the monarchs and princes of Europe redrew their boundaries, to the advantage of Prussia (in Saxony and the Ruhr), Austria (in Illyria and Venetia), and Russia (in Poland and Finland). British conquest of Dutch and French colonies (S Africa, Ceylon, Mauritius) was recognized. France, under the restored Bourbons, retained its expanded 1792 borders. The settlement brought 50 years of international peace to Europe.

But the Congress was unable to check the advance of liberal ideals and of nationalism among the smaller European nations. The 1825 **Decembrist uprising** by liberal officers in Russia was easily suppressed. But an independence movement in **Greece**, stirred by commercial prosperity and a cultural revival, succeeded in expelling Ottoman rule by 1831, with the aid of Britain, France, and Russia.

A constitutional monarchy was secured in France by the **1830 Revolution**; Louis Philippe became king. The revolutionary contagion spread to **Belgium**, which gained its independence (1830) from the Dutch monarchy, to **Poland**, whose rebellion was defeated (1830-31) by Russia, and to Germany.

Romanticism. A new style in intellectual and artistic life replaced Neoclassicism and Rococo after the mid-18th cent. By the early 19th cent., Romanticism prevailed in Europe.

Rousseau had begun the reaction against rationalism; in education (*Émile*, 1762) he stressed subjective spontaneity over regularized instruction. German writers (Lessing, 1729-81; Herder, 1744-1803) favorably compared the German folk song to classical forms and began a cult of Shakespeare, whose passion and "natural" wisdom was a model for the romantic *Sturm und Drang* (Storm and Stress) movement. **Goethe**'s *Sorrows of Young Werther* (1774) set the model for the tragic, passionate genius.

A new interest in **Gothic architecture** in England after 1760 (Walpole, 1717-97) spread through Europe, associated with an aesthetic Christian and mystic revival (**Blake**, 1757-1827). Celtic, Norse, and German mythology and folk tales were revived or imitated (Grimm's Fairy Tales, 1812-22). The medieval revival (Scott's *Ivanhoe*, 1819) led to a new interest in history, stressing national differences and organic growth (**Carlyle**, 1795-1881; Michelet, 1798-1874), corresponding to theories of natural evolution (Lamarck's *Philosophie Zoologique*, 1809; Lyell's *Geology*, 1830-33). A reaction against classicism characterized the English **romantic poets** (beginning with **Wordsworth**, 1770-1850). Revolution and war fed an emphasis on freedom and conflict, expressed by both poets (**Byron**, 1788-1824; **Hugo**, 1802-85) and philosophers (**Hegel**, 1770-1831).

Wild gardens replaced the formal French variety, and painters favored rural, stormy, and mountainous landscapes (**Turner**, 1775-1851; **Constable**, 1776-1837). Clothing became freer, with wigs, hoops, and ruffles discarded. Originality and genius were expected in the life and work of inspired artists (Murger's *Scenes From Bohemian Life*, 1847-49). Exotic locales and themes (as in Gothic horror stories) were used in art and literature (Delacroix, 1798-1863; **Poe**, 1809-49). Music exhibited the new dramatic style and a breakdown of classical forms (**Beethoven**, 1770-1827). The use of folk melodies and modes aided the growth of distinct national traditions (Glinka in Russia, 1804-57).

Latin America. François **Toussaint L'Ouverture** led a successful slave revolt in Haiti, which subsequently became the first Caribbean state to achieve independence (1804). The mainland Spanish colonies won their independence (1810-24) under such leaders as Simón **Bolívar** (1783-1830). Brazil became an independent empire (1822) under the Portuguese prince regent. A new class of military officers divided power with large landholders and the church.

United States. Territory under U.S. control nearly doubled in size with the **Louisiana Purchase** (1803). Heavy immigration and exploitation of ample natural resources fueled rapid economic growth. The spread of the franchise, public education, and antislavery sentiment were signs of a widespread democratic ethic.

China. Failure to keep pace with Western arms technology exposed China to greater European influence and hampered efforts to bar imports of opium, which had damaged Chinese society and drained wealth overseas. In the **Opium War** (1839-42), Britain forced China to expand trade opportunities and to cede Hong Kong.

New Complexities: Reforms and Imperialism: 1840-80

Idea of progress. As a result of the cumulative scientific, economic, and political changes of the preceding eras, the idea took hold among literate people in the West that continuing growth and improvement constituted the usual state of human and natural life.

Charles **Darwin**'s statement of the **theory of evolution** and survival of the fittest (*On the Origin of Species*, 1859), defended by intellectuals and scientists against theological objections, was taken as confirmation that progress was the natural direction of life. The controversy helped define popular ideas of the dedicated scientist and of science's increasing control over the world (Foucault's demonstration of Earth's rotation, 1851; **Pasteur**'s germ theory, 1861).

Liberals following Ricardo (1772-1823) in their faith that unrestrained competition would bring continuous economic expansion sought to adjust political life to new social realities and believed that unregulated competition of ideas would yield truth (**Mill**, 1806-73). In England, successive reform bills (1832, 1867, 1884) gave representation to the new industrial towns and extended the franchise to the middle and lower classes and to Catholics, Dissenters, and Jews. On both sides of the Atlantic, reformists tried to improve conditions for the mentally ill (**Dix**, 1802-87), women (Anthony, 1820-1906), and prisoners. Slavery was barred in the British Empire (1833), the U.S. (1865), and Brazil (1888).

Socialist theories based on ideas of human perfectibility or progress were widely disseminated. Utopian socialists such as Saint-Simon (1760-1825) envisaged an orderly, just society directed by a technocratic elite. A model factory town, New Lanark, Scotland, was set up by utopian Robert Owen (1771-1858), and communal experiments were tried in the U.S. (Brook Farm, MA, 1841-47). Bakunin's (1814-76) anarchism represented the opposite extreme of total freedom. Karl **Marx** (1818-83) posited the inevitable triumph of socialism in industrial countries through a dialectical process of class conflict. Effective development of oceanic steamship lines (Cunard Lines, 1840s) and the opening of the **Suez Canal** accelerated shipping and commerce. Telegraph lines (Australia-Europe, 1871) sped communication. International organizations included the General (later Universal) Postal Union (1874) and conferences to limit epidemics like cholera. The initial **Geneva Convention** (1864) regulated treatment of prisoners of war.

Spread of industry. The technical processes and managerial innovations of the English industrial revolution spread to Europe (especially Germany) and the U.S., causing an explosion of industrial production, demand for raw materials, and competition for markets. Inventors, both trained and self-taught, provided means for larger-scale production (Bessemer steel, 1856; sewing machine, 1846). Many inventions were shown at the universal prosperity-themed 1851 London Great Exhibition at the **Crystal Palace**.

Local specialization and long-distance trade were aided by a revolution in transportation and communication. Railroads were first introduced in the 1820s in England and the U.S. Over 150,000 mi of track had been laid worldwide by 1880, with another 100,000 mi laid in the next decade. Steamships were improved (*Savannah* crossed Atlantic, 1819). The **telegraph**, perfected by 1844 (Morse), connected the Old and New Worlds by cable in 1866 and quickened the pace of international commerce and politics. The first commercial **telephone** exchange went into operation in the U.S. in 1878.

The new class of industrial workers, uprooted from their rural homes, lacked job security and suffered from dangerous overcrowding at work and at home. Many responded by organizing **trade unions** (legalized in England, 1824; France, 1884). The U.S. Knights of Labor had 700,000 members by 1886. The First International (1864-76) tried to unite workers worldwide around a Marxist program. The quasi-Socialist Paris Commune uprising (1871) was violently suppressed. Acts to reduce child labor and regulate conditions were passed (1833-50 in England). Social security measures were introduced by the Bismarck regime (1883-89) in Germany.

Revolutions of 1848. Among the causes of the continent-wide revolutions were an international collapse of credit and resulting unemployment, bad harvests in 1845-47, and a cholera epidemic. The new urban proletariat and expanding bourgeoisie demanded greater political roles. Republics were proclaimed in France, Rome, and Venice. Nationalist feelings reached fever pitch in the Habsburg empire, as Hungary declared independence under Kossuth, a Slav Congress demanded equality, and Piedmont tried to drive Austria from Lombardy. A national liberal assembly at Frankfurt called for German unification.

But riots fueled bourgeois fear of socialism (**Marx** and **Engels**, *Communist Manifesto*, 1848), and peasants remained conservative. The old establishment—the Papacy, the Habsburgs with the help of the Tsarist Russian army—was able to rout the revolutionaries by 1849. The French Republic succumbed to a renewed monarchy by 1852 (Emperor Napoleon III).

Great nations unified. Using the "blood and iron" tactics of Bismarck from 1862, Prussia controlled N Germany by 1867 (war with Denmark, 1864; Austria, 1866). After defeating France in 1870 (annexation of Alsace-Lorraine), it won the allegiance of S German states. A new **German Empire** was proclaimed (1871). **Italy**, inspired by Giuseppe Mazzini (1805-72) and Giuseppe Garibaldi (1807-82), was unified by the reformed Piedmont kingdom through uprisings, plebiscites, and war.

The **United States** expanded its area after the 1846-48 Mexican War and defeated (1861-65) a secession attempt by Southern states in the **Civil War**. Canadian provinces were united in an autonomous **Dominion of Canada** (1867). Control in **India** was removed from the East India Co. and centralized under British administration after the 1857-58 Sepoy rebellion, laying the groundwork for the modern Indian state. Queen Victoria was named Empress of India (1876).

Europe dominates Asia. The Ottoman Empire began to weaken in the face of Balkan nationalisms and European imperial incursions in N Africa (**Suez Canal**, 1869). The Ottomans had lost control of most of both regions by 1882. Russia completed its expansion S by 1884 (despite the temporary setback of the **Crimean War** with Turkey, Britain, and France, 1853-56), taking Turkestan, all the Caucasus, and Chinese areas in the E and sponsoring Balkan Slavs against the Turks. A succession of reformist and reactionary regimes presided over a slow modernization (serfs freed, 1861). Persian independence suffered as Russia and British India competed for influence.

China was forced to sign a series of unequal treaties with European powers and Japan. Overpopulation and an inefficient dynasty brought misery and caused rebellions (Taiping, Muslims) leaving tens of millions dead. **Japan** was forced by the U.S. (Commodore Perry's visits, 1853-54) and Europe to end its isolation. The Meiji restoration (1868) gave power to a Westernizing oligarchy, abolishing feudalism and expanding education. Intensified empire-building gave Burma to Britain (1824-85) and Indochina to France (1862-95). Christian missionary activity followed imperial and trade expansion in Asia.

Arts. The official **Beaux Arts** school in Paris set an international style of imposing public buildings (Paris Opera, 1861-74; Vienna Opera, 1861-69) and uplifting statues (Bartholdi's Statue of Liberty, 1884). Realist painting, influenced by photography

(Daguerre, 1837), appealed to a new mass audience with social or historical narrative (Wilkie, 1785-1841; Poynter, 1836-1919) or with serious religious, moral, or social messages (pre-Raphaelites, Millet's *Angelus*, 1858), often drawn from ordinary life. The **Impressionists** (Monet, 1840-1926; Pissarro, 1830-1903; Renoir, 1841-1919) rejected the formalism, sentimentality, and precise techniques of academic art in favor of a spontaneous, undetailed rendering of the world through careful representation of the effect of natural light on objects. They were strongly influenced by Asian and African styles.

Realistic **novelists** presented the full panorama of social classes and personalities but retained sentimentality and moral judgment (**Dickens**, 1812-70; **Eliot**, 1819-80; **Tolstoy**, 1828-1910; **Balzac**, 1799-1850).

Veneer of Stability: 1880-1900

Imperialism triumphant. The vast **African** interior, visited by European explorers (Barth, 1821-65; Livingstone, 1813-73), was conquered by the European powers in rapid, competitive thrusts from their coastal bases after 1880, mostly for domestic political and international strategic reasons. W African Muslim kingdoms (Fulani), Arab slave traders (Zanzibar), and Bantu military confederations (Zulu) were alike subdued. Only Christian Ethiopia (defeat of Italy, 1896) and Liberia resisted successfully. France (W Africa) and Britain ("Cape to Cairo," **Boer War**, 1899-1902) were the major beneficiaries. The ideology of "the white man's burden" (Kipling, *Barrack Room Ballads*, 1892) justified the conquests, which in fact reflected Europe's weapons superiority.

W European foreign capital investment soared to nearly $40 billion by 1914, but most was in E Europe (France, Germany), the Americas (Britain), and Europe's colonies. The foundation of the modern interdependent world economy was laid, with cartels dominating raw material trade. Global developments included a new agreement on international patents (1883), the modern Olympics (1896), and the worldwide spread of department stores.

An industrious world. Industrial and technological proficiency characterized the two new great powers—Germany and the U.S. Coal and iron deposits enabled Germany to reach second- or third-place status in iron, steel, and shipbuilding by the 1900s. German electrical and chemical industries were world leaders. The U.S. post-Civil War boom (interrupted by financial panics—1873, 1884, and 1893) was shaped by massive immigration from S and E Europe from 1880, government subsidy of railroads, and huge private monopolies (Standard Oil, 1870; U.S. Steel, 1901). The **Spanish-American War**, 1898 (Philippine Insurrection, 1899-1902), and the **Open Door policy** in China (1899) made the U.S. a world power.

England led in **urbanization**, with London the world capital of finance, insurance, and shipping. Sewer systems (Paris, 1850s), electric subways (London, 1890), parks, and bargain department stores helped improve living standards for most of the urban population of the industrial world. Birthrates declined in the West while infant mortality rates plunged (demographic transition, 1880-1920).

Upheavals in Asia. Asian reaction to European economic, military, and religious incursions took the form of imitation of Western techniques and adoption of Western ideas of progress and freedom. The Chinese "self-strengthening" movement of the 1860s and 1870s included rail, port, and arsenal improvements and metal and textile mills. Reformers such as **K'ang** Yu-wei (1858-1927) won liberalizing reforms in 1898, right after the European and Japanese "scramble for concessions."

A universal education system in Japan and importation of foreign industrial, scientific, and military experts aided Japan's rapid modernization after 1868 under the authoritarian Meiji regime. Japan's victory in the **Sino-Japanese War** (1894-95) put Formosa and Korea in its power. Industrialization began in earnest by 1890.

In India, the British alliance with the remaining princely states masked reform sentiment among the Westernized urban elite; higher education had been conducted largely in English for 50 years. The **Indian National Congress**, founded in 1885, demanded a larger government role for Indians.

***Fin-de-siècle* sophistication.** **Naturalist** writers pushed realism to its extreme limits, adopting a quasi-scientific attitude and writing about formerly taboo subjects such as sex, crime, extreme poverty, and corruption (Flaubert, 1821-80; Zola, 1840-1902; Hardy, 1840-1928). Unseen or repressed psychological motivations were explored in the clinical and theoretical works of Sigmund **Freud** (1856-1939) and in works of fiction (**Dostoyevsky**, 1821-81; Henry James, 1843-1916; Schnitzler, 1862-1931).

A contempt for bourgeois life or a desire to shock a complacent audience was shared by the French **symbolist** poets (Verlaine, 1844-96; Rimbaud, 1854-91), by neopagan English writers (Swinburne, 1837-1909), by continental dramatists (**Ibsen**, 1828-1906), and by satirists (**Wilde**, 1854-1900). The German philosopher Friedrich **Nietzsche** (1844-1900) was influential in his elitism and pessimism.

Postimpressionist art neglected long-cherished conventions of representation (**Cézanne**, 1839-1906) and showed a willingness to learn from primitive and non-European art (**Gauguin**, 1848-1903; Japanese prints).

Racism. Gobineau (1816-82) gave a pseudobiological foundation to modern racist theories, which spread in Europe in the latter 19th cent., along with **Social Darwinism**, the belief that societies are and should be organized as a struggle for survival of the fittest. The medieval period was interpreted as an era of natural Germanic rule (Chamberlain, 1855-1927), and notions of racial superiority were associated with German national aspirations (Treitschke, 1834-96). **Anti-Semitism**, with a new racist rationale, became a significant political force in Germany (Anti-Semitic Petition, 1880), Austria (Lueger, 1844-1910), and France (**Dreyfus affair**, 1894-1906).

Imperialism's High Point: 1900-09

Alliances. While the peace of Europe (and its dependencies) continued to hold (1907 **Hague Conference** extended the rules of war and international arbitration procedures), imperial rivalries, protectionist trade practices (in Germany and France), and the escalating arms race (British *Dreadnought* battleship launched; Germany widens Kiel canal, 1906) exacerbated minor disputes (German-French Moroccan "crises," 1905, 1911).

Security was sought through balance-of-power alliances: **Triple Alliance** (Germany, Austria-Hungary, Italy; renewed in 1902 and 1907); Anglo-Japanese Alliance (1902), Franco-Russian Alliance (1899), **Entente Cordiale** (Britain, France, 1904), Anglo-Russian Treaty (1907), German-Ottoman friendship. Global developments included the establishment of an international court in The Hague, the first transatlantic radio transmission (1901), and the creation of the first international association for European football (1904).

Ottomans decline. The Ottoman government was unable to resist further loss of territory, and earlier reform efforts gave way to greater authoritarianism. Nearly all European lands were lost in 1912 to Serbia, Greece, Montenegro, and Bulgaria. Italy took Libya and the Dodecanese islands the same year. Britain took Kuwait (1899) and the Sinai (1906). The **Young Turk** revolution in 1908 forced the sultan to restore a constitution, and it introduced some social reform and secularization.

British Empire. British trade and cultural influence remained dominant in the empire, but constitutional reforms presaged its eventual dissolution. The colonies of **Australia** were united in 1901 under a self-governing commonwealth. **New Zealand** acquired dominion status in 1907. The old Boer republics joined Cape Colony and Natal in the self-governing Union of **South Africa** in 1910.

The 1909 Indian Councils Act enhanced the role of elected province legislatures in **India**. The Muslim League (founded 1906) sought separate communal representation.

East Asia. Japan exploited its growing industrial power to expand its empire. Victory in the 1904-05 war against Russia (naval battle of Tsushima, 1905) assured Japan's domination of **Korea** (annexed 1910) and Manchuria (Port Arthur taken, 1905).

In China, central authority began to crumble (empress died, 1908). Reforms (Confucian exam system ended 1905, modernization of the army, building of railroads) were inadequate, and secret societies of reformers and nationalists, inspired by the Westernized **Sun** Yat-sen (1866-1925), fomented periodic uprisings in the S.

Siam, whose independence had been guaranteed by Britain and France in 1896, was split into spheres of influence by those countries in 1907.

Russia. The population of the Russian Empire approached 150 million in 1900. Reforms in education, in law, and in local institutions (*zemstvos*) and an industrial boom starting in the 1880s (oil, railroads) created the beginnings of a modern society, despite the autocratic tsarist regime. Liberals (1903 Union of Liberation), Socialists (Social Democrats founded 1898, Bolsheviks split off 1903), and populists (Social Revolutionaries founded 1901) were periodically repressed, and national minorities were persecuted (anti-Jewish pogroms, 1903, 1905-06).

An industrial crisis after 1900 and harvest failures aggravated poverty among urban workers, and the 1904-05 defeat by Japan (which checked Russia's Asian expansion) sparked the **Revolution of 1905-06**. A **Duma** (parliament) was created under Tsar Nicholas II. Agricultural reform (under Stolypin, prime minister, 1906-11) created a large class of land-owning peasants (*kulaks*).

The world shrinks. Developments in transportation and communication and mass population movements helped create an awareness of an interdependent world. Early **automobiles** (Daimler, Benz, 1885) were experimental or were designed as luxuries. Assembly-line mass production (Ford Motor Co., 1903) made the invention practical, and by 1910 nearly 500,000 motor vehicles were registered in the U.S. alone. **Heavier-than-air flights** began in 1903 in the U.S. (Wright brothers' *Flyer*), preceded by glider, balloon, and model plane advances in several countries. Trade was advanced by improvements in **ship design** (gyrocompass, 1910), speed (*Lusitania* crossed Atlantic in five days, 1907), and reach (Panama Canal begun, 1904).

The first transatlantic **radio** telegraphic transmission occurred in 1901, six years after Marconi discovered radio. Radio transmission of human speech had been made in 1900. Telegraphic transmission of photos was achieved in 1904, lending immediacy to news reports. **Phonographs**, popularized by Caruso's recordings (starting 1902), made for quick international spread of musical styles (ragtime). **Motion pictures**, perfected in the 1890s (Dickson, Lumière brothers), became a popular and artistic medium after 1900; newsreels appeared in 1909.

Emigration from crowded European centers soared in the decade: 9 million migrated to the U.S., and millions more went to Siberia, Canada, Argentina, Australia, South Africa, and Algeria. Some 70 million Europeans emigrated in the century before 1914. Several million Chinese, Indians, and Japanese migrated to SE Asia, where their urban skills often enabled them to take a predominant economic role.

Social reform. The social and economic problems of the poor were kept in the public eye by realist fiction writers (Dreiser's *Sister Carrie*, 1900; Gorky's *Lower Depths*, 1902; Sinclair's *The Jungle*, 1906), journalists (U.S. **muckrakers**—Steffens, Tarbell), and artists (Ashcan school). Frequent labor strikes and occasional assassinations by anarchists or radicals (Empress Elizabeth of Austria, 1898; King Umberto I of Italy, 1900; U.S. Pres. McKinley, 1901; Russian Interior Min. Plehve, 1904; Portugal's King Carlos, 1908) added to social tension and fear of revolution. Feminist agitators for the vote surfaced in several countries.

Emigration from densely populated European countries to the Americas soared in the early 20th century; many landed on Ellis Island, in New York Harbor, en route to U.S. cities.

But democratic reformism responded in part. In Germany, Bernstein's (1850-1932) **revisionist Marxism**, downgrading revolution, was accepted by the powerful Social Democrats and trade unions. The British Fabian Society (the Webbs, Shaw) and the Labour Party (founded 1906) worked for reforms such as social security and union rights (1906), while woman suffragists grew more militant. U.S. **progressives** fought big business (Pure Food and Drug Act, 1906). In France, the 10-hour workday (1904) and separation of church and state (1905) were reform victories, as was universal suffrage in Austria (1907).

Arts. An unprecedented period of experimentation, centered in France, produced several new **painting styles**: Fauvism exploited bold color areas (Matisse, *Woman With Hat*, 1905); expressionism reflected powerful inner emotions (Brücke group, 1905); Cubism combined several views of an object on one flat surface (Picasso, *Demoiselles*, 1906-07); futurism tried to depict speed and motion (Italian Futurist Manifesto, 1910). **Architects** explored new uses of steel structures, with facades either neoclassical (Adler and Sullivan in U.S.), curvilinear Art Nouveau (Gaudi's Casa Mila, 1905-10), or functionally streamlined (Wright's Robie House, 1909).

Music and dance shared the experimental spirit. Ruth St. Denis (1877-1968) and Isadora Duncan (1878-1927) pioneered modern dance, while Sergei Diaghilev in Paris revitalized classic ballet from 1909. Composers explored atonal music (Debussy, 1862-1918) and dissonance (Schoenberg, 1874-1951) or revolutionized classical forms (Stravinsky, 1882-1971), often showing jazz or folk music influences.

War and Revolution: 1910-19

War threatens. Germany under Wilhelm II sought a political and imperial role consonant with its industrial strength, challenging Britain's world supremacy and threatening France, which was still resenting the loss (1871) of Alsace-Lorraine. Austria wanted to curb an expanded Serbia (after 1912) and the threat it posed to its own Slav lands. Russia feared Austrian and German political and economic aims in the Balkans and Turkey.

An accelerated arms race resulted from these circumstances. The German standing army rose to more than 2 million men by 1914. Russia and France had more than a million each, and Austria and the British Empire nearly a million each. Dozens of enormous battleships were built by the powers after 1906.

The **assassination of Austrian Archduke Franz Ferdinand** by a Serbian nationalist, June 28, 1914, was the trigger for war. The system of alliances made the conflict Europe-wide; Germany's invasion of Belgium to outflank France forced Britain to enter the war. Patriotic fervor was nearly unanimous among all classes in most countries.

War unfolds. German forces were stopped in France in one month. The rival armies dug **trench networks**. Artillery and improved machine guns prevented either side from any lasting advance despite repeated assaults (600,000 dead at **Verdun**, Feb.-July 1916). German deployment of poisonous chlorine gas (Ypres, 1915) was first major use of lethal **chemical weapons**. The entrance of more than 1 million U.S. troops tipped the balance after mid-1917, forcing Germany to sue for peace the next year. The formal armistice was signed on Nov. 11, 1918, and the German emperor abdicated.

In the E, the Russian armies were thrown back (battle of **Tannenberg**, Aug. 20, 1914), and the war grew unpopular in Russia. An allied attempt to relieve Russia through Turkey failed (**Gallipoli**, 1915). The **Russian Revolution** (1917) abolished the monarchy. The new Bolshevik regime signed the capitulatory Brest-Litovsk peace in Mar. 1918. Italy entered the war on the allied side in May 1915 but was pushed back by Oct. 1917. A renewed offensive with Allied aid in Oct.-Nov. 1918 forced Austria to surrender.

The British Navy successfully blockaded Germany, which responded with submarine U-boat attacks; **unrestricted submarine warfare** against neutrals after Jan. 1917 helped bring the U.S. into the war. Other battlefields included Palestine and Mesopotamia, both of which Britain wrested from the Turks in 1917, and the African and Pacific colonies of Germany, most of which fell to Britain, France, Australia, Japan, and South Africa.

Settlement. At the **Paris Peace Conference** (Jan.-June 1919), concluded by the **Treaty of Versailles**, and in subsequent negotiations and local wars (Russian-Polish War, 1920), the **map of Europe** was redrawn with a nod to U.S. Pres. Woodrow Wilson's principle of self-determination. Austria and Hungary were separated, and much of their land was given to Yugoslavia

Both sides in World War I developed elaborate networks of dug-in trenches from which to fight.

(formerly Serbia), Romania, Italy, and the newly independent Poland and Czechoslovakia. Germany lost territory in the W, N, and E, while Finland and the Baltic states were detached from Russia. The Ottoman Empire ended (1922) and most of its Arab lands went to British-sponsored Arab states or to direct French and British rule. Belgium's sovereignty was recognized.

From 1916, the civilian populations and economies of both sides were mobilized to an unprecedented degree. Hardships intensified among fighting nations in 1917 (French mutiny crushed in May). More than 10 million soldiers died in the war.

A huge **reparations** burden and partial demilitarization were imposed on Germany. Pres. Wilson proposed a League of Nations, but the U.S. Senate voted against U.S. involvement.

Pandemic. The presence and movement of World War I troops facilitated the spread of a deadly form of **influenza** caused by an H1N1 virus, its place of origin not clearly known. With no vaccine or drug treatment available, an estimated 500 million people, about one-third of the world population, were infected, 1918-19, and some 50 million believed to have died, in the worst pandemic of recent history.

Russian revolution. Military defeats and high casualties caused a contagious lack of confidence in Tsar Nicholas, who was forced to abdicate Mar. 1917. A liberal provisional government failed to end the war, and massive desertions, riots, and fighting between factions followed. A moderate socialist government under Aleksandr Kerensky was overthrown (Nov. 1917) in a violent coup by the **Bolsheviks** in Petrograd under **Lenin**, who later disbanded the elected Constituent Assembly.

The Bolsheviks brutally suppressed all opposition and ended the war with Germany in Mar. 1918. **Civil war** broke out in the summer between the Red Army (the Bolsheviks and their supporters), and monarchists, anarchists, minority nationalities (Ukrainians, Georgians, Poles), and others. Small U.S., British, French, and Japanese units also opposed the Bolsheviks (1918-19; Japan in Vladivostok to 1922). The civil war, anarchy, and pogroms devastated the country until the 1920 Red Army victory. The **Communist Party** leadership retained absolute power.

Other European revolutions. An unpopular monarchy in **Portugal** was overthrown in 1910. The new republic took severe anticlerical measures in 1911.

After a century of Home Rule agitation, during which **Ireland** was devastated by famine (1 million dead, 1846-47) and emigration, republican militants staged an unsuccessful uprising in Dublin during **Easter 1916**. The execution of the leaders and mass arrests by the British won popular support for the rebels. The **Irish Free State**, comprising all but the six northern counties, achieved dominion status in 1922.

In the aftermath of the world war, radical revolutions were attempted in Germany (**Spartacist** uprising, Jan. 1919), **Hungary** (Kun regime, 1919), and elsewhere. All were suppressed or failed for lack of support.

Chinese revolution. The Qinq, or Manchu, Dynasty was overthrown and a republic proclaimed, 1911-12. Revolutionary leader Sun Yat-sen, who organized the nationalist **Kuomintang** party and led a provisional republican government in Nanjing, resigned in a unification compromise with former imperial viceroy Yuan Shikai. Yuan became president upon the abdication of the emperor in Feb. 1912.

Students launched protests on May 4, 1919, against League of Nations concessions in China to Japan. Nationalist, liberal, and socialist ideas and political groups spread. The **Chinese Communist Party** was founded in 1921. A Communist regime took power in Mongolia with Soviet support in 1921.

India restive. Indian objections to British rule erupted in nationalist riots as well as in the nonviolent tactics of Mahatma **Gandhi** (1869-1948). Nearly 400 unarmed demonstrators were shot at **Amritsar** in Apr. 1919. Britain approved limited self-rule that year.

Mexican revolution. Under the long **Díaz** dictatorship (1877-1911) the economy advanced, but Indian and mestizo lands were confiscated, and concessions to foreigners (mostly U.S.) damaged the middle class. A revolution in 1910 led to civil wars and U.S. intervention (1914, 1916-17). Land reform and a more democratic constitution (1917) were achieved.

Sciences. Scientific specialization continued to advance, with key discoveries especially in **physics**. Physicists challenged common-sense views of causality, observation, and a mechanistic universe, putting science further beyond popular grasp (**Einstein**'s general theory of relativity, 1915-16; Bohr's quantum mechanics, 1913; Heisenberg's uncertainty principle, 1927).

Aftermath of War: 1920-29

U.S. Easy credit, technological ingenuity, and war-related industrial decline in Europe caused a long economic boom, in which ownership of new products—**autos**, **phones**, **radios**—became more democratized. **Prosperity**, an increase in women workers, women's suffrage (19th Amendment ratified, 1920), and drastic change in fashion (**flappers**, mannish bob for women, clean-shaven men) created a wide perception of social change despite prohibition of alcoholic beverages (1919-33). Union membership and strikes increased. Fear of radicals led to Palmer raids (1919-20) and the Sacco-Vanzetti case (1921-27).

Europe sorts itself out. Germany's liberal **Weimar constitution** (1919) could not guarantee a stable government in the face of rightist violence (Foreign Min. Rathenau assassinated, 1922) and Communist refusal to cooperate with Socialists. Reparations and Allied occupation of the Rhineland caused staggering inflation that destroyed middle-class savings, but economic expansion resumed after mid-decade, aided by U.S. loans. A sophisticated, **innovative culture** developed in architecture and design (Bauhaus, 1919-28), film (Lang, *M*, 1931), painting (Grosz), music (Weill, *Threepenny Opera*, 1928), theater (Brecht, *A Man's a Man*, 1926), criticism (Benjamin), philosophy (Jung), and fashion. This culture was considered decadent and socially disruptive by rightists.

England elected its first Labour governments (Jan. 1924, June 1929). A 10-day general strike in support of coal miners failed in May 1926. In **Italy**, strikes, political chaos, and violence by small Fascist bands culminated in the Oct. 1922 Fascist March on Rome, which established **Mussolini**'s dictatorship. Strikes were outlawed (1926), and Italian influence was pressed in the Balkans (Albania made a protectorate, 1926). A conservative dictatorship was also established in **Portugal** in a 1926 military coup.

Czechoslovakia, the only stable democracy to emerge from the war in Central or E Europe, faced opposition from Germans (in the Sudetenland), Ruthenians, and some Slovaks. As the industrial heartland of the old Habsburg empire, it remained fairly prosperous. With French backing, it formed the Little Entente with Yugoslavia (1920) and **Romania** (1921) to block Austrian or Hungarian irredentism. Croats and Slovenes in **Yugoslavia** demanded a federal state until King Alexander I proclaimed (1929) a royal dictatorship. Poland faced internal nationality problems as well (Germans, Ukrainians, Jews); Pilsudski ruled as dictator from 1926. The Baltic states were threatened by traditionally dominant ethnic Germans and by Soviet-supported Communists.

An economic collapse and famine in **Russia** (1921-22) claimed 5 million lives. The New Economic Policy (1921) allowed land ownership by peasants and some private commerce and industry. **Stalin** was absolute ruler within four years of Lenin's death (1924). He inaugurated a brutal collectivization program (1929-32) and used foreign Communist parties for Soviet state advantage. Industrialization advanced rapidly.

Internationalism. Revulsion against World War I led to pacifist agitation, to the Kellogg-Briand Pact renouncing aggressive war (1928), and to **naval disarmament** pacts (Washington, 1922; London, 1930). But the League of Nations was able to arbitrate only minor disputes (Greece-Bulgaria, 1925). A number of countries pulled back from global contacts, as with American isolationism and Russia's separation from international capitalism.

Middle East. Mustafa Kemal (**Ataturk**) led **Turkish** nationalists in resisting Italian, French, and Greek military advances (1919-23). The sultanate was abolished (1922), and elaborate reforms were passed, including secularization of law and adoption of the Latin alphabet. Ethnic conflict led to persecution of **Armenians** (more than 1 million dead in 1915, 1 million expelled), Greeks (forced Greek-Turk population exchange, 1923), and Kurds (1925 uprising).

With evacuation of the Turks from **Arab** lands, the puritanical Wahabi dynasty of E Arabia conquered (1919-25) what is now Saudi Arabia. British, French, and Arab dynastic and nationalist maneuvering resulted in the creation of two more Arab monarchies in 1921—Iraq and Transjordan (both under British control)—and two French mandates—Syria and Lebanon. Jewish immigration into British-mandated **Palestine**, inspired by the Zionist movement, was resisted by Arabs, at times violently (1921, 1929 riots).

Reza Khan ruled **Persia** after his 1921 coup (shah from 1925), centralized control, and created the trappings of a modern secular state.

In 1922, English archaeologist Howard Carter discovered the tomb of the boy pharaoh **Tutankhamun** in the Valley of the Kings in Egypt.

China. The Kuomintang under **Chiang Kai-shek** (1887-1975) subdued the warlords by 1928. The Communists were brutally suppressed after their alliance with the Kuomintang was broken in 1927. Relative peace thereafter allowed for industrial and financial improvements, with some Russian, British, and U.S. cooperation.

Arts. Nearly all bounds of subject matter, style, and attitude were broken in the arts of the period. **Abstract** art first took inspiration from natural forms or narrative themes (Kandinsky from 1911) and then worked free of any representational aims (Malevich's suprematism, 1915-19; Mondrian's geometric style from 1917). The **Dada** movement (from 1916) mocked artistic pretension with absurd collages and constructions. Paradox, illusion, and psychological taboos were exploited by **surrealists** by the late 1920s (Dali, Magritte). Architectural schools celebrated industrial values, whether vigorous abstract constructivism (Tatlin, *Monument to the Third International*, 1919) or the machined, streamlined **Bauhaus** style, which was extended to many design fields (Helvetica typeface).

Prose writers explored revolutionary narrative modes related to dreams (Kafka's *Trial*, 1925), internal monologue (Joyce's ***Ulysses***, 1922), and word play (Stein's *Making of Americans*, 1925). Poets and novelists wrote of modern alienation (Eliot's ***Waste Land***, 1922) and aimlessness ("The Lost Generation").

Rise of Totalitarians: 1930-39

Depression. A worldwide financial panic and economic depression began with the Oct. 1929 U.S. stock market crash and the May 1931 failure of the Austrian Credit-Anstalt. A credit crunch caused international bankruptcies and **unemployment**: 12 million jobless by 1932 in the U.S., 5.6 million in Germany, 2.7 million in England. Governments responded with **tariff restrictions** (Smoot-Hawley Act, 1930; Ottawa Imperial Conference, 1932), which dried up world trade. Government public works programs were vitiated by deflationary budget balancing.

Germany. As **Nazi Party** leader, **Adolf Hitler** built up a mass movement (feeding on economic hardship, ideas of racial superiority, fear of leftist influence). With a plurality in the Reichstag, he persuaded Pres. **Hindenburg** to name him chancellor (Jan. 1933); Hindenburg further granted him emergency powers after the Reichstag fire in Feb. Other parties and most forms of opposition, including strikes, were banned, and the media and most aspects of life fell under Nazi control. Severe persecution of Jews began (**Nuremberg Laws**, Sept. 1935). Many Jews, political opponents, and others were sent to concentration camps (Dachau, 1933), where thousands died or were killed. Public works, renewed conscription (1935), arms production, and a four-year plan (1936) all but ended unemployment.

Hitler's expansionism started with reincorporation of the Saar (1935), occupation of the **Rhineland** (Mar. 1936), and annexation of Austria (Mar. 1938). At **Munich** (Sept. 1938) Britain and France attempted to appease Hitler and avoid war by successfully encouraging Czechoslovakia's surrender of the Sudetenland territory.

Russia. Rapid industrialization was achieved through successive **five-year plans** starting in 1928, using severe labor discipline and mass forced labor. Industry was financed by exploitation of agriculture, which was almost totally collectivized by the early 1930s. Millions perished in a series of manufactured disasters: extermination (1929-34) of kulaks (peasant landowners), severe famine (1932-33), party purges and show trials (Great Purge, 1936-38), suppression of nationalities, and poor conditions in labor camps. Purges also increased Stalin's power in the Communist party.

Spain. An industrial revolution during World War I created an urban proletariat, which was attracted to socialism and anarchism; Catalan nationalists challenged central authority. The five years after King Alfonso left Spain in Apr. 1931 were dominated by tension between intermittent leftist and anticlerical governments and clericals, monarchists, and other rightists. Anarchist and Communist rebellions were crushed, but a July 1936 extreme right rebellion led by Gen. Francisco **Franco** and aided by Nazi Germany and Fascist Italy succeeded after a three-year **civil war** (more than 1 million dead in battles and atrocities). The war polarized international public opinion.

Italy. Despite propaganda for the ideal of the Corporate State, few domestic reforms were attempted. An entente with Hungary and Austria (Mar. 1934), a pact with Germany and Japan (Nov. 1937), and intervention by 50,000-75,000 troops in Spain (1936-39) sealed Italy's identification with the fascist bloc (anti-Semitic laws after Mar. 1938). Ethiopia was conquered (1935-36) and Albania annexed (Jan. 1939) in conscious imitation of ancient Rome.

Eastern Europe. Repressive regimes fought for power against an active opposition (liberals, socialists, Communists, peasants, Nazis). Minority groups and Jews were restricted

Mahatma Gandhi (right) led efforts for Indian autonomy and independence for more than 25 years.

within national boundaries that did not coincide with ethnic population patterns. In the destruction of **Czechoslovakia**, Hungary occupied S Slovakia (Nov. 1938) and Ruthenia (Mar. 1939), and a pro-Nazi regime took power in the rest of Slovakia. Other boundary disputes (e.g., Poland-Lithuania, Yugoslavia-Bulgaria, and Romania-Hungary) doomed attempts to build joint fronts against Germany or Russia. Economic depression was severe.

East Asia. After a period of liberalism in **Japan**, nativist militarists dominated the government with peasant support. Manchuria was seized (Sept. 1931-Feb. 1932), and a puppet state was set up (Manchukuo). Adjacent Jehol (Inner Mongolia) was occupied in 1933. **China** proper was invaded in July 1937; large areas were conquered by Oct. 1938. Hundreds of thousands of rapes, murders, and other atrocities were attributed to the Japanese.

Communist forces left Kuomintang-besieged strongholds in the S of China in a Long March (1934-35) to the N. The Kuomintang-Communist civil war was suspended in Jan. 1937 in the face of threatening Japan.

Democracies. The Franklin Roosevelt administration, in office Mar. 1933, embarked on an extensive program of **New Deal** social reform and economic stimulation, including protection for labor unions (heavy industries organized), Social Security, public works, wage-and-hour laws, and assistance to farmers. Isolationist sentiment (1937 Neutrality Act) prevented U.S. intervention in Europe, but military expenditures were increased in 1939.

French political instability and polarization prevented resolution of economic and international security questions. The **Popular Front** government under Léon Blum (June 1936-Apr. 1938) passed social reforms (40-hour work week) and raised arms spending. National coalition governments, which ruled Britain from Aug. 1931, brought economic recovery but failed to define a consistent international policy until Chamberlain's government (from May 1937), which practiced **appeasement** of Germany and Italy.

India. Twenty years of agitation for autonomy and then for independence (Gandhi's **salt march**, 1930) achieved some constitutional reform (extended provincial powers, 1935) despite Muslim-Hindu strife. Social issues assumed prominence with peasant uprisings (1921), strikes (1928), Gandhi's efforts for untouchables (1932 "fast unto death"), and social and agrarian reform by the provinces after 1937.

Arts. The streamlined, geometric design motifs of Art Deco (from 1925) prevailed through the 1930s. **Abstract art** flourished (Moore sculptures from 1931) alongside a new **realism** related to social and political concerns (Socialist Realism, the official Soviet style from 1934; Mexican muralist Rivera, 1886-1957; Orozco, 1883-1949), which were also expressed in fiction and poetry (Steinbeck's *Grapes of Wrath*, 1939; Sandburg's *The People, Yes*, 1936). Modern architecture (International Style, 1932) was unchallenged in its use of artificial materials (concrete, glass), lack of decoration, and monumentality (Rockefeller Center, 1929-40). Larger-than-life U.S.-made films captured a worldwide audience *(Gone With the Wind, The Wizard of Oz*, both 1939).

War, Hot and Cold: 1940-49

War in Asia-Pacific. Japan occupied Indochina in Sept. 1940, dominated Thailand in Dec. 1941, and attacked Hawaii (**Pearl Harbor**), the Philippines, Hong Kong, and Malaya on Dec. 7, 1941 (precipitating U.S. entrance into the war). Indonesia was attacked in Jan. 1942, and Burma was conquered in Mar. 1942. The Battle of **Midway** (June 1942) turned back the Japanese advance. "Island-hopping" battles (**Guadalcanal**, Aug. 1942-Jan. 1943; **Leyte Gulf**, Oct. 1944; **Iwo Jima**, Feb.-Mar. 1945; **Okinawa**, Apr. 1945) and massive bombing raids on Japan from June 1944 wore out Japanese defenses. U.S. atom bombs, dropped Aug. 6 and 9 on **Hiroshima** and **Nagasaki**, forced Japan to agree, on Aug. 14, to surrender; formal surrender was on Sept. 2, 1945.

The U.S. bombing of Hiroshima and Nagasaki, Japan, in 1945 demonstrated the deadly, destructive power of atomic weapons.

War in Europe. The **Nazi-Soviet nonaggression** pact (Aug. 1939) freed Germany to attack Poland (Sept. 1939). Britain and France, which had guaranteed Polish independence, declared war on Germany. Russia seized E Poland (Sept. 1939), attacked Finland (Nov. 1939), and took the Baltic states (July 1940). Mobile German forces staged *blitzkrieg* attacks during Apr.-June 1940, conquering neutral Belgium, Denmark, Luxembourg, Netherlands, and Norway and defeating France; 350,000 British and French troops were evacuated at **Dunkirk**, France (May). The **Battle of Britain** (June-Dec. 1940) denied Germany air superiority. German-Italian campaigns won the Balkans by Apr. 1941. Three million Axis troops **invaded Russia** in June 1941, marching through Ukraine to the Caucasus, and through White Russia and the Baltic republics to Moscow and Leningrad.

Russian winter counterthrusts (1941-42 and 1942-43) stopped the German advance (**Stalingrad**, Sept. 1942-Feb. 1943). Sustaining great casualties, the Russians drove the Axis from all E Europe and the Balkans in the next two years. Invasions of N Africa (Nov. 1942), Italy (Sept. 1943), and **Normandy** (launched on D-Day, June 6, 1944) brought U.S., British, Free French, and allied troops to Germany by spring 1945. In Feb. 1945, the three Allied leaders, Winston **Churchill** (Britain), Joseph **Stalin** (USSR), and Franklin D. **Roosevelt** (U.S.), met in **Yalta** to discuss strategy and resolve political issues, including the postwar Allied occupation of Germany. Germany surrendered May 7, 1945.

Atrocities. The war brought 20th-cent. cruelty to its peak. The Nazi regime systematically killed an estimated 5-6 million Jews, including some 3 million who died in death camps (e.g., **Auschwitz**). The Nazis also killed Roma (also known as Gypsies), political opponents, people with mental or physical disabilities, homosexuals, others deemed undesirable, and vast numbers of Slavs.

German bombs killed 70,000 British civilians. More than 100,000 Chinese civilians were killed by Japanese forces in the capture and occupation of Nanking. Severe retaliation by the Soviet army, E European partisans, Free French, and others took a heavy toll. U.S. and British bombing of Germany killed hundreds of thousands, as did U.S. bombing of Japan (80,000-200,000 at Hiroshima alone). Some 45 million people died in the war.

Settlement. The **United Nations** charter was signed in San Francisco on June 26, 1945, by 50 nations. The International Tribunal at **Nuremberg** convicted 22 German leaders for war crimes in Sept. 1946; 23 Japanese leaders were convicted in Nov. 1948. Postwar border changes included large gains in territory for the USSR, losses for Germany, a shift to the W in Polish borders, and minor losses for Italy. Communist regimes, supported by Soviet troops, took power in most of Eastern Europe, including Soviet-occupied Germany (GDR, a.k.a. East Germany, proclaimed Oct. 1949). Japan lost all overseas lands. Global developments involved establishing new economic coordinating bodies like the International Monetary Fund (1944) and the Universal Declaration of Human Rights (1948).

Recovery. Basic political and social changes were imposed on Japan and W Germany by the Western allies (Japan constitution adopted, Nov. 1946; W German basic law, May 1949). U.S. **Marshall Plan** aid ($12 billion, 1947-51) spurred W European economic recovery after a period of severe inflation and strikes in Europe and the U.S. The British Labour Party introduced a national health service and nationalized basic industries in 1946.

Cold War. Western fears of further Soviet advances (Cominform formed in Oct. 1947; Czechoslovakia coup, Feb. 1948; Berlin blockade, Apr. 1948-Sept. 1949) led to the formation of **NATO**. Civil war in Greece and Soviet pressure on Turkey led to U.S. aid under the **Truman Doctrine** (Mar. 1947). Other anti-Communist security pacts were the Organization of American States (Apr. 1948) and the SE Asia Treaty Organization (Sept. 1954). A new wave of **Soviet purges** and repression intensified in the last years of Stalin's rule, extending to E Europe (Slansky trial in Czechoslovakia, 1951). Only Yugoslavia resisted Soviet control (expelled by Cominform, June 1948; U.S. aid, June 1949).

China, Korea. Communist forces emerged from World War II strengthened by the Soviet takeover of industrial Manchuria. In four years of fighting, the Kuomintang was driven from the mainland; the People's Republic of China was proclaimed Oct. 1, 1949. Korea was divided by USSR and U.S. occupation forces. Separate republics were proclaimed in the two zones in Aug.-Sept. 1948.

India. India and Pakistan became independent dominions on Aug. 15, 1947. Millions of Hindu and Muslim refugees were created by the partition. Riots (1946-47) took hundreds of thousands of lives. Mahatma **Gandhi** was assassinated in Jan. 1948. Burma became completely independent in Jan. 1948; Ceylon (later Sri Lanka) took dominion status in Feb.

Middle East. The UN approved partition of Palestine into Jewish and Arab states. **Israel** was proclaimed a state, May 14, 1948. Arabs rejected partition, but failed to defeat Israel in war (May 1948-July 1949). Immigration from Europe and the Middle East swelled Israel's Jewish population. British and French forces left Lebanon and Syria in 1946. Transjordan occupied most of Arab Palestine.

Southeast Asia. Communists and others fought against restoration of French rule in **Indochina** from 1946; a non-Communist government was recognized by France in Mar. 1949, but fighting continued. Both Indonesia and the Philippines became independent; the former in 1949 after four years of war with the Netherlands, the latter in 1946. Philippine economic and military ties with the U.S. remained strong; a Communist-led peasant rising was checked in 1948.

Arts. New York City became the center of the world art market; **abstract expressionism** was the chief mode (Pollock from 1943, de Kooning from 1947). Literature and philosophy explored **existentialism** (Camus's *The Stranger*, 1942; Sartre's *Being and Nothingness*, 1943). Non-Western attempts to revive or create regional styles (Senghor's Négritude, Mishima's novels) were responses to global cultural influences. Radio and phonograph records spread American popular music (swing, bebop) around the world.

The Cold War Decade: 1950-59

Decolonization. The relatively peaceful decline of European political and military power in Asia and Africa accelerated in the 1950s. Nearly all of **N Africa** was freed by 1956, but France fought bitterly to retain Algeria, with its large European minority, until 1962. **Ghana**, independent in 1957, led a parade of new self-led African nations (more than two dozen by 1962), which altered the political character of the UN. Ethnic, political, and other factional disputes often exploded in the new nations after decolonization (UN troops in Cyprus, 1964; **Nigerian civil war**, 1967-70). Leaders of the new states, mostly sharing socialist ideologies, tried to create an Afro-Asian bloc (Bandung Conference, 1955), but Western economic influence and U.S. political ties remained strong (Baghdad Pact, 1955).

Trade. World trade volume soared, in an atmosphere of monetary stability assured by international accords (**Bretton Woods**, 1944). In Europe, economic integration advanced (**European Economic Community**, 1957; European Free Trade Association, 1960). Comecon (1949) coordinated the economies of Soviet-bloc countries. Global developments included transcontinental jet travel (first South Africa to Britain flight, 1952; introduction of term "jet lag," 1965) and the increasing spread of English in global business, sports, and transportation.

U.S. Economic growth produced an abundance of consumer goods (9.3 million motor vehicles sold, 1955). Suburban housing changed life patterns for middle and working classes (Levittown, NY, 1947-51). Pres. Dwight **Eisenhower**'s landslide election victories (1952, 1956) reflected consensus politics. A system of alliances and military bases bolstered U.S. influence on all continents. Trade and payments surpluses were balanced by overseas investments and foreign aid ($50 billion, 1950-59).

USSR. In the "thaw" after Stalin's death in 1953, relations with the West improved (evacuation of Vienna, Geneva summit conference, both 1955). Repression of scientific and cultural life eased, and many prisoners were freed culminating in **de-Stalinization** (1956). Nikita **Khrushchev**'s leadership aimed at consumer sector growth, but farm production lagged, despite the virgin lands program (from 1954). Soviet crushing of the 1956 Hungarian revolution, the 1960 U-2 spy plane episode, and other incidents renewed E-W tension and domestic curbs.

Eastern Europe. Resentment of Russian domination and Stalinist repression combined with nationalist, economic, and religious factors to produce periodic violence. E Berlin workers rioted (1953), Polish workers rioted in Poznan (June 1956), and a broad-based **revolution** broke out in **Hungary** (Oct. 1956). All were suppressed by Soviet force or threats (at least 7,000 dead in Hungary), but Poland was allowed to restore private ownership of farms, and a degree of personal and economic freedom returned to Hungary. Yugoslavia experimented with worker self-management and a market economy.

Korea. The 1945 division of Korea along the 38th parallel left industry in the N, which was organized into a militant regime and armed by the USSR. The S was politically disunited. More than 60,000 N Korean troops invaded the S on June 25, 1950. The U.S., backed by the UN Security Council, sent troops. **UN troops** reached the Chinese border in Nov. Some 200,000 Chinese troops crossed the Yalu R. and drove back UN forces. By spring 1951, battle lines had become stabilized near the original 38th parallel border, but heavy fighting continued. Finally, an armistice was signed on July 27, 1953. U.S. troops remained in the S, and U.S. economic and military aid continued. The war stimulated rapid economic recovery in Japan.

China. Starting in 1952, industry, agriculture, and social institutions were forcibly collectivized. In a massive purge, as many as several million people were executed as Kuomintang supporters or as class and political enemies. The **Great Leap Forward** (1958-60) unsuccessfully tried to force the pace of development by substituting labor for investment.

Southeast Asia. Ho Chi Minh's forces, aided by the USSR and the new Chinese Communist government, fought French and pro-French Vietnamese forces to a standstill and captured the strategic **Dien Bien Phu** camp in May 1954. The Geneva Agreements divided Vietnam in half pending elections (never held) and recognized Laos and Cambodia as independent. The U.S. aided the anti-Communist Republic of Vietnam in the S.

Middle East. Arab revolutions placed leftist, militantly nationalist regimes in power in Egypt (1952) and Iraq (1958). But Arab unity attempts failed (United Arab Republic joined Egypt, Syria, Yemen, 1958-61). Arab refusal to recognize Israel (Arab League economic blockade began Sept. 1951) led to a permanent **state of war**, with repeated incidents (Gaza, 1955). Israel occupied Sinai, and Britain and France took (Oct. 1956) the Suez Canal, but were replaced by the UN Emergency Force. The Mossadegh government in Iran nationalized (May 1951) the British-owned oil industry in May, but was overthrown (Aug. 1953) in a U.S.-aided coup.

Latin America. Argentinian dictator Juan **Perón**, in office 1946, crushed opposition and enforced land reform, some nationalization, welfare state measures, and curbs on the Roman Catholic Church. A Sept. 1955 coup deposed Perón. The 1952 revolution in Bolivia brought land reform, nationalization of tin mines, and improvement in the status of the Indigenous population, who nevertheless remained poor. The Batista regime in Cuba was overthrown (Jan. 1959) by Fidel **Castro**, who imposed a Communist dictatorship, aligned Cuba with the USSR, and improved education and health care. A U.S.-backed anti-Castro invasion (**Bay of Pigs**, Apr. 1961) was crushed. Self-government advanced in the British Caribbean.

Technology. Large outlays on research and development in the U.S. and the USSR focused on military applications (H-bomb in U.S., 1952; USSR, 1953; Britain, 1957; intercontinental missiles, late 1950s). Soviet launching of the **Sputnik** satellite (Oct. 4, 1957) spurred increases in U.S. science education funds (National Defense Education Act).

Literature and film. Alienation from social and literary conventions reached an extreme in the theater of the absurd (Beckett's *Waiting for Godot*, 1952), the "new novel" (Robbe-Grillet's *Voyeur*, 1955), and avant-garde film (Antonioni's *L'Avventura*, 1960). U.S. beatniks (Kerouac's *On the Road*, 1957) and others rejected the supposed conformism of Americans (Riesman's *The Lonely Crowd*, 1950).

Rising Expectations and New Protests: 1960-69

Global economy. The longest sustained economic boom on record spanned almost the entire decade in the capitalist world; the closely watched GNP figure doubled (1960-70) in the U.S., fueled by **Vietnam War**-related budget deficits. The **General Agreement on Tariffs and Trade** (1967) stimulated Western European prosperity, which spread to peripheral areas (Spain, Italy, E Germany). Japan became a top economic power. Foreign investment aided the industrialization of Brazil. There were limited Soviet economic reform attempts. Outside the Soviet zone the global economy was marked by the growing role of multinational corporations (3,000 in 1914; 6,000 by 1970). International nongovernmental organizations (NGOs) also multiplied rapidly (Amnesty International, 1961).

Reform and radicalization. Pres. John F. **Kennedy**, inaugurated 1961, emphasized youthful idealism and vigor; his assassination Nov. 22, 1963, was a national trauma. Political and social reform movements took root in U.S. and other countries. Blacks demonstrated nonviolently and with partial success against segregation and poverty (1963 March on Washington; 1964 **Civil Rights Act**), but some urban areas erupted in riots (Watts, 1965; Detroit, 1967; more than 100 cities following **Martin Luther King Jr.** assassination, Apr. 4, 1968). New concern for the poor (Harrington's *Other America*, 1963) helped lead to Pres. Lyndon Johnson's **"Great Society"** programs (Medicare, Water Quality Act, Higher Education Act, all 1965). Concern for the **environment** surged (Carson's *Silent Spring*, 1962).

Feminism revived as a cultural and political movement (Friedan's *Feminine Mystique*, 1963; National Organization for Women founded, 1966), and a movement for homosexual rights emerged (Stonewall riot in NYC, 1969). Pope John XXIII called the **Second Vatican Council** (1962-65), which liberalized Roman Catholic liturgy and some other aspects of Catholicism.

Opposition to U.S. involvement in Vietnam, especially among university students (**Moratorium** protest, Nov. 1969), turned violent (Weatherman Chicago riots, Oct. 1969). **New Left** and Marxist theories became popular, and membership in radical groups (Students for a Democratic Society, Black Panthers) increased. Maoist groups, especially in Europe, called for total transformation of society. In France, students sparked a nationwide strike affecting 10 million workers in May-June 1968.

East Germany in 1961 began construction on a barrier to slow the exodus of its population to West Berlin.

China. China's revolutionary militancy under **Mao** Zedong led to border disputes and other conflict with the USSR under "revisionist" Khrushchev, starting in 1960. The **"Great Proletarian Cultural Revolution"** tried to impose a utopian egalitarian program in China and spread revolution abroad; political struggle, often violent, convulsed China in 1965-68.

Southeast Asia. Communist-led guerrillas aided by N Vietnam fought from 1960 against the S Vietnam government of Ngo Dinh Diem (killed 1963). The U.S. military role increased after the 1964 **Tonkin Gulf** incident. Laotian and Cambodian neutrality were threatened by Communist insurgencies, with N Vietnamese aid, and U.S. intrigues.

Developing world. A bloc of authoritarian leftist regimes among the newly independent nations came to dominate the conference of nonaligned nations (Belgrade, 1961; Cairo, 1964; Lusaka, 1970). Soviet political ties and military bases were established in Cuba, Egypt, Algeria, Guinea, and other countries. Some leaders were ousted in coups by pro-Western groups—Dem. Rep. of the Congo's Patrice Lumumba (killed 1961), Ghana's Kwame Nkrumah (exiled 1966), and Indonesia's Sukarno (effectively ousted in 1965 after a Communist coup failed).

Middle East. Arab-Israeli tension erupted into a brief war June 1967. Israel emerged from the war as a major regional power. Military shipments before and after the war increased Soviet influence in much of the Arab world. Most Arab states broke U.S. diplomatic ties, while Communist countries cut their ties to Israel. Intra-Arab disputes continued: Egypt and Saudi Arabia supported rival factions in a bloody Yemen civil war 1962-70; Lebanese troops fought Palestinian commandos 1969.

Eastern Europe. To stop the large-scale exodus of citizens, E German authorities built (Aug. 1961) a fortified **wall across Berlin** that enclosed West Berlin. Soviet sway in the Balkans was weakened by Albania's realignment with China (USSR broke ties with Albania in Dec. 1961) and Romania's assertion (1964) of limited autonomy. Liberalization (spring 1968) in **Czechoslovakia** was crushed with massive force by troops of five Warsaw Pact countries. W German treaties (1970) with the USSR and Poland facilitated transfer of German technology and confirmed postwar boundaries.

Arts and styles. The boundary between fine and popular arts was blurred to some extent by Pop Art (Warhol) and rock musicals (*Hair*, 1968). Informality and exaggeration prevailed in fashion (beards, miniskirts). A nonpolitical "counterculture" developed, rejecting traditional bourgeois life goals and personal habits, and use of marijuana and hallucinogens spread (**Woodstock** festival, Aug. 1969). **The Beatles** brought unprecedented sophistication to rock music.

Science. The decade saw great scientific and technological progress, epitomized by landing of **U.S. astronauts on the Moon** (July 1969). There were major advances in **electronics** (lasers, integrated circuits), **agriculture** ("green revolution"), **medicine** (heart transplants, 1967), and other areas, as well as attempts to control spread of **nuclear weapons** (1963 Limited Test Ban Treaty, 1968 Nuclear Nonproliferation Treaty).

New Global Balances and Religious Revivals: 1970-79

U.S. trends. The decade was marked by a sluggish economy, energy shortages, and environmental problems. Communist forces' takeover of **South Vietnam** (evacuation of U.S. civilians, Apr. 1975), revelations of **CIA** misdeeds (Rockefeller Commission report, June 1975), and **Watergate** scandal (Nixon resignation, Aug. 1974) reduced faith in U.S. influence and leadership. Social issues spurred controversy—school busing and racial quotas were challenged (**Bakke** case decided by Supreme Court, June 1978), and proposed **Equal Rights Amendment**, sent to states for approval in Mar. 1972, fell short of ratification. **Three Mile Island** nuclear reactor accident (Mar. 1979) reinforced fears of nuclear energy.

Economic woes. The 1960s boom faltered in the 1970s; a severe **recession** in U.S. and Europe (1974-75) followed a huge oil price hike (Dec. 1973), precipitated by the Oct. 1973 Arab **oil embargo**. Monetary instability (U.S. cut ties to gold, 1971), decline of the dollar, and protectionist moves by industrial countries (1977-78) threatened trade. Business investment declined. Severe **inflation** plagued many countries (25% in Britain, 1975; 18% in U.S., 1979).

China readjusts. After the 1976 deaths of **Mao** Zedong and **Zhou** Enlai, relative pragmatists won the struggle for leadership. Orthodox Maoists were purged; Mao's widow and other members of the so-called **Gang of Four** were arrested. New leaders freed many political prisoners. Political and trade ties to Japan, Europe, and the U.S. (Nixon visit, 1972) expanded, as relations with the USSR, Cuba, and Vietnam eventually worsened (four-week invasion by China, 1979). Some ideological restrictions were reversed (bonuses to workers, exams for college entrance allowed, 1977); some restrictions on cultural expression were eased.

Europe. European unity (**EEC-EFTA** trade accord, 1972) faltered as economic problems developed (Britain floated pound, 1972; France floated franc, 1974). Germany and Switzerland curbed guest workers from S Europe, while Greece and Turkey quarreled over Cyprus and Aegean oil rights. The authoritarian regime in **Portugal** was overthrown (Apr. 1974), **Greece**'s seven-year military dictatorship yielded power (July 1974), and **Spain** held free elections (June 1977) after Francisco Franco's death.

A surge of terrorist attacks in **Germany** and elsewhere (1972 **Munich Olympics** killings) raised security concerns. France's Socialist-Communist coalition lost 1978 election bid. Disruptive strikes in **Britain** (1978-79 "winter of discontent") contributed to Labour government defeat in May 1979 elections, bringing Conservative Margaret **Thatcher** to power as UK's first woman prime minister.

Religion and politics. Along with the growth of Arab oil wealth, there was a resurgence of activism, often religiously motivated. Libyan dictator Muammar al-**Qaddafi** mixed Islamic laws with socialism. The illegal **Muslim Brotherhood** in Egypt was accused of violence, while extreme groups bombed (1977) theaters to protest Western and secular values. In **Turkey**, the National Salvation Party became the first Islamic group to win a share in power (1974) since secularization in the 1920s. In **Iran**, Ayatollah Ruhollah **Khomeini** led a revolution that deposed the secular shah (Jan. 1979) and created an Islamic republic. Religiously motivated insurrectionists in **Saudi Arabia** briefly seized (1979) the Grand Mosque in Mecca. Muslim puritan opposition to **Pakistan** Pres. Zulfikar Ali-**Bhutto** contributed to his overthrow in July 1977. Bengali nationalism was a driving force behind a successful fight for the independence of Pakistan's eastern province (**Bangladesh**) in Dec. 1971, after a bloody civil war.

Muslim and Hindu opposition to coerced sterilization in **India** helped defeat the Indira **Gandhi** government, to be replaced (Mar. 1977) by a coalition including Hindu religious parties. Muslims in the S **Philippines**, aided by Libya, rebelled against central rule from 1973. The **Buddhist** Soka Gakkai movement launched (1964) the Komeito party in **Japan**, a major opposition party in 1972 and 1976 elections. Israel's secularist **Israeli** Labor party was ousted in 1977 by conservatives led by Menachem **Begin**; religious militants founded settlements on the disputed **West Bank**, part of biblically promised Israel.

Religious wars raged in **Northern Ireland** (Catholic vs. Protestant, 1969-97) and **Lebanon** (Christian vs. Muslim, 1975-90), while religious militancy complicated the Israel-Arab dispute (1973 Israel-Arab war). The **Camp David Accords**, negotiated in 1978 by Egyptian Pres. Anwar al-**Sadat**, Israeli Prime Min. Menachem **Begin**, and U.S. Pres. Jimmy **Carter**, facilitated landmark 1979 **Egypt-Israel peace treaty**, but increased militancy on the West Bank impeded further progress. **Evangelical Protestant** groups grew in influence in the U.S. Reform **Judaism** in U.S. expanded and ordained first woman rabbi (1972).

Latin America. Right-wing forces strengthened their hold, with a violent coup against the elected (Sept. 1973) leftist **Allende** government in **Chile**, a military coup in **Argentina** (1976), and coups against left-wing regimes in **Bolivia** (1971, 1979) and **Peru** (1976). In Central America, increasing liberal and leftist militancy led to ouster (1979) of the **Somoza** regime of **Nicaragua** and to civil conflict in **El Salvador**.

Southeast Asia. Communist victories in Vietnam, Cambodia, and Laos by May 1975 led to new turmoil. **Pol Pot**'s **Khmer Rouge** regime in **Cambodia** ordered millions to resettle in rural areas, in a program of forced labor and terrorism that cost more than 1 million lives (1975-79) and caused hundreds of thousands to flee. The Vietnamese invasion of Cambodia (1979) swelled the refugee population and contributed to widespread starvation.

Russian expansion. Soviet influence, checked in some countries (troops ousted by **Egypt**, 1972), was projected farther afield (**Angola**, 1975-89; **Ethiopia**, 1977-88). **Détente** with the West—1972 Berlin pact, 1972 strategic arms pact (**SALT**)—was marred in the late 1970s by revelations of Soviet atrocities (Solzhenitsyn's *Gulag Archipelago*, 1974) and the 1979 Soviet invasion of **Afghanistan**.

Africa. The last European colonies won independence (**Spanish Sahara**, 1976; **Djibouti**, 1977), and, after 10 years of civil war, a Black government took over (1979) in **Zimbabwe** (Rhodesia); white domination remained in **South Africa**. Ethnic or tribal conflicts were widespread, with European intervention in local wars (France in **Chad**, **Zaire**, **Mauritania**) and heavy involvement of Cuban troops. Dominant figures included Ugandan dictator Idi **Amin**, toppled in Apr. 1979 after eight years of chaotic rule.

The Vietnam War, in which an estimated 2 million Vietnamese and 58,000 Americans died, ended with the dramatic evacuation of Saigon.

End of the Cold War and Demand for Democracy: 1980-89

Global developments. International contacts accelerated thanks to **new openness** in China (from 1978) and USSR (from 1985). **Global consumerism** was symbolized by rapid spread of McDonald's restaurants (Japan, 1971; Russia, 1990). New forms of home media proliferated (VCRs, personal computers, video gaming systems). HIV/AIDS was identified; WHO estimated 400,000 cases worldwide by 1989.

USSR, Eastern Europe. The late 1980s saw the remaking of the Soviet state and the beginning of the disintegration of the Soviet empire. After the deaths of Gen. Sec. Leonid **Brezhnev** (1982) and two successors, emigration restrictions and repression of dissent were eased. Gen. Sec. Mikhail **Gorbachev** (in office 1985-91) promoted ***glasnost*** and ***perestroika***—economic, political, and social reform. Four Reagan-Gorbachev **summits** (1985-88) yielded the **INF disarmament treaty** (1987; expired 2019). Military withdrawal from **Afghanistan** was completed in Feb. 1989, and the Soviet people chose (Mar. 1989) part of the new Congress of People's Deputies from competing candidates.

In **Poland**, Solidarity, the labor union founded (1980) by Lech **Walesa**, was outlawed in 1982 but legalized in 1988, after years of unrest. Free elections (June 1989) brought in a Walesa adviser as prime minister in a government with the Communists. In fall 1989 failing Marxist economies in **Hungary**, **East Germany**, **Czechoslovakia**, **Bulgaria**, and **Romania** brought the collapse of the Communist monopoly and a demand for democracy. In a historic step, the **Berlin Wall** was opened in Nov. 1989.

U.S. Under Pres. Ronald **Reagan** (1981-88) conservative economic policies yielded budget and tax cuts, deregulation, "junk bond" financing, leveraged buyouts, and mergers. Federal budget deficits rose, and a stock market crash in Oct. 1987 (Black Monday) had global repercussions. Foreign policy took a **strong anti-Communist** turn, with increased defense spending, invasion of Cuba-threatened **Grenada** (Oct. 1983), a **"Star Wars"** missile defense program, and the **Iran-contra scandal**.

Middle East. The Middle East remained militarily unstable, with sharp divisions along economic, political, racial, and religious lines. The 1979 Islamic revolution in **Iran**, bringing Ayatollah Ruhollah **Khomeini** to power, fueled antagonism toward U.S. and the West (**hostage crisis**, Nov. 1979-Jan. 1981; first U.S. sanctions imposed). In Sept. 1980, **Iraq** repudiated its border agreement with Iran, and hostilities between the two countries led to an eight-year war in which hundreds of thousands died. After the death of Khomeini (June 1989), his chosen successor, former Pres. Ali Hosseini **Khamenei**, became Iran's supreme leader, retaining office over the next three decades and beyond. **Libya**'s support for **terrorism** poisoned relations with the West; U.S. closed (1981) its diplomatic mission there and embargoed Libyan oil (1982). Following an attack on a West Berlin disco frequented by U.S. military (Apr. 1986, 3 killed), U.S. bombed targets in Libya.

Israel affirmed (July 1980) all **Jerusalem** as its capital, destroyed (June 1981) an **Iraqi atomic reactor**, and invaded **Lebanon**, citing terrorism from the Palestine Liberation Organization; PLO withdrew from Lebanon after cease-fire.

The Chinese government responded to pro-democracy demonstrations in Tiananmen Square with force (1989).

Palestinian uprising began (Dec. 1987) in Israeli-occupied Gaza and spread to the West Bank; troops responded with force, leaving hundreds dead and thousands in detention camps. Israel began (Feb. 1985) withdrawal from **war-torn Lebanon**; artillery duels (Mar.-Apr. 1989) between Christian East Beirut and Muslim West Beirut left 200 dead.

Latin America. In **Nicaragua**, the leftist **Sandinista** National Liberation Front, in power after the 1979 civil war, gave military aid to guerrillas in El Salvador, while U.S. aided anti-Sandinista **contras**, utilizing profits from secret arms sales to Iran (**Iran-contra scandal**), and the **CIA** directed the mining of Nicaraguan ports. In **El Salvador**, a military coup (Oct. 1979) failed to halt a leftist insurgency armed by Cuba and Nicaragua. Salvadoran Archbishop Oscar **Romero**, advocate for poor, was assassinated Mar. 1980; right-wing death squads killed thousands in ensuing decade of civil war. In **Chile**, Gen. Augusto **Pinochet**—in power since 1973, and known for harsh measures against leftists and dissidents—yielded the presidency after elections (Dec. 1989) but remained head of the army. In **Panama**, U.S. troops overthrew dictator Manuel **Noriega** (Dec. 1989); later convicted on drug and human rights charges, he served time in the U.S., France, and Panama.

Africa. African countries suffered severe hardship, fueled by accelerating desertification, heavy foreign debt, worldwide recession, rapid population growth, and wars and political instability. Some 60 million Africans faced prolonged hunger in 1981, and severe **drought** in 1983 left one-third of the population, or about 150 million, near **famine**. Western nations sent aid, and **Live Aid**, a marathon rock concert (July 1985), raised relief funds. Wars in **Ethiopia** and **Sudan** and military strife in several other nations continued.

Anti-apartheid sentiment gathered force in **South Africa**, with demonstrations meeting violent police response. White voters approved (Nov. 1983) the first constitution to give Asians and people of mixed-race backgrounds a voice, while still excluding the Black majority. Twelve nations imposed economic **sanctions** in Aug.-Sept. 1985, and Pres. P. W. **Botha** was succeeded (Sept. 1989) by F.W. **de Klerk**, who promised negotiation with the Black population.

Asia and Pacific. Benazir **Bhutto** became the first woman to lead a majority-Muslim nation as prime minister of **Pakistan** (Dec. 1988). "People power" revolt in the **Philippines** ousted Ferdinand **Marcos** (Feb. 1986) after two decades as president; he was replaced by Corazon **Aquino**. Trade imbalances favoring **Japan** dominated that nation's foreign relations.

During the 1980s **China**'s Communist government and paramount leader **Deng** Xiaoping expanded ties to the West and the role of market forces. But in Apr. 1989 pro-democracy demonstrators camped out in **Tiananmen Square**, Beijing, and peaceful protest marches spread to at least 20 other cities. Troops and tanks crushed the demonstration in and around Tiananmen Square (June 3-4), leaving an estimated 500-7,000 dead; up to 10,000 were arrested, 31 tried and executed. The conciliatory Communist Party chief was ousted; the Politburo adopted (1989) reforms against official corruption.

Europe. With the addition of Greece, Portugal, and Spain, the **European Community** became a common market of more than 300 million people. In the UK, Conservative Margaret **Thatcher** won three elections (1979, 1983, 1987) to serve as prime minister; she pursued a policy of deregulation and privatization, and presided over British victory in the 1982 **Falklands war**. **France** elected (1981) its first socialist president, François **Mitterrand** (reelected, 1988). Elections in 1983 brought **Italy** its first socialist premier, Bettino **Craxi**.

International terrorism. With the 1979 overthrow of the shah of **Iran** and instability in the **Middle East** and elsewhere, terrorism became a prominent tactic. In 1979-81, Iranian militants held 52 **U.S. hostages** in Iran for 444 days. In Oct. 1983, in **Lebanon**, truck bombs exploded at U.S. Marine headquarters, killing 241 Americans, and at a French paratrooper barracks, killing 58. The ***Achille Lauro*** cruise ship was hijacked in Oct. 1985. **Assassinated leaders** included Egypt's Pres. Anwar al-**Sadat** (1981), India's Prime Min. Indira **Gandhi** (1984), and Lebanese Prem. Rashid **Karami** (1987).

New Regional Tensions in a Post-Cold War World: 1990-99

Soviet Empire collapse. Breakup of the Soviet Union into 15 independent states began with declarations of independence by **Lithuania**, **Latvia**, and **Estonia** during abortive coup against Mikhail **Gorbachev** (Aug. 1991). Other republics followed. In Dec. 1991, **Russia**, **Ukraine**, and **Belarus** declared the Soviet Union dead; Gorbachev resigned. The **Warsaw Pact** and Council for Mutual Economic Assistance (**Comecon**) disbanded. Most former Soviet republics joined in loose confederation (**Commonwealth of Independent States**). Hardship ensued as Russia, under Pres. Boris **Yeltsin**, moved to reboot the economy under a free-market system. When the Muslim-majority Russian republic of **Chechnya** declared independence, Russian forces invaded (Dec. 1994), causing massive destruction and civilian casualties before withdrawing after a 1996 cease-fire. In 1999, Russia forcibly suppressed Muslim insurgents in Russian republic of **Dagestan** and again invaded Chechnya, with heavy civilian casualties. **Yeltsin** resigned Russia's presidency, Dec. 1999, with Prime Min. Vladimir **Putin** becoming acting president.

Europe. **Yugoslavia** broke apart, and hostilities ensued along ethnic and religious lines. **Croatia**, **Slovenia**, and **Macedonia** declared independence (1991), followed by **Bosnia-Herzegovina** (1992). **Serbia** and **Montenegro** remained as the republic of Yugoslavia. Bitter fighting followed, especially in Bosnia; Serbian forces laid siege to the town of **Srebrenica**, slaughtering more than 7,000 Bosnian Muslim men and boys (July 1995), and expelling some 20,000 people in an **ethnic cleansing** of the Muslim population; peace plan (**Dayton accord**, reached Nov. 1995) was brokered by the U.S., with **NATO** policing its implementation. In spring 1999, NATO conducted a bombing campaign aimed at stopping Yugoslavia from driving ethnic Albanians from the **Kosovo** region; a June accord brought in NATO peacekeepers.

The **two Germanys were reunited** after 45 years, in Oct. 1990. Czechoslovakia broke apart (Jan. 1993) into the **Czech Republic** and **Slovakia**. Labor leader Lech **Walesa** was elected president of **Poland** (Dec. 1991). In Jan. 1994, NATO approved the **Partnership for Peace**, coordinating defense of E and Central European countries; Russia later joined. NATO signed pact with **Russia** (May 1997) allowing for NATO expansion into former Soviet-bloc countries; Czech Republic, **Hungary**, and **Poland** joined NATO in Jan. 1999. Efforts toward European unity continued with adoption of a single market (Jan. 1993) and conversion of the European Community to the **European Union** as the **Maastricht Treaty** took effect (Nov. 1993). The **euro** was launched as common currency, Jan. 1999, initially only for non-cash uses, in 12 EU countries.

An intraparty revolt forced Margaret **Thatcher** out as UK prime minister, to be succeeded by John **Major** (Nov. 1990); Labour took power under Tony **Blair** (May 1997). Prince **Charles** and **Diana** divorced (Aug. 1996); Diana died in car crash a year later. Talks on **Northern Ireland** led to **peace plan**, approved in all-Ireland vote (May 1998). In Dec. 1999, Northern Ireland was granted home rule. Voters in **Scotland** (overwhelmingly) and **Wales** (narrowly) approved creation of regional legislatures (1997). In **France**, socialist Pres. François **Mitterrand** declined to run for a third term and conservative Jacques **Chirac** was elected (May 1995) to the office.

Middle East. In Aug. 1990, **Iraq's Saddam Hussein** ordered troops to invade **Kuwait**. A UN-approved international force, led by U.S., bombed Iraq (Jan. 1991) and launched a land attack, crushing the invasion. After a cease-fire, agreed to, Apr. 1991, the UN extended sanctions on Iraq for failure to abide by its terms. Iraq's reported failure to cooperate with UN inspectors seeking to eliminate **weapons of mass destruction** led to airstrikes by U.S. and Britain (1998).

Israel and the **PLO** signed peace accord (Sept. 1993) providing for Palestinian self-government in **West Bank** and **Gaza** Strip; Prime Min. Yitzhak **Rabin** and Foreign Min. Shimon **Peres** of Israel and Yasir **Arafat** of the PLO shared 1994 Nobel Peace Prize. Six Arab nations relaxed boycott against Israel (1994), and Israel and **Jordan** signed peace treaty (Oct. 1994). Rabin was assassinated (Nov. 1995) by an Israeli extremist; Benjamin **Netanyahu** became prime minister (May 1996).

Asia and Pacific. Longtime **North Korean** dictator **Kim Il Sung** died (July 1994) and was succeeded by son **Kim Jong Il**. In Oct. 1994 North Korea signed agreement with U.S. setting timetable for ending **nuclear weapons** program (deal collapsed in 2002). Well over 200,000 (perhaps more than 2 million) North Koreans died in the 1990s from **famine**. **Palau** achieved independence, Oct. 1994. **Hong Kong** was returned to **China** (July 1997), after 156 years as a British colony, and **Macau** reverted to China (Dec. 1999) after over 400 years of Portuguese rule. **Jiang** Zemin, general secretary of the Chinese Communist Party, also became China's president (Mar. 1993). China released several well-known dissidents but continued to jail and execute many. U.S. and China signed trade pact (Nov. 1999). In **Japan** members of a religious cult released the nerve gas sarin on **Tokyo subway**, killing 12 and injuring over 5,500 (Mar. 1995).

After years of growing prosperity, **Thailand**, **Indonesia**, and **South Korea** in 1997 began to suffer economic reverses, with worldwide ripple effect, and received IMF **bailout** packages. In Indonesia, protests over mismanagement led to the resignation of Pres. **Suharto** (May 1998) after 32 years of rule. In a referendum (Aug. 1999), **East Timorese** voted for independence; pro-Indonesian militias rampaged, but a multinational peacekeeping force helped restore order (Sept. 1999).

In **Afghanistan** the radical Islamist **Taliban** gained control of Kabul (Sept. 1996) and, eventually, most of the country. **Indian** forces repeatedly clashed with pro-independence demonstrators in the disputed majority-Muslim region of **Kashmir**, exacerbating relations with **Pakistan**. India and Pakistan both conducted **nuclear tests** in 1998. Conflict between government and the military led to a **bloodless coup** in Pakistan (Oct. 1999).

Africa. **South Africa**'s Pres. F. W. **de Klerk** released dissident Black leader Nelson **Mandela** from prison (Feb. 1990) after 27 years, and the white minority government repealed **apartheid** laws (1990, 1991); also dismantled its **nuclear weapons** program. The African National Congress won in multiracial elections (Apr. 1994), making Mandela president, and a new constitution became law (Dec. 1996). **Namibia** became independent in Mar. 1990, after long UN trusteeship. **Eritrea** won independence from **Ethiopia**, July 1993, after over 30 years of war. **Mobutu** Sese Seko, longtime ruler of **Zaire**, was deposed (May 1997) by rebel forces under Laurent **Kabila**, who changed country's name back to **Democratic Republic of the Congo**. In **Nigeria**, former Gen. Olusegun **Obasanjo** was elected (Feb. 1999) as the nation's first civilian leader in 15 years.

Civil war broke out in **Liberia** (Dec. 1989) and lasted, with interruptions, through the 1990s and beyond, leaving hundreds of thousands dead. Factional fighting erupted in **Somalia** (Jan. 1991); a U.S.-led UN peacekeeping force failed to restore order and left (Mar. 1995). In **Algeria**, the army canceled parliamentary elections (Jan. 1992) when the Islamic party won a first round; after ensuing civil war, a peace and amnesty plan was approved in a Sept. 1999 referendum. Assassination of **Burundi**'s president (June 1993) renewed ethnic violence between **Hutus** and **Tutsis** there. A suspicious plane crash that killed the

South Africa abandoned apartheid and transitioned to a nonracial democratic government, with Nelson Mandela (pictured, with U.S. Pres. Bill Clinton) elected president in 1994.

presidents of Burundi and Rwanda (Apr. 1994) led to **genocide** in **Rwanda**; some 800,000 died, mostly Tutsis massacred by Hutu militias.

North America. U.S. Pres. Bill **Clinton** (D) (elected 1992, 1996) presided over growing economy, promoted free trade, intervened in Bosnia. Impeached by House (Dec. 1998) on charges stemming from affair with intern, he was acquitted by the Senate. In **Canada**, Liberal Jean **Chrétien** became prime minister (Nov. 1993; reelected 1997). The Canadian territory of **Nunavut** was created, Apr. 1999. In **Mexico**, Ernesto **Zedillo** of the ruling PRI party was elected president (July 1994) after PRI's first candidate was assassinated. The country weathered a **monetary crisis** with the help of a 1995 U.S. bailout. The North American Free Trade Agreement (**NAFTA**), liberalizing trade between U.S., Canada, and Mexico, took effect Jan. 1994. Globalization trends drew protests from radical activists (**World Trade Org.** meeting, Nov.-Dec. 1999).

Central America and Caribbean. In **Haiti**, Jean-Bertrand **Aristide** was elected president, Dec. 1990; ousted in Sept. 1991 military coup, he was restored to office (Oct. 1994) through U.S.-led negotiations. In Feb. 1990 elections in **Nicaragua** the opposition won a surprise victory over **Sandinista** Pres. Daniel **Ortega**. A 12-year civil war in **El Salvador** ended with peace treaty, Jan. 1992, between government and leftist rebels. In Dec. 1999, Panama assumed full control of the **Panama Canal**, in accord with 1977 treaty with U.S.

South America. Alberto **Fujimori** was elected president of **Peru** in June 1990; condemned for human rights abuses but popular for reducing terrorism; reelected in 1995. Leftist guerrillas took hostages in Lima (Dec. 1996); one hostage killed during rescue operation (Apr. 1997). Peronist Pres. Carlos Saúl **Menem** was **Argentina**'s president for much of the decade, imposing economic austerity. Former **Chilean** Pres. Augusto **Pinochet** was arrested in London (Oct. 1998) and charged with human-rights violations but judged unfit for trial. In **Brazil**, Fernando Henrique **Cardoso** was elected president (Oct. 1994) and reelected in 1998 despite economic slump; the IMF announced a $42-billion aid package (Nov. 1998). In **Venezuela** two coups were thwarted (1992), but leftist coup leader Hugo **Chávez** was elected president, Dec. 1998.

Terrorism. A bomb exploded in garage beneath New York City's **World Trade Center**, killing six (Feb. 1993); six Islamic fundamentalists were convicted. Bombs outside U.S. embassies in **Kenya** and **Tanzania** killed over 220 (Aug. 1998); U.S. retaliated with airstrikes in Afghanistan and Sudan. Anti-government U.S. radicals bombed a federal building in **Oklahoma City**, OK (Apr. 1995), killing 168.

Science, technology, environment. Hubble Space Telescope was launched, Apr. 1990. U.S. space shuttle ***Atlantis*** docked with the orbiting Russian space station ***Mir*** (June 1995) in first of several joint missions. In Nov. 1998 the first component for a new **International Space Station** was launched into space from Kazakhstan. Scottish scientists announced (Feb. 1997) **cloning** of a sheep. Tim **Berners-Lee** launched first **World Wide Web** server (1990); user-friendly graphical browsers (Mosaic, 1993; Netscape, 1994) and consumer internet service providers followed, beginning a global transformation of communications and information access. Efforts to limit **global climate change** intensified with tentative agreements adopted in **Kyoto**, Japan (Dec. 1997). In 1999, World Health Org. announced 33 million people were living with **HIV**, and **AIDS** was fourth leading cause of death worldwide (No. 1 cause in Africa), with an estimated 14 million deaths since the epidemic began.

Globalization and Global Realignments: 2000-09

Terrorism. In Oct. 2000, 17 U.S. Navy sailors were killed aboard the USS *Cole* in Aden, **Yemen**, in suicide bombing tied to **al-Qaeda** terrorist network, based in Afghanistan. Hijackers on Sept. 11, 2001, crashed two jetliners into the twin towers of the **World Trade Center** in New York City and another into the **Pentagon** outside Washington, DC, with a fourth crashing in a Pennsylvania field. The attacks, linked to al-Qaeda and its leader, **Osama bin Laden**, killed nearly 3,000.

The attacks of Sept. 11, 2001, killed more than 2,750 people in New York.

Islamic radicals also planted a car bomb on the Indonesian island of **Bali** (Oct. 2002; over 200 killed) and bombed mass transit systems in **Madrid** (Mar. 2004; some 200 killed), **London** (July 2005; 56 killed), and **Mumbai** (July 2006; over 180 killed). Jihadists in Mumbai attacked sites frequented by foreigners in Nov. 2008 (over 160 died). **Chechen** separatist guerrillas were implicated in an attack on a **Moscow** movie theater (Oct. 2002; at least 120 hostages died) and takeover of a school in Beslan (Sept. 2004; over 330 killed). Bombing attacks on **Yazidi** towns in **Iraq** (Aug. 2007) killed at least 500.

Economic crisis. Rapid economic growth in **China** and other developing countries contrasted with sluggish rates in traditional economic powers. A global **recession**, beginning in late 2007, combined with **financial meltdown** (Sept. 2008). **Iceland**'s banking system collapsed (Oct. 2008); rescued by loans and austerity. **Dubai**'s state-controlled investment company was bailed out (Dec. 2009) by Abu Dhabi. Soaring food and fuel prices sparked unrest in **Egypt** and **Haiti** (Apr. 2008). **Austerity** measures spurred protests in Europe.

War in Iraq and Afghanistan. The U.S., with the UK, invaded **Iraq** (Mar. 2003) to oust the regime of Saddam **Hussein**. U.S. Pres. George W. **Bush** declared major combat ended by May, but insurgents caused continuing casualties. Though cited as grounds for the invasion, **weapons of mass destruction** were not found. Hussein was captured by U.S. troops (Dec. 2003) and executed by Iraq (2006) for crimes against humanity. Iraqi **elections** led to a **Shiite coalition government** under Prime Min. Nouri al-**Maliki** (May 2006). With **insurgent** violence intensifying, Bush announced (Jan. 2007) a **"surge"** of additional U.S. troops; casualties fell sharply, aided by changing sectarian aims. In **Afghanistan**, a U.S.-led military coalition ousted the **Taliban** regime. A transitional government was installed (Dec. 2001), and NATO assumed control of multinational forces (Aug. 2003).

Afghans elected Hamid **Karzai** president (Nov. 2004; reelected 2009); Taliban and other Islamist militants stepped up attacks.

Middle East. **Palestinian suicide bombings** continued, and **Israel** mounted a major offensive (Mar. 2002), reoccupying much of the **West Bank**. The U.S., Russia, UN, and EU introduced (Apr. 2003) **"road map"** for peace negotiations, but made little progress. After Palestinian leader Yasir **Arafat** died (Nov. 2004), Mahmoud **Abbas** was elected in his place; in Jan. 2006 the militant Palestinian party **Hamas** won a parliamentary majority. Israel launched attacks on **Lebanon** (July 2006) after a raid by Lebanon-based **Hezbollah** guerrillas, and in reaction to **Hamas** launched an offensive in the **Gaza Strip** (Dec. 2008), with heavy Palestinian casualties. Feb. 2009 elections in Israel led to a coalition government headed by conservative former Prime Min. Benjamin **Netanyahu**. In **Yemen**, U.S. used drones to kill suspected **al-Qaeda** terrorists (Nov. 2002), and the government, from 2004 onward, battled a growing insurgency from **Shiite Houthi** rebels, believed aided by Iran.

Asia and Pacific. Gen. Pervez **Musharraf**, brought to power in Oct. 1999 coup, assumed **Pakistan**'s presidency, June 2001; former Prime Min. Benazir **Bhutto** was assassinated, Dec. 2007. Riots in the mostly Hindu state of Gujarat, **India** (Feb.-Apr. 2002), left more than 1,200 dead, mostly Muslims. Pakistan and **India** restored ties (May 2003) and declared cease-fire in disputed **Kashmir** (Nov. 2003); relations remained tense.

Leaders of **North** and **South Korea** met (June 2000) in first-ever summit. But North Korea withdrew from nuclear nonproliferation treaty Jan. 2003. The country agreed, Feb. 2007, to end **nuclear weapons** development in exchange for aid, but reneged in 2009. East Timor (**Timor-Leste**) achieved independence, May 2002. In **China**, **Hu** Jintao succeeded **Jiang** Zemin as party chief (Nov. 2002) and president (Mar. 2003).

The UN Intl. Atomic Energy Agency (IAEA) censured **Iran** (Dec. 2003) for covering up aspects of its nuclear program; UN sanctions imposed, Dec. 2006, after Iran continued enriching uranium. Hardline Pres. Mahmoud **Ahmadinejad** was declared landslide winner in June 2009 Iranian elections widely perceived as rigged; massive protests were crushed, with dozens killed, hundreds jailed, some tortured. In **Kyrgyzstan**, protests (Mar. 2005) against election fraud brought down Pres. Askar **Akayev** in **"tulip revolution." Myanmar**'s military junta cracked down on hundreds of thousands of protesters (Sept. 2007). In **Australia** the center-left Labor Party won landslide victory in Nov. 2007 elections. **Tamil** guerrillas in **Sri Lanka**, soundly defeated in bloody battles against government forces, ended their rebellion (May 2009), which in 26 years had claimed at least 80,000 lives.

In Dec. 2004 a **tsunami** devastated Indian Ocean nations, leaving some 228,000 dead. **Earthquakes** struck the Indian subcontinent (Oct. 2005; nearly 80,000 died) and China's Sichuan province (May 2008; nearly 70,000 died). Over 80,000 died in a May 2008 **cyclone** in Myanmar.

Europe. The **European Union** admitted 12 E European nations by Jan. 2007. Voters in France and Netherlands rejected treaty to establish a new EU constitution (May-June 2005); modified plan (**Treaty of Lisbon**) came into force Dec. 2009. **Yugoslav** strongman Slobodan **Milosevic** yielded power in Oct. 2000 and died, Mar. 2006, while on trial for **war crimes**. **Serbia** and **Montenegro** separated into two independent nations, May-June 2006. **Kosovo** declared independence, Feb. 2008.

Vladimir **Putin**, elected Mar. 2000, began long tenure as Russian president, interrupted (2008-12) when his protégé, Dmitri **Medvedev**, held that office. Russians captured capital of **Chechnya** (Feb. 2000) and established direct rule, but the insurgency continued. In **Ukraine**, a tainted presidential runoff election (Nov. 2004) led to the country's "orange revolution"; recount gave power to nationalist Viktor **Yushchenko**.

British Labour Prime Min. Tony **Blair** won reelection twice (2001, 2005). Angela **Merkel**, of the center-right Christian Democratic Union, began (Nov. 2005) her long tenure as German chancellor. Riots broke out in **France**'s immigrant community, Nov. 2005. French voters elected conservative Nicolas **Sarkozy** president (May 2007), and France rejoined **NATO** military command (Apr. 2009) after more than 40 years.

Vladimir Putin is sworn in as Russia's president May 7, 2000, pledging to restore Russia as a great world power.

Netherlands became first country to legalize **same-sex marriage**, effective Apr. 2001.

Africa. **Ethiopia** and **Eritrea** signed peace treaty (Dec. 2000), ending two-year border war, but clashes continued. Laurent **Kabila**, president of Dem. Rep. of the Congo (**DRC**), was assassinated, Jan. 2001. A peace agreement in DRC (Apr. 2003) did not end violence there. Pres. Charles **Taylor** went into exile (Aug. 2003) in deal to end 14-year civil war in **Liberia**; other accords aimed at ending civil wars in **Angola** (Apr. 2002) and **Côte d'Ivoire** (Jan. 2003). In **Sudan** the Muslim-led government and rebels from the Christian south signed power-sharing agreement, Jan. 2005. Rebellion in the **Darfur** area of W Sudan led to large-scale violence, especially by Arab militias (**janjaweed**) reportedly backed by the government; over 2 million people were displaced and 300,000 killed. The Intl. Criminal Court issued an arrest warrant for Sudanese Pres. Omar al-**Bashir** for war crimes (Mar. 2009), to no avail. Disputed elections sparked violence in **Kenya** (Jan. 2008) and **Zimbabwe** (Apr. 2008). Under longtime Pres. Robert **Mugabe**, Zimbabwe sustained soaring unemployment and hyperinflation. **Guinea-Bissau**'s defense chief and president were assassinated, Mar. 2009.

Americas and the Caribbean. George W. **Bush** (R) served as U.S. president, 2001-09, after close election. He pursued wars in Afghanistan and Iraq following Sept. 2001 terror attack. Barack **Obama** (D), first-ever Black U.S. president, elected in 2008, pledged to end Afghanistan and Iraq conflicts. The long-supreme Institutional Revolutionary Party (**PRI**) lost power in **Mexico** with election of center-right presidents Vicente

Fox (2000) and Felipe **Calderón** (2006); drug violence claimed over 30,000 lives. After 12 years in power, **Canada**'s Liberal Party was defeated in Jan. 2006 elections.

Leftists held power in **Chile** under Ricardo **Lagos** Escobar (from 2000) and Michelle **Bachelet** (from 2006), in **Brazil** under Luiz Inácio **Lula** da Silva (elected 2002; reelected 2006), and in **Bolivia** under Evo **Morales** (elected 2005). In **Venezuela**, leftist populist Pres. Hugo **Chávez** regained power after a failed coup (2002). Peronist Néstor **Kirchner** was elected president of **Argentina** (Apr. 2003); his wife **Cristina** was elected (2007) to succeed him. In **Honduras**, leftist leader Manuel **Zelaya** was elected president (Nov. 2005) but was ousted by the military (June 2009). In **Nicaragua** Sandinista leader Daniel **Ortega** won back the presidency, Nov. 2006, and strengthened ties with Cuba and Iran.

In **Peru**, right-wing Pres. Alberto **Fujimori** was reelected (May 2000) but fled the country; he was extradited (2007) and convicted on human rights and corruption charges. **Haiti** was wracked by antigovernment protests, leading to resignation of Jean-Bertrand **Aristide** in Feb. 2004; a UN peacekeeping mission was brought in. Ailing Pres. **Fidel Castro**, **Cuba**'s strongman leader since 1959, ceded powers (July 2006) to his brother, **Raúl**.

Religion. **John Paul II** died, Apr. 2005, after 26 years as pope; German Cardinal Joseph Ratzinger succeeded him, under the name **Benedict XVI**. The Catholic Church was shaken by **sexual abuse scandal**.

Science and technology. The U.S. **space shuttle** ***Columbia*** broke up on reentering Earth's atmosphere (Feb. 2003), killing seven crewmembers. NASA landed two rovers, *Spirit* and *Opportunity*, on **Mars** (Jan. 2004); **China** launched its first manned space flight, Oct. 2003. **Internet** penetration and access to technology expanded exponentially; online commerce, use of **social media** (Facebook, 2004; Twitter, 2006), mobile computing (iPhone, 2007), and file-sharing services became common.

Environment and health. Under the **Kyoto Protocol** (effective Feb. 2005), most industrialized nations agreed to specific reductions in emissions of **greenhouse gases** linked to global warming. Worldwide **AIDS** estimates showed (Nov. 2007) new infections had peaked in the late 1990s. A pandemic of **swine flu**, or influenza A (H1N1), broke out in **Mexico** (Apr. 2009) and spread, killing more than 150,000.

Searching for Resolutions: 2010-19

Middle East. UN General Assembly granted observer-state status to **Palestine** (Nov. 2012). **Israel** launched airstrikes on **Gaza** (July-Aug. 2014) after sustaining rocket attacks; heavy Palestinian casualties were recorded.

Poverty, religious and ethnic conflict, and government corruption and repression fueled revolts against entrenched Arab regimes ("**Arab Spring**"), yielding mixed results. In **Tunisia**, protests forced out Pres. Zine al-Abidine **Ben Ali** (Jan. 2011); elections and a new constitution followed. In **Egypt**, mass demonstrations led to overthrow of longtime Pres. Hosni **Mubarak** (Feb. 2011), but the elected **Muslim Brotherhood**-dominated government fell in a military coup, July 2013; coup leader Abdel Fattah al-**Sisi** was elected president (May 2014). In **Libya**, insurgents backed by NATO overthrew Muammar al-**Qaddafi**, who was killed (Oct. 2011), but Libya became a battleground for rival Islamist factions and a hub for extralegal migration to Europe. In **Yemen**, Pres. Ali Abdullah **Saleh** yielded power, Feb. 2012, after protests; **Houthi** rebels, backed by Iran, took over the capital, Sept. 2014. A **Saudi**-led coalition of Arab states (Mar. 2015) launched bombings against Houthi, with massive casualties. In Oct. 2018 Saudi dissident journalist Jamal **Khashoggi** was killed inside Saudi consulate in Istanbul; a 2021 CIA report implicated the Saudi crown prince.

In **Iraq**, U.S. military left, Dec. 2011. Death toll, 2003-11: about 4,500 U.S. service members, 300 from allied countries, over 100,000 civilians. Government forces and Shia militia continued to fight the Sunni extremist Islamic State in Iraq and Syria (**ISIS**). U.S. and allies conducted airstrikes against ISIS and sent in advisers; separatist **Kurds** fought ISIS on the ground. ISIS imposed strict Islamic law, murdered minorities and resisters, and sponsored terrorism, but by Dec. 2017 was routed from virtually all its territory in Iraq.

Ashraf **Ghani** was sworn in, Sept. 2014, as president of **Afghanistan**, in power-sharing government (reelected 2020). U.S. and NATO ended combat operations against Taliban insurgents, Dec. 2014, but troops remained in support roles. In **Syria**, Pres. Bashar al-**Assad**, Mar. 2011, launched offensive against protesters, giving rise to **civil war**. After about 1,400 people died in **chemical attacks**, the government, Sept. 2013, agreed to a Russian-backed plan for surrender of chemical weapons; fighting and sporadic chemical attacks continued. U.S.-backed rebels conquered last remnant of **ISIS** territory in Syria, Mar. 2019.

Iran, July 2015, accepted multinational agreement to cut back **nuclear weapons** capability in return for lifting of sanctions and release of over $100 bil in frozen assets; U.S. withdrew from agreement, 2018, and Iran reduced compliance. Iran was shaken by antigovernment protests, Nov. 2019 (many allegedly tortured, hundreds killed).

Terrorism. Despite killing of leader Osama **bin Laden**, in U.S. raid in **Pakistan** (May 2011), **al-Qaeda** remained entrenched along Afghan-Pakistan border, while **ISIS** and al-Qaeda affiliates were active on a wide scale. **Al-Shabab** militants were behind Oct. 2017 bombings in **Somalia** and repeated attacks in **Kenya**. In **Yemen**, al-Qaeda in the Arabian Peninsula (**AQAP**) attacked military parade rehearsal (May 2012). **Boko Haram** jihadists abducted over 200 schoolgirls in **Nigeria** (Apr. 2014). **Taliban** gunmen in **Pakistan** attacked a Peshawar school (Dec. 2014).

Terrorists possibly linked to AQAP killed 17 in and around **Paris**, Jan. 2015, most at offices of a magazine considered hostile to Islam. Jihadists linked to ISIS murdered 130 in or near Paris, Nov. 2015. Islamists also launched attacks in **U.S.**, **Belgium**, **Tunisia**, **Egypt**, **Turkey**, and **Sri Lanka**.

An anti-Muslim extremist killed 77 people in **Norway**, July 2011, and a white supremacist killed over 50 at two mosques in **New Zealand**, Mar. 2019.

Europe. The EU, with IMF help, provided loans to bail out **Greece** (beginning May 2010). Also receiving **bailouts** were **Ireland** (2010), **Portugal** (2011), **Spain** (2013), and **Cyprus** (2013). **Croatia** became 28th EU member, July 2013; **Lithuania** became 19th nation to adopt the **euro**, Jan. 2015. Millions of **migrants**, from Mideast and Africa, sought asylum in Europe; thousands drowned attempting to cross the Mediterranean. Migrant influx helped fuel **anti-EU sentiment** and support for right-wing parties.

Apr. 2010 elections in **Hungary** brought right-wing former Prime Min. Viktor **Orbán** back into office (reelected 2014, 2018). Conservatives returned to power in **UK**, under David

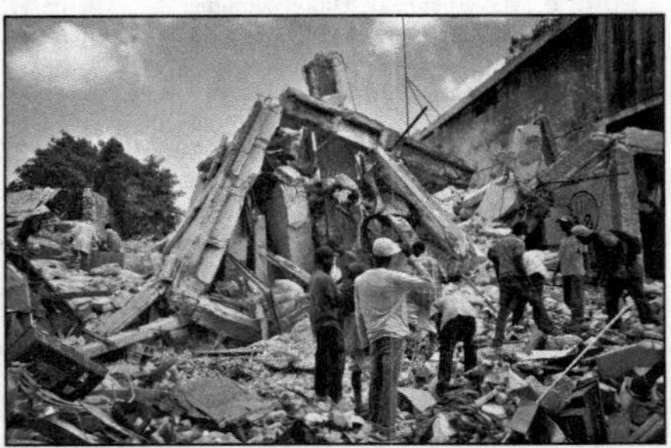

In one of the deadliest natural disasters in history, over 300,000 people were killed in a massive earthquake in Haiti (2010).

Fleeing violence, overcrowded camps, or poverty in Northern Africa, the Middle East, and Afghanistan, millions of refugees and migrants sought refuge in Europe in a wave that peaked 2014-16.

Cameron, May 2010, but he resigned after British voters, in a June 2016 referendum, opted to leave the EU (**"Brexit"**). His successor, Conservative Prime Min. Theresa **May**, left office over her Brexit plan, but Conservatives, led by Boris **Johnson**, won a big majority in a snap general election (Dec. 2019), and Parliament approved his Brexit agreement.

Emmanuel **Macron** was elected president of **France**, May 2017; **"yellow-vest"** mass protests followed, initially targeting fuel-tax hike. In **Turkey**, Recep Tayyip **Erdogan**, prime minister since 2003, was term-limited. But elected president (2014, 2018); he expanded presidential powers, cracked down on opposition following a July 2016 coup attempt (160,000 jailed), and launched offensives against Kurds in N Syria. ETA, the **Basque** separatist group responsible for over 800 deaths in **Spain** over some 40 years, announced its dissolution, May 2018.

After an interregnum as prime minister, Vladimir **Putin** was reelected as **Russia**'s president (Mar. 2012), beginning what was to be a long tenure. He sent troops to annex Ukrainian territory of **Crimea**, Mar. 2014.

Hundreds were arrested in Russian anti-corruption protests, June 2017. Pro-Russian Viktor **Yanukovych**, elected president of **Ukraine** in Feb. 2010, fled in Feb. 2014 after mass protests. War soon broke out in E Ukraine between Ukrainian forces and pro-Russian separatists, aided by Russia.

Ireland became first country to legalize **same-sex marriage** by popular vote, May 2015. Over 20 years after the **Srebrenica massacre** in **Bosnia**, former Bosnian Serb leader Radovan **Karadzic** (Mar. 2016) and commander Ratko **Mladic** (Nov. 2017) were convicted of war crimes.

Asia and Pacific. An **earthquake** and **tsunami** (Mar. 2011) struck **Japan**, killing more than 16,000 and leading to meltdowns at nuclear reactors. Over 8,500 were killed in two earthquakes in **Nepal** (Apr.-May 2015); over 2,000 in **Indonesia** quake and tsunami (Sept. 2018).

Kyrgyzstan's president was ousted, Apr. 2010, after clashes with protesters; up to 2,000 killed in ethnic violence; voters (Dec. 2016) approved strengthening executive power. In **Kazakhstan**, autocratic Pres. Nursultan **Nazarbayev**, in office since 1990, resigned, Mar. 2019, but retained some power.

North Korean dictator **Kim Jong Il** died, Dec. 2011; his son and successor **Kim Jong Un** resumed missile tests, leading to international sanctions. In **Indonesia, Joko Widodo** was elected president, July 2014 (reelected 2019), and introduced reforms.

In **South Korea**, Pres. **Park** Geun-hye was removed, Mar. 2017 (later convicted of corruption); replaced by center-left **Moon** Jae-in. Moon and Kim met in historic summits, Apr.-Sept. 2018. **Myanmar**'s military-backed party lost Nov. 2015 election to party of dissident leader Aung San **Suu Kyi**, but sectarian and government violence against **Rohingya** Muslims surged.

In **China**, **Xi** Jinping succeeded **Hu** Jintao as Communist party chief, Nov. 2012, and president, Mar. 2013; term limit on presidency removed, Mar. 2018. Mass demonstrations in **Hong Kong** opposed new anti-democratic policies ("umbrella" protests, 2014; extradition law protests, from Apr. 2019). UN human rights panel (Aug. 2018) denounced China's mass confinement of **Uyghur** minorities. First reported cases of new coronavirus known aa **COVID-19** emerged in **Wuhan**, China, Dec. 2019.

Hindu nationalists won majority in May 2014 elections in **India**; Narendra **Modi** became prime minister (reelected 2019). Anti-crime hardliner Rodrigo **Duterte** was elected **Philippines** president, May 2016; thousands of alleged drug dealers and users were killed in Duterte **anti-drug campaign**.

Thailand's King **Bhumibol** Adulyadej died Oct. 2016, ending 70-year reign; new king **Vajiralongkorn** signed army-drafted constitution. In **Japan**, Prince **Naruhito** acceded to the throne, May 2019, following abdication of Emperor **Akihito**.

Trans-Pacific Partnership (TPP), trade pact covering 12 Pacific nations, was signed Feb. 2016; after new U.S. administration repudiated it, remaining nations signed replacement, Mar. 2018.

Africa. Coups ousted **Niger**'s president (Feb. 2010) and ended elections in **Guinea-Bissau** (Apr. 2012); in both cases, civilian rule returned. Drought conditions triggered famine in **Somalia** (2010-12); more than 250,000 died. Southerners in **Sudan** (mostly Christian or indigenous religion) voted overwhelmingly for separation from the north (mostly Arab Muslim), and **South Sudan** was granted independence, as of July 2011; civil war there (2013-18) left thousands dead, millions displaced. Following a Mar. 2012 coup, **Mali's** junta ceded power to civilians, but Islamic rebels seized control in the north. French and West African forces intervened; a peace deal (June 2013) proved fragile. Armed attackers killed mostly Islamic villagers in central Mali, Mar. 2019; ISIS attacked military posts in Mali and **Niger**, Sept.-Dec. 2019. Former **Liberian** Pres. Charles **Taylor** was convicted of war crimes, Apr. 2012. The Muslim Seleka coalition seized power in **Central African Republic** (Mar. 2013), precipitating civil war; UN peacekeepers were brought in; new president elected, Feb. 2016.

In **Burkina Faso**, longtime Pres. Blaise **Campaoré** fled amid protests (Oct. 2014); elections in Dec. 2015 brought in new government. In **Nigeria**, former dictator Muhammadu **Buhari** was elected president, Mar. 2015; reelected 2019. During the decade, thousands of Nigerians were killed in attacks by **Boko Haram** jihadists and in conflicts between mostly Christian farmers and mostly Muslim herders.

An African Union court, June 2016, convicted Hissène **Habré** of crimes against humanity while ruler of **Chad** in the 1980s. In **Gambia** longtime Pres. Yahya **Jammeh** reluctantly yielded power, Jan. 2017, after election defeat. In **Zimbabwe** Pres. Robert **Mugabe**, in power since 1980, resigned, Nov. 2017, after house arrest by military and impeachment threat. In **South Africa**, Jacob **Zuma**, president since 2009, resigned Feb. 2018, amid corruption charges. **Ethiopia** and **Eritrea** opened their common border, closed for 20 years (Sept. 2018). Ailing **Algerian** Pres. Abdelaziz **Bouteflika** stepped down, Apr. 2019, following protests over his plans to seek fifth term. Omar al-**Bashir**, president of **Sudan** since a 1989 coup, was deposed in Apr. 2019 and imprisoned; protests demanding civilian rule were repressed; a power-sharing agreement, July 2019, led to transitional government. Bashir was convicted of money laundering and corruption, Dec. 2019.

An **Ebola** epidemic in W Africa (2014-15) caused over 11,000 deaths, mostly in Guinea, Liberia, and Sierra Leone.

Americas and the Caribbean. In **Haiti** an earthquake (Jan. 2010) killed over 300,000; lingering **cholera** epidemic introduced by aid workers left thousands more dead, with violence and political instability continuing. Entrepreneur Jovenel **Moïse** became Haiti's president, Feb. 2017, after disputed election. Poverty and violence fueled by drug cartels spurred **migration** to the U.S. from **Mexico**, **El Salvador**, **Honduras**, and **Guatemala**.

Cuba and U.S. restored relations, July 2015; Miguel **Díaz-Canel** succeeded Raúl Castro as Cuba's president, Apr. 2018. Real estate magnate Donald **Trump** won election, Nov. 2016, as

U.S. president; he campaigned on illegal immigration, deregulation, and "America First" stance.

In **Canada**, Conservatives won a majority in May 2011 elections. Liberals came back in Oct. 2015 under party leader Justin **Trudeau**.

Left and right factions battled in Latin America: **Chilean** Pres. Michelle **Bachelet** was replaced by billionaire conservative Sebastián **Piñera** following Jan. 2010 election; after she returned for second term, Piñera regained office, Dec. 2017. In **Nicaragua** leftist Pres. Daniel **Ortega** twice won reelections challenged as flawed (2011, 2016); protests were violently suppressed. In **Venezuela**, Pres. Hugo **Chávez** died Mar. 2013. Under his ally and successor Nicolás **Maduro** Moros, the economy collapsed and millions fled; results of a legislative election (Dec. 2015) won by the opposition were cast aside; mass protests saw heavy casualties. Maduro was installed for new term, Jan. 2019, after reelection denounced as fraudulent. In **Mexico**, leftist anti-establishment candidate Andrés Manuel **López Obrador** was elected president, July 2018, following a campaign season during which over 100 politicians were murdered. In **Brazil**, after leftist presidents **Lula** da Silva and Dilma **Rousseff** were damaged by corruption scandals, far-right populist Jair **Bolsonaro** was elected president, Oct. 2018. In Bolivia longtime leftist Pres. Evo **Morales** resigned, Nov. 2019, amid protests over his disputed reelection; leftist Luis **Arce** was subsequently elected president (Oct. 2020).

Argentine voters ended 12 years of Peronist rule, choosing center-right candidate Mauricio **Macri** as president (Nov. 2015). The **Colombian** government signed peace accord (Nov. 2016) with Revolutionary Army of Colombia (**FARC**) guerrillas; conflicts continued.

Uruguay (Dec. 2013) and **Canada** (June 2018) became first countries to fully legalize **marijuana.**

Miscellaneous. After 30 years, NASA's **space shuttle** program ended with return of *Atlantis* to Earth (July 2011). NASA's rover *Curiosity* landed on **Mars**, Aug. 2012; **China** landed unmanned *Yulu* rover on moon, Dec. 2013, and space probe on moon's far side, Dec. 2018. NASA's Kepler/K2 missions ended, Oct. 2018, having found over 2,600 **exoplanets**. **Ransomware** emerged as increasing global threat with launch of CryptoLocker (Sept. 2013) and other cyberattacks. Scientists, Feb. 2016, reported direct observation of **gravitational waves**, confirming Einstein prediction. Two new **Boeing 737 Max 8 jets** with automated anti-stall system crashed after takeoff (Oct. 2018, Mar. 2019; 346 died); model was temporarily grounded.

Pope **Benedict XVI** resigned, Feb. 2013; Argentinean Cardinal Jorge Mario Bergoglio was elected to succeed him, taking the name **Francis**. He stressed poverty, environment, and migrant rights as concerns, along with clerical sex abuse.

Representatives of 195 nations, meeting in Paris (Dec. 2015), committed to individual plans for reducing greenhouse gas emissions linked to **climate change**. **Global Climate Strike** protests (Sept. 2019) drew millions of participants around the world. Europe experienced **floods** and **heat waves**, breaking temperature records (2019).

Conflicts in a Divided World, 2020-mid 2024

COVID Pandemic. In Mar. 2020, WHO declared **COVID-19** to be a global pandemic, with some 120,000 cases worldwide. **China** (where it originated), **Iran**, **Italy**, and **South Korea** accounted for over 90% of very early cases; by Mar. 2020 the U.S. had recorded the most. Global health resources were severely strained. **Vaccines** were developed rapidly and distributed beginning Dec. 2020. By mid-2022 the world had recorded over 6 mil COVID deaths. **China** imposed severe restrictions, which were eased starting Dec. 2022, following protests. In May 2023, with new cases and deaths declining, WHO declared an end to the **public emergency** phase.

Ukraine War. In Feb. 2022, **Russia invaded Ukraine**, in what Pres. Vladimir **Putin** called a "special military operation" to "denazify" the country. Millions fled as artillery shelled cities and towns, and invading troops killed and terrorized civilians. The **UN General Assembly** condemned the invasion; Western nations imposed economic sanctions. Stirred by Ukrainian Pres. Volodymyr **Zelenskyy** and bolstered by Western military aid and intelligence, Ukrainian forces turned massing Russian troops away from **Kyiv** but surrendered the port city of **Mariupol**, May 2022. Russians sought to consolidate gains in the east (Sievierodonetsk surrendered, June 2022) and took full control of the devastated city of **Bakhmut** (May 2023). A short-lived rebellion by Russia's paramilitary **Wagner Group** in June 2023 ended in a settlement, though group leaders were killed in a suspicious plane crash two months later. Ukrainian troops began a long-planned **counteroffensive** in mid-2023, which stalled, due in part to shortages of armaments. In first half 2024 Russians seized about 300 sq mi of territory. Much of the country's infrastructure was destroyed and casualties were heavy.

Israel-Hamas War. Hamas militants from the **Gaza Strip**, in a brutal Oct. 2023 surprise attack on **Israel**, broke through the Israeli border and targeted and killed some 1,200 people, also taking some 250 hostages. Israel launched a massive counterattack aimed at destroying Hamas. Tens of thousands of Palestinians died and hundreds of thousands were displaced, with humanitarian aid crippled. Some 70 hostages were released by Hamas and about 180 prisoners freed by Israel, as part of a temporary truce, Nov. 2023. In spring 2024 Israeli forces launched an attack on **Rafah**. **UN Security Council**, June 2024, called for three-phase truce to end the war.

Americas and Caribbean. Former Vice Pres. Joe **Biden** defeated incumbent Pres. Donald **Trump** to win the Nov. 2020 U.S. presidential election. Trump disputed the result, and a mob of his supporters, Jan. 2021, broke into the **Capitol** by force, seeking to prevent certification of the vote. The new Biden administration wrestled with the COVID-19 pandemic and bitter political divisions. Poverty and gang violence fueled an influx of Latin American **migrants** at the southern U.S. border, creating a humanitarian crisis.

Justin **Trudeau** won third term as **Canadian** prime minister following 2021 elections. **Mass graves** found in Canada, beginning May 2021, brought attention to abuses at former residential schools for Indigenous children. **Wildfires** spread through Canada in 2023, generating toxic smoke that reached far into the U.S.

Leftist **Venezuelan** Pres. Nicolás **Maduro** survived coup attempt, May 2020. **Haitian** Pres. Jovenel **Moïse** was assassinated, July 2021; the following month an **earthquake** killed over 2,200 Haitians. Drug gangs enjoyed virtual control of the country. Protests in **Cuba**, July 2021, met with beatings and arrests.

Pedro **Castillo**, a leftist and political novice, won the presidency in sharply divided **Peru** (June 2021). Ousted by Congress and arrested after attempting to rule by decree (Dec. 2022), he was replaced by his vice pres., Dina **Boluarte**. **Colombia** acquired its first left-wing president with the election of former rebel Gustavo **Petro** (June 2022). In **Brazil**, right-wing populist Jair **Bolsonaro** lost his bid for reelection (Oct. 2022), as leftist Luiz Inácio **Lula** da Silva returned to power. A mob of Bolsonaro supporters stormed government buildings, Jan. 2023, in protest

In **Argentina** amid hyperinflation, populist conservative Javier **Milei** won the presidency, Nov. 2023, and introduced austerity reforms. **Mexico**, June 2024, elected Claudia **Sheinbaum**, a protege of outgoing leftist Pres. Andrés Manuel **López Obrador**; she became the nation's first woman and first Jewish president.

Europe. **UK** formalized **Brexit** terms and left the EU Jan. 2020; replacement trade agreement reached, Dec. 2020. **European Central Bank** cut interest rates, June 2024, for the first time since 2019, as **inflation** cooled. UK Prime Min. Boris **Johnson** resigned amid scandal, July 2022, to be succeeded briefly by Liz **Truss** and in Oct. 2022 by Rishi **Sunak**. After 14 years of Conservative UK leadership, **Labour** took power following July 2024 elections, installing Keir **Starmer** as prime min. Britain's **Queen Elizabeth II** died in Sept. 2022; her eldest son was crowned **King Charles III**, May 2023.

After Sept. 2021 elections, Olaf **Scholz**, of the SPD, was sworn in as **German** chancellor; he replaced Angela **Merkel**, of the CDU, who retired after 16 years. Centrist **French** Pres. Emmanuel **Macron** was reelected Apr. 2022, defeating far-right populist Marine **Le Pen**. But far-right gains in European Parliament elections, June 2024, shook political landscapes in several countries.

Right-wing Euroskeptic populist Viktor **Orbán** continued as prime minister of **Hungary**, following Apr. 2022 elections. **Italy's** first center-right coalition government since World War II came to power following Sept. 2022 elections.

Frederik X assumed the throne of **Denmark**, Jan. 2024, following the abdication of his mother, **Queen Margrethe II**, after over five decades as monarch.

Russian anticorruption activist and opposition leader Alexei **Navalny** was poisoned by a nerve agent, Aug. 2020; Russian agents implicated. Returning to Russia, he was imprisoned, Jan. 2021, and died there from unknown causes, Feb. 2024.

Intl. Criminal Court issued arrest warrant for Pres. Vladimir **Putin**, Mar. 2023, in connection with forced deportation of Ukrainian children to Russia. In Mar. 2024, with no credible opponents able to run, Putin was elected to a **fifth term**, allowing him to remain in power until 2030.

In **Belarus**, longtime authoritarian Pres. Aleksandr **Lukashenko** retained power after Aug. 2020 election widely considered rigged. A UN war crimes tribunal, June 2021, convicted two top **Serbian** officials in 1990s **ethnic cleansing** in the Balkans.

Finland joined NATO, Apr. 2023; **Sweden** followed in Mar. 2024.

Middle East. U.S. drone strike, Jan. 2020, killed Qassem **Soleimani**, leader of Iran's powerful Quds Force.

"Abraham Accords," signed Sept. 2020, normalized relations between **Israel** and two Arab nations, **UAE** and **Bahrain**. Over 250 Palestinians died, along with 12 Israeli civilians, in May 2021 violence between **Hamas** and Israel. Longtime Israeli Prime Min. Benjamin **Netanyahu** was ousted June 2021 amid corruption charges. Though still on trial, he was returned to office after Nov. 2022 elections, heading a sharply conservative coalition government

Death of a woman arrested for dress code violations triggered protests in **Iran**, Sept. 2022. Ebrahim **Raisi**, elected president of Iran, June 2021, died along with the foreign minister, in May 2024 helicopter crash. Masoud **Pezeshkian**, a reformist, was elected president of Iran in July 2024. U.S. raid in NW **Syria**, Feb. 2022, took down **ISIS** leader Abu Ibrahim al-Hashimi **al-Qurayshi**.

Earthquake, Feb. 2023, killed over 50,000 people in **Turkey** and over 8,000 in **Syria**. Longtime authoritarian Turkish Pres. Recep Tayyip **Erdogan** won reelection, May 2023. Ireland, Norway, and Spain recognized **Palestinian statehood**, May 2024, joining some 140 mostly non-European nations.

Asia and Pacific. A **U.S.-Taliban peace agreement**, Feb. 2020, called for phased U.S. withdrawal from **Afghanistan** with Taliban prisoner releases and intra-Afghan talks, which failed.

The bumpy, deadly withdrawal of U.S. forces (2021) marked an end to 20 years of war in Afghanistan.

With little resistance, Taliban forces captured most provincial capitals and retook Kabul, Aug. 2021, as Pres. Ashraf **Ghani** fled. At a fixed Aug. 31, 2021, deadline, the last foreign forces left, amid chaotic evacuation (over 180 killed in airport bombing; many left behind). Taliban imposed **sharia law** and suppressed protests.

China's parliament, June 2020, approved sweeping security law for **Hong Kong**. Chinese Pres. **Xi** Jinping secured third five-year term as party leader, Oct. 2022; unanimously elected president for third term by ceremonial National People's Congress, 2023. UN-backed tribunal in **Cambodia** ended its long tenure, Sept. 2022, having convicted two **Khmer Rouge** leaders and a prison commandant of 1970s war crimes.

After **Myanmar**'s ruling party, led by Aung San **Suu Kyi**, won landslide victory in Nov. 2020 elections, the military staged a coup (Feb. 2021); protests were crushed, leaders arrested, and hundreds killed.

Monsoon flooding, June-Oct. 2022, devastated **Pakistan**, leaving over 1,700 dead. Pakistani Prime Min. Imran **Khan** ousted in no-confidence vote, Apr. 2022, and arrested in May 2023, sparking demonstrations.

Ferdinand **Marcos** Jr., son of the late dictator, won May 2022 presidential election in the **Philippines**. Former **Japanese** Prime Min. Shinzo **Abe** was assassinated, July 2022. Over 2,000 people buried, May 2024, in **Papua New Guinea landslide**.

India surpassed China as world's most populous nation in 2023. In June 2024, India's nationalist Prime Min. Narendra **Modi** won a third straight term, but heavy losses to his party required him to form a coalition government.

Africa. Transitional unity government formed in **South Sudan**, Feb. 2020, as unrest continued. In **Sudan**, peace agreement was reached, Oct. 2020, with most rebel groups, but the transitional government was deposed in a military coup (Oct. 2021); a power-sharing arrangement followed.

Heavy fighting broke out, Apr. 2023, between Sudan's military (**SAF**) and the paramilitary Rapid Support Forces (**RSF**) and allies, amid reports of rapes and other war crimes, especially against non-Arab civilians. Millions were displaced and threatened by famine.

Libya's UN-backed government reached cease-fire with rival factions, Oct. 2020, ending six-year civil war. Hostilities broke out in **Ethiopia**, Nov. 2020, between Tigray separatists and Ethiopian and Eritrean troops; millions were displaced, as famine spread and atrocities were reported; a truce was reached, Nov. 2022.

W Africa saw repeated attacks by Islamic terrorists, as well as political instability. **Mali**'s Pres. Ibrahim Boubacar **Keita** was removed in an Aug. 2020 military coup; a transitional government went down in a second coup, May 2021. Longtime **Chad** Pres. Idriss **Déby** was killed Apr. 2021, while visiting troops fighting rebels. Military coups took down governments in **Guinea** (Sept. 2021), **Burkina Faso** (Jan. 2022), and **Gabon** (Aug. 2023). **Niger** saw its first-ever democratic transfer of power, with the inauguration of pro-Western Pres. Mohamed **Bazoum** in Apr. 2021, but he was deposed in a military coup in July 2023.

Autocratic **Ugandan** Pres. Yoweri **Museveni** was returned, Jan. 2021, for sixth term, after disputed elections. After long delay, lawmakers in **Somalia** elected a new president, May 2022, amid continuing violence by **al-Shabab** rebels. **Uganda** enacted a new **anti-gay law**, with harsh penalties, May 2023.

WHO, Oct. 2021, endorsed a vaccine for **malaria**, fatal to hundreds of thousands of African children every year.

Miscellaneous. **SpaceX** became the first private company to launch humans into orbit, May 2020. **China** landed a robotic *Chang'e 5* spacecraft on the **moon**, Dec. 2020, and its *Tianwen-1* spacecraft on **Mars**, May 2021; *Chang'e 6* landed on the moon's far side, June 2024. **NASA's** ***Perseverance*** rover landed on Mars, Feb. 2021. **India's** unmanned *Chandrayaan-3* spacecraft landed near the moon's South Pole, Aug. 2023. **ChatGPT**, an artificial intelligence chatbot, was launched, Nov. 2022.

The average **global temperature** for 2023 was the highest so far on record. At **UN Climate Change Conference** (COP28), Dec. 2023 in Dubai, delegates endorsed a goal of transitioning from **fossil fuels**, without endorsing a phaseout plan.

HISTORICAL FIGURES

Note: Information accurate as of Sept. 2024.

Ancient Greeks and Romans

Greeks

Aeschines, orator, 389-314 BCE
Aeschylus, dramatist, 525-456 BCE
Aesop, fableist, c. 620-c. 560 BCE
Alcibiades, politician, 450-404 BCE
Anacreon, poet, c. 582-c. 485 BCE
Anaxagoras, philosopher, c. 500-428 BCE
Anaximander, philosopher, 611-546 BCE
Anaximenes, philosopher, c. 570-500 BCE
Antiphon, speechwriter, c. 480-411 BCE
Apollonius, mathematician, c. 265-170 BCE
Archimedes, mathematician, 287-212 BCE
Aristophanes, dramatist, c. 448-380 BCE
Aristotle, philosopher, 384-322 BCE
Athenaeus, scholar, fl. c. 200
Callicrates, architect, fl. 5th cent. BCE
Callimachus, poet, c. 305-240 BCE
Cratinus, comic dramatist, 520-421 BCE
Democritus, philosopher, c. 460-370 BCE
Demosthenes, orator, 384-322 BCE
Diodorus, historian, fl. 20 BCE
Diogenes, philosopher, c. 400-c. 325 BCE
Dionysius, historian, d. c. 7 BCE
Empedocles, philosopher, c. 490-430 BCE
Epicharmus, dramatist, c. 530-440 BCE
Epictetus, philosopher, c. 55-c. 135
Epicurus, philosopher, 341-270 BCE
Eratosthenes, scientist, 276-194 BCE
Euclid, mathematician, fl. c. 300 BCE
Euripides, dramatist, c. 484-406 BCE
Galen, physician, 129-200
Heraclitus, philosopher, c. 540-c. 480 BCE
Herodotus, historian, c. 484-420 BCE
Hesiod, poet, 8th cent. BCE
Hippocrates, physician, c. 460-377 BCE
Homer, poet, fl. c. 8th cent. BCE
Isocrates, orator, 436-338 BCE
Menander, dramatist, 342-292 BCE
Parmenides, philosopher, c. 515-440 BCE
Pericles, statesman, c. 495-429 BCE
Phidias, sculptor, fl. 490-430 BCE
Pindar, poet, c. 518-c. 438 BCE
Plato, philosopher, c. 428-347 BCE
Plutarch, biographer, c. 46-120
Polybius, historian, c. 200-c. 118 BCE
Praxiteles, sculptor, 400-330 BCE
Pythagoras, phil., math., c. 580-c. 500 BCE
Sappho, poet, c. 610-c. 580 BCE
Simonides, poet, 556-c. 468 BCE
Socrates, philosopher, 469-399 BCE
Solon, statesman, 640-560 BCE
Sophocles, dramatist, c. 496-406 BCE
Strabo, geographer, c. 63 BCE-24 CE
Thales, philosopher, c. 634-546 BCE
Themistocles, politician, c. 524-c. 460 BCE
Theocritus, poet, c. 310-250 BCE
Theophrastus, phil., c. 372-c. 287 BCE
Thucydides, historian, fl. 5th cent. BCE
Timon, philosopher, c. 320-c. 230 BCE
Xenophon, historian, c. 434-c. 355 BCE
Zeno, philosopher, c. 335-c. 263 BCE

Romans

Ammianus, historian, c. 330-395
Apuleius, satirist, c. 124-c. 170
Boethius, scholar, c. 480-524
Caesar, Julius, leader, 100-44 BCE
Catiline, politician, c. 108-62 BCE
Cato (Elder), statesman, 234-149 BCE
Catullus, poet, c. 84-54 BCE
Cicero, orator, 106-43 BCE
Claudian, poet, c. 370-c. 404
Ennius, poet, 239-170 BCE
Gellius, author, c. 130-c. 165
Horace, poet, 65-8 BCE
Juvenal, satirist, 60-127
Livy, historian, 59 BCE-17 CE
Lucan, poet, 39-65
Lucilius, poet, c. 180-c.102 BCE
Lucretius, poet, c. 99-c. 55 BCE
Martial, epigrammatist, c. 38-c. 103
Nepos, historian, c. 100-c. 25 BCE
Ovid, poet, 43 BCE-17 CE
Persius, satirist, 34-62
Plautus, dramatist, c. 254-c. 184 BCE
Pliny the Elder, scholar, 23-79
Pliny the Younger, author, 62-113
Quintilian, rhetorician, c. 35-c. 97
Sallust, historian, 86-34 BCE
Seneca, philosopher, 4 BCE-65 CE
Silius, poet, c. 25-101
Statius, poet, c. 45-c. 96
Suetonius, biographer, c. 69-c. 122
Tacitus, historian, 56-120
Terence, dramatist, 195/185-c. 159 BCE
Tibullus, poet, c. 55-c. 19 BCE
Virgil (or Vergil), poet, 70-19 BCE
Vitruvius, architect, fl. late 1st cent. BCE

Roman Rulers

From Romulus to the end of the Empire in the West (Rome). Rulers in the East sat in Constantinople and, for a brief period, in Nicaea, until the capture of Constantinople by the Turks in 1453, when Byzantium was succeeded by the Ottoman Empire.

The Kingdom

BCE
753 Romulus (Quirinus)
715 Numa Pompilius
673 Tullus Hostilius
641 Ancus Marcius
616 L. Tarquinius Priscus
579 Servius Tullius
534 L. Tarquinius Superbus

The Republic

509 Consulate established; Quaestorship instituted
498 Dictatorship introduced
494 Plebeian Tribunate created; Plebeian Aedileship created
444 Consular Tribunate organized
435 Censorship instituted
366 Praetorship established; Curule Aedileship created
362 Military Tribunate elected
326 Proconsulate introduced
311 Naval Duumvirate elected
217 Dictatorship of Fabius Maximus
133 Tribunate of Tiberius Gracchus
123 Tribunate of Gaius Gracchus
82 Dictatorship of Sulla
60 First Triumvirate formed (Caesar, Pompeius, Crassus)
47 Dictatorship of Caesar
43 Second Triumvirate formed (Octavianus, Antonius, Lepidus)

The Empire

27 Augustus (or Octavian)
CE
14 Tiberius
37 Caligula
41 Claudius
54 Nero
68 Galba
69 Otho; Vitellius; Vespasian, established Flavian Dynasty
79 Titus
81 Domitian, end of Flavian Dynasty
96 Nerva
98 Trajan
117 Hadrian
138 Antoninus Pius
161 Marcus Aurelius and Lucius Verus
169 Marcus Aurelius (alone)
177 Marcus Aurelius and Commodus
180 Commodus
193 Pertinax
193 Didius Julianus
193 Septimius Severus, founded Severan Dynasty
211 Caracalla and Geta
212 Caracalla (alone)
217 Macrinus
218 Elagabalus (or Heliogabalus)
222 Alexander Severus, end of dynasty
235 Maximinus (the Thracian)
238 Gordian I and Gordian II
238 Pupienus and Balbinus
238 Gordian III
244 Philip (the Arabian)
249 Decius
251 Gallus and Volusianus
253 Aemilian
253 Valerian and Gallienus
258 Gallienus (alone)
268 Claudius II (or Claudius Gothicus)
270 Quintillus
270 Aurelian
275 Tacitus
276 Florian
276 Probus
282 Carus
283 Carinus and Numerian
284 Diocletian
286 Diocletian and Maximian
305 Galerius and Constantius I
306 Galerius, Maximinus (or Maximinus Daia), Severus
307 Galerius, Maximinus (Daia), Constantine I, Licinius, Maxentius
311 Maximinus (Daia), Constantine I, Licinius, Maxentius
314 Constantine I, Licinius
324 Constantine I (the Great), first Christian emperor
337 Constantine II, Constans I, Constantius II
340 Constantius II and Constans I
353 Constantius II (alone)
361 Julian (the Apostate)
363 Jovian

West (Rome) and East (Constantinople)

364 Valentinian I (West), Valens (East)
367 Valentinian I with Gratian (W), Valens (E)
375 Gratian with Valentinian II (W), Valens (E)
379 Gratian with Valentinian II (W), Theodosius I (E)
383 Magnus Maximus and Valentinian II (W), Theodosius I (E)
388 Valentinian II (W), Theodosius I (E)
392 Eugenius (W), Theodosius I (E)
394 Theodosius I (the Great)
395 Honorius (W), Arcadius (E)
408 Honorius (W), Theodosius II (E)
423 Valentinian III (W), Theodosius II (E)
450 Valentinian III (W), Marcian (E)
455 Petronius Maximus (W), Marcian (E)
455 Avitus (W), Marcian (E)
457 Majorian (W), Leo I (E)
461 Libius Severus (W), Leo I (E)
467 Anthemius (W), Leo I (E)
472 Olybrius (W), Leo I (E)
473 Glycerius (W), Leo I (E)
474 Julius Nepos (W), Leo II (E)
475 Romulus Augustulus (W), Zeno (E)
476 End of Empire in W when Romulus Augustulus deposed by Germanic chief Odoacer, who was later murdered by King Theodoric of Ostrogoths, 493

Rulers of England and the United Kingdom

Reign began	England: Saxons and Danes	Age at death[1]
829	Egbert, king of Wessex, won allegiance of all English	NA
839	Ethelwulf, son, king of Wessex, Sussex, Kent, Essex	NA
858	Ethelbald, eldest son, displaced father in Wessex	NA
860	Ethelbert, 2nd son of Ethelwulf, united Kent and Wessex	NA
866	Ethelred I, 3rd son of Ethelwulf, king of Wessex, fought Danes	NA
871	Alfred (the Great), 4th son of Ethelwulf, defeated Danes, fortified London	52
899	Edward (the Elder), son, united English, claimed Scotland	55
924	Athelstan (the Glorious), eldest son, king of Mercia, Wessex	45
940	Edmund, 3rd son of Edward, king of Wessex, Mercia	25
946	Edred, 4th son of Edward	32
955	Edwy (the Fair), eldest son of Edmund, king of Wessex	18
959	Edgar (the Peaceful), 2nd son of Edmund, ruled all English	32
975	Edward (the Martyr), eldest son, murdered by stepmother	17
978; 1014[2]	Ethelred II (the Unready), 2nd son of Edgar, married Emma of Normandy	48
1016	Edmund II (Ironside), son, king of London	27
1016	Canute (the Dane), son of Sweyn, who conquered English territory; gave Wessex to Edmund II; married Emma, Ethelred II's widow	40
1035	Harold I (Harefoot), illegitimate son	NA
1040	Hardecanute, son of Canute by Emma, also king of Denmark	24
1042	Edward (the Confessor), son of Ethelred II, canonized 1161	62
1066	Harold II, brother-in-law, last Saxon king	44
	England: House of Normandy	
1066	William I (the Conqueror), son of Duke Robert I of Normandy, defeated Harold II at Hastings	60
1087	William II (Rufus), 3rd son, killed by arrow while hunting in possible assassination	43
1100	Henry I (Beauclerc), youngest son of William I	67
	England: House of Blois	
1135	Stephen, son of Adela, daughter of William I, and Count of Blois	50
	England: House of Plantagenet	
1154	Henry II, son of Geoffrey Plantagenet (Angevin) by Matilda, daughter of Henry I	56
1189	Richard I (Coeur de Lion), son, crusader	42
1199	John (Lackland), son of Henry II, approved Magna Carta, 1215	50
1216	Henry III, son, acceded at 9, under regency until 1227	65
1272	Edward I (Longshanks), son	68
1307	Edward II, son, deposed by Parliament	43
1327	Edward III (of Windsor), son	65
1377	Richard II, grandson of Edward III, deposed	33
	England: House of Lancaster	
1399	Henry IV (of Bolingbroke), son of John of Gaunt, duke of Lancaster, son of Edward III	47
1413	Henry V, son, victor over French at Agincourt	34
1422; 1470	Henry VI, son, overthrown by Edward IV in 1461 but was returned to throne in 1470. Deposed, died in Tower of London, 1471	49
	England: House of York	
1461; 1471	Edward IV, great-great-grandson of Edward III, son of duke of York. Acclaimed king by Parliament, 1461. Driven into exile in 1470 but regained throne, 1471	40
1483	Edward V, son, murdered in Tower of London	13
1483	Richard III, brother of Edward IV, fell in battle at Bosworth Field against Henry Tudor	32

Reign began	England: House of Tudor	Age at death[1]
1485	Henry VII, son of Edmund Tudor, earl of Richmond, whose father had married Henry V's widow. Descended from Edward III through mother, Margaret Beaufort, via John of Gaunt. Married Elizabeth of York, eldest daughter of Edward IV, to unite Lancaster and York	53
1509	Henry VIII, 2nd son, by Elizabeth	56
1547	Edward VI, son, by Jane Seymour, his 3rd queen. Was persuaded by John Dudley to name Lady Jane Grey, his cousin and Dudley's daughter-in-law, his successor. Council of State proclaimed her queen, July 10, 1553, but she ruled only nine days before Mary Tudor overthrew her	16
1553	Mary I, daughter of Henry VIII, by his 1st wife, Catherine of Aragon	43
1558	Elizabeth I, daughter of Henry VIII, by his 2nd wife, Anne Boleyn	69
	Great Britain: House of Stuart	
1603	James I (James VI of Scotland), son of Mary, Queen of Scots. First to call self king of Great Britain; this became official with Acts of Union, 1707	59
1625	Charles I, only surviving son of James I	48
	Great Britain: Commonwealth	
1649	Declared upon execution of Charles I	NA
	Great Britain: Protectorate	
1653	Oliver Cromwell, served on Council of State, executive body of Commonwealth, following overthrow of monarchy. Named Lord Protector upon creation of Protectorate by 1653 Instrument of Government	59
1658	Richard Cromwell, 3rd son, resigned as Lord Protector amid civil war, 1659	86
	Great Britain: House of Stuart (restored)	
1660	Charles II, eldest son of Charles I, acceded to throne by Restoration, died without issue	55
1685	James II, 2nd son of Charles I, deposed 1688	68
1689	William III, son of William, Prince of Orange, by Mary, daughter of Charles I. Offered joint rule of throne with wife by Parliament	51
1689	Mary II, eldest daughter of James II and wife of William III, died 1694	33
1702	Anne, 2nd daughter of James II, sister-in-law of William III, assumed throne on William's death	49
	United Kingdom of Great Britain[3]: House of Hanover	
1714	George I, son of Elector of Hanover by Sophia, granddaughter of James I	67
1727	George II, only son, married Caroline of Brandenburg	77
1760	George III, grandson, married Charlotte of Mecklenburg	81
1820	George IV, eldest son, prince regent from Feb. 1811	67
1830	William IV, 3rd son of George III, married Adelaide of Saxe-Meiningen	71
1837	Victoria, daughter of Edward, 4th son of George III; married Prince Albert of Saxe-Coburg and Gotha, 1840	81
	United Kingdom of Great Britain[3]: House of Saxe-Coburg-Gotha	
1901	Edward VII, eldest son, married Alexandra, Princess of Denmark	68
	United Kingdom of Great Britain[3]: House of Windsor[4]	
1910	George V, 2nd son, married Princess Mary of Teck	70
1936	Edward VIII, eldest son, acceded Jan. 20, abdicated Dec. 11	77
1936	George VI, 2nd son of George V, married Lady Elizabeth Bowes-Lyon	56
1952	Elizabeth II, elder daughter, acceded Feb. 6	96
2022	Charles III, eldest son, acceded Sept. 8	NA

NA = Age/birthdate not certain or not applicable. (1) Except where noted, year of death is the same year the next ruler's reign began. (2) King Sweyn I of Denmark invaded England in 1013 and declared himself king. Ethelred II reclaimed the throne upon Sweyn's death in 1014. (3) Officially the United Kingdom of Great Britain and Ireland after Act of Union 1801 and the United Kingdom of Great Britain and Northern Ireland after Anglo-Irish Treaty of 1921 (name formalized 1927). (4) Name adopted by proclamation of George V, July 17, 1917, because of anti-German feeling during World War I.

Rulers of Scotland

Reign began	Name
846	Kenneth I, first Scot to rule both Scots and Picts
1005	Malcolm II, son of Kenneth II
1034	Duncan I, grandson, first general ruler
1040	Macbeth, seized kingdom, slain by Malcolm Canmore
1057	Malcolm III (Canmore), eldest son of Duncan I
1093	Donald III (the Fair), younger brother
1094	Duncan II, eldest son of Malcolm III by first wife
1095	Donald III (restored)
1097	Edgar, 4th son of Malcolm III and Queen Margaret
1107	Alexander I, brother
1124	David I, brother
1153	Malcolm IV (the Maiden), grandson
1165	William (the Lion), brother
1214	Alexander II, son
1249	Alexander III, son
1286	Margaret (Maid of Norway), granddaughter; died 1290 at age 8. (Interregnum, 1290-92)
1292	John Balliol, proclaimed king of Scotland by Edward I of England. (Interregnum, 1296-1306[1])
1306	Robert I (the Bruce), victor at Bannockburn, 1314. Treaty with England and secured throne, 1328
1329	David II, only surviving son
1371	Robert II (the Steward), son of Robert I's daughter Marjorie and Walter, steward of Scotland. First of Stewart line
1390	Robert III, son
1406	James I, son, assassinated
1437	James II, son
1460	James III, eldest son, possibly assassinated
1488	James IV, eldest son
1513	James V, eldest son, died at Battle of Flodden
1542	Mary (Queen of Scots), daughter, became queen before she was 1 week old. Married Francis II (d. 1560), son of King Henry II of France, 1558. Married her cousin, Henry Stewart, Lord Darnley (d. 1567), 1565. Married James Hepburn, Earl of Bothwell, 1567. Imprisoned by her cousin Elizabeth I of England, 1568; beheaded, 1587
1567	James VI, son of Mary and Lord Darnley, became James I, king of England, on Elizabeth's death, 1603. (Legislative union of Scotland and England as United Kingdom of Great Britain not official until Acts of Union, 1707)

Note: Not all rulers before 1005 are shown. (1) Edward I decreed annexation of Scotland to England, 1296, after defeating Balliol in battle. William Wallace led resistance, 1297-1305.

Prime Ministers of the United Kingdom

Titles are given on first mention only. C = Conservative; La. = Labour; Li. = Liberal; P = Peelite; T = Tory; W = Whig.

Entered office	Name (party)
1721	Sir Robert Walpole (W)[1]
1742	Spencer Compton, 1st Earl of Wilmington (W)
1743	Henry Pelham (W)
1754	Thomas Pelham-Holles, 1st Duke of Newcastle (W)
1756	William Cavendish, 4th Duke of Devonshire (W)
1757	Thomas Pelham-Holles (W)
1762	John Stuart, 3rd Earl of Bute (T)
1763	George Grenville (W)
1765	Charles Watson-Wentworth, 2nd Marquess of Rockingham (W)
1766	William Pitt the Elder, 1st Earl of Chatham (W)
1768	Augustus Henry Fitzroy, 3rd Duke of Grafton (W)
1770	Lord Frederick North (T)
1782	Charles Watson-Wentworth (W)
1782	William Petty, 2nd Earl of Shelburne (W)
1783	William Cavendish-Bentinck, 3rd Duke of Portland (W[2])
1783	William Pitt the Younger (T)
1801	Henry Addington (T)
1804	William Pitt the Younger (T)
1806	William Wyndham Grenville, 1st Baron Grenville (W)
1807	William Cavendish-Bentinck (T)
1809	Spencer Perceval (T)
1812	Robert Banks Jenkinson, 2nd Earl of Liverpool (T)
1827	George Canning (T)
1827	Frederick John Robinson, Viscount Goderich (T)
1828	Arthur Wellesley, 1st Duke of Wellington (T)
1830	Charles Grey, 2nd Earl Grey (W)
1834	William Lamb, 2nd Viscount Melbourne (W)
1834	Arthur Wellesley (T)
1834	Sir Robert Peel, 2nd Baronet (C)
1835	William Lamb (W)
1841	Sir Robert Peel (C)
1846	John Russell, 1st Earl Russell (W)
1852	Edward Stanley, 14th Earl of Derby (C)
1852	George Hamilton Gordon, 4th Earl of Aberdeen (P[2])
1855	Henry John Temple, 3rd Viscount Palmerston (W-Li.)
1858	Edward Stanley (C)
1859	Henry John Temple (W-Li.)
1865	John Russell (Li.)
1866	Edward Stanley (C)
1868	Benjamin Disraeli (C)
1868	William E. Gladstone (Li.)
1874	Benjamin Disraeli (C)
1880	William E. Gladstone (Li.)
1885	Robert Gascoyne-Cecil, 3rd Marquess of Salisbury (C)
1886	William E. Gladstone (Li.)
1886	Robert Gascoyne-Cecil (C)
1892	William E. Gladstone (Li.)
1894	Archibald Primrose, 5th Earl of Rosebery (Li.)
1895	Robert Gascoyne-Cecil (C)
1902	Arthur James Balfour (C)
1905	Sir Henry Campbell-Bannerman (Li.)
1908	Herbert Henry Asquith (Li.[2])
1916	David Lloyd George (Li.[2])
1922	Andrew Bonar Law (C)
1923	Stanley Baldwin (C)
1924	Ramsay MacDonald (La.)
1924	Stanley Baldwin (C)
1929	Ramsay MacDonald (La.[2])
1935	Stanley Baldwin (C[2])
1937	Neville Chamberlain (C[2])
1940	Winston Churchill (C[2])
1945	Clement Attlee (La.)
1951	Winston Churchill (C)
1955	Anthony Eden (C)
1957	Harold Macmillan (C)
1963	Alec Douglas-Home (C)
1964	Harold Wilson (La.)
1970	Edward Heath (C)
1974	Harold Wilson (La.)
1976	James Callaghan (La.)
1979	Margaret Thatcher (C)
1990	John Major (C)
1997	Tony Blair (La.)
2007	Gordon Brown (La.)
2010	David Cameron (C[2])
2016	Theresa May (C)
2019	Boris Johnson (C)
2022	Liz Truss (C)
2022	Rishi Sunak (C)
2024	Keir Starmer (La.)

Note: Prime ministers prior to 1801 are for Great Britain. The Conservative Party was formed in 1834, an outgrowth of the Tory party. (1) Walpole is traditionally regarded as the first prime minister of Britain though the title was not commonly used then and did not become official until 1905. (2) Led a coalition government for all or part of time in office.

Prime Ministers of Canada

C = Conservative; Lib. = Liberal; PC = Progressive Conservative; U = Unionist

Entered office	Name (party)
1867	John A. Macdonald (C)
1873	Alexander Mackenzie (Lib.)
1878	John A. Macdonald (C)
1891	John Abbott (C)
1892	John Thompson (C)
1894	Mackenzie Bowell (C)
1896[1]	Charles Tupper (C)
1896	Wilfrid Laurier (Lib.)
1911	Robert Borden (C/U)[2]
1920	Arthur Meighen (U)
1921	W. L. Mackenzie King (Lib.)
1926[3]	Arthur Meighen (C)
1926	W. L. Mackenzie King (Lib.)
1930	Richard Bedford Bennett (C)
1935	W. L. Mackenzie King (Lib.)
1948	Louis St. Laurent (Lib.)
1957	John G. Diefenbaker (PC)
1963	Lester B. Pearson (Lib.)
1968	Pierre Trudeau (Lib.)
1979	Joe Clark (PC)
1980	Pierre Trudeau (Lib.)
1984[3]	John Turner (Lib.)
1984	Brian Mulroney (PC)
1993[4]	Kim Campbell (PC)
1993	Jean Chrétien (Lib.)
2003	Paul Martin (Lib.)
2006	Stephen Harper (C)
2015	Justin Trudeau (Lib.)

(1) May-July. (2) Conservative 1911-17, Unionist 1917-20. (3) June-Sept. (4) June-Nov.

Rulers of France

Caesar to Charlemagne

Julius Caesar subdued the Gauls, native tribes of Gaul (France), 58 to 51 BCE. The Romans ruled 500 years. The Franks, a Teutonic tribe, reached the Somme from the east c. 250 CE. By the 5th cent., the Merovingian Franks ousted the Romans. In 451, with the help of Visigoths, Burgundians, and others, they defeated Attila and the Huns at Châlons-sur-Marne.

Childeric I became leader of the Merovingians, 458. After son Clovis I (crowned 481) defeated the Alemanni (Germans), 496, he was baptized a Christian and made Paris his capital. Line ended when Childeric III was deposed, 751.

The West Merovingians were called Neustrians, the eastern Austrasians. Pepin of Herstal (687-714), major domus (head of the palace) of Austrasia, took over Neustria as dux (leader) of the Franks. Pepin's son, Charles, called Martel (the Hammer), defeated the Saracens at Tours-Poitiers, 732; was succeeded in 741 by his sons, Pepin the Short and Carloman (abdicated 747). Pepin deposed Childeric III and ruled as king until 768.

His son, Charlemagne, or Charles the Great (742-814), became king of the Franks, 768, with his brother Carloman (751-71). Charlemagne ruled France, Germany, parts of Italy, Spain, and Austria, and enforced Christianity. Crowned Emperor of the Romans by Pope Leo III in Rome, 800. Succeeded by son, Louis I (the Pious), 814. At death, 840, Louis left empire to sons Lothair (Roman emperor), Pepin I (king of Aquitaine), Louis II (the German), and Charles II (the Bald, of France). They quarreled and, by the Treaty of Verdun, 843, divided the empire.

The date preceding each entry is year of accession.

Carolingian Dynasty

843 Charles II (the Bald), Roman emperor, 875
877 Louis II (the Stammerer), son
879 Louis III (d. 882), son, and brother Carloman
885 Charles III (the Fat), son of Louis the German, Roman emperor, 881
888 Eudes (Odo), son of Robert the Strong, elected by nobles
898 Charles III (the Simple), son of Louis II the Stammerer, deposed
922 Robert I, brother of Eudes, defeated forces of Charles III but died in battle
923 Rudolph (Raoul), Robert I's son-in-law, duke of Burgundy
936 Louis IV, son of Charles III (the Simple); struggled with Hugh the Great, son of Robert I
954 Lothair, son, dominated by Hugh the Great
986 Louis V (the Sluggard), left no heirs

House of Capet

987 Hugh Capet, son of Hugh the Great
996 Robert II (the Pious), son
1031 Henry I, son
1060 Philip I (the Fair), son
1108 Louis VI (the Fat), son
1137 Louis VII (the Younger), son
1180 Philip II Augustus, son, crowned at Reims
1223 Louis VIII (the Lion), son
1226 Louis IX, son, arbitrated disputes with English King Henry III; led crusades, 1248 (captured in Egypt, 1250) and 1270, when he died of plague in Tunis. Canonized as St. Louis, 1297
1270 Philip III (the Bold), son
1285 Philip IV (the Fair), son, king at 17
1314 Louis X (the Headstrong), son. His posthumous son, John I, lived and reigned only five days.
1316 Philip V (the Tall), brother of Louis X
1322 Charles IV (the Fair), brother of Louis X

House of Valois

1328 Philip VI (of Valois), grandson of Philip III
1350 John II (the Good), son, retired to England
1364 Charles V (the Wise), son
1380 Charles VI (the Beloved), son
1422 Charles VII (the Victorious), son. In 1429, Joan of Arc defeated English at Orleans and Patay and had Charles crowned at Reims. Joan was captured, 1430, and executed, 1431, at Rouen for heresy.
1461 Louis XI (the Cruel), son, civil reformer
1483 Charles VIII (the Affable), son
1498 Louis XII, great-grandson of Charles V
1515 Francis I, of Angouleme, nephew, son-in-law. Fought four major wars, was patron of the arts
1547 Henry II, son, killed at joust. Husband of Catherine (daughter of Lorenzo) de Médicis and lover of Diane de Poitiers. By marriage to Henry II, Catherine became the mother of Francis II, Charles IX, Henry III, and Queen Margaret (Reine Margot), wife of Henry IV (of Navarre).
1559 Francis II, son. Betrothed in 1548 at age 4 to Mary, Queen of Scots, aged 6; they were married 1558. Francis died 1560, aged 16. Mary returned to rule Scotland, 1561.
1560 Charles IX, brother
1574 Henry III, brother, assassinated

House of Bourbon

1589 Henry IV (of Navarre), grandson of Queen Margaret of Navarre. Made enemies when he gave tolerance to Protestants by Edict of Nantes, 1598. Married Margaret of Valois, daughter of Henry II and Catherine de Médicis; was divorced. Married Marie de Médicis, 1600. She became regent upon Henry's assassination, 1610-17, for her son, Louis XIII; she was exiled by Richelieu, 1631.
1610 Louis XIII (the Just), son, married Anne of Austria. His chief minister (1622-42), Cardinal Richelieu, determined his policies.
1643 Louis XIV (the Sun King), son; was king 72 years. Until 1661, Anne of Austria was regent with Cardinal Mazarin as chief minister; Louis then ruled absolutely. Known for lavish court and arts patronage, he exhausted the economy with wars for territory.
1715 Louis XV (the Beloved), great-grandson. Married a Polish princess, lost Canada to England. Favorite mistresses Mme. de Pompadour and Mme. Du Barry influenced policies. Pompadour's saying "Après moi, le déluge" (After me, the deluge) is often incorrectly attributed to Louis XV.
1774 Louis XVI, grandson, married Marie Antoinette, daughter of Empress Maria Therese of Austria. Couple executed by guillotine in French Revolution, 1793. Louis XVII, son, never ruled and died in prison.

First Republic

1792 National Convention of the French Revolution
1795 Directory, under Viscount of Barras and others
1799 Consulate, Napoleon Bonaparte, first consul. Elected consul for life, 1802

First Empire

1804 Napoleon I (Napoleon Bonaparte), emperor. Josephine (de Beauharnais), empress, 1804-09; Marie Louise, empress, 1810-14. Son, Napoleon II (1811-32), titular king of Rome, later duke of Reichstadt, never ruled. Napoleon I abdicated 1814; died in exile, 1821.

House of Bourbon (restored)

1814 Louis XVIII, brother of Louis XVI, king
1824 Charles X, brother, reactionary, deposed by the July Revolution, 1830

House of Orleans

1830 Louis-Philippe (the Citizen King)

Second Republic

1848 Louis Napoleon Bonaparte, nephew of Napoleon I, president

Second Empire

1852 Napoleon III (Louis Napoleon Bonaparte), emperor; Eugenie (de Montijo) (d. 1920), empress. Lost Franco-Prussian war, deposed 1870. Son, Prince Imperial (1856-79), died in Zulu War.

Third Republic

1871 Adolphe Thiers (1797-1877), president
1873 Patrice de Mac-Mahon (1808-93)
1879 Jules Grévy (1807-91)
1887 Sadi Carnot (1837-94), assassinated
1894 Jean Casimir-Périer (1847-1907)
1895 Félix Faure (1841-99)
1899 Émile Loubet (1838-1929)
1906 Armand Fallières (1841-1931)
1913 Raymond Poincaré (1860-1934)
1920 Paul Deschanel (1855-1922)
1920 Alexandre Millerand (1859-1943)
1924 Gaston Doumergue (1863-1937)
1931 Paul Doumer (1857-1932), assassinated
1932 Albert Lebrun (1871-1950), resigned 1940

Vichy Regime

1940 Philippe Pétain (1856-1951), chief of state, 1940-44, under German armistice

Provisional Government

1944 Charles de Gaulle (1890-1970)
1946 Félix Gouin (1884-1977)
1946 Georges Bidault (1899-1983)

Fourth Republic

1947 Vincent Auriol (1884-1966), president
1954 René Coty (1882-1962)

Fifth Republic

1959 Charles de Gaulle (1890-1970), president; resigned 1969. Alain Poher (1909-96), interim pres., Apr.-June 1969
1969 Georges Pompidou (1911-74); Poher, interim pres., Apr.-May 1974
1974 Valéry Giscard d'Estaing (1926-2020)
1981 François Mitterrand (1916-96)
1995 Jacques Chirac (1932-2019)
2007 Nicolas Sarkozy (1955-)
2012 François Hollande (1954-)
2017 Emmanuel Macron (1977-)

Rulers of Middle Europe and Germany

Carolingian Dynasty

Charles I (the Great), or Charlemagne, made Roman emperor by pope in Rome, 800. Ruled France, Italy, and Middle Europe; established Ostmark (later Austria). Died 814.

Louis I (Ludwig) (the Pious), son, crowned co-emperor by Charlemagne, 813. Divided empire among sons. Died 840; sons fought for control.

Louis II (the German), son, succeeded to East Francia (Germany), 843-76, with Treaty of Verdun.

Charles III (the Fat), son, inherited Swabia, 876. With brothers' deaths, acquired East Francia and West Francia (France), reuniting empire. Crowned emperor by pope, 881; deposed 887.

Arnulf, nephew, 887-99, took over East Francia; partition of empire.

Louis IV (the Child), son, 900-11, last direct descendant of Charlemagne.

Conrad I, duke of Franconia, first elected German king, 911-18.

Saxon Dynasty; First Reich

Henry I (the Fowler), duke of Saxony, elected king 919-36.

Otto I (the Great), son, 936-73, crowned Holy Roman Emperor by pope, 962.

Otto II, son, 961-83, ruled with Otto I as king, then emperor, 967.

Otto III, son, 983-1002, crowned Holy Roman Emperor, 996.

Henry II (the Saint), great-grandson of Otto the Great, duke of Bavaria, 1002-24. Crowned emperor, 1014.

Salian Dynasty

Conrad II, 1024-39, elected king of Germany.

Henry III (the Black), son, 1039-56, deposed three popes; annexed Burgundy.

Henry IV, son, 1056-1106, with mother, Agnes of Poitou, as regent in early years. He and Pope Gregory VII tried to depose each other. Civil war lasted about 20 years.

Henry V, son, 1106-25, last of Salian Dynasty.

Lothair, duke of Saxony, elected king 1125-37. Crowned emperor in Rome, 1133.

Hohenstaufen Dynasty

Conrad III, duke of Franconia, 1138-52, in Second Crusade.

Frederick I (Barbarossa, Italian for "Redbeard"), nephew, 1152-90.

Henry VI, son, 1190-97, gained kingdom of Sicily through marriage.

Philip of Swabia, brother, 1197-1208. Otto IV, nephew of King Richard I of England, 1198-1215, was elected rival king. Philip's murder, in 1208, led to Otto's win in new election same year. Civil war followed before Otto was deposed, 1215.

Frederick II, son of Henry VI, elected 1212-50. Had earlier succeeded father as king of Sicily; crowned himself king of Jerusalem, 1229, in Sixth Crusade.

Conrad IV, son, 1250-54. Conquered Naples.

(Interregnum, 1254-73. Conradin, son of Conrad IV and last legitimate Hohenstaufen, defeated by Charles of Anjou—brother of King Louis IX of France—and executed, 1268. Rise of electors of German monarch.)

Transition

Rudolf I, of Habsburg, 1273-91, defeated King Ottocar II of Bohemia, 1278. Bequeathed duchies of Austria and Styria to sons.

Adolf of Nassau, 1292-98, killed in war with Albert I.

Albert I, elder son of Rudolf I, 1298-1308, assassinated.

Henry VII, of Luxemburg, 1308-13. Gained Bohemia, 1310; crowned Holy Roman Emperor, 1312.

Louis IV, of Wittelsbach, 1314-46. Also elected was a son of Albert I, Frederick of Austria, whom Louis defeated in 1322. Rejected need for papal confirmation of elected German king.

Charles IV, of Luxemburg, grandson of Henry VII, 1346-78. Took Brandenburg.

Wenceslaus, son, 1378-1400; deposed.

Rupert, of Wittelsbach, elector palatine, 1400-10.

Sigismund, brother of Wenceslaus, 1410-37.

Habsburg Dynasty

Albert II, duke of Austria, son-in-law of Sigismund, elected German king, 1438-39; king of Hungary and Holy Roman Emperor.

Frederick III, cousin, 1440-93, fought Turks.

Maximilian I, son, 1493-1519, archduke of Austria.

Charles V, grandson, 1519-58. King of Spain; assumed title of Holy Roman Emperor. Martin Luther, who had been excommunicated by pope, appeared at Diet of Worms, 1521. Charles attempted church reform and conciliation between Catholicism and Protestantism; abdicated.

Ferdinand I, brother, 1558-64; king of Hungary and Bohemia, 1526 (successive leaders through Maria Theresa will rule these lands as well).

Maximilian II, son, 1564-76.

Rudolf II, son, 1576-1612.

Matthias, brother, 1612-19.

Ferdinand II, grandson of Ferdinand I, 1619-37. Bohemian Protestants, unhappy with Ferdinand's support of Catholic Counter-Reformation, crowned Frederick V, elector palatine. Frederick became known as "Winter King" with defeat in battle, 1620; start of Thirty Years' War.

Ferdinand III, son, 1637-57. Treaties signed, 1648, in Peace of Westphalia ended war.

Leopold I, son, 1658-1705.

Joseph I, son, 1705-11.

Charles VI, brother, 1711-40; died without male heir.

Maria Theresa, daughter, 1740-80. Appointed husband, Francis Stephen of Lorraine, co-regent. Dispute over her inheritance led to War of the Austrian Succession. Charles VII, also known as Charles Albert, elected in opposition to Francis, 1742-45. After Charles's death, Maria Theresa obtained election of her husband as Holy Roman Emperor Francis I, 1745-65. Fought Seven Years' War with Frederick II of Prussia.

Habsburg-Lorraine Dynasty

Joseph II, son, 1765-90, reformer. Ruled jointly with Maria Theresa until her death. Participated in first partition of Poland, with Prussia and Russia.

Leopold II, brother, 1790-92; king of Hungary and Bohemia.

Francis II, son, 1792-1806; king of Hungary and Bohemia. Proclaimed first emperor of Austria, 1804-35. Unsuccessfully fought against Napoleon; forced to abdicate, 1806, as Holy Roman Emperor, last use of title.

Ferdinand, son, 1835-48, emperor of Austria; king of Hungary and Bohemia. Abdicated in favor of nephew after revolution broke out in Vienna.

Austro-Hungarian Monarchy

Francis Joseph I, nephew, 1848-1916, emperor of Austria and king of Hungary. Defeated in Austro-Prussian War, 1866. Formed dual monarchy of Austria-Hungary, 1867. After Serbian nationalist assassinated Francis Joseph's nephew and heir, Archduke Francis Ferdinand, June 28, 1914, Austrian diplomacy precipitated World War I.

Charles I, grandnephew, 1916-18, last emperor of Austria and king of Hungary. Abdicated Nov. 1918; died in exile, 1922.

Second and Third Reichs

William I, brother of Frederick William IV, 1861-88, king of Prussia. Appointed Otto von Bismarck chancellor, 1862. Franco-Prussian War, also known as Franco-German War, 1870-71, unified German states. William proclaimed German emperor, 1871; beginning of Second Reich.

Frederick III, son, 1888.

William II, son, 1888-1918, led Germany into World War I. Abdicated Nov. 1918; died in exile in the Netherlands, 1941.

Germany adopted constitution at Weimar, July 1, 1919, setting up Weimar Republic. Presidents included Friedrich Ebert, 1919-25, and Paul von Hindenburg, 1925-34, field marshal in World War I. Hindenburg appointed Adolf Hitler chancellor, 1933, at beginning of Third Reich. Following Hindenburg's death, Hitler succeeded as Führer and chancellor, 1934-45, with dictatorial powers. Annexed Austria, 1938. Precipitated World War II, 1939-45. Hitler committed suicide, 1945.

Germany After 1945

After World War II, Germany was split between democratic West and Soviet-dominated East. West German chancellors: Konrad Adenauer, 1949-63; Ludwig Erhard, 1963-66; Kurt Georg Kiesinger, 1966-69; Willy Brandt, 1969-74; Helmut Schmidt, 1974-82; Helmut Kohl, 1982-90. East German Communist party leaders: Walter Ulbricht, 1950-71; Erich Honecker, 1971-89; Egon Krenz, 1989. (Berlin Wall fell, Nov. 1989.)

Germany reunited Oct. 3, 1990. Post-reunification chancellors: Helmut Kohl, 1990-98; Gerhard Schröder, 1998-2005; Angela Merkel, 2005-21; Olaf Scholz, 2021- .

Rulers of Hungary

The first king of Hungary was Stephen I, of the Arpad Dynasty, 1000-38. Feuds followed his death.

Charles I, also known as Charles Robert, became king, 1308-42.

Louis I (the Great), son, 1342-82. Succeeded uncle Casimir III as ruler of Poland, 1370.

Mary, elder daughter, 1382-95, ruled with husband, Sigismund of Luxemburg, 1387-1437, who also became king of Bohemia, Germany and Holy Roman Emperor. Hedwig (Jadwiga), younger daughter of Louis I, became queen of Poland. (See **Rulers of Poland**.)

Albert II, duke of Austria, son-in-law of Sigismund, 1438-39. Also king of Germany and Holy Roman Emperor.

Vladislaus I, 1440-44, king of Poland.

Ladislaus V, posthumous son of Albert II, 1444-57, not crowned until 1453. Janos Hunyadi acted as governor under young king, 1446-52; fought Turks.

Matthias I (Corvinus), son of Janos Hunyadi, 1458-90. Shared title of king of Bohemia. Captured Vienna, 1485; annexed Styria, Carinthia.

Vladislaus II, 1490-1516, king of Bohemia.

Louis II, son, 1516-26. Died in Battle of Mohács against Suleiman (the Magnificent), head of Ottoman Empire.

Ferdinand I, of Austria, brother-in-law, and John I, also known as John Zapolya of Transylvania, elected rival kings. Suleiman claimed part of Hungary for Ottoman Empire. Hungary partitioned. (Refer to **Habsburg Dynasty** for continuation.)

Rulers of Prussia

Nucleus of Prussia was the margravate of Brandenburg, an electorate of the Holy Roman Empire. Frederick VI, burgrave of Nuremberg, was made elector of Brandenburg, 1415. Rise of Hohenzollern Dynasty in territory that included Brandenburg and duchy of Prussia.

Frederick William (the Great Elector), 1640-88, elector of Brandenburg.

Frederick III, son, 1688-1713, elector of Brandenburg. Crowned Frederick I, king in Prussia, 1701.

Frederick William I, son, 1713-40.

Frederick II (the Great), son, 1740-86; military strategist who expanded Prussia's holdings.

Frederick William II, nephew, 1786-97.

Frederick William III, son, 1797-1840; Napoleonic Wars.

Frederick William IV, son, 1840-61. Revolution of 1848; constitution adopted, 1850. (Refer to **Second and Third Reichs** for continuation.)

Rulers of Poland

House of Piast

Mieszko I, c. 963-92, duke of Poland; Poland Christianized, 966. Expansion under three with name Boleslaus (reigns not consecutive): Boleslaus I (the Brave), son, 992-1025, crowned first king of Poland, 1025; Boleslaus II (the Bold), great-grandson, 1058-79, exiled after killing bishop of Krakow, Stanislaus (who became a patron saint of Poland); Boleslaus III (the Wry-Mouthed), nephew, 1102-38, divided Poland among four sons with oldest also in control of crown. Period of feudal division followed.

A Polish duke, Conrad of Masovia, asked the Teutonic Knights—a German military religious order—to crusade against Prussia, 1226. Teutonic Knights conquered lands; thereafter warred with Poland. Mongols/Tatars invaded Poland, 1241.

Vladislaus I, 1306-33, reunited most Polish territories; crowned king, 1320. Casimir III (the Great), son, 1333-70, developed economy, cultural life, foreign policy. No male heir. Succeeded by Louis I, nephew, 1370-82, who was also Louis I (the Great) of Hungary.

Jadwiga, daughter, 1384-99.

House of Jagiello

Vladislaus Jagiello, grand duke of Lithuania, married Jadwiga, 1386, and ruled jointly as Vladislaus II, 1386-1434. Poland and Lithuania united; Lithuania converted to Christianity. Defeated Teutonic Knights at Grunwald (Tannenberg), 1410.

Vladislaus III, son, 1434-44, also king of Hungary. Fought Turks; killed in Battle of Varna, 1444.

Casimir IV, brother, 1447-92, put son Vladislaus on throne of Bohemia and Hungary. Victorious over Teutonic Knights; signed treaty, 1466, after 13-year war.

John I, son, 1492-1501.

Alexander I, brother, 1501-05.

Sigismund I, brother, 1506-48, patronized sciences and arts; his and son's reign were golden age. Grand Master of Teutonic Order, Albert Hohenzollern, converted to Protestantism; secularized his state and made first duke of Prussia by Sigismund, 1525.

Sigismund II, son, 1548-72; Union of Lublin, 1569, established dual state of Poland and Lithuania. No male heir.

Elective Kings

Henry of Valois, 1573-74, first king elected by nobility. Left Poland to assume crown of France after brother's death. Interregnum.

Stephen Bathory, 1576-86, prince of Transylvania, married Anna, sister of Sigismund II. Fought Russians.

Sigismund III Vasa, nephew of Sigismund II and son of king of Sweden, 1587-1632. Fought to reclaim Swedish crown, which he'd lost because of his Catholicism; battled Russians and Turks.

Vladislaus IV Vasa, son, 1632-48.

John II Casimir Vasa, brother, 1648-68. Fought Cossacks, Swedish, Russians, Turks, Tatars; period of invasions known as "the Deluge."

Michael Korybut Wisniowiecki, 1669-73.

John III Sobieski, 1674-96, freed Vienna from besieging Turks, 1683.

Augustus II (the Strong), 1697-1733, elector of Saxony.

Augustus III, son, 1733-63, elector of Saxony.

Stanislaus II, 1764-95, last king. Encouraged reforms; first modern constitution in Europe, 1791. Poland lost territory to Russia, Austria, and Prussia in three partitions (1772, 1793, 1795). Thaddeus Kosciusko, American-Polish general, attempted unsuccessful insurrection, 1794.

Poland Under Foreign Rule

Grand duchy of Warsaw created by Napoleon I out of Prussian (formerly Polish) territory. Frederick Augustus I, king of Saxony, ruled grand duchy, 1807-15. Defeat of Napoleon led to Congress of Vienna, 1814-15; part of Poland claimed as kingdom by Russia. Polish uprisings against Russia (1830, 1863) and Austria (1846) repressed. Poland regained independence following World War I.

Second Republic

Jozef Pilsudski, 1918-22, head of state. Presidents: Gabriel Narutowicz, 1922, assassinated by extremist; Stanislaus Wojciechowski, 1922-26, resigned after coup d'état by Pilsudski; Ignacy Moscicki, 1926-39, ruled with Pilsudski (d. 1935) and Pilsudski's military colleagues as virtual dictator during what came to be known as Sanacja (meaning "cleansing" or "healing") regime.

Poland Under Foreign Occupation, Influence

After Hitler and Stalin signed nonaggression pact, Germany invaded Poland Sept. 1, 1939; Russia invaded Sept. 17. Polish government-in-exile was in France, then England. Vladislaus Raczkiewicz, 1939-47, president; Gen. Vladislaus Sikorski, 1939-43, and Stanislaus Mikolajczyk, 1943-44, prime ministers. Polish residents were sent to German concentration camps and Soviet labor camps; about 3 million Jewish Poles were killed in the Holocaust. Thousands of Polish prisoners of war, mostly military officers, massacred in Katyn Forest by Soviet secret police, 1940. Soviet-sponsored Polish Committee of National Liberation took formative role in new government, 1945, renamed Polish People's Republic in 1952. Communist Polish United Workers' Party ruled the country. Brief period of liberalization followed Stalin's death in 1953. Vladislaus Gomulka, 1956-70, and Edward Gierek, 1970-80, led country as first secretary of Polish United Workers' Party.

Election of Cardinal Karol Wojtyla, archbishop of Krakow, as pope (John Paul II) inspired Poles, 1978. Strikes in 1980 prompted creation of Solidarity, an independent trade union headed by Lech Walesa. Solidarity gained control of government in partly free elections, 1985.

Third Republic

Presidents: Lech Walesa, 1990-95; Aleksander Kwasniewski, 1995-2005; Lech Kaczynski, 2005-10, died in plane crash; Bronislaus Komorowski and Grzegorz Schetyna, acting, 2010; Komorowski, 2010-15; Andrzej Duda, 2015- .

Rulers of Denmark, Sweden, Norway

Denmark

Canute (the Great) ruled area that included England, Denmark, and Norway, 1016-35. Valdemar IV Atterdag reunited Denmark, 1361. Margrethe I, daughter, married to Haakon VI, king of Norway, 1363. After Valdemar's death, Olaf, Margrethe's infant son, made king of Denmark, 1375. He was also crowned king of Norway after death of Haakon, 1380. Following Olaf's death, 1387, Margrethe served as regent of Denmark, Norway, and Sweden. She effected the Union of Kalmar of the three kingdoms, 1397. She had her grandnephew, Eric of Pomerania, crowned (she held actual power until her death, 1412).

Succeeding rulers were unable to enforce their claims on Sweden until Christian II, 1512-23, conquered the country, 1520. He was soon deposed; accession of Gustav I as king of Sweden, 1523, ended Kalmar Union. Denmark continued to dominate Norway until the Napoleonic Wars when Frederik VI, 1808-39, allied with Napoleon I after Danish fleet was attacked by Britain, 1807. By 1814 treaty, Denmark was forced to cede Norway to Sweden.

Succession: House of Oldenborg (began with Christian I, 1448): Christian VIII, 1839-48; Frederik VII, son, 1848-63. House of Glücksborg: Christian IX, 1863-1906; Frederik VIII, son, 1906-12; Christian X, son, 1912-47; Frederik IX, son, 1947-72; Margrethe II, daughter, 1972-2024; Frederik X, son, 2024- .

Sweden

Under King Magnus Ladulas, hereditary nobility established around 1280. Swedish nobles opposed to Albrekt of Mecklenburg accepted Margareta (Margrethe), regent of Denmark, as ruler, 1389. Sweden joined Kalmar Union, 1397. After internal unrest, Sweden was conquered anew by Denmark's Kristian II, 1520. Execution of Kristian's opponents in "Stockholm Bloodbath" led to uprising under Gustav I Eriksson (Vasa), who was elected Swedish king, 1523-60. Gustav established an independent kingdom with centralized power, state church, and hereditary throne. Gustav II Adolf (Lion of the North), 1611-32, fought Russia, Poland, Germany; died in battle.

Later rulers: Kristina, daughter, 1632-54, abdicated; Karl X Gustav, cousin, 1654-60; Karl XI, son, 1660-97; Karl XII, son, 1697-1718; Ulrika Eleonora, sister, 1718-20, abdicated; Fredrik I, of Hesse, husband, 1720-51; Adolf Fredrik, 1751-71; Gustaf III, son, 1771-92; Gustaf IV Adolf, son, 1792-1809, deposed; Karl XIII, uncle, 1809-18. Karl XIV Johan (born Jean Baptiste Bernadotte, a general under Napoleon I), 1818-44, founded House of Bernadotte.

Succession: Oskar I, son, 1844-59; Karl XV, son, 1859-72; Oskar II, brother, 1872-1907; Gustaf V, son, 1907-50; Gustaf VI Adolf, son, 1950-73; Carl XVI Gustaf, grandson, 1973- .

Norway

Harald I (Fairhair) overcame rivals to become first king of Norway, c. 885-c. 933. Olaf II Haraldsson, 1015-28, Christianized country; became patron saint of Norway. Haakon V Magnusson, 1299-1319, died without male heir. His daughter Ingeborg was married to Erik, a son of the Norwegian king; their son Magnus VII Eriksson became ruler of Norway, 1319-55, and Sweden, 1319-63. Haakon VI Magnusson, son, 1355-80, married Margaret of Denmark. Olaf IV, son, became king of Norway, 1380-87, and Denmark, 1375-87, with mother as regent. Margaret took over rule upon his death, 1387. Union of Kalmar, 1397, united Norway, Denmark, and Sweden.

After Napoleonic Wars, Denmark ceded Norway to Sweden, 1814. A strong nationalist movement forced Sweden to recognize Norway as an independent kingdom under the Swedish kings. Norwegian constitution, adopted 1814, allowed for creation of the Storting (Norwegian parliament), which governed country domestically. In 1905, the union was dissolved. Prince Charles of Denmark elected king of Norway as Haakon VII, 1905-57; founded House of Glücksburg. Succession: Olav V, son, 1957-91; Harald V, son, 1991- .

Rulers of the Netherlands and Belgium

The Netherlands

Willem I, son of Prince Willem V of Orange, came to power after French rule ended in the Netherlands, 1813; crowned king with approval of Congress of Vienna, 1815. Started House of Orange-Nassau. Northern Netherlands was known as Holland. Belgians, in southern Netherlands, rebelled against the Dutch and seceded, Oct. 4, 1830. Dutch formally recognized Belgian independence, Apr. 19, 1839. Willem I abdicated, 1840.

Succession: Willem II, son, 1840-49; Willem III, son, 1849-90; Wilhelmina, daughter, 1890-1948; Juliana, daughter, 1948-80; Beatrix, daughter, 1980-2013; Willem-Alexander, son, 2013- .

Belgium

A national congress elected Prince Leopold of Saxe-Coburg as king. He took the throne July 21, 1831, as Leopold I.

Succession: Leopold II, son, 1865-1909; Albert I, nephew, 1909-34; Leopold III, son, 1934-51, in exile after Germany invaded Belgium, later abdicated; Prince Charles, brother, acted as regent 1944-50; Baudouin I, son of Leopold III, 1951-93; Albert II, brother, 1993-2013; Philippe, son, 2013- .

Rulers of Modern Italy

After the fall of Napoleon, the Congress of Vienna, 1814-15, restored Italy as a political patchwork, comprising the Kingdom of the Two Sicilies (Naples and Sicily), the Papal States, and smaller units. King Victor Emmanuel I of Savoy ruled Sardinia, Piedmont, and Genoa.

Victor Emmanuel I abdicated 1821. Charles Felix, brother, 1821-31, died without issue. Succeeded by Charles Albert, 1831-49; he abdicated upon defeat by the Austrians. Succeeded by Victor Emmanuel II, son, 1849-61. United Italy emerged under Camillo Benso di Cavour, prime minister of the Kingdom of Sardinia, 1852-61. Giuseppe Mazzini and Giuseppe Garibaldi were also figures in Risorgimento ("resurgence") period before Italy's unification.

In 1859, France forced Austria to cede Lombardy to Sardinia. In 1860, Garibaldi led more than 1,000 volunteers in a campaign against King Francis II of the Two Sicilies, taking Sicily and Naples. The House of Savoy subsequently annexed the Two Sicilies, Tuscany, Parma, Modena, Romagna, the Marches, and Umbria. Victor Emmanuel II assumed leadership of a united Kingdom of Italy, Mar. 17, 1861.

In 1866, Victor Emmanuel II allied with Prussia in the Austro-Prussian War and, with Prussia's victory, received Venetia. On Sept. 20, 1870, Italian troops entered Rome, ending the temporal power of the Roman Catholic Church. (The 1929 Lateran Treaty established papal sovereignty in Vatican City.)

Succession: Umberto I, son, 1878-1900, assassinated; Victor Emmanuel III, son, 1900-46; Umberto II, son, 1946, ruled only one month before voters in a referendum chose to establish a republic. In 1919, Benito Mussolini helped found the nationalist Fasci di Combattimento (Fighting Leagues), or Fascists. After Mussolini organized March on Rome, 1922, Victor Emmanuel III agreed to a coalition government. Mussolini eventually became dictator (Il Duce). He entered World War II as an ally of Hitler, 1940. He was dismissed by the king, 1943; captured and executed by partisans, 1945.

At a plebiscite, 1946, voters approved a republic. Prime minister Alcide de Gasperi was chief of state, 1945-53; Enrico de Nicola was provisional president. Successive presidents: Luigi Einaudi, 1948-55; Giovanni Gronchi, 1955-62; Antonio Segni, 1962-64; Giuseppe Saragat, 1964-71; Giovanni Leone, 1971-78; Alessandro Pertini, 1978-85; Francesco Cossiga, 1985-92; Oscar Luigi Scalfaro, 1992-99; Carlo Azeglio Ciampi, 1999-2006; Giorgio Napolitano, 2006-15; Sergio Mattarella, 2015- .

Rulers of Spain

From 8th to 11th centuries, Spain was dominated by the Moors (Muslims from North Africa of Arab and Berber origin). A number of small kingdoms—Aragon, Asturias, Castile, Catalonia, Leon, Navarre, and Valencia—undertook a Christian reconquest. In 1474, Isabella I became Queen of Castile and Leon. By the Catholic Monarchs' request, Pope Sixtus IV authorized the Inquisition, 1478. Isabella's husband, Ferdinand V, acceded to the throne of Aragon, 1479. Last Moorish kingdom, Granada, seized 1492. Spain sponsored Christopher Columbus, who led European exploration of New World, 1492. Isabella was succeeded by daughter, Joanna (the Mad), but Ferdinand acted as regent until his death, 1516.

Charles I, son of Joanna and grandson of Habsburg Emperor Maximilian I, became Holy Roman Emperor as Charles V, 1520;

abdicated 1556. Philip II, son, 1556-98, inherited only part of empire. He conquered Portugal, fought against Ottoman Empire, sent Armada in unsuccessful invasion of England. Succession: Philip III, son, 1598-1621; Philip IV, son, 1621-65; Charles II, son, 1665-1700, no issue, left Spain to Philip of Anjou, grandson of Louis XIV of France. As Philip V, he was first of Bourbon dynasty in Spain, 1700-46 (his son Louis ruled briefly in 1724); Ferdinand VI, son, 1746-59; Charles III, brother, 1759-88; Charles IV, son, 1788-1808, abdicated.

Joseph Bonaparte made king of Spain, 1808-13, by his brother Napoleon. Ferdinand VII, son of Charles IV, 1808, 1814-33, lost American colonies except Cuba, Puerto Rico. Maria Christina of the Two Sicilies, wife, was regent until 1843 for Isabella II, daughter, who was driven into exile by revolution, 1868. Amadeo of Savoy elected king by the Cortes (parliament), 1870-73. First Republic, 1873-74. Alfonso XII, son of Isabella II, 1875-85; Alfonso XIII, posthumous son, 1901-31, with mother Maria Christina as regent before he assumed throne. Spain ceded territory after loss in Spanish-American War, 1898. Primo de Rivera ruled as dictator, 1923-30, after military coup but was forced to resign after losing support. Alfonso agreed to exile without formal abdication. Monarchy abolished; Second Republic established with socialist backing. Presidents: Niceto Alcala Zamora, 1931-36; Manuel Azaña, 1936-39.

Revolt by military started Spanish Civil War, 1936-39. Gen. Francisco Franco ruled as head of Nationalist regime, 1939-73. Monarchy restored after 1947 referendum. Juan Carlos, grandson of Alfonso XIII, acceded to throne after Franco's death in 1975; abdicated, 2014. Felipe VI, son, 2014- .

Leaders in the South American Wars of Liberation

Francisco de Miranda, José de San Martín, and Simón Bolívar led early 19th-cent. struggles of South American nations to free themselves from Spain.

Miranda (1750-1816), a Venezuelan, served as an officer in the Spanish army. After a dispute with the army, he fled to the U.S., 1783, where he met leaders of the American Revolution. He traveled seeking support for South American independence from other world leaders. Miranda unsuccessfully attempted a revolt in Venezuela, 1806. Napoleon's invasion of Spain, 1808, prompted the start of a revolution in Venezuela. Miranda returned, 1810, and headed the revolution with dictatorial powers. Venezuela declared independence, 1811. Overcome by royalist forces, 1812, Miranda surrendered and was arrested; he died in a Spanish prison.

San Martín (1778-1850) was born in present-day Argentina. He served in Spanish campaigns in Europe until 1811. He returned to Argentina and joined the independence movement, 1812. In 1817, he invaded Chile through the Andean mountain passes. He and Bernardo O'Higgins defeated the Spanish at Chacabuco, 1817. Chile gained independence, 1819; O'Higgins became first director of Chile, 1817-23. In 1821, San Martín entered Lima and took the port of Callao; he became protector of an independent Peru.

Bolívar (1783-1830) was born into an aristocratic family in Venezuela. He served under Miranda until Miranda's surrender in 1812. Bolívar continued to fight; he captured Caracas and was named Liberator, 1813. But he was forced to flee by royalist forces, 1814. In 1817, Bolívar again fought for control of Venezuela. With Francisco de Paula Santander and José Antonio Páez, he defeated the Spanish at the Battle of Boyacá, 1819, freeing New Granada (present-day Colombia). New Granada, Venezuela, and the area that is now Panama and Ecuador were joined as the Republic of Colombia, or Gran Colombia, with Bolívar as president later that same year, though parts of the republic remained under Spanish control. He decisively defeated the Spanish in the Battle of Carabobo in Venezuela, 1821.

Antonio José de Sucre, Bolívar's chief lieutenant, overcame Spanish forces at the Battle of Pichincha in Ecuador, 1822. Bolívar convinced San Martín to resign as protector of Peru. Peru was declared independent after Bolívar and Sucre won the Battle of Junin, Aug. 1824, and Sucre triumphed at the Battle of Ayacucho, Dec. 1824.

Sucre organized Upper Peru as Republica Bolívar (now Bolivia), 1825, and acted as president in place of Bolívar, who wrote its constitution.

Civil strife caused the Colombian federation to break apart. Bolívar gave up the presidency, 1830.

Rulers of Russia; Leaders of the USSR and Russian Federation

The Varangian (Viking) prince Rurik is considered to be the first leader of the Russians; he established himself at Novgorod, c. 862 CE. His successor, Oleg, and those who followed Oleg ruled as princes of Kiev. Vladimir I, or Saint Vladimir, married sister of Byzantine emperor and converted to Christianity, 988. Yaroslav I (the Wise), brother, 1019-54, was important organizer and lawgiver; his daughters married kings of Norway, Hungary, and France. In 1169, Andrew Bogolyubsky conquered Kiev and began the line of Vladimir.

Daniel, a son of grand prince of Vladimir, Alexander Nevsky, was first to be called prince of Muscovy (Moscow), 1263-1303. Dmitri Ivanovich (Donskoi), prince of Moscow, defeated the Tatars at the Battle of Kulikovo, 1380. His successors were grand princes of Moscow. Ivan III (the Great), 1462-1505, achieved considerable territorial expansion.

Ivan III married Sofia Palaeologus, niece of the last Byzantine emperor. Succession: Vasily III, son. Ivan IV (the Terrible), son, crowned 1547 as Tsar of Russia. Fyodor I, son, reigned 1584-98, but his brother-in-law Boris Godunov had real control before becoming tsar himself, 1598-1605. After years of internal strife ("Time of Troubles"), the Russians united under 16-year-old Michael Romanov, distantly related to Ivan IV's first wife. He ruled 1613-45, establishing the Romanov line.

Tsars, or emperors, of Russia (Romanovs): Peter I (the Great), 1682-1725, with Ivan V, brother, as co-ruler, 1682-96. Catherine I, his widow, 1725-27. Peter II, grandson of Peter I, 1727-30. Anna, daughter of Ivan V and niece of Peter I, 1730-40. Ivan VI, nephew, 1740-41; deposed by Elizabeth, daughter of Peter I, 1741-62. Peter III, nephew, 1762; deposed by his wife, Catherine II (the Great), former princess of Anhalt Zerbst (Germany), 1762-96. Paul I, son, 1796-1801, assassinated. Alexander I, son, 1801-25, defeated Napoleon. Nicholas I, brother, 1825-55. Alexander II, son, 1855-81, assassinated. Alexander III, son, 1881-94. Nicholas II, son, 1894-1917, last tsar of Russia, was forced to abdicate by revolutionaries following losses to Germany in WWI. The tsar, empress, tsarevich (crown prince), and tsar's four daughters were murdered by the Bolsheviks, July 1918.

Premiers of provisional government: Prince Georgi Lvov, followed by Alexander Kerensky, 1917.

Union of Soviet Socialist Republics

Bolshevik Revolution, Nov. 7, 1917, (also known as the October Revolution, based on Russia's then use of the Julian calendar) removed Kerensky from power. Council of People's Commissars formed with Lenin (Vladimir Ilyich Ulyanov) as chair (or premier), 1917-24. Aleksei Rykov (executed 1938) and Vyacheslav M. Molotov held the office, but effective ruler was Joseph Stalin (Joseph Vissarionovich Dzhugashvili), general secretary of the Communist Party. Stalin was chair of the Council of People's Commissars from 1941 until his death in 1953. Succeeded by Georgi M. Malenkov, who also briefly served as general secretary of the Communist Party before being ousted from the position by Nikita S. Khrushchev. Malenkov was forced to resign as premier, 1955, and was expelled from the Communist Party, 1961. Nikolai A. Bulganin was premier, 1955-58, until his replacement by Khrushchev, 1958-64.

Leonid I. Brezhnev ousted Khrushchev as general secretary of the party, a post he held until his death in 1982. Aleksei N. Kosygin was premier, 1964-80. The Central Committee elected former KGB (state security) head Yuri V. Andropov general secretary, 1982-84. After Andropov's death, Konstantin U. Chernenko was chosen for the position, 1984-85. Upon Chernenko's death, he was succeeded by Mikhail Gorbachev. Gorbachev assumed the newly created position of president of the Soviet Union, 1990. Boris Yeltsin was sworn in July 1991 as the Russian Republic's first elected president. Under Yeltsin, Russia became a founding member of the Commonwealth of Independent States. Gorbachev resigned the presidency, Dec. 25, 1991, and the Soviet Union officially disbanded Dec. 31. Each of the 15 former Soviet constituent republics became independent.

Post-Soviet Russia

Presidents of the Russian Federation: Boris Yeltsin, 1991-99; Vladimir Putin, 2000-08; Dmitry Medvedev, 2008-12; Putin, 2012- .

Rulers of China

Where dynastic dates overlap, the rulers or events referred to appeared in different areas of China.

Years in power	Dynasty/ruler(s)
c. 1994-c. 1766 BCE	Xia dynasty, first hereditary Chinese dynasty
c. 1766-c. 1045 BCE	Shang dynasty, first Chinese dynasty with historical records
c. 1045-771 BCE	Western Zhou dynasty, capital near present-day Xi'an
770-256 BCE	Eastern Zhou dynasty, new capital established at Luoyang. During Chunqiu (Spring and Autumn) period (722-481 BCE), Zhou began to lose authority. Period of the Warring States (403-221 BCE) involved major powers of Qi, Chu, Yan, Han, Zhao, Wei, and Qin
221-207 BCE	Qin dynasty, quasi-feudal states unified for first time under self-proclaimed Shi Huang Di, or First Emperor. Prefectures/counties organized under central govt., uniform laws; written language, weights standardized
206 BCE-9 CE	Earlier, or Western Han dynasty, founded by rebel leader Liu Bang. Expansion under Emperor Wudi (born Liu Che), 140-87 BCE; civil service system established
9-23	Xin dynasty, established by Wang Mang, who deposed infant emperor for whom he was regent
25-220	Later, or Eastern Han dynasty
220-265[1]	Wei dynasty, established by son of Han general Cao Cao
221-263[1]	Shu Han dynasty in SW China
222-280[1]	Wu dynasty in SE China
265-317	Western Jin dynasty, established by Sima Yan, Wei dynasty general
317-420	Eastern Jin dynasty, established by prince of Sima family
420-589	Southern dynasties, four short-lived dynasties with capital at Jiankang (present-day Nanjing)
581-618	Sui dynasty, reunified China; established by Emperor Wendi (born Yang Jian), military appointee who usurped throne of non-Chinese Northern Zhou, 581
618-906	Tang dynasty, founded by Li Yuan (known as Emperor Gaozu of Tang), who led rebellion against the Sui. Notable rulers include former imperial concubine Empress Wu, 683-705; Xuanzong, 712-56
907-960	Five Dynasties. Period of disunion with short-lived dynasties in N; Ten Kingdoms (states) in S and W
907-1125	Liao dynasty, of Khitan Mongols, capital at Yanjing (present-day Beijing)
960-1126	Northern Song dynasty, established by military leader Zhao Kuangyin (Emperor Taizu), capital at Kaifeng
1122-1234	Jin dynasty, of Juchen people of Manchuria; drove Song out of N China
1127-1279	Southern Song dynasty, capital at Lin'an (present-day Hangzhou)
1279-1368	Yuan, or Mongol dynasty; Kublai Khan, grandson of Genghis Khan, high point of Mongol power
1368-1644	Ming dynasty, founded by Buddhist monk turned rebel general Zhu Yuanzhang. Country again under Chinese rule; capital in present-day Nanjing, then Beijing after Mongolian tribes' defeat
1644-1912	Qing, or Manchu dynasty, under rule of Manchu people. Last imperial dynasty; Emperor Xuantong, or Puyi, last emperor. Sun Yat-sen organized Kuomintang (Nationalist party) and led provisional republican government in Nanjing, 1911-12. Sun resigned in unification compromise with former imperial viceroy Yuan Shikai, who became president upon emperor's abdication in Feb. 1912
1912-1949	Rep. of China, power passed to provincial warlords upon Yuan's death, 1916. Gen. Chiang Kai-shek sought to reunify China under Kuomintang with new government at Nanjing, 1928. War with Japan, then civil war, led to Nationalist authority collapse, Communist declaration of People's Rep. of China, 1949

(1) Also known as the period of the Three Kingdoms because of warfare between the Wei, Shu Han, and Wu dynasties.

Leaders of People's Republic of China

Name	Title/position, years in power
Mao Zedong	People's Rep. of China (PRC) Chairman, 1949-59; Chinese Communist Party (CCP) Chairman, 1949-76
Zhou Enlai	Premier, 1949-76
Liu Shaoqi	PRC Chairman, 1959-68; one-time Mao successor removed from power during Cultural Revolution (1966-76)
Lin Biao	Red Army cmdr. designated Mao's successor, 1966; govt. reported his death in plane crash, 1971, after coup attempt
Hua Guofeng	Premier, 1976-80; CCP Chairman, 1976-81
Deng Xiaoping	"Paramount leader," 1977-97
Hu Yaobang	CCP General Secretary, 1980-87; CCP Chairman, 1981-82
Zhao Ziyang	Premier, 1980-87; CCP General Secretary, 1987-89
Li Xiannian	President, 1983-88
Yang Shangkun	President, 1988-93
Li Peng	Premier, 1988-98
Jiang Zemin	CCP General Secretary, 1989-2002; President, 1993-2003
Zhu Rongji	Premier, 1998-2003
Hu Jintao	CCP General Secretary, 2002-12; President, 2003-13
Wen Jiabao	Premier, 2003-13
Xi Jinping	CCP General Secretary, 2012- ; President, 2013-
Li Keqiang	Premier, 2013-23
Li Qiang	Premier, 2023-

Historical Periods of Japan

Years in power	Period	Founding event
c. 300-592	Yamato	The Yamato clan united various Japanese states. Also called Tumulus, or Tomb, period for its large burial mounds
593-710	Asuka	Accession of Empress Suiko, with her nephew Prince Shotoku as regent. The Taika reforms (from 645) established a centralized government under the emperor; capital moved to Asuka
710-794	Nara	Capital moved to Nara
794-1185	Heian	Capital moved to Heian (present-day Kyoto) by Emperor Kammu
858-1160	Fujiwara	Fujiwara no Yoshifusa became regent for his grandson
1160-1185	Taira	Taira no Kiyomoro assumed control; Minamoto no Yoritomo defeated Taira, 1185
1192-1333	Kamakura	Yoritomo became shogun, head of military government, with the emperor as titular leader
1334-1392	Namboku	Emperor Go-Daigo returned to power in Kemmu Restoration; 1336 revolt drove him from Kyoto to establish Southern Court at Yoshino
1392-1573	Muromachi	Unification of Southern and Northern Courts; Ashikaga family dominates
1467-1600	Sengoku	Onin War began; also known as Warring States period
1573-1603	Momoyama	Oda Nobunaga entered Kyoto, 1568, deposed last Ashikaga shogun, 1573. Tokugawa Ieyasu victor at Battle of Sekigahara, 1600
1603-1867	Edo	Ieyasu established Tokugawa shogunate, became shogun
1868-1912	Meiji	Meiji Restoration of imperial power, with Meiji (reign name of Mutsuhito) ascending throne; Charter Oath, 1868, led to Westernization
1912-1926	Taisho	Accession of Emperor Taisho (reign name of Yoshihito)
1926-1989	Showa	Accession of Emperor Hirohito (posthumous name Showa)
1989-2019	Heisei	Accession of Emperor Akihito[1]
2019-	Reiwa	Accession of Emperor Naruhito[1]

(1) A 2017 law allowed Akihito to abdicate, the first Japanese emperor to do so in about 200 years, on Apr. 30, 2019, and assume the title of emperor emeritus. His eldest son acceded to the throne the next day.

WORLD EXPLORATION AND GEOGRAPHY

Early Explorers of the Western Hemisphere

Genetic evidence suggests that humans reached the Americas by sailing along the Pacific coast or by crossing the Bering Land Bridge between Siberia and Alaska. Scientists dated fossilized footprints in New Mexico's White Sands National Park to 21,000-23,000 years before the present (BP), in a study published in 2021. Previously discovered remains of early arrivals include Anzick-1 (c. 12,600 BP), a male infant of the Clovis people found buried in present-day Montana; Xach'itee'aanenh T'eede Gaay (Sunrise Girl-Child) (c. 11,500 BP) of the Ancient Beringians, in Alaska; Luzia Woman (11,500 BP) in Brazil; and Kennewick Man (8,500 BP), in Washington. Modern Native Americans appear to be descended from peoples indigenous to N and Central Asia who split into two Native American populations—Northern and Southern—as they dispersed across the continents.

The Americas were populated mostly by hunter-gatherers and small-scale horticulturalists, but complex chiefdoms and state-level societies appeared in a few areas (SE U.S., Mesoamerica, coastal Chile). The earliest known state in the Americas, established by the Caral, or Caral-Supe, civilization, spanned 700 sq mi across river valleys in coastal Peru about 5,000 BP.

The Norse, led by Leif Ericson, are usually credited as being the first Europeans to reach America, with at least five voyages occurring about 1000 CE to areas they called Helluland, Markland, and Vinland—possibly present-day Baffin Island, Labrador, and either Newfoundland or New England. L'Anse aux Meadows, Newfoundland, is the only documented settlement, with evidence of a village dating to c. 1000 CE.

Sustained contact between the hemispheres began with Christopher Columbus (born Cristoforo Colombo, c. 1451, near Genoa, Italy), who made four voyages to the Americas with funding from the Spanish monarchs and private investors. He left Spain, Aug. 3, 1492, with 88 men and a fleet of three vessels—the *Niña*, *Pinta*, and *Santa María*—and landed on the island of San Salvador in present-day Bahamas on Oct. 12, 1492. He also visited Cuba, Hispaniola, and many smaller Caribbean islands, then populated by the Taíno. A second expedition, in 1493, reached the island of Dominica in the Lesser Antilles; a third, in 1498, took Columbus to Trinidad and the adjacent S American coast. A fourth voyage reached Mexico, Honduras, Panama, and what he christened Santiago (the present-day island of Jamaica) in 1502.

In 1497 and 1499, Amerigo Vespucci (for whom the Americas are named), an Italian sailing for Spain, passed along the N and E coasts of S America. He was the first to claim these lands were previously unknown and not part of Asia. Some early explorations are listed below.

Year	Explorer	Nationality (sponsor, if different)	Area reached or explored
1497	John Cabot	Italian (English)	Newfoundland, possibly Nova Scotia
1497-98	Vasco da Gama	Portuguese	Cape of Good Hope (Africa), India
1499	Alonso de Ojeda	Spanish	Northern S Amer. coast, Venezuela
1500	Vicente Yañez Pinzón	Spanish	S American coast, Amazon R.
1500	Pedro Álvarez Cabral	Portuguese	Brazil
1501	Rodrigo de Bastidas	Spanish	Central America
1513	Vasco Núñez de Balboa	Spanish	Panama, Pacific Ocean
1513	Juan Ponce de León	Spanish	Florida, Yucatán Peninsula
1515	Juan de Solis	Spanish	Río de la Plata
1519	Alonso de Pineda	Spanish	Mouth of Mississippi R.
1519	Hernán Cortés	Spanish	Mexico
1519-20	Ferdinand Magellan	Portuguese (Spanish)	Straits of Magellan, Tierra del Fuego
1524	Giovanni da Verrazano	Italian (French)	Atlantic coast, incl. New York Harbor
1528	Álvar Núñez Cabeza de Vaca	Spanish	Texas coast and interior
1532	Francisco Pizarro	Spanish	Peru
1534	Jacques Cartier	French	Canada, Gulf of St. Lawrence
1536	Pedro de Mendoza	Spanish	Up Río de la Plata, Buenos Aires
1539	Francisco de Ulloa	Spanish	California coast
1539	Marcos de Niza	Italian (Spanish)	SW United States
1539-41	Hernando de Soto	Spanish	Mississippi R., near Memphis, TN
1540	Francisco de Coronado	Spanish	SW United States
1540	Hernando de Alarcón	Spanish	Colorado R.
1540	Garcia Lopez de Cárdenas	Spanish	Colorado, Grand Canyon
1541	Francisco de Orellana	Spanish	Amazon R.
1542	Juan Rodriguez Cabrillo	Portuguese (Spanish)	Western Mexico, San Diego Harbor
1565	Pedro Menéndez de Avilés	Spanish	St. Augustine, FL
1576	Sir Martin Frobisher	English	Frobisher Bay, Canada
1577-80	Sir Francis Drake	English	CA coast, on voyage around world
1582	Antonio de Espejo	Spanish	SW U.S. (New Mexico)
1584	Philip Amadas and Arthur Barlowe (for Raleigh)	English	Virginia, Roanoke Isl.
1585-87	Sir Walter Raleigh's men	English	Roanoke Isl., NC
1595	Sir Walter Raleigh	English	Orinoco R., Venezuela
1603-09	Samuel de Champlain	French	Canadian interior, Lake Champlain
1607	John Smith	English	Atlantic coast
1609-10	Henry Hudson	English (Dutch)	Hudson R., Hudson Bay
1634	Jean Nicolet	French	Lake Michigan, Wisconsin
1673	Jacques Marquette and Louis Jolliet	French	Mississippi R., south to Arkansas
1682	René-Robert Cavelier, sieur de La Salle	French	Mississippi R., south to Gulf of Mexico
1727-29	Vitus Bering	Danish (Russian)	Bering Strait, Alaska
1789	Sir Alexander Mackenzie	Canadian	NW Canada
1804-06	Meriwether Lewis and William Clark	American	Missouri R., Rocky Mts., Columbia R.

Arctic Exploration

1596-97: Willem Barents (Dutch) touched Spitsbergen, 79°49´N, and rounded Novaya Zemlya, where he and crew were forced to winter ashore, first W Europeans to successfully do so in the Arctic.

1610: Henry Hudson (Eng.) explored Hudson Strait, Hudson Bay on search for Northwest Passage. After winter ashore, crew mutinied, 1611, and set him, his son, and some others adrift on small boat.

1733-43: Great Northern Expedition (Russ.), led by Vitus Bering (Dan./Russ.), surveyed Siberian Arctic coast. Bering had sailed through what would become known as Bering Strait, 1728, but this second expedition proved that Asia and North America were separate.

1827: William Edward Parry (Eng.), attempting to reach North Pole, made it to 82°45´N via sledge, setting record for farthest north.

1831: James Clark Ross (Eng.) was first to north magnetic pole.

1878-79: Baron Adolf Erik Nordenskiöld (Swed.) was first to navigate Northeast Passage—ocean route connecting Europe's North Sea to Pacific O.

1881-84: Adolphus Greely led 25-person U.S. expedition to Ellesmere Isl. as part of first Intl. Polar Year (1882-83). Only he and five others survived scurvy and starvation after relief ships failed to reach them.

1893-96: Fridtjof Nansen (Nor.) deliberately allowed *Fram* to become icebound and drift from New Siberian Isls. Leaving others in charge of ship, he tried polar dash in 1895 but only reached 86°14´N.

1903-06: Roald Amundsen (Nor.) was first to sail length of Northwest Passage—route linking Atlantic and Pacific via Canada's marine waterways.

1909: Robert E. Peary (U.S.) began dash for North Pole, Mar. 1, from Ellesmere Isl. Reportedly reached the pole, 90°N, Apr. 6, with Matthew Henson and four Inuit. Research suggests he may have fallen short of goal by c. 30-60 mi. (Dr. Frederick Cook [U.S.] claimed to have reached the North Pole in 1908.)

1926: Richard E. Byrd and Floyd Bennett (both U.S.) reputedly flew over North Pole, May 9. Amundsen, Lincoln Ellsworth (U.S.), and Umberto Nobile (Ital.) flew over North Pole May 12 in dirigible *Norge*.

1958: Nuclear-powered submarine USS *Nautilus* crossed the North Pole beneath the ice.

1968: Ralph Plaisted (U.S.) and three amateur explorers on snowmobiles became first independently confirmed surface expedition to reach North Pole.

1978: Naomi Uemura (Jpn.) became first person to reach the North Pole alone, traveling by dog sled in 54-day, 600-mi trek.

1982: Ranulph Fiennes (Eng.) and Charles Burton (S. Afr.-UK) reached the North Pole and became first to circle the Earth from pole to pole. They had reached the South Pole 16 months earlier. The 52,000-mi trek took three years at an est. cost of $18 mil.

1995: Richard Weber (Can.) and Mikhail Malakhov (Russ.) became first to North Pole and back without any mechanical assistance. The 940-mi trip on skis took 121 days.

Antarctic Exploration

Research published in 2021 suggests Polynesian (Māori) explorer Hui Te Rangiora and his crew may have sighted Antarctica in the early 600s. Western explorers have approached Antarctica since 1773-75, when Capt. James Cook (Eng.) reached 71°10´S. Fabian von Bellingshausen (Russ.) mapped the region on an expedition for Tsar Alexander I, 1819-21. In 1823, James Weddell (Brit.) reached 74°15´S and found the Weddell Sea.

First to announce existence of the continent of Antarctica was Charles Wilkes (U.S.), who followed the coast for 1,500 mi, 1840. Ross Ice Shelf was found by James Clark Ross (Brit.), 1841-42.

1895: Leonard Kristensen (Nor.) landed a party on Victoria Land, first ashore on main continental mass. C. E. Borchgrevink, a member of that party, returned in 1899 with a Brit. expedition, first to winter on Antarctica.

1901-04: Robert Falcon Scott (Eng.), commander of Brit. Natl. Antarctic Expedition, crossed Ross Ice Shelf to 82°17´S, farthest south then reached.

1911: Roald Amundsen (Nor.) with four men and dog teams were first to South Pole, Dec. 14. Scott and four companions reached South Pole on Jan. 17, 1912; they died on return trip.

1929: Richard E. Byrd (U.S.) crossed South Pole, Nov. 29, with three others on 1,600-mi airplane flight.

1934-35: Byrd led second expedition to Little America base camp, explored 450,000 sq mi, wintered alone at 80°08´S.

1935: Lincoln Ellsworth (U.S.) made first transcontinental crossing by air, flying south along E coast of Palmer Peninsula then across to Little America.

1946-48: Ronne Antarctic Research Expedition Cmdr. Finn Ronne determined Antarctic to be one continent with no strait between Weddell and Ross Seas.

1955-57: Supporting U.S. scientific efforts for Intl. Geophysical Year (IGY), the U.S. Navy's Operation Deep Freeze, led by Byrd, established five coastal stations and three interior stations; explored more than 1 mil sq mi in Wilkes Land.

1957-58: During the IGY, scientists from 12 countries conducted research within network of some 60 stations on Antarctica. Vivian E. Fuchs (Eng.) led 12-person Trans-Antarctic Expedition on first land crossing of Antarctica; completed in Mar. 1958 after traveling 2,158 mi in 99 days.

1959: Argentina, Australia, Belgium, Chile, France, Japan, New Zealand, Norway, South Africa, USSR, UK, and U.S. signed a treaty (in force 1961) affirming the use of Antarctica (specifically the area south of 60°S) "for peaceful purposes only." Territorial claims suspended.

1961-62: Scientists discovered Bentley Trench, running from Ross Ice Shelf into Marie Byrd Land, near the end of the Ellsworth Mts., toward Weddell Sea.

1985: Ocean Drilling Project finds that E Antarctic Ice Sheet is 37 mil years old, W Antarctic Ice Sheet 8 mil years old.

1991: Protocol to the Antarctic Treaty on Environmental Protection, or Madrid Protocol, adopted (in force 1998); it banned activities, except research, related to mineral resources.

1995: After 1994 solo expedition to North Pole, Borge Ousland (Nor.) reached South Pole on skis, becoming first to reach both poles alone. He later became the first to traverse both Antarctica (1996-97) and the Arctic (2001) solo.

2018: Colin O'Brady (U.S.) makes first solo Antarctic crossing without assistance or wind aid (54 days). Louis Rudd (Brit.) completed the same feat a little over two days later (56 days).

Volcanoes

Source: *Volcanoes of the World*, Geoscience Press; Global Volcanism Program, Smithsonian Institution, volcano.si.edu

Eruptions have been confirmed in some 859 volcanoes. More than half to three-quarters of historically active volcanoes can be found on the so-called **Ring of Fire**, which runs along the W coast of the Americas from the southern tip of Chile to Alaska, down the E coast of Asia from Kamchatka to Indonesia, and continues from New Guinea to New Zealand. The Ring of Fire marks boundaries between tectonic plates underlying the Pacific Ocean and the surrounding continents. Volcanic activity also occurs along rift zones like Iceland, where plates pull apart, or over hot spots such as Hawaii, where molten material rises from the mantle to Earth's crust. The majority of Earth's volcanism takes place at submarine rift zones, on the seafloor.

Notable Volcanic Eruptions

In approximately 5,700 BC, Mount Mazama, in southern Oregon, erupted violently, ejecting large amounts of ash and pumice and sending out pyroclastic flows (mixture of volcanic debris and gases). The top of the mountain collapsed, leaving a caldera about 6 mi across and 1 mi deep. This depression filled with water from rain and snow to form Crater Lake.

Date	Volcano	Est. deaths
Aug. 24, 79 CE	Vesuvius, Italy	16,000[1]
1586	Kelut, Java, Indon.	10,000
Dec. 15, 1631	Vesuvius, Italy	4,000
Aug. 12, 1772	Papandayan, Java, Indon.	3,000
June 8, 1783	Laki, Iceland	9,350
May 21, 1792	Unzen, Japan	14,500
Apr. 10-12, 1815	Tambora, Sumbawa, Indon.	92,000[2]
Aug. 26-27, 1883	Krakatau, Indon.	36,000[3]
Apr. 24, 1902	Santa María, Guatemala	1,000[4]
May 8, 1902	Pelée, Martinique	28,000
Jan. 30, 1911	Taal, Philippines	1,400
June 6-8, 1912	Novarupta, AK, U.S.[5]	1
May 19, 1919	Kelut, Java, Indon.	5,000
Jan. 17-21, 1951	Lamington, Papua New Guinea	3,000
May 18, 1980	St. Helens, WA, U.S.	57
Mar. 28, 1982	El Chichón, Mexico	1,880
Nov. 13, 1985	Nevado del Ruiz, Colombia	23,000
Aug. 21, 1986	Lake Nyos, Cameroon	1,700[6]
June 15, 1991	Pinatubo, Luzon, Philippines	800[7]

(1) Heated mud and ash engulfed Pompeii, Herculaneum, and Stabiae with debris more than 60 ft deep. About 10% of the three towns' pop. were killed. (2) Of these, about 10,000 were directly related to the eruption. Released gases and particles altered the global climate, leading to additional deaths from starvation and disease when crops failed. (3) At least 2,000 died in pyroclastic flows, Aug. 26. Collapse of volcano, Aug. 27, sank most of island, killing over 3,000. Resulting tsunamis were responsible for the majority of deaths, in Java and Sumatra. (4) An additional 3,000 deaths due to a malaria outbreak are sometimes attributed to the eruption. (5) Biggest eruption of 20th cent. by volume. (6) Caused by release of massive amount of carbon dioxide from crater lake. (7) Of these, about 500 were associated with post-eruption lahars (volcanic mudflows).

Notable Active Volcanoes

Source: Global Volcanism Program, Smithsonian Inst.; Volcano Hazards Program, U.S. Geological Survey, U.S. Dept. of the Interior

Active volcanoes display a wide range of activity, including the production of ash plumes and seismic swarms. An eruption may involve the explosive ejection of fragmental material and escape of liquid lava. Year of a volcano's last known or confirmed eruption, as of mid-2024, is given. Volcanoes are listed by elevation, which does not reflect eruptive magnitude. Submarine volcanoes are not included.

Volcano (last eruption)	Location	Elev. (ft)
Africa		
Cameroon (2000)	Cameroon	13,435
Nyiragongo (2023)	Dem. Rep. of the Congo	11,385
Nyamuragira (2024)	Dem. Rep. of the Congo	10,033
Ol Doinyo Lengai (2024)	Tanzania	9,718
Fogo (2015)	Cape Verde Isls.	9,281
Piton de la Fournaise (2023)	Réunion Isl. (Fr.), Indian O.	8,635
Karthala (2007)	Comoros	7,746
Nabro (2012)	Eritrea	7,277
Antarctica		
Erebus (2024)	Ross Isl.	12,448
Melbourne (1892)	Victoria Land	8,963
Asia and Oceania		
Ararat (1840)	Turkey	16,946
Klyuchevskoy (2023)	Kamchatka, Russia	15,597
Kerinci (2020)	Sumatra, Indon.	12,467
Fuji (1708)	Honshu, Japan	12,388
Rinjani (2016)	Lombok, Indon.	12,224
Semeru (2024)	Java, Indon.	11,998
Tolbachik (2013)	Kamchatka, Russia	11,847
Koryaksky (2009)	Kamchatka, Russia	11,253
Slamet (2014)	Java, Indon.	11,247
Shiveluch (Sheveluch) (2024)	Kamchatka, Russia	10,771
Raung (2022)	Java, Indon.	10,696
Dempo (2023)	Sumatra, Indon.	10,308
Ontake (2014)	Honshu, Japan	10,062
Agung (2019)	Bali, Indon.	9,833
Merapi (2024)	Java, Indon.	9,547
Zhupanovsky (2016)	Kamchatka, Russia	9,511
Marapi (2024)	Sumatra, Indon.	9,465
Bezymianny (2024)	Kamchatka, Russia	9,455
Ruapehu (2007)	North Isl., New Zealand	9,177
Heard (2024)	Heard Isl., Australia	9,006
Changbaishan (1903)	China-North Korea	9,003
Avachinsky (2001)	Kamchatka, Russia	8,914
Papandayan (2002)	Java, Indon.	8,743
Talang (2007)	Sumatra, Indon.	8,448
Asama (2019)	Honshu, Japan	8,425
Dieng Volcanic Complex (2021)	Java, Indon.	8,415
Mayon (2024)	Luzon, Philippines	8,077
Sinabung (2021)	Sumatra, Indon.	8,071
Kanlaon (2017)	Negros, Philippines	7,989
Niigata-Yakeyama (1998)	Honshu, Japan	7,874
Kizimen (2013)	Kamchatka, Russia	7,657
Ulawun (2023)	Papua New Guinea	7,657
Tengger Caldera (2020)	Java, Indon.	7,641
Alaid (2022)	Kuril Isls., Russia	7,497
Chokai (1974)	Honshu, Japan	7,336
Galunggung (1984)	Java, Indon.	7,113
Kusatsu-Shirane (2018)	Honshu, Japan	7,103
Sorikmarapi (1986)	Sumatra Isl., Indon.	7,037
Kambalny (2017)	Kamchatka, Russia	6,942
Tangkubanparahu (2019)	Java, Indon.	6,837
Tongariro (2012)	North Isl., New Zealand	6,490
Azuma (1977)	Honshu, Japan	6,394
Kaba (2000)	Sumatra Isl., Indon.	6,365
Nasu (1963)	Honshu, Japan	6,283
Sangeang Api (2022)	Lesser Sunda Isls., Indon.	6,273
Bagana (2024)	Papua New Guinea	6,086
Karkar (2014)	Papua New Guinea	6,033
Chachadake (Tiatia) (1981)	Kunashir Isl., Japan-admin. by Russia	5,978
Bandai (1888)	Honshu, Japan	5,958
Manam (2024)	Papua New Guinea	5,928
Gorely (2010)	Kamchatka, Russia	5,902
Karangetang (Api Siau) (2024)	Siau Isl., Indon.	5,896
Kuju (1996)	Kyushu, Japan	5,876
Soputan (2020)	Sulawesi, Indon.	5,856
Chikurachki (2022)	Kuril Isls., Russia	5,843
Kelut (2014)	Java, Indon.	5,679
Adatara (1996)	Honshu, Japan	5,669
Batur (2000)	Bali, Indon.	5,633
Gamalama (2018)	Ternate, Indon.	5,627
Lewotobi (2024)	Flores Isl., Indon.	5,587
Kirishima (2018)	Kyushu, Japan	5,577
Egon (2008)	Flores, Indon.	5,449
Gamkonora (2007)	Halmahera, Indon.	5,364
Aso (2020)	Kyushu, Japan	5,223
Lokon-Empung (2015)	Sulawesi, Indon.	5,184
Bulusan (2022)	Luzon, Philippines	5,036
Karymsky (2022)	Kamchatka, Russia	4,964
Akan (2008)	Hokkaido, Japan	4,918
Pinatubo (2021)	Luzon, Philippines	4,875
Central America and West Indies		
Tacaná (1986)	Mexico-Guatemala	13,333
Acatenango (1972)	Guatemala	13,045
Fuego (2024)	Guatemala	12,346
Santa María (2024)	Guatemala	12,287
Irazú (1994)	Costa Rica	11,260
Turrialba (2022)	Costa Rica	10,958
Poás (2024)	Costa Rica	8,848
Pacaya (2020)	Guatemala	8,428
Santa Ana (2005)	El Salvador	7,812
San Miguel (2023)	El Salvador	6,988
Rincón de la Vieja (2024)	Costa Rica	6,286
San Cristóbal (2023)	Nicaragua	5,725
Concepción (2011)	Nicaragua	5,577
Arenal (2010)	Costa Rica	5,479
Soufrière Guadeloupe (1977)	Guadeloupe (France)	4,813
Pelée (1932)	Martinique (France)	4,573
Momotombo (2016)	Nicaragua	4,167
North America		
Pico de Orizaba (1846)	Mexico	18,406
Popocatépetl (2024)	Mexico	17,694
Rainier (1450)	Washington	14,409
Shasta (1250)	California	14,163
Wrangell (1912)	Alaska	14,035
Colima (2019)	Mexico	12,631
Hood (1866)	Oregon	11,240
Spurr (1992)	Alaska	11,070
Lassen Peak (1917)	California	10,456
Redoubt (2009)	Alaska	10,197
Iliamna (1876)	Alaska	10,016
Shishaldin (2023)	Unimak Isl., Aleutians, AK	9,373
St. Helens (2008)	Washington	8,363
Veniaminof (2021)	Alaska	8,225
Pavlof (2022)	Alaska	8,179
Fourpeaked (2006)	Alaska	6,906
Katmai (1912)	Alaska	6,716
Makushin (1995)	Unalaska Isl., Aleutians, AK	5,906
Great Sitkin (2024)	Great Sitkin Isl., Aleutians, AK	5,709
Cleveland (2020)	Chuginadak Isl., Aleutians, AK	5,676
South America		
Llullaillaco (1877)	Chile-Argentina	22,110
San Pedro-San Pablo (1960)	Chile	20,151
Guallatiri (1960)	Chile	19,918
San José (1960)	Chile-Argentina	19,915
Sabancaya (2024)	Peru	19,554
Cotopaxi (2023)	Ecuador	19,393
El Misti (1985)	Peru	19,101
Ubinas (2023)	Peru	18,609
Tupungatito (1987)	Chile-Argentina	18,570
Láscar (2023)	Chile	18,346
Nevado del Huila (2012)	Colombia	17,598
Sangay (2024)	Ecuador	17,343
Nevado del Ruiz (2024)	Colombia	17,320
Irruputuncu (1995)	Chile-Bolivia	16,939
Tungurahua (2016)	Ecuador	16,480
Guagua Pichincha (2002)	Ecuador	15,696
Puracé (2023)	Colombia	15,256
Galeras (2014)	Colombia	14,029
Planchón-Peteroa (2019)	Chile	13,048
Lautaro (1979)	Chile	11,834
Reventador (2024)	Ecuador	11,686
Nevados de Chillán (2022)	Chile	10,433
Llaima (2009)	Chile	10,253
Europe		
Etna (2024)	Italy	11,014
Vesuvius (1944)	Italy	4,203
Stromboli (2024)	Italy	3,031
Mid-Atlantic		
La Palma (2021)	Canary Isls. (Spain)	7,959
Beerenberg (1985)	Jan Mayen (Norway)	7,208
Bardarbunga (2015)	Iceland	6,562
Grímsvötn (2011)	Iceland	5,640
Eyjafjallajökull (2010)	Iceland	5,417
Hekla (2000)	Iceland	4,888
Mid-Pacific		
Mauna Loa (2022)	Hawaii, HI	13,681
Haleakala (1750)	Maui, HI	10,023
Kilauea (2023)	Hawaii, HI	4,009

Mountains

North America

Source: U.S. Geological Survey, U.S. Dept. of the Interior; National Geodetic Survey, NOAA, U.S. Dept. of Commerce; Natural Resources Canada. Survey dates and elevation sources may differ.

Peak, state/prov., country	Height (ft)	Peak, state/prov., country	Height (ft)	Peak, state/prov., country	Height (ft)
Denali (fmr. McKinley), AK	20,308	La Malinche (Matlalcuéyetl), Mexico	14,636	Wilson, CO	14,246
Logan, Yukon, Canada	19,551	Hunter, AK	14,573	Cameron, CO	14,238
Pico de Orizaba, Mexico	18,406	Browne Tower, AK	14,530	Shavano, CO	14,231
St. Elias, AK-YT, U.S.-Can.	18,009	Whitney, CA	14,505	Princeton, CO	14,204
Popocatépetl, Mexico	17,802	Alverstone, AK-YT, U.S.-Can.	14,500	Belford, CO	14,203
Foraker, AK	17,400	University Peak, AK	14,470	Yale, CO	14,200
Iztaccíhuatl, Mexico	17,159	Elbert, CO	14,440	Crestone Needle, CO	14,197
Lucania, YT, Canada	17,146	Massive, CO	14,421	Bross, CO	14,172
King Peak, YT, Canada	16,972	Harvard, CO	14,421	Kit Carson, CO	14,165
Steele, YT, Canada	16,624	Rainier, WA	14,410	Point Success, WA	14,164
Bona, AK	16,500	Williamson, CA	14,376	Shasta, CA	14,163
Blackburn, AK	16,390	Blanca Peak, CO	14,345	Wrangell, AK	14,163
Sanford, AK	16,237	La Plata Peak, CO	14,336	Maroon Peak, CO	14,163
South Buttress, AK	15,885	Uncompahgre Peak, CO	14,321	Tabeguache, CO	14,162
Wood, YT, Canada	15,873	Crestone Peak, CO	14,294	Oxford, CO	14,160
Vancouver, AK-YT, U.S.-Can.	15,699	Lincoln, CO	14,293	El Diente Peak, CO	14,159
Churchill, AK	15,638	Castle Peak, CO	14,279	Sill, CA	14,159
Nevado de Toluca (Xinantécatl), Mexico	15,354	Grays Peak, CO	14,278	Democrat, CO	14,155
Fairweather, AK-BC, U.S.-Can.	15,299	Antero, CO	14,276	Sneffels, CO	14,150
Macaulay, YT, Canada	15,299	Torreys Peak, CO	14,275	Capitol Peak, CO	14,130
Slaggard, YT, Canada	15,299	Quandary Peak, CO	14,271	Liberty Cap, WA	14,118
Hubbard, AK-YT, U.S.-Can.	15,016	Evans, CO	14,265	Pikes Peak, CO	14,115
Bear, AK	14,831	Longs Peak, CO	14,259	Snowmass, CO	14,099
Walsh, YT, Canada	14,780	McArthur, YT, Canada	14,253	Russell, CA	14,094
East Buttress, AK	14,730	White Mountain Peak, CA	14,252	Eolus, CO	14,083
		North Palisade, CA	14,248	Windom, CO	14,082
				Challenger Point, CO	14,081

Note: The highest point in the West Indies is Pico Duarte (10,417 ft), in the Dominican Republic.

Other Notable U.S. Mountains

Peak, state	Height (ft)	Peak, state	Height (ft)	Peak, state	Height (ft)
Gannett, WY	13,810	Adams, WA	12,281	Mitchell, NC	6,683
Grand Teton, WY	13,775	San Gorgonio, CA	11,503	Clingmans Dome, NC-TN	6,644
Kings, UT	13,518	Hood, OR	11,247	Washington, NH	6,289
Cloud, WY	13,171	Cleveland, MT	10,466	Rogers, VA	5,729
Wheeler, NM	13,167	Lassen, CA	10,461	Marcy, NY	5,343
Boundary, NV	13,146	Granite, CA	10,325	Katahdin, ME	5,269
Granite, MT	12,807	Guadalupe, TX	8,751	Spruce Knob, WV	4,863
Borah, ID	12,668	Olympus, WA	7,973	Mansfield, VT	4,395
Humphreys, AZ	12,637	Harney, SD	7,244	Black Mountain, KY	4,139

South America

Peak, country	Height (ft)	Peak, country	Height (ft)	Peak, country	Height (ft)
Aconcagua, Argentina	22,835	Coropuna, Peru	21,083	Solo, Argentina	20,492
Ojos del Salado, Arg.-Chile	22,569	Laudo, Argentina	20,997	Polleras, Argentina	20,456
Bonete, Argentina	22,546	Ancohuma, Bolivia	20,958	Pular, Chile	20,423
Tupungato, Argentina-Chile	22,310	Ausangate, Peru	20,945	Chani, Argentina	20,341
Pissis, Argentina	22,241	Toro, Argentina-Chile	20,932	Aucanquilcha, Chile	20,295
Mercedario, Argentina	22,211	Illampu, Bolivia	20,873	Juncal, Argentina-Chile	20,276
Huascarán, Peru	22,205	Tres Cruces, Argentina-Chile	20,853	Negro, Argentina	20,184
Llullaillaco, Argentina-Chile	22,110	Huandoy, Peru	20,852	Quela, Argentina	20,128
El Libertador, Argentina	22,047	Parinacota, Bolivia-Chile	20,768	Condoriri, Bolivia	20,095
Cachi, Argentina	22,047	Tortolas, Argentina-Chile	20,745	Palermo, Argentina	20,079
Yerupajá, Peru	21,765	Ampato, Peru	20,702	Solimana, Peru	20,068
Incahuasi, Argentina-Chile	21,720	El Condor, Argentina	20,669	San Juan, Argentina-Chile	20,049
Galan, Argentina	21,654	Salcantay, Peru	20,574	Sierra Nevada, Argentina-Chile	20,023
Nevado Sajama, Bolivia	21,463	Chimborazo, Ecuador	20,564	Antofalla, Argentina	20,013
El Muerto, Argentina-Chile	21,457	Huancarhuas, Peru	20,531	Marmolejo, Argentina-Chile	20,013
Nacimiento, Argentina	21,302	Famatina, Argentina	20,505	Chachani, Peru	19,931
Illimani, Bolivia	21,201	Pumasillo, Peru	20,492		

Africa

Peak, country	Height (ft)	Peak, country	Height (ft)	Peak, country	Height (ft)
Kilimanjaro, Tanzania	19,341	Karisimbi, Congo-Rwanda	14,787	Guna, Ethiopia	13,881
Kenya, Kenya	17,057	Tullu Dimtu, Ethiopia	14,360	Gughe, Ethiopia	13,780
Margherita Pk., Uganda-Congo	16,765	Elgon, Kenya-Uganda	14,178	Jebel Toubkal, Morocco	13,665
Meru, Tanzania	14,977	Batu, Ethiopia	14,131	Cameroon, Cameroon	13,435
Ras Dashen, Ethiopia	14,872				

Australia, New Zealand, SE Asian Islands

Peak, country	Height (ft)	Peak, country	Height (ft)	Peak, country	Height (ft)
Jaya, New Guinea, Indon.	16,024	Wilhelm, Papua New Guinea	14,793	Aoraki/Cook, New Zealand	12,218
Trikora, New Guinea, Indon.	15,585	Kinabalu, Malaysia	13,436	Semeru, Java, Indon.	12,060
Mandala, New Guinea, Indon.	15,420	Kerinci, Sumatra, Indon.	12,467	Kosciusko, Australia	7,313

Height of Mount Everest

Mt. Everest, the world's highest mountain, was considered 29,002 ft when Edmund Hillary and Tenzing Norgay became the first to scale it, in 1953. In 1954, the Surveyor General of the Republic of India set the height at 29,028 ft, plus or minus 10 ft because of snow. In 1999, a team of climbers sponsored by Boston's Museum of Science and the National Geographic Society measured the height at the summit using satellite-based technology. The new measurement, of 29,035 ft, was accepted by other authorities, including the U.S. National Imagery and Mapping Agency, but not by Nepal. Government surveyors from Nepal and China, in 2019 and 2020, respectively, ascended Everest in order to determine a new official height. They jointly announced Everest's height as 29,031.693 ft (8,848.86 m) in Dec 2020.

Climbers typically ascend Everest on its north (Tibet) or south face (Nepal). By the end of the 2023 climbing season, which runs from April through May, a total of about 6,664 different climbers had made successful ascents; around 327 climbers had died, including 16 Sherpas killed in 2014 when falling ice set off an avalanche. A 7.8 magnitude earthquake hit Nepal Apr. 25, 2015, triggering avalanches that swept through Everest Base Camp on the south side, killing 19. The 2015 season was subsequently canceled, making it the first year since 1974 that no one reached the top. The 2019 climbing season included 11 deaths, raising concerns about overcrowding and the number of permits issued to inexperienced climbers. The COVID-19 pandemic forced the closure of the 2020 climbing season. Lax procedures and poor communication led to a COVID-19 outbreak in spring 2021 at Everest Base Camp in Nepal. In 2023, 17 people died or were presumed dead climbing to and from Mt. Everest. Nepal issued 478 permits for climbing parties in 2024. The estimated cost to climb in 2024 was $30,000-$75,000.

Europe

Peak, country	Height (ft)
Alps	
Mont Blanc, France-Italy	15,774
Dufourspitze (highest of Monte Rosa group), Switzerland	15,203
Dom, Switzerland	14,911
Liskamm, It.-Switzerland	14,852
Weisshorn, Switzerland	14,780
Taschhorn, Switzerland	14,733
Matterhorn, It.-Switzerland	14,692
Dent Blanche, Switzerland	14,293
Nadelhorn, Switzerland	14,196
Grand Combin, Switzerland	14,154
Lenzpitze, Switzerland	14,088
Finsteraarhorn, Switzerland	14,022
Castor, Switzerland	13,865
Zinalrothorn, Switzerland	13,849
Hohberghom, Switzerland	13,842
Alphubel, Switzerland	13,799
Rimpfischhom, Switzerland	13,776
Aletschorn, Switzerland	13,763
Strahlhorn, Switzerland	13,747
Dent D'Herens, Switzerland	13,686
Breithorn, It.-Switzerland	13,665
Bishorn, Switzerland	13,645
Jungfrau, Switzerland	13,642
Ecrins, France	13,461
Monch, Switzerland	13,448
Pollux, Switzerland	13,422
Schreckhorn, Switzerland	13,379
Ober Gabelhorn, Switzerland	13,330
Gran Paradiso, Italy	13,323
Bernina, It.-Switzerland	13,284
Fiescherhorn, Switzerland	13,283
Grunhorn, Switzerland	13,266
Lauteraarhorn, Switzerland	13,261
Durrenhorn, Switzerland	13,238
Allalinhorn, Switzerland	13,213
Weissmies, Switzerland	13,199
Lagginhorn, Switzerland	13,156
Zupo, Switzerland	13,120
Fletschhorn, Switzerland	13,110
Adlerhorn, Switzerland	13,081
Gletscherhorn, Switzerland	13,068
Schalihorn, Switzerland	13,040
Scerscen, Switzerland	13,028
Eiger, Switzerland	13,025
Jagerhorn, Switzerland	13,024
Rottalhorn, Switzerland	13,022
Pyrenees	
Aneto, Spain	11,168
Posets, Spain	11,073
Perdido, Spain	11,007
Vignemale, France-Spain	10,820
Long, Spain	10,479
Estats, Spain	10,304
Montcalm, Spain	10,105
Caucasus (Europe-Asia)	
Elbrus, Russia	18,481
Shkhara, Georgia	17,064
Dykh Tau, Russia	17,054
Kashtan Tau, Russia	16,877
Janqi, Georgia	16,565
Kazbek, Georgia	16,558

Asia (Mainland)

Peak, country/region	Height (ft)
Everest, Nepal-Tibet	29,032
K2 (Godwin Austen), Kashmir	28,251
Kanchenjunga, India-Nepal	28,169
Lhotse I (Everest), Nepal-Tibet	27,923
Makalu I, Nepal-Tibet	27,824
Lhotse II (Everest), Nepal-Tibet	27,560
Dhaulagiri, Nepal	26,795
Manaslu I, Nepal	26,781
Cho Oyu, Nepal-Tibet	26,750
Nanga Parbat, Kashmir	26,660
Annapurna I, Nepal	26,545
Annapurna II, Nepal	26,545
Gasherbrum, Kashmir	26,470
Broad, Kashmir	26,400
Gosainthan, Nepal-Tibet	26,287
Gyachung Kang, Nepal-Tibet	25,910
Disteghil Sar, Kashmir	25,868
Himalchuli, Nepal	25,801
Nuptse (Everest), Nepal-Tibet	25,726
Masherbrum, Kashmir	25,660
Nanda Devi, India	25,645
Rakaposhi, Kashmir	25,550
Kamet, India-Tibet	25,447
Namcha Barwa, Tibet	25,445
Gurla Mandhata, Tibet	25,355
Kungur, Xinjiang, China	25,325
Tirich Mir, Pakistan	25,230
Makalu II, Nepal-Tibet	25,120
Minya Konka, China	24,900
Annapurna III, Nepal	24,786
Kula Gangri, Bhutan-Tibet	24,784
Changtse (Everest), Nepal-Tibet	24,780
Muztagh Ata, Xinjiang, China	24,757
Skyang Kangri, Kashmir	24,750
Annapurna IV, Nepal	24,688
Ismail Samani Peak, Tajikistan	24,590
Noshaq, Afghanistan	24,580
Jongsong Peak, India-Nepal-China	24,472
Jengish Chokusu, Xinjiang, China-Kyrgyzstan	24,406
Sia Kangri, Kashmir	24,350
Haramosh Peak, Pakistan	24,270
Istoro Nal, Pakistan	24,240
Kirat Chuli, India-Nepal	24,165
Chomo Lhari, Bhutan-Tibet	24,040
Chamlang, Nepal	24,012
Kabru, India-Nepal	24,002
Alung Gangri, Tibet	24,000
Baltoro Kangri, Kashmir	23,990
Mana, India	23,860
Baruntse, Nepal	23,688
Nepal Peak, India-Nepal	23,500
Amne Machin, China	23,490
Gauri Sankar, Nepal-Tibet	23,440
Badrinath, India	23,420
Nunkun, Kashmir	23,410
Lenin Peak, Tajikistan	23,406
Pyramid, India-Nepal	23,400
Api, Nepal	23,399
Pauhunri, India-Tibet	23,385
Trisul, India	23,360
Kangto, India-Tibet	23,260
Nyenchen Thanglha, Tibet	23,255
Trisuli, India	23,210
Pumori, Nepal-Tibet	23,190
Dunagiri, India	23,184
Lombo Kangra, Tibet	23,165
Saipal, Nepal	23,100
Macha Pucchare, Nepal	22,958
Khan Tengri, Kazakhstan-Kyrgyzstan-Xinjiang, China	22,949
Ulugh Muztagh, Xinjiang, China-Tibet	22,877
Numbar, Nepal	22,817
Kanjiroba, Nepal	22,580
Ama Dablam, Nepal	22,350
Cho Polu, Nepal	22,093
Lingtren, Nepal-Tibet	21,972
Khumbutse, Nepal-Tibet	21,785
Hlako Gangri, Tibet	21,266

Antarctica

Peak	Height (ft)
Vinson Massif	16,066
Tyree	15,919
Shinn	15,750
Gardner	15,375
Epperly	15,100
Kirkpatrick	14,855
Elizabeth	14,698
Markham	14,290
Bell	14,117
Mackellar	14,098
Anderson	13,957
Bentley	13,934
Kaplan	13,878
Andrew Jackson	13,750
Sidley	13,720
Ostenso	13,710
Minto	13,668
Miller	13,650
Long Gables	13,620
Dickerson	13,517
Giovinetto	13,412
Wade	13,400
Fisher	13,386
Fridtjof Nansen	13,350
Wexler	13,202
Lister	13,200
Shear	13,100
Odishaw	13,008
Donaldson	12,894
Ray	12,808
Sellery	12,779
Waterman	12,730
Anne	12,703
Press	12,566
Falla	12,549
Rucker	12,520
Goldthwait	12,510
Morris	12,500
Erebus	12,448

Notable Islands and Their Areas

Figures are for total area in square miles. Boldface figures in parentheses show rank among the world's 10 largest individual islands. Only the largest islands in an island group are shown. Table does not include islands smaller than 10 sq mi in area. Canada's Manitoulin Island (1,068 sq mi), in Lake Huron, is the world's largest island in a freshwater lake.

Antarctica	
Adelaide	1,400
Alexander	16,700
Berkner	18,500
Roosevelt	2,900

Arctic Ocean	
Amund Ringnes, NU, Can.	2,029
Axel Heiberg, NU, Can.	16,671
Baffin, NU, Can. **(5)**	195,928
Banks, NT, Can.	27,038
Bathurst, NU, Can.	6,194
Bolshoy Lyakhovsky, Russia	1,776
Borden, NT-NU, Can.	1,079
Bylot, NU, Can.	4,273
Coats, NU, Can.	2,123
Cornwallis, NU, Can.	2,701
Devon, NU, Can.	21,331
Disko, Greenland, Denmark	3,312
Ellef Ringnes, NU, Can.	4,361
Ellesmere, NU, Can. **(10)**	75,767
Faddayevskiy, Russia	1,930
Franz Josef Land, Russia	8,000
Iturup (Etorofu), Russia	2,596
King William, NU, Can.	5,062
Kotelny, Russia	4,504
Mackenzie King, NT, Can.	1,949
Melville, NT-NU, Can.	16,274
Milne Land, Greenland, Den.	1,400
New Siberian Isls., Russia	14,500
Novaya Zemlya, Russia (2 isls.)	31,730
Prince Charles, NT, Can.	3,676
Prince Patrick, NT, Can.	6,119
Prince of Wales, NU, Can.	12,872
Severnaya Zemlya, Russia (tot. group)	14,175
Bol'shevik	4,368
Komsomolets	3,477
Oktyabr'skoy Revolyutsii	5,471
Somerset, NU, Can.	9,570
Southampton, NU, Can.	15,913
Svalbard, Norway (tot. group)	23,561
Nordaustlandet	5,576
Spitsbergen	14,546
Traill, Greenland, Denmark	1,300
Victoria, NT-NU, Can. **(8)**	83,897
Wrangel, Russia	2,937

Atlantic Ocean	
Anticosti, QC, Can.	3,066
Ascension, UK	35
Azores, Portugal (tot. group)	868
Faial	67
San Miguel	291
Bahama Isls. (tot. group)	5,382
Andros	2,300
Bermuda Isls., UK (tot. group)	21
Bioko Isl., Equatorial Guinea	785
Block Island, RI, U.S.	21
Cabo Verde	1,557
Canary Isls., Spain (tot. group)	2,807
Fuerteventura	688
Gran Canaria	592
Tenerife	795
Cape Breton, NS, Can.	3,981
Caviana, Pará, Brazil	1,918
Channel Isls., UK (tot. group)	75
Guernsey	24
Jersey	45
Falkland Isls., UK (tot. group)	4,700
East Falkland	2,550
West Falkland	1,750
Faroe Isls., Denmark	538
Great Britain, UK **(9)**	80,823
Greenland, Denmark **(1)**	836,330
Gurupá, Pará, Brazil	1,878
Hebrides, Scotland, UK	2,744
Iceland	39,958
Ireland, Ireland-UK	32,589
Isle of Man, UK	221
Isle of Wight, England, UK	147
Long Island, NY, U.S.	1,320
Madeira Isls., Portugal	306
Marajó, Brazil	15,444
Martha's Vineyard, MA, U.S.	89
Mount Desert, ME, U.S.	104
Nantucket, MA, U.S.	45
Newfoundland, Canada	42,031
Orkney Isls., Scotland, UK	383
Prince Edward Isl. (main), Can.	2,170
St. Helena, UK	47
Shetland Isls., Scotland, UK	555
Skye, Scotland, UK	647
South Georgia, UK	1,450
Tierra del Fuego, Chile-Arg.	18,800
Tristan da Cunha, UK	38

Baltic Sea	
Aland Isls., Finland	610
Bornholm, Denmark	227
Funen, Denmark	1,154
Gotland, Sweden	1,159
Zealand, Denmark	2,722

Caribbean Sea	
Antigua	108
Aruba, Netherlands	69
Barbados	166
Cayman Isls., UK (tot. group)	102
Cuba	40,285
Isle of Youth	934
Curaçao, Netherlands	171
Dominica	290
Guadeloupe, France	687
Hispaniola (Haiti and Dominican Rep.)	29,389
Jamaica	4,244
Martinique, France	436
Montserrat, UK	39
Nevis	36
Puerto Rico, U.S.	3,425
St. Kitts	65
St. Lucia	238
St. Vincent	133
Tobago	116
Trinidad	1,864
Virgin Isls., UK	59
Virgin Isls., U.S.	134

East Indies	
Bali, Indonesia	2,171
Bangka, Indonesia	4,375
Borneo, Indonesia-Malaysia-Brunei **(3)**	290,321
Bougainville, Papua New Guinea	3,880
Buru, Indonesia	3,670
Flores, Indonesia	5,500
Halmahera, Indonesia	6,865
Java (Jawa), Indonesia	48,900
Madura, Indonesia	2,113
Moluccas, Indonesia	32,307
New Britain, PNG	14,093
New Guinea, Indon.-PNG **(2)**	303,381
New Ireland, PNG	3,707
Seram, Indonesia	6,621
Sulawesi (Celebes), Indonesia	69,000
Sumatra, Indonesia **(6)**	182,543
Sumba, Indonesia	4,306
Sumbawa, Indonesia	5,965
Timor, Indon.–Timor-Leste	13,094
Yos Sudarsa, Indonesia	4,500

Indian Ocean	
Andaman Isls., India	2,500
Kerguelen, France	2,247
Madagascar **(4)**	226,917
Mauritius	720
Pemba, Tanzania	380
Réunion, France	970
Seychelles	176
Sri Lanka	25,332
Zanzibar, Tanzania	640

Mediterranean Sea	
Balearic Isls., Spain	1,927
Corfu, Greece	229
Corsica, France	3,369
Crete, Greece	3,189
Cyprus	3,572
Elba, Italy	86
Euboea, Greece	1,411
Malta	95
Rhodes, Greece	540
Sardinia, Italy	9,301
Sicily, Italy	9,926

Pacific Ocean	
Admiralty, AK, U.S.	1,709
Aleutian Isls., AK, U.S. (tot. group)	6,912
Adak	275
Attu	350
Tanaga	195
Umnak	686
Unalaska	1,051
Unimak	1,571
Baranof, AK, U.S.	1,636
Chichagof, AK, U.S.	2,062
Chiloe, Chile	3,241
Easter Isl. (Rapa Nui), Chile	63
Fiji (tot. group)	7,056
Vanua Levu	2,242
Viti Levu	4,109
Galapagos Isls., Ecuador	3,043
Graham Isl., BC, Can.	2,456
Guadalcanal, Solomon Isls.	2,180
Guam, U.S.	210
Hainan, China	13,000
Hawaiian Isls., HI, U.S. (tot. group)	6,428
Hawaii	4,028
Oahu	597
Hong Kong, China	31
Hoste, Chile	1,590
Japan (tot. group)	145,937
Hokkaido	32,210
Honshu **(7)**	89,280
Kyushu	16,305
Okinawa	881
Shikoku	7,260
Kangaroo, South Australia	1,705
Kiritimati (Christmas), Kiribati	150
Kodiak, AK, U.S.	3,485
Kupreanof, AK, U.S.	1,084
Marquesas Isls., France	492
Marshall Islands	70
Melville, Northern Terr., Australia	2,234
Micronesia	271
New Caledonia, France	6,530
New Zealand (tot. group)	103,362
Chatham Isls.	372
North	44,075
South	58,076
Stewart	649
Northern Mariana Isls., U.S.	179
Nunivak, AK, U.S.	1,600
Palau	188
Philippines (tot. group)	115,831
Leyte	2,787
Luzon	40,680
Mindanao	36,775
Mindoro	3,690
Negros	4,907
Palawan	4,554
Panay	4,446
Samar	5,050
Prince of Wales, AK, U.S.	2,770
Revillagigedo, AK, U.S.	1,134
Riesco, Chile	1,973
St. Lawrence, AK, U.S.	1,780
Sakhalin, Russia	29,500
Samoa Isls. (tot. group)	1,177
American Samoa, U.S.	77
Savaii, Samoa	659
Tutuila, U.S.	55
Upolu, Samoa	432
Santa Catalina, CA, U.S.	75
Santa Ines, Chile	1,407
Tahiti, France	402
Taiwan (tot. group)	13,892
Jinmen Dao (Quemoy)	56
Tasmania, Australia	26,178
Tonga	288
Vancouver Isl., BC, Can.	12,079
Vanuatu	4,707
Wellington, Chile	2,549

Persian Gulf	
Bahrain	295

Notable Deserts of the World

Deserts are defined as regions of the Earth receiving less than 10 in. of precipitation annually, usually in combination with an evaporation rate exceeding precipitation.

In addition to areas listed below, the continent of Antarctica, with an area of about 5.48 mil sq mi (of which 110,039 sq mi are ice free), is generally considered a desert. Average annual precipitation for the continent as a whole is 2-6 in., with most precipitation falling along the coast; there is little evaporation.

Arabian, 899,618 sq mi, spanning almost all of Arabian Peninsula
Atacama, 600-mi-long area rich in nitrate and copper deposits in northern Chile
Chihuahuan, 139,769 sq mi in TX, NM, AZ, and Mexico
Dasht-e Kavir, approx. 500 mi long by 200 mi wide in north-central Iran
Dasht-e Lut, approx. 300 mi long by 200 mi wide in south-central Iran
Death Valley, 3,300 sq mi in CA and NV
Eastern (Arabian), 86,000 sq mi in Egypt between the Nile R. and Red Sea, extending south into Sudan
Gibson, 60,232 sq mi in the interior of western Australia
Gobi, 500,002 sq mi in Mongolia and China
Great Sandy, 103,186 sq mi in western Australia
Great Victoria, 134,653 sq mi in southwestern Australia
Kalahari, 347,492 sq mi in southern Africa
Karakum, 135,136 sq mi in Turkmenistan
Kyzyl Kum, 115,000 sq mi in Kazakhstan and Uzbekistan
Libyan, 425,000 sq mi in the Sahara, extending from Libya through southwestern Egypt into Sudan
Mojave, 15,000 sq mi in southern CA
Namib, long narrow area (varies 30-100 mi wide) extending 800 mi along SW coast of Africa
Nubian, 157,000 sq mi in the Sahara in northeastern Sudan
Painted Desert, section of high plateau in northern AZ extending 200 mi southeast from Grand Canyon
Patagonia, 259,847 sq mi in southern Argentina
Rub al-Khali (Empty Quarter), 250,000 sq mi in the S Arabian Peninsula
Sahara, 3,552,140 sq mi in N Africa, extending west to the Atlantic. Largest desert in the world
Sonoran, 120,000 sq mi in southwestern AZ and southeastern CA extending into NW Mexico
Syrian, 193,051 sq mi over much of northern Saudi Arabia, eastern Jordan, southern Syria, and western Iraq
Taklamakan, 130,000 sq mi in Xinjiang Prov., China
Tanami, 71,236 sq mi in northern Australia
Thar (Great Indian), 100,000-sq-mi area extending 400 mi along India-Pakistan border

Areas and Average Depths of Oceans, Seas, and Gulfs

Four major bodies of water were historically recognized: the Pacific, Atlantic, Indian, and Arctic Oceans. The Atlantic and Pacific Oceans are considered divided at the equator into N and S. The Arctic Ocean is the name for waters north of the continental landmasses in the region of the Arctic Circle. The International Hydrographic Organization (IHO) delimited a fifth world ocean—the Southern (Antarctic)—in 2000. The Southern Ocean extends from the coast of Antarctica north to 60°S latitude, encompassing portions of the Atlantic, Indian, and Pacific Oceans, although its boundaries have yet to be agreed on by all IHO member countries. A Woods Hole Oceanographic Institution study published in 2010 calculated a mean depth of 12,081 ft for the world's oceans.

Body of water	Area (sq mi)	Avg. depth (ft)
Pacific Ocean	60,060,893	14,040
Atlantic Ocean	29,637,974	11,810
Indian Ocean	26,469,620	12,800
Southern Ocean	7,848,299	14,450
Arctic Ocean	5,427,052	4,300
South China Sea	1,388,385	4,802
Caribbean Sea	1,094,214	8,448
Bering Sea	972,977	4,893
Mediterranean Sea	953,286	4,926
Gulf of Mexico	582,100	5,297
Sea of Okhotsk	537,500	3,192
Sea of Japan	391,100	5,468
Hudson Bay	281,900	305
East China Sea	256,600	620
Andaman Sea	218,100	3,667
Black Sea	196,100	3,906
Red Sea	174,900	1,764
North Sea	164,900	308
Baltic Sea	147,500	180
Yellow Sea	113,500	121
Persian Gulf	88,800	328
Gulf of California	59,100	2,375

Principal Ocean Depths

Source: Intl. Hydrographic Org. (IHO); Intergovernmental Oceanographic Commission (IOC) of UNESCO; National Geospatial-Intelligence Agency, U.S. Dept. of Defense

Body of water	Location (lat.)	(long.)	Depth (meters)	(fathoms)	(feet)
Pacific Ocean					
Mariana Trench	11°22′ N	142°36′ E	10,994	6,012	36,069
Tonga Trench	23°16′ S	174°44′ W	10,800	5,906	35,433
Philippine Trench	10°38′ N	126°36′ E	10,057	5,499	32,995
Kermadec Trench	31°53′ S	177°21′ W	10,047	5,494	32,963
Bonin Trench	24°30′ N	143°24′ E	9,994	5,464	32,788
Kuril Trench	44°15′ N	150°34′ E	9,750	5,331	31,988
Izu Trench	31°05′ N	142°10′ E	9,695	5,301	31,808
New Britain Trench	06°19′ S	153°45′ E	8,940	4,888	29,331
Yap Trench	08°33′ N	138°02′ E	8,527	4,663	27,976
Japan Trench	36°08′ N	142°43′ E	8,412	4,600	27,599
Peru-Chile Trench	23°18′ S	71°14′ W	8,064	4,409	26,457
Palau Trench	07°52′ N	134°56′ E	8,054	4,404	26,424
Aleutian Trench	50°51′ N	177°11′ E	7,679	4,199	25,194
New Hebrides Trench	20°36′ S	168°37′ E	7,570	4,139	24,836
North Ryukyu Trench	24°00′ N	126°48′ E	7,181	3,927	23,560
Middle America Trench	14°02′ N	93°39′ W	6,662	3,643	21,857
Atlantic Ocean					
Puerto Rico Trench	19°55′ N	65°27′ W	8,605	4,705	28,232
South Sandwich Trench	55°42′ S	25°56′ W	8,325	4,552	27,313
Romanche Gap	0°13′ S	18°26′ W	7,728	4,226	25,354
Cayman Trench	19°12′ N	80°00′ W	7,535	4,120	24,721
Brazil Basin	09°10′ S	23°02′ W	6,119	3,346	20,076
Indian Ocean					
Java Trench	10°19′ S	109°58′ E	7,125	3,896	23,376
Ob' Trench	09°45′ S	67°18′ E	6,874	3,759	22,553
Diamantina Trench	35°50′ S	105°14′ E	6,602	3,610	21,660
Vema Trench	09°08′ S	67°15′ E	6,402	3,501	21,004
Agulhas Basin	45°20′ S	26°50′ E	6,195	3,387	20,325
Arctic Ocean					
Eurasia Basin	82°23′ N	19°31′ E	5,450	2,980	17,881
Mediterranean Sea					
Ionian Basin	36°32′ N	21°06′ E	5,150	2,816	16,896

Note: Greater depths have been reported in some areas but have not been officially confirmed by research vessels.

Major World Rivers

North American rivers are listed in a separate table.

River	Source or upper limit of length	Outflow	Length (mi)
Africa			
Chari	Bamingui-Bangoran region, Central African Republic	Lake Chad	650
Congo	Junction of Lualaba and Luvua Rivers, Dem. Rep. of Congo	Atlantic Ocean	2,720
Cubango (fmr. Okavango)	Central Angola	Okavango Delta	1,000
Gambia	Fouta Djallon Highlands, Guinea	Atlantic Ocean	700
Kasai	Central Angola	Congo River	1,100
Limpopo	Junction of Marico and Ngotwane Rivers, South Africa	Indian Ocean	1,100
Lualaba	Southeastern Dem. Rep. of Congo	Congo River	1,100
Niger	Fouta Djallon Highlands, Guinea	Gulf of Guinea	2,600
Nile	Luvironza River, Burundi	Mediterranean Sea	4,132
Orange	Maluti Mountains, northern Lesotho	Atlantic Ocean	1,300
Sénégal	Junction of Bafing and Bakoy Rivers, Mali	Atlantic Ocean	1,000
Ubangi	Junction of Uele and Bomu Rivers, Dem. Rep. of Congo	Congo River	700
Zambezi	Northwestern Zambia	Indian Ocean	1,700
Asia			
Amu Darya	Junction of Vakhsh and Panj Rivers, Afghanistan-Tajikistan	Aral Sea	1,660
Amur	Junction of Shilka and Argun Rivers, China-Russia	Tartar Strait	1,780
Angara	Lake Baikal, Russia	Yenisei River	1,150
Ayeyarwady (fmr. Irrawaddy)	Junction of Mali and Nmai Rivers, Myanmar	Andaman Sea	1,000
Brahmaputra	Kailas Range, Himalayas, southwestern Tibet	Bay of Bengal	1,800
Chang-Jiang	Tibetan Plateau, southwestern Qinghai, China	East China Sea	3,450
Euphrates	Junction of Kara (Sarasu) and Murat Rivers, Turkey	Shatt al-Arab	1,700
Ganges	Gangotri glacier, Himalayas, India	Bay of Bengal	1,560
Godavari	Western Ghats, Maharashtra, India	Bay of Bengal	900
Hsi (see Xi He)			
Huang-He	Kunlun Mountains, Qinghai, China	Yellow Sea	3,000
Indus	Kailas Range, Himalayas, Tibet	Arabian Sea	1,900
Irtysh	Kazakhstan-Russia	Ob River	2,650
Jordan	Junction of Dan, Banias, and Hazbani streams, Israel	Dead Sea	200
Kolyma	Kolyma and Cherskogo Ranges, Russia	Arctic Ocean	1,500
Krishna	Western Ghats, Maharashtra, India	Bay of Bengal	800
Kura	Northeastern Turkey	Caspian Sea	950
Lena	Western Baikal Range, Russia	Laptev Sea	2,734
Mekong	Eastern Tibetan Plateau, China	South China Sea	2,700
Narmada	Madhya Pradesh, India	Arabian Sea	775
Ob	Junction of Biya and Katun Rivers, Russia	Gulf of Ob	2,300
Salween	Eastern Tibet, China	Gulf of Martaban	1,750
Songhua Jiang	Changbai Mountains, Jilin, China	Amur River	1,150
Sungari (see Songhua Jiang)			
Sutlej	Kailas Range, Himalayas, Tibet	Indus River	900
Syr	Junction of Naryn and Kara Darya Rivers, Uzbekistan	Aral Sea	1,380
Tarim	Junction of Kashi and Yarkant Rivers, China	Lop Nor	1,300
Tigris	Taurus Mountains, Turkey	Shatt al-Arab	1,150
Xi He	Eastern Yunnan, China	South China Sea	1,250
Yamuna	Yamnotri glacier, Uttarakhand, India	Ganges River	850
Yangtze (see Chang-Jiang)			
Yellow (see Huang-He)			
Yenisei	Kyzyl, Tuva Republic, Russia	Kara Sea	2,500
Australia			
Darling	Eastern Highlands, NE New South Wales/SE Queensland	Murray River	1,703
Murray	Australian Alps, SE New South Wales	Southern Ocean	1,558
Murrumbidgee	Australian Alps, SE New South Wales	Murray River	923
Europe			
Buh, Southern	Podolian Upland, Ukraine	Black Sea	532
Buh, Western	Western Ukraine	Vistula River	500
Danube	Brege and Brigach Rivers, Black Forest, southwestern Germany	Black Sea	1,770
Dnieper	Valdai Hills, western Russia	Black Sea	1,420
Dniester	Carpathian Mountains, Ukraine	Black Sea	850
Don	SE of Tula, Russia	Sea of Azov	1,200
Drava	Carnic Alps, northern Italy	Danube River	450
Dvina, North	Near Veliki Ustyug, Vologda, Russia	White Sea	465
Dvina, West	Valdai Hills, Russia	Gulf of Riga	635
Ebro	Cantabrian Mountains, northern Spain	Mediterranean Sea	575
Elbe	Giant Mountains, northwestern Czechia	North Sea	725
Garonne	Central Pyrenees, Spain	Bay of Biscay	402
Kama	Ural Mountains, N of Kuliga, Russia	Volga River	1,260
Loire	Mt. Gerbier-de-Jonc, Vivrais Mountains, France	Atlantic Ocean	630
Marne	Langres Plateau, northeastern France	Seine River	325
Meuse	Langres Plateau, northeastern France	North Sea	560
Oder	Sudetes Mountains, northeastern Czechia	Baltic Sea	562
Oka	S of Orël, Russia	Volga River	925
Pechora	Northern Ural Mountains, Russia	Barents Sea	1,120
Po	Cottian Alps, Piedmont, northwestern Italy	Adriatic Sea	405
Rhine	Swiss Alps	North Sea	766

River	Source or upper limit of length	Outflow	Length (mi)
Rhône	Rhône glacier, northeastern Valais, Switzerland	Mediterranean Sea	505
Seine	Langres Plateau, northern Burgundy, France	English Channel	480
Shannon	Near Cuilcagh Mountain, northwestern Cavan County, Ireland	Atlantic Ocean	240
Tagus	E of Madrid, Spain	Atlantic Ocean	585
Thames	4 headstreams in the Cotswold Hills, Gloucestershire, England, UK	North Sea	215
Tiber	Etruscan Apennines, Italy	Tyrrhenian Sea	251
Tisza	N of Rakhiv, western Ukraine	Danube River	700
Ural	Southern Ural Mountains, northeastern Bashkortostan, Russia	Caspian Sea	1,580
Vistula (Wisla)	W Beskid range, Carpathian Mountains, southwestern Poland	Gulf of Gdansk	665
Volga	Valdai Hills, Smolensk, Russia	Caspian Sea	2,290
Weser	Junction of Fulda and Werra Rivers, Germany	North Sea	273
South America			
Amazon	Junction of Ucayali and Marañón Rivers, Andes Mountains, Peru	Atlantic Ocean	4,000
Araguaía	Serra das Araras, Goiás-Mato Grosso, Brazil	Tocantins River	1,100
Beni	Cordillera Real, La Paz, Bolivia	Madeira River	1,000
Caquetá-Japura	Andes Mountains, southwestern Colombia	Amazon River	1,750
Juruá	Cerros de Canchyuaya, eastern Peru	Amazon River	1,500
Madeira	Junction of Beni and Mamoré Rivers, Bolivia	Amazon River	2,100
Magdalena	Cordillera Central, southwestern Colombia	Caribbean Sea	1,000
Negro	Southeastern Colombia	Amazon River	1,400
Orinoco	Near Mt. Delgado Chalbaud, Guiana Highlands, S Venezuela	Atlantic Ocean	1,600
Paraguay	Central Mato Grosso highlands, Brazil	Paraná River	1,584
Paraná	Junction of Paranaíba and Rio Grande Rivers, SE Brazil	Río de la Plata	2,485
Pilcomayo	E of Lake Poopó, Bolivia	Paraguay River	1,000
Purus	Andes Mountains, eastern Peru	Amazon River	2,100
Putumayo	Andes Mountains, southern Colombia	Amazon River	1,000
Río de la Plata	Estuary of Paraná and Uruguay Rivers, Argentina-Uruguay	Atlantic Ocean	170
São Francisco	Serra de Canastra, southwestern Minas Gerais, Brazil	Atlantic Ocean	1,800
Tocantins	South-central Goiás, Brazil	Para River	1,640
Ucayali	Junction of Apurímac and Urubamba Rivers, eastern Peru	Marañón River	1,000
Uruguay	Southern Brazil	Río de la Plata	1,000
Xingu	Central Mato Grosso, Brazil	Amazon River	1,230

Major Rivers in North America

River	Source or upper limit of length	Outflow	Length (mi)
Alabama	Gilmer County, GA	Mobile River	729
Albany	Lake St. Joseph, ON, Can.	James Bay	610
Allegheny	Potter County, PA	Ohio River, Pittsburgh, PA	325
Altamaha-Ocmulgee	Junction of Yellow and South Rivers, Newton Co., GA	Atlantic Ocean	392
Apalachicola-Chattahoochee	Towns County, GA	Gulf of Mexico	524
Arkansas	Lake County, CO	Mississippi River	1,459
Assiniboine	Eastern Saskatchewan, Can.	Red River	450
Athabasca	Columbia Icefield, AB, Can.	Lake Athabasca	765
Attawapiskat	Attawapiskat, ON, Can.	James Bay	465
Back (NT)	Contwoyto Lake, NT, Can.	Chantrey Inlet, Arctic Ocean	605
Big Black	Webster County, MS	Mississippi River	330
Brazos	Junction of Salt and Double Mountain Forks, Stonewall Co., TX	Gulf of Mexico	1,280
Canadian	Las Animas County, CO	Arkansas River	906
Cedar (IA)	Dodge County, MN	Iowa River	329
Cheyenne	Junction of Antelope Creek and Dry Fork, Converse Co., WY	Missouri River	290
Churchill, Labrador	Lake Ashuanipi, NL, Can.	Atlantic Ocean	532
Churchill, Manitoba	Methy Lake, SK, Can.	Hudson Bay	1,000
Cimarron	Colfax County, NM	Arkansas River	600
Colorado (AZ)	Rocky Mountain Natl. Park, CO	Gulf of California	1,450
Colorado (TX)	Dawson County, TX	Matagorda Bay	862
Columbia	Columbia Lake, BC, Can.	Pacific Ocean, Astoria, OR	1,243
Columbia, Upper	Columbia Lake, BC, Can.	Mouth of Snake River	890
Connecticut	Third Connecticut Lake, NH	Long Island Sound, CT	407
Coppermine	Lac de Gras, NT, Can.	Coronation Gulf, Arctic Ocean	525
Cumberland	Letcher County, KY	Ohio River	720
Delaware	Schoharie County, NY	Liston Point, Delaware Bay	390
Fraser	Near Mount Robson (on Continental Divide)	Strait of Georgia	851
Gila	Catron County, NM	Colorado River	649
Green (UT-WY)	Junction of Wells and Trail Creeks, Sublette County, WY	Colorado River	730
Hudson	Henderson Lake, Essex County, NY	Upper New York Bay	306
Illinois	St. Joseph County, IN	Mississippi River	420
James (ND-SD)	Wells County, ND	Missouri River	710
James (VA)	Junction of Jackson and Cowpasture Rivers, Botetourt Co., VA	Hampton Roads	340
Kanawha-New	Junction of North and South Forks of New River, NC	Ohio River	352
Kentucky	Junction of North and Middle Forks, Lee County, KY	Ohio River	259
Klamath	Lake Ewauna, Klamath Falls, OR	Pacific O., Klamath, CA	250

River	Source or upper limit of length	Outflow	Length (mi)
Kootenay (Kootenai)	Rocky Mountains, BC, Can.	Columbia River	485
Koyukuk	Endicott Mountains, AK	Yukon River	470
Kuskokwim	Alaska Range	Kuskokwim Bay	724
Liard	Southern Yukon, AK	Mackenzie River	693
Little Missouri	Crook County, WY	Missouri River	560
Mackenzie	Great Slave Lake, NT, Can.	Arctic Ocean	2,635
Milk	Junction of North and South Forks, AB, Can.	Missouri River	624
Minnesota	Big Stone Lake, MN	Mississippi River	332
Mississippi	Lake Itasca, Clearwater County, MN	Gulf of Mexico	2,340
Mississippi-Missouri-Red Rock	Source of Red Rock, Beaverhead County, MT	Gulf of Mexico	3,710
Missouri	Junction of Jefferson, Madison, and Gallatin Rivers, Gallatin County, MT	Mississippi River	2,315
Missouri-Red Rock	Source of Red Rock, Beaverhead County, MT	Mississippi River	2,540
Mobile-Alabama-Coosa	Gilmer County, GA	Mobile Bay	774
Nelson	Lake Winnipeg, MB, Can.	Hudson Bay	400
Neosho	Morris County, KS	Arkansas River, OK	460
Niobrara	Niobrara County, WY	Missouri River, NE	431
North Canadian	Union County, NM	Canadian River, OK	800
North Platte	Junction of Grizzly and Little Grizzly Creeks, Jackson Co., CO	Platte River, NE	618
Ohio	Junction of Allegheny and Monongahela Rivers, Pittsburgh, PA	Mississippi River, Cairo, IL	981
Osage	East-central Kansas	Missouri River	500
Ottawa	Lake Capimitchigama, QC, Can.	St. Lawrence River	790
Ouachita	Polk County, AR	Black River	605
Peace	Junction of Finlay and Parsnip Rivers, BC, Can.	Slave River	1,195
Pearl	Neshoba County, MS	Gulf of Mexico	411
Pecos	Mora County, NM	Rio Grande	926
Pee Dee-Yadkin	Watauga County, NC	Winyah Bay	435
Pend Oreille-Clark Fork	Near Butte, MT	Columbia River	531
Platte	Junction of North Platte and South Platte Rivers, NE	Missouri River	990
Porcupine	West-central Yukon, Can.	Yukon River, AK	569
Potomac	Garrett County, MD	Chesapeake Bay	383
Powder	Junction of South and Middle Forks, WY	Yellowstone River	375
Red (River of the South)	Curry County, NM	Atchafalaya River, LA	1,290
Red River of the North	Junction of Otter Tail and Bois de Sioux Rivers, Wilkin Co., MN	Lake Winnipeg	545
Republican	Junction of North Fork and Arikaree Rivers, NE	Kansas River	445
Rio Grande (Rio Bravo)	San Juan County, CO	Gulf of Mexico	1,900
Roanoke	Junction of North and South Forks, Montgomery Co., VA	Albemarle Sound	380
Rock (IL-WI)	Dodge County, WI	Mississippi River	300
Sabine	Junction of South and Caddo Forks, Hunt Co., TX	Sabine Lake	380
Sacramento	Siskiyou County, CA	Suisun Bay	377
Saguenay	Lake St. John, QC, Can.	St. Lawrence River	434
St. Francis	Iron County, MO	Mississippi River	425
St. John	Northwestern Maine	Bay of Fundy	418
St. Lawrence	Lake Ontario, NY-ON, Can.	Gulf of St. Lawrence, Atlantic Ocean	800
Salmon (ID)	Custer County, ID	Snake River	420
San Joaquin	Junction of South and Middle Forks, Madera Co., CA	Suisun Bay	350
San Juan	Silver Lake, Archuleta County, CO	Colorado River	360
Santee-Wateree-Catawba	McDowell County, NC	Atlantic Ocean	538
Saskatchewan, North	Rocky Mountains, AB, Can.	Saskatchewan R.	800
Saskatchewan, South	Rocky Mountains, AB, Can.	Saskatchewan R.	865
Savannah	Junction of Seneca and Tugaloo Rivers, Anderson Co., SC	Atlantic Ocean, GA-SC	314
Severn (ON)	Sandy Lake, ON, Can.	Hudson Bay	610
Smoky Hill	Cheyenne County, CO	Kansas River, KS	540
Snake	Teton County, WY	Columbia River, WA	1,038
South Platte	Junction of South and Middle Forks, Park County, CO	Platte River	424
Susitna	Alaska Range	Cook Inlet	313
Susquehanna	Otsego Lake, Otsego County, NY	Chesapeake Bay	447
Tallahatchie	Tippah County, MS	Yazoo River	301
Tanana	Wrangell Mountains, AK	Yukon River	659
Tennessee	Junction of French Broad and Holston Rivers, TN	Ohio River	652
Tennessee-French Broad	Courthouse Creek, Transylvania County, NC	Ohio River	886
Tombigbee	Prentiss County, MS	Mobile River	525
Trinity	N of Dallas, TX	Galveston Bay	360
Usumacinta	Junction of Pasión and Chixoy Rivers, Guatemala	Bay of Campeche, Mex.	600
Wabash	Darke County, OH	Ohio River	512
Washita	Hemphill County, TX	Red River, OK	500
White (AR-MO)	Madison County, AR	Mississippi River	722
Willamette	Douglas County, OR	Columbia River	309
Wind-Bighorn	Junction of Wind and Little Wind Rivers, Fremont Co., WY (source of Wind R. is Togwotee Pass, Teton Co., WY)	Yellowstone River	338
Wisconsin	Lac Vieux Desert, Vilas County, WI	Mississippi River	430
Yellowstone	Park County, WY	Missouri River	682
Yukon	McNeil River, YT, Can.	Bering Sea	1,979

Major Natural Lakes of the World

Source: U.S. Geological Survey, U.S. Dept. of the Interior; Natural Resources Canada

A lake is generally defined as a body of water surrounded by land. By this definition some bodies of water that are called seas, such as the Caspian Sea and the Aral Sea, are really lakes. In the following table, the word "lake" is omitted when it is part of the name.

Name	Continent	Area (sq mi)	Length (mi)	Maximum depth (ft)	Elevation (ft)
Caspian Sea[1]	Asia-Europe	144,402	760	3,363	–92
Superior	North America	31,700	350	1,333	601
Victoria	Africa	26,828	210	270	3,720
Huron	North America	23,000	206	750	578
Michigan	North America	22,300	307	923	578
Tanganyika	Africa	12,700	420	4,823	2,534
Baikal	Asia	12,162	395	5,315	1,493
Great Bear	North America	12,096	192	1,463	512
Nyasa (Malawi)	Africa	11,150	360	2,280	1,550
Great Slave	North America	11,030	298	2,014	512
Erie	North America	9,910	241	210	569
Winnipeg	North America	9,416	266	200	712
Ontario	North America	7,340	193	802	243
Balkhash[1]	Asia	7,115	376	85	1,115
Ladoga	Europe	6,835	124	738	13
Maracaibo	South America	5,217	133	115	sea level
Aral Sea[1,2]	Asia	4,040	260	180	175
Onega	Europe	3,710	145	328	108
Eyre[1]	Australia	3,600[3]	90	4	–49
Titicaca	South America	3,200	122	922	12,500
Nicaragua	North America	3,100	102	230	102
Athabasca	North America	3,064	208	407	699
Reindeer	North America	2,568	143	720	1,106
Tonle Sap	Asia	2,500[3]	70	45	NA
Turkana (Rudolf)	Africa	2,473	154	240	1,230
Issyk Kul[1]	Asia	2,355	115	2,303	5,279
Torrens[1]	Australia	2,230[3]	130	NA[3]	92
Vänern	Europe	2,181	91	328	144
Nettilling	North America	2,140	67	NA[3]	98
Winnipegosis	North America	2,075	141	38	833
Albert	Africa	2,075	100	168	2,030
Nipigon	North America	1,872	72	540	853
Gairdner[1]	Australia	1,840[3]	90	NA[3]	112
Manitoba	North America	1,799	140	21	813
Urmia[1]	Asia	888	90	49	4,177
Chad	Africa	521[4]	175	24	787

NA = Not available. (1) Salt lake. (2) The diversion of its two feeder rivers since the 1960s has devastated the Aral—once the world's fourth-largest lake (26,000 sq mi) with length, max. depth, and elevation shown. By 2000, the Aral had effectively become three lakes, with the total area shown. (3) Subject to great seasonal variation. (4) Once fourth-largest lake in Africa (about 10,000 sq mi in the 1960s), Chad had shrunk to around 5% of its original size by 2006 as a result of irrigation and long-term drought.

The Great Lakes

Source: National Ocean Service, National Oceanic and Atmospheric Administration, U.S. Dept. of Commerce

The Great Lakes form the world's **largest freshwater body** (in surface area) and with their connecting waterways are the largest inland water transportation unit. Draining the north-central basin of the U.S., they enable shipping to get to the Atlantic via their outlet, the St. Lawrence R.; the Gulf of Mexico can be reached via the Illinois Waterway, between Lake Michigan and the Mississippi R. A third outlet connects with the Hudson R. and then the Atlantic via the New York State Barge Canal System. Illinois Waterway and NYS Barge Canal System traffic is limited to recreational boating and small shipping vessels.

Only Lake Michigan is wholly in the U.S.; the other lakes are shared with Canada. Ships move from the shores of Lake Superior to Whitefish Bay in the east, then through the Soo Locks in Sault Ste. Marie, MI, onto St. Mary's R. and into Lake Huron. To reach the Port of Indiana-Burns Harbor and South Chicago, IL, ships travel west from Lake Huron to Lake Michigan through the Straits of Mackinac. Low water datum is based on the International Great Lakes Datum (1985), with Rimouski, Quebec, as the reference zero point. The distance between Duluth, MN, and Lake Ontario's east end is 1,156 mi.

	Superior	Michigan	Huron	Erie	Ontario
Length (mi)	350	307	206	241	193
Breadth (mi)	160	118	183	57	53
Deepest soundings (ft)	1,333	923	750	210	802
Volume of water (cu mi)	2,935	1,180	850	116	393
Area (sq mi) water surface—U.S.	20,600	22,300	9,100	4,980	3,460
Canada	11,100	NA	13,900	4,930	3,880
Area (sq mi) entire drainage basin—U.S.	16,900	45,600	16,200	18,000	15,200
Canada	32,400	NA	35,500	4,720	12,100
Total area (sq mi), U.S. and Canada	**81,000**	**67,900**	**74,700**	**32,630**	**34,850**
Low water datum above mean water level at Rimouski, QC, avg. level (ft)	601.10	577.50	577.50	569.20	243.30
Latitude, N	46°25′	41°37′	43°00′	41°23′	43°11′
	49°00′	46°06′	46°17′	42°52′	44°15′
Longitude, W	84°22′	84°45′	79°43′	78°51′	76°03′
	92°06′	88°02′	84°45′	83°29′	79°53′
National boundary line (mi)	282.8	NA	260.8	251.5	174.6
U.S. shoreline (mainland only) (mi)	863	1,400	580	431	300

NA = Not applicable.

Notable Waterfalls

The magnitude of a waterfall is determined not only by height but also by volume and steadiness of flow, crest width, the angle of a drop, and the number of leaps it may make. A series of low falls over a considerable distance is known as a cascade. Waterfalls are highly variable and few authoritative figures exist. For more information and some alternative measurements, see the World Waterfall Database at www.worldwaterfalldatabase.com.

Estimated mean annual flow (ft³/sec): Niagara, 205,000; Paulo Afonso, 100,000; Iguazú, 61,000; Victoria, 35,400.

Height is total drop in feet in one or more leaps. If river name is not shown, it is the same as the waterfall. # = more than one leap; * = diminishes greatly seasonally; ** = reduces to a trickle or is dry for part of each year; R. = river; (C) = cascade.

Name, location	Height (ft)
Africa	
Angola-Namibia	
Ruacana, Cunene R.	352
Lesotho	
Maletsunyane*	610
South Africa	
Augrabies, Orange R.*	183
Tugela#	3,110
Tanzania-Zambia	
Kalambo*	726
Zimbabwe-Zambia	
Victoria, Zambezi R.*	344
Asia and Oceania	
Australia	
New South Wales	
Wentworth	615
Wollomombi	738
Queensland	
Tully**	525
Wallaman, Stony Creek	879
India	
Jog, Sharavati R.*	829
Sivasamudram	320
Japan	
Kegon, Lake Chuzenji*	318
New Zealand	
Helena	722
Sutherland, Arthur R.#	1,904
Europe	
Austria	
Gastein#	420
Krimml#	1,248
France	
Gavarnie*	1,384
Italy	
Toce (C)	469
Norway	
Mardalsfossen#**	2,116
Skykje**	1,135
Vetti, Morka-Koldedola R.	902
Sweden	
Handol#	345
Switzerland	
Giessbach (C)	825
Reichenbach#	525
Staubbach	1,025
Trümmelbach#	460
United Kingdom	
Glomach, Scotland	370
Pistyll Rhaeadr, Wales	240
North America	
Canada	
Alberta	
Panther, Nigel Creek	218
British Columbia	
Della#	1,443
Takakkaw, Daly Glacier#	992
Ontario	
Niagara (Horseshoe)	167
Québec	
Montmorency	253
United States	
Alabama	
Noccalula Falls	90
California	
Feather*	410
Yosemite National Park	
Bridalveil*	620
Nevada, Merced R.*	594
Ribbon**	1,612
Silver Strand, Meadow Brook**	574
Vernal, Merced R.*	317
Wapama	1,310
Yosemite#**	2,425
Colorado	
Seven Falls, S. Cheyenne Creek#	175
Hawaii	
Akaka, Kolekole Stream	422
Idaho	
Shoshone, Snake R.**	212
Kentucky	
Cumberland	68
Maryland	
Great, Potomac R. (C)*	47
Minnesota	
Minnehaha**	53
New Jersey	
Great, Passaic R.	77
New York	
Kaaterskill, Lake Creek*	231
Niagara (American)	120
Taughannock*	209
Oregon	
Multnomah#	620
Tennessee	
Fall Creek	203
Washington	
Colonial Creek	2,568
Sluiskin, Paradise R.	155
Snoqualmie**	268
Wisconsin	
Big Manitou, Black R. (C)*	165
Wyoming	
Tower	111
Yellowstone (lower)*	308
Yellowstone (upper)*	109
South America	
Argentina-Brazil	
Iguazú	269
Brazil	
Cachoeira da Fumaça*	1,115
Paulo Afonso, São Francisco R.	275
Colombia	
Tequendama, Bogota R.*	482
Ecuador	
Agoyan, Pastaza R.*	200
Guyana	
Kaieteur, Potaro R.	741
King George VI, Kamarang R.	524
Marina, Ipobe R.#	500
Venezuela	
Angel (Kerepakupai Merú), Churún#*	2,648
Cuquenan (Kukenaam)	2,211

Latitude and Longitude of World Cities

Source: National Geospatial-Intelligence Agency, U.S. Dept. of Defense

City, country	Lat. °	Lat. ′	Long. °	Long. ′
Athens, Greece	37	59 N	23	43 E
Bangkok, Thailand	13	45 N	100	30 E
Beijing, China	39	54 N	116	23 E
Berlin, Germany	52	31 N	13	24 E
Bogotá, Colombia	4	36 N	74	4 W
Buenos Aires, Argentina	34	36 S	58	22 W
Cairo, Egypt	30	3 N	31	14 E
Jakarta, Indonesia	6	12 S	106	50 E
Jerusalem, Israel	31	46 N	35	12 E
Johannesburg, South Africa	26	11 S	28	2 E
Kyiv, Ukraine	50	27 N	30	31 E
Lagos, Nigeria	6	27 N	3	24 E
London, UK (Greenwich)	51	28 N	0	0
Manila, Philippines	14	36 N	120	58 E
Mexico City, Mexico	19	25 N	99	7 W
Moscow, Russia	55	45 N	37	36 E
Mumbai, India	19	4 N	72	52 E
New Delhi, India	28	37 N	77	12 E
Paris, France	48	51 N	2	20 E
Rio de Janeiro, Brazil	22	54 S	43	10 W
Rome, Italy	41	53 N	12	30 E
Santiago, Chile	33	27 S	70	38 W
Seoul, South Korea	37	33 N	126	58 E
Sydney, Australia	33	52 S	151	12 E
Tehran, Iran	35	41 N	51	25 E
Tokyo, Japan	35	41 N	139	41 E

Highest and Lowest Continental Elevations

Continent	Highest point	Elev. (ft)
Asia	Everest, Nepal-Tibet	29,032
South America	Aconcagua, Argentina	22,835
North America	Denali (fmr. McKinley), Alaska, U.S.	20,308
Africa	Kilimanjaro, Tanzania	19,341
Europe	Elbrus, Russia	18,481
Antarctica	Vinson Massif	16,066
Australia	Kosciusko, New South Wales	7,313

Continent	Lowest point	Ft below sea level
Antarctica	Denman Glacier	11,483
Asia	Dead Sea, Israel-Jordan	1,414
Africa	Lake Assal, Djibouti	509
South America	Laguna del Carbón, Argentina	344
North America	Death Valley, California, U.S.	282
Europe	Caspian Sea, Azer.-Kazakh.-Russ.	92
Australia	Lake Eyre, South Australia	49

Latitude, Longitude, and Elevation of U.S. and Canadian Cities

Source: U.S. geographic positions and altitudes provided by U.S. Geological Survey, U.S. Dept. of the Interior. Canadian geographic positions and altitudes provided by Natural Resources Canada.

City, state/province	Lat. N °	′	″	Long. W °	′	″	Elev. (ft)
Albany, NY	42	39	9	73	45	22	149
Albuquerque, NM	35	5	4	106	39	4	4,956
Anchorage, AK	61	13	5	149	54	1	104
Annapolis, MD	38	58	42	76	29	32	43
Atlanta, GA	33	44	56	84	23	17	1,050
Augusta, GA	33	28	15	81	58	29	141
Augusta, ME	44	18	38	69	46	46	123
Austin, TX	30	16	2	97	44	35	489
Baltimore, MD	39	17	25	76	36	44	36
Baton Rouge, LA	30	27	3	91	9	16	46
Billings, MT	45	47	0	108	30	2	3,124
Birmingham, AL	33	31	14	86	48	9	610
Bismarck, ND	46	48	30	100	47	1	1,695
Boise, ID	43	36	49	116	12	12	2,699
Boston, MA	42	21	30	71	3	35	45
Buffalo, NY	42	53	11	78	52	42	600
Burlington, VT	44	28	33	73	12	43	196
Calgary, AB	51	2	45	114	3	27	3,557
Carson City, NV	39	9	50	119	46	3	4,681
Casper, WY	42	52	0	106	18	47	5,105
Cedar Rapids, IA	42	0	30	91	38	39	808
Charleston, SC	32	46	36	79	55	51	11
Charleston, WV	38	20	59	81	37	57	596
Charlotte, NC	35	13	38	80	50	35	762
Charlottetown, PE	46	14	25	63	8	5	160
Cheyenne, WY	41	8	24	104	49	13	6,087
Chicago, IL	41	51	0	87	39	0	586
Churchill, MB	58	46	51	94	11	13	94
Cleveland, OH	41	29	58	81	41	43	653
Colorado Springs, CO	38	50	2	104	49	17	6,010
Columbia, SC	34	0	3	81	2	5	300
Columbus, OH	39	57	40	82	59	56	780
Concord, NH	43	12	29	71	32	15	273
Corpus Christi, TX	27	48	2	97	23	47	7
Dallas, TX	32	46	59	96	48	24	421
Denver, CO	39	44	21	104	59	5	5,277
Des Moines, IA	41	36	2	93	36	33	873
Detroit, MI	42	19	53	83	2	45	598
Dover, DE	39	9	29	75	31	27	28
Durham, NC	35	59	39	78	53	55	400
Edmonton, AB	53	32	4	113	29	25	2,200
El Paso, TX	31	45	31	106	29	13	3,717
Eugene, OR	44	3	7	123	5	12	430
Evansville, IN	37	58	29	87	33	21	388
Fairbanks, AK	64	50	16	147	42	59	445
Fargo, ND	46	52	38	96	47	23	902
Ft. Smith, AR	35	23	9	94	23	55	440
Ft. Wayne, IN	41	7	50	85	7	44	810
Ft. Worth, TX	32	43	31	97	19	15	653
Frankfort, KY	38	12	3	84	52	24	507
Fredericton, NB	45	56	43	66	40	0	67
Greensboro, NC	36	4	21	79	47	31	827
Greenville, SC	34	51	9	82	23	38	984
Gulfport, MS	30	22	3	89	5	34	21
Halifax, NS	44	52	0	63	42	58	477
Hamilton, ON	43	14	34	79	59	22	780
Harrisburg, PA	40	16	25	76	53	4	332
Hartford, CT	41	45	49	72	41	6	29
Helena, MT	46	35	34	112	2	10	4,047
Hilo, HI	19	43	47	155	5	24	59
Honolulu, HI	21	18	25	157	51	30	17
Houston, TX	29	45	48	95	21	48	37
Idaho Falls, ID	43	28	0	112	2	3	4,705
Indianapolis, IN	39	46	6	86	9	29	720
Iqaluit, NU	63	45	0	68	31	0	112
Jackson, MS	32	17	56	90	11	5	280
Jacksonville, FL	30	19	56	81	39	20	15
Jefferson City, MO	38	34	36	92	10	25	630
Jersey City, NJ	40	43	41	74	4	40	34
Juneau, AK	58	18	7	134	25	11	33
Kansas City, MO	39	5	59	94	34	43	898
Knoxville, TN	35	57	38	83	55	15	904
Lansing, MI	42	43	57	84	33	20	853
Laredo, TX	27	30	23	99	30	27	415
Las Vegas, NV	36	10	30	115	8	14	2,001
Lexington, KY	37	59	19	84	28	40	968
Lincoln, NE	40	48	0	96	40	0	1,200
Little Rock, AR	34	44	47	92	17	23	333
Los Angeles, CA	34	3	8	118	14	37	291
Louisville, KY	38	15	15	85	45	34	466
Madison, WI	43	4	23	89	24	4	873
Manchester, NH	42	59	44	71	27	17	258
Memphis, TN	35	8	58	90	2	56	260
Miami, FL	25	46	27	80	11	37	8
Milwaukee, WI	43	2	20	87	54	23	615
Minneapolis, MN	44	58	48	93	15	50	830
Mobile, AL	30	41	40	88	2	35	10
Montgomery, AL	32	22	0	86	18	0	238
Montpelier, VT	44	15	36	72	34	31	526
Montréal, QC	45	31	0	73	39	0	221
Nashville, TN	36	9	57	86	47	4	567
New Orleans, LA	29	57	17	90	4	30	1
New York, NY	40	42	51	74	0	22	35
Newark, NJ	40	44	8	74	10	21	32
Nome, AK	64	30	4	165	24	23	37
Oklahoma City, OK	35	28	3	97	30	59	1,198
Olympia, WA	47	2	16	122	54	3	93
Omaha, NE	41	15	31	95	56	16	1,059
Ottawa, ON	45	20	0	75	35	3	382
Overland Park, KS	38	58	56	94	40	15	1,084
Philadelphia, PA	39	57	8	75	9	50	45
Phoenix, AZ	33	26	54	112	4	27	1,085
Pierre, SD	44	22	6	100	21	3	1,479
Pittsburgh, PA	40	26	26	79	59	45	766
Portland, OR	45	31	24	122	40	34	33
Providence, RI	41	49	26	71	24	46	9
Provo, UT	40	14	2	111	39	31	4,551
Québec, QC	46	49	0	71	13	0	244
Raleigh, NC	35	46	20	78	38	19	315
Rapid City, SD	44	4	50	103	13	52	3,243
Regina, SK	50	27	17	104	36	24	1,894
Reno, NV	39	31	47	119	48	50	4,505
Richmond, VA	37	33	14	77	27	37	213
Rochester, NY	43	9	17	77	36	56	504
Sacramento, CA	38	34	54	121	29	40	27
St. John's, NL	47	28	56	52	47	49	461
St. Louis, MO	38	37	38	90	11	52	464
St. Paul, MN	44	56	34	93	5	36	789
Salem, OR	44	56	35	123	2	6	157
Salt Lake City, UT	40	45	39	111	53	28	4,265
San Antonio, TX	29	25	27	98	29	37	649
San Diego, CA	32	42	55	117	9	26	63
San Francisco, CA	37	46	30	122	25	10	54
San Jose, CA	37	20	22	121	53	42	82
San Juan, PR	18	27	59	66	6	21	26
Santa Fe, NM	35	41	13	105	56	16	6,995
Saskatoon, SK	52	8	23	106	41	10	1,653
Savannah, GA	32	5	1	81	5	59	20
Seattle, WA	47	36	22	122	19	55	177
Shreveport, LA	32	31	31	93	45	1	151
Sioux City, IA	42	30	0	96	24	1	1,201
Sioux Falls, SD	43	33	0	96	42	1	1,473
Spokane, WA	47	39	35	117	25	45	1,732
Springfield, IL	39	48	6	89	38	37	600
Tacoma, WA	47	15	10	122	26	39	250
Tampa, FL	27	56	51	82	27	30	15
Topeka, KS	39	2	54	95	40	41	948
Toronto, ON	43	44	30	79	22	24	251
Trenton, NJ	40	13	1	74	44	35	61
Tucson, AZ	32	13	18	110	55	35	2,490
Tulsa, OK	36	9	14	95	59	34	721
Vancouver, BC	49	15	40	123	6	50	14
Victoria, BC	48	25	42	123	21	53	63
Virginia Beach, VA	36	51	11	75	58	41	11
Washington, DC	38	53	42	77	2	11	24
Whitehorse, YT	60	41	46	135	4	51	2,305
Wichita, KS	37	41	32	97	20	15	1,302
Wilmington, DE	39	44	45	75	32	48	91
Wilmington, NC	34	13	33	77	56	41	36
Winnipeg, MB	49	53	4	97	8	47	783
Yakima, WA	46	36	7	120	30	21	1,068
Yellowknife, NT	62	27	13	114	22	12	675

Religious Affiliation in the U.S., 2025

Source: Gina A. Zurlo, ed., *World Religion Database* (Leiden/Boston: Brill, July 2024)

Affiliation	2025 pop.	Percent	Affiliation	2025 pop.	Percent	Affiliation	2025 pop.	Percent
Agnostics	62,220,858	18.1%	Christians	247,885,133	72.1%	Muslims	5,389,455	1.6%
Atheists	11,140,539	3.2	Daoists	14,216	—	New religionists	1,830,854	0.5
Baha'is	632,788	0.2	Ethnic religionists	1,254,531	0.4	Shintoists	71,777	—
Buddhists	4,724,121	1.4	Hindus	1,800,632	0.5	Sikhs	484,414	0.1
Chinese folk-religionists	124,385	—	Jains	104,187	—	Spiritists	262,709	0.1
			Jews	5,642,613	1.6	Zoroastrians	20,193	—

— = Less than 0.05%.

Religious Group Membership in the U.S., 2020

Source: Gina A. Zurlo and Todd M. Johnson, eds., *World Christian Database* (Leiden/Boston: Brill, July 2024)

Figures generally are based on collected reports made by each denomination as of 2020 and include only persons affiliated with a congregation of the denomination. Reporting practices vary from one denomination to another but generally include all members, not only full communicants. Denominations with fewer than 28,000 members not generally shown. Broad religious groups are indicated in **boldface**.

Group (congregations)	Members
African Methodist Episcopal Church (9,000)	2,700,000
African Methodist Episcopal Zion Church (3,500)	1,800,000
Agnosticism	**55,894,000**
Albanian Orthodox Archdiocese in America (11)	33,700
American Baptist Assn. (770)	180,000
American Baptist Churches in the USA (4,800)	1,546,000
Antiochian Orthodox Christian (260)	500,000
Apostolic Assemblies of Christ Intl. (280)	54,800
Apostolic Assembly of the Faith in Christ Jesus (780)	94,400
Armenian Apostolic Church of America (32)	370,000
Armenian Church of North America (89)	370,000
Armenian Evangelical Union of Churches (26)	43,600
Assemblies of God USA (15,000)	4,148,000
Assemblies of the Lord Jesus Christ (33)	75,800
Assembly of Christian Churches (150)	29,800
Associate Reformed Presbyterian Church (250)	54,000
Assyrian Church of the East (46)	115,000
Atheism	**9,655,000**
Baha'i Faith	**580,000**
Baptist Bible Fellowship Intl. (4,500)	1,765,000
Baptist General Conference (880)	687,000
Baptist Missionary Assn. of America (1,100)	226,000
Brethren in Christ Church (240)	29,200
Buddhism	**4,380,000**
Calvary Chapels Intl. (100)	543,000
Catholic Church in the USA[1] (17,200)	73,164,000
Charis Fellowship (260)	38,400
Chinese folk-religions[2]	**118,000**
Christian and Missionary Alliance (1,800)	508,000
Christian Brethren (Open) (840)	118,000
Christian Church (Disciples of Christ) (3,100)	488,000
Christian Churches and Churches of Christ (4,800)	1,692,000
Christian Congregation (69)	140,000
Christian Intl. Ministries (160)	37,500
Christian Methodist Episcopal Church (1,300)	1,200,000
Christian Reformed Church in N. America (790)	183,000
Christianity	**249,623,000**
Church of Christ, Scientist (310)	120,000
Church of God (Anderson, IN) (1,900)	427,000
Church of God (Cleveland, OH) (5,900)	1,066,000
Church of God (Huntsville, AL) (1,600)	79,800
Church of God in Christ (25,000)	8,100,000
Church of God of Prophecy (1,600)	115,000
Church of Jesus Christ (420)	102,000
Church of Jesus Christ of Latter-day Saints (14,600)	6,721,000
Church of Our Lord Jesus Christ of Apostolic Faith (530)	105,000
Church of the Brethren (920)	134,000
Church of the Living God (110)	41,400
Church of the Nazarene (5,200)	906,000
Churches of Christ (Non-Instrumental) (11,900)	1,422,000
Churches of God General Conference (300)	38,300
Churches of God (Holiness) (30)	29,600
Churches on the Rock Intl. (110)	103,000
Community of Christ (620)	163,000
Conservative Baptist Assn. of America (1,000)	139,000
Conservative Congregational Christian Conference (310)	51,100
Coptic Orthodox Church (280)	600,000
Covenant Ministries Intl. (41)	98,500
Crenshaw Christian Center (2)	33,000
Cumberland Presbyterian Church (610)	64,900
Czechoslovak Hussite Church (20)	49,300
Daoism	**13,400**
Defenders of the Christian Faith (100)	30,500
Elim Assemblies Fellowship (240)	44,800
Episcopal Church in the USA (6,400)	1,577,000
Ethiopian Orthodox Church in the USA (200)	96,400
Ethnic religions[2]	**1,174,000**
Evangelical Covenant Church of America (860)	189,000
Evangelical Fellowship Intl. (330)	99,500
Evangelical Free Church of America (1,600)	399,000
Evangelical Friends Intl. (240)	42,900
Evangelical Lutheran Church in America (8,900)	3,139,000
Evangelical Presbyterian Church (630)	182,000
Evangelistic Messengers Assn. (700)	69,400
Faith Christian Fellowship Intl. (160)	79,200
Fellowship of Christian Believers (75)	30,500
Free Lutheran Congregations, Assn. of (250)	43,900
Free Methodist Church of North America (620)	71,600
Friends United Meeting (600)	38,000
Full Gospel Baptist Church Fellowship (820)	170,000
Full Gospel Fellowship of Churches and Ministers (500)	461,000
General Assn. of General Baptists (110)	41,600
General Assn. of Regular Baptist Churches (940)	219,000
Global Christian Ministry Forum (80)	39,600
Global Network of Christian Ministries (290)	49,800
Grace Intl. (120)	139,000
Greater Emmanuel Intl. Fellowship of Churches & Ministries (53)	52,400
Greek Orthodox Archdiocese of America (530)	1,500,000
Gulf States Pastors & Churches Fellowship (380)	29,800
Hinduism	**1,626,000**
Independent Assemblies Fellowship (560)	84,000
Independent Assemblies of God Intl. (310)	122,000
Independent Fundamental Churches of America (610)	56,200
Intl. Church of the Foursquare Gospel (1,600)	446,000
Intl. Churches of Christ (180)	65,800
Intl. Convention of Faith Ministries (430)	108,000
Intl. Council of Community Churches (57)	65,200
Intl. Gospel Assemblies, Assn. of (32)	266,000
Intl. Pentecostal Holiness Church (1,600)	221,000
Islam[3]	**4,630,000**
Jainism	**95,700**
Jehovah's Witnesses (12,200)	2,888,000
Judaism[4]	**5,662,000**
Korean American Presbyterian Church (650)	80,000
Korean Full Gospel Churches of America (900)	266,000
Korean Presbyterian Church in America (320)	67,900
Korean Presbyterian Church of America (650)	80,000
Latin American Council of Christian Churches (220)	37,500
Lutheran Church-Missouri Synod (5,900)	1,803,000
Malankara Orthodox Syrian Church of the East (110)	50,000
Mennonite Church USA (550)	87,200
Ministers Fellowship Intl. (210)	56,200
Missionary Church (460)	57,600
Moravian Church in America (150)	39,700
Native American Church of North America (400)	250,000
Natl. Assn. of Free Will Baptists (1,900)	193,000
Natl. Baptist Convention of America (12,700)	4,300,000
Natl. Baptist Convention, USA (40,000)	9,100,000
Natl. Missionary Baptist Conv. of America (260)	2,981,000
Natl. Primitive Baptist Convention (1,600)	600,000
New Apostolic Church USA (190)	32,300
New religions[2]	**1,736,000**
North American Baptist Conference (410)	65,000

Group (congregations)	Members
North American Old Roman Catholic Church (9)	66,000
Old Order & Wisler Mennonite Church (68)	31,300
Old Order Amish Mennonite Church (1,100)	142,000
Open Bible Churches (240)	38,100
Orthodox Church in America (560)	3,000,000
Orthodox Presbyterian Church (340)	35,400
Pentecostal Assemblies of the World (1,600)	1,300,000
Pentecostal Church of God (990)	105,000
Pentecostal Churches of the Apostolic Faith (500)	76,900
Potter's House (10)	36,500
Presbyterian Church (USA) (8,900)	1,492,000
Presbyterian Church in America (1,900)	373,000
Primitive Baptists (450)	51,800
Progressive Natl. Baptist Convention (1,200)	1,800,000
Redeemed Christian Church of God (820)	40,200
Reformed Church in America (910)	235,000
Rhema Bible Churches (640)	188,000
Romanian Orthodox Episcopate of America (100)	114,000
Salvation Army (1,100)	400,000
Serbian Orthodox Church in N. and S. Amer. (120)	59,500
Seventh-day Adventist Church (6,000)	1,550,000
Shintoism	**67,900**
Sikhism	**423,000**
Southern Baptist Convention (51,400)	17,649,000
Spiritism	**244,000**
Spiritual Life Concepts (550)	29,500
Unitarian Universalist Assn. (1,000)	202,000
United Baptist Churches (390)	51,400
United Church of Christ (4,800)	925,000
United Church of Jesus Christ (Apostolic) (130)	33,600
United Free Will Baptist Church (680)	95,700
United House of Prayer for All People (130)	1,800,000
United Methodist Church (30,100)	8,019,000
United Pentecostal Church Intl. (4,500)	956,000
Unity School of Christianity (700)	149,000
U.S. Conference Mennonite Brethren Churches (220)	53,100
Vineyard Churches (USA) (750)	168,000
Way of the Cross Church of Christ (78)	84,000
Wesleyan Church (1,500)	306,000
Willow Creek Assn. of Churches (2,400)	477,000
Wisconsin Evangelical Lutheran Synod (1,200)	408,000
World Council of Independent Christian Churches (250)	41,500
World Harvest Ministerial Alliance (150)	41,500
Zoroastrianism	**19,100**

(1) According to the U.S. Center for Applied Research in the Apostolate, there were 75.0 mil self-identified Catholics in the U.S. in 2023. (2) **Chinese folk-religionists** include followers of traditional Chinese religion; it may involve worship of local deities, ancestor veneration, Confucian ethics, divination, and Buddhist or Taoist elements, among other beliefs and practices. **Ethnic religionists** include followers of local, tribal, animistic, or shamanistic religions, generally belonging to a single ethnic group. **New religionists** include followers of Asian new religions, neoreligious movements, radical new crisis religions, and syncretistic mass religions. (3) Other sources vary. In 2017, the Council on American-Islamic Relations estimated a total of 2,000 mosques and 6-7 mil Muslims in the U.S., and a 2021 Pew Research Center report estimated the U.S. Muslim pop. at 3.85 mil in 2020. (4) Includes Jewish Reconstructionist Communities (about 90), Union of Orthodox Jewish Congregations of America (500), Other Orthodox congregations (1,200), Chabad (over 2,000), Union for Reform Judaism (850), and United Synagogue of Conservative Judaism (580). Among Jewish adherents in the U.S., about 35% classify themselves as Reform, 18% as Conservative, 10% as Orthodox, 2% as Reconstructionist, the rest as "just Jewish." Source: Arnold Dashefsky and Ira M. Sheskin, "United States Jewish Population, 2020," in *The American Jewish Year Book* (Dordrecht: Springer, 2023). (This source estimates the total American Jewish population at 7.6 mil.)

World Adherents of Religions by Continental Area, 2025

Source: Gina A. Zurlo, ed., *World Religion Database* (Leiden/Boston: Brill, July 2024). All adherents figures are midyear estimates, in thous.

Religion (no. of countries/territories)	Africa	Asia	Europe	Latin America	Northern America	Oceania	World	% of world pop.
Baha'is (227)	3,360	4,594	182	1,070	707	178	10,090	0.1%
Buddhists (153)	422	527,921	2,087	989	5,454	1,300	538,173	6.6
Chinese folk-religionists (121)	282	445,688	829	235	1,001	248	448,283	5.5
Christians (237)	754,229	416,786	551,934	620,116	271,779	30,472	2,645,317	32.3
Catholics (237)	271,605	160,370	239,184	506,576	84,331	10,709	1,272,775	15.5
Protestants (234)	298,918	122,895	72,179	70,176	53,188	11,505	628,862	7.7
Independents (234)	141,937	132,763	12,199	65,873	54,257	2,397	409,425	5.0
Orthodox (142)	62,321	17,257	201,379	1,420	8,031	1,170	291,580	3.6
Confucianists (19)	43	8,846	22	9	—	93	9,012	0.1
Daoists (7)	—	9,524	—	—	14	19	9,558	0.1
Ethnic religionists (148)	119,883	167,669	1,275	4,039	1,425	509	294,801	3.6
Hindus (147)	3,967	1,119,224	1,829	872	2,341	922	1,129,155	13.8
Jains (21)	145	6,334	43	2	122	11	6,657	0.1
Jews (149)	91	7,427	1,304	397	6,013	125	15,357	0.2
Muslims (221)	636,395	1,362,220	53,491	1,900	6,679	1,033	2,061,718	25.2
Sunnis (218)	629,654	1,156,118	50,637	1,390	4,597	787	1,843,183	22.5
Shiites (150)	1,242	195,596	2,811	495	1,314	242	201,700	2.5
New religionists (123)	217	62,884	390	2,082	1,945	171	67,690	0.8
Shintoists (9)	—	2,702	—	9	72	1	2,784	—
Sikhs (65)	107	29,167	826	9	1,112	213	31,433	0.4
Spiritists (61)	4	2	176	14,709	284	11	15,186	0.2
Zoroastrians (29)	1	171	6	—	28	3	210	—
All religious adherents (237)	**1,519,146**	**4,171,160**	**614,394**	**646,438**	**298,977**	**35,306**	**7,285,421**	**88.9**
Nonreligious (236)	10,885	645,089	126,652	28,424	84,184	11,333	906,567	11.1
Agnostics (236)	10,024	532,816	111,728	25,102	72,005	9,418	761,092	9.3
Atheists (226)	861	112,273	14,924	3,323	12,179	1,915	145,475	1.8

— = Less than 500 adherents or 0.05% of world pop. **Note:** Figures may not add up to totals due to rounding. Continental areas are as per UN demographic terminology; "Asia" is defined to include the former Soviet Central Asian states, while "Europe" includes all of Russia, extending to the Pacific coast. Figures in parentheses indicate the number of countries/territories where the religion or type of belief has a significant following. **Buddhists** include Mahayana (70%), Theravada or Hinayana (26%), and Tantrayana (incl. Lamaists, Tibetans) (4%). **Chinese folk-religionists** are followers of traditional Chinese religion; it may involve worship of local deities, ancestor veneration, Confucian ethics, divination, and Buddhist or Taoist elements, among other beliefs and practices. **Christians** are usually baptized members of a church belonging to one of the major Christian traditions shown here. Those characterized as Independents belong to groups that consider themselves independent of historical mainstream institutionalized Christianity; these include groups such as Unitarians, Church of Jesus Christ of Latter-day Saints, and Jehovah's Witnesses. **Confucianists** are followers of Confucius, mostly living in China or elsewhere in East/Southeast Asia. **Ethnic religionists** are followers of local, tribal, animistic, or shamanistic religions, generally belonging to a single ethnic group. **Hindus** include Vaishnavites (37%); Shaivites (35%); and Shaktas, neo-Hindi, and reformed Hindi (28%). **New religionists** include followers of Asian new religions, neoreligious movements, radical new crisis religions, and syncretistic mass religions.

Episcopal Church Liturgical Colors and Calendar, 2024-28

The most common liturgical colors in the Episcopal Church are as follows: **White**—Christmas Day through first Sunday after Epiphany; Maundy Thursday (as an alternative to crimson at the Eucharist); from the Vigil of Easter to the Day of Pentecost (Whitsunday); Trinity Sunday; Feasts of the Lord (except Holy Cross Day); the Confession of St. Peter; the Conversion of St. Paul; St. Joseph; St. Mary Magdalene; St. Mary the Virgin; St. Michael and All Angels; All Saints' Day; St. John the Evangelist; memorials of other saints who were not martyred; Independence Day and Thanksgiving Day; weddings and funerals. **Red**—the Day of Pentecost; Holy Cross Day; feasts of apostles and evangelists (except those previously mentioned); feasts and memorials of martyrs (including Holy Innocents' Day). **Violet**—Advent and Lent. **Crimson** or oxblood (dark red)—Holy Week. **Green**—the seasons after Epiphany and after Pentecost. **Black**—optional alternative for funerals and Good Friday.

The days of fasting are Ash Wednesday and Good Friday. Other days of special devotion (penitence) include the 40 days of Lent. Ember days are days of prayer for the church's ministry. They fall on the Wednesday, Friday, and Saturday after the first Sunday in Lent, the Day of Pentecost, Holy Cross Day, and Dec. 13. Rogation Days, the three days before Ascension Day, are days of prayer for God's blessing on the crops, on commerce and industry, and for conservation of the Earth's resources.

Holy days and other variables	2024	2025	2026	2027	2028
Golden Number	11	12	13	14	15
Sunday Letter	G/F	E	D	C	B/A
Sundays after Epiphany	6	8	6	5	8
Ash Wednesday	Feb. 14	Mar. 5	Feb. 18	Feb. 10	Mar. 1
First Sunday in Lent	Feb. 18	Mar. 9	Feb. 22	Feb. 14	Mar. 5
Passion/Palm Sunday	Mar. 24	Apr. 13	Mar. 29	Mar. 21	Apr. 9
Good Friday	Mar. 29	Apr. 18	Apr. 3	Mar. 26	Apr. 14
Easter Day	Mar. 31	Apr. 20	Apr. 5	Mar. 28	Apr. 16
Ascension Day	May 9	May 29	May 14	May 6	May 25
Day of Pentecost	May 19	June 8	May 24	May 16	June 4
Trinity Sunday	May 26	June 15	May 31	May 23	June 11
Numbered Proper of 2 Pentecost	#4	#7	#5	#4	#6
First Sunday of Advent	Dec. 1	Nov. 30	Nov. 29	Nov. 28	Dec. 3

Greek Orthodox Movable Ecclesiastical Dates, 2024-28

Feast days and fasting days are determined annually on the basis of the date of Holy Pascha (Easter). Western Easter dates are also included for reference. This ecclesiastical cycle begins with the first day of the Triodion and ends with the Sunday of All Saints, a total of 18 weeks. In years where Pascha falls on or after May 3, Fast of Holy Apostles lasts zero days.

Holy days and observances	2024	2025	2026	2027	2028
Triodion begins	Feb. 25	Feb. 9	Feb. 1	Feb. 21	Feb. 6
1st Saturday of Souls	Mar. 9	Feb. 22	Feb. 14	Mar. 6	Feb. 19
Meat-Fare Sunday	Mar. 10	Feb. 23	Feb. 15	Mar. 7	Feb. 20
2nd Saturday of Souls	Mar. 16	Mar. 1	Feb. 21	Mar. 13	Feb. 26
Lent begins	Mar. 18	Mar. 3	Feb. 23	Mar. 15	Feb. 28
St. Theodore—3rd Saturday of Souls	Mar. 23	Mar. 8	Feb. 28	Mar. 20	Mar. 4
Sunday of Orthodoxy	Mar. 24	Mar. 9	Mar. 1	Mar. 21	Mar. 5
Saturday of Lazarus	Apr. 27	Apr. 12	Apr. 4	Apr. 24	Apr. 8
Palm Sunday	Apr. 28	Apr. 13	Apr. 5	Apr. 25	Apr. 9
Holy (Good) Friday	May 3	Apr. 18	Apr. 10	Apr. 30	Apr. 14
Western Easter	Mar. 31	Apr. 20	Apr. 5	Mar. 28	Apr. 16
Orthodox Pascha (Easter)	May 5	Apr. 20	Apr. 12	May 2	Apr. 16
Ascension	June 13	May 29	May 21	June 10	May 25
Saturday of Souls	June 22	June 7	May 30	June 19	June 3
Pentecost	June 23	June 8	May 31	June 20	June 4
All Saints	June 30	June 15	June 7	June 27	June 11
Fast of Holy Apostles (first day)	NA	June 16	June 8	June 28	June 12
Fast of Holy Apostles lasts—	0 days	13 days	21 days	1 day	17 days

Jewish Holy Days, 5784-5788 (2023-28)

The Jewish calendar consists of 12 lunar months, alternating between 29 and 30 days. It is lunisolar and adjusts for the solar cycle by adding an extra month (Adar II) in the 3rd, 6th, 8th, 11th, 14th, 17th, and 19th years of a 19-year cycle. The calendar starts on the day of Creation, reckoned in the 2nd-3rd cent. BCE as Tishrei 1, 3,761 years before the common era.

The religious calendar begins with the month Nisan, from which all other months are counted, and the civil calendar with Tishrei. The months are 1) Nisan, 2) Iyar, 3) Sivan, 4) Tammuz, 5) Av (also Abh), 6) Elul, 7) Tishrei, 8) Cheshvan (also Marcheshvan), 9) Kislev, 10) Tevet (also Tebeth), 11) Shevat (also Shebhat), 12) Adar, and 12a) Adar Sheni (II), added in leap years.

All holidays listed below begin at sunset of the previous day and end at nightfall on the last day shown.

Holiday	Date on Jewish cal.	5784 (2023-24)		5785 (2024-25)		5786 (2025-26)		5787 (2026-27)		5788 (2027-28)	
Rosh Hashanah (New Year)	Tishrei 1	Sept. 16	Sat.	Oct. 3	Thu.	Sept. 23	Tue.	Sept. 12	Sat.	Oct. 2	Sat.
	Tishrei 2	Sept. 17	Sun.	Oct. 4	Fri.	Sept. 24	Wed.	Sept. 13	Sun.	Oct. 3	Sun.
Yom Kippur (Day of Atonement)	Tishrei 10	Sept. 25	Mon.	Oct. 12	Sat.	Oct. 2	Thu.	Sept. 21	Mon.	Oct. 11	Mon.
Sukkot	Tishrei 15	Sept. 30	Sat.	Oct. 17	Thu.	Oct. 7	Tue.	Sept. 26	Sat.	Oct. 16	Sat.
	Tishrei 21	Oct. 6	Fri.	Oct. 23	Wed	Oct. 13	Mon.	Oct. 2	Fri.	Oct. 22	Fri.
Shemini Atzeret	Tishrei 22	Oct. 7	Sat.	Oct. 24	Thu.	Oct. 14	Tue.	Oct. 3	Sat.	Oct. 23	Sat.
Simchat Torah	Tishrei 23	Oct. 8	Sun.	Oct. 25	Fri.	Oct. 15	Wed.	Oct. 4	Sun.	Oct. 24	Sun.
Hanukkah	Kislev 25	Dec. 8	Fri.	Dec. 26	Thu.	Dec. 15	Mon.	Dec. 5	Sat.	Dec. 25	Sat.
	Tevet 2 or 3	Dec. 15	Fri.	Jan. 2	Thu.	Dec. 22	Mon.	Dec. 12	Sat.	Jan. 1	Sat.
Purim	Adar 14	Mar. 24	Sun.	Mar. 14	Fri.	Mar. 3	Tue.	Mar. 23	Tue.	Mar. 12	Sun.
Pesach (Passover)	Nisan 15	Apr. 23	Tue.	Apr. 13	Sun.	Apr. 2	Thu.	Apr. 22	Thu.	Apr. 11	Tue.
	Nisan 22	Apr. 30	Tue.	Apr. 20	Sun.	Apr. 9	Thu.	Apr. 29	Thu.	Apr. 18	Tue.
Shavuot	Sivan 6	June 12	Wed.	June 2	Mon.	May 22	Fri.	June 11	Fri.	May 31	Wed.
	Sivan 7	June 13	Thu.	June 3	Tue.	May 23	Sat.	June 12	Sat.	June 1	Thu.
Fast of the 9th of Av	Av 9	Aug. 13	Tue.	Aug. 3	Sun.	July 23	Thu.	Aug. 12	Thu.	Aug. 1	Tue.

Hindu Festivals, 2024-28

There are various traditional lunisolar Hindu calendars. Most have similar names for the 12 lunar months, with days beginning at dawn or sunrise, but they differ in various ways, including the numbering of years and the starting point of months. The Indian civil (Saka) calendar, adopted in 1957, is solar-based, and begins Mar. 22 (Mar. 21 in leap years). There are many Hindu holidays and festivals; some are observed only in certain regions. Below are three of the most widely observed.

Festival	2024	2025	2026	2027	2028
Maha Shivaratri (Night of Shiva)[1]	Mar. 8	Feb. 26	Feb. 15	Mar. 6	Feb. 23
Holi (Festival of Color)	Mar. 25	Mar. 14	Mar. 3	Mar. 22	Mar. 11
Diwali (Festival of Lights)	Oct. 31	Oct. 20	Nov. 8	Oct. 29	Oct. 17

(1) Begins the night of the previous day.

Islamic Holy Days, 1445-1449 AH (2023-28)

The Islamic calendar is a strict lunar calendar reckoned from the year of the Hijra (anno Hegirae, or AH)—Muhammad's flight from Mecca to Medina, in 622 CE. Each year consists of 12 lunar months of 29 or 30 days beginning and ending with each new moon's visible crescent. Common years have 354 days; leap years have 355 days. Some Muslim countries employ a conventionalized calendar with the leap day added to the last month, Dhu'l-Hijja, but for religious purposes the leap date is taken into account by tracking each new moon sighting.

Holy days begin at sunset of the day previous to the day cited. The actual dates may vary slightly from what is shown below, depending on the locality and the times of actual moon sightings as determined by different authorities.

Holy day (date)	1445 (2023-24)	1446 (2024-25)	1447 (2025-26)	1448 (2026-27)	1449 (2027-28)
New Year's Day (Muharram 1)	July 19, 2023	July 7, 2024	June 26, 2025	June 16, 2026	June 6, 2027
Ashura (Muharram 10)	July 28, 2023	July 16, 2024	July 5, 2025	June 25, 2026	June 15, 2027
Mawlid (Rabi' I 12)	Sept. 27, 2023	Sept. 15, 2024	Sept. 4, 2025	Aug. 25, 2026	Aug. 14, 2027
Ramadan begins (Ramadan 1)	Mar. 11, 2024	Mar. 1, 2025	Feb. 18, 2026	Feb. 8, 2027	Jan. 28, 2028
Eid al-Fitr (Shawwal 1)	Apr. 10, 2024	Mar. 30, 2025	Mar. 20, 2026	Mar. 9, 2027	Feb. 26, 2028
Eid al-Adha (Dhu'l-Hijja 10)	June 17, 2024	June 6, 2025	May 27, 2026	May 16, 2027	May 5, 2028

Ash Wednesday and Easter Sunday (Western Churches), 2001-2100

Year	Ash Wed.	Easter Sunday	Year	Ash Wed.	Easter Sunday	Year	Ash Wed.	Easter Sunday	Year	Ash Wed.	Easter Sunday	Year	Ash Wed.	Easter Sunday
2001	Feb. 28	Apr. 15	2021	Feb. 17	Apr. 4	2041	Mar. 6	Apr. 21	2061	Feb. 23	Apr. 10	2081	Feb. 12	Mar. 30
2002	Feb. 13	Mar. 31	2022	Mar. 2	Apr. 17	2042	Feb. 19	Apr. 6	2062	Feb. 8	Mar. 26	2082	Mar. 4	Apr. 19
2003	Mar. 5	Apr. 20	2023	Feb. 22	Apr. 9	2043	Feb. 11	Mar. 29	2063	Feb. 28	Apr. 15	2083	Feb. 17	Apr. 4
2004	Feb. 25	Apr. 11	2024	Feb. 14	Mar. 31	2044	Mar. 2	Apr. 17	2064	Feb. 20	Apr. 6	2084	Feb. 9	Mar. 26
2005	Feb. 9	Mar. 27	2025	Mar. 5	Apr. 20	2045	Feb. 22	Apr. 9	2065	Feb. 11	Mar. 29	2085	Feb. 28	Apr. 15
2006	Mar. 1	Apr. 16	2026	Feb. 18	Apr. 5	2046	Feb. 7	Mar. 25	2066	Feb. 24	Apr. 11	2086	Feb. 13	Mar. 31
2007	Feb. 21	Apr. 8	2027	Feb. 10	Mar. 28	2047	Feb. 27	Apr. 14	2067	Feb. 16	Apr. 3	2087	Mar. 5	Apr. 20
2008	Feb. 6	Mar. 23	2028	Mar. 1	Apr. 16	2048	Feb. 19	Apr. 5	2068	Mar. 7	Apr. 22	2088	Feb. 25	Apr. 11
2009	Feb. 25	Apr. 12	2029	Feb. 14	Apr. 1	2049	Mar. 3	Apr. 18	2069	Feb. 27	Apr. 14	2089	Feb. 16	Apr. 3
2010	Feb. 17	Apr. 4	2030	Mar. 6	Apr. 21	2050	Feb. 23	Apr. 10	2070	Feb. 12	Mar. 30	2090	Mar. 1	Apr. 16
2011	Mar. 9	Apr. 24	2031	Feb. 26	Apr. 13	2051	Feb. 15	Apr. 2	2071	Mar. 4	Apr. 19	2091	Feb. 21	Apr. 8
2012	Feb. 22	Apr. 8	2032	Feb. 11	Mar. 28	2052	Mar. 6	Apr. 21	2072	Feb. 24	Apr. 10	2092	Feb. 13	Mar. 30
2013	Feb. 13	Mar. 31	2033	Mar. 2	Apr. 17	2053	Feb. 19	Apr. 6	2073	Feb. 8	Mar. 26	2093	Feb. 25	Apr. 12
2014	Mar. 5	Apr. 20	2034	Feb. 22	Apr. 9	2054	Feb. 11	Mar. 29	2074	Feb. 28	Apr. 15	2094	Feb. 17	Apr. 4
2015	Feb. 18	Apr. 5	2035	Feb. 7	Mar. 25	2055	Mar. 3	Apr. 18	2075	Feb. 20	Apr. 7	2095	Mar. 9	Apr. 24
2016	Feb. 10	Mar. 27	2036	Feb. 27	Apr. 13	2056	Feb. 16	Apr. 2	2076	Mar. 4	Apr. 19	2096	Feb. 29	Apr. 15
2017	Mar. 1	Apr. 16	2037	Feb. 18	Apr. 5	2057	Mar. 7	Apr. 22	2077	Feb. 24	Apr. 11	2097	Feb. 13	Mar. 31
2018	Feb. 14	Apr. 1	2038	Mar. 10	Apr. 25	2058	Feb. 27	Apr. 14	2078	Feb. 16	Apr. 3	2098	Mar. 5	Apr. 20
2019	Mar. 6	Apr. 21	2039	Feb. 23	Apr. 10	2059	Feb. 12	Mar. 30	2079	Mar. 8	Apr. 23	2099	Feb. 25	Apr. 12
2020	Feb. 26	Apr. 12	2040	Feb. 15	Apr. 1	2060	Mar. 3	Apr. 18	2080	Feb. 21	Apr. 7	2100	Feb. 10	Mar. 28

Roman Catholic Church Hierarchy

The Roman Catholic Church is headed by the pope, or bishop of Rome. He is assisted and advised by members of the College of Cardinals. The church is governed through a central administrative body, the Roman Curia. Dioceses around the world are headed by bishops appointed by the pope; collectively they also play a part in leadership of the church as a whole.

The Papacy

Roman Catholics consider Peter the Apostle to have been the first bishop of Rome and first in a line of popes extending to the present. He is said to have arrived in Rome c. 42 CE and to have been martyred there c. 67; he was later canonized as a saint. Popes through history have had both religious and secular roles. The pope today is the head of state of Vatican City as well as leader of the church.

German-born Pope **Benedict XVI**, formerly Cardinal Joseph Ratzinger, who was elected in Apr. 2005, resigned effective Feb. 28, 2013, citing his age (85) and declining health. Assuming the title of supreme pontiff emeritus, he took up residence in a restored convent near the Vatican. He died Dec. 31, 2022.

At a papal conclave in Mar. 2013, 115 cardinals from 48 countries chose Argentinean Cardinal Jorge Mario Bergoglio as pope. He took the name **Francis**, after St. Francis of Assisi (1182-1226), known for his life of poverty and devotion to the poor. Pope Francis was the first member of the Society of Jesus (Jesuits), a Roman Catholic order, to become pope, and the first born outside Europe since Syrian-born Gregory III, who died in 741.

Chronological List of Popes

Source: *Annuario Pontificio*

Table lists year of accession of each pope. * = antipope, an illegitimate claimant to the papal throne.

Year	Pope	Year	Pope	Year	Pope	Year	Pope	Year	Pope
NA	St. Peter	530	Boniface II	884	St. Adrian III	1102	Albert*	1431	Eugene IV
67	St. Linus	530	Dioscorus*	885	Stephen V (VI)	1105	Sylvester IV*	1439	Felix V*
76	St. Anacletus, or Cletus	533	John II	891	Formosus	1118	Gelasius II	1447	Nicholas V
88	St. Clement I	535	St. Agapitus I	896	Boniface VI	1118	Gregory VIII*	1455	Callistus III
97	St. Evaristus	536	St. Silverius, Martyr	896	Stephen VI (VII)	1119	Callistus II	1458	Pius II
105	St. Alexander I	537	Vigilius	897	Romanus	1124	Honorius II	1464	Paul II
115	St. Sixtus I	556	Pelagius I	897	Theodore II	1124	Celestine II*	1471	Sixtus IV
125	St. Telesphorus	561	John III	898	John IX	1130	Innocent II	1484	Innocent VIII
136	St. Hyginus	575	Benedict I	900	Benedict IV	1130	Anacletus II*	1492	Alexander VI
140	St. Pius I	579	Pelagius II	903	Leo V	1138	Victor IV*	1503	Pius III
155	St. Anicetus	590	St. Gregory I	903	Christopher*	1143	Celestine II	1503	Julius II
166	St. Soter	604	Sabinian	904	Sergius III	1144	Lucius II	1513	Leo X
175	St. Eleutherius	607	Boniface III	911	Anastasius III	1145	Bl. Eugene III	1522	Adrian VI
189	St. Victor I	608	St. Boniface IV	913	Landus	1153	Anastasius IV	1523	Clement VII
199	St. Zephyrinus	615	St. Deusdedit, or Adeodatus	914	John X	1154	Adrian IV	1534	Paul III
217	St. Callistus I	619	Boniface V	928	Leo VI	1159	Alexander III	1550	Julius III
217	St. Hippolytus*	625	Honorius I	928	Stephen VII (VIII)	1159	Victor IV*	1555	Marcellus II
222	St. Urban I	640	Severinus	931	John XI	1164	Paschal III*	1555	Paul IV
230	St. Pontian	640	John IV	936	Leo VII	1168	Callistus III*	1559	Pius IV
235	St. Anterus	642	Theodore I	939	Stephen VIII (IX)	1179	Innocent III*	1566	St. Pius V
236	St. Fabian	649	St. Martin I, Martyr	942	Marinus II	1181	Lucius III	1572	Gregory XIII
251	St. Cornelius	654	St. Eugene I	946	Agapitus II	1185	Urban III	1585	Sixtus V
251	Novatian*	657	St. Vitalian	955	John XII	1187	Clement III	1590	Urban VII
253	St. Lucius I	672	Adeodatus II	963	Leo VIII	1187	Gregory VIII	1590	Gregory XIV
254	St. Stephen I	676	Donus	964	Benedict V	1191	Celestine III	1591	Innocent IX
257	St. Sixtus II	678	St. Agatho	965	John XIII	1198	Innocent III	1592	Clement VIII
259	St. Dionysius	682	St. Leo II	973	Benedict VI	1216	Honorius III	1605	Leo XI
269	St. Felix I	684	St. Benedict II	974	Boniface VII*	1227	Gregory IX	1605	Paul V
275	St. Eutychian	685	John V	974	Benedict VII	1241	Celestine IV	1621	Gregory XV
283	St. Caius	686	Conon	983	John XIV	1243	Innocent IV	1623	Urban VIII
296	St. Marcellinus	687	Theodore*	984	Boniface VII*	1254	Alexander IV	1644	Innocent X
308	St. Marcellus I	687	Paschal*	985	John XV	1261	Urban IV	1655	Alexander VII
309	St. Eusebius	687	St. Sergius I	996	Gregory V	1265	Clement IV	1667	Clement IX
311	St. Melchiades	701	John VI	997	John XVI*	1271	Bl. Gregory X	1670	Clement X
314	St. Sylvester I	705	John VII	999	Sylvester II	1276	Bl. Innocent V	1676	Bl. Innocent XI
336	St. Marcus	708	Sisinnius	1003	John XVII	1276	Adrian V	1689	Alexander VIII
337	St. Julius I	708	Constantine	1004	John XVIII	1276	John XXI	1691	Innocent XII
352	Liberius	715	St. Gregory II	1009	Sergius IV	1277	Nicholas III	1700	Clement XI
355	Felix II*	731	St. Gregory III	1012	Benedict VIII	1281	Martin IV	1721	Innocent XIII
366	St. Damasus I	741	St. Zachary	1012	Gregory*	1285	Honorius IV	1724	Benedict XIII
366	Ursinus*	752	Stephen II (III)[1]	1024	John XIX	1288	Nicholas IV	1730	Clement XII
384	St. Siricius	757	St. Paul I	1032	Benedict IX	1294	St. Celestine V	1740	Benedict XIV
399	St. Anastasius I	767	Constantine*	1045	Sylvester III	1294	Boniface VIII	1758	Clement XIII
401	St. Innocent I	768	Philip*	1045	Benedict IX	1303	Bl. Benedict XI	1769	Clement XIV
417	St. Zosimus	768	Stephen III (IV)	1045	Gregory VI	1305	Clement V	1775	Pius VI
418	St. Boniface I	772	Adrian I	1046	Clement II	1316	John XXII	1800	Pius VII
418	Eulalius*	795	St. Leo III	1047	Benedict IX	1328	Nicholas V*	1823	Leo XII
422	St. Celestine I	816	Stephen IV (V)	1048	Damasus II	1334	Benedict XII	1829	Pius VIII
432	St. Sixtus III	817	St. Paschal I	1049	St. Leo IX	1342	Clement VI	1831	Gregory XVI
440	St. Leo I	824	Eugene II	1055	Victor II	1352	Innocent VI	1846	Pius IX
461	St. Hilary	827	Valentine	1057	Stephen IX (X)	1362	Bl. Urban V	1878	Leo XIII
468	St. Simplicius	827	Gregory IV	1058	Benedict X*	1370	Gregory XI	1903	St. Pius X
483	St. Felix III (II)	844	John*	1059	Nicholas II	1378	Urban VI	1914	Benedict XV
492	St. Gelasius I	844	Sergius II	1061	Alexander II	1378	Clement VII*	1922	Pius XI
496	Anastasius II	847	St. Leo IV	1061	Honorius II*	1389	Boniface IX	1939	Pius XII
498	St. Symmachus	855	Benedict III	1073	St. Gregory VII	1394	Benedict XIII*	1958	St. John XXIII
498	Lawrence* (also in 501-505)	855	Anastasius*	1080	Clement III*	1404	Innocent VII	1963	Paul VI
514	St. Hormisdas	858	St. Nicholas I	1086	Bl. Victor III	1406	Gregory XII	1978	John Paul I
523	St. John I, Martyr	867	Adrian II	1088	Bl. Urban II	1409	Alexander V*	1978	St. John Paul II
526	St. Felix IV (III)	872	John VIII	1099	Paschal II	1410	John XXIII*	2005	Benedict XVI
		882	Marinus I	1100	Theodoric*	1417	Martin V	2013	Francis

NA = Not available. Bl. = Blessed. (1) A Roman priest named Stephen was elected but died before assuming the papacy. Another Stephen was then elected to succeed St. Zachary, as Stephen II. He is sometimes listed as Stephen III.

Pope Francis

Pope Francis was born Jorge Mario Bergoglio in Buenos Aires, Argentina, Dec. 17, 1936; his parents were Italian immigrants. He joined the Jesuits in 1958 and was ordained a priest in 1969. Bergoglio served as a parish priest, theology professor, and college administrator. Ordained a bishop in 1992, he was named archbishop of Buenos Aires in 1998 and made a cardinal in 2001.

Soon after his election in 2013, Francis approved measures for reform of the scandal-ridden Vatican Bank and established a commission on clerical sex abuse. In 2015, Francis released an encyclical focusing on consumerism and the environment, and the next year addressed family life, divorce, and inclusion. A 2018 publication offered guidance on holy behavior, including the need to care for poor, sick, and migrant populations. Francis convened a summit on clergy sex abuse in Rome in Feb. 2019 and in May 2019 issued guidance mandating that church officials worldwide report clergy sexual abuse and cover-ups to their church superiors. A Dec. 2023 declaration from the Vatican announced Francis had approved the blessing of same-sex couples while reserving the rites of marriage for unions between a man and a woman.

College of Cardinals

Members of the Sacred College of Cardinals are chosen by the pope to be his chief assistants and advisers in the administration of the church. Among their duties is the election of the pope.

In its present form, the College of Cardinals dates from the 12th century. The first cardinals, from about the 6th century, were deacons and priests of the leading churches of Rome and were bishops of neighboring dioceses. The title of cardinal was limited to members of the college in 1567. The number of cardinals was set at 70 in 1586. Pope John XXIII began to increase the number in 1959; however, the number eligible to participate in papal elections was limited to 120. Previous limitations were set aside by Pope John Paul II when he created new cardinals. In 1918, the Code of Canon Law specified that all cardinals must be priests. Pope John XXIII in 1962 ruled that cardinals must ordinarily be bishops. In 1971, Pope Paul VI decreed that at age 80, cardinals must retire from curial departments and offices and cannot be summoned to participate in papal elections.

As of Sept. 2024, there were 236 cardinals from 90 countries, of whom 123 from 66 countries remained eligible to vote.

North American Cardinals

Name	Office	Born	Named cardinal
Carlos Aguiar Retes	Archbishop of Mexico City	1950	2016
Felipe Arizmendi Esquivel[2]	Bishop emeritus of San Cristóbal de las Casas, Mexico	1940	2020
Raymond L. Burke	Archbishop emeritus of St. Louis	1948	2010
Thomas C. Collins	Archbishop of Toronto, Canada	1947	2012
Blase J. Cupich	Archbishop of Chicago	1949	2016
Michael Czerny	Dicastery for Promoting Integral Human Development	1946	2019
Daniel N. DiNardo	Archbishop of Galveston-Houston	1949	2007
Timothy M. Dolan	Archbishop of New York	1950	2012
Kevin J. Farrell	Prefect, Dicastery for Laity, Family, and Life; bishop emer. of Dallas	1947	2016
Wilton Daniel Gregory	Archbishop of Washington, DC	1947	2020
James M. Harvey	Archpriest of St. Paul Outside-the-Walls	1949	2012
Gérald Cyprien Lacroix[1]	Archbishop of Québec, Canada	1957	2014
Roger Mahony[2]	Archbishop emeritus of Los Angeles	1936	1991
Adam Joseph Maida[2]	Archbishop emeritus of Detroit	1930	1994
Robert Walter McElroy	Bishop of San Diego	1954	2022
Edwin F. O'Brien[2]	Archbishop emeritus of Baltimore	1939	2012
Sean O'Malley[3]	Archbishop of Boston	1944	2006
Marc Ouellet[2]	Prefect emeritus, Dicastery for Bishops; pres. emeritus, Pontifical Commission for Latin America	1944	2003
Robert Francis Prevost	Prefect, Dicastery for Bishops, pres., Pontifical Commission for Latin America	1955	2023
Justin F. Rigali[2]	Archbishop emeritus of Philadelphia	1935	2003
Norberto Rivera Carrera[2]	Archbishop emeritus of Mexico City, Mexico	1942	1998
José Francisco Robles Ortega	Archbishop of Guadalajara, Mexico	1949	2007
Juan Sandoval Íñiguez[2]	Archbishop emeritus of Guadalajara, Mexico	1933	1994
James F. Stafford[2]	Archbishop emeritus of Denver	1932	1998
Alberto Suárez Inda[2]	Archbishop emeritus of Morelia, Mexico	1939	2015
Joseph W. Tobin[1]	Archbishop of Newark	1952	2016
Donald W. Wuerl[2,4]	Archbishop emeritus of Washington, DC	1940	2010

Note: (1) Member, Council for the Economy. (2) Ineligible to vote in a papal conclave because of age. (3) Member, Council of Cardinals and Pres., Pontifical Commission for the Protection of Minors. (4) Resigned as archbishop in Oct. 2018 after allegations he concealed clergy sexual abuse.

The Ten Commandments

In the Hebrew Bible (Old Testament) the Ten Commandments (also called the Decalogue, from the Greek meaning "ten words") were revealed by God to Moses on Mt. Sinai. They form the covenant between God and the Israelites and the moral code that is the basis for the Jewish and Christian religions. The Ten Commandments appear in two places in the Old Testament—Exodus 20:1-17 and Deuteronomy 5:6-21.

Most Protestant, Anglican, and Orthodox Christians follow Jewish tradition, as shown here, which considers the introduction ("I am the Lord ...") the first commandment and makes the prohibition against idolatry the second. Roman Catholic and Lutheran traditions combine I and II and split the last commandment into two that separately prohibit coveting of a neighbor's wife and of a neighbor's goods. This arrangement alters the numbering of the other commandments by one.

Following is the text as it appears in Exodus 20:1-17 in the King James version of the Bible [Roman numerals added]:

And God spake all these words, saying,

I. I *am* the LORD thy God, which have brought thee out of the land of Egypt, out of the house of bondage. Thou shalt have no other gods before me.

II. Thou shalt not make unto thee any graven image, or any likeness of *any thing* that *is* in heaven above, or that *is* in the earth beneath, or that *is* in the water under the earth. Thou shalt not bow down thyself to them, nor serve them: for I the LORD thy God *am* a jealous God, visiting the iniquity of the fathers upon the children unto the third and fourth *generation* of them that hate me; and shewing mercy unto thousands of them that love me, and keep my commandments.

III. Thou shalt not take the name of the LORD thy God in vain: for the LORD will not hold him guiltless that taketh his name in vain.

IV. Remember the sabbath day, to keep it holy. Six days shalt thou labour, and do all thy work: but the seventh day *is* the sabbath of the LORD thy God: *in it* thou shalt not do any work, thou, nor thy son, nor thy daughter, thy manservant, nor thy maidservant, nor thy cattle, nor thy stranger that *is* within thy gates: for *in* six days the LORD made heaven and earth, the sea, and all that in them *is*, and rested the seventh day: wherefore the LORD blessed the sabbath day, and hallowed it.

V. Honour thy father and thy mother: that thy days may be long upon the land which the LORD thy God giveth thee.

VI. Thou shalt not kill.

VII. Thou shalt not commit adultery.

VIII. Thou shalt not steal.

IX. Thou shalt not bear false witness against thy neighbour.

X. Thou shalt not covet thy neighbour's house, thou shalt not covet thy neighbour's wife, nor his manservant, nor his maidservant, nor his ox, nor his ass, nor any thing that *is* thy neighbour's.

Major Christian Denominations:

Brackets indicate some features that tend to

Denomination	Origins	Organization	Authority	Special rites
Baptists	In radical Reformation, objections to infant baptism, demands for church and state separation; John Smyth, English Separatist, in 1609; Roger Williams, 1638, Providence, RI.	Congregational; each local church is autonomous.	Scripture; some Baptists, particularly in the South, interpret the Bible literally.	[Baptism, usually early teen years and after, by total immersion]; Lord's Supper.
Church of Christ (Disciples)	Among evangelical Presbyterians in KY (1804) and PA (1809), in distress over Protestant factionalism and decline of fervor; organized in 1832.	Congregational.	["Where the Scriptures speak, we speak; where the Scriptures are silent, we are silent."]	Adult baptism; Lord's Supper (weekly).
Episcopalians	Henry VIII separated English Catholic Church from Rome, 1534, for political reasons; Protestant Episcopal Church in U.S. founded in 1789.	[Diocesan bishops, in apostolic succession, are elected by parish representatives; the national Church is headed by General Convention and Presiding Bishop; part of the Anglican Communion.]	Scripture as interpreted by tradition, especially 39 Articles (1563); tri-annual convention of bishops, priests, and lay people.	Infant baptism, Eucharist, and other sacraments; sacrament taken to be symbolic, but as having real spiritual effect.
Jehovah's Witnesses	Founded in 1870 in PA by Charles Taze Russell; incorporated as Watch Tower Bible and Tract Society of PA, 1884; name Jehovah's Witnesses adopted in 1931.	A governing body located in NY coordinates worldwide activities; each congregation cared for by a body of elders; each Witness considered a minister.	The Bible.	Baptism by immersion; annual Lord's Meal ceremony.
Latter-day Saints (Mormons)	In a vision of the Father and the Son reported by Joseph Smith (1820s) in NY; Smith also reported receiving new scripture on golden tablets: the Book of Mormon.	Theocratic; 1st Presidency (church president, two counselors), 12 Apostles preside over international church; local congregations headed by lay priesthood leaders.	Revelation to living prophet (church president). The Bible, Book of Mormon, and other revelations to Smith and his successors.	Baptism at age 8; laying on of hands (which confers the gift of the Holy Ghost); Lord's Supper; temple rites: baptism for the dead, marriage for eternity, others.
Lutherans	Begun by Martin Luther in Wittenberg, Germany, in 1517; objection to Catholic doctrine of salvation and sale of indulgences; break complete, 1519.	Varies from congregational to episcopal; in U.S., a combination of regional synods and congregational polities is most common.	Scripture alone; the *Book of Concord* (1580), which includes the three Ecumenical Creeds, is subscribed to as a correct exposition of Scripture.	Infant baptism; Lord's Supper; Christ's true body and blood present "in, with, and under the bread and wine."
Methodists	Rev. John Wesley began movement in 1738, within Church of England; first U.S. denomination in Baltimore (1784).	Conference and superintendent system; [in United Methodist Church, general superintendents are bishops—not a priestly order, only an office—who are elected for life].	Scripture as interpreted by tradition, reason, and experience.	Baptism of infants or adults; Lord's Supper commanded; other rites: marriage, ordination, solemnization of personal commitments.
Orthodox	Developed in original Christian proselytizing; broke with Rome in 1054 after centuries of doctrinal disputes and diverging traditions.	Synods of bishops in autonomous, usually national, churches elect a patriarch, archbishop, or metropolitan; these men, as a group, are the heads of the church.	Scripture, tradition, and the first seven church councils up to Nicaea II in 787; bishops in council have authority in doctrine and policy.	Seven sacraments: infant baptism and anointing, Eucharist, ordination, penance, marriage, and anointing of the sick.
Pentecostal	In Topeka, KS (1901) and Los Angeles (1906), in reaction to perceived loss of evangelical fervor among Methodists and others.	Originally a movement, not a formal organization, Pentecostalism now has a variety of organized forms and continues also as a movement.	Scripture; individual charismatic leaders, the teachings of the Holy Spirit.	[Spirit baptism, especially as shown in "speaking in tongues"; faith healing; sometimes exorcism]; adult baptism; Lord's Supper.
Presbyterians	In 16th-cent. Calvinist reformation; differed with Lutherans over sacraments, church government; John Knox founded Scotch Presbyterian church about 1560.	[Highly structured representational system of ministers and lay persons (presbyters) in local, regional, and national bodies (synods).]	Scripture.	Infant baptism; Lord's Supper; bread and wine symbolize Christ's spiritual presence.
Roman Catholics	Traditionally, founded by Jesus who named St. Peter the first vicar; developed in early Christian proselytizing, especially after the conversion of imperial Rome in the 4th cent.	[Hierarchy with supreme power vested in pope elected by cardinals]; councils of bishops advise on matters of doctrine and policy.	[The pope, when speaking for the whole church in matters of faith and morals, and tradition (which is expressed in church councils and in part contained in Scripture).]	Mass; seven sacraments: baptism, reconciliation, Eucharist, confirmation, marriage, ordination, and anointing of the sick (unction).
United Church of Christ	By ecumenical union, in 1957, of Congregationalists and Evangelical and Reformed, representing both Calvinist and Lutheran traditions.	Congregational; a General Synod, representative of all congregations, sets general policy.	Scripture.	Infant baptism; Lord's Supper.

How Do They Differ?

distinguish a denomination sharply from others.

Practice	Ethics	Doctrine	Other	Denomination
Worship style varies from staid to evangelistic; extensive missionary activity.	Usually opposed to alcohol and tobacco; some tendency toward a perfectionist ethical standard.	[No creed; true church is of believers only, who are all equal.]	Believing no authority can stand between the believer and God, the Baptists are strong supporters of church and state separation.	**Baptists**
Tries to avoid any rite not considered part of the 1st-cent. church; some congregations may reject instrumental music.	Some tendency toward perfectionism; increasing interest in social action programs.	Simple New Testament faith; avoids any elaboration not firmly based on Scripture.	Highly tolerant in doctrinal and religious matters; strongly supportive of scholarly education.	**Church of Christ (Disciples)**
Formal, based on *Book of Common Prayer*, updated 1979; services range from austerely simple to highly liturgical.	Tolerant, sometimes permissive; some social action programs.	Scripture; the "historic creeds," which include the Apostles, Nicene, and Athanasian, and the *Book of Common Prayer*; ranges from Anglo-Catholic to low church, with Calvinist influences.	Strongly ecumenical, holding talks with many branches of Christendom.	**Episcopalians**
Meetings are held in Kingdom Halls and members' homes for study and worship; [extensive door-to-door visitations].	High moral code; stress on marital fidelity and family values; avoidance of tobacco and blood transfusions.	[God, by his first creation, Christ, will soon destroy all wickedness; 144,000 faithful ones will rule in heaven with Christ over others on a paradise earth.]	Total allegiance proclaimed only to God's kingdom or heavenly government by Christ.	**Jehovah's Witnesses**
Simple service with prayers, hymns, sermon; private temple ceremonies may be more elaborate.	Temperance; strict moral code; [tithing]; a strong work ethic with communal self-reliance; [strong missionary activity]; family emphasis.	Jesus Christ is the Son of God, the Eternal Father. Jesus's atonement saves all humans; those who are obedient to God's laws may become joint-heirs with Christ in God's kingdom.	Mormons believe theirs is the true church of Jesus Christ, restored by God through Joseph Smith. Official name: The Church of Jesus Christ of Latter-day Saints.	**Latter-day Saints (Mormons)**
Relatively simple, formal liturgy with emphasis on the sermon.	Generally conservative in personal and social ethics; doctrine of "two kingdoms" (worldly and holy) supports conservatism in secular affairs.	Salvation by grace alone through faith; Lutheranism has made major contributions to Protestant theology.	Though still somewhat divided along ethnic lines (German, Swedish, etc.), main divisions are between fundamentalists and liberals.	**Lutherans**
Worship style varies widely by denomination, local church, geography.	Originally pietist and perfectionist; always strong social activist elements.	No distinctive theological development; 25 articles abridged from Church of England's 39, not binding.	In 1968, The United Methodist Church was formed by the union of The Methodist Church and The Evangelical United Brethren Church.	**Methodists**
Elaborate liturgy, usually in the vernacular, though extremely traditional; the liturgy is the essence of Orthodoxy; veneration of icons.	Tolerant; little stress on social action; divorce, remarriage permitted in some cases; bishops are celibate; priests need not be.	Emphasis on Christ's resurrection, rather than crucifixion; the Holy Spirit proceeds from God the Father only.	Orthodox Church in America originally under Patriarch of Moscow, was granted autonomy in 1970; Greek Orthodox do not recognize this autonomy.	**Orthodox**
Loosely structured service with rousing hymns and sermons, culminating in spirit baptism.	Usually, emphasis on perfectionism, with varying degrees of tolerance.	Simple traditional beliefs, usually Protestant, with emphasis on the immediate presence of God in the Holy Spirit.	Once appealed mostly to lower classes; formation of charismatic fellowships in mainline churches expanded reach.	**Pentecostal**
A simple, sober service in which the sermon is central.	Traditionally, a tendency toward strictness, with firm church- and self-discipline; otherwise tolerant.	Emphasizes the sovereignty and justice of God; no longer dogmatic.	Although traces of belief in predestination (that God has foreordained salvation for the "elect") remain, this idea is no longer a central element in Presbyterianism.	**Presbyterians**
Relatively elaborate ritual centered on the Mass; also rosary recitation, novenas.	Traditionally strict but increasingly tolerant in practice; divorce and remarriage not accepted, but annulments sometimes granted; celibate clergy, except in Eastern rite.	Highly elaborated; salvation by merit gained through grace; dogmatic; special veneration of Mary, the mother of Jesus.	Relatively rapid changes followed Vatican Council II (1962-65). Mass held in vernacular instead of Latin; more stress on social action, tolerance, ecumenism.	**Roman Catholics**
Usually simple service with emphasis on the sermon.	Tolerant; some social action emphasis.	Standard Protestant; Statement of Faith (1959) is not binding.	Two main churches in the 1957 union represented earlier unions with small groups of almost every Protestant denomination.	**United Church of Christ**

Books of the Bible

Old Testament—Standard Protestant List

Genesis	I Kings	Ecclesiastes	Obadiah
Exodus	II Kings	Song of Solomon	Jonah
Leviticus	I Chronicles	Isaiah	Micah
Numbers	II Chronicles	Jeremiah	Nahum
Deuteronomy	Ezra	Lamentations	Habakkuk
Joshua	Nehemiah	Ezekiel	Zephaniah
Judges	Esther	Daniel	Haggai
Ruth	Job	Hosea	Zechariah
I Samuel	Psalms	Joel	Malachi
II Samuel	Proverbs	Amos	

New Testament List

Matthew	Ephesians	Hebrews
Mark	Philippians	James
Luke	Colossians	I Peter
John	I Thessalonians	II Peter
Acts	II Thessalonians	I John
Romans	I Timothy	II John
I Corinthians	II Timothy	III John
II Corinthians	Titus	Jude
Galatians	Philemon	Revelation

The standard Protestant Old Testament consists of the same 39 books as in the Bible of Judaism, but the latter is organized differently. The Old Testament used by Roman Catholics has 7 additional deuterocanonical books, plus some additional parts of books. The 7 are **Tobit**, **Judith**, **Wisdom**, **Sirach (Ecclesiasticus)**, **Baruch**, **I Maccabees**, and **II Maccabees**. Both Catholic and Protestant versions of the New Testament have 27 books with the same names.

Figures in the Hebrew Bible (Old Testament)

Aaron: First of Hebrew high priests; brother of Moses and Miriam.
Abel: Second son of Adam and Eve; slain by Cain.
Abraham: Founder of monotheism; patriarch; also called Abram.
Adam: First human according to Genesis.
Amos: Herdsman; prophesized against social injustice and oppression of the poor.
Bathsheba: Seduced by King David; mother of King Solomon.
Cain: First son of Adam and Eve; killed his brother Abel.
Cyrus: Persian ruler; sent Jews home to Jerusalem from exile.
Daniel: Cast into lion's den for violating decree of King Darius; saved.
David: Israel's greatest king; shepherd, warrior, musician, psalmist.
Deborah: Prophet and judge; ruled over Israel.
Elijah: Great prophet; was victorious over the priests of the Phoenician god Baal.
Elisha: Prophet; successor to Elijah.
Esther: Jewish wife of the king of Persia; saved Jews from annihilation.
Eve: First woman according to Genesis.
Ezekiel: Visionary; prophesized hope to exiled Jews in Babylon.
Ezra: Great Jewish leader; rededicated worship and Torah law after exile.
Goliath: Giant Philistine warrior; slain by David.
Hannah: Childless; promised child to God; mother to the prophet Samuel.
Hosea: Enacted prophecy; asked God's forgiveness for Israel's unfaithfulness.
Isaac: Son of Abraham and Sarah; saved from sacrificial altar.
Isaiah: Highly educated prophet; avoided war with Assyria; Israel destroyed; Jerusalem survived.
Jacob: Son of Isaac; father of the Twelve Tribes; renamed "Israel" by angel.
Jeremiah: Confronted leaders and urged surrender to Babylon.
Jezebel: Phoenician queen of King Ahab of Israel; had Israelite prophets killed.
Job: "Blameless" man; allowed by God to lose family, health, and possessions in a test of his faith.
Jonah: Swallowed by a great fish; prophesied destruction of the city of Nineveh, averted when the people repented.
Jonathan: Son of King Saul; friend of David.
Joseph: Favorite of Jacob; interpreted Pharaoh's dreams; brought Hebrews to Egypt.
Joshua: Successor of Moses; led Hebrews into Canaan.
Josiah: Reformist king; repaired Solomon's Temple; restored worship; reintroduced Passover.
Leah: Matriarch; older sister of Rachel; Jacob's wife.
Micah: Prophet; predicted the end of war and beginning of peace.
Miriam: Prophet and great leader of the Hebrews; sister to Moses and Aaron.
Moses: Most important Hebrew prophet; leader of the Israelites; received the Torah.
Nathan: Prophet; confronted King David over his seduction of the married Bathsheba.
Nebuchadnezzar: Babylonian king; destroyed Jerusalem.
Nehemiah: Led Jews back to Jerusalem from Babylonian exile.
Noah: Man of great faith who, according to Genesis, saved his family and two of every living thing on Earth from a great flood.
Rachel: Matriarch; younger sister of Leah; Jacob's wife; Joseph's mother.
Rebecca: Matriarch; wife of Isaac; mother of Jacob.
Ruth: Moabite convert; ancestor of David.
Samson: Judge and military leader of Israel; possessed superhuman strength.
Samuel: Prophet; anointed Saul king of Israel and later anointed David to succeed him.
Sarah: First matriarch of Israel; wife of Abraham; mother of Isaac.
Saul: First king of Israel; father of Jonathan.
Solomon: King of Israel at its zenith; known for great wisdom.
Zechariah: Prophet; encouraged rebuilding of Solomon's Temple, which had been destroyed by Babylonians.

Figures in the New Testament

Andrew: One of the Twelve Apostles; brother of Peter and former fisherman; one of the earlier disciples.
Barabbas: Imprisoned with Jesus; set free by Pilate on Passover.
Barnabas: Disciple of Jesus; closely connected with Paul.
Bartholomew: A lesser-known member of the Twelve Apostles; cheerful and prayed often.
Cornelius: Roman convert; defended by Peter, allowing Gentiles to become Christians.
Elizabeth: Mother of John the Baptist; relation of the Virgin Mary.
Gabriel: Archangel; appeared to the Virgin Mary to announce that she was to give birth to the Messiah.
Herod: May refer to Herod the Great, who ordered the death of children after Jesus's birth, or to his son, Herod, who had John the Baptist beheaded.
James: May refer to either of two apostles: James, son of Zebedee, brother of John the Apostle, or the lesser-known James, son of Alphaeus.
Jesus: Central figure of the Gospels; believed to be the Messiah and son of God; crucified by the Romans.
John (Apostle): Beloved disciple of Jesus; one of the Twelve Apostles; possible author of fourth Gospel; brother of James.
John (Baptist): Known as John the Baptist; important prophet and forerunner to Jesus; relation of the Virgin Mary.
Joseph: Husband of the Virgin Mary; descendant of King David.
Judas Iscariot: Betrayer of Jesus; prominent member of the Apostles; committed suicide.
Judas Thaddeus: One of the Twelve Apostles; also called Jude to distinguish him from Judas Iscariot.
Lazarus: Brother of the disciples Martha and Mary of Bethany; raised from the dead by Jesus at their request; possibly the same Lazarus who appears in Jesus's parable of the rich man.
Luke: Traditional author of the Gospel of Luke; possibly a follower of Paul.
Mark: Traditional author of the Gospel of Mark; possibly a disciple of Peter.
Mary, the mother of Jesus: Traditionally believed to be a virgin who conceived without sin; wife of Joseph.
Mary Magdalene: Important female disciple of Jesus; witness to his death and resurrection.
Matthew: One of the Twelve Apostles; possible author of the Gospel of Matthew; former tax collector.
Matthias: Often included on lists of the Twelve Apostles as the apostle who replaced Judas Iscariot after his betrayal.
Paul (Saul): Writer of nearly a quarter of the New Testament; a former persecutor of Christians, converted after a vision; played a significant role in spreading Christianity.
Peter: Considered the foremost of the Twelve Apostles; traditionally the first pope and "rock" of the Christian church; author of epistles; also called Simon and Simon Peter.
Philip: One of the Twelve; considered pragmatic and sensible.
Pilate, Pontius: A Roman prefect; played large role in the trial and crucifixion of Jesus.
Simon: One of the Twelve Apostles; known as "the Zealot" to distinguish from Simon Peter.
Stephen: Fervently preached that Jesus was the Messiah; stoned to death by angry mob, including Saul (Paul); important figure in Saul's conversion.
Thomas: One of the Twelve Apostles; known as "Doubting Thomas" because he did not believe Jesus was risen until he could touch him.
Timothy: A disciple closely connected with Paul; recipient of epistles.
Zacharias: Father of John the Baptist; husband of Elizabeth; struck dumb when he doubted his barren wife could become pregnant.

Major Religions

Islam

Founded: Muhammad received his first revelation in 610 CE.

Founder: Muhammad (c. 570-632 CE), the Prophet.

Sacred texts: Two texts constitute the Muslim sacred canon, the *Quran* (Koran) and the *Hadith*. The Quran provides the foundation for Islamic religion and culture. It is regarded as the final, perfect, and complete word of God as revealed to Muhammad over the course of his life. Received by Muhammad in the Arabic language, it is memorized in Arabic by adherents regardless of their native language. It is divided into 114 chapters of unequal length, the shortest containing only 3 verses, and the longest containing 286 verses. The Quran is the ultimate source of everything Islamic, from metaphysics to theology to sacred history, to ethics and law, to art. The Hadith, which describes Muhammad's actions, attitudes, and teachings, complements the Quran. Due to its long history of oral transmission, the Hadith's lessons are seen as somewhat vulnerable to human error. It is not said to contain God's unadulterated voice as is the Quran but functions as a powerful spiritual and behavioral code nonetheless.

Organization: Muhammad was both the last prophet and a statesman. Muslim leaders have often assumed both civil and moral functions within Islamic states. Within the larger community, there are cultural and national groups, held together by a common religious law, the *Sharia*. Muslims believe that God is the ultimate lawgiver and that human beings cannot devise laws that oppose divine laws. Still, the Sharia is approached differently in different parts of the Islamic world. Over the centuries, Sunnis have developed four major schools of law: the Hanafi, the Shafi'i, the Hanbali, and the Maliki. The Ja'fari is the most important and well-known Shiite school. Before the 20th century, religious scholars known as the *ulama* held much legal power. Judges (*qadis*) and law-interpreters (*muftis*) are people learned in religious law who lead congregational prayers in mosques and perform other religious duties.

Practice: Five duties (of both men and women), known as the Pillars of Islam, are regarded as cardinal in Islam and as central to the life of the Islamic community. In accordance with Islam's absolute commitment to monotheism, the first duty is the profession of faith (the *Shahadah*): "There is no God but Allah and Muhammad is His Prophet." A Muslim must profess this belief publicly at least once in his or her lifetime; it defines the membership of an individual in the Islamic community. The second duty is that of five daily prayers organized in intervals throughout the day: sunrise, early afternoon, late afternoon, immediately after sunset, and before midnight. During prayer, Muslims face the Kaaba, a small, cube-shaped structure in the courtyard of al-Haram (the "inviolate place"), at the Grand Mosque of Mecca in Saudi Arabia. All five prayers in Islam are congregational and are to be offered in a mosque, but they may be offered individually if one cannot be present with a congregation. Congregational prayer is required only at the early afternoon prayer on Friday for men. The third cardinal duty of a Muslim is to pay alms, or *zakat*, which should be 2.5% of one's total wealth. This was originally the tax levied by Muhammad on the wealthy members of the community, primarily to help the poor. Only when zakat has been paid is the rest of a Muslim's property considered purified and legitimate. The fourth duty is the fast of the lunar month of Ramadan. During the fasting month, one must abstain from eating, drinking, smoking, impure thoughts, and sexual intercourse from dawn until sunset, and feed at least one poor person, if able. The fifth duty is the pilgrimage to the Kaaba, known as the hajj, which a Muslim must undertake, with exceptions for poverty and ill health, at least once during his or her lifetime.

Divisions: There are two major groups: the majority **Sunni** (85%-90% of the worldwide Muslim population) and the minority Shiites. Sects first appeared in Islam at the time of Muhammad's death. The group that came to be known as Sunni accepted Abu Bakr, an early convert, as his successor (caliph), while a smaller number, which became the Shia, believed that Ali ibn Abi Talib, the son-in-law and first cousin of the prophet, should have become his successor (Imam). Imams are believed to interpret the Quran infallibly. **Shiites** fall into three major branches: Fivers, Seveners, and Twelvers, reflecting the number of Imams they recognize. Twelvers believe that the 12th Imam has lived an invisible existence since 874, and will return as the Mahdi (a messiah figure) who will usher in a 1,000-year reign of peace and justice. **Sufism** (mystical dimension of Islam) emphasizes personal relation to God and obedience informed by love of God; it is prevalent among both Sunni and Shiites.

Location: W Africa to Philippines, across a band including E Africa, Central Asia and western China, India, Malaysia, Indonesia. Islam has several million adherents in North America and about 30 mil in Europe.

Beliefs: Strictly monotheistic. God is creator of the universe, omnipotent, omniscient, just, forgiving, and merciful. God revealed the Quran to Muhammad to guide humanity to truth and justice. Those who sincerely "submit" (literal meaning of "Islam") to God attain salvation.

World's Largest Muslim Populations, 2025

Source: Gina A. Zurlo, ed., *World Religion Database* (Leiden/Boston: Brill, July 2024).

Rank	Country	Muslim population	% of country's pop.
1.	Pakistan	238,085,000	95.3%
2.	Indonesia	219,304,000	77.8
3.	India	199,536,000	13.7
4.	Bangladesh	156,531,000	88.7
5.	Nigeria	108,279,000	46.2
6.	Egypt	104,966,000	90.3
7.	Iran	88,692,000	98.1
8.	Turkey	84,992,000	98.0
9.	Sudan	46,486,000	91.8
10.	Iraq	46,344,000	97.5
11.	Algeria	46,002,000	98.0
12.	Afghanistan	44,452,000	99.9
13.	Ethiopia	43,635,000	32.8
14.	Morocco	38,438,000	99.7
15.	Yemen	35,720,000	99.2
16.	Uzbekistan	34,354,000	95.0
17.	Saudi Arabia	34,273,000	90.2
18.	China	28,412,000	2.0
19.	Niger	28,040,000	95.6
20.	Syria	24,269,000	95.4
21.	Tanzania	23,678,000	33.1
22.	Mali	21,666,000	87.5
23.	Somalia	19,253,000	99.8
24.	Malaysia	19,239,000	54.9
25.	Senegal	17,085,000	91.4

Baha'i

Founded: Mid-19th century.

Founder: Mirza Husayn-Ali Nuri (1817-92), later known as Baha'u'llah (Arabic for "Glory of God").

Sacred texts: The writings of Baha'u'llah and of his herald the Bab (Siyyid Ali-Muhammad, 1819-50). The primary text is *Kitab-i-Aqdas* (Most Holy Book).

Organization: The Baha'i administrative system consists of elected nine-member councils at the local, national, and international levels. There are also more than 180 National Spiritual Assemblies and an elected, international governing body known as the Universal House of Justice.

Practice: Prayer, meditation, and fasting are key components of the Baha'i Faith. Work performed in a spirit of service to humanity is considered an important form of worship. The Baha'i Faith has no clergy and minimal ritual and congregational worship.

Divisions: In a religion in which unity is perhaps the central spiritual value, the Baha'i Faith has avoided separating into sects with differentiated theologies and practices.

Location: Worldwide.

Beliefs: God has progressively revealed His will and purpose through a series of Divine manifestations including Jesus, Buddha, Muhammad, Zoroaster, and Baha'u'llah. Baha'u'llah's teachings include the oneness of humanity, the equality of men and women, the harmony of science and religion, and the need to abandon all forms of prejudice and eliminate extremes of poverty and wealth.

Buddhism

Founded: About 525 BCE, reportedly near Benares, India.

Founder: Gautama Siddhartha (c. 563-483 BCE), the Buddha, who achieved enlightenment through intense meditation.

Sacred texts: The *Tripitaka*, a collection of the Buddha's teachings, rules of monastic life, and philosophical commentaries on the teachings; also a vast body of Buddhist teachings and commentaries, many of which are called *sutras*.

Organization: The basic institution is the *sangha*, or monastic order, through which traditions are passed down. Monastic life tends to be democratic and antiauthoritarian.

Practice: Varies widely according to the sect and ranges from austere meditation to magical chanting and elaborate temple rites. Many practices, such as exorcism of devils, reflect pre-Buddhist beliefs.

Divisions: A variety of sects grouped into three primary branches: Theravada, which emphasizes the importance of pure thought and deed; Mahayana (includes Zen and Soka-gakkai), which ranges from philosophical schools to belief in the saving grace of higher beings or ritual practices and to practical meditative disciplines; and Vajrayana, or Tantrism, a combination of belief in ritual magic and sophisticated philosophy.

Location: Mainly in Asia, from Sri Lanka to Japan.

Beliefs: Life is suffering, and there is no ultimate reality behind it. The cycle of birth and rebirth continues because of desire and attachment to the unreal "self." Meditation and deeds will end the cycle and achieve Nirvana (nothingness, enlightenment).

Hinduism

Founded: About 1500 BCE to 300 CE as a religion and *dharma* (way of life); a diverse synthesis of primarily Indian traditions, practices, and beliefs.

Sacred texts: The *Vedas* (Rig, Sama, Yajur, Atharva); the *Upanishads*, a collection of rituals and commentaries; a vast number of epic stories about gods, heroes, and saints, including the *Puranas*, *Ramayana*, and *Mahabharata*; the *Bhagavad Gita*; and the *Agamas*.

Organization: None, strictly speaking. No single founder, establishment date, authoritative scripture, or central religious organization exist.

Practice: *Sanskara*, or rites of passage (e.g., initiation, marriage, death), and devotionals (*bhakti*). Bhakti may be practiced privately, as at a household shrine, or in a group.

Divisions: There is no concept of orthodoxy in Hinduism, which presents a variety of sects. Three major traditions are those devoted to the gods Vishnu and Shiva and to the goddess Shakti, but others believe in *brahman* (the All) as a more impersonal but infinite spiritual core. Numerous beliefs and practices, often in amalgamation, exist side by side with various philosophical schools.

Location: Mainly India, Nepal, Malaysia, Mauritius, Guyana, Suriname, and Sri Lanka.

Beliefs: Two basic tenets of Hinduism include a belief in the unity of existence as well as in the process of transmigration and rebirth (*samsara*) with no clear beginning or end. Life in all its forms is an aspect or manifestation of the divine or of divine qualities.

Judaism

Founded: About 2000 BCE.

Founder: Abraham is regarded as the founding patriarch.

Sacred texts: The five books of Moses (the Torah), the basic source of teachings.

Organization: Originally theocratic, Judaism has evolved into a congregational polity. The basic institution is the local synagogue or temple, operated by the congregation and led by a rabbi of their choice. Chief rabbis in France and Great Britain have authority only over those who accept it; in Israel, the two chief rabbis (one each from the Sephardic Jewish and Ashkenazi Jewish communities) have civil authority in family law.

Practice: Among traditional practitioners, almost all areas of life are governed by strict discipline. Sabbath and holidays are marked by observances, and attendance at public worship is considered especially important. Chief annual observances are Passover, celebrating liberation of the Israelites from Egypt and marked by the Seder meal in homes, and the 10 days from Rosh Hashanah (New Year) to Yom Kippur (Day of Atonement), a period of penitence.

Divisions: Judaism is an unbroken spectrum from ultraconservative to ultraliberal, largely reflecting different points of view regarding the binding character of the prohibitions and duties—particularly the dietary and Sabbath observations—traditionally prescribed for the daily life of the Jew.

Location: Mainly in Israel and the U.S.

Beliefs: Strictly monotheistic. God is the creator and ruler of the universe. God established a particular relationship with the Hebrew people: by obeying a divine law God gave them, they would be a special witness to God's mercy and justice. Judaism stresses ethical behavior (and, among the traditional, careful ritual obedience) as true worship of God.

Sikhism

Founded: Late 15th century in South Asia.

Founder: Guru Nanak Dev ji, Sikhism's first Guru.

Sacred texts: The *Guru Granth Sahib* was compiled by the Sikh Gurus and contains their experiences of the Divine. It also contains writings by other saintly figures of different faiths.

Organization: Each Sikh must make her or his own spiritual journey and not depend on clergy. Congregational prayer led by both men and women takes place in local *Gurdwaras* ("doorway to the Guru"). Harmandir Sahib in Amritsar, Punjab (northern India), is the central place of worship.

Practice: Prayers are required in the morning, evening, and before sleeping. The most important mode of congregational prayer is the singing of hymns from the Guru Granth Sahib. The "Five Ks" are five articles of faith required of all Sikhs: *Kes* (uncut hair), *Kangha* (comb), *Kara* (steel bracelet), *Kirpan* (sword), and *Kaccha* (short pants).

Divisions: The last living Guru, Guru Gobind Singh (1666-1708), crystallized the practices and beliefs of the faith and determined that no future living Guru was needed. Today the religion is guided by joint sovereignty of Guru Granth and Guru Panth. Guru Granth is the Sikh scripture, as the spiritual manifestation of the Guru, while the Guru Panth is the collectivity of all initiated Sikhs worldwide, as the physical manifestation of the Guru.

Location: Many Sikhs have Punjabi backgrounds. The Punjab region was divided between India and Pakistan with the end of British rule.

Beliefs: Sikhism preaches a message of devotion, remembrance of God at all times, truthful living, equality between all human beings, and social justice, while denouncing what is considered superstition and blind ritualism. Sikhism is a monotheistic religion based on revelation.

LANGUAGE

New Words in English

The following new words and definitions were provided by Merriam-Webster, Inc., publishers of *Merriam-Webster's Collegiate Dictionary, Eleventh Edition*, and other language references. The words are among those added in 2024 by Merriam-Webster's editors to the digital version of the dictionary, available as the *Merriam-Webster Dictionary* app and online at www.merriam-webster.com.

agua fresca: a beverage consisting of water and sugar with fruits, grains, or seeds added for flavoring
Anthropocene: the period of time during which human activities have had an environmental impact on the Earth regarded as constituting a distinct geological time interval
badassery *chiefly U.S., informal + sometimes impolite* **1:** the state or condition of being a badass: a badass quality or character **2:** the actions or behaviors characteristic of a badass
barbacoa: a flavorful Mexican dish of shredded meat (such as beef, lamb, or goat) made by slow-cooking the meat in a marinade
beach read: a usually light work of escapist fiction (such as a thriller or romance)
bhaji 1: an Indian food consisting of a small mass of chopped, battered vegetables that has been deep-fried **2:** a dish of Indian origin featuring fried or sautéed vegetables in a curry sauce
bolillo: a large, elongated crusty roll of Mexican origin used especially for sandwiches
cipher 1: a circle formed by performers (such as rappers or hip-hop dancers) who take turns improvising in the middle, often as part of a competition **2:** a hip-hop song that features multiple rappers taking turns delivering verses
crybully: a person who falsely claims to be a victim or who feigns emotional pain in order to manipulate, coerce, or threaten others
esport: a multiplayer video game used as the basis for an organized competition; *also*: the activity of engaging in esports
For You page: a social media feed that contains personalized content based on the user's interests
headhunting *sports*: the practice of physically intimidating or harming one's opponent
International Bitterness Unit: a unit of measurement used to assess the concentration of a bitter compound found in hops in order to provide information about how bitter a beer is
katana: a slightly curved, single-edged sword historically worn by the Japanese samurai
land acknowledgment: a usually brief statement (such as one made at a public gathering) that recognizes the surrounding land as the ancestral, traditional, or contemporary homeland of one or more Indigenous peoples
Mexican street corn 1: grilled corn on the cob that is coated with a creamy spread (such as mayonnaise, sour cream, or crema) and garnished with toppings **2:** boiled, grilled, or sautéed corn kernels mixed with assorted ingredients (such as lime juice, mayonnaise, cotija cheese, and chili powder)
money grab: the greedy pursuit of an opportunity for making money especially when done without regard for ethics, concerns, or consequences
nepo baby: a person who gains success or opportunities through familial connections
neurodivergent: having or relating to a disorder or condition (such as autism spectrum disorder, attention deficit hyperactivity disorder, dyslexia, or obsessive-compulsive disorder) that impacts the way the brain processes information: exhibiting or characteristic of variations in typical neurological development
rehome: to provide (someone or something) with a different home or location
representation: the participation of people from groups who have historically been excluded or discriminated against (as due to race, gender, sexuality, or ability); *also*: the inclusion of characters, perspectives, etc. from such groups
saditty *African American English:* putting on or marked by airs of superiority
shadow ban: to cause (a user or their content) to be hidden from some or all other users usually without the user's knowledge
single-use: intended or designed to be used once and then discarded
throw shade *informal:* to express contempt or disrespect for someone or something especially in an indirect or subtle way
true crime: a nonfiction genre of literature, film, podcasts, etc. that depicts and examines real crime cases
turn-based: of, relating to, or being a game or part of a game in which the players take turns or in which a single player takes turns with an AI opponent
Uber 1: to use a rideshare service and especially the Uber rideshare service **2:** to drive a car for the Uber rideshare service
ultra-processed *of foods and beverages:* containing or made primarily with highly processed ingredients including artificial additives (such as coloring, flavoring, and preservatives) and typically having high levels of fat, sugar, or salt
unhoused: not having a dwelling place, shelter, or permanent place of residence; *also:* of, relating to, or involving people who are unhoused

National Spelling Bee

The Scripps National Spelling Bee, conducted each year since 1925, allows students under age 16 in 8th grade or lower to compete for a chance to advance to national championship finals in Washington, DC. After announcing it was running out of challenging words, the competition named eight spellers co-champions in 2019; the 2020 Bee was canceled due to the COVID-19 pandemic. The contest format has changed repeatedly to help avert ties that had become increasingly common in recent years. In 2024, Bruhat Soma, a 12-year-old from St. Petersburg, FL, was named the winner after spelling 29 words correctly during the 90-second lightning round. The runner-up, 12-year-old Faizan Zaki of Allen, TX, spelled 20 lightning round words correctly.

Here are the last words given and spelled correctly at the National Spelling Bee in recent years:

Year	Word	Year	Word	Year	Word	Year	Word	Year	Word
1982	psoriasis	1992	lyceum	2002	prospicience	2012	guetapens	2019	auslaut, erysipelas, palama, aiguillette, odylic, cernuous, pendeloque, bougainvillea
1983	purim	1993	kamikaze	2003	pococurante	2013	knaidel	2021	murraya
1984	luge	1994	antediluvian	2004	autochthonous	2014	feuilleton stichomythia	2022	moorhen
1985	milieu	1995	xanthosis	2005	appoggiatura	2015	scherenschnitte nunatak	2023	psammophile
1986	odontalgia	1996	vivisepulture	2006	Ursprache	2016	Feldenkrais gesellschaft	2024	abseil
1987	staphylococci	1997	euonym	2007	serrefine	2017	marocain		
1988	elegiacal	1998	chiaroscurist	2008	guerdon	2018	koinonia		
1989	spoliator	1999	logorrhea	2009	Laodicean				
1990	fibranne	2000	demarche	2010	stromuhr				
1991	antipyretic	2001	succedaneum	2011	cymotrichous				

Non-English Words and Phrases Commonly Used by English Speakers

A = Arabic; F = French; Ger = German; Gr = Greek; I = Italian; J = Japanese; L = Latin; R = Russian; S = Spanish; Y = Yiddish

ad hoc (L; ad-HOK): for the end or purpose at hand; impromptu
ad hominem (L; ad-HOH-mee-nem): argument that criticizes an opponent, often unfairly, rather than addressing an issue directly
al fresco (I; ahl-FRAYS-koh): outdoors
anime (J: A-nuh-may): Japanese-style animation
apparatchik (R: ap-per-AT-chik): functionary; blindly devoted official or working member of a party/other organization
au courant (F; oh-koo-RAHN): up-to-date, fashionable
belles lettres (F; bel-LET-truh): writing aspiring to artistic merit
bête noire (F; bet-NWAHR): literally, black beast; a thing or person viewed with particular dislike or fear
bildungsroman (Ger; BIL-doongs-roh-mahn): novel embodying coming-of-age story
bodega (S; boh-DAY-gah): grocery store
bon vivant (F; bon-vee-VAHN): a person with refined tastes, esp. for food and drink
bonhomie (F; boh-noh-MEE): friendliness
bourgeois (F; boo-ZHWAH): middle-class; materialistic
carte blanche (F; kahrt-BLANSH): full discretionary power
cause célèbre (F; kawz-suh-LEB): a notorious incident
chutzpah (Y, HUHTS-pah): audacity, nerve
coup de grâce (F; kooh-duh-GRAHS): the decisive final blow
cum laude/magna cum laude/summa cum laude (L; kuhm-LOU-day; MAG-na ... ; SOO-ma ...): with praise or honor/with great praise or honor/with the highest praise or honor
de facto (L; day-FAK-toh): in fact, if not by law
de jure (L; dee-JOOR-ee, day-YOOR-ay): by right or by law
de rigueur (F; duh-ree-GUR): required by convention or etiquette
détente (F; day-TAHNT): an easing of strained relations
deus ex machina (L; DAY-uhs-eks-MAH-keh-nah): person/event that provides a solution unexpectedly or suddenly, esp. (in literature) a contrived solution to a plot
doppelgänger (Ger; DAH-pul-gang-ur): a double or ghostly counterpart of a person
double entendre (F; DOO-blahn-TAHN-druh): expression with a double meaning, one meaning of which is often risqué
e pluribus unum (L; eh-PLOO-ree-boos-OO-noom): out of many, one (U.S. motto)
éminence grise (F; ay-meh-nahns-GREEZ): one who wields power behind the scenes
ennui (F; ah-NOOEE): boredom; world-weariness; annoyance
ersatz (Ger; EHR-zats): artificial; being a (usually inferior) substitute
ex post facto (L; eks-pohst-FAK-toh): retroactive(ly)
fait accompli (F; fayt-uh-kom-PLEE): an accomplished fact
fatwa (A; FAHT-wah): in Islam, a legal or religious decree
faux pas (F; foh-PAH): false step; breach of etiquette
habeas corpus (L; HAY-bee-ahs-KOR-pus): an order for a prisoner to be brought to court to challenge his or her detention
hoi polloi (Gr; hoy-puh-LOY): the masses

impresario (I; im-prah-SAH-ri-oh): manager, promoter, or sponsor of a musical or theatrical program or company
imprimatur (L; im-prah-MAH-toor): approval or official permission to print, esp. by the Roman Catholic church
in loco parentis (L; in-LOH-koh-puh-REN-tis): in place of a parent
in medias res (L; in-MAY-dee-oos-rays): into the middle of things
intelligentsia (R; in-te-luh-JEN-see-uh): elite social class made up of intellectuals and educated people
ipso facto (L; ip-soh-FAK-toh): by that fact itself
je ne sais quoi (F; zhuh-nuh-say-KWAH): literally, "I don't know what"; the little something that eludes description
jihad (A; jih-HAHD): Islamic holy war; struggle in devotion to Islam
joie de vivre (F; zhwah-duh-VEEV-ruh): zest for life
kvetch (Y; Kuh-VETCH): complain, gripe
leitmotif (Ger; lyt-moh-TEEF): the central theme or idea, particularly in art and literature
mano a mano (S; MAH-noh-ah-MAH-noh): hand to hand; in direct combat
mea culpa (L; MAY-uh-CUL-puh): through my fault
mensch (Y; MENTSCH): an upright, noble, admirable person
modus operandi (L; MOH-duhs-op-uh-RAN-dee): method of operation
mujahedeen (A; moo-jah-ha-DEEN): Islamic holy warrior
noblesse oblige (F; noh-BLES-oh-BLEEZH): the obligation of nobility to help the less fortunate
nolo contendere (L; NOH-loh-kohn-TEN-duh-ree): a plea of no contest to charges, without admitting guilt
non compos mentis (L; non-KOM-puhs-MEN-tis): not of sound mind
non sequitur (L; non-SEH-kwi-tour): a conclusion that does not logically follow from what preceded it
nouveau riche (F; noo-voh-REESH): a newly rich person, esp. one who spends money conspicuously
ombudsman (Swedish; AHM-budz-muhn): person who receives, investigates, and settles complaints
pariah (Tamil; par-EYE-ah): an outcast; member of low caste in India
persona non grata (L; per-SOH-nah-non-GRAH-tah): unwelcome person
pièce de résistance (F; pee-es-duh-ray-ZEES-tonz): the outstanding item in a series or group
prima facie (L; pry-muh-FAY-shee-ee; pry-muh-FAY-shuh): true at first glance; presumptively valid
pro bono (L; proh-BOH-noh): (work) donated for the public good
quid pro quo (L; kwid-proh-KWOH): something given or received for something else
raison d'être (F; RAY-zohnn-DET-ruh): reason for being
savoir faire (F; sav-wahr-FAIR): dexterity in social affairs
schadenfreude (Ger; SHAH-duhn-froy-deh): joy at another's misfortune
semper fidelis (L; SEM-puhr-fee-DAY-lis): always faithful
sobriquet (F; SOH-bri-kay): nickname or informal descriptive name for someone
sotto voce (I; sah-toh-VOH-chee); in a low voice
sui generis (L; soo-ee-JEN-er-is); unique; one of a kind
terra firma (L; TER-uh-FUR-muh): solid ground
verboten (Ger; ver-BOH-ten): forbidden
vis-à-vis (F; vee-zuh-VEE): compared with; with regard to
voir dire (F; vwar-DEER): examination by lawyers or judge to determine the suitability of a witness or a prospective juror
zeitgeist (Ger; ZITE-gyste): the general intellectual, moral, and cultural climate of an era

Names for Animal Young

calf: cattle, elephant, hippo, camel, others
cheeper: grouse, partridge, quail
chick: chicken, penguin, other birds
cockerel: rooster
codling, sprag: codfish
colt: horse, zebra (male)
cria: llama, alpaca
cub: lion, bear, shark, fox, others
cygnet: swan
duckling: duck
elver: eel
ephyra: jellyfish
eyas: hawk, other birds
fawn: deer, antelope
filly: horse, zebra (female)
fingerling, fry: fish generally
fledgling, nestling: birds generally
foal: horse, zebra, others
gosling: goose
heifer: cow
hoglet: hedgehog
joey: kangaroo, opossum, wombat
kid: goat
kit: beaver, rabbit, ferret, others
kitten: cat, other small mammals
lamb: sheep
larva: frog, sea urchin, insects generally
parr, smolt, grilse: salmon
piglet, shoat, farrow, suckling: pig
polliwog, tadpole: frog
poult: turkey
pullet: hen
pup: dog, fox, seal, rat, others
spat: oyster, other bivalves
spiderling: spider
spike, blinker, tinker: mackerel
squab: pigeon
whelp: dog, tiger, other carnivores
yearling: cattle, sheep, horse, others

Names for Animal Collectives

alligators: congregation
ants: army, colony, swarm
apes: shrewdness, troop
bears: sleuth, sloth
bees: colony, swarm, hive
birds: flight, volery
buffalo: gang, obstinacy
butterflies: flutter
buzzards: wake
camels: caravan, flock, train
cats: clowder, cluster, pounce
cattle: drove
cheetahs: coalition
cockroaches: intrusion
cranes: sedge, siege
crocodiles: bask, nest, float
crows: murder, horde
dolphins: pod
doves: dule, pitying
ducks: brace, team
eagles: convocation, aerie
ferrets: business
finches: charm
fish: school, shoal
flamingos: stand, flamboyance
foxes: skulk
geese: flock, gaggle, skein
giraffes: corps, herd, tower
goats: tribe, trip
gorillas: band, troop, whoop
grasshoppers: cloud
hawks: cast, kettle
hedgehogs: array, prickle
hippopotamuses: bloat
horses: pair, team
hounds: cry, mute, pack
hyenas: cackle
iguanas: mess
jellyfish: smack
kangaroos: mob, troop
larks: exaltation
leopards: leap
lions: pride
locusts: plague, swarm
mice, rats: mischief
moles: labor
monkeys: troop
mules: barren, span
nightingales: watch
otters: romp
owls: parliament
oxen: yoke
peacocks: muster
pheasants: nest, nide, bouquet
ponies: string
raccoons: gaze
ravens: unkindness
rhinoceroses: crash
seals: pod
sheep: flock, drove, hurtle
snakes: nest
squirrels: dray, scurry
starlings: flock, murmuration
swans: bevy
tigers: streak
toads: knot
trout: hover
turkeys: rafter
turtles: bale
vultures: committee
whales: gam, herd, pod
woodchucks: fall
woodpeckers: descent
zebras: herd, zeal

Some Common Abbreviations

(See also Abbreviations in the General Index.) Abbreviations include acronyms, pronounceable words formed from first letters, or syllables, of other words, e.g., AIDS. Some acronyms are words coined as abbreviations and written in lowercase (e.g., sonar). Italicized words below are Latin unless otherwise noted.

A: ampere
AA: Alcoholics Anonymous
ABA: American Bar Association
AC: alternating current; air-conditioning
ACA: Affordable Care Act
ACLU: American Civil Liberties Union
AD: *anno Domini* (in the year of the Lord)
AD(H)D: attention deficit (hyperactivity) disorder
AFL-CIO: American Federation of Labor-Congress of Industrial Organizations
AFSCME: American Federation of State, County, and Municipal Employees
AFT: American Federation of Teachers
AI: artificial intelligence
AIDS: acquired immune deficiency syndrome
ALA: American Library Association
a.m. or **AM:** *ante meridiem* (before noon)
AP: Associated Press
APO: army post office
APR: annual percentage rate
AQAP: al-Qaeda in the Arabian Peninsula
ARM: adjustable rate mortgage
ASAP: as soon as possible
ASCAP: American Society of Composers, Authors, and Publishers
ASCII: American Standard Code for Information Interchange
ATM: automated teller machine
Ave.: Avenue
AWOL: absent without leave
BA: Bachelor of Arts
bbl: barrel(s)
BC: before Christ
BCE: before Common, or Christian, Era
Benelux: Belgium, Netherlands, Luxembourg
bpd or **b/d:** barrels per day
BRB: be right back
Brexit: BRitish EXIT (from the EU)
BS: Bachelor of Science
Btu: British thermal unit(s)
BTW: by the way
B2B: business-to-business (company)
bu: bushel(s)
BYOB: bring your own bottle
C: Celsius, centigrade
c.: *circa* (about); copyright
C(A)T: computerized (axial) tomography
CD: compact disc

CDC: Centers for Disease Control and Prevention; Community Development Corporation
CE: Common Era; Christian Era
CEO: chief executive officer
cf.: *confer* (compare)
CFO: chief financial officer
CIA: Central Intelligence Agency
COBRA: Consolidated Omnibus Budget Reconciliation Act (health insurance continuation)
COD: cash (or collect) on delivery
COL or **Col.:** Colonel
COLA: cost of living adjustment
COO: chief operating officer
CPA: certified public accountant
CPI: consumer price index
CPL or **Cpl.:** Corporal
CPR: cardiopulmonary resuscitation
CPU: central processing unit
CRT: critical race theory
CST: central standard time
CV: curriculum vitae
DA: district attorney
DACA: Deferred Action for Childhood Arrivals
DC: direct current
DD: Doctor of Divinity
DDS: Doctor of Dental Surgery
DEA: Drug Enforcement Administration
DHS: Department of Homeland Security
DJ or **deejay:** disc jockey
DM: direct message
DMD: Doctor of Dental Medicine
DMZ: demilitarized zone
DNA: deoxyribonucleic acid
DNC: Democratic National Committee
DNR: do not resuscitate
DOA: dead on arrival
DOB: date of birth
DoD: Department of Defense
dpi: dots per inch
DPT: diphtheria, pertussis, tetanus
DUI: driving under the influence
DVD: digital video disc
DVM: Doctor of Veterinary Medicine
DWI: driving while intoxicated
ECB: European Central Bank
ed.: edited; edition; editor
EEG: electroencephalogram
e.g.: *exempli gratia* (for example)
EKG or **ECG:** electrocardiogram
EMT: emergency medical technician
EOE: equal opportunity employer
EP: extended play
EPA: Environmental Protection Agency
ERA: Equal Rights Amendment; earned run average
ESL: English as a second language
ESP: extrasensory perception
Esq.: Esquire
EST: eastern standard time
et al.: *et alii* (and others)
etc.: *et cetera* (and so forth)
EU: European Union
F: Fahrenheit
Fannie Mae: Federal National Mortgage Association
FAQ: frequently asked questions
FBI: Federal Bureau of Investigation
FDA: Food and Drug Administration
FDIC: Federal Deposit Insurance Corporation
FEC: Federal Election Commission
FEMA: Federal Emergency Management Agency
ff.: and those following
FICA: Federal Insurance Contributions Act (Social Security)
FIFA: Fédération Internationale de Football Association
fl.: *floruit* (flourished), used for historical figures when life dates uncertain
FLOTUS: First Lady of the United States
FOMO: fear of missing out
Freddie Mac: Federal Home Loan Mortgage Corporation
FTP: file transfer protocol
FWIW: for what it's worth
FY: fiscal year
FYI: for your information
GB: gigabyte(s)
GDP: gross domestic product
GED: general equivalency diploma
GMO: genetically modified organism
GMT: Greenwich mean time
GOP: Grand Old Party (Republican Party)
GPS: Global Positioning System
GTG: got to go
GUI: graphical user interface
ha: hectare
hazmat: HAZardous MATerial
HDTV: high-definition television
HIV: human immunodeficiency virus
HMO: health maintenance organization
HMS: His/Her Majesty's Ship (UK)
Hon.: the Honorable
HOV: high-occupancy vehicle
HRH: Her (His) Royal Highness (UK)
HTML: hypertext markup language
HTTP: hypertext transfer protocol
HUD: Department of Housing and Urban Development
HVAC: heating, ventilating, and air-conditioning
Hz: hertz
ibid.: *ibidem* (in the same place)
ICE: Immigration and Customs Enforcement (agency)
ICU: intensive care unit
ICYMI: in case you missed it
i.e.: *id est* (that is)
IM: instant messaging
IMF: International Monetary Fund
IM(H)O: in my (humble) opinion
INS: Immigration and Naturalization Service
IPO: initial public offering
IQ: intelligence quotient
IRA: individual retirement account; Irish Republican Army
IRS: Internal Revenue Service
ISBN: International Standard Book Number
ISIL or **ISIS:** Islamic State of Iraq in the Levant, or of Iraq and Syria
ISP: Internet service provider
IVF: in vitro fertilization
JD: *Juris Doctor* (Doctor of Law)
k: karat; **K:** Kelvin
kWh: kilowatt-hour(s)
laser: Light Amplification by Stimulated Emission of Radiation
lb: pound
LGBT(QIA): lesbian, gay, bisexual, transgender (queer/questioning, intersex, asexual)
LLP: limited liability partnership
loc. cit.: *loco citato* (in the place cited)
LOL: laughing out loud
LSAT: Law School Admission Test
LT or **Lt.:** Lieutenant
MA: Master of Arts
MB: megabyte(s)
MBA: Master of Business Administration
MCAT: Medical College Admission Test
MD: *Medicinae Doctor* (Doctor of Medicine)
MIA: missing in action
modem: MOdulator-DEModulator
MP: member of Parliament (UK)
mph: miles per hour
MRI: magnetic resonance imaging
ms, mss: manuscript(s)
MS: Master of Science; multiple sclerosis
MSG: monosodium glutamate
MST: mountain standard time
MVP: most valuable player
MYOB: mind your own business
NA: not applicable; not available
NAACP: National Association for the Advancement of Colored People
NAFTA: North American Free Trade Agreement
NASA: National Aeronautics and Space Administration
NATO: North Atlantic Treaty Organization
NB or **n.b.:** *nota bene* (note carefully)
NCAA: National Collegiate Athletic Association
NEA: National Education Association; National Endowment for the Arts
NFT: non-fungible token
NIH: National Institutes of Health
NIMBY: not in my backyard
NOW: National Organization for Women
NPR: National Public Radio
NRA: National Rifle Association
NSA: National Security Agency
NSC: National Security Council
obs.: obsolete
OECD: Organization for Economic Cooperation and Development
OED: Oxford English Dictionary
OMB: Office of Management and Budget
OMG: Oh my goodness/gosh/God!
op., opp.: *opus* (work[s])
OPEC: Organization of Petroleum Exporting Countries
OTC: over-the-counter
oz: ounce
p., pp.: page(s)
PA: public address
PAC: political action committee
PC: personal computer; politically correct
PDA: personal digital assistant
PET: positron emission tomography
PETA: People for the Ethical Treatment of Animals
PhD: *Philosophiae Doctor* (Doctor of Philosophy)
PIN: personal identification number
p.m. or **PM:** *post meridiem* (after noon)
PM: private message; prime minister
POTUS: President of the United States
PPE: personal protective equipment
PPO: preferred provider organization, a type of health-care provider network
PS: *post scriptum* (postscript)
PST: Pacific standard time
pt: part(s); pint(s); point(s)
PT: physical therapy/training
PTSD: post-traumatic stress disorder
PVT or **Pvt.:** Private
QC: Queen's Council (UK)
QED: *quod erat demonstrandum* (which was to be demonstrated)
radar: RAdio Detecting And Ranging
RAM: random access memory
RC: Roman Catholic
RCMP: Royal Canadian Mounted Police
REM: rapid eye movement
Rev.: Reverend
rev.: revised; reviewed
RIP: *requiescat in pace* (may he/she rest in peace)
RN: registered nurse
RNA: ribonucleic acid
RNC: Republican National Committee
ROFL: rolling on the floor laughing
ROM: read only memory
ROTC: Reserve Officers' Training Corps

rpm: revolutions per minute
RSVP: *répondez s'il vous plaît* (Fr.) (please reply)
SARS: severe acute respiratory syndrome
SCOTUS: Supreme Court of the United States
scuba: self-contained underwater breathing apparatus
SEC: Securities and Exchange Commission
SEO: search engine optimization
SETI: Search for Extraterrestrial Intelligence
SGT or **Sgt.:** Sergeant
SIDS: sudden infant death syndrome
SJ: Society of Jesus (Jesuits)
SMH: shaking my head
sonar: SOund NAvigation and Ranging
SOTU: State of the Union
SPCA: Society for the Prevention of Cruelty to Animals
SSI: Supplementary Security Income
St.: Saint; Street
STEM: science, technology, engineering, math
TB: tuberculosis; terabyte(s)
TBA/TBD: to be announced/determined
tbsp: tablespoon
TBT: Throwback Thursday
TEFL: teaching English as a foreign language
TIA: transient ischemic attack
TMI: too much information
TPP: Trans-Pacific Partnership (trade agreement)
TSA: Transportation Security Administration
tsp: teaspoon
UFO: unidentified flying object
UPC: Universal Product Code
URL: Universal Resource Locator
USDA: United States Department of Agriculture
USS: United States ship
UTC: coordinated universal time
VA: Department of Veterans Affairs
VAT: value-added tax
VCR: videocassette recorder
VISTA: Volunteers in Service to America
viz: *videlicet* (namely)
VP: vice president
W: watt(s)
WHO: World Health Organization
WMD: weapon of mass destruction
WPM: words per minute
WTF: what the f--- [expletive]
WTO: World Trade Organization
WWW: World Wide Web
YMCA/YWCA: Young Men's/Women's Christian Association
YOLO: you only live once
YTD: year to date
yuppie: young urban professional
ZIP: zone improvement plan (U.S. Postal Service)

Most Popular U.S. First Names by Decade or Year of Birth

Source: U.S. Social Security Administration

All names are from Social Security card applications for births that occurred in the United States after 1879. Rankings are based on one spelling of the name; variant spellings and similar sounding names are considered separate names.

BOYS	
1880-1889	John, William, James, George, Charles, Frank, Joseph, Henry, Robert, Thomas
1890-1899	John, William, James, George, Charles, Joseph, Frank, Robert, Edward, Henry
1900-1909	John, William, James, George, Charles, Robert, Joseph, Frank, Edward, Thomas
1910-1919	John, William, James, Robert, Joseph, George, Charles, Edward, Frank, Thomas
1920-1929	Robert, John, James, William, Charles, George, Joseph, Richard, Edward, Donald
1930-1939	Robert, James, John, William, Richard, Charles, Donald, George, Thomas, Joseph
1940-1949	James, Robert, John, William, Richard, David, Charles, Thomas, Michael, Ronald
1950-1959	Michael, David, James, John, Robert, Mark, William, Richard, Thomas, Jeffrey
1960-1969	Michael, David, John, James, Robert, Mark, William, Richard, Thomas, Jeffrey
1970-1979	Michael, Christopher, Jason, David, James, John, Robert, Brian, William, Matthew
1980-1989	Michael, Christopher, Matthew, Joshua, David, James, Daniel, Robert, John, Joseph
1990-1999	Michael, Christopher, Matthew, Joshua, Jacob, Nicholas, Andrew, Daniel, Tyler, Joseph
2000-2009	Jacob, Michael, Joshua, Matthew, Daniel, Christopher, Andrew, Ethan, Joseph, William
2010-2019	Noah, Liam, Jacob, William, Mason, Ethan, Michael, Alexander, James, Elijah
2023	Liam, Noah, Oliver, James, Elijah, Mateo, Theodore, Henry, Lucas, William
GIRLS	
1880-1889	Mary, Anna, Emma, Elizabeth, Margaret, Minnie, Ida, Bertha, Clara, Alice
1890-1899	Mary, Anna, Margaret, Helen, Elizabeth, Ruth, Florence, Ethel, Emma, Marie
1900-1909	Mary, Helen, Margaret, Anna, Ruth, Elizabeth, Dorothy, Marie, Florence, Mildred
1910-1919	Mary, Helen, Dorothy, Margaret, Ruth, Mildred, Anna, Elizabeth, Frances, Virginia
1920-1929	Mary, Dorothy, Helen, Betty, Margaret, Ruth, Virginia, Doris, Mildred, Frances
1930-1939	Mary, Betty, Barbara, Shirley, Patricia, Dorothy, Joan, Margaret, Nancy, Helen
1940-1949	Mary, Linda, Barbara, Patricia, Carol, Sandra, Nancy, Sharon, Judith, Susan
1950-1959	Mary, Linda, Patricia, Susan, Deborah, Barbara, Debra, Karen, Nancy, Donna
1960-1969	Lisa, Mary, Susan, Karen, Kimberly, Patricia, Linda, Donna, Michelle, Cynthia
1970-1979	Jennifer, Amy, Melissa, Michelle, Kimberly, Lisa, Angela, Heather, Stephanie, Nicole
1980-1989	Jessica, Jennifer, Amanda, Ashley, Sarah, Stephanie, Melissa, Nicole, Elizabeth, Heather
1990-1999	Jessica, Ashley, Emily, Sarah, Samantha, Amanda, Brittany, Elizabeth, Taylor, Megan
2000-2009	Emily, Madison, Emma, Olivia, Hannah, Abigail, Isabella, Samantha, Elizabeth, Ashley
2010-2019	Emma, Olivia, Sophia, Isabella, Ava, Mia, Abigail, Emily, Charlotte, Madison
2023	Olivia, Emma, Charlotte, Amelia, Sophia, Mia, Isabella, Ava, Evelyn, Luna

Words and Expressions in Common Languages

English	Arabic	Chinese[1]	French	German	Hebrew	Russian	Spanish
Hello/hi	Salam	Ni hao	Bonjour	Hallo	Shalom	Privet (informal)	Hola
Good morning	Sabah el kheer	Zao shang hao	Bonjour	Guten Morgen	Boker tov	Dobraye utra	Buenos días
Good night	Tosbeho ʻala khair	Wan an	Bonne nuit	Gute Nacht	Layla tov	Spakoynay noci	Buenas noches
Goodbye	Maʻa salama	Zai jian	Au revoir	Auf wiedersehen	Lehitraot	Da svidan'ya	Adiós
Please	Men fadlek	Qing	S'il vous plaît	Bitte	Bevakasha	Pazhalusta	Por favor
Thank you very much	Shokran jazeelan	Xie xie	Merci beaucoup	Danke schön	Toda raba	Spasiba	Muchas gracias
You're welcome	Alʻ afw	Huan ying	De rien/pas de quoi	Bitte schön	Bevakasha	Pazhalusta	De nada
How are you?	Kaifa haloka?	Ni hao?	Comment allez-vous?	Wie geht's dir/Ihnen?	Ma shelomkha?	Kak dela?	¿Cómo estás?
I'm fine	Ana bekhair	Hen hao	Je vais bien	Mir geht's gut	Tov	Harasho	Estoy bien
I'm sorry	Aasef	Bao qian	Je suis désolé	Entschuldigung	Ani mamash mitstaer	Prastite	Lo siento
Excuse me	Almaʻderah	Bao qian	Pardon	Darf ich mal vorbei?	Selikha	Izvinite	Perdone
yes	naʻam	shi [it is so]	oui	ja	ken	da	sí
no	laa	bu [not]	non	nein	lo	nyet	no
one	wahed	yi	un	eins	ekhad	adin	uno
two	ithnaan	er	deux	zwei	shenayim	dva	dos
three	thalatha	san	trois	drei	shelosha	tri	tres
four	arbaʻa	si	quatre	vier	arbaa	chityri	cuatro
five	khamsa	wu	cinq	fünf	khamisha	p'at	cinco

Note: Actual form or usage of some words and expressions may vary depending on dialect, grammar, or circumstances. Transliterations for languages not in Latin alphabet vary. (1) Mandarin.

Principal Languages of the World

Source: Used by permission. © 2024 SIL International, from *Ethnologue: Languages of the World, 27th Edition*

Languages shown in italics are macrolanguages, or language groups that are equivalent in some ways to individual languages. Each language group consists of a number of variants, which may be mutually unintelligible; these variants, when they have 2.5 mil speakers or more, appear in the larger table below, and occasionally have the same name as the macrolanguage. Numbers are estimates and count only speakers for whom the language is a first language, or mother tongue.

Languages Spoken by the Most People

Language	Speakers (mil)	Language	Speakers (mil)	Language	Speakers (mil)
Chinese	1,348.5	Marathi	83.2	Hausa	53.8
Spanish	485.5	Telugu	82.8	Bhojpuri	52.5
Arabic	382.7	*Malay*	82.3	*Oromo*	45.5
English	380.2	Korean	81.1	Yoruba	45.2
Hindi	345.1	Tamil	78.7	*Pushto*	44.2
Bengali	236.9	German, Standard	76.4	Kannada	43.7
Portuguese	236.5	French	73.7	Polish	39.7
Russian	147.6	*Persian*	72.0	*Fulah*	37.3
Japanese	123.4	Urdu	69.6	*Oriya*	37.1
Lahnda	118.5	Javanese	68.3	Malayalam	37.0
Vietnamese	85.4	Italian	63.5	Amharic	34.6
Turkish	84.1	Gujarati	57.6		

Languages With at Least 2.5 Million Speakers

Primary country is country of origin, not necessarily the country where the most speakers reside (e.g., Portugal is the primary country for Portuguese, but more Portuguese speakers live in Brazil). Number of speakers is worldwide total for each language.

Primary country	Language	Countries	Speakers (mil)
Afghanistan	Pashto, Southern	4	14.9
	Dari	3	10.4
	Hazaragi	3	4.0
	Uzbek, Southern	2	3.5
Albania	*Albanian*	8	6.4
	Albanian, Gheg	6	4.9
Algeria	Arabic, Algerian	2	35.7
	Kabyle	2	7.8
	Tachawit	2	2.6
Angola	Umbundu	1	7.8
	Kikongo	1	2.8
	Chokwe	3	2.7
Armenia	Armenian	4	3.8
Austria	Bavarian	4	14.7
Azerbaijan	Azerbaijani, North	4	10.3
Bangladesh	Bengali	4	236.9
	Chittagonian	1	13.0
	Rangpuri	2	10.5
	Sylheti	2	10.0
Bosnia and Herzegovina	Bosnian	6	2.7
Botswana	Setswana	4	5.9
Brazil	Hunsrik	1	3.0
Bulgaria	Bulgarian	8	6.7
Burkina Faso	Moore	5	11.9
Burundi	Rundi	1	13.2
Cambodia	Khmer	2	16.6
Cameroon	Fulfulde, Adamawa	5	3.0
China	*Chinese*	25	1,348.5
	Chinese, Mandarin	18	940.9
	Chinese, Yue	15	86.1
	Chinese, Wu	1	83.4
	Chinese, Min Nan	10	50.6
	Chinese, Jinyu	1	48.0
	Chinese, Hakka	14	43.9
	Chinese, Xiang	1	38.1
	Chinese, Gan	1	22.6
	Zhuang	2	14.9
	Chinese, Min Bei	2	11.7
	Chinese, Min Dong	6	10.9
	Uyghur	6	10.5
	Hmong	6	8.1
	Chinese, Huizhou	1	5.4
	Chinese Sign Language	1	4.2
	Chinese, Min Zhong	1	3.7
	Mongolian, Peripheral	2	3.4
	Chinese, Pu-Xian	3	3.2
	Bouyei	3	3.0
Congo, Dem. Rep of the	Lingala	2	20.5
	Kituba	1	11.6
	Kongo	3	9.3
	Luba-Kasai	2	6.4
	Koongo	2	3.0
Côte d'Ivoire	Baoulé	1	5.3
	Jula	3	2.6
Croatia	Croatian	8	5.1
Czechia	Czech	8	9.6
Denmark	Danish	4	5.8
Egypt	Arabic, Egyptian	2	78.4
	Arabic, Sa'idi	1	25.1
	Arabic, Eastern Egyptian Bedawi	4	3.0
Eritrea	Tigrigna	3	9.7
Ethiopia	*Oromo*	3	45.5
	Amharic	2	34.6
	Oromo, West Central	1	24.7
	Oromo, Eastern	1	11.1
	Oromo, Borana-Arsi-Guji	3	9.6
	Sidamo	1	4.9
	Wolaytta	1	2.7
	Afar	3	2.6
Finland	Finnish	5	5.0
France	French	102	73.7
Georgia	Georgian	4	3.8
Germany	German, Standard	45	76.4
Ghana	Akan	1	8.9
	Éwé	2	5.0
Greece	Greek	11	13.1
Guinea	*Mandingo*	7	9.1
	Pular	5	4.9
	Maninkakan, Eastern	3	3.7
Haiti	Haitian Creole	5	13.2
Hungary	Hungarian	9	12.4
India	Hindi	5	345.1
	Marathi	1	83.2
	Telugu	4	82.8
	Tamil	11	78.7
	Gujarati	8	57.6
	Bhojpuri	3	52.5
	Kannada	1	43.7
	Oriya	1	37.1
	Malayalam	2	37.0
	Odia	1	34.5
	Punjabi, Eastern	5	33.4
	Maithili	2	21.7
	Magahi	2	20.9
	Marwari	3	20.6
	Chhattisgarhi	1	16.3
	Rajasthani	3	16.2
	Assamese	1	15.3
	Deccan	1	12.8
	Bajjika	2	12.6
	Haryanvi	1	9.8
	Marwari	2	7.9
	Santhali	3	7.6
	Kashmiri	2	7.1
	Varhadi-Nagpuri	1	7.0
	Indian Sign Language	2	6.8
	Kanauji	1	6.0
	Konkani	2	5.9
	Bundeli	1	5.6
	Malvi	1	5.4
	Sadri	2	5.1
	Lambadi	1	5.1
	Awadhi	2	4.7
	Mewari	1	4.2

Primary country	Language	Countries	Speakers (mil)
India (cont.)	Merwari	1	3.9
	Konkani, Goan	2	3.7
	Dogri	1	3.7
	Wagdi	1	3.4
	Bhili	1	3.3
	Shekhawati	1	3.0
	Godwari	1	3.0
	Haroti	1	2.9
	Bagheli	1	2.7
	Sambalpuri	1	2.6
	Dogri	1	2.6
Indonesia	Javanese	3	68.3
	Indonesian	2	43.7
	Sunda	1	32.4
	Madura	2	7.8
	Betawi	1	5.0
	Minangkabau	1	4.9
	Bugis	2	3.9
	Banjar	2	3.7
	Bali	1	3.3
	Musi	1	3.1
	Aceh	1	2.8
Iran	*Persian*	9	72.0
	Persian, Iranian	7	61.6
	Azerbaijani	8	22.0
	Azerbaijani, South	5	11.7
	Kurdish, Southern	2	4.3
Iraq	*Kurdish*	9	26.1
	Arabic, Mesopotamian	4	17.5
	Arabic, North Mesopotamian	4	10.5
	Kurdish, Central	2	5.3
Israel	Hebrew	3	6.0
Italy	Italian	18	63.5
	Napoletano	1	5.7
	Sicilian	1	4.7
	Lombard	2	3.9
	Venetian	5	3.9
Jamaica	Jamaican English Creole	3	3.1
Japan	Japanese	5	123.4
Kazakhstan	Kazakh	6	16.4
Kenya	Gikuyu	1	8.2
	Dholuo	2	5.3
	Kamba	2	4.7
	Kalenjin	3	4.6
	Oluluyia	3	3.3
	Ekegusii	2	2.7
Korea	Korean	7	81.1
Kuwait	Arabic, Gulf	10	10.9
Kyrgyzstan	Kyrgyz	5	5.4
Laos	Lao	3	3.7
Lesotho	Sotho, Southern	2	5.6
Libya	Arabic, Libyan	3	5.6
Lithuania	Lithuanian	2	2.8
Madagascar	*Malagasy*	2	18.1
	Malagasy, Merina	2	7.5
Malawi	Chichewa	4	14.4
	Lomwe, Malawi	1	4.0
	Yao	4	3.7
Malaysia	*Malay*	8	82.3
	Malay	3	16.2
	Malay, Kedah	2	2.6
Mali	Bamanankan	3	4.2
	Tamashek	6	2.8
Mauritania	Hassaniyya	7	5.2
Mongolia	*Mongolian*	3	6.2
	Mongolian, Halh	2	2.8
Morocco	Arabic, Moroccan	4	29.4
	Tachelhit	4	5.8
	Tamazight, Central Atlas	1	3.1
Mozambique	Makhuwa	2	4.0
	Lomwe	1	2.5
Myanmar	Burmese	1	33.2
	Shan	3	4.7
	Rohingya	2	2.5
Nepal	*Nepali*	3	19.0
	Nepali	3	18.5
Netherlands	Dutch	9	23.7
Niger	Zarma	4	6.1
	Fulfulde, Western Niger	4	3.1
Nigeria	Hausa	9	53.8
	Yoruba	3	45.2
	Igbo	1	30.9
	Fulfulde, Nigerian	3	16.6
	Kanuri	5	9.6
	Kanuri, Yerwa	5	8.6
	Ibibio	1	6.3
	Pidgin, Nigerian	1	4.7
Nigeria (cont.)	Tiv	2	4.6
	Anaang	1	2.9
Norway	Norwegian	1	5.4
Oman	Arabic, Omani	4	3.2
Pakistan	*Lahnda*	3	118.5
	Punjabi, Western	2	82.3
	Urdu	9	69.6
	Pushto	6	44.2
	Sindhi	4	32.5
	Saraiki	2	25.6
	Pashto, Northern	4	22.9
	Baluchi	7	8.8
	Pashto, Central	1	6.4
	Hindko, Northern	1	5.3
	Balochi, Southern	4	3.6
	Pahari-Potwari	2	3.5
	Balochi, Eastern	2	2.9
	Brahui	3	2.8
Paraguay	*Guaraní*	4	6.7
	Guaraní, Paraguayan	1	6.5
Peru	*Quechua*	6	7.3
Philippines	Tagalog	5	29.2
	Cebuano	1	16.0
	Ilocano	1	6.5
	Hiligaynon	1	6.3
	Waray-Waray	1	2.6
Poland	Polish	10	39.7
Portugal	Portuguese	16	236.5
Romania	Romanian	5	25.2
Russia	Russian	23	147.6
	Tatar	4	4.0
Rwanda	Kinyarwanda	3	14.8
Saudi Arabia	*Arabic*	43	382.7
	Arabic, Najdi	5	18.5
	Arabic, Hijazi	4	10.8
Senegal	*Fulah*	19	37.3
	Wolof	3	7.1
	Pulaar	6	6.3
Serbia	*Serbo-Croatian*	11	18.2
	Serbian	10	10.1
Sierra Leone	Mende	2	2.5
Slovakia	Slovak	8	5.4
Somalia	Somali	4	23.8
	Maay	1	2.8
South Africa	Zulu	5	12.1
	Xhosa	3	8.2
	Afrikaans	6	7.8
	Tsonga	4	6.6
	Sotho, Northern	1	4.6
South Sudan	*Dinka*	1	4.2
Spain	Spanish	43	485.5
	Catalan	4	4.2
	Galician	3	3.1
Sri Lanka	Sinhala	2	15.9
Sudan	Arabic, Sudanese	5	37.4
	Bedawiyet	3	2.8
Sweden	Swedish	4	10.0
Switzerland	German, Swiss	6	6.5
Syria	Arabic, Levantine	9	51.2
Tajikistan	Tajik	5	10.0
Tanzania	Sukuma	1	8.1
	Swahili	10	5.2
	Swahili	8	3.2
Thailand	Thai	2	21.1
	Thai, Northeastern	1	15.0
	Thai, Northern	2	6.0
	Thai, Southern	1	4.5
Tunisia	Arabic, Tunisian	2	12.0
Turkey	Turkish	13	84.1
	Kurdish, Northern	9	16.5
Turkmenistan	Turkmen	5	6.1
Uganda	Ganda	1	5.8
	Nyankore	2	3.4
	Soga	1	3.0
	Ateso	2	2.8
Ukraine	Ukrainian	10	32.9
United Kingdom	English	171	380.2
Uzbekistan	*Uzbek*	8	32.5
	Uzbek, Northern	6	29.1
Vietnam	Vietnamese	5	85.4
Yemen	Arabic, Sanaani	1	12.6
	Arabic, Ta'izzi-Adeni	3	12.2
	Arabic, Hadrami	1	5.1
Zambia	Bemba	2	4.1
Zimbabwe	Shona	3	7.4

BUILDINGS, BRIDGES, AND TUNNELS

100 Tallest Buildings in the World

Source: SKYDB, www.skydb.net; Council on Tall Buildings and Urban Habitat (CTBUH), www.ctbuh.org

Only buildings that are completed or under construction and topped out as of Oct. 2024 are shown here. Structures under construction and topped out architecturally are denoted by an asterisk (*). Year in parentheses is date of completion or projected completion. Height is generally measured from the lowest significant open-air pedestrian entrance to the architectural top, including spires and other decorative features that are an integral part of the design, but not including flagpoles and antennae. Stories generally counted from street level. NA = Not available.

Building	Ht. (ft)	Stories
Burj Khalifa, Dubai, United Arab Emirates (2010)	2,717	163
Merdeka 118, Kuala Lumpur, Malaysia (2023)	2,227	118
Shanghai Tower, Shanghai, China (2015)	2,074	128
Makkah Royal Clock Tower Hotel, Mecca, Saudi Arabia (2013)	1,972	120
Ping An Finance Center, Shenzhen, China (2016)	1,965	115
*Goldin Finance 117, Tianjin, China (on hold)	1,957	128
Lotte World Tower, Seoul, South Korea (2017)	1,819	123
One World Trade Center, New York, NY, U.S. (2014)	1,782	94
CTF Finance Center, Guangzhou, China (2016)	1,739	111
Tianjin CTF Finance Center, Tianjin, China (2019)	1,739	97
Citic Tower, Beijing, China (2018)	1,732	108
Taipei 101, Taipei, Taiwan (2004)	1,667	101
Shanghai World Financial Center, Shanghai, China (2008)	1,614	101
International Commerce Centre, Hong Kong, China (2010)	1,588	108
Wuhan Greenland Center, Wuhan, China (2023)	1,560	97
Central Park Tower, New York, NY, U.S. (2021)	1,550	95
Lakhta Center, St. Petersburg, Russia (2019)	1,516	87
Vincom Landmark 81, Ho Chi Minh City, Vietnam (2018)	1,513	81
*International Land-Sea Center, Chongqing, China (2025)	1,503	98
The Exchange 106, Kuala Lumpur, Malaysia (2019)	1,488	97
Changsha IFS Tower T1, Changsha, China (2018)	1,483	94
Petronas Tower I, Kuala Lumpur, Malaysia (1998)	1,483	88
Petronas Tower II, Kuala Lumpur, Malaysia (1998)	1,483	88
Suzhou IFS, Suzhou, China (2019)	1,476	95
Zifeng Tower, Nanjing, China (2010)	1,476	66
Wuhan Center, Wuhan, China (2019)	1,454	88
Willis (fmr. Sears) Twr., Chicago, IL, U.S. (1974)	1,451	108
KK100, Shenzhen, China (2011)	1,449	100
Guangzhou International Finance Center, Guangzhou, China (2010)	1,439	103
111 West 57th St., New York, NY, U.S. (2021)	1,428	82
*Shandong IFC, Jinan, China (2025)	1,404	88
Minying International Trade Center T2, Dongguan, China (2021)	1,401	88
One Vanderbilt, New York, NY, U.S. (2020)	1,401	62
432 Park Avenue, New York, NY, U.S. (2015)	1,397	85
Marina 101, Dubai, UAE (2017)	1,394	101
Trump Intl. Hotel & Tower, Chicago, IL, U.S. (2009)	1,389	98
*JPMorgan Chase World Headquarters, New York, NY, U.S. (2025)	1,388	63
Jin Mao Tower, Shanghai, China (1999)	1,380	88
*Nanjing Financial City Phase II Tower 1, Nanjing, China (2026)	1,367	88
Princess Tower, Dubai, UAE (2012)	1,356	101
Al Hamra Tower, Kuwait City, Kuwait (2011)	1,354	80
Two International Finance Centre, Hong Kong, China (2003)	1,352	88
LCT Landmark Tower, Busan, South Korea (2019)	1,350	101
*Ningbo Central Plaza Tower 1, Ningbo, China (2024)	1,342	80
Guangxi China Resources Tower, Nanning, China (2020)	1,321	85
Guiyang Financial Ctr. Twr. 1, Guiyang, China (2021)	1,316	79
Iconic Tower, Cairo, Egypt (2024)	1,292	80
China Resources HQ, Shenzhen, China (2018)	1,288	66
23 Marina, Dubai, UAE (2012)	1,287	88
CITIC Plaza, Guangzhou, China (1997)	1,280	80
Citimark Center, Shenzhen, China (2023)	1,274	70
Sum Yip Upperhills Twr. 1, Shenzhen, China (2020)	1,273	80
*China Merchant Bank Headquarters Tower 1, Shenzhen, China (2025)	1,271	77
30 Hudson Yards, New York, NY (2019)	1,268	73
PIF Tower, Riyadh, Saudi Arabia (2021)	1,260	76
Shun Hing Square, Shenzhen, China (1996)	1,260	69
Eton Place Dalian Tower 1, Dalian, China (2016)	1,257	80
Autograph Tower, Jakarta, Indonesia (2022)	1,256	75
Burj Mohammed Bin Rashid Tower, Abu Dhabi, UAE (2014)	1,251	88
Logan Century Center 1, Nanning, China (2019)	1,251	82
Empire State Building, New York, NY, U.S. (1931)	1,250	102
Elite Residence, Dubai, UAE (2012)	1,248	87
1 Corporate Avenue, Wuhan, China (2021)	1,234	73
Shenzhen Center, Shenzhen, China (2021)	1,232	71
*Guangdong Business Center, Guangzhou, China (2024)	1,232	60
Central Plaza, Hong Kong, China (1992)	1,227	78
Vostok, Moscow, Russia (2017)	1,226	93
*Hengfeng Guiyang Ctr. Twr. 1, Guiyang, China (on hold)	1,225	77
Dalian Intl. Trade Center, Dalian, China (2019)	1,214	86
*Shanghai Intl. Trade Center Tower 1, Shanghai, China (2025)	1,214	67
Hai Tian Center Tower 2, Qingdao, China (2021)	1,211	72
Golden Eagle Tiandi Tower A, Nanjing, China (2019)	1,207	76
Address Boulevard, Dubai, UAE (2017)	1,207	72
Bank of China Tower, Hong Kong, China (1989)	1,205	72
Bank of America Twr., New York, NY, U.S. (2009)	1,200	55
*Ciel Tower, Dubai, UAE (2024)	1,199	81
St. Regis Chicago, Chicago, IL, U.S. (2020)	1,191	101
Almas Tower, Dubai, UAE (2008)	1,181	68
Ping'an Finance Ctr. Twr. 1, Jinan, China (2023)	1,181	63
Huiyin Center, Shenzhen, China (2023)	1,178	80
Hanking Center, Shenzhen, China (2018)	1,177	65
*Greenland Group Suzhou Center, Suzhou, China (2024)	1,175	77
Gevora Hotel, Dubai, UAE (2017)	1,169	76
Il Primo Tower 1, Dubai, UAE (2023)	1,168	79
Galaxy World Tower 1, Shenzhen, China (2023)	1,168	71
Galaxy World Tower 2, Shenzhen, China (2023)	1,168	71
JW Marriott Marquis Hotel Dubai Tower 2, Dubai, UAE (2013)	1,166	82
JW Marriott Marquis Hotel Dubai Tower 1, Dubai, UAE (2012)	1,166	82
Chongqing Raffles City T3N, Chongqing, China (2019)	1,163	81
Chongqing Raffles City T4N, Chongqing, China (2019)	1,163	81
Emirates Office Tower, Dubai, UAE (2000)	1,163	54
OKO South Tower, Moscow, Russia (2015)	1,162	90
The Torch, Dubai, UAE (2011)	1,155	86
*Central Bank of the Republic of Turkey, Istanbul, Turkey (2024)	1,155	59
Forum 66 Tower 1, Shenyang, China (2015)	1,150	67
The Pinnacle, Guangzhou, China (2012)	1,149	60
Glory-Xi'an Intl. Finance Ctr., Xi'an, China (2022)	1,148	75
Spring City 66, Kunming, China (2019)	1,145	61
Tuntex Sky Tower, Kaohsiung, Taiwan (1998)	1,140	85
Shimao Hunan Center, Changsha, China (2019)	1,138	76

Tallest Free-Standing Towers in the World

Source: SKYDB, www.skydb.net; Council on Tall Buildings and Urban Habitat (CTBUH), www.ctbuh.org
Year is date of completion or projected completion. As of Oct. 2024.

Tower	Ht. (ft)	Year
Tokyo Sky Tree, Tokyo, Japan	2,080	2012
Canton Tower, Guangzhou, China	1,969	2010
CN Tower, Toronto, ON, Canada	1,815	1976
Ostankino Tower, Moscow, Russia	1,772	1967
Oriental Pearl Television Tower, Shanghai, China	1,535	1995
Milad Tower, Tehran, Iran	1,427	2008
Manara Kuala Lumpur, Kuala Lumpur, Malaysia	1,379	1996
Tianjin Radio & TV Tower, Tianjin, China	1,362	1991
Central Radio & TV Tower, Beijing, China	1,347	1992
Henan Province Radio & Television Emission Tower, Zhengzhou, China	1,273	2010
Kiev TV Tower, Kiev, Ukraine	1,263	1974
Tashkent Tower, Tashkent, Uzbekistan	1,230	1985
Liberation Tower, Kuwait City, Kuwait	1,220	1996
Alma-Ata Tower, Almaty, Kazakhstan	1,217	1982
Camlica TV Tower, Istanbul, Turkey	1,211	2019
TV Tower, Riga, Latvia	1,208	1987
Berliner Fernsehturm, Berlin, Germany	1,207	1969
Stratosphere Tower, Las Vegas, NV, U.S.	1,149	1996
Lotus Tower, Colombo, Sri Lanka	1,148	2019
West Pearl Tower, Chengdu, China	1,112	2004
Macau Tower, Macau, China	1,109	2001
Europaturm, Frankfurt, Germany	1,106	1979
Dragon Tower, Harbin, China	1,102	2000

Tall Buildings in Selected North American Cities

Source: SKYDB, www.skydb.net; Council on Tall Buildings and Urban Habitat (CTBUH), www.ctbuh.org

List includes freestanding towers and other structures that do not have stories and are not technically considered buildings. Structures under construction and topped out architecturally as of Oct. 2024 are denoted by an asterisk (*). Year in parentheses is date of completion or projected completion. Height is generally measured from the lowest significant open-air pedestrian entrance to the architectural top, including penthouses, spires, and other decorative features that are an integral part of the design, but not including flagpoles and antennae. Stories generally counted from street level. NA = Not applicable/available.

Atlanta, GA

Building/structure	Ht. (ft)	Stories
Bank of America Plaza (incl. spire), 600 Peachtree St. NE (1992)	1,023	55
Truist Plaza, 303 Peachtree St. NE[1] (1993)	867	60
One Atlantic Center, 1201 W. Peachtree St. (1987)	820	50
191 Peachtree Tower (1991)	770	50
*1072 W. Peachtree St. (2026)	733	61
Westin Peachtree Plz., 210 Peachtree St. NW[2] (1976)	723	73
Georgia Pacific Tower, 133 Peachtree St. NE (1981)	697	51
Promenade II (incl. spire), 1230 Peachtree St. NE (1989)	691	40
AT&T Bldg., 675 W. Peachtree St. (1980)	677	47
Sovereign, 3344 Peachtree (2008)	665	48
1180 Peachtree (2006)	657	41
GLG Grand/Four Seasons Hotel, 75 14th St. NE (1992)	609	53
The Mansion on Peachtree, 3376 Peachtree Rd. NE (2008)	580	42
Atlantic, 270 17th St. NW (2009)	577	46
State of Georgia Bldg., 2 Peachtree St. NW[3] (1967)	556	44
Marriott Marquis, 265 Peachtree Ctr. Ave. NE (1985)	554	52

(1) 902 ft incl. antenna. (2) 883 ft incl. antenna. (3) 599 ft incl. antenna.

Austin, TX

Building/structure	Ht. (ft)	Stories
*Waterline, 98 Red River St. (2026)	1,021	74
6 X Guadalupe, 400 W. 6th St. (2023)	874	66
*The Republic, 308 Guadalupe St. (2025)	710	46
The Independent, 301 West Ave. (2019)	694	58
Austonian, 200 Congress Ave. (2010)	683	56
*ATX Tower, 325 W. 6th St. (2025)	675	58
*Modern Austin, 90 Rainey St. (2025)	655	55
*415 Colorado (2025)	633	47
*The Travis Phase I, 80 Red River St. (2025)	594	52
601 W. 2nd St. (2022)	594	35
Fairmont Austin (incl. spire), 101 Red River St. (2018)	591	36
360 Condominiums (incl. spire), 360 Nueces St. (2008)	581	45
44 East Avenue (2023)	573	49
*Paseo, 80 Rainey St. (2025)	567	48
Indeed Tower, 200 W. 6th St. (2021)	542	36
Hanover Republic Square, 305 W. 5th St. (2022)	516	44
Hanover, 300 Brazos (2024)	513	45
Frost Bank Tower, 401 N. Congress Ave. (2004)	510	33
*700 River (2025)	500	42

Boston, MA

Building/structure	Ht. (ft)	Stories
200 Clarendon (1976)	790	62
Prudential Tower, 800 Boylston St.[1] (1964)	750	52
Four Seasons Hotel and Private Residences One Dalton Street (2020)	743	61
115 Winthrop Square (2023)	691	48
Millennium Tower, 426 Washington St. (2016)	681	54
*South Station Tower (2025)	678	51
Federal Reserve Bldg., 600 Atlantic Ave. (1978)	604	32
BNY Mellon Center at One Boston Place, 201 Washington St. (1970)	602	41
One International Place, 100 Oliver St. (1987)	600	46
One Congress Street Tower 2 (2023)	600	43
100 Federal St. (1971)	591	37
One Financial Center, 10 Dewey Square (1984)	590	46
111 Huntington Ave. (2002)	564	36

(1) 920 ft incl. antenna.

Burnaby, BC, Canada

Building/structure	Ht. (ft)	Stories
*Grand Tower at Sky Park, 4750 Kingsway (2025)	755	65
Two Gilmore Place (2024)	708	64
*Solo District-Aerius (2026)	666	52
Solo District-Altus, 2880 Skyline Ct. (2017)	616	49
Brentwood One, 4610 Halifax St. (2019)	611	53
Brentwood Two, 1955 Alpha St. (2019)	611	53
Brentwood Three, 4615 Lougheed Hwy. (2021)	597	55
Hillside East C, 4880 Lougheed Hwy. (2024)	597	55
Highline, 6511 Sussex Ave. (2023)	581	53
Station Square V, 6000 McKay Ave. (2022)	564	52
One Gilmore Place (2024)	564	51
*Central Tower at Sky Park, 4750 Kingsway (2025)	542	45
4670 Assembly Way (2018)	535	48
The City of Lougheed Tower One (2023)	520	55
Sovereign, 4509 Kingsway (2014)	511	45

Calgary, AB, Canada

Building/structure	Ht. (ft)	Stories
Brookfield Place Tower One, 225 6th Ave. (2017)	810	56
The Bow, 510 Centre St. (2012)	779	57
Telus Sky (2019)	737	59
Petro Canada Centre West Tower, 150 6th Ave. SW (1984)	705	53
Eighth Avenue Place East Tower, 8th Ave. & 5th St. SW (2011)	696	49
Bankers Hall West Tower, 888 3rd St. SW (2000)	645	50
Bankers Hall East Tower, 855 2nd St. SW (1989)	645	50
Calgary Tower, 101 9th Ave. SW (1967)	626	NA
Centennial Place 1 (incl. spire), 520 3rd Ave. SW (2010)	599	40
TransCanada Tower, 450 1st St. SW (2001)	581	38
Canterra Tower, 400 3rd Ave. SW (1988)	580	46
Eighth Avenue Place West Tower, 8th Ave. & 5th St. SW (2014)	580	40
Jamieson Place (incl. spires), 302 4th Ave. SW (2009)	568	38
First Canadian Centre, 350 7th Ave. SW (1982)	547	41
Western Canadian Place-North Tower, 707 6th St. SW (1983)	538	41
Canada Trust, Calgary Eatons Centre, 421 7th Ave. SW (1991)	530	40

Charlotte, NC

Building/structure	Ht. (ft)	Stories
Bank of America Corp. Center, 100 N. Tryon St. (1992)	871	60
Duke Energy Center, 534 S. Tryon St. (2010)	786	48
Hearst Tower, 214 N. Tryon St. (2002)	659	47
Bank of America Tower, 620 Tryon St. (2019)	632	33
Charlotte Metro, S. Tryon St. (2023)	629	40
One Wells Fargo Center, 301 S. College St. (1988)	588	42
The Vue, 400 W. 5th St. (2010)	574	50
Bank of America Plaza, 101 S. Tryon St. (1974)	503	40

Chicago, IL

Building/structure	Ht. (ft)	Stories
Willis (fmr. Sears) Tower, 233 S. Wacker Dr.[1] (1974)	1,451	108
Trump International Hotel & Tower (incl. spire), 401 N. Wabash Ave. (2009)	1,389	98
St. Regis Chicago, 381 E. Wacker Dr. (2020)	1,191	101
Aon Center, 200 E. Randolph St. (1973)	1,136	83
875 N. Michigan Ave. (fmr. John Hancock Ctr.)[2] (1969)	1,128	100
Franklin Center-North Tower (incl. spires), 227 W. Monroe St. (1989)	1,007	60
Two Prudential Plaza (incl. spire), 180 N. Stetson Ave. (1990)	978	64
One Chicago Square East Tower, 732 N. State St. (2022)	971	78
311 S. Wacker Drive (1990)	961	65
NEMA Chicago, 1200 S. Indiana Ave. (2019)	896	81
900 N. Michigan Ave. (1989)	871	66
Chase Tower, 21 S. Clark St. (1969)	868	61
Aqua at Lakeshore East, 225 N. Columbus Dr. (2009)	859	86
Water Tower Place, 845 N. Michigan Ave. (1976)	859	74
*400 N. Lake Shore Dr. North Tower (2027)	858	72
Park Tower, 800 N. Michigan Ave. (2000)	844	68
One Bennett Park, 451 E. Grand Ave. (2018)	837	67
Salesforce Tower, 333 Wolf Point Plaza (2023)	835	60
The Legacy at Millennium Park, 60 E. Monroe St. (2010)	818	73
110 N. Wacker Dr. (2020)	817	55
1000M, 1000 S. Michigan Ave. (2024)	805	73
300 N. LaSalle (2009)	785	60
3 First National Plaza, 70 W. Madison St. (1981)	767	57
Grant Thornton Tower, 161 N. Clark St. (1992)	756	50
Blue Cross Headquarters, 300 E. Randolph St. (2010)	744	54
River Point, 444 W. Lake St. (2017)	732	52
Olympia Centre, 737 N. Michigan Ave. (1986)	731	63
BMO Tower, 310 S. Canal St. (2021)	727	50
One Museum Park, 1215 S. Prairie Ave. (2009)	726	62
150 North Riverside (2017)	725	53
AMA Plaza, 330 N. Wabash Ave. (1973)	695	52
Waldorf Astoria Chicago, 940 N. Rush St. (2009)	686	60
111 S. Wacker Dr. (2005)	681	51
181 W. Madison St. (1990)	680	50
71 S. Wacker (2005)	679	48
One Magnificent Mile, 980 N. Michigan Ave. (1983)	673	57
340 on the Park, 340 E. Randolph St. (2007)	672	64
Wolf Point East Tower, 350 N. Orleans St. (2020)	668	60
United Bldg., 77 W. Wacker Dr. (1992)	668	49
UBS Tower, 1 N. Wacker Dr. (2001)	652	50
Daley Center, 55 W. Washington St. (1965)	648	31
55 E. Erie St. (2004)	647	56
Lake Point Tower, 505 N. Lake Shore Dr. (1968)	645	70
River East Center, 350 E. Illinois St. (2001)	644	58
Grand Plaza I (incl. spire), 540 N. State St. (2003)	641	57
155 N. Wacker Dr. (2009)	638	45
Leo Burnett Bldg., 35 W. Wacker Dr. (1989)	635	46
The Heritage at Millennium Park, 125 N. Wabash Ave. (2005)	631	57
NBC Tower (incl. spire), 455 N. Cityfront Plaza Dr. (1989)	627	37
353 N. Clark (2009)	623	44
OneEleven, 111 West Wacker (2014)	616	58

Building/structure	Ht. (ft)	Stories
Millennium Centre, 33 W. Ontario St. (2003)	610	58
Board of Trade (incl. statue), 141 W. Jackson Blvd. (1930)	609	44
Chicago Place, 700 N. Michigan Ave. (1991)	608	49
Essex on the Park, 812 S. Michigan Ave. (2019)	607	56
CNA Plaza, 325 S. Wabash St. (1972)	601	44
One Prudential Plaza, 130 E. Randolph St.[3] (1955)	601	41
500 W. Monroe St. (1992)	600	45
One Madison Plaza, 200 W. Madison St. (1982)	599	44
The Grant, 201 E. Roosevelt Rd. (2010)	595	54
1000 Lake Shore Plaza (1964)	590	55
The Clare at Water Tower, 55 East Pearson St. (2008)	589	52
Marina City I, 300 N. State St. (1964)	588	61
Marina City II, 301 N. Dearborn St. (1964)	588	61
Accenture Tower, 500 W. Madison St. (1987)	588	42
Optima Signature, 220 E. Illinois St. (2017)	587	57
The Park Monroe, 65 E. Monroe St. (1972)	583	49
Crain Communications Bldg., 150 N. Michigan Ave. (1983)	582	41
North Pier Apts., 474 N. Lake Shore Dr. (1990)	581	61
Citadel Center, 131 S. Dearborn St. (2003)	580	39
The Fordham, 25 E. Superior St. (2003)	574	52
23 W. Chicago Ave. (2022)	574	49
190 S. LaSalle St. (1987)	573	40
One S. Dearborn (2005)	571	39
Onterie Center, 446 E. Ontario St. (1986)	570	58
Loews Chicago Hotel, 455 North Park Dr. (2015)	569	52
Chicago Temple, 77 W. Washington St. (1924)	568	23
Palmolive Bldg. (incl. beacon), 919 N. Michigan Ave. (1929)	565	37
Kluczynski Federal Bldg., 230 S. Dearborn St. (1974)	562	42
Huron Plaza Apts., 30 E. Huron St. (1983)	560	56
Boeing International Headquarters, 100 N. Riverside Plaza (1990)	560	36
Cirrus, 211 N. Harbor Dr. (2021)	559	47
The Parkshore, 195 N. Harbor Dr. (1991)	556	56
North Harbor Tower, 175 N. Harbor Dr. (1988)	556	55
Civic Opera Bldg., 20 N. Wacker Dr. (1929)	555	45
Streeter Place, 351 E. Ohio St. (2009)	554	55
Harbor Point, 155 N. Harbor Dr. (1975)	554	54
Newberry Plaza, 1000 N. State St. (1974)	553	53
Michigan Plaza South, 205 N. Michigan Ave. (1985)	553	46
30 N. LaSalle St. (1975)	553	44
Pittsfield Bldg., 55 E. Washington St. (1927)	551	38
One S. Wacker Dr. (1982)	550	40

(1) 1,729 ft incl. antenna. (2) 1,499 ft incl. antenna. (3) 912 ft incl. antenna.

Cleveland, OH

Building/structure	Ht. (ft)	Stories
Key Tower (incl. spire), 127 Public Sq. (1991)	947	57
Terminal Tower, 50 Public Sq.[1] (1928)	708	52
200 Public Square (1985)	658	46
*Sherwin-Williams HQ, 145 W. 3rd St. (2024)	616	36
Tower at Erieview, 1301 E. 9th St. (1964)	529	40

(1) 771 ft incl. flagpole.

Columbus, OH

Building/structure	Ht. (ft)	Stories
James A. Rhodes State Office Tower, 30 E. Broad St. (1973)	624	41
Leveque-Lincoln Tower, 50 W. Broad St. (1927)	555	47
William Green Bldg., 30 W. Spring St. (1990)	530	33
Huntington Center, 41 S. High St. (1983)	512	37
Vern Riffe State Office Tower, 77 S. High St. (1988)	503	33

Dallas, TX

Building/structure	Ht. (ft)	Stories
Bank of America Plaza, 901 Main St. (1985)	921	72
Renaissance Tower (incl. spire), 1201 Elm St. (1974)	886	56
Comerica Bank Tower, 1717 Main St. (1987)	787	60
Dallas Arts Tower, 2200 Ross Ave. (1987)	738	55
Fountain Place, 1445 Ross Ave. (1986)	720	58
2001 Ross Ave. (1984)	686	50
1700 Pacific Ave. (1983)	655	50
Santander Tower, 1600 Pacific Ave. (1982)	645	50
Energy Plaza, 1601 Bryan St. (1983)	629	49
The Drever, 1401 Elm St. (1965)	628	52
Gables Republic Tower (incl. spire), 300 N. Ervay (1954)	602	36
Republic Center Tower II, 325 N. St. Paul (1964)	598	50
One AT&T Plaza, 208 S. Akard St. (1984)	580	37
Ross Tower, 500 N. Akard St. (1984)	579	45
AMLI Fountain Place, 1800 N. Field St. (2020)	562	46
Museum Tower, 2112 Flora St. (2013)	560	42
Tower at Cityplace, 2711 N. Haskell Ave. (1989)	560	42
Reunion Tower, 300 Reunion Blvd. (1976)	560	NA
Sheraton Dallas Hotel Center Tower, 400 Olive St. (1959)	550	42
Mercantile Bldg. (incl. spire), 1700 Main St. (1943)	523	31
Bryan Tower, 2001 Bryan St. (1973)	512	40

Denver, CO

Building/structure	Ht. (ft)	Stories
Republic Plaza, 330 17th St. (1984)	714	56
1801 California Street (1982)	709	52
Wells Fargo Center, 1700 Lincoln Ave. (1983)	698	50
Four Seasons Hotel & Private Residences, 1111 14th St. (2010)	639	45
1144 Fifteenth (2018)	602	42
1999 Broadway (1985)	544	43
707 17th St. (1981)	522	42
555 17th St. (1978)	507	40

Detroit, MI

Building/structure	Ht. (ft)	Stories
Marriott Hotel, Renaissance Center I[1] (1977)	727	70
*Hudsons Tower, 1246 Woodward Ave. (2025)	685	51
One Detroit Center, 500 Woodward Ave. (1991)	619	43
Penobscot Bldg., 633 Griswold Ave.[2] (1928)	565	47

(1) 755 ft incl. antenna. (2) 665 ft incl. antenna.

Houston, TX

Building/structure	Ht. (ft)	Stories
600 Travis St. (1982)	1,002	75
Wells Fargo Plaza, 1000 Louisiana St. (1983)	992	71
Williams Tower, 2800 Post Oak Blvd. (1982)	901	64
TC Energy Center, 700 Louisiana St. (1983)	780	56
Texaco Heritage Plaza, 1111 Bagby St. (1987)	762	53
Enterprise Plaza, 1100 Louisiana St.[1] (1980)	756	55
609 Main at Texas (2017)	755	48
Centerpoint Energy Plaza, 1111 Louisiana St. (1996)	741	53
Texas Tower, 801 Texas Ave. (2021)	735	47
1600 Smith St. (1984)	732	55
Fulbright Tower, 1301 McKinney St. (1982)	725	52
One Shell Plaza, 900 Louisiana St.[2] (1970)	714	50
1400 Smith St. (1983)	691	50
3 Allen Center, 333 Clay St. (1980)	685	50
LyondellBassell Tower, 1221 McKinney St. (1978)	678	47
First City Tower, 1001 Fannin St. (1984)	662	47
BG Group Place, 811 Main St. (2011)	632	46
San Felipe Plaza, 5847 San Felipe Blvd. (1984)	625	45
ExxonMobil Bldg., 800 Bell Ave. (1962)	606	44
1500 Louisiana St. (2002)	600	40
America General Center, 2929 Allen Pkwy. (1983)	590	42
Two Houston Center, 909 Fannin St. (1974)	579	40
San Jacinto Monument, La Porte (1939)	570	NA
Marathon Oil Tower, 5555 San Felipe Blvd. (1983)	562	41
1415 Louisiana (1983)	550	44
KBR Tower, 601 Jefferson St. (1973)	550	40

(1) 782 ft incl. antenna. (2) 999 ft incl. antenna.

Huixquilucan, Mexico

Building/structure	Ht. (ft)	Stories
*Nua Interlomas Torre 1 (2025)	591	47
*Nua Interlomas Torre 2 (2025)	591	47
Bosque Real Residence Torre 3-4 (2021)	558	52
Bosque Real Residence Torre 1-2 (2019)	558	52

Jersey City, NJ

Building/structure	Ht. (ft)	Stories
99 Hudson St. (2020)	889	76
30 Hudson St. (2004)	781	42
Journal Squared 2, 537 Summit Ave. (2021)	759	72
*One Journal Square Tower I (2026)	710	64
*One Journal Square Tower II (2026)	710	64
URL Harborside Tower 1 (2016)	700	70
*400 Marin Blvd. (NA)	634	60
Journal Squared 3 (2024)	633	60
Haus25, 25 Columbus Dr. (2022)	626	57
Journal Squared 1, 615 Pavonia Ave. (2016)	574	53
101 Hudson St. (1992)	548	42
235 Grand St. (2019)	537	45
Trump Plaza I, 88 Morgan St. (2008)	532	55
Newport Tower, 525 Washington Blvd. (1990)	531	37
90 Columbus (2018)	529	50
70 Columbus (2015)	529	50

Las Vegas, NV

Building/structure	Ht. (ft)	Stories
Stratosphere Twr., 2000 Las Vegas Blvd. S. (1996)	1,149	NA
The Fontainebleau Las Vegas, 2755 Las Vegas Blvd. S. (2023)	735	63
Resorts World Las Vegas Tower I, 3000 Las Vegas Blvd. S. (2021)	674	57
The Palazzo, 3339 Las Vegas Blvd. S. (2007)	642	53
Encore at Wynn Las Vegas, 3145 Las Vegas Blvd. S. (2008)	631	52
Trump International Hotel and Tower 1, 3128 Las Vegas Blvd. S. (2008)	622	64
Wynn Las Vegas, 3145 Las Vegas Blvd. S. (2005)	613	45
Cosmopolitan Casino Spa Tower, Las Vegas Blvd. S. and Harmon Ave. (2010)	603	52
Cosmopolitan Beach Resort Twr., Las Vegas Blvd. S. and Harmon Ave. (2010)	603	50
Aria Resort & Casino (2009)	600	60
Elara-Hilton Grand Vacations Hotel, 3667 Las Vegas Blvd. S. (2009)	597	50
VDARA, 2551 W. Harmon Ave. (2009)	556	55
Eiffel Tower, Paris Hotel and Casino, 3645 Las Vegas Blvd. S. (1998)	540	NA
Mandarin Oriental Hotel Las Vegas, 3750 Las Vegas Blvd. S. (2009)	539	47
New York, New York Hotel & Casino, 3790 Las Vegas Blvd. S. (1997)	529	48

Los Angeles, CA

Building/structure	Ht. (ft)	Stories
Wilshire Grand Center, 900 Wilshire Blvd. (2017)	1,100	62
US Bank Tower, 633 W. 5th St. (1990)	1,018	72
Aon Center, 707 Wilshire Blvd. (1974)	858	62
Two California Plaza, 350 S. Grand Ave. (1992)	750	52
Gas Company Tower, 555 W. 5th St. (1991)	749	52

Building/structure	Ht. (ft)	Stories
Wells Fargo North Tower, 333 S. Grand Ave. (1983)	740	54
Bank of America Plaza, 333 S. Hope St. (1975)	735	55
777 Tower, 777 S. Figueroa St. (1991)	725	53
Figueroa at Wilshire, 601 S. Figueroa St. (1989)	717	52
City National Tower, 555 S. Flower St. (1971)	699	52
Paul Hastings Tower, 515 S. Flower St. (1971)	699	52
Beaudry, 945 W. 8th St. (2023)	695	64
*Oceanwide Plaza Tower I (on hold)	677	53
Ritz Carlton/Marriott Marquis Los Angeles, 900 W. Olympic Blvd. (2010)	667	54
Thea at Metropolis Tower 3, 1000 W. 8th St. (2019)	627	56
FourFortyFour South Flower (1982)	625	48
611 W. 6th St. (1969)	620	42
Wells Fargo South Tower, 355 S. Grand Ave. (1984)	606	45
*1000 S. Hill St. (2025)	590	54
One California Plaza, 300 S. Grand Ave. (1985)	578	42
Century Plaza Tower 1, 2029 Century Park East (1973)	571	44
Century Plaza Tower 2, 2049 Century Park East (1973)	571	44
*Century City Center, 1950 Ave. of the Stars (2026)	564	37
825 S. Hill (2019)	563	53

Mexico City, Mexico

Building/structure	Ht. (ft)	Stories
Torre Mitikah, Rio Churubusco 601 (2022)	877	67
Torre Reforma, Paseo de la Reforma 483 (2016)	807	57
Chapultepec Uno, Paseo de la Reforma 509 (2019)	789	59
Torre BBVA, Paseo de la Reforma 506 (2015)	771	50
Torre Mayor, Paseo de la Reforma 505 (2003)	738	55
Torre Ejecutiva Pemex, Marina Nacional 329 Col. Huasteca (1984)	693	51
*The University Tower, Paseo de la Reforma 150 (2025)	666	58
*Expansion Antara (2025)	660	42
*Rosewood Mexico City (2025)	659	48
Downtown & Be Grand Reforma, La Fragura 7 (2023)	657	50
Torre Paradox, Av. Santa Fe 562 (2018)	644	60
Torre Reforma Latino, Paseo de la Reforma 296 (2016)	599	47
Torre Cuarzo, Paseo de la Reforma 26 (2017)	591	40
Torre M, Rio Churubusco 601 (2019)	577	35
Torre 300, Santa Fe 578 (2019)	574	51
Torre Altus, Paseo de los Laureles 416 (1998)	571	47
World Trade Center, Montecito 38 Col. Napoles (1972)	565	50
Miyana Torre Chapulin, Av. Ejecito Nacional (2020)	563	49
Siroco Elite Residences, Av. Santa Fe 482 (2015)	561	43
Sofitel Hotel Mexico City, Paseo de la Reforma 297 (2019)	558	41
Torre Latino Americana, Eje Central Lazaro Cardenas 2[1] (1956)	545	44

(1) 595 ft incl. antenna.

Miami, FL

Building/structure	Ht. (ft)	Stories
*Waldorf Astoria Hotel and Residences, 300 Biscayne Blvd. (2028)	1,038	98
*Cipriani Residences, 1420 S. Miami Ave. (2028)	939	80
*Okan Tower, 501 N. Miami Ave. (2026)	890	70
*Baccarat Residences, 99 SE 5th St. (2026)	848	75
Panorama Tower, 1101 Brickell Ave. (2018)	828	81
Aston Martin Residences, 300 Biscayne Blvd. Way (2024)	817	66
Four Seasons Hotel & Tower, 1441 Brickell Ave. (2003)	789	64
*Mercedes Benz Places, 1133 SW 2nd Ave. (2027)	773	64
Wachovia Financial Ctr., 200 S. Biscayne Blvd. (1983)	764	55
*830 Brickell, 830 SE 1st Ave. (2024)	724	55
Paramount Miami Worldcenter, 129 NE 8th St. (2019)	706	57
Marquis, 1100 Biscayne Blvd. (2009)	702	63
*E11even Hotel & Residences (2026)	699	65
One Thousand Museum, 1000 Biscayne Blvd. (2019)	699	60
Brickell Flatiron, 1001 S. Miami Ave. (2019)	698	64
*Legacy Hotel & Residences, 942 NE 1st Ave. (2026)	690	51
Wells Fargo Tower, 200 SE 3rd St. (2010)	655	47
900 Biscayne Bay, 900 Biscayne Blvd. (2008)	650	63
Missoni Baia, 700 NE 26th Ter. (2023)	646	57
Elysee, 700 NE 23rd St. (2021)	644	57
*Miami River Phase 1, 265 SW 6th St. (2025)	640	54
Echo Brickell, 1451 Brickell Ave. (2017)	637	57
Mint at Riverfront, 90 SW 3rd St. (2009)	631	55
Infinity at Brickell, 60 W. 13th St. (2008)	630	52
Miami Tower, 100 SE Second St. (1987)	625	47
Marinablue, 888 Biscayne Blvd. (2007)	615	57
*Una Residences, 175 SE 25th Rd. (2025)	613	47
Plaza on Brickell Tower I, 901 Brickell Ave. (2007)	610	56
Epic Residences & Hotel, 300 Biscayne Blvd. Way (2009)	601	54
One Paraiso, 620 NE 31st St. (2018)	601	53
SLS Brickell, 1300 S. Miami Ave. (2016)	599	52
SLS Lux Brickell, 801 S. Miami Ave. (2018)	595	57
Natiivo, 159 NE 6th St. (2024)	588	51
Icon Brickell North Tower, 495 Brickell Ave. (2008)	586	58
Icon Brickell South Tower, 495 Brickell Ave. (2008)	586	58
*Miami World Towers 1 (2024)	579	52
*Lofty Brickell, 99 SW 7th St. (2026)	574	44
400 Biscayne (2022)	573	49
Downtown 1st, 34 SW 1st St. (2023)	560	57
Paramount at Edgewater Square, 2066 N. Bayshore Dr. (2009)	555	47
50 Biscayne Blvd. (2007)	554	55
Quantum on the Bay South Tower, 1900 N. Bayshore Dr. (2008)	554	51
Biscayne Beach, 701 NE 29th St. (2017)	550	51
Solitair Brickell, 80 SW 8th St. (2018)	550	49

Minneapolis, MN

Building/structure	Ht. (ft)	Stories
IDS Center, 80 8th St. South[1] (1973)	792	55
Capella Tower, 225 South Sixth (1992)	776	56
Wells Fargo Center, 90 7th St. South (1988)	775	56
33 South Sixth St. (1983)	668	52
Two22 Tower, 222 9th St. South (1985)	582	42
US Bank Plaza I, 200 6th St. South (1981)	561	40
Eleven, 1111 West River Parkway (2022)	547	44
RBC Plaza, 60 6th St. South (1992)	539	40

(1) 910 ft incl. antenna.

Mississauga, ON, Canada

Building/structure	Ht. (ft)	Stories
*M City Tower 3 (2026)	854	81
*Exchange District Condos, EX3 (2026)	761	72
*M City Tower 4 (2026)	707	67
*Exchange District Condos, EX1 (2025)	659	60
*M City Tower 2, 3883 Quartz Rd. (2023)	650	62
*M City Tower 1, 3980 Burnhamthorpe Rd. (2023)	650	62
Absolute World 56, 50 Absolute Ave. (2012)	576	56
*Oro at Edge Towers (2025)	558	51
*Avia-PSV (2024)	518	50
Absolute World 50, 30 Absolute Ave. (2012)	518	50
Pinnacle Grand Park II (2017)	500	48

Monterrey, Mexico

Building/structure	Ht. (ft)	Stories
*Torre Rise (2026)	1,558	94
T.Op Corporativo (2020)	1,002	64
Torre Koi, San Pedro Garza Garcia (2017)	916	65
*Sohl, Constitucion 999 (2026)	879	62
Hotel Safi Metropolitan, San Pedro Garza Garcia (2020)	764	56
Pabellon M (2015)	681	47
Santa Maria Torre 6 (2020)	620	43
*Torre ¡LoLa! (2025)	604	44
Metropolitan Center Torre II, San Pedro Garza Garcia (2017)	594	52
Centro de Gobierno Plaza Civica (2010)	591	36
*Libertad HO, Hidalgo 450 Pte. (2026)	574	48
*Ikon Tower, Av. Lazaro Cardenas 2305, San Pedro Garza Garcia (2024)	574	38
LIU East, San Pedro Garza Garcia (2013)	564	39

Montréal, QC, Canada

Building/structure	Ht. (ft)	Stories
1250 Boulevard Rene-Levesque O. (incl. spire) (1992)	743	47
1000 Rue de la Gauchetiere (1992)	673	51
*1 Square Phillips, 539 Rue St. Catherine O. (2024)	658	61
*Le 900 Saint James (2025)	656	62
Victoria Sur le Parc, 700 Rue Saint James (2024)	656	58
Banque Nationale HQ, 800 Rue Saint James (2024)	656	40
Maestra Tour B (2024)	651	58
Tour de la Bourse, 800 Place Victoria (1964)	624	47
1 Place Villa Marie (1962)	616	43
Maestra Tour A (2023)	606	55
L'Avenue, 1175 Avenue des Canadiens (2017)	605	51
La Tour CIBC, 1155 Boul. Rene-Levesque O.[1] (1962)	604	45
Montreal Tower (1987)	574	NA
Tour des Canadiens 3, 1250 Rue St. Antoine O. (2021)	551	53
Tour des Canadiens 2, 1150 Rue St. Antoine O. (2019)	551	53
Tour des Canadiens, 1288 Ave. des Canadiens (2016)	548	50

(1) 740 ft incl. antenna.

Nashville, TN

Building/structure	Ht. (ft)	Stories
*1010 Tower, 1010 Church St. (2027)	750	60
AT&T Building, 333 Commerce St. (1994)	617	33
*Amazon Tower 3, 1001 Church St. (2025)	609	43
Four Season Hotel & Residences, 151 1st Ave. South (2022)	539	40
*Pinnacle Tower (NA)	525	34
505, 505 Church St. (2018)	524	46

New Orleans, LA

Building/structure	Ht. (ft)	Stories
Hancock Whitney Center, 701 Poydras St. (1972)	697	51
CapitalOne Center, 201 St. Charles Ave. (1985)	645	53
Plaza Tower, 1001 Howard Ave. (1969)	531	45
Energy Centre, 1100 Poydras St. (1984)	530	39

New York, NY

Building/structure	Ht. (ft)	Stories
One World Trade Center (incl. spire) (2014)	1,782	94
Central Park Tower, 217 W. 57th St. (2021)	1,550	98
111 W. 57th St. (2021)	1,428	82
One Vanderbilt Place, 51 E. 42nd St. (2020)	1,401	62
432 Park Avenue (2015)	1,397	85
*JPMorgan Chase World HQ, 270 Park Ave. (2025)	1,389	60
30 Hudson Yards (2019)	1,268	73
Empire State Building, 350 5th Ave.[1] (1931)	1,250	102
Bank of America Tower (incl. spire), One Bryant Park (2009)	1,200	55
Three World Trade Center, 175 Greenwich St. (2018)	1,079	69
*The Torch, 740 8th Ave. (on hold)	1,067	52
53 West 53rd (2019)	1,050	77
Chrysler Bldg. (incl. spire), 405 Lexington Ave. (1930)	1,046	77
New York Times Twr. (incl. spire), 620 8th Ave. (2007)	1,046	52
The Brooklyn Tower, 340 Flatbush Ext., Brooklyn (2023)	1,035	74

Building/structure	Ht. (ft)	Stories
The Spiral, 435 10th Ave. (2023)	1,031	66
One57, 157 W. 57th St. (2014)	1,005	75
*520 5th Ave. (2026)	1,000	76
35 Hudson Yards (2019)	1,000	72
One Manhattan West, 401 9th Ave. (2019)	996	67
50 Hudson Yards, 504 W. 34th St. (2022)	981	58
4 World Trade Center, 150 Greenwich St. (2014)	977	65
220 Central Park South (2019)	952	70
70 Pine (incl. spire) (1932)	952	67
Two Manhattan West, 401 W. 31st St. (2023)	935	58
The Trump Bldg., 40 Wall St. (1930)	927	71
30 Park Place, 99 Church St. (2016)	926	67
Citigroup Center, 153 E. 53rd St. (1977)	915	63
15 Hudson Yards (2019)	914	70
*125 Greenwich St. (2024)	912	72
10 Hudson Yards (2016)	878	50
New York by Gehry at Eight Spruce Street (2011)	870	76
Trump World Tower, 845 UN Plaza (2001)	861	72
*262 5th Ave. (2025)	860	54
425 Park Avenue (2021)	860	44
Comcast Bldg., 30 Rockefeller Center (1933)	850	70
One Manhattan Square, 250 South St. (2019)	847	72
Sutton 58, 428-432 E. 58th St. (2022)	847	65
Cityspire Center, 150 W. 56th St. (1987)	814	75
28 Liberty (1961)	813	60
56 Leonard St. (2016)	813	57
4 Times Square[2] (1999)	809	48
MetLife Bldg., 200 Park Ave. (1963)	808	59
Bloomberg Tower, 731 Lexington Ave.[3] (2005)	806	54
Madison House, 126 Madison Ave. (2022)	805	56
The Centrale, 138 E. 50th St. (2019)	803	64
*42-02 Orchard St., Queens (2026)	794	69
Woolworth Building, 233 Broadway (1913)	792	58
111 Murray St. (2019)	788	60
520 Park Avenue (2018)	781	52
50 West, 50 West St. (2018)	779	64
Madison Square Park Tower, 41 E. 22nd St. (2017)	778	61
55 Hudson Yards (2019)	778	51
1 Worldwide Plaza, 935 8th Ave. (1989)	778	47
*50 W. 66th St. (2025)	775	52
Skyline Tower, 23-15 44th Dr., Queens (2021)	762	67
19 Dutch St. (2018)	758	63
Carnegie Hall Tower, 152 W. 57th St. (1991)	757	60
Sven, 29-55 Northern Blvd., Queens (2021)	755	67
The Wall Street Tower, 130 William St. (2021)	755	61
383 Madison Ave. (2001)	755	47
1717 Broadway (2013)	753	67
AXA Center, 787 7th Ave. (1985)	752	51
One Penn Plaza, 250 W. 34th St. (1972)	750	57
1251 Ave. of the Americas (1971)	750	54
Time Warner Center North Tower, 10 Columbus Cir. (2004)	749	55
Time Warner Center South Tower, 10 Columbus Cir. (2004)	749	55
Goldman Sachs HQ, 200 Murray St. (2010)	749	44
60 Wall Street (1989)	745	55
One Astor Plaza, 1515 Broadway (1972)	745	54
*100 W. 37th St. (2026)	743	68
One Liberty Plaza, 165 Broadway (1972)	743	54
7 World Trade Center, 250 Greenwich St. (2006)	743	49
Twenty Exchange, 20 Exchange Pl. (1931)	741	57
Three World Financial Center, 200 Vesey St. (1986)	739	51
ARO, 242 W. 53rd St. (2018)	738	62
*43-30 24th St., Queens (2026)	732	66
1540 Broadway (incl. spire) (1990)	732	42
Times Square Tower, 1459 Broadway (2004)	726	47
Brooklyn Point, 138 Willoughby St., Brooklyn (2020)	723	57
Metropolitan Tower, 142 W. 57th St. (1985)	716	68
252 E. 57th St. (2016)	715	59
*111 Washington St. (2026)	712	64
100 E. 53rd St. (2018)	711	61
General Motors Bldg., 767 5th Ave. (1968)	705	50
The Eugene, 401 W. 31st St. (2017)	702	64
25 Park Row (2020)	702	54
Metropolitan Life Tower, 1 Madison Ave. (1909)	700	50
500 5th Ave. (1931)	697	59
Americas Tower, 1177 Ave. of the Americas (1992)	692	48
Solow Bldg., 9 W. 57th St. (1974)	689	49
Marine Midland Bldg., 140 Broadway (1967)	688	52
55 Water St. (1972)	687	53
277 Park Ave. (1963)	687	50
The Beekman Hotel & Residences, 5 Beekman St. (2017)	687	47
1585 Broadway (1989)	685	42
Random House/Park Imperial, 1739 Broadway (2003)	684	52
Four Seasons Hotel, 57 E. 57th St. (1993)	682	52
Sky, 605 W. 42nd St (2015)	676	61
McGraw-Hill Bldg., 1221 Ave. of the Americas (1972)	674	51
Barclay Tower, 10 Barclay St. (2007)	673	56
One Grand Central Place, 60 E. 42nd St. (1930)	673	53
277 5th Ave. (2019)	673	52
One Court Square, Queens (1990)	673	50
*One Seaport, 161 Maiden Ln. (on hold)	670	60

Building/structure	Ht. (ft)	Stories
Paramount Plaza, 1633 Broadway (1970)	670	48
200 Amsterdam Ave. (2021)	668	55
*45 Park Place (on hold)	667	43
Trump Tower, 725 5th Ave. (1982)	664	58
Bank of New York Bldg., 1 Wall St. (1932)	654	50
Silver Towers East, 600 W. 42nd St. (2009)	653	58
Silver Towers West, 600 W. 42nd St. (2009)	653	58
599 Lexington Ave. (1986)	653	51
712 5th Ave. (1990)	650	53
Chanin Bldg., 122 E. 42nd St. (1929)	649	56
245 Park Avenue (1967)	648	47
550 Madison Avenue (1983)	647	37
Two World Financial Center, 225 Liberty St. (1986)	645	44
1095 Ave. of the Americas (1974)	645	43
*Aloft Hotel, 450 11th Ave. (2025)	642	51
570 Lexington Ave. (1931)	642	50
1 New York Plaza, 1 Water St. (1969)	640	50
Rose Hill, 30 E. 29th St. (2021)	639	45
1 MiMA Tower, 440 W. 42nd St. (2011)	638	63
Tower 28, 42-12 28th St., Queens (2017)	638	58
3Eleven, 311 11th Ave. (2022)	637	59
1 Dag Hammarskjold Plaza, 885 2nd Ave. (1972)	637	48
345 Park Ave. (1968)	634	44
Langham Place, 400 5th Ave. (2010)	632	58
Mercantile Bldg., 10 E. 40th St. (1929)	632	48
W New York Downtown Hotel & Residences, 123 Washington St. (2010)	631	57
Grace Plaza, 1114 Ave. of the Americas (1972)	630	50
Home Insurance Plaza, 59 Maiden Ln. (1966)	630	44
101 Park Ave. (1982)	629	49
Central Park Place, 301 W. 57th St. (1988)	628	56
888 7th Ave. (1971)	628	45
11 Hoyt St., Brooklyn (2020)	626	51
Burlington House, 1345 Ave. of the Americas (1969)	625	50
Waldorf Astoria New York, 301 Park Ave. (1931)	625	47
Avalon Willoughby West, 100 Willoughby St., Brooklyn (2015)	624	57
Trump Palace, 200 E. 69th St. (1991)	623	54
One Madison Park, 20 E. 23rd St. (2010)	621	51
Olympic Tower, 645 5th Ave. (1976)	620	51
425 Fifth Ave. (2003)	618	55
The Epic, 125 W. 31st St. (2007)	615	61
919 3rd Ave. (1970)	615	47
Tower 49, 12 E. 49th St. (1985)	615	44
750 7th Ave. (incl. spire) (1989)	615	35
New York Life, 51 Madison Ave. (1928)	615	33
835 6th Ave. (2010)	614	53
Gotham Point, 1-15 57th Ave., Queens (2023)	612	57
551 10th Ave. (2016)	612	52
*98 DeKalb Ave., Brooklyn (2025)	612	49
Baccarat Hotel & Residences, 20 W. 53rd St. (2014)	610	46
Credit Lyonnais Bldg., 1301 Ave. of the Amer. (1964)	609	46
The Orion, 350 W. 42nd St. (2006)	604	58
590 Madison Ave. (1983)	603	41
The Hub, 333 Schermerhorn St., Brooklyn (2017)	602	54
250 W. 55th St. (2013)	602	40
Eleven Times Square, 644 8th Ave. (2011)	601	40
1166 Avenue of the Americas (1974)	600	44
Eagle Lofts, 43-22 Queens St., Queens (2018)	598	55
Hawthorn Park, 160 W. 62nd St. (2014)	598	54
Hearst Magazine Tower, 959 8th Ave. (2006)	597	46
3 Lincoln Center, 160 W. 66th St. (1993)	595	60
Celanese Bldg., 1211 Ave. of the Amer. (1973)	592	45
The London NYC, 151 W. 54th St. (1990)	590	54
388 Bridge St., Brooklyn (2014)	590	51
Thurgood Marshall U.S. Courthouse, 505 Pearl St. (1936)	590	37
Museum Tower Apts., 21 W. 53rd St. (1985)	589	52
The Millennium Hilton Hotel, 55 Church St. (1992)	588	58
Sky House, 11 E. 29th St. (2008)	588	55
Hunter's Point South Phase 2 Tower A, 52-03 Center Blvd., Queens (2022)	587	56
1271 Ave. of the Americas (1959)	587	48
451 10th Ave. Residential Tower (2022)	587	45
Jacob K. Javits Federal Bldg., 26 Federal Plz. (1967)	587	41
W Times Square, 1567 Broadway (2000)	584	53
Trump Intl. Hotel & Twr., 15 Columbus Cir. (1970)	583	44
3 Jackson Park, 28-30 Jackson Ave., Queens (2018)	581	54
Stevens Tower, 1185 Ave. of the Amer. (1971)	580	42
Ritz-Carlton NoMad, 1185 Broadway (2022)	580	40
Municipal Bldg., 1 Centre St. (1914)	580	34
520 Madison Ave. (1981)	577	43
One World Financial Center, 200 Liberty St. (1985)	577	37
Merchandise Mart, 41 Madison Ave. (1973)	576	42
One Domino Square, 5 S. 5th St., Brooklyn (2024)	575	52
*The Brook, 589 Fulton St., Brooklyn (2025)	575	51
Park Ave. Plaza, 55 E. 52nd St. (1981)	575	44
300 Madison Ave. (2003)	575	38
Lehman Bldg., 745 7th Ave. (2001)	575	38
32 Old Slip (1987)	575	37
Marriott Marquis Times Sq., 1531 Broadway (1985)	574	50
299 Park Ave. (1967)	574	42
5 Times Square, 590 7th Ave. (2002)	574	40
Socony Mobil Bldg., 150 E. 42nd St. (1956)	572	42

Building/structure	Ht. (ft)	Stories
Lyra, 555 W. 38th St. (2022)	571	52
1290 Ave. of the Americas (1963)	571	43
780 3rd Ave. (1983)	570	49
600 3rd Ave. (1971)	570	42
The Ashland, 590 Fulton St., Brooklyn (2016)	568	51
450 Lexington Ave. (1991)	568	38
Paramount Tower, 240 E. 39th St. (1998)	567	51
230 Park Ave. (1928)	565	35
New York Palace Hotel, 455 Madison Ave. (1980)	563	51
Continental Bank Bldg., 30 Broad St. (1932)	562	48
Turkevi Center, 821 UN Plaza (2021)	561	36
Park Ave. Tower, 65 E. 55th St. (1986)	561	36
Nelson Tower, 450 7th Ave. (1931)	560	46
Sherry-Netherland, 781 5th Ave. (1927)	560	40
623 5th Ave. (1990)	560	36
South Park Tower, 124 W. 60th St. (1986)	558	51
100 UN Plaza, 327 E. 48th St. (1986)	557	52
Continental Can, 633 3rd Ave. (1962)	557	39
Summit New York, 222 E. 44th St. (2018)	556	42
3 Park Ave. (1975)	556	42
Continental Center, 180 Maiden Ln. (1983)	555	41
330 Madison Ave. (1964)	555	41
Equitable Bldg., 120 Broadway (1915)	555	38
3 Times Square[4] (2001)	555	30
Tower 111, 885 6th Ave. (2011)	554	48
Instrada Nomad, 10 E. 29th St. (1999)	554	48
Inmont Bldg., 1133 Ave. of the Americas (1970)	553	44
One Willoughby Square, 420 Albee Sq., Brooklyn (2021)	552	35
Downtown by Philippe Starck, 15 Broad St. (1927)	551	42
*3 W. 29th St. (on hold)	551	34
Hyatt Times Square, 135 W. 45th St. (2013)	550	53
Biltmore Tower, 267 W. 47th St. (2003)	550	51
Unisys Bldg., 605 3rd Ave. (1963)	550	44
The Tower at 15 Central Park West (2008)	550	35
AT&T Long Lines Bldg., 33 Thomas St. (1974)	550	29

(1) 1,455 ft incl. antenna. (2) 1,118 ft incl. antenna. (3) 941 ft incl. antenna. (4) 659 ft incl. antenna.

Philadelphia, PA

Building/structure	Ht. (ft)	Stories
Comcast Technology Center, 1800 Arch St. (2018)	1,121	59
Comcast Center, 1701 JFK Blvd. (2008)	974	57
One Liberty Place (incl. spire), 1650 Market St. (1987)	945	61
Two Liberty Place (incl. spire), 1601 Chestnut St. (1989)	848	58
BNY Mellon Bank Center, 1735 Market St. (1990)	792	54
Three Logan, 1717 Arch St. (1991)	739	55
FMC Tower at Cira Centre South (2017)	730	49
G. Fred DiBona Jr. Bldg., 1901 Market St. (1990)	625	45
The W Philadelphia and Element, 1441 Chestnut St. (2019)	617	51
The Laurel, 1911 Walnut St. (2022)	599	50
Commerce Square #1, 2005 Market St. (1990)	572	40
Commerce Square #2, 2001 Market St. (1992)	572	40
City Hall (incl. statue) (1901)	548	7
Arthaus, 309 S. Broad St. (2022)	528	47

Pittsburgh, PA

Building/structure	Ht. (ft)	Stories
US Steel Tower, 600 Grant St. (1970)	841	64
BNY Mellon Center, 500 Grant St. (1983)	725	54
One PPG Place (1984)	635	40
Fifth Ave. Place, 120 5th Ave. (1987)	616	32
One Oxford Centre, 301 Grant St. (1982)	615	46
Gulf Tower, 707 Grant St. (1932)	582	44
The Tower at PNC Plaza (2015)	545	33
University of Pittsburgh Cathedral of Learning, 4200 5th Ave. (1936)	535	42
3 Mellon Bank Center, 525 Wm. Penn Way (1951)	520	41
K & L Gates Center, 210 6th Ave. (1968)	511	39

Portland, OR

Building/structure	Ht. (ft)	Stories
Wells Fargo Center, 1300 SW 5th Ave. (1973)	546	40
Park Avenue West (incl. spire), 728 SW 9th Ave. (2016)	537	30
U.S. Bancorp Tower, 111 SW 5th Ave. (1983)	536	42
Koin Center, 222 SW Columbia St. (1984)	509	31

Puebla, Mexico

Building/structure	Ht. (ft)	Stories
*Oak 58 Torre Orso, San Andres Cholula (on hold)	761	58
Inxignia (2023)	738	45
*Torre NVBOLA (on hold)	650	40
*Oak 58 Torre Lupo, San Andres Cholula (on hold)	630	48

St. Louis, MO

Building/structure	Ht. (ft)	Stories
Gateway Arch, 11 N. 4th St. (1965)	630	NA
Metropolitan Square Tower, 211 N. Broadway (1988)	593	42
900 Pine St. (1986)	588	44
Thomas F. Eagleton Federal Courthouse, 111 S. 10th St. (2000)	557	29

San Francisco, CA

Building/structure	Ht. (ft)	Stories
Salesforce Tower, 415 Mission St. (2018)	1,070	61
Sutro Tower (1972)	977	NA
Transamerica Pyramid, 600 Montgomery St. (1972)	853	48
181 Fremont (2018)	810	56
555 California St. (1969)	779	52
345 California Center (1986)	695	48
Millennium Tower, 301 Mission St. (2009)	645	58
The Avery, 400 Folsom St. (2019)	618	56
One Rincon Hill South Tower, 425 First St. (2008)	605	54
Park Tower at Transbay (2018)	605	43
101 California St. (1982)	600	48
50 Fremont Center (1985)	600	43
575 Market St. (1975)	573	40
Four Embarcadero Center, 55 Clay St. (1984)	570	45
One Embarcadero Center, 355 Clay St. (1970)	569	45
44 Montgomery St. (1967)	565	43
Spear Tower, 1 Market St. (1976)	565	42
One Sansome Street (1984)	550	43

Seattle, WA

Building/structure	Ht. (ft)	Stories
Columbia Center, 701 5th Ave. (1985)	933	76
Rainier Square Tower, 1301 5th Ave. (2020)	852	58
1201 Third Avenue Tower, 1201 3rd Ave. (1988)	772	55
Two Union Square, 601 Union St. (1989)	740	56
Seattle Municipal Tower, 700 5th Ave. (1990)	722	57
F5 Tower, 811 5th Ave. (2017)	660	44
Safeco Plaza, 1001 4th Ave. (1969)	630	50
City Centre, 1420 5th Ave. (1989)	606	44
Space Needle, 203 6th Ave. (1962)	605	NA
Russell Investments Center, 1301 2nd Ave. (2006)	598	42
Wells Fargo Center, 999 3rd Ave. (1983)	574	47
Madison Centre, 505 Madison St. (2017)	560	36

Sunny Isles Beach, FL

Building/structure	Ht. (ft)	Stories
Estates at Acqualina Boutique North Tower, 17901 Collins Ave. (2023)	672	52
Estates at Acqualina South Tower, 17901 Collins Ave. (2022)	672	52
Turnberry Ocean Club, 18501 Collins Ave. (2020)	649	52
Muse, 17141 Collins Ave. (2018)	649	47
Porsche Design Tower, 18555 Collins Ave. (2016)	644	58
Mansions at Acqualina, 17749 Collins Ave. (2015)	643	46
The Ritz-Carlton Residences, 15701 Collins Ave. (2020)	642	52
Residences by Armani Casa, 18975 Collins Ave. (2019)	639	55
Jade Signature, 16901 Collins Ave. (2017)	636	57
Jade on the Beach Condominiums, 17001 Collins Ave. (2008)	574	51
Trump Royale, 18201 Collins Ave. (2008)	551	43
Trump Palace, 18101 Collins Ave. (2005)	551	43
Acqualina Resort & Spa, 17875 Collins Ave. (2004)	550	51
Jade Ocean, 17121 Collins Ave. (2009)	543	51

Tampa, FL

Building/structure	Ht. (ft)	Stories
Regions Bldg., 100 N. Tampa St. (1992)	579	42
Bank of America Plaza, 101 E. Kennedy Blvd. (1986)	577	42
One Tampa City Center, 201 N. Franklin St. (1981)	537	39
Truist Place, 401 E. Jackson St. (1992)	525	36

Toronto, ON, Canada

Building/structure	Ht. (ft)	Stories
CN Tower, 310 Front St. West (1976)	1,815	NA
*Sky Tower at Pinnacle One Yonge, 1 Yonge St. (2026)	1,132	105
*The One, 1 Bloor St. West (2025)	1,077	91
*Concord Sky, 385 Yonge St. (2027)	985	85
First Canadian Place, 100 King St. West[1] (1975)	978	72
The St. Regis Toronto (incl. spire), 325 Bay St. (2012)	908	63
Scotia Tower, 40 King St. West (1989)	902	68
Aura at College Park, 388 Yonge St. (2014)	892	78
*Forma East, 260 King St. West (2026)	874	73
Brookfield Place (incl. spire), 161 Bay St. (1990)	856	53
Number One Bloor, 1 Bloor St. East (2017)	844	75
*CIBC Square II, 141 Bay St. (2025)	792	53
TD Terrace, 160 Front St. (2024)	787	46
Commerce Court West, 199 Bay St.[2] (1973)	784	57
CIBC Square I, 81 Bay St. (2021)	780	49
Ice Condos at York Centre 2, 16 York St. (2015)	768	67
Harbour Plaza Residences E., 90 Harbour St. (2017)	764	71
*Canada House 1, 23 Spadina Ave. (2025)	759	69
Sugar Wharf Tower D, 95 Lakeshore East (2023)	755	70
Eau de Soleil Sky Tower, 2183 Lake Shore Blvd. W., Etobicoke (2019)	747	67
Harbour Plaza Residences W., 90 Harbour St. (2017)	735	67
Ten York (2018)	735	65
TD Centre-Toronto Dominion Bank Tower, 66 Wellington St. West (1967)	730	56
Sugar Wharf Tower E, 95 Lakeshore East (2023)	717	65
*8 Elm St. (2026)	716	69
The Prestige at Pinnacle One Yonge (2022)	712	65
*The Pemberton, 33 Yorkville Ave. (2026)	708	68
Bay-Adelaide Center West Twr., 335 Bay St. (2010)	704	52
Living Shangri-La Toronto, 180 University Ave. (2012)	702	65
*11 YV, 11 Yorkville Ave. (2025)	699	62
Ritz-Carlton Hotel and Residences, 185 Wellington St. West (2011)	687	54
The Residences of 488 University Avenue (2019)	679	58
BCE Place, Bay-Wellington Tower, 181 Bay St. (1991)	679	49

Building/structure	Ht. (ft)	Stories
L Tower, 1 Front St. (2014)	673	59
Massey Tower, 199 Yonge St. (2019)	670	62
88 Scott St. (2017)	669	58
Four Seasons Private Residences West, 48 Yorkville Ave. (2012)	669	55
YC Condos, 460 Yonge St. (2018)	664	60
*Canada House 2, 23 Spadina Ave. (2025)	663	59
Ice Condos at York Centre 1, 16 York St. (2014)	663	57
Bay-Adelaide Center East Twr., 40 Adelaide St. (2016)	643	44
E Condos South, 8 Eglington Ave. (2019)	642	58
Wellesley on the Park, 11 Wellesley St. W. (2021)	637	60
22I21 Yonge, 2221 Yonge St. (2021)	632	58
EY Tower, 100 Adelaide St. West (2017)	617	40
19 Duncan St. (2024)	612	58
*QueenChurch, 60 Queen St. East (2028)	611	57
Rosedale on Bloor, 403 Bloor St. East (2023)	610	55
*Water's Edge at the Cove, 38 The Marginal Blvd., Etobicoke (2024)	607	56
RBC Centre, 155 Wellington St. West (2009)	607	42
*United Bldg., 481 University Ave. (2026)	606	54
CASA II, 42 Charles St. East (2016)	605	57
U Condominiums East Tower, 50 St. Joseph St. (2016)	604	55
One Yorkville (2020)	601	58
TD North Tower, 77 King St. West (1969)	600	46
*8 Wellesley West (2025)	595	55
Maple Leaf Square North Tower, 65 Bremmer Blvd. (2010)	595	54
Eau de Soleil Water Tower, 2183 Lake Shore Blvd. West, Etobicoke (2019)	593	49
CASA III, 50 Charles St. East (2018)	589	55
Vita on the Lake, 2165 Lake Shore Blvd. West, Etobicoke (2022)	587	55
INDX Condominiums, 70 Temperance St. (2016)	585	54
1 King West (2005)	578	51
The Well Office Tower, 410 Front St. West (2022)	571	38
Success Tower 2, 33 Bay St. (2010)	569	55
Royal Bank Plaza-South Tower, 200 Bay St. (1976)	567	41
Maple Leaf Square South Tower, 55 Bremmer Blvd. (2010)	562	50
Teahouse Condominiums South, 501 Yonge St. (2022)	561	52
The Selby Condominiums, 592 Shelbourne St. (2019)	560	51
Eight Cumberland, 826 Yonge St. (2024)	557	51
Hullmark Centre I, 4789 Yonge St. (2015)	557	45
*4800 Yonge (2025)	552	49
Lago at the Waterfront, 2151 Lake Shore Blvd. W., Etobicoke (2016)	550	49

(1) 1,116 ft incl. antenna. (2) 942 ft incl. antenna.

Tulsa, OK

Building/structure	Ht. (ft)	Stories
BOK Tower, 1 E. 2nd St. (1975)	667	52
Cityplex Central Tower, 2448 E. 81st St. (1979)	648	60
First Place Tower, 15 E. 5th St. (1973)	516	40
Mid-Continent Tower, 401 S. Boston St. (1984)	513	36

Vancouver, BC, Canada

Building/structure	Ht. (ft)	Stories
Shangri-La Vancouver, 1120 W. Georgia St. (2009)	659	59
Paradox Hotel and Residences, 1133 W. Georgia (2016)	616	58
The Butterfly, 969 Burrard St. (2024)	586	57
One Burrard Place (2021)	551	54
The Stack, 1133 Melville St. (2023)	550	37

Vaughan, ON, Canada

Building/structure	Ht. (ft)	Stories
*Festival Tower A (2024)	620	59
*CG Tower, 2900 Hwy. 7 (2025)	608	60
Transit City Condos 3 (2021)	587	55
*Festival Tower C (2024)	585	55
Transit City Condos 1 (2021)	575	55
Transit City Condos 2 (2021)	575	55
TC4 (2023)	546	50

Other Tall Buildings in North America

Building/structure	City	Ht. (ft)	Stories
Devon Energy Center (2012)	Oklahoma City, OK	844	52
Stantec Tower (2019)	Edmonton, AB, Can.	816	66
RSA Battle House Tower (incl. spire) (2007)	Mobile, AL	745	35
Ocean Resort Casino (2012)	Atlantic City, NJ	718	53
Salesforce Tower[1] (1990)	Indianapolis, IN	701	49
*Mutual of Omaha HQ (2026)	Omaha, NE	677	44
Hotel Riu Plaza Guadalajara (incl. spire) (2011)	Guadalajara, Mexico	669	42
Great American Twr. at Queen City Square (2011)	Cincinnati, OH	665	40
The Tower at First National Center (2002)	Omaha, NE	634	45
801 Grand (1991)	Des Moines, IA	630	44
JW Marriott-Legends Private Residences (2019)	Edmonton, AB, Can.	627	56
*Legend (2029)	Zapopan, Mexico	623	52
One Kansas City Place (incl. spire) (1988)	Kansas City, MO	623	42
Tower of the Americas (1968)	San Antonio, TX	622	NA
Bank of America Tower (1990)	Jacksonville, FL	617	42
U.S. Bank Center (1973)	Milwaukee, WI	601	42
*Bellevue 600 (2025)	Bellevue, WA	600	43
Amazon Sonic (2023)	Bellevue, WA	600	42
Town Pavilion (1986)	Kansas City, MO	591	38
Erastus Corning II Twr. (1973)	Albany, NY	589	44
*Pier West 1 (2024)	New West., BC, Can.	584	53
Hilton Cincinnati Netherland Plaza[2] (1931)	Cincinnati, OH	574	49
Concourse Corporate Ctr. V (incl. spire) (1988)	Sandy Springs, GA	570	34
Hyatt Regency Andares (2017)	Zapopan, Mexico	568	41
Burnett Plaza (1983)	Fort Worth, TX	567	40
*VuPoint Tower 1 (2025)	Pickering, ON, Can.	565	53
*The Halo Tower 1 (2025)	Newark, NJ	565	52
Torre Aura Altitude (2008)	Zapopan, Mexico	563	44
Blue Diamond Tower (2000)	Miami Beach, FL	559	44
Green Diamond Tower (2000)	Miami Beach, FL	559	44
*Parkway II (2025)	Surrey, BC, Can.	555	50
Washington Monument (1884)	Washington, DC	555	NA
Concourse Corporate Ctr. VI (incl. spire) (1991)	Sandy Springs, GA	553	34
Northwestern Mutual Tower (2017)	Milwaukee, WI	550	33
400 West Market (1992)	Louisville, KY	549	35
D.R. Horton Tower (1984)	Fort Worth, TX	547	38
Five Park (2024)	Miami Beach, FL	546	44
Simmons Tower (1986)	Little Rock, AR	546	40
Marriott Rivercenter (incl. spires) (1988)	San Antonio, TX	546	38
PNC Plaza (incl. spire) (2008)	Raleigh, NC	538	32
City Place I (1980)	Hartford, CT	535	38
Modis Tower (1975)	Jacksonville, FL	535	37
One America Tower (1982)	Indianapolis, IN	533	38
Niagara Falls Hilton Phase 2 (2009)	Niagara Falls, ON, Can.	532	50
567 Clarke + Como (2021)	Coquitlam, BC, Can.	532	49
Corporativo Bansi (2019)	Guadalajara, Mexico	532	32
Torre 40 Residencial Gran Jardin (2020)	León, Mexico	531	44
Transamerica Tower (1973)	Baltimore, MD	529	40
Seneca One (1970)	Buffalo, NY	529	38
*Highpoint (2024)	Coquitlam, BC, Can.	528	50
*VuPoint Tower 2 (2025)	Pickering, ON, Can.	527	49
Travelers Tower (1919)	Hartford, CT	527	24
Vehicle Assembly Bldg. (1965)	Cape Canaveral, FL	526	40
Harrah's Waterfront Twr. (2008)	Atlantic City, NJ	525	44
Carter Burgess Plaza (1982)	Fort Worth, TX	525	40
*The Sky (2025)	Mérida, Mexico	525	37
Goodwin Square (1990)	Hartford, CT	522	30
Skylon (1965)	Niagara Falls, ON, Can.	520	NA
3 Civic Plaza (2018)	Surrey, BC, Can.	516	50
*The Residences at 400 Central (2025)	St. Petersburg, FL	515	46
*Pine & Glen T1 (2026)	Coquitlam, BC, Can.	514	49
PNC Tower (1972)	Louisville, KY	512	40
*UBCO Downtown (2027)	Kelowna, BC, Can.	510	46
Hospital San Jose Moscati (2022)	Queretaro, Mexico	509	40
Bank of America (1929)	Baltimore, MD	509	37
The Westin Virginia Beach Town Ctr. & Res. (2007)	Virginia Beach, VA	508	38
*Myriad By Concert (2024)	Coquitlam, BC, Can.	507	50
*The Couture (2025)	Milwaukee, WI	507	44
The Beach Club Tower 2 (2006)	Hallandale Beach, FL	505	50
*Emerald Tower (on hold)	Edmonton, AB, Can.	504	45
One Indiana Square (1970)	Indianapolis, IN	504	36
414 Light St. (2018)	Baltimore, MD	500	44
Cotter Ranch Tower (1971)	Oklahoma City, OK	500	36
One American Plaza (1991)	San Diego, CA	500	34

(1) 811 ft incl. antenna. (2) 623 ft incl. antenna.

Selected Bridge Styles

Bridges support weight through tension (pulling), compression (pushing), or a combination of both. **Suspension** and **cable-stayed** bridges are characterized by cables under tension. While the deck of a suspension bridge hangs from suspenders, that of a cable-stayed bridge ties directly to a bridge tower. The elements of a **truss** form triangles, which distribute the forces of tension and compression. Truss bridges can thus carry more weight than beam bridges. Steel plates can be welded or bolted together to make a **plate girder**, a kind of beam. A common form is the **box girder**.

A bridge can have a **simple** configuration, whereby its load is supported at both ends. If a bridge is **continuous**, its load extends across multiple supports. In a **cantilever** configuration, structural elements (e.g., trusses or girders) supported at one end project out, or cantilever, to carry a span.

Notable North American Bridges

Source: World Almanac research; Office of Bridge Technology, Federal Highway Administration, U.S. Dept. of Transportation

Asterisk (*) designates a bridge that carries railroads only. All other bridges carry roads or roads and rail unless otherwise noted. Year is date of completion or projected completion. Span of bridge is the distance between its main supports. As of mid-2024.

Suspension

Year	Bridge	Location	Main span (ft)
1964	Verrazzano-Narrows	New York, NY	4,260
1937	Golden Gate	San Francisco Bay, CA	4,200
1957	Mackinac	Straits of Mackinac, MI	3,800
1931	George Washington	New York, NY-Fort Lee, NJ	3,500
1950/2007	Tacoma Narrows (twin)	Tacoma, WA	2,800
2003	Al Zampa Mem. (New Carquinez) (westbound)	Carquinez Strait, CA	2,388
1936	San Francisco-Oakland Bay (West Span)[1]	San Francisco-Yerba Buena Isl., CA	2,310
1939	Bronx-Whitestone	East R., New York, NY	2,300
1970	Pierre Laporte	Quebec City, QC, Can.	2,190
1951/68	Delaware Mem. (twin)	Pennsville, NJ-New Castle, DE	2,150
1957	Walt Whitman	Philadelphia, PA-NJ	2,000
1929	Ambassador	Detroit, MI-Windsor, ON, Can.	1,850
1961	Throgs Neck	New York, NY	1,801
1926	Benjamin Franklin	Phila., PA-Camden, NJ	1,750
1924	Bear Mountain	Hudson R., Peekskill, NY	1,632
1969	Claiborne Pell/Newport	Narragansett Bay, RI	1,600
1952/73	William Preston Lane Jr. Memorial (twin)	Sandy Point, MD	1,600
1903	Williamsburg	East R., New York, NY	1,600
1883	Brooklyn	East R., New York, NY	1,596
1938	Lions Gate	Vancouver, BC, Can.	1,549
1963	Vincent Thomas	L.A. Harbor, CA	1,500
1930	Mid-Hudson	Poughkeepsie, NY	1,495
1909	Manhattan	East R., New York, NY	1,470
1955	Angus L. Macdonald	Halifax, NS, Can.	1,447
1970	A. Murray MacKay	Halifax, NS, Can.	1,400
1936	Triborough (Harlem R. Lift/Bronx Crossing/East R. Suspension)	East R., New York, NY	1,380
2013	San Francisco-Oakland Bay (SAS)[2]	San Francisco Bay, CA	1,263

Cantilever

Year	Bridge	Location	Main span (ft)
1917	Quebec	Quebec City, QC, Can.	1,800
1974	Commodore Barry	Chester, PA-Bridgeport, NJ	1,644
1958/88	Crescent City Connection (twin)	Mississippi R., New Orleans, LA	1,575
1995	Veterans Memorial	Gramercy, LA	1,460
1968	Baton Rouge	Mississippi R., LA	1,235
1930	Lewis and Clark	Longview, WA-Rainier, OR	1,200
1909	Queensboro	East R., New York, NY	1,182
1958	Carquinez (eastbound)	San Francisco Bay, CA	1,100
1930	Jacques Cartier	Montreal, QC, Can.	1,097
1968	Isaiah D. Hart	Jacksonville, FL	1,088
1956	Richmond-San Rafael (twin)	San Francisco Bay, CA	1,070
1963/80	Newburgh-Beacon (twin)	Hudson R., NY	1,000

Truss[3]

Year	Bridge	Location	Main span (ft)
1966	Astoria-Megler (U.S. 101)	Columbia R., OR-WA	1,232
1981	Ravenswood	Ohio R., Ravenswood, WV	902
1995	Taylor-Southgate, Ohio R.	Cincinnati, OH-Newport, KY	850
1943	Julien Dubuque (U.S. 20)	Mississippi R., IA-IL	845
1966	Charles Braga	Fall River, MA	840
1963	Brent Spence (I-71/I-75)	Ohio R., OH-KY	831
1956	Shawneetown (KY 56) (twin)	Ohio R., IL-KY	825
1953	John E. Mathews	Jacksonville, FL	810
1992	Cooper R.	Charleston, SC	800
1957	Kingston-Rhinecliff	Hudson R., NY	800
1950	Maurice J. Tobin	Boston, MA	800
1988	Phil G. McDonald (Glade Creek)	Beckley, WV	784
1986	Rochester-Monaca	Rochester-Monaca, PA	780
1973/88	Atchafalaya R. (U.S. 190) (twin)	Krotz Springs, LA	780
1917	*Sciotoville RR (twin)	Sciotoville, OH-KY	775
1981	Sewickley	Sewickley, PA	750
1977	Jennings Randolph	Chester, WV-E. Liverpool, OH	750
1974	Carroll C. Cropper (I-275)	Ohio R., IN-KY	750
1940	Glover Cary	Ohio R., Owensboro, KY-IN	750
1984	13th Street	Ohio R., Ashland, KY-OH	740
1959	Monaca-E. Rochester	Monaca-E. Rochester, PA	730
1976	Betsy Ross	Phila., PA-Pennsauken, NJ	729
2013	Milton-Madison (U.S. 421)	Ohio R., KY-IN	727
1967	Matthew E. Welsh	Ohio R., Mauckport, IN-KY	725
1994	Robert C. Byrd	Huntington, WV	720
1971	Atchafalaya R. (LA 1)	Simmesport, LA	720
1962	U.S. 41 Twin	Ohio R., Evansville, IN-Henderson, KY	720
1929	Irvin S. Cobb (U.S. 45)	Ohio R., Brookport, IL-Paducah, KY	716
1970	Vanport	Vanport, PA	715
1973	Girard Point	Philadelphia, PA	700
1963	John F. Kennedy (I-65)	Ohio R., Louisville, KY-Jeffersonville, IN	700
1923	*Mears Mem., Tanana R.	Nenana, AK	700

Plate and Box Girder

Year	Bridge	Location	Main span (ft)
1997	Confederation[4]	Prince Edward Isl.-NB, Can.	820
2010	Kanawha R. (I-64)	S. Charleston-Dunbar, WV	760
1982	Jesse H. Jones Memorial	Houston, TX	750
1977	LA 27, Intracoastal Canal	Gibbstown, LA	750
1976	LA 82, Intracoastal Canal	Forked Isl., LA	750
1967	San Mateo-Hayward	San Francisco Bay, CA	750
1992	Jamestown-Verrazano	Narragansett Bay, RI	674
2002	Vietnam Veterans Mem.	James R., Richmond, VA	672
1986	Umatilla	Columbia R., OR-WA	660
1969	San Diego-Coronado (twin)	San Diego Bay, CA	660
2007	Benicia-Martinez (new)	Carquinez Strait, CA	659

Cable-Stayed

Year	Bridge	Location	Main span (ft)
2025	Gordie Howe Intl.	Detroit, MI-Windsor, ON, Can.	2,798
2012	Baluarte Bicentennial	Sinaloa-Durango, Mex.	1,706
2025	New Harbor (U.S. 181)	Corpus Christi Ship Channel, TX	1,661
2011	John James Audubon	Miss. R., St. Francisville, LA	1,583
2005	Arthur Ravenel Jr.	Charleston, SC	1,546
2012	Port Mann	Vancouver, BC, Can.	1,542
1986	Alex Fraser	Vancouver, BC, Can.	1,526
2014	Stan Musial Veterans Memorial (I-70)	Miss. R., St. Louis, MO-IL	1,500
2010	Greenville (U.S. 82)	MS-Lake Village, AR	1,378
1994	Clark	Alton, IL-MO	1,360
1989	Dames Point	Jacksonville, FL	1,300
2003	Sidney Lanier	Brunswick, GA	1,250
1995	Fred Hartman	Houston Ship Channel, Baytown, TX	1,250
2007	Veterans' Glass City Skyway	Maumee R., Toledo, OH	1,225
1983	Hale Boggs Memorial	Luling, LA	1,222
2017	Mario Cuomo (I-287) (twin)	Hudson R., Tarrytown-Nyack, NY	1,200
2002	William Natcher, Ohio R.	Owensboro, KY-IN	1,200
1987	Sunshine Skyway (I-275)	Tampa Bay, FL	1,200
2012	Margaret Hunt Hill	Trinity R., Dallas, TX	1,197
1988	Tampico	Panuco R., Mex.	1,181
2006	Penobscot Narrows	Bucksport, ME	1,161
2003	Bill Emerson Memorial	Cape Girardeau, MO-IL	1,150
1988	Skybridge	Vancouver, BC, Can.	1,115
1991	Talmadge Memorial	Savannah, GA	1,100
2000	Maysville (Wm. H. Harsha)	Ohio R., KY-Aberdeen, OH	1,050

Steel Arch

Year	Bridge	Location	Main span (ft)
1977	New River Gorge	Fayetteville, WV	1,700
1931	Bayonne (Kill Van Kull)	Bayonne, NJ-New York, NY	1,675
1973	Fremont	Portland, OR	1,255
1964	Port Mann	Vancouver, BC, Can.	1,200
1967	Laviolette	Trois-Rivières, QC, Can.	1,100
1990	Roosevelt Lake	Roosevelt Lake, AZ	1,080
1959	Glen Canyon	Page, AZ	1,028
1962	Lewiston-Queenston	NY-ON, Can.	1,001
1976	Perrine	Twin Falls, ID	993
1916	*Hell Gate	East R., New York, NY	978
1941	Rainbow	Niagara Falls, NY-ON, Can.	950
1997	Second Blue Water	Port Huron, MI-ON, Can.	922
1977	Moundsville	Ohio R., WV	912

Year	Bridge	Location	Main span (ft)
1983/92	Jefferson Barracks (I-255) (twin)	Mississippi R., IL-MO	910
1973	Hernando DeSoto (I-40) (two spans)	Mississippi R., AR-TN	900
2008	Blennerhassett (U.S. 50)	Parkersburg, WV-OH	878
1936	Henry Hudson	Harlem R., New York, NY	840
2023	Wellsburg, Ohio R.	WV-Brilliant, OH	830
1966	Bob Cummings Lincoln Trail	Ohio R., IN-KY	825
1978	I-57, Mississippi R.	Cairo, IL	821
1980	I-65, Mobile R.	Mobile, AL	800
1962	Sherman Minton (I-64)	IN-Louisville, KY	800
1978	I-470, Ohio R.	Wheeling, WV	780
1932	West End	Pittsburgh, PA	780
1971	Piscataqua R. (I-95 High Level)	Portsmouth, NH-Kittery, ME	756
1959	Fort Pitt	Pittsburgh, PA	750

Movable Bridges

Vertical Lift

Year	Bridge	Location	Main span (ft)
1959	*Arthur Kill	New York, NY-Elizabeth, NJ	558
1935	*Cape Cod Canal	Buzzards Bay, MA	544
1896	*Delair[5]	Pennsauken, NJ-Phila., PA	542
1937	Marine Pkwy. Hodges Mem.	Jamaica Bay, New York, NY	540
1931	Burlington-Bristol	Delaware R., NJ-PA	540
1908	*Burlington Northern RR[6]	Portland, OR	516
1968	*Second Narrows Railway	Vancouver, BC, Can.	499
1911	*Armour-Swift-Burlington	Missouri R., Kansas City, MO	428

Bascule

Year	Bridge	Location	Main span (ft)
1940	Charles Berry Memorial	Lorain, OH	333
1917	Market St./Ch. John Ross.	Chattanooga, TN	310
2003	SW 2nd Avenue	Miami, FL	302

Swing

Year	Bridge	Location	Main span (ft)
1927	Fort Madison (Santa Fe)	Mississippi R., IA	525
1952	George P. Coleman Mem.	Yorktown, VA	500
1991	SW Spokane St.	Seattle, WA	480
1899	*Illinois Central RR	Chicago, IL	479
1914	*Coos Bay RR	Coos Bay, OR	458
1913	East Haddam (Rt. 82)	Connecticut R., CT	458

Floating Pontoon[7]

Year	Bridge	Location	Main span (ft)
2016	New SR 520	Seattle, WA	7,709
1993	Lacey V. Murrow (I-90)	Seattle, WA	6,620
1961	Hood Canal (SR 104)	Kitsap-Jefferson Cos., WA	6,521
1989	Homer M. Hadley (I-90)	Seattle, WA	5,811

Other Notable North American Bridges

Year	Bridge	Type	Location	Tot. length (ft)
1956/69	Lake Pontchartrain Causeway[8]	Twin concrete trestle	Metairie-Mandeville, LA	126,055
1979	Manchac Swamp	Twin concrete trestle	Manchac, LA	120,384
1973	Atchafalaya Basin (I-10)	Twin concrete trestle	Baton Rouge, LA	95,040
1982	Seven Mile (Overseas Hwy., U.S. 1)	Segmental concrete	Florida Keys	35,867
2009/11	I-10 Twin Spans	Twin concrete trestle	Slidell-New Orleans, LA	29,040
2002	Croatan Sound	Continuous post-tensioned girder	Manteo, NC	27,000
1993	Choctawhatchee Mid-Bay	Segmental concrete	Destin-Niceville, FL	19,265
1962	International	Arch truss	Sault Ste. Marie, MI-ON, Can.	9,278
2009	Walkway Over the Hudson[9]	Pedestrian	Poughkeepsie-Highland, NY	6,768
1874	Eads, Mississippi R.[10]	Steel arch	St. Louis, MO-IL	6,442
2013	San Francisco-Oakland Bay (Skyway)	Segmental concrete box girder	San Francisco Bay, CA	6,336
1987	Powder Point	Tropical hardwood	Duxbury, MA	2,200
1969	Silver Memorial, Ohio R.[11]	Cantilever	Pt. Pleasant, WV-OH	1,964
2010	O'Callaghan-Tillman Mem. (U.S. 93)[12]	Concrete arch	Colorado R., AZ-NV	1,900
1994	Natchez Trace Parkway	Concrete arch	Franklin, TN	1,572
1901	Hartland[13]	Covered	St. John R., Hartland, NB, Can.	1,282

(1) Two complete bridges each 2,310-ft long, which share an anchor point. (2) Self-Anchored Suspension Span (SAS); world's longest single-tower, self-anchored suspension bridge. (3) The Francis Scott Key Bridge (1,200-ft main span) in Baltimore, MD, collapsed after it was struck by a cargo ship on Mar. 26, 2024. (4) World's longest bridge crossing ice-covered water, with total length of 8 mi. (5) Vertical-lift span replaced fixed span of swing bridge in 1959. (6) Vertical lift replaced swing span in 1989. (7) Length listed is of bridge's floating section. (8) World's longest continuous spans over water. (9) Opened in 1889 as a railroad bridge. (10) World's first major structure made of alloy steel. (11) Replaced Silver Bridge, the collapse of which in 1967 led to the creation of National Bridge Inspection Standards in the U.S. (12) Longest single-span concrete arch in Western Hemisphere. (13) World's longest covered bridge.

Oldest U.S. Bridges in Continuous Use

Built in 1697, the stone-arch Frankford Ave. Bridge (U.S. 13) crosses Pennypack Creek in Philadelphia, PA. It is 73-ft long and consists of three spans. The bridge was constructed as part of the King's Road, which connected Philadelphia to New York.

The oldest covered bridge, completed in 1829, is the double-span, 256-ft-long Bath-Haverhill Bridge, which spans the Ammonoosuc River between the towns of Bath and Haverhill, NH. The bridge was bypassed in 1999. It has since reopened to pedestrian traffic only.

Notable World Bridges

Source: World Almanac research; as of mid-2024

Year is date of completion or projected completion. Span of bridge is the distance between its main supports.

Suspension

Year	Bridge	Location	Main span (ft)
2022	Çanakkale 1915	Turkey	6,637
1998	Akashi Kaikyo	Japan	6,532
2019	Yangsigang	China	5,577
2019	Nansha	China	5,538
2024	Lingdingyang (ShenZhong Link)	China	5,466
2009	Xihoumen	China	5,413
1998	Storebælt (Great Belt, East Bridge)	Denmark	5,328
2016	Osman Gazi (Izmit Bay)	Turkey	5,085
2012	Yi Sun-sin (Gwangyang)	South Korea	5,069
2005	Runyang Yangtze R. (south)	China	4,888
2018	Second Dingtinghu	China	4,854
2012	Nanjing Fourth Yangtze R.	China	4,652
1981	Humber	England	4,625
2016	Yavuz Sultan Selim (Bosporus III)	Turkey	4,619
2021	Jin'an	China	4,547
1999	Jiangyin Yangtze R.	China	4,544
1997	Tsing Ma	China	4,518
2013	Hardanger	Norway	4,298
2007	Yangluo Yangtze R.	China	4,199
1997	Höga Kusten	Sweden	3,970
2019	Hongjun Chishulhe	China	3,937
2019	Dasha	China	3,937
2016	Longjian	China	3,924
2012	Aizhai	China	3,858
2015	Ulsan Grand	South Korea	3,773
2018	Halogaland	Norway	3,756
2015	Qingshui R.	China	3,710
2008	Huangpu	China	3,635
2018	Xingkang	China	3,609
1988	Minami Bisan-Seto	Japan	3,609
1988	Fatih Sultan Mehmet (Bosporus II)	Turkey	3,576
2009	Baling R.	China	3,570
2012	Taizhou Yangtze R.[1]	China	3,543
1973	July 15 Martyrs' (Bosporus)	Turkey	3,524
2017	Fuma Yangtze R.	China	3,445
1999	Kurushima III	Japan	3,379
1999	Kurushima II	Japan	3,346
1966	Ponte 25 de Abril, Tagus R.	Portugal	3,323
1964	Forth Road	Scotland	3,300

(1) Two consecutive spans of equal length.

Steel Arch

Year	Bridge	Location	Main span (ft)
2009	Chaotianmen Yangtze R.	China	1,811
2003	Lupu	China	1,804
2012	Bosideng	China	1,739
1932	Sydney Harbour	Australia	1,650
2005	Wushan Yangtze R.	China	1,614
2024	Chenab (rail)[1]	India	1,532
2013	Xijiang (rail)	China	1,476

Year	Bridge	Location	Main span (ft)
2007	Xinguang	China	1,404
2007	Caiyuanba	China	1,378
2010	Daning R.	China	1,312
2007	Lianxiang	China	1,312
2010	Hiroshima Airport	Japan	1,247
1959	Sloboda	Croatia	1,224
2007	Maocao Street	China	1,207

(1) World's highest rail bridge (1,178 ft).

Concrete Arch

Year	Bridge	Location	Main span (ft)
2016	Beipanjiang	China	1,460
1997	Wanxian Yangtze R.	China	1,378
2015	Nanpanjiang (rail)	China	1,365
1980	Krk I (one of Krk's two arches)	Croatia	1,280
2016	Almonte Viaduct	Spain	1,260

Cantilever

Year	Bridge	Location	Main span (ft)
1890	Forth Rail[1]	Scotland	1,710
1974	Minato	Japan	1,673
1943	Rabindra Setu (Howrah)	India	1,500

(1) Two spans of equal length.

Plate and Box Girder

Year	Bridge	Location	Main span (ft)
2006	Shibanpo	China	1,083
1998	Stolmasundet	Norway	988
1974	Pres. Costa e Silva (Rio-Niterói)	Brazil	984
1998	Raftsund	Norway	978

Cable-Stayed

Year	Bridge	Location	Main span (ft)
2012	Russky Island	Russia	3,622
2020	Hutong	China	3,583
2008	Sutong Yangtze R.	China	3,570
2009	Stonecutters	China	3,340
2009	Edong	China	3,038
2018	Jiayu Yangtze R.	China	3,018
1999	Tatara	Japan	2,920
1995	Normandy	France	2,808
2019	Chizhou Yangtze R.	China	2,717
2019	Shishou Yangtze R.	China	2,690
2013	Jiujiang Yangtze R. Expressway	China	2,684
2010	Jingyue Yangtze R.	China	2,677
2017	Second Wuhu Yangtze R.	China	2,644
2009	Incheon	South Korea	2,625

Year	Bridge	Location	Main span (ft)
2016	Yachi R.	China	2,600
2013	Xiamen Zhangzhou Cross-sea	China	2,559
2012	Zolotoy Rog	Russia	2,418
2009	Shanghai Yangtze R.	China	2,395
2009	Minpu	China	2,323
2017	Queensferry	Scotland	2,132
2005	Third Nanjing Yangtze R.	China	2,126
2001	Second Nanjing Yangtze R.	China	2,060
2000	Third Wuhan Yangtze R. (Baishazhou)	China	2,028
2002	Qingzhou Minjiang R.	China	1,985
1993	Yangpu	China	1,975
1998	Meiko Chuo	Japan	1,936
1997	Xupu	China	1,936
2024	Msikaba	South Africa	1,902
2004	Rion-Antirion	Greece	1,837
2015	La Pepa	Spain	1,772
2014	Bukhang	South Korea	1,772

Other Notable World Bridges[1]

Year	Bridge	Location	Length (ft)
2011	Danyang-Kunshan Grand (rail)[2]	China	538,000
2007	Changhua-Kaohsiung Viaduct (rail)	Taiwan	516,076
2011	Tianjin Grand (rail)	China	373,824
2000	Bang Na Expressway[3]	Thailand	180,446
2010	Beijing Grand (rail)	China	157,982
2007	Yangcun (rail)	China	117,493
2007	Hangzhou Bay	China	117,037
2011	Qingdao-Haiwan (Jiaozhou Bay)	China	87,598
2018	Hong Kong-Zhuhai-Macau Main[4]	China	75,131
2013	Jiashao[5]	China	33,136
2018	Maputo-Katembe[6]	Mozambique	9,977
2004	Millau Viaduct[7]	France	8,071
1978	Demerara Harbour (floating)	Guyana	6,074
1991	Ikitsuki[8]	Japan	1,312

(1) Total bridge length listed unless otherwise noted. (2) World's longest bridge. (3) World's longest road bridge. (4) World's longest sea bridge in aggregate; part of HZMB link. (5) World's longest multispan cable-stayed bridge. (6) Africa's longest suspension bridge. (7) World's tallest bridge; max. height 1,125 ft from top of pylon to valley floor. (8) Length of main span; world's longest continuous truss span.

World's Longest Railway Tunnels

Source: World Almanac research

Year is date of opening or projected opening unless otherwise noted. As of mid-2024.

Year	Tunnel	Location	Operating railway	Length (mi)
2032	Brenner Base (twin)	Austria-Italy	Austrian Federal Railways (ÖBB) and Ferrovie dello Stato (FS)	39.8
2016	Gotthard Base (twin)	Switzerland-Italy	Swiss Federal Railways (SBB)	35.4/35.5
1988	Seikan	Japan	Japan Railways Group	33.5
1994	English Channel (Chunnel) (twin)	UK-France	Eurotunnel	31.5
2016	Yulhyeon	South Korea	SR/Korea Railroad Corporation (Korail)	31.2
2016	Songshan Lake	China	Dongguan-Huizhou Intercity Railway	24.0
2007	Lötschberg Base (twin)	Switzerland	BLS Lötschbergbahn AG	21.5
2025	Koralm (twin)	Austria	Austrian Federal Railways (ÖBB)	20.5
2014	New Guanjiao	China	Qinghai-Tibet Railway Company	20.3
2007	Guadarrama (twin)	Spain	Renfe	17.6
2016	West Qinling	China	Chongqing-Lanzhou Railway	17.5
2009	Taihang (twin)	China	China's Ministry of Railways	17.3
1940	Northern Line	UK	London Underground	17.3
2005	Hakkoda	Japan	Japan Railways Group	16.4
2018	Guangzhou-Shenzhen-Hong Kong Express Rail Link (XRL), Hong Kong section	China	MTR Corporation	16.2
2002	Iwate-Ichinohe	Japan	Japan Railways Group	16.0
2023	Pajares (twin)	Spain	Renfe	15.3
2015	Iiyama	Japan	Japan Railways Group	13.8
1982	Daishimizu	Japan	Japan Railways Group	13.8
2022	Crossrail (twin)	UK	Transport for London	13.0
2008-09	Geumjeong	South Korea	Korea Railroad Corporation (Korail)	12.6
2006	Wushaoling (twin)	China	China's Ministry of Railways	12.5
1906/22	Simplon No. 1 and 2	Switzerland-Italy	BLS Lötschbergbahn AG	12.3
2022	Blix (Follo Line) (twin)	Norway	Vy (Norwegian State Railways)	12.1
1999	Vereina	Switzerland	Rhätische Bahn (RhB)	11.8
1975	Shin-Kanmon (twin)	Japan	Japan Railways Group	11.6
1934	Apennine	Italy	Ferrovie dello Stato (FS)	11.5
2029	Fehmarnbelt[1]	Denmark-Germany	DSB (Danish State Railways)	11.2

(1) Would be world's longest immersed tunnel for rail and auto.

Underwater U.S. Vehicular Tunnels

Source: National Tunnel Inventory, Federal Highway Administration, U.S. Dept. of Transportation (year is date of opening)

Year	Name	Location	Waterway	Length (ft)
1950	Hugh L. Carey (twin)	Brooklyn-Manhattan, New York, NY	East River	9,137
1927	Holland	New York, NY-Jersey City, NJ	Hudson River	8,556
1937/45/57	Lincoln (center/north/south tubes)	New York, NY-Weehawken, NJ	Hudson River	8,216/7,482/8,006
1958	Baltimore Harbor (twin)	Baltimore, MD	Baltimore Harbor	7,651
1957/1976	Hampton Roads (westbound, eastbound)[1]	Norfolk-Hampton, VA	Hampton Roads Harbor	7,479/7,315
1985	Fort McHenry (twin)	Baltimore, MD	Patapsco River	7,209
1940	Queens Midtown (twin)	Queens-Manhattan, New York, NY	East River	6,272
2004	Silver Line	Boston, MA	Boston Harbor	6,233
1964	Thimble Shoal[2]	Virginia Beach, VA	Chesapeake Bay	5,738
1934	Sumner	Boston, MA	Boston Harbor	5,655
1964	Chesapeake Channel	Northampton Co., VA	Chesapeake Bay	5,424
1930	Detroit-Windsor	Detroit, MI-Windsor, ON, Canada	Detroit River	5,160
1961	Callahan	Boston, MA	Boston Harbor	5,070

(1) As part of an expansion project, twin tunnels are under construction with target completion of 2027. (2) A Parallel Thimble Shoal tunnel is under construction with expected completion in 2027.

Land Vehicular Tunnels in the U.S.

Source: World Almanac research; Federal Highway Administration, U.S. Dept. of Transportation

Name	Location	Length (ft)
Anton Anderson Memorial[1]	Whittier, AK	13,300
SR 99 (Alaskan Way)	Seattle, WA	12,244
Edwin C. Johnson Memorial	I-70, Clear Creek Co.-Summit Co., CO	8,877
Eisenhower Memorial	I-70, Clear Creek Co.-Summit Co., CO	8,856
Ted Williams[2]	MA Turnpike, Boston, MA	8,448
Thomas P. O'Neill Jr.	I-93, Boston, MA	7,920
Tetsuo Harano (twin)	Oahu, HI	6,336
Allegheny (twin)	Somerset Co., PA	6,069
Liberty (twin)	PA Turnpike, Pittsburgh, PA	5,898
East River Mountain (twin)	I-77, Rocky Gap, VA-Bluefield, WV	5,661
Zion-Mount Carmel	Zion Natl. Park, UT	5,613
Tuscarora Mountain (twin)	Franklin Co.-Huntingdon Co., PA	5,324
Cumberland Gap (twin)	U.S. 25E, KY-TN	4,860
Kittatinny Mountain (twin)	Franklin Co., PA	4,727
Lehigh (twin)	Lehigh Co.-Carbon Co., PA	4,383
Tom Lantos/Devil's Slide (twin)	San Mateo Co., CA	4,342/4,265
Blue Mountain (twin)	Newburg, PA	4,340
Wawona	Yosemite Natl. Pk., CA	4,237
Big Walker Mountain (twin)	Bland Co., VA	4,228
Squirrel Hill (twin)	Pittsburgh, PA	4,225
Hanging Lake (twin)	Glenwood Canyon, CO	4,035/3,941
Cave Rock (eastbound)	Douglas Co., NV	3,915
Wabash HOV	Pittsburgh, PA	3,661
Caldecott (4 tubes)	Oakland, CA	3,616/3,610/3,371/3,399
Fort Pitt (twin)	Pittsburgh, PA	3,614
Mount Washington Transit	Pittsburgh, PA	3,549
I-395 Mall (Third St.)	Washington, DC	3,400

(1) Vehicles and trains take turns using the tunnel's one lane. (2) Total length of tunnel is 8,448 ft, of which 3,960 ft is underwater.

Major U.S. Dams and Reservoirs

Source: National Inventory of Dams, U.S. Army Corps of Engineers

Highest U.S. Dams

Rank	Dam (year completed)	River	Location	Type	Height (ft)
1.	Oroville (1968)	Feather	California	Embankment earthfill	770
2.	Hoover (1935)	Colorado	Nevada-Arizona	Arch-Gravity	730
3.	Dworshak (1973)	N. Fork Clearwater	Idaho	Gravity	717
4.	Glen Canyon (1963)	Colorado	Arizona	Arch	710
5.	New Bullards Bar (1970)	North Yuba	California	Arch	645
6.	New Melones (1979)	Stanislaus	California	Embankment rockfill	625
7.	Mossyrock (1968)	Cowlitz	Washington	Arch	606
8.	Shasta (1945)	Sacramento	California	Gravity	602
9.	Don Pedro (1971)	Tuolumne	California	Embankment earthfill	585
10.	Hungry Horse (1952)	S. Fork Flathead	Montana	Arch	564

Note: The height of a dam is the vertical distance between the original streambed or excavated foundation and the dam's crest, parapet wall, or maximum design water level. Tailings and other mining dams (i.e., dams built from the waste generated by mining operations) are not included in this list.

Largest U.S. Embankment Dams

Rank	Dam (year completed)	River	Location	Volume in cubic yards (thous.)
1.	Fort Peck (1957)	Missouri	Montana	125,628
2.	Oahe (1966)	Missouri	South Dakota	92,000
3.	Oroville (1968)	Feather	California	80,000
4.	B. F. Sisk (San Luis) (1967)	San Luis Creek	California	77,664
5.	Garrison (1953)	Missouri	North Dakota	66,500
6.	Scotts Flat (1948)	Deer Creek	California	66,300
7.	Cochiti (1975)	Rio Grande	New Mexico	65,000
8.	Herbert Hoover (1965)	Kissimmee River Basin	Florida	54,700
9.	Fort Randall (1954)	Missouri	South Dakota	50,200
10.	Castaic (1973)	Castaic Creek	California	44,000

Note: An embankment dam is any dam constructed with excavated material, including earth, rocks, and mining or other industrial waste. (In contrast, gravity, arch, and buttress dams are generally made out of concrete or masonry.) The majority of the world's dams are embankment dams. All dams in this list are earthfill, or formed primarily out of layers of compacted earth.

Largest-Capacity U.S. Reservoirs

Rank	Dam (year completed)	Reservoir	Location	Maximum capacity (thous. acre-feet)
1.	Hoover (1935)	Lake Mead	Nevada-Arizona	30,237
2.	Glen Canyon (1963)	Lake Powell	Arizona	29,875
3.	Garrison (1953)	Lake Sakakawea	North Dakota	26,000
4.	Oahe (1966)	Lake Oahe	South Dakota	23,600
5.	Fort Peck (1957)	Fort Peck Lake	Montana	19,100
6.	Grand Coulee (1941)	Lake Roosevelt	Washington	9,562
7.	Herbert Hoover (1965)	Lake Okeechobee	Florida	8,519
8.	Kentucky (1944)	Kentucky Lake	Kentucky	7,535
9.	Sam Rayburn (1965)	Sam Rayburn Lake	Texas	6,520
10.	Wright Patman (1954)	Wright Patman Lake	Texas	6,505

Note: A reservoir is a body of water created by a dam for storage. This water may serve a single or multiple purposes, such as irrigation, flood reduction, and electricity generation.

Major Dams and Reservoirs of the World

Source: World Register of Dams, Intl. Commission on Large Dams (ICOLD)
Asterisk (*) designates structure is planned or under construction as of mid-2024. NA = Not available.

World's Highest Dams

Rank	Dam	Country	Meters	Feet
1.	*Rogun	Tajikistan	335	1,099
2.	*Shuangjiangkou	China	315	1,033
3.	Jinping 1	China	305	1,001
4.	Nurek	Tajikistan	300	984
5.	*Lianghekou	China	295	968
6.	Xiaowan	China	294	965
7.	Baihetan	China	289	948
8.	Xiluodu	China	286	938
9.	Grande Dixence	Switzerland	285	935
10.	*Bakhtiyari	Iran	275	902
11.	Yusufeli	Turkey	275	902
12.	Enguri	Georgia	272	892
13.	*Diamer-Bhasha	Pakistan	272	892
14.	Wudongde	China	270	886
15.	Vajont	Italy	262	860

World's Largest-Capacity Reservoirs

Rank	Dam	Country	Max. capacity (thous. cubic meters)
1.	Kariba	Zambia/Zimbabwe	180,600,000
2.	Bratsk	Russia	169,000,000
3.	Akosombo	Ghana	150,000,000
4.	Daniel Johnson	Canada	141,851,350
5.	Guri	Venezuela	135,000,000
6.	High Aswan	Egypt	132,000,000
7.	W.A.C. Bennett	Canada	74,300,000
8.	*Grand Ethiopian Renaissance	Ethiopia	74,000,000
9.	Krasnoyarsk	Russia	73,300,000
10.	Zeya	Russia	68,400,000
11.	Robert-Bourassa	Canada	61,400,000
12.	La Grande-3	Canada	59,994,000
13.	Ust-Ilimsk	Russia	59,300,000
14.	Cutarm Creek	Canada	58,595,982
15.	Boguchany	Russia	58,200,000

World's Largest-Capacity Hydroelectric Plants

Rank	Dam	Country	Installed capacity (MW)	Energy generated (GWh/year)
1.	Sanxia (Three Gorges)	China	22,500	98,100
2.	*Baihetan	China	16,000	51,500
3.	Itaipu	Brazil/Paraguay	14,000	98,300
4.	Xiluodu	China	13,860	57,120
5.	Belo Monte	Brazil	11,000	NA
6.	Guri	Venezuela	10,235	53,400
7.	Wudongde	China	10,200	38,910
8.	Tucurui	Brazil	8,370	41,400
9.	Robert-Bourassa	Canada	7,722	37,400
10.	Grand Coulee	U.S.	6,809	21,403
11.	Xiangjiaba	China	6,488	30,747
12.	Grand Ethiopian Renaissance	Ethiopia	6,420	NA
13.	Sayano-Shushenskaya	Russia	6,400	22,800
14.	Longtan	China	6,300	18,710
15.	Krasnoyarsk	Russia	6,000	20,400

Dams by Purpose, Worldwide

	Single-purpose dams		Multi-purpose dams	
Purpose	Number	% distrib. by purpose	Number	% distrib. by purpose
Irrigation	14,537	46.6%	6,590	23.2%
Hydropower	6,082	19.5	4,358	15.3
Water supply	3,388	10.9	4,918	17.3
Flood control	2,502	8.0	5,180	18.2
Recreation	1,524	4.9	3,259	11.5
Fish farming, navigation, tailing, and others	3,134	10.1	4,101	14.4

Note: Based on a survey of 31,167 single-purpose dams and 11,002 multi-purpose dams registered with ICOLD. Percentages may not sum to 100 due to rounding.

Timeline of Selected Architectural Styles and Structures

Asterisk (*) denotes part of a UNESCO World Heritage site as of mid-2024.

Style and period	Location; characteristics; significant examples
Mesopotamian c. 3500-539 BCE	City-states of Sumer, Akkad, Babylon, Assyria (modern-day Iraq). Mud-brick rectangular temples on oval platforms with simple corbel vaults, later ziggurats. Painted terra-cotta mosaics and murals; carved reliefs on columns and walls. **Ziggurat of Nanna**, Ur (Muqayyar, Iraq), ordered by Ur-Nammu, c. 2100 BCE **Anu Ziggurat and White Temple**, Uruk (Warka, Iraq), c. 3000 BCE
Egyptian c. 3000-30 BCE	Along Nile R. Mud-brick and limestone tombs and massive, geometric pyramids, post-and-lintel construction. Highly decorative with colorful hieroglyphics, carvings, columns, obelisks, paintings, and sculpture. ***Stepped Pyramid of Pharaoh Djoser** (Saqqara, Egypt), by Imhotep, c. 2737-2717 BCE ***Great Pyramid of Khufu** (Giza, Egypt), c. 2250 BCE ***Great Temple of Amon-Ra** (Karnak, Egypt), c. 1530-300 BCE ***Mortuary Temple of Queen Hatshepsut**, Deir el-Bahari (Thebes, Egypt), by Senenmut, c. 1479-1458 BCE
Three Dynasties c. 2100-221 BCE	China. Single-level mud-brick or mud-smeared timber structures on earthen platforms with thatched roofs. Later, bracketed wooden-framed structures with brick-tiled floors, roofs with overhanging eaves. **City of Erlitou** (Yanshi, China), c. 1900-1500 BCE

Style and period	Location; characteristics; significant examples
Minoan c. 1800-1450 BCE	Crete. Palaces, tombs in monumental style adapted from Mesopotamia and Egypt. Multilevel stone palaces with large central court, no fortifications. Walls made of doors (*polythyron*); stone porticoes and lintels; wooden ceilings and columns; beehive-shaped tombs (*tholi*). **Palace at Knossos** (Heraklion, Crete, Greece), c. 1700 BCE
Mycenaean c. 1600-1100 BCE	Greece. Adapted Minoan style, with large stone masonry, huge walls, and fortified citadels with complex palaces (*megaron*). ***Treasury of Atreus** (Mycenae, Greece), c. 1250 BCE
Olmec c. 1200-400 BCE	Mexico Gulf Coast. Many religious structures, including stone temple-pyramids centered in cities; also large stone sculptures and mosaic pavement with natural and animistic themes. **Great Pyramid** (La Venta, Mexico), c. 800-400 BCE
Mayan c. 900 BCE-900 CE	Central America. Religious structures with plaster-surfaced stone temple-pyramids with stairs containing tombs. Decorative animistic and geometric relief sculptures, lintels, and stone monuments with hieroglyphics. ***Pyramid of the Magician** (Uxmal, Mexico), c. 700-910 CE ***North Acropolis** (Tikal, Guatemala), c. 200 BCE
Greek c. 750-323 BCE	Greek peninsula, Asia Minor, North Africa, western Mediterranean. Religious, civic buildings in monumental style, inspired by Egypt, based on strict rules of form and human proportion; many ornamental details. Marble and limestone structures (including rectangular temples) with pediment, colonnaded porticoes in diverse regional styles, defined by orders of architecture like Ionic, Doric, Corinthian. Most early buildings with timber supports; solid stone in later temples. ***Parthenon, Acropolis** (Athens, Greece), by Ictinus and Callicrates, 447-436 BCE ***Temple of Zeus** (Olympia, Greece), by Libon of Elis, mid-5th cent. BCE **Mausoleum of Halicarnassus** (Bodrum, Turkey), by Pythis, c. 353 BCE (destroyed) ***Temple of Apollo Epicurius** (Bassae, Greece), by Ictinus, c. 420 BCE
Achaemenid c. 550-334 BCE	Persian Empire (Eastern Mediterranean to Indus R.). Palatial complexes influenced by cultures absorbed by the empire; limestone and mud-brick complexes on raised stone terraces with ornamental stairways, rectangular pillared audience halls with porticoes and corner towers; pleasure gardens (*bâgh*) as focal point of architecture. ***Pasargadae** (Iran), founded by Cyrus II, after 547 BCE ***Persepolis** (Iran), founded by Darius I, around 518 BCE
Roman c. 500 BCE-400 CE	Roman Empire. Civic and religious structures with grandiose limestone brick and concrete construction in systematic, practical layout. Adapted Greek orders in many structures, including circular temples and large covered halls (basilica), but emphasized movement with rounded arches and domes, geometric vaults. ***Pantheon** (Rome, Italy), ordered by Emperor Hadrian, 118-128 CE ***Colosseum** (Rome, Italy), ordered by Emperor Vespasian, 70-82 CE ***Roman Forum** (Rome, Italy), 500s BCE-608 CE
Qin and Han c. 221 BCE-220 CE	China. Massive public works, palaces, tombs, and planned cities; systematic layout and design determined by divination techniques (geomancy). Multistoried timber palace complexes with gardens, courtyards laid along a long hall with a south-north axis for weather; decorative roof with overhanging eaves. ***The Great Wall** (China), ordered by Qin Shi Huang, 220 BCE-c. 1600 CE ***Mausoleum of the First Qin Emperor** (Xianyang [Xi'an], China), c. 210 BCE
Sassanian 226-651	Iran. Mud-brick, mortared rubble, and stone palaces on platforms. Tall, vaulted entry chambers with one open side (*iwans*). Three-aisled hall chambers covered with rudimentary barrel vaults. Parabolic domes abandoned for square courtyards in later Sassanian period. ***Palace of Ardashir I** (Firuzabad, Iran), c. 224 **Taq-i Kisra** [Arch of Khosrau] (Ctesiphon, Iraq), c. 260 or c. 550
Byzantine 330-1453	Byzantine Empire, Italy, Russia. Religious structures with masonry construction based on Roman architecture, many salvaged pieces. Centralized cross-in-square layout, with large central dome supported by vaults. Highly decorative, with iconographic frescoes, glass mosaics. ***Hagia Sophia** (Istanbul, Turkey), by Anthemius and Isidorus, 532-37 ***St. Mark's Basilica** (Venice, Italy), ordered by Domenico Contarini, 1063-94
Sui and Tang 581-906	China. Includes influences from other cultures; geomancy used to enhance harmony and social status. Rectangular, multistory modular timber structures with interlinking corridors; single-eaved roofs with exposed beams. **Daming Palace** (Xi'an, China), 634 (destroyed) ***Hall of the Great Buddha**, Foguang Temple (Mount Wutai, China), ordered rebuilt by Xuan Zhong, 857
Early Islamic (Umayyad) 692-c. 1000	Syria, Middle East, North Africa, southern Spain. Mosques in adapted Sassanian style. Austere exteriors; simple columned halls with minarets and mihrabs (prayer niches), walled courtyards and gardens, onion domes. Highly decorative interiors with patterned marble, mosaics. ***Dome of the Rock** [Qubbat al-Sakhra] (Jerusalem), ordered by Abd al-Malik, 692 ***Great Mosque of Córdoba** (Spain), ordered by Abd al-Rahman I, 784-86
Khmer c. 880-1200s	Indochina. Hindu or Buddhist temple complexes, including brick, later sandstone beehive-shaped shrines with arches atop terraced temple "mountains" symbolizing Mount Meru, Hindu and Buddhist center of the universe, where the gods dwell. Concentric layout of structures mimics the cosmos, relating religious narrative in carved reliefs. ***Angkor Wat** (Cambodia), ordered by Suryavarman II, 12th cent.
Romanesque (Norman) c. 900s-1100s	Western Europe. Churches and monasteries in localized Roman style; many reused material from Roman structures. Austere, heavy, simple masonry construction with thick walls, concealed buttresses, small windows, barrel arches, and vaults. Churches like Roman basilica with arched central nave, lower side aisles, apse, transept formed Latin cross. Monumental art and ornaments with Christian narrative throughout, especially on façade and portals. ***Durham Cathedral** (England, UK), ordered by Bishop William de Saint-Calais, 1093-1133 ***Cathedral, Baptistery, and "Leaning" Tower** (Pisa, Italy), by various architects, begun in 1063, tower not completed until 1372
Gothic c. 1100s-1500s	France, Europe. Cathedrals meant to inspire spirituality with design like Roman basilica: pointed arches and spires that reach toward heavens, skeletal masonry, revealed structure like flying buttresses, ribbed vaults to allow better lighting, large stained-glass windows. **Abbey Church of Saint-Denis** (France), ordered by Abbot Suger, 1135-44 ***Cathedral of Notre-Dame** (Paris, France), ordered by Bishop Maurice de Sully, 1163-1351 ***Cologne Cathedral** (Cologne, Germany), ordered by Archbishop Konrad von Hochstaden, 1248-1880 ***St. Vitus Cathedral** (Prague, Czech Republic), by Matthias of Arras, later Peter Parler, 1344-1929
Yuan and Ming 1279-1644	China. Mongol-influenced timber and some brick structures influenced by geomancy. Emphasized monumental mass in low-lying, sprawling structures with simple rectangular pavilions, great halls, elaborate wooden latticework, carved and painted details. ***Forbidden City** (Beijing, China), ordered by Emperor Yongle, 1406-20

Style and period	Location; characteristics; significant examples
Renaissance 1420s-1520s	Italy. The rebirth or rediscovery of ancient Roman design, grounded in a scholarly approach to architecture. Followed rules of proportion in perspective and symmetry, classical orders, and simple but perfected geometric forms; emphasis on human scale. ***Pazzi Chapel** (Florence, Italy), by Filippo Brunelleschi, 1429-61 ***Palazzo Medici-Riccardi** (Florence, Italy), by Michelozzo di Bartolomeo, 1444-60 ***Tempietto San Pietro** (Rome, Italy), by Donato Bramante, 1502-10 ***Villa Almerico Capra, or La Rotonda** (near Vicenza, Italy), by Andrea Palladio, later Vincenzo Scamozzi, 1566-1610
Mughal 1526-1858	India. Monumental palaces and mosques blending Hindu and Islamic architecture. Sandstone with marble inlay; highly decorative, with semiprecious stones, vegetal and Koranic motifs. Formulaic four-part pleasure gardens (*charbâgh*), exemplified by grounds of Taj Mahal. ***Humayun's Tomb** (Delhi, India), by Sayyid Muhammad, 1562-72 ***Taj Mahal** (Agra, India), ordered by Emperor Shah Jahan, 1631-48
Baroque 1630s-1700s	Italy, later Western Europe. Elaborate and theatrical religious and civic structures, focused on dramatic overall effect. Complex geometric shapes and elaborate sculptures meant to be viewed from many angles. **St. Carlo alle Quattro Fontane** (Rome, Italy), by Francesco Borromini, 1638-41 ***Palace of Versailles** (Versailles, France), royal hunting lodge (built 1631-34) expanded under Louis XIV, 1661-1710 **Church of San Lorenzo** (Turin, Italy), by Guarino Guarini, 1666-79 **Church of St. John of Nepomuk, or Asamkirche** (Munich, Germany), by Cosmas Damian and Egid Quirin Asam, 1733-46
Rococo 1690s-1700s	Europe. Mostly interior, simplified but still fanciful Baroque designs; ornate with natural motifs, gold trim, light and creamy colors, asymmetrical designs, and unusual materials. ***Sanssouci Palace** (Potsdam, Germany), by Georg Wenzeslaus von Knobelsdorff, 1745-47
Neoclassicism 1750-1830	Europe, Americas. Civic, commercial, and religious structures; chaste, non-decorative designs in reaction to Baroque excess. Grounded in Enlightenment-era principles and simple, strict adherence to classic (Greek, Roman, Renaissance) forms and details. Palladian style in England, Federal style in U.S. **Chiswick House** (Chiswick, England, UK), by Richard Boyle, 1725-29 ***Monticello** (Charlottesville, VA), by Thomas Jefferson, 1768-1809
Neo-Gothic 1837-1900s	Britain, U.S. Civic, commercial, and religious structures utilizing Gothic forms in new commercial enterprises like railway stations and hotels. Traditional masonry façade disguised modern structural material like iron and glass. ***Westminster Palace** (London, England, UK), by Charles Barry and A.W.N. Pugin, 1840-47 **Hotel fronting St. Pancras Railway Station** (London, England, UK), by George Gilbert Scott, 1865-71
Arts and Crafts 1850s-1930s	England, U.S. Residential structures made of brick and other indigenous materials with pastoral and traditional elements like gabled roofs. Conceived as a reaction against homogenization of style following the Industrial Revolution. **Red House** (Bexley Heath, England, UK), by Philip Webb, 1859 **Tigbourne Court** (Surrey, England, UK), by Edwin Lutyens, 1898
Beaux-Arts 1870s-1930s	France, U.S. Grandiose, highly decorative style, using a mix of classical forms taught at the École des Beaux-Arts (School of Fine Arts) in Paris: columns, wall projections, elaborate rooftops, high-relief decoration. **Boston Public Library** (Boston, MA), by McKim, Mead, and White, 1888-95 **Grand Central Terminal** (New York, NY), Reed & Stem and Warren & Wetmore, 1903-13
Art Nouveau 1884-1905	Europe (esp. Brussels, Belgium; France). Civic and residential structures using industrial products like metal and glass to mimic natural forms; airy, fluid, and ornate. ***Hôtel Tassel** (Brussels, Belgium), by Victor Horta, 1892-93 **Entrances to Métro (subway)** (Paris, France), by Hector Guimard, 1900
Prairie 1893-1917	U.S. Mostly residences, some civic buildings in adapted Arts and Crafts style. Inspired by American Midwest and small-town values. Frank Lloyd Wright most notable architect of the style. Buildings centered on chimney, with overhanging eaves and horizontal emphasis, long bands of windows. ***Robie House** (Chicago, IL), by Frank Lloyd Wright, 1908-10 **National Farmer's Bank** (Owatonna, MN), by Louis Sullivan, 1906-08
Futurism 1913-14	Italy. Purely theoretical style that produced no actual structures. Emphasized concrete, glass, and steel construction; pure geometric forms and straight lines; and exposed structure and utilities. **La Città Nuova (The New City)** (sketches), by Antonio Sant'Elia, 1913
Constructivism 1914-20s	Russia, Europe. Public buildings based on socialist philosophies. Purely utilitarian industrial design, modern materials. **Rusakov Club** (Moscow, Russia), by Konstantin Melnikov, 1927-28
De Stijl 1917-31	Netherlands. Building and fixtures designed as a complete, sculpture-like piece of art; emphasis on primary colors, simple but asymmetrical geometry. Name is Dutch for "The Style." ***Schröder House** (Utrecht, Netherlands), by Gerrit Thomas Rietveld, 1924
Bauhaus 1919-33	Weimar Republic Germany. Art and design school founded by Walter Gropius with philosophy that the machine is the modern medium. Concrete, glass, and steel construction that united industrial crafts and fine arts with simple geometric forms and colors. ***Bauhaus** (Dessau, Germany), by Walter Gropius, 1925-26
International Style 1920s-70s	Asia, Europe, North America. Reinforced concrete and steel structures, mostly commercial buildings with some residences and civic structures. Post-and-slab construction meant walls no longer supported weight so façades could be continuous strip (ribbon) glass "curtain-walls" with modular interiors. Emphasis on simple forms; glass, marble, and stainless steel; minimal decoration. **Philadelphia Savings Fund Society Building** (Philadelphia, PA), by George Howe and William Lescaze, 1926-32 ***Villa Savoye** (Poissy, France), by Le Corbusier, 1928-31 **Seagram Building** (New York, NY), by Ludwig Mies Van Der Rohe with Philip Johnson, 1954-58
Art Deco 1925-30s	Europe, U.S. Traditional, symmetric, elegant construction like Beaux-Arts whimsically mixed with modern styles like geometric forms and steel or chrome features. **Chrysler Building** (New York, NY), by William van Alen, 1928-30 **Empire State Building** (New York, NY), by Shreve, Lamb & Harmon, 1930-31
Postmodernism 1970s-present	Asia, Europe, North America. Playful reaction against generic, mainstream "orthodox modern architecture," according to Robert Venturi. Token references to traditional architectural elements like pediments or gables on houses; aim to present, Venturi wrote, "old clichés in new settings." **Vanna Venturi House** (Philadelphia, PA), by Robert Venturi, 1962-64 **Portland Building** (Portland, OR), by Michael Graves, 1980-82 **Nara Centennial Hall** (Nara, Japan), by Arata Isozaki, 1992-99

World Population Growth

There were perhaps 50 mil people in the world in 1000 BCE. The United Nations (UN) Population Division estimates a figure of 300 mil for 1 CE. This diagram shows estimated population growth since then.

Although different sources may provide varying numbers, they agree that the world's population began growing more rapidly in the 18th and 19th centuries and increased at an even greater rate in the 20th century. According to the UN, the total population reached 1 bil in 1804; rose to 2 bil 123 years later, in 1927; and went up to 3 bil 33 years after that, in 1960. It reached additional milestones in the years shown in the graph.

The UN put the world population in mid-2024 at 8.2 bil. It projected that the population would continue to grow until it peaks at 10.3 bil people in the mid-2080s before starting to decline gradually. By 2080, the global number of persons age 65 and over would exceed the number of children under age 18. These demographic changes are being driven by factors such as declines in fertility in some of the most populous countries, like China.

1 CE 300 mil
1250 400 mil
1500 500 mil
1804 1 bil
1927 2 bil
1960 3 bil
1975 4 bil
1987 5 bil
1999 6 bil
2011 7 bil
2022 8 bil

Area and Population of the World by Continent, 1950-2050

Source: International Data Base, International Programs Center, U.S. Census Bureau, U.S. Dept. of Commerce; *The World Factbook*, Central Intelligence Agency (CIA)

Continent/ region	Land area (sq mi)	Land area (sq km)	% of Earth's land	Population (midyear) 1950	1975	2000	2024	% of world total, 2024	2050[1]
Asia	11,922,585	30,879,354	21.2	1,437,565,483	2,412,768,719	3,727,396,405	4,736,387,098	58.8	5,265,738,526
Africa	11,533,768	29,872,321	20.5	229,049,683	417,042,317	808,149,205	1,485,428,913	18.4	2,529,555,804
Europe[2]	8,559,255	22,168,368	15.2	547,140,324	678,635,710	731,606,159	742,080,956	9.2	715,078,409
N. America	7,880,737	20,411,014	14.0	166,348,602	239,291,685	313,388,419	380,893,904	4.7	433,053,921
Lat. Amer./Carib.	7,712,209	19,974,529	13.7	165,442,794	320,977,717	521,659,054	666,921,546	8.3	751,989,444
Oceania	3,277,072	8,487,578	5.8	12,476,128	21,181,359	30,808,618	45,523,826	0.6	59,423,135
Antarctica[3]	5,482,651	14,200,000	9.7	NA	NA	NA	NA	NA	NA
World[4]	**56,368,276**	**145,993,164**	**100.0**	**2,558,023,014**	**4,089,897,507**	**6,133,007,860**	**8,057,236,243**	**100.0**	**9,754,839,239**

NA = Not applicable. **Note:** Composition of geographical (continental) regions are as defined by the United Nations. Figures may not add up to totals due to rounding. (1) Projected. (2) Includes all of Russia. (3) Antarctica has no indigenous inhabitants, though people are present at permanent and seasonal research stations. Only an est. 110,039 sq mi are ice free. (4) Total pops. do not include countries for which ests. or projections are not available.

Population of the World's Largest Urban Areas, 1975-2035

Source: *World Urbanization Prospects: The 2018 Revision*, Dept. of Economic and Social Affairs, UN Population Division

Population figures are midyear estimates or projections for urban agglomerations, i.e., whole metropolitan areas comprising an urban center and surrounding settlements of lower density. In 2024, 57.9% of the world's population lived in an urban area. That proportion is expected to increase to an est. 62.5% in 2035.

Data may differ from figures elsewhere in *The World Almanac*. MMA = Major Metropolitan Area.

(ranked by mid-2024 population)

Rank	Urban area, country	Population (thous.) 1975	2000	2024	2035	Rate of change (%) 1975-2000	2000-24	2024-35	Pop. of urban area as % of country's 2024 pop.
1.	Tokyo, Japan	26,615	34,450	37,115	36,014	29.4%	7.7%	–3.0%	29.7%
2.	Delhi, India	4,436	15,692	33,807	43,345	253.7	115.4	28.2	2.3
3.	Shanghai, China	5,658	14,247	29,868	34,341	151.8	109.7	15.0	2.1
4.	Dhaka, Bangladesh	2,221	10,285	23,936	31,234	363.1	132.7	30.5	13.6
5.	São Paulo, Brazil	9,614	17,014	22,807	24,490	77.0	34.0	7.4	10.4
6.	Cairo, Egypt	6,450	13,626	22,624	28,504	111.3	66.0	26.0	20.6
7.	Mexico City, Mexico	10,734	18,457	22,505	25,415	72.0	21.9	12.9	16.1
8.	Beijing, China	4,828	10,285	22,189	25,366	113.0	115.7	14.3	1.5
9.	Mumbai (Bombay), India	7,685	16,147	21,673	27,343	110.1	34.2	26.2	1.5
10.	New York, NY-Newark, NJ, U.S.	15,880	17,813	19,034	20,817	12.2	6.9	9.4	5.6
11.	Kinki MMA (Osaka), Japan	16,298	18,660	18,967	18,346	14.5	1.6	–3.3	15.2
12.	Chongqing, China	2,545	7,863	17,774	20,531	209.0	126.0	15.5	1.2
13.	Karachi, Pakistan	3,989	9,825	17,649	23,128	146.3	79.6	31.0	7.9
14.	Kinshasa, Dem. Rep. of the Congo	1,482	6,140	17,032	26,682	314.4	177.4	56.7	16.8
15.	Lagos, Nigeria	1,890	7,281	16,536	24,419	285.3	127.1	47.7	7.3
16.	Istanbul, Turkey	3,600	8,744	16,047	17,986	142.9	83.5	12.1	18.7
17.	Buenos Aires, Argentina	9,143	12,504	15,618	17,128	36.8	24.9	9.7	33.2
18.	Kolkata (Calcutta), India	8,166	13,097	15,571	19,564	60.4	18.9	25.6	1.1
19.	Manila, Philippines	4,999	9,958	14,942	18,649	99.2	50.1	24.8	12.9
20.	Guangzhou, Guangdong, China	1,698	7,812	14,590	16,741	360.0	86.8	14.7	1.0
21.	Tianjin, China	3,527	6,989	14,471	16,446	98.1	107.1	13.6	1.0
22.	Lahore, Pakistan	2,399	5,576	14,407	19,117	132.5	158.4	32.7	6.5
23.	Bangalore, India	2,111	5,581	14,008	18,066	164.4	151.0	29.0	1.0
24.	Rio de Janeiro, Brazil	7,733	11,307	13,824	14,810	46.2	22.3	7.1	6.3
25.	Shenzhen, China	36	6,550	13,312	15,185	18,327.5	103.2	14.1	0.9
26.	Moscow, Russia	7,623	10,005	12,712	12,823	31.2	27.1	0.9	8.9
27.	Los Angeles-Long Beach-Santa Ana, CA, U.S.	8,926	11,798	12,598	13,778	32.2	6.8	9.4	3.7
28.	Chennai (Madras), India	3,594	6,593	12,054	15,376	83.5	82.8	27.6	0.8
29.	Bogotá, Colombia	3,040	6,329	11,658	12,753	108.2	84.2	9.4	22.6
30.	Jakarta, Indonesia	4,813	8,390	11,436	13,688	74.3	36.3	19.7	4.0

National Rankings by Population, Area, Population Density, 2024

Source: International Data Base (IDB), International Programs Center, U.S. Census Bureau, U.S. Dept. of Commerce; *The World Factbook*, Central Intelligence Agency (CIA)

Pop. figures are for midyear. In mid-2024, the world had an estimated pop. of 8.06 bil, of which China and India each represented one-sixth. (The IDB projected that India's pop. will overtake China's by 2025; the UN Population Division estimated that date occurred in mid-2023.) Pop. density is calculated using land area, which does not include inland water.

Largest Populations

Rank	Country	Population
1.	China[1]	1,416,043,270
2.	India	1,409,128,296
3.	United States	341,963,408
4.	Indonesia	281,562,465
5.	Pakistan	252,363,571
6.	Nigeria	236,747,130
7.	Brazil	220,051,512
8.	Bangladesh	168,697,184
9.	Russia	140,820,810
10.	Mexico	130,739,927

Smallest Populations

Rank	Country	Population
1.	Vatican City[2]	1,000
2.	Nauru	9,892
3.	Tuvalu	11,733
4.	Palau	21,864
5.	Monaco	31,813
6.	San Marino	35,095
7.	Liechtenstein	40,272
8.	Saint Kitts and Nevis	55,133
9.	Dominica	74,661
10.	Marshall Islands	82,011

Largest Land Areas

Rank	Country	Area (sq mi)	Area (sq km)
1.	Russia	6,323,482	16,377,742
2.	China[1]	3,600,947	9,326,410
3.	United States	3,533,269	9,151,125
4.	Canada	3,511,023	9,093,507
5.	Brazil	3,227,096	8,358,140
6.	Australia	2,966,153	7,682,300
7.	India	1,147,956	2,973,193
8.	Argentina	1,056,642	2,736,690
9.	Kazakhstan	1,042,360	2,699,700
10.	Algeria	919,595	2,381,740

Smallest Land Areas

Rank	Country	Area (sq mi)	Area (sq km)
1.	Vatican City	0.17	0.44
2.	Monaco	0.77	2
3.	Nauru	8	21
4.	Tuvalu	10	26
5.	San Marino	24	61
6.	Liechtenstein	62	160
7.	Marshall Islands	70	181
8.	Saint Kitts and Nevis	101	261
9.	Maldives	115	298
10.	Malta	122	316

Most Densely Populated

Rank	Country	Persons per sq mi	Persons per sq km
1.	Monaco	41,197.6	15,906.5
2.	Singapore	22,022.1	8,502.8
3.	Vatican City[2]	5,886.3	2,272.7
4.	Bahrain	5,339.8	2,061.7
5.	Malta	3,850.0	1,486.5
6.	Maldives	3,379.7	1,304.9
7.	Bangladesh	3,356.6	1,296.0
8.	Taiwan	1,894.3	731.4
9.	Barbados	1,831.9	707.3
10.	Mauritius	1,672.0	645.6

Least Densely Populated

Rank	Country	Persons per sq mi	Persons per sq km
1.	Mongolia	5.47	2.11
2.	Namibia	8.82	3.41
3.	Australia	9.02	3.48
4.	Iceland	9.40	3.63
5.	Guyana	10.45	4.03
6.	Suriname	10.74	4.15
7.	Libya	10.84	4.18
8.	Mauritania	10.88	4.20
9.	Canada	11.05	4.27
10.	Botswana	11.20	4.32

(1) Does not include Hong Kong (mid-2024 pop., 7,297,821; area, 414 sq mi) and Macau (644,426; 11 sq mi). (2) 2022 pop. est.

Current Population and Projections for Countries and Other Areas

Source: International Data Base, International Programs Center, U.S. Census Bureau, U.S. Dept. of Commerce; *The World Factbook*, Central Intelligence Agency (CIA)

(midyear figures)

Country/area	2024	2035	2050
Afghanistan	40,121,552	49,971,066	63,197,340
Albania	3,107,100	3,088,040	2,894,358
Algeria	47,022,473	54,222,378	63,881,021
American Samoa	43,895	37,849	31,305
Andorra	85,370	83,961	78,031
Angola	37,202,061	53,282,768	82,021,832
Anguilla	19,416	23,061	27,546
Antigua and Barbuda	102,634	114,077	124,705
Argentina	46,994,384	50,803,301	54,950,409
Armenia	2,976,765	2,813,532	2,521,147
Aruba	125,063	138,571	153,739
Australia	26,768,598	29,791,638	33,374,282
Austria	8,967,982	9,202,329	9,383,858
Azerbaijan	10,650,239	11,096,353	11,362,533
Bahamas, The	410,862	457,965	502,118
Bahrain	1,566,888	1,700,439	1,847,256
Bangladesh	168,697,184	183,161,334	194,343,726
Barbados	304,139	307,710	298,257
Belarus	9,501,451	9,048,412	8,448,423
Belgium	11,977,634	12,539,867	13,095,652
Belize	415,789	481,755	555,669
Benin	14,697,052	20,785,031	32,070,919
Bermuda	72,800	74,001	71,717
Bhutan	884,546	968,448	1,047,471
Bolivia	12,311,974	13,504,069	14,596,934
Bosnia and Herzegovina	3,798,671	3,649,137	3,303,663
Botswana	2,450,668	2,795,948	3,199,855
Brazil	220,051,512	232,129,523	238,435,974
Brunei	491,900	563,881	646,799
Bulgaria	6,782,659	6,315,986	5,740,967
Burkina Faso	23,042,199	29,082,087	36,938,704
Burundi	13,590,102	18,294,904	25,611,635
Cabo Verde	611,014	680,565	745,776
Cambodia	17,063,669	18,651,681	20,202,507
Cameroon	30,966,105	41,067,264	57,310,971
Canada	38,794,813	41,420,185	44,002,894
Cayman Islands	66,653	78,906	93,381
Central African Republic	5,650,957	6,771,878	8,322,885
Chad	19,093,595	26,161,691	37,418,108
Chile	18,664,652	19,631,668	20,126,545
China	1,416,043,270	1,419,797,578	1,361,613,688
Colombia	49,588,357	51,529,656	51,491,975
Comoros	900,141	1,026,481	1,172,195
Congo, Dem. Rep of the	115,403,027	160,911,174	240,710,111
Congo Republic	6,097,665	7,815,317	10,275,163
Cook Islands	7,761	6,328	5,392
Costa Rica	5,265,575	5,677,653	5,975,331
Croatia	4,150,116	3,939,174	3,623,602
Cuba	10,966,038	10,703,968	10,100,436
Curaçao	153,289	155,690	153,245
Cyprus	1,320,525	1,413,331	1,428,212
Czechia	10,837,890	10,760,383	10,693,275
Côte d'Ivoire	29,981,758	37,217,421	46,939,672
Denmark	5,973,136	6,215,716	6,416,507
Djibouti	994,974	1,189,701	1,391,020
Dominica	74,661	73,032	66,443
Dominican Republic	10,815,857	11,645,804	12,344,447
Ecuador	18,309,984	20,154,794	22,041,749
Egypt	111,247,248	127,733,072	150,738,197
El Salvador	6,628,702	6,693,932	6,492,154
Equatorial Guinea	1,795,834	2,399,813	3,052,647
Eritrea	6,343,956	7,353,464	8,921,842

Country/area	2024	2035	2050
Estonia	1,193,791	1,093,594	970,580
Eswatini (Swaziland)	1,138,089	1,216,135	1,309,186
Ethiopia	118,550,298	150,787,873	195,558,207
Faroe Islands	52,933	55,974	58,360
Fiji	951,611	986,402	1,018,845
Finland	5,626,414	5,671,447	5,620,077
France	68,374,591	69,898,077	70,728,538
French Polynesia	303,540	320,833	330,218
Gabon	2,455,105	3,132,314	4,081,893
Gambia, The	2,523,327	3,101,196	3,826,233
Gaza Strip	2,141,643	2,611,485	3,185,102
Georgia	4,900,961	4,737,968	4,619,863
Germany	84,119,100	82,632,717	79,776,607
Ghana	34,589,092	43,079,646	55,437,373
Gibraltar	29,683	29,806	28,946
Greece	10,461,091	10,066,836	9,504,172
Greenland	57,751	56,560	53,424
Grenada	114,621	116,330	116,072
Guam	169,532	168,908	159,508
Guatemala	18,255,216	21,096,354	24,442,800
Guernsey	67,787	68,819	68,777
Guinea	13,986,179	18,812,686	27,517,931
Guinea-Bissau	2,132,325	2,817,191	4,036,411
Guyana	794,099	830,909	843,728
Haiti	11,753,943	13,265,381	14,925,766
Honduras	9,529,188	10,813,479	12,014,761
Hong Kong	7,297,821	7,271,766	6,890,901
Hungary	9,855,745	9,497,398	8,932,065
Iceland	364,036	391,869	417,620
India	1,409,128,296	1,522,819,483	1,622,372,511
Indonesia	281,562,465	301,603,148	318,393,046
Iran	88,386,937	95,163,155	100,972,304
Iraq	42,083,436	51,251,890	63,087,363
Ireland	5,233,461	5,672,192	6,132,190
Isle of Man	92,269	95,321	95,693
Israel	9,402,617	11,082,091	13,325,409
Italy	60,964,931	60,887,498	61,036,680
Jamaica	2,823,713	2,869,074	2,972,457
Japan	123,201,945	116,494,761	106,156,887
Jersey	103,387	107,852	110,111
Jordan	11,174,024	13,207,868	15,735,443
Kazakhstan	20,260,006	22,125,625	25,119,957
Kenya	58,246,378	71,838,265	89,573,347
Kiribati	116,545	128,289	139,289
Korea, North	26,298,666	27,169,227	27,383,844
Korea, South	52,081,799	52,598,115	50,217,135
Kosovo	1,977,093	2,121,219	2,243,316
Kuwait	3,138,355	3,492,016	3,896,539
Kyrgyzstan	6,172,101	6,635,711	7,097,955
Laos	7,953,556	8,934,325	9,920,518
Latvia	1,801,246	1,586,003	1,341,195
Lebanon	5,364,482	5,652,938	5,744,987
Lesotho	2,227,548	2,423,048	2,638,694
Liberia	5,437,249	6,832,525	8,628,813
Libya	7,361,263	8,369,582	9,734,776
Liechtenstein	40,272	42,897	44,924
Lithuania	2,628,186	2,346,636	2,050,440
Luxembourg	671,254	769,014	884,664
Macau	644,426	679,863	697,801
Madagascar	29,452,714	36,418,409	45,355,015
Malawi	21,763,309	27,022,619	33,877,000
Malaysia	34,564,810	37,957,793	41,286,972
Maldives	388,858	416,544	449,604
Mali	21,990,607	29,679,103	41,603,635
Malta	469,730	484,290	490,187
Marshall Islands	82,011	92,725	103,319
Mauritania	4,328,040	5,249,163	6,467,891
Mauritius	1,310,504	1,305,007	1,232,670
Mexico	130,739,927	142,051,813	152,646,592
Micronesia, Federated States of	99,603	90,317	74,899
Moldova	3,599,528	3,372,140	3,049,227
Monaco	31,813	33,636	32,661
Mongolia	3,281,676	3,497,963	3,699,569
Montenegro	599,849	563,539	494,545
Montserrat	5,468	5,707	5,546
Morocco	37,387,585	40,402,356	43,116,499
Mozambique	33,350,954	44,206,049	63,366,021
Myanmar (Burma)	57,527,139	61,366,234	64,228,536
Namibia	2,803,660	3,354,953	4,077,509
Nauru	9,892	10,351	11,329
Nepal	31,122,387	33,250,249	35,274,683
Netherlands	17,772,378	18,328,410	18,603,894
New Caledonia	304,167	339,444	376,851
New Zealand	5,161,211	5,591,053	5,990,813
Nicaragua	6,676,948	7,275,957	7,738,971
Niger	26,342,784	38,971,565	62,099,731
Nigeria	236,747,130	310,623,710	428,438,012
North Macedonia	2,135,622	2,135,941	2,074,629
Northern Mariana Islands	51,118	49,497	45,315
Norway	5,509,733	5,844,962	6,215,043
Oman	3,901,992	4,594,402	5,421,335
Pakistan	252,363,571	303,043,639	366,569,839
Palau	21,864	22,628	22,478
Panama	4,470,241	5,123,749	5,796,506
Papua New Guinea	10,046,233	12,576,047	15,933,221
Paraguay	7,522,549	8,305,805	8,954,539
Peru	32,600,249	35,145,177	37,977,511
Philippines	118,277,063	137,176,759	158,108,572
Poland	38,746,310	35,997,391	32,900,075
Portugal	10,207,177	10,083,359	9,728,863
Puerto Rico	3,019,450	2,646,152	2,163,684
Qatar	2,552,088	2,587,812	2,586,967
Romania	18,148,155	16,854,271	15,560,475
Russia	140,820,810	133,744,190	124,975,435
Rwanda	13,623,302	16,065,002	19,133,170
Saint Barthélemy	7,086	6,997	6,721
Saint Helena, Ascension, and Tristan da Cunha	7,943	7,935	7,569
Saint Kitts and Nevis	55,133	57,569	57,519
Saint Lucia	168,038	171,168	167,817
Saint Martin	32,996	34,033	35,182
Saint Pierre and Miquelon	5,132	4,475	3,685
Saint Vincent and the Grenadines	100,647	98,989	95,383
Samoa	208,853	224,906	246,912
San Marino	35,095	36,771	36,514
São Tomé and Príncipe	223,561	258,415	306,603
Saudi Arabia	36,544,431	42,536,636	47,966,097
Senegal	18,847,519	23,938,019	30,635,314
Serbia	6,652,212	6,238,163	5,692,788
Seychelles	98,187	102,137	101,082
Sierra Leone	9,121,049	11,399,388	14,356,255
Singapore	6,028,459	6,536,522	6,959,346
Sint Maarten	46,215	50,943	54,257
Slovakia	5,563,649	5,457,446	5,182,624
Slovenia	2,097,893	2,059,546	1,983,776
Solomon Islands	726,799	855,336	1,006,932
Somalia	13,017,273	16,987,551	22,655,319
South Africa	60,442,647	66,747,605	73,710,707
South Sudan	12,703,714	17,304,109	23,592,886
Spain	47,280,433	47,798,695	47,250,516
Sri Lanka	21,982,608	22,393,780	22,004,518
Sudan	50,467,278	66,369,914	88,749,624
Suriname	646,758	716,199	784,492
Sweden	10,589,835	11,108,774	11,771,380
Switzerland	8,860,574	9,495,428	10,098,275
Syria	23,865,423	28,091,447	33,355,509
Taiwan	23,595,274	23,481,565	22,132,472
Tajikistan	10,394,063	12,654,917	16,021,762
Tanzania	67,462,121	89,502,233	124,222,573
Thailand	69,920,998	70,086,586	66,768,316
Timor-Leste	1,506,909	1,824,351	2,184,155
Togo	8,917,994	11,447,738	15,344,759
Tonga	104,889	100,169	90,196
Trinidad and Tobago	1,408,966	1,409,512	1,359,882
Tunisia	12,048,847	12,553,077	12,895,172
Turkey (Türkiye)	84,119,531	88,693,414	90,656,580
Turkmenistan	5,744,151	6,216,739	6,627,470
Turks and Caicos Islands	60,439	71,821	86,092
Tuvalu	11,733	12,551	13,341
Uganda	49,283,041	67,953,747	96,972,729
Ukraine	35,661,826	35,633,410	30,945,857
United Arab Emirates	10,032,213	10,965,355	12,429,115
United Kingdom	68,459,055	71,307,950	74,268,354
United States	341,963,408	364,862,145	388,922,201
Uruguay	3,425,330	3,504,442	3,560,420
Uzbekistan	36,520,593	41,151,788	46,455,743
Vanuatu	318,007	370,413	432,719
Vatican City[1]	1,000	NA	NA
Venezuela	31,250,306	34,187,388	36,513,281
Vietnam	105,758,975	114,434,819	121,027,926
Virgin Islands, British	40,102	47,666	56,060
Virgin Islands, U.S.	104,377	96,072	82,348
Wallis and Futuna	15,964	16,126	15,971
West Bank	3,243,369	3,958,281	4,801,797
Yemen	32,140,443	38,207,444	45,693,399
Zambia	20,799,116	27,807,418	38,476,482
Zimbabwe	17,150,352	20,699,038	25,696,160
World[2]	**8,057,236,243**	**8,843,341,278**	**9,754,839,239**

NA = Not available. **Note:** Figures for countries do not include the population of any dependencies listed separately in this table. For example, China's population estimate and projections do not include Hong Kong or Macau. (1) 2022 pop. est. (2) Total projected populations do not include countries for which projections were not available.

Countries Ranked by Gross Domestic Product and Per Capita GDP, 2023

Source: The World Bank

Estimates of gross domestic product (GDP)—the value of all final goods and services that a country produced in a year—were made based on purchasing power parity exchange rates. Per capita GDP is calculated using the estimated population size as of July 1 in a given year. GDP figures are 2023 ests. unless otherwise noted.

GDP (in mil)				Per capita GDP			
Highest		Lowest		Highest		Lowest	
1. China[1]	$34,643,707	1. Tuvalu	$66	1. Luxembourg	$143,341	1. Burundi	$951
2. U.S.	27,360,935	2. Nauru	162	2. Singapore	141,500	2. Central African Republic	1,130
3. India	14,537,384	3. Marshall Islands	315	3. Ireland	127,623	3. Somalia	1,611
4. Russia	6,452,309	4. Palau	316	4. Qatar[2]	121,125	4. Mozambique	1,657
5. Japan	6,251,559	5. Kiribati	470	5. Norway	104,460	5. Congo, Dem. Rep. of	1,671
6. Germany	5,857,856	6. Micronesia, Fed. States	486	6. Switzerland	92,980	6. Niger	1,817
7. Brazil	4,454,930	7. Tonga[2]	750	7. Brunei	86,446	7. Liberia	1,819
8. Indonesia	4,333,084	8. Vanuatu	1,109	8. United Arab Emirates	83,903	8. Sierra Leone	1,847
9. France	4,169,071	9. Dominica	1,285	9. U.S.	81,695	9. Malawi	1,868
10. UK	4,026,241	10. São Tomé and Príncipe	1,406	10. Netherlands	78,215	10. Madagascar	1,875
11. Turkey (Türkiye)	3,767,230	11. Samoa	1,508	11. Iceland	77,567	11. Chad	1,969
12. Italy	3,452,506	12. St. Kitts and Nevis	1,595	12. Denmark	76,688	12. Afghanistan[2]	2,093
13. Mexico	3,288,671	13. St. Vincent and the Grenadines	2,061	13. Austria	73,751	13. Guinea-Bissau	2,630
14. South Korea	2,794,196	14. San Marino[3]	2,218	14. Andorra	71,587	14. Mali	2,726
15. Spain	2,553,108	15. Grenada	2,228	15. Belgium	70,456	15. Burkina Faso	2,727
16. Canada	2,469,314	16. Solomon Islands	2,247	16. Sweden	70,207	16. Lesotho	2,794
17. Egypt	2,120,932	17. Antigua and Barbuda	2,999	17. Germany	69,338	17. Syria[3]	2,915
18. Saudi Arabia	2,031,781	18. Comoros	3,285	18. Australia	69,115	18. Solomon Islands	3,035
19. Australia	1,841,116	19. Seychelles	3,916	19. San Marino[3]	65,718	19. Uganda	3,098
20. Poland	1,814,629	20. St. Lucia	4,529	20. Finland	65,061	20. Ethiopia	3,109

(1) Does not include Hong Kong ($538.7 bil GDP) or Macau ($79.7 bil GDP). (2) 2022 est. (3) 2021 est.

Budget Deficits as Percent of GDP in Selected Countries, 1995-2024

Source: *OECD Economic Outlook*, Organisation for Economic Co-operation and Development (OECD); as of Apr. 24, 2024

Country	1995	2000	2005	2010	2015	2020	2021	2022	2023	2024
Australia	–1.8%	0.9%	2.2%	–4.2%	–1.0%	–11.5%	–4.0%	–1.4%	–0.8%	–1.8%
Austria	–6.1	–2.4	–2.5	–4.4	–1.0	–8.0	–5.8	–3.3	–2.7	–2.8
Belgium	–4.5	–0.1	–2.7	–4.1	–2.4	–9.0	–5.4	–3.6	–4.5	–4.7
Brazil*	NA	–3.3	–3.5	–2.4	–10.2	–13.3	–4.5	–4.5	–8.7	–6.4
Canada	–5.5	2.6	1.6	–4.7	–0.1	–10.9	–2.9	0.1	–0.6	–0.7
China*	–1.0	–2.6	–0.6	–0.4	–1.2	–6.8	–6.4	–6.5	–6.7	–7.5
Colombia	NA	–4.7	–2.5	–0.8	–3.4	–8.8	–7.8	–5.1	–4.2	–5.3
Czechia	–12.4	–3.6	–3.0	–4.2	–0.6	–5.8	–5.1	–3.2	–3.7	–2.3
Denmark	–3.6	1.9	5.0	–2.7	–1.3	0.4	4.1	3.3	3.1	2.5
Estonia	1.0	–0.1	1.1	0.2	0.1	–5.4	–2.5	–1.0	–3.4	–3.2
Finland	–5.9	6.9	2.7	–2.5	–2.4	–5.6	–2.8	–0.4	–2.7	–4.3
France	–5.1	–1.3	–3.5	–7.2	–3.9	–8.9	–6.6	–4.8	–5.5	–5.2
Germany	–9.4	–1.6	–3.3	–4.4	1.0	–4.3	–3.6	–2.5	–2.1	–1.5
Greece	–8.7	–4.0	–6.2	–11.4	–5.9	–9.8	–6.9	–2.5	–1.6	–0.6
Hungary	–8.6	–3.0	–7.8	–4.4	–2.0	–7.6	–7.2	–6.2	–6.7	–4.5
Iceland	–2.9	1.4	5.0	–6.7	–0.3	–8.8	–8.3	–3.9	–2.0	–0.4
India*	–6.5	–9.4	–6.6	–7.0	–6.9	–13.1	–9.5	–9.6	–8.8	–7.9
Ireland	–2.1	4.9	1.6	–32.1	–2.0	–5.0	–1.5	1.7	1.7	1.6
Israel	NA	–0.8	–2.7	–3.7	–1.2	–10.7	–3.4	0.4	–4.1	–6.6
Italy	–7.2	–2.4	–4.1	–4.2	–2.6	–9.4	–8.7	–8.6	–7.4	–4.4
Japan	–4.3	–7.3	–4.4	–9.1	–3.7	–9.1	–6.2	–4.2	–3.9	–3.0
Korea, South	2.8	4.2	1.4	0.9	1.2	–2.7	–0.3	–1.8	–1.8	–1.6
Latvia	–1.4	–2.7	–0.5	–8.6	–1.5	–4.4	–7.2	–4.6	–2.2	–2.9
Lithuania	–1.5	–3.2	–0.3	–6.9	–0.3	–6.5	–1.1	–0.6	–0.8	–2.8
Luxembourg	2.7	5.5	–0.2	–0.3	1.3	–3.4	0.5	–0.3	–1.2	–1.2
Netherlands	–8.7	1.2	–0.5	–5.3	–1.9	–3.7	–2.2	–0.1	–0.3	–1.0
New Zealand	2.4	1.7	4.8	–6.8	0.2	–7.7	–4.1	–3.2	–3.2	–3.7
Norway	3.1	15.0	14.7	10.9	6.0	–2.6	10.3	25.6	16.3	11.3
Poland	–4.3	–4.0	–3.9	–7.5	–2.6	–6.9	–1.8	–3.4	–5.1	–4.3
Portugal	–5.2	–3.2	–6.1	–11.4	–4.4	–5.8	–2.9	–0.3	1.2	0.3
Slovakia	–3.5	–12.6	–2.9	–7.5	–2.7	–5.3	–5.2	–1.7	–4.9	–5.8
Slovenia	–8.1	–3.6	–1.3	–5.6	–2.8	–7.6	–4.6	–3.0	–2.5	–3.1
South Africa*	–3.1	–2.1	–1.3	–3.1	–3.7	–10.1	–6.4	–4.8	–7.2	–5.2
Spain	–6.8	–1.2	1.2	–9.5	–5.3	–10.1	–6.7	–4.7	–3.6	–3.3
Sweden	–7.0	3.1	1.8	–0.1	0.0	–2.8	0.0	1.2	–0.6	–1.1
Switzerland	–1.9	0.3	–0.6	0.4	0.5	–3.1	–0.3	1.2	0.5	0.3
United Kingdom	–5.1	1.3	–2.9	–9.3	–4.6	–13.0	–7.9	–4.6	–5.4	–4.6
United States	–4.7	0.3	–4.5	–12.5	–4.7	–14.8	–11.5	–4.0	–8.0	–7.6
OECD countries	**–5.2**	**–0.9**	**–2.9**	**–8.1**	**–3.1**	**–10.2**	**–7.1**	**–3.3**	**–4.8**	**–4.5**

* = Not an OECD member nation; excluded from OECD country total. NA = Not available.

Gold Reserves of Selected Central Banks and Governments, 1975-2023

Source: *International Financial Statistics*, International Monetary Fund (IMF)
(in mil fine troy ounces)

Year-end	World[1]	Brazil	China[2]	France	Germany[3]	India	IMF	Japan	Russia	Saudi Arabia	Switzer-land	Turkey (Türkiye)	U.S.
1975	1,179.8	1.3	NA	100.9	117.6	7.0	153.4	21.1	NA	3.1	83.2	3.6	274.7
1980	1,152.9	1.9	12.8	81.9	95.2	8.6	103.4	24.2	NA	4.6	83.3	3.8	264.3
1985	1,146.7	3.1	12.7	81.9	95.2	9.4	103.4	24.2	NA	4.6	83.3	3.9	262.7
1990	1,144.2	4.6	12.7	81.9	95.2	10.7	103.4	24.2	NA	4.6	83.3	4.1	261.9
1995	1,114.7	4.6	12.7	81.9	95.2	12.8	103.4	24.2	9.4	4.6	83.3	3.7	261.7
2000	1,067.8	2.1	12.7	97.2	111.5	11.5	103.4	24.5	12.4	4.6	77.8	3.7	261.6
2005	992.9	1.1	19.3	90.9	110.2	11.5	103.4	24.6	12.4	4.6	41.5	3.7	261.6
2008	964.6	1.1	19.3	80.1	109.7	11.5	103.4	24.6	16.7	10.4	33.4	3.7	261.5
2010	991.8	1.1	33.9	78.3	109.3	17.9	90.5	24.6	25.4	10.4	33.4	3.7	261.5
2012	1,018.8	2.2	33.9	78.3	109.0	17.9	90.5	24.6	30.8	10.4	33.4	11.6	261.5
2014	1,037.5	2.2	33.9	78.3	108.8	17.9	90.5	24.6	38.8	10.4	33.4	17.0	261.5
2016	1,080.1	2.2	59.2	78.3	108.6	17.9	90.5	24.6	51.9	10.4	33.4	12.1	261.5
2018	1,100.6	2.2	59.6	78.3	108.3	19.3	90.5	24.6	67.9	10.4	33.4	15.7	261.5
2019	1,118.3	2.2	62.6	78.3	108.2	20.4	90.5	24.6	73.0	10.4	33.4	17.8	261.5
2020	1,134.5	2.2	62.6	78.3	108.1	21.8	90.5	24.6	73.9	10.4	33.4	23.0	261.5
2021	1,141.7	4.2	62.6	78.3	108.0	24.2	90.5	27.2	74.0	10.4	33.4	21.1	261.5
2022	1,140.8	4.2	64.6	78.3	107.9	25.3	90.5	27.2	75.0	10.4	33.4	25.3	261.5
2023	1,156.4	4.2	71.9	78.4	107.8	25.8	90.5	27.2	75.0	10.4	33.4	23.4	261.5

IMF = International Monetary Fund. NA = Not available. (1) Includes countries and international organizations not shown here. (2) Figures are for mainland China only and do not include Hong Kong (0.07 mil oz t in 2023) or Macau. (3) West Germany prior to 1991.

Unemployment Rates in Selected Countries, 1960-2024

Source: *OECD Economic Outlook*, Organisation for Economic Co-operation and Development (OECD); as of Apr. 24, 2024

Year	Brazil*	Canada	France	Germany	Greece	Italy	Japan	South Korea	Mexico	Turkey (Türkiye)	UK	U.S.	OECD countries[1]
1960	NA	6.9%	1.3%	NA	NA	4.0%	1.6%	NA	NA	8.8%	2.8%	5.6%	3.4%
1965	NA	3.9	1.4	NA	NA	3.8	1.2	7.3%	NA	9.1	2.7	4.5	3.1
1970	NA	5.7	2.2	NA	NA	3.8	1.2	4.4	NA	5.7	3.5	5.0	3.2
1975	NA	6.9	3.6	NA	NA	4.1	1.9	4.1	NA	6.9	4.5	8.5	5.0
1980	NA	7.5	5.6	NA	NA	5.4	2.0	5.2	NA	7.5	6.8	7.2	5.4
1985	NA	10.5	9.1	NA	NA	8.3	2.6	4.0	NA	6.6	11.4	7.2	7.3
1990	NA	8.2	8.0	NA	NA	8.8	2.1	2.4	NA	7.5	7.1	5.6	5.7
1995	4.7%	9.5	10.0	8.2%	9.7%	11.3	3.1	2.1	7.9%	7.1	8.6	5.6	7.4
2000	7.2	6.8	8.6	7.9	11.6	10.1	4.7	4.4	3.6	6.0	5.5	4.0	6.2
2005	10.6	6.7	8.9	11.0	10.0	7.7	4.4	3.7	3.6	9.5	4.8	5.1	6.8
2010	8.7	8.1	9.3	6.6	12.7	8.5	5.0	3.7	5.4	11.1	7.9	9.6	8.5
2012	7.4	7.4	9.8	5.1	24.4	10.9	4.3	3.2	5.0	8.4	8.0	8.1	8.1
2014	6.9	7.0	10.3	4.7	26.5	12.7	3.6	3.5	4.8	9.9	6.2	6.2	7.5
2016	11.6	7.0	10.1	3.9	23.5	11.7	3.1	3.7	3.9	10.9	4.9	4.9	6.5
2018	12.4	5.8	9.1	3.2	19.3	10.6	2.4	3.9	3.3	10.9	4.2	3.9	5.5
2020	13.7	9.7	8.1	3.7	16.3	9.3	2.8	4.0	4.4	13.1	4.7	8.1	7.2
2021	13.2	7.5	7.9	3.6	14.7	9.5	2.8	3.6	4.1	12.0	4.6	5.4	6.2
2022	9.3	5.3	7.3	3.1	12.4	8.1	2.6	2.9	3.3	10.5	3.9	3.6	5.0
2023	8.0	5.4	7.3	3.0	11.1	7.6	2.6	2.7	2.8	9.4	4.0	3.6	4.8
2024	7.8	5.9	7.7	3.1	9.8	7.4	2.5	2.9	2.9	9.3	4.5	3.9	5.0

* = Not an OECD member nation; excl. from OECD country total. NA = Not available. **Note:** Labor market data are subject to differences in definitions across countries. Because of changes in methodology, some data may not be fully comparable over time. (1) Total incl. countries not shown here.

Personal Tax Rates in Selected Countries, 2023

Source: *Taxing Wages*, Organisation for Economic Co-operation and Development (OECD)
Rates are averages for a single person without children at the income level of the average full-time worker.
(as % of gross wage earnings before taxes in U.S. dollars with equal purchasing power; ranked by gross wage earnings)

Country	Total payment[1]	Income tax	Employee soc. sec. contribs.	Gross wage earnings
Switzerland	18.6%	12.2%	6.4%	$100,048
Luxembourg	33.2	20.9	12.3	83,741
Norway	28.1	20.2	7.9	82,880
Denmark	36.0	36.0	0.0	82,383
Belgium	39.9	26.0	14.0	81,461
Germany	37.4	17.0	20.5	81,439
Netherlands	27.3	16.4	11.0	78,201
Ireland	28.0	24.0	4.0	77,006
Iceland	27.4	27.3	0.1	76,597
Austria	32.9	15.0	18.0	76,127
Canada	25.6	19.2	6.4	73,102
Australia	24.9	24.9	0.0	70,154
United Kingdom	23.7	14.8	8.9	69,143
United States	24.2	16.6	7.7	67,264
South Korea	16.2	6.8	9.4	66,806
Finland	31.6	21.1	10.5	64,833
France	27.5	16.2	11.3	60,922
Sweden	23.9	16.9	7.0	57,235
Japan	22.6	7.9	14.7	53,673
Italy	27.7	22.1	5.6	52,734
New Zealand	21.1%	21.1%	0.0%	$51,149
Israel	18.8	10.8	8.0	49,235
Spain	22.1	15.6	6.5	48,836
Lithuania	37.8	18.3	19.5	46,124
Turkey (Türkiye)	27.6	12.6	15.0	46,011
Slovenia	34.2	12.1	22.1	45,465
Greece	24.8	10.9	13.9	43,840
Poland	23.6	5.7	17.8	42,696
Portugal	28.6	17.6	11.0	41,048
Hungary	33.5	15.0	18.5	39,916
Czechia	20.0	9.0	11.0	38,122
Estonia	18.9	17.3	1.6	36,052
Latvia	27.1	16.6	10.5	35,043
Slovakia	24.3	10.9	13.4	29,872
Chile	7.1	0.1	7.0	29,325
Costa Rica	10.7	0.0	10.7	27,695
Mexico	11.0	9.6	1.4	16,845
Colombia	0.0	0.0	0.0	16,615
OECD avg.[2]	**24.9**	**15.4**	**9.6**	**56,306**

(1) Income tax and soc. sec. contribs. may not add up to total due to rounding. (2) The 38 countries shown here.

Inflation Rates in Selected Countries, 1975-2023

Source: *International Financial Statistics*, International Monetary Fund (IMF)
(annual average consumer price % change)

Country	1975-80	1980-85	1985-90	1990-95	1995-2000	2000-05	2005-10	2010-15	2015-19	2019-20	2020-21	2021-22	2022-23
Brazil	NA	151.1%	1,076.6%	1,090.8%	7.6%	8.7%	4.7%	6.7%	4.9%	3.2%	8.3%	9.3%	4.6%
Canada	8.8%	7.5	4.5	2.3	1.7	2.3	1.7	1.7	1.8	0.7	3.4	6.8	3.9
China[1]	NA	NA	11.8[2]	13.1	1.9	1.3	3.0	2.8	2.1	2.4	1.0	2.0	0.2
France	10.5	9.7	3.0	2.2	1.2	1.9	1.5	1.1	1.0	0.5	1.6	5.2	4.9
Germany	4.0	3.9	1.4	3.6	1.3	1.5	1.6	1.4	1.3	0.1	3.1	6.9	5.9
Greece	16.3	20.7	17.4	13.9	4.9	3.4	3.2	0.2	0.3	–1.2	1.2	9.6	3.5
India	4.2	9.3	8.6	10.5	7.6	4.0	8.7	8.0	4.0	6.6	5.1	6.7	5.6
Japan	6.6	2.8	1.4	1.4	0.3	–0.4	–0.1	0.7	0.5	–0.02	–0.2	2.5	3.3
Pakistan	8.7	7.2	6.8	11.2	7.3	5.2	12.5	7.8	5.9	9.7	9.5	19.9	30.8
Turkey (Türkiye)	52.6	38.3	53.2	79.3	74.1	27.5	8.7	7.9	12.6	12.3	19.6	72.3	53.9
United Kingdom	14.4	7.2	5.1	3.9	2.0	1.6	2.6	2.1	1.9	1.0	2.5	7.9	6.8
United States	8.9	5.5	4.0	3.1	2.5	2.6	2.2	1.7	1.9	1.2	4.7	8.0	4.1

NA = Not available. (1) Figures for mainland China only and do not include Hong Kong (2.1% in 2022-23) or Macau (1.0% in 2021-22). (2) For 1986-90.

Number of Days Off Work Per Year in Selected Countries

Source: Organisation for Economic Co-operation and Development (OECD); Center for Economic and Policy Research

Entitlements are generally for full-time, full-year private-sector employees working a five-day week who have been with their current employer for at least one year. The U.S. is the only OECD country without a national statute that entitles workers to a minimum number of days off per year.

Country	Paid days off[1]	Public holidays[2]	Total minimum days off
Australia	20	8	28
Austria	25	13	38
Belgium	20	10	30
Bulgaria	20	12	32
Canada	10	9	19
Chile	15	5	20
Colombia	15	18	33
Costa Rica	10	11	21
Croatia	20	13	33
Cyprus	20	14-17	34-37
Czechia	20	13	33
Denmark	25	11	36
Estonia	20	11	31
Finland	24	11	35
France	25	11	36
Germany	20	10-14	30-34
Greece	20	11	31
Hungary	20	11	31
Iceland	24	12	36
Ireland	20	9	29
Israel	16	9	25
Italy	20	12	32
Japan	10	16	26
Korea, South	15	15	30
Latvia	20	15	35
Lithuania	20	15	35
Luxembourg	26	10	36
Malta	24	14	38
Mexico	6	8	14
Netherlands	20	9	29
New Zealand	20	11	31
Norway	21	10	31
Poland	20	13	33
Portugal	22	13	35
Romania	20	13	33
Slovakia	20	15	35
Slovenia	20	13	33
Spain	22	14	36
Sweden	25	11	36
Switzerland	20	9-13	29
Turkey (Türkiye)	14	15	29
UK	28	8	28
U.S.	0	NA[3]	0

NA = Not applicable. (1) Statutory minimum. (2) Generally set at the national or federal level. May vary at the state level. In some countries, including the U.S., public holidays do not have to be given as paid leave. (3) The government designates 11 federal holidays per year (Inauguration Day is also a holiday for federal employees in the Washington, DC, metro area). Private sector employers decide how much paid leave to offer.

International Migrants by Destination and Origin, 2000, 2020

Source: *International Migrant Stock 2020*, Dept. of Economic and Social Affairs, UN Population Division
(numbers in thousands)

Places hosting the most international migrants

	2020 Country/terr.	2020 Migrants	2000 Country/terr.	2000 Migrants
1.	U.S.	50,632.8	U.S.	34,814.1
2.	Germany	15,762.5	Russia	11,900.3
3.	Saudi Arabia	13,454.8	Germany	8,992.6
4.	Russia	11,636.9	India	6,411.3
5.	UK	9,359.6	France	6,278.7
6.	UAE	8,716.3	Ukraine	5,527.1
7.	France	8,524.9	Canada	5,511.9
8.	Canada	8,049.3	Saudi Arabia	5,263.4
9.	Australia	7,685.9	UK	4,730.2
10.	Spain	6,842.2	Australia	4,386.3
11.	Italy	6,387.0	Pakistan	4,181.9
12.	Turkey (Türkiye)	6,052.7	Kazakhstan	2,874.2
13.	Ukraine	4,997.4	Hong Kong	2,669.1
14.	India	4,878.7	Iran	2,476.5
15.	Kazakhstan	3,732.1	UAE	2,447.0
16.	Thailand	3,632.5	Côte d'Ivoire	2,163.6
17.	Malaysia	3,476.6	Italy	2,121.7
18.	Jordan	3,457.7	Jordan	1,927.8
19.	Pakistan	3,276.6	Israel	1,851.3
20.	Kuwait	3,110.2	Japan	1,686.4
21.	Hong Kong	2,962.5	Spain	1,657.3
22.	South Africa	2,860.5	Switzerland	1,570.8
23.	Iran	2,797.2	Netherlands	1,556.3
24.	Japan	2,771.0	Argentina	1,540.2
25.	Côte d'Ivoire	2,564.9	Malaysia	1,463.6
26.	Singapore	2,523.6	Uzbekistan	1,406.5
27.	Switzerland	2,491.2	Singapore	1,351.7
28.	Oman	2,372.8	Turkey (Türkiye)	1,281.0
29.	Netherlands	2,358.3	Belgium	1,268.4
30.	Argentina	2,281.7	Thailand	1,257.8
	World	**280,598.1**	**World**	**173,230.6**

(1) Not incl. Hong Kong or Macau.

Places of origin with the largest diaspora populations

	2020 Country/terr.	2020 Migrants	2000 Country/terr.	2000 Migrants
1.	India	17,869.5	Russia	10,664.8
2.	Mexico	11,185.7	Mexico	9,562.9
3.	Russia	10,756.7	India	7,928.1
4.	China[1]	10,461.2	China[1]	5,884.9
5.	Syria	8,457.2	Ukraine	5,596.5
6.	Bangladesh	7,401.8	Bangladesh	5,441.1
7.	Pakistan	6,328.4	Afghanistan	4,750.7
8.	Ukraine	6,139.1	UK	3,860.0
9.	Philippines	6,094.3	Kazakhstan	3,554.5
10.	Afghanistan	5,853.8	Pakistan	3,406.4
11.	Venezuela	5,415.3	Germany	3,235.2
12.	Poland	4,825.1	Italy	3,067.5
13.	UK	4,732.5	Philippines	3,062.7
14.	Indonesia	4,601.4	Turkey (Türkiye)	2,847.3
15.	Kazakhstan	4,203.9	Palestine	2,767.3
16.	Palestine	4,022.8	Indonesia	2,415.1
17.	Romania	3,987.1	Vietnam	2,158.5
18.	Germany	3,855.3	Morocco	2,077.0
19.	Myanmar	3,711.8	Poland	2,047.6
20.	Egypt	3,610.5	Portugal	1,993.8
21.	Turkey (Türkiye)	3,411.4	U.S.	1,979.3
22.	Vietnam	3,392.0	South Korea	1,875.4
23.	Morocco	3,262.2	Egypt	1,708.3
24.	Italy	3,258.8	Belarus	1,685.6
25.	Colombia	3,024.3	Azerbaijan	1,630.6
26.	U.S.	2,996.2	Puerto Rico	1,600.1
27.	Nepal	2,599.7	Uzbekistan	1,576.0
28.	South Sudan	2,575.9	France	1,555.4
29.	France	2,341.9	Bosnia and Herzegovina	1,496.7
30.	South Korea	2,204.6	Colombia	1,433.9
	World	**280,598.1**	**World**	**173,230.6**

Refugees and Other Populations of Concern, 2014-23

Source: *UNHCR Global Trends*, United Nations High Commissioner for Refugees (UNHCR)

Refugees are persons recognized under the 1951 UN Refugee Convention/1967 Protocol, the 1969 OAU (Org. of African Unity) Refugee Convention, the refugee definition in the 1984 Cartagena Declaration as incorporated into national laws, those recognized in accordance with the UNHCR Statute, and persons granted or receiving protection. The UNHCR also extends assistance to internally displaced persons (IDPs), although they legally remain under their home country's protection. Stateless persons are not considered nationals under any state under the operation of its laws. Others of concern comprises persons who do not necessarily belong in any one category. All data are provisional; population as of year-end.

Category	2014	2016	2018	2020	2021	2022	2023	% change, 2022-23
Refugees	14,384,289	17,184,286	20,359,553	20,661,846	21,327,285	29,429,078	31,637,408	7.5%
Asylum-seekers	1,794,704	2,729,521	3,501,629	4,184,926	4,616,135	5,442,319	6,858,499	26.0
Other people in need of intl. protection[1]	NA	NA	2,592,947	3,862,102	4,406,432	5,217,456	5,755,363	10.3
Returned refugees[2]	126,767	552,219	519,321	250,951	429,234	1,356,261	1,052,074	–22.4
IDPs[3]	32,274,619	36,627,127	41,425,168	48,557,439	51,322,623	57,321,197	63,251,367	10.3
Returned IDPs[2]	1,822,591	6,511,144	2,312,926	3,184,118	5,265,622	8,324,166	5,092,064	–38.8
Stateless persons	3,492,255	3,242,206	3,851,981	4,179,331	4,338,192	4,428,314	4,358,188	–1.6
Others of concern[1]	1,052,746	803,084	1,182,756	3,939,756	4,223,095	6,008,804	5,945,550	–1.1
Total	**54,947,971**	**67,649,587**	**75,746,281**	**88,820,469**	**95,928,618**	**117,527,595**	**123,950,513**	**5.5**

NA = Value is zero or not available. (1) Other people in need of intl. protection are those who have not been reported under other categories but who likely need international protection. Prior to 2018, they were included among Others of concern. (2) Persons who have returned to their place of origin in that calendar year. (3) Conflict-generated only, of concern to UNHCR.

Refugees and People in a Refugee-Like Situation, 2023

Source: *UNHCR Global Trends*, United Nations High Commissioner for Refugees (UNHCR)

Refugees are persons recognized under the 1951 UN Refugee Convention/1967 Protocol, 1969 OAU (Org. of African Unity) Refugee Convention, the refugee definition in the 1984 Cartagena Declaration as incorporated into national laws, those recognized in accordance with the UNHCR Statute, and persons granted/receiving protection. Persons in a refugee-like situation have not yet had their status ascertained. Only countries hosting 100,000 or more refugees/people in a refugee-like situation are shown; of those countries, only places originating 10,000 or more persons are given, in decreasing order. Data are provisional and as of year-end.

Place of asylum	Origin of most refugees (excl. asylum-seekers with pending cases)	Number
Africa		**8,226,204**
Cameroon	Central African Republic, Nigeria	485,285
Chad	Sudan, Central African Republic, Cameroon, Nigeria	1,100,921
Congo, Dem. Rep. of the	Central African Republic, Rwanda, South Sudan, Burundi	523,392
Egypt	Syria, Sudan, South Sudan, Eritrea	240,507
Ethiopia	South Sudan, Somalia, Eritrea, Sudan	979,846
Kenya	Somalia, South Sudan, Dem. Rep. of the Congo, Ethiopia	538,899
Mauritania	Mali	112,549
Niger	Nigeria, Mali	269,996
Rwanda	Dem. Rep. of the Congo, Burundi	115,643
South Sudan	Sudan, Dem. Rep. of the Congo	381,236
Sudan	South Sudan, Eritrea, Ethiopia, Syria, Central African Republic	922,474
Tanzania	Burundi, Dem. Rep. of the Congo	188,953
Uganda	South Sudan, Dem. Rep. of the Congo, Somalia, Burundi, Eritrea, Rwanda, Sudan	1,577,498
Asia		**12,688,667**
Armenia	Azerbaijan	150,080
Bangladesh	Myanmar (Burma)	971,984
India	Sri Lanka, Myanmar (Burma), China, Afghanistan	252,867
Iran	Afghanistan, Iraq	3,764,517
Iraq	Syria	286,480
Jordan	Syria, Iraq	684,066
Lebanon	Syria	788,472
Malaysia	Myanmar (Burma)	135,872
Pakistan	Afghanistan	1,988,231
Turkey (Türkiye)	Syria, Iraq, Afghanistan	3,251,127
Europe		**9,589,094**
Austria	Syria, Ukraine, Afghanistan	257,811
Belgium	Ukraine, various/unknown, Syria	167,831
Czechia	Ukraine	377,120
France	Afghanistan, Ukraine, Syria, Dem. Rep. of the Congo, Russia, Sri Lanka, Sudan, Guinea, Turkey (Türkiye), Serbia-Kosovo, Côte d'Ivoire, Iraq, Somalia, Eritrea, China, Albania, Cambodia, Bangladesh	664,366
Germany	Ukraine, Syria, Afghanistan, Iraq, Eritrea, Iran, Turkey (Türkiye), various/unknown, Somalia, Russia, stateless[2], Nigeria	2,593,007
Greece	Syria, Afghanistan, Ukraine, Iraq, Palestinian[1], various/unknown	192,384
Ireland	Ukraine	113,902
Italy	Ukraine, Nigeria, Afghanistan, Pakistan, Mali	298,296
Moldova	Ukraine	120,947
Netherlands	Ukraine, Syria, Eritrea, Turkey (Türkiye)	237,767
Norway	Ukraine, Syria	103,606
Poland	Ukraine	971,478
Russia	Ukraine	1,230,131
Slovakia	Ukraine	126,866
Spain	Ukraine, Venezuela, Syria	385,701
Sweden	Syria, Ukraine, Afghanistan, Eritrea, stateless[2]	237,632
Switzerland	Ukraine, Eritrea, Syria, Afghanistan, Turkey (Türkiye)	192,507
United Kingdom	Ukraine, Afghanistan, Iran, Eritrea, Syria, Sudan, Iraq	448,620
Latin America		**503,797**
Brazil	Venezuela, Haiti	235,765
Mexico	Honduras, Venezuela, El Salvador	124,784
North America and the Caribbean		**582,769**
Canada	Ukraine	169,448
United States	China, El Salvador, Afghanistan, Guatemala, Venezuela, Honduras, Haiti, India, Mexico, Egypt	409,202
Oceania		**46,877**
Total		**31,637,408**

(1) Palestinians under the UNHCR mandate only. (2) Persons not considered nationals by any state under the operation of its laws.

Internally Displaced Persons, 2023

Source: Internal Displacement Monitoring Centre, Norwegian Refugee Council

Internally displaced persons (IDPs) are people who have been forced to move due to conflict or natural disasters but who have not crossed into another country. As such, they are not protected by international refugee law and legally remain under the protection of their home country. Estimates shown are of those displaced by conflict and violence only as of year end; they may comprise only registered IDPs or those displaced from a certain area of a country.

Country/territory	Number	Country/territory	Number	Country/territory	Number
Abyei Area[1]	42,000	Honduras	101,000	Palestine[2]	1,710,000
Afghanistan	4,187,000	India	613,000	Papua New Guinea	87,000
Armenia	7,600	Indonesia	55,000	Peru	75,000
Azerbaijan	658,000	Iraq	1,124,000	Philippines	113,000
Bangladesh	426,000	Israel	200,000	Russia	60,000
Benin	8,800	Kazakhstan	120	Senegal	8,400
Bosnia and Herzegovina	91,000	Kenya	40,000	Serbia	194,000
Brazil	16,000	Kosovo	16,000	Sierra Leone	3,000
Burkina Faso	2,063,000	Kyrgyzstan	4,000	Solomon Islands	1,000
Burundi	8,100	Lebanon	74,000	Somalia	3,862,000
Cameroon	1,044,000	Libya	119,000	South Africa	620
Central African Republic	512,000	Madagascar	2,800	South Sudan	1,121,000
Chad	452,000	Mali	344,000	Sri Lanka	12,000
Colombia	5,077,000	Mexico	392,000	Sudan	9,053,000
Congo, Dem. Rep. of	6,734,000	Mozambique	592,000	Syria	7,248,000
Cyprus	248,000	Myanmar (Burma)	2,625,000	Thailand	41,000
El Salvador	49,000	New Caledonia (France)	150	Togo	18,000
Ethiopia	2,852,000	Nicaragua	1,300	Turkey (Türkiye)	1,099,000
Gambia, The	5,700	Niger	347,000	Uganda	4,800
Georgia	311,000	Nigeria	3,340,000	Ukraine	3,689,000
Ghana	3,800	North Macedonia	110	Yemen	4,516,000
Guatemala	242,000	Pakistan	23,000	**Total**	**68.3 mil**
Haiti	311,000				

(1) Disputed territory between Sudan and South Sudan. (2) In the West Bank, East Jerusalem, and Gaza.

Countries With Highest Mortality Rates by Selected Causes of Death

Source: *World Health Statistics 2024*, World Health Organization (WHO)
(per 100,000 live births or 100,000 population)

Rank	Country/area	Maternal mortality ratio, 2020[1]	Rank	Country/area	Suicide mortality rate, 2021	Rank	Country/area	Mortality rate due to homicide, 2021
1.	South Sudan	1,223	1.	Lesotho	30.4	1.	El Salvador	94.3
2.	Chad	1,063	2.	South Korea	27.5	2.	Honduras	77.1
3.	Nigeria	1,047	3.	Eswatini	27.5	3.	Venezuela	62.8
4.	Central African Rep.	835	4.	Guyana	25.1	4.	Jamaica	51.9
5.	Guinea-Bissau	725	5.	Uruguay	24.7	5.	Bahamas, The	43.9
6.	Liberia	652	6.	Lithuania	22.3	6.	Lesotho	39.8
7.	Somalia	621	7.	South Africa	22.3	7.	Belize	38.5
8.	Afghanistan	620	8.	Suriname	22.2	8.	Trinidad and Tobago	37.3
9.	Lesotho	566	9.	Russia	21.4	9.	Colombia	35.6
10.	Guinea	553	10.	Ukraine	21.0	10.	St. Vincent and the Grenadines	34.6
11.	Congo, Dem. Rep. of	547	11.	Micronesia, Fed. States	20.3	11.	South Africa	32.8
12.	Kenya	530	12.	Solomon Islands	19.1	12.	Brazil	32.5
13.	Benin	523	13.	Slovenia	18.9	13.	Mexico	28.5
14.	Burundi	494	14.	Mongolia	18.5	14.	Guatemala	26.2
15.	Côte d'Ivoire	480	15.	Belgium	18.4	15.	Puerto Rico	23.5
16.	Mauritania	464	16.	Japan	17.5	16.	Haiti	20.9
17.	Gambia, The	458	17.	Zimbabwe	17.4	17.	Panama	20.2
18.	Sierra Leone	443	18.	Kiribati	17.2	18.	St. Lucia	20.1
19.	Niger	441	19.	France	16.6	19.	Dominican Rep.	19.7
20.	Mali	440	20.	Hungary	16.5	20.	Central African Rep.	19.0
	Global	**223**		**Global**	**9.1**		**Global**	**6.1**

(1) Ranking excl. some countries with small pops.

Global HIV/AIDS Status, 2023

Source: HIV Justice Network, Joint United Nations Programme on HIV/AIDS (UNAIDS)

The annual number of AIDS-related deaths has dropped approximately 69% between 2004—when the number of such deaths reached a peak of 2.1 million—and 2023. The number of new infections each year has also decreased (60%), from a high of 3.3 million in 1995 to 1.3 million in 2023. The risk of HIV infection remained high and access to services was inadequate for what UNAIDS considers key population groups. Median HIV prevalence in the adult population (ages 15-49) worldwide was 0.8% in 2023, but median prevalence was higher in certain groups because of marginalization, discrimination, or even criminalization: people in prisons (1.3%), sex workers (3%), people who inject drugs (5%), gay men and other men who have sex with men (7.7%), and transgender persons (9.2%). In 2023, about 77% of all people living with HIV were accessing antiretroviral therapy. Laws criminalizing nondisclosure, exposure, or transmission of HIV existed in 96 countries; 34 U.S. states criminalized actions taken by people with HIV through HIV- or STD-specific laws.

An estimated $562.6 billion was spent on the HIV/AIDS epidemic in 2000-15 according to a study published in *The Lancet* in 2018. At year-end 2023, $19.8 billion (in constant 2019 U.S. dollars) was available to low- and middle-income countries in responding to AIDS, short of the $29.3 billion UNAIDS estimated would be needed in 2025 to get on track to end AIDS as a public health threat.

Current and New HIV/AIDS Cases and Deaths by Region, 2023

Source: Joint United Nations Programme on HIV/AIDS (UNAIDS)

Region	Number living with HIV	Percent of world total[1]	Number newly infected with HIV	AIDS-related deaths
Asia and the Pacific	6,700,000	16.8%	300,000	150,000
Caribbean	340,000	0.9	15,000	5,100
Eastern and Southern Africa	20,800,000	52.1	450,000	260,000
Eastern Europe and Central Asia	2,100,000	5.3	140,000	44,000
Latin America	2,300,000	5.8	120,000	30,000
Middle East and North Africa	210,000	0.5	23,000	6,200
Western and Central Africa	5,100,000	12.8	190,000	130,000
Western and Central Europe and North America[2]	2,300,000	5.8	56,000	13,000
World[3]	**39,900,000**	**100.0**	**1,300,000**	**630,000**

(1) Population within a region living with HIV as a percentage of population worldwide living with HIV. (2) Numbers do not include estimates for children (aged 0-14 years). (3) Figures may not add up to totals because of rounding.

Drinking Water, Sanitation, and Hygiene, 2022

Source: WHO/UNICEF Joint Monitoring Programme for Water Supply, Sanitation, and Hygiene (JMP)

In 2022, an estimated 91.2% of the world's population had access to at least basic drinking water services, up from 82% in 2000. A gap remained, however, between coverage in urban (96.6%) and rural areas (84.0%). Having basic drinking water service means access to an off-premise improved water source, collecting water from which takes up to 30 min. roundtrip. As of the same year, 80.8% of people worldwide, compared to 56% in 2000, used at least basic sanitation services; 11.0% of the rural population and <1% of the urban population still practiced open defecation. Those without access to improved sanitation facilities, which are designed to prevent contact with human waste, are at increased risk of contracting a variety of infectious and parasitic diseases such as diarrhea, malaria, and hepatitis A.

High-income countries had near-universal (99% or greater) access to at least basic water and sanitation services in 2022. In comparison, while 97.1% of the population of Russia (upper middle income) had access to at least basic drinking water services, only 89.4% had access to at least basic sanitation services. In China (also upper middle income), the figures were 97.6% and 95.9%, respectively.

In 2022, only 75.2% of the world population had access to basic hygiene services at home, specifically a basic handwashing facility with soap and water available.

Lowest Access to Basic Drinking Water Services, 2022

Source: WHO/UNICEF Joint Monitoring Programme for Water Supply, Sanitation, and Hygiene (JMP)

A person who spends up to 30 min. roundtrip collecting water from an off-premise improved water source is said to have basic access to drinking water. Improved water sources protect from outside contamination and include piped water, boreholes or tubewells, dug wells, rainwater, and packaged or delivered water.

(ranked by % of total pop. with at least basic access)

Rank	Country/area	% of pop. with access: Total	Rural	Urban
1.	Dem. Rep. of the Congo	35.1%	13.8%	59.3%
2.	Central African Republic	36.3	27.4	48.1
3.	South Sudan	41.2	33.6	70.0
4.	Niger	48.9	40.9	88.3
5.	Burkina Faso	49.5	34.8	80.9
6.	Papua New Guinea	50.2	44.5	86.9
7.	Ethiopia	51.5	42.2	83.2
8.	Eritrea[1]	51.8	27.8	89.7
9.	Chad	52.0	43.8	77.9
10.	Madagascar	53.5	36.0	79.8
11.	Angola	57.7	27.8	71.7
12.	Somalia	58.3	38.6	80.1
13.	Uganda	59.3	51.8	80.3
14.	Tanzania	60.8	49.0	81.1
15.	Yemen	61.8	51.8	77.2
16.	Guinea-Bissau	61.8%	52.5%	73.1%
17.	Zimbabwe	62.3	47.7	92.8
18.	Burundi	62.4	57.7	90.7
19.	Kenya	62.9	53.3	86.4
20.	Mozambique	63.2	48.3	87.3
	Australia and New Zealand	>99.0	>99.0	>99.0
	Central and Southern Asia	93.3	91.7	96.0
	Eastern and South-Eastern Asia	96.7	93.9	98.4
	Europe and Northern America	98.9	97.3	>99.0
	Latin America and the Caribbean	97.6	91.6	>99.0
	Northern Africa and Western Asia	91.9	84.4	96.3
	Oceania	59.9	50.9	92.8
	Sub-Saharan Africa	65.0	50.1	85.3
	World	**91.2**	**84.0**	**96.6**

(1) 2016 ests.

Lowest Access to Basic Sanitation Services, 2022

Source: WHO/UNICEF Joint Monitoring Programme for Water Supply, Sanitation, and Hygiene (JMP)

Improved sanitation facilities are those designed to hygienically prevent human contact with feces and urine, including sewer or septic system connections, ventilated improved pit latrines, and composting toilets, and are not shared with other households. If human waste is not safely managed on- or off-site, then access to sanitation services is considered basic.

(ranked by % of total pop. with at least basic access)

Rank	Country/area	% of pop. with access: Total	Rural	Urban
1.	Ethiopia	9.3%	5.5%	22.3%
2.	Eritrea[1]	11.9	5.6	22.0
3.	Chad	12.9	4.5	39.5
4.	Central African Republic	13.8	5.7	24.5
5.	Madagascar	14.8	10.2	21.6
6.	South Sudan	16.1	9.3	41.8
7.	Dem. Rep. of the Congo	16.2	11.2	21.8
8.	Niger	16.4	9.0	52.8
9.	Togo	19.2	9.1	32.1
10.	Papua New Guinea	19.3	14.7	48.8
11.	Benin	19.5	9.6	29.5
12.	Congo Republic[2]	20.6	6.3	27.2
13.	Uganda	21.0	17.9	29.9
14.	Liberia	22.5	9.2	34.3
15.	Sierra Leone	22.9	13.9	34.5
16.	Burkina Faso	24.8%	16.6%	42.2%
17.	Guinea-Bissau	27.8	16.2	42.1
18.	Ghana	28.6	21.4	33.7
19.	Tanzania	30.6	21.3	46.8
20.	Guinea	31.3	21.7	47.0
	Australia and New Zealand	>99.0	NA	NA
	Central and Southern Asia	76.9	73.2	83.0
	Eastern and South-Eastern Asia	93.8	89.7	96.4
	Europe and Northern America	97.6	93.8	98.7
	Latin America and the Caribbean	89.5	74.6	93.3
	Northern Africa and Western Asia	92.9	86.4	96.5
	Oceania	33.3	22.9	69.0
	Sub-Saharan Africa	34.7	24.3	48.7
	World	**80.8**	**70.1**	**88.9**

NA = Not available. (1) 2016 ests. (2) 2021 ests.

Foreign Development Aid Donors, 2021-23

Source: Development Assistance Committee (DAC), Organisation for Economic Co-operation and Development (OECD)

The amount of official development assistance (ODA), in the form of grants or loans, each DAC member country disbursed to developing countries is given here. Net ODA are disbursements less repayments on earlier loans. The OECD uses the ODA grant equivalent to better reflect donor effort, with more generous loans having a higher ODA value.

(ranked by size of ODA grant equivalent as % of 2023 gross national income [GNI]; 2023 figures are prelim.)

Rank	Donor	ODA as % of GNI 2023	Net ODA in mil of current U.S. dollars 2021	2022	2023
1.	Norway	1.09%	$4,673.0	$5,161.0	$5,292.9
2.	Luxembourg	0.99	539.4	530.1	580.1
3.	Sweden	0.91	5,934.2	5,458.0	5,466.2
4.	Germany	0.79	32,455.6	36,444.7	35,191.7
5.	Denmark	0.74	2,913.7	2,764.3	3,014.1
6.	Ireland	0.67	1,154.9	2,410.2	2,815.2
7.	Netherlands	0.66	5,265.9	6,450.2	7,281.4
8.	Switzerland	0.60	3,911.4	4,496.4	5,141.3
9.	UK	0.58	16,277.8	15,761.3	18,661.7
10.	Finland	0.52	1,497.6	1,615.1	1,626.8
11.	France	0.50	16,721.9	17,558.9	16,679.3
12.	Belgium	0.44	2,649.2	2,687.5	2,885.7
	Japan	0.44	15,767.0	16,747.4	18,662.4
14.	Austria	0.38	1,492.2	1,836.1	1,826.5
	Canada	0.38	6,257.7	9,274.1	9,197.2
16.	Iceland	0.36	70.8	94.4	115.5
17.	Poland	0.34	971.2	3,481.3	2,594.5
18.	New Zealand	0.30	685.3	515.2	746.4
19.	Estonia	0.28%	$60.2	$200.9	$109.3
	Lithuania	0.28	86.4	243.3	190.7
21.	Italy	0.27	6,271.8	6,705.9	5,908.5
22.	Czechia	0.24	366.1	1,051.3	788.1
	Slovenia	0.24	116.2	168.7	162.9
	Spain	0.24	3,358.5	4,046.5	3,596.4
	U.S.	0.24	47,528.2	60,328.7	65,886.7
26.	Australia	0.19	3,546.4	3,078.8	3,220.5
	Portugal	0.19	447.0	439.6	450.0
28.	South Korea	0.18	2,997.9	2,906.3	3,267.3
29.	Hungary	0.15	435.1	371.3	304.3
30.	Greece	0.14	340.9	360.4	325.3
	Slovakia	0.14	155.3	171.9	174.5
	Total DAC countries	**0.37**	**184,948.4**	**213,359.5**	**222,163.6**
	G7 countries[1]	**0.36**	**141,279.9**	**162,821.0**	**170,187.5**
	EU institutions	**NA**	**20,639.1**	**27,165.9**	**37,680.3**
	Total non-DAC countries[2]	**NA**	**18,894.5**	**17,735.5**	**11,225.9**

NA = Not applicable/available. (1) Canada, France, Germany, Italy, Japan, the UK, and the U.S. (2) Countries not shown here.

Recipients of U.S. Official Development Assistance, 2021-22

Source: Development Assistance Committee (DAC), Organisation for Economic Co-operation and Development (OECD)

(net flows of official development assistance, in mil of current U.S. dollars; ranked by 2022 numbers)

Rank	Country	2021	2022
1.	Ukraine	$304.72	$9,238.05
2.	Ethiopia	1,324.63	1,437.01
3.	Afghanistan	1,480.72	1,296.00
4.	Yemen	900.57	982.54
5.	South Sudan	799.29	949.82
6.	Nigeria	912.51	772.35
7.	Syria	801.62	649.81
8.	Uganda	630.78	615.97
9.	Dem. Rep. of the Congo	898.85	598.40
10.	Kenya	701.44	590.77
11.	Sudan	734.12	578.78
12.	Colombia	$673.18	$568.80
13.	Mozambique	573.86	527.95
14.	South Africa	697.57	527.48
15.	Somalia	469.79	519.29
16.	Tanzania	506.86	429.45
17.	Zambia	399.98	408.52
18.	Bangladesh	443.83	375.63
19.	Jordan	1,267.98	323.79
20.	Malawi	285.39	300.28
21.	Lebanon	270.82	291.93
	Total developing countries	**38,229.28**	**52,001.97**

Nuclear Powers of the World

As of Sept. 2024, eight countries were acknowledged nuclear weapons states: the **U.S., UK, France, China, India, Pakistan, Russia,** and **North Korea**. **Israel** was presumed to have an arsenal.

All of the more than 40 nations with the knowledge or technology to produce nuclear weapons have signed the Nuclear Non-Proliferation Treaty (NPT) with the exception of Israel, India, and Pakistan. After expelling Intl. Atomic Energy Agency (IAEA) inspectors in Dec. 2002, North Korea announced on Jan. 10, 2003, its withdrawal from the NPT effective the following day.

Iran argued for the right to pursue the peaceful application of nuclear technology, but the IAEA maintained the country had violated the NPT. In 2015, the so-called P5+1 (the five permanent members of the UN Security Council plus Germany) signed a Joint Comprehensive Plan of Action (JCPOA) with Iran, which agreed to curb its ability to enrich uranium as well as reduce its current stockpile of the material. Nuclear-related sanctions on Iran were lifted in Jan. 2016, after the IAEA certified the country had implemented key measures. The U.S., under Pres. Donald Trump, pulled out of the JCPOA in May 2018, and reimposed sanctions that Nov. The other JCPOA states maintained their commitment. In 2019, Iran resumed enriching uranium, increasing its stockpile beyond what the deal allowed.

North Korea conducted six nuclear tests between 2006 and 2017. In 2017, it held two intercontinental ballistic missile tests, which appeared to indicate North Korean missiles were capable of reaching the U.S. In response, the UN Security Council unanimously approved new sanctions on North Korea. The country resumed missile testing in 2019. Although Trump and North Korean leader Kim Jong Un met multiple times in 2018-19, no formal agreement on denuclearization was reached. North Korean state media reported passage of a law in Sept. 2022 making the country's nuclear status "irreversible" and authorizing preemptive nuclear strikes.

Estimated Numbers of Nuclear Weapons by Country, 1945-2024

Source: Hans M. Kristensen, Matt Korda, Eliana Johns, and Mackenzie Knight, Federation of American Scientists (FAS)

Year	United States	USSR/Russia	United Kingdom	France	China	Israel[1]	India	Pakistan	Total[2]
1945	6	—	—	—	—	—	—	—	**6**
1950	369	5	—	—	—	—	—	—	**374**
1960	20,434	1,605	30	—	—	—	—	—	**22,069**
1970	26,662	11,643	280	36	75	8	—	—	**38,696**
1980	24,304	30,062	350	250	280	31	—	—	**55,246**
1990	21,004	37,000	300	505	430	53	—	—	**59,239**
2000	10,577	21,000	185	470	400	72	—	—	**32,632**
2010	9,400	12,300	225	300	240	60-80	60-80	70-90	**22,400**
2020	5,800	6,372	195	290	320	90	150	160	**13,410**
2024[3]	5,044	5,580	225	290	500	90	172	170	**12,121**

(1) Israel is widely presumed to have a nuclear stockpile although it has never confirmed nor denied its nuclear status. (2) Numbers may not add up due to rounding and include deployed warheads, those in reserve or in a military stockpile, and retired warheads awaiting dismantlement. (3) As of mid-2024, North Korea was estimated to have produced sufficient material for up to 90 warheads and have about 50 assembled warheads.

Nuclear Arms Treaties and Negotiations: A Historical Overview

Aug. 5, 1963: Partial (Limited) Test Ban Treaty signed by the UK, U.S., and USSR, went into effect Oct. 10, 1963. Prohibits its parties from testing or participating in the testing of nuclear weapons in the atmosphere, in outer space, and under water.

July 1, 1968: Nuclear Non-Proliferation Treaty (NPT) opened to signatures, went into effect Mar. 5, 1970. With the UK, U.S., and USSR as major signers, the parties agree not to help non-nuclear nations get or make nuclear weapons, though such nations can pursue the peaceful application of nuclear energy. On May 11, 1995, parties to the treaty voted to extend it indefinitely. As of Sept. 2023, 191 states were party to the treaty, not including North Korea, which withdrew in 2003. Israel, India, and Pakistan were not signatories.

May 26, 1972: The **Strategic Arms Limitation Talks (SALT I)** led to the signing of two agreements by the U.S. and USSR: the **Treaty on the Limitation of Anti-Ballistic Missile Systems** (or **ABM Treaty**) and an interim agreement. These agreements cap the numbers of intercontinental ballistic missile (ICBM) launchers and submarine-launched ballistic missile (SLBM) launchers.

July 3, 1974: Treaty on the Limitation of Underground Nuclear Weapon Tests (or **Threshold Test Ban Treaty**) signed by the U.S. and USSR. Limits underground testing of nuclear weapons to yields of 150 kilotons or less. On May 28, 1976, U.S. and Russia signed the **Peaceful Nuclear Explosions Treaty**, governing explosions outside weapons test sites. Both treaties entered into force Dec. 11, 1990.

June 18, 1979: Strategic Offensive Arms Limitation Treaty (or **SALT II**) signed by the U.S. and USSR. Limited each side to 2,400 missile launchers and heavy bombers; ceiling to apply until Jan. 1, 1985. Never ratified; superseded by START I.

Dec. 8, 1987: Intermediate-Range Nuclear Forces (INF) Treaty signed by the U.S. and USSR. Eliminated all U.S. and Soviet intermediate- and shorter-range nuclear missiles, the first time a treaty banned an entire category of nuclear weapons. Entered into force June 1, 1988. The treaty lapsed Aug. 2, 2019, after the U.S., citing Russian "noncompliance," gave formal notice of its withdrawal on Feb. 2, 2019, and Russia responded by suspending its participation.

July 31, 1991: Strategic Arms Reduction Treaty (START I) signed by the USSR and U.S. to reduce long-range nuclear forces no later than seven years after the treaty entered into force. This was the first treaty to mandate reductions in so-called strategic nuclear weapons by the superpowers.

With the Soviet Union breakup in Dec. 1991, four former republics became independent nations with strategic nuclear arms: Russia, Ukraine, Kazakhstan, and Belarus. Under the **Lisbon Protocol** of May 1992, Ukraine, Kazakhstan, and Belarus agreed to accede to the NPT as non-nuclear-weapon states, to destroy or transfer their nuclear weapons to Russia, and to ratify START I. START I expired on Dec. 5, 2009.

Jan. 3, 1993: START II signed by the U.S. and Russia, ratified by the two on Jan. 26, 1996, and Apr. 14, 2000, respectively. Called for further reductions in their long-range nuclear arsenals. Both sides withdrew before the treaty went into force.

Sept. 24, 1996: Comprehensive Nuclear-Test-Ban Treaty (CTBT) signed by 71 countries, including the five nuclear-weapons states (China, France, Russia, UK, U.S.). It bans all nuclear explosions and is intended to prevent the nuclear powers from developing more advanced weapons while limiting other states' ability to acquire such devices. As of Sept. 2024, the CTBT had been signed by 187 nations and ratified by 178 of them. It will enter into force only after all Annex 2 states—the 44 states with nuclear capabilities at the time of the treaty's final negotiations—have signed and ratified it. Only 35 have done so to date. Six Annex 2 countries (China, Egypt, Iran, Israel, Russia, U.S.) have yet to ratify the CTBT, and three (India, North Korea, Pakistan) have yet to sign it.

Dec. 13, 2001: The U.S. announced its intention to withdraw from the **ABM Treaty** in 180 days, arguing that it hindered the government in protecting itself from "future terrorist or rogue state missile attacks." Russia responded by withdrawing from **START II**, stating that U.S. withdrawal from the ABM Treaty effectively invalidated START II.

May 24, 2002: Strategic Offensive Reductions Treaty (SORT or **Moscow Treaty)** signed by the U.S. and Russia, entered into force June 1, 2003. Committed both countries to cutting nuclear arsenals to 1,700-2,200 warheads each by Dec. 31, 2012. SORT lapsed upon entry into force of the New START Treaty.

Apr. 8, 2010: New START Treaty signed by the U.S. and Russia, entered into force Feb. 5, 2011. It limits each country's arsenal of deployed strategic nuclear warheads to 1,550. Both countries agreed in Feb. 2021 to a five-year extension. In Feb. 2023, Russia announced the suspension of its participation in the treaty and began to withhold data mandated by the treaty. The U.S. in turn ceased sharing data with Russia that June. In a Feb. 2024 speech, Russian Pres. Putin indicated there would be no discussions on strategic stability as long as the U.S. provided military aid to Ukraine, which Russia invaded in 2022.

Major International Organizations

African Union (AU), inaugurated July 9, 2002, following disbanding of the Organization of African Unity (OAU). Africa's 55 countries make up its members. (Morocco withdrew in 1984 after the OAU admitted Western Sahara [Sahrawi Arab Dem. Rep.], a territory it claimed, but rejoined in 2017.) **Headquarters:** Addis Ababa, Ethiopia. **Website:** au.int

Asia-Pacific Economic Cooperation (APEC), founded Nov. 1989. Its 21 member economies are Australia, Brunei, Canada, Chile, China, Hong Kong, Indonesia, Japan, Malaysia, Mexico, New Zealand, Papua New Guinea, Peru, Philippines, Russia, Singapore, South Korea, Taiwan, Thailand, the U.S., and Vietnam. **Secretariat:** Singapore. **Website:** www.apec.org

Association of Southeast Asian Nations (ASEAN), formed Aug. 8, 1967. Its 10 members are Brunei, Cambodia, Indonesia, Laos, Malaysia, Myanmar, Philippines, Singapore, Thailand, and Vietnam. **Secretariat:** Jakarta, Indonesia. **Website:** asean.org

The Commonwealth, originally called the British Commonwealth of Nations, then the Commonwealth of Nations, in 1949, is an association of nations and dependencies, most part of the former British Empire. King Charles III, the current British monarch, is the symbolic head of the Commonwealth. The secretary-general is chosen by Commonwealth leaders.

There are 56 independent, sovereign nations in the Commonwealth as of Sept. 2024. Among them are the UK and 14 other nations, known as Commonwealth Realms, that recognize the British monarch as their head of state. **Secretariat:** London, UK. **Website:** thecommonwealth.org

Commonwealth of Independent States (CIS), established in Dec. 1991 as an alliance of former Soviet constituent republics. Its members are Armenia, Azerbaijan, Belarus, Kazakhstan, Kyrgyzstan, Moldova, Russia, Tajikistan, and Uzbekistan; Turkmenistan is an associate member. Georgia and Ukraine have withdrawn from the organization, and Moldova expressed its intent to withdraw by year-end 2024. **Headquarters:** Minsk, Belarus. **Website:** cis.minsk.by

European Union (EU), known as the European Community (EC) until 1993. The Treaty on European Union (Maastricht Treaty) was signed on Feb. 7, 1992 (in effect Nov. 1993). As of Jan. 1, 1993, there has been a single market, with no restrictions on the movement of people, goods, services, and money, within the EU.

The EU has its origins in the European Coal and Steel Community (ECSC), European Economic Community (EEC, or Common Market), and European Atomic Energy Community (Euratom). A merger of the three communities' executives went into effect in 1967. As of Sept. 2024, there were 27 EU members: 11 of the 12 original members (Belgium, Denmark, France, Germany, Greece, Ireland, Italy, Luxembourg, Netherlands, Portugal, Spain); 3 that joined in 1995 (Austria, Finland, Sweden); 10 in 2004 (Cyprus, Czechia, Estonia, Hungary, Latvia, Lithuania, Malta, Poland, Slovakia, Slovenia); 2 in 2007 (Bulgaria, Romania); and 1 in 2013 (Croatia). The euro is the official currency in 20 of these 27 countries. Albania, Bosnia and Herzegovina, Georgia, Moldova, Montenegro, North

Macedonia, Serbia, Turkey (Türkiye), and Ukraine have been granted candidate status. The UK, one of the original EU members, withdrew from the organization, Jan. 31, 2020, after UK citizens voted in favor of Brexit in 2016. **De facto capital:** Brussels, Belgium. **Website:** europa.eu

Group of Seven (G7), forum of major industrialized countries. France, Germany, Italy, Japan, the UK, and the U.S. first met in 1975 as the Group of Six. Canada joined in 1976. In 2014, group members boycotted a planned G8 summit in Russia (joined 1998) in condemnation of its annexation of Crimea. The EU is represented at summits. The **Group of Twenty (G20)**, which first gathered in 1999, comprises 19 countries, the EU, and the African Union.

International Criminal Police Organization (INTERPOL), created 1923, is the world's largest intergovernmental police organization. There were 196 member nations as of Sept. 2024. **General Secretariat:** Lyon, France. **Website:** www.interpol.int

League of Arab States (Arab League), created Mar. 22, 1945. Its 22 members are Algeria, Bahrain, Comoros, Djibouti, Egypt, Iraq, Jordan, Kuwait, Lebanon, Libya, Mauritania, Morocco, Oman, Palestine (considered an independent state by the League), Qatar, Saudi Arabia, Somalia, Sudan, Syria (membership suspended since 2011), Tunisia, United Arab Emirates, and Yemen. **Headquarters:** Cairo, Egypt. **Website:** www.lasportal.org

North Atlantic Treaty Organization (NATO), created with the signing of what is popularly known as the Washington Treaty Apr. 4, 1949 (in effect Aug. 24, 1949). Its 32 members as of Sept. 2024 are Albania, Belgium, Bulgaria, Canada, Croatia, Czechia, Denmark, Estonia, Finland, France, Germany, Greece, Hungary, Iceland, Italy, Latvia, Lithuania, Luxembourg, Montenegro, Netherlands, North Macedonia, Norway, Poland, Portugal, Romania, Slovakia, Slovenia, Spain, Sweden, Turkey (Türkiye), UK, and U.S. **Headquarters:** Brussels, Belgium. **Website:** www.nato.int

With the end of the Cold War in the early 1990s, members put greater stress on political action and on creating a force that could rapidly deploy to local crises. A NATO-led multinational force was deployed to help keep the peace in Bosnia and Herzegovina in 1995. In 1999, a force was deployed in Kosovo. NATO's first mission outside Europe was in Afghanistan in 2003.

Organization of American States (OAS), which describes itself as the world's oldest regional organization, was officially formed by the signing of a charter on Apr. 30, 1948. The OAS's 34 members are Antigua and Barbuda, Argentina, The Bahamas, Barbados, Belize, Bolivia, Brazil, Canada, Chile, Colombia, Costa Rica, Cuba, Dominica, Dominican Republic, Ecuador, El Salvador, Grenada, Guatemala, Guyana, Haiti, Honduras, Jamaica, Mexico, Panama, Paraguay, Peru, St. Kitts and Nevis, St. Lucia, St. Vincent and the Grenadines, Suriname, Trinidad and Tobago, U.S., Uruguay, and Venezuela. **Headquarters:** Washington, DC. **Website:** www.oas.org

Organization for Economic Cooperation and Development (OECD), established Dec. 14, 1960. Its 38 members, as of Sept. 2024, are Australia, Austria, Belgium, Canada, Chile, Colombia, Costa Rica, Czechia, Denmark, Estonia, Finland, France, Germany, Greece, Hungary, Iceland, Ireland, Israel, Italy, Japan, Latvia, Lithuania, Luxembourg, Mexico, Netherlands, New Zealand, Norway, Poland, Portugal, Slovakia, Slovenia, South Korea, Spain, Sweden, Switzerland, Turkey, UK, and the U.S. Brazil, China, India, Indonesia, and South Africa are OECD key partners. **Headquarters:** Paris, France. **Website:** www.oecd.org

Organization of the Petroleum Exporting Countries (OPEC), created Sept. 14, 1960, by Iran, Iraq, Kuwait, Saudi Arabia, and Venezuela. In addition to the founding countries, members as of Sept. 2024 include Algeria, Congo Republic, Equatorial Guinea, Gabon, Libya, Nigeria, and United Arab Emirates. Angola, Ecuador, Indonesia, and Qatar are former members. **Secretariat/headquarters:** Vienna, Austria. **Website:** www.opec.org

Organization for Security and Cooperation in Europe (OSCE), established in 1972 by NATO and Warsaw Pact members. There were 57 member states from Europe, Central Asia, and North America as of Sept. 2024, making it the world's largest regional security organization. **Secretariat:** Vienna, Austria. **Website:** www.osce.org

United Nations

The 79th regular session of the UN General Assembly opened on Sept. 10, 2024, attended by delegates from 193 member states. The UN headquarters is located on 18 acres, considered international territory, in New York, NY.

Proposals to establish an organization for maintaining world peace led to the convening of the United Nations Conference on International Organization in San Francisco, Apr. 25-June 26, 1945, where the UN charter was drawn. It was signed June 26 by 50 nations and on Oct. 15 by Poland. It went into effect Oct. 24, 1945, upon ratification by the permanent members of the Security Council and a majority of the other signatories.

Purposes. To maintain international peace and security; to promote sustained economic growth and sustainable development; to achieve international cooperation in solving economic, social, cultural, and humanitarian problems; to protect human rights; and to advance justice and international law.

Visitors to the UN. Normally, the UN headquarters is open every day except New Year's Day, Good Friday, Eid al-Fitr, Memorial Day, Eid al-Adha, Independence Day, Labor Day, Thanksgiving, and Christmas. It is typically closed to the public during the UN general debate and for meetings of heads of state and government.

As of Sept. 2024, the UN offered a one-hour in-person guided tour or a virtual tour with a live guide to groups of up to 20-30 people. Specialty tours with a focus on art, architecture, or Black history, among other subjects, were also available. Groups can also book an in-house or online briefing with a UN expert. Children under 5 years of age are not permitted on tours; the UN offers a children's tour for ages 5-10. Guided tours at the UN's other headquarters—in Geneva, Switzerland; Vienna, Austria; and Nairobi, Kenya—are also available. For updates, visit the UN website. **Website:** www.un.org/visit

Six Main Organs of the United Nations

General Assembly. The General Assembly comprises representatives from all member nations. Each nation is entitled to one vote. The General Assembly meets in Sept. for an annual session; the Security Council or a majority of UN members can convoke a special session. Decisions on important issues, such as security, require a two-thirds majority of the General Assembly; a simple majority can decide other issues.

The General Assembly must approve the UN budget and apportion expenses among members. A member in arrears can lose its vote if the amount of arrears equals or exceeds the amount of the contributions due for the preceding two full years. **Website:** www.un.org/en/ga/

Security Council. The Security Council has primary responsibility within the UN for maintaining peace and security. It consists of 15 members, five of whom (China, France, Russia, United Kingdom, U.S.) have permanent seats. Ten are elected for two-year terms by the General Assembly. Nonpermanent members with terms expiring Dec. 31, 2024, are Ecuador, Japan, Malta, Mozambique, and Switzerland; those with terms expiring Dec. 31, 2025, are Algeria, Guyana, Sierra Leone, Slovenia, and South Korea. Denmark, Greece, Pakistan, Panama, and Somalia have been elected to two-year terms starting on Jan. 1, 2025.

Any UN member may participate in Council discussions at its invitation. Decisions on procedural questions are made by an affirmative vote of nine members. On all other matters the affirmative vote of nine members must include the concurring votes of all permanent members (giving them veto power).

The Security Council directs the various peacekeeping forces deployed throughout the world. **Website:** www.un.org/securitycouncil/

Secretariat. The Secretariat is responsible for the UN's day-to-day operations. It is headed by the secretary-general, who is appointed by the General Assembly, on the recommendation of the Security Council, for a five-year, renewable term. The secretary-general reports to the General Assembly and may bring to the attention of the Security Council any matter that threatens international peace. The Secretariat maintained an international staff of 36,791 as of Dec. 31, 2022. **Website:** www.un.org/en/about-us/secretariat

United Nations Secretaries General

Took office	Secretary, nation
1946	Trygve Lie, Norway
1953	Dag Hammarskjöld, Sweden
1961	U Thant, Burma (Myanmar)
1972	Kurt Waldheim, Austria
1982	Javier Pérez de Cuéllar, Peru
1992	Boutros Boutros-Ghali, Egypt
1997	Kofi Annan, Ghana
2007	Ban Ki-moon, South Korea
2017	António Guterres, Portugal

Economic and Social Council. ECOSOC consists of 54 members elected by the General Assembly to overlapping three-year terms. The council is responsible for economic, social, and environmental issues in relation to sustainable development. It conducts multiple substantive sessions throughout the year, meeting with policymakers, parliamentarians, academics, nongovernmental organizations, private-sector representatives, and youth. **Website:** www.un.org/ecosoc/

International Court of Justice (World Court). The International Court of Justice is the principal judicial organ of the UN. The Court has jurisdiction over cases that UN members or parties to the court's statute submit to it. In addition to rendering judgments, the Court issues advisory opinions.

The court's 15 judges are elected to nine-year terms by the General Assembly and the Security Council. No two judges may come from the same nation, and they should represent the world's principal legal systems. Once elected, the judges no longer act as representatives of a government. The Court remains permanently in session, except during vacations. All questions are decided by a majority. The International Court of Justice sits in The Hague, Netherlands. **Website:** www.icj-cij.org

Trusteeship Council. The Trusteeship Council, made up of the five permanent Security Council members, supervised the administration of UN trust territories. All 11 trust territories have since attained their right to self-determination. The Council formally suspended its work on Nov. 1, 1994, with Palau's independence.

The text of the **UN Charter** is online at www.un.org/en/about-us/un-charter/.

Ongoing UN Peacekeeping Missions, 2024

Source: Dept. of Peacekeeping Operations (DPKO), Dept. of Field Support, Dept. of Management; United Nations Secretariat

Unless otherwise noted, numbers are for peacekeeping operations only (not including political and peacebuilding missions) as of Mar. 31, 2024. Year given in graphic is the year each mission started.

Uniformed personnel (troops, police, military observers, and staff officers)	62,519
Countries contributing uniformed personnel	121
Civilian personnel	7,792
Total personnel serving in 11 current peacekeeping operations	71,417
Approved budget for July 1, 2024-June 30, 2025 (excl. UNTSO and UNMOGIP, financed by UN regular budget[1])	$5.59 bil
Peacekeeping operations since 1948	71
Total fatalities in all peace operations since 1948 (as of June 30, 2024)	4,383
Est. total cost of operations, 1948 to June 30, 2010	$69 bil

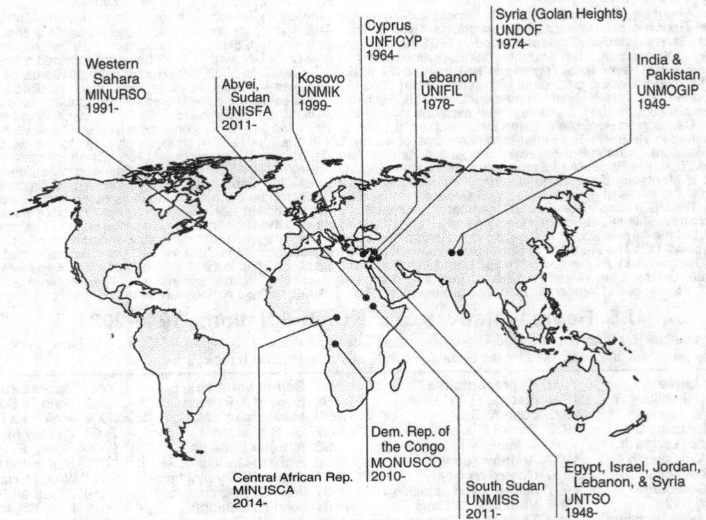

(1) The UN Security Council June 30, 2023, terminated the mandate for the Multidimensional Integrated Stabilization Mission in Mali (MINUSMA). The UN authorized funding in its 2024-25 budget to support the conclusion of the mission's operations by year-end 2024.

Roster of the United Nations

Listed below are the 193 members of the United Nations, with the years in which they were admitted (as of Sept. 2024). Vatican City (Holy See), Kosovo, and China (Taiwan)[1] are not members. Taiwan's repeated bids for UN membership have so far been unsuccessful. Palestine and Vatican City are non-member states of the UN with permanent observer status.

Member	Year
Afghanistan	1946
Albania	1955
Algeria	1962
Andorra	1993
Angola	1976
Antigua and Barbuda	1981
Argentina	1945
Armenia	1992
Australia	1945
Austria	1955
Azerbaijan	1992
Bahamas, The	1973
Bahrain	1971
Bangladesh	1974
Barbados	1966
Belarus	1945
Belgium	1945
Belize	1981
Benin	1960
Bhutan	1971
Bolivia	1945
Bosnia and Herzegovina[2]	1992
Botswana	1966
Brazil	1945
Brunei	1984
Bulgaria	1955
Burkina Faso	1960
Burundi	1962
Cabo Verde	1975
Cambodia	1955
Cameroon	1960
Canada	1945
Central African Rep.	1960
Chad	1960
Chile	1945
China[1]	1945
Colombia	1945
Comoros	1975
Congo, Dem. Rep. of	1960
Congo Republic	1960
Costa Rica	1945
Côte d'Ivoire	1960
Croatia[2]	1992
Cuba	1945
Cyprus	1960
Czechia[3]	1993
Denmark	1945
Djibouti	1977
Dominica	1978
Dominican Republic	1945
Ecuador	1945
Egypt[4]	1945
El Salvador	1945
Equatorial Guinea	1968
Eritrea	1993
Estonia	1991
Ethiopia	1945
Fiji	1970
Finland	1955
France	1945
Gabon	1960
Gambia, The	1965
Georgia	1992
Germany[5]	1973
Ghana	1957
Greece	1945
Grenada	1974
Guatemala	1945
Guinea	1958
Guinea-Bissau	1974
Guyana	1966
Haiti	1945
Honduras	1945
Hungary	1955
Iceland	1946
India	1945
Indonesia[6]	1950
Iran	1945
Iraq	1945
Ireland	1955
Israel	1949
Italy	1955
Jamaica	1962
Japan	1956
Jordan	1955
Kazakhstan	1992
Kenya	1963
Kiribati	1999
Korea, North	1991
Korea, South	1991
Kuwait	1963
Kyrgyzstan	1992
Laos	1955
Latvia	1991
Lebanon	1945
Lesotho	1966
Liberia	1945
Libya	1955
Liechtenstein	1990
Lithuania	1991
Luxembourg	1945
Madagascar	1960
Malawi	1964
Malaysia[7]	1957
Maldives	1965
Mali	1960
Malta	1964
Marshall Islands	1991
Mauritania	1961
Mauritius	1968
Mexico	1945
Micronesia, Fed. States	1991
Moldova	1992
Monaco	1993
Mongolia	1961
Montenegro[2,8]	2006
Morocco	1956
Mozambique	1975
Myanmar (Burma)	1948
Namibia	1990
Nauru	1999
Nepal	1955
Netherlands	1945
New Zealand	1945
Nicaragua	1945
Niger	1960
Nigeria	1960
North Macedonia[2,9]	1993
Norway	1945
Oman	1971
Pakistan	1947
Palau	1994
Panama	1945
Papua New Guinea	1975
Paraguay	1945
Peru	1945
Philippines	1945
Poland	1945
Portugal	1955
Qatar	1971
Romania	1955
Russia[10]	1945
Rwanda	1962
Saint Kitts and Nevis	1983
Saint Lucia	1979
Saint Vincent and the Grenadines	1980
Samoa	1976
San Marino	1992
São Tomé and Príncipe	1975
Saudi Arabia	1945
Senegal	1960
Serbia[2,9]	2000
Seychelles	1976
Sierra Leone	1961
Singapore[8]	1965
Slovakia[3]	1993
Slovenia[2]	1992
Solomon Islands	1978
Somalia	1960
South Africa[11]	1945
South Sudan[12]	2011
Spain	1955
Sri Lanka	1955
Sudan[12]	1956
Suriname	1975
Swaziland	1968
Sweden	1946
Switzerland	2002
Syria[3]	1945
Tajikistan	1992
Tanzania[13]	1961
Thailand	1946
Timor-Leste	2002
Togo	1960
Tonga	1999
Trinidad and Tobago	1962
Tunisia	1956
Turkey (Türkiye)	1945
Turkmenistan	1992
Tuvalu	2000
Uganda	1962
Ukraine	1945
United Arab Emirates	1971
United Kingdom	1945
United States	1945
Uruguay	1945
Uzbekistan	1992
Vanuatu	1981
Venezuela	1945
Vietnam	1977
Yemen[14]	1947
Zambia	1964
Zimbabwe	1980

(1) The General Assembly (GA) voted in 1971 to expel the Chinese government in Taiwan and admit the government in Beijing. (2) The Socialist Federal Republic of Yugoslavia was an original UN member. After four of its six republics (Bosnia and Herzegovina, Croatia, Macedonia, and Slovenia) declared independence in 1991-92, the two remaining republics, Montenegro and Serbia, reconstituted as the Federal Republic of Yugoslavia. They sought to take over the former Yugoslavia's UN seat in 1992 but were expelled a few months later by GA vote. The Federal Republic of Yugoslavia was granted membership in 2000. In 2003, the country changed its name to Serbia and Montenegro. (3) Czechoslovakia, an original UN member from 1945 to 1992, was succeeded by both the Czech Republic and Slovakia in 1993. (4) Egypt and Syria were original UN members. In 1958, Egypt and Syria established the United Arab Republic and continued under a single UN membership. In 1961, Syria resumed separate membership following independence. (5) The Federal Republic of Germany and the German Democratic Republic became UN members in 1973. In 1990, the two formed one sovereign state. (6) Withdrew from the UN in 1965; rejoined in 1966. (7) The Federation of Malaya joined the UN in 1957. In 1963, it changed its name to Malaysia following the accession of Singapore, Sabah, and Sarawak. Singapore became an independent UN member in 1965. (8) After Montenegro declared independence in 2006, the Republic of Serbia continued Serbia and Montenegro's UN membership. Montenegro was admitted to the UN as the Republic of Montenegro the same month. (9) Admitted to the UN under the provisional name of the former Yugoslav Republic of Macedonia. Under the terms of an agreement with Greece in force Feb. 12, 2019, the country changed its name to the Republic of North Macedonia. (10) The USSR was an original UN member. After the USSR's dissolution in 1991, Russia informed the UN it would continue the Soviet Union's membership in the Security Council and all other UN organs with the support of the Commonwealth of Independent States (comprising most of the former Soviet republics). (11) Readmitted in 1994. Its delegation had been suspended from participation in 1974 because of apartheid. (12) The Republic of South Sudan seceded from the Republic of the Sudan in 2011 and was admitted to the UN the same year. (13) Tanganyika (UN member from 1961) and Zanzibar (from 1963), merged in 1964 to form the United Republic of Tanganyika and Zanzibar, later renamed the United Republic of Tanzania. It continued a single UN membership. (14) The Yemen Arab Republic was admitted in 1947; the People's Democratic Republic of Yemen in 1967. In 1990, the two nations formed the Republic of Yemen.

U.S. Representatives to the United Nations, 1946-2024

The U.S. Permanent Representative to the United Nations is head of the U.S. Mission to the UN in New York. He or she is appointed by the president and confirmed by the Senate. Year given is the year each took office.

Year	Representative
1946	Edward R. Stettinius Jr.
1946	Herschel V. Johnson[1]
1947	Warren R. Austin
1953	Henry Cabot Lodge Jr.
1960	James J. Wadsworth
1961	Adlai E. Stevenson
1965	Arthur J. Goldberg
1968	George W. Ball
1968	James Russell Wiggins
1969	Charles W. Yost
1971	George H. W. Bush
1973	John A. Scali
1975	Daniel P. Moynihan
1976	William W. Scranton
1977	Andrew Young
1979	Donald McHenry
1981	Jeane J. Kirkpatrick
1985	Vernon A. Walters
1989	Thomas R. Pickering
1992	Edward J. Perkins
1993	Madeleine K. Albright
1997	Bill Richardson
1998	A. Peter Burleigh[1]
1999	Richard C. Holbrooke
2001	James B. Cunningham[1]
2001	John D. Negroponte
2004	John C. Danforth
2005	Anne W. Patterson[1]
2005	John R. Bolton
2006	Alejandro D. Wolff[1]
2007	Zalmay M. Khalilzad
2009	Susan E. Rice
2013	Samantha Power
2017	Nikki R. Haley
2019	Jonathan R. Cohen[1]
2019	Kelly Craft
2021	Linda Thomas-Greenfield

(1) Acting.

International Criminal Court

The International Criminal Court (ICC) was created when 120 nations signed the Rome Statute on July 17, 1998. Its mission is to try individuals accused of genocide, war crimes, and crimes against humanity. The statute came into force on July 1, 2002. As of Sept. 2024, 124 nations were state parties to the Rome Statute of the ICC. China, Russia, and the U.S. are among those countries that have not yet signed or ratified the treaty.

The ICC, unlike the International Court of Justice (World Court), is not part of the UN. It is an independent international agency with its own administration and budget, which is made up of funds from member states and voluntary contributions by other institutions, international groups, individuals, and corporations. It consists of 18 judges elected by state parties to 9-year, nonrenewable terms. An absolute majority of these 18 judges elect 3 from among themselves to serve as president and first and second vice presidents. A Registry handles the nonjudicial aspects of administration. The Office of the Prosecutor reviews, investigates, and prosecutes cases referred to it by a state or by the UN Security Council.

As of June 2024, 32 cases had been brought before the ICC. The Office of the Prosecutor was investigating situations in Afghanistan, Bangladesh/Myanmar (Burma), Burundi, Côte d'Ivoire, Dem. Rep. of the Congo, Libya, Mali, Palestine, the Philippines, Sudan (Darfur), Ukraine, and Venezuela. The court issued its first-ever conviction in 2012, when it found the warlord Thomas Lubanga Dyilo guilty of war crimes for his use of child soldiers in the Dem. Rep. of the Congo. In Mar. 2023, the ICC issued arrest warrants for Russian Pres. Vladimir Putin and another Russian government official for the alleged war crime of unlawful deportation and transfer of children from occupied Ukraine to Russia.

Though jurisdiction is limited to member nations, the ICC is a court of last resort. It may also initiate cases involving non-member nations if it deems the country's authorities have not taken steps to investigate or prosecute a case. The ICC is headquartered in The Hague, Netherlands, though it may sit elsewhere.

Website: www.icc-cpi.int

Geneva Conventions

The Geneva Conventions are four international treaties governing the protection of civilians and medical and religious personnel in times of war, the treatment of prisoners of war, and the care of the wounded and sick in the armed forces. The first convention, covering the sick and wounded in war, was concluded in Geneva, Switzerland, in 1864. The convention was amended and expanded in 1906. In 1929, two more conventions covering the wounded and prisoners of war were signed. Outrage at the treatment of prisoners and civilians during WWII by some belligerents, notably Germany and Japan, prompted the conclusion, on Aug. 12, 1949, of four new conventions. Three of these restated and strengthened the previous conventions.

The fourth Geneva Convention of 1949 codified general principles of international law governing the treatment of civilians in wartime, with special safeguards for wounded persons, children under 15 years of age, pregnant women, and the elderly. Discrimination on racial, religious, national, or political grounds was forbidden. Torture, collective punishment, unwarranted destruction of property, and forced use of civilians for an occupier's armed forces were prohibited. Also included was a pledge for the humane treatment, adequate feeding, and delivery of supplies to prisoners. Two additional protocols, adopted in June 1977, increased protections for victims of international and non-international armed conflicts (e.g., civil wars). (A third protocol, adopted in 2005, created the Red Crystal emblem for use along with the Red Cross and Red Crescent.)

Nearly all countries have formally accepted all or most international humanitarian law as binding. However, there is no permanent international machinery in place to enforce these treaties.

Genocide

Source: Convention on the Prevention and Punishment of the Crime of Genocide, United Nations Treaty Series 277; Rome Statute of the International Criminal Court (ICC)

The term "genocide" (which combines Greek and Latin roots to mean "murder of a race") was coined by Polish-Jewish lawyer Raphael Lemkin in 1944 to describe the intentional or attempted destruction of a national, ethnic, racial, or religious group. Genocide is defined as killing members of a group, causing serious bodily harm to members of a group, or otherwise attempting to bring about a group's destruction, including efforts to prevent births or transfer children away from a group. The definition of genocide does not extend to political groups, but the term is often used colloquially to refer to large-scale political violence.

The prohibition against genocide is part of customary international law and is codified in the Convention on the Prevention and Punishment of the Crime of Genocide, which entered into force on Jan. 12, 1951. As of Sept. 2024, 153 nations, including the U.S., were parties to it. Genocide is also prohibited by the domestic laws of many nations.

The first modern trials for genocide were conducted by the Allies after WWII. Although the charter of the Nuremberg Tribunal—the international court set up to try Nazi war criminals—did not use the term genocide, its definition of "crimes against humanity" included persecution on racial or religious grounds. More recently, the UN Security Council created ad hoc tribunals to try those responsible for genocide and other serious crimes in former Yugoslavia and in Rwanda. The ICC also has jurisdiction to try perpetrators. Sudanese Pres. Omar Hassan al-Bashir is the first person the ICC has charged with the crime of genocide, for the violence in Darfur against the Fur, Masalit, and Zaghawa people. Bashir was deposed in Apr. 2019, but Sudan had yet to turn him over to the ICC as of mid-2024.

The ICC in 2019 authorized an investigation into the genocide of Myanmar's Rohingya population. At least 6,700 Rohingya are estimated to have been killed by armed government forces in Aug.-Sept. 2017.

Examples of Genocides Since 1900

Year	Event	Location	Est. deaths
1915	Extermination of Armenians by the nationalist Young Turks	Turkey/Ottoman Empire	1,000,000+
1930s	Intentional infliction of famine on Ukraine	Soviet Union (Ukraine)	6,000,000-7,000,000
1933-45	Attempted destruction of European Jewry (Holocaust)	Europe	6,000,000
1939-45	Attempted destruction of European Roma	Europe	250,000-500,000
1975-79	Khmer Rouge campaign of extermination under Pol Pot[1]	Cambodia	1,500,000-2,000,000
1981-83	Army and paramilitary killings of indigenous Mayan during civil war	Guatemala	200,000+
1988	Anfal Campaign (named by the Iraqi government) against Iraqi Kurds	Iraq	100,000-200,000
1992-95	Ethnic killings during the breakup of Yugoslavia, chiefly Serbs against Bosnian Muslims (known as Bosniaks)	Bosnia-Herzegovina, Serbia, Croatia	200,000
1994	Hutu massacre of Tutsis	Rwanda	800,000
2003-present	Govt. forces and Arab militia (Janjaweed) attacks on non-Arab southern tribes, mainly Fur, Masalit, Zaghawa[2]; more recently, paramilitary (RSF) attacks on non-Arab civilian pop.	Darfur region, Sudan	300,000-600,000
2014-19	Self-proclaimed Islamic State (ISIS) against Yazidi, Christian, and Shia Muslim population	Iraq, Syria	5,000+

Note: Ests. based on historical evidence. The legal definition of "genocide" does not include politically motivated mass killings. Therefore, instances of mass violence against political or class enemies, such as Josef Stalin's purges of some 20 mil Soviets in the 1930s, and Mao Zedong's Cultural Revolution, which killed several million Chinese, are not included. (1) Though many of the murders committed by the Khmer Rouge regime were politically or class motivated, a UN-backed tribunal, Nov. 2018, found two senior officials guilty of genocide of Vietnamese in Cambodia and the Cham ethnic group. (2) In 2005, a UN commission concluded that although the "international offenses ... that have been committed in Darfur may be no less serious and heinous than genocide," it did not term the situation a genocide.

NATIONS OF THE WORLD

As of mid-2024, there were **196 nations** in the world. This number includes three nations that are not United Nations (UN) members—Kosovo, Taiwan, and Vatican City (Holy See). Certain regions and territories can be found under the entry for their governing nation. **Sources:** FAOSTAT and AQUASTAT, Food and Agric. Org. of the UN (FAO); Intl. Data Base, U.S. Census Bureau, U.S. Dept. of Commerce; Energy Information Administration, U.S. Dept. of Energy; *International Financial Statistics*, Intl. Monetary Fund (IMF); Joint UN Programme on HIV/AIDS (UNAIDS); ILOSTAT, International Labour Organization; *The Military Balance*, Intl. Inst. for Strategic Studies; *Oil & Gas Journal*, Endeavor Business Media; *International Migrant Stock* and *World Urbanization Prospects*, Population Div., UN Dept. of Economic and Social Affairs; UN Educational, Scientific, and Cultural Org. (UNESCO); UNWTO World Tourism Barometer © World Tourism Org.; U.S. Dept. of State; Wards Intelligence, a div. of Informa; WHO COVID-19 Dashboard, World Health Organization; The World Bank; *The World Factbook*, Central Intelligence Agency (CIA); Gina A. Zurlo, ed., *World Religion Database* (Leiden/Boston: Brill, July 2024); ITU DataHub, Intl. Telecommunication Union; Xe.com.

Note: Because of rounding or incomplete enumeration, percentages may not add up to 100%. FY = Fiscal year. NA = Not available/applicable. Figures are for years noted below unless otherwise indicated within a country's profile. **Population**, **age distrib.**, and **pop. density** are mid-2024 ests. **Growth** gives the avg. annual percent change in the pop. resulting from **births** and **deaths** at midyear 2024 as well as the flow of migrants into and out of a country. International **migrants**, including foreign-born citizens and refugees, as a percent of the total pop. is for mid-2020. Percent of total pop. living in **urban** areas, as defined by each country, are projections for mid-2024. **Ethnic groups** are given in descending order of size; data are most recent available. **Languages** are listed with those most widely spoken or official given first. **Arable land** is given as percentage of country's land area. Pop. of **capitals** and **cities** are projected ests. for urban agglomerations as of mid-2018 or mid-2024. **Defense budget** and **active troops** are for 2023. Selected **industries** are ranked by descending value of annual output. Selected **chief agric.** products are most important by annual tonnage. Total renewable **water** resources per inhabitant is for 2021. Reserves of **crude oil** (incl. lease condensate) are as of Jan. 1, 2021; countries without this entry lack reserves. **Electricity prod.** indicates net, not gross, generated in 2022. **Labor force** percentages are for 2022; **unemployment** (percentage of total labor force age 15 and older currently available for and seeking work) are 2023 ests. **Monetary unit** exchange rate is as of Aug. 27, 2024. **GDP** and **per capita GDP**, 2023 ests., are based on purchasing power parity exchange rates; **GDP growth** is annual percent change between 2022 and 2023. Value of **imports** and **exports**, calculated on an exchange rate basis, are from 2023; 2022 trade partners are listed in descending order of importance by percentage of total dollar value. **Tourism** is 2023 receipts from intl. visitors; data not available for all countries. **Budget** calculated on an exchange rate basis, not purchasing power parity terms, is 2019 expenditures. **Inflation** is measured by the percent change in the consumer price index (or avg. consumer cost for certain goods and services) between 2022 and 2023. Total length of a country's **railway** network is the latest available. **Motor vehicle** statistics, for cars and comm. vehicles in operation based on registrations, are for 2022. The number of active **airports** or airfields (civilian and military) are for 2024. Number of **mobile**-cellular telephone subscriptions offering voice communications and active mobile-**broadband** subscriptions are for 2023. Percentage of pop. accessing the **internet**, regardless of device used, are for 2022. Current health **expend.** (both government and private) is given as a percentage of GDP in 2021. **Life expect.** is in avg. number of years at birth for persons born in 2024. **Infant mortality** measures the probability of a child dying between birth and exact age 1 in 2024. **Undernourished**, the prevalence of undernourishment, is the proportion of the population in 2021-23 whose habitual food consumption is insufficient for an active, healthy life. **HIV** prevalence is the percentage of a country's pop. of 15- to 49-year-olds living with HIV in 2023. **COVID-19** data were reported to WHO as of Aug. 11, 2024 (confirmed cases/deaths) or Dec. 31, 2023 (those who received a complete primary series of any COVID vaccine); all data subject to continuous verification and change. Note that figures do not necessarily reflect actual COVID-19 numbers as a number of countries have stopped reporting or changed their frequency of reporting. **Education** and **literacy** rate ests. are latest available. Literacy measures the percent of the pop. age 15 and older able to read and write simple statements; some countries define as literate those who have completed certain schooling. Current events as of Oct. 1, 2024.

See pages 489-504 for full-color maps and flags of all nations.

Afghanistan

Islamic Emirate of Afghanistan

People: Population: 40,121,552 (36). **Age distrib.:** <15: 39.6%; 65+: 2.9%. **Growth:** 2.2%. **Migrants:** 0.4%. **Pop. density:** 159.3 per sq mi, 61.5 per sq km. **Urban:** 27.3%. **Ethnic groups:** Pashtun, Tajik, Hazara, Uzbek; smaller numbers of 10 other constitutionally recognized ethnic groups. **Languages:** Afghan Persian or Dari (official, lingua franca), Pashto (official); Uzbeki, English, Turkmani, Urdu. **Religions:** Muslim 99.9% (Sunni 88%, Shia 12%).

Geography: Total area: 251,827 sq mi, 652,230 sq km (41); **Land area:** 251,827 sq mi, 652,230 sq km. **Location:** SW Asia, NW of Indian subcontinent. Pakistan on E, S; Iran on W; Turkmenistan, Uzbekistan, Tajikistan on N. NE tip touches China. **Topography:** Landlocked and mountainous, much of it over 4,000 ft above sea level. The Hindu Kush Mts. tower 16,000 ft above Kabul and reach a height of 25,000 ft to the E. Dry climate with extreme temperatures; large desert regions. **Arable land:** 12.0%. **Capital:** Kabul, 4,728,384. **Cities:** Herat, 724,172; Mazare Sharif, 653,486; Kandahar, 559,349.

Government: Type: Theocratic; U.S. does not recognize the Taliban govt. **Head of state and govt.:** Taliban leader Haibatullah Akhundzada; in office: Aug. 15, 2021. **Local divisions:** 34 provinces. **Defense budget** (2021): $2.1 bil. **Active troops:** 150,000 (Taliban).

Economy: Industries: small-scale prod. of bricks, textiles, soap, furniture, shoes, fertilizer, apparel, food prods. **Chief agric.:** wheat, milk, watermelons, grapes, potatoes, cantaloupes/melons. **Natural resources:** nat. gas, petroleum, coal, copper, chromite, talc, barites, sulfur, lead, zinc, iron ore, salt, prec./semiprec. stones. **Water:** 1,629 cu m per capita. **Electricity prod.:** 830.8 mil kWh. **Labor force:** agric. 46.6%, industry 18.3%, services 35.1%. **Unemployment:** 14.4%.

Finance: Monetary unit: Afghani (AFN) (70.73 = $1 U.S.). **GDP** (2022): $86.1 bil; **per capita GDP** (2022): $2,093; **GDP growth** (2022): –6.2%. **Imports** (2020): $7.0 bil; UAE 21%, Kazakhstan 17%, Pakistan 17%, China 9%, Uzbekistan 9%. **Exports** (2020): $1.5 bil; Pakistan 57%, India 28%. **Tourism** (2020): $65 mil. **Budget:** $5.3 bil. **Inflation** (2018-19): 2.3%.

Transport: Motor vehicles: 44.7 per 1,000 pop. **Airports:** 67.

Communications: Mobile: 55.5 per 100 pop. **Broadband:** 55.5 per 100 pop. **Internet** (2019): 17.6%.

Health: Expend.: 21.8%. **Life expect.:** 52.8 male; 56.1 female. **Births:** 34.2 per 1,000 pop. **Deaths:** 11.8 per 1,000 pop. **Infant mortality:** 101.3 per 1,000 live births. **Undernourished:** 30.4%. **HIV:** <0.1%. **COVID-19:** 7,998 deaths; rates per 100,000: 604 cases, 21 deaths. 47% vaccinated.

Education: Compulsory: ages 7-15. **Literacy:** 37.3%.

Website: moj.gov.af/en/ or www.state.gov/countries-areas/afghanistan/

Afghanistan, occupying a favored invasion route since antiquity, has been variously known as Ariana or Bactria (in ancient times) and Khorasan (in the Middle Ages). Foreign empires alternated rule with local emirs and kings until the 18th cent., when a unified kingdom was established. In 1973, a military coup ushered in a republic.

Pro-Soviet leftists took power in a bloody 1978 coup. In Dec. 1979 the USSR began a massive airlift into Kabul and backed a new coup, leading to the installation of a more pro-Soviet leader. Soviet forces fanned out over Afghanistan and waged a protracted guerrilla war against Muslim rebels (aided by the U.S.); some 15,000 Soviet troops reportedly died.

A UN-mediated agreement was signed Apr. 14, 1988, providing for withdrawal of Soviet troops, a neutral Afghan state, and repatriation of refugees. Afghan rebels rejected the pact. The Soviets completed their troop withdrawal Feb. 15, 1989; fighting between Afghan rebels and government forces ensued. Communist Pres. Najibullah resigned Apr. 16, 1992, as competing guerrilla forces advanced on Kabul. The rebels achieved power Apr. 28. More than 2 mil Afghans had been killed, and 6 mil had left the country since 1979.

Clashes between moderates and Islamic fundamentalist forces followed the rebel victory. The Taliban, an insurgent radical-Islamist faction, captured Kabul in Sept. 1996 and empowered religious police to enforce strict Islamic codes of dress and behavior.

Victories in the north, Aug. 1998, essentially gave the Taliban control over the entire country. On Aug. 20, 1998, U.S. cruise missiles struck SE of Kabul, hitting facilities the U.S. said were terrorist training camps run by al-Qaeda leader Osama bin Laden.

After the Sept. 11, 2001, attacks on the World Trade Center and Pentagon, the U.S., blaming bin Laden, demanded that the Taliban surrender him and shut down his al-Qaeda terrorist network. When the Taliban refused, the U.S., with British assistance, began bombing Afghanistan Oct. 7, and sent in ground troops as part of Operation Enduring Freedom (OEF).

Supported by the U.S., the opposition Northern Alliance captured Kabul in Nov.; Taliban forces abandoned Kandahar, their last stronghold, to southern tribal fighters Dec. 7. A power-sharing agreement signed by four anti-Taliban factions, including the Northern Alliance, provided for an interim government headed by Hamid Karzai, a Pashtun tribal leader.

A new constitution, approved in Jan. 2004, included protections for women's rights denied under Taliban rule. Karzai won the Oct. 9, 2004, presidential election.

Although the U.S. announced the end of major combat operations in Afghanistan, May 1, 2003, resistance continued. NATO officially assumed control of peacekeeping forces—the Intl. Security Assistance Force (ISAF)—Aug. 11, 2003.

The most intense fighting in more than 4 years erupted Mar. 2006 with a new wave of attacks and other strikes by Taliban insurgents. Operating from sanctuaries in Pakistan, Islamist suicide bombers and Taliban insurgents stepped up their activities, 2007-11. Karzai was sworn in for a second term Nov. 19, 2009.

Ending a decade-long manhunt, U.S. commandos killed bin Laden shortly after midnight May 2, 2011, in Abbottabad, Pakistan. Ayman al-Zawahiri, who helped plan the Sept. 11 and other attacks on the U.S., succeeded bin Laden as head of al-Qaeda. (A U.S. drone strike, July 31, 2022, killed al-Zawahiri in Kabul.)

Between Jan. 2009 and June 2011, the number of U.S. troops in Afghanistan rose from about 36,000 to 101,000, while the number of allied foreign forces under ISAF increased from nearly 32,000 to more than 42,000. The U.S., June 22, 2011, outlined a timetable for drawing down troops and ending their combat role, with a residual force focusing on combating Islamic extremists and training and advising Afghan troops. OEF and ISAF officially ended Dec. 28, 2014; since Oct. 2001, 2,215 U.S. and 1,270 allied troops had been killed. The NATO-led Resolute Support Mission (RSM) to aid Afghan forces began Jan. 1, 2015.

A June 14, 2014, presidential runoff election was marred by allegations of electoral fraud. Ashraf Ghani Ahmadzai was declared the winner Sept. 21. Fighting between government and Taliban forces continued. Beginning in 2014, an affiliate of the Sunni extremist group ISIS was active in eastern Afghanistan. Following the death of his predecessor in a 2016 U.S. drone strike, Haibatullah Akhundzada became head of the Taliban.

A U.S. report estimated that, in late 2018, the government effectively controlled only about half of the country's districts. Ghani won a Sept. 28, 2019, presidential election. U.S. intelligence officials concluded, by early 2020, that Russia had paid bounties to Taliban-linked forces to kill U.S. and allied troops.

Combat, including airstrikes, and terrorist attacks caused high civilian casualties. The UN reported over 26,000 conflict-related civilian deaths, Jan. 2014-June 2021.

Under a U.S.-Taliban bilateral agreement signed Feb. 29, 2020, in return for a Taliban pledge that Afghanistan would not be a base for anti-U.S. terrorism, the U.S. pledged to withdraw its troops (then about 12,000). U.S. Pres. Joe Biden announced, Apr. 14, 2021, that withdrawal of the remaining 2,500-3,500 U.S. troops would begin May 1, to be completed by Sept. Remaining non-U.S. RSM forces also began withdrawing May 1.

Direct Taliban-Afghan government talks began in Qatar, Sept. 12, 2020, but made little progress, and the Taliban stepped up its attacks. With the U.S. withdrawal nearing completion in mid-2021, Taliban offensives rapidly captured provinces and major cities nationwide. Taliban forces entered and effectively took control of Kabul, Aug. 15, and Ghani fled the country.

The U.S. sent thousands of troops to evacuate people from Kabul's airport. By the time U.S. and coalition-partner flights ended Aug. 30 and the last U.S. troops left, about 123,000 civilians had been evacuated, including 6,000 Americans, other foreign nationals, and Afghans who had assisted the U.S. and its allies since 2001. As thousands of Afghans seeking (often unsuccessfully) to leave gathered outside the airport, an ISIS suicide bombing, Aug. 26, resulted in the deaths of 13 U.S. troops and some 170 others.

The new Taliban government severely limited women's rights—including restricting access to education, work opportunities, public places, and travel; imposing strict dress codes; and limiting a woman's right to speak outside their homes. Other freedoms were also restricted. The U.S. and many other nations did not recognize the Taliban government; foreign aid fell, though humanitarian aid through NGOs continued. Drought followed by 2024 flooding and aid cuts contributed to a humanitarian crisis. As of mid-2024, more than 14 mil Afghans faced acute food insecurity. As of Dec. 31, 2023, the UNHCR estimated that more than 5.8 mil Afghans were refugees in neighboring countries.

Albania

Republic of Albania

People: Population: 3,107,100 (135). **Age distrib.:** <15: 18.0%; 65+: 15.1%. **Growth:** 0.2%. **Migrants:** 1.7%. **Pop. density:** 293.7 per sq mi, 113.4 per sq km. **Urban:** 65.4%. **Ethnic groups:** Albanian 82.6%. **Languages:** Albanian (official). **Religions:** Muslim 65.2% (Sunni 61%), Christian 32.9% (Orthodox 18.0%, Catholic 13.4%).

Geography: Total area: 11,100 sq mi, 28,748 sq km (141); **Land area:** 10,578 sq mi, 27,398 sq km. **Location:** SE Europe, on SE coast of Adriatic Sea. Greece on S; Montenegro, Kosovo on N; North Macedonia on E. **Topography:** Narrow coastal plain; hills and mountains covered with scrub forest, cut by small E-W rivers. **Arable land:** 21.8%. **Capital:** Tirana, 528,127.

Government: Type: Parliamentary republic. **Head of state:** Pres. Bajram Begaj; b. 1967; in office: July 24, 2022. **Head of govt.:** Prime Min. Edi Rama; b. 1964; in office: Sept. 15, 2013. **Local divisions:** 12 counties. **Defense budget:** $401 mil. **Active troops:** 7,500.

Economy: Industries: food; footwear, apparel, clothing; lumber. **Chief agric.:** milk, maize, tomatoes, potatoes, watermelons, wheat. **Natural resources:** petroleum, nat. gas, coal, bauxite, chromite, copper, iron ore, nickel, salt, timber, hydropower. **Water:** 10,579 cu m per capita. **Crude oil reserves:** 150 mil bbls. **Electricity prod.:** 7.0 bil kWh. **Labor force:** agric. 34.9%, industry 21.4%, services 43.7%. **Unemployment:** 11.6%.

Finance: Monetary unit: Lek (ALL) (89.67 = $1 U.S.). **GDP:** $58.8 bil; **per capita GDP:** $21,395; **GDP growth:** 3.4%. **Imports:** $10.4 bil; Italy 25%, Turkey (Türkiye) 14%, Greece 12%, China 10%, Germany 5%. **Exports:** $9.2 bil; Italy 41%, Greece 10%, Spain 7%, Germany 5%. **Tourism:** $4.5 bil. **Budget:** $4.5 bil. **Inflation** (2021-22): 6.7%.

Transport: Railways: 263 mi. **Airports:** 3.

Communications: Mobile: 93.0 per 100 pop. **Broadband:** 74.1 per 100 pop. **Internet** (2023): 83.1%.

Health: Expend.: 7.3%. **Life expect.:** 77.3 male; 82.8 female. **Births:** 12.3 per 1,000 pop. **Deaths:** 7.4 per 1,000 pop. **Infant mortality:** 10.3 per 1,000 live births. **Undernourished:** 4.5%. **HIV:** <0.1%. **COVID-19:** 3,605 deaths; rates per 100,000: 11,642 cases, 125 deaths. 44% vaccinated.

Education: Compulsory: ages 6-14. **Literacy:** 98.5%.

Website: www.kryeministria.al

Ancient Illyria was conquered by Romans, Slavs, and Turks (15th cent.); the Turks Islamized the population. Independent Albania was proclaimed in 1912. Italy invaded in 1939.

Communist partisans took over in 1944 and allied Albania with the USSR but broke with the USSR in 1960 over de-Stalinization. Billions of dollars in Chinese financial assistance was cut off in 1978 when Albania attacked China's policies. Large-scale purges of officials occurred during the 1970s.

Enver Hoxha, the nation's ruler for four decades, died Apr. 11, 1985. The new regime introduced some liberalization.

Albania's former Communists were routed in elections Mar. 1992, amid economic collapse and social unrest. Sali Berisha was elected as the first non-Communist president since WWII. Berisha's party claimed a landslide victory in disputed parliamentary elections, May 26 and June 2, 1996. Public protests over the collapse of fraudulent investment schemes in Jan. 1997 led to armed rebellion. The UN Security Council, Mar. 28, authorized a 7,000-member force to restore order. Socialists and their allies won parliamentary elections, June 29 and July 6, 1997.

During NATO's air war against Yugoslavia, Mar.-June 1999, Albania hosted some 465,000 Kosovar refugees. A pro-Berisha coalition victory in July 3, 2005, elections ended eight years of Socialist rule. Albania became a full member of NATO Apr. 1, 2009. Socialists won June 23, 2013, parliamentary elections, and Edi Rama became prime min. Rama's Socialists won 2017 and 2021 parliamentary elections. Rama pledged to reduce organized crime and political corruption, key issues for EU membership; EU membership negotiations began in 2022. Albania's parliament, Feb. 22, 2024, approved a Nov. 2023 agreement with Italy under which migrants intercepted trying to reach Italy by sea could be sent to Albania pending asylum claims.

Algeria

People's Democratic Republic of Algeria

People: Population: 47,022,473 (33). **Age distrib.:** <15: 30.8%; 65+: 6.9%. **Growth:** 1.5%. **Migrants:** 0.6%. **Pop. density:** 51.1 per sq mi, 19.7 per sq km. **Urban:** 75.7%. **Ethnic groups:** Arab-Amazigh 99%. **Languages:** Arabic (official), French (lingua franca), Tamazight (official). **Religions:** Muslim (official) 98.0% (Sunni).

Geography: Total area: 919,595 sq mi, 2,381,740 sq km (10); **Land area:** 919,595 sq mi, 2,381,740 sq km. **Location:** NW Africa, from Medit. Sea into Sahara. Morocco, Western Sahara on W; Mauritania, Mali, Niger on S; Libya, Tunisia on E. **Topography:** The Tell, on the coast, comprises fertile plains 50-100 mi wide with a moderate climate and adequate rain. Two major chains of Atlas Mts., running roughly E-W and reaching 7,000 ft, enclose a dry plateau region. The Sahara lies below. **Arable land:** 3.2%. **Capital:** Algiers, 2,952,115. **Cities:** Oran, 950,768.

Government: Type: Presidential republic. **Head of state:** Pres. Abdelmadjid Tebboune; b. 1945; in office: Dec. 12, 2019. **Head of govt.:** Prime Min. Nadir Larbaoui; b. 1949; in office: Nov. 11, 2023. **Local divisions:** 58 provinces. **Defense budget:** $18.3 bil. **Active troops:** 139,000.

Economy: Industries: petroleum, nat. gas, light industries, mining, electrical, petrochemical, food proc. **Chief agric.:** potatoes, wheat, milk, watermelons, onions, tomatoes. **Natural resources:** petroleum, nat. gas, iron ore, phosphates, uranium, lead, zinc. **Water:** 264 cu m per capita. **Crude oil reserves:** 12.2 bil bbls. **Electricity prod.:** 88.2 bil kWh. **Labor force:** agric. 9.7%, industry 30.9%, services 59.4%. **Unemployment:** 11.8%.

Finance: Monetary unit: Dinar (DZD) (134.06 = $1 U.S.). **GDP:** $776.5 bil; **per capita GDP:** $17,027; **GDP growth:** 4.1%. **Imports:** $51.5 bil; China 18%, France 14%, Italy 7%, Turkey (Türkiye) 6%, Brazil 6%. **Exports:** $58.8 bil; Italy 29%, Spain 12%, France 12%, U.S. 5%, South Korea 5%. **Tourism** (2022): $176 mil. **Budget:** $64.7 bil. **Inflation:** 9.3%.

Transport: Railways: 2,498 mi. **Motor vehicles:** 134.4 per 1,000 pop. **Airports:** 85.

Communications: Mobile: 111.6 per 100 pop. **Broadband:** 104 per 100 pop. **Internet:** 71.2%.

Health: Expend.: 5.5%. **Life expect.:** 77.2 male; 78.7 female. **Births:** 20.2 per 1,000 pop. **Deaths:** 4.4 per 1,000 pop. **Infant mortality:** 18.7 per 1,000 live births. **Undernourished:** <2.5%. **HIV:**

<0.1%. **COVID-19:** 6,881 deaths; rates per 100,000: 621 cases, 16 deaths. 15% vaccinated.

Education: Compulsory: ages 6-15. **Literacy:** 81.4%.

Website: www.el-mouradia.dz, www.algerianembassy.org

Earliest known inhabitants were ancestors of Berbers, followed by Phoenicians, Romans, Vandals, and Arabs. Turkey ruled 1518-1830, when France took control. Large-scale European immigration followed. Arab nationalists launched a guerrilla war, 1954, that more than 400,000 French troops were unable to suppress. After French Pres. Charles de Gaulle came to power, 1958, colonial rule ended, nearly all Europeans left, and Algeria declared independence July 5, 1962. Ahmed Ben Bella ruled until 1965, when an army coup installed Col. Houari Boumedienne, a former guerrilla leader who held power until his death in 1978.

Hundreds died in anti-government riots protesting economic hardship, Oct. 1988. The government canceled the Jan. 1992 elections and banned all nonreligious activities at Algeria's 10,000 mosques. Pres. Mohammed Boudiaf was assassinated June 29, 1992. Over the next seven years, Muslim fundamentalists attacked high-ranking officials, security forces, and foreigners; pro-government death squads were active.

Liamine Zeroual won the Nov. 16, 1995, presidential election. A new constitution banning Islamic political parties and increasing the president's powers passed in a Nov. 1996 referendum. Abdelaziz Bouteflika, who became president after a flawed Apr. 15, 1999, election, reconciled with rebels. Bouteflika was reelected Apr. 8, 2004, though opponents charged fraud.

Under a reconciliation plan approved by referendum Sept. 2005, the government in Mar. 2006 began freeing Islamists jailed for their role in the 1990s civil war, which left up to 200,000 people dead and 8,000 "disappeared."

Radical Islamists bombed police stations in Oct. 2006 and Feb. 2007. A group known as al-Qaeda in the Islamic Maghreb (AQIM) carried out terrorist attacks, 2007-08, that killed more than 200 people.

Bouteflika claimed more than 90% of the vote in a 2009 election denounced as fraudulent by opposition parties. During Arab Spring uprisings in early 2011, Bouteflika's government suppressed street protests in Algiers, Feb. 12. The country's governing party, the Natl. Liberation Front (FLN), strengthened its hold on power in May 10, 2012, parliamentary elections that opposition groups called fraudulent.

AQIM members seized the In Amenas gas facility Jan. 16, 2013, holding about 40 foreign workers hostage for 4 days and demanding the release of about 100 Islamist prisoners; 38 hostages died, as well as some 29 militants, as Algerian special forces attempted to liberate the facility.

The 77-year-old Bouteflika, who had suffered a stroke in 2013, won a fourth term as president with 81.5% of the vote in the Apr. 17, 2014, election. The FLN won May 4, 2017, parliamentary elections.

Large-scale protests following the Feb. 2019 announcement that Bouteflika would seek a fifth term led to his forced resignation Apr. 2, 2019. In a Dec. 12, 2019, presidential election, boycotted by many government opponents, FLN candidate Abdelmadjid Tebboune won with 58% of the vote. The FLN won June 12, 2021, parliamentary elections. Tebboune was reelected on Sept. 7, 2024, with 84.3% of the vote; initial count of 94.7% was contested by candidates.

Andorra

Principality of Andorra

People: Population: 85,370 (186). **Age distrib.:** <15: 12.0%; 65+: 20.4%. **Growth:** –0.1%. **Migrants:** 59.0%. **Pop. density:** 472.5 per sq mi, 182.4 per sq km. **Urban:** 87.7%. **Ethnic groups** (by birth country): Spanish 34.3%, Andorran 32.1%, Portuguese 10%, French 5.6%. **Languages:** Catalan (official), Castilian, Portuguese, French. **Religions:** Christian 88.1% (Catholic 87.1%), agnostic 8.4%.

Geography: Total area: 181 sq mi, 468 sq km (180); **Land area:** 181 sq mi, 468 sq km. **Location:** SW Europe, in Pyrenees Mts. Spain on S, France on N. **Topography:** High mountains and narrow valleys across country. **Arable land:** 1.6%. **Capital:** Andorra la Vella, 22,614.

Government: Type: Parliamentary democracy. **Heads of state:** President of France and Bishop of Urgell (Spain), as co-princes. **Head of govt.:** Prime Min. Xavier Espot Zamora; in office: May 16, 2019. **Local divisions:** 7 parishes. **Defense budget/active troops:** NA.

Economy: Industries: tourism (skiing), banking, timber, furniture. **Chief agric.:** small quantities of rye, wheat, barley, oats, vegetables, tobacco. **Natural resources:** hydropower, mineral water, timber, iron ore, lead. **Water:** 3,993 cu m per capita. **Labor force:** NA. **Unemployment:** NA.

Finance: Monetary unit: Euro (EUR) (0.90 = $1 U.S.). **GDP:** $5.7 bil; **per capita GDP:** $71,588; **GDP growth:** 1.4%. **Imports** (2022): $2.4 bil; Spain 66%, France 12%. **Exports** (2022): $2.7 bil; Spain 73%, France 6%. **Tourism** (2022): $2.2 bil. **Budget** (2016): $2.1 bil. **Inflation:** NA.

Transport: NA.

Communications: Mobile: 156.1 per 100 pop. **Broadband:** 107 per 100 pop. **Internet:** 94.5%.

Health: Expend.: 8.3%. **Life expect.:** 81.6 male; 86.2 female. **Births:** 6.9 per 1,000 pop. **Deaths:** 8.1 per 1,000 pop. **Infant mortality:** 3.3 per 1,000 live births. **Undernourished:** NA. **HIV:** NA. **COVID-19:** 159 deaths; rates per 100,000: 62,143 cases, 206 deaths. 69% vaccinated.

Education: Compulsory: ages 6-15. **Literacy:** 100.0%.

Website: www.govern.ad

France and the bishop of Urgell held joint sovereignty over Andorra from 1278 to 1993. Voters chose to adopt a parliamentary system Mar. 14, 1993, although co-princes remain heads of state. Tourism, especially skiing, and banking are economic mainstays. For years, Andorra served as a tax haven, but it began reforms in 2008 and was removed by the OECD from its list of uncooperative tax havens, May 27, 2009. In Mar. 2015, the government seized control of Banca Privada d'Andorra (BPA) and arrested its chief executive after money laundering accusations. The parliament approved, Nov. 30, 2016, a measure to end, in stages, banking secrecy for foreigners' accounts.

Angola

Republic of Angola

People: Population: 37,202,061 (40). **Age distrib.:** <15: 46.9%; 65+: 2.4%. **Growth:** 3.3%. **Migrants:** 2.0%. **Pop. density:** 77.3 per sq mi, 29.8 per sq km. **Urban:** 69.3%. **Ethnic groups:** Ovimbundu 37%, Kimbundu 25%, Bakongo 13%, mestico (mixed European/native African) 2%. **Languages:** Portuguese (official), Umbundu, Kikongo, Kimbundu, Chokwe, Nhaneca, Nganguela. **Religions:** Christian 92.0% (Catholic 54.7%, Protestant 28.9%), ethnic religionist 5.7%.

Geography: Total area: 481,354 sq mi, 1,246,700 sq km (22); **Land area:** 481,354 sq mi, 1,246,700 sq km. **Location:** SW Africa on the Atlantic. Namibia on S, Zambia on E, Dem. Rep. of the Congo on N; Cabinda, an exclave separated by short Atlantic coast of the DRC, borders Rep. of the Congo. **Topography:** Mostly plateau 3,000-5,000 ft above sea level, rising from a narrow coastal strip. Temperate highland area in the W-central region, a desert in S, and a tropical rain forest in Cabinda. **Arable land:** 4.3%. **Capital:** Luanda, 9,651,032. **Cities:** Lubango, 1,003,016; Cabinda, 947,634.

Government: Type: Presidential republic. **Head of state and govt.:** Pres. João Lourenço; b. 1954; in office: Sept. 26, 2017. **Local divisions:** 18 provinces. **Defense budget:** $1.3 bil. **Active troops:** 107,000.

Economy: Industries: petroleum, diamonds, cement, metal prods., fish/food proc. **Chief agric.:** cassava, bananas, maize, sweet potatoes, sugarcane, pineapples. **Natural resources:** petroleum, diamonds, iron ore, phosphates, copper, feldspar, gold, bauxite, uranium. **Water:** 4,301 cu m per capita. **Crude oil reserves:** 7.8 bil bbls. **Electricity prod.:** 16.9 bil kWh. **Labor force:** agric. 56.3%, industry 5.7%, services 38.0%. **Unemployment:** 14.6%.

Finance: Monetary unit: Kwanza (AOA) (918.05 = $1 U.S.). **GDP:** $295.0 bil; **per capita GDP:** $8,041; **GDP growth:** 0.9%. **Imports:** $23.7 bil; China 24%, Portugal 10%, Netherlands 8%, UAE 5%. **Exports:** $37.0 bil; China 40%, India 9%, Netherlands 7%, France 7%, UAE 7%. **Tourism:** $8 mil. **Budget:** $17.2 bil. **Inflation:** 13.6%.

Transport: Railways: 1,716 mi. **Motor vehicles:** 5.8 per 1,000 pop. **Airports:** 106.

Communications: Mobile: 70.1 per 100 pop. **Broadband:** 30.3 per 100 pop. **Internet:** 39.3%.

Health: Expend.: 3.0%. **Life expect.:** 60.8 male; 65.1 female. **Births:** 41.1 per 1,000 pop. **Deaths:** 7.6 per 1,000 pop. **Infant mortality:** 55.6 per 1,000 live births. **Undernourished:** 23.2%. **HIV:** 1.5%. **COVID-19:** 1,937 deaths; rates per 100,000: 327 cases, 6 deaths. 29% vaccinated.

Education: Compulsory: ages 6-11. **Literacy:** 72.4%.

Website: www.governo.gov.ao

From the early centuries CE to 1500, Bantu tribes penetrated most of the region. Portuguese came in 1583, allied with the Bakongo kingdom in the north, and developed the slave trade. Large-scale colonization began in the 20th cent., when 400,000 Portuguese immigrated.

A guerrilla war, 1961-75, ended when Portugal granted Angola independence. Fighting then erupted among rival rebel groups, including the Soviet-backed Popular Movement for the Liberation of Angola (MPLA) and the National Union for the Total Independence of Angola (UNITA), aided by the U.S. and South Africa. Cuban troops helped the MPLA win control of most of the country by 1976, but fighting continued. The UN estimated that the civil war had claimed some 1 mil lives and left another 2.5 mil people homeless by mid-2001. Government troops killed rebel leader Jonas Savimbi Feb. 22, 2002. UNITA agreed to a truce Apr. 4, 2002. Separatist rebels in oilrich Cabinda agreed to a cease-fire July 2006.

With proven petroleum reserves estimated at 9 bil barrels, Angola is among Africa's leading oil producers. Wealth is extremely unevenly distributed, and corruption has been widespread. The ruling MPLA claimed victory in voting Sept. 2008, in Angola's first parliamentary elections in 16 years. Parliament approved Jan. 21, 2010, a new constitution augmenting the power of MPLA leader José Eduardo dos Santos, Angola's president since 1979. The MPLA won flawed elections, Aug 31, 2012, giving dos Santos another 5-year term. The MPLA won disputed Aug. 23, 2017, elections, and João Lourenço took office as president, Sept. 26. On Nov. 15, Lourenço dismissed as head of the state oil company dos Santos's daughter, Isabel dos Santos, suspected of misappropriating up to $1 bil of government funds. On Jan. 11, 2018, Lourenço removed as head of the country's sovereign wealth fund dos Santos's son, José Filomeno dos Santos; he was sentenced, Aug. 2020, to 5 years in prison for embezzlement.

A new penal code, approved Jan. 23, 2019, decriminalized same-sex relationships and prohibited discrimination based on sexual orientation.

The MPLA was declared the winner by a slim margin of Aug. 24, 2022, parliamentary elections, giving Lourenço another term as president.

Angola, which joined OPEC in 2007, terminated its membership as of Jan. 1, 2024, opposing production ceilings.

Antigua and Barbuda

People: Population: 102,634 (182). **Age distrib.:** <15: 21.8%; 65+: 10.5%. **Growth:** 1.1%. **Migrants:** 30.0%. **Pop. density:** 600.0 per sq mi, 231.7 per sq km. **Urban:** 24.3%. **Ethnic groups:** African descent 87.3%, mixed 4.7%, Hispanic 2.7%. **Languages:** English (official), Antiguan Creole. **Religions:** Christian 91.3% (Protestant 76.8%, Catholic 9.5%), Spiritist 3.8%.

Geography: Total area: 171 sq mi, 443 sq km (Antigua, 108 sq mi, 280 sq km; Barbuda, 62 sq mi, 161 sq km) (183); **Land area:** 171 sq mi, 443 sq km. **Location:** E Caribbean. St. Kitts and Nevis to W, Guadeloupe (Fr.) to S. **Topography:** Mostly low-lying and limestone coral islands. Antigua is mostly hilly with an indented coast; Barbuda is a flat island with a large lagoon on W. **Arable land:** 9.1%. **Capital:** St. John's, 20,764.

Government: Type: Parliamentary democracy under constitutional monarchy. **Head of state:** King Charles III, rep. by Gov.-Gen. Rodney Williams; b. 1947; in office: Aug. 14, 2014. **Head of govt.:** Prime Min. Gaston Browne; b. 1967; in office: June 13, 2014. **Local divisions:** 6 parishes, 2 dependencies. **Defense budget:** $8 mil. **Active troops:** 200.

Economy: Industries: tourism, constr., light mfg. **Chief agric.:** tropical fruits, milk, mangoes/guavas, eggs, lemons/limes, pumpkins/squash. **Natural resources:** negligible. **Water:** 558 cu m per capita. **Electricity prod.:** 356.2 mil kWh. **Labor force:** NA. **Unemployment:** NA.

Finance: Monetary unit: East Caribbean Dollar (XCD) (2.70 = $1 U.S.). **GDP:** $3.0 bil; **per capita GDP:** $31,802; **GDP growth:** 3.9%. **Imports:** $1.3 bil; U.S. 57%, China 7%. **Exports:** $1.2 bil; Suriname 28%, Poland 20%, Germany 13%, UK 8%, Barbados 5%. **Tourism:** $723 mil. **Budget** (2020): $357 mil. **Inflation:** 5.1%.

Transport: Airports: 3.

Communications: Mobile (2022): 201.0 per 100 pop. **Broadband** (2022): 51.7 per 100 pop. **Internet:** 91.4%.

Health: Expend.: 5.9%. **Life expect.:** 76.1 male; 80.5 female. **Births:** 14.9 per 1,000 pop. **Deaths:** 5.7 per 1,000 pop. **Infant mortality:** 13.6 per 1,000 live births. **Undernourished:** NA. **HIV:** NA. **COVID-19:** 146 deaths; rates per 100,000: 9,299 cases, 149 deaths. 64% vaccinated.

Education: Compulsory: ages 5-15. **Literacy:** 99.0%.

Website: ab.gov.ag

Christopher Columbus landed on Antigua in 1493. The British colonized it in 1632. The British-associated state of Antigua achieved independence as Antigua and Barbuda on Nov. 1, 1981. Tourism generally accounts for well over half of GDP. The worldwide recession caused the economy to shrink in 2009-11. With the economy still weak, the opposition Antigua and Barbuda Labour Party (ABLP) won June 12, 2014, parliamentary elections. ABLP leader Gaston Browne became prime minister and supported development projects opposed by environmental groups. Hurricane Irma caused massive damage on Barbuda, Sept. 5-6, 2017.

The ABLP easily retained power in Mar. 21, 2018, elections. With the economy not fully recovered from the sharp decline in tourism, 2020-21, caused by the COVID-19 pandemic and the country dealing with high inflation, the ABLP only narrowly won Jan. 18, 2023, elections.

Argentina

Argentine Republic

People: Population: 46,994,384 (34). **Age distrib.:** <15: 23.3%; 65+: 12.8%. **Growth:** 0.8%. **Migrants:** 5.0%. **Pop. density:** 44.5 per sq mi, 17.2 per sq km. **Urban:** 92.6%. **Ethnic groups:** European (mostly Spanish/Italian descent) and mestizo (mixed European/Indigenous) 97.2%, Indigenous 2.4%. **Languages:** Spanish (official), Italian, English, German, French, Indigenous (Quechua, Guarani, Mapudungun). **Religions:** Christian 87.7% (Catholic 74.6%), agnostic 7.7%, Muslim 2.3%.

Geography: Total area: 1,073,518 sq mi, 2,780,400 sq km (8); **Land area:** 1,056,642 sq mi, 2,736,690 sq km. **Location:** Occupies most of southern S America. Chile on W; Bolivia, Paraguay on N; Brazil, Uruguay on NE. **Topography:** Andean, Central, Misiones, and Southern mountain ranges in W. Aconcagua (22,831 ft) is highest peak in Western Hemisphere. Gran Chaco, heavily wooded plains, are E of Andes in the N; fertile, treeless Pampas in the central region. Patagonia, in S, is bleak and arid. Rio de la Plata, an estuary in NE, 170 by 140 mi, is mostly freshwater, from 2,485-mi Paraná and 1,000-mi Uruguay Rivers. **Arable land:** 15.7%. **Capital:** Buenos Aires, 15,618,288. **Cities:** Córdoba, 1,625,937; Rosario, 1,613,041; Mendoza, 1,242,319.

Government: Type: Presidential republic. **Head of state and govt.:** Pres. Javier Gerardo Milei; b. 1970; in office: Dec. 10, 2023. **Local divisions:** 23 provinces, 1 autonomous city. **Defense budget:** $2.9 bil. **Active troops:** 72,100.

Economy: Industries: food proc., motor vehicles, consumer durables, textiles, chemicals and petrochemicals. **Chief agric.:** maize, soybeans, wheat, sugarcane, milk, barley. **Natural resources:** lead, zinc, tin, copper, iron ore, manganese, petroleum, uranium. **Water:** 19,353 cu m per capita. **Crude oil reserves:** 2.5 bil bbls. **Electricity prod.:** 145.0 bil kWh. **Labor force:** agric. 7.2%, industry 20.0%, services 72.8%. **Unemployment:** 6.2%.

Finance: Monetary unit: Peso (ARS) (948.76 = $1 U.S.). **GDP:** $1.4 tril; **per capita GDP:** $29,363; **GDP growth:** –1.6%. **Imports:** $92.6 bil; China 21%, Brazil 20%, U.S. 14%. **Exports:** $83.4 bil; Brazil 15%, China 9%, U.S. 8%, Chile 6%, India 5%. **Tourism:** $5.4 bil. **Budget:** $170.7 bil. **Inflation** (2016-17): 25.7%.

Transport: Railways: 11,101 mi. **Motor vehicles:** 306.2 per 1,000 pop. **Airports:** 756.

Communications: Mobile: 137.7 per 100 pop. **Broadband** (2022): 76.2 per 100 pop. **Internet** (2023): 89.2%.

Health: Expend.: 9.7%. **Life expect.:** 75.8 male; 82.0 female. **Births:** 15.2 per 1,000 pop. **Deaths:** 7.3 per 1,000 pop. **Infant mortality:** 9.0 per 1,000 live births. **Undernourished:** 3.2%. **HIV:** 0.4%. **COVID-19:** 130,664 deaths; rates per 100,000: 22,350 cases, 289 deaths. 84% vaccinated.

Education: Compulsory: ages 4-17. **Literacy:** 99.0%.

Website: www.argentina.gob.ar

Nomadic Indians roamed the Pampas when Spaniards arrived, 1515-16, led by Juan Díaz de Solís. Nearly all the Indians were killed by the late 19th cent. The colonists won independence, 1816. A long period of disorder ended in a strong centralized government.

Large-scale Italian, German, and Spanish immigration in the decades after 1880 spurred modernization. Social reforms were enacted in the 1920s, but military coups prevailed, 1930-46, until Gen. Juan Perón was elected president.

Perón, with his wife, Eva Duarte (d. 1952), introduced labor reforms but suppressed speech and press freedoms, closed religious schools, and ran the country into debt. A 1955 coup exiled Perón. A series of military and civilian regimes followed. Perón returned in 1973 and was again elected president. He died 10 months later. His wife and vice president, Isabel, succeeded him.

A military junta ousted Isabel Perón in 1976 amid charges of corruption. Under a continuing state of siege, the army conducted a "dirty war" against guerrillas and leftists. An estimated 30,000 people "disappeared."

Argentine troops seized control of the British-held Falkland Islands (Islas Malvinas) on Apr. 2, 1982. The British imposed an air and sea blockade around the Falklands. Fighting began May 1. British troops landed on East Falkland May 21. Argentine troops surrendered, June 14.

Democratic rule returned in 1983. On Dec. 9, 1985, five former junta members were found guilty of murder and human rights abuses during the "dirty war" period. Buenos Aires Mayor Fernando de la Rúa won the presidential election Oct. 24, 1999, but resigned in 2001 after a prolonged recession resulted in debt of more than $130 bil. Congress, Jan. 1, 2002, chose a Peronist, Eduardo Alberto Duhalde, to finish de la Rúa's term. Further economic decline and renewed protests led Duhalde, July 2, to schedule an early presidential election for Mar. 2003; another Peronist, Néstor Kirchner, took office May 25, 2003. A new IMF aid deal, approved Sept. 10, 2003, rescued Argentina from default.

The Supreme Court, June 14, 2005, overturned amnesty laws that had barred prosecution for "dirty war" crimes committed while the military ruled Argentina. In July 2010, Argentina became the first Latin American country to extend full marriage rights to same-sex couples.

Cristina Fernández de Kirchner ran as the Peronist candidate after her husband and was elected president Oct. 28, 2007. She was reelected Oct. 23, 2011. In 2013, special prosecutor Alberto Nisman accused Fernández de Kirchner of interfering with his investigation of Iranian involvement in a 1994 Jewish community center bombing in Buenos Aires that killed 85 people. Nisman was found shot dead in his home, Jan. 18, 2015. A border police investigation concluded, Nov. 2017, that Nisman had been murdered.

Buenos Aires Archbishop Jorge Mario Bergoglio was elected pope Mar. 13, 2013; he was the first pope from the Americas. He took the name Francis.

Defeating Peronist candidate Daniel Scioli in a runoff, Mauricio Macri of the center-right Republican Proposal Party was elected president Nov. 22, 2015. Pres. Macri, Sept. 3, 2018, announced austerity measures to stem a budget deficit and a sharp drop in the value of the peso. With economic problems continuing, Peronist Alberto Fernández defeated Macri in the Oct. 27, 2019, presidential election. Argentina's Congress, Dec. 30, 2020, completed legislation legalizing abortion in the first 14 weeks of pregnancy.

With the economy in recession and inflation in triple digits, rightist Javier Milei won the Nov. 19, 2023, presidential runoff election. Milei's austerity measures, as well as June 2024 legislation providing for privatization, deregulation to spur foreign investment, and increased presidential control over the economy, sparked strikes and large-scale protests.

Armenia

Republic of Armenia

People: Population: 2,976,765 (136). **Age distrib.:** <15: 17.7%; 65+: 15.3%. **Growth:** –0.4%. **Migrants:** 6.4%. **Pop. density:** 273.4 per sq mi, 105.5 per sq km. **Urban:** 63.9%. **Ethnic groups:** Armenian 98.1%, Yezidi 1.1%. **Languages:** Armenian (official). **Religions:** Christian 95.0% (Orthodox 79.8%, Catholic 8.2%, Protestant 4.0%), agnostic 2.7%.

Geography: Total area: 11,484 sq mi, 29,743 sq km (139); **Land area:** 10,889 sq mi, 28,203 sq km. **Location:** SW Asia. Georgia on N, Azerbaijan on E, Iran on S, Turkey on W. **Topography:** Mountainous with many peaks above 10,000 ft. **Arable land:** 15.6%. **Capital:** Yerevan, 1,097,542.

Government: Type: Parliamentary democracy. **Head of state:** Pres. Vahagn Khachaturyan; b. 1959; in office: Mar. 13, 2022. **Head of govt.:** Prime Min. Nikol Pashinyan; b. 1975; in office: Sept. 10, 2021. **Local divisions:** 11 provinces. **Defense budget:** $1.3 bil. **Active troops:** 42,900.

Economy: Industries: brandy, mining, diamond proc., metal-cutting machine tools, forging/pressing machines, elec. motors, knitted wear. **Chief agric.:** milk, potatoes, grapes, tomatoes, vegetables, wheat. **Natural resources:** gold, copper, molybdenum, zinc, bauxite. **Water:** 2,784 cu m per capita. **Electricity prod.:** 8.8 bil kWh. **Labor force:** agric. 52.4%, industry 14.0%, services 33.5%. **Unemployment:** 8.6%.

Finance: Monetary unit: Dram (AMD) (386.08 = $1 U.S.). **GDP:** $64.0 bil; **per capita GDP:** $23,055; **GDP growth:** 8.7%. **Imports:** $14.3 bil; Russia 23%, UAE 19%, China 10%, Georgia 5%, Iran 5%. **Exports:** $14.1 bil; Russia 41%, UAE 9%, China 7%. **Tourism:** $3.0 bil. **Budget:** $3.4 bil. **Inflation:** 2.0%.

Transport: Railways: 426 mi. **Airports:** 11.

Communications: Mobile: 134.5 per 100 pop. **Broadband:** 103 per 100 pop. **Internet:** 77%.

Health: Expend.: 12.3%. **Life expect.:** 73.4 male; 80.1 female. **Births:** 10.5 per 1,000 pop. **Deaths:** 9.6 per 1,000 pop. **Infant mortality:** 11.6 per 1,000 live births. **Undernourished:** <2.5%. **HIV:** 0.4%. **COVID-19:** 8,777 deaths; rates per 100,000: 15,263 cases, 296 deaths. 35% vaccinated.

Education: Compulsory: ages 6-17. **Literacy:** 99.8%.

Website: www.gov.am

Ancient Armenia extended into parts of what are now Turkey and Iran. Present-day Armenia was set up as a Soviet republic Apr. 2, 1921. It joined Georgian and Azerbaijan SSRs Mar. 12, 1922, to form the Transcaucasian SFSR, which became part of the USSR Dec. 30, 1922. Armenia became a constituent republic of the USSR Dec. 5, 1936. An earthquake struck Armenia Dec. 7, 1988; approximately 25,000 were killed.

Armenia became an independent state when the USSR disbanded Dec. 26, 1991. Nagorno-Karabakh, an enclave in Azerbaijan with an ethnic Armenian majority, seceded from Azerbaijan in 1988. A 1992-94 war that cost 30,000 lives ended in a cease-fire with Armenian forces in control of Nagorno-Karabakh and adjacent areas. Deadly clashes between Armenian and Azerbaijani forces occurred in 2015-16 in and near Nagorno-Karabakh. After Azerbaijani victories in heavy fighting beginning in Sept. 2020, Armenia agreed, in a Nov. 9 cease-fire, to cede areas in Azerbaijan it had controlled since 1994. A new offensive by Azerbaijan in Sept. 2023 gave it complete control of Nagorno-Karabakh, prompting more than 100,000 ethnic Armenians (most of the Armenian pop.) in the region to flee to Armenia.

Voters approved, July 5, 1995, a new constitution increasing presidential powers. Pres. Levon Ter-Petrosian won reelection Sept. 22, 1996, amid claims of fraud. He resigned Feb. 3, 1998, and Robert Kocharian, a nationalist born in Nagorno-Karabakh, won the presidency Mar. 30, 1998. Gunmen stormed Parliament Oct. 27, 1999, killing Prime Min. Vazgen Sarkissian and 7 others. Kocharian won a second term Mar. 5, 2003.

Prime Min. Serzh Sargsyan defeated Ter-Petrosian in a Feb. 19, 2008, presidential election. Armenia did not ratify an Oct. 2009 treaty it had approved with Turkey over the 1915-18 killing of more than 1 mil Armenians by Ottoman Turks, due to renewed friction between the countries in 2010. Sargsyan won reelection Feb. 18, 2013. Constitutional revisions transitioned the government to a parliamentary system as of 2018. Opposition leader Nikol Pashinyan was elected prime min. by parliament May 8. Pashinyan's party won a landslide victory in Dec. 9, 2018, parliamentary elections. Blamed for Armenia's defeat in 2020 fighting against Azerbaijan, Pashinyan resigned Apr. 25, 2021, but retained office after winning June 20 elections; the opposition charged electoral fraud.

Australia

Commonwealth of Australia

People: Population: 26,768,598 (54). **Age distrib.:** <15: 18.3%; 65+: 17.0%. **Growth:** 1.1%. **Migrants:** 30.1%. **Pop. density:** 9.0 per sq mi, 3.5 per sq km. **Urban:** 86.8%. **Ethnic groups:** English 33%, Australian 29.9%, Irish 9.5%, Scottish 8.6%, Chinese 5.5%, Italian 4.4%, German 4%, Indian 3.1%, Australian Aboriginal 2.9%. **Languages:** English, Chinese (Mandarin, Cantonese), Arabic, Vietnamese. **Religions:** Christian 53.5% (Catholic 26.6%, Protestant 19.0%), agnostic 27.0%, atheist 6.8%, Buddhist 4.1%, Muslim 3.2% (Sunni 2%).

Geography: Total area: 2,988,902 sq mi, 7,741,220 sq km (6); **Land area:** 2,966,153 sq mi, 7,682,300 sq km. **Location:** SE of Asia. Surrounded by Indian O. on W and S, Pacific O. (Coral, Tasman Seas) in E. Tasmania lies 150 mi S of Victoria state, across Bass Strait. Nearest are Indonesia, Papua New Guinea on N; Solomons, Fiji, and New Zealand on E. **Topography:** An island continent. The Great Dividing Range along the E coast has Mt. Kosciusko (7,310 ft). The Western Plateau rises to 2,000 ft, with arid areas in the Great Sandy and Great Victoria Deserts. The NW part of Western Australia and Northern Terr. are arid and hot. The NE has heavy rainfall. Jungles in Cape York Peninsula. **Arable land:** 4.1%. **Capital:** Canberra, 477,567. **Cities:** Melbourne, 5,315,600; Sydney, 5,184,896; Brisbane, 2,536,449; Perth, 2,143,491; Adelaide, 1,379,280.

Government: Type: Federal parliamentary democracy under constitutional monarchy. **Head of state:** King Charles III, rep. by Gov.-Gen. Samantha (Sam) Mostyn; b. 1965; in office: July 1, 2024. **Head of govt.:** Prime Min. Anthony Albanese; b. 1963; in office: May 23, 2022. **Local divisions:** 6 states, 2 territories. **Defense budget:** $34.4 bil. **Active troops:** 59,800.

Economy: Industries: mining, industrial and transp. equip., food proc., chemicals, steel. **Chief agric.:** wheat, sugarcane, barley, milk, rapeseed, cotton. **Natural resources:** alumina, coal, iron ore, copper, lithium, tin, gold, silver, uranium, nickel, tungsten, rare earth elements, mineral sands, lead, zinc, diamonds, opals, nat. gas, petroleum. **Water:** 18,981 cu m per capita. **Crude oil reserves:** 2.4 bil bbls. **Electricity prod.:** 261.5 bil kWh. **Labor force:** agric. 2.2%, industry 18.6%, services 79.2%. **Unemployment:** 3.7%.

Finance: Monetary unit: Dollar (AUD) (1.48 = $1 U.S.). **GDP:** $1.8 tril; **per capita GDP:** $69,115; **GDP growth:** 3.0%. **Imports:** $363.6 bil; China 28%, U.S. 10%, South Korea 6%, Japan 6%, Singapore 5%. **Exports:** $447.5 bil; China 29%, Japan 19%, South Korea 10%, India 7%, Taiwan 6%. **Tourism:** $46.6 bil. **Budget:** $532.6 bil. **Inflation:** 5.6%.

Transport: Railways: 20,260 mi. **Motor vehicles:** 751.4 per 1,000 pop. **Airports:** 2,180.

Communications: Mobile: 110.2 per 100 pop. **Broadband:** 126 per 100 pop. **Internet:** 94.9%.

Health: Expend.: 10.5%. **Life expect.:** 81.3 male; 85.7 female. **Births:** 12.2 per 1,000 pop. **Deaths:** 6.8 per 1,000 pop. **Infant mortality:** 2.9 per 1,000 live births. **Undernourished:** <2.5%. **HIV:** <0.1%. **COVID-19:** 25,236 deaths; rates per 100,000: 46,515 cases, 99 deaths. 85% vaccinated.

Education: Compulsory: ages 6-16. **Literacy:** NA.

Website: www.australia.gov.au

Australia harbors many plant and animal species not found elsewhere, including kangaroos, koalas, platypuses, dingoes (wild dogs), Tasmanian devils, wombats, and barking and frilled lizards.

Aboriginal peoples first reached Australia, from SE Asia, at least 45,000-50,000 years ago and perhaps thousands of years earlier. British Capt. James Cook explored the eastern coast in 1770, when the entire continent and its offshore islands were inhabited by Indigenous peoples. The first European settlers, beginning in 1788, were mostly convicts, soldiers, and government officials. By 1830, Britain had claimed the entire continent, and the immigration of free settlers accelerated. The Commonwealth was proclaimed Jan. 1, 1901. Northern Terr. was granted limited self-rule July 1, 1978.

State/territory, capital	Tot. area (sq mi)	Pop.
New South Wales, Sydney	309,326	8,434,754
Victoria, Melbourne	87,817	6,905,978
Queensland, Brisbane	667,857	5,528,292
Western Australia, Perth	975,685	2,927,888
South Australia, Adelaide	380,048	1,866,318
Tasmania, Hobart	26,410	574,705
Australian Capital Terr., Canberra	910	470,232
Northern Terr., Darwin	520,385	253,634

Note: Estimated pop. as of Dec. 31, 2023. (Source: Australian Bureau of Statistics)

In a 1967 referendum, Australians voted to change parts of the country's constitution that discriminated against Aboriginal Australians. Racially discriminatory immigration policies ended in 1973, after 3 mil Europeans (half British) had entered since 1945.

Australia is among the top exporters of lamb, wool, and wheat. Major mineral deposits, including coal, have been developed, largely for export. Slumping commodity prices and sluggish exports to China impacted the economy beginning in 2016. By 2019, the government instituted various economic stimulus measures to boost sagging GDP growth.

Australian troops fought in U.S.-led military operations in Afghanistan (beginning 2001) and Iraq (beginning 2003); the last Australian troops left Afghanistan in 2021. Some 2,000 Australian peacekeepers began arriving in the Solomon Isls., July 24, 2003; nearly all were withdrawn by mid-2005. In race riots in Sydney suburbs, Dec. 11-12, 2005, thousands of youths assaulted people of Middle Eastern ancestry, who then retaliated. Australian troops were dispatched, 2006, to suppress disorder in the Solomon Isls. in Apr. and Timor in May. The last Australian troops in Timor returned home on Mar. 27, 2013.

Australian warplanes joined the U.S.-led air campaign in Iraq (2014-18) and Syria (2015-18) against the Sunni extremist group ISIS. About 23,000 refugees fleeing warfare in Syria and Iraq arrived in Australia 2015-17.

The Labor Party's Julia Gillard became, June 24, 2010, Australia's first female prime minister. Downpours from Cyclone Tasha and other storms caused severe flooding in Queensland, Dec. 2010-Jan. 2011. Prime Min. Gillard, Mar. 20, 2013, officially apologized for Australia's forced adoption policy (in effect late 1950s-70s), in which the state took the babies of single, teenage, or "unfit" mothers, often under duress. Labor's Kevin Rudd replaced Gillard June 26, 2013.

The conservatives returned to power after Sept. 7, 2013, elections, making Tony Abbott prime min. Malcolm Turnbull replaced Abbott as prime min., Sept. 15, 2015, after defeating him in a vote for Liberal Party leader. Turnbull's Liberal/National Party coalition won a narrow victory in July 2, 2016, elections. Liberal Scott Morrison replaced Turnbull as prime min., Aug. 24, 2018.

National and state governments instituted travel restrictions and lockdown measures, beginning in 2020, to combat the COVID-19 pandemic; violent anti-vaccination, anti-lockdown protests took place in Melbourne, Sept. 2021. As of Sept. 2024, Australia had recorded nearly 12 mil total confirmed COVID-19 cases (14th-highest in the world).

Under a 2021 agreement, elaborated in 2023, Australia would first buy from the U.S. and then build, with U.S. and UK assistance, nuclear-powered submarines, countering China's growing sea power.

May 21, 2022, elections returned Labor to power, with a slim House of Representatives majority; Anthony Albanese became prime min. An Oct. 2023 referendum defeated a proposed constitutional amendment to create an Indigenous advisory body, Voice to Parliament.

Australian External Territories

Norfolk Isl., area 14.3 sq mi, pop. (2021 census) 2,188, was taken over, 1914. The soil is very fertile, suitable for citrus, bananas, and coffee. Many of the inhabitants are descended from Pitcairn Islanders who moved to Norfolk in 1856 after the British abandoned an attempted penal colony. Australia offered the island limited home rule in 1979 but revoked its autonomy in 2015. The island's legislative assembly was replaced by an elected regional council in 2016. **Website:** www.norfolkisland.gov.nf

The only inhabitants of **Coral Sea Isls.**, area 2.7 sq mi, are meteorological staff on Willis Isl.

Ashmore and Cartier Isls., area 1.9 sq mi, in the Indian O., came under Australian authority in 1934. **Heard Isl. and McDonald Isls.**, area 159.1 sq mi, are administered by the Australian Antarctic Division.

Cocos (Keeling) Isls. are 27 coral islands in the Indian O. about 1,833 mi NW of Australia. Area 5.4 sq mi; pop. (2021 census) 593. The residents voted to become part of Australia, Apr. 1984. **Website:** www.shire.cc

Christmas Isl., area 52.1 sq mi, pop. (2021 census) 1,692; 230 mi S of Java, was transferred by Britain in 1958. Phosphate mining is the main economic activity, though high-grade phosphate deposits are nearly depleted. **Website:** www.shire.gov.cx

Australian Antarctic Territory was claimed by the UK and then transferred to Australian sovereignty in 1933. It comprises some 2.2 mil sq mi of territory S of 60th parallel S lat. between 45°E and 160°E (not incl. France's Adelie Coast) and between 136°E and 142°E.

Austria
Republic of Austria

People: Population: 8,967,982 (100). **Age distrib.:** <15: 14.1%; 65+: 21.2%. **Growth:** 0.3%. **Migrants:** 19.3%. **Pop. density:** 281.7 per sq mi, 108.8 per sq km. **Urban:** 59.8%. **Ethnic groups** (by birth country): Austrian 80.8%, German 2.6%. **Languages:** German (official), Turkish, Serbian, Croatian (official in one state). **Religions:** Christian 67.3% (Catholic 59.1%, Protestant 4.0%), agnostic 22.4%, Muslim 7.7% (Sunni), atheist 2.0%.

Geography: Total area: 32,383 sq mi, 83,871 sq km (112); **Land area:** 31,832 sq mi, 82,445 sq km. **Location:** S Central Europe. Switzerland, Liechtenstein on W; Germany, Czechia on N; Slovakia, Hungary on E; Slovenia, Italy on S. **Topography:** Primarily mountainous, with the Alps and foothills covering the western and southern provinces. The eastern provinces and Vienna are located in the Danube River Basin. **Arable land:** 16.0%. **Capital:** Vienna, 1,990,487.

Government: Type: Federal parliamentary republic. **Head of state:** Pres. Alexander Van der Bellen; b. 1944; in office: Jan. 26, 2017. **Head of govt.:** Chancellor Karl Nehammer; b. 1972; in office: Dec. 6, 2021. **Local divisions:** 9 states. **Defense budget:** $4.4 bil. **Active troops:** 22,200.

Economy: Industries: constr., machinery, vehicles and parts, food, metals, chemicals, lumber and paper, electronics, tourism. **Chief agric.:** milk, sugar beets, maize, wheat, barley, potatoes. **Natural resources:** oil, coal, lignite, timber, iron ore, copper, zinc, antimony, magnesite, tungsten, graphite, salt, hydropower. **Water:** 8,709 cu m per capita. **Crude oil reserves:** 35 mil bbls. **Electricity prod.:** 59.7 bil kWh. **Labor force:** agric. 3.5%, industry 26.4%, services 70.1%. **Unemployment:** 5.2%.

Finance: Monetary unit: Euro (EUR) (0.90 = $1 U.S.). **GDP:** $673.5 bil; **per capita GDP:** $73,751; **GDP growth:** –0.8%. **Imports:** $288.1 bil; Germany 40%, Italy 7%, Czechia 5%, Switzerland 5%. **Exports:** $306.5 bil; Germany 28%, U.S. 7%, Italy 7%, Switzerland 5%, Hungary 5%. **Tourism:** $25.0 bil. **Budget:** $215.5 bil. **Inflation:** 7.8%.

Transport: Railways: 3,805 mi. **Motor vehicles:** 641.1 per 1,000 pop. **Airports:** 61.

Communications: Mobile: 121.7 per 100 pop. **Broadband:** 125 per 100 pop. **Internet** (2023): 95.3%.

Health: Expend.: 12.1%. **Life expect.:** 80.1 male; 85.4 female. **Births:** 9.3 per 1,000 pop. **Deaths:** 9.9 per 1,000 pop. **Infant mortality:** 3.2 per 1,000 live births. **Undernourished:** <2.5%. **HIV:** NA. **COVID-19:** 22,534 deaths; rates per 100,000: 68,334 cases, 253 deaths. 75% vaccinated.

Education: Compulsory: ages 5-17. **Literacy:** NA.

Website: www.bundeskanzleramt.gv.at

Rome conquered Austrian lands from Celtic tribes around 15 BCE. In 788 the territory was incorporated into Charlemagne's empire. By 1300, the House of Habsburg had gained control; it added vast territories in all parts of Europe to the realm in the next few hundred years.

Austrian dominance of Germany was undermined in the 18th cent. and ended by Prussia by 1866. But the Congress of Vienna, 1815, confirmed Austrian control of a large empire in SE Europe consisting of Germans, Hungarians, Slavs, Italians, and others. The dual Austro-Hungarian monarchy was established in 1867, giving autonomy to Hungary and almost 50 years of peace.

World War I, which started after the June 28, 1914, assassination of Archduke Franz Ferdinand, the Habsburg heir, by a Serbian nationalist, destroyed the empire. By 1918 Austria was reduced to a small republic, with the borders it has today.

Nazi Germany, ruled by the Austrian-born Adolf Hitler, annexed Austria Mar. 13, 1938. The republic was reestablished in 1945, under Allied occupation. Full independence and neutrality were restored in 1955. Austria joined the EU Jan. 1, 1995.

The right-wing, anti-immigrant Austrian Freedom Party (FPO) challenged the dominance of the Social Democratic Party (SPO) beginning in the late 1990s. However, the SPO won parliamentary elections in 2006, 2008, and 2013. About 125,000 migrants fleeing war and hardship in Syria and elsewhere applied for asylum in Austria in 2015-16; government actions in 2016 sharply limited future asylum claims.

Former Green Party leader Alexander Van der Bellen defeated FPO candidate Norbert Hofer in a Dec. 4, 2016, presidential runoff election. The conservative Austrian People's Party (OVP) won Oct. 15, 2017, parliamentary elections and formed a coalition with the FPO. After the coalition collapsed, the OVP won Sept. 29, 2019, elections and formed a new coalition with the Green Party. Under investigation for corruption, OVP leader Sebastian Kurz announced his resignation as chancellor, Oct. 9, 2021; the OVP's Karl Nehammer succeeded him. Van der Bellen won reelection, Oct. 9, 2022. The FPO won more than 25% of the Austrian vote (the most of any party) in June 2024 EU parliamentary elections. The FPO won again in Sept. 29, 2024, national elections, with over 29% of the vote, though its likelihood of governing was uncertain.

Authorities foiled a terrorist plot by people loyal to ISIS against scheduled Taylor Swift concerts in Vienna, Aug. 8-10, 2024; the concerts were canceled.

Azerbaijan
Republic of Azerbaijan

People: Population: 10,650,239 (88). **Age distrib.:** <15: 22.3%; 65+: 9.0%. **Growth:** 0.4%. **Migrants:** 2.5%. **Pop. density:** 333.8 per sq mi, 128.9 per sq km. **Urban:** 58.0%. **Ethnic groups:** Azerbaijani 91.6%, Lezghin 2%. **Languages:** Azerbaijani (Azeri) (official), Russian, Armenian. **Religions:** Muslim 96.3% (Shia 66%, Sunni 30%), Christian 2.4% (Orthodox).

Geography: Total area: 33,436 sq mi, 86,600 sq km (111); **Land area:** 31,903 sq mi, 82,629 sq km. **Location:** SW Asia. Russia, Georgia on N; Iran on S; Armenia on W; Caspian Sea on E. **Topography:** The Great Caucasus Mts. in N, Karabakh Upland in W border the Kur-Araz lowland. Arid climate except in subtropical SE. **Arable land:** 25.3%. **Capital:** Baku, 2,464,162.

Government: Type: Presidential republic. **Head of state:** Pres. Ilham Aliyev; b. 1961; in office: Oct. 31, 2003. **Head of govt.:** Prime

Min. Ali Asadov; b. 1956; in office: Oct. 8, 2019. **Local divisions:** 66 districts, 11 cities. **Defense budget:** $3.1 bil. **Active troops:** 64,050.

Economy: Industries: petroleum/petroleum prods., nat. gas, oil field equip.; steel, iron ore; cement. **Chief agric.:** milk, wheat, potatoes, barley, tomatoes, watermelons. **Natural resources:** petroleum, nat. gas, iron ore, nonferrous metals, bauxite. **Water:** 3,362 cu m per capita. **Crude oil reserves:** 7 bil bbls. **Electricity prod.:** 28.9 bil kWh. **Labor force:** agric. 35.6%, industry 14.9%, services 49.5%. **Unemployment:** 5.6%.

Finance: Monetary unit: Manat (AZN) (1.70 = $1 U.S.). **GDP:** $239.5 bil; **per capita GDP:** $23,686; **GDP growth:** 1.1%. **Imports:** $25.0 bil; Russia 17%, Turkey (Türkiye) 17%, China 10%, UAE 5%, Georgia 5%. **Exports:** $35.5 bil; Italy 47%, Turkey (Türkiye) 9%. **Tourism:** $1.5 bil. **Budget:** $16 bil. **Inflation:** 8.8%.

Transport: Railways: 1,830 mi. **Motor vehicles:** 148.1 per 1,000 pop. **Airports:** 32.

Communications: Mobile: 106.6 per 100 pop. **Broadband:** 85.4 per 100 pop. **Internet:** 88%.

Health: Expend.: 4.7%. **Life expect.:** 73.5 male; 78.6 female. **Births:** 11.2 per 1,000 pop. **Deaths:** 6.4 per 1,000 pop. **Infant mortality:** 10.9 per 1,000 live births. **Undernourished:** <2.5%. **HIV:** 0.1%. **COVID-19:** 10,353 deaths; rates per 100,000: 8,244 cases, 102 deaths. 48% vaccinated.

Education: Compulsory: ages 5-14. **Literacy:** 99.8%.

Website: www.president.az

Azerbaijan was home to Scythian tribes and part of the Roman Empire. Overrun by Turks in the 11th cent. and conquered by Russia in 1806 and 1813, it joined the USSR Dec. 30, 1922, and became a constituent republic in 1936. Azerbaijan gained independence when the Soviet Union disbanded Dec. 26, 1991.

Nagorno-Karabakh, an enclave with a majority population of ethnic Armenians, seceded from Azerbaijan in 1988. A war between mostly Muslim Azerbaijan and mostly Christian Armenia, 1992-94, in which 30,000 died, left Armenia-backed separatists in control of Nagorno-Karabakh; hundreds of thousands of Azeris were expelled from the region. After heavy fighting Sept.-Nov. 2020, Azerbaijan regained control of much of the territory lost in the early 1990s. In a new offensive, Sept. 2023, Azerbaijan regained full control of Nagorno-Karabakh.

Voters approved a new constitution expanding presidential powers, Nov. 12, 1995. Pres. Haydar Aliyev, a pro-Russian former Communist, was reelected Oct. 11, 1998, but international monitors called the vote seriously flawed. His son Ilham Aliyev won a flawed Oct. 15, 2003, presidential election. He responded to violent protests Oct. 16 by arresting hundreds of opposition leaders and their supporters.

The opening May 25, 2005, of the Baku-Tbilisi-Ceyhan pipeline, providing an outlet for Azerbaijan's vast Caspian oil reserves, transformed the nation's economy. Construction began in 2014 on new pipelines to carry natural gas from Caspian Sea deposits in Azerbaijan to Georgia, Turkey, and Europe. An agreement announced July 18, 2022, would significantly increase Azerbaijani gas exports to the EU.

Pres. Ilham Aliyev won flawed 2008, 2013, 2018, and 2024 elections.

The European Parliament voted, Sept. 2017, to investigate a so-called Azerbaijani Laundromat scheme, in which almost $3 bil was reportedly sent out of Azerbaijan, including money allegedly paid to European officials to influence policy toward Azerbaijan.

The Bahamas

Commonwealth of The Bahamas

People: Population: 410,862 (171). **Age distrib.:** <15: 21.4%; 65+: 8.6%. **Growth:** 1.1%. **Migrants:** 16.2%. **Pop. density:** 106.3 per sq mi, 41.0 per sq km. **Urban:** 83.8%. **Ethnic groups** (by racial group): African descent 90.6%, white 4.7%, mixed 2.1%. **Languages:** English (official), Creole (among Haitian immigrants). **Religions:** Christian 92.6% (Protestant 72.0%, Catholic 12.6%), agnostic 4.5%, spiritist 2.1%.

Geography: Total area: 5,359 sq mi, 13,880 sq km (156); **Land area:** 3,865 sq mi, 10,010 sq km. **Location:** In Atlantic O., SE of Florida. U.S. is on W, Cuba to SW. **Topography:** Nearly 700 islands (30 inhabited) and over 2,000 cays in the W Atlantic O. extend 760 mi NW to SE. **Arable land:** 0.8%. **Capital:** Nassau, 279,668.

Government: Type: Parliamentary democracy under constitutional monarchy. **Head of state:** King Charles III, rep. by Gov.-Gen. Cynthia A. Pratt; b. 1945; in office: Sept. 1, 2023. **Head of govt.:** Prime Min. Philip Davis; b. 1951; in office: Sept. 18, 2021. **Local divisions:** 31 districts. **Defense budget:** $106 mil. **Active troops:** 1,500.

Economy: Industries: tourism, banking, oil bunkering, maritime, transshipment and logistics, salt, aragonite. **Chief agric.:** sugarcane, grapefruits, vegetables, bananas, tomatoes, chicken. **Natural resources:** salt, aragonite, timber. **Water:** 1,716 cu m per capita. **Electricity prod.:** 2.0 bil kWh. **Labor force:** agric. 3.0%, industry 11.8%, services 85.2%. **Unemployment:** 9.2%.

Finance: Monetary unit: Dollar (BSD) (1.00 = $1 U.S.). **GDP:** $14.7 bil; **per capita GDP:** $35,555; **GDP growth:** 2.6%. **Imports** (2022): $5.7 bil; U.S. 59%, South Korea 6%, Germany 6%, China 5%. **Exports** (2022): $4.7 bil; U.S. 49%, Côte d'Ivoire 20%, Germany 9%, Thailand 7%. **Tourism** (2022): $4.2 bil. **Budget** (2020): $2.9 bil. **Inflation:** 3.1%.

Transport: Motor vehicles: 394.0 per 1,000 pop. **Airports:** 55.

Communications: Mobile: 100.0 per 100 pop. **Broadband:** 100 per 100 pop. **Internet:** 94.4%.

Health: Expend.: 7.1%. **Life expect.:** 75.1 male; 78.4 female. **Births:** 13.1 per 1,000 pop. **Deaths:** 5.6 per 1,000 pop. **Infant mortality:** 9.4 per 1,000 live births. **Undernourished:** NA. **HIV:** 1.1%. **COVID-19:** 849 deaths; rates per 100,000: 9,950 cases, 216 deaths. 42% vaccinated.

Education: Compulsory: ages 5-16. **Literacy:** NA.

Website: www.bahamas.gov.bs

Christopher Columbus likely first set foot in the Americas on San Salvador (Watling Isl.) in 1492, when Arawak Indians inhabited the islands. British settlement began in 1647; the islands became a British colony in 1783. Independence was attained July 10, 1973. Tourism and international finance are major industries. Hurricane Dorian, Sept. 1-3, 2019, devastated the northern Bahamas. The COVID-19 pandemic hurt the tourism industry; real GDP fell more than 16% in 2020, before rebounding in 2021. The impact of the pandemic hurt the governing party in Sept. 16, 2021, parliamentary elections; Philip Davis of the opposition Progressive Liberal Party became prime minister after the PLP won 32 of 39 lower house seats.

Bahrain

Kingdom of Bahrain

People: Population: 1,566,888 (151). **Age distrib.:** <15: 18.1%; 65+: 4.3%. **Growth:** 0.8%. **Migrants:** 55.0%. **Pop. density:** 5,339.8 per sq mi, 2,061.7 per sq km. **Urban:** 90.0%. **Ethnic groups:** Bahraini 47.4%, Asian 43.4%, other Arab 4.9%. **Languages:** Arabic (official), English, Farsi, Urdu. **Religions:** Muslim 77.5% (Shia 44%, Sunni 34%), Christian 12.1% (Catholic 9.8%), Hindu 8.5%.

Geography: Total area: 293 sq mi, 760 sq km (174); **Land area:** 293 sq mi, 760 sq km. **Location:** SW Asia, in Persian Gulf. Saudi Arabia on W, Qatar on E. **Topography:** Bahrain Island and several adjacent, smaller islands are flat, hot, and humid with little rain. **Arable land:** 2.7%. **Capital:** Manama, 726,505.

Government: Type: Constitutional monarchy. **Head of state:** King Hamad bin Isa al-Khalifa; b. 1950; in office: as emir Mar. 6, 1999; as king Feb. 14, 2002. **Head of govt.:** Prime Min. Salman bin Hamad al-Khalifa; b. 1969; in office: Nov. 11, 2020. **Local divisions:** 4 governorates. **Defense budget:** $1.4 bil. **Active troops:** 8,200.

Economy: Industries: petroleum proc. and refining, aluminum smelting, iron pelletization, fertilizers, Islamic and offshore banking, insurance. **Chief agric.:** lamb/mutton, dates, milk, chicken, tomatoes, fruits. **Natural resources:** oil, nat. gas, fish, pearls. **Water:** 79 cu m per capita. **Crude oil reserves:** 187 mil bbls. **Electricity prod.:** 35.5 bil kWh. **Labor force:** agric. 0.9%, industry 34.8%, services 64.3%. **Unemployment:** 1.2%.

Finance: Monetary unit: Dinar (BHD) (0.38 = $1 U.S.). **GDP:** $94.8 bil; **per capita GDP:** $63,848; **GDP growth:** 2.5%. **Imports:** $32.4 bil; China 15%, UAE 12%, Brazil 9%, Australia 8%, India 7%. **Exports:** $40.3 bil; Saudi Arabia 15%, UAE 10%, U.S. 9%, Japan 5%. **Tourism** (2022): $4.1 bil. **Budget:** $12.6 bil. **Inflation:** 0.1%.

Transport: Motor vehicles: 464.1 per 1,000 pop. **Airports:** 3.

Communications: Mobile: 153.9 per 100 pop. **Broadband:** 142 per 100 pop. **Internet** (2023): 100%.

Health: Expend.: 4.3%. **Life expect.:** 78.1 male; 82.7 female. **Births:** 12.2 per 1,000 pop. **Deaths:** 2.8 per 1,000 pop. **Infant mortality:** 9.7 per 1,000 live births. **Undernourished:** NA. **HIV:** NA. **COVID-19:** 1,536 deaths; rates per 100,000: 40,939 cases, 90 deaths. 72% vaccinated.

Education: Compulsory: ages 6-14. **Literacy:** 97.9%.

Website: www.bahrain.bh

Long ruled by the Khalifa family, Bahrain was a British protectorate from 1861 to Aug. 15, 1971, when it regained independence. Oil was discovered in 1932. Natural gas output has more than doubled since 1990. A major offshore oil and gas field discovery was announced in Apr. 2018.

Emir Hamad bin Isa al-Khalifa proclaimed himself king Feb. 14, 2002. Local elections in May 2002 marked the first time Bahraini women were allowed to vote and run for office. The monarchy suppressed Arab Spring demonstrations Feb.-Mar. 2011. Protests, however, continued, largely by members of the country's Shiite majority against the mostly Sunni ruling elite. A 2015 Human Rights Watch report accused the government of torturing detained dissidents. Forced labor and sexual exploitation of Asian and African immigrants also gained international attention. Court rulings, 2016-17, ordered the dissolution of leading opposition groups. Crown prince Salman bin Hamad al-Khalifa became prime minister, Nov. 11, 2020.

Bahrain was one of a Saudiled group of nations that broke diplomatic relations and embargoed trade with Qatar, June 2017-Jan. 2021. Bahrain and Israel agreed, Sept. 15, 2020, to establish diplomatic relations. Bahrain signed a security agreement with the U.S., Sept. 13, 2023. An Apr. 2024 royal pardon freed over 1,500, including hundreds of political prisoners.

Bangladesh

People's Republic of Bangladesh

People: Population: 168,697,184 (8). **Age distrib.:** <15: 25.1%; 65+: 7.8%. **Growth:** 0.9%. **Migrants:** 1.3%. **Pop. density:** 3,356.6 per sq mi, 1,296.0 per sq km. **Urban:** 41.2%. **Ethnic groups:**

Bengali 99%+ (27 Indigenous ethnic groups recognized by govt.). **Languages:** Bangla or Bengali (official). **Religions:** Muslim 88.7% (Sunni), Hindu 9.2%.

Geography: Total area: 57,321 sq mi, 148,460 sq km (92); **Land area:** 50,259 sq mi, 130,170 sq km. **Location:** S Asia, on N bend of Bay of Bengal. India nearly surrounds country on W, N, E; Myanmar on SE. **Topography:** Mostly a low plain cut by the Ganges and Brahmaputra R. and their delta. Alluvial and marshy along the coast. Hilly only in the extreme SE and NE. Its tropical monsoon climate makes country among the world's rainiest. **Arable land:** 60.5%. **Capital:** Dhaka, 23,935,652. **Cities:** Chittagong, 5,513,609.

Government: Type: Parliamentary republic. **Head of state:** Pres. Mohammad Shahabuddin Chuppi; b. 1949; in office: Apr. 24, 2023. **Head of govt.:** vacant as of Aug. 5, 2024. **Local divisions:** 8 divisions. **Defense budget:** $4.0 bil. **Active troops:** 171,250.

Economy: Industries: cotton, garments, jute, tea, paper, cement, fertilizer, sugar, light engineering. **Chief agric.:** rice, milk, potatoes, maize, sugarcane, onions. **Natural resources:** nat. gas, timber, coal. **Water:** 7,245 cu m per capita. **Crude oil reserves:** 28 mil bbls. **Electricity prod.:** 102.0 bil kWh. **Labor force:** agric. 36.9%, industry 21.9%, services 41.3%. **Unemployment:** 5.1%.

Finance: Monetary unit: Taka (BDT) (119.49 = $1 U.S.). **GDP:** $1.6 tril; **per capita GDP:** $9,066; **GDP growth:** 5.8%. **Imports:** $73.2 bil; China 32%, India 17%, Singapore 6%, Malaysia 5%, Indonesia 5%. **Exports:** $58.9 bil; U.S. 18%, Germany 16%, UK 8%, Spain 7%, Poland 6%. **Tourism:** $453 mil. **Budget:** $46.4 bil. **Inflation:** 9.9%.

Transport: Railways: 1,529 mi. **Motor vehicles:** 3.2 per 1,000 pop. **Airports:** 17.

Communications: Mobile: 111.3 per 100 pop. **Broadband:** 57.8 per 100 pop. **Internet** (2023): 44.5%.

Health: Expend.: 2.4%. **Life expect.:** 73.1 male; 77.5 female. **Births:** 17.3 per 1,000 pop. **Deaths:** 5.5 per 1,000 pop. **Infant mortality:** 28.8 per 1,000 live births. **Undernourished:** 11.9%. **HIV:** <0.1%. **COVID-19:** 29,499 deaths; rates per 100,000: 1,246 cases, 18 deaths. 86% vaccinated.

Education: Compulsory: ages 6-10. **Literacy:** 76.4%.

Website: bangladesh.gov.bd

Muslim invaders conquered the formerly Hindu area in the 12th cent. British rule lasted from the 18th cent. to 1947, when East Bengal became part of Pakistan.

Opposing domination by West Pakistan, the Awami League, based in the East, won control of the National Assembly in 1971. Assembly sessions were postponed; riots broke out. Pakistani troops attacked, Mar. 25; Bangladesh independence was proclaimed the next day. In the ensuing civil war, 1 mil died and 10 mil fled to India. War between India and Pakistan broke out Dec. 3, 1971. Pakistan surrendered in the East on Dec. 16. Mujibur Rahman, known as Sheikh Mujib, became prime min.; he was killed in a coup Aug. 15, 1975.

Army rivals killed Pres. Ziaur Rahman in an unsuccessful coup attempt, May 1981. Vice Pres. Abdus Sattar assumed the presidency but was ousted in a coup led by army chief of staff Gen. H. M. Ershad, Mar. 1982. A parliamentary system of government was adopted in 1991. A cyclone, Apr. 1991, killed over 131,000 people.

Political turmoil led to the resignation, Mar. 1996, of Prime Min. Khaleda Zia, Ziaur Rahman's widow. Sheikh Mujib's daughter, known as Sheikh Hasina, led the country after the June 1996 election. Khaleda Zia returned to power following parliamentary elections, Oct. 1, 2001. Bangladeshi economist Muhammad Yunus won the 2006 Nobel Peace Prize for using very small loans (microcredit) to help alleviate the nation's severe poverty.

Amid escalating political violence, Pres. Iajuddin Ahmed declared a state of emergency, Jan. 11, 2007, and a military-backed caretaker government took office. Cyclone Sidr struck Nov. 15, 2007, damaging more than 1.5 mil homes and leaving about 3,400 dead.

The Awami League triumphed in parliamentary elections Dec. 2008, and Sheikh Hasina returned as prime min. Jan. 6, 2009. She remained in office when her party won 2014 and 2018 elections. Her political rival, Khaleda Zia, was convicted in 2018 on embezzlement charges Zia claimed were politically motivated. In 2022-23, the government intensified crackdowns on opposition parties, rights activists, and media. Sheikh Hasina's Awami League won Jan. 7, 2024, parliamentary elections boycotted by the opposition.

Hundreds died and over 10,000 were arrested in student-led protests, met with a lethal response, that began mid-2024 following a court decision reinstating a quota system for government jobs. Although the Supreme Court, July 21, 2024, reduced jobs subject to quotas, protests continued, focusing on Hasina's authoritarian rule. Sheikh Hasina resigned and left the country Aug 5; some violence followed her departure. Muhammad Yunus became head of an interim government Aug. 8, 2024.

Rana Plaza, a building near Dhaka that housed garment factories, collapsed Apr. 24, 2013, killing more than 1,100 workers. The owner of Rana Plaza was among dozens of people charged, in 2016, with murder in connection with the disaster. After lengthy procedural delays, the murder trial resumed in early 2022.

Assassinations of non-Muslims and activists, attributed to Islamist militants, escalated in 2016. In an attack in Dhaka, July 1-2, 2016, for which ISIS claimed responsibility, 20 people, mostly foreigners, held hostage inside a restaurant were killed, as well as 2 police officers and 5 terrorist gunmen.

Beginning in late 2016, recurrent military and vigilante attacks in neighboring Myanmar caused much of the Rohingya population to seek refuge in Bangladesh. Anti-Rohingya violence in Myanmar peaked in Aug.-Sept. 2017, leading hundreds of thousands to flee. As of Aug. 31, 2024, almost 994,000 Rohingya refugees were in Bangladesh.

Barbados

People: Population: 304,139 (175). **Age distrib.:** <15: 16.6%; 65+: 16.3%. **Growth:** 0.2%. **Migrants:** 12.1%. **Pop. density:** 1,831.9 per sq mi, 707.3 per sq km. **Urban:** 31.5%. **Ethnic groups:** African descent 92.4%, mixed 3.1%, white 2.7%. **Languages:** English (official), Bajan (English-based Creole). **Religions:** Christian 94.5% (Protestant 79.4%, independent 10.2%).

Geography: Total area: 166 sq mi, 430 sq km (184); **Land area:** 166 sq mi, 430 sq km. **Location:** In Atlantic O., farthest E of West Indies. Nearest neighbors are St. Lucia and St. Vincent and the Grenadines to the W. **Topography:** Almost completely surrounded by coral reefs. Highest point is Mt. Hillaby (1,102 ft). **Arable land:** 16.3%. **Capital:** Bridgetown, 89,201.

Government: Type: Parliamentary republic. **Head of state:** Pres. Sandra Mason; b. 1949; in office: Nov. 30, 2021. **Head of govt.:** Prime Min. Mia Mottley; b. 1965; in office: May 25, 2018. **Local divisions:** 11 parishes, 1 city. **Defense budget:** $44 mil. **Active troops:** 610.

Economy: Industries: tourism, sugar, light mfg., component assembly for export. **Chief agric.:** sugarcane, chicken, vegetables, milk, eggs, sweet potatoes. **Natural resources:** petroleum, fish, nat. gas. **Water:** 285 cu m per capita. **Crude oil reserves:** 2 mil bbls. **Electricity prod.:** 1.1 bil kWh. **Labor force:** agric. 2.7%, industry 16.5%, services 80.8%. **Unemployment:** 8.0%.

Finance: Monetary unit: Dollar (BBD) (2.00 = $1 U.S.). **GDP:** $5.5 bil; **per capita GDP:** $19,357; **GDP growth:** 4.5%. **Imports** (2021): $2.1 bil; U.S. 43%, China 8%, Trinidad and Tobago 7%, UK 5%. **Exports** (2017): $2.2 bil; U.S. 23%, Jamaica 11%, Trinidad and Tobago 9%, Guyana 8%, Poland 6%. **Tourism:** $1.1 bil. **Budget** (2020): $1.5 bil. **Inflation:** 9.8%.

Transport: Motor vehicles: 434.8 per 1,000 pop. **Airports:** 2.

Communications: Mobile (2022): 114.6 per 100 pop. **Broadband** (2022): 64.7 per 100 pop. **Internet:** 76.2%.

Health: Expend.: 8.1%. **Life expect.:** 76.3 male; 81.8 female. **Births:** 10.7 per 1,000 pop. **Deaths:** 8.1 per 1,000 pop. **Infant mortality:** 9.6 per 1,000 live births. **Undernourished:** 3.5%. **HIV:** 0.9%. **COVID-19:** 593 deaths; rates per 100,000: 37,805 cases, 206 deaths. 54% vaccinated.

Education: Compulsory: ages 5-15. **Literacy:** 99.6%.

Website: www.gov.bb

Barbados was probably named by Portuguese sailors in reference to bearded fig trees. An English ship visited in 1605, and English settlers arrived on the uninhabited island in 1627. Enslaved labor was forced to work the sugarcane plantations until slavery was abolished in 1834. Barbados became independent Nov. 30, 1966. Tourism, banking, and manufacturing have surpassed sugarcane in economic importance since the 1990s. Ousting the ruling Democratic Labour Party, the Barbados Labour Party (BLP) won all 30 House of Assembly seats in May 24, 2018, elections, making Mia Mottley the country's first female prime min.

Barbados became a republic, Nov. 30, 2021, ending the role of the British monarch as head of state. Elected by Parliament, Oct. 20, 2021, Sandra Mason became the country's first president. Mottley's BLP again won all 30 seats in Jan. 19, 2022, elections. Barbados's High Court, Dec. 12, 2022, struck down laws criminalizing gay sex.

Belarus

Republic of Belarus

People: Population: 9,501,451 (97). **Age distrib.:** <15: 16.1%; 65+: 17.8%. **Growth:** –0.4%. **Migrants:** 11.3%. **Pop. density:** 121.3 per sq mi, 46.8 per sq km. **Urban:** 81.1%. **Ethnic groups:** Belarusian 83.7%, Russian 8.3%, Polish 3.1%. **Languages:** Russian, Belarusian (both official). **Religions:** Christian 82.3% (Orthodox 62.7%, Catholic 16.0%), agnostic 15.5%.

Geography: Total area: 80,155 sq mi, 207,600 sq km (84); **Land area:** 78,340 sq mi, 202,900 sq km. **Location:** Eastern Europe. Poland on W; Latvia, Lithuania on N; Russia on E; Ukraine on S. **Topography:** Landlocked country consisting mostly of hilly lowland with significant marsh areas in S. **Arable land:** 27.6%. **Capital:** Minsk, 2,064,733.

Government: Type: Presidential republic in name; in fact a dictatorship. **Head of state:** Pres. Aleksandr Lukashenko; b. 1954; in office: July 20, 1994. **Head of govt.:** Prime Min. Roman Golovchenko; b. 1973; in office: June 4, 2020. **Local divisions:** 6 regions, 1 municipality. **Defense budget:** $994 mil. **Active troops:** 48,600.

Economy: Industries: metal-cutting machine tools, tractors, trucks, earthmovers. **Chief agric.:** milk, sugar beets, potatoes, wheat, triticale, barley. **Natural resources:** timber, peat, oil, nat. gas, granite, dolomitic limestone, marl, chalk, sand, gravel, clay.

Water: 6,045 cu m per capita. **Crude oil reserves:** 198 mil bbls. **Electricity prod.:** 38.6 bil kWh. **Labor force:** agric. 10.6%, industry 30.4%, services 59.0%. **Unemployment:** 3.6%.

Finance: Monetary unit: Ruble (BYN) (3.27 = $1 U.S.). **GDP:** $282.2 bil; **per capita GDP:** $30,752; **GDP growth:** 3.9%. **Imports:** $47.4 bil; China 26%, Poland 15%, Germany 12%, Lithuania 12%, Turkey (Türkiye) 9%. **Exports:** $47.9 bil; China 15%, Ukraine 12%, Poland 9%, Kazakhstan 8%, Lithuania 8%. **Tourism** (2021): $427 mil. **Budget:** $24.2 bil. **Inflation:** 5.0%.

Transport: Railways: 3,435 mi. **Motor vehicles:** 368.3 per 1,000 pop. **Airports:** 46.

Communications: Mobile: 129.0 per 100 pop. **Broadband:** 104 per 100 pop. **Internet** (2023): 91.5%.

Health: Expend.: 6.6%. **Life expect.:** 69.8 male; 80.0 female. **Births:** 8.3 per 1,000 pop. **Deaths:** 13.3 per 1,000 pop. **Infant mortality:** 2.1 per 1,000 live births. **Undernourished:** <2.5%. **HIV:** 0.4%. **COVID-19:** 7,118 deaths; rates per 100,000: 10,520 cases, 75 deaths. 67% vaccinated.

Education: Compulsory: ages 6-16. **Literacy:** 99.9%.

Website: www.belarus.by

Belarus became a constituent republic of the USSR in 1922. Overrun by German armies in 1941, Belarus was recaptured by Soviet troops in 1944. Following WWII, Belarus increased in area through Soviet annexation of part of NE Poland. Belarus became independent when the Soviet Union disbanded Dec. 26, 1991.

Russia and Belarus signed a pact, Apr. 2, 1996, linking their political and economic systems. Sept. 2021 talks strengthened economic ties.

An authoritarian constitution enacted in Nov. 1996 gave Pres. Aleksandr Lukashenko (elected 1994) vast new powers. He retained office in five flawed elections, 2001-20. Weeks of large-scale protests followed the Aug. 9, 2020, elections; a brutal government response included thousands of arrests and reported torture of prisoners. Leading dissidents were jailed or exiled. Belarus supported Russia's 2022 invasion of Ukraine; Russian ground troops entered N Ukraine from Belarus, and Russian air attacks were launched from Belarus. Lukashenko claimed to have negotiated an end to a June 2023 mutiny in Russia by forces of the mercenary Wagner Group.

Belgium

Kingdom of Belgium

People: Population: 11,977,634 (82). **Age distrib.:** <15: 16.9%; 65+: 20.2%. **Growth:** 0.5%. **Migrants:** 17.3%. **Pop. density:** 1,024.6 per sq mi, 395.6 per sq km. **Urban:** 98.2%. **Ethnic groups:** Belgian 75.2%, Italian 4.1%, Moroccan 3.7%, French 2.4%, Turkish 2%, Dutch 2%. **Languages:** Dutch, French, German (all official). **Religions:** Christian 61.5% (Catholic 59.3%), agnostic 26.2%, Muslim 9.0% (Sunni), atheist 2.3%.

Geography: Total area: 11,787 sq mi, 30,528 sq km (137); **Land area:** 11,690 sq mi, 30,278 sq km. **Location:** Western Europe, on North Sea. France on W and S, Luxembourg on SE, Germany on E, Netherlands on N. **Topography:** Mostly flat; trisected by the Scheldt and Meuse, major commercial rivers. The land becomes hilly and forested in the Ardennes region to the SE. **Arable land:** 28.3%. **Capital:** Brussels, 2,132,178. **Cities:** Antwerpen, 1,061,089.

Government: Type: Federal parliamentary democracy under constitutional monarchy. **Head of state:** King Philippe; b. 1960; in office: July 21, 2013. **Head of govt.:** Prime Min. Alexander De Croo; b. 1975; in office: Oct. 1, 2020. **Local divisions:** 3 regions. **Defense budget:** $5.6 bil. **Active troops:** 22,900.

Economy: Industries: engineering and metal prods., motor vehicle assembly, transp. equip., scientific instruments, processed food/beverages. **Chief agric.:** sugar beets, milk, potatoes, wheat, pork, lettuce. **Natural resources:** constr. materials, silica sand, carbonates. **Water:** 1,576 cu m per capita. **Electricity prod.:** 90.9 bil kWh. **Labor force:** agric. 0.9%, industry 19.1%, services 80.0%. **Unemployment:** 5.5%.

Finance: Monetary unit: Euro (EUR) (0.90 = $1 U.S.). **GDP:** $833.0 bil; **per capita GDP:** $70,456; **GDP growth:** 1.4%. **Imports:** $545.5 bil; Netherlands 19%, Germany 12%, France 9%, U.S. 6%, China 6%. **Exports:** $535.2 bil; Germany 19%, France 15%, Netherlands 14%, U.S. 6%, Italy 5%. **Tourism:** $7.6 bil. **Budget:** $277.5 bil. **Inflation:** 4.1%.

Transport: Railways: 2,238 mi. **Motor vehicles:** 581.5 per 1,000 pop. **Airports:** 49.

Communications: Mobile: 103.3 per 100 pop. **Broadband:** 98.8 per 100 pop. **Internet** (2023): 94.6%.

Health: Expend.: 11.0%. **Life expect.:** 79.7 male; 85.0 female. **Births:** 10.8 per 1,000 pop. **Deaths:** 9.5 per 1,000 pop. **Infant mortality:** 3.1 per 1,000 live births. **Undernourished:** <2.5%. **HIV:** NA. **COVID-19:** 34,339 deaths; rates per 100,000: 42,299 cases, 298 deaths. 79% vaccinated.

Education: Compulsory: ages 6-17. **Literacy:** NA.

Website: www.belgium.be

Belgium derives its name from the Belgae, the first recorded inhabitants, probably Celts. The land was ruled for 1,800 years by conquerors, including Rome, the Franks, Burgundy, Spain, Austria, and France. After 1815, Belgium was made a part of the Netherlands but became an independent constitutional monarchy in 1830.

King Leopold III surrendered to Germany, May 28, 1940. After WWII, he was forced to abdicate. Philippe, grandson of Leopold III, became king July 21, 2013.

The Flemings of northern Belgium speak Dutch, while the Walloons in the south speak French. The language difference is a source of controversy between the two groups. Parliament has passed measures transferring power from the central government to three regions—Wallonia, Flanders, and Brussels. Constitutional changes in 1993 made Belgium a federal state. After elections June 2007, rivalries between Flemings and Walloons created a 9-month political stalemate. June 2010 elections led to an 18-month political deadlock. After May 25, 2014, elections, Charles Michel was sworn in as prime min. Oct. 11, heading a center-right coalition.

Islamist extremists living in Belgium planned and took part in terrorist attacks in France, Nov. 13, 2015, that killed 130. In Mar. 22, 2016, attacks for which the Sunni extremist group ISIS claimed responsibility, 3 suicide bombers killed 32 others and wounded more than 300 in a Brussels subway station and at the city's airport (6 men were convicted of murder, July 25, 2023, for their roles in the 2016 attacks).

Michel's coalition collapsed, Dec. 2018, over immigration policy. After inconclusive May 26, 2019, elections, Sophie Wilmès became caretaker prime min., Oct. 27—Belgium's first female head of government. A 7-party coalition headed by Prime Min. Alexander De Croo took office Oct. 1, 2020. In June 9, 2024, elections, the New Flemish Alliance (N-VA), advocating greater autonomy for Flanders, won the largest share of the vote, followed by the Flemish separatist, anti-immigration Vlaams Belang. De Croo continued as caretaker prime minister, pending negotiations to form a new government.

Belize

People: Population: 415,789 (170). **Age distrib.:** <15: 27.7%; 65+: 5.5%. **Growth:** 1.5%. **Migrants:** 15.6%. **Pop. density:** 47.2 per sq mi, 18.2 per sq km. **Urban:** 46.8%. **Ethnic groups:** mestizo 52.9%, Creole 25.9%, Maya 11.3%, Garifuna 6.1%, East Indian 3.9%, Mennonite 3.6%. **Languages:** English (official), Spanish, Creole, Maya, German, Garifuna. **Religions:** Christian 91.1% (Catholic 57.1%, Protestant 27.9%), Hindu 2.9%, Baha'i 2.6%.

Geography: Total area: 8,867 sq mi, 22,966 sq km (148); **Land area:** 8,805 sq mi, 22,806 sq km. **Location:** Eastern coast of Central America. Mexico on N, Guatemala on W and S. **Topography:** Swampy lowlands in N, Maya Mts. in S, coral reefs and cays near coast. Tropical climate. **Arable land:** 4.4%. **Capital:** Belmopan, 22,964.

Government: Type: Parliamentary democracy under constitutional monarchy. **Head of state:** King Charles III, rep. by Gov.-Gen. Froyla Tzalam; in office: May 27, 2021. **Head of govt.:** Prime Min. John Briceño; b. 1960; in office: Nov. 12, 2020. **Local divisions:** 6 districts. **Defense budget:** $28 mil. **Active troops:** 1,500.

Economy: Industries: garment prod., food proc., tourism, constr. **Chief agric.:** sugarcane, maize, bananas, oranges, soybeans, sorghum. **Natural resources:** timber, fish, hydropower. **Water:** 54,331 cu m per capita. **Crude oil reserves:** 7 mil bbls. **Electricity prod.:** 303 mil kWh. **Labor force:** agric. 16.8%, industry 19.6%, services 63.6%. **Unemployment:** 8.3%.

Finance: Monetary unit: Dollar (BZD) (2.02 = $1 U.S.). **GDP:** $5.8 bil; **per capita GDP:** $14,195; **GDP growth:** 4.5%. **Imports:** $1.6 bil; U.S. 33%, China 23%, Guatemala 9%, Mexico 8%. **Exports:** $1.5 bil; U.S. 22%, UK 16%, Guatemala 10%, Spain 7%, Honduras 5%. **Tourism:** $717 mil. **Budget:** $656 mil. **Inflation:** 4.4%.

Transport: Motor vehicles: 122.3 per 1,000 pop. **Airports:** 27.

Communications: Mobile (2022): 67.2 per 100 pop. **Broadband** (2022): 44.3 per 100 pop. **Internet:** 70.4%.

Health: Expend.: 5.0%. **Life expect.:** 72.6 male; 76.1 female. **Births:** 17.7 per 1,000 pop. **Deaths:** 5.0 per 1,000 pop. **Infant mortality:** 11.3 per 1,000 live births. **Undernourished:** 4.6%. **HIV:** 1.1%. **COVID-19:** 688 deaths; rates per 100,000: 17,961 cases, 173 deaths. 56% vaccinated.

Education: Compulsory: ages 5-12. **Literacy:** NA.

Website: www.belize.gov.bz

Belize (formerly British Honduras) gained independence from Great Britain Sept. 21, 1981. Belize has become a transshipment point for illicit drugs bound for North America. Ending 12 years of United Democratic Party governance, the People's United Party swept Nov. 11, 2020, elections, making PUP leader John Briceño prime minister.

Benin

Republic of Benin

People: Population: 14,697,052 (74). **Age distrib.:** <15: 45.3%; 65+: 2.5%. **Growth:** 3.3%. **Migrants:** 3.3%. **Pop. density:** 344.1 per sq mi, 132.9 per sq km. **Urban:** 50.7%. **Ethnic groups:** Fon/related 38.4%, Adja/related 15.1%, Yoruba/related 12%, Bariba/related 9.6%, Fulani/related 8.6%, Ottamari/related 6.1%, Yoa-Lokpa/related 4.3%, Dendi/related 2.9%. **Languages:** French (official), Fon, Yom, Yoruba in S; Bariba, Fulfulde in N. **Religions:**

Christian 44.9% (Catholic 24.7%, independent 11.8%, Protestant 8.5%), Muslim 30.0% (Sunni), ethnic religionist 24.7%.

Geography: Total area: 43,484 sq mi, 112,622 sq km (100); **Land area:** 42,711 sq mi, 110,622 sq km. **Location:** W Africa on Gulf of Guinea. Togo on W; Burkina Faso, Niger on N; Nigeria on E. **Topography:** Mostly flat and covered with dense vegetation. The coast is hot, humid, and rainy. **Arable land:** 31.4%. **Capital:** Cotonou (seat), 738,444; Porto-Novo (constitutional), 285,328. **Cities:** Abomey-Calavi, 1,314,916.

Government: Type: Presidential republic. **Head of state and govt.:** Pres. Patrice Talon; b. 1958; in office: Apr. 6, 2016. **Local divisions:** 12 departments. **Defense budget:** $129 mil. **Active troops:** 12,300.

Economy: Industries: textiles, food proc., constr. materials, cement. **Chief agric.:** cassava, yams, maize, oil palm fruit, cotton, rice. **Natural resources:** offshore oil, limestone, marble, timber. **Water:** 2,030 cu m per capita. **Crude oil reserves:** 8 mil bbls. **Electricity prod.:** 1.1 bil kWh. **Labor force:** agric. 28.4%, industry 22.3%, services 49.3%. **Unemployment:** 1.5%.

Finance: Monetary unit: CFA Franc (XOF) (587.79 = $1 U.S.). **GDP:** $58.3 bil; **per capita GDP:** $4,248; **GDP growth:** 6.4%. **Imports** (2021): $4.9 bil; China 24%, India 14%, U.S. 6%, UAE 6%, France 5%. **Exports** (2021): $4.2 bil; India 27%, Bangladesh 24%, UAE 23%. **Tourism** (2021): $244 mil. **Budget:** $2.1 bil. **Inflation:** 2.7%.

Transport: Railways: 272 mi. **Motor vehicles:** 3.8 per 1,000 pop. **Airports:** 10.

Communications: Mobile: 116.0 per 100 pop. **Broadband:** 50.1 per 100 pop. **Internet:** 33.8%.

Health: Expend.: 2.6%. **Life expect.:** 61.1 male; 65.0 female. **Births:** 40.3 per 1,000 pop. **Deaths:** 7.6 per 1,000 pop. **Infant mortality:** 52.9 per 1,000 live births. **Undernourished:** 10.3%. **HIV:** 0.7%. **COVID-19:** 163 deaths; rates per 100,000: 231 cases, 1 death. 23% vaccinated.

Education: Compulsory: ages 6-11. **Literacy:** 47.1%.

Website: www.gouv.bj

The Kingdom of Abomey, rising to power in the 17th cent., came under French domination in the late 19th cent. and was incorporated into French West Africa by 1904. Under the name Dahomey, the country gained independence Aug. 1, 1960; it became Benin in 1975. In the fifth coup since independence, Mathieu (Ahmed) Kérékou took power in 1972; he ruled until 1991, when democracy was restored, and served as elected president 1996-2006.

Patrice Talon won a presidential runoff election Mar. 20, 2016. Rule changes to help Talon loyalists in Apr. 28, 2019, legislative elections, as well as a crackdown on dissent, led to violent protests. With opposition suppressed, Talon won reelection, Apr. 11, 2021, with more than 86% of the vote.

Benin's parliament, Oct. 20, 2021, adopted legislation to legalize abortion in most cases. Parties supporting Talon won more open Jan. 8, 2023, legislative elections; an opposition party gained 28 seats.

Bhutan

Kingdom of Bhutan

People: Population: 884,546 (161). **Age distrib.:** <15: 23.1%; 65+: 6.7%. **Growth:** 1.0%. **Migrants:** 6.9%. **Pop. density:** 59.7 per sq mi, 23.0 per sq km. **Urban:** 45.0%. **Ethnic groups:** Ngalop or Bhote 50%, ethnic Nepali (predom. Lhotshampas) 35%, Indigenous or migrant tribes 15%. **Languages:** Sharchopkha, Dzongkha (official), Lhotshamkha. **Religions:** Buddhist 82.6% (Lamaist), Hindu 11.3% (Shaivite 5%, Vaishnavite 5%), ethnic religionist 3.3%, Christian 2.5%.

Geography: Total area: 14,824 sq mi, 38,394 sq km (133); **Land area:** 14,824 sq mi, 38,394 sq km. **Location:** S Asia, in eastern Himalayan Mts. India (Sikkim state) on W and S, China on N. **Topography:** Very high mountains in the N, fertile valleys in the center, and thick forests in the Duar Plain in the S. **Arable land:** 1.8%. **Capital:** Thimphu, 203,297.

Government: Type: Constitutional monarchy. **Head of state:** King Jigme Khesar Namgyel Wangchuck; b. 1980; in office: Dec. 14, 2006. **Head of govt.:** Prime Min. Tshering Tobgay; b. 1965; in office: Jan. 28, 2024. **Local divisions:** 20 districts. **Defense budget/ active troops:** NA.

Economy: Industries: cement, wood prods., processed fruits, alcoholic beverages, calcium carbide, tourism. **Chief agric.:** milk, rice, root vegetables, potatoes, maize, oranges. **Natural resources:** timber, hydropower, gypsum, calcium carbonate. **Water:** 100,323 cu m per capita. **Electricity prod.:** 9.0 bil kWh. **Labor force:** agric. 44.0%, industry 15.2%, services 40.8%. **Unemployment:** 5.7%.

Finance: Monetary unit: Ngultrum (BTN) (83.92 = $1 U.S.). **GDP** (2022): $11.8 bil; **per capita GDP** (2022): $15,022; **GDP growth** (2022): 5.2%. **Imports:** $1.8 bil; India 75%, China 12%, Indonesia 5%. **Exports:** $815.1 mil; India 88%, Italy 5%. **Tourism:** $89 mil. **Budget** (2020): $777 mil (nearly one-quarter financed by India's govt.). **Inflation:** 4.2%.

Transport: Airports: 4.

Communications: Mobile: 95.6 per 100 pop. **Broadband:** 96.8 per 100 pop. **Internet:** 86.8%.

Health: Expend.: 3.9%. **Life expect.:** 72.5 male; 75.0 female. **Births:** 15.3 per 1,000 pop. **Deaths:** 5.9 per 1,000 pop. **Infant mortality:** 24.3 per 1,000 live births. **Undernourished:** NA. **HIV:** 0.2%. **COVID-19:** 21 deaths; rates per 100,000: 8,125 cases, 3 deaths. 88% vaccinated.

Education: Compulsory: NA. **Literacy:** 72.1%.

Website: www.bhutan.gov.bt

The region came under Tibetan rule in the 16th cent. British influence grew in the 19th cent. A Buddhist monarchy was set up in 1907. After a 1910 treaty, Britain guided Bhutan's external affairs, while the country remained internally self-governing. Upon independence the treaty was revised, 1949, to allow India to assume Britain's role.

Isolated for much of its history, Bhutan has taken steps toward modernization. King Jigme Singye Wangchuck, in power since 1972, stepped down Dec. 14, 2006, in favor of his son, Jigme Khesar Namgyel Wangchuck. Multiparty parliamentary elections took place Mar. 24, 2008. A new constitution, ratified July 18, made Bhutan a democratic constitutional monarchy. The People's Democratic Party (PDP) won July 13, 2013, parliamentary elections. After the United Party of Bhutan won Oct. 18, 2018, elections, Jan. 9, 2024, voting returned the PDP to power.

Bolivia

Plurinational State of Bolivia

People: Population: 12,311,974 (80). **Age distrib.:** <15: 28.5%; 65+: 7.0%. **Growth:** 1.0%. **Migrants:** 1.4%. **Pop. density:** 29.4 per sq mi, 11.4 per sq km. **Urban:** 71.5%. **Ethnic groups:** mestizo (mixed white/Indigenous) 68%, Indigenous 20%, white 5%, Cholo/ Chola 2%. **Languages:** Spanish, Quechua, Aymara, Guarani (all official). **Religions:** Christian 92.8% (Catholic 80.1%, Protestant 7.9%), ethnic religionist 2.7%, Baha'i 2.2%, agnostic 2.0%.

Geography: Total area: 424,164 sq mi, 1,098,581 sq km (27); **Land area:** 418,265 sq mi, 1,083,301 sq km. **Location:** W central South America, in the Andes Mts. One of two landlocked countries in S America. Peru, Chile on W; Argentina, Paraguay on S; Brazil on E and N. **Topography:** The great central plateau, more than 500 mi long at an elevation of 12,000 ft, lies between two cordilleras having three of the highest peaks in S America. Lake Titicaca, on Peruvian border, is world's highest lake (12,500 ft) navigable by large boats. The E central region has semitropical forests; the llanos, or Amazon-Chaco lowlands, are in E. **Arable land:** 5.1%. **Capital:** La Paz (administrative), 1,965,570; Sucre (constitutional), 277,910. **Cities:** Santa Cruz, 1,855,732; Cochabamba, 1,430,688.

Government: Type: Presidential republic. **Head of state and govt.:** Pres. Luis Alberto Arce Catacora; b. 1963; in office: Nov. 8, 2020. **Local divisions:** 9 departments. **Defense budget:** $473 mil. **Active troops:** 34,100.

Economy: Industries: mining, smelting, electricity, petroleum, food/beverages, handicrafts, clothing, jewelry. **Chief agric.:** sugarcane, soybeans, potatoes, maize, rice, sorghum. **Natural resources:** lithium, tin, nat. gas, petroleum, zinc, tungsten, antimony, silver, iron, lead, gold, timber, hydropower. **Water:** 47,519 cu m per capita. **Crude oil reserves:** 241 mil bbls. **Electricity prod.:** 11.5 bil kWh. **Labor force:** agric. 27.0%, industry 20.6%, services 52.4%. **Unemployment:** 3.1%.

Finance: Monetary unit: Boliviano (BOB) (6.88 = $1 U.S.). **GDP:** $132.9 bil; **per capita GDP:** $10,727; **GDP growth:** 2.4%. **Imports:** $13.1 bil; Brazil 20%, China 19%, Chile 13%, Peru 9%, Argentina 6%. **Exports:** $12.0 bil; India 16%, Brazil 14%, Argentina 13%, Colombia 8%, Japan 7%. **Tourism:** $775 mil. **Budget:** $14.8 bil. **Inflation:** 2.6%.

Transport: Railways: 2,461 mi. **Motor vehicles:** 84.5 per 1,000 pop. **Airports:** 200.

Communications: Mobile (2022): 101.6 per 100 pop. **Broadband** (2022): 89.9 per 100 pop. **Internet:** 73.3%.

Health: Expend.: 8.2%. **Life expect.:** 71.0 male; 74.0 female. **Births:** 17.6 per 1,000 pop. **Deaths:** 6.6 per 1,000 pop. **Infant mortality:** 22.3 per 1,000 live births. **Undernourished:** 23.0%. **HIV:** 0.4%. **COVID-19:** 22,387 deaths; rates per 100,000: 10,384 cases, 192 deaths. 54% vaccinated.

Education: Compulsory: ages 4-17. **Literacy:** 93.9%.

Website: www.bolivia.gob.bo

The Incas conquered the region's earlier Indian inhabitants in the 13th cent. Spanish colonial rule began in the 1530s and lasted until Aug. 6, 1825. The country is named after independence fighter Simón Bolívar. In a series of wars, Bolivia lost its Pacific coast to Chile, the oil-bearing Chaco to Paraguay, and rubber-growing areas to Brazil, 1879-1935.

Economic unrest, especially among militant mine workers, led to continuing political instability. A reformist government under Victor Paz Estenssoro, 1951-64, nationalized tin mines and attempted to improve conditions for the Indian majority but was overthrown by a military junta. A series of coups and countercoups continued until constitutional government was restored in 1982.

U.S. pressure on the government to reduce production of coca, the raw material for cocaine, led to clashes between police and growers. Gen. Hugo Banzer Suárez, who ruled as a dictator, 1971-78, later governed as president, 1997-2001.

Leftist Juan Evo Morales Ayma won the presidential election, Dec. 2005. Bolivia's first Indigenous president, he nationalized the hydrocarbon sector and launched a land-redistribution program. Voters, Jan. 25, 2009, approved a new constitution strengthening the rights of Bolivia's Indigenous majority. Morales won a second term Dec. 6, 2009. His government nationalized major utility companies in 2012. Morales won reelection Oct. 12, 2014.

After Morales appeared to narrowly win a fourth term in Oct. 20, 2019, elections, large-scale protests and allegations of fraud forced his resignation, Nov. 10; second Senate Vice Pres. Jeanine Áñez Chavez became acting president, Nov. 12, in a process later criticized by the OAS. In a new election, Oct. 18, 2020, Luis Alberto Arce Catacora of Morales's leftist party easily won the presidency. Áñez was convicted of assuming the presidency illegally and sentenced to 10 years in prison, June 10, 2022; additional charges were pending. Luis Fernando Camacho, a losing candidate in the 2020 election, was arrested in Dec. 2022 on charges related to Morales's ouster.

In the early 2020s, Bolivia was severely affected by the COVID-19 pandemic.

An attempted military coup was thwarted, June 26, 2024; Arce denied allegations he staged the event.

Bosnia and Herzegovina

People: Population: 3,798,671 (130). **Age distrib.:** <15: 13.1%; 65+: 18.6%. **Growth:** –0.3%. **Migrants:** 1.1%. **Pop. density:** 192.2 per sq mi, 74.2 per sq km. **Urban:** 50.7%. **Ethnic groups:** Bosniak 50.1%, Serb 30.8%, Croat 15.4%. **Languages:** Bosnian, Serbian, Croatian (all official). **Religions:** Christian 50.0% (Orthodox 39.4%, Catholic 10.4%), Muslim 45.7% (Sunni), agnostic 3.7%.

Geography: Total area: 19,767 sq mi, 51,197 sq km (125); **Land area:** 19,763 sq mi, 51,187 sq km. **Location:** Balkan Peninsula in SE Europe. Serbia, Montenegro on E and SE; Croatia on N and W. **Topography:** Hilly with some mountains. **Arable land:** 19.7%. **Capital:** Sarajevo, 346,859.

Government: Type: Parliamentary republic. **Heads of state:** Collective presidency with rotating leadership every 8 months. **Head of govt.:** Chair of the Council of Ministers Borjana Kristo; b. 1961; in office: Jan. 25, 2023. **Local divisions:** 3 first-order admin. divisions. **Defense budget:** $849 mil. **Active troops:** 10,500.

Economy: Industries: steel, coal, iron ore, lead, zinc, manganese, bauxite, aluminum, motor vehicle assembly, textiles, tobacco prods. **Chief agric.:** maize, milk, vegetables, potatoes, plums, wheat. **Natural resources:** coal, iron ore, antimony, bauxite, copper, lead, zinc, chromite, cobalt, manganese, nickel, clay, gypsum, salt, sand, timber, hydropower. **Water:** 11,465 cu m per capita. **Electricity prod.:** 17.0 bil kWh. **Labor force:** agric. 16.9%, industry 33.5%, services 49.6%. **Unemployment:** 10.4%.

Finance: Monetary unit: Convertible Mark (BAM) (1.75 = $1 U.S.). **GDP:** $73.4 bil; **per capita GDP:** $22,846; **GDP growth:** 1.7%. **Imports:** $15.4 bil; Croatia 16%, Serbia 13%, Germany 8%, Italy 8%, China 7%. **Exports:** $11.9 bil; Croatia 14%, Germany 14%, Serbia 13%, Italy 10%, Austria 9%. **Tourism:** $1.6 bil. **Budget:** $8.2 bil. **Inflation** (2020-21): 2.0%.

Transport: Railways: 600 mi. **Airports:** 13.

Communications: Mobile: 121.6 per 100 pop. **Broadband:** 69.4 per 100 pop. **Internet** (2023): 83.4%.

Health: Expend.: 9.6%. **Life expect.:** 75.5 male; 81.6 female. **Births:** 8.2 per 1,000 pop. **Deaths:** 10.3 per 1,000 pop. **Infant mortality:** 5.0 per 1,000 live births. **Undernourished:** <2.5%. **HIV:** <0.1%. **COVID-19:** 16,392 deaths; rates per 100,000: 12,304 cases, 500 deaths. 14% vaccinated.

Education: Compulsory: ages 6-14. **Literacy:** 98.3%.

Website: fbihvlada.gov.ba

Bosnia was ruled by Croatian kings c. 958 CE, and by Hungary 1000-1200. It became organized c. 1200 and later took control of Herzegovina. The kingdom disintegrated after 1391, with the southern part becoming the independent duchy of Herzegovina. It was conquered by Turks in 1463 and made a Turkish province. The area was placed under control of Austria-Hungary in 1878 and made part of the province of Bosnia and Herzegovina, which was formally annexed to Austria-Hungary, 1908. Bosnia became a province of Yugoslavia in 1918. It was reunited with Herzegovina as a federated republic under the 1946 Yugoslav constitution.

Bosnia and Herzegovina declared sovereignty Oct. 15, 1991. A referendum for independence was passed Feb. 29, 1992. Ethnic Serbs' opposition to the referendum spurred violent clashes and bombings. The U.S. and EU recognized the republic Apr. 7. Fierce three-way fighting continued between Bosnia's Serbs, Muslims, and Croats. Serb forces engaged in ethnic cleansing, killing thousands of Bosnian Muslims (Bosniaks) and expelling Muslims and other non-Serbs from areas under Bosnian Serb control. Muslims and Croats in Bosnia began a cease-fire Feb. 23, 1994, and signed an accord, Mar. 18, to create a Muslim-Croat confederation in Bosnia.

As fighting continued in 1995, the balance of power shifted toward the Muslim-Croat alliance. Massive NATO airstrikes on Bosnian Serb targets beginning Aug. 30 triggered a new round of peace talks. These talks produced an agreement to create autonomous regions within Bosnia, with the Serb region (Republika Srpska) constituting 49% of the country.

A peace agreement was signed in Paris, Dec. 14, 1995, by leaders of Bosnia, Croatia, and Serbia. Some 60,000 NATO troops (about 20,000 from the U.S.) moved in to police the accord. Meanwhile, a UN tribunal—the International Criminal Tribunal for the Former Yugoslavia (ICTY), established in 1993 at The Hague, Netherlands—began bringing charges against suspected war criminals. Elections were held Sept. 14, 1996, for a 3-person collective presidency, for seats in a federal parliament, and for regional offices. In Dec. a revamped NATO Stabilization Force (SFOR) of over 30,000 members (more than 8,000 from the U.S.) received an 18-month mandate, which was later extended.

The ICTY found Radislav Krstic, a Bosnian Serb general, guilty in 2001, in connection with the genocide of thousands of Muslims at Srebrenica in 1995. An EU peacekeeping force (EUFOR), initially with 7,000 members, assumed responsibility from SFOR, Dec. 2, 2004. Accused of complicity in the Srebrenica and other atrocities, former Bosnian Serb leader Radovan Karadzic was convicted, Mar. 24, 2016, by the ICTY of genocide, war crimes, and crimes against humanity; he was ultimately sentenced to life in prison. Gen. Ratko Mladic, the former Bosnian Serb military commander accused of directing the Srebrenica massacre, was convicted by the ICTY, Nov. 22, 2017, of genocide, war crimes, and crimes against humanity and sentenced to life in prison. An ICTY successor tribunal at The Hague convicted, June 30, 2021, two former high-ranking Serbian security officials of abetting war crimes in Bosnia. EUFOR strength in Bosnia was about 1,100 in 2024. The EU Council, Mar. 21, 2024, agreed to open EU membership negotiations with Bosnia.

Bosnia ranked among the hardest-hit countries by per capita deaths during the COVID-19 pandemic that began in 2020.

Botswana

Republic of Botswana

People: Population: 2,450,668 (143). **Age distrib.:** <15: 28.7%; 65+: 6.1%. **Growth:** 1.3%. **Migrants:** 4.7%. **Pop. density:** 11.2 per sq mi, 4.3 per sq km. **Urban:** 73.5%. **Ethnic groups:** Tswana or Setswana 79%, Kalanga 11%, Basarwa 3%. **Languages:** Setswana, Sekalanga, Shekgalagadi, English (official). **Religions:** Christian 71.9% (independent 48.0%, Protestant 16.8%, Catholic 7.2%), ethnic religionist 26.5%.

Geography: Total area: 224,607 sq mi, 581,730 sq km (48); **Land area:** 218,816 sq mi, 566,730 sq km. **Location:** Southern Africa. Namibia on N and W, Zambia on N, Zimbabwe on NE, South Africa on S. **Topography:** The Kalahari Desert, supporting nomadic peoples and wildlife, spreads over SW. Swamplands and farming areas in N; rolling plains in E where livestock are grazed. **Arable land:** 0.5%. **Capital:** Gaborone, 269,338.

Government: Type: Parliamentary republic. **Head of state and govt.:** Pres. Mokgweetsi Masisi; b. 1962; in office: Apr. 1, 2018. **Local divisions:** 10 districts, 6 town councils. **Defense budget:** $547 mil. **Active troops:** 9,000.

Economy: Industries: diamonds, copper, nickel, salt, soda ash, potash, coal, iron ore, silver. **Chief agric.:** milk, root vegetables, vegetables, maize, sorghum, beef. **Natural resources:** diamonds, copper, nickel, salt, soda ash, potash, coal, iron ore, silver. **Water:** 4,729 cu m per capita. **Electricity prod.:** 2.6 bil kWh. **Labor force:** agric. 17.6%, industry 15.7%, services 66.7%. **Unemployment:** 23.4%.

Finance: Monetary unit: Pula (BWP) (13.28 = $1 U.S.). **GDP:** $51.9 bil; **per capita GDP:** $19,383; **GDP growth:** 2.7%. **Imports** (2022): $8.7 bil; South Africa 61%, Namibia 9%, Belgium 5%. **Exports** (2022): $8.9 bil; UAE 27%, Belgium 18%, India 15%, South Africa 10%, Hong Kong 6%. **Tourism** (2022): $370 mil. **Budget** (2020): $6 bil. **Inflation:** 5.1%.

Transport: Railways: 552 mi. **Motor vehicles:** 240.2 per 1,000 pop. **Airports:** 122.

Communications: Mobile: 179.0 per 100 pop. **Broadband:** 107 per 100 pop. **Internet:** 77.3%.

Health: Expend.: 6.3%. **Life expect.:** 64.4 male; 68.6 female. **Births:** 19.6 per 1,000 pop. **Deaths:** 8.9 per 1,000 pop. **Infant mortality:** 23.7 per 1,000 live births. **Undernourished:** 24.3%. **HIV:** 16.6%. **COVID-19:** 2,801 deaths; rates per 100,000: 14,062 cases, 119 deaths. 71% vaccinated.

Education: Compulsory: NA. **Literacy:** 88.5%.

Website: www.gov.bw

First inhabited by San people, then Bantus, the region became the British protectorate of Bechuanaland in 1886. The country became fully independent Sept. 30, 1966. Mining, especially of diamonds, has contributed to economic growth. Pres. Festus Mogae transferred power Apr. 1, 2008, to Seretse Khama Ian Khama, son of Botswana's independence leader and first president (1966-80), Sir Seretse Khama. Mokgweetsi Eric Masisi became president, Apr. 1, 2018. In power since independence, the Botswana Democratic Party won Oct. 23, 2019, legislative elections—keeping the BDP's Masisi in office.

The High Court, June 11, 2019, struck down 1965 penal code provisions criminalizing same-sex relationships. During the COVID-19 pandemic that began in 2020, Botswana had one of the highest vaccination rates of any African country.

Brazil

Federative Republic of Brazil

People: Population: 220,051,512 (7). **Age distrib.:** <15: 19.6%; 65+: 10.9%. **Growth:** 0.6%. **Migrants:** 0.5%. **Pop. density:** 68.2 per sq mi, 26.3 per sq km. **Urban:** 88.0%. **Ethnic groups:** mixed

45.3%, white 43.5%, Black 10.2%. **Languages:** Portuguese (official). **Religions:** Christian 90.5% (Catholic 62.3%, Protestant 15.3%, independent 12.7%), Spiritist 4.8%, agnostic 2.9%.

Geography: Total area: 3,287,957 sq mi, 8,515,770 sq km (5); **Land area:** 3,227,096 sq mi, 8,358,140 sq km. **Location:** Occupies eastern half of S America. French Guiana, Suriname, Guyana, Venezuela on N; Colombia, Peru, Bolivia, Paraguay on W; Argentina, Uruguay on S. **Topography:** Atlantic coastline stretches 4,603 mi. Heavily wooded Amazon basin covers N half of country. Vast network of navigable rivers. The Amazon R. flows 2,093 mi in Brazil. The NE region is semiarid scrubland, heavily settled and poor. Almost half of pop. resides in S central region. Most major cities are in the narrow coastal belt. Almost the entire country has a tropical or semitropical climate. **Arable land:** 6.7%. **Capital:** Brasília, 4,935,274. **Cities:** São Paulo, 22,806,704; Rio de Janeiro, 13,824,347; Belo Horizonte, 6,300,409.

Government: Type: Federal presidential republic. **Head of state and govt.:** Pres. Luiz Inácio Lula da Silva; b. 1945; in office: Jan. 1, 2023. **Local divisions:** 26 states, 1 federal district. **Defense budget:** $24.2 bil. **Active troops:** 366,500.

Economy: Industries: textiles, shoes, chemicals, cement, lumber, iron ore, tin, steel, aircraft, motor vehicles and parts. **Chief agric.:** sugarcane, soybeans, maize, milk, cassava, oranges. **Natural resources:** alumina, bauxite, beryllium, gold, iron ore, manganese, nickel, niobium, phosphates, platinum, tantalum, tin, rare earth elements, uranium, petroleum. **Water:** 40,345 cu m per capita. **Crude oil reserves:** 12.7 bil bbls. **Electricity prod.:** 674.3 bil kWh. **Labor force:** agric. 8.7%, industry 20.5%, services 70.8%. **Unemployment:** 8.0%.

Finance: Monetary unit: Real (BRL) (5.51 = $1 U.S.). **GDP:** $4.5 tril; **per capita GDP:** $20,584; **GDP growth:** 2.9%. **Imports:** $346.6 bil; China 24%, U.S. 18%, Germany 5%, Argentina 5%. **Exports:** $389.6 bil; China 26%, U.S. 11%, Argentina 5%. **Tourism:** $6.9 bil. **Budget** (2020): $617.3 bil. **Inflation:** 4.6%.

Transport: Railways: 18,548 mi. **Motor vehicles:** 213.5 per 1,000 pop. **Airports:** 4,919.

Communications: Mobile: 101.0 per 100 pop. **Broadband:** 97.5 per 100 pop. **Internet** (2023): 84.2%.

Health: Expend.: 9.9%. **Life expect.:** 72.6 male; 80.1 female. **Births:** 13.2 per 1,000 pop. **Deaths:** 7.0 per 1,000 pop. **Infant mortality:** 12.9 per 1,000 live births. **Undernourished:** 3.9%. **HIV:** 0.6%. **COVID-19:** 702,116 deaths; rates per 100,000: 17,648 cases, 330 deaths. 81% vaccinated.

Education: Compulsory: ages 4-17. **Literacy:** 94.7%.

Website: www.brasil.gov.br

Pedro Álvares Cabral, a Portuguese navigator, is generally credited as the first European to reach Brazil, in 1500. The country was thinly settled by various Indigenous groups. Only a few survive today, mostly in the Amazon Basin.

In the next centuries, Portuguese colonists gradually pushed inland, bringing along large numbers of enslaved Africans. (Slavery was not abolished until 1888.) The king of Portugal, fleeing Napoleon's army, moved the seat of government to Brazil in 1808. Brazil thereupon became a kingdom under Dom Joao VI. After Joao VI returned to Portugal, his son Pedro proclaimed Brazil's independence, Sept. 7, 1822, and was crowned emperor. The second emperor, Dom Pedro II, was deposed in 1889, and a republic proclaimed.

A military junta took control in 1930; Getulio Vargas assumed dictatorial power. The military forced him out in 1945. A democratic regime prevailed 1945-64, during which time the capital was moved from Rio de Janeiro to Brasília. Military-backed governments ruled Brazil for the next 20 years. Censorship was imposed, and the opposition was suppressed. Democratic presidential elections held in 1985 brought back civilian rule.

By the 1990s, Brazil had one of the world's largest economies (7th-largest in 2023). Income is unevenly distributed, however, and poverty widespread. Development has destroyed much of the Amazon ecosystem.

A new civil code guaranteeing legal equality for women was enacted Aug. 15, 2001. Luiz Inácio Lula da Silva, a union leader and reformer, won a presidential runoff, Oct. 2002. Brazil's space program launched its first rocket into space Oct. 23, 2004.

Despite political corruption scandals, Lula won a second presidential term, Oct. 2006. The nation reported huge offshore oil finds in 2007-08. Lula's former chief of staff, Dilma Rousseff, won a runoff election Oct. 31, 2010, to become Brazil's first woman president. She narrowly won reelection in an Oct. 26, 2014, runoff.

A Zika virus outbreak and related microcephaly caused 2,952 confirmed microcephaly cases and 369,013 confirmed or suspected Zika infections, 2015-17.

A $3-bil bribery and corruption scandal involving Petrobras (the national oil company), Pres. Rousseff's Workers' Party, and high-level government officials led to the resignations of Petrobras's top executives in Feb. 2015. José Dirceu, Lula's former chief of staff, was sentenced, May 18, 2016, to 23 years in prison for money laundering and other Petrobras-related offenses. Former Pres. Lula was convicted, July 12, 2017, of bribery and money laundering in connection with the Petrobras scandal; Mar. 2021 court rulings essentially overturned his convictions.

As Brazil suffered an economic downturn, the lower house of Congress, Apr. 17, 2016, charged Pres. Rousseff with illegally manipulating the federal budget. Her Senate impeachment trial, Aug. 25-31, ended with her conviction and removal from office. Former lower house speaker Eduardo Cunha was sentenced, Mar. 30, 2017, to more than 15 years in prison following his conviction on Petrobras-related corruption charges.

Campaigning against corruption and pledging to boost the economy (including through further Amazon development), far-right candidate Jair Bolsonaro won an Oct. 28, 2018, presidential runoff election. Amazon deforestation accelerated beginning in 2019 but fell sharply in 2023 after Bolsonaro left office.

Bolsonaro belittled the threat of the COVID-19 pandemic that began in 2020, and his government was slow to respond. Brazil was affected by the pandemic worse than almost any other country. As of Sept. 2024, Brazil had about 37.5 mil total confirmed COVID-19 cases (6th-highest in the world) and 702,000 recorded deaths (2nd-highest).

Lula narrowly defeated Bolsonaro in an Oct. 30, 2022, presidential runoff election, but Bolsonaro repeatedly claimed voting irregularities. On Jan. 8, 2023, one week after Lula's inauguration, rightist pro-Bolsonaro rioters briefly seized government buildings in Brasília, in an apparent attempt to overturn the election result.

Torrential rains and flooding in southern Brazil, Apr.-May 2024—perhaps related to climate change—claimed at least 169 lives and displaced hundreds of thousands. In the 2020s, hotter, drier weather in the Pantanal region and parts of the Amazon, likely climate-change related, contributed to increased wildfires.

Brunei

Brunei Darussalam

People: Population: 491,900 (168). **Age distrib.:** <15: 21.7%; 65+: 7.5%. **Growth:** 1.4%. **Migrants:** 25.6%. **Pop. density:** 242.0 per sq mi, 93.4 per sq km. **Urban:** 79.4%. **Ethnic groups:** Malay 67.4%, Chinese 9.6%. **Languages:** Malay (Bahasa Melayu) (official), English, Chinese dialects. **Religions:** Muslim (official) 58.6% (Sunni), Christian 12.1%, ethnic religionist 9.8%, Buddhist 9.5% (Mahayanist 7%), Chinese folk-religionist 5.2%, Confucianist 2.0%.

Geography: Total area: 2,226 sq mi, 5,765 sq km (165); **Land area:** 2,033 sq mi, 5,265 sq km. **Location:** SE Asia, on the N coast of the island of Borneo. It is surrounded on its landward side by the Malaysian state of Sarawak. **Topography:** Narrow coastal plain with mountains in E, hilly lowlands in W. Swamps in W and NE. Tropical climate. **Arable land:** 0.8%. **Capital:** Bandar Seri Begawan, 40,781.

Government: Type: Absolute monarchy or sultanate. **Head of state and govt.:** Sultan and Prime Min. Sir Hassanal Bolkiah Mu'izzaddin Waddaulah; b. 1946; in office: Jan. 1, 1984 (sultan since Oct. 5, 1967). **Local divisions:** 4 districts. **Defense budget:** $485 mil. **Active troops:** 7,200.

Economy: Industries: petroleum, petroleum refining, liquefied nat. gas, constr. **Chief agric.:** chicken, eggs, fruits, rice, vegetables, beans. **Natural resources:** petroleum, nat. gas, timber. **Water:** 19,085 cu m per capita. **Crude oil reserves:** 1.1 bil bbls. **Electricity prod.:** 5.8 bil kWh. **Labor force:** agric. 1.4%, industry 24.2%, services 74.4%. **Unemployment:** 5.3%.

Finance: Monetary unit: Dollar (BND) (1.30 = $1 U.S.). **GDP:** $39.1 bil; **per capita GDP:** $86,446; **GDP growth:** 1.4%. **Imports** (2022): $10.1 bil; Malaysia 22%, UAE 11%, China 10%, Singapore 7%, Qatar 6%. **Exports** (2022): $14.4 bil; Australia 19%, Japan 17%, China 16%, Singapore 14%, Malaysia 10%. **Tourism** (2022): $14 mil. **Budget** (2020): $3.2 bil. **Inflation:** 0.4%.

Transport: Motor vehicles: 570.4 per 1,000 pop. **Airports:** 2.

Communications: Mobile: 117.8 per 100 pop. **Broadband:** 119 per 100 pop. **Internet:** 99%.

Health: Expend.: 2.2%. **Life expect.:** 76.5 male; 81.3 female. **Births:** 15.8 per 1,000 pop. **Deaths:** 3.9 per 1,000 pop. **Infant mortality:** 10.0 per 1,000 live births. **Undernourished:** NA. **HIV:** NA. **COVID-19:** 180 deaths; rates per 100,000: 79,537 cases, 41 deaths. 100% vaccinated.

Education: Compulsory: ages 6-14. **Literacy:** 97.6%.

Website: www.gov.bn

The Sultanate of Brunei was a powerful state in the early 16th cent., with authority over all of the island of Borneo as well as parts of the Sulu Islands and the Philippines. In 1888, a treaty placed the state under the protection of Great Britain.

Brunei became a fully sovereign and independent state on Jan. 1, 1984. A new penal code based on Islamic law, implemented in stages 2014-19, imposed harsh physical punishments for crimes such as theft, as well as for adultery and gay sex. Brunei outlawed public Christmas celebrations and displays in 2015.

Oil and natural gas account for significant portions of GDP and exports. Brunei's GDP per capita is among the world's highest.

Bulgaria

Republic of Bulgaria

People: Population: 6,782,659 (106). **Age distrib.:** <15: 13.8%; 65+: 21.0%. **Growth:** –0.7%. **Migrants:** 2.7%. **Pop. density:** 161.9

per sq mi, 62.5 per sq km. **Urban:** 77.0%. **Ethnic groups:** Bulgarian 78.5%, Turkish 7.8%, Roma 4.1% (Romani pop. usually underestimated; may represent 9%-11% of pop.). **Languages:** Bulgarian (official), Turkish, Romani. **Religions:** Christian 83.5% (Orthodox 79.7%), Muslim 13.0% (Sunni 12%), agnostic 2.6%.

Geography: Total area: 42,811 sq mi, 110,879 sq km (103); **Land area:** 41,888 sq mi, 108,489 sq km. **Location:** SE Europe, in E Balkan Peninsula on Black Sea. Romania on N; Serbia, North Macedonia on W; Greece, Turkey on S. **Topography:** The Stara Planina (Balkan) Mts. stretch E-W across the center of country, with the Danubian plain on N, the Rhodope Mts. on SW, and Thracian Plain on SE. **Arable land:** 31.9%. **Capital:** Sofia, 1,287,540.

Government: Type: Parliamentary republic. **Head of state:** Pres. Rumen Radev; b. 1963; in office: Jan. 22, 2017. **Head of govt.:** Caretaker Prime Min. Dimitar Glavchev; b. 1963; in office: Apr. 9, 2024. **Local divisions:** 28 provinces. **Defense budget:** $1.7 bil. **Active troops:** 36,950.

Economy: Industries: electricity, gas, water; food, beverages, tobacco; machinery and equip. **Chief agric.:** wheat, maize, sunflower seeds, milk, barley, rapeseed. **Natural resources:** bauxite, copper, lead, zinc, coal, timber. **Water:** 3,093 cu m per capita. **Crude oil reserves:** 15 mil bbls. **Electricity prod.:** 50.2 bil kWh. **Labor force:** agric. 6.4%, industry 30.0%, services 63.5%. **Unemployment:** 4.3%.

Finance: Monetary unit: Lev (BGN) (1.75 = $1 U.S.). **GDP:** $248.8 bil; **per capita GDP:** $38,690; **GDP growth:** 1.8%. **Imports:** $58.8 bil; Germany 10%, Russia 10%, Turkey (Türkiye) 9%, Romania 7%, Greece 6%. **Exports:** $62.1 bil; Germany 13%, Romania 13%, Italy 7%, Turkey (Türkiye) 6%, Greece 6%. **Tourism:** $4.0 bil. **Budget** (2020): $26.5 bil. **Inflation:** 9.4%.

Transport: Railways: 2,504 mi. **Motor vehicles:** 487.9 per 1,000 pop. **Airports:** 111.

Communications: Mobile: 117.9 per 100 pop. **Broadband:** 118 per 100 pop. **Internet** (2023): 80.4%.

Health: Expend.: 8.6%. **Life expect.:** 72.9 male; 79.4 female. **Births:** 7.9 per 1,000 pop. **Deaths:** 14.2 per 1,000 pop. **Infant mortality:** 7.7 per 1,000 live births. **Undernourished:** <2.5%. **HIV:** 0.1%. **COVID-19:** 38,701 deaths; rates per 100,000: 19,138 cases, 557 deaths. 30% vaccinated.

Education: Compulsory: ages 5-15. **Literacy:** 98.4%.

Website: www.gob.bg

Bulgaria was settled by Slavs in the 6th cent. Turkic Bulgars arrived in the 7th cent., merged with the Slavs, became Christians by the 9th cent., and set up powerful empires in the 10th and 12th cents. Ottomans took over in 1396 and ruled for nearly 500 years.

An 1876 revolt led to an independent kingdom in 1908. Bulgaria expanded after the first Balkan War but lost its Aegean coastline in WWI, when it sided with Germany. Bulgaria joined the Axis in WWII but withdrew in 1944. Communists took power with Soviet aid; the monarchy was abolished Sept. 8, 1946.

On Nov. 10, 1989, Communist Party leader and head of state Todor Zhivkov resigned after 35 years. In Jan. 1990, Parliament voted to revoke the constitutionally guaranteed dominant role of the Communist Party. A new constitution took effect July 13, 1991.

Bulgaria became a full member of NATO, Apr. 2, 2004, and entered the EU, Jan. 1, 2007.

A terrorist blew up a bus carrying Israeli tourists, July 18, 2012, leaving 5 Israelis, the Bulgarian bus driver, and the bomber dead. An investigation ending Feb. 5, 2013, blamed the Muslim militant group Hezbollah, which denied involvement.

Worsening economic conditions in 2012-13 inspired protests that led center-right, pro-EU Prime Min. Boyko Borisov to submit his government's resignation Feb. 20, 2013. After Oct. 5, 2014, elections, Borisov again became prime min. Construction began in 2015 on the second phase of a security fence along the Turkish border, intended to stop Middle Eastern, SW Asian, and African migrants from entering Bulgaria; about 30,000 entered in 2015.

Socialist-backed, pro-Moscow candidate Rumen Radev won Bulgaria's presidential runoff election Nov. 13, 2016. Radev was reelected, Nov. 21, 2021.

Borisov's GERB party won Mar. 26, 2017, parliamentary elections. After inconclusive Apr. 4 and July 11, 2021, parliamentary elections, in which widespread corruption hurt GERB, a new anti-corruption party won Nov. 14 elections. Kiril Petkov became prime min. but resigned, June 27, 2022, after losing a no-confidence vote. After inconclusive Oct. 2, 2022, elections, GERB and the reformist, pro-EU bloc We Continue the Change won the most seats in Apr. 2, 2023, elections and formed a coalition government. After the coalition collapsed and inconclusive June 9, 2024, elections (no party could form a government), new elections were scheduled for Oct. 27.

Burkina Faso

People: Population: 23,042,199 (59). **Age distrib.:** <15: 41.6%; 65+: 3.2%. **Growth:** 2.4%. **Migrants:** 3.5%. **Pop. density:** 218.0 per sq mi, 84.2 per sq km. **Urban:** 33.2%. **Ethnic groups:** Mossi 53.7%, Fulani (Peuhl) 6.8%, Gurunsi 5.9%, Bissa 5.4%, Gurma 5.2%, Bobo 3.4%, Senufo 2.2%. **Languages:** Mossi, Fula, Gourmantche, Dyula, Bissa, Gurunsi, French (official). **Religions:** Muslim 56.1% (Sunni), Christian 26.4% (Catholic 16.0%, Protestant 10.0%), ethnic religionist 16.8%.

Geography: Total area: 105,869 sq mi, 274,200 sq km (74); **Land area:** 105,715 sq mi, 273,800 sq km. **Location:** W Africa, S of the Sahara. Mali on NW; Niger on NE; Benin, Togo, Ghana, Côte d'Ivoire on S. **Topography:** Landlocked in the savanna region of W Africa. The N is arid, hot, and thinly populated. **Arable land:** 28.9%. **Capital:** Ouagadougou, 3,358,934. **Cities:** Bobo-Dioulasso, 1,185,053.

Government: Type: Presidential republic. **Head of state:** Interim Pres. Ibrahim Traoré; in office: Oct. 6, 2022. **Head of govt.:** Prime Min. Joachim Kylem de Tambela; in office: Oct. 21, 2022. **Local divisions:** 13 regions. **Defense budget:** $832 mil. **Active troops:** 7,000.

Economy: Industries: cotton lint, beverages, agric. proc., soap, cigarettes, textiles. **Chief agric.:** sorghum, maize, fruits, vegetables, millet, cowpeas. **Natural resources:** gold, manganese, zinc, limestone, marble, phosphates, pumice, salt. **Water:** 611 cu m per capita. **Electricity prod.:** 781.4 mil kWh. **Labor force:** agric. 74.2%, industry 7.0%, services 18.8%. **Unemployment:** 5.3%.

Finance: Monetary unit: CFA Franc (XOF) (587.79 = $1 U.S.). **GDP:** $63.4 bil; **per capita GDP:** $2,727; **GDP growth:** 3.0%. **Imports** (2022): $6.8 bil; Côte d'Ivoire 16%, China 12%, Russia 7%, France 7%, Ghana 5%. **Exports** (2022): $5.8 bil; Switzerland 74%, UAE 7%. **Tourism** (2022): $76 mil. **Budget:** $3.8 bil. **Inflation:** 0.7%.

Transport: Railways: 386 mi. **Motor vehicles:** 20.9 per 1,000 pop. **Airports:** 49.

Communications: Mobile (2022): 119.5 per 100 pop. **Broadband** (2022): 72.3 per 100 pop. **Internet:** 19.9%.

Health: Expend.: 6.4%. **Life expect.:** 62.3 male; 66.1 female. **Births:** 31.9 per 1,000 pop. **Deaths:** 7.3 per 1,000 pop. **Infant mortality:** 47.0 per 1,000 live births. **Undernourished:** 15.4%. **HIV:** 0.6%. **COVID-19:** 400 deaths; rates per 100,000: 106 cases, 2 deaths. 25% vaccinated.

Education: Compulsory: ages 6-15. **Literacy:** 34.5%.

Website: www.gouvernement.gov.bf, burkina-usa.org

The Mossi people entered Burkina Faso in the 11th-13th cents. Their kingdoms ruled until they were defeated by the Mali and Songhai empires. French control came by 1896, but Upper Volta (renamed Burkina Faso on Aug. 4, 1984) was not established as a separate territory until 1947. Independence came Aug. 5, 1960. The military seized power in 1980. After a 1987 coup, Blaise Compaoré became sole ruler by 1989. Violent protests in 2014 led to his resignation, Oct. 31. Former center-left Prime Min. Roch Marc Christian Kaboré was elected president, Nov. 29, 2015.

Islamist extremists attacked a café and hotel in Ouagadougou Jan. 15-16, 2016, leaving 30 victims dead. By mid-2019, insurgents allied with Islamist extremists controlled parts of northern and eastern Burkina Faso, and extremist violence subsequently escalated.

Kaboré, who had won reelection Nov. 22, 2020, was ousted in a military coup, Jan. 24, 2022. Coup leader Lt. Col. Paul-Henri Sandaogo Damiba pledged stronger action against insurgents, but attacks by Islamist extremists continued. A coup led by Capt. Ibrahim Traoré, Sept. 30-Oct. 2, 2022, ousted Damiba. Extremist attacks, as well as alleged atrocities by government forces, continued in 2023-24. Russian military trainers began arriving in Burkina Faso in late 2023. As of Mar. 31, 2023, more than 2 mil people were internally displaced.

Burma

See Myanmar.

Burundi

Republic of Burundi

People: Population: 13,590,102 (77). **Age distrib.:** <15: 42.3%; 65+: 3.4%. **Growth:** 2.8%. **Migrants:** 2.9%. **Pop. density:** 1,370.6 per sq mi, 529.2 per sq km. **Urban:** 15.2%. **Ethnic groups:** Hutu, Tutsi, Twa, South Asian. **Languages:** Kirundi, French, English (all official). **Religions:** Christian 93.8% (Catholic 60.1%, Protestant 30.0%), ethnic religionist 3.8%, Muslim 2.1% (Sunni).

Geography: Total area: 10,745 sq mi, 27,830 sq km (143); **Land area:** 9,915 sq mi, 25,680 sq km. **Location:** Central Africa. Rwanda on N, Dem. Rep. of the Congo on W, Tanzania on E and S. **Topography:** Mostly grassy highland, with mountains reaching 8,900 ft. The southernmost source of the White Nile is located in Burundi. Lake Tanganyika is the world's second deepest lake (max. depth 4,823 ft). **Arable land:** 50.4%. **Capital:** Bujumbura, 1,277,050.

Government: Type: Presidential republic. **Head of state and govt.:** Pres. Evariste Ndayishimiye; b. 1968; in office: June 18, 2020. **Local divisions:** 18 provinces. **Defense budget:** $65 mil. **Active troops:** 30,050.

Economy: Industries: light consumer goods, cement, assembly of imported components, public works constr., food proc. (fruits). **Chief agric.:** cassava, bananas, sweet potatoes, vegetables, beans, potatoes. **Natural resources:** nickel, uranium, rare earth oxides, peat, cobalt, copper, platinum, vanadium, hydropower, niobium, tantalum, gold, tin, tungsten, kaolin, limestone. **Water:** 999 cu m per capita. **Electricity prod.:** 354.2 mil kWh. **Labor force:** agric. 85.1%, industry 3.1%, services 11.8%. **Unemployment:** 0.9%.

Finance: Monetary unit: Franc (BIF) (2,885.80 = $1 U.S.). **GDP:** $12.6 bil; **per capita GDP:** $951; **GDP growth:** 2.7%. **Imports** (2018): $905.3 mil; China 15%, UAE 14%, Saudi Arabia 13%, Tanzania 12%, India 7%. **Exports** (2018): $285.1 mil; UAE 32%, Dem. Rep. of the Congo 14%, China 5%, Sudan 5%. **Tourism** (2022): $3 mil. **Budget** (2020): $1.1 bil. **Inflation:** 26.9%.

Transport: Motor vehicles: 7.7 per 1,000 pop. **Airports:** 6.

Communications: Mobile: 63.2 per 100 pop. **Broadband:** 10.3 per 100 pop. **Internet:** 11.3%.

Health: Expend.: 9.1%. **Life expect.:** 66.0 male; 70.3 female. **Births:** 34.6 per 1,000 pop. **Deaths:** 5.7 per 1,000 pop. **Infant mortality:** 35.7 per 1,000 live births. **Undernourished:** NA. **HIV:** 0.9%. **COVID-19:** 15 deaths; rates per 100,000: 459 cases.

Education: Compulsory: NA. **Literacy:** 75.5%.

Website: presidence.gov.bi, burundiembassy-usa.com

The Pygmy Twa people were the first inhabitants, followed by Bantu Hutus, who were conquered in the 16th cent. by the Tutsi, probably from Ethiopia. Germany gained control in 1899. Belgium took over in 1916, successively exercising a League of Nations mandate and UN trusteeship over Ruanda-Urundi (now the two countries of Rwanda and Burundi). Burundi became independent July 1, 1962.

An unsuccessful Hutu rebellion in 1972-73 left 10,000 Tutsi and 150,000 Hutu dead. Over 100,000 Hutu fled to Tanzania and Zaire (now Dem. Rep. of the Congo). In the 1980s, Burundi's Tutsi-dominated regime pledged itself to ethnic reconciliation and democratic reform. In the nation's first democratic presidential election, June 1993, a Hutu, Melchior Ndadaye, was elected. He was killed in an attempted coup, Oct. 21, 1993. At least 150,000 Burundians died in ethnic conflicts over the next three years. Pres. Cyprien Ntaryamira, elected Jan. 1994, and the president of Rwanda were killed when missiles shot down their plane, Apr. 6. The incident sparked massive carnage in Rwanda; violence in Burundi, initially far more limited, intensified in 1995. Ethnic strife continued after a military coup, July 25, 1996. Most warring groups signed a draft peace treaty, Aug. 2000. A power-sharing government headed by Pierre Buyoya was sworn in Nov. 1, 2001, but clashes with rebels continued.

Domitien Ndayizeye, a Hutu, became president Apr. 2003. The UN Security Council authorized, May 2004, a peacekeeping force (ONUB) for Burundi. Approval of a power-sharing constitution by referendum, Feb. 28, 2005, paved the way for local and parliamentary elections. Chosen by parliament, Pierre Nkurunziza, former leader of a Hutu rebel group, became president Aug. 2005. Under a reconciliation accord reached Dec. 4, 2008, remaining Hutu rebels began to demobilize. Candidates opposing Nkurunziza dropped out of the June 2010 presidential election, claiming the vote was rigged. The government was accused of ordering extrajudicial killings, 2010-11.

The mission of UN successor offices to ONUB ended in 2014. Violent protests began after Nkurunziza's Apr. 2015 decision to seek a constitutionally dubious third term, which he won, July 21, despite a coup attempt. Political violence and harsh government repression continued in Nkurunziza's third term, leading hundreds of thousands to flee the country. Evariste Ndayishimiye, of Nkurunziza's ruling party, won the May 20, 2020, election, which the opposition claimed was rigged. Nkurunziza died June 8, 2020, before the end of his term. Sporadic violence by some Hutu rebels continued in the 2020s.

Cabo Verde

Republic of Cabo Verde

People: Population: 611,014 (166). **Age distrib.:** <15: 26.4%; 65+: 6.4%. **Growth:** 1.2%. **Migrants:** 2.8%. **Pop. density:** 392.4 per sq mi, 151.5 per sq km. **Urban:** 68.4%. **Ethnic groups:** Creole (mulatto) 71%, African 28%. **Languages:** Portuguese (official), Crioulo (Portuguese-based Creole). **Religions:** Christian 94.7% (Catholic 79.7%, independent 10.7%), Muslim 2.9% (Sunni).

Geography: Total area: 1,557 sq mi, 4,033 sq km (167); **Land area:** 1,557 sq mi, 4,033 sq km. **Location:** In Atlantic O., off W tip of Africa. Nearest neighbors are Mauritania, Senegal to E. **Topography:** 15 Cabo Verde islands, volcanic in origin (active crater on Fogo). Landscape is eroded and stark, with vegetation mostly in interior valleys. **Arable land:** 12.4%. **Capital:** Praia, 167,504.

Government: Type: Parliamentary republic. **Head of state:** Pres. José Maria Neves; b. 1960; in office: Nov. 9, 2021. **Head of govt.:** Prime Min. José Ulisses Correia e Silva; b. 1962; in office: Apr. 22, 2016. **Local divisions:** 22 municipalities. **Defense budget:** $459 mil. **Active troops:** 1,200.

Economy: Industries: food and beverages, fish proc., shoes and garments, salt mining, ship repair. **Chief agric.:** sugarcane, tomatoes, coconuts, pulses, goat milk, vegetables. **Natural resources:** salt, basalt rock, limestone, kaolin, fish, clay, gypsum. **Water:** 510 cu m per capita. **Electricity prod.:** 433 mil kWh. **Labor force:** agric. 10.1%, industry 22.0%, services 67.9%. **Unemployment:** 12.0%.

Finance: Monetary unit: Escudo (CVE) (98.81 = $1 U.S.). **GDP:** $5.4 bil; **per capita GDP:** $9,086; **GDP growth:** 5.1%. **Imports:** $1.4 bil; Portugal 41%, Spain 12%, China 8%, Netherlands 7%, Togo 5%. **Exports:** $951.2 mil; Spain 56%, Portugal 12%, Italy 9%, U.S. 6%, India 5%. **Tourism** (2022): $400 mil. **Budget:** $619 mil. **Inflation** (2021-22): 7.9%.

Transport: Airports: 10.

Communications: Mobile: 113.0 per 100 pop. **Broadband:** 98.8 per 100 pop. **Internet:** 72.1%.

Health: Expend.: 6.9%. **Life expect.:** 72.0 male; 76.7 female. **Births:** 17.9 per 1,000 pop. **Deaths:** 5.7 per 1,000 pop. **Infant mortality:** 22.4 per 1,000 live births. **Undernourished:** 12.6%. **HIV:** 1.0%. **COVID-19:** 417 deaths; rates per 100,000: 11,596 cases, 75 deaths. 56% vaccinated.

Education: Compulsory: ages 6-15. **Literacy:** 91.0%.

Website: www.governo.cv

The first Portuguese colonists landed in 1462; enslaved African workers were brought soon after, and most Cabo Verdeans descend from both groups. Independence for Cabo Verde (known as Cape Verde until Oct. 2013) came July 5, 1975. Remittances from Cabo Verdean emigrants are a major source of income.

The nation's first free presidential election was held Feb. 17, 1991. Jorge Carlos Fonseca, of the center-right MFD party, won presidential elections in 2011 and 2016. José Maria Neves, of the leftist PAICV, won the Oct. 17, 2021, presidential election. The WHO certified, Jan. 2024, that Cabo Verde had become malaria-free.

Cambodia

Kingdom of Cambodia

People: Population: 17,063,669 (73). **Age distrib.:** <15: 28.9%; 65+: 5.3%. **Growth:** 1.0%. **Migrants:** 0.5%. **Pop. density:** 250.4 per sq mi, 96.7 per sq km. **Urban:** 26.0%. **Ethnic groups:** Khmer 95.4%, Cham 2.4%. **Languages:** Khmer (official). **Religions:** Buddhist (official) 86.6% (Theravadin), ethnic religionist 3.8%, Christian 3.2%, Chinese folk-religionist 2.3%.

Geography: Total area: 69,898 sq mi, 181,035 sq km (88); **Land area:** 68,153 sq mi, 176,515 sq km. **Location:** SE Asia, on Indochina Peninsula. Thailand on W and N, Laos on NE, Vietnam on E. **Topography:** The central area, formed by the Mekong R. basin and Tonle Sap Lake, is level. Hills and mountains in SE; long escarpment in NW separates the country from Thailand. **Arable land:** 23.3%. **Capital:** Phnum Pénh (Phnom Penh), 2,352,680.

Government: Type: Parliamentary constitutional monarchy. **Head of state:** King Norodom Sihamoni; b. 1953; in office: Oct. 29, 2004. **Head of govt.:** Prime Min. Hun Manet; b. 1977; in office: Aug. 22, 2023. **Local divisions:** 24 provinces, 1 municipality. **Defense budget:** $1.2 bil. **Active troops:** 124,300.

Economy: Industries: tourism, garments, constr., rice milling, fishing, wood and wood prods., rubber, cement, gem mining, textiles. **Chief agric.:** cassava, rice, maize, sugarcane, vegetables, oil palm fruit. **Natural resources:** oil and gas, timber, gems, iron ore, manganese, phosphates. **Water:** 28,700 cu m per capita. **Electricity prod.:** 8.8 bil kWh. **Labor force:** agric. 36.6%, industry 26.6%, services 36.8%. **Unemployment:** 0.2%.

Finance: Monetary unit: Riel (KHR) (4,067.44 = $1 U.S.). **GDP:** $95.3 bil; **per capita GDP:** $5,624; **GDP growth:** 5.4%. **Imports:** $29.4 bil; China 30%, Thailand 19%, Singapore 18%, Vietnam 13%. **Exports:** $27.8 bil; U.S. 36%, Vietnam 10%, Germany 7%, Japan 5%, Canada 5%. **Tourism:** $3.1 bil. **Budget:** $6.5 bil. **Inflation:** 2.1%.

Transport: Railways: 399 mi (under restoration). **Airports:** 13.

Communications: Mobile (2022): 113.4 per 100 pop. **Broadband** (2022): 99.4 per 100 pop. **Internet:** 56.7%.

Health: Expend.: 7.5%. **Life expect.:** 69.6 male; 73.3 female. **Births:** 18.2 per 1,000 pop. **Deaths:** 5.7 per 1,000 pop. **Infant mortality:** 27.9 per 1,000 live births. **Undernourished:** 4.6%. **HIV:** 0.5%. **COVID-19:** 3,056 deaths; rates per 100,000: 833 cases, 18 deaths. 88% vaccinated.

Education: Compulsory: NA. **Literacy:** 83.8%.

Website: en.cnv.org.kh

Early kingdoms dating from that of Funan in the 1st cent. CE culminated in the great Khmer empire that flourished from the 9th cent. to the 13th, encompassing present-day Thailand, Cambodia, Laos, and southern Vietnam. The peripheral areas were lost to invading Siamese and Vietnamese. France established a protectorate in 1863. Independence came in 1953.

Prince Norodom Sihanouk, king (1941-55) and head of state from 1960, tried to maintain neutrality during the Vietnam War. The U.S. bombed Cambodia, 1969-73, targeting suspected border sanctuaries of Vietnamese insurgents.

In 1970, pro-U.S. Prem. Lon Nol seized power, demanded removal of 40,000 North Vietnamese troops, and abolished the monarchy. Open war began between Lon Nol's government and Communist Khmer Rouge guerrillas, led by Pol Pot and supported by Vietnam and China. The U.S. provided Lon Nol with military and economic aid.

Khmer Rouge forces captured Phnom Penh Apr. 17, 1975. Cities were depopulated with the stated goal of making Cambodia a classless agrarian society; Cambodians were executed or forced to work on cooperative farms. An estimated 1.7 mil people died in "killing fields" or from other hardships under Khmer Rouge rule, 1975-79.

Border fighting in 1978 developed into a full-fledged Vietnamese invasion. Formation of a Vietnamese-backed government was announced, Jan. 8, 1979, one day after Phnom Penh was seized. Thousands of refugees fled to Thailand; widespread starvation was reported. Vietnamese troops remained in Cambodia until Sept. 1989 to combat resistance from Khmer Rouge guerrillas.

Following 1993 UN-sponsored elections, two leading parties agreed to share power in an interim government. On Sept. 21, the National Assembly adopted a constitution reestablishing a monarchy with Sihanouk as king. The Khmer Rouge insurgency weakened and splintered by 1996.

Co-Prime Min. Hun Sen staged a coup July 5, 1997, ousting his rival, Prince Norodom Ranariddh. Pol Pot was denounced by his former comrades at a show trial, July 25, 1997, and sentenced to house arrest; he died Apr. 15, 1998. Sihanouk abdicated because of poor health and was succeeded, Oct. 2004, by his son Norodom Sihamoni. A UN-backed war crimes tribunal convicted a former prison warden known as Duch July 2010 for overseeing the killing and torture of more than 14,000 inmates under the Khmer Rouge.

Hun Sen's Cambodian People's Party (CPP) retained power through a series of flawed elections and repressive policies. The political party of opposition leader Kem Sokha was dissolved in Nov. 2017, and several media outlets were shut down. Trials of more than 100 opposition figures resulted in prison terms, 2021-22. Kem Sokha was convicted of treason and sentenced to 27 years' confinement, Mar. 3, 2023. A new opposition party was barred, May 15, 2023, from participating in July 23 elections swept by the CPP. Hun Sen transferred the premiership, Aug. 22, 2023, to his son Hun Manet but remained CPP head and became, Apr. 3, 2024, Senate president.

In recent years, Chinese investment, military and other aid, and tourism have increased sharply.

Cameroon

Republic of Cameroon

People: Population: 30,966,105 (51). **Age distrib.:** <15: 41.5%; 65+: 3.2%. **Growth:** 2.7%. **Migrants:** 2.2%. **Pop. density:** 169.7 per sq mi, 65.5 per sq km. **Urban:** 59.9%. **Ethnic groups:** Bamileke-Bamu 22.2%, Biu-Mandara 16.4%, Arab-Choa/Hausa/Kanuri 13.5%, Beti/Bassa, Mbam 13.1%, Grassfields 9.9%, Adamawa-Ubangi 9.8%, Cotier/Ngoe/Oroko 4.6%, Southwestern Bantu 4.3%, Kako/Meka 2.3%. **Languages:** English, French (both official); 24 major African lang. groups. **Religions:** Christian 58.0% (Catholic 27.9%, Protestant 23.3%), Muslim 21.8% (Sunni), ethnic religionist 19.1%.

Geography: Total area: 183,568 sq mi, 475,440 sq km (54); **Land area:** 182,514 sq mi, 472,710 sq km. **Location:** Between W and central Africa. Nigeria on NW; Chad, Central African Rep. on E; Rep. of the Congo, Gabon, Equatorial Guinea on S. **Topography:** Low coastal plain with rain forests in S; plateaus in center lead to forested mountains in W, including Mt. Cameroon (13,435 ft). Grasslands in N, marshes around Lake Chad. **Arable land:** 13.1%. **Capital:** Yaoundé, 4,681,768. **Cities:** Douala, 4,203,108.

Government: Type: Presidential republic. **Head of state:** Pres. Paul Biya; b. 1933; in office: Nov. 6, 1982. **Head of govt.:** Prime Min. Joseph Dion Ngute; b. 1954; in office: Jan. 4, 2019. **Local divisions:** 10 regions. **Defense budget:** $15 mil. **Active troops:** 25,400.

Economy: Industries: petroleum prod./refining, aluminum prod., food proc., light consumer goods, textiles, lumber, ship repair. **Chief agric.:** cassava, plantains, oil palm fruit, maize, taro, tomatoes. **Natural resources:** petroleum, bauxite, iron ore, timber, hydropower. **Water:** 10,410 cu m per capita. **Crude oil reserves:** 200 mil bbls. **Electricity prod.:** 8.1 bil kWh. **Labor force:** agric. 42.2%, industry 15.4%, services 42.4%. **Unemployment:** 3.6%.

Finance: Monetary unit: Central African CFA Franc (XAF) (587.79 = $1 U.S.). **GDP:** $154.1 bil; **per capita GDP:** $5,380; **GDP growth:** 4.0%. **Imports** (2022): $9.8 bil; China 39%, France 8%, India 6%. **Exports** (2022): $8.6 bil; Netherlands 19%, France 15%, India 14%, Spain 10%, China 8%. **Tourism** (2022): $541 mil. **Budget:** $7.4 bil. **Inflation:** 7.4%.

Transport: Railways: 613 mi. **Motor vehicles:** 18.3 per 1,000 pop. **Airports:** 37.

Communications: Mobile: 92.4 per 100 pop. **Broadband:** 35.3 per 100 pop. **Internet:** 43.9%.

Health: Expend.: 3.8%. **Life expect.:** 62.3 male; 66.1 female. **Births:** 34.7 per 1,000 pop. **Deaths:** 7.4 per 1,000 pop. **Infant mortality:** 46.1 per 1,000 live births. **Undernourished:** 5.7%. **HIV:** NA. **COVID-19:** 1,974 deaths; rates per 100,000: 472 cases, 7 deaths. 12% vaccinated.

Education: Compulsory: ages 6-11. **Literacy:** 78.2%.

Website: www.spm.gov.cm

Portuguese sailors were the first Europeans to reach Cameroon, in the 15th cent. The European and American slave trade was very active in the area. German control lasted from 1884 to 1916, when France and Britain divided the territory. French Cameroon became independent Jan. 1, 1960; one part of British Cameroon joined Nigeria in 1961 while the other part joined Cameroon. Pres. Paul Biya has retained power since 1982 in a series of elections that were boycotted by opposition parties or disputed as fraudulent.

More than a dozen French citizens were kidnapped during 2013, allegedly in retaliation for France's intervention in Mali, by the Nigerian-based jihadist group Boko Haram. Kidnappings and attacks by Boko Haram in northern Cameroon continued in subsequent years. Beginning in 2015, Cameroon troops fought in Nigeria against Islamist-extremist forces; a 2017 Amnesty Intl. report accused the Cameroon military of torturing detainees.

Beginning in late 2016, government forces violently suppressed protesters and fought separatists in Anglophone areas of western Cameroon. As a result of violence in the north and west, more than 1 mil people were internally displaced as of Aug. 31, 2024.

Canada

People: Population: 38,794,813 (37). **Age distrib.:** <15: 15.5%; 65+: 21.0%. **Growth:** 0.7%. **Migrants:** 21.3%. **Pop. density:** 11.0 per sq mi, 4.3 per sq km. **Urban:** 82.0%. **Ethnic groups:** Canadian 15.6%, English 14.7%, Scottish 12.1%, Irish 12.1%, French 11%, German 8.1%, Chinese 4.7%, Italian 4.3%, Indian 3.7%, Ukrainian 3.5%, First Nations 1.7%. **Languages:** English, French (both official); Chinese langs., Spanish, Punjabi, Arabic, Tagalog. **Religions:** Christian 59.9% (Catholic 42.7%, Protestant 9.5%), agnostic 25.1%, Muslim 3.3% (Sunni), atheist 2.6%, Chinese folk-religionist 2.2%, Buddhist 1.9% (Mahayanist), Sikh 1.6%, Hindu 1.4%.

Geography: Total area: 3,855,103 sq mi, 9,984,670 sq km (2); **Land area:** 3,511,023 sq mi, 9,093,507 sq km. **Location:** Extends 3,426 mi E-W and S from the North Pole to the U.S. **Topography:** Seacoast includes 36,356 mi of mainland and 115,133 mi of islands, including the Arctic islands almost from Greenland to near the Alaskan border. Generally temperate, though varies from freezing winter cold to blistering summer heat. **Arable land:** 4.4%. **Capital:** Ottawa, 1,451,571. **Cities:** Toronto, 6,431,430; Montréal, 4,341,638; Vancouver, 2,682,509; Calgary, 1,665,023; Edmonton, 1,567,615; Québec, 851,061; Winnipeg, 849,251; Halifax, 422,891; Victoria, 401,577.

Government: Type: Federal parliamentary democracy under constitutional monarchy. **Head of state:** King Charles III, rep. by Gov.-Gen. Mary Simon; b. 1947; in office: July 26, 2021. **Head of govt.:** Prime Min. Justin Trudeau; b. 1971; in office: Nov. 4, 2015. **Local divisions:** 10 provinces, 3 territories. **Defense budget:** $24.2 bil. **Active troops:** 62,300.

Economy: Industries: transp. equip., chemicals, minerals, food prods., wood and paper prods., fish prods. **Chief agric.:** wheat, rapeseed, maize, barley, milk, soybeans. **Natural resources:** bauxite, iron ore, nickel, zinc, copper, gold, lead, uranium, rare earth elements, molybdenum, potash, diamonds, silver, fish, timber, wildlife, coal, petroleum, nat. gas. **Water:** 76,058 cu m per capita. **Crude oil reserves:** 170.3 bil bbls. **Electricity prod.:** 638.0 bil kWh. **Labor force:** agric. 1.3%, industry 19.2%, services 79.6%. **Unemployment:** 5.4%.

Finance: Monetary unit: Dollar (CAD) (1.35 = $1 U.S.). **GDP:** $2.5 tril; **per capita GDP:** $61,582; **GDP growth:** 1.1%. **Imports:** $726.1 bil; U.S. 56%, China 11%. **Exports:** $717.7 bil; U.S. 75%. **Tourism:** $39.2 bil. **Budget** (2020): $862.0 bil. **Inflation:** 3.9%.

Transport: Railways: 30,709 mi. **Motor vehicles:** 675.6 per 1,000 pop. **Airports:** 1,425.

Communications: Mobile: 93.0 per 100 pop. **Broadband:** 87.8 per 100 pop. **Internet:** 94%.

Health: Expend. (2022): 11.2%. **Life expect.:** 81.9 male; 86.6 female. **Births:** 10.0 per 1,000 pop. **Deaths:** 8.2 per 1,000 pop. **Infant mortality:** 4.3 per 1,000 live births. **Undernourished:** <2.5%. **HIV:** NA. **COVID-19:** 55,282 deaths; rates per 100,000: 12,768 cases, 146 deaths. 83% vaccinated.

Education: Compulsory: ages 6-15. **Literacy:** NA.

Website: www.canada.ca

Indigenous people have lived in Canada for at least 12,000 years. Vikings reached and briefly settled in part of Newfoundland in the 10th cent. Italian seaman Giovanni Caboto (a.k.a. John Cabot) claimed parts of the Atlantic coast for England in 1497 and 1498. After French explorer Jacques Cartier reached the Gulf of St. Lawrence in 1534, France pioneered Canadian settlement by Western Europeans, establishing Québec City (1608) and Montréal (1642) and declaring New France a colony in 1663.

Britain acquired Acadia (later Nova Scotia) in 1717 and defeated French forces in Canada to gain control of all of New France by 1763. The French, through the Quebec Act of 1774, retained rights to their language, religion, and civil law. During the American Revolution, many colonials, calling themselves United Empire Loyalists, moved north to Canada. Fur traders and explorers led Canadians of European origin westward across the continent. Sir Alexander Mackenzie reached the Pacific in 1793 and scrawled on a rock, "From Canada by land."

In Upper and Lower Canada (later called Ontario and Quebec) and in the Maritimes, legislative assemblies were formed in the 18th cent. Upper Canada was involved in the War of 1812 between Great Britain and the U.S.

In 1837 political agitation for a more democratic government culminated in rebellions in Upper and Lower Canada and the union of the two into the colony of Canada in 1839. The union lasted until the 1867 British North America Act (now known as the Constitution Act, 1867) launched the Dominion of Canada, consisting of Ontario, Quebec, and the former colonies of Nova Scotia and New Brunswick.

The British North America Act, which was the basis for the country's written constitution, established a federal system of government modeled on the British parliament and cabinet structure under the crown. Canada was proclaimed a self-governing dominion within the British Empire in 1931. The Constitution Act, 1982,

Canada's Provinces and Territories

Province/territory	Joined confed.	Tot. area (sq mi)	Pop. ests. (2023)	Capital	Premier	Party	In office
Alberta	1905	255,541	4,695,290	Edmonton	Danielle Smith	United Cons.	2022
British Columbia	1871	364,764	5,519,013	Victoria	David Eby	New Democratic	2022
Manitoba	1870	250,116	1,454,902	Winnipeg	Wab Kinew	New Democratic	2023
New Brunswick	1867	28,150	834,691	Fredericton	Blaine Higgs	Prog. Cons.	2018
Newfoundland and Labrador	1949	156,453	538,605	St. John's	Andrew Furey	Liberal	2020
Nova Scotia	1867	21,345	1,058,694	Halifax	Tim Houston	Prog. Cons.	2021
Ontario	1867	415,598	15,608,369	Toronto	Doug Ford	Prog. Cons.	2018
Prince Edward Island	1873	2,185	173,787	Charlottetown	Dennis King	Prog. Cons.	2019
Québec	1867	595,391	8,874,683	Québec	François Legault	Coalition Avenir Québec	2018
Saskatchewan	1905	251,366	1,209,107	Regina	Scott Moe	Saskatchewan	2018
Northwest Territories[1]	1871	519,734	44,972	Yellowknife	R.J. Simpson	Nonpartisan	2023
Nunavut[1,2]	1999	808,185	40,673	Iqaluit	P.J. Akeeagok	Nonpartisan	2021
Yukon[1]	1898	186,272	44,975	Whitehorse	Ranj Pillai	Liberal	2023

Note: Census pop. as of Jan. 1. (Source: Statistics Canada.) (1) Territories also have federally appointed commissioners to represent federal interests. (2) Territory created in 1999 from eastern portion of Northwest Territories.

gave Canada the right to amend its constitution, thereby severing its last legislative link with Britain.

Failure in 1990 of the so-called Meech Lake Accord, which would have assured constitutional protection for Quebec's efforts to preserve its French language and culture, sparked a separatist revival in Quebec. The Charlottetown agreement, calling for constitutional changes, such as recognition of Quebec as a "distinct society" within the Canadian confederation, was defeated by a national referendum Oct. 1992. A Quebec referendum on secession, Oct. 1995, also failed.

On Jan. 7, 1998, the government apologized to Indigenous peoples for 150 years of mistreatment. Nunavut ("Our Land"), carved from the Northwest Territories as a homeland for the Inuit, was established Apr. 1, 1999. A national commission concluded in 2015 that the forced removal, 1883-1996, of thousands of Indigenous children to residential schools (including Roman Catholic and other religious schools), where some students suffered abuse, constituted "cultural genocide"; in mid-2021, the remains of more than 1,000 children were found on the grounds of several former schools.

Same-sex marriage (already permitted in 8 provinces) became legal throughout the country July 2005. Marijuana was legalized nationally for medical purposes in 2001 and for recreational use in 2018.

Twelve years of Liberal Party rule ended when the Conservatives won parliamentary elections, Jan. 23, 2006. Elections Oct. 19, 2015, returned Liberals to power, and Justin Trudeau, son of former Prime Min. Pierre Trudeau, became prime min. After Oct. 21, 2019, and Sept. 20, 2021, elections, Justin Trudeau continued as prime minister, although the Liberals fell short of a majority each time.

The Canadian government approved, Nov. 29, 2016, a major expansion (opposed by environmental groups) of the Trans Mountain pipeline to transport oil from Alberta to British Columbia. Plans to build the Keystone XL pipeline, to carry Alberta oil to the Gulf of Mexico, were abandoned in 2021, after U.S. approval was rescinded.

On Oct. 22, 2014, a terrorist gunman in Ottawa, apparently inspired by the Islamist extremist group ISIS, killed a soldier at the Canadian War Memorial and opened fire in the Parliament building before being shot to death. Canada joined the U.S.-led campaign of airstrikes against ISIS forces in Iraq (2014-16) and Syria (2015-16). Canada resettled, 2015-16, almost 40,000 refugees fleeing Syria's civil war. Following the Aug. 2021 Taliban takeover of Afghanistan, Canada announced, Sept. 27, it would accept 40,000 Afghan refugees. By Apr. 1, 2024, when a special visa program ended, about 300,000 Ukrainians had arrived in Canada since Russia's Feb. 2022 invasion of Ukraine.

The North American Free Trade Agreement (NAFTA) among Canada, Mexico, and the U.S. went into effect Jan. 1, 1994. A revised agreement—renamed the U.S.-Mexico-Canada Agreement (USMCA)—including auto industry changes and increased U.S. access to the Canadian dairy market, went into effect July 1, 2020.

A Canada-EU trade agreement eliminating almost all tariffs was signed Oct. 30, 2016. Canada signed, Mar. 8, 2018, an 11-nation trans-Pacific trade-liberalization agreement.

The COVID-19 pandemic reached Canada by early 2020. Large-scale protests by truckers and their supporters, Jan.-Feb. 2022, against vaccination requirements and other COVID-19 restrictions, blocked downtown Ottawa as well as Canada-U.S. border crossings, severely disrupting trade.

Canada had its worst wildfire season on record in summer 2023, likely linked to climate change. The fires caused dangerous levels of air pollution across large areas of Canada (and the U.S.); in mid-Aug., Yellowknife and other communities in NWT and British Columbia were told to evacuate. In summer 2024, wildfires devastated parts of Jasper, Alberta, and Jasper National Park.

Canada accused India of assassinating an India-born, Canadian Sikh community leader in British Columbia June 18, 2023, which India denied.

Central African Republic

People: Population: 5,650,957 (116). **Age distrib.:** <15: 38.5%; 65+: 3.5%. **Growth:** 1.8%. **Migrants:** 1.8%. **Pop. density:** 23.5 per sq mi, 9.1 per sq km. **Urban:** 44.1%. **Ethnic groups:** Baya 28.8%, Banda 22.9%, Mandjia 9.9%, Sara 7.9%, M'Baka-Bantu 7.9%, Arab-Fulani (Peuhl) 6%, Mbum 6%, Ngbanki 5.5%, Zande-Nzakara 3%, other Central African Republic ethnic groups 2%. **Languages:** French (official), Sangho (lingua franca and national lang.), tribal langs. **Religions:** Christian 74.7% (Catholic 44.0%, Protestant 15.5%, independent 15.2%), Muslim 14.0% (Sunni), ethnic religionist 10.4%.

Geography: Total area: 240,535 sq mi, 622,984 sq km (45); **Land area:** 240,535 sq mi, 622,984 sq km. **Location:** Central Africa. Chad on N, Cameroon on W, Rep. of the Congo and the DRC on S, South Sudan and Sudan on E. **Topography:** Mostly rolling plateau, avg. elevation 2,000 ft, with rivers draining S to the Congo and N to Lake Chad. Open, well-watered savanna covers most of area, with an arid area in NE and tropical rain forest in SW. **Arable land:** 2.9%. **Capital:** Bangui, 985,965.

Government: Type: Presidential republic. **Head of state:** Pres. Faustin-Archange Touadéra; b. 1957; in office: Mar. 30, 2016. **Head of govt.:** Prime Min. Félix Moloua; in office: Feb. 7, 2022. **Local divisions:** 14 prefectures, 2 economic prefectures, 1 commune. **Defense budget:** $63 mil. **Active troops:** 9,150.

Economy: Industries: gold and diamond mining, logging, brewing, sugar refining. **Chief agric.:** cassava, groundnuts, yams, coffee, maize, sesame seeds. **Natural resources:** diamonds, uranium, timber, gold, oil, hydropower. **Water:** 25,838 cu m per capita. **Electricity prod.:** 151.1 mil kWh. **Labor force:** agric. 70.8%, industry 6.3%, services 22.9%. **Unemployment:** 6.3%.

Finance: Monetary unit: Central African CFA Franc (XAF) (587.79 = $1 U.S.). **GDP:** $6.5 bil; **per capita GDP:** $1,130; **GDP growth:** 0.9%. **Imports** (2022): $784.7 mil; Cameroon 28%, U.S. 8%, China 7%, France 6%, South Korea 5%. **Exports** (2022): $293.1 mil; UAE 40%, Italy 11%, Pakistan 10%, China 10%, France 6%. **Tourism** (2020): $30 mil. **Budget:** $385 mil. **Inflation:** 3.0%.

Transport: Motor vehicles: 1.3 per 1,000 pop. **Airports:** 43.

Communications: Mobile (2022): 38.8 per 100 pop. **Broadband** (2022): 5.5 per 100 pop. **Internet** (2019): 7.5%.

Health: Expend.: 9.1%. **Life expect.:** 55.1 male; 57.7 female. **Births:** 31.9 per 1,000 pop. **Deaths:** 11.3 per 1,000 pop. **Infant mortality:** 80.5 per 1,000 live births. **Undernourished:** 23.5%. **HIV:** NA. **COVID-19:** 113 deaths; rates per 100,000: 320 cases, 2 deaths. 51% vaccinated.

Education: Compulsory: ages 6-15. **Literacy:** 37.5%.

Website: www.gouv.cf or www.usrcaembassy.org

Various Bantu peoples migrated through the region for centuries before French control was asserted in the late 19th cent., when the region was named Ubangi-Shari. Independence was attained Aug. 13, 1960.

Pres. Jean-Bedel Bokassa, who seized power in a 1965 military coup, proclaimed himself emperor Dec. 1976. Bokassa's rule was characterized by ruthless authoritarianism. He was ousted in a bloodless coup aided by France, Sept. 20, 1979. In 1981, Gen. André Kolingba became head of state in another bloodless coup. Elections in Aug. and Sept. 1993 led to civilian rule under Pres. Ange-Félix Patassé.

Patassé was ousted Mar. 15, 2003, by rebels under former army chief François Bozizé. Bozizé won a presidential runoff election May 8, 2005, but insurgent activity by Patassé loyalists and others continued in the north. A national peace conference, Dec. 8-20, 2008, enabled the installation of a unity government Jan. 19, 2009. Pres. Bozizé won reelection Jan. 23, 2011, but was ousted when the largely Muslim rebel group Seleka, led by Michel Djotodia, seized the capital Mar. 24, 2013. Bozizé supporters and Christian militias clashed with pro-Djotodia and Muslim fighters, resulting in thousands of deaths. A National Transitional Council elected Catherine

Samba-Panza interim pres. Jan. 20, 2014. France sent peacekeeping troops (2014-16). A UN peacekeeping force (MINUSCA) was authorized Apr. 10, 2014.

Faustin-Archange Touadéra, a Christian, won a UN-supervised presidential runoff election, Feb. 14, 2016. Violence between Muslims and Christians, as well as between rival militias and ethnic groups, continued. The government signed peace agreements with rebel groups Feb. 6 and Apr. 9, 2019. But violence persisted, and rebels at times controlled large areas of the country. Russian mercenaries began, in 2018, assisting CAR troops fighting rebels. Touadéra won reelection, Dec. 27, 2020. A new constitution, approved in a July 30, 2023, referendum boycotted by opposition groups, eliminated presidential term limits.

More than 17,000 MINUSCA uniformed personnel were in the CAR as of July 31, 2024. About 453,000 people were internally displaced as of June 2024, and 656,000 were refugees in neighboring countries.

Chad

Republic of Chad

People: Population: 19,093,595 (65). **Age distrib.:** <15: 45.8%; 65+: 2.5%. **Growth:** 3.0%. **Migrants:** 3.3%. **Pop. density:** 39.3 per sq mi, 15.2 per sq km. **Urban:** 24.7%. **Ethnic groups:** Sara (Ngambaye/Sara/Madjingaye/Mbaye) 30.5%, Kanembu/Bornu/Buduma 9.8%, Arab 9.7%, Wadai/Maba/Masalit/Mimi 7%, Gorane 5.8%, Masa/Musseye/Musgum 4.9%, Bulala/Medogo/Kuka 3.7%, Marba/Lele/Mesme 3.5%, Mundang 2.7%, Bidiyo/Migaama/Kenga/Dangleat 2.5%, Dadjo/Kibet/Muro 2.4%. **Languages:** French, Arabic (both official); Sara in S; 120+ langs. and dialects. **Religions:** Muslim 60.4% (Sunni), Christian 31.7% (Catholic 18.0%, Protestant 9.1%), ethnic religionist 6.5%.

Geography: Total area: 495,755 sq mi, 1,284,000 sq km (20); **Land area:** 486,180 sq mi, 1,259,200 sq km. **Location:** Central N Africa. Libya on N; Niger, Nigeria, Cameroon on W; Central African Republic on S; Sudan on E. **Topography:** Wooded savanna, steppe, and desert in the S; part of the Sahara in the N. Southern rivers flow N to Lake Chad, surrounded by marshland. **Arable land:** 4.2%. **Capital:** N'Djaména, 1,655,618.

Government: Type: Presidential republic. **Head of state:** Pres. Mahamat Idriss Déby Itno; b. 1984; in office: May 23, 2024. **Head of govt.:** Prime Min. Allamaye Halina; b. 1967; in office: May 23, 2024. **Local divisions:** 23 provinces. **Defense budget:** $352 mil. **Active troops:** 33,250.

Economy: Industries: oil, cotton textiles, brewing, natron (sodium carbonate), soap, cigarettes, constr. materials. **Chief agric.:** sorghum, groundnuts, millet, cereals, beef, sugarcane. **Natural resources:** petroleum, uranium, natron, kaolin, fish, gold, limestone, sand/gravel, salt. **Water:** 2,660 cu m per capita. **Crude oil reserves:** 1.5 bil bbls. **Electricity prod.:** 349.8 mil kWh. **Labor force:** agric. 69.2%, industry 9.6%, services 21.2%. **Unemployment:** 1.1%.

Finance: Monetary unit: Central African CFA Franc (XAF) (587.79 = $1 U.S.). **GDP:** $36.0 bil; **per capita GDP:** $1,969; **GDP growth:** 4.1%. **Imports** (2022): $5.0 bil; China 25%, UAE 20%, France 7%, U.S. 7%, Belgium 7%. **Exports** (2022): $6.5 bil; Germany 25%, China 21%, UAE 20%, Taiwan 12%, France 10%. **Budget** (2020): $2.1 bil. **Inflation:** 10.8%.

Transport: Airports: 42.

Communications: Mobile (2022): 65.4 per 100 pop. **Broadband** (2022): 3.3 per 100 pop. **Internet:** 12.2%.

Health: Expend.: 5.2%. **Life expect.:** 58.1 male; 62.0 female. **Births:** 39.2 per 1,000 pop. **Deaths:** 9.0 per 1,000 pop. **Infant mortality:** 62.5 per 1,000 live births. **Undernourished:** 35.1%. **HIV:** 1.0%. **COVID-19:** 194 deaths; rates per 100,000: 47 cases, 1 death. 31% vaccinated.

Education: Compulsory: ages 6-15. **Literacy:** 27.3%.

Website: presidence.td

Chad was the site of Paleolithic and Neolithic cultures before the Sahara Desert formed. A succession of kingdoms and Arab slave traders dominated Chad until France took control around 1900. Independence came Aug. 11, 1960. Northern Muslim rebels fought animist and Christian southern government and French troops from 1966.

Rebel forces led by Hissène Habré captured the capital and forced Pres. Goukouni Oueddei to flee the country in June 1982. In Dec. 1990, a Libyan-supported insurgent group, the Patriotic Salvation Movement, overthrew Habré, who went into exile in Senegal. (Accused of killing and torturing thousands in the 1980s, Habré was convicted in Senegal, May 30, 2016, of crimes against humanity and sentenced to life in prison. Habré died Aug. 24, 2021.)

After approval of a new constitution Mar. 1996, Chad's first multiparty presidential election was held in June and July.

Violence along the Sudan border escalated in 2006, as Sudanese janjaweed militias and Chadian rebels attacked civilians, and Darfur rebels preyed on refugee camps. On Jan. 15, 2010, Chad and Sudan signed an accord aimed at normalizing relations and suppressing cross-border activities by rebel groups. Escalating violence in Sudan, 2023-24, brought over 637,000 new refugees into Chad by Sept. 2024.

After Islamist groups took over northern Mali and imposed a repressive regime in late 2012, Chad contributed roughly 2,000 soldiers to aid French, Malian, and other African forces in a military intervention. On Apr. 15, 2013, Chad announced it would begin pulling its troops out of Mali. Beginning in 2015, Chad periodically sent troops into Nigeria to fight Boko Haram Islamist extremists; extremist fighters and suicide bombers staged attacks in Chad.

Pres. Idriss Déby, who won reelection for a sixth term, Apr. 11, 2021, died 9 days later from injuries suffered while he was with government troops fighting rebels in northern Chad. His son, Mahamat Idriss Déby, succeeded him and was declared the winner of a delayed May 6, 2024, presidential election; the main opposition candidate disputed the result.

Chile

Republic of Chile

People: Population: 18,664,652 (67). **Age distrib.:** <15: 19.2%; 65+: 13.6%. **Growth:** 0.6%. **Migrants:** 8.6%. **Pop. density:** 65.0 per sq mi, 25.1 per sq km. **Urban:** 88.1%. **Ethnic groups:** white and non-Indigenous 88.9%, Mapuche 9.1%. **Languages:** Spanish (official), English, Indigenous. **Religions:** Christian 86.8% (Catholic 61.0%, independent 22.0%), agnostic 9.4%, atheist 2.6%.

Geography: Total area: 291,933 sq mi, 756,102 sq km (37); **Land area:** 287,187 sq mi, 743,812 sq km. **Location:** W coast of southern S America. Peru on N, Bolivia on NE, Argentina on E. **Topography:** Andes Mts., with some of world's highest peaks, on E border; on W is 2,650-mi Pacific coast. Width varies 100-250 mi. Atacama Desert in N. **Arable land:** 1.7%. **Capital:** Santiago, 6,950,952; Valparaíso (legislative seat), 1,016,585. **Cities:** Concepción, 920,916.

Government: Type: Presidential republic. **Head of state and govt.:** Pres. Gabriel Boric; b. 1986; in office: Mar. 11, 2022. **Local divisions:** 16 regions. **Defense budget:** $4.4 bil. **Active troops:** 68,500.

Economy: Industries: copper, lithium, other minerals, foodstuffs, fish proc., iron and steel, wood and wood prods., transp. equip., cement. **Chief agric.:** grapes, milk, apples, wheat, potatoes, chicken. **Natural resources:** copper, timber, iron ore, nitrates, prec. metals, molybdenum, hydropower. **Water:** 47,353 cu m per capita. **Crude oil reserves:** 150 mil bbls. **Electricity prod.:** 90.9 bil kWh. **Labor force:** agric. 6.3%, industry 22.8%, services 70.9%. **Unemployment:** 9.0%.

Finance: Monetary unit: Peso (CLP) (907.00 = $1 U.S.). **GDP:** $653.4 bil; **per capita GDP:** $33,285; **GDP growth:** 0.2%. **Imports:** $99.8 bil; China 26%, U.S. 22%, Brazil 10%, Argentina 5%. **Exports:** $104.3 bil; China 39%, U.S. 14%, Japan 8%, South Korea 6%, Brazil 5%. **Tourism:** $2.4 bil. **Budget** (2020): $73.2 bil. **Inflation:** 7.6%.

Transport: Railways: 4,525 mi. **Motor vehicles:** 316.4 per 1,000 pop. **Airports:** 374.

Communications: Mobile: 135.9 per 100 pop. **Broadband:** 109 per 100 pop. **Internet** (2023): 94.1%.

Health: Expend. (2022): 9.0%. **Life expect.:** 77.3 male; 83.3 female. **Births:** 12.4 per 1,000 pop. **Deaths:** 6.6 per 1,000 pop. **Infant mortality:** 6.3 per 1,000 live births. **Undernourished:** <2.5%. **HIV:** 0.7%. **COVID-19:** 62,734 deaths; rates per 100,000: 28,255 cases, 328 deaths. 93% vaccinated.

Education: Compulsory: ages 6-17. **Literacy:** 97.2%.

Website: www.gob.cl

Northern Chile was under Inca rule before the Spanish conquest, 1536-40. The southern Araucanian Indians resisted until the late 19th cent. Independence was gained 1810-18 under José de San Martin and Bernardo O'Higgins; the latter, as supreme director 1817-23, sought social and economic reforms until deposed. Chile defeated Peru and Bolivia in 1836-39 and 1879-84, gaining mineral-rich northern land. Chile is the world's largest producer of copper, responsible for about one-fourth of the world total; copper exports are a mainstay of the economy.

In 1970, Salvador Allende Gossens, a Marxist, became president. His government improved conditions for the poor, but property seizures by left-wing extremists, poorly planned socialist economic programs, and a destabilization campaign backed by the U.S. led to political and financial chaos. A U.S.-backed military junta seized power Sept. 11, 1973; Allende apparently killed himself. The junta, headed by Gen. Augusto Pinochet Ugarte, implemented plans to privatize the economy and "exterminate Marxism." Repression continued into the 1980s.

In Dec. 1989 voters elected a civilian president. In Mar. 1994, a Chilean human rights group estimated that more than 3,100 people were killed or "disappeared" during Pinochet's rule.

Ricardo Lagos Escobar, Chile's first Socialist president since the 1973 coup, took office Mar. 11, 2000. Michelle Bachelet Jeria, also a Socialist, won a runoff election Jan. 2006 and took office in Mar. as Chile's first woman president.

Billionaire businessman Sebastián Piñera Echenique, a conservative, won a presidential runoff election Jan. 2010. An earthquake and tsunami, Feb. 27, 2010, killed at least 521 people and caused up to $30 bil in property damage. Low wages sparked protests against the Piñera government. Bachelet returned to the presidency after winning a runoff election Dec. 15, 2013. Chile legalized civil unions between same-sex couples, Oct. 22, 2015, and abortion in very limited circumstances, Aug. 2, 2017.

With the Socialists' popularity hurt by a sluggish economy, Piñera returned as president after winning a Dec. 17, 2017, runoff. Pope Francis, Apr. 11, 2018, apologized for "grave errors" in the handling by Catholic Church officials in Chile of numerous allegations of child sex abuse by clergy. Months of large-scale demonstrations, beginning Oct. 2019, protested economic inequality. A harsh police response resulted in more than 30 deaths and thousands of injuries. Progressive Gabriel Boric defeated a rightist candidate in a Dec. 19, 2021, runoff to become Chile's youngest elected president.

In an Oct. 25, 2020, plebiscite, Chileans voted to rewrite the country's Pinochetera constitution. However, a new progressive constitution was voted down in a Sept. 4, 2022, plebiscite, and a new more conservative constitution was voted down Dec. 17, 2023. Severe wildfires in central Chile, Feb. 2024, killed more than 130.

Tierra del Fuego is the largest (18,800 sq mi) island in the archipelago of the same name at the southern tip of S America. It was visited 1520 by Magellan and named Land of Fire because of its many Indian bonfires. Part of the island is in Chile, part in Argentina. Punta Arenas, on a mainland peninsula, is the world's southernmost city; Puerto Williams is the southernmost settlement.

China

People's Republic of China

(Statistical data do not include Hong Kong or Macau.)

People: Population: 1,416,043,270 (1). **Age distrib.:** <15: 16.3%; 65+: 14.4%. **Growth:** 0.2%. **Migrants:** 0.1%. **Pop. density:** 393.2 per sq mi, 151.8 per sq km. **Urban:** 65.5%. **Ethnic groups:** Han Chinese 91.1%, ethnic minorities (incl. Zhang, Hui, Manchu, Uighur, Miao, Yi, Tujia, Tibetan, Mongol, Dong, Buyei, Yao, Bai, Korean, other nationalities) 8.9%. **Languages:** Standard Chinese or Mandarin (official; Putonghua, based on Beijing dialect), Yue (Cantonese), Wu (Shanghainese), Minbei (Fuzhou), Minnan (Hokkien-Taiwanese), Xiang, Gan, Hakka dialects. **Religions:** agnostic 31.5%, Chinese folk-religionist 29.2%, Buddhist 15.8% (Mahayanist), Christian 9.0%, atheist 6.6%, ethnic religionist 5.1%, Muslim 2.0% (Sunni).

Geography: Total area: 3,705,407 sq mi, 9,596,960 sq km (4); **Land area:** 3,600,947 sq mi, 9,326,410 sq km. **Location:** Occupies most of the habitable mainland of E Asia. Mongolia on N; Russia on NE and NW; Kazakhstan, Kyrgyzstan, Tajikistan, Afghanistan, Pakistan on W; India, Nepal, Bhutan, Myanmar, Laos, Vietnam on S; North Korea on NE. **Topography:** Two-thirds of territory is mountainous or desert. The Da Xing'an Ling Mts. in N separate Manchuria and Mongolia. Other ranges incl. the Tien Shan in Xinjiang and the Himalayan and Kunlun Mts. in the SW and in Tibet. Three great river systems—the Chang (Yangtze), Huang (Yellow), and Xi—cross the country's eastern half. **Arable land:** 11.5%. **Capital:** Beijing, 22,189,082. **Cities:** Shanghai, 29,867,918; Chongqing, 17,773,923; Guangzhou, Guangdong, 14,590,096; Tianjin, 14,470,873; Shenzhen, 13,311,855; Nanjing, Jiangsu, 9,947,548; Chengdu, 9,828,110; Xi'an, Shaanxi, 9,013,837.

Government: Type: Communist party-led state. **Head of state:** Pres. Xi Jinping; b. 1953; in office: Mar. 14, 2013 (gen. sec. of Communist Party since Nov. 15, 2012). **Head of govt.:** Prem. Li Qiang; b. 1959; in office: Mar. 11, 2023. **Local divisions:** 22 provinces (not incl. Taiwan), 5 autonomous regions, 4 municipalities, special admin. regions of Hong Kong (as of July 1, 1997) and Macau (as of Dec. 20, 1999). **Defense budget:** $219.5 bil. **Active troops:** 2,035,000.

Economy: Industries: mining and ore proc., iron, steel, aluminum, other metals, coal; machine building; armaments; textiles and apparel; petroleum; cement; chemicals; fertilizer; consumer prods.; food proc.; transp. equip.; telecom equip.; comm. space launch vehicles, satellites. **Chief agric.:** maize, rice, vegetables, wheat, sugarcane, potatoes. **Natural resources:** coal, iron ore, helium, petroleum, nat. gas, arsenic, bismuth, cobalt, cadmium, ferrosilicon, aluminum, lead, zinc, rare earth elements, uranium. **Water:** 1,948 cu m per capita. **Crude oil reserves:** 26 bil bbls. **Electricity prod.:** 8.9 tril kWh. **Labor force:** agric. 22.6%, industry 32.2%, services 45.3%. **Unemployment:** 4.7%.

Finance: Monetary unit: Yuan Renminbi (CNY) (7.13 = $1 U.S.). **GDP:** $34.6 tril; **per capita GDP:** $24,558; **GDP growth:** 5.2%. **Imports:** $3.1 tril; U.S. 7%, South Korea 7%, Japan 6%, Australia 6%, Taiwan 6%. **Exports:** $3.5 tril; U.S. 15%, Hong Kong 7%, Japan 5%. **Tourism:** $24.8 bil. **Budget:** $4.9 tril. **Inflation:** 0.2%.

Transport: Railways: 93,206 mi. **Motor vehicles:** 224.5 per 1,000 pop. **Airports:** 531.

Communications: Mobile: 127.1 per 100 pop. **Broadband:** 114 per 100 pop. **Internet** (2023): 77.5%.

Health: Expend.: 5.4%. **Life expect.:** 76.0 male; 81.7 female. **Births:** 10.2 per 1,000 pop. **Deaths:** 7.7 per 1,000 pop. **Infant mortality:** 6.2 per 1,000 live births. **Undernourished:** <2.5%. **HIV:** NA. **COVID-19:** 122,309 deaths; rates per 100,000: 6,754 cases, 8 deaths. 87% vaccinated.

Education: Compulsory: ages 6-14. **Literacy:** 96.7%.

Website: www.gov.cn

Remains of various humanlike creatures who lived as early as several hundred thousand years ago have been found in many parts of China. Neolithic agricultural settlements dotted the Huang (Yellow) R. basin from about 5000 BCE. Their language, religion, and art were the sources of later Chinese civilization.

Bronze metallurgy reached a peak and Chinese pictographic writing, similar to today's, was in use in the more developed culture of the Shang Dynasty (c. 1766 BCE-c. 1045 BCE), which ruled much of North China.

A succession of dynasties and interdynastic warring kingdoms ruled China for the next 3,000 years. They expanded Chinese political and cultural domination to the south and west, and developed a technologically and culturally advanced society that was unaffected by foreign rule (Mongols in the Yuan Dynasty, 1279-1368, and Manchus in the Qing Dynasty, 1644-1912).

Rebellions in the 19th cent. left tens of millions dead. Russia, Japan, Britain, and other powers exercised political and economic control in large parts of the country. China became a republic in 1912, when the Qing emperor Puyi abdicated following the Wuchang Uprising inspired by Dr. Sun Yat-sen, founder of the Kuomintang (Nationalist) party. By 1928, the Kuomintang, led by Chiang Kaishek, succeeded in nominal reunification of China. About the same time, a bloody purge of Communists from the ranks of the Kuomintang fomented hostilities.

For over 50 years, 1894-1945, China was involved in conflicts with Japan. In 1895, China ceded Korea, Taiwan, and other areas. On Sept. 18, 1931, Japan seized the Northeastern Provinces (Manchuria) and set up a puppet state called Manchukuo. Taking advantage of Chinese dissension, Japan invaded China proper July 7, 1937. On Nov. 20 the retreating Nationalist government moved its capital to Chongqing (Chungking) from Nanjing (Nanking), which Japanese troops then ravaged Dec. 13.

From 1939 the Sino-Japanese War (1937-45) became part of the broader world conflict. After its defeat in World War II, Japan relinquished China. Within China, conflicts involving the Kuomintang, Communists, and other factions resumed. China came under the domination of Communist armies, 1949-50. The Kuomintang government fled to Taiwan, Dec. 8, 1949.

The People's Republic of China was proclaimed in Beijing (Peking) Oct. 1, 1949, under Mao Zedong. China and the USSR signed a 30-year treaty of "friendship, alliance, and mutual assistance," Feb. 15, 1950. The U.S. refused to recognize the new regime. On Nov. 26, 1950, the People's Republic sent armies into Korea against U.S. troops and forced a stalemate in the Korean War.

Frequent drastic changes in policy and violent factionalism 1949-52 interfered with economic development. In 1957, Mao admitted an estimated 800,000 people had been executed 1949-54; opponents claimed much higher figures. The Great Leap Forward, 1958-60, tried to accelerate economic development through intensive labor on huge new rural communes and emphasis on ideological purity. Many resisted, and the program was largely abandoned.

By the 1960s, relations with the USSR deteriorated, and the USSR canceled aid accords. The Great Proletarian Cultural Revolution, 1965, an attempt to instruct a new generation in revolutionary principles, resulted in massive purges. Millions of urban teenagers were relocated to rural areas. By 1968 the movement had run its course; many purged officials returned to office in subsequent years, and several ideological reforms were gradually weakened.

On Oct. 25, 1971, the UN General Assembly ousted the Taiwan government from the UN and seated the People's Republic. U.S. Pres. Richard Nixon visited China Feb. 21-28, 1972. China and the U.S. opened liaison offices in each other's capitals, May-June 1973. The U.S., Dec. 15, 1978, formally recognized the People's Republic of China as the sole legal government of China; diplomatic relations were established, Jan. 1, 1979.

Mao died Sept. 9, 1976. By 1978, Vice Prem. Deng Xiaoping had consolidated power, succeeding Mao as "paramount leader" of China. The new ruling group modified Maoist policies in education, culture, and industry, and sought better ties with non-Communist countries. By the mid-1980s, China had enacted farreaching economic reforms, including market-oriented incentives, although close government-industry coordination continued.

Some 100,000 students and workers marched in Beijing to demand political reforms, May 4, 1989. As the unrest spread, martial law was imposed, May 20. Troops entered Beijing, June 3-4, and crushed the pro-democracy protests, as tanks and armored personnel carriers rolled through Tiananmen Square. It is estimated that hundreds died and thousands were injured, and hundreds of students and workers were arrested.

Deng Xiaoping died Feb. 19, 1997. Hong Kong reverted to Chinese sovereignty July 1, 1997. Portugal returned Macau to China Dec. 20, 1999.

China, Oct. 15-16, 2003, became the third nation (after the U.S. and USSR) to send a person into space. In Dec. 2013, China became the third nation to reach the moon with a spacecraft that made a soft landing. In 2021, China landed a rover on Mars and sent its first astronauts to a space station in Earth orbit. In June 2024, China's *Chang'e 6* mission became the first to return soil samples from the far side of the moon.

China's industries, exports, and energy demand have increased rapidly since the 1980s. China became the world's largest producer and consumer of coal. In part to diversify energy production, China completed construction in 2006 of the world's largest hydroelectric dam, the Three Gorges Dam on the Yangtze R. China announced,

Sept. 3, 2016, that it had ratified the 195-nation agreement to limit climate change negotiated in Paris in Dec. 2015. However, in subsequent years, China remained the largest source of greenhouse gas emissions.

An earthquake in Sichuan prov. May 12, 2008, left 69,226 dead and 17,923 missing. The Nobel Peace Prize was awarded Oct. 8, 2010, to Liu Xiaobo, an incarcerated human rights activist; Liu died of cancer in government custody, July 13, 2017. Xi Jinping was chosen Communist Party general secretary, Nov. 15, 2012. In Mar. 2013, the National People's Congress (NPC) elected Xi as president of China and Li Keqiang as premier. They were reelected Mar. 2018. The NPC elected Xi to a third term, Mar. 10, 2023; Xi ally Li Qiang was elected premier by the NPC, Mar. 11.

Western experts Jan.-Feb. 2010 blamed hackers in China for cyberattacks on Google and other firms. Hackers in China were suspected in two attacks on U.S. government computer systems in 2014. The U.S., July 19, 2021, accused China of orchestrating cyberattacks on companies and organizations in the U.S. and around the world.

After double-digit gains for many years since the 1980s, China's GDP growth slowed beginning in 2012. However, by 2014, China's GDP (measured by purchasing power parity) was the largest in the world. Since 2010, China has been the world's largest exporter. Since 2013, partly under the $1-tril Belt and Road Initiative, China has been financing and building infrastructure projects in many developing countries worldwide.

The U.S. accused China in 2017 of unfair trade practices. In 2018-19, the U.S. implemented tariffs on hundreds of billions of dollars' worth of Chinese products; China retaliated with tariffs on U.S. goods. The U.S. trade in goods deficit with China was $279 bil in 2023, down from $418 bil in 2018. U.S. tariffs on Chinese electric vehicles and other technology products were increased sharply in 2024.

To stem population growth, a requirement that families have a maximum of one child was implemented in 1980. Subsequently, amid concerns about worker shortages and an aging population, the limit was changed to two children by 2016 and three children in 2021.

China has occupied the Paracel Isls., in the South China Sea, since 1974. Taiwan and Vietnam also claim the resource-rich islands. The Spratly Isls. are similarly in dispute with Taiwan, Vietnam, Malaysia, and the Philippines. The international Permanent Court of Arbitration in The Hague, July 12, 2016, rejected China's claim to most of the South China Sea as territorial waters and ruled that China's building of artificial islands—in some cases militarized—in disputed areas violated international law. China had the world's largest navy by 2017.

A new coronavirus, causing the disease COVID-19, emerged in late 2019 in Wuhan; its severity may have been initially concealed, especially by local officials. The origin of the virus was uncertain. By Feb. 2020, the virus was spreading worldwide. As of Sept. 2024, the COVID-19 pandemic had caused about 776 mil confirmed cases globally (over 99 mil in China) and more than 7 mil confirmed deaths (about 122,000 in China). Strict lockdown measures, under the Chinese government's "zero COVID" policy, hurt the economy. Large protests against lockdown restrictions took place in many cities, Nov. 2022. By Dec., most restrictions had been eased or eliminated. Sharp spikes in cases and deaths occurred Dec. 2022-Jan. 2023.

Amid heightened Chinese-U.S. tensions, an apparent Chinese spy balloon that had flown across the U.S. was shot down off the U.S. east coast, Feb. 4, 2023.

Autonomous Regions

Guangxi Zhuang is in SE China, bounded on the N by Guizhou and Hunan provinces, E and S by Guangdong, on the SW by Vietnam, and on the W by Yunnan. It produces rice and forest products. Pop. (2020 census) 50,126,804. Capital: Nanning; pop. (2024 est.) 4,291,463.

Inner Mongolia was organized by the People's Republic in 1947. Its boundaries were later expanded, to an area of 454,600 sq mi, allegedly to dilute the minority Mongol population. Han Chinese greatly outnumber Mongols. China began, Sept. 1, 2020, replacing Mongolian- with Mandarin-language instruction in schools. Pop. (2020 census) 24,049,155. Capital: Hohhot; pop. (2024 est.) 2,443,686.

Ningxia Hui, in N central China, is about 60,000 sq mi. Pop. (2020) 7,202,654. Capital: Yinchuan; pop. (2024 est.) 1,757,699. The climate is mostly semiarid, with desert areas in the N. The Huang (Yellow) R. furnishes water for irrigation. The majority of the population is Han. The Hui, most of whom follow Islam, constitute about one-third of the population; a crackdown on Muslim practices began in the late 2010s.

Xinjiang Uighur, in Central Asia, is 635,900 sq mi, pop. (2020 census) 25,852,345 (75% Uighurs, a Turkic Muslim group, with a heavy Han Chinese increase in recent years). Capital: Urumqi; pop. (2024 est.) 5,005,964. It is China's richest region in strategic minerals. In recent decades, China has moved to suppress Uighur cultural and religious practices and to crack down on Uighur separatists. Legislation effective Apr. 1, 2017, placed new restrictions on women wearing face veils in public. Chinese authorities reportedly destroyed mosques, removed children from Uighur families, forced birth control measures on Uighur women, and carried out intensive electronic surveillance of the Uighur population. The number of people sentenced to prison terms began increasing sharply in 2017. In addition, by 2019, an estimated 1-1.5 mil Uighurs had been interned in "re-education" or labor camps; large-scale use of forced labor was reported. China alleged that, by the end of 2019, most camps had been closed, but dissidents and others reported that large numbers of Uighurs subsequently remained in detention. U.S. anti-forced-labor legislation in 2022 essentially barred imports of products with supply chains linked to Xinjiang.

Tibet, 471,700 sq mi, is a thinly populated region of high plateaus and massive mountains, the Himalayas on the S, the Kunluns on the N. Capital: Lhasa. Avg. elevation is 15,000 ft. Jiachan, 15,870 ft, is believed to be the highest inhabited town on Earth. Pop. (2020 census) 3,648,100 (of whom about 500,000 are Chinese). Millions of Tibetans live in vast adjacent areas that have long been incorporated into China.

China ruled all of Tibet from the 18th cent. Independence came in 1911, but China reasserted control in 1951, and a Communist government was installed in 1953. Serfdom was abolished, but all land remained collectivized. A Tibetan uprising within China in 1956 spread to Lhasa in 1959. The rebellion was crushed by Chinese troops, and Buddhism was almost totally suppressed. The Dalai Lama and 100,000 Tibetans fled to India. Efforts by Chinese authorities to halt peaceful demonstrations by Tibetan monks led to anti-Chinese riots in Lhasa, Mar. 14, 2008—crushed by Chinese government troops. Protests (including about 160 self-immolations since 2009), as well as government repression and coerced assimilation, continued in subsequent years.

Hong Kong

Hong Kong (Xianggang), located at the mouth of the Zhu Jiang (Pearl R.) in SE China, 90 mi S of Guangzhou, was a British dependency from 1842 until July 1, 1997, when it became a Special Administrative Region of China. Its nucleus is Hong Kong Isl., 31 sq mi, occupied by the British in 1841 and formally ceded to them in 1842, on which is located the seat of government. Opposite is Kowloon Peninsula, 3 sq mi, and Stonecutters Isl., added to the territory in 1860. An additional 355 sq mi known as the New Territories, a mainland area and islands, were leased from China, 1898, for 99 years. Area 428 sq mi (total); 414 sq mi (land); pop. (2024 est.) 7,297,821. **Website:** www.gov.hk

Hong Kong is a major trade and banking center. Per capita GDP, over $70,000 in 2023, is among the highest in the world. Principal industries are textiles and apparel, tourism ($21.1 bil in international receipts in 2023), banking, shipping, and electronics. A majority of tourists are from mainland China.

Hong Kong harbor was long an important British naval station and one of the world's great transshipment ports. The colony often provided refuge for exiles from mainland China. It was occupied by Japan during WWII.

From 1949 to 1962, Hong Kong absorbed more than 1 mil refugees fleeing Communist China. Starting in the 1950s, cheap labor led to a boom in light manufacturing, while liberal tax policies attracted foreign investment. Hong Kong became one of the wealthiest, most productive areas in the Far East. In recent years, manufacturing has been shifting from Hong Kong to mainland China.

With the end of the 99-year lease on the New Territories drawing near, Britain and China signed an agreement, Dec. 19, 1984, under which all of Hong Kong was to be returned to China in 1997; under this agreement Hong Kong was to be allowed to keep its capitalist system for 50 years. Following the transfer of government, Hong Kong retained its currency, the Hong Kong dollar; in recent years, a growing portion of financial transactions use the Chinese renminbi. Cantonese, English, and Mandarin are official languages.

Pro-Beijing candidate Carrie Lam was chosen chief executive by an election committee of about 1,200 members, Mar. 26, 2017. China's foreign ministry stated, June 30, 2017, that the 1984 agreement with Britain no longer had binding force.

Large-scale protests (up to 2 mil people) in 2019 opposed proposed legislation authorizing Hong Kong to extradite suspects to mainland China. Police often used force against sometimes-violent demonstrations. Lam, Sept. 4, withdrew the extradition bill. Protests continued, demanding greater democracy and an investigation of police tactics. The Chinese government enacted a broad Hong Kong security law, in effect as of June 30, 2020, that was used to crack down on speech, peaceful protests, media outlets, and political activists. Mar. 2021 electoral-law changes reduced the number of directly elected seats on Hong Kong's Legislative Council and instituted vetting of candidates for compliance with the 2020 security law. In Dec. 19, 2021, Legislative Council elections marked by low turnout, pro-Beijing candidates won virtually all seats at stake. The election committee, May 8, 2022, chose former security chief John Lee as Hong Kong's new chief executive. Mar. 2024 security legislation, passed by the Legislative Council, further strengthened authorities' powers to crack down on dissent.

Macau

Macau, area of 11 sq mi, is a peninsula and two small islands at the mouth of the Xi (Pearl) R. in China. It was established as a Portuguese trading colony in 1557. In 1849, Portugal claimed sovereignty over the territory; this claim was accepted by China in an 1887 treaty. Portugal granted broad autonomy in 1976. Under a 1987 agreement, Macau reverted to China Dec. 20, 1999. The

Chinese government guaranteed Macau it would not interfere in its way of life for a period of 50 years. However, pro-democracy candidates were barred from running in Sept. 12, 2021, legislative elections. Tourism, including casino gambling, is a mainstay of the economy ($32.6 bil in international receipts in 2023); most tourists are from mainland China. Per capita GDP was $113,183 in 2023, nearly back to its level in 2019 after COVID-19 severely hurt tourism, but rebounded to over $113,000 in 2023. Pop. (2024 est.) 644,426. **Website:** www.gov.mo

Colombia

Republic of Colombia

People: Population: 49,588,357 (30). **Age distrib.:** <15: 22.3%; 65+: 11.2%. **Growth:** 0.5%. **Migrants:** 3.7%. **Pop. density:** 123.6 per sq mi, 47.7 per sq km. **Urban:** 82.7%. **Ethnic groups:** mestizo and white 87.6%, Afro-Colombian (incl. mulatto, Raizal, Palenquero) 6.8%, Indigenous 4.3%. **Languages:** Spanish (official), 65 Indigenous langs. **Religions:** Christian 94.9% (Catholic 83.5%), agnostic 3.0%.

Geography: Total area: 439,736 sq mi, 1,138,910 sq km (25); **Land area:** 401,044 sq mi, 1,038,700 sq km. **Location:** NW corner of S America. Panama on NW, Ecuador and Peru on S, Brazil and Venezuela on E. **Topography:** Three Andes ranges—Western, Central, and Eastern Cordilleras—run N-S. The eastern range consists mostly of high tablelands. The Magdalena R. rises in the Andes, flows N to Caribbean through a rich alluvial plain. Sparsely settled plains in E are drained by Orinoco and Amazon systems. **Arable land:** 2.2%. **Capital:** Bogotá, 11,658,211. **Cities:** Medellín, 4,137,386; Cali, 2,890,433; Barranquilla, 2,373,302.

Government: Type: Presidential republic. **Head of state and govt.:** Pres. Gustavo Petro; b. 1960; in office: Aug. 7, 2022. **Local divisions:** 32 departments, 1 capital district. **Defense budget:** $5.4 bil. **Active troops:** 257,450.

Economy: Industries: textiles, food proc., oil, clothing and footwear, beverages, chemicals, cement. **Chief agric.:** sugarcane, oil palm fruit, milk, rice, potatoes, bananas. **Natural resources:** petroleum, nat. gas, coal, iron ore, nickel, gold, copper, emeralds, hydropower. **Water:** 45,811 cu m per capita. **Crude oil reserves:** 2 bil bbls. **Electricity prod.:** 85.2 bil kWh. **Labor force:** agric. 14.6%, industry 20.3%, services 65.0%. **Unemployment:** 9.6%.

Finance: Monetary unit: Peso (COP) (4,045.65 = $1 U.S.). **GDP:** $1.1 tril; **per capita GDP:** $21,548; **GDP growth:** 0.6%. **Imports:** $76.0 bil; U.S. 26%, China 25%, Brazil 7%, Mexico 5%. **Exports:** $67.8 bil; U.S. 26%, Panama 10%, Netherlands 6%. **Tourism:** $7.6 bil. **Budget:** $103.1 bil. **Inflation:** 11.7%.

Transport: Railways: 1,330 mi. **Motor vehicles:** 114.1 per 1,000 pop. **Airports:** 662.

Communications: Mobile: 167.0 per 100 pop. **Broadband:** 85.2 per 100 pop. **Internet:** 72.8%.

Health: Expend.: 9.0%. **Life expect.:** 71.3 male; 78.7 female. **Births:** 14.9 per 1,000 pop. **Deaths:** 8.0 per 1,000 pop. **Infant mortality:** 11.7 per 1,000 live births. **Undernourished:** 4.2%. **HIV:** 0.6%. **COVID-19:** 142,727 deaths; rates per 100,000: 12,563 cases, 281 deaths. 73% vaccinated.

Education: Compulsory: ages 5-16. **Literacy:** 95.6%.

Website: id.presidencia.gov.co

Spain subdued the local Indian kingdoms (Funza, Tunja) by the 1530s and ruled Colombia and neighboring areas as New Granada for 300 years. Independence was won by 1819. Venezuela and Ecuador broke away in 1829-30, and Panama withdrew in 1903.

In the 20th and early 21st cents., Colombia was plagued by rural and urban violence. "La Violencia" of 1948-58 claimed 200,000 lives. Guerrilla warfare and terrorist attacks by leftist rebels, including the Revolutionary Armed Forces of Colombia (FARC), began in the 1960s. Violence by right-wing paramilitary groups became widespread by the 1980s. Government activity against drug cartels sparked retaliation killings of politicians and judges. The FARC engaged in drug trafficking and kidnappings for ransom to finance its operations.

Álvaro Uribe Vélez, a hardliner, won a presidential election, May 2002, and launched a new government offensive against the FARC. Uribe won reelection, May 2006. Key political figures were arrested in 2007 on charges of colluding with paramilitary death squads. Former Defense Min. Juan Manuel Santos Calderón won presidential elections, June 2010 and June 2014. A peace accord with the FARC, providing for FARC disarmament and reintegration into civilian life, went into effect Dec. 1, 2016. On Oct. 7, 2016, Santos won the Nobel Peace Prize. On June 27, 2017, about 7,000 FARC rebels finished surrendering weapons, but violence by criminal gangs, former FARC members, and other rebels continued. New ceasefires by some armed groups were announced Sept. 28, 2022, and June 9, 2023. Millions of Colombians were internally displaced by decades of conflict and violence—almost 7 mil as of July 31, 2024.

Iván Duque, a conservative, won a June 17, 2018, presidential runoff election. A series of national strikes, Nov.-Dec. 2019, protested government economic policies, failure to fully implement the FARC accord, and killings of Indigenous and other rights activists. Weeks of demonstrations began Apr. 2021, protesting poverty, inequality, and proposed tax hikes. Promising economic changes, leftist Gustavo Petro won the June 19, 2022, presidential runoff election. Nicolás Petro, the president's son, was charged, July 29, 2023, with money laundering related to drug trafficking.

A ruling by Colombia's Constitutional Court, Feb. 21, 2022, legalized most abortions.

Beginning in 2015, large numbers of Venezuelans fleeing hardship and repression entered Colombia. By July 31, 2024, more than 2.8 mil Venezuelan refugees were in Colombia, which granted many of them temporary legal status.

Comoros

Union of the Comoros

People: Population: 900,141 (160). **Age distrib.:** <15: 32.6%; 65+: 4.6%. **Growth:** 1.3%. **Migrants:** 1.4%. **Pop. density:** 1,043.1 per sq mi, 402.7 per sq km. **Urban:** 30.4%. **Ethnic groups:** Antalote, Cafre, Makoa, Oimatsaha, Sakalava. **Languages:** Arabic, French, Shikomoro (Comorian) (similar to Swahili) (all official). **Religions:** Muslim 98.0% (Sunni).

Geography: Total area: 863 sq mi, 2,235 sq km (170); **Land area:** 863 sq mi, 2,235 sq km. **Location:** 3 islands—Grande Comore (Njazidja), Anjouan (Nzwani), and Moheli (Mwali)—in the Mozambique Channel between NW Madagascar and SE Africa. Nearest neighbor is Mozambique on W. **Topography:** Of volcanic origin; an active volcano on Grande Comore. **Arable land:** 34.9%. **Capital:** Moroni, 62,351.

Government: Type: Federal presidential republic. **Head of state and govt.:** Pres. Azali Assoumani; b. 1959; in office: May 26, 2016. **Local divisions:** 3 islands. **Defense budget/active troops:** NA.

Economy: Industries: fishing, tourism, perfume distillation. **Chief agric.:** coconuts, bananas, cassava, yams, maize, taro. **Natural resources:** fish. **Water:** 1,461 cu m per capita. **Electricity prod.:** 135.2 mil kWh. **Labor force:** agric. 34.6%, industry 15.0%, services 50.4%. **Unemployment:** 5.8%.

Finance: Monetary unit: Franc (KMF) (440.84 = $1 U.S.). **GDP:** $3.3 bil; **per capita GDP:** $3,855; **GDP growth:** 2.7%. **Imports** (2022): $479.9 mil; UAE 25%, China 19%, India 12%, France 8%, Tanzania 7%. **Exports** (2022): $165.3 mil; Turkey (Türkiye) 23%, India 19%, UAE 9%, U.S. 9%, Indonesia 8%. **Tourism** (2022): $84 mil. **Budget** (2018): $228 mil. **Inflation** (2016-17): 1%.

Transport: Airports: 3.

Communications: Mobile: 109.9 per 100 pop. **Broadband:** 81.8 per 100 pop. **Internet** (2019): 16.4%.

Health: Expend.: 6.3%. **Life expect.:** 65.5 male; 70.2 female. **Births:** 21.6 per 1,000 pop. **Deaths:** 6.4 per 1,000 pop. **Infant mortality:** 54.9 per 1,000 live births. **Undernourished:** 16.9%. **HIV:** <0.1%. **COVID-19:** 160 deaths; rates per 100,000: 1,047 cases, 18 deaths. 46% vaccinated.

Education: Compulsory: ages 6-11. **Literacy:** 61.7%.

Website: beit-salam.km

France acquired the islands from Muslim sultans, 1841-1909. The islands were granted internal autonomy in 1961. In a 1974 referendum, all islands favored independence except Mayotte. The Comorian government declared independence July 6, 1975, with Ahmed Abdallah as its president. In a 1976 referendum, Mayotte voted to remain French.

A leftist regime that seized power from Abdallah in 1975 was deposed in a pro-French 1978 coup in which he regained the presidency. In Nov. 1989, Pres. Abdallah was assassinated; soon after, a multiparty system was instituted.

Anjouan and Moheli seceded from the Comoros in 1997. Unrest on Grande Comore culminated in a military coup, Apr. 1999. A constitution adopted in a referendum Dec. 2001 that went into effect the following year reunited Anjouan and Moheli with Grande Comore, granting each a semi-autonomous status and its own president.

Irregularities marred the Apr. 2002 runoff election for national president, won by Azali Assoumani, who led the 1999 coup. Having left office in 2006, Assoumani was again elected president in an Apr. 10, 2016, runoff. After changing the constitution to permit him to run again, Assoumani won new terms in flawed elections, Mar. 24, 2019, and Jan. 14, 2024.

Congo, Democratic Republic of the (DRC)

Democratic Republic of the Congo

(Former Zaire, now commonly called the DRC, is also known as Congo-Kinshasa. The Republic of the Congo is also known as Congo [Brazzaville].)

People: Population: 115,403,027 (14). **Age distrib.:** <15: 45.7%; 65+: 2.5%. **Growth:** 3.1%. **Migrants:** 1.1%. **Pop. density:** 131.8 per sq mi, 50.9 per sq km. **Urban:** 48.1%. **Ethnic groups:** 200+ groups, majority Bantu; four largest groups (Mongo, Luba, Kongo [all Bantu], and Mangbetu-Azande [Hamitic]) 45%. **Languages:** French (official), Lingala (trade lang.), Kingwana (Kiswahili or Swahili dialect), Kikongo, Tshiluba. **Religions:** Christian 95.2% (Catholic 51.0%, independent 25.0%, Protestant 19.1%), ethnic religionist 2.3%.

Geography: Total area: 905,355 sq mi, 2,344,858 sq km (11); **Land area:** 875,312 sq mi, 2,267,048 sq km. **Location:** Central Africa. Congo (Brazzaville) on W; Central African Republic, South

Sudan on N; Uganda, Rwanda, Burundi, Tanzania on E; Zambia, Angola on S. **Topography:** Includes the bulk of the Congo R. basin. Central region is a low-lying plateau covered by rain forest. Mountainous terraces in the W, savannas in the S and SE, grasslands toward the N, and Ruwenzori Mts. on the E. A short strip of territory borders the Atlantic O. **Arable land:** 6.6%. **Capital:** Kinshasa, 17,032,322. **Cities:** Mbuji-Mayi, 3,022,855; Lubumbashi, 2,933,962; Kananga, 1,738,716.

Government: Type: Semi-presidential republic. **Head of state:** Pres. Felix Tshisekedi; b. 1963; in office: Jan. 24, 2019. **Head of govt.:** Prime Min. Judith Suminwa Tuluka; b. 1967; in office: May 29, 2024. **Local divisions:** 26 provinces. **Defense budget:** $765 mil. **Active troops:** 134,250.

Economy: Industries: mining, mineral proc., consumer prods., metal prods., processed foods and beverages, timber, cement. **Chief agric.:** cassava, plantains, sugarcane, oil palm fruit, maize, rice. **Natural resources:** cobalt, copper, niobium, tantalum, petroleum, diamonds, gold, silver, zinc, manganese, tin, uranium, coal, hydropower, timber. **Water:** 13,379 cu m per capita. **Crude oil reserves:** 180 mil bbls. **Electricity prod.:** 11.0 bil kWh. **Labor force:** agric. 56.1%, industry 10.2%, services 33.7%. **Unemployment:** 4.5%.

Finance: Monetary unit: Franc (CDF) (2,840.58 = $1 U.S.). **GDP:** $170.9 bil; **per capita GDP:** $1,671; **GDP growth:** 8.6%. **Imports** (2021): $22.2 bil; China 33%, Zambia 10%, South Africa 10%, UAE 5%. **Exports** (2021): $22.4 bil; China 55%, Singapore 5%, UAE 5%. **Tourism** (2021): $108 mil. **Budget:** $6.4 bil. **Inflation** (2016-17): 41.5%.

Transport: Railways: 2,490 mi. **Motor vehicles:** 25.3 per 1,000 pop. **Airports:** 272.

Communications: Mobile (2022): 48.7 per 100 pop. **Broadband** (2022): 25.3 per 100 pop. **Internet:** 27.2%.

Health: Expend.: 3.8%. **Life expect.:** 60.7 male; 64.6 female. **Births:** 39.2 per 1,000 pop. **Deaths:** 7.6 per 1,000 pop. **Infant mortality:** 57.4 per 1,000 live births. **Undernourished:** 37.0%. **HIV:** 0.7%. **COVID-19:** 1,474 deaths; rates per 100,000: 113 cases, 2 deaths. 16% vaccinated.

Education: Compulsory: ages 6-11. **Literacy:** 80.5%.

Website: www.presidence.cd

The earliest inhabitants of Congo may have been the Pygmies, followed by Bantus from the east and Nilotic people from the north. The large Bantu Bakongo kingdom ruled much of Congo and Angola when Portuguese explorers visited in the 15th cent.

Leopold II, king of the Belgians, formed an international group to exploit the Congo region in 1876. In 1877, British explorer Henry M. Stanley traveled the Congo R, and in 1879, in the service of Leopold II, he returned to help colonize the region. The Conference of Berlin, 1884-85, established the Congo Free State with Leopold as king and chief owner. The colony became known as the Belgian Congo in 1908 when Leopold sold it to the Belgian government. Millions of Congolese rubber plantation workers were exploited and died under brutal European rule between 1880 and 1920. (On June 30, 2020, Belgium's king expressed "deepest regrets for the wounds of the past.")

Belgian and Congolese leaders agreed Jan. 27, 1960, that Congo would become independent. In May 31 elections, Patrice Lumumba's party won a plurality in the National Assembly. The Republic of the Congo was proclaimed June 30. Europeans and others fled widespread violence. The UN Security Council, Aug. 9, called on Belgium to withdraw its troops and sent a UN contingent. Lumumba was dismissed as premier in Sept. and murdered Jan. 17, 1961. The last UN troops left the Congo June 30, 1964.

In late 1965, Gen. Joseph D. Mobutu was named president. He later changed his name to Mobutu Sese Seko and ruled as a dictator. The country became the Democratic Republic of the Congo (DRC, 1966) and the Republic of Zaire (1971). Under Mobutu, economic decline and government corruption plagued the country.

During 1994, Zaire was inundated with refugees from the massive ethnic bloodshed in Rwanda. Ethnic violence spread to eastern Zaire in 1996. In Oct., militant Hutus, who dominated in the refugee camps, fought rebels (mostly Tutsis) in Zaire, precipitating intervention by government troops. The rebels, led by Gen. Laurent Kabila, moved west across Zaire. On May 17, 1997, Kabila's troops entered Kinshasa, and Mobutu went into exile. The country again became the DRC.

Kabila, who ruled by decree, alienated UN officials, international aid donors, and former allies. Rebels assisted by Rwanda and Uganda threatened Kinshasa in Aug. 1998 but were turned back with help from Angola, Namibia, and Zimbabwe. Rebel groups agreed to a cease-fire, Aug. 31, 1999, but the truce was widely violated. Kabila was assassinated Jan. 16, 2001, and was succeeded by his son Joseph.

The estimated death toll from the civil war and related causes was 3.3 mil through Nov. 2002. By then, Rwanda and Uganda had agreed to pull out their remaining troops. A power-sharing accord signed Apr. 2, 2003, led to the installation of a new DRC government in July. Under a new constitution in effect as of Feb. 18, 2006, a UN peacekeeping force (MONUC), established in 1999, oversaw July 2006 elections. Kabila defeated former rebel leader Jean-Pierre Bemba in a presidential runoff election, Oct. 2006.

Tutsi rebel Gen. Laurent Nkunda, head of a militia in eastern DRC that launched an offensive in Aug. 2008, was arrested by Rwandan authorities Jan. 2009.

Kabila was reelected, Nov. 28, 2011. A June 2011 study estimated that more than 1,000 women were raped in the DRC every day. The Intl. Criminal Court (ICC) at The Hague convicted Congolese warlord Thomas Lubanga Dyilo Mar. 2012 of war crimes for conscripting child soldiers during the country's civil war. The ICC, May 23, 2014, sentenced rebel leader Germain Katanga to 12 years in prison in connection with a 2003 massacre of more than 200 villagers.

The MONUC peacekeeping mission was reconstituted and renamed MONUSCO as of July 1, 2010. Eleven African nations signed a peace plan Feb. 24, 2013, designed to end the violence in the DRC. Rebel leader Bosco Ntaganda surrendered in Rwanda Mar. 18, 2013, to face charges of war crimes and crimes against humanity; he was convicted by the ICC, July 8, 2019. A peace agreement with the M23 militia group was reached in Dec. 2013. About 8,000 rebels laid down their arms, but other fighters remained active. With Kabila legally required to leave office in Dec. 2016, protests occurred, 2016-17, over government delays in scheduling the next presidential election. After a Dec. 30, 2018, election—in which widespread voting irregularities were reported—Félix Tshisekedi was declared the winner. Tshisekedi won reelection in Dec. 20, 2023, voting; the opposition claimed irregularities. An apparent coup attempt was foiled, May 19, 2024. On May 29, 2024, Judith Suminwa became the DRC's first female prime minister.

In the 2020s, political and ethnic violence continued in eastern DRC, involving various armed rebel groups—including a resurgent M23 (reportedly backed by Rwanda) and an ISIS affiliate. Ethnic conflict in western DRC left thousands dead. MONUSCO had more than 12,000 uniformed personnel as of July 31, 2024. As of July 31, 2024, more than 6.4 mil Congolese were internally displaced.

A severe Ebola outbreak occurred in eastern DRC, 2018-20. The DRC was affected, in the 2020s, by the COVID-19 pandemic. An mpox outbreak concentrated in the DRC led the WHO to declare a global health emergency, Aug. 14, 2024.

Congo, Republic of the

Republic of the Congo

(Also known as Congo [Brazzaville]. The Democratic Republic of the Congo [formerly Zaire], now commonly called the DRC, is also known as Congo-Kinshasa.)

People: Population: 6,097,665 (112). **Age distrib.:** <15: 37.8%; 65+: 4.3%. **Growth:** 2.4%. **Migrants:** 7.0%. **Pop. density:** 46.2 per sq mi, 17.9 per sq km. **Urban:** 69.6%. **Ethnic groups:** Kongo (Bakongo) 40.5%, Teke 16.9%, Mbochi 13.1%, foreigner 8.2%, Sangha 5.6%, Mbere/Mbeti/Kele 4.4%, Punu 4.3%. **Languages:** French (official); French Lingala, Monokutuba (trade langs.); many local langs., dialects (Kikongo most widespread). **Religions:** Christian 84.1% (Catholic 59.0%, Protestant 12.7%, independent 12.4%), agnostic 8.8%, ethnic religionist 4.9%.

Geography: Total area: 132,047 sq mi, 342,000 sq km (63); **Land area:** 131,854 sq mi, 341,500 sq km. **Location:** W central Africa. Gabon and Cameroon on W, Central African Republic on N, Dem. Rep. of the Congo on E, Angola on SW. **Topography:** Thick forests across much of country. A coastal plain leads to the fertile Niari Valley. The Congo R. basin consists of flood plains in the lower portion and savanna in the upper. **Arable land:** 1.6%. **Capital:** Brazzaville, 2,724,566. **Cities:** Pointe-Noire, 1,379,368.

Government: Type: Presidential republic. **Head of state:** Pres. Denis Sassou-Nguesso; b. 1943; in office: Oct. 25, 1997. **Head of govt.:** Prime Min. Anatole Collinet Makosso; b. 1965; in office: July 22, 2021. **Local divisions:** 12 departments. **Defense budget:** $288 mil. **Active troops:** 10,000.

Economy: Industries: petroleum extraction, cement, lumber, brewing, sugar, palm oil, soap. **Chief agric.:** cassava, sugarcane, oil palm fruit, bananas, plantains, root vegetables. **Natural resources:** petroleum, timber, potash, lead, zinc, uranium, copper, phosphates, gold, magnesium, nat. gas, hydropower. **Water:** 142,568 cu m per capita. **Crude oil reserves:** 2.9 bil bbls. **Electricity prod.:** 4.0 bil kWh. **Labor force:** agric. 32.3%, industry 22.2%, services 45.6%. **Unemployment:** 20.1%.

Finance: Monetary unit: Central African CFA Franc (XAF) (587.79 = $1 U.S.). **GDP:** $42.3 bil; **per capita GDP:** $6,933; **GDP growth:** 1.9%. **Imports** (2021): $4.5 bil; China 26%, France 9%, UAE 6%, Belgium 6%, India 5%. **Exports** (2021): $7.8 bil; China 39%, India 20%, UAE 15%, Italy 5%. **Tourism** (2020): $4 mil. **Budget** (2018): $2.6 bil. **Inflation:** 4.3%.

Transport: Railways: 317 mi. **Motor vehicles:** 20.1 per 1,000 pop. **Airports:** 56.

Communications: Mobile: 94.9 per 100 pop. **Broadband:** 57.5 per 100 pop. **Internet:** 36.2%.

Health: Expend.: 3.9%. **Life expect.:** 71.5 male; 74.3 female. **Births:** 28.7 per 1,000 pop. **Deaths:** 4.8 per 1,000 pop. **Infant mortality:** 30.6 per 1,000 live births. **Undernourished:** 26.8%. **HIV:** 3.2%. **COVID-19:** 389 deaths; rates per 100,000: 457 cases, 7 deaths. 12% vaccinated.

Education: Compulsory: ages 6-15. **Literacy:** 80.6%.

Website: presidence.cg, www.ambacongo-us.org

The Loango kingdom flourished in the 15th cent., as did the Anzico kingdom of the Batekes; by the late 17th cent. they had weakened. By 1885, France controlled the region. The Republic of the Congo gained independence Aug. 15, 1960.

After a 1963 coup, the country adopted a Marxist-Leninist stance. However, France remained a dominant trade partner and source of technical assistance, and French-owned private enterprise retained a major economic role. In 1970, the country was renamed People's Republic of the Congo. Since the 1980s, oil has dominated the economy. In June 2018, the country joined OPEC.

In 1990, Marxism was renounced and opposition parties were legalized. In 1991 the country's name was changed back to Rep. of the Congo. A democratically elected government came into office in 1992. Factional fighting broke out in Brazzaville, June 1997. Troops loyal to former Marxist dictator Denis Sassou-Nguesso took control of the city Oct. 15, 1997; he claimed lopsided victories in 2002 and 2009 presidential elections. After 2015 constitutional changes allowed him to run again, Sassou-Nguesso was reelected Mar. 20, 2016, and Mar. 21, 2021—in the latter case, with almost 90% of the vote after some opposition groups boycotted the election and the main opposition candidate died of COVID-19 on election day.

Costa Rica

Republic of Costa Rica

People: Population: 5,265,575 (122). **Age distrib.:** <15: 18.8%; 65+: 11.1%. **Growth:** 0.7%. **Pop. density:** 267.1 per sq mi, 103.1 per sq km. **Urban:** 83.2%. **Ethnic groups:** white or mestizo 83.6%, mulatto 6.7%, Indigenous 2.4%. **Languages:** Spanish (official), English. **Religions:** Christian 94.6% (Catholic 76.3%, independent 10.0%, Protestant 8.3%), agnostic 3.9%.

Geography: Total area: 19,730 sq mi, 51,100 sq km (126); **Land area:** 19,714 sq mi, 51,060 sq km. **Location:** Central America. Nicaragua on N, Panama on S. **Topography:** Tropical lowlands by the Caribbean. The interior plateau, at an elevation of about 4,000 ft, is temperate. **Arable land:** 3.8%. **Capital:** San José, 1,482,460.

Government: Type: Presidential republic. **Head of state and govt.:** Pres. Rodrigo Chaves Robles; b. 1961; in office: May 8, 2022. **Local divisions:** 7 provinces. **Defense budget:** $493 mil (paramilitary budget). **Active troops:** No armed forces. 9,950 paramilitary-style police and coast guard only.

Economy: Industries: medical equip., food proc., textiles and clothing, constr. materials, fertilizer, plastic prods. **Chief agric.:** sugarcane, pineapples, bananas, milk, oil palm fruit, fruits. **Natural resources:** hydropower. **Water:** 21,925 cu m per capita. **Electricity prod.:** 12.5 bil kWh. **Labor force:** agric. 13.4%, industry 19.0%, services 67.6%. **Unemployment:** 8.3%.

Finance: Monetary unit: Colon (CRC) (523.98 = $1 U.S.). **GDP:** $145.7 bil; **per capita GDP:** $27,953; **GDP growth:** 5.1%. **Imports:** $28.4 bil; U.S. 39%, China 14%, Mexico 5%. **Exports:** $33.7 bil; U.S. 40%, Netherlands 7%, Guatemala 5%, Belgium 5%. **Tourism:** $4.8 bil. **Budget:** $14 bil. **Inflation:** 0.5%.

Transport: Railways: 173 mi (some sections rehabilitated after entire network fell into disrepair). **Motor vehicles:** 250.4 per 1,000 pop. **Airports:** 129.

Communications: Mobile: 145.8 per 100 pop. **Broadband:** 102 per 100 pop. **Internet** (2023): 85.1%.

Health: Expend.: 7.6%. **Life expect.:** 77.7 male; 82.9 female. **Births:** 10.8 per 1,000 pop. **Deaths:** 5.3 per 1,000 pop. **Infant mortality:** 6.7 per 1,000 live births. **Undernourished:** <2.5%. **HIV:** 0.5%. **COVID-19:** 9,373 deaths; rates per 100,000: 24,246 cases, 184 deaths. 86% vaccinated.

Education: Compulsory: ages 4-16. **Literacy:** 98.0%.

Website: www.presidencia.gob.cr

Guaymi Indians inhabited the area when Spaniards arrived, 1502. Independence came in 1821. Costa Rica seceded from the Central American Federation in 1838. Since the civil war of 1948-49, free political institutions have been preserved.

Nobel Peace Prize-winner Óscar Arias Sánchez, president 1986-90, won a second term in 2006. In 2010, the ruling party's Laura Chinchilla Miranda became the nation's first female president. The opposition Citizen Action Party (PAC) won 2014 and 2018 presidential elections. Beginning in 2018, Nicaraguan asylum seekers fleeing political violence and repression entered Costa Rica—over 175,000 were in Costa Rica as of mid-2024.

The important tourism industry was hurt by travel restrictions and business closures to combat the COVID-19 epidemic, which had spread worldwide by 2020.

Economist and political outsider Rodrigo Chavez won the Apr. 3, 2022, presidential runoff election.

Côte d'Ivoire

Republic of Côte d'Ivoire

People: Population: 29,981,758 (52). **Age distrib.:** <15: 36.1%; 65+: 3.0%. **Growth:** 2.1%. **Migrants:** 9.7%. **Pop. density:** 244.2 per sq mi, 94.3 per sq km. **Urban:** 53.6%. **Ethnic groups:** Akan 38%, Voltaique or Gur 22%, Northern Mande 22%, Kru 9.1%, Southern Mande 8.6%. **Languages:** French (official), 60 native dialects (Dioula most widely spoken). **Religions:** Christian 39.0% (Catholic 23.0%, Protestant 11.8%), Muslim 36.1% (Sunni), ethnic religionist 24.5%.

Geography: Total area: 124,504 sq mi, 322,463 sq km (68); **Land area:** 122,782 sq mi, 318,003 sq km. **Location:** S coast of W Africa. Liberia, Guinea on W; Mali, Burkina Faso on N; Ghana on E. **Topography:** Forests cover W half of country. A sparse inland plain leads to low mountains in NW. **Arable land:** 13.5%. **Capital:** Abidjan (administrative), 5,866,704; Yamoussoukro (official), 231,072.

Government: Type: Presidential republic. **Head of state:** Pres. Alassane Ouattara; b. 1942; in office: Apr. 11, 2011 (sworn in Dec. 4, 2010). **Head of govt.:** Prime Min. Robert Beugré Mambé; b. 1952; in office: Oct. 17, 2023. **Local divisions:** 12 districts, 2 autonomous districts. **Defense budget:** $687 mil. **Active troops:** 27,400.

Economy: Industries: foodstuffs, beverages, wood prods., oil refining, gold mining, truck and bus assembly, textiles, fertilizer. **Chief agric.:** yams, cassava, oil palm fruit, cocoa beans, sugarcane, plantains. **Natural resources:** petroleum, nat. gas, diamonds, manganese, iron ore, cobalt, bauxite, copper, gold, nickel, tantalum, silica sand, clay, cocoa beans, coffee, palm oil, hydropower. **Water:** 3,062 cu m per capita. **Crude oil reserves:** 100 mil bbls. **Electricity prod.:** 11.1 bil kWh. **Labor force:** agric. 45.6%, industry 10.5%, services 44.0%. **Unemployment:** 2.4%.

Finance: Monetary unit: CFA Franc (XOF) (587.79 = $1 U.S.). **GDP:** $224.9 bil; **per capita GDP:** $7,791; **GDP growth:** 6.5%. **Imports** (2022): $19.9 bil; China 18%, Nigeria 11%, France 8%, India 5%. **Exports** (2022): $17.2 bil; Switzerland 9%, Mali 8%, Netherlands 8%, U.S. 6%, France 5%. **Tourism** (2022): $335 mil. **Budget:** $10.1 bil. **Inflation:** 4.4%.

Transport: Railways: 410 mi. **Motor vehicles:** 29.8 per 1,000 pop. **Airports:** 29.

Communications: Mobile: 172.0 per 100 pop. **Broadband:** 93.6 per 100 pop. **Internet:** 38.4%.

Health: Expend.: 3.1%. **Life expect.:** 60.9 male; 65.4 female. **Births:** 27.5 per 1,000 pop. **Deaths:** 7.3 per 1,000 pop. **Infant mortality:** 52.5 per 1,000 live births. **Undernourished:** 9.6%. **HIV:** 1.8%. **COVID-19:** 835 deaths; rates per 100,000: 335 cases, 3 deaths. 46% vaccinated.

Education: Compulsory: ages 6-15. **Literacy:** 89.9%.

Website: www.gouv.ci

A French protectorate from 1842, Côte d'Ivoire became independent in 1960. The name was officially changed from Ivory Coast, Oct. 1985.

Students and workers protested, Feb. 1990, demanding the ouster of longtime Pres. Félix Houphouët-Boigny. Côte d'Ivoire held its first multiparty presidential election Oct. 1990, which Houphouët-Boigny won. He died Dec. 7, 1993. His successor, Henri Konan Bédié, was reelected Oct. 1995 but ousted in a military coup Dec. 24, 1999. The coup leader, Robert Guéi, lost a presidential vote Oct. 2000 but claimed victory anyway. After mass protests, he fled, and Laurent Gbagbo became president. Guéi was killed in Abidjan Sept. 19, 2002.

Agreement on power sharing was reached in Mar. 2003, and Gbagbo and former rebel leaders declared an end to their war July 5. The country remained divided, however. Rebels held the north and government forces controlled the south. Under a new accord reached Mar. 2007, rebel leader Guillaume Soro became prime min.

After apparently losing a presidential runoff election, Nov. 28, 2010, to former Prime Min. Alassane Ouattara, Gbagbo clung to power. A violent power struggle followed, claiming several thousand lives and displacing at least 1 mil people. Ouattara loyalists captured Gbagbo in Abidjan, Apr. 2011. After Ouattara took power, Gbagbo supporters were killed and tortured. Ouattara won reelection Oct. 25, 2015. Legislative elections were held and a new constitution approved in 2016. Amid violent clashes over the legality of his candidacy, Ouattara won reelection, Oct. 31, 2020.

The ICC tried Gbagbo for crimes against humanity. He was acquitted, Jan. 15, 2019. His wife, Simone Gbagbo, was sentenced, Mar. 10, 2015, by a Côte d'Ivoire court to 20 years in prison for her role in the violence that followed the 2010 election. (She was released in Aug. 2018.) In attacks, Mar. 13, 2016, for which al-Qaeda in the Islamic Maghreb claimed responsibility, gunmen killed 19 people and wounded more than 30 at three resort hotels in Grand-Bassam.

Croatia

Republic of Croatia

People: Population: 4,150,116 (128). **Age distrib.:** <15: 13.8%; 65+: 23.1%. **Growth:** –0.5%. **Migrants:** 12.9%. **Pop. density:** 192.0 per sq mi, 74.1 per sq km. **Urban:** 58.9%. **Ethnic groups:** Croat 91.6%, Serb 3.2%, other (incl. Bosniak, Romani, Albanian, Italian, Hungarian) 3.9%. **Languages:** Croatian (official). **Religions:** Christian 93.9% (Catholic 86.5%), agnostic 2.8%, Muslim 1.9% (Sunni).

Geography: Total area: 21,851 sq mi, 56,594 sq km (124); **Land area:** 21,612 sq mi, 55,974 sq km. **Location:** SE Europe, on the Balkan Peninsula. Slovenia, Hungary on N; Bosnia and Herzegovina, Serbia, Montenegro on E. **Topography:** Flat plains in NE; highlands, low mts. along Adriatic. **Arable land:** 15.2%. **Capital:** Zagreb, 684,142.

Government: Type: Parliamentary republic. **Head of state:** Pres. Zoran Milanovic; b. 1966; in office: Feb. 18, 2020. **Head of govt.:** Prime Min. Andrej Plenkovic; b. 1970; in office: Oct. 19, 2016. **Local divisions:** 20 counties, 1 city with special county status. **Defense budget:** $1.1 bil. **Active troops:** 16,800.

Economy: Industries: chemicals and plastics, machine tools, fabricated metal, electronics. **Chief agric.:** maize, wheat, sugar beets, milk, barley, soybeans. **Natural resources:** oil, coal, bauxite, iron ore, calcium, gypsum, natural asphalt, silica, mica, clays, salt, hydropower. **Water:** 25,984 cu m per capita. **Crude oil reserves:** 71 mil bbls. **Electricity prod.:** 14.1 bil kWh. **Labor force:** agric. 5.9%, industry 28.4%, services 65.7%. **Unemployment:** 6.1%.

Finance: Monetary unit: Euro (EUR) (0.90 = $1 U.S.). **GDP:** $176.9 bil; **per capita GDP:** $45,910; **GDP growth:** 3.1%. **Imports:** $46.6 bil; Italy 14%, Germany 12%, Slovenia 11%, Hungary 7%, U.S. 7%. **Exports:** $45.0 bil; Italy 13%, Slovenia 11%, Germany 11%, Hungary 10%, Bosnia and Herzegovina 9%. **Tourism:** $15.8 bil. **Budget:** $211.1 bil. **Inflation:** 7.9%.

Transport: Railways: 1,626 mi. **Motor vehicles:** 495.2 per 1,000 pop. **Airports:** 40.

Communications: Mobile: 117.1 per 100 pop. **Broadband:** 140 per 100 pop. **Internet** (2023): 83.2%.

Health: Expend.: 8.1%. **Life expect.:** 74.6 male; 81.0 female. **Births:** 8.5 per 1,000 pop. **Deaths:** 13.1 per 1,000 pop. **Infant mortality:** 8.4 per 1,000 live births. **Undernourished:** <2.5%. **HIV:** <0.1%. **COVID-19:** 18,754 deaths; rates per 100,000: 32,616 cases, 462 deaths. 55% vaccinated.

Education: Compulsory: ages 7-14. **Literacy:** 99.5%.

Website: vlada.gov.hr

From the 7th cent. the area was inhabited by Croats, a south Slavic people. It was formed into a kingdom under Tomislav in 924, and joined with Hungary in 1102. The Croats became westernized and separated from Slavs under Austro-Hungarian influence. Croatia united with other Yugoslav areas to proclaim the Kingdom of Serbs, Croats, and Slovenes in 1918. A nominally independent state between 1941 and 1945, it became a constituent republic of Yugoslavia in the 1946 constitution.

On June 25, 1991, Croatia declared independence from Yugoslavia. Fighting began between ethnic Serbs and Croats. The Serbs gained control of some Croatian territory, but Croatian troops recaptured most of it Aug. 1995. A peace accord was signed in Dec. The last Serbheld enclave, E Slavonia, was returned to Croatia in 1998. Croatia became a full NATO member Apr. 1, 2009. It joined the EU July 1, 2013, and began using the euro as its currency Jan. 1, 2023.

Kolinda Grabar-Kitarovic of the conservative Croatian Democratic Union (HDZ) party won a runoff election, Jan. 11, 2015, to become Croatia's first woman president. Zoran Milanovic of the center-left Social Democratic Party defeated her in a Jan. 5, 2020, presidential runoff.

The HDZ won the most seats in Sept. 11, 2016, parliamentary elections, and party leader Andrej Plenkovic formed a coalition government, Oct. 19. Plenkovic's HDZ increased its number of seats in July 5, 2020, elections. HDZ again won the most seats in Apr. 17, 2024, elections, and Plenkovic formed a new coalition government, May 17.

Beginning Sept. 2015, tens of thousands of Middle Eastern, Asian, and African refugees and other migrants—most trying to reach N Europe—entered Croatia from Serbia. Croatia announced that as of Mar. 9, 2016, it would block virtually all migrants from transiting through the country.

Cuba

Republic of Cuba

People: Population: 10,966,038 (85). **Age distrib.:** <15: 16.3%; 65+: 17.2%. **Growth:** –0.2%. **Migrants:** 0.03%. **Pop. density:** 258.6 per sq mi, 99.9 per sq km. **Urban:** 77.7%. **Ethnic groups:** white 64.1%, mulatto or mixed 26.6%, Black 9.3%. **Languages:** Spanish (official). **Religions:** Christian 61.4% (Catholic 54.2%), Spiritist 17.1%, agnostic 16.7%, atheist 4.2%.

Geography: Total area: 42,803 sq mi, 110,860 sq km (104); **Land area:** 42,402 sq mi, 109,820 sq km. **Location:** In Caribbean, westernmost of West Indies. The Bahamas, U.S. to N; Mexico to W; Jamaica to S; Haiti to E. **Topography:** Coastline is about 2,500 mi. The N coast is steep and rocky, the S coast low and marshy. Low hills and fertile valleys cover more than half the country. Three mountain ranges. **Arable land:** 28.0%. **Capital:** Havana, 2,152,518.

Government: Type: Communist state. **Head of state:** Pres. Miguel Díaz-Canel Bermúdez; b. 1960; in office: Apr. 19, 2018. **Head of govt.:** Prime Min. Manuel Marrero Cruz; b. 1963; in office: Dec. 21, 2019. **Local divisions:** 15 provinces, 1 special municipality. **Defense budget:** NA. **Active troops:** 49,000.

Economy: Industries: petroleum, nickel, cobalt, pharmaceuticals, tobacco, constr., steel, cement, agric. machinery, sugar. **Chief agric.:** sugarcane, cassava, plantains, vegetables, mangoes/guavas, milk. **Natural resources:** cobalt, nickel, iron ore, chromium, copper, salt, timber, silica, petroleum. **Water:** 3,387 cu m per capita. **Crude oil reserves:** 124 mil bbls. **Electricity prod.:** 18.2 bil kWh. **Labor force:** agric. 17.1%, industry 16.6%, services 66.3%. **Unemployment:** 1.2%.

Finance: Monetary unit: Peso (CUP) (23.90 = $1 U.S.). **GDP:** NA; **per capita GDP:** NA; **GDP growth** (2022): 1.8%. **Imports** (2020): $8.1 bil; Spain 23%, China 12%, U.S. 10%, Brazil 8%, Netherlands 6%. **Exports** (2020): $8.8 bil; China 40%, Spain 13%, Germany 5%. **Tourism** (2022): $1.0 bil. **Budget** (2017): $64.6 bil. **Inflation** (2016-17): 5.5%.

Transport: Railways: 5,199 mi. **Motor vehicles:** 53.5 per 1,000 pop. **Airports:** 123.

Communications: Mobile: 69.6 per 100 pop. **Broadband:** 48.6 per 100 pop. **Internet:** 73.2%.

Health: Expend.: 13.8%. **Life expect.:** 77.8 male; 82.6 female. **Births:** 9.9 per 1,000 pop. **Deaths:** 9.5 per 1,000 pop. **Infant mortality:** 4.0 per 1,000 live births. **Undernourished:** <2.5%. **HIV:** 0.6%. **COVID-19:** 8,530 deaths; rates per 100,000: 9,832 cases, 75 deaths. 89% vaccinated.

Education: Compulsory: ages 6-14. **Literacy:** 99.7%.

Website: www.presidencia.gob.cu

Some 50,000 Indigenous people lived in Cuba when Christopher Columbus reached it in 1492. Except for British occupation of Havana, 1762-63, Cuba remained Spanish until 1898. A sugar plantation economy, built primarily on enslaved labor, developed from the 18th cent. Sugar remains a leading agricultural product. Spain failed to deliver on rights guaranteed in 1878, prompting a full-scale liberation movement under Jose Martí in 1895.

The Spanish-American War began Apr. 1898, following the Feb. sinking of the USS *Maine* in Havana harbor. Spain lost the war and gave up all claims to Cuba. U.S. troops withdrew in 1902, but under 1903 and 1934 agreements, the U.S. continued to lease a site at Guantánamo Bay in the SE as a naval base. U.S. and other foreign investors dominated the economy. In 1952, former Pres. Fulgencio Batista established a dictatorship, which grew increasingly harsh and corrupt. Fidel Castro began a rebellion in 1956. Batista fled Jan. 1, 1959, and Castro took power.

Government-instituted economic and social changes failed to restore promised liberties. Opponents were imprisoned or executed. Some 700,000 Cubans emigrated in the first years after Castro's takeover, mostly to the U.S. By 1960, all banks and industrial companies had been nationalized, including over $1-bil worth of U.S.-owned properties, mostly without compensation. U.S. economic sanctions became a complete trade embargo under legislation passed by Congress in 1961. The U.S. broke diplomatic relations with Cuba in Jan. 1961.

In Apr. 1961, some 1,400 Cubans, trained and backed by the U.S. Central Intelligence Agency, unsuccessfully tried to overthrow the regime. On Oct. 22, 1962, U.S. Pres. John F. Kennedy ordered a naval blockade around Cuba and demanded that Soviet-installed nuclear missiles be withdrawn. The crisis ended Oct. 28 when Soviet Prem. Nikita S. Khrushchev agreed to withdraw the missiles; the U.S. pledged not to invade Cuba and removed its own missiles from Turkey.

In 1978 and 1980, the U.S. agreed to accept political prisoners released by Cuba, some of whom were criminals and mental patients. A 1987 agreement provided for 20,000 Cubans to emigrate to the U.S. each year. Cuba's support for left-wing regimes and liberation movements in Central America, Africa, and the Caribbean contributed to poor relations with the U.S.

Cuba's economy, hobbled by U.S. sanctions and dependent on aid from other Communist countries, was shaken by the collapse of the Communist bloc in the late 1980s. Anti-government demonstrations in Aug. 1994 prompted Castro to loosen emigration restrictions. A new U.S.-Cuba accord in Sept. ended the exodus of "boat people" after more than 30,000 had left Cuba.

On July 31, 2006, the ailing Fidel Castro yielded power to his 75-year-old brother Raúl. (Fidel Castro, age 90, died Nov. 25, 2016.) The U.S. in 2009 eased restrictions on remittances and family travel to Cuba. The Cuban government announced, Sept. 2010, economic restructuring plans involving cutting more than 500,000 public jobs. A Communist Party conference, Apr. 2011, approved an expansion of private property rights and private ownership of some small businesses. Legislation to encourage foreign investment was adopted in Mar. 2014.

The U.S., Jan. 11, 2002, began using its naval base at Guantánamo Bay to detain prisoners captured in Afghanistan and other suspected Islamist fighters or terrorists. The indefinite detention, as well as aggressive interrogation of prisoners in the early 2000s, was criticized by human rights groups. After about 750 prisoner releases to other countries, the detention center held 30 men as of Sept. 1, 2024. A 2023 report by a UN investigator found detention conditions to be "cruel, inhuman, and degrading."

Under Pres. Barack Obama, the U.S. restored full diplomatic relations with Cuba, July 20, 2015. Some travel and economic restrictions were eased. Scheduled U.S. commercial flights to Cuba, suspended since the early 1960s, resumed Aug. 31, 2016. The Trump administration, 2017-20, tightened travel regulations and economic sanctions—some of which were again eased by the Biden administration in 2022-24.

The U.S. announced, Sept. 29, 2017, the withdrawal of nonessential personnel from its Havana embassy, after staff and family members developed various medical problems. A U.S. study concluded in 2020 that "directed, pulsed radiofrequency energy" could have caused "Havana syndrome" illnesses (which also affected U.S. personnel in other countries), although much uncertainty remained.

Elected by the National Assembly, Miguel Díaz-Canel Bermúdez became head of state Apr. 19, 2018, succeeding Raúl Castro. A new constitution, approved in a Feb. 24, 2019, referendum, created a new office of prime minister. Díaz-Canel succeeded Raúl Castro as Communist Party head in Apr. 2021. Díaz-Canel was reelected president, Apr. 19, 2023.

Large demonstrations in several cities, July 11, 2021, protesting food shortages and other hardships were met with hundreds of arrests and other government measures to suppress dissent. Continuing economic hardship and repression sparked a new upsurge in immigration to the U.S., 2021-24.

July 2022 legislation, approved by voters in a Sept. 25 referendum, permitted same-sex couples to marry and adopt children.

Cyprus

Republic of Cyprus

People: Population: 1,320,525 (154). **Age distrib.:** <15: 15.6%; 65+: 14.4%. **Growth:** 1.0%. **Migrants:** 15.8%. **Pop. density:** 370.1 per sq mi, 142.9 per sq km. **Urban:** 67.1%. **Ethnic groups:** Greek 98.8% (Greek-Cypriot citizens in Republic of Cyprus only). **Languages:** Greek, Turkish (both official); English, Romanian, Russian, Bulgarian. **Religions:** Christian 70.3% (Orthodox 66.7%), Muslim 23.1% (Sunni), agnostic 3.8%.

Geography: Total area: 3,572 sq mi, 9,251 sq km (164); **Land area:** 3,568 sq mi, 9,241 sq km. **Location:** Eastern Mediterranean Sea, off Turkish coast. Nearest neighbors are Turkey to N, Syria and Lebanon to E. **Topography:** Two mountain ranges run E-W, separated by a wide, fertile plain. **Arable land:** 10.3%. **Capital:** Nicosia (Lefkosia), 269,469.

Government: Type: Presidential republic. **Head of state and govt.:** Pres. Nikos Christodoulides; b. 1973; in office: Feb. 28, 2023. **Local divisions:** 6 districts. **Defense budget:** $571 mil. **Active troops:** 12,000.

Economy: Industries: tourism, food and beverage proc., cement and gypsum, ship repair and refurb., textiles, light chemicals, metal prods. **Chief agric.:** milk, potatoes, sheep milk, pork, goat milk, wheat. **Natural resources:** copper, pyrites, asbestos, gypsum, timber, salt, marble, clay earth pigment. **Water:** 627 cu m per capita. **Electricity prod.:** 5.3 bil kWh. **Labor force:** agric. 2.4%, industry 17.2%, services 80.5%. **Unemployment:** 6.0%.

Finance: Monetary unit: Euro (EUR) (0.90 = $1 U.S.). **GDP:** $53.0 bil; **per capita GDP:** $57,101; **GDP growth:** 2.5%. **Imports:** $29.1 bil; Greece 19%, Turkey (Türkiye) 12%, Italy 9%, China 9%, Israel 5%. **Exports:** $28.8 bil; Hong Kong 10%, Greece 10%, Lebanon 7%, UK 6%, Liberia 5%. **Tourism:** $3.2 bil. **Budget:** $10.0 bil. **Inflation:** 3.5%.

Transport: Motor vehicles: 507.1 per 1,000 pop. **Airports:** 13.

Communications: Mobile: 155.7 per 100 pop. **Broadband:** 88.3 per 100 pop. **Internet** (2023): 91.2%.

Health: Expend.: 9.4%. **Life expect.:** 77.4 male; 83.1 female. **Births:** 10.2 per 1,000 pop. **Deaths:** 7.0 per 1,000 pop. **Infant mortality:** 8.1 per 1,000 live births. **Undernourished:** <2.5%. **HIV:** NA. **COVID-19:** 1,451 deaths; rates per 100,000: 78,424 cases, 163 deaths. 74% vaccinated.

Education: Compulsory: ages 5-14. **Literacy:** 99.4%.

Website: www.cyprus.gov.cy

The Ottoman Empire held Cyprus, 1571-1878, until it yielded control to Britain. Agitation for enosis (union) with Greece, which the Turkish minority opposed, increased after WWII and led to violence in 1955-56. In 1959, Britain, Greece, Turkey, and Cypriot leaders approved a plan for an independent republic, with constitutional guarantees for the Turkish minority.

Archbishop Makarios III was elected president, and full independence became final Aug. 16, 1960. Strife between Greek Cypriot and Turkish Cypriot communities prompted the UN to send a peacekeeping force (UNFICYP) in 1964; more than 850 UNFICYP uniformed personnel were in Cyprus as of July 31, 2024.

The Cypriot National Guard, led by officers from the Greek army, seized the government July 15, 1974. On July 20, Turkey invaded the island, and by Aug. 16, Turkish forces had occupied the northeastern 40%. Turkish troops remained in northern Cyprus in 2024.

Turkish Cyprus opened its border with Greek Cyprus Apr. 23, 2003, for the first time since partition. In separate referendums Apr. 2004, 65% of Turkish Cypriot voters accepted a UN-sponsored reunification plan, but 76% of Greek Cypriots rejected it. Still divided, Cyprus became a full member of the EU on May 1, 2004. Greek Cyprus began using the euro as its currency in 2008. The conservative candidate and head of the Democratic Rally party, Nicos Anastasiades, won 2013 and 2018 presidential elections.

In part because Cypriot banks held large amounts of Greek bonds, Cyprus suffered a banking crisis in 2013. A $13 bil bailout package was agreed upon Mar. 5, 2013, by the Intl. Monetary Fund, the European Central Bank, and eurozone countries. Cyprus agreed to stringent banking reforms and economic austerity; large depositors lost some of their money.

Independent Nikos Christodoulides, with center-right backing, won a Feb. 12, 2023, presidential runoff election.

Turkish Republic of Northern Cyprus

A declaration of independence was announced by Turkish-Cypriot leader Rauf Denktash, Nov. 15, 1983. The state, a parliamentary republic with enhanced presidency, is not internationally recognized but has trade relations with some countries. Political moderate Mustafa Akinci won an Apr. 26, 2015, presidential runoff election. New UN-sponsored reunification talks began in June 2015, but after several rounds of negotiations, the UN announced, July 7, 2017, that talks had failed. Akinci was defeated for reelection in an Oct. 18, 2020, presidential runoff by Turkish nationalist Ersin Tatar. UN-sponsored meetings, 2021-24, on restarting unification negotiations failed to make progress. Area 1,295 sq mi; pop. (2011 census) 286,257, nearly all ethnically Turkish. Capital: Nicosia (Lefkosia). Local divisions: 5 districts. Active troops: 3,000. **Website:** www.kktcb.org

Czechia

Czech Republic

(As of May 17, 2016, the country's official short form name in English was Czechia.)

People: Population: 10,837,890 (86). **Age distrib.:** <15: 15.7%; 65+: 20.5%. **Growth:** 0.04%. **Migrants:** 5.1%. **Pop. density:** 363.4 per sq mi, 140.3 per sq km. **Urban:** 74.7%. **Ethnic groups:** Czech 57.3%, Moravian 3.4%. **Languages:** Czech (official). **Religions:** agnostic 59.2%, Christian 33.9% (Catholic 29.7%), atheist 6.0%.

Geography: Total area: 30,451 sq mi, 78,867 sq km (114); **Land area:** 29,825 sq mi, 77,247 sq km. **Location:** E central Europe. Poland on N, Germany on N and W, Austria on S, Slovakia on E and SE. **Topography:** Bohemia, in W, is a plateau surrounded by mountains; Moravia is hilly. **Arable land:** 32.1%. **Capital:** Prague, 1,327,947.

Government: Type: Parliamentary republic. **Head of state:** Pres. Petr Pavel; b. 1961; in office: Mar. 9, 2023. **Head of govt.:** Prime Min. Petr Fiala; b. 1964; in office: Dec. 17, 2021. **Local divisions:** 13 regions, 1 capital city. **Defense budget:** $5.1 bil. **Active troops:** 26,600.

Economy: Industries: motor vehicles, metallurgy, machinery and equip., glass, armaments. **Chief agric.:** wheat, sugar beets, milk, barley, rapeseed, potatoes. **Natural resources:** coal, kaolin, clay, graphite, timber. **Water:** 1,251 cu m per capita. **Crude oil reserves:** 15 mil bbls. **Electricity prod.:** 79.0 bil kWh. **Labor force:** agric. 2.5%, industry 36.4%, services 61.0%. **Unemployment:** 2.6%.

Finance: Monetary unit: Koruna (CZK) (22.41 = $1 U.S.). **GDP:** $585.2 bil; **per capita GDP:** $53,817; **GDP growth:** –0.3%. **Imports:** $219.4 bil; Germany 24%, China 13%, Poland 10%, Slovakia 6%. **Exports:** $236.7 bil; Germany 32%, Slovakia 8%, Poland 7%, France 5%, Austria 5%. **Tourism:** $7.9 bil. **Budget:** $103.2 bil. **Inflation:** 10.7%.

Transport: Railways: 5,933 mi. **Motor vehicles:** 670.6 per 1,000 pop. **Airports:** 243.

Communications: Mobile: 126.0 per 100 pop. **Broadband:** 106 per 100 pop. **Internet** (2023): 86%.

Health: Expend.: 9.5%. **Life expect.:** 75.6 male; 81.8 female. **Births:** 9.8 per 1,000 pop. **Deaths:** 12.0 per 1,000 pop. **Infant mortality:** 2.6 per 1,000 live births. **Undernourished:** <2.5%. **HIV:** <0.1%. **COVID-19:** 43,510 deaths; rates per 100,000: 44,537 cases, 407 deaths. 64% vaccinated.

Education: Compulsory: ages 5-14. **Literacy:** 99.0%.

Website: www.vlada.cz

Bohemia and Moravia were part of the Great Moravian Empire in the 9th cent. and later became part of the Holy Roman Empire. Under the kings of Bohemia, Prague in the 14th cent. was the cultural center of Central Europe. Bohemia and Hungary became part of Austria-Hungary.

In 1914-18, Thomas G. Masaryk and Eduard Benes formed a provisional government with the support of Slovak leaders, including Milan Stefanik. They proclaimed the Republic of Czechoslovakia Oct. 28, 1918.

By 1938, Nazi Germany had generated disaffection among German-speaking citizens in Sudetenland and demanded its cession. British Prime Min. Neville Chamberlain signed with Adolf Hitler at Munich, Sept. 30, 1938, an agreement to the cession, with a guarantee of peace by Hitler and Italian dictator Benito Mussolini. Germany occupied Sudetenland Oct. 1-2. Hitler on Mar. 15, 1939, dissolved Czechoslovakia, made protectorates of Bohemia and Moravia, and supported the autonomy of Slovakia, proclaimed independent Mar. 14, 1939.

Soviet troops with some Czechoslovak contingents entered eastern Czechoslovakia in 1944 and reached Prague in May 1945; Benes returned as president. In May 1946 elections, the Communist Party won 38% of the votes. In Feb. 1948, the Communists seized power in advance of scheduled elections. The country was renamed the Czechoslovak Socialist Republic. A harsh Stalinist period followed; all opposition was suppressed.

In Jan. 1968 a liberalization movement spread through Czechoslovakia. Long-time Stalinist ruler Antonin Novotny was deposed; the democrat Slovak Alexander Dubcek succeeded him. On

Aug. 20, troops from the USSR and 4 Warsaw Pact nations invaded Czechoslovakia. Despite demonstrations and riots by students and workers, press censorship was imposed and liberal leaders were ousted. On Apr. 17, 1969, Dubcek resigned as Communist Party leader and was succeeded by Gustav Husak. Censorship was tightened, and the Communist Party expelled a third of its members.

More than 700 leading Czechoslovak intellectuals and former party leaders signed a human rights manifesto in 1977, called Charter 77, prompting a renewed crackdown by the regime.

The police crushed a massive protest in Prague, Nov. 17, 1989. As protesters demanded free elections, the Communist Party leadership resigned Nov. 24; millions went on strike Nov. 27.

On Dec. 10, 1989, the first cabinet in 41 years without a Communist majority took power; Vaclav Havel, playwright and human rights campaigner, was chosen president, Dec. 29. In Mar. 1990 the country was officially renamed the Czech and Slovak Federal Republic. A Slovakled coalition blocked Havel's bid to win reelection July 1992.

Slovakia declared sovereignty, July 17, 1992. Czech and Slovak leaders agreed, July 23, on a plan for a peaceful division of Czechoslovakia. It split into two separate states—the Czech Republic and Slovakia—Jan. 1, 1993. Havel was elected president of the Czech Republic on Jan. 26. The country became a full member of NATO in 1999.

Vaclav Klaus replaced the retiring Havel, 2003. The nation became a full EU member May 1, 2004.

Center-right parties made a strong showing in May 2010 parliamentary elections. Conservative Milos Zeman was elected president, Jan. 26, 2013; running on an anti-immigration, anti-EU platform, Zeman narrowly won reelection, Jan. 2018.

Billionaire Andrej Babis became prime minister, Dec. 13, 2017, after his new, anti-immigration party ANO won the most seats in Oct. elections. The center-right Together bloc, headed by Petr Fiala, narrowly outpolled ANO in Oct. 2021 elections; Fiala formed a coalition government and became prime minister Dec. 17, 2021. Pro-Western retired general Petr Pavel defeated Babis in a Jan. 28, 2023, presidential runoff election.

Following Russia's Feb. 2022 invasion of Ukraine, Czechia sent military aid to Ukraine. More than 370,000 Ukrainian refugees were in Czechia as of Aug. 2024. Soaring energy costs related to the Ukraine war contributed to high inflation, 2022-23; inflation eased significantly in 2024.

Denmark

Kingdom of Denmark

People: Population: 5,973,136 (114). **Age distrib.:** <15: 16.2%; 65+: 20.8%. **Growth:** 0.4%. **Migrants:** 12.4%. **Pop. density:** 364.6 per sq mi, 140.8 per sq km. **Urban:** 88.6%. **Ethnic groups:** Danish (incl. Greenlandic [predom. Inuit] and Faroese) 84.2%, Turkish 1.1%, other (incl. Polish, Romanian, Syrian, Ukrainian, German, Iraqi) 14.7%. **Languages:** Danish, Faroese, Greenlandic (Inuit dialect), English (predom. second lang.). **Religions:** Evangelical Lutheran (official); Christian 76.5% (Protestant 74.1%), agnostic 15.2%, Muslim 6.0% (Sunni).

Geography: Total area: 16,639 sq mi, 43,094 sq km (130); **Land area:** 16,384 sq mi, 42,434 sq km. **Location:** Northern Europe, separating North and Baltic Seas. Germany on S, Norway on NW, Sweden on NE. **Topography:** Consists of the Jutland Peninsula and more than 400 islands; flat and gently rolling plains. **Arable land:** 59.0%. **Capital:** Copenhagen, 1,391,205.

Government: Type: Parliamentary constitutional monarchy. **Head of state:** King Frederik X; b. 1968; in office: Jan. 14, 2024. **Head of govt.:** Prime Min. Mette Frederiksen; b. 1977; in office: June 27, 2019. **Local divisions:** 5 regions. **Defense budget:** $5.3 bil. **Active troops:** 15,400.

Economy: Industries: wind turbines, pharmaceuticals, medical equip., shipbuilding and refurb., iron, steel, nonferrous metals, chemicals, food proc., machinery and transp. equip., textiles and clothing. **Chief agric.:** milk, wheat, barley, potatoes, sugar beets, pork. **Natural resources:** petroleum, nat. gas, fish, salt, limestone, chalk, stone, gravel and sand. **Water:** 1,025 cu m per capita. **Crude oil reserves:** 441 mil bbls. **Electricity prod.:** 33.7 bil kWh. **Labor force:** agric. 2.1%, industry 19.1%, services 78.8%. **Unemployment:** 5.1%.

Finance: Monetary unit: Krone (DKK) (6.69 = $1 U.S.). **GDP:** $456.1 bil; **per capita GDP:** $76,688; **GDP growth:** 1.9%. **Imports:** $240.3 bil; Germany 20%, Sweden 12%, China 9%, Netherlands 8%, Norway 5%. **Exports:** $278.9 bil; Germany 15%, U.S. 11%, Sweden 10%, Netherlands 6%, Norway 5%. **Tourism:** $10.3 bil. **Budget:** $172.4 bil. **Inflation:** 3.3%.

Transport: Railways: 1,667 mi. **Motor vehicles:** 544.0 per 1,000 pop. **Airports:** 99.

Communications: Mobile: 126.1 per 100 pop. **Broadband:** 145 per 100 pop. **Internet** (2023): 98.8%.

Health: Expend. (2022): 9.5%. **Life expect.:** 80.2 male; 84.1 female. **Births:** 11.3 per 1,000 pop. **Deaths:** 9.6 per 1,000 pop. **Infant mortality:** 3.0 per 1,000 live births. **Undernourished:** <2.5%. **HIV:** <0.1%. **COVID-19:** 9,693 deaths; rates per 100,000: 59,004 cases, 166 deaths. 82% vaccinated.

Education: Compulsory: ages 6-15. **Literacy:** NA.

Website: denmark.dk

Most of the Viking raiders in the early Middle Ages were Danes. The Danish kingdom was a major power until the 17th cent., when it lost its land in southern Sweden. Norway was separated in 1815, and Schleswig-Holstein in 1864. Northern Schleswig was returned in 1920. Nazi Germany occupied Denmark, Apr. 1940-May 1945, but Danes helped more than 7,200 Jews escape to safety in Sweden, Sept. 1943.

The Danish newspaper Jyllands-Posten published, Sept. 30, 2005, cartoon images of the prophet Muhammad, offensive to Muslims; the caricatures, republished elsewhere, triggered violent protests and a boycott of Danish products in Islamic countries.

After Sept. 2011 parliamentary elections, Helle Thorning-Schmidt of the center-left Social Democrats became Denmark's first female prime min. A bill granting marriage rights to same-sex couples was voted into law, June 7, 2012. In 2014-16, in part as a result of the Syrian refugee crisis, almost 50,000 migrants sought asylum in Denmark. A center-right coalition returned to power in June 2015 elections in which the anti-immigration Danish People's Party won 21% of the vote. Asylum applications fell sharply beginning in 2017. May 2018 legislation banned wearing a face-covering garment such as a burqa or niqab in public. Dec. 2018 legislation required preschool education, including "Danish values" lessons, in largely immigrant areas. After the Social Democrats won June 5, 2019, elections, party leader Mette Frederiksen became prime min. The Social Democrats won the most seats in Nov. 1, 2022, elections, and Frederiksen formed a broad coalition government with center-right parties. After 52 years on the throne, making her Denmark's longest-serving monarch, Margrethe II abdicated, Jan. 14, 2024, in favor of her son, who became King Frederik X.

The **Faroe Islands** in the N Atlantic, about 300 mi NW of the Shetlands, and 850 mi from Denmark proper, 18 inhabited, have an area of 538 sq mi and pop. (2024 est.) of 52,933. They are an administrative division of Denmark, self-governing in most matters. Capital: Tórshavn; pop. (2018 est.) 20,817. Fish is a primary export. **Website:** www.government.fo

Kalaallit Nunaat (Greenland)

Greenland, an island between the North Atlantic and the Arctic Oceans, is separated from the North American continent by Davis Strait and Baffin Bay. Total area is 836,330 sq mi, about 79% of which is ice-capped. Most of the island is a lofty plateau 9,000-10,000 ft in elevation. The average thickness of the cap is 1,000 ft. Scientists point to accelerated melting of Greenland's ice sheet—about 4 tril tons of ice lost 1994-2017, according to a 2021 study—as evidence of global warming. The pop. (2024 est.) was 57,751. Ethnic groups: Greenlandic 89.1%, Danish 7.5%. Under the 1953 Danish constitution, the colony gained representatives in the Folketing (Danish legislature). The Danish parliament, 1978, approved home rule for Greenland, effective May 1, 1979. With home rule, Greenlandic place names came into official use. The name for its capital is Nuuk (2018 est. pop., 18,406), rather than Godthab. Voters approved a new Self-Government Act in Nov. 2008. Per capita GDP was $41,800 (2015 est.). The labor force is distributed as follows: agric. 15.9%, industry 10.1%, services 73.9%. Fish and fish products account for over 90% of exports. Other natural resources include coal, iron ore, lead, zinc, molybdenum, diamonds, gold, platinum, uranium, and hydropower. **Website:** naalakkersuisut.gl

Djibouti

Republic of Djibouti

People: Population: 994,974 (158). **Age distrib.:** <15: 28.4%; 65+: 4.2%. **Growth:** 1.9%. **Migrants:** 12.1%. **Pop. density:** 111.2 per sq mi, 42.9 per sq km. **Urban:** 78.7%. **Ethnic groups:** Somali 60%, Afar 35%, other (mostly Yemeni Arab, also French, Ethiopian, Italian) 5%. **Languages:** French, Arabic (both official); Somali, Afar. **Religions:** Muslim 97.7% (Sunni).

Geography: Total area: 8,958 sq mi, 23,200 sq km (147); **Land area:** 8,950 sq mi, 23,180 sq km. **Location:** E coast of Africa, separated from Arabian Peninsula by strategically vital strait of Bab el-Mandeb. Eritrea on NW, Ethiopia on W and SW, Somalia on SE. **Topography:** Low coastal plain with mountains behind and an interior plateau. Arid, sandy, and desolate. Hot and dry climate. **Arable land:** 0.1%. **Capital:** Djibouti, 607,804.

Government: Type: Presidential republic. **Head of state:** Pres. Ismail Omar Guelleh; b. 1947; in office: May 8, 1999. **Head of govt.:** Prime Min. Abdoulkader Kamil Mohamed; b. 1951; in office: Apr. 1, 2013. **Local divisions:** 6 districts. **Defense budget:** NA. **Active troops:** 8,450.

Economy: Industries: constr., agric. proc., shipping. **Chief agric.:** vegetables, beans, milk, beef, camel milk, lemons/limes. **Natural resources:** potential geothermal power, gold, clay, granite, limestone, marble, salt, diatomite, gypsum, pumice, petroleum. **Water:** 271 cu m per capita. **Electricity prod.:** 133 mil kWh. **Labor force:** agric. 1.2%, industry 6.0%, services 92.9%. **Unemployment:** 26.3%.

Finance: Monetary unit: Franc (DJF) (177.55 = $1 U.S.). **GDP:** $8.2 bil; **per capita GDP:** $7,204; **GDP growth:** 6.7%. **Imports** (2022): $5.1 bil; China 38%, UAE 20%, India 10%, Morocco 6%,

Turkey (Türkiye) 6%. **Exports** (2022): $5.7 bil; Ethiopia 61%, China 17%, India 7%. **Tourism** (2022): $45 mil. **Budget:** $754 mil. **Inflation:** 1.5%.

Transport: Railways: 60 mi (Djibouti segment of Addis Ababa-Djibouti railway). **Airports:** 10.

Communications: Mobile: 49.8 per 100 pop. **Broadband:** 34.9 per 100 pop. **Internet:** 65%.

Health: Expend.: 2.9%. **Life expect.:** 63.4 male; 68.5 female. **Births:** 21.8 per 1,000 pop. **Deaths:** 7.0 per 1,000 pop. **Infant mortality:** 45.2 per 1,000 live births. **Undernourished:** 12.9%. **HIV:** 0.8%. **COVID-19:** 189 deaths; rates per 100,000: 1,588 cases, 19 deaths. 36% vaccinated.

Education: Compulsory: ages 6-15. **Literacy:** NA.

Website: www.presidence.dj

France gained control of the territory in stages between 1862 and 1900. As French Somaliland, it became an overseas French territory in 1945; in 1967 it was renamed the French Territory of the Afars and the Issas. Ethiopia and Somalia renounced their claims to the area, but each accused the other of trying to gain control. There were clashes between Afars (ethnically related to Ethiopians) and Issas (related to Somalis) in 1976. Immigrants from both countries continued to enter Djibouti until independence on June 27, 1977.

Post-independence economic support has come from France, Arab countries, the U.S., and China. A peace accord Dec. 1994 ended a 3-year Afar rebel uprising. The U.S. announced, May 5, 2014, the signing of a new 20-year lease for its military base in Djibouti. A 460-mi Chinese-built railroad linking Addis Ababa, Ethiopia, with Djibouti City began service Oct. 5, 2016. China opened a naval base in Djibouti, Aug. 1, 2017. Pres. Ismail Omar Guelleh won a fifth term in Apr. 9, 2021, elections largely boycotted by the opposition. In the 2020s, Djibouti became a major transit point for African migrants trying to reach the Middle East.

Dominica

Commonwealth of Dominica

People: Population: 74,661 (188). **Age distrib.:** <15: 20.7%; 65+: 13.7%. **Growth:** –0.01%. **Migrants:** 11.5%. **Pop. density:** 257.5 per sq mi, 99.4 per sq km. **Urban:** 72.3%. **Ethnic groups:** African descent 84.5%, mixed 9%, Indigenous 3.8%. **Languages:** English (official), French patois. **Religions:** Christian 94.2% (Catholic 50.4%, Protestant 40.8%), Spiritist 2.6%, Baha'i 1.8%.

Geography: Total area: 290 sq mi, 751 sq km (175); **Land area:** 290 sq mi, 751 sq km. **Location:** E Caribbean, most northerly Windward Isl. Guadeloupe to N, Martinique to S (both French terr.). **Topography:** Central ridge runs N-S, terminating in cliffs. Volcanic in origin, with numerous thermal springs. **Arable land:** 8.0%. **Capital:** Roseau, 14,942.

Government: Type: Parliamentary republic. **Head of state:** Pres. Sylvanie Burton; in office: Oct. 2, 2023. **Head of govt.:** Prime Min. Roosevelt Skerrit; b. 1972; in office: Jan. 8, 2004. **Local divisions:** 10 parishes. **Defense budget/active troops:** NA.

Economy: Industries: soap, coconut oil, tourism, copra, furniture, cement blocks, shoes. **Chief agric.:** taro, grapefruits, yams, bananas, plantains, coconuts. **Natural resources:** timber, hydropower. **Water:** 2,762 cu m per capita. **Electricity prod.:** 170.8 mil kWh. **Labor force:** NA. **Unemployment:** NA.

Finance: Monetary unit: East Caribbean Dollar (XCD) (2.70 = $1 U.S.). **GDP:** $1.3 bil; **per capita GDP:** $17,599; **GDP growth:** 4.7%. **Imports:** $414.1 mil; U.S. 51%, China 9%. **Exports:** $185.1 mil; Bahamas 12%, Guyana 8%, Antigua and Barbuda 7%, Dominican Republic 7%, Barbados 6%. **Tourism:** $72 mil. **Budget** (2021): $184 mil. **Inflation:** 3.5%.

Transport: Airports: 2.

Communications: Mobile (2022): 85.2 per 100 pop. **Broadband** (2022): 78 per 100 pop. **Internet:** 83.4%.

Health: Expend.: 6.5%. **Life expect.:** 75.8 male; 81.8 female. **Births:** 13.3 per 1,000 pop. **Deaths:** 8.1 per 1,000 pop. **Infant mortality:** 10.7 per 1,000 live births. **Undernourished:** 13.4%. **HIV:** NA. **COVID-19:** 74 deaths; rates per 100,000: 22,290 cases, 103 deaths. 43% vaccinated.

Education: Compulsory: ages 5-16. **Literacy:** NA.

Website: dominica.gov.dm

A British colony since 1805, Dominica was granted self-government in 1967. Independence was achieved Nov. 3, 1978. Hurricanes and other tropical storms periodically devastate the island.

Coups were attempted in 1980 and 1981. Prime Min. Pierre Charles died Jan. 6, 2004, and was succeeded by Roosevelt Skerrit. The COVID-19 pandemic hurt the important tourism industry beginning in 2020. Elected by parliament Sept. 27, 2023, Sylvanie Burton became Dominica's first female president and first head of state of Kalinago (or Carib) descent.

Dominican Republic

People: Population: 10,815,857 (87). **Age distrib.:** <15: 25.5%; 65+: 7.6%. **Growth:** 0.8%. **Migrants:** 5.6%. **Pop. density:** 579.7 per sq mi, 223.8 per sq km. **Urban:** 85.0%. **Ethnic groups:** mixed 70.4% (mestizo/indio 58%, mulatto 12.4%), Black 15.8%, white 13.5%. **Languages:** Spanish (official). **Religions:** Christian 94.7% (Catholic 81.1%, Protestant 8.2%), agnostic 2.4%, Spiritist 2.2%.

Geography: Total area: 18,792 sq mi, 48,670 sq km (128); **Land area:** 18,656 sq mi, 48,320 sq km. **Location:** W Indies, sharing isl. of Hispaniola with Haiti on W, Puerto Rico (U.S.) to E. **Topography:** The Cordillera Central range crosses center, rising to over 10,000 ft, highest in the Caribbean. Cibao Valley to N. **Arable land:** 18.2%. **Capital:** Santo Domingo, 3,587,402.

Government: Type: Presidential republic. **Head of state and govt.:** Pres. Luis Rodolfo Abinader Corona; b. 1967; in office: Aug. 16, 2020. **Local divisions:** 10 regions. **Defense budget:** $894 mil. **Active troops:** 56,800.

Economy: Industries: tourism, sugar proc., gold mining, textiles, cement, tobacco. **Chief agric.:** sugarcane, bananas, papayas, plantains, rice, milk. **Natural resources:** nickel, bauxite, gold, silver. **Water:** 2,114 cu m per capita. **Electricity prod.:** 21.5 bil kWh. **Labor force:** agric. 7.7%, industry 20.3%, services 72.0%. **Unemployment:** 5.6%.

Finance: Monetary unit: Peso (DOP) (59.67 = $1 U.S.). **GDP:** $290.2 bil; **per capita GDP:** $25,611; **GDP growth:** 2.4%. **Imports:** $34.5 bil; U.S. 44%, China 15%. **Exports:** $25.8 bil; U.S. 50%, Switzerland 8%, Haiti 7%. **Tourism:** $9.8 bil. **Budget:** $14.5 bil. **Inflation:** 4.8%.

Transport: Railways: 308 mi. **Motor vehicles:** 208.3 per 1,000 pop. **Airports:** 32.

Communications: Mobile: 91.9 per 100 pop. **Broadband:** 72.8 per 100 pop. **Internet:** 84.4%.

Health: Expend.: 4.9%. **Life expect.:** 71.0 male; 74.3 female. **Births:** 17.3 per 1,000 pop. **Deaths:** 7.1 per 1,000 pop. **Infant mortality:** 21.7 per 1,000 live births. **Undernourished:** 4.6%. **HIV:** 1.0%. **COVID-19:** 4,384 deaths; rates per 100,000: 6,094 cases, 40 deaths. 57% vaccinated.

Education: Compulsory: ages 3-17. **Literacy:** 95.5%.

Website: www.dominicana.gob.do

Carib and Arawak Indians inhabited the island of Hispaniola when Christopher Columbus landed in 1492. The city of Santo Domingo, founded 1496, is the oldest European settlement in the Western Hemisphere.

France took over the western third of the island (now Haiti) in 1697 and Santo Domingo in 1795. Spain returned intermittently 1803-21, as several native republics came and went. Haiti ruled again, 1822-44; Spanish occupation occurred 1861-63. U.S. Marines occupied the country 1916-24.

In 1930, Gen. Rafael Leonidas Trujillo Molina was elected president. The brutal Trujillo era ended with his assassination in 1961. Pres. Joaquín Balaguer, appointed by Trujillo in 1960, resigned under pressure in 1962.

Juan Bosch, elected president in the first free elections in 38 years, was overthrown in 1963. On Apr. 24, 1965, Bosch's followers and others, including a few Communists, launched a revolt. Four days later U.S. Marines intervened against pro-Bosch forces. A provisional government supervised a June 1966 election in which Balaguer defeated Bosch. Balaguer remained in office for most of the next 28 years, but his May 1994 reelection was widely denounced as fraudulent. He called for new elections but did not run, and Leonel Fernández Reyna was elected June 1996. After a presidential election defeat in 2000, Fernández again won the presidency in 2004 and 2008. Fernández ally Danilo Medina Sánchez, of the center-left Dominican Liberation Party (PLD), was elected in 2012 and 2016. In the July 5, 2020, presidential election, businessman Luis Rodolfo Abinader defeated the PLD candidate. Abinader won reelection, May 19, 2024, and his party won sizable majorities in both houses of Congress the same day.

The Constitutional Court ruled, Sept. 23, 2013, that people born in the Dominican Rep. after 1929 to undocumented immigrant parents were not entitled to citizenship. The decision affected perhaps 200,000 people, most of Haitian descent. In 2015, the government required undocumented immigrants—estimated at more than 500,000, most of them Haitian—to register or face deportation. By the end of 2017, more than 250,000 Haitians had left the country voluntarily or been deported. As undocumented emigration from Haiti, largely to escape violence and hardship, increased in the 2020s, the Dominican Rep. stepped up deportations and tightened border security, including by constructing a border wall.

Ecuador

Republic of Ecuador

People: Population: 18,309,984 (68). **Age distrib.:** <15: 26.8%; 65+: 9.1%. **Growth:** 0.9%. **Migrants:** 4.4%. **Pop. density:** 171.3 per sq mi, 66.1 per sq km. **Urban:** 65.0%. **Ethnic groups:** mestizo (mixed Indigenous/white) 77.5%, Montubio 7.7%, Indigenous 7.7%, white 2.2%, Afroecuadorian 2%. **Languages:** Spanish (Castilian) (official), Indigenous (incl. Quechua). **Religions:** Christian 94.4% (Catholic 83.4%), agnostic 4.3%.

Geography: Total area: 109,484 sq mi, 283,561 sq km (73); **Land area:** 106,889 sq mi, 276,841 sq km. **Location:** NW S America, on Pacific coast, astride the equator. Colombia on N, Peru on E and S. **Topography:** Two Andes ranges run N-S, splitting country into 3 zones: hot, humid lowlands on coast;

temperate highlands between ranges; and rainy, tropical lowlands to E. **Arable land:** 3.9%. **Capital:** Quito, 1,986,667. **Cities:** Guayaquil, 3,193,267.

Government: Type: Presidential republic. **Head of state and govt.:** Pres. Daniel Noboa; in office: Nov. 23, 2023. **Local divisions:** 24 provinces. **Defense budget:** $1.7 bil. **Active troops:** 39,600.

Economy: Industries: petroleum, food proc., textiles, wood prods., chemicals. **Chief agric.:** sugarcane, bananas, oil palm fruit, milk, maize, rice. **Natural resources:** petroleum, fish, timber, hydropower. **Water:** 24,857 cu m per capita. **Crude oil reserves:** 8.3 bil bbls. **Electricity prod.:** 32.6 bil kWh. **Labor force:** agric. 31.5%, industry 17.3%, services 51.1%. **Unemployment:** 3.4%.

Finance: Monetary unit: U.S. Dollar (USD) (1.00 = $1 U.S.). **GDP:** $288.7 bil; **per capita GDP:** $15,870; **GDP growth:** 2.4%. **Imports:** $34.4 bil; U.S. 26%, China 23%, Colombia 6%. **Exports:** $34.6 bil; U.S. 27%, China 17%, Panama 14%. **Tourism:** $2.0 bil. **Budget:** $39.3 bil. **Inflation:** 2.2%.

Transport: Railways: 600 mi. **Motor vehicles:** 101.1 per 1,000 pop. **Airports:** 310.

Communications: Mobile: 101.0 per 100 pop. **Broadband:** 63.1 per 100 pop. **Internet** (2023): 72.7%.

Health: Expend.: 8.3%. **Life expect.:** 69.7 male; 80.4 female. **Births:** 17.7 per 1,000 pop. **Deaths:** 7.2 per 1,000 pop. **Infant mortality:** 11.2 per 1,000 live births. **Undernourished:** 13.9%. **HIV:** 0.4%. **COVID-19:** 36,050 deaths; rates per 100,000: 6,108 cases, 204 deaths. 81% vaccinated.

Education: Compulsory: ages 3-17. **Literacy:** 94.0%.

Website: www.presidencia.gob.ec

The region, which was the northern Inca empire, was conquered by Spain in 1533. Liberation forces defeated the Spanish May 24, 1822, near Quito. Ecuador became part of the Great Colombia Republic but seceded, May 13, 1830.

Ecuadoran Indigenous peoples, demanding greater rights, staged protests in the 1990s. A border war with Peru flared Jan. 26-Mar. 1, 1995. Elected president, July 1996, Abdalá Bucaram imposed stiff price increases and other austerity measures; the National Assembly, Feb. 1997, dismissed him for "mental incapacity."

Jamil Mahuad Witt won a presidential runoff election July 1998. Opposed by Indian groups and military leaders, he was ousted Jan. 2000, and succeeded by Vice Pres. Gustavo Noboa Bejarano. Noboa enacted a plan introduced by Mahuad to replace the sucre with the U.S. dollar as Ecuador's currency. Lucio Gutiérrez Borbúa, a leader in the 2000 coup, won a presidential runoff Nov. 2002.

Gutiérrez imposed economic austerity measures, purged opponents from the Supreme Court, Dec. 2004, and then dissolved it, Apr. 2005. The National Assembly ousted Gutiérrez Apr. 20. In May 2006, Ecuador took over oil assets belonging to U.S.-based Occidental Petroleum.

Rafael Correa, a left-wing economist, won a presidential runoff vote Nov. 2006. Correa initially boosted development spending and aid to poor families; later, as oil revenue dropped, Ecuador in Dec. 2008 defaulted on part of its $10-bil foreign debt. Correa was reelected in 2009 and 2013.

Ecuador granted asylum, Aug. 16, 2012, to Julian Assange, the founder of WikiLeaks. Assange was in Ecuador's UK embassy in London avoiding possible extradition, including to the U.S. in connection with the hacking and publication of classified information. After Ecuador withdrew asylum, Assange was arrested at the embassy, Apr. 11, 2019, and jailed in the UK; legal appeals blocked his extradition to the U.S. for over 5 years. Under a plea agreement, Assange pleaded guilty, June 26, 2024, to one U.S. espionage charge and returned to his native Australia.

Beginning in 2015, large numbers of Venezuelans fleeing economic hardship and repression entered Ecuador. About 475,000 Venezuelan refugees were in Ecuador as of mid-2024.

Following a 2021 court decision, regulations in effect in 2022 permitted abortion in limited circumstances for rape victims. Voters, Aug. 20, 2023, approved a referendum measure to block oil drilling in part of the Amazon.

Drug trafficking and crime by drug gangs has increased sharply in recent years. Facing impeachment on corruption charges, Pres. Guillermo Lasso Mendoza (elected Apr. 11, 2021) dissolved the National Assembly, May 17, 2023. New first-round presidential elections were scheduled for Aug. 20, 2023. Presidential candidate Fernando Villavicencio, outspoken about drug crime and corruption, was shot and killed at a campaign event Aug. 9. Businessman Daniel Noboa defeated Luisa González, of Correa's party, in an Oct. 15, 2023, presidential runoff. In Jan. 2024, Noboa deployed the military to combat escalating gang violence. Security measures approved in an Apr. 21, 2024, referendum increased his powers.

The **Galápagos Islands**, pop. (2020 est.) 33,042, about 600 mi to the W, are the home of giant tortoises and other distinctive animals. The Galápagos are vulnerable to the impacts of climate change. Ecuador announced, Nov. 2, 2021, it would increase by almost 50% the size of a protected marine reserve.

Egypt

Arab Republic of Egypt

People: Population: 111,247,248 (15). **Age distrib.:** <15: 33.8%; 65+: 5.6%. **Growth:** 1.5%. **Migrants:** 0.5%. **Pop. density:** 289.4 per sq mi, 111.8 per sq km. **Urban:** 43.3%. **Ethnic groups** (by nationality): Egyptian 99.7%. **Languages:** Arabic (official), English and French widely understood by educated classes. **Religions:** Muslim 90.3% (Sunni), Christian 8.8% (Orthodox).

Geography: Total area: 386,662 sq mi, 1,001,450 sq km (29); **Land area:** 384,345 sq mi, 995,450 sq km. **Location:** NE corner of Africa. Libya on W; Sudan on S; Israel, Gaza Strip on E. **Topography:** Almost entirely desolate and barren with hills and mountains in E and along Nile. Most people live in 550-mi-long Nile Valley. **Arable land:** 3.1%. **Capital:** Cairo, 22,623,874. **Cities:** Alexandria, 5,696,131.

Government: Type: Presidential republic. **Head of state:** Pres. Abdel Fattah al-Sisi; b. 1954; in office: June 8, 2014. **Head of govt.:** Prime Min. Mostafa Madbouly; in office: June 7, 2018. **Local divisions:** 27 governorates. **Defense budget:** $3.6 bil. **Active troops:** 438,500.

Economy: Industries: textiles, food proc., tourism, chemicals, pharmaceuticals, hydrocarbons, constr., cement, metals, light manufactures. **Chief agric.:** sugarcane, sugar beets, wheat, maize, tomatoes, potatoes. **Natural resources:** petroleum, nat. gas, iron ore, phosphates, manganese, limestone, gypsum, talc, asbestos, lead, rare earth elements, zinc. **Water:** 526 cu m per capita. **Crude oil reserves:** 3.3 bil bbls. **Electricity prod.:** 215.8 bil kWh. **Labor force:** agric. 18.7%, industry 28.4%, services 53.0%. **Unemployment:** 7.3%.

Finance: Monetary unit: Pound (EGP) (48.70 = $1 U.S.). **GDP:** $2.1 tril; **per capita GDP:** $18,817; **GDP growth:** 3.8%. **Imports** (2022): $97.1 bil; China 17%, U.S. 7%, Saudi Arabia 7%, UAE 6%, Turkey (Türkiye) 5%. **Exports** (2022): $76.3 bil; Turkey (Türkiye) 8%, Italy 6%, U.S. 6%, Spain 6%, India 5%. **Tourism:** $14.1 bil. **Budget** (2020): $100.3 bil. **Inflation:** 33.9%.

Transport: Railways: 3,160 mi. **Motor vehicles:** 61.3 per 1,000 pop. **Airports:** 73.

Communications: Mobile: 92.8 per 100 pop. **Broadband:** 69.1 per 100 pop. **Internet:** 72.2%.

Health: Expend.: 4.6%. **Life expect.:** 73.8 male; 76.2 female. **Births:** 19.5 per 1,000 pop. **Deaths:** 4.3 per 1,000 pop. **Infant mortality:** 16.8 per 1,000 live births. **Undernourished:** 8.5%. **HIV:** <0.1%. **COVID-19:** 24,830 deaths; rates per 100,000: 504 cases, 24 deaths. 41% vaccinated.

Education: Compulsory: ages 6-17. **Literacy:** 74.5%.

Website: www.egypt.gov.eg

Archaeological records of ancient Egyptian civilization date back to 4000 BCE. A unified kingdom arose around 3200 BCE and extended south into Nubia and as far north as Syria. A high culture of rulers and priests was built on an economic base of serfdom, fertile soil, and annual flooding of the Nile.

Imperial decline facilitated conquest by Asian invaders (Hyksos, Assyrians). The last native dynasty fell in 341 BCE to the Persians, who were in turn replaced by Greeks (Alexander and the Ptolemies), Romans, Byzantines, and Arabs, who introduced Islam and the Arabic language. The ancient Egyptian language is preserved only in Coptic Christian liturgy.

Egypt was ruled as part of larger Islamic empires for many centuries. Britain intervened in Egypt in 1882 and ruled the country as a protectorate, 1914-22. A 1936 treaty strengthened Egyptian autonomy, but Britain retained bases in Egypt and a condominium (joint rule with Egypt) over Sudan. When the state of Israel was proclaimed in 1948, Egypt joined other Arab nations invading Israel and was defeated. In 1951 Egypt abrogated the 1936 treaty; Sudan became independent in 1956.

A July 1952 uprising overthrew King Farouk and established a republic. Lt. Col. Gamal Abdel Nasser rose to power, becoming premier in 1954 and president in 1956. Nasser pushed construction of Egypt's Aswan High Dam, completed in 1970.

After guerrilla raids across its border, Israel invaded Egypt's Sinai Peninsula, Oct. 29, 1956. Egypt rejected a cease-fire demand by Britain and France; on Oct. 31 the two nations dropped bombs and on Nov. 5-6 landed forces. Egypt and Israel accepted a UN cease-fire; fighting ended Nov. 7. Full-scale war with Israel broke out again, June 5, 1967; before it ended under a UN cease-fire June 10, Israel had captured Gaza and the Sinai Peninsula and taken control of the E bank of the Suez Canal.

Nasser died Sept. 28, 1970, and was replaced by Vice Pres. Anwar Sadat. In a surprise attack Oct. 6, 1973, Egyptian forces crossed the Suez Canal into the Sinai. (At the same time, Syrian forces attacked Israelis on the Golan Heights.) Israel counterattacked, crossed the canal, and surrounded Suez City. A UN cease-fire took effect Oct. 24. Under an agreement signed Jan. 1974, Israeli forces withdrew from the canal's W bank; limited numbers of Egyptian forces occupied a strip along the E bank. A second accord was signed in 1975, with Israel yielding Sinai oil fields.

Pres. Sadat's surprise visit to Jerusalem, Nov. 1977, opened the prospect of peace with Israel. On Mar. 26, 1979, Egypt and Israel signed a formal peace treaty, ending 30 years of war and establishing diplomatic relations. On Oct. 6, 1981, Muslim extremists within the army assassinated Pres. Sadat, who was succeeded by Hosni Mubarak. Israel returned control of the Sinai to Egypt in Apr. 1982.

Egyptian security forces battled Islamist violence in the 1990s and early 2000s. On Nov. 17, 1997, near Luxor, Muslim extremists killed 58 foreign tourists and 4 Egyptians. Bombs Oct. 7, 2004, in and near Taba, a Sinai tourist site popular with Israelis, killed at least 35 people. Another 88 people were killed in bombings July 23, 2005, at Sharm el Sheikh, a Red Sea resort city. Suicide bombings at the Sinai resort town of Dahab, Apr. 24, 2006, killed at least 18 people; security forces May 9 killed Nasser Khamis al-Mallahi, leader of the group blamed for the Taba, Sharm el Sheikh, and Dahab attacks.

Following 18 days of mass protests in which at least 846 people died in clashes between Arab Spring dissidents and Mubarak loyalists, Mubarak surrendered power Feb. 11, 2011. A transitional military regime prepared for elections. Mubarak was convicted on corruption charges, May 9, 2015, and sentenced to three years in prison. Released, Mar. 24, 2017, from a military hospital, Mubarak died Feb. 25, 2020.

Islamist candidate Mohammed Morsi of the Muslim Brotherhood was declared winner of the presidential election, June 2012. On Oct. 8, 2012, Morsi pardoned select political prisoners detained during the Arab Spring uprising. Violent clashes between Morsi supporters and opponents erupted Nov. 23 after Morsi announced an edict interpreted as a powergrab. The proposal of a new Islamist constitution prompted demonstrations throughout Dec.; it passed Dec. 23, 2012.

The military forced Morsi out of office July 3, 2013, and cracked down violently, Aug. 14, on pro-Morsi protesters. More than 600 protesters and at least 40 police officers died in confrontations. The military outlawed the Muslim Brotherhood as a terrorist organization Dec. 25, 2013. Under a new constitution approved in a Jan. 2014 referendum, former Gen. Abdel Fattah al-Sisi, one of the leaders in ousting Morsi, won a May presidential election. Violence between Morsi supporters and security forces continued, causing hundreds of deaths on both sides. Muslim Brotherhood leader Mohamed Badie was sentenced to death June 21, 2014, in connection with July 2013 violence; the sentence was reduced to life in prison Aug. 30, 2014. Morsi was sentenced to 20 years in prison, Apr. 21, 2015, in a trial related to Dec. 2012 street violence. He died, June 17, 2019, after collapsing in court while facing separate espionage charges.

The Sisi government carried out arrests of dissidents and journalists, and it suppressed protests and free expression. Sisi won a new term as president in a Mar. 2018 election from which opposition candidates were essentially barred. Constitutional changes approved in an Apr. 2019 referendum extended the president's term to 6 years and increased presidential power over the judiciary. Sisi won reelection (with 90% of the vote) in Dec. 2023.

Beginning in 2013, Islamist militants battled security forces and seized territory in the northern Sinai. Terrorist attacks occurred at major tourist sites in Luxor and Giza in June 2015. A Russian airliner crashed in the Sinai, Oct. 31, 2015, apparently after a bomb onboard exploded, killing all 224 on board; Sinai Province, an ISIS-affiliated Islamist group, claimed responsibility. Egypt announced, Aug. 4, 2016, that it had killed Sinai Province's leader in an airstrike. A suicide bombing, for which ISIS claimed responsibility, killed about 30 people at a Coptic Christian chapel in Cairo, Dec. 11, 2016. About 75 people were killed in three attacks on Coptic Christians, Apr.-May 2017. Militant attacks killed scores of Egyptian soldiers and police July-Oct. 2017. An attack on a Sufi mosque in the northern Sinai, Nov. 24, 2017, left more than 300 dead. An Egyptian military offensive, launched Feb. 2018, against Islamist militants in the Sinai and other areas somewhat reduced militant attacks.

A WHO May 2022 report estimated about 250,000 excess deaths in Egypt in 2020-21 related to the COVID-19 pandemic, compared with fewer than 25,000 officially reported COVID-19 deaths as of Sept. 2024.

The Suez Canal, 103 mi long, links the Mediterranean and Red Seas. It was built by a French corporation 1859-69, but Britain obtained controlling interest in 1875. On July 26, 1956, Egypt nationalized the canal.

El Salvador

Republic of El Salvador

People: Population: 6,628,702 (109). **Age distrib.:** <15: 25.3%; 65+: 8.4%. **Growth:** 0.3%. **Migrants:** 0.7%. **Pop. density:** 828.5 per sq mi, 319.9 per sq km. **Urban:** 76.0%. **Ethnic groups:** mestizo 86.3%, white 12.7%. **Languages:** Spanish (official), Nawat. **Religions:** Christian 96.3% (Catholic 64.4%, independent 16.6%, Protestant 15.3%), agnostic 2.9%.

Geography: Total area: 8,124 sq mi, 21,041 sq km (150); **Land area:** 8,000 sq mi, 20,721 sq km. **Location:** Central America. Guatemala on W, Honduras on N. **Topography:** A hot Pacific coastal plain in S rises to a cooler plateau and valley region, densely populated. The N is mountainous with many volcanoes. **Arable land:** 34.8%. **Capital:** San Salvador, 1,123,376.

Government: Type: Presidential republic. **Head of state and govt.:** Pres. Nayib Bukele; b. 1981; in office: June 1, 2019. **Local divisions:** 14 departments. **Defense budget:** $251 mil. **Active troops:** 24,500.

Economy: Industries: food proc., beverages, petroleum, chemicals, fertilizer, textiles, furniture, light metals. **Chief agric.:** sugarcane, maize, milk, chicken, beans, sorghum. **Natural resources:** hydropower, geothermal power, petroleum. **Water:** 4,160 cu m per capita. **Electricity prod.:** 6.4 bil kWh. **Labor force:** agric. 15.0%, industry 23.4%, services 61.6%. **Unemployment:** 2.8%.

Finance: Monetary unit: Colon (SVC) (8.75 = $1 U.S.). **GDP:** $79.8 bil; **per capita GDP:** $12,542; **GDP growth:** 3.5%. **Imports:** $17.0 bil; U.S. 30%, China 16%, Guatemala 12%, Mexico 8%, Honduras 6%. **Exports:** $10.6 bil; U.S. 38%, Guatemala 16%, Honduras 16%, Nicaragua 7%. **Tourism:** $2.8 bil. **Budget:** $7.3 bil. **Inflation:** 4.1%.

Transport: Railways: 8 mi. **Motor vehicles:** 53.8 per 1,000 pop. **Airports:** 27.

Communications: Mobile (2022): 183.2 per 100 pop. **Broadband** (2022): 75.5 per 100 pop. **Internet:** 62.9%.

Health: Expend.: 9.7%. **Life expect.:** 72.4 male; 79.5 female. **Births:** 17.1 per 1,000 pop. **Deaths:** 5.9 per 1,000 pop. **Infant mortality:** 11.7 per 1,000 live births. **Undernourished:** 6.8%. **HIV:** 0.5%. **COVID-19:** 4,230 deaths; rates per 100,000: 3,113 cases, 65 deaths. 68% vaccinated.

Education: Compulsory: ages 1-15. **Literacy:** 90.0%.

Website: www.presidencia.gob.sv

El Salvador became independent of Spain in 1821 and of the Central American Federation in 1839.

After a military coup in 1979, a military-civilian junta failed to quell a rebellion by leftist insurgents, armed by Cuba and Nicaragua. Right-wing death squads killed thousands of suspected leftists in the 1980s. The U.S. supported the government with military aid. After taking the lives of some 75,000 people (with thousands more "disappeared"), the civil war ended Jan. 16, 1992, as the government and leftist rebels signed a peace treaty.

The right-wing ARENA party held the presidency, 1989-2009, and the leftist FMLN, 2009-19. Rejecting both major parties, voters elected Nayib Bukele, who pledged to reduce corruption, in the Feb. 3, 2019, presidential election. Bukele's party and allies won a sweeping victory in Feb. 28, 2021, legislative elections.

Beginning in 2013, tens of thousands of migrants or asylum seekers from El Salvador tried to enter the U.S. from Mexico; many were fleeing widespread gang violence. Amid continuing violence, the Legislative Assembly, Mar. 2022, granted the government emergency powers, including suspension of civil liberties. Subsequently, gang violence dropped sharply, but more than 80,000 people had been arrested by mid-2024, amid hundreds of suspicious deaths in prisons and reports of arbitrary arrests as well as physical abuse. Bukele won reelection, Feb. 4, 2024, with 85% of the vote, and his party won 90% of legislative seats (opposition parties charged fraud).

Equatorial Guinea

Republic of Equatorial Guinea

People: Population: 1,795,834 (150). **Age distrib.:** <15: 35.6%; 65+: 5.0%. **Growth:** 3.2%. **Migrants:** 16.4%. **Pop. density:** 165.8 per sq mi, 64.0 per sq km. **Urban:** 74.9%. **Ethnic groups:** Fang 78.1%, Bubi 9.4%, Ndowe 2.8%, Nanguedambo 2.7%. **Languages:** Spanish, French, Portuguese (all official); Fang, Bubi. **Religions:** Christian 88.1% (Catholic 82.3%), Muslim 4.1% (Sunni), agnostic 3.9%.

Geography: Total area: 10,831 sq mi, 28,051 sq km (142); **Land area:** 10,831 sq mi, 28,051 sq km. **Location:** Bioko Isl. off W Africa coast in Gulf of Guinea. Rio Muni, mainland enclave, has Gabon on S, Cameroon on E and N. **Topography:** Bioko Isl. consists of 2 volcanic mountains and connecting valley. Rio Muni, with over 90% of area, has coastal plain and low hills. **Arable land:** 1.9%. **Capital:** Malabo, 296,770. **Cities:** Bata, 493,731.

Government: Type: Presidential republic. **Head of state:** Pres. Teodoro Obiang Nguema Mbasogo; b. 1942; in office: Aug. 3, 1979. **Head of govt.:** Prime Min. Manuela Roka Botey; in office: Feb. 1, 2023. **Local divisions:** 8 provinces. **Defense budget:** NA. **Active troops:** 1,750.

Economy: Industries: petroleum, nat. gas, sawmilling. **Chief agric.:** sweet potatoes, cassava, plantains, oil palm fruit, root vegetables, bananas. **Natural resources:** petroleum, nat. gas, timber, gold, bauxite, diamonds, tantalum, sand and gravel, clay. **Water:** 15,907 cu m per capita. **Crude oil reserves:** 1.1 bil bbls. **Electricity prod.:** 1.5 bil kWh. **Labor force:** agric. 55.5%, industry 13.1%, services 31.3%. **Unemployment:** 8.7%.

Finance: Monetary unit: Central African CFA Franc (XAF) (587.79 = $1 U.S.). **GDP:** $32.1 bil; **per capita GDP:** $18,724; **GDP growth:** –5.7%. **Imports** (2022): $4.3 bil; Zambia 38%, China 14%, Spain 10%, Nigeria 7%. **Exports** (2022): $6.2 bil; Zambia 21%, Spain 15%, China 15%, India 10%, Italy 6%. **Budget** (2018): $2.5 bil. **Inflation** (2021-22): 4.8%.

Transport: Airports: 7.

Communications: Mobile (2022): 49.5 per 100 pop. **Broadband** (2022): 0.8 per 100 pop. **Internet:** 66.8%.

Health: Expend.: 3.4%. **Life expect.:** 61.6 male; 66.2 female. **Births:** 29.0 per 1,000 pop. **Deaths:** 8.9 per 1,000 pop. **Infant mortality:** 77.4 per 1,000 live births. **Undernourished:** NA. **HIV:** NA. **COVID-19:** 183 deaths; rates per 100,000: 1,221 cases, 13 deaths. 15% vaccinated.

Education: Compulsory: ages 7-12. **Literacy:** 95.3%.
Website: www.guineaecuatorialpress.com

Fernando Po (now Bioko) Island was reached by Portugal in the late 15th cent. and ceded to Spain in 1778. Independence came Oct. 12, 1968. Anti-Spanish riots erupted in 1969 in Rio Muni province on the mainland.

Masie Nguema Biyogo, a mainlander, became president for life in 1972. His reign, among the most brutal in Africa, left the nation bankrupt; most of the nation's 7,000 Europeans emigrated. He was ousted in a military coup, Aug. 1979. Teodoro Obiang Nguema Mbasogo, leader of the coup, became president. Presidential elections in 1996, 2002, 2009, 2016, and 2022 were seriously flawed.

The economy is dependent on oil exports. As a result of government misuse and embezzlement of oil revenue, poverty remains widespread.

Human Rights Watch reported in 2012 that the regime "tortures and arbitrarily detains" dissidents. The seat of government was officially moved, Feb. 2017, from Malabo (on Bioko) to Ciudad de la Paz on the mainland. Obiang, Jan. 31, 2023, named Manuela Roka Botey the country's first female prime min.

Eritrea

State of Eritrea

People: Population: 6,343,956 (110). **Age distrib.:** <15: 35.7%; 65+: 4.0%. **Growth:** 1.1%. **Migrants:** 0.4%. **Pop. density:** 162.7 per sq mi, 62.8 per sq km. **Urban:** 43.9%. **Ethnic groups:** Tigrinya 50%, Tigre 30%, Saho 4%, Afar 4%, Kunama 4%, Bilen 3%, Hedareb/Beja 2%, Nara 2%. **Languages:** Tigrinya, Arabic, English (all official); Tigre, Kunama, Afar. **Religions:** Muslim 53.6% (Sunni 52%), Christian 44.2% (Orthodox 37.6%).

Geography: Total area: 45,406 sq mi, 117,600 sq km (99); **Land area:** 38,996 sq mi, 101,000 sq km. **Location:** E Africa, on SW coast of Red Sea. Sudan on W, Ethiopia on S, Djibouti on SE. **Topography:** Includes many islands of Dahlak Archipelago. Low coastal plains in S, mountain range with peaks to 9,000 ft in N. **Arable land:** 5.7%. **Capital:** Asmara, 1,111,748.

Government: Type: Presidential republic. **Head of state and govt.:** Pres. Isaias Afwerki; b. 1946; in office: June 8, 1993. **Local divisions:** 6 regions. **Defense budget:** NA. **Active troops:** 301,750.

Economy: Industries: food proc., beverages, clothing and textiles, light mfg., salt, cement. **Chief agric.:** sorghum, milk, barley, vegetables, root vegetables, cereals. **Natural resources:** gold, potash, zinc, copper, salt, fish. **Water:** 2,021 cu m per capita. **Electricity prod.:** 387.7 mil kWh. **Labor force:** agric. 64.0%, industry 9.0%, services 27.0%. **Unemployment:** 5.9%.

Finance: Monetary unit: Nakfa (ERN) (15.00 = $1 U.S.). **GDP:** NA; **per capita GDP:** NA; **GDP growth:** NA. **Imports** (2017): $1.1 bil; China 34%, UAE 26%, Turkey (Türkiye) 12%, U.S. 7%. **Exports** (2017): $624.3 mil; China 52%, UAE 33%, South Korea 9%. **Budget** (2018): $549 mil. **Inflation** (2016-17): 9%.

Transport: Railways: 190 mi. **Airports:** 10.

Communications: Mobile (2022): 59.1 per 100 pop. **Broadband** (2022): 29.2 per 100 pop. **Internet:** 26.6%.

Health: Expend.: 4.2%. **Life expect.:** 64.9 male; 70.2 female. **Births:** 26.3 per 1,000 pop. **Deaths:** 6.5 per 1,000 pop. **Infant mortality:** 39.8 per 1,000 live births. **Undernourished:** NA. **HIV:** 0.4%. **COVID-19:** 103 deaths; rates per 100,000: 287 cases, 3 deaths.

Education: Compulsory: ages 6-13. **Literacy:** 76.6%.
Website: shabait.com

Eritrea was part of the Ethiopian kingdom of Aksum. It was an Italian colony from 1890 to 1941, when it was captured by the British. Following a period of British and UN supervision, Eritrea was awarded to Ethiopia as part of a federation in 1952. Ethiopia annexed Eritrea as a province in 1962. After a 31-year struggle, Eritrea formally declared its independence May 24, 1993. A constitution was ratified in 1997 but not implemented.

A border war with Ethiopia erupted in June 1998. Although a peace treaty was signed Dec. 12, 2000, border disputes and tensions continued. Agreements signed July 9, 2018, ended the "state of war between Ethiopia and Eritrea" and restored diplomatic relations as well as communications, transportation, and commercial links.

Many thousands have fled repressive conditions and forced labor in Eritrea. Tens of thousands of Eritreans were among migrants reaching or trying to reach Europe beginning in 2014. Thousands migrated to Ethiopia after the border reopened in 2018.

Beginning in 2020, Eritrean troops fought in northern Ethiopia, assisting government forces fighting Tigrayan rebels. Eritrean soldiers were widely accused of atrocities against civilians. After a Nov. 2022 peace deal between the Ethiopian government and Tigray rebels, Eritrean troops remained in parts of northern Ethiopia in 2024.

Estonia

Republic of Estonia

People: Population: 1,193,791 (156). **Age distrib.:** <15: 15.2%; 65+: 22.6%. **Growth:** –0.8%. **Migrants:** 15.0%. **Pop. density:** 72.9 per sq mi, 28.2 per sq km. **Urban:** 70.0%. **Ethnic groups:** Estonian 69.1%, Russian 23.7%, Ukrainian 2.1%. **Languages:** Estonian (official), Russian. **Religions:** agnostic 58.1%, Christian 36.8% (Orthodox 18.2%, Protestant 16.5%), atheist 4.6%.

Geography: Total area: 17,463 sq mi, 45,228 sq km (129); **Land area:** 16,366 sq mi, 42,388 sq km. **Location:** Eastern Europe, bordering Baltic Sea and Gulf of Finland. Russia on E, Latvia on S. **Topography:** Marshy lowland with numerous lakes and swamps. Elongated hills show evidence of former glaciation. More than 800 islands on Baltic coast. **Arable land:** 16.5%. **Capital:** Tallinn, 456,184.

Government: Type: Parliamentary republic. **Head of state:** Pres. Alar Karis; b. 1958; in office: Oct. 11, 2021. **Head of govt.:** Prime Min. Kaja Kallas; b. 1977; in office: Jan. 26, 2021. **Local divisions:** 15 urban municipalities, 64 rural municipalities. **Defense budget:** $1.2 bil. **Active troops:** 7,100.

Economy: Industries: food, engineering, electronics, wood/wood prods., textiles, information tech., telecom. **Chief agric.:** wheat, milk, barley, rapeseed, oats, peas. **Natural resources:** oil shale, peat, rare earth elements, phosphorite, clay, limestone, sand, dolomite, sea mud. **Water:** 9,638 cu m per capita. **Electricity prod.:** 7.0 bil kWh. **Labor force:** agric. 2.6%, industry 28.6%, services 68.8%. **Unemployment:** 6.3%.

Finance: Monetary unit: Euro (EUR) (0.90 = $1 U.S.). **GDP:** $66.9 bil; **per capita GDP:** $48,992; **GDP growth:** –3.0%. **Imports:** $31.7 bil; Finland 13%, Germany 10%, Lithuania 8%, Latvia 8%, Russia 8%. **Exports:** $31.9 bil; Finland 13%, Latvia 12%, Sweden 8%, Lithuania 7%, Russia 6%. **Tourism:** $1.5 bil. **Budget:** $12.3 bil. **Inflation:** 9.2%.

Transport: Railways: 895 mi. **Airports:** 26.

Communications: Mobile: 150.2 per 100 pop. **Broadband:** 189 per 100 pop. **Internet** (2023): 93.2%.

Health: Expend. (2022): 6.9%. **Life expect.:** 73.8 male; 83.2 female. **Births:** 8.2 per 1,000 pop. **Deaths:** 13.2 per 1,000 pop. **Infant mortality:** 3.3 per 1,000 live births. **Undernourished:** <2.5%. **HIV:** 0.8%. **COVID-19:** 2,998 deaths; rates per 100,000: 45,935 cases, 226 deaths. 63% vaccinated.

Education: Compulsory: ages 7-15. **Literacy:** 99.9%.
Website: www.eesti.ee

Estonia, a province of imperial Russia before World War I, was independent between World Wars I and II. The USSR conquered it in 1940 and incorporated it as the Estonian SSR. Estonia, Aug. 20, 1991, declared independence, which the Soviet Union recognized Sept. 1991. The first free elections in over 50 years were held Sept. 20, 1992. The last occupying Russian troops departed Aug. 31, 1994.

Estonia became a full member of the EU and NATO, 2004, and adopted the euro, 2011.

The Reform Party's Kaja Kallas became, Jan. 26, 2021, Estonia's first post-Soviet female prime minister. Alar Karis, backed by Kallas, was elected president by parliament, Aug. 31, 2021. Kallas's Reform Party won Mar. 5, 2023, elections. After Kallas resigned, July 15, 2024, to take the EU's top foreign policy post, Kristen Michal of the Reform Party succeeded her July 23, 2024.

An act of parliament effective Jan. 1, 2024, legalized same-sex marriage.

Following Russia's Feb. 2022 invasion of Ukraine, a June 2022 NATO summit agreed to strengthen forces defending Estonia. Estonia provided weapons to Ukraine and, as of Aug. 30, 2024, hosted over 36,000 Ukrainian refugees.

Eswatini

Kingdom of Eswatini

(King Mswati III announced, Apr. 19, 2018, that he was changing the country's name from Swaziland to "Eswatini" to celebrate the 50th anniversary of its independence.)

People: Population: 1,138,089 (157). **Age distrib.:** <15: 31.6%; 65+: 4.0%. **Growth:** 0.7%. **Migrants:** 2.8%. **Pop. density:** 171.3 per sq mi, 66.2 per sq km. **Urban:** 25.0%. **Ethnic groups:** predom. Swazi; smaller pops. of Zulu, people of European ancestry. **Languages:** English (used in govt.), siSwati (both official). **Religions:** Christian 87.9% (independent 65.8%, Protestant 16.6%, Catholic 5.6%), ethnic religionist 9.6%.

Geography: Total area: 6,704 sq mi, 17,364 sq km (154); **Land area:** 6,643 sq mi, 17,204 sq km. **Location:** Southern Africa, near Indian O. coast. South Africa on N, W, S; Mozambique on E. **Topography:** Descends W-E in broad belts, becoming more arid in low veld region, then rising to plateau in E. **Arable land:** 10.3%. **Capital:** Mbabane (administrative), 68,010; Lobamba (legislative).

Government: Type: Absolute monarchy. **Head of state:** King Mswati III; b. 1968; in office: Apr. 25, 1986. **Head of govt.:** Prime Min. Russell Dlamini; in office: Nov. 6, 2023. **Local divisions:** 4 regions. **Defense budget/active troops:** NA.

Economy: Industries: soft drink concentrates, coal, forestry, sugar proc., textiles, apparel. **Chief agric.:** sugarcane, maize, root vegetables, grapefruits, oranges, milk. **Natural resources:** asbestos, coal, clay, cassiterite, hydropower, forests, small gold/diamond deposits, quarry stone, talc. **Water:** 3,783 cu m per capita.

Electricity prod.: 585.9 mil kWh. **Labor force:** agric. 13.4%, industry 24.0%, services 62.6%. **Unemployment:** 37.6%.

Finance: Monetary unit: Lilangeni (SZL) (17.75 = $1 U.S.). **GDP:** $14.2 bil; **per capita GDP:** $11,741; **GDP growth:** 4.8%. **Imports** (2022): $2.3 bil; South Africa 76%. **Exports** (2022): $2.1 bil; South Africa 66%, Kenya 5%. **Tourism** (2022): $11 mil. **Budget** (2020): $1.5 bil. **Inflation** (2018-19): 2.6%.

Transport: Railways: 187 mi. **Airports:** 16.

Communications: Mobile: 123.5 per 100 pop. **Broadband:** 103 per 100 pop. **Internet:** 58.3%.

Health: Expend.: 7.0%. **Life expect.:** 58.7 male; 62.8 female. **Births:** 22.3 per 1,000 pop. **Deaths:** 9.4 per 1,000 pop. **Infant mortality:** 36.7 per 1,000 live births. **Undernourished:** 12.4%. **HIV:** 25.1%. **COVID-19:** 1,427 deaths; rates per 100,000: 6,495 cases, 123 deaths. 37% vaccinated.

Education: Compulsory: ages 6-12. **Literacy:** 89.3%.

Website: www.gov.sz

The royal house of Eswatini traces back 400 years. The Zulus drove the Swazis, a Bantu people, from lands to the N, 1820. Britain and Transvaal (later part of South Africa) later guaranteed their autonomy, and Britain assumed control after 1903. Independence came Sept. 6, 1968. In 1973, the king repealed the constitution and assumed full powers.

A new constitution banning political parties took effect Oct. 13, 1978. Under a revised constitution effective Feb. 8, 2006, non-partisan parliamentary elections were permitted. The pro-democracy People's United Democratic Movement (PU-DEMO) was outlawed as a terrorist group in 2008. Anti-monarchy protests and looting in mid-2021 were suppressed.

In recent decades, Eswatini has suffered from an AIDS epidemic. AIDS-related deaths and new HIV infections fell sharply due to antiretroviral medications, but as of 2022, almost 26% of adults were HIV positive, the highest rate in the world.

Ethiopia

Federal Democratic Republic of Ethiopia

People: Population: 118,550,298 (12). **Age distrib.:** <15: 38.7%; 65+: 3.4%. **Growth:** 2.4%. **Migrants:** 0.9%. **Pop. density:** 280.0 per sq mi, 108.1 per sq km. **Urban:** 23.7%. **Ethnic groups:** Oromo 35.8%, Amhara 24.1%, Somali 7.2%, Tigray 5.7%, Sidama 4.1%, Guragie 2.6%, Welaita 2.3%, Afar 2.2%. **Languages:** Oromo (official regional working lang.); Amharic (official nationally); Somali, Tigrigna (both official regional working langs.); Sidamo, Wolaytta, Gurage. **Religions:** Christian 61.4% (Orthodox 39.5%, Protestant 19.0%), Muslim 32.8% (Sunni), ethnic religionist 5.7%.

Geography: Total area: 426,373 sq mi, 1,104,300 sq km (26); **Land area:** 423,388 sq mi, 1,096,570 sq km. **Location:** E Africa. Sudan, South Sudan on W; Kenya on S; Somalia, Djibouti on E; Eritrea on N. **Topography:** A central plateau, 6,000-10,000 ft high, rises to mountains near the Great Rift Valley, cutting in from SW. Blue Nile and other rivers cross the plateau, which descends to plains on W and SE. **Arable land:** 14.5%. **Capital:** Addis Ababa, 5,703,628.

Government: Type: Federal parliamentary republic. **Head of state:** Pres. Sahle-Work Zewde; b. 1950; in office: Oct. 25, 2018. **Head of govt.:** Prime Min. Abiy Ahmed; b. 1976; in office: Apr. 2, 2018. **Local divisions:** 12 regional states (ethnically based), 2 chartered cities. **Defense budget:** $1.5 bil. **Active troops:** 503,000.

Economy: Industries: food proc., beverages, textiles, leather, garments, chemicals, metals proc., cement. **Chief agric.:** maize, wheat, cereals, sorghum, milk, barley. **Natural resources:** gold, platinum, copper, potash, nat. gas, hydropower. **Water:** 1,014 cu m per capita. **Crude oil reserves:** 428,000 bbls. **Electricity prod.:** 15.4 bil kWh. **Labor force:** agric. 62.8%, industry 6.5%, services 30.7%. **Unemployment:** 3.5%.

Finance: Monetary unit: Birr (ETB) (108.41 = $1 U.S.). **GDP:** $393.4 bil; **per capita GDP:** $3,109; **GDP growth:** 6.5%. **Imports:** $23.0 bil; China 24%, U.S. 9%, India 8%, UAE 6%. **Exports:** $10.9 bil; UAE 17%, U.S. 13%, Germany 6%, Saudi Arabia 6%, Somalia 6%. **Tourism** (2022): $1.2 bil. **Budget** (2020): $14.0 bil. **Inflation:** 30.2%.

Transport: Railways: 409 mi (Ethiopian segment of Addis Ababa-Djibouti railroad). **Motor vehicles:** 2.0 per 1,000 pop. **Airports:** 57.

Communications: Mobile (2022): 57.0 per 100 pop. **Broadband** (2022): 26.5 per 100 pop. **Internet:** 19.4%.

Health: Expend.: 3.2%. **Life expect.:** 65.4 male; 70.0 female. **Births:** 29.6 per 1,000 pop. **Deaths:** 5.8 per 1,000 pop. **Infant mortality:** 32.6 per 1,000 live births. **Undernourished:** 22.2%. **HIV:** 0.7%. **COVID-19:** 7,574 deaths; rates per 100,000: 436 cases, 7 deaths. 38% vaccinated.

Education: Compulsory: ages 7-14. **Literacy:** 51.8%.

Website: www.ethiopia.gov.et

Ethiopian culture was influenced by Egypt and Greece. Italy invaded the region in 1880, but Ethiopia maintained its independence until the Italian invasion of 1936. British forces freed the country in 1941.

A series of droughts in the 1970s killed hundreds of thousands. An army mutiny, strikes, and student demonstrations led to the 1974 dethronement of Ethiopia's Emperor, Haile Selassie I, ending his 58-year reign. The ruling junta, known as the Dergue, dissolved parliament, abolished the monarchy, established a socialist state, redistributed land, curbed the influence of the Coptic Church, and violently suppressed opposition.

The regime, torn by bloody coups, faced uprisings by tribal and political groups aided in part by Sudan and Somalia. In 1978, Soviet advisers and Cuban troops helped defeat Somali forces. Ethiopia and Somalia signed a peace agreement in 1988. A worldwide relief effort began in 1984, as an extended drought precipitated famine; up to 1 mil people died.

The Ethiopian People's Revolutionary Democratic Front (EPRDF) launched a major push against government forces in 1991, prompting Pres. Mengistu Haile Mariam's resignation. The EPRDF set up a transitional government. It won five parliamentary elections, 1995-2015.

Eritrea, a province on the Red Sea, declared its independence May 24, 1993. Fighting along the border with Eritrea, which erupted in 1998, intensified in May 2000. Although a peace treaty was signed Dec. 12, 2000, tensions and border conflicts persisted until a July 9, 2018, accord.

Violent protests by members of the Oromo ethnic group claimed hundreds of lives in 2016. Successive droughts caused severe food shortages in 2015-17, affecting about 18 mil people. Amid continuing ethnic violence in eastern Ethiopia and anti-government protests, Prime Min. Hailemariam Desalegn resigned, Feb. 15, 2018. New Prime Min. Abiy Ahmed, the country's first Oromo leader, implemented some economic and political reforms. For his domestic policies and 2018 peace accord with Eritrea, Abiy was awarded the Nobel Peace Prize, Oct. 11, 2019. However, political repression subsequently increased.

Elected by parliament, Oct. 25, 2018, Sahle-Work Zewde became Ethiopia's first female president.

A Nov. 2020 attack on a military base in the opposition-controlled northern Tigray region led to a large-scale government offensive against the Tigray People's Liberation Front (TPLF). As fighting continued, widespread atrocities against civilians were reported. A TPLF offensive pushed back government troops in mid-2021. By then, hundreds of thousands in Tigray faced famine, as drought plagued the region and the Abiy government reportedly blocked aid shipments. TPLF forces advanced into the neighboring Amhara and Afar regions, before being largely beaten back by government troops and allied militias. After two years of war in which hundreds of thousands died and millions were displaced, negotiations in South Africa produced a Nov. 2, 2022, cease-fire agreement, calling for disarmament of Tigrayan rebels and the free flow of humanitarian aid into Tigray.

A government crackdown began in May 2022 against militia forces in Amhara, though activists were also swept up. Mid-2022 massacres in the Oromia region were blamed on the rebel Oromo Liberation Army (OLA), which denied responsibility. Government-rebel fighting in Amhara and Oromia, as well as atrocities against civilians, continued in 2023-24.

As a result of drought and conflict, some 13 mil people nationwide faced food insecurity in mid-2024; 4.5 mil Ethiopians were internally displaced.

Ethiopia began construction, Apr. 2, 2011, of Africa's largest dam, the Grand Renaissance Dam across the Blue Nile. Power generation began in 2022.

Fiji

Republic of Fiji

People: Population: 951,611 (159). **Age distrib.:** <15: 24.7%; 65+: 8.9%. **Growth:** 0.4%. **Migrants:** 1.6%. **Pop. density:** 134.9 per sq mi, 52.1 per sq km. **Urban:** 59.2%. **Ethnic groups:** iTaukei (predom. Melanesian with Polynesian admixture) 56.8%, Indo-Fijian 37.5%. **Languages:** English, iTaukei, Fiji Hindi (all official). **Religions:** Christian 64.3% (Protestant 40.5%, independent 12.0%, Catholic 11.8%), Hindu 27.4% (Shaivite 11%, Vaishnavite 10%), Muslim 6.1% (Sunni).

Geography: Total area: 7,056 sq mi, 18,274 sq km (152); **Land area:** 7,056 sq mi, 18,274 sq km. Viti Levu, largest island of group, has over half the total land area. **Location:** Western S Pacific O. Nearest neighbors are Vanuatu to W, Tonga to E. **Topography:** 322 isls. (about 110 inhabited), many mountainous, with tropical forests and large fertile areas. **Arable land:** 4.2%. **Capital:** Suva, 178,339.

Government: Type: Parliamentary republic. **Head of state:** Pres. Wiliame Katonivere; b. 1964; in office: Nov. 12, 2021. **Head of govt.:** Prime Min. Sitiveni Rabuka; b. 1948; in office: Dec. 24, 2022. **Local divisions:** 14 provinces, 1 dependency. **Defense budget:** $49 mil. **Active troops:** 4,040.

Economy: Industries: tourism, sugar proc., clothing, copra. **Chief agric.:** sugarcane, cassava, taro, chicken, vegetables, coconuts. **Natural resources:** timber, fish, gold, copper, hydropower. **Water:** 30,878 cu m per capita. **Electricity prod.:** 1.0 bil kWh. **Labor force:** agric. 28.8%, industry 14.2%, services 57.0%. **Unemployment:** 4.3%.

Finance: Monetary unit: Dollar (FJD) (2.20 = $1 U.S.). **GDP:** $14.1 bil; **per capita GDP:** $15,047; **GDP growth:** 8.0%. **Imports** (2022): $3.4 bil; Singapore 23%, China 16%, Australia 13%, New Zealand 11%, South Korea 8%. **Exports** (2022): $2.4 bil; U.S. 39%, Australia 11%, Tonga 5%, New Zealand 5%. **Tourism:** $1.1 bil. **Budget** (2020): $1.5 bil. **Inflation** (2021-22): 4.5%.

Transport: Railways: 371 mi. **Motor vehicles:** 152.3 per 1,000 pop. **Airports:** 26.

Communications: Mobile (2022): 111.7 per 100 pop. **Broadband** (2022): 81.4 per 100 pop. **Internet:** 85.2%.

Health: Expend.: 5.4%. **Life expect.:** 72.2 male; 77.6 female. **Births:** 15.9 per 1,000 pop. **Deaths:** 6.5 per 1,000 pop. **Infant mortality:** 9.7 per 1,000 live births. **Undernourished:** 7.8%. **HIV:** 0.4%. **COVID-19:** 885 deaths; rates per 100,000: 7,702 cases, 99 deaths. 72% vaccinated.

Education: Compulsory: NA. **Literacy:** 99.1%.

Website: www.fiji.gov.fj

A British colony since 1874, Fiji became independent Oct. 10, 1970. Cultural differences between Indo-Fijians (mostly descendants of contract laborers brought to the islands from India in the 19th cent.) and Indigenous Fijians have led to political tensions. More than 100,000 people of Indian descent left Fiji after a 1987 coup deposed an Indo-Fijian-majority government.

The country's first Indo-Fijian prime minister, Mahendra Chaudhry, and other government officials were taken captive May 19, 2000, by Indigenous Fijian gunmen, culminating in a military takeover, May 29, led by Frank Bainimarama. An interim military-backed government was installed in July 2000. Prime Min. Laisenia Qarase headed an elected civilian government, 2001-06, but was ousted in a military coup Dec. 5, 2006. Bainimarama took office as interim prime min. After a court ruled in 2009 that the 2006 coup was illegal, Fiji's president abrogated the constitution, dissolved the judiciary, and reappointed Bainimarama. He accepted a new draft constitution released Mar. 22, 2013, and he retained office in democratic elections Sept. 17, 2014. Bainimarama's party narrowly won Nov. 18, 2018, elections.

The COVID-19 pandemic severely hurt the important tourism industry in 2020-21.

In Dec. 14, 2022, elections, Bainimarama's party lost its majority. Opposition parties formed a coalition government, and Sitiveni Rabuka became prime minister Dec. 24, 2022. On June 14, 2023, Fiji signed a defense agreement with New Zealand, seen as a move to counter growing Chinese influence in the Pacific.

Finland
Republic of Finland

People: Population: 5,626,414 (117). **Age distrib.:** <15: 16.2%; 65+: 23.5%. **Growth:** 0.2%. **Migrants:** 7.0%. **Pop. density:** 48.0 per sq mi, 18.5 per sq km. **Urban:** 85.9%. **Ethnic groups:** Finnish, Swedish, Russian, Estonian, Romani, Sami. **Languages:** Finnish, Swedish (both official). **Religions:** Christian 75.8% (Protestant 73.5%), agnostic 16.6%, Muslim 4.0% (Sunni 3%), atheist 1.9%.

Geography: Total area: 130,559 sq mi, 338,145 sq km (64); **Land area:** 117,304 sq mi, 303,815 sq km. **Location:** Northern Europe. Norway on N, Sweden on W, Russia on E. **Topography:** Flat with low hills and many lakes in S and center. The N has mountainous areas 3,000-4,000 ft above sea level. **Arable land:** 7.4%. **Capital:** Helsinki, 1,346,810.

Government: Type: Parliamentary republic. **Head of state:** Pres. Alexander Stubb; b. 1968; in office: Mar. 1, 2024. **Head of govt.:** Prime Min. Petteri Orpo; b. 1969; in office: June 20, 2023. **Local divisions:** 19 regions. **Defense budget:** $6.6 bil. **Active troops:** 23,850.

Economy: Industries: metals/metal prods., electronics, machinery and scientific instruments, shipbuilding, pulp and paper, foodstuffs, chemicals, textiles. **Chief agric.:** milk, barley, oats, wheat, potatoes, sugar beets. **Natural resources:** timber, iron ore, copper, lead, zinc, chromite, nickel, gold, silver, limestone. **Water:** 19,870 cu m per capita. **Electricity prod.:** 70.2 bil kWh. **Labor force:** agric. 3.8%, industry 21.4%, services 74.8%. **Unemployment:** 7.2%.

Finance: Monetary unit: Euro (EUR) (0.90 = $1 U.S.). **GDP:** $363.3 bil; **per capita GDP:** $65,061; **GDP growth:** –1.0%. **Imports:** $124.2 bil; Sweden 15%, Germany 14%, China 8%, Norway 7%, Netherlands 6%. **Exports:** $123.0 bil; Germany 11%, U.S. 10%, Sweden 10%, Netherlands 7%, China 5%. **Tourism:** $2.7 bil. **Budget** (2020): $153.6 bil (central govt.). **Inflation:** 6.3%.

Transport: Railways: 3,677 mi. **Motor vehicles:** 569.1 per 1,000 pop. **Airports:** 98.

Communications: Mobile: 127.5 per 100 pop. **Broadband:** 159 per 100 pop. **Internet** (2023): 93.5%.

Health: Expend.: 10.3%. **Life expect.:** 79.3 male; 85.2 female. **Births:** 10.2 per 1,000 pop. **Deaths:** 10.4 per 1,000 pop. **Infant mortality:** 2.1 per 1,000 live births. **Undernourished:** <2.5%. **HIV:** NA. **COVID-19:** 11,466 deaths; rates per 100,000: 27,143 cases, 208 deaths. 79% vaccinated.

Education: Compulsory: ages 6-17. **Literacy:** NA.

Website: valtioneuvosto.fi

Early Finns may have migrated from the Ural region and other areas about 6,000 years ago. Swedish settlers brought the country into Sweden, 1154 to 1809, when Finland became an autonomous grand duchy of the Russian Empire. On Dec. 6, 1917, Finland declared its independence, and in 1919 it became a republic. On Nov. 30, 1939, the Soviet Union invaded, and Finland was forced to cede 16,173 sq mi of territory. After World War II, further cessions were exacted.

Finland entered the EU Jan. 1, 1995. More than 32,000 migrants applied for asylum in Finland in 2015. The government, 2016, announced it would deport rejected applicants and concluded agreements with Russia to reduce border crossings.

The Social Democratic Party (SDP) won Apr. 14, 2019, parliamentary elections and formed a coalition government. The SDP's Sanna Marin became prime minister, Dec. 10, after her predecessor resigned.

Following Russia's Feb. 2022 invasion of Ukraine, Finland applied to join NATO; it was officially admitted Apr. 4, 2023.

The conservative National Coalition Party won Apr. 2, 2023, elections. Party leader Petteri Orpo formed a coalition government, including the right-wing, anti-immigration Finns Party, and became prime minister June 20, 2023. Alexander Stubb, of Orpo's party, was elected president, Feb. 11, 2024.

Aland, or Ahvenanmaa, an autonomous, Swedish-speaking province, is a group of small islands, 590 sq mi, in the Gulf of Bothnia, 25 mi from Sweden, 15 mi from Finland. Mariehamn is the chief port and seat of government. **Website:** www.aland.ax

France
French Republic

People: Population: 68,374,591 (22). **Age distrib.:** <15: 17.3%; 65+: 22.0%. **Growth:** 0.2%. **Migrants:** 13.1%. **Pop. density:** 276.5 per sq mi, 106.8 per sq km. **Urban:** 82.0%. **Ethnic groups:** Celtic and Latin with Teutonic, Slavic, North African (Algerian, Moroccan, Tunisian), Indochinese, Basque minorities. **Languages:** French (official), declining regional dialects and langs. (Provençal, Breton, Alsatian, Corsican, Catalan, Basque, Flemish, Occitan, Picard). **Religions:** Christian 62.2% (Catholic 58.0%), agnostic 19.9%, Muslim 11.2% (Sunni), atheist 4.2%.

Geography: Total area: 248,573 sq mi, 643,801 sq km (incl. overseas departments) (43); **Land area:** 247,270 sq mi, 640,427 sq km (incl. overseas departments). **Location:** Western Europe, between Atlantic O. and Medit. Sea. Spain, Andorra, Monaco on S; Italy, Switzerland, Germany on E; Luxembourg, Belgium on N. **Topography:** A wide plain covers more than half of the country, in N and W, drained to W by Seine, Loire, Garonne Rivers. The Alps (Mt. Blanc is tallest in W Europe at 15,781 ft), the lower Jura range, and forested Vosges are in E. The Rhone flows from Lake Geneva to Mediterranean. Pyrenees are on SW border. **Arable land:** 34.1%. **Capital:** Paris, 11,276,701. **Cities:** Lyon, 1,774,395; Marseille-Aix-en-Provence, 1,635,707; Lille, 1,085,199; Toulouse, 1,070,746; Bordeaux, 1,009,594.

Government: Type: Semi-presidential republic. **Head of state:** Pres. Emmanuel Macron; b. 1977; in office: May 14, 2017. **Head of govt.:** Prime Min. Michel Barnier; b. 1951; in office: Sept. 5, 2024. **Local divisions:** 13 metropolitan regions, 5 overseas regions. **Defense budget:** $60.0 bil. **Active troops:** 203,850.

Economy: Industries: machinery, chemicals, automobiles, metallurgy, aircraft, electronics, textiles, food proc., tourism. **Chief agric.:** wheat, sugar beets, milk, barley, maize, potatoes. **Natural resources:** coal, iron ore, bauxite, zinc, uranium, antimony, arsenic, potash, feldspar, fluorspar, gypsum, timber, fish. **Water:** 3,270 cu m per capita. **Crude oil reserves:** 62 mil bbls. **Electricity prod.:** 446.3 bil kWh. **Labor force:** agric. 2.6%, industry 19.3%, services 78.2%. **Unemployment:** 7.3%.

Finance: Monetary unit: Euro (EUR) (0.90 = $1 U.S.). **GDP:** $4.2 tril; **per capita GDP:** $61,157; **GDP growth:** 0.7%. **Imports:** $1.1 tril; Germany 15%, Belgium 9%, Spain 8%, Italy 8%, Netherlands 8%. **Exports:** $1.1 tril; Germany 13%, Italy 9%, U.S. 8%, Belgium 8%, Spain 8%. **Tourism:** $68.6 bil. **Budget:** $1.5 tril. **Inflation:** 4.9%.

Transport: Railways: 17,311 mi. **Motor vehicles:** 712.4 per 1,000 pop. **Airports:** 689.

Communications: Mobile: 116.5 per 100 pop. **Broadband:** 109 per 100 pop. **Internet** (2023): 86.8%.

Health: Expend.: 12.3%. **Life expect.:** 79.8 male; 85.5 female. **Births:** 10.9 per 1,000 pop. **Deaths:** 10.0 per 1,000 pop. **Infant mortality:** 3.1 per 1,000 live births. **Undernourished:** <2.5%. **HIV:** 0.3%. **COVID-19:** 168,091 deaths; rates per 100,000: 59,960 cases, 258 deaths. 82% vaccinated.

Education: Compulsory: ages 3-15. **Literacy:** NA.

Website: www.gouvernement.fr

Julius Caesar conquered Celtic Gaul 58-51 bce; Romans ruled for 500 years. Under Charlemagne, Frankish rule extended over much of Europe. After his death (in 814), France emerged as one of the successor kingdoms.

The monarchy was overthrown in the French Revolution (1789-93) and succeeded by the First Republic, followed by the First Empire under Napoleon I (1804-15), a monarchy (1814-48), the Second Republic (1848-52), the Second Empire (1852-70), the Third Republic (1871-1946), the Fourth Republic (1946-58), and the Fifth Republic (1958-present).

France suffered severe losses in people and wealth in WWI (1914-18) when it was invaded by Germany. By the Treaty of Versailles, 1919, France exacted return of Alsace and Lorraine, provinces seized by Germany in 1871 after it defeated France in the Franco-Prussian War. During WWII (1939-45), Germany invaded France in May 1940 and signed an armistice with a government based in Vichy. After the Allies liberated France in 1944, Gen. Charles de Gaulle became head of the provisional government, serving until 1946. De Gaulle again became premier in 1958, during a crisis over Algeria, and obtained voter approval for a new constitution, ushering in the Fifth Republic. He then became president.

France withdrew from Indochina in 1954 and from Morocco and Tunisia in 1956. Most of its remaining African territories, including Algeria, were freed 1958-62.

In May 1968, students in Paris and other centers rioted, battled police, and were joined by workers who launched nationwide strikes. De Gaulle resigned from office in Apr. 1969, after losing a nationwide referendum on constitutional reform. Georges Pompidou was elected to succeed him. After Pompidou's death, in 1974, Valery Giscard d'Estaing was elected president; he continued his predecessors' conservative policies.

In 1981, France elected Socialist François Mitterrand president. Under Mitterrand the government nationalized industries and banks. After 1986, however, when rightists won a narrow victory in the National Assembly, France pursued a privatization program, selling many state-owned companies. Mitterrand won a second 7-year term in 1988.

Conservative Jacques Chirac won the presidency in 1995 and was reelected in 2002. A summer 2003 heat wave caused an est. 15,000 deaths. Parliament gave final approval in 2004 to a law barring the wearing of Islamic head scarves and other religious symbols in public schools. A state of emergency was declared Nov. 8, 2005, after 12 days of riots that began in Paris and spread to some 300 French cities and towns; rioters were mainly young immigrants from N and W Africa.

The conservative Nicolas Sarkozy won the 2007 presidential runoff election. With France's economy struggling, the Socialist François Hollande won a presidential runoff over Sarkozy in 2012. Hollande, May 18, 2013, signed a bill that legalized same-sex marriage and allowed gay couples to adopt children.

After forming a new party in 2016, centrist Emmanuel Macron was elected president, May 7, 2017, defeating Marine Le Pen of the far-right, anti-immigration National Front (renamed National Rally in 2018) in a runoff. Macron pledged reforms to improve GDP growth and reduce unemployment. His party won June 2017 parliamentary elections. Months of large "yellow vest" demonstrations began Nov. 17, 2018, protesting economic conditions. Macron again defeated Le Pen (by a narrower margin) in an Apr. 24, 2022, presidential runoff to win a second term. Macron's party and its allies lost their National Assembly majority in June 2022 elections; the National Rally took 89 seats (a gain of 81). Legislation in 2023 raising the retirement age for many workers sparked months of strikes and demonstrations.

Amid discontent over the economy and immigration, Macron named a new prime minister, Gabriel Attal, Jan. 9, 2024. After the National Rally won the most votes in June European parliament elections, Macron called new National Assembly elections. Following July 7 second-round voting, an alliance of leftist parties had the most seats, followed by Macron's bloc; the National Rally, which again won the largest share of the vote, controlled over 140 seats. No group had a National Assembly majority. Macron rejected the leftist candidate and appointed Michel Barnier, of the fourth-place Republican party, as prime minister Sept. 5, 2024, in hopes of breaking the two-month deadlock amid fervent leftist criticism.

France took part in the U.S.-led campaign of airstrikes against the Sunni extremist group ISIS in Iraq (beginning 2014) and in Syria (beginning 2015). French troops entered the conflict between government forces in Mali and Islamist militants Jan. 11, 2013. France maintained a counterterrorism force in the region, but in the 2020s, France withdrew troops, often in response to requests from some African governments.

On Jan. 7, 2015, two Islamist-extremist French gunmen of Algerian descent attacked the Paris offices of the magazine Charlie Hebdo (which had published satirical images of Muhammad), killing 12 people. A third gunman, who claimed loyalty to ISIS, killed 5 people Jan. 8-9. On Nov. 13, 2015, in coordinated attacks in and near Paris for which ISIS claimed responsibility, terrorists killed 130, many in Paris's Bataclan concert hall. In a July 14, 2016, attack ISIS claimed to have inspired, a Tunisian-born French resident drove a truck through a Bastille Day fireworks crowd in Nice, killing 86.

France ratified, June 15, 2016, a global agreement to reduce greenhouse gas emissions negotiated at a UN climate conference in Paris, Dec. 2015. A fire, Apr. 15, 2019, heavily damaged Paris's Notre-Dame Cathedral, largely built in the 12th and 13th cents. Extreme summer heat, linked by many scientists to climate change, gripped the country in 2019 and the 2020s.

France was one of the countries hardest hit, beginning in 2020, by the COVID-19 pandemic, recording about 39 mil total confirmed cases by Sept. 2024—4th-highest in the world. The pandemic had a severe impact on the economy, including the important tourism industry.

Paris hosted the 2024 Summer Olympics, July 26-Aug. 11. Arson attacks disrupted many of France's high-speed rail lines on July 26; far-left extremists were suspected. Some communications lines were sabotaged July 29.

The island of **Corsica** in the Mediterranean, W of Italy and N of Sardinia, is a territorial collectivity and region of France comprising two departments. It elects 2 senators and 3 deputies to the French Parliament. Area 3,369 sq mi; pop. (2023 est.) 352,851. The capital is Ajaccio, birthplace of Napoleon I. Violence by Corsican separatist groups was common in the 1980s and 1990s. Corsicans rejected, 51%-49%, a limited autonomy plan in a referendum July 6, 2003. **Website:** www.isula.corsica

French Overseas Departments

French Guiana is on the NE coast of South America with Suriname on the W and Brazil on the E and S. Its area is 35,135 sq mi (total), 34,421 sq mi (land); pop. (2023 est.) 292,892. Guiana sends 1 senator and 2 deputies to the French Parliament. Guiana is administered by a prefect and has a Council General of 16 elected members; capital is Cayenne, pop. (2020 est.) 61,645.

The famous penal colony, Devil's Island, was phased out between 1938 and 1951. The European Space Agency helps to maintain a satellite-launching center (est. 1964 by France), in the city of Kourou.

Immense forests of rich timber cover much of the land. Fishing (especially shrimp), forestry, and gold mining are the most important industries. Natural resources include petroleum, kaolin, niobium, tantalum, and clay.

Guadeloupe, in the West Indies' Leeward Isls., consists of two large islands, Basse-Terre and Grande-Terre, separated by the Salt R., plus Marie Galante and the Saintes group to the S and Desirade to the N. A French possession since 1635, the department is represented in the French Parliament; administration consists of a prefect (governor) as well as an elected general and regional councils.

Area of the islands is 525 sq mi; pop. (2023 est.) 380,469, mainly descendants of enslaved people; capital is Basse-Terre (2018 est. pop. 58,397) on Basse-Terre Island. The land is fertile; sugar, rum, and bananas are exported. Tourism is an important industry.

Martinique, the northernmost of the Windward Islands, in the West Indies, has been a possession since 1635, and a department since Mar. 1946. It is represented in the French Parliament by 2 senators and 4 deputies. The island was the birthplace of Napoleon's first wife, Empress Josephine.

It has an area of 425 sq mi (total), 409 sq mi (land); pop. (2023 est.) 353,444, mostly descendants of enslaved laborers. The capital is Fort-de-France; pop. (2018 est.) 79,361. It is a popular tourist destination with international receipts in 2022 of $535 mil. The chief exports are rum, bananas, and petroleum products. **Website:** www.collectivitedemartinique.mq

Mayotte, claimed by Comoros and administered by France, voted in 1976 to become a territorial collectivity of France. An island NW of Madagascar, area is 144 sq mi, pop. (2023 est.) 309,901. The capital is Mamoudzou; pop. (2018 est.) 6,180. In a Mar. 29, 2009, referendum, 95% of voters endorsed a plan under which Mayotte became an overseas department of France as of Mar. 31, 2011.

Réunion is a volcanic island in the Indian O. about 420 mi E of Madagascar, and has belonged to France since 1665. Area, 972 sq mi (total), 968 sq mi (land); pop. (2023 est.) 880,766. Capital: Saint-Denis; pop. (2018 est.) 147,209. The chief export is sugar. Tourism contributes to the economy with international receipts in 2022 of $439 mil. Réunion elects 5 deputies, 3 senators to the French Parliament. **Website:** regionreunion.com

French Overseas Territorial Authorities

French Polynesia, comprises 130 islands widely scattered among 5 archipelagos in the S Pacific; administered by a Council of Ministers (headed by a president). Territorial Assembly and the Council have headquarters at Papeete (2018 est. pop., 136,005), on Tahiti, one of the Society Islands (which include the Windward Isls. and Leeward Isls.). Two deputies and a senator are elected to the French Parliament.

Other groups are the Marquesas Isls.; the Tuamotu Archipelago; the Gambier Isls.; and the Austral, or Tubuai, Isls.

Total area of the islands administered from Tahiti is 1,609 sq mi (total), 1,478 sq mi (land); pop. (2024 est.) 303,540. Tahiti is mountainous with a productive coastline bearing coconuts, citrus, pineapples, and vanilla. Tourism is the largest industry.

Tahiti was visited by Capt. James Cook in 1769 and by Capt. Bligh in the *Bounty*, 1788-89. Its beauty impressed Herman Melville, Paul Gauguin, and Charles Darwin. A UN General Assembly resolution May 17, 2013, called on France to grant French Polynesia independence. Anti-independence parties won 2013 and 2018 general elections, but a pro-independence party won in 2023.

A 2013-14 Zika virus outbreak affected about 28,000 people. **Website:** www.presidence.pf

St. Pierre and Miquelon became a territorial collectivity in 1985. It consists of two groups of rocky islands near the SW coast of Newfoundland. Fish products are the chief export. The St. Pierre group has an area of 10 sq mi; Miquelon, 83 sq mi. Total pop. (2024 est.) 5,132. Capital: Saint-Pierre, pop. (2018 est.) 5,723. Both Mayotte and St. Pierre and Miquelon elect a deputy and a senator to the French Parliament.

St. Barthélemy and **St. Martin**, both formerly part of Guadeloupe, voted for secession in 2003 and became overseas territorial collectivities in 2007. Both suffered severe damage from Hurricane Irma, Sept. 6, 2017, which caused at least 11 deaths. Total area 10 sq mi and 19 sq mi; total pop. (2024 est.) 7,086 and 32,996 respectively.

The territorial collectivity of **Wallis and Futuna** comprises two island groups in the SW Pacific S of Tuvalu, N of Fiji, and W of Samoa. It became an overseas territory July 29, 1961. The islands have a total area of 55 sq mi and pop. (2024 est.) of 15,964. Alofi, attached to Futuna, is uninhabited. Capital: Mata-Utu; pop. (2018 est.) 1,025. Chief exports are copra, chemicals, and construction materials. A senator and a deputy are elected to the French Parliament. **Website:** www.assembleeterritoriale.wf

Overseas Territory and Special Collectivity

The territory of the **French Southern and Antarctic Lands** comprises island groups in the Indian O. Area: 2,991 sq mi (total), 2,960 sq mi (land).

The U.S. does not recognize French claim to Adelie Land, an area of about 193,051 sq mi on Antarctica. Adelie, reached 1840, has a 185-mi coastline and tapers 1,240 mi inland to the S Pole. It has a research station. The area includes the Ninnis and Mertz glaciers.

The Indian O. groups are as follows: Kerguelen Archipelago, visited 1772, consists of one large and 300 small islands. The chief is 87 mi long, 74 mi wide, and has Mt. Ross (6,429 ft). Principal research station is Port-aux-Français. There are seals, blue whales, coal, peat, semiprecious stones. Crozet Archipelago, reached 1772, covers 136 sq mi. Eastern Island rises to 6,560 ft. Volcanic Saint Paul, in southern Indian O., has warm springs. Amsterdam Island is nearby; both produce cod and rock lobster. Military garrisons and meteorological stations are located on the Scattered Isls.

The special collectivity of **New Caledonia** and Dependencies is a group of islands in the Pacific O. about 1,115 mi E of Australia and approx. the same distance NW of New Zealand. Dependencies are the Loyalty Isls., Isle of Pines, Belep Archipelago, and Huon Isls.

The largest island, New Caledonia, is 6,530 sq mi. Total area of the territory is 7,172 sq mi (total), 7,056 sq mi (land); pop. (2024 est.) 304,167. The group was acquired by France in 1853.

The territory is administered by a High Commissioner. There is a popularly elected Territorial Congress. Two deputies and two senators are elected to the French Parliament. Capital: Nouméa; pop. (2018 est.) 197,787.

Mining is a key industry. New Caledonia is one of the world's largest nickel producers. Chrome, iron, cobalt, manganese, silver, gold, lead, and copper are also found. Tourism is an important industry.

In 1987, New Caledonian voters chose by referendum to remain within France. French and Melanesians (Kanaks) clashed in 1988. An agreement (the Nouméa Accord) signed May 5, 1998, between France and rival New Caledonian factions specified a 20-year period of shared sovereignty and up to three referenda on independence. Voters rejected independence in 2018, 2020, and 2021 referenda. A French government proposal to change voter rolls, diluting the Kanak vote in any future referendum, sparked violent protests in 2024.

Website: gouv.nc

Gabon

Gabonese Republic

People: Population: 2,455,105 (142). **Age distrib.:** <15: 34.6%; 65+: 4.3%. **Growth:** 2.4%. **Migrants:** 18.7%. **Pop. density:** 24.7 per sq mi, 9.5 per sq km. **Urban:** 91.3%. **Ethnic groups:** Fang 23.5%, Shira-Punu'Vii 20.6%, Nzabi-Duma 11.2%, Mbede-Teke 5.6%, Myene 4.4%, Kota-Kele 4.3%. **Languages:** French (official), Fang, Myene, Nzebi, Bapounou/Eschira, Bandjabi. **Religions:** Christian 84.2% (Catholic 53.6%, independent 16.1%, Protestant 14.6%), Muslim 10.5% (Sunni), ethnic religionist 3.2%.

Geography: Total area: 103,347 sq mi, 267,667 sq km (76); **Land area:** 99,486 sq mi, 257,667 sq km. **Location:** Atlantic coast of W central Africa. Equatorial Guinea, Cameroon on N; Rep. of the Congo on E and S. **Topography:** Heavily forested, consisting of coastal lowlands; plateaus in N, E, and S; mountains in N, SE, and center. The Ogooue R. system covers most of Gabon. **Arable land:** 1.3%. **Capital:** Libreville, 883,920.

Government: Type: Presidential republic. **Head of state:** Interim Pres. Brice Oligui Nguema; in office: Sept. 4, 2023. **Head of govt.:** Interim Prime Min. Raymond Ndong Sima; in office: Sept. 7, 2023. **Local divisions:** 9 provinces. **Defense budget:** $267 mil. **Active troops:** 4,700.

Economy: Industries: petroleum extraction and refining; manganese, gold; chemicals, ship repair, food and beverages, textiles. **Chief agric.:** plantains, cassava, sugarcane, yams, taro, vegetables. **Natural resources:** petroleum, nat. gas, diamonds, niobium, manganese, uranium, gold, timber, iron ore, hydropower. **Water:** 70,904 cu m per capita. **Crude oil reserves:** 2 bil bbls. **Electricity prod.:** 2.4 bil kWh. **Labor force:** agric. 29.3%, industry 16.2%, services 54.5%. **Unemployment:** 20.4%.

Finance: Monetary unit: Central African CFA Franc (XAF) (587.79 = $1 U.S.). **GDP:** $53.5 bil; **per capita GDP:** $21,947; **GDP growth:** 2.3%. **Imports** (2022): $3.5 bil; China 22%, France 21%, UAE 5%, U.S. 5%. **Exports** (2022): $12.9 bil; China 43%, South Korea 8%, Italy 7%, India 7%, Indonesia 5%. **Budget:** $2.9 bil. **Inflation:** 3.6%.

Transport: Railways: 403 mi. **Airports:** 40.

Communications: Mobile (2022): 123.2 per 100 pop. **Broadband** (2022): 92.8 per 100 pop. **Internet:** 73.7%.

Health: Expend.: 2.7%. **Life expect.:** 68.6 male; 72.1 female. **Births:** 25.7 per 1,000 pop. **Deaths:** 5.5 per 1,000 pop. **Infant mortality:** 26.9 per 1,000 live births. **Undernourished:** 20.1%. **HIV:** 3%. **COVID-19:** 307 deaths; rates per 100,000: 2,204 cases, 14 deaths. 12% vaccinated.

Education: Compulsory: ages 6-15. **Literacy:** 85.7%.

Website: www.gouvernement.ga

France established control over the region in the second half of the 19th cent. Gabon became independent Aug. 17, 1960. Backed by France, Pres. Albert-Bernard Bongo (later Omar Bongo Ondimba) ruled the country 1967-2009, greatly enriching himself and his family. After he died June 8, 2009, his son Ali Bongo Ondimba claimed victory in a disputed 2009 presidential election. He claimed a disputed reelection victory in 2016. Government forces put down a Jan. 7, 2019, attempted coup.

Gabon has abundant natural resources (including oil), although there is extreme income inequality. Gabon joined the Commonwealth in 2022. After Bongo was declared the winner of a flawed Aug. 26, 2023, presidential election, military officers led by Gen. Brice Oligui Nguema announced, Aug. 30, Bongo's overthrow in a coup; a transitional government was set up.

The Gambia

Republic of The Gambia

People: Population: 2,523,327 (141). **Age distrib.:** <15: 38.2%; 65+: 3.7%. **Growth:** 2.2%. **Migrants:** 8.9%. **Pop. density:** 645.8 per sq mi, 249.3 per sq km. **Urban:** 65.1%. **Ethnic groups:** Mandinka/Jahanka 33.3%, Fulani/Tukulur/Lorobo 18.2%, Wolof 12.9%, Jola/Karoninka 11%, Serahuleh 7.2%, Serer 3.5%, non-Gambian 9.9%. **Languages:** English (official), Mandinka, Wolof, Fula, other Indigenous vernaculars. **Religions:** Muslim 88.5% (Sunni), Christian 5.0%, ethnic religionist 5.0%.

Geography: Total area: 4,363 sq mi, 11,300 sq km (160); **Land area:** 3,907 sq mi, 10,120 sq km. **Location:** Atlantic coast near W tip of Africa. Surrounded on 3 sides by Senegal. **Topography:** Narrow strip of land on each side of lower Gambia R. **Arable land:** 43.5%. **Capital:** Banjul, 495,099.

Government: Type: Presidential republic. **Head of state and govt.:** Pres. Adama Barrow; b. 1965; in office: Jan. 19, 2017. **Local divisions:** 5 regions, 1 city, 1 municipality. **Defense budget:** $14 mil. **Active troops:** 4,100.

Economy: Industries: peanuts, fish, hides, tourism, beverages, agric. machinery assembly. **Chief agric.:** groundnuts, milk, rice, millet, oil palm fruit, maize. **Natural resources:** fish, clay, silica sand, titanium, tin, zircon. **Water:** 3,030 cu m per capita. **Electricity prod.:** 509.6 mil kWh. **Labor force:** agric. 47.5%, industry 7.5%, services 45.0%. **Unemployment:** 6.5%.

Finance: Monetary unit: Dalasi (GMD) (70.19 = $1 U.S.). **GDP:** $8.8 bil; **per capita GDP:** $3,163; **GDP growth:** 5.3%. **Imports** (2022): $829.5 mil; China 31%, Senegal 12%, India 8%, Brazil 8%, U.S. 5%. **Exports** (2022): $267.4 mil; India 31%, China 23%, Italy 7%, Chile 7%, Portugal 5%. **Tourism** (2022): $154 mil. **Budget** (2018): $353 mil. **Inflation:** 17.0%.

Transport: Airports: 1.

Communications: Mobile (2022): 106.8 per 100 pop. **Broadband** (2022): 60.1 per 100 pop. **Internet:** 54.2%.

Health: Expend.: 3.2%. **Life expect.:** 66.7 male; 70.1 female. **Births:** 27.3 per 1,000 pop. **Deaths:** 5.6 per 1,000 pop. **Infant mortality:** 35.7 per 1,000 live births. **Undernourished:** 20.5%. **HIV:** 1.4%. **COVID-19:** 372 deaths; rates per 100,000: 522 cases, 15 deaths. 22% vaccinated.

Education: Compulsory: ages 7-15. **Literacy:** 58.7%.

Website: op.gov.gm

The peoples of The Gambia were at one time associated with the West African empires of Ghana, Mali, and Songhai. The area became Britain's first African possession in 1588.

Independence came Feb. 18, 1965; republic status within the Commonwealth was achieved in 1970. The country suffered from severe famine in the 1970s. Senegambia, a confederation with Senegal, lasted from 1982 to 1989.

On July 22, 1994, after 24 years in power, Pres. Dawda K. Jawara was deposed in a bloodless coup by a military officer, Yahya Jammeh. Jammeh barred political activity, detained opponents, and governed by decree. There was a nominal return to constitutional government in 1996. Jammeh won a fourth 5-year term in 2011. After businessman Adama Barrow defeated Jammeh in the Dec. 1, 2016, presidential election, Jammeh rejected the results. Barrow was sworn in, Jan. 19, 2017, in Senegal. Under pressure from ECOWAS and the UN, Jammeh went into exile, Jan. 21, 2017. Barrow won reelection, Dec. 4, 2021.

Georgia

People: Population: 4,900,961 (125). **Age distrib.:** <15: 20.6%; 65+: 16.7%. **Growth:** –0.5%. **Migrants:** 2.0%. **Pop. density:** 182.1 per sq mi, 70.3 per sq km. **Urban:** 61.2% (incl. Abkhazia and South Ossetia). **Ethnic groups:** Georgian 86.8%, Azeri 6.3%, Armenian 4.5%. **Languages:** Georgian (official), Azeri, Armenian. **Religions:** Christian 86.1% (Orthodox [official] 80.6%), Muslim 10.9% (Shia 6%, Sunni 5%), agnostic 2.5%.

Geography: Total area: 26,911 sq mi, 69,700 sq km (119). (About 18% is occupied by Russia.) **Land area:** 26,911 sq mi, 69,700 sq km. **Location:** SW Asia, on E coast of Black Sea. Russia on N and NE, Turkey and Armenia on S, Azerbaijan on SE. **Topography:** Main range of Caucasus Mts. in NE separates country from Russia. **Arable land:** 4.5%. **Capital:** Tbilisi, 1,084,471.

Government: Type: Semi-presidential republic. **Head of state:** Pres. Salome Zourabichvili; b. 1952; in office: Dec. 16, 2018. **Head of govt.:** Prime Min. Irakli Kobakhidze; in office: Feb. 8, 2024. **Local divisions:** 9 regions, 1 city, 2 autonomous republics. **Defense budget:** $481 mil. **Active troops:** 20,650.

Economy: Industries: steel, machine tools, elec. appliances, mining, chemicals, wood prods., wine. **Chief agric.:** milk, grapes, potatoes, wheat, maize, apples. **Natural resources:** timber, hydropower, manganese, iron ore, copper, minor coal/oil deposits. **Water:** 16,852 cu m per capita. **Crude oil reserves:** 35 mil bbls. **Electricity prod.:** 14.2 bil kWh. **Labor force:** agric. 39.9%, industry 13.8%, services 46.3%. **Unemployment:** 11.6%.

Finance: Monetary unit: Lari (GEL) (2.69 = $1 U.S.). **GDP:** $92.8 bil; **per capita GDP:** $24,681; **GDP growth:** 7.5%. **Imports:** $17.8 bil; Turkey (Türkiye) 17%, Russia 12%, China 8%, U.S. 8%, Germany 5%. **Exports:** $15.2 bil; China 11%, Azerbaijan 10%, Russia 9%, Armenia 8%, Bulgaria 7%. **Tourism:** $4.1 bil. **Budget:** $5.1 bil. **Inflation:** 2.5%.

Transport: Railways: 847 mi. **Airports:** 19.

Communications: Mobile: 155.3 per 100 pop. **Broadband:** 113 per 100 pop. **Internet** (2023): 81.9%.

Health: Expend. (2022): 7.4%. **Life expect.:** 68.7 male; 77.2 female. **Births:** 12.0 per 1,000 pop. **Deaths:** 13.3 per 1,000 pop. **Infant mortality:** 21.7 per 1,000 live births. **Undernourished:** 4.0%. **HIV:** 0.4%. **COVID-19:** 17,150 deaths; rates per 100,000: 46,717 cases, 430 deaths. 30% vaccinated.

Education: Compulsory: ages 6-14. **Literacy:** 99.6%.

Website: www.gov.ge

The region, which contained the ancient kingdoms of Colchis and Iberia, was Christianized in the 4th cent. and conquered by Arabs in the 8th cent. Annexed by Russia in 1801, Georgia was forcibly incorporated into the USSR in 1922.

Georgia gained independence when the Soviet Union disbanded Dec. 26, 1991. After a power struggle, former Soviet Foreign Min. Eduard A. Shevardnadze became president. He survived several coup attempts and won reelection in 1995 and 2000. Parliamentary elections Nov. 2, 2003, denounced as fraudulent sparked massive anti-government protests, causing Shevardnadze to resign Nov. 23. Opposition leader Mikhail Saakashvili won the 2004 presidential election. He survived an apparent assassination attempt along with U.S. Pres. George W. Bush in Tbilisi May 10, 2005. He suppressed an alleged coup plot, Sept. 6, 2006, and cracked down violently on anti-government protests, Nov. 2007. He called early elections, Jan. 2008, which he won. Barred by term limits from seeking reelection in 2013, he left the country. In 2018, he was convicted of abuse of power, and he was imprisoned following his return to Georgia in 2021.

Giorgi Margvelashvili of the recently formed Georgian Dream coalition, which won 2012 parliamentary elections, was elected president Oct. 27, 2013. Constitutional changes that went into effect in 2013 greatly increased the powers of the prime minister. Georgian Dream won Oct. 2016 parliamentary elections. Independent Salome Zurabishvili, backed by Georgian Dream, won a disputed Nov. 28, 2018, presidential election, becoming Georgia's first female president. Georgian Dream won disputed Oct.-Nov. 2020 parliamentary elections.

Georgia completed a cooperation agreement with the EU in 2014. It applied for EU membership, Mar. 3, 2022.

A "foreign agents" law enacted by Parliament in May 2024—modeled on Russian legislation and perceived by opponents as a government effort to suppress dissent—sparked large-scale protests.

After independence, secessionist movements in South Ossetia and Abkhazia, supported by Russia, rejected the Tbilisi government. Open warfare erupted in Aug. 2008 between Georgia and Russia, which dispatched forces to South Ossetia and Abkhazia and attacked key Georgian cities. After a cease-fire signed Aug. 15-16, Russian troops remained in the breakaway regions. Russia, Aug. 2008, formally recognized South Ossetia and Abkhazia's independence; almost all other nations have not.

Germany

Federal Republic of Germany

People: Population: 84,119,100 (19). **Age distrib.:** <15: 13.8%; 65+: 23.7%. **Growth:** –0.1%. **Migrants:** 18.8%. **Pop. density:** 624.8 per sq mi, 241.3 per sq km. **Urban:** 77.9%. **Ethnic groups** (by nationality): German 85.4%, Turkish 1.8%, Ukrainian 1.4%, Syrian 1.1%, Romanian 1%, Polish 1%. **Languages:** German (official); Danish, Frisian, Sorbian, Romani (all official minority langs.). **Religions:** Christian 60.0% (Catholic 30.7%, Protestant 23.8%), agnostic 29.8%, Muslim 7.2% (Sunni 6%), atheist 2.5%.

Geography: Total area: 137,847 sq mi, 357,022 sq km (62); **Land area:** 134,623 sq mi, 348,672 sq km. **Location:** Central Europe. Denmark on N; Netherlands, Belgium, Luxembourg, France on W; Switzerland, Austria on S; Czechia, Poland on E. **Topography:** Flat in N, hilly in center and W, and mountainous in Bavaria in the S. Chief rivers—Elbe, Weser, Ems, Rhine, and Main—flow toward North Sea; Danube flows toward Black Sea. **Arable land:** 33.4%. **Capital:** Berlin, 3,576,873. **Cities:** Hamburg, 1,787,280; Munich, 1,584,507; Cologne, 1,149,014.

Government: Type: Federal parliamentary republic. **Head of state:** Pres. Frank-Walter Steinmeier; b. 1956; in office: Mar. 22, 2017. **Head of govt.:** Chancellor Olaf Scholz; b. 1958; in office: Dec. 8, 2021. **Local divisions:** 16 states. **Defense budget:** $63.7 bil. **Active troops:** 181,000.

Economy: Industries: iron, steel, coal, cement, chemicals, machinery, vehicles, machine tools, electronics, automobiles, food and beverages. **Chief agric.:** milk, sugar beets, wheat, barley, potatoes, pork. **Natural resources:** coal, lignite, nat. gas, iron ore, copper, nickel, uranium, potash, salt, constr. materials, timber. **Chief agric.:** milk, sugar beets, wheat, barley, potatoes, pork. **Water:** 1,846 cu m per capita. **Crude oil reserves:** 115 mil bbls. **Electricity prod.:** 560.8 bil kWh. **Labor force:** agric. 1.2%, industry 26.9%, services 71.9%. **Unemployment:** 3.0%.

Finance: Monetary unit: Euro (EUR) (0.90 = $1 U.S.). **GDP:** $5.9 tril; **per capita GDP:** $69,338; **GDP growth:** –0.3%. **Imports:** $1.9 tril; China 10%, Netherlands 9%, Poland 6%, Belgium 6%, Italy 5%. **Exports:** $2.1 tril; U.S. 10%, France 7%, China 7%, Netherlands 7%, Italy 6%. **Tourism:** $37.4 bil. **Budget** (2020): $1.9 tril. **Inflation:** 5.9%.

Transport: Railways: 24,469 mi. **Motor vehicles:** 629.3 per 1,000 pop. **Airports:** 838.

Communications: Mobile: 124.7 per 100 pop. **Broadband:** 94.4 per 100 pop. **Internet** (2023): 92.5%.

Health: Expend. (2022): 12.7%. **Life expect.:** 79.6 male; 84.4 female. **Births:** 8.9 per 1,000 pop. **Deaths:** 12.0 per 1,000 pop. **Infant mortality:** 3.1 per 1,000 live births. **Undernourished:** <2.5%. **HIV:** NA. **COVID-19:** 174,979 deaths; rates per 100,000: 46,218 cases, 210 deaths. 76% vaccinated.

Education: Compulsory: ages 6-18. **Literacy:** NA.

Website: www.deutschland.de

Julius Caesar defeated Germanic tribes, 55 and 53 BCE, but Roman expansion north of the Rhine was stopped in 9 CE. Charlemagne, ruler of the Franks, consolidated Saxon, Bavarian, Rhenish, Frankish, and other lands; after him the eastern part became the German Empire. The Thirty Years' War, 1618-48, split Germany into small principalities and kingdoms.

Otto von Bismarck, Prussian chancellor, formed the North German Confederation, 1867. In 1870 Bismarck maneuvered Napoleon III into declaring war. After the quick defeat of France, Bismarck formed the German Empire and on Jan. 18, 1871, in Versailles, proclaimed King Wilhelm I of Prussia the German emperor (Deutscher kaiser).

The German Empire reached its peak before WWI in 1914, with 208,780 sq mi, plus overseas colonies. After losing the war in 1918, Germany ceded Alsace-Lorraine to France, West Prussia and Posen (Poznan) province to Poland, and part of Schleswig to Denmark. It lost all colonies and the ports of Memel and Danzig.

Republic of Germany, 1919-33, adopted the Weimar constitution; met reparation payments and elected Friedrich Ebert and Gen. Paul von Hindenburg presidents.

Third Reich, 1933-45: Adolf Hitler led the National Socialist German Workers' (Nazi) party after WWI. Pres. von Hindenburg named Hitler chancellor in 1933; on Aug. 3, 1934, the day after Hindenburg's death, the cabinet joined the offices of president and chancellor and made Hitler *führer* (leader). Hitler abolished freedom of speech and assembly, and began a long series of persecutions culminating in the murder of millions of Jews and others in the Holocaust.

He repudiated the Versailles treaty and reparations agreements, remilitarized the Rhineland (1936), and annexed Austria (Anschluss, 1938). At Munich he made an agreement with British Prime Min. Neville Chamberlain, which permitted Germany to annex part of Czechoslovakia. He declared war on Poland Sept. 1, 1939, precipitating WWII. With total defeat near, Hitler committed suicide in Berlin Apr. 1945. The victorious Allies voided all acts and annexations of Hitler's Reich.

Germany was sectioned into four zones of occupation, administered by the Allied Powers (U.S., USSR, UK, and France). The USSR took control of many E German states. The territory E of the so-called Oder-Neisse line was assigned to, and later annexed by, Poland. The USSR annexed Northern East Prussia (now Kaliningrad). Greater Berlin, within but not part of the Soviet zone, was administered by the four occupying powers under the Allied Command. In 1948 the USSR withdrew, established its single command in East Berlin, and cut off supplies. The Western Allies utilized a gigantic airlift to bring food to West Berlin, 1948-49.

In 1949, two separate German states were established. The zones administered by the Western Allies became West Germany; the Soviet sector became East Germany. West Berlin was considered a West German enclave, a status the Soviet bloc disputed.

East Germany. The German Democratic Republic (East Germany) was proclaimed in the Soviet sector of Berlin Oct. 7, 1949. It was declared fully sovereign in 1954, but Soviet troops remained.

Coincident with the entrance of West Germany into the European defense community in 1952, the East German government decreed a prohibited zone 3 mi deep along its 600-mi border with West Germany. East Germany also erected a fortified wall dividing Berlin in 1961, after over 3 mil East Germans had fled to the West. The oppressive Communist regime maintained control through the state security police, known as the Stasi.

By the early 1970s, the economy of East Germany was highly industrialized, and the nation was credited with the highest standard of living among Warsaw Pact countries. Growth slowed in the late 1970s because of shortages of natural resources and labor and huge debt. Comparison with the lifestyle in the West caused many young people to emigrate.

In the late 1980s the government firmly resisted following the USSR's policy of openness (*glasnost*) but was faced with nationwide demonstrations demanding reform. Pres. Erich Honecker, in office since 1976, was forced to resign Oct. 18, 1989. On Nov. 9, the East German government announced its decision to open the border with the West, signaling the end of the Berlin Wall. On Aug. 23, 1990, the East German parliament agreed to reunite with West Germany.

West Germany. The Federal Republic of Germany (West Germany) was proclaimed May 23, 1949, in Bonn. The occupying powers—the U.S., Britain, and France—restored civil status, Sept. 21. The Western Allies ended the state of war with Germany in 1951, while the USSR did so in 1955. The republic became fully independent May 5, 1955. The U.S. maintained military bases.

Dr. Konrad Adenauer, a Christian Democrat, was made chancellor 1949 and was reelected 1953, 1957, and 1961. Willy Brandt, heading a coalition of Social Democrats and Free Democrats, became chancellor 1969 and pursued a policy of *Ostpolitik*, or rapprochement with East Germany and the USSR. Brandt resigned May 1974 after a spy scandal. Terrorist acts on German soil in the 1970s included activities of the Baader-Meinhof gang, also known as the Red Army Faction, and the murder of Israeli athletes by Palestinian commandos at the Olympic Games in Munich, Sept. 5, 1972.

Helmut Kohl became chancellor in 1982 and led the Christian Democratic Union (CDU) and its Bavarian sister party Christian Social Union (CSU) to victory in 1983 and 1987.

Unified Germany. In May 1990, NATO ministers voted to make the united Germany a full member of NATO and barred the new Germany from having its own nuclear, chemical, or biological weapons. The merger of the two Germanys took place Oct. 3, and the first all-German elections since 1932 were held Dec. 2, with Kohl confirmed as leader of the unified nation. Eastern Germany received over $1 tril in public and private funds from western Germany, 1990-95. In 1991, Berlin again became Germany's capital. The Christian Democrats lost parliamentary elections, Sept. 27, 1998, and Gerhard Schröder, of the Social Democratic Party (SPD), became chancellor. The Christian Democrats, led by Angela Merkel, won a razor-thin plurality in 2005 parliamentary elections, and she became chancellor Nov. 22, heading a "grand coalition" that included the SPD.

Responding to the global recession, the government passed a 50-bil euro economic stimulus plan in early 2009. Merkel led a center-right coalition to victory in 2009 national elections. Merkel led the response to the European debt crisis beginning in late 2009; debtor nations were required to adopt stern austerity measures.

Merkel's Christian Democrats won Sept. 22, 2013, parliamentary elections but fell short of a majority. She formed a new coalition, including the SPD, in Dec.

Germany was the destination in 2015-16 for many migrants reaching Europe after fleeing war or hardship in the Middle East, SW Asia, or Africa. More than 1.2 mil migrants applied for asylum, 2015-16. Germany expedited asylum applications and began repatriating migrants judged not to be refugees. Germany played a key role in negotiating a Mar. 2016 EU-Turkey agreement to stem the flow of migrants to Europe. In an attack for which ISIS claimed responsibility, a Tunisian migrant killed 12 when he stole a truck and drove it into a crowded Berlin outdoor market, Dec. 19, 2016.

Legislation legalizing same-sex marriage was signed into law by Germany's president, July 21, 2017.

Merkel's CDU/CSU won a plurality in Sept. 24, 2017, elections; the far-right, anti-immigration Alternative for Germany (AfD) party won 12.6% of the vote. Merkel reached agreement, Feb. 2018, on a new coalition with the SPD. Far-right protests and rioting in Chemnitz in Aug. included attacks on apparent immigrants.

A study commissioned by the German Catholic Church, released Sept. 2018, found evidence that more than 3,600 children had been sexually abused, 1946-2014, by over 1,600 members of the clergy.

German Defense Min. Ursula von der Leyen became, Dec. 1, 2019, the first woman to head the European Commission. She was reelected by the European Parliament to a second term, July 18, 2024.

In Sept. 26, 2021, parliamentary elections, the SPD increased its vote share and outpolled the CDU/CSU, with the Greens and center-right Free Democrats also increasing their support (AfD won about 10% of the vote). SPD leader Olaf Scholz formed a coalition with the Greens and Free Democrats; he became chancellor Dec. 8.

Heavily dependent on Russian energy imports, Germany joined EU sanctions against Russia over its 2022 invasion of Ukraine. Germany also blocked the opening of a new natural gas pipeline (Nord Stream 2) from Russia, Feb. 22, 2022, and essentially ended Russian oil imports by the end of the year. As of July 31, 2024, almost 1.2 mil Ukrainian refugees were in Germany.

German authorities announced, Dec. 7, 2022, the arrests of 25 far-right extremists, said to be plotting the violent overthrow of the government. AfD won almost 16% of the vote in June 2024 European Parliament elections, outpolling the SPD.

Severely affected by the COVID-19 pandemic, Germany had a total of 38.4 mil confirmed cases as of Aug. 2024, 5th-highest in the world.

Helgoland, an island of 0.66 sq mi in the North Sea, was taken from Denmark by a British naval force in 1807 and ceded to Germany in 1890. The island was surrendered to the UK, May 23, 1945, and returned to then-West Germany, Mar. 1, 1952.

Ghana

Republic of Ghana

People: Population: 34,589,092 (44). **Age distrib.:** <15: 37.4%; 65+: 4.4%. **Growth:** 2.2%. **Migrants:** 1.5%. **Pop. density:** 393.7 per sq mi, 152.0 per sq km. **Urban:** 59.9%. **Ethnic groups:** Akan 45.7%, Mole-Dagbani 18.5%, Ewe 12.8%, Ga-Dangme 7.1%, Gurma 6.4%, Guan 3.2%, Grusi 2.7%, Mande 2%. **Languages:** Asante, Ewe, Fante, Boron (Brong), Dagomba, Dangme, Dagarte (Dagaba), Kokomba, Akyem, Ga, English (official). **Religions:** Christian 72.0% (Protestant 36.3%, independent 20.9%, Catholic 14.8%), Muslim 18.8% (Sunni 12%, Islamic schismatic 7%), ethnic religionist 8.6%.

Geography: Total area: 92,098 sq mi, 238,533 sq km (80); **Land area:** 87,851 sq mi, 227,533 sq km. **Location:** S coast of W Africa. Côte d'Ivoire on W, Burkina Faso on N, Togo on E. **Topography:** Mostly low fertile plains and scrubland, cut by rivers and by the artificial Lake Volta. **Arable land:** 20.7%. **Capital:** Accra, 2,721,165. **Cities:** Kumasi, 3,903,481; Sekondi Takoradi, 1,119,534.

Government: Type: Presidential republic. **Head of state and govt.:** Pres. Nana Addo Dankwa Akufo-Addo; b. 1944; in office: Jan. 7, 2017. **Local divisions:** 16 regions. **Defense budget:** $335 mil. **Active troops:** 19,000.

Economy: Industries: mining, lumbering, light mfg., aluminum smelting, food proc., cement, small comm. shipbuilding. **Chief agric.:** cassava, yams, plantains, maize, oil palm fruit, taro. **Natural resources:** gold, timber, industrial diamonds, bauxite, manganese, fish, rubber, hydropower, petroleum, silver, salt, limestone. **Water:** 1,712 cu m per capita. **Crude oil reserves:** 660 mil bbls. **Electricity prod.:** 22.5 bil kWh. **Labor force:** agric. 39.7%, industry 18.9%, services 41.4%. **Unemployment:** 3.1%.

Finance: Monetary unit: Cedi (GHS) (15.62 = $1 U.S.). **GDP:** $254.8 bil; **per capita GDP:** $7,466; **GDP growth:** 2.9%. **Imports** (2022): $26.3 bil; China 41%, Netherlands 7%, India 5%, U.S. 5%. **Exports** (2022): $25.7 bil; UAE 24%, Switzerland 17%, U.S. 14%, India 10%, China 10%. **Tourism** (2022): $830 mil. **Budget** (2018): $14.1 bil. **Inflation:** 38.1%.

Transport: Railways: 588 mi. **Motor vehicles:** 6.7 per 1,000 pop. **Airports:** 11.

Communications: Mobile: 98.8 per 100 pop. **Broadband:** 56.5 per 100 pop. **Internet:** 69.8%.

Health: Expend.: 4.2%. **Life expect.:** 68.4 male; 71.8 female. **Births:** 27.6 per 1,000 pop. **Deaths:** 5.9 per 1,000 pop. **Infant mortality:** 31.2 per 1,000 live births. **Undernourished:** 6.2%. **HIV:** 1.5%. **COVID-19:** 1,462 deaths; rates per 100,000: 554 cases, 5 deaths. 35% vaccinated.

Education: Compulsory: ages 4-14. **Literacy:** 80.4%.

Website: www.ghana.gov.gh

Named for an African empire along the Niger R., 400-1240 CE, Ghana was ruled by Britain for 113 years as the Gold Coast. The UN in 1956 approved merger with the British Togoland trust territory. Independence came Mar. 6, 1957, and republic status within the Commonwealth in 1960.

Pres. Kwame Nkrumah built hospitals and schools and promoted development projects but ran the country into debt, jailed opponents, and was accused of corruption. A 1964 referendum gave Nkrumah dictatorial powers and set up a one-party socialist state. A police-army coup overthrew Nkrumah in 1966. Elections were held in 1969, but four further coups occurred in 1972, 1978, 1979, and 1981. A new constitution, allowing multiparty politics, was approved in Apr. 1992. Former coup leader Jerry Rawlings won the 1996 presidential election.

Opposition leader John Agyekum Kufuor won a 2000 runoff vote and was sworn in Jan. 7, 2001, marking Ghana's first peaceful transfer of power from one elected president to another. A major offshore oil and gas find was announced June 2007. Nana Addo Dankwa Akufo-Addo won the Dec. 7, 2016, presidential election and was reelected, Dec. 7, 2020. Akufo-Addo signed, Aug. 2, 2023, legislation abolishing the death penalty for most crimes.

Greece
Hellenic Republic

People: Population: 10,461,091 (90). **Age distrib.:** <15: 13.8%; 65+: 23.6%. **Growth:** –0.4%. **Migrants:** 12.9%. **Pop. density:** 207.4 per sq mi, 80.1 per sq km. **Urban:** 81.0%. **Ethnic groups** (citizenship): Greek 91.6%, Albanian 4.4%. Greece does not collect ethnicity data. **Languages:** Greek (official). **Religions:** Christian 88.8% (Orthodox 86.1%), Muslim 6.1% (Sunni), agnostic 4.3%.

Geography: Total area: 50,949 sq mi, 131,957 sq km (95); **Land area:** 50,443 sq mi, 130,647 sq km. **Location:** S end of Balkan Peninsula in SE Europe. Albania, North Macedonia, Bulgaria on N; Turkey on E. **Topography:** About three-quarters is non-arable, with mountains in all areas incl. N-S Pindus Mts. Heavily indented coastline is 9,385 mi long. About 2,000 islands, only 169 inhabited, among them Crete, Rhodes, Milos, Kerkira (Corfu), Chios, Lesbos, Samos, Euboea, Delos, Mykonos. **Arable land:** 14.1%. **Capital:** Athens, 3,154,463. **Cities:** Thessaloniki, 814,980.

Government: Type: Parliamentary republic. **Head of state:** Pres. Katerina Sakellaropoulou; b. 1956; in office: Mar. 13, 2020. **Head of govt.:** Prime Min. Kyriakos Mitsotakis; b. 1968; in office: July 8, 2019. **Local divisions:** 13 regions, 1 autonomous monastic state. **Defense budget:** $7.4 bil. **Active troops:** 132,200.

Economy: Industries: tourism, food and tobacco proc., textiles, chemicals, metal prods. **Chief agric.:** maize, wheat, sheep milk, peaches/nectarines, oranges, grapes. **Natural resources:** lignite, petroleum, iron ore, bauxite, lead, zinc, nickel, magnesite, marble, salt. **Water:** 6,548 cu m per capita. **Crude oil reserves:** 10 mil bbls. **Electricity prod.:** 49.2 bil kWh. **Labor force:** agric. 11.2%, industry 15.6%, services 73.3%. **Unemployment:** 11.0%.

Finance: Monetary unit: Euro (EUR) (0.90 = $1 U.S.). **GDP:** $426.7 bil; **per capita GDP:** $41,187; **GDP growth:** 2.0%. **Imports:** $117.9 bil; China 12%, Germany 9%, Russia 9%, Italy 7%, Iraq 7%. **Exports:** $106.7 bil; Italy 10%, Bulgaria 7%, Germany 6%, Cyprus 5%, Turkey (Türkiye) 5%. **Tourism:** $22.3 bil. **Budget:** $97.3 bil. **Inflation:** 3.5%.

Transport: Railways: 1,457 mi. **Motor vehicles:** 677.7 per 1,000 pop. **Airports:** 81.

Communications: Mobile: 110.8 per 100 pop. **Broadband:** 105 per 100 pop. **Internet** (2023): 85%.

Health: Expend.: 9.2%. **Life expect.:** 79.4 male; 84.6 female. **Births:** 7.4 per 1,000 pop. **Deaths:** 12.0 per 1,000 pop. **Infant mortality:** 3.4 per 1,000 live births. **Undernourished:** <2.5%. **HIV:** 0.2%. **COVID-19:** 39,296 deaths; rates per 100,000: 52,985 cases, 367 deaths. 72% vaccinated.

Education: Compulsory: ages 5-14. **Literacy:** 97.9%.

Website: primeminister.gr

The achievements of ancient Greece in art, architecture, science, mathematics, philosophy, drama, literature, and democracy became legacies for succeeding ages. Greece reached the height of its power, particularly in the Athenian city-state, in the 5th cent. BCE. Greece fell under Roman rule in the 2nd and 1st cents. BCE. In the 4th cent. CE, it became part of the Byzantine Empire and, after the fall of Constantinople to the Turks in 1453, part of the Ottoman Empire.

Greece won its war of independence from Turkey, 1821-29, and became a kingdom. A republic was established 1924; the monarchy was restored, 1935. In Oct. 1940, Greece rejected an ultimatum from Italy, but the country was defeated and occupied by German, Italian, and Bulgarian forces. By the end of 1944 the invaders withdrew. Communist resistance forces were overcome by Royalist and British troops. A plebiscite restored the monarchy.

Communists waged guerrilla war 1947-49 against the government but were defeated with the aid of the U.S. A period of reconstruction and rapid development followed, mainly with conservative governments under Prem. Constantine Karamanlis. The Center Union, led by Georgios Papandreou, won elections in 1963 and 1964, but King Constantine forced Papandreou to resign. A period of political maneuvers ended with Col. George Papadopoulos's military takeover Apr. 1967. King Constantine tried to reverse the consolidation of the harsh dictatorship, Dec. 1967, but failed and fled to Italy. Papadopoulos was ousted Nov. 1973.

Greek army officers serving in the Cyprus National Guard staged a coup on the island July 15, 1974. Turkey invaded Cyprus a week later, precipitating the collapse of the Greek junta. Democratic government returned, and in 1975 the monarchy was abolished.

The 1981 electoral victory of the Panhellenic Socialist Movement (Pasok) of Andreas Papandreou (Georgios's son) substantially changed Greece's internal and external policies. A scandal contributed to the 1989 defeat of the Socialists at the polls. Papandreou, who was acquitted Jan. 1992 of corruption charges, led the Socialists to a comeback victory in 1993 general elections. The Socialists retained power in 1996 and 2000 elections.

The conservative New Democracy (ND) party won 2004 parliamentary elections, and Konstantinos (Costas) Karamanlis became prime min. Beset by scandals and an ailing economy, Karamanlis called early elections for Oct. 4, 2009, won by Pasok under the leadership of the U.S.-born George A. Papandreou (Andreas's son). The IMF and eurozone countries agreed in 2010 on a 110-bil euro loan package to prevent Greece from defaulting on its debt; in return, Greek leaders implemented an austerity plan. As the debt crisis continued, parliament passed, amid violent anti-austerity protests, new austerity measures, Feb. 2012, to obtain a second, 130-bil euro bailout in Mar. The conservative, pro-bailout Antonis Samaras of ND became prime min., June 2012. Recession and austerity measures, 2007-13, caused Greece's GDP to shrink by 26%. In 2014, 36% of people lived below the poverty line.

Campaigning against austerity, the leftist Syriza party won Jan. 25, 2015, elections. Syriza's Alexis Tsipras became prime min. In a July 5 referendum, Greek voters decisively rejected further austerity. However, negotiations after the referendum produced an 86-bil euro third bailout agreement with tough austerity terms. As austerity measures were implemented, unemployment was over 20% in 2016 and 2017. After negotiating extended debt repayment, Greece exited the bailout program, Aug. 20, 2018. Syriza lost July 7, 2019, elections to ND, and Kyriakos Mitsotakis became prime min. Elected by parliament, Jan. 22, 2020, Katerina Sakellaropoulou took office, Mar. 13, as Greece's first woman president. ND won June 25, 2023, elections, giving Mitsotakis a second term as prime min.

In 2015, more than 861,000 migrants from the Middle East, SW Asia, and Africa trying to reach the EU arrived in Greece. A 2016 EU-Turkey agreement reduced the number of undocumented migrants reaching Greece, but more than 463,000 arrived from 2016 to Sept. 1, 2024. Most migrants tried to continue to N Europe. More than 105,000 refugees and asylum seekers (from all countries) were in Greece as of Mar. 31, 2024. Greece has been accused in recent years of forcibly preventing migrants from entering the country and of forcing out some who had arrived. Hundreds died, June 14, 2023, when an overcrowded boat carrying migrants sank near the Greek coast, prompting questions about the assistance provided by the Greek Coast Guard.

Severe summer heat waves and associated widespread wildfires, 2021-24, were likely related to climate change.

Legislation approved, Feb. 15, 2024, by Greece's Parliament legalized same-sex marriage.

Grenada

People: Population: 114,621 (180). **Age distrib.:** <15: 21.9%; 65+: 12.8%. **Growth:** 0.3%. **Migrants:** 6.4%. **Pop. density:** 863.0 per sq mi, 333.2 per sq km. **Urban:** 37.3%. **Ethnic groups:** African descent 82.4%, mixed 13.3%, East Indian 2.2%. **Languages:** English (official), French patois. **Religions:** Christian 96.4% (Catholic 50.8%, Protestant 39.3%).

Geography: Total area: 133 sq mi, 344 sq km (186); **Land area:** 133 sq mi, 344 sq km. **Location:** In Caribbean, 90 mi N of Venezuela. Trinidad and Tobago to S, St. Vincent and the Grenadines to N. **Topography:** Main island is mountainous. Country also comprises Carriacou and Petit Martinique Isls. **Arable land:** 8.8%. **Capital:** St. George's, 39,297.

Government: Type: Parliamentary democracy under constitutional monarchy. **Head of state:** King Charles III, rep. by Gov.-Gen. Cécile La Grenade; b. 1952; in office: May 7, 2013. **Head of govt.:** Prime Min. Dickon Mitchell; b. 1978; in office: June 24, 2022. **Local divisions:** 6 parishes, 1 dependency. **Defense budget/active troops:** NA.

Economy: Industries: food and beverages, textiles, light assembly operations, tourism, constr., education, call-center operations. **Chief agric.:** coconuts, sugarcane, eggs, bananas, vegetables, fruits. **Natural resources:** timber, tropical fruit. **Water:** 1,605 cu m per capita. **Electricity prod.:** 240.6 mil kWh. **Labor force:** NA. **Unemployment:** NA.

Finance: Monetary unit: East Caribbean Dollar (XCD) (2.70 = $1 U.S.). **GDP:** $2.2 bil; **per capita GDP:** $17,654; **GDP growth:** 4.8%. **Imports:** $1.0 bil; U.S. 37%, Trinidad and Tobago 11%, Cayman Islands 11%, China 5%. **Exports:** $899.2 mil; U.S. 33%, Antigua and Barbuda 10%. **Tourism:** $327 mil. **Budget:** $263 mil. **Inflation:** 2.7%.

Transport: Airports: 2.

Communications: Mobile (2022): 95.8 per 100 pop. **Broadband** (2022): 60.2 per 100 pop. **Internet:** 79.9%.

Health: Expend.: 5.7%. **Life expect.:** 73.7 male; 79.1 female. **Births:** 13.3 per 1,000 pop. **Deaths:** 8.4 per 1,000 pop. **Infant mortality:** 9.0 per 1,000 live births. **Undernourished:** NA. **HIV:** NA. **COVID-19:** 238 deaths; rates per 100,000: 17,501 cases, 212 deaths. 35% vaccinated.

Education: Compulsory: ages 5-16. **Literacy:** 98.6%.

Website: www.gov.gd

Christopher Columbus sighted Grenada in 1498. The first European settlers were French, 1650. The island was held alternately by France and England until final British occupation, 1784. Grenada became fully independent Feb. 7, 1974, during a general strike.

On Oct. 14, 1983, a military coup ousted Prime Min. Maurice Bishop, who was executed Oct. 19. A largely U.S. force invaded Grenada, Oct. 25. Resistance from the Grenadian army and Cuban advisors was quickly overcome, and U.S. troops left Grenada in June 1985.

Hurricane Ivan slammed into Grenada, Sept. 7, 2004, killing 39 and damaging an estimated 90% of the buildings. The center-right New National Party (NNP) won 2013 and 2018 legislative elections.

In June 23, 2022, elections, the center-left National Democratic Congress (NDC) defeated the NNP. The NDC's Dickon Mitchell became prime min., June 24, 2022.

Guatemala

Republic of Guatemala

People: Population: 18,255,216 (69). **Age distrib.:** <15: 31.5%; 65+: 5.4%. **Growth:** 1.5%. **Migrants:** 0.5%. **Pop. density:** 441.2 per sq mi, 170.4 per sq km. **Urban:** 53.5%. **Ethnic groups:** mestizo or Ladino (mixed Indigenous/Spanish) 56%, Maya 41.7%. **Languages:** Spanish (official), Maya langs. (incl. Q'eqchi', K'iche, Mam, Kaqchikel). **Religions:** Christian 97.2% (Catholic 65.8%, Protestant 18.1%, independent 12.1%).

Geography: Total area: 42,042 sq mi, 108,889 sq km (105); **Land area:** 41,374 sq mi, 107,159 sq km. **Location:** Central America. Mexico on N and W, El Salvador on S, Honduras and Belize on E. **Topography:** Central highland and mountain areas bordered by a narrow Pacific coast and lowlands and fertile river valleys on the Caribbean. Numerous volcanoes in S, more than half a dozen over 11,000 ft. **Arable land:** 14.5%. **Capital:** Guatemala City, 3,159,631.

Government: Type: Presidential republic. **Head of state and govt.:** Pres. Bernardo Arévalo; b. 1958; in office: Jan. 15, 2024. **Local divisions:** 22 departments. **Defense budget:** $412 mil. **Active troops:** 18,050.

Economy: Industries: sugar, textiles/clothing, furniture, chemicals, petroleum, metals, rubber, tourism. **Chief agric.:** sugarcane, bananas, oil palm fruit, maize, cantaloupes/melons, potatoes. **Natural resources:** petroleum, nickel, rare woods, fish, chicle, hydropower. **Water:** 7,264 cu m per capita. **Crude oil reserves:** 86 mil bbls. **Electricity prod.:** 13.1 bil kWh. **Labor force:** agric. 27.1%, industry 22.0%, services 50.8%. **Unemployment:** 2.7%.

Finance: Monetary unit: Quetzal (GTQ) (7.71 = $1 U.S.). **GDP:** $247.6 bil; **per capita GDP:** $14,067; **GDP growth:** 3.5%. **Imports:** $33.0 bil; U.S. 34%, China 18%, Mexico 9%. **Exports:** $17.3 bil; U.S. 32%, El Salvador 12%, Honduras 10%, Nicaragua 6%. **Tourism:** $1.4 bil. **Budget:** $10.4 bil. **Inflation:** 6.2%.

Transport: Railways: 497 mi (rail service suspended in 2007). **Motor vehicles:** 144.8 per 1,000 pop. **Airports:** 58.

Communications: Mobile: 113.7 per 100 pop. **Broadband** (2022): 17 per 100 pop. **Internet:** 54.4%.

Health: Expend.: 6.9%. **Life expect.:** 71.5 male; 75.6 female. **Births:** 21.4 per 1,000 pop. **Deaths:** 4.9 per 1,000 pop. **Infant mortality:** 25.0 per 1,000 live births. **Undernourished:** 12.6%. **HIV:** 0.2%. **COVID-19:** 20,203 deaths; rates per 100,000: 6,979 cases, 113 deaths. 40% vaccinated.

Education: Compulsory: NA. **Literacy:** 84.3%.

Website: guatemala.gob.gt, www.presidencia.gob.gt

A Mayan Indian empire flourished in present-day Guatemala for over 1,000 years before Spaniards came. Guatemala was a Spanish colony 1524-1821. A republic was established in 1839.

In 1954, the U.S. Central Intelligence Agency engineered the overthrow of elected Pres. Jacobo Arbenz Guzmán, a left-wing reformer. Since then, the country has experienced a variety of military and civilian governments and periods of insurgency, repression, paramilitary violence, and civil war.

The Guatemalan government and leftist rebels signed a peace accord Dec. 29, 1996. During more than 35 years of armed conflict, some 200,000 people were killed or "disappeared"; most casualties were attributed to the government and its paramilitary allies. Gen. Efraín Ríos Montt, dictator in 1982-83, was found guilty of genocide May 10, 2013, but the Constitutional Court overturned his conviction May 20; Ríos Montt died, Apr. 1, 2018, during a retrial.

Former Pres. Alfonso Portillo was extradited to the U.S. May 24, 2013, and pleaded guilty to money laundering, Mar. 18, 2014. Drug trafficking, arms smuggling, police corruption, and gang violence posed threats to national stability. Hundreds of thousands of Guatemalans were among the asylum seekers and other migrants detained trying to enter the U.S. from Mexico 2013-24.

Vice Pres. Roxana Baldetti resigned, May 2015, and was convicted on fraud charges, Oct. 9, 2018. Following large-scale protests, Pres. Otto Pérez Molina resigned Sept. 2, 2015, amid corruption allegations. Pérez Molina and Baldetti were convicted on corruption charges, Dec. 7, 2022.

Former comedian Jimmy Ernesto Morales Cabrera won a runoff election for president, Oct. 25, 2015. He blocked an investigation by a UN-sponsored anti-corruption panel, 2018-19. Conservative Alejandro Giammattei won an Aug. 11, 2019, presidential runoff election. Despite a crackdown on journalists, judges, and the political opposition, Bernardo Arévalo, running on an anti-corruption platform, defeated conservative Sandra Torres in an Aug. 20, 2023, presidential runoff. Overcoming congressional and other efforts to block his inauguration, Arévalo was sworn in Jan. 15, 2024.

Guinea

Republic of Guinea

People: Population: 13,986,179 (75). **Age distrib.:** <15: 40.9%; 65+: 4.0%. **Growth:** 2.7%. **Migrants:** 0.9%. **Pop. density:** 147.4 per sq mi, 56.9 per sq km. **Urban:** 38.5%. **Ethnic groups:** Fulani (Peuhl) 33.4%, Malinke 29.4%, Susu 21.2%, Guerze 7.8%, Kissi 6.2%. **Languages:** French (official), ethnic group-specific langs. **Religions:** Muslim 86.4% (Sunni), ethnic religionist 9.9%, Christian 3.5%.

Geography: Total area: 94,926 sq mi, 245,857 sq km (77); **Land area:** 94,872 sq mi, 245,717 sq km. **Location:** Atlantic coast of W Africa. Guinea-Bissau, Senegal, Mali on N; Côte d'Ivoire on E; Liberia, Sierra Leone on S. **Topography:** Narrow coastal belt leads to mountainous middle region, source of the Gambia, Senegal, and Niger R. Upper Guinea, farther inland, is cooler upland. The SE is forested. **Arable land:** 20.7%. **Capital:** Conakry, 2,178,596.

Government: Type: Presidential republic. **Head of state:** Pres. Mamady Doumbouya; b. 1980; in office: Oct. 1, 2021. **Head of govt.:** Prime Min. Mamadou Oury Bah; in office: Feb. 27, 2024. **Local divisions:** 7 administrative regions, 1 governorate. **Defense budget:** $501 mil. **Active troops:** 9,700.

Economy: Industries: bauxite, gold, diamonds, iron ore; light mfg.; agric. proc. **Chief agric.:** cassava, rice, groundnuts, oil palm fruit, maize, fonio. **Natural resources:** bauxite, iron ore, diamonds, gold, uranium, hydropower, fish, salt. **Water:** 16,701 cu m per capita. **Electricity prod.:** 3.0 bil kWh. **Labor force:** agric. 60.3%, industry 7.2%, services 32.4%. **Unemployment:** 5.3%.

Finance: Monetary unit: Franc (GNF) (8,616.35 = $1 U.S.). **GDP:** $62.9 bil; **per capita GDP:** $4,429; **GDP growth:** 7.1%. **Imports** (2022): $5.7 bil; China 37%, India 10%, Netherlands 8%. **Exports** (2022): $8.9 bil; China 37%, India 27%, UAE 25%. **Tourism** (2022): $11 mil. **Budget:** $2.0 bil. **Inflation:** 7.8%.

Transport: Railways: 675 mi. **Airports:** 16.

Communications: Mobile (2022): 108.9 per 100 pop. **Broadband** (2022): 23.1 per 100 pop. **Internet:** 33.9%.

Health: Expend.: 3.8%. **Life expect.:** 62.7 male; 66.6 female. **Births:** 35.3 per 1,000 pop. **Deaths:** 7.8 per 1,000 pop. **Infant mortality:** 47.0 per 1,000 live births. **Undernourished:** 10.3%. **HIV:** 1.3%. **COVID-19:** 468 deaths; rates per 100,000: 294 cases, 4 deaths. 45% vaccinated.

Education: Compulsory: ages 7-12. **Literacy:** 45.3%.

Website: www.primature.gov.gn

Guinea, a French colony, attained independence Oct. 2, 1958. Sékou Touré, Guinea's first president (1958-84), turned to Communist nations for support and set up a one-party state. Thousands of opponents were jailed and tortured, and many were killed in the 1970s after an unsuccessful Portuguese invasion.

The military took control in a bloodless coup after the Mar. 1984 death of Touré. A new constitution was approved in 1991, but movement toward democracy was slow. Gen. Lansana Conté, the incumbent, won a long-awaited presidential election in Dec. 1993, which outside monitors called flawed. Conté won reelection in 1998.

Major opposition parties boycotted the 2003 presidential election, in which the ailing Conté won 95.6% of the vote. More than 120 died in Jan.-Feb. 2007 strikes and protests that pressured Conté to name a new prime min.; protests followed Prime Min. Lansana Kouyate's ouster by Conté in May 2008. After Conté's death Dec. 22, a military junta took power. More than 150 people were reportedly killed Sept. 28, 2009, when Guinean troops fired into a crowd of about 50,000 anti-government protesters in Conakry. After an assassination attempt Dec. 3, 2009, by a former aide left Pres. Moussa Dadis Camara seriously wounded, Vice Pres. Sékouba Konaté became interim head of state.

Presidential elections June-Nov. 2010 brought a civilian government headed by Alpha Condé to power. The largest known outbreak of Ebola virus disease, 2013-16, began in Guinea and spread rapidly to Liberia and Sierra Leone. Condé won reelection, Oct. 11, 2015. A new constitution, approved in a Mar. 22, 2020, referendum boycotted by the opposition, permitted Condé to seek a third term. He won a disputed Oct. 18, 2020, election. Demonstrations before and after election day left dozens dead. Condé was ousted in a Sept. 5, 2021, military coup led by Col. Mamady Doumbouya. Amid unrest over rising prices, Doumbouya named a new prime minister, Feb. 27, 2024. Former Pres. Camara was convicted, July 31, 2024, of crimes against humanity in connection with the 2009 massacre of protesters.

Guinea-Bissau

Republic of Guinea-Bissau

People: Population: 2,132,325 (146). **Age distrib.:** <15: 42.3%; 65+: 3.1%. **Growth:** 2.5%. **Migrants:** 0.9%. **Pop. density:** 196.4 per sq mi, 75.8 per sq km. **Urban:** 45.9%. **Ethnic groups:** Balanta 30%, Fulani 30%, Manjaco 14%, Mandinga 13%, Papel 7%. **Languages:** Portuguese-based Creole, Portuguese (official), Pular, Mandingo. **Religions:** Muslim 45.5% (Sunni), ethnic religionist 39.8%, Christian 13.4% (Catholic 9.4%).

Geography: Total area: 13,948 sq mi, 36,125 sq km (134); **Land area:** 10,857 sq mi, 28,120 sq km. **Location:** Atlantic coast of W Africa. Senegal on N, Guinea on E and S. **Topography:** A swampy coastal plain covers most of country. Low savanna region to E. **Arable land:** 14.0%. **Capital:** Bissau, 686,623.

Government: Type: Semi-presidential republic. **Head of state:** Pres. Umaro Cissoko Embaló; b. 1972; in office: Feb. 27, 2020. **Head of govt.:** Prime Min. Rui Duarte de Barros; in office: Dec. 20, 2023.

Local divisions: 9 regions. **Defense budget:** $26 mil. **Active troops:** 4,450.

Economy: Industries: agric. prods. proc., beer, soft drinks. **Chief agric.:** rice, groundnuts, cashews, root vegetables, oil palm fruit, plantains. **Natural resources:** fish, timber, phosphates, bauxite, clay, granite, limestone. **Water:** 15,237 cu m per capita. **Electricity prod.:** 84.9 mil kWh. **Labor force:** agric. 50.3%, industry 10.6%, services 39.1%. **Unemployment:** 3.2%.

Finance: Monetary unit: CFA Franc (XOF) (587.79 = $1 U.S.). **GDP:** $5.7 bil; **per capita GDP:** $2,630; **GDP growth:** 4.2%. **Imports** (2022): $577.9 mil; Portugal 34%, Senegal 22%, China 14%, Netherlands 6%. **Exports** (2022): $280.1 mil; India 92%. **Tourism** (2021): $16 mil. **Budget:** $278 mil. **Inflation** (2021-22): 9.4%.

Transport: Airports: 7.

Communications: Mobile: 128.1 per 100 pop. **Broadband:** 73.5 per 100 pop. **Internet:** 31.6%.

Health: Expend.: 8.2%. **Life expect.:** 62.2 male; 66.8 female. **Births:** 36.0 per 1,000 pop. **Deaths:** 7.2 per 1,000 pop. **Infant mortality:** 46.4 per 1,000 live births. **Undernourished:** 32.2%. **HIV:** 2.3%. **COVID-19:** 177 deaths; rates per 100,000: 489 cases, 9 deaths. 28% vaccinated.

Education: Compulsory: ages 6-14. **Literacy:** 53.9%.

Website: www.gov.gw

Portuguese mariners explored the area in the mid-15th cent.; the slave trade flourished in the 17th and 18th cents., and colonization began in the 19th. Independence came Sept. 10, 1974, ending 13 years of guerrilla warfare against the Portuguese regime.

A Nov. 1980 coup gave army chief João Bernardo Vieira absolute power. Multiparty elections were held in 1994. A 1998 army uprising triggered a civil war; rebel troops ousted Vieira on May 7, 1999.

Civilian rule returned with 1999-2000 elections, but top military officers staged a coup Sept. 14, 2003. Vieira won a presidential runoff election, July 24, 2005. A group of soldiers murdered Vieira, Mar. 2, 2009. In the 2009 presidential election, the ruling party (PAIGC) candidate, Malam Bacai Sanhá, won a runoff vote July 26. He died Jan. 9, 2012. A coup was staged, Apr. 12, 2012. Drug trafficking increased substantially, with the support of the military. José Mário Vaz of the PAIGC won a May 18, 2014, presidential runoff. In a Dec. 29, 2019, presidential runoff, Umaro Sissoco Embaló defeated the candidate of the PAIGC, which disputed the result. Forces loyal to Embaló put down a coup attempt, Feb. 1, 2022. Accusing legislators of corruption, Embaló dissolved parliament, May 16, 2022. New elections were held June 4, 2023. After charging an attempted coup, Embaló dissolved parliament again in Dec. 2023.

Guyana

Cooperative Republic of Guyana

People: Population: 794,099 (162). **Age distrib.:** <15: 23.5%; 65+: 8.1%. **Growth:** 0.3%. **Migrants:** 4.0%. **Pop. density:** 10.4 per sq mi, 4.0 per sq km. **Urban:** 27.3%. **Ethnic groups:** East Indian 39.8%, African descent 29.3%, mixed 19.9%, Indigenous 10.5%. **Languages:** English (official), Guyanese Creole, Amerindian langs., Indian langs., Chinese. **Religions:** Christian 54.4% (Protestant 33.9%, independent 12.9%, Catholic 6.1%), Hindu 30.7% (Saktist 14%, Vaishnavite 8%, Shaivite 8%), Muslim 7.4% (Sunni 6%), ethnic religionist 2.3%.

Geography: Total area: 83,000 sq mi, 214,969 sq km (83); **Land area:** 76,004 sq mi, 196,849 sq km. **Location:** N coast of S America. Venezuela on W, Brazil on S, Suriname on E. **Topography:** Dense tropical forests cover much of land. A grassy savanna divides it from flat coastal area, where 90% of the pop. lives, with its rich alluvial soil. **Arable land:** 2.1%. **Capital:** Georgetown, 109,934.

Government: Type: Parliamentary republic. **Head of state and govt.:** Pres. Mohammed Irfaan Ali; b. 1980; in office: Aug. 2, 2020. **Local divisions:** 10 regions. **Defense budget:** $97 mil. **Active troops:** 3,400.

Economy: Industries: bauxite, sugar, rice milling, timber, textiles, gold mining. **Chief agric.:** sugarcane, rice, plantains, papayas, cassava, pumpkins/squash. **Natural resources:** bauxite, gold, diamonds, hardwood timber, shrimp, fish. **Water:** 336,827 cu m per capita. **Electricity prod.:** 1.1 bil kWh. **Labor force:** agric. 11.9%, industry 25.4%, services 62.7%. **Unemployment:** 12.4%.

Finance: Monetary unit: Dollar (GYD) (207.95 = $1 U.S.). **GDP:** $45.0 bil; **per capita GDP:** $55,263; **GDP growth:** 33.0%. **Imports** (2022): $7.1 bil; U.S. 28%, China 14%, Brazil 7%, Trinidad and Tobago 7%. **Exports** (2022): $11.5 bil; Panama 32%, Netherlands 15%, U.S. 13%, UAE 6%, Italy 6%. **Tourism** (2022): $51 mil. **Budget:** $1.5 bil. **Inflation:** 2.8%.

Transport: Motor vehicles: 137.9 per 1,000 pop. **Airports:** 51.

Communications: Mobile (2022): 112.6 per 100 pop. **Broadband** (2022): 32.5 per 100 pop. **Internet:** 85.3%.

Health: Expend.: 4.9%. **Life expect.:** 70.6 male; 74.3 female. **Births:** 16.7 per 1,000 pop. **Deaths:** 7.0 per 1,000 pop. **Infant mortality:** 21.1 per 1,000 live births. **Undernourished:** <2.5%. **HIV:** 1.6%. **COVID-19:** 1,302 deaths; rates per 100,000: 9,467 cases, 166 deaths. 49% vaccinated.

Education: Compulsory: ages 6-11. **Literacy:** 90.0%.

Website: parliament.gov.gy

Guyana became a Dutch possession in the 17th cent., but sovereignty passed to Britain in 1815. Indentured servants from India soon outnumbered the enslaved African population. Guyana became independent May 26, 1966.

The Port Kaituma ambush of U.S. Rep. Leo J. Ryan and others investigating mistreatment of American followers of the Rev. Jim Jones's Peoples Temple cult triggered a mass suicide-execution of more than 900 at their commune in Jonestown, Nov. 18, 1978.

An Oct. 1992 election victory began more than two decades of People's Progressive Party/Civic (PPP/C) governance. An opposition coalition won May 11, 2015, elections, but a Mar. 2, 2020, election returned the PPP/C to power.

Major offshore oil discoveries beginning in 2015 spurred rapid GDP growth by the 2020s. Venezuela claims Guyana's large, resource-rich Essequibo region.

Haiti

Republic of Haiti

People: Population: 11,753,943 (83). **Age distrib.:** <15: 30.5%; 65+: 4.2%. **Growth:** 1.2%. **Migrants:** 0.2%. **Pop. density:** 1,104.6 per sq mi, 426.5 per sq km. **Urban:** 60.5%. **Ethnic groups:** Black 95%, mixed and white 5%. **Languages:** French, Creole (both official). **Religions:** Christian 93.9% (Catholic 66.5%, Protestant 19.7%), agnostic 2.9%, Spiritist 2.8%.

Geography: Total area: 10,714 sq mi, 27,750 sq km (144); **Land area:** 10,641 sq mi, 27,560 sq km. **Location:** In Caribbean; occupies western third of isl. of Hispaniola. Dominican Republic on E, Cuba to W. **Topography:** About two-thirds is mountainous. Much of rest is semiarid. Coastal areas are warm and moist. **Arable land:** 36.5%. **Capital:** Port-au-Prince, 3,060,169.

Government: Type: Semi-presidential republic. **Head of govt.:** Prime Min. Garry Conille; in office: June 3, 2024. A Presidential Transitional Council was sworn in Apr. 25, 2024, with presidential powers. **Local divisions:** 10 departments. **Defense budget:** $19 mil. **Active troops:** 700.

Economy: Industries: textiles, sugar refining, flour milling, cement, light assembly using imported parts. **Chief agric.:** sugarcane, cassava, mangoes/guavas, plantains, bananas, maize. **Natural resources:** bauxite, copper, calcium carbonate, gold, marble, hydropower. **Water:** 1,225 cu m per capita. **Electricity prod.:** 1.0 bil kWh. **Labor force:** agric. 45.5%, industry 12.3%, services 42.2%. **Unemployment:** 14.6%.

Finance: Monetary unit: Gourde (HTG) (131.29 = $1 U.S.). **GDP:** $38.2 bil; **per capita GDP:** $3,256; **GDP growth:** –1.9%. **Imports** (2022): $5.5 bil; U.S. 31%, Dominican Republic 26%, China 16%. **Exports** (2022): $1.4 bil; U.S. 84%. **Tourism** (2022): $73 mil. **Budget** (2020): $1.5 bil. **Inflation:** 36.8%.

Transport: Motor vehicles: 9.7 per 1,000 pop. **Airports:** 17.

Communications: Mobile (2022): 65.2 per 100 pop. **Broadband** (2022): 28.8 per 100 pop. **Internet** (2019): 39.3%.

Health: Expend.: 3.5%. **Life expect.:** 63.8 male; 67.4 female. **Births:** 21.2 per 1,000 pop. **Deaths:** 7.3 per 1,000 pop. **Infant mortality:** 36.8 per 1,000 live births. **Undernourished:** 50.4%. **HIV:** 1.6%. **COVID-19:** 860 deaths; rates per 100,000: 302 cases, 8 deaths. 3% vaccinated.

Education: Compulsory: ages 6-11. **Literacy:** 61.7%.

Website: www.primature.gouv.ht, www.haiti.org

Haiti, visited by Christopher Columbus in 1492 and a French colony from 1697, attained its independence, 1804, following a rebellion led by formerly enslaved Toussaint L'Ouverture. After a period of political violence, the U.S. occupied the country 1915-34.

François Duvalier, known as Papa Doc, was elected president in 1957; in 1964 he was named president for life. Upon his death in 1971, he was succeeded by his son, Jean Claude Duvalier, known as Baby Doc. Following weeks of unrest, Jean Claude fled Haiti aboard a U.S. Air Force jet Feb. 7, 1986. His departure ended the Duvalier family's brutal 28-year dictatorship, but political violence, corruption, poverty, and disease have continued to plague Haiti.

Jean-Bertrand Aristide was elected president in 1990, but the military arrested and expelled him from the country in Sept. 1991. Tens of thousands of Haitian refugees tried to enter the U.S. in the early 1990s.

A UN-authorized, U.S.-led invasion of Haiti was averted, Sept. 18, 1994, when military leaders agreed to step down. Aristide was restored to office Oct. 15. A UN peacekeeping force exercised responsibility in Haiti from 1995 to 1997. Aristide transferred power to his elected successor, René Préval, in 1996.

Aristide won the 2000 presidency in an election boycotted by opposition groups. An armed uprising in early 2004 and pressure from France and the U.S. toppled Aristide, who went into exile Feb. 29. A U.S.-led contingent, sent in after the upheaval, yielded authority June 1, 2004, to a UN stabilization force (MINUSTAH). MINUSTAH's mission ended Oct. 15, 2017.

Préval was again elected president in 2006. Skyrocketing prices for food imports sparked riots and mass protests in Apr. 2008. A succession of hurricanes and tropical storms, Aug.-Sept. 2008, left up to 1 mil homeless.

An earthquake Jan. 12, 2010, near Port-au-Prince caused cataclysmic damage. More than 220,000 people were killed, at least 300,000 were injured, and more than 1.5 mil were left homeless. In the following years, rebuilding proceeded slowly. A severe cholera epidemic began soon after the 2010 earthquake; through 2018, about 820,000 total cases had been reported and almost 9,800 people had died. The UN publicly acknowledged responsibility for the epidemic Dec. 1, 2016.

Michel Martelly, an entertainer, won a Mar. 20, 2011, presidential runoff election. After allegations of widespread fraud in the Oct. 25, 2015, first-round election for a new president, an electoral commission ruled that the balloting should be held again. The Nov. 20, 2016, re-vote was won by businessman Jovenel Moise. Protests against corruption and economic hardship occurred in 2019. Gang violence and anti-government protests plagued Haiti in early 2021.

Pres. Moise was assassinated, July 7, 2021, apparently by Colombian mercenaries. On July 20, 2021, Ariel Henry, designated by Moise shortly before the assassination to become prime minister, took office as prime minister and acting president. A powerful earthquake, Aug. 14, 2021, in SW Haiti killed more than 2,200 and caused widespread damage and suffering. Gang violence and kidnappings for ransom intensified in late 2021 and continued in 2022-24, accompanied by retaliatory violence against gang members. A coalition of gangs that controlled much of Port-au-Prince by early 2024 prevented Henry's return from a foreign trip; Henry resigned Apr. 24. A transitional council named Garry Conille prime minister May 28, 2024.

Eleven people were charged in the U.S. with planning, financing, or facilitating the plot against Moise. By mid-2024, 6 had pleaded guilty to various offenses.

The UN approved, Oct. 2, 2023, a Kenya-led mission in which Kenyan and other nations' security forces would work to reduce violence in Haiti. Kenyan police began arriving in Haiti June 25, 2024. Nearly half the population was facing acute hunger as of Oct. 2024.

Honduras
Republic of Honduras

People: Population: 9,529,188 (96). **Age distrib.:** <15: 28.7%; 65+: 5.6%. **Growth:** 1.3%. **Migrants:** 0.4%. **Pop. density:** 220.6 per sq mi, 85.2 per sq km. **Urban:** 60.8%. **Ethnic groups:** mestizo (mixed Indigenous/European) 90%, Indigenous 7%, African descent 2%. **Languages:** Spanish (official), Amerindian dialects. **Religions:** Christian 95.5% (Catholic 70.3%, Protestant 16.6%), agnostic 2.0%.

Geography: Total area: 43,278 sq mi, 112,090 sq km (101); **Land area:** 43,201 sq mi, 111,890 sq km. **Location:** Central America. Guatemala on W; El Salvador, Nicaragua on S. **Topography:** Caribbean coast is 500 mi long. Pacific coast, on Gulf of Fonseca, is 40 mi long. Mountainous with wide fertile valleys and rich forests. **Arable land:** 9.1%. **Capital:** Tegucigalpa, 1,609,261. **Cities:** San Pedro Sula, 1,008,220.

Government: Type: Presidential republic. **Head of state and govt.:** Pres. Iris Xiomara Castro de Zelaya; b. 1959; in office: Jan. 27, 2022. **Local divisions:** 18 departments. **Defense budget:** $426 mil. **Active troops:** 14,950.

Economy: Industries: sugar proc., coffee, woven and knit apparel, wood prods., cigars. **Chief agric.:** sugarcane, oil palm fruit, milk, maize, bananas, coffee. **Natural resources:** timber, gold, silver, copper, lead, zinc, iron ore, antimony, coal, fish, hydropower. **Water:** 8,967 cu m per capita. **Electricity prod.:** 12.0 bil kWh. **Labor force:** agric. 24.2%, industry 23.4%, services 52.3%. **Unemployment:** 6.1%.

Finance: Monetary unit: Lempira (HNL) (24.80 = $1 U.S.). **GDP:** $76.4 bil; **per capita GDP:** $7,211; **GDP growth:** 3.6%. **Imports:** $17.9 bil; U.S. 47%, Guatemala 10%, China 10%, El Salvador 7%. **Exports:** $9.7 bil; U.S. 51%, Nicaragua 8%, El Salvador 8%, Guatemala 5%. **Tourism:** $722 mil. **Budget:** $6.5 bil. **Inflation:** 6.7%.

Transport: Railways: 434 mi. **Motor vehicles:** 23.8 per 1,000 pop. **Airports:** 129.

Communications: Mobile: 74.4 per 100 pop. **Broadband:** 50.1 per 100 pop. **Internet:** 59.7%.

Health: Expend.: 9.2%. **Life expect.:** 69.6 male; 76.8 female. **Births:** 19.9 per 1,000 pop. **Deaths:** 5.4 per 1,000 pop. **Infant mortality:** 15.4 per 1,000 live births. **Undernourished:** 20.4%. **HIV:** 0.2%. **COVID-19:** 11,114 deaths; rates per 100,000: 4,775 cases, 112 deaths. 59% vaccinated.

Education: Compulsory: ages 5-16. **Literacy:** 88.5%.

Website: www.presidencia.gob.hn

Mayan civilization flourished in Honduras in the 1st millennium CE. Columbus arrived in 1502. Honduras became independent after freeing itself from Spain, 1821, and from the Fed. of Central America, 1838.

In 1975, the army ousted Gen. Oswaldo Lopez Arellano, president for most of the time since 1963, over charges of pervasive bribery by United Brands Co. of the U.S. An elected civilian government took power in 1982.

Hurricane Mitch, Oct. 1998, killed at least 5,600.

Juan Orlando Hernández of the conservative National Party won the Nov. 2013 presidential election. He won reelection, Nov. 26, 2017.

Honduras has become a transshipment point for illegal drugs being smuggled to the U.S. Pres. Hernández's brother was convicted in the U.S, Oct. 18, 2019, of drug-related crimes. Drug-gang violence contributed to an increase in Hondurans trying to enter the U.S. along the Mexican border, 2013-24. A government-declared state of emergency, beginning Dec. 2022, to counter gang violence suspended some constitutional rights.

In Mar. 2016, environmental activist Berta Cáceres was shot to death, a murder apparently ordered by a company facing delays on a dam project. The NGO Global Witness estimated in mid-2017 that more than 120 environmental activists or opponents of land seizures for development had been killed since 2009.

Leftist Xiomara Castro won the Nov. 28, 2021, election to become Honduras's first woman president. The government announced, Mar. 25, 2023, that Honduras was switching diplomatic relations from Taiwan to the People's Republic of China. Former Pres. Hernández, extradited to the U.S. in 2022, was convicted, Mar. 8, 2024, on drug-related charges.

Hungary

People: Population: 9,855,745 (95). **Age distrib.:** <15: 14.6%; 65+: 21.5%. **Growth:** –0.3%. **Migrants:** 6.1%. **Pop. density:** 284.9 per sq mi, 110.0 per sq km. **Urban:** 73.2%. **Ethnic groups:** Hungarian 84.3%, Romani 2.1% (Romani pop. usually underestimated; may represent 5%-10% of pop.). **Languages:** Hungarian (official), English, German, Russian. **Religions:** Christian 87.1% (Catholic 59.2%, Protestant 23.4%), agnostic 7.6%, atheist 4.2%.

Geography: Total area: 35,918 sq mi, 93,028 sq km (108); **Land area:** 34,598 sq mi, 89,608 sq km. **Location:** E central Europe. Ukraine, Slovakia on N; Austria on W; Slovenia, Croatia, Serbia on S; Romania on E. **Topography:** Danube R. forms Slovak border in NW, then swings S to bisect country. Eastern half of country is mainly a great fertile plain, the Alfold. Hilly in W and N. **Arable land:** 45.6%. **Capital:** Budapest, 1,780,391.

Government: Type: Parliamentary republic. **Head of state:** Pres. Tamas Sulyok; b. 1956; in office: Mar. 5, 2024. **Head of govt.:** Prime Min. Viktor Orbán; b. 1963; in office: May 29, 2010. **Local divisions:** 19 counties, 25 cities with county rights, 1 capital city. **Defense budget:** $4.0 bil. **Active troops:** 32,150.

Economy: Industries: mining, metallurgy, constr. materials, processed foods, textiles, chemicals (espec. pharmaceuticals), motor vehicles. **Chief agric.:** wheat, maize, milk, barley, sunflower seeds, rapeseed. **Natural resources:** bauxite, coal, nat. gas. **Water:** 10,711 cu m per capita. **Crude oil reserves:** 12 mil bbls. **Electricity prod.:** 33.8 bil kWh. **Labor force:** agric. 4.4%, industry 31.4%, services 64.3%. **Unemployment:** 4.1%.

Finance: Monetary unit: Forint (HUF) (352.31 = $1 U.S.). **GDP:** $440.6 bil; **per capita GDP:** $45,942; **GDP growth:** –0.9%. **Imports:** $161.6 bil; Germany 21%, China 7%, Austria 7%, Slovakia 6%, Poland 6%. **Exports:** $172.5 bil; Germany 24%, Italy 6%, Romania 5%, Slovakia 5%. **Tourism:** $8.0 bil. **Budget:** $74.1 bil. **Inflation:** 17.1%.

Transport: Railways: 4,776 mi. **Motor vehicles:** 471.7 per 1,000 pop. **Airports:** 109.

Communications: Mobile: 105.1 per 100 pop. **Broadband:** 86.2 per 100 pop. **Internet** (2023): 91.5%.

Health: Expend.: 7.4%. **Life expect.:** 72.9 male; 79.3 female. **Births:** 9.1 per 1,000 pop. **Deaths:** 14.5 per 1,000 pop. **Infant mortality:** 4.7 per 1,000 live births. **Undernourished:** <2.5%. **HIV:** NA. **COVID-19:** 49,053 deaths; rates per 100,000: 22,836 cases, 502 deaths. 63% vaccinated.

Education: Compulsory: ages 4-16. **Literacy:** 99.1%.

Website: kormany.hu

Earliest settlers, chiefly Slav and Germanic, were overrun by Magyars from the east. Stephen I (997-1038) was made king by Pope Sylvester II in 1000 CE. The country suffered repeated Turkish invasions in the 15th-17th cents. After the Turks were defeated, 1686-97, Austria dominated, but Hungary obtained concessions, and regained internal independence in 1867 under a dual monarchy with the emperor of Austria. Defeated with the Central Powers at the end of WWI in 1918, Hungary lost Transylvania to Romania, Croatia and Bacska to Yugoslavia, and Slovakia and Carpatho-Ruthenia to Czechoslovakia. All had large Hungarian minorities. A republic under Michael Karolyi and a Bolshevist revolt under Bela Kun were followed by a vote for a monarchy in 1920 with Adm. Nicholas Horthy as regent.

Hungary allied with Germany in WWII (1939-45). Russian troops captured the country, 1944-45.

A republic was declared Feb. 1, 1946. In 1947 a hard-line Communist, pro-Soviet government was installed. Demonstrations against Communist rule developed into open revolt in 1956. Soviet forces launched a massive attack Nov. 4 against Budapest. About 200,000 persons fled the country. Thousands were arrested and executed.

Major economic reforms were launched early in 1968, switching from a central planning system to one based on market forces and profit. In 1989 Parliament legalized freedom of assembly and association as Hungary shifted away from Communism. In Oct. the Communist Party was formally dissolved. The last Soviet troops left

June 19, 1991. Hungary became a full member of NATO in 1999 and of the EU in 2004.

The center-right Fidesz party ousted the Socialists in 2010 parliamentary elections, and Viktor Orbán became prime min. A fiscally and socially conservative constitution went into force Jan. 1, 2012. Fidesz won Apr. 6, 2014, elections.

Hungary was a major transit route in 2015 for migrants from the Balkans, SW Asia, the Middle East, and Africa trying to reach N Europe; more than 411,000 migrants entered or tried to enter Hungary by the end of Oct., when Hungary completed more than 300 mi of security fencing along its southern border. The government refused to participate in a 2015 EU refugee resettlement program.

After an anti-immigration campaign, Fidesz increased its majority in Apr. 8, 2018, voting. The EU in 2018 began consideration of disciplinary measures against Hungary, in part over limits on press and other freedoms. Dec. 2018 Hungarian legislation limited judicial independence. Legislation in 2020 and 2021 repealed legal rights of transgender people and restricted information about gay people in educational materials or media for minors. The EU, in 2021, began withholding grant payments to Hungary.

Elected by parliament, Mar. 10, 2022, Fidesz's Katalin Novák became Hungary's first woman president. Benefitting from gerrymandering and media control, Fidesz won Apr. 3, 2022, elections. Dec. 2023 "sovereignty" legislation increased government powers to investigate individuals, media outlets, and other groups suspected of acting under foreign influence. Tamas Sulyok replaced Novák as president in 2024.

Iceland

People: Population: 364,036 (173). **Age distrib.:** <15: 19.8%; 65+: 17.1%. **Growth:** 0.9%. **Migrants:** 19.2%. **Pop. density:** 9.4 per sq mi, 3.6 per sq km. **Urban:** 94.1%. **Ethnic groups** (by birth country): Icelandic 78.7%, Polish 5.8%. **Languages:** Icelandic, English, Polish, Nordic langs., German. **Religions:** Evangelical Lutheran Church of Iceland (official); Christian 86.9% (Protestant 75.8%), agnostic 10.3%.

Geography: Total area: 39,769 sq mi, 103,000 sq km (106); **Land area:** 38,707 sq mi, 100,250 sq km. **Location:** Isl. at N end of Atlantic O. Nearest neighbor is Greenland (Den.) to W. **Topography:** Recent volcanic origin. Three-quarters of surface is wasteland: glaciers, lakes, a lava desert, geysers, and hot springs. The climate is moderated by the Gulf Stream. **Arable land:** 1.2%. **Capital:** Reykjavík, 216,364.

Government: Type: Unitary parliamentary republic. **Head of state:** Pres. Halla Tomasdottir; b. 1968; in office: Aug. 1, 2024. **Head of govt.:** Prime Min. Bjarni Benediktsson; b. 1970; in office: Apr. 9, 2024. **Local divisions:** 64 municipalities. **Defense budget:** $41 mil (Coast Guard budget). **Active troops:** No standing armed forces; 250 Coast Guard. Relies on NATO allies for air policing and defense.

Economy: Industries: tourism, fish proc., aluminum smelting, geothermal power, hydropower, medical/pharmaceutical prods. **Chief agric.:** milk, chicken, barley, lamb/mutton, potatoes, pork. **Natural resources:** fish, hydropower, geothermal power, diatomite. **Water:** 459,044 cu m per capita. **Electricity prod.:** 19.9 bil kWh. **Labor force:** agric. 4.1%, industry 18.0%, services 77.9%. **Unemployment:** 3.6%.

Finance: Monetary unit: Krona (ISK) (137.01 = $1 U.S.). **GDP:** $30.5 bil; **per capita GDP:** $77,567; **GDP growth:** 4.1%. **Imports:** $13.5 bil; Norway 12%, Netherlands 10%, Denmark 8%, Germany 8%, China 7%. **Exports:** $13.5 bil; Netherlands 27%, UK 9%, U.S. 8%, Germany 8%, France 6%. **Tourism:** $3.1 bil. **Budget** (2018): $11.5 bil. **Inflation:** 8.7%.

Transport: Motor vehicles: 923.4 per 1,000 pop. **Airports:** 83.

Communications: Mobile: 123.0 per 100 pop. **Broadband:** 125 per 100 pop. **Internet:** 99.9%.

Health: Expend. (2022): 8.6%. **Life expect.:** 81.8 male; 86.3 female. **Births:** 12.6 per 1,000 pop. **Deaths:** 6.6 per 1,000 pop. **Infant mortality:** 1.6 per 1,000 live births. **Undernourished:** <2.5%. **HIV:** 0.1%. **COVID-19:** 186 deaths; rates per 100,000: 57,780 cases, 51 deaths. 82% vaccinated.

Education: Compulsory: ages 6-15. **Literacy:** NA.

Website: www.government.is

Iceland was an independent republic from 930 to 1262, when it joined with Norway. Its language has maintained its purity for 1,000 years. The Althing, or assembly, established in 930, is the world's oldest surviving parliament. Danish rule lasted 1380-1918; the last ties with the Danish crown were severed in 1944.

Iceland's banking system and currency collapsed amid the global financial crisis in Oct. 2008. More than $10 bil in loans from the IMF and European governments restored financial stability; austerity measures were imposed, and the nation entered a deep recession. An Apr. 2010 eruption of the Eyjafjallajökull volcano disrupted European air traffic. Following Oct. 28, 2017, elections, the Left-Green Movement formed a coalition with center-right parties. The same coalition won Sept. 25, 2021, elections. Volcanic eruptions in S Iceland, beginning Dec. 2023 and continuing in 2024, prompted evacuations and disrupted the economy.

Iceland's glaciers have been shrinking, an apparent effect of climate change.

India

Republic of India

People: Population: 1,409,128,296 (2). **Age distrib.:** <15: 24.5%; 65+: 6.8%. **Growth:** 0.7%. **Migrants:** 0.4%. **Pop. density:** 1,227.5 per sq mi, 473.9 per sq km. **Urban:** 36.9%. **Ethnic groups:** Indo-Aryan 72%, Dravidian 25%. **Languages:** Hindi (most widely spoken); 22 other official langs. (incl. Bengali, Marathi, Telugu, Tamil, Gujarati, Urdu); English (subsidiary official lang.; most important for natl., political, commercial communication); Hindustani (variant of Hindi/Urdu) widely spoken throughout N. **Religions:** Hindu 73.2% (Vaishnavite 27%, Shaivite 26%, Saktist 21%), Muslim 13.7% (Sunni 13%), Christian 5.0%, ethnic religionist 3.1%, Sikh 1.8%, agnostic 1.5%.

Geography: Total area: 1,269,219 sq mi, 3,287,263 sq km (7); **Land area:** 1,147,956 sq mi, 2,973,193 sq km. **Location:** Occupies most of Indian subcontinent in S Asia. Pakistan on W; China, Nepal, Bhutan on N; Myanmar, Bangladesh on E. **Topography:** The Himalayan Mts., highest in world, stretch across northern borders. The Ganges Plain below is among the world's most densely populated regions. The climate varies from tropical heat in S to near-Arctic cold in N. Rajasthan Desert in NW. NE Assam Hills get 400 in. of rain a year. **Arable land:** 51.9%. **Capital:** Delhi, 33,807,403. **Cities:** Mumbai (Bombay), 21,673,149; Kolkata (Calcutta), 15,570,786; Bangalore, 14,008,262; Chennai (Madras), 12,053,697; Hyderabad, 11,068,877; Ahmadabad, 8,854,444; Surat, 8,330,528; Pune (Poona), 7,345,848.

Government: Type: Federal parliamentary republic. **Head of state:** Pres. Droupadi Murmu; b. 1958; in office: July 25, 2022. **Head of govt.:** Prime Min. Narendra Modi; b. 1950; in office: May 26, 2014. **Local divisions:** 28 states, 8 union territories. **Defense budget:** $73.6 bil. **Active troops:** 1,475,750.

Economy: Industries: textiles, chemicals, food proc., steel, transp. equip., cement, mining, petroleum, machinery, software, pharmaceuticals. **Chief agric.:** sugarcane, rice, milk, wheat, bison milk, potatoes. **Natural resources:** coal, antimony, iron ore, lead, manganese, mica, bauxite, rare earth elements, titanium ore, chromite, nat. gas, diamonds, petroleum, limestone. **Water:** 1,358 cu m per capita. **Crude oil reserves:** 4.6 bil bbls. **Electricity prod.:** 1.8 tril kWh. **Labor force:** agric. 42.9%, industry 26.1%, services 31.0%. **Unemployment:** 4.2%.

Finance: Monetary unit: Rupee (INR) (83.92 = $1 U.S.). **GDP:** $14.5 tril; **per capita GDP:** $10,176; **GDP growth:** 7.6%. **Imports:** $859.5 bil; China 15%, UAE 7%, U.S. 7%, Saudi Arabia 6%, Russia 6%. **Exports:** $773.2 bil; U.S. 18%, UAE 7%. **Tourism:** $32.2 bil. **Budget** (2020): $818.9 bil. **Inflation:** 5.6%.

Transport: Railways: 40,733 mi. **Motor vehicles:** 58.9 per 1,000 pop. **Airports:** 311.

Communications: Mobile: 80.6 per 100 pop. **Broadband:** 60.2 per 100 pop. **Internet** (2020): 43.4%.

Health: Expend.: 3.3%. **Life expect.:** 66.5 male; 70.1 female. **Births:** 16.2 per 1,000 pop. **Deaths:** 9.1 per 1,000 pop. **Infant mortality:** 30.4 per 1,000 live births. **Undernourished:** 13.7%. **HIV:** 0.2%. **COVID-19:** 533,626 deaths; rates per 100,000: 3,264 cases, 39 deaths. 69% vaccinated.

Education: Compulsory: ages 6-13. **Literacy:** 76.3%.

Website: www.india.gov.in

India has one of the oldest civilizations in the world. Excavations trace the Indus Valley civilization back for at least 5,000 years. Paintings in the mountain caves of Ajanta, richly carved temples, the Taj Mahal in Agra, and the Kutab Minar in Delhi are among treasured relics of the past.

Aryan tribes, speaking Sanskrit, invaded from the NW around 1500 BCE. Asoka ruled most of the Indian subcontinent in the 3rd cent. BCE and established Buddhism. But Hinduism revived and eventually predominated. Under the Guptas, 4th-6th cent. CE, science, literature, and the arts enjoyed a golden age. Arab invaders established a Muslim foothold in the west in the 8th cent., and Turkish Muslims gained control of North India by 1200. The Mughal emperors ruled 1526-1857.

Vasco da Gama established Portuguese trading posts 1498-1503. The Dutch followed. The British East India Co. sent Capt. William Hawkins, 1609, to get concessions from the Mughal emperor for spices and textiles. Operating as the East India Co., the British gained control of most of India. The British parliament assumed political direction; under Lord Bentinck, 1828-35, rule by rajahs (princes) was curbed. After the Sepoy troops mutinied, 1857-58, the British supported the native rulers.

Nationalism grew after WWI. The Indian National Congress and the Muslim League demanded constitutional reform. A leader emerged in Mohandas K. Gandhi (called Mahatma, or Great Soul) (b. Oct. 2, 1869), who advocated self-rule, nonviolence, and an end to caste discrimination against "untouchables." In 1930 he launched a program of civil disobedience, boycotting British goods and rejecting taxes without representation. He was assassinated Jan. 30, 1948.

In 1935, Britain gave India a constitution providing a bicameral federal congress. Muhammad Ali Jinnah, head of the Muslim League, sought creation of a Muslim nation, Pakistan.

The British government partitioned British India into the dominions of India and Pakistan. India became a member of the UN in 1945, a self-governing member of the Commonwealth in 1947, and a democratic republic, Jan. 26, 1950. More than 12 mil Hindu and Muslim refugees crossed the India-Pakistan borders in 1947; about 200,000 were killed in communal fighting.

After Pakistan troops began attacks on Bengali separatists in East Pakistan, Mar. 25, 1971, some 10 mil refugees fled to India. India and Pakistan went to war Dec. 3, 1971, on both the east and west fronts. Pakistan troops, Dec. 16, surrendered in the east, which became Bangladesh; Pakistan agreed to a cease-fire in the west Dec. 17.

Indira Gandhi, India's prime minister since Jan. 1966, invoked emergency powers in June 1975. Thousands of opponents were arrested and press censorship imposed. These and other actions, including population control through forced vasectomies, were widely resented. Opposition parties, united in the Janata coalition, won the 1977 elections.

Gandhi became prime minister for the second time in 1980. She was assassinated by two of her Sikh bodyguards Oct. 31, 1984, in response to the government suppression in June 1984 of a Sikh uprising in Punjab, which included an assault on the Golden Temple at Amritsar, the holiest Sikh shrine. Widespread rioting followed the assassination; thousands of Sikhs were killed and some 50,000 left homeless. Rajiv, Indira Gandhi's son, replaced her as prime min. A gas leak at a Union Carbide chemical plant in Bhopal, Dec. 1984, eventually killed some 14,000 people.

Many died in religious, ethnic, and political conflicts during the late 1980s and early '90s. To suppress the Sikh insurgency in Punjab, Indian government troops attacked the Golden Temple again in 1988. Rajiv Gandhi, swept from office in 1989, was assassinated May 21, 1991. Nationwide riots followed the destruction of a 16th-cent. mosque in Ayodhya by Hindu militants in Dec. 1992. Ethnic clashes in Assam, in NE India, killed thousands in Feb. 1993. Bombs jolted Mumbai and Kolkata, Mar. 12-19, killing over 300.

India conducted a series of nuclear tests in mid-May 1998, raising tensions with Pakistan. India blamed Pakistani-sponsored terrorist groups for an Oct. 1, 2001, suicide attack on the state legislature in Jammu and Kashmir (see below), in which at least 40 people died, and a Dec. 13 assault on the Indian parliament in New Delhi that left 13 people dead. Hindu-Muslim clashes in Gujarat Feb.-Mar. 2002 claimed more than 1,000 lives.

The Congress Party won the most seats in 2004 parliamentary elections.

The Indian Ocean tsunami of Dec. 26, 2004, left more than 16,000 people dead and over 647,000 displaced in India. Islamic extremists set off 7 bombs on commuter trains in Mumbai, July 11, 2006, killing some 200 people.

Chandrayaan-1, India's first lunar survey mission, was launched into space Oct. 22, 2008. *Chandrayaan-3* was the first mission from any nation to make a soft landing, Aug. 23, 2023, in the Moon's south polar region.

Ten Pakistanis linked to a Kashmir militant group stormed several sites in Mumbai, Nov. 2008, killing 163 people.

In 2009 parliamentary elections, the United Progressive Alliance, headed by the Congress Party, gained a resounding victory. Electricity blackouts July 30-31, 2012, left 670 mil people without power.

Several rapes in New Delhi in Nov.-Dec. 2012 prompted protests for their mishandling by police and government inaction. Tougher laws against sexual violence were passed Feb. 4, 2013. The Hindu nationalist Bharatiya Janata party (BJP) won a large majority in Apr.-May 2014 parliamentary elections; Narendra Modi became prime min.

Development of high-tech industries has propelled rapid economic growth in most years since the 1990s; hundreds of millions have emerged from extreme poverty, although distribution of wealth remains highly uneven. Since 2011, India has had the world's third-largest GDP. To combat climate change, the government released a plan, Oct. 1, 2015, for reducing the rate of growth in India's carbon emissions.

The Supreme Court, Sept. 6, 2018, struck down a 19th-cent. law that made consensual gay sex a criminal offense. The BJP increased its majority in Apr.-May 2019 elections. A check of citizenship status in Assam produced a list, released Aug. 31, 2019, of 1.9 mil people, mostly Muslim ethnic Bengalis, judged to be noncitizens and subject to deportation. Dec. 2019 legislation facilitating citizenship excluded Muslims. On Aug. 5, 2020, Modi participated in a groundbreaking ceremony for a Hindu temple on the site of the destroyed Ayodhya mosque. Anti-Muslim violence increased in the early 2020s.

A Sept. 22, 2021, Supreme Court ruling opened India's elite military academy to women. In one of the country's worst rail disasters, more than 290 people died in a multitrain accident, June 2, 2023, in the eastern state of Odisha. In the northeastern state of Manipur, ethnic violence beginning in May 2023 and continuing in 2024 left over 200 dead and displaced tens of thousands.

Severe heatwaves, likely related to climate change, gripped northern India in the 2020s.

The COVID-19 pandemic that began in 2020 impacted India more severely than almost any other country. Spikes in new cases at times overwhelmed the health care system. By Sept. 2024, India had a total of about 45 mil confirmed cases (3rd-highest in the world). A WHO report released in May 2022 estimated that India had more than 4.7 mil excess deaths in 2020-21 associated with COVID-19.

According to UN estimates, India's population surpassed China's in 2023, making India the world's most populous nation.

The BJP won the most seats but fell well short of a majority in Apr.-June 2024 parliamentary elections. Modi formed a coalition and was sworn in for a new term as prime min., June 9, 2024.

Sikkim, bordered by Tibet, Bhutan, and Nepal, formerly British protected, became a protectorate of India in 1950. Area 2,740 sq mi; pop. (2011 census) 610,577; capital is Gangtok. In Sept. 1974, India's parliament voted to make Sikkim an associate Indian state, absorbing it into India.

Kashmir is a predominantly Muslim region in the NW that borders India, Pakistan, Afghanistan, and China. Muslim rule of the previously Hindu kingdom began in 1341; after almost 200 years under the Mughals, the area was incorporated into British India in 1846. Fighting broke out in the region between India and Pakistan in 1947 following independence from Britain. A cease-fire was negotiated by the UN Jan. 1, 1949; it gave Pakistan control of one-third of the area as Azad Kashmir, in the W and NW, and India the remaining two-thirds, as the Indian state of Jammu and Kashmir. Area 39,146 sq mi; pop. (2011 census) 12,541,302. Capitals: Srinagar (summer), pop. (2023 est.) 1,698,277; Jammu (winter), pop. (2023 est.) 726,618. Fighting in the area resumed during 1965 and 1971. China occupied about 14,000 sq mi in the Ladakh district after a war with India in 1962. India separated Ladakh from Jammu and Kashmir in 2019.

Since 1989, Indian security forces in Jammu and Kashmir have battled Islamic separatist fighters. India has charged Pakistan with aiding the separatists. A cease-fire between Indian and Pakistani troops along the line of control took effect Nov. 2003 (later renewed). Some breaches have occurred, and fighting between Indian forces and Islamic militants has continued. More than 40 Indian paramilitary troops in Kashmir were killed in a terrorist bombing, Feb. 14, 2019. Estimates of conflict-related deaths since 1989 range from 40,000 to over 80,000.

The Indian government revoked statehood for Jammu and Kashmir, effective Oct. 31, 2019, to create two federally administered territories; India increased security forces and reportedly detained thousands. In accordance with a Dec. 2023 Supreme Court ruling, elections for a regional legislature in Jammu and Kashmir were scheduled for Sept.-Oct. 2024.

France, 1952-54, peacefully yielded to India its five colonies, former French India: Pondicherry, Karikal, Mahe, and Yanaon were merged to become Pondicherry, now Puducherry, area 185 sq mi; pop. (2011 census) 1,247,953. The colony of Chandernagor was incorporated into the state of West Bengal.

Indonesia

Republic of Indonesia

People: Population: 281,562,465 (4). **Age distrib.:** <15: 23.8%; 65+: 8.0%. **Growth:** 0.7%. **Migrants:** 0.1%. **Pop. density:** 402.5 per sq mi, 155.4 per sq km. **Urban:** 59.2%. **Ethnic groups:** Javanese 40.1%, Sundanese 15.5%, Malay 3.7%, Batak 3.6%, Madurese 3%, Betawi 2.9%, Minangkabau 2.7%, Buginese 2.7%, Bantenese 2%. **Languages:** Bahasa Indonesia (official; modified form of Malay), English, Dutch, local dialects (Javanese most widely spoken). **Religions:** Muslim 77.8% (Sunni), Christian 13.0% (Protestant 7.4%, Catholic 3.2%, indep. 2.4%), new religionist 2.1%, ethnic religionist 2.1%.

Geography: Total area: 735,358 sq mi, 1,904,569 sq km (14); **Land area:** 699,451 sq mi, 1,811,569 sq km. **Location:** Archipelago SE of Asian mainland along the equator. Malaysia on N, Papua New Guinea on E, Timor-Leste on S. **Topography:** Comprises 17,508 islands (about 6,000 inhabited), incl. Java, Sumatra, Kalimantan (most of Borneo), Sulawesi (Celebes), and West Irian (Irian Jaya, the W half of New Guinea). Also Bangka, Belitung, Madura, Bali, Timor. Cooler climate in mountains and plateaus on the major isls.; tropical lowlands. **Arable land:** 9.5%. **Capital:** Jakarta, 11,436,004 (new capital of Nusantara, on the island of Borneo, is still in development). **Cities:** Bekasi, 3,830,678; Depok, 3,133,298; Surabaya, 3,088,748; Bandung, 2,714,215; Tangerang, 2,570,980.

Government: Type: Presidential republic. **Head of state and govt.:** Pres. Joko Widodo; b. 1961; in office: Oct. 20, 2014. **Local divisions:** 35 provinces, 1 autonomous province, 1 special region, 1 national capital district. **Defense budget:** $8.8 bil. **Active troops:** 404,500.

Economy: Industries: petroleum and nat. gas, textiles, automotive, elec. appliances, apparel, footwear, mining, cement, medical instruments and appliances. **Chief agric.:** oil palm fruit, rice, sugarcane, maize, coconuts, cassava. **Natural resources:** petroleum, tin, nat. gas, nickel, timber, bauxite, copper, coal, gold, silver. **Water:** 7,374 cu m per capita. **Crude oil reserves:** 2.5 bil bbls. **Electricity prod.:** 337.2 bil kWh. **Labor force:** agric. 29.3%, industry 21.9%, services 48.8%. **Unemployment:** 3.4%.

Finance: Monetary unit: Rupiah (IDR) (15,497.98 = $1 U.S.). **GDP:** $4.3 tril; **per capita GDP:** $15,613; **GDP growth:** 5.0%. **Imports:** $264.4 bil; China 31%, Singapore 10%, Japan 6%,

Malaysia 5%, Thailand 5%. **Exports:** $292.8 bil; China 21%, U.S. 10%, Japan 8%, India 8%, Malaysia 5%. **Tourism:** $14.0 bil. **Budget** (2020): $193.0 bil. **Inflation:** 3.7%.

Transport: Railways: 5,070 mi (only partly operational). **Motor vehicles:** 82.7 per 1,000 pop. **Airports:** 513.

Communications: Mobile: 125.2 per 100 pop. **Broadband:** 118 per 100 pop. **Internet** (2023): 69.2%.

Health: Expend.: 3.7%. **Life expect.:** 71.3 male; 76.0 female. **Births:** 14.8 per 1,000 pop. **Deaths:** 6.8 per 1,000 pop. **Infant mortality:** 18.9 per 1,000 live births. **Undernourished:** 7.2%. **HIV:** 0.4%. **COVID-19:** 162,059 deaths; rates per 100,000: 2,497 cases, 59 deaths. 64% vaccinated.

Education: Compulsory: ages 7-15. **Literacy:** 96.0%.

Website: www.indonesia.go.id

Hindu and Buddhist civilization from India reached Indonesia nearly 2,000 years ago, taking root especially in Java. Islam spread along the maritime trade routes in the 15th cent. and became predominant by the 16th cent. The Dutch replaced the Portuguese as the area's most important European trade power in the 17th cent., securing territorial control over Java by 1750. The other islands were subdued in the early 20th cent.

Following Japanese occupation, 1942-45, nationalists led by Sukarno and Hatta declared independence. The Netherlands ceded sovereignty in 1949. A republic was declared, Aug. 17, 1950, with Sukarno as president.

Irian Jaya, on New Guinea, remained under Dutch control but was transferred by the UN to Indonesia in 1963; it became the provinces of Papua and West Papua in the early 2000s. Pro-independence protests and an armed separatist movement were met by a harsh government crackdown in the late 2010s and 2020s, including allegations of atrocities against civilians. Tens of thousands were displaced.

Sukarno suspended parliament in 1960 and was named president for life in 1963. He made close alliances with Communist governments. In Sept. 1965 an attempted coup was successfully put down, but Sukarno was forced to cede power to the army, led by Gen. Suharto. The regime blamed the coup on the Communist Party; more than 300,000 alleged Communists were killed in army-initiated massacres.

Parliament reelected Suharto to a seventh consecutive presidential term in 1998, as a severe economic downturn focused public anger on nepotism, cronyism, and corruption in the Suharto regime. Suharto resigned May 21, 1998. Abdurrahman Wahid, leader of Indonesia's largest Muslim organization, was elected president in 1999. In Aug. 2000, under pressure from the legislature, he agreed to share power with Vice Pres. Megawati Sukarnoputri, the daughter of the late Pres. Sukarno. Charging Wahid with incompetence and corruption, the legislature ousted him July 23, 2001, and Megawati became Indonesia's first woman president.

Clashes between Muslims and Christians in the Maluku (Molucca) Isls., 1999-2002, claimed about 5,000 lives. East Timor, a former Portuguese colony that Indonesia invaded in Dec. 1975 and controlled until Oct. 1999, became a fully independent country May 20, 2002, as Timor-Leste.

Separatists in Aceh, NW Sumatra, fought government troops, 1980s-2000s. A peace agreement granting Aceh greater autonomy was signed Aug. 15, 2005. Aceh adopted a strict penal code based on sharia law and sometimes enforced by vigilantes; prohibited conduct was punished by public canings.

Investigators blamed Islamic terrorists for bombings that killed 202 people, mostly foreign tourists, at nightclubs in Bali, Oct. 12, 2002, and 12 people at a Marriott hotel in Jakarta, Aug. 5, 2003. Susilo Bambang Yudhoyono, a retired general, defeated Megawati in a 2004 direct presidential runoff vote.

A massive earthquake off NW Sumatra, Dec. 26, 2004, triggered tsunamis that wreaked havoc in the Indian Ocean region. The death toll in Indonesia alone exceeded 165,000.

Pres. Yudhoyono won a second 5-year term July 8, 2009.

The General Elections Commission, July 22, 2014, declared populist Jakarta governor Joko Widodo the presidential election winner. All 162 people aboard an AirAsia Indonesia flight were killed, Dec. 28, 2014, when the plane crashed into the Java Sea near Borneo.

Assaults by terrorist gunmen and bombers in Jakarta, Jan. 14, 2016, left 8 dead, including 4 attackers; ISIS claimed responsibility. A series of ISIS-inspired suicide bombings at churches and attacks on police, May 2018, left 13 victims dead.

Rainforest destruction and air pollution from fires to clear areas for agriculture have been major environmental problems in recent years.

All 189 on board an Indonesian Lion Air flight were killed, Oct. 29, 2018, when the Boeing 737 Max 8 plane crashed shortly after takeoff from Jakarta.

Pres. Widodo won reelection in Apr. 17, 2019, voting. The COVID-19 pandemic that began in 2020 had a devastating impact in Indonesia. A 2022 WHO report estimated more than 1 mil excess deaths in Indonesia in 2020-21, far exceeding the recorded death toll from COVID-19. Dec. 2022 penal code revisions criminalized extramarital sex and limited free expression.

Former general Prabowo Subianto, accused of past human rights abuses, was declared the winner of the Feb. 14, 2024, presidential election.

Iran

Islamic Republic of Iran

People: Population: 88,386,937 (17). **Age distrib.:** <15: 23.3%; 65+: 7.0%. **Growth:** 0.9%. **Migrants:** 3.3%. **Pop. density:** 149.5 per sq mi, 57.7 per sq km. **Urban:** 77.7%. **Ethnic groups:** Persian, Azeri, Kurd, Lur, Baloch, Arab, Turkmen, Turkic tribes. **Languages:** Persian Farsi (official), Azeri and other Turkic dialects, Kurdish, Gilaki and Mazandarani, Luri, Balochi, Arabic. **Religions:** Muslim (official) 98.1% (Shia 80%, Sunni 17%).

Geography: Total area: 636,372 sq mi, 1,648,195 sq km (17); **Land area:** 591,352 sq mi, 1,531,595 sq km. **Location:** Between the Middle East and S Asia. Iraq, Turkey on W; Armenia, Azerbaijan, Turkmenistan on N; Afghanistan, Pakistan on E. **Topography:** Interior highlands and plains surrounded by high mountains, up to 18,000 ft. Large salt deserts cover much of area; some oases and forests. Most of pop. inhabits N and NW. **Arable land:** 9.7%. **Capital:** Tehran, 9,616,007. **Cities:** Mashhad, 3,415,532; Esfahan, 2,294,589; Shiraz, 1,742,750; Tabriz, 1,678,028; Karaj, 1,603,011.

Government: Type: Theocratic republic. **Religious head:** Ayatollah Sayyed Ali Khamenei; b. 1939; in office: June 4, 1989. **Head of state and govt.:** Pres. Masoud Pezeshkian; in office: July 30, 2024. **Local divisions:** 31 provinces. **Defense budget:** $7.4 bil. **Active troops:** 610,000.

Economy: Industries: petroleum, petrochemicals, gas, fertilizer, caustic soda, textiles, cement and other constr. materials. **Chief agric.:** wheat, sugarcane, milk, sugar beets, tomatoes, barley. **Natural resources:** petroleum, nat. gas, coal, chromium, copper, iron ore, lead, manganese, zinc, sulfur. **Water:** 1,559 cu m per capita. **Crude oil reserves:** 208.6 bil bbls. **Electricity prod.:** 360.7 bil kWh. **Labor force:** agric. 15.1%, industry 34.2%, services 50.7%. **Unemployment:** 9.1%.

Finance: Monetary unit: Rial (IRR) (42,157.75 = $1 U.S.). **GDP:** $1.6 tril; **per capita GDP:** $17,922; **GDP growth:** 5.0%. **Imports** (2022): $102.5 bil; China 28%, UAE 19%, Brazil 13%, Turkey (Türkiye) 9%, India 6%. **Exports** (2022): $110.9 bil; China 36%, Turkey (Türkiye) 20%, Kuwait 6%, Pakistan 5%. **Budget:** $90.2 bil. **Inflation:** 44.6%.

Transport: Railways: 5,271 mi. **Motor vehicles:** 82.8 per 1,000 pop. **Airports:** 173.

Communications: Mobile: 166.3 per 100 pop. **Broadband:** 120 per 100 pop. **Internet:** 81.7%.

Health: Expend.: 5.8%. **Life expect.:** 74.3 male; 77.1 female. **Births:** 14.3 per 1,000 pop. **Deaths:** 5.3 per 1,000 pop. **Infant mortality:** 14.3 per 1,000 live births. **Undernourished:** 6.5%. **HIV:** <0.1%. **COVID-19:** 146,837 deaths; rates per 100,000: 9,082 cases, 175 deaths. 70% vaccinated.

Education: Compulsory: ages 6-14. **Literacy:** 89.0%.

Website: www.president.ir

Ancestors of inhabitants of Iran, formerly known as Persia, came from the east during the second millennium BCE; they were an Indo-European group related to the Aryans of India. In 549 BCE, Cyrus the Great united the Medes and Persians in the Persian Empire; he conquered Babylonia in 538 BCE, and restored Jerusalem to the Jews. Alexander the Great conquered Persia in 333 BCE, but Persians regained independence in the next century under the Parthians, themselves succeeded by Sassanian Persians in 226 CE. Arabs brought Islam to Persia in the 7th cent., replacing the Indigenous Zoroastrian faith. After Persian political and cultural autonomy was reasserted in the 9th cent., arts and sciences flourished.

Turks and Mongols ruled Persia in turn from the 11th cent. to 1502, when Ismael I established the Iranian Safavid dynasty and made Shiite Islam the official religion. The dynasty lasted until 1722. The British and Russian empires vied for influence in the 19th cent.; Britain severed Afghanistan from Iran in 1857.

Reza Khan, a military officer, became prime min., 1923, and shah in 1925. He began modernization, curbed foreign influence, and officially changed the country's name from Persia to Iran in 1935. Fearing the shah's Axis sympathies, British and Soviet troops forced him to abdicate, 1941; he was succeeded by his son, Mohammad Reza Pahlavi. The U.S. Central Intelligence Agency had a major role in the ouster, 1953, of Prime Min. Muhammad Mossadegh, who had nationalized the oil industry.

With U.S. backing, the shah brought economic and social change to Iran (White Revolution), but repression of opposition groups grew severe. Violent protests in 1978 eventually forced the shah to depart, Jan. 16, 1979 (he died in Egypt, July 27, 1980). Forces loyal to Shiite leader Ayatollah Ruhollah Khomeini defeated government troops, Feb 11, 1979. Khomeini established an Islamic theocracy.

Iranian militants seized the U.S. embassy in Tehran Nov. 4, 1979, and took hostages, including 62 Americans. Despite international condemnations and U.S. efforts, including an abortive Apr. 1980 rescue attempt, the crisis continued until Jan. 20, 1981, when an accord, involving the release of frozen Iranian assets, was reached.

War between Iran and Iraq, 1980-88, killed hundreds of thousands. In Nov. 1986 it became known that the U.S., which had generally sided with Iraq during the war, had secretly shipped arms to Iran to gain help in obtaining the release of U.S. hostages held in Lebanon.

A U.S. Navy warship shot down an Iranian airliner, July 3, 1988, after mistaking it for an F-14 fighter jet; all 290 aboard died.

An earthquake struck northern Iran June 21, 1990, killing more than 45,000 and leaving 400,000 homeless. Some 1 mil Kurdish refugees fled from Iraq to Iran following the Persian Gulf War of 1991. To curb Iran's alleged support for international terrorism, the U.S. in 1996 authorized sanctions on foreign companies that invested there.

An earthquake Dec. 26, 2003, in Bam, SE Iran, killed about 26,000 people.

The religiously conservative mayor of Tehran, Mahmoud Ahmadinejad, defeated former Pres. Hashemi Rafsanjani in a 2005 runoff election. U.S. Pres. George W. Bush's administration accused Iran of seeking to build nuclear weapons. Seeking to halt Iran's uranium-enrichment program, the UN Security Council imposed sanctions, 2006-07.

Seeking to halt Iran's uranium-enrichment program, the UN Security Council imposed sanctions, 2006-07.

Ahmadinejad won the 2009 presidential election. His main opponent claimed the vote count was fraudulent. Huge post-election protests were crushed. Tensions with the U.S. and European governments were heightened in 2009 by disclosures that Iran had been secretly enriching uranium and by Iranian tests of medium-range missiles.

The UN and U.S. toughened sanctions, June-July 2010. Iran accused Israel, the U.S., and other Western powers of carrying out cyberattacks against the country's nuclear facilities and of assassinating Iranian scientists. Iran announced, Jan. 2012, it was enriching uranium at its underground Fordo nuclear facility.

The moderate cleric Hassan Rouhani was elected president June 14, 2013. An agreement—signed July 14, 2015, by the U.S., UK, France, Germany, Russia, China, Iran, and the EU—required Iran to limit and partly dismantle its nuclear program and submit to international inspections in return for the lifting of most sanctions. Rouhani won reelection as president, May 19, 2017. Large-scale protests, mainly against poor economic conditions, occurred in dozens of cities around Iran, Dec. 2017-Jan. 2018, until suppressed by forces of the Islamic Revolutionary Guard Corps (IRGC). Pres. Donald Trump announced, May 8, 2018, that the U.S. would withdraw from the 2015 nuclear agreement and reimpose U.S. sanctions. Beginning in July 2019, Iran took nuclear program actions in violation of the 2015 accord.

Playing a role in regional conflicts, Iran supported the Syrian government in its civil war, beginning 2012. In recent decades, Iran has also given significant support to Shiite militias in Iraq, Hezbollah forces in Lebanon, Hamas in the Palestinian Territories, and Houthi rebels in Yemen.

Widespread demonstrations protesting economic conditions were suppressed, Nov. 2019; up to 1,500 protesters may have been killed.

A U.S. drone strike in Iraq, Jan. 3, 2020, killed IRGC general Qassem Soleimani, in charge of the corps' foreign operations. Iran, Jan. 7, fired missiles at two Iraqi military bases housing U.S. troops. On Jan. 8, Iran mistakenly shot down a Ukrainian airliner shortly after its takeoff from Tehran, killing all 176 onboard.

An explosion and fire caused extensive damage, July 2, 2020, at a key Iranian nuclear facility; Israeli sabotage was suspected. Similar disasters occurred, 2020-21, at Iranian industrial, nuclear, and infrastructure sites or aboard warships. A leading Iranian nuclear scientist was assassinated, Nov. 27, 2020.

Iran was hardhit by the COVID-19 pandemic that began in 2020; health care facilities were at times severely strained.

In an election marked by low turnout, hardliner Ebrahim Raisi was elected president, June 18, 2021.

The death in custody, Sept. 16, 2022, of a woman arrested for a dress-code violation sparked nationwide, sometimes violent protests, met with a lethal response by security forces. Iran's parliament approved, Sept. 20, 2023, legislation toughening penalties for dress-code violations.

Iran and Saudi Arabia announced, Mar. 10, 2023, they would restore diplomatic relations (severed in 2016). Iran released, Sept. 18, 2023, 5 imprisoned Americans; the U.S. unfroze $6 bil of Iranian assets, to be used for humanitarian purposes.

Suicide bombings, Jan. 3, 2024, for which a branch of ISIS claimed responsibility, killed more than 80. An Israeli airstrike killed 7 IRGC officers in Damascus, Apr. 1, 2024. In retaliation, Iran attacked Israel, Apr. 13, with hundreds of missiles and drones; almost all were intercepted. Pres. Raisi died, May 19, in a helicopter crash. Masoud Pezeshkian, running as a moderate, won a July 5 runoff to succeed Raisi. Iran blamed Israel for the assassination in Tehran, July 31, 2024, of a top Hamas leader.

In response to Israel's killing of Hezbollah leader Hassan Nasrallah and "limited" ground invasion of southern Lebanon in late Sept. 2024, Iran fired nearly 200 ballistic missiles at Israel, Oct. 2, 2024; they were mostly intercepted by Israeli and U.S. forces.

Iraq

Republic of Iraq

People: Population: 42,083,436 (35). **Age distrib.:** <15: 34.6%; 65+: 3.6%. **Growth:** 2.0%. **Migrants:** 0.9%. **Pop. density:** 249.2 per sq mi, 96.2 per sq km. **Urban:** 71.9%. **Ethnic groups:** Arab 75%-80%, Kurdish 15%-20%, other (incl. Turkmen, Yezidi, Shabak, Kaka'i) 5%. **Languages:** Arabic, Kurdish (both official); Turkmen, Syriac both official where native speakers present. **Religions:** Muslim (official) 97.5% (Shia 61%, Sunni 35%).

Geography: Total area: 169,235 sq mi, 438,317 sq km (58); **Land area:** 168,868 sq mi, 437,367 sq km. **Location:** Middle East, occupying most of historic Mesopotamia. Jordan, Syria on W; Turkey on N; Iran on E; Kuwait, Saudi Arabia on S. **Topography:** Mostly an alluvial plain, including the Tigris and Euphrates Rivers, descending from mountains in N to desert in SW. Persian Gulf region is marshland. **Arable land:** 11.4%. **Capital:** Baghdad, 7,921,134. **Cities:** Mosul, 1,847,691; Basra, 1,485,156; Kirkuk, 1,100,390.

Government: Type: Federal parliamentary republic. **Head of state:** Pres. Abdul Latif Rashid; b. 1944; in office Oct. 13, 2022. **Head of govt.:** Prime Min. Mohammed Shia al-Sudani; b. 1970; in office: Oct. 27, 2022. **Local divisions:** 18 governorates (3 administered by Kurdistan Regional Govt.). **Defense budget:** $10.3 bil. **Active troops:** 193,000.

Economy: Industries: petroleum, chemicals, textiles, leather, constr. materials, food proc., fertilizer, metal fabrication/proc. **Chief agric.:** wheat, dates, tomatoes, maize, watermelons, grapes. **Natural resources:** petroleum, nat. gas, phosphates, sulfur. **Water:** 2,064 cu m per capita. **Crude oil reserves:** 145 bil bbls. **Electricity prod.:** 133.5 bil kWh. **Labor force:** agric. 8.4%, industry 27.5%, services 64.1%. **Unemployment:** 15.5%.

Finance: Monetary unit: Dinar (IQD) (1,309.62 = $1 U.S.). **GDP:** $635.6 bil; **per capita GDP:** $13,969; **GDP growth:** –2.9%. **Imports** (2022): $69.2 bil; UAE 32%, China 21%, Turkey (Türkiye) 20%. **Exports** (2022): $127.1 bil; India 32%, China 28%, U.S. 8%, South Korea 7%, Greece 5%. **Tourism** (2022): $4.7 bil. **Budget** (2020): $85.5 bil. **Inflation** (2021-22): 5.0%.

Transport: Railways: 1,412 mi. **Motor vehicles:** 72.9 per 1,000 pop. **Airports:** 71.

Communications: Mobile: 101.4 per 100 pop. **Broadband:** 52.8 per 100 pop. **Internet:** 78.7%.

Health: Expend.: 5.3%. **Life expect.:** 71.9 male; 75.7 female. **Births:** 23.7 per 1,000 pop. **Deaths:** 3.9 per 1,000 pop. **Infant mortality:** 18.7 per 1,000 live births. **Undernourished:** 16.1%. **HIV:** <0.1%. **COVID-19:** 25,375 deaths; rates per 100,000: 6,130 cases, 63 deaths. 20% vaccinated.

Education: Compulsory: ages 6-11. **Literacy:** 85.6%.

Website: www.pmo.iq

The Tigris-Euphrates valley, formerly called Mesopotamia, was the site of one of the earliest civilizations in the world. Mesopotamia ceased to be a separate entity after Persian, Greek, and Arab conquests. The Arabs founded Baghdad, from where the caliph ruled a vast Islamic empire in the 8th and 9th cents. Mongol and Turkish conquests led to a decline in the region's population, economy, cultural life, and irrigation system.

Britain secured a League of Nations mandate over Iraq after WWI. Independence under a king came in 1932. Rebellious army officers killed King Faisal II, July 1958, and established a leftist, pan-Arab republic. The Baath Arab Socialist Party increasingly dominated successive regimes. A Baath leader, Saddam Hussein, became president in 1979. He ruled as a dictator for more than two decades, repressing Iraq's Kurds and Shiites. Israeli planes destroyed a nuclear reactor near Baghdad in 1981, claiming it could be used to produce nuclear weapons.

After skirmishing intermittently for 10 months, Iraq and Iran entered into open warfare on Sept. 22, 1980. Iran repulsed early Iraqi advances, producing a long and costly stalemate; hundreds of thousands of Iraqis lost their lives during the 8-year conflict. Saddam used poison gas against Iraqi Kurds in 1988, killing more than 5,000 people in Halabja, the first mass use of poison gas against civilians since the Holocaust.

Iraq invaded Kuwait in 1990. Backed by the UN, a U.S.-led coalition launched air and missile attacks on Iraq, Jan. 16, 1991, and began a ground attack to retake Kuwait Feb. 23. Iraqi forces were defeated in four days. Some 175,000 Iraqis were taken prisoner, and Iraqi casualties were estimated at over 85,000. As part of the cease-fire agreement, Iraq agreed to scrap all poison gas and germ weapons and allow UN observers to inspect the sites.

Iraqi cooperation with UN weapons inspection teams was intermittent throughout the 1990s. Standoffs over inspections culminated in intensive U.S. and British aerial bombardment of Iraqi military targets, Dec. 16-19, 1998. After two years of sporadic activity, U.S. and British warplanes struck sites near Baghdad mid-Feb. 2001.

Despite opposition from some countries, including France, Germany, and Russia, a U.S.-led coalition invaded Iraq Mar. 19, 2003. By Apr. 6 the British controlled Basra and other areas in the south, and the U.S. entered Baghdad Apr. 7. Saddam disappeared, the Iraqi government collapsed, and most of Iraq's armed forces dissolved into the civilian population. On May 1, U.S. Pres. George W. Bush declared the end of major combat. Searches failed to find chemical, biological, or nuclear weapons that the U.S. and other countries claimed Iraq had stockpiled.

The U.S.-led Coalition Provisional Authority was unable to maintain order following Saddam's fall. Reconstruction efforts were hampered by guerrilla attacks from Baath remnants, Islamic extremists, and others. U.S. troops killed two of Saddam's sons, Uday and Qusay, July 22, 2003, in Mosul. Saddam Hussein was captured in an underground hideout mid-Dec. 2003; tried and convicted for committing crimes against humanity in the 1980s, he was executed Dec. 30, 2006.

Photographs released in Apr. 2004 showed instances of physical abuse and sexual humiliation of Iraqi inmates by U.S. military personnel at Baghdad's Abu Ghraib prison in 2003.

On June 28, 2004, U.S. authorities transferred sovereignty to a transitional Iraqi government. Despite insurgent threats, an estimated 8 mil people in Iraq, mostly Shiites and Kurds, cast ballots Jan. 30, 2005, for a transitional national assembly. Insurgents launched new waves of attacks. Rumors of a suicide bomber set off a stampede by Shiite pilgrims in northern Baghdad Aug. 31, killing close to 1,000 people. The U.S. blamed Jordanian militant Abu Musab al-Zarqawi, leader of al-Qaeda in Iraq, for directing a series of kidnappings, beheadings, and suicide bombings. He was killed by a U.S. airstrike, June 2006.

A new government elected in legislative elections Dec. 15, 2005, was installed May 20, 2006, headed by Shiite leader Nouri Kamel al-Maliki. The Iraqi civilian death toll averaged more than 2,800 per month in 2006.

A 2007 "surge" elevated U.S. troop strength from 132,000 in Jan. to 171,000 in Oct. Military and civilian casualties began dropping after mid-2007. A cease-fire by Shiite militias and a shift by Sunni clan leaders against al-Qaeda in Iraq contributed to the reduction in violence.

A Nov. 2008 agreement called for all U.S. forces to leave Iraq by Dec. 31, 2011. Inconclusive legislative elections were held Mar. 7, 2010. On Aug. 31, Pres. Barack Obama formally declared an end to the U.S. combat role, and Operation Iraqi Freedom was succeeded by Operation New Dawn. More than 9 months of political deadlock ended when Prime Min. Maliki was sworn in for a second term Dec. 21.

U.S. troops completed their withdrawal from Iraq Dec. 15, 2011. From Mar. 2003 through Dec. 2011, more than 4,500 U.S. service members died in operations in Iraq; another 32,000 were wounded. British troop losses totaled 179; other allies, 139. More than 115,000 Iraqi civilians and over 10,000 police and security forces were killed. U.S. budgeted costs of the Iraq war exceeded $820 bil for the 2003-12 period.

Tensions manifested between Sunnis and Shiites after the U.S. departure. The Sunni insurgent group al-Qaeda in Iraq was blamed for ongoing violence. About 25,000 civilians were killed, 2012-14.

In parliamentary elections Apr. 30, 2014, Maliki's coalition won the largest bloc of seats. Shiite Haider al-Abadi, of Maliki's Dawa Party, became prime min. Sept. 8.

In Dec. 2013, the Sunni extremist Islamic State in Iraq and Syria (ISIS) began crossing from Syria into Iraq and seizing territory. The ISIS offensive intensified beginning in June 2014. The group took control of large areas of northern and central Iraq, including the cities of Mosul (Iraq's second-largest) and Tikrit, where ISIS killed 1,700 captured Shiite soldiers. ISIS imposed Islamic law, with harsh punishments, in areas it controlled while suppressing, killing, and sexually assaulting civilians who were non-Sunni Muslims or members of the Yazidi sect and other religious minorities. (Nadia Murad, a Yazidi sexual assault survivor, shared the 2018 Nobel Peace Prize for her activism against sexual violence in war.) The U.S., later joined by other nations, began, Aug. 8, 2014, airstrikes against ISIS targets; the U.S. provided military aid, including ground troops (beginning in 2014), to Iraqi government forces and Kurdish fighters opposing ISIS.

Forces fighting ISIS in 2015-17 included government troops, Shiite militias (often backed by Iran), Sunni tribal militias, and Kurdish troops. Kurdish fighters made gains in northern Iraq, and government and Shiite forces completed recapturing Tikrit, Apr. 1, 2015. Abadi proclaimed the recapture of Mosul, July 9, 2017, and announced, Dec. 9, that all ISIS territory in Iraq had been retaken. However, thousands of ISIS fighters remained in the country, attacking civilians and security forces.

In a Sept. 25, 2017, referendum, called by the Kurdistan Regional Government—but deemed illegal by the Iraqi government—92.7% of participants voted for Kurdistan's independence from Iraq. Iraqi-government and Shiitemilitia forces responded by driving Kurdish troops from territory outside the Kurdistan autonomous region that the Kurds had occupied during the fight against ISIS.

The U.S. deactivated, Apr. 30, 2018, its land forces command in Baghdad, but more than 5,000 U.S. troops remained in Iraq—reduced to about 2,500 by late 2020. Combat missions by U.S. troops were officially ended in 2021.

After May 12, 2018, parliamentary elections, on Oct. 2, 2018, parliament elected Kurdish politician Barham Salih as president, and Shiite consensus candidate Adel Abdul Mahdi was designated prime min. After protests against economic conditions, corruption, and Iranian influence—in which hundreds were killed by security forces—the prime min. resigned, Nov. 29, 2019. Protests continued into 2020. Iran-backed militia forces attacked the U.S. embassy in Baghdad, Dec. 31, 2019. Mustafa al-Kadhimi became prime min., May 7, 2020.

Following Oct. 10, 2021, parliamentary elections, political disputes delayed formation of a new government. A government was approved by parliament Oct. 27, 2022; Mohammed Shia al-Sudani became prime minister, heading a coalition of pro-Iran groups. Kurdish politician Abdul Latif Rashid was elected president by parliament, Oct. 13, 2022.

Beginning in late 2023, attacks increased, largely by Iran-backed militias, on U.S. troops in Iraq (and neighboring countries), prompting retaliatory U.S. strikes. After 8 months of negotiations, the U.S. and Iraqi government announced a Sept. 27, 2024, deal to end the U.S.-led coalition mission in Iraq within the year, with some U.S. troops remaining through at least 2026 to support anti-ISIS operations in Syria.

Ireland

People: Population: 5,233,461 (123). **Age distrib.:** <15: 18.6%; 65+: 15.8%. **Growth:** 0.9%. **Migrants:** 17.6%. **Pop. density:** 196.8 per sq mi, 76.0 per sq km. **Urban:** 64.8%. **Ethnic groups:** Irish 76.6%, other white 9.9%, Asian 3.3%. **Languages:** English (official; generally used), Irish (Gaelic or Gaeilge) (official; spoken by about 37.7% of pop.). **Religions:** Christian 90.4% (Catholic 82.3%, Protestant 6.0%), agnostic 7.4%, Muslim 1.5% (Sunni).

Geography: Total area: 27,133 sq mi, 70,273 sq km (118); **Land area:** 26,596 sq mi, 68,883 sq km. **Location:** Atlantic O. just W of Great Britain. Northern Ireland (UK) on E. **Topography:** Central plateau surrounded by isolated groups of hills and mountains. Heavily indented Atlantic coastline. **Arable land:** 6.5%. **Capital:** Dublin, 1,284,551.

Government: Type: Parliamentary republic. **Head of state:** Pres. Michael D. Higgins; b. 1941; in office: Nov. 11, 2011. **Head of govt.:** Prime Min. Simon Harris; b. 1986; in office: Apr. 9, 2024. **Local divisions:** 28 counties, 3 cities. **Defense budget:** $1.3 bil. **Active troops:** 7,700.

Economy: Industries: pharmaceuticals, chemicals, computer hardware and software, food prods., beverages and brewing, medical devices. **Chief agric.:** milk, barley, wheat, beef, potatoes, pork. **Natural resources:** nat. gas, peat, copper, lead, zinc, silver, barite, gypsum, limestone, dolomite. **Water:** 10,428 cu m per capita. **Electricity prod.:** 33.0 bil kWh. **Labor force:** agric. 4.0%, industry 19.2%, services 76.8%. **Unemployment:** 4.3%.

Finance: Monetary unit: Euro (EUR) (0.90 = $1 U.S.). **GDP:** $671.6 bil; **per capita GDP:** $127,623; **GDP growth:** –3.2%. **Imports:** $548.8 bil; UK 26%, U.S. 16%, Germany 9%, China 6%, Netherlands 6%. **Exports:** $731.8 bil; U.S. 30%, Germany 12%, UK 8%, Belgium 7%, China 7%. **Tourism:** $7.6 bil. **Budget:** $97.7 bil. **Inflation:** 6.3%.

Transport: Railways: 1,049 mi. **Motor vehicles:** 534.1 per 1,000 pop. **Airports:** 100.

Communications: Mobile: 110.8 per 100 pop. **Broadband:** 118 per 100 pop. **Internet:** 95.6%.

Health: Expend. (2022): 6.1%. **Life expect.:** 80.3 male; 83.9 female. **Births:** 11.1 per 1,000 pop. **Deaths:** 7.4 per 1,000 pop. **Infant mortality:** 3.3 per 1,000 live births. **Undernourished:** <2.5%. **HIV:** 0.3%. **COVID-19:** 9,759 deaths; rates per 100,000: 35,163 cases, 197 deaths. 82% vaccinated.

Education: Compulsory: ages 6-15. **Literacy:** NA.

Website: www.gov.ie

Celtic tribes invaded the islands about the 4th cent. bce; their Gaelic culture and literature flourished in the 5th cent. ce, the same century in which St. Patrick converted the Irish to Christianity. Norse invasions began in the 8th cent., ending with defeat of the Danes by the Irish King Brian Boru in 1014. English invasions started in the 12th cent. For over 700 years the Anglo-Irish struggle continued with bitter rebellions and savage repressions. In the Irish Potato Famine, failure of the staple potato crop, 1845-49, caused 1 mil deaths from starvation and related diseases; up to 2 mil people emigrated, many to the U.S.

The Easter Monday Rebellion in 1916 failed but was followed by guerrilla warfare and harsh reprisals by British troops called the Black and Tans. The Dail Eireann (Irish parliament) reaffirmed independence in Jan. 1919. The British offered dominion status to Ulster (6 counties) and southern Ireland (26 counties) Dec. 1921. The constitution of the Irish Free State, a British dominion, was adopted Dec. 11, 1922. Northern Ireland remained part of the UK (*see* United Kingdom—Northern Ireland).

A new constitution adopted by plebiscite came into operation Dec. 29, 1937. It declared the name of the state Eire in the Irish language (Ireland in the English) and declared it a sovereign democratic state. On Dec. 21, 1948, the country was declared a republic rather than a dominion and withdrew from the Commonwealth. The British Parliament recognized both actions, 1949, but the six northeastern counties remained in the UK.

Irish governments have favored peaceful unification of all Ireland and cooperated with Britain against terrorist groups. After negotiators in Northern Ireland approved a peace settlement on Good Friday, Apr. 10, 1998, voters in the Irish Republic endorsed the accord, on May 22, and the Irish gave up their constitution's territorial claims on the north.

Expansion of educational opportunities and foreign investment in high-tech industries in the 1990s boosted Ireland's prosperity. In 1990, Mary Robinson became Ireland's first woman president.

Responding to allegations of child sex abuse by Catholic clergy in Ireland, Pope Benedict XVI issued a public apology to victims and their families Mar. 2010.

After a 2008-10 financial crisis, the EU approved an 85-bil euro emergency loan package that obligated Ireland to impose unpopular austerity measures. Fianna Fáil, the party that had dominated Irish politics since the 1930s, was defeated in Feb. 2011 elections, and the center-right Fine Gael formed a government. In a national referendum, May 22, 2015, voters legalized same-sex marriage. In a May 25, 2018, referendum, voters essentially legalized almost all abortions.

Inconclusive Feb. 8, 2020, elections saw the nationalist Sinn Féin party make gains. On June 27, a coalition government of Fianna Fáil, Fine Gael, and the Green Party took office. Facing declining popularity, including over undocumented immigration, Prime Min. Leo Varadkar of Fine Gael announced his resignation, Mar. 20, 2024. He was succeeded, Apr. 9, 2024, by Fine Gael's Simon Harris.

Israel

State of Israel

People: Population: 9,402,617 (98). **Age distrib.:** <15: 27.5%; 65+: 12.3%. **Growth:** 1.6%. **Migrants:** 22.6%. **Pop. density:** 1,132.8 per sq mi, 437.4 per sq km. **Urban:** 92.9%. **Ethnic groups:** Jewish 73.5% (Israel-born 79.7%, Europe/America/Oceania-born 14.3%, Africa-born 3.9%, Asia-born 2.1%), Arab 21.1%. **Languages:** Hebrew (official), Arabic, English. **Religions:** Jewish 70.0%, Muslim 22.3% (Sunni), agnostic 4.5%, Christian 1.9%.

Geography: Total area: 8,470 sq mi, 21,937 sq km (149); **Land area:** 8,300 sq mi, 21,497 sq km. **Location:** Middle East, on E end of Mediterranean Sea. Lebanon on N; Syria, West Bank, Jordan on E; Gaza Strip, Egypt on W. **Topography:** The Mediterranean coastal plain is fertile and well-watered. Judean Plateau in center. Semi-desert Negev region extends to apex at head of Gulf of Aqaba. The E border drops sharply into the Jordan Rift Valley, which incl. Lake Tiberias (Sea of Galilee) and the Dead Sea (1,339 ft below sea level), lowest point in Asia. **Arable land:** 17.2%. **Capital:** Jerusalem, 983,097. **Cities:** Tel Aviv-Jaffa, 4,495,727; Haifa, 1,186,475.

Government: Type: Parliamentary democracy. **Head of state:** Pres. Isaac Herzog; b. 1960; in office: July 7, 2021. **Head of govt.:** Prime Min. Benjamin Netanyahu; b. 1949; in office: Dec. 29, 2022. **Local divisions:** 6 districts. **Defense budget:** $19.2 bil. **Active troops:** 169,500.

Economy: Industries: high-tech prods. (incl. aviation, communications, computer-aided design and manufactures, medical electronics, fiber optics), wood and paper prods. **Chief agric.:** milk, chicken, potatoes, tomatoes, avocados, bananas. **Natural resources:** timber, potash, copper ore, nat. gas, phosphate rock, magnesium bromide, clays, sand. **Water:** 200 cu m per capita. **Crude oil reserves:** 13 mil bbls. **Electricity prod.:** 75.9 bil kWh. **Labor force:** agric. 0.8%, industry 15.7%, services 83.5%. **Unemployment:** 3.4%.

Finance: Monetary unit: Shekel (ILS) (3.68 = $1 U.S.). **GDP:** $521.3 bil; **per capita GDP:** $53,434; **GDP growth:** 2.0%. **Imports:** $137.6 bil; China 14%, U.S. 11%, Turkey (Türkiye) 7%, Germany 6%, India 5%. **Exports:** $156.2 bil; U.S. 25%, China 7%, West Bank/Gaza Strip 6%, Ireland 5%. **Tourism:** $6.0 bil. **Budget:** $154.9 bil. **Inflation:** 4.2%.

Transport: Railways: 930 mi. **Motor vehicles:** 419.4 per 1,000 pop. **Airports:** 37.

Communications: Mobile (2022): 151.1 per 100 pop. **Broadband:** 143 per 100 pop. **Internet:** 91.9%.

Health: Expend.: 7.9%. **Life expect.:** 81.1 male; 85.1 female. **Births:** 19.1 per 1,000 pop. **Deaths:** 5.2 per 1,000 pop. **Infant mortality:** 2.8 per 1,000 live births. **Undernourished:** <2.5%. **HIV:** 0.1%. **COVID-19:** 12,707 deaths; rates per 100,000: 55,936 cases, 147 deaths. 74% vaccinated.

Education: Compulsory: ages 3-17. **Literacy:** 97.8%.

Website: www.gov.il

Occupying the southwest corner of the ancient Fertile Crescent, Israel contains some of the oldest known evidence of agriculture and of primitive town life. The Hebrews probably arrived early in the 2nd millennium BCE. Under King David and his successors (c. 1000 BCE-597 BCE), Judaism was developed and secured. After conquest by Babylonians, Persians, and Greeks, an independent Jewish kingdom was revived, 168 BCE, but Rome took over in the next century, suppressed Jewish revolts in 70 CE and 135 CE, and renamed Judea Palestine, after the earlier coastal inhabitants, the Philistines.

Arab invaders conquered Palestine in 636. The Arabic language and Islam prevailed within a few centuries, but a Jewish minority remained. The land was ruled from the 11th cent. as a part of non-Arab empires by Seljuks, Mamluks, and Ottomans (with a Crusader interval, 1098-1291).

After four centuries of Ottoman rule, the land was taken in 1917 by Britain, which pledged in the Balfour Declaration to support a Jewish homeland there. In 1920 a British Palestine Mandate was recognized; in 1922 the land east of the Jordan R. was detached.

Jewish immigration, begun in the late 19th cent., swelled in the 1930s and 1940s with refugees from Nazi Germany and survivors of the Holocaust; heavy Arab immigration from Syria and Lebanon also occurred. Arab opposition to Jewish immigration turned violent in 1920, 1921, 1929, and 1936. The UN General Assembly voted in 1947 to partition Palestine into an Arab and a Jewish state. Britain withdrew in May 1948.

Israel was declared independent May 14, 1948; Arabs rejected partition. Egypt, Jordan, Syria, Lebanon, Iraq, and Saudi Arabia invaded but failed to destroy the Jewish state, which gained territory. Separate armistices with the Arab nations were signed in 1949; Jordan occupied the West Bank, Egypt occupied Gaza. Neither granted Palestinian autonomy.

After persistent terrorist raids, Israel invaded Egypt's Sinai, Oct. 29, 1956, aided briefly by British and French forces. A UN cease-fire was arranged Nov. 6.

An uneasy truce between Israel and the Arab countries lasted until 1967, when Egypt closed the Gulf of Aqaba to Israeli shipping. In the Six-Day War, starting June 5, the Israelis took the Gaza Strip, occupied the Sinai Peninsula to the Suez Canal, and captured East Jerusalem, Syria's Golan Heights, and Jordan's West Bank.

Egypt and Syria attacked Israel, Oct. 6, 1973 (Yom Kippur, the most solemn day in the Jewish calendar). Israel counterattacked, driving the Syrians back, and crossed the Suez Canal. A cease-fire took effect Oct. 24. Under a 1974 disengagement agreement, Israel withdrew from the canal's west bank. Israeli forces raided Entebbe, Uganda, in 1976 and rescued 103 hostages who had been seized by Arab and German terrorists.

Israel's prime ministers, including David Ben-Gurion, Golda Meir, and Yitzhak Rabin, pursued a moderate socialist program, 1948-77. In 1977, the conservative opposition, led by Menachem Begin, was voted into office for the first time. Egypt's Pres. Anwar al-Sadat visited Jerusalem in 1977, and on Mar. 26, 1979, Egypt and Israel signed a formal peace treaty, ending 30 years of war. Israel returned the Sinai to Egypt in 1982.

Israeli forces invaded Lebanon, June 6, 1982, to destroy Palestine Liberation Organization (PLO) strongholds. After massive Israeli bombing of West Beirut, the PLO agreed to evacuate the city. Israeli troops entered West Beirut Sept. 14. Israel drew widespread condemnation when Lebanese Christian forces, Sept. 16, entered two West Beirut refugee camps and slaughtered hundreds of Palestinians.

In 1989, violence escalated over the Israeli military occupation of the West Bank and Gaza Strip. In a series of uprisings known as the first intifada, Palestinian protesters defied Israeli troops, who forcibly retaliated.

Ongoing peace talks led to historic agreements between Israel and the PLO, Sept. 1993. The PLO recognized Israel's right to exist; Israel recognized the PLO as the Palestinians' representative. The two sides then signed, Sept. 13, an agreement (known as the Oslo Accord) for limited Palestinian self-rule in the West Bank and Gaza. A follow-up Sept. 1995 agreement (Oslo II) essentially divided the West Bank into areas under Israeli or Palestinian control. Israel and Jordan signed, July 25, 1994, in Washington, DC, a declaration ending their 46-year state of war.

On Nov. 4, 1995, an Orthodox Jewish Israeli assassinated Labor Party Prime Min. Yitzhak Rabin in Tel Aviv. Support for Rabin's successor, Shimon Peres, was shaken by a series of suicide bombings and rocket attacks by Islamic militants. Emphasizing security issues, the candidate of the conservative Likud bloc, Benjamin Netanyahu, was elected prime minister on May 29, 1996.

Under an interim accord signed by Netanyahu and PLO leader Yasir Arafat, Oct. 23, 1998, Israel agreed to yield more West Bank territory to the Palestinians, in exchange for new security guarantees. After May 1999 elections, the Labor Party's Ehud Barak replaced Netanyahu as prime minister.

Israel pulled virtually all its troops out of southern Lebanon in May 2000. Marathon summit talks in the U.S. between Barak and Arafat, July 11-25, failed. A second intifada began in late Sept. in Israel and the Palestinian territories. Barak called new elections for prime minister but lost Feb. 2001 to Ariel Sharon, a hardliner. The bloodshed intensified during the summer, as Palestinian suicide bombers attacked Israeli civilians, and Israel struck at Palestinian-controlled territory attempting to assassinate suspected terrorists.

Israel launched a major West Bank offensive Mar. 29, 2002, two days after a suicide bomber killed 26 Israeli Jews at a Passover celebration in Netanya. Palestinian-Israeli violence in the West Bank flared periodically in subsequent years.

Sharon's decision to pull all Israeli settlers and troops out of Gaza was approved by the cabinet Feb. 2005. Sharon and Deputy Prime Min. Ehud Olmert then formed the centrist Kadima Party. Sharon suffered a massive stroke Jan. 4, 2006. Olmert became prime minister, led Kadima to victory in Mar. elections, and formed a broad coalition government.

Clashes in mid-2006 along the Gaza and Lebanon borders rapidly escalated into full-scale war. By Aug. 14, a UN-sponsored cease-fire had taken hold. Olmert, targeted in multiple corruption inquiries, announced his resignation July 30, 2008. (He was convicted on bribery charges, 2014 and 2015.) After Feb. 2009 elections, on Mar. 31, Netanyahu became prime min. for a second time.

Israel's relations with allies were strained when the Israeli government announced in Mar. 2010 that it would build 1,600 homes in Ramat Shlomo (a Jewish settlement in mostly Arab East Jerusalem) and when 10 Turkish pro-Palestinian activists died as a result of clashes with Israeli commandos May 31 on board the *Mavi Marmara*, part of a flotilla seeking to break Israel's blockade of Gaza.

Netanyahu stayed in office after Jan. 22, 2013, and Mar. 17, 2015, parliamentary elections.

Conflict between Israel and Hamas escalated in 2014. Rocket attacks from Gaza into Israel increased beginning in June. Israel began air and artillery attacks, then sent ground forces into Gaza, July 17-Aug. 5, in part to destroy tunnels used to infiltrate fighters into Israel. Israeli ground and air attacks caused high civilian casualties.

Tensions between Iran and Israel have grown over Iran's nuclear and missile programs, which Israel sees as existential threats, as well as over Iranian support for regional anti-Israel militias and governments. Israeli airstrikes have targeted Iranian military assets or Iranian-backed forces in countries including Syria, Iraq, and Lebanon.

On May 14, 2018, the U.S. officially moved its embassy from Tel Aviv, where most embassies are located, to Jerusalem. A proclamation signed Mar. 25, 2019, by U.S. Pres. Donald Trump recognized Israeli sovereignty over the Golan Heights.

Controversial July 2018 legislation declared that "the Jewish people ... have an exclusive right to national self-determination" in Israel. With Netanyahu plagued by corruption scandals, two inconclusive 2019 elections were followed by a third, Mar. 2, 2020. Netanyahu and centrist Benny Gantz then reached a power-sharing agreement, with Netanyahu initially continuing as prime minister. The Netanyahu-Gantz coalition collapsed, Dec. 22, 2020. Following a fourth inconclusive election, Mar. 23, 2021, rightist Naftali Bennett became prime minister, June 13, 2021.

Normalizations of relations between Israel and the United Arab Emirates and Bahrain were announced Aug. and Sept. 2020, respectively.

Renewed heavy fighting between Hamas (backed by Iran) and Israel occurred May 2021—and between Islamic Jihad in Gaza and Israel Aug. 2022 and May 2023.

Deadly clashes between Palestinians and Israeli security forces in the West Bank intensified beginning in 2022, as well as attacks on Israeli civilians, amid more aggressive actions by security forces and militant Israeli settlers. Violence further escalated in 2024, following Hamas's Oct. 7, 2023, attacks on Israel and Israel's subsequent invasion of Gaza.

Bennett's coalition collapsed, June 2022. A right-wing coalition headed by Likud won new elections, Nov. 1, and Netanyahu again became prime minister, Dec. 29, 2022. Government plans to limit the powers and independence of the judiciary sparked months of large-scale demonstrations and strikes in 2023. Legislation narrowing judicial review won final passage July 24, 2023, but was struck down by the Supreme Court, Jan. 1, 2024.

At least 1,200 people, most of them Israelis, were killed in unprecedented, highly coordinated attacks by Hamas and allied fighters, launched from Gaza Oct. 7, 2023, against targets in Israel. About 250 hostages were taken to Gaza. Israel vowed to destroy Hamas and launched air and artillery strikes and a ground offensive into Gaza. The Israeli offensive caused high civilian casualties and widespread destruction and displaced most Gazans, many of whom faced famine. Hamas fighters were believed embedded near, in, or in tunnels under residential areas and sites such as schools, hospitals, and civilian evacuation zones. As of Aug. 15, 2024, the Gaza Health Ministry claimed that more than 40,000 Gazans had been killed; Israel claimed it had killed over 17,000 Hamas or allied fighters. After prisoner exchanges, rescues, and recovery of bodies, about 100 hostages (one-third presumed dead) remained in Gaza as of Aug. 31, 2024. After Israel recovered the bodies of six recently killed hostages, Israel's largest labor union launched a general strike Sept. 2, 2024, to increase pressure on Netanyahu to reach a cease-fire deal.

Cross-border attacks between Iran-backed Hezbollah fighters in Lebanon and Israeli forces increased significantly after Israel launched its Oct. 2023 offensive into Gaza. Iran-backed Houthi rebels in Yemen fired hundreds of missiles and drones toward Israel, most of which were intercepted. After an Israeli airstrike killed 7 Iranian Revolutionary Guard officers in Syria, Iran fired hundreds of missiles and drones toward Israel, Apr. 13, 2024, almost all intercepted by Israeli, U.S., European, or Jordanian forces. Iran blamed Israel for the assassination, July 31, 2024, of a top Hamas leader in Tehran.

In late Sept. 2024, Israel killed Hezbollah leader Hassan Nasrallah and launched a ground incursion into southern Lebanon targeting Hezbollah militants. In response, Iran fired nearly 200 ballistic missiles at Israel on Oct. 2, 2024, most of which were intercepted, while Israel vowed to retaliate.

Palestinian Territories

The Palestinian territories comprise the Gaza Strip, often called Gaza, and the West Bank, both occupied by Israel in 1967. Since 1996 the Palestinian Authority has been responsible for civil government in the territories. Elected president Jan. 20, 1996, PLO leader Yasir Arafat headed the Palestinian Authority until his death Nov. 11, 2004. Mahmoud Abbas, of the PLO's Fatah faction, was elected president Jan. 2005. A victory by Hamas militants in Jan. 2006 legislative elections led to a power struggle with Abbas. In bitter fighting, Hamas ousted Fatah from Gaza, June 2007, but Abbas retained power in the West Bank.

The UN General Assembly voted, Nov. 29, 2012, to make Palestine a non-member observer state.

The **Gaza Strip** extends NE from the Sinai Peninsula for 25 mi, with the Mediterranean Sea to the W and Israel to the E. Nearly all the inhabitants are Palestinian Arabs. Area 139 sq mi; pop. (2024 est.) 2,141,643. Hamas's security force, the Izz al-Din al-Qassam Brigades, numbered 30,000 as of Oct. 2023.

Israel captured Gaza from Egypt in the 1967 war. It remained under Israeli occupation until May 1994, when the Israeli Defense Forces largely withdrew. Israel forcibly evacuated all 9,000 Jewish settlers from Gaza by Aug. 22, 2005, and established a fortified barrier on its Gaza border intended to block Palestinian infiltrators.

After the Hamas takeover, Israel declared Gaza a "hostile entity," Sept. 19, 2007, and intensified military and economic pressures. Hamas, Jan. 2008, blew up part of the border wall between Gaza and Egypt. Retaliating for Hamas rocket and mortar attacks, Israel launched an aerial assault and ground offensive in Gaza, Dec. 2008-Jan. 2009. After the *Mavi Marmara* incident, Israel June 2010 eased some restrictions on the flow of goods to Gaza. Egypt's military government closed the Gaza border in 2013 and sought to destroy tunnels dug by Hamas to bring military and other equipment into Gaza. Egypt began opening the Gaza border intermittently in 2015.

In 2017, Israel began building a below-ground barrier on the Gaza border in an effort to block Hamas tunneling. Large-scale, sometimes violent protests occurred, Mar.-May 2018, on the Gaza side of the Israeli border wall, accompanied by attempts to storm the wall and firing across the border into Israel. After Oct. 7, 2023, Israel investigated how such a large-scale Hamas attack into Israel from Gaza could have been planned and launched undetected.

The **West Bank** is located W of the Jordan R. and Dead Sea, bounded by Jordan on the E and by Israel on the N, W, and S. The Palestinian Authority administers several major cities, but Israel retains control over much land, including Jewish settlements. Total area 2,263 sq mi, land area 2,178 sq mi; pop. (2024 est.) 3,243,369. The Palestinian Authority's Security Forces maintain internal security in Palestinian-controlled areas of the West Bank.

In June 2002 the Israeli government began building a controversial security barrier in the West Bank to restrict Palestinian access to Israel and reduce infiltration by suicide bombers. In a nonbinding ruling, July 9, 2004, the World Court said the barrier violated international law. Israel has continued to allow the expansion of Jewish settlements—accelerated by the Netanyahu government, as well as aggressive actions by settlers, in 2023 and 2024. By 2024, more than 500,000 Jewish settlers were living in the West Bank (not including about 340,000 in East Jerusalem, which Israel annexed in 1967).

Italy

Italian Republic

People: Population: 60,964,931 (24). **Age distrib.:** <15: 11.9%; 65+: 23.6%. **Growth:** –0.1%. **Migrants:** 10.6%. **Pop. density:** 536.8 per sq mi, 207.3 per sq km. **Urban:** 72.3%. **Ethnic groups:** Italian (incl. small clusters of German-, French-, and Slovene-Italians in N; Albanian-, Croat-, and Greek-Italians in S). **Languages:** Italian (official), German, French, Slovene. **Religions:** Christian 75.4% (Catholic 70.6%), agnostic 14.2%, Muslim 5.8% (Sunni), atheist 3.6%.

Geography: Total area: 116,348 sq mi, 301,340 sq km (71); **Land area:** 113,568 sq mi, 294,140 sq km. **Location:** Southern Europe, jutting into Mediterranean Sea. France on W; Switzerland, Austria on N; Slovenia on E. **Topography:** Long boot-shaped peninsula, with Apennine Mts. running SE its length, from the Alps into Mediterranean, with islands of Sicily and Sardinia offshore. The alluvial Po Valley drains most of N. Rest of the country is rugged and mountainous, except for intermittent coastal plains like the Campania S of Rome. **Arable land:** 24.0%. **Capital:** Rome, 4,331,974. **Cities:** Milan, 3,160,631; Naples, 2,180,027; Turin, 1,805,727.

Government: Type: Parliamentary republic. **Head of state:** Pres. Sergio Mattarella; b. 1941; in office: Feb. 3, 2015. **Head of govt.:** Prime Min. Giorgia Meloni; b. 1977; in office: Oct. 22, 2022. **Local divisions:** 20 regions (5 autonomous). **Defense budget:** $32.8 bil. **Active troops:** 160,900.

Economy: Industries: tourism, machinery, iron and steel, chemicals, food proc., textiles, motor vehicles, clothing, footwear. **Chief agric.:** milk, grapes, wheat, tomatoes, maize, apples. **Natural resources:** coal, antimony, mercury, zinc, potash, marble, barite, asbestos, pumice, fluorspar, feldspar, pyrite (sulfur), nat. gas/crude oil reserves, fish. **Water:** 3,229 cu m per capita. **Crude oil reserves:** 498 mil bbls. **Electricity prod.:** 274.2 bil kWh. **Labor force:** agric. 3.8%, industry 26.9%, services 69.3%. **Unemployment:** 7.6%.

Finance: Monetary unit: Euro (EUR) (0.90 = $1 U.S.). **GDP:** $3.5 tril; **per capita GDP:** $58,755; **GDP growth:** 0.9%. **Imports:** $756.2 bil; Germany 14%, France 8%, China 8%, Netherlands 5%, Spain 5%. **Exports:** $793.6 bil; Germany 12%, U.S. 11%, France 10%, Spain 5%. **Tourism:** $55.9 bil. **Budget** (2020): $1.1 tril. **Inflation:** 5.6%.

Transport: Railways: 11,480 mi. **Motor vehicles:** 747.8 per 1,000 pop. **Airports:** 636.

Communications: Mobile: 131.9 per 100 pop. **Broadband:** 98.4 per 100 pop. **Internet** (2023): 87%.

Health: Expend. (2022): 9.0%. **Life expect.:** 80.7 male; 85.5 female. **Births:** 7.1 per 1,000 pop. **Deaths:** 11.2 per 1,000 pop. **Infant mortality:** 3.1 per 1,000 live births. **Undernourished:**

<2.5%. **HIV:** 0.2%. **COVID-19:** 197,307 deaths; rates per 100,000: 44,903 cases, 331 deaths. 83% vaccinated.

Education: Compulsory: ages 6-17. **Literacy:** 99.4%.

Website: www.governo.it

Rome emerged as the major power in Italy after 500 BCE, dominating the Etruscans to the north and Greeks to the south. Under the Empire, which lasted until the 5th cent. CE, Rome ruled most of Western Europe, the Balkans, the Middle East, and North Africa. After Rome fell, Italy became a patchwork of kingdoms, principalities, and city-states until reunified, 1870.

The Fascist leader Benito Mussolini came to power, 1922, and aligned Italy with Nazi Germany in WWII. After Fascism was overthrown in 1943, Italy declared war on Germany and Japan and contributed to the Allied victory. It surrendered conquered lands and lost its colonies. Mussolini was killed by partisans Apr. 28, 1945. Victor Emmanuel III abdicated May 9, 1946; his son Humbert II was king until June 10, when Italy became a republic after a referendum, June 2-3. In the postwar decades, Italy had a succession of short-lived governments.

Christian Democratic leader and former Prime Min. Aldo Moro was abducted and murdered in 1978 by Red Brigade terrorists. A wave of left-wing political violence continued into the 1980s.

In Mar. 1994 voting, right-wing parties won a majority, dislodging Italy's long-powerful Christian Democratic Party. Italy led a 7,000-member peacekeeping force in Albania, Apr.-Aug. 1997.

Supporters of Silvio Berlusconi, a multibillionaire media magnate, won the 2001 parliamentary elections. Berlusconi lost 2006 parliamentary elections but returned at the head of a center-right coalition after Apr. 2008 elections. Sluggish economic growth and rising public debt raised investors' concerns about Italy's financial stability. Berlusconi resigned Nov. 12, 2011, but Italy's economic problems worsened. After Feb. 25, 2013, elections, a coalition government was announced Apr. 27, 2013, led by the center-left Democratic Party (PD). Berlusconi was convicted in 2012 of tax fraud and in 2015 of bribing a senator. Legalization of civil unions between same-sex couples won final parliamentary approval, May 11, 2016.

About 625,000 migrants, largely from Africa or Asia, fleeing violence and economic hardship crossed the Mediterranean from North Africa (mainly Libya) to Italy, 2014-17. More than 13,000 died trying to make the crossing. Beginning in 2017, Italy and the EU worked with various Libyan authorities and other N African governments to reduce migrant crossings. However, the pace of crossings increased again in the 2020s: over 330,000 migrant arrivals 2021-23; over 4,900 dead or missing. Italy signed an agreement with Albania, Nov. 6, 2023, under which migrants intercepted at sea by Italy could be sent to detention centers in Albania while their asylum applications were processed. By late Sept. 2024, more than 49,000 migrants had arrived in Italy by sea.

In Mar. 4, 2018, elections, the populist Five Star Movement (M5S) and the anti-immigration League made strong showings. A League-M5S coalition government took office June 1, 2018. With League-M5S disputes increasing and the economy stagnant, the government resigned, Aug. 20, 2019. M5S and the PD agreed, Aug. 28, to form a new coalition. Defections from his coalition forced Mario Draghi, prime minister since Feb. 2021, to resign, July 21, 2022. In Sept. 25, 2022, elections, a rightist, anti-immigration coalition won a majority of seats—led by the Brothers of Italy party of Giorgia Meloni. She became, Oct. 22, 2022, Italy's first female prime minister, heading a government that also included the League and Berlusconi's Forza Italia party (Berlusconi died June 12, 2023).

Italy was one of the first European countries severely impacted, in early 2020, by COVID-19. Health care facilities were strained, and GDP fell 9% in 2020. Severe heat waves in the 2020s were likely related to climate change.

Sicily, 9,927 sq mi, pop. (2014 est.) 5,094,937, is an island 180 by 120 mi, seat of an autonomous region that embraces the island of Pantelleria, 32 sq mi, and the Lipari group, 44 sq mi, including two active volcanoes: Vulcano (1,637 ft) and Stromboli (3,031 ft). From prehistoric times Sicily has been settled by various peoples; a Greek state had its capital at Syracuse. Rome took Sicily from Carthage 215 BCE. Mt. Etna, a 10,925-ft active volcano, is its tallest peak.

Sardinia, 9,301 sq mi, pop. (2014 est.) 1,663,859, lies in the Mediterranean, 115 mi W of Italy and 7½ mi S of Corsica. It is 160 mi long, 68 mi wide, and mountainous. Mining, historically important, has declined in recent decades, and tourism has increased. In 1720, Sardinia was added to the possessions of the Dukes of Savoy in Piedmont and Savoy to form the Kingdom of Sardinia. Elba, 86 sq mi, lies 6 mi W of Tuscany. Napoleon I lived in exile on Elba 1814-15.

Jamaica

People: Population: 2,823,713 (137). **Age distrib.:** <15: 23.8%; 65+: 10.4%. **Growth:** 0.1%. **Migrants:** 0.8%. **Pop. density:** 675.2 per sq mi, 260.7 per sq km. **Urban:** 57.8%. **Ethnic groups:** Black 92.1%, mixed 6.1%. **Languages:** English, Jamaican patois. **Religions:** Christian 83.9% (Protestant 59.5%, independent 19.8%), Spiritist 10.6%, agnostic 4.3%.

Geography: Total area: 4,244 sq mi, 10,991 sq km (161); **Land area:** 4,182 sq mi, 10,831 sq km. **Location:** W Indies. Cuba to N, Haiti to E. **Topography:** Four-fifths of country is covered by mountains. **Arable land:** 11.1%. **Capital:** Kingston, 600,225.

Government: Type: Parliamentary democracy under constitutional monarchy. **Head of state:** King Charles III, rep. by Gov.-Gen. Patrick Allen; b. 1951; in office: Feb. 26, 2009. **Head of govt.:** Prime Min. Andrew Holness; b. 1972; in office: Mar. 3, 2016. **Local divisions:** 14 parishes. **Defense budget:** $232 mil. **Active troops:** 5,950.

Economy: Industries: agriculture, mining, manufacture, constr., financial and insurance services, tourism, telecom. **Chief agric.:** sugarcane, yams, goat milk, chicken, coconuts, oranges. **Natural resources:** bauxite, alumina, gypsum, limestone. **Water:** 3,828 cu m per capita. **Electricity prod.:** 4.6 bil kWh. **Labor force:** agric. 15.3%, industry 17.2%, services 67.5%. **Unemployment:** 4.4%.

Finance: Monetary unit: Dollar (JMD) (155.96 = $1 U.S.). **GDP:** $32.4 bil; **per capita GDP:** $11,475; **GDP growth:** 2.2%. **Imports** (2022): $9.7 bil; U.S. 36%, China 12%, Trinidad and Tobago 6%, Brazil 5%. **Exports** (2022): $6.4 bil; U.S. 57%, Russia 5%. **Tourism** (2022): $3.6 bil. **Budget** (2020): $4.6 bil. **Inflation:** 6.5%.

Transport: Motor vehicles: 78.8 per 1,000 pop. **Airports:** 20.

Communications: Mobile: 115.1 per 100 pop. **Broadband:** 70.5 per 100 pop. **Internet:** 85.1%.

Health: Expend.: 7.2%. **Life expect.:** 74.5 male; 78.1 female. **Births:** 15.6 per 1,000 pop. **Deaths:** 7.5 per 1,000 pop. **Infant mortality:** 10.7 per 1,000 live births. **Undernourished:** 7.3%. **HIV:** 1.1%. **COVID-19:** 3,611 deaths; rates per 100,000: 5,309 cases, 122 deaths. 26% vaccinated.

Education: Compulsory: ages 6-11. **Literacy:** 88.7%.

Website: jis.gov.jm

Jamaica was visited by Christopher Columbus, 1494, and ruled by Spain (under whom Arawak Indians died out) until seized by Britain, 1655. Use of enslaved African labor, begun by the Spanish, expanded significantly under British rule. Jamaica won independence Aug. 6, 1962. The island's rich musical innovations include ska and reggae. Rastafarianism is an influential religious movement.

In 1976, Jamaica's socialist government acquired 50% ownership of U.S. and Canadian companies' bauxite mines. Rudimentary welfare state measures were passed. Relations with the U.S. improved in the 1980s when Jamaican politics entered a more conservative phase.

Portia Simpson-Miller of the People's National Party (PNP) became Jamaica's first female prime min., Mar. 30, 2006. The Jamaica Labour Party (JLP) won Sept. 3, 2007, elections. While trying to arrest alleged gang leader Christopher (Dudus) Coke, police and soldiers clashed with residents in a section of Kingston in May 2010, leaving 76 people dead. Coke pleaded guilty in the U.S. to racketeering charges in 2011. The PNP won Dec. 2011 elections; Simpson-Miller again became prime min. After she implemented unpopular austerity measures to obtain IMF aid, the JLP won Feb. 25, 2016, elections; Andrew Holness became prime min. The JLP won Sept. 3, 2020, elections.

Japan

People: Population: 123,201,945 (11). **Age distrib.:** <15: 12.1%; 65+: 29.5%. **Growth:** –0.4%. **Migrants:** 2.2%. **Pop. density:** 875.5 per sq mi, 338.0 per sq km. **Urban:** 92.1%. **Ethnic groups** (by nationality): Japanese 97.5%. **Languages:** Japanese. **Religions:** Buddhist 55.2% (Mahayanist), new religionist 26.2%, agnostic 10.5%, atheist 2.9%, Christian 2.2%, Shintoist 2.2%.

Geography: Total area: 145,914 sq mi, 377,915 sq km (61); **Land area:** 140,728 sq mi, 364,485 sq km. Consists of 4 main islands: Honshu ("mainland"), 87,805 sq mi; Hokkaido, 30,144 sq mi; Kyushu, 14,114 sq mi; Shikoku, 7,049 sq mi. **Location:** Archipelago off E coast of Asia. Russia to N, N. Korea and S. Korea to W. **Topography:** Deeply indented coast. The northern islands are continuation of the Sakhalin Mts. China's Kunlun range continues into southern islands. The ranges meet in Japanese Alps. Group of mostly extinct or inactive volcanoes, incl. Mt. Fuji (Fujiyama) (12,388 ft), cross Honshu E-W in a vast transverse fissure. **Arable land:** 11.2%. **Capital:** Tokyo, 37,115,035. **Cities:** Kinki MMA (Osaka), 18,967,459; Chukyo MMA (Nagoya), 9,556,879; Kitakyushu-Fukuoka MMA, 5,478,076.

Government: Type: Parliamentary constitutional monarchy. **Head of state:** Emperor Naruhito; b. 1960; in office: May 1, 2019. **Head of govt.:** Prime Min. Shigeru Ishiba, b. 1957; in office Oct. 1, 2024. **Local divisions:** 47 prefectures. **Defense budget:** $49.0 bil. **Active troops:** 247,000.

Economy: Industries: motor vehicles, electronic equip., machine tools, steel and nonferrous metals, ships, chemicals. **Chief agric.:** rice, milk, sugar beets, vegetables, eggs, chicken. **Natural resources:** negligible mineral resources, fish. **Water:** 3,451 cu m per capita. **Crude oil reserves:** 44 mil bbls. **Electricity prod.:** 991.4 bil kWh. **Labor force:** agric. 3.1%, industry 23.6%, services 73.3%. **Unemployment:** 2.6%.

Finance: Monetary unit: Yen (JPY) (144.29 = $1 U.S.). **GDP:** $6.3 tril; **per capita GDP:** $50,207; **GDP growth:** 1.9%. **Imports:** $989.8 bil; China 22%, Australia 10%, U.S. 10%, UAE 5%. **Exports:** $920.7 bil; U.S. 19%, China 19%, South Korea 7%, Taiwan 7%. **Tourism:** $38.6 bil. **Budget** (2021): $1.9 tril. **Inflation:** 3.3%.

SPORTS

OUT OF THE BLUE
The Michigan Wolverines claimed the CFP Championship Jan. 8, 2024, defeating the Washington Huskies 34-13.

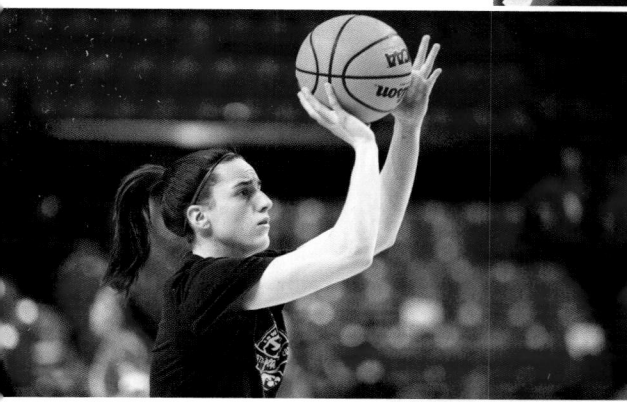

SHARPSHOOTER
Iowa Hawkeyes point guard Caitlin Clark claimed multiple all-time NCAA scoring records during her senior season, ending her collegiate career Apr. 7, 2024, with a record 3,951 points.

UNSTOPPABLE
The undefeated South Carolina Gamecocks outlasted the Iowa Hawkeyes, 87-75, Apr. 7, 2024, to claim the NCAA women's championship.

COMEBACK KING
Patrick Mahomes led Kansas City to a win in Super Bowl LVIII Feb. 11, 2024, defeating the San Francisco 49ers, 25-22, in overtime.

SPORTS

SWEET EIGHTEEN Jaylen Brown and the Boston Celtics captured the franchise's record 18th NBA title June 17, 2024, with a Game Five win, 106-88, over the Dallas Mavericks.

CALL IT A WIN-WIN? The Florida Panthers claimed the Stanley Cup June 24, 2024, but Edmonton Oilers captain Connor McDavid was awarded the Conn Smythe Trophy as the top postseason performer.

THE REST IS HISTORY Oscar Charleston, Josh Gibson, Ted Page, and Judy Johnson were among hundreds of Negro League players whose statistics were officially incorporated into the MLB record books and leader lists as of May 2024.

BACK-TO-BACK Tristen Newton was named most outstanding player of the Final Four as UConn took down Purdue in the NCAA men's Division I championship game, 75-60, Apr. 8, 2024.

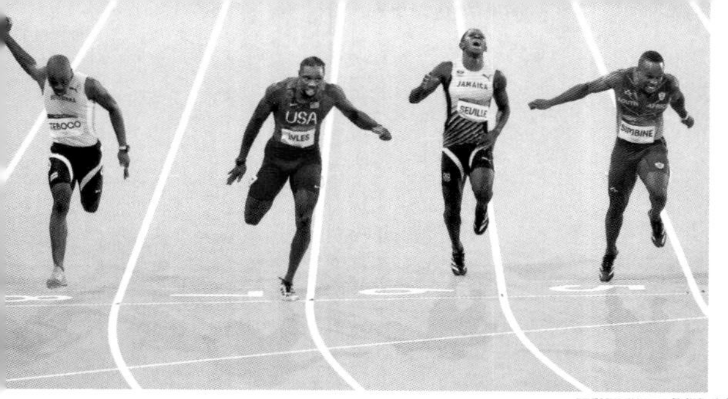

PHOTO FINISH Noah Lyles was the first American sprinter to win the Olympic 100-m title in 20 years Aug. 4, 2024, setting a personal best and winning by a mere 0.005 seconds.

A WINNING RECORD Appearing at her fourth Olympic Games, U.S. swimmer Katie Ledecky took home four more medals, including gold in the 800-m and 1500-m freestyle.

GREATEST OF ALL TIME Already the most decorated gymnast ever, Simone Biles claimed four more Olympic medals in Paris, including the individual all-around gold on Aug. 1, 2024.

GOLD AGAIN Mallory Swanson and Team USA claimed the Olympic gold medal in soccer for the first time since 2012, defeating Brazil, 1-0, Aug. 10, 2024.

ARTS

TAKE IT TO THE LIMIT The 17,600-seat Sphere in Las Vegas provided a site for shows from Dead & Company and Eagles in 2024 that made use of the venue's unique visual displays both inside and out.

RAP BATTLE Rappers Kendrick Lamar and Drake turned their talents against each other, each targeting the other in pointed lyrics on multiple songs released Mar.-May 2024.

GOOD AS GOLD Oscar winners on Mar. 10, 2024, included *Oppenheimer* stars Robert Downey Jr. and Cillian Murphy, *The Holdovers*' Da'Vine Joy Randolph, and *Poor Things*' Emma Stone.

WORLD TRAVELER Taylor Swift's Eras Tour continued to dazzle on its international leg, including eight sold-out shows at London's Wembley Stadium in June and Aug. 2024.

PEOPLE

WITH FRIENDS LIKE THESE Ippei Mizuhara, interpreter for Shohei Ohtani, pleaded guilty to bank and tax fraud June 4, 2024, after admitting he stole over $16 million from the two-time AL MVP's bank account to cover his own gambling losses.

ROAD TO RECOVERY Princess Kate attended Wimbledon July 14, 2024, after being out of the UK public eye for much of the year receiving cancer treatment.

SAFE SPACE NASA astronauts Butch Wilmore and Suni Williams found their return from the Intl. Space Station unexpectedly delayed from June 2024 to Feb. 2025 by technical issues with their Boeing Starliner spacecraft.

SEEKING JUSTICE Music mogul Sean "Diddy" Combs was arrested Sept. 16, 2024, following a federal indictment on racketeering and sex trafficking charges.

FAREWELL

JOHN AMOS
Dec. 27, 1939-Aug. 21, 2024

ANDRE BRAUGHER
July 1, 1962-Dec. 11, 2023

ROSALYNN CARTER
Aug. 18, 1927-Nov. 19, 2023

DABNEY COLEMAN
Jan. 3, 1932-May 16, 2024

SHANNEN DOHERTY
Apr. 12, 1971-July 13, 2024

PHIL DONAHUE
Dec. 21, 1935-Aug. 18, 2024

SHELLEY DUVALL
July 7, 1949-July 11, 2024

LOUIS GOSSETT JR.
May 27, 1936-Mar. 29, 2024

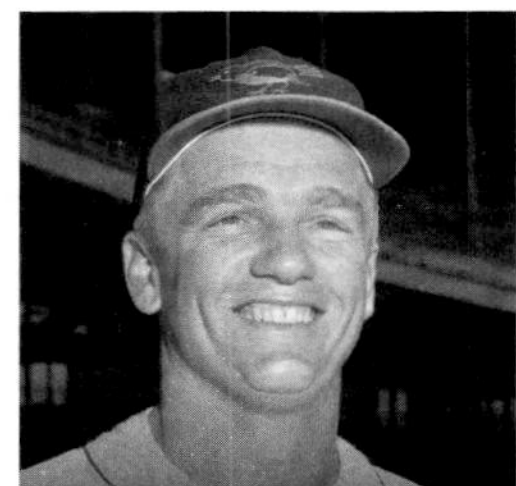

WHITEY HERZOG
Nov. 9, 1931-Apr. 15, 2024

JAMES EARL JONES
Jan. 17, 1931-Sept. 9, 2024

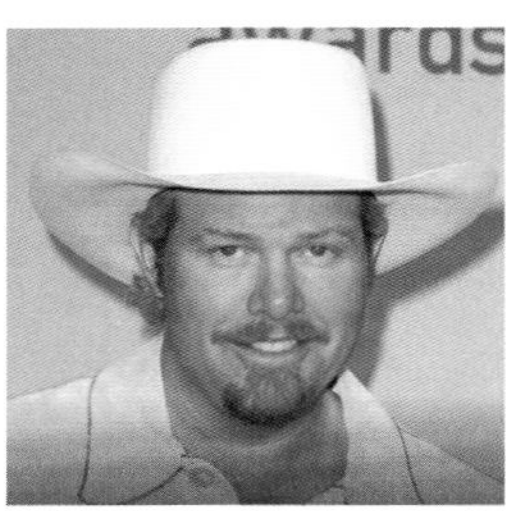

TOBY KEITH
July 8, 1961-Feb. 5, 2024

HENRY KISSINGER
May 27, 1923-Nov. 29, 2023

KRIS KRISTOFFERSON
June 22, 1936-Sept. 28, 2024

NORMAN LEAR
July 27, 1922-Dec. 5, 2023

RICHARD LEWIS
June 29, 1947-Feb. 27, 2024

JOE LIEBERMAN
Feb. 24, 1942-Mar. 27, 2024

WILLIE MAYS
May 6, 1931-June 18, 2024

MARTIN MULL
Aug. 18, 1943-June 27, 2024

ALICE MUNRO
July 10, 1931-May 13, 2024

DIKEMBE MUTOMBO
June 25, 1966-Sept. 30, 2024

ALEXEI NAVALNY
June 4, 1976-Feb. 16, 2024

BOB NEWHART
Sept. 5, 1929-July 18, 2024

SANDRA DAY O'CONNOR
Mar. 26, 1930-Dec. 1, 2023

RYAN O'NEAL
Apr. 20, 1941-Dec. 8, 2023

FAREWELL

MATTHEW PERRY
Aug. 19, 1969-Oct. 28, 2023

FAITH RINGGOLD
Oct. 8, 1930-Apr. 13, 2024

CHITA RIVERA
Jan. 23, 1933-Jan. 30, 2024

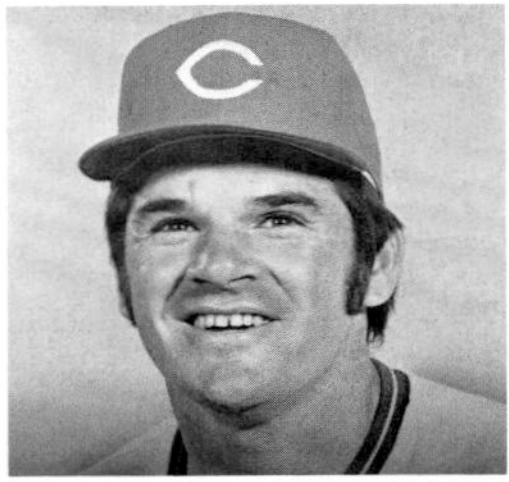

PETE ROSE
Apr. 14, 1941-Sept. 30, 2024

GENA ROWLANDS
June 19, 1930-Aug. 14, 2024

RICHARD SIMMONS
July 12, 1948-July 13, 2024

O. J. SIMPSON
July 9, 1947-Apr. 10, 2024

MAGGIE SMITH
Dec. 28, 1934-Sept. 27, 2024

DONALD SUTHERLAND
July 17, 1935-June 20, 2024

BILL WALTON
Nov. 5, 1952-May 27, 2024

CARL WEATHERS
Jan. 14, 1948-Feb. 2, 2024

RUTH WESTHEIMER
June 4, 1928-July 12, 2024

Transport: Railways: 16,970 mi. **Motor vehicles:** 632.6 per 1,000 pop. **Airports:** 279.

Communications: Mobile: 175.9 per 100 pop. **Broadband:** 246 per 100 pop. **Internet:** 84.9%.

Health: Expend.: 10.8%. **Life expect.:** 82.3 male; 88.2 female. **Births:** 6.9 per 1,000 pop. **Deaths:** 11.9 per 1,000 pop. **Infant mortality:** 1.9 per 1,000 live births. **Undernourished:** 3.4%. **HIV:** NA. **COVID-19:** 74,694 deaths; rates per 100,000: 26,727 cases, 59 deaths. 82% vaccinated.

Education: Compulsory: ages 6-14. **Literacy:** NA.

Website: www.japan.go.jp

According to Japanese legend, the empire was founded by Emperor Jimmu, 660 BCE, but earliest records of a unified Japan date from 1,000 years later. Chinese influence was strong in the formation of Japanese civilization. Buddhism was introduced before the 6th cent. CE.

A feudal system, with locally powerful noble families and their samurai warrior retainers, dominated from 1192. Central power was held by successive families of shoguns (military dictators), 1192-1867, until recovered by Emperor Meiji, 1868. The Portuguese and Dutch had minor trade with Japan in the 16th and 17th cents.; U.S. Commodore Matthew C. Perry opened the country to U.S. trade in a treaty ratified 1854. Industrialization began in the late 19th cent. Military conflicts won Taiwan from China, 1894-95, and the southern half of Sakhalin from Russia, 1904-05. Japan annexed Korea, 1910.

In WWI Japan ousted Germany from Shandong in China and took over German Pacific islands. Japan took Manchuria in 1931 and launched full-scale war in China in 1937. In WWII, Japan attacked Pearl Harbor, Dec. 7, 1941, launching war with the U.S. The U.S. dropped atomic bombs on Hiroshima, Aug. 6, and Nagasaki, Aug. 9, 1945. Japan surrendered Aug. 14.

In a new constitution adopted May 3, 1947, Japan renounced the right to wage war; the emperor renounced claims to divinity; and the Diet became the sole lawmaking authority. The U.S. and 48 other non-Communist nations signed a peace treaty with Japan on Sept. 8, 1951; on the same day, the U.S. signed a bilateral defense agreement with Japan. The peace treaty restored Japan's sovereignty effective Apr. 28, 1952.

Rebuilding after WWII, Japan emerged as one of the most powerful economies in the world.

In 1968, the U.S. returned control of the Bonin Isls., Volcano Isls. (including Iwo Jima), and Marcus Isls to Japan. In 1972, the U.S. returned Okinawa, the other Ryukyu Isls., and the Daito Isls., but the U.S. continued to maintain military bases on Okinawa.

The Liberal Democratic Party (LDP) governed Japan from the mid-1950s through early 1990s. In 1994, Tomiichi Murayama became Japan's first Socialist premier since 1947-48. With the country mired in a lengthy recession, the LDP regained power in 1996.

For the first time since WWII, Japan sent troops to an overseas war zone, when about 600 noncombat troops served in Iraq Feb. 2004-July 2006. Legislation formalizing a new constitutional interpretation allowing the military to take offensive action to aid an ally, such as the U.S., won final passage Sept. 19, 2015.

The 2008-09 global recession hit Japan hard, prompting a series of economic stimulus plans. The LDP suffered a crushing defeat in 2009 parliamentary elections, won by the opposition Democratic Party of Japan (DPJ).

A 9.0 magnitude earthquake and tsunami off Japan's east coast Mar. 11, 2011, left almost 21,000 people dead. The Fukushima Daiichi nuclear power plant experienced meltdowns, spewing radiation over a large area. (On Aug. 24, 2023, despite opposition, Japan began releasing treated wastewater used to cool nuclear fuel rods.)

Elections swept LDP candidates into office in Dec. 2012, and former Prime Min. Shinzo Abe became prime minister. Abe's LDP won Dec. 14, 2014, and Oct. 22, 2017, elections.

Japan signed, Mar. 8, 2018, an 11-nation trans-Pacific trade pact. Japan and the EU signed, July 17, 2018, a trade liberalization agreement.

Emperor Akihito, 85, abdicated, Apr. 30, 2019; he was succeeded, May 1, by his son Naruhito. Abe announced, Aug. 28, 2020, that he would resign because of ill health. The LDP's Yoshihide Suga became prime minister Sept. 16.

The COVID-19 pandemic reached Japan by Jan. 2020. The 2020 Summer Olympics in Tokyo were delayed until 2021. Prime Min. Suga, facing declining popularity, announced, Sept. 3, 2021, he would resign. Former foreign min. Fumio Kishida became prime minister, Oct. 4, 2021, and led the LDP to victory in Oct. 31 elections.

Former Prime Min. Abe was shot to death, July 8, 2022, at a political rally; LDP ties to the Unification Church was the assassin's apparent motivation. Enhanced Japan-U.S.-South Korea security cooperation was agreed to, Aug. 18, 2023, at a summit meeting in the U.S. Japan signed new military cooperation agreements with the U.S. and the Philippines in 2024. Prime Min. Kishida stepped down amid political scandal and inflation pressures; Shigeru Ishiba took office Oct. 1, 2024, promising to counter security threats with closer ties to allies.

Jordan

Hashemite Kingdom of Jordan

People: Population: 11,174,024 (84). **Age distrib.:** <15: 30.9%; 65+: 4.2%. **Growth:** 0.8%. **Migrants:** 33.9%. **Pop. density:** 325.9 per sq mi, 125.8 per sq km. **Urban:** 92.2%. **Ethnic groups** (by nationality): Jordanian 69.3%, Syrian 13.3%, Palestinian 6.7%, Egyptian 6.7%. **Languages:** Arabic (official), English (widely understood among upper/middle classes). **Religions:** Muslim (official) 95.6% (Sunni 93%), agnostic 2.5%.

Geography: Total area: 34,495 sq mi, 89,342 sq km (110); **Land area:** 34,287 sq mi, 88,802 sq km. **Location:** Middle East. Israel, West Bank on W; Saudi Arabia on S; Iraq on E; Syria on N. **Topography:** Mostly arid. Fertile areas in W. Only port is on short Aqaba Gulf coast. Country shares Dead Sea (1,339 ft below sea level) with Israel. **Arable land:** 2.3%. **Capital:** Amman, 2,252,688.

Government: Type: Parliamentary constitutional monarchy. **Head of state:** King Abdullah II; b. 1962; in office: Feb. 7, 1999. **Head of govt.:** Prime Min. Jafar Hassan; b. 1968; in office: Sept. 15, 2024. **Local divisions:** 12 governorates. **Defense budget:** $1.9 bil. **Active troops:** 100,500.

Economy: Industries: tourism, information tech., clothing, fertilizer, potash, phosphate mining, pharmaceuticals. **Chief agric.:** tomatoes, milk, chicken, potatoes, cucumbers/gherkins, olives. **Natural resources:** phosphates, potash, shale oil. **Water:** 84 cu m per capita. **Crude oil reserves:** 1 mil bbls. **Electricity prod.:** 21.9 bil kWh. **Labor force:** agric. 3.2%, industry 18.2%, services 78.6%. **Unemployment:** 17.9%.

Finance: Monetary unit: Dinar (JOD) (0.71 = $1 U.S.). **GDP:** $118.5 bil; **per capita GDP:** $10,452; **GDP growth:** 2.6%. **Imports** (2022): $30.0 bil; China 17%, UAE 12%, Saudi Arabia 12%, India 6%. **Exports** (2022): $20.3 bil; U.S. 20%, India 14%, Saudi Arabia 7%, China 6%, Iraq 6%. **Tourism:** $7.4 bil. **Budget:** $13.5 bil. **Inflation:** 2.1%.

Transport: Railways: 316 mi. **Motor vehicles:** 164.3 per 1,000 pop. **Airports:** 17.

Communications: Mobile: 67.5 per 100 pop. **Broadband:** 67.5 per 100 pop. **Internet:** 90.5%.

Health: Expend.: 7.3%. **Life expect.:** 75.0 male; 78.1 female. **Births:** 22.2 per 1,000 pop. **Deaths:** 3.5 per 1,000 pop. **Infant mortality:** 13.2 per 1,000 live births. **Undernourished:** 17.9%. **HIV:** <0.1%. **COVID-19:** 14,122 deaths; rates per 100,000: 17,122 cases, 138 deaths. 45% vaccinated.

Education: Compulsory: ages 6-15. **Literacy:** 98.4%.

Website: portal.jordan.gov.jo

From ancient times to 1922 the lands to the east of the Jordan R. were culturally and politically united with the lands to the W. Arabs conquered the area in the 7th cent.; the Ottomans took control in the 16th. Britain's 1920 Palestine Mandate covered both sides of the Jordan. In 1921, Abdullah, son of the ruler of Hejaz in Arabia, was installed by Britain as emir of an autonomous Transjordan, covering two-thirds of Palestine. An independent kingdom was proclaimed, 1946.

During the 1948 Arab-Israeli war, the West Bank and East Jerusalem were added to the kingdom, which changed its name to Jordan. These territories were lost to Israel in 1967, which swelled the number of Arab refugees on the East Bank.

Jordan and Israel signed a peace treaty, Oct. 26, 1994. King Hussein died Feb. 7, 1999, ending a nearly 47-year reign; his eldest son assumed the throne as Abdullah II. The king responded to Arab Spring protests, 2011-12, by somewhat liberalizing parliamentary election laws. Low turnout (32%) and anger over the war in Gaza resulted in Islamist gains in Sept. 10, 2024, parliamentary elections.

In 2014, Jordan joined the U.S.-led military campaign against ISIS in Syria and Iraq. About 621,000 Syrians fleeing civil war were living in Jordan as of Sept. 30, 2024. Jordan intercepted missiles and drones in its airspace during Iranian missile attacks on Israel Apr. 13, 2024, and Oct. 2, 2024.

Kazakhstan

Republic of Kazakhstan

People: Population: 20,260,006 (64). **Age distrib.:** <15: 27.6%; 65+: 9.6%. **Growth:** 0.9%. **Migrants:** 19.9%. **Pop. density:** 19.4 per sq mi, 7.5 per sq km. **Urban:** 58.4%. **Ethnic groups:** Kazakh 71%, Russian 14.9%, Uzbek 3.3%. **Languages:** Kazakh or Qazaq, Russian, English. **Religions:** Muslim 78.1% (Sunni), Christian 18.0% (Orthodox 16.4%), agnostic 3.0%.

Geography: Total area: 1,052,090 sq mi, 2,724,900 sq km (9); **Land area:** 1,042,360 sq mi, 2,699,700 sq km. **Location:** Central Asia. Russia on N; China on E; Kyrgyzstan, Uzbekistan, Turkmenistan on S. **Topography:** Extends from lower reaches of Volga in Europe to Altay Mts. on Chinese border. **Arable land:** 11.0%. **Capital:** Astana, 1,324,111. **Cities:** Almaty, 2,015,209; Shimkent, 1,181,020.

Government: Type: Presidential republic. **Head of state:** Pres. Kassym-Jomart Tokayev; b. 1953; in office: Mar. 20, 2019. **Head of govt.:** Prime Min. Olzhas Bektenov; b. 1980; in office: Feb. 6, 2024. **Local divisions:** 17 provinces, 4 cities. **Defense budget:** $2.5 bil. **Active troops:** 39,000.

Economy: Industries: oil, coal, iron ore, manganese, chromite, lead, zinc, copper, titanium, bauxite, gold, silver, phosphates, sulfur, uranium. **Chief agric.:** wheat, milk, potatoes, barley, watermelons, sunflower seeds. **Natural resources:** petroleum, nat. gas, coal, iron ore, manganese, chrome ore, nickel, cobalt, copper, molybdenum, lead, zinc, bauxite, gold, uranium. **Water:** 5,647 cu m per capita. **Crude oil reserves:** 30 bil bbls. **Electricity prod.:** 118.9 bil kWh. **Labor force:** agric. 12.9%, industry 21.5%, services 65.6%. **Unemployment:** 4.8%.

Finance: Monetary unit: Tenge (KZT) (480.67 = $1 U.S.). **GDP:** $782.7 bil; **per capita GDP:** $39,332; **GDP growth:** 5.1%. **Imports:** $71.8 bil; Russia 29%, China 28%, Germany 5%. **Exports:** $90.2 bil; China 14%, Italy 13%, Russia 9%, UK 8%, Netherlands 6%. **Tourism:** $2.3 bil. **Budget** (2020): $42.0 bil. **Inflation:** 14.7%.

Transport: Railways: 10,337 mi. **Airports:** 132.

Communications: Mobile: 127.1 per 100 pop. **Broadband:** 101 per 100 pop. **Internet** (2023): 92.9%.

Health: Expend.: 3.9%. **Life expect.:** 69.0 male; 77.9 female. **Births:** 17.2 per 1,000 pop. **Deaths:** 8.1 per 1,000 pop. **Infant mortality:** 8.0 per 1,000 live births. **Undernourished:** <2.5%. **HIV:** 0.3%. **COVID-19:** 19,072 deaths; rates per 100,000: 8,012 cases, 102 deaths. 70% vaccinated.

Education: Compulsory: ages 6-14. **Literacy:** 99.8%.

Website: egov.kz

The region came under the Mongols' rule in the 13th cent. and gradually came under Russian rule, 1730-1853. It was admitted to the USSR as a constituent republic in 1936.

Kazakhstan became independent when the Soviet Union dissolved Dec. 26, 1991. The Communist Party chief, Nursultan Nazarbayev, was elected president unopposed. Dissent was suppressed. Nazarbayev encouraged Western investment in the oil industry, helping the economy. Regular production began, Oct. 2016, at the large Kashagan oil field in the Caspian Sea.

Kazakhstan agreed, Feb. 1994, to dismantle nuclear missiles. Private land ownership was legalized Dec. 1995.

Pres. Nazarbayev was reelected in 1999, 2005, 2011, and 2015. His Nur Otan party won 2016 and 2021 parliamentary elections. Nazarbayev resigned, Mar. 20, 2019, retaining influence as "first president." Kassym-Jomart Tokayev of Nur Otan became acting president and won a June 9, 2019, presidential election.

Sparked by a rise in fuel prices, violent protests over economic conditions and corruption—and a harsh crackdown by security forces—left over 230 dead in Jan. 2022. In a June 5 referendum, voters approved constitutional changes including limits on the official powers of former Pres. Nazarbayev. Tokayev was reelected, Nov. 20, 2022. The ruling party, renamed from Nur Otan to Amanat in 2022, dominated Mar. 19, 2023, parliamentary elections.

Kenya

Republic of Kenya

People: Population: 58,246,378 (26). **Age distrib.:** <15: 35.8%; 65+: 3.4%. **Growth:** 2.1%. **Migrants:** 2.0%. **Pop. density:** 265.1 per sq mi, 102.3 per sq km. **Urban:** 30.0%. **Ethnic groups:** Kikuyu 17.1%, Luhya 14.3%, Kalenjin 13.4%, Luo 10.7%, Kamba 9.8%, Somali 5.8%, Kisii 5.7%, Mijikenda 5.2%, Meru 4.2%, Maasai 2.5%, Turkana 2.1%. **Languages:** English, Kiswahili (both official); numerous Indigenous langs. **Religions:** Christian 79.8% (Protestant 37.1%, Catholic 21.9%, independent 20.1%), Muslim 10.5% (Sunni), ethnic religionist 7.8%.

Geography: Total area: 224,081 sq mi, 580,367 sq km (49); **Land area:** 219,746 sq mi, 569,140 sq km. **Location:** E Africa, on coast of Indian O. Uganda on W, Tanzania on S, Somalia on E, Ethiopia on N, South Sudan on NW. **Topography:** Northern three-fifths of country is arid. A low coastal area and a plateau 3,000-10,000-ft high is in S. The Great Rift Valley enters the country N-S, flanked by high mountains. **Arable land:** 11.1%. **Capital:** Nairobi, 5,541,172. **Cities:** Mombasa, 1,495,223.

Government: Type: Presidential republic. **Head of state and govt.:** Pres. William Ruto; b. 1966; in office: Sept. 13, 2022. **Local divisions:** 47 counties. **Defense budget:** $1.3 bil. **Active troops:** 24,100.

Economy: Industries: agric., transp., services, mfg., constr., telecom, tourism, retail. **Chief agric.:** sugarcane, milk, maize, tea, bananas, potatoes. **Natural resources:** limestone, soda ash, salt, gems, fluorspar, zinc, diatomite, gypsum, wildlife, hydropower. **Water:** 579 cu m per capita. **Electricity prod.:** 12.4 bil kWh. **Labor force:** agric. 32.6%, industry 15.6%, services 51.8%. **Unemployment:** 5.7%.

Finance: Monetary unit: Shilling (KES) (128.99 = $1 U.S.). **GDP:** $348.4 bil; **per capita GDP:** $6,324; **GDP growth:** 5.4%. **Imports** (2022): $24.4 bil; China 26%, UAE 14%, India 11%. **Exports** (2022): $13.9 bil; U.S. 10%, Uganda 9%, Pakistan 7%, Netherlands 7%, Rwanda 6%. **Tourism:** $1.0 bil. **Budget:** $24.3 bil. **Inflation:** 7.7%.

Transport: Railways: 2,373 mi. **Motor vehicles:** 35.9 per 1,000 pop. **Airports:** 370.

Communications: Mobile: 120.6 per 100 pop. **Broadband:** 66 per 100 pop. **Internet:** 40.8%.

Health: Expend.: 4.5%. **Life expect.:** 68.6 male; 72.2 female. **Births:** 25.6 per 1,000 pop. **Deaths:** 4.9 per 1,000 pop. **Infant mortality:** 26.1 per 1,000 live births. **Undernourished:** 34.5%. **HIV:** 3.2%. **COVID-19:** 5,689 deaths; rates per 100,000: 640 cases, 11 deaths. 21% vaccinated.

Education: Compulsory: ages 6-17. **Literacy:** 82.9%.

Website: www.president.go.ke

Arab colonies exported spices and slaves from the Kenya coast as early as the 8th cent. Britain obtained control in the 19th cent. Kenya won independence Dec. 12, 1963, four years after the end of the violent Mau Mau uprising. Jomo Kenyatta, the country's leader since independence, died Aug. 22, 1978. He was succeeded by his vice president, Daniel arap Moi.

Tribal clashes in the western provinces in the 1990s claimed thousands of lives. Pres. Moi won a fourth term in Dec. 1997, in an election plagued by irregularities. A truck bomb explosion at the U.S. embassy in Nairobi, Aug. 7, 1998, killed more than 200 people and injured about 5,000. The U.S. blamed the attack on al-Qaeda.

Pres. Moi was succeeded, Dec. 2002, by Mwai Kibaki of the opposition Democratic Party. After a disputed election Dec. 2007, Kenya's electoral commission declared Kibaki the winner over challenger Raila Odinga. Weeks of factional violence followed, leaving some 1,500 people dead and 600,000 displaced. Uhuru Kenyatta (Jomo Kenyatta's son) was declared, Mar. 10, 2013, the winner over Odinga in the Mar. 4 presidential election, amid accusations of vote-rigging. On Aug. 11, 2017, Kenyatta was again declared the victor over Odinga in Aug. 8 presidential voting; Odinga charged electoral fraud. After the Supreme Court, Sept. 1, nullified the result, Kenyatta won an Oct. 26 re-vote boycotted by Odinga.

Kenya sent troops into Somalia in 2011 (they joined with an African Union force in 2012) to combat the Somali Islamist extremist group al-Shabab. Al-Shabab carried out a series of deadly terrorist attacks in Kenya. An Apr. 2, 2015, attack on Garissa Univ. College killed 148. About 435,000 Somali refugees were living in Kenya as of June 30, 2024 (in the mid-2010s, tens of thousands were repatriated to Somalia, amid allegations of forced returns).

Vice Pres. William Ruto, with 50.5% of the vote, was declared the winner over Odinga in the Aug. 9, 2022, presidential election. Soaring prices and tax increases sparked violent protests (over 30 dead) in July 2023.

Kenya agreed to lead a multinational security force (approved by the UN, Oct. 2, 2023) intended to reduce violence in Haiti. Kenyan police began arriving in Haiti June 25, 2024.

Proposed tax increases touched off weeks of violent youth-led protests met with a lethal security response beginning in June 2024, leaving at least 60 dead.

Kiribati

Republic of Kiribati

People: Population: 116,545 (179). **Age distrib.:** <15: 26.8%; 65+: 5.4%. **Growth:** 1.0%. **Migrants:** 2.6%. **Pop. density:** 372.2 per sq mi, 143.7 per sq km. **Urban:** 58.4%. **Ethnic groups:** I-Kiribati 95.8%, I-Kiribati/mixed 3.8%. **Languages:** Gilbertese, English (official). **Religions:** Christian 96.7% (Catholic 48.1%, Protestant 31.6%, independent 17.0%), Baha'i 2.5%.

Geography: Total area: 313 sq mi, 811 sq km (173); **Land area:** 313 sq mi, 811 sq km. **Location:** 33 atolls (Gilbert, Line, and Phoenix Isls.) in mid-Pacific scattered over an area of about 1.35 mil sq mi around the point where the International Date Line formerly crossed the Equator. The Date Line was moved in 1997 to follow Kiribati's E border. Nearest neighbors are Nauru to SW, Tuvalu and Tokelau Isls. (N.Z.) to S. **Topography:** Except Banaba (Ocean) Isl., all are low-lying, with soil of coral sand and rock fragments, and erratic rainfall. **Arable land:** 2.5%. **Capital:** Tarawa, 64,011.

Government: Type: Presidential republic. **Head of state and govt.:** Pres. Taneti Maamau; b. 1960; in office: Mar. 11, 2016. **Local divisions:** 3 geographical units (no first-order admin. divisions). **Defense budget/active troops:** NA.

Economy: Industries: fishing, handicrafts. **Chief agric.:** coconuts, bananas, vegetables, taro, tropical fruits, pork. **Natural resources:** phosphate (prod. discontinued in 1979), coconuts, fish. **Water:** 0 cu m per capita. **Electricity prod.:** 31.2 mil kWh. **Labor force:** NA. **Unemployment:** NA.

Finance: Monetary unit: Australian Dollar (AUD) (1.48 = $1 U.S.). **GDP:** $470.2 mil; **per capita GDP:** $3,522; **GDP growth:** 4.3%. **Imports** (2022): $254.4 mil; Taiwan 25%, China 22%, Fiji 13%, Australia 9%, South Korea 7%. **Exports** (2022): $19.7 mil; Thailand 55%, Philippines 15%, Japan 10%, Indonesia 8%. **Tourism** (2022): $2 mil. **Budget** (2017): $205 mil. **Inflation** (2020-21): 2.1%.

Transport: Airports: 21.

Communications: Mobile: 53.0 per 100 pop. **Broadband:** 53.4 per 100 pop. **Internet:** 54.4%.

Health: Expend.: 14.8%. **Life expect.:** 65.9 male; 71.3 female. **Births:** 19.7 per 1,000 pop. **Deaths:** 6.9 per 1,000 pop. **Infant mortality:** 31.5 per 1,000 live births. **Undernourished:** 3.7%. **HIV:** NA. **COVID-19:** 24 deaths; rates per 100,000: 4,257 cases, 20 deaths. 68% vaccinated.

Education: Compulsory: ages 6-14. **Literacy:** NA.

Website: www.president.gov.ki

A British protectorate since 1892, the Gilbert and Ellice Islands colony was completed with the inclusion of the Phoenix Islands, 1937. Tarawa Atoll was the scene of some of the bloodiest fighting in the Pacific during WWII.

Self-rule was granted 1971; the Ellice Islands separated from the colony in 1975 and became independent Tuvalu, 1978. Kiribati (pronounced *Kiribass*) independence was attained July 12, 1979. Kiribati's land area is shrinking as a result of rising sea levels; in 2014, the government began buying land in Fiji for agriculture and possible future resettlement.

Opposition candidate Taneti Maamau won the Mar. 9, 2016, presidential election. With Chinese investment increasing, Kiribati broke relations with Taiwan, Sept. 20, 2019. Maamau won a second term as president, June 22, 2020.

Korea, North

Democratic People's Republic of Korea

People: Population: 26,298,666 (56). **Age distrib.:** <15: 19.9%; 65+: 11.2%. **Growth:** 0.4%. **Migrants:** 0.2%. **Pop. density:** 565.7 per sq mi, 218.4 per sq km. **Urban:** 63.5%. **Ethnic groups:** racially homogeneous; small Chinese community, a few ethnic Japanese. **Languages:** Korean. **Religions:** agnostic 56.9%, atheist 15.5%, new religionist 12.8%, ethnic religionist 12.2%, Buddhist 2.1% (Mahayanist).

Geography: Total area: 46,540 sq mi, 120,538 sq km (97); **Land area:** 46,490 sq mi, 120,408 sq km. **Location:** Northern E Asia. China and Russia on N, S. Korea on S. **Topography:** Mountains and hills cover nearly entire country, with narrow valleys and small plains in between. N and E coasts are most rugged areas. **Arable land:** 19.1%. **Capital:** P'yongyang, 3,183,135.

Government: Type: Dictatorship, single-party communist state. **Head of state:** State Affairs Commission Pres. Kim Jong Un; b. 1983; officially assumed post Dec. 17, 2011. **Head of govt.:** Supreme People's Assembly Pres. Choe Ryong Hae; b. 1950; in office: Apr. 11, 2019. **Local divisions:** 9 provinces, 4 special administration cities. **Defense budget:** NA. **Active troops:** 1,280,000.

Economy: Industries: military prods.; machine building, elec. power, chemicals; mining, metallurgy; textiles, food proc.; tourism. **Chief agric.:** maize, rice, vegetables, apples, cabbages, fruits. **Natural resources:** coal, iron ore, limestone, magnesite, graphite, copper, zinc, lead, prec. metals, hydropower. **Water:** 2,971 cu m per capita. **Electricity prod.:** 22.3 bil kWh. **Labor force:** agric. 44.6%, industry 13.0%, services 42.4%. **Unemployment:** 3.0%.

Finance: Monetary unit: Won (KPW) (900.00 = $1 U.S.). **GDP:** NA; **per capita GDP:** NA; **GDP growth:** NA. **Imports** (2018): $2.3 bil; China 98%. **Exports** (2018): $222.0 mil; China 53%, Senegal 11%, Nigeria 6%. **Budget** (2007): $3.3 bil. **Inflation:** NA.

Transport: Railways: 4,620 mi. **Airports:** 83.

Communications: Mobile (2022): 24.1 per 100 pop. **Broadband** (2022): 20.7 per 100 pop. **Internet:** NA.

Health: Expend.: NA. **Life expect.:** 70.2 male; 77.0 female. **Births:** 13.2 per 1,000 pop. **Deaths:** 9.2 per 1,000 pop. **Infant mortality:** 15.4 per 1,000 live births. **Undernourished** (2017-19): 45.3%. **HIV:** NA. **COVID-19:** NA.

Education: Compulsory: ages 6-17. **Literacy:** 100.0%.

Permanent UN mission: 820 Second Ave., 13th Fl., New York, NY 10017; (212) 972-3105.

Website: naenara.com.kp

The Democratic People's Republic of Korea was founded May 1, 1948, in the zone occupied by Russia after WWII. Its armies tried to conquer the south, 1950. After three years of fighting, with Chinese and U.S. intervention, a cease-fire was proclaimed. A demilitarized zone (DMZ) was established, straddling the cease-fire line.

For the next four decades, a hard-line Communist regime headed by Kim Il Sung kept tight control over the nation's political, economic, and cultural life. The nation used its mineral and hydroelectric resources to develop its military strength. By the early 1990s, North Korea was widely believed to be developing nuclear weapons. The U.S. and North Korea signed an agreement, Oct. 21, 1994, providing for phased dismantling of North Korea's nuclear development program in return for U.S. energy aid and improved ties with the U.S.

Kim Il Sung died July 8, 1994. He was succeeded by his son, Kim Jong Il. Defections by high officials, a deteriorating economy, and severe food shortages plagued North Korea, beginning in the late 1990s. North Korea and Japan agreed to normalize relations in a Sept. 2002 summit.

In Oct. 2002, North Korea admitted to pursuing a secret nuclear weapons program in violation of past agreements. During 2003-09, as six-nation talks sponsored by China sought to resolve the nuclear issue, North Korea alternately stopped and resumed its nuclear program. North Korea conducted its first nuclear explosion Oct. 9, 2006.

In Apr.-May 2009, North Korea suspended participation in the six-nation talks, expelled IAEA inspectors, tested multiple missiles, and exploded a nuclear device underground. The UN Security Council June 12 toughened sanctions on North Korea.

Kim Jong Il died Dec. 17, 2011. He was succeeded by his son Kim Jong Un. In Dec. 2013, Kim Jong Un ordered the execution of his politically powerful uncle, Jang Song Thaek.

North Korea conducted a nuclear test Feb. 10, 2013, and it negated, Mar. 11, 2013, the cease-fire agreement with the South that ended the Korean War. It conducted numerous short- and medium-range missile tests 2013-15. North Korea was apparently responsible for cyberattacks on Sony Pictures Entertainment, Nov. 2014, related to a comedy film about Kim Jong Un. North Korea conducted its fourth nuclear weapons test on Jan. 6, 2016, and its fifth on Sept. 9. North Korea continued missile tests, 2016-17, including its first ICBM launch, July 4, 2017. U.S. and UN sanctions were strengthened in 2016 and again in 2017. North Korea conducted its sixth nuclear test, Sept. 3, 2017.

North Korea said it destroyed, May 24, 2018, its nuclear test site. At a June 12 summit meeting in Singapore with U.S. Pres. Donald Trump, Kim made a general denuclearization pledge. However, U.S. officials, and an Aug. 2018 UN report, concluded that North Korea was continuing its nuclear and missile programs. Two Trump-Kim summits in 2019 produced no progress. Beginning May 2019, North Korea fired a number of short-range missiles, its first missile tests since 2017. Tests of various types of missiles continued in 2020-24. Following Russia's 2022 invasion of Ukraine, North Korea reportedly provided military equipment to Russia for use in the war in exchange for military technology and other aid from Russia.

North Korea initially maintained it had no cases of COVID-19, which began spreading worldwide in early 2020. Protective measures, such as closing the border in 2020 with key trading partner China, contributed to a severe economic crisis; some imports from China resumed in early 2022. In May 2022, North Korea acknowledged for the first time that COVID-19 was spreading in the country. Millions of cases had likely occurred by the time Kim Jong Un declared victory over COVID-19 on Aug. 11; the claim met with widespread international skepticism.

Korea, South

Republic of Korea

People: Population: 52,081,799 (28). **Age distrib.:** <15: 11.3%; 65+: 19.3%. **Growth:** 0.2%. **Migrants:** 3.4%. **Pop. density:** 1,391.8 per sq mi, 537.4 per sq km. **Urban:** 81.5%. **Ethnic groups:** homogeneous. **Languages:** Korean, English. **Religions:** Christian 32.9% (independent 13.4%, Protestant 12.3%, Catholic 7.2%), Buddhist 24.6% (Mahayanist), ethnic religionist 15.1%, new religionist 14.2%, Confucianist 10.9%.

Geography: Total area: 38,502 sq mi, 99,720 sq km (107); **Land area:** 37,421 sq mi, 96,920 sq km. **Location:** Northern E Asia. N. Korea on N. **Topography:** Mountainous, with a rugged E coast. W and S coasts are deeply indented, with many islands and harbors. **Arable land:** 13.5%. **Capital:** Seoul, 10,004,840; Sejong (administrative capital for some of govt.). **Cities:** Busan, 3,477,419; Incheon, 2,861,686; Daegu, 2,179,929; Daejon, 1,581,705; Gwangju, 1,532,902.

Government: Type: Presidential republic. **Head of state and govt.:** Pres. Yoon Suk-yeol; b. 1960; in office: May 10, 2022. **Local divisions:** 9 provinces, 6 metropolitan cities, 1 special city, 1 special self-governing city. **Defense budget:** $43.8 bil. **Active troops:** 500,000.

Economy: Industries: electronics, telecom, auto prod., chemicals, shipbuilding, steel. **Chief agric.:** rice, vegetables, cabbages, milk, pork, onions. **Natural resources:** coal, tungsten, graphite, molybdenum, lead. **Water:** 1,345 cu m per capita. **Electricity prod.:** 606.8 bil kWh. **Labor force:** agric. 5.4%, industry 24.5%, services 70.1%. **Unemployment:** 2.6%.

Finance: Monetary unit: Won (KRW) (1,331.21 = $1 U.S.). **GDP:** $2.8 tril; **per capita GDP:** $54,033; **GDP growth:** 1.4%. **Imports:** $761.1 bil; China 23%, U.S. 11%, Japan 8%, Australia 6%, Saudi Arabia 5%. **Exports:** $769.5 bil; China 21%, U.S. 16%, Vietnam 9%. **Tourism:** $15.3 bil. **Budget:** $372.4 bil. **Inflation:** 3.6%.

Transport: Railways: 2,472 mi. **Motor vehicles:** 498.8 per 1,000 pop. **Airports:** 89.

Communications: Mobile: 162.1 per 100 pop. **Broadband:** 122 per 100 pop. **Internet** (2023): 97.4%.

Health: Expend. (2022): 9.7%. **Life expect.:** 80.3 male; 86.6 female. **Births:** 7.0 per 1,000 pop. **Deaths:** 7.4 per 1,000 pop. **Infant mortality:** 2.8 per 1,000 live births. **Undernourished:** <2.5%. **HIV:** NA. **COVID-19:** 35,934 deaths; rates per 100,000: 67,432 cases, 70 deaths. 87% vaccinated.

Education: Compulsory: ages 6-14. **Literacy:** 98.8%.

Website: www.korea.net

The recorded history of Korea, once called the Hermit Kingdom, dates back to the 1st cent. BCE. It was united in a kingdom under the Silla Dynasty, 668 CE. It was at times associated with the Chinese empire; the treaty that concluded the Sino-Japanese war of 1894-95 recognized Korea's complete independence. In 1910 Japan forcibly annexed Korea, controlling it until 1945. (Japan's exploitation of forced labor and "comfort women" while it occupied Korea strained Japanese-South Korean relations in subsequent decades.)

At the Potsdam conference, July 1945, near the end of WWII, the 38th parallel was designated as the line dividing Soviet (north) and U.S. (south) occupation zones. Soviet and U.S. troops entered Korea.

The South Koreans formed the Republic of Korea in May 1948. Dr. Syngman Rhee was chosen president. A separate, Communist regime was formed in the North; its army (later aided by Chinese troops) attacked the south in June 1950, initiating the Korean War. UN troops, largely U.S. and under U.S. command, supported South Korea in the war, which ended in an armistice (July 1953) leaving Korea divided by a demilitarized zone (DMZ) along the 38th parallel. The U.S. kept troops in South Korea (about 28,500 in 2024).

Rhee's authoritarian rule became increasingly unpopular, forcing his resignation Apr. 26, 1960. In an army coup May 16, 1961, Gen. Park Chung-hee became chairman of a ruling junta. First elected president, 1963, Park was assassinated by the chief of the Korean intelligence agency, Oct. 26, 1979.

In May 1980, Gen. Chun Doo-hwan, head of military intelligence, ordered the brutal suppression of pro-democracy demonstrations in Kwangju. Chun became president, Aug. 27, 1980. On July 1, 1987, following anti-government protests, Chun agreed to democratic reforms. In Dec., Roh Tae-woo, a longtime ally of Chun's, was elected president.

Pres. Kim Young-sam took office in 1993. Convicted of mutiny, treason, and corruption, Chun was sentenced to death by a Seoul court, Aug. 26, 1996, for his role in the 1979 coup and 1980 Kwangju massacre; Roh received a 225-year prison sentence. Kim Dae-jung, a longtime dissident, won the presidential election Dec. 18, 1997. Chun and Roh were released and pardoned Dec. 22.

For seeking improved relations with North Korea, Kim Dae-jung was named, Oct. 13, 2000, winner of the Nobel Peace Prize. Roh Moo-hyun won the 2002 presidential election.

The IAEA, Sept. 2, 2004, said South Korea had acknowledged having secretly processed a small amount of uranium to near weapons-grade level in 2000 (North Korea, 2006-17, conducted 6 nuclear weapons tests).

A U.S.-South Korea trade liberalization agreement went into effect Mar. 15, 2012. Conservative Park Geun-hye became South Korea's first female president in Dec. 19, 2012, elections. Pres. Park was impeached for corruption by the National Assembly, Dec. 9, 2016, and removed from office, Mar. 10, 2017. A criminal trial ended, Apr. 6, 2018, in a conviction and prison sentence; she was pardoned and released in Dec. 2021.

Following a series of North Korean missile tests, a U.S.-South Korean agreement to deploy an advanced U.S. missile defense system known as THAAD in South Korea was announced July 8, 2016.

Moon Jae-in of the Democratic Party (DP), who campaigned on a policy of diplomatic engagement with North Korea, won the May 9, 2017, presidential election. Moon met with North Korean leader Kim Jong Un in the DMZ, Apr. 27, 2018, but North-South tensions subsequently increased.

After a Constitutional Court decision, abortion was decriminalized as of Jan. 1, 2021. Amid economic problems and a lack of results from engagement with North Korea, conservative Yoon Suk-yeol narrowly defeated the DP candidate in the Mar. 9, 2022, presidential election. Concerned by aggressive Chinese and North Korean military actions, the Yoon government sought improved relations with Japan; at an Aug. 2023 summit meeting, South Korea, the U.S., and Japan agreed to increase security cooperation. The opposition DP swept Apr. 10, 2024, National Assembly elections.

South Korea was affected by late Jan. 2020 by the COVID-19 pandemic. Total confirmed cases as of Sept. 2024 were 7th-highest in the world.

Kosovo

Republic of Kosovo

People: Population: 1,977,093 (148). **Age distrib.:** <15: 22.7%; 65+: 8.4%. **Growth:** 0.7%. **Migrants:** NA. **Pop. density:** 470.3 per sq mi, 181.6 per sq km. **Urban:** NA. **Ethnic groups:** Albanian 92.9%, Bosniak 1.6%, Serb 1.5%. **Languages:** Albanian, Serbian (both official); Bosnian. **Religions:** Muslim 92.4% (Sunni), Christian 7.0%.

Geography: Total area: 4,203 sq mi, 10,887 sq km (162); **Land area:** 4,203 sq mi, 10,887 sq km. **Location:** SE Europe. Serbia on N, Montenegro on NW, Albania on SW, North Macedonia on SE. **Topography:** Low flood basins surrounded by several high mountain ranges. **Arable land:** 27.4%. **Capital:** Pristina.

Government: Type: Parliamentary republic. **Head of state:** Pres. Vjosa Osmani; b. 1982; in office: Apr. 4, 2021. **Head of govt.:** Prime Min. Albin Kurti; b. 1975; in office: Mar. 22, 2021. **Local divisions:** 38 municipalities. **Defense budget:** NA. **Active troops:** 3,000 Kosovo Security Force (nonmilitary) only.

Economy: Industries: mineral mining, constr. materials, base metals, leather, machinery, appliances, foodstuffs and beverages. **Chief agric.:** wheat, corn, berries, potatoes, peppers, fruit. **Natural resources:** nickel, lead, zinc, magnesium, lignite, kaolin, chrome, bauxite. **Water:** NA. **Electricity prod.:** 7.0 bil kWh. **Labor force:** NA. **Unemployment:** NA.

Finance: Monetary unit: Euro (EUR) (0.90 = $1 U.S.). **GDP:** $26.4 bil; **per capita GDP:** $15,029; **GDP growth:** 3.3%. **Imports:** $7.4 bil; (2021) Germany 13%, Turkey (Türkiye) 13%, China 10%, Serbia 7%, Italy 6%. **Exports:** $4.2 bil; (2021) U.S. 16%, Albania 15%, North Macedonia 12%, Germany 8%, Italy 8%. **Budget** (2020): $2.5 bil. **Inflation:** 4.9%.

Transport: Railways: 272 mi. **Airports:** 4.

Communications: Mobile (2022): 34.5 per 100 pop. **Broadband:** NA. **Internet** (2018): 89.4%.

Health: Expend.: NA. **Life expect.:** 71.0 male; 75.5 female. **Births:** 14.4 per 1,000 pop. **Deaths:** 7.2 per 1,000 pop. **Infant mortality:** 22.9 per 1,000 live births. **Undernourished:** NA. **HIV:** NA. **COVID-19:** 3,212 deaths; rates per 100,000: 15,274 cases, 179 deaths. 46% vaccinated.

Education: Compulsory: ages 6-14. **Literacy:** NA.

Website: www.rks-gov.net

Kosovo was part of the Roman and Byzantine empires before Serbs, a Slavic people, took control in the Middle Ages. After Ottoman Turks defeated Serb forces, 1389, Kosovo's population became predominantly Muslim and Kosovar (ethnic Albanian). Serbia regained control in the First Balkan War (1912-13). Kosovo entered the Kingdom of Serbs, Croats, and Slovenes as part of Serbia after World War I and became an autonomous province of Serbia, a constituent republic of Yugoslavia, after World War II.

Revoking provincial autonomy, Serbia began ruling Kosovo by force in 1989. Albanian secessionists proclaimed an independent Republic of Kosovo in July 1990. As Yugoslavia collapsed, the republics of Serbia (incl. Kosovo) and Montenegro proclaimed a new Federal Republic of Yugoslavia, 1992. Guerrilla attacks by the Kosovo Liberation Army (KLA) in 1997 brought a ferocious counter-offensive by Serbian authorities.

Fearful that the Serbs were employing "ethnic cleansing" tactics, NATO launched an air war against Yugoslavia, Mar.-June 1999; the Serbs retaliated by terrorizing the Kosovars. Hundreds of thousands fled, mostly to Albania and Macedonia (now North Macedonia). A 50,000-member multinational force (KFOR) entered Kosovo in June, and most refugees returned by Sept. 1, 1999.

From June 1999, Kosovo was administered by a UN mission (UNMIK). Kosovo declared independence, Feb. 17, 2008. More than 100 nations, including the U.S. and most EU members, have recognized Kosovo; Serbia and Russia have not.

An EU special prosecutor reported, July 29, 2014, evidence of ethnic cleansing against Serbs by the KLA in the late 1990s. Prime Min. Hashim Thaçi, who headed the KLA at that time, had denied any wrongdoing. Thaçi was replaced as prime min., Dec. 9, 2014. Parliament elected Thaçi president of Kosovo, Feb. 26, 2016. An indictment against Thaçi for war crimes was announced June 24, 2020; he resigned Nov. 5. Parliament speaker Vjosa Osmani became acting head of state and was elected president by parliament, Apr. 4, 2021. After his party swept Feb. 14, 2021, parliamentary elections, Albin Kurti became prime minister.

Tensions between ethnic Serbs and Albanians in northern Kosovo remained high, prompting KFOR to increase its troop strength in 2023. (About 4,500 KFOR troops were in Kosovo as of June 2024.

Kuwait

State of Kuwait

People: Population: 3,138,355 (134). **Age distrib.:** <15: 23.0%; 65+: 3.6%. **Growth:** 1.1%. **Migrants:** 72.8%. **Pop. density:** 456.2 per sq mi, 176.1 per sq km. **Urban:** 100.0%. **Ethnic groups:** Asian 40.3%, Kuwaiti 30.4%, other Arab 27.4%. **Languages:** Arabic (official), English widely spoken. **Religions:** Muslim (official) 78.0% (Sunni 67%, Shia 11%), Christian 14.6%, Hindu 5.0%.

Geography: Total area: 6,880 sq mi, 17,818 sq km (153); **Land area:** 6,880 sq mi, 17,818 sq km. **Location:** Middle East, at N end of Persian Gulf. Iraq on N, Saudi Arabia on S. **Topography:** Flat, very dry, and extremely hot. **Arable land:** 0.4%. **Capital:** Kuwait City, 3,353,602.

Government: Type: Constitutional monarchy (emirate). **Head of state:** Emir Sheikh Meshal al-Ahmad al-Jaber al-Sabah; b. 1940; in office: Dec. 16, 2023. **Head of govt.:** Prime Min. Sheikh Ahmad Abdullah al-Ahmad al-Sabah; b. 1952; in office: May 15, 2024. **Local divisions:** 6 governorates. **Defense budget:** $7.8 bil. **Active troops:** 17,500.

Economy: Industries: petroleum, petrochemicals, cement, shipbuilding and repair, water desalination, food proc., constr. materials. Chief agric.: eggs, dates, tomatoes, cucumbers, poultry, milk. **Chief agric.:** tomatoes, dates, cucumbers/gherkins, eggs, milk, chicken. **Water:** 5 cu m per capita. **Crude oil reserves:** 101.5 bil bbls (incl. half of Neutral Zone reserves with Saudi Arabia). **Electricity prod.:** 86.4 bil kWh. **Labor force:** agric. 1.9%, industry 25.2%, services 72.9%. **Unemployment:** 2.1%.

Finance: Monetary unit: Dinar (KWD) (0.31 = $1 U.S.). **GDP:** $243.0 bil; **per capita GDP:** $56,386; **GDP growth:** –2.2%. **Imports:** $63.4 bil; UAE 20%, China 16%, Saudi Arabia 9%,

U.S. 7%. **Exports:** $95.5 bil; China 24%, India 15%, South Korea 11%, Japan 9%, Taiwan 7%. **Tourism:** $1.7 bil. **Budget:** $72.0 bil. **Inflation:** 3.6%.

Transport: Motor vehicles: 774.4 per 1,000 pop. **Airports:** 6.

Communications: Mobile: 167.7 per 100 pop. **Broadband:** 136 per 100 pop. **Internet** (2023): 99.7%.

Health: Expend.: 5.8%. **Life expect.:** 78.1 male; 81.1 female. **Births:** 17.5 per 1,000 pop. **Deaths:** 2.3 per 1,000 pop. **Infant mortality:** 7.2 per 1,000 live births. **Undernourished:** <2.5%. **HIV:** <0.1%. **COVID-19:** 2,570 deaths; rates per 100,000: 15,625 cases, 60 deaths. 78% vaccinated.

Education: Compulsory: ages 6-14. **Literacy:** 96.5%.

Website: www.pm.gov.kw

Kuwait is ruled by the Sabah dynasty, founded 1759. Britain ran foreign relations and defense from 1899 until independence in 1961. More than two-thirds of the population is non-Kuwaiti, including many Palestinians and non-Arab Asians, and cannot vote.

Oil exports provide most of Kuwait's income. Oil pays for free medical care and education for citizens. There is no income tax. Government efforts to diversify the economy proceeded slowly.

Kuwait was attacked and overrun by Iraqi forces Aug. 1990. In Operation Desert Storm a U.S.-led coalition began bombing Iraq and Iraqi forces in Kuwait, Jan. 1991, then launched a ground assault Feb. 23. By Feb. 27, Iraqi forces were routed and Kuwait liberated.

Political rights were extended to women, May 16, 2005; the first female cabinet member was appointed June 12. A suicide bomber killed 27 people and wounded more than 200 at a Shiite mosque, June 26, 2015; an ISIS-affiliated Sunni extremist group claimed responsibility.

Nawaf al-Ahmad al-Jabir al-Sabah, emir since 2020, died Dec. 16, 2023. His half-brother, Crown Prince Meshal al-Ahmad al-Sabah, succeeded him. Following Apr. 4, 2024, legislative elections in which opposition candidates won a majority, the new emir, May 10, suspended the National Assembly and parts of the constitution.

Kyrgyzstan

Kyrgyz Republic

People: Population: 6,172,101 (111). **Age distrib.:** <15: 29.1%; 65+: 6.9%. **Growth:** 0.8%. **Migrants:** 3.1%. **Pop. density:** 83.3 per sq mi, 32.2 per sq km. **Urban:** 38.2%. **Ethnic groups:** Kyrgyz 73.8%, Uzbek 14.8%, Russian 5.1%, other (incl. Uyghur, Tajik, Turk, Kazakh, Tatar, Ukrainian, Korean, German) 5.2%. **Languages:** Kyrgyz, Russian (both official); Uzbek. **Religions:** Muslim 90.0% (Sunni), agnostic 4.7%, Christian 3.1%.

Geography: Total area: 77,202 sq mi, 199,951 sq km (85); **Land area:** 74,055 sq mi, 191,801 sq km. **Location:** Central Asia. Kazakhstan on N, China on E, Uzbekistan on W, Tajikistan on S. **Topography:** Landlocked country nearly covered by Tien Shan and Pamir Mts.; avg. elevation 9,020 ft. Issyk-Kul, a large salt lake in NE, is 1 mi above sea level. **Arable land:** 6.7%. **Capital:** Bishkek, 1,127,721.

Government: Type: Parliamentary republic. **Head of state and govt.:** Pres. Sadyr Japarov; b. 1968; in office: Jan. 28, 2021. **Local divisions:** 7 provinces, 2 cities. **Defense budget:** NA. **Active troops:** 10,900.

Economy: Industries: small machinery, textiles, food proc., cement, shoes, lumber, refrigerators, furniture, elec. motors. **Chief agric.:** milk, potatoes, maize, wheat, barley, sugar beets. **Natural resources:** hydropower, gold, rare earth metals, coal, oil, nat. gas, nepheline, mercury, bismuth, lead, zinc. **Water:** 3,618 cu m per capita. **Crude oil reserves:** 40 mil bbls. **Electricity prod.:** 13.9 bil kWh. **Labor force:** agric. 24.6%, industry 24.6%, services 50.9%. **Unemployment:** 4.0%.

Finance: Monetary unit: Som (KGS) (85.14 = $1 U.S.). **GDP:** $50.4 bil; **per capita GDP:** $7,103; **GDP growth:** 6.2%. **Imports** (2022): $10.7 bil; China 64%, Russia 10%. **Exports** (2022): $3.6 bil; Russia 43%, Kazakhstan 18%, Uzbekistan 10%, Turkey (Türkiye) 6%. **Tourism** (2022): $756 mil. **Budget:** $2.9 bil. **Inflation:** 10.8%.

Transport: Railways: 263 mi. **Airports:** 28.

Communications: Mobile: 108.6 per 100 pop. **Broadband:** 92.1 per 100 pop. **Internet:** 79.8%.

Health: Expend.: 5.4%. **Life expect.:** 68.9 male; 77.2 female. **Births:** 18.7 per 1,000 pop. **Deaths:** 6.0 per 1,000 pop. **Infant mortality:** 24.5 per 1,000 live births. **Undernourished:** 6.1%. **HIV:** 0.3%. **COVID-19:** 1,024 deaths; rates per 100,000: 1,363 cases, 16 deaths. 21% vaccinated.

Education: Compulsory: ages 6-15. **Literacy:** 99.6%.

Website: www.gov.kg

The region was inhabited around the 13th cent. by the Kyrgyz. It was annexed to Russia, 1864, and became a constituent republic of the USSR in 1936. Kyrgyzstan declared independence Aug. 31, 1991, ahead of the USSR disbanding Dec. 26, 1991.

In power since 1990, Pres. Askar Akayev won a third 5-year term in the 2000 election. Fraud by Akayev loyalists in parliamentary elections Feb.-Mar. 2005 sparked protests. Akayev fled the country, Mar. 24, and formally resigned, Apr. 4. His interim successor, former Prime Min. Kurmanbek Bakiyev, a leader of the "tulip revolution," won the 2005 presidential vote. He was reelected, 2009, but was ousted by opposition parties Apr. 7, 2010.

Fighting in mid-June 2010 between majority Kyrgyz and minority Uzbeks in the southern cities of Osh and Jalalabad claimed up to 2,000 lives. Former Prime Min. Sooronbay Jeenbekov won the Oct. 15, 2017, presidential election. Violent protests against alleged widespread fraud followed Oct. 4, 2020, parliamentary elections. The results, favoring parties supporting Pres. Jeenbekov, were annulled, and Jeenbekov resigned Oct. 15. Sadyr Japarov, until recently jailed for abducting a political rival, succeeded Jeenbekov and won a landslide victory in a Jan. 10, 2021, presidential election. A new constitution approved in an Apr. 11, 2021, referendum gave Kyrgyzstan a presidential rather than parliamentary system of government. Kyrgyzstan-Tajikistan fighting in a disputed border region flared in Apr. 2021 and again in Sept. 2022.

Laos

Lao People's Democratic Republic

People: Population: 7,953,556 (103). **Age distrib.:** <15: 30.1%; 65+: 4.8%. **Growth:** 1.3%. **Migrants:** 0.7%. **Pop. density:** 89.3 per sq mi, 34.5 per sq km. **Urban:** 38.9%. **Ethnic groups:** Lao 53.2%, Khmou 11%, Hmong 9.2%, Phouthay 3.4%, Tai 3.1%, Makong 2.5%, Katong 2.2%, Lue 2%. **Languages:** Lao (official), French, English, ethnic langs. **Religions:** Buddhist 54.2% (Theravadin), ethnic religionist 40.7%, Christian 2.9% (Protestant).

Geography: Total area: 91,429 sq mi, 236,800 sq km (82); **Land area:** 89,112 sq mi, 230,800 sq km. **Location:** Indochina Peninsula in SE Asia. Myanmar, China on N; Vietnam on E; Cambodia on S; Thailand on W. **Topography:** Landlocked, dominated by jungle. Mountains along E border are source of E-W rivers. Mekong R. defines most of W border. **Arable land:** 5.3%. **Capital:** Vientiane, 737,750.

Government: Type: Communist party-led state. **Head of state:** Pres. Thongloun Sisoulith; b. 1945; in office: Mar. 22, 2021. **Head of govt.:** Prime Min. Sonxai Siphandon; in office: Dec. 30, 2022. **Local divisions:** 17 provinces, 1 prefecture. **Defense budget:** NA. **Active troops:** 29,100.

Economy: Industries: mining, timber, elec. power, agric. proc., rubber, constr., garments. **Chief agric.:** cassava, root vegetables, rice, sugarcane, vegetables, bananas. **Natural resources:** timber, hydropower, gypsum, tin, gold, gems. **Water:** 44,915 cu m per capita. **Electricity prod.:** 46.0 bil kWh. **Labor force:** agric. 69.6%, industry 7.2%, services 23.3%. **Unemployment:** 1.2%.

Finance: Monetary unit: Kip (LAK) (21,949.32 = $1 U.S.). **GDP:** $71.2 bil; **per capita GDP:** $9,326; **GDP growth:** 3.8%. **Imports** (2022): $7.8 bil; Thailand 56%, China 26%, Vietnam 8%. **Exports** (2022): $8.6 bil; Thailand 35%, China 29%, Vietnam 10%. **Tourism** (2022): $265 mil. **Budget:** $3.8 bil. **Inflation:** 31.2%.

Transport: Railways: 262 mi. **Airports:** 18.

Communications: Mobile (2022): 63.4 per 100 pop. **Broadband** (2022): 60.3 per 100 pop. **Internet:** 66.2%.

Health: Expend.: 2.7%. **Life expect.:** 67.4 male; 70.7 female. **Births:** 19.8 per 1,000 pop. **Deaths:** 6.2 per 1,000 pop. **Infant mortality:** 35.4 per 1,000 live births. **Undernourished:** 5.4%. **HIV:** 0.4%. **COVID-19:** 671 deaths; rates per 100,000: 3,011 cases, 9 deaths. 78% vaccinated.

Education: Compulsory: ages 6-14. **Literacy:** 87.5%.

Website: na.gov.la

Laos became a French protectorate in 1893, but regained independence as a constitutional monarchy July 19, 1949. Conflicts among neutralist, Communist, and conservative factions created a chaotic political situation. Armed conflict increased after 1960.

The three factions formed a coalition government in June 1962 with neutralist Prince Souvanna Phouma as premier. A 14-nation conference in Geneva signed agreements, 1962, guaranteeing independence. By 1964 the leftist Pathet Lao had withdrawn from the coalition, and, with aid from North Vietnamese troops, renewed attacks. During the Vietnam War, U.S. planes (1964-73) dropped more than 2 mil tons of bombs on targets in Laos, principally the Ho Chi Minh trail, a supply line from North Vietnam to Communist forces in Laos, South Vietnam, and Cambodia. (Beginning in the 1990s, the U.S., other nations, and the UN provided aid to dismantle unexploded bombs.)

After Pathet Lao military gains in Laos, Souvanna Phouma, May 1975, ordered government troops to cease fighting; the Pathet Lao took control. The Lao People's Democratic Republic was proclaimed Dec. 3, 1975.

From the mid-1970s through the 1980s, Laos relied on Vietnam for military and financial aid. After easing its finance laws in 1988, Laos attracted investment from Thailand, China, South Korea, the U.S., and other nations. Laos was admitted to the Assn. of SE Asian Nations in 1997. The U.S. Congress approved normalization of trade with Laos in 2004.

Despite environmental and safety concerns, since the 1990s, dozens of dams have been built or planned on Mekong R. tributaries, providing hydroelectricity for domestic use and export. A dam collapse, July 23, 2018, killed at least 35.

Latvia

Republic of Latvia

People: Population: 1,801,246 (149). **Age distrib.:** <15: 14.7%; 65+: 22.2%. **Growth:** –1.1%. **Migrants:** 12.7%. **Pop. density:** 74.9 per sq mi, 28.9 per sq km. **Urban:** 68.8%. **Ethnic groups:** Latvian 62.7%, Russian 24.5%, Belarusian 3.1%, Ukrainian 2.2%, Polish 2%. **Languages:** Latvian (official), Russian. **Religions:** Christian 82.9% (Protestant 39.0%, Orthodox 23.5%, Catholic 19.8%), agnostic 13.1%, atheist 3.2%.

Geography: Total area: 24,938 sq mi, 64,589 sq km (122); **Land area:** 24,034 sq mi, 62,249 sq km. **Location:** E Europe, on Baltic Sea. Estonia on N; Russia on E; Belarus, Lithuania on S. **Topography:** Lowland with numerous lakes, marshes, and peat bogs. Principal river is W. Dvina (Daugava). Glacial hills in E. **Arable land:** 21.8%. **Capital:** Riga, 618,560.

Government: Type: Parliamentary republic. **Head of state:** Pres. Edgars Rinkevics; b. 1973; in office, July 8, 2023. **Head of govt.:** Evika Silina; b. 1975; in office, Sept. 15, 2023. **Local divisions:** 36 municipalities, 7 state cities. **Defense budget:** $1.1 bil. **Active troops:** 6,600.

Economy: Industries: processed foods, processed wood prods., textiles, processed metals, pharmaceuticals, railroad cars, synthetic fibers. **Chief agric.:** wheat, milk, rapeseed, barley, oats, potatoes. **Natural resources:** peat, limestone, dolomite, amber, hydropower, timber. **Water:** 18,645 cu m per capita. **Electricity prod.:** 4.0 bil kWh. **Labor force:** agric. 6.8%, industry 23.7%, services 69.5%. **Unemployment:** 6.5%.

Finance: Monetary unit: Euro (EUR) (0.90 = $1 U.S.). **GDP:** $80.0 bil; **per capita GDP:** $42,501; **GDP growth:** –0.3%. **Imports:** $29.6 bil; Lithuania 22%, Estonia 10%, Germany 9%, Poland 9%, Russia 6%. **Exports:** $27.9 bil; Lithuania 18%, Estonia 10%, Germany 6%, Russia 6%, Sweden 5%. **Tourism:** $1.3 bil. **Budget** (2020): $14.2 bil. **Inflation:** 8.9%.

Transport: Railways: 1,377 mi. **Motor vehicles:** 472.8 per 1,000 pop. **Airports:** 56.

Communications: Mobile: 119.9 per 100 pop. **Broadband:** 121 per 100 pop. **Internet** (2023): 92.2%.

Health: Expend.: 9.0%. **Life expect.:** 72.0 male; 81.0 female. **Births:** 8.3 per 1,000 pop. **Deaths:** 14.7 per 1,000 pop. **Infant mortality:** 4.7 per 1,000 live births. **Undernourished:** <2.5%. **HIV:** 0.6%. **COVID-19:** 7,475 deaths; rates per 100,000: 51,254 cases, 392 deaths. 68% vaccinated.

Education: Compulsory: ages 5-15. **Literacy:** 99.9%.

Website: www.mk.gov.lv

Prior to 1918, Latvia was occupied by the Russians and Germans. It was an independent republic, 1918-39. The Aug. 1939 Soviet-German agreement assigned Latvia to the Soviet sphere of influence. It was officially absorbed by the USSR in 1940. It was overrun by the German army in 1941, but retaken in 1945.

Latvia declared independence, Aug. 21, 1991. The last Russian troops in Latvia withdrew by Aug. 31, 1994. Responding to international pressure, Latvian voters, 1998, eased citizenship laws that had discriminated against some 500,000 ethnic Russians. Latvia joined the EU and NATO in 2004. It began using the euro as its currency Jan. 1, 2014.

After more than 50 people died, Nov. 21, 2013, in a Riga supermarket roof collapse, Prime Min. Valdis Dombrovskis (of the center-right Unity Party) resigned. Laimdota Straujuma became Latvia's first woman prime min., Jan. 22, 2014. She resigned, Dec. 7, 2015, after agreeing to an unpopular EU refugee resettlement program. NATO announced, Feb. 5, 2016, it would station troops in Latvia to deter Russian aggression. After money-laundering scandals, populist parties did well in inconclusive Oct. 6, 2018, elections. Krisjanis Karins of New Unity formed a coalition and became prime min., Jan. 23, 2019. Following Russia's Feb. 2022 invasion of Ukraine, a June 2022 NATO summit pledged to increase troops defending Latvia, and Latvia began providing military aid to Ukraine. New Unity won the most votes in Oct. 1, 2022, elections. Elected by parliament, May 31, 2023, Edgars Rinkevics became Latvia's first openly gay president. Disputes within his coalition led Karins to resign, Aug. 17, 2023. Evika Silina of New Unity became prime min. in Sept.

Lebanon

Lebanese Republic

People: Population: 5,364,482 (121). **Age distrib.:** <15: 18.9%; 65+: 9.5%. **Growth:** 0.6%. **Migrants:** 25.1%. **Pop. density:** 1,358.2 per sq mi, 524.4 per sq km. **Urban:** 89.6%. **Ethnic groups:** Arab 95%, Armenian 4%. (Many Christian Lebanese identify not as Arab but as Phoenician, descendants of ancient Canaanites.) **Languages:** Arabic (official), French, English, Armenian. **Religions:** Muslim 60.5% (Shia 30%, Sunni 25%, Islamic schismatic 5%), Christian 33.5% (Catholic 26.0%), agnostic 3.0%, Buddhist 2.0% (Theravadin).

Geography: Total area: 4,015 sq mi, 10,400 sq km (163); **Land area:** 3,950 sq mi, 10,230 sq km. **Location:** Middle East, on E end of Mediterranean Sea. Syria on E, Israel on S. **Topography:** Narrow coastal strip. Two N-S mountain ranges enclose the fertile Beqaa Valley. The Litani R. runs S through the valley. **Arable land:** 13.6%. **Capital:** Beirut, 2,402,485.

Government: Type: Parliamentary democratic republic. **Head of state:** Vacant. **Head of govt.:** Caretaker Prime Min. Najib Mikati; b. 1955; in office: Sept. 10, 2021. **Local divisions:** 8 governorates. **Defense budget** (2022): $263 mil. **Active troops:** 60,000.

Economy: Industries: banking, tourism, real estate and constr., food proc., wine, jewelry, cement, textiles, mineral and chem. prods., wood and furniture prods. **Chief agric.:** potatoes, milk, tomatoes, apples, oranges, olives. **Natural resources:** limestone, iron ore, salt, water (surplus in a water-deficit region). **Water:** 805 cu m per capita. **Electricity prod.:** 10.0 bil kWh. **Labor force:** agric. 3.5%, industry 20.4%, services 76.0%. **Unemployment:** 11.6%.

Finance: Monetary unit: Pound (LBP) (90,181.32 = $1 U.S.). **GDP** (2022): $70.6 bil; **per capita GDP** (2022): $12,853; **GDP growth:** –0.2%. **Imports:** $23.3 bil; China 14%, Turkey (Türkiye) 13%, Greece 9%, UAE 7%, Italy 5%. **Exports:** $11.8 bil; UAE 22%, Syria 8%, Egypt 5%, U.S. 5%. **Tourism:** $5.4 bil. **Budget:** $16.6 bil. **Inflation:** 221.3%.

Transport: Railways: 249 mi (unusable due to damage from fighting). **Motor vehicles:** 195.6 per 1,000 pop. **Airports:** 8.

Communications: Mobile (2022): 74.0 per 100 pop. **Broadband** (2022): 85.4 per 100 pop. **Internet:** 90.1%.

Health: Expend.: 10.1%. **Life expect.:** 77.8 male; 80.7 female. **Births:** 12.6 per 1,000 pop. **Deaths:** 5.6 per 1,000 pop. **Infant mortality:** 6.7 per 1,000 live births. **Undernourished:** 9.6%. **HIV:** <0.1%. **COVID-19:** 10,947 deaths; rates per 100,000: 18,166 cases, 160 deaths. 35% vaccinated.

Education: Compulsory: ages 6-15. **Literacy:** 87.3%.

Website: www.pcm.gov.lb, www.presidency.gov.lb

Formed from five former Turkish Empire districts, Lebanon became independent Sept. 1, 1920, and was administered under French mandate 1920-41. French troops withdrew in 1946.

Under the 1943 National Covenant, all public positions were divided among the various religious communities, with Christians in the majority. By the 1970s, Muslims became the majority and demanded a larger political and economic role.

U.S. Marines intervened, May-Oct. 1958, during a Syrian-aided revolt. Continued raids against Israeli civilians, 1970-75, brought Israeli retaliation in southern Lebanon.

An estimated 60,000 were killed in a 1975-76 civil war. Palestinian units and leftist Muslims fought against Maronite militia (the Phalange) and other Christians. Several Arab countries provided support to various factions, while Israel aided Christian forces. Syria, which intervened in 1976 to fight Palestinian groups, largely policed a cease-fire.

Israeli forces invaded Lebanon June 6, 1982, attacking strongholds of the Palestine Liberation Organization (PLO). Israeli and Syrian forces engaged in the Bekaa Valley. On Aug. 21, the PLO evacuated W Beirut after massive Israeli bombings. Israeli troops entered W Beirut following the Sept. 14 assassination of newly elected Lebanese Pres. Bashir Gemayel. On Sept. 16, 1982, Lebanese Christian troops entered the Sabra and Shatila refugee camps and massacred hundreds of Palestinian civilians. An agreement May 17, 1983, between Lebanon, Israel, and the U.S. (but not Syria) provided for the withdrawal of Israeli troops; at least 30,000 Syrian troops remained in Lebanon, and Israel held onto a "security zone" in the south.

In 1983, some 50 people were killed in an explosion at the U.S. embassy, Apr. 18; 241 U.S. service members and 58 French soldiers died in separate Islamist suicide attacks, Oct. 23. The 1980s witnessed kidnappings of U.S., British, French, and Soviet citizens by Islamic militants.

A treaty signed May 22, 1991, between Lebanon and Syria recognized Lebanon as a separate state for the first time since 1943.

Israeli forces conducted air raids and artillery strikes against guerrilla bases and villages in southern Lebanon, causing over 200,000 to flee their homes July 25-29, 1993. Some 500,000 civilians fled in Apr. 1996 when Israel struck suspected guerrilla bases in the south. Israel withdrew virtually all its troops from southern Lebanon by May 2000, leaving Hezbollah, an Iranian-backed Shiite Muslim guerrilla group, in control of much of the region.

Rafik al-Hariri, a former prime min. (1992-98, 2000-04), was killed by a truck bomb, Feb. 14, 2005. Many Lebanese blamed Syria or Hezbollah. As anti-Syrian protests mounted, Syrian troops left Lebanon.

Beginning July 2006, Hezbollah bombarded northern Israel with thousands of rockets, and Israeli air and ground forces assaulted suspected Hezbollah strongholds in southern Lebanon and southern Beirut. A UN-sponsored cease-fire took hold, Aug. 14, 2006. To enforce the truce, thousands of Lebanese troops moved into southern Lebanon, and the small UN force already in Lebanon (UNIFIL) was expanded. UNIFIL had about 9,700 uniformed personnel in Lebanon as of July 31, 2024.

A 2008 power-sharing accord between the government and Hezbollah eased factional violence and paved the way for Gen. Michel Suleiman to become president, ending an 18-month stalemate. Factional disputes in parliament led to a lengthy delay in electing a successor when Suleiman's term expired in May 2014. Maronite Christian Michel Aoun was elected president Oct. 31, 2016. Saad al-Hariri, a Sunni Muslim, became prime min., Dec. 18, 2016. Hezbollah and allied Shiite parties made gains in May 6, 2018, parliamentary elections.

The Syrian civil war, in which Hezbollah fighters supported Syria's government (dominated by followers of the Alawite sect of Shiite Islam), spilled over into Lebanon beginning in 2012. As of June 30, 2024, about 775,000 Syrian refugees were in Lebanon.

Months of protests against deteriorating economic conditions began in Oct. 2019. Prime Min. Hariri resigned, Oct. 29. Hassan Diab replaced him, Jan. 21, 2020.

A massive explosion in Beirut, Aug. 4, 2020, at a warehouse storing dangerous chemicals caused more than 200 deaths and about 6,500 injuries and displaced 300,000. Protests against government corruption and inefficiency followed, and the country's economic crisis continued to worsen. Diab resigned Aug. 10, 2020. Former Prime Min. Najib Mikati became prime minister Sept. 10, 2021. After May 15, 2022, elections, Mikati became caretaker prime minister. When Pres. Aoun's term ended, Oct. 2022, parliamentary deadlocks delayed the selection of a successor.

After Israel launched a large-scale offensive, Oct. 2023, against Iran-backed Hamas forces in Gaza (following Hamas terrorist attacks in Israel, Oct. 7, that left 1,200 dead), Hezbollah significantly increased cross-border strikes into Israel—and Israel sharply increased strikes into Lebanon. By Aug. 2024, more than 110,000 people had been evacuated from or fled southern Lebanon, and over 500 Hezbollah fighters and other Lebanese had been killed. Israeli airstrikes killed a top Hezbollah official near Beirut July 30, 2024, and its longtime leader, Hassan Nasrallah, on Sept. 27, 2024. Israel launched a ground offensive against Hezbollah in southern Lebanon Oct. 1, 2024.

Lesotho
Kingdom of Lesotho

People: Population: 2,227,548 (144). **Age distrib.:** <15: 32.0%; 65+: 5.4%. **Growth:** 0.8%. **Migrants:** 0.6%. **Pop. density:** 190.1 per sq mi, 73.4 per sq km. **Urban:** 30.9%. **Ethnic groups:** Sotho 99.7%. **Languages:** Sesotho, English (both official); Phuthi; Xhosa, Zulu. **Religions:** Christian 92.4% (Catholic 49.3%, Protestant 33.2%), ethnic religionist 6.4%.

Geography: Total area: 11,720 sq mi, 30,355 sq km (138); **Land area:** 11,720 sq mi, 30,355 sq km. **Location:** Southern Africa. Completely surrounded by South Africa. **Topography:** Landlocked and mountainous, 5,000 to 11,000 ft in elevation. **Arable land:** 8.8%. **Capital:** Maseru, 201,851.

Government: Type: Parliamentary constitutional monarchy. **Head of state:** King Letsie III; b. 1963; in office: Feb. 7, 1996. **Head of govt.:** Prime Min. Ntsokoane Samuel Matekane; b. 1958; in office: Oct. 28, 2022. **Local divisions:** 10 districts. **Defense budget:** $34 mil. **Active troops:** 2,000.

Economy: Industries: food, beverages, textiles, apparel assembly, handicrafts, constr., tourism. **Chief agric.:** milk, potatoes, maize, vegetables, fruits, beans. **Natural resources:** water, diamonds, sand, clay, building stone. **Water:** 1,325 cu m per capita. **Electricity prod.:** 502.1 mil kWh. **Labor force:** agric. 29.4%, industry 35.0%, services 35.6%. **Unemployment:** 16.5%.

Finance: Monetary unit: Loti (LSL) (17.75 = $1 U.S.). **GDP:** $6.5 bil; **per capita GDP:** $2,794; **GDP growth:** 0.9%. **Imports:** $2.1 bil; South Africa 77%, China 6%, Taiwan 5%. **Exports:** $886.3 mil; South Africa 37%, U.S. 28%, Belgium 19%, UAE 6%. **Tourism:** $9 mil. **Budget** (2020): $1.2 bil. **Inflation:** 6.3%.

Transport: Airports: 33.

Communications: Mobile: 69.4 per 100 pop. **Broadband:** 61 per 100 pop. **Internet:** 47%.

Health: Expend.: 10.2%. **Life expect.:** 58.1 male; 62.3 female. **Births:** 22.9 per 1,000 pop. **Deaths:** 10.8 per 1,000 pop. **Infant mortality:** 45.7 per 1,000 live births. **Undernourished:** NA. **HIV:** 18.5%. **COVID-19:** 709 deaths; rates per 100,000: 1,687 cases, 33 deaths. 44% vaccinated.

Education: Compulsory: ages 6-12. **Literacy:** 82.0%.

Website: www.gov.ls

Lesotho (once called Basutoland) became a British protectorate in 1868. Independence came Oct. 4, 1966. Livestock raising is a major industry; textiles, clothing, and diamonds are leading exports. Cultivation of marijuana is a significant source of income.

Letsie III became king Nov. 12, 1990. In Mar. 1993, Ntsu Mokhehle, a civilian, was elected prime minister, ending 23 years of military rule. After a series of violent disturbances, the king dismissed the Mokhehle government Aug. 17, 1994; constitutional rule was restored Sept. 14.

Letsie abdicated, Jan. 25, 1995. King Moshoeshoe died, Jan. 15, 1996, and Letsie returned to power Feb. 7. After parliamentary elections May 26, 2012, the left-leaning Thomas Motsoahae Thabane became prime min. He fled to South Africa, Aug.-Sept. 2014, when units of the military attacked police forces loyal to Thabane. June 3, 2017, elections returned Thabane to office. He resigned May 19, 2020, after allegations he was involved in the 2017 murder of his wife. Finance Min. Moeketsi Majoro became prime min. May 20.

Lesotho suffered a spike in COVID-19 cases with the emergence of the Omicron variant in late 2021-early 2022. After his party won the most seats in Oct. 7, 2022, elections, Samuel Matekane became prime min. Oct. 28, 2022.

Liberia
Republic of Liberia

People: Population: 5,437,249 (120). **Age distrib.:** <15: 38.9%; 65+: 3.2%. **Growth:** 2.3%. **Migrants:** 1.7%. **Pop. density:** 146.2 per sq mi, 56.4 per sq km. **Urban:** 54.1%. **Ethnic groups:** Kpelle 20.2%, Bassa 13.6%, Grebo 9.9%, Gio 7.9%, Mano 7.2%, Kru 5.5%, Lorma 4.8%, Krahn 4.5%, Kissi 4.3%, Mandingo 4.2%, Vai 3.8%, Gola 3.8%, Gbandi 2.9%. **Languages:** English (official), 27 Indigenous langs. **Religions:** Christian 41.8% (Protestant 16.3%, independent 14.6%, Catholic 10.9%), ethnic religionist 39.8%, Muslim 16.4% (Sunni).

Geography: Total area: 43,000 sq mi, 111,369 sq km (102); **Land area:** 37,189 sq mi, 96,320 sq km. **Location:** SW coast of W Africa. Sierra Leone on W, Guinea on N, Côte d'Ivoire on E. **Topography:** Marshy Atlantic coastline rises to low mountains and plateaus in forested interior. Six major rivers flow in parallel courses to the ocean. **Arable land:** 5.2%. **Capital:** Monrovia, 1,735,365.

Government: Type: Presidential republic. **Head of state and govt.:** Pres. Joseph Boakai; b. 1944; in office: Jan. 22, 2024. **Local divisions:** 15 counties. **Defense budget:** $16 mil. **Active troops:** 2,010.

Economy: Industries: mining, rubber and palm oil proc., diamonds. **Chief agric.:** cassava, rice, sugarcane, oil palm fruit, bananas, rubber. **Natural resources:** iron ore, timber, diamonds, gold, hydropower. **Water:** 44,672 cu m per capita. **Electricity prod.:** 795.2 mil kWh. **Labor force:** agric. 39.3%, industry 8.3%, services 52.4%. **Unemployment:** 2.9%.

Finance: Monetary unit: Dollar (LRD) (194.99 = $1 U.S.). **GDP:** $9.9 bil; **per capita GDP:** $1,819; **GDP growth:** 4.7%. **Imports** (2022): $2.0 bil; China 42%, South Korea 23%, Japan 15%, Germany 5%. **Exports** (2022): $1.2 bil; Switzerland 28%, France 8%, Germany 8%, UK 8%, Poland 6%. **Tourism** (2022): $4 mil. **Budget:** $6 mil. **Inflation** (2017-18): 23.6%.

Transport: Railways: 267 mi (mostly inoperable due to damage from fighting). **Motor vehicles:** 17.6 per 1,000 pop. **Airports:** 19.

Communications: Mobile (2022): 32.1 per 100 pop. **Broadband** (2022): 40.7 per 100 pop. **Internet:** 30.1%.

Health: Expend.: 16.6%. **Life expect.:** 59.9 male; 63.3 female. **Births:** 32.4 per 1,000 pop. **Deaths:** 8.3 per 1,000 pop. **Infant mortality:** 55.7 per 1,000 live births. **Undernourished:** 38.4%. **HIV:** 0.9%. **COVID-19:** 294 deaths; rates per 100,000: 157 cases, 6 deaths. 74% vaccinated.

Education: Compulsory: ages 6-11. **Literacy:** 48.3%.

Website: www.emansion.gov.lr

Liberia was founded in 1822 by freed Black slaves from the U.S. who settled at Monrovia with the aid of colonization societies. It became a republic July 26, 1847, with a constitution modeled on that of the U.S. Descendants of freed slaves dominated politics for much of the 19th and 20th cents.

Under Pres. William V. S. Tubman, Liberia was a founding member of the UN in 1945. Tubman died in 1971 and was succeeded by his vice president, William R. Tolbert Jr. Charging rampant corruption, an Army Redemption Council of enlisted men staged a bloody predawn coup, Apr. 12, 1980, killing Pres. Tolbert and installing Sgt. Samuel Doe, an Indigenous African, as head of state. In 1985, Doe was chosen president in a disputed election.

A civil war began Dec. 1989. In Sept. 1990, Pres. Doe was executed. Despite the introduction of a multinational peacekeeping force, the conflict intensified. Factional fighting devastated Monrovia in Apr. 1996. Ruth Perry became modern Africa's first female head of state Sept. 3, 1996, leading a transitional government. By then, the civil war had claimed more than 150,000 lives.

Former rebel leader Charles Taylor was elected president July 1997. The UN imposed sanctions in 2001, to punish Liberia for aiding an insurgency in Sierra Leone.

A UN-sponsored war crimes tribunal indicted Taylor, June 2003, for his role in the Sierra Leone conflict. With Liberian rebels threatening Monrovia, Taylor resigned Aug. 11 and went into exile. The UN authorized a 15,000-member peacekeeping force (UNMIL) Sept. 19. (UNMIL officially ended Mar. 30, 2018.) Charles Gyude Bryant, was sworn in Oct. 14, 2003, to head an interim government. Ellen Johnson-Sirleaf won presidential elections in 2005 and 2011, and shared the 2011 Nobel Peace Prize. Charles Taylor was convicted at The Hague in 2012 of aiding and abetting war crimes and crimes against humanity. Former soccer star George Weah succeeded Johnson-Sirleaf after winning a Dec. 26, 2017, presidential runoff election. His reelection bid hurt by corruption allegations and economic problems, Weah narrowly lost to former Vice Pres. Joseph Boakai in a Nov. 14, 2023, runoff.

Liberia was seriously affected, 2014-16, by an Ebola virus epidemic. The country was affected by the COVID-19 pandemic beginning in 2020.

Libya
State of Libya

People: Population: 7,361,263 (105). **Age distrib.:** <15: 32.3%; 65+: 4.6%. **Growth:** 1.4%. **Migrants:** 12.0%. **Pop. density:** 10.8

per sq mi, 4.2 per sq km. **Urban:** 81.9%. **Ethnic groups:** Amazigh and Arab 97%, other (incl. Egyptian, Greek, Indian, Italian, Maltese, Pakistani, Tunisian, Turkish) 3%. **Languages:** Arabic (official), Italian, English, Tamazight. **Religions:** Muslim (official) 99.0% (Sunni 94%, Islamic schismatic 5%).

Geography: Total area: 679,362 sq mi, 1,759,540 sq km (16); **Land area:** 679,362 sq mi, 1,759,540 sq km. **Location:** Mediterranean coast of N Africa. Tunisia, Algeria on W; Niger, Chad on S; Sudan, Egypt on E. **Topography:** Desert and semidesert regions cover 92% of land with low mountains in N, higher mountains in S, and a narrow coastal zone. **Arable land:** 1.0%. **Capital:** Tripoli, 1,192,436. **Cities:** Misratah, 1,011,119; Banghazi, 870,502.

Government: Type: In transition. **Head of state:** Pres. Mohammed Al Menfi; b. 1976; in office: Feb. 5, 2021. **Head of govt.:** Prime Min. Abdul Hamid Dbeibeh; b. 1959; in office: Feb. 5, 2021. **Local divisions:** 22 governorates. **Defense budget/active troops:** NA.

Economy: Industries: petroleum, petrochemicals, aluminum, iron and steel, food proc., textiles, handicrafts, cement. **Chief agric.:** potatoes, watermelons, tomatoes, onions, dates, milk. **Natural resources:** petroleum, nat. gas, gypsum. **Water:** 104 cu m per capita. **Crude oil reserves:** 48.4 bil bbls. **Electricity prod.:** 30.3 bil kWh. **Labor force:** agric. 9.2%, industry 22.8%, services 68.0%. **Unemployment:** 18.7%.

Finance: Monetary unit: Dinar (LYD) (4.76 = $1 U.S.). **GDP:** $135.3 bil; **per capita GDP:** $19,641; **GDP growth:** –1.7%. **Imports** (2021): $25.4 bil; Turkey (Türkiye) 15%, China 12%, Italy 12%, Greece 10%, UAE 7%. **Exports** (2021): $32.4 bil; Italy 26%, Spain 10%, Germany 9%, China 7%, France 6%. **Tourism** (2020): $28 mil. **Budget:** $37.5 bil. **Inflation:** 2.4%.

Transport: Motor vehicles: 558.4 per 1,000 pop. **Airports:** 66.

Communications: Mobile (2022): 193.0 per 100 pop. **Broadband** (2022): 118 per 100 pop. **Internet:** 88.4%.

Health: Expend.: NA. **Life expect.:** 75.5 male; 80.0 female. **Births:** 20.3 per 1,000 pop. **Deaths:** 3.5 per 1,000 pop. **Infant mortality:** 10.7 per 1,000 live births. **Undernourished:** 11.4%. **HIV:** 0.1%. **COVID-19:** 6,437 deaths; rates per 100,000: 7,382 cases, 94 deaths. 18% vaccinated.

Education: Compulsory: ages 6-14. **Literacy:** 91.0%.

Website: www.embassyoflibyadc.org

First settled by Berbers, Libya was ruled in succession by Carthage, Rome, the Vandals, and the Ottomans. Italy ruled from 1912, and Britain and France after WWII. Libya became an independent constitutional monarchy Jan. 2, 1952. In 1969 a junta led by Col. Muammar al-Qaddafi seized power.

Under Qaddafi's dictatorship, dissent was suppressed and wars were waged with Egypt and Chad. During the 1980s, Libya was accused of promoting terrorism, such as the Apr. 5, 1986, bombing of a West Berlin nightclub, which killed 3, including a U.S. serviceman. The U.S. attacked what it called "terrorist-related targets" in Libya, Apr. 14, including Qaddafi's barracks.

Libyan agents were accused of planting bombs that blew up Pan Am Flight 103 over Lockerbie, Scotland, killing 270 people Dec. 21, 1988, and French UTA Flight 772 over Niger, killing 170 people Sept. 19, 1989.

Libya agreed in 2003 to renounce terrorism and settle compensation cases for the families of the Lockerbie and UTA bombing victims. The UN lifted sanctions in Sept., and in Dec., Libya renounced nuclear, chemical, and biological weapons and long-range missiles.

Arab Spring rebels fought Qaddafi's forces throughout the spring of 2011. With diplomatic backing from the Arab League and the UN, NATO forces imposed an arms embargo and no-fly zone against Qaddafi. Aided by NATO, rebels took control of Tripoli Aug. 23, 2011. Rebels killed Qaddafi Oct. 20, 2011. Ansar al-Shariah terrorists attacked the U.S. consulate and a CIA base in Benghazi Sept. 11, 2012, killing Ambassador J. Christopher Stephens and three other Americans.

As violence between Islamists, rival militia groups, and pro-government forces continued, parliamentary elections were held June 25, 2014. The new parliament met in Tobruk because of Islamist militia control of Tripoli. A UN-backed Government of National Accord (GNA), formed in Jan. 2016, largely took control in Tripoli, but was not recognized by the Tobruk government. ISIS seized territory in Libya by early 2016. An offensive by pro-GNA and other militia forces, aided by the U.S., had retaken most ISIS territory by Dec. 2016. By mid-2017, forces led by former Libyan army Gen. Khalifa Haftar gained control of eastern Libya.

Haftar's forces began, Apr. 2019, an offensive toward Tripoli; they were supported by Russian military aid but ended their unsuccessful offensive June 2020. Forces that opposed Haftar, received Turkish military support. UN-sponsored talks produced a ceasefire, Oct. 23, 2020, followed by agreement, Feb. 5, 2021, on a new interim government in Tripoli, charged with preparing for nationwide elections. However, planned Dec. 2021 elections were postponed, and conflict between rival groups and political deadlock continued in subsequent years.

Beginning in 2014, Libya was a major transit route for African, Asian, and other migrants trying to reach Europe. By mid-2017, efforts by Italy and other EU nations reduced migrant crossings of the Mediterranean, but crossing attempts increased again in 2021-23. By mid-2024, more than 761,000 migrants from dozens of countries were estimated to be in Libya. Thousands of migrants were in Libyan detention centers, where they often faced harsh conditions.

Torrential rains, Sept. 2023, in NE Libya caused two dams in poor repair to collapse and led to catastrophic flooding in and near the coastal city of Derna. Thousands died, and tens of thousands were displaced.

Liechtenstein

Principality of Liechtenstein

People: Population: 40,272 (190). **Age distrib.:** <15: 15.3%; 65+: 20.8%. **Growth:** 0.7%. **Migrants:** 67.9%. **Pop. density:** 651.9 per sq mi, 251.7 per sq km. **Urban:** 14.7%. **Ethnic groups** (by nationality): Liechtensteiner 65.6%, Swiss 9.6%, Austrian 5.8%, German 4.5%, Italian 3.1%. **Languages:** German (official). **Religions:** Christian 88.3% (Catholic [official] 75.5%, Protestant 10.9%), agnostic 6.1%, Muslim 5.4% (Sunni).

Geography: Total area: 62 sq mi, 160 sq km (191); **Land area:** 62 sq mi, 160 sq km. **Location:** Central Europe, in Alps. Switzerland on W, Austria on E. **Topography:** Rhine Valley occupies one-third of country, Alps in the rest. **Arable land:** 10.8%. **Capital:** Vaduz, 5,470.

Government: Type: Constitutional monarchy. **Head of state:** Prince Hans-Adam II; b. 1945; in office: Nov. 13, 1989. **Head of govt.:** Prime Min. Daniel Risch; b. 1978; in office: Mar. 25, 2021. **Local divisions:** 11 communes. **Defense budget/active troops:** NA.

Economy: Industries: electronics, metal mfg., dental prods., ceramics, pharmaceuticals, food prods., precision instruments, tourism, optical instruments. **Chief agric.:** wheat, barley, corn, potatoes; livestock, dairy products. **Natural resources:** hydroelectric potential. **Water:** 0 cu m per capita. **Labor force:** NA. **Unemployment:** NA.

Finance: Monetary unit: Swiss Franc (CHF) (0.84 = $1 U.S.). **GDP:** NA; **per capita GDP:** NA; **GDP growth:** NA. **Imports** (2014): $2.2 bil. **Exports** (2015): $3.2 bil. **Budget** (2011): $890.4 mil. **Inflation** (2015-16): –0.4%.

Transport: Railways: 6 mi (owned by Austrian Railway System).

Communications: Mobile: 127.2 per 100 pop. **Broadband:** 125 per 100 pop. **Internet:** 96.8%.

Health: Expend.: NA. **Life expect.:** 80.7 male; 85.8 female. **Births:** 10.3 per 1,000 pop. **Deaths:** 8.2 per 1,000 pop. **Infant mortality:** 3.9 per 1,000 live births. **Undernourished:** NA. **HIV:** NA. **COVID-19:** 89 deaths; rates per 100,000: 55,715 cases, 230 deaths.

Education: Compulsory: ages 7-15. **Literacy:** NA.

Website: www.liechtenstein.li

Liechtenstein became sovereign in 1806. It is united with Switzerland by a customs and monetary union. Many workers commute daily from Austria, Switzerland, and Germany.

On Aug. 15, 2004, Prince Hans-Adam II assigned day-to-day responsibilities to his son, Crown Prince Alois. Long a tax haven, Liechtenstein took steps, 2008-13, to ease banking secrecy laws.

Lithuania

Republic of Lithuania

People: Population: 2,628,186 (139). **Age distrib.:** <15: 15.2%; 65+: 22.2%. **Growth:** –1.1%. **Migrants:** 5.3%. **Pop. density:** 108.6 per sq mi, 41.9 per sq km. **Urban:** 68.9%. **Ethnic groups:** Lithuanian 84.6%, Polish 6.5%, Russian 5%. **Languages:** Lithuanian (official), Russian, Polish. **Religions:** Christian 89.7% (Catholic 82.2%), agnostic 9.4%.

Geography: Total area: 25,212 sq mi, 65,300 sq km (121); **Land area:** 24,201 sq mi, 62,680 sq km. **Location:** Eastern Europe, on SE coast of Baltic. Latvia on N; Belarus on E, S; Poland, Russia on W. **Topography:** Lowland with hills in W and S. Many small lakes and rivers with marshes espec. in N and W. **Arable land:** 36.6%. **Capital:** Vilnius, 541,505.

Government: Type: Semi-presidential republic. **Head of state:** Gitanas Nauseda; b. 1964; in office: July 12, 2019. **Head of govt.:** Prime Min. Ingrida Simonyte; b. 1974; in office: Dec. 11, 2020. **Local divisions:** 60 municipalities. **Defense budget:** $2.0 bil. **Active troops:** 25,300.

Economy: Industries: metal-cutting machine tools, elec. motors, TVs, refrigerators and freezers, petroleum refining, shipbuilding, furniture. **Chief agric.:** wheat, milk, rapeseed, sugar beets, barley, potatoes. **Natural resources:** peat, amber. **Water:** 8,792 cu m per capita. **Crude oil reserves:** 12 mil bbls. **Electricity prod.:** 3.5 bil kWh. **Labor force:** agric. 5.5%, industry 25.7%, services 68.8%. **Unemployment:** 7.0%.

Finance: Monetary unit: Euro (EUR) (0.90 = $1 U.S.). **GDP:** $149.0 bil; **per capita GDP:** $51,877; **GDP growth:** –0.3%. **Imports:** $58.1 bil; Poland 12%, Germany 11%, Latvia 8%, U.S. 6%, Russia 5%. **Exports:** $61.1 bil; Latvia 13%, Poland 8%, Germany 8%, Russia 6%, U.S. 6%. **Tourism:** $1.8 bil. **Budget:** $18.5 bil. **Inflation:** 9.1%.

Transport: Railways: 1,187 mi. **Motor vehicles:** 614.9 per 1,000 pop. **Airports:** 65.

Communications: Mobile: 137.2 per 100 pop. **Broadband:** 137 per 100 pop. **Internet** (2023): 88.5%.

Health: Expend. (2022): 7.5%. **Life expect.:** 70.8 male; 81.7 female. **Births:** 8.9 per 1,000 pop. **Deaths:** 15.2 per 1,000 pop. **Infant mortality:** 3.6 per 1,000 live births. **Undernourished:** <2.5%. **HIV:** 0.2%. **COVID-19:** 9,810 deaths; rates per 100,000: 49,059 cases, 351 deaths. 68% vaccinated.

Education: Compulsory: ages 6-16. **Literacy:** 99.8%.

Website: lrvk.lrv.lt

Lithuania, briefly occupied by the German army, 1914-18, was annexed by the Soviet Union until 1919. In 1939 it rejoined the Soviet sphere of influence and was annexed by the USSR Aug. 3, 1940.

Lithuania declared its independence Mar. 11, 1990. The country became a full member of NATO and the EU in 2004; it began using the euro as its currency, Jan. 1, 2015. Independent Gitanas Nauseda won a presidential runoff election, May 26, 2019. With COVID-19 cases spiking and the economy faltering, center-right parties won Oct. 2020 parliamentary elections. Ingrida Simonyte of Homeland Union became prime minister, Nov. 24, ending center-left governance. Nauseda won reelection in a presidential runoff, May 26, 2024.

NATO, which first stationed troops in Lithuania in 2017, decided at a June 2022 summit meeting (following Russia's Feb. 2022 invasion of Ukraine) to increase troop strength defending Lithuania.

Luxembourg

Grand Duchy of Luxembourg

People: Population: 671,254 (164). **Age distrib.:** <15: 16.7%; 65+: 16.1%. **Growth:** 1.5%. **Migrants:** 47.6%. **Pop. density:** 672.3 per sq mi, 259.6 per sq km. **Urban:** 92.3%. **Ethnic groups** (by nationality): Luxembourger 52.9%, Portuguese 14.5%, French 7.6%, Italian 3.7%, Belgian 3%, German 2%. **Languages:** Luxembourgish (national lang.), French, German (all official admin. and judicial langs.); Portuguese; Italian; English. **Religions:** Christian 72.9% (Catholic 70.2%), agnostic 21.3%, Muslim 3.7% (Sunni).

Geography: Total area: 998 sq mi, 2,586 sq km (169); **Land area:** 998 sq mi, 2,586 sq km. **Location:** Western Europe. Belgium on W, France on S, Germany on E. **Topography:** Heavy forests (Ardennes) cover N. Low, open plateau in S. **Arable land:** 24.1%. **Capital:** Luxembourg, 119,752.

Government: Type: Constitutional monarchy. **Head of state:** Grand Duke Henri; b. 1955; in office: Oct. 7, 2000. **Head of govt.:** Prime Min. Luc Frieden; b. 1963; in office: Nov. 17, 2023. **Local divisions:** 12 cantons. **Defense budget:** $1.2 bil. **Active troops:** 900.

Economy: Industries: banking and financial services, constr., real estate services, iron, metals, steel, information tech., telecom, cargo transp. and logistics. **Chief agric.:** milk, wheat, barley, triticale, potatoes, pork. **Natural resources:** iron ore (no longer exploited). **Water:** 5,475 cu m per capita. **Electricity prod.:** 763.5 mil kWh. **Labor force:** agric. 1.1%, industry 9.1%, services 89.8%. **Unemployment:** 5.2%.

Finance: Monetary unit: Euro (EUR) (0.90 = $1 U.S.). **GDP:** $95.8 bil; **per capita GDP:** $143,341; **GDP growth:** –1.1%. **Imports:** $146.8 bil; Belgium 26%, Germany 26%, France 11%, Netherlands 6%. **Exports:** $176.1 bil; Germany 20%, France 15%, Belgium 10%, Netherlands 8%. **Tourism:** $6.3 bil. **Budget:** $30.0 bil. **Inflation:** 3.7%.

Transport: Railways: 168 mi. **Motor vehicles:** 777.9 per 1,000 pop. **Airports:** 3.

Communications: Mobile: 144.5 per 100 pop. **Broadband:** 117 per 100 pop. **Internet** (2023): 99.3%.

Health: Expend. (2022): 5.5%. **Life expect.:** 80.9 male; 85.9 female. **Births:** 11.6 per 1,000 pop. **Deaths:** 7.1 per 1,000 pop. **Infant mortality:** 3.2 per 1,000 live births. **Undernourished:** <2.5%. **HIV:** 0.3%. **COVID-19:** 1,000 deaths; rates per 100,000: 62,885 cases, 160 deaths. 74% vaccinated.

Education: Compulsory: ages 4-15. **Literacy:** NA.

Website: gouvernement.lu

Luxembourg, founded about 963, was ruled by Burgundy, Spain, Austria, and France from 1448 to 1815. It left the Germanic Confederation in 1866. Overrun by Germany in two world wars, Luxembourg ended its neutrality in 1948, when a customs union with Belgium and the Netherlands was adopted. Luxembourg was a founding member of NATO (1949) and of what became the European Union (1951).

After Oct. 20, 2013, elections, Xavier Bettel of the Democratic Party (DP) formed a center-left coalition. Same-sex marriage was legalized in 2014. Bettel's coalition retained power in 2018 elections.

To reduce traffic, the government made public transportation free as of Mar. 1, 2020. The center-right Christian Social People's Party (CSV) won Oct. 8, 2023, elections; the CSV and DP formed a coalition, and the CSV's Luc Frieden became prime minister.

Madagascar

Republic of Madagascar

People: Population: 29,452,714 (53). **Age distrib.:** <15: 37.0%; 65+: 3.9%. **Growth:** 2.2%. **Migrants:** 0.1%. **Pop. density:** 131.2 per sq mi, 50.6 per sq km. **Urban:** 41.2%. **Ethnic groups:** Malayo-Indonesian (Merina and related Betsileo), Cotiers (mixed African/Malayo-Indonesian/Arab ancestry), French, Indian, Creole, Comoran. **Languages:** Malagasy, French (both official); English. **Religions:** Christian 60.2% (Protestant 33.9%, Catholic 22.9%), ethnic religionist 37.0%, Muslim 2.2% (Sunni).

Geography: Total area: 226,658 sq mi, 587,041 sq km (47); **Land area:** 224,534 sq mi, 581,540 sq km. **Location:** In Indian O., off SE coast of Africa. Comoro Isls. to NW, Mozambique to W. **Topography:** Humid coastal strip in E, fertile valleys in mountainous center plateau region, and a wider coastal strip on W. **Arable land:** 5.2%. **Capital:** Antananarivo, 4,048,666.

Government: Type: Semi-presidential republic. **Head of state:** Pres. Andry Rajoelina; b. 1974; in office: Dec. 16, 2023. **Head of govt.:** Prime Min. Christian Ntsay; b. 1961; in office: June 6, 2018. **Local divisions:** 6 provinces. **Defense budget:** $107 mil. **Active troops:** 13,500.

Economy: Industries: meat proc., seafood, soap, beer, leather, sugar, textiles, glassware, cement, auto assembly. **Chief agric.:** rice, sugarcane, cassava, sweet potatoes, milk, bananas. **Natural resources:** graphite, chromite, coal, bauxite, rare earth elements, salt, quartz, tar sands, semiprec. stones, mica, fish, hydropower. **Water:** 11,655 cu m per capita. **Electricity prod.:** 2.4 bil kWh. **Labor force:** agric. 70.1%, industry 9.9%, services 20.1%. **Unemployment:** 3.1%.

Finance: Monetary unit: Ariary (MGA) (4,563.03 = $1 U.S.). **GDP:** $56.9 bil; **per capita GDP:** $1,875; **GDP growth:** 4.0%. **Imports** (2022): $6.0 bil; China 24%, India 10%, France 9%, Oman 6%, South Africa 6%. **Exports** (2022): $4.7 bil; U.S. 18%, France 15%, China 13%, Japan 11%. **Tourism** (2022): $367 mil. **Budget** (2020): $2.1 bil. **Inflation:** 9.9%.

Transport: Railways: 519 mi. **Motor vehicles:** 15.5 per 1,000 pop. **Airports:** 91.

Communications: Mobile: 81.4 per 100 pop. **Broadband:** 25.7 per 100 pop. **Internet:** 20.6%.

Health: Expend.: 3.5%. **Life expect.:** 67.3 male; 70.3 female. **Births:** 27.6 per 1,000 pop. **Deaths:** 5.8 per 1,000 pop. **Infant mortality:** 37.5 per 1,000 live births. **Undernourished:** 39.7%. **HIV:** 0.4%. **COVID-19:** 1,428 deaths; rates per 100,000: 248 cases, 5 deaths. 9% vaccinated.

Education: Compulsory: ages 6-10. **Literacy:** 77.5%.

Website: www.primature.gov.mg

Madagascar was settled 2,000 years ago by Malayan-Indonesian people, whose descendants still predominate. A unified kingdom ruled in the 18th and 19th cent. The island became a French protectorate, 1885, and a colony, 1896. Independence came June 26, 1960.

Discontent with inflation and French domination led to a coup in 1972. The new regime nationalized French-owned financial interests, closed French bases and a U.S. space-tracking station, and obtained Chinese aid. The government conducted a program of arrests, expulsion of foreigners, and repression of strikes in 1979.

In 1990, Madagascar ended a ban on multiparty politics that had existed since 1975. A 1993 presidential election ended the 17-year rule of Adm. Didier Ratsiraka.

Marc Ravalomanana won 2001 and 2006 presidential elections. A power struggle between Ravalomanana and the military-backed Andry Rajoelina led to Rajoelina's installation as head of a transitional regime, Mar. 17, 2009. Out of office since 2013, Rajoelina defeated Ravalomanana in a disputed Dec. 19, 2018, presidential runoff.

The government attempted to limit media coverage of the COVID-19 pandemic that began in 2020. Years of drought were compounded by severe cyclone damage in early 2023. After a disputed Nov. 16, 2023, election, the High Constitutional Court ruled, Dec. 1, that Rajoelina had won reelection.

Malawi

Republic of Malawi

People: Population: 21,763,309 (62). **Age distrib.:** <15: 37.7%; 65+: 3.9%. **Growth:** 2.2%. **Migrants:** 1.0%. **Pop. density:** 599.1 per sq mi, 231.3 per sq km. **Urban:** 18.6%. **Ethnic groups:** Chewa 34.3%, Lomwe 18.8%, Yao 13.2%, Ngoni 10.4%, Tumbuka 9.2%, Sena 3.8%, Mang'anja 3.2%. **Languages:** English (official), Chewa (dominant), Lambya, Lomwe, Ngoni, Nkhonde. **Religions:** Christian 79.4% (Catholic 37.9%, Protestant 33.0%), Muslim 14.7% (Sunni), ethnic religionist 5.2%.

Geography: Total area: 45,747 sq mi, 118,484 sq km (98); **Land area:** 36,324 sq mi, 94,080 sq km. **Location:** SE Africa. Zambia on W, Mozambique on S and E, Tanzania on N. **Topography:** 560 mi N-S along Lake Nyasa (Lake Malawi), most of which belongs to Malawi. High plateaus and mountains line the Rift Valley along length of nation. **Arable land:** 42.4%. **Capital:** Lilongwe, 1,333,096. **Cities:** Blantyre-Limbe, 1,070,625.

Government: Type: Presidential republic. **Head of state and govt.:** Pres. Lazarus Chakwera; b. 1955; in office: June 28, 2020. **Local divisions:** 28 districts. **Defense budget:** $62 mil. **Active troops:** 10,700.

Economy: Industries: tobacco, tea, sugar, sawmill prods., cement, consumer goods. **Chief agric.:** sweet potatoes, cassava, maize, sugarcane, mangoes/guavas, potatoes. **Natural resources:** limestone; hydropower; unexploited deposits of uranium, coal, bauxite. **Water:** 869 cu m per capita. **Electricity prod.:** 1.4 bil kWh. **Labor force:** agric. 62.1%, industry 8.1%, services 29.8%. **Unemployment:** 5.0%.

Finance: Monetary unit: Kwacha (MWK) (1,734.02 = $1 U.S.). **GDP:** $39.1 bil; **per capita GDP:** $1,868; **GDP growth:** 1.5%. **Imports** (2022): $3.7 bil; South Africa 20%, China 15%, UAE 11%, India 6%, Kuwait 5%. **Exports** (2022): $1.5 bil; UAE 21%, Belgium 12%, Tanzania 6%, Kenya 5%, South Africa 5%. **Tourism** (2021): $27 mil. **Budget:** $2.1 bil. **Inflation:** 28.8%.

Transport: Railways: 477 mi. **Motor vehicles:** 2.5 per 1,000 pop. **Airports:** 28.

Communications: Mobile: 61.1 per 100 pop. **Broadband:** 40.2 per 100 pop. **Internet** (2023): 18%.

Health: Expend.: 7.4%. **Life expect.:** 69.9 male; 76.1 female. **Births:** 26.6 per 1,000 pop. **Deaths:** 4.5 per 1,000 pop. **Infant mortality:** 31.9 per 1,000 live births. **Undernourished:** 19.9%. **HIV:** 6.7%. **COVID-19:** 2,686 deaths; rates per 100,000: 466 cases, 14 deaths. 22% vaccinated.

Education: Compulsory: ages 6-13. **Literacy:** 68.1%.

Website: www.malawi.gov.mw

Bantus came to the land in the 16th cent., Arab slavers in the 19th. The area became the British protectorate Nyasaland in 1891. It became independent July 6, 1964, and a republic in 1966. After three decades as a one-party state, Malawi adopted a new constitution and held multiparty elections, 1994.

Ruling-party candidate Bingu wa Mutharika won a disputed 2004 presidential election. He won reelection May 2009. Joyce Banda became Malawi's first female pres. after the death of Mutharika Apr. 5, 2012. In May 20-22, 2014, presidential elections, Peter Mutharika (the former president's brother) was declared the winner. Drought affected up to 8 mil in 2016. Peter Mutharika appeared to narrowly win reelection, May 21, 2019, but the Constitutional Court, Feb. 3, 2020, annulled the result. Opposition candidate Lazarus Chakwera won a June 23, 2020, re-vote.

Affected by the COVID-19 pandemic that began in 2020, Malawi experienced widespread vaccine resistance. The country's worst known cholera outbreak began in Mar. 2022; nearly 2,000 died before the outbreak was brought under control in mid-2023. More than 1,000 died when Cyclone Freddy struck Malawi in Mar. 2023. Drought caused food shortages and acute hunger in 2024.

Malaysia

People: Population: 34,564,810 (45). **Age distrib.:** <15: 22.2%; 65+: 8.4%. **Growth:** 1.0%. **Migrants:** 10.7%. **Pop. density:** 272.4 per sq mi, 105.2 per sq km. **Urban:** 79.2%. **Ethnic groups:** Bumiputera 63.8% (Malay 52.8% and Indigenous, incl. Orang Asli, Dayak, Anak Negeri, 11%), Chinese 20.6%, Indian 6%. **Languages:** Bahasa Malaysia (official), English, Chinese, Tamil, Telugu, Malayalam, Panjabi, Thai. **Religions:** Muslim (official) 54.9% (Sunni), Chinese folk-religionist 18.8%, Christian 9.5%, Hindu 6.8%, Buddhist 5.3% (Mahayanist), ethnic religionist 3.6%.

Geography: Total area: 127,355 sq mi, 329,847 sq km (66); **Land area:** 126,895 sq mi, 328,657 sq km. **Location:** SE tip of Asia, plus N coast of the island of Borneo. Thailand, Brunei on N; Indonesia on S. **Topography:** Most of W is covered by tropical jungle, including a central mountain range that runs N-S through the peninsula. Marshy W coast, sandy E coast. Wide swampy coastal plain with interior jungles and mountains in E. **Arable land:** 2.5%. **Capital:** Kuala Lumpur, 8,815,630; Putrajaya (administrative). **Cities:** Johor Bahru, 1,107,001.

Government: Type: Federal parliamentary constitutional monarchy. **Head of state:** King Sultan Ibrahim Iskandar; b. 1958; in office: Jan. 31, 2024. **Head of govt.:** Prime Min. Anwar Ibrahim; b. 1947; in office: Nov. 24, 2022. **Local divisions:** 13 states, 1 federal territory. **Defense budget:** $4.0 bil. **Active troops:** 113,000.

Economy: Industries: rubber and palm oil proc. and mfg., petroleum and nat. gas, light mfg., pharmaceuticals, medical tech., logging. **Chief agric.:** oil palm fruit, rice, chicken, eggs, coconuts, tropical fruits. **Natural resources:** tin, petroleum, timber, copper, iron ore, nat. gas, bauxite. **Water:** 17,275 cu m per capita. **Crude oil reserves:** 3.6 bil bbls. **Electricity prod.:** 194.3 bil kWh. **Labor force:** agric. 10.0%, industry 28.1%, services 61.9%. **Unemployment:** 3.9%.

Finance: Monetary unit: Ringgit (MYR) (4.35 = $1 U.S.). **GDP:** $1.3 tril; **per capita GDP:** $37,248; **GDP growth:** 3.7%. **Imports** (2022): $283.6 bil; China 28%, Singapore 12%, U.S. 6%, Taiwan 6%, Japan 5%. **Exports** (2022): $312.9 bil; Singapore 14%, China 13%, U.S. 12%, Japan 6%, Hong Kong 6%. **Tourism:** $14.8 bil. **Budget:** $85.9 bil. **Inflation:** 2.5%.

Transport: Railways: 1,150 mi. **Motor vehicles:** 533.5 per 1,000 pop. **Airports:** 102.

Communications: Mobile: 142.7 per 100 pop. **Broadband:** 129 per 100 pop. **Internet** (2023): 97.7%.

Health: Expend.: 4.4%. **Life expect.:** 75.0 male; 78.4 female. **Births:** 14.2 per 1,000 pop. **Deaths:** 5.8 per 1,000 pop. **Infant mortality:** 6.4 per 1,000 live births. **Undernourished:** <2.5%. **HIV:** 0.3%. **COVID-19:** 37,351 deaths; rates per 100,000: 16,404 cases, 115 deaths. 85% vaccinated.

Education: Compulsory: ages 6-11. **Literacy:** 95.0%.

Website: www.malaysia.gov.my

European traders visited in the 16th cent.; Britain established control in 1867. Malaysia was created Sept. 16, 1963. It included Malaya (which gained independence in 1957 after the suppression of Communist rebels), plus the formerly British Singapore, Sabah (N Borneo), and Sarawak (NW Borneo). Singapore was separated in 1965.

Malaysia has abundant natural resources, though rainforest destruction has become a major environmental problem. Work on a federal administrative center at Putrajaya, south of Kuala Lumpur, was completed in 1999.

National Front leader Najib Razak took over the premiership in 2009. In a close election (deemed fraudulent by the opposition), May 5, 2013, the governing coalition was returned to power.

A Malaysia Airlines flight, carrying 239 passengers and crew, lost contact with air traffic control Mar. 8, 2014, and was presumed lost in the Indian Ocean. On July 17, 2014, a Malaysia Airlines flight from Amsterdam to Kuala Lumpur was shot down over separatist-controlled eastern Ukraine; all 298 people onboard were killed.

A security law enacted Dec. 3, 2015, gave the Malaysian government sweeping powers to conduct surveillance and searches and to suppress protests.

Beginning in 2015, Malaysian authorities (and other countries) investigated possible misappropriation of more than $4.5 bil from a government development fund (1MDB), including up to $1 bil in transfers to bank accounts controlled by Prime Min. Najib. After the National Front lost May 9, 2018, elections and new Prime Min. Mahathir Mohamad took office, Najib was charged, in 2018, with dozens of corruption-related offenses. He was convicted, July 28, 2020, on 7 corruption counts. With his coalition fracturing, Mahathir resigned, Feb. 24, 2020. Muhyiddin Yassin, backed by Najib's party, became prime minister Mar. 1. Criticized for his handling of the COVID-19 pandemic, Muhyiddin resigned Aug. 16, 2021. Ismail Sabri Yaakob, of Najib's party, became prime minister Aug. 21.

After losing appeals of his 2020 conviction, Najib was imprisoned, Aug. 23, 2022. A progressive coalition headed by Anwar Ibrahim won the most seats in Nov. 19, 2022, elections, and he became prime minister.

Maldives

Republic of Maldives

People: Population: 388,858 (172). **Age distrib.:** <15: 22.4%; 65+: 6.1%. **Growth:** –0.2%. **Migrants:** 13.0%. **Pop. density:** 3,379.7 per sq mi, 1,304.9 per sq km. **Urban:** 42.4%. **Ethnic groups:** homogeneous mix of Sinhalese, Dravidian, Arab, Australasian, African. **Languages:** Dhivehi (official), English (spoken by most govt. officials). **Religions:** Muslim 98.7% (Sunni [official]).

Geography: Total area: 115 sq mi, 298 sq km (188); **Land area:** 115 sq mi, 298 sq km. **Location:** In Indian O. Nearest neighbor is India to NE. **Topography:** 19 atolls with 1,190 islands, 200 inhabited. None of the islands are over 5 sq mi in area; all are nearly flat. **Arable land:** 13.0%. **Capital:** Male, 176,851.

Government: Type: Presidential republic. **Head of state and govt.:** Pres. Mohamed Muizzu; b. 1978; in office: Nov. 17, 2023. **Local divisions:** 21 admin. atolls. **Defense budget:** $110 mil. **Active troops:** 4,000.

Economy: Industries: tourism, fish proc., shipping, boat building, coconut proc., woven mats, rope. **Chief agric.:** fruits, vegetables, nuts, tomatoes, bananas. **Natural resources:** fish. **Water:** 58 cu m per capita. **Electricity prod.:** 847.3 mil kWh. **Labor force:** agric. 7.3%, industry 25.2%, services 67.5%. **Unemployment:** 4.1%.

Finance: Monetary unit: Rufiyaa (MVR) (15.41 = $1 U.S.). **GDP:** $12.9 bil; **per capita GDP:** $24,809; **GDP growth:** 4.0%. **Imports** (2022): $4.9 bil; India 16%, China 16%, UAE 10%, Oman 9%, Malaysia 6%. **Exports** (2022): $5.1 bil; India 71%, Thailand 12%. **Tourism** (2022): $4.5 bil. **Budget** (2020): $1.8 bil. **Inflation:** 2.9%.

Transport: Airports: 19.

Communications: Mobile: 141.6 per 100 pop. **Broadband:** 52.5 per 100 pop. **Internet:** 83.9%.

Health: Expend.: 10.0%. **Life expect.:** 75.1 male; 79.9 female. **Births:** 15.1 per 1,000 pop. **Deaths:** 4.3 per 1,000 pop. **Infant mortality:** 24.4 per 1,000 live births. **Undernourished:** NA. **HIV:** NA. **COVID-19:** 316 deaths; rates per 100,000: 34,538 cases, 58 deaths. 71% vaccinated.

Education: Compulsory: ages 6-12. **Literacy:** 97.9%.

Website: presidency.gov.mv

A British protectorate since 1887, the nation achieved independence July 26, 1965; long a sultanate, the Maldives became a republic in 1968. Rising sea levels threaten the island nation. The Indian Ocean tsunami of Dec. 26, 2004, killed at least 82 people in the Maldives.

Pres. Maumoon Abdul Gayoom, in office 1978-2008, lost a 2008 runoff election to pro-democracy leader and former political prisoner Mohamed (Anni) Nasheed. Following protests over the arrest of a judge, Nasheed resigned Feb. 2012. Abdulla Yameen Abdul Gayoom (the former president's half-brother) won a Nov. 16, 2013, presidential runoff. In 2017, the government detained political opponents. Opposition candidate Ibrahim Mohamed Solih defeated Yameen in the Sept. 23, 2018, presidential election. Solih's party won Apr. 6, 2019, parliamentary elections. Nasheed was severely injured in an assassination attempt, May 6, 2021. Yameen was convicted on corruption charges in 2022, but a 2024 court ruling ordered further trial proceedings. Mohamed Muizzu, of Yameen's party, defeated Solih in a Sept. 30, 2023, presidential runoff election. In an apparent endorsement of the president's pro-China policies, Muizzu's party swept Apr. 21, 2024, parliamentary elections.

Mali

Republic of Mali

People: Population: 21,990,607 (60). **Age distrib.:** <15: 46.8%; 65+: 3.1%. **Growth:** 2.9%. **Migrants:** 2.4%. **Pop. density:** 46.7 per sq mi, 18.0 per sq km. **Urban:** 46.9%. **Ethnic groups:** Bambara 33.3%, Fulani (Peuhl) 13.3%, Sarakole/Soninke/Marka 9.8%, Senufo/Manianka 9.6%, Malinke 8.8%, Dogon 8.7%, Sonrai 5.9%, Bobo 2.1%. **Languages:** Bambara (official), French, Peuhl/Foulfoulbe/Fulani, Dogon, Maraka/Soninke, Malinke, Sonrhai/Djerma, Minianka, Tamacheq. **Religions:** Muslim 87.5% (Sunni), ethnic religionist 8.7%, Christian 3.6% (Catholic 2%).

Geography: Total area: 478,841 sq mi, 1,240,192 sq km (23); **Land area:** 471,118 sq mi, 1,220,190 sq km. **Location:** W Africa. Mauritania, Senegal on W; Guinea, Côte d'Ivoire, Burkina Faso on S; Niger on E; Algeria on N. **Topography:** Landlocked grassy plain in upper basins of the Senegal and Niger R., extending N into the Sahara. **Arable land:** 6.8%. **Capital:** Bamako, 3,050,570.

Government: Type: Semi-presidential republic. **Head of state:** Transitional Pres. Assimi Goïta; b. 1983; in office: June 7, 2021. **Head of govt.:** Transitional Prime Min. Choguel Kokalla Maiga; b. 1958; in office: June 7, 2021. **Local divisions:** 10 regions, 1 district. **Defense budget:** $1.1 bil. **Active troops:** 21,000.

Economy: Industries: food proc., constr., phosphate and gold mining. **Chief agric.:** maize, rice, millet, sorghum, okra, sugarcane. **Natural resources:** gold, phosphates, kaolin, salt, limestone, uranium, gypsum, granite, hydropower. **Water:** 5,478 cu m per capita. **Electricity prod.:** 3.8 bil kWh. **Labor force:** agric. 68.0%, industry 10.1%, services 21.9%. **Unemployment:** 3.0%.

Finance: Monetary unit: CFA Franc (XOF) (587.79 = $1 U.S.). **GDP:** $63.5 bil; **per capita GDP:** $2,726; **GDP growth:** 5.2%. **Imports** (2022): $7.9 bil; Côte d'Ivoire 24%, Senegal 19%, China 10%, France 6%, Burkina Faso 5%. **Exports** (2022): $5.9 bil; UAE 74%, Switzerland 17%, Australia 5%. **Tourism** (2022): $142 mil. **Budget** (2018): $3.5 bil. **Inflation:** 2.1%.

Transport: Railways: 368 mi. **Motor vehicles:** 2.0 per 1,000 pop. **Airports:** 30.

Communications: Mobile (2022): 112.1 per 100 pop. **Broadband** (2022): 57.3 per 100 pop. **Internet:** 33.1%.

Health: Expend.: 4.5%. **Life expect.:** 60.9 male; 65.6 female. **Births:** 40.0 per 1,000 pop. **Deaths:** 8.1 per 1,000 pop. **Infant mortality:** 57.4 per 1,000 live births. **Undernourished:** 9.6%. **HIV:** 0.8%. **COVID-19:** 743 deaths; rates per 100,000: 164 cases, 4 deaths. 18% vaccinated.

Education: Compulsory: ages 7-15. **Literacy:** 30.8%.

Website: primature.ml

Until the 15th cent. the area was part of the great Mali Empire. Timbuktu (Tombouctou) was a center of Islamic study. French rule was secured, 1898. The Sudanese Rep. and Senegal became independent as the Mali Federation in 1960, but Senegal withdrew, and the Sudanese Rep. was renamed Mali.

A coup toppled a socialist regime led, 1960-68, by Pres. Modibo Keita. Famine struck in 1973-74, killing as many as 100,000 people.

The military, Mar. 1991, overthrew Pres. Moussa Traoré, who had ruled since 1968. The government and a Tuareg rebel group signed a peace accord in 1994, but Taureg separatists remained active in the north.

Amadou Toumani Touré, who led the 1991 coup, was elected president in 2002 and reelected 2007. After a Mar. 2012 coup, Islamist rebels, allied with Taureg groups, seized control of the country's north. In Jan. 2013, France and West African regional forces entered the fight against the Islamists, who were pushed out of most areas they had seized. The UN Stabilization Mission in Mali (MINUSMA) was approved Apr. 25, 2013. Ibrahim Boubacar Keita was elected president Aug. 11, 2013. Attacks by Taureg rebels and fights against Islamists continued in 2014 and early 2015. A new peace agreement with Taureg fighters was signed mid-2015, but violence continued. Islamists linked to al-Qaeda and ISIS remained active. Violence in central Mali left hundreds dead in 2019.

Beginning in June 2020, large-scale demonstrations protested corruption, economic conditions, and disputed Mar.-Apr. parliamentary elections. Keita and his prime minister, Boubou Cissé, were ousted, Aug. 18, 2020, in a military coup led by Col. Assimi Goïta. On May 24, 2021, Goïta ousted civilian transitional leaders, and he became transitional president June 7.

Fighting against Islamists and separatists persisted in 2022-24. Its relations with the Goïta government strained, France withdrew its troops from Mali in 2022. By 2022, Russian mercenaries were fighting alongside government troops. Following a Mali government request, the UN Security Council voted, June 30, 2023, to end the MINUSMA mission. The Mali government ended, Jan. 2024, the 2015 peace agreement with Taureg groups. An al-Qaeda-linked military group led attacks on the capital, Sept. 17, 2024, killing at least 50 Malian soldiers.

Malta

Republic of Malta

People: Population: 469,730 (169). **Age distrib.:** <15: 14.5%; 65+: 23.1%. **Growth:** 0.5%. **Migrants:** 26.0%. **Pop. density:** 3,850.0 per sq mi, 1,486.5 per sq km. **Urban:** 95.0%. **Ethnic groups:** Maltese (descendants of ancient Carthaginians and Phoenicians with Italian, other Mediterranean stock). **Languages:** Maltese, English (both official). **Religions:** Christian 91.8% (Catholic [official] 89.7%), agnostic 4.5%, Muslim 3.4% (Sunni).

Geography: Total area: 122 sq mi, 316 sq km (187); **Land area:** 122 sq mi, 316 sq km. Island of Malta is 95 sq mi. Gozo, 26 sq mi, and Comino, 1 sq mi, are other islands in group. **Location:** Center of Mediterranean Sea. Nearest neighbor is Italy to N. **Topography:** Heavily indented coastline. Low hills cover interior. **Arable land:** 24.4%. **Capital:** Valletta, 212,768.

Government: Type: Parliamentary republic. **Head of state:** Pres. Myriam Spiteri Debono; b. 1952; in office: Apr. 4, 2024. **Head of govt.:** Prime Min. Robert Abela; b. 1977; in office: Jan. 13, 2020. **Local divisions:** 68 localities. **Defense budget:** $80 mil. **Active troops:** 1,700.

Economy: Industries: tourism, electronics, shipbuilding and repair, constr., food/beverages, pharmaceuticals, footwear. **Chief agric.:** milk, tomatoes, onions, potatoes, cauliflower/broccoli, pork. **Natural resources:** limestone, salt. **Water:** 96 cu m per capita. **Electricity prod.:** 2.2 bil kWh. **Labor force:** agric. 0.8%, industry 17.2%, services 82.0%. **Unemployment:** 3.1%.

Finance: Monetary unit: Euro (EUR) (0.90 = $1 U.S.). **GDP:** $34.5 bil; **per capita GDP:** $62,446; **GDP growth:** 5.6%. **Imports** (2022): $23.9 bil; Italy 14%, China 11%, South Korea 11%, Germany 10%, Canada 5%. **Exports** (2022): $25.4 bil; Germany 12%, Italy 6%, France 6%, Japan 5%, Singapore 5%. **Tourism:** $2.1 bil. **Budget:** $5.6 bil. **Inflation:** 5.1%.

Transport: Motor vehicles: 808.2 per 1,000 pop. **Airports:** 1.

Communications: Mobile: 140.6 per 100 pop. **Broadband:** 129 per 100 pop. **Internet** (2023): 91.9%.

Health: Expend.: 10.6%. **Life expect.:** 81.5 male; 85.8 female. **Births:** 9.4 per 1,000 pop. **Deaths:** 8.8 per 1,000 pop. **Infant mortality:** 4.4 per 1,000 live births. **Undernourished:** <2.5%. **HIV:** 0.3%. **COVID-19:** 922 deaths; rates per 100,000: 23,877 cases, 179 deaths. 86% vaccinated.

Education: Compulsory: ages 5-15. **Literacy:** 94.9%.

Website: www.gov.mt

Malta was ruled by Phoenicians, Romans, Arabs, Normans, the Knights of Malta, France, and Britain (since 1814). It became independent Sept. 21, 1964, and a republic in 1974.

Malta became a full member of the EU May 1, 2004. Same-sex marriage was legalized in 2017.

The Labour Party won June 3, 2017, elections, called early by Prime Min. Joseph Muscat in the face of corruption allegations. Daphne Caruana Galizia, a journalist reporting on corruption, was killed by a car bomb, Oct. 16, 2017. Labour's Robert Abela replaced Muscat in Jan. 2020. Labour won Mar. 26, 2022, elections.

Marshall Islands

Republic of the Marshall Islands

People: Population: 82,011 (187). **Age distrib.:** <15: 30.0%; 65+: 5.7%. **Growth:** 1.3%. **Migrants:** 5.6%. **Pop. density:** 1,173.5 per sq mi, 453.1 per sq km. **Urban:** 79.2%. **Ethnic groups:** Marshallese 95.6%. **Languages:** Marshallese, English (both official). **Religions:** Christian 95.1% (Protestant 70.3%, independent 15.6%), Baha'i 2.7%.

Geography: Total area: 70 sq mi, 181 sq km (190); **Land area:** 70 sq mi, 181 sq km. **Location:** In N Pacific O.; made up of two 800-mi-long island chains, including atolls of Bikini, Enewetak, Kwajalein, Majuro, Rongelap, and Utirik. Nearest neighbors are Micronesia to W, Nauru and Kiribati to S. **Topography:** Low coral limestone and sand islands. **Arable land:** 2.8%. **Capital:** Majuro, 30,661.

Government: Type: Mixed presidential-parliamentary system in free association with U.S. **Head of state and govt.:** Pres. Hilda C. Heine; b. 1951; in office: Jan. 3, 2023. **Local divisions:** 24 municipalities. **Defense budget/active troops:** NA.

Economy: Industries: copra, tuna proc., tourism, craft items. **Chief agric.:** coconuts. **Natural resources:** coconut prods., marine prods., deep-seabed minerals. **Water:** 0 cu m per capita. **Labor force:** NA. **Unemployment:** NA.

Finance: Monetary unit: U.S. Dollar (USD) (1.00 = $1 U.S.). **GDP:** $314.6 mil; **per capita GDP:** $7,491; **GDP growth:** 3.2%. **Imports** (2021): $206.0 mil; China 33%, South Korea 31%, Japan 12%. **Exports** (2021): $130.0 mil; Germany 30%, Denmark 15%, UK 14%, Malta 6%, Indonesia 5%. **Tourism** (2020): $4 mil. **Budget:** $153 mil. **Inflation** (2016-17): 0%.

Transport: Airports: 33.

Communications: Mobile (2022): 39.7 per 100 pop. **Broadband:** NA. **Internet:** 73.2%.

Health: Expend.: 12.5%. **Life expect.:** 73.0 male; 77.5 female. **Births:** 21.2 per 1,000 pop. **Deaths:** 4.3 per 1,000 pop. **Infant mortality:** 20.6 per 1,000 live births. **Undernourished:** NA. **HIV:** NA. **COVID-19:** 17 deaths; rates per 100,000: 27,532 cases, 29 deaths.

Education: Compulsory: ages 5-17. **Literacy:** 98.3%.

Website: rmiparliament.org

The Marshall Islands were a German possession until WWI and were administered by Japan between the World Wars. After WWII, they were administered by the U.S. During 1946-58, Bikini and Enewetak Atolls were used as test sites for U.S. nuclear weapons.

A Compact of Free Association (COFA), ratified by the U.S. in 1986, gave the islands their independence; the U.S. agreed to provide financial aid to the islands, maintain their defense, and compensate victims of nuclear testing. The COFA was amended in 2003 and 2023, extending and increasing financial aid through 2043.

Elected by parliament, Hilda Heine served as the country's first female president, 2016-20 and again beginning in 2024. The Marshall Islands is vulnerable to rising sea levels resulting from climate change.

Mauritania

Islamic Republic of Mauritania

People: Population: 4,328,040 (127). **Age distrib.:** <15: 35.7%; 65+: 4.4%. **Growth:** 1.9%. **Migrants:** 3.9%. **Pop. density:** 10.9 per sq mi, 4.2 per sq km. **Urban:** 58.5%. **Ethnic groups:** Black Moor (Haratine—Arab-speaking descendants of African origin who are or were enslaved by white Moors) 40%, white Moor (Arab-Amazigh descent, known as Beydane) 30%, Sub-Saharan Mauritanian (non-Arabic speaking) 30%. **Languages:** Arabic (official and national); Pular, Soninke, Wolof (all national langs.); French. **Religions:** Muslim (official) 99.3% (Sunni).

Geography: Total area: 397,955 sq mi, 1,030,700 sq km (28); **Land area:** 397,955 sq mi, 1,030,700 sq km. **Location:** NW Africa. Western Sahara on N; Algeria, Mali on E; Senegal on S. **Topography:** Fertile Senegal R. valley in S gives way to wide central region of sandy plains and scrub trees. N is arid and extends into the Sahara. **Arable land:** 0.4%. **Capital:** Nouakchott, 1,552,146.

Government: Type: Presidential republic. **Head of state:** Pres. Mohamed Ould Ghazouani; b. 1956; in office: Aug. 1, 2019. **Head of govt.:** Prime Min. Mohamed Ould Bilal; b. 1963; in office: Aug. 6, 2020. **Local divisions:** 15 regions. **Defense budget:** $244 mil. **Active troops:** 15,850.

Economy: Industries: fish proc., oil prod., mining. **Chief agric.:** rice, milk, sorghum, goat milk, sheep milk, lamb/mutton. **Natural resources:** iron ore, gypsum, copper, phosphate, diamonds, gold, oil, fish. **Water:** 2,470 cu m per capita. **Crude oil reserves:** 20 mil bbls. **Electricity prod.:** 1.7 bil kWh. **Labor force:** agric. 33.0%, industry 14.7%, services 52.3%. **Unemployment:** 10.5%.

Finance: Monetary unit: Ouguiya (MRU) (39.58 = $1 U.S.). **GDP:** $33.7 bil; **per capita GDP:** $6,934; **GDP growth:** 3.4%. **Imports** (2022): $5.8 bil; China 18%, Spain 7%, Morocco 6%, UAE 6%, Indonesia 6%. **Exports** (2022): $4.1 bil; China 24%, Canada 12%, UAE 12%, Spain 9%, Turkey (Türkiye) 6%. **Tourism** (2022): $10 mil. **Budget:** $1.4 bil. **Inflation:** 5.0%.

Transport: Railways: 452 mi. **Motor vehicles:** 9.4 per 1,000 pop. **Airports:** 25.

Communications: Mobile (2022): 109.9 per 100 pop. **Broadband** (2022): 71.3 per 100 pop. **Internet:** 44.4%.

Health: Expend.: 4.1%. **Life expect.:** 63.4 male; 68.5 female. **Births:** 27.2 per 1,000 pop. **Deaths:** 7.2 per 1,000 pop. **Infant mortality:** 48.9 per 1,000 live births. **Undernourished:** 9.3%. **HIV:** 0.2%. **COVID-19:** 997 deaths; rates per 100,000: 1,374 cases, 21 deaths. 33% vaccinated.

Education: Compulsory: ages 6-14. **Literacy:** 67.0%.

Website: primature.gov.mr

A French protectorate from 1903, Mauritania became independent Nov. 28, 1960. It annexed the south of former Spanish Sahara (now Morocco-claimed Western Sahara) in 1976 but renounced its claim to the region after signing a peace treaty with the Saharan guerrillas of the Polisario Front, 1979.

Up to 10,000 people tried to emigrate in handmade boats to Spain's Canary Islands Jan.-June 2006; more than 1,700 died. After decades of military rule, civilian rule was restored, 2006-07, but a 2008 military coup toppled the elected government. The coup leader, Gen. Mohamed Ould Abdel Aziz, won disputed presidential elections in 2009 and 2014. Mohamed Ould Ghazouani, backed by Aziz, won a disputed June 22, 2019, presidential election. Ghazouani won reelection, June 29, 2024.

In 2013, U.S. troops began training and equipping Mauritanian counterterrorism forces combatting Islamic extremists.

Major oil finds have recently been developed. Slavery, though repeatedly abolished, continues to exist in Mauritania.

More than 135,000 refugees and asylum seekers fleeing violence in neighboring Mali were in Mauritania as of June 30, 2024. In the 2020s, Mauritania was again a major embarkation point for migrants trying to reach the Canary Islands.

Mauritius

Republic of Mauritius

People: Population: 1,310,504 (155). **Age distrib.:** <15: 15.1%; 65+: 13.9%. **Growth:** 0.1%. **Migrants:** 2.3%. **Pop. density:** 1,672.0 per sq mi, 645.6 per sq km. **Urban:** 40.9%. **Ethnic groups:** Indo-Mauritian (approx. two-thirds of pop.), Creole, Sino-Mauritian, Franco-Mauritian. **Languages:** Creole, Bhojpuri, French, English (one of two official langs. of National Assembly). **Religions:** Hindu 44.0% (Shaivite 15%, Vaishnavite 15%, Saktist 14%), Christian 33.0% (Catholic 21.9%, Protestant 10.3%), Muslim 16.9% (Sunni 13%), agnostic 2.0%.

Geography: Total area: 788 sq mi, 2,040 sq km (171); **Land area:** 784 sq mi, 2,030 sq km. **Location:** In Indian O., 500 mi E of Madagascar, its nearest neighbor. **Topography:** A volcanic island nearly surrounded by coral reefs. A central plateau is encircled by peaks. **Arable land:** 37.6%. **Capital:** Port Louis, 149,365.

Government: Type: Parliamentary republic. **Head of state:** Pres. Prithvirajsing Roopun; b. 1959; in office: Dec. 2, 2019. **Head of govt.:** Prime Min. Pravind Jugnauth; b. 1961; in office: Jan. 23, 2017. **Local divisions:** 9 districts, 3 dependencies. **Defense budget:** $242 mil. **Active troops:** No standing armed forces; 2,550 paramilitary. Special Mobile Force and coast guard (with support from India)—both part of police—provide security.

Economy: Industries: food proc. (largely sugar milling), textiles, clothing, mining, chemicals, metal prods. **Chief agric.:** sugarcane, chicken, pumpkins/squash, eggs, potatoes, tomatoes. **Natural resources:** fish. **Water:** 2,118 cu m per capita. **Electricity prod.:** 3.5 bil kWh. **Labor force:** agric. 5.1%, industry 21.5%, services 73.4%. **Unemployment:** 6.1%.

Finance: Monetary unit: Rupee (MUR) (46.13 = $1 U.S.). **GDP:** $37.2 bil; **per capita GDP:** $29,498; **GDP growth:** 7.0%. **Imports:** $8.0 bil; China 16%, South Africa 10%, UAE 9%, India 9%, Oman 8%. **Exports:** $5.5 bil; Zimbabwe 11%, South Africa 11%, France 10%, Madagascar 8%, U.S. 7%. **Tourism:** $1.9 bil. **Budget** (2020): $3.7 bil. **Inflation:** 7.1%.

Transport: Motor vehicles: 271.3 per 1,000 pop. **Airports:** 4.

Communications: Mobile: 165.3 per 100 pop. **Broadband:** 125 per 100 pop. **Internet:** 75.5%.

Health: Expend.: 6.4%. **Life expect.:** 72.6 male; 78.4 female. **Births:** 9.8 per 1,000 pop. **Deaths:** 9.0 per 1,000 pop. **Infant mortality:** 11.6 per 1,000 live births. **Undernourished:** 5.9%. **HIV:** 1.5%. **COVID-19:** 1,073 deaths; rates per 100,000: 25,804 cases, 84 deaths. 86% vaccinated.

Education: Compulsory: ages 5-15. **Literacy:** 92.2%.

Website: govmu.org

Mauritius was uninhabited when settled in 1638 by the Dutch, who introduced sugarcane. France took over in 1721, bringing African slaves. Britain ruled from 1810, bringing Indian workers. Mauritius became independent, Mar. 12, 1968, and a republic, Mar. 12, 1992.

Prime Min. Pravind Jugnauth's party won Nov. 7, 2019, legislative elections. An oil tanker ran aground off the SE coast, July 25, 2020, spilling 1,000 tons of fuel.

Mexico

United Mexican States

People: Population: 130,739,927 (10). **Age distrib.:** <15: 23.3%; 65+: 8.2%. **Growth:** 0.7%. **Migrants:** 0.9%. **Pop. density:** 174.2 per sq mi, 67.3 per sq km. **Urban:** 81.9%. **Ethnic groups:** mestizo (Indigenous-Spanish) 62%, predom. Indigenous 21%, Indigenous 7%. **Languages:** Spanish, Indigenous langs. (incl. Mayan, Nahuatl). **Religions:** Christian 95.2% (Catholic 84.2%), agnostic 3.4%.

Geography: Total area: 758,449 sq mi, 1,964,375 sq km (13); **Land area:** 750,561 sq mi, 1,943,945 sq km. **Location:** Southern N America. U.S. on N, Guatemala and Belize on S. **Topography:** The Sierra Madre Occidental Mts. run NW-SE near the W coast; the Sierra Madre Oriental Mts. are near Gulf of Mexico. They join S of Mexico City. In between lies a dry central plateau (5,000-8,000 ft) with temperate vegetation. Coastal lowlands are tropical. About 45% of land is arid. **Arable land:** 9.8%. **Capital:** Mexico City, 22,505,315. **Cities:** Guadalajara, 5,499,678; Monterrey, 5,195,355; Puebla, 3,394,342; Toluca de Lerdo, 2,674,336; Tijuana, 2,297,216.

Government: Type: Federal presidential republic. **Head of state and govt.:** Pres. Claudia Sheinbaum; b. 1962; in office: Oct. 1, 2024. **Local divisions:** 32 states. **Defense budget:** $7.8 bil. **Active troops:** 216,000.

Economy: Industries: food/beverages, tobacco, chemicals, iron and steel, petroleum, mining, textiles, clothing, motor vehicles. **Chief agric.:** sugarcane, maize, milk, oranges, sorghum, tomatoes. **Natural resources:** petroleum, silver, antimony, copper, gold, lead, zinc, nat. gas, timber. **Water:** 3,645 cu m per capita. **Crude oil reserves:** 5.8 bil bbls. **Electricity prod.:** 333.1 bil kWh. **Labor force:** agric. 12.6%, industry 25.0%, services 62.3%. **Unemployment:** 2.8%.

Finance: Monetary unit: Peso (MXN) (19.66 = $1 U.S.). **GDP:** $3.3 tril; **per capita GDP:** $25,602; **GDP growth:** 3.2%. **Imports:** $673.8 bil; U.S. 56%, China 17%. **Exports:** $649.3 bil; U.S. 77%,

Canada 4%. **Tourism:** $30.8 bil. **Budget** (2020): $313.4 bil. **Inflation:** 5.5%.

Transport: Railways: 14,533 mi. **Motor vehicles:** 347.7 per 1,000 pop. **Airports:** 1,485.

Communications: Mobile: 107.6 per 100 pop. **Broadband:** 93.5 per 100 pop. **Internet** (2023): 81.2%.

Health: Expend.: 6.1%. **Life expect.:** 71.6 male; 77.7 female. **Births:** 14.3 per 1,000 pop. **Deaths:** 6.5 per 1,000 pop. **Infant mortality:** 12.1 per 1,000 live births. **Undernourished:** 3.1%. **HIV:** 0.4%. **COVID-19:** 334,586 deaths; rates per 100,000: 5,910 cases, 260 deaths. 63% vaccinated.

Education: Compulsory: ages 4-17. **Literacy:** 95.3%.

Website: www.gob.mx

Mexico was the site of advanced civilizations. The Mayans, an agricultural people, moved up from Yucatan, built huge stone pyramids, and invented a calendar. The Toltecs were overcome by the Aztecs, who founded Tenochtitlan 1325 ce, now Mexico City. Hernán Cortés, Spanish conquistador, destroyed the Aztec empire, 1519-21. After three centuries of Spanish rule the people revolted, beginning in 1810. Spain recognized Mexican independence, 1821. A republic was declared in 1823.

Mexican territory extended into the present-day United States. Texas established a republic in 1836, and Mexico lost California and most of the SW in the U.S.-Mexican War, 1846-48.

The French supported an Austrian archduke on the Mexican throne as Maximilian I, 1864-67. He was deposed in an uprising led by Benito Juárez. Dictatorial rule by Porfirio Díaz, president 1877-80, 1884-1911, led to a period of rebellion and factional fighting. A new constitution in 1917 brought reform.

The Institutional Revolutionary Party (PRI) dominated politics from 1929 until the late 1990s. Gains in agriculture, industry, and social services were achieved, but poverty remained widespread. Vast oil reserves were discovered, 1970s-80s. About 10,000 people died when a magnitude 8.0 earthquake struck near Mexico City, Sept. 19, 1985.

The National Action Party won the 2000 and 2006 presidential elections. Despite a government crackdown on drug cartels, drug-related violence intensified. Enrique Peña Nieto (PRI) won the 2012 presidential election. Notorious Sinaloa drug cartel leader Joaquín Guzmán Loera, known as El Chapo, was extradited to the U.S., Jan. 19, 2017, and convicted, Feb. 12, 2019, of drug trafficking.

Leftist Andrés Manuel López Obrador of the Morena party easily won the July 1, 2018, presidential election. Drug cartel and other violence continued; tens of thousands were murdered or "disappeared" during López Obrador's presidency.

A Supreme Court decision, June 3, 2015, in effect legalized same-sex marriage nationwide. The Court held, Sept. 6, 2023, that federal laws criminalizing abortion were unconstitutional, making abortion legal nationwide at least in federal health care facilities; at the time of the ruling, abortion was legal under state law in 12 of the country's 32 states.

The North American Free Trade Agreement (NAFTA) with the U.S. and Canada took effect Jan. 1, 1994. A revised pact—renamed the U.S.-Mexico-Canada Agreement (USMCA)—came into force July 1, 2020. It strengthened labor and environmental provisions.

With hundreds of thousands of Central American asylum-seekers and other migrants crossing from Mexico into the U.S. in 2019, Mexico agreed, June 7, to increase troops at its southern border with Guatemala. By 2021, under a 2019 U.S. policy, tens of thousands of asylum seekers were forced to wait in Mexico, often in harsh conditions, while their U.S. cases were pending. The U.S. "wait in Mexico" policy ended in 2022. Border crossings were at high levels, 2022 through mid-2024, then fell after new U.S. restrictions on asylum seekers were announced, June 4, 2024.

Hard-hit by the COVID-19 pandemic, Mexico officially recorded the world's 5th highest death toll as of Sept. 2024.

Claudia Sheinbaum of Morena easily won the June 2, 2024, election to succeed López Obrador, becoming the first woman and first Jewish president of Mexico on Oct. 1, 2024. With smuggling of illicit drugs, including fentanyl, from Mexico into the U.S. continuing at high levels, Sinaloa cartel leader Ismael Zambada García was arrested in the U.S., July 25, 2024. A controversial constitutional amendment, enacted by outgoing president López Obrador, Sept. 15. 2024, required judges at every level to be elected by popular vote.

Micronesia, Fed. States of

Federated States of Micronesia

People: Population: 99,603 (184). **Age distrib.:** <15: 27.0%; 65+: 5.7%. **Growth:** –0.7%. **Migrants:** 2.5%. **Pop. density:** 367.5 per sq mi, 141.9 per sq km. **Urban:** 23.6%. **Ethnic groups:** Chuukese/Mortlockese 49.3%, Pohnpeian 29.8%, Kosraean 6.3%, Yapese 5.7%, Yap outer islander 5.1%. **Languages:** English (official), Chuukese, Kosrean, Pohnpeian, Yapese, Ulithian, Woleaian, Nukuoro, Kapingamarangi. **Religions:** Christian 94.8% (Catholic 53.0%, Protestant 33.6%), ethnic religionist 2.7%.

Geography: Total area: 271 sq mi, 702 sq km (178); **Land area:** 271 sq mi, 702 sq km. **Location:** Consists of 607 islands in four major island groups in W Pacific O. **Topography:** Mountainous islands and coral atolls; volcanic outcroppings on Pohnpei, Kosrae, and Truk. Tropical climate. **Arable land:** 2.9%. **Capital:** Palikir, 6,996.

Government: Type: Federal republic in free association with U.S. **Head of state and govt.:** Pres. Wesley W. Simina; b. 1961; in office: May 12, 2023. **Local divisions:** 4 states. **Defense budget/active troops:** NA.

Economy: Industries: tourism, constr., specialized aquaculture, craft items. **Chief agric.:** coconuts, cassava, vegetables, sweet potatoes, bananas, pork. **Natural resources:** timber, marine prods., deep-seabed minerals, phosphate. **Water:** 0 cu m per capita. **Labor force:** NA. **Unemployment:** NA.

Finance: Monetary unit: U.S. Dollar (USD) (1.00 = $1 U.S.). **GDP:** $485.8 mil; **per capita GDP:** $4,217; **GDP growth:** 0.8%. **Imports** (2021): $126.0 mil; U.S. 37%, China 21%, Japan 10%, South Korea 8%, Taiwan 5%. **Exports** (2021): $179.0 mil; Thailand 78%, Philippines 12%, Japan 5%. **Budget** (2018): $223 mil. **Inflation** (2021-22): 5.4%.

Transport: Airports: 7.

Communications: Mobile (2022): 20.0 per 100 pop. **Broadband:** NA. **Internet:** 40.5%.

Health: Expend.: 11.0%. **Life expect.:** 72.9 male; 77.2 female. **Births:** 17.8 per 1,000 pop. **Deaths:** 4.2 per 1,000 pop. **Infant mortality:** 20.9 per 1,000 live births. **Undernourished:** NA. **HIV:** NA. **COVID-19:** 65 deaths; rates per 100,000: 27,616 cases, 57 deaths.

Education: Compulsory: ages 6-13. **Literacy:** NA.

Website: gov.fm

Micronesia, formerly known as the Caroline Islands, was ruled successively by Spain, Germany, Japan, and the U.S. The nation gained independence under a Compact of Free Association (COFA) with the U.S., Nov. 1986. Micronesia is vulnerable to rising sea levels linked to climate change. Amid U.S. efforts to counter Chinese influence in the Pacific, the U.S. and Micronesia signed agreements in 2023 to extend U.S. financial aid under COFA.

Moldova

Republic of Moldova

People: Population: 3,599,528 (131). **Age distrib.:** <15: 14.8%; 65+: 15.0%. **Growth:** –0.6%. **Migrants:** 2.6%. **Pop. density:** 283.4 per sq mi, 109.4 per sq km. **Urban:** 43.6%. **Ethnic groups:** Moldovan 75.1%, Romanian 7%, Ukrainian 6.6%, Gagauz 4.6%, Russian 4.1%. **Languages:** Moldovan/Romanian (official), Russian, Gagauz, Ukrainian. **Religions:** Christian 96.2% (Orthodox 90.6%), agnostic 2.6%.

Geography: Total area: 13,070 sq mi, 33,851 sq km (136); **Land area:** 12,699 sq mi, 32,891 sq km. **Location:** Eastern Europe. Romania on W; Ukraine on N, E, and S. **Topography:** Landlocked; mainly hilly plains with steppelands in S near Black Sea. **Arable land:** 52.4%. **Capital:** Chisinau, 485,636.

Government: Type: Parliamentary republic. **Head of state:** Pres. Maia Sandu; b. 1972; in office: Dec. 24, 2020. **Head of govt.:** Prime Min. Dorin Recean; b. 1974; in office: Feb. 16, 2023. **Local divisions:** 32 raions, 3 municipalities, 2 territorial units (1 autonomous). **Defense budget:** $87 mil. **Active troops:** 5,150.

Economy: Industries: sugar proc., vegetable oil, food proc., agric. machinery, foundry equip., refrigerators and freezers. **Chief agric.:** wheat, maize, sunflower seeds, grapes, sugar beets, apples. **Natural resources:** lignite, phosphorites, gypsum, limestone. **Water:** 4,008 cu m per capita. **Electricity prod.:** 5.3 bil kWh. **Labor force:** agric. 55.4%, industry 12.7%, services 31.9%. **Unemployment:** 1.6%.

Finance: Monetary unit: Leu (MDL) (17.36 = $1 U.S.). **GDP:** $43.2 bil; **per capita GDP:** $17,384; **GDP growth:** 0.8%. **Imports:** $9.9 bil; Romania 23%, Russia 11%, Ukraine 10%, China 8%, Turkey (Türkiye) 7%. **Exports:** $5.9 bil; Romania 27%, Ukraine 15%, Italy 7%, Turkey (Türkiye) 6%, Germany 5%. **Tourism:** $660 mil. **Budget:** $3.8 bil. **Inflation:** 13.4%.

Transport: Railways: 728 mi. **Airports:** 11.

Communications: Mobile: 130.8 per 100 pop. **Broadband:** 94.6 per 100 pop. **Internet:** 63.5%.

Health: Expend.: 7.7%. **Life expect.:** 66.1 male; 74.4 female. **Births:** 8.4 per 1,000 pop. **Deaths:** 14.2 per 1,000 pop. **Infant mortality:** 13.8 per 1,000 live births. **Undernourished:** <2.5%. **HIV:** 0.9%. **COVID-19:** 12,248 deaths; rates per 100,000: 15,838 cases, 304 deaths. 27% vaccinated.

Education: Compulsory: ages 6-15. **Literacy:** 99.6%.

Website: moldova.md

In 1918, Romania annexed Bessarabia, west of the Dniester (Nistru) R. In 1924, the Soviet Union established the Moldavian Autonomous Soviet Socialist Republic on the eastern bank of the river (Trans-Dniester region, or Transnistria). It was merged with the Romanian-speaking districts of Bessarabia in 1940 to form the Moldavian SSR. During WWII, Romania, allied with Germany, occupied the area. It was recaptured by the USSR in 1944. Moldova declared independence Aug. 27, 1991, prior to the dissolution of the USSR Dec. 26, 1991.

Fighting erupted Mar. 1992 in Transnistria between Moldovan security forces and Slavic separatists—including ethnic Russians. Defying the Moldovan government, voters in the breakaway Transnistria held legislative elections and approved a separatist constitution in 1995. A peace accord with Transnistria separatists was signed in Moscow in 1997. In a 2006 referendum, Transnistria voters overwhelmingly supported independence from Moldova and eventual union with Russia. About 2,000 Russian troops were in Transnistria in 2024.

Pro-Western parties won Moldova's parliamentary elections in 2009, 2010, and 2014. In Moldova's first direct presidential election, pro-Russian candidate Igor Dodon won a Nov. 13, 2016, runoff. Following Feb. 24, 2019, parliamentary elections, pro-EU Maia Sandu became prime min. in June, but she lost a no-confidence vote in Nov. Sandu defeated Dodon in a Nov. 15, 2020, runoff to become Moldova's first woman president. Sandu's party swept July 11, 2021, parliamentary elections. The EU, June 23, 2022, officially made Moldova a candidate for membership.

In the wake of Russia's Feb. 2022 invasion of Ukraine, Moldova hosted about 123,000 Ukrainian refugees as of Sept. 2024. After high inflation and energy shortages related to the Ukraine war sparked protests, pro-EU politician Dorin Recean replaced Natalia Gavrilita as prime minister, Feb. 16, 2023.

Monaco
Principality of Monaco

People: Population: 31,813 (192). **Age distrib.:** <15: 9.1%; 65+: 37.1%. **Growth:** 0.7%. **Migrants:** 67.8%. **Pop. density:** 41,197.6 per sq mi, 15,906.5 per sq km. **Urban:** 100.0%. **Ethnic groups** (by birth country): Monegasque 32.1%, French 19.9%, Italian 15.3%, British 5%, Belgian 2.3%, Swiss 2%. **Languages:** French (official), English, Italian, Monegasque. **Religions:** Christian 87.1% (Catholic [official] 84.2%), agnostic 8.8%, atheist 2.2%, Jewish 1.4%.

Geography: Total area: 0.77 sq mi, 2 sq km (195); **Land area:** 0.77 sq mi, 2 sq km. **Location:** NW Mediterranean coast. France to W, N, and E. **Topography:** Principality rises from port up to Monaco-Ville on a high promontory. **Arable land:** 0%. **Capital:** Monaco, 38,897.

Government: Type: Constitutional monarchy. **Head of state:** Prince Albert II; b. 1958; in office: Apr. 6, 2005. **Head of govt.:** Min. of State Didier Guillaume; b. 1959; in office: Sept. 2, 2024. **Local divisions:** no first-order admin. divisions. **Defense budget/active troops:** NA.

Economy: Industries: banking, insurance, tourism, constr. **Chief agric.:** none. **Natural resources:** none. **Water:** NA. **Labor force:** NA. **Unemployment:** NA.

Finance: Monetary unit: Euro (EUR) (0.90 = $1 U.S.). **GDP:** NA; **per capita GDP:** NA; **GDP growth** (2022): 11.1%. **Imports** (2017): $1.4 bil; (2021) Italy, Switzerland, United Kingdom, Germany, China. **Exports** (2017): $964.6 mil; (2021) Italy, Switzerland, Germany, Belgium, Spain. **Budget** (2011): $953.6 mil. **Inflation:** NA.

Transport: Railways: Only one railway station; France operates service in Monaco.

Communications: Mobile: 104.1 per 100 pop. **Broadband:** 101 per 100 pop. **Internet:** 98.4%.

Health: Expend.: 3.7%. **Life expect.:** 86.0 male; 93.7 female. **Births:** 6.5 per 1,000 pop. **Deaths:** 11.1 per 1,000 pop. **Infant mortality:** 1.7 per 1,000 live births. **Undernourished:** NA. **HIV:** NA. **COVID-19:** 67 deaths; rates per 100,000: 43,780 cases, 171 deaths. 64% vaccinated.

Education: Compulsory: ages 6-16. **Literacy:** NA.

Website: www.gouv.mc

Monaco has belonged to the House of Grimaldi almost continuously since 1297. It was annexed by France in 1793 and was placed under the protectorate of Sardinia in 1815. An 1861 treaty restored independence. The Prince of Monaco was an absolute ruler until the 1911 constitution. Monaco is noted for its climate, scenery, casinos, and Formula One Grand Prix auto race. The country is a tourist destination and tax haven for the wealthy. Prince Rainier III, ruler from 1949, died in 2005 and was succeeded by his son, Albert II.

Mongolia

People: Population: 3,281,676 (133). **Age distrib.:** <15: 25.7%; 65+: 5.9%. **Growth:** 0.8%. **Migrants:** 0.7%. **Pop. density:** 5.5 per sq mi, 2.1 per sq km. **Urban:** 69.3%. **Ethnic groups:** Khalkh 83.8%, Kazak 3.8%, Durvud 2.6%, Bayad 2%. **Languages:** Mongolian (official) (Khalkha dialect predom.), Turkic, Russian. **Religions:** Buddhist 59.4% (Lamaist), ethnic religionist 18.2%, agnostic 12.6%, Muslim 5.3% (Sunni), Christian 2.1%.

Geography: Total area: 603,909 sq mi, 1,564,116 sq km (18); **Land area:** 599,831 sq mi, 1,553,556 sq km. **Location:** E Central Asia. Russia on N, China on E, W, and S. **Topography:** Mostly high plateau with mountains, salt lakes, and vast grasslands. Gobi Desert in S. **Arable land:** 0.7%. **Capital:** Ulaanbaatar, 1,699,363.

Government: Type: Semi-presidential republic. **Head of state:** Pres. Ukhnaa Khurelsukh; b. 1968; in office: June 5, 2021. **Head of govt.:** Prime. Min. Luvsannamsrai Oyun-Erdene; b. 1980; in office: Jan. 27, 2021. **Local divisions:** 21 provinces, 1 municipality. **Defense budget:** $92 mil. **Active troops:** 9,700.

Economy: Industries: constr. and constr. materials, mining, oil, food/beverages, animal prods. proc., cashmere and natural fiber mfg. **Chief agric.:** milk, wheat, potatoes, lamb/mutton, goat milk, beef. **Natural resources:** oil, coal, copper, molybdenum, tungsten, phosphates, tin, nickel, zinc, fluorspar, gold, silver, iron. **Water:** 10,395 cu m per capita. **Electricity prod.:** 7.8 bil kWh. **Labor force:** agric. 26.3%, industry 22.1%, services 51.6%. **Unemployment:** 6.1%.

Finance: Monetary unit: Tughrik (MNT) (3,401.67 = $1 U.S.). **GDP:** $62.4 bil; **per capita GDP:** $18,108; **GDP growth:** 7.0%. **Imports:** $13.5 bil; China 36%, Russia 29%, Japan 7%, South Korea 5%. **Exports:** $15.5 bil; China 78%, Switzerland 15%. **Tourism:** $531 mil. **Budget** (2020): $5.0 bil. **Inflation:** 10.3%.

Transport: Railways: 1,128 mi. **Airports:** 35.

Communications: Mobile: 141.1 per 100 pop. **Broadband:** 120 per 100 pop. **Internet:** 83.9%.

Health: Expend.: 6.9%. **Life expect.:** 67.8 male; 76.3 female. **Births:** 14.9 per 1,000 pop. **Deaths:** 6.4 per 1,000 pop. **Infant mortality:** 19.4 per 1,000 live births. **Undernourished:** <2.5%. **HIV:** <0.1%. **COVID-19:** 2,136 deaths; rates per 100,000: 30,854 cases, 65 deaths. 67% vaccinated.

Education: Compulsory: ages 6-17. **Literacy:** 99.2%.

Website: mongolia.gov.mn, president.mn

Mongolia reached the zenith of its power in the 13th cent. when Genghis Khan and his successors conquered all of China and extended their influence as far west as Hungary and Poland. In later centuries, the empire dissolved, and Mongolia became a province of China.

With the advent of the 1911 Chinese revolution, Mongolia, with Russian backing, declared its independence. A Communist regime was established, 1921. The Mongolian People's Revolutionary Party (MPRP) yielded its monopoly on power, 1990. A new constitution took effect, 1992.

Riots followed 2008 parliamentary elections, won by the ruling MPRP (renamed the Mongolian People's Party, or MPP, in 2010). The Democratic Party (DP) won the 2009 presidential election and 2012 legislative elections. With the economy slumping, the MPP won June 29, 2016, parliamentary elections. The IMF approved a $5.5-bil bailout package, May 24, 2017. The MPP won June 24, 2020, legislative elections. Following protests over the government's response to the COVID-19 pandemic, Prime Min. Ukhnaa Khurelsukh (of the MPP) resigned, Jan. 21, 2021; he then won the June 9 presidential election. The MPP won June 28, 2024, parliamentary elections.

Montenegro

People: Population: 599,849 (167). **Age distrib.:** <15: 17.7%; 65+: 17.9%. **Growth:** –0.4%. **Migrants:** 11.3%. **Pop. density:** 115.5 per sq mi, 44.6 per sq km. **Urban:** 68.8%. **Ethnic groups:** Montenegrin 45%, Serbian 28.7%, Bosniak 8.7%, Albanian 4.9%, Muslim 3.3%. **Languages:** Serbian, Montenegrin (official), Bosnian, Albanian, Serbo-Croat. **Religions:** Christian 78.7% (Orthodox 71.4%), Muslim 18.0% (Sunni), agnostic 2.7%.

Geography: Total area: 5,333 sq mi, 13,812 sq km (157); **Land area:** 5,194 sq mi, 13,452 sq km. **Location:** Balkan Peninsula in SE Europe. Bosnia and Herzegovina on N and W, Serbia on E, Albania on SE, Croatia on W. **Topography:** Mostly rugged and mountainous, with few arable regions, mostly along the Zeta R. Highly indented narrow coastline. **Arable land:** 0.7%. **Capital:** Podgorica, 177,177.

Government: Type: Parliamentary republic. **Head of state:** Pres. Jakov Milatovic; b. 1986; in office: May 20, 2023. **Head of govt.:** Prime. Min. Milojko Spajic; b. 1987; in office: Oct. 31, 2023. **Local divisions:** 25 municipalities. **Defense budget:** $123 mil. **Active troops:** 2,885.

Economy: Industries: steelmaking, aluminum, agric. proc., consumer goods, tourism. **Chief agric.:** milk, potatoes, grapes, watermelons, sheep milk, cabbages. **Natural resources:** bauxite, hydroelectricity. **Water:** NA. **Electricity prod.:** 3.3 bil kWh. **Labor force:** agric. 7.2%, industry 18.5%, services 74.3%. **Unemployment:** 15.3%.

Finance: Monetary unit: Euro (EUR) (0.90 = $1 U.S.). **GDP:** $19.2 bil; **per capita GDP:** $31,216; **GDP growth:** 6.0%. **Imports:** $5.2 bil; Serbia 24%, China 8%, Italy 8%, Croatia 7%, Greece 7%. **Exports:** $3.8 bil; South Korea 24%, Serbia 12%, Italy 9%, Switzerland 9%, Bosnia and Herzegovina 7%. **Tourism:** $1.6 bil. **Budget** (2020): $2.6 bil. **Inflation:** 8.6%.

Transport: Railways: 155 mi. **Airports:** 5.

Communications: Mobile: 207.2 per 100 pop. **Broadband:** 112 per 100 pop. **Internet:** 88.2%.

Health: Expend.: 10.6%. **Life expect.:** 75.8 male; 80.7 female. **Births:** 10.9 per 1,000 pop. **Deaths:** 10.3 per 1,000 pop. **Infant mortality:** 3.2 per 1,000 live births. **Undernourished:** <2.5%. **HIV:** 0.1%. **COVID-19:** 2,654 deaths; rates per 100,000: 40,009 cases, 423 deaths. 40% vaccinated.

Education: Compulsory: ages 6-14. **Literacy:** 99.0%.

Website: www.gov.me

Part of the medieval Serbian Kingdom, Montenegro preserved its autonomy for centuries because of its mountainous terrain. After WWI, it was part of the Kingdom of Serbs, Croats, and Slovenes, later renamed Yugoslavia. Italian forces occupied parts of Montenegro during WWII. In 1945, with the establishment of a federal Yugoslavia under Communist rule, Montenegro became one of six constituent republics.

In Apr. 1992, after four other republics had declared independence, Montenegro and Serbia became the Federal Republic of Yugoslavia. On June 3, 2006, Montenegro declared independence. The governing, pro-Western Democratic Party of Socialists (DPS) won the most seats in Oct. 16, 2016, parliamentary elections. Montenegro became a member of NATO, June 5, 2017. The DPS's Milo Djukanovic won the Apr. 15, 2018, presidential election. Parliament legalized same-sex partnerships, July 1, 2020. In Aug. 30, 2020, parliamentary elections, a coalition of opposition parties won a slim majority, but governments were unstable. Jakov Milatovic of the Europe Now Movement (PES) defeated Djukanovic in an Apr. 2, 2023, presidential runoff election. In new parliamentary elections, June 11, 2023, PES won the most votes, and Milojko Spajic of PES formed a coalition government and became prime minister Oct. 31. EU accession negotiations were ongoing in 2024.

Morocco

Kingdom of Morocco

People: Population: 37,387,585 (39). **Age distrib.:** <15: 25.7%; 65+: 8.4%. **Growth:** 0.8%. **Migrants:** 0.3%. **Pop. density:** 135.2 per sq mi, 52.2 per sq km. **Urban:** 65.6%. **Ethnic groups:** Arab-Amazigh 99%. **Languages:** Arabic (official), Tamazight langs. (incl. Tamazight [official]), French (lang. of business, govt., diplomacy). **Religions:** Muslim (official) 99.7% (Sunni).

Geography: Total area: 276,662 sq mi, 716,550 sq km (39); **Land area:** 276,565 sq mi, 716,300 sq km. Total/land area incl. Western Sahara (102,703 sq mi, 266,000 sq km). **Location:** NW coast of Africa. Western Sahara on S, Algeria on E, Spain to N. **Topography:** Five natural regions: mountain ranges (Riff in N, Middle Atlas, Upper Atlas, and Anti-Atlas); rich plains in W; alluvial plains in SW; well-cultivated plateaus in center; pre-Sahara arid zone extending from SE. **Arable land:** 16.8%. **Capital:** Rabat, 1,989,197. **Cities:** Casablanca, 3,950,408; Tanger, 1,348,848; Fès, 1,313,311; Marrakech, 1,067,172.

Government: Type: Parliamentary constitutional monarchy. **Head of state:** King Mohammed VI; b. 1963; in office: July 30, 1999. **Head of govt.:** Prime Min. Aziz Akhannouch; b. 1961; in office: Oct. 7, 2021. **Local divisions:** 11 regions (not incl. 12th claimed region that lies within territory of disputed Western Sahara). **Defense budget:** $6.5 bil. **Active troops:** 195,800.

Economy: Industries: automotive parts, phosphate mining and proc., aerospace, food proc., leather goods. **Chief agric.:** wheat, milk, olives, sugar beets, potatoes, tomatoes. **Natural resources:** phosphates, iron ore, manganese, lead, zinc, fish, salt. **Water:** 782 cu m per capita. **Crude oil reserves:** 684,000 bbls. **Electricity prod.:** 41.2 bil kWh. **Labor force:** agric. 30.8%, industry 24.0%, services 45.3%. **Unemployment:** 9.1%.

Finance: Monetary unit: Dirham (MAD) (9.65 = $1 U.S.). **GDP:** $374.4 bil; **per capita GDP:** $9,743; **GDP growth:** 3.2%. **Imports** (2022): $73.8 bil; Spain 18%, France 10%, China 10%, U.S. 6%, Saudi Arabia 6%. **Exports** (2022): $58.6 bil; Spain 18%, France 17%, India 6%, Italy 5%. **Tourism:** $10.3 bil. **Budget:** $35.6 bil. **Inflation:** 6.1%.

Transport: Railways: 1,284 mi. **Motor vehicles:** 138.2 per 1,000 pop. **Airports:** 49.

Communications: Mobile: 148.2 per 100 pop. **Broadband:** 94.6 per 100 pop. **Internet:** 89.9%.

Health: Expend.: 5.7%. **Life expect.:** 72.5 male; 76.0 female. **Births:** 16.8 per 1,000 pop. **Deaths:** 6.6 per 1,000 pop. **Infant mortality:** 18.3 per 1,000 live births. **Undernourished:** 6.9%. **HIV:** <0.1%. **COVID-19:** 16,305 deaths; rates per 100,000: 3,465 cases, 44 deaths. 64% vaccinated.

Education: Compulsory: ages 6-14. **Literacy:** 77.4%.

Website: www.egov.ma

Berbers were the region's original inhabitants, followed by Carthaginians and Romans. Arabs conquered it in 683. In the 11th and 12th cents., a Berber empire ruled all NW Africa and most of Spain from Morocco.

Part of Morocco came under Spanish rule in the 19th cent.; France controlled the rest in the early 20th. Tribal uprisings lasted from 1911 to 1933. Independence was achieved Mar. 2, 1956. Tangier, an internationalized seaport, was incorporated into Morocco, 1956. Ifni, a Spanish enclave, was ceded in 1969.

King Hassan II assumed the throne in 1961, reigning until his death in 1999; he was succeeded by his eldest son. A bicameral legislature was established in 1997.

Five terrorist attacks, linked to al-Qaeda, in Casablanca May 16, 2003, left 45 dead. Following a series of suicide bombings in 2007, the government stepped up its campaign against militant Islamists. After Arab Spring street demonstrations Feb.-Mar. 2011, the monarchy implemented modest constitutional reforms. Throughout 2011, Moroccans staged protests over persistent unemployment, alleged unjust detentions, and lack of free speech. The moderate Islamist Justice and Development Party (PJD) won a plurality in Oct. 7, 2016, parliamentary elections. Large protests in the impoverished Rif region, 2017-18, prompted a harsh response by security forces. Morocco completed, Dec. 2018, one of the world's largest concentrated solar power complexes. Morocco and Israel agreed, Dec. 10, 2020, to establish diplomatic relations. The National Rally of Independents (RNI) party won Sept. 8, 2021, parliamentary elections; the RNI's Aziz Akhannouch became prime minister. An earthquake near Marrakesh, Sept. 8, 2023, left more than 2,900 dead.

Western Sahara

Western Sahara, formerly the protectorate of Spanish Sahara, is bounded on the N by Morocco, the NE by Algeria, the E and S by Mauritania, and the W by the Atlantic O. Phosphates are the major resource. Pop. (2024 est.) 590,506. Capital is Laayoune; pop. (2018 est.) 232,388.

Spain withdrew in Feb. 1976. On Apr. 14, 1976, Morocco annexed over 70,000 sq mi, with the remainder annexed by Mauritania. The Polisario Front guerrilla movement, which proclaimed the region independent Feb. 27, launched attacks with Algerian support. After Mauritania signed a treaty with Polisario Aug. 5, 1979, Morocco occupied Mauritania's portion of Western Sahara.

After years of bitter fighting, Morocco controlled the main urban and coastal areas, with Polisario controlling the sparsely populated desert interior. The two sides implemented a cease-fire in 1991, when a UN peacekeeping force (MINURSO) was established with a mandate to prepare for a referendum on self-determination, which was not held. Morocco proposed, 2007, an autonomy plan under Moroccan sovereignty for Western Sahara—rejected by Polisario. Following military clashes, Polisario ended the cease-fire Nov. 14, 2020. MINURSO had about 200 military personnel in Western Sahara as of July 31, 2024.

Mozambique

Republic of Mozambique

People: Population: 33,350,954 (46). **Age distrib.:** <15: 44.7%; 65+: 2.9%. **Growth:** 2.5%. **Migrants:** 1.1%. **Pop. density:** 109.8 per sq mi, 42.4 per sq km. **Urban:** 39.3%. **Ethnic groups:** African (incl. Makhuwa, Tsonga, Lomwe, Sena) 99%. **Languages:** Makhuwa, Portuguese (official), Tsonga, Nyanja, Sena, Lomwe, Chuwabo, Ndau, Tswa, other Mozambican langs. **Religions:** Christian 57.6% (Catholic 30.9%, Protestant 14.3%, independent 12.4%), ethnic religionist 23.9%, Muslim 17.9% (Sunni).

Geography: Total area: 308,642 sq mi, 799,380 sq km (34); **Land area:** 303,623 sq mi, 786,380 sq km. **Location:** SE coast of Africa. Tanzania on N; Malawi, Zambia, Zimbabwe on W; South Africa, Eswatini on S. **Topography:** Coastal lowlands comprise nearly half the country with plateaus rising in steps to mountains along western border. **Arable land:** 7.2%. **Capital:** Maputo, 1,193,253. **Cities:** Matola, 1,915,035; Nampula, 1,012,582.

Government: Type: Presidential republic. **Head of state:** Pres. Filipe Jacinto Nyusi; b. 1959; in office: Jan. 15, 2015. Head of govt.: Prime Min. Adriano Afonso Maleiane; b. 1949; in office: Mar. 3, 2022. **Local divisions:** 10 provinces, 1 city. **Defense budget:** $195 mil. **Active troops:** 11,200.

Economy: Industries: aluminum, petroleum prods., chemicals, textiles, cement, glass, asbestos, tobacco, food, beverages. **Chief agric.:** cassava, sugarcane, maize, tomatoes, sweet potatoes, beans. **Natural resources:** coal, titanium, nat. gas, hydropower, tantalum, graphite. **Water:** 6,768 cu m per capita. **Electricity prod.:** 19.0 bil kWh. **Labor force:** agric. 70.1%, industry 9.1%, services 20.8%. **Unemployment:** 3.5%.

Finance: Monetary unit: Metical (MZN) (63.90 = $1 U.S.). **GDP:** $56.2 bil; **per capita GDP:** $1,657; **GDP growth:** 5.0%. **Imports:** $11.2 bil; South Africa 23%, South Korea 20%, China 12%, India 10%, Dem. Rep. of the Congo 5%. **Exports:** $9.3 bil; India 22%, South Africa 9%, South Korea 8%, Italy 7%, China 6%. **Tourism:** $221 mil. **Budget:** $4.6 bil. **Inflation:** 7.1%.

Transport: Railways: 2,975 mi. **Motor vehicles:** 3.9 per 1,000 pop. **Airports:** 92.

Communications: Mobile (2022): 45.8 per 100 pop. **Broadband** (2022): 23.4 per 100 pop. **Internet:** 21.2%.

Health: Expend.: 9.1%. **Life expect.:** 57.1 male; 59.6 female. **Births:** 36.5 per 1,000 pop. **Deaths:** 9.6 per 1,000 pop. **Infant mortality:** 58.2 per 1,000 live births. **Undernourished:** 24.8%. **HIV:** 11.5%. **COVID-19:** 2,252 deaths; rates per 100,000: 748 cases, 7 deaths. 68% vaccinated.

Education: Compulsory: NA. **Literacy:** 63.4%.

Website: www.portaldogoverno.gov.mz

The first Portuguese post on the Mozambique coast was established in 1505 on the trade route to Asia. Mozambique became independent June 25, 1975, after a 10-year war against Portuguese rule led by Frelimo (Front for the Liberation of Mozambique).

The Frelimo government, headed by Pres. Samora Machel, transitioned to a Communist system. Most of the country's whites emigrated. In the 1980s, severe drought and civil war caused famine and heavy loss of life. Pres. Machel was killed in a plane crash, Oct. 19, 1986. Frelimo formally abandoned Marxist-Leninism in 1989, and a new constitution, effective Nov. 30, 1990, established multiparty elections and a free-market economy.

A 1992 peace agreement ended 15 years of hostilities (up to 1 mil killed) between the government and the Mozambique National Resistance (Renamo), which became the main opposition party. Repatriation of 1.7 mil Mozambican refugees ended June 1995.

Frelimo retained power under Pres. Joaquim Chissano (1986-2005) and Pres. Armando Guebuza (2005-15). Filipe Jacinto Nyusi of Frelimo won the Oct. 15, 2014, presidential election. Clashes began in 2013 between government forces and Renamo, which challenged

2014 election results. A truce beginning Dec. 2016 paved the way for May 2018 constitutional amendments decentralizing political power. Cyclone Idai, Mar. 2019, killed more than 600 and displaced hundreds of thousands. Nyusi was reelected Oct. 15, 2019.

Natural gas reserves are estimated at more than 100 tril cu ft (third-largest in Africa). Beginning Oct. 2017, Islamist militants staged a series of attacks in the gas-rich northern Cabo Delgado region. Violence escalated in 2020-21. By mid-2021, Rwandan and other African forces were aiding Mozambican troops. Islamist attacks in Cabo Delgado and neighboring areas continued in 2022-24. The UNHCR reported, as of Jan. 2024, almost 600,000 people in northern Mozambique were internally displaced by the conflict.

Myanmar
(Burma)
Union of Myanmar

People: Population: 57,527,139 (27). **Age distrib.:** <15: 24.4%; 65+: 7.1%. **Growth:** 0.7%. **Migrants:** 0.1%. **Pop. density:** 228.0 per sq mi, 88.0 per sq km. **Urban:** 32.5%. **Ethnic groups:** Burman (Bamar) 68%, Shan 9%, Karen 7%, Rakhine 4%, Chinese 3%, Indian 2%, Mon 2%. **Languages:** Burmese (official). **Religions:** Buddhist 73.8% (Theravadin), ethnic religionist 9.3%, Christian 8.8%, Muslim 3.9% (Sunni).

Geography: Total area: 261,228 sq mi, 676,578 sq km (40); **Land area:** 252,321 sq mi, 653,508 sq km. **Location:** Between S and SE Asia, on Bay of Bengal. Bangladesh, India on W; China, Laos, Thailand on E. **Topography:** Surrounding mountains on W, N, and E. Dense forests cover much of nation. N-S rivers provide habitable valleys, espec. the Irrawaddy, navigable for 900 mi. Tropical monsoon climate. **Arable land:** 16.8%. **Capital:** Nay Pyi Taw (administrative), 757,823. **Cities:** Yangon, 5,709,678; Mandalay, 1,563,021.

Government: Type: Military regime. **Head of state and govt.:** Prime Min. Senior Gen. Min Aung Hlaing (self-appointed head of a "caretaker govt." set up by the military); b. 1956; in office: Aug. 1, 2021. **Local divisions:** 7 regions, 7 states, 1 union territory. **Defense budget:** $3.1 bil. **Active troops:** 201,000.

Economy: Industries: agric. proc.; wood/wood prods.; copper, tin, tungsten, iron; cement, constr. materials; pharmaceuticals; fertilizer. **Chief agric.:** rice, sugarcane, vegetables, beans, maize, groundnuts. **Natural resources:** petroleum, timber, tin, antimony, zinc, copper, tungsten, lead, coal, marble, limestone, prec. stones, nat. gas, hydropower. **Water:** 21,707 cu m per capita. **Crude oil reserves:** 139 mil bbls. **Electricity prod.:** 20.4 bil kWh. **Labor force:** agric. 45.5%, industry 18.8%, services 35.7%. **Unemployment:** 2.8%.

Finance: Monetary unit: Kyat (MMK) (2,099.24 = $1 U.S.). **GDP:** $322.3 bil; **per capita GDP:** $5,905; **GDP growth:** 1.0%. **Imports** (2021): $23.1 bil; China 45%, Thailand 16%, Singapore 14%. **Exports** (2021): $20.4 bil; China 36%, Thailand 13%, Germany 6%, Japan 6%. **Tourism** (2019): $2.5 bil. **Budget** (2020): $18 bil. **Inflation** (2018-19): 8.8%.

Transport: Railways: 3,126 mi. **Motor vehicles:** 0.9 per 1,000 pop. **Airports:** 73.

Communications: Mobile: 121.0 per 100 pop. **Broadband:** 109 per 100 pop. **Internet** (2019): 48.1%.

Health: Expend.: 5.6%. **Life expect.:** 68.5 male; 72.1 female. **Births:** 15.7 per 1,000 pop. **Deaths:** 7.3 per 1,000 pop. **Infant mortality:** 32.1 per 1,000 live births. **Undernourished:** 5.3%. **HIV:** 0.9%. **COVID-19:** 19,494 deaths; rates per 100,000: 1,182 cases, 36 deaths. 66% vaccinated.

Education: Compulsory: ages 5-9. **Literacy:** 89.1%.

Website: www.myanmar.gov.mm

The Burmese arrived from Tibet before the 9th cent., displacing earlier cultures, and a Buddhist monarchy was established by the 11th cent. Burma was conquered by China's Mongol dynasty in 1272, then ruled by the Shan people as a Chinese tributary until the 16th cent. Britain subjugated Burma in three wars, 1824-84, and ruled the country as part of India until 1937, when Burma became self-governing. Full independence was achieved Jan. 4, 1948.

Gen. Ne Win dominated politics from 1962 to 1988, first as military ruler, then as constitutional president, advancing policies that increased economic socialization and international isolation. Ne Win resigned July 1988, following antigovernment riots. In Sept., the military seized power, under Gen. Saw Maung. In 1989 the country's name was changed to Myanmar.

Although the main opposition party won a decisive victory in 1990 multiparty elections, the military refused to surrender power. A key opposition leader, Aung San Suu Kyi, was held under house arrest, 1989-95, 2000-02, and 2003-10.

In late Sept. 2007, thousands of Buddhist monks led mass protests in Yangon; security forces cracked down by raiding monasteries, arresting monks, and firing on demonstrators. Cyclone Nargis, May 2-3, 2008, killed more than 138,000.

Suu Kyi's National League for Democracy (NLD) won 43 of 45 parliamentary seats in an Apr. 1, 2012, election, and Suu Kyi traveled to Oslo, Norway, to accept the Nobel Peace Prize (awarded in 1991). The NLD won Nov. 8, 2015, parliamentary elections. NLD candidates were elected president by the parliament, 2016 and 2018. Suu Kyi, constitutionally barred from the presidency, assumed the newly created post of state counsellor, Apr. 6, 2016, becoming the country's de facto leader. The NLD swept Nov. 8, 2020, parliamentary elections.

A military coup, Feb. 1, 2021, ousted the civilian government. Suu Kyi and other NLD leaders were arrested (Suu Kyi was subsequently convicted of various offenses), and Nov. 2020 election results were annulled. Protests against the coup were met with a deadly crackdown. At least hundreds of protesters were killed. Thousands were arrested; hundreds were estimated to have died in detention, and others were tortured. The first executions of pro-democracy activists occurred July 2022. Opponents of the coup began an armed rebellion against the military regime. With the rebels making gains in 2024, the military increased air attacks in rebel-held areas, causing high civilian casualties. As a result of the rebellion and various ethnic conflicts, about 3.2 mil people in Myanmar were internally displaced as of mid-2024.

Violence against Rohingya Muslims, in Rakhine state in the W, intensified beginning in 2012. Almost all of Myanmar's Rohingya are not recognized as citizens by the government. Widespread military and vigilante attacks on Rohingya in which at least 10,000 were killed led almost three-quarters of a million Rohingya to flee to Bangladesh beginning in Aug. 2017. As of Aug. 31, 2024, Bangladesh hosted a total of over 994,000 Rohingya refugees. Rebel forces that gained control of parts of Rakhine state also attacked Rohingya Muslim villages in 2024.

Namibia
Republic of Namibia

People: Population: 2,803,660 (138). **Age distrib.:** <15: 34.1%; 65+: 3.9%. **Growth:** 1.7%. **Migrants:** 4.3%. **Pop. density:** 8.8 per sq mi, 3.4 per sq km. **Urban:** 55.8%. **Ethnic groups:** Ovambo 50%, Kavangos 9%, Herero 7%, Damara 7%, mixed European/African ancestry 6.5%, European 6%, Nama 5%, Caprivian 4%, San 3%, Baster 2%. **Languages:** Oshiwambo langs., Nama/Damara, Kavango langs., Afrikaans, Herero langs., Zambezi langs., English (official). **Religions:** Christian 90.9% (Protestant 64.6%, Catholic 17.1%), ethnic religionist 5.6%, agnostic 2.6%.

Geography: Total area: 318,261 sq mi, 824,292 sq km (33); **Land area:** 317,874 sq mi, 823,290 sq km. **Location:** Southern Africa on Atlantic coast. Angola on N; Botswana, Zambia on E; South Africa on S. **Topography:** Three distinct regions incl. Namib Desert along the Atlantic, a mountainous central plateau with woodland savanna, and Kalahari Desert in E. True forests found in NE. Four rivers but little other surface water. **Arable land:** 1.0%. **Capital:** Windhoek, 494,085.

Government: Type: Presidential republic. **Head of state and govt.:** Acting Pres. Nangolo Mbumba; b. 1941; in office: Feb. 4, 2024. **Local divisions:** 14 regions. **Defense budget:** $350 mil. **Active troops:** 9,900.

Economy: Industries: mining, tourism, fishing, agric. **Chief agric.:** root vegetables, milk, maize, millet, grapes, beef. **Natural resources:** diamonds, copper, uranium, gold, silver, lead, tin, lithium, cadmium, tungsten, zinc, salt, hydropower, fish. **Water:** 15,774 cu m per capita. **Electricity prod.:** 1.4 bil kWh. **Labor force:** agric. 21.6%, industry 16.6%, services 61.9%. **Unemployment:** 19.4%.

Finance: Monetary unit: Dollar (NAD) (17.75 = $1 U.S.). **GDP:** $33.2 bil; **per capita GDP:** $12,757; **GDP growth:** 4.2%. **Imports:** $8.3 bil; South Africa 41%, China 7%, Nigeria 5%. **Exports:** $5.6 bil; South Africa 28%, Botswana 11%, China 10%, Zambia 5%. **Tourism:** $348 mil. **Budget:** $4.7 bil. **Inflation:** 5.9%.

Transport: Railways: 1,633 mi. **Motor vehicles:** 140.2 per 1,000 pop. **Airports:** 255.

Communications: Mobile: 87.7 per 100 pop. **Broadband:** 58.5 per 100 pop. **Internet:** 62.2%.

Health: Expend.: 9.4%. **Life expect.:** 64.2 male; 67.6 female. **Births:** 24.3 per 1,000 pop. **Deaths:** 7.1 per 1,000 pop. **Infant mortality:** 27.9 per 1,000 live births. **Undernourished:** 22.2%. **HIV:** 9.7%. **COVID-19:** 4,108 deaths; rates per 100,000: 6,790 cases, 162 deaths. 22% vaccinated.

Education: Compulsory: ages 7-13. **Literacy:** 92.3%.

Website: www.gov.na

Namibia was declared a German protectorate in 1890 and officially called South-West Africa. German troops putting down a rebellion killed tens of thousands of Herero and Nama people, 1904-08 (Germany, in 2021, acknowledged the "genocide"). South Africa seized the territory in 1915 during WWI. In 1966, the Marxist South-West Africa People's Organization (SWAPO) launched a guerrilla war for independence, aided by Angola and Cuba. The UN General Assembly named the area Namibia in 1968.

A 1988 U.S.-mediated agreement ended South African administration. A constitution providing for multiparty government was adopted Feb. 9, 1990, and Namibia gained independence Mar. 21.

Walvis Bay, the principal deepwater port, was returned to Namibia by South Africa in 1994.

SWAPO, the leading political group since independence, won Nov. 2019 presidential and parliamentary elections. Pres. Hage Geingob died Feb. 4, 2024, before the end of his term; he was succeeded by Vice Pres. Nangolo Mbumba.

Nauru

Republic of Nauru

People: Population: 9,892 (195). **Age distrib.:** <15: 29.6%; 65+: 4.4%. **Growth:** 0.4%. **Migrants:** 20.3%. **Pop. density:** 1,220.0 per sq mi, 471.0 per sq km. **Urban:** 100.0%. **Ethnic groups:** Nauruan 94.6%, I-Kiribati 2.2%. **Languages:** Nauruan (official), English (used in govt. and commerce). **Religions:** Christian 74.8% (Protestant 43.2%, Catholic 24.3%), Chinese folk-religionist 10.6%, Baha'i 8.8%, agnostic 4.4%.

Geography: Total area: 8.1 sq mi, 21 sq km (194); **Land area:** 8.1 sq mi, 21 sq km. **Location:** In W Pacific O. just S of equator. Nearest neighbor is Kiribati to E. **Topography:** Mostly a plateau bearing high-grade phosphate deposits, surrounded by a sandy shore and coral reef in concentric rings. **Arable land:** 0%. **Capital:** Nauru, 11,312.

Government: Type: Parliamentary republic. **Head of state and govt.:** Pres. David Adeang; b. 1969; in office: Oct. 30, 2023. **Local divisions:** 14 districts. **Defense budget/active troops:** NA.

Economy: Industries: phosphate mining, offshore banking, coconut prods. **Chief agric.:** coconuts, tropical fruits, pork, eggs, pork offal, pork fat. **Natural resources:** phosphates, fish. **Water:** 799 cu m per capita. **Electricity prod.:** 41.4 mil kWh. **Labor force:** NA. **Unemployment:** NA.

Finance: Monetary unit: Australian Dollar (AUD) (1.48 = $1 U.S.). **GDP:** $161.9 mil; **per capita GDP:** $12,671; **GDP growth:** 0.7%. **Imports** (2021): $94.2 mil; Australia 47%, China 17%, Japan 12%, Fiji 11%. **Exports** (2021): $187.0 mil; Thailand 59%, Philippines 19%, South Korea 11%. **Budget** (2020): $158 mil. **Inflation** (2016-17): 5.1%.

Transport: Airports: 1.

Communications: Mobile (2022): 87.2 per 100 pop. **Broadband** (2022): 33.8 per 100 pop. **Internet:** 82.7%.

Health: Expend.: 13.1%. **Life expect.:** 65.0 male; 72.3 female. **Births:** 20.2 per 1,000 pop. **Deaths:** 6.5 per 1,000 pop. **Infant mortality:** 7.6 per 1,000 live births. **Undernourished:** NA. **HIV:** NA. **COVID-19:** 1 death; rates per 100,000: 49,778 cases, 9 deaths. 100% vaccinated.

Education: Compulsory: ages 4-17. **Literacy:** NA.

Website: naurugov.nr

The British reached the island in 1798, but it was annexed to the German Empire in 1886. After WWI, Australia administered Nauru under a League of Nations mandate. Japan occupied the island during WWII. In 1947 Nauru was made a UN trust territory, administered by Australia. It became an independent republic Jan. 31, 1968.

Phosphate exports provided Nauru with high per capita revenues. Phosphate reserves, however, are nearly depleted, and environmental damage from strip mining has been severe. Rising sea levels linked to global climate change have eroded Nauru's coastline.

A 2012 Amnesty Intl. report found inhumane living conditions at Australia's detention center on Nauru for migrants intercepted trying to enter Australia by boat. A 2015 Australian government report confirmed abuse of detainees. After refugees were resettled in the U.S. or other countries, returned to their country of origin, or moved to Australia for medical treatment or temporary detention, by mid-2023 no refugees remained in the Nauru detention center. However, Australia again sent migrants to the detention center starting in Sept. 2023 and continuing in 2024.

Nauru, Jan. 2024, announced it would switch diplomatic relations from Taiwan to China.

Nepal

People: Population: 31,122,387 (50). **Age distrib.:** <15: 25.8%; 65+: 6.4%. **Growth:** 0.7%. **Migrants:** 1.7%. **Pop. density:** 562.3 per sq mi, 217.1 per sq km. **Urban:** 22.4%. **Ethnic groups:** Chhettri 16.5%, Brahman-Hill 11.3%, Magar 6.9%, Tharu 6.2%, Tamang 5.6%, Bishwokarma 5%, Musalman 4.9%, Newar 4.6%, Yadav 4.2%, Rai 2.2%. **Languages:** Nepali (official), Maithali, Bhojpuri, Tharu, Tamang, Bajjika (123 langs. reported as mother tongue in 2021 census). **Religions:** Hindu 64.0% (Shaivite 29%, Vaishnavite 29%), ethnic religionist 13.4%, Buddhist 12.3% (Lamaist 11%), Christian 5.6%, Muslim 4.2% (Sunni).

Geography: Total area: 56,827 sq mi, 147,181 sq km (93); **Land area:** 55,348 sq mi, 143,351 sq km. **Location:** Astride Himalaya Mts. China on N, India on S. **Topography:** The Himalayas across the N, hill country with fertile valleys across the center. S border region is part of flat, subtropical Ganges Plain. **Arable land:** 12.6%. **Capital:** Kathmandu, 1,621,642.

Government: Type: Federal parliamentary republic. **Head of state:** Pres. Ram Chandra Poudel; b. 1944; in office: Mar. 13, 2023. **Head of govt.:** Prime Min. Khadga Prasad Sharma Oli; b. 1952; in office: July 15, 2024. **Local divisions:** 7 provinces. **Defense budget:** $424 mil. **Active troops:** 96,600.

Economy: Industries: tourism, carpets, textiles; small rice, jute, sugar, oilseed mills; cigarettes, cement/brick prod. **Chief agric.:** rice, vegetables, potatoes, sugarcane, maize, wheat. **Natural resources:** quartz, water, timber, hydropower; small deposits of lignite, copper, cobalt, iron ore. **Water:** 6,999 cu m per capita. **Electricity prod.:** 9.8 bil kWh. **Labor force:** agric. 61.4%, industry 17.5%, services 21.2%. **Unemployment:** 10.7%.

Finance: Monetary unit: Rupee (NPR) (134.34 = $1 U.S.). **GDP:** $160.1 bil; **per capita GDP:** $5,182; **GDP growth:** 2.0%. **Imports:** $14.1 bil; India 64%, China 13%. **Exports:** $3.0 bil; India 67%, U.S. 11%. **Tourism:** $558 mil. **Budget** (2020): $9.0 bil. **Inflation:** 7.1%.

Transport: Railways: 37 mi. **Airports:** 51.

Communications: Mobile (2022): 133.3 per 100 pop. **Broadband** (2022): 91.5 per 100 pop. **Internet:** 49.6%.

Health: Expend.: 5.4%. **Life expect.:** 72.2 male; 73.7 female. **Births:** 17.0 per 1,000 pop. **Deaths:** 5.6 per 1,000 pop. **Infant mortality:** 24.0 per 1,000 live births. **Undernourished:** 5.7%. **HIV:** 0.1%. **COVID-19:** 12,031 deaths; rates per 100,000: 3,444 cases, 41 deaths. 84% vaccinated.

Education: Compulsory: ages 4-12. **Literacy:** 71.2%.

Website: nepal.gov.np

Nepal was originally a group of principalities, with the Gurkha principality becoming dominant about 1769. In 1951 King Tribhubana Bir Bikram, member of the Shah family, ended the system of rule by hereditary premiers of the Ranas family, who had kept the kings virtual prisoners, and established a cabinet system of government. Polygamy, child marriage, and the caste system were officially abolished in 1963. Political parties were legalized in 1990.

Nine members of Nepal's royal family, including King Birendra, died in a June 1, 2001, massacre. The killings were blamed on a 10th family member, Crown Prince Dipendra, who reportedly killed himself, allowing Birendra's brother Gyanendra Bir Bikram Shah Dev to take the throne.

Citing a Maoist insurgency, King Gyanendra assumed absolute authority, Feb. 1, 2005, but after protests, he agreed, Apr. 24, 2006, to reinstate parliament. A new government signed a peace accord with Maoist rebels Nov. 21 ending a decade-long civil war that claimed 13,000 lives. A constituent assembly voted May 2008 to abolish the monarchy and make Nepal a republic.

A new constitution, establishing a federal system with seven states, was adopted Sept. 20, 2015. Khadga Prasad Sharma Oli, leader of a non-Maoist Communist party, became prime min. Oct. 11, 2015. Bidhya Devi Bhandari (of Oli's party) was elected by parliament, Oct. 28, 2015, as Nepal's first female president. Oli, facing a no-confidence vote, announced his resignation, July 23, 2016. A coalition of Communist parties won late 2017 legislative elections, and Oli returned as prime min., Feb. 15, 2018. After Oli lost support within his coalition, opposition leader Sher Bahadur Deuba became prime min. July 13, 2021. Following Nov. 20, 2022, elections, former Maoist guerrilla Pushpa Kamal Dahal became prime min. Dec. 26. Ram Chandra Poudel, backed by Dahal, became president Mar. 13, 2023. After Dahal lost a no-confidence vote, Oli formed a coalition with the Nepali Congress party and again became prime min. July 15, 2024; he pursued policies to more closely align Nepal with China.

A magnitude 7.8 earthquake near Kathmandu, Apr. 25, 2015, displaced 2.8 mil. Historic temples were heavily damaged. After a second quake, May 12, 2015, the combined death toll exceeded 8,600.

Nepal did not permit climbing on Mount Everest in the 2020 season because of the COVID-19 pandemic. Crowding and trash have become problems on Everest in recent years.

Netherlands

Kingdom of the Netherlands

People: Population: 17,772,378 (71). **Age distrib.:** <15: 15.2%; 65+: 20.7%. **Growth:** 0.4%. **Migrants:** 13.8%. **Pop. density:** 1,358.1 per sq mi, 524.4 per sq km. **Urban:** 93.5%. **Ethnic groups:** Dutch 75.4%, EU (excl. Dutch) 6.4%, Turkish 2.4%, Moroccan 2.4%, Surinamese 2.1%, Indonesian 2%. **Languages:** Dutch (official). **Religions:** Christian 53.3% (Catholic 30.5%, Protestant 19.3%), agnostic 33.2%, Muslim 8.2% (Sunni), atheist 2.8%.

Geography: Total area: 16,040 sq mi, 41,543 sq km (131); **Land area:** 13,086 sq mi, 33,893 sq km. **Location:** NW Europe on North Sea. Germany on E, Belgium on S. **Topography:** Land is flat with avg. elevation of 37 ft above sea level; much of land reclaimed and protected by some 1,500 mi of dikes. **Arable land:** 29.8%. **Capital:** Amsterdam, 1,181,817; s-Gravenhage (The Hague) (seat), 720,085. **Cities:** Rotterdam, 1,021,919.

Government: Type: Parliamentary constitutional monarchy. **Head of state:** King Willem-Alexander; b. 1967; in office: Apr. 30, 2013. **Head of govt.:** Prime Min. Dick Schoof; b. 1957; in office: July 2, 2024. **Local divisions:** 12 provinces, 3 public entities. **Defense budget:** $16.8 bil. **Active troops:** 33,600.

Economy: Industries: agroindustries, metal/engineering prods., electrical machinery/equip., chemicals. **Chief agric.:** milk, sugar beets, potatoes, pork, onions, wheat. **Natural resources:** nat. gas, petroleum, peat, limestone, salt, sand and gravel. **Water:** 5,199 cu m per capita. **Crude oil reserves:** 138 mil bbls. **Electricity prod.:** 120.8 bil kWh. **Labor force:** agric. 1.9%, industry 14.0%, services 84.1%. **Unemployment:** 3.6%.

Finance: Monetary unit: Euro (EUR) (0.90 = $1 U.S.). **GDP:** $1.4 tril; **per capita GDP:** $78,215; **GDP growth:** 0.1%. **Imports:** $825.8 bil; Germany 14%, China 12%, U.S. 9%, Belgium 9%, UK 5%.

Exports: $950.0 bil; Germany 19%, Belgium 14%, France 9%, UK 6%, Italy 5%. **Tourism:** $20.2 bil. **Budget:** $374.2 bil. **Inflation:** 3.8%.

Transport: Railways: 1,898 mi. **Motor vehicles:** 580.5 per 1,000 pop. **Airports:** 45.

Communications: Mobile: 117.4 per 100 pop. **Broadband:** 123 per 100 pop. **Internet** (2023): 97%.

Health: Expend.: 11.3%. **Life expect.:** 80.3 male; 83.5 female. **Births:** 10.6 per 1,000 pop. **Deaths:** 9.7 per 1,000 pop. **Infant mortality:** 3.6 per 1,000 live births. **Undernourished:** <2.5%. **HIV:** NA. **COVID-19:** 22,986 deaths; rates per 100,000: 49,637 cases, 132 deaths. 71% vaccinated.

Education: Compulsory: ages 5-17. **Literacy:** NA.

Website: www.government.nl

Julius Caesar conquered the region in 55 BCE, when it was inhabited by Celtic and Germanic tribes. After the empire of Charlemagne fell apart, the Netherlands (Holland, Belgium, Flanders) split among counts, dukes, and bishops, passed to Burgundy and thence to Spain. William the Silent, prince of Orange, led a confederation of the northern provinces, called Estates, in the Union of Utrecht, 1579; in 1581 they repudiated allegiance to Spain. The rise of the Dutch republic to naval, economic, and artistic eminence came in the 17th cent.

After a period of French hegemony, 1795-1813, the Congress of Vienna in 1815 formed a kingdom of the Netherlands, including Belgium, under William I. In 1830, Belgium seceded.

The Netherlands maintained its neutrality in WWI but was invaded during WWII and occupied by Germany, 1940-45. In 1949, after several years of fighting, the Netherlands granted independence to Indonesia.

On Apr. 30, 2009, an attempt to assassinate Queen Beatrix failed (but left 8 dead). Beatrix, 75, abdicated the throne to her son, Willem-Alexander, Apr. 30, 2013. A Malaysia Airlines flight from Amsterdam to Kuala Lumpur was shot down over eastern Ukraine, July 17, 2014; nearly 200 Dutch passport holders were among 298 killed.

Prime Min. Mark Rutte's center-right People's Party (VVD) won Mar. 15, 2017, parliamentary elections, holding off a challenge from the anti-Islamic, right-wing Freedom Party (PVV). Rutte's party won Mar. 17, 2021, elections, and a new coalition government headed by Rutte was sworn in Jan. 10, 2022. Rutte's coalition collapsed in July 2023 in a dispute about immigration policy; new elections, Nov. 22, saw the Freedom Party win the most seats. A coalition of four centrist to far-right parties (including the VVD and PVV) was formed, and Dick Schoof became prime minister July 2, 2024.

On July 1, 2023, the 150th anniversary of the abolition of slavery in the Netherlands' American possessions, King Willem-Alexander apologized for the Dutch role in bringing enslaved Africans to the Americas and keeping them in bondage.

Dutch Dependencies

Constitutional changes effective Oct. 10, 2010, dissolved the political entity known as the Netherlands Antilles. Curaçao (area 171 sq mi), an island near the coast of Venezuela, and Sint Maarten (13 sq mi), occupying the southern one-third of the island of St. Martin, SE of Puerto Rico, were elevated to the status of autonomous countries. Bonaire, Saba, and Sint Eustatius became special municipalities. Pop. of **Curaçao**, 153,289 (2024 est.); that of its capital, Willemstad, 144,037 (2018 est.). **Sint Maarten**, pop. 46,215 (2024 est.); capital is Philipsburg, pop. 40,552 (2018 est.). Principal industries: Curaçao, tourism, petroleum refining and transshipment, light mfg.; Sint Maarten, tourism, light industry. International tourism receipts were $988 mil (2022) for Curaçao, $956 mil (2022) for Sint Maarten. Per capita GDP of Sint Maarten was $51,527 (2023), Curaçao, $29,524 (2022). **Websites:** gobiernu.cw (Curaçao); www.sintmaartengov.org (Sint Maarten)

Aruba, about 26 mi west of Curaçao, was separated from the Netherlands Antilles on Jan. 1, 1986; it is an autonomous component of the Netherlands, with a status similar to Curaçao and Sint Maarten. Area: 69 sq mi; pop. (2024 est.) 125,063. Capital: Oranjestad; pop. (2018 est.) 29,877. Chief industries are tourism ($2.3 bil in international receipts in 2022), petroleum transshipment facilities, banking. Website: www.kabga.aw

New Zealand

People: Population: 5,161,211 (124). **Age distrib.:** <15: 19.0%; 65+: 16.9%. **Growth:** 1.0%. **Migrants:** 28.7%. **Pop. density:** 50.5 per sq mi, 19.5 per sq km. **Urban:** 87.1%. **Ethnic groups:** European 64.1%, Maori 16.5%, Chinese 4.9%, Indian 4.7%, Samoan 3.9%. **Languages:** English (de facto official), Maori (de jure official), Samoan, Northern Chinese. **Religions:** Christian 50.3% (Protestant 28.5%, Catholic 12.8%), agnostic 37.7%, Buddhist 3.7% (Mahayanist), Hindu 2.7%, Muslim 1.7% (Sunni), atheist 1.5%.

Geography: Total area: 103,799 sq mi, 268,838 sq km (75); **Land area:** 102,138 sq mi, 264,537 sq km. **Location:** SW Pacific O. Nearest neighbors are Australia to W, Fiji and Tonga to N. **Topography:** Two main islands (North and South Isls.) are hilly and mountainous. The E coasts consist of fertile plains, incl. Canterbury Plains on South Isl. Volcanic plateau in center of North Isl. Glaciers and 15 peaks over 10,000 ft on South Isl. **Arable land:** 2.0%. **Capital:** Wellington, 424,441. **Cities:** Auckland, 1,692,770.

Government: Type: Parliamentary democracy under constitutional monarchy. **Head of state:** King Charles III, rep. by Gov.-Gen. Cindy Kiro; b. 1958; in office: Oct. 21, 2021. **Head of govt.:** Prime Min. Christopher Luxon; b. 1970; in office: Nov. 27, 2023. **Local divisions:** 16 regions, 1 territory. **Defense budget:** $3.7 bil. **Active troops:** 8,700.

Economy: Industries: agric., forestry, fishing, logs and wood articles, mfg., mining, constr., financial services, real estate services, tourism. **Chief agric.:** milk, beef, kiwifruit, apples, grapes, lamb/mutton. **Natural resources:** nat. gas, iron ore, sand, coal, timber, hydropower, gold, limestone. **Water:** 63,746 cu m per capita. **Crude oil reserves:** 41 mil bbls. **Electricity prod.:** 44.2 bil kWh. **Labor force:** agric. 6.0%, industry 20.8%, services 73.2%. **Unemployment:** 3.7%.

Finance: Monetary unit: Dollar (NZD) (1.60 = $1 U.S.). **GDP:** $282.6 bil; **per capita GDP:** $54,110; **GDP growth:** 0.6%. **Imports:** $68.4 bil; China 21%, Australia 14%, U.S. 8%, South Korea 7%, Singapore 6%. **Exports:** $59.0 bil; China 28%, Australia 11%, U.S. 11%, Japan 6%. **Tourism:** $7.9 bil. **Budget** (2020): $88.6 bil. **Inflation:** 5.7%.

Transport: Railways: 2,565 mi. **Motor vehicles:** 889.4 per 1,000 pop. **Airports:** 202.

Communications: Mobile: 126.9 per 100 pop. **Broadband:** 102 per 100 pop. **Internet:** 95.7%.

Health: Expend.: 10.0%. **Life expect.:** 81.2 male; 84.8 female. **Births:** 12.6 per 1,000 pop. **Deaths:** 6.9 per 1,000 pop. **Infant mortality:** 3.3 per 1,000 live births. **Undernourished:** <2.5%. **HIV:** <0.1%. **COVID-19:** 4,299 deaths; rates per 100,000: 54,757 cases, 89 deaths. 85% vaccinated.

Education: Compulsory: ages 6-15. **Literacy:** NA.

Website: www.govt.nz

New Zealand comprises North Island, 43,911 sq mi; South Island, 58,084 sq mi; Stewart Island, 649 sq mi; Chatham Isls., 373 sq mi; and several groups of smaller islands. The Maori, a Polynesian group from the eastern Pacific, reached New Zealand before and during the 14th cent. The first European to sight New Zealand was Dutch navigator Abel Janszoon Tasman. The Maori refused to allow him to land. British Capt. James Cook explored the coasts, 1769-70.

British sovereignty was proclaimed and Maori land rights were recognized in the Treaty of Waitangi, 1840, with organized British settlement beginning the same year. Representative institutions were granted in 1853. The Maori Wars, or New Zealand Wars, ended in 1870 with British victory. The colony became a dominion in 1907 and gained full independence in 1947.

A progressive tradition in politics began in the 19th cent. Much of the nation's economy has been deregulated since the 1980s. Jenny Shipley of the National Party became the nation's first female prime min., Dec. 8, 1997. The Labour Party won 1999 elections.

A measure establishing a supreme court and ending appeals to the UK Privy Council passed Oct. 14, 2003. A major settlement of Maori land claims was signed June 25, 2008.

A Christchurch earthquake, Feb. 22, 2011, killed 181 people and caused extensive damage. Parliament legalized same-sex marriage Apr. 17, 2013.

After the National Party (in office since 2008) fell short of a majority in Sept. 23, 2017, elections, Labour Party head Jacinda Ardern formed a coalition government.

A gunman killed 51 in attacks at two Christchurch-area mosques, Mar. 15, 2019. Parliament, Apr. 10, outlawed many types of semiautomatic weapons. Mar. 2020 legislation legalized most abortions. Labour won 2020 elections.

New Zealand at times used strict lockdown measures and vaccine mandates to counter the COVID-19 pandemic that began in 2020; some measures were met with violent protests. Ardern resigned as prime minister in Jan. 2023. In Oct. 14, 2023, elections in which inflation was a major issue, the National Party won the most seats; it formed a coalition government, and party leader Christopher Luxon became prime minister Nov. 27, 2023.

A government report, July 24, 2024, found that since 1950 some 200,000 people in government, religious, or foster care had been victims of abuse.

In 1965, the **Cook Islands** (area: 91 sq mi; 2024 est. pop.: 7,761), halfway between New Zealand and Hawaii, became self-governing. Capital: Rarotonga, pop. 13,067 (2018 est.). New Zealand retained responsibility for defense and foreign affairs. **Niue** (area: 100 sq mi; 2022 est. pop.: 2,000) attained the same status in 1974; capital: Alofi, pop. 727 (2018 est.). It lies about 675 mi W of Cook Isls. The U.S. announced, Sept. 25, 2023, it would establish diplomatic relations with the Cook Islands and Niue. **Tokelau** (area: 4.6 sq mi; 2019 est. pop.: 1,647) comprises three atolls 300 mi N of Samoa. **Ross Dependency**, administered by New Zealand since 1923, comprises 160,000 sq mi of Antarctic territory. **Websites:** www.cookislands.gov.ck; www.gov.nu; www.tokelau.org.nz

Nicaragua

Republic of Nicaragua

People: Population: 6,676,948 (107). **Age distrib.:** <15: 25.1%; 65+: 6.0%. **Growth:** 1.0%. **Migrants:** 0.6%. **Pop. density:** 144.1 per sq mi, 55.6 per sq km. **Urban:** 60.2%. **Ethnic groups:** mestizo (mixed Indigenous/white) 69%, white 17%, Black 9%, Indigenous 5%. **Languages:** Spanish (official), Indigenous. **Religions:** Christian 94.8% (Catholic 66.5%, Protestant 21.2%), agnostic 2.8%.

Geography: Total area: 50,336 sq mi, 130,370 sq km (96); **Land area:** 46,328 sq mi, 119,990 sq km. **Location:** Central America. Honduras on N, Costa Rica on S. **Topography:** Both Caribbean and Pacific coasts are over 200 mi long. Cordillera Mts., with many volcanic peaks, run NW-SE through middle of country. **Arable land:** 12.5%. **Capital:** Managua, 1,107,118.

Government: Type: Presidential republic. **Head of state and govt.:** Pres. Daniel Ortega Saavedra; b. 1945; in office: Jan. 10, 2007. **Local divisions:** 15 departments, 2 autonomous regions. **Defense budget:** $95 mil. **Active troops:** 12,000.

Economy: Industries: food proc., chemicals, machinery and metal prods., knit and woven apparel, petroleum refining/distrib. **Chief agric.:** sugarcane, milk, rice, oil palm fruit, maize, plantains. **Natural resources:** gold, silver, copper, tungsten, lead, zinc, timber, fish. **Water:** 24,016 cu m per capita. **Electricity prod.:** 4.3 bil kWh. **Labor force:** agric. 27.7%, industry 18.2%, services 54.1%. **Unemployment:** 4.8%.

Finance: Monetary unit: Cordoba (NIO) (36.80 = $1 U.S.). **GDP:** $56.7 bil; **per capita GDP:** $8,044; **GDP growth:** 4.6%. **Imports:** $10.5 bil; U.S. 26%, China 11%, Honduras 10%, Guatemala 9%, Mexico 9%. **Exports:** $8.3 bil; U.S. 52%, Mexico 12%, Honduras 7%, El Salvador 6%. **Tourism:** $739 mil. **Budget:** $3.5 bil. **Inflation:** 8.4%.

Transport: Motor vehicles: 73.4 per 1,000 pop. **Airports:** 39.

Communications: Mobile: 105.8 per 100 pop. **Broadband:** 70.7 per 100 pop. **Internet:** 61.1%.

Health: Expend.: 9.7%. **Life expect.:** 73.2 male; 76.4 female. **Births:** 16.4 per 1,000 pop. **Deaths:** 5.1 per 1,000 pop. **Infant mortality:** 14.4 per 1,000 live births. **Undernourished:** 19.6%. **HIV:** 0.3%. **COVID-19:** 245 deaths; rates per 100,000: 244 cases, 4 deaths. 92% vaccinated.

Education: Compulsory: ages 5-11. **Literacy:** 82.6%.

Website: www.asamblea.gob.ni

Nicaragua, inhabited by various Indian tribes, was conquered by Spain in 1552. After gaining independence from Spain, 1821, Nicaragua was united for a short period with Mexico, then with the United Provinces of Central America, before becoming an independent republic, 1838. U.S. Marines occupied the country at times in the early 20th cent., the last time from 1926 to 1933.

Gen. Anastasio Somoza Debayle held the presidency 1967-72, 1974-79. Martial law was imposed in Dec. 1974, after officials were kidnapped by Marxist Sandinista guerrillas. Nationwide strikes touched off a civil war, 1978, which ended when Somoza fled Nicaragua and the Sandinistas took control of Managua, July 1979. Somoza was assassinated in Paraguay, Sept. 17, 1980.

Relations with the U.S. were strained as a result of Nicaragua's aid to leftist guerrillas in El Salvador and U.S. backing of anti-Sandinista contra guerrilla groups, which fought the Sandinista government throughout the 1980s. In 1985 the U.S. House rejected Pres. Ronald Reagan's request for military aid to the contras. The U.S. later secretly diverted funds to the contras.

In a stunning upset, Violeta Barrios de Chamorro defeated Sandinista leader Daniel Ortega Saavedra in national elections, Feb. 25, 1990. Conservative candidates won the 1996 and 2001 presidential elections. Drought and a drop in coffee prices precipitated an economic crisis in 2001.

Ortega won the Nov. 2006 presidential election. He was reelected Nov. 6, 2011, and Nov. 6, 2016. In 2016, Rosario Murillo Zambrana, Ortega's wife, was elected vice president.

Months of protests, beginning Apr. 2018, against government policies and authoritarian rule resulted in hundreds of deaths, most at the hands of security forces or allied paramilitary groups. Hundreds were arrested, some reportedly tortured in detention. By early 2021, more than 100,000 Nicaraguans had fled the country. In the months leading up to the Nov. 7, 2021, presidential election, opposition leaders, activists, and critics of the government were arrested; Ortega and Murillo were reelected.

Seeking Chinese aid, Nicaragua established diplomatic relations with China, Dec. 10, 2021, breaking ties with Taiwan.

The government continued its crackdown on dissent in 2022-24, including arresting Catholic clerics and shutting down thousands of Catholic, Protestant, and other organizations. Nicaraguans continued to leave the country, many for neighboring Costa Rica.

Niger

Republic of Niger

People: Population: 26,342,784 (55). **Age distrib.:** <15: 49.5%; 65+: 2.7%. **Growth:** 3.7%. **Migrants:** 1.4%. **Pop. density:** 53.9 per sq mi, 20.8 per sq km. **Urban:** 17.2%. **Ethnic groups:** Hausa 53.1%, Zarma/Songhai 21.2%, Tuareg 11%, Fulani (Peuhl) 6.5%, Kanuri 5.9%. **Languages:** Hausa, Zarma, French (official). **Religions:** Muslim 95.6% (Sunni), ethnic religionist 4.0%.

Geography: Total area: 489,191 sq mi, 1,267,000 sq km (21); **Land area:** 489,076 sq mi, 1,266,700 sq km. **Location:** Interior of N Africa. Libya, Algeria on N; Mali, Burkina Faso on W; Benin, Nigeria on S; Chad on E. **Topography:** Mostly arid desert and mountains. Narrow savanna in S and Niger R. basin in the SW. **Arable land:** 14.0%. **Capital:** Niamey, 1,496,258.

Government: Type: Formerly semi-presidential republic. **Head of state:** Pres. Gen. Abdourahamane Tchiani; in office: July 28, 2023. **Head of govt.:** Prime Min. Ali Mahaman Lamine Zeine; in office: Aug. 9, 2023. **Local divisions:** 7 regions, 1 capital district. **Defense budget:** $334 mil. **Active troops:** 39,100.

Economy: Industries: uranium mining, petroleum, cement, brick, soap, textiles, food proc., chemicals, slaughterhouses. **Chief agric.:** millet, cowpeas, sorghum, onions, milk, groundnuts. **Natural resources:** uranium, coal, iron ore, tin, phosphates, gold, molybdenum, gypsum, salt, petroleum. **Water:** 1,348 cu m per capita. **Crude oil reserves:** 150 mil bbls. **Electricity prod.:** 785.7 mil kWh. **Labor force:** agric. 70.9%, industry 7.4%, services 21.7%. **Unemployment:** 0.6%.

Finance: Monetary unit: CFA Franc (XOF) (587.79 = $1 U.S.). **GDP:** $49.4 bil; **per capita GDP:** $1,817; **GDP growth:** 2.5%. **Imports** (2022): $4.2 bil; China 22%, France 14%, Nigeria 8%, Germany 5%, UAE 5%. **Exports** (2022): $1.4 bil; UAE 69%, France 9%, China 9%. **Tourism** (2022): $121 mil. **Budget:** $2.8 bil. **Inflation:** 3.7%.

Transport: Motor vehicles: 15.0 per 1,000 pop. **Airports:** 26.

Communications: Mobile (2022): 64.0 per 100 pop. **Broadband** (2022): 29 per 100 pop. **Internet:** 16.9%.

Health: Expend.: 5.8%. **Life expect.:** 59.3 male; 62.5 female. **Births:** 46.6 per 1,000 pop. **Deaths:** 9.5 per 1,000 pop. **Infant mortality:** 64.3 per 1,000 live births. **Undernourished:** 13.3%. **HIV:** 0.2%. **COVID-19:** 315 deaths; rates per 100,000: 39 cases, 1 death. 23% vaccinated.

Education: Compulsory: NA. **Literacy:** 38.1%.

Website: www.gouv.ne

Niger was part of ancient and medieval African empires. European explorers reached the area in the late 18th cent. The French colony of Niger was established 1900-22 after the defeat of Tuareg fighters, who had invaded the area from the north a century before. The country became independent Aug. 3, 1960.

In 1993, Niger held its first free and open elections since independence. A peace accord Apr. 24, 1995, ended a Tuareg rebellion that began in 1990. After a coup, Jan. 27, 1996, the military retained control. Oct.-Nov. 1999 elections, under a new constitution, restored civilian rule.

Popularly elected in 1999 and 2004, Pres. Mamadou Tandja invoked emergency powers in 2009 to remain in office. He was overthrown by a military junta Feb. 18, 2010. Civilian rule returned following 2011 elections. Pres. Mahamadou Issoufou won reelection in 2016. Mohamed Bazoum, of Issoufou's party, won a Feb. 21, 2021, presidential runoff.

Beginning in Feb. 2015, the Nigeria-based Islamist extremist group Boko Haram staged attacks in southern Niger. Islamist extremists based in Mali staged attacks in W Niger; an attack by ISIS-affiliated militants, Oct. 4, 2017, killed 9, including 4 U.S. special operations troops. As Islamist violence increased, by Aug. 31, 2024, Niger had more than 500,000 internally displaced persons.

A military coup led by Gen. Abdourahamane Tchiani overthrew Pres. Bazoum, July 26, 2023. Coup leaders demanded that France and the U.S. withdraw their troops from Niger; both complied. Russian military equipment and instructors began arriving in Niger in Apr. 2024.

Nigeria

Federal Republic of Nigeria

People: Population: 236,747,130 (6). **Age distrib.:** <15: 40.4%; 65+: 3.4%. **Growth:** 2.5%. **Migrants:** 0.6%. **Pop. density:** 673.2 per sq mi, 259.9 per sq km. **Urban:** 55.0%. **Ethnic groups:** More than 250, incl. Hausa 30%, Yoruba 15.5%, Igbo (Ibo) 15.2%, Fulani 6%, Tiv 2.4%, Kanuri/Beriberi 2.4%. **Languages:** English (official), Hausa, Yoruba, Igbo (Ibo), Fulani, 500+ Indigenous langs. **Religions:** Christian 46.5% (Protestant 24.9%, independent 10.6%, Catholic 11.0%), Muslim 46.2% (Sunni), ethnic religionist 7.0%.

Geography: Total area: 356,669 sq mi, 923,768 sq km (31); **Land area:** 351,649 sq mi, 910,768 sq km. **Location:** S coast of W Africa. Benin on W, Niger on N, Chad and Cameroon on E. **Topography:** 4 E-W regions: a coastal mangrove swamp, a tropical rain forest, a plateau of savanna and open woodland, and semi-desert in N. **Arable land:** 40.5%. **Capital:** Abuja, 4,025,735. **Cities:** Lagos, 16,536,018; Kano, 4,490,734; Ibadan, 4,004,316; Port Harcourt, 3,636,547.

Government: Type: Federal presidential republic. **Head of state and govt.:** Pres. Bola Ahmed Adekunle Tinubu; b. 1952; in office: May 29, 2023. **Local divisions:** 36 states, 1 territory. **Defense budget:** $2.0 bil. **Active troops:** 143,000.

Economy: Industries: crude oil, coal, tin, columbite; rubber prods., wood; hides/skins, textiles, cement and other constr. materials. **Chief agric.:** yams, cassava, maize, oil palm fruit, rice, taro. **Natural resources:** nat. gas, petroleum, tin, iron ore, coal, limestone, niobium, lead, zinc. **Water:** 1,341 cu m per capita. **Crude oil reserves:** 36.9 bil bbls. **Electricity prod.:** 37.0 bil kWh. **Labor force:** agric. 38.0%, industry 14.6%, services 47.5%. **Unemployment:** 3.1%.

Finance: Monetary unit: Naira (NGN) (1,589.95 = $1 U.S.). **GDP:** $1.4 tril; **per capita GDP:** $6,318; **GDP growth:** 2.9%. **Imports:** $72.3 bil; China 32%, Belgium 11%, Netherlands 10%, India 8%, U.S. 5%. **Exports:** $60.3 bil; Spain 13%, India 12%, France 7%, U.S. 7%, Netherlands 6%. **Tourism:** $672 mil. **Budget:** $59.9 bil. **Inflation:** 24.7%.

Transport: Railways: 2,360 mi (majority in severe disrepair). **Motor vehicles:** 9.4 per 1,000 pop. **Airports:** 47.

Communications: Mobile: 98.5 per 100 pop. **Broadband:** 41.6 per 100 pop. **Internet:** 35.5%.

Health: Expend.: 4.1%. **Life expect.:** 60.4 male; 64.2 female. **Births:** 33.8 per 1,000 pop. **Deaths:** 8.4 per 1,000 pop. **Infant mortality:** 53.7 per 1,000 live births. **Undernourished:** 18.0%. **HIV:** 1.3%. **COVID-19:** 3,155 deaths; rates per 100,000: 130 cases, 2 deaths. 39% vaccinated.

Education: Compulsory: ages 6-14. **Literacy:** 62.0%.

Website: nigeria.gov.ng

Early cultures in Nigeria date back to at least 700 BCE. From the 12th to the 14th cent., more advanced cultures developed in the Yoruba area, at Ife, and in the north, where Muslim influence prevailed. Portuguese and British slavers appeared in the 15th-16th cent. Britain seized Lagos, 1861, and gradually extended control inland until 1900. Nigeria became independent Oct. 1, 1960, and a republic Oct. 1, 1963.

On May 30, 1967, the Eastern Region seceded, proclaiming itself the Republic of Biafra, plunging the country into civil war. Casualties were estimated at over 1 mil, including many Biafrans (mostly Igbos) who died of starvation despite international relief efforts. The secessionists capitulated Jan. 12, 1970.

Nigeria emerged as one of the world's leading oil exporters in the 1970s, but much of the revenue has been squandered through corruption and mismanagement. Oil spills have polluted much of the Niger Delta region.

After 13 years of military rule, the nation made a peaceful return to civilian government Oct. 1979. Military rule resumed Dec. 31, 1983. A coup brought Gen. Sani Abacha to power in 1993. His brutal rule ended June 8, 1998, when he died of an apparent heart attack. Olusegun Obasanjo won a presidential election Feb. 27, 1999, to lead a civilian government.

The imposition of strict Islamic law in northern states led to clashes, Jan.-Mar. 2000, in which at least 800 people died. Fighting between Muslims and Christians in the early 2000s claimed hundreds of lives. Vice Pres. Goodluck Jonathan, a southern Christian, became president in 2010 when his predecessor died. Jonathan won reelection Apr. 16, 2011, over Muhammadu Buhari, a northern-based Muslim.

Boko Haram, a radical Islamist group based in NE Nigeria seeking to establish an Islamist state, began terrorist attacks in 2009 against government forces and civilian targets. The group gained control of a large area in the NE and terrorist attacks escalated, 2013-15. Boko Haram split, in 2016, into ISIS-affiliated and non-affiliated factions.

Vowing tougher action against Boko Haram, Buhari defeated Jonathan in the Mar. 28-29, 2015, presidential election. Subsequent government offensives retook much of the territory Boko Haram had seized, but Boko Haram forces, including the ISIS-affiliated militants, continued to control areas of NE Nigeria and stage deadly attacks against civilians and security forces in the NE and elsewhere in the country.

Amid ongoing Islamist, as well as other religious and ethnic violence (including in Biafra), Buhari won reelection, Feb. 23, 2019. Boko Haram leader Abubakar Shekau died, May 2021, in a conflict with ISIS-affiliated fighters, as the ISIS forces became the dominant extremist group in the NE.

Islamist extremists, as well as other groups apparently seeking ransom, have kidnapped thousands of Nigerians and foreigners since 2014, including a number of mass abductions of schoolchildren.

The Council on Foreign Relations estimated that, as of July 1, 2023, more than 98,000 people had been killed since 2011 as a result of Islamist extremist attacks, clashes with security forces, and actions by other armed groups. With Islamist extremist and other violence continuing, the UNHCR estimated that, as of Sept. 30, 2024, more than 383,000 Nigerian refugees were in Niger, Cameroon, or Chad and about 2.3 mil Nigerians were internally displaced.

Bola Tinubu (of Buhari's party) was declared the winner of the Feb. 25, 2023, presidential election; opposition candidates disputed the result. A government decision to reduce fuel subsidies contributed to skyrocketing inflation, widespread hunger, and nationwide protests in 2024.

North Macedonia

Republic of North Macedonia

(Under the Prespa Agreement, in force as of Feb. 12, 2019, Macedonia and Greece agreed to recognize the former under the name North Macedonia, ending a longstanding regional dispute.)

People: Population: 2,135,622 (145). **Age distrib.:** <15: 16.0%; 65+: 15.6%. **Growth:** 0.1%. **Migrants:** 6.3%. **Pop. density:** 217.5 per sq mi, 84.0 per sq km. **Urban:** 59.9%. **Ethnic groups:** Macedonian 58.4%, Albanian 24.3%, Turkish 3.9%, Romani 2.5% (Romani pop. usually underestimated and may represent 6.5%-13% of pop.). **Languages:** Macedonian, Albanian (both official); Turkish; minority langs (incl. Romani, Aromanian, Serbian) co-official in certain municipalities. **Religions:** Christian 63.8% (Orthodox 61.8%), Muslim 32.7% (Sunni), agnostic 3.2%.

Geography: Total area: 9,928 sq mi, 25,713 sq km (146); **Land area:** 9,820 sq mi, 25,433 sq km. **Location:** SE Europe. Bulgaria on E, Greece on S, Albania on W, Serbia on N. **Topography:** Landlocked, mostly mountainous with deep river valleys, 3 large lakes. Country is bisected by Vardar R. **Arable land:** 16.5%. **Capital:** Skopje, 616,039.

Government: Type: Parliamentary republic. **Head of state:** Pres. Gordana Siljanovska-Davkova; b. 1953; in office: May 12, 2024. **Head of govt.:** Prime Min. Hristijan Mickoski; in office: June 23, 2024. **Local divisions:** 80 municipalities, 1 city. **Defense budget:** $275 mil. **Active troops:** 8,000.

Economy: Industries: food proc., beverages, textiles, chemicals, iron, steel, cement, energy, pharmaceuticals. **Chief agric.:** milk, grapes, chilies/peppers, wheat, potatoes, apples. **Natural resources:** iron ore, copper, lead, zinc, chromite, manganese, nickel, tungsten, gold, silver, asbestos, gypsum, timber. **Water:** 3,043 cu m per capita. **Electricity prod.:** 5.4 bil kWh. **Labor force:** agric. 9.7%, industry 30.4%, services 59.9%. **Unemployment:** 13.1%.

Finance: Monetary unit: Denar (MKD) (54.98 = $1 U.S.). **GDP:** $45.1 bil; **per capita GDP:** $24,873; **GDP growth:** 1.0%. **Imports:** $12.7 bil; UK 16%, Greece 13%, Germany 9%, Serbia 8%, China 6%. **Exports:** $10.7 bil; Germany 42%, Serbia 8%, Greece 7%, Bulgaria 5%. **Tourism:** $599 mil. **Budget** (2020): $4.5 bil. **Inflation:** 9.4%.

Transport: Railways: 434 mi. **Airports:** 13.

Communications: Mobile: 104.8 per 100 pop. **Broadband:** 81.3 per 100 pop. **Internet:** 84.2%.

Health: Expend.: 8.5%. **Life expect.:** 75.3 male; 79.6 female. **Births:** 10.2 per 1,000 pop. **Deaths:** 9.6 per 1,000 pop. **Infant mortality:** 7.0 per 1,000 live births. **Undernourished:** <2.5%. **HIV:** <0.1%. **COVID-19:** 9,979 deaths; rates per 100,000: 16,852 cases, 479 deaths. 40% vaccinated.

Education: Compulsory: ages 6-18. **Literacy:** 98.4%.

Website: vlada.mk

Muslim Turks ruled present-day North Macedonia from 1389 to 1912. In 1913, the area was incorporated into Serbia, which in 1918 became part of the Kingdom of Serbs, Croats, and Slovenes (later Yugoslavia). In 1946, the area, then called Macedonia, became a constituent republic of Yugoslavia.

Macedonia declared its independence Sept. 8, 1991, and was admitted to the UN in 1993. For decades, Greece, objecting to Macedonia's use of what it considered a Hellenic name, blocked Macedonia's bids to join NATO and the EU.

Ethnic Albanian guerrillas launched an offensive Mar. 2001 in NW Macedonia. An accord signed Aug. 13 paved the way for a NATO peacekeeping force. A law broadening the rights of ethnic Albanians was enacted Jan. 2002.

In 2015 and early 2016, tens of thousands of migrants from the Middle East and SW Asia who landed in Greece tried to cross Macedonia on their way to N Europe. Macedonia announced, Mar. 9, 2016, that its border with Greece was closed to migrants.

Macedonia and Greece reached an agreement, effective as of Feb. 12, 2019, for the former to change its name to North Macedonia. Pro-EU, pro-NATO candidate Stevo Pendarovski won a May 5 presidential runoff election. North Macedonia joined NATO Mar. 27, 2020. Conservative Gordana Siljanovska-Davkova defeated Pendarovski in a May 8, 2024, runoff to become North Macedonia's first woman president. In parliamentary elections the same day, the governing Social Democrats lost to the conservative Party for Macedonian National Unity (VMRO-DPMNE) and its allies, and Hristijan Mickoski of VMRO-DPMNE became prime min., June 23, 2024.

Norway

Kingdom of Norway

People: Population: 5,509,733 (119). **Age distrib.:** <15: 16.3%; 65+: 19.1%. **Growth:** 0.6%. **Migrants:** 15.7%. **Pop. density:** 46.9 per sq mi, 18.1 per sq km. **Urban:** 84.3%. **Ethnic groups:** Norwegian (incl. Sami) 81.5%, other European 8.9%. **Languages:** Bokmal Norwegian, Nynorsk Norwegian (both official); Sami (official in some municipalities). **Religions:** Church of Norway (Evangelical Lutheran) (official); Christian 84.0% (Protestant 77.6%), Muslim 7.0% (Sunni), agnostic 7.0%.

Geography: Total area: 125,021 sq mi, 323,802 sq km (67); **Land area:** 117,484 sq mi, 304,282 sq km. **Location:** W part of Scandinavian peninsula in NW Europe (extends farther N than any European land). Sweden, Finland, Russia on E. **Topography:** Highly indented coast lined with tens of thousands of islands. Mountains and plateaus cover most of country, which is only 33% forested. **Arable land:** 2.2%. **Capital:** Oslo, 1,100,868.

Government: Type: Parliamentary constitutional monarchy. **Head of state:** King Harald V; b. 1937; in office: Jan. 17, 1991. **Head of govt.:** Prime Min. Jonas Gahr Store; b. 1960; in office: Oct. 14, 2021. **Local divisions:** 12 counties. **Defense budget:** $7.3 bil. **Active troops:** 25,400.

Economy: Industries: petroleum and gas, shipping, fishing, aquaculture, food proc., shipbuilding, pulp/paper prods. **Chief agric.:** milk, barley, wheat, potatoes, oats, pork. **Natural resources:** petroleum, nat. gas, iron ore, copper, lead, zinc, titanium, pyrites, nickel, fish, timber, hydropower. **Water:** 72,737 cu m per capita. **Crude oil reserves:** 8.1 bil bbls. **Electricity prod.:** 143.4 bil kWh. **Labor force:** agric. 2.2%, industry 19.3%, services 78.5%. **Unemployment:** 3.6%.

Finance: Monetary unit: Krone (NOK) (10.49 = $1 U.S.). **GDP:** $576.6 bil; **per capita GDP:** $104,460; **GDP growth:** 0.5%. **Imports:** $157.0 bil; Sweden 18%, Germany 11%, China 10%, Denmark 6%, Netherlands 6%. **Exports:** $228.6 bil; Germany 27%, UK 21%, France 9%, Belgium 7%, Sweden 6%. **Tourism:** $6.2 bil. **Budget** (2020): $210.5 bil. **Inflation:** 5.5%.

Transport: Railways: 2,391 mi. **Motor vehicles:** 644.6 per 1,000 pop. **Airports:** 145.

Communications: Mobile (2022): 111.7 per 100 pop. **Broadband** (2022): 117 per 100 pop. **Internet** (2023): 99%.

Health: Expend. (2022): 8.1%. **Life expect.:** 81.3 male; 84.6 female. **Births:** 10.4 per 1,000 pop. **Deaths:** 8.4 per 1,000 pop. **Infant mortality:** 1.8 per 1,000 live births. **Undernourished:** <2.5%. **HIV:** NA. **COVID-19:** 5,732 deaths; rates per 100,000: 28,195 cases, 107 deaths. 76% vaccinated.

Education: Compulsory: ages 6-15. **Literacy:** NA.

Website: www.regjeringen.no

The first ruler of Norway was Harald the Fairhaired, who came to power in 872 CE. Between 800 and 1000, Norway's Vikings raided and occupied widely dispersed parts of Europe. The country was united with Denmark, 1381-1814, and with Sweden, 1814-1905. In 1905, the country became independent with Prince Charles of Denmark as king.

Norway remained neutral during WWI. In WWII, Germany attacked Norway Apr. 9, 1940, and held it until liberation May 8, 1945. The country abandoned its neutrality after the war and joined NATO. In a referendum Nov. 28, 1994, Norwegian voters rejected European Union membership.

Norway has one of the highest living standards in the world. Hydropower accounts for more than 90% of electricity production. In the early 2000s, the country became a leading producer and exporter of oil and natural gas, with extensive reserves in the North Sea. Norway used oil and gas revenue to build up the world's largest sovereign wealth fund (about $1.76 tril as of Sept. 1, 2024).

A right-wing extremist, Anders Behring Breivik, confessed to killing 8 people with a car bomb in central Oslo and murdering 69 at a camp sponsored by the Labor Party's youth wing July 22, 2011. Parliament, June 18, 2013, made military service compulsory for women as well as men. Rightist and anti-immigration parties won the most seats in Sept. 9, 2013, elections; Conservative Party leader Erna Solberg became prime min. In 2015, about 31,000 migrants from the Middle East, SW Asia, and Africa applied for asylum. Solberg's coalition won 2017 elections. After a campaign in which climate change was a key issue, Labor won the most seats in Sept. 13, 2021, elections; party leader Jonas Gahr Store became prime minister Oct. 14.

Svalbard is a group of mountainous islands in the Arctic O., area 23,956 sq mi, pop. (2021 est.) 2,926. The largest, Spitsbergen (formerly called West Spitsbergen), 14,546 sq mi, seat of the governor, is about 370 mi N of Norway. By the 1920 Svalbard Treaty (in force 1925), major European powers recognized Norway's sovereignty over the archipelago.

Jan Mayen, area 146 sq mi, is a volcanic island located about 565 mi W-NW of Norway; it was annexed in 1929. The only people on Jan Mayen are military personnel and researchers. Norway operates a research station on volcanic Bouvet Isl. (annexed 1930), area 19 sq mi, in the South Atlantic O., about midway between South Africa and Antarctica.

Oman

Sultanate of Oman

People: Population: 3,901,992 (129). **Age distrib.:** <15: 29.8%; 65+: 4.0%. **Growth:** 1.8%. **Migrants:** 46.5%. **Pop. density:** 32.7 per sq mi, 12.6 per sq km. **Urban:** 89.0%. **Ethnic groups:** Arab, Baluchi, South Asian (Indian, Pakistani, Sri Lankan, Bangladeshi), African. **Languages:** Arabic (official), English, Baluchi, Swahili, Urdu, Indian dialects. **Religions:** Muslim 88.7% (Sunni 47%, Islamic schismatic 35%), Hindu 5.4%, Christian 4.0%.

Geography: Total area: 119,499 sq mi, 309,500 sq km (70); **Land area:** 119,499 sq mi, 309,500 sq km. **Location:** SE coast of Arabian peninsula. United Arab Emirates, Saudi Arabia, Yemen on W. **Topography:** A narrow coastal plain, a range of barren mountains reaching 9,900 ft, and a wide, stony, mostly waterless plateau, avg. elevation 1,000 ft. An exclave at the tip of the Musandam peninsula controls access to the Persian Gulf. **Arable land:** 0.3%. **Capital:** Muscat, 1,676,167.

Government: Type: Absolute monarchy. **Head of state and govt.:** Sultan and Prime Min. Haitham bin Tariq bin Taimur al-Said; b. 1954; in office: Jan. 11, 2020. **Local divisions:** 11 governorates. **Defense budget:** $6.5 bil. **Active troops:** 42,600.

Economy: Industries: crude oil prod. and refining, nat. and liquefied nat. gas prod., constr., cement, copper, steel, chemicals, optic fiber. **Chief agric.:** dates, tomatoes, milk, sorghum, vegetables, goat milk. **Natural resources:** petroleum, copper, asbestos, marble, limestone, chromium, gypsum, nat. gas. **Water:** 310 cu m per capita. **Crude oil reserves:** 5.4 bil bbls. **Electricity prod.:** 43.1 bil kWh. **Labor force:** agric. 6.1%, industry 46.9%, services 47.0%. **Unemployment:** 1.5%.

Finance: Monetary unit: Rial (OMR) (0.38 = $1 U.S.). **GDP:** $206.3 bil; **per capita GDP:** $44,421; **GDP growth:** 1.3%. **Imports** (2022): $46.3 bil; UAE 27%, Saudi Arabia 11%, India 10%, China 9%, Qatar 5%. **Exports** (2022): $69.7 bil; China 40%, India 11%, South Korea 6%. **Tourism** (2022): $1.6 bil. **Budget** (2018): $36.0 bil. **Inflation:** 0.9%.

Transport: Motor vehicles: 401.7 per 1,000 pop. **Airports:** 36.

Communications: Mobile: 135.2 per 100 pop. **Broadband:** 117 per 100 pop. **Internet** (2023): 95.3%.

Health: Expend.: 4.4%. **Life expect.:** 75.5 male; 79.4 female. **Births:** 21.1 per 1,000 pop. **Deaths:** 3.2 per 1,000 pop. **Infant mortality:** 13.9 per 1,000 live births. **Undernourished:** 5.7%. **HIV:** <0.1%. **COVID-19:** 4,628 deaths; rates per 100,000: 7,822 cases, 91 deaths. 60% vaccinated.

Education: Compulsory: ages 6-15. **Literacy:** 97.3%.

Website: www.oman.om

Oman was originally called Muscat and Oman. A long history of rule by other lands, including Portugal in the 16th cent., ended with the ouster of the Persians in 1744. By the early 19th cent., Muscat and Oman controlled much of the Persian and Pakistan coasts.

A British protectorate since 1881, Muscat and Oman became independent under a 1951 treaty with the UK. Britain helped suppress an uprising by interior tribes in the 1950s.

On July 23, 1970, Sultan Qaboos bin Said al-Said became ruler. He changed the nation's name to Sultanate of Oman. Petroleum and natural gas are major sources of income. After Arab Spring protests Feb. 2011, Sultan Qaboos expanded the powers of the lower house of parliament. Sultan Qaboos died, Jan. 10, 2020; he was succeeded the next day by his cousin Haitham bin Tariq al-Said. Heavy rainfall, Apr. 2024, caused flooding and left at least 19 dead.

Pakistan

Islamic Republic of Pakistan

People: Population: 252,363,571 (5). **Age distrib.:** <15: 34.4%; 65+: 4.9%. **Growth:** 1.9%. **Migrants:** 1.5%. **Pop. density:** 847.9 per sq mi, 327.4 per sq km. **Urban:** 38.4%. **Ethnic groups:** Punjabi 44.7%, Pashtun (Pathan) 15.4%, Sindhi 14.1%, Saraiki 8.4%, Muhajir 7.6%, Baloch 3.6%. **Languages:** Punjabi, Pashto or Pashtu, Sindhi, Saraiki, Urdu, Balochi, Hindko, English (official; lingua franca of elite and most govt. ministries). **Religions:** Muslim (official) 95.3% (Sunni 86%, Shia 8%), Christian 1.9%, Hindu 1.4%.

Geography: Total area: 307,374 sq mi, 796,095 sq km (35); **Land area:** 297,637 sq mi, 770,875 sq km. **Location:** W part of S Asia. Iran on W, Afghanistan and China on N, India on E. **Topography:** The Indus R. rises in the Hindu Kush and Himalaya Mts. in the N, then flows 1,000 mi into Arabian Sea. Thar Desert, Eastern Plains flank Indus Valley. **Arable land:** 39.2%. **Capital:** Islamabad, 1,266,792. **Cities:** Karachi, 17,648,555; Lahore, 14,407,074; Faisalabad, 3,800,193; Peshawar, 2,480,546; Gujranwala, 2,479,058; Rawalpindi, 2,430,388.

Government: Type: Federal parliamentary republic. **Head of state:** Pres. Asif Ali Zardari; in office: Mar. 10, 2024. **Head of govt.:** Prime Min. Shehbaz Sharif; in office: Mar. 3, 2024. **Local divisions:** 4 provinces, 1 capital territory, 2 admin. areas (Azad Kashmir and Gilgit-Baltistan) in Pakistan-administered part of disputed region. **Defense budget:** $11.1 bil. **Active troops:** 660,000.

Economy: Industries: textiles and apparel, food proc., pharmaceuticals, surgical instruments, constr. materials, paper prods., fertilizer, shrimp. **Chief agric.:** sugarcane, bison milk, wheat, milk, rice, maize. **Natural resources:** nat. gas, limited petroleum, poor quality coal, iron ore, copper, salt, limestone. **Water:** 1,067 cu m per capita. **Crude oil reserves:** 540 mil bbls. **Electricity prod.:** 168.5 bil kWh. **Labor force:** agric. 36.4%, industry 25.5%, services 38.1%. **Unemployment:** 5.5%.

Finance: Monetary unit: Rupee (PKR) (278.57 = $1 U.S.). **GDP:** $1.5 tril; **per capita GDP:** $6,212; **GDP growth:** 0.0%. **Imports:** $57.8 bil; China 28%, UAE 8%, Indonesia 6%, Saudi Arabia 6%, Kuwait 5%. **Exports:** $36.4 bil; U.S. 17%, Germany 7%, China 7%, UAE 7%, UK 6%. **Tourism:** $859 mil. **Budget** (2020): $59.6 bil. **Inflation:** 30.8%.

Transport: Railways: 7,383 mi. **Motor vehicles:** 20.1 per 1,000 pop. **Airports:** 116.

Communications: Mobile: 76.5 per 100 pop. **Broadband:** 51.6 per 100 pop. **Internet:** 32.9%.

Health: Expend.: 2.9%. **Life expect.:** 68.2 male; 72.5 female. **Births:** 25.5 per 1,000 pop. **Deaths:** 5.9 per 1,000 pop. **Infant mortality:** 51.5 per 1,000 live births. **Undernourished:** 20.7%. **HIV:** 0.2%. **COVID-19:** 30,656 deaths; rates per 100,000: 716 cases, 14 deaths. 64% vaccinated.

Education: Compulsory: ages 5-16. **Literacy:** 58.0%.

Website: pakistan.gov.pk

Pakistan shares the 5,000-year history of the India-Pakistan subcontinent. At present-day Harappa and Mohenjo Daro, the Indus Valley civilization, with large cities and elaborate irrigation systems, flourished c. 4,000-2,500 BCE. Aryan invaders from the northwest conquered the region around 1,500 BCE, forging the Vedic civilization that dominated the region for over a thousand years. The first Arab invasion, 712 CE, introduced Islam. Present-day Pakistan and India were part of the Mughal Empire from 1526 to 1857. Muslim power faded by the end of the 19th cent. as the British gained control.

Muhammad Ali Jinnah (1876-1948) was the principal architect of Pakistan. When the British withdrew, Aug. 14, 1947, two largely Islamic regions of British India acquired self-government as Pakistan, with dominion status in the Commonwealth. Pakistan consisted of West Pakistan and East Pakistan, nearly 1,000 mi apart on opposite sides of India. Kashmir, a predominantly Muslim region divided between Pakistan and India, has remained a source of conflict between the two countries.

Rioting and strikes broke out in the East after Pakistan's government, Mar. 1, 1971, postponed the constituent assembly, dominated by supporters of regional autonomy for East Pakistan. Armed conflict between East and West lasted from Mar. to Dec. 1971, with India siding with Easterners, who proclaimed the independent nation of Bangladesh. Thousands were killed, and some 10 mil Easterners fled to India. Full-scale war erupted between India and Pakistan. A day after Pakistan troops in the East surrendered, Pakistan agreed to a cease-fire in the West Dec. 17, 1971. On July 3, 1972, Pakistan and India signed a pact providing for troop withdrawals.

Zulfikar Ali Bhutto, who became president in 1971 and prime min. in 1973, was overthrown in a military coup July 1977. Convicted of complicity in a 1974 political murder, he was executed Apr. 4, 1979.

Millions of Afghan refugees entered Pakistan after the USSR invaded Afghanistan Dec. 1979, after U.S.-led forces began fighting the Taliban in Afghanistan in 2001, and after the Taliban regained control in Afghanistan in 2021. Although millions of refugees were repatriated, about 2 mil Afghan refugees were estimated to be living in Pakistan at the end of 2023. Pakistan announced, Oct. 2023, that undocumented immigrants had to leave the country or face deportation; about 733,000 Afghans had returned to Afghanistan by mid-Sept. 2024.

Pres. Mohammad Zia ul-Haq was killed when his plane exploded in Aug. 1988. Following Nov. elections, Benazir Bhutto, daughter of Zulfikar Ali Bhutto, became prime min. and the first elected woman leader of a Muslim nation. She was accused of corruption and dismissed by the president, Aug. 1990. Bhutto returned to power Oct. 1993 but was dismissed Nov. 1996 amid further corruption charges. Responding to India's nuclear weapons tests, Pakistan conducted its own tests in 1998.

Prime Min. Nawaz Sharif fired, Oct. 1999, army chief Gen. Pervez Musharraf, whose supporters staged a bloodless coup. Musharraf assumed the presidency June 20, 2001. Following the Sept. 11, 2001, terrorist attacks on the U.S., Pres. Musharraf pledged cooperation with the U.S. in fighting Taliban and al-Qaeda militants within Pakistan and in neighboring Afghanistan. An earthquake that rocked Pakistan and the Pakistani-held region of Kashmir Oct. 8, 2005, killed about 80,000 people.

More than 140 people died Oct. 18, 2007, when suicide bombers struck Benazir Bhutto's convoy upon her return from more than eight years in exile. Musharraf, who had won the Oct. 6 presidential election, gave up his army post Nov. 25 and was sworn in as civilian president the next day. Bhutto was assassinated Dec. 27, 2007, after a rally in Rawalpindi.

Headed by Bhutto's widower, Asif Ali Zardari, the Pakistan Peoples Party (PPP) led in parliamentary elections Feb. 18, 2008. Musharraf resigned Aug. 18 under threat of impeachment, and Zardari became president Sept. 9. Amid deteriorating security, U.S. and Pakistani forces clashed with the Taliban near the Afghan border, and Islamists carried out new suicide attacks. A 2009 government offensive against the Taliban in the strategic Swat Valley displaced nearly 2 mil civilians. Catastrophic floods and monsoon rains, July-Aug. 2010, inundated one-fifth of Pakistan, leaving more than 1,750 people dead and displacing up to 20 mil.

On May 2, 2011, U.S. commandos killed al-Qaeda leader Osama bin Laden in Abbottabad. The raid was carried out without prior warning to Pakistan; the U.S. suspected some Pakistani military and other officials of covert links and assistance to Islamist extremist groups such as the Taliban and al-Qaeda.

On Oct. 9, 2012, 15-year-old Malala Yousafzai, who advocated for education rights for girls in Pakistan, was shot by the Taliban, sparking worldwide outrage. After treatment at a British hospital, she resumed her advocacy, for which she shared the 2014 Nobel Peace Prize. A terrorist attack on a Peshawar school, Dec. 16, 2014, left about 150 dead. In 2007-14, an estimated 7,500 people died in terrorist attacks. Fighting between Pakistani forces and Islamic extremists resulted in more than 17,000 fatalities, 2007-14.

Musharraf, charged with treason in 2014, was convicted in absentia, Dec. 2019. He had been allowed to leave the country in 2016. Former Prime Min. Nawaz Sharif was returned to office in May 11, 2013, elections. With Sharif accused of corruption, a Supreme Court ruling, July 28, 2017, forced him to step down as prime min.

The party of former cricket star Imran Khan, the Pakistan Movement for Justice (PTI), with apparent backing from the military, won the most seats in July 25, 2018, parliamentary elections; Khan became prime min. Aug. 18. Arif Alvi, from Khan's party, was elected president Sept. 4, 2018. Hurt by economic problems and a loss of military support, Khan lost a no-confidence vote and was removed from office, Apr. 10, 2022. Shehbaz Sharif (brother of Nawaz Sharif) became prime minister, Apr. 11.

Following the 2021 Taliban victory in Afghanistan, attacks increased sharply in Pakistan by Islamist and other militants, some apparently using sanctuaries in eastern Afghanistan. Unusually heavy monsoon rains, perhaps related to climate change, beginning in June 2022 caused flooding that inundated one-third of the country and killed over 1,700; more than 33 mil people were displaced.

Shehbaz Sharif was replaced, Aug. 14, 2023, by a caretaker prime minister to prepare for new parliamentary elections. Jailed and convicted on multiple charges, former Prime Min. Khan was barred from running. In the Feb. 8, 2024, voting—marred by irregularities—candidates backed by the PTI won the most seats at stake, but Shehbaz Sharif's PML-N party and the PPP formed a coalition, and Shehbaz Sharif became prime minister, Mar. 3. Chosen by parliament, Asif Ali Zardari of the PPP became president, Mar. 10, 2024.

Palau

Republic of Palau

People: Population: 21,864 (193). **Age distrib.:** <15: 17.5%; 65+: 11.2%. **Growth:** 0.4%. **Migrants:** 28.1%. **Pop. density:** 123.4 per sq mi, 47.6 per sq km. **Urban:** 82.8%. **Ethnic groups:** Palauan (Micronesian with Malayan/Melanesian admixtures) 70.6%, Asian 26.5%. **Languages:** Palauan (official on most islands), English (official), Filipino. **Religions:** Christian 91.5% (Catholic 44.7%, Protestant 34.3%, independent 12.5%), agnostic 3.2%, Muslim 2.8% (Sunni).

Geography: Total area: 177 sq mi, 459 sq km (181); **Land area:** 177 sq mi, 459 sq km. **Location:** Archipelago (26 islands, more than 300 islets) in W Pacific O., about 530 mi SE of the Philippines. Micronesia to E, Indonesia to S. **Topography:** A mountainous main island and low coral atolls, usually fringed with large barrier reefs. **Arable land:** 0.7%. **Capital:** Ngerulmud.

Government: Type: Presidential republic in free association with U.S. **Head of state and govt.:** Pres. Surangel Whipps Jr.; b. 1968; in office: Jan. 21, 2021. **Local divisions:** 16 states. **Defense budget/active troops:** NA.

Economy: Industries: tourism, fishing, subsistence agriculture. **Chief agric.:** coconuts, cassava (manioc, tapioca), sweet potatoes; fish, pigs, chickens. **Natural resources:** forests, minerals (espec. gold), marine prods., deep-seabed minerals. **Water:** 0 cu m per capita. **Labor force:** NA. **Unemployment:** NA.

Finance: Monetary unit: U.S. Dollar (USD) (1.00 = $1 U.S.). **GDP:** $315.8 mil; **per capita GDP:** $17,491; **GDP growth:** 0.5%. **Imports** (2022): $216.7 mil; China 35%, U.S. 14%, South Korea 13%, Japan 8%, Italy 6%. **Exports** (2022): $24.5 mil; Greece 27%, Japan 26%, France 18%, Taiwan 8%, U.S. 7%. **Tourism** (2022): $15 mil. **Budget:** $121 mil. **Inflation:** 12.8%.

Transport: Airports: 3.

Communications: Mobile: 135.4 per 100 pop. **Broadband:** NA. **Internet:** NA.

Health: Expend.: 16.4%. **Life expect.:** 72.0 male; 78.5 female. **Births:** 11.6 per 1,000 pop. **Deaths:** 8.4 per 1,000 pop. **Infant mortality:** 10.8 per 1,000 live births. **Undernourished:** NA. **HIV:** NA. **COVID-19:** 10 deaths; rates per 100,000: 35,220 cases, 55 deaths. 100% vaccinated.

Education: Compulsory: ages 6-17. **Literacy:** 96.6%.

Website: www.palaugov.pw

Spain acquired the Palau Islands, 1886, and sold them to Germany, 1899. Japan seized them in 1914. U.S. forces occupied the islands in 1944; in 1947, they became part of a U.S.-administered UN trust territory. In 1981, Palau became an autonomous republic. It ratified a Compact of Free Association (COFA) with the U.S. in 1993 and became independent Oct. 1, 1994. Oct. 2015 legislation created a 193,000 sq mi marine sanctuary. Agreements signed in 2018 and 2023 extended U.S. financial aid to Palau under the COFA.

Palau is vulnerable to rising sea levels and stronger storms resulting from climate change.

Panama

Republic of Panama

People: Population: 4,470,241 (126). **Age distrib.:** <15: 25.0%; 65+: 10.1%. **Growth:** 1.5%. **Migrants:** 7.3%. **Pop. density:** 155.7 per sq mi, 60.1 per sq km. **Urban:** 69.9%. **Ethnic groups:** mestizo (mixed Indigenous/white) 65%, Indigenous (incl. Ngabe, Kuna) 12.3%, Black or African descent 9.2%, mulatto 6.8%, white 6.7%. **Languages:** Spanish (official), Indigenous langs. **Religions:** Christian 89.6% (Catholic 72.3%, Protestant 10.6%), agnostic 4.1%.

Geography: Total area: 29,120 sq mi, 75,420 sq km (116); **Land area:** 28,703 sq mi, 74,340 sq km. **Location:** Central America. Costa Rica on W, Colombia on E. **Topography:** Two mountain ranges run length of isthmus. Tropical rain forests cover the Caribbean coast and E. **Arable land:** 7.6%. **Capital:** Panama City, 2,015,735.

Government: Type: Presidential republic. **Head of state and govt.:** Pres. José Raúl Mulino; b. 1959; in office: July 1, 2024. **Local divisions:** 10 provinces, 4 Indigenous regions. **Defense budget:** $903 mil. **Active troops:** No armed forces. 27,700 paramilitary only.

Economy: Industries: constr., brewing, cement/other constr. materials, sugar milling. **Chief agric.:** sugarcane, bananas, rice, oranges, oil palm fruit, plantains. **Natural resources:** copper, mahogany forests, shrimp, hydropower. **Water:** 32,015 cu m per capita. **Electricity prod.:** 13.4 bil kWh. **Labor force:** agric. 15.3%, industry 16.7%, services 68.0%. **Unemployment:** 6.7%.

Finance: Monetary unit: Balboa (PAB) (1.00 = $1 U.S.). **GDP:** $177.4 bil; **per capita GDP:** $39,695; **GDP growth:** 7.3%. **Imports:** $36.1 bil; China 20%, U.S. 20%, Guyana 11%, Colombia 11%, Ecuador 9%. **Exports:** $36.6 bil; China 17%, Japan 12%, South Korea 8%, U.S. 5%, Spain 5%. **Tourism:** $5.5 bil. **Budget** (2020): $15.1 bil. **Inflation:** 1.5%.

Transport: Railways: 48 mi. **Motor vehicles:** 211.5 per 1,000 pop. **Airports:** 76.

Communications: Mobile: 156.6 per 100 pop. **Broadband:** 106 per 100 pop. **Internet:** 73.6%.

Health: Expend.: 9.7%. **Life expect.:** 76.4 male; 82.2 female. **Births:** 17.4 per 1,000 pop. **Deaths:** 5.7 per 1,000 pop. **Infant mortality:** 14.2 per 1,000 live births. **Undernourished:** 5.6%. **HIV:** 1.0%. **COVID-19:** 8,753 deaths; rates per 100,000: 24,217 cases, 203 deaths. 74% vaccinated.

Education: Compulsory: ages 4-14. **Literacy:** 95.7%.

Website: www.presidencia.gob.pa

The Caribbean coast of Panama was sighted by Rodrigo de Bastidas, sailing with Columbus for Spain in 1501, and was visited by Columbus in 1502. Vasco Núñez de Balboa crossed the isthmus and "discovered" the Pacific Ocean, Sept. 13, 1513. Spanish colonies were ravaged by Francis Drake, 1572-95, and Henry Morgan, 1668-71. Morgan destroyed the old city of Panama, which was founded in 1519. Freed from Spain, Panama joined Colombia in 1821.

Panama declared independence from Colombia Nov. 3, 1903, and granted control of the Canal Zone to the U.S. Feb. 26, 1904. The U.S.-built Panama Canal opened Aug. 15, 1914. A 1978 treaty provided for its gradual return to Panama—completed Dec. 31, 1999. A $5.3-bil canal expansion was completed in 2016.

Pres. Eric Arturo Delvalle was ousted by the National Assembly, Feb. 26, 1988, after he tried to fire Gen. Manuel Antonio Noriega, who was under a U.S. indictment on drug charges. U.S. troops invaded Panama Dec. 20, 1989, and Noriega surrendered Jan. 3, 1990.

Information published beginning Apr. 3, 2016, from "Panama Papers" documents—leaked from a Panama City law firm—linked public officials and others in various countries to offshore bank accounts and companies created to conceal wealth or avoid taxes. Vowing to fight corruption, Laurentino Cortizo of the Democratic Revolutionary Party narrowly won the May 5, 2019, presidential election. Pledging to boost the economy, José Raúl Mulino won the May 5, 2024, presidential election.

In the 2020s, hundreds of thousands of migrants heading north from South America transited Panama, including the remote Darién Gap region, en route to the U.S.—more than 500,000 in 2023 alone. Under a July 1, 2024, agreement, the U.S. would assist Panama with intercepting and deporting migrants.

Papua New Guinea

Independent State of Papua New Guinea

People: Population: 10,046,233 (93). **Age distrib.:** <15: 37.1%; 65+: 4.0%. **Growth:** 2.3%. **Migrants:** 0.3%. **Pop. density:** 57.5 per sq mi, 22.2 per sq km. **Urban:** 13.9%. **Ethnic groups:** Melanesian, Papuan, Negrito, Micronesian, Polynesian. **Languages:** Tok Pisin, English, Hiri Motu (all official); some 839 Indigenous langs. **Religions:** Christian 95.1% (Protestant 57.4%, Catholic 31.5%), ethnic religionist 2.9%.

Geography: Total area: 178,704 sq mi, 462,840 sq km (55); **Land area:** 174,850 sq mi, 452,860 sq km. **Location:** SE Asia; E half of island of New Guinea and about 600 nearby islands. Indonesia on W, Australia on S. **Topography:** Thickly forested mountains cover much of center, with lowlands along the coasts. Incl. some islands of Bismarck and Solomon groups, such as Admiralty Isls., New Ireland, New Britain, and Bougainville. **Arable land:** 0.7%. **Capital:** Port Moresby, 420,419.

Government: Type: Parliamentary democracy under constitutional monarchy. **Head of state:** King Charles III, rep. by Gov.-Gen. Bob Dadae; in office: Feb. 28, 2017. **Head of govt.:** Prime Min. James Marape; in office: May 30, 2019. **Local divisions:** 20 provinces, 1 autonomous region, 1 district. **Defense budget:** $98 mil. **Active troops:** 4,000.

Economy: Industries: oil and gas, mining, palm oil proc., plywood and wood chip prod., copra crushing, constr., tourism. **Chief agric.:** oil palm fruit, coconuts, bananas, fruits, sweet potatoes, game meat. **Natural resources:** gold, copper, silver, nat. gas, timber, oil, fisheries. **Water:** 80,507 cu m per capita. **Crude oil reserves:** 160 mil bbls. **Electricity prod.:** 4.8 bil kWh. **Labor force:** agric. 18.5%, industry 11.5%, services 70.0%. **Unemployment:** 2.7%.

Finance: Monetary unit: Kina (PGK) (3.94 = $1 U.S.). **GDP:** $47.6 bil; **per capita GDP:** $4,607; **GDP growth:** 2.7%. **Imports** (2021): $6.3 bil; China 26%, Australia 23%, Singapore 16%, Malaysia 9%. **Exports** (2021): $11.6 bil; Japan 26%, China 22%, Australia 11%, South Korea 10%, Taiwan 9%. **Tourism** (2022): $1 mil. **Budget:** $5.1 bil. **Inflation:** 2.3%.

Transport: Motor vehicles: 17.5 per 1,000 pop. **Airports:** 535.

Communications: Mobile (2022): 49.2 per 100 pop. **Broadband** (2022): 11 per 100 pop. **Internet:** 27%.

Health: Expend.: 2.3%. **Life expect.:** 68.3 male; 71.9 female. **Births:** 28.1 per 1,000 pop. **Deaths:** 5.4 per 1,000 pop. **Infant mortality:** 32.0 per 1,000 live births. **Undernourished:** 27.7%. **HIV:** 1.0%. **COVID-19:** 670 deaths; rates per 100,000: 524 cases, 7 deaths. 4% vaccinated.

Education: Compulsory: NA. **Literacy:** 64.2%.

Website: www.pm.gov.pg

Human remains dating back at least 10,000 years have been found in the interior of New Guinea. European colonization began in the 19th cent., when the Dutch took control of the island's western half (now part of Indonesia). The southern half of eastern New Guinea was claimed by Britain in 1884 and transferred to Australia in 1905. Germany claimed the northern half in 1884, but Australia captured it in WWI. Self-government was achieved Dec. 1, 1973, and independence Sept. 16, 1975.

Secessionist rebels clashed with government forces on Bougainville 1988-97, claiming some 20,000 lives. A Bougainville autonomy agreement was signed Aug. 30, 2001. In a late-2019 nonbinding referendum, 98% of Bougainville voters favored independence. Independence advocate and former rebel leader Ishmael Toroama was elected president of Bougainville in Sept. 2020.

Sir Michael Somare, the nation's first prime min. (1975-80, 1982-85), regained the office in 2002. Somare took indefinite medical leave Apr. 2011. After June-July 2012 parliamentary elections, Peter O'Neill served as prime minister. Losing support over economic conditions and corruption, O'Neill resigned, May 26, 2019. James Marape was elected prime minister by parliament, May 30, 2019. After July 2022 elections marred by violence (at least 50 deaths) and apparent fraud, Marape was reelected by parliament, Aug. 9. Inter-tribal and other violence continued in 2023-24.

The Supreme Court, Apr. 26, 2016, ruled illegal Australia's detention center on Manus Island for migrants intercepted trying to reach Australia by boat. The center, where detainees endured harsh living conditions, was closed Oct. 31, 2017. About 600 detainees were relocated; after most had gone to other countries, about 70 remained in Papua New Guinea as of mid-2024.

The country has extensive energy resources. Shipments of liquefied natural gas through a new facility near Port Moresby began in May 2014.

With Chinese influence growing in the Pacific, Papua New Guinea and the U.S. signed a new defense agreement, May 22, 2023; a security agreement with Australia was signed Dec. 7, 2023.

A landslide in western Enga Province, May 24, 2024, left hundreds dead.

Paraguay

Republic of Paraguay

People: Population: 7,522,549 (104). **Age distrib.:** <15: 22.2%; 65+: 9.4%. **Growth:** 1.1%. **Migrants:** 2.4%. **Pop. density:** 49.0 per sq mi, 18.9 per sq km. **Urban:** 63.5%. **Ethnic groups:** mestizo (mixed Spanish/Indigenous ancestry) 95%. **Languages:** Spanish, Guaraní (both official). **Religions:** Christian 95.4% (Catholic 84.5%), ethnic religionist 2.0%.

Geography: Total area: 157,048 sq mi, 406,752 sq km (59); **Land area:** 153,399 sq mi, 397,302 sq km. **Location:** Landlocked country in central S America. Bolivia on N, Argentina on S, Brazil on E. **Topography:** Paraguay R. bisects country. Fertile plains, wooded slopes, grasslands to E. Gran Chaco plain, with marshes and scrub trees, to W. Extreme W is arid. **Arable land:** 11.5%. **Capital:** Asunción, 3,568,830.

Government: Type: Presidential republic. **Head of state and govt.:** Pres. Santiago Peña Palacios; b. 1978; in office: Aug. 15, 2023. **Local divisions:** 17 departments, 1 capital city. **Defense budget:** $300 mil. **Active troops:** 13,950.

Economy: Industries: sugar proc., cement, textiles, beverages, wood prods., steel. **Chief agric.:** sugarcane, maize, soybeans, cassava, rice, wheat. **Natural resources:** hydropower, timber, iron ore, manganese, limestone. **Water:** 57,843 cu m per capita. **Electricity prod.:** 44.0 bil kWh. **Labor force:** agric. 17.4%, industry 18.7%, services 63.8%. **Unemployment:** 5.8%.

Finance: Monetary unit: Guarani (PYG) (7,565.73 = $1 U.S.). **GDP:** $119.8 bil; **per capita GDP:** $17,466; **GDP growth:** 4.7%. **Imports:** $17.9 bil; China 28%, Brazil 23%, U.S. 11%, Argentina 8%. **Exports:** $18.7 bil; Brazil 36%, Argentina 19%, Chile 12%. **Tourism:** $633 mil. **Budget:** $8.7 bil. **Inflation:** 4.6%.

Transport: Railways: 19 mi. **Motor vehicles:** 182.1 per 1,000 pop. **Airports:** 83.

Communications: Mobile: 126.6 per 100 pop. **Broadband:** 75 per 100 pop. **Internet** (2023): 78.1%.

Health: Expend.: 8.0%. **Life expect.:** 76.2 male; 81.6 female. **Births:** 15.9 per 1,000 pop. **Deaths:** 4.9 per 1,000 pop. **Infant mortality:** 22.0 per 1,000 live births. **Undernourished:** 4.5%. **HIV:** 0.5%. **COVID-19:** 19,880 deaths; rates per 100,000: 10,316 cases, 279 deaths. 50% vaccinated.

Education: Compulsory: ages 5-17. **Literacy:** 94.5%.

Website: www.presidencia.gov.py

Guaraní Indians preceded Europeans in Paraguay, which was visited by Sebastian Cabot in 1527 and became a Spanish possession in 1535. Paraguay gained independence from Spain in 1811. It lost half its population and much of its territory to Brazil, Uruguay, and Argentina in the War of the Triple Alliance, 1865-70. Large areas were won from Bolivia in the Chaco War, 1932-35. Gen. Alfredo Stroessner held the presidency 1954-89, until his ouster in a military coup.

Power struggles ensued between civilian and military leaders, 1993-97. The assassination of Vice Pres. Luis María Argaña, Mar. 23, 1999, was widely attributed to Pres. Raúl Cubas Grau and triggered protests and an impeachment vote; Cubas resigned Mar. 28. An attempted military coup was suppressed May 18, 2000.

Nicanor Duarte Frutos of the conservative Colorado Party won the presidency, Apr. 27, 2003.

Paraguayan authorities blamed a leftist group for the Sept. 2004 kidnapping and subsequent murder of Cecilia Cubas, daughter of former Pres. Cubas. Fernando Lugo, a former Catholic cleric known as the "bishop of the poor," won a presidential election Apr. 20, 2008, ending over six decades of Colorado rule. On June 22, 2012, Lugo was removed from office after his handling of a dispute between landless peasants and police left 17 dead June 15. Colorado candidates won the presidency in 2013 and 2018 elections. Santiago Peña of the Colorado Party won the Apr. 30, 2023, presidential election.

Peru

Republic of Peru

People: Population: 32,600,249 (47). **Age distrib.:** <15: 25.8%; 65+: 8.0%. **Growth:** 0.5%. **Migrants:** 3.7%. **Pop. density:** 66.0 per sq mi, 25.5 per sq km. **Urban:** 79.1%. **Ethnic groups:** mestizo (mixed Indigenous/white) 60.2%, Indigenous 25.8%, white 5.9%, African descent 3.6%. **Languages:** Spanish, Quechua, Aymara (all official). **Religions:** Christian 96.5% (Catholic 82.9%).

Geography: Total area: 496,225 sq mi, 1,285,216 sq km (19); **Land area:** 494,209 sq mi, 1,279,996 sq km. **Location:** Pacific coast of S America. Ecuador, Colombia on N; Brazil, Bolivia on E; Chile on S. **Topography:** An arid coastal strip, 10-100 mi wide. The Andes cover one-quarter of land area. The uplands are well-watered, as are the eastern slopes reaching the Amazon Basin, which covers half of country. **Arable land:** 3.1%. **Capital:** Lima, 11,361,938. **Cities:** Arequipa, 971,296.

Government: Type: Presidential republic. **Head of state and govt.** Pres. Dina Boluarte; b. 1962; in office: Dec. 7, 2022. **Local divisions:** 25 regions, 1 province. **Defense budget:** $1.9 bil. **Active troops:** 81,000.

Economy: Industries: mining/refining of minerals; steel, metal fabrication; petroleum extraction/refining, nat. gas and nat. gas liquefaction; fishing/fish proc., cement, glass, textiles. **Chief agric.:** sugarcane, potatoes, rice, bananas, milk, chicken. **Natural resources:** copper, silver, gold, petroleum, timber, fish, iron ore, coal, phosphate, potash, hydropower, nat. gas. **Water:** 55,755 cu m per capita. **Crude oil reserves:** 859 mil bbls. **Electricity prod.:** 57.6 bil kWh. **Labor force:** agric. 25.7%, industry 17.5%, services 56.8%. **Unemployment:** 4.8%.

Finance: Monetary unit: Sol (PEN) (3.74 = $1 U.S.). **GDP:** $574.3 bil; **per capita GDP:** $16,717; **GDP growth:** –0.6%. **Imports:** $63.0 bil; China 27%, U.S. 24%, Brazil 6%. **Exports:** $73.3 bil; China 30%, U.S. 15%. **Tourism:** $2.6 bil. **Budget:** $49.1 bil. **Inflation:** 6.5%.

Transport: Railways: 1,152 mi. **Motor vehicles:** 78.6 per 1,000 pop. **Airports:** 166.

Communications: Mobile: 122.0 per 100 pop. **Broadband:** 90.4 per 100 pop. **Internet:** 74.7%.

Health: Expend.: 6.2%. **Life expect.:** 65.4 male; 72.7 female. **Births:** 16.7 per 1,000 pop. **Deaths:** 10.9 per 1,000 pop. **Infant mortality:** 10.8 per 1,000 live births. **Undernourished:** 7.0%. **HIV:** 0.5%. **COVID-19:** 220,975 deaths; rates per 100,000: 13,730 cases, 670 deaths. 87% vaccinated.

Education: Compulsory: ages 3-16. **Literacy:** 94.5%.

Website: www.peru.gob.pe

The powerful Inca Empire had its seat at Cuzco in the Andes and covered much of western S America. A civil war had weakened the empire when Spaniard Francisco Pizarro began raiding Peru for its wealth, 1532. In 1533 he executed the Inca ruler, Atahualpa, and enslaved the people.

José de San Martin captured Lima from the Spanish in 1821; Simón Bolívar routed Spanish forces in 1824, and for much of the 19th cent., the country was governed by military leaders. Chile defeated Peru in the War of the Pacific, 1879-83. Right-wing groups allied with the military and the leftist APRA party vied for power in the first half of the 20th cent.

Peru returned to democratic leadership in 1980 but was plagued by economic problems and by leftist Shining Path (Sendero Luminoso) guerrillas. Conflict between guerrillas and government troops, 1980-2000, killed more than 69,000.

Elected president in June 1990, Alberto Fujimori dissolved Congress, suspended parts of the constitution, and initiated press censorship, Apr. 1992. The leader of Shining Path was captured Sept. 12. Fujimori won reelection in 1995 and 2000, but his repressive antiterrorism tactics drew international criticism. Scandals involving a top aide led Fujimori to leave office, Nov. 2000. He was convicted, 2007-15, on various charges.

In a presidential runoff election June 5, 2011, leftist Ollanta Humala Tasso defeated Keiko Fujimori, daughter of the former president. Pedro Pablo Kuczynski defeated Keiko Fujimori, June 5, 2016. Facing impeachment over a corruption scandal, Kuczynski resigned and was replaced, Mar. 2018, by Vice Pres. Martín Vizcarra. Accused of corruption, Vizcarra was impeached by Congress, Nov. 9, 2020.

In a June 6, 2021, presidential runoff, leftist José Pedro Castillo Terrones narrowly defeated Keiko Fujimori. Corruption scandals and protests over rising prices marred Castillo's administration. Castillo was removed from office and arrested, Dec. 7, 2022, after an unsuccessful attempt to dissolve Congress to avoid impeachment; First Vice Pres. Dina Boluarte became Peru's first female head of state. Castillo's arrest touched off sometimes-violent protests, met with a lethal response by security forces that left dozens dead.

As of May 2024, about 1.5 mil Venezuelan migrants were in Peru, having fled economic hardship and repression.

In the early 2020s, Peru was one of the worst affected countries in Latin America by the COVID-19 pandemic, which at times severely strained the health care system.

Philippines

Republic of the Philippines

People: Population: 118,277,063 (13). **Age distrib.:** <15: 30.2%; 65+: 5.6%. **Growth:** 1.6%. **Migrants:** 0.2%. **Pop. density:** 1,027.4 per sq mi, 396.7 per sq km. **Urban:** 48.6%. **Ethnic groups:** Tagalog 26%, Bisaya/Binisaya 14.3%, Ilocano 8%, Cebuano 8%, Ilonggo 7.9%, Bikol/Bicol 6.5%, Waray 3.8%, Kapampangan 3%. **Languages:** Filipino (based on Tagalog), English (both official); 8 major dialects (incl. Tagalog). **Religions:** Christian 89.9% (Catholic 67.8%, independent 16.8%), Muslim 6.3% (Sunni), ethnic religionist 2.2%.

Geography: Total area: 115,831 sq mi, 300,000 sq km (72); **Land area:** 115,124 sq mi, 298,170 sq km. **Location:** Archipelago in SE Asia. Malaysia, Indonesia on S; Taiwan on N. **Topography:** Comprises some 7,107 islands stretching 1,100 mi N-S. About 95% of area and pop. are on 11 largest islands, which are mountainous, except for the heavily indented coastlines and central plain on Luzon. **Arable land:** 18.7%. **Capital:** Manila, 14,941,953. **Cities:** Davao City, 1,991,457; Cebu City, 1,042,613.

Government: Type: Presidential republic. **Head of state and govt.:** Pres. Ferdinand "Bongbong" Romualdez Marcos Jr.; b. 1957; in office: June 30, 2022. **Local divisions:** 81 provinces, 38 chartered cities. **Defense budget:** $6.2 bil. **Active troops:** 146,250.

Economy: Industries: semiconductors and electronics assembly, business process outsourcing, food/beverage mfg., constr. **Chief agric.:** sugarcane, rice, coconuts, maize, bananas, vegetables. **Natural resources:** timber, petroleum, nickel, cobalt, silver, gold, salt, copper. **Water:** 4,206 cu m per capita. **Crude oil reserves:** 139 mil bbls. **Electricity prod.:** 113.0 bil kWh. **Labor force:** agric. 23.7%, industry 18.9%, services 57.4%. **Unemployment:** 2.2%.

Finance: Monetary unit: Peso (PHP) (56.27 = $1 U.S.). **GDP:** $1.3 tril; **per capita GDP:** $10,755; **GDP growth:** 5.6%. **Imports:** $150.3 bil; China 32%, Indonesia 8%, South Korea 7%, Japan 7%, Singapore 6%. **Exports:** $103.6 bil; U.S. 14%, China 14%, Hong Kong 11%, Japan 10%, Singapore 6%. **Tourism:** $9.1 bil. **Budget** (2020): $91.0 bil. **Inflation:** 6.0%.

Transport: Railways: 48 mi. **Motor vehicles:** 46.7 per 1,000 pop. **Airports:** 246.

Communications: Mobile: 117.3 per 100 pop. **Broadband:** 73.7 per 100 pop. **Internet:** 75.2%.

Health: Expend. (2022): 5.1%. **Life expect.:** 67.3 male; 74.5 female. **Births:** 22.1 per 1,000 pop. **Deaths:** 6.2 per 1,000 pop. **Infant mortality:** 22.0 per 1,000 live births. **Undernourished:** 5.9%. **HIV:** 0.3%. **COVID-19:** 66,864 deaths; rates per 100,000: 3,778 cases, 61 deaths. 72% vaccinated.

Education: Compulsory: ages 5-17. **Literacy:** 98.5%.

Website: www.gov.ph

Originally inhabited by Malay peoples, the archipelago was visited by Magellan, 1521. The Spanish founded Manila, 1571. Spain ceded the islands, named for King Philip II of Spain, to the U.S. for $20 mil, 1898, following the Spanish-American War. U.S. troops suppressed a guerrilla uprising in a brutal war, 1899-1905. Japan attacked the Philippines Dec. 8, 1941, and occupied the islands during WWII. Independence was proclaimed, July 4, 1946. A republic was established.

The repressive and corrupt regime of Pres. Ferdinand Marcos and his wife, Imelda, was in place 1965-86. The assassination of prominent opposition leader Benigno S. Aquino Jr., Aug. 21, 1983, sparked calls for Marcos's resignation. Marcos defeated Corazon Aquino, widow of the slain opposition leader, Feb. 16, 1986, in an allegedly fraudulent election. Mass protests and international pressure forced Marcos to flee the country Feb. 25, and Aquino became president.

Her government was plagued by a weak economy, widespread poverty, and Communist and Muslim insurgencies. Fidel Ramos won the May 1992 presidential election. A treaty with Muslim separatist guerrillas providing for expansion and development of an autonomous Muslim region on Mindanao, in the southern Philippines, was signed Sept. 2, 1996.

Joseph (Erap) Estrada, a former movie actor, won the presidential election, May 11, 1998, but was impeached on bribery and corruption charges Nov. 13, 2000. Vice Pres. Gloria Macapagal Arroyo became president Jan. 20, 2001, and won reelection May 10, 2004. After Estrada was convicted in 2007 of taking more than $85 mil in bribes and kickbacks while in office, then pardoned, Benigno "NoyNoy" Aquino III, the son of former Pres. Aquino, defeated Estrada in the May 10, 2010, presidential election.

The government, 2012 and 2014, signed new peace and autonomy deals with Muslim rebels on Mindanao; violence had persisted after the 1996 accord. However, the Abu Sayyaf Islamist guerrilla group and the rebel group Maute, both of which claimed allegiance to ISIS, continued to stage attacks.

Typhoon Haiyan, Nov. 8, 2013, killed more than 6,200 people and displaced over 4 mil.

Vowing a tough crackdown on drug crime, Rodrigo Duterte was elected president, May 9, 2016. The death toll in the war on drugs, largely from extrajudicial killings by police or vigilantes, was estimated as high as 30,000 by 2021.

Muslim rebels held part of the city of Marawi, May-Oct. 2017. Jan. 21 and Feb. 6, 2019, referenda in the south endorsed a new Bangsamoro autonomous region, although extremist attacks continued. Duterte signed, July 3, 2020, an antiterrorism bill giving security forces sweeping powers. Prosecuted in the Philippines, journalist Maria Ressa shared the 2021 Nobel Peace Prize.

Ferdinand "Bongbong" Marcos Jr., the former dictator's son, easily won the May 9, 2022, presidential election. Sara Duterte, the outgoing president's daughter, was elected vice president.

The Philippines was severely affected by the COVID-19 pandemic that began in 2020. Schools fully reopened in Aug. 2022 after more than two years of pandemic shutdown.

Amid concerns about growing Chinese power and aggression in the South China Sea, the Philippines and U.S. announced, Feb. 2023, an agreement giving the U.S. increased access to military bases in the Philippines. A Philippines-Japan defense cooperation agreement was signed July 8, 2024.

Poland

Republic of Poland

People: Population: 38,746,310 (38). **Age distrib.:** <15: 14.2%; 65+: 19.8%. **Growth:** –1.0%. **Migrants:** 2.2%. **Pop. density:** 329.8 per sq mi, 127.3 per sq km. **Urban:** 60.3%. **Ethnic groups:** Polish 96.9%. **Languages:** Polish (official). **Religions:** Christian 95.4% (Catholic 92.8%), agnostic 4.2%.

Geography: Total area: 120,728 sq mi, 312,685 sq km (69); **Land area:** 117,474 sq mi, 304,255 sq km. **Location:** On Baltic Sea in E central Europe. Germany on W; Czechia, Slovakia on S; Lithuania, Belarus, Ukraine on E; Russia on N. **Topography:** Mostly lowlands forming part of the Northern European Plain. The Carpathian Mts. along S border rise to 8,200 ft. **Arable land:** 36.5%. **Capital:** Warsaw, 1,799,451. **Cities:** Cracow, 769,396.

Government: Type: Parliamentary republic. **Head of state:** Pres. Andrzej Duda; b. 1972; in office: Aug. 6, 2015. **Head of govt.:** Prime Min. Donald Tusk; b. 1957; in office: Dec. 11, 2023. **Local divisions:** 16 provinces. **Defense budget:** $23.5 bil. **Active troops:** 100,400.

Economy: Industries: machine building, iron and steel, coal mining, chemicals, shipbuilding, food proc., glass, beverages, textiles. **Chief agric.:** milk, sugar beets, wheat, maize, potatoes, triticale. **Natural resources:** coal, sulfur, copper, nat. gas, silver, lead, salt, amber. **Water:** 1,579 cu m per capita. **Crude oil reserves:** 113 mil bbls. **Electricity prod.:** 167.2 bil kWh. **Labor force:** agric. 8.3%, industry 30.8%, services 60.9%. **Unemployment:** 2.9%.

Finance: Monetary unit: Zloty (PLN) (3.84 = $1 U.S.). **GDP:** $1.8 tril; **per capita GDP:** $49,464; **GDP growth:** 0.2%. **Imports:** $419.7 bil; Germany 23%, China 11%, Italy 5%, Netherlands 5%. **Exports:** $469.3 bil; Germany 27%, Czechia 6%, France 6%, UK 5%, Netherlands 5%. **Tourism:** $15.0 bil. **Budget:** $248.9 bil. **Inflation:** 11.5%.

Transport: Railways: 12,093 mi. **Motor vehicles:** 803.9 per 1,000 pop. **Airports:** 288.

Communications: Mobile: 135.1 per 100 pop. **Broadband:** 202 per 100 pop. **Internet** (2023): 86.4%.

Health: Expend. (2022): 6.7%. **Life expect.:** 72.8 male; 80.9 female. **Births:** 8.4 per 1,000 pop. **Deaths:** 12.2 per 1,000 pop. **Infant mortality:** 4.9 per 1,000 live births. **Undernourished:** <2.5%. **HIV:** NA. **COVID-19:** 120,734 deaths; rates per 100,000: 17,583 cases, 318 deaths. 60% vaccinated.

Education: Compulsory: ages 6-15. **Literacy:** 99.8%.

Website: www.gov.pl

Slavic tribes in the area were converted to Latin Christianity in the 10th cent. Poland was a great power from the 14th to the 17th cent. In three partitions (1772, 1793, 1795) it was apportioned among Prussia, Russia, and Austria. Overrun by the Austro-German armies in WWI, it declared its independence on Nov. 11, 1918, and was recognized as independent by the Treaty of Versailles, June 28, 1919. Large territories to the east were taken in a war with Russia, 1921.

Germany and the USSR invaded Poland Sept. 1939 and divided the country. During the war, Nazis killed some 6 mil Polish citizens, half of them Jews. (Controversial 2018 legislation outlawed attributing to Poland any role in Nazi atrocities.) In compensation for territory ceded to the USSR when WWII ended, Poland received German territory comprising Silesia, Pomerania, West Prussia, and part of East Prussia. Communists, who aligned themselves with the USSR, dominated the 1947 election.

In 12 years of rule by Stalinists, large estates were abolished, industries nationalized, schools secularized, and Roman Catholic prelates jailed. Farm production fell off. Harsh working conditions caused a riot in Poznan, June 28-29, 1956. A new Politburo, committed to a more independent Polish Communism, was named Oct. 1956. Collectivization of farms was ended and religious liberty increased.

Independent trade union Solidarity gained strength in the 1980s. Led by Lech Walesa, Solidarity helped to win political and economic reforms, including free elections, in an Apr. 5, 1989, accord. Candidates endorsed by Solidarity swept the parliamentary elections, June 4. Walesa became president Dec. 22, 1990.

Policies to transform the economy into a free-market system led to inflation, unemployment, and a return to the political left in 1993 parliamentary elections. A former Communist, Aleksander Kwasniewski, succeeded Walesa as president, 1995. Poland became a full member of NATO, Mar. 12, 1999, and entered the European Union May 1, 2004.

Andrzej Duda of the conservative Law and Justice (PiS) party won a May 24, 2015, presidential runoff. PiS won Oct. 25, 2015, parliamentary elections. Beginning in 2015, PiS governments resisted EU resettlement programs for non-European migrants entering the EU. July 2017 legislation allowing the justice minister to appoint judges drew EU criticism as a threat to judicial independence. Legislation effective July 2018 to force the retirement of some Supreme Court judges prompted widespread protests. PiS won a slim majority in Oct. 13, 2019, parliamentary elections. Duda narrowly won reelection, July 12, 2020. Following an Oct. 2020 court ruling, and despite massive protests, a ban on almost all abortions went into effect Jan. 27, 2021. The EU, in 2021, began withholding some grant funding to Poland.

NATO increased troop strength in Poland in response to Russia's Feb. 2022 invasion of Ukraine. Poland provided military aid to Ukraine. As of Sept. 2024, Poland hosted over 970,000 Ukrainian refugees.

In Oct. 15, 2023, elections, PiS lost its parliamentary majority. Opposition parties, led by former Prime Min. Donald Tusk's centrist Civic Platform, formed a coalition, and Tusk again became prime min. Dec. 11. The new government announced a plan in Feb. 2024 to restore judicial independence, and the EU, in May, ended efforts to sanction Poland for rule-of-law violations.

Portugal

Portuguese Republic

People: Population: 10,207,177 (92). **Age distrib.:** <15: 12.7%; 65+: 22.3%. **Growth:** –0.1%. **Migrants:** 9.8%. **Pop. density:** 289.0 per sq mi, 111.6 per sq km. **Urban:** 68.4%. **Ethnic groups:** Portuguese 95%; citizens from Portugal's former colonies and other foreign born 5%. **Languages:** Portuguese, Mirandese (both official). **Religions:** Christian 88.2% (Catholic 82.6%), agnostic 8.9%.

Geography: Total area: 35,556 sq mi, 92,090 sq km (109); **Land area:** 35,317 sq mi, 91,470 sq km. **Location:** SW extreme of Europe. Spain on N, E. **Topography:** Tajus R. bisects country NE-SW. N is cool and rainy, mountainous. S is drier, with warm climate and rolling plains. **Arable land:** 10.2%. **Capital:** Lisbon, 3,014,607. **Cities:** Porto, 1,329,301.

Government: Type: Semi-presidential republic. **Head of state:** Pres. Marcelo Rebelo de Sousa; b. 1948; in office: Mar. 9, 2016. **Head of govt.:** Prime Min. Luís Montenegro; b. 1973; in office: Apr. 2, 2024. **Local divisions:** 18 districts, 2 autonomous regions. **Defense budget:** $2.8 bil. **Active troops:** 26,050.

Economy: Industries: textiles, clothing, footwear, wood and cork, paper and pulp, chemicals, fuels and lubricants, automobiles/auto parts, base metals. **Chief agric.:** milk, tomatoes, grapes, olives, maize, oranges. **Natural resources:** fish, forests (cork), iron ore, copper, zinc, tin, tungsten, silver, gold, uranium, marble, clay, gypsum, salt, hydropower. **Water:** 7,522 cu m per capita. **Electricity prod.:** 45.5 bil kWh. **Labor force:** agric. 5.0%, industry 24.0%, services 71.0%. **Unemployment:** 6.5%.

Finance: Monetary unit: Euro (EUR) (0.90 = $1 U.S.). **GDP:** $513.2 bil; **per capita GDP:** $48,759; **GDP growth:** 2.3%. **Imports:** $133.0 bil; Spain 31%, Germany 11%, France 6%, China 5%, Italy 5%. **Exports:** $136.6 bil; Spain 25%, France 12%, Germany 11%, U.S. 7%, UK 5%. **Tourism:** $27.2 bil. **Budget:** $101.9 bil. **Inflation:** 4.3%.

Transport: Railways: 1,570 mi. **Motor vehicles:** 670.0 per 1,000 pop. **Airports:** 130.

Communications: Mobile: 123.0 per 100 pop. **Broadband:** 100 per 100 pop. **Internet** (2023): 85.8%.

Health: Expend. (2022): 10.6%. **Life expect.:** 78.8 male; 85.2 female. **Births:** 8.0 per 1,000 pop. **Deaths:** 10.9 per 1,000 pop. **Infant mortality:** 2.4 per 1,000 live births. **Undernourished:** <2.5%. **HIV:** 0.5%. **COVID-19:** 28,840 deaths; rates per 100,000: 55,022 cases, 280 deaths. 87% vaccinated.

Education: Compulsory: ages 6-17. **Literacy:** 96.8%.

Website: www.portugal.gov.pt

Portugal, an independent state since the 12th cent., was a kingdom until a 1910 revolution drove out King Manoel II and a republic was proclaimed. Prime Min. Antonio de Oliveira Salazar headed a repressive government, 1932-68.

On Apr. 25, 1974, a military junta led by Gen. Antonio de Spinola seized the government; Spinola became president. The new government granted independence to Guinea-Bissau, Mozambique, Cabo Verde, Angola, and São Tomé and Príncipe.

With the economy lagging, the Socialists won 2005 and 2009 parliamentary elections. After Portugal was given a 78-bil euro bailout package from international lenders to avert default, the center-right Social Democratic Party (PSD) won parliamentary elections June 2011. Austerity cuts caused widespread protests in Nov. 2012. After parliamentary elections Oct. 4, 2015, Socialist António Costa became prime min., and he retained office after 2019 and 2022 elections. Costa resigned, Nov. 7, 2023, amid a corruption scandal. In Mar. 10, 2024, elections, an alliance including the PSD outpolled the Socialists, and the far-right Chega party made substantial gains. The PSD's Luís Montenegro became prime min., Apr. 2, heading a minority government not including Chega.

In recent years, Portugal has experienced extreme heat, drought, and wildfires likely related to climate change.

Azores Isls., in the Atlantic, 740 mi W of Portugal, have an area of 868 sq mi and a pop. (2014 est.) of 246,353. The **Madeira Isls.**, 350 mi off the NW coast of Africa, have an area of 306 sq mi and a pop. (2014 est.) of 258,686. Both groups were offered partial autonomy in 1976.

Qatar

State of Qatar

People: Population: 2,552,088 (140). **Age distrib.:** <15: 13.1%; 65+: 1.5%. **Growth:** 0.7%. **Migrants:** 77.3%. **Pop. density:** 570.5 per sq mi, 220.3 per sq km. **Urban:** 99.4%. **Ethnic groups:** non-Qatari 88.4%, Qatari 11.6%. **Languages:** Arabic (official), English. **Religions:** Muslim 65.4% (Sunni 62%), Hindu 16.3% (Shaivite 7%, Vaishnavite 7%), Christian 14.0% (Catholic 12.6%), Buddhist 2.0% (Theravadin).

Geography: Total area: 4,473 sq mi, 11,586 sq km (159); **Land area:** 4,473 sq mi, 11,586 sq km. **Location:** Middle East, occupying peninsula on W coast of Persian Gulf. Saudi Arabia on S. **Topography:** Mostly flat desert with some limestone ridges; scarce vegetation. **Arable land:** 1.8%. **Capital:** Doha, 665,597. **Cities:** Ar-Rayyan, 815,869.

Government: Type: Absolute monarchy. **Head of state:** Sheikh Tamim bin Hamad al-Thani; b. 1980; in office: June 25, 2013. **Head of govt.:** Prime Min. Muhammad bin Abd al-Rahman Al Thani; b. 1980; in office: Mar. 7, 2023. **Local divisions:** 8 municipalities. **Defense budget:** $9.0 bil. **Active troops:** 16,500.

Economy: Industries: liquefied nat. gas, crude oil prod./refining, ammonia, fertilizer, petrochemicals, steel reinforcing bars. **Chief agric.:** tomatoes, dates, chicken, cucumbers/gherkins, camel milk, eggs. **Natural resources:** petroleum, fish, nat. gas. **Water:** 22 cu m per capita. **Crude oil reserves:** 25.2 bil bbls. **Electricity prod.:** 54.0 bil kWh. **Labor force:** agric. 1.3%, industry 40.0%, services 58.7%. **Unemployment:** 0.1%.

Finance: Monetary unit: Riyal (QAR) (3.64 = $1 U.S.). **GDP** (2022): $326.4 bil; **per capita GDP** (2022): $121,125; **GDP growth** (2022): 4.2%. **Imports:** $72.2 bil; UAE 13%, China 11%, U.S. 10%, UK 8%, India 5%. **Exports:** $128.7 bil; China 18%, India 15%, Japan 10%, South Korea 9%, UK 6%. **Tourism:** $8.8 bil. **Budget:** $57.3 bil. **Inflation:** 3.0%.

Transport: Motor vehicles: 769.8 per 1,000 pop. **Airports:** 8.

Communications: Mobile: 157.8 per 100 pop. **Broadband:** 155 per 100 pop. **Internet:** 100%.

Health: Expend.: 2.9%. **Life expect.:** 78.2 male; 82.4 female. **Births:** 9.2 per 1,000 pop. **Deaths:** 1.4 per 1,000 pop. **Infant mortality:** 6.4 per 1,000 live births. **Undernourished:** NA. **HIV:** <0.1%. **COVID-19:** 690 deaths; rates per 100,000: 17,859 cases, 24 deaths. 99% vaccinated.

Education: Compulsory: ages 6-17. **Literacy:** 97.8%.

Website: hukoomi.gov.qa

Qatar was under Bahrain's control until the Ottoman Turks took power, 1872 to 1915. In a treaty signed 1916, Qatar gave Great Britain responsibility for its defense and foreign relations. Qatar declared itself independent, Sept. 1, 1971. In municipal elections held Mar. 8, 1999, women participated for the first time as candidates and voters. Qatar's emir, Sheikh Hamad bin Khalifa al-Thani, abdicated in favor of his son, Sheikh Tamim bin Hamad al-Thani, June 25, 2013. A major producer and exporter of oil and natural gas, Qatar is one of the world's wealthiest nations per capita.

Since the early 2000s, Qatar has hosted U.S. military facilities and forces. Beginning June 5, 2017, a Saudi-led group of Arab nations, alleging Qatari support for terrorist and sectarian groups, broke diplomatic relations with Qatar and imposed a travel and trade ban. On Aug. 24, Qatar restored full diplomatic relations with Iran (severed in 2016). A member of OPEC since 1961, Qatar left the organization Jan. 1, 2019. An agreement to end the Saudi-led boycott was signed Jan. 5, 2021. Qatar held its first elections, Oct. 2, 2021, for some members of a national advisory council.

Qatar hosted the men's World Cup soccer tournament, Nov.-Dec. 2022. The host country was widely criticized for exploitation and abuse of migrant workers in World Cup-related construction and service jobs.

Romania

People: Population: 18,148,155 (70). **Age distrib.:** <15: 15.4%; 65+: 22.6%. **Growth:** –0.9%. **Migrants:** 3.7%. **Pop. density:** 204.5 per sq mi, 78.9 per sq km. **Urban:** 54.9%. **Ethnic groups:** Romanian 89.3%, Hungarian 6%, Romani 3.4% (Romani pop. usually underestimated; may represent 5%-11% of pop.). **Languages:** Romanian (official), Hungarian. **Religions:** Christian 98.5% (Orthodox 82.7%, Protestant 8.1%).

Geography: Total area: 92,043 sq mi, 238,391 sq km (81); **Land area:** 88,761 sq mi, 229,891 sq km. **Location:** SE Europe, on the Black Sea. Moldova on E, Ukraine on N, Hungary and Serbia on W, Bulgaria on S. **Topography:** The Carpathian Mts. surround the N central Transylvanian plateau. The lower reaches of the Danube river system flow through plains S and E of the mountains. **Arable land:** 35.7%. **Capital:** Bucharest, 1,767,520.

Government: Type: Semi-presidential republic. **Head of state:** Pres. Klaus Iohannis; b. 1959; in office: Dec. 21, 2014. **Head of govt.:** Prime Min. Ion-Marcel Ciolacu; b. 1967; in office: June 15, 2023. **Local divisions:** 41 counties, 1 municipality. **Defense budget:** $8.5 bil. **Active troops:** 69,900.

Economy: Industries: elec. machinery/equip., auto assembly, textiles/footwear, light machinery, metallurgy, chemicals, food proc. **Chief agric.:** wheat, maize, milk, sunflower seeds, barley, potatoes. **Natural resources:** petroleum, timber, nat. gas, coal, iron ore, salt, hydropower. **Water:** 10,969 cu m per capita. **Crude oil reserves:** 600 mil bbls. **Electricity prod.:** 54.8 bil kWh. **Labor force:** agric. 18.0%, industry 32.8%, services 49.2%. **Unemployment:** 5.6%.

Finance: Monetary unit: Leu (RON) (4.46 = $1 U.S.). **GDP:** $912.9 bil; **per capita GDP:** $47,903; **GDP growth:** 2.2%. **Imports:** $154.1 bil; Germany 17%, Italy 8%, Hungary 6%, Turkey (Türkiye) 6%, Poland 6%. **Exports:** $137.3 bil; Germany 19%, Italy 10%, Hungary 7%, France 6%. **Tourism:** $5.0 bil. **Budget:** $83.6 bil. **Inflation:** 10.4%.

Transport: Railways: 6,604 mi. **Motor vehicles:** 484.9 per 1,000 pop. **Airports:** 82.

Communications: Mobile (2022): 121.1 per 100 pop. **Broadband:** 97.8 per 100 pop. **Internet** (2023): 89.2%.

Health: Expend.: 6.5%. **Life expect.:** 73.4 male; 80.5 female. **Births:** 8.5 per 1,000 pop. **Deaths:** 14.6 per 1,000 pop. **Infant mortality:** 5.5 per 1,000 live births. **Undernourished:** <2.5%. **HIV:** 0.2%. **COVID-19:** 68,841 deaths; rates per 100,000: 18,349 cases, 356 deaths. 42% vaccinated.

Education: Compulsory: ages 7-16. **Literacy:** 99.2%.

Website: www.gov.ro

Romania's earliest known people merged with invading Proto-Thracians, preceding by centuries the Dacians. Rome occupied the Dacian kingdom, 106-271 CE; people and language were Romanized. The Turkey-dominated principalities of Wallachia and Moldavia were united in 1859, became Romania in 1861, and gained recognition as an independent kingdom, 1881.

After WWI, Romania acquired Bessarabia, Bukovina, Transylvania, and Banat. In 1940 it ceded Bessarabia and Northern Bukovina to the USSR, part of southern Dobrudja to Bulgaria, and northern Transylvania to Hungary. In 1941, Prem. Marshal Ion Antonescu led Romania in support of Germany against the USSR. He was overthrown in 1944, and Romania joined the Allies. After occupation by Soviet troops, a People's Republic was proclaimed, Dec. 30, 1947.

The domestic policies of Nicolae Ceausescu (in power 1965) were repressive. All industry was state-owned, and state farms and cooperatives owned almost all arable land. Ceausescu's security forces fired on anti-government demonstrators, Dec. 1989, killing hundreds, but when the army sided with the protesters, his regime fell. Ceausescu and his wife were executed Dec. 25, 1989.

A new constitution providing for a multiparty system took effect Dec. 8, 1991. Many state-owned companies were privatized in 1996. Romania became a full NATO member in 2004. It entered the European Union Jan. 1, 2007.

The Social Democratic Party's (PSD) Victor-Viorel Ponta became prime min. May 7, 2012. He ran for president in 2014 but lost the runoff to centrist Klaus Iohannis. Large protests over government incompetence led to Ponta's resignation, Nov. 4, 2015. The PSD's Viorica Dancila became Romania's first female prime min. Jan. 29, 2018. After Dancila, Oct. 10, 2019, lost a no-confidence vote, Ludovic Orban of the center-right National Liberal Party (PNL) became prime min., Nov. 4. Iohannis won reelection in a Nov. 24 presidential runoff (defeating Dancila). After Dec. 6, 2020, parliamentary elections, Nicolae Ciuca of the PNL became prime min., Nov. 25, 2021, heading a broad coalition with the PSD; as agreed, in June 2023, Ciuca resigned and was replaced by the PSD's Ion-Marcel Ciolacu.

Russia

Russian Federation

People: Population: 140,820,810 (9). **Age distrib.:** <15: 16.5%; 65+: 17.8%. **Growth:** –0.5%. **Migrants:** 8.0%. **Pop. density:** 22.3 per sq mi, 8.6 per sq km. **Urban:** 75.5%. **Ethnic groups:** Russian 77.7%, Tatar 3.7%. **Languages:** Russian (official), Tatar. **Religions:** Christian 82.2% (Orthodox 79.5%), Muslim 10.8% (Sunni), agnostic 5.1%.

Geography: Total area: 6,601,668 sq mi, 17,098,242 sq km (1); **Land area:** 6,323,482 sq mi, 16,377,742 sq km, about 76% of total area of the former USSR and the largest country in the world. **Location:** Stretches from Eastern Europe across N Asia to the Pacific O. Finland, Norway, Estonia, Latvia, Belarus, Ukraine on W; Georgia, Azerbaijan, Kazakhstan, China, Mongolia, N. Korea on S; Kaliningrad exclave bordered by Poland on the S, Lithuania on the N and E. **Topography:** Every type of climate except distinctly tropical. European portion is low plain, grassy in S, wooded in N, with Ural Mts. on E and Caucasus Mts. on S. Urals stretch N-S for 2,500 mi. Asiatic portion is vast plain, with mountains on S and in E; tundra covers extreme N with forest belt below; plains, marshes in W, desert in SW. **Arable land:** 7.4%. **Capital:** Moscow, 12,712,305. **Cities:** Saint Petersburg, 5,581,707; Novosibirsk, 1,701,510; Yekaterinburg, 1,532,970; Kazan, 1,296,232; Nizhniy Novgorod, 1,250,302; Chelyabinsk, 1,243,883.

Government: Type: Semi-presidential federation. **Head of state:** Pres. Vladimir Putin; b. 1952; in office: May 7, 2012. **Head of govt.:** Prime Min. Mikhail Mishustin; b. 1966; in office: Jan. 16, 2020. **Local divisions:** 46 provinces (oblasts), 21 republics, 4 autonomous okrugs, 9 krays, 2 federal cities, 1 autonomous oblast. **Defense budget:** $74.8 bil. **Active troops:** 1,100,000.

Economy: Industries: coal, oil, gas, chemicals, metals; machine building; defense (incl. radar, missile prod.); shipbuilding; road, rail transp. equip.; communications equip.; agric. machinery, tractors, constr. equip. **Chief agric.:** wheat, sugar beets, milk, barley, potatoes, sunflower seeds. **Natural resources:** oil, nat. gas, coal, minerals, bauxite, rare earth elements, timber. Climate, terrain, and distance are obstacles to resource exploitation. **Water:** 31,188 cu m per capita. **Crude oil reserves:** 80 bil bbls. **Electricity prod.:** 1.1 tril kWh. **Labor force:** agric. 5.7%, industry 26.6%, services 67.8%. **Unemployment:** 3.3%.

Finance: Monetary unit: Ruble (RUB) (91.50 = $1 U.S.). **GDP:** $6.5 tril; **per capita GDP:** $44,104; **GDP growth:** 3.6%. **Imports:** $378.6 bil; China 39%, Germany 8%, Turkey (Türkiye) 5%, Kazakhstan 5%. **Exports:** $465.4 bil; China 21%, India 8%, Germany 6%, Turkey (Türkiye) 5%, Italy 5%. **Tourism:** $6.7 bil. **Budget:** $571.5 bil. **Inflation** (2020-21): 6.7%.

Transport: Railways: 53,124 mi. **Motor vehicles:** 484.2 per 1,000 pop. **Airports:** 904.

Communications: Mobile (2022): 168.5 per 100 pop. **Broadband** (2022): 110 per 100 pop. **Internet** (2023): 92.2%.

Health: Expend.: 7.4%. **Life expect.:** 67.4 male; 77.4 female. **Births:** 8.4 per 1,000 pop. **Deaths:** 14.0 per 1,000 pop. **Infant mortality:** 6.5 per 1,000 live births. **Undernourished:** <2.5%. **HIV:** NA. **COVID-19:** 403,202 deaths; rates per 100,000: 16,637 cases, 276 deaths. 55% vaccinated.

Education: Compulsory: ages 7-17. **Literacy:** 99.9%.

Website: government.ru

Slavic tribes began migrating into present-day Russia from the W in the 5th cent. Scandinavian chieftains controlled much of today's western Russia beginning in the 9th cent. In the 13th cent., Mongols overran the area. Under the grand dukes and princes of Muscovy, or Moscow, Mongol control was ended by 1480. Ivan the Terrible was proclaimed Tsar of Russia, 1547. Peter the Great (1682-1725) extended the domain and, in 1721, founded the Russian empire. Western ideas and the beginnings of modernization spread through the empire in the 19th and early 20th cent.

Military reverses in the 1905 war with Japan and in WWI led to the breakdown of the Tsarist regime. The 1917 Revolution began in Mar. with a series of sporadic strikes for higher wages by factory workers. A provisional democratic government under Prince Georgi Lvov was established but a second provisional government, under Alexander Kerensky, followed in May. Vladimir Ilyich Lenin, Nov. 7, overthrew the Kerensky government and the freely elected Constituent Assembly in a Communist coup.

Soviet Union. Lenin's death Jan. 21, 1924, led to an internal power struggle won by Joseph Stalin. His brutal tactics, including purge trials, mass executions, and exile to work camps, resulted in millions of deaths.

Despite a Germany-USSR non-aggression pact signed in Aug. 1939, Germany invaded the Soviet Union, June 1941. Russian winter counterthrusts, 1941-42 and 1942-43; victory at Stalingrad (now Volgograd), Feb. 2, 1943 (2 mil total casualties); and resistance to the siege of Leningrad (now St. Petersburg) stopped the German advance. Russian armies drove the Germans from Russia, Eastern Europe, and the Balkans in the next two years.

After WWII, Communists took over in countries throughout the region, extending the Soviet sphere of influence. The USSR and the U.S., the world's leading nuclear superpowers, became Cold War rivals. After Stalin died, Mar. 5, 1953, Nikita Khrushchev gained power and denounced Stalin, 1956, beginning "de-Stalinization."

Under Khrushchev the open antagonism of Poles and Hungarians toward Moscow's domination was suppressed in 1956. He aided the Cuban revolution under Fidel Castro but withdrew Soviet missiles from Cuba during a confrontation with U.S. Pres. John Kennedy, Sept.-Oct. 1962. Khrushchev was deposed, Oct. 1964, and replaced by Leonid I. Brezhnev. In Aug. 1968, Soviet forces invaded Czechoslovakia, crushing liberalization there.

Massive Soviet military aid to North Vietnam in the late 1960s and early 1970s helped ensure Communist victories throughout Indochina. In Dec. 1979, Soviet forces entered Afghanistan to support a pro-Soviet regime against U.S.-supported Muslim resistance fighters. In Apr. 1988, the Soviets agreed to withdraw their troops, ending a futile 8-year war.

Mikhail Gorbachev was chosen Communist Party gen. sec., Mar. 1985. In 1987 he initiated a program of political and economic reforms through openness (*glasnost*) and restructuring (*perestroika*). Gorbachev faced economic problems as well as ethnic and nationalist unrest in the republics. A coup by Communist hardliners Aug. 1991 was foiled with help from Russian Republic Pres. Boris Yeltsin. On Aug. 24, Gorbachev resigned as leader of the Communist Party. Several republics declared their independence. On Aug. 29, the Soviet Parliament voted to suspend all activities of the Communist Party. The Soviet Union officially broke up Dec. 26, 1991.

Russian Federation. Under Pres. Yeltsin, Russia took steps toward privatization, which caused inflation and a severe economic downturn. In June 1992, Yeltsin and U.S. Pres. George H. W. Bush agreed to massive arms reductions. Russian troops fought rebels in the breakaway republic of Chechnya Dec. 1994-Aug. 1996, when a peace accord temporarily ended the conflict.

An Aug. 1999 operation to suppress Islamic rebels in the republic of Dagestan reignited the war in neighboring Chechnya, where Russia launched a full-scale assault. Yeltsin unexpectedly resigned Dec. 31, 1999, naming Prime Min. Vladimir Putin as his interim successor. Putin won presidential elections Mar. 2000 and Mar. 2004. Putin's allies won legislative elections, Dec. 2003.

After Chechen rebels, Sept. 1, 2004, seized control of a school in Beslan, North Ossetia, Russian troops stormed the school Sept. 3; more than 330 people, including 186 children, died. Putin cited the terrorist threat Sept. 13 in proposing a government overhaul that tightened his control over parliament and regional officeholders. Russian forces killed Chechen rebel leader Aslan Maskhadov, Mar. 8, 2005, and Chechen guerrilla leader Shamil Basayev, organizer of the Beslan attack, July 10, 2006.

Constitutionally barred from seeking another term, Pres. Putin backed his protégé Prime Min. Dmitri Medvedev, who won the presidential election Mar. 2, 2008. Medvedev named Putin as prime min. Russian troops, Aug. 2008, supported secessionists in Georgia's enclaves of South Ossetia and Abkhazia, which Russia recognized as independent, Aug. 26.

Russia declared, Apr. 16, 2009, that it had ended counterterrorism operations in Chechnya; from June through Aug., there was an upsurge of insurgent violence in Chechnya and neighboring Dagestan and Ingushetia. Suicide bombers from Dagestan struck two Moscow subway stations Mar. 29, 2010, killing 40 people.

Medvedev and U.S. Pres. Barack Obama, Apr. 8, 2010, signed a nuclear arms reduction treaty known as New START. Putin won the Mar. 4, 2012, presidential election, though there were claims of fraud. Putin signed a law, June 30, 2013, effectively making it illegal to advocate publicly for gay rights. Persecution of LBGTQ people increased in subsequent years. A 2020 constitutional amendment defined marriage as only between a man and a woman.

In 2014, Russia sent troops into Ukraine's Crimean Peninsula and annexed Crimea Mar. 18. Russia also provided military support to pro-Russian separatists in eastern Ukraine beginning in Apr. 2014.

Russia supported Pres. Bashar al-Assad in Syria's civil war beginning in 2011. Russian airstrikes, starting in 2015, against various rebel forces, including ISIS, and rebel-held areas caused high civilian casualties. An ISIS-affiliated group claimed responsibility for planting a bomb on a Russian airliner that crashed in Egypt, Oct. 31, 2015, killing all 224 onboard.

Putin's United Russia party won Sept. 18, 2016, parliamentary elections. With the media tightly controlled and amid allegations of fraud, Putin won a new 6-year term as president, Mar. 18, 2018; leading dissident Alexei Navalny was barred from running. Constitutional changes approved in 2020 allowed Putin to serve two more terms as president.

U.S. government security agencies concluded in Dec. 2016 that Russia attempted to interfere in the 2016 U.S. presidential election, apparently to assist the candidacy of Donald Trump, using tactics including cyberattacks and manipulation of social media. U.S. officials concluded that Russia attempted to interfere in the 2018, 2020, and 2022 elections as well. The U.S. State Dept. estimated in Sept.

2022 that Russia had spent at least $300 mil since 2014 to influence politics in more than two dozen countries around the world.

Russian agents were apparently responsible for the poisoning, in the UK in Mar. 2018, of a former Russian intelligence officer. Navalny was apparently poisoned, Aug. 20, 2020. He was arrested, Jan. 17, 2021, subsequently sentenced to prison on various charges, and died in prison Feb. 16, 2024.

Beginning in 2014, the U.S. accused Russia of violating the 1987 Intermediate-Range Nuclear Forces (INF) Treaty. The U.S. withdrew from the INF treaty Aug. 2, 2019. A 5-year extension, agreed to by Russia and the U.S., of the New START treaty went into effect Feb. 2021, but Putin announced, Feb. 21, 2023, that Russia would suspend participation.

Putin's party swept Sept. 2021 parliamentary elections. Opposition leaders charged fraud. Russia was one of the world's most severely affected countries by the COVID-19 pandemic. A May 2022 WHO report estimated 1 mil excess COVID-related deaths in Russia in 2020-21, more than triple its reported number.

On Feb. 24, 2022, Russia launched a large-scale invasion of Ukraine. The U.S., the EU, and other nations imposed sanctions that hurt the Russian economy. Russia gained control of extensive areas of eastern and southern Ukraine. Russian attacks caused high Ukrainian civilian casualties, and Russian troops were accused of war crimes. After sham referenda in Russian-controlled parts of four eastern and southern Ukrainian provinces, Putin signed legislation, Oct. 5, 2022, to annex the four regions. Beginning in 2023, Ukraine increasingly launched drone and other attacks against targets in Russia—including a ground offensive, started Aug. 6, 2024, into the Kursk region. By mid-2024, the U.S. estimated that Russian troops killed or wounded in Ukraine totaled about 350,000.

On June 23-24, 2023, mercenaries in the Wagner Group (which had been fighting in Ukraine), led by Yevgeny Prigozhin, mutinied and advanced toward Moscow before withdrawing. Prigozhin died, Aug. 23, 2023, when his plane apparently exploded midflight. In a sham election, Mar. 2024, Putin won a new term as president. At least 145 died in a terrorist attack on a concert hall near Moscow, Mar. 22; a branch of ISIS claimed responsibility.

In recent years, authorities have arrested a number of Americans in Russia. WNBA star Brittney Griner was convicted on a drug charge, Aug. 4, 2022, but freed in a prisoner exchange Dec. 8, 2022. A multinational prisoner exchange, Aug. 1, 2024, freed several Americans (including journalist Evan Gershkovich, convicted of espionage, which he denied), Russian dissidents, and others.

Rwanda

Republic of Rwanda

People: Population: 13,623,302 (76). **Age distrib.:** <15: 37.2%; 65+: 3.1%. **Growth:** 1.6%. **Migrants:** 4.0%. **Pop. density:** 1,430.4 per sq mi, 552.3 per sq km. **Urban:** 18.1%. **Ethnic groups:** Hutu, Tutsi, Twa. **Languages:** Kinyarwanda (universal Bantu vernacular), French, English, Swahili/Kiswahili (all official). **Religions:** Christian 91.8% (Catholic 41.3%, Protestant 35.7%, independent 14.8%), Muslim 4.9% (Sunni), ethnic religionist 2.8%.

Geography: Total area: 10,169 sq mi, 26,338 sq km (145); **Land area:** 9,524 sq mi, 24,668 sq km. **Location:** E central Africa. Uganda on N, Dem. Rep. of the Congo on W, Burundi on S, Tanzania on E. **Topography:** Grassy uplands and hills cover most of country, with chain of volcanoes in NW. Nile R. source is in headwaters of the Kagera (Akagera) R. **Arable land:** 51.4%. **Capital:** Kigali, 1,287,952.

Government: Type: Presidential republic. **Head of state:** Pres. Paul Kagame; b. 1957; in office: Apr. 22, 2000 (de facto from Mar. 24). **Head of govt.:** Prime Min. Edouard Ngirente; b. 1973; in office: Aug. 30, 2017. **Local divisions:** 4 provinces, 1 city. **Defense budget:** $193 mil. **Active troops:** 33,000.

Economy: Industries: cement, agric. prods., small-scale beverages, soap, furniture, shoes, plastic goods, textiles, cigarettes. **Chief agric.:** bananas, cassava, sweet potatoes, potatoes, plantains, maize. **Natural resources:** gold, tin ore, tungsten ore, methane, hydropower. **Water:** 988 cu m per capita. **Electricity prod.:** 979.9 mil kWh. **Labor force:** agric. 56.0%, industry 14.4%, services 29.6%. **Unemployment:** 14.9%.

Finance: Monetary unit: Franc (RWF) (1,332.01 = $1 U.S.). **GDP:** $47.4 bil; **per capita GDP:** $3,361; **GDP growth:** 8.2%. **Imports:** $5.8 bil; China 19%, Tanzania 11%, Kenya 10%, UAE 10%, India 7%. **Exports:** $3.5 bil; UAE 32%, Dem. Rep. of the Congo 25%, Thailand 5%. **Tourism:** $564 mil. **Budget:** $2.9 bil. **Inflation:** 19.8%.

Transport: Airports: 8.

Communications: Mobile: 91.5 per 100 pop. **Broadband:** 66.5 per 100 pop. **Internet:** 34.4%.

Health: Expend.: 7.3%. **Life expect.:** 64.6 male; 68.6 female. **Births:** 25.0 per 1,000 pop. **Deaths:** 5.7 per 1,000 pop. **Infant mortality:** 24.9 per 1,000 live births. **Undernourished:** 31.4%. **HIV:** 2.2%. **COVID-19:** 1,468 deaths; rates per 100,000: 1,029 cases, 11 deaths. 80% vaccinated.

Education: Compulsory: ages 6-11. **Literacy:** 78.8%.

Website: www.gov.rw

For centuries, the Tutsi dominated the Hutu majority. A civil war broke out in 1959 and Tutsi power was ended. Many Tutsi went into exile. Rwanda, which had been part of the Belgian UN trusteeship of Rwanda-Urundi, became independent July 1, 1962.

A large-scale massacre of Tutsi occurred in 1963. Hutu rivalries led to a bloodless coup July 1973 in which Hutu army officer Juvénal Habyarimana took power. After an invasion and coup attempt by Tutsi exiles in 1990, a multiparty democracy was established.

Renewed ethnic strife led to an Aug. 1993 peace accord between the government and rebels of the Tutsi-led Rwandan Patriotic Front (RPF). But after Habyarimana and Burundi Pres. Cyprien Ntaryamira were killed Apr. 6, 1994, in a suspicious plane crash, violence broke out. More than 1 mil may have died in massacres, mostly of Tutsi by Hutu militias, and in civil warfare as the RPF sought power. About 2 mil Tutsi and Hutu fled to camps in Zaire (now Dem. Rep. of the Congo, or DRC) and other countries; many died of disease. French troops under a UN mandate temporarily moved into SW Rwanda June 23 to establish a safe zone. The RPF claimed victory, installing a government led by a moderate Hutu president in July. More than 1 mil refugees, mostly Hutu, returned to Rwanda in Nov.-Dec. 1996.

Former Prime Min. Jean Kambanda pleaded guilty to genocide, May 1, 1998, before the UN-backed Intl. Criminal Tribunal for Rwanda (ICTR); he received a life sentence Sept. 4, 1998. RPF leader Maj. Gen. Paul Kagame became Rwanda's first Tutsi president Apr. 22, 2000.

Rwandans approved a new constitution, May 26, 2003, and reelected Pres. Kagame, Aug. 25. Rwanda cut diplomatic ties with France Nov. 24, 2006, after a French judge linked Kagame to the 1994 deaths of Habyarimana and Ntaryamira. The country restored relations with France, Nov. 2009, the same month Rwanda joined the Commonwealth. Accused of being one of the architects of the 1994 genocide, Col. Theoneste Bagosora was convicted and sentenced to prison by the ICTR, Dec. 18, 2008. A Rwandan court Jan. 20, 2009, sentenced former Justice Min. Agnes Ntamabyariro to life in prison for her role in inciting the massacres. Up to 4,000 Rwandan troops fought that month alongside Congolese forces against Hutu militias in eastern DRC. After a campaign criticized as repressive by human rights groups, Pres. Kagame won reelection Aug. 9, 2010.

An Oct. 17, 2012, UN report found that the Rwanda military was backing a rebellion (2012-13) by the mostly-Tutsi M23 group in the DRC. In the 2020s, M23, again apparently backed by Rwanda, increased military operations in the eastern DRC.

Suppressing political opposition, Kagame won—with almost 99% of the vote—a new term as president in an Aug. 4, 2017, election. Dissident Paul Rusesabagina, whose protection of over 1,200 Tutsi from the 1994 genocide was dramatized in the film *Hotel Rwanda*, was arrested, Aug. 2020, on terrorism charges. He was convicted and sentenced to 25 years in prison, Sept. 20, 2021. After widespread criticism of Rwanda's actions, the sentence was commuted and Rusesabagina was released, Mar. 24, 2023. Kagame won reelection, officially with over 99% of the vote, July 15, 2024.

Saint Kitts and Nevis

Federation of Saint Kitts and Nevis

People: Population: 55,133 (189). **Age distrib.:** <15: 19.2%; 65+: 12.7%. **Growth:** 0.6%. **Migrants:** 14.5%. **Pop. density:** 547.1 per sq mi, 211.2 per sq km. **Urban:** 31.2%. **Ethnic groups:** African descent 92.5%, mixed 3%, white 2.1%. **Languages:** English (official). **Religions:** Christian 94.5% (Protestant 75.2%, independent 12.0%).

Geography: Total area: 101 sq mi, 261 sq km (189); **Land area:** 101 sq mi, 261 sq km. **Location:** In N part of the Leeward group of Lesser Antilles in E Caribbean Sea. Antigua and Barbuda to E. **Topography:** Forested volcanic slopes on St. Kitts; beaches rising to central peak on Nevis. Tropical climate moderated by sea breezes. **Arable land:** 19.2%. **Capital:** Basseterre, 14,434.

Government: Type: Federal parliamentary democracy under constitutional monarchy. **Head of state:** King Charles III, rep. by Gov.-Gen. Marcella Liburd; in office: Feb. 1, 2023. **Head of govt.:** Prime Min. Terrance Drew; b. 1976; in office: Aug. 6, 2022. **Local divisions:** 14 parishes. **Defense budget/active troops:** NA.

Economy: Industries: tourism, cotton, salt, copra, clothing, footwear, beverages. **Chief agric.:** coconuts, tropical fruits, root vegetables, vegetables, eggs, pulses. **Water:** 504 cu m per capita. **Electricity prod.:** 217.0 mil kWh. **Labor force:** NA. **Unemployment:** NA.

Finance: Monetary unit: East Caribbean Dollar (XCD) (2.70 = $1 U.S.). **GDP:** $1.6 bil; **per capita GDP:** $33,403; **GDP growth:** 3.4%. **Imports:** $674.1 mil; U.S. 47%, Italy 9%, Turkey (Türkiye) 6%, Trinidad and Tobago 6%, China 5%. **Exports:** $577.6 mil; U.S. 61%, India 7%, Trinidad and Tobago 5%. **Tourism:** $159 mil. **Budget** (2020): $324 mil. **Inflation:** 3.6%.

Transport: Railways: 31 mi. **Airports:** 2.

Communications: Mobile: 118.9 per 100 pop. **Broadband** (2022): 119 per 100 pop. **Internet:** 76.5%.

Health: Expend.: 6.2%. **Life expect.:** 75.2 male; 80.1 female. **Births:** 11.8 per 1,000 pop. **Deaths:** 7.4 per 1,000 pop. **Infant mortality:** 8.0 per 1,000 live births. **Undernourished:** NA. **HIV:** NA. **COVID-19:** 46 deaths; rates per 100,000: 12,421 cases, 86 deaths. 51% vaccinated.

Education: Compulsory: ages 5-16. **Literacy:** NA.
Website: www.gov.kn

St. Kitts (formerly St. Christopher; known by Indigenous peoples as Liamuiga) and Nevis were reached by Columbus in 1493. They were settled by Britain in 1623 (ownership was disputed with France until 1713). The colony achieved self-government in 1967, becoming independent, Sept. 19, 1983. Twenty years of Labour Party governments ended when an opposition coalition won Feb. 16, 2015, legislative elections. The coalition won June 5, 2020, elections, but Aug. 5, 2022, elections returned Labour to power.

Saint Lucia

People: Population: 168,038 (178). **Age distrib.:** <15: 17.9%; 65+: 15.4%. **Growth:** 0.3%. **Migrants:** 4.5%. **Pop. density:** 718.2 per sq mi, 277.3 per sq km. **Urban:** 19.3%. **Ethnic groups:** Black/African descent 85.3%, mixed 10.9%, East Indian 2.2%. **Languages:** English (official), Saint Lucian Creole. **Religions:** Christian 95.5% (Catholic 69.8%, Protestant 22.5%).

Geography: Total area: 238 sq mi, 616 sq km (179); **Land area:** 234 sq mi, 606 sq km. **Location:** E Caribbean, second largest of Windward Isls. Martinique (Fr.) to N, St. Vincent to S. **Topography:** Mountainous, volcanic in origin; Soufrière Volcanic Centre in S. Wooded mountains run N-S. **Arable land:** 4.4%. **Capital:** Castries, 22,258.

Government: Type: Parliamentary democracy under constitutional monarchy. **Head of state:** King Charles III, rep. by Acting Gov.-Gen. Errol Charles, in office: Nov. 11, 2021. **Head of govt.:** Prime Min. Philip J. Pierre; in office: July 28, 2021. **Local divisions:** 10 districts. **Defense budget/active troops:** NA.

Economy: Industries: tourism, clothing, electronic components assembly, beverages, corrugated cardboard boxes, lime proc. **Chief agric.:** coconuts, bananas, tropical fruits, fruits, plantains, root vegetables. **Natural resources:** forests, sandy beaches, pumice, mineral springs. **Water:** 1,670 cu m per capita. **Electricity prod.:** 391.4 mil kWh. **Labor force:** agric. 10.5%, industry 16.8%, services 72.7%. **Unemployment:** 11.1%.

Finance: Monetary unit: East Caribbean Dollar (XCD) (2.70 = $1 U.S.). **GDP:** $4.5 bil; **per capita GDP:** $25,129; **GDP growth:** 3.2%. **Imports:** $1.3 bil; U.S. 76%. **Exports:** $1.4 bil; U.S. 17%, Guyana 16%, Trinidad and Tobago 14%, Barbados 9%, Suriname 7%. **Tourism:** $1.2 bil. **Budget** (2020): $516 mil. **Inflation:** 4.1%.

Transport: Airports: 2.

Communications: Mobile (2022): 98.7 per 100 pop. **Broadband** (2022): 63.6 per 100 pop. **Internet:** 74.2%.

Health: Expend.: 6.2%. **Life expect.:** 76.7 male; 82.3 female. **Births:** 11.4 per 1,000 pop. **Deaths:** 8.3 per 1,000 pop. **Infant mortality:** 11.5 per 1,000 live births. **Undernourished:** NA. **HIV:** NA. **COVID-19:** 410 deaths; rates per 100,000: 16,492 cases, 223 deaths. 30% vaccinated.

Education: Compulsory: ages 5-14. **Literacy:** NA.
Website: www.govt.lc

St. Lucia, ceded to Britain by France with the Treaty of Paris, 1814, gained independence Feb. 22, 1979. The conservative United Workers Party (UWP) defeated the governing St. Lucia Labor Party (SLP) in June 6, 2016, elections. The SLP returned to power following July 26, 2021, elections.

The COVID-19 pandemic severely hurt the important tourism industry. GDP began recovering in 2021 after a 20% drop in 2020.

Saint Vincent and the Grenadines

People: Population: 100,647 (183). **Age distrib.:** <15: 18.8%; 65+: 13.0%. **Growth:** –0.2%. **Migrants:** 4.3%. **Pop. density:** 670.1 per sq mi, 258.7 per sq km. **Urban:** 54.7%. **Ethnic groups:** African descent 71.2%, mixed 23%, Indigenous 3%. **Languages:** English, Vincentian Creole English, French patois. **Religions:** Christian 88.7% (Protestant 62.2%, independent 21.5%), Hindu 3.3%, agnostic 2.6%.

Geography: Total area: 150 sq mi, 389 sq km (185); **Land area:** 150 sq mi, 389 sq km. **Location:** E Caribbean; St. Vincent (133 sq mi) and the northern islets of the Grenadines form a part of Windward chain. St. Lucia to N, Barbados to E, Grenada to S. **Topography:** St. Vincent is volcanic, with a ridge of thickly wooded mountains running its length. **Arable land:** 5.1%. **Capital:** Kingstown, 26,636.

Government: Type: Parliamentary democracy under constitutional monarchy. **Head of state:** King Charles III, rep. by Gov.-Gen. Susan Dougan; in office: Aug. 1, 2019. **Head of govt.:** Prime Min. Ralph Gonsalves; b. 1946; in office: Mar. 29, 2001. **Local divisions:** 6 parishes. **Defense budget/active troops:** NA.

Economy: Industries: tourism, food proc., cement, furniture, clothing, starch. **Chief agric.:** bananas, root vegetables, plantains, vegetables, fruits, coconuts. **Natural resources:** hydropower. **Water:** 958 cu m per capita. **Electricity prod.:** 173.2 mil kWh. **Labor force:** agric. 9.7%, industry 19.9%, services 70.4%. **Unemployment:** 18.7%.

Finance: Monetary unit: East Caribbean Dollar (XCD) (2.70 = $1 U.S.). **GDP:** $2.1 bil; **per capita GDP:** $19,876; **GDP growth:** 6.0%. **Imports:** $566.5 mil; U.S. 40%, Trinidad and Tobago 10%, China 6%, UK 6%, Turkey (Türkiye) 5%. **Exports:** $347.8 mil; Malaysia 34%, U.S. 10%, Greece 9%, Barbados 8%, Spain 6%. **Tourism:** $209 mil. **Budget** (2020): $288 mil. **Inflation:** 4.6%.

Transport: Airports: 5.

Communications: Mobile: 101.6 per 100 pop. **Broadband:** 62.3 per 100 pop. **Internet:** 77.7%.

Health: Expend.: 5.4%. **Life expect.:** 75.2 male; 79.3 female. **Births:** 11.9 per 1,000 pop. **Deaths:** 7.7 per 1,000 pop. **Infant mortality:** 12.3 per 1,000 live births. **Undernourished:** 4.8%. **HIV:** NA. **COVID-19:** 124 deaths; rates per 100,000: 8,720 cases, 112 deaths. 29% vaccinated.

Education: Compulsory: ages 5-16. **Literacy:** NA.
Website: www.gov.vc

St. Vincent received its name because of the unsupported belief that Christopher Columbus landed there on Jan. 22, 1498 (St. Vincent's Day). Britain and France laid claim to the island in the 17th and 18th cent.; the Treaty of Versailles, 1783, ceded it to Britain. Independence came Oct. 27, 1979.

Samoa
Independent State of Samoa

People: Population: 208,853 (177). **Age distrib.:** <15: 26.9%; 65+: 7.2%. **Growth:** 0.7%. **Migrants:** 2.0%. **Pop. density:** 191.8 per sq mi, 74.0 per sq km. **Urban:** 17.4%. **Ethnic groups** (by citizenship): Samoan 96%, Samoan/New Zealander 2%. **Languages:** Samoan (Polynesian), English (both official). **Religions:** Christian 98.8% (Protestant 49.7%, independent 34.3%, Catholic 14.7%).

Geography: Total area: 1,093 sq mi, 2,831 sq km (168); **Land area:** 1,089 sq mi, 2,821 sq km. **Location:** S Pacific O. Nearest neighbors are Fiji to SW, Tonga to S. **Topography:** Main islands, Savaii (659 sq mi) and Upolu (432 sq mi), both ruggedly mountainous. Small islands of Manono and Apolima. **Arable land:** 4.1%. **Capital:** Apia, 36,066.

Government: Type: Parliamentary republic. **Head of state:** Tuimaleali'ifano Va'aletoa Sualauvi II; b. 1947; in office: July 21, 2017. **Head of govt.:** Prime Min. Fiame Naomi Mata'afa; b. 1957; in office: July 28, 2021. **Local divisions:** 11 districts. **Defense budget/active troops:** NA.

Economy: Industries: food proc., building materials, auto parts. **Chief agric.:** coconuts, taro, bananas, tropical fruits, pineapples, mangoes/guavas. **Natural resources:** hardwood forests, fish, hydropower. **Water:** 0 cu m per capita. **Electricity prod.:** 194.5 mil kWh. **Labor force:** agric. 20.1%, industry 16.3%, services 63.6%. **Unemployment:** 9.7%.

Finance: Monetary unit: Tala (WST) (2.71 = $1 U.S.). **GDP:** $1.5 bil; **per capita GDP:** $6,681; **GDP growth:** 8.0%. **Imports:** $560.5 mil; China 25%, Singapore 16%, New Zealand 14%, South Korea 7%, U.S. 7%. **Exports:** $347.2 mil; India 23%, U.S. 19%, New Zealand 12%, Hungary 8%, Poland 6%. **Tourism:** $220 mil. **Budget** (2020): $263 mil. **Inflation:** 8.1%.

Transport: Airports: 3.

Communications: Mobile (2022): 62.4 per 100 pop. **Broadband** (2022): 34.8 per 100 pop. **Internet:** 75.3%.

Health: Expend.: 6.8%. **Life expect.:** 72.8 male; 78.7 female. **Births:** 18.8 per 1,000 pop. **Deaths:** 5.4 per 1,000 pop. **Infant mortality:** 17.3 per 1,000 live births. **Undernourished:** 5.4%. **HIV:** NA. **COVID-19:** 31 deaths; rates per 100,000: 8,597 cases, 16 deaths. 90% vaccinated.

Education: Compulsory: ages 5-12. **Literacy:** 99.1%.
Website: www.samoagovt.ws

Samoa (formerly Western Samoa) was a German colony, 1899 to 1914, when New Zealand landed troops and took over. It became a New Zealand mandate under the League of Nations and, in 1945, a New Zealand UN Trusteeship. An elected local government took office in Oct. 1959, and the country became fully independent Jan. 1, 1962. In 2011, Samoa moved west of the Intl. Date Line to reduce time differences with Australia and New Zealand. A new party headed by Fiame Naomi Mata'afa defeated the party of Prime Min. Tuila'epa Sailele Malielegaoi (in office more than two decades) in Apr. 9, 2021, elections. After a constitutional crisis in which Tuila'epa refused to concede, Fiame became Samoa's first female prime minister. Samoa and China signed a cooperation agreement, May 28, 2022.

San Marino
Republic of San Marino

People: Population: 35,095 (191). **Age distrib.:** <15: 14.2%; 65+: 21.5%. **Growth:** 0.6%. **Migrants:** 16.3%. **Pop. density:** 1,490.1 per sq mi, 575.3 per sq km. **Urban:** 97.9%. **Ethnic groups:** Sammarinese, Italian. **Languages:** Italian. **Religions:** Christian 91.3% (Catholic), agnostic 5.8%.

Geography: Total area: 24 sq mi, 61 sq km (192); **Land area:** 24 sq mi, 61 sq km. **Location:** Completely surrounded by Italy, in N center of that country, near Adriatic coast. **Topography:** On slopes of Mt. Titano. **Arable land:** 33.1%. **Capital:** San Marino, 4,465.

Government: Type: Parliamentary republic. **Heads of state:** Two captains regent, elected by parliament from among its members, to 6-month term. **Head of govt.:** Sec. of State for Foreign and Political Affairs Luca Beccari; b. 1974; in office: Jan. 8, 2020. **Local divisions:** 9 municipalities. **Defense budget/active troops:** NA.

Economy: Industries: tourism, banking, textiles, electronics, ceramics, cement, wine. **Chief agric.:** wheat, grapes, corn, olives; cattle, pigs. **Natural resources:** building stone. **Water:** NA. **Labor force:** NA. **Unemployment:** NA.

Finance: Monetary unit: Euro (EUR) (0.90 = $1 U.S.). **GDP** (2021): $2.2 bil; **per capita GDP** (2021): $65,718; **GDP growth** (2021): 8.5%. **Imports** (2021): $2.9 bil; Italy 22%, Germany 20%, Poland 7%, Spain 7%, Netherlands 7%. **Exports** (2021): $3.4 bil; U.S. 10%, Germany 9%, France 9%, Austria 9%, Romania 7%. **Tourism** (2021): $225 mil. **Budget:** $363 mil. **Inflation** (2016-17): 1.0%.

Transport: Airports: 1.

Communications: Mobile (2022): 120.3 per 100 pop. **Broadband** (2022): 135 per 100 pop. **Internet:** 85.1%.

Health: Expend.: 8.0%. **Life expect.:** 81.7 male; 87.0 female. **Births:** 9.0 per 1,000 pop. **Deaths:** 8.9 per 1,000 pop. **Infant mortality:** 6.2 per 1,000 live births. **Undernourished:** NA. **HIV:** NA. **COVID-19:** 126 deaths; rates per 100,000: 74,524 cases, 371 deaths. 70% vaccinated.

Education: Compulsory: ages 6-15. **Literacy:** 99.9%.

Website: www.gov.sm

San Marino, founded in the 4th cent., claims to be the world's oldest republic. It has a treaty of friendship with Italy. In 2021, referendum voters approved legalizing abortion in the first 12 weeks of pregnancy. An alliance led by the Sammarinese Christian Democratic Party and socialist parties did well in June 9, 2024, parliamentary elections and formed a coalition government.

São Tomé and Príncipe

Democratic Republic of São Tomé and Príncipe

People: Population: 223,561 (176). **Age distrib.:** <15: 36.4%; 65+: 3.2%. **Growth:** 1.4%. **Migrants:** 1.0%. **Pop. density:** 600.6 per sq mi, 231.9 per sq km. **Urban:** 77.0%. **Ethnic groups:** mestico, angolares (descendants of Angolan slaves), forros (descendants of freed slaves), servicais (contract laborers fr. Angola, Mozambique, Cabo Verde), tongas (children of servicais born on the islands), Europeans (primarily Portuguese), Asians (mostly Chinese). **Languages:** Portuguese (official), Forro, Cabo Verdian, French, Angolar, English. **Religions:** Christian 95.9% (Catholic 73.6%, independent 15.9%), Baha'i 2.3%.

Geography: Total area: 372 sq mi, 964 sq km (172); **Land area:** 372 sq mi, 964 sq km. **Location:** Gulf of Guinea about 125 mi off W central Africa. Gabon, Equatorial Guinea to E. **Topography:** Part of an extinct volcano chain; lush forests and croplands. **Arable land:** 4.2%. **Capital:** São Tomé, 80,099.

Government: Type: Semi-presidential republic. **Head of state:** Pres. Carlos Vila Nova; b. 1956; in office: Oct. 2, 2021. **Head of govt.:** Prime Min. Patrice Trovoada; b. 1962; in office: Nov. 11, 2022. **Local divisions:** 6 districts, 1 autonomous region. **Defense budget/active troops:** NA.

Economy: Industries: light constr., textiles, soap, beer, fish proc., timber. **Chief agric.:** plantains, oil palm fruit, taro, bananas, fruits, cocoa beans. **Natural resources:** fish, hydropower. **Water:** 9,771 cu m per capita. **Electricity prod.:** 136.2 mil kWh. **Labor force:** agric. 17.1%, industry 20.0%, services 62.8%. **Unemployment:** 14.2%.

Finance: Monetary unit: Dobra (STN) (22.14 = $1 U.S.). **GDP:** $1.4 bil; **per capita GDP:** $6,064; **GDP growth:** –0.5%. **Imports** (2022): $219.3 mil; Portugal 35%, Angola 18%, Togo 13%, China 6%, Italy 5%. **Exports** (2022): $97.0 mil; Netherlands 26%, France 11%, Belgium 11%, Portugal 8%, Angola 6%. **Tourism** (2022): $48 mil. **Budget:** $102 mil. **Inflation:** 21.3%.

Transport: Airports: 2.

Communications: Mobile: 65.9 per 100 pop. **Broadband:** 42 per 100 pop. **Internet:** 57%.

Health: Expend.: 7.8%. **Life expect.:** 66.0 male; 69.4 female. **Births:** 26.7 per 1,000 pop. **Deaths:** 6.0 per 1,000 pop. **Infant mortality:** 42.6 per 1,000 live births. **Undernourished:** 16.4%. **HIV:** NA. **COVID-19:** 80 deaths; rates per 100,000: 3,090 cases, 37 deaths. 51% vaccinated.

Education: Compulsory: ages 6-11. **Literacy:** 93.8%.

Website: www.parlamento.st

The Portuguese reached the islands in 1471 and brought the first inhabitants—convicts and exiled Jews. Sugarcane planting was replaced by the slave trade as the chief economic activity until coffee and cocoa were introduced in the 19th cent.

Portugal agreed, 1974, to turn the colony over to the Gabon-based Movement for the Liberation of São Tomé and Príncipe; its East German-trained leader, Manuel Pinto da Costa, became the country's first president. Independence came July 12, 1975. Democratic reforms were instituted in 1987.

The country, one of the world's poorest, has sought to develop oil deposits in the Gulf of Guinea and tourism. Seeking aid and investment, São Tomé broke diplomatic ties with Taiwan and established relations with China, Dec. 2016. Carlos Vila Nova of the Independent Democratic Action (ADI) party won a Sept. 5, 2021, presidential runoff election. The ADI, formerly in opposition, won the most votes in Sept. 25, 2022, parliamentary elections; the ADI's Patrice Trovoada became prime minister Nov. 11, 2022.

Saudi Arabia

Kingdom of Saudi Arabia

People: Population: 36,544,431 (41). **Age distrib.:** <15: 22.9%; 65+: 4.4%. **Growth:** 1.7%. **Migrants:** 38.6%. **Pop. density:** 44.0 per sq mi, 17.0 per sq km. **Urban:** 85.2%. **Ethnic groups:** Arab 90%, Afro-Asian 10%. **Languages:** Arabic (official). **Religions:** Muslim (official) 90.2% (Sunni 81%, Shia 9%), Christian 6.1% (Catholic), Hindu 2.1%.

Geography: Total area: 830,000 sq mi, 2,149,690 sq km (12); **Land area:** 830,000 sq mi, 2,149,690 sq km. **Location:** Occupies most of Arabian Peninsula in Middle East. Kuwait, Iraq, Jordan on N; Yemen, Oman on S; UAE, Qatar on E. **Topography:** Bordered by Red Sea on W. Highlands in W slope as barren desert to the Persian Gulf on E. **Arable land:** 1.6%. **Capital:** Riyadh, 7,820,551. **Cities:** Jiddah, 4,943,210; Mecca, 2,184,560; Medina, 1,598,976; Ad-Dammam, 1,352,912.

Government: Type: Absolute monarchy. **Head of state:** King Salman bin Abdul Aziz; b. 1924; in office: Jan. 23, 2015. **Head of govt.:** Mohammed bin Salman; b. 1985; in office: Sept. 27, 2022. **Local divisions:** 13 regions. **Defense budget:** $69.1 bil. **Active troops:** 257,000.

Economy: Industries: crude oil prod., petroleum refining, basic petrochemicals, ammonia, industrial gases, caustic soda, cement, fertilizer. **Chief agric.:** milk, dates, chicken, wheat, tomatoes, potatoes. **Natural resources:** petroleum, nat. gas, iron ore, gold, copper. **Water:** 67 cu m per capita. **Crude oil reserves:** 258.6 bil bbls (incl. half of Neutral Zone reserves with Kuwait). **Electricity prod.:** 431.9 bil kWh. **Labor force:** agric. 2.9%, industry 16.9%, services 80.2%. **Unemployment:** 4.9%.

Finance: Monetary unit: Riyal (SAR) (3.75 = $1 U.S.). **GDP:** $2.0 tril; **per capita GDP:** $54,992; **GDP growth:** –0.8%. **Imports:** $291.6 bil; China 22%, UAE 16%, U.S. 6%, India 6%. **Exports:** $371.0 bil; China 19%, India 13%, Japan 10%, South Korea 10%, U.S. 7%. **Tourism:** $36.0 bil. **Budget:** $282.4 bil. **Inflation:** 2.3%.

Transport: Railways: 3,362 mi. **Motor vehicles:** 277.1 per 1,000 pop. **Airports:** 86.

Communications: Mobile: 157.8 per 100 pop. **Broadband:** 169 per 100 pop. **Internet** (2023): 100%.

Health: Expend.: 6.0%. **Life expect.:** 75.6 male; 78.8 female. **Births:** 13.6 per 1,000 pop. **Deaths:** 3.5 per 1,000 pop. **Infant mortality:** 11.7 per 1,000 live births. **Undernourished:** 3.0%. **HIV:** <0.1%. **COVID-19:** 9,646 deaths; rates per 100,000: 2,417 cases, 28 deaths. 73% vaccinated.

Education: Compulsory: ages 6-14. **Literacy:** 97.6%.

Website: www.my.gov.sa

Arabia was divided among numerous warring groups and small kingdoms before Muhammad united it in the early 7th cent. His successors conquered the entire Middle East and North Africa, bringing Islam and the Arabic language. But Arabia soon returned to its former status.

Nejd, in central Arabia, long an independent state and center of the Wahhabi sect, fell under Turkish rule in the 18th cent. Ibn Saud, founder of the Saudi dynasty, overthrew the Turks, 1913. He captured Hasa, a Turkish province in eastern Arabia, also 1913; the Hejaz region in western Arabia, 1925; and most of Asir, in SW Arabia, by 1926. The discovery of oil in the 1930s transformed the nation. The Hejaz contains the holy cities of Islam—Medina and Mecca.

Ibn Saud reigned until his death, Nov. 1953. Subsequent kings as of mid-2024 have been his sons. King Salman, June 21, 2017, named as crown prince (heir to the throne) his son Mohammed bin Salman. Known as MBS, the crown prince took on increasing responsibilities. He became Saudi Arabia's prime minister Sept. 27, 2022.

The Islamic religious code is the law of the land. Alcohol and public entertainments are restricted. Dissent is repressed.

Saudi Arabia has often allied itself with and purchased arms from the U.S. and other Western nations. Saudi units, nevertheless, fought against Western ally Israel in the 1948 and 1973 Arab-Israeli wars. Saudi Arabia played a leading role in the 1973-74 Arab oil embargo against the U.S. and other nations.

After Iraq invaded Kuwait, Aug. 2, 1990, Saudi Arabia accepted the Kuwait royal family and more than 400,000 Kuwaiti refugees. Western and Arab troops also deployed on Saudi soil before and during the 1991 Persian Gulf War.

When 15 of the 19 al-Qaeda hijackers who carried out the Sept. 11, 2001, attacks on the U.S. were found to be Saudi, some in the U.S. blamed the Saudi government for allowing Muslim extremism to flourish in Saudi Arabia.

In 2012, Saudi women competed in the Olympics for the first time. A royal decree, Jan. 11, 2013, permitted women to hold 30 of the 150 seats on the government's advisory Shura council. Women were allowed to vote and run for office in municipal elections for the first time in 2015. The male guardianship system that subordinated women was loosened in the late 2010s. A royal decree, effective June 24, 2018, made it legal for women to drive. Decrees issued Aug. 2, 2019, gave women the rights to obtain passports and travel freely, as well as increasing rights in employment and family matters.

Middle East Respiratory Syndrome (MERS), a disease caused by a coronavirus, was first recognized in Saudi Arabia in 2012 and had spread to 26 other countries as of mid-2024.

Beginning in 2014, Saudi warplanes participated in U.S.-led airstrikes against ISIS in Syria. ISIS staged terrorist attacks inside Saudi Arabia in 2014 and subsequent years.

Saudi Arabia led a coalition of Sunni nations that began airstrikes, Mar. 25, 2015, and took other military action against Iran-backed Shiite Houthi rebels in Yemen, causing high civilian casualties. Rebels launched drone and missile strikes on targets in Saudi Arabia and claimed credit for attacks, Sept. 14, 2019, on two major oil installations; Saudi Arabia blamed Iran for the Sept. 14 attacks. A truce in Yemen beginning Apr. 2, 2022, significantly reduced violence.

King Salman announced, Apr. 25, 2016, a plan for economic diversification and privatization by the year 2030. In what was said to be a government anti-corruption campaign, hundreds of business leaders and royal family members were detained, Nov. 2017-Jan. 2018, and more than $100 bil in assets taken.

Saudi dissident and journalist Jamal Khashoggi was killed, Oct. 2, 2018, inside the Saudi consulate in Istanbul, Turkey. A CIA assessment concluded with "high confidence" in Nov. 2018 that MBS ordered the killing.

The Saudi-backed LIV Golf tour, widely perceived as intended to boost Saudi Arabia's international image, launched in 2022; men's pro golfers received huge fees to join the tour. A potential merger of LIV and the PGA Tour was announced June 6, 2023. In recent years, Saudi Arabia's sovereign wealth fund has also invested heavily in other sports.

To combat COVID-19 spread, Saudi Arabia barred foreign residents (usually numbering about 2 mil) from making the hajj, or pilgrimage, to Mecca in 2020 and 2021. Amid extreme heat during the 2024 hajj, more than 1,300 pilgrims died.

Saudi Arabia and Iran announced, Mar. 10, 2023, an agreement to restore diplomatic relations, severed by Saudi Arabia in 2016. A Human Rights Watch report, issued Aug. 21, 2023, accused Saudi border guards of systematically killing or maiming Ethiopian and other East African migrants trying to enter the kingdom through Yemen.

Senegal

Republic of Senegal

People: Population: 18,847,519 (66). **Age distrib.:** <15: 40.7%; 65+: 3.4%. **Growth:** 2.5%. **Migrants:** 1.6%. **Pop. density:** 253.5 per sq mi, 97.9 per sq km. **Urban:** 50.1%. **Ethnic groups:** Wolof 39.7%, Pular 27.5%, Sereer 16%, Mandinka 4.9%, Jola 4.2%, Soninke 2.4%, other (incl. Europeans, persons of Lebanese descent) 5.4%. **Languages:** French (official), Wolof, Pular, Jola, Mandinka, Serer, Soninke. **Religions:** Muslim 91.4% (Sunni), Christian 5.0% (Catholic), ethnic religionist 3.1%.

Geography: Total area: 75,955 sq mi, 196,722 sq km (86); **Land area:** 74,336 sq mi, 192,530 sq km. **Location:** W extreme of Africa. Mauritania on N, Mali on E, Guinea and Guinea-Bissau on S; surrounds The Gambia on three sides. **Topography:** Mostly low rolling plains, rising somewhat in SE. Swamp and jungles in SW. **Arable land:** 19.9%. **Capital:** Dakar, 3,540,462.

Government: Type: Presidential republic. **Head of state:** Pres. Bassirou Diomaye Faye; b. 1980; in office: Apr. 2, 2024. **Head of govt.:** Prime Min. Ousmane Sonko; b. 1974; in office: Apr. 2, 2024. **Local divisions:** 14 regions. **Defense budget:** $452 mil. **Active troops:** 13,600.

Economy: Industries: agric. and fish proc., phosphate mining, fertilizer prod., petroleum refining, zircon and gold mining, constr. materials, ship constr./repair. **Chief agric.:** groundnuts, watermelons, rice, cassava, sugarcane, millet. **Natural resources:** fish, phosphates, iron ore. **Water:** 2,309 cu m per capita. **Electricity prod.:** 7.8 bil kWh. **Labor force:** agric. 21.5%, industry 22.6%, services 55.8%. **Unemployment:** 2.9%.

Finance: Monetary unit: CFA Franc (XOF) (587.79 = $1 U.S.). **GDP:** $85.8 bil; **per capita GDP:** $4,833; **GDP growth:** 3.7%. **Imports** (2021): $12.3 bil; China 22%, India 8%, France 7%, Belgium 5%. **Exports** (2021): $6.8 bil; Mali 18%, India 16%, Switzerland 11%, U.S. 8%. **Tourism** (2021): $360 mil. **Budget:** $5.7 bil. **Inflation** (2021-22): 9.7%.

Transport: Railways: 563 mi. **Airports:** 19.

Communications: Mobile: 123.9 per 100 pop. **Broadband:** 108 per 100 pop. **Internet:** 60%.

Health: Expend.: 4.4%. **Life expect.:** 68.8 male; 72.4 female. **Births:** 30.2 per 1,000 pop. **Deaths:** 4.9 per 1,000 pop. **Infant mortality:** 31.1 per 1,000 live births. **Undernourished:** 4.6%. **HIV:** 0.3%. **COVID-19:** 1,971 deaths; rates per 100,000: 534 cases, 12 deaths. 9% vaccinated.

Education: Compulsory: ages 6-16. **Literacy:** 57.7%.

Website: www.sec.gouv.sn

Portuguese settlers arrived in the 15th cent., but French control grew from the 17th cent. The last independent Muslim state was subdued in 1893. Senegal became an independent republic Aug. 20, 1960, but French political and economic influence remained strong. Senegambia, 1982-89, was a loose confederation of Senegal and The Gambia.

A Senegalese ferry capsized Sept. 26, 2002, killing at least 1,863 people.

Macky Sall won the Mar. 26, 2012, presidential election. After a campaign marred by violence, Sall's coalition won July 30, 2017, legislative elections. Sall won the Feb. 24, 2019, presidential election; leading opposition candidates were barred. Sall's coalition put together a one-seat majority after July 31, 2022, legislative elections.

Opposition leader Ousmane Sonko was convicted, June 1, 2023, on a charge of corrupting youth. Sonko was released in an amnesty 10 days before delayed Mar. 24, 2024, presidential elections, won by Bassirou Diomaye Faye (backed by Sonko and also recently released). Faye named Sonko prime minister.

Serbia

Republic of Serbia

People: Population: 6,652,212 (108). **Age distrib.:** <15: 14.4%; 65+: 20.0%. **Growth:** –0.6%. **Migrants:** 9.4%. **Pop. density:** 222.4 per sq mi, 85.9 per sq km. **Urban:** 57.4% (incl. Kosovo). **Ethnic groups:** Serb 83.3%, Hungarian 3.5%, Romani 2.1% (Romani pop. usually underestimated; may represent 5%-11% of pop.), Bosniak 2%. **Languages:** Serbian (official), Hungarian. **Religions:** Christian 90.0% (Orthodox 82.9%), Muslim 6.9% (Sunni), agnostic 2.5%.

Geography: Total area: 29,913 sq mi, 77,474 sq km (115); **Land area:** 29,913 sq mi, 77,474 sq km. **Location:** Balkan Peninsula in SE Europe. Croatia, Bosnia and Herzegovina on W; Hungary on N; Romania, Bulgaria on E; Montenegro, Albania, North Macedonia on S. **Topography:** Terrain varies widely—fertile plains drained by Danube, other rivers in N; limestone basins in E; mountains, hills in SE. **Arable land:** 30.9%. **Capital:** Belgrade, 1,410,697.

Government: Type: Parliamentary republic. **Head of state:** Pres. Aleksandar Vucic; b. 1970; in office: May 31, 2017. **Head of govt.:** Prime Min. Milos Vucevic; b. 1974; in office: May 2, 2024. **Local divisions:** 117 municipalities, 28 cities (of which 37 municipalities and 8 cities comprise the autonomous province of Vojvodina). **Defense budget:** $1.5 bil. **Active troops:** 28,150.

Economy: Industries: automobiles, base metals, furniture, food proc., machinery, chemicals, sugar, tires. **Chief agric.:** maize, wheat, sugar beets, milk, sunflower seeds, potatoes. **Natural resources:** oil, gas, coal, iron ore, copper, zinc, antimony, chromite, gold, silver, magnesium, pyrite, limestone, marble, salt. **Water:** 22,229 cu m per capita. **Crude oil reserves:** 78 mil bbls. **Electricity prod.:** 32.5 bil kWh. **Labor force:** agric. 13.6%, industry 29.1%, services 57.4%. **Unemployment:** 8.7%.

Finance: Monetary unit: Dinar (RSD) (104.87 = $1 U.S.). **GDP:** $181.3 bil; **per capita GDP:** $27,402; **GDP growth:** 2.5%. **Imports:** $48.2 bil; Germany 11%, China 8%, Hungary 8%, Russia 7%, Italy 6%. **Exports:** $44.3 bil; Germany 13%, Bosnia and Herzegovina 7%, Italy 7%, Hungary 6%. **Tourism:** $2.8 bil. **Budget** (2020): $25.7 bil (central and local govts.). **Inflation:** 12.4%.

Transport: Railways: 2,071 mi. **Motor vehicles:** 391.1 per 1,000 pop. **Airports:** 43.

Communications: Mobile: 128.5 per 100 pop. **Broadband:** 114 per 100 pop. **Internet** (2023): 85.4%.

Health: Expend.: 10.0%. **Life expect.:** 72.7 male; 78.1 female. **Births:** 8.8 per 1,000 pop. **Deaths:** 14.9 per 1,000 pop. **Infant mortality:** 4.5 per 1,000 live births. **Undernourished:** <2.5%. **HIV:** <0.1%. **COVID-19:** 18,057 deaths; rates per 100,000: 37,297 cases, 261 deaths. 48% vaccinated.

Education: Compulsory: ages 7-14. **Literacy:** 99.5%.

Website: www.srbija.gov.rs

Serbia was a vassal principality of Turkey from 1389 to 1878, when the Treaty of Berlin established it as an independent kingdom. After the Balkan wars, Serbia annexed Old Serbia and Macedonia, 1913.

When the Austro-Hungarian empire collapsed after WWI, the Kingdom of Serbs, Croats, and Slovenes—Yugoslavia after 1929—was formed from the provinces of Croatia, Dalmatia, Bosnia, Herzegovina, Slovenia, Vojvodina, and the independent state of Montenegro.

After Nazi Germany's occupation 1941-45, Yugoslavia became a federal republic, headed by Josip Broz, a Communist, known as Marshal Tito. He rejected Stalin's dictatorship and accepted economic and military aid from the West. After Tito died in 1980, Yugoslavia held together for a decade before breaking apart. During 1991-95, Serbia, under Pres. Slobodan Milosevic, supported ethnic Serb fighters in Croatia and in Bosnia and Herzegovina, which had declared independence. The republics of Serbia and Montenegro proclaimed a new Federal Republic of Yugoslavia, Apr. 17, 1992. The UN imposed sanctions on the newly reconstituted Yugoslavia to end the bloodshed in Bosnia.

A peace agreement was reached in 1995. A UN-backed war crimes tribunal began in May 1996 to try suspects from the former Yugoslavia. Barred from running for a third term as Serbian president, Milosevic became president of Yugoslavia, July 23, 1997.

Serbian efforts to suppress a secessionist movement in Kosovo led in Mar.-June 1999 to a war with the U.S. and its NATO allies; they accused Milosevic of pursuing a policy of ethnic cleansing against the predominantly Muslim Kosovars (ethnic Albanians).

Milosevic initially refused to accept defeat in a 2000 presidential election but resigned Oct. 6 after mass demonstrations. He was extradited June 28, 2001, to The Hague, Netherlands, where a UN tribunal had indicted him for war crimes. He was found dead in prison Mar. 11, 2006, before his trial was completed.

A pact to reconstitute Yugoslavia as a new union of Serbia and Montenegro took effect Feb. 4, 2003. Zoran Djindjic, premier of the Republic of Serbia, was assassinated Mar. 12 in Belgrade, triggering a roundup of more than 4,500 people associated with organized crime and the Milosevic regime. Montenegrins voted for separation in a referendum May 21, 2006, and Montenegro became an independent republic June 3.

Kosovo declared independence from Serbia Feb. 17, 2008, but Serbia refused to recognize the new country. Following parliamentary elections in Serbia May 11, a pro-Western government took office. To meet a requirement for future EU membership, Serbia arrested, in 2008, former Bosnian Serb leader Radovan Karadzic; he was convicted at The Hague of genocide and crimes against humanity, Mar. 24, 2016. Serbia's parliament passed a resolution Mar. 31, 2010, apologizing for the 1995 massacre of 8,000 Bosniaks (primarily Muslim ethnic group) by Bosnian Serbs at Srebrenica. Bosnian Serb military commander Ratko Mladic, accused of directing the Srebrenica massacre, was arrested in Serbia, May 2011, and sent to The Hague; he was convicted, Nov. 22, 2017, of genocide, war crimes, and crimes against humanity. Aleksandar Vucic, an advocate of EU membership and also close ties to Russia, became prime min. following Mar. 16, 2014, elections.

An estimated 900,000 migrants, largely from the Middle East and SW Asia, passed through Serbia in 2015-16, before the government essentially closed Serbia's borders Mar. 9, 2016.

Vucic was elected president, Apr. 2, 2017. Ana Brnabic took office, June 29, as Serbia's first female prime min. Months of anti-Vucic demonstrations began in late 2018, protesting authoritarian policies and control of the media. In June 21, 2020, parliamentary elections boycotted by leading opposition parties, Vucic's coalition won a landslide victory. Vucic won reelection, Apr. 3, 2022, and his coalition won parliamentary elections.

Two mass shootings in early May 2023 that left 18 dead led to large-scale protests and new parliamentary elections. The Dec. 17, 2023, elections, marred by irregularities, were again won by Vucic's coalition, and Milos Vucevic became prime min., May 2, 2024.

Government approval, July 2024, of a lithium mining operation in W Serbia prompted large-scale protests, mainly over concerns about pollution.

Vojvodina (8,304 sq mi) is a nominally autonomous province in northern Serbia with a pop. (2011 census) of 1,931,809, mostly Serbian. The capital is Novi Sad. **Website:** www.vojvodina.gov.rs

Seychelles

Republic of Seychelles

People: Population: 98,187 (185). **Age distrib.:** <15: 17.7%; 65+: 10.0%. **Growth:** 0.6%. **Migrants:** 13.3%. **Pop. density:** 558.9 per sq mi, 215.8 per sq km. **Urban:** 59.2%. **Ethnic groups:** predominantly creole (mainly East African/Malagasy heritage); also French, Indian, Chinese, Arab pops. **Languages:** Seychellois Creole, English, French (all official). **Religions:** Christian 94.6% (Catholic 83.1%, Protestant 10.4%), agnostic 2.3%.

Geography: Total area: 176 sq mi, 455 sq km (182); **Land area:** 176 sq mi, 455 sq km. **Location:** In Indian O. 700 mi NE of Madagascar. Nearest neighbors are Madagascar and Somalia on NW. **Topography:** Archipelago of over 116 islands. One group is composed of coral; the Mahe group of isls., predominantly mountainous, is granite. **Arable land:** 0.3%. **Capital:** Victoria, 28,091.

Government: Type: Presidential republic. **Head of state and govt.:** Pres. Wavel Ramkalawan; b. 1961; in office: Oct. 26, 2020. **Local divisions:** 27 admin. districts. **Defense budget:** NA. **Active troops:** 420.

Economy: Industries: fishing, tourism, beverages. **Chief agric.:** coconuts, vegetables, bananas, eggs, chicken, pork. **Natural resources:** fish, coconuts, cinnamon trees. **Water:** 0 cu m per capita. **Electricity prod.:** 615.3 mil kWh. **Labor force:** NA. **Unemployment:** NA.

Finance: Monetary unit: Rupee (SCR) (13.50 = $1 U.S.). **GDP:** $3.9 bil; **per capita GDP:** $32,694; **GDP growth:** 3.2%. **Imports:** $2.4 bil; UAE 22%, Netherlands 14%, Cayman Islands 7%, France 6%, China 6%. **Exports:** $2.4 bil; UAE 18%, France 17%, UK 9%, Mauritius 9%, Japan 8%. **Tourism:** $989 mil. **Budget:** $586 mil. **Inflation:** –1.0%.

Transport: Airports: 16.

Communications: Mobile: 129.2 per 100 pop. **Broadband:** 80.3 per 100 pop. **Internet:** 86.7%.

Health: Expend.: 5.3%. **Life expect.:** 72.2 male; 81.1 female. **Births:** 11.8 per 1,000 pop. **Deaths:** 7.0 per 1,000 pop. **Infant mortality:** 10.2 per 1,000 live births. **Undernourished:** <2.5%. **HIV:** NA. **COVID-19:** 172 deaths; rates per 100,000: 52,758 cases, 175 deaths. 85% vaccinated.

Education: Compulsory: ages 6-15. **Literacy:** 96.2%.

Website: www.egov.sc

The islands were occupied by France in 1768 and seized by Britain in 1794. Seychelles declared independence June 29, 1976. Tourism, a major driver of economic growth, was hurt by the COVID-19 pandemic in 2020, before rebounding in 2021.

The country's first president was ousted in a 1977 coup by socialist leader France Albert René. A 1993 constitution provided for a multiparty state. René resigned in 2004. Vice Pres. James Michel succeeded him and won 2006, 2011, and 2015 elections. After Michel resigned in 2016, Vice Pres. Danny Faure became president. Opposition candidate Wavel Ramkalawan defeated Faure in the Oct. 2020 presidential election, ending more than four decades of rule by Faure's party.

Sierra Leone

Republic of Sierra Leone

People: Population: 9,121,049 (99). **Age distrib.:** <15: 40.1%; 65+: 2.5%. **Growth:** 2.3%. **Migrants:** 0.7%. **Pop. density:** 329.8 per sq mi, 127.4 per sq km. **Urban:** 44.8%. **Ethnic groups:** Temne 35.4%, Mende 30.8%, Limba 8.8%, Kono 4.3%, Korankoh 4%, Fullah 3.8%, Mandingo 2.8%, Loko 2%. **Languages:** English (official), Mende (principal vernacular in S), Temne (principal vernacular in N), Krio (English-based Creole). **Religions:** Muslim 68.0% (Sunni), ethnic religionist 19.0%, Christian 11.4%.

Geography: Total area: 27,699 sq mi, 71,740 sq km (117); **Land area:** 27,653 sq mi, 71,620 sq km. **Location:** W coast of W Africa. Guinea on N and E, Liberia on S. **Topography:** Mangrove swamps in heavily indented, 210-mi coastline. Wooded hills rise to a plateau and mountains in E. **Arable land:** 21.9%. **Capital:** Freetown, 1,347,559.

Government: Type: Presidential republic. **Head of state and govt.:** Pres. Julius Maada Bio; b. 1964; in office: Apr. 4, 2018. **Local divisions:** 4 provinces, 1 area. **Defense budget:** $20 mil. **Active troops:** 8,500.

Economy: Industries: diamond mining, iron ore, rutile and bauxite mining, small-scale mfg. (beverages, textiles, footwear). **Chief agric.:** cassava, rice, oil palm fruit, vegetables, sweet potatoes, milk. **Natural resources:** diamonds, titanium ore, bauxite, iron ore, gold, chromite. **Water:** 19,001 cu m per capita. **Electricity prod.:** 198.2 mil kWh. **Labor force:** agric. 43.3%, industry 12.0%, services 44.6%. **Unemployment:** 3.2%.

Finance: Monetary unit: Leone (SLE) (22.55 = $1 U.S.). **GDP:** $16.2 bil; **per capita GDP:** $1,847; **GDP growth:** 3.4%. **Imports** (2022): $2.0 bil; China 33%, India 12%, Turkey (Türkiye) 9%, U.S. 6%, UAE 5%. **Exports** (2022): $1.2 bil; China 54%, Belgium 12%, UAE 6%. **Tourism** (2022): $20 mil. **Budget:** $867 mil. **Inflation:** 47.6%.

Transport: Motor vehicles: 5.1 per 1,000 pop. **Airports:** 8.

Communications: Mobile (2022): 107.9 per 100 pop. **Broadband** (2022): 25.8 per 100 pop. **Internet:** 30.4%.

Health: Expend.: 8.6%. **Life expect.:** 57.8 male; 61.0 female. **Births:** 30.8 per 1,000 pop. **Deaths:** 9.0 per 1,000 pop. **Infant mortality:** 71.2 per 1,000 live births. **Undernourished:** 28.4%. **HIV:** 1.4%. **COVID-19:** 125 deaths; rates per 100,000: 100 cases, 2 deaths. 62% vaccinated.

Education: Compulsory: ages 6-14. **Literacy:** 48.6%.

Website: statehouse.gov.sl

The British founded Freetown, 1787, as a haven for freed slaves. Full independence arrived Apr. 27, 1961. A one-party state was established by referendum in 1978.

Mutinous soldiers ousted Pres. Joseph Momoh, Apr. 30, 1992. A coup, Jan. 16, 1996, paved the way for multiparty elections and a return to civilian rule. A peace accord, signed Nov. 30 with the Revolutionary United Front (RUF), brought a temporary halt to a civil war that had claimed over 10,000 lives in five years.

After a May 25, 1997, coup, Nigeria's military restored Pres. Ahmad Tejan Kabbah to power on Mar. 10, 1998, but RUF rebels mounted a guerrilla counteroffensive, killing thousands of civilians and mutilating thousands more. A power-sharing agreement between the Kabbah government and the RUF, July 1999, collapsed in early May 2000, but rebel leader Foday Sankoh was captured in Freetown, May 17. Government and rebel leaders declared an official end to the war Jan. 18, 2002; more than 50,000 people had died in the conflict. Kabbah won the May 14, 2002, presidential election.

Opposition leader Ernest Bai Koroma won a presidential runoff vote, Sept. 8, 2007. A 2012 cholera epidemic caused about 23,000 cases and 300 deaths. Koroma won reelection Nov. 17, 2012. An Ebola virus epidemic caused 14,124 cases and 3,956 deaths in Sierra Leone, 2013-16. After a campaign marred by violence, Julius Maada Bio, a leader of the 1992 mutiny and 1996 coup, was declared the winner, Apr. 4, 2018, of a presidential runoff election. On Feb. 7, 2019, Bio declared a national emergency in response to the high incidence of rape and other sexual violence against women. Parliament voted, July 23, 2021, to abolish capital punishment. Soaring inflation in 2022 led to violent protests in Aug. 2022, met with a deadly government response. Amid a continuing economic crisis, Bio was declared the winner of the June 24, 2023, presidential election; the opposition charged irregularities. An apparent attempted coup was thwarted, Nov. 26, 2023.

Singapore
Republic of Singapore

People: Population: 6,028,459 (113). **Age distrib.:** <15: 14.6%; 65+: 14.3%. **Growth:** 0.9%. **Migrants:** 43.1%. **Pop. density:** 22,015.8 per sq mi, 8,500.4 per sq km. **Urban:** 100.0%. **Ethnic groups:** Chinese 74.2%, Malay 13.7%, Indian 8.9%, other (incl. Eurasian, Caucasian, Japanese, Filipino, Vietnamese) 3.2%. **Languages:** English, Mandarin, Malay, Tamil (all official); other Chinese dialects (incl. Hokkien, Cantonese, Teochew, Hakka). **Religions:** Chinese folk-religionist 36.3%, Christian 22.4%, Muslim 14.9% (Sunni), Buddhist 14.7% (Mahayanist 13%), Hindu 5.1% (Shaivite 3%, Vaishnavite 2%), agnostic 4.5%.

Geography: Total area: 278 sq mi, 719 sq km (177); **Land area:** 274 sq mi, 709 sq km. **Location:** Off tip of Malayan Peninsula in SE Asia. Nearest neighbors are Malaysia on N, Indonesia on S. **Topography:** Flat, formerly swampy island with 40 nearby islets. **Arable land:** 0.8%. **Capital:** Singapore, 6,119,203.

Government: Type: Parliamentary republic. **Head of state:** Pres. Tharman Shanmugaratnam; in office: Sept. 14, 2023. **Head of govt.:** Prime Min. Lawrence Wong; b. 1972; in office: May 15, 2024. **Local divisions:** no first-order admin. divisions. **Defense budget:** $13.4 bil. **Active troops:** 51,000.

Economy: Industries: electronics, chemicals, financial services, oil drilling equip., petroleum refining, biomedical prods., scientific instruments. **Chief agric.:** chicken, eggs, pork, vegetables, duck, spinach. **Natural resources:** fish, deepwater ports. **Water:** 101 cu m per capita. **Electricity prod.:** 57.7 bil kWh. **Labor force:** agric. 0.1%, industry 14.2%, services 85.7%. **Unemployment:** 3.5%.

Finance: Monetary unit: Dollar (SGD) (1.30 = $1 U.S.). **GDP:** $837.3 bil; **per capita GDP:** $141,500; **GDP growth:** 1.1%. **Imports:** $686.7 bil; China 17%, Malaysia 13%, U.S. 10%, Taiwan 9%, South Korea 5%. **Exports:** $874.0 bil; Hong Kong 14%, China 13%, Malaysia 9%, U.S. 8%, Indonesia 6%. **Tourism:** $21.1 bil. **Budget** (2020): $90.3 bil (operational and development expenditures). **Inflation:** 4.8%.

Transport: Motor vehicles: 144.1 per 1,000 pop. **Airports:** 9.

Communications: Mobile: 166.7 per 100 pop. **Broadband:** 167 per 100 pop. **Internet** (2023): 94.3%.

Health: Expend.: 5.6%. **Life expect.:** 84.0 male; 89.5 female. **Births:** 8.8 per 1,000 pop. **Deaths:** 4.3 per 1,000 pop. **Infant mortality:** 1.5 per 1,000 live births. **Undernourished:** NA. **HIV:** 0.1%. **COVID-19:** 2,024 deaths; rates per 100,000: 51,384 cases, 35 deaths. 90% vaccinated.

Education: Compulsory: ages 6-11. **Literacy:** 97.7%.

Website: www.gov.sg

Founded in 1819 by Sir Thomas Stamford Raffles, Singapore was a British colony until 1959, when it became autonomous within the Commonwealth. On Sept. 16, 1963, it joined with Malaya, Sarawak, and Sabah to form the Federation of Malaysia. Tensions between Malays, dominant in the federation, and ethnic Chinese, dominant in Singapore, led to an accord under which Singapore became a separate nation, Aug. 9, 1965.

Singapore is a major port and manufacturing, banking, and commerce center. Asian immigrant workers hold many low-paying jobs. The government, dominated by the People's Action Party (PAP), has taken strong actions to keep order and suppress dissent.

Singapore's first prime min., Lee Kuan Yew (in office 1959-90), was credited with building the country's strong economy. His oldest child, Lee Hsien Loong, took office as prime min., Aug. 12, 2004. Halimah Yacob became Singapore's first female president, Sept. 14, 2017.

Nov. 2022 legislation decriminalized consensual sex between men. Tharman Shanmugaratnam won the Sept. 1, 2023, presidential election. On May 15, 2024, Lawrence Wong of the PAP succeeded Lee as prime min.

Slovakia
Slovak Republic

People: Population: 5,563,649 (118). **Age distrib.:** <15: 15.3%; 65+: 18.1%. **Growth:** –0.1%. **Migrants:** 3.6%. **Pop. density:** 299.5 per sq mi, 115.7 per sq km. **Urban:** 54.2%. **Ethnic groups** (by nationality): Slovak 83.8%, Hungarian 7.8%, Romani 1.2% (Romani pop. usually underestimated; may represent 7%-11% of pop.). **Languages:** Slovak (official), Hungarian. **Religions:** Christian 83.5% (Catholic 72.6%), agnostic 12.7%, atheist 3.7%.

Geography: Total area: 18,933 sq mi, 49,035 sq km (127); **Land area:** 18,573 sq mi, 48,105 sq km. **Location:** E central Europe. Poland on N, Hungary on S, Austria and Czechia on W, Ukraine on E. **Topography:** Carpathian Mts. in N, fertile Danube plain in S. **Arable land:** 27.9%. **Capital:** Bratislava, 442,306.

Government: Type: Parliamentary republic. **Head of state:** Pres. Peter Pellegrini; b. 1975; in office: June 15, 2024. **Head of govt.:** Prime Min. Robert Fico; b. 1964; in office: Oct. 25, 2023. **Local divisions:** 8 regions. **Defense budget:** $2.7 bil. **Active troops:** 17,850.

Economy: Industries: automobiles; metal and metal prods.; electricity, gas, coke, oil, nuclear fuel; chemicals, synthetic fibers, wood and paper prods.; machinery. **Chief agric.:** wheat, sugar beets, milk, maize, barley, rapeseed. **Natural resources:** lignite, iron ore, copper and manganese ore, salt. **Water:** 9,197 cu m per capita. **Crude oil reserves:** 9 mil bbls. **Electricity prod.:** 26.2 bil kWh. **Labor force:** agric. 2.5%, industry 35.9%, services 61.6%. **Unemployment:** 5.8%.

Finance: Monetary unit: Euro (EUR) (0.90 = $1 U.S.). **GDP:** $242.3 bil; **per capita GDP:** $44,650; **GDP growth:** 1.6%. **Imports:** $118.9 bil; Czechia 18%, Germany 15%, Poland 9%, Russia 7%, Austria 7%. **Exports:** $121.2 bil; Germany 20%, Czechia 11%, Hungary 9%, Poland 7%, France 6%. **Tourism:** $1.6 bil. **Budget:** $44.9 bil. **Inflation:** 10.5%.

Transport: Railways: 2,254 mi. **Motor vehicles:** 531.3 per 1,000 pop. **Airports:** 114.

Communications: Mobile: 138.2 per 100 pop. **Broadband:** 94.6 per 100 pop. **Internet** (2023): 87.2%.

Health: Expend.: 7.8%. **Life expect.:** 73.7 male; 81.0 female. **Births:** 10.0 per 1,000 pop. **Deaths:** 11.2 per 1,000 pop. **Infant mortality:** 5.1 per 1,000 live births. **Undernourished:** 3.6%. **HIV:** <0.1%. **COVID-19:** 21,228 deaths; rates per 100,000: 34,411 cases, 389 deaths. 51% vaccinated.

Education: Compulsory: ages 5-15. **Literacy:** NA.

Website: www.government.gov.sk

Settled by Illyrian, Celtic, and Germanic peoples, Slovakia was incorporated into Great Moravia in the 9th cent. It became part of Hungary in the 11th cent. Overrun by Czech Hussites in the 15th cent., it was restored to Hungarian rule in 1526. After WWI, the Slovaks joined the Czechs of Bohemia to form the Republic of Czechoslovakia, Oct. 28, 1918.

Germany invaded Czechoslovakia, 1939, and declared Slovakia independent. Slovakia rejoined Czechoslovakia in 1945. Czechoslovakia split into two separate states—the Czech Republic and Slovakia—on Jan. 1, 1993.

Slovakia joined the EU and NATO in 2004. After a corruption scandal, Peter Pellegrini replaced Robert Fico (both then of the Smer party) as prime min., Mar. 22, 2018. Anti-corruption activist Zuzana Caputová won a Mar. 30, 2019, runoff election to become Slovakia's first female president. The center-right Ordinary People (OP) party won Feb. 29, 2020, legislative elections. In Sept. 30, 2023, elections, Smer (led by Fico, who campaigned on pro-Russia positions) gained the most seats; Fico formed a coalition and became prime min., Oct. 25, 2023. Pellegrini, also taking pro-Russia positions, was elected president in an Apr. 6, 2024, runoff. Fico was seriously wounded but survived an assassination attempt, May 15, 2024.

Slovenia
Republic of Slovenia

People: Population: 2,097,893 (147). **Age distrib.:** <15: 14.3%; 65+: 23.2%. **Growth:** –0.1%. **Migrants:** 13.4%. **Pop. density:** 269.6 per sq mi, 104.1 per sq km. **Urban:** 56.4%. **Ethnic groups:** Slovene 83.1%, Serb 2%. **Languages:** Slovene (official), Croatian; Hungarian, Italian (official in certain municipalities). **Religions:** Christian 83.0% (Catholic 76.9%), agnostic 10.6%, Muslim 4.0% (Sunni), atheist 2.4%.

Geography: Total area: 7,827 sq mi, 20,273 sq km (151); **Land area:** 7,780 sq mi, 20,151 sq km. **Location:** SE Europe. Italy on W, Austria on N, Hungary on NE, Croatia on SE, S. **Topography:** Mostly hilly; more than half forested. **Arable land:** 8.9%. **Capital:** Ljubljana, 286,491.

Government: Type: Parliamentary republic. **Head of state:** Pres. Natasa Pirc Musar; b. 1968; in office: Dec. 23, 2023. **Head of govt.:** Prime Min. Robert Golob; b. 1967; in office: June 1, 2022. **Local divisions:** 200 municipalities, 12 urban municipalities. **Defense budget:** $1.0 bil. **Active troops:** 6,400.

Economy: Industries: ferrous metallurgy and aluminum prods., lead and zinc smelting, electronics (incl. military), trucks, automobiles, elec. power equip., wood prods. **Chief agric.:** milk, maize, wheat, barley, grapes, chicken. **Natural resources:** lignite, lead, zinc, building stone, hydropower, forests. **Water:** 15,037 cu m per capita. **Electricity prod.:** 12.5 bil kWh. **Labor force:** agric. 4.3%, industry 30.2%, services 65.5%. **Unemployment:** 3.6%.

Finance: Monetary unit: Euro (EUR) (0.90 = $1 U.S.). **GDP:** $116.5 bil; **per capita GDP:** $54,947; **GDP growth:** 1.6%. **Imports:** $52.8 bil; Switzerland 17%, China 11%, Italy 10%, Germany 10%, Austria 7%. **Exports:** $57.5 bil; Switzerland 18%, Germany 14%, Italy 11%, Croatia 8%, Austria 7%. **Tourism:** $3.5 bil. **Budget:** $23.5 bil. **Inflation:** 7.4%.

Transport: Railways: 750 mi. **Motor vehicles:** 643.4 per 1,000 pop. **Airports:** 42.

Communications: Mobile: 129.0 per 100 pop. **Broadband:** 98.4 per 100 pop. **Internet** (2023): 90.4%.

Health: Expend. (2022): 8.8%. **Life expect.:** 79.4 male; 85.2 female. **Births:** 8.0 per 1,000 pop. **Deaths:** 10.5 per 1,000 pop. **Infant mortality:** 1.5 per 1,000 live births. **Undernourished:** <2.5%. **HIV:** <0.1%. **COVID-19:** 10,083 deaths; rates per 100,000: 64,735 cases, 481 deaths. 57% vaccinated.

Education: Compulsory: ages 6-14. **Literacy:** 99.7%.

Website: www.gov.si

The Slovenes settled in their current territory during the 6th to 8th cent. They fell under German domination in the 9th cent. After 1848, the Slovenes, divided among several Austrian provinces, began their struggle for unification. In 1918 a majority of Slovenes became part of the Kingdom of Serbs, Croats, and Slovenes, later renamed Yugoslavia.

Slovenia declared independence June 25, 1991; attained full membership in the EU and NATO in 2004; and adopted the euro Jan. 1, 2007. About 474,000 migrants (many from the Middle East and SW Asia) entered Slovenia Oct. 1, 2015-Mar. 8, 2016; Slovenia, Mar. 8, essentially closed its border to migrants. The rightist, anti-immigration Slovenian Democratic Party (SDS) won the most seats in June 3, 2018, National Assembly elections. Five center-left parties formed a coalition minority government but couldn't pass legislation. Janez Jansa of SDS became prime minister, Mar. 13, 2020. The environmentalist, pro-democracy Freedom Movement (GS) outpolled the SDS in Apr. 24, 2022, elections; Robert Golob of GS became prime minister, heading a center-left coalition government. Independent Natasa Pirc Musar, backed by Golob, defeated the SDS candidate in a Nov. 13, 2022, runoff to become Slovenia's first woman president.

Solomon Islands

People: Population: 726,799 (163). **Age distrib.:** <15: 30.6%; 65+: 5.3%. **Growth:** 1.7%. **Migrants:** 0.4%. **Pop. density:** 67.3 per sq mi, 26.0 per sq km. **Urban:** 26.5%. **Ethnic groups:** Melanesian 95.3%, Polynesian 3.1%. **Languages:** Melanesian pidgin (lingua franca in much of country), English (official), 120 Indigenous langs. **Religions:** Christian 95.4% (Protestant 67.8%, Catholic 20.3%), ethnic religionist 3.1%.

Geography: Total area: 11,157 sq mi, 28,896 sq km (140); **Land area:** 10,805 sq mi, 27,986 sq km. **Location:** Melanesian Archipelago in W Pacific O. Nearest neighbor is Papua New Guinea to W. **Topography:** 10 large volcanic, rugged islands; 4 groups of smaller islands. **Arable land:** 0.8%. **Capital:** Honiara, 81,801.

Government: Type: Parliamentary democracy under constitutional monarchy. **Head of state:** King Charles III, rep. by Gov.-Gen. David Tiva Kapu; in office: July 7, 2024. **Head of govt.:** Prime Min. Jeremiah Manele; b. 1968; in office: May 2, 2024. **Local divisions:** 9 provinces, 1 city. **Defense budget/active troops:** NA.

Economy: Industries: fish (tuna), mining, timber. **Chief agric.:** oil palm fruit, coconuts, sweet potatoes, taro, yams, fruits. **Natural resources:** fish, forests, gold, bauxite, phosphates, lead, zinc, nickel. **Water:** 63,149 cu m per capita. **Electricity prod.:** 109.1 mil kWh. **Labor force:** agric. 37.3%, industry 11.4%, services 51.3%. **Unemployment:** 1.5%.

Finance: Monetary unit: Dollar (SBD) (8.31 = $1 U.S.). **GDP:** $2.2 bil; **per capita GDP:** $3,035; **GDP growth:** 3.0%. **Imports:** $883.6 mil; China 37%, Singapore 16%, Malaysia 12%, Australia 10%. **Exports:** $546.0 mil; China 51%, India 9%, Italy 8%, Australia 5%. **Tourism:** $23 mil. **Budget:** $537 mil. **Inflation:** 5.9%.

Transport: Airports: 35.

Communications: Mobile (2022): 62.1 per 100 pop. **Broadband** (2022): 16.8 per 100 pop. **Internet:** 45%.

Health: Expend.: 4.8%. **Life expect.:** 74.6 male; 80.0 female. **Births:** 22.0 per 1,000 pop. **Deaths:** 3.9 per 1,000 pop. **Infant mortality:** 19.1 per 1,000 live births. **Undernourished:** 19.4%. **HIV:** NA. **COVID-19:** 199 deaths; rates per 100,000: 3,779 cases, 29 deaths. 37% vaccinated.

Education: Compulsory: NA. **Literacy:** NA.

Website: www.parliament.gov.sb

The Solomon Isls. were inhabited by Melanesians. Britain established a protectorate in the 1890s over most of the group. The islands, including Guadalcanal, saw major WWII battles. They achieved self-government, Jan. 2, 1976, and formal independence, July 7, 1978.

To restore order after years of factional violence, an Australian-led regional security force (RAMSI) arrived in July 2003.

Former prime min. Manasseh Sogavare (2000-01, 2006-07) again became head of government following Nov. 19, 2014, parliamentary elections. RAMSI formally ended June 2017. Sogavare, Nov. 6, 2017, lost a no-confidence vote but returned as prime min. after his OUR Party won Apr. 3, 2019, elections.

Seeking Chinese aid, the government in 2019 switched diplomatic relations from Taiwan to China. A security agreement with China was signed in 2022. The U.S., in 2023, reopened an embassy in the Solomon Islands, ending a 30-year absence. OUR fell short of a majority in delayed Apr. 17, 2024, elections; Jeremiah Manele of OUR formed a coalition and became prime min. May 2.

Somalia

Federal Republic of Somalia

People: Population: 13,017,273 (78). **Age distrib.:** <15: 41.4%; 65+: 2.8%. **Growth:** 2.6%. **Migrants:** 0.4%. **Pop. density:** 53.7 per sq mi, 20.8 per sq km. **Urban:** 48.5%. **Ethnic groups:** predom. Somali with lesser numbers of Arab, Bantu, others. **Languages:** Somali, Arabic (both official); Italian; English. **Religions:** Muslim 99.8% (Sunni 98%).

Geography: Total area: 246,201 sq mi, 637,657 sq km (44); **Land area:** 242,216 sq mi, 627,337 sq km. **Location:** Eastern horn of Africa. Djibouti, Ethiopia, Kenya on W. **Topography:** Coastline extends for 1,700 mi. Hills cover the N; center and S are flat. **Arable land:** 1.8%. **Capital:** Mogadishu, 2,726,815. **Cities:** Hargeysa, 1,176,617.

Government: Type: Federal parliamentary republic. **Head of state:** Pres. Hassan Sheikh Mohamud; b. 1955; in office: May 23, 2022. **Head of govt.:** Prime Min. Hamza Abdi Barre; in office: June 25, 2022. **Local divisions:** 18 regions. **Defense budget:** NA. **Active troops:** 13,900.

Economy: Industries: light industries incl. sugar refining, textiles, wireless communication. **Chief agric.:** camel milk, milk, goat milk, sheep milk, sugarcane, fruits. **Natural resources:** uranium, largely unexploited reserves of iron ore, tin, gypsum, bauxite, copper, salt, nat. gas. **Water:** 861 cu m per capita. **Electricity prod.:** 378.4 mil kWh. **Labor force:** agric. 25.9%, industry 17.8%, services 56.3%. **Unemployment:** 19.0%.

Finance: Monetary unit: Shilling (SOS) (566.42 = $1 U.S.). **GDP:** $29.2 bil; **per capita GDP:** $1,611; **GDP growth:** 3.1%. **Imports** (2018): $94.4 bil; UAE 33%, China 19%, India 16%, Turkey (Türkiye) 7%, Ethiopia 5%. **Exports** (2014): $819.0 mil; UAE 50%, Oman 30%. **Budget** (2014): $151.1 mil. **Inflation** (2016-17): 1.5%.

Transport: Airports: 38.

Communications: Mobile (2022): 49.7 per 100 pop. **Broadband** (2022): 2.5 per 100 pop. **Internet:** 27.6%.

Health: Expend.: NA. **Life expect.:** 54.1 male; 59.0 female. **Births:** 37.4 per 1,000 pop. **Deaths:** 11.2 per 1,000 pop. **Infant mortality:** 83.6 per 1,000 live births. **Undernourished:** 51.3%. **HIV:** <0.1%. **COVID-19:** 1,361 deaths; rates per 100,000: 172 cases, 9 deaths. 48% vaccinated.

Education: Compulsory: 6-13. **Literacy:** 41.0%.

Website: villasomalia.gov.so

British Somaliland (present-day N Somalia) was formed in the 19th cent., as was Italian Somaliland (now central and S Somalia). Italy lost its African colonies in WWII. British Somaliland gained independence, June 26, 1960, and by prearrangement, merged, July 1, with the UN Trust Territory of Somalia to create the independent Somali Republic.

On Oct. 15, 1969, Somalia's first civilian president, Abdirashid Ali Sharmarke, was assassinated. Six days later, Maj. Gen. Muhammad Siad Barre led a military coup. In 1970, he declared the country a socialist state.

Somalia has laid claim to Ogaden, the huge eastern region of Ethiopia, peopled mostly by Somalis. Some 11,000 Cuban troops with Soviet arms defeated Somali army troops and ethnic Somali rebels in Ethiopia, 1978. Guerrilla fighting in Ogaden continued until 1988, when a peace agreement was reached with Ethiopia.

Fighting in Mogadishu led Siad Barre to flee the capital, Jan. 1991. Fighting between rival factions caused 40,000 casualties, 1991-92, and by mid-1992, the civil war, drought, and banditry combined to produce a famine that threatened some 1.5 mil people.

U.S. troops and the UN worked to safeguard food delivery, 1991-93, resulting in significant U.S. and other casualties; a failed mission Oct. 3-4, 1993, left 18 U.S. troops and more than 500 Somalis dead. The U.S. withdrew its peacekeeping forces Mar. 25, 1994.

When the last UN troops pulled out, Mar. 3, 1995, armed factions controlled different regions. A peace deal Jan. 29, 2004, led to the Aug. 22 inauguration of a transitional parliament, Somalia's first legislature in 13 years. Meeting in Nairobi, Kenya, the parliament chose Abdullahi Yusuf Ahmed as president. On June 5, 2005, an Islamist militia took over Mogadishu. Islamists held much of the central and southern regions.

With aid from Ethiopian troops, transitional govt. forces recaptured Mogadishu in Dec. 2006. The UN Security Council authorized, Feb. 20, 2007, an African Union peacekeeping mission to Somalia (AMISOM). An upsurge of fighting in Mogadishu, Feb.-Apr., killed hundreds of people and caused 350,000 to flee. Bombings and kidnappings escalated in 2007-08; many of the attacks on transitional authorities and their allies were blamed on al-Shabab, an al-Qaeda ally.

After Pres. Yusuf resigned Dec. 29, 2008, the transitional parliament, meeting in Djibouti Jan. 31, 2009, elected a moderate Islamist, Sheikh Sharif Sheikh Ahmed. Meanwhile, pirates carried out more than 200 attacks off the Horn of Africa in 2009. Pirates and Islamist insurgents continued to disrupt famine relief efforts in 2010-11. Pressured by AMISOM forces, al-Shabab pulled out of Mogadishu, Aug. 6, 2011, but continued to control much of southern Somalia. A caretaker government was sworn in Aug. 20, 2012, and the new parliament elected Hassan Sheikh Mohamud president Sept. 10. Bombings and other attacks by al-Shabab, in Mogadishu and elsewhere, continued.

Delayed by violence, late 2016 indirect elections resulted in the seating of a new bicameral parliament Dec. 27. Parliament, Feb. 8, 2017, elected former Prime Min. Mohamed Abdullahi Mohamed (2010-11) as Somalia's president. He pledged stronger action against Islamist militants, but combat and al-Shabab terrorist attacks continued. A truck bombing in Mogadishu, Oct. 14, 2017, killed more than 500.

U.S. forces assisted Somali government forces and AMISOM troops. AMISOM had about 19,000 troops in Somalia on Apr. 1, 2022, when its mission officially ended. It was replaced by the African Union Transition Mission in Somalia (ATMIS), under which Somali government forces would, over time, take the lead role in fighting al-Shabab.

Delayed indirect legislative elections were completed Apr. 2022, and on May 15, Hassan Sheikh Mohamud was again elected president by legislators. Ongoing drought and warfare left millions of Somalis facing food insecurity in 2022. Al-Shabab car bombings in Mogadishu, Oct. 29, 2022, left more than 100 dead. Heavy rains and flooding in central Somalia, May 2023, displaced more than 245,000. With combat in S and central Somalia continuing in 2024, an al-Shabab terrorist attack in Mogadishu's Lido beach area, Aug. 2-3, left at least 37 dead.

South Africa

Republic of South Africa

People: Population: 60,442,647 (25). **Age distrib.:** <15: 27.2%; 65+: 7.5%. **Growth:** 1.1%. **Migrants:** 4.8%. **Pop. density:** 128.9 per sq mi, 49.8 per sq km. **Urban:** 69.3%. **Ethnic groups:** Black African 81.4%, colored (South African term for persons of mixed-race ancestry) 8.2%, white 7.3%, Indian/Asian 2.7%. **Languages:** isiZulu, isiXhosa, Afrikaans, Sepedi, Setswana, English, Sesotho, Xitsonga, siSwati, Tshivenda, isiNdebele (all official). **Religions:** Christian 81.2% (independent 49.4%, Protestant 24.3%), ethnic religionist 7.2%, agnostic 5.7%, Hindu 2.4%.

Geography: Total area: 470,693 sq mi, 1,219,090 sq km (24); **Land area:** 468,909 sq mi, 1,214,470 sq km. **Location:** Southern extreme of Africa. Namibia, Botswana, Zimbabwe on N; Mozambique, Eswatini on E; surrounds Lesotho. **Topography:** Large interior plateau reaches close to the country's 1,739-mi coastline. Few major rivers or lakes. Rainfall is sparse in W, more plentiful in E. **Arable land:** 9.9%. **Capital:** Cape Town (legislative), 4,977,833; Pretoria (administrative), 2,889,899; Bloemfontein (judicial), 608,655. **Cities:** Johannesburg, 6,324,351; Ekurhuleni, 4,190,832; Durban (Ethekwini), 3,262,128.

Government: Type: Parliamentary republic. **Head of state and govt.:** Pres. Cyril Ramaphosa; b. 1952; in office: Feb. 15, 2018. **Local divisions:** 9 provinces. **Defense budget:** $2.9 bil. **Active troops:** 69,200.

Economy: Industries: mining (platinum, gold, chromium), auto assembly, metalworking, machinery, textiles, iron and steel, chemicals, fertilizer, foodstuffs. **Chief agric.:** sugarcane, maize, milk, potatoes, wheat, grapes. **Natural resources:** gold, chromium, antimony, coal, iron ore, manganese, nickel, phosphates, tin, rare earth elements, uranium, gem diamonds, platinum, copper, vanadium, salt, nat. gas. **Water:** 865 cu m per capita. **Crude oil reserves:** 15 mil bbls. **Electricity prod.:** 229.5 bil kWh. **Labor force:** agric. 19.3%, industry 18.1%, services 62.7%. **Unemployment:** 28.0%.

Finance: Monetary unit: Rand (ZAR) (17.75 = $1 U.S.). **GDP:** $957.4 bil; **per capita GDP:** $15,847; **GDP growth:** 0.6%. **Imports:** $123.5 bil; China 21%, Germany 9%, India 7%, U.S. 5%. **Exports:** $124.7 bil; China 16%, U.S. 7%, Germany 7%, India 6%, Japan 6%. **Tourism:** $5.7 bil. **Budget** (2020): $121.2 bil. **Inflation:** 6.1%.

Transport: Railways: 18,890 mi. **Motor vehicles:** 282.0 per 1,000 pop. **Airports:** 575.

Communications: Mobile: 171.5 per 100 pop. **Broadband:** 131 per 100 pop. **Internet:** 74.7%.

Health: Expend.: 8.3%. **Life expect.:** 70.3 male; 73.5 female. **Births:** 17.7 per 1,000 pop. **Deaths:** 6.9 per 1,000 pop. **Infant mortality:** 21.9 per 1,000 live births. **Undernourished:** 8.1%. **HIV:** 17.1%. **COVID-19:** 102,595 deaths; rates per 100,000: 6,867 cases, 173 deaths. 35% vaccinated.

Education: Compulsory: ages 7-15. **Literacy:** 90.0%.

Website: www.gov.za

San and KhoiKhoi people were the original inhabitants. Bantus, including Zulu, Xhosa, Swazi, and Sotho, occupied the area from northeastern to southern South Africa before the 17th cent.

The Dutch settled the Cape of Good Hope area, beginning in the 17th cent. Britain seized the Cape, 1806. Many Dutch trekked north and founded two republics, Transvaal and Orange Free State. Diamonds were discovered, 1867, and gold, 1886. The Dutch (Boers) resented encroachments by the British and others; the Anglo-Boer War followed, 1899-1902. Britain won and created, May 31, 1910, the Union of South Africa, incorporating two British colonies (Cape and Natal) with Transvaal and Orange Free State. After a referendum, the Union became the Republic of South Africa, May 31, 1961, and withdrew from the Commonwealth (it rejoined in 1994).

Daniel Malan's National Party, elected in 1948, made the policy of separate development of the races, or apartheid, official. Under apartheid, the majority-Black population was restricted to living and working in designated areas, attended separate schools, could hold only certain jobs, and were paid less than whites for similar work. Only whites could vote or run for public office. Persons of Asian Indian ancestry and those of mixed race ("coloureds") had limited political rights.

Protests against apartheid were suppressed. At Sharpeville on Mar. 21, 1960, government troops killed 69 Black protesters. At least 600 persons, mostly Bantus, were killed in 1976 anti-apartheid riots. In 1986, Nobel Peace Prize winner Bishop Desmond Tutu called for Western nations to apply sanctions against South Africa to force an end to apartheid. On May 19, 1986, South Africa attacked guerrilla strongholds of the anti-apartheid African National Congress (ANC) in neighboring countries.

Some 2 mil South African Black workers staged a strike, June 6-8, 1988. Pres. P. W. Botha, head of the government since 1978, resigned Aug. 14, 1989, and was replaced by F. W. de Klerk. In 1990 the government lifted its ban on the ANC. Anti-apartheid leader Nelson Mandela was freed Feb. 11 after more than 27 years in prison.

In 1993 negotiators agreed on basic principles for a new democratic constitution, and Mandela and de Klerk shared the Nobel Peace Prize. South Africa's partially self-governing Black territories, or "homelands," were incorporated into a national system of nine provinces. The ANC won elections Apr. 26-29, 1994, making Mandela president. The predominantly-Zulu Inkatha Freedom Party won control of the legislature in a mainly Zulu province. By then, fighting between the ANC and Inkatha had killed more than 14,000 people in the Zulu region.

A post-apartheid constitution became law Dec. 10, 1996. The ANC won elections, June 2, 1999, and ANC leader Thabo Mbeki became president. South Africa, Nov. 30, 2006, became the first African country to legalize same-sex marriage.

Mbeki's former deputy president, Jacob Zuma, became president after Apr. 22, 2009, elections. Despite corruption charges, Zuma was reelected president by the National Assembly, May 21, 2014. With the economy weak and claims of corruption continuing, Zuma resigned Feb. 14, 2018. The ANC's Cyril Ramaphosa replaced him. The ANC retained a parliamentary majority in May 8, 2019, elections, and the National Assembly reelected Ramaphosa president, May 22.

In the early 2020s, South Africa was the African country hit hardest by the COVID-19 pandemic, in terms of both total confirmed cases and total confirmed deaths.

At least 76 people died after an arson fire gutted an illegally occupied, overcrowded, and unsafe building in Johannesburg, Aug. 31, 2023.

Hurt by a continuing weak economy, the ANC lost its National Assembly majority in May 29, 2024, elections. After the ANC formed a coalition, the National Assembly reelected Ramaphosa president, June 14, 2024.

South Sudan

Republic of South Sudan

People: Population: 12,703,714 (79). **Age distrib.:** <15: 42.1%; 65+: 2.6%. **Growth:** 4.7%. **Migrants:** 7.9%. **Pop. density:** 52.1 per sq mi, 20.1 per sq km. **Urban:** 21.6%. **Ethnic groups:** Dinka (Jieng) 35%-40%, Nuer (Naath) 15%, Shilluk (Chollo), Azande, Bari, Kakwa, Kuku, Murle, Mandari, Didinga. **Languages:** English (official), Arabic (incl. Juba, Sudanese variants), ethnic langs. **Religions:** Christian 61.0% (Catholic 38.5%, Protestant 21.2%), ethnic religionist 32.1%, Muslim 6.4% (Sunni).

Geography: Total area: 248,777 sq mi, 644,329 sq km (42). **Location:** NE Africa. Sudan on N, Uganda and Kenya on S, Ethiopia on E, Central African Rep. and Dem. Rep. of the Congo on W. **Topography:** The White Nile R. flows N through center of country and feeds the Sudd, a swampy area occupying more than 15% of the country's center; it is one of the world's largest wetlands. **Arable land:** 3.8%. **Capital:** Juba, 479,359.

Government: Type: Presidential republic. **Head of state and govt.:** Pres. Salva Kiir Mayardit; b. 1951; in office: July 9, 2011. **Local divisions:** 10 states. **Defense budget:** $48 mil. **Active troops:** 90,000.

Economy: Chief agric.: milk, cassava, sorghum, goat milk, vegetables, fruits. **Natural resources:** hydropower, gold, diamonds, petroleum, hardwoods, limestone, iron ore, copper, chromium ore, zinc, tungsten, mica, silver. **Water:** 4,605 cu m per capita. **Electricity prod.:** 620.1 mil kWh. **Labor force:** agric. 60.3%, industry 13.7%, services 26.0%. **Unemployment:** 12.3%.

Finance: Monetary unit: Pound (SSP) (2,290.94 = $1 U.S.). **GDP:** NA; **per capita GDP:** NA; **GDP growth:** NA. **Imports** (2022): $6.4 bil; UAE 39%, Kenya 18%, China 17%. **Exports** (2022): $5.8 bil; China 44%, Italy 26%, Singapore 12%, Japan 9%, UAE 8%. **Budget:** $1.9 bil. **Inflation:** 2.4%.

Transport: Railways: 154 mi. **Airports:** 82.

Communications: Mobile: 53.7 per 100 pop. **Broadband:** 6.6 per 100 pop. **Internet:** 12.1%.

Health: Expend.: 5.9%. **Life expect.:** 58.4 male; 62.2 female. **Births:** 36.4 per 1,000 pop. **Deaths:** 8.9 per 1,000 pop. **Infant mortality:** 60.1 per 1,000 live births. **Undernourished:** 19.6%. **HIV:** 1.6%. **COVID-19:** 147 deaths; rates per 100,000: 168 cases, 1 death. 38% vaccinated.

Education: Compulsory: ages 6-13. **Literacy:** 34.5%.
Website: www.eservices.gov.ss

South Sudan was a region of the Republic of the Sudan when that country became independent in 1956. Northerners (mostly Arab Muslims) dominated, while southerners (mostly Black Africans who practiced Christianity or traditional religions) were marginalized. Southern rebels waged war against the north, 1955-72, until an agreement was reached offering regional self-government for the south. Oil was discovered in the south in 1978.

Civil war broke out again in 1983. Fighting and related famine cost an estimated 2 mil lives and displaced millions of southerners. A peace accord was signed in 2005. A power-sharing agreement allowed for an independence referendum.

Almost 99% of southern Sudanese who voted in the referendum, Jan. 9-15, 2011, supported secession. The UN Security Council, July 8, authorized a peacekeeping force (UNMISS) for the area. South Sudan attained full independence July 9, 2011.

Pres. Salva Kiir fired Vice Pres. Riek Machar, July 23, 2013. Heavy fighting broke out in Dec. 2013 between government troops and rebels led by Machar. Forces of Kiir and Machar battled throughout the country until a peace accord was signed Aug. 2015. Renewed heavy fighting began July 7, 2016. A new peace agreement was signed Sept. 12, 2018. A U.S.-funded study reported, Sept. 26, 2018, that South Sudan's civil war had caused about 383,000 "excess deaths" since late 2013. After Kiir and Machar agreed in Feb. 2020 on a new transitional government, Machar was sworn in as first vice president Feb. 22. Some violence continued. As of July 2024, about 2 mil South Sudanese were internally displaced. Almost 2.3 mil were refugees in neighboring countries as of Sept. 30, 2024. As of July 31, 2024, UNMISS had more than 15,000 uniformed personnel in South Sudan. Millions of South Sudanese faced hunger in 2023-24 as a result of drought, floods, and sharply increased food prices. Warfare in Sudan beginning Apr. 2023 caused over 600,000 South Sudanese to return home and about 180,000 Sudanese to become refugees in South Sudan as of late Aug. 2024.

Spain

Kingdom of Spain

People: Population: 47,280,433 (32). **Age distrib.:** <15: 13.0%; 65+: 20.9%. **Growth:** 0.1%. **Migrants:** 14.6%. **Pop. density:** 245.4 per sq mi, 94.8 per sq km. **Urban:** 81.8%. **Ethnic groups** (by birth country): Spanish 84.8%, Moroccan 1.7%. **Languages:** Castilian Spanish (official); Catalan, Galician, Basque (all official in areas). **Religions:** Christian 84.6% (Catholic 80.9%), agnostic 9.7%, Muslim 3.3% (Sunni).

Geography: Total area: 195,124 sq mi, 505,370 sq km (52); **Land area:** 192,657 sq mi, 498,980 sq km. **Location:** SW Europe. Portugal on W; France, Andorra on N; Morocco to S. **Topography:** High, arid plateau broken by mountain ranges and river valleys in interior. The NW is heavily watered, the S has lowlands and a Medit. climate. **Arable land:** 23.4%. **Capital:** Madrid, 6,783,241. **Cities:** Barcelona, 5,711,917.

Government: Type: Parliamentary constitutional monarchy. **Head of state:** King Felipe VI; b. 1968; in office: June 19, 2014. **Head of govt.:** Pres. Pedro Sánchez Pérez-Castejón; b. 1972; in office: June 2, 2018. **Local divisions:** 17 autonomous communities, 2 autonomous cities. **Defense budget:** $19.0 bil. **Active troops:** 124,150.

Economy: Industries: textiles/apparel (incl. footwear), food/beverages, metals/metal manufactures, chemicals, shipbuilding, automobiles, machine tools, tourism. **Chief agric.:** milk, barley, wheat, grapes, pork, olives. **Natural resources:** coal, lignite, iron ore, copper, lead, zinc, uranium, tungsten, mercury, pyrites, magnesite, fluorspar, gypsum, sepiolite, kaolin, potash, hydropower. **Water:** 2,348 cu m per capita. **Crude oil reserves:** 150 mil bbls. **Electricity prod.:** 278.7 bil kWh. **Labor force:** agric. 3.8%, industry 20.1%, services 76.1%. **Unemployment:** 12.1%.

Finance: Monetary unit: Euro (EUR) (0.90 = $1 U.S.). **GDP:** $2.6 tril; **per capita GDP:** $52,779; **GDP growth:** 2.5%. **Imports:** $550.6 bil; Germany 11%, China 10%, France 10%, Italy 7%, U.S. 6%. **Exports:** $615.8 bil; France 17%, Germany 10%, Portugal 9%, Italy 8%, UK 6%. **Tourism:** $92.0 bil. **Budget:** $586.0 bil. **Inflation:** 3.5%.

Transport: Railways: 9,624 mi. **Motor vehicles:** 639.2 per 1,000 pop. **Airports:** 363.

Communications: Mobile: 127.7 per 100 pop. **Broadband:** 113 per 100 pop. **Internet** (2023): 95.4%.

Health: Expend.: 10.7%. **Life expect.:** 80.3 male; 85.8 female. **Births:** 7.1 per 1,000 pop. **Deaths:** 10.0 per 1,000 pop. **Infant mortality:** 2.4 per 1,000 live births. **Undernourished:** <2.5%. **HIV:** 0.2%. **COVID-19:** 121,852 deaths; rates per 100,000: 29,536 cases, 257 deaths. 79% vaccinated.

Education: Compulsory: ages 6-15. **Literacy:** 98.6%.
Website: www.lamoncloa.gob.es

Settled by Iberians, Basques, and Celts, Spain was successively ruled (wholly or in part) by Carthage, Rome, and the Visigoths. Muslims invaded Iberia from N Africa in 711. Reconquest of the peninsula by Christians from the N laid the foundations of modern Spain. In 1469 the kingdoms of Aragon and Castile were united by the marriage of Ferdinand II and Isabella I. Moorish rule ended with the fall of Granada, 1492, the year Spain's large Jewish community was expelled.

Spain established a colonial empire after Columbus's 1492 "discovery" of America. Cortés conquered Mexico, and Pizarro conquered Peru. Spain lost most of its American colonies in the early 19th cent. and Cuba, the Philippines, and Puerto Rico in the Spanish-American War, 1898.

Primo de Rivera became dictator, 1923. King Alfonso XIII revoked the dictatorship, 1930, but was forced into exile in 1931. A republic was proclaimed, which disestablished the church, curtailed its privileges, and secularized education. A Popular Front of socialists, Communists, republicans, and anarchists governed 1936-39.

Army officers under Francisco Franco revolted, 1936. Some 500,000 to 1 mil died in the Spanish Civil War before Franco's Nationalist forces won a complete victory Apr. 1, 1939. Franco ruled as a dictator. Spain was officially neutral in WWII but had cordial relations with Nazi Germany for most of the war.

After Franco's death, Nov. 20, 1975, Prince Juan Carlos became king. In free elections, June 1977, moderates and democratic socialists won the most votes. The king thwarted a 1981 coup attempt by right-wing military officers. The Socialist Workers' Party (PSOE), under Felipe González Márquez, won four consecutive general elections, 1982-93, but lost to a coalition of conservative and regional parties, 1996.

Islamic extremists bombed four commuter trains in central Madrid, Mar. 11, 2004, killing 191 people. The PSOE won elections three days later. Spain legalized same-sex marriage in 2005.

Spain's economy suffered during the worldwide financial crisis that began in 2008; in May 2010, as the budget deficit mounted, the government introduced austerity measures to reassure international lenders. Mariano Rajoy's conservative Popular Party (PP) won Nov. 2011 elections. Spain received a 100-bil euro EU bailout for its ailing banks in 2012. Spain's unemployment rate surpassed 26% in 2013. GDP began growing in 2014, after five years of decline.

Juan Carlos abdicated in favor of his son, who became King Felipe VI, June 19, 2014. Hurt by corruption scandals, the PP lost support in Dec. 20, 2015, and June 26, 2016, legislative elections, but Rajoy formed a minority govt., Oct. 31, 2016.

In one of a series of events linked by police to an Islamist extremist cell in Catalonia, 14 people were killed and more than 100 injured in Barcelona, Aug. 17, 2017, when a terrorist drove a van through a crowded pedestrian area.

Rajoy lost a no-confidence vote, June 1, 2018; the PSOE's Pedro Sánchez became prime min. After Apr. 28 and Nov. 10, 2019, elections, Sánchez formed a new coalition minority government, Jan. 7, 2020.

Spain was the European entry point for over 272,000 African and Middle Eastern migrants (most arriving by boat), 2018-23. In 2024, over 42,000 had arrived by Sept. 29 (over two-thirds reaching the Canary Isls.). Thousands died attempting dangerous sea crossings.

Spain (incl. the Canary Isls.) experienced extreme summer heat, drought, and wildfires in the 2020s, a possible impact of climate change.

In July 23, 2023, elections, the PP won more seats than Sánchez's PSOE, but Sánchez formed a new coalition government, approved by parliament Nov. 16.

With a 1-0 victory over England, Aug. 20, 2023, Spain won the FIFA Women's World Cup soccer tournament. Spanish soccer federation chief Luis Rubiales was charged with sexual assault over kissing a player after the game.

Catalonia and the **Basque Country** were granted autonomy, Jan. 1980, following approval in referendums. But Basque extremists pushed for independence, and the separatist group ETA carried out a series of bombings. ETA declared a unilateral cease-fire in 2011 and said in 2018 that it was disbanding.

In Catalonia, voters approved expanded home-rule, June 18, 2006. Separatist parties won Catalonia's regional parliamentary elections Sept. 27, 2015. Spanish authorities took steps to interfere with a separation referendum, Oct. 1, 2017. After the regional parliament, Oct. 27, voted to declare independence, the national government dissolved the parliament and removed pro-independence regional president Carles Puigdemont from office. In new regional parliamentary elections, Dec. 21, separatists again won a majority.

In Feb. 14, 2021, elections, pro-independence parties won a majority. The Socialists won the most seats in May 12, 2024, elections, and regional party leader Salvador Illa, an ally of Sánchez, formed a coalition govt. and became regional president Aug. 10. **Website:** web.gencat.cat

The **Balearic Isls.** in the W Mediterranean, 1,927 sq mi, is an autonomous community of Spain; the islands include Majorca (Mallorca; capital Palma de Mallorca), Minorca, Cabrera, Ibiza, and Formentera. The **Canary** Isls., 2,807 sq mi, an autonomous community in the Atlantic W of Morocco, includes the islands of Tenerife, La Palma, La Gomera, El Hierro, Gran Canaria, Fuerteventura, and Lanzarote; Las Palmas and Santa Cruz are thriving ports.

Ceuta and **Melilla**, small Spanish enclaves on Morocco's Mediterranean coast, gained limited autonomy in Sept. 1994. In 2014-24, thousands of African and Middle Eastern migrants crossed the borders between Morocco and the enclaves.

Spain has sought the return of **Gibraltar**, in British hands since 1704.

Sri Lanka
Democratic Socialist Republic of Sri Lanka

People: Population: 21,982,608 (61). **Age distrib.:** <15: 22.6%; 65+: 12.4%. **Growth:** 0.4%. **Migrants:** 0.2%. **Pop. density:** 880.9 per sq mi, 340.1 per sq km. **Urban:** 19.4%. **Ethnic groups:** Sinhalese 74.9%, Sri Lankan Tamil 11.2%, Sri Lankan Moor 9.2%, Indian Tamil 4.2%. **Languages:** Sinhala, Tamil (both official); English (commonly used in govt.). **Religions:** Buddhist (official) 67.4% (Theravadin), Hindu 12.9% (Shaivite 9%), Christian 10.1%, Muslim 9.0% (Sunni).

Geography: Total area: 25,332 sq mi, 65,610 sq km (120); **Land area:** 24,954 sq mi, 64,630 sq km. **Location:** Indian O. off SE coast of India. **Topography:** Coastal area and N half are flat; S central area is hilly and mountainous. **Arable land:** 22.2%. **Capital:** Colombo (commercial), 639,818; Sri Jayewardenepura Kotte (legislative), 103,248.

Government: Type: Presidential republic. **Head of state:** Pres. Anura Kumara Dissanayake; b. 1968; in office: Sept. 23, 2024. **Head of govt.:** Prime Min. Harini Amarasuriya; b. 1970; in office: Sept. 24, 2024. **Local divisions:** 9 provinces. **Defense budget:** $1.3 bil. **Active troops:** 265,900.

Economy: Industries: proc. of rubber, tea, coconuts, tobacco and other agric. commodities; tourism, clothing and textiles; mining. **Chief agric.:** rice, coconuts, plantains, tea, sugarcane, milk. **Natural resources:** limestone, graphite, mineral sands, gems, phosphates, clay, hydropower. **Water:** 2,425 cu m per capita. **Electricity prod.:** 12.0 bil kWh. **Labor force:** agric. 26.4%, industry 27.0%, services 46.5%. **Unemployment:** 6.4%.

Finance: Monetary unit: Rupee (LKR) (300.34 = $1 U.S.). **GDP:** $318.6 bil; **per capita GDP:** $14,455; **GDP growth:** –2.3%. **Imports:** $18.8 bil; India 34%, China 19%, UAE 5%. **Exports:** $17.3 bil; U.S. 24%, India 8%, UK 7%, Germany 6%. **Tourism:** $2.1 bil. **Budget:** $17.5 bil. **Inflation:** 16.5%.

Transport: Railways: 971 mi. **Motor vehicles:** 68.8 per 1,000 pop. **Airports:** 18.

Communications: Mobile: 130.7 per 100 pop. **Broadband:** 72.3 per 100 pop. **Internet:** 50.1%.

Health: Expend.: 4.1%. **Life expect.:** 73.7 male; 79.9 female. **Births:** 14.5 per 1,000 pop. **Deaths:** 7.5 per 1,000 pop. **Infant mortality:** 6.8 per 1,000 live births. **Undernourished:** 4.1%. **HIV:** <0.1%. **COVID-19:** 16,907 deaths; rates per 100,000: 3,142 cases, 79 deaths. 69% vaccinated.

Education: Compulsory: ages 5-15. **Literacy:** 92.5%.

Website: www.gov.lk

The island was known to the ancient world as Taprobane (Greek for copper-colored) and later as Serendip (from Arabic). Colonists from N India subdued the Indigenous Veddahs about 543 BCE; their descendants, the Buddhist Sinhalese, still form most of the population. Hindu descendants of Tamil immigrants from S India are the largest minority ethnic group.

Parts were occupied by the Portuguese in 1505 and the Dutch in 1658. The British seized the island in 1796. It became an independent member of the Commonwealth as Ceylon in 1948 before changing its name to Sri Lanka May 22, 1972.

Prime Min. Solomon W. R. D. Bandaranaike was assassinated Sept. 25, 1959. His widow, Sirimavo Bandaranaike, served as prime min. 1960-65, 1970-77, 1994-2000. In the 1970s, thousands of ultra-leftists were executed, while massive land reform and nationalization of foreign-owned plantations took place.

Tensions between Sinhalese and Tamil separatists erupted in the early 1980s and turned into a 20-year civil war that killed more than 60,000; another 20,000, mostly young Tamils, "disappeared" while in government custody. Pres. Ranasinghe Premadasa was assassinated May 1, 1993, by a Tamil rebel. A truce intended to bring an end to the civil war was signed Feb. 22, 2002.

More than 31,000 died in the Dec. 26, 2004, Indian Ocean tsunami. Prime Min. Mahinda Rajapaksa won the 2005 presidential election and was reelected in 2010. Thousands died during more than three years of fighting among government forces, paramilitary groups, and Tamil rebels beginning in Dec. 2005. Tamil leader Velupillai Prabhakaran was killed May 18-19, 2009, and Pres. Rajapaksa formally declared victory. Maithripala Sirisena defeated Rajapaksa in the Jan. 8, 2015, presidential election.

Loans and investments from China have financed large infrastructure projects in recent years. More than 260 died Easter Sunday, Apr. 21, 2019, in suicide bombings at churches and other sites carried out by Islamist extremists. Gotabaya Rajapaksa, brother of the former president, won the Nov. 16, 2019, presidential election. He named Mahinda Rajapaksa prime min.

Amid a financial crisis and violent protests against widespread shortages and mismanagement of the economy, Mahinda Rajapaksa resigned, May 9, 2022, and was replaced as prime min., May 12, by Ranil Wickremesinghe. As protests intensified, Gotabaya Rajapaksa resigned, July 14. Wickremesinghe, July 20, was elected president by parliament. He declared a state of emergency and cracked down on protesters and their leaders. Sri Lanka, which defaulted on debt payments in 2022, obtained a $3-bil IMF bailout in Mar. 2023.

Leftist politician Anura Kumara Dissanayake was elected president Sept. 21, 2024, pledging to revive the economy and fight corruption.

Sudan
Republic of the Sudan

People: Population: 50,467,278 (29). **Age distrib.:** <15: 40.1%; 65+: 3.2%. **Growth:** 2.6%. **Migrants:** 3.1%. **Pop. density:** 75.5 per sq mi, 29.1 per sq km. **Urban:** 36.8%. **Ethnic groups:** over 500, incl. Sudanese Arab (approx. 70%), Fur, Beja, Nuba, Ingessana. **Languages:** Arabic, English (both official); Nubian; Ta Bedawie; Fur. **Religions:** Muslim 91.8% (Sunni), Christian 4.4%, ethnic religionist 2.6%.

Geography: Total area: 718,723 sq mi, 1,861,484 sq km (15); Land area: 668,602 sq mi, 1,731,671 sq km. **Location:** E end of Sahara desert zone. Egypt on N; Libya, Chad, Central African Republic on W; South Sudan on S; Ethiopia, Eritrea on E. **Topography:** The N consists of Libyan Desert in W and the mountainous Nubia Desert in E, with narrow Nile Valley between. Large rainy areas with fields, pastures, and forests in center. The S has rich soil, heavy rain. **Arable land:** 11.2%. **Capital:** Khartoum, 6,542,070. **Cities:** Nyala, 1,101,314.

Government: Type: Presidential republic. **Head of state and govt.:** Sovereign Council Chair Gen. Abdel Fattah al-Burhan; b. 1960; in office: Aug. 21, 2019. **Local divisions:** 18 states. **Defense budget:** NA. **Active troops:** 104,300.

Economy: Industries: oil, cotton ginning, textiles, cement, edible oils, sugar, soap distilling, shoes, petroleum refining, pharmaceuticals, armaments. **Chief agric.:** sorghum, sugarcane, milk, groundnuts, millet, onions. **Natural resources:** petroleum; small reserves of iron ore, copper, chromium ore, zinc, tungsten, mica, silver, gold; hydropower. **Water:** 828 cu m per capita. **Crude oil reserves:** 5 bil bbls. **Electricity prod.:** 17.9 bil kWh. **Labor force:** agric. 40.4%, industry 14.5%, services 45.0%. **Unemployment:** 11.4%.

Finance: Monetary unit: Pound (SDG) (601.44 = $1 U.S.). **GDP:** $150.9 bil; **per capita GDP:** $3,137; **GDP growth:** –12.1%. **Imports** (2022): $11.6 bil; China 22%, UAE 20%, India 18%, Egypt 9%, Turkey (Türkiye) 5%. **Exports** (2022): $5.9 bil; UAE 43%, China 16%, Italy 8%, Egypt 8%. **Tourism** (2022): $1.1 bil. **Budget:** $8.3 bil. **Inflation** (2021-22): 138.8%.

Transport: Railways: 4,506 mi. **Motor vehicles:** 3.3 per 1,000 pop. **Airports:** 41.

Communications: Mobile (2022): 70.2 per 100 pop. **Broadband** (2022): 45.2 per 100 pop. **Internet:** 28.7%.

Health: Expend.: 2.8%. **Life expect.:** 65.5 male; 70.2 female. **Births:** 33.1 per 1,000 pop. **Deaths:** 6.1 per 1,000 pop. **Infant mortality:** 40.6 per 1,000 live births. **Undernourished:** 11.4%. **HIV:** 0.2%. **COVID-19:** 5,046 deaths; rates per 100,000: 146 cases, 12 deaths. 31% vaccinated.

Education: Compulsory: ages 6-13. **Literacy:** 60.7%.

Website: www.presidency.gov.sd

Northern Sudan, ancient Nubia, was settled by Egyptians in antiquity. The population was converted to Coptic Christianity in the 6th cent. Arab conquests brought Islam to the area in the 15th cent. In the 1820s, Egypt took over Sudan. In the 1880s, Muhammad Ahmad, who called himself the Mahdi (leader of the faithful), and his followers, the dervishes, led a revolution. An Anglo-Egyptian force crushed the Mahdi's successors, 1898.

Sudan gained independence Jan. 1, 1956. In 1969, a Revolutionary Council took power, led by authoritarian Pres. Gaafar al-Nimeiry. He was overthrown, Apr. 6, 1985. Sudan held democratic elections in 1986. Brig. Omar Hassan Ahmad al-Bashir staged a coup, June 30, 1989. He became president in 1993.

During 1955-72 and 1983-2005, rebels in the south (primarily Christians and followers of traditional religions) fought against government domination by mostly Arab-Muslim northern Sudan. War and famine cost an estimated 2 mil lives. An accord largely ended the rebellion Jan. 9, 2005, but violence continued.

A rebellion in the Darfur region of western Sudan caused a new crisis, 2003-11. Marauding Arab militias, the janjaweed, reportedly acting in collusion with Sudanese government troops, looted and burned homes in Darfur. By Sept. 2009, the Darfur war had killed about 300,000 people and displaced another 2.7 mil.

After southern Sudanese voted overwhelmingly for secession, Jan. 9-15, 2011, South Sudan attained full independence July 9. Conflict in Darfur flared up again in 2014-16. A UN-AU peacekeeping mission in Darfur (UNAMID) was established. The government signed a peace agreement, Oct. 3, 2020, with some Darfur and southern rebel groups. The UNAMID mission ended Dec. 31, 2020, but violence in Darfur persisted.

After months of deadly protests triggered by economic hardship, Bashir was ousted in a military coup, Apr. 11, 2019. Protests continued, demanding civilian rule. An Aug. 17, 2019, agreement provided for a power-sharing transition government, followed by elections.

In an Oct. 25, 2021, coup led by transition government head Gen. Abdel Fattah al-Burhan, the military seized full power; it cracked down violently on anti-coup protesters.

Fierce fighting in and around Khartoum began Apr. 15, 2023, between the Sudanese armed forces and the formerly allied paramilitary Rapid Support Forces (RSF). The fighting quickly spread to other regions, including Darfur, where the RSF (with links to the janjaweed) was widely accused of atrocities. By Sept. 2024, over 8 mil Sudanese had been internally displaced since fighting began in Apr. 2023; over 2 mil Sudanese had become refugees in neighboring countries. Perhaps 25 mil Sudanese faced acute hunger or famine. Tens of thousands had been killed in the conflict.

Suriname

Republic of Suriname

People: Population: 646,758 (165). **Age distrib.:** <15: 22.5%; 65+: 7.5%. **Growth:** 1.1%. **Migrants:** 8.1%. **Pop. density:** 10.7 per sq mi, 4.1 per sq km. **Urban:** 66.5%. **Ethnic groups:** Hindustani or East Indian (descended fr. 19th-cent. emigrants fr. northern India) 27.4%, Maroon (descendants of escaped African slaves) 21.7%, Creole (mixed white/Black) 15.7%, Javanese 13.7%, mixed 13.4%. **Languages:** Dutch (official), English (widely spoken), Sranang Tongo (Surinamese), Caribbean Hindustani, Javanese. **Religions:** Christian 52.6% (Catholic 33.9%, Protestant 12.1%), Hindu 19.1% (Vaishnavite 7%, Saktist 7%, Shaivite 7%), Muslim 15.7% (Sunni), agnostic 4.4%, Spiritist 2.7%, ethnic religionist 2.7%.

Geography: Total area: 63,251 sq mi, 163,820 sq km (90); **Land area:** 60,232 sq mi, 156,000 sq km. **Location:** N shore of S America. Guyana on W, Brazil on S, French Guiana on E. **Topography:** Flat Atlantic coast, where dikes permit agriculture. Inland is forest belt. Hills cover three-fourths of country in S. **Arable land:** 0.3%. **Capital:** Paramaribo, 239,457.

Government: Type: Presidential republic. **Head of state and govt.:** Pres. Chandrikapersad Santokhi; b. 1959; in office: July 16, 2020. **Local divisions:** 10 districts. **Defense budget:** NA. **Active troops:** 1,840.

Economy: Industries: gold mining, oil, lumber, food proc., fishing. **Chief agric.:** rice, sugarcane, oranges, chicken, plantains, vegetables. **Natural resources:** timber, hydropower, fish, kaolin, shrimp, bauxite, gold; small amounts of nickel, copper, platinum, iron ore. **Water:** 161,505 cu m per capita. **Crude oil reserves:** 89 mil bbls. **Electricity prod.:** 2.1 bil kWh. **Labor force:** agric. 7.5%, industry 26.4%, services 66.0%. **Unemployment:** 7.7%.

Finance: Monetary unit: Dollar (SRD) (28.99 = $1 U.S.). **GDP:** $13.1 bil; **per capita GDP:** $21,047; **GDP growth:** 2.1%. **Imports:** $2.2 bil; U.S. 25%, China 15%, Netherlands 13%, Trinidad and Tobago 6%. **Exports:** $2.5 bil; Switzerland 39%, UAE 21%, Belgium 10%, Guyana 5%. **Tourism:** $29 mil. **Budget:** $1.6 bil. **Inflation** (2021-22): 52.4%.

Transport: Motor vehicles: 301.4 per 1,000 pop. **Airports:** 55.

Communications: Mobile: 157.2 per 100 pop. **Broadband:** 138 per 100 pop. **Internet:** 75.8%.

Health: Expend.: 5.7%. **Life expect.:** 69.0 male; 76.7 female. **Births:** 14.9 per 1,000 pop. **Deaths:** 6.7 per 1,000 pop. **Infant mortality:** 29.6 per 1,000 live births. **Undernourished:** 10.1%. **HIV:** 1.6%. **COVID-19:** 1,406 deaths; rates per 100,000: 14,064 cases, 240 deaths. 41% vaccinated.

Education: Compulsory: ages 7-12. **Literacy:** 95.0%.

Website: www.gov.sr or www.surinameembassy.org

The Netherlands acquired Suriname in 1667 from Britain. The 1954 Dutch constitution raised the colony to a level of equality with the Netherlands. Independence was granted Nov. 25, 1975; some 40% of the population (mostly E Indians, who opposed independence) immigrated to the Netherlands.

Désire "Dési" Bouterse, who masterminded coups in 1982 and 1990, was elected president by the National Assembly, July 19, 2010. Bouterse had been convicted in absentia in the Netherlands, 1999, for drug trafficking. Named by the U.S. as a transshipment point for cocaine, Suriname agreed in 2012 to improve shipping inspections. Bouterse's son Dino pleaded guilty in the U.S., Aug. 29, 2014, to drug trafficking and terrorism charges. Bouterse was reelected by the National Assembly, July 14, 2015. He was convicted, in Suriname Nov. 29, 2019, of murder in connection with the 1982 coup; after losing his appeal, Dec. 20, 2023, Bouterse failed to report, Jan. 12, 2024, to start his prison sentence.

Following an opposition victory in May 25, 2020, elections, the new National Assembly elected Chandrikapersad Santokhi president, July 13.

Sweden

Kingdom of Sweden

People: Population: 10,589,835 (89). **Age distrib.:** <15: 17.1%; 65+: 20.8%. **Growth:** 0.5%. **Migrants:** 19.8%. **Pop. density:** 66.8 per sq mi, 25.8 per sq km. **Urban:** 89.0%. **Ethnic groups** (by birth country): Swedish 79.6%, Syrian 1.9%, Iraqi 1.4%, Finnish 1.3%; Indigenous Sami. **Languages:** Swedish (official). **Religions:** Christian 57.1% (Protestant 54.0%), agnostic 20.6%, Muslim 10.7% (Sunni 8%), atheist 10.4%.

Geography: Total area: 173,860 sq mi, 450,295 sq km (56); **Land area:** 158,431 sq mi, 410,335 sq km. **Location:** Scandinavian Peninsula in N Europe. Norway on W, Denmark on S (across Kattegat strait), Finland on E. **Topography:** Mountains along NW border cover 25% of Sweden. Flat or rolling terrain with several large lakes across central and southern areas. **Arable land:** 6.2%. **Capital:** Stockholm, 1,719,604.

Government: Type: Parliamentary constitutional monarchy. **Head of state:** King Carl XVI Gustaf; b. 1946; in office: Sept. 15, 1973. **Head of govt.:** Prime Min. Ulf Kristersson; b. 1963; in office: Oct. 18, 2022. **Local divisions:** 21 counties. **Defense budget:** $9.2 bil. **Active troops:** 14,850.

Economy: Industries: iron and steel, precision equip. (bearings, radio/phone parts, armaments), wood pulp and paper prods., processed foods, motor vehicles. **Chief agric.:** wheat, milk, sugar beets, barley, potatoes, oats. **Natural resources:** iron ore, copper, lead, zinc, gold, silver, tungsten, uranium, arsenic, feldspar, timber, hydropower. **Water:** 16,624 cu m per capita. **Electricity prod.:** 173.8 bil kWh. **Labor force:** agric. 1.9%, industry 17.2%, services 80.9%. **Unemployment:** 7.6%.

Finance: Monetary unit: Krona (SEK) (10.18 = $1 U.S.). **GDP:** $739.7 bil; **per capita GDP:** $70,207; **GDP growth:** –0.2%. **Imports:** $296.8 bil; Germany 16%, Netherlands 10%, Norway 9%, China 7%, Denmark 6%. **Exports:** $324.1 bil; Germany 10%, Norway 10%, U.S. 9%, Denmark 8%, Finland 7%. **Tourism:** $9.8 bil. **Budget:** $256.5 bil. **Inflation:** 8.5%.

Transport: Railways: 6,779 mi. **Motor vehicles:** 542.7 per 1,000 pop. **Airports:** 203.

Communications: Mobile: 140.4 per 100 pop. **Broadband:** 132 per 100 pop. **Internet** (2023): 95.7%.

Health: Expend. (2022): 10.7%. **Life expect.:** 81.2 male; 84.7 female. **Births:** 10.7 per 1,000 pop. **Deaths:** 9.6 per 1,000 pop. **Infant mortality:** 2.3 per 1,000 live births. **Undernourished:** <2.5%. **HIV:** NA. **COVID-19:** 27,433 deaths; rates per 100,000: 26,686 cases, 266 deaths. 72% vaccinated.

Education: Compulsory: ages 6-15. **Literacy:** NA.

Website: sweden.se

The Swedes have lived in present-day Sweden for at least 5,000 years. Gothic tribes from Sweden played a major role in the disintegration of the Roman Empire. Swedish chieftains controlled much of present-day western Russia and Ukraine in the 9th cent. The Swedes were Christianized from the 11th cent., and a strong centralized monarchy developed. The Riksdag, the first European parliament to represent all classes of society, was first called in 1435.

A revolt led by Gustavus I in 1521-23 freed Sweden from Danish rule (dating from 1397); he built up the government and military and established the Lutheran Church. In the 17th cent. Sweden was a major European power, gaining most of the Baltic seacoast. The Napoleonic wars, 1799-1815, in which Sweden acquired Norway (it became independent 1905), were the last in which Sweden participated.

The Social Democratic Party (SAP) has governed Sweden for most of the period since World War II. Prime Min. Olof Palme was shot to death in Stockholm, Feb. 28, 1986. Sweden entered the EU, Jan. 1, 1995. A center-right alliance defeated the SAP in 2006 and 2010 parliamentary elections. Parliament voted Apr. 1, 2009, to legalize same-sex marriage. The SAP won Sept. 14, 2014, elections, in which the right-wing, anti-immigration Sweden Democrats (SD) won 49 seats.

About 238,000 migrants, mostly from the Middle East, SW Asia, and Africa, applied for asylum in Sweden in 2015-18. Legislation tightening asylum rules was enacted June 21, 2016. Of applications decided, 2015-18, about 50% were approved.

In Sept. 9, 2018, elections, an SAP-led coalition fell short of a majority but retained power; the SD won 62 seats. As the COVID-19 pandemic spread in 2020, Sweden's government resisted strict lockdowns to combat transmission. In Nov. 2021, the SAP's Magdalena Andersson became Sweden's first female prime min. In Sept. 11, 2022, elections center-right parties, including the SD (which won 73 seats and over 20% of the vote), narrowly defeated the SAP-led coalition. The Moderate Party's Ulf Kristersson formed a coalition government that officially did not include the SD but would rely on SD support in parliament.

Following Russia's Feb. 2022 invasion of Ukraine, Sweden applied to join NATO; it was admitted Mar. 7, 2024.

Switzerland

Swiss Confederation

People: Population: 8,860,574 (102). **Age distrib.:** <15: 15.1%; 65+: 20.3%. **Growth:** 0.8%. **Migrants:** 28.8%. **Pop. density:** 573.8 per sq mi, 221.5 per sq km. **Urban:** 74.3%. **Ethnic groups** (by birth country): Swiss 69.2%, German 4.2%, Italian 3.2%, Portuguese 2.5%, French 2.1%. **Languages:** German, French, Italian, Romansh (all official); English; Portuguese; Albanian; Serbo-Croatian; Spanish. **Religions:** Christian 73.4% (Catholic 39.3%, Protestant 29.8%), agnostic 16.4%, Muslim 7.5% (Sunni).

Geography: Total area: 15,937 sq mi, 41,277 sq km (132); **Land area:** 15,443 sq mi, 39,997 sq km. **Location:** In Alps Mts. in central Europe. France on W; Italy on S; Liechtenstein, Austria on E; Germany on N. **Topography:** The Alps cover 60% of land area; the Jura, near France, 10%. The midlands run NE-SW in-between. **Arable land:** 10.0%. **Capital:** Bern, 444,530. **Cities:** Zurich, 1,443,349.

Government: Type: Federal republic (formally a confederation). **Head of state and govt.:** President chosen on rotating basis from among 7-member Federal Council for 1-year term. **Local divisions:** 26 cantons. **Defense budget:** $5.9 bil. **Active troops:** 21,300.

Economy: Industries: machinery, chemicals, watches, textiles, precision instruments, tourism, banking, insurance. **Chief agric.:** milk, sugar beets, wheat, potatoes, pork, apples. **Natural resources:** timber, salt. **Water:** 6,156 cu m per capita. **Electricity prod.:** 58.7 bil kWh. **Labor force:** agric. 2.3%, industry 20.3%, services 77.4%. **Unemployment:** 4.1%.

Finance: Monetary unit: Franc (CHF) (0.84 = $1 U.S.). **GDP:** $822.9 bil; **per capita GDP:** $92,980; **GDP growth:** 0.7%. **Imports:** $554.4 bil; Germany 21%, U.S. 10%, Italy 8%, France 6%, China 5%. **Exports:** $661.6 bil; U.S. 15%, Germany 13%, China 11%, Italy 6%, France 5%. **Tourism:** $21.1 bil. **Budget** (2018): $230.4 bil (federal, cantonal, and municipal). **Inflation:** 2.1%.

Transport: Railways: 3,291 mi. **Motor vehicles:** 639.5 per 1,000 pop. **Airports:** 62.

Communications: Mobile: 122.9 per 100 pop. **Broadband:** 106 per 100 pop. **Internet** (2023): 97.3%.

Health: Expend.: 11.8%. **Life expect.:** 82.0 male; 85.8 female. **Births:** 10.1 per 1,000 pop. **Deaths:** 8.5 per 1,000 pop. **Infant mortality:** 3.0 per 1,000 live births. **Undernourished:** <2.5%. **HIV:** 0.2%. **COVID-19:** 14,170 deaths; rates per 100,000: 51,514 cases, 164 deaths. 66% vaccinated.

Education: Compulsory: ages 4-14. **Literacy:** NA.

Website: www.ch.ch

Switzerland, the former Roman province of Helvetia, traces its modern history to 1291, when three cantons created a defensive league. Other cantons were subsequently admitted to the Swiss Confederation, which obtained its independence from the Holy Roman Empire through the Peace of Westphalia (1648). The cantons were joined under a federal constitution in 1848.

Switzerland has maintained an armed neutrality since 1815 and has not been involved in a foreign war since 1515. It is the seat of many UN and other international agencies but only became a full UN member on Sept. 10, 2002.

Switzerland is a world banking center. The government announced, Mar. 1997, a $4.7-bil fund to compensate victims of the Nazi Holocaust and other catastrophes. Swiss banks agreed Aug. 12, 1998, to pay $1.25 bil in reparations. A June 2002 referendum decriminalized abortion. Referenda in 2005 harmonized many policies with the EU.

In a Nov. 2009 referendum, voters approved a constitutional ban on construction of new minarets on mosques. A Mar. 2021 referendum banned face coverings such as a burqa in public.

Switzerland officially opened the 35-mi Gotthard Base Tunnel, the world's longest railway tunnel, June 1, 2016. In a May 19, 2019, referendum, voters approved stricter gun controls. Dec. 18, 2020, egislation legalized same-sex marriage, ratified by voters in a Sept. 26, 2021, referendum. UBS, Switzerland's largest bank, agreed in Mar. 2023 to acquire its scandal-plagued rival Credit Suisse.

In recent years, glaciers in the Swiss Alps have been shrinking as a result of climate change—including a 10% total volume loss in the hot summers of 2022 and 2023.

Syria

Syrian Arab Republic

People: Population: 23,865,423 (57). **Age distrib.:** <15: 33.0%; 65+: 4.2%. **Growth:** 1.7%. **Migrants:** 5.0%. **Pop. density:** 332.5 per sq mi, 128.4 per sq km. **Urban:** 58.0%. **Ethnic groups:** Arab 50%, Alawite 15%, Kurd 10%, Levantine 10%, other (incl. Druze, Ismaili, Imami, Nusairi, Assyrian, Turkoman, Armenian) 15%. **Languages:** Arabic (official), Kurdish, Armenian, Aramaic, Circassian, French, English. **Religions:** Muslim (official) 95.4% (Sunni 80%, Shia 14%), Christian 2.7%.

Geography: Total area: 72,370 sq mi, 187,437 sq km (87); **Land area:** 71,771 sq mi, 185,887 sq km. (500 sq mi of area is occupied by Israel.) **Location:** Middle East, at E end of Medit. Sea. Lebanon, Israel on W; Jordan on S; Iraq on E; Turkey on N. **Topography:** A short Medit. coastline stretches E and S with fertile lowlands and plains, alternating with mountains and large desert areas. **Arable land:** 23.8%. **Capital:** Damascus, 2,685,361. **Cities:** Aleppo, 2,317,650; Homs, 1,499,603.

Government: Type: Presidential republic; highly authoritarian regime. **Head of state:** Pres. Bashar al-Assad; b. 1965; in office: July 17, 2000. **Head of govt.:** Prime Min. Hussein Arnous; b. 1953; in office: Aug. 31, 2020. **Local divisions:** 14 provinces. **Defense budget:** NA. **Active troops:** 169,000. (Est. 50,000 Syrian Democratic Forces in territory where govt. does not exercise effective control.)

Economy: Industries: petroleum, textiles, food proc., beverages, tobacco, phosphate rock mining, cement. **Chief agric.:** wheat, milk, olives, sheep milk, tomatoes, potatoes. **Natural resources:** petroleum, phosphates, chrome and manganese ores, asphalt, iron ore, rock salt, marble, gypsum, hydropower. **Water:** 788 cu m per capita. **Crude oil reserves:** 2.5 bil bbls. **Electricity prod.:** 16.9 bil kWh. **Labor force:** agric. 15.5%, industry 22.7%, services 61.8%. **Unemployment:** 13.5%.

Finance: Monetary unit: Pound (SYP) (13,002.12 = $1 U.S.). **GDP** (2021): $62.2 bil; **per capita GDP** (2021): $2,915; **GDP growth** (2021): 1.3%. **Imports** (2021): $6.6 bil; Turkey (Türkiye) 45%, UAE 10%, China 9%, Lebanon 8%, Egypt 7%. **Exports** (2021): $2.2 bil; Turkey (Türkiye) 29%, Kuwait 15%, Lebanon 14%, Jordan 8%, Egypt 7%. **Budget** (2017): $3.2 bil. **Inflation** (2016-17): 28.1%.

Transport: Railways: 1,275 mi. **Motor vehicles:** 154.7 per 1,000 pop. **Airports:** 39.

Communications: Mobile: 64.1 per 100 pop. **Broadband:** 31.2 per 100 pop. **Internet** (2019): 34.7%.

Health: Expend.: NA. **Life expect.:** 73.4 male; 76.4 female. **Births:** 21.7 per 1,000 pop. **Deaths:** 4.0 per 1,000 pop. **Infant mortality:** 15.1 per 1,000 live births. **Undernourished:** 34.0%. **HIV:** <0.1%. **COVID-19:** 3,163 deaths; rates per 100,000: 328 cases, 18 deaths. 13% vaccinated.

Education: Compulsory: ages 6-14. **Literacy:** 94.4%.

Website: www.egov.sy

Syria was the center of the Seleucid Empire but later was absorbed into the Roman and Arab empires. Ottoman rule prevailed for four cents., until the end of WWI.

The state of Syria was formed from former Turkish districts, separated by the Treaty of Sevres, 1920, and divided into the states of Syria and Greater Lebanon. Both were administered under a French League of Nations mandate, 1920-41. The occupying French proclaimed Syria a republic Sept. 16, 1941; independence came Apr. 17, 1946. Syria joined the Arab invasion of Israel in 1948.

Syria belonged to the United Arab Republic from Feb. 1958 to Sept. 1961. The Socialist Baath party seized power Mar. 1963 and became the only legal party. The Alawite minority has dominated the government (Alawism is a sect of Shiite Islam).

In the June 1967 Arab-Israeli war, Israel seized and occupied the Golan Heights, from which Syria had shelled Israeli settlements. On Oct. 6, 1973, Syria and Egypt attacked Israel but failed to recapture the Golan Heights. Syrian troops entered Lebanon in 1976, during the Lebanese civil war, and remained a strong presence in the country. Syria sided with Iran during the Iran-Iraq War, 1980-88.

Thousands died in the city of Hama Feb. 1982 when government forces crushed a Muslim Brotherhood uprising. Following Israel's invasion of Lebanon, June 6, 1982, Israeli planes destroyed Syrian planes and antiaircraft missile batteries in the Bekaa Valley, June 9.

Hafez al-Assad, president of Syria since 1971, died June 10, 2000, and was succeeded by his son Bashar al-Assad. Syria aided fighters of the Lebanon-based Shiite group Hezbollah in their conflict with Israel and gave about 180,000 Lebanese temporary refuge when Israeli forces targeted Hezbollah, July-Aug. 2006. On Sept. 6, 2007, Israel bombed a secret site in N Syria where the Israelis believed Syria and North Korea were developing a nuclear facility; both countries denied the claim.

The Assad regime used troops and tanks during Arab Spring demonstrations in Mar. 2011, but the confrontations escalated into outright rebellion. A number of armed opposition groups fought Assad's forces and each other for control of territory. Hezbollah forces fought on the side of the Assad government, which was also backed by Iran.

International intelligence communities announced, May 2013, increasing evidence that Assad's forces had used chemical and biological weapons. A chemical attack on an opposition-controlled Damascus suburb Aug. 21, 2013, killed more than 1,400. Russian and U.S. negotiators reached an agreement with Syria requiring the Assad government to relinquish chemical weapons. Assad's forces continued using chlorine gas (not covered by the 2013 agreement). Syrian aircraft dropped chemical weapons prohibited by the 2013 agreement on a rebel-held town, Apr. 4, 2017; the U.S., Apr. 6, launched a cruise missile attack on the air base used by the planes. Israeli warplanes reportedly attacked, Sept. 7, 2017, Syrian military sites producing chemical weapons and missiles. An apparent chemical attack, Apr. 7, 2018, that killed dozens in a then-rebel-held area east of Damascus prompted U.S., UK, and French retaliatory airstrikes, Apr. 13.

By summer 2014, the Sunni extremist group ISIS (Islamic State in Iraq and Syria) controlled large areas in eastern and northern Syria. The night of Sept. 22-23, 2014, the U.S. began a campaign of airstrikes against ISIS and other Islamist extremist groups in Syria, supported by several Middle East countries and European and other allies. Russia, which backed Assad, sent warplanes and troops to Syria in Sept. 2015 and began its own air campaign, Sept. 30, against anti-government forces. Heavy Russian airstrikes helped the Assad regime regain control of large areas, 2016-18, often with high civilian casualties. Syrian Kurdish and other rebel groups making up the Syrian Democratic Forces (SDF), with support from U.S. airstrikes and special operations troops, retook territory in northern and eastern Syria from ISIS, 2015-17, including Raqqa (ISIS's self-proclaimed capital), Oct. 2017. The SDF said it captured the last ISIS-controlled area in Mar. 2019, although ISIS continued to stage attacks. ISIS leader Abu Bakr al-Baghdadi died (an apparent suicide) in a U.S. raid on his N Syria compound, Oct. 26, 2019. Three subsequent ISIS leaders were killed in Syria, 2022-23.

The U.S., in early 2019, announced plans to reduce its ground troops in Syria (about 800 remained in 2024).

Beginning in 2016, Turkish troops and groups aligned with them attacked Syrian Kurdish forces and tried to limit Kurdish-controlled areas in northern Syria. When the U.S., Oct. 2019, pulled back troops in northern Syria, Turkish and allied forces launched a new attack on the SDF, displacing tens of thousands of people and shrinking Kurdish-controlled territory.

By 2019, non-Kurdish rebels had largely retreated to Idlib Province in NW Syria; a Syrian government offensive, supported by Russian airstrikes, began Apr. 2019; Turkish troops supported some Idlib rebel groups. A Mar. 2020 cease-fire reduced violence somewhat.

Estimates of the total death toll in Syria's civil war since Mar. 2011 varied widely; the Syrian Observatory for Human Rights issued an overall estimate of about 618,000, including over 507,000 it said it had documented, as of Mar. 2024. The UNHCR reported the number of Syrian refugees in Turkey, the Middle East, and North Africa at about 5 mil as of Sept. 2024. More than 1 mil Syrians had applied for asylum in Europe. Over 7 mil people were displaced within Syria in 2024 according to UNHCR estimates.

A powerful earthquake centered in south-central Turkey, Feb. 6, 2023, plus aftershocks, caused massive damage in northern Syria. More than 8,400 died in Syria, and the Assad government apparently blocked some aid shipments to rebel-held areas already suffering from shortages of food, shelter, and medical facilities.

The Arab League agreed, May 7, 2023, to readmit Syria (expelled in 2011).

The removal of fuel subsidies, Aug. 2023, sparked demonstrations, largely in southern Syria, protesting economic hardship and calling of Assad's ouster.

Taiwan

People: Population: 23,595,274 (58). **Age distrib.:** <15: 12.1%; 65+: 18.8%. **Growth:** 0.03%. **Migrants:** NA. **Pop. density:** 1,894.3 per sq mi, 731.4 per sq km. **Urban:** 80.4%. **Ethnic groups:** Han Chinese (incl. Holo [approx. 70% of pop.], Hakka, other groups originating in mainland China) 95%+, Indigenous Malayo-Polynesian peoples 2.3%. **Languages:** Mandarin (official), Min Nan, Hakka dialects, about 16 Indigenous langs. **Religions:** Chinese folk-religionist 42.3%, Buddhist 26.4% (Mahayanist), Daoist 12.6%, Christian 6.8%, new religionist 6.7%, agnostic 4.3%.

Geography: Total area: 13,892 sq mi, 35,980 sq km (135); **Land area:** 12,456 sq mi, 32,260 sq km. **Location:** Off SE coast of China, between E and S China Seas. **Topography:** A mountain range forms backbone of island. The eastern half is very steep and craggy; western slope is flat, fertile, and well cultivated. **Arable land:** 16.7%. **Capital:** Taibei, 2,766,334. **Cities:** Xinbei, 4,534,877; Taoyuan, 2,338,724; Gaoxiong, 1,559,085.

Government: Type: Semi-presidential republic. **Head of state:** Pres. Lai Ching-te; b. 1959; in office: May 20, 2024. **Head of govt.:** Prem. Cho Jung-tai; b. 1959; in office: May 20, 2024. **Local divisions:** 13 counties, 3 cities, 6 special municipalities. **Defense budget:** $18.9 bil. **Active troops:** 169,000.

Economy: Industries: electronics, communications and information tech. prods., petroleum refining, chemicals, textiles, iron and steel, machinery, cement, food proc. **Chief agric.:** rice, vegetables, pork, chicken, cabbages, sugarcane. **Natural resources:** coal, nat. gas, limestone, marble, asbestos. **Water:** NA. **Crude oil reserves:** 2 mil bbls. **Electricity prod.:** 283.6 bil kWh. **Labor force:** agric. 4.7%, industry 36.3%, services 59.0%. **Unemployment:** 3.7%.

Finance: Monetary unit: New Dollar (TWD) (31.93 = $1 U.S.). **GDP:** NA; **per capita GDP:** NA; **GDP growth:** NA. **Imports** (2019): $308.7 bil; China 19%, Japan 12%, U.S. 10%, South Korea 7%, Australia 6%. **Exports** (2019): $388.5 bil; China 22%, U.S. 15%, Hong Kong 12%, Singapore 7%, Japan 6%. **Tourism:** $8.7 bil. **Budget:** $105.8 bil. **Inflation** (2018-19): 0.5%.

Transport: Railways: 1,002 mi. **Motor vehicles:** 360.2 per 1,000 pop. **Airports:** 53.

Communications: Mobile: 128.6 per 100 pop. **Broadband:** 122 per 100 pop. **Internet** (2023): 93.1%.

Health: Expend.: NA. **Life expect.:** 78.6 male; 84.7 female. **Births:** 7.3 per 1,000 pop. **Deaths:** 8.1 per 1,000 pop. **Infant mortality:** 3.8 per 1,000 live births. **Undernourished:** 3.7%. **HIV:** NA. **COVID-19:** 17,668 deaths; rates per 100,000: 43,866 cases, 76 deaths. 89% vaccinated.

Education: Compulsory: ages 6-15. **Literacy:** 98.5%.

Website: www.taiwan.gov.tw

Large-scale immigration from China began in the 17th cent. The island came under mainland control after an interval of Dutch rule, 1620-62. Japan ruled Taiwan (also called Formosa), 1895-1945. The Kuomintang (Chinese Nationalist Party) government fled to Taiwan in 1949 and established the Republic of China under Chiang Kai-shek, who ruled until his death in 1975. The U.S. provided military aid to deter a Communist invasion.

In 1971, the UN expelled Taiwan and recognized the mainland government. The U.S. acknowledged the People's Republic of China, Dec. 15, 1978, and severed diplomatic relations with Taiwan. The U.S. and Taiwan have maintained strong economic, defense, and unofficial ties. After opportunities for Chinese aid and investment led a number of countries to break relations in the 2010s and 2020s, Taiwan maintained diplomatic ties with 12 countries as of Aug. 31, 2024.

Land reform, government planning, U.S. aid and investment, and free universal education brought advances in industry, agriculture, and living standards. In 1987 martial law was lifted after 38 years, and in 1991 more than four decades of emergency rule ended. Taiwan held its first direct presidential election Mar. 23, 1996.

Five decades of Kuomintang rule ended when Chen Shui-bian, leader of the pro-independence Democratic Progressive Party (DPP), won the Mar. 2000 presidential election. Chen was wounded in an apparent assassination attempt Mar. 19, 2004, one day before he won a second term as president. Promising increased cooperation with China, Kuomintang candidate Ma Ying-jeou won the 2008 and 2012 presidential elections.

The People's Republic considers Taiwan a rebel province of the mainland; in 1991, the Kuomintang dropped its claim to be the sole government of both. The first formal talks between Taiwan and China were held Feb. 11, 2014. Concern over recent Kuomintang pro-China policies helped the DPP win the Jan. 16, 2016, presidential election; Tsai Ingwen became Taiwan's first female president. She was reelected, Jan. 11, 2020.

In accordance with a Constitutional Court ruling, legislation legalizing same-sex marriage went into effect May 24, 2019.

Objecting to an Aug. 2022 visit to Taiwan by U.S. House Speaker Nancy Pelosi, China staged large-scale military exercises near Taiwan. Chinese military shows of force near Taiwan increased in 2023-24. The DPP's Lai Ching-te won Taiwan's Jan. 13, 2024, presidential election (although with only 40% of the vote); in legislative elections the same day, the DPP lost its majority.

The Penghu Isls. (Pescadores), 49 sq mi, pop. (2011 est.) 96,597, lie between Taiwan and the mainland. Kinmen, fmr. Quemoy, pop. (2011 est.) 99,691, and Matsu, pop. (2011 est.) 10,106, lie just off the mainland.

Tajikistan

Republic of Tajikistan

People: Population: 10,394,063 (91). **Age distrib.:** <15: 36.9%; 65+: 3.9%. **Growth:** 1.9%. **Migrants:** 2.9%. **Pop. density:** 190.2 per sq mi, 73.5 per sq km. **Urban:** 28.5%. **Ethnic groups:** Tajik (incl. Pamiri and Yagnobi) 84.3%, Uzbek 13.8%, other (incl. Kyrgyz, Russian, Turkmen, Tatar, Arab) 2%. **Languages:** Tajik (official), Uzbek, Russian (used in govt. and business). **Religions:** Muslim 97.9% (Sunni 88%, Shia 10%).

Geography: Total area: 55,637 sq mi, 144,100 sq km (94); **Land area:** 54,637 sq mi, 141,510 sq km. **Location:** Central Asia. Uzbekistan on N and W, Kyrgyzstan on N, China on E, Afghanistan on S. **Topography:** Mountainous; contains the Pamirs, Trans-Alai mountain system. **Arable land:** 6.0%. **Capital:** Dushanbe, 1,012,794.

Government: Type: Presidential republic. **Head of state:** Pres. Emomali Rahmon; b. 1952; in office: Nov. 6, 1994. **Head of govt.:** Prime Min. Qohir Rasulzoda; b. 1961; in office: Nov. 23, 2013. **Local divisions:** 2 provinces, 1 autonomous province, 1 capital region, 1 area (Districts Under Republic Admin.). **Defense budget:** $141 mil. **Active troops:** 8,800.

Economy: Industries: aluminum, cement, coal, gold, silver. **Chief agric.:** milk, potatoes, wheat, watermelons, onions, cotton. **Natural resources:** hydropower, petroleum, uranium, mercury, brown coal, lead, zinc, antimony, tungsten, silver, gold. **Water:** 2,247 cu m per capita. **Crude oil reserves:** 12 mil bbls. **Electricity prod.:** 20.9 bil kWh. **Labor force:** agric. 43.5%, industry 20.8%, services 35.7%. **Unemployment:** 7.0%.

Finance: Monetary unit: Somoni (TJS) (10.66 = $1 U.S.). **GDP:** $51.6 bil; **per capita GDP:** $5,082; **GDP growth:** 8.3%. **Imports:** $5.9 bil; China 33%, Russia 22%, Kazakhstan 13%, Uzbekistan 6%, Turkey (Türkiye) 6%. **Exports:** $2.1 bil; Kazakhstan 20%, Switzerland 19%, China 17%, Turkey (Türkiye) 8%, Uzbekistan 8%. **Tourism:** $20 mil. **Budget:** $2.4 bil. **Inflation** (2018-19): 7.7%.

Transport: Railways: 423 mi. **Airports:** 19.

Communications: Mobile (2022): 126.2 per 100 pop. **Broadband** (2022): 39.1 per 100 pop. **Internet:** 36.1%.

Health: Expend.: 8.0%. **Life expect.:** 70.1 male; 73.8 female. **Births:** 25.8 per 1,000 pop. **Deaths:** 4.7 per 1,000 pop. **Infant mortality:** 21.7 per 1,000 live births. **Undernourished:** 8.7%. **HIV:** 0.2%. **COVID-19:** 125 deaths; rates per 100,000: 186 cases, 1 death. 54% vaccinated.

Education: Compulsory: ages 7-15. **Literacy:** 99.8%.

Website: www.president.tj

Societies were settled in the region from about 3000 bce. Invaders have included Iranians, Arabs (who converted the population to Islam), Mongols, Uzbeks, Afghans, and Russians. The USSR gained control 1918-25, making the region a part of the Uzbek SSR until the Tajik SSR was proclaimed, 1929.

Tajikistan declared independence Sept. 9, 1991. Factional fighting led to the installation of a pro-Communist regime, Jan. 1993. A new constitution establishing a presidential system was approved by referendum in 1994.

About 55,000 died in clashes between Muslim rebels and loyalist troops (supported by Russia) by mid-1997. Pres. Emomali Rakhmonov, first elected in 1994, won a Nov. 1999 election called a farce by human-rights observers. Leading opposition groups boycotted the Nov. 2006 election, again won by Rakhmonov (who changed his name to Rahmon in 2007). He won reelection in Nov. 2013 and Oct. 2020.

Poverty and corruption are widespread in Tajikistan. After rebels murdered a Tajik general, July 21, 2012, the army killed about 30 militants, July 24. A former warlord surrendered, Aug. 13, in exchange for a troop withdrawal. In the 2010s, an est. 1,300 Tajiks joined ISIS forces in Syria and Iraq. Islamist militant prison riots in Tajikistan, Nov. 2018 and May 2019, left at least 55 dead. Fighting erupted in a disputed area of the border with Kyrgyzstan, Apr. 2021 and Sept. 2022. Dozens died, 2021-22, when security forces cracked down violently on rights demonstrators in eastern Tajikistan. Four men from Tajikistan were accused of a terrorist attack near Moscow, Mar. 22, 2024, that left at least 145 dead; ISIS-K, based in Afghanistan, claimed responsibility—and in the 2020s recruited a large number of Tajiks.

Tanzania

United Republic of Tanzania

People: Population: 67,462,121 (23). **Age distrib.:** <15: 41.2%; 65+: 3.4%. **Growth:** 2.7%. **Migrants:** 0.7%. **Pop. density:** 197.3 per sq mi, 76.2 per sq km. **Urban:** 38.1%. **Ethnic groups:** African 99% (of which 95% are Bantu consisting of 130+ tribes); Arab, African, mixed Arab/African on Zanzibar. **Languages:** Kiswahili or Swahili, English (primary lang. of commerce, admin., higher ed.) (both official); Arabic. **Religions:** Christian 55.5% (Protestant 32.6%, Catholic 22.0%), Muslim 33.1% (Sunni), ethnic religionist 9.6%.

Geography: Total area: 365,755 sq mi, 947,300 sq km (30); **Land area:** 342,009 sq mi, 885,800 sq km. **Location:** Coast of E Africa. Kenya, Uganda on N; Rwanda, Burundi, Dem. Rep. of the Congo on W; Zambia, Malawi, Mozambique on S. **Topography:** Hot, arid central plateau surrounded by lake region in W. Temperate highlands in N and S; coastal plains. Mt. Kilimanjaro (19,341 ft) is highest in Africa. **Arable land:** 15.2%. **Capital:** Dar es Salaam (de facto), 8,161,231; Dodoma (legislative), 261,645. **Cities:** Mwanza, 1,378,014.

Government: Type: Presidential republic. **Head of state and govt.:** Pres. Samia Suluhu Hassan; b. 1960; in office: Mar. 19, 2021. **Local divisions:** 31 regions. **Defense budget:** $1.1 bil. **Active troops:** 27,000.

Economy: Industries: agric. proc.; mining; salt, soda ash; cement, oil refining, shoes, apparel, wood prods., fertilizer. **Chief agric.:** cassava, maize, sweet potatoes, sugarcane, bananas, milk. **Natural resources:** hydropower, tin, phosphates, iron ore, coal, diamonds, gems, gold, nat. gas, nickel. **Water:** 1,514 cu m per capita. **Electricity prod.:** 9.0 bil kWh. **Labor force:** agric. 65.5%, industry 8.5%, services 26.0%. **Unemployment:** 2.6%.

Finance: Monetary unit: Shilling (TZS) (2,704.98 = $1 U.S.). **GDP:** $259.7 bil; **per capita GDP:** $3,973; **GDP growth:** 5.2%. **Imports** (2022): $16.7 bil; China 30%, India 18%, UAE 11%, Dem. Rep. of the Congo 5%. **Exports** (2022): $12.0 bil; India 27%, UAE 11%, South Africa 9%, Kenya 5%, Rwanda 5%. **Tourism:** $3.4 bil. **Budget:** $10.0 bil. **Inflation:** 3.8%.

Transport: Railways: 2,546 mi. **Motor vehicles:** 2.1 per 1,000 pop. **Airports:** 206.

Communications: Mobile: 105.4 per 100 pop. **Broadband:** 32.3 per 100 pop. **Internet:** 31.9%.

Health: Expend.: 3.4%. **Life expect.:** 69.0 male; 72.6 female. **Births:** 32.5 per 1,000 pop. **Deaths:** 5.0 per 1,000 pop. **Infant mortality:** 29.6 per 1,000 live births. **Undernourished:** 23.8%. **HIV:** 3.8%. **COVID-19:** 846 deaths; rates per 100,000: 72 cases, 1 death. 54% vaccinated.

Education: Compulsory: ages 7-13. **Literacy:** 82.0%.

Website: www.tanzania.go.tz

Arab colonization and slaving in Tanganyika began in the 8th cent.; Portuguese sailors explored the coast around 1500. Other Europeans followed.

In 1885 Germany established German East Africa, of which Tanganyika formed the bulk. Under Britain, it became a League of Nations mandate and after 1946, a UN trust territory. It became independent, Dec. 9, 1961, and a republic within the Commonwealth a year later.

Zanzibar, area 640 sq mi, lies 23 mi off mainland Tanzania. The island of Pemba, area 380 sq mi, is 25 mi to the NE. Ethnic groups in Zanzibar include Arabs and Africans. Zanzibar and Pemba are major producers of cloves and clove oil.

Zanzibar was for centuries the center for Arab slave traders. Portugal ruled the region for two centuries until ousted by Arabs around 1700. Zanzibar became a British Protectorate in 1890; independence came Dec. 10, 1963. Revolutionary forces overthrew the Sultan, Jan. 12, 1964. The new government ousted Western diplomats and journalists, slaughtered thousands of Arabs, and nationalized farms.

The Republic of Tanganyika and the Republic of Zanzibar joined to form the United Republic of Tanzania, Apr. 26, 1964. Zanzibar retains internal self-government.

Until resigning as president in 1985, Julius K. Nyerere, a former Tanganyikan independence leader, dominated Tanzania's single-party government, which emphasized government planning and economic control. A multiparty system was established in 1992, and the economy was privatized in the 1990s.

A bomb at the U.S. embassy in Dar es Salaam, Aug. 7, 1998, killed 11 and injured at least 70. The U.S. blamed the attack on Islamic terrorists associated with Osama bin Laden.

John Magufuli, of the ruling party, won the Oct. 25, 2015, presidential election. Magufuli suppressed press freedom and political opposition. He won a second term in an Oct. 28, 2020, election dismissed as fraudulent by the opposition. Magufuli falsely denied the COVID-19 pandemic was a problem in Tanzania.

Magufuli died Mar. 17, 2021. Vice Pres. Samia Suluhu Hassan became Tanzania's first woman president. She encouraged COVID-19 vaccination and somewhat eased restrictions on journalists, but hundreds of opposition-party supporters were arrested in Aug. 2024.

Large natural gas deposits (57 tril cu ft) have been discovered in recent years.

Thailand

Kingdom of Thailand

People: Population: 69,920,998 (20). **Age distrib.:** <15: 15.8%; 65+: 15.1%. **Growth:** 0.2%. **Migrants:** 5.2%. **Pop. density:** 354.5 per sq mi, 136.9 per sq km. **Urban:** 54.3%. **Ethnic groups** (by nationality): Thai 97.5%, Burmese 1.3%. **Languages:** Thai (official), English is secondary lang. among elite. **Religions:** Buddhist 86.5% (Theravadin 79%), Muslim 5.9% (Sunni), ethnic religionist 2.3%.

Geography: Total area: 198,117 sq mi, 513,120 sq km (51); **Land area:** 197,256 sq mi, 510,890 sq km. **Location:** On Indochinese and Malayan peninsulas in SE Asia. Myanmar on W and N, Laos on N, Cambodia on E, Malaysia on S. **Topography:** A plateau dominates NE third of Thailand, dropping to fertile alluvial valley of Chao Phraya R. in center. Forested mountains with narrow fertile valleys in N. Rain forests cover S peninsula region. **Arable land:** 33.6%. **Capital:** Krung Thep (Bangkok), 11,233,869. **Cities:** Chon Buri, 1,472,709; Samut Prakan, 1,376,146; Chiang Mai, 1,228,773.

Government: Type: Constitutional monarchy. **Head of state:** King Vajiralongkorn; b. 1952; in office: Dec. 1, 2016. **Head of govt.:** Prime Min. Paetongtarn Shinawatra; b. 1986; in office: Aug. 18, 2024. **Local divisions:** 76 provinces, 1 municipality. **Defense budget:** $5.7 bil. **Active troops:** 360,850.

Economy: Industries: tourism, textiles and garments, agric. proc., beverages, tobacco, cement, light mfg. (jewelry, elec. appliances, computers and parts, integrated circuits, furniture). **Chief agric.:** sugarcane, rice, cassava, oil palm fruit, maize, rubber. **Natural resources:** tin, rubber, nat. gas, tungsten, tantalum, timber, lead, fish, gypsum, lignite, fluorite. **Water:** 6,126 cu m per capita. **Crude oil reserves:** 253 mil bbls. **Electricity prod.:** 181.9 bil kWh. **Labor force:** agric. 30.4%, industry 22.2%, services 47.3%. **Unemployment:** 0.9%.

Finance: Monetary unit: Baht (THB) (34.02 = $1 U.S.). **GDP:** $1.7 tril; **per capita GDP:** $23,423; **GDP growth:** 1.9%. **Imports:** $328.0 bil; China 26%, Japan 11%, UAE 6%, U.S. 5%, Malaysia 5%. **Exports:** $336.9 bil; U.S. 17%, China 11%, Japan 8%. **Tourism:** $29.7 bil. **Budget** (2020): $128.6 bil. **Inflation:** 1.2%.

Transport: Railways: 2,564 mi. **Motor vehicles:** 269.6 per 1,000 pop. **Airports:** 108.

Communications: Mobile: 168.6 per 100 pop. **Broadband:** 124 per 100 pop. **Internet** (2023): 89.5%.

Health: Expend.: 5.2%. **Life expect.:** 75.2 male; 81.3 female. **Births:** 9.9 per 1,000 pop. **Deaths:** 8.0 per 1,000 pop. **Infant mortality:** 6.3 per 1,000 live births. **Undernourished:** 5.6%. **HIV:** 1.1%. **COVID-19:** 34,719 deaths; rates per 100,000: 6,876 cases, 50 deaths. 78% vaccinated.

Education: Compulsory: ages 6-14. **Literacy:** 94.1%.

Website: www.soc.go.th

Thais began migrating from southern China during the 11th cent. and established a unified Thai kingdom, 1350. Known as Siam until 1939, Thailand is the only country in SE Asia never colonized by Europeans. King Mongkut and his son King Chulalongkorn, ruling successively from 1851 to 1910, modernized the country and signed trade treaties with Britain and France. A bloodless revolution in 1932 limited the monarchy. Thailand was an ally of Japan during WWII and of the U.S. during the postwar period. For decades, the military had a dominant role in governing the country.

By the end of the 1990s, more than 750,000 people in Thailand had HIV/AIDS. A prevention campaign reduced the number of new HIV infections.

Beginning in 2004, security forces tried to suppress a Muslim insurgency in southern Thailand. By 2024, more than 7,500 people, mostly civilians, had been killed.

Following elections in Jan. 2001, Thaksin Shinawatra became prime min. A military junta took power in a bloodless coup Sept. 19, 2006. Thaksin supporters won Dec. 2007 elections, and Samak Sundaravej became prime min. after civilian rule was restored Jan. 22, 2008. Thailand's Constitutional Court ousted Samak in

Sept., and Thaksin's brother-in-law Somchai Wongsawat became prime min. Sept. 18. But a Constitutional Court ruling, Dec. 2, barred him from politics.

In 2010, after Thaksin supporters, known as Red Shirts, staged mass rallies and began to build a fortified compound in Bangkok, a crackdown by Thai security forces, May 14-19, left more than 90 people dead. Thaksin's sister, Yingluck Shinawatra, became Thailand's first female prime min. after parliamentary elections July 3, 2011. On May 7, 2014, she was removed from office by the Constitutional Court, and the military seized power in a May 22 coup. Gen. Prayut Chan-ocha became prime min. in Aug. 2014.

A 2015 investigation resulted in charges against more than 100, including government and military officials, for involvement in human trafficking of migrants from Myanmar and Bangladesh. More than 60 traffickers were convicted, July 19, 2017.

In an Aug. 7, 2016, referendum (opposition campaigning had been barred), voters approved a military-drafted new constitution and a companion measure giving the military a strong role in selecting prime ministers after a return to civilian rule.

King Bhumibol, monarch since June 1946, died Oct. 13, 2016; crown prince Maha Vajiralongkorn succeeded him Dec. 1.

Following disputed Mar. 24, 2019, legislative elections, the National Assembly, June 5, elected Prayut to remain prime min. Months of large student-led protests, 2020-21, demanded political reforms. In May 14, 2023, lower-house elections, opposition partiesled by Move Forward and Pheu Thai (Thaksin's party)-won a majority of seats. After the largely military-appointed Senate blocked Move Forward's reformist leader from becoming prime minister, businessman Srettha Thavisin of Pheu Thai gained military backing and was elected prime minister by the National Assembly Aug. 22, 2023. The Constitutional Court, Aug. 7, 2024, ordered Move Forward disbanded (it re-formed as the People's Party). On Aug. 14, the Court ordered Prime Min. Srettha removed from office. Paetongtarn Shinawatra, Thaksin's daughter, became prime minister Aug. 18, 2024.

Thailand became the first Southeast Asian nation to legalize same-sex marriage with a bill passed in June 2024, to take effect in Jan. 2025.

Timor-Leste

Democratic Republic of Timor-Leste

People: Population: 1,506,909 (152). **Age distrib.:** <15: 38.7%; 65+: 4.5%. **Growth:** 2.0%. **Migrants:** 0.6%. **Pop. density:** 262.4 per sq mi, 101.3 per sq km. **Urban:** 32.8%. **Ethnic groups:** Austronesian (Malayo-Polynesian), Melanesian-Papuan, small Chinese minority. **Languages:** Tetun Prasa, Portuguese (both official); Indonesian, English (working langs.); about 32 Indigenous langs. **Religions:** Christian 87.8% (Catholic 83.9%), ethnic religionist 7.3%, Muslim 3.8% (Sunni).

Geography: Total area: 5,743 sq mi, 14,874 sq km (155); **Land area:** 5,743 sq mi, 14,874 sq km. **Location:** E half of Timor Isl. in SW Pacific O. Indonesia on W half of island. **Topography:** Rugged terrain, rising to 9,721 ft at Mt. Ramelau. **Arable land:** 7.5%. **Capital:** Dili, 281,135.

Government: Type: Semi-presidential republic. **Head of state:** Pres. José Ramos-Horta; b. 1949; in office: May 20, 2022. **Head of govt.:** Prime Min. Kay Rala Xanana Gusmão; b. 1946; in office: July 1, 2023. **Local divisions:** 12 municipalities, 1 special admin. region. **Defense budget:** $55 mil. **Active troops:** 2,250.

Economy: Industries: printing, soap mfg., handicrafts, woven cloth. **Chief agric.:** maize, rice, coconuts, root vegetables, vegetables, cassava. **Natural resources:** gold, petroleum, nat. gas, manganese, marble. **Water:** 6,219 cu m per capita. **Electricity prod.:** 514.8 mil kWh. **Labor force:** agric. 39.2%, industry 11.8%, services 49.0%. **Unemployment:** 1.5%.

Finance: Monetary unit: U.S. Dollar (USD) (1.00 = $1 U.S.). **GDP:** $7.0 bil; **per capita GDP:** $5,109; **GDP growth:** –14.4%. **Imports:** $1.2 bil; Indonesia 27%, China 23%, Singapore 9%, Australia 6%, Malaysia 6%. **Exports:** $701.8 mil; China 25%, Indonesia 20%, Japan 14%, South Korea 13%, Thailand 7%. **Tourism:** $51 mil. **Budget:** $1.4 bil. **Inflation** (2018-19): 1.0%.

Transport: Airports: 10.

Communications: Mobile: 112.6 per 100 pop. **Broadband:** 29 per 100 pop. **Internet:** 40.8%.

Health: Expend.: 11.4%. **Life expect.:** 68.9 male; 72.3 female. **Births:** 29.7 per 1,000 pop. **Deaths:** 5.5 per 1,000 pop. **Infant mortality:** 32.2 per 1,000 live births. **Undernourished:** 15.9%. **HIV:** 0.2%. **COVID-19:** 138 deaths; rates per 100,000: 1,779 cases, 10 deaths. 61% vaccinated.

Education: Compulsory: ages 6-14. **Literacy:** 69.9%.

Website: timor-leste.gov.tl

The collapse of Portuguese rule in East Timor led to factional fighting, Aug. 1975, and an invasion by Indonesia in Dec. Indonesia annexed East Timor in 1976. In over two decades, some 200,000 Timorese died due to civil war, famine, and persecution by Indonesian authorities. In a referendum held Aug. 1999 under UN auspices, Timorese voted overwhelmingly for independence but were then terrorized by pro-Indonesian militias. An international peacekeeping force entered in Sept.; a UN interim administration formally took command Oct. 26, 1999. Pro-independence forces won elections for a constituent assembly Aug. 2001. Xanana Gusmão, a former guerrilla leader, won the presidential election Apr. 2002. As Timor-Leste, the territory became independent May 20.

José Ramos-Horta, a Nobel Peace Prize laureate, won a presidential runoff vote May 2007. Ramos-Horta chose Gusmão as prime min. Gusmão-supported independent Taur Matan Ruak became president in a May 2012 runoff election. Gusmão's CNRT party won July parliamentary elections. The UN peacekeeping mission ended Dec. 31, 2012.

Beginning in 2005, much of East Timor's budget consisted of revenue from offshore oil and natural gas deposits. Lower oil prices beginning in 2014, as well as depletion of oil fields and costly infrastructure projects, hurt the economy. Gusmão resigned Feb. 6, 2015, and was replaced as prime min. by a member of the Fretilin party. Fretilin's Francisco Guterres won the Mar. 20, 2017, presidential election. A coalition including the CNRT won parliamentary elections, May 12, 2018; Taur Matan Ruak became prime min.

Timor-Leste and Australia signed a treaty, Mar. 6, 2018, establishing the boundary between them in an oil- and gas-rich area of the Timor Sea. Ramos-Horta again became president after defeating Guterres in an Apr. 2022 runoff election. The CNRT won May 21, 2023, parliamentary elections, and Gusmão again became prime min.

Togo

Togolese Republic

People: Population: 8,917,994 (101). **Age distrib.:** <15: 38.7%; 65+: 4.3%. **Growth:** 2.4%. **Migrants:** 3.4%. **Pop. density:** 424.7 per sq mi, 164.0 per sq km. **Urban:** 45.1%. **Ethnic groups:** est. 37, incl. Adja-Ewe/Mina 42.4%, Kabye/Tem 25.9%, Para-Gourma/Akan 17.1%, Akposso/Akebu 4.1%, Ana-Ife 3.2%. **Languages:** French (official; lang. of commerce), Ewe and Mina (in S), Kabye and Dagomba (in N). **Religions:** Christian 50.4% (Catholic 33.5%, Protestant 13.4%), ethnic religionist 32.1%, Muslim 16.5% (Sunni).

Geography: Total area: 21,925 sq mi, 56,785 sq km (123); **Land area:** 20,998 sq mi, 54,385 sq km. **Location:** S coast of W Africa. Ghana on W, Burkina Faso on N, Benin on E. **Topography:** Hills running SW-NE split Togo into two savanna plains regions. **Arable land:** 48.7%. **Capital:** Lomé, 2,042,734.

Government: Type: Presidential republic. **Head of state:** Pres. Faure Gnassingbé b. 1966; in office: May 4, 2005. **Head of govt.:** Prime Min. Victoire Tomegah-Dogbé b. 1959; in office: Sept. 28, 2020. **Local divisions:** 5 regions. **Defense budget:** $198 mil. **Active troops:** 13,750.

Economy: Industries: phosphate mining, agric. proc., cement, handicrafts, textiles, beverages. **Chief agric.:** cassava, yams, maize, oil palm fruit, sorghum, soybeans. **Natural resources:** phosphates, limestone, marble. **Water:** 1,700 cu m per capita. **Electricity prod.:** 887.3 mil kWh. **Labor force:** agric. 30.8%, industry 20.0%, services 49.2%. **Unemployment:** 2.0%.

Finance: Monetary unit: CFA Franc (XOF) (587.79 = $1 U.S.). **GDP:** $28.6 bil; **per capita GDP:** $3,155; **GDP growth:** 6.4%. **Imports** (2020): $2.4 bil; India 30%, China 16%, South Korea 13%. **Exports** (2020): $1.7 bil; UAE 26%, India 11%, Côte d'Ivoire 11%, South Africa 6%, Burkina Faso 6%. **Tourism** (2020): $77 mil. **Budget:** $1.2 bil. **Inflation** (2021-22): 8.0%.

Transport: Railways: 353 mi. **Motor vehicles:** 32.4 per 1,000 pop. **Airports:** 7.

Communications: Mobile: 75.8 per 100 pop. **Broadband:** 43 per 100 pop. **Internet:** 37.6%.

Health: Expend.: 5.6%. **Life expect.:** 69.5 male; 74.7 female. **Births:** 30.9 per 1,000 pop. **Deaths:** 5.1 per 1,000 pop. **Infant mortality:** 38.4 per 1,000 live births. **Undernourished:** 12.8%. **HIV:** 1.6%. **COVID-19:** 290 deaths; rates per 100,000: 477 cases, 4 deaths. 19% vaccinated.

Education: Compulsory: ages 6-15. **Literacy:** 66.5%.

Website: primature.gouv.tg

Togoland was administered by Germany and then by France and Britain. The French sector became the republic of Togo Apr. 27, 1960. In office since 1967, Pres. Gnassingbé Eyadéma died Feb. 5, 2005. His son, Faure Gnassingbé, was installed as president and won a disputed Apr. 24 election; protests led to violent clashes in Lomé.

Kpatcha Gnassingbé, the president's brother, was arrested Apr. 12, 2009, and accused of plotting a coup. Pres. Gnassingbé won reelection Mar. 4, 2010. Anti-government protests led the prime min. to resign, July 13, 2012. Pres. Gnassingbé won a third term in disputed Apr. 25, 2015, elections. More than a dozen people died in anti-government protests, beginning Aug. 2017. Gnassingbé's party (UNIR) won Dec. 20, 2018, legislative elections, and Gnassingbé won a new term as president, Feb. 22, 2020. Victoire Tomegah-Dogbé became Togo's first woman prime minister, Sept. 28, 2020. Togo joined the Commonwealth in 2022.

UNIR won almost all seats in Apr. 29, 2024, legislative elections (disputed by the opposition). Under 2024 constitutional changes, the National Assembly will elect the head of state.

Tonga
Kingdom of Tonga

People: Population: 104,889 (181). **Age distrib.:** <15: 29.3%; 65+: 7.4%. **Growth:** –0.3%. **Migrants:** 3.5%. **Pop. density:** 378.9 per sq mi, 146.3 per sq km. **Urban:** 23.2%. **Ethnic groups:** Tongan 96.5%, other (incl. European, Fijian, Samoan, Indian, Chinese, other Pacific Islander, other Asian) 3.5%. **Languages:** Tongan. **Religions:** Christian 94.8% (independent 62.9%, Protestant 25.1%), Baha'i 3.4%.

Geography: Total area: 288 sq mi, 747 sq km (176); **Land area:** 277 sq mi, 717 sq km. **Location:** Western S Pacific O. Nearest neighbors are Fiji to NW, Samoa to NE. **Topography:** Comprises 170 volcanic and coral islands, 36 inhabited. **Arable land:** 27.8%. **Capital:** Nuku'alofa, 22,904.

Government: Type: Constitutional monarchy. **Head of state:** King Tupou VI; b. 1959; in office: Mar. 18, 2012. **Head of govt.:** Prime Min. Siaosi Sovaleni; b. 1970; in office: Dec. 27, 2021. **Local divisions:** 5 island divisions. **Defense budget:** $9 mil. **Active troops:** 600.

Economy: Industries: tourism, constr., fishing. **Chief agric.:** coconuts, pumpkins/squash, cassava, sweet potatoes, vegetables, yams. **Natural resources:** fish. **Water:** 0 cu m per capita. **Electricity prod.:** 75.1 mil kWh. **Labor force:** agric. 26.9%, industry 27.6%, services 45.5%. **Unemployment:** 2.3%.

Finance: Monetary unit: Pa'anga (TOP) (2.35 = $1 U.S.). **GDP** (2022): $749.8 mil; **per capita GDP** (2022): $7,016; **GDP growth** (2022): –2.0%. **Imports** (2022): $332.7 mil; Fiji 28%, China 23%, New Zealand 21%, Australia 6%, U.S. 5%. **Exports** (2022): $59.9 mil; U.S. 31%, Australia 19%, New Zealand 12%, Hong Kong 8%, Belgium 8%. **Tourism** (2022): $10 mil. **Budget:** $196 mil. **Inflation:** 6.4%.

Transport: Airports: 6.

Communications: Mobile (2022): 61.7 per 100 pop. **Broadband** (2022): 63.6 per 100 pop. **Internet** (2021): 57.5%.

Health: Expend.: 6.3%. **Life expect.:** 76.4 male; 79.7 female. **Births:** 19.7 per 1,000 pop. **Deaths:** 5.0 per 1,000 pop. **Infant mortality:** 11.8 per 1,000 live births. **Undernourished:** NA. **HIV:** NA. **COVID-19:** 13 deaths; rates per 100,000: 16,074 cases, 12 deaths. 73% vaccinated.

Education: Compulsory: ages 4-18. **Literacy:** 99.4%.

Website: www.gov.to

First inhabited by ancestors of Polynesians c. 2000 bce, Tonga was visited by the Dutch in the early 17th cent. and by British explorer James Cook in the 1770s. A series of civil wars ended, 1845, with establishment of the Tupou dynasty. In 1900, Tonga became a British protectorate. Tonga gained independence June 1970 and joined the Commonwealth. Elections in Nov. 2010 gave the country its first democratically elected parliament. George Tupou VI became king Mar. 18, 2012.

In recent years, Tonga has relied on borrowing from China to fund development projects. The U.S., in 2023, opened an embassy in Tonga.

Trinidad and Tobago
Republic of Trinidad and Tobago

People: Population: 1,408,966 (153). **Age distrib.:** <15: 18.7%; 65+: 14.1%. **Growth:** 0.1%. **Migrants:** 5.6%. **Pop. density:** 711.6 per sq mi, 274.8 per sq km. **Urban:** 53.6%. **Ethnic groups:** East Indian 35.4%, African descent 34.2%, mixed-other 15.3%, mixed African/East Indian 7.7%. **Languages:** English (official), Trinidadian Creole English, Tobagonian Creole English, Caribbean Hindustani, Trinidadian Creole French, Spanish, Chinese. **Religions:** Christian 63.6% (Catholic 27.8%, Protestant 23.9%, independent 11.1%), Hindu 24.0% (Saktist 10%, Shaivite 8%, Vaishnavite 7%), Muslim 6.3% (Sunni), agnostic 2.4%.

Geography: Total area: 1,980 sq mi, 5,128 sq km (166); **Land area:** 1,980 sq mi, 5,128 sq km. **Location:** In Caribbean, off E coast of Venezuela. **Topography:** Three low mountain ranges cross Trinidad E-W, with a well-watered plain between N and central ranges. Parts of E and W coasts are swamps. Tobago, 116 sq mi, lies 20 mi NE. **Arable land:** 4.9%. **Capital:** Port of Spain, 545,707.

Government: Type: Parliamentary republic. **Head of state:** Pres. Christine Kangaloo; b. 1961; in office: Mar. 20, 2023. **Head of govt.:** Prime Min. Keith Rowley; b. 1949; in office: Sept. 9, 2015. **Local divisions:** 9 regions, 3 boroughs, 2 cities, 1 ward. **Defense budget:** $512 mil. **Active troops:** 4,650.

Economy: Industries: petroleum and petroleum prods., liquefied nat. gas, methanol, ammonia, urea, steel prods., beverages. **Chief agric.:** chicken, fruits, coconuts, citrus fruits, plantains, maize. **Natural resources:** petroleum, nat. gas, asphalt. **Water:** 2,517 cu m per capita. **Crude oil reserves:** 243 mil bbls. **Electricity prod.:** 9.4 bil kWh. **Labor force:** agric. 3.0%, industry 26.7%, services 70.3%. **Unemployment:** 4.2%.

Finance: Monetary unit: Dollar (TTD) (6.76 = $1 U.S.). **GDP:** $48.5 bil; **per capita GDP:** $31,572; **GDP growth:** 2.1%. **Imports** (2022): $10.7 bil; U.S. 40%, China 9%, Italy 7%. **Exports** (2022): $17.6 bil; U.S. 35%, Belgium 6%, Morocco 5%. **Tourism** (2022): $324 mil. **Budget** (2020): $7.5 bil. **Inflation:** 4.6%.

Transport: Motor vehicles: 330.4 per 1,000 pop. **Airports:** 3.

Communications: Mobile: 134.2 per 100 pop. **Broadband** (2022): 56 per 100 pop. **Internet:** 80%.

Health: Expend.: 7.0%. **Life expect.:** 74.6 male; 78.4 female. **Births:** 10.5 per 1,000 pop. **Deaths:** 8.6 per 1,000 pop. **Infant mortality:** 15.1 per 1,000 live births. **Undernourished:** 12.6%. **HIV:** NA. **COVID-19:** 4,390 deaths; rates per 100,000: 13,683 cases, 314 deaths. 51% vaccinated.

Education: Compulsory: ages 5-11. **Literacy:** 99.0%.

Website: www.ttconnect.gov.tt

Christopher Columbus sighted Trinidad in 1498. It became a British possession in 1802; in the 1800s tens of thousands of indentured servants and their families were brought from India to work in agriculture. Trinidad and Tobago won independence Aug. 31, 1962. It became a republic in 1976. The nation, among the most prosperous in the Caribbean, produces oil and natural gas. In recent years, drug-related crime and other violent crime, especially against women, has increased.

Basdeo Panday was the nation's first prime min. of Indian ancestry (1995-2001). The country's first female prime min., Kamla Persad-Bissessar, took office May 26, 2010. After Sept. 7, 2015, elections, Keith Rowley of the People's National Movement (PNM) became prime min. On Mar. 19, 2018, Paula-Mae Weekes became Trinidad's first female president. The PNM narrowly won Aug. 10, 2020, elections. Christine Kangaloo succeeded Weekes as president, Mar. 20, 2023.

Tunisia
Republic of Tunisia

People: Population: 12,048,847 (81). **Age distrib.:** <15: 24.4%; 65+: 10.4%. **Growth:** 0.6%. **Migrants:** 0.5%. **Pop. density:** 200.9 per sq mi, 77.6 per sq km. **Urban:** 70.9%. **Ethnic groups:** Arab 98%, European 1%. **Languages:** Arabic (official), French (used in commerce), Tamazight. **Religions:** Muslim (official) 99.5% (Sunni 98%, Islamic schismatic 2%).

Geography: Total area: 63,170 sq mi, 163,610 sq km (91); **Land area:** 59,985 sq mi, 155,360 sq km. **Location:** N coast of Africa. Algeria on W, Libya on E. **Topography:** The N is wooded and fertile. Grazing lands and orchards are in central coastal plains. The S is arid, approaching Sahara Desert. **Arable land:** 18.2%. **Capital:** Tunis, 2,510,673. **Cities:** Safaqis, 657,791.

Government: Type: Parliamentary republic. **Head of state:** Pres. Kais Saied; b. 1958; in office: Oct. 23, 2019. **Head of govt.:** Prime Min. Kamel Maddouri; b. 1974; in office: Aug. 7, 2024. **Local divisions:** 24 governorates. **Defense budget:** $1.2 bil. **Active troops:** 35,800.

Economy: Industries: petroleum, mining, tourism, textiles, footwear, agribusiness, beverages. **Chief agric.:** milk, olives, tomatoes, wheat, barley, watermelons. **Natural resources:** petroleum, phosphates, iron ore, lead, zinc, salt. **Water:** 376 cu m per capita. **Crude oil reserves:** 425 mil bbls. **Electricity prod.:** 21.2 bil kWh. **Labor force:** agric. 14.0%, industry 33.4%, services 52.6%. **Unemployment:** 15.1%.

Finance: Monetary unit: Dinar (TND) (3.03 = $1 U.S.). **GDP:** $170.4 bil; **per capita GDP:** $13,682; **GDP growth:** 0.4%. **Imports** (2022): $22.5 bil; Italy 14%, France 14%, China 9%, Germany 7%, Turkey (Türkiye) 6%. **Exports** (2022): $17.3 bil; France 22%, Italy 16%, Germany 14%. **Tourism:** $2.5 bil. **Budget:** $12.4 bil. **Inflation:** 9.3%.

Transport: Railways: 1,350 mi (only partly operational). **Motor vehicles:** 181.1 per 1,000 pop. **Airports:** 14.

Communications: Mobile: 134.1 per 100 pop. **Broadband:** 95.1 per 100 pop. **Internet:** 73.8%.

Health: Expend.: 7.0%. **Life expect.:** 75.7 male; 79.1 female. **Births:** 13.5 per 1,000 pop. **Deaths:** 6.4 per 1,000 pop. **Infant mortality:** 11.3 per 1,000 live births. **Undernourished:** 3.2%. **HIV:** 0.1%. **COVID-19:** 29,423 deaths; rates per 100,000: 9,759 cases, 249 deaths. 54% vaccinated.

Education: Compulsory: ages 6-14. **Literacy:** 82.7%.

Website: www.tunisie.gov.tn or www.pm.gov.tn

Site of ancient Carthage and a former Barbary state under the suzerainty of Turkey, Tunisia became a protectorate of France, May 12, 1881. The nation became independent Mar. 20, 1956, and ended the monarchy the following year. Habib Bourguiba, an independence leader, served as president until 1987, when he was deposed by his prime min., Zine al-Abidine Ben Ali, who then won five presidential elections, 1989-2009, all tightly controlled.

Arab Spring protests, which began Dec. 2010, ousted Ben Ali, Jan. 14, 2011. The moderate Islamist Ennahda party won Oct. 2011 elections but failed to institute promised reforms. The secular Nida Tunis party won 2014 legislative and presidential elections.

Three Islamist extremist gunmen attacked a museum in Tunis, Mar. 18, 2015, killing 22. A gunman killed 38 foreign tourists at a resort hotel in Sousse, June 26; ISIS claimed responsibility.

July 2017 legislation gave women greater protection from abuse and sexual harassment.

In an Oct. 13, 2019, presidential runoff, law professor Kais Saied, an independent, won election. A decade-long weak economy was aggravated, beginning in 2020, by the impact of the COVID-19 pandemic. On July 25, 2021, Pres. Saied took on expanded powers. He announced, Sept. 22, increased powers to rule by decree, and he dissolved the legislature, Mar. 30, 2022. In a July 25 referendum boycotted by the opposition, a new constitution was approved centralizing power in the presidency. Most parties and voters boycotted Dec. 2022-Jan. 2023 elections for a new parliament. In 2023-24, journalists and opposition figures were arrested, and opponents were barred from running in the Oct. 6, 2024, presidential election.

In recent years, a growing number of African and other migrants trying to reach Europe by boat have embarked from Tunisia. Under a Tunisia-EU agreement announced July 16, 2023, Tunisia would crack down on migrants and people smugglers in exchange for badly needed economic aid.

Turkey (Türkiye)
Republic of Turkey

(As of June 1, 2022, the country formally changed its name to Türkiye [tur-KEE-yeh], using the Turkish-language spelling.)

People: Population: 84,119,531 (18). **Age distrib.:** <15: 21.7%; 65+: 9.6%. **Growth:** 0.6%. **Migrants:** 7.2%. **Pop. density:** 283.1 per sq mi, 109.3 per sq km. **Urban:** 77.9%. **Ethnic groups:** Turkish 70%-75%, Kurdish 19%. **Languages:** Turkish (official), Kurdish. **Religions:** Muslim 98.0% (Sunni 83%, Shia 15%).

Geography: Total area: 302,535 sq mi, 783,562 sq km (36); **Land area:** 297,157 sq mi, 769,632 sq km. **Location:** Asia Minor, stretching into continental Europe; borders on Medit. and Black Seas. Bulgaria, Greece on W; Georgia, Armenia on N; Iran on E; Iraq, Syria on S. **Topography:** Center has wide plateaus with hot, dry summers and cold winters. High mountains ring the interior on all but W, with more than 20 peaks over 10,000 ft. Rolling plains in W; mild, fertile coastal plains in S and W. **Arable land:** 26.2%. **Capital:** Ankara, 5,477,087. **Cities:** Istanbul, 16,047,350; Izmir, 3,120,340; Bursa, 2,115,513.

Government: Type: Presidential republic. **Head of state and govt.:** Pres. Recep Tayyip Erdogan; b. 1954; in office: Aug. 28, 2014. (The position of prime minister was eliminated in June 2018.) **Local divisions:** 81 provinces. **Defense budget:** $9.7 bil. **Active troops:** 355,200.

Economy: Industries: textiles, food proc., automobiles, electronics, mining, steel, petroleum, constr., lumber, paper. **Chief agric.:** milk, wheat, sugar beets, tomatoes, barley, maize. **Natural resources:** coal, iron ore, copper, chromium, antimony, mercury, gold, barite, borate, strontium, emery, feldspar, limestone, magnesite, marble, perlite, pumice, pyrites (sulfur), clay, hydropower. **Water:** 2,496 cu m per capita. **Crude oil reserves:** 366 mil bbls. **Electricity prod.:** 308.2 bil kWh. **Labor force:** agric. 16.7%, industry 27.7%, services 55.6%. **Unemployment:** 9.4%.

Finance: Monetary unit: Lira (TRY) (34.03 = $1 U.S.). **GDP:** $3.8 tril; **per capita GDP:** $44,151; **GDP growth:** 4.5%. **Imports:** $386.8 bil; China 13%, Germany 9%, Russia 8%, U.S. 5%, Italy 5%. **Exports:** $352.5 bil; Germany 8%, U.S. 7%, Iraq 5%, UK 5%, Italy 5%. **Tourism:** $49.5 bil. **Budget** (2020): $249.3 bil. **Inflation:** 53.9%.

Transport: Railways: 7,144 mi. **Motor vehicles:** 242.8 per 1,000 pop. **Airports:** 115.

Communications: Mobile: 105.7 per 100 pop. **Broadband:** 84.5 per 100 pop. **Internet** (2023): 86%.

Health: Expend.: 4.6%. **Life expect.:** 74.4 male; 79.2 female. **Births:** 13.8 per 1,000 pop. **Deaths:** 6.1 per 1,000 pop. **Infant mortality:** 18.4 per 1,000 live births. **Undernourished:** <2.5%. **HIV:** NA. **COVID-19:** 101,419 deaths; rates per 100,000: 20,162 cases, 120 deaths. 63% vaccinated.

Education: Compulsory: ages 6-17. **Literacy:** 96.7%.

Website: www.tccb.gov.tr

Ancient inhabitants of Turkey were among the world's first agriculturalists. Such civilizations as the Hittite, Phrygian, and Lydian flourished in Asiatic Turkey (Asia Minor), as did much of Greek civilization. After the fall of Rome in the 5th cent., Constantinople (now Istanbul) was the capital of the Byzantine Empire for 1,000 years. It fell in 1453 to Ottoman Turks, who ruled a vast empire for over 400 years.

Just before WWI, Turkey, or the Ottoman Empire, ruled what is now Syria, Lebanon, Iraq, Jordan, Israel, Saudi Arabia, Yemen, and islands in the Aegean Sea. Turkey joined Germany and Austria in WWI, and its defeat resulted in the loss of territory and the fall of the sultanate. A secular republic was established Oct. 29, 1923. The first pres., Mustafa Kemal (later Kemal Ataturk), led Turkey until his death in 1938.

Turkey kept neutral during most of WWII. The country became a full member of NATO in 1952. Military coups overthrew civilian governments in 1960 and 1980. Turkey invaded nearby Cyprus July 20, 1974, to prevent that country from uniting with Greece, and Cyprus was divided into Greek and Turkish zones.

Turkey joined the U.S.-led force that ousted Iraq from Kuwait, 1991. Millions of Iraqi Kurdish refugees fled to Turkey's SE border region after the war. Turkish offensives in Kurdish areas of Turkey caused heavy casualties among separatist guerrillas and civilians. Kurdish militants raided Turkish diplomatic missions in some 25 Western European cities, June 24, 1993.

Tansu Ciller became Turkey's first woman prime min. July 5, 1993. The Islamic Welfare Party gained strength in the 1990s, and in June 1996, a coalition with Ciller's True Path Party was formed. The pro-Islamic government resigned June 18, 1997, under pressure from the military, which stepped up its campaign against Islamic fundamentalism in 1998.

Kurdish rebel leader Abdullah Öcalan was captured Feb. 15, 1999, and convicted of terrorism June 29. His organization, the Kurdistan Workers' Party (PKK), announced in 1999 that it would abandon its 14-year-old insurgency. Violence continued at a lower level, however.

Earthquakes in Apr. and Nov. 1999 killed over 17,000 people. The Islamic Justice and Development Party (AKP) led by Recep Tayyip Erdogan won Nov. 3, 2002, parliamentary elections. Erdogan became prime min., May 14, 2003. His party scored a landslide win in 2007 parliamentary elections.

Erdogan won an Aug. 10, 2014, election to become Turkey's first popularly elected president. In an Apr. 16, 2017, referendum, accompanied by allegations of irregularities, voters narrowly approved constitutional amendments strengthening the president's powers and abolishing the post of prime minister after the next elections. Erdogan won the June 24, 2018, presidential election; the AKP won parliamentary elections the same day.

During Syria's civil war (2011-), Turkey became a haven for Syrian refugees (more than 3.7 mil by mid-2022; over 3 mil remained as of Sept. 2024). Turkey was also a major transit route for Syrian and other migrants trying to reach Europe. Under a Turkey-EU agreement, effective Mar. 20, 2016, Turkey pledged, in return for EU aid, to crack down on smugglers ferrying migrants to Greece. Migrant crossings decreased.

Turkish government forces launched a new offensive against the PKK in SE Turkey, beginning in mid-2015, and Kurdish extremists staged terrorist attacks in Turkish cities, as well as attacks on government troops. Turkey began airstrikes, July 24, 2015, against PKK strongholds in N Iraq and later launched attacks on Syrian Kurdish fighters said to be affiliated with the PKK. Turkish ground troops fought in Syria beginning in 2016, mainly to limit areas controlled by Syrian Kurds (allied with the U.S. in fighting ISIS in Syria). After the U.S., Oct. 2019, pulled back troops from N Syria, a new offensive by Turkish and allied Syrian militia forces drove Syrian Kurdish fighters out of areas near the Turkish border.

Terrorist attacks within Turkey attributed to ISIS included suicide bombings at Istanbul's main airport, June 28, 2016, that killed at least 45. On Aug. 20, a suicide bomber killed at least 54 at a wedding in SE Turkey.

A coup attempt against Erdogan by elements of the military, July 15-16, 2016, was put down by loyal military units. The government blamed the coup on Muslim cleric Fethullah Gülen, living in the U.S. The abortive coup left at least 240 dead, and some 50,000 soldiers, government officials, and civilians (including journalists) were detained. Intensifying an ongoing crackdown on dissent, the government closed more than 100 media outlets and fired or suspended tens of thousands of judges, government officials, and teachers. July 2020 legislation increased government control of social media platforms in Turkey.

Tensions in U.S.-Turkish relations, along with economic problems, contributed to a sharp drop in the lira's value, 2018-19. Under a July 2020 decree issued by Erdogan, Istanbul's Hagia Sophia—built as a Christian church in the 6th cent., used as a mosque 1453-1934, and a museum since 1934—once again was converted to a mosque.

A continuing weak economy and currency were aggravated by high inflation in 2022-24. In the early 2020s, the COVID-19 pandemic also hurt the economy. To curb inflation, interest rates were raised to around 50% by 2024.

A powerful Feb. 6, 2023, earthquake in south-central Turkey, plus aftershocks, killed over 50,000 and caused widespread destruction. Taking advantage of tightly controlled media, Erdogan narrowly won a new term as president in a May 28, 2023, runoff. The AKP and allied parties won a majority in parliamentary elections the same month.

Turkmenistan

People: Population: 5,744,151 (115). **Age distrib.:** <15: 24.5%; 65+: 6.9%. **Growth:** 0.9%. **Migrants:** 3.2%. **Pop. density:** 31.7 per sq mi, 12.2 per sq km. **Urban:** 54.5%. **Ethnic groups:** Turkmen 85%, Uzbek 5%, Russian 4%. **Languages:** Turkmen (official), Russian, Uzbek. **Religions:** Muslim 95.1% (Sunni 94%), agnostic 2.8%.

Geography: Total area: 188,456 sq mi, 488,100 sq km (53); **Land area:** 181,441 sq mi, 469,930 sq km. **Location:** Central Asia. Kazakhstan on N; Uzbekistan on N and E; Afghanistan, Iran on S. **Topography:** Kara Kum Desert occupies 80% of country. Bordered on W by Caspian Sea. **Arable land:** 3.4%. **Capital:** Ashgabat, 921,601.

Government: Type: Presidential republic; authoritarian. **Head of state and govt.:** Pres. Serdar Berdimuhamedov; b. 1981; in office: Mar. 19, 2022. **Local divisions:** 5 provinces, 1 independent city. **Defense budget:** NA. **Active troops:** 36,500.

Economy: Industries: nat. gas, oil, petroleum prods., textiles, food proc. **Chief agric.:** milk, cotton, wheat, potatoes, watermelons, tomatoes. **Natural resources:** petroleum, nat. gas, sulfur, salt.

Water: 3,905 cu m per capita. **Crude oil reserves:** 600 mil bbls. **Electricity prod.:** 23.1 bil kWh. **Labor force:** agric. 22.7%, industry 33.7%, services 43.6%. **Unemployment:** 4.1%.

Finance: Monetary unit: Manat (TMT) (3.50 = $1 U.S.). **GDP** (2019): $105.3 bil; **per capita GDP** (2019): $17,100; **GDP growth:** 6.3%. **Imports** (2021): $6.3 bil; UAE 27%, Turkey (Türkiye) 24%, China 19%, Kazakhstan 7%. **Exports** (2021): $10.3 bil; China 71%, Turkey (Türkiye) 7%, Uzbekistan 5%. **Budget:** $6.1 bil. **Inflation** (2016-17): 8%.

Transport: Railways: 3,177 mi. **Airports:** 23.

Communications: Mobile (2021): 88.2 per 100 pop. **Broadband** (2022): 44.5 per 100 pop. **Internet** (2017): 21.3%.

Health: Expend.: 5.6%. **Life expect.:** 69.4 male; 75.5 female. **Births:** 16.8 per 1,000 pop. **Deaths:** 6.0 per 1,000 pop. **Infant mortality:** 35.9 per 1,000 live births. **Undernourished:** 4.1%. **HIV:** NA. **COVID-19:** NA. 76% vaccinated.

Education: Compulsory: ages 6-17. **Literacy:** 99.7%.

Website: turkmenistan.gov.tm

The region has been inhabited by Turkic peoples since the 10th cent. It became part of Russian Turkestan in 1881, and a constituent republic of the USSR in 1925. Turkmenistan declared independence Oct. 27, 1991, and became an independent state when the USSR disbanded Dec. 26, 1991.

Turkmenistan has extensive natural gas reserves and also oil reserves. Political power centers on the former Communist Party apparatus and authoritarian leadership. Gurbanguly Berdimuhamedov won the Feb. 2007 presidential election, considered fraudulent by international observers. He was reelected with 97% of the vote in 2012 and 98% in 2017. After the president announced in Feb. 2022 he would step down, his son, Serdar Berdimuhamedov, was declared the winner of the Mar. 12 election.

Tuvalu

People: Population: 11,733 (194). **Age distrib.:** <15: 29.2%; 65+: 7.6%. **Growth:** 0.8%. **Migrants:** 2.0%. **Pop. density:** 1,168.8 per sq mi, 451.3 per sq km. **Urban:** 66.9%. **Ethnic groups:** Tuvaluan 97%, Tuvaluan/I-Kiribati 1.6%. **Languages:** Tuvaluan, English (both official); Samoan. **Religions:** Christian 94.7% (Protestant 85.3%), agnostic 3.1%.

Geography: Total area: 10 sq mi, 26 sq km (193); **Land area:** 10 sq mi, 26 sq km. **Location:** 9 islands forming NW-SE chain 360 mi long in SW Pacific O. Nearest neighbors are Kiribati to NE, Fiji to S. **Topography:** All low-lying atolls, no more than 15 ft above sea level, composed of coral reefs. **Arable land:** 0%. **Capital:** Funafuti, 7,042.

Government: Type: Parliamentary democracy under constitutional monarchy. **Head of state:** King Charles III, rep. by Gov.-Gen. Tofiga Falani; in office: Sept. 28, 2021. **Head of govt.:** Prime Min. Feleti Penitala Teo; b. 1962; in office: Feb. 27, 2024. **Local divisions:** 7 island councils, 1 town council. **Defense budget/active troops:** NA.

Economy: Industries: fishing. **Chief agric.:** coconuts, vegetables, tropical fruits, bananas, root vegetables, pork. **Natural resources:** fish, coconuts. **Water:** 0 cu m per capita. **Labor force:** NA. **Unemployment:** NA.

Finance: Monetary unit: Tuvaluan Dollar (TVD), equivalent to the Australian Dollar (AUD) (1.48 = $1 U.S.). **GDP:** $65.7 mil; **per capita GDP:** $5,763; **GDP growth:** 3.9%. **Imports** (2022): $57.4 mil; China 34%, Japan 27%, Fiji 20%, New Zealand 5%, Australia 5%. **Exports** (2022): $2.2 mil; Thailand 69%, Croatia 21%. **Tourism** (2022): $1 mil. **Budget:** $88 mil. **Inflation** (2016-17): 4.1%.

Transport: Airports: 1.

Communications: Mobile (2022): 98.9 per 100 pop. **Broadband:** NA. **Internet:** 81.2%.

Health: Expend.: 20.0%. **Life expect.:** 66.5 male; 71.6 female. **Births:** 22.0 per 1,000 pop. **Deaths:** 7.8 per 1,000 pop. **Infant mortality:** 27.8 per 1,000 live births. **Undernourished:** NA. **HIV:** NA. **COVID-19:** 1 death; rates per 100,000: 24,958 cases, 8 deaths. 81% vaccinated.

Education: Compulsory: ages 6-13. **Literacy:** NA.

Website: www.tuvalu.tv

The Ellice Islands separated from the British Gilbert and Ellice Islands Colony in 1975 and became Tuvalu; independence came Oct. 1, 1978.

Following Sept. 9, 2019, elections, the legislature elected Kausea Natano prime minister, Sept. 19. After Natano lost his seat in Jan. 26, 2024, elections, Feleti Teo became prime minister Feb. 27.

Rising sea levels due to climate change are threatening to submerge the tiny island nation. Australia, Nov. 2023, agreed to allow some Tuvalu residents displaced by climate change to relocate to Australia.

Uganda

Republic of Uganda

People: Population: 49,283,041 (31). **Age distrib.:** <15: 47.0%; 65+: 2.4%. **Growth:** 3.2%. **Migrants:** 3.8%. **Pop. density:** 647.6 per sq mi, 250.0 per sq km. **Urban:** 27.4%. **Ethnic groups:** Baganda 16.5%, Banyankole 9.6%, Basoga 8.8%, Bakiga 7.1%, Iteso 7%, Langi 6.3%, Bagisu 4.9%, Acholi 4.4%, Lugbara 3.3%. **Languages:** English, Swahili (both official); Ganda or Luganda (most widely used Niger-Congo lang.). **Religions:** Christian 83.5% (Protestant 43.3%, Catholic 38.4%), Muslim 12.9% (Sunni).

Geography: Total area: 93,065 sq mi, 241,038 sq km (79); **Land area:** 76,101 sq mi, 197,100 sq km. **Location:** E Central Africa. South Sudan on N, Dem. Rep. of the Congo on W, Rwanda and Tanzania on S, Kenya on E. **Topography:** Mostly high plateau 3,000-6,000 ft high, with Ruwenzori Range in W (Mt. Margherita, 16,765 ft), volcanoes in SW. NE is arid, W and SW rainy. Lakes Victoria, Edward, Albert form much of borders. **Arable land:** 34.4%. **Capital:** Kampala, 4,050,826.

Government: Type: Presidential republic. **Head of state:** Pres. Yoweri Kaguta Museveni; b. 1944; in office: Jan. 29, 1986. **Head of govt.:** Prime Min. Robinah Nabbanja; b. 1969; in office: June 14, 2021. **Local divisions:** 134 districts, 1 capital city. **Defense budget:** $1.0 bil. **Active troops:** 45,000.

Economy: Industries: sugar proc., brewing, tobacco, cotton textiles, cement, steel prod. **Chief agric.:** plantains, sugarcane, maize, cassava, milk, sweet potatoes. **Natural resources:** copper, cobalt, hydropower, limestone, salt, gold. **Water:** 1,311 cu m per capita. **Crude oil reserves:** 2.5 bil bbls. **Electricity prod.:** 5.4 bil kWh. **Labor force:** agric. 66.3%, industry 7.3%, services 26.4%. **Unemployment:** 2.8%.

Finance: Monetary unit: Shilling (UGX) (3,714.14 = $1 U.S.). **GDP:** $150.5 bil; **per capita GDP:** $3,098; **GDP growth:** 5.2%. **Imports** (2022): $11.1 bil; China 23%, Kenya 15%, India 13%, UAE 7%, Tanzania 6%. **Exports** (2022): $6.1 bil; UAE 31%, India 12%, Hong Kong 9%, Kenya 8%, Italy 7%. **Tourism:** $1.3 bil. **Budget:** $6.9 bil. **Inflation:** 5.4%.

Transport: Railways: 773 mi. **Motor vehicles:** 13.7 per 1,000 pop. **Airports:** 39.

Communications: Mobile: 86.5 per 100 pop. **Broadband:** 61.7 per 100 pop. **Internet** (2021): 10%.

Health: Expend.: 4.7%. **Life expect.:** 67.5 male; 72.0 female. **Births:** 39.6 per 1,000 pop. **Deaths:** 4.7 per 1,000 pop. **Infant mortality:** 28.5 per 1,000 live births. **Undernourished:** 36.9%. **HIV:** 5.1%. **COVID-19:** 3,632 deaths; rates per 100,000: 376 cases, 8 deaths. 29% vaccinated.

Education: Compulsory: ages 6-12. **Literacy:** 80.6%.

Website: www.gou.go.ug

Britain obtained a protectorate over Uganda in 1894. The country became independent Oct. 9, 1962, and a republic within the Commonwealth a year later. In 1967, the traditional kingdoms, including the powerful Buganda state, were abolished.

Gen. Idi Amin seized power from Prime Min. Milton Obote in 1971. During his 8-year dictatorship, he was responsible for the deaths of up to 300,000 of his opponents. In 1972 he expelled nearly all of Uganda's 45,000 Asians. Tanzanian troops and Ugandan exiles and rebels ousted Amin, Apr. 11, 1979.

Obote, president from Dec. 1980, was ousted in a military coup July 1985. Guerrilla war and rampant human rights abuses had plagued Uganda under Obote's regime.

Yoweri Museveni took power in Jan. 1986. In 1993 the Buganda and other traditional monarchies were restored for ceremonial purposes. Uganda helped Laurent Kabila seize power in the Dem. Rep. of the Congo (DRC; formerly Zaire) in 1997 but sent troops in 1998 to aid insurgents seeking his ouster. A withdrawal accord was signed Sept. 2002.

Pres. Museveni won flawed 2001, 2006, 2011, and 2016 elections. Opposition politicians were arrested, Aug. 2018; anti-government protests were violently suppressed. Museveni was declared the winner of the Jan. 14, 2021, presidential election. His main opponent, Robert Kyagulanyi (a former entertainer known as Bobi Wine) charged fraud. Hundreds of Wine's supporters were arrested and beaten.

The rebel Lord's Resistance Army (LRA), led by Joseph Kony, began an insurgency against the Museveni government in 1986 and abducted tens of thousands of children to serve as soldiers and sex slaves. According to UN estimates, the LRA, 1987-2012, killed more than 100,000 people and displaced some 2.5 mil in Uganda and neighboring countries. Peace talks began in 2006, and LRA violence in Uganda diminished. A cease-fire accord was signed Feb. 23, 2008.

In 2007, Uganda began supplying troops to the African Union's peacekeeping force in Somalia. Suicide bombings July 11, 2010, killed 76 people in Kampala; al-Shabab, a Somali al-Qaeda-linked Islamist group, claimed responsibility. In recent years, the DRC-based, ISIS-affiliated Allied Democratic Forces has staged attacks in Uganda; a June 16, 2023, attack on a school left at least 41 dead.

The UNHCR estimated that, as of July 31, 2024, Uganda hosted more than 1.7 mil refugees and asylum seekers, including over 953,000 from South Sudan and 531,000 from the DRC.

Legislation signed by Museveni May 29, 2023, toughened penalties for homosexuality (already illegal), including life imprisonment for engaging in gay sex—and the death penalty in some cases.

Ukraine

People: Population: 35,661,826 (43). **Age distrib.:** <15: 12.3%; 65+: 19.9%. **Growth:** 2.4%. **Migrants:** 11.4%. **Pop. density:** 159.4 per sq mi, 61.6 per sq km. **Urban:** 70.3% (incl. Crimea). **Ethnic**

groups: Ukrainian 77.8%, Russian 17.3%. **Languages:** Ukrainian (official), Russian (regional lang.). **Religions:** Christian 86.7% (Orthodox 71.2%, Catholic 12.4%), agnostic 9.9%.

Geography: Total area: 233,032 sq mi, 603,550 sq km (about 7.1% was occupied by Russia as of Sept. 2023) (46); **Land area:** 223,681 sq mi, 579,330 sq km. **Location:** Eastern Europe. Belarus on N; Russia on NE and E; Moldova, Romania on SW; Hungary, Slovakia, Poland on W. **Topography:** Part of E European plain with arable black soil. Carpathians in the SW, Crimean chain in the S. **Arable land:** 56.8%. **Capital:** Kyiv, 3,020,228. **Cities:** Kharkiv, 1,418,978; Odesa, 1,007,596; Dnipro, 936,766.

Government: Type: Semi-presidential republic. **Head of state:** Pres. Volodymyr Zelenskyy; b. 1978; in office: May 20, 2019. **Head of govt.:** Prime Min. Denys Shmyhal; b. 1975; in office: Mar. 4, 2020. **Local divisions:** 24 provinces, 1 autonomous republic, 2 municipalities. **Defense budget:** $30.9 bil. **Active troops:** 500,000-800,000.

Economy: Industries: industrial machinery, metals, auto and aircraft components, electronics, chemicals. **Chief agric.:** maize, potatoes, wheat, sunflower seeds, sugar beets, milk. **Natural resources:** iron ore, coal, manganese, nat. gas, oil, salt, sulfur, graphite, titanium, magnesium, kaolin, nickel, mercury, timber. **Water:** 4,027 cu m per capita. **Crude oil reserves:** 395 mil bbls. **Electricity prod.:** 112.2 bil kWh. **Labor force:** NA. **Unemployment** (2021): 9.8%.

Finance: Monetary unit: Hryvnia (UAH) (41.31 = $1 U.S.). **GDP:** $621.3 bil; **per capita GDP:** $18,007; **GDP growth:** 5.3%. **Imports:** $88.5 bil; Poland 17%, China 12%, Germany 9%, Turkey (Türkiye) 6%. **Exports:** $51.1 bil; Poland 14%, Romania 8%, Turkey (Türkiye) 6%, China 6%, Germany 5%. **Tourism:** $857 mil. **Budget** (2021): $35.8 bil. **Inflation:** 12.8%.

Transport: Railways: 13,504 mi. **Motor vehicles:** 294.7 per 1,000 pop. **Airports:** 148.

Communications: Mobile: 122.8 per 100 pop. **Broadband:** 81.6 per 100 pop. **Internet** (2021): 79.2%.

Health: Expend.: 8.0%. **Life expect.:** 65.4 male; 75.8 female. **Births:** 6.0 per 1,000 pop. **Deaths:** 18.6 per 1,000 pop. **Infant mortality:** 8.7 per 1,000 live births. **Undernourished:** 5.8%. **HIV:** NA. **COVID-19:** 109,923 deaths; rates per 100,000: 12,652 cases, 251 deaths. 36% vaccinated.

Education: Compulsory: ages 6-16. **Literacy:** 100.0%.

Website: www.kmu.gov.ua

Ukrainians' Slavic ancestors inhabited the region well before the 1st cent. CE. In the 9th cent., the princes of Kyiv established a strong state called Kyivan Rus, which included much of present-day Ukraine. Internal conflicts led to the disintegration of the Ukrainian state by the 13th cent. Mongol rule was supplanted by Poland and Lithuania in the 14th and 15th cent. The N Black Sea coast and Crimea came under Turkish control in 1478. Ukrainian Cossacks, starting in the late 16th cent., rebelled against the occupiers of Ukraine: Russia, Poland, and Turkey.

An independent Ukrainian National Republic was proclaimed on Jan. 22, 1918. But in 1921, Ukraine's neighbors occupied and divided Ukrainian territory. In 1922, Ukraine became a constituent republic of the USSR. In 1932-33, the Soviet government engineered a famine in eastern Ukraine, and 6-7 mil Ukrainians died. During WWII the Ukrainian nationalist underground fought Nazi and Soviet forces. Over 5 mil Ukrainians died in the war. The reoccupation of Ukraine by Soviet troops in 1944 brought a renewed wave of repression.

The world's worst nuclear power plant disaster occurred in Chernobyl, Ukraine, in Apr. 1986; many thousands were killed or disabled as a result of the radiation leak.

Ukrainian independence was restored, Dec. 1991, with the Soviet Union's dissolution. Following a 1994 accord with Russia and the U.S., Ukraine's large nuclear arsenal was transferred to Russia for destruction.

Russian-backed Prime Min. Viktor Yanukovych was declared the winner in Nov. of the 2004 presidential election. Massive protests (the Orange Revolution) forced an election rerun, Dec. 26, won by Viktor Yushchenko. Yanukovych was the winner in the Feb. 2010 presidential election.

Large anti-Yanukovych protests began in Nov. 2013, following his decision not to sign a free trade pact with the EU. Parliament removed Yanukovych from office, Feb. 22, 2014. Pro-EU candidate Petro Poroshenko won a May 25, 2014, presidential election. The EU agreement was completed Sept. 16.

Hurt by corruption and a weak economy, Poroshenko lost an Apr. 21, 2019, presidential runoff election to entertainer and businessman Volodymyr Zelenskyy. Zelenskyy's party won July 21, 2019, parliamentary elections.

Russian forces entered Crimea in Mar. 2014, and Russia annexed the region Mar. 18. Fighting began in Apr. 2014 in eastern Ukraine between Ukrainian forces and pro-Russian separatists, aided by Russia. A missile shot down a Malaysian airliner over separatist-controlled eastern Ukraine, July 17, 2014, killing all 298 on board.

On Feb. 24, 2022, Russia launched a large-scale invasion of Ukraine. The U.S., as well as many European and other nations, provided extensive military aid to Ukraine, which defeated an initial Russian advance toward Kyiv. By Aug. 2022, Russia controlled large portions of four eastern and southern Ukrainian provinces; Russia annexed them in Oct. Despite Ukrainian counteroffensives, as of mid-2024, Russia controlled almost one-fifth of Ukrainian territory. Ukraine's combat casualties perhaps totaled over 130,000 killed, wounded, or missing as of mid-2024.

Russia repeatedly attacked civilian targets, causing widespread destruction and high civilian casualties, and there was evidence that Russian troops committed war crimes. The IOM estimated that, as of June 2024, more than 3.3 mil Ukrainians were internally displaced. The UNHCR estimated, as of Sept. 2024, that over 6 mil Ukrainians were refugees in European or other nations (excluding Russia and Belarus); Russia was believed to have forcibly deported large numbers of Ukrainians.

Aug. 2024 legislation barred Orthodox Christian and other churches with links to Russia.

United Arab Emirates

People: Population: 10,032,213 (94). **Age distrib.:** <15: 16.4%; 65+: 2.2%. **Growth:** 0.6%. **Migrants:** 88.1%. **Pop. density:** 310.8 per sq mi, 120.0 per sq km. **Urban:** 88.0%. **Ethnic groups:** South Asian 59.4% (incl. Indian 38.2%, Bangladeshi 9.5%, Pakistani 9.4%), Emirati 11.6%, Egyptian 10.2%, Filipino 6.1%. **Languages:** Arabic (official), English, Hindi, Malayalam, Urdu, Pashto, Tagalog, Persian. **Religions:** Muslim (official) 74.5% (Sunni 63%, Shia 7%, Islamic schismatic 4%), Christian 12.9% (Catholic 11.5%), Hindu 6.2%, Buddhist 3.2%.

Geography: Total area: 32,278 sq mi, 83,600 sq km (113); **Land area:** 32,278 sq mi, 83,600 sq km. **Location:** Middle East, on S shore of the Persian Gulf. Saudi Arabia on W and S, Oman on E. **Topography:** A barren, flat coastal plain gives way to uninhabited sand dunes on S. Hajar Mts. in E. **Arable land:** 0.7%. **Capital:** Abu Dhabi, 1,593,284. **Cities:** Dubai, 3,051,016; Sharjah, 1,872,199.

Government: Type: Federation of monarchies. **Head of state:** Pres. Sheikh Mohamed bin Zayed al Nahyan; b. 1961; in office: May 14, 2022. **Head of govt.:** Prime Min. Sheikh Muhammad bin Rashid al-Maktum; b. 1949; in office: Jan. 5, 2006. **Local divisions:** 7 emirates: Abu Dhabi, Ajman, Dubai, Fujaira, Ras al-Khaimah, Sharjah, Umm al-Qaiwain. **Defense budget:** $20.7 bil. **Active troops:** 63,000.

Economy: Industries: petroleum and petrochemicals, fishing, aluminum, cement, fertilizer, comm. ship repair, constr. materials. **Chief agric.:** dates, cucumbers/gherkins, camel milk, goat milk, tomatoes, eggs. **Natural resources:** petroleum, nat. gas. **Water:** 16 cu m per capita. **Crude oil reserves:** 97.8 bil bbls. **Electricity prod.:** 169.2 bil kWh. **Labor force:** agric. 1.4%, industry 29.6%, services 69.0%. **Unemployment:** 2.7%.

Finance: Monetary unit: Dirham (AED) (3.67 = $1 U.S.). **GDP:** $798.5 bil; **per capita GDP:** $83,903; **GDP growth:** 3.4%. **Imports** (2020): $246.9 bil; China 18%, India 10%, U.S. 6%. **Exports** (2020): $335.2 bil; India 13%, Japan 10%, China 8%, Saudi Arabia 7%, Iraq 5%. **Tourism:** $51.9 bil. **Budget:** $127.3 bil (excl. emirate-level spending in Abu Dhabi and Dubai). **Inflation** (2021-22): 4.8%.

Transport: Motor vehicles: 406.1 per 1,000 pop. **Airports:** 42.

Communications: Mobile: 199.4 per 100 pop. **Broadband:** 199 per 100 pop. **Internet** (2023): 100%.

Health: Expend.: 5.3%. **Life expect.:** 78.6 male; 81.4 female. **Births:** 10.7 per 1,000 pop. **Deaths:** 1.7 per 1,000 pop. **Infant mortality:** 5.0 per 1,000 live births. **Undernourished:** 2.7%. **HIV:** <0.1%. **COVID-19:** 2,349 deaths; rates per 100,000: 10,789 cases, 24 deaths. 99% vaccinated.

Education: Compulsory: ages 6-17. **Literacy:** 98.3%.

Website: u.ae

The 7 "Trucial Sheikdoms" gave Britain control of defense and foreign relations in the 19th cent. They merged to become an independent state Dec. 2, 1971. Oil revenues have made the UAE one of the world's wealthiest countries. Banking, construction, and tourism have also become economically important.

In Mar. 2015, the UAE joined a Saudi-led coalition conducting military operations against Shiite Houthi rebels in Yemen's civil war. A truce beginning in 2022 reduced violence in Yemen's civil war.

The UAE and Israel signed an agreement, Sept. 15, 2020, to normalize relations.

Sheikh Khalifa bin Zayed al Nahyan, president since 2004, died May 13, 2022. He was succeeded, May 14, by his half-brother Sheikh Mohamed bin Zayed al Nahyan.

In 2023-24, the UAE was widely reported to be providing military aid to the Rapid Support Forces in Sudan's civil war.

United Kingdom

United Kingdom of Great Britain and Northern Ireland

People: Population: 68,459,055 (21). **Age distrib.:** <15: 16.7%; 65+: 19.3%. **Growth:** 0.5%. **Migrants:** 13.8%. **Pop. density:** 732.9 per sq mi, 283.0 per sq km. **Urban:** 84.9%. **Ethnic groups:** white 87.2%, Black/African/Caribbean/Black British 3%, Asian/Asian British: Indian 2.3%. **Languages:** English; Scots, Scottish Gaelic, Welsh, Irish, Cornish (all recognized regional langs.). **Religions:** Christian 63.2% (Protestant 44.3%, Catholic 12.0%), agnostic 24.6%, Muslim 6.8% (Sunni).

Geography: Total area: 94,058 sq mi, 243,610 sq km (78); **Land area:** 93,410 sq mi, 241,930 sq km. **Location:** Off NW coast of Europe, across English Channel, Strait of Dover, North Sea. Ireland to W, France to SE. **Topography:** England is mostly rolling land, rising to Uplands of southern Scotland. Lowlands in center of Scotland, granite highlands in N. British Isles have milder climate than N Europe due to Gulf Stream and ample rainfall. Severn, 220 mi, and Thames, 215 mi, are longest rivers. **Arable land:** 24.8%. **Capital:** London, 9,748,033. **Cities:** Manchester, 2,811,756; Birmingham (West Midlands), 2,684,807; West Yorkshire, 1,942,470; Glasgow, 1,708,147; Southampton/Portsmouth (South Hampshire), 959,202; Liverpool, 922,871; Newcastle upon Tyne, 828,712; Nottingham, 813,078; Sheffield, 751,303; Bristol, 713,884; Belfast, 647,438; Brighton-Worthing-Littlehampton, 627,524; Leicester, 570,858; Edinburgh, 558,676; Bournemouth/Poole, 522,736; Cardiff, 491,755.

Government: Type: Parliamentary constitutional monarchy. **Head of state:** King Charles III, b. 1948; in office: Sept. 8, 2022. **Head of govt.:** Prime Min. Keir Starmer; b. 1962; in office: July 5, 2024. **Local divisions:** 229 local authorities (England: 152; Wales: 22; Scotland: 32; Northern Ireland: 11; 12 other dependent areas). **Defense budget:** $73.5 bil. **Active troops:** 144,400.

Economy: Industries: machine tools, elec. power equip., automation equip., railroad equip., shipbuilding, aircraft, motor vehicles and parts, electronics and communications equip. **Chief agric.:** milk, wheat, barley, sugar beets, potatoes, chicken. **Natural resources:** coal, petroleum, nat. gas, iron ore, lead, zinc, gold, tin, limestone, salt, clay, chalk, gypsum, potash, silica sand, slate. **Water:** 2,185 cu m per capita. **Crude oil reserves:** 2.5 bil bbls. **Electricity prod.:** 318.6 bil kWh. **Labor force:** agric. 1.0%, industry 18.1%, services 80.9%. **Unemployment:** 4.1%.

Finance: Monetary unit: Pound (GBP) (0.76 = $1 U.S.). **GDP:** $4.0 tril; **per capita GDP:** $58,906; **GDP growth:** 0.1%. **Imports:** $1.1 tril; China 12%, Germany 10%, U.S. 10%, Norway 8%, Netherlands 5%. **Exports:** $1.1 tril; U.S. 13%, Netherlands 9%, Germany 9%, China 8%, Ireland 7%. **Tourism:** $73.9 bil. **Budget** (2020): $1.4 tril. **Inflation:** 6.8%.

Transport: Railways: 10,184 mi. **Motor vehicles:** 600.7 per 1,000 pop. **Airports:** 1,043.

Communications: Mobile: 122.8 per 100 pop. **Broadband:** 115 per 100 pop. **Internet:** 95.3%.

Health: Expend. (2022): 11.3%. **Life expect.:** 80.1 male; 84.4 female. **Births:** 10.8 per 1,000 pop. **Deaths:** 9.2 per 1,000 pop. **Infant mortality:** 3.8 per 1,000 live births. **Undernourished:** <2.5%. **HIV:** NA. **COVID-19:** 232,112 deaths; rates per 100,000: 36,792 cases, 342 deaths. 75% vaccinated.

Education: Compulsory: ages 5-15. **Literacy:** NA.

Website: www.gov.uk

The United Kingdom of Great Britain and Northern Ireland comprises England, Wales, Scotland, and Northern Ireland.

Royal Family. Since 1901, ruling sovereigns have been members of the House of Windsor. Elizabeth II (b. Apr. 21, 1926) succeeded King George VI to the throne Feb. 6, 1952. Elizabeth II, who became Britain's longest-reigning monarch in 2015, died Sept. 8, 2022.

Charles Philip Arthur George (b. Nov. 14, 1948), Elizabeth II's eldest son, immediately succeeded her as King Charles III (coronation: May 6, 2023). His second wife, Camilla (married Apr. 9, 2005), became Queen. (Charles's first wife, Diana—married 1981, divorced 1996—died in a car crash in Paris, Aug. 31, 1997.)

Charles III's first son, William Philip Arthur Louis (b. June 21, 1982), is the Prince of Wales and heir apparent. William married Catherine (Kate) Middleton, Apr. 29, 2011. Their son George Alexander Louis (b. July 22, 2013) is second in line to the throne; Charlotte Elizabeth Diana (b. May 2, 2015) is third; Louis Arthur Charles (b. Apr. 23, 2018) is fourth. On May 19, 2018, King Charles's younger son, Henry Charles Albert David (Harry, b. Sept. 15, 1984; fifth in line) married American actor Meghan Markle. Their son Archie Harrison was born May 6, 2019; daughter Lilibet Diana was born June 4, 2021. Harry and Meghan withdrew from official duties as of Mar. 31, 2020. Prince Andrew, younger brother of Charles III, stepped back from official duties Nov. 20, 2019, following allegations related to his friendship with convicted sex offender Jeffrey Epstein.

Parliament is the UK's legislative body, with certain powers over dependent units. It consists of two houses. The House of Commons has 650 members, elected by direct ballot and divided as follows (mid-2024): England, 543; Wales, 32; Scotland, 57; Northern Ireland, 18. The House of Lords (Sept. 1, 2024) comprised 805 members: 88 hereditary peers, 692 life peers, and 25 archbishops and bishops of the Church of England.

Resources and Industries. Great Britain is a global trade and financial services center. Service industries account for about four-fifths of GDP; industry for most of the rest; agriculture for less than 1%. Manufacturing, historically important since the Industrial Revolution, has declined in economic significance, while finance, centered in London, has grown in importance. Coal production, also historically important, has declined by more than 90% since 1970. Large oil and gas fields in the North Sea began commercial production in 1975, but proved reserves and production were declining in the 21st cent. Large offshore wind farms have been constructed in the North Sea.

Religion and Education. The Church of England is Protestant Episcopal. The monarch is its temporal head. There are two provinces, Canterbury and York, each headed by an archbishop. Westminster Abbey (1050-1760) is the site of coronations and the tombs of Elizabeth I, Mary, Queen of Scots, kings, poets, and the Unknown Warrior (buried Nov. 11, 1920). Celebrated British universities Oxford and Cambridge each date to the 13th cent.

History. Britain was separated from the European continent at least 200,000 years ago by catastrophic flooding that created the English Channel. Migrants across the Channel included the Celts, who arrived 2,500 to 3,000 years ago. Their language survives in Welsh and Gaelic enclaves.

England was part of the Roman Empire 43-410 CE, after which waves of Jutes, Angles, and Saxons arrived from German lands, followed by Danish raiders from the 8th through 11th cent. French-speaking Normans invaded in 1066, uniting the country with their dominions in France.

Opposition by nobles to royal authority forced King John to agree to the Magna Carta in 1215, a guarantee of rights and the rule of law. In the ensuing decades, the foundations of the parliamentary system were laid.

English dynastic claims to large parts of France led to the Hundred Years War, 1338-1453, an unsuccessful campaign. A long civil war, the War of the Roses, 1455-85, ended with the establishment of the Tudor monarchy. The economy prospered over long periods of domestic peace unmatched in continental Europe. The Church of England separated from the authority of the pope, 1534.

During the reign of Queen Elizabeth I, 1558-1603, England became a major naval power, leading to the founding of colonies in the New World and the expansion of trade with Europe and Asia. Scotland and England shared a single monarch after James VI of Scotland was crowned James I of England in 1603.

A struggle between Parliament and the Stuart kings led to a civil war, 1642-49, and the establishment of a republic under the Puritan Oliver Cromwell. The monarchy was restored in 1660, but the Glorious Revolution of 1688 confirmed the sovereignty of Parliament: a Bill of Rights was granted 1689. Scotland was united with England after the ratification of the Articles of Union of Scotland and England, May 1707.

Technological and entrepreneurial innovations led to the Industrial Revolution in the 18th cent. The 13 N American colonies were lost but replaced by growing empires in Canada, India, Australia, and elsewhere. Britain's role in the defeat of Napoleon, 1815, strengthened its position as the leading world power.

The limited extension of voting rights in 1832, 1867, and 1884; the formation of trade unions; and the development of universal public education were among the social changes that accompanied the spread of industrialization and urbanization in the 19th cent. (Men gained full voting rights in 1918 and women in 1928.) Large parts of Africa and Asia were added to the empire during the reign of Queen Victoria, 1837-1901.

Though victorious in WWI, Britain suffered huge casualties and economic dislocation. Ireland became independent in 1921, and independence movements became active in India and other colonies. The country suffered major bombing damage in WWII but rallied behind Prime Min. Winston Churchill and held off Germany until Allied victory was achieved, 1945.

In the postwar period, Britain lost its world leadership position to other powers. Labour governments nationalized some basic industries and expanded social welfare programs. In 1973, the UK joined the European Economic Community, which became the European Union (EU). Prime Min. Margaret Thatcher's Conservative governments, 1979-90, fostered private enterprise and began denationalization of key industries. The Channel Tunnel linking Britain to the Continent was opened May 6, 1994.

After the Sept. 11 attacks on the U.S., the UK participated, beginning in 2001, in the Afghanistan war; the last British troops left in 2021. Labour Prime Min. Tony Blair committed British troops to the 2003 U.S.-led invasion of Iraq. UK forces, which numbered 46,000 at the height of combat operations, almost entirely pulled out by mid-2009.

Suicide bombings on 3 London underground trains and a bus, July 7, 2005, left 56 people dead.

Legislation in 2005 established a Supreme Court, to replace the House of Lords as the UK's highest court. Blair, who had won three elections, was succeeded by Labour's Gordon Brown, June 2007.

In the wake of Britain's deepest recession since WWII, voters rejected the Labour Party in May 2010 elections. Conservative Prime Min. David Cameron responded to the fiscal crisis with austerity measures. Parliament voted in favor of same-sex marriage July 16, 2013. The Conservatives won May 7, 2015, elections. Tens of thousands of migrants to Europe from Africa, the Middle East, and SW Asia in 2015 tried to enter Britain. Anti-immigrant sentiment, including concerns about immigration from elsewhere in the EU, contributed to a 51.9%-48.1% referendum vote, June 23, 2016, favoring Britain's exit from the EU ("Brexit"). Conservative Theresa May replaced Cameron, July 13.

A suicide bomber apparently with ISIS connections killed 22 victims and injured more than 100 at a concert in Manchester, May 22,

2017. In London, June 3, three attackers fatally ran down with a van or stabbed 8 victims; ISIS claimed responsibility.

Prime Min. May and EU leaders completed, Nov. 2018, a separation agreement, but Parliament, Jan.-Mar. 2019, rejected it three times. Conservative Boris Johnson, a Brexit hardliner, replaced May as prime min., July 24, 2019, and negotiated a revised EU agreement. It included a provision ("the Northern Ireland protocol") that kept Northern Ireland largely aligned with EU policies, to prevent a "hard" border between Northern Ireland and the Irish Republic (an EU member), while requiring customs checks between Britain and Northern Ireland. Campaigning to "get Brexit done," Johnson and the Conservatives won a sweeping victory in Dec. 12 elections. Britain formally exited the EU Jan. 31, 2020. A UK-EU agreement ("the Windsor framework"), reducing customs checks of goods entering Northern Ireland from the rest of the UK, was adopted in Mar. 2023.

Britain was one of the hardest-hit countries by the COVID-19 pandemic that began in 2020. Confirmed cases by Sept. 2024 totaled 25 mil (10th-highest in the world); 232,000 had died (6th highest). By the end of 2021, GDP had largely recovered from a pandemic-related 2020 decline of over 9%, but stagnant growth, inflation, and high interest rates plagued the economy in the following years.

Facing declining popularity and a revolt in the Conservative Party, Johnson announced, July 7, 2022, that he would step down. Conservative Liz Truss became prime min. Sept. 6, but stepped down after just 45 days, amid a financial and political crisis. Conservative Rishi Sunak became prime min. Oct. 25, 2022.

The UK experienced severe heat waves in summer 2022, including the highest temperature ever recorded in the country: 40.3°C (104.5°F) on July 19.

Ending 14 years of Conservative governance, Labour won a sweeping victory in July 4, 2024, elections; Labour Party leader Keir Starmer became prime min. July 5.

With migrant crossings of the English Channel to the UK increasing in the 2020s, the UK announced in Apr. 2022 a program to deport migrants to Rwanda. After court challenges delayed implementation, the Starmer government canceled the program in July 2024.

A knife attack at a children's dance class near Liverpool, July 29, 2024, led to anti-immigrant, anti-Muslim riots, largely in N England, apparently touched off by misinformation on social media that the accused attacker (born in the UK) was a recent migrant.

When Cyprus gained independence, the UK retained the sovereign base areas of Akrotiri (47 sq mi) and Dhekelia (51 sq mi) on the island.

Wales

The Principality of Wales in western Britain has an area of 8,019 sq mi and a population (2021 census) of 3,107,500. Cardiff is the capital, pop. (2024 est.) 491,755.

The creation of a 60-seat elected Welsh assembly with limited powers passed by a thin margin in a Sept. 18, 1997, referendum.

Early Anglo-Saxon invaders drove Celtic peoples into the mountains of Wales, where they developed a distinct nationality. Members of the ruling house of Gwynedd in the 13th cent. fought England but were crushed, 1283. Edward of Caernarvon, son of Edward I of England, was created Prince of Wales, 1301. **Website:** gov.wales

Scotland

Scotland occupies the northern 37% of the main British island, and the Hebrides, Orkney, Shetland, and smaller islands. Length 275 mi, breadth approx. 150 mi, area 30,414 sq mi, pop. (2022 census) 5,439,842.

The Lowlands, a belt of land approx. 60 mi wide from the Firth of Clyde to the Firth of Forth, divide the farming region of the Southern Uplands from the granite Highlands of the N; they contain 75% of the population and most of the industry. The Highlands, famous for hunting and fishing, have been opened to industry by many hydroelectric power stations.

Edinburgh, pop. (2024 est.) 558,676, is the capital. Glasgow, pop. (2024 est.) 1,708,147, is Scotland's major port and shipbuilding center and has developed a services-based economy in the 21st cent., including financial services, health care, and engineering. Aberdeen, pop. (2019 est.) 228,670, is a major port and center of granite, fish-processing, and North Sea oil industries. Dundee, pop. (2019 est.) 149,320, NE of Edinburgh, is an industrial and fish-processing center.

History. Scotland was called Caledonia by the Romans who battled early Celtic tribes and occupied southern areas from the 1st to the 4th cent. Missionaries from England introduced Christianity in the 4th cent.; St. Columba, an Irish monk, converted most of Scotland in the 6th cent.

The Kingdom of Scotland was founded in 1018. William Wallace and Robert Bruce both defeated English armies 1297 and 1314, respectively. In 1603, James VI of Scotland, son of Mary, Queen of Scots, succeeded to the English throne as James I, and effected the Union of the Crowns. In 1707 Scotland received representation in the British Parliament. A 1997 proposal to create a regional legislature passed by a landslide; the Scottish Parliament has limited taxing authority and autonomy in areas such as education and social welfare. In 2011 elections for the 129-seat parliament, the pro-independence Scottish National Party (SNP) won a majority. In a referendum on independence Sept. 18, 2014, 55% of Scottish voters opposed separating from the UK. The SNP remained in power but narrowly fell short of a majority in 2016 and 2021 parliamentary elections.

Memorials of Robert Burns, Sir Walter Scott, John Knox, and Mary, Queen of Scots, draw many tourists, as do the beauties of the Trossachs, Loch Katrine, Loch Lomond, and abbey ruins.

Industries. Engineering products are a key industry, with growing emphasis on office machinery, autos, electronics, and other consumer goods. Support industries for offshore energy production (oil, gas, and wind turbines) have grown in recent decades.

Scotland produces fine woolens, worsteds, tweeds, silks, fine linens, and jute. It is known for its special breeds of cattle and sheep. Commercial fishing is an important industry. Whisky is a major export.

The Hebrides are a group of about 500 islands, 100 inhabited, off the W coast. The **Inner Hebrides** include Skye, Mull, and Iona, the last famous for the arrival of St. Columba, 563 CE. The **Outer Hebrides** include Lewis and Harris. Industries include sheep raising and weaving. The approx. 70 **Orkney Isls.** are to the NE. The capital is Kirkwall, on Pomona Isl. Fish curing, sheep raising, and weaving are occupations. NE of Orkney are the 200 **Shetland Isls.**, 24 inhabited, home of Shetland ponies. Orkney and Shetland are centers for the North Sea oil industry. **Website:** www.gov.scot

Northern Ireland

Northern Ireland was constituted in 1920 from 6 of the 9 counties of Ulster, the NE corner of Ireland. Area 5,452 sq mi, pop. (2021 census) 1,903,100. Capital and chief industrial center, Belfast, pop. (2024 est.) 647,438.

Industries. Shipbuilding, including large tankers, has long been an important industry, centered in Belfast, the largest port. Linen is manufactured, along with apparel, rope, and twine. Growing diversification has added engineering products, synthetic fibers, and electronics. Major farm products include livestock, poultry, potatoes, and dairy foods.

Government and History. An act of the British Parliament, 1920, divided Northern from Southern Ireland, each with a parliament and government. When Ireland became a dominion, 1921, and later a republic, Northern Ireland chose to remain a part of the UK.

During 1968-69, Roman Catholics, then a smaller portion of the pop. than Protestants, claimed discrimination in voting rights, housing, and employment. Violence and terrorism intensified, involving branches of the Irish Republican Army (IRA; outlawed in the Irish Republic), Protestant groups, police, and British troops. Between 1969 and 2001, more than 3,500 were killed in sectarian violence in Northern Ireland, Ireland, England, and elsewhere. For most of this period, Britain imposed direct rule.

A settlement reached on Good Friday, Apr. 10, 1998, and approved May 22 by voters in Northern Ireland and the Irish Republic, restored home rule and election of a 108-member assembly with safeguards for the rights of different communities. Both Ireland and Great Britain agreed to relinquish constitutional claims on Northern Ireland. IRA dissidents detonated a bomb at Omagh Aug. 15 that killed 29 people and injured over 330.

London transferred authority to a Northern Ireland power-sharing government in 1999. The IRA July 2005 renounced violence; Britain reduced its military presence. A dispute between the pro-UK Democratic Unionist Party (DUP) and the Irish nationalist party Sinn Féin caused the government to collapse in Jan. 2017. A new power-sharing government was not formed until Jan. 2020. Same-sex marriage and most abortions became legal in Northern Ireland in 2020. Sinn Féin won the largest bloc of seats in May 5, 2022, elections for the Northern Ireland assembly; the DUP, which finished second, delayed a new power-sharing government, seeking changes to the Northern Ireland protocol. After the 2023 Windsor framework, the DUP agreed in 2024 to a new power-sharing government; Sinn Féin's Michelle O'Neill became first minister Feb. 3, 2024.

Religion and Education. According to the 2021 census, the population of Northern Ireland was about 42.3% Catholic, 37.4% Protestant and other Christian, 1.3% other non-Christian religions, 17.4% no religion, and 1.6% not stated. Education is compulsory between the ages of 4 and 16 years. **Website:** www.northernireland.gov.uk

Channel Islands

The Channel Islands, area 75 sq mi, off the NW coast of France, the only parts of the former Dukedom of Normandy belonging to England, are Jersey, Guernsey, and the dependencies of Guernsey—Alderney, Brecqhou, Herm, Jethou, Lihou, and Sark. The Bailiwicks of **Jersey**, area 45 sq mi, pop. (2024 est.) 103,387, capital St. Helier (2018 est. pop., 34,386), and **Guernsey**, area 30 sq mi, pop. (2024 est.) 67,787, capital St. Peter Port (2018 est. pop., 16,271), have separate legal existences and lieutenant governors named by the Crown. The islands were the only British soil occupied by German troops in WWII. **Websites:** www.gov.je; www.gov.gg

Isle of Man

The Isle of Man, area 221 sq mi, pop. (2024 est.) 92,269, is in the Irish Sea, 20 mi from Scotland, 30 mi from Cumberland. It is rich in lead and iron. The island has its own laws and a lieutenant governor appointed by the Crown. The Tynwald (legislature) consists of the Legislative Council, partly elected, and House of Keys, elected. Capital: Douglas; pop. (2021 census) 26,677. Leading employment sectors in 2016 were professional, education, medical, and scientific services 22.6%; insurance, banking, finance, and business services 20.9%; and misc. services 9.3%. Man is famous for the Manx tailless cat. **Website:** www.gov.im

Gibraltar

A dependency on the S coast of Spain, Gibraltar guards the entrance to the Mediterranean. Known as the Rock, Gibraltar has been in British possession since 1704. It is 3 mi long and 0.75 mi wide (total area, 2.25 sq mi) and reaches a max. elevation of 1,396 ft. A narrow isthmus connects it with the rest of the Iberian Peninsula. Pop. (2024 est.) 29,683.

Gibraltar has historically been—and remains—an object of contention between Britain and Spain. In 1967, residents voted almost unanimously to remain under British rule. A 1969 constitution increased Gibraltarian control of domestic affairs. Voters rejected a plan for the UK and Spain to share sovereignty, Nov. 7, 2002. Residents approved a new constitution Nov. 30, 2006. **Website:** www.gibraltar.gov.gi

British West Indies

A number of the Leeward Isls. are self-governing British possessions. Universal suffrage was instituted 1951-54; ministerial systems were set up 1956-60.

The Leeward Isls. associated with the UK are **Montserrat**, area 39 sq mi, pop. (2024 est.) 5,468. Brades Estate (2018 est. pop., 472) is de facto capital after Plymouth was abandoned in 1997 due to volcanic activity. The **British Virgin Isls.**, 58 sq mi, pop. (2024 est.) 40,102, capital Road Town (2018 est. pop., 15,137); and **Anguilla**, 35 sq mi, pop. (2024 est.) 19,416, capital The Valley (2018 est. pop., 1,402). Montserrat was devastated by the Soufrière Hills volcano, which began erupting July 18, 1995. In the 2020s, Anguilla had significant revenue from companies applying for domain names ending in ".ai."

The three **Cayman Isls.**, a dependency, lie S of Cuba, NW of Jamaica. Pop. (2024 est.) 66,653, most of it on Grand Cayman. It is a free port; in the 1970s Grand Cayman became a tax-free refuge for foreign funds and branches of many Western banks were opened there. International tourism receipts in 2019 were $919 mil. Total area 102 sq mi. Capital: George Town; pop. (2018 est.) 34,875.

The **Turks and Caicos Isls.** are a dependency at the SE end of the Bahama Islands. Of about 40 islands, only 8 are inhabited; area 366 sq mi, pop. (2023 est.) 60,439; capital Cockburn Town (Grand Turk), pop. 5,447 (2018 est.). Salt, shellfish, and conch shells are the main exports.

In Sept. 2017, Anguilla, the British Virgin Isls., and the Turks and Caicos Isls. suffered severe damage from Hurricane Irma. Hurricane Maria further damaged the Turks and Caicos Isls.

Bermuda

Bermuda is a British dependency governed by a royal governor and an assembly, dating from 1620, the oldest legislative body among British dependencies. It is a group of about 150 small islands of coral formation, 20 inhabited, comprising 21 sq mi in the western Atlantic, 580 mi E of N. Carolina. Pop. (2024 est.) 72,800 (about 54% of African descent). Pop. density is high. Capital: Hamilton; pop. (2018 est.) 10,073.

Tourism is the major industry; tourism receipts in 2022 were $342 mil. Bermuda is also a haven for the offshore insurance industry. Exports include petroleum products, medicine. GDP per capita in 2022 exceeded $122,000. In a referendum Aug. 15, 1995, voters rejected independence. **Website:** www.gov.bm

South Atlantic Territories

The **Falkland Isls.**, a dependency, lie 300 mi E of the Strait of Magellan at the southern end of S America.

The Falklands include 2 large islands and about 200 smaller ones, area 4,700 sq mi, pop. (2016 est.) 3,198. Capital Stanley, pop. (2018 est.) 2,269. The licensing of foreign fishing vessels is a major source of revenue. Fishing, tourism, and sheep farming are main industries; wool is the leading export. There are indications of large oil and gas deposits. Argentina claims the islands as Islas Malvinas; 97% of inhabitants are of British origin. Argentina invaded the islands Apr. 2, 1982. A British military task force forced an Argentine surrender at Port Stanley, June 14, 1982. **Website:** www.falklands.gov.fk

British Antarctic Territory, S of 60° S lat., formerly a dependency of the Falkland Isls., was made a separate colony in 1962 and includes the South Shetland Isls., the South Orkney Isls., and the Antarctic Peninsula. A chain of meteorological stations is maintained.

South Georgia and the **South Sandwich Isls.**, formerly administered by the Falklands Isls., became a separate dependency in 1985. Total area of 1,507 sq mi. South Georgia, with no permanent population, is about 800 mi SE of the Falklands; the South Sandwich Isls. are uninhabited, about 470 mi SE of South Georgia. **Website:** www.gov.gs

St. Helena, an island 1,200 mi off the W coast of Africa and 1,800 mi E of S America, 47 sq mi. Total area of St. Helena, Ascension, and Tristan da Cunha is 152 sq mi; total pop. (2024 est.) 7,943. Construction, crafts, fishing are chief industries. After Napoleon Bonaparte was defeated at Waterloo the Allies exiled him to St. Helena, where he lived from Oct. 16, 1815, to his death, May 5, 1821. Capital: Jamestown; pop. (2018 est.) 603. **Website:** www.sainthelena.gov.sh

Tristan da Cunha is the principal island, area 38 sq mi, in a group of islands of volcanic origin, total area 71 sq mi, halfway between the Cape of Good Hope and S America. The islands are part of the British overseas territory of St. Helena, Ascension, and Tristan da Cunha.

Ascension is an island of volcanic origin, 34 sq mi in area, 700 mi NW of St. Helena. It is part of the British overseas territory of St. Helena, Ascension, and Tristan da Cunha. It is a communications relay center for Britain and has a U.S. satellite tracking center. The island is noted for sea turtles. **Website:** www.ascension.gov.ac

British Indian Ocean Territory (BIOT)

Formed Nov. 1965, with islands formerly dependencies of Mauritius (the Chagos Archipelago, including Diego Garcia) or Seychelles (Aldabra, Farquhar, and Des Roches—later transferred back to Seychelles). Total area 21,004 sq mi, land area 23 sq mi. The Chagos civilian population was removed by the UK by the 1970s to make way for expansion of the U.S. military base on Diego Garcia. The UK has opposed islanders' efforts to return home. Mauritius claims the archipelago. UN courts have found UK control of the Chagos illegal.

Pacific Ocean Territories

Pitcairn Isl. is in the Pacific, halfway between S America and Australia. The island was reached in 1767 by British sea captain Philip Carteret but was not inhabited until 23 years later when the mutineers of the *Bounty* landed there. Pop. (2021 est.) 50; descendants of mutineers and their Tahitian wives. It is administered by a British High Commissioner in New Zealand and a local Council. The uninhabited islands of Henderson, Ducie, and Oeno are in the Pitcairn group, area 18 sq mi. **Website:** www.government.pn

United States

United States of America

(Figures for U.S. may differ elsewhere in **The World Almanac.***)*

People: Population: 341,963,408 (3). **Age distrib.:** <15: 18.1%; 65+: 18.5%. **Growth:** 0.7%. **Migrants:** 15.3%. **Pop. density:** 96.8 per sq mi, 37.4 per sq km. **Urban:** 83.5%. **Ethnic groups:** white 61.6%, Black 12.4%, Asian 6%, Indigenous/Alaska native 1.1%. An est. 18.7% of pop. is Hispanic (any race). **Languages:** English, Spanish; Hawaiian official in Hawaii, 20 Indigenous langs. official in Alaska. No official natl. lang. **Religions:** Christian 72.1% (Catholic 28.3%, independent 21.2%, Protestant 20.0%, Orthodox 2.7%), agnostic 18.1%, atheist 3.2%, Jewish 1.6%, Muslim 1.6% (Sunni), Buddhist 1.4% (Mahayanist).

Geography: Total area: 3,796,742 sq mi, 9,833,517 sq km (3); **Land area:** 3,531,905 sq mi, 9,147,593 sq km. (Area is for 50 states and DC only.) **Location:** Primarily N America. Canada on N, Mexico on S; Pacific on W, Atlantic on E. **Topography:** Vast central plain, mountains in W, hills and low mountains in E. **Arable land:** 16.6%. **Capital:** Washington, DC, 5,545,186.

Government: Type: Constitutional federal republic. **Head of state and govt.:** Pres. Joseph R. Biden Jr.; b. 1942; in office: Jan. 20, 2021. **Local divisions:** 50 states, 1 district. **Defense budget:** $905.5 bil. **Active troops:** 1,326,050.

Economy: Industries: petroleum, steel, motor vehicles, aerospace, telecom, chemicals, electronics, food proc., consumer goods, lumber, mining. **Chief agric.:** maize, soybeans, milk, wheat, sugarcane, sugar beets. **Natural resources:** coal, copper, lead, molybdenum, phosphates, rare earth elements, uranium, bauxite, gold, iron, mercury, nickel, potash, silver, tungsten, zinc, petroleum, nat. gas, timber. **Water:** 9,107 cu m per capita. **Crude oil reserves** (2020): 47.1 bil bbls. **Electricity prod.:** 4.3 tril kWh. **Labor force:** agric. 1.6%, industry 19.3%, services 79.1%. **Unemployment:** 3.6%.

Finance: Monetary unit: Dollar (USD) (1.00 = $1 U.S.). **GDP:** $27.4 tril; **per capita GDP:** $81,695; **GDP growth:** 2.5%. **Imports:** $3.8 tril; China 18%, Canada 14%, Mexico 14%, Germany 5%, Japan 4%. **Exports:** $3.1 tril; Canada 16%, Mexico 15%, China 8%, Japan 4%, UK 4%. **Tourism:** $175.9 bil. **Budget:** $7.6 tril. **Inflation:** 4.1%.

Transport: Railways: 182,412 mi. **Motor vehicles:** 905.0 per 1,000 pop. **Airports:** 15,873.

Communications: Mobile: 112.4 per 100 pop. **Broadband:** 185 per 100 pop. **Internet:** 97.1%.

Health: Expend. (2022): 16.6%. **Life expect.:** 78.7 male; 83.1 female. **Births:** 12.2 per 1,000 pop. **Deaths:** 8.5 per 1,000 pop. **Infant mortality:** 5.1 per 1,000 live births. **Undernourished:** <2.5%. **HIV:** NA. **COVID-19:** 1,194,158 deaths; rates per 100,000: 31,250 cases, 361 deaths. 70% vaccinated.

Education: Compulsory: ages 6-17. **Literacy:** NA.

Website: www.usa.gov

See also U.S. History chapter; Chronology of the Year's Events.

Uruguay

Oriental Republic of Uruguay

People: Population: 3,425,330 (132). **Age distrib.:** <15: 18.9%; 65+: 15.7%. **Growth:** 0.3%. **Migrants:** 3.1%. **Pop. density:** 50.7 per sq mi, 19.6 per sq km. **Urban:** 95.9%. **Ethnic groups:** white 87.7%, Black 4.6%, Indigenous 2.4%. **Languages:** Spanish (official). **Religions:** Christian 62.4% (Catholic 49.5%), agnostic 29.8%, atheist 6.8%.

Geography: Total area: 68,037 sq mi, 176,215 sq km (89); **Land area:** 67,574 sq mi, 175,015 sq km. **Location:** Southern S America, on Atlantic O. Argentina on W, Brazil on N. **Topography:** Rolling, grassy plains and hills, well-watered by rivers flowing W to Uruguay R. **Arable land:** 12.1%. **Capital:** Montevideo, 1,781,363.

Government: Type: Presidential republic. **Head of state and govt.:** Pres. Luis Alberto Lacalle Pou; b. 1973; in office: Mar. 1, 2020. **Local divisions:** 19 departments. **Defense budget:** $573 mil. **Active troops:** 21,100.

Economy: Industries: food proc., electrical machinery, transp. equip., petroleum prods., textiles, chemicals, beverages. **Chief agric.:** milk, rice, wheat, barley, soybeans, beef. **Natural resources:** hydropower, minor minerals, fish. **Water:** 50,259 cu m per capita. **Electricity prod.:** 15.2 bil kWh. **Labor force:** agric. 8.4%, industry 18.1%, services 73.6%. **Unemployment:** 8.4%.

Finance: Monetary unit: Peso (UYU) (40.25 = $1 U.S.). **GDP:** $116.6 bil; **per capita GDP:** $34,062; **GDP growth:** 0.4%. **Imports:** $18.9 bil; Brazil 20%, China 18%, U.S. 15%, Argentina 11%. **Exports:** $21.3 bil; China 24%, Brazil 14%, Argentina 8%, U.S. 7%, Netherlands 5%. **Tourism:** $2.5 bil. **Budget** (2020): $17.6 bil. **Inflation:** 5.9%.

Transport: Railways: 1,040 mi (operational; govt. claims 1,840 mi total length). **Motor vehicles:** 396.4 per 1,000 pop. **Airports:** 64.

Communications: Mobile: 141.7 per 100 pop. **Broadband:** 110 per 100 pop. **Internet:** 89.9%.

Health: Expend.: 9.4%. **Life expect.:** 75.8 male; 82.1 female. **Births:** 12.6 per 1,000 pop. **Deaths:** 9.1 per 1,000 pop. **Infant mortality:** 8.0 per 1,000 live births. **Undernourished:** <2.5%. **HIV:** 0.6%. **COVID-19:** 7,682 deaths; rates per 100,000: 29,978 cases, 221 deaths. 84% vaccinated.

Education: Compulsory: ages 4-17. **Literacy:** 98.8%.

Website: www.gub.uy

Spanish settlers began to supplant the Indigenous Charrua Indians in 1624. Uruguay was attached to the Spanish Viceroyalty of Rio de la Plata in the 18th cent. Rebels fought against Spain beginning in 1810, with independence declared Aug. 25, 1825. To suppress Tupamaro guerrilla activities, a repressive military regime took power in 1973. Constitutional government was restored in 1985.

Same-sex marriage and marijuana use were legalized in 2013.

José (Pepe) Mujica, a former guerrilla, transformed his Marxist Tupamaro movement into a mainstream political party. Tabaré Vázquez, the candidate of Mujica's Broad Front coalition, won a presidential runoff election, Nov. 30, 2014. Conservative Luis Lacalle Pou narrowly defeated the Broad Front candidate in a Nov. 24, 2019, runoff.

Uzbekistan

Republic of Uzbekistan

People: Population: 36,520,593 (42). **Age distrib.:** <15: 29.6%; 65+: 6.7%. **Growth:** 1.4%. **Migrants:** 3.5%. **Pop. density:** 222.4 per sq mi, 85.9 per sq km. **Urban:** 50.6%. **Ethnic groups:** Uzbek 83.8%, Tajik 4.8%, Kazakh 2.5%, Russian 2.3%, Karakalpak 2.2%. **Languages:** Uzbek (official), Russian, Tajik. **Religions:** Muslim 95.0% (Sunni), agnostic 2.7%.

Geography: Total area: 172,742 sq mi, 447,400 sq km (57); **Land area:** 164,248 sq mi, 425,400 sq km. **Location:** Central Asia. Kazakhstan on N and W; Kyrgyzstan, Tajikistan on E; Afghanistan, Turkmenistan on S. **Topography:** Mostly plains and desert. **Arable land:** 9.1%. **Capital:** Tashkent, 2,633,661.

Government: Type: Presidential republic; highly authoritarian. **Head of state:** Pres. Shavkat Mirziyoyev; b. 1957; in office: Dec. 14, 2016. **Head of govt.:** Prime Min. Abdulla Aripov; b. 1961; in office: Dec. 14, 2016. **Local divisions:** 12 provinces, 1 autonomous republic, 3 cities. **Defense budget:** NA. **Active troops:** 48,000.

Economy: Industries: textiles, food proc., machine building, metallurgy, mining, hydrocarbon extraction, chemicals. **Chief agric.:** milk, wheat, carrots/turnips, cotton, potatoes, tomatoes. **Natural resources:** nat. gas, petroleum, coal, gold, uranium, silver, copper, lead, zinc, tungsten, molybdenum. **Water:** 1,434 cu m per capita. **Crude oil reserves:** 594 mil bbls. **Electricity prod.:** 74.8 bil kWh. **Labor force:** agric. 25.9%, industry 24.2%, services 49.9%. **Unemployment:** 4.5%.

Finance: Monetary unit: Som (UZS) (12,616.91 = $1 U.S.). **GDP:** $354.1 bil; **per capita GDP:** $9,725; **GDP growth:** 6.0%. **Imports:** $42.1 bil; China 24%, Russia 19%, Kazakhstan 12%, South Korea 8%, Turkey (Türkiye) 6%. **Exports:** $24.5 bil; Switzerland 25%, Russia 15%, China 12%, Turkey (Türkiye) 9%, Kazakhstan 7%. **Tourism:** $2.2 bil. **Budget:** $16.3 bil. **Inflation** (2021-22): 11.4%.

Transport: Railways: 2,884 mi. **Motor vehicles:** 81.7 per 1,000 pop. **Airports:** 74.

Communications: Mobile: 105.2 per 100 pop. **Broadband:** 107 per 100 pop. **Internet** (2023): 89%.

Health: Expend.: 7.7%. **Life expect.:** 73.6 male; 79.0 female. **Births:** 20.5 per 1,000 pop. **Deaths:** 5.1 per 1,000 pop. **Infant mortality:** 18.2 per 1,000 live births. **Undernourished:** <2.5%. **HIV:** 0.2%. **COVID-19:** 1,016 deaths; rates per 100,000: 523 cases, 3 deaths. 55% vaccinated.

Education: Compulsory: ages 7-18. **Literacy:** 100.0%.

Website: www.gov.uz

The region was overrun by the Mongols under Genghis Khan in 1220. In the 14th cent., Uzbekistan became the center of a native Timurid empire. In later centuries Muslim feudal states emerged. Russian military conquest began in the 19th cent. The Uzbek SSR became a Soviet republic in 1925.

Uzbekistan gained independence when the Soviet Union disbanded Dec. 26, 1991, and was led by the authoritarian government of a former Communist, Islam A. Karimov.

Attacks by Islamic militants, Mar.-July 2004, killed more than 50 people. In June 2004, Russia's OAO Lukoil signed a $1-bil deal to develop Uzbekistan's natural gas fields.

After armed dissidents at Andizhan attacked government buildings and freed hundreds of prisoners, May 2005, security forces killed many rebels and unarmed demonstrators. Karimov then launched a general crackdown on human rights activists.

Karimov remained in office following the expiration of his presidential term Jan. 22, 2007, despite a two-term constitutional limit. He won a third term Dec. 23 (88.1% of the vote) and a fourth term, Mar. 29, 2015 (90.4%). The government announced, Sept. 2, 2016, that Karimov had died. Prime Min. Shavkat Mirziyoyev became interim president and won a flawed Dec. 4 presidential election. Mirziyoyev took steps to reduce repression, including freeing some jailed dissidents and reducing forced labor in the cotton harvests. Mirziyoyev won an Oct. 24, 2021, presidential election from which several opposition candidates were barred. Constitutional changes in 2023 allowed Mirziyoyev to serve two more 7-year terms; he won a sham presidential election, July 9, 2023.

Vanuatu

Republic of Vanuatu

People: Population: 318,007 (174). **Age distrib.:** <15: 31.1%; 65+: 5.0%. **Growth:** 1.6%. **Migrants:** 1.1%. **Pop. density:** 67.6 per sq mi, 26.1 per sq km. **Urban:** 26.1%. **Ethnic groups:** Ni-Vanuatu 99%. **Languages:** 100+ Indigenous langs.; Bislama (creole), English, French (all official). **Religions:** Christian 93.7% (Protestant 67.0%, Catholic 14.5%, independent 12.3%), ethnic religionist 4.2%.

Geography: Total area: 4,706 sq mi, 12,189 sq km (158); **Land area:** 4,706 sq mi, 12,189 sq km. **Location:** More than 80 islands (about 65 inhabited) in SW Pacific, 1,200 mi NE of Brisbane, Australia. Fiji to E, Solomon Isls. to NW. **Topography:** Dense forest with narrow coastal strips of cultivated land. **Arable land:** 1.6%. **Capital:** Port Vila, 52,690.

Government: Type: Parliamentary republic. **Head of state:** Pres. Nikenike Vurobaravu; b. 1964; in office: July 23, 2022. **Head of govt.:** Prime Min. Charlot Salwai; b. 1963; in office: Oct. 6, 2023. **Local divisions:** 6 provinces. **Defense budget/active troops:** NA.

Economy: Industries: food and fish freezing, wood proc., meat canning. **Chief agric.:** coconuts, root vegetables, bananas, vegetables, fruits, pork. **Natural resources:** manganese, hardwood forests, fish. **Water:** 31,335 cu m per capita. **Electricity prod.:** 73.3 mil kWh. **Labor force:** agric. 42.3%, industry 11.2%, services 46.4%. **Unemployment:** 5.1%.

Finance: Monetary unit: Vatu (VUV) (118.50 = $1 U.S.). **GDP:** $1.1 bil; **per capita GDP:** $3,315; **GDP growth:** 2.2%. **Imports** (2022): $579.3 mil; China 24%, Australia 15%, Malaysia 12%, New Zealand 9%, Fiji 8%. **Exports** (2022): $152.1 mil; Thailand 42%, Japan 27%, South Korea 7%, Philippines 6%, China 5%. **Tourism** (2022): $39 mil. **Budget:** $355 mil. **Inflation** (2021-22): 6.7%.

Transport: Motor vehicles: 58.1 per 1,000 pop. **Airports:** 31.

Communications: Mobile (2022): 81.6 per 100 pop. **Broadband** (2022): 339 per 100 pop. **Internet:** 69.9%.

Health: Expend.: 4.4%. **Life expect.:** 74.0 male; 77.4 female. **Births:** 20.8 per 1,000 pop. **Deaths:** 4.0 per 1,000 pop. **Infant mortality:** 13.7 per 1,000 live births. **Undernourished:** 7.9%. **HIV:** NA. **COVID-19:** 14 deaths; rates per 100,000: 3,913 cases, 5 deaths. 53% vaccinated.

Education: Compulsory: NA. **Literacy:** 89.1%.

Website: www.gov.vu

The Anglo-French condominium of the New Hebrides, administered jointly since 1906, became the independent Republic of Vanuatu on July 30, 1980. Cyclone Pam, Mar. 13-14, 2015, destroyed 96% of crops and left 166,000 people in need of aid. The COVID-19 pandemic hurt tourism revenue, 2020-21. Following Oct. 13, 2022, elections, Alatoi Ishmael Kalsakau formed a coalition government. After he and his successor lost no-confidence votes, Sept.-Oct. 2023, Charlot Salwai became prime minister Oct. 6, 2023.

Vanuatu is vulnerable to climate change effects such as rising sea levels and stronger storms. Aid from China has increased in recent years.

Vatican City

The Holy See (Vatican City State)

People: Population (2022): 1,000 (196). **Age distrib.:** NA. **Growth:** NA. **Migrants:** 100.0%. **Pop. density** (2022): 5,886.3 per sq mi, 2,272.7 per sq km. **Urban:** 100.0%. **Ethnic groups:** Italian, Swiss, Argentinian, other nationalities from around the world. **Languages:** Italian, Latin, French. **Religions:** Christian 100.0% (Catholic [official]).

Geography: Total area: 0.17 sq mi, 0.44 sq km (196); **Land area:** 0.17 sq mi, 0.44 sq km. **Location:** Within the city of Rome, completely surrounded by Italy. **Arable land:** 0%. **Capital:** Vatican City.

Government: Ecclesiastical elective monarchy; self-described as "absolute monarchy."

Economy: Industries: printing; coin, medal, postage stamp prod.; mosaics, staff uniforms; worldwide banking, financial activities. **Water:** 0 cu m per capita. **Labor force:** NA. **Unemployment:** NA.

Finance: Monetary unit: Euro (EUR) (0.90 = $1 U.S.). **GDP:** NA; **per capita GDP:** NA; **GDP growth:** NA. **Budget** (2013): $348 mil.

Communications: Internet: 85.1%.

Health: COVID-19: 0 deaths; rates per 100,000: 3,214 cases.

Apostolic Nunciature: 3339 Massachusetts Ave. NW 20008; 333-7171.

Website: www.vatican.va or www.vaticanstate.va

The popes for many centuries, with brief interruptions, held temporal sovereignty over mid-Italy (the so-called Papal States), comprising an area of some 16,000 sq mi, with a population in the 19th cent. of more than 3 mil. This territory was incorporated in the new Kingdom of Italy (1861), the sovereignty of the pope being confined to the palaces of the Vatican and the Lateran in Rome and the villa of Castel Gandolfo, by an Italian law, May 13, 1871.

A Treaty of Conciliation, a concordat, and a financial convention with Italy were signed Feb. 11, 1929. They established the independent state of Vatican City and gave the Roman Catholic Church special status in Italy. The treaty was incorporated into Italy's Constitution in 1947. Italy and the Vatican signed an agreement in 1984 eliminating Roman Catholicism as the state religion and ending required religious education in Italian schools.

Vatican City includes the Basilica of Saint Peter, the Vatican Palace and Museum, the Vatican gardens, and neighboring buildings; 13 buildings in Rome, outside the boundaries, enjoy extraterritorial rights. The legal system is based on the code of canon law, the apostolic constitutions, and laws especially promulgated for Vatican City by the pope.

Pope Benedict XVI, elected Apr. 19, 2005, became, Feb. 28, 2013, the first pontiff to resign since 1415 (Benedict died Dec. 31, 2022). Cardinal Jorge Mario Bergoglio, from Argentina, was elected Mar. 13, taking the name Francis. He became the first Latin American and first Jesuit pope.

Cardinal George Pell, prefect of the Vatican's Secretariat for the Economy, was convicted in Australia in 2018 of child sex abuse; his conviction was overturned on appeal, Apr. 7, 2020. Former cardinal and archbishop of Washington, DC, Theodore McCarrick was defrocked by the Vatican, Feb. 2019, for sexual abuse of minors. A May 9, 2019, papal edict required priests and nuns to report to church authorities sexual abuse or attempted cover-ups. A new constitution, 2022, somewhat strengthened the role of women and increased protections against sexual abuse.

Venezuela

Bolivarian Republic of Venezuela

People: Population: 31,250,306 (49). **Age distrib.:** <15: 25.0%; 65+: 9.1%. **Growth:** 2.3%. **Migrants:** 4.7%. **Pop. density:** 91.8 per sq mi, 35.4 per sq km. **Urban:** 88.5%. **Ethnic groups:** Spanish, Italian, Portuguese, Arab, German, African, Indigenous. **Languages:** Spanish (official), Indigenous. **Religions:** Christian 92.1% (Catholic 74.7%, Protestant 11.5%), agnostic 4.8%.

Geography: Total area: 352,144 sq mi, 912,050 sq km (32); **Land area:** 340,561 sq mi, 882,050 sq km. **Location:** Carib. coast of S America. Colombia on W, Brazil on S, Guyana on E. **Topography:** Plains, called llanos, extend between Andes Mts. and Orinoco Delta. Orinoco stretches 1,600 mi and drains 80% of country. **Arable land:** 2.9%. **Capital:** Caracas, 2,991,727. **Cities:** Maracaibo, 2,400,826; Valencia, 2,007,265.

Government: Type: Federal presidential republic. **Head of state and govt.:** Pres. Nicolás Maduro Moros; b. 1962; in office: Apr. 19, 2013. (The U.S. does not recognize Maduro.) **Local divisions:** 23 states, 1 capital district, 1 federal dependency (with 11 federally controlled island groups). **Defense budget:** NA. **Active troops:** 123,000.

Economy: Industries: agric. prods., livestock, raw materials, machinery and equip., transp. equip., constr. materials, medical equip., pharmaceuticals. **Chief agric.:** milk, sugarcane, maize, plantains, oil palm fruit, bananas. **Natural resources:** petroleum, nat. gas, iron ore, gold, bauxite, hydropower, diamonds. **Water:** 46,986 cu m per capita. **Crude oil reserves:** 303.8 bil bbls. **Electricity prod.:** 84.6 bil kWh. **Labor force:** agric. 11.5%, industry 17.9%, services 70.6%. **Unemployment:** 5.5%.

Finance: Monetary unit: Bolivar (VES) (36.52 = $1 U.S.). **GDP:** NA; **per capita GDP:** NA; **GDP growth:** NA. **Imports** (2018): $18.4 bil; China 31%, U.S. 23%, Brazil 14%, Colombia 7%. **Exports** (2018): $83.4 bil; China 16%, Turkey (Türkiye) 14%, Spain 12%, U.S. 10%, Brazil 8%. **Tourism** (2022): $271 mil. **Budget** (2017): $76 mil. **Inflation** (2018-19): 146,101.7%.

Transport: Railways: 278 mi. **Motor vehicles:** 133.5 per 1,000 pop. **Airports:** 502.

Communications: Mobile (2022): 66.5 per 100 pop. **Broadband** (2022): 52.3 per 100 pop. **Internet** (2017): 61.6%.

Health: Expend.: 4.0%. **Life expect.:** 71.5 male; 77.7 female. **Births:** 16.7 per 1,000 pop. **Deaths:** 6.5 per 1,000 pop. **Infant mortality:** 13.9 per 1,000 live births. **Undernourished:** 17.6%. **HIV:** 0.5%. **COVID-19:** 5,856 deaths; rates per 100,000: 1,944 cases, 21 deaths. 50% vaccinated.

Education: Compulsory: NA. **Literacy:** 97.6%.

Website: www.state.gov/countries-areas/venezuela/

Columbus first set foot on the South American continent on the peninsula of Paria, Aug. 1498. Alonso de Ojeda, 1499, called the land Venezuela, or Little Venice, because the native people had houses on stilts. Spanish colonialists dominated Venezuela until Simón Bolívar's victory near Carabobo in June 1821. The republic was formed after secession from the Colombian Federation in 1830. Military strongmen ruled Venezuela for much of its history. Beginning in 1959, the country had democratically elected governments.

Venezuela has the world's largest crude oil reserves, and the economy in recent decades has been heavily dependent on oil revenues. The government, Jan. 1, 1976, nationalized the oil industry. The country also has large reserves of natural gas.

Two attempted coups were thwarted by loyalist troops in Feb. and Nov. 1992. Coup leader Hugo Chávez, who ran as a populist, was elected president Dec. 1998. That month, voters approved a new constitution greatly increasing his powers.

Popular among the poor, Chávez alienated middle- and upper-class Venezuelans with economic and political reforms, and his foreign policy antagonized the U.S. With the economy surging, he won the Dec. 2006 presidential election. Suffering from cancer, Chávez won reelection, Oct. 7, 2012. He died Mar. 5, 2013, before he could be sworn in. Vice Pres. Nicolás Maduro Moros won a narrow victory in Apr. 14, 2013, elections.

With the economy hurt by low oil prices, declining oil production, and tight currency and price controls, GDP declined sharply beginning in 2014 and inflation soared. Shortages of food, medicine, and other goods were widespread. A political crisis intensified economic problems. Beginning in 2015, millions of Venezuelans emigrated, largely to other Latin American nations, the U.S., and Spain—7.7 mil by the end of 2023.

Large anti-Maduro protests, Feb.-June 2014, were met with a harsh crackdown. An opposition coalition won Dec. 6, 2015, National Assembly elections, but the Supreme Court often overturned legislation. Looting and sometimes violent demonstrations were widespread in 2016-17. In a flawed election, May 20, 2018, Maduro won a new term as president. National Assembly head Juan Guaidó, Jan. 23, 2019, declared himself interim president. Dozens of countries, including the U.S., recognized Guaidó, but Maduro clung to power. The military cracked down on protesters. UN reports in 2019 and 2020 concluded that detainees were being tortured and that security forces and death squads had committed thousands of extrajudicial killings. Pro-Maduro candidates swept Dec. 6, 2020, National Assembly elections boycotted by the opposition. In the 2020s, extreme poverty and deprivation remained widespread.

With Maduro apparently entrenched in power, opposition groups voted in Dec. 2022 to dissolve the interim government that Guaidó had headed.

After opposition coalition leader María Corina Machado was barred from running, Edmundo González, backed by Machado, opposed Maduro in the July 28, 2024, presidential election. Official results, disputed by opposition tallies, gave Maduro a victory. The

U.S., Aug. 1, recognized González as the winner. More than 2,000 were arrested for disputing the official results.

Vietnam

Socialist Republic of Vietnam

People: Population: 105,758,975 (16). **Age distrib.:** <15: 23.2%; 65+: 8.3%. **Growth:** 0.9%. **Migrants:** 0.1%. **Pop. density:** 883.4 per sq mi, 341.1 per sq km. **Urban:** 40.2%. **Ethnic groups:** 54 recognized by govt., incl. Kinh (Viet) 85.3%. **Languages:** Vietnamese (official), English, French, Chinese, Khmer. **Religions:** Buddhist 48.0% (Mahayanist 47%), agnostic 11.8%, ethnic religionist 11.5%, new religionist 10.9%, Christian 10.0%, atheist 6.1%.

Geography: Total area: 127,881 sq mi, 331,210 sq km (65); **Land area:** 119,719 sq mi, 310,070 sq km. **Location:** SE Asia, on E coast of Indochinese Peninsula. China on N; Laos, Cambodia on W. **Topography:** Long and narrow, with 1,400-mi coast. Densely settled Red R. Valley in N; narrow coastal plains in center; wide, often marshy Mekong R. Delta in S. Semi-arid plateaus and barren mountains, with some stretches of tropical rain forest, in rest of country. **Arable land:** 21.5%. **Capital:** Hà Noi, 5,431,801. **Cities:** Thành Pho Ho Chí Minh (Ho Chi Minh City), 9,567,656; Can Tho, 1,938,915; Hai Phòng, 1,463,650.

Government: Type: Communist party-led state. **Head of state:** Pres. To Lam; b. 1957; in office: May 22, 2024. **Head of govt.:** Prime Min. Pham Minh Chinh; b. 1958; in office: Apr. 5, 2021. **Local divisions:** 58 provinces, 5 municipalities. **Defense budget:** $7.4 bil. **Active troops:** 450,000.

Economy: Industries: food proc., garments, shoes, machine-building, mining, coal, steel, cement, chemical fertilizer. **Chief agric.:** rice, vegetables, sugarcane, cassava, maize, pork. **Natural resources:** antimony, phosphates, coal, manganese, rare earth elements, bauxite, chromate, offshore oil/gas deposits, timber, hydropower. **Water:** 9,071 cu m per capita. **Crude oil reserves:** 4.4 bil bbls. **Electricity prod.:** 267.7 bil kWh. **Labor force:** agric. 33.6%, industry 30.6%, services 35.8%. **Unemployment:** 1.6%.

Finance: Monetary unit: Dong (VND) (24,862.63 = $1 U.S.). **GDP:** $1.5 tril; **per capita GDP:** $15,194; **GDP growth:** 5.1%. **Imports:** $339.8 bil; China 38%, South Korea 17%, Japan 5%. **Exports:** $374.3 bil; U.S. 29%, China 15%, South Korea 6%, Japan 6%. **Tourism:** $9.2 bil. **Budget:** $75.8 bil. **Inflation:** 3.3%.

Transport: Railways: 1,616 mi. **Motor vehicles:** 6.9 per 1,000 pop. **Airports:** 42.

Communications: Mobile: 131.0 per 100 pop. **Broadband:** 99.8 per 100 pop. **Internet** (2023): 78.1%.

Health: Expend.: 4.6%. **Life expect.:** 73.5 male; 78.9 female. **Births:** 14.9 per 1,000 pop. **Deaths:** 5.8 per 1,000 pop. **Infant mortality:** 14.1 per 1,000 live births. **Undernourished:** 5.2%. **HIV:** 0.3%. **COVID-19:** 43,206 deaths; rates per 100,000: 11,942 cases, 44 deaths. 88% vaccinated.

Education: Compulsory: ages 5-14. **Literacy:** 96.1%.

Website: vietnam.gov.vn

Settled by Viets from central China, Vietnam was held by China, 111 BCE-939 CE, and was a vassal state during subsequent periods. Conquest by France began in 1858 and ended in 1884 with the protectorates of Tonkin and Annam in the N and the colony of Cochin-China in the S.

Japan occupied Vietnam in 1940. Several groups formed the Vietminh (Independence) League, headed by Communist guerrilla leader Ho Chi Minh. In Aug. 1945, the Vietminh forced out Bao Dai, former emperor of Annam and head of a Japan-sponsored regime. France, seeking to reestablish colonial control, unsuccessfully battled Communist and nationalist forces, 1946-54.

Separate states formed in N. and S. Vietnam, with Communists under Ho Chi Minh (backed by Russia and China) controlling N. Vietnam and a non-Communist government (backed by the U.S.) controlling S. Vietnam. N. Vietnam aided Vietcong guerrillas who sought to take over S. Vietnam. U.S. troops and the S. Vietnamese army fought N. Vietnamese and Vietcong forces, including in border areas of Laos and Cambodia. Combat deaths: U.S. 47,434 (Aug. 4, 1964-Jan. 27, 1973); S. Vietnam more than 200,000; other allied forces 5,225. Total U.S. fatalities exceeded 58,000. Vietnamese civilian casualties were more than 1 mil. The war displaced more than 6.5 mil in S. Vietnam.

A never-implemented cease-fire agreement was signed in Paris Jan. 27, 1973, by the U.S., N. and S. Vietnam, and the Vietcong. The last U.S. troops left Vietnam Mar. 27, 1973. S. Vietnam surrendered Apr. 30, 1975. N. Vietnam assumed control. The country was officially reunited July 2, 1976.

Heavy fighting with Cambodia took place, 1977-80. Reacting to Vietnam's 1979 invasion of Cambodia, China attacked four Vietnamese border provinces, Feb. 1979.

Vietnam announced in 1987 reforms aimed at reducing central control of the economy. The U.S. ended, Feb. 1994, a 19-year embargo on trade with Vietnam, and it extended full diplomatic recognition to Vietnam July 11, 1995. The U.S. lifted in 2016 its embargo on lethal arms sales to Vietnam.

As part of an ongoing anti-corruption campaign, Vietnam's president resigned in Jan. 2023. In 2024, the new president resigned Mar. 20, and the head of the National Assembly resigned Apr. 26. The powerful head of the Communist Party died, July 19, 2024. To Lam became president May 22 and Communist Party head Aug. 3, 2024.

Yemen

Republic of Yemen

People: Population: 32,140,443 (48). **Age distrib.:** <15: 34.4%; 65+: 3.4%. **Growth:** 1.8%. **Migrants:** 1.3%. **Pop. density:** 157.7 per sq mi, 60.9 per sq km. **Urban:** 40.5%. **Ethnic groups:** predom. Arab; also Afro-Arab, South Asian, European. **Languages:** Arabic (official). **Religions:** Muslim (official) 99.2% (Shia 55%, Sunni 44%).

Geography: Total area: 203,850 sq mi, 527,968 sq km (50); **Land area:** 203,850 sq mi, 527,968 sq km. **Location:** Middle East, on S coast of the Arabian Peninsula. Saudi Arabia on N, Oman on E. **Topography:** Sandy coastal strip; well-watered fertile mountains in interior. **Arable land:** 2.2%. **Capital:** Sana'a, 3,407,814. **Cities:** Aden, 1,116,193.

Government: Type: In transition. **Chief of state:** Presidential Council Chair Rashad Mohammed Al-Alimi; in office: Apr. 19, 2022. **Head of govt.:** Prime Min. Ahmad Awad bin Mubarek; in office: Feb. 5, 2024. **Local divisions:** 22 governorates. **Defense budget:** NA. **Active troops:** 40,000. (Est. 20,000 insurgent forces, incl. Houthi and tribes, in territory where govt. does not exercise effective control.)

Economy: Industries: crude oil prod. and petroleum refining; small-scale prod. of cotton textiles, leather goods; food proc.; handicrafts; aluminum prods. **Chief agric.:** mangoes/guavas, potatoes, onions, milk, sorghum, spices. **Natural resources:** petroleum; fish; rock salt; marble; small deposits of coal, gold, lead, nickel, copper. **Water:** 64 cu m per capita. **Crude oil reserves:** 3 bil bbls. **Electricity prod.:** 3.0 bil kWh. **Labor force:** agric. 29.3%, industry 11.7%, services 59.0%. **Unemployment:** 17.2%.

Finance: Monetary unit: Rial (YER) (250.40 = $1 U.S.). **GDP:** NA; **per capita GDP:** NA; **GDP growth:** NA. **Imports** (2017): $4.1 bil; China 26%, UAE 14%, Turkey (Türkiye) 10%, India 10%. **Exports** (2017): $384.5 mil; China 32%, Thailand 20%, India 12%, UAE 7%, Oman 5%. **Budget:** $3.6 bil. **Inflation** (2016-17): 24.7%.

Transport: Motor vehicles: 35.0 per 1,000 pop. **Airports:** 36.

Communications: Mobile: 50.9 per 100 pop. **Broadband:** 34.3 per 100 pop. **Internet:** 17.7%.

Health: Expend.: NA. **Life expect.:** 65.8 male; 70.6 female. **Births:** 23.4 per 1,000 pop. **Deaths:** 5.5 per 1,000 pop. **Infant mortality:** 44.6 per 1,000 live births. **Undernourished:** 39.5%. **HIV:** <0.1%. **COVID-19:** 2,159 deaths; rates per 100,000: 40 cases, 7 deaths. 3% vaccinated.

Education: Compulsory: ages 6-14. **Literacy:** 70.1%.

Website: www.yemenembassy.org

Yemen's territory once was part of the ancient biblical Kingdom of Sheba, or Saba. Yemen became independent in 1918, after centuries of Ottoman Turkish rule.

Imam Yahya ibn Muhammad ruled, 1904-48, and after his assassination was succeeded by his son, Imam Ahmed, 1948-62. Army officers headed by Brig. Gen. Abdullah al-Salal declared the country the Yemen Arab Republic, Sept. 1962. Ahmed's heir, the Imam Mohamad al-Badr, fled to the mountains where tribesmen joined royalist forces, aided by the Saudi monarchy. Fighting between royalists and republicans killed about 150,000 people until hostilities ended in 1970.

South Yemen, formed from the British colony of Aden and the British protectorate of South Arabia, became independent Nov. 1967. A Marxist state and a Soviet ally, it took the name People's Democratic Republic of Yemen in 1970. More than 300,000 Yemenis fled from the S to the N after independence, contributing to two decades of hostility between the two states.

The two countries were formally united May 21, 1990, but regional clan-based rivalries led to full-scale civil war in 1994. Northern troops captured the former southern capital of Aden in July.

While on a refueling stop in Aden, Oct. 12, 2000, the destroyer USS Cole was bombed, killing 17 Americans; the U.S. blamed the attack on al-Qaeda terrorists.

Clashes began in June 2004 between Yemeni government forces and Shiite rebels led by an anti-U.S. cleric, Hussein al-Houthi. The government announced Sept. 10 that Yemeni troops had killed al-Houthi.

During 2007-10, Shiite rebels in the northwest, secessionists in the south, Sunni militants in the east affiliated with al-Qaeda in the Arabian Peninsula (AQAP), and pirates in coastal waters challenged Yemeni government authority. Pres. Ali Abdullah Saleh was severely wounded June 3, 2011, in a rocket attack. Vice Pres. Abd Rabbuh Mansur Hadi became acting president and won an uncontested Feb. 2012 election. Anwar al-Awlaki, a U.S. citizen and radical Muslim cleric linked to several plots against the U.S., was killed Sept. 30, 2011, by a U.S. missile in northern Yemen.

Shiite rebels known as Houthis took over Sanaa in Sept. 2014 and gained control of much of western Yemen. A coalition of Sunni nations led by Saudi Arabia, which backed Hadi, began, Mar. 25, 2015, airstrikes against Houthi fighters and Houthi-controlled areas. The U.S. provided logistical support (ended in 2021). UAE ground troops aided forces combating Houthi rebels. Airstrikes and other fighting caused high civilian casualties. Houthi rebels were aided by Iran. AQAP was active in southern Yemen, and the Sunni extremist group ISIS staged attacks. Houthi forces launched missile and drone attacks on targets in Saudi Arabia and the UAE. A UN-mediated cease-fire went into effect Apr. 2, 2022. Hadi transferred power, in Apr. 2022, to an 8-member Presidential Council. Although the cease-fire expired, Oct. 2, 2022, a lull in fighting continued.

By the beginning of 2022, the UN estimated total deaths in Yemen's civil war since 2014 at 377,000, including 154,000 resulting from combat and other violence and 223,000 from indirect causes such as famine. As of Feb. 2024, more than 4.5 mil people were internally displaced, and over 18 mil needed humanitarian assistance in 2024. A cholera epidemic that began in late 2016 caused millions of cases and thousands of deaths in the following years.

After Israel's offensive in Gaza began (following the Oct. 7, 2023, Hamas attacks in Israel), the Houthis began attacking shipping in the Gulf of Aden and Red Sea (pathway to the Suez Canal) and also firing missiles and drones at Israel, 2023-24. The U.S., UK, and Israel launched retaliatory attacks against Houthi targets in Yemen.

Zambia

Republic of Zambia

People: Population: 20,799,116 (63). **Age distrib.:** <15: 42.1%; 65+: 2.8%. **Growth:** 2.8%. **Migrants:** 1.0%. **Pop. density:** 72.5 per sq mi, 28.0 per sq km. **Urban:** 46.9%. **Ethnic groups:** Bemba 21%, Tonga 13.6%, Chewa 7.4%, Lozi 5.7%, Nsenga 5.3%, Tumbuka 4.4%, Ngoni 4%, Lala 3.1%, Kaonde 2.9%, Namwanga 2.8%, Lunda (northwestern) 2.6%, Mambwe 2.5%, Luvale 2.2%, Lamba 2.1%. **Languages:** Bantu langs. (incl. Bemba, Nyanja, Tonga, Lozi, Chewa, Nsenga, Tumbuka); English (official). **Religions:** Christian 86.9% (Catholic 40.7%, Protestant 30.8%, independent 15.3%), ethnic religionist 9.6%, Baha'i 2.2%.

Geography: Total area: 290,587 sq mi, 752,618 sq km (38); **Land area:** 287,028 sq mi, 743,398 sq km. **Location:** S central Africa. Dem. Rep. of the Congo on N; Tanzania, Malawi, Mozambique on E; Zimbabwe, Namibia on S; Angola on W. **Topography:** Mostly high plateau with thick forests, drained by several important rivers including the Zambezi. **Arable land:** 5.1%. **Capital:** Lusaka, 3,324,219.

Government: Type: Presidential republic. **Head of state and govt.:** Pres. Hakainde Hichilema; b. 1962; in office: Aug. 24, 2021. **Local divisions:** 10 provinces. **Defense budget:** $411 mil. **Active troops:** 15,100.

Economy: Industries: copper mining and proc., emerald mining, constr., foodstuffs, beverages, chemicals, textiles, fertilizer, horticulture. **Chief agric.:** sugarcane, cassava, maize, milk, soybeans, vegetables. **Natural resources:** copper, cobalt, zinc, lead, coal, emeralds, gold, silver, uranium, hydropower. **Water:** 5,382 cu m per capita. **Electricity prod.:** 19.5 bil kWh. **Labor force:** agric. 57.3%, industry 10.3%, services 32.3%. **Unemployment:** 5.9%.

Finance: Monetary unit: Kwacha (ZMW) (25.83 = $1 U.S.). **GDP:** $84.9 bil; **per capita GDP:** $4,126; **GDP growth:** 5.8%. **Imports** (2022): $10.0 bil; South Africa 26%, Equatorial Guinea 18%, China 14%, UAE 7%, Dem. Rep. of the Congo 6%. **Exports** (2022): $12.4 bil; Switzerland 30%, China 18%, Dem. Rep. of the Congo 10%, Pitcairn Islands 10%, UAE 7%. **Tourism:** $801 mil. **Budget:** $7.0 bil. **Inflation:** 10.9%.

Transport: Railways: 1,942 mi (incl. 1,156 mi of Tanzania-Zambia Railway Authority). **Motor vehicles:** 24.2 per 1,000 pop. **Airports:** 119.

Communications: Mobile: 102.1 per 100 pop. **Broadband:** 60.2 per 100 pop. **Internet:** 31.2%.

Health: Expend.: 6.6%. **Life expect.:** 65.2 male; 68.7 female. **Births:** 34.1 per 1,000 pop. **Deaths:** 5.9 per 1,000 pop. **Infant mortality:** 35.6 per 1,000 live births. **Undernourished:** 35.4%. **HIV:** 9.8%. **COVID-19:** 4,077 deaths; rates per 100,000: 1,903 cases, 22 deaths. 50% vaccinated.

Education: Compulsory: ages 7-13. **Literacy:** 87.5%.

Website: www.parliament.gov.zm

Ruled by the British as Northern Rhodesia, the country became the independent republic of Zambia within the Commonwealth Oct. 24, 1964. Independence leader Kenneth Kaunda governed as president, 1964-91. A Zambian government corporation in 1970 took over 51% of two foreign-owned copper-mining companies. Privately held land and other enterprises were nationalized in 1975. In the 1980s and 1990s, lowered copper prices hurt the economy and severe drought caused famine.

Oct. 1991 elections brought an end to Kaunda's one-party rule. The new government sought to sell state enterprises, including the copper industry. Pres. Frederick Chiluba won reelection Nov. 1996. In 2001, Chiluba endorsed Levy Patrick Mwanawasa, who won a disputed Dec. election. Food shortages threatened more than 2 mil Zambians in 2002. Mwanawasa won a second term in 2006.

Pres. Mwanawasa died Aug. 19, 2008. Vice Pres. Rupiah Banda became acting pres. He narrowly won the presidency in the Oct. 2008 election but lost to opposition leader Michael Sata Sept. 2011. Sata died in office, Oct. 28, 2014. Edgar Lungu of Sata's Patriotic Front party narrowly won a Jan. 2015 special election. Lungu narrowly won a new term in Aug. 11, 2016, elections that his main opponent claimed were marred by fraud. With inflation and unemployment high, Hakainde Hichilema defeated Lungu in the Aug. 12, 2021, presidential election.

The country has made progress in treating HIV/AIDS, but in 2022, almost 11% of Zambians ages 15-49 were HIV positive.

Drought caused hydroelectric power shortages as well as acute hunger in 2024.

Zimbabwe

Republic of Zimbabwe

People: Population: 17,150,352 (72). **Age distrib.:** <15: 38.3%; 65+: 3.9%. **Growth:** 1.9%. **Migrants:** 2.8%. **Pop. density:** 114.8 per sq mi, 44.3 per sq km. **Urban:** 32.7%. **Ethnic groups:** African (predom. Shona; Ndebele is second-largest) 99.6%. **Languages:** Shona, Ndebele (both official and most widely spoken); English (official, used in business), 13 official minority langs. **Religions:** Christian 82.3% (independent 35.6%, Protestant 35.0%, Catholic 11.7%), ethnic religionist 15.3%.

Geography: Total area: 150,872 sq mi, 390,757 sq km (60); **Land area:** 149,362 sq mi, 386,847 sq km. **Location:** Southern Africa. Zambia on N, Botswana on W, South Africa on S, Mozambique on E. **Topography:** High plateau rising to mountains on E border, sloping down on other borders. **Arable land:** 8.1%. **Capital:** Harare, 1,603,201.

Government: Type: Presidential republic. **Head of state and govt.:** Pres. Emmerson Mnangagwa; b. 1942; in office: Nov. 24, 2017. **Local divisions:** 8 provinces, 2 cities with provincial status. **Defense budget:** $96 mil. **Active troops:** 29,000.

Economy: Industries: mining, steel, wood prods., cement, chemicals, fertilizer, clothing/footwear, foodstuffs, beverages. **Chief agric.:** sugarcane, maize, beef, milk, cassava, wheat. **Natural resources:** coal, chromium ore, asbestos, gold, nickel, copper, iron ore, vanadium, lithium, tin, platinum group metals. **Water:** 1,251 cu m per capita. **Electricity prod.:** 8.9 bil kWh. **Labor force:** agric. 52.6%, industry 13.8%, services 33.6%. **Unemployment:** 8.8%.

Finance: Monetary unit: Gold (ZWG) (14.02 = $1 U.S.). **GDP:** $65.0 bil; **per capita GDP:** $3,900; **GDP growth:** 5.0%. **Imports** (2022): $10.1 bil; South Africa 39%, China 15%, Singapore 12%, UAE 6%. **Exports** (2022): $7.7 bil; UAE 57%, South Africa 17%, China 7%. **Tourism** (2020): $63 mil. **Budget** (2018): $23 mil. **Inflation** (2021-22): 104.7%.

Transport: Railways: 2,129 mi. **Motor vehicles:** 50.6 per 1,000 pop. **Airports:** 144.

Communications: Mobile: 91.6 per 100 pop. **Broadband:** 67.6 per 100 pop. **Internet:** 32.6%.

Health: Expend.: 2.8%. **Life expect.:** 65.6 male; 68.8 female. **Births:** 28.8 per 1,000 pop. **Deaths:** 6.5 per 1,000 pop. **Infant mortality:** 33.4 per 1,000 live births. **Undernourished:** 38.1%. **HIV:** 10.5%. **COVID-19:** 5,740 deaths; rates per 100,000: 1,792 cases, 39 deaths. 38% vaccinated.

Education: Compulsory: ages 6-12. **Literacy:** 89.9%.

Website: www.zim.gov.zw

Britain took over the area as Southern Rhodesia in 1923 from the British South Africa Co. (which, under Cecil Rhodes, had conquered it by 1897) and granted internal self-government. A 1961 constitution restricted voting to keep whites in power.

On Nov. 11, 1965, Prime Min. Ian D. Smith unilaterally declared independence. Britain termed the act illegal and demanded that the country (known as Rhodesia until 1980) enfranchise the Black African majority. The UN imposed sanctions, and Black nationalists launched guerrilla attacks.

After the country held its first universal-franchise election, Apr. 21, 1979, all parties accepted a cease-fire, Dec. 5. The country changed its name to Zimbabwe upon independence, Apr. 18, 1980. Robert Mugabe, the nation's first prime min., became executive president in 1987. From the late 1990s, Mugabe's rule became increasingly repressive. A land redistribution campaign triggered violent attacks in Apr. 2000 against some white farmers (white landowners had controlled 70% of the land). Production of corn, the nation's food staple, subsequently declined sharply. Mugabe, relying on fraud and intimidation, won the Mar. 9-11, 2002, presidential election. During 2006-08, inflation soared to a yearly rate of more than 100,000%.

Mugabe clung to power after a widely discredited 2008 presidential election and intensified a crackdown on dissidents. Mugabe won the July 31, 2013, presidential election.

Drought caused food shortages in 2016. Police suppressed strikes and demonstrations protesting economic conditions. Mugabe lost the support of the military and his ZANU-PF party, and he resigned, Nov. 21, 2017. Vice Pres. Emmerson Mnangagwa became president, Nov. 24, and narrowly won a disputed July 30, 2018, presidential election. Security forces cracked down violently after Jan. 2019 protests and looting, triggered by food and fuel shortages. As economic hardship and repression continued, Mnangagwa won a disputed Aug. 23-24, 2023, presidential election. Drought again threatened food supplies in 2024.

WORLD ALMANAC EDITORS' PICKS: MEMORABLE SPORTS DUOS

Batman and Robin; Butch and Sundance; Thelma and Louise; the movies are full of dynamic duos. And so are sports. Here are some of our favorites throughout the years.

Wayne Gretzky and Mark Messier

Wayne Gretzky made everyone around him better. But so did his lifelong friend—and his literal wing man—Mark Messier. The two future Hall of Famers became teammates as teenagers in 1979 on the expansion Edmonton Oilers, and immediately paid dividends, taking the team to the playoffs in their first season together. Starting in 1983-84, they propelled the Oilers to four Stanley Cup championships over a five-year span. During one six-year span with the Oilers, Gretzky led the league every year but one in goals, assists, and points. A five-time All-Star, Messier never led the league in anything throughout his 25-year career, but he does outrank the Great One in one category: Stanley Cups won. A year after the Oilers traded Gretzky to Los Angeles, Messier in 1989-90 took Edmonton to its fifth title. And in 1994, he became the first (and so far, only) player to captain two different teams to a Stanley Cup, leading the NY Rangers to their first title in more than 50 years.

Martina Navratilova and Pam Shriver

Martina Navratilova (18 titles) and Pam Shriver (none) might not have won as many Grand Slam singles championships as the Williams sisters (30 between them). But put them together and they were a better combination than peanut butter and jelly. They are the only women to win all four Grand Slam doubles events in the same year (1984), part of a stretch in which they captured eight straight major championships and an astounding 109 straight matches. They captured three of the four majors in 1983 and 1987, and two in 1982, 1985, 1986, and 1988. Their total of 20 Grand Slam wins is a record in the Open era, and includes 7 Australian Opens, 4 French Opens, 5 Wimbledons, and 4 US Opens. By comparison, the Williams sisters won "just" 14 doubles majors.

Alan Trammell and Lou Whitaker

These Detroit Tiger middle infielders made their debut in the same game in 1977 and played together for 19 years. Whitaker retired after the 1995 season, and Trammell called it quits a year later. They weren't exactly Babe Ruth and Lou Gehrig at the plate: Whitaker hit .276 over his career, with 244 total homers, while Trammell batted .285 with 185 round-trippers. But this pair was the foundation of Detroit's 1984 World Series championship and in the Tigers' lineup together for nearly two decades. They are the longest double-play combination in baseball history. Between them, they won seven Gold Gloves (four for Trammel, three for Whitaker) and seven Silver Slugger awards (four for Whitaker, three for Trammel). Whitaker won the Rookie of the Year in 1978, while Trammell finished fourth in the voting. Trammell was inducted into the Baseball Hall of Fame in 2018; Whitaker fell off the ballot in 2021 after failing to receive 75% of votes from the Modern Baseball Era Committee but will be eligible again in 2025.

Torvill and Dean

No skaters of any stripe captured the imagination—or the TV audience—like Britain's Jayne Torvill and Christopher Dean. Winners of the three previous Ice Dancing World Championships, they were the odds-on favorites to win gold at Sarajevo in 1984. And indeed, the pair had a comfortable lead after the compulsory portions of the competition. But it was their free dance program that revolutionized the sport. Skating to Ravel's *Bolero* is somewhat common today, but the choice was risqué in 1984, and the pair went to great lengths to shoehorn the 4:28 piece into the maximum length of 4:10 for an Olympic event. The stunning scoring results—12 perfect 6.0s and six 5.9s—were the highest ever for a figure skating program, and the broadcast was watched by more than 24 million people in Britain, still one of the biggest TV audiences in British history.

Scottie Pippen and Michael Jordan

For the first three years of his career, Michael Jordan was the scoring machine who couldn't bring home an NBA title. Then came Scottie Pippen, a largely unheralded college player from Central Arkansas. The Chicago teammates advanced a little bit farther in the playoffs in each of Pippen's first three seasons, and finally won the franchise's first NBA title in 1991. That was the first of six Bulls championships over the next eight years, a run that might have extended to eight straight had Jordan not taken off the 1993-94 season and part of 1994-95 to pursue an ill-fated career in baseball. Pippen was traded after the final championship in 1997-98, and neither player won another title. Ironically, since their playing days, the NBA's greatest duo has been in a years-long feud that started in 2020 when Pippen felt the Jordan-sanctioned documentary *The Last Dance* overlooked his contributions to the Bulls dynasty and escalated in 2022 when Jordan's son began an on-and-off relationship with Pippen's ex-wife.

Kerri Walsh Jennings and Misty May-Treanor

With its two-person teams, beach volleyball lends itself to dynamic duos, and no partners were more dominant than these two Californians. For three straight Summer Olympic Games (2004-12), they dominated like no other team before or since. They won 21 straight Olympic matches over that period, losing just a single set on the way to their three gold medals. They also won the Beach Volleyball World Championships in 2003, 2005, and 2007, and finished second in 2011. From 2007-09, they won 112 consecutive matches and 19 straight tournament titles. After May-Treanor retired in 2012, Walsh Jennings and new partner April Ross went on to win 12 more tournaments, including a bronze medal at the 2016 Olympics. But she never again reached the same heights as she did with her legendary teammate. May-Treanor was inducted into the International Volleyball Hall of Fame in 2016; Walsh Jennings, who is the woman with the most career victories (135), joined her there six years later.

Venus and Serena Williams

The Williamses aren't just the most successful sisters in tennis; they're the most accomplished siblings of arguably any sport. Both have won multiple grand slam titles (7 for Venus, 23 for Serena), and both were ranked No. 1 in the world multiple times (Venus for a total of 11 weeks in 2002, Serena for a whopping 319 weeks overall, including 186 straight weeks from 2013-16). In addition to their monumental solo accomplishments, the pair were a doubles juggernaut. They won all four major championships two or more times, and captured Wimbledon a record six times in the Open era. The sisters won three gold medals together in Olympic doubles competition, and each won a gold medal in singles (Venus in 2000, Serena in 2012). Venus just barely outshines Serena as the most decorated tennis player in modern Olympic history, thanks to a silver medal in mixed doubles in 2016.

Tom Brady and... Anyone?

Peyton Manning and Marvin Harrison hold the official record for touchdowns by a quarterback-receiver combo, with 112. But Brady gets the nod here because he made so many receivers into stars. Wes Welker, for example, had 37 of his 50 career TDs as a Patriot. When Welker left New England for free agency in 2013, Julian Edelman slid into his spot and wound up notching 36 career touchdowns. In his 3-plus seasons in New England, Randy Moss revived his career, adding 50 touchdowns to his career total of 156, and leading the league twice. Brady's favorite receiver, however, was tight end Rob Gronkowski, who came out of retirement in 2020 to join his former teammate in Tampa Bay, where the two went on to win their fourth Super Bowl together. Over their careers, Brady found Gronk in the end zone a total of 90 times during the regular season (second all-time to Manning and Harrison), and another 15 times in the playoffs (since surpassed by Kansas City's Travis Kelce and Patrick Mahomes, who had 16 before the 2024 season began).

OLYMPIC GAMES

General Olympic Information

The modern Olympic Games, first held in Athens, Greece, in 1896, were the result of efforts by Baron Pierre de Coubertin, a French educator, to promote interest in education and culture and to foster better international understanding through love of athletics. His inspiration was the ancient Greek Olympic Games, most notable of the four Panhellenic celebrations. The games were combined patriotic, religious, and athletic festivals held every four years. The first such recorded festival was held in 776 BCE, when the Greeks began to keep their calendar by "Olympiads," or four-year spans between the games.

Coubertin enlisted 14 nations to send athletes to the first modern Olympics. Now athletes from more than 200 nations and territories compete in the Summer Olympics. The Winter Olympic Games, started in 1924, draw competitors from about 90 countries and territories.

Symbol: Five rings or circles, linked to represent the sporting friendship of all peoples. They also symbolize five geographic areas—Africa, America, Asia, Australia, and Europe. Each ring is a different color—blue, yellow, black, green, and red—which, with the color white, represent the colors of the world's flags.

Flag: The five-ring symbol on a plain white background.

Creed: "The most important thing in the Olympic Games is not to win but to take part, just as the most important thing in life is not the triumph but the struggle. The essential thing is not to have conquered but to have fought well."

Motto: Citius, Altius, Fortius. ("Faster, higher, stronger" in Latin.) Updated in 2021 to "Citius, Altius, Fortius – Communiter" ("Faster, higher, stronger – together").

Oath: "In the name of all the competitors I promise that we shall take part in these Olympic Games, respecting and abiding by the rules which govern them, committing ourselves to a sport without doping and without drugs, in the true spirit of sportsmanship, for the glory of sport and the honor of our teams."

Flame: The modern version of the flame was adopted in 1936. The torch used to kindle it is first lit by the sun's rays in Olympia, Greece, then carried to the site of the Games by relays of runners. Ships and planes are used when necessary.

Winter Olympic Games Sites, 1924-2034

1924 Chamonix, France
1928 St. Moritz, Switzerland
1932 Lake Placid, NY, U.S.
1936 Garmisch-Partenkirchen, Germany
1948 St. Moritz, Switzerland
1952 Oslo, Norway
1956 Cortina d'Ampezzo, Italy
1960 Squaw Valley, CA, U.S.
1964 Innsbruck, Austria
1968 Grenoble, France
1972 Sapporo, Japan
1976 Innsbruck, Austria
1980 Lake Placid, NY, U.S.
1984 Sarajevo, Yugoslavia
1988 Calgary, AB, Canada
1992 Albertville, France
1994 Lillehammer, Norway
1998 Nagano, Japan
2002 Salt Lake City, UT, U.S.
2006 Turin, Italy
2010 Vancouver, BC, Can.
2014 Sochi, Russia
2018 Pyeongchang, South Korea
2022 Beijing, China
2026 Milan-Cortina, Italy
2030 French Alps, France
2034 Salt Lake City, UT, U.S.

Summer Olympic Games Sites, 1896-2032

1896 Athens, Greece
1900 Paris, France
1904 St. Louis, MO, U.S.
1906 Athens, Greece*
1908 London, England, UK
1912 Stockholm, Sweden
1920 Antwerp, Belgium
1924 Paris, France
1928 Amsterdam, Netherlands
1932 Los Angeles, CA, U.S.
1936 Berlin, Germany
1948 London, England, UK
1952 Helsinki, Finland
1956 Melbourne, Australia
1960 Rome, Italy
1964 Tokyo, Japan
1968 Mexico City, Mexico
1972 Munich, W. Germany
1976 Montréal, QC, Canada
1980 Moscow, USSR
1984 Los Angeles, CA, U.S.
1988 Seoul, South Korea
1992 Barcelona, Spain
1996 Atlanta, GA, U.S.
2000 Sydney, Australia
2004 Athens, Greece
2008 Beijing, China
2012 London, England, UK
2016 Rio de Janeiro, Brazil
2020 Tokyo, Japan
2024 Paris, France
2028 Los Angeles, CA, U.S.
2032 Brisbane, Australia

* = Games not recognized by International Olympic Committee. **Note:** Games VI (1916), XII (1940), and XIII (1944) were not celebrated.

2026 Winter Olympic Games: Preview

Milan and Cortina d'Ampezzo, Italy, Feb. 6-Feb. 22, 2026

The XXV Olympic Winter Games are scheduled to take place in Milan and Cortina d'Ampezzo, Italy, in Feb. 2026, two decades after the country hosted the XX Winter Games, and 70 years since Cortina d'Ampezzo hosted the 1956 Games. They will be the fourth Games hosted by Italy, and they are the first Games ever hosted by two cities. Some competitions will take place at the same sites used in the 1956 Games. Competitions in 195 medal events across 16 sports, including 9 new events: men's and women's dual moguls (in the sport of freestyle skiing); men's and women's double luge; women's individual large hill ski jumping, men's super team ski jumping; ski mountaineering, with a men's and women's sprint and mixed relay events; and mixed team skeleton. As of Sept. 2024, 93 nations were expected to compete.

2024 Summer Olympic Games

Paris, France, July 26-Aug. 11, 2024

More than 10,700 athletes represented 206 nations, in addition to a team of refugees and independent athletes competing under a neutral flag, at the third Olympic Games in history to be held in Paris, France. Thirty-nine venues hosted 329 events in 32 different sports, including new sport breaking.

U.S. swimmer Katie Ledecky continued her winning streak, earning two golds, one silver, and one bronze, extending her status as the most decorated U.S. female Olympian in history. U.S. gymnast Simone Biles won three gold medals and one silver in her third Olympic appearance, making her the U.S. gymnast with the most Olympic medals. U.S. swimmers Torri Huske and Regan Smith were the most decorated athletes at these Games for Team USA with five medals apiece. The U.S. women's and men's basketball teams won their eighth and fifth consecutive Olympic gold medals, respectively. U.S. runner Noah Lyles won gold in the 100-m final by 0.005 of a second; he tested positive for coronavirus two days later but went on to take the bronze in the 200-m. In a controversy that extended beyond the Games, U.S. gymnast Jordan Chiles, who had been awarded the bronze medal in the women's floor exercise after an inquiry from her coach elevated her from fifth to third place, was stripped of the medal by the International Olympic Committee after the Court of Arbitration for Sport ruled to invalidate her coach's inquiry, claiming it was filed 4 seconds beyond the 1-minute deadline.

Russian and Belorussian athletes were banned from participating due to the war in Ukraine, but a total of 32 athletes, 15 of them Russian, participated in the Games as AIN, Individual Neutral Athletes.

2024 Summer Olympic Games: Final Medal Standings

(G = Gold, S = Silver, B = Bronze, T = Total medals)

Country	G	S	B	T
United States	40	44	42	126
China	40	27	24	91
Great Britain	14	22	29	65
France	16	26	22	64
Australia	18	19	16	53
Japan	20	12	13	45
Italy	12	13	15	40
Netherlands	15	7	12	34
Germany	12	13	8	33
South Korea	13	9	10	32
Canada	9	7	11	27
New Zealand	10	7	3	20
Brazil	3	7	10	20
Hungary	6	7	6	19
Spain	5	4	9	18
Uzbekistan	8	2	3	13
Iran	3	6	3	12
Ukraine	3	5	4	12
Sweden	4	4	3	11
Kenya	4	2	5	11
Belgium	3	1	6	10
Poland	1	4	5	10
Romania	3	4	2	9
Denmark	2	2	5	9
Cuba	2	1	6	9
Norway	4	1	3	8
Switzerland	1	2	5	8
Greece	1	1	6	8
Turkey (Türkiye)	0	3	5	8
Ireland	4	0	3	7
Georgia	3	3	1	7
Bulgaria	3	1	3	7
Azerbaijan	2	2	3	7
Croatia	2	2	3	7
Taiwan	2	0	5	7
Israel	1	5	1	7
Kazakhstan	1	3	3	7
Jamaica	1	3	2	6
South Africa	1	3	2	6
Thailand	1	3	2	6
Kyrgyzstan	0	2	4	6
North Korea	0	2	4	6
India	0	1	5	6
Serbia	3	1	1	5
Czechia	3	0	2	5
Austria	2	0	3	5
Ecuador	1	2	2	5
Mexico	0	3	2	5
Bahrain	2	1	1	4
Hong Kong	2	0	2	4
Philippines	2	0	2	4
Ethiopia	1	3	0	4
Portugal	1	2	1	4
Armenia	0	3	1	4
Colombia	0	3	1	4
Lithuania	0	2	2	4
Moldova	0	1	3	4
Slovenia	2	1	0	3
Algeria	2	0	1	3
Indonesia	2	0	1	3
Argentina	1	1	1	3
Egypt	1	1	1	3
Tunisia	1	1	1	3
Dominican Republic	1	0	2	3
Tajikistan	0	0	3	3
Botswana	1	1	0	2
Chile	1	1	0	2
Saint Lucia	1	1	0	2
Uganda	1	1	0	2
Guatemala	1	0	1	2
Morocco	1	0	1	2
Kosovo	0	1	1	2
Albania	0	0	2	2
Grenada	0	0	2	2
Malaysia	0	0	2	2
Puerto Rico	0	0	2	2
Dominica	1	0	0	1
Pakistan	1	0	0	1
Cyprus	0	1	0	1
Fiji	0	1	0	1
Jordan	0	1	0	1
Mongolia	0	1	0	1
Panama	0	1	0	1
Cabo Verde	0	0	1	1
Côte d'Ivoire	0	0	1	1
Peru	0	0	1	1
Qatar	0	0	1	1
Refugee Olympic Team	0	0	1	1
Singapore	0	0	1	1
Slovakia	0	0	1	1
Zambia	0	0	1	1

2024 Summer Olympic Medal Winners

G = Gold, S = Silver, B = Bronze. AIN = Russian and Belorussian athletes competing as Individual Neutral Athletes. EOR = Refugee Olympic Team consisting of athletes from 11 nations

Archery

Men's Individual: G–Kim Woo-jin, South Korea; S–Brady Ellison, United States; B–Lee Woo-seok, South Korea
Women's Individual: G–Lim Si-hyeon, South Korea; S–Nam Su-hyeon, South Korea; B–Lisa Barbelin, France
Men's Team: G–South Korea; S–France; B–Turkey
Women's Team: G–South Korea; S–China; B–Mexico
Mixed Team: G–South Korea; S–Germany; B–United States

Badminton

Men's Singles: G–Viktor Axelsen, Denmark; S–Kunlavut Vitidsarn, Thailand; B–Lee Zii Jia, Malaysia
Men's Doubles: G–Lee Yang & Wang Chi-lin, Taiwan; S–Liang Wei Keng & Wang Chang, China; B–Aaron Chia & Soh Wooi Yik, Malaysia
Women's Singles: G–An Se-young, South Korea; S–He Bing Jiao, China; B–Gregoria Mariska Tunjung, Indonesia
Women's Doubles: G–Chen Qingchen & Jia Yifan, China; S–Liu Shengshu & Tan Ning, China; B–Nami Matsuyama & Chiharu Shida, Japan
Mixed Doubles: G–Zheng Siwei & Huang Ya Qiong, China; S–Kim Won-ho & Jeong Na-eun, South Korea; B–Yuta Watanabe & Arisa Higashino, Japan

Basketball

Men: G–U.S.; S–France; B–Serbia
Women: G–U.S.; S–France; B–Australia

3x3 Basketball

Men: G–Netherlands; S–France; B–Lithuania
Women: G–Germany; S–Spain; B–U.S.

Beach Volleyball

Men: G–David Ahman & Jonatan Hellvig, Sweden; S–Nils Ehlers & Clemens Wickler, Germany; B–Anders Mol & Christian Sørum, Norway
Women: G–Ana Patricia Silva Ramos & Eduarda Santos Lisboa, Brazil; S–Melissa Humana-Paredes & Brandie Wilkerson, Canada; B–Tanja Hüberli & Nina Brunner, Switzerland

Boxing

Men

Flyweight (48-52 kg/106-115 lbs): G–Hasanboy Dusmatov, Uzbekistan; S–Billal Bennama, France; B–Daniel Varela de Pina, Cabo Verde; B–Junior Alcántara, Dominican Republic
Featherweight (52-57 kg/115-126 lbs): G–Abdumalik Khalokov, Uzbekistan; S–Munarbek Seiitbek Uulu, Kyrgyzstan; B–Charlie Senior, Australia; B–Javier Ibanez Diaz, Bulgaria
Lightweight (57-63.5 kg/126-140 lbs): G–Erislandy Álvarez, Cuba; S–Sofiane Oumiha, France; B–Lasha Guruli, Georgia; B–Wyatt Sanford, Canada
Welterweight (63.5-71 kg/139-157 lbs): G–Asadkhuja Muydinkhujaev, Uzbekistan; S–Marco Verde, Mexico; B–Omari Jones, U.S.; B–Lewis Richardson, Great Britain
Light Heavyweight (71-80 kg/165-176 lbs): G–Oleksandr Khyzhniak, Ukraine; S–Nurbek Oralbay, Kazakhstan; B–Arlen López, Cuba; B–Cristian Pinales, Dominican Republic
Heavyweight (80-92 kg/176-203 lbs): G–Lazizbek Mullojonov, Uzbekistan; S–Loren Alfonso, Azerbaijan; B–Davlat Boltaev, Tajikistan; B–Enmanuel Reyes, Spain
Super Heavyweight (92+ kg/203+ lbs): G–Bakhodir Jalolov, Uzbekistan; S–Ayoub Ghadfa, Spain; B–Nelvie Tiafack, Germany; B–Djamili-Dini Aboudou Moindze, France

Women

Flyweight (48-50 kg/106-110 lbs): G–Wu Yu, China; S–Buse Naz Çakıroğlu, Turkey; B–Nazym Kyzaibay, Kazakhstan; B–Aira Villegas, Philippines
Bantamweight (50-54 kg/110-119 lbs): G–Chang Yuan, China; S–Hatice Akbaş, Turkey; B–Pang Chol Mi, North Korea; B–Im Ae-ji, South Korea
Featherweight (54-57 kg/119-126 lbs): G–Lin Yu-ting, Taiwan; S–Julia Szeremeta, Poland; B–Esra Yildiz, Turkey; B–Nesthy Petecio, Philippines
Lightweight (57-60 kg/126-134 lbs): G–Kellie Harrington, Ireland; S–Yang Wenlu, China; B–Beatriz Ferreira, Brazil; B–Wu Shih-yi, Taiwan
Welterweight (60-66 kg/134-146 lbs): G–Imane Khelif, Algeria; S–Yang Liu, China; B–Janjaem Suwannapheng, Thailand; B–Chen Nien-chin, Taiwan
Middleweight (66-75 kg/146-165 lbs): G–Li Qian, China; S–Atheyna Bylon, Panama; S–Caitlin Parker, Australia; B–Cindy Ngamba, Refugee Olympic Team

Breaking

Boys: G–Phil Wizard (Philip Kim), Canada; S–Dany Dann (Danis Civil), France; B–Victor (Victor Montalvo), U.S.
Girls: G–Ami (Ami Yuasa), Japan; S–Nicka (Dominika Banevič), Lithuania; B–671 (Liu Qingyi), China

Canoe/Kayak—Slalom

Canoe Single Men: G–Nicolas Gestin, France; S–Adam Burgess, Great Britain; B–Matej Beňuš, Slovakia
Canoe Single Women: G–Jessica Fox, Australia; S–Elena Lilik, Germany; B–Evy Leibfarth, U.S.
Kayak Men: G–Giovanni De Gennaro, Italy; S–Titouan Castryck, France; B–Pau Echaniz, Spain
Kayak Women: G–Jessica Fox, Australia; S–Klaudia Zwolińska, Poland; B–Kimberley Woods, Great Britain
Kayak Cross Men: G–Finn Butcher, New Zealand; S–Joseph Clarke, Great Britain; B–Noah Hegge, Germany
Kayak Cross Women: G–Noemie Fox, Australia; S–Angèle Hug, France; B–Kimberley Woods, Great Britain

Canoe/Kayak—Sprint

Men

Canoe Single 1000-m: G–Martin Fuksa, Czechia; S–Isaquias Queiroz, Brazil; B–Serghei Tarnovschi, Moldova
Canoe Double 500-m: G–Liu Hao & Ji Bowen, China; S–Gabriele Casadei & Carlo Tacchini, Italy; B–Joan Antoni Moreno & Diego Domínguez, Spain
Kayak Single 1000-m: G–Josef Dostál, Czechia; S–Ádám Varga, Hungary; B–Bálint Kopasz, Hungary
Kayak Double 500-m: G–Jacob Schopf & Max Lemke, Germany; S–Bence Nádas & Sándor Tótka, Hungary; B–Jean van der Westhuyzen & Tom Green, Australia
Kayak Four 500-m: G–Germany; S–Australia; B–Brazil

Women

Canoe Single 200-m: G–Katie Vincent, Canada; S–Nevin Harrison, U.S.; B–Yarisleidis Cirilo, Cuba
Canoe Double 500-m: G–Xu Shixiao & Sun Mengya, China; S–Liudmyla Luzan & Anastasila Rybachok, Ukraine; B–Sloan MacKenzie & Katie Vincent, Canada
Kayak Single 500-m: G–Lisa Carrington, New Zealand; S–Tamara Csipes, Hungary; B–Emma Jørgensen, Denmark
Kayak Double 500-m: G–Lisa Carrington & Alicia Hoskin, New Zealand; S–Tamara Csipes & Alida Dóra Gazsó, Hungary; B–Paulina Paszek & Jule Hake, Germany; B–Noémi Pupp & Sára Fojt, Hungary
Kayak Four 500-m: G–New Zealand; S–Germany; B–Hungary

Cycling—BMX Freestyle

Men: G–José Torres Gil, Argentina; S–Kieran Reilly, Great Britain; B–Anthony Jeanjean, France
Women: G–Deng Yawen, China; S–Perris Benegas, U.S.; B–Natalya Diehm, Australia

Cycling—BMX Racing

Men: G–Joris Daudet, France; S–Sylvain André, France; B–Romain Mahieu, France
Women: G–Saya Sakakibara, Australia; S–Manon Veenstra, Netherlands; B–Zoé Claessens, Switzerland

Cycling—Mountain Bike

Men's Cross-Country: G–Tom Pidcock, Great Britain; S–Victor Koretzky, France; B–Alan Hatherly, South Africa
Women's Cross-Country: G–Pauline Ferrand-Prévot, France; S–Haley Batten, U.S.; B–Jenny Rissveds, Sweden

Cycling—Road

Men's Road Race: G–Remco Evenepoel, Belgium; S–Valentin Madouas, France; B–Christophe Laporte, France
Men's Individual Time Trial: G–Remco Evenepoel, Belgium; S–Filippo Ganna, Italy; B–Wout van Aert, Belgium
Women's Road Race: G–Kristen Faulkner, U.S.; S–Marianne Vos, Netherlands; B–Lotte Kopecky, Belgium
Women's Individual Time Trial: G–Grace Brown, Australia; S–Anna Henderson, Great Britain; B–Chloé Dygert, U.S.

Cycling—Track

Men

Sprint: G–Harrie Lavreysen, Netherlands; S–Matthew Richardson, Australia; B–Jack Carlin, Great Britain
Team Sprint: G–Netherlands; S–Great Britain; B–Australia
Keirin: G–Harrie Lavreysen, Netherlands; S–Matthew Richardson, Australia; B–Matthew Glaetzer, Australia
Team Pursuit: G–Australia; S–Great Britain; B–Italy
Omnium: G–Benjamin Thomas, France; S–Iúri Leitão, Portugal; B–Fabio Van den Bossche, Belgium
Madison: G–Iúri Leitão & Rui Oliveira, Portugal; S–Simone Consonni & Elia Viviani, Italy; B–Niklas Larsen & Michael Mørkøv, Denmark

Women

Sprint: G–Ellesse Andrews, New Zealand; S–Lea Friedrich, Germany; B–Emma Finucane, Great Britain
Team Sprint: G–Great Britain; S–New Zealand; B–Germany
Keirin: G–Ellesse Andrews, New Zealand; S–Hetty van de Wouw, Netherlands; B–Emma Finucane, Great Britain
Team Pursuit: G–U.S.; S–New Zealand; B–Great Britain
Omnium: G–Jennifer Valente, U.S.; S–Daria Pikulik, Poland; B–Ally Wollaston, New Zealand
Madison: G–Chiara Consonni & Vittoria Guazzini, Italy; S–Elinor Barker & Neah Evans, Great Britain; B–Lisa van Belle & Maike van der Duin, Netherlands

Diving

Men

Springboard: G–Xie Siyi, China; S–Wang Zongyuan, China; B–Osmar Olvera, Mexico
Platform: G–Cao Yuan, China; S–Rikuto Tamai, Japan; B–Noah Williams, Great Britain
Synchronized Springboard: G–Long Daoyi & Wang Zongyuan, China; S–Juan Celaya & Osmar Olvera, Mexico; B–Anthony Harding & Jack Laugher, Great Britain
Synchronized Platform: G–Lian Junjie & Yang Hao, China; S–Tom Daley & Noah Williams, Great Britain; B–Rylan Wiens & Nathan Zsombor-Murray, Canada

Women

Springboard: G–Chen Yiwen, China; S–Maddison Keeney, Australia; B–Chang Yani, China
Platform: G–Quan Hongchan, China; S–Chen Yuxi, China; B–Kim Mi Rae, North Korea
Synchronized Springboard: G–Chang Yani & Chen Yiwen, China; S–Sarah Bacon & Kassidy Cook, U.S.; B–Yasmin Harper & Scarlett Mew Jensen, Great Britain
Synchronized Platform: G–Chen Yuxi & Quan Hongchan, China; S–Jo Jin Mi & Kim Mi Rae, North Korea; B–Andrea Spendolini-Sirieix & Lois Toulson, Great Britain

Equestrian

Eventing Individual: G–Michael Jung, Germany; S–Christopher Burton, Australia; B–Laura Collett, Great Britain
Eventing Team: G–Great Britain; S–France; B–Japan
Dressage Individual: G–Jessica von Bredow-Werndl, Germany; S–Isabell Werth, Germany; B–Charlotte Fry, Great Britain
Dressage Team: G–Germany; S–Denmark; B–Great Britain
Jumping Individual: G–Christian Kukuk, Germany; S–Steve Guerdat, Switzerland; B–Maikel van der Vleuten, Netherlands
Jumping Team: G–Great Britain; S–U.S.; B–France

Fencing

Men

Foil Individual: G–Cheung Ka Long, Hong Kong; S–Filippo Macchi, Italy; B–Nick Itkin, U.S.
Épée Individual: G–Koki Kano, Japan; S–Yannick Borel, France; B–Mohamed El-Sayed, Egypt
Sabre Individual: G–Oh Sang-uk, South Korea; S–Farès Ferjani, Tunisia; B–Luigi Samele, Italy
Foil Team: G–Japan; S–Italy; B–France
Épée Team: G–Hungary; S–Japan; B–Czechia
Sabre Team: G–South Korea; S–Hungary; B–France

Women

Foil Individual: G–Lee Kiefer, U.S.; S–Lauren Scruggs, U.S.; B–Eleanor Harvey, Canada
Épée Individual: G–Vivian Kong, Hong Kong; S–Auriane Mallo-Breton, France; B–Eszter Muhari, Hungary
Sabre Individual: G–Manon Apithy-Brunet, France; S–Sara Balzer, France; B–Olga Kharlan, Ukraine
Foil Team: G–U.S.; S–Italy; B–Japan
Épée Team: G–Italy; S–France; B–Poland
Sabre Team: G–Ukraine; S–South Korea; B–Japan

Field Hockey

Men: G–Netherlands; S–Germany; B–India
Women: G–Netherlands; S–China; B–Argentina

Golf

Men's Individual Stroke Play: G–Scottie Scheffler, U.S.; S–Tommy Fleetwood, Great Britain; B–Hideki Matsuyama, Japan
Women's Individual Stroke Play: G–Lydia Ko, New Zealand; S–Esther Henseleit, Germany; B–Lin Xiyu, China

Gymnastics—Artistic

Men

Team: G–Japan; S–China; B–U.S.
Individual All-Around: G–Shinnosuke Oka, Japan; S–Zhang Boheng, China; B–Xiao Ruoteng, China
Horizontal Bar: G–Shinnosuke Oka, Japan; S–Ángel Barajas, Colombia; B–Zhang Boheng, China; B–Tang Chia-hung, Taiwan
Parallel Bars: G–Zou Jingyuan, China; S–Illia Kovtun, Ukraine; B–Shinnosuke Oka, Japan
Floor Exercise: G–Carlos Yulo, Philippines; S–Artem Dolgopyat, Israel; B–Jake Jarman, Great Britain
Pommel Horse: G–Rhys McClenaghan, Ireland; S–Nariman Kurbanov, Kazakhstan; B–Stephen Nedoroscik, U.S.
Rings: G–Liu Yang, China; S–Zou Jingyuan, China; B–Eleftherios Petrounias, Greece
Vault: G–Carlos Yulo, Philippines; S–Artur Davtyan, Armenia; B–Harry Hepworth, Great Britain

Women

Team: G–U.S.; S–Italy; B–Brazil
Individual All-Around: G–Simone Biles, U.S.; S–Rebeca Andrade, Brazil; B–Sunisa Lee, U.S.
Balance Beam: G–Alice D'Amato, Italy; S–Zhou Yaqin, China; B–Manila Esposito, Italy
Floor Exercise: G–Rebeca Andrade, Brazil; S–Simone Biles, U.S.; B–Ana Bărbosu, Romania
Uneven Bars: G–Kaylia Nemour, Algeria; S–Qiu Qiyuan, China; B–Sunisa Lee, U.S.
Vault: G–Simone Biles, U.S.; S–Rebeca Andrade, Brazil; B–Jade Carey, U.S.

Gymnastics—Rhythmic

Individual All-Around: G–Darja Varfolomeev, Germany; S–Boryana Kaleyn, Bulgaria; B–Sofia Raffaeli, Italy
Group All-Around: G–China; S–Israel; B–Italy

Gymnastics—Trampoline

Men: G–Ivan Litvinovich, AIN; S–Wang Zisai, China; B–Yan Langyu, China
Women: G–Bryony Page, Great Britain; S–Viyaleta Bardzilouskaya, AIN; B–Sophiane Méthot, Canada

Handball

Men: G–Denmark; S–Germany; B–Spain
Women: G–Norway; S–France; B–Denmark

Judo

Men

60 kg/132 lbs: G–Yeldos Smetov, Kazakhstan; S–Luka Mkheidze, France; B–Ryuju Nagayama, Japan; B–Francisco Garrigós, Spain
66 kg/146 lbs: G–Hifumi Abe, Japan; S–Willian Lima, Brazil; B–Gusman Kyrgyzbayev, Kazakhstan; B–Denis Vieru, Moldova
73 kg/161 lbs: G–Hidayet Heydarov, Azerbaijan; S–Joan-Benjamin Gaba, France; B–Adil Osmanov, Moldova; B–Soichi Hashimoto, Japan
81 kg/179 lbs: G–Takanori Nagase, Japan; S–Tato Grigalashvili, Georgia; B–Lee Joon-hwan, South Korea; B–Somon Makhmadbekov, Tajikistan
90 kg/198 lbs: G–Lasha Bekauri, Georgia; S–Sanshiro Murao, Japan; B–Maxime-Gaël Ngayap Hambou, France; B–Theodoros Tselidis, Greece
100 kg/220 lbs: G–Zelym Kotsoiev, Azerbaijan; S–Ilia Sulamanidze, Georgia; B–Peter Paltchik, Israel; B–Muzaffarbek Turoboyev, Uzbekistan
100+ kg/220+ lbs: G–Teddy Riner, France; S–Kim Min-jong, South Korea; B–Temur Rakhimov, Tajikistan; B–Alisher Yusupov, Uzbekistan

Women

48 kg/106 lbs: G–Natsumi Tsunoda, Japan; S–Bavuudorjiin Baasankhüü, Mongolia; B–Shirine Boukli, France; B–Tara Babulfath, Sweden
52 kg/115 lbs: G–Diyora Keldiyorova, Uzbekistan; S–Distria Krasniqi, Kosovo; B–Larissa Pimenta, Brazil; B–Amandine Buchard, France
57 kg/126 lbs: G–Christa Deguchi, Canada; S–Huh Mimi, South Korea; B–Haruka Funakubo, Japan; B–Sarah-Léonie Cysique, France
63 kg/139 lbs: G–Andreja Leški, Slovenia; S–Prisca Awiti Alcaraz, Mexico; B–Clarisse Agbegnenou, France; B–Laura Fazliu, Kosovo
70 kg/154 lbs: G–Barbara Matić, Croatia; S–Miriam Butkereit, Germany; B–Michaela Polleres, Austria; B–Gabriella Willems, Belgium
78 kg/172 lbs: G–Alice Bellandi, Italy; S–Inbar Lanir, Israel; B–Ma Zhenzhao, China; B–Patrícia Sampaio, Portugal
78+ kg/172+ lbs: G–Beatriz Souza, Brazil; S–Raz Hershko, Israel; B–Kim Ha-yun, South Korea; B–Romane Dicko, France
Mixed Team: G–France; S–Japan; B–Brazil; B–South Korea

Modern Pentathlon

Men: G–Ahmed El-Gendy, Egypt; S–Taishu Sato, Japan; B–Giorgio Malan, Italy
Women: G–Michelle Gulyás, Hungary; S–Élodie Clouvel, France; B–Seong Seung-min, South Korea

Rowing

Men

Single Sculls: G–Oliver Zeidler, Germany; S–Yauheni Zalaty, AIN; B–Simon van Dorp, Netherlands
Double Sculls: G–Andrei Cornea & Marian Enache, Romania; S–Melvin Twellaar & Stef Broenink, Netherlands; B–Daire Lynch & Philip Doyle, Ireland
Pair: G–Martin Sinković & Valent Sinković, Croatia; S–Oliver Wynne-Griffith & Tom George, Great Britain; B–Roman Röösli & Andrin Gulich, Switzerland
Four: G–U.S.; S–New Zealand; B–Great Britain
Lightweight Double Sculls: G–Fintan McCarthy & Paul O'Donovan, Ireland; S–Stefano Oppo & Gabriel Soares, Italy; B–Antonios Papakonstantinou & Petros Gkaidatzis, Greece
Quadruple Sculls: G–Netherlands; S–Italy; B–Poland
Eight: G–Great Britain; S–Netherlands; B–U.S.

Women

Single Sculls: G–Karolien Florijn, Netherlands; S–Emma Twigg, New Zealand; B–Viktorija Senkutė, Lithuania
Double Sculls: G–Brooke Francis & Lucy Spoors, New Zealand; S–Ancuța Bodnar & Simona Radiș, Romania; B–Mathilda Hodgkins-Byrne & Rebecca Wilde, Great Britain
Pair: G–Ymkje Clevering & Veronique Meester, Netherlands; S–Ioana Vrînceanu & Roxana Anghel, Romania; B–Jessica Morrison & Annabelle McIntyre, Australia
Four: G–Netherlands; S–Great Britain; B–New Zealand
Lightweight Double Sculls: G–Emily Craig & Imogen Grant, Great Britain; S–Gianina van Groningen & Ionela Cozmiuc, Romania; B–Dimitra Kontou & Zoi Fitsiou, Greece
Quadruple Sculls: G–Great Britain; S–Netherlands; B–Germany
Eight: G–Romania; S–Canada; B–Great Britain

Rugby Sevens

Men: G–France; S–Fiji; B–South Africa
Women: G–New Zealand; S–Canada; B–U.S.

Sailing

Men's Windsurfing: G–Tom Reuveny, Israel; S–Grae Morris, Australia; B–Luuc van Opzeeland, Netherlands
Women's Windsurfing: G–Marta Maggetti, Italy; S–Sharon Kantor, Israel; B–Emma Wilson, Great Britain
Men's Kite: G–Valentin Bontus, Austria; S–Toni Vodišek, Slovenia; B–Maximilian Maeder, Singapore
Women's Kite: G–Ellie Aldridge, Great Britain; S–Lauriane Nolot, France; B–Annelous Lammerts, Netherlands
Men's Dinghy: G–Matt Wearn, Australia; S–Pavlos Kontides, Cyprus; B–Stefano Peschiera, Peru
Women's Dinghy: G–Marit Bouwmeester, Netherlands; S–Anne-Marie Rindom, Denmark; B–Line Flem Høst, Norway
Mixed Dinghy: G–Lara Vadlau & Lukas Mähr, Austria; S–Keiju Okada & Miho Yoshioka, Japan; B–Anton Dahlberg & Lovisa Karlsson, Sweden
Men's Skiff: G–Diego Botín & Florián Trittel, Spain; S–Isaac McHardie & William McKenzie, New Zealand; B–Ian Barrows & Hans Henken, U.S.
Women's Skiff: G–Odile van Aanholt & Annette Duetz, Netherlands; S–Vilma Bobeck & Rebecca Netzler, Sweden; B–Sarah Steyaert & Charline Picon, France
Mixed Multihull: G–Ruggero Tita & Caterina Banti, Italy; S–Mateo Majdalani & Eugenia Bosco, Argentina; B–Micah Wilkinson & Erica Dawson, New Zealand

Shooting

Men

50-m Rifle 3 Positions: G–Liu Yukun, China; S–Serhiy Kulish, Ukraine; B–Swapnil Kusale, India
10-m Air Rifle: G–Sheng Lihao, China; S–Victor Lindgren, Sweden; B–Miran Maričić, Croatia
25-m Rapid Fire Pistol: G–Li Yuehong, China; S–Cho Yeong-jae, South Korea; B–Wang Xinjie, China

10-m Air Pistol: G–Xie Yu, China; S–Federico Nilo Maldini, Italy; B–Paolo Monna, Italy
Trap: G–Nathan Hales, Great Britain; S–Qi Ying, China; B–Jean Pierre Brol, Guatemala
Skeet: G–Vincent Hancock, U.S.; S–Conner Prince, U.S.; B–Lee Meng-yuan, Taiwan

Women

50-m Rifle 3 Positions: G–Chiara Leone, Switzerland; S–Sagen Maddalena, U.S.; B–Zhang Qiongyue, China
10-m Air Rifle: G–Ban Hyo-jin, South Korea; S–Huang Yuting, China; B–Audrey Gogniat, Switzerland
25-m Pistol: G–Yang Ji-in, South Korea; S–Camille Jedrzejewski, France; B–Veronika Major, Hungary
10-m Air Pistol: G–Oh Ye-jin, South Korea; S–Kim Ye-ji, South Korea; B–Manu Bhaker, India
Trap: G–Adriana Ruano, Guatemala; S–Silvana Stanco, Italy; B–Penny Smith, Australia
Skeet: G–Francisca Crovetto, Chile; S–Amber Rutter, Great Britain; B–Austen Smith, U.S.

Mixed

10-m Air Rifle Team: G–Huang Yuting & Sheng Lihao, China; S–Keum Ji-hyeon & Park Ha-jun, South Korea; B–Alexandra Le & Islam Satpayev, Kazakhstan
10-m Air Pistol Team: G–Zorana Arunović & Damir Mikec, Serbia; S–Şevval İlayda Tarhan & Yusuf Dikeç, Turkey; B–Manu Bhaker & Sarabjot Singh, India
Skeet Team: G–Diana Bacosi & Gabriele Rossetti, Italy; S–Austen Smith & Vincent Hancock, U.S.; B–Jiang Yiting & Lyu Jianlin, China

Skateboarding

Men

Park: G–Keegan Palmer, Australia; S–Tom Schaar, U.S.; B–Augusto Akio, Brazil
Street: G–Yuto Horigome, Japan; S–Jagger Eaton, U.S.; B–Nyjah Huston, U.S.

Women

Park: G–Arisa Trew, Australia; S–Cocona Hiraki, Japan; B–Sky Brown, Great Britain
Street: G–Coco Yoshizawa, Japan; S–Liz Akama, Japan; B–Rayssa Leal, Brazil

Soccer

Men: G–Spain; S–France; B–Morocco
Women: G–U.S.; S–Brazil; B–Germany

Sport Climbing

Men's Boulder & Lead: G–Toby Roberts, Great Britain; S–Sorato Anraku, Japan; B–Jakob Schubert, Austria
Women's Boulder & Lead: G–Janja Garnbret, Slovenia; S–Brooke Raboutou, U.S.; B–Jessica Pilz, Austria
Men's Speed: G–Veddriq Leonardo, Indonesia; S–Wu Peng, China; B–Sam Watson, U.S.
Women's Speed: G–Aleksandra Mirosław, Poland; S–Deng Lijuan, China; B–Aleksandra Kałucka, Poland

Surfing

Men: G–Kauli Vaast, France; S–Jack Robinson, Australia; B–Gabriel Medina, Brazil
Women: G–Caroline Marks, U.S.; S–Tatiana Weston-Webb, Brazil; B–Johanne Defay, France

Swimming

Men

50-m Freestyle: G–Cameron McEvoy, Australia; S–Ben Proud, Great Britain; B–Florent Manaudou, France
100-m Freestyle: G–Pan Zhanle, China; S–Kyle Chalmers, Australia; B–David Popovici, Romania
200-m Freestyle: G–David Popovici, Romania; S–Matthew Richards, Great Britain; B–Luke Hobson, U.S.
400-m Freestyle: G–Lukas Märtens, Germany; S–Elijah Winnington, Australia; B–Kim Woo-min, South Korea
800-m Freestyle: G–Daniel Wiffen, Ireland; S–Bobby Finke, U.S.; B–Gregorio Paltrinieri, Italy
1500-m Freestyle: G–Bobby Finke, U.S.; S–Gregorio Paltrinieri, Italy; B–Daniel Wiffen, Ireland
100-m Backstroke: G–Thomas Ceccon, Italy; S–Xu Jiayu, China; B–Ryan Murphy, U.S.
200-m Backstroke: G–Hubert Kós, Hungary; S–Apostolos Christou, Greece; B–Roman Mityukov, Switzerland
100-m Breaststroke: G–Nicolò Martinenghi, Italy; S–Adam Peaty, Great Britain; S–Nic Fink, U.S.
200-m Breaststroke: G–Léon Marchand, France; S–Zac Stubblety-Cook, Australia; Caspar Corbeau, Netherlands
100-m Butterfly: G–Kristóf Milák, Hungary; S–Josh Liendo, Canada; B–Ilya Kharun, Canada
200-m Butterfly: G–Léon Marchand, France; S–Kristóf Milák, Hungary; B–Ilya Kharun, Canada
200-m Individual Medley: G–Léon Marchand, France; S–Duncan Scott, Great Britain; B–Wang Shun, China
400-m Individual Medley: G–Léon Marchand, France; S–Tomoyuki Matsushita, Japan; B–Carson Foster, U.S.
4×100-m Freestyle Relay: G–U.S.; S–Australia; B–Italy
4×200-m Freestyle Relay: G–Great Britain; S–U.S.; B–Australia
4×100-m Medley Relay: G–China; S–U.S.; B–France

Women

50-m Freestyle: G–Sarah Sjöström, Sweden; S–Meg Harris, Australia; B–Zhang Yufei, China
100-m Freestyle: G–Sarah Sjöström, Sweden; S–Torri Huske, U.S.; B–Siobhán Haughey, Hong Kong
200-m Freestyle: G–Mollie O'Callaghan, Australia; S–Ariarne Titmus, Australia; B–Siobhán Haughey, Hong Kong
400-m Freestyle: G–Ariarne Titmus, Australia; S–Summer McIntosh, Canada; B–Katie Ledecky, U.S.
800-m Freestyle: G–Katie Ledecky, U.S.; S–Ariarne Titmus, Australia; B–Paige Madden, U.S.
1500-m Freestyle: G–Katie Ledecky, U.S.; S–Anastasiia Kirpichnikova, France; B–Isabel Marie Gose, Germany
100-m Backstroke: G–Kaylee McKeown, Australia; S–Regan Smith, U.S.; B–Katharine Berkoff, U.S.
200-m Backstroke: G–Kaylee McKeown, Australia; S–Regan Smith, U.S.; B–Kylie Masse, Canada
100-m Breaststroke: G–Tatjana Smith, South Africa; S–Tang Qianting, China; B–Mona McSharry, Ireland
200-m Breaststroke: G–Kate Douglass, U.S.; S–Tatjana Smith, U.S.; B–Tes Schouten, Netherlands
100-m Butterfly: G–Torri Huske, U.S.; S–Gretchen Walsh, U.S.; B–Zhang Yufei, China
200-m Butterfly: G–Summer McIntosh, Canada; S–Regan Smith, U.S.; B–Zhang Yufei, China
200-m Individual Medley: G–Summer McIntosh, Canada; S–Kate Douglass, U.S.; B–Kaylee McKeown, Australia
400-m Individual Medley: G–Summer McIntosh, Canada; S–Katie Grimes, U.S.; B–Emma Weyant, U.S.
4×100-m Freestyle Relay: G–Australia; S–U.S.; B–China
4×200-m Freestyle Relay: G–Australia; S–U.S.; B–China
4×100-m Medley Relay: G–U.S.; S–Australia; B–China

Mixed

4x100-m Medley Relay: G–U.S.; S–China; B–Australia

Artistic Swimming

Duets: G–Wang Liuyi & Wang Qianyi, China; S–Kate Shortman & Isabelle Thorpe, Great Britain; B–Bregje de Brouwer & Noortje de Brouwer, Netherlands
Teams: G–China; S–U.S.; B–Spain

Marathon Swimming

Men's 10-km: G–Kristóf Rasovszky, Hungary; S–Oliver Klemet, Germany; B–Dávid Betlehem, Hungary
Women's 10-km: G–Sharon van Rouwendaal, Netherlands; S–Moesha Johnson, Australia; B–Ginevra Taddeucci, Italy

Table Tennis

Men's Singles: G–Fan Zhendong, China; S–Truls Möregårdh, Sweden; B–Félix Lebrun, France
Women's Singles: G–Chen Meng, China; S–Sina Yingsha, China; B–Hina Hayata, Japan
Men's Team: G–China; S–Sweden; B–France
Women's Team: G–China; S–Japan; B–South Korea
Mixed Doubles: G–Wang Chuqin & Sun Yingsha, China; S–Ri Jong Sik & Kim Kum Yong, North Korea; B–Lim Jong-hoon & Shin Yu-bin, South Korea

Taekwondo

Men

58 kg/128 lbs: G–Park Tae-joon, South Korea; S–Gashim Magomedov, Azerbaijan; B–Cyrian Ravet, France; B–Mohamed Khalil Jendoubi, Tunisia
68 kg/150 lbs: G–Ulugbek Rashitov, Uzbekistan; S–Zaid Kareem, Jordan; B–Edival Pontes, Brazil; B–Liang Yushuai, China
80 kg/176 lbs: G–Firas Katoussi, Tunisia; S–Mehran Barkhordari, Iran; B–Edi Hrnic, Denmark; B–Simone Alessio, Italy
80+ kg/176+ lbs: G–Arian Salimi, Iran; S–Caden Cunningham, Great Britain; B–Cheick Sallah Cissé, Côte d'Ivoire; B–Rafael Alba, Cuba

Women

49 kg/108 lbs: G–Panipak Wongpattanakit, Thailand; S–Guo Qing, China; B–Lena Stojković, Croatia; B–Mobina Nematzadeh, Iran

57 kg/126 lbs: G–Kim Yu-jin, South Korea; S–Nahid Kiyanichandeh, Iran; B–Kimia Alizadeh, Bulgaria; B–Skylar Park, Canada

67 kg/148 lbs: G–Viviana Márton, Hungary; S–Aleksandra Perišić, Serbia; B–Sarah Chaâri, Belgium; B–Kristina Teachout, U.S.

67+ kg/148+ lbs: G–Althéa Laurin, France; S–Svetlana Osipova, Uzbekistan; B–Lee Da-bin, South Korea; B–Nafia Kuş, Turkey

Tennis

Men's Singles: G–Novak Djokovic, Serbia; S–Carlos Alcaraz, Spain; B–Lorenzo Musetti, Italy

Men's Doubles: G–Matthew Ebden & John Peers, Australia; S–Austin Krajicek & Rajeev Ram, U.S.; B–Taylor Fritz & Tommy Paul, U.S.

Women's Singles: G–Zheng Qinwen, China; S–Donna Vekić, Croatia; B–Iga Świątek, Poland

Women's Doubles: G–Sara Errani & Jasmine Paolini, Italy; S–Mirra Andreeva & Diana Shnaider, AIN; B–Cristina Bucșa & Sara Sorribes Tormo, Spain

Mixed Doubles: G–Kateřina Siniaková & Tomáš Macháč, Czechia; S–Wang Xinyu & Zhang Zhizhen, China; B–Gabriela Dabrowski & Félix Auger-Aliassime, Canada

Track and Field

Men

100-m: G–Noah Lyles, U.S.; S–Kishane Thompson, Jamaica; B–Fred Kerley, U.S.

200-m: G–Letsile Tebogo, Botswana; S–Kenny Bednarek, U.S.; B–Noah Lyles, U.S.

400-m: G–Quincy Hall, U.S.; S–Matthew Hudson-Smith, Great Britain; B–Muzala Samukonga, Zambia

800-m: G–Emmanuel Wanyonyi, Kenya; S–Marco Arop, Canada; B–Djamel Sedjati, Algeria

1500-m: G–Cole Hocker, U.S.; S–Josh Kerr, Great Britain; B–Yared Nuguse, U.S.

5000-m: G–Jakob Ingebrigtsen, Norway; S–Ronald Kwemoi, Kenya; B–Grant Fisher, U.S.

10,000-m: G–Joshua Cheptegei, Uganda; S–Berihu Aregawi, Ethiopia; B–Grant Fisher, U.S.

Marathon: G–Tamirat Tola, Ethiopia; S–Bashir Abdi, Belgium; B–Benson Kipruto, Kenya

3000-m Steeplechase: G–Soufiane El Bakkali, Morocco; S–Kenneth Rooks, U.S.; B–Abraham Kibiwot, Kenya

110-m Hurdles: G–Grant Holloway, U.S.; S–Daniel Roberts, U.S.; B–Rasheed Broadbell, Jamaica

400-m Hurdles: G–Rai Benjamin, U.S.; S–Karsten Warholm, Norway; B–Alison dos Santos, Brazil

High Jump: G–Hamish Kerr, New Zealand; S–Shelby McEwen, U.S.; B–Mutaz Essa Barshim, Qatar

Pole Vault: G–Armand Duplantis, Sweden; S–Sam Kendricks, U.S.; B–Emmanouil Karalis, Greece

Long Jump: G–Miltiadis Tentoglou, Greece; S–Wayne Pinnock, Jamaica; B–Mattia Furlani, Italy

Triple Jump: G–Jordan Diaz, Spain; S–Pedro Pichardo, Portugal; B–Andy Diaz, Italy

Shot Put: G–Ryan Crouser, U.S.; S–Joe Kovacs, U.S.; B–Rajindra Campbell, Jamaica

Discus Throw: G–Rojé Stona, Jamaica; S–Mykolas Alekna, Lithuania; B–Matthew Denny, Australia

Hammer Throw: G–Ethan Katzberg, Canada; S–Bence Halász, Hungary; B–Mykhaylo Kokhan, Ukraine

Javelin Throw: G–Arshad Nadeem, Pakistan; S–Neeraj Chopra, India; B–Anderson Peters, Grenada

Decathlon: G–Markus Rooth, Norway; S–Leo Neugebauer, Germany; B–Lindon Victor, Grenada

20-km Walk: G–Brian Pintado, Ecuador; S–Caio Bonfim, Brazil; B–Álvaro Martín, Spain

4x100-m Relay: G–Canada; S–South Africa; B–Great Britain

4x400-m Relay: G–U.S.; S–Botswana; B–Great Britain

Women

100-m: G–Julien Alfred, Saint Lucia; S–Sha'Carri Richardson, U.S.; B–Melissa Jefferson, U.S.

200-m: G–Gabrielle Thomas, U.S.; S–Julien Alfred, Saint Lucia; B–Brittany Brown, U.S.

400-m: G–Marileidy Paulino, Dominican Republic; S–Salwa Eid Naser, Bahrain; B–Natalia Kaczmarek, Poland

800-m: G–Keely Hodgkinson, Great Britain; S–Tsige Duguma, Ethiopia; B–Mary Moraa, Kenya

1500-m: G–Faith Kipyegon, Kenya; S–Jessica Hull, Australia; B–Georgia Bell, Great Britain

5000-m: G–Beatrice Chebet, Kenya; S–Faith Kipyegon, Kenya; B–Sifan Hassan, Netherlands

10,000-m: G–Beatrice Chebet, Kenya; S–Nadia Battocletti, Italy; B–Sifan Hassan, Netherlands

Marathon: G–Sifan Hassan, Netherlands; S–Tigst Assefa, Ethiopia; B–Hellen Obiri, Kenya

3000-m Steeplechase: G–Winfred Yavi, Bahrain; S–Peruth Chemutai, Uganda; B–Faith Cherotich, Kenya

100-m Hurdles: G–Masai Russell, U.S.; S–Cyréna Samba-Mayela, France; B–Jasmine Camacho-Quinn, Puerto Rico

400-m Hurdles: G–Sydney McLaughlin-Levrone, U.S.; S–Anna Cockrell, U.S.; B–Femke Bol, Netherlands

High Jump: G–Yaroslava Mahuchikh, Ukraine; S–Nicola Olyslagers, Australia; B–Iryna Gerashchenko, Ukraine; B–Eleanor Patterson, Australia

Pole Vault: G–Nina Kennedy, Australia; S–Katie Moon, U.S.; B–Alysha Newman, Canada

Long Jump: G–Tara Davis-Woodhall, U.S.; S–Malaika Mihambo, Germany; B–Jasmine Moore, U.S.

Triple Jump: G–Thea LaFond, Dominica; S–Shanieka Ricketts, Jamaica; B–Jasmine Moore, U.S.

Shot Put: G–Yemisi Ogunleye, Germany; S–Maddison-Lee Wesche, New Zealand; B–Song Jiayuan, China

Discus Throw: G–Valarie Allman, U.S.; S–Feng Bin, China; B–Sandra Elkasević, Croatia

Hammer Throw: G–Camryn Rogers, Canada; S–Annette Echikunwoke, U.S.; B–Zhao Jie, China

Javelin Throw: G–Haruka Kitaguchi, Japan; S–Jo-Ane van Dyk, South Africa; B–Nikola Ogrodníková, Czechia

Heptathlon: G–Nafissatou Thiam, Belgium; S–Katarina Johnson-Thompson, Great Britain; B–Noor Vidts, Belgium

20-km Walk: G–Yang Jiayu, China; S–María Pérez, Spain; B–Jemima Montag, Australia

4x100-m Relay: G–U.S.; S–Great Britain; B–Germany

4x400-m Relay: G–U.S.; S–Netherlands; B–Great Britain

Mixed

4 x 400m Relay: G–Netherlands; S–U.S.; B–Great Britain

Marathon Race Walk Relay: G–Álvaro Martín & María Pérez, Spain; S–Brian Pintado & Glenda Morejón, Ecuador; B–Rhydian Cowley & Jemima Montag, Australia

Triathlon

Men: G–Alex Yee, Great Britain; S–Hayden Wilde, New Zealand; B–Léo Bergère, France

Women: G–Cassandre Beaugrand, France; S–Julie Derron, Switzerland; B–Beth Potter, Great Britain

Mixed Relay: G–Germany; S–U.S.; B–Great Britain

Volleyball

Men: G–France; S–Poland; B–U.S.

Women: G–Italy; S–U.S.; B–Brazil

Water Polo

Men: G–Serbia; S–Croatia; B–U.S.

Women: G–Spain; S–Australia; B–Netherlands

Weightlifting

Men

61 kg/134 lbs: G–Li Fabin, China; S–Theerapong Silachai, Thailand; B–Hampton Morris, U.S.

73 kg/161 lbs: G–Rizki Juniansyah, Indonesia; S–Weeraphon Wichuma, Thailand; B–Bozhidar Andreev, Bulgaria

89 kg/196 lbs: G–Karlos Nasar, Bulgaria; S–Yeison López, Colombia; B–Antonino Pizzolato, Italy

102 kg/224 lbs: G–Liu Huanhua, China; S–Akbar Djuraev, Uzbekistan; B–Yauheni Tsikhantsou, AIN

102+ kg/224+ lbs: G–Lasha Talakhadze, Georgia; S–Varazdat Lalayan, Armenia; B–Gor Minasyan, Bahrain

Women

49 kg/108 lbs: G–Hou Zhihui, China; S–Mihaela Cambei, Romania; B–Surodchana Khambao, Thailand

59 kg/130 lbs: G–Luo Shifang, China; S–Maude Charron, Canada; B–Kuo Hsing-chun, Taiwan

71 kg/157 lbs: G–Olivia Reeves, U.S.; S–Mari Sánchez, Colombia; B–Angie Palacios, Ecuador

81 kg/179 lbs: G–Solfrid Koanda, Norway; S–Sara Ahmed, Egypt; B–Neisi Dajomes, Ecuador

81+ kg/179+ lbs: G–Li Wenwen, China; S–Park Hye-jeong, South Korea; B–Emily Campbell, Great Britain

Wrestling

Men

Greco-Roman 60 kg/132 lbs: G–Kenichiro Fumita, Japan; S–Cao Liguo, China; B–Zholaman Sharshenbekov, Kyrgyzstan; B–Ri Se Ung, North Korea

Greco-Roman 67 kg/148 lbs: G–Saeid Esmaeili Leivesi, Iran; S–Parviz Nasibov, Ukraine; B–Hasrat Jafarov, Azerbaijan; B–Luis Orta, Cuba

Greco-Roman 77 kg/170 lbs: G–Nao Kusaka, Japan; S–Demeu Zhadrayev, Kazakhstan; B–Malkhas Amoyan, Armenia; B–Akzhol Makhmudov, Kyrgyzstan

Greco-Roman 87 kg/192 lbs: G–Semen Novikov, Bulgaria; S–Alireza Mohmadipiani, Iran; B–Zhan Beleniuk, Ukraine; B–Turpal Bisultanov, Denmark

Greco-Roman 97 kg/214 lbs: G–Mohammadhadi Saravi, Iran; S–Artur Aleksanyan, Armenia; B–Gabriel Rosillo, Cuba; B–Uzur Dzhuzupbekov, Kyrgyzstan

Greco-Roman 130 kg/287 lbs: G–Mijaín López, Cuba; S–Yasmani Acosta, Chile; B–Amin Mirzazadeh, Iran; B–Meng Lingzhe, China

Freestyle 57 kg/125 lbs: G–Rei Higuchi, Japan; S–Spencer Lee, U.S.; B–Aman Sehrawat, India; B–Gulomjon Abdullaev, Uzbekistan

Freestyle 65 kg/143 lbs: G–Kotaro Kiyooka, Japan; S–Rahman Amouzad, Iran; B–Sebastian Rivera, Puerto Rico; B–Islam Dudaev, Albania

Freestyle 74 kg/163 lbs: G–Razambek Jamalov, Uzbekistan; S–Daichi Takatani, Japan; B–Kyle Dake, U.S.; B–Chermen Valiev, Albania

Freestyle 86 kg/190 lbs: G–Magomed Ramazanov, Bulgaria; S–Hassan Yazdani, Iran; B–Aaron Brooks, U.S.; B–Dauren Kurugliev, Greece

Freestyle 97 kg/214 lbs: G–Akhmed Tazhudinov, Bahrain; S–Givi Matcharashvili, Georgia; B–Magomedkhan Magomedov, Azerbaijan; B–Amirali Azarpira, Iran

Freestyle 125 kg/276 lbs: G–Geno Petriashvili, Georgia; S–Amir Hossein Zare, Iran; B–Taha Akgül, Turkey; B–Giorgi Meshvildishvili, Azerbaijan

Women

Freestyle 50 kg/110 lbs: G–Sarah Hildebrandt, U.S.; S–Yusneylys Guzmán, Cuba; B–Yui Susaki, Japan; B–Feng Ziqi, China

Freestyle 53 kg/117 lbs: G–Akari Fujinami, Japan; S–Lucía Yépez, Ecuador; B–Choe Hyo Gyong, North Korea; B–Pang Qianyu, China

Freestyle 57 kg/126 lbs: G–Tsugumi Sakurai, Japan; S–Anastasia Nichita, Moldova; B–Helen Maroulis, U.S.; B–Hong Kexin, China

Freestyle 62 kg/137 lbs: G–Sakura Motoki, Japan; S–Iryna Koliadenko, Ukraine; B–Aisuluu Tynybekova, Kyrgyzstan; B–Grace Bullen, Norway

Freestyle 68 kg/150 lbs: G–Amit Elor, U.S.; S–Meerim Zhumanazarova, Kyrgyzstan; B–Buse Tosun Çavuşoğlu, Turkey; B–Nonoka Ozaki, Japan

Freestyle 76 kg/168 lbs: G–Yuka Kagami, Japan; S–Kennedy Blades, U.S.; B–Milaimys Marín, Cuba; B–Tatiana Rentería, Colombia

Summer Olympic Games Champions, 1896-2024

* = Olympic record; (w) wind-aided; times are shown in hour:minute:sec.

The 1980 Games were boycotted by 62 nations, including the U.S. The 1984 Games were boycotted by the USSR and most Eastern bloc nations. East and West Germany competed separately, 1968-88. The 1992 Unified Team consisted of 12 former Soviet republics. The 1992 Independent Olympic Participants (IOP) were from Serbia, Montenegro, and Macedonia. In the 2020 Games, delayed until 2021 by the COVID-19 pandemic, Russian athletes competed as the Russian Olympic Committee (ROC). In 2024, Russian and Belorussian athletes competed as Individual Neutral Athletes (AIN), and athletes from Iran, Afghanistan, Cameroon, Cuba, Democratic Republic of the Congo, Eritrea, Ethiopia, South Sudan, Sudan, Syria, and Venezuela participated as the Refugee Olympic Team (EOR).

Not all sports are listed here, and many events are omitted, even within listed sports, particularly if the event has not been held in more recent Games. Point systems for scoring events have changed many times. Points shown are those under the point system in use at the time.

Basketball

Men

1936	United States, Canada, Mexico
1948	United States, France, Brazil
1952	United States, USSR, Uruguay
1956	United States, USSR, Uruguay
1960	United States, USSR, Brazil
1964	United States, USSR, Brazil
1968	United States, Yugoslavia, USSR
1972	USSR, United States, Cuba
1976	United States, Yugoslavia, USSR
1980	Yugoslavia, Italy, USSR
1984	United States, Spain, Yugoslavia
1988	USSR, Yugoslavia, United States
1992	United States, Croatia, Lithuania
1996	United States, Yugoslavia, Lithuania
2000	United States, France, Lithuania
2004	Argentina, Italy, United States
2008	United States, Spain, Argentina
2012	United States, Spain, Russia
2016	United States, Serbia, Spain
2020	United States, France, Australia
2024	United States, France, Serbia

Women

1976	USSR, United States, Bulgaria
1980	USSR, Bulgaria, Yugoslavia
1984	United States, South Korea, China
1988	United States, Yugoslavia, USSR
1992	Unified Team, China, United States
1996	United States, Brazil, Australia
2000	United States, Australia, Brazil
2004	United States, Australia, Russia
2008	United States, Australia, Russia
2012	United States, France, Australia
2016	United States, Spain, Serbia
2020	United States, Japan, France
2024	United States, France, Australia

3 x 3 Men

2020	Lativia, ROC, Serbia
2024	Netherlands, France, Lithuania

3 x 3 Women

2020	United States, ROC, China
2024	Germany, Spain, United States

Boxing—Men

Weight class limits have changed many times since the first Olympic boxing events were held in 1904. The limits shown were used in the 2024 Olympic Games. The Super Heavyweight class was known as Heavyweight 1904-80.

Lt. Flyweight (49 kg/108 lbs)

1968	Francisco Rodriguez, Venezuela
1972	Gyorgy Gedo, Hungary
1976	Jorge Hernandez, Cuba
1980	Shamil Sabyrov, USSR
1984	Paul Gonzalez, United States
1988	Ivailo Hristov, Bulgaria
1992	Rogelio Marcelo, Cuba
1996	Daniel Petrov, Bulgaria
2000	Brahim Asloum, France
2004	Yan Bhartelemy Varela, Cuba
2008	Zou Shiming, China
2012	Zou Shiming, China
2016	Hasanboy Dusmatov, Uzbekistan

Flyweight (51 kg/112 lbs)

1904	George Finnegan, United States
1920	Frank Di Gennara, United States
1924	Fidel LaBarba, United States
1928	Antal Kocsis, Hungary
1932	Istvan Enekes, Hungary
1936	Willi Kaiser, Germany
1948	Pascual Perez, Argentina
1952	Nathan Brooks, United States
1956	Terence Spinks, Great Britain
1960	Gyula Török, Hungary
1964	Fernando Atzori, Italy
1968	Ricardo Delgado, Mexico
1972	Georgi Kostadinov, Bulgaria

Flyweight (51 kg/112 lbs)

1976	Leo Randolph, United States
1980	Peter Lesov, Bulgaria
1984	Steve McCrory, United States
1988	Kim Kwang-sun, S. Korea
1992	Choi Chol Su, N. Korea
1996	Maikro Romero, Cuba
2000	Wijan Ponlid, Thailand
2004	Yuriorkis Gamboa Toledano, Cuba
2008	Somjit Jongjohor, Thailand
2012	Robeisy Ramírez, Cuba
2016	Shakhobidin Zoirov, Uzbekistan
2020	Galal Yafai, Great Britain
2024	Hasanboy Dusmatov, Uzbekistan

Bantamweight (56 kg/123 lbs)

1904 Oliver Kirk, United States
1908 A. Henry Thomas, Great Britain
1920 Clarence Walker, South Africa
1924 William Smith, South Africa
1928 Vittorio Tamagnini, Italy
1932 Horace Gwynne, Canada
1936 Ulderico Sergo, Italy
1948 Tibor Csik, Hungary
1952 Pentti Hamalainen, Finland
1956 Wolfgang Behrendt, E. Germany
1960 Oleg Grigoryev, USSR
1964 Takao Sakurai, Japan
1968 Valery Sokolov, USSR
1972 Orlando Martinez, Cuba
1976 Gu Yong Ju, N. Korea
1980 Juan Hernandez, Cuba
1984 Maurizio Stecca, Italy
1988 Kennedy McKinney, United States
1992 Joel Casamayor, Cuba
1996 Istvan Kovacs, Hungary
2000 Guillermo Rigondeaux, Cuba
2004 Guillermo Rigondeaux, Cuba
2008 Badar-Uugan Enkhbat, Mongolia
2012 Luke Campbell, Great Britain
2016 Robeisy Ramírez, Cuba

Featherweight (57 kg/126 lbs)

1904 Oliver Kirk, United States
1908 Richard Gunn, Great Britain
1920 Paul Fritsch, France
1924 John Fields, United States
1928 Lambertus van Klaveren, Netherlands
1932 Carmelo Robledo, Argentina
1936 Oscar Casanovas, Argentina
1948 Ernesto Formenti, Italy
1952 Jan Zachara, Czechoslovakia
1956 Vladimir Safronov, USSR
1960 Francesco Musso, Italy
1964 Stanislav Stephashkin, USSR
1968 Antonio Roldan, Mexico
1972 Boris Kousnetsov, USSR
1976 Angel Herrera, Cuba
1980 Rudi Fink, E. Germany
1984 Meldrick Taylor, United States
1988 Giovanni Parisi, Italy
1992 Andreas Tews, Germany
1996 Somluck Kamsing, Thailand
2000 Bekzat Sattarkhanov, Kazakhstan
2004 Alexey Tishchenko, Russia
2008 Vasyl Lomachenko, Ukraine
2020 Albert Batyrgaziev, ROC
2024 Abdumalik Khalokov, Uzbekistan

Lightweight (63.5 kg/140 lbs)

1904 Harry Spanger, United States
1908 Frederick Grace, Great Britain
1920 Samuel Mosberg, United States
1924 Hans Nielsen, Denmark
1928 Carlo Orlandi, Italy
1932 Lawrence Stevens, South Africa
1936 Imre Harangi, Hungary
1948 Gerald Dreyer, South Africa
1952 Aureliano Bolognesi, Italy
1956 Richard McTaggart, Great Britain
1960 Kazimierz Pazdzior, Poland
1964 Jozef Grudzien, Poland
1968 Ronald Harris, United States
1972 Jan Szczepanski, Poland
1976 Howard Davis, United States
1980 Angel Herrera, Cuba
1984 Pernell Whitaker, United States
1988 Andreas Zülow, E. Germany
1992 Oscar De La Hoya, United States
1996 Hocine Soltani, Algeria
2000 Mario Kindelan, Cuba
2004 Mario Kindelan, Cuba
2008 Alexey Tishchenko, Russia
2012 Vasyl Lomachenko, Ukraine
2016 Robson Conceição, Brazil

Lightweight (63.5 kg/140 lbs)

2020 Andy Cruz, Cuba
2024 Erislandy Álvarez, Cuba

Lt. Welterweight (64 kg/141 lbs)

1952 Charles Adkins, United States
1956 Vladimir Yengibaryan, USSR
1960 Bohumil Nemecek, Czechoslovakia
1964 Jerzy Kulej, Poland
1968 Jerzy Kulej, Poland
1972 Ray Seales, United States
1976 Ray Leonard, United States
1980 Patrizio Oliva, Italy
1984 Jerry Page, United States
1988 Viatcheslav Janovski, USSR
1992 Hector Vinent, Cuba
1996 Hector Vinent, Cuba
2000 Mahamadkadyz Abdullaev, Uzbekistan
2004 Manus Boonjumnong, Thailand
2008 Felix Diaz, Dominican Republic
2012 Roniel Iglesias, Cuba
2016 Fazliddin Gaibnazarov, Uzbekistan

Welterweight (71 kg/157 lbs)

1904 Albert Young, United States
1920 Albert Schneider, Canada
1924 Jean Delarge, Belgium
1928 Edward Morgan, New Zealand
1932 Edward Flynn, United States
1936 Sten Suvio, Finland
1948 Julius Torma, Czechoslovakia
1952 Zygmunt Chychia, Poland
1956 Nicolae Linca, Romania
1960 Giovanni Benvenuti, Italy
1964 Marian Kasprzyk, Poland
1968 Manfred Wolke, E. Germany
1972 Emilio Correa, Cuba
1976 Jochen Bachfeld, E. Germany
1980 Andres Aldama, Cuba
1984 Mark Breland, United States
1988 Robert Wangila, Kenya
1992 Michael Carruth, Ireland
1996 Oleg Saitov, Russia
2000 Oleg Saitov, Russia
2004 Bakhtiyar Artayev, Kazakhstan
2008 Bakhyt Sarsekbayev, Kazakhstan
2012 Serik Sapiyev, Kazakhstan
2016 Daniyar Yeleussinov, Kazakhstan
2020 Roniel Iglesias, Cuba
2024 Asadkhuja Muydinkhujaev, Uzbekistan

Lt. Middleweight (71 kg/156 lbs)

1952 Laszlo Papp, Hungary
1956 Laszlo Papp, Hungary
1960 Wilbert McClure, United States
1964 Boris Lagutin, USSR
1968 Boris Lagutin, USSR
1972 Dieter Kottysch, W. Germany
1976 Jerzy Rybicki, Poland
1980 Armando Martinez, Cuba
1984 Frank Tate, United States
1988 Park Si-hun, S. Korea
1992 Juan Lemus, Cuba
1996 David Reid, United States
2000 Yermakhan Ibraimov, Kazakhstan

Middleweight (75 kg/165 lbs)

1904 Charles Mayer, United States
1908 John Douglas, Great Britain
1920 Harry Mallin, Great Britain
1924 Harry Mallin, Great Britain
1928 Piero Toscani, Italy
1932 Carmen Barth, United States
1936 Jean Despeaux, France
1948 Laszlo Papp, Hungary
1952 Floyd Patterson, United States
1956 Gennady Schatkov, USSR
1960 Edward Crook, United States
1964 Valery Popenchenko, USSR
1968 Christopher Finnegan, Great Britain
1972 Vyacheslav Lemechev, USSR
1976 Michael Spinks, United States

Middleweight (75 kg/165 lbs)

1980 Jose Gomez, Cuba
1984 Shin Joon-sup, S. Korea
1988 Henry Maske, E. Germany
1992 Ariel Hernandez, Cuba
1996 Ariel Hernandez, Cuba
2000 Jorge Gutierrez, Cuba
2004 Gaydarbek Gaydarbekov, Russia
2008 James Degale, Great Britain
2012 Ryota Murata, Japan
2016 Arlen López, Cuba
2020 Hebert Conceição, Brazil

Lt. Heavyweight (80 kg/176 lbs)

1920 Edward Eagan, United States
1924 Harry Mitchell, Great Britain
1928 Victor Avendaño, Argentina
1932 David Carstens, South Africa
1936 Roger Michelot, France
1948 George Hunter, South Africa
1952 Norvel Lee, United States
1956 James Boyd, United States
1960 Cassius Clay, United States
1964 Cosimo Pinto, Italy
1968 Dan Poznyak, USSR
1972 Mate Parlov, Yugoslavia
1976 Leon Spinks, United States
1980 Slobodan Kacar, Yugoslavia
1984 Anton Josipovic, Yugoslavia
1988 Andrew Maynard, United States
1992 Torsten May, Germany
1996 Vassili Jirov, Kazakhstan
2000 Alexander Lebziak, Russia
2004 Andre Ward, United States
2008 Zhang Xiaoping, China
2012 Yegor Mekhontsev, Russia
2016 Julio César la Cruz, Cuba
2020 Arlen López, Cuba
2024 Oleksandr Khyzhniak, Ukraine

Heavyweight (92 kg/203 lbs)

1984 Henry Tillman, United States
1988 Ray Mercer, United States
1992 Felix Savon, Cuba
1996 Felix Savon, Cuba
2000 Felix Savon, Cuba
2004 Odlanier Solis Fonte, Cuba
2008 Rakhim Chakhkiev, Russia
2012 Oleksandr Usik, Ukraine
2016 Evgeny Tishchenko, Russia
2020 Julio César la Cruz, Cuba
2024 Lazizbek Mullojonov, Uzbekistan

Super Heavyweight (92+ kg/203+ lbs)

1904 Samuel Berger, United States
1908 Albert Oldham, Great Britain
1920 Ronald Rawson, Great Britain
1924 Otto von Porat, Norway
1928 Arturo Rodriguez Jurado, Argentina
1932 Santiago Lovell, Argentina
1936 Herbert Runge, Germany
1948 Rafael Iglesias, Argentina
1952 H. Edward Sanders, United States
1956 T. Peter Rademacher, United States
1960 Franco De Piccoli, Italy
1964 Joe Frazier, United States
1968 George Foreman, United States
1972 Teofilo Stevenson, Cuba
1976 Teofilo Stevenson, Cuba
1980 Teofilo Stevenson, Cuba
1984 Tyrell Biggs, United States
1988 Lennox Lewis, Canada
1992 Roberto Balado, Cuba
1996 Vladimir Klitchko, Ukraine
2000 Audley Harrison, Great Britain
2004 Alexander Povetkin, Russia
2008 Roberto Cammarelle, Italy
2012 Anthony Joshua, Great Britain
2016 Tony Yoka, France
2020 Bakhodir Jalolov, Uzbekistan
2024 Bakhodir Jalolov, Uzbekistan

Boxing—Women

Flyweight (50 kg/110 lbs)

2012 Nicola Adams, Great Britain
2016 Nicola Adams, Great Britain
2020 Stoyka Krasteva, Bulgaria
2024 Wu Yu, China

Bantamweight (54 kg/119 lbs)

2024 Chang Yuan, China

Featherweight (57 kg/126 lbs)

2020 Sena Irie, Japan
2024 Lin Yu-ting, Taiwan

Lightweight (60 kg/132 lbs)

2012 Katie Taylor, Ireland
2016 Estelle Mossely, France
2020 Kellie Harrington, Ireland
2024 Kellie Harrington, Ireland

Welterweight (66 kg/146 lbs)

2020 Busenaz Sürmeneli, Turkey
2024 Imane Khelif, Algeria

Middleweight (75 kg/165 lbs)

2012 Claressa Shields, United States
2016 Claressa Shields, United States
2020 Lauren Price, Great Britain
2024 Li Qian, China

Gymnastics—Men

Floor Exercise

1932 István Pelle, Hungary
1936 Georges Miez, Switzerland
1948 Ferenc Pataki, Hungary
1952 William Thoresson, Sweden
1956 Valentin Muratov, USSR
1960 Nobuyuki Aihara, Japan
1964 Franco Menichelli, Italy
1968 Sawao Kato, Japan
1972 Nikolay Andrianov, USSR
1976 Nikolay Andrianov, USSR
1980 Roland Brückner, E. Germany
1984 Li Ning, China
1988 Sergei Kharkov, USSR
1992 Li Xiaoshuang, China
1996 Ioannis Melissanidis, Greece
2000 Igors Vihrovs, Latvia
2004 Kyle Shewfelt, Canada
2008 Zou Kai, China
2012 Zou Kai, China
2016 Max Whitlock, Great Britain
2020 Artem Dolgopyat, Israel
2024 Carlos Yulo, Philippines

Horizontal Bar

1896 Hermann Weingärtner, Germany
1904 Anton Heida, United States; Edward Hennig, United States (tie)
1924 Leon Stukelj, Yugoslavia
1928 Georges Miez, Switzerland
1932 Dallas Denver Bixler, United States
1936 Aleksanteri Saarvala, Finland
1948 Josef Stalder, Switzerland
1952 Jakob "Jack" Günthard, Switzerland
1956 Takashi Ono, Japan
1960 Takashi Ono, Japan
1964 Boris Shakhlin, USSR
1968 Akinori Nakayama, Japan; Mikhail Voronin, USSR (tie)
1972 Mitsuo Tsukahara, Japan
1976 Mitsuo Tsukahara, Japan
1980 Stoyan Deltchev, Bulgaria
1984 Shinji Morisue, Japan
1988 Vladimir Artemov, USSR; Valeri Liukin, USSR (tie)
1992 Trent Dimas, United States
1996 Andreas Wecker, Germany
2000 Alexei Nemov, Russia
2004 Igor Cassina, Italy
2008 Zou Kai, China
2012 Epke Zonderland, Netherlands
2016 Fabian Hambüchen, Germany
2020 Daiki Hashimoto, Japan
2024 Shinnosuke Oka, Japan

Individual All-Around

1900 Gustave Sandras, France
1904 Julius Lenhart, United States
1908 G. Alberto Braglia, Italy
1912 G. Alberto Braglia, Italy
1920 Giorgio Zampori, Italy
1924 Leon Stukelj, Yugoslavia
1928 Georges Miez, Switzerland
1932 Romeo Neri, Italy
1936 Karl-Alfred Schwarzmann, Germany
1948 Veikko Huhtanen, Finland
1952 Viktor Ivanovich Chukarin, USSR
1956 Viktor Ivanovich Chukarin, USSR
1960 Boris Shakhlin, USSR
1964 Yukio Endo, Japan
1968 Sawao Kato, Japan
1972 Sawao Kato, Japan
1976 Nikolay Andrianov, USSR
1980 Aleksandr Dityatin, USSR
1984 Koji Gushiken, Japan
1988 Vladimir Artemov, USSR
1992 Vitaly Scherbo, Unified Team (Belarus)
1996 Li Xiaoshuang, China
2000 Alexei Nemov, Russia
2004 Paul Hamm, United States
2008 Yang Wei, China
2012 Kohei Uchimura, Japan
2016 Kohei Uchimura, Japan

Individual All-Around

2020 Daiki Hashimoto, Japan
2024 Shinnosuke Oka, Japan

Parallel Bars

1896 Alfred Flatow, Germany
1904 George Eyser, United States
1924 August Güttinger, Switzerland
1928 Ladislav Vacha, Czechoslovakia
1932 Romeo Neri, Italy
1936 Konrad Frey, Germany
1948 Michael Reusch, Switzerland
1952 Hans Eugster, Switzerland
1956 Viktor Ivanovich Chukarin, USSR
1960 Boris Shakhlin, USSR
1964 Yukio Endo, Japan
1968 Akinori Nakayama, Japan
1972 Sawao Kato, Japan
1976 Sawao Kato, Japan
1980 Aleksandr Tkachev, USSR
1984 Bart Conner, United States
1988 Vladimir Artemov, USSR
1992 Vitaly Scherbo, Unified Team (Belarus)
1996 Roustam Sharipov, Ukraine
2000 Li Xiaopeng, China
2004 Valeri Goncharov, Ukraine
2008 Li Xiaopeng, China
2012 Feng Zhe, China
2016 Oleg Verniaiev, Ukraine
2020 Zou Jingyuan, China
2024 Zou Jingyuan, China

Pommel Horse

1896 Louis Zutter, Switzerland
1904 Anton Heida, United States
1924 Josef Wilhelm, Switzerland
1928 Hermann Hänggi, Switzerland
1932 István Pelle, Hungary
1936 Konrad Frey, Germany
1948 Paavo Johannes Aaltonen, Finland; Veikko Huhtanen, Finland; Heikki Savolainen, Finland (tie)
1952 Viktor Ivanovich Chukarin, USSR
1956 Boris Shakhlin, USSR
1960 Eugen Georg Oskar Ekman, Finland; Boris Shakhlin, USSR (tie)
1964 Miroslav Cerar, Yugoslavia
1968 Miroslav Cerar, Yugoslavia
1972 Viktor Klimenko, USSR
1976 Zoltan Magyar, Hungary
1980 Zoltan Magyar, Hungary
1984 Li Ning, China; Peter Glen Vidmar, United States (tie)
1988 Dmitri Bilozerchev, USSR; Zsolt Borkai, Hungary; Lubomir Geraskov, Bulgaria (tie)
1992 Pae Gil Su, N. Korea; Vitaly Scherbo, Unified Team (Belarus) (tie)
1996 Li Donghua, Switzerland
2000 Marius Daniel Urzica, Romania
2004 Teng Haibin, China
2008 Xiao Qin, China
2012 Krisztián Berki, Hungary
2016 Max Whitlock, Great Britain
2020 Max Whitlock, Great Britain
2024 Rhys McClenaghan, Ireland

Rings

1896 Ioannis Mitropoulos, Greece
1904 Hermann Glass, United States
1924 Francesco Martino, Italy
1928 Leon Stukelj, Yugoslavia
1932 George Gulack, United States
1936 Alois Hudec, Czechoslovakia
1948 Karl Frei, Switzerland
1952 Grant Shaginyan, USSR
1956 Albert Azaryan, USSR
1960 Albert Azaryan, USSR
1964 Takuji Hayata, Japan

Rings

1968 Akinori Nakayama, Japan
1972 Akinori Nakayama, Japan
1976 Nikolay Andrianov, USSR
1980 Aleksandr Dityatin, USSR
1984 Koji Gushiken, Japan; Li Ning, China (tie)
1988 Holger Behrendt, E. Germany; Dmitri Bilozerchev, USSR (tie)
1992 Vitaly Scherbo, Unified Team (Belarus)
1996 Juri Chechi, Italy
2000 Szilveszter Csollany, Hungary
2004 Dimosthenis Tampakos, Greece
2008 Chen Yibing, China
2012 Arthur Zanetti, Brazil
2016 Eleftherios Petrounias, Greece
2020 Liu Yang, China
2024 Liu Yang, China

Team Competition

1904 United States, United States, United States
1908 Sweden, Norway, Finland
1912 Italy, Hungary, Great Britain
1920 Italy, Belgium, France
1924 Italy, France, Switzerland
1928 Switzerland, Czechoslovakia, Yugoslavia
1932 Italy, United States, Finland
1936 Germany, Switzerland, Finland
1948 Finland, Switzerland, Hungary
1952 USSR, Switzerland, Finland
1956 USSR, Japan, Finland
1960 Japan, USSR, Italy
1964 Japan, USSR, Unified Team of Germany
1968 Japan, USSR, E. Germany
1972 Japan, USSR, E. Germany
1976 Japan, USSR, E. Germany
1980 USSR, E. Germany, Hungary
1984 United States, China, Japan
1988 USSR, E. Germany, Japan
1992 Unified Team, China, Japan
1996 Russia, China, Ukraine
2000 China, Ukraine, Russia
2004 Japan, United States, Romania
2008 China, Japan, United States
2012 China, Japan, Great Britain
2016 Japan, Russia, China
2020 ROC, Japan, China
2024 Japan, China, United States

Vault

1896 Carl Schuhmann, Germany
1904 George Eyser, United States; Anton Heida, United States (tie)
1924 Frank Kriz, United States
1928 Eugen Mack, Switzerland
1932 Savino Guglielmetti, Italy
1936 Karl-Alfred Schwarzmann, Germany
1948 Paavo Johannes Aaltonen, Finland
1952 Viktor Ivanovich Chukarin, USSR
1956 Helmut Bantz, Unified Team of Germany; Valentin Muratov, USSR (tie)
1960 Takashi Ono, Japan; Boris Shakhlin, USSR (tie)
1964 Haruhiro Yamashita, Japan
1968 Mikhail Voronin, USSR
1972 Klaus Köste, E. Germany
1976 Nikolay Andrianov, USSR
1980 Nikolay Andrianov, USSR
1984 Lou Yun, China
1988 Lou Yun, China
1992 Vitaly Scherbo, Unified Team (Belarus)
1996 Alexei Nemov, Russia
2000 Gervasio Deferr, Spain
2004 Gervasio Deferr, Spain
2008 Leszek Blanik, Poland
2012 Yang Hak-seon, South Korea
2016 Ri Se Gwang, North Korea
2020 Shin Jeahwan, South Korea
2024 Carlos Yulo, Philippines

Gymnastics—Women

Balance Beam

1952 Nina Bocharova, USSR
1956 Agnes Keleti, Hungary
1960 Eva Vechtova-Bosakova, Czechoslovakia
1964 Vera Caslavska, Czechoslovakia
1968 Natalya Kuchinskaya, USSR
1972 Olga Korbut, USSR
1976 Nadia Comaneci, Romania
1980 Nadia Comaneci, Romania
1984 Ecaterina Szabo, Romania; Simona Pauca, Romania (tie)
1988 Daniela Silivas, Romania
1992 Tatiana Lyssenko, Unified Team (Ukraine)
1996 Shannon Miller, United States
2000 Liu Xuan, China
2004 Catalina Ponor, Romania
2008 Shawn Johnson, United States
2012 Deng Linlin, China
2016 Sanne Wevers, Netherlands
2020 Guan Chenchen, China
2024 Alice D'Amato, Italy

Floor Exercise

1952 Agnes Keleti, Hungary
1956 Agnes Keleti, Hungary; Larisa Latynina, USSR (tie)
1960 Larisa Latynina, USSR
1964 Larisa Latynina, USSR
1968 Vera Caslavska, Czechoslovakia; Larisa Petrik, USSR (tie)
1972 Olga Korbut, USSR
1976 Nelli Kim, USSR
1980 Nelli Kim, USSR; Nadia Comaneci, Romania (tie)
1984 Ecaterina Szabo, Romania
1988 Daniela Silivas, Romania
1992 Lavinia Milosovici, Romania
1996 Lilia Podkopayeva, Ukraine
2000 Elena Zamolodchikova, Russia
2004 Catalina Ponor, Romania
2008 Sandra Izbasa, Romania
2012 Aly Raisman, United States
2016 Simone Biles, United States
2020 Jade Carey, United States
2024 Rebeca Andrade, Brazil

Individual All-Around

1952 Mariya Gorokhovskaya, USSR
1956 Larisa Latynina, USSR
1960 Larisa Latynina, USSR
1964 Vera Caslavska, Czechoslovakia
1968 Vera Caslavska, Czechoslovakia
1972 Lyudmila Turischeva, USSR
1976 Nadia Comaneci, Romania
1980 Elena Davydova, USSR
1984 Mary-Lou Retton, United States
1988 Elena Shushunova, USSR
1992 Tatiana Gutsu, Unified Team (Ukraine)
1996 Lilia Podkopayeva, Ukraine
2000 Simona Amanar, Romania
2004 Carly Patterson, United States
2008 Nastia Liukin, United States
2012 Gabby Douglas, United States
2016 Simone Biles, United States
2020 Sunisa Lee, United States
2024 Simone Biles, United States

Team Competition

1928 Netherlands, Italy, Great Britain
1936 Germany, Czechoslovakia, Hungary
1948 Czechoslovakia, Hungary, United States
1952 USSR, Hungary, Czechoslovakia
1956 USSR, Hungary, Romania
1960 USSR, Czechoslovakia, Romania
1964 USSR, Czechoslovakia, Japan
1968 USSR, Czechoslovakia, E. Germany
1972 USSR, E. Germany, Hungary
1976 USSR, Romania, E. Germany
1980 USSR, Romania, E. Germany
1984 Romania, United States, China
1988 USSR, Romania, E. Germany
1992 Unified Team, Romania, United States
1996 United States, Russia, Romania
2000 Romania, Russia, United States
2004 Romania, United States, Russia
2008 China, United States, Romania
2012 United States, Russia, Romania
2016 United States, Russia, China
2020 ROC, United States, Great Britain
2024 United States, Italy, Brazil

Uneven Bars

1952 Margit Korondi, Hungary
1956 Agnes Keleti, Hungary
1960 Polina Astakhova, USSR
1964 Polina Astakhova, USSR
1968 Vera Caslavska, Czechoslovakia
1972 Karin Janz, E. Germany
1976 Nadia Comaneci, Romania
1980 Maxi Gnauck, E. Germany
1984 Julianne McNamara, United States; Yan-Hong Ma, China (tie)
1988 Daniela Silivas, Romania
1992 Lu Li, China
1996 Svetlana Khorkina, Russia
2000 Svetlana Khorkina, Russia
2004 Emilie LePennec, France
2008 He Kexin, China
2012 Aliya Mustafina, Russia
2016 Aliya Mustafina, Russia
2020 Nina Derwael, Belgium
2024 Kaylia Nemour, Algeria

Vault

1952 Ekaterina Kalinchuk, USSR
1956 Larisa Latynina, USSR
1960 Margarita Nikolaeva, USSR
1964 Vera Caslavska, Czechoslovakia
1968 Vera Caslavska, Czechoslovakia
1972 Karin Janz, E. Germany
1976 Nelli Kim, USSR
1980 Natalia Shaposhnikova, USSR
1984 Ecaterina Szabo, Romania
1988 Svetlana Boginskaya, USSR
1992 Henrietta Onodi, Hungary; Lavinia Milosovici, Romania (tie)
1996 Simona Amanar, Romania
2000 Elena Zamolodchikova, Russia
2004 Monica Rosu, Romania
2008 Hong Un Jong, N. Korea
2012 Sandra Izbaşa, Romania
2016 Simone Biles, United States
2020 Rebeca Andrade, Brazil
2024 Simone Biles, United States

Soccer

Men

1900 Great Britain, France, Belgium
1904 Canada, United States, United States
1908 Great Britain, Denmark, Netherlands
1912 Great Britain, Denmark, Netherlands
1920 Belgium, Spain, Netherlands
1924 Uruguay, Switzerland, Sweden
1928 Uruguay, Argentina, Italy
1936 Italy, Austria, Norway
1948 Sweden, Yugoslavia, Denmark
1952 Hungary, Yugoslavia, Sweden
1956 USSR, Yugoslavia, Bulgaria
1960 Yugoslavia, Denmark, Hungary
1964 Hungary, Czechoslovakia, Unified Team of Germany
1968 Hungary, Bulgaria, Japan
1972 Poland; Hungary; USSR, E. Germany (tie for bronze)
1976 E. Germany, Poland, USSR
1980 Czechoslovakia, E. Germany, USSR
1984 France, Brazil, Yugoslavia
1988 USSR, Brazil, W. Germany
1992 Spain, Poland, Ghana
1996 Nigeria, Argentina, Brazil
2000 Cameroon, Spain, Chile
2004 Argentina, Paraguay, Italy
2008 Argentina, Nigeria, Brazil
2012 Mexico, Brazil, South Korea
2016 Brazil, Germany, Nigeria
2020 Brazil, Spain, Mexico
2024 Spain, France, Morocco

Women

1996 United States, China, Norway
2000 Norway, United States, Germany
2004 United States, Brazil, Germany
2008 United States, Brazil, Germany
2012 United States, Japan, Canada
2016 Germany, Sweden, Canada
2020 Canada, Sweden, United States
2024 United States, Brazil, Germany

Swimming and Diving—Men

50-Meter Freestyle

		Time
1988	Matt Biondi, United States	0:22.14
1992	Aleksandr Popov, Unified Team (Rus.)	0:21.91
1996	Aleksandr Popov, Russia	0:22.13
2000	Anthony Ervin, United States	0:21.98
	Gary Hall Jr., United States (tie)	0:21.98
2004	Gary Hall Jr., United States	0:21.93
2008	Cesar Cielo Filho, Brazil	0:21.30
2012	Florent Manaudou, France	0:21.34
2016	Anthony Ervin, United States	0:21.40
2020	Caeleb Dressel, United States	0:21.07*
2024	Cameron McEvoy, Australia	0:21.25

100-Meter Freestyle

		Time
1896	Alfred Hajos, Hungary	1:22.2
1904	Zoltan de Halmay, Hungary (100 yds)	1:02.8
1908	Charles Daniels, United States	1:05.6
1912	Duke P. Kahanamoku, United States	1:03.4
1920	Duke P. Kahanamoku, United States	1:01.4
1924	Johnny Weissmuller, United States	0:59.0
1928	Johnny Weissmuller, United States	0:58.6
1932	Yasuji Miyazaki, Japan	0:58.2
1936	Ferenc Csik, Hungary	0:57.6
1948	Wally Ris, United States	0:57.3
1952	Clarke Scholes, United States	0:57.4
1956	Jon Henricks, Australia	0:55.4
1960	John Devitt, Australia	0:55.2
1964	Don Schollander, United States	0:53.4
1968	Mike Wenden, Australia	0:52.2
1972	Mark Spitz, United States	0:51.22
1976	Jim Montgomery, United States	0:49.99
1980	Jorg Woithe, E. Germany	0:50.40
1984	Ambrose "Rowdy" Gaines, United States	0:49.80
1988	Matt Biondi, United States	0:48.63
1992	Aleksandr Popov, Unified Team (Rus.)	0:49.02
1996	Aleksandr Popov, Russia	0:48.74
2000	Pieter van den Hoogenband, Netherlands	0:48.30
2004	Pieter van den Hoogenband, Netherlands	0:48.17
2008	Alain Bernard, France	0:47.21
2012	Nathan Adrian, United States	0:47.52
2016	Kyle Chalmers, Australia	0:47.58
2020	Caeleb Dressel, United States	0:47.02
2024	Pan Zhanle, China	0:46.40*

	200-Meter Freestyle	Time
1968	Mike Wenden, Australia	1:55.2
1972	Mark Spitz, United States	1:52.78
1976	Bruce Furniss, United States	1:50.29
1980	Sergei Kopliakov, USSR	1:49.81
1984	Michael Gross, W. Germany	1:47.44
1988	Duncan Armstrong, Australia	1:47.25
1992	Yevgeny Sadovyi, Unified Team (Rus.)	1:46.70
1996	Danyon Loader, New Zealand	1:47.63
2000	Pieter van den Hoogenband, Netherlands	1:45.35
2004	Ian Thorpe, Australia	1:44.71
2008	Michael Phelps, United States	1:42.96*
2012	Yannick Agnel, France	1:43.14
2016	Sun Yang, China	1:44.65
2020	Thomas Dean, Great Britain	1:44.22
2024	David Popovici, Romania	1:44.72

	400-Meter Freestyle	Time
1904	C. M. Daniels, United States (440 yds)	6:16.2
1908	Henry Taylor, Great Britain	5:36.8
1912	George Hodgson, Canada	5:24.4
1920	Norman Ross, United States	5:26.8
1924	Johnny Weissmuller, United States	5:04.2
1928	Albert Zorilla, Argentina	5:01.6
1932	Clarence Crabbe, United States	4:48.4
1936	Jack Medica, United States	4:44.5
1948	William Smith, United States	4:41.0
1952	Jean Boiteux, France	4:30.7
1956	Murray Rose, Australia	4:27.3
1960	Murray Rose, Australia	4:18.3
1964	Don Schollander, United States	4:12.2
1968	Mike Burton, United States	4:09.0
1972	Brad Cooper, Australia	4:00.27
1976	Brian Goodell, United States	3:51.93
1980	Vladimir Salnikov, USSR	3:51.31
1984	George DiCarlo, United States	3:51.23
1988	Uwe Dassler, E. Germany	3:46.95
1992	Yevgeny Sadovyi, Unified Team (Rus.)	3:45.00
1996	Danyon Loader, New Zealand	3:47.97
2000	Ian Thorpe, Australia	3:40.59
2004	Ian Thorpe, Australia	3:43.10
2008	Park Tae-hwan, S. Korea	3:41.86
2012	Sun Yang, China	3:40.14*
2016	Mack Horton, Australia	3:41.55
2020	Ahmed Hafnaoui, Tunisia	3:43.36
2024	Lukas Märtens, Germany	3:41.78

	800-Meter Freestyle	Time
2020	Robert Finke, United States	7:41.87
2024	Daniel Wiffen, Ireland	7:38.19*

	1500-Meter Freestyle	Time
1908	Henry Taylor, Great Britain	22:48.4
1912	George Hodgson, Canada	22:00.0
1920	Norman Ross, United States	22:23.2
1924	Andrew Charlton, Australia	20:06.6
1928	Arne Borg, Sweden	19:51.8
1932	Kusuo Kitamura, Japan	19:12.4
1936	Noboru Terada, Japan	19:13.7
1948	James McLane, United States	19:18.5
1952	Ford Konno, United States	18:30.3
1956	Murray Rose, Australia	17:58.9
1960	John Konrads, Australia	17:19.6
1964	Robert Windle, Australia	17:01.7
1968	Mike Burton, United States	16:38.9
1972	Mike Burton, United States	15:52.58
1976	Brian Goodell, United States	15:02.40
1980	Vladimir Salnikov, USSR	14:58.27
1984	Michael O'Brien, United States	15:05.20
1988	Vladimir Salnikov, USSR	15:00.40
1992	Kieren Perkins, Australia	14:43.48
1996	Kieren Perkins, Australia	14:56.40
2000	Grant Hackett, Australia	14:48.33
2004	Grant Hackett, Australia	14:43.40
2008	Oussama Mellouli, Tunisia	14:40.84
2012	Sun Yang, China	14:31.02
2016	Gregorio Paltrinieri, Italy	14:34.57
2020	Robert Finke, United States	14:39.65
2024	Bobby Finke, United States	14:30.67*

	100-Meter Backstroke	Time
1904	Walter Brack, Germany (100 yds)	1:16.8
1908	Arno Bieberstein, Germany	1:24.6
1912	Harry Hebner, United States	1:21.2
1920	Warren Kealoha, United States	1:15.2
1924	Warren Kealoha, United States	1:13.2
1928	George Kojac, United States	1:08.2
1932	Masaji Kiyokawa, Japan	1:08.6
1936	Adolph Kiefer, United States	1:05.9
1948	Allen Stack, United States	1:06.4
1952	Yoshi Oyakawa, United States	1:05.4
1956	David Theile, Australia	1:02.2
1960	David Theile, Australia	1:01.9
1968	Roland Matthes, E. Germany	0:58.7
1972	Roland Matthes, E. Germany	0:56.58
1976	John Naber, United States	0:55.49
1980	Bengt Baron, Sweden	0:56.33
1984	Rick Carey, United States	0:55.79
1988	Daichi Suzuki, Japan	0:55.05
1992	Mark Tewksbury, Canada	0:53.98
1996	Jeff Rouse, United States	0:54.10
2000	Lenny Krayzelburg, United States	0:53.72
2004	Aaron Peirsol, United States	0:54.06
2008	Aaron Peirsol, United States	0:52.54
2012	Matt Grevers, United States	0:52.16
2016	Ryan Murphy, United States	0:51.97*
2020	Evgeny Rylov, ROC	0:51.98
2024	Thomas Ceccon, Italy	0:52.00

	200-Meter Backstroke	Time
1964	Jed Graef, United States	2:10.3
1968	Roland Matthes, E. Germany	2:09.6
1972	Roland Matthes, E. Germany	2:02.82
1976	John Naber, United States	1:59.19
1980	Sandor Wladar, Hungary	2:01.93
1984	Rick Carey, United States	2:00.23
1988	Igor Polyanski, USSR	1:59.37
1992	Martin Lopez-Zubero, Spain	1:58.47
1996	Brad Bridgewater, United States	1:58.54
2000	Lenny Krayzelburg, United States	1:56.76
2004	Aaron Peirsol, United States	1:54.95
2008	Ryan Lochte, United States	1:53.94
2012	Tyler Clary, United States	1:53.41
2016	Ryan Murphy, United States	1:53.62
2020	Evgeny Rylov, ROC	1:53.27*
2024	Hubert Kós, Hungary	1:54.26

	100-Meter Breaststroke	Time
1968	Don McKenzie, United States	1:07.79
1972	Nobutaka Taguchi, Japan	1:04.94
1976	John Hencken, United States	1:03.11
1980	Duncan Goodhew, Great Britain	1:03.44
1984	Steve Lundquist, United States	1:01.65
1988	Adrian Moorhouse, Great Britain	1:02.04
1992	Nelson Diebel, United States	1:01.50
1996	Fred Deburghgraeve, Belgium	1:00.60
2000	Domenico Fioravanti, Italy	1:00.46
2004	Kosuke Kitajima, Japan	1:00.08
2008	Kosuke Kitajima, Japan	0:58.91
2012	Cameron van der Burgh, South Africa	0:58.46
2016	Adam Peaty, Great Britain	0:57.13*
2020	Adam Peaty, Great Britain	0:57.37
2024	Nicolò Martinenghi, Italy	0:59.03

	200-Meter Breaststroke	Time
1908	Frederick Holman, Great Britain	3:09.2
1912	Walter Bathe, Germany	3:01.8
1920	Hakan Malmrot, Sweden	3:04.4
1924	Robert Skelton, United States	2:56.6
1928	Yoshiyuki Tsuruta, Japan	2:48.8
1932	Yoshiyuki Tsuruta, Japan	2:45.4
1936	Tetsuo Hamuro, Japan	2:41.5
1948	Joseph Verdeur, United States	2:39.3
1952	John Davies, Australia	2:34.4
1956	Masura Furukawa, Japan	2:34.7
1960	William Mulliken, United States	2:37.4
1964	Ian O'Brien, Australia	2:27.8
1968	Felipe Muñoz, Mexico	2:28.7
1972	John Hencken, United States	2:21.55
1976	David Wilkie, Great Britain	2:15.11
1980	Robertas Zhulpa, USSR	2:15.85
1984	Victor Davis, Canada	2:13.34
1988	Jozsef Szabo, Hungary	2:13.52
1992	Mike Barrowman, United States	2:10.16
1996	Norbert Rozsa, Hungary	2:12.57
2000	Domenico Fioravanti, Italy	2:10.87
2004	Kosuke Kitajima, Japan	2:09.44
2008	Kosuke Kitajima, Japan	2:07.64
2012	Dániel Gyurta, Hungary	2:07.28
2016	Dmitriy Balandin, Kazakhstan	2:07.46
2020	Izaac Stubblety-Cook, Australia	2:06.38
2024	Léon Marchand, France	2:05.85*

	100-Meter Butterfly	Time
1968	Doug Russell, United States	0:55.9
1972	Mark Spitz, United States	0:54.27
1976	Matt Vogel, United States	0:54.35
1980	Par Arvidsson, Sweden	0:54.92
1984	Michael Gross, W. Germany	0:53.08
1988	Anthony Nesty, Suriname	0:53.00
1992	Pablo Morales, United States	0:53.32
1996	Denis Pankratov, Russia	0:52.27
2000	Lars Froelander, Sweden	0:52.00
2004	Michael Phelps, United States	0:51.25
2008	Michael Phelps, United States	0:50.58
2012	Michael Phelps, United States	0:51.21
2016	Joseph Schooling, Singapore	0:50.39
2020	Caeleb Dressel, United States	0:49.45*
2024	Kristóf Milák, Hungary	0:49.90

	200-Meter Butterfly	Time
1956	William Yorzyk, United States	2:19.3
1960	Michael Troy, United States	2:12.8
1964	Kevin J. Berry, Australia	2:06.6
1968	Carl Robie, United States	2:08.7
1972	Mark Spitz, United States	2:00.70
1976	Mike Bruner, United States	1:59.23
1980	Sergei Fesenko, USSR	1:59.76
1984	Jon Sieben, Australia	1:57.04
1988	Michael Gross, W. Germany	1:56.94
1992	Mel Stewart, United States	1:56.26
1996	Denis Pankratov, Russia	1:56.51
2000	Tom Malchow, United States	1:55.35
2004	Michael Phelps, United States	1:54.04
2008	Michael Phelps, United States	1:52.03
2012	Chad le Clos, South Africa	1:52.96
2016	Michael Phelps, United States	1:53.36
2020	Kristóf Milák, Hungary	1:51.25
2024	Léon Marchand, France	1:51.21*

	200-Meter Individual Medley	Time
1968	Charles Hickcox, United States	2:12.0
1972	Gunnar Larsson, Sweden	2:07.17
1984	Alex Baumann, Canada	2:01.42
1988	Tamas Darnyi, Hungary	2:00.17
1992	Tamas Darnyi, Hungary	2:00.76
1996	Attila Czene, Hungary	1:59.91
2000	Massimiliano Rosolino, Italy	1:58.98
2004	Michael Phelps, United States	1:57.14
2008	Michael Phelps, United States	1:54.23
2012	Michael Phelps, United States	1:54.27
2016	Michael Phelps, United States	1:54.66
2020	Wang Shun, China	1:55.00
2024	Léon Marchand, France	1:54.06*

	400-Meter Individual Medley	Time
1964	Dick Roth, United States	4:45.4
1968	Charles Hickcox, United States	4:48.4
1972	Gunnar Larsson, Sweden	4:31.98
1976	Rod Strachan, United States	4:23.68
1980	Aleksandr Sidorenko, USSR	4:22.89
1984	Alex Baumann, Canada	4:17.41
1988	Tamas Darnyi, Hungary	4:14.75
1992	Tamas Darnyi, Hungary	4:14.23
1996	Tom Dolan, United States	4:14.90
2000	Tom Dolan, United States	4:11.76
2004	Michael Phelps, United States	4:08.26
2008	Michael Phelps, United States	4:03.84
2012	Ryan Lochte, United States	4:05.18
2016	Kosuke Hagino, Japan	4:06.05
2020	Chase Kalisz, United States	4:09.42
2024	Léon Marchand, France	4:02.95*

	4x100-Meter Freestyle Relay	Time
1964	United States	3:31.2
1968	United States	3:31.7
1972	United States	3:26.42
1984	United States	3:19.03
1988	United States	3:16.53
1992	United States	3:16.74
1996	United States	3:15.41
2000	Australia	3:13.67
2004	South Africa	3:13.17
2008	United States	3:08.24*
2012	France	3:09.93
2016	United States	3:09.92
2020	United States	3:08.97
2024	United States	3:09.28

	4x200-Meter Freestyle Relay	Time
1908	Great Britain	10:55.6
1912	Australasia (Australia and New Zealand)	10:11.6
1920	United States	10:04.4
1924	United States	9:53.4
1928	United States	9:36.2
1932	Japan	8:58.4
1936	Japan	8:51.5
1948	United States	8:46.0
1952	United States	8:31.1
1956	Australia	8:23.6
1960	United States	8:10.2
1964	United States	7:52.1
1968	United States	7:52.33
1972	United States	7:35.78
1976	United States	7:23.22
1980	USSR	7:23.50
1984	United States	7:15.69
1988	United States	7:12.51
1992	Unified Team	7:11.95
1996	United States	7:14.84
2000	Australia	7:07.05
2004	United States	7:07.33
2008	United States	6:58.56*
2012	United States	6:59.70
2016	United States	7:00.66
2020	Great Britain	6:58.58
2024	Great Britain	6:59.43

	4x100-Meter Medley Relay	Time
1960	United States	4:05.4
1964	United States	3:58.4
1968	United States	3:54.9
1972	United States	3:48.16
1976	United States	3:42.22
1980	Australia	3:45.70
1984	United States	3:39.30
1988	United States	3:36.93
1992	United States	3:36.93
1996	United States	3:34.84
2000	United States	3:33.73
2004	United States	3:30.68
2008	United States	3:29.34
2012	United States	3:29.35
2016	United States	3:27.95
2020	United States	3:26.78*
2024	China	3:27.46

	10-Kilometer Marathon	Time
2008	Maarten van der Weijden, Netherlands	1:51:51.6
2012	Oussama Mellouli, Tunisia	1:49:55.1
2016	Ferry Weertman, Netherlands	1:52:59.8
2020	Florian Wellbrock, Germany	1:48:33.7
2024	Kristóf Rasovszky, Hungary	1:50:52.7

	Platform Diving	Points
1904	Dr. G. E. Sheldon, United States	112.75
1908	Hjalmar Johansson, Sweden	183.75
1912	Erik Adlerz, Sweden	73.94
1920	Clarence Pinkston, United States	100.67
1924	Albert White, United States	97.46
1928	Pete Desjardins, United States	98.74
1932	Harold Smith, United States	124.80
1936	Marshall Wayne, United States	113.58
1948	Sammy Lee, United States	130.05
1952	Sammy Lee, United States	156.28
1956	Joaquin Capilla, Mexico	152.44
1960	Robert Webster, United States	165.56
1964	Robert Webster, United States	148.58
1968	Klaus Dibiasi, Italy	164.18
1972	Klaus Dibiasi, Italy	504.12
1976	Klaus Dibiasi, Italy	600.51
1980	Falk Hoffmann, E. Germany	835.65
1984	Greg Louganis, United States	710.91
1988	Greg Louganis, United States	638.61
1992	Sun Shuwei, China	677.31
1996	Dmitri Sautin, Russia	692.34
2000	Tian Liang, China	724.53
2004	Hu Jia, China	748.08
2008	Matthew Mitcham, Australia	537.95
2012	David Boudia, United States	568.65
2016	Chen Aisen, China	545.35
2020	Cao Yuan, China	582.35
2024	Cao Yuan, China	547.50

	Springboard Diving	Points
1908	Albert Zurner, Germany	85.50
1912	Paul Guenther, Germany	79.23
1920	Louis Kuehn, United States	675.40
1924	Albert White, United States	97.46
1928	Pete Desjardins, United States	185.04
1932	Michael Galitzen, United States	161.38
1936	Richard Degener, United States	163.57
1948	Bruce Harlan, United States	163.64
1952	David Browning, United States	205.29
1956	Robert Clotworthy, United States	159.56
1960	Gary Tobian, United States	170.00
1964	Kenneth Sitzberger, United States	159.90
1968	Bernie Wrightson, United States	170.15
1972	Vladimir Vasin, USSR	594.09
1976	Phil Boggs, United States	619.52
1980	Aleksandr Portnov, USSR	905.02
1984	Greg Louganis, United States	754.41
1988	Greg Louganis, United States	730.80
1992	Mark Lenzi, United States	676.53
1996	Xiong Ni, China	701.46
2000	Xiong Ni, China	708.72
2004	Peng Bo, China	787.30
2008	He Chong, China	572.90
2012	Ilya Zakharov, Russia	555.90
2016	Cao Yuan, China	547.60
2020	Xie Siyi, China	558.75
2024	Xie Siyi, China	543.60

	Synchronized Platform Diving	Points
2004	Tian Liang & Yang Jinghui, China	383.88
2008	Lin Yue & Huo Liang, China	468.18
2012	Cao Yuan & Zhang Yanquan, China	486.78
2016	Chen Aisen & Lin Yue, China	496.98
2020	Tom Daley & Matty Lee, Great Britain	471.81
2024	Lian Junjie & Yang Hao, China	490.35

	Synchronized Springboard Diving	Points
2004	Nikolaos Siranidis & Thomas Bimis, Greece	353.34
2008	Wang Feng & Qin Kai, China	469.08
2012	Luo Yutong & Qin Kai, China	477.00
2016	Jack Laugher & Chris Mears, Great Britain	454.32
2020	Xie Siyi & Wang Zongyuan, China	467.82
2024	Long Daoyi & Wang Zongyuan, China	446.10

Swimming and Diving—Women

50-Meter Freestyle

Year	Winner	Time
1988	Kristin Otto, E. Germany	0:25.49
1992	Yang Wenyi, China	0:24.76
1996	Amy Van Dyken, United States	0:24.87
2000	Inge de Bruijn, Netherlands	0:24.32
2004	Inge de Bruijn, Netherlands	0:24.58
2008	Britta Steffen, Germany	0:24.06
2012	Ranomi Kromowidjojo, Netherlands	0:24.05
2016	Pernille Blume, Denmark	0:24.07
2020	Emma McKeon, Australia	0:23.81*
2024	Sarah Sjöström, Sweden	0:23.71

100-Meter Freestyle

Year	Winner	Time
1912	Fanny Durack, Australia	1:22.2
1920	Ethelda Bleibtrey, United States	1:13.6
1924	Ethel Lackie, United States	1:12.4
1928	Albina Osipowich, United States	1:11.0
1932	Helene Madison, United States	1:06.8
1936	Hendrika Mastenbroek, Netherlands	1:05.9
1948	Greta Andersen, Denmark	1:06.3
1952	Katalin Szoke, Hungary	1:06.8
1956	Dawn Fraser, Australia	1:02.0
1960	Dawn Fraser, Australia	1:01.2
1964	Dawn Fraser, Australia	0:59.5
1968	Jan Henne, United States	1:00.0
1972	Sandra Neilson, United States	0:58.59
1976	Kornelia Ender, E. Germany	0:55.65
1980	Barbara Krause, E. Germany	0:54.79
1984	Carrie Steinseifer, United States	0:55.92
	Nancy Hogshead, United States (tie)	0:55.92
1988	Kristin Otto, E. Germany	0:54.93
1992	Zhuang Yong, China	0:54.64
1996	Li Jingyi, China	0:54.50
2000	Inge de Bruijn, Netherlands	0:53.83
2004	Jodie Henry, Australia	0:53.84
2008	Britta Steffen, Germany	0:53.12
2012	Ranomi Kromowidjojo, Netherlands	0:53.00
2016	Simone Manuel, United States	0:52.70
	Penny Oleksiak, Canada (tie)	0:52.70
2020	Emma McKeon, Australia	0:51.96*
2024	Sarah Sjöström, Sweden	0:52.16

200-Meter Freestyle

Year	Winner	Time
1968	Debbie Meyer, United States	2:10.5
1972	Shane Gould, Australia	2:03.56
1976	Kornelia Ender, E. Germany	1:59.26
1980	Barbara Krause, E. Germany	1:58.33
1984	Mary Wayte, United States	1:59.23
1988	Heike Friedrich, E. Germany	1:57.65
1992	Nicole Haislett, United States	1:57.90
1996	Claudia Poll, Costa Rica	1:58.16
2000	Susan O'Neill, Australia	1:58.24
2004	Camelia Potec, Romania	1:58.03
2008	Federica Pellegrini, Italy	1:54.82
2012	Allison Schmitt, United States	1:53.61
2016	Katie Ledecky, United States	1:53.73
2020	Ariarne Titmus, Australia	1:53.50
2024	Mollie O'Callaghan, Australia	1:53.27*

400-Meter Freestyle

Year	Winner	Time
1924	Martha Norelius, United States	6:02.2
1928	Martha Norelius, United States	5:42.8
1932	Helene Madison, United States	5:28.5
1936	Hendrika Mastenbroek, Netherlands	5:26.4
1948	Ann Curtis, United States	5:17.8
1952	Valerie Gyenge, Hungary	5:12.1
1956	Lorraine Crapp, Australia	4:54.6
1960	Chris von Saltza, United States	4:50.6
1964	Virginia Duenkel, United States	4:43.3
1968	Debbie Meyer, United States	4:31.8
1972	Shane Gould, Australia	4:19.44
1976	Petra Thuemer, E. Germany	4:09.89
1980	Ines Diers, E. Germany	4:08.76
1984	Tiffany Cohen, United States	4:07.10
1988	Janet Evans, United States	4:03.85
1992	Dagmar Hase, Germany	4:07.18
1996	Michelle Smith, Ireland	4:07.25
2000	Brooke Bennett, United States	4:05.80
2004	Laure Manaudou, France	4:05.34
2008	Rebecca Adlington, Great Britain	4:03.22
2012	Camille Muffat, France	4:01.45
2016	Katie Ledecky, United States	3:56.46*
2020	Ariarne Titmus, Australia	3:56.69
2024	Ariarne Titmus, Australia	3:57.49

800-Meter Freestyle

Year	Winner	Time
1968	Debbie Meyer, United States	9:24.0
1972	Keena Rothhammer, United States	8:53.68
1976	Petra Thuemer, E. Germany	8:37.14
1980	Michelle Ford, Australia	8:28.90
1984	Tiffany Cohen, United States	8:24.95
1988	Janet Evans, United States	8:20.20
1992	Janet Evans, United States	8:25.52
1996	Brooke Bennett, United States	8:27.89
2000	Brooke Bennett, United States	8:19.67
2004	Ai Shibata, Japan	8:24.54
2008	Rebecca Adlington, Great Britain	8:14.10
2012	Katie Ledecky, United States	8:14.63
2016	Katie Ledecky, United States	8:04.79*
2020	Katie Ledecky, United States	8:12.57
2024	Katie Ledecky, United States	8:11.04

1500-Meter Freestyle

Year	Winner	Time
2020	Katie Ledecky, United States	15:37.34
2024	Katie Ledecky, United States	15:30.02*

100-Meter Backstroke

Year	Winner	Time
1924	Sybil Bauer, United States	1:23.2
1928	Marie Braun, Netherlands	1:22.0
1932	Eleanor Holm, United States	1:19.4
1936	Dina Senff, Netherlands	1:18.9
1948	Karen Harup, Denmark	1:14.4
1952	Joan Harrison, South Africa	1:14.3
1956	Judy Grinham, Great Britain	1:12.9
1960	Lynn Burke, United States	1:09.3
1964	Cathy Ferguson, United States	1:07.7
1968	Kaye Hall, United States	1:06.2
1972	Melissa Belote, United States	1:05.78
1976	Ulrike Richter, E. Germany	1:01.83
1980	Rica Reinisch, E. Germany	1:00.86
1984	Theresa Andrews, United States	1:02.55
1988	Kristin Otto, E. Germany	1:00.89
1992	Krisztina Egerszegi, Hungary	1:00.68
1996	Beth Botsford, United States	1:01.19
2000	Diana Mocanu, Romania	1:00.21
2004	Natalie Coughlin, United States	1:00.37
2008	Natalie Coughlin, United States	0:58.96
2012	Missy Franklin, United States	0:58.33
2016	Katinka Hosszú, Hungary	0:58.45
2020	Kaylee McKeown, Australia	0:57.47
2024	Kaylee McKeown, Australia	0:57.33

200-Meter Backstroke

Year	Winner	Time
1968	Lillian "Pokey" Watson, United States	2:24.8
1972	Melissa Belote, United States	2:19.19
1976	Ulrike Richter, E. Germany	2:13.43
1980	Rica Reinisch, E. Germany	2:11.77
1984	Jolanda de Rover, Netherlands	2:12.38
1988	Krisztina Egerszegi, Hungary	2:09.29
1992	Krisztina Egerszegi, Hungary	2:07.06
1996	Krisztina Egerszegi, Hungary	2:07.83
2000	Diana Mocanu, Romania	2:08.16
2004	Kirsty Coventry, Zimbabwe	2:09.19
2008	Kirsty Coventry, Zimbabwe	2:05.24
2012	Missy Franklin, United States	2:04.06
2016	Maya DiRado, United States	2:05.99
2020	Kaylee McKeown, Australia	2:04.68
2024	Kaylee McKeown, Australia	2:03.73*

100-Meter Breaststroke

Year	Winner	Time
1968	Djurdjica Bjedov, Yugoslavia	1:15.8
1972	Cathy Carr, United States	1:13.58
1976	Hannelore Anke, E. Germany	1:11.16
1980	Ute Geweniger, E. Germany	1:10.22
1984	Petra Van Staveren, Netherlands	1:09.88
1988	Tania Dangalakova, Bulgaria	1:07.95
1992	Yelena Rudkovskaya, Unified Team (Belarus)	1:08.00
1996	Penny Heyns, South Africa	1:07.73
2000	Megan Quann, United States	1:07.05
2004	Luo Xuejuan, China	1:06.64
2008	Leisel Jones, Australia	1:05.17
2012	Ruta Meilutyte, Lithuania	1:05.47
2016	Lilly King, United States	1:04.93
2020	Lydia Jacoby, United States	1:04.95
2024	Tatjana Smith, South Africa	1:05.28

200-Meter Breaststroke

Year	Winner	Time
1924	Lucy Morton, Great Britain	3:33.2
1928	Hilde Schrader, Germany	3:12.6
1932	Clare Dennis, Australia	3:06.3
1936	Hideko Maehata, Japan	3:03.6
1948	Nelly Van Vliet, Netherlands	2:57.2
1952	Eva Szekely, Hungary	2:51.7
1956	Ursula Happe, Germany	2:53.1
1960	Anita Lonsbrough, Great Britain	2:49.5
1964	Galina Prozumenshchikova, USSR	2:46.4
1968	Sharon Wichman, United States	2:44.4
1972	Beverly Whitfield, Australia	2:41.71
1976	Marina Koshevaia, USSR	2:33.35
1980	Lina Kachushite, USSR	2:29.54
1984	Anne Ottenbrite, Canada	2:30.38
1988	Silke Hoerner, E. Germany	2:26.71
1992	Kyoko Iwasaki, Japan	2:26.65
1996	Penny Heyns, South Africa	2:25.41

	200-Meter Breaststroke	Time
2000	Agnes Kovacs, Hungary	2:24.35
2004	Amanda Beard, United States	2:23.37
2008	Rebecca Soni, United States	2:20.22
2012	Rebecca Soni, United States	2:19.59
2016	Rie Kaneto, Japan	2:20.30
2020	Tatjana Schoenmaker, South Africa	2:18.95*
2024	Kate Douglass, United States	2:19.24

	100-Meter Butterfly	Time
1956	Shelley Mann, United States	1:11.0
1960	Carolyn Schuler, United States	1:09.5
1964	Sharon Stouder, United States	1:04.7
1968	Lynn McClements, Australia	1:05.5
1972	Mayumi Aoki, Japan	1:03.34
1976	Kornelia Ender, E. Germany	1:00.13
1980	Caren Metschuck, E. Germany	1:00.42
1984	Mary T. Meagher, United States	0:59.26
1988	Kristin Otto, E. Germany	0:59.00
1992	Qian Hong, China	0:58.62
1996	Amy Van Dyken, United States	0:59.13
2000	Inge de Bruijn, Netherlands	0:56.61
2004	Petria Thomas, Australia	0:57.72
2008	Lisbeth Trickett, Australia	0:56.73
2012	Dana Vollmer, United States	0:55.98
2016	Sarah Sjöström, Sweden	0:55.48*
2020	Maggie MacNeil, Canada	0:55.59
2024	Torri Huske, United States	0:55.59

	200-Meter Butterfly	Time
1968	Ada Kok, Netherlands	2:24.7
1972	Karen Moe, United States	2:15.57
1976	Andrea Pollack, E. Germany	2:11.41
1980	Ines Geissler, E. Germany	2:10.44
1984	Mary T. Meagher, United States	2:06.90
1988	Kathleen Nord, E. Germany	2:09.51
1992	Summer Sanders, United States	2:08.67
1996	Susan O'Neill, Australia	2:07.76
2000	Misty Hyman, United States	2:05.88
2004	Otylia Jedrzejczak, Poland	2:06.05
2008	Liu Zige, China	2:04.18
2012	Jiao Liuyang, China	2:04.06
2016	Mireia Belmonte, Spain	2:04.85
2020	Zhang Yufei, China	2:03.86
2024	Summer McIntosh, Canada	2:03.03*

	200-Meter Individual Medley	Time
1968	Claudia Kolb, United States	2:24.7
1972	Shane Gould, Australia	2:23.07
1984	Tracy Caulkins, United States	2:12.64
1988	Daniela Hunger, E. Germany	2:12.59
1992	Lin Li, China	2:11.65
1996	Michelle Smith, Ireland	2:13.93
2000	Yana Klochkova, Ukraine	2:10.68
2004	Yana Klochkova, Ukraine	2:11.14
2008	Stephanie Rice, Australia	2:08.45
2012	Ye Shiwen, China	2:07.57
2016	Katinka Hosszú, Hungary	2:06.58
2020	Yui Ohashi, Japan	2:08.52
2024	Summer McIntosh, Canada	2:06.56*

	400-Meter Individual Medley	Time
1964	Donna de Varona, United States	5:18.7
1968	Claudia Kolb, United States	5:08.5
1972	Gail Neall, Australia	5:02.97
1976	Ulrike Tauber, E. Germany	4:42.77
1980	Petra Schneider, E. Germany	4:36.29
1984	Tracy Caulkins, United States	4:39.24
1988	Janet Evans, United States	4:37.76
1992	Krisztina Egerszegi, Hungary	4:36.54
1996	Michelle Smith, Ireland	4:39.18
2000	Yana Klochkova, Ukraine	4:33.59
2004	Yana Klochkova, Ukraine	4:34.83
2008	Stephanie Rice, Australia	4:29.45
2012	Ye Shiwen, China	4:28.43
2016	Katinka Hosszú, Hungary	4:26.36*
2020	Yui Ohashi, Japan	4:32.08
2024	Summer McIntosh, Canada	4:27.71

	4x100-Meter Freestyle Relay	Time
1912	Great Britain	5:52.8
1920	United States	5:11.6
1924	United States	4:58.8
1928	United States	4:47.6
1932	United States	4:38.0
1936	Netherlands	4:36.0
1948	United States	4:29.2
1952	Hungary	4:24.4
1956	Australia	4:17.1
1960	United States	4:08.9
1964	United States	4:03.8
1968	United States	4:02.5
1972	United States	3:55.19
1976	United States	3:44.82

	4x100-Meter Freestyle Relay	Time
1980	East Germany	3:42.71
1984	United States	3:43.43
1988	East Germany	3:40.63
1992	United States	3:39.46
1996	United States	3:39.29
2000	United States	3:36.61
2004	Australia	3:35.94
2008	Netherlands	3:33.76
2012	Australia	3:33.15
2016	Australia	3:30.65
2020	Australia	3:29.69
2024	Australia	3:28.92*

	4x200-Meter Freestyle Relay	Time
1996	United States	7:59.87
2000	United States	7:57.80
2004	United States	7:53.42
2008	Australia	7:44.31
2012	United States	7:42.92
2016	United States	7:43.03
2020	China	7:40.33
2024	Australia	7:38.08*

	4x100-Meter Medley Relay	Time
1960	United States	4:41.1
1964	United States	4:33.9
1968	United States	4:28.3
1972	United States	4:20.75
1976	East Germany	4:07.95
1980	East Germany	4:06.67
1984	United States	4:08.34
1988	East Germany	4:03.74
1992	United States	4:02.54
1996	United States	4:02.88
2000	United States	3:58.30
2004	Australia	3:57.32
2008	Australia	3:52.69
2012	United States	3:52.05
2016	United States	3:53.13
2020	Australia	3:51.60
2024	United States	3:49.63*

	10-Kilometer Marathon	Time
2008	Larisa Ilchenko, Russia	1:59:27.7
2012	Éva Risztov, Hungary	1:57:38.2
2016	Sharon van Rouwendaal, Netherlands	1:56:32.1
2020	Ana Marcela Cunha, Brazil	1:59:30.8
2024	Sharon van Rouwendaal, Netherlands	2:03:34.2

	Platform Diving	Points
1912	Greta Johansson, Sweden	39.90
1920	Stefani Fryland-Clausen, Denmark	34.60
1924	Caroline Smith, United States	33.20
1928	Elizabeth B. Pinkston, United States	31.60
1932	Dorothy Poynton, United States	40.26
1936	Dorothy Poynton Hill, United States	33.93
1948	Victoria M. Draves, United States	68.87
1952	Patricia McCormick, United States	79.37
1956	Patricia McCormick, United States	84.85
1960	Ingrid Kramer, Germany	91.28
1964	Lesley Bush, United States	99.80
1968	Milena Duchkova, Czechoslovakia	109.59
1972	Ulrika Knape, Sweden	390.00
1976	Elena Vaytsekhouskaya, USSR	406.59
1980	Martina Jaschke, E. Germany	596.25
1984	Zhou Jihong, China	435.51
1988	Xu Yanmei, China	445.20
1992	Fu Mingxia, China	461.43
1996	Fu Mingxia, China	521.58
2000	Laura Wilkinson, United States	543.75
2004	Chantelle Newbery, Australia	590.31
2008	Chen Ruolin, China	447.70
2012	Chen Ruolin, China	422.30
2016	Ren Qian, China	439.25
2020	Quan Hongchan, China	466.20
2024	Quan Hongchan, China	425.60

	Springboard Diving	Points
1920	Aileen Riggin, United States	539.90
1924	Elizabeth Becker, United States	474.50
1928	Helen Meany, United States	78.62
1932	Georgia Coleman, United States	87.52
1936	Marjorie Gestring, United States	89.27
1948	Victoria M. Draves, United States	108.74
1952	Patricia McCormick, United States	147.30
1956	Patricia McCormick, United States	142.36
1960	Ingrid Kramer, Germany	155.81
1964	Ingrid Engel-Kramer, Germany	145.00
1968	Sue Gossick, United States	150.77
1972	Micki King, United States	450.03

	Springboard Diving	Points
1976	Jenni Chandler, United States	506.19
1980	Irina Kalinina, USSR	725.91
1984	Sylvie Bernier, Canada	530.70
1988	Gao Min, China	580.23
1992	Gao Min, China	572.40
1996	Fu Mingxia, China	547.68
2000	Fu Mingxia, China	609.42
2004	Guo Jingjing, China	633.15
2008	Guo Jingjing, China	415.35
2012	Wu Minxia, China	414.00
2016	Shi Tingmao, China	406.05
2020	Shi Tingmao, China	383.50
2024	Chen Yiwen, China	376.00

	Synchronized Platform Diving	Points
2004	Lao Lishi & Li Ting, China	352.14
2008	Wang Xin & Chen Ruolin, China	363.54
2012	Chen Ruolin & Wang Hao, China	368.40
2016	Chen Ruolin & Liu Huixia, China	354.00
2020	Chen Yuxi & Zhang Jiaqi, China	363.78
2024	Chen Yuxi & Quan Hongchan, China	359.10

	Synchronized Springboard Diving	Points
2004	Wu Minxia & Guo Jingjing, China	336.90
2008	Guo Jingjing & Wu Minxia, China	343.50
2012	He Zi & Wu Minxia, China	346.20
2016	Wu Minxia & Shi Tingmao, China	345.60
2020	Shi Tingmao & Wang Han, China	326.40
2024	Chang Yani & Chen Yiwen, China	337.68

Swimming—Mixed

	4x100-Meter Medley Relay	Time
2020	Great Britain	3:37.58
2024	United States	3:37.43*

Tennis

Men's Singles

1896 John Boland, Great Britain
1900 Hugh Lawrence Doherty, Great Britain
1904 Beals Wright, United States
1908 Josiah George Ritchie, Great Britain
1912 Charles Lyndhurst Winslow, South Africa
1920 Louis Raymond, South Africa
1924 Vincent Richards, United States
1988 Miloslav Mecir, Czechoslovakia
1992 Marc Rosset, Switzerland
1996 Andre Agassi, United States
2000 Yevgeny Kafelnikov, Russia
2004 Nicolas Massu, Chile
2008 Rafael Nadal, Spain
2012 Andy Murray, Great Britain
2016 Andy Murray, Great Britain
2020 Alexander Zverev, Germany
2024 Novak Djokovic, Serbia

Men's Doubles

1896 John Boland, Great Britain & Friedrick Traun, Germany
1900 Hugh Lawrence Doherty & Reginald Frank Doherty, Great Britain
1904 Edgar Leonard & Beals Wright, U.S.
1908 George Whiteside Hillyard & Reginald Frank Doherty, Great Britain
1912 Harry Austin Kitson & Charles Lyndhurst Winslow, South Africa
1920 Noel Turnbull & Maxwell Woosnam, Great Britain
1924 Vincent Richards & Francis Townsend Hunter, U.S.
1988 Kenneth Flach & Robert A. Seguso, United States
1992 Boris Becker & Michael Stich, Germany
1996 Mark Woodforde & Todd Woodbridge, Australia
2000 Sebastien Lareau & Daniel Nestor, Canada
2004 Fernando Gonzales & Nicolas Massu, Chile
2008 Roger Federer & Stanislas Wawrinka, Switzerland
2012 Mike Bryan & Bob Bryan, United States
2016 Marc López & Rafael Nadal, Spain
2020 Nikola Mektić & Mate Pavić, Croatia
2024 Matthew Ebden & John Peers, Australia

Women's Singles

1900 Charlotte Cooper, Great Britain
1908 Dorothy Katherine Chambers, Great Britain
1912 Marguerite Broquedis, France
1920 Suzanne Lenglen, France
1924 Helen Wills, United States
1988 Steffi Graf, W. Germany
1992 Jennifer Capriati, United States
1996 Lindsay Davenport, United States
2000 Venus Williams, United States
2004 Justine Henin-Hardenne, Belgium
2008 Elena Dementieva, Russia
2012 Serena Williams, United States
2016 Monica Puig, Puerto Rico
2020 Belinda Bencic, Switzerland
2024 Zheng Qinwen, China

Women's Doubles

1920 Winifred Margaret McNair & Kathleen McKane, Great Britain
1924 Hazel Virginia Wightman & Helen Wills, United States
1988 Pam Shriver & Zina Garrison, United States
1992 Gigi Fernandez & Mary Joe Fernandez, United States
1996 Gigi Fernandez & Mary Joe Fernandez, United States
2000 Venus Williams & Serena Williams, United States
2004 Ting Li & Tian Tian Sun, China
2008 Serena Williams & Venus Williams, United States
2012 Serena Williams & Venus Williams, United States
2016 Ekaterina Makarova & Elena Vesnina, Russia
2020 Barbora Krejčíková & Kateřina Siniaková, Czech Republic
2024 Sara Errani & Jasmine Paolini, Italy

Mixed Doubles

2012 Victoria Azarenka & Max Mirnyi, Belarus
2016 Bethanie Mattek-Sands & Jack Sock, United States
2020 Anastasia Pavlyuchenkova & Andrey Rublev, ROC
2024 Kateřina Siniaková & Tomáš Macháč, Czechia

Track and Field—Men

	100-Meter Run	Time
1896	Thomas Burke, United States	0:12.0
1900	Francis Jarvis, United States	0:11.0
1904	Archie Hahn, United States	0:11.0
1908	Reginald Walker, South Africa	0:10.8
1912	Ralph Craig, United States	0:10.8
1920	Charles Paddock, United States	0:10.8
1924	Harold Abrahams, Great Britain	0:10.6
1928	Percy Williams, Canada	0:10.8
1932	Eddie Tolan, United States	0:10.3
1936	Jesse Owens, United States	0:10.3
1948	Harrison Dillard, United States	0:10.3
1952	Lindy Remigino, United States	0:10.4
1956	Bobby Morrow, United States	0:10.5
1960	Armin Hary, Germany	0:10.2
1964	Bob Hayes, United States	0:10.0
1968	Jim Hines, United States	0:09.95
1972	Valery Borzov, USSR	0:10.14
1976	Hasely Crawford, Trinidad and Tobago	0:10.06
1980	Allan Wells, Great Britain	0:10.25
1984	Carl Lewis, United States	0:09.99
1988	Carl Lewis, United States	0:09.92
1992	Linford Christie, Great Britain	0:09.96
1996	Donovan Bailey, Canada	0:09.84
2000	Maurice Greene, United States	0:09.87
2004	Justin Gatlin, United States	0:09.85
2008	Usain Bolt, Jamaica	0:09.69
2012	Usain Bolt, Jamaica	0:09.63*
2016	Usain Bolt, Jamaica	0:09.81
2020	Marcell Jacobs, Italy	0:09:80
2024	Noah Lyles, United States	0:09.79

	200-Meter Run	Time
1900	Walter Tewksbury, United States	0:22.2
1904	Archie Hahn, United States	0:21.6
1908	Robert Kerr, Canada	0:22.6
1912	Ralph Craig, United States	0:21.7
1920	Allan Woodring, United States	0:22.0
1924	Jackson Scholz, United States	0:21.6
1928	Percy Williams, Canada	0:21.8
1932	Eddie Tolan, United States	0:21.2
1936	Jesse Owens, United States	0:20.7
1948	Mel Patton, United States	0:21.1

	200-Meter Run	Time
1952	Andrew Stanfield, United States	0:20.7
1956	Bobby Morrow, United States	0:20.6
1960	Livio Berruti, Italy	0:20.5
1964	Henry Carr, United States	0:20.3
1968	Tommie Smith, United States	0:19.83
1972	Valery Borzov, USSR	0:20.00
1976	Donald Quarrie, Jamaica	0:20.23
1980	Pietro Mennea, Italy	0:20.19
1984	Carl Lewis, United States	0:19.80
1988	Joe DeLoach, United States	0:19.75
1992	Mike Marsh, United States	0:20.01
1996	Michael Johnson, United States	0:19.32
2000	Konstantinos Kenteris, Greece	0:20.09
2004	Shawn Crawford, United States	0:19.79
2008	Usain Bolt, Jamaica	0:19.30*
2012	Usain Bolt, Jamaica	0:19.32
2016	Usain Bolt, Jamaica	0:19.78
2020	Andre De Grasse, Canada	0:19.62
2024	Letsile Tebogo, Botswana	0:19.46

	400-Meter Run	Time
1896	Thomas Burke, United States	0:54.2
1900	Maxwell Long, United States	0:49.4
1904	Harry Hillman, United States	0:49.2
1908	Wyndham Halswelle, Gr. Brit. (walkover)	0:50.0
1912	Charles Reidpath, United States	0:48.2
1920	Bevil Rudd, South Africa	0:49.6
1924	Eric Liddell, Great Britain	0:47.6
1928	Ray Barbuti, United States	0:47.8
1932	William Carr, United States	0:46.2
1936	Archie Williams, United States	0:46.5
1948	Arthur Wint, Jamaica	0:46.2
1952	George Rhoden, Jamaica	0:45.9
1956	Charles Jenkins, United States	0:46.7
1960	Otis Davis, United States	0:44.9
1964	Michael Larrabee, United States	0:45.1
1968	Lee Evans, United States	0:43.86
1972	Vincent Matthews, United States	0:44.66
1976	Alberto Juantorena, Cuba	0:44.26
1980	Viktor Markin, USSR	0:44.60
1984	Alonzo Babers, United States	0:44.27
1988	Steve Lewis, United States	0:43.87
1992	Quincy Watts, United States	0:43.50
1996	Michael Johnson, United States	0:43.49
2000	Michael Johnson, United States	0:43.84
2004	Jeremy Wariner, United States	0:44.00
2008	LaShawn Merritt, United States	0:43.75
2012	Kirani James, Grenada	0:43.94
2016	Wayde van Niekerk, South Africa	0:43.03*
2020	Steven Gardiner, Bahamas	0:43.85
2024	Quincy Hall, United States	0:43.40

	800-Meter Run	Time
1896	Edwin Flack, Australia	2:11.0
1900	Alfred Tysoe, Great Britain	2:01.2
1904	James Lightbody, United States	1:56.0
1908	Mel Sheppard, United States	1:52.8
1912	James "Ted" Meredith, United States	1:51.9
1920	Albert Hill, Great Britain	1:53.4
1924	Douglas Lowe, Great Britain	1:52.4
1928	Douglas Lowe, Great Britain	1:51.8
1932	Thomas Hampson, Great Britain	1:49.8
1936	John Woodruff, United States	1:52.9
1948	Mal Whitfield, United States	1:49.2
1952	Mal Whitfield, United States	1:49.2
1956	Tom Courtney, United States	1:47.7
1960	Peter Snell, New Zealand	1:46.3
1964	Peter Snell, New Zealand	1:45.1
1968	Ralph Doubell, Australia	1:44.3
1972	Dave Wottle, United States	1:45.9
1976	Alberto Juantorena, Cuba	1:43.50
1980	Steve Ovett, Great Britain	1:45.40
1984	Joaquim Cruz, Brazil	1:43.00
1988	Paul Ereng, Kenya	1:43.45
1992	William Tanui, Kenya	1:43.66
1996	Vebjørn Rodal, Norway	1:42.58
2000	Nils Schumann, Germany	1:45.08
2004	Yuriy Borzakovskiy, Russia	1:44.45
2008	Wilfred Bungei, Kenya	1:44.65
2012	David Lekuta Rudisha, Kenya	1:40.91*
2016	David Lekuta Rudisha, Kenya	1:42.15
2020	Emmanuel Korir, Kenya	1:45.06
2024	Emmanuel Wanyonyi, Kenya	1:41.19

	1500-Meter Run	Time
1896	Edwin Flack, Australia	4:33.2
1900	Charles Bennett, Great Britain	4:06.2
1904	James Lightbody, United States	4:05.4
1908	Mel Sheppard, United States	4:03.4
1912	Arnold Jackson, Great Britain	3:56.8
1920	Albert Hill, Great Britain	4:01.8
1924	Paavo Nurmi, Finland	3:53.6
1928	Harry Larva, Finland	3:53.2
1932	Luigi Beccali, Italy	3:51.2
1936	Jack Lovelock, New Zealand	3:47.8
1948	Henry Eriksson, Sweden	3:49.8
1952	Joseph Barthel, Luxembourg	3:45.2
1956	Ron Delany, Ireland	3:41.2
1960	Herb Elliott, Australia	3:35.6
1964	Peter Snell, New Zealand	3:38.1
1968	Kipchoge Keino, Kenya	3:34.91
1972	Pekka Vasala, Finland	3:36.33
1976	John Walker, New Zealand	3:39.17
1980	Sebastian Coe, Great Britain	3:38.4
1984	Sebastian Coe, Great Britain	3:32.53
1988	Peter Rono, Kenya	3:35.96
1992	Fermin Cacho Ruiz, Spain	3:40.12
1996	Noureddine Morceli, Algeria	3:35.78
2000	Noah Ngeny, Kenya	3:32.07
2004	Hicham El Guerrouj, Morocco	3:34.18
2008	Asbel Kiprop, Kenya[1]	3:33.11
2012	Taoufik Makhloufi, Algeria	3:34.08
2016	Matthew Centrowitz, United States	3:50.00
2020	Jakob Ingebrigtsen, Norway	3:28.32
2024	Cole Hocker, United States	3:27.65*

(1) Originally won by Rashid Ramzi, Bahrain, who was stripped of the gold in 2009 due to doping.

	3000-Meter Steeplechase	Time
1920	Percy Hodge, Great Britain	10:00.4
1924	Ville Ritola, Finland	9:33.6
1928	Toivo Loukola, Finland	9:21.8
1932	Volmari Iso-Hollo, Finland (about 3,450 m; extra lap by error)	10:33.4
1936	Volmari Iso-Hollo, Finland	9:03.8
1948	Tore Sjöstrand, Sweden	9:04.6
1952	Horace Ashenfelter, United States	8:45.4
1956	Chris Brasher, Great Britain	8:41.2
1960	Zdzislaw Krzyszkowiak, Poland	8:34.2
1964	Gaston Roelants, Belgium	8:30.8
1968	Amos Biwott, Kenya	8:51.0
1972	Kipchoge Keino, Kenya	8:23.64
1976	Anders Garderud, Sweden	8:08.02
1980	Bronislaw Malinowski, Poland	8:09.7
1984	Julius Korir, Kenya	8:11.80
1988	Julius Kariuki, Kenya	8:05.51
1992	Matthew Birir, Kenya	8:08.84
1996	Joseph Keter, Kenya	8:07.12
2000	Reuben Kosgei, Kenya	8:21.43
2004	Ezekiel Kemboi, Kenya	8:05.81
2008	Brimin Kiprop Kirpruto, Kenya	8:10.34
2012	Ezekiel Kemboi, Kenya	8:18.56
2016	Conseslus Kipruto, Kenya	8:03.28*
2020	Soufiane El Bakkali, Morocco	8:08.90
2024	Soufiane El Bakkali, Morocco	8:06.05

	5000-Meter Run	Time
1912	Hannes Kolehmainen, Finland	14:36.6
1920	Joseph Guillemot, France	14:55.6
1924	Paavo Nurmi, Finland	14:31.2
1928	Ville Ritola, Finland	14:38.0
1932	Lauri Lehtinen, Finland	14:30.0
1936	Gunnar Höckert, Finland	14:22.2
1948	Gaston Reiff, Belgium	14:17.6
1952	Emil Zatopek, Czechoslovakia	14:06.6
1956	Vladimir Kuts, USSR	13:39.6
1960	Murray Halberg, New Zealand	13:43.4
1964	Bob Schul, United States	13:48.8
1968	Mohamed Gammoudi, Tunisia	14:05.0
1972	Lasse Viren, Finland	13:26.4
1976	Lasse Viren, Finland	13:24.76
1980	Miruts Yifter, Ethiopia	13:20.91
1984	Said Aouita, Morocco	13:05.59
1988	John Ngugi, Kenya	13:11.70
1992	Dieter Baumann, Germany	13:12.52
1996	Venuste Niyongabo, Burundi	13:07.96
2000	Million Wolde, Ethiopia	13:35.49
2004	Hicham El Guerrouj, Morocco	13:14.39
2008	Kenenisa Bekele, Ethiopia	12:57.82*
2012	Mo Farah, Great Britain	13:41.66
2016	Mo Farah, Great Britain	13:03.30
2020	Joshua Cheptegei, Uganda	12:58.15
2024	Jakob Ingebrigtsen, Norway	13:13.66

10,000-Meter Run

		Time
1912	Hannes Kolehmainen, Finland	31:20.8
1920	Paavo Nurmi, Finland	31:45.8
1924	Ville Ritola, Finland	30:23.2
1928	Paavo Nurmi, Finland	30:18.8
1932	Janusz Kusocinski, Poland	30:11.4
1936	Ilmari Salminen, Finland	30:15.4
1948	Emil Zatopek, Czechoslovakia	29:59.6
1952	Emil Zatopek, Czechoslovakia	29:17.0
1956	Vladimir Kuts, USSR	28:45.6
1960	Pyotr Bolotnikov, USSR	28:32.2
1964	Billy Mills, United States	28:24.4
1968	Naftali Temu, Kenya	29:27.4
1972	Lasse Viren, Finland	27:38.4
1976	Lasse Viren, Finland	27:40.38
1980	Miruts Yifter, Ethiopia	27:42.7
1984	Alberto Cova, Italy	27:47.54
1988	Brahim Boutayeb, Morocco	27:21.46
1992	Khalid Skah, Morocco	27:46.70
1996	Haile Gebrselassie, Ethiopia	27:07.34
2000	Haile Gebrselassie, Ethiopia	27:18.20
2004	Kenenisa Bekele, Ethiopia	27:05.10
2008	Kenenisa Bekele, Ethiopia	27:01.17
2012	Mo Farah, Great Britain	27:30.42
2016	Mo Farah, Great Britain	27:05.17
2020	Selemon Barega, Ethiopia	27:43.22
2024	Joshua Cheptegei, Uganda	26:43.14*

Marathon

		Time
1896	Spyridon Louis, Greece	2:58:50
1900	Michel Theato, France	2:59:45.0
1904	Thomas Hicks, United States	3:28:53.0
1908	John Hayes, United States	2:55:18.4
1912	Kenneth McArthur, South Africa	2:36:54.8
1920	Hannes Kolehmainen, Finland	2:32:35.8
1924	Albin Stenroos, Finland	2:41:22.6
1928	Boughera El Ouafi, France	2:32.57
1932	Juan Zabala, Argentina	2:31:36
1936	Kee-chung Sohn, Japan[1]	2:29:19.2
1948	Delfo Cabrera, Argentina	2:34:51.6
1952	Emil Zatopek, Czechoslovakia	2:23:03.2
1956	Alain Mimoun, France	2:25:00.0
1960	Abebe Bikila, Ethiopia	2:15:16.2
1964	Abebe Bikila, Ethiopia	2:12:11.2
1968	Mamo Wolde, Ethiopia	2:20:26.4
1972	Frank Shorter, United States	2:12:19.8
1976	Waldemar Cierpinski, E. Germany	2:09:55.0
1980	Waldemar Cierpinski, E. Germany	2:11:03.0
1984	Carlos Lopes, Portugal	2:09:21
1988	Gelindo Bordin, Italy	2:10:32
1992	Hwang Young-cho, S. Korea	2:13:23
1996	Josia Thugwane, South Africa	2:12:36
2000	Gezahegne Abera, Ethiopia	2:10:11
2004	Stefano Baldini, Italy	2:10:55
2008	Samuel Kamau Wanjiru, Kenya	2:06:32
2012	Stephen Kiprotich, Uganda	2:08:01
2016	Eliud Kipchoge, Kenya	2:08:44
2020	Eliud Kipchoge, Kenya	2:08:38
2024	Tamirat Tola, Ethiopia	2:06:26*

(1) Korean runner who competed under Japanese name Kitei Son.

4x100-Meter Relay

		Time
1912	Great Britain	0:42.4
1920	United States	0:42.2
1924	United States	0:41.0
1928	United States	0:41.0
1932	United States	0:40.0
1936	United States	0:39.8
1948	United States	0:40.6
1952	United States	0:40.1
1956	United States	0:39.5
1960	Germany (U.S. disqualified)	0:39.5
1964	United States	0:39.0
1968	United States	0:38.24
1972	United States	0:38.19
1976	United States	0:38.33
1980	USSR	0:38.26
1984	United States	0:37.83
1988	USSR (U.S. disqualified)	0:38.19
1992	United States	0:37.40
1996	Canada	0:37.69
2000	United States	0:37.61
2004	Great Britain	0:38.07
2008	Trinidad and Tobago[1]	0:38.06
2012	Jamaica	0:36.84*
2016	Jamaica	0:37.27
2020	Italy	0:37.50
2024	Canada	0:37.50

(1) Due to team member Nesta Carter's doping, Jamaica was stripped of the victory in 2017.

4x400-Meter Relay

		Time
1908	United States	3:29.4
1912	United States	3:16.6
1920	Great Britain	3:22.2
1924	United States	3:16.0
1928	United States	3:14.2
1932	United States	3:08.2
1936	Great Britain	3:09.0
1948	United States	3:10.4
1952	Jamaica	3:03.9
1956	United States	3:04.8
1960	United States	3:02.2
1964	United States	3:00.7
1968	United States	2:56.16
1972	Kenya	2:59.8
1976	United States	2:58.65
1980	USSR	3:01.1
1984	United States	2:57.91
1988	United States	2:56.16
1992	United States	2:55.74
1996	United States	2:55.99
2000	Nigeria[1]	2:58.68
2004	United States	2:55.91
2008	United States	2:55.39
2012	The Bahamas	2:56.72
2016	United States	2:57.30
2020	United States	2:55.70
2024	United States	2:54.43*

(1) The U.S. was stripped of the medal in 2012 after team member Antonio Pettigrew admitted to doping.

20-Kilometer Walk

		Time
1956	Leonid Spirin, USSR	1:31:27.4
1960	Vladimir Golubnichy, USSR	1:34:07.2
1964	Kenneth Matthews, Great Britain	1:29:34.0
1968	Vladimir Golubnichy, USSR	1:33:58.4
1972	Peter Frenkel, E. Germany	1:26:42.4
1976	Daniel Bautista, Mexico	1:24:40.6
1980	Maurizio Damilano, Italy	1:23:35.5
1984	Ernesto Canto, Mexico	1:23:13
1988	Jozef Pribilinec, Czechoslovakia	1:19.57
1992	Daniel Plaza Montero, Spain	1:21:45
1996	Jefferson Perez, Ecuador	1:20:07
2000	Robert Korzeniowski, Poland	1:18:59
2004	Ivano Brugnetti, Italy	1:19:40
2008	Valeriy Borchin, Russia	1:19:01
2012	Chen Ding, China	1:18:46*
2016	Wang Zhen, China	1:19:44
2020	Massimo Stano, Italy	1:21:05
2024	Brian Pintado, Ecuador	1:18:55

50-Kilometer Walk

		Time
1932	Thomas "Tommy" Green, Great Britain	4:50.10
1936	Harold Whitlock, Great Britain	4:30:41.4
1948	John Ljunggren, Sweden	4:41.52
1952	Giuseppe Dordoni, Italy	4:28:07.8
1956	Norman Read, New Zealand	4:30:42.8
1960	Donald Thompson, Great Britain	4:25:30
1964	Abdon Pamich, Italy	4:11:12.4
1968	Christoph Höhne, E. Germany	4:20:13.6
1972	Bernd Kannenberg, W. Germany	3:56:11.6
1980	Hartwig Gauder, E. Germany	3:49:24.0
1984	Raúl González, Mexico	3:47:26
1988	Vyacheslav Ivanenko, USSR	3:38.29
1992	Andrey Perlov, Unified Team (Rus.)	3:50:13
1996	Robert Korzeniowski, Poland	3:43:30
2000	Robert Korzeniowski, Poland	3:42:22
2004	Robert Korzeniowski, Poland	3:38:46
2008	Alex Schwazer, Italy	3:37:09
2012	Jared Tallent, Australia[1]	3:36:53*
2016	Matej Tóth, Slovakia	3:40:58
2020	Dawid Tomala, Poland	3:50:08

(1) Russia's Sergey Kirdyapkin was stripped of the gold medal in 2016 for doping.

110-Meter Hurdles

		Time
1896	Thomas Curtis, United States	0:17.6
1900	Alvin Kraenzlein, United States	0:15.4
1904	Frederick Schule, United States	0:16.0
1908	Forrest Smithson, United States	0:15.0
1912	Frederick Kelly, United States	0:15.1
1920	Earl Thomson, Canada	0:14.8
1924	Daniel Kinsey, United States	0:15.0
1928	Sydney Atkinson, South Africa	0:14.8
1932	George Saling, United States	0:14.6
1936	Forrest Towns, United States	0:14.2
1948	William Porter, United States	0:13.9
1952	Harrison Dillard, United States	0:13.7
1956	Lee Calhoun, United States	0:13.5

110-Meter Hurdles

Year	Champion	Time
1960	Lee Calhoun, United States	0:13.8
1964	Hayes Jones, United States	0:13.6
1968	Willie Davenport, United States	0:13.33
1972	Rod Milburn, United States	0:13.24
1976	Guy Drut, France	0:13:30
1980	Thomas Munkelt, E. Germany	0:13.39
1984	Roger Kingdom, United States	0:13.20
1988	Roger Kingdom, United States	0:12.98
1992	Mark McKoy, Canada	0:13.12
1996	Allen Johnson, United States	0:12.95
2000	Anier Garcia, Cuba	0:13.00
2004	Liu Xiang, China	0:12.91*
2008	Dayron Robles, Cuba	0:12.93
2012	Aries Merritt, United States	0:12.92
2016	Omar McLeod, Jamaica	0:13.05
2020	Hansle Parchment, Jamaica	0:13.04
2024	Grant Holloway, United States	0:12.99

400-Meter Hurdles

Year	Champion	Time
1900	Walter Tewksbury, United States	0:57.6
1904	Harry Hillman, United States	0:53.0
1908	Charles Bacon, United States	0:55.0
1920	Frank Loomis, United States	0:54.0
1924	F. Morgan Taylor, United States	0:52.6
1928	David, Lord Burghley, Great Britain	0:53.4
1932	Bob Tisdall, Ireland	0:51.7
1936	Glenn Hardin, United States	0:52.4
1948	Roy Cochran, United States	0:51.1
1952	Charles Moore, United States	0:50.8
1956	Glenn Davis, United States	0:50.1
1960	Glenn Davis, United States	0:49.3
1964	Rex Cawley, United States	0:49.6
1968	David Hemery, Great Britain	0:48.12
1972	John Akii-Bua, Uganda	0:47.82
1976	Edwin Moses, United States	0:47.64
1980	Volker Beck, E. Germany	0:48.70
1984	Edwin Moses, United States	0:47.75
1988	Andre Phillips, United States	0:47.19
1992	Kevin Young, United States	0:46.78
1996	Derrick Adkins, United States	0:47.54
2000	Angelo Taylor, United States	0:47.50
2004	Félix Sánchez, Dominican Republic	0:47.63
2008	Angelo Taylor, United States	0:47.25
2012	Félix Sánchez, Dominican Republic	0:47.63
2016	Kerron Clement, United States	0:47.73
2020	Karsten Warholm, Norway	0:45.94*
2024	Rai Benjamin, United States	0:46.46

Note: Event not held in 1912.

Discus Throw

Year	Champion	Dist.	
1896	Robert Garrett, United States	29.15m	(95' 7")
1900	Rudolf Bauer, Hungary	36.04m	(118' 3")
1904	Martin Sheridan, United States	39.28m	(128' 10")
1908	Martin Sheridan, United States	40.89m	(134' 1")
1912	Armas Taipale, Finland	45.21m	(148' 3")
1920	Elmer Niklander, Finland	44.68m	(146' 7")
1924	Clarence "Bud" Houser, U.S.	46.15m	(151' 4")
1928	Clarence "Bud" Houser, U.S.	47.32m	(155' 3")
1932	John Anderson, United States	49.49m	(162' 4")
1936	Ken Carpenter, United States	50.48m	(165' 7")
1948	Adolfo Consolini, Italy	52.78m	(173' 2")
1952	Sim Iness, United States	55.03m	(180' 6")
1956	Al Oerter, United States	56.36m	(184' 11")
1960	Al Oerter, United States	59.18m	(194' 2")
1964	Al Oerter, United States	61.00m	(200' 1")
1968	Al Oerter, United States	64.78m	(212' 6")
1972	Ludvik Danek, Czechoslovakia	64.40m	(211' 3")
1976	Mac Wilkins, United States	67.50m	(221' 5")
1980	Viktor Rashchupkin, USSR	66.64m	(218' 8")
1984	Rolf Danneberg, W. Germany	66.60m	(218' 6")
1988	Jürgen Schult, E. Germany	68.82m	(225' 9")
1992	Romas Ubartas, Lithuania	65.12m	(213' 8")
1996	Lars Riedel, Germany	69.40m	(227' 8")
2000	Virgilijus Alekna, Lithuania	69.30m	(227' 4")
2004	Virgilijus Alekna, Lithuania	69.89m	(228' 9¾")
2008	Gerd Kanter, Estonia	68.82m	(225' 9½")
2012	Robert Harting, Germany	68.27m	(224')
2016	Christoph Harting, Germany	68.37m	(224' 3¾")
2020	Daniel Ståhl, Sweden	68.90m	(226' ½")
2024	Rojé Stona, Jamaica	70.00m	(229' 8")*

Hammer Throw

Year	Champion	Dist.	
1900	John Flanagan, United States	49.73m	(163' 1")
1904	John Flanagan, United States	51.23m	(168' 1")
1908	John Flanagan, United States	51.92m	(170' 4")
1912	Matt McGrath, United States	54.74m	(179' 7")
1920	Pat Ryan, United States	52.875m	(173' 5¾")
1924	Fred Tootell, United States	53.295m	(174' 10")
1928	Patrick O'Callaghan, Ireland	51.39m	(168' 7")
1932	Patrick O'Callaghan, Ireland	53.92m	(176' 11")
1936	Karl Hein, Germany	56.49m	(185' 4")
1948	Imre Németh, Hungary	56.07m	(183' 11½")
1952	József Csérmák, Hungary	60.34m	(197' 11")
1956	Harold Connolly, United States	63.19m	(207' 3")
1960	Vasily Rudenkov, USSR	67.10m	(202' 0")
1964	Romuald Klim, USSR	69.74m	(228' 10")
1968	Gyula Zsivótzky, Hungary	73.36m	(240' 8")
1972	Anatoly Bondarchuk, USSR	75.50m	(247' 8")
1976	Yuri Sedykh, USSR	77.52m	(254' 4")
1980	Yuri Sedykh, USSR	81.80m	(268' 4")
1984	Juha Tiainen, Finland	78.08m	(256' 2")
1988	Sergei Litvinov, USSR	84.80m	(278' 2")*
1992	Andrey Abduvaliyev, Unified Team	82.54m	(270' 9")
1996	Balázs Kiss, Hungary	81.24m	(266' 6")
2000	Szymon Ziolkowski, Poland	80.02m	(262' 6")
2004	Koji Murofushi, Japan	82.91m	(272')
2008	Primoz Kozmus, Slovenia	82.02m	(269' 1")
2012	Krisztián Pars, Hungary	80.59m	(264' 5")
2016	Dilshod Nazarov, Tajikistan	78.68m	(258' 1¾")
2020	Wojciech Nowicki, Poland	82.52m	(270' 8¾")
2024	Ethan Katzberg, Canada	84.12m	(275' 11¾")

High Jump

Year	Champion	Height	
1896	Ellery Clark, United States	1.81m	(5' 11¼")
1900	Irving Baxter, United States	1.90m	(6' 2¾")
1904	Samuel Jones, United States	1.80m	(5' 11")
1908	Harry Porter, United States	1.90m	(6' 2¾")
1912	Alma Richards, United States	1.93m	(6' 4")
1920	Richmond Landon, United States	1.94m	(6' 4¼")
1924	Harold Osborn, United States	1.98m	(6' 6")
1928	Robert "Bob" King, United States	1.94m	(6' 4¼")
1932	Duncan McNaughton, Canada	1.97m	(6' 5½")
1936	Cornelius Johnson, United States	2.03m	(6' 8")
1948	John Winter, Australia	1.98m	(6' 6")
1952	Walter Davis, United States	2.04m	(6' 8¼")
1956	Charles Dumas, United States	2.12m	(6' 11½")
1960	Robert Shavlakadze, USSR	2.16m	(7' 1")
1964	Valery Brumel, USSR	2.18m	(7' 1¾")
1968	Dick Fosbury, United States	2.24m	(7' 4¼")
1972	Jüri Tarmak, USSR	2.23m	(7' 3¾")
1976	Jacek Wszola, Poland	2.25m	(7' 4½")
1980	Gerd Wessig, E. Germany	2.36m	(7' 8¾")
1984	Dietmar Mögenburg, W. Germany	2.35m	(7' 8½")
1988	Gennadi Avdeyenko, USSR	2.38m	(7' 9¾")
1992	Javier Sotomayor, Cuba	2.34m	(7' 8")
1996	Charles Austin, United States	2.39m	(7' 10")*
2000	Sergey Klyugin, Russia	2.35m	(7' 8½")
2004	Stefan Holm, Sweden	2.36m	(7' 8¾")
2008	Andrey Silnov, Russia	2.36m	(7' 8¾")
2012	Erik Kynard, United States[1]	2.33m	(7' 7¾")
2016	Derek Drouin, Canada	2.38m	(7' 9¾")
2020	Mutaz Essa Barshim, Qatar & Gianmarco Tamberi, Italy (tie)	2.37m	(7' 9¼")
2024	Hamish Kerr, New Zealand	2.36m	(7' 8¾")

(1) Ivan Ukhov, Russia, was stripped of the gold medal in 2019 due to doping.

Javelin Throw

Year	Champion	Dist.	
1908	Eric Lemming, Sweden	54.82m	(179' 10")
1912	Eric Lemming, Sweden	60.64m	(198' 11")
1920	Jonni Myyrä, Finland	65.78m	(215' 9¾")
1924	Jonni Myyrä, Finland	62.96m	(206' 7")
1928	Erik Lundkvist, Sweden	66.60m	(218' 6")
1932	Matti Järvinen, Finland	72.71m	(238' 6½")
1936	Gerhard Stöck, Germany	71.84m	(235' 8")
1948	Kaj Tapio Rautavaara, Finland	69.77m	(228' 11")
1952	Cy Young, United States	73.78m	(242' 1")
1956	Egil Danielsen, Norway	85.71m	(281' 2½")
1960	Viktor Tsybulenko, USSR	84.64m	(277' 8")
1964	Pauli Nevala, Finland	82.66m	(271' 2")
1968	Janis Lusis, USSR	90.10m	(295' 7")
1972	Klaus Wolfermann, W. Germany	90.48m	(296' 10")
1976	Miklós Németh, Hungary	94.58m	(310' 4")
1980	Dainis Kula, USSR	91.20m	(299' 2")
1984	Arto Härkönen, Finland	86.76m	(284' 8")
1988	Tapio Korjus, Finland	84.28m	(276' 6")
1992	Jan Zelezny, Czechoslovakia	89.66m	(294' 2")
1996	Jan Zelezny, Czech Republic	88.16m	(289' 3")
2000	Jan Zelezny, Czech Republic	90.17m	(295' 9½")
2004	Andreas Thorkildsen, Norway	86.50m	(283' 10")
2008	Andreas Thorkildsen, Norway	90.57m	(297' 1¾")
2012	Keshorn Walcott, Trinidad & Tobago	84.58m	(277' 6")
2016	Thomas Röhler, Germany	90.30m	(296' 3")

Javelin Throw		Dist.	
2020	Neeraj Chopra, India	87.58m	(287' 4")
2024	Arshad Nadeem, Pakistan	92.97m	(305' ¼")*

Long Jump		Dist.	
1896	Ellery Clark, United States	6.35m	(20' 10")
1900	Alvin Kraenzlein, United States	7.18m	(23' 6¾")
1904	Meyer Prinstein, United States	7.34m	(24' 1")
1908	Frank Irons, United States	7.48m	(24' 6½")
1912	Albert Gutterson, United States	7.60m	(24' 11¼")
1920	William Petersson, Sweden	7.15m	(23' 5½")
1924	William DeHart Hubbard, U.S.	7.45m	(24' 5¼")
1928	Ed Hamm, United States	7.73m	(25' 4½")
1932	Edward Gordon, United States	7.64m	(25' ¾")
1936	Jesse Owens, United States	8.06m	(26' 5½")
1948	Willie Steele, United States	7.82m	(25' 8")
1952	Jerome Biffle, United States	7.57m	(24' 10")
1956	Gregory Bell, United States	7.83m	(25' 8¼")
1960	Ralph Boston, United States	8.12m	(26' 7¾")
1964	Lynn Davies, Great Britain	8.07m	(26' 5¾")
1968	Bob Beamon, United States	8.90m	(29' 2½")*
1972	Randy Williams, United States	8.24m	(27' ½")
1976	Arnie Robinson, United States	8.35m	(27' 4¾")
1980	Lutz Dombrowski, E. Germany	8.54m	(28' ¼")
1984	Carl Lewis, United States	8.54m	(28' ¼")
1988	Carl Lewis, United States	8.72m	(28' 7½")
1992	Carl Lewis, United States	8.67m	(28' 5½")
1996	Carl Lewis, United States	8.50m	(27' 10¾")
2000	Ivan Pedroso, Cuba	8.55m	(28' ¾")
2004	Dwight Phillips, United States	8.59m	(28' 2¼")
2008	Irving Saladino, Panama	8.34m	(27' 4¼")
2012	Greg Rutherford, Great Britain	8.31m	(27' 3¼")
2016	Jeff Henderson, United States	8.38m	(27' 6")
2020	Miltiadis Tentoglou, Greece	8.41m	(27' 7")
2024	Miltiadis Tentoglou, Greece	8.48m	(27' 10")

Pole Vault		Height	
1896	William Welles Hoyt, United States	3.30m	(10' 10")
1900	Irving Baxter, United States	3.30m	(10' 10")
1904	Charles Dvorak, United States	3.50m	(11' 6")
1908	Edward Cooke, United States	3.71m	(12' 2")
	Alfred Gilbert, United States (tie)	3.71m	(12' 2")
1912	Harry Stoddard Babcock, U.S.	3.95m	(12' 11½")
1920	Frank Foss, United States	4.09m	(13' 5")
1924	Lee Barnes, United States	3.95m	(12' 11½")
1928	Sabin Carr, United States	4.20m	(13' 9¼")
1932	Bill Miller, United States	4.31m	(14' 1¾")
1936	Earle Meadows, United States	4.35m	(14' 3¼")
1948	Guinn Smith, United States	4.30m	(14' 1¼")
1952	Robert Richards, United States	4.55m	(14' 11¼")
1956	Robert Richards, United States	4.56m	(14' 11½")
1960	Don Bragg, United States	4.70m	(15' 5")
1964	Fred Hansen, United States	5.10m	(16' 8¾")
1968	Bob Seagren, United States	5.40m	(17' 8½")
1972	Wolfgang Nordwig, E. Germany	5.50m	(18' ½")
1976	Tadeusz Slusarski, Poland	5.50m	(18' ½")
1980	Wladyslaw Kozakiewicz, Poland	5.78m	(18' 11½")
1984	Pierre Quinon, France	5.75m	(18' 10¼")
1988	Sergei Bubka, USSR	5.90m	(19' 4¼")
1992	Maksim Tarasov, Unified Team (Rus.)	5.80m	(19' ¼")
1996	Jean Galfione, France	5.92m	(19' 5")
2000	Nick Hysong, United States	5.90m	(19' 4¼")
2004	Timothy Mack, United States	5.95m	(19' 6¼")
2008	Steve Hooker, Australia	5.96m	(19' 6¾")
2012	Renaud Lavillenie, France	5.97m	(19' 7")
2016	Thiago Braz, Brazil	6.03m	(19' 9½")
2020	Armand Duplantis, Sweden	6.02m	(19' 9¼")
2024	Armand Duplantis, Sweden	6.25m	(20' 6")*

Shot Put		Dist.	
1896	Robert Garrett, United States	11.22m	(36' 9¾")
1900	Richard Sheldon, United States	14.10m	(46' 3¼")
1904	Ralph Rose, United States	14.81m	(48' 7")
1908	Ralph Rose, United States	14.21m	(46' 7½")
1912	Pat McDonald, United States	15.34m	(50' 4")
1920	Ville Pörhölä, Finland	14.81m	(48' 7¼")
1924	Clarence "Bud" Houser, United States	14.99m	(49' 2¼")
1928	John Kuck, United States	15.87m	(52' ¾")
1932	Leo Sexton, United States	16.00m	(52' 6")
1936	Hans Woellke, Germany	16.20m	(53' 1¾")
1948	Wilbur Thompson, United States	17.12m	(56' 2")
1952	W. Parry O'Brien, United States	17.41m	(57' 1½")
1956	W. Parry O'Brien, United States	18.57m	(60' 11¼")
1960	Bill Nieder, United States	19.68m	(64' 6¾")
1964	Dallas Long, United States	20.33m	(66' 8½")
1968	Randy Matson, United States	20.54m	(67' 4¾")
1972	Wladyslaw Komar, Poland	21.18m	(69' 6")
1976	Udo Beyer, E. Germany	21.05m	(69' ¾")
1980	Vladimir Kiselyov, USSR	21.35m	(70' ½")
1984	Alessandro Andrei, Italy	21.26m	(69' 9")
1988	Ulf Timmermann, E. Germany	22.47m	(73' 8¾")
1992	Michael Stulce, United States	21.70m	(71' 2½")
1996	Randy Barnes, United States	21.62m	(70' 11¼")
2000	Arsi Harju, Finland	21.29m	(69' 10¼")
2004	Adam Nelson, United States[1]	21.16m	(69' 5¼")
2008	Tomasz Majewski, Poland	21.51m	(70' 6¾")
2012	Tomasz Majewski, Poland	21.89m	(71' 9¾")
2016	Ryan Crouser, United States	22.52m	(73' 10½")
2020	Ryan Crouser, United States	23.30m	(76' 5¼")*
2024	Ryan Crouser, United States	22.90m	(75' 1½")

(1) Yuriy Bilonog, Ukraine, was stripped of the gold medal in 2012 due to doping.

Triple Jump		Dist.	
1896	James Connolly, United States	13.71m	(44' 11¾")
1900	Meyer Prinstein, United States	14.47m	(47' 5¾")
1904	Meyer Prinstein, United States	14.35m	(47' 1")
1908	Tim Ahearne, Gr. Brit.-Ireland	14.92m	(48' 11½")
1912	Gustaf Lindblom, Sweden	14.76m	(48' 5")
1920	Vilho Tuulos, Finland	14.505m	(47' 7")
1924	Anthony Winter, Australia	15.525m	(50' 11¼")
1928	Mikio Oda, Japan	15.21m	(49' 11")
1932	Chuhei Nambu, Japan	15.72m	(51' 7")
1936	Naoto Tajima, Japan	16.00m	(52' 6")
1948	Arne Ahman, Sweden	15.40m	(50' 6¼")
1952	Adhemar Ferreira da Silva, Brazil	16.22m	(53' 2¾")
1956	Adhemar Ferreira da Silva, Brazil	16.35m	(53' 7¾")
1960	Jozef Schmidt, Poland	16.81m	(55' 1½")
1964	Jozef Schmidt, Poland	16.85m	(55' 3½")
1968	Viktor Saneyev, USSR	17.39m	(57' ¾")
1972	Viktor Saneyev, USSR	17.35m	(56' 11¼")
1976	Viktor Saneyev, USSR	17.29m	(56' 8¾")
1980	Jaak Uudmäe, USSR	17.35m	(56' 11")
1984	Al Joyner, United States	17.26m	(56' 7½")
1988	Khristo Markov, Bulgaria	17.61m	(57' 9½")
1992	Mike Conley, United States	18.17m	(59' 7½")(w)
1996	Kenny Harrison, United States	18.09m	(59' 4¼")*
2000	Jonathan Edwards, Great Britain	17.71m	(58' 1¼")
2004	Christian Olsson, Sweden	17.79m	(58' 4½")
2008	Nelson Evora, Portugal	17.67m	(57' 11¾")
2012	Christian Taylor, United States	17.81m	(58' 5¼")
2016	Christian Taylor, United States	17.86m	(58' 7¼")
2020	Pedro Pichardo, Portugal	17.98m	(58' 11¾")
2024	Jordan Díaz, Spain	17.86m	(58' 7¼")

Decathlon		Points
1904	Thomas F. Kiely, Ireland	6,036
1912	Jim Thorpe, United States[1]	8,412.995
1920	Helge Lovland, Norway	6,804.355
1924	Harold Osborn, United States	7,710.775
1928	Paavo Yrjölä, Finland	8,053.29
1932	James Bausch, United States	8,462.23
1936	Glenn Morris, United States	7,900
1948	Robert Mathias, United States	7,139
1952	Robert Mathias, United States	7,887
1956	Milton Campbell, United States	7,937
1960	Rafer Johnson, United States	8,392
1964	Willi Holdorf, Germany	7,887
1968	Bill Toomey, United States	8,193
1972	Nikolai Avilov, USSR	8,454
1976	Bruce Jenner, United States	8,618
1980	Daley Thompson, Great Britain	8,495
1984	Daley Thompson, Great Britain	8,797
1988	Christian Schenk, E. Germany	8,488
1992	Robert Zmelik, Czechoslovakia	8,611
1996	Dan O'Brien, United States	8,824
2000	Erki Nool, Estonia	8,641
2004	Roman Sebrle, Czech Republic	8,893
2008	Bryan Clay, United States	8,791
2012	Ashton Eaton, United States	8,869
2016	Ashton Eaton, United States	8,893
2020	Damian Warner, Canada	9,018*
2024	Markus Rooth, Norway	8,796

Note: Event not held in 1908. (1) Thorpe had been stripped of his medal for playing pro baseball prior to the Olympics. The Intl. Olympic Committee in 1982 posthumously restored him as co-champion, and in 2022 named him the sole gold medal winner in both pentathlon and decathlon.

Track and Field—Women

100-Meter Run

	100-Meter Run	Time
1928	Elizabeth Robinson, United States	0:12.2
1932	Stella Walsh, Poland	0:11.9
1936	Helen Stephens, United States	0:11.5
1948	Fanny Blankers-Koen, Netherlands	0:11.9
1952	Marjorie Jackson, Australia	0:11.5
1956	Betty Cuthbert, Australia	0:11.5
1960	Wilma Rudolph, United States	0:11.0
1964	Wyomia Tyus, United States	0:11.4
1968	Wyomia Tyus, United States	0:11.08
1972	Renate Stecher, E. Germany	0:11.07
1976	Annegret Richter, W. Germany	0:11.08
1980	Lyudmila Kondratyeva, USSR	0:11.06
1984	Evelyn Ashford, United States	0:10.97
1988	Florence Griffith-Joyner, United States	0:10.54
1992	Gail Devers, United States	0:10.82
1996	Gail Devers, United States	0:10.94
2000	No winner[1]	NA
2004	Yuliya Nestsiarenka, Belarus	0:10.93
2008	Shelly-Ann Fraser, Jamaica	0:10.78
2012	Shelly-Ann Fraser-Pryce, Jamaica	0:10.75
2016	Elaine Thompson, Jamaica	0:10.71
2020	Elaine Thompson-Herah, Jamaica	0:10.61*
2024	Julien Alfred, Saint Lucia	0:10.72

(1) Marion Jones, U.S., was stripped of her gold medal in 2007 due to doping; the Intl. Olympic Committee declined to award the medal to the runner-up, who was also suspected of doping.

200-Meter Run

	200-Meter Run	Time
1948	Fanny Blankers-Koen, Netherlands	0:24.4
1952	Marjorie Jackson, Australia	0:23.7
1956	Betty Cuthbert, Australia	0:23.4
1960	Wilma Rudolph, United States	0:24.0
1964	Edith McGuire, United States	0:23.0
1968	Irena Szewinska, Poland	0:22.5
1972	Renate Stecher, E. Germany	0:22.40
1976	Bärbel Eckert, E. Germany	0:22.37
1980	Bärbel Wöckel, E. Germany	0:22.03
1984	Valerie Brisco-Hooks, United States	0:21.81
1988	Florence Griffith-Joyner, United States	0:21.34*
1992	Gwen Torrence, United States	0:21.81
1996	Marie-Jose Perec, France	0:22.12
2000	Pauline Davis-Thompson, The Bahamas[1]	0:22.27
2004	Veronica Campbell, Jamaica	0:22.05
2008	Veronica Campbell-Brown, Jamaica	0:21.74
2012	Allyson Felix, United States	0:21.88
2016	Elaine Thompson, Jamaica	0:21.78
2020	Elaine Thompson-Herah, Jamaica	0:21.53
2024	Gabrielle Thomas, United States	0:21.83

(1) Originally won by Marion Jones, U.S., who was stripped of the gold in 2007 due to doping.

400-Meter Run

	400-Meter Run	Time
1964	Betty Cuthbert, Australia	0:52.0
1968	Colette Besson, France	0:52.0
1972	Monika Zehrt, E. Germany	0:51.08
1976	Irena Szewinska, Poland	0:49.29
1980	Marita Koch, E. Germany	0:48.88
1984	Valerie Brisco-Hooks, United States	0:48.83
1988	Olga Bryzgina, USSR	0:48.65
1992	Marie-Jose Perec, France	0:48.83
1996	Marie-Jose Perec, France	0:48.25
2000	Cathy Freeman, Australia	0:49.11
2004	Tonique Williams-Darling, The Bahamas	0:49.41
2008	Christine Ohuruogu, Great Britain	0:49.62
2012	Sanya Richards-Ross, United States	0:49.55
2016	Shaunae Miller, The Bahamas	0:49.44
2020	Shaunae Miller-Uibo, The Bahamas	0:48.36
2024	Marileidy Paulino, Dominican Republic	0:48.17*

800-Meter Run

	800-Meter Run	Time
1928	Lina Radke, Germany	2:16.8
1960	Lyudmila Shevtsova, USSR	2:04.3
1964	Ann Packer, Great Britain	2:01.1
1968	Madeline Manning, United States	2:00.9
1972	Hildegard Falck, W. Germany	1:58.55
1976	Tatyana Kazankina, USSR	1:54.94
1980	Nadezhda Olizarenko, USSR	1:53.43*
1984	Doina Melinte, Romania	1:57.60
1988	Sigrun Wodars, E. Germany	1:56.10
1992	Ellen Van Langen, Netherlands	1:55.54
1996	Svetlana Masterkova, Russia	1:57.73
2000	Maria Mutola, Mozambique	1:56.15
2004	Kelly Holmes, Great Britain	1:56.38
2008	Pamela Jelimo, Kenya	1:54.87
2012	Caster Semenya, South Africa[1]	1:57.23
2016	Caster Semenya, South Africa	1:55.28
2020	Athing Mu, United States	1:55.21
2024	Keely Hodgkinson, Great Britain	1:56.72

(1) Russia's Mariya Savinova was stripped of the gold medal for doping.

1500-Meter Run

	1500-Meter Run	Time
1972	Lyudmila Bragina, USSR	4:01.04
1976	Tatyana Kazankina, USSR	4:05.48
1980	Tatyana Kazankina, USSR	3:56.06
1984	Gabriella Dorio, Italy	4:03.25
1988	Paula Ivan, Romania	3:53.96
1992	Hassiba Boulmerka, Algeria	3:55.30
1996	Svetlana Masterkova, Russia	4:00.83
2000	Nouria Merah-Benida, Algeria	4:05.10
2004	Kelly Holmes, Great Britain	3:57.90
2008	Nancy Jebet Langat, Kenya	4:00.23
2012	Gamze Bulut, Turkey[1]	4:10.40
2016	Faith Chepngetich Kipyegon, Kenya	4:08.92
2020	Faith Chepngetich Kipyegon, Kenya	3:53.11
2024	Faith Kipyegon, Kenya	3:51.29*

(1) Turkey's Asli Cakir Alpetkin was stripped of the gold medal for doping.

3000-Meter Run

	3000-Meter Run	Time
1984	Maricica Puica, Romania	8:35.96
1988	Tatyana Samolenko, USSR	8:26.53*
1992	Elena Romanova, Unified Team (Rus.)	8:46.04

3000-Meter Steeplechase

	3000-Meter Steeplechase	Time
2008	Gulnara Galkina-Samitova, Russia	8:58.81
2012	Habiba Ghribi, Tunisia[1]	9:08.37
2016	Ruth Jebet, Bahrain	8:59.75
2020	Peruth Chemutai, Uganda	9:01.45
2024	Winfred Yavi, Bahrain	8:52.76*

(1) Russia's Yuliya Zaripova was stripped of the gold medal in 2016 for doping.

5000-Meter Run

	5000-Meter Run	Time
1996	Wang Junxia, China	14:59.88
2000	Gabriela Szabo, Romania	14:40.79
2004	Meseret Defar, Ethiopia	14:45.65
2008	Tirunesh Dibaba, Ethiopia	15:41.40
2012	Meseret Defar, Ethiopia	15:04.25
2016	Vivian Cheruiyot, Kenya	14:26.17*
2020	Sifan Hassan, Netherlands	14:36.79
2024	Beatrice Chebet, Kenya	14:28.56

10,000-Meter Run

	10,000-Meter Run	Time
1988	Olga Bondarenko, USSR	31:05.21
1992	Derartu Tulu, Ethiopia	31:06.02
1996	Fernanda Ribeiro, Portugal	31:01.63
2000	Derartu Tulu, Ethiopia	30:17.49
2004	Xing Huina, China	30:24.36
2008	Tirunesh Dibaba, Ethiopia	29:54.66
2012	Tirunesh Dibaba, Ethiopia	30:20.75
2016	Almaz Ayana, Ethiopia	29:17.45*
2020	Sifan Hassan, Netherlands	29:55.32
2024	Beatrice Chebet, Kenya	30:43.25

Marathon

	Marathon	Time
1984	Joan Benoit, United States	2:24:52
1988	Rosa Mota, Portugal	2:25:40
1992	Valentina Yegorova, Unified Team (Rus.)	2:32:41
1996	Fatuma Roba, Ethiopia	2:26:05
2000	Naoko Takahashi, Japan	2:23:14
2004	Mizuki Noguchi, Japan	2:26:20
2008	Constantina Tomescu, Romania	2:26:44
2012	Tiki Gelana, Ethiopia	2:23:07
2016	Jemima Jelagat Sumgong, Kenya	2:24:04
2020	Peres Jepchirchir, Kenya	2:27:20
2024	Sifan Hassan, Netherlands	2:22:55*

4x100-Meter Relay

	4x100-Meter Relay	Time
1928	Canada	0:48.4
1932	United States	0:46.9
1936	United States	0:46.9
1948	Netherlands	0:47.5
1952	United States	0:45.9
1956	Australia	0:44.5
1960	United States	0:44.5
1964	Poland	0:43.6
1968	United States	0:42.8
1972	West Germany	0:42.81

4x100-Meter Relay

		Time
1976	East Germany	0:42.55
1980	East Germany	0:41.60
1984	United States	0:41.65
1988	United States	0:41.98
1992	United States	0:42.11
1996	United States	0:41.95
2000	The Bahamas	0:41.95
2004	Jamaica	0:41.73
2008	Russia	0:42.31
2012	United States	0:40.82*
2016	United States	0:41.01
2020	Jamaica	0:41.02
2024	United States	0:41.78

4x400-Meter Relay

		Time
1972	East Germany	3:23.0
1976	East Germany	3:19.23
1980	USSR	3:20.2
1984	United States	3:18.29
1988	USSR	3:15.18*
1992	Unified Team	3:20.20
1996	United States	3:20.91
2000	United States[1]	3:22.62
2004	United States[2]	3:19.01
2008	United States	3:18.54
2012	United States	3:16.87
2016	United States	3:19.06
2020	United States	3:16.85
2024	United States	3:15.27

(1) Due to team member Marion Jones's doping, the U.S. was stripped of the victory in 2008. Jones's teammates won an appeal in 2010 to have their medals restored. (2) Team member Crystal Cox was stripped of her gold medal in 2012 due to doping.

20-Kilometer Walk

		Time
2000	Wang Liping, China	1:29:05
2004	Athanasia Tsoumeleka, Greece	1:29:12
2008	Olga Kaniskina, Russia	1:26:31
2012	Shijie Qieyang, China[1]	1:25:16*
2016	Liu Hong, China	1:28:35
2020	Antonella Palmisano, Italy	1:29:12
2024	Yang Jiayu, China	1:25:54

(1) Russia's Elena Lashmanova was stripped of the gold medal for doping in 2022.

100-Meter Hurdles

		Time
1972	Annelie Ehrhardt, E. Germany	0:12.59
1976	Johanna Schaller, E. Germany	0:12.77
1980	Vera Komisova, USSR	0:12.56
1984	Benita Fitzgerald-Brown, United States	0:12.84
1988	Yordanka Donkova, Bulgaria	0:12.38
1992	Paraskevi Patoulidou, Greece	0:12.64
1996	Ludmila Engquist, Sweden	0:12.58
2000	Olga Shishigina, Kazakhstan	0:12.65
2004	Joanna Hayes, United States	0:12.37
2008	Dawn Harper, United States	0:12.54
2012	Sally Pearson, Australia	0:12.35*
2016	Brianna Rollins, United States	0:12.48
2020	Jasmine Camacho-Quinn, Puerto Rico	0:12.37
2024	Masai Russell, United States	0:12.33

400-Meter Hurdles

Year	Athlete	Time
1984	Nawal El Moutawakel, Morocco	0:54.61
1988	Debra Flintoff-King, Australia	0:53.17
1992	Sally Gunnell, Great Britain	0:53.23
1996	Deon Hemmings, Jamaica	0:52.82
2000	Irina Privalova, Russia	0:53.02
2004	Faní Halkia, Greece	0:52.82
2008	Melaine Walker, Jamaica	0:52.64
2012	Natalya Antyukh, Russia	0:52.70
2016	Dalilah Muhammad, United States	0:53.13
2020	Sydney McLaughlin, United States	0:51.46
2024	Sydney McLaughlin-Levrone, United States	0:50.37*

Discus Throw

		Dist.	
1928	Halina Konopacka, Poland	39.62m	(130' 0")
1932	Lillian Copeland, United States	40.58m	(133' 2")
1936	Gisela Mauermayer, Germany	47.63m	(156' 3")
1948	Micheline Ostermeyer, France	41.92m	(137' 6")
1952	Nina Ponomareva, USSR	51.42m	(168' 8")
1956	Olga Fikotová, Czechoslovakia	53.69m	(176' 1¾")
1960	Nina Ponomareva, USSR	55.10m	(180' 9")
1964	Tamara Press, USSR	57.27m	(187' 10¾")
1968	Lia Manoliu, Romania	58.28m	(191' 2")
1972	Faina Melnik, USSR	66.62m	(218' 7")
1976	Evelin Jahl, E. Germany	69.00m	(226' 4")
1980	Evelin Jahl, E. Germany	69.96m	(229' 6")
1984	Ria Stalman, Netherlands	65.36m	(214' 5")
1988	Martina Hellmann, E. Germany	72.30m	(237' 2")*
1992	Maritza Martén, Cuba	70.06m	(229' 10")
1996	Ilke Wyludda, Germany	69.66m	(228' 6")
2000	Ellina Zvereva, Belarus	68.40m	(224' 5")
2004	Natalya Sadova, Russia	67.02m	(219' 8¾")
2008	Stephanie Brown Trafton, U.S.	64.74m	(212' 4¾")
2012	Sandra Perkovic, Croatia	69.11m	(226' 9")
2016	Sandra Perkovic, Croatia	69.21m	(227' ¾")
2020	Valarie Allman, United States	68.98m	(226' 3¾")
2024	Valarie Allman, United States	69.50m	(228' ¼")

Hammer Throw

		Dist.	
2000	Kamila Skolimowska, Poland	71.16m	(233' 5¾")
2004	Olga Kuzenkova, Russia	75.02m	(246' 1")
2008	Yipsi Moreno, Cuba[1]	75.20m	(246' 8¾")
2012	Anita Wlodarczyk, Poland[2]	77.60m	(254' 7")
2016	Anita Wlodarczyk, Poland	82.29m	(269' 11¾")*
2020	Anita Wlodarczyk, Poland	78.48m	(257' 5¾")
2024	Camryn Rogers, Canada	76.97m	(252' 6¼")

(1) Belarus's Aksana Miankova was stripped of the gold medal for doping in 2016. (2) Russia's Tatyana Lysenko was stripped of the gold medal for doping in 2016.

High Jump

		Height	
1928	Ethel Catherwood, Canada	1.59m	(5' 2½")
1932	Jean Shiley, United States	1.67m	(5' 5½")
1936	Ibolya Csák, Hungary	1.60m	(5' 3")
1948	Alice Coachman, United States	1.68m	(5' 6")
1952	Esther Brand, South Africa	1.67m	(5' 5¾")
1956	Mildred McDaniel, United States	1.76m	(5' 9¼")
1960	Iolanda Balas, Romania	1.85m	(6' ¾")
1964	Iolanda Balas, Romania	1.90m	(6' 2¾")
1968	Miloslava Rezková, Czech.	1.82m	(5' 11½")
1972	Ulrike Meyfarth, W. Germany	1.92m	(6' 3½")
1976	Rosemarie Ackermann, E. Germany	1.93m	(6' 4")
1980	Sara Simeoni, Italy	1.97m	(6' 5½")
1984	Ulrike Meyfarth, W. Germany	2.02m	(6' 7½")
1988	Louise Ritter, United States	2.03m	(6' 8")
1992	Heike Henkel, Germany	2.02m	(6' 7½")
1996	Stefka Kostadinova, Bulgaria	2.05m	(6' 8¾")
2000	Yelena Yelesina, Russia	2.01m	(6' 7")
2004	Yelena Slesarenko, Russia	2.06m	(6' 9")*
2008	Tia Hellebaut, Belgium	2.05m	(6' 8¾")
2012	Anna Chicherova, Russia	2.05m	(6' 8¾")
2016	Ruth Beitia, Spain	1.97m	(6' 5½")
2020	Mariya Lasitskene, ROC	2.04m	(6' 8¼")
2024	Yaroslava Mahuchikh, Ukraine	2.00m	(6' 6¾")

Javelin Throw

		Dist.	
1932	"Babe" Didrikson, United States	43.68m	(143' 4")
1936	Tilly Fleischer, Germany	45.18m	(148' 3")
1948	Herma Bauma, Austria	45.57m	(149' 6")
1952	Dana Zátopková, Czechoslovakia	50.47m	(165' 7")
1956	Inese Jaunzeme, USSR	53.86m	(176' 8")
1960	Elvira Ozolina, USSR	55.98m	(183' 8")
1964	Mihaela Penes, Romania	60.54m	(198' 7")
1968	Angéla Németh, Hungary	60.36m	(198' 0")
1972	Ruth Fuchs, E. Germany	63.88m	(209' 7")
1976	Ruth Fuchs, E. Germany	65.94m	(216' 4")
1980	Maria Colón, Cuba	68.40m	(224' 5")
1984	Tessa Sanderson, Great Britain	69.56m	(228' 2")
1988	Petra Felke, E. Germany	74.68m	(245' 0")
1992	Silke Renk, Germany	68.34m	(224' 2")
1996	Heli Rantanen, Finland	67.94m	(222' 11")
2000	Trine Hattestad, Norway	68.91m	(226' 1")
2004	Osleidys Menendez, Cuba	71.53m	(234' 8")*
2008	Barbora Spotáková, Czech Republic	71.42m	(234' ¾")
2012	Barbora Spotáková, Czech Republic	69.55m	(228' 2¼")
2016	Sara Kolak, Croatia	66.18m	(217' 1½")
2020	Liu Shiying, China	66.34m	(217' 7¾")
2024	Haruka Kitaguchi, Japan	65.80m	(215' 10½")

Note: New records were kept after javelin was modified in 1999.

Long Jump

		Dist.	
1948	Olga Gyarmati, Hungary	5.69m	(18' 8")
1952	Yvette Williams, New Zealand	6.24m	(20' 5¼")
1956	Elzbieta Krzesinska, Poland	6.35m	(20' 10")
1960	Vera Krepkina, USSR	6.37m	(20' 10¾")
1964	Mary Rand, Great Britain	6.76m	(22' 2¼")
1968	Viorica Viscopoleanu, Romania	6.82m	(22' 4½")
1972	Heidemarie Rosendahl, W. Germany	6.78m	(22' 3")
1976	Angela Voigt, E. Germany	6.72m	(22' ¾")
1980	Tatyana Kolpakova, USSR	7.06m	(23' 2")
1984	Anisoara Cusmir-Stanciu, Romania	6.96m	(22' 10")
1988	Jackie Joyner-Kersee, United States	7.40m	(24' 3½")*
1992	Heike Drechsler, Germany	7.14m	(23' 5¼")
1996	Chioma Ajunwa, Nigeria	7.12m	(23' 4¼")
2000	Heike Drechsler, Germany	6.99m	(22' 11¼")
2004	Tatyana Lebedeva, Russia	7.07m	(23' 2½")
2008	Maurren Higa Maggi, Brazil	7.04m	(23' 1¼")
2012	Brittney Reese, United States	7.12m	(23' 4¼")

	Long Jump	Dist.	
2016	Tianna Bartoletta, United States	7.17m	(23' 6¼")
2020	Malaika Mihambo, Germany	7.00m	(22' 11½")
2024	Tara Davis-Woodhall, United States	7.10m	(23' 3½")

	Pole Vault	Height	
2000	Stacy Dragila, United States	4.60m	(15' 1")
2004	Elena Isinbayeva, Russia	4.91m	(16' 1¼')
2008	Elena Isinbayeva, Russia	5.05m	(16' 6¾")*
2012	Jennifer Suhr, United States	4.75m	(15' 7")
2016	Ekateríni Stefanídi, Greece	4.85m	(15' 11")
2020	Katie Nageotte, United States	4.90m	(16' 1")
2024	Nina Kennedy, Australia	4.90m	(16' 1")

	Shot Put	Dist.	
1948	Micheline Ostermeyer, France	13.75m	(45' 1½")
1952	Galina Zybina, USSR	15.28m	(50' 1½")
1956	Tamara Tyshkevich, USSR	16.59m	(54' 5¼")
1960	Tamara Press, USSR	17.32m	(56' 10")
1964	Tamara Press, USSR	18.14m	(59' 6¼")
1968	Margitta Gummel, E. Germany	19.61m	(64' 4")
1972	Nadezhda Chizhova, USSR	21.03m	(69' 0")
1976	Ivanka Khristova, Bulgaria	21.16m	(69' 5¼")
1980	Ilona Slupianek, E. Germany	22.41m	(73' 6¼")*
1984	Claudia Losch, W. Germany	20.48m	(67' 2")
1988	Natalya Lisovskaya, USSR	22.24m	(72' 11¾")
1992	Svetlana Krivelyova, Unified Team	21.06m	(69' 1¼")
1996	Astrid Kumbernuss, Germany	20.56m	(67' 5½")
2000	Yanina Karolchik, Belarus	20.56m	(67' 5½")
2004	Yumileidi Cumbá, Cuba	19.59m	(64' 3¼")

	Shot Put	Dist.	
2008	Valerie Vili, New Zealand	20.56m	(67' 5½")
2012	Valerie Adams, New Zealand	20.70m	(67' 11")
2016	Michelle Carter, United States	20.63m	(67' 8¼")
2020	Gong Lijiao, China	20.58m	(67' 6¼")
2024	Yemisi Ogunleye, Germany	20.00m	(65' 7½")

	Triple Jump	Dist.	
1996	Inessa Kravets, Ukraine	15.33m	(50' 3½")
2000	Tereza Marinova, Bulgaria	15.20m	(49' 10½")
2004	Francoise Mbango Etone, Cameroon	15.30m	(50' 2¼")
2008	Francoise Mbango Etone, Cameroon	15.39m	(50' 6")
2012	Olga Rypakova, Kazakhstan	14.98m	(49' 1¾")
2016	Caterine Ibargüen, Colombia	15.17m	(49' 9¼")
2020	Yulimar Rojas, Venezuela	15.67m	(51' 5")*
2024	Thea LaFond, Dominica	15.02m	(49' 3½")

	Heptathlon	Points
1984	Glynis Nunn, Australia	6,390
1988	Jackie Joyner-Kersee, United States	7,291*
1992	Jackie Joyner-Kersee, United States	7,044
1996	Ghada Shouaa, Syria	6,780
2000	Denise Lewis, Great Britain	6,584
2004	Carolina Kluft, Sweden	6,952
2008	Natallia Dobrynska, Ukraine	6,733
2012	Jessica Ennis, Great Britain	6,955
2016	Nafissatou Thiam, Belgium	6,810
2020	Nafissatou Thiam, Belgium	6,791
2024	Nafissatou Thiam, Belgium	6,880

Track and Field—Mixed

	4x400-Meter Relay	
2020	Poland	3:09.87
2024	Netherlands	3:07.43*

	Marathon Race Walk Relay	
2024	Álvaro Martín & María Pérez, Spain	2:50:31

2022 Winter Olympic Games

Beijing, China, Feb. 4-20, 2022

Nearly, 3,000 (2,871) athletes representing 91 nations met in Beijing, China, to compete in a record 109 events in 15 disciplines during the XXIV Olympic Winter Games Feb. 4-20, 2022. These were the second Games held during the worldwide COVID-19 pandemic. China was hosting the Games for the first time since the 2008 Summer Games, repurposing five of the seven structures created for those Games. Norway once again dominated the Games with 37 medals, including 16 gold, to top the final medal count, followed by Russian Olympic Committee athletes (32 medals, 6 gold), Germany (27, 12), Canada (26, 4), and the U.S. (25, 8).

The human rights violations and the Uyghur genocide of the host country China caused several countries, including the U.S. and the United Kingdom, to conduct a diplomatic boycott, refusing to send any official representation to the Games. China's close ally, North Korea, did not attend the Games, citing the pandemic and "hostile forces," but the Intl. Olympic Committee (IOC) had already suspended the country. The IOC ruling barring Russia from competing due a state-sponsored doping scandal was still in effect, but Russian athletes were granted exemptions to compete under the designation Russian Olympic Committee (ROC).

At 18, American-born Eileen Gu, competing for China, became the youngest Olympic champion in freestyle skiing, winning gold in the halfpipe and big air, and silver in slopestyle. Sui Wenjing and Han Cong of China won gold in the figure skating pairs competition; they were the 2018 silver medalists. Germany swept the two-man bobsled competition by winning gold, silver, and bronze. The controversial decision by the Court of Arbitration for Sport to allow 15-year-old ROC athlete Kamila Valieva to skate after a delayed report for testing positive for a banned substance in Dec. 2021, left in question the ROC's earlier victory in the figure skating team event. In Jan. 2024, CAS disqualified Valieva for four years (backdated to 2021) and removed her points from the ROC totals. The United States was upgraded to gold and ROC downgraded to bronze. Favored to win the women's singles event, Valieva had failed to medal.

Three-time world champion U.S. figure skater Nathan Chen performed five clean quadruple jumps on his way to winning gold in men's singles. U.S. snowboarder Lindsey Jacobellis, a 36-year-old veteran of four previous Olympic Games, won gold and her first Olympic medal since 2006 with 40-year-old teammate Nick Baumgartner in mixed team snowboard cross. American speed skater Erin Jackson won gold in the women's 500-m speed skating event, becoming the first Black woman to medal in Olympic speed skating. After finishing fourth in the snowboard halfpipe, five-time Olympian Shaun White announced his retirement.

Seven new medal events were introduced in 2022: men's and women's big air freestyle; women's monobob; mixed relay in short-track speed skating; and mixed team competitions in freestyle skiing aerials, ski jumping, and snowboard cross.

2022 Winter Olympic Games: Final Medal Standings

(G = Gold, S = Silver, B = Bronze, T = Total medals)

Country	G	S	B	T	Country	G	S	B	T	Country	G	S	B	T
Norway	16	8	13	37	Italy	2	7	8	17	Great Britain	1	1	0	2
Russian Olympic					China	9	4	2	15	Belgium	1	0	1	2
Committee	5	12	15	32	Switzerland	7	2	5	14	Czech Republic	1	0	1	2
Germany	12	10	5	27	France	5	7	2	14	Slovakia	1	0	1	2
Canada	4	8	14	26	South Korea	2	5	2	9	Belarus	0	2	0	2
United States	9	9	7	25	Finland	2	2	4	8	Spain	0	1	0	1
Sweden	8	5	5	18	Slovenia	2	3	2	7	Ukraine	0	1	0	1
Austria	7	7	4	18	Australia	1	2	1	4	Estonia	0	0	1	1
Japan	3	6	9	18	New Zealand	2	1	0	3	Latvia	0	0	1	1
Netherlands	8	5	4	17	Hungary	1	0	2	3	Poland	0	0	1	1

Winter Olympic Games Champions, 1924-2022

East and West Germany competed separately, 1968-88. In 1992, the Unified Team represented the former Soviet republics of Russia, Ukraine, Belarus, Kazakhstan, and Uzbekistan. In 2018, Russian athletes competed under the designation Olympic Athlete(s) from Russia (OAR); in 2022, Russian athletes competed under the designation Russian Olympic Committee (ROC); Russia was banned from competition due to a state-sponsored doping scandal. Not all sports are listed here, and many events are omitted. Point systems used for scoring have changed many times; those shown are of the point system in use at those Games. Times are shown in hour:minute:sec.

Alpine Skiing

Team

	Team
2018	Switzerland, Austria, Norway
2022	Austria, Germany, Norway

Men's Downhill

	Men's Downhill	Time
1948	Henri Oreiller, France	2:55.0
1952	Zeno Colo, Italy	2:30.8
1956	Toni Sailer, Austria	2:52.2
1960	Jean Vuarnet, France	2:06.0
1964	Egon Zimmermann, Austria	2:18.16
1968	Jean-Claude Killy, France	1:59.85
1972	Bernhard Russi, Switzerland	1:51.43
1976	Franz Klammer, Austria	1:45.73
1980	Leonhard Stock, Austria	1:45.50
1984	Bill Johnson, United States	1:45.59
1988	Pirmin Zurbriggen, Switzerland	1:59.63
1992	Patrick Ortlieb, Austria	1:50.37
1994	Tommy Moe, United States	1:45.75
1998	Jean-Luc Cretier, France	1:50.11
2002	Fritz Strobl, Austria	1:39.13
2006	Antoine Deneriaz, France	1:48.80
2010	Didier Defago, Switzerland	1:54.31
2014	Matthias Mayer, Austria	2:06.23
2018	Aksel Lund Svindal, Norway	1:40.25
2022	Beat Feuz, Switzerland	1:42.69

Men's Giant Slalom

	Men's Giant Slalom	Time
1952	Stein Eriksen, Norway	2:25.0
1956	Toni Sailer, Austria	3:00.1
1960	Roger Staub, Switzerland	1:48.3
1964	François Bonlieu, France	1:46.71
1968	Jean-Claude Killy, France	3:29.28
1972	Gustavo Thoeni, Italy	3:09.62
1976	Heini Hemmi, Switzerland	3:26.97
1980	Ingemar Stenmark, Sweden	2:40.74
1984	Max Julen, Switzerland	2:41.18
1988	Alberto Tomba, Italy	2:06.37
1992	Alberto Tomba, Italy	2:06.98
1994	Markus Wasmeier, Germany	2:52.46
1998	Hermann Maier, Austria	2:38.51
2002	Stephan Eberharter, Austria	2:23.28
2006	Benjamin Raich, Austria	2:35.00
2010	Carlo Janka, Switzerland	2:37.83
2014	Ted Ligety, United States	2:45.29
2018	Marcel Hirscher, Austria	2:18.04
2022	Marco Odermatt Switzerland	2:09.35

Men's Slalom

	Men's Slalom	Time
1948	Edi Reinalter, Switzerland	2:10.3
1952	Othmar Schneider, Austria	2:00.0
1956	Toni Sailer, Austria	3:14.7
1960	Ernst Hinterseer, Austria	2:08.9
1964	Josef Stiegler, Austria	2:11.13
1968	Jean-Claude Killy, France	1:39.73
1972	Francisco Fernandez-Ochoa, Spain	1:49.27
1976	Piero Gros, Italy	2:03.29
1980	Ingemar Stenmark, Sweden	1:44.26
1984	Phil Mahre, United States	1:39.41
1988	Alberto Tomba, Italy	1:39.47
1992	Finn Christian Jagge, Norway	1:44.39
1994	Thomas Stangassinger, Austria	2:02.02
1998	Hans-Petter Buraas, Norway	1:49.31
2002	Jean-Pierre Vidal, France	1:41.06
2006	Benjamin Raich, Austria	1:43.14
2010	Giuliano Razzoli, Italy	1:39.32
2014	Mario Matt, Austria	1:41.84
2018	Andre Myhrer, Sweden	1:38.99
2022	Clément Noël, France	1:44.09

Men's Combined

	Men's Combined	Time
1936	Franz Pfnür, Germany	99.25 (pts.)
1948	Henri Oreiller, France	3.27 (pts.)
1988	Hubert Strolz, Austria	36.55 (pts.)
1992	Josef Polig, Italy	14.58 (pts.)
1994	Lasse Kjus, Norway	3:17.53
1998	Mario Reiter, Austria	3:08.06
2002	Kjetil André Aamodt, Norway	3:17.56
2006	Ted Ligety, United States	3:09.35
2010	Bode Miller, United States	2:44.92
2014	Sandro Viletta, Switzerland	2:45.20
2018	Marcel Hirscher, Austria	2:06.52
2022	Johannes Strolz, Austria	2:31.43

Men's Super Giant Slalom

	Men's Super Giant Slalom	Time
1988	Franck Piccard, France	1:39.66
1992	Kjetil André Aamodt, Norway	1:13.04
1994	Markus Wasmeier, Germany	1:32.53
1998	Hermann Maier, Austria	1:34.82
2002	Kjetil André Aamodt, Norway	1:21.58
2006	Kjetil André Aamodt, Norway	1:30.65
2010	Aksel Lund Svindal, Norway	1:30.34
2014	Kjetil Jansrud, Norway	1:18.14
2018	Matthias Mayer, Austria	1:24.44
2022	Matthias Mayer, Austria	1:19.94

Women's Downhill

	Women's Downhill	Time
1948	Hedi Schlunegger, Switzerland	2:28.3
1952	Trude Beiser-Jochum, Austria	1:47.1
1956	Madeleine Berthod, Switzerland	1:40.7
1960	Heidi Biebl, Germany	1:37.6
1964	Christl Haas, Austria	1:55.39
1968	Olga Pall, Austria	1:40.87
1972	Marie-Theres Nadig, Switzerland	1:36.68
1976	Rosi Mittermaier, W. Germany	1:46.16
1980	Annemarie Moser-Proell, Austria	1:37.52
1984	Michela Figini, Switzerland	1:13.36
1988	Marina Kiehl, W. Germany	1:25.86
1992	Kerrin Lee-Gartner, Canada	1:52.55
1994	Katja Seizinger, Germany	1:35.93
1998	Katja Seizinger, Germany	1:28.89
2002	Carole Montillet, France	1:39.56
2006	Michaela Dorfmeister, Austria	1:56.49
2010	Lindsey Vonn, United States	1:44.19
2014	Tina Maze, Slovenia	1:41.57
	Dominique Gisin, Switzerland (tie)	1:41.57
2018	Sofia Goggia, Italy	1:39.22
2022	Corinne Suter, Switzerland	1:31.87

Women's Giant Slalom

	Women's Giant Slalom	Time
1952	Andrea Mead Lawrence, United States	2:06.8
1956	Ossi Reichert, Germany	1:56.5
1960	Yvonne Ruegg, Switzerland	1:39.9
1964	Marielle Goitschel, France	1:52.24
1968	Nancy Greene, Canada	1:51.97
1972	Marie-Theres Nadig, Switzerland	1:29.90
1976	Kathy Kreiner, Canada	1:29.13
1980	Hanni Wenzel, Liechtenstein	2:41.66
1984	Debbie Armstrong, United States	2:20.98
1988	Vreni Schneider, Switzerland	2:06.49
1992	Pernilla Wiberg, Sweden	2:12.74
1994	Deborah Compagnoni, Italy	2:30.97
1998	Deborah Compagnoni, Italy	2:50.59
2002	Janica Kostelic, Croatia	2:30.01
2006	Julia Mancuso, United States	2:09.19
2010	Viktoria Rebensburg, Germany	2:27.11
2014	Tina Maze, Slovenia	2:36.87
2018	Mikaela Shiffrin, United States	2:20.02
2022	Sara Hector, Sweden	1:55.69

Note: Beginning in 1980, the event time combined two runs.

Women's Slalom

	Women's Slalom	Time
1948	Gretchen Fraser, United States	1:57.2
1952	Andrea Mead Lawrence, United States	2:10.6
1956	Renee Colliard, Switzerland	1:52.3
1960	Anne Heggtveit, Canada	1:49.6
1964	Christine Goitschel, France	1:29.86
1968	Marielle Goitschel, France	1:25.86
1972	Barbara Ann Cochran, United States	1:31.24
1976	Rosi Mittermaier, W. Germany	1:30.54
1980	Hanni Wenzel, Liechtenstein	1:25.09
1984	Paoletta Magoni, Italy	1:36.47
1988	Vreni Schneider, Switzerland	1:36.69
1992	Petra Kronberger, Austria	1:32.68
1994	Vreni Schneider, Switzerland	1:56.01
1998	Hilde Gerg, Germany	1:32.40
2002	Janica Kostelic, Croatia	1:46.10
2006	Anja Paerson, Sweden	1:29.04
2010	Maria Riesch, Germany	1:42.89
2014	Mikaela Shiffrin, United States	1:44.54
2018	Frida Hansdotter, Sweden	1:38.63
2022	Petra Vlhová, Slovakia	1:44.98

Women's Combined

	Women's Combined	Time
1936	Christl Cranz, Germany	97.06 (pts.)
1948	Trude Beiser-Jochum, Austria	6.58 (pts.)
1988	Anita Wachter, Austria	29.25 (pts.)
1992	Petra Kronberger, Austria	2.55 (pts.)
1994	Pernilla Wiberg, Sweden	3:05.16

Women's Combined — Time

		Time
1998	Katja Seizinger, Germany	2:40.74
2002	Janica Kostelic, Croatia	2:43.28
2006	Janica Kostelic, Croatia	2:51.08
2010	Maria Riesch, Germany	2:09.14
2014	Maria Hoefl-Riesch, Germany	2:34.62
2018	Michelle Gisin, Switzerland	2:20.90
2022	Michelle Gisin, Switzerland	2:25.67

Note: In 2010, a one-day super combined event replaced the traditional two-day combined event.

Women's Super Giant Slalom

		Time
1988	Sigrid Wolf, Austria	1:19.03
1992	Deborah Compagnoni, Italy	1:21.22
1994	Diann Roffe (Steinrotter), United States	1:22.15
1998	Picabo Street, United States	1:18.02
2002	Daniela Ceccarelli, Italy	1:13.59
2006	Michaela Dorfmeister, Austria	1:32.47
2010	Andrea Fischbacher, Austria	1:20.14
2014	Anna Fenninger, Austria	1:25.52
2018	Ester Ledecká, Czech Republic	1:21.11
2022	Lara Gut-Behrami, Switzerland	1:13.51

Bobsled

(Driver/pilot in parentheses.)

Two-Man Bobsled

		Time
1932	United States (Hubert Stevens)	8:14.74
1936	United States (Ivan Brown)	5:29.29
1948	Switzerland (Felix Endrich)	5:29.20
1952	Germany (Andreas Ostler)	5:24.54
1956	Italy (Dalla Costa)	5:30.14
1964	Great Britain (Anthony Nash)	4:21.90
1968	Italy (Eugenio Monti)	4:41.54
1972	W. Germany (Wolfgang Zimmerer)	4:57.07
1976	E. Germany (Meinhard Nehmer)	3:44.42
1980	Switzerland (Erich Schaerer)	4:09.36
1984	E. Germany (Wolfgang Hoppe)	3:25.56
1988	USSR (Janis Kipours)	3:54.19
1992	Switzerland (Gustav Weber)	4:03.26
1994	Switzerland (Gustav Weber)	3:30.81
1998	Canada (Pierre Lueders)	3:37.24
	Italy (Guenther Huber) (tie)	3:37.24
2002	Germany II (Christoph Langen)	3:10.11
2006	Germany (Andre Lange)	3:43.38
2010	Germany (Andre Lange)	3:26.65
2014	Switzerland (Beat Hefti)[1]	3:46.05
2018	Canada (Justin Kripps)	3:16.86
	Germany (Francesco Friedrich) (tie)	3:16.86
2022	Germany (Francesco Friedrich)	3:56.89

Four-Man Bobsled

		Time
1924	Switzerland (Eduard Scherrer)	5:45.54
1928	United States (William Fiske) (5-man)	3:20.50
1932	United States (William Fiske)	7:53.68
1936	Switzerland (Pierre Musy)	5:19.85
1948	United States (Francis Tyler)	5:20.10
1952	Germany (Andreas Ostler)	5:07.84
1956	Switzerland (Franz Kapus)	5:10.44
1964	Canada (Victor Emery)	4:14.46
1968	Italy (Eugenio Monti) (2 heats)	2:17.39
1972	Switzerland (Jean Wicki)	4:43.07
1976	E. Germany (Meinhard Nehmer)	3:40.43
1980	E. Germany (Meinhard Nehmer)	3:59.92
1984	E. Germany (Wolfgang Hoppe)	3:20.22
1988	Switzerland (Ekkehard Fasser)	3:47.51
1992	Austria (Ingo Appelt)	3:53.90
1994	Germany (Wolfgang Hoppe)	3:27.28
1998	Germany II (Christoph Langen)	2:39.41
2002	Germany II (Andre Lange)	3:07.51
2006	Germany (Andre Lange)	3:40.42
2010	United States (Steven Holcomb)	3:24.46
2014	Latvia (Oskars Melbardis)[1]	3:40.69
2018	Germany (Francesco Friedrich)	3:15.85
2022	Germany (Francesco Friedrich)	3:54.30

Two-Woman Bobsled

		Time
2002	United States II (Jill Bakken)	1:37.76
2006	Germany (Sandra Kiriasis)	3:49.98
2010	Canada (Kaillie Humphries)	3:32.28
2014	Canada (Kaillie Humphries)	3:50.61
2018	Germany (Mariama Jamanka)	3:22.45
2022	Germany (Laura Nolte)	4:03.96

(1) Awarded gold after Russia's Alexander Zubkov was stripped of medals in both events due to doping.

Women's Monobob

		Time
2022	Kaillie Humphries, United States	4:19.27

Cross-Country Skiing

Men's Individual Sprint

		Time
2002	Tor Arne Hetland, Norway (1.5 km)	2:56.9
2006	Bjoern Lind, Sweden (1.3 km)	2:26.5
2010	Nikita Kriukov, Russia	3:36.3
2014	Ola Vigen Hattestad, Norway	3:38.39
2018	Johannes Hoesflot Klaebo, Norway	3:05.75
2022	Johannes Hoesflot Klaebo, Norway	2:58.06

Men's 10 Kilometers

		Time
1992	Vegard Ulvang, Norway	27:36.0
1994	Bjoern Daehlie, Norway	24:20.1
1998	Bjoern Daehlie, Norway	27:24.5

Men's 15 Kilometers

		Time
1924	Thorleif Haug, Norway	1:14:31
1928	Johan Grottumsbraaten, Norway	1:37:01
1932	Sven Utterstrom, Sweden	1:23:07
1936	Erik-August Larsson, Sweden	1:14:38
1948	Martin Lundstrom, Sweden	1:13:50
1952	Hallgeir Brenden, Norway	1:01:34
1956	Hallgeir Brenden, Norway	0:49:39.0
1960	Haakon Brusveen, Norway	0:51:55.5
1964	Eero Maentyranta, Finland	0:50:54.1
1968	Harald Groenningen, Norway	0:47:54.2
1972	Sven-Ake Lundback, Sweden	0:45:28.24
1976	Nikolai Balukov, USSR	0:43:58.47
1980	Thomas Wassberg, Sweden	0:41:57.63
1984	Gunde Svan, Sweden	0:41:25.6
1988	Mikhail Deviatiarov, USSR	0:41:18.9
1992	Bjoern Daehlie, Norway	0:38:01.9
1994	Bjoern Daehlie, Norway	0:35:48.8
1998	Thomas Alsgaard, Norway	1:07:01.7
2002	Andrus Veerpalu, Estonia	0:37:07.4
2006	Andrus Veerpalu, Estonia	0:38:01.3
2010	Dario Cologna, Switzerland	0:33:36.3
2014	Dario Cologna, Switzerland	0:38:29.7
2018	Dario Cologna, Switzerland	0:33:43.9
2022	Iivo Niskanen, Finland	0:37:54.8

Note: Approx. 18-km course 1924-52.

Men's 30-Kilometer

		Time
1956	Veikko Hakulinen, Finland	1:44:06.0
1960	Sixten Jernberg, Sweden	1:51:03.9
1964	Eero Maentyranta, Finland	1:30:50.7
1968	Franco Nones, Italy	1:35:39.2
1972	Vyacheslav Vedenine, USSR	1:36:31.15
1976	Sergei Saveliev, USSR	1:30:29.38
1980	Nikolai Zimyatov, USSR	1:27:02.80
1984	Nikolai Zimyatov, USSR	1:28:56.3
1988	Aleksei Prokourorov, USSR	1:24:26.3
1992	Vegard Ulvang, Norway	1:22:27.8
1994	Thomas Alsgaard, Norway	1:12:26.4
1998	Mika Myllylae, Finland	1:33:55.8
2002	Christian Hoffmann, Austria[1]	1:11:31.0
2006	Eugeni Dementiev, Russia	1:17:00.8
2010	Marcus Hellner, Sweden	1:15:11.4
2022	Alexander Bolshunov, ROC	1:16:09.8

(1) Awarded gold after Johann Muehlegg of Spain was stripped of gold for a drug offense.

Men's Skiathlon

		Time
2014	Dario Cologna, Switzerland	1:08:15.4
2018	Simen Hegstad Krüger, Norway	1:16:20.0
2022	Alexander Bolshunov, ROC	1:16:09.8

Men's 50-Kilometer

		Time
1924	Thorleif Haug, Norway	3:44:32.0
1928	Per Erik Hedlund, Sweden	4:52:03.0
1932	Veli Saarinen, Finland	4:28:00.0
1936	Elis Wiklund, Sweden	3:30:11.0
1948	Nils Karlsson, Sweden	3:47:48.0
1952	Veikko Hakulinen, Finland	3:33:33.0
1956	Sixten Jernberg, Sweden	2:50:27.0
1960	Kalevi Hamalainen, Finland	2:59:06.3
1964	Sixten Jernberg, Sweden	2:43:52.6
1968	Ole Ellefsaeter, Norway	2:28:45.8
1972	Paal Tyldum, Norway	2:43:14.75
1976	Ivar Formo, Norway	2:37:30.05
1980	Nikolai Zimyatov, USSR	2:27:24.60
1984	Thomas Wassberg, Sweden	2:15:55.8
1988	Gunde Svan, Sweden	2:04:30.9
1992	Bjoern Daehlie, Norway	2:03:41.5
1994	Vladimir Smirnov, Kazakhstan	2:07:20.3
1998	Bjoern Daehlie, Norway	2:05:08.2
2002	Mikhail Ivanov, Russia	2:06:20.8
2006	Giorgio di Centa, Italy	2:06:11.8
2010	Petter Northug, Norway	2:05:35.5
2014	Alexander Legkov, Russia	1:46:55.2
2018	Iivo Niskanen, Finland	2:08:22.1
2022*	Alexander Bolshunov, ROC	1:11:32.7

* = Shortened to 28.4 km due to weather.

Men's 4x10-Kilometer Relay

		Time
1936	Finland, Norway, Sweden	2:41:33.0
1948	Sweden, Finland, Norway	2:32:08.0

	Men's 4x10-Kilometer Relay	Time
1952	Finland, Norway, Sweden	2:20:16.0
1956	USSR, Finland, Sweden	2:15:30.0
1960	Finland, Norway, USSR	2:18:45.6
1964	Sweden, Finland, USSR	2:18:34.6
1968	Norway, Sweden, Finland	2:08:33.5
1972	USSR, Norway, Switzerland	2:04:47.94
1976	Finland, Norway, USSR	2:07:59.72
1980	USSR, Norway, Finland	1:57:03.46
1984	Sweden, USSR, Finland	1:55:06.30
1988	Sweden, USSR, Czechoslovakia	1:43:58.60
1992	Norway, Italy, Finland	1:39:26.00
1994	Italy, Norway, Finland	1:41:15.00
1998	Norway, Italy, Finland	1:40:55.70
2002	Norway, Italy, Germany	1:32:45.5
2006	Italy, Germany, Sweden	1:43:45.7
2010	Sweden, Norway, Czech Republic	1:45:05.4
2014	Sweden, Russia, France	1:28:42.0
2018	Norway, OAR, France	1:33:04.9
2022	ROC, Norway, France	1:54:50.7

	Men's Team Sprint	Time
2006	Bjoern Lind & Thobias Fredriksson, Sweden	17:02.9
2010	Oeystein Pettersen & Petter Northug, Norway	19:01.0
2014	Sami Jauhojaervi & Iivo Niskanen, Finland	23:14.89
2018	Martin Johnsrud Sundby & Johannes Hoesflot Klaebo, Norway	15:56.26
2022	Erik Valnes & Johannes Hoesflot Klaebo, Norway	19:22.99

	Women's Individual Sprint	Time
2002	Julia Tchepalova, Russia (1.5 km)	3:10.6
2006	Chandra Crawford, Canada (1.1 km)	2:12.3
2010	Marit Bjoergen, Norway	3:39.2
2014	Maiken Caspersen Falla, Norway	2:35.49
2018	Stina Nilsson, Sweden	3:03.84
2022	Jonna Sundling, Sweden	3:09.68

	Women's 5 Kilometers	Time
1964	Claudia Boyarskikh, USSR	17:50.5
1968	Toini Gustafsson, Sweden	16:45.2
1972	Galina Koulacova, USSR	17:00.50
1976	Helena Takalo, Finland	15:48.69
1980	Raisa Smetanina, USSR	15:06.92
1984	Marja-Liisa Hamalainen, Finland	17:04.0
1988	Marjo Matikainen, Finland	15:04.0
1992	Marjut Lukkarinen, Finland	14:13.8
1994	Lyubov Yegorova, Russia	14:08.8
1998	Larissa Lazutina, Russia	17:37.9
2002	Beckie Scott, Canada[1]	25:09.9

(1) Awarded gold after Olga Danilova of Russia was stripped of gold and Larissa Lazutina of Russia was stripped of silver for drug offenses.

	Women's 10 Kilometers	Time
1952	Lydia Wideman, Finland	41:40.0
1956	Lyubov Kosyreva, USSR	38:11.0
1960	Maria Gusakova, USSR	39:46.6
1964	Claudia Boyarskikh, USSR	40:24.3
1968	Toini Gustafsson, Sweden	36:46.5
1972	Galina Koulacova, USSR	34:17.82
1976	Raisa Smetanina, USSR	30:13.41
1980	Barbara Petzold, E. Germany	30:31.54
1984	Marja-Liisa Hamalainen, Finland	31:44.2
1988	Vida Ventsene, USSR	30:08.3
1992	Lyubov Yegorova, Unified Team (Rus.)	25:53.7
1994	Lyubov Yegorova, Russia	27:30.1
1998	Larissa Lazutina, Russia	46.06.9
2002	Bente Skari, Norway	28:05.6
2006	Kristina Smigun, Estonia	27:51.4
2010	Charlotte Kalla, Sweden	24:58.4
2014	Justyna Kowalczyk, Poland	28:17.8
2018	Ragnhild Haga, Norway	25:00.5
2022	Therese Johaug, Norway	28:06.3

	Women's 15-Kilometer	Time
1992	Lyubov Yegorova, Unified Team (Rus.)	42:20.8
1994	Manuela Di Centa, Italy	39:44.5
1998	Olga Danilova, Russia	46:55.4
2002	Stefania Belmondo, Italy	39:54.4
2006	Kristina Smigun, Estonia	42:48.7
2010	Marit Bjoergen, Norway	39:58.1

	Women's Skiathlon	Time
2014	Marit Bjoergen, Norway	38:33.6
2018	Charlotte Kalla, Sweden	40:44.9
2022	Therese Johaug, Norway	44:13.7

	Women's 30-Kilometer	Time
1992	Stefania Belmondo, Italy	1:22:30.1
1994	Manuela Di Centa, Italy	1:25:41.6
1998	Julija Tchepalova, Russia	1:22:01.5
2002	Gabriella Paruzzi, Italy	1:30:57.1
2006	Katerina Neumannova, Czech Republic	1:22:25.4
2010	Justyna Kowalczyk, Poland	1:30:33.7
2014	Marit Bjoergen, Norway	1:11:05.2
2018	Marit Bjoergen, Norway	1:22:17.6
2022	Therese Johaug, Norway	1:24:54.0

	Women's 4x5-Kilometer Relay	Time
1956	Finland, USSR, Sweden (3x5-km)	1:09:01.0
1960	Sweden, USSR, Finland (3x5-km)	1:04:21.4
1964	USSR, Sweden, Finland (3x5-km)	0:59:20.2
1968	Norway, Sweden, USSR (3x5-km)	0:57:30.0
1972	USSR, Finland, Norway (3x5-km)	0:48:46.15
1976	USSR, Finland, E. Germany	1:07:49.75
1980	E. Germany, USSR, Norway	1:02:11.1
1984	Norway, Czechoslovakia, Finland	1:06:49.7
1988	USSR, Norway, Finland	0:59:51.1
1992	Unified Team, Norway, Italy	0:59:34.8
1994	Russia, Norway, Italy	0:57:12.5
1998	Russia, Norway, Italy	0:55:13.5
2002	Germany, Norway, Switzerland	0:49:30.6
2006	Russia, Germany, Italy	0:54:47.7
2010	Norway, Germany, Finland	0:55:19.5
2014	Sweden, Finland, Germany	0:53:02.7
2018	Norway, Sweden, OAR	0:51:24.3
2022	ROC, Germany, Sweden	0:53:41.0

	Women's Team Sprint	Time
2006	Lina Andersson & Anna Dahlberg, Sweden	16:36.9
2010	Evi Sachenbacher-Stehle & Claudia Nystad, Germany	18:03.7
2014	Marit Bjoergen & Ingvild Flugstad Oestberg, Norway	16:04.05
2018	Kikkan Randall & Jessie Diggins, United States	15:56.47
2022	Katharina Hennig & Victoria Carl, Germany	22:09.85

Curling

Men

1998 Switzerland, Canada, Norway
2002 Norway, Canada, Switzerland
2006 Canada, Finland, United States
2010 Canada, Norway, Switzerland
2014 Canada, Great Britain, Sweden
2018 United States, Sweden, Switzerland
2022 Sweden, Great Britain, Canada

Women

1998 Canada, Denmark, Sweden
2002 Britain, Switzerland, Canada
2006 Sweden, Switzerland, Canada
2010 Sweden, Canada, China
2014 Canada, Sweden, Great Britain
2018 Sweden, S. Korea, Japan
2022 Great Britain, Japan, Sweden

Mixed

2018 Canada, Switzerland, Norway
2022 Italy, Norway, Sweden

Figure Skating

Men's Singles

1908[1] Ulrich Salchow, Sweden
1920[1] Gillis Grafstrom, Sweden
1924 Gillis Grafstrom, Sweden
1928 Gillis Grafstrom, Sweden
1932 Karl Schaefer, Austria
1936 Karl Schaefer, Austria
1948 Richard Button, United States
1952 Richard Button, United States
1956 Hayes Alan Jenkins, United States
1960 David W. Jenkins, United States
1964 Manfred Schnelldorfer, Germany
1968 Wolfgang Schwartz, Austria
1972 Ondrej Nepela, Czechoslovakia
1976 John Curry, Great Britain
1980 Robin Cousins, Great Britain
1984 Scott Hamilton, United States
1988 Brian Boitano, United States
1992 Viktor Petrenko, Unified Team (Ukr.)
1994 Aleksei Urmanov, Russia
1998 Ilya Kulik, Russia
2002 Alexei Yagudin, Russia
2006 Yevgeny Plushenko, Russia
2010 Evan Lysacek, United States
2014 Yuzuru Hanyu, Japan
2018 Yuzuru Hanyu, Japan
2022 Nathan Chen, United States

(1) Event held during Summer Olympic Games.

Women's Singles

1908[1] Madge Syers, Great Britain
1920[1] Magda Julin-Mauroy, Sweden
1924 Herma von Szabo-Planck, Austria
1928 Sonja Henie, Norway
1932 Sonja Henie, Norway
1936 Sonja Henie, Norway
1948 Barbara Ann Scott, Canada
1952 Jeanette Altwegg, Great Britain

Women's Singles

1956 Tenley Albright, United States
1960 Carol Heiss, United States
1964 Sjoukje Dijkstra, Netherlands
1968 Peggy Fleming, United States
1972 Beatrix Schuba, Austria
1976 Dorothy Hamill, United States
1980 Anett Poetzsch, E. Germany
1984 Katarina Witt, E. Germany
1988 Katarina Witt, E. Germany
1992 Kristi Yamaguchi, United States
1994 Oksana Baiul, Ukraine
1998 Tara Lipinski, United States
2002 Sarah Hughes, United States
2006 Shizuka Arakawa, Japan
2010 Kim Yu-na, South Korea
2014 Adelina Sotnikova, Russia
2018 Alina Zagitova, OAR
2022 Anna Shcherbakova, ROC

(1) Event held during Summer Olympic Games.

Pairs

1908[1] Anna Hubler & Heinrich Burger, Germany
1920[1] Ludovika Jakobsson & Walter Jakobsson, Finland
1924 Helene Engelman & Alfred Berger, Austria
1928 Andree Joly & Pierre Brunet, France
1932 Andree Joly & Pierre Brunet, France
1936 Maxi Herber & Ernst Baier, Germany
1948 Micheline Lannoy & Pierre Baugniet, Belgium
1952 Ria Falk & Paul Falk, Germany
1956 Elisabeth Schwartz & Kurt Oppelt, Austria
1964 Ludmila Beloussova & Oleg Protopopov, USSR
1968 Ludmila Beloussova & Oleg Protopopov, USSR
1972 Irina Rodnina & Alexei Ulanov, USSR
1976 Irina Rodnina & Aleksandr Zaitzev, USSR
1980 Irina Rodnina & Aleksandr Zaitzev, USSR
1984 Elena Valova & Oleg Vassiliev, USSR
1988 Ekaterina Gordeeva & Sergei Grinkov, USSR
1992 Natalia Mishkutienok & Artur Dimitriev, Unified Team (Rus.)
1994 Ekaterina Gordeeva & Sergei Grinkov, Russia
1998 Oksana Kazakova & Artur Dmitriev, Russia
2002 Elena Berezhnaya & Anton Sikharulidze, Russia; Jamie Salé & David Pelletier, Canada (tie)
2006 Tatyana Totmianina & Maxim Marinin, Russia
2010 Shen Xue & Zhao Hongbo, China
2014 Tatiana Volosozhar & Maxim Trankov, Russia
2018 Aljona Savchenko & Bruno Massot, Germany
2022 Sui Wenjing & Han Cong, China

(1) Event held during Summer Olympic Games.

Ice Dancing

1976 Ludmila Pakhomova & Aleksandr Gorschkov, USSR
1980 Natalya Linichuk & Gennadi Karponosov, USSR
1984 Jayne Torvill & Christopher Dean, Great Britain
1988 Natalia Bestemianova & Andrei Bukin, USSR
1992 Marina Klimova & Sergei Ponomarenko, Unified Team (Rus.)
1994 Pasha Grishuk & Evgeny Platov, Russia
1998 Pasha Grishuk & Evgeny Platov, Russia
2002 Marina Anissina & Gwendal Peizerat, France
2006 Tatyana Navka & Roman Kostomarov, Russia
2010 Tessa Virtue & Scott Moir, Canada
2014 Meryl Davis & Charlie White, United States
2018 Tessa Virtue & Scott Moir, Canada
2022 Gabriella Papadakis & Guillaume Cizeron, France

Mixed Team

2014 Russia, Canada, United States
2018 Canada, OAR, United States
2022 United States, Japan, ROC

Freestyle Skiing

Men's Aerials		Points
1994	Andreas Schoenbaechler, Switzerland	234.67
1998	Eric Bergoust, United States	255.64
2002	Ales Valenta, Czech Republic	257.02
2006	Xiaopeng Han, China	250.77
2010	Alexei Grishin, Belarus	248.41
2014	Anton Kushnir, Belarus	134.50
2018	Oleksandr Abramenko, Ukraine	128.51
2022	Qi Guangpu, China	129.00

Men's Big Air		Points
2022	Birk Ruud, Norway	187.75

Men's Moguls		Points
1992	Edgar Grospiron, France	25.81
1994	Jean-Luc Brassard, Canada	27.24
1998	Jonny Moseley, United States	26.93
2002	Janne Lahtela, Finland	27.97
2006	Dale Begg-Smith, Australia	26.77
2010	Alex Bilodeau, Canada	26.75
2014	Alex Bilodeau, Canada	26.31
2018	Mikaël Kingsbury, Canada	86.63
2022	Walter Wallberg, Sweden	83.23

Men's Ski Cross

2010 Michael Schmid, Switzerland
2014 Jean Frederic Chapuis, France
2018 Brady Leman, Canada
2022 Ryan Regez, Switzerland

Men's Ski Halfpipe		Points
2014	David Wise, United States	92.00
2018	David Wise, United States	97.20
2022	Nico Porteous, New Zealand	93.00

Men's Ski Slopestyle		Points
2014	Joss Christensen, United States	95.80
2018	Oystein Braaten, Norway	95.00
2022	Alexander Hall, United States	90.01

Women's Aerials		Points
1994	Lina Tcherjazova, Uzbekistan	166.84
1998	Nikki Stone, United States	193.00
2002	Alisa Camplin, Australia	193.47
2006	Evelyne Leu, Switzerland	202.55
2010	Lydia Lassila, Australia	214.74
2014	Alla Tsuper, Belarus	98.01
2018	Hanna Huskova, Belarus	96.14
2022	Xu Mengtao, China	108.61

Women's Big Air		Points
2022	Eileen Gu, China	188.25

Women's Moguls		Points
1992	Donna Weinbrecht, United States	23.69
1994	Stine Lise Hattestad, Norway	25.97
1998	Tae Satoya, Japan	25.06
2002	Kari Traa, Norway	25.94
2006	Jennifer Heil, Canada	26.50
2010	Hannah Kearney, United States	26.63
2014	Justine Dufour-Lapointe, Canada	22.44
2018	Perrine Laffont, France	78.65
2022	Jakara Anthony, Australia	83.09

Women's Ski Cross

2010 Ashleigh McIvor, Canada
2014 Marielle Thompson, Canada
2018 Kelsey Serwa, Canada
2022 Sandra Naeslund, Sweden

Women's Ski Halfpipe		Points
2014	Maddie Bowman, United States	89.00
2018	Cassie Sharpe, Canada	95.80
2022	Eileen Gu, China	95.25

Women's Ski Slopestyle		Points
2014	Dara Howell, Canada	94.20
2018	Sarah Höfflin, Switzerland	91.20
2022	Mathilde Gremaud, Switzerland	86.56

Mixed Team Aerials		Points
2022	United States, China, Canada	338.34

Ice Hockey

Men

1920[1] Canada, United States, Czechoslovakia
1924 Canada, United States, Great Britain
1928 Canada, Sweden, Switzerland
1932 Canada, United States, Germany
1936 Great Britain, Canada, United States
1948 Canada, Czechoslovakia, Switzerland
1952 Canada, United States, Sweden
1956 USSR, United States, Canada
1960 United States, Canada, USSR
1964 USSR, Sweden, Czechoslovakia
1968 USSR, Czechoslovakia, Canada
1972 USSR, United States, Czechoslovakia
1976 USSR, Czechoslovakia, W. Germany
1980 United States, USSR, Sweden
1984 USSR, Czechoslovakia, Sweden
1988 USSR, Finland, Sweden
1992 Unified Team, Canada, Czechoslovakia
1994 Sweden, Canada, Finland
1998 Czech Republic, Russia, Finland
2002 Canada, United States, Russia
2006 Sweden, Finland, Czech Republic
2010 Canada, United States, Finland
2014 Canada, Sweden, Finland
2018 OAR, Germany, Canada
2022 Finland, ROC, Slovakia

(1) Event held during Summer Olympic Games.

Women

1998 United States, Canada, Finland
2002 Canada, United States, Sweden

Women

2006	Canada, Sweden, United States
2010	Canada, United States, Finland
2014	Canada, United States, Switzerland
2018	United States, Canada, Finland
2022	Canada, United States, Finland

Luge

	Men's Singles	Time
1964	Thomas Keohler, E. Germany	3:27.77
1968	Manfred Schmid, Austria	2:52.48
1972	Wolfgang Scheidel, E. Germany	3:27.58
1976	Detlef Guenther, E. Germany	3:27.688
1980	Bernhard Glass, E. Germany	2:54.796
1984	Paul Hildgartner, Italy	3:04.258
1988	Jens Mueller, E. Germany	3:05.548
1992	Georg Hackl, Germany	3:02.363
1994	Georg Hackl, Germany	3:21.571
1998	Georg Hackl, Germany	3:18.436
2002	Armin Zoeggeler, Italy	2:57.941
2006	Armin Zoeggeler, Italy	3:26.088
2010	Felix Loch, Germany	3:13.085
2014	Felix Loch, Germany	3:27.526
2018	David Gleirscher, Austria	3:10.702
2022	Johannes Ludwig, Germany	3:48.735

	Men's Doubles	Time
1964	Austria	1:41.62
1968	E. Germany	1:35.85
1972	Italy, E. Germany (tie)	1:28.35
1976	E. Germany	1:25.604
1980	E. Germany	1:19.331
1984	W. Germany	1:23.620
1988	E. Germany	1:31.940
1992	Germany	1:32.053
1994	Italy	1:36.720
1998	Germany	1:41.105
2002	Germany	1:26.082
2006	Austria	1:34.497
2010	Austria	1:22.705
2014	Germany	1:38.933
2018	Germany	1:31.697
2022	Germany	1:56.554

	Women's Singles	Time
1964	Ortun Enderlein, Germany	3:24.67
1968	Erica Lechner, Italy	2:28.66
1972	Anna M. Muller, E. Germany	2:59.18
1976	Margit Schumann, E. Germany	2:50.621
1980	Vera Zozulya, USSR	2:36.537
1984	Steffi Martin, E. Germany	2:46.570
1988	Steffi (Martin) Walter, E. Germany	3:03.973
1992	Doris Neuner, Austria	3:06.696
1994	Gerda Weissensteiner, Italy	3:15.517
1998	Silke Kraushaar, Germany	3:23.779
2002	Sylke Otto, Germany	2:52.464
2006	Sylke Otto, Germany	3:07.979
2010	Tatjana Huefner, Germany	2:46.524
2014	Natalie Geisenberger, Germany	3:19.768
2018	Natalie Geisenberger, Germany	3:05.232
2022	Natalie Geisenberger, Germany	3:53.454

	Mixed Team Relay	Time
2014	Germany, Russia, Latvia	2:45.649
2018	Germany, Canada, Austria	2:24.517
2022	Germany, Austria, Latvia	3:03.406

Ski Jumping

	Men's Normal Hill	Points
1964	Veikko Kankkonen, Finland	229.9
1968	Jiri Raska, Czechoslovakia	216.5
1972	Yukio Kasaya, Japan	244.2
1976	Hans-Georg Aschenbach, E. Germany	252.0
1980	Toni Innauer, Austria	266.3
1984	Jens Weissflog, E. Germany	215.2
1988	Matti Nykaenen, Finland	230.5
1992	Ernst Vettori, Austria	222.8
1994	Espen Bredesen, Norway	282.0
1998	Jani Soininen, Finland	234.5
2002	Simon Ammann, Switzerland	269.0
2006	Lars Bystoel, Norway	266.5
2010	Simon Ammann, Switzerland	276.5
2014	Kamil Stoch, Poland	278.0
2018	Andreas Wellinger, Germany	259.3
2022	Ryoyu Kobayashi, Japan	275.0

	Men's Large Hill	Points
1924	Jacob Tullin Thams, Norway	18.960
1928	Alfred Andersen, Norway	19.208
1932	Birger Ruud, Norway	228.1
1936	Birger Ruud, Norway	232.0
1948	Petter Hugsted, Norway	228.1
1952	Arnfinn Bergmann, Norway	226.0
1956	Antti Hyvarinen, Finland	227.0
1960	Helmut Recknagel, E. Germany	227.2
1964	Toralf Engan, Norway	230.7
1968	Vladimir Beloussov, USSR	231.3
1972	Wojciech Fortuna, Poland	219.9
1976	Karl Schnabl, Austria	234.8
1980	Jouko Tormanen, Finland	271.0
1984	Matti Nykaenen, Finland	231.2
1988	Matti Nykaenen, Finland	224.0
1992	Toni Nieminen, Finland	239.5
1994	Jens Weissflog, Germany	274.5
1998	Kazuyoshi Funaki, Japan	272.3
2002	Simon Ammann, Switzerland	281.4
2006	Thomas Morgenstern, Austria	276.9
2010	Simon Ammann, Switzerland	283.6
2014	Kamil Stoch, Poland	278.7
2018	Kamil Stoch, Poland	285.7
2022	Marius Lindvik, Norway	296.1

	Men's Team	Points
1988	Finland, Yugoslavia, Norway	634.4
1992	Finland, Austria, Czechoslovakia	644.4
1994	Germany, Japan, Austria	970.1
1998	Japan, Germany, Austria	933.0
2002	Germany, Finland, Slovenia	974.1
2006	Austria, Finland, Norway	984.0
2010	Austria, Germany, Norway	1,107.9
2014	Germany, Austria, Japan	1,041.1
2018	Norway, Germany, Poland	1,098.5
2022	Austria, Slovenia, Germany	942.7

	Women's Normal Hill	Points
2014	Carina Vogt, Germany	247.4
2018	Maren Lundby, Norway	264.6
2022	Ursa Bogataj, Slovenia	239.0

	Mixed Team	Points
2022	Slovenia, ROC, Canada	1,001.5

Snowboarding

	Men's Big Air	Points
2018	Sebastien Toutant, Canada	174.25
2022	Su Yiming, China	182.50

	Men's Halfpipe	Points
1998	Gian Simmen, Switzerland	85.2
2002	Ross Powers, United States	46.1
2006	Shaun White, United States	46.8
2010	Shaun White, United States	48.4
2014	Iouri Podladtchikov, Switzerland	94.75
2018	Shaun White, United States	97.75
2022	Ayumu Hirano, Japan	96.0

Men's Parallel Giant Slalom

1998	Ross Rebagliati, Canada
2002	Philipp Schoch, Switzerland
2006	Philipp Schoch, Switzerland
2010	Jasey Jay Anderson, Canada
2014	Vic Wild, Russia
2018	Nevin Galmarini, Switzerland
2022	Benjamin Karl, Austria

Note: In 2002, the Giant Slalom became the Parallel Giant Slalom.

Men's Parallel Slalom

2014	Vic Wild, Russia

	Men's Slopestyle	Points
2014	Sage Kotsenburg, United States	93.50
2018	Red Gerard, United States	87.16
2022	Max Parrot, Canada	90.96

Men's Snowboard Cross

2006	Seth Wescott, United States
2010	Seth Wescott, United States
2014	Pierre Vaultier, France
2018	Pierre Vaultier, France
2022	Alessandro Haemmerle, Austria

	Women's Big Air	Points
2018	Anna Gasser, Austria	185.00
2022	Anna Gasser, Austria	185.50

	Women's Halfpipe	Points
1998	Nicola Thost, Germany	74.6
2002	Kelly Clark, United States	47.9
2006	Hannah Teter, United States	46.4
2010	Torah Bright, Australia	45.0
2014	Kaitlyn Farrington, United States	91.75
2018	Chloe Kim, United States	98.25
2022	Chloe Kim, United States	94.0

Women's Parallel Giant Slalom

1998	Karine Ruby, France
2002	Isabelle Blanc, France

Women's Parallel Giant Slalom

2006 Daniela Meuli, Switzerland
2010 Nicolien Sauerbreij, Netherlands
2014 Patrizia Kummer, Switzerland
2018 Ester Ledecká, Czech Republic
2022 Ester Ledecká, Czech Republic

Note: In 2002, the Giant Slalom became the Parallel Giant Slalom.

Women's Parallel Slalom

2014 Julia Dujmovits, Austria

Year	Women's Slopestyle	Points
2014	Jamie Anderson, United States	95.25
2018	Jamie Anderson, United States	83.00
2022	Zoi Sadowski-Synnott, New Zealand	92.88

Women's Snowboard Cross

2006 Tanja Frieden, Switzerland
2010 Maelle Ricker, Canada
2014 Eva Samková, Czech Republic
2018 Michela Moioli, Italy
2022 Lindsey Jacobellis, United States

Mixed Team Snowboard Cross

2022 United States, Italy, Canada

Speed Skating

* = Olympic record

Year	Men's 500 Meters	Time
1924	Charles Jewtraw, United States	0:44.0
1928	C. Thunberg, Finland; B. Evensen, Norway (tie)	0:43.4
1932	John A. Shea, United States	0:43.4
1936	Ivar Ballangrud, Norway	0:43.4
1948	Finn Helgesen, Norway	0:43.1
1952	Kenneth Henry, United States	0:43.2
1956	Evgeniy Grishin, USSR	0:40.2
1960	Evgeniy Grishin, USSR	0:40.2
1964	Terry McDermott, United States	0:40.1
1968	Erhard Keller, W. Germany	0:40.3
1972	Erhard Keller, W. Germany	0:39.44
1976	Evgeny Kulikov, USSR	0:39.17
1980	Eric Heiden, United States	0:38.03
1984	Sergei Fokichev, USSR	0:38.19
1988	Uwe-Jens Mey, E. Germany	0:36.45
1992	Uwe-Jens Mey, Germany	0:37.14
1994	Aleksandr Golubev, Russia	0:36.33
1998	Hiroyasu Shimizu, Japan	0:35.59
2002	Casey FitzRandolph, United States	0:34.42
2006	Joey Cheek, United States	0:34.82
2010	Mo Tae-bum, S. Korea	0:69.82
2014	Michel Mulder, Netherlands	0:69.312
2018	Havard Lorentzen, Norway	0:34.41
2022	Gao Tingyu, China	0.34.32*

Note: In 2010 and 2014, results include the total of two 500-km race times.

Year	Men's 1000 Meters	Time
1976	Peter Mueller, United States	1:19.32
1980	Eric Heiden, United States	1:15.18
1984	Gaetan Boucher, Canada	1:15.80
1988	Nikolai Guiliaev, USSR	1:13.03
1992	Olaf Zinke, Germany	1:14.85
1994	Dan Jansen, United States	1:12.43
1998	Ids Postma, Netherlands	1:10.64
2002	Gerard van Velde, Netherlands	1:07.18*
2006	Shani Davis, United States	1:08.89
2010	Shani Davis, United States	1:08.94
2014	Stefan Groothuis, Netherlands	1:08.39
2018	Kjeld Nuis, Netherlands	1:07.95
2022	Thomas Krol, Netherlands	1:07.92

Year	Men's 1500 Meters	Time
1924	Clas Thunberg, Finland	2:20.8
1928	Clas Thunberg, Finland	2:21.1
1932	John A. Shea, United States	2:57.5
1936	Charles Mathiesen, Norway	2:19.2
1948	Sverre Farstad, Norway	2:17.6
1952	Hjalmar Andersen, Norway	2:20.4
1956	Y. Grishin, USSR; Y. Mikhailov, USSR (tie)	2:08.6
1960	R. Aas, Norway; Y. Grishin, USSR (tie)	2:10.4
1964	Ants Anston, USSR	2:10.3
1968	Cornetis Verkerk, Netherlands	2:03.4
1972	Ard Schenk, Netherlands	2:02.96
1976	Jan Egil Storholt, Norway	1:59.38
1980	Eric Heiden, United States	1:55.44
1984	Gaetan Boucher, Canada	1:58.36
1988	Andre Hoffmann, E. Germany	1:52.06
1992	Johann Koss, Norway	1:54.81
1994	Johann Koss, Norway	1:51.29
1998	Aadne Sondral, Norway	1:47.87
2002	Derek Parra, United States	1:43.95
2006	Enrico Fabris, Italy	1:45.97
2010	Mark Tuitert, Netherlands	1:45.57
2014	Zbigniew Brodka, Poland	1:45.006
2018	Kjeld Nuis, Netherlands	1:44.01
2022	Kjeld Nuis, Netherlands	1:43.21*

Year	Men's 5000 Meters	Time
1924	Clas Thunberg, Finland	8:39.0
1928	Ivar Ballangrud, Norway	8:50.5
1932	Irving Jaffee, United States	9:40.8
1936	Ivar Ballangrud, Norway	8:19.6
1948	Reidar Liaklev, Norway	8:29.4
1952	Hjalmar Andersen, Norway	8:10.6
1956	Boris Shilkov, USSR	7:48.7
1960	Viktor Kosichkin, USSR	7:51.3
1964	Knut Johannesen, Norway	7:38.4
1968	F. Anton Maier, Norway	7:22.4
1972	Ard Schenk, Netherlands	7:23.61
1976	Sten Stensen, Norway	7:24.48
1980	Eric Heiden, United States	7:02.29
1984	Tomas Gustafson, Sweden	7:12.28
1988	Tomas Gustafson, Sweden	6:44.63
1992	Geir Karlstad, Norway	6:59.97
1994	Johann Koss, Norway	6:34.96
1998	Gianni Romme, Netherlands	6:22.20
2002	Jochem Uytdehaage, Netherlands	6:14.66
2006	Chad Hedrick, United States	6:14.68
2010	Sven Kramer, Netherlands	6:14.60
2014	Sven Kramer, Netherlands	6:10.76
2018	Sven Kramer, Netherlands	6:09.76
2022	Nils van der Poel, Sweden	6:08.84*

Year	Men's 10,000 Meters	Time
1924	Julius Skutnabb, Finland	18:04.8
1928	Event not held because of thawing of ice	
1932	Irving Jaffee, United States	19:13.6
1936	Ivar Ballangrud, Norway	17:24.3
1948	Ake Seyffarth, Sweden	17:26.3
1952	Hjalmar Andersen, Norway	16:45.8
1956	Sigvard Ericsson, Sweden	16:35.9
1960	Knut Johannesen, Norway	15:46.6
1964	Jonny Nilsson, Sweden	15:50.1
1968	Jonny Hoeglin, Sweden	15:23.6
1972	Ard Schenk, Netherlands	15:01.35
1976	Piet Kleine, Netherlands	14:50.59
1980	Eric Heiden, United States	14:28.13
1984	Igor Malkov, USSR	14:39.90
1988	Tomas Gustafson, Sweden	13:48.20
1992	Bart Veldkamp, Netherlands	14:12.12
1994	Johann Koss, Norway	13:30.55
1998	Gianni Romme, Netherlands	13:15.33
2002	Jochem Uytdehaage, Netherlands	12:58.92
2006	Bob de Jong, Netherlands	13:01.57
2010	Lee Seung-hoon, S. Korea	12:58.55
2014	Jorrit Bergsma, Netherlands	12:44.45
2018	Ted-Jan Bloemen, Canada	12:39.77
2022	Nils van der Poel, Sweden	12:30.74*

Men's Mass Start

2018 Lee Seung-hoon, S. Korea
2022 Bart Swings, Belgium

Year	Men's Team Pursuit	Time
2006	Italy, Canada, Netherlands	3:44.46
2010	Canada, United States, Netherlands	3:41.37
2014	Netherlands, S. Korea, Poland	3:37.71
2018	Norway, S. Korea, Netherlands	3:37.32
2022	Norway, ROC, United States	3:38.08

Year	Women's 500 Meters	Time
1960	Helga Haase, Germany	0:45.9
1964	Lydia Skoblikova, USSR	0:45.0
1968	Ludmila Titova, USSR	0:46.1
1972	Anne Henning, United States	0:43.33
1976	Sheila Young, United States	0:42.76
1980	Karin Enke, E. Germany	0:41.78
1984	Christa Rothenburger, E. Germany	0:41.02
1988	Bonnie Blair, United States	0:39.10
1992	Bonnie Blair, United States	0:40.33
1994	Bonnie Blair, United States	0:39.25
1998	Catriona Le May Doan, Canada	0:38.21
2002	Catriona Le May Doan, Canada	0:37.30
2006	Svetlana Zhurova, Russia	0:38.23
2010	Lee Sang-hwa, S. Korea	0:76.09
2014	Lee Sang-hwa, S. Korea	0:74.70
2018	Nao Kodaira, Japan	0:36.94*
2022	Erin Jackson, United States	0.37.04

Note: In 2010 and 2014, results include the total of two 500-km race times.

Year	Women's 1000 Meters	Time
1960	Klara Guseva, USSR	1:34.1
1964	Lydia Skoblikova, USSR	1:33.2
1968	Carolina Geijssen, Netherlands	1:32.6
1972	Monika Pflug, W. Germany	1:31.40
1976	Tatiana Averina, USSR	1:28.43
1980	Natalya Petruseva, USSR	1:24.10
1984	Karin Enke, E. Germany	1:21.61
1988	Christa Rothenburger, E. Germany	1:17.65

	Women's 1000 Meters	Time
1992	Bonnie Blair, United States	1:21.90
1994	Bonnie Blair, United States	1:18.74
1998	Marianne Timmer, Netherlands	1:16.51
2002	Chris Witty, United States	1:13.83
2006	Marianne Timmer, Netherlands	1:16.05
2010	Christine Nesbitt, Canada	1:16.56
2014	Zhang Hong, China	1:14.02
2018	Jorien ter Mors, Netherlands	1:13.56
2022	Miho Takagi, Japan	1:13.19*

	Women's 1500 Meters	Time
1960	Lydia Skoblikova, USSR	2:52.2
1964	Lydia Skoblikova, USSR	2:22.6
1968	Kaija Mustonen, Finland	2:22.4
1972	Dianne Holum, United States	2:20.85
1976	Galina Stepanskaya, USSR	2:16.58
1980	Anne Borckink, Netherlands	2:10.95
1984	Karin Enke, E. Germany	2:03.42
1988	Yvonne van Gennip, Netherlands	2:00.68
1992	Jacqueline Boerner, Germany	2:05.87
1994	Emese Hunyady, Austria	2:02.19
1998	Marianne Timmer, Netherlands	1:57.58
2002	Anni Friesinger, Germany	1:54.02
2006	Cindy Klassen, Canada	1:55.27
2010	Ireen Wüst, Netherlands	1:56.89
2014	Jorien ter Mors, Netherlands	1:53.51
2018	Ireen Wüst, Netherlands	1:54.35
2022	Ireen Wüst, Netherlands	1:53.28*

	Women's 3000 Meters	Time
1960	Lydia Skoblikova, USSR	5:14.3
1964	Lydia Skoblikova, USSR	5:14.9
1968	Johanna Schut, Netherlands	4:56.2
1972	Christina Baas-Kaiser, Netherlands	4:52.14
1976	Tatiana Averina, USSR	4:45.19
1980	Bjoerg Eva Jensen, Norway	4:32.13
1984	Andrea Schoene, E. Germany	4:24.79
1988	Yvonne van Gennip, Netherlands	4:11.94
1992	Gunda Niemann, Germany	4:19.90
1994	Svetlana Bazhanova, Russia	4:17.43
1998	Gunda Niemann-Stirnemann, Germany	4:07.29
2002	Claudia Pechstein, Germany	3:57.70
2006	Ireen Wüst, Netherlands	4:02.43
2010	Martina Sablikova, Czech Republic	4:02.53
2014	Ireen Wüst, Netherlands	4:00.34
2018	Carlijn Achtereekte, Netherlands	3:59.21
2022	Irene Schouten, Netherlands	3:56.93*

	Women's 5000 Meters	Time
1988	Yvonne van Gennip, Netherlands	7:14.13
1992	Gunda Niemann, Germany	7:31.57
1994	Claudia Pechstein, Germany	7:14.37
1998	Claudia Pechstein, Germany	6:59.61
2002	Claudia Pechstein, Germany	6:46.91
2006	Clara Hughes, Canada	6:59.07
2010	Martina Sablikova, Czech Republic	6:50.91
2014	Martina Sablikova, Czech Republic	6:51.54
2018	Esmee Visser, Netherlands	6:50.23
2022	Irene Schouten, Netherlands	6:43.51*

	Women's Mass Start
2018	Nana Takagi, Japan
2022	Irene Schouten, Netherlands

	Women's Team Pursuit	Time
2006	Germany, Canada, Russia	3:01.25
2010	Germany, Japan, Poland	3:02.82
2014	Netherlands, Poland, Russia	2:58.05
2018	Japan, Netherlands, United States	2:53.89
2022	Canada, Japan, Netherlands	2:53.44*

Speed Skating (Short Track)

* = Olympic record

	Men's 500 Meters	Time
1998	Takafumi Nishitani, Japan	0:42.862
2002	Marc Gagnon, Canada	0:41.802
2006	Apolo Anton Ohno, United States	0:41.935
2010	Charles Hamelin, Canada	0:40.981
2014	Victor An, Russia	0:41.312
2018	Wu Dajing, China	0:39.584*
2022	Shaoang Liu, Hungary	0.40.388

	Men's 1000 Meters	Time
1992	Kim Ki-hoon, S. Korea	1:30.76
1994	Kim Ki-hoon, S. Korea	1:34.57
1998	Kim Dong-sung, S. Korea	1:32.375
2002	Steven Bradbury, Australia	1:29.109
2006	Ahn Hyun-soo, S. Korea	1:26.739
2010	Lee Jung-su, S. Korea	1:23.747
2014	Victor An, Russia	1:25.325
2018	Samuel Girard, Canada	1:24.650
2022	Ren Ziwei, China	1:26.768

	Men's 1500 Meters	Time
2002	Apolo Anton Ohno, United States	2:18.541
2006	Ahn Hyun-soo, S. Korea	2:25.341
2010	Lee Jung-su, S. Korea	2:17.611
2014	Charles Hamelin, Canada	2:14.985
2018	Lim Hyo-jun, S. Korea	2:10.485
2022	Hwang Dae-heon, S. Korea	2:09.219

	Men's 5000-Meter Relay	Time
1992	S. Korea, Canada, Japan	7:14.02
1994	Italy, United States, Australia	7:11.74
1998	Canada, S. Korea, China	7:06.075
2002	Canada, Italy, China	6:51.579
2006	S. Korea, Canada, United States	6:43.376
2010	Canada, S. Korea, United States	6:44.224
2014	Russia, United States, China	6:42.100
2018	Hungary, China, Canada	6:31.971*
2022	Canada, S. Korea, Italy	6:41.257

	Women's 500 Meters	Time
1992	Cathy Turner, United States	0:47.04
1994	Cathy Turner, United States	0:45.98
1998	Annie Perreault, Canada	0:46.568
2002	Yang Yang (A), China	0:44.187
2006	Wang Meng, China	0:44.345
2010	Wang Meng, China	0:43.048
2014	Li Jianrou, China	0:45.263
2018	Arianna Fontana, Italy	0:42.569
2022	Arianna Fontana, Italy	0.42.488

	Women's 1000 Meters	Time
1998	Chun Lee-kyung, S. Korea	1:42.776
2002	Yang Yang (A), China	1:36.391
2006	Jin Sun-yu, S. Korea	1:32.859
2010	Wang Meng, China	1:29.213
2014	Park Seung-hi, S. Korea	1:30.761
2018	Suzanne Schulting, Netherlands	1:29.778
2022	Suzanne Schulting, Netherlands	1:28.391

	Women's 1500 Meters	Time
2002	Ko Gi-hyun, S. Korea	2:31.581
2006	Jin Sun-yu, S. Korea	2:23.494
2010	Zhou Yang, China	2:16.993
2014	Zhou Yang, China	2:19.140
2018	Choi Min-jeong, S. Korea	2:24.948
2022	Choi Min-jeong, S. Korea	2:17.789

	Women's 3000-Meter Relay	Time
1992	Canada, United States, Unified Team	4:36.62
1994	S. Korea, Canada, United States	4:26.64
1998	S. Korea, China, Canada	4:16.26
2002	S. Korea, China, Canada	4:12.793
2006	S. Korea, Canada, Italy	4:17.040
2010	China, Canada, United States	4:06.610*
2014	S. Korea, Canada, Italy	4:09.498
2018	S. Korea, Italy, Netherlands	4:07.361
2022	Netherlands, S. Korea, China	4:03.409*

	Mixed 2000-Meter Relay	Time
2022	China, Italy, Hungary	2:37.348

Paralympic Games

Aug. 28-Sept. 8, 2024

Around 4,400 athletes from 167 countries, plus the Refugee Team and Neutral Paralympic Athletes from Russia and Belarus, met at the XVII Paralympic Summer Games, held Aug. 28-Sept. 8, 2024, in Paris, France. A total of 549 gold medals were awarded in 22 sports. China claimed 220 total medals, outpacing Great Britain (124) and the United States (105). The XIII Paralympic Winter Games were held Mar. 4-13, 2022, in the same Olympic venues that hosted the 2022 Winter Games in Beijing, China. A record 564 athletes from 46 delegations competed in 78 medal events across 6 sports. China led the medal tally with 61 total (18 gold), followed by Ukraine with 29 (11 gold), Canada with 25 (8 gold), and France with 12 (7 gold). The 2026 Winter Paralympics were expected to be held in Mar. in Milan and Cortina d'Ampezzo, Italy.

The first Olympic Games for athletes with an impairment were held in Rome after the 1960 Summer Olympics; use of the name "paralympic" began with the 1964 Games in Tokyo. The Paralympics are held by the Olympic host country in the same year and usually the same city and venue or venues. In 1976, the first Winter Paralympics were held in Ornskoldsvik, Sweden.

COLLEGE FOOTBALL

2023 CFP Championship: Undefeated Michigan Takes Down Washington

The Univ. of Michigan Wolverines dominated the Univ. of Washington Huskies, 34-13, at NRG Stadium in Houston, TX, Jan. 8, 2024, to claim the 2023 College Football Playoff Championship. The vaunted Wolverines defense held Huskies QB (and Heisman Trophy runner-up) Michael Penix Jr. to 27-of-51 passing, one touchdown, and two interceptions. Led by head coach Jim Harbaugh, who was suspended for three games on two separate occasions during the season, Big Blue still went undefeated—including a 27-20 win over Alabama at the Rose Bowl—on its path to claiming the school's first title since 1997.

2023 College Football Final Rankings

College Football Playoff Rankings

Rank, team	Rank, team
1. Michigan	14. Arizona
2. Washington	15. Louisville
3. Texas	16. Notre Dame
4. Alabama	17. Iowa
5. Florida St.	18. NC State
6. Georgia	19. Oregon St.
7. Ohio St.	20. Oklahoma St.
8. Oregon	21. Tennessee
9. Missouri	22. Clemson
10. Penn St.	23. Liberty
11. Mississippi	24. SMU
12. Oklahoma	25. Kansas St.
13. LSU	

Associated Press Poll

Rank, team	Rank, team
1. Michigan	14. Notre Dame
2. Washington	15. Oklahoma
3. Texas	16. Oklahoma St.
4. Georgia	17. Tennessee
5. Alabama	18. Kansas State
6. Oregon	19. Louisville
7. Florida St.	20. Clemson
8. Missouri	21. NC State
9. Mississippi	22. SMU
10. Ohio State	23. Kansas
11. Arizona	24. Iowa
12. LSU	25. Liberty
13. Penn St.	

USA Today Coaches Poll

Rank, team	Rank, team
1. Michigan	14. Notre Dame
2. Washington	15. Oklahoma
3. Georgia	16. Oklahoma St.
4. Texas	17. Tennessee
5. Alabama	18. Louisville
6. Florida St.	19. Kansas St.
7. Oregon	20. Clemson
8. Missouri	21. NC State
9. Mississippi	22. Iowa
10. Ohio State	23. Kansas
11. Arizona	24. SMU
12. LSU	25. West Virginia
13. Penn State	

Note: College Football Playoff ranking is through games Dec. 2, 2023. Final AP poll and Coaches poll include games through Jan. 8, 2024 (after all bowls and championship game).

National College Football Championship Game Results, 1998-2023

The Bowl Championship Series (BCS) National Championship game (BCS ranked No. 1 vs. BCS No. 2) determined the NCAA's Football Bowl Subdivision (Div. I-A) champion in 1998-2013. The College Football Playoff (CFP) replaced the BCS at the end of the 2014 regular season. The four-team CFP consisted of a semifinal round (rotating among the following six bowl games: Sugar, Rose, Orange, Cotton, Peach, and Fiesta) and a championship game played on a Monday night. A 12-team playoff was expected to begin in Dec. 2024, replacing the four-team CFP. Years shown here are for regular season, not year in which championship was played.

Year	Result
1998	Tennessee 23, Florida St. 16
1999	Florida St. 46, Virginia Tech 29
2000	Oklahoma 13, Florida St. 2
2001	Miami (FL) 37, Nebraska 14
2002	Ohio St. 31, Miami (FL) 24
2003[1]	LSU 21, Oklahoma 14
2004[2]	USC 55, Oklahoma 19
2005	Texas 41, USC 38
2006	Florida 41, Ohio St. 14
2007	LSU 38, Ohio St. 24
2008	Florida 24, Oklahoma 14
2009	Alabama 37, Texas 21
2010	Auburn 22, Oregon 19
2011	Alabama 21, LSU 0
2012	Alabama 42, Notre Dame 14
2013	Florida St. 34, Auburn 31
2014	Ohio St. 42, Oregon 20
2015	Alabama 45, Clemson 40
2016	Clemson 35, Alabama 31
2017	Alabama 26, Georgia 23 (OT)
2018	Clemson 44, Alabama 16
2019	LSU 42, Clemson 25
2020	Alabama 52, Ohio St. 24
2021	Georgia 33, Alabama 18
2022	Georgia 65, TCU 7
2023	Michigan 34, Washington 13

(1) AP named USC No. 1 in its final poll despite its not appearing in the BCS No. 1 vs. No. 2 matchup. (2) The BCS's Presidential Oversight Committee vacated USC's 2004 championship due to rules violations.

National College Football Champions, 1936-1997

Unofficial champion(s), as selected by the AP poll of writers and a separate poll of coaches. Where the polls disagreed, both teams are listed with the AP winner first. The AP poll started in 1936, the coaches poll in 1950.

Year	Champion(s)
1936	Minnesota
1937	Pittsburgh
1938	Texas Christian
1939	Texas A&M
1940	Minnesota
1941	Minnesota
1942	Ohio St.
1943	Notre Dame
1944	Army
1945	Army
1946	Notre Dame
1947	Notre Dame
1948	Michigan
1949	Notre Dame
1950	Oklahoma
1951	Tennessee
1952	Michigan St.
1953	Maryland
1954	Ohio St./UCLA
1955	Oklahoma
1956	Oklahoma
1957	Auburn/Ohio St.
1958	LSU
1959	Syracuse
1960	Minnesota
1961	Alabama
1962	USC
1963	Texas
1964	Alabama
1965	Alabama/Mich. St.
1966	Notre Dame
1967	USC
1968	Ohio St.
1969	Texas
1970	Nebraska/Texas
1971	Nebraska
1972	USC
1973	Notre Dame/ Alabama
1974	Oklahoma/USC
1975	Oklahoma
1976	Pittsburgh
1977	Notre Dame
1978	Alabama/USC
1979	Alabama
1980	Georgia
1981	Clemson
1982	Penn St.
1983	Miami (FL)
1984	Brigham Young
1985	Oklahoma
1986	Penn St.
1987	Miami (FL)
1988	Notre Dame
1989	Miami (FL)
1990	Colorado/GA Tech
1991	Miami (FL)/Wash.
1992	Alabama
1993	Florida St.
1994	Nebraska
1995	Nebraska
1996	Florida
1997	Mich./Nebraska

Results of Major Bowl Games

Date indicates year the game was played; bowl games are generally played in late Dec. or early Jan. CFP = College Football Playoff semifinal game.

Rose Bowl Results, 1902-2024

Year	Result
1902	(Jan.) Michigan 49, Stanford 0
1916	Washington St. 14, Brown 0
1917	Oregon 14, Pennsylvania 0
1918-19	Service teams
1920	Harvard 7, Oregon 6
1921	California 28, Ohio St. 0
1922	Washington & Jefferson 0, California 0
1923	USC 14, Penn St. 3
1924	Navy 14, Washington 14
1925	Notre Dame 27, Stanford 10
1926	Alabama 20, Washington 19
1927	Alabama 7, Stanford 7
1928	Stanford 7, Pittsburgh 6
1929	Georgia Tech 8, California 7
1930	USC 47, Pittsburgh 14
1931	Alabama 24, Washington St. 0
1932	USC 21, Tulane 12
1933	USC 35, Pittsburgh 0
1934	Columbia 7, Stanford 0
1935	Alabama 29, Stanford 13
1936	Stanford 7, SMU 0
1937	Pittsburgh 21, Washington 0
1938	California 13, Alabama 0
1939	USC 7, Duke 3
1940	USC 14, Tennessee 0
1941	Stanford 21, Nebraska 13
1942	Oregon St. 20, Duke 16
1943	Georgia 9, UCLA 0
1944	USC 29, Washington 0
1945	USC 25, Tennessee 0
1946	Alabama 34, USC 14
1947	Illinois 45, UCLA 14
1948	Michigan 49, USC 0
1949	Northwestern 20, California 14
1950	Ohio St. 17, California 14
1951	Michigan 14, California 6
1952	Illinois 40, Stanford 7
1953	USC 7, Wisconsin 0

1954	Michigan St. 28, UCLA 20
1955	Ohio St. 20, USC 7
1956	Michigan St. 17, UCLA 14
1957	Iowa 35, Oregon St. 19
1958	Ohio St. 10, Oregon 7
1959	Iowa 38, California 12
1960	Washington 44, Wisconsin 8
1961	Washington 17, Minnesota 7
1962	Minnesota 21, UCLA 3
1963	USC 42, Wisconsin 37
1964	Illinois 17, Washington 7
1965	Michigan 34, Oregon St. 7
1966	UCLA 14, Michigan St. 12
1967	Purdue 14, USC 13
1968	USC 14, Indiana 3
1969	Ohio St. 27, USC 16
1970	USC 10, Michigan 3
1971	Stanford 27, Ohio St. 17
1972	Stanford 13, Michigan 12
1973	USC 42, Ohio St. 17
1974	Ohio St. 42, USC 21
1975	USC 18, Ohio St. 17
1976	UCLA 23, Ohio St. 10
1977	USC 14, Michigan 6
1978	Washington 27, Michigan 20
1979	USC 17, Michigan 10
1980	USC 17, Ohio St. 16
1981	Michigan 23, Washington 6
1982	Washington 28, Iowa 0
1983	UCLA 24, Michigan 14
1984	UCLA 45, Illinois 9
1985	USC 20, Ohio St. 17
1986	UCLA 45, Iowa 28
1987	Arizona St. 22, Michigan 15
1988	Michigan St. 20, USC 17
1989	Michigan 22, USC 14
1990	USC 17, Michigan 10
1991	Washington 46, Iowa 34
1992	Washington 34, Michigan 14
1993	Michigan 38, Washington 31
1994	Wisconsin 21, UCLA 16
1995	Penn St. 38, Oregon 20
1996	USC 41, Northwestern 32
1997	Ohio St. 20, Arizona St. 17
1998	Michigan 21, Washington St. 16
1999	Wisconsin 38, UCLA 31
2000	Wisconsin 17, Stanford 9
2001	Washington 34, Purdue 24
2002	Miami (FL) 37, Nebraska 14
2003	Oklahoma 34, Washington St. 14
2004	USC 28, Michigan 14
2005	Texas 38, Michigan 37
2006	Texas 41, USC 38
2007	USC 32, Michigan 18
2008	USC 49, Illinois 17
2009	USC 38, Penn St. 24
2010	Ohio St. 26, Oregon 17
2011	TCU 21, Wisconsin 19
2012	Oregon 45, Wisconsin 38
2013	Stanford 20, Wisconsin 14
2014	Michigan St. 24, Stanford 20
2015	Oregon 59, Florida St. 20 (CFP)
2016	Stanford 45, Iowa 16
2017	USC 52, Penn St. 49
2018	Georgia 54, Oklahoma 48 (2 OT)(CFP)
2019	Ohio St. 28, Washington 23
2020	Oregon 28, Wisconsin 27
2021	Alabama 31, Notre Dame 14 (CFP)
2022	Ohio St. 48, Utah 45
2023	Penn St. 35, Utah 21
2024	Michigan 27, Alabama 20 (OT) (CFP)

Orange Bowl Results, 1935-2023

1935	(Jan.) Bucknell 26, Miami (FL) 0
1936	Catholic 20, Mississippi 19
1937	Duquesne 13, Mississippi St. 12
1938	Auburn 6, Michigan St. 0
1939	Tennessee 17, Oklahoma 0
1940	Georgia Tech 21, Missouri 7
1941	Mississippi St. 14, Georgetown 7
1942	Georgia 40, TCU 26
1943	Alabama 37, Boston College 21
1944	LSU 19, Texas A&M 14
1945	Tulsa 26, Georgia Tech 12
1946	Miami (FL) 13, Holy Cross 6
1947	Rice 8, Tennessee 0
1948	Georgia Tech 20, Kansas 14
1949	Texas 41, Georgia 28
1950	Santa Clara 21, Kentucky 13
1951	Clemson 15, Miami (FL) 14
1952	Georgia Tech 17, Baylor 14
1953	Alabama 61, Syracuse 6
1954	Oklahoma 7, Maryland 0
1955	Duke 34, Nebraska 7
1956	Oklahoma 20, Maryland 6
1957	Colorado 27, Clemson 21
1958	Oklahoma 48, Duke 21
1959	Oklahoma 21, Syracuse 6
1960	Georgia 14, Missouri 0
1961	Missouri 21, Navy 14
1962	LSU 25, Colorado 7
1963	Alabama 17, Oklahoma 0
1964	Nebraska 13, Auburn 7
1965	Texas 21, Alabama 17
1966	Alabama 39, Nebraska 28
1967	Florida 27, Georgia Tech 12
1968	Oklahoma 26, Tennessee 24
1969	Penn St. 15, Kansas 14
1970	Penn St. 10, Missouri 3
1971	Nebraska 17, LSU 12
1972	Nebraska 38, Alabama 6
1973	Nebraska 40, Notre Dame 6
1974	Penn St. 16, LSU 9
1975	Notre Dame 13, Alabama 11
1976	Oklahoma 14, Michigan 6
1977	Ohio St. 27, Colorado 10
1978	Arkansas 31, Oklahoma 6
1979	Oklahoma 31, Nebraska 24
1980	Oklahoma 24, Florida St. 7
1981	Oklahoma 18, Florida St. 17
1982	Clemson 22, Nebraska 15
1983	Nebraska 21, LSU 20
1984	Miami (FL) 31, Nebraska 30
1985	Washington 28, Oklahoma 17
1986	Oklahoma 25, Penn St. 10
1987	Oklahoma 42, Arkansas 8
1988	Miami (FL) 20, Oklahoma 14
1989	Miami (FL) 23, Nebraska 3
1990	Notre Dame 21, Colorado 6
1991	Colorado 10, Notre Dame 9
1992	Miami (FL) 22, Nebraska 0
1993	Florida St. 27, Nebraska 14
1994	Florida St. 18, Nebraska 16
1995	Nebraska 24, Miami (FL) 17
1996	Florida St. 31, Notre Dame 26
1996	(Dec.) Nebraska 41, Virginia Tech 21
1998	(Jan.) Nebraska 42, Tennessee 17
1999	Florida 31, Syracuse 10
2000	Michigan 35, Alabama 34 (OT)
2001	Oklahoma 13, Florida St. 2
2002	Florida 56, Maryland 23
2003	USC 38, Iowa 17
2004	Miami (FL) 16, Florida St. 14
2005	USC 55, Oklahoma 19
2006	Penn St. 26, Florida St. 23 (3 OT)
2007	Louisville 24, Wake Forest 13
2008	Kansas 24, Virginia Tech 21
2009	Virginia Tech 20, Cincinnati 7
2010	Iowa 24, Georgia Tech 14
2011	Stanford 40, Virginia Tech 12
2012	West Virginia 70, Clemson 33
2013	Florida St. 31, Northern Illinois 10
2014	Clemson 40, Ohio St. 35
2014	(Dec.) Georgia Tech 49, Mississippi St. 34
2015	Clemson 37, Oklahoma 17 (CFP)
2016	Florida St. 33, Michigan 32
2017	Wisconsin 34, Miami (FL) 24
2018	Alabama 45, Oklahoma 34 (CFP)
2019	Florida 36, Virginia 28
2021	(Jan.) Texas A&M 41, North Carolina 27
2021	(Dec.) Georgia 34, Michigan 11 (CFP)
2022	Tennessee 31, Clemson 14
2023	Georgia 63, Florida St. 3

Sugar Bowl Results, 1935-2024

1935	(Jan.) Tulane 20, Temple 14
1936	TCU 3, LSU 2
1937	Santa Clara 21, LSU 14
1938	Santa Clara 6, LSU 0
1939	TCU 15, Carnegie Tech 7
1940	Texas A&M 14, Tulane 13
1941	Boston College 19, Tennessee 13
1942	Fordham 2, Missouri 0
1943	Tennessee 14, Tulsa 7
1944	Georgia Tech 20, Tulsa 18
1945	Duke 29, Alabama 26
1946	Oklahoma A&M 33, St. Mary's (CA) 13
1947	Georgia 20, N. Carolina 10
1948	Texas 27, Alabama 7
1949	Oklahoma 14, N. Carolina 6
1950	Oklahoma 35, LSU 0
1951	Kentucky 13, Oklahoma 7
1952	Maryland 28, Tennessee 13
1953	Georgia Tech 24, Mississippi 7
1954	Georgia Tech 42, West Virginia 19
1955	Navy 21, Mississippi 0
1956	Georgia Tech 7, Pittsburgh 0
1957	Baylor 13, Tennessee 7
1958	Mississippi 39, Texas 7
1959	LSU 7, Clemson 0
1960	Mississippi 21, LSU 0
1961	Mississippi 14, Rice 6
1962	Alabama 10, Arkansas 3
1963	Mississippi 17, Arkansas 13
1964	Alabama 12, Mississippi 7
1965	LSU 13, Syracuse 10
1966	Missouri 20, Florida 18
1967	Alabama 34, Nebraska 7
1968	LSU 20, Wyoming 13
1969	Arkansas 16, Georgia 2
1970	Mississippi 27, Arkansas 22
1971	Tennessee 34, Air Force 13
1972	Oklahoma 40, Auburn 22
1972	(Dec.) Oklahoma 14, Penn St. 0
1973	Notre Dame 24, Alabama 23
1974	Nebraska 13, Florida 10
1975	Alabama 13, Penn St. 6
1977	(Jan.) Pittsburgh 27, Georgia 3
1978	Alabama 35, Ohio St. 6
1979	Alabama 14, Penn St. 7
1980	Alabama 24, Arkansas 9
1981	Georgia 17, Notre Dame 10
1982	Pittsburgh 24, Georgia 20
1983	Penn St. 27, Georgia 23
1984	Auburn 9, Michigan 7
1985	Nebraska 28, LSU 10
1986	Tennessee 35, Miami (FL) 7
1987	Nebraska 30, LSU 15
1988	Syracuse 16, Auburn 16
1989	Florida St. 13, Auburn 7
1990	Miami (FL) 33, Alabama 25
1991	Tennessee 23, Virginia 22
1992	Notre Dame 39, Florida 28
1993	Alabama 34, Miami (FL) 13
1994	Florida 41, West Virginia 7
1995	Florida St. 23, Florida 17
1995	(Dec.) Virginia Tech 28, Texas 10
1997	(Jan.) Florida 52, Florida St. 20
1998	Florida St. 31, Ohio St. 14
1999	Ohio St. 24, Texas A&M 14
2000	Florida St. 46, Virginia Tech 29
2001	Miami (FL) 37, Florida 20
2002	LSU 47, Illinois 34
2003	Georgia 26, Florida St. 13
2004	LSU 21, Oklahoma 14
2005	Auburn 16, Virginia Tech 13
2006	West Virginia 38, Georgia 35
2007	LSU 41, Notre Dame 14
2008	Georgia 41, Hawaii 10
2009	Utah 31, Alabama 17
2010	Florida 51, Cincinnati 24
2011	Ohio St. 31, Arkansas 26
2012	Michigan 23, Virginia Tech 20
2013	Louisville 33, Florida 23
2014	Oklahoma 45, Alabama 31
2015	Ohio St. 42, Alabama 35 (CFP)
2016	Mississippi 48, Oklahoma St. 20
2017	Oklahoma 35, Auburn 19
2018	Alabama 24, Clemson 6 (CFP)
2019	Texas 28, Georgia 21
2020	Georgia 26, Baylor 14
2021	Ohio St. 49, Clemson 28 (CFP)
2022	(Jan.) Baylor 21, Mississippi 7
2022	(Dec.) Alabama 45, Kansas St. 20
2024	(Jan.) Washington 37, Texas 31 (CFP)

Cotton Bowl Results, 1937-2023

1937 (Jan.) TCU 16, Marquette 6
1938 Rice 28, Colorado 14
1939 St. Mary's 20, Texas Tech 13
1940 Clemson 6, Boston College 3
1941 Texas A&M 13, Fordham 12
1942 Alabama 29, Texas A&M 21
1943 Texas 14, Georgia Tech 7
1944 Randolph Field 7, Texas 7
1945 Oklahoma A&M 34, TCU 0
1946 Texas 40, Missouri 27
1947 Arkansas 0, LSU 0
1948 SMU 13, Penn St. 13
1949 SMU 21, Oregon 13
1950 Rice 27, N. Carolina 13
1951 Tennessee 20, Texas 14
1952 Kentucky 20, TCU 7
1953 Texas 16, Tennessee 0
1954 Rice 28, Alabama 6
1955 Georgia Tech 14, Arkansas 6
1956 Mississippi 14, TCU 13
1957 TCU 28, Syracuse 27
1958 Navy 20, Rice 7
1959 TCU 0, Air Force 0
1960 Syracuse 23, Texas 14
1961 Duke 7, Arkansas 6
1962 Texas 12, Mississippi 7
1963 LSU 13, Texas 0
1964 Texas 28, Navy 6
1965 Arkansas 10, Nebraska 7
1966 LSU 14, Arkansas 7
1966 (Dec.) Georgia 24, SMU 9
1968 (Jan.) Texas A&M 20, Alabama 16
1969 Texas 36, Tennessee 13
1970 Texas 21, Notre Dame 17
1971 Notre Dame 24, Texas 11
1972 Penn St. 30, Texas 6
1973 Texas 17, Alabama 13
1974 Nebraska 19, Texas 3
1975 Penn St. 41, Baylor 20
1976 Arkansas 31, Georgia 10
1977 Houston 30, Maryland 21
1978 Notre Dame 38, Texas 10
1979 Notre Dame 35, Houston 34
1980 Houston 17, Nebraska 14
1981 Alabama 30, Baylor 2
1982 Texas 14, Alabama 12
1983 SMU 7, Pittsburgh 3
1984 Georgia 10, Texas 9
1985 Boston College 45, Houston 28
1986 Texas A&M 36, Auburn 16
1987 Ohio St. 28, Texas A&M 12
1988 Texas A&M 35, Notre Dame 10
1989 UCLA 17, Arkansas 3
1990 Tennessee 31, Arkansas 27
1991 Miami (FL) 46, Texas 3
1992 Florida St. 10, Texas A&M 2
1993 Notre Dame 28, Texas A&M 3
1994 Notre Dame 24, Texas A&M 21
1995 USC 55, Texas Tech 14
1996 Colorado 38, Oregon 6
1997 Brigham Young 19, Kansas St. 15
1998 UCLA 29, Texas A&M 23
1999 Texas 38, Mississippi St. 11
2000 Arkansas 27, Texas 6
2001 Kansas St. 35, Tennessee 21
2002 Oklahoma 10, Arkansas 3
2003 Texas 35, LSU 20
2004 Mississippi 31, Oklahoma St. 28
2005 Tennessee 38, Texas A&M 7
2006 Alabama 13, Texas Tech 10
2007 Auburn 17, Nebraska 14
2008 Missouri 38, Arkansas 7
2009 Mississippi 47, Texas Tech 34
2010 Mississippi 21, Oklahoma St. 7
2011 LSU 41, Texas A&M 24
2012 Arkansas 29, Kansas St. 16
2013 Texas A&M 41, Oklahoma 13
2014 Missouri 41, Oklahoma St. 31
2015 Michigan St. 42, Baylor 41
2015 (Dec.) Alabama 38, Michigan St. 0 (CFP)
2017 (Jan.) Wisconsin 24, W. Michigan 16
2017 (Dec.) Ohio St. 24, USC 7
2018 Clemson 30, Notre Dame 3 (CFP)
2019 Penn St. 53, Memphis 39
2020 Oklahoma 55, Florida 20
2021 Alabama 27, Cincinnati 6 (CFP)
2023 (Jan.) Tulane 46, USC 45
2023 (Dec.) Missouri 14, Ohio St. 3

Peach Bowl Results, 1968-2023

1968 (Dec.) LSU 31, Florida St. 27
1969 West Virginia 14, S. Carolina 3
1970 Arizona St. 48, N. Carolina 26
1971 Mississippi 41, Georgia Tech 18
1972 N. Carolina St. 49, West Virginia 13
1973 Georgia 17, Maryland 16
1974 Vanderbilt 6, Texas Tech 6
1975 West Virginia 13, N. Carolina St. 10
1976 Kentucky 21, N. Carolina 0
1977 N. Carolina St. 24, Iowa St. 14
1978 Purdue 41, Georgia Tech 21
1979 Baylor 24, Clemson 18
1981 (Jan.) Miami (FL) 20, Virginia Tech 10
1981 (Dec.) West Virginia 26, Florida 6
1982 Iowa 28, Tennessee 22
1983 Florida St. 28, N. Carolina 3
1984 Virginia 27, Purdue 22
1985 Army 31, Illinois 29
1986 Virginia Tech 25, N. Carolina St. 24
1988 (Jan.) Tennessee 27, Indiana 22
1988 (Dec.) N. Carolina St. 28, Iowa 23
1989 Syracuse 19, Georgia 18
1990 Auburn 27, Indiana 23
1992 (Jan.) E. Carolina 37, N. Carolina St. 34
1993 N. Carolina 21, Mississippi St. 17
1993 (Dec.) Clemson 14, Kentucky 13
1995 (Jan.) N. Carolina St. 28, Mississippi St. 24
1995 (Dec.) Virginia 34, Georgia 27
1996 LSU 10, Clemson 7
1998 (Jan.) Auburn 21, Clemson 17
1998 (Dec.) Georgia 35, Virginia 33
1999 Mississippi St. 27, Clemson 7
2000 LSU 28, Georgia Tech 14
2001 N. Carolina 16, Auburn 10
2002 Maryland 30, Tennessee 3
2004 (Jan.) Clemson 27, Tennessee 14
2004 (Dec.) Miami (FL) 27, Florida 10
2005 LSU 40, Miami (FL) 3
2006 Georgia 31, Virginia Tech 24
2007 Auburn 23, Clemson 20 (OT)
2008 LSU 38, Georgia Tech 3
2009 Virginia Tech 37, Tennessee 14
2010 Florida St. 26, S. Carolina 17
2011 Auburn 43, Virginia 24
2012 Clemson 25, LSU 24
2013 Texas A&M 52, Duke 48
2014 TCU 42, Mississippi 3
2015 Houston 38, Florida St. 24
2016 Alabama 24, Washington 7 (CFP)
2018 (Jan.) Central Florida 34, Auburn 27
2018 (Dec.) Florida 41, Michigan 15
2019 LSU 63, Oklahoma 28 (CFP)
2021 (Jan.) Georgia 24, Cincinnati 21
2021 (Dec.) Michigan St. 31, Pittsburgh 21
2022 Georgia 42, Ohio St. 41 (CFP)
2023 Mississippi 38, Penn St. 25

Fiesta Bowl Results, 1971-2024

1971 (Dec.) Arizona St. 45, Florida St. 38
1972 Arizona St. 49, Missouri 35
1973 Arizona St. 28, Pittsburgh 7
1974 Oklahoma St. 16, Brigham Young 6
1975 Arizona St. 17, Nebraska 14
1976 Oklahoma 41, Wyoming 7
1977 Penn St. 42, Arizona St. 30
1978 UCLA 10, Arkansas 10
1979 Pittsburgh 16, Arizona 10
1980 Penn St. 31, Ohio St. 19
1982 (Jan.) Penn St. 26, USC 10
1983 Arizona St. 32, Oklahoma 21
1984 Ohio St. 28, Pittsburgh 23
1985 UCLA 39, Miami (FL) 37
1986 Michigan 27, Nebraska 23
1987 Penn St. 14, Miami (FL) 10
1988 Florida St. 31, Nebraska 28
1989 Notre Dame 34, West Virginia 21
1990 Florida St. 41, Nebraska 17
1991 Louisville 34, Alabama 7
1992 Penn St. 42, Tennessee 17
1993 Syracuse 26, Colorado 22
1994 Arizona 29, Miami (FL) 0
1995 Colorado 41, Notre Dame 24
1996 Nebraska 62, Florida 24
1997 Penn St. 38, Texas 15
1997 (Dec.) Kansas St. 35, Syracuse 18
1999 (Jan.) Tennessee 23, Florida St. 16
2000 Nebraska 31, Tennessee 21
2001 Oregon St. 41, Notre Dame 9
2002 Oregon 38, Colorado 16
2003 Ohio St. 31, Miami (FL) 24 (2 OT)
2004 Ohio St. 35, Kansas St. 28
2005 Utah 35, Pittsburgh 7
2006 Ohio St. 34, Notre Dame 20
2007 Boise St. 43, Oklahoma 42 (OT)
2008 West Virginia 48, Oklahoma 28
2009 Texas 24, Ohio St. 21
2010 Boise St. 17, TCU 10
2011 Oklahoma 48, Connecticut 20
2012 Oklahoma St. 41, Stanford 38 (OT)
2013 Oregon 35, Kansas St. 17
2014 UCF 52, Baylor 42
2014 (Dec.) Boise St. 38, Arizona 30
2016 (Jan.) Ohio St. 44, Notre Dame 28
2016 (Dec.) Clemson 31, Ohio St. 0 (CFP)
2017 Penn St. 35, Washington 28
2019 (Jan.) LSU 40, UCF 32
2019 (Dec.) Clemson 29, Ohio St. 23 (CFP)
2021 Iowa St. 34, Oregon 17
2022 (Jan.) Oklahoma St. 37, Notre Dame 35
2022 (Dec.) TCU 51, Michigan 45 (CFP)
2024 (Jan.) Oregon 45, Liberty 6

All-Time NCAA Bowl Subdivision (FBS) Statistical Leaders

Career Rushing Yards

Player, team	Yrs	Carries	Yds	Avg
Donnel Pumphrey, San Diego St.	2013-16	1,059	6,405	6.05
Ron Dayne, Wisconsin	1996-99	1,115	6,397	5.74
Ricky Williams, Texas	1995-98	1,011	6,279	6.21
Jonathan Taylor, Wisconsin	2017-19	926	6,174	6.67
Tony Dorsett, Pittsburgh	1973-76	1,074	6,082	5.66
DeAngelo Williams, Memphis	2002-05	969	6,026	6.22
Royce Freeman, Oregon	2014-17	947	5,621	5.94
Charles White, USC	1976-79	1,023	5,598	5.47
Travis Prentice, Miami (OH)	1996-99	1,138	5,596	4.92
Cedric Benson, Texas	2001-04	1,112	5,540	4.98

Career Rushing Yards/Game (min. 2,500 yds)

Player, team	Yrs	Carries	Yds	Avg/game
Ed Marinaro, Cornell	1969-71	918	4,715	174.6
O.J. Simpson, USC	1967-68	621	3,124	164.4
Herschel Walker, Georgia	1980-82	994	5,259	159.4
Garrett Wolfe, N. Illinois	2004-06	807	5,164	156.5
LeShon Johnson, N. Illinois	1992-93	592	3,314	150.6
Jonathan Taylor, Wisconsin	2017-19	926	6,174	150.6
Ron Dayne, Wisconsin	1996-99	1,115	6,397	148.8
Marshall Faulk, San Diego St.	1991-93	766	4,589	148.0
George Jones, San Diego St.	1995-96	486	2,810	147.9
Tony Dorsett, Pittsburgh	1973-76	1,074	6,082	141.4
Troy Davis, Iowa St.	1994-96	782	4,382	141.4

Career Passing Yards

Player, team	Yrs	Comp/att	Yds
Case Keenum, Houston	2007-11	1,546/2,229	19,217
Timmy Chang, Hawaii	2000-04	1,388/2,436	17,072
Landry Jones, Oklahoma	2009-12	1,388/2,183	16,646
Graham Harrell, Texas Tech	2005-08	1,403/2,010	15,793
*Sam Hartman, Wake Forest-Notre Dame	2018-23	1,135/1,898	15,656
Bo Nix, Auburn-Oregon	2019-23	1,286/1,936	15,351
Ty Detmer, BYU	1988-91	958/1,530	15,031
Dillon Gabriel, UCF-Oklahoma	2019-23	1,050/1,664	14,865
Kellen Moore, Boise St.	2008-11	1,157/1,658	14,667
Baker Mayfield, Texas Tech/Oklahoma	2013, '15-'17	1,026/1,497	14,607

Career Receiving Yards

Player, team	Yrs	Rec	Yds	Yds/G
Corey Davis, W. Michigan	2013-16	332	5,285	105.7
Trevor Insley, Nevada	1996-99	298	5,005	113.8
Ryan Broyles, Oklahoma	2008-11	349	4,586	95.5
Justin Hardy, E. Carolina	2011-14	387	4,541	92.7
Marcus Harris, Wyoming	1993-96	259	4,518	98.2
Patrick Edwards, Houston	2008-11	291	4,507	93.9
Jacob Cowing, UTEP-Arizona	2019-23	316	4,477	77.2
James Washington, Oklahoma St.	2014-17	225	4,467	85.9
Rashaun Woods, Oklahoma St.	2000-03	293	4,414	92.0
Ryan Yarborough, Wyoming	1990-93	229	4,357	94.7

* = Includes stats from season(s) with an FCS team. **Note:** As of end of 2023 season. Prior to 2002, postseason games were not included in NCAA final football statistics or records. Career rushing yards per game rankings do not include active players.

All-Time NCAA Bowl Subdivision (FBS) Team Won-Lost Records

Team	Years	W	L	T	Total games	Pct.
Ohio St.*	134	964	333	53	1,350	0.734
Michigan	144	1004	353	36	1,393	0.734
Alabama*	129	965	337	43	1,345	0.733
Notre Dame*	134	948	337	42	1,327	0.730
Oklahoma	129	944	341	53	1,338	0.725
Boise St.	56	490	187	2	679	0.723
Texas	131	948	392	33	1,373	0.702
USC*	130	875	368	54	1,297	0.695
Penn St.	137	930	409	41	1,380	0.689
Nebraska	134	917	424	40	1,381	0.678
Florida St.*	77	581	281	17	879	0.671
Tennessee	127	865	414	53	1,332	0.669
Georgia	130	881	429	54	1,364	0.666
LSU	130	843	434	47	1,324	0.654
Appalachian State	94	664	354	29	1,047	0.648
Miami (FL)	98	663	388	19	1,070	0.629
Florida	117	758	445	40	1,243	0.626
Auburn	131	799	471	47	1,317	0.625
Clemson	128	798	472	45	1,315	0.624
Ga. Southern*	60	418	253	10	681	0.621
Washington	134	775	466	50	1,291	0.620
Texas A&M	129	778	504	48	1,330	0.603
Virginia Tech	130	772	505	46	1,323	0.601
Arizona St.	111	638	424	24	1,086	0.599
Utah	130	719	482	31	1,232	0.596
Michigan St.	127	730	487	44	1,261	0.596
Miami (OH)	135	724	484	44	1,252	0.596
West Virginia	131	781	526	45	1,352	0.594
Fresno St.	102	645	446	27	1,118	0.589
Western Ky.	105	615	426	30	1,071	0.588
Central Mich.	123	647	450	36	1,133	0.587

* = Record adjusted by action of the NCAA Committee on Infractions. **Note:** As of end of 2023 season. Includes records as senior college only. Bowl and playoff games are included, and each tie game is computed as half won and half lost. Teams must have been in Div. I for at least 25 years to qualify. Tiebreaker rule began with 1996 season.

Heisman Trophy Winners, 1935-2023

The Heisman Memorial Trophy is awarded annually to the nation's outstanding college football player by the Downtown Athletic Club.

Year	Winner, school, position
1935	Jay Berwanger, Chicago, HB
1936	Larry Kelley, Yale, E
1937	Clinton Frank, Yale, HB
1938	David O'Brien, Texas Christian, QB
1939	Nile Kinnick, Iowa, HB
1940	Tom Harmon, Michigan, HB
1941	Bruce Smith, Minnesota, HB
1942	Frank Sinkwich, Georgia, HB
1943	Angelo Bertelli, Notre Dame, QB
1944	Leslie Horvath, Ohio St., QB
1945	Felix Blanchard, Army, FB
1946	Glenn Davis, Army, HB
1947	John Lujack, Notre Dame, QB
1948	Doak Walker, SMU, HB
1949	Leon Hart, Notre Dame, E
1950	Vic Janowicz, Ohio St., HB
1951	Richard Kazmaier, Princeton, HB
1952	Billy Vessels, Oklahoma, HB
1953	John Lattner, Notre Dame, HB
1954	Alan Ameche, Wisconsin, FB
1955	Howard Cassady, Ohio St., HB
1956	Paul Hornung, Notre Dame, QB
1957	John Crow, Texas A&M, HB
1958	Pete Dawkins, Army, HB
1959	Billy Cannon, LSU, HB
1960	Joe Bellino, Navy, HB
1961	Ernest Davis, Syracuse, HB
1962	Terry Baker, Oregon St., QB
1963	Roger Staubach, Navy, QB
1964	John Huarte, Notre Dame, QB
1965	Mike Garrett, USC, HB
1966	Steve Spurrier, Florida, QB
1967	Gary Beban, UCLA, QB
1968	O.J. Simpson, USC, RB
1969	Steve Owens, Oklahoma, RB
1970	Jim Plunkett, Stanford, QB
1971	Pat Sullivan, Auburn, QB
1972	Johnny Rodgers, Nebraska, RB-WR
1973	John Cappelletti, Penn St., RB
1974	Archie Griffin, Ohio St., RB
1975	Archie Griffin, Ohio St., RB
1976	Tony Dorsett, Pittsburgh, RB
1977	Earl Campbell, Texas, RB
1978	Billy Sims, Oklahoma, RB
1979	Charles White, USC, RB
1980	George Rogers, S. Carolina, RB
1981	Marcus Allen, USC, RB
1982	Herschel Walker, Georgia, RB
1983	Mike Rozier, Nebraska, RB
1984	Doug Flutie, Boston College, QB
1985	Bo Jackson, Auburn, RB
1986	Vinny Testaverde, Miami (FL), QB
1987	Tim Brown, Notre Dame, WR
1988	Barry Sanders, Oklahoma St., RB
1989	Andre Ware, Houston, QB
1990	Ty Detmer, BYU, QB
1991	Desmond Howard, Michigan, WR
1992	Gino Torretta, Miami (FL), QB
1993	Charlie Ward, Florida St., QB
1994	Rashaan Salaam, Colorado, RB
1995	Eddie George, Ohio St., RB
1996	Danny Wuerffel, Florida, QB
1997	Charles Woodson, Michigan, CB
1998	Ricky Williams, Texas, RB
1999	Ron Dayne, Wisconsin, RB
2000	Chris Weinke, Florida St., QB
2001	Eric Crouch, Nebraska, QB
2002	Carson Palmer, USC, QB
2003	Jason White, Oklahoma, QB
2004	Matt Leinart, USC, QB
2005	Reggie Bush, USC, RB
2006	Troy Smith, Ohio St., QB
2007	Tim Tebow, Florida, QB
2008	Sam Bradford, Oklahoma, QB
2009	Mark Ingram, Alabama, RB
2010	Cam Newton, Auburn, QB
2011	Robert Griffin III, Baylor, QB
2012	Johnny Manziel, Texas A&M, QB
2013	Jameis Winston, Florida St., QB
2014	Marcus Mariota, Oregon, QB
2015	Derrick Henry, Alabama, RB
2016	Lamar Jackson, Louisville, QB
2017	Baker Mayfield, Oklahoma, QB
2018	Kyler Murray, Oklahoma, QB
2019	Joe Burrow, LSU, QB
2020	DeVonta Smith, Alabama, WR
2021	Bryce Young, Alabama, QB
2022	Caleb Williams, USC, QB
2023	Jayden Daniels, LSU, QB

College Football Coach of the Year, 1957-2023

The Coach of the Year has been selected by the American Football Coaches Assn. (AFCA) since 1935 as well as the Football Writers Assn. of America (FWAA) since 1957. When polls disagree, both winners are indicated.

1957 Woody Hayes, Ohio St.
1958 Paul Dietzel, LSU
1959 Ben Schwartzwalder, Syracuse
1960 Murray Warmath, Minnesota
1961 Paul "Bear" Bryant, Alabama (AFCA); Darrell Royal, Texas (FWAA)
1962 John McKay, USC
1963 Darrell Royal, Texas
1964 Ara Parseghian, Notre Dame & Frank Broyles, Arkansas (AFCA); Ara Parseghian, Notre Dame (FWAA)
1965 Tommy Prothro, UCLA (AFCA); Duffy Daugherty, Mich. St. (FWAA)
1966 Tom Cahill, Army
1967 John Pont, Indiana
1968 Joe Paterno, Penn St. (AFCA); Woody Hayes, Ohio St. (FWAA)
1969 Bo Schembechler, Michigan
1970 Charles McClendon, LSU & Darrell Royal, Texas (AFCA); Alex Agase, Northwestern (FWAA)
1971 Paul "Bear" Bryant, Alabama (AFCA); Bob Devaney, Nebraska (FWAA)
1972 John McKay, USC
1973 Paul "Bear" Bryant, Alabama (AFCA); Johnny Majors, Pittsburgh (FWAA)
1974 Grant Teaff, Baylor
1975 Frank Kush, Arizona St. (AFCA); Woody Hayes, Ohio St. (FWAA)
1976 Johnny Majors, Pittsburgh
1977 Don James, Washington (AFCA); Lou Holtz, Arkansas (FWAA)
1978 Joe Paterno, Penn St.
1979 Earle Bruce, Ohio St.
1980 Vince Dooley, Georgia
1981 Danny Ford, Clemson
1982 Joe Paterno, Penn St.
1983 Ken Hatfield, Air Force (AFCA); Howard Schnellenberger, Miami (FL) (FWAA)
1984 LaVell Edwards, Brigham Young
1985 Fisher De Berry, Air Force
1986 Joe Paterno, Penn St.
1987 Dick MacPherson, Syracuse
1988 Don Nehlen, W. Virginia (AFCA); Lou Holtz, Notre Dame (FWAA)
1989 Bill McCartney, Colorado
1990 Bobby Ross, Georgia Tech
1991 Don James, Washington
1992 Gene Stallings, Alabama
1993 Barry Alvarez, Wisconsin (AFCA); Terry Bowden, Auburn (FWAA)
1994 Tom Osborne, Nebraska (AFCA); Rich Brooks, Oregon (FWAA)
1995 Gary Barnett, Northwestern
1996 Bruce Snyder, Arizona St.
1997 Mike Price, Washington St.
1998 Phillip Fulmer, Tennessee
1999 Frank Beamer, Virginia Tech
2000 Bob Stoops, Oklahoma
2001 Larry Coker, Miami (FL) & Ralph Friedgen, Maryland (AFCA); Ralph Friedgen, Maryland (FWAA)
2002 Jim Tressel, Ohio St.
2003 Pete Carroll, USC (AFCA); Nick Saban, LSU (FWAA)
2004 Tommy Tuberville, Auburn (AFCA); Urban Meyer, Utah (FWAA)
2005 Joe Paterno, Penn St. (AFCA); Charlie Weis, Notre Dame (FWAA)
2006 Jim Grobe, Wake Forest (AFCA); Greg Schiano, Rutgers (FWAA)
2007 Mark Mangino, Kansas
2008 Kyle Whittingham, Utah (AFCA); Nick Saban, Alabama (FWAA)
2009 Gary Patterson, TCU
2010 Chip Kelly, Oregon
2011 Les Miles, LSU (AFCA); Mike Gundy, Oklahoma St. (FWAA)
2012 Brian Kelly, Notre Dame
2013 David Cutcliffe, Duke (AFCA); Gus Malzahn, Auburn (FWAA)
2014 Gary Patterson, TCU
2015 Dabo Swinney, Clemson (AFCA); Kirk Ferentz, Iowa (FWAA)
2016 Mike MacIntyre, Colorado
2017 Scott Frost, UCF
2018 Mike Leach, Washington St. (AFCA); Bill Clark, UAB (FWAA)
2019 Ed Orgeron, LSU
2020 Tom Allen, Indiana (AFCA); Jamey Chadwell, Coastal Carolina (FWAA)
2021 Luke Fickell, Cincinnati
2022 Sonny Dykes, TCU
2023 Kalen DeBoer, Washington

COLLEGE BASKETBALL

2024 NCAA Men's Basketball: UConn Claims Second Straight Title

The Univ. of Connecticut Huskies repeated as champions and claimed their sixth NCAA men's basketball title since 1999 on Apr. 8, 2024, defeating the Purdue Univ. Boilermakers, 75-60, at State Farm Stadium in Glendale, AZ. Huskies senior Tristen Newton scored 20 points with 7 assists and 5 rebounds and was named the most outstanding player of the Final Four. No. 1-seed UConn dominated their 2024 tournament run, winning their six games by an average of 23.33 points per game.

NCAA Men's Basketball Division I Champions, 1939-2024

No tournament was held in 2020 due to the COVID-19 pandemic.

Year	Champion	Final opponent	Score	Most outstanding player	Winning coach	Site
1939	Oregon	Ohio St.	46-33	Jimmy Hull, Ohio St.	Howard Hobson	Evanston, IL
1940	Indiana	Kansas	60-42	Marv Huffman, Indiana	Branch McCracken	Kansas City, MO
1941	Wisconsin	Washington St.	39-34	John Kotz, Wisconsin	Bud Foster	Kansas City, MO
1942	Stanford	Dartmouth	53-38	Howie Dallmar, Stanford	Everett Dean	Kansas City, MO
1943	Wyoming	Georgetown	46-34	Ken Sailors, Wyoming	Everett Shelton	New York, NY
1944	Utah	Dartmouth	42-40[1]	Arnold Ferrin, Utah	Vadal Peterson	New York, NY
1945	Oklahoma St.[2]	NYU	49-45	Bob Kurland, Oklahoma St.	Henry Iba	New York, NY
1946	Oklahoma St.[2]	North Carolina	43-40	Bob Kurland, Oklahoma St.	Henry Iba	New York, NY
1947	Holy Cross	Oklahoma	58-47	George Kaftan, Holy Cross	Alvin Julian	New York, NY
1948	Kentucky	Baylor	58-42	Alex Groza, Kentucky	Adolph Rupp	New York, NY
1949	Kentucky	Oklahoma St.	46-36	Alex Groza, Kentucky	Adolph Rupp	Seattle, WA
1950	CCNY	Bradley	71-68	Irwin Dambrot, CCNY	Nat Holman	New York, NY
1951	Kentucky	Kansas St.	68-58	Bill Spivey, Kentucky	Adolph Rupp	Minneapolis, MN
1952	Kansas	St. John's (NY)	80-63	Clyde Lovellette, Kansas	Forrest Allen	Seattle, WA
1953	Indiana	Kansas	69-68	B. H. Born, Kansas	Branch McCracken	Kansas City, MO
1954	La Salle	Bradley	92-76	Tom Gola, La Salle	Kenneth Loeffler	Kansas City, MO
1955	San Francisco	La Salle	77-63	Bill Russell, San Francisco	Phil Woolpert	Kansas City, MO
1956	San Francisco	Iowa	83-71	Hal Lear, Temple	Phil Woolpert	Evanston, IL
1957	North Carolina	Kansas	54-53[1]	Wilt Chamberlain, Kansas	Frank McGuire	Kansas City, MO
1958	Kentucky	Seattle	84-72	Elgin Baylor, Seattle	Adolph Rupp	Louisville, KY
1959	California	West Virginia	71-70	Jerry West, West Virginia	Pete Newell	Louisville, KY
1960	Ohio St.	California	75-55	Jerry Lucas, Ohio St.	Fred Taylor	San Francisco, CA
1961	Cincinnati	Ohio St.	70-65[1]	Jerry Lucas, Ohio St.	Edwin Jucker	Kansas City, MO
1962	Cincinnati	Ohio St.	71-59	Paul Hogue, Cincinnati	Edwin Jucker	Louisville, KY
1963	Loyola (IL)	Cincinnati	60-58[1]	Art Heyman, Duke	George Ireland	Louisville, KY
1964	UCLA	Duke	98-83	Walt Hazzard, UCLA	John Wooden	Kansas City, MO
1965	UCLA	Michigan	91-80	Bill Bradley, Princeton	John Wooden	Portland, OR
1966	UTEP[3]	Kentucky	72-65	Jerry Chambers, Utah	Don Haskins	College Park, MD
1967	UCLA	Dayton	79-64	Lew Alcindor[4], UCLA	John Wooden	Louisville, KY
1968	UCLA	North Carolina	78-55	Lew Alcindor[4], UCLA	John Wooden	Los Angeles, CA
1969	UCLA	Purdue	92-72	Lew Alcindor[4], UCLA	John Wooden	Louisville, KY
1970	UCLA	Jacksonville	80-69	Sidney Wicks, UCLA	John Wooden	College Park, MD
1971	UCLA	Villanova*	68-62	Howard Porter, Villanova*	John Wooden	Houston, TX
1972	UCLA	Florida St.	81-76	Bill Walton, UCLA	John Wooden	Los Angeles, CA
1973	UCLA	Memphis[5]	87-66	Bill Walton, UCLA	John Wooden	St. Louis, MO
1974	North Carolina St.	Marquette	76-64	David Thompson, NC State	Norm Sloan	Greensboro, NC
1975	UCLA	Kentucky	92-85	Richard Washington, UCLA	John Wooden	San Diego, CA
1976	Indiana	Michigan	86-68	Kent Benson, Indiana	Bob Knight	Philadelphia, PA

Year	Champion	Final opponent	Score	Most outstanding player	Winning coach	Site
1977	Marquette	North Carolina	67-59	Butch Lee, Marquette	Al McGuire	Atlanta, GA
1978	Kentucky	Duke	94-88	Jack Givens, Kentucky	Joe Hall	St. Louis, MO
1979	Michigan St.	Indiana St.	75-64	Magic Johnson, Michigan St.	Jud Heathcote	Salt Lake City, UT
1980	Louisville	UCLA*	59-54	Darrell Griffith, Louisville	Denny Crum	Indianapolis, IN
1981	Indiana	North Carolina	63-50	Isiah Thomas, Indiana	Bob Knight	Philadelphia, PA
1982	North Carolina	Georgetown	63-62	James Worthy, N. Carolina	Dean Smith	New Orleans, LA
1983	North Carolina St.	Houston	54-52	Hakeem Olajuwon, Houston	Jim Valvano	Albuquerque, NM
1984	Georgetown	Houston	84-75	Patrick Ewing, Georgetown	John Thompson	Seattle, WA
1985	Villanova	Georgetown	66-64	Ed Pinckney, Villanova	Rollie Massimino	Lexington, KY
1986	Louisville	Duke	72-69	Pervis Ellison, Louisville	Denny Crum	Dallas, TX
1987	Indiana	Syracuse	74-73	Keith Smart, Indiana	Bob Knight	New Orleans, LA
1988	Kansas	Oklahoma	83-79	Danny Manning, Kansas	Larry Brown	Kansas City, MO
1989	Michigan	Seton Hall	80-79[1]	Glen Rice, Michigan	Steve Fisher	Seattle, WA
1990	UNLV	Duke	103-73	Anderson Hunt, UNLV	Jerry Tarkanian	Denver, CO
1991	Duke	Kansas	72-65	Christian Laettner, Duke	Mike Krzyzewski	Indianapolis, IN
1992	Duke	Michigan	71-51	Bobby Hurley, Duke	Mike Krzyzewski	Minneapolis, MN
1993	North Carolina	Michigan	77-71	Donald Williams, N. Carolina	Dean Smith	New Orleans, LA
1994	Arkansas	Duke	76-72	Corliss Williamson, Arkansas	Nolan Richardson	Charlotte, NC
1995	UCLA	Arkansas	89-78	Ed O'Bannon, UCLA	Jim Harrick	Seattle, WA
1996	Kentucky	Syracuse	76-67	Tony Delk, Kentucky	Rick Pitino	E. Rutherford, NJ
1997	Arizona	Kentucky	84-79[1]	Miles Simon, Arizona	Lute Olson	Indianapolis, IN
1998	Kentucky	Utah	78-69	Jeff Sheppard, Kentucky	Tubby Smith	San Antonio, TX
1999	Connecticut	Duke	77-74	Richard Hamilton, Connecticut	Jim Calhoun	St. Petersburg, FL
2000	Michigan St.	Florida	89-76	Mateen Cleaves, Michigan St.	Tom Izzo	Indianapolis, IN
2001	Duke	Arizona	82-72	Shane Battier, Duke	Mike Krzyzewski	Minneapolis, MN
2002	Maryland	Indiana	64-52	Juan Dixon, Maryland	Gary Williams	Atlanta, GA
2003	Syracuse	Kansas	81-78	Carmelo Anthony, Syracuse	Jim Boeheim	New Orleans, LA
2004	Connecticut	Georgia Tech	82-73	Emeka Okafor, Connecticut	Jim Calhoun	San Antonio, TX
2005	North Carolina	Illinois	75-70	Sean May, N. Carolina	Roy Williams	St. Louis, MO
2006	Florida	UCLA	73-57	Joakim Noah, Florida	Billy Donovan	Indianapolis, IN
2007	Florida	Ohio St.	84-75	Corey Brewer, Florida	Billy Donovan	Atlanta, GA
2008	Kansas	Memphis	75-68[1]	Mario Chalmers, Kansas	Bill Self	San Antonio, TX
2009	North Carolina	Michigan St.	89-72	Wayne Ellington, N. Carolina	Roy Williams	Detroit, MI
2010	Duke	Butler	61-59	Kyle Singler, Duke	Mike Krzyzewski	Indianapolis, IN
2011	Connecticut	Butler	53-41	Kemba Walker, Connecticut	Jim Calhoun	Houston, TX
2012	Kentucky	Kansas	67-59	Anthony Davis, Kentucky	John Calipari	New Orleans, LA
2013[6]	Louisville	Michigan	82-76	Luke Hancock, Louisville	Rick Pitino	Atlanta, GA
2014	Connecticut	Kentucky	60-54	Shabazz Napier, Connecticut	Kevin Ollie	Arlington, TX
2015	Duke	Wisconsin	68-63	Tyus Jones, Duke	Mike Krzyzewski	Indianapolis, IN
2016	Villanova	North Carolina	77-74	Ryan Arcidiacono, Villanova	Jay Wright	Houston, TX
2017	North Carolina	Gonzaga	71-65	Joel Berry II, N. Carolina	Roy Williams	Glendale, AZ
2018	Villanova	Michigan	79-62	Donte DiVincenzo, Villanova	Jay Wright	San Antonio, TX
2019	Virginia	Texas Tech	85-77[1]	Kyle Guy, Virginia	Tony Bennett	Minneapolis, MN
2021	Baylor	Gonzaga	86-70	Jared Butler, Baylor	Scott Drew	Indianapolis, IN
2022	Kansas	North Carolina	72-69	Ochai Agbaji, Kansas	Bill Self	New Orleans, LA
2023	Connecticut	San Diego St.	76-59	Adama Sanogo, Connecticut	Dan Hurley	Houston, TX
2024	Connecticut	Purdue	75-60	Tristen Newton, Connecticut	Dan Hurley	Glendale, AZ

* = Declared ineligible after the tournament. (1) Overtime. (2) Then known as Oklahoma A&M. (3) Then known as Texas Western. (4) Changed name to Kareem Abdul-Jabbar in 1971. (5) Then known as Memphis State. (6) Title vacated by the NCAA Committee on Infractions in 2018.

All-Time Winningest Men's NCAA Division I Basketball Teams

Team	Yrs	Won	Lost	Pct.
Kentucky	121	2,398	758	0.760
N. Carolina	114	2,372	860	0.734
Kansas	126	2,408	896	0.729
Duke	119	2,300	929	0.712
UCLA	105	2,002	905	0.689
UNLV	66	1,349	627	0.683
Syracuse	123	1,993	976	0.671
W. Kentucky	110	1,894	985	0.658
Arizona	119	1,889	986	0.657
Villanova	104	1,882	989	0.656
VCU	54	1,075	568	0.654
Murray St.	99	1,736	954	0.645
Norfolk St.	71	1,326	729	0.645
Connecticut	121	1,837	1,015	0.644
Illinois	119	1,907	1,061	0.643
Purdue	126	1,929	1,080	0.641
Arkansas	101	1,799	1,014	0.640
Cincinnati	123	1,911	1,079	0.639
Notre Dame	121	1,963	1,109	0.639
St. John's (NY)	117	1,942	1,098	0.639
Louisville	110	1,784	1,011	0.638
Utah	116	1,897	1,082	0.637
Memphis	103	1,675	965	0.634
Indiana	124	1,932	1,116	0.634
Lipscomb	74	1,318	762	0.634
Temple	128	1,994	1,155	0.633
UAB	46	936	548	0.631
Weber St.	62	1,149	678	0.629
Texas	118	1,900	1,139	0.625
Missouri St.	112	1,760	1,057	0.625

Note: Winningest teams by percentage. Minimum 25 years as Div. I program.

National Invitation Tournament Champions, 1938-2024

The National Invitation Tournament (NIT), first played in 1938, is the oldest U.S. basketball tournament. The first National Collegiate Athletic Association (NCAA) national championship tournament was played one year later. In 2005, the NCAA purchased the NIT from the five New York City-area colleges that had run it. No tournament was held in 2020 in response to the COVID-19 outbreak.

Year	Champion
1938	Temple
1939	Long Island Univ.
1940	Colorado
1941	Long Island Univ.
1942	West Virginia
1943	St. John's (NY)
1944	St. John's (NY)
1945	DePaul
1946	Kentucky
1947	Utah
1948	St. Louis
1949	San Francisco
1950	CCNY
1951	Brigham Young
1952	La Salle
1953	Seton Hall
1954	Holy Cross
1955	Duquesne
1956	Louisville
1957	Bradley
1958	Xavier (OH)
1959	St. John's (NY)
1960	Bradley
1961	Providence
1962	Dayton
1963	Providence
1964	Bradley
1965	St. John's (NY)
1966	Brigham Young
1967	Southern Illinois
1968	Dayton
1969	Temple
1970	Marquette
1971	North Carolina
1972	Maryland
1973	Virginia Tech
1974	Purdue
1975	Princeton
1976	Kentucky
1977	St. Bonaventure
1978	Texas
1979	Indiana
1980	Virginia
1981	Tulsa
1982	Bradley
1983	Fresno State
1984	Michigan
1985	UCLA
1986	Ohio State
1987	Southern Miss
1988	Connecticut
1989	St. John's (NY)
1990	Vanderbilt
1991	Stanford
1992	Virginia
1993	Minnesota
1994	Villanova
1995	Virginia Tech
1996	Nebraska
1997	Michigan
1998	Minnesota
1999	California
2000	Wake Forest
2001	Tulsa
2002	Memphis
2003	St. John's (NY)
2004	Michigan
2005	South Carolina
2006	South Carolina
2007	West Virginia
2008	Ohio State
2009	Penn State
2010	Dayton
2011	Wichita State
2012	Stanford
2013	Baylor
2014	Minnesota
2015	Stanford
2016	George Washington
2017	TCU
2018	Penn State
2019	Texas
2021	Memphis
2022	Xavier
2023	North Texas
2024	Seton Hall

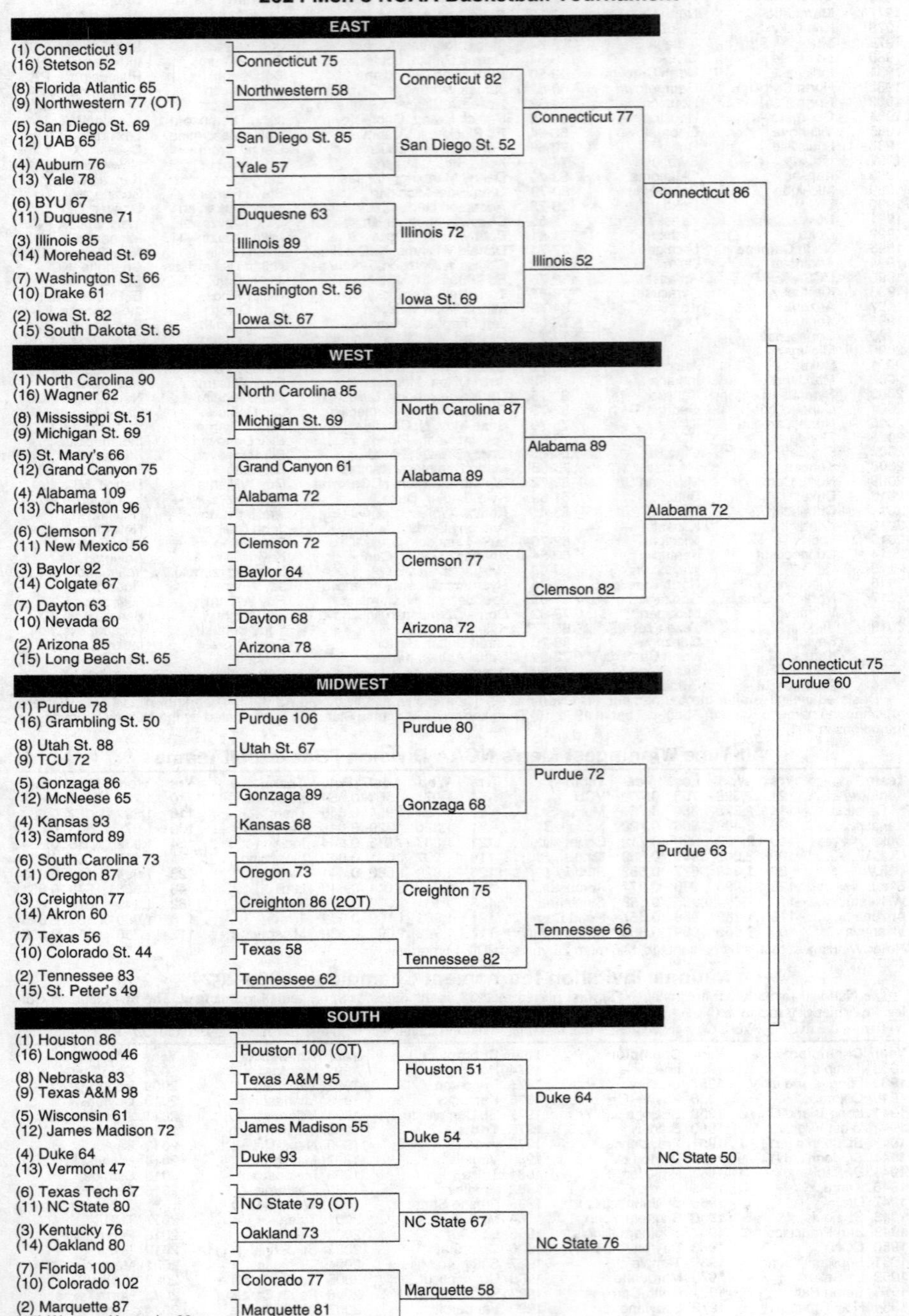
2024 Men's NCAA Basketball Tournament
EAST
(1) Connecticut 91
(16) Stetson 52
(8) Florida Atlantic 65
(9) Northwestern 77 (OT)
(5) San Diego St. 69
(12) UAB 65
(4) Auburn 76
(13) Yale 78
(6) BYU 67
(11) Duquesne 71
(3) Illinois 85
(14) Morehead St. 69
(7) Washington St. 66
(10) Drake 61
(2) Iowa St. 82
(15) South Dakota St. 65
Connecticut 75
Northwestern 58
San Diego St. 85
Yale 57
Duquesne 63
Illinois 89
Washington St. 56
Iowa St. 67
Connecticut 82
San Diego St. 52
Illinois 72
Iowa St. 69
Connecticut 77
Illinois 52
Connecticut 86
WEST
(1) North Carolina 90
(16) Wagner 62
(8) Mississippi St. 51
(9) Michigan St. 69
(5) St. Mary's 66
(12) Grand Canyon 75
(4) Alabama 109
(13) Charleston 96
(6) Clemson 77
(11) New Mexico 56
(3) Baylor 92
(14) Colgate 67
(7) Dayton 63
(10) Nevada 60
(2) Arizona 85
(15) Long Beach St. 65
North Carolina 85
Michigan St. 69
Grand Canyon 61
Alabama 72
Clemson 72
Baylor 64
Dayton 68
Arizona 78
North Carolina 87
Alabama 89
Clemson 77
Arizona 72
Alabama 89
Clemson 82
Alabama 72
Connecticut 75
Purdue 60
MIDWEST
(1) Purdue 78
(16) Grambling St. 50
(8) Utah St. 88
(9) TCU 72
(5) Gonzaga 86
(12) McNeese 65
(4) Kansas 93
(13) Samford 89
(6) South Carolina 73
(11) Oregon 87
(3) Creighton 77
(14) Akron 60
(7) Texas 56
(10) Colorado St. 44
(2) Tennessee 83
(15) St. Peter's 49
Purdue 106
Utah St. 67
Gonzaga 89
Kansas 68
Oregon 73
Creighton 86 (2OT)
Texas 58
Tennessee 62
Purdue 80
Gonzaga 68
Creighton 75
Tennessee 82
Purdue 72
Tennessee 66
Purdue 63
SOUTH
(1) Houston 86
(16) Longwood 46
(8) Nebraska 83
(9) Texas A&M 98
(5) Wisconsin 61
(12) James Madison 72
(4) Duke 64
(13) Vermont 47
(6) Texas Tech 67
(11) NC State 80
(3) Kentucky 76
(14) Oakland 80
(7) Florida 100
(10) Colorado 102
(2) Marquette 87
(15) Western Kentucky 69
Houston 100 (OT)
Texas A&M 95
James Madison 55
Duke 93
NC State 79 (OT)
Oakland 73
Colorado 77
Marquette 81
Houston 51
Duke 54
NC State 67
Marquette 58
Duke 64
NC State 76
NC State 50

NCAA Men's Basketball Division I All-Time Leaders

Season points

Player, school (season)	G	FG	3-FG	FT	PTS
Pete Maravich, LSU (1970)	31	522	NA	337	1,381
Elvin Hayes, Houston (1968)	33	519	NA	176	1,214
Frank Selvy, Furman (1954)	29	427	NA	355	1,209
Pete Maravich, LSU (1969)	26	433	NA	282	1,148
Pete Maravich, LSU (1968)	26	432	NA	274	1,138
Bo Kimble, Loyola Marymount (1990)	32	404	92	231	1,131
Hersey Hawkins, Bradley (1988)	31	377	87	284	1,125
Austin Carr, Notre Dame (1970)	29	444	NA	218	1,106
Austin Carr, Notre Dame (1971)	29	430	NA	241	1,101
Otis Birdsong, Houston (1977)	36	452	NA	186	1,090

Career points

Player, school (seasons)	G	FG	3-FG	FT	PTS
Pete Maravich, LSU (1968-70)	83	1,387	NA	893	3,667
Antoine Davis, Detroit Mercy (2018-23)	144	1,219	588	638	3,664
Freeman Williams, Portland St. (1975-78)	106	1,369	NA	511	3,249
Chris Clemons, Campbell (2016-19)	130	1,024	444	733	3,225
Lionel Simmons, La Salle (1987-90)	131	1,244	56	673	3,217
Alphonso Ford, Mississippi Valley St. (1990-93)	109	1,121	333	590	3,165
Doug McDermott, Creighton (2011-14)	145	1,141	274	594	3,150
Max Abmas, Oral Roberts-Texas (2019-24)	157	1,035	512	550	3,132
Mike Daum, South Dakota St. (2016-19)	137	1,005	271	786	3,067
Harry Kelly, Texas Southern (1980-83)	110	1,234	NA	598	3,066

NA = Not available.

Season points per game

Player, school (season)	G	FG	FT	PTS	PPG
Pete Maravich, LSU (1970)	31	522	337	1,381	44.5
Pete Maravich, LSU (1969)	26	433	282	1,148	44.2
Pete Maravich, LSU (1968)	26	432	274	1,138	43.8
Frank Selvy, Furman (1954)	29	427	355	1,209	41.7
Johnny Neumann, Mississippi (1971)	23	366	191	923	40.1
Freeman Williams, Portland St. (1977)	26	417	176	1,010	38.8
Billy McGill, Utah (1962)	26	394	221	1,009	38.8
Calvin Murphy, Niagara (1968)	24	337	242	916	38.2
Austin Carr, Notre Dame (1970)	29	444	218	1,106	38.1
Austin Carr, Notre Dame (1971)	29	430	241	1,101	38.0

Career points per game

Player, school (seasons)	G	FG	FT	PTS	PPG
Pete Maravich, LSU (1968-70)	83	1,387	893	3,667	44.2
Austin Carr, Notre Dame (1969-71)	74	1,017	526	2,560	34.6
Oscar Robertson, Cincinnati (1958-60)	88	1,052	869	2,973	33.8
Calvin Murphy, Niagara (1968-70)	77	947	654	2,548	33.1
Bo Lamar, La.-Lafayette (1972-73)	57	768	326	1,862	32.7
Frank Selvy, Furman (1952-54)	78	922	694	2,538	32.5
Rick Mount, Purdue (1968-70)	72	910	503	2,323	32.3
Darrell Floyd, Furman (1954-56)	71	868	545	2,281	32.1
Nick Werkman, Seton Hall (1962-64)	71	812	649	2,273	32.0
Willie Humes, Idaho St. (1970-71)	48	565	380	1,510	31.5

John R. Wooden Award Winners, 1977-2024

Awarded to the nation's outstanding men's college basketball player by the Los Angeles Athletic Club since 1977; awarded under the same name to women since 2004.

Year	Player, school
1977	Marques Johnson, UCLA
1978	Phil Ford, North Carolina
1979	Larry Bird, Indiana State
1980	Darrell Griffith, Louisville
1981	Danny Ainge, Brigham Young
1982	Ralph Sampson, Virginia
1983	Ralph Sampson, Virginia
1984	Michael Jordan, North Carolina
1985	Chris Mullin, St. John's (NY)
1986	Walter Berry, St. John's (NY)
1987	David Robinson, Navy
1988	Danny Manning, Kansas
1989	Sean Elliott, Arizona
1990	Lionel Simmons, La Salle
1991	Larry Johnson, UNLV
1992	Christian Laettner, Duke
1993	Calbert Cheaney, Indiana
1994	Glenn Robinson, Purdue
1995	Ed O'Bannon, UCLA
1996	Marcus Camby, Massachusetts
1997	Tim Duncan, Wake Forest
1998	Antawn Jamison, North Carolina
1999	Elton Brand, Duke
2000	Kenyon Martin, Cincinnati
2001	Shane Battier, Duke
2002	Jay Williams, Duke
2003	T. J. Ford, Texas
2004	(M) Jameer Nelson, St. Joseph's
	(W) Alana Beard, Duke
2005	(M) Andrew Bogut, Utah
	(W) Seimone Augustus, LSU
2006	(M) J. J. Redick, Duke
	(W) Seimone Augustus, LSU
2007	(M) Kevin Durant, Texas
	(W) Candace Parker, Tennessee
2008	(M) Tyler Hansbrough, N. Carolina
	(W) Candace Parker, Tennessee
2009	(M) Blake Griffin, Oklahoma
	(W) Maya Moore, Connecticut
2010	(M) Evan Turner, Ohio State
	(W) Tina Charles, Connecticut
2011	(M) Jimmer Fredette, Brigham Young
	(W) Maya Moore, Connecticut
2012	(M) Anthony Davis, Kentucky
	(W) Brittney Griner, Baylor
2013	(M) Trey Burke, Michigan
	(W) Brittney Griner, Baylor
2014	(M) Doug McDermott, Creighton
	(W) Chiney Ogwumike, Stanford
2015	(M) Frank Kaminsky, Wisconsin
	(W) Breanna Stewart, Connecticut
2016	(M) Buddy Hield, Oklahoma
	(W) Breanna Stewart, Connecticut
2017	(M) Frank Mason III, Kansas
	(W) Kelsey Plum, Washington
2018	(M) Jalen Brunson, Villanova
	(W) A'ja Wilson, South Carolina
2019	(M) Zion Williamson, Duke
	(W) Sabrina Ionescu, Oregon
2020	(M) Obi Toppin, Dayton
	(W) Sabrina Ionescu, Oregon
2021	(M) Luka Garza, Iowa
	(W) Paige Bueckers, Connecticut
2022	(M) Oscar Tshiebwe, Kentucky
	(W) Aliyah Boston, South Carolina
2023	(M) Zach Edey, Purdue
	(W) Caitlin Clark, Iowa
2024	(M) Zach Edey, Purdue
	(W) Caitlin Clark, Iowa

Naismith Coach of the Year, 1987-2024

Year	Men's coach, school	Women's coach, school
1987	Bob Knight, Indiana	Pat Summitt, Tennessee
1988	Larry Brown, Kansas	Leon Barmore, Louisiana Tech
1989	Mike Krzyzewski, Duke	Pat Summitt, Tennessee
1990	Bobby Cremins, Georgia Tech	Tara VanDerveer, Stanford
1991	Randy Ayers, Ohio St.	Debbie Ryan, Virginia
1992	Mike Krzyzewski, Duke	Chris Weller, Maryland
1993	Dean Smith, North Carolina	Vivian Stringer, Iowa
1994	Nolan Richardson, Arkansas	Pat Summitt, Tennessee
1995	Jim Harrick, UCLA	Geno Auriemma, UConn
1996	John Calipari, UMass	Andy Landers, Georgia
1997	Roy Williams, Kansas	Geno Auriemma, UConn
1998	Bill Guthridge, North Carolina	Pat Summitt, Tennessee
1999	Mike Krzyzewski, Duke	Carolyn Peck, Purdue
2000	Mike Montgomery, Stanford	Geno Auriemma, UConn
2001	Rod Barnes, Mississippi	Muffet McGraw, Notre Dame
2002	Ben Howland, Pittsburgh	Geno Auriemma, UConn
2003	Tubby Smith, Kentucky	Gail Goestenkors, Duke
2004	Phil Martelli, St. Joseph's	Pat Summitt, Tennessee
2005	Bruce Weber, Illinois	Pokey Chatman, LSU
2006	Jay Wright, Villanova	Sylvia Hatchell, North Carolina
2007	Tony Bennett, Washington St.	Gail Goestenkors, Duke
2008	John Calipari, Memphis	Geno Auriemma, UConn
2009	Jamie Dixon, Pittsburgh	Geno Auriemma, UConn
2010	Jim Boeheim, Syracuse	Connie Yori, Nebraska
2011	Steve Fisher, San Diego St.	Tara VanDerveer, Stanford
2012	Bill Self, Kansas	Kim Mulkey, Baylor
2013	Jim Larrañaga, Miami (FL)	Muffet McGraw, Notre Dame
2014	Gregg Marshall, Wichita St.	Muffet McGraw, Notre Dame
2015	John Calipari, Kentucky	Courtney Banghart, Princeton
2016	Jay Wright, Villanova	Geno Auriemma, UConn
2017	Mark Few, Gonzaga	Geno Auriemma, UConn
2018	Tony Bennett, Virginia	Vic Schaefer, Mississippi St.
2019	Rick Barnes, Tennessee	Lisa Bluder, Iowa
2020	Anthony Grant, Dayton	Dawn Staley, South Carolina
2021	Mark Few, Gonzaga	Tara VanDerveer, Stanford
2022	Ed Cooley, Providence	Dawn Staley, South Carolina
2023	Jerome Tang, Kansas St.	Dawn Staley, South Carolina
2024	Dan Hurley, UConn	Dawn Staley, South Carolina

2024 Women's NCAA Basketball Tournament

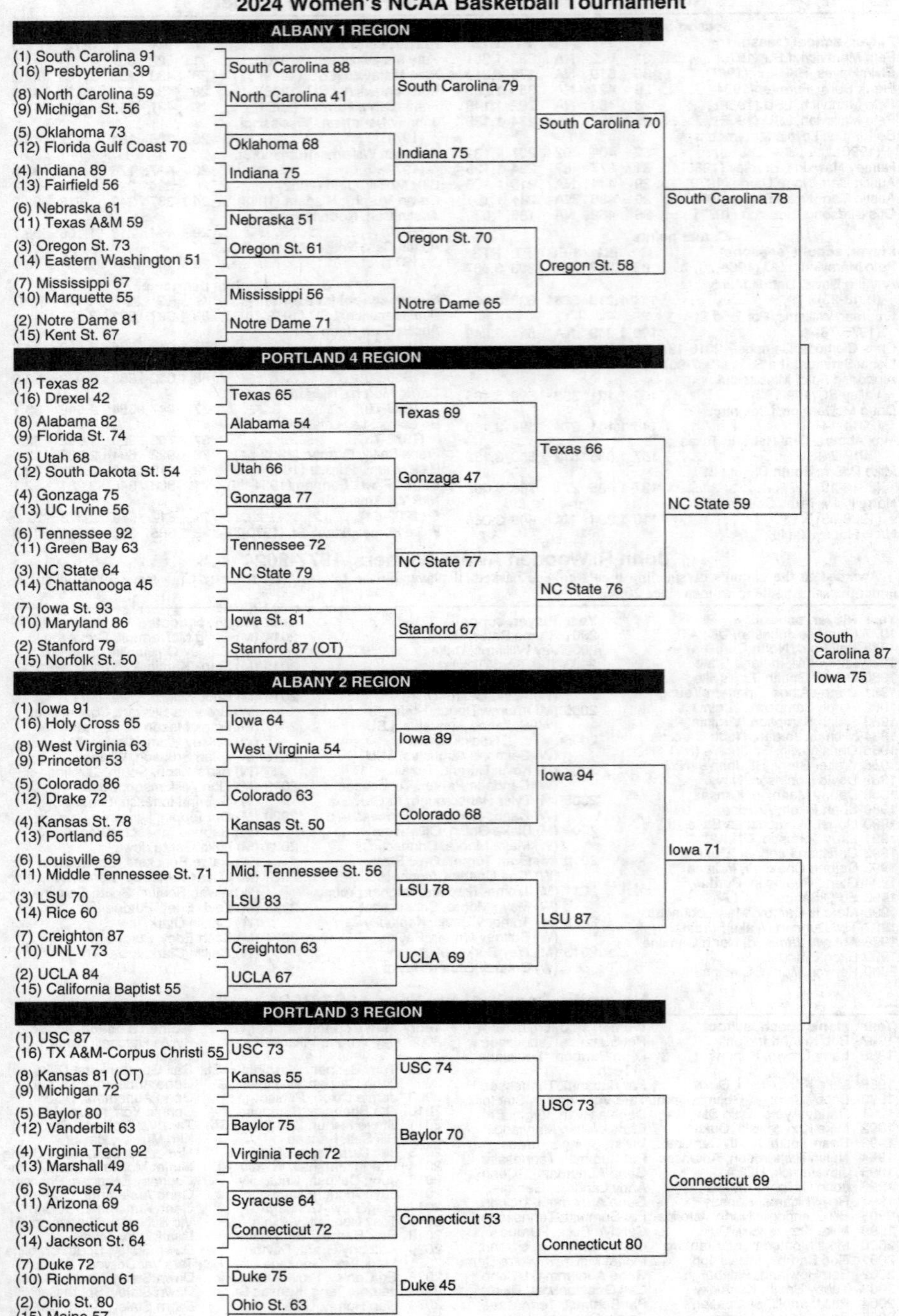
ALBANY 1 REGION
(1) South Carolina 91
(16) Presbyterian 39
(8) North Carolina 59
(9) Michigan St. 56
(5) Oklahoma 73
(12) Florida Gulf Coast 70
(4) Indiana 89
(13) Fairfield 56
(6) Nebraska 61
(11) Texas A&M 59
(3) Oregon St. 73
(14) Eastern Washington 51
(7) Mississippi 67
(10) Marquette 55
(2) Notre Dame 81
(15) Kent St. 67
South Carolina 88
North Carolina 41
Oklahoma 68
Indiana 75
Nebraska 51
Oregon St. 61
Mississippi 56
Notre Dame 71
South Carolina 79
Indiana 75
Oregon St. 70
Notre Dame 65
South Carolina 70
Oregon St. 58
South Carolina 78
PORTLAND 4 REGION
(1) Texas 82
(16) Drexel 42
(8) Alabama 82
(9) Florida St. 74
(5) Utah 68
(12) South Dakota St. 54
(4) Gonzaga 75
(13) UC Irvine 56
(6) Tennessee 92
(11) Green Bay 63
(3) NC State 64
(14) Chattanooga 45
(7) Iowa St. 93
(10) Maryland 86
(2) Stanford 79
(15) Norfolk St. 50
Texas 65
Alabama 54
Utah 66
Gonzaga 77
Tennessee 72
NC State 79
Iowa St. 81
Stanford 87 (OT)
Texas 69
Gonzaga 47
NC State 77
Stanford 67
Texas 66
NC State 76
NC State 59
South Carolina 87
Iowa 75
ALBANY 2 REGION
(1) Iowa 91
(16) Holy Cross 65
(8) West Virginia 63
(9) Princeton 53
(5) Colorado 86
(12) Drake 72
(4) Kansas St. 78
(13) Portland 65
(6) Louisville 69
(11) Middle Tennessee St. 71
(3) LSU 70
(14) Rice 60
(7) Creighton 87
(10) UNLV 73
(2) UCLA 84
(15) California Baptist 55
Iowa 64
West Virginia 54
Colorado 63
Kansas St. 50
Mid. Tennessee St. 56
LSU 83
Creighton 63
UCLA 67
Iowa 89
Colorado 68
LSU 78
UCLA 69
Iowa 94
LSU 87
Iowa 71
PORTLAND 3 REGION
(1) USC 87
(16) TX A&M-Corpus Christi 55
(8) Kansas 81 (OT)
(9) Michigan 72
(5) Baylor 80
(12) Vanderbilt 63
(4) Virginia Tech 92
(13) Marshall 49
(6) Syracuse 74
(11) Arizona 69
(3) Connecticut 86
(14) Jackson St. 64
(7) Duke 72
(10) Richmond 61
(2) Ohio St. 80
(15) Maine 57
USC 73
Kansas 55
Baylor 75
Virginia Tech 72
Syracuse 64
Connecticut 72
Duke 75
Ohio St. 63
USC 74
Baylor 70
Connecticut 53
Duke 45
USC 73
Connecticut 80
Connecticut 69

2024 NCAA Women's Basketball: South Carolina Topples Iowa

The South Carolina Gamecocks claimed the women's NCAA basketball title, defeating the Univ. of Iowa Hawkeyes, 87-75, Apr. 7, 2024, at Rocket Mortgage FieldHouse in Cleveland, OH. South Carolina head coach Dawn Staley led the Gamecocks to an undefeated season despite not having a single returning starter and claimed her third NCAA title. Iowa star Caitlin Clark, who set scoring records throughout the season while appearing before record-setting crowds, scored 30 points with 8 rebounds in her final college game. South Carolina center Kamilla Cardoso scored 15 points with 17 rebounds and was named most outstanding player.

NCAA Women's Basketball Division I Champions, 1982-2024

No tournament was held in 2020 due to the COVID-19 pandemic.

Year	Champion	Final opponent	Score	Most outstanding player	Winning coach	Site
1982	Louisiana Tech	Cheyney	76-62	Janice Lawrence, LA Tech	Sonja Hogg	Norfolk, VA
1983	USC	Louisiana Tech	69-67	Cheryl Miller, USC	Linda Sharp	Norfolk, VA
1984	USC	Tennessee	72-61	Cheryl Miller, USC	Linda Sharp	Los Angeles, CA
1985	Old Dominion	Georgia	70-65	Tracy Claxton, Old Dominion	Marianne Stanley	Austin, TX
1986	Texas	USC	97-81	Clarissa Davis, Texas	Jody Conradt	Lexington, KY
1987	Tennessee	Louisiana Tech	67-44	Tonya Edwards, Tennessee	Pat Summitt	Austin, TX
1988	Louisiana Tech	Auburn	56-54	Erica Westbrooks, LA Tech	Leon Barmore	Tacoma, WA
1989	Tennessee	Auburn	76-60	Bridgette Gordon, Tennessee	Pat Summitt	Tacoma, WA
1990	Stanford	Auburn	88-81	Jennifer Azzi, Stanford	Tara VanDerveer	Knoxville, TN
1991	Tennessee	Virginia	70-67 (OT)	Dawn Staley, Virginia	Pat Summitt	New Orleans, LA
1992	Stanford	W. Kentucky	78-62	Molly Goodenbour, Stanford	Tara VanDerveer	Los Angeles, CA
1993	Texas Tech	Ohio St.	84-82	Sheryl Swoopes, Texas Tech	Marsha Sharp	Atlanta, GA
1994	North Carolina	Louisiana Tech	60-59	Charlotte Smith, North Carolina	Sylvia Hatchell	Richmond, VA
1995	Connecticut	Tennessee	70-64	Rebecca Lobo, Connecticut	Geno Auriemma	Minneapolis, MN
1996	Tennessee	Georgia	83-65	Michelle Marciniak, Tennessee	Pat Summitt	Charlotte, NC
1997	Tennessee	Old Dominion	68-59	Chamique Holdsclaw, Tennessee	Pat Summitt	Cincinnati, OH
1998	Tennessee	Louisiana Tech	93-75	Chamique Holdsclaw, Tennessee	Pat Summitt	Kansas City, MO
1999	Purdue	Duke	62-45	Ukari Figgs, Purdue	Carolyn Peck	San Jose, CA
2000	Connecticut	Tennessee	71-52	Shea Ralph, Connecticut	Geno Auriemma	Philadelphia, PA
2001	Notre Dame	Purdue	68-66	Ruth Riley, Notre Dame	Muffet McGraw	St. Louis, MO
2002	Connecticut	Oklahoma	82-70	Swin Cash, Connecticut	Geno Auriemma	San Antonio, TX
2003	Connecticut	Tennessee	73-68	Diana Taurasi, Connecticut	Geno Auriemma	Atlanta, GA
2004	Connecticut	Tennessee	70-61	Diana Taurasi, Connecticut	Geno Auriemma	New Orleans, LA
2005	Baylor	Michigan St.	84-62	Sophia Young, Baylor	Kim Mulkey-Robertson	Indianapolis, IN
2006	Maryland	Duke	78-75 (OT)	Laura Harper, Maryland	Brenda Frese	Boston, MA
2007	Tennessee	Rutgers	59-46	Candace Parker, Tennessee	Pat Summitt	Cleveland, OH
2008	Tennessee	Stanford	64-48	Candace Parker, Tennessee	Pat Summitt	Tampa Bay, FL
2009	Connecticut	Louisville	76-54	Tina Charles, Connecticut	Geno Auriemma	St. Louis, MO
2010	Connecticut	Stanford	53-47	Maya Moore, Connecticut	Geno Auriemma	San Antonio, TX
2011	Texas A&M	Notre Dame	76-70	Danielle Adams, Texas A&M	Gary Blair	Indianapolis, IN
2012	Baylor	Notre Dame	80-61	Brittney Griner, Baylor	Kim Mulkey	Denver, CO
2013	Connecticut	Louisville	93-60	Breanna Stewart, Connecticut	Geno Auriemma	New Orleans, LA
2014	Connecticut	Notre Dame	79-58	Breanna Stewart, Connecticut	Geno Auriemma	Nashville, TN
2015	Connecticut	Notre Dame	63-53	Breanna Stewart, Connecticut	Geno Auriemma	Tampa, FL
2016	Connecticut	Syracuse	82-51	Breanna Stewart, Connecticut	Geno Auriemma	Indianapolis, IN
2017	South Carolina	Mississippi St.	67-55	A'ja Wilson, South Carolina	Dawn Staley	Dallas, TX
2018	Notre Dame	Mississippi St.	61-58	Arike Ogunbowale, Notre Dame	Muffet McGraw	Columbus, OH
2019	Baylor	Notre Dame	82-81	Chloe Jackson, Baylor	Kim Mulkey	Tampa, FL
2021	Stanford	Arizona	54-53	Haley Jones, Stanford	Tara VanDerveer	San Antonio, TX
2022	South Carolina	Connecticut	64-49	Aliyah Boston, South Carolina	Dawn Staley	Minneapolis, MN
2023	LSU	Iowa	102-85	Angel Reese, LSU	Kim Mulkey	Dallas, TX
2024	South Carolina	Iowa	87-75	Kamilla Cardoso, South Carolina	Dawn Staley	Cleveland, OH

NCAA Women's Basketball Division I All-Time Leaders

Season points

Player, school (season)	G	FG	3-FG	FT	PTS
Caitlin Clark, Iowa (2024)	39	403	201	227	1,234
Kelsey Plum, Washington (2017)	35	379	115	236	1,109
Maddy Siegrist, Villanova (2023)	37	403	52	223	1,081
Jackie Stiles, Missouri St. (2001)	35	365	65	267	1,062
Caitlin Clark, Iowa (2023)	38	338	140	239	1,055
Odyssey Sims, Baylor (2014)	37	362	98	232	1,054
Megan Gustafson, Iowa (2019)	36	412	1	176	1,001
Cindy Brown, Long Beach St. (1987)	35	362	NA	250	974
Jerica Coley, FIU (2014)	33	345	51	231	972
Genia Miller, Cal St. Fullerton (1991)	33	376	0	217	969

Season points per game

Player, school (season)	G	FG	3-FG	FT	PTS	PPG
Patricia Hoskins, Mississippi Valley St. (1989)	27	345	13	205	908	33.6
Andrea Congreaves, Mercer (1992)	28	353	77	142	925	33.0
Kelsey Plum, Washington (2017)	35	379	115	236	1,109	31.7
Caitlin Clark, Iowa (2024)	39	403	201	227	1,234	31.6
Deborah Temple, Delta St. (1984)	28	373	NA	127	873	31.2
Andrea Congreaves, Mercer (1993)	26	302	51	150	805	31.0
Wanda Ford, Drake (1986)	30	390	NA	139	919	30.6
Anucha Browne, Northwestern (1985)	28	341	NA	173	855	30.5
LeChandra LeDay, Grambling (1988)	28	334	36	146	850	30.4
Jackie Stiles, Missouri St. (2001)	35	365	65	267	1,062	30.3

Career points

Player, school (seasons)	G	FG	3-FG	FT	PTS
Caitlin Clark, Iowa (2020-24)	139	1,293	548	817	3,951
Kelsey Plum, Washington (2014-17)	139	1,136	343	912	3,527
Dyaisha Fair, Buffalo-Syracuse (2019-24)	153	1,159	430	655	3,403
Kelsey Mitchell, Ohio St. (2015-18)	139	1,120	497	665	3,402
Jackie Stiles, Missouri St. (1998-2001)	129	1,160	221	852	3,393
Brittney Griner, Baylor (2010-13)	148	1,247	2	787	3,283
Patricia Hoskins, Mississippi Valley St. (1986-89)	110	1,196	24	706	3,122
Lorri Bauman, Drake (1981-84)	120	1,104	NA	907	3,115
Jerica Coley, FIU (2011-14)	131	1,099	160	749	3,107
Rachel Banham, Minnesota (2012-16)	144	1,081	354	577	3,093
Ashley Joens, Iowa St. (2018-23)	158	988	344	740	3,060
Elena Delle Donne, Delaware (2010-13)	114	1,030	206	773	3,039
Maya Moore, Connecticut (2008-11)	154	1,171	311	383	3,036

Career points per game

Player, school (seasons)	G	FG	3-FG	FT	PTS	PPG
Patricia Hoskins, Mississippi Valley St. (1986-89)	110	1,196	24	706	3,122	28.4
Caitlin Clark, Iowa (2020-24)	139	1,293	548	817	3,951	28.4
Sandra Hodge, New Orleans (1981-84)	107	1,194	NA	472	2,860	26.7
Elena Delle Donne, Delaware (2010-13)	114	1,030	206	773	3,039	26.7
Jackie Stiles, Missouri St. (1998-2001)	129	1,160	221	852	3,393	26.3
Lorri Bauman, Drake (1981-84)	120	1,104	NA	907	3,115	26.0
Andrea Congreaves, Mercer (1990-93)	108	1,107	153	429	2,796	25.9
Cindy Blodgett, Maine (1995-98)	118	1,055	219	676	3,005	25.5
Valorie Whiteside, Appalachian St. (1985-88)	116	1,153	0	638	2,944	25.4
Kelsey Plum, Washington (2014-17)	139	1,136	343	912	3,527	25.4

NA = Not available. **Note:** Career leaders played at least three seasons (in a four-year career) or two (in a three-season career) since official NCAA record-keeping began (1981-82).

Wade Trophy Winners, 1978-2024

Awarded by the National Assn. for Girls and Women in Sport and the Women's Basketball Coaches Assn. (WBCA) to the best college women's basketball player in terms of character, leadership, and player performance.

Year	Player, school
1978	Carol Blazejowski, Montclair St.
1979	Nancy Lieberman, Old Dominion
1980	Nancy Lieberman, Old Dominion
1981	Lynette Woodard, Kansas
1982	Pam Kelly, Louisiana Tech
1983	LaTaunya Pollard, Long Beach St.
1984	Janice Lawrence, Louisiana Tech
1985	Cheryl Miller, USC
1986	Kamie Ethridge, Texas
1987	Shelly Pennefeather, Villanova
1988	Teresa Weatherspoon, Louisiana Tech
1989	Clarissa Davis, Texas
1990	Jennifer Azzi, Stanford
1991	Daedra Charles, Tennessee
1992	Susan Robinson, Penn St.
1993	Karen Jennings, Nebraska
1994	Carol Ann Shudlick, Minnesota
1995	Rebecca Lobo, Connecticut
1996	Jennifer Rizzotti, Connecticut
1997	DeLisha Milton, Florida
1998	Ticha Penicheiro, Old Dominion
1999	Stephanie White-McCarty, Purdue
2000	Edwina Brown, Texas
2001	Jackie Stiles, Missouri St.
2002	Sue Bird, Connecticut
2003	Diana Taurasi, Connecticut
2004	Alana Beard, Duke
2005	Seimone Augustus, LSU
2006	Seimone Augustus, LSU
2007	Candace Parker, Tennessee
2008	Candice Wiggins, Stanford
2009	Maya Moore, Connecticut
2010	Maya Moore, Connecticut
2011	Maya Moore, Connecticut
2012	Brittney Griner, Baylor
2013	Brittney Griner, Baylor
2014	Odyssey Sims, Baylor
2015	Breanna Stewart, Connecticut
2016	Breanna Stewart, Connecticut
2017	Kelsey Plum, Washington
2018	A'ja Wilson, South Carolina
2019	Sabrina Ionescu, Oregon
2020	Sabrina Ionescu, Oregon
2021	NaLyssa Smith, Baylor
2022	Aliyah Boston, South Carolina
2023	Caitlin Clark, Iowa
2024	Caitlin Clark, Iowa

NCAA Men's Baseball Division I Champions, 1947-2024

Year	Champion
1947	California
1948	USC
1949	Texas
1950	Texas
1951	Oklahoma
1952	Holy Cross
1953	Michigan
1954	Missouri
1955	Wake Forest
1956	Minnesota
1957	California
1958	USC
1959	Oklahoma St.
1960	Minnesota
1961	USC
1962	Michigan
1963	USC
1964	Minnesota
1965	Arizona St.
1966	Ohio St.
1967	Arizona St.
1968	USC
1969	Arizona St.
1970	USC
1971	USC
1972	USC
1973	USC
1974	USC
1975	Texas
1976	Arizona
1977	Arizona St.
1978	USC
1979	Cal St. Fullerton
1980	Arizona
1981	Arizona St.
1982	Miami (FL)
1983	Texas
1984	Cal St. Fullerton
1985	Miami (FL)
1986	Arizona
1987	Stanford
1988	Stanford
1989	Wichita St.
1990	Georgia
1991	LSU
1992	Pepperdine
1993	LSU
1994	Oklahoma
1995	Cal St. Fullerton
1996	LSU
1997	LSU
1998	USC
1999	Miami (FL)
2000	LSU
2001	Miami (FL)
2002	Texas
2003	Rice
2004	Cal St. Fullerton
2005	Texas
2006	Oregon St.
2007	Oregon St.
2008	Fresno St.
2009	LSU
2010	South Carolina
2011	South Carolina
2012	Arizona
2013	UCLA
2014	Vanderbilt
2015	Virginia
2016	Coastal Carolina
2017	Florida
2018	Oregon St.
2019	Vanderbilt
2020	No champion
2021	Mississippi St.
2022	Mississippi
2023	LSU
2024	Tennessee

NCAA Women's Softball Division I Champions, 1982-2024

Year	Champion
1982	UCLA
1983	Texas A&M
1984	UCLA
1985	UCLA
1986	Cal St. Fullerton
1987	Texas A&M
1988	UCLA
1989	UCLA
1990	UCLA
1991	Arizona
1992	UCLA
1993	Arizona
1994	Arizona
1995	UCLA
1996	Arizona
1997	Arizona
1998	Fresno St.
1999	UCLA
2000	Oklahoma
2001	Arizona
2002	California
2003	UCLA
2004	UCLA
2005	Michigan
2006	Arizona
2007	Arizona
2008	Arizona St.
2009	Washington
2010	UCLA
2011	Arizona St.
2012	Alabama
2013	Oklahoma
2014	Florida
2015	Florida
2016	Oklahoma
2017	Oklahoma
2018	Florida St.
2019	UCLA
2020	No champion
2021	Oklahoma
2022	Oklahoma
2023	Oklahoma
2024	Oklahoma

NCAA Men's Hockey Division I Champions, 1948-2024

Year	Champion	Year	Champion	Year	Champion	Year	Champion	Year	Champion
1948	Michigan	1964	Michigan	1980	North Dakota	1995	Boston Univ.	2010	Boston College
1949	Boston College	1965	Michigan Tech	1981	Wisconsin	1996	Michigan	2011	Minnesota Duluth
1950	Colorado College	1966	Michigan St.	1982	North Dakota	1997	North Dakota	2012	Boston College
1951	Michigan	1967	Cornell	1983	Wisconsin	1998	Michigan	2013	Yale
1952	Michigan	1968	Denver	1984	Bowling Green	1999	Maine	2014	Union College
1953	Michigan	1969	Denver	1985	Rensselaer	2000	North Dakota	2015	Providence
1954	Rensselaer	1970	Cornell	1986	Michigan St.	2001	Boston College	2016	North Dakota
1955	Michigan	1971	Boston Univ.	1987	North Dakota	2002	Minnesota	2017	Denver
1956	Michigan	1972	Boston Univ.	1988	Lake Superior St.	2003	Minnesota	2018	Minnesota Duluth
1957	Colorado College	1973	Wisconsin	1989	Harvard	2004	Denver	2019	Minnesota Duluth
1958	Denver	1974	Minnesota	1990	Wisconsin	2005	Denver	2020	No champion
1959	North Dakota	1975	Michigan Tech	1991	North Michigan	2006	Wisconsin	2021	Massachusetts
1960	Denver	1976	Minnesota	1992	Lake Superior St.	2007	Michigan St.	2022	Denver
1961	Denver	1977	Wisconsin	1993	Maine	2008	Boston College	2023	Quinnipiac
1962	Michigan Tech	1978	Boston Univ.	1994	Lake Superior St.	2009	Boston Univ.	2024	Denver
1963	North Dakota	1979	Minnesota						

NCAA Women's Hockey Champions, 2001-24

Year	Champion	Year	Champion	Year	Champion	Year	Champion	Year	Champion
2001	Minnesota Duluth	2006	Wisconsin	2011	Wisconsin	2016	Minnesota	2021	Wisconsin
2002	Minnesota Duluth	2007	Wisconsin	2012	Minnesota	2017	Clarkson	2022	Ohio St.
2003	Minnesota Duluth	2008	Minnesota Duluth	2013	Minnesota	2018	Clarkson	2023	Wisconsin
2004	Minnesota	2009	Wisconsin	2014	Clarkson	2019	Wisconsin	2024	Ohio St.
2005	Minnesota	2010	Minnesota Duluth	2015	Minnesota	2020	No champion		

NCAA Division I Lacrosse Champions, 1982-2024

Year	Men	Women	Year	Men	Women	Year	Men	Women
1982	North Carolina	Massachusetts	1997	Princeton	Maryland	2011	Virginia	Northwestern
1983	Syracuse	Delaware	1998	Princeton	Maryland	2012	Loyola (MD)	Northwestern
1984	Johns Hopkins	Temple	1999	Virginia	Maryland	2013	Duke	North Carolina
1985	Johns Hopkins	New Hampshire	2000	Syracuse	Maryland	2014	Duke	Maryland
1986	North Carolina	Maryland	2001	Princeton	Maryland	2015	Denver	Maryland
1987	Johns Hopkins	Penn St.	2002	Syracuse	Princeton	2016	North Carolina	North Carolina
1988	Syracuse	Temple	2003	Virginia	Princeton	2017	Maryland	Maryland
1989	Syracuse	Penn St.	2004	Syracuse	Virginia	2018	Yale	James Madison
1990	Syracuse[1]	Harvard	2005	Johns Hopkins	Northwestern	2019	Virginia	Maryland
1991	North Carolina	Virginia	2006	Virginia	Northwestern	2020	No champion	No champion
1992	Princeton	Maryland	2007	Johns Hopkins	Northwestern	2021	Virginia	Boston Coll.
1993	Syracuse	Virginia	2008	Syracuse	Northwestern	2022	Maryland	North Carolina
1994	Princeton	Princeton	2009	Syracuse	Northwestern	2023	Notre Dame	Northwestern
1995	Syracuse	Maryland	2010	Duke	Maryland	2024	Notre Dame	Boston Coll.
1996	Princeton	Maryland						

Note: NCAA Championships began in 1971 for men, in 1982 for women. (1) Vacated due to an NCAA rules violation.

NCAA Division I Soccer Champions, 1982-2023

Year	Men	Women	Year	Men	Women	Year	Men	Women
1982	Indiana	North Carolina	1996	St. John's (NY)	North Carolina	2010	Akron	Notre Dame
1983	Indiana	North Carolina	1997	UCLA	North Carolina	2011	North Carolina	Stanford
1984	Clemson	North Carolina	1998	Indiana	Florida	2012	Indiana	North Carolina
1985	UCLA	George Mason	1999	Indiana	North Carolina	2013	Notre Dame	UCLA
1986	Duke	North Carolina	2000	Connecticut	North Carolina	2014	Virginia	Florida St.
1987	Clemson	North Carolina	2001	North Carolina	Santa Clara	2015	Stanford	Penn St.
1988	Indiana	North Carolina	2002	UCLA	Portland	2016	Stanford	USC
1989	Santa Clara;		2003	Indiana	North Carolina	2017	Stanford	Stanford
	Virginia (tie)	North Carolina	2004	Indiana	Notre Dame	2018	Maryland	Florida St.
1990	UCLA	North Carolina	2005	Maryland	Portland	2019	Georgetown	Stanford
1991	Virginia	North Carolina	2006	UC Santa Barbara	North Carolina	2020	Marshall	Santa Clara
1992	Virginia	North Carolina	2007	Wake Forest	USC	2021	Clemson	Florida St.
1993	Virginia	North Carolina	2008	Maryland	North Carolina	2022	Syracuse	UCLA
1994	Virginia	North Carolina	2009	Virginia	North Carolina	2023	Clemson	Florida St.
1995	Wisconsin	Notre Dame						

Note: NCAA Championships began in 1959 for men, in 1982 for women.

NCAA Division I Wrestling Champions, 1964-2024

Year	Champion	Year	Champion	Year	Champion	Year	Champion	Year	Champion
1964	Oklahoma St.	1977	Iowa St.	1989	Oklahoma St.	2001	Minnesota	2013	Penn St.
1965	Iowa St.	1978	Iowa	1990	Oklahoma St.	2002	Minnesota	2014	Penn St.
1966	Oklahoma St.	1979	Iowa	1991	Iowa	2003	Oklahoma St.	2015	Ohio St.
1967	Michigan St.	1980	Iowa	1992	Iowa	2004	Oklahoma St.	2016	Penn St.
1968	Oklahoma St.	1981	Iowa	1993	Iowa	2005	Oklahoma St.	2017	Penn St.
1969	Iowa St.	1982	Iowa	1994	Oklahoma St.	2006	Oklahoma St.	2018	Penn St.
1970	Iowa St.	1983	Iowa	1995	Iowa	2007	Minnesota	2019	Penn St.
1971	Oklahoma St.	1984	Iowa	1996	Iowa	2008	Iowa	2020	No champion
1972	Iowa St.	1985	Iowa	1997	Iowa	2009	Iowa	2021	Iowa
1973	Iowa St.	1986	Iowa	1998	Iowa	2010	Iowa	2022	Penn St.
1974	Oklahoma	1987	Iowa St.	1999	Iowa	2011	Penn St.	2023	Penn St.
1975	Iowa	1988	Arizona St.	2000	Iowa	2012	Penn St.	2024	Penn St.
1976	Iowa								

FOOTBALL

NFL 2023: Chiefs Prove Swift and Sure in Super Bowl Repeat

Super Bowl LVIII—the Feb. 11, 2024, rematch of Super Bowl LIV between Kansas City and San Francisco—ended with the same results, a Chiefs comeback win, this time 25-22 in overtime at Allegiant Stadium in Las Vegas, NV. The Chiefs became the ninth team ever to win consecutive Super Bowls. Kansas City tight end Travis Kelce's well-documented romance with pop singer Taylor Swift brought even more eyes to the NFL in 2023. TV ratings rose significantly, even factoring in streaming services, with the Super Bowl the most watched TV program ever with 123.7 million viewers. The average TV audience of 17.9 million per game during the regular season was the highest since 2015, and that number doubled for the playoffs.

Kansas City uncharacteristically stumbled down the stretch in Dec. 2023. The Chiefs went 4-4 in the second half to close the regular season at 11-6—still enough for an eighth straight AFC West title. Kansas City's lone home playoff game was a 26-7 wild-card win against the Dolphins, on a frigid –4-degree night Jan. 13. The Chiefs then hit the road and upset Buffalo, 27-24, then Baltimore, 17-10, to claim the AFC title Jan. 28. San Francisco was home for its two playoff games, winning by a field goal against both Green Bay and Detroit.

The Lions were one of the biggest surprises in the NFL in 2023. Detroit's 12 wins tied its tally for 1991, the last year the Lions reached the NFC Championship Game. After beating the Rams and Buccaneers at home in the playoffs, Detroit took a commanding 24-10 lead in San Francisco Jan. 28, but head coach Dan Campbell twice went on fourth down instead of attempting field goals as the 49ers rallied to win, 34-31. It was the closest the Lions have ever gotten to a Super Bowl, falling to 0-12 in road playoff games since Detroit's last championship in 1957, a decade before the first Super Bowl.

In Miami's 70-20 win Sept. 24 over the Denver Broncos, Miami became the first team with five passing and five rushing touchdowns in the same game, and the most points in an NFL game since 1966—the year the Dolphins were founded. Four days after being shut out by the Vikings, 3-0, on Dec. 10, the Las Vegas Raiders scored six touchdowns in the first half and set a franchise record of 63 points—an avalanche that also set a Los Angeles Chargers record for most points allowed. Philadelphia's Jalen Hurts and Buffalo's Josh Allen shared the record for most rushing touchdowns as quarterbacks in a season with 15 apiece; Allen also set a record with 10 straight games with at least one touchdown run and one TD pass.

The New England Patriots endured their worst season (4-13) since 1992, but Bill Belichick became the third coach to win 300 games in his 24th and final season with the Pats. He also ended 2023 with 165 losses, tied for the most in history. Led by the NFL's stingiest defense led by Defensive Player of the Year Myles Garrett, Cleveland won 11 games for just the second time since playing for Belichick in 1994. The 10-7 Pittsburgh Steelers joined the 1965-85 Dallas Cowboys as teams with 20 consecutive seasons of .500 W-L records or better. The AFC North was the first division in 88 years to have every team finish with a winning record.

Houston's 22-year-old C.J. Stroud became the youngest starting quarterback to win a playoff game, beating Cleveland, 45-14. The Texans had NFL Rookies of the Year on Offense (Stroud) and Defense (end Will Anderson). The Baltimore Ravens, led by NFL MVP Lamar Jackson, defeated Houston in the Divisional Round, 34-10. Green Bay matched a franchise playoff record with 48 points in Dallas; the upset marked the first time a No. 7-seed won a postseason game.

NFL Playoff Results, 2023

AFC Wild Card Games: Kansas City 26, Miami 7; Buffalo 31, Pittsburgh 17; Houston 45, Cleveland 14.
NFC Wild Card Games: Tampa Bay 32, Philadelphia 9; Detroit 24, L.A. Rams 23; Green Bay 48, Dallas 32.
AFC Divisional Playoff Games: Kansas City 27, Buffalo 24; Baltimore 34, Houston 10.
NFC Divisional Playoff Games: Detroit 31, Tampa Bay 23; San Francisco 24, Green Bay 21.
AFC Championship Game: Kansas City 17, Baltimore 10.
NFC Championship Game: San Francisco 34, Detroit 31.
Super Bowl LVIII: Kansas City 25, San Francisco 22 (OT).

Super Bowl LVIII: Kansas City 25, San Francisco 22

The Kansas City Chiefs became the NFL's first repeat champion since 2005, battling from behind to tie the score in regulation and—after falling behind again in overtime—scored on a 3-yard pass from Patrick Mahomes to Mecole Hardman to defeat the San Francisco 49ers in Super Bowl LVIII on Feb. 11, 2024. Allegiant Stadium hosted the first Super Bowl ever in Las Vegas. The game marked the fourth Super Bowl victory in six tries for Kansas City; three of those victories have come since 2019, all with Mahomes named MVP—two against the 49ers. The New England Patriots, the last team to repeat before Kansas City, were the only previous overtime Super Bowl winner, in Super Bowl LI.

The Chiefs trailed by double digits in a Super Bowl for the fourth time under head coach Andy Reid. A field goal by rookie Jake Moody and a touchdown pass thrown by receiver Jauan Jennings gave San Francisco a 10-0 lead. Harrison Butker's field goal shortly before halftime gave Kansas City its first points.

A 57-yard field goal by Butker in the third quarter became the longest field goal in Super Bowl history, breaking the mark of 55 yards set by Moody a quarter earlier. Kansas City recovered a muffed punt at the San Francisco 16. Mahomes hit Marquez Valdes-Scantling for a touchdown on the next play for a 13-10 lead. Another special teams mistake cost the 49ers points when Moody's extra point try was blocked following a 10-yard touchdown pass from Brock Purdy to Jennings, who became the second player to catch and throw a touchdown in the same Super Bowl (Philadelphia quarterback Nick Fowles did it in Super Bowl LII).

An exchange of field goals gave the 49ers the lead with 1:53 to play. Travis Kelce hauled in a 22-yard pass and got out of bounds at the 11. With three seconds left, Butker's fourth field goal sent the game to overtime. The 49ers won the coin toss and Christian McCaffrey accounted for 50 of the 66 yards on the drive. Moody's third field goal gave the 49ers a 22-19 lead. Mahomes got the needed yards on fourth down and later scrambled for 19 yards, setting up a confetti explosion when he hit Hardman in the end zone.

	Quarters					
Team	**1**	**2**	**3**	**4**	**OT**	**Final**
Kansas City	0	3	10	6	6	25
San Francisco	0	10	0	9	3	22

Total attendance: 61,629
Game length: 4:06

Team Statistics

	Kansas City	**San Francisco**
First downs	24	23
Total net yards	455	382
Rushes-yards	30-130	33-110
Passing yards, net	325	272
Punt returns-yards	4-12	2-0
Kickoff returns-yards	0-0	0-0
Interception returns-yards	0-0	1-0
Field goals made-attempts	4/4	3/3
Pass attempts-completions-interceptions	34-46-333-2-1	24-39-276-2-0
Sacked-yards lost	3-8	1-4
Punts-average	5-50.8	5-50.8
Fumbles-lost	5-1	2-2
Penalties-yards	6-55	6-40
Time of possession	36:26	38:31

Scoring

San Francisco: Jake Moody, 55-yard field goal
San Francisco: Christian McCaffrey, 21-yard pass from Jauan Jennings (Moody PAT)
Kansas City: Harrison Butker, 28-yard field goal
Kansas City: Butker, 57-yard field goal
Kansas City: Marquez Valdes-Scantling, 16-yard pass from Patrick Mahomes (Butker PAT)
San Francisco: Jennings, 10-yard pass from Brock Purdy (Moody kick failed)
Kansas City: Butker, 24-yard field goal
San Francisco: Moody, 53-yard field goal
Kansas City: Butker, 29-yard field goal
San Francisco: Moody, 27-yard field goal
Kansas City: Mecole Hardman, 3-yard pass from Mahomes

Individual Statistics

Rushing

Kansas City: Mahomes, 9-66; Isiah Pacheco, 18-59; Rashee Rice, 2-5.
San Francisco: McCaffrey, 22-80; Purdy, 3-12; Deebo Samuel, 3-8; Elijah Mitchell, 2-8; Kyle Juszczyk, 1-2.

Passing

Kansas City: Mahomes, 34-46, 333 yards, 2 TD, 1 int.
San Francisco: Purdy, 23-38, 255 yards, 1 TD, 0 int.; Jennings, 1-1, 21 yards, 1 TD, 0 int.

Receiving

Kansas City: Travis Kelce, 9-93; Hardman, 3-57, 1 TD; Justin Watson, 3-54; Rice, 6-39; Pacheco, 6-33; Noah Gray, 2-22; Valdes-Scantling, 3-20, 1 TD; Jerick McKinnon, 2-15.
San Francisco: McCaffrey, 8-80, 1 TD; Brandon Aiyuk, 3-49; Jennings, 4-42, 1 TD; Samuel, 3-33; Juszczyk, 2-31; Ray-Ray McCloud, 1-19; Chris Conley, 1-18; George Kittle, 2-4.

NFL Final Standings, 2023

(playoff seeding in parentheses; * = wild card qualifier for playoffs)

AMERICAN FOOTBALL CONFERENCE

	W	L	T	Pct	PF	PA	Div
East Division							
Buffalo (2)	11	6	0	0.647	451	311	4-2
Miami* (6)	11	6	0	0.647	496	391	4-2
NY Jets	7	10	0	0.412	268	355	2-4
New England	4	13	0	0.235	236	366	2-4
North Division							
Baltimore (1)	13	4	0	0.765	483	280	3-3
Cleveland* (5)	11	6	0	0.647	396	362	3-3
Pittsburgh* (7)	10	7	0	0.588	304	324	5-1
Cincinnati	9	8	0	0.529	366	384	1-5
South Division							
Houston (4)	10	7	0	0.588	377	353	4-2
Jacksonville	9	8	0	0.529	377	371	4-2
Indianapolis	9	8	0	0.529	396	415	3-3
Tennessee	6	11	0	0.353	305	367	1-5
West Division							
Kansas City (3)	11	6	0	0.647	371	294	4-2
Las Vegas	8	9	0	0.471	332	331	4-2
Denver	8	9	0	0.471	357	413	3-3
L.A. Chargers	5	12	0	0.294	346	398	1-5

NATIONAL FOOTBALL CONFERENCE

	W	L	T	Pct	PF	PA	Div
East Division							
Dallas (2)	12	5	0	0.706	509	315	5-1
Philadelphia* (5)	11	6	0	0.647	433	428	4-2
NY Giants	6	11	0	0.353	266	407	3-3
Washington	4	13	0	0.235	329	518	0-6
North Division							
Detroit (3)	12	5	0	0.706	461	395	4-2
Green Bay* (7)	9	8	0	0.529	383	350	4-2
Minnesota	7	10	0	0.412	344	362	2-4
Chicago	7	10	0	0.412	360	379	2-4
South Division							
Tampa Bay (4)	9	8	0	0.529	348	325	4-2
New Orleans	9	8	0	0.529	402	327	4-2
Atlanta	7	10	0	0.412	321	373	3-3
Carolina	2	15	0	0.118	236	416	1-5
West Division							
San Francisco (1)	12	5	0	0.706	491	298	5-1
L.A. Rams* (6)	10	7	0	0.588	404	377	5-1
Seattle	9	8	0	0.529	364	402	2-4
Arizona	4	13	0	0.235	330	455	0-6

NFL Individual Leaders: American Football Conference, 2023

(* = rookie)

PASSING

Player, team	Att	Comp	Pct comp	Yds	Yds/Att	Long	TD	Pct TD	Int	Rating
Lamar Jackson, Baltimore	457	307	67.2	3,678	8.1	80	24	5.2	7	102.7
Tua Taglovailoa, Miami	560	388	69.3	4,624	8.3	78	29	5.2	14	101.1
*C.J. Stroud, Houston	499	319	63.9	4,108	8.2	75	23	4.6	5	100.8
*Jake Browning, Cincinnati	243	171	70.4	1,936	8.0	80	12	4.9	7	98.4
Russell Wilson, Denver	447	297	66.4	3,070	6.9	60	26	5.8	8	98.0
Justin Hebert, L.A. Chargers	456	297	65.1	3,134	6.9	60	20	4.4	7	93.2
Patrick Mahomes, Kansas City	597	401	67.2	4,183	7.0	67	27	4.5	14	92.6
Josh Allen, Buffalo	579	385	66.5	4,306	7.4	81	29	5.0	18	92.2
Joe Burrow, Cincinnati	365	244	66.8	2,309	6.3	64	15	4.1	6	91.0
Trevor Lawrence, Jacksonville	564	370	65.6	4,016	7.1	65	21	3.7	14	88.5
Gardner Minshew, Indianapolis	490	305	62.2	3,305	6.7	75	15	3.1	9	84.6
*Will Levis, Tennessee	255	149	58.4	1,808	7.1	61	8	3.1	4	84.2
*Aidan O'Connell, Las Vegas	343	213	62.1	2,218	6.5	50	12	3.5	7	83.9
Kenny Pickett. Pittsburgh	324	201	62.0	2,070	6.4	72	6	1.9	4	81.4
Zach Wilson, NY Jets	368	221	60.0	2,271	6.2	68	8	2.2	7	77.2
Mac Jones, New England	345	224	64.9	2,120	6.1	58	10	2.9	12	77.0

RUSHING YARDS

Player, team	Yds	Att	Avg	Long	TD
Derrick Henry, Tennessee	1,167	280	4.2	69	12
James Cook, Buffalo	1,122	237	4.7	42	2
Najee Harris, Pittsburgh	1,035	255	4.1	25	8
Joe Mixon, Cincinnati	1,034	257	4.0	44	9
Raheem Mostert, Miami	1,012	209	4.8	49	18
Travis Etienne, Jacksonville	1,008	267	3.8	62T	11
Breece Hall, NY Jets	994	223	4.5	83	5
Isiah Pacheco, Kansas City	935	205	4.6	48T	7
Devin Singletary, Houston	898	216	4.2	24	4
Lamar Jackson, Baltimore	821	148	5.6	30	5

RECEPTIONS

Player, team	Rec	Yds	Avg	Long	TD
Tyreek Hill, Miami	119	1,799	15.1	78T	13
Evan Engram, Jacksonville	114	963	8.5	34	4
Michael Pittman, Indianapolis	109	1,152	10.6	75T	4
Keenan Allen L.A. Chargers	108	1,243	11.5	42	7
Stefon Diggs, Buffalo	107	1,183	11.1	55T	8
Davante Adams, Las Vegas	103	1,144	11.1	46T	8
Ja'Marr Chase, Cincinnati	100	1,216	12.2	76T	7
Garrett Wilson, NY Jets	95	1,042	11.0	68T	3
Travis Kelce, Kansas City	93	984	10.6	53	5
David Njoku, Cleveland	81	882	10.9	43	6

SCORING—KICKERS

Player, team	PAT	FG	Long	Pts
Justin Tucker, Baltimore	51	32	50	147
Harrison Butker, Kansas City	38	33	60	137
Matt Gay, Indianapolis	35	33	57	134
Jason Sanders, Miami	58	24	57	130
Cameron Dicker, L.A. Chargers	35	31	55	128
Brandon McManus, Jacksonville	35	30	56	125
Dustin Hopkins, Cleveland	24	33	58	123
Tyler Bass, Buffalo	49	24	54	121
Greg Zuerlein, NY Jets	15	35	55	120
Wil Lutz, Denver	29	30	52	119

SCORING—NON-KICKERS

Player, team	TD	Rush	Rec	2-Pt	Pts
Raheem Mostert, Miami	21	18	3	0	126
Josh Allen, Buffalo	15	15	0	0	90
Gus Edwards, Baltimore	13	13	0	1	80
Tyreek Hill, Miami	13	0	13	0	78
Travis Etienne, Jacksonville	12	11	1	2	76
Joe Mixon, Cincinnati	12	9	3	1	74
Derrick Henry, Tennessee	12	12	0	0	72
*De'Von Achane, Miami	11	8	3	0	66
Jakobi Meyers, Las Vegas	10	2	8	0	60
Courtland Sutton, Denver	10	0	10	0	60

INTERCEPTIONS

Player, team	No.	Yds	Avg	Long	TD
Geno Stone, Baltimore	7	101	14.4	36	0
Derek Stingley, Houston	5	17	3.4	14	0

(Ten players tied with 4)

KICKOFF RETURNS

Player, team	No.	Yds	Avg	Long	TD
*Xavier Gipson, NY Jets	22	511	23.2	34	0
Braxton Berrios, Miami	18	441	24.5	33	0
*Derius Davis, L.A. Chargers	17	374	22.0	46	0
*Marvin Mims, Denver	15	397	26.5	99T	1
Jamal Agnew, Jacksonville	15	391	26.1	53	0

PUNT RETURNS

Player, team	No.	Yds	Avg	Long	TD
*Derius Davis, L.A. Chargers	24	385	16.0	87T	1
Devin Duvernay, Baltimore	23	290	12.6	70	0
Deonte Harty, Buffalo	26	323	12.4	96T	1
*Charlie Jones, Cincinnati	23	248	10.8	81T	1
Braxton Berrios, Miami	23	235	10.2	19	0
DeAndre Carter, Las Vegas	24	232	9.7	32	0
*Xavier Gipson, NY Jets	33	319	9.7	65T	1

PUNTING

Player, team	No.	Yds	Long	Avg
Ryan Stonehouse, Tennessee	53	2,812	74	53.1
A.J. Cole III, Las Vegas	75	3,783	83	50.4
Corey Bojorquez, Cleveland	87	4,294	73	49.4
Thomas Morstead, NY Jets	99	4,831	62	48.8
Rigoberto Sanchez, Indianapolis	68	3,281	69	48.2
Jordan Stout, Baltimore	66	3,158	67	47.9
Cameron Johnston, Houston	66	3,145	74	47.6
Logan Cooke, Jacksonville	61	2,893	65	47.4
Tommy Townsend, Kansas City	59	2,776	68	47.0
*Bryce Baringer, New England	98	4,598	79	46.9

SACKS

Player, team	No.
T.J. Watt, Pittsburgh	19.0
Josh Allen, Jacksonville	17.5
Trey Hendrickson, Cincinnati	17.5
Khalil Mack, L.A. Chargers	17.0
Maxx Crosby, Las Vegas	14.5
Myles Garrett, Cleveland	14.0
Justin Madubuike, Baltimore	13.0
Jonathan Greenard, Houston	12.5
Denico Autry, Tennessee	11.5
Bradley Chubb, Miami	11.0

NFL Individual Leaders: National Football Conference, 2023

(* = rookie)

PASSING

Player, team	Att	Comp	Pct comp	Yds	Yds/Att	Long	TD	Pct TD	Int	Rating
Brock Purdy, San Francisco	444	308	69.4	4,280	9.6	76	31	7.0	11	113.0
Dak Prescott, Dallas	590	410	69.5	4,516	7.7	92	36	6.1	9	105.9
Kirk Cousins, Minnesota	311	216	69.5	2,331	7.5	62	18	5.8	5	103.8
Jared Goff, Detroit	605	407	67.3	4,575	7.6	70	30	5.0	12	97.9
Derek Carr, New Orleans	548	375	68.4	3,878	7.1	58	25	4.6	8	97.7
Jordan Love, Green Bay	579	372	64.2	4,159	7.2	77	32	5.5	11	96.1
Baker Mayfield, Tampa Bay	566	364	64.3	4,044	7.1	75	28	5.0	10	94.6
Matthew Stafford, L.A. Rams	521	326	62.6	3,965	7.6	80	24	4.6	11	92.5
Geno Smith, Seattle	499	323	64.7	3,624	7.3	73	20	4.0	9	92.1
Kyler Murray, Arizona	268	176	65.7	1,799	6.7	48	10	3.7	5	89.4
Jalen Hurts, Philadelphia	538	352	65.4	3,858	7.2	63	23	4.3	15	89.1
Justin Fields, Chicago	370	227	61.4	2,562	6.9	58	16	4.3	9	86.3
Desmond Ridder, Atlanta	388	249	64.2	2,836	7.3	71	12	3.1	12	83.4
Joshua Dobbs, Arizona-Minnesota	417	262	62.8	2,464	5.9	69	13	3.1	10	79.5
Sam Howell, Washington	612	388	63.4	3,946	6.5	51	21	3.4	21	78.9
*Bryce Young, Carolina	527	315	59.8	2,877	5.5	48	11	2.1	10	73.7

RUSHING YARDS

Player, team	Yds	Att	Avg	Long	TD
Christian McCaffrey, San Francisco	1,459	272	5.4	72	14
Kyren Williams, L.A. Rams	1,144	228	5.0	56	12
D'Andre Swift, Philadelphia	1,049	229	4.6	43	5
James Conner, Arizona	1,040	208	5.0	44	7
David Montgomery, Detroit	1,015	219	4.6	75T	13
Tony Pollard, Dallas	1,005	252	4.0	31	6
Rachaad White, Tampa Bay	990	272	3.6	38	6
*Bijan Robinson, Atlanta	976	214	4.6	38	4
Saquon Barkley, NY Giants	962	247	3.9	36	6
*Jahmyr Gibbs, Detroit	945	182	5.2	36	10

RECEPTIONS

Player, team	Rec	Yds	Avg	Long	TD
CeeDee Lamb, Dallas	135	1,749	13.0	92T	12
Amon-Ra St. Brown, Detroit	119	1,515	12.7	70T	10
A.J. Brown, Philadelphia	106	1,456	13.7	59T	7
*Puka Nacua, L.A. Rams	105	1,486	14.2	80	6
Adam Thielen, Carolina	103	1,014	9.8	32	4
D.J. Moore, Chicago	96	1,364	14.2	58	8
T.J. Hockenson, Minnesota	95	960	10.1	29	5
Chris Olave, New Orleans	87	1,123	12.9	51	5
*Sam LaPorta, Detroit	86	889	10.3	48	10
Chris Godwin, Tampa Bay	83	1,024	12.3	47T	2

SCORING—KICKERS

Player, team	PAT	FG	Long	Pts
*Brandon Aubrey, Dallas	49	36	60	157
Jason Myers, Seattle	33	35	55	138
Cairo Santos, Chicago	31	35	55	136
Jake Elliott, Philadelphia	45	30	61	135
*Blake Grupe, New Orleans	40	30	55	130
*Jake Moody, San Francisco	60	21	57	123
Younghoe Koo, Atlanta	27	32	54	123
Chase McLaughlin, Tampa Bay	33	29	57	120
*Anders Carlson, Green Bay	34	27	53	115
Greg Joseph, Minnesota	36	24	54	108

SCORING—NON-KICKERS

Player, team	TD	Rush	Rec	2-Pt	Pts
Christian McCaffrey, San Francisco	21	14	7	0	126
Kyren Williams, L.A. Rams	15	12	3	1	92
Jalen Hurts, Philadelphia	15	15	0	0	90
CeeDee Lamb, Dallas	14	2	12	1	86
David Montgomery, Detroit	13	13	0	1	80
Mike Evans, Tampa Bay	13	0	13	0	78
Deebo Samuel, San Francisco	12	5	7	0	72
*Jahmyr Gibbs, Detroit	11	10	1	0	66
*Sam LaPorta, Detroit	10	0	10	2	64
Saquon Barkley, NY Giants	10	6	4	1	62
*Jayden Reed, Green Bay	10	2	8	1	62

INTERCEPTIONS

Player, team	No.	Yds	Avg	Long	TD
DaRon Bland, Dallas	9	209	23.2	63T	5
Jessie Bates III, Atlanta	6	95	15.8	92T	1
Charvarius Ward, San Francisco	5	91	18.2	66T	1
(Nine players tied with 4)					

KICKOFF RETURNS

Player, team	No.	Yds	Avg	Long	TD
Keisean Nixon, Green Bay	30	782	26.1	51	0
Rashid Shaheed, New Orleans	18	384	21.3	18	0
Greg Dortch, Arizona	17	360	21.2	40	0
DeeJay Dallas, Seattle	17	440	25.9	34	0
Velus Jones, Chicago	16	435	27.2	37	0
Deven Thompkins, Tampa Bay	16	327	20.4	32	0
Raheem Blackshear, Carolina	16	430	26.9	52	0

PUNT RETURNS

Player, team	No.	Yds	Avg	Long	TD
Britain Covey, Philadelphia	29	417	14.4	54	0
Rashid Shaheed, New Orleans	25	339	13.6	76T	1
Gunner Olszewski, NY Giants	23	273	11.9	94T	1
Kalif Raymond, Detroit	29	331	11.4	42	0
DeeJay Dallas, Seattle	25	265	10.6	32	0
Greg Dortch, Arizona	29	275	9.5	49	0
Deven Thompkins, Tampa Bay	25	234	9.4	51	0
Ihmir Smith-Marsette, Carolina	37	322	8.7	79T	1

PUNTING

Player, team	No.	Yds	Long	Avg
Bryan Anger, Dallas	44	2,262	63	51.4
Blake Gillikin, Arizona	51	2,580	77	50.6
Jake Camarda, Tampa Bay	77	3,854	74	50.0
Michael Dickson, Seattle	66	3,303	73	50.0
Braden Mann, Philadelphia	44	2,190	63	49.8
*Ethan Evans, L.A. Rams	63	3,101	72	49.2
Ryan Wright, Minnesota	59	2,873	68	48.7
Mitch Wishnowsky, San Francisco	52	2,480	67	47.7
Bradley Pinion, Atlanta	75	3,523	66	47.0
Johnny Hekker, Carolina	82	3,838	69	46.8

SACKS

Player, team	No.
Danielle Hunter, Minnesota	16.5
Micah Parsons, Dallas	14.0
Montez Sweat, Washington/Chicago	12.5
Aidan Hutchinson, Detroit	11.5
Kayvon Thibodeaux, NY Giants	11.5
Haason Reddick, Philadelphia	11.0
Nick Bosa, San Francisco	10.5
Rashan Gary, Green Bay	9.0
Boye Mafe, Seattle	9.0
*Kobie Turner, L.A. Rams	9.0

Super Bowl, 1967-2024

The Super Bowl was created as a condition of the merger between the American Football League (AFL, formed in 1959) and National Football League (NFL, formed in 1920). Announced June 8, 1966, the merger agreement stipulated that the leagues would play separate regular season schedules through the 1969 season but meet in an AFL-NFL Championship Game, unofficially dubbed the Super Bowl. The first Super Bowl, played at the Memorial Coliseum in Los Angeles on Jan. 15, 1967, did not sell out, unlike every Super Bowl game since. Each player on the victorious Green Bay Packers earned $15,000 for the win; the defeated Kansas City Chiefs each collected $7,500.

No.	Year	Winner	Opponent	Winning coach	Site
I	1967	*Green Bay Packers, 35	Kansas City Chiefs, 10	Vince Lombardi	Memorial Coliseum, Los Angeles, CA
II	1968	Green Bay Packers, 33	*Oakland Raiders, 14	Vince Lombardi	Orange Bowl, Miami, FL
III	1969	*NY Jets, 16	Baltimore Colts, 7	Weeb Ewbank	Orange Bowl, Miami, FL
IV	1970	Kansas City Chiefs, 23	*Minnesota Vikings, 7	Hank Stram	Tulane Stadium, New Orleans, LA
V	1971	Baltimore Colts, 16	*Dallas Cowboys, 13	Don McCafferty	Orange Bowl, Miami, FL
VI	1972	Dallas Cowboys, 24	*Miami Dolphins, 3	Tom Landry	Tulane Stadium, New Orleans, LA
VII	1973	*Miami Dolphins, 14	Washington Redskins, 7	Don Shula	Memorial Coliseum, Los Angeles, CA
VIII	1974	*Miami Dolphins, 24	Minnesota Vikings, 7	Don Shula	Rice Stadium, Houston, TX
IX	1975	*Pittsburgh Steelers, 16	Minnesota Vikings, 6	Chuck Noll	Tulane Stadium, New Orleans, LA
X	1976	Pittsburgh Steelers, 21	*Dallas Cowboys, 17	Chuck Noll	Orange Bowl, Miami, FL
XI	1977	*Oakland Raiders, 32	Minnesota Vikings, 14	John Madden	Rose Bowl, Pasadena, CA
XII	1978	*Dallas Cowboys, 27	Denver Broncos, 10	Tom Landry	Superdome, New Orleans, LA
XIII	1979	Pittsburgh Steelers, 35	*Dallas Cowboys, 31	Chuck Noll	Orange Bowl, Miami, FL
XIV	1980	Pittsburgh Steelers, 31	*L.A. Rams, 19	Chuck Noll	Rose Bowl, Pasadena, CA
XV	1981	Oakland Raiders, 27	*Philadelphia Eagles, 10	Tom Flores	Superdome, New Orleans, LA
XVI	1982	*San Francisco 49ers, 26	Cincinnati Bengals, 21	Bill Walsh	Silverdome, Pontiac, MI
XVII	1983	Washington Redskins, 27	*Miami Dolphins, 17	Joe Gibbs	Rose Bowl, Pasadena, CA
XVIII	1984	*L.A. Raiders, 38	Washington Redskins, 9	Tom Flores	Tampa Stadium, Tampa, FL
XIX	1985	*San Francisco 49ers, 38	Miami Dolphins, 16	Bill Walsh	Stanford Stadium, Stanford, CA
XX	1986	*Chicago Bears, 46	New England Patriots, 10	Mike Ditka	Superdome, New Orleans, LA
XXI	1987	NY Giants, 39	*Denver Broncos, 20	Bill Parcells	Rose Bowl, Pasadena, CA
XXII	1988	*Washington Redskins, 42	Denver Broncos, 10	Joe Gibbs	Jack Murphy Stadium, San Diego, CA
XXIII	1989	*San Francisco 49ers, 20	Cincinnati Bengals, 16	Bill Walsh	Joe Robbie Stadium, Miami, FL
XXIV	1990	San Francisco 49ers, 55	*Denver Broncos, 10	George Seifert	Superdome, New Orleans, LA
XXV	1991	NY Giants, 20	*Buffalo Bills, 19	Bill Parcells	Tampa Stadium, Tampa, FL
XXVI	1992	*Washington Redskins, 37	Buffalo Bills, 24	Joe Gibbs	Metrodome, Minneapolis, MN
XXVII	1993	Dallas Cowboys, 52	*Buffalo Bills, 17	Jimmy Johnson	Rose Bowl, Pasadena, CA
XXVIII	1994	*Dallas Cowboys, 30	Buffalo Bills, 13	Jimmy Johnson	Georgia Dome, Atlanta, GA
XXIX	1995	*San Francisco 49ers, 49	San Diego Chargers, 26	George Seifert	Joe Robbie Stadium, Miami, FL
XXX	1996	*Dallas Cowboys, 27	Pittsburgh Steelers, 17	Barry Switzer	Sun Devil Stadium, Tempe, AZ
XXXI	1997	Green Bay Packers, 35	*New England Patriots, 21	Mike Holmgren	Superdome, New Orleans, LA
XXXII	1998	Denver Broncos, 31	*Green Bay Packers, 24	Mike Shanahan	Qualcomm Stadium, San Diego, CA
XXXIII	1999	Denver Broncos, 34	*Atlanta Falcons, 19	Mike Shanahan	Pro Player Stadium, Miami, FL
XXXIV	2000	*St. Louis Rams, 23	Tennessee Titans, 16	Dick Vermeil	Georgia Dome, Atlanta, GA
XXXV	2001	Baltimore Ravens, 34	*NY Giants, 7	Brian Billick	Raymond James Stadium, Tampa, FL
XXXVI	2002	New England Patriots, 20	*St. Louis Rams, 17	Bill Belichick	Superdome, New Orleans, LA
XXXVII	2003	*Tampa Bay Buccaneers, 48	Oakland Raiders, 21	Jon Gruden	Qualcomm Stadium, San Diego, CA
XXXVIII	2004	New England Patriots, 32	*Carolina Panthers, 29	Bill Belichick	Reliant Stadium, Houston, TX
XXXIX	2005	New England Patriots, 24	*Philadelphia Eagles, 21	Bill Belichick	Alltel Stadium, Jacksonville, FL
XL	2006	Pittsburgh Steelers, 21	*Seattle Seahawks, 10	Bill Cowher	Ford Field, Detroit, MI
XLI	2007	Indianapolis Colts, 29	*Chicago Bears, 17	Tony Dungy	Dolphin Stadium, Miami Gardens, FL
XLII	2008	*NY Giants, 17	New England Patriots, 14	Tom Coughlin	Univ. of Phoenix Stadium, Glendale, AZ
XLIII	2009	Pittsburgh Steelers, 27	**Arizona Cardinals, 23	Mike Tomlin	Raymond James Stadium, Tampa, FL
XLIV	2010	*New Orleans Saints, 31	Indianapolis Colts, 17	Sean Payton	Sun Life Stadium, Miami Gardens, FL
XLV	2011	**Green Bay Packers, 31	Pittsburgh Steelers, 25	Mike McCarthy	Cowboys Stadium, Arlington, TX
XLVI	2012	NY Giants, 21	**New England Patriots, 17	Tom Coughlin	Lucas Oil Stadium, Indianapolis, IN
XLVII	2013	**Baltimore Ravens, 34	San Francisco 49ers, 31	John Harbaugh	Mercedes-Benz Superdome, New Orleans, LA
XLVIII	2014	**Seattle Seahawks, 43	Denver Broncos, 8	Pete Carroll	MetLife Stadium, East Rutherford, NJ
XLIX	2015	New England Patriots, 28	**Seattle Seahawks, 24	Bill Belichick	Univ. of Phoenix Stadium, Glendale, AZ
50 (L)	2016	Denver Broncos, 24	**Carolina Panthers, 10	Gary Kubiak	Levi's Stadium, Santa Clara, CA
LI	2017	New England Patriots, 34 (OT)	**Atlanta Falcons, 28	Bill Belichick	NRG Stadium, Houston, TX
LII	2018	Philadelphia Eagles, 41	**New England Patriots, 33	Doug Pederson	U.S. Bank Stadium, Minneapolis, MN
LIII	2019	New England Patriots, 13	**L.A. Rams, 3	Bill Belichick	Mercedes-Benz Stadium, Atlanta, GA
LIV	2020	Kansas City Chiefs, 31	**San Francisco 49ers, 20	Andy Reid	Hard Rock Stadium, Miami Gardens, FL
LV	2021	Tampa Bay Buccaneers, 31	**Kansas City Chiefs, 9	Bruce Arians	Raymond James Stadium, Tampa, FL
LVI	2022	L.A. Rams, 23	**Cincinnati Bengals, 20	Sean McVay	SoFi Stadium, Inglewood, CA
LVII	2023	**Kansas City Chiefs, 38	Philadelphia Eagles, 35	Andy Reid	State Farm Stadium, Glendale, AZ
LVIII	2024	**Kansas City Chiefs 25 (OT)	San Francisco 49ers 22	Andy Reid	Allegiant Stadium, Las Vegas, NV

* = Team won the coin toss and elected to receive. ** = Team won the coin toss and elected to receive in the second half. OT = Overtime.

Super Bowl Sites, 2025-27

No.	Site	Date
LIX	Caesars Superdome, New Orleans, LA	Feb. 9, 2025
LX	Levi's Stadium, Santa Clara, CA	Feb. 8, 2026
LXI	SoFi Stadium, Inglewood, CA	Feb. 14, 2027

Super Bowl MVPs, 1967-2024

Year	Most valuable player, team	Year	Most valuable player, team	Year	Most valuable player, team
1967	Bart Starr, Green Bay	1987	Phil Simms, NY Giants	2006	Hines Ward, Pittsburgh
1968	Bart Starr, Green Bay	1988	Doug Williams, Washington	2007	Peyton Manning, Indianapolis
1969	Joe Namath, NY Jets	1989	Jerry Rice, San Francisco	2008	Eli Manning, NY Giants
1970	Len Dawson, Kansas City	1990	Joe Montana, San Francisco	2009	Santonio Holmes, Pittsburgh
1971	Chuck Howley, Dallas	1991	Ottis Anderson, NY Giants	2010	Drew Brees, New Orleans
1972	Roger Staubach, Dallas	1992	Mark Rypien, Washington	2011	Aaron Rodgers, Green Bay
1973	Jake Scott, Miami	1993	Troy Aikman, Dallas	2012	Eli Manning, NY Giants
1974	Larry Csonka, Miami	1994	Emmitt Smith, Dallas	2013	Joe Flacco, Baltimore
1975	Franco Harris, Pittsburgh	1995	Steve Young, San Francisco	2014	Malcolm Smith, Seattle
1976	Lynn Swann, Pittsburgh	1996	Larry Brown, Dallas	2015	Tom Brady, New England
1977	Fred Biletnikoff, Oakland	1997	Desmond Howard, Green Bay	2016	Von Miller, Denver
1978	Randy White, Harvey Martin; Dallas	1998	Terrell Davis, Denver	2017	Tom Brady, New England
1979	Terry Bradshaw, Pittsburgh	1999	John Elway, Denver	2018	Nick Foles, Philadelphia
1980	Terry Bradshaw, Pittsburgh	2000	Kurt Warner, St. Louis	2019	Julian Edelman, New England
1981	Jim Plunkett, Oakland	2001	Ray Lewis, Baltimore	2020	Patrick Mahomes, Kansas City
1982	Joe Montana, San Francisco	2002	Tom Brady, New England	2021	Tom Brady, Tampa Bay
1983	John Riggins, Washington	2003	Dexter Jackson, Tampa Bay	2022	Cooper Kupp, L.A. Rams
1984	Marcus Allen, L.A. Raiders	2004	Tom Brady, New England	2023	Patrick Mahomes, Kansas City
1985	Joe Montana, San Francisco	2005	Deion Branch, New England	2024	Patrick Mahomes, Kansas City
1986	Richard Dent, Chicago				

Super Bowl Single-Game Statistical Leaders

PASSING YARDS

Player, team	Year	Att/comp	Yds	TD
Tom Brady, New England	2018	48/28	505	3
Tom Brady, New England	2017	62/43	466	2
Kurt Warner, St. Louis	2000	45/24	414	2
Kurt Warner, Arizona	2009	43/31	377	3
Nick Foles, Philadelphia	2018	43/28	373	3
Kurt Warner, St. Louis	2002	44/28	365	1
Donovon McNabb, Philadelphia	2005	51/30	357	3
Joe Montana, San Francisco	1989	36/23	357	2

RECEIVING YARDS

Player, team	Year	Rec	Yds	TD
Jerry Rice, San Francisco	1989	11	215	1
Ricky Sanders, Washington	1988	9	193	2
Isaac Bruce, St. Louis	2000	6	162	1

RUSHING YARDS

Player, team	Year	Att	Yds	TD
Timmy Smith, Washington	1988	22	204	2
Marcus Allen, L.A. Raiders	1984	20	191	2
John Riggins, Washington	1983	38	166	1

PASSING TOUCHDOWNS

Player, team	Year	Att/comp	Yds	TD
Steve Young, San Francisco	1995	36/24	325	6
Joe Montana, San Francisco	1990	29/22	297	5
Tom Brady, New England	2015	50/37	328	4
Troy Aikman, Dallas	1993	30/22	273	4
Doug Williams, Washington	1988	29/18	340	4
Terry Bradshaw, Pittsburgh	1979	30/17	318	4

SCORING

Player, team	Year	Pts	
Jalen Hurts, Philadelphia	2023	20	(3 TDs, 1 2-pt)
James White, New England	2017	20	(3 TDs, 1 2-pt)
Terrell Davis, Denver	1998	18	(3 TDs)
Jerry Rice, San Francisco	1995	18	(3 TDs)
Ricky Watters, San Francisco	1995	18	(3 TDs)
Jerry Rice, San Francisco	1990	18	(3 TDs)
Roger Craig, San Francisco	1985	18	(3 TDs)
Don Chandler, Green Bay	1968	15	(4 FGs, 3 PATs)
Kevin Butler, Chicago Bears	1986	14	(3 FGs, 5 PATs)
Ray Wersching, San Francisco	1982	14	(4 FGs, 2 PATs)

First-Round Selections in the 2024 NFL Draft

Held Apr. 25-27, 2024 in Detroit, MI

Team	Player	Pos.	College
1. Chicago Bears[1]	Caleb Williams	QB	USC
2. Washington Commanders	Jayden Daniels	QB	LSU
3. New England Patriots	Drake Maye	QB	North Carolina
4. Arizona Cardinals	Marvin Harrison Jr.	WR	Ohio St.
5. L.A. Chargers	Joe Alt	OT	Notre Dame
6. NY Giants	Malik Nabers	WR	LSU
7. Tennessee Titans	JC Latham	OT	Alabama
8. Atlanta Falcons	Michael Penix Jr.	QB	Washington
9. Chicago Bears	Rome Odunze	WR	Washington
10. Minnesota Vikings[2]	J.J. McCarthy	QB	Michigan
11. NY Jets[3]	Olu Fashanu	OT	Penn St.
12. Denver Broncos	Bo Nix	QB	Oregon
13. Las Vegas Raiders	Brock Bowers	TE	Georgia
14. New Orleans Saints	Taliese Fuaga	OT	Oregon St.
15. Indianapolis Colts	Laiatu Latu	DE	UCLA
16. Seattle Seahawks	Byron Murphy II	DT	Texas
17. Minnesota Vikings[4]	Dallas Turner	DE	Alabama
18. Cincinnati Bengals	Amarius Mims	OT	Georgia
19. L.A. Rams	Jared Verse	DE	Florida St.
20. Pittsburgh Steelers	Troy Fautanu	OT	Washington
21. Miami Dolphins	Chop Robinson	DE	Penn St.
22. Philadelphia Eagles	Quinyon Mitchell	CB	Toledo
23. Jacksonville Jaguars[5]	Brian Thomas Jr.	WR	LSU
24. Detroit Lions[6]	Terrion Arnold	CB	Alabama
25. Green Bay Packers	Jordan Morgan	OT	Arizona
26. Tampa Bay Buccaneers	Graham Barton	C	Duke
27. Arizona Cardinals[7]	Darius Robinson	DE	Missouri
28. Kansas City Chiefs[8]	Xavier Worthy	WR	Texas
29. Dallas Cowboys[9]	Tyler Guyton	OT	Oklahoma
30. Baltimore Ravens	Nate Wiggins	CB	Clemson
31. San Francisco 49ers	Ricky Pearsall	WR	Florida
32. Carolina Panthers[10]	Xavier Legette	WR	South Carolina

(1) From Carolina. (2) From NY Jets. (3) From Minnesota. (4) From Jacksonville. (5) From Cleveland via Houston and Minnesota. (6) From Dallas. (7) From Houston. (8) From Buffalo. (9) From Detroit. (10) From Kansas City via Buffalo.

Number One NFL Draft Choices, 1980-2024

Year	Team	Player, pos., college
1980	Detroit	Billy Sims, RB, Oklahoma
1981	New Orleans	George Rogers, RB, South Carolina
1982	New England	Kenneth Sims, DT, Texas
1983	Baltimore Colts	John Elway, QB, Stanford
1984	New England	Irving Fryar, WR, Nebraska
1985	Buffalo	Bruce Smith, DE, Virginia Tech
1986	Tampa Bay	Bo Jackson, RB, Auburn
1987	Tampa Bay	Vinny Testaverde, QB, Miami (FL)
1988	Atlanta	Aundray Bruce, LB, Auburn
1989	Dallas	Troy Aikman, QB, UCLA
1990	Indianapolis	Jeff George, QB, Illinois
1991	Dallas	Russell Maryland, DL, Miami (FL)
1992	Indianapolis	Steve Emtman, DL, Washington
1993	New England	Drew Bledsoe, QB, Washington St.
1994	Cincinnati	Dan Wilkinson, DT, Ohio St.
1995	Cincinnati	Ki-Jana Carter, RB, Penn St.
1996	NY Jets	Keyshawn Johnson, WR, USC
1997	St. Louis	Orlando Pace, OT, Ohio St.
1998	Indianapolis	Peyton Manning, QB, Tennessee
1999	Cleveland	Tim Couch, QB, Kentucky
2000	Cleveland	Courtney Brown, DE, Penn St.
2001	Atlanta	Michael Vick, QB, Virginia Tech
2002	Houston	David Carr, QB, Fresno St.
2003	Cincinnati	Carson Palmer, QB, USC
2004	San Diego	Eli Manning, QB, Mississippi
2005	San Francisco	Alex D. Smith, QB, Utah
2006	Houston	Mario Williams, DE, NC State
2007	Oakland	JaMarcus Russell, QB, LSU
2008	Miami	Jake Long, OT, Michigan
2009	Detroit	Matthew Stafford, QB, Georgia
2010	St. Louis	Sam Bradford, QB, Oklahoma
2011	Carolina	Cam Newton, QB, Auburn
2012	Indianapolis	Andrew Luck, QB, Stanford
2013	Kansas City	Eric Fisher, OT, Central Michigan
2014	Houston	Jadeveon Clowney, DE, South Carolina
2015	Tampa Bay	Jameis Winston, QB, Florida St.
2016	L.A. Rams	Jared Goff, QB, California
2017	Cleveland	Myles Garrett, DE, Texas A&M
2018	Cleveland	Baker Mayfield, QB, Oklahoma
2019	Arizona	Kyler Murray, QB, Oklahoma
2020	Cincinnati	Joe Burrow, QB, LSU
2021	Jacksonville	Trevor Lawrence, QB, Clemson
2022	Jacksonville	Travon Walker, DE, Georgia
2023	Carolina	Bryce Young, QB, Alabama
2024	Chicago	Caleb Williams, QB, USC

American Football League Champions, 1960-69

Year	Eastern (W-L-T)	Western (W-L-T)	Championship
1960	Houston Oilers (10-4-0)	L.A. Chargers (10-4-0)	Houston 24, L.A. 16
1961	Houston Oilers (10-3-1)	San Diego Chargers (12-2-0)	Houston 10, San Diego 3
1962	Houston Oilers (11-3-0)	Dallas Texans (11-3-0)	Dallas 20, Houston 17 (2 OT)
1963	Boston Patriots (7-6-1)[1]	San Diego Chargers (11-3-0)	San Diego 51, Boston 10
1964	Buffalo Bills (12-2-0)	San Diego Chargers (8-5-1)	Buffalo 20, San Diego 7
1965	Buffalo Bills (10-3-1)	San Diego Chargers (9-2-3)	Buffalo 23, San Diego 0
1966	Buffalo Bills (9-4-1)	Kansas City Chiefs (11-2-1)	Kansas City 31, Buffalo 7
1967	Houston Oilers (9-4-1)	Oakland Raiders (13-1-0)	Oakland 40, Houston 7
1968	NY Jets (11-3-0)	Oakland Raiders (12-2-0)[2]	NY Jets 27, Oakland 23
1969	NY Jets (10-4-0)	Oakland Raiders (12-1-1)	Kansas City 17, Oakland 7[3]

(1) Defeated conference champion Buffalo Bills in divisional playoff. (2) Defeated conference champion Kansas City Chiefs in divisional playoff. (3) Kansas City Chiefs defeated NY Jets, and Oakland Raiders defeated Houston Oilers in divisional playoffs.

National Football League Champions, 1933-69

Year	Eastern (W-L-T)	Western (W-L-T)	Championship
1933	NY Giants (11-3-0)	Chicago Bears (10-2-1)	Chicago Bears 23, NY Giants 21
1934	NY Giants (8-5-0)	Chicago Bears (13-0-0)	NY Giants 30, Chicago Bears 13
1935	NY Giants (9-3-0)	Detroit Lions (7-3-2)	Detroit 26, NY Giants 7
1936	Boston Redskins (7-5-0)	Green Bay Packers (10-1-1)	Green Bay 21, Boston 6
1937	Washington Redskins (8-3-0)	Chicago Bears (9-1-1)	Washington 28, Chicago Bears 21
1938	NY Giants (8-2-1)	Green Bay Packers (8-3-0)	NY Giants 23, Green Bay 17
1939	NY Giants (9-1-1)	Green Bay Packers (9-2-0)	Green Bay 27, NY Giants 0
1940	Washington Redskins (9-2-0)	Chicago Bears (8-3-0)	Chicago Bears 73, Washington 0
1941	NY Giants (8-3-0)	Chicago Bears (10-1-0)[1]	Chicago Bears 37, NY Giants 9
1942	Washington Redskins (10-1-0)	Chicago Bears (11-0-0)	Washington 14, Chicago Bears 6
1943	Washington Redskins (6-3-1)[1]	Chicago Bears (8-1-1)	Chicago Bears, 41, Washington 21
1944	NY Giants (8-1-1)	Green Bay Packers (8-2-0)	Green Bay 14, NY Giants 7
1945	Washington Redskins (8-2-0)	Cleveland Rams (9-1-0)	Cleveland Rams 15, Washington 14
1946	NY Giants (7-3-1)	Chicago Bears (8-2-1)	Chicago Bears 24, NY Giants 14
1947	Philadelphia Eagles (8-4-0)[1]	Chicago Cardinals (9-3-0)	Chicago Cardinals 28, Philadelphia 21
1948	Philadelphia Eagles (9-2-1)	Chicago Cardinals (11-1-0)	Philadelphia 7, Chicago Cardinals 0
1949	Philadelphia Eagles (11-1-0)	L.A. Rams (8-2-2)	Philadelphia 14, L.A. Rams 0
1950	Cleveland Browns (10-2-0)[1]	L.A. Rams (9-3-0)[1]	Cleveland Browns 30, L.A. Rams 28
1951	Cleveland Browns (11-1-0)	L.A. Rams (8-4-0)	L.A. Rams 24, Cleveland Browns 17
1952	Cleveland Browns (8-4-0)	Detroit Lions (9-3-0)[1]	Detroit 17, Cleveland Browns 7
1953	Cleveland Browns (11-1-0)	Detroit Lions (10-2-0)	Detroit 17, Cleveland Browns 16
1954	Cleveland Browns (9-3-0)	Detroit Lions (9-2-1)	Cleveland Browns 56, Detroit 10
1955	Cleveland Browns (9-2-1)	L.A. Rams (8-3-1)	Cleveland Browns 38, L.A. Rams 14
1956	NY Giants (8-3-1)	Chicago Bears (9-2-1)	NY Giants 47, Chicago Bears 7
1957	Cleveland Browns (9-2-1)	Detroit Lions (8-4-0)[1]	Detroit 59, Cleveland Browns 14
1958	NY Giants (9-3-0)[1]	Baltimore Colts (9-3-0)	Baltimore 23, NY Giants 17[2]
1959	NY Giants (10-2-0)	Baltimore Colts (9-3-0)	Baltimore 31, NY Giants 16
1960	Philadelphia Eagles (10-2-0)	Green Bay Packers (8-4-0)	Philadelphia 17, Green Bay 13
1961	NY Giants (10-3-1)	Green Bay Packers (11-3-0)	Green Bay 37, NY Giants 0
1962	NY Giants (12-2-0)	Green Bay Packers (13-1-0)	Green Bay 16, NY Giants 7
1963	NY Giants (11-3-0)	Chicago Bears (11-1-2)	Chicago 14, NY Giants 10
1964	Cleveland Browns (10-3-1)	Baltimore Colts (12-2-0)	Cleveland Browns 27, Baltimore 0
1965	Cleveland Browns (11-3-0)	Green Bay Packers (10-3-1)[1]	Green Bay 23, Cleveland Browns 12
1966	Dallas Cowboys (10-3-1)	Green Bay Packers (12-2-0)	Green Bay 34, Dallas 27
1967	Dallas Cowboys (9-5-0)	Green Bay Packers (9-4-1)	Green Bay 21, Dallas 17
1968	Cleveland Browns (10-4-0)	Baltimore Colts (13-1-0)	Baltimore 34, Cleveland Browns 0
1969	Cleveland Browns (10-3-1)	Minnesota Vikings (12-2-0)	Minnesota 27, Cleveland Browns 7

Note: Conference title games preceded NFL Championship from 1967-69. (1) Won divisional or conference playoff. (2) Won at 8:15 of sudden death overtime period.

NFL Divisional Champions and Wild Cards, 1970-95

The American Football League and National Football League officially merged in 1966. At the beginning of the 1970 season, the two leagues became the AFC and NFC conferences in the new NFL. Regular-season (W-L-T) records are in parentheses.

AMERICAN FOOTBALL CONFERENCE

Year	Eastern	Central	Western	Wild card
1970	Baltimore Colts (11-2-1)	Cincinnati Bengals (8-6-0)	Oakland Raiders (8-4-2)	Miami Dolphins (10-4-0)
1971	Miami Dolphins (10-3-1)	Cleveland Browns (9-5-0)	Kansas City Chiefs (10-3-1)	Baltimore Colts (10-4-0)
1972	Miami Dolphins (14-0-0)	Pittsburgh Steelers (11-3-0)	Oakland Raiders (10-3-1)	Cleveland Browns (10-4-0)
1973	Miami Dolphins (12-2-0)	Cincinnati Bengals (10-4-0)	Oakland Raiders (9-4-1)	Pittsburgh Steelers (10-4-0)
1974	Miami Dolphins (11-3-0)	Pittsburgh Steelers (10-3-1)	Oakland Raiders (12-2-0)	Buffalo Bills (9-5-0)
1975	Baltimore Colts (10-4-0)	Pittsburgh Steelers (12-2-0)	Oakland Raiders (11-3-0)	Cincinnati Bengals (11-3-0)
1976	Baltimore Colts (11-3-0)	Pittsburgh Steelers (10-4-0)	Oakland Raiders (13-1-0)	New England Patriots (11-3-0)
1977	Baltimore Colts (10-4-0)	Pittsburgh Steelers (9-5-0)	Denver Broncos (12-2-0)	Oakland Raiders (11-3-0)
1978	New England Patriots (11-5-0)	Pittsburgh Steelers (14-2-0)	Denver Broncos (10-6-0)	Houston Oilers (10-6-0) Miami Dolphins (11-5-0)
1979	Miami Dolphins (10-6-0)	Pittsburgh Steelers (12-4-0)	San Diego Chargers (12-4-0)	Houston Oilers (11-5-0) Denver Broncos (10-6-0)
1980	Buffalo Bills (11-5-0)	Cleveland Browns (11-5-0)	San Diego Chargers (11-5-0)	Houston Oilers (11-5-0) Oakland Raiders (11-5-0)
1981	Miami Dolphins (11-4-1)	Cincinnati Bengals (12-4-0)	San Diego Chargers (10-6-0)	Buffalo Bills (10-6-0) NY Jets (10-5-1)
1982	Strike abbreviated season. See note.			
1983	Miami Dolphins (12-4-0)	Pittsburgh Steelers (10-6-0)	L.A. Raiders (12-4-0)	Denver Broncos (9-7-0) Seattle Seahawks (9-7-0)
1984	Miami Dolphins (14-2-0)	Pittsburgh Steelers (9-7-0)	Denver Broncos (13-3-0)	L.A. Raiders (11-5-0) Seattle Seahawks (12-4-0)
1985	Miami Dolphins (12-4-0)	Cleveland Browns (8-8-0)	L.A. Raiders (12-4-0)	New England Patriots (11-5-0) NY Jets (11-5-0)
1986	New England Patriots (11-5-0)	Cleveland Browns (12-4-0)	Denver Broncos (11-5-0)	Kansas City Chiefs (10-6-0) NY Jets (10-6-0)
1987	Indianapolis Colts (9-6-0)	Cleveland Browns (10-5-0)	Denver Broncos (10-4-1)	Houston Oilers (9-6-0) Seattle Seahawks (9-6-0)
1988	Buffalo Bills (12-4-0)	Cincinnati Bengals (12-4-0)	Seattle Seahawks (9-7-0)	Cleveland Browns (10-6-0) Houston Oilers (10-6-0)
1989	Buffalo Bills (9-7-0)	Cleveland Browns (9-6-1)	Denver Broncos (11-5-0)	Houston Oilers (9-7-0) Pittsburgh Steelers (9-7-0)
1990	Buffalo Bills (13-3-0)	Cincinnati Bengals (9-7-0)	L.A. Raiders (12-4-0)	Houston Oilers (9-7-0) Kansas City Chiefs (11-5-0) Miami Dolphins (12-4-0)
1991	Buffalo Bills (13-3-0)	Houston Oilers (11-5-0)	Denver Broncos (12-4-0)	Kansas City Chiefs (10-6-0) L.A. Raiders (9-7-0) NY Jets (8-8-0)
1992	Miami Dolphins (11-5-0)	Pittsburgh Steelers (11-5-0)	San Diego Chargers (11-5-0)	Buffalo Bills (11-5-0) Houston Oilers (10-6-0) Kansas City Chiefs (10-6-0)
1993	Buffalo Bills (12-4-0)	Houston Oilers (12-4-0)	Kansas City Chiefs (11-5-0)	Denver Broncos (9-7-0) L.A. Raiders (10-6-0) Pittsburgh Steelers (9-7-0)
1994	Miami Dolphins (10-6-0)	Pittsburgh Steelers (12-4-0)	San Diego Chargers (11-5-0)	Cleveland Browns (11-5-0) Kansas City Chiefs (9-7-0) New England Patriots (10-6-0)
1995	Buffalo Bills (10-6-0)	Pittsburgh Steelers (11-5-0)	Kansas City Chiefs (13-3-0)	Miami Dolphins (9-7-0) Indianapolis Colts (9-7-0) San Diego Chargers (9-7-0)

NATIONAL FOOTBALL CONFERENCE

Year	Eastern	Central	Western	Wild card
1970	Dallas Cowboys (10-4-0)	Minnesota Vikings (12-2-0)	San Francisco 49ers (10-3-1)	Detroit Lions (10-4-0)
1971	Dallas Cowboys (11-3-0)	Minnesota Vikings (11-3-0)	San Francisco 49ers (9-5-0)	Washington Redskins (9-4-1)
1972	Washington Redskins (11-3-0)	Green Bay Packers (10-4-0)	San Francisco 49ers (8-5-1)	Dallas Cowboys (10-4-0)
1973	Dallas Cowboys (10-4-0)	Minnesota Vikings (12-2-0)	L.A. Rams (12-2-0)	Washington Redskins (10-4-0)
1974	St. Louis Cardinals (10-4-0)	Minnesota Vikings (10-4-0)	L.A. Rams (10-4-0)	Washington Redskins (10-4-0)
1975	St. Louis Cardinals (11-3-0)	Minnesota Vikings (12-2-0)	L.A. Rams (12-2-0)	Dallas Cowboys (10-4-0)
1976	Dallas Cowboys (11-3-0)	Minnesota Vikings (11-2-1)	L.A. Rams (10-3-1)	Washington Redskins (10-4-0)
1977	Dallas Cowboys (12-2-0)	Minnesota Vikings (9-5-0)	L.A. Rams (10-4-0)	Chicago Bears (9-5-0)
1978	Dallas Cowboys (12-4-0)	Minnesota Vikings (8-7-1)	L.A. Rams (12-4-0)	Atlanta Falcons (9-7-0) Philadelphia Eagles (9-7-0)
1979	Dallas Cowboys (11-5-0)	Tampa Bay Buccaneers (10-6-0)	L.A. Rams (9-7-0)	Chicago Bears (10-6-0) Philadelphia Eagles (11-5-0)
1980	Philadelphia Eagles (12-4-0)	Minnesota Vikings (9-7-0)	Atlanta Falcons (12-4-0)	Dallas Cowboys (12-4-0) L.A. Rams (11-5-0)

Year	Eastern	Central	Western	Wild card
1981	Dallas Cowboys (12-4-0)	Tampa Bay Buccaneers (9-7-0)	San Francisco 49ers (13-3-0)	NY Giants (9-7-0) Philadelphia Eagles (10-6-0)
1982	Strike abbreviated season. See note.			
1983	Washington Redskins (14-2-0)	Detroit Lions (9-7-0)	San Francisco 49ers (10-6-0)	Dallas Cowboys (12-4-0) L.A. Rams (9-7-0)
1984	Washington Redskins (11-5-0)	Chicago Bears (10-6-0)	San Francisco 49ers (15-1-0)	L.A. Rams (10-6-0) NY Giants (9-7-0)
1985	Dallas Cowboys (10-6-0)	Chicago Bears (15-1-0)	L.A. Rams (11-5-0)	NY Giants (10-6-0) San Francisco 49ers (10-6-0)
1986	NY Giants (14-2-0)	Chicago Bears (14-2-0)	San Francisco 49ers (10-5-1)	L.A. Rams (10-6-0) Washington Redskins (12-4-0)
1987	Washington Redskins (11-4-0)	Chicago Bears (11-4-0)	San Francisco 49ers (13-2-0)	Minnesota Vikings (8-7-0) New Orleans Saints (12-3-0)
1988	Philadelphia Eagles (10-6-0)	Chicago Bears (12-4-0)	San Francisco 49ers (10-6-0)	L.A. Rams (10-6-0) Minnesota Vikings (11-5-0)
1989	NY Giants (12-4-0)	Minnesota Vikings (10-6-0)	San Francisco 49ers (14-2-0)	L.A. Rams (11-5-0) Philadelphia Eagles (11-5-0)
1990	NY Giants (13-3-0)	Chicago Bears (11-5-0)	San Francisco 49ers (14-2-0)	New Orleans Saints (8-8-0) Philadelphia Eagles (10-6-0) Washington Redskins (10-6-0)
1991	Washington Redskins (14-2-0)	Detroit Lions (12-4-0)	New Orleans Saints (11-5-0)	Atlanta Falcons (10-6-0) Chicago Bears (11-5-0) Dallas Cowboys (11-5-0)
1992	Dallas Cowboys (13-3-0)	Minnesota Vikings (11-5-0)	San Francisco 49ers (14-2-0)	New Orleans Saints (12-4-0) Philadelphia Eagles (11-5-0) Washington Redskins (9-7-0)
1993	Dallas Cowboys (12-4-0)	Detroit Lions (10-6-0)	San Francisco 49ers (10-6-0)	Green Bay Packers (9-7-0) Minnesota Vikings (9-7-0) NY Giants (11-5-0)
1994	Dallas Cowboys (12-4-0)	Minnesota Vikings (10-6-0)	San Francisco 49ers (13-3-0)	Chicago Bears (9-7-0) Detroit Lions (9-7-0) Green Bay Packers (9-7-0)
1995	Dallas Cowboys (12-4-0)	Green Bay Packers (11-5-0)	San Francisco 49ers (11-5-0)	Philadelphia Eagles (10-6-0) Detroit Lions (10-6-0) Atlanta Falcons (9-7-0)

Note: A strike shortened the 1982 season from 16 to 9 games. The top eight teams in each conference played in a tournament to determine the conference champion.

NFL Division Winners and Playoff Results, 1996-2023

Year	Conference	Division	Winner (W-L-T)	Playoffs[1]	Year
1996	American	Eastern	New England Patriots (11-5-0)	Jacksonville* 30, Denver 27	1996
		Central	Pittsburgh Steelers (10-6-0)	New England 28, Pittsburgh 3	
		Western	Denver Broncos (13-3-0)	New England 20, Jacksonville* 6	
	National	Eastern	Dallas Cowboys (10-6-0)	Green Bay 35, San Francisco* 14	
		Central	Green Bay Packers (13-3-0)	Carolina 26, Dallas 17	
		Western	Carolina Panthers (12-4-0)	Green Bay 30, Carolina 13	
1997	American	Eastern	New England Patriots (10-6-0)	Pittsburgh 7, New England 6	1997
		Central	Pittsburgh Steelers (11-5-0)	Denver* 14, Kansas City 10	
		Western	Kansas City Chiefs (13-3-0)	Denver* 24, Pittsburgh 21	
	National	Eastern	NY Giants (10-5-1)	San Francisco 38, Minnesota* 22	
		Central	Green Bay Packers (13-3-0)	Green Bay 21, Tampa Bay* 7	
		Western	San Francisco 49ers (13-3-0)	Green Bay 23, San Francisco 10	
1998	American	Eastern	NY Jets (12-4-0)	Denver 38, Miami* 3	1998
		Central	Jacksonville Jaguars (11-5-0)	NY Jets 34, Jacksonville 24	
		Western	Denver Broncos (14-2-0)	Denver 23, NY Jets 10	
	National	Eastern	Dallas Cowboys (10-6-0)	Atlanta 20, San Francisco* 18	
		Central	Minnesota Vikings (15-1-0)	Minnesota 41, Arizona* 21	
		Western	Atlanta Falcons (14-2-0)	Atlanta 30, Minnesota 27 (OT)	
1999	American	Eastern	Indianapolis Colts (13-3-0)	Jacksonville 62, Miami* 7	1999
		Central	Jacksonville Jaguars (14-2-0)	Tennessee* 19, Indianapolis 16	
		Western	Seattle Seahawks (9-7-0)	Tennessee* 33, Jacksonville 14	
	National	Eastern	Washington Redskins (10-6-0)	Tampa Bay 14, Washington 13	
		Central	Tampa Bay Buccaneers (11-5-0)	St. Louis 49, Minnesota* 37	
		Western	St. Louis Rams (13-3-0)	St. Louis 11, Tampa Bay 6	
2000	American	Eastern	Miami Dolphins (11-5-0)	Oakland 27, Miami 0	2000
		Central	Tennessee Titans (13-3-0)	Baltimore* 24, Tennessee 10	
		Western	Oakland Raiders (12-4-0)	Baltimore* 16, Oakland 3	
	National	Eastern	NY Giants (12-4-0)	Minnesota 34, New Orleans 16	
		Central	Minnesota Vikings (11-5-0)	NY Giants 20, Philadelphia* 10	
		Western	New Orleans Saints (10-6-0)	NY Giants 41, Minnesota 0	
2001	American	Eastern	New England Patriots (11-5-0)	New England 16, Oakland 13 (OT)	2001
		Central	Pittsburgh Steelers (13-3-0)	Pittsburgh 27, Baltimore* 10	
		Western	Oakland Raiders (10-6-0)	New England 24, Pittsburgh 17	
	National	Eastern	Philadelphia Eagles (11-5-0)	Philadelphia 33, Chicago 19	
		Central	Chicago Bears (13-3-0)	St. Louis 45, Green Bay* 17	
		Western	St. Louis Rams (14-2-0)	St. Louis 29, Philadelphia 24	

Year	Conference	Division	Winner (W-L-T)	Playoffs[1]	Year
2002	American	East	NY Jets (9-7-0)		2002
		North	Pittsburgh Steelers (10-5-1)	Oakland 30, NY Jets 10	
		South	Tennessee Titans (11-5-0)	Tennessee 34, Pittsburgh 31 (OT)	
		West	Oakland Raiders (11-5-0)	Oakland 41, Tennessee 24	
	National	East	Philadelphia Eagles (12-4-0)		
		North	Green Bay Packers (12-4-0)	Philadelphia 20, Atlanta* 6	
		South	Tampa Bay Buccaneers (12-4-0)	Tampa Bay 31, San Francisco 6	
		West	San Francisco 49ers (10-6-0)	Tampa Bay 27, Philadelphia 10	
2003	American	East	New England Patriots (14-2-0)		2003
		North	Baltimore Ravens (10-6-0)	Indianapolis 38, Kansas City 31	
		South	Indianapolis Colts (12-4-0)	New England 17, Tennessee* 14	
		West	Kansas City Chiefs (13-3-0)	New England 24, Indianapolis 14	
	National	East	Philadelphia Eagles (12-4-0)		
		North	Green Bay Packers (10-6-0)	Carolina 29, St. Louis 23 (2 OT)	
		South	Carolina Panthers (11-5-0)	Philadelphia 20, Green Bay 17 (OT)	
		West	St. Louis Rams (12-4-0)	Carolina 14, Philadelphia 3	
2004	American	East	New England Patriots (14-2-0)		2004
		North	Pittsburgh Steelers (15-1-0)	Pittsburgh 20, NY Jets* 17 (OT)	
		South	Indianapolis Colts (12-4-0)	New England 20, Indianapolis 3	
		West	San Diego Chargers (12-4-0)	New England 41, Pittsburgh 27	
	National	East	Philadelphia Eagles (13-3-0)		
		North	Green Bay Packers (10-6-0)	Atlanta 47, St. Louis* 17	
		South	Atlanta Falcons (11-5-0)	Philadelphia 27, Minnesota* 14	
		West	Seattle Seahawks (9-7-0)	Philadelphia 27, Atlanta 10	
2005	American	East	New England Patriots (10-6-0)		2005
		North	Cincinnati Bengals (11-5-0)	Denver 27, New England 13	
		South	Indianapolis Colts (14-2-0)	Pittsburgh* 21, Indianapolis 18	
		West	Denver Broncos (13-3-0)	Pittsburgh* 34, Denver 17	
	National	East	NY Giants (11-5-0)		
		North	Chicago Bears (11-5-0)	Seattle 20, Washington* 10	
		South	Tampa Bay Buccaneers (11-5-0)	Carolina* 29, Chicago 21	
		West	Seattle Seahawks (13-3-0)	Seattle 34, Carolina* 14	
2006	American	East	New England Patriots (12-4-0)		2006
		North	Baltimore Ravens (13-3-0)	Indianapolis 15, Baltimore 6	
		South	Indianapolis Colts (12-4-0)	New England 24, San Diego 21	
		West	San Diego Chargers (14-2-0)	Indianapolis 38, New England 34	
	National	East	Philadelphia Eagles (10-6-0)		
		North	Chicago Bears (13-3-0)	New Orleans 27, Philadelphia 24	
		South	New Orleans Saints (10-6-0)	Chicago 27, Seattle 24 (OT)	
		West	Seattle Seahawks (9-7-0)	Chicago 39, New Orleans 14	
2007	American	East	New England Patriots (16-0-0)		2007
		North	Pittsburgh Steelers (10-6-0)	New England 31, Jacksonville* 20	
		South	Indianapolis Colts (13-3-0)	San Diego 28, Indianapolis 24	
		West	San Diego Chargers (11-5-0)	New England 21, San Diego 12	
	National	East	Dallas Cowboys (13-3-0)		
		North	Green Bay Packers (13-3-0)	Green Bay 42, Seattle 20	
		South	Tampa Bay Buccaneers (9-7-0)	NY Giants* 21, Dallas 17	
		West	Seattle Seahawks (10-6-0)	NY Giants* 23, Green Bay 20 (OT)	
2008	American	East	Miami Dolphins (11-5-0)		2008
		North	Pittsburgh Steelers (12-4-0)	Baltimore* 13, Tennessee 10	
		South	Tennessee Titans (13-3-0)	Pittsburgh 35, San Diego 24	
		West	San Diego Chargers (8-8-0)	Pittsburgh 23, Baltimore* 14	
	National	East	NY Giants (12-4-0)		
		North	Minnesota Vikings (10-6-0)	Arizona 33, Carolina 13	
		South	Carolina Panthers (12-4-0)	Philadelphia* 23, NY Giants 11	
		West	Arizona Cardinals (9-7-0)	Arizona 32, Philadelphia* 25	
2009	American	East	New England Patriots (10-6-0)		2009
		North	Cincinnati Bengals (10-6-0)	Indianapolis 20, Baltimore* 3	
		South	Indianapolis Colts (14-2-0)	NY Jets* 17, San Diego 14	
		West	San Diego Chargers (13-3-0)	Indianapolis 30, NY Jets* 17	
	National	East	Dallas Cowboys (11-5-0)		
		North	Minnesota Vikings (12-4-0)	New Orleans 45, Arizona 14	
		South	New Orleans Saints (13-3-0)	Minnesota 34, Dallas 3	
		West	Arizona Cardinals (10-6-0)	New Orleans 31, Minnesota 28 (OT)	
2010	American	East	New England Patriots (14-2-0)		2010
		North	Pittsburgh Steelers (12-4-0)	Pittsburgh 31, Baltimore* 24	
		South	Indianapolis Colts (10-6-0)	NY Jets* 28, New England 21	
		West	Kansas City Chiefs (10-6-0)	Pittsburgh 24, NY Jets* 19	
	National	East	Philadelphia Eagles (10-6-0)		
		North	Chicago Bears (11-5-0)	Green Bay* 48, Atlanta 21	
		South	Atlanta Falcons (13-3-0)	Chicago 35, Seattle 24	
		West	Seattle Seahawks (7-9-0)	Green Bay* 21, Chicago 14	
2011	American	East	New England Patriots (13-3-0)		2011
		North	Baltimore Ravens (12-4-0)	New England 45, Denver 10	
		South	Houston Texans (10-6-0)	Baltimore 20, Houston 13	
		West	Denver Broncos (8-8-0)	New England 23, Baltimore 20	
	National	East	NY Giants (9-7-0)		
		North	Green Bay Packers (15-1-0)	San Francisco 36, New Orleans 32	
		South	New Orleans Saints (13-3-0)	NY Giants 37, Green Bay 20	
		West	San Francisco 49ers (13-3-0)	NY Giants 20, San Francisco 17 (OT)	

Year	Conference	Division	Winner (W-L-T)	Playoffs[1]	Year
2012	American	East	New England Patriots (12-4-0)		2012
		North	Baltimore Ravens (10-6-0)	Baltimore 38, Denver 35 (2 OT)	
		South	Houston Texans (12-4-0)	New England 41, Houston 28	
		West	Denver Broncos (13-3-0)	Baltimore 28, New England 13	
	National	East	Washington Redskins (10-6-0)		
		North	Green Bay Packers (11-5-0)	San Francisco 45, Green Bay 31	
		South	Atlanta Falcons (13-3-0)	Atlanta 30, Seattle* 28	
		West	San Francisco 49ers (11-4-1)	San Francisco 28, Atlanta 24	
2013	American	East	New England Patriots (12-4-0)		2013
		North	Cincinnati Bengals (11-5-0)	New England 43, Indianapolis 22	
		South	Indianapolis Colts (11-5-0)	Denver 24, San Diego* 17	
		West	Denver Broncos (13-3-0)	Denver 26, New England 16	
	National	East	Philadelphia Eagles (10-6-0)		
		North	Green Bay Packers (8-7-1)	Seattle 23, New Orleans* 15	
		South	Carolina Panthers (12-4-0)	San Francisco* 23, Carolina 10	
		West	Seattle Seahawks (13-3-0)	Seattle 23, San Francisco* 17	
2014	American	East	New England Patriots (12-4-0)		2014
		North	Pittsburgh Steelers (11-5-0)	New England 35, Baltimore* 31	
		South	Indianapolis Colts (11-5-0)	Indianapolis 24, Denver 13	
		West	Denver Broncos (12-4-0)	New England 45, Indianapolis 7	
	National	East	Dallas Cowboys (12-4-0)		
		North	Green Bay Packers (12-4-0)	Seattle 31, Carolina 17	
		South	Carolina Panthers (7-8-1)	Green Bay 26, Dallas 21	
		West	Seattle Seahawks (12-4-0)	Seattle 28, Green Bay 22 (OT)	
2015	American	East	New England Patriots (12-4-0)		2015
		North	Cincinnati Bengals (12-4-0)	New England 27, Kansas City* 20	
		South	Houston Texans (9-7-0)	Denver 23, Pittsburgh* 16	
		West	Denver Broncos (12-4-0)	Denver 20, New England 18	
	National	East	Washington Redskins (9-7-0)		
		North	Minnesota Vikings (11-5-0)	Arizona 26, Green Bay* 20 (OT)	
		South	Carolina Panthers (15-1-0)	Carolina 31, Seattle* 24	
		West	Arizona Cardinals (13-3-0)	Carolina 49, Arizona 15	
2016	American	East	New England Patriots (14-2-0)		2016
		North	Pittsburgh Steelers (11-5-0)	New England 34, Houston 16	
		South	Houston Texans (9-7-0)	Pittsburgh 18, Kansas City 16	
		West	Kansas City Chiefs (12-4-0)	New England 36, Pittsburgh 17	
	National	East	Dallas Cowboys (13-3-0)		
		North	Green Bay Packers (10-6-0)	Atlanta 36, Seattle 20	
		South	Atlanta Falcons (11-5-0)	Green Bay 34, Dallas 31	
		West	Seattle Seahawks (10-5-1)	Atlanta 44, Green Bay 21	
2017	American	East	New England Patriots (13-3-0)		2017
		North	Pittsburgh Steelers (13-3-0)	New England 35, Tennessee* 14	
		South	Jacksonville Jaguars (10-6-0)	Jacksonville 45, Pittsburgh 42	
		West	Kansas City Chiefs (10-6-0)	New England 24, Jacksonville 20	
	National	East	Philadelphia Eagles (13-3-0)		
		North	Minnesota Vikings (13-3-0)	Philadelphia 15, Atlanta* 10	
		South	New Orleans Saints (11-5-0)	Minnesota 29, New Orleans 24	
		West	Los Angeles Rams (11-5-0)	Philadelphia 38, Minnesota 7	
2018	American	East	New England Patriots (11-5-0)		2018
		North	Baltimore Ravens (10-6-0)	Kansas City 31, Indianapolis* 13	
		South	Houston Texans (11-5-0)	New England 41, L.A. Chargers* 28	
		West	Kansas City Chiefs (12-4-0)	New England 37, Kansas City 31 (OT)	
	National	East	Dallas Cowboys (10-6-0)		
		North	Chicago Bears (12-4-0)	L.A. Rams 30, Dallas 22	
		South	New Orleans Saints (13-3-0)	New Orleans 20, Philadelphia* 14	
		West	L.A. Rams (13-3-0)	L.A. Rams 26, New Orleans 23 (OT)	
2019	American	East	New England Patriots (12-4-0)		2019
		North	Baltimore Ravens (14-2-0)	Tennessee* 28, Baltimore 12	
		South	Houston Texans (10-6-0)	Kansas City 51, Houston 31	
		West	Kansas City Chiefs (12-4-0)	Kansas City 35, Tennessee* 24	
	National	East	Philadelphia Eagles (9-7-0)		
		North	Green Bay Packers (13-3-0)	San Francisco 27, Minnesota* 10	
		South	New Orleans Saints (13-3-0)	Green Bay 28, Seattle* 23	
		West	San Francisco 49ers (13-3-0)	San Francisco 37, Green Bay 20	
2020	American	East	Buffalo Bills (13-3-0)		2020
		North	Pittsburgh Steelers (12-4-0)	Buffalo 17, Baltimore* 3	
		South	Tennessee Titans (11-5-0)	Kansas City 22, Cleveland* 17	
		West	Kansas City Chiefs (14-2-0)	Kansas City 38, Buffalo 24	
	National	East	Washington (7-9-0)		
		North	Green Bay Packers (13-3-0)	Green Bay 32, L.A. Rams 18	
		South	New Orleans Saints (12-4-0)	Tampa Bay* 30, New Orleans 20	
		West	Seattle Seahawks (12-4-0)	Tampa Bay* 31, Green Bay 26	
2021	American	East	Buffalo Bills (11-6-0)		2021
		North	Cincinnati Bengals (10-7-0)	Cincinnati 19, Tennessee 16	
		South	Tennessee Titans (12-5-0)	Kansas City 42, Buffalo 36 (OT)	
		West	Kansas City Chiefs (12-5-0)	Cincinnati 27, Kansas City 24 (OT)	
	National	East	Dallas Cowboys (12-5-0)		
		North	Green Bay Packers (13-4-0)	San Francisco* 13, Green Bay 10	
		South	Tampa Bay Buccaneers (13-4-0)	L.A. Rams 30, Tampa Bay 27	
		West	L.A. Rams (12-5-0)	L.A. Rams 20, San Francisco* 17	
2022	American	East	Buffalo Bills (13-3-0)		2022
		North	Cincinnati Bengals (12-4-0)	Kansas City 27, Jacksonville 20	
		South	Jacksonville Jaguars (9-8-0)	Cincinnati 27, Buffalo 10	
		West	Kansas City Chiefs (14-3-0)	Kansas City 23, Cincinnati 20	
	National	East	Philadelphia Eagles (14-3-0)		
		North	Minnesota Vikings (13-4-0)	Philadelphia 38, NY Giants* 7	
		South	Tampa Bay Buccaneers (8-9-0)	San Francisco 19, Dallas* 12	
		West	San Francisco 49ers (13-4-0)	Philadelphia 31, San Francisco 7	
2023	American	East	Buffalo Bills (11-6)		2023
		North	Baltimore Ravens (13-4)	Baltimore 34, Houston 10	
		South	Houston Texans (10-7)	Kansas City 27, Buffalo 24	
		West	Kansas City Chiefs (11-6)	Kansas City 17, Baltimore 10	
	National	East	Dallas Cowboys (12-5)		
		North	Detroit Lions (12-5)	San Francisco 24, Green Bay 21	
		South	Tampa Bay Buccaneers (9-8)	Detroit 31, Tampa Bay 23	
		West	San Francisco 49ers (12-5)	San Francisco 34, Detroit 31	

* = Wild card team. (1) Only the final two conference playoff rounds are shown.

American Football Conference Leaders, 1960-2023

(American Football League, 1960-69)

PASSING (BASED ON QB RATING POINTS)

Player, team	Rating	Att	Comp	Yds	TD	Year
Jack Kemp, L.A. Chargers	NA	406	211	3,018	20	**1960**
George Blanda, Houston Oilers	NA	362	187	3,330	36	**1961**
Len Dawson, Dallas Texans	NA	310	189	2,759	29	**1962**
Tobin Rote, San Diego	NA	286	170	2,510	20	**1963**
Len Dawson, Kansas City	NA	354	199	2,879	30	**1964**
John Hadl, San Diego	NA	348	174	2,798	20	**1965**
Len Dawson, Kansas City	NA	284	159	2,527	26	**1966**
Daryle Lamonica, Oakland	NA	425	220	3,228	30	**1967**
Len Dawson, Kansas City	NA	224	131	2,109	17	**1968**
Greg Cook, Cincinnati	NA	197	106	1,854	15	**1969**
Daryle Lamonica, Oakland	NA	356	179	2,516	22	**1970**
Bob Griese, Miami	NA	263	145	2,089	19	**1971**
Earl Morrall, Miami	NA	150	83	1,360	11	**1972**
Ken Stabler, Oakland	88.3	260	163	1,997	14	**1973**
Ken Anderson, Cincinnati	95.7	328	213	2,667	18	**1974**
Ken Anderson, Cincinnati	93.9	377	228	3,169	21	**1975**
Ken Stabler, Oakland	103.4	291	194	2,737	27	**1976**
Bob Griese, Miami	87.8	307	180	2,252	22	**1977**
Terry Bradshaw, Pittsburgh	84.7	368	207	2,915	28	**1978**
Dan Fouts, San Diego	82.6	530	332	4,082	24	**1979**
Brian Sipe, Cleveland	91.4	554	337	4,132	30	**1980**
Ken Anderson, Cincinnati	98.4	479	300	3,754	29	**1981**
Ken Anderson, Cincinnati	95.3	309	218	2,495	12	**1982**
Dan Marino, Miami	96.0	296	173	2,210	20	**1983**
Dan Marino, Miami	108.9	564	362	5,084	48	**1984**
Ken O'Brien, NY Jets	96.2	488	297	3,888	25	**1985**
Dan Marino, Miami	92.5	623	378	4,746	44	**1986**
Bernie Kosar, Cleveland	95.4	389	241	3,033	22	**1987**
Boomer Esiason, Cincinnati	97.4	388	223	3,572	28	**1988**
Boomer Esiason, Cincinnati	92.1	455	258	3,525	28	**1989**
Jim Kelly, Buffalo	101.2	346	219	2,829	24	**1990**
Jim Kelly, Buffalo	97.6	474	304	3,844	33	**1991**
Warren Moon, Houston Oilers	89.3	346	224	2,521	18	**1992**
John Elway, Denver	92.8	551	348	4,030	25	**1993**
Dan Marino, Miami	89.2	615	385	4,453	30	**1994**
Jim Harbaugh, Indianapolis	100.7	314	200	2,575	17	**1995**
John Elway, Denver	89.2	466	287	3,328	26	**1996**
Mark Brunell, Jacksonville	91.2	435	264	3,281	18	**1997**
Vinny Testaverde, NY Jets	101.6	421	259	3,256	29	**1998**
Peyton Manning, Indianapolis	90.7	533	331	4,135	26	**1999**
Brian Griese, Denver	102.9	336	216	2,688	19	**2000**
Rich Gannon, Oakland	95.5	549	361	3,828	27	**2001**
Chad Pennington, NY Jets	104.2	399	275	3,120	22	**2002**
Steve McNair, Tennessee	100.4	400	250	3,215	24	**2003**
Peyton Manning, Indianapolis	121.1	497	336	4,557	49	**2004**
Peyton Manning, Indianapolis	104.1	453	305	3,747	28	**2005**
Peyton Manning, Indianapolis	101.0	557	362	4,397	31	**2006**
Tom Brady, New England	117.2	578	398	4,806	50	**2007**
Philip Rivers, San Diego	105.5	478	312	4,009	34	**2008**
Philip Rivers, San Diego	104.4	486	317	4,254	28	**2009**
Tom Brady, New England	111.0	492	324	3,900	36	**2010**
Tom Brady, New England	105.6	611	401	5,235	39	**2011**
Peyton Manning, Denver	105.8	583	400	4,659	37	**2012**
Peyton Manning, Denver	115.1	659	450	5,477	55	**2013**
Ben Roethlisberger, Pittsburgh	103.3	608	408	4,952	32	**2014**
Andy Dalton, Cincinnati	106.2	386	255	3,250	25	**2015**
Tom Brady, New England	112.2	432	291	3,554	28	**2016**
Alex Smith, Kansas City	104.7	505	341	4,042	26	**2017**
Patrick Mahomes, Kansas City	113.8	580	383	5,097	50	**2018**
Ryan Tannehill, Tennessee	117.5	286	201	2,742	22	**2019**
Deshaun Watson, Houston	112.4	544	382	4,823	33	**2020**
Joe Burrow, Cincinnati	108.3	520	366	4,611	34	**2021**
Tua Tagovailoa, Miami	105.5	400	259	3,548	25	**2022**
Lamar Jackson, Baltimore	102.7	457	307	3,678	24	**2023**

RECEPTIONS

Year	Player, team	Rec	Yds	TD
1960	Lionel Taylor, Denver	92	1,235	12
1961	Lionel Taylor, Denver	100	1,176	4
1962	Lionel Taylor, Denver	77	908	4
1963	Lionel Taylor, Denver	78	1,101	10
1964	Charley Hennigan, Houston Oilers	101	1,546	8
1965	Lionel Taylor, Denver	85	1,131	6
1966	Lance Alworth, San Diego	73	1,383	13
1967	George Sauer, NY Jets	75	1,189	6
1968	Lance Alworth, San Diego	68	1,312	10
1969	Lance Alworth, San Diego	64	1,003	4
1970	Marlin Briscoe, Buffalo	57	1,036	8
1971	Fred Biletnikoff, Oakland	61	929	9
1972	Fred Biletnikoff, Oakland	58	802	7
1973	Fred Willis, Houston Oilers	57	371	1
1974	Lydell Mitchell, Baltimore Colts	72	544	2
1975	Reggie Rucker, Cleveland	60	770	3
	Lydell Mitchell, Baltimore Colts	60	544	4
1976	MacArthur Lane, Kansas City	66	686	1
1977	Lydell Mitchell, Baltimore Colts	71	620	4
1978	Steve Largent, Seattle	71	1,168	8
1979	Joe Washington, Baltimore Colts	82	750	3
1980	Kellen Winslow, San Diego	89	1,290	9
1981	Kellen Winslow, San Diego	88	1,075	10
1982	Kellen Winslow, San Diego	54	721	6
1983	Todd Christensen, L.A. Raiders	92	1,247	12
1984	Ozzie Newsome, Cleveland	89	1,001	5
1985	Lionel James, San Diego	86	1,027	6
1986	Todd Christensen, L.A. Raiders	95	1,153	8
1987	Al Toon, NY Jets	68	976	5
1988	Al Toon, NY Jets	93	1,067	5
1989	Andre Reed, Buffalo	88	1,312	9
1990	Haywood Jeffires, Houston Oilers	74	1,048	8
	Drew Hill, Houston Oilers	74	1,019	5
1991	Haywood Jeffires, Houston Oilers	100	1,181	7
1992	Haywood Jeffires, Houston Oilers	90	913	9
1993	Reggie Langhorne, Indianapolis	85	1,038	3
1994	Ben Coates, New England	96	1,174	7
1995	Carl Pickens, Cincinnati	99	1,234	17
1996	Carl Pickens, Cincinnati	100	1,180	12
1997	Tim Brown, Oakland	104	1,408	5
1998	O.J. McDuffie, Miami	90	1,050	7
1999	Jimmy Smith, Jacksonville	116	1,636	6
2000	Marvin Harrison, Indianapolis	102	1,413	14
2001	Rod Smith, Denver	113	1,343	11
2002	Marvin Harrison, Indianapolis	143	1,722	11
2003	LaDainian Tomlinson, San Diego	100	725	4
2004	Tony Gonzalez, Kansas City	102	1,258	7
2005	Chad Johnson, Cincinnati	97	1,432	9
2006	Andre Johnson, Houston	103	1,147	5
2007	Wes Welker, New England	112	1,175	8
	T.J. Houshmandzadeh, Cincinnati	112	1,143	12
2008	Andre Johnson, Houston	115	1,575	8
2009	Wes Walker, New England	123	1,348	4
2010	Reggie Wayne, Indianapolis	111	1,355	6
2011	Wes Welker, New England	122	1,569	9
2012	Wes Welker, New England	118	1,354	6
2013	Antonio Brown, Pittsburgh	110	1,499	8
2014	Antonio Brown, Pittsburgh	129	1,698	13
2015	Antonio Brown, Pittsburgh	136	1,834	10
2016	Antonio Brown, Pittsburgh	106	1,284	12
2017	Jarvis Landry, Miami	112	987	9
2018	DeAndre Hopkins, Houston	115	1,572	11
2019	Keenan Allen, L.A. Chargers	104	1,199	6
	DeAndre Hopkins, Houston	104	1,165	7
2020	Stefon Diggs, Buffalo	127	1,535	8
2021	Tyreek Hill, Kansas City	111	1,239	9
2022	Tyreek Hill, Miami	119	1,710	7
2023	Tyreek Hill, Miami	119	1,799	13

SCORING

Player, team	TD	XPM	FGM	Pts	Year
Gene Mingo, Denver	6	33	18	123	**1960**
Gino Cappelletti, Boston	8	48	17	147	**1961**
Gene Mingo, Denver	4	32	27	137	**1962**
Gino Cappelletti, Boston	2	35	22	113	**1963**
Gino Cappelletti, Boston	7	36	25	155	**1964**
Gino Cappelletti, Boston	9	27	17	132	**1965**
Gino Cappelletti, Boston	6	35	16	119	**1966**
George Blanda, Oakland	0	56	20	116	**1967**
Jim Turner, NY Jets	0	43	34	145	**1968**

RUSHING YARDS

Year	Player, team	Yds	Att	TD
1960	Abner Haynes, Dallas Texans	875	156	9
1961	Billy Cannon, Houston Oilers	948	200	6
1962	Cookie Gilchrist, Buffalo	1,096	214	13
1963	Clem Daniels, Oakland	1,099	215	3
1964	Cookie Gilchrist, Buffalo	981	230	6
1965	Paul Lowe, San Diego	1,121	222	7
1966	Jim Nance, Boston	1,458	299	11
1967	Jim Nance, Boston	1,216	269	7
1968	Paul Robinson, Cincinnati	1,023	238	8

SCORING						RUSHING YARDS			
Player, team	TD	XPM	FGM	Pts	Year	Player, team	Yds	Att	TD
Jim Turner, NY Jets	0	33	32	129	**1969**	Dickie Post, San Diego	873	182	6
Jan Stenerud, Kansas City	0	26	30	116	**1970**	Floyd Little, Denver	901	209	3
Garo Yepremian, Miami	0	33	28	117	**1971**	Floyd Little, Denver	1,133	284	6
Bobby Howfield, NY Jets	0	40	27	121	**1972**	O.J. Simpson, Buffalo	1,251	292	6
Roy Gerela, Pittsburgh	0	36	29	123	**1973**	O.J. Simpson, Buffalo	2,003	332	12
Roy Gerela, Pittsburgh	0	33	20	93	**1974**	Otis Armstrong, Denver	1,407	263	9
O.J. Simpson, Buffalo	23	0	0	138	**1975**	O.J. Simpson, Buffalo	1,817	329	16
Toni Linhart, Baltimore Colts	0	49	20	109	**1976**	O.J. Simpson, Buffalo	1,503	290	8
Errol Mann, Oakland	0	39	20	99	**1977**	Mark van Eeghen, Oakland	1,273	324	7
Pat Leahy, NY Jets	0	41	22	107	**1978**	Earl Campbell, Houston Oilers	1,450	302	13
John Smith, New England	0	46	23	115	**1979**	Earl Campbell, Houston Oilers	1,697	368	19
John Smith, New England	0	51	26	129	**1980**	Earl Campbell, Houston Oilers	1,934	373	13
Jim Breech, Cincinnati	0	49	22	115	**1981**	Earl Campbell, Houston Oilers	1,376	361	10
Nick Lowery, Kansas City	0	37	26	115					
Marcus Allen, L.A. Raiders	14	0	0	84	**1982**	Freeman McNeil, NY Jets	786	151	6
Gary Anderson, Pittsburgh	0	38	27	119	**1983**	Curt Warner, Seattle	1,449	335	13
Gary Anderson, Pittsburgh	0	45	24	117	**1984**	Earnest Jackson, San Diego	1,179	296	8
Gary Anderson, Pittsburgh	0	40	33	139	**1985**	Marcus Allen, L.A. Raiders	1,759	380	11
Tony Franklin, New England	0	44	32	140	**1986**	Curt Warner, Seattle	1,481	319	13
Jim Breech, Cincinnati	0	25	24	97	**1987**	Eric Dickerson, L.A. Rams-Ind.	1,288*	283	6
Scott Norwood, Buffalo	0	33	32	129	**1988**	Eric Dickerson, Indianapolis	1,659	388	14
David Treadwell, Denver	0	39	27	120	**1989**	Christian Okoye, Kansas City	1,480	370	12
Nick Lowery, Kansas City	0	37	34	139	**1990**	Thurman Thomas, Buffalo	1,297	271	11
Pete Stoyanovich, Miami	0	28	31	121	**1991**	Thurman Thomas, Buffalo	1,407	288	7
Pete Stoyanovich, Miami	0	34	30	124	**1992**	Barry Foster, Pittsburgh	1,690	390	11
Jeff Jaeger, L.A. Raiders	0	27	35	132	**1993**	Thurman Thomas, Buffalo	1,315	355	6
John Carney, San Diego	0	33	34	135	**1994**	Chris Warren, Seattle	1,545	333	9
Norm Johnson, Pittsburgh	0	39	34	141	**1995**	Curtis Martin, New England	1,487	368	14
Cary Blanchard, Indianapolis	0	27	36	135	**1996**	Terrell Davis, Denver	1,538	345	13
Mike Hollis, Jacksonville	0	41	31	134	**1997**	Terrell Davis, Denver	1,750	369	15
Steve Christie, Buffalo	0	41	33	140	**1998**	Terrell Davis, Denver	2,008	392	21
Mike Vanderjagt, Indianapolis	0	43	34	145	**1999**	Edgerrin James, Indianapolis	1,553	369	13
Matt Stover, Baltimore	0	30	35	135	**2000**	Edgerrin James, Indianapolis	1,709	387	13
Mike Vanderjagt, Indianapolis	0	41	28	125	**2001**	Priest Holmes, Kansas City	1,555	327	8
Priest Holmes, Kansas City	24	0	0	144	**2002**	Ricky Williams, Miami	1,853	383	16
Priest Holmes, Kansas City	27	0	0	162	**2003**	Jamal Lewis, Baltimore	2,066	387	14
Adam Vinatieri, New England	0	48	31	141	**2004**	Curtis Martin, NY Jets	1,697	371	12
Shayne Graham, Cincinnati	0	47	28	131	**2005**	Larry Johnson, Kansas City	1,750	336	20
LaDainian Tomlinson, San Diego	31	0	0	186	**2006**	LaDainian Tomlinson, San Diego	1,815	348	28
Randy Moss, New England	23	0	0	138	**2007**	LaDainian Tomlinson, San Diego	1,474	315	15
Stephen Gostkowski, New England	0	40	36	148	**2008**	Thomas Jones, NY Jets	1,312	290	13
Nate Kaeding, San Diego	0	50	32	146	**2009**	Chris Johnson, Tennessee	2,006	358	14
Sebastian Janikowski, Oakland	0	43	33	142	**2010**	Arian Foster, Houston	1,616	327	16
Stephen Gostkowski, New England	0	59	28	143	**2011**	Maurice Jones-Drew, Jacksonville	1,606	343	8
Stephen Gostkowski, New England	0	66	29	153	**2012**	Jamaal Charles, Kansas City	1,509	285	5
Stephen Gostkowski, New England	0	44	38	158	**2013**	Jamaal Charles, Kansas City	1,287	259	12
Stephen Gostkowski, New England	0	51	35	156	**2014**	Le'Veon Bell, Pittsburgh	1,361	290	8
Stephen Gostkowski, New England	0	52	33	151	**2015**	Chris Ivory, NY Jets	1,070	247	7
Justin Tucker, Baltimore	0	27	38	141	**2016**	DeMarco Murray, Tennessee	1,287	293	9
Stephen Gostkowski, New England	0	45	37	156	**2017**	Kareem Hunt, Kansas City	1,327	272	8
Ka'imi Fairbairn, Houston	0	39	37	150	**2018**	Joe Mixon, Cincinnati	1,168	237	8
Harrison Butker, Kansas City	0	45	34	147	**2019**	Derrick Henry, Tennessee	1,540	303	16
Daniel Carlson, Las Vegas	0	45	33	144	**2020**	Derrick Henry, Tennessee	2,027	378	17
Jason Sanders, Miami	0	36	36	144					
Daniel Carlson, Las Vegas	0	30	40	150	**2021**	Jonathan Taylor, Indianapolis	1,811	332	18
Nick Folk, New England	0	42	36	150					
Justin Tucker, Baltimore	0	31	37	142	**2022**	Josh Jacobs, Las Vegas	1,653	340	12
Justin Tucker, Baltimore	0	51	32	147	**2023**	Derrick Henry, Tennessee	1,167	280	12

* = Includes 277 yards after being traded to NFC; 1,011 yards led AFC. NA = Not applicable/available. **Note:** Passer ratings for years prior to 1973 were determined by different measures and are not directly comparable to current passer ratings.

National Football Conference Leaders, 1960-2023

(National Football League, 1960-69)

PASSING (BASED ON QB RATING POINTS)							RECEPTIONS			
Player, team	Rating	Att	Comp	Yds	TD	Year	Player, team	Rec	Yds	TD
Milt Plum, Cleveland	NA	250	151	2,297	21	**1960**	Raymond Berry, Baltimore Colts	74	1,298	10
Milt Plum, Cleveland	NA	302	177	2,416	18	**1961**	Jim Phillips, L.A. Rams	78	1,092	5
Bart Starr, Green Bay	NA	285	178	2,438	12	**1962**	Bobby Mitchell, Washington	72	1,384	11
Y. A. Tittle, NY Giants	NA	367	221	3,145	36	**1963**	Bobby Joe Conrad, St. Louis Cardinals	73	967	10
Bart Starr, Green Bay	NA	272	163	2,144	15	**1964**	Johnny Morris, Chicago	93	1,200	10
Rudy Bukich, Chicago	NA	312	176	2,641	20	**1965**	Dave Parks, San Francisco	80	1,344	12
Bart Starr, Green Bay	NA	251	156	2,257	14	**1966**	Charley Taylor, Washington	72	1,119	12
Sonny Jurgensen, Washington	NA	508	288	3,747	31	**1967**	Charley Taylor, Washington	70	990	9
Earl Morrall, Baltimore Colts	NA	317	182	2,909	26	**1968**	Clifton McNeil, San Francisco	71	994	7
Sonny Jurgensen, Washington	NA	442	274	3,102	22	**1969**	Dan Abramowicz, New Orleans	73	1,015	7
John Brodie, San Francisco	NA	378	223	2,941	24	**1970**	Dick Gordon, Chicago	71	1,026	13
Roger Staubach, Dallas	NA	211	126	1,882	15	**1971**	Bob Tucker, NY Giants	59	791	4
Norm Snead, NY Giants	NA	325	196	2,307	17	**1972**	Harold Jackson, Philadelphia	62	1,048	4
Roger Staubach, Dallas	94.6	286	179	2,428	23	**1973**	Harold Carmichael, Philadelphia	67	1,116	9
Sonny Jurgensen, Washington	94.5	167	107	1,185	11	**1974**	Charles Young, Philadelphia	63	696	3

PASSING (BASED ON QB RATING POINTS) / **RECEPTIONS**

Player, team	Rating	Att	Comp	Yds	TD	Year	Player, team	Rec	Yds	TD
Fran Tarkenton, Minnesota	91.8	425	273	2,994	25	**1975**	Chuck Foreman, Minnesota	73	691	9
James Harris, L.A. Rams	89.6	158	91	1,460	8	**1976**	Drew Pearson, Dallas	58	806	6
Roger Staubach, Dallas	87.0	361	210	2,620	18	**1977**	Ahmad Rashad, Minnesota	51	681	2
Roger Staubach, Dallas	84.9	413	231	3,190	25	**1978**	Rickey Young, Minnesota	88	704	5
Roger Staubach, Dallas	92.3	461	267	3,586	27	**1979**	Ahmad Rashad, Minnesota	80	1,156	9
Ron Jaworski, Philadelphia	91.0	451	257	3,529	27	**1980**	Earl Cooper, San Francisco	83	567	4
Joe Montana, San Francisco	88.4	488	311	3,565	19	**1981**	Dwight Clark, San Francisco	85	1,105	4
Joe Theismann, Washington	91.3	252	161	2,033	13	**1982**	Dwight Clark, San Francisco	60	913	5
Steve Bartkowski, Atlanta	97.6	432	274	3,167	22	**1983**	Roy Green, St. Louis Cardinals	78	1,227	14
							Charlie Brown, Washington	78	1,225	8
							Earnest Gray, NY Giants	78	1,139	5
Joe Montana, San Francisco	102.9	432	279	3,630	28	**1984**	Art Monk, Washington	106	1,372	7
Joe Montana, San Francisco	91.3	494	303	3,653	27	**1985**	Roger Craig, San Francisco	92	1,016	6
Tommy Kramer, Minnesota	92.6	372	208	3,000	24	**1986**	Jerry Rice, San Francisco	86	1,570	15
Joe Montana, San Francisco	102.1	398	266	3,054	31	**1987**	J. T. Smith, St. Louis Cardinals	91	1,117	8
Wade Wilson, Minnesota	91.5	332	204	2,746	15	**1988**	Henry Ellard, L.A. Rams	86	1,414	10
Joe Montana, San Francisco	112.4	386	271	3,521	26	**1989**	Sterling Sharpe, Green Bay	90	1,423	12
Phil Simms, NY Giants	92.7	311	184	2,284	15	**1990**	Jerry Rice, San Francisco	100	1,502	13
Steve Young, San Francisco	101.8	279	180	2,517	17	**1991**	Michael Irvin, Dallas	93	1,523	8
Steve Young, San Francisco	107.0	402	268	3,465	25	**1992**	Sterling Sharpe, Green Bay	108	1,461	13
Steve Young, San Francisco	101.5	462	314	4,023	29	**1993**	Sterling Sharpe, Green Bay	112	1,274	11
Steve Young, San Francisco	112.8	461	324	3,969	35	**1994**	Cris Carter, Minnesota	122	1,256	7
Brett Favre, Green Bay	99.5	570	359	4,413	38	**1995**	Herman Moore, Detroit	123	1,686	14
Steve Young, San Francisco	97.2	316	214	2,410	14	**1996**	Jerry Rice, San Francisco	108	1,254	8
Steve Young, San Francisco	104.7	356	241	3,029	19	**1997**	Herman Moore, Detroit	104	1,293	8
Randall Cunningham, Minnesota	106.0	425	259	3,704	34	**1998**	Frank Sanders, Arizona	89	1,145	3
Kurt Warner, St. Louis	109.2	499	325	4,353	41	**1999**	Muhsin Muhammad, Carolina	96	1,253	8
Trent Green, St. Louis	101.8	240	145	2,063	16	**2000**	Muhsin Muhammad, Carolina	102	1,183	6
Kurt Warner, St. Louis	101.4	546	375	4,830	36	**2001**	Keyshawn Johnson, Tampa Bay	106	1,266	1
Brad Johnson, Tampa Bay	92.9	451	281	3,049	22	**2002**	Randy Moss, Minnesota	106	1,347	7
Daunte Culpepper, Minnesota	96.4	454	295	3,479	25	**2003**	Torry Holt, St. Louis	117	1,696	12
Daunte Culpepper, Minnesota	110.9	548	379	4,717	39	**2004**	Joe Horn, New Orleans	94	1,399	11
							Torry Holt, St. Louis	94	1,372	10
Matt Hasselbeck, Seattle	98.2	449	294	3,459	24	**2005**	Steve Smith, Carolina	103	1,563	12
							Larry Fitzgerald, Arizona	103	1,409	10
Drew Brees, New Orleans	96.2	554	356	4,418	26	**2006**	Mike Furrey, Detroit	98	1,086	6
Tony Romo, Dallas	97.4	520	335	4,211	36	**2007**	Larry Fitzgerald, Arizona	100	1,409	10
Kurt Warner, Arizona	96.9	598	401	4,583	30	**2008**	Larry Fitzgerald, Arizona	96	1,431	12
Drew Brees, New Orleans	109.6	514	363	4,388	34	**2009**	Steve Smith, NY Giants	107	1,220	7
Aaron Rodgers, Green Bay	101.2	475	312	3,922	28	**2010**	Roddy White, Atlanta	115	1,389	10
Aaron Rodgers, Green Bay	122.5	502	343	4,643	45	**2011**	Roddy White, Atlanta	100	1,296	8
Aaron Rodgers, Green Bay	108.0	552	371	4,295	39	**2012**	Calvin Johnson, Detroit	122	1,964	5
Nick Foles, Philadelphia	119.2	317	203	2,891	27	**2013**	Pierre Garcon, Washington	113	1,346	5
Tony Romo, Dallas	113.2	435	304	3,705	34	**2014**	Julio Jones, Atlanta	104	1,593	6
Russell Wilson, Seattle	110.1	483	329	4,024	34	**2015**	Julio Jones, Atlanta	136	1,871	8
Matt Ryan, Atlanta	117.1	534	373	4,944	38	**2016**	Larry Fitzgerald, Arizona	107	1,023	6
Drew Brees, New Orleans	103.9	536	386	4,334	23	**2017**	Larry Fitzgerald, Arizona	109	1,156	6
Drew Brees, New Orleans	115.7	489	364	3,992	32	**2018**	Michael Thomas, New Orleans	125	1,405	9
Drew Brees, New Orleans	116.3	378	281	2,979	27	**2019**	Michael Thomas, New Orleans	149	1,725	9
Aaron Rodgers, Green Bay	121.5	526	372	4,299	48	**2020**	DeAndre Hopkins, Arizona	115	1,407	6
							Davante Adams, Green Bay	115	1,374	18
Aaron Rodgers, Green Bay	111.9	531	366	4,115	37	**2021**	Cooper Kupp, L.A. Rams	145	1,947	16
Jimmy Garoppolo, San Francisco	103.0	308	207	2,437	16	**2022**	Justin Jefferson, Minnesota	128	1,809	8
Brock Purdy, San Francisco	113.0	444	308	4,280	31	**2023**	CeeDee Lamb, Dallas	135	1,749	12

SCORING / **RUSHING YARDS**

Player, team	TD	XPM	FGM	Pts	Year	Player, team	Yds	Att	TD
Paul Hornung, Green Bay	15	41	15	176	**1960**	Jim Brown, Cleveland	1,257	215	9
Paul Hornung, Green Bay	10	41	15	146	**1961**	Jim Brown, Cleveland	1,408	305	8
Jim Taylor, Green Bay	19	0	0	114	**1962**	Jim Taylor, Green Bay	1,474	272	19
Don Chandler, NY Giants	0	52	18	106	**1963**	Jim Brown, Cleveland	1,863	291	12
Lenny Moore, Baltimore Colts	20	0	0	120	**1964**	Jim Brown, Cleveland	1,446	280	7
Gale Sayers, Chicago	22	0	0	132	**1965**	Jim Brown, Cleveland	1,544	289	17
Bruce Gossett, L.A. Rams	0	29	28	113	**1966**	Gale Sayers, Chicago	1,231	229	8
Jim Bakken, St. Louis Cardinals	0	36	27	117	**1967**	Leroy Kelly, Cleveland	1,205	235	11
Leroy Kelly, Cleveland	20	0	0	120	**1968**	Leroy Kelly, Cleveland	1,239	248	16
Fred Cox, Minnesota	0	43	26	121	**1969**	Gale Sayers, Chicago	1,032	236	8
Fred Cox, Minnesota	0	35	30	125	**1970**	Larry Brown, Washington	1,125	237	5
Curt Knight, Washington	0	27	29	114	**1971**	John Brockington, Green Bay	1,105	216	4
Chester Marcol, Green Bay	0	29	33	128	**1972**	Larry Brown, Washington	1,216	285	8
David Ray, L.A. Rams	0	40	30	130	**1973**	John Brockington, Green Bay	1,144	265	3
Chester Marcol, Green Bay	0	19	25	94	**1974**	Lawrence McCutcheon, L.A. Rams	1,109	236	3
Chuck Foreman, Minnesota	22	0	0	132	**1975**	Jim Otis, St. Louis Cardinals	1,076	269	5
Mark Moseley, Washington	0	31	22	97	**1976**	Walter Payton, Chicago	1,390	311	13
Walter Payton, Chicago	16	0	0	96	**1977**	Walter Payton, Chicago	1,852	339	14
Frank Corral, L.A. Rams	0	31	29	118	**1978**	Walter Payton, Chicago	1,395	333	11
Mark Moseley, Washington	0	39	25	114	**1979**	Walter Payton, Chicago	1,610	369	14
Ed Murray, Detroit	0	35	27	116	**1980**	Walter Payton, Chicago	1,460	317	6
Ed Murray, Detroit	0	46	25	121	**1981**	George Rogers, New Orleans	1,674	378	13
Rafael Septien, Dallas	0	40	27	121					
Wendell Tyler, L.A. Rams	13	0	0	78	**1982**	Tony Dorsett, Dallas	745	177	5
Mark Moseley, Washington	0	62	33	161	**1983**	Eric Dickerson, L.A. Rams	1,808	390	18

SCORING						RUSHING YARDS			
Player, team	TD	XPM	FGM	Pts	Year	Player, team	Yds	Att	TD
Ray Wersching, San Francisco	0	56	25	131	**1984**	Eric Dickerson, L.A. Rams	2,105	379	14
Kevin Butler, Chicago	0	51	31	144	**1985**	Gerald Riggs, Atlanta	1,719	397	10
Kevin Butler, Chicago	0	36	28	120	**1986**	Eric Dickerson, L.A. Rams	1,821	404	11
Jerry Rice, San Francisco	23	0	0	138	**1987**	Charles White, L.A. Rams	1,374	324	11
Mike Cofer, San Francisco	0	40	27	121	**1988**	Herschel Walker, Dallas	1,514	361	5
Mike Cofer, San Francisco	0	49	29	136	**1989**	Barry Sanders, Detroit	1,470	280	14
Chip Lohmiller, Washington	0	41	30	131	**1990**	Barry Sanders, Detroit	1,304	255	13
Chip Lohmiller, Washington	0	56	31	149	**1991**	Emmitt Smith, Dallas	1,563	365	12
Morten Andersen, New Orleans	0	33	29	120	**1992**	Emmitt Smith, Dallas	1,713	373	18
Chip Lohmiller, Washington	0	30	30	120					
Jason Hanson, Detroit	0	28	34	130	**1993**	Emmitt Smith, Dallas	1,486	283	9
Fuad Reveiz, Minnesota	0	30	34	132	**1994**	Barry Sanders, Detroit	1,883	331	7
Emmitt Smith, Dallas	22	0	0	132					
Emmitt Smith, Dallas	25	0	0	150	**1995**	Emmitt Smith, Dallas	1,773	377	25
John Kasay, Carolina	0	34	37	145	**1996**	Barry Sanders, Detroit	1,553	307	11
Richie Cunningham, Dallas	0	24	34	126	**1997**	Barry Sanders, Detroit	2,053	335	11
Gary Anderson, Minnesota	0	59	35	164	**1998**	Jamal Anderson, Atlanta	1,846	410	14
Jeff Wilkins, St. Louis	0	64	20	124	**1999**	Stephen Davis, Washington	1,405	290	17
Marshall Faulk, St. Louis	26	0	0	160	**2000**	Robert Smith, Minnesota	1,521	295	7
Marshall Faulk, St. Louis	21	0	0	128	**2001**	Stephen Davis, Washington	1,432	356	5
Jay Feely, Atlanta	0	42	32	138	**2002**	Deuce McAllister, New Orleans	1,388	325	13
Jeff Wilkins, St. Louis	0	46	39	163	**2003**	Ahman Green, Green Bay	1,883	355	15
David Akers, Philadelphia	0	41	27	122	**2004**	Shaun Alexander, Seattle	1,696	353	16
Shaun Alexander, Seattle	28	0	0	168	**2005**	Shaun Alexander, Seattle	1,880	370	27
Robbie Gould, Chicago	0	47	32	143	**2006**	Frank Gore, San Francisco	1,695	312	8
Mason Crosby, Green Bay	0	48	31	141	**2007**	Adrian Peterson, Minnesota	1,341	238	12
David Akers, Philadelphia	0	45	33	144	**2008**	Adrian Peterson, Minnesota	1,760	363	10
David Akers, Philadelphia	0	43	32	139	**2009**	Steven Jackson, St. Louis	1,416	324	4
David Akers, Philadelphia	0	47	32	143	**2010**	Michael Turner, Atlanta	1,371	334	12
David Akers, San Francisco	0	34	44	166	**2011**	Michael Turner, Atlanta	1,340	301	11
Lawrence Tynes, NY Giants	0	46	33	145	**2012**	Adrian Peterson, Minnesota	2,097	348	12
Steven Hauschka, Seattle	0	44	33	143	**2013**	LeSean McCoy, Philadelphia	1,607	314	9
Cody Parkey, Philadelphia	0	54	32	150	**2014**	DeMarco Murray, Dallas	1,845	392	13
Graham Gano, Carolina	0	56	30	146	**2015**	Adrian Peterson, Minnesota	1,485	327	11
Matt Bryant, Atlanta	0	56	34	158	**2016**	Ezekiel Elliott, Dallas	1,631	322	15
Greg Zuerlein, L.A. Rams	0	44	38	158	**2017**	Todd Gurley, L.A. Rams	1,305	279	13
Wil Lutz, New Orleans	0	52	28	136	**2018**	Ezekiel Elliott, Dallas	1,434	304	6
Wil Lutz, New Orleans	0	48	32	144	**2019**	Christian McCaffrey, Carolina	1,387	287	15
Younghoe Koo, Atlanta	0	33	37	144	**2020**	Dalvin Cook, Minnesota	1,557	312	16
Matt Gay, L.A. Rams	0	48	32	144	**2021**	Dalvin Cook, Minnesota	1,159	249	6
Jason Myers, Seattle	0	41	34	143	**2022**	Saquon Barkley, NY Giants	1,312	295	10
Brandon Aubrey, Dallas	0	49	36	157	**2023**	Christian McCaffrey, San Francisco	1,459	272	14

NA = Not applicable/available. **Note:** Passer ratings for years prior to 1973 were determined by different measures and are not directly comparable to current passer ratings.

NFL Most Valuable Player, 1957-2023

The Most Valuable Player is one of many awards given out annually by the Associated Press. Many other organizations give out annual awards honoring the NFL's best players, and those winners may differ from this list.

Year	Player, team
1957	Jim Brown, Cleveland
1958	Jim Brown, Cleveland
1959	Charlie Conerly, NY Giants
1960	Norm Van Brocklin, Philadelphia
1961	Paul Hornung, Green Bay
1962	Jim Taylor, Green Bay
1963	Y. A. Tittle, NY Giants
1964	Johnny Unitas, Baltimore
1965	Jim Brown, Cleveland
1966	Bart Starr, Green Bay
1967	Johnny Unitas, Baltimore
1968	Earl Morrall, Baltimore
1969	Roman Gabriel, Los Angeles
1970	John Brodie, San Francisco
1971	Alan Page, Minnesota
1972	Larry Brown, Washington
1973	O.J. Simpson, Buffalo
1974	Ken Stabler, Oakland
1975	Fran Tarkenton, Minnesota
1976	Bert Jones, Baltimore
1977	Walter Payton, Chicago
1978	Terry Bradshaw, Pittsburgh
1979	Earl Campbell, Houston
1980	Brian Sipe, Cleveland
1981	Ken Anderson, Cincinnati
1982	Mark Moseley, Washington
1983	Joe Theismann, Washington
1984	Dan Marino, Miami
1985	Marcus Allen, Los Angeles
1986	Lawrence Taylor, NY Giants
1987	John Elway, Denver
1988	Boomer Esiason, Cincinnati
1989	Joe Montana, San Francisco
1990	Joe Montana, San Francisco
1991	Thurman Thomas, Buffalo
1992	Steve Young, San Francisco
1993	Emmitt Smith, Dallas
1994	Steve Young, San Francisco
1995	Brett Favre, Green Bay
1996	Brett Favre, Green Bay
1997	Brett Favre, Green Bay; Barry Sanders, Detroit
1998	Terrell Davis, Denver
1999	Kurt Warner, St. Louis
2000	Marshall Faulk, St. Louis
2001	Kurt Warner, St. Louis
2002	Rich Gannon, Oakland
2003	Peyton Manning, Indianapolis; Steve McNair, Tennessee
2004	Peyton Manning, Indianapolis
2005	Shaun Alexander, Seattle
2006	LaDainian Tomlinson, San Diego
2007	Tom Brady, New England
2008	Peyton Manning, Indianapolis
2009	Peyton Manning, Indianapolis
2010	Tom Brady, New England
2011	Aaron Rodgers, Green Bay
2012	Adrian Peterson, Minnesota
2013	Peyton Manning, Denver
2014	Aaron Rodgers, Green Bay
2015	Cam Newton, Carolina
2016	Matt Ryan, Atlanta
2017	Tom Brady, New England
2018	Patrick Mahomes, Kansas City
2019	Lamar Jackson, Baltimore
2020	Aaron Rodgers, Green Bay
2021	Aaron Rodgers, Green Bay
2022	Patrick Mahomes, Kansas City
2023	Lamar Jackson, Baltimore

All-Time Professional (NFL and AFL) Football Records

(at end of 2023 season; * = active in 2023; (a) includes AFL statistics; ** = includes one 2-pt conversion)

All-Time Defensive Leaders

Interceptions, career: 81, Paul Krause, Washington-Minnesota, 1964-79.

Interceptions, season: 14, Dick "Night Train" Lane, L.A. Rams, 1952.

Interception touchdowns, career: 12, Rod Woodson, Pittsburgh-San Francisco-Baltimore Ravens-Oakland, 1987-2003.

Interception touchdowns, season: 5, DaRon Bland, Dallas, 2023.

Sacks, career (since 1982): 200.0, Bruce Smith, Buffalo-Washington, 1985-2003.

Sacks, season (since 1982): 22.5; Michael Strahan, NY Giants, 2001; T.J. Watt, Pittsburgh, 2021.

All-Time Scoring Leaders by Points

Player	Yrs	TD	PAT	FG	Total
Adam Vinatieri	24	0	874	599	2,673**
Morten Andersen	25	0	849	565	2,544
Gary Anderson	23	0	820	538	2,434
Jason Hanson	21	0	665	495	2,150
John Carney	23	0	628	478	2,062
Matt Stover	19	0	591	471	2,004
George Blanda (a)	26	9	943	335	2,002
Jason Elam	17	0	675	436	1,983
John Kasay	20	0	587	461	1,970
Robbie Gould	18	0	620	447	1,961
Mason Crosby*	17	0	739	400	1,939
Sebastian Janikowski	18	0	605	436	1,913
Stephen Gostkowski	15	0	699	392	1,875
Phil Dawson	20	1	518	441	1,847
Matt Prater*	17	0	577	401	1,780

Points, season: 186, LaDainian Tomlinson, San Diego, 2006 (31 TDs).
Points, game: 40, Ernie Nevers, Chicago Cardinals vs. Chicago Bears, Nov. 28, 1929 (6 TDs, 4 PATs).
Touchdowns, season: 31, LaDainian Tomlinson, San Diego, 2006.
Touchdowns, game: 6; Ernie Nevers, Chicago Cardinals vs. Chicago Bears, Nov. 28, 1929 (6 rushing); Dub Jones, Cleveland Browns vs. Chicago Bears, Nov. 25, 1951 (4 rushing, 2 pass receptions); Gale Sayers, Chicago Bears vs. San Francisco, Dec. 12, 1965 (4 rushing, 1 pass reception, 1 punt return); Alvin Kamara, New Orleans vs. Minnesota, Dec. 25, 2020 (6 rushing).

All-Time Scoring Leaders by Touchdowns

Player	Yrs	Rush	Rec	Ret	TD
Jerry Rice	20	10	197	1	208
Emmitt Smith	15	164	11	0	175
LaDainian Tomlinson	11	145	17	0	162
Randy Moss	14	0	156	1	157
Terrell Owens	15	3	153	0	156
Marcus Allen	16	123	21	1	145
Marshall Faulk	12	100	36	0	136
Cris Carter	16	0	130	1	131
Marvin Harrison	13	0	128	0	128
Jim Brown	9	106	20	0	126
Adrian Peterson	15	120	6	0	126
Walter Payton	13	110	15	0	125
Larry Fitzgerald	17	0	121	0	121
Antonio Gates	16	0	116	0	116
John Riggins	14	104	12	0	116

Points after TD, season: 75, Matt Prater, Denver, 2013.
Consecutive points after TD: 523, Stephen Gostkowski, New England, 2006-16.
Field goals, career: 599, Adam Vinatieri, New England-Indianapolis, 1996-2019.
Field goals, season: 44, David Akers, San Francisco, 2011.
Field goals, game: 8, Rob Bironas, Tennessee vs. Houston, Oct. 21, 2007.
Longest field goal: 66 yards, Justin Tucker, Baltimore vs. Detroit, Sept. 26, 2021.

All-Time Rushing Leaders

(ranked by rushing yards)

Player	Yrs	Att	Yds	Avg	Long	TD
Emmitt Smith	15	4,409	18,355	4.2	75T	164
Walter Payton	13	3,838	16,726	4.4	76	110
Frank Gore	16	3,735	16,000	4.3	80T	81
Barry Sanders	10	3,062	15,269	5.0	85	99
Adrian Peterson	15	3,230	14,918	4.6	90T	120
Curtis Martin	11	3,518	14,101	4.0	70T	90
LaDainian Tomlinson	11	3,174	13,684	4.3	85T	145
Jerome Bettis	13	3,479	13,662	3.9	71T	91
Eric Dickerson	11	2,996	13,259	4.4	85T	90
Tony Dorsett	12	2,936	12,739	4.3	99T	77
Jim Brown	9	2,359	12,312	5.2	80T	106
Marshall Faulk	12	2,836	12,279	4.3	71T	100
Edgerrin James	11	3,028	12,246	4.0	72	80
Marcus Allen	16	3,022	12,243	4.1	61T	123
Franco Harris	13	2,949	12,120	4.1	75T	91
Thurman Thomas	13	2,877	12,074	4.2	80T	65
Fred Taylor	13	2,534	11,695	4.6	80T	66
Steven Jackson	12	2,764	11,438	4.1	59T	69
John Riggins	14	2,916	11,352	3.9	66T	104
Corey Dillon	10	2,618	11,241	4.3	96T	82

Yards gained, season: 2,105, Eric Dickerson, L.A. Rams, 1984.
Yards gained, game: 296, Adrian Peterson, Minnesota vs. San Diego, Nov. 4, 2007.
Rushing TDs, career: 164, Emmitt Smith, Dallas-Arizona, 1990-2004.
Rushing TDs, season: 28, LaDainian Tomlinson, San Diego, 2006.
Rushing TDs, game: 6; Ernie Nevers, Chicago Cardinals vs. Chicago Bears, Nov. 28, 1929; Alvin Kamara, New Orleans Saints vs. Minnesota Vikings, Dec. 25, 2020.
Rushing attempts, game: 45, Jamie Morris, Washington vs. Cincinnati, Dec. 17, 1988 (OT).
Longest run from scrimmage: 99 yards (TD); Tony Dorsett, Dallas vs. Minnesota, Jan. 3, 1983; Derrick Henry, Tennessee vs. Jacksonville, Dec. 6, 2018.

All-Time Receiving Leaders

(ranked by number of receptions)

Player	Yrs	No.	Yds	Avg	Long	TD
Jerry Rice	20	1,549	22,895	14.8	96T	197
Larry Fitzgerald	17	1,432	17,492	12.2	80T	121
Tony Gonzalez	17	1,325	15,127	11.4	73T	111
Jason Witten	17	1,228	13,046	10.6	69	74
Marvin Harrison	13	1,102	14,580	13.2	80T	128
Cris Carter	16	1,101	13,899	12.6	80T	130
Tim Brown	17	1,094	14,934	13.7	80T	100
Terrell Owens	15	1,078	15,934	14.8	98T	153
Anquan Boldin	14	1,076	13,779	12.8	79T	82
Reggie Wayne	14	1,070	14,345	13.4	80	82
Andre Johnson	14	1,062	14,185	13.4	77T	70
Steve Smith Sr.	16	1,031	14,731	14.3	80T	81
Isaac Bruce	16	1,024	15,208	14.9	80T	91
Hines Ward	14	1,000	12,083	12.1	85T	85
Randy Moss	14	982	15,292	15.6	82T	156
Brandon Marshall	13	970	12,351	12.7	75T	83
Antonio Gates	16	955	11,841	12.4	72T	116
Andre Reed	16	951	13,198	13.9	83T	87
Derrick Mason	15	943	12,061	12.8	79T	66
Art Monk	16	940	12,721	13.5	79T	68

Yards gained, career: 22,895, Jerry Rice, San Francisco-Oakland-Seattle, 1985-2004.
Yards gained, season: 1,964, Calvin Johnson, Detroit, 2012.
Yards gained, game: 336, Willie "Flipper" Anderson, L.A. Rams vs. New Orleans, Nov. 26, 1989 (OT).
Pass receptions, season: 149, Michael Thomas, New Orleans, 2019.
Pass receptions, game: 21, Brandon Marshall, Denver vs. Indianapolis, Dec. 13, 2009.
Touchdown receptions, career: 197, Jerry Rice, San Francisco-Oakland-Seattle, 1985-2004.
Touchdown receptions, season: 23, Randy Moss, New England, 2007.
Touchdown receptions, game: 5; Bob Shaw, Chicago Cardinals vs. Baltimore Colts, Oct. 2, 1950; Kellen Winslow, San Diego vs. Oakland, Nov. 22, 1981; Jerry Rice, San Francisco vs. Atlanta, Oct. 14, 1990.

All-Time Passing Leaders

(minimum 1,500 attempts; ranked by quarterback rating points)

Player	Yrs	Att	Comp	Yds	TD	Int	Rate[1]
Aaron Rodgers*	19	7,661	5,001	59,055	475	105	103.6
Patrick Mahomes*	7	3,590	2,386	28,424	219	63	103.5
Deshaun Watson*	6	2,089	1,390	16,756	118	45	100.8
Russell Wilson*	12	5,665	3,668	43,653	334	106	100.0
Dak Prescott*	8	3,873	2,595	29,459	202	74	99.0
Drew Brees	20	10,551	7,142	80,358	571	243	98.7
Joe Burrow*	4	1,895	1,288	14,083	97	37	98.6
Kirk Cousins*	12	5,177	3,465	39,471	270	110	98.2
Lamar Jackson*	6	2,112	1,362	15,887	125	45	98.0
Jimmy Garoppolo*	10	1,895	1,277	15,494	94	51	97.6
Tom Brady	23	12,050	7,753	89,214	649	212	97.2
Tony Romo	13	4,335	2,829	34,183	248	117	97.1
Tua Tagovailoa*	4	1,638	1,096	12,639	81	37	97.1
Steve Young	15	4,149	2,667	33,124	232	107	96.8
Peyton Manning	17	9,380	6,125	71,940	539	251	96.5
Justin Herbert*	4	2,422	1,613	17,223	114	42	95.7
Philip Rivers	17	8,134	5,277	63,440	421	209	95.2
Kurt Warner	12	4,070	2,666	32,344	208	128	93.7
Jared Goff*	8	4,107	2,657	30,429	185	82	93.6
Matt Ryan	15	8,464	5,551	62,792	381	183	93.6

(1) Rating points based on performances in the following categories: percentage of completions, percentage of touchdown passes, percentage of interceptions, and average gain per pass attempt.

Yards gained, career: 89,214, Tom Brady, New England-Tampa Bay, 2000-22.
Yards gained, season: 5,477, Peyton Manning, Denver, 2013.
Yards gained, game: 554, Norm Van Brocklin, L.A. Rams vs. NY Yanks, Sept. 28, 1951 (27 completions in 41 attempts).
Touchdowns passing, career: 649, Tom Brady, New England-Tampa Bay, 2000-22.
Touchdowns passing, season: 55, Peyton Manning, Denver, 2013.
Touchdowns passing, game: 7; Sid Luckman, Chicago Bears vs. NY Giants, Nov. 14, 1943; Adrian Burk, Philadelphia vs. Washington, Oct. 17, 1954; George Blanda, Houston vs. NY Titans, Nov. 19, 1961; Y. A. Tittle, NY Giants vs. Washington, Oct. 28, 1962; Joe Kapp, Minnesota vs. Baltimore Colts, Sept. 28, 1969; Peyton Manning, Denver vs. Baltimore, Sept. 5, 2013; Nick Foles, Philadelphia vs. Oakland, Nov. 3, 2013; Drew Brees, New Orleans vs. NY Giants, Nov. 1, 2015.
Passes completed, career: 7,753, Tom Brady, New England-Tampa Bay, 2000-22.
Passes completed, season: 490, Tom Brady, Tampa Bay, 2022.
Passes completed, game: 47, Ben Roethlisberger, Pittsburgh vs. Cleveland, Jan. 10, 2021.
Passes completed, game (reg. season): 45; Drew Bledsoe, New England vs. Minnesota, Nov. 13, 1994 (OT); Jared Goff, L.A. Rams vs. Tampa Bay, Sept. 29, 2019.

National Football League Franchise Origins and Name History

(Team: founding year, league. Franchise name history.)

Arizona Cardinals: 1920, American Professional Football Association (APFA)[1]. Chicago Cardinals, 1920-43, 1945-59; Card-Pitt[2], 1944; St. Louis Cardinals, 1960-87; Phoenix Cardinals, 1988-93; Arizona Cardinals, 1994-present.
Atlanta Falcons: 1966, NFL. 1966-present.
Baltimore Ravens: 1996, NFL. 1996-present[3].
Buffalo Bills: 1960, American Football League (AFL)[4]. 1960-present.
Carolina Panthers: 1995, NFL. 1996-present.
Chicago Bears: 1920, APFA. Decatur Staleys, 1920; Chicago Staleys, 1921; Chicago Bears, 1922-present.
Cincinnati Bengals: 1968, AFL. 1968-present.
Cleveland Browns: 1946, All-America Football Conference (AAFC)[5]. 1946-95[3], 1999-present.
Dallas Cowboys: 1960, NFL. 1960-present.
Denver Broncos: 1960, AFL. 1960-present.
Detroit Lions: 1930, NFL. Portsmouth Spartans, 1930-33; Detroit Lions, 1934-present.
Green Bay Packers: 1921, APFA. 1921-present.
Houston Texans: 2002, NFL. 2002-present.
Indianapolis Colts: 1953, NFL[5]. Baltimore Colts, 1953-83; Indianapolis Colts, 1984-present.
Jacksonville Jaguars: 1995, NFL. 1995-present.
Kansas City Chiefs: 1960, AFL. Dallas Texans, 1960-62; Kansas City Chiefs, 1963-present.
Las Vegas Raiders: 1960, AFL. Oakland Raiders, 1960-81, 1995-2019; Los Angeles Raiders, 1982-94; Las Vegas Raiders, 2020-present.
Los Angeles Chargers: 1960, AFL. Los Angeles Chargers, 1960, 2017-present; San Diego Chargers, 1961-2016.
Los Angeles Rams: 1937, NFL. Cleveland Rams, 1937-45; Los Angeles Rams, 1946-94, 2016-present; St. Louis Rams, 1995-2015.
Miami Dolphins: 1966, AFL. 1966-present.
Minnesota Vikings: 1961, NFL. 1961-present.
New England Patriots: 1960, AFL. Boston Patriots, 1960-70; New England Patriots, 1971-present.
New Orleans Saints: 1967, NFL. 1967-present.
New York Giants: 1925, NFL. 1925-present.
New York Jets: 1960, AFL. New York Titans, 1960-62; New York Jets, 1963-present.
Philadelphia Eagles: 1933, NFL. Philadelphia Eagles, 1933-42, 1944-present; Phil-Pitt "Steagles"[6], 1943.
Pittsburgh Steelers: 1933, NFL. Pittsburgh Pirates, 1933-39; Pittsburgh Steelers, 1940-42, 1945-present; Phil-Pitt "Steagles"[6], 1943; Card-Pitt[2], 1944.
San Francisco 49ers: 1946, AAFC. 1946-present.
Seattle Seahawks: 1976, NFL. 1976-present.
Tampa Bay Buccaneers: 1976, NFL. 1976-present.
Tennessee Titans: 1960, AFL. Houston Oilers, 1960-96; Tennessee Oilers, 1996-97; Tennessee Titans, 1998-present.
Washington Commanders: 1932, NFL. Boston Braves, 1932; Boston Redskins 1933-36; Washington Redskins, 1937-2019; Washington Football Team, 2020-21; Washington Commanders, 2022-present.

(1) The American Professional Football Association (APFA) was formed in 1920 to standardize the rules of professional football. In 1922, the name was changed to the National Football League (NFL). (2) In 1944, the Chicago Cardinals and the Pittsburgh Steelers temporarily merged because numerous players were lost to military service. (3) In 1995, Cleveland Browns owner Art Modell moved the franchise to Baltimore and the team was rechristened the Ravens. In 1999, a new Cleveland Browns team joined the NFL, but it is considered a continuation of the original Browns franchise. (4) The most successful of four leagues called the American Football League, or AFL (1926; 1936-37; 1940-41; 1960-69). Congress approved an NFL/AFL merger in 1966. Baltimore, Cleveland, and Pittsburgh agreed to join the 10 incoming AFL teams to form the American Football Conference. The unified NFL began play in 1970 with 26 teams. (5) The All-America Football Conference (AAFC), 1946-49. In 1950, three of its teams joined the NFL (Baltimore, Cleveland, and San Francisco). The Baltimore franchise failed, but the NFL awarded the city a second one, also called the Colts, in 1953. (6) In 1943, the Philadelphia Eagles and the Pittsburgh Steelers temporarily merged because numerous players were lost to military service. The team was informally known as the Steagles.

NFL Stadiums

(**A** = A-Turf Titan, **F** = FieldTurf, **G** = Grass, **M** = Matrix Turf, **SI** = SISGrass, **TNM** = Turf Nation-M6, **U** = Act Global Xtreme Turf)

Team: stadium, location, surface (year built)	Capacity
Bears: Soldier Field[1], Chicago, IL, G (1924)	61,500
Bengals: Paycor Stadium, Cincinnati, OH, F (2000)	65,656
Bills: Highmark Stadium, Orchard Park, NY, A (1973)	71,621
Broncos: Empower Field at Mile High, Denver, CO, G (2001)	76,125
Browns: Cleveland Browns Stadium, Cleveland, OH, G (1999)	67,827
Buccaneers: Raymond James Stadium, Tampa, FL, G (1998)	65,844
Cardinals: State Farm Stadium, Glendale, AZ, G (2006)	65,000
Chargers: SoFi Stadium, Inglewood, CA, M (2020)	71,500
Chiefs: GEHA Field at Arrowhead Stadium, Kansas City, MO, G (1972; fully renovated 2010)	73,426
Colts: Lucas Oil Stadium, Indianapolis, IN, M (2008)	63,000
Commanders: Commanders Field, Landover, MD, G (1997)	67,617
Cowboys: AT&T Stadium, Arlington, TX, M (2009)	80,000
Dolphins: Hard Rock Stadium, Miami Gardens, FL, G (1987)	64,992
Eagles: Lincoln Financial Field, Philadelphia, PA, G (2003)	69,879
Falcons: Mercedes-Benz Stadium, Atlanta, GA, F (2017)	72,000
49ers: Levi's Stadium, Santa Clara, CA, G (2014)	68,500
Giants: MetLife Stadium, East Rutherford, NJ, F (2010)	82,500
Jaguars: EverBank Stadium, Jacksonville, FL, G (1995)	67,838
Jets: MetLife Stadium, East Rutherford, NJ, F (2010)	82,500
Lions: Ford Field, Detroit, MI, F (2002)	64,500
Packers: Lambeau Field[2], Green Bay, WI, SI (1957)	81,041
Panthers: Bank of America Stadium, Charlotte, NC, F (1996)	73,778
Patriots: Gillette Stadium, Foxborough, MA, F (2002)	64,628
Raiders: Allegiant Stadium, Las Vegas, NV, G (2020)	65,000
Rams: SoFi Stadium, Inglewood, CA, M (2020)	71,500
Ravens: M&T Bank Stadium, Baltimore, MD, G (1998)	70,765
Saints: Caesars Superdome, New Orleans, LA, TNM (1975)	73,000
Seahawks: Lumen Field, Seattle, WA, F (2002)	68,740
Steelers: Acrisure Stadium, Pittsburgh, PA, G (2001)	68,400
Texans: NRG Stadium, Houston, TX, M (2002)	71,995
Titans: Nissan Stadium, Nashville, TN, M (1999)	69,143
Vikings: U.S. Bank Stadium, Minneapolis, MN, U (2016)	67,202

Note: As of 2023-24 season. (1) Renovation in 2002 replaced interior of stadium. (2) Renovation completed in 2003 added 11,625 seats.

Pro Football Hall of Fame

Located in Canton, OH. * = Member elected in Feb. 2024 and inducted in Aug. 2024. www.profootballhof.com

Herb Adderley
Troy Aikman
George Allen
Larry Allen
Marcus Allen
Lance Alworth
Morten Andersen
Doug Atkins
Steve Atwater
Morris "Red" Badgro
Champ Bailey
Ronde Barber
Lem Barney
Cliff Battles
Sammy Baugh
Bobby Beathard
Chuck Bednarik
Bert Bell
Bobby Bell
Raymond Berry
Elvin Bethea
Jerome Bettis
Charles Bidwill
Fred Biletnikoff
George Blanda
Mel Blount
Tony Boselli
Pat Bowlen
Terry Bradshaw
Cliff Branch
Gil Brandt
Robert Brazile
Derrick Brooks
Bob Brown
Jim Brown
Paul Brown
Roosevelt Brown
Tim Brown
Willie Brown
Isaac Bruce
Junious "Buck" Buchanan
Nick Buoniconti
Dick Butkus
Jack Butler
LeRoy Butler
Earl Campbell
Tony Canadeo
Harold Carmichael
Joe Carr
Harry Carson
Cris Carter
Dave Casper
Guy Chamberlin
Jack Christiansen
Earl "Dutch" Clark
George Connor
Jim Conzelman
Don Coryell
Jimbo Covert
Bill Cowher
Lou Creekmur
Larry Csonka
Curley Culp
Al Davis
Terrell Davis
Willie Davis
Dermontti Dawson
Len Dawson
Fred Dean
Edward DeBartolo Jr.
Joe DeLamielleure
Richard Dent
Eric Dickerson
Dan Dierdorf
Bobby Dillon
Mike Ditka
Chris Doleman
Art Donovan
Tony Dorsett
John "Paddy" Driscoll
Bill Dudley
Tony Dungy
Kenny Easley
Glen "Turk" Edwards
Carl Eller
John Elway
Weeb Ewbank
Alan Faneca
Marshall Faulk
Brett Favre
Tom Fears
Jim Finks
Ray Flaherty
Tom Flores
Len Ford
Dr. Daniel Fortmann
Dan Fouts
*Dwight Freeney
Benny Friedman
Frank Gatski
Bill George
Joe Gibbs
Frank Gifford
Sid Gillman
Tony Gonzalez
*Randy Gradishar
Otto Graham
Harold "Red" Grange
Bud Grant
Darrell Green
Joe Greene
Kevin Greene
Forrest Gregg
Bob Griese
Russ Grimm
Lou Groza
Ray Guy
Joe Guyon
George Halas
Charles Haley
Jack Ham
Dan Hampton
Chris Hanburger
John Hannah
Cliff Harris
Franco Harris
Marvin Harrison
Bob Hayes
Mike Haynes
Ed Healey
Mel Hein
Ted Hendricks
Wilbur "Pete" Henry
Arnold Herber
*Devin Hester
Bill Hewitt
Gene Hickerson
Winston Hill
Clarke Hinkle
Elroy "Crazylegs" Hirsch
Paul Hornung
Ken Houston
Chuck Howley
Robert "Cal" Hubbard
Sam Huff
Claude Humphrey
Lamar Hunt
Steve Hutchinson
Don Hutson
Michael Irvin
Rickey Jackson
Edgerrin James
*Andre Johnson
Calvin Johnson
Jimmy Johnson
Jimmy Johnson (coach)
John Henry Johnson
Charlie Joiner
David "Deacon" Jones
Jerry Jones
Stan Jones
Walter Jones
Henry Jordan
Sonny Jurgensen
Alex Karras
Jim Kelly
Leroy Kelly
Cortez Kennedy
Walt Kiesling
Frank "Bruiser" Kinard
Joe Klecko
Jerry Kramer
Paul Krause
Earl "Curly" Lambeau
Jack Lambert
Tom Landry
Dick "Night Train" Lane
Jim Langer
Willie Lanier
Steve Largent
Yale Lary
Dante Lavelli
Ty Law
Bobby Layne
Dick LeBeau
Alphonse "Tuffy" Leemans
Marv Levy
Ray Lewis
Bob Lilly
Floyd Little
Larry Little
James Lofton
Vince Lombardi
Howie Long
Ronnie Lott
Sid Luckman
Roy "Link" Lyman
John Lynch
Tom Mack
John Mackey
John Madden
Peyton Manning
Tim Mara
Wellington Mara
Gino Marchetti
Dan Marino
George Preston Marshall
Curtis Martin
Ollie Matson
Bruce Matthews
Kevin Mawae
Don Maynard
George McAfee
Mike McCormack
Randall McDaniel
Tommy McDonald
Hugh McElhenny
*Steve McMichael
Art McNally
Johnny "Blood" McNally
Mike Michalske
Wayne Millner
Sam Mills
Bobby Mitchell
Ron Mix
Art Monk
Joe Montana
Warren Moon
Lenny Moore
Randy Moss
Marion Motley
Mike Munchak
Anthony Muñoz
George Musso
Bronko Nagurski
Joe Namath
Earle "Greasy" Neale
Ernie Nevers
Ozzie Newsome
Ray Nitschke
Chuck Noll
Leo Nomellini
Bill Nunn
Jonathan Ogden
Merlin Olsen
Jim Otto
Steve Owen
Terrell Owens
Orlando Pace
Alan Page
Bill Parcells
Clarence "Ace" Parker
Jim Parker
Walter Payton
Drew Pearson
*Julius Peppers
Joe Perry
Pete Pihos
Troy Polamalu
Bill Polian
Fritz Pollard
John Randle
Hugh "Shorty" Ray
Andre Reed
Ed Reed
Dan Reeves
Mel Renfro
Darrelle Revis
Jerry Rice
Les Richter
John Riggins
Ken Riley
Jim Ringo
Willie Roaf
Dave Robinson
Johnny Robinson
Andy Robustelli
Art Rooney
Dan Rooney
Pete Rozelle
Ed Sabol
Steve Sabol
Bob St. Clair
Barry Sanders
Charlie Sanders
Deion Sanders
Warren Sapp
Gale Sayers
Joe Schmidt
Tex Schramm
Junior Seau
Lee Roy Selmon
Richard Seymour
Shannon Sharpe
Billy Shaw
Art Shell
Donnie Shell
Will Shields
Don Shula
O.J. Simpson
Mike Singletary
Duke Slater
Jackie Slater
Bruce Smith
Emmitt Smith
Jackie Smith
Mac Speedie
Ed Sprinkle
Ken Stabler
John Stallworth
Dick Stanfel
Bart Starr
Roger Staubach
Ernie Stautner
Jan Stenerud
Dwight Stephenson
Michael Strahan
Hank Stram
Ken Strong
Joe Stydahar
Lynn Swann
Paul Tagliabue
Fran Tarkenton
Charley Taylor
Jason Taylor
Jim Taylor
Lawrence "LT" Taylor
Derrick Thomas
Emmitt Thomas
Joe Thomas
Thurman Thomas
Zach Thomas
Jim Thorpe
Mick Tingelhoff
Andre Tippett
Y. A. Tittle
LaDainian Tomlinson
George Trafton
Charley Trippi
Emlen Tunnell
Clyde "Bulldog" Turner
Johnny Unitas
Gene Upshaw
Brian Urlacher
Norm Van Brocklin
Steve Van Buren
Dick Vermeil
Doak Walker
Bill Walsh
DeMarcus Ware
Paul Warfield
Kurt Warner
Bob Waterfield
Mike Webster
Roger Wehrli
Arnie Weinmeister
Randy White
Reggie White
Dave Wilcox
Aeneas Williams
Bill Willis
*Patrick Willis
Larry Wilson
Ralph Wilson Jr.
Kellen Winslow
Alex Wojciechowicz
Ron Wolf
Willie Wood
Charles Woodson
Rod Woodson
Rayfield Wright
Ron Yary
Bryant Young
George Young
Steve Young
Jack Youngblood
Gary Zimmerman

All-Time NFL Coaching Victories

(at end of 2023 season; ranked by overall career wins; * = active in 2023)

			Regular Season				Overall			
Coach	**Team**	**Yrs**	**W**	**L**	**T**	**Pct**	**W**	**L**	**T**	**Pct**
Don Shula	Colts, Dolphins	33	328	156	6	.677	347	173	6	.666
Bill Belichick*	Browns, Patriots	29	302	165	0	.647	333	178	0	.652
George Halas	Bears	40	318	148	31	.682	324	151	31	.682
Andy Reid*	Eagles, Chiefs	25	258	144	1	.641	284	160	1	.640
Tom Landry	Cowboys	29	250	162	6	.607	270	178	6	.603
Earl (Curly) Lambeau	Packers, Cardinals, Washington	33	226	132	22	.631	229	134	22	.631
Chuck Noll	Steelers	23	193	148	1	.566	209	156	1	.572
Marty Schottenheimer	Browns, Chiefs, Washington, Chargers	21	200	126	1	.613	205	139	1	.596
Dan Reeves	Broncos, Giants, Falcons	23	190	165	2	.535	201	174	2	.536
Chuck Knox	L.A. Rams, Bills, Seahawks	22	186	147	1	.558	193	158	1	.550
Bill Parcells	Giants, Patriots, Jets, Cowboys	19	172	130	1	.569	183	138	1	.570
Tom Coughlin	Jaguars, Giants	20	170	150	0	.531	182	157	0	.537
Mike Shanahan	L.A. Raiders, Broncos, Washington	20	170	138	0	.552	178	144	0	.553
Jeff Fisher	Houston/Tennessee Oilers, Titans, St. Louis/L.A. Rams	22	173	165	1	.512	178	171	1	.510
Mike Holmgren	Packers, Seahawks	17	161	111	0	.592	174	122	0	.588

Note: Official NFL records do not include All-America Football Conference statistics.

BASEBALL

Playoff Results, 2024

American League

Wild Card Series: Detroit 2, Houston 0; Kansas City 2, Baltimore 0.
Division Series (ALDS): Cleveland 3, Detroit 2; NY Yankees 3, Kansas City 1.
Championship Series (ALCS): NY Yankees 4, Cleveland 1.

National League

Wild Card Series: NY Mets 2, Milwaukee 1; San Diego 2, Atlanta 1.
Division Series (NLDS): NY Mets 3, Philadelphia 1; L.A. Dodgers 3, San Diego 2.
Championship Series (NLCS): L.A. Dodgers 4, NY Mets 2.

World Series 2024: Freeman Leads Dodgers Past Yankees

The Los Angeles Dodgers won their eighth World Series in five games against the New York Yankees on Oct. 30, 2024, at Yankee Stadium in the Bronx, NY. This marked the 12th World Series between the two storied franchises and their first since 1981. Freddie Freeman homered in each of the first four games and tied a record with 12 RBI in a single World Series to earn MVP. Freeman, playing on a severely sprained ankle, didn't homer in Game 5, but his two-run single helped L.A. erase a 5-0 deficit, the biggest comeback in a clinching World Series game.

With the Dodgers down to their last out and the bases loaded in the 10th inning of Game 1 at Dodger Stadium in Los Angeles Oct. 25, 2024, Freeman crushed a home run for the first walkoff grand slam in World Series history. Yankees left fielder Alex Verdugo had tumbled into the stands to grab the second out in the bottom of the 10th inning with two men on. Since Verdugo left the field of play, the runners were entitled to move up a base—setting the stage for the Yankees to intentionally walk Mookie Betts to pitch to Freeman.

The Dodgers won Games 2 and 3 by the same 4-2 score. New York grabbed the lead in Game 4 on Anthony Volpe's grand slam. Gleyber Torres hit a three-run homer as the Yankees scored five in the eighth for an 11-4 victory. Gerrit Cole, who pitched brilliantly in the opener for the Yankees, left with a lead in Game 5, only to see the bullpen surrender it. Cole had nearly pitched out of a bases-loaded, no-out jam in the fifth, but he failed to cover first base on a grounder that could have ended the inning. All five runs that inning were unearned. Two sacrifice flies in the eighth gave L.A. the lead. Walker Buehler, who started and won Game 3, pitched the ninth for the Series-clinching save. Megastar Shohei Ohtani, in the first year of a 10-year contract with the Dodgers after winning two MVP awards with the L.A. Angels, went 2-for-19 in his first World Series after partially dislocating his shoulder in Game 2.

Before the Dodgers could face the New York Yankees in the World Series, they had to beat New York Mets. The Dodgers set a postseason record by drawing 42 walks in a six-game NLCS victory over the Mets. Championship Series MVP Tommy Edman, a midseason acquisition, batted .407 with 11 RBI against the Mets. The Dodgers reeled off a postseason record-tying 33 straight shutout innings: blanking San Diego in the last two NLDS games and the Mets in the NLCS opener.

Game 1

On Oct. 25 at Dodger Stadium, Los Angeles, CA. Attendance: 52,394. Game time: 3:27.

	1	2	3	4	5	6	7	8	9	10	R	H	E
New York Yankees	0	0	0	0	0	2	0	0	0	1	3	10	1
Los Angeles Dodgers	0	0	0	0	1	0	0	1	0	4	6	7	1

Winning pitcher: Blake Treinen
Losing pitcher: Jake Cousins

Game 2

On Oct. 26 at Dodger Stadium, Los Angeles, CA. Attendance: 52,725. Game Time: 2:53.

	1	2	3	4	5	6	7	8	9	R	H	E
New York Yankees	0	0	1	0	0	0	0	0	1	2	4	0
Los Angeles Dodgers	0	1	3	0	0	0	0	0	X	4	8	0

Winning pitcher: Yoshinobu Yamamoto
Losing pitcher: Carlos Rodón
Save: Alex Vesia

Game 3

On Oct. 28 at Yankee Stadium, Bronx, NY. Attendance: 49,368. Game time: 3:25.

	1	2	3	4	5	6	7	8	9	R	H	E
Los Angeles Dodgers	2	0	1	0	0	1	0	0	0	4	5	0
New York Yankees	0	0	0	0	0	0	0	0	2	2	5	1

Winning pitcher: Walker Buehler
Losing pitcher: Clarke Schmidt

Game 4

On Oct. 29 at Yankee Stadium, Bronx, NY. Attendance: 49,354. Game time: 3:16.

	1	2	3	4	5	6	7	8	9	R	H	E
Los Angeles Dodgers	2	0	0	0	2	0	0	0	0	4	6	1
New York Yankees	0	1	4	0	0	1	0	5	X	11	9	0

Winning pitcher: Clay Holmes
Losing pitcher: Daniel Hudson

Game 5

On Oct. 30 at Yankee Stadium, Bronx, NY. Attendance: 49,263. Game time: 3:42.

	1	2	3	4	5	6	7	8	9	R	H	E
Los Angeles Dodgers	0	0	0	0	5	0	0	2	0	7	7	0
New York Yankees	3	1	1	0	0	1	0	0	0	6	8	3

Winning pitcher: Blake Treinen
Losing pitcher: Tommy Kahnle
Save: Walker Buehler

MLB 2024: Ohtani's 50-50 and White Flag Sox Represent Season's Highs and Lows

Elbow surgery prevented L.A. Dodger Shohei Ohtani from taking the mound in 2024, but he certainly earned his paycheck in the first year of a massive contract that lured him away from the L.A. Angels. Ohtani, who played 159 games as designated hitter, became the first 50-50 man in baseball history: 54 home runs (the most in the National League in 2024) and 59 steals. He also led the National League with 130 RBI, among other categories. NY Yankee Aaron Judge led the majors in homers (58) and RBI (144), but like Ohtani he missed the Triple Crown. Kansas City's Bobby Witt Jr. won the American League batting title; Luis Arráez, traded by the Miami Marlins to the San Diego Padres in May, hit .314 and became the first player to win three successive batting crowns with three different teams.

In the second season after the institution of several rule changes to speed up play, the average 2024 nine-inning game time of 2:36 was the fastest in the majors since 1984. Across the league, baserunners stole 3,617 bases—the most since 1915.

MLB traveled well in 2024. The Dodgers and Padres opened the season Mar. 20-21 at Gocheok Sky Dome in Seoul, South Korea. The Houston Astros and Colorado Rockies played in Mexico City Apr. 27-28, and the NY Mets and Philadelphia Phillies hopped across the pond to London June 8-9.

A June 20 game between the San Francisco Giants and St. Louis Cardinals at historic Rickwood Field in Birmingham, AL, was played two days after legend Willie Mays died at 93. The Alabama-born Mays began his pro career at Rickwood, helping the Birmingham Black Barons reach the Negro League World Series as a 17-year-old in 1948. Hall of Famer Reggie Jackson, who played in the minors in Birmingham in 1967, told the game's broadcast viewers about being Black and playing baseball in the segregated South in unsparing detail.

The Arizona Diamondbacks won five more regular-season games in 2024 than their pennant-winning squad did in 2023, but the 2024 D-Backs wound up on the outside looking in when it came to the postseason. Two postponed Mets-Braves games were played in a doubleheader in Atlanta Sept. 30 to decide the final two Wild Card spots. The Mets scored twice in the ninth to win the first game, 8-7, and the Braves won the nightcap, 3-0. The Braves, Diamondbacks, and Mets all went 89-73, but Arizona was shut out of the postseason because Atlanta and New York bested them in head-to-head meetings.

The hapless 2024 Chicago White Sox broke the 62-year-old record for most losses in a season established by the expansion 1962 Mets. Playing their 123rd season in MLB, Chicago's record-setting 121st loss Sept. 27 in Detroit also clinched the Tigers' Wild Card spot. The White Sox finished with just 41 wins—one more than the 1962 Mets, who played two fewer games. The American League won its 10th All-Star Game in 11 tries, 5-3, on July 16 at Globe Life Field in Arlington, TX. Ohtani launched a three-run home run to give the NL the lead, but All-Star MVP Jarren Duran of the Boston Red Sox broke a tie with a two-run shot.

National League Final Standings, 2024

(* = wild card)

Eastern Division

Team	W	L	PCT	GB	Home	Road	vs. East	vs. Central	vs. West	vs. AL
Philadelphia	95	67	.586	–	54-27	41-40	29-23	18-14	22-10	26-20
Atlanta*	89	73	.549	6	46-35	43-38	28-24	13-17	17-17	31-15
NY Mets*	89	73	.549	6	46-35	43-38	30-22	18-14	17-15	24-22
Washington	71	91	.438	24	38-43	33-48	25-27	15-18	10-21	21-25
Miami	62	100	.383	33	30-51	32-49	18-34	12-21	13-18	19-27

Central Division

Team	W	L	PCT	GB	Home	Road	vs. East	vs. Central	vs. West	vs. AL
Milwaukee	93	69	.574	–	47-34	46-35	15-15	32-20	15-19	31-15
Chicago Cubs	83	79	.512	10	44-37	39-42	17-16	23-29	16-15	27-19
St. Louis	83	79	.512	10	44-37	39-42	15-16	26-26	18-15	24-22
Cincinnati	77	85	.475	16	39-42	38-43	17-15	24-28	15-17	21-25
Pittsburgh	76	86	.469	17	39-42	37-44	20-14	25-27	10-20	21-25

Western Division

Team	W	L	PCT	GB	Home	Road	vs. East	vs. Central	vs. West	vs. AL
L.A. Dodgers	98	64	.605	–	52-29	46-35	19-12	18-15	31-21	30-16
San Diego*	93	69	.574	5	45-36	48-33	17-15	22-10	27-25	27-19
Arizona	89	73	.549	9	44-37	45-36	18-15	19-12	28-24	24-22
San Francisco	80	82	.494	18	42-39	38-43	16-17	15-16	26-26	23-23
Colorado	61	101	.377	37	37-44	24-57	11-20	12-21	18-34	20-26

Note: Atlanta and NY Mets received Wild Cards instead of Arizona because Braves and Mets had better head-to-head records against Diamondbacks.

American League Final Standings, 2024

(* = wild card)

Eastern Division

Team	W	L	PCT	GB	Home	Road	vs. East	vs. Central	vs. West	vs. NL
NY Yankees	94	68	.580	–	44-37	50-31	26-26	24-7	21-12	23-23
Baltimore*	91	71	.562	3	44-37	47-34	32-20	21-11	18-14	20-26
Boston	81	81	.500	13	38-43	43-38	25-27	16-17	19-12	21-25
Tampa Bay	80	82	.494	14	42-39	38-43	26-26	14-18	14-18	26-20
Toronto	74	88	.457	20	39-42	35-46	21-31	13-19	20-12	20-26

Central Division

Team	W	L	PCT	GB	Home	Road	vs. East	vs. Central	vs. West	vs. NL
Cleveland	92	69	.571	–	50-30	42-39	18-15	30-22	20-10	24-22
Kansas City*	86	76	.531	6.5	45-36	41-40	14-18	33-19	16-16	23-23
Detroit*	86	76	.531	6.5	43-38	43-38	20-12	28-24	16-16	22-24
Minnesota	82	80	.506	10.5	43-38	39-42	10-21	29-23	25-8	18-28
Chicago White Sox	41	121	.253	51.5	23-58	18-63	10-22	10-42	10-22	11-35

Western Division

Team	W	L	PCT	GB	Home	Road	vs. East	vs. Central	vs. West	vs. NL
Houston	88	73	.547	–	46-35	42-38	19-14	18-12	29-23	22-24
Seattle	85	77	.525	3.5	49-32	36-45	13-19	14-18	32-20	26-20
Texas	78	84	.481	10.5	44-37	34-47	14-17	20-13	25-27	19-27
Oakland	69	93	.426	19.5	38-43	31-50	12-20	10-22	23-29	24-22
L.A. Angels	63	99	.389	25.5	32-49	31-50	10-22	10-22	21-31	22-44

National League Team Statistics, 2024

Team Batting

Team	AVG	AB	R	H	HR	RBI
San Diego Padres	.263	5,526	760	1,456	190	726
Arizona Diamondbacks	.263	5,522	886	1,452	211	845
L.A. Dodgers	.258	5,522	842	1,423	233	815
Philadelphia Phillies	.257	5,534	784	1,423	198	750
Milwaukee Brewers	.248	5,472	777	1,359	177	742
St. Louis Cardinals	.248	5,507	672	1,363	165	639
NY Mets	.246	5,510	768	1,357	207	735
Miami Marlins	.244	5,522	637	1,347	150	611
Atlanta Braves	.243	5,481	704	1,333	213	674
Washington Nationals	.243	5,374	660	1,306	135	621
Chicago Cubs	.242	5,441	736	1,318	170	696
Colorado Rockies	.242	5,454	682	1,319	179	655
San Francisco Giants	.239	5,460	693	1,303	177	661
Pittsburgh Pirates	.234	5,477	665	1,283	160	643
Cincinnati Reds	.231	5,325	699	1,230	174	663

Team Pitching

Team	ERA	IP	H	BB	K	SV
Atlanta Braves	3.49	1,443.1	1,277	449	1,553	40
Milwaukee Brewers	3.65	1,446.0	1,289	494	1,373	53
Chicago Cubs	3.78	1,432.1	1,302	485	1,348	38
Philadelphia Phillies	3.85	1,442.2	1,339	444	1,433	37
San Diego Padres	3.86	1,439.1	1,296	462	1,453	44
L.A. Dodgers	3.90	1,445.2	1,273	501	1,390	50
NY Mets	3.96	1,442.1	1,232	586	1,455	39
St. Louis Cardinals	4.04	1,444.0	1,363	454	1,308	55
Cincinnati Reds	4.09	1,428.0	1,302	487	1,370	36
San Francisco Giants	4.10	1,433.2	1,339	526	1,436	36
Pittsburgh Pirates	4.15	1,438.2	1,369	515	1,356	43
Washington Nationals	4.30	1,434.0	1,429	473	1,314	40
Arizona Diamondbacks	4.62	1,443.1	1,468	481	1,313	38
Miami Marlins	4.73	1,437.1	1,431	556	1,317	33
Colorado Rockies	5.47	1,426.2	1,604	563	1,118	37

American League Team Statistics, 2024

Team Batting

Team	AVG	AB	R	H	HR	RBI
Houston Astros	.262	5,530	740	1,448	190	701
Boston Red Sox	.252	5,577	751	1,404	194	724
Baltimore Orioles	.250	5,567	786	1,391	235	759
NY Yankees	.248	5,450	815	1,352	237	782
Kansas City Royals	.248	5,421	735	1,343	170	711
Minnesota Twins	.246	5,490	742	1,352	183	702
Toronto Blue Jays	.241	5,410	671	1,306	156	640
Texas Rangers	.238	5,472	683	1,302	176	652
Cleveland Guardians	.238	5,310	708	1,263	185	670
Detroit Tigers	.234	5,442	682	1,273	162	656
Oakland Athletics	.233	5,432	643	1,267	196	619
Tampa Bay Rays	.230	5,389	604	1,241	147	564
L.A. Angels	.229	5,357	635	1,227	165	596
Seattle Mariners	.224	5,330	676	1,195	185	642
Chicago White Sox	.221	5,383	507	1,187	133	485

Team Pitching

Team	ERA	IP	H	BB	K	SV
Seattle Mariners	3.49	1,433.0	1,174	369	1,416	34
Cleveland Guardians	3.61	1,428.0	1,224	492	1,410	53
Detroit Tigers	3.61	1,447.0	1,265	416	1,354	45
Houston Astros	3.74	1,432.0	1,238	544	1,479	43
NY Yankees	3.74	1,452.2	1,272	533	1,457	45
Kansas City Royals	3.76	1,428.0	1,303	472	1,339	41
Tampa Bay Rays	3.77	1,440.2	1,286	445	1,406	51
Baltimore Orioles	3.94	1,442.0	1,303	481	1,380	46
Boston Red Sox	4.04	1,452.2	1,363	461	1,353	40
Minnesota Twins	4.26	1,440.1	1,333	433	1,500	43
Toronto Blue Jays	4.29	1,427.1	1,316	503	1,314	36
Texas Rangers	4.35	1,427.2	1,323	530	1,371	38
Oakland Athletics	4.37	1,436.2	1,385	530	1,263	35
L.A. Angels	4.56	1,431.0	1,328	601	1,252	35
Chicago White Sox	4.67	1,420.0	1,397	643	1,366	21

Major League Leaders, 2024

National League Leaders, 2024

Batting Average: Luis Arráez, Miami-San Diego, .314; Shohei Ohtani, L.A. Dodgers, .310; Marcell Ozuna, Atlanta, .302; Trea Turner, Philadelphia, .295; Jackson Merrill, San Diego, .292; Ketel Marte, Arizona, .292; Mookie Betts, L.A. Dodgers, .289; Bryce Harper, Philadelphia, .285; Seiya Suzuki, Chicago Cubs, .283; Freddie Freeman, L.A. Dodgers, .282; Luis García, Washington, .282.

On-Base Percentage: Shohei Ohtani, L.A. Dodgers, .390; Jurickson Profar, San Diego, .380; Marcell Ozuna, Atlanta, .378; Freddie Freeman, L.A. Dodgers, .378; Bryce Harper, Philadelphia, .373; Ketel Marte, Arizona, .372; Mookie Betts, L.A. Dodgers, .372; Seiya Suzuki, Chicago Cubs, .366; Kyle Schwarber, Philadelphia, .366; William Contreras, Milwaukee, .365.

Slugging: Shohei Ohtani, L.A. Dodgers, .646; Ketel Marte, Arizona, .560; Marcell Ozuna, Atlanta, .546; Bryce Harper, Philadelphia, .525; Teoscar Hernández, L.A. Dodgers, .501; Francisco Lindor, NY Mets, .500; Jackson Merrill, San Diego, .500; Mookie Betts, L.A. Dodgers, .491; Kyle Schwarber, Philadelphia, .485; Seiya Suzuki, Chicago Cubs, .482.

Runs Scored: Shohei Ohtani, L.A. Dodgers, 134; Corbin Carroll, Arizona, 121; Kyle Schwarber, Philadelphia, 110; Francisco Lindor, NY Mets, 107; Elly De La Cruz, Cincinnati, 105; William Contreras, Milwaukee, 99; Matt Chapman, San Francisco, 98; Marcell Ozuna, Atlanta, 96; Jurickson Profar, San Diego, 94; Willy Adames, Milwaukee, 93; Ketel Marte, Arizona, 93.

Runs Batted In: Shohei Ohtani, L.A. Dodgers, 130; Willy Adames, Milwaukee, 112; Manny Machado, San Diego, 105; Marcell Ozuna, Atlanta, 104; Kyle Schwarber, Philadelphia, 104; Eugenio Suárez, Arizona, 101; Teoscar Hernández, L.A. Dodgers, 99; Matt Olson, Atlanta, 98; Alec Bohm, Philadelphia, 97; Ketel Marte, Arizona, 95.

Hits: Luis Arráez, Miami-San Diego, 200; Shohei Ohtani, L.A. Dodgers, 197; Marcell Ozuna, Atlanta, 183; Ezequiel Tovar, Colorado, 176; Bryan Reynolds, Pittsburgh, 171; Francisco Lindor, NY Mets, 169; William Contreras, Milwaukee, 167; Brendan Donovan, St. Louis, 163; Manny Machado, San Diego, 163; Jackson Merrill, San Diego, 162.

Doubles: Ezequiel Tovar, Colorado, 45; Alec Bohm, Philadelphia, 44; Bryce Harper, Philadelphia, 42; Matt Chapman, San Francisco, 39; Francisco Lindor, NY Mets, 39; Shohei Ohtani, L.A. Dodgers, 38; William Contreras, Milwaukee, 37; Matt Olson, Atlanta, 37; Elly De La Cruz, Cincinnati, 36; Freddie Freeman, L.A. Dodgers, 35; Nico Hoerner, Chicago Cubs, 35.

Triples: Corbin Carroll, Arizona, 14; Elly De La Cruz, Cincinnati, 10; Mike Yastrzemski, San Francisco, 9; Jake McCarthy, Arizona, 7; Shohei Ohtani, L.A. Dodgers, 7; C.J. Abrams, Washington, 6; Pete Crow-Armstrong, Chicago Cubs, 6; Jackson Merrill, San Diego, 6; Joey Ortiz, Milwaukee, 6; Seiya Suzuki, Chicago Cubs, 6.

Home Runs: Shohei Ohtani, L.A. Dodgers, 54; Marcell Ozuna, Atlanta, 39; Kyle Schwarber, Philadelphia, 38; Ketel Marte, Arizona, 36; Pete Alonso, NY Mets, 34; Teoscar Hernández, L.A. Dodgers, 33; Francisco Lindor, NY Mets, 33; Willy Adames, Milwaukee, 32; Bryce Harper, Philadelphia, 30; Eugenio Suárez, Arizona, 30.

Stolen Bases: Elly De La Cruz, Cincinnati, 67; Shohei Ohtani, L.A. Dodgers, 59; Brice Turang, Milwaukee, 50; Corbin Carroll, Arizona, 35; Jacob Young, Washington, 33; Bryson Stott, Philadelphia, 32; C.J. Abrams, Washington, 31; Xavier Edwards, Miami, 31; Nico Hoerner, Chicago Cubs, 31; Brenton Doyle, Colorado, 30.

Pitching Wins: Chris Sale, Atlanta, 18; Zack Wheeler, Philadelphia, 16; Shota Imanaga, Chicago Cubs, 15; Dylan Cease, San Diego, 14; Zac Gallen, Arizona, 14; Aaron Nola, Philadelphia, 14; Sonny Gray, St. Louis, 13; Michael King, San Diego, 13; Logan Webb, San Francisco, 13.

Earned Run Average: Chris Sale, Atlanta, 2.38; Zack Wheeler, Philadelphia, 2.57; Shota Imanaga, Chicago Cubs, 2.91; Michael King, San Diego, 2.95; Max Fried, Atlanta, 3.25; Jameson Taillon, Chicago Cubs, 3.27; Cristopher Sánchez, Philadelphia, 3.32; Dylan Cease, San Diego, 3.47; Sean Manaea, NY Mets, 3.47; Logan Webb, San Francisco, 3.47.

Strikeouts: Chris Sale, Atlanta, 225; Dylan Cease, San Diego, 224; Zack Wheeler, Philadelphia, 224; Sonny Gray, St. Louis, 203; Michael King, San Diego, 201; Freddy Peralta, Milwaukee, 200; Aaron Nola, Philadelphia, 197; Brandon Pfaadt, Arizona, 185; Sean Manaea, NY Mets, 184; MacKenzie Gore, Washington, 181.

Saves: Ryan Helsley, St. Louis, 49; Kyle Finnegan, Washington, 38; Robert Suárez, San Diego, 36; Raisel Iglesias, Atlanta, 34; Alexis Díaz, Cincinnati, 28; David Bednar, Pittsburgh, 23; Camilo Doval, San Francisco, 23; Tanner Scott, Miami-San Diego, 22; Trevor Megill, Milwaukee, 21; Edwin Díaz, NY Mets, 20.

A Note on Historical Baseball Statistics

Major League Baseball announced Dec. 16, 2020, that it was integrating its official record books with the statistics of the Negro Leagues, including more than 3,400 players' performances, from 1920 to 1948. The all-time records reflect what is listed by mlb.com as of publication.

American League Leaders, 2024

Batting Average: Bobby Witt Jr., Kansas City, .332; Vladimir Guerrero Jr., Toronto, .323; Aaron Judge, NY Yankees, .322; Yordan Alvarez, Houston, .308; Yainer Diaz, Houston, .299; Jose Altuve, Houston, .295; Brent Rooker, Oakland, .293; Steven Kwan, Cleveland, .292; Juan Soto, NY Yankees, .288; Jarren Duran, Boston, .285.

On-Base Percentage: Aaron Judge, NY Yankees, .458; Juan Soto, NY Yankees, .419; Vladimir Guerrero Jr., Toronto, .396; Yordan Alvarez, Houston, .392; Bobby Witt Jr., Kansas City, .389; Steven Kwan, Cleveland, .368; Brent Rooker, Oakland, .365; Gunnar Henderson, Baltimore, .364; Nathaniel Lowe, Texas, .361; Rafael Devers, Boston, .354; Justin Turner, Toronto-Seattle, .354.

Slugging: Aaron Judge, NY Yankees, .701; Bobby Witt Jr., Kansas City, .588; Juan Soto, NY Yankees, .569; Yordan Alvarez, Houston, .567; Brent Rooker, Oakland, .562; Vladimir Guerrero Jr., Toronto, .544; José Ramírez, Cleveland, .537; Gunnar Henderson, Baltimore, .529; Rafael Devers, Boston, .516; Corey Seager, Texas, .512.

Runs Scored: Juan Soto, NY Yankees, 128; Bobby Witt Jr., Kansas City, 125; Aaron Judge, NY Yankees, 122; Gunnar Henderson, Baltimore, 118; José Ramírez, Cleveland, 114; Jarren Duran, Boston, 111; Marcus Semien, Texas, 101; Vladimir Guerrero Jr., Toronto, 98; Jose Altuve, Houston, 94; Anthony Santander, Baltimore, 91.

Runs Batted In: Aaron Judge, NY Yankees, 144; José Ramírez, Cleveland, 118; Brent Rooker, Oakland, 112; Juan Soto, NY Yankees, 109; Bobby Witt Jr., Kansas City, 109; Josh Naylor, Cleveland, 108; Salvador Perez, Kansas City, 104; Vladimir Guerrero Jr., Toronto, 103; Anthony Santander, Baltimore, 102; Cal Raleigh, Seattle, 100.

Hits: Bobby Witt Jr., Kansas City, 211; Vladimir Guerrero Jr., Toronto, 199; Jarren Duran, Boston, 191; Jose Altuve, Houston, 185; Aaron Judge, NY Yankees, 180; Gunnar Henderson, Baltimore, 177; Yainer Diaz, Houston, 175; José Ramírez, Cleveland, 173; Yordan Alvarez, Houston, 170; Juan Soto, NY Yankees, 166.

Doubles: Jarren Duran, Boston, 48; Bobby Witt Jr., Kansas City, 45; Vladimir Guerrero Jr., Toronto, 44; J.J. Bleday, Oakland, 43; José Ramírez, 39; Aaron Judge, NY Yankees, 36; Yordan Alvarez, Houston, 34; Rafael Devers, Boston, 34; Zach Neto, L.A. Angels, 34; Wilyer Abreu, Boston, 33; Randy Arozarema, Tampa Bay-Seattle, 33.

Triples: Jarren Duran, Boston, 14; Bobby Witt Jr., Kansas City, 11; Kyle Isbel, Kansas City, 8; Gunnar Henderson, Baltimore, 7; Daulton Varsho, Toronto, 7; Anthony Volpe, NY Yankees, 7; Riley Greene, Detroit, 6; Parker Meadows, Detroit, 6; Wenceel Pérez, Detroit, 6.

Home Runs: Aaron Judge, NY Yankees, 58; Anthony Santander, Baltimore, 44; Juan Soto, NY Yankees, 41; José Ramírez, Cleveland, 39; Brent Rooker, Oakland, 39; Gunnar Henderson, Baltimore, 37; Yordan Alvarez, Houston, 35; Cal Raleigh, Seattle, 34; Bobby Witt Jr., Kansas City, 32; Josh Naylor, Cleveland, 31; Tyler O'Neill, Boston, 31.

Stolen Bases: José Caballero, Tampa Bay, 44; José Ramírez, Cleveland, 41; Maikel Garcia, Kansas City, 37; Jarren Duran, Boston, 34; David Hamilton, Boston, 33; Dylan Moore, Seattle, 32; Cedric Mullins, Baltimore, 32; Dairon Blanco, Kansas City, 31; Bobby Witt Jr., Kansas City, 31.

Pitching Wins: Tarik Skubal, Detroit, 18; José Berríos, Toronto, 16; Seth Lugo, Kansas City, 16; Carlos Rodón, NY Yankees, 16; Corbin Burnes, Baltimore, 15; Luis Gil, NY Yankees, 15; Pablo López, Minnesota, 15; Framber Valdez, Houston, 15; Brayan Bello, Boston, 14; Kevin Gausman, Toronto, 14; George Kirby, Seattle, 14.

Earned Run Average: Tarik Skubal, Detroit, 2.39; Ronel Blanco, Houston, 2.80; Framber Valdez, Houston, 2.91; Corbin Burnes, Baltimore, 2.92; Bryce Miller, Seattle, 2.94; Seth Lugo, Kansas City, 3.00; Tanner Houck, Boston, 3.12; Cole Ragans, Kansas City, 3.14; Logan Gilbert, Seattle, 3.23; Michael Wacha, Kansas City, 3.35.

Strikeouts: Tarik Skubal, Detroit, 228; Cole Ragans, Kansas City, 223; Logan Gilbert, Seattle, 220; Garrett Crochet, Chicago White Sox, 209; Yusei Kikuchi, Houston, 206; Pablo López, Minnesota, 198; Carlos Rodón, NY Yankees, 195; Bailey Ober, Minnesota, 191; Tanner Bibee, Cleveland, 187; Corbin Burnes, Baltimore, 181; Seth Lugo, Kansas City, 181.

Saves: Emmanuel Clase, Cleveland, 47; Josh Hader, Houston, 34; Kirby Yates, Texas, 33; Clay Holmes, NY Yankees, 30; Jason Foley, Detroit, 28; Mason Miller, Oakland, 28; Kenley Jansen, Boston, 27; Jhoan Duran, Minnesota, 23; Pete Fairbanks, Tampa Bay, 23; Craig Kimbrel, Baltimore, 23.

All-Time Major League Single-Season Leaders

Source: www.mlb.com; * = Active in 2024 season; records for "modern" era beginning in 1901.

Home Runs

Barry Bonds (2001)	73
Mark McGwire (1998)	70
Sammy Sosa (1998)	66
Mark McGwire (1999)	65
Sammy Sosa (2001)	64
Sammy Sosa (1999)	63
Aaron Judge* (2022)	62
Roger Maris (1961)	61
Babe Ruth (1927)	60

Runs Scored

Babe Ruth (1921)	177
Lou Gehrig (1936)	167
Lou Gehrig (1931)	163
Babe Ruth (1928)	163
Chuck Klein (1930)	158
Babe Ruth (1920, 1927)	158
Rogers Hornsby (1929)	156
Kiki Cuyler (1930)	155

Hits

Ichiro Suzuki (2004)	262
George Sisler (1920)	257
Lefty O'Doul (1929)	254
Bill Terry (1930)	254
Al Simmons (1925)	253
Rogers Hornsby (1922)	250
Chuck Klein (1930)	250
Ty Cobb (1911)	248

Runs Batted In

Hack Wilson (1930)	191
Lou Gehrig (1931)	184
Hank Greenberg (1937)	183
Jimmie Foxx (1938)	175
Lou Gehrig (1927)	175
Lou Gehrig (1930)	174
Babe Ruth (1921)	171
Hank Greenburg (1935)	170
Chuck Klein (1930)	170

Batting Average

Josh Gibson (1943)	.466
Charlie Smith (1929)	.451
Oscar Charleston (1921)	.434
Charlie Blackwell (1921)	.432
Oscar Charleston (1925)	.427
Mule Suttles (1926)	.425
Rogers Hornsby (1924)	.424
Biz Mackey (1923)	.423

Stolen Bases

Rickey Henderson (1982)	130
Lou Brock (1974)	118
Vince Coleman (1985)	110
Vince Coleman (1987)	109
Rickey Henderson (1983)	108
Vince Coleman (1986)	107
Maury Wills (1962)	104
Rickey Henderson (1980)	100

Walks (Batter)

Barry Bonds (2004)	232
Barry Bonds (2002)	198
Barry Bonds (2001)	177
Babe Ruth (1923)	170
Mark McGwire (1998)	162
Ted Williams (1947, 1949)	162
Ted Williams (1946)	156

Strikeouts (Batter)

Mark Reynolds (2009)	223
Adam Dunn (2012)	222
Chris Davis (2016)	219
Elly De La Cruz* (2024)	218
Yoán Moncada* (2018)	217
Kyle Schwarber* (2023)	215
Eugenio Suárez* (2023)	214
Joey Gallo* (2021)	213
Chris Carter (2013)	212
Teoscar Hernández* (2023)	211
Mark Reynolds (2010)	211
Giancarlo Stanton* (2018)	211

Earned Run Average

Dutch Leonard (1914)	0.96
Satchel Paige (1944)	1.01
Mordecai "Three Finger" Brown (1906)	1.04
Bob Gibson (1968)	1.12
Christy Mathewson (1909)	1.14
Walter Johnson (1913)	1.14
Jack Pfiester (1907)	1.15
Addie Joss (1908)	1.16

Wins (Pitcher)

Jack Chesbro (1904)	41
Ed Walsh (1908)	40
Christy Mathewson (1908)	37
Walter Johnson (1913)	36
Joe McGinnity (1904)	35
Smoky Joe Wood (1912)	34
Grover Alexander (1916)	33
Walter Johnson (1912)	33
Cristy Mathewson (1904)	33
Cy Young (1901)	33

Strikeouts (Pitcher)

Nolan Ryan (1973)	383
Sandy Koufax (1965)	382
Randy Johnson (2001)	372
Nolan Ryan (1974)	367
Randy Johnson (1999)	364
Rube Waddell (1904)	349
Bob Feller (1946)	348
Randy Johnson (2000)	347

Saves

Francisco Rodríguez (2008)	62
Edwin Díaz* (2018)	57
Bobby Thigpen (1990)	57
Eric Gagne (2003)	55
John Smoltz (2002)	55
Trevor Hoffman (1998)	53
Randy Myers (1993)	53
Mariano Rivera (2004)	53

All-Time Major League Leaders

Source: www.mlb.com; * = Active in 2024 season; career records for players in "modern" era beginning in 1901 may include statistics from preceding years.

Games

Pete Rose	3,562
Carl Yastrzemski	3,308
Hank Aaron	3,298
Rickey Henderson	3,081
Albert Pujols	3,080
Ty Cobb	3,035
Eddie Murray	3,026
Stan Musial	3,026
Willie Mays	3,005
Cal Ripken Jr.	3,001

At Bats

Pete Rose	14,053
Hank Aaron	12,364
Carl Yastrzemski	11,988
Cal Ripken Jr.	11,551
Ty Cobb	11,429
Albert Pujols	11,421
Eddie Murray	11,336
Derek Jeter	11,195
Adrián Beltré	11,068
Robin Yount	11,008

Runs Batted In

Hank Aaron	2,297
Albert Pujols	2,218
Babe Ruth	2,213
Alex Rodriguez	2,086
Barry Bonds	1,996
Lou Gehrig	1,995
Stan Musial	1,951
Ty Cobb	1,938
Jimmie Foxx	1,922
Eddie Murray	1,917

Runs

Rickey Henderson	2,295
Ty Cobb	2,246
Barry Bonds	2,227
Hank Aaron	2,174
Babe Ruth	2,174
Pete Rose	2,165
Willie Mays	2,068
Alex Rodriguez	2,021
Stan Musial	1,949
Derek Jeter	1,923

Stolen Bases

Rickey Henderson	1,406
Lou Brock	938
Billy Hamilton	912
Ty Cobb	892
Tim Raines	808
Vince Coleman	752
Eddie Collins	745
Arlie Latham	739
Max Carey	738
Honus Wagner	722

Triples

Sam Crawford	309
Ty Cobb	297
Honus Wagner	252
Jake Beckley	243
Roger Connor	233
Tris Speaker	222
Fred Clarke	220
Dan Brouthers	205
Joe Kelley	194
Paul Waner	191

Batting Average

Josh Gibson	.372
Ty Cobb	.367
Oscar Charleston	.363
Rogers Hornsby	.358
Jud Wilson	.350
Turkey Stearnes	.348
Ed Delahanty	.346
Buck Leonard	.345
Tris Speaker	.345
Ted Williams	.344
Billy Hamilton	.344

Walks (Batter)

Barry Bonds	2,558
Rickey Henderson	2,190
Babe Ruth	2,062
Ted Williams	2,019
Joe Morgan	1,865
Carl Yastrzemski	1,845
Jim Thome	1,747
Mickey Mantle	1,733
Mel Ott	1,708
Frank Thomas	1,667

Strikeouts (Pitcher)

Player	SO
Nolan Ryan	5,714
Randy Johnson	4,875
Roger Clemens	4,672
Steve Carlton	4,136
Bert Blyleven	3,701
Tom Seaver	3,640
Don Sutton	3,574
Gaylord Perry	3,534
Walter Johnson	3,508
Justin Verlander*	3,416

Saves

Player	Saves
Mariano Rivera	652
Trevor Hoffman	601
Lee Smith	478
Kenley Jansen*	447
Craig Kimbrel*	440
Francisco Rodríguez	437
John Franco	424
Billy Wagner	422
Dennis Eckersley	390
Joe Nathan	377

Shutouts

Walter Johnson	110
Grover Alexander	90
Christy Mathewson	79
Cy Young	76
Eddie Plank	69
Warren Spahn	63
Nolan Ryan	61
Tom Seaver	61
Bert Blyleven	60
Don Sutton	58

Losses

Cy Young	316
Nolan Ryan	292
Walter Johnson	279
Phil Niekro	274
Gaylord Perry	265
Don Sutton	256
Jack Powell	254
Eppa Rixey	251
Bert Blyleven	250
Robin Roberts	245
Warren Spahn	245

All-Time Home Run Leaders

Source: www.mlb.com; * = Active in 2024 season.

Player	HR
Barry Bonds	762
Hank Aaron	755
Babe Ruth	714
Albert Pujols	703
Alex Rodriguez	696
Willie Mays	660
Ken Griffey Jr.	630
Jim Thome	612
Sammy Sosa	609
Frank Robinson	586
Mark McGwire	583
Harmon Killebrew	573
Rafael Palmeiro	569
Reggie Jackson	563
Manny Ramirez	555
Mike Schmidt	548
David Ortiz	541
Mickey Mantle	536
Jimmie Foxx	534
Willie McCovey	521
Frank Thomas	521
Ted Williams	521
Ernie Banks	512
Eddie Mathews	512
Miguel Cabrera	511
Mel Ott	511
Gary Sheffield	509
Eddie Murray	504
Lou Gehrig	493
Fred McGriff	493
Adrián Beltré	477
Stan Musial	475
Willie Stargell	475
Carlos Delgado	473
Chipper Jones	468
Dave Winfield	465
Nelson Cruz	464
Jose Canseco	462
Adam Dunn	462
Carl Yastrzemski	452
Jeff Bagwell	449
Vladimir Guerrero	449
Dave Kingman	442
Jason Giambi	440
Paul Konerko	439
Andre Dawson	438
Carlos Beltrán	435
Juan Gonzalez	434
Andruw Jones	434
Cal Ripken Jr.	431
Giancarlo Stanton*	429
Mike Piazza	427
Billy Williams	426
Edwin Encarnación	424
Darrell Evans	414
Alfonso Soriano	412
Mark Teixeira	409

Players With 3,000 Major League Hits

Source: www.mlb.com; * = Active in 2024 season.

Player	Hits
Pete Rose	4,256
Ty Cobb	4,191
Hank Aaron	3,771
Stan Musial	3,630
Tris Speaker	3,515
Derek Jeter	3,465
Honus Wagner	3,430
Carl Yastrzemski	3,419
Albert Pujols	3,384
Paul Molitor	3,319
Eddie Collins	3,314
Willie Mays	3,293
Eddie Murray	3,255
Nap Lajoie	3,252
Cal Ripken Jr.	3,184
Miguel Cabrera	3,174
Adrián Beltré	3,166
George Brett	3,154
Paul Waner	3,152
Robin Yount	3,142
Tony Gwynn	3,141
Alex Rodriguez	3,115
Dave Winfield	3,110
Ichiro Suzuki	3,089
Craig Biggio	3,060
Rickey Henderson	3,055
Rod Carew	3,053
Lou Brock	3,023
Rafael Palmeiro	3,020
Cap Anson	3,011
Wade Boggs	3,010
Al Kaline	3,007
Roberto Clemente	3,000

50 Home Run Club

Only Barry Bonds and Mark McGwire hit 70 or more home runs in a season. Six players—including Babe Ruth and Roger Maris—hit 60 or more, a feat Sammy Sosa accomplished for the third time in 2001.

HR	Player, team	Year
73	Barry Bonds, San Francisco Giants	2001
70	Mark McGwire, St. Louis Cardinals	1998
66	Sammy Sosa, Chicago Cubs	1998
65	Mark McGwire, St. Louis Cardinals	1999
64	Sammy Sosa, Chicago Cubs	2001
63	Sammy Sosa, Chicago Cubs	1999
62	Aaron Judge, NY Yankees	2022
61	Roger Maris, NY Yankees	1961
60	Babe Ruth, NY Yankees	1927
59	Babe Ruth, NY Yankees	1921
59	Giancarlo Stanton, Miami Marlins	2017
58	Jimmie Foxx, Philadelphia Athletics	1932
58	Hank Greenberg, Detroit Tigers	1938
58	Ryan Howard, Philadelphia Phillies	2006
58	Aaron Judge, NY Yankees	2024
58	Mark McGwire, Oakland A's/St. Louis Cardinals	1997
57	Luis Gonzalez, Arizona Diamondbacks	2001
57	Alex Rodriguez, Texas Rangers	2002
56	Ken Griffey Jr., Seattle Mariners	1997
56	Ken Griffey Jr., Seattle Mariners	1998
56	Hack Wilson, Chicago Cubs	1930
54	José Bautista, Toronto Blue Jays	2010
54	Ralph Kiner, Pittsburgh Pirates	1949
54	Mickey Mantle, NY Yankees	1961
54	Shohei Ohtani, L.A. Dodgers	2024
54	Matt Olson, Atlanta Braves	2023
54	David Ortiz, Boston Red Sox	2006
54	Alex Rodriguez, NY Yankees	2007
54	Babe Ruth, NY Yankees	1920
54	Babe Ruth, NY Yankees	1928
53	Pete Alonso, NY Mets	2019
53	Chris Davis, Baltimore Orioles	2013
52	George Foster, Cincinnati Reds	1977
52	Aaron Judge, NY Yankees	2017
52	Mickey Mantle, NY Yankees	1956
52	Willie Mays, San Francisco Giants	1965
52	Mark McGwire, Oakland A's	1996
52	Alex Rodriguez, Texas Rangers	2001
52	Jim Thome, Cleveland Indians	2002
51	Cecil Fielder, Detroit Tigers	1990
51	Andruw Jones, Atlanta Braves	2005
51	Ralph Kiner, Pittsburgh Pirates	1947
51	Willie Mays, NY Giants	1955
51	Johnny Mize, NY Giants	1947
50	Brady Anderson, Baltimore Orioles	1996
50	Albert Belle, Cleveland Indians	1995
50	Prince Fielder, Milwaukee Brewers	2007
50	Jimmie Foxx, Boston Red Sox	1938
50	Sammy Sosa, Chicago Cubs	2000
50	Greg Vaughn, San Diego Padres	1998

Pitchers With 300 Major League Wins

Source: www.mlb.com

Pitcher	Wins
Cy Young	511
Walter Johnson	417
Grover Alexander	373
Christy Mathewson	373
Warren Spahn	363
James "Pud" Galvin	361
Charles "Kid" Nichols	361
Greg Maddux	355
Roger Clemens	354
Tim Keefe	342
Steve Carlton	329
John Clarkson	328
Eddie Plank	326
Nolan Ryan	324
Don Sutton	324
Phil Niekro	318
Gaylord Perry	314
Tom Seaver	311
Charley Radbourn	309
Mickey Welch	307
Tom Glavine	305
Randy Johnson	303
Robert "Lefty" Grove	300
Early "Gus" Wynn	300

Official Major League Perfect Games Since 1901

Date	Pitcher	Teams
5/5/1904	Cy Young	Boston 3 vs. Phil. 0 (AL)
10/2/1908	Addie Joss	Clev. 1 vs. Chicago 0 (AL)
4/30/1922	Charlie Robertson	Chicago 2 vs. Detroit 0 (AL)
10/8/1956	Don Larsen	NY 2 (AL) vs. Brooklyn 0* (NL)
6/21/1964	Jim Bunning	Phil. 6 vs. NY 0 (NL)
9/9/1965	Sandy Koufax	L.A. 1 vs. Chicago 0 (NL)
5/8/1968	Jim "Catfish" Hunter	Oakland 4 vs. Minn. 0 (AL)
5/15/1981	Len Barker	Clev. 3 vs. Toronto 0 (AL)
9/30/1984	Mike Witt	California 1 vs. Texas 0 (AL)
9/16/1988	Tom Browning	Cincinnati 1 vs. L.A. 0 (NL)
7/28/1991	Dennis Martinez	Montréal 2 vs. L.A. 0 (NL)
7/28/1994	Kenny Rogers	Texas 4 vs. California 0 (AL)
5/17/1998	David Wells	NY 4 vs. Minn. 0 (AL)
7/18/1999	David Cone	NY 6 vs. Montréal 0 (AL)
5/18/2004	Randy Johnson	Arizona 2 vs. Atlanta 0 (NL)
7/23/2009	Mark Buehrle	Chicago 5 vs. Tampa Bay 0 (AL)
5/9/2010	Dallas Braden	Oakland 4 vs. Tampa Bay 0 (AL)
5/29/2010	Roy Halladay	Phil. 1 vs. Florida 0 (NL)
4/21/2012	Philip Humber	Chicago 4 vs. Seattle 0 (AL)
6/13/2012	Matt Cain	S.F. 10 vs. Houston 0 (NL)
8/15/2012	Felix Hernandez	Seattle 1 vs. Tampa Bay 0 (AL)
6/28/2023	Domingo Germán	NY 11 vs. Oakland 0 (AL)

* = World Series game. **Note:** Two pre-1901 National League pitchers are also credited with perfect games. Within one week in 1880, Lee Richmond (June 12, Worcester 1, Cleveland 0) and John "Monte" Ward (June 17, Providence 5, Buffalo 0) each threw a perfect game.

Most Career Major League No-Hitters

No.	Pitcher
7	Nolan Ryan
4	Sandy Koufax
3	Larry Corcoran, Bob Feller, Justin Verlander, Cy Young
2	Jake Arrieta, Al Atkinson, Homer Bailey, Theodore Breitenstein, Mark Buehrle, Jim Bunning, Steve Busby, Carl Erskine, Mike Fiers, Bob Forsch, James "Pud" Galvin, Roy Halladay, Ken Holtzman, Randy Johnson, Addie Joss, Dutch Leonard, Tim Lincecum, Jim Maloney, Christy Mathewson, Hideo Nomo, Allie Reynolds, Max Scherzer, Frank Smith, Warren Spahn, Bill Stoneman, Adonis Terry, Virgil Trucks, Johnny Vander Meer, Don Wilson

Home Run Leaders by Season, 1901-2024

* = All-time single-season record for league since beginning of "modern" era in 1901.

	National League			American League	
Year	Player, team	HR	Year	Player, team	HR
1901	Sam Crawford, Cincinnati	16	1901	Nap Lajoie, Philadelphia	14
1902	Thomas Leach, Pittsburgh	6	1902	Socks Seybold, Philadelphia	16
1903	James Sheckard, Brooklyn	9	1903	Buck Freeman, Boston	13
1904	Harry Lumley, Brooklyn	9	1904	Harry Davis, Philadelphia	10
1905	Fred Odwell, Cincinnati	9	1905	Harry Davis, Philadelphia	8
1906	Timothy Jordan, Brooklyn	12	1906	Harry Davis, Philadelphia	12
1907	David Brain, Boston	10	1907	Harry Davis, Philadelphia	8
1908	Timothy Jordan, Brooklyn	12	1908	Sam Crawford, Detroit	7
1909	Red Murray, New York	7	1909	Ty Cobb, Detroit	9
1910	Fred Beck, Boston; Frank Schulte, Chicago	10	1910	Jake Stahl, Boston	10
1911	Frank Schulte, Chicago	21	1911	J. Franklin Baker, Philadelphia	11
1912	Henry Zimmerman, Chicago	14	1912	J. Franklin Baker, Phil.; Tris Speaker, Boston	10
1913	Gavvy Cravath, Philadelphia	19	1913	J. Franklin Baker, Philadelphia	12
1914	Gavvy Cravath, Philadelphia	19	1914	J. Franklin Baker, Philadelphia	9
1915	Gavvy Cravath, Philadelphia	24	1915	Robert Roth, Chicago-Cleveland	7

National League

Year	Player, team	HR
1916	Dave Robertson, NY; Fred "Cy" Williams, Chicago	12
1917	Gavvy Cravath, Phil.; Dave Robertson, NY	12
1918	Gavvy Cravath, Philadelphia	8
1919	Gavvy Cravath, Philadelphia	12
1920	Cy Williams, Philadelphia	15
1921	George Kelly, New York	23
1922	Rogers Hornsby, St. Louis	42
1923	Cy Williams, Philadelphia	41
1924	Jacques Fournier, Brooklyn	27
1925	Rogers Hornsby, St. Louis	39
1926	Hack Wilson, Chicago	21
1927	Hack Wilson, Chicago; Cy Williams, Philadelphia	30
1928	Hack Wilson, Chicago; Jim Bottomley, St. Louis	31
1929	Chuck Klein, Philadelphia	43
1930	Hack Wilson, Chicago	56
1931	Chuck Klein, Philadelphia	31
1932	Chuck Klein, Philadelphia; Mel Ott, New York	38
1933	Chuck Klein, Philadelphia	28
1934	Rip Collins, St. Louis; Mel Ott, New York	35
1935	Walter Berger, Boston	34
1936	Mel Ott, New York	33
1937	Joe Medwick, St. Louis; Mel Ott, New York	31
1938	Mel Ott, New York	36
1939	John Mize, St. Louis	28
1940	John Mize, St. Louis	43
1941	Dolph Camilli, Brooklyn	34
1942	Mel Ott, New York	30
1943	Bill Nicholson, Chicago	29
1944	Bill Nicholson, Chicago	33
1945	Tommy Holmes, Boston	28
1946	Ralph Kiner, Pittsburgh	23
1947	Ralph Kiner, Pittsburgh; John Mize, New York	51
1948	Ralph Kiner, Pittsburgh; John Mize, New York	40
1949	Ralph Kiner, Pittsburgh	54
1950	Ralph Kiner, Pittsburgh	47
1951	Ralph Kiner, Pittsburgh	42
1952	Ralph Kiner, Pittsburgh; Hank Sauer, Chicago	37
1953	Ed Mathews, Milwaukee	47
1954	Ted Kluszewski, Cincinnati	49
1955	Willie Mays, New York	51
1956	Duke Snider, Brooklyn	43
1957	Hank Aaron, Milwaukee	44
1958	Ernie Banks, Chicago	47
1959	Ed Mathews, Milwaukee	46
1960	Ernie Banks, Chicago	41
1961	Orlando Cepeda, San Francisco	46
1962	Willie Mays, San Francisco	49
1963	Hank Aaron, Milwaukee; Willie McCovey, S.F.	44
1964	Willie Mays, San Francisco	47
1965	Willie Mays, San Francisco	52
1966	Hank Aaron, Atlanta	44
1967	Hank Aaron, Atlanta	39
1968	Willie McCovey, San Francisco	36
1969	Willie McCovey, San Francisco	45
1970	Johnny Bench, Cincinnati	45
1971	Willie Stargell, Pittsburgh	48
1972	Johnny Bench, Cincinnati	40
1973	Willie Stargell, Pittsburgh	44
1974	Mike Schmidt, Philadelphia	36
1975	Mike Schmidt, Philadelphia	38
1976	Mike Schmidt, Philadelphia	38
1977	George Foster, Cincinnati	52
1978	George Foster, Cincinnati	40
1979	Dave Kingman, Chicago	48
1980	Mike Schmidt, Philadelphia	48
1981	Mike Schmidt, Philadelphia	31
1982	Dave Kingman, New York	37
1983	Mike Schmidt, Philadelphia	40
1984	Dale Murphy, Atlanta; Mike Schmidt, Philadelphia	36
1985	Dale Murphy, Atlanta	37
1986	Mike Schmidt, Philadelphia	37
1987	Andre Dawson, Chicago	49
1988	Darryl Strawberry, New York	39
1989	Kevin Mitchell, San Francisco	47
1990	Ryne Sandberg, Chicago	40

American League

Year	Player, team	HR
1916	Wally Pipp, New York	12
1917	Wally Pipp, New York	9
1918	Babe Ruth, Boston; Tilly Walker, Philadelphia	11
1919	Babe Ruth, Boston	29
1920	Babe Ruth, New York	54
1921	Babe Ruth, New York	59
1922	Ken Williams, St. Louis	39
1923	Babe Ruth, New York	41
1924	Babe Ruth, New York	46
1925	Bob Meusel, New York	33
1926	Babe Ruth, New York	47
1927	Babe Ruth, New York	60
1928	Babe Ruth, New York	54
1929	Babe Ruth, New York	46
1930	Babe Ruth, New York	49
1931	Lou Gehrig, New York; Babe Ruth, New York	46
1932	Jimmie Foxx, Philadelphia	58
1933	Jimmie Foxx, Philadelphia	48
1934	Lou Gehrig, New York	49
1935	Jimmie Foxx, Phil.; Hank Greenberg, Detroit	36
1936	Lou Gehrig, New York	49
1937	Joe DiMaggio, New York	46
1938	Hank Greenberg, Detroit	58
1939	Jimmie Foxx, Boston	35
1940	Hank Greenberg, Detroit	41
1941	Ted Williams, Boston	37
1942	Ted Williams, Boston	36
1943	Rudy York, Detroit	34
1944	Nick Etten, New York	22
1945	Vern Stephens, St. Louis	24
1946	Hank Greenberg, Detroit	44
1947	Ted Williams, Boston	32
1948	Joe DiMaggio, New York	39
1949	Ted Williams, Boston	43
1950	Al Rosen, Cleveland	37
1951	Gus Zernial, Chicago-Philadelphia	33
1952	Larry Doby, Cleveland	32
1953	Al Rosen, Cleveland	43
1954	Larry Doby, Cleveland	32
1955	Mickey Mantle, New York	37
1956	Mickey Mantle, New York	52
1957	Roy Sievers, Washington	42
1958	Mickey Mantle, New York	42
1959	Rocky Colavito, Clev.; Harmon Killebrew, Wash.	42
1960	Mickey Mantle, New York	40
1961	Roger Maris, New York	61*
1962	Harmon Killebrew, Minnesota	48
1963	Harmon Killebrew, Minnesota	45
1964	Harmon Killebrew, Minnesota	49
1965	Tony Conigliaro, Boston	32
1966	Frank Robinson, Baltimore	49
1967	Harmon Killebrew, Minn.; Carl Yastrzemski, Boston	44
1968	Frank Howard, Washington	44
1969	Harmon Killebrew, Minnesota	49
1970	Frank Howard, Washington	44
1971	Bill Melton, Chicago	33
1972	Dick Allen, Chicago	37
1973	Reggie Jackson, Oakland	32
1974	Dick Allen, Chicago	32
1975	Reggie Jackson, Oak.; George Scott, Milw.	36
1976	Graig Nettles, New York	32
1977	Jim Rice, Boston	39
1978	Jim Rice, Boston	46
1979	Gorman Thomas, Milwaukee	45
1980	Reggie Jackson, New York; Ben Oglivie, Milw.	41
1981	Tony Armas, Oakland; Dwight Evans, Boston; Bobby Grich, Cal.; Eddie Murray, Baltimore	22
1982	Gorman Thomas, Milw.; Reggie Jackson, Cal.	39
1983	Jim Rice, Boston	39
1984	Tony Armas, Boston	43
1985	Darrell Evans, Detroit	40
1986	Jesse Barfield, Toronto	40
1987	Mark McGwire, Oakland	49
1988	Jose Canseco, Oakland	42
1989	Fred McGriff, Toronto	36
1990	Cecil Fielder, Detroit	51

National League			American League		
Year	**Player, team**	**HR**	**Year**	**Player, team**	**HR**
1991	Howard Johnson, New York	38	1991	Jose Canseco, Oakland; Cecil Fielder, Detroit	44
1992	Fred McGriff, San Diego	35	1992	Juan Gonzalez, Texas	43
1993	Barry Bonds, San Francisco	46	1993	Juan Gonzalez, Texas	46
1994	Matt Williams, San Francisco	43	1994	Ken Griffey Jr., Seattle	40
1995	Dante Bichette, Colorado	40	1995	Albert Belle, Cleveland	50
1996	Andres Galarraga, Colorado	47	1996	Mark McGwire, Oakland	52
1997[1]	Larry Walker, Colorado	49	1997[1]	Ken Griffey Jr., Seattle	56
1998	Mark McGwire, St. Louis	70	1998	Ken Griffey Jr., Seattle	56
1999	Mark McGwire, St. Louis	65	1999	Ken Griffey Jr., Seattle	48
2000	Sammy Sosa, Chicago	50	2000	Troy Glaus, Anaheim	47
2001	Barry Bonds, San Francisco	73*	2001	Alex Rodriguez, Texas	52
2002	Sammy Sosa, Chicago	49	2002	Alex Rodriguez, Texas	57
2003	Jim Thome, Philadelphia	47	2003	Alex Rodriguez, Texas	47
2004	Adrián Beltré, Los Angeles	48	2004	Manny Ramirez, Boston	43
2005	Andruw Jones, Atlanta	51	2005	Alex Rodriguez, New York	48
2006	Ryan Howard, Philadelphia	58	2006	David Ortiz, Boston	54
2007	Prince Fielder, Milwaukee	50	2007	Alex Rodriguez, New York	54
2008	Ryan Howard, Philadelphia	48	2008	Miguel Cabrera, Detroit	37
2009	Albert Pujols, St. Louis	47	2009	Carlos Peña, Tampa Bay; Mark Teixeira, New York	39
2010	Albert Pujols, St. Louis	42	2010	José Bautista, Toronto	54
2011	Matt Kemp, Los Angeles	39	2011	José Bautista, Toronto	43
2012	Ryan Braun, Milwaukee	41	2012	Miguel Cabrera, Detroit	44
2013	Pedro Alvarez, Pitt.; Paul Goldschmidt, Arizona	36	2013	Chris Davis, Baltimore	53
2014	Giancarlo Stanton, Miami	37	2014	Nelson Cruz, Baltimore	40
2015	Nolan Arenado, Colorado; Bryce Harper, Washington	42	2015	Chris Davis, Baltimore	47
2016	Nolan Arenado, Colorado; Chris Carter, Milwaukee	41	2016	Mark Trumbo, Baltimore	47
2017	Giancarlo Stanton, Miami	59	2017	Aaron Judge, New York	52
2018	Nolan Arenado, Colorado	38	2018	Khris Davis, Oakland	48
2019	Pete Alonso, New York	53	2019	Jorge Soler, Kansas City	48
2020	Marcell Ozuna, Atlanta	18	2020	Luke Voit, New York	22
2021	Fernando Tatís Jr., San Diego	42	2021	Vladimir Guerrero Jr., Toronto	48
2022	Kyle Schwarber, Philadelphia	46	2022	Aaron Judge, New York	62
2023	Matt Olson, Atlanta	54	2023	Shohei Ohtani, Los Angeles	44
2024	Shohei Ohtani, Los Angeles	54	2024	Aaron Judge, New York	58

(1) In 1997, Mark McGwire hit 58 home runs, 34 with the Oakland Athletics (AL) and 24 with the St. Louis Cardinals (NL).

Batting Champions by Season, 1901-2024

* = All-time single-season record for league since beginning of "modern" era in 1901.

National League			American League		
Year	**Player, team**	**AVG**	**Year**	**Player, team**	**AVG**
1901	Jesse C. Burkett, St. Louis	.376	1901[1]	Nap Lajoie, Philadelphia	.426*
1902	Clarence Beaumont, Pittsburgh	.357	1902	Ed Delahanty, Washington	.376
1903	Honus Wagner, Pittsburgh	.355	1903	Nap Lajoie, Cleveland	.357
1904	Honus Wagner, Pittsburgh	.349	1904	Nap Lajoie, Cleveland	.382
1905	James Seymour, Cincinnati	.377	1905	Elmer Flick, Cleveland	.308
1906	Honus Wagner, Pittsburgh	.339	1906	George Stone, St. Louis	.358
1907	Honus Wagner, Pittsburgh	.350	1907	Ty Cobb, Detroit	.350
1908	Honus Wagner, Pittsburgh	.354	1908	Ty Cobb, Detroit	.324
1909	Honus Wagner, Pittsburgh	.339	1909	Ty Cobb, Detroit	.377
1910	Sherwood Magee, Philadelphia	.331	1910[2]	Ty Cobb, Detroit	.385
1911	Honus Wagner, Pittsburgh	.334	1911	Ty Cobb, Detroit	.420
1912	Henry Zimmerman, Chicago	.372	1912	Ty Cobb, Detroit	.410
1913	Jacob Daubert, Brooklyn	.350	1913	Ty Cobb, Detroit	.390
1914	Jacob Daubert, Brooklyn	.329	1914	Ty Cobb, Detroit	.368
1915	Larry Doyle, New York	.320	1915	Ty Cobb, Detroit	.369
1916	Hal Chase, Cincinnati	.339	1916	Tris Speaker, Cleveland	.386
1917	Edd Roush, Cincinnati	.341	1917	Ty Cobb, Detroit	.383
1918	Zack Wheat, Brooklyn	.335	1918	Ty Cobb, Detroit	.382
1919	Edd Roush, Cincinnati	.321	1919	Ty Cobb, Detroit	.384
1920	Rogers Hornsby, St. Louis	.370	1920	George Sisler, St. Louis	.407
1921	Rogers Hornsby, St. Louis	.397	1921	Harry Heilmann, Detroit	.394
1922	Rogers Hornsby, St. Louis	.401	1922	George Sisler, St. Louis	.420
1923	Rogers Hornsby, St. Louis	.384	1923	Harry Heilmann, Detroit	.403
1924	Rogers Hornsby, St. Louis	.424*	1924	Babe Ruth, New York	.378
1925	Rogers Hornsby, St. Louis	.403	1925	Harry Heilmann, Detroit	.393
1926	Eugene Hargrave, Cincinnati	.353	1926	Henry Manush, Detroit	.378
1927	Paul Waner, Pittsburgh	.380	1927	Harry Heilmann, Detroit	.398
1928	Rogers Hornsby, Boston	.387	1928	Goose Goslin, Washington	.379
1929	Lefty O'Doul, Philadelphia	.398	1929	Lew Fonseca, Cleveland	.369
1930	Bill Terry, New York	.401	1930	Al Simmons, Philadelphia	.381
1931	Chick Hafey, St. Louis	.349	1931	Al Simmons, Philadelphia	.390
1932	Lefty O'Doul, Brooklyn	.368	1932	Dale Alexander, Detroit-Boston	.367
1933	Chuck Klein, Philadelphia	.368	1933	Jimmie Foxx, Philadelphia	.356
1934	Paul Waner, Pittsburgh	.362	1934	Lou Gehrig, New York	.363
1935	Arky Vaughan, Pittsburgh	.385	1935	Buddy Myer, Washington	.349
1936	Paul Waner, Pittsburgh	.373	1936	Luke Appling, Chicago	.388
1937	Joe Medwick, St. Louis	.374	1937	Charlie Gehringer, Detroit	.371
1938	Ernie Lombardi, Cincinnati	.342	1938	Jimmie Foxx, Boston	.349

National League

Year	Player, team	AVG
1939	John Mize, St. Louis	.349
1940	Debs Garms, Pittsburgh	.355
1941	Pete Reiser, Brooklyn	.343
1942	Ernie Lombardi, Boston	.330
1943	Stan Musial, St. Louis	.357
1944	Dixie Walker, Brooklyn	.357
1945	Phil Cavarretta, Chicago	.355
1946	Stan Musial, St. Louis	.365
1947	Harry Walker, St. Louis-Philadelphia	.363
1948	Stan Musial, St. Louis	.376
1949	Jackie Robinson, Brooklyn	.342
1950	Stan Musial, St. Louis	.346
1951	Stan Musial, St. Louis	.355
1952	Stan Musial, St. Louis	.336
1953	Carl Furillo, Brooklyn	.344
1954	Willie Mays, New York	.345
1955	Richie Ashburn, Philadelphia	.338
1956	Hank Aaron, Milwaukee	.328
1957	Stan Musial, St. Louis	.351
1958	Richie Ashburn, Philadelphia	.350
1959	Hank Aaron, Milwaukee	.355
1960	Dick Groat, Pittsburgh	.325
1961	Roberto Clemente, Pittsburgh	.351
1962	Tommy Davis, Los Angeles	.346
1963	Tommy Davis, Los Angeles	.326
1964	Roberto Clemente, Pittsburgh	.339
1965	Roberto Clemente, Pittsburgh	.329
1966	Matty Alou, Pittsburgh	.342
1967	Roberto Clemente, Pittsburgh	.357
1968	Pete Rose, Cincinnati	.335
1969	Pete Rose, Cincinnati	.348
1970	Rico Carty, Atlanta	.366
1971	Joe Torre, St. Louis	.363
1972	Billy Williams, Chicago	.333
1973	Pete Rose, Cincinnati	.338
1974	Ralph Garr, Atlanta	.353
1975	Bill Madlock, Chicago	.354
1976	Bill Madlock, Chicago	.339
1977	Dave Parker, Pittsburgh	.338
1978	Dave Parker, Pittsburgh	.334
1979	Keith Hernandez, St. Louis	.344
1980	Bill Buckner, Chicago	.324
1981	Bill Madlock, Pittsburgh	.341
1982	Al Oliver, Montréal	.331
1983	Bill Madlock, Pittsburgh	.323
1984	Tony Gwynn, San Diego	.351
1985	Willie McGee, St. Louis	.353
1986	Tim Raines, Montréal	.334
1987	Tony Gwynn, San Diego	.370
1988	Tony Gwynn, San Diego	.313
1989	Tony Gwynn, San Diego	.336
1990	Willie McGee, St. Louis	.335
1991	Terry Pendleton, Atlanta	.319
1992	Gary Sheffield, San Diego	.330
1993	Andres Galarraga, Colorado	.370
1994	Tony Gwynn, San Diego	.394
1995	Tony Gwynn, San Diego	.368
1996	Tony Gwynn, San Diego	.353
1997	Tony Gwynn, San Diego	.372
1998	Larry Walker, Colorado	.363
1999	Larry Walker, Colorado	.379
2000	Todd Helton, Colorado	.372
2001	Larry Walker, Colorado	.350
2002	Barry Bonds, San Francisco	.370
2003	Albert Pujols, St. Louis	.359
2004	Barry Bonds, San Francisco	.362
2005	Derrek Lee, Chicago	.335
2006	Freddy Sanchez, Pittsburgh	.344
2007	Matt Holliday, Colorado	.340
2008	Chipper Jones, Atlanta	.364
2009	Hanley Ramirez, Florida	.342
2010	Carlos Gonzalez, Colorado	.336
2011	José Reyes, New York	.337
2012	Buster Posey, San Francisco	.336
2013	Michael Cuddyer, Colorado	.331
2014	Justin Morneau, Colorado	.319

American League

Year	Player, team	AVG
1939	Joe DiMaggio, New York	.381
1940	Joe DiMaggio, New York	.352
1941	Ted Williams, Boston	.406
1942	Ted Williams, Boston	.356
1943	Luke Appling, Chicago	.328
1944	Lou Boudreau, Cleveland	.327
1945	George Stirnweiss, New York	.309
1946	Mickey Vernon, Washington	.353
1947	Ted Williams, Boston	.343
1948	Ted Williams, Boston	.369
1949	George Kell, Detroit	.343
1950	Billy Goodman, Boston	.354
1951	Ferris Fain, Philadelphia	.344
1952	Ferris Fain, Philadelphia	.327
1953	Mickey Vernon, Washington	.337
1954	Roberto Avila, Cleveland	.341
1955	Al Kaline, Detroit	.340
1956	Mickey Mantle, New York	.353
1957	Ted Williams, Boston	.388
1958	Ted Williams, Boston	.328
1959	Harvey Kuenn, Detroit	.353
1960	Pete Runnels, Boston	.320
1961	Norm Cash, Detroit	.361
1962	Pete Runnels, Boston	.326
1963	Carl Yastrzemski, Boston	.321
1964	Tony Oliva, Minnesota	.323
1965	Tony Oliva, Minnesota	.321
1966	Frank Robinson, Baltimore	.316
1967	Carl Yastrzemski, Boston	.326
1968	Carl Yastrzemski, Boston	.301
1969	Rod Carew, Minnesota	.332
1970	Alex Johnson, California	.329
1971	Tony Oliva, Minnesota	.337
1972	Rod Carew, Minnesota	.318
1973	Rod Carew, Minnesota	.350
1974	Rod Carew, Minnesota	.364
1975	Rod Carew, Minnesota	.359
1976	George Brett, Kansas City	.333
1977	Rod Carew, Minnesota	.388
1978	Rod Carew, Minnesota	.333
1979	Fred Lynn, Boston	.333
1980	George Brett, Kansas City	.390
1981	Carney Lansford, Boston	.336
1982	Willie Wilson, Kansas City	.332
1983	Wade Boggs, Boston	.361
1984	Don Mattingly, New York	.343
1985	Wade Boggs, Boston	.368
1986	Wade Boggs, Boston	.357
1987	Wade Boggs, Boston	.363
1988	Wade Boggs, Boston	.366
1989	Kirby Puckett, Minnesota	.339
1990	George Brett, Kansas City	.329
1991	Julio Franco, Texas	.341
1992	Edgar Martinez, Seattle	.343
1993	John Olerud, Toronto	.363
1994	Paul O'Neill, New York	.359
1995	Edgar Martinez, Seattle	.356
1996	Alex Rodriguez, Seattle	.358
1997	Frank Thomas, Chicago	.347
1998	Bernie Williams, New York	.339
1999	Nomar Garciaparra, Boston	.357
2000	Nomar Garciaparra, Boston	.372
2001	Ichiro Suzuki, Seattle	.350
2002	Manny Ramirez, Boston	.349
2003	Bill Mueller, Boston	.326
2004	Ichiro Suzuki, Seattle	.372
2005	Michael Young, Texas	.331
2006	Joe Mauer, Minnesota	.347
2007	Magglio Ordoñez, Detroit	.363
2008	Joe Mauer, Minnesota	.328
2009	Joe Mauer, Minnesota	.365
2010	Josh Hamilton, Texas	.359
2011	Miguel Cabrera, Detroit	.344
2012	Miguel Cabrera, Detroit	.330
2013	Miguel Cabrera, Detroit	.348
2014	José Altuve, Houston	.341

National League			American League		
Year	**Player, team**	**AVG**	**Year**	**Player, team**	**AVG**
2015	Dee Gordon, Miami	.333	2015	Miguel Cabrera, Detroit	.338
2016	DJ LeMahieu, Colorado	.348	2016	José Altuve, Houston	.338
2017	Charlie Blackmon, Colorado	.331	2017	José Altuve, Houston	.346
2018	Christian Yelich, Milwaukee	.326	2018	Mookie Betts, Boston	.346
2019	Christian Yelich, Milwaukee	.329	2019	Tim Anderson, Chicago	.335
2020	Juan Soto, Washington	.351	2020	DJ LeMahieu, New York	.364
2021	Trea Turner, Washington-Los Angeles	.328	2021	Yuli Gurriel, Houston	.319
2022	Jeff McNeil, New York	.326	2022	Luis Arráez, Minnesota	.316
2023	Luis Arráez, Miami	.354	2023	Yandy Díaz, Tampa Bay	.330
2024	Luis Arráez, Miami-San Diego	.314	2024	Bobby Witt Jr., Kansas City	.332

(1) Nap Lajoie's 1901 batting average varies in historical records from .421 to .426. (2) Some baseball researchers have concluded that Ty Cobb actually hit .382 in 1910 while Nap Lajoie, Cleveland, hit .383.

Earned Run Average Leaders by Season, 1977-2024

National League					American League				
Year	**Pitcher, team**	**G**	**IP**	**ERA**	**Year**	**Pitcher, team**	**G**	**IP**	**ERA**
1977	John Candelaria, Pittsburgh	33	230.2	2.34	1977	Frank Tanana, California	31	241.1	2.54
1978	Craig Swan, New York	29	207.1	2.43	1978	Ron Guidry, New York	35	273.2	1.74
1979	J. R. Richard, Houston	38	292.1	2.71	1979	Ron Guidry, New York	33	236.1	2.78
1980	Don Sutton, Los Angeles	32	212.1	2.20	1980	Rudy May, New York	41	175.1	2.46
1981	Nolan Ryan, Houston	21	149.0	1.69	1981	Sammy Stewart, Baltimore	29	112.1	2.32
1982	Steve Rogers, Montréal	35	277.0	2.40	1982	Rick Sutcliffe, Cleveland	34	216.0	2.96
1983	Atlee Hammaker, San Francisco	23	172.1	2.25	1983	Rick Honeycutt, Texas	25	174.2	2.42
1984	Alejandro Peña, Los Angeles	28	199.1	2.48	1984	Mike Boddicker, Baltimore	34	261.1	2.79
1985	Dwight Gooden, New York	35	276.2	1.53	1985	Dave Stieb, Toronto	36	265.0	2.48
1986	Mike Scott, Houston	37	275.1	2.22	1986	Roger Clemens, Boston	33	254.0	2.48
1987	Nolan Ryan, Houston	34	211.2	2.76	1987	Jimmy Key, Toronto	36	261.0	2.76
1988	Joe Magrane, St. Louis	24	165.1	2.18	1988	Allan Anderson, Minnesota	30	202.1	2.45
1989	Scott Garrelts, San Francisco	30	193.1	2.28	1989	Bret Saberhagen, Kansas City	36	262.1	2.16
1990	Danny Darwin, Houston	48	162.2	2.21	1990	Roger Clemens, Boston	31	228.1	1.93
1991	Dennis Martinez, Montréal	31	222.0	2.39	1991	Roger Clemens, Boston	35	271.1	2.62
1992	Bill Swift, San Francisco	30	164.2	2.08	1992	Roger Clemens, Boston	32	246.2	2.41
1993	Greg Maddux, Atlanta	36	267.0	2.36	1993	Kevin Appier, Kansas City	34	238.2	2.56
1994	Greg Maddux, Atlanta	25	202.0	1.56	1994	Steve Ontiveros, Oakland	27	115.1	2.65
1995	Greg Maddux, Atlanta	28	209.2	1.63	1995	Randy Johnson, Seattle	30	214.1	2.48
1996	Kevin Brown, Florida	32	233.0	1.89	1996	Juan Guzmán, Toronto	27	187.2	2.93
1997	Pedro Martinez, Montréal	31	241.1	1.90	1997	Roger Clemens, Toronto	34	264.0	2.05
1998	Greg Maddux, Atlanta	34	251.0	2.22	1998	Roger Clemens, Toronto	33	234.2	2.65
1999	Randy Johnson, Arizona	35	271.2	2.48	1999	Pedro Martinez, Boston	31	213.1	2.07
2000	Kevin Brown, Los Angeles	33	230.0	2.58	2000	Pedro Martinez, Boston	29	217.0	1.74
2001	Randy Johnson, Arizona	35	249.2	2.49	2001	Freddy Garcia, Seattle	34	238.2	3.05
2002	Randy Johnson, Arizona	35	260.0	2.32	2002	Pedro Martinez, Boston	30	199.1	2.26
2003	Jason Schmidt, San Francisco	29	207.2	2.34	2003	Pedro Martinez, Boston	29	186.2	2.22
2004	Jake Peavy, San Diego	27	166.1	2.27	2004	Johan Santana, Minnesota	34	228.0	2.61
2005	Roger Clemens, Houston	32	211.1	1.87	2005	Kevin Millwood, Cleveland	30	192.0	2.86
2006	Roy Oswalt, Houston	33	220.2	2.98	2006	Johan Santana, Minnesota	34	233.2	2.77
2007	Jake Peavy, San Diego	34	223.1	2.54	2007	John Lackey, Los Angeles	33	224.0	3.01
2008	Johan Santana, New York	34	234.1	2.53	2008	Cliff Lee, Cleveland	31	223.1	2.54
2009	Chris Carpenter, St. Louis	28	192.2	2.24	2009	Zack Greinke, Kansas City	33	229.1	2.16
2010	Josh Johnson, Florida	28	183.2	2.30	2010	Felix Hernandez, Seattle	34	249.2	2.27
2011	Clayton Kershaw, Los Angeles	33	233.1	2.28	2011	Justin Verlander, Detroit	34	251.0	2.40
2012	Clayton Kershaw, Los Angeles	33	227.2	2.53	2012	David Price, Tampa Bay	31	211.0	2.56
2013	Clayton Kershaw, Los Angeles	33	236.0	1.83	2013	Anibal Sanchez, Detroit	29	182.0	2.57
2014	Clayton Kershaw, Los Angeles	27	198.1	1.77	2014	Felix Hernandez, Seattle	34	236.0	2.14
2015	Zack Greinke, Los Angeles	32	222.2	1.66	2015	David Price, Detroit-Toronto	32	220.1	2.45
2016	Kyle Hendricks, Chicago	31	190.0	2.13	2016	Aaron Sanchez, Toronto	30	192.0	3.00
2017	Clayton Kershaw, Los Angeles	27	175.0	2.31	2017	Corey Kluber, Cleveland	29	203.2	2.25
2018	Jacob deGrom, New York	32	217.0	1.70	2018	Blake Snell, Tampa Bay	31	180.2	1.89
2019	Hyun-jin Ryu, Los Angeles	29	182.2	2.32	2019	Gerrit Cole, Houston	33	212.1	2.50
2020	Trevor Bauer, Cincinnati	11	73.0	1.73	2020	Shane Bieber, Cleveland	12	77.1	1.63
2021	Corbin Burnes, Milwaukee	28	167.0	2.43	2021	Robbie Ray, Toronto	32	193.1	2.84
2022	Julio Urías, Los Angeles	31	175.0	2.16	2022	Justin Verlander, Houston	28	175.0	1.75
2023	Blake Snell, San Diego	32	180.0	2.25	2023	Gerrit Cole, New York	33	209.0	2.63
2024	Chris Sale, Atlanta	29	177.2	2.38	2024	Tarik Skubal, Detroit	31	192.0	2.39

Strikeout Leaders by Season, 1901-2024

* = All-time single-season record for league since beginning of "modern" era in 1901.

National League			American League		
Year	**Pitcher, team**	**SO**	**Year**	**Pitcher, team**	**SO**
1901	Noodles Hahn, Cincinnati	239	1901	Cy Young, Boston	158
1902	Vic Willis, Boston	225	1902	Rube Waddell, Philadelphia	210
1903	Christy Mathewson, New York	267	1903	Rube Waddell, Philadelphia	302
1904	Christy Mathewson, New York	212	1904	Rube Waddell, Philadelphia	349
1905	Christy Mathewson, New York	206	1905	Rube Waddell, Philadelphia	287
1906	Fred Beebe, Chicago-St. Louis	171	1906	Rube Waddell, Philadelphia	196
1907	Christy Mathewson, New York	178	1907	Rube Waddell, Philadelphia	232
1908	Christy Mathewson, New York	259	1908	Ed Walsh, Chicago	269
1909	Orval Overall, Chicago	205	1909	Frank Smith, Chicago	177
1910	Earl Moore, Philadelphia	185	1910	Walter Johnson, Washington	313

National League

Year	Pitcher, team	SO
1911	Rube Marquard, New York	237
1912	Grover Alexander, Philadelphia	195
1913	Tom Seaton, Philadelphia	168
1914	Grover Alexander, Philadelphia	214
1915	Grover Alexander, Philadelphia	241
1916	Grover Alexander, Philadelphia	167
1917	Grover Alexander, Philadelphia	200
1918	Hippo Vaughn, Chicago	148
1919	Hippo Vaughn, Chicago	141
1920	Grover Alexander, Chicago	173
1921	Burleigh Grimes, Brooklyn	136
1922	Dazzy Vance, Brooklyn	134
1923	Dazzy Vance, Brooklyn	197
1924	Dazzy Vance, Brooklyn	262
1925	Dazzy Vance, Brooklyn	221
1926	Dazzy Vance, Brooklyn	140
1927	Dazzy Vance, Brooklyn	184
1928	Dazzy Vance, Brooklyn	200
1929	Pat Malone, Chicago	166
1930	Bill Hallahan, St. Louis	177
1931	Bill Hallahan, St. Louis	159
1932	Dizzy Dean, St. Louis	191
1933	Dizzy Dean, St. Louis	199
1934	Dizzy Dean, St. Louis	195
1935	Dizzy Dean, St. Louis	190
1936	Van Lingle Mungo, Brooklyn	238
1937	Carl Hubbell, New York	159
1938	Clay Bryant, Chicago	135
1939	Claude Passeau, Philadelphia-Chicago; Bucky Walters, Cincinnati	137
1940	Kirby Higbe, Philadelphia	137
1941	John Vander Meer, Cincinnati	202
1942	John Vander Meer, Cincinnati	186
1943	John Vander Meer, Cincinnati	174
1944	Bill Voiselle, New York	161
1945	Preacher Roe, Pittsburgh	148
1946	Johnny Schmitz, Chicago	135
1947	Ewell Blackwell, Cincinnati	193
1948	Harry Brecheen, St. Louis	149
1949	Warren Spahn, Boston	151
1950	Warren Spahn, Boston	191
1951	Warren Spahn, Boston; Don Newcombe, Brooklyn	164
1952	Warren Spahn, Boston	183
1953	Robin Roberts, Philadelphia	198
1954	Robin Roberts, Philadelphia	185
1955	Sam Jones, Chicago	198
1956	Sam Jones, Chicago	176
1957	Jack Sanford, Philadelphia	188
1958	Sam Jones, St. Louis	225
1959	Don Drysdale, Los Angeles	242
1960	Don Drysdale, Los Angeles	246
1961	Sandy Koufax, Los Angeles	269
1962	Don Drysdale, Los Angeles	232
1963	Sandy Koufax, Los Angeles	306
1964	Bob Veale, Pittsburgh	250
1965	Sandy Koufax, Los Angeles	382*
1966	Sandy Koufax, Los Angeles	317
1967	Jim Bunning, Philadelphia	253
1968	Bob Gibson, St. Louis	268
1969	Ferguson Jenkins, Chicago	273
1970	Tom Seaver, New York	283
1971	Tom Seaver, New York	289
1972	Steve Carlton, Philadelphia	310
1973	Tom Seaver, New York	251
1974	Steve Carlton, Philadelphia	240
1975	Tom Seaver, New York	243
1976	Tom Seaver, New York	235
1977	Phil Niekro, Atlanta	262
1978	J. R. Richard, Houston	303
1979	J. R. Richard, Houston	313
1980	Steve Carlton, Philadelphia	286
1981	Fernando Valenzuela, Los Angeles	180
1982	Steve Carlton, Philadelphia	286
1983	Steve Carlton, Philadelphia	275
1984	Dwight Gooden, New York	276
1985	Dwight Gooden, New York	268
1986	Mike Scott, Houston	306
1987	Nolan Ryan, Houston	270
1988	Nolan Ryan, Houston	228

American League

Year	Pitcher, team	SO
1911	Ed Walsh, Chicago	255
1912	Walter Johnson, Washington	303
1913	Walter Johnson, Washington	243
1914	Walter Johnson, Washington	225
1915	Walter Johnson, Washington	203
1916	Walter Johnson, Washington	228
1917	Walter Johnson, Washington	188
1918	Walter Johnson, Washington	162
1919	Walter Johnson, Washington	147
1920	Stan Coveleski, Cleveland	133
1921	Walter Johnson, Washington	143
1922	Urban Shocker, St. Louis	149
1923	Walter Johnson, Washington	130
1924	Walter Johnson, Washington	158
1925	Lefty Grove, Philadelphia	116
1926	Lefty Grove, Philadelphia	194
1927	Lefty Grove, Philadelphia	174
1928	Lefty Grove, Philadelphia	183
1929	Lefty Grove, Philadelphia	170
1930	Lefty Grove, Philadelphia	209
1931	Lefty Grove, Philadelphia	175
1932	Red Ruffing, New York	190
1933	Lefty Gomez, New York	163
1934	Lefty Gomez, New York	158
1935	Tommy Bridges, Detroit	163
1936	Tommy Bridges, Detroit	175
1937	Lefty Gomez, New York	194
1938	Bob Feller, Cleveland	240
1939	Bob Feller, Cleveland	246
1940	Bob Feller, Cleveland	261
1941	Bob Feller, Cleveland	260
1942	Tex Hughson, Boston; Bobo Newsom, Washington	113
1943	Allie Reynolds, Cleveland	151
1944	Hal Newhouser, Detroit	187
1945	Hal Newhouser, Detroit	212
1946	Bob Feller, Cleveland	348
1947	Bob Feller, Cleveland	196
1948	Bob Feller, Cleveland	164
1949	Virgil Trucks, Detroit	153
1950	Bob Lemon, Cleveland	170
1951	Vic Raschi, New York	164
1952	Allie Reynolds, New York	160
1953	Billy Pierce, Chicago	186
1954	Bob Turley, Baltimore	185
1955	Herb Score, Cleveland	245
1956	Herb Score, Cleveland	263
1957	Early Wynn, Cleveland	184
1958	Early Wynn, Chicago	179
1959	Jim Bunning, Detroit	201
1960	Jim Bunning, Detroit	201
1961	Camilo Pascual, Minnesota	221
1962	Camilo Pascual, Minnesota	206
1963	Camilo Pascual, Minnesota	202
1964	Al Downing, New York	217
1965	Sam McDowell, Cleveland	325
1966	Sam McDowell, Cleveland	225
1967	Jim Lonborg, Boston	246
1968	Sam McDowell, Cleveland	283
1969	Sam McDowell, Cleveland	279
1970	Sam McDowell, Cleveland	304
1971	Mickey Lolich, Detroit	308
1972	Nolan Ryan, California	329
1973	Nolan Ryan, California	383*
1974	Nolan Ryan, California	367
1975	Frank Tanana, California	269
1976	Nolan Ryan, California	327
1977	Nolan Ryan, California	341
1978	Nolan Ryan, California	260
1979	Nolan Ryan, California	223
1980	Len Barker, Cleveland	187
1981	Len Barker, Cleveland	127
1982	Floyd Bannister, Seattle	209
1983	Jack Morris, Detroit	232
1984	Mark Langston, Seattle	204
1985	Bert Blyleven, Cleveland-Minnesota	206
1986	Mark Langston, Seattle	245
1987	Mark Langston, Seattle	262
1988	Roger Clemens, Boston	291

National League			American League		
Year	**Pitcher, team**	**SO**	**Year**	**Pitcher, team**	**SO**
1989	Jose DeLeon, St. Louis	201	1989	Nolan Ryan, Texas	301
1990	David Cone, New York	233	1990	Nolan Ryan, Texas	232
1991	David Cone, New York	241	1991	Roger Clemens, Boston	241
1992	John Smoltz, Atlanta	215	1992	Randy Johnson, Seattle	241
1993	José Rijo, Cincinnati	227	1993	Randy Johnson, Seattle	308
1994	Andy Benes, San Diego	189	1994	Randy Johnson, Seattle	204
1995	Hideo Nomo, Los Angeles	236	1995	Randy Johnson, Seattle	294
1996	John Smoltz, Atlanta	276	1996	Roger Clemens, Boston	257
1997	Curt Schilling, Philadelphia	319	1997	Roger Clemens, Toronto	292
1998	Curt Schilling, Philadelphia	300	1998	Roger Clemens, Toronto	271
1999	Randy Johnson, Arizona	364	1999	Pedro Martinez, Boston	313
2000	Randy Johnson, Arizona	347	2000	Pedro Martinez, Boston	284
2001	Randy Johnson, Arizona	372	2001	Hideo Nomo, Boston	220
2002	Randy Johnson, Arizona	334	2002	Pedro Martineż, Boston	239
2003	Kerry Wood, Chicago	266	2003	Esteban Loaiza, Chicago	207
2004	Randy Johnson, Arizona	290	2004	Johan Santana, Minnesota	265
2005	Jake Peavy, San Diego	216	2005	Johan Santana, Minnesota	238
2006	Aaron Harang, Cincinnati	216	2006	Johan Santana, Minnesota	245
2007	Jake Peavy, San Diego	240	2007	Scott Kazmir, Tampa Bay	239
2008	Tim Lincecum, San Francisco	265	2008	A. J. Burnett, Toronto	231
2009	Tim Lincecum, San Francisco	261	2009	Justin Verlander, Detroit	269
2010	Tim Lincecum, San Francisco	231	2010	Jered Weaver, Los Angeles	233
2011	Clayton Kershaw, Los Angeles	248	2011	Justin Verlander, Detroit	250
2012	R.A. Dickey, New York	230	2012	Justin Verlander, Detroit	239
2013	Clayton Kershaw, Los Angeles	232	2013	Yu Darvish, Texas	277
2014	Johnny Cueto, Cincinnati; Stephen Strasburg, Washington	242	2014	David Price, Tampa Bay-Detroit	271
2015	Clayton Kershaw, Los Angeles	301	2015	Chris Sale, Chicago	274
2016	Max Scherzer, Washington	284	2016	Justin Verlander, Detroit	254
2017	Max Scherzer, Washington	268	2017	Chris Sale, Boston	308
2018	Max Scherzer, Washington	300	2018	Justin Verlander, Houston	290
2019	Jacob deGrom, New York	255	2019	Gerrit Cole, Houston	326
2020	Jacob deGrom, New York	104	2020	Shane Bieber, Cleveland	122
2021	Zack Wheeler, Philadelphia	247	2021	Robbie Ray, Toronto	248
2022	Corbin Burnes, Milwaukee	243	2022	Gerrit Cole, New York	257
2023	Spencer Strider, Atlanta	281	2023	Kevin Gausman, Toronto	237
2024	Chris Sale, Atlanta	225	2024	Tarik Skubal, Detroit	228

Cy Young Award Winners, 1956-2023

Year	Pitcher, team
1956	Don Newcombe, Brooklyn
1957	Warren Spahn, Milwaukee
1958	Bob Turley, NY Yankees
1959	Early Wynn, Chicago White Sox
1960	Vernon Law, Pittsburgh
1961	Whitey Ford, NY Yankees
1962	Don Drysdale, L.A. Dodgers
1963	Sandy Koufax, L.A. Dodgers
1964	Dean Chance, L.A. Angels
1965	Sandy Koufax, L.A. Dodgers
1966	Sandy Koufax, L.A. Dodgers
1967	(NL) Mike McCormick, S.F.
	(AL) Jim Lonborg, Boston
1968	(NL) Bob Gibson, St. Louis
	(AL) Denny McLain, Detroit
1969	(NL) Tom Seaver, NY
	(AL) Denny McLain, Detroit; Mike Cuellar, Baltimore
1970	(NL) Bob Gibson, St. Louis
	(AL) Jim Perry, Minnesota
1971	(NL) Ferguson Jenkins, Chicago
	(AL) Vida Blue, Oakland
1972	(NL) Steve Carlton, Philadelphia
	(AL) Gaylord Perry, Cleveland
1973	(NL) Tom Seaver, NY
	(AL) Jim Palmer, Baltimore
1974	(NL) Mike Marshall, L.A.
	(AL) Jim "Catfish" Hunter, Oakland
1975	(NL) Tom Seaver, NY
	(AL) Jim Palmer, Baltimore
1976	(NL) Randy Jones, San Diego
	(AL) Jim Palmer, Baltimore
1977	(NL) Steve Carlton, Philadelphia
	(AL) Sparky Lyle, NY
1978	(NL) Gaylord Perry, San Diego
	(AL) Ron Guidry, NY
1979	(NL) Bruce Sutter, Chicago
	(AL) Mike Flanagan, Baltimore
1980	(NL) Steve Carlton, Philadelphia
	(AL) Steve Stone, Baltimore

Year	Pitcher, team
1981	(NL) Fernando Valenzuela, L.A.
	(AL) Rollie Fingers, Milwaukee
1982	(NL) Steve Carlton, Philadelphia
	(AL) Pete Vuckovich, Milwaukee
1983	(NL) John Denny, Philadelphia
	(AL) LaMarr Hoyt, Chicago
1984	(NL) Rick Sutcliffe, Chicago
	(AL) Willie Hernandez, Detroit
1985	(NL) Dwight Gooden, NY
	(AL) Bret Saberhagen, Kansas City
1986	(NL) Mike Scott, Houston
	(AL) Roger Clemens, Boston
1987	(NL) Steve Bedrosian, Phil.
	(AL) Roger Clemens, Boston
1988	(NL) Orel Hershiser, L.A.
	(AL) Frank Viola, Minnesota
1989	(NL) Mark Davis, San Diego
	(AL) Bret Saberhagen, Kansas City
1990	(NL) Doug Drabek, Pittsburgh
	(AL) Bob Welch, Oakland
1991	(NL) Tom Glavine, Atlanta
	(AL) Roger Clemens, Boston
1992	(NL) Greg Maddux, Chicago
	(AL) Dennis Eckersley, Oakland
1993	(NL) Greg Maddux, Atlanta
	(AL) Jack McDowell, Chicago
1994	(NL) Greg Maddux, Atlanta
	(AL) David Cone, Kansas City
1995	(NL) Greg Maddux, Atlanta
	(AL) Randy Johnson, Seattle
1996	(NL) John Smoltz, Atlanta
	(AL) Pat Hentgen, Toronto
1997	(NL) Pedro Martinez, Montréal
	(AL) Roger Clemens, Toronto
1998	(NL) Tom Glavine, Atlanta
	(AL) Roger Clemens, Toronto
1999	(NL) Randy Johnson, Arizona
	(AL) Pedro Martinez, Boston
2000	(NL) Randy Johnson, Arizona
	(AL) Pedro Martinez, Boston
2001	(NL) Randy Johnson, Arizona
	(AL) Roger Clemens, NY

Year	Pitcher, team
2002	(NL) Randy Johnson, Arizona
	(AL) Barry Zito, Oakland
2003	(NL) Eric Gagne, L.A.
	(AL) Roy Halladay, Toronto
2004	(NL) Roger Clemens, Houston
	(AL) Johan Santana, Minnesota
2005	(NL) Chris Carpenter, St. Louis
	(AL) Bartolo Colon, L.A.
2006	(NL) Brandon Webb, Arizona
	(AL) Johan Santana, Minnesota
2007	(NL) Jake Peavy, San Diego
	(AL) CC Sabathia, Cleveland
2008	(NL) Tim Lincecum, S.F.
	(AL) Cliff Lee, Cleveland
2009	(NL) Tim Lincecum, S.F.
	(AL) Zack Greinke, Kansas City
2010	(NL) Roy Halladay, Philadelphia
	(AL) Felix Hernandez, Seattle
2011	(NL) Clayton Kershaw, L.A.
	(AL) Justin Verlander, Detroit
2012	(NL) R.A. Dickey, NY
	(AL) David Price, Tampa Bay
2013	(NL) Clayton Kershaw, L.A.
	(AL) Max Scherzer, Detroit
2014	(NL) Clayton Kershaw, L.A.
	(AL) Corey Kluber, Cleveland
2015	(NL) Jake Arrieta, Chicago
	(AL) Dallas Keuchel, Houston
2016	(NL) Max Scherzer, Washington
	(AL) Rick Porcello, Boston
2017	(NL) Max Scherzer, Washington
	(AL) Corey Kluber, Cleveland
2018	(NL) Jacob deGrom, NY
	(AL) Blake Snell, Tampa Bay
2019	(NL) Jacob deGrom, NY
	(AL) Justin Verlander, Houston
2020	(NL) Trevor Bauer, Cincinnati
	(AL) Shane Bieber, Cleveland
2021	(NL) Corbin Burnes, Milwaukee
	(AL) Robbie Ray, Toronto
2022	(NL) Sandy Alcantara, Miami
	(AL) Justin Verlander, Houston
2023	(NL) Blake Snell, San Diego
	(AL) Gerrit Cole, NY

Most Valuable Players, 1931-2023

As selected by the Baseball Writers' Assn. of America. Prior to 1931, MVP honors were named by various sources.

National League

Year	Player, team
1931	Frank Frisch, St. Louis
1932	Chuck Klein, Philadelphia
1933	Carl Hubbell, New York
1934	Dizzy Dean, St. Louis
1935	Gabby Hartnett, Chicago
1936	Carl Hubbell, New York
1937	Joe Medwick, St. Louis
1938	Ernie Lombardi, Cincinnati
1939	Bucky Walters, Cincinnati
1940	Frank McCormick, Cincinnati
1941	Dolph Camilli, Brooklyn
1942	Mort Cooper, St. Louis
1943	Stan Musial, St. Louis
1944	Martin Marion, St. Louis
1945	Phil Cavarretta, Chicago
1946	Stan Musial, St. Louis
1947	Bob Elliott, Boston
1948	Stan Musial, St. Louis
1949	Jackie Robinson, Brooklyn
1950	Jim Konstanty, Philadelphia
1951	Roy Campanella, Brooklyn
1952	Hank Sauer, Chicago
1953	Roy Campanella, Brooklyn
1954	Willie Mays, New York
1955	Roy Campanella, Brooklyn
1956	Don Newcombe, Brooklyn
1957	Hank Aaron, Milwaukee
1958	Ernie Banks, Chicago
1959	Ernie Banks, Chicago
1960	Dick Groat, Pittsburgh
1961	Frank Robinson, Cincinnati
1962	Maury Wills, Los Angeles
1963	Sandy Koufax, Los Angeles
1964	Ken Boyer, St. Louis
1965	Willie Mays, San Francisco
1966	Roberto Clemente, Pittsburgh
1967	Orlando Cepeda, St. Louis
1968	Bob Gibson, St. Louis
1969	Willie McCovey, San Francisco
1970	Johnny Bench, Cincinnati
1971	Joe Torre, St. Louis
1972	Johnny Bench, Cincinnati
1973	Pete Rose, Cincinnati
1974	Steve Garvey, Los Angeles
1975	Joe Morgan, Cincinnati
1976	Joe Morgan, Cincinnati
1977	George Foster, Cincinnati
1978	Dave Parker, Pittsburgh
1979	Keith Hernandez, St. Louis; Willie Stargell, Pittsburgh
1980	Mike Schmidt, Philadelphia
1981	Mike Schmidt, Philadelphia
1982	Dale Murphy, Atlanta
1983	Dale Murphy, Atlanta
1984	Ryne Sandberg, Chicago
1985	Willie McGee, St. Louis
1986	Mike Schmidt, Philadelphia
1987	Andre Dawson, Chicago
1988	Kirk Gibson, Los Angeles
1989	Kevin Mitchell, San Francisco
1990	Barry Bonds, Pittsburgh
1991	Terry Pendleton, Atlanta
1992	Barry Bonds, Pittsburgh
1993	Barry Bonds, San Francisco
1994	Jeff Bagwell, Houston
1995	Barry Larkin, Cincinnati
1996	Ken Caminiti, San Diego
1997	Larry Walker, Colorado
1998	Sammy Sosa, Chicago
1999	Chipper Jones, Atlanta
2000	Jeff Kent, San Francisco
2001	Barry Bonds, San Francisco
2002	Barry Bonds, San Francisco
2003	Barry Bonds, San Francisco
2004	Barry Bonds, San Francisco
2005	Albert Pujols, St. Louis
2006	Ryan Howard, Philadelphia
2007	Jimmy Rollins, Philadelphia
2008	Albert Pujols, St. Louis
2009	Albert Pujols, St. Louis
2010	Joey Votto, Cincinnati
2011	Ryan Braun, Milwaukee
2012	Buster Posey, San Francisco
2013	Andrew McCutchen, Pittsburgh
2014	Clayton Kershaw, Los Angeles
2015	Bryce Harper, Washington
2016	Kris Bryant, Chicago
2017	Giancarlo Stanton, Miami
2018	Christian Yelich, Milwaukee
2019	Cody Bellinger, Los Angeles
2020	Freddie Freeman, Atlanta
2021	Bryce Harper, Philadelphia
2022	Paul Goldschmidt, St. Louis
2023	Ronald Acuña, Atlanta

American League

Year	Player, team
1931	Lefty Grove, Philadelphia
1932	Jimmie Foxx, Philadelphia
1933	Jimmie Foxx, Philadelphia
1934	Mickey Cochrane, Detroit
1935	Hank Greenberg, Detroit
1936	Lou Gehrig, New York
1937	Charlie Gehringer, Detroit
1938	Jimmie Foxx, Boston
1939	Joe DiMaggio, New York
1940	Hank Greenberg, Detroit
1941	Joe DiMaggio, New York
1942	Joe Gordon, New York
1943	Spurgeon "Spud" Chandler, New York
1944	Hal Newhouser, Detroit
1945	Hal Newhouser, Detroit
1946	Ted Williams, Boston
1947	Joe DiMaggio, New York
1948	Lou Boudreau, Cleveland
1949	Ted Williams, Boston
1950	Phil Rizzuto, New York
1951	Yogi Berra, New York
1952	Bobby Shantz, Philadelphia
1953	Al Rosen, Cleveland
1954	Yogi Berra, New York
1955	Yogi Berra, New York
1956	Mickey Mantle, New York
1957	Mickey Mantle, New York
1958	Jackie Jensen, Boston
1959	Nellie Fox, Chicago
1960	Roger Maris, New York
1961	Roger Maris, New York
1962	Mickey Mantle, New York
1963	Elston Howard, New York
1964	Brooks Robinson, Baltimore
1965	Zoilo Versalles, Minnesota
1966	Frank Robinson, Baltimore
1967	Carl Yastrzemski, Boston
1968	Denny McLain, Detroit
1969	Harmon Killebrew, Minnesota
1970	John "Boog" Powell, Baltimore
1971	Vida Blue, Oakland
1972	Dick Allen, Chicago
1973	Reggie Jackson, Oakland
1974	Jeff Burroughs, Texas
1975	Fred Lynn, Boston
1976	Thurman Munson, New York
1977	Rod Carew, Minnesota
1978	Jim Rice, Boston
1979	Don Baylor, California
1980	George Brett, Kansas City
1981	Rollie Fingers, Milwaukee
1982	Robin Yount, Milwaukee
1983	Cal Ripken Jr., Baltimore
1984	Willie Hernandez, Detroit
1985	Don Mattingly, New York
1986	Roger Clemens, Boston
1987	George Bell, Toronto
1988	Jose Canseco, Oakland
1989	Robin Yount, Milwaukee
1990	Rickey Henderson, Oakland
1991	Cal Ripken Jr., Baltimore
1992	Dennis Eckersley, Oakland
1993	Frank Thomas, Chicago
1994	Frank Thomas, Chicago
1995	Mo Vaughn, Boston
1996	Juan Gonzalez, Texas
1997	Ken Griffey Jr., Seattle
1998	Juan Gonzalez, Texas
1999	Ivan Rodriguez, Texas
2000	Jason Giambi, Oakland
2001	Ichiro Suzuki, Seattle
2002	Miguel Tejada, Oakland
2003	Alex Rodriguez, Texas
2004	Vladimir Guerrero, Anaheim
2005	Alex Rodriguez, New York
2006	Justin Morneau, Minnesota
2007	Alex Rodriguez, New York
2008	Dustin Pedroia, Boston
2009	Joe Mauer, Minnesota
2010	Josh Hamilton, Texas
2011	Justin Verlander, Detroit
2012	Miguel Cabrera, Detroit
2013	Miguel Cabrera, Detroit
2014	Mike Trout, Los Angeles
2015	Josh Donaldson, Toronto
2016	Mike Trout, Los Angeles
2017	José Altuve, Houston
2018	Mookie Betts, Boston
2019	Mike Trout, Los Angeles
2020	José Abreu, Chicago
2021	Shohei Ohtani, Los Angeles
2022	Aaron Judge, New York
2023	Shohei Ohtani, Los Angeles

Rookie of the Year, 1949-2023

(as selected by the Baseball Writers' Assn. of America)

1947: Jackie Robinson, Brooklyn, 1B (combined selection); 1948: Alvin Dark, Boston (NL), SS (combined selection).

National League

Year	Player, team, position
1949	Don Newcombe, Brooklyn, P
1950	Sam Jethroe, Boston, OF
1951	Willie Mays, NY, OF
1952	Joe Black, Brooklyn, P
1953	Jim Gilliam, Brooklyn, 2B
1954	Wally Moon, St. Louis, OF
1955	Bill Virdon, St. Louis, OF
1956	Frank Robinson, Cincinnati, OF
1957	Jack Sanford, Philadelphia, P
1958	Orlando Cepeda, San Francisco, 1B
1959	Willie McCovey, San Francisco, 1B
1960	Frank Howard, L.A., OF
1961	Billy Williams, Chicago, OF
1962	Ken Hubbs, Chicago, 2B
1963	Pete Rose, Cincinnati, 2B
1964	Richie Allen, Philadelphia, 3B
1965	Jim Lefebvre, L.A., 2B
1966	Tommy Helms, Cincinnati, 2B
1967	Tom Seaver, NY, P
1968	Johnny Bench, Cincinnati, C
1969	Ted Sizemore, L.A., 2B
1970	Carl Morton, Montréal, P
1971	Earl Williams, Atlanta, C
1972	Jon Matlack, NY, P
1973	Gary Matthews, San Francisco, OF
1974	Bake McBride, St. Louis, OF
1975	John Montefusco, San Francisco, P
1976	Butch Metzger, San Diego, P; Pat Zachry, Cincinnati, P
1977	Andre Dawson, Montréal, OF
1978	Bob Horner, Atlanta, 3B
1979	Rick Sutcliffe, L.A., P
1980	Steve Howe, L.A., P
1981	Fernando Valenzuela, L.A., P
1982	Steve Sax, L.A., 2B
1983	Darryl Strawberry, NY, OF
1984	Dwight Gooden, NY, P
1985	Vince Coleman, St. Louis, OF
1986	Todd Worrell, St. Louis, P
1987	Benito Santiago, San Diego, C
1988	Chris Sabo, Cincinnati, 3B
1989	Jerome Walton, Chicago, OF
1990	Dave Justice, Atlanta, 1B
1991	Jeff Bagwell, Houston, 1B
1992	Eric Karros, L.A., 1B
1993	Mike Piazza, L.A., C
1994	Raul Mondesi, L.A., OF
1995	Hideo Nomo, L.A., P
1996	Todd Hollandsworth, L.A., OF
1997	Scott Rolen, Philadelphia, 3B
1998	Kerry Wood, Chicago, P
1999	Scott Williamson, Cincinnati, P
2000	Rafael Furcal, Atlanta, SS
2001	Albert Pujols, St. Louis, OF
2002	Jason Jennings, Colorado, P
2003	Dontrelle Willis, Florida, P
2004	Jason Bay, Pittsburgh, OF
2005	Ryan Howard, Philadelphia, 1B
2006	Hanley Ramirez, Florida, SS
2007	Ryan Braun, Milwaukee, 3B
2008	Geovany Soto, Chicago, C
2009	Chris Coghlan, Florida, OF
2010	Buster Posey, San Francisco, C
2011	Craig Kimbrel, Atlanta, P
2012	Bryce Harper, Washington, OF
2013	José Fernández, Miami, P
2014	Jacob deGrom, NY, P
2015	Kris Bryant, Chicago, 3B
2016	Corey Seager, L.A., SS
2017	Cody Bellinger, L.A., 1B
2018	Ronald Acuña Jr., Atlanta, OF
2019	Pete Alonso, NY, 1B
2020	Devin Williams, Milwaukee, P
2021	Jonathan India, Cincinnati, 2B
2022	Michael Harris II, Atlanta, OF
2023	Corbin Carroll, Arizona, OF

American League

Year	Player, team, position
1949	Roy Sievers, St. Louis, OF
1950	Walt Dropo, Boston, 1B
1951	Gil McDougald, NY, 3B
1952	Harry Byrd, Philadelphia, P
1953	Harvey Kuenn, Detroit, SS
1954	Bob Grim, NY, P
1955	Herb Score, Cleveland, P
1956	Luis Aparicio, Chicago, SS
1957	Tony Kubek, NY, IF-OF
1958	Albie Pearson, Washington, OF
1959	Bob Allison, Washington, OF
1960	Ron Hansen, Baltimore, SS
1961	Don Schwall, Boston, P
1962	Tom Tresh, NY, IF-OF
1963	Gary Peters, Chicago, P
1964	Tony Oliva, Minnesota, OF
1965	Curt Blefary, Baltimore, OF
1966	Tommie Agee, Chicago, OF
1967	Rod Carew, Minnesota, 2B
1968	Stan Bahnsen, NY, P
1969	Lou Piniella, Kansas City, OF
1970	Thurman Munson, NY, C
1971	Chris Chambliss, Cleveland, 1B
1972	Carlton Fisk, Boston, C
1973	Al Bumbry, Baltimore, OF
1974	Mike Hargrove, Texas, 1B
1975	Fred Lynn, Boston, OF
1976	Mark Fidrych, Detroit, P
1977	Eddie Murray, Baltimore, DH
1978	Lou Whitaker, Detroit, 2B
1979	John Castino, Minnesota, 3B; Alfredo Griffin, Toronto, SS
1980	Joe Charboneau, Cleveland, OF
1981	Dave Righetti, NY, P
1982	Cal Ripken Jr., Baltimore, SS
1983	Ron Kittle, Chicago, OF
1984	Alvin Davis, Seattle, 1B
1985	Ozzie Guillen, Chicago, SS
1986	Jose Canseco, Oakland, OF
1987	Mark McGwire, Oakland, 1B
1988	Walt Weiss, Oakland, SS
1989	Gregg Olson, Baltimore, P
1990	Sandy Alomar Jr., Cleveland, C
1991	Chuck Knoblauch, Minnesota, 2B
1992	Pat Listach, Milwaukee, SS
1993	Tim Salmon, California, OF
1994	Bob Hamelin, Kansas City, DH
1995	Marty Cordova, Minnesota, OF
1996	Derek Jeter, NY, SS
1997	Nomar Garciaparra, Boston, SS
1998	Ben Grieve, Oakland, OF
1999	Carlos Beltran, Kansas City, OF
2000	Kazuhiro Sasaki, Seattle, P
2001	Ichiro Suzuki, Seattle, OF
2002	Eric Hinske, Toronto, 3B
2003	Angel Berroa, Kansas City, SS
2004	Bobby Crosby, Oakland, SS
2005	Huston Street, Oakland, P
2006	Justin Verlander, Detroit, P
2007	Dustin Pedroia, Boston, 2B
2008	Evan Longoria, Tampa Bay, 3B
2009	Andrew Bailey, Oakland, P
2010	Neftali Feliz, Texas, P
2011	Jeremy Hellickson, Tampa Bay, P
2012	Mike Trout, L.A., OF
2013	Wil Myers, Tampa Bay, OF
2014	José Abreu, Chicago, 1B
2015	Carlos Correa, Houston, SS
2016	Michael Fulmer, Detroit, P
2017	Aaron Judge, NY, OF
2018	Shohei Ohtani, L.A., DH/P
2019	Yordan Álvarez, Houston, OF
2020	Kyle Lewis, Seattle, OF
2021	Randy Arozarena, Tampa Bay, OF
2022	Julio Rodríguez, Seattle, OF
2023	Gunnar Henderson, Baltimore, SS

Major League Pennant Winners, 1901-75

National League						American League					
Year	Winner	W	L	PCT	Manager	Year	Winner	W	L	PCT	Manager
1901	Pittsburgh	90	49	.647	Clarke	1901	Chicago	83	53	.610	Griffith
1902	Pittsburgh	103	36	.741	Clarke	1902	Philadelphia	83	53	.610	Mack
1903	Pittsburgh	91	49	.650	Clarke	1903	Boston	91	47	.659	Collins
1904	New York	106	47	.693	McGraw	1904	Boston	95	59	.617	Collins
1905	New York	105	48	.686	McGraw	1905	Philadelphia	92	56	.622	Mack
1906	Chicago	116	36	.763	Chance	1906	Chicago	93	58	.616	Jones
1907	Chicago	107	45	.704	Chance	1907	Detroit	92	58	.613	Jennings
1908	Chicago	99	55	.643	Chance	1908	Detroit	90	63	.588	Jennings
1909	Pittsburgh	110	42	.724	Clarke	1909	Detroit	98	54	.645	Jennings
1910	Chicago	104	50	.675	Chance	1910	Philadelphia	102	48	.680	Mack
1911	New York	99	54	.647	McGraw	1911	Philadelphia	101	50	.669	Mack
1912	New York	103	48	.682	McGraw	1912	Boston	105	47	.691	Stahl
1913	New York	101	51	.664	McGraw	1913	Philadelphia	96	57	.627	Mack
1914	Boston	94	59	.614	Stallings	1914	Philadelphia	99	53	.651	Mack
1915	Philadelphia	90	62	.592	Moran	1915	Boston	101	50	.669	Carrigan
1916	Brooklyn	94	60	.610	Robinson	1916	Boston	91	63	.591	Carrigan
1917	New York	98	56	.636	McGraw	1917	Chicago	100	54	.649	Rowland
1918	Chicago	84	45	.651	Mitchell	1918	Boston	75	51	.595	Barrow
1919	Cincinnati	96	44	.686	Moran	1919	Chicago	88	52	.629	Gleason
1920	Brooklyn	93	61	.604	Robinson	1920	Cleveland	98	56	.636	Speaker

National League

Year	Winner	W	L	PCT	Manager
1921	New York	94	59	.614	McGraw
1922	New York	93	61	.604	McGraw
1923	New York	95	58	.621	McGraw
1924	New York	93	60	.608	McGraw
1925	Pittsburgh	95	58	.621	McKechnie
1926	St. Louis	89	65	.578	Hornsby
1927	Pittsburgh	94	60	.610	Bush
1928	St. Louis	95	59	.617	McKechnie
1929	Chicago	98	54	.645	McCarthy
1930	St. Louis	92	62	.597	Street
1931	St. Louis	101	53	.656	Street
1932	Chicago	90	64	.584	Hornsby, Grimm
1933	New York	91	61	.599	Terry
1934	St. Louis	95	58	.621	Frisch
1935	Chicago	100	54	.649	Grimm
1936	New York	92	62	.597	Terry
1937	New York	95	57	.625	Terry
1938	Chicago	89	63	.586	Grimm, Hartnett
1939	Cincinnati	97	57	.630	McKechnie
1940	Cincinnati	100	53	.654	McKechnie
1941	Brooklyn	100	54	.649	Durocher
1942	St. Louis	106	48	.688	Southworth
1943	St. Louis	105	49	.682	Southworth
1944	St. Louis	105	49	.682	Southworth
1945	Chicago	98	56	.636	Grimm
1946	St. Louis	98	58	.628	Dyer
1947	Brooklyn	94	60	.610	Shotton
1948	Boston	91	62	.595	Southworth
1949	Brooklyn	97	57	.630	Shotton
1950	Philadelphia	91	63	.591	Sawyer
1951	New York	98	59	.624	Durocher
1952	Brooklyn	96	57	.627	Dressen
1953	Brooklyn	105	49	.682	Dressen
1954	New York	97	57	.630	Durocher
1955	Brooklyn	98	55	.641	Alston
1956	Brooklyn	93	61	.604	Alston
1957	Milwaukee	95	59	.617	Haney
1958	Milwaukee	92	62	.597	Haney
1959	Los Angeles	88	68	.564	Alston
1960	Pittsburgh	95	59	.617	Murtaugh
1961	Cincinnati	93	61	.604	Hutchinson
1962	San Francisco	103	62	.624	Dark
1963	Los Angeles	99	63	.611	Alston
1964	St. Louis	93	69	.574	Keane
1965	Los Angeles	97	65	.599	Alston
1966	Los Angeles	95	67	.586	Alston
1967	St. Louis	101	60	.627	Schoendienst
1968	St. Louis	97	65	.599	Schoendienst
1969	New York	100	62	.617	Hodges
1970	Cincinnati	102	60	.630	Anderson
1971	Pittsburgh	97	65	.599	Murtaugh
1972	Cincinnati	95	59	.617	Anderson
1973	New York	82	79	.509	Berra
1974	Los Angeles	102	60	.630	Alston
1975	Cincinnati	108	54	.667	Anderson

American League

Year	Winner	W	L	PCT	Manager
1921	New York	98	55	.641	Huggins
1922	New York	94	60	.610	Huggins
1923	New York	98	54	.645	Huggins
1924	Washington	92	62	.597	Harris
1925	Washington	96	55	.636	Harris
1926	New York	91	63	.591	Huggins
1927	New York	110	44	.714	Huggins
1928	New York	101	53	.656	Huggins
1929	Philadelphia	104	46	.693	Mack
1930	Philadelphia	102	52	.662	Mack
1931	Philadelphia	107	45	.704	Mack
1932	New York	107	47	.695	McCarthy
1933	Washington	99	53	.651	Cronin
1934	Detroit	101	53	.656	Cochrane
1935	Detroit	93	58	.616	Cochrane
1936	New York	102	51	.667	McCarthy
1937	New York	102	52	.662	McCarthy
1938	New York	99	53	.651	McCarthy
1939	New York	106	45	.702	McCarthy
1940	Detroit	90	64	.584	Baker
1941	New York	101	53	.656	McCarthy
1942	New York	103	51	.669	McCarthy
1943	New York	98	56	.636	McCarthy
1944	St. Louis	89	65	.578	Sewell
1945	Detroit	88	65	.575	O'Neill
1946	Boston	104	50	.675	Cronin
1947	New York	97	57	.630	Harris
1948	Cleveland	97	58	.626	Boudreau
1949	New York	97	57	.630	Stengel
1950	New York	98	56	.636	Stengel
1951	New York	98	56	.636	Stengel
1952	New York	95	59	.617	Stengel
1953	New York	99	52	.656	Stengel
1954	Cleveland	111	43	.721	Lopez
1955	New York	96	58	.623	Stengel
1956	New York	97	57	.630	Stengel
1957	New York	98	56	.636	Stengel
1958	New York	92	62	.597	Stengel
1959	Chicago	94	60	.610	Lopez
1960	New York	97	57	.630	Stengel
1961	New York	109	53	.673	Houk
1962	New York	96	66	.593	Houk
1963	New York	104	57	.646	Houk
1964	New York	99	63	.611	Berra
1965	Minnesota	102	60	.630	Mele
1966	Baltimore	97	63	.606	Bauer
1967	Boston	92	70	.568	Williams
1968	Detroit	103	59	.636	Smith
1969	Baltimore	109	53	.673	Weaver
1970	Baltimore	108	54	.667	Weaver
1971	Baltimore	101	57	.639	Weaver
1972	Oakland	93	62	.600	Williams
1973	Oakland	94	68	.580	Williams
1974	Oakland	90	72	.556	Dark
1975	Boston	95	65	.594	Johnson

Major League Pennant Winners, 1976-2024

National League

Year	East winner	W	L	PCT	Manager	West winner	W	L	PCT	Manager	Pennant winner
1976	Philadelphia	101	61	.623	Ozark	Cincinnati	102	60	.630	Anderson	Cincinnati
1977	Philadelphia	101	61	.623	Ozark	Los Angeles	98	64	.605	Lasorda	Los Angeles
1978	Philadelphia	90	72	.556	Ozark	Los Angeles	95	67	.586	Lasorda	Los Angeles
1979	Pittsburgh	98	64	.605	Tanner	Cincinnati	90	71	.559	McNamara	Pittsburgh
1980	Philadelphia	91	71	.562	Green	Houston	93	70	.571	Virdon	Philadelphia
1981(a)	Philadelphia	34	21	.618	Green	Los Angeles	36	21	.632	Lasorda	(c)
1981(b)	Montréal	30	23	.566	Williams, Fanning	Houston	33	20	.623	Virdon	Los Angeles
1982	St. Louis	92	70	.568	Herzog	Atlanta	89	73	.549	Torre	St. Louis
1983	Philadelphia	90	72	.556	Corrales, Owens	Los Angeles	91	71	.562	Lasorda	Philadelphia
1984	Chicago	96	65	.596	Frey	San Diego	92	70	.568	Williams	San Diego
1985	St. Louis	101	61	.623	Herzog	Los Angeles	95	67	.586	Lasorda	St. Louis
1986	New York	108	54	.667	Johnson	Houston	96	66	.593	Lanier	New York
1987	St. Louis	95	67	.586	Herzog	San Francisco	90	72	.556	Craig	St. Louis
1988	New York	100	60	.625	Johnson	Los Angeles	94	67	.584	Lasorda	Los Angeles
1989	Chicago	93	69	.574	Zimmer	San Francisco	92	70	.568	Craig	San Francisco
1990	Pittsburgh	95	67	.586	Leyland	Cincinnati	91	71	.562	Piniella	Cincinnati
1991	Pittsburgh	98	64	.605	Leyland	Atlanta	94	68	.580	Cox	Atlanta

Year	East winner	W	L	PCT	Manager	West winner	W	L	PCT	Manager	Pennant winner
1992	Pittsburgh	96	66	.593	Leyland	Atlanta	98	64	.605	Cox	Atlanta
1993	Philadelphia	97	65	.599	Fregosi	Atlanta	104	58	.642	Cox	Philadelphia

Year	Division	Winner	W	L	PCT	Manager	Playoffs	Pennant winner
1994(d)	East	Montréal	74	40	.649	Alou	—	—
	Central	Cincinnati	66	48	.579	Johnson		
	West	Los Angeles	58	56	.509	Lasorda		
1995	East	Atlanta	90	54	.625	Cox	Atlanta 3, Colorado* 1	Atlanta
	Central	Cincinnati	85	59	.590	Johnson	Cincinnati 3, Los Angeles 0	
	West	Los Angeles	78	66	.542	Lasorda	Atlanta 4, Cincinnati 0	
1996	East	Atlanta	96	66	.593	Cox	Atlanta 3, Los Angeles* 0	Atlanta
	Central	St. Louis	88	74	.543	La Russa	St. Louis 3, San Diego 0	
	West	San Diego	91	71	.562	Bochy	Atlanta 4, St. Louis 3	
1997	East	Atlanta	101	61	.623	Cox	Atlanta 3, Houston 0	Florida* (Leyland)
	Central	Houston	84	78	.519	Dierker	Florida* 3, San Francisco 0	
	West	San Francisco	90	72	.556	Baker	Florida* 4, Atlanta 2	
1998	East	Atlanta	106	56	.654	Cox	Atlanta 3, Chicago* 0	San Diego
	Central	Houston	102	60	.630	Dierker	San Diego 3, Houston 1	
	West	San Diego	98	64	.605	Bochy	San Diego 4, Atlanta 2	
1999	East	Atlanta	103	59	.636	Cox	Atlanta 3, Houston 1	Atlanta
	Central	Houston	97	65	.599	Dierker, Galante	New York* 3, Arizona 1	
	West	Arizona	100	62	.617	Showalter	Atlanta 4, New York* 2	
2000	East	Atlanta	95	67	.586	Cox	St. Louis 3, Atlanta 0	New York* (Valentine)
	Central	St. Louis	95	67	.586	La Russa	New York* 3, San Francisco 1	
	West	San Francisco	97	65	.599	Baker	New York* 4, St. Louis 1	
2001	East	Atlanta	88	74	.543	Cox	Atlanta 3, Houston 0	Arizona
	Central	Houston	93	69	.574	Dierker	Arizona 3, St. Louis* 2	
	West	Arizona	92	70	.568	Brenly	Arizona 4, Atlanta 1	
2002	East	Atlanta	101	59	.631	Cox	St. Louis 3, Arizona 0	San Francisco* (Baker)
	Central	St. Louis	97	65	.599	La Russa	San Francisco* 3, Atlanta 2	
	West	Arizona	98	64	.605	Brenly	San Francisco* 4, St. Louis 1	
2003	East	Atlanta	101	61	.623	Cox	Chicago 3, Atlanta 2	Florida* (McKeon, Torborg)
	Central	Chicago	88	74	.543	Baker	Florida* 3, San Francisco 1	
	West	San Francisco	100	61	.621	Alou	Florida* 4, Chicago 3	
2004	East	Atlanta	96	66	.593	Cox	Houston* 3, Atlanta 2	St. Louis
	Central	St. Louis	105	57	.648	La Russa	St. Louis 3, Los Angeles 1	
	West	Los Angeles	93	69	.574	Tracy	St. Louis 4, Houston* 3	
2005	East	Atlanta	90	72	.556	Cox	St. Louis 3, San Diego 0	Houston* (Garner)
	Central	St. Louis	100	62	.617	La Russa	Houston* 3, Atlanta 1	
	West	San Diego	82	80	.506	Bochy	Houston* 4, St. Louis 2	
2006	East	New York	97	65	.599	Randolph	New York 3, Los Angeles* 0	St. Louis
	Central	St. Louis	83	78	.516	La Russa	St. Louis 3, San Diego 1	
	West	San Diego	88	74	.543	Bochy	St. Louis 4, New York 3	
2007	East	Philadelphia	89	73	.549	Manuel	Colorado* 3, Philadelphia 0	Colorado* (Hurdle)
	Central	Chicago	85	77	.525	Piniella	Arizona 3, Chicago 0	
	West	Arizona	90	72	.556	Melvin	Colorado* 4, Arizona 0	
2008	East	Philadelphia	92	70	.568	Manuel	Philadelphia 3, Milwaukee* 1	Philadelphia
	Central	Chicago	97	64	.602	Piniella	Los Angeles 3, Chicago 0	
	West	Los Angeles	84	78	.519	Torre	Philadelphia 4, Los Angeles 1	
2009	East	Philadelphia	93	69	.574	Manuel	Philadelphia 3, Colorado* 1	Philadelphia
	Central	St. Louis	91	71	.562	La Russa	Los Angeles 3, St. Louis 0	
	West	Los Angeles	95	67	.586	Torre	Philadelphia 4, Los Angeles 1	
2010	East	Philadelphia	97	65	.599	Manuel	San Francisco 3, Atlanta* 1	San Francisco
	Central	Cincinnati	91	71	.562	Baker	Philadelphia 3, Cincinnati 0	
	West	San Francisco	92	70	.568	Bochy	San Francisco 4, Philadelphia 2	
2011	East	Philadelphia	102	60	.630	Manuel	Milwaukee 3, Arizona 2	St. Louis* (La Russa)
	Central	Milwaukee	96	66	.593	Roenicke	St. Louis* 3, Philadelphia 2	
	West	Arizona	94	68	.580	Gibson	St. Louis* 4, Milwaukee 2	
2012	East	Washington	98	64	.605	Johnson	#St. Louis* 3, Washington 2	San Francisco
	Central	Cincinnati	97	65	.599	Baker	San Francisco 3, Cincinnati 2	
	West	San Francisco	94	68	.580	Bochy	San Francisco 4, St. Louis* 3	
2013	East	Atlanta	96	66	.593	González	St. Louis 3, #Pittsburgh* 2	St. Louis
	Central	St. Louis	97	65	.599	Matheny	Los Angeles 3, Atlanta 1	
	West	Los Angeles	92	70	.568	Mattingly	St. Louis 4, Los Angeles 2	
2014	East	Washington	96	66	.593	Williams	#San Francisco* 3, Washington 1	San Francisco* (Bochy)
	Central	St. Louis	90	72	.556	Matheny	St. Louis 3, Los Angeles 1	
	West	Los Angeles	94	68	.580	Mattingly	San Francisco* 4, St. Louis 1	
2015	East	New York	90	72	.556	Collins	#Chicago* 3, St. Louis 1	New York
	Central	St. Louis	100	62	.617	Matheny	New York 3, Los Angeles 2	
	West	Los Angeles	92	70	.568	Mattingly	New York 4, Chicago* 0	
2016	East	Washington	95	67	.586	Baker	Chicago 3, #San Francisco* 1	Chicago
	Central	Chicago	103	58	.640	Maddon	Los Angeles 3, Washington 2	
	West	Los Angeles	91	71	.562	Roberts	Chicago 4, Los Angeles 2	
2017	East	Washington	97	65	.599	Baker	Chicago 3, Washington 2	Los Angeles
	Central	Chicago	92	70	.568	Maddon	Los Angeles 3, #Arizona* 0	
	West	Los Angeles	104	58	.642	Roberts	Los Angeles 4, Chicago 1	
2018	East	Atlanta	90	72	.556	Snitker	Milwaukee 3, #Colorado* 0	Los Angeles
	Central	Milwaukee	96	67	.589	Counsell	Los Angeles 3, Atlanta 1	
	West	Los Angeles	92	71	.564	Roberts	Los Angeles 4, Milwaukee 3	
2019	East	Atlanta	97	65	.599	Snitker	St. Louis 3, Atlanta 2	Washington* (Martinez)
	Central	St. Louis	91	71	.562	Shildt	#Washington* 3, Los Angeles 2	
	West	Los Angeles	106	56	.654	Roberts	Washington* 4, St. Louis 0	
2020	East	Atlanta	35	25	.583	Snitker	Los Angeles 3, San Diego* 0	Los Angeles
	Central	Chicago	34	26	.567	Ross	Atlanta 3, Miami* 0	
	West	Los Angeles	43	17	.717	Roberts	Los Angeles 4, Atlanta 3	
2021	East	Atlanta	88	73	.547	Snitker	Los Angeles* 3, San Francisco 2	Atlanta
	Central	Milwaukee	95	67	.586	Counsell	#Atlanta 3, Milwaukee 1	
	West	San Francisco	107	55	.660	Kapler	Atlanta 4, Los Angeles* 2	
2022	East	Atlanta	101	61	.623	Snitker	**Philadelphia 2, St. Louis 0	Philadelphia* (Thomson)
	Central	St. Louis	93	69	.574	Marmol	**San Diego 2, New York 1	
	West	Los Angeles	111	51	.685	Roberts	Philadelphia* 3, Atlanta 1	
							San Diego* 3, Los Angeles 1	
							Philadelphia* 4, San Diego* 1	

Year	Division	Winner	W	L	PCT	Manager	Playoffs	Pennant winner
2023	East	Atlanta	104	58	.642	Snitker	**Philadelphia 2, Miami 0	Arizona*
	Central	Milwaukee	92	70	.568	Counsell	**Arizona 2, Milwaukee 0	(Lovullo)
	West	Los Angeles	100	62	.617	Roberts	Philadelphia* 3, Atlanta 1	
							Arizona* 3, Los Angeles 0	
							Arizona* 4, Philadelphia* 3	
2024	East	Philadelphia	95	67	.586	Thomson	**New York 2, Milwaukee 1	Los Angeles
	Central	Milwaukee	93	69	.574	Murphy	**San Diego 2, Atlanta 1	
	West	Los Angeles	98	64	.605	Roberts	New York* 3, Philadelphia 1	
							Los Angeles 3, San Diego* 2	
							Los Angeles 4, New York* 2	

American League

Year	East winner	W	L	PCT	Manager	West winner	W	L	PCT	Manager	Pennant winner
1976	New York	97	62	.610	Martin	Kansas City	90	72	.556	Herzog	New York
1977	New York	100	62	.617	Martin	Kansas City	102	60	.630	Herzog	New York
1978	New York	100	63	.613	Martin, Lemon	Kansas City	92	70	.568	Herzog	New York
1979	Baltimore	102	57	.642	Weaver	California	88	74	.543	Fregosi	Baltimore
1980	New York	103	59	.636	Howser	Kansas City	97	65	.599	Frey	Kansas City
1981(a)	New York	34	22	.607	Michael, Lemon	Oakland	37	23	.617	Martin	(c)
1981(b)	Milwaukee	31	22	.585	Rodgers	Kansas City	30	23	.566	Frey, Howser	New York
1982	Milwaukee	95	67	.586	Rodgers, Kuenn	California	93	69	.574	Mauch	Milwaukee
1983	Baltimore	98	64	.605	Altobelli	Chicago	99	63	.611	La Russa	Baltimore
1984	Detroit	104	58	.642	Anderson	Kansas City	84	78	.519	Howser	Detroit
1985	Toronto	99	62	.615	Cox	Kansas City	91	71	.562	Howser	Kansas City
1986	Boston	95	66	.590	McNamara	California	92	70	.568	Mauch	Boston
1987	Detroit	98	64	.605	Anderson	Minnesota	85	77	.525	Kelly	Minnesota
1988	Boston	89	73	.549	McNamara, Morgan	Oakland	104	58	.642	La Russa	Oakland
1989	Toronto	89	73	.549	Williams, Gaston	Oakland	99	63	.611	La Russa	Oakland
1990	Boston	88	74	.543	Morgan	Oakland	103	59	.636	La Russa	Oakland
1991	Toronto	91	71	.562	Gaston, Tenace	Minnesota	95	67	.586	Kelly	Minnesota
1992	Toronto	96	66	.593	Gaston	Oakland	96	66	.593	La Russa	Toronto
1993	Toronto	95	67	.586	Gaston	Chicago	94	68	.580	Lamont	Toronto

Year	Division	Winner	W	L	PCT	Manager	Playoffs	Pennant winner
1994(d)	East	New York	70	43	.619	Showalter	—	—
	Central	Chicago	67	46	.593	Lamont		
	West	Texas	52	62	.456	Kennedy		
1995	East	Boston	86	58	.597	Kennedy	Cleveland 3, Boston 0	Cleveland
	Central	Cleveland	100	44	.694	Hargrove	Seattle 3, New York* 2	
	West	Seattle	79	66	.545	Piniella	Cleveland 4, Seattle 2	
1996	East	New York	92	70	.568	Torre	Baltimore* 3, Cleveland 1	New York
	Central	Cleveland	99	62	.615	Hargrove	New York 3, Texas 1	
	West	Texas	90	72	.556	Oates	New York 4, Baltimore* 1	
1997	East	Baltimore	98	64	.605	Johnson	Baltimore 3, Seattle 1	Cleveland
	Central	Cleveland	86	75	.534	Hargrove	Cleveland 3, New York* 2	
	West	Seattle	90	72	.556	Piniella	Cleveland 4, Baltimore 2	
1998	East	New York	114	48	.704	Torre	New York 3, Texas 0	New York
	Central	Cleveland	89	73	.549	Hargrove	Cleveland 3, Boston* 1	
	West	Texas	88	74	.543	Oates	New York 4, Cleveland 2	
1999	East	New York	98	64	.605	Torre	New York 3, Texas 0	New York
	Central	Cleveland	97	65	.599	Hargrove	Boston* 3, Cleveland 2	
	West	Texas	95	67	.586	Oates	New York 4, Boston* 1	
2000	East	New York	87	74	.540	Torre	New York 3, Oakland 2	New York
	Central	Chicago	95	67	.586	Manuel	Seattle* 3, Chicago 0	
	West	Oakland	91	70	.565	Howe	New York 4, Seattle* 2	
2001	East	New York	95	65	.594	Torre	Seattle 3, Cleveland 2	New York
	Central	Cleveland	91	71	.562	Manuel	New York 3, Oakland* 2	
	West	Seattle	116	46	.716	Piniella	New York 4, Seattle 1	
2002	East	New York	103	58	.640	Torre	Anaheim* 3, New York 1	Anaheim*
	Central	Minnesota	94	67	.584	Gardenhire	Minnesota 3, Oakland 2	(Scioscia)
	West	Oakland	103	59	.636	Howe	Anaheim* 4, Minnesota 1	
2003	East	New York	101	61	.623	Torre	New York 3, Minnesota 1	New York
	Central	Minnesota	90	72	.556	Gardenhire	Boston* 3, Oakland 2	
	West	Oakland	96	66	.593	Macha	New York 4, Boston* 3	
2004	East	New York	101	61	.623	Torre	New York 3, Minnesota 1	Boston*
	Central	Minnesota	92	70	.568	Gardenhire	Boston* 3, Anaheim 0	(Francona)
	West	Anaheim	92	70	.568	Scioscia	Boston* 4, New York 3	
2005	East	New York	95	67	.586	Torre	Chicago 3, Boston* 0	Chicago
	Central	Chicago	99	63	.611	Guillen	Los Angeles 3, New York 2	
	West	Los Angeles	95	67	.586	Scioscia	Chicago 4, Los Angeles 1	
2006	East	New York	97	65	.599	Torre	Oakland 3, Minnesota 0	Detroit*
	Central	Minnesota	96	66	.593	Gardenhire	Detroit* 3, New York 1	(Leyland)
	West	Oakland	93	69	.574	Macha	Detroit* 4, Oakland 0	
2007	East	Boston	96	66	.593	Francona	Boston 3, Los Angeles 0	Boston
	Central	Cleveland	96	66	.593	Wedge	Cleveland 3, New York* 1	
	West	Los Angeles	94	68	.580	Scioscia	Boston 4, Cleveland 3	
2008	East	Tampa Bay	97	65	.599	Maddon	Tampa Bay 3, Chicago 1	Tampa Bay
	Central	Chicago	89	74	.546	Guillen	Boston* 3, Los Angeles 1	
	West	Los Angeles	100	62	.617	Scioscia	Tampa Bay 4, Boston* 3	
2009	East	New York	103	59	.636	Girardi	New York 3, Minnesota 0	New York
	Central	Minnesota	87	76	.534	Gardenhire	Los Angeles 3, Boston* 0	
	West	Los Angeles	97	65	.599	Scioscia	New York 4, Los Angeles 2	
2010	East	Tampa Bay	96	66	.593	Maddon	New York* 3, Minnesota 0	Texas
	Central	Minnesota	94	68	.580	Gardenhire	Texas 3, Tampa Bay 2	
	West	Texas	90	72	.556	Washington	Texas 4, New York* 2	
2011	East	New York	97	65	.599	Girardi	Detroit 3, New York 2	Texas
	Central	Detroit	95	67	.586	Leyland	Texas 3, Tampa Bay* 1	
	West	Texas	96	66	.593	Washington	Texas 4, Detroit 2	
2012	East	New York	95	67	.586	Girardi	New York 3, #Baltimore* 2	Detroit
	Central	Detroit	88	74	.543	Leyland	Detroit 3, Oakland 2	
	West	Oakland	94	68	.580	Melvin	Detroit 4, New York 0	
2013	East	Boston	97	65	.599	Farrell	Boston 3, #Tampa Bay* 1	Boston
	Central	Detroit	93	69	.574	Leyland	Detroit 3, Oakland 2	
	West	Oakland	96	66	.593	Melvin	Boston 4, Detroit 2	

Year	Division	Winner	W	L	PCT	Manager	Playoffs	Pennant winner
2014	East	Baltimore	96	66	.593	Showalter	#Kansas City* 3, Los Angeles 0	Kansas City* (Yost)
	Central	Detroit	90	72	.556	Ausmus	Baltimore 3, Detroit 0	
	West	Los Angeles	98	64	.605	Scioscia	Kansas City* 4, Baltimore 0	
2015	East	Toronto	93	69	.574	Gibbons	Kansas City 3, #Houston* 2	Kansas City
	Central	Kansas City	95	67	.586	Yost	Toronto 3, Texas 2	
	West	Texas	88	74	.543	Banister	Kansas City 4, Toronto 2	
2016	East	Boston	93	69	.574	Farrell	#Toronto* 3, Texas 0	Cleveland
	Central	Cleveland	94	67	.584	Francona	Cleveland 3, Boston 0	
	West	Texas	95	67	.586	Banister	Cleveland 4, Toronto* 1	
2017	East	Boston	93	69	.574	Farrell	Houston 3, Boston 1	Houston
	Central	Cleveland	102	60	.630	Francona	#New York* 3, Cleveland 2	
	West	Houston	101	61	.623	Hinch	Houston 4, New York* 3	
2018	East	Boston	108	54	.667	Cora	Boston 3, #New York* 1	Boston
	Central	Cleveland	91	71	.562	Francona	Houston 3, Cleveland 0	
	West	Houston	103	59	.636	Hinch	Boston 4, Houston 1	
2019	East	New York	103	59	.636	Boone	New York 3, Minnesota 0	Houston
	Central	Minnesota	101	61	.623	Baldelli	Houston 3, #Tampa Bay* 2	
	West	Houston	107	55	.660	Hinch	Houston 4, New York 2	
2020	East	Tampa Bay	40	20	.667	Cash	Tampa Bay 3, New York* 2	Tampa Bay
	Central	Minnesota	36	24	.600	Baldelli	Houston* 3, Oakland 1	
	West	Oakland	36	24	.600	Melvin	Tampa Bay 4, Houston* 3	
2021	East	Tampa Bay	100	62	.617	Cash	#Boston* 3, Tampa Bay 1	Houston
	Central	Chicago	93	69	.574	La Russa	Houston 3, Chicago 1	
	West	Houston	95	67	.586	Baker	Houston 4, Boston* 2	
2022	East	New York	99	63	.611	Boone	**Cleveland 2, Tampa Bay 0	Houston
	Central	Cleveland	92	70	.568	Francona	**Seattle 2, Toronto 0	
	West	Houston	106	56	.654	Baker	Houston 3, Seattle* 0	
							New York 3, Cleveland* 2	
							Houston 4, New York 0	
2023	East	Baltimore	101	61	.623	Hyde	**Minnesota 2, Toronto 0	Texas* (Bochy)
	Central	Minnesota	87	75	.537	Baldelli	**Texas 2, Tampa Bay 0	
	West	Houston	90	72	.556	Baker	Houston 3, Minnesota 1	
							Texas* 3, Baltimore 0	
							Texas* 4, Houston 3	
2024	East	New York	94	68	.580	Boone	**Detroit 2, Houston 0	New York
	Central	Cleveland	92	69	.571	Vogt	**Kansas City 2, Baltimore 0	
	West	Houston	88	73	.547	Espada	New York 3, Kansas City* 1	
							Cleveland 3, Detroit* 2	
							New York 4, Cleveland 1	

* = Wild-card team. If pennant winner is wild-card team, manager's name is given in parentheses. # = Single-game wild-card playoff winner (2012-21). ** = Best-of-three wild-card series (debuted in 2022). **Note:** In 2020, a best-of-three wild-card round included 8 teams in each league. (a) First half. (b) Second half. (c) Montréal, L.A., NY Yankees, and Oakland won the divisional playoffs. (d) In Aug. 1994, a players' strike began that caused the cancelation of the remainder of the season, the playoffs, and the World Series. Teams listed as division "winners" for 1994 were leading their divisions at the time of the strike.

World Series Results, 1903-2024

1903 Boston AL 5, Pittsburgh NL 3
1904 No series
1905 New York NL 4, Philadelphia AL 1
1906 Chicago AL 4, Chicago NL 2
1907 Chicago NL 4, Detroit AL 0, 1 tie
1908 Chicago NL 4, Detroit AL 1
1909 Pittsburgh NL 4, Detroit AL 3
1910 Philadelphia AL 4, Chicago NL 1
1911 Philadelphia AL 4, New York NL 2
1912 Boston AL 4, New York NL 3, 1 tie
1913 Philadelphia AL 4, New York NL 1
1914 Boston NL 4, Philadelphia AL 0
1915 Boston AL 4, Philadelphia NL 1
1916 Boston AL 4, Brooklyn NL 1
1917 Chicago AL 4, New York NL 2
1918 Boston AL 4, Chicago NL 2
1919 Cincinnati NL 5, Chicago AL 3
1920 Cleveland AL 5, Brooklyn NL 2
1921 New York NL 5, New York AL 3
1922 New York NL 4, New York AL 0, 1 tie
1923 New York AL 4, New York NL 2
1924 Washington AL 4, New York NL 3
1925 Pittsburgh NL 4, Washington AL 3
1926 St. Louis NL 4, New York AL 3
1927 New York AL 4, Pittsburgh NL 0
1928 New York AL 4, St. Louis NL 0
1929 Philadelphia AL 4, Chicago NL 1
1930 Philadelphia AL 4, St. Louis NL 2
1931 St. Louis NL 4, Philadelphia AL 3
1932 New York AL 4, Chicago NL 0
1933 New York NL 4, Washington AL 1
1934 St. Louis NL 4, Detroit AL 3
1935 Detroit AL 4, Chicago NL 2
1936 New York AL 4, New York NL 2
1937 New York AL 4, New York NL 1
1938 New York AL 4, Chicago NL 0
1939 New York AL 4, Cincinnati NL 0
1940 Cincinnati NL 4, Detroit AL 3
1941 New York AL 4, Brooklyn NL 1
1942 St. Louis NL 4, New York AL 1
1943 New York AL 4, St. Louis NL 1
1944 St. Louis NL 4, St. Louis AL 2
1945 Detroit AL 4, Chicago NL 3
1946 St. Louis NL 4, Boston AL 3
1947 New York AL 4, Brooklyn NL 3
1948 Cleveland AL 4, Boston NL 2
1949 New York AL 4, Brooklyn NL 1
1950 New York AL 4, Philadelphia NL 0
1951 New York AL 4, New York NL 2
1952 New York AL 4, Brooklyn NL 3
1953 New York AL 4, Brooklyn NL 2
1954 New York NL 4, Cleveland AL 0
1955 Brooklyn NL 4, New York AL 3
1956 New York AL 4, Brooklyn NL 3
1957 Milwaukee NL 4, New York AL 3
1958 New York AL 4, Milwaukee NL 3
1959 Los Angeles NL 4, Chicago AL 2
1960 Pittsburgh NL 4, New York AL 3
1961 New York AL 4, Cincinnati NL 1
1962 New York AL 4, San Francisco NL 3
1963 Los Angeles NL 4, New York AL 0
1964 St. Louis NL 4, New York AL 3
1965 Los Angeles NL 4, Minnesota AL 3
1966 Baltimore AL 4, Los Angeles NL 0
1967 St. Louis NL 4, Boston AL 3
1968 Detroit AL 4, St. Louis NL 3
1969 New York NL 4, Baltimore AL 1
1970 Baltimore AL 4, Cincinnati NL 1
1971 Pittsburgh NL 4, Baltimore AL 3
1972 Oakland AL 4, Cincinnati NL 3
1973 Oakland AL 4, New York NL 3
1974 Oakland AL 4, Los Angeles NL 1
1975 Cincinnati NL 4, Boston AL 3
1976 Cincinnati NL 4, New York AL 0
1977 New York AL 4, Los Angeles NL 2
1978 New York AL 4, Los Angeles NL 2
1979 Pittsburgh NL 4, Baltimore AL 3
1980 Philadelphia NL 4, Kansas City AL 2
1981 Los Angeles NL 4, New York AL 2
1982 St. Louis NL 4, Milwaukee AL 3
1983 Baltimore AL 4, Philadelphia NL 1
1984 Detroit AL 4, San Diego NL 1
1985 Kansas City AL 4, St. Louis NL 3
1986 New York NL 4, Boston AL 3
1987 Minnesota AL 4, St. Louis NL 3
1988 Los Angeles NL 4, Oakland AL 1
1989 Oakland AL 4, San Francisco NL 0
1990 Cincinnati NL 4, Oakland AL 0
1991 Minnesota AL 4, Atlanta NL 3
1992 Toronto AL 4, Atlanta NL 2
1993 Toronto AL 4, Philadelphia NL 2
1995 Atlanta NL 4, Cleveland AL 2
1996 New York AL 4, Atlanta NL 2
1997 Florida NL 4, Cleveland AL 3
1998 New York AL 4, San Diego NL 0
1999 New York AL 4, Atlanta NL 0
2000 New York AL 4, New York NL 1
2001 Arizona NL 4, New York AL 3
2002 Anaheim AL 4, San Francisco NL 3
2003 Florida NL 4, New York AL 2
2004 Boston AL 4, St. Louis NL 0
2005 Chicago AL 4, Houston NL 0
2006 St. Louis NL 4, Detroit AL 1
2007 Boston AL 4, Colorado NL 0
2008 Philadelphia NL 4, Tampa Bay AL 1
2009 New York AL 4, Philadelphia NL 2
2010 San Francisco NL 4, Texas AL 1
2011 St. Louis NL 4, Texas AL 3
2012 San Francisco NL 4, Detroit AL 0
2013 Boston AL 4, St. Louis NL 2
2014 San Fran. NL 4, Kansas City AL 3
2015 Kansas City AL 4, New York NL 1
2016 Chicago NL 4, Cleveland AL 3
2017 Houston AL 4, Los Angeles NL 3
2018 Boston AL 4, Los Angeles NL 1
2019 Washington NL 4, Houston AL 3
2020 Los Angeles NL 4, Tampa Bay AL 2
2021 Atlanta NL 4, Houston AL 2
2022 Houston AL 4, Philadelphia NL 2
2023 Texas AL 4, Arizona NL 1
2024 Los Angeles NL 4, New York AL 1

World Series Most Valuable Player, 1955-2024

Year	Player, position, team
1955	Johnny Podres, P, Brooklyn
1956	Don Larsen, P, NY (AL)
1957	Lew Burdette, P, Milwaukee (NL)
1958	Bob Turley, P, NY (AL)
1959	Larry Sherry, P, Los Angeles (NL)
1960[1]	Bobby Richardson, 2B, NY (AL)
1961	Whitey Ford, P, NY (AL)
1962	Ralph Terry, P, NY (AL)
1963	Sandy Koufax, P, Los Angeles (NL)
1964	Bob Gibson, P, St. Louis
1965	Sandy Koufax, P, Los Angeles (NL)
1966	Frank Robinson, OF, Baltimore
1967	Bob Gibson, P, St. Louis
1968	Mickey Lolich, P, Detroit
1969	Donn Clendenon, 1B, NY (NL)
1970	Brooks Robinson, 3B, Baltimore
1971	Roberto Clemente, OF, Pittsburgh
1972	Gene Tenace, C, Oakland
1973	Reggie Jackson, OF, Oakland
1974	Rollie Fingers, P, Oakland
1975	Pete Rose, 3B, Cincinnati
1976	Johnny Bench, C, Cincinnati
1977	Reggie Jackson, OF, NY (AL)
1978	Bucky Dent, SS, NY (AL)
1979	Willie Stargell, 1B, Pittsburgh
1980	Mike Schmidt, 3B, Philadelphia
1981	Ron Cey, 3B, Los Angeles (NL); Pedro Guerrero, OF, Los Angeles; Steve Yeager, C, Los Angeles
1982	Darrell Porter, C, St. Louis
1983	Rick Dempsey, C, Baltimore
1984	Alan Trammell, SS, Detroit
1985	Bret Saberhagen, P, Kansas City
1986	Ray Knight, 3B, NY (NL)
1987	Frank Viola, P, Minnesota
1988	Orel Hershiser, P, Los Angeles (NL)
1989	Dave Stewart, P, Oakland
1990	José Rijo, P, Cincinnati
1991	Jack Morris, P, Minnesota
1992	Pat Borders, C, Toronto
1993	Paul Molitor, DH, Toronto
1995	Tom Glavine, P, Atlanta
1996	John Wetteland, P, NY (AL)
1997	Livan Hernandez, P, Florida
1998	Scott Brosius, 3B, NY (AL)
1999	Mariano Rivera, P, NY (AL)
2000	Derek Jeter, SS, NY (AL)
2001	Curt Schilling, P, Arizona; Randy Johnson, P, Arizona
2002	Troy Glaus, 3B, Anaheim
2003	Josh Beckett, P, Florida
2004	Manny Ramirez, OF, Boston
2005	Jermaine Dye, OF, Chicago (AL)
2006	David Eckstein, SS, St. Louis
2007	Mike Lowell, 3B, Boston
2008	Cole Hamels, P, Philadelphia
2009	Hideki Matsui, DH, NY (AL)
2010	Edgar Renteria, SS, San Francisco
2011	David Freese, 3B, St. Louis
2012	Pablo Sandoval, 3B, San Francisco
2013	David Ortiz, DH, Boston
2014	Madison Bumgarner, P, San Francisco
2015	Salvador Pérez, C, Kansas City
2016	Ben Zobrist, OF, Chicago (NL)
2017	George Springer, OF, Houston
2018	Steve Pearce, 1B, Boston
2019	Stephen Strasburg, P, Washington
2020	Corey Seager, SS, Los Angeles (NL)
2021	Jorge Soler, OF, Atlanta
2022	Jeremy Peña, SS, Houston
2023	Corey Seager, SS, Texas
2024	Freddie Freeman, 1B, Los Angeles (NL)

World Series Won-Lost Records, by Franchise

Since beginning of "modern" era in 1901. Figures represent overall Series wins, not individual games.

Team	Wins	Losses
New York Yankees	27	14
St. Louis Cardinals	11	8
Boston Red Sox	9	4
Philadelphia/Kansas City/Oakland A's	9	5
New York/San Francisco Giants	8	12
Brooklyn/Los Angeles Dodgers	8	14
Pittsburgh Pirates	5	2
Cincinnati Reds	5	4
Boston/Milwaukee/Atlanta Braves	4	6
Detroit Tigers	4	7
Chicago White Sox	3	2
Washington Senators/Minnesota Twins	3	3
St. Louis Browns/Baltimore Orioles	3	4
Chicago Cubs	3	8
Florida/Miami Marlins	2	0
Toronto Blue Jays	2	0
Kansas City Royals	2	2
Houston Astros	2	3
New York Mets	2	3
Cleveland Indians/Guardians	2	4
Philadelphia Phillies	2	6
L.A./California/Anaheim/L.A. Angels	1	0
Montréal Expos/Washington Nationals	1	0
Arizona Diamondbacks	1	1
Texas Rangers	1	2
Colorado Rockies	0	1
Seattle Pilots/Milwaukee Brewers	0	1
San Diego Padres	0	2
Tampa Bay Rays	0	2
Seattle Mariners	0	0

All-Time World Series Career Leaders

(through 2024)

World Series Batting Leaders

Batter (min. 50 PA)	H	AB	AVG
1. David Ortiz	20	44	.455
2. Pablo Sandoval	20	47	.426
3. Johnny "Pepper" Martin	23	55	.418
4. Paul Molitor[1]	23	55	.418
5. Lance Berkman	16	39	.410
6. Hal McRae	18	45	.400
7. Lou Brock	34	87	.391
8. Marquis Grissom	30	77	.390
9. Thurman Munson	25	67	.373
10. George Brett	19	51	.373

Games Played	
Yogi Berra	75
Mickey Mantle	65
Elston Howard	54
Hank Bauer	53
Gil McDougald	53
Phil Rizzuto	52
Joe DiMaggio	51
Frankie Frisch	50
Pee Wee Reese	44
Roger Maris	41
Babe Ruth	41

Runs Batted In	
Mickey Mantle	40
Yogi Berra	39
Lou Gehrig	35
Babe Ruth	33
Joe DiMaggio	30
Bill Skowron	29
Duke Snider	26

Hits	
Yogi Berra	71
Mickey Mantle	59
Frankie Frisch	58
Joe DiMaggio	54
Derek Jeter	50
Hank Bauer	46
Pee Wee Reese	46
Gil McDougald	45
Phil Rizzuto	45
Lou Gehrig	43

Home Runs	
Mickey Mantle	18
Babe Ruth	15
Yogi Berra	12
Duke Snider	11
Lou Gehrig	10
Reggie Jackson	10
Joe DiMaggio	8
Frank Robinson	8
Bill Skowron	8

Runs	
Mickey Mantle	42
Yogi Berra	41
Babe Ruth	37
Derek Jeter	32
Lou Gehrig	30
Joe DiMaggio	27
Roger Maris	26
Elston Howard	25
Gil McDougald	23
Jackie Robinson	22

Stolen Bases	
Lou Brock	14
Eddie Collins	14
Dave Lopes	10
Phil Rizzuto	10
Frank Chance	9
Frankie Frisch	9
Kenny Lofton	9
Honus Wagner	9

(1) Some records show Molitor with 22 career World Series hits (.400 AVG).

World Series Pitching Leaders

Games Pitched		Wins		Strikeouts		Saves	
Mariano Rivera	24	Whitey Ford	10	Whitey Ford	94	Mariano Rivera	11
Whitey Ford	22	Bob Gibson	7	Bob Gibson	92	Rollie Fingers	6
Mike Stanton	20	Allie Reynolds	7	Allie Reynolds	62	Johnny Murphy	4
Rollie Fingers	16	Red Ruffing	7	Sandy Koufax	61	Robb Nen	4
Ryan Madson	16	Chief Bender	6	Red Ruffing	61	Allie Reynolds	4
Jeff Nelson	16	Lefty Gomez	6	Chief Bender	59	John Wetteland	4
Allie Reynolds	15	Waite Hoyt	6	George Earnshaw	56	Roy Face	3
Bob Turley	15	Three Finger Brown	5	Andy Pettitte	56	Neftali Feliz	3
Clay Carroll	14	Jack Coombs	5	John Smoltz	52	Firpo Marberry	3
Clem Labine	13	Catfish Hunter	5	Justin Verlander	50	Will McEnaney	3
Andy Pettitte	13	Christy Mathewson	5	Roger Clemens	49	Tug McGraw	3
Mark Wohlers	13	Herb Pennock	5	Waite Hoyt	49	Jonathan Papelbon	3
Jeremy Affeldt	12	Andy Pettitte	5	Christy Mathewson	48	Herb Pennock	3
Waite Hoyt	12	Vic Raschi	5	Bob Turley	46	Troy Percival	3
Catfish Hunter	12					Sergio Romo	3
Art Nehf	12					Kent Tekulve	3
Ryan Pressly	12					Todd Worrell	3

MLB Stadiums, 2024

Team	Stadium (year opened)	Surface	Distances (ft) LF	Center	RF	Seating capacity[1]
Arizona Diamondbacks	Chase Field (1998)	Turf	330	407	335	48,330
Atlanta Braves	Truist Park (2017)	Grass	335	400	325	41,184
Chicago Cubs	Wrigley Field (1914)	Grass	355	400	353	41,649
Cincinnati Reds	Great American Ball Park (2003)	Grass	328	404	325	45,814
Colorado Rockies	Coors Field (1995)	Grass	347	415	350	46,896
Los Angeles Dodgers	Dodger Stadium (1962)	Grass	330	395	330	56,000
Miami Marlins	loanDepot Park (2012)	Turf	344	400	335	37,442
Milwaukee Brewers	American Family Field (2001)	Grass	342	400	345	41,700
New York Mets	Citi Field (2009)	Grass	335	408	330	41,922
Philadelphia Phillies	Citizens Bank Park (2004)	Grass	329	401	330	42,901
Pittsburgh Pirates	PNC Park (2001)	Grass	325	399	320	38,362
St. Louis Cardinals	Busch Stadium (2006)	Grass	336	400	335	44,158
San Diego Padres	Petco Park (2004)	Grass	336	396	322	39,860
San Francisco Giants	Oracle Park (2000)	Grass	339	404	309	42,300
Washington Nationals	Nationals Park (2008)	Grass	336	402	335	41,373
Baltimore Orioles	Oriole Park at Camden Yards (1992)	Grass	333	410	318	44,487
Boston Red Sox	Fenway Park (1912)	Grass	310	390	302	37,105[2]
Chicago White Sox	Guaranteed Rate Field (1991)	Grass	330	400	335	40,615
Cleveland Guardians	Progressive Field (1994)	Grass	325	405	325	35,041
Detroit Tigers	Comerica Park (2000)	Grass	342	412	330	40,988
Houston Astros	Minute Maid Park (2000)	Grass	315	409	326	41,000
Kansas City Royals	Kauffman Stadium (1973)	Grass	330	410	330	37,903
Los Angeles Angels	Angel Stadium of Anaheim (1966)	Grass	347	396	348	45,603
Minnesota Twins	Target Field (2010)	Grass	339	404	328	38,544
New York Yankees	Yankee Stadium (2009)	Grass	318	408	314	46,537
Oakland Athletics	Oakland-Alameda County Coliseum (1966)	Grass	330	400	330	46,847
Seattle Mariners	T-Mobile Park (1999)	Grass	331	402	326	47,943
Tampa Bay Rays	Tropicana Field (1990)	Turf	315	404	322	25,025
Texas Rangers	Globe Life Field (2020)	Turf	329	407	326	40,518
Toronto Blue Jays	Rogers Centre (1989)	Astroturf	328	400	328	39,150

(1) As of 2024 season. (2) For day games; night game capacity is 37,555.

Major League Franchise Shifts and Additions Since 1904

1953: Boston Braves (NL) became Milwaukee Braves.
1954: St. Louis Browns (AL) became Baltimore Orioles.
1955: Philadelphia Athletics (AL) became Kansas City Athletics.
1958: New York Giants (NL) became San Francisco Giants.
1958: Brooklyn Dodgers (NL) became L.A. Dodgers.
1961: Washington Senators (AL) became Minnesota Twins.
1961: L.A. Angels enfranchised by the AL.
1961: Washington Senators II enfranchised by the AL, replacing Washington Senators I, whose franchise moved to Minneapolis-St. Paul and became Minnesota Twins.
1962: Houston Colt .45s enfranchised by the NL.
1962: New York Mets enfranchised by the NL.
1966: Milwaukee Braves (NL) became Atlanta Braves.
1968: Kansas City Athletics (AL) became Oakland Athletics.
1969: Kansas City Royals and Seattle Pilots enfranchised by the AL; Montréal Expos and San Diego Padres enfranchised by the NL.
1970: Seattle Pilots (AL) became Milwaukee Brewers.
1972: Washington Senators II (AL) became Texas Rangers (Dallas-Fort Worth area).
1977: Toronto Blue Jays and Seattle Mariners enfranchised by the AL.
1993: Colorado Rockies (Denver) and Florida Marlins (Miami) enfranchised by the NL.
1998: Tampa Bay Devil Rays began play in the AL; Arizona Diamondbacks (Phoenix) began play in the NL (both teams enfranchised in 1995). Milwaukee Brewers moved from the AL to the NL.
2005: Montréal Expos (NL) became Washington Nationals.
2013: Houston Astros moved from the NL to the AL.

National Baseball Hall of Fame and Museum

Located in Cooperstown, NY. # = Player chosen in first year of eligibility (five seasons after retirement) or earlier.
* = 2024 inductee. www.baseballhall.org

#Aaron, Hank
Alexander, Grover
Alomar, Roberto
Alston, Walt
Anderson, George
Anson, Cap
Aparicio, Luis
Appling, Luke
Ashburn, Richie
Averill, Earl
Bagwell, Jeff
Baines, Harold
Baker, Frank "Home Run"
Bancroft, Dave
#Banks, Ernie
Barlick, Al
Barrow, Edward G.
Beckley, Jake
Bell, James "Cool Papa"
*#Beltré, Adrián
#Bench, Johnny
Bender, Charles "Chief"
Berra, Lawrence "Yogi"
Biggio, Craig
Blyleven, Bert
#Boggs, Wade
Bottomley, Jim
Boudreau, Lou
Bresnahan, Roger
#Brett, George
#Brock, Lou
Brouthers, Dan
Brown, Mordecai
Brown, Ray
Brown, Willard
Bulkeley, Morgan C.
Bunning, Jim
Burkett, Jesse C.
Campanella, Roy
#Carew, Rod
Carey, Max
#Carlton, Steve
Carter, Gary
Cartwright, Alexander
Cepeda, Orlando
Chadwick, Henry
Chance, Frank
Chandler, Albert "Happy"
Charleston, Oscar
Chesbro, John
Chylak, Nestor
Clarke, Fred
Clarkson, John
#Clemente, Roberto
Cobb, Ty[1]
Cochrane, Mickey
Collins, Eddie
Collins, James
Combs, Earle
Comiskey, Charles A.
Conlan, John "Jocko"
Connolly, Thomas H.
Connor, Roger
Cooper, Andy
Coveleski, Stan
Cox, Bobby
Crawford, Sam
Cronin, Joe
Cummings, W. A. "Candy"
Cuyler, Hazen "Kiki"

Dandridge, Ray
Davis, George
Dawson, Andre
Day, Leon
Dean, Jay Hanna "Dizzy"
Delahanty, Ed
Dickey, Bill
Dihigo, Martín
#DiMaggio, Joe
#Doby, Larry
Doerr, Bobby
Dreyfuss, Barney
Drysdale, Don
Duffy, Hugh
Durocher, Leo
#Eckersley, Dennis
Evans, Billy
Evers, John
Ewing, Buck
Faber, Urban "Red"
#Feller, Bob
Ferrell, Rick
Fingers, Rollie
Fisk, Carlton
Flick, Elmer H.
Ford, Whitey
Foster, Andrew "Rube"
Foster, Bill
Fowler, Bud (born John W. Jackson)
Fox, Nellie
Foxx, Jimmie
Frick, Ford
Frisch, Frank
Galvin, James "Pud"
#Gehrig, Lou
Gehringer, Charles
#Gibson, Bob
Gibson, Josh
Giles, Warren
Gillick, Pat
#Glavine, Tom
Gomez, Lefty
Gordon, Joe
Goslin, Leon "Goose"
Gossage, Rich
Grant, Frank
Greenberg, Hank
#Griffey, Ken, Jr.
Griffith, Clark
Grimes, Burleigh
Grove, Lefty
Guerrero, Vladimir
#Gwynn, Tony
Hafey, Charles "Chick"
Haines, Jesse
#Halladay, Roy
Hamilton, Bill
Hanlon, Ned
Harridge, Will
Harris, Bucky
Hartnett, Gabby
Harvey, Doug
Heilmann, Harry
*Helton, Todd
#Henderson, Rickey
Herman, Billy
Herzog, Whitey
Hill, Pete
Hodges, Gil

Hoffman, Trevor
Hooper, Harry
Hornsby, Rogers
Hoyt, Waite
Hubbard, Cal
Hubbell, Carl
Huggins, Miller
Hulbert, William
Hunter, James "Catfish"
Irvin, Monte
#Jackson, Reggie
Jackson, Travis
Jenkins, Ferguson
Jennings, Hugh
#Jeter, Derek
Johnson, Byron "Ban"
#Johnson, Randy
Johnson, Walter[1]
Johnson, William "Judy"
#Jones, Chipper
Joss, Addie
Kaat, Jim
#Kaline, Al
Keefe, Timothy
Keeler, William
Kell, George
Kelley, Joe
Kelly, George
Kelly, King
Killebrew, Harmon
Kiner, Ralph
Klein, Chuck
Klem, Bill
#Koufax, Sandy
Kuhn, Bowie
La Russa, Tony
Lajoie, Nap
Landis, Kenesaw M.
Larkin, Barry
Lasorda, Tommy
Lazzeri, Tony
Lemon, Bob
Leonard, Buck
*Leyland, Jim
Lindstrom, Fred
Lloyd, Pop
Lombardi, Ernie
Lopez, Al
Lyons, Ted
Mack, Connie
Mackey, James "Biz"
MacPhail, Larry
MacPhail, Lee
#Maddux, Greg
Manley, Effa
#Mantle, Mickey
Manush, Henry
Maranville, Walter
Marichal, Juan
Marquard, Rube
Martinez, Edgar
#Martinez, Pedro
Mathews, Eddie
Mathewson, Christy[1]
*#Mauer, Joe
#Mays, Willie
Mazeroski, Bill
McCarthy, Joe
McCarthy, Thomas

#McCovey, Willie
McGinnity, Joe
McGowan, Bill
McGraw, John
McGriff, Fred
McKechnie, Bill
McPhee, John "Bid"
Medwick, Joe
Mendez, Jose
Miller, Marvin
Miñoso, Minnie
Mize, Johnny
#Molitor, Paul
#Morgan, Joe
Morris, Jack
#Murray, Eddie
#Musial, Stan
Mussina, Mike
Newhouser, Hal
Nichols, Kid
Niekro, Phil
O'Day, Hank
Oliva, Tony
O'Malley, Walter
O'Neil, John "Buck"
O'Rourke, Jim
#Ortiz, David
Ott, Mel
Paige, Satchel
#Palmer, Jim
Pennock, Herb
Perez, Tony
Perry, Gaylord
Piazza, Mike
Plank, Ed
Pompez, Alex
Posey, Cum(berland)
#Puckett, Kirby
Radbourn, Charlie
Raines, Tim
Reese, Pee Wee
Rice, Jim
Rice, Sam
Rickey, Branch
#Ripken, Cal, Jr.
#Rivera, Mariano
Rixey, Eppa
Rizzuto, Phil "Scooter"
Roberts, Robin
#Robinson, Brooks
#Robinson, Frank
#Robinson, Jackie
Robinson, Wilbert
#Rodríguez, Iván
Rogan, Joe "Bullet"
Rolen, Scott
Roush, Edd
Ruffing, Red
Ruppert, Jacob
Rusie, Amos
#Ruth, Babe[1]
#Ryan, Nolan
Sandberg, Ryne
Santo, Ron
Santop, Louis
Schalk, Ray
#Schmidt, Mike
Schoendienst, Red
Schuerholz, John

#Seaver, Tom
Selee, Frank
Selig, Bud
Sewell, Joe
Simmons, Al
Simmons, Ted
Sisler, George
Slaughter, Enos
Smith, Hilton
Smith, Lee
#Smith, Ozzie
#Smoltz, John
Snider, Duke
Southworth, Billy
#Spahn, Warren
Spalding, Albert
Speaker, Tris
#Stargell, Willie
Stearnes, Norman
Stengel, Casey
Sutter, Bruce
Suttles, George "Mule"
Sutton, Don
Taylor, Ben
Terry, Bill
#Thomas, Frank
#Thome, Jim
Thompson, Sam
Tinker, Joe
Torre, Joe
Torriente, Cristobal
Trammell, Alan
Traynor, Harold J. "Pie"
Vance, Arthur "Dazzy"
Vaughan, Joseph "Arky"
Veeck, Bill
Waddell, Rube
Wagner, Honus[1]
Walker, Larry
Wallace, Roderick
Walsh, Ed
Waner, Lloyd
Waner, Paul
Ward, John
Weaver, Earl
Weiss, George
Welch, Mickey
Wells, Willie
Wheat, Zach
White, Deacon
White, Sol
Wilhelm, Hoyt
Wilkinson, J. L.
Williams, Billy
Williams, Dick
Williams, Joe
#Williams, Ted
Willis, Vic
Wilson, Hack
Wilson, Jud
#Winfield, Dave
Wright, George
Wright, Harry
Wynn, Early
#Yastrzemski, Carl
Yawkey, Tom
Young, Cy
Youngs, Ross
#Yount, Robin

(1) Player inducted in 1936, the year of the first Hall of Fame election.

World Baseball Classic Results, 2006-23

Year	Champion	Runner-up	Final score	Final game location	Third place team
2006	Japan	Cuba	10-6	Petco Park, San Diego, CA	South Korea
2009	Japan	South Korea	5-3 (10)	Dodger Stadium, Los Angeles, CA	U.S.
2013	Dominican Republic	Puerto Rico	3-0	AT&T Park, San Francisco, CA	Netherlands
2017	U.S.	Puerto Rico	8-0	Dodger Stadium, Los Angeles, CA	Japan
2023	Japan	U.S.	3-2	loanDepot Park, Miami, FL	Mexico

Celtics Claim Record 18th NBA Title

The Boston Celtics captured their record 18th NBA championship with a 106-88 victory in Game 5 over the Dallas Mavericks at TD Garden in Boston, on June 17, 2024. The Celtics had set a record over the previous seven-year span with 61 playoff wins without winning a title, but this time Boston would not be denied. After a dominant 64-18 season to win the Atlantic Division by 14 games, the Celtics finished the 2024 postseason with a 16-3 record, losing just one game each to the Miami Heat and Cleveland Cavaliers before sweeping the Indiana Pacers in the Eastern Conference Finals. Rhode Island-born 35-year-old Celtics head coach Joe Mazzulla, in only his second year, became the youngest head coach to win a title since Bill Russell won with the Celtics in 1969. The 2024 Bill Russell Award for Finals MVP went to Boston's Jaylen Brown, who edged out teammate Jayson Tatum, the leading scorer in the series (22.2 points).

Boston's 18th title broke a tie with the Los Angeles Lakers for most championships, but the Lakers became the first team to win the new NBA Cup in-season tournament, beating the Pacers, 123-109, at T-Mobile Arena in Las Vegas on Dec. 9, 2023. Though it was the lone game to not count in the season standings, each player on the winning team received a $500,000 bonus. Lakers star LeBron James added yet another award to his storied career as the first in-season tournament MVP. In his 21st NBA season, James also became the first player to reach 40,000 career points and appear in 20 All-Star Games; the East won the highest-scoring All-Star Game in history, 211-186, in Indianapolis on Feb. 18, 2024.

In the two international games the Atlanta Hawks nipped the Orlando Magic, 120-119, at Arena CDMX in Mexico City, Nov. 9, 2023, and the Cavaliers downed the Brooklyn Nets, 111-102, at Accor Arena in Paris, Jan. 11, 2024. The NBA's rookie French sensation, first overall pick Victor Wembanyama with the San Antonio Spurs, at 19 years old became the youngest player in NBA history to have at least 20 points and 20 rebounds in a game on Dec. 8, 2023. Milwaukee Bucks star Giannis Antetokounmpo Dec. 13, 2023 notched 64 points without a 3-point field goal in a 140-126 victory against the Pacers, the most points in an NBA game without a three-pointer since the rule allowing the shot was introduced in 1979-80.

Dallas guard Luka Dončić, who became the first European NBA scoring leader in 2023-24, recorded 73 points in a 148-143 victory, Jan. 26, 2024, over the Hawks, the most points in an NBA game since an 81-point performance by Kobe Bryant of the Lakers in 2006. The No. 5-seed Mavericks upset three teams on their way to the Finals, defeating the No. 4-seed Los Angeles Clippers, top seed Oklahoma City Thunder, and 3-seed Minnesota Timberwolves in the Western Conference Finals.

Nikola Jokić of the Denver Nuggets won his third MVP Award in four years. Center Rudy Gobert of Minnesota received his fourth career Defensive Player of the Year Award, and teammate Naz Reid won Sixth Man for the first time. Mark Daigneault of the Oklahoma City Thunder was the NBA's Coach of the Year.

NBA Final Standings, 2023-24

Teams with the 7th-10th highest winning percentages in each conference qualified for a play-in tournament held Apr. 16-19, 2024. (playoff seeding in parentheses)

Eastern Conference

Atlantic Division	W	L	PCT	GB
Boston Celtics (1)	64	18	0.780	—
New York Knicks (2)	50	32	0.610	14
Philadelphia 76ers (7)	47	35	0.573	17
Brooklyn Nets	32	50	0.390	32
Toronto Raptors	25	57	0.305	39

Central Division	W	L	PCT	GB
Milwaukee Bucks (3)	49	33	0.598	—
Cleveland Cavaliers (4)	48	34	0.585	1
Indiana Pacers (6)	47	35	0.573	2
Chicago Bulls (9)	39	43	0.476	10
Detroit Pistons	14	68	0.171	35

Southeast Division	W	L	PCT	GB
Orlando Magic (5)	47	35	0.573	—
Miami Heat (8)	46	36	0.561	1
Atlanta Hawks (10)	36	46	0.439	11
Charlotte Hornets	21	61	0.256	26
Washington Wizards	15	67	0.183	32

Western Conference

Northwest Division	W	L	PCT	GB
Oklahoma City Thunder (1)	57	25	0.695	—
Denver Nuggets (2)	57	25	0.695	—
Minnesota Timberwolves (3)	56	26	0.683	1
Utah Jazz	31	51	0.378	26
Portland Trail Blazers	21	61	0.256	36

Pacific Division	W	L	PCT	GB
L.A. Clippers (4)	51	31	0.622	—
Phoenix Suns (6)	49	33	0.598	2
L.A. Lakers (8)	47	35	0.573	4
Sacramento Kings (9)	46	36	0.561	5
Golden State Warriors (10)	46	36	0.561	5

Southwest Division	W	L	PCT	GB
Dallas Mavericks (5)	50	32	0.610	—
New Orleans Pelicans (7)	49	33	0.598	1
Houston Rockets	41	41	0.500	9
Memphis Grizzlies	27	55	0.329	23
San Antonio Spurs	22	60	0.268	28

Note: Oklahoma City took the No. 1 seed over Denver due to a better division won-lost percentage.

NBA Playoff Results, 2024

Eastern Conference

Boston defeated Miami, 4 games to 1
Cleveland defeated Orlando, 4 games to 3
Indiana defeated Milwaukee, 4 games to 2
New York defeated Philadelphia, 4 games to 2
Boston defeated Cleveland, 4 games to 1
Indiana defeated New York, 4 games to 3
Boston defeated Indiana, 4 games to 0

Western Conference

Oklahoma City defeated New Orleans, 4 games to 0
Dallas defeated L.A. Clippers, 4 games to 2
Minnesota defeated Phoenix, 4 games to 0
Denver defeated L.A. Lakers, 4 games to 1
Dallas defeated Oklahoma City, 4 games to 2
Minnesota defeated Denver, 4 games to 3
Dallas defeated Minnesota, 4 games to 1

NBA Finals

Boston defeated Dallas, 4 games to 1 (107-89, 105-98, 106-99, 84-122, 106-88)

NBA Regular Season Individual Highs, 2023-24

Minutes, game: 54, Tyrese Maxey, Philadelphia v. San Antonio, Apr. 7 (2 OT)
Points, game: 73, Luka Dončić, Dallas v. Atlanta, Jan. 26
Field goals, game: 25, Luka Dončić, Dallas v. Atlanta, Jan. 26; Jalen Brunson, New York v. San Antonio, Mar. 29 (OT)
Field goal attempts, game: 47, Jalen Brunson, New York v. San Antonio, Mar. 29 (OT)
3-pointers, game: 12, Keegan Murray, Sacramento v. Utah, Dec. 16
3-point attempts, game: 23, Stephen Curry, Golden State v. Atlanta, Feb. 3 (OT)
Free throws, game: 24, Giannis Antetokounmpo, Milwaukee v. Indiana, Dec. 13
Free throw attempts, game: 32, Giannis Antetokounmpo, Milwaukee v. Indiana, Dec. 13
Rebounds, game: 31, Jusuf Nurkić, Phoenix v. Oklahoma City, Mar. 3
Assists, game: 23, Tyrese Haliburton, Indiana v. New York, Dec. 30
Steals, game: 7, Shai Gilgeous-Alexander, Oklahoma City v. San Antonio, Nov. 14; Herbert Jones, New Orleans v. Houston, Feb. 22; Anthony Davis, L.A. Lakers v. Minnesota, Mar. 10; Tre Mann, Charlotte v. Atlanta, Apr. 10
Blocks, game: 10, Victor Wembanyama, San Antonio v. Toronto, Feb. 12
Minutes played, season: 2,989, DeMar DeRozan, Chicago
Off. rebounds, season: 335, Clint Capela, Atlanta
Def. rebounds, season: 826, Domantas Sabonis, Sacramento
Personal fouls, season: 254, Jusuf Nurkić , Phoenix

NBA Finals MVP, 1969-2024

Year	Player, team
1969	Jerry West, L.A. Lakers
1970	Willis Reed, New York
1971	Lew Alcindor (Kareem Abdul-Jabbar), Milwaukee
1972	Wilt Chamberlain, L.A. Lakers
1973	Willis Reed, New York
1974	John Havlicek, Boston
1975	Rick Barry, Golden State
1976	Jo Jo White, Boston
1977	Bill Walton, Portland
1978	Wes Unseld, Washington
1979	Dennis Johnson, Seattle
1980	Magic Johnson, L.A. Lakers
1981	Cedric Maxwell, Boston
1982	Magic Johnson, L.A. Lakers
1983	Moses Malone, Philadelphia
1984	Larry Bird, Boston
1985	Kareem Abdul-Jabbar, L.A. Lakers
1986	Larry Bird, Boston
1987	Magic Johnson, L.A. Lakers
1988	James Worthy, L.A. Lakers
1989	Joe Dumars, Detroit
1990	Isiah Thomas, Detroit
1991	Michael Jordan, Chicago
1992	Michael Jordan, Chicago
1993	Michael Jordan, Chicago
1994	Hakeem Olajuwon, Houston
1995	Hakeem Olajuwon, Houston
1996	Michael Jordan, Chicago
1997	Michael Jordan, Chicago
1998	Michael Jordan, Chicago
1999	Tim Duncan, San Antonio
2000	Shaquille O'Neal, L.A. Lakers
2001	Shaquille O'Neal, L.A. Lakers
2002	Shaquille O'Neal, L.A. Lakers
2003	Tim Duncan, San Antonio
2004	Chauncey Billups, Detroit
2005	Tim Duncan, San Antonio
2006	Dwyane Wade, Miami
2007	Tony Parker, San Antonio
2008	Paul Pierce, Boston
2009	Kobe Bryant, L.A. Lakers
2010	Kobe Bryant, L.A. Lakers
2011	Dirk Nowitzki, Dallas
2012	LeBron James, Miami
2013	LeBron James, Miami
2014	Kawhi Leonard, San Antonio
2015	Andre Iguodala, Golden State
2016	LeBron James, Cleveland
2017	Kevin Durant, Golden State
2018	Kevin Durant, Golden State
2019	Kawhi Leonard, Toronto
2020	LeBron James, L.A. Lakers
2021	Giannis Antetokounmpo, Milwaukee
2022	Stephen Curry, Golden State
2023	Nikola Jokić, Denver
2024	Jaylen Brown, Boston

NBA Finals All-Time Statistical Leaders

(* = Active in 2023-24 season; minimum 10 games played.)

Scoring average	GP	FG	FT	PTS	AVG
Rick Barry	10	138	87	363	36.3
Michael Jordan	35	438	258	1,176	33.6
Jerry West	55	612	455	1,679	30.5
*Kevin Durant	15	160	92	455	30.3
Shaquille O'Neal	30	340	185	865	28.8
Bob Pettit	25	241	227	709	28.4
*LeBron James	55	588	285	1,562	28.4
Hakeem Olajuwon	17	187	91	467	27.5
*Stephen Curry	34	300	176	928	27.3
Elgin Baylor	44	442	277	1,161	26.4

Games Played

Bill Russell	70
Sam Jones	64
Kareem Abdul-Jabbar	56
Jerry West	55
*LeBron James	55

Points

Player	Points
Jerry West	1,679
*LeBron James	1,562
Kareem Abdul-Jabbar	1,317
Michael Jordan	1,176
Elgin Baylor	1,161

Rebounds

Player	Rebounds
Bill Russell	1,718
Wilt Chamberlain	862
Elgin Baylor	593
*LeBron James	561
Kareem Abdul-Jabbar	507

Assists

Player	Assists
Magic Johnson	584
*LeBron James	430
Jerry West	306
Bill Russell	265
Bob Cousy	239

NBA Most Valuable Player, 1956-2024

Year	Player, team
1956	Bob Pettit, St. Louis
1957	Bob Cousy, Boston
1958	Bill Russell, Boston
1959	Bob Pettit, St. Louis
1960	Wilt Chamberlain, Philadelphia
1961	Bill Russell, Boston
1962	Bill Russell, Boston
1963	Bill Russell, Boston
1964	Oscar Robertson, Cincinnati
1965	Bill Russell, Boston
1966	Wilt Chamberlain, Philadelphia
1967	Wilt Chamberlain, Philadelphia
1968	Wilt Chamberlain, Philadelphia
1969	Wes Unseld, Baltimore
1970	Willis Reed, New York
1971	Lew Alcindor (Abdul-Jabbar), Milw.
1972	Kareem Abdul-Jabbar, Milwaukee
1973	Dave Cowens, Boston
1974	Kareem Abdul-Jabbar, Milwaukee
1975	Bob McAdoo, Buffalo
1976	Kareem Abdul-Jabbar, L.A. Lakers
1977	Kareem Abdul-Jabbar, L.A. Lakers
1978	Bill Walton, Portland
1979	Moses Malone, Houston
1980	Kareem Abdul-Jabbar, L.A. Lakers
1981	Julius Erving, Philadelphia
1982	Moses Malone, Houston
1983	Moses Malone, Philadelphia
1984	Larry Bird, Boston
1985	Larry Bird, Boston
1986	Larry Bird, Boston
1987	Magic Johnson, L.A. Lakers
1988	Michael Jordan, Chicago
1989	Magic Johnson, L.A. Lakers
1990	Magic Johnson, L.A. Lakers
1991	Michael Jordan, Chicago
1992	Michael Jordan, Chicago
1993	Charles Barkley, Phoenix
1994	Hakeem Olajuwon, Houston
1995	David Robinson, San Antonio
1996	Michael Jordan, Chicago
1997	Karl Malone, Utah
1998	Michael Jordan, Chicago
1999	Karl Malone, Utah
2000	Shaquille O'Neal, L.A. Lakers
2001	Allen Iverson, Philadelphia
2002	Tim Duncan, San Antonio
2003	Tim Duncan, San Antonio
2004	Kevin Garnett, Minnesota
2005	Steve Nash, Phoenix
2006	Steve Nash, Phoenix
2007	Dirk Nowitzki, Dallas
2008	Kobe Bryant, L.A. Lakers
2009	LeBron James, Cleveland
2010	LeBron James, Cleveland
2011	Derrick Rose, Chicago
2012	LeBron James, Miami
2013	LeBron James, Miami
2014	Kevin Durant, Oklahoma City
2015	Stephen Curry, Golden State
2016	Stephen Curry, Golden State
2017	Russell Westbrook, Oklahoma City
2018	James Harden, Houston
2019	Giannis Antetokounmpo, Milwaukee
2020	Giannis Antetokounmpo, Milwaukee
2021	Nikola Jokić, Denver
2022	Nikola Jokić, Denver
2023	Joel Embiid, Philadelphia
2024	Nikola Jokić, Denver

NBA Scoring Leaders, 1947-2024

(Average points per game; minimum games for eligibility varied.)

Year	Player, team	PTS	AVG
1947	Joe Fulks, Philadelphia	1,389	23.2
1948	Max Zaslofsky, Chicago	1,007	21.0
1949	George Mikan, Minneapolis	1,698	28.3
1950	George Mikan, Minneapolis	1,865	27.4
1951	George Mikan, Minneapolis	1,932	28.4
1952	Paul Arizin, Philadelphia	1,674	25.4
1953	Neil Johnston, Philadelphia	1,564	22.3
1954	Neil Johnston, Philadelphia	1,759	24.4
1955	Neil Johnston, Philadelphia	1,631	22.7
1956	Bob Pettit, St. Louis	1,849	25.7
1957	Paul Arizin, Philadelphia	1,817	25.6
1958	George Yardley, Detroit	2,001	27.8
1959	Bob Pettit, St. Louis	2,105	29.2
1960	Wilt Chamberlain, Philadelphia	2,707	37.6
1961	Wilt Chamberlain, Philadelphia	3,033	38.4
1962	Wilt Chamberlain, Philadelphia	4,029	50.4
1963	Wilt Chamberlain, San Francisco	3,586	44.8
1964	Wilt Chamberlain, San Francisco	2,948	36.9
1965	Wilt Chamberlain, San Francisco-Phil.	2,534	34.7
1966	Wilt Chamberlain, Philadelphia	2,649	33.5
1967	Rick Barry, San Francisco	2,775	35.6
1968	Dave Bing, Detroit	2,142	27.1
1969	Elvin Hayes, San Diego	2,327	28.4
1970	Jerry West, L.A. Lakers	2,309	31.2
1971	Lew Alcindor (Kareem Abdul-Jabbar), Milw.	2,596	31.7
1972	Kareem Abdul-Jabbar, Milwaukee	2,822	34.8
1973	Nate Archibald, Kansas City-Omaha	2,719	34.0
1974	Bob McAdoo, Buffalo	2,261	30.6
1975	Bob McAdoo, Buffalo	2,831	34.5
1976	Bob McAdoo, Buffalo	2,427	31.1
1977	Pete Maravich, New Orleans	2,273	31.1
1978	George Gervin, San Antonio	2,232	27.2
1979	George Gervin, San Antonio	2,365	29.6
1980	George Gervin, San Antonio	2,585	33.1
1981	Adrian Dantley, Utah	2,452	30.7
1982	George Gervin, San Antonio	2,551	32.3
1983	Alex English, Denver	2,326	28.4
1984	Adrian Dantley, Utah	2,418	30.6
1985	Bernard King, New York	1,809	32.9
1986	Dominique Wilkins, Atlanta	2,366	30.3
1987	Michael Jordan, Chicago	3,041	37.1
1988	Michael Jordan, Chicago	2,868	35.0
1989	Michael Jordan, Chicago	2,633	32.5
1990	Michael Jordan, Chicago	2,753	33.6
1991	Michael Jordan, Chicago	2,580	31.5
1992	Michael Jordan, Chicago	2,404	30.1
1993	Michael Jordan, Chicago	2,541	32.6
1994	David Robinson, San Antonio	2,383	29.8

Year	Player, team	PTS	AVG
1995	Shaquille O'Neal, Orlando	2,315	29.3
1996	Michael Jordan, Chicago	2,491	30.4
1997	Michael Jordan, Chicago	2,431	29.6
1998	Michael Jordan, Chicago	2,357	28.7
1999	Allen Iverson, Philadelphia	1,284	26.8
2000	Shaquille O'Neal, L.A. Lakers	2,344	29.7
2001	Allen Iverson, Philadelphia	2,207	31.1
2002	Allen Iverson, Philadelphia	1,883	31.4
2003	Tracy McGrady, Orlando	2,407	32.1
2004	Tracy McGrady, Orlando	1,878	28.0
2005	Allen Iverson, Philadelphia	2,302	30.7
2006	Kobe Bryant, L.A. Lakers	2,832	35.4
2007	Kobe Bryant, L.A. Lakers	2,430	31.6
2008	LeBron James, Cleveland	2,250	30.0
2009	Dwyane Wade, Miami	2,386	30.2
2010	Kevin Durant, Oklahoma City	2,472	30.1
2011	Kevin Durant, Oklahoma City	2,161	27.7
2012	Kevin Durant, Oklahoma City	1,850	28.0
2013	Carmelo Anthony, New York	1,920	28.7
2014	Kevin Durant, Oklahoma City	2,593	32.0
2015	Russell Westbrook, Oklahoma City	1,886	28.1
2016	Stephen Curry, Golden State	2,375	30.1
2017	Russell Westbrook, Oklahoma City	2,558	31.6
2018	James Harden, Houston	2,191	30.4
2019	James Harden, Houston	2,818	36.1
2020	James Harden, Houston	2,335	34.3
2021	Stephen Curry, Golden State	2,015	32.0
2022	Joel Embiid, Philadelphia	2,079	30.6
2023	Joel Embiid, Philadelphia	2,183	33.1
2024	Luka Dončić, Dallas	2,370	33.9

NBA Champions, 1947-2024

	Regular season		Playoffs		
Year	Eastern champion	Western champion	Champion	Winning coach	Opponent
1947	Washington Capitols	Chicago Stags	Philadelphia	Ed Gottlieb	Chicago
1948	Philadelphia Warriors	St. Louis Bombers	Baltimore	Buddy Jeannette	Philadelphia
1949	Washington Capitols	Rochester	Minneapolis	John Kundla	Washington
1950[1]	Syracuse	Indianapolis	Minneapolis	John Kundla	Syracuse
1951	Philadelphia Warriors	Minneapolis	Rochester	Lester Harrison	New York
1952	Syracuse	Rochester	Minneapolis	John Kundla	New York
1953	New York	Minneapolis	Minneapolis	John Kundla	New York
1954	New York	Minneapolis	Minneapolis	John Kundla	Syracuse
1955	Syracuse	Ft. Wayne	Syracuse	Al Cervi	Ft. Wayne
1956	Philadelphia Warriors	Ft. Wayne	Philadelphia	George Senesky	Ft. Wayne
1957	Boston	St. Louis	Boston	Red Auerbach	St. Louis
1958	Boston	St. Louis	St. Louis	Alex Hannum	Boston
1959	Boston	St. Louis	Boston	Red Auerbach	Minneapolis
1960	Boston	St. Louis	Boston	Red Auerbach	St. Louis
1961	Boston	St. Louis	Boston	Red Auerbach	St. Louis
1962	Boston	L.A. Lakers	Boston	Red Auerbach	L.A. Lakers
1963	Boston	L.A. Lakers	Boston	Red Auerbach	L.A. Lakers
1964	Boston	San Francisco	Boston	Red Auerbach	San Francisco
1965	Boston	L.A. Lakers	Boston	Red Auerbach	L.A. Lakers
1966	Philadelphia	L.A. Lakers	Boston	Red Auerbach	L.A. Lakers
1967	Philadelphia	San Francisco	Philadelphia	Alex Hannum	San Francisco
1968	Philadelphia	St. Louis	Boston	Bill Russell	L.A. Lakers
1969	Baltimore	L.A. Lakers	Boston	Bill Russell	L.A. Lakers
1970	New York	Atlanta	New York	Red Holzman	L.A. Lakers

Year	Atlantic	Central	Midwest	Pacific	Champion	Winning coach	Opponent
1971	New York	Baltimore	Milwaukee	L.A. Lakers	Milwaukee	Larry Costello	Baltimore
1972	Boston	Baltimore	Milwaukee	L.A. Lakers	L.A. Lakers	Bill Sharman	New York
1973	Boston	Baltimore	Milwaukee	L.A. Lakers	New York	Red Holzman	L.A. Lakers
1974	Boston	Capital	Milwaukee	L.A. Lakers	Boston	Tom Heinsohn	Milwaukee
1975	Boston	Washington	Chicago	Golden State	Golden State	Al Attles	Washington
1976	Boston	Cleveland	Milwaukee	Golden State	Boston	Tom Heinsohn	Phoenix
1977	Philadelphia	Houston	Denver	L.A. Lakers	Portland	Jack Ramsay	Philadelphia
1978	Philadelphia	San Antonio	Denver	Portland	Washington	Dick Motta	Seattle
1979	Washington	San Antonio	Kansas City	Seattle	Seattle	Len Wilkens	Washington
1980	Boston	Atlanta	Milwaukee	L.A. Lakers	L.A. Lakers	Paul Westhead	Philadelphia
1981	Boston	Milwaukee	San Antonio	Phoenix	Boston	Bill Fitch	Houston
1982	Boston	Milwaukee	San Antonio	L.A. Lakers	L.A. Lakers	Pat Riley	Philadelphia
1983	Philadelphia	Milwaukee	San Antonio	L.A. Lakers	Philadelphia	Billy Cunningham	L.A. Lakers
1984	Boston	Milwaukee	Utah	L.A. Lakers	Boston	K. C. Jones	L.A. Lakers
1985	Boston	Milwaukee	Denver	L.A. Lakers	L.A. Lakers	Pat Riley	Boston
1986	Boston	Milwaukee	Houston	L.A. Lakers	Boston	K. C. Jones	Houston
1987	Boston	Atlanta	Dallas	L.A. Lakers	L.A. Lakers	Pat Riley	Boston
1988	Boston	Detroit	Denver	L.A. Lakers	L.A. Lakers	Pat Riley	Detroit
1989	New York	Detroit	Utah	L.A. Lakers	Detroit	Chuck Daly	L.A. Lakers
1990	Philadelphia	Detroit	San Antonio	L.A. Lakers	Detroit	Chuck Daly	Portland
1991	Boston	Chicago	San Antonio	Portland	Chicago	Phil Jackson	L.A. Lakers
1992	Boston	Chicago	Utah	Portland	Chicago	Phil Jackson	Portland
1993	New York	Chicago	Houston	Phoenix	Chicago	Phil Jackson	Phoenix
1994	New York	Atlanta	Houston	Seattle	Houston	Rudy Tomjanovich	New York
1995	Orlando	Indiana	San Antonio	Phoenix	Houston	Rudy Tomjanovich	Orlando
1996	Orlando	Chicago	San Antonio	Seattle	Chicago	Phil Jackson	Seattle
1997	Miami	Chicago	Utah	Seattle	Chicago	Phil Jackson	Utah
1998	Miami	Chicago	Utah	L.A. Lakers	Chicago	Phil Jackson	Utah
1999	Miami	Indiana	San Antonio	Portland	San Antonio	Gregg Popovich	New York
2000	Miami	Indiana	Utah	L.A. Lakers	L.A. Lakers	Phil Jackson	Indiana
2001	Philadelphia	Milwaukee	San Antonio	L.A. Lakers	L.A. Lakers	Phil Jackson	Philadelphia
2002	New Jersey	Detroit	San Antonio	Sacramento	L.A. Lakers	Phil Jackson	New Jersey
2003	New Jersey	Detroit	San Antonio	Sacramento	San Antonio	Gregg Popovich	New Jersey
2004	New Jersey	Indiana	Minnesota	L.A. Lakers	Detroit	Larry Brown	L.A. Lakers

Year	Atlantic	Central	Southeast	Northwest	Pacific	Southwest	Champion	Winning coach	Opponent
2005	Boston	Detroit	Miami	Seattle	Phoenix	San Antonio	San Antonio	Gregg Popovich	Detroit
2006	New Jersey	Detroit	Miami	Denver	Phoenix	San Antonio	Miami	Pat Riley	Dallas
2007	Toronto	Detroit	Miami	Utah	Phoenix	Dallas	San Antonio	Gregg Popovich	Cleveland
2008	Boston	Detroit	Orlando	Utah	L.A. Lakers	New Orleans	Boston	Glenn "Doc" Rivers	L.A. Lakers
2009	Boston	Cleveland	Orlando	Denver	L.A. Lakers	San Antonio	L.A. Lakers	Phil Jackson	Orlando
2010	Boston	Cleveland	Orlando	Denver	L.A. Lakers	Dallas	L.A. Lakers	Phil Jackson	Boston
2011	Boston	Chicago	Miami	OK City	L.A. Lakers	San Antonio	Dallas	Rick Carlisle	Miami
2012	Boston	Chicago	Miami	OK City	L.A. Lakers	San Antonio	Miami	Erik Spoelstra	OK City
2013	New York	Indiana	Miami	OK City	L.A. Clippers	San Antonio	Miami	Erik Spoelstra	San Antonio
2014	Toronto	Indiana	Miami	OK City	L.A. Clippers	San Antonio	San Antonio	Gregg Popovich	Miami
2015	Toronto	Cleveland	Atlanta	Portland	Golden State	Houston	Golden State	Steve Kerr	Cleveland
2016	Toronto	Cleveland	Miami	OK City	Golden State	San Antonio	Cleveland	Tyronn Lue	Golden State
2017	Boston	Cleveland	Washington	Utah	Golden State	San Antonio	Golden State	Steve Kerr	Cleveland
2018	Toronto	Cleveland	Miami	Portland	Golden State	Houston	Golden State	Steve Kerr	Cleveland
2019	Toronto	Milwaukee	Orlando	Denver	Golden State	Houston	Toronto	Nick Nurse	Golden State
2020	Toronto	Milwaukee	Miami	Denver	L.A. Lakers	Houston	L.A. Lakers	Frank Vogel	Miami
2021	Philadelphia	Milwaukee	Atlanta	Utah	Phoenix	Dallas	Milwaukee	Mike Budenholzer	Phoenix
2022	Boston	Milwaukee	Miami	Utah	Phoenix	Memphis	Golden State	Steve Kerr	Boston
2023	Boston	Milwaukee	Miami	Denver	Sacramento	Memphis	Denver	Michael Malone	Miami
2024	Boston	Milwaukee	Orlando	OK City	L.A. Clippers	Dallas	Boston	Joe Mazzulla	Dallas

(1) The newly formed NBA combined the 11-team BAA (Basketball Assn. of Amer.) and six NBL (Natl. Basketball League) teams in the 1949-50 season and had three divisions for one year. The Minneapolis Lakers were co-champions of the soon-defunct Central Division.

All-NBA and All-Defensive Teams, 2023-24

All-NBA Team		All-Defensive Team	
First Team	**Second Team**	**First Team**	**Second Team**
Giannis Antetokounmpo, Milwaukee	Kevin Durant, Phoenix	Anthony Davis, L.A. Lakers	Jaden McDaniels, Minnesota
Jayson Tatum, Boston	Kawhi Leonard, L.A. Clippers	Herbert Jones, New Orleans	Jalen Suggs, Orlando
Nikola Jokić, Denver	Anthony Davis, L.A. Lakers	Victor Wembanyama, San Antonio	Derrick White, Boston
Shai Gilgeous-Alexander, Oklahoma City	Jalen Brunson, New York	Rudy Gobert, Minnesota	Jrue Holiday, Boston
Luka Dončić, Dallas	Anthony Edwards, Minnesota	Bam Adebayo, Miami	Alex Caruso, Chicago

NBA Statistical Leaders, 2023-24

To qualify for averaged categories, player must be on pace to play 58 games in an 82-game season. Minimums in 2023-24 based on team games played.

Scoring Average

Player, team	GP	FG	FT	PTS	AVG
Luka Dončić, Dallas	70	804	478	2,370	33.9
Giannis Antetokounmpo, Milwaukee	73	837	514	2,222	30.4
Shai Gilgeous-Alexander, Oklahoma City	75	796	567	2,254	30.1
Jalen Brunson, New York	77	790	421	2,212	28.7
Devin Booker, Phoenix	68	642	405	1,841	27.1
Kevin Durant, Phoenix	75	751	362	2,032	27.1
Jayson Tatum, Boston	74	672	414	1,987	26.9
De'Aaron Fox, Sacramento	74	720	312	1,966	26.6
Stephen Curry, Golden State	74	650	299	1,956	26.4
Nikola Jokić, Denver	79	822	358	2,085	26.4

Field Goal Percentage
(Minimum 300 field goals made)

Player, team	FGM	FGA	PCT
Daniel Gafford, Washington-Dallas	348	480	0.725
Rudy Gobert, Minnesota	406	614	0.661
Ivica Zubac, L.A. Clippers	337	519	0.649
Jarrett Allen, Cleveland	519	819	0.634
Nic Claxton, Brooklyn	366	582	0.629
Jalen Duren, Detroit	349	564	0.619
Giannis Antetokounmpo, Milwaukee	837	1,369	0.611
Moritz Wagner, Orlando	332	552	0.601
Domantas Sabonis, Sacramento	634	1,068	0.594
Nikola Jokić, Denver	822	1,411	0.583

Free Throw Percentage
(Minimum 125 free throws made)

Player, team	FTM	FTA	PCT
Klay Thompson, Golden State	127	137	0.927
Stephen Curry, Golden State	299	324	0.923
Bogdan Bogdanović, Atlanta	151	164	0.921
Damian Lillard, Milwaukee	473	514	0.920
Anfernee Simons, Portland	163	178	0.916
Paul George, L.A. Clippers	264	291	0.907
Kyrie Irving, Dallas	190	210	0.905
Derrick White, Boston	137	152	0.901
Lauri Markkanen, Utah	249	277	0.899
Devin Booker, Phoenix	405	457	0.886

3-Point Field Goal Percentage
(Minimum 82 3-point field goals made)

Player, team	3FGM	3FGA	PCT
Grayson Allen, Phoenix	205	445	0.461
Luke Kennard, Memphis	107	238	0.450
Mike Conley, Minnesota	179	405	0.442
Garrison Mathews, Atlanta	85	193	0.440
Noman Powell, L.A. Clippers	167	384	0.435
Bradley Beal, Phoenix	101	235	0.430
Jrue Holiday, Boston	138	322	0.429
C.J. McCollum, New Orleans	239	557	0.429
Jalen Williams, Oklahoma City	103	241	0.427
Jamal Murray, Denver	145	341	0.425

Rebounds per Game

Player, team	GP	OFF	DEF	TOT	AVG
Domantas Sabonis, Sacramento	82	294	826	1,120	13.7
Rudy Gobert, Minnesota	76	285	697	982	12.9
Anthony Davis, L.A. Lakers	76	239	722	961	12.6
Nikola Jokić, Denver	79	223	753	976	12.4
Jalen Duren, Detroit	61	192	517	709	11.6
Giannis Antetokounmpo, Milwaukee	73	196	645	841	11.5
Jusuf Nurkić, Phoenix	76	224	613	837	11.0
Victor Wembanyama, San Antonio	71	161	594	755	10.6
Clint Capela, Atlanta	73	335	441	776	10.6
Jarrett Allen, Cleveland	77	243	568	811	10.5
Nikola Vučević, Chicago	76	210	591	801	10.5

Assists per Game

Player, team	GP	AST	APG
Tyrese Haliburton, Indiana	69	752	10.9
Luka Dončić, Dallas	70	686	9.8
Nikola Jokić, Denver	79	708	9.0
James Harden, L.A. Clippers	72	614	8.5
LeBron James, L.A. Lakers	71	589	8.3
Domantas Sabonis, Sacramento	82	673	8.2
Fred VanVleet, Houston	73	589	8.1
Cade Cunningham, Detroit	62	464	7.5
Tyus Jones, Washington	66	485	7.3
Damian Lillard, Milwaukee	73	508	7.0

Steals per Game

Player, team	GP	STL	AVG
De'Aaron Fox, Sacramento	74	150	2.0
Shai Gilgeous-Alexander, Oklahoma City	75	150	2.0
Alex Caruso, Chicago	71	120	1.7
Matisse Thybulle, Portland	65	113	1.7
Kawhi Leonard, L.A. Clippers	68	111	1.6
Paul George, L.A. Clippers	74	113	1.5

Blocked Shots per Game

Player, team	GP	BLK	AVG
Victor Wembanyama, San Antonio	71	254	3.6
Walker Kessler, Utah	64	154	2.4
Brook Lopez, Milwaukee	79	189	2.4
Anthony Davis. L.A. Lakers	76	178	2.3
Chet Holmgren, Oklahoma City	82	190	2.3
Nic Claxton, Brooklyn	71	146	2.1
Daniel Gafford, Washington-Dallas	74	153	2.1
Rudy Gobert, Minnesota	76	162	2.1
Myles Turner, Indiana	77	144	1.9
Jaren Jackson Jr., Memphis	66	106	1.6

NBA Defensive Player of the Year, 1983-2024

Year	Player, team
1983	Sidney Moncrief, Milwaukee
1984	Sidney Moncrief, Milwaukee
1985	Mark Eaton, Utah
1986	Alvin Robertson, San Antonio
1987	Michael Cooper, L.A. Lakers
1988	Michael Jordan, Chicago
1989	Mark Eaton, Utah
1990	Dennis Rodman, Detroit
1991	Dennis Rodman, Detroit
1992	David Robinson, San Antonio
1993	Hakeem Olajuwon, Houston
1994	Hakeem Olajuwon, Houston
1995	Dikembe Mutombo, Denver
1996	Gary Payton, Seattle
1997	Dikembe Mutombo, Atlanta
1998	Dikembe Mutombo, Atlanta
1999	Alonzo Mourning, Miami
2000	Alonzo Mourning, Miami
2001	Dikembe Mutombo, Philadelphia-Atlanta
2002	Ben Wallace, Detroit
2003	Ben Wallace, Detroit
2004	Ron Artest, Indiana
2005	Ben Wallace, Detroit
2006	Ben Wallace, Detroit
2007	Marcus Camby, Denver
2008	Kevin Garnett, Boston
2009	Dwight Howard, Orlando
2010	Dwight Howard, Orlando
2011	Dwight Howard, Orlando
2012	Tyson Chandler, New York
2013	Marc Gasol, Memphis
2014	Joakim Noah, Chicago
2015	Kawhi Leonard, San Antonio
2016	Kawhi Leonard, San Antonio
2017	Draymond Green, Golden State
2018	Rudy Gobert, Utah
2019	Rudy Gobert, Utah
2020	Giannis Antetokounmpo, Milwaukee
2021	Rudy Gobert, Utah
2022	Marcus Smart, Boston
2023	Jaren Jackson Jr., Memphis
2024	Rudy Gobert, Minnesota

NBA Rookie of the Year, 1953-2024

Year	Player, team
1953	Don Meineke, Ft. Wayne
1954	Ray Felix, Baltimore
1955	Bob Pettit, Milwaukee
1956	Maurice Stokes, Rochester
1957	Tom Heinsohn, Boston
1958	Woody Sauldsberry, Philadelphia
1959	Elgin Baylor, Minneapolis
1960	Wilt Chamberlain, Philadelphia
1961	Oscar Robertson, Cincinnati
1962	Walt Bellamy, Chicago
1963	Terry Dischinger, Chicago
1964	Jerry Lucas, Cincinnati
1965	Willis Reed, New York
1966	Rick Barry, San Francisco
1967	Dave Bing, Detroit
1968	Earl Monroe, Baltimore
1969	Wes Unseld, Baltimore
1970	Lew Alcindor (Kareem Abdul-Jabbar), Milwaukee
1971	Dave Cowens, Boston; Geoff Petrie, Portland
1972	Sidney Wicks, Portland
1973	Bob McAdoo, Buffalo
1974	Ernie DiGregorio, Buffalo
1975	Jamaal Wilkes, Golden State
1976	Alvan Adams, Phoenix
1977	Adrian Dantley, Buffalo
1978	Walter Davis, Phoenix
1979	Phil Ford, Kansas City
1980	Larry Bird, Boston
1981	Darrell Griffith, Utah
1982	Buck Williams, New Jersey
1983	Terry Cummings, San Diego
1984	Ralph Sampson, Houston
1985	Michael Jordan, Chicago
1986	Patrick Ewing, New York
1987	Chuck Person, Indiana
1988	Mark Jackson, New York
1989	Mitch Richmond, Golden State
1990	David Robinson, San Antonio
1991	Derrick Coleman, New Jersey
1992	Larry Johnson, Charlotte
1993	Shaquille O'Neal, Orlando
1994	Chris Webber, Golden State
1995	Grant Hill, Detroit; Jason Kidd, Dallas
1996	Damon Stoudamire, Toronto
1997	Allen Iverson, Philadelphia
1998	Tim Duncan, San Antonio
1999	Vince Carter, Toronto
2000	Elton Brand, Chicago; Steve Francis, Houston
2001	Mike Miller, Orlando
2002	Pau Gasol, Memphis
2003	Amar'e Stoudemire, Phoenix
2004	LeBron James, Cleveland
2005	Emeka Okafor, Charlotte
2006	Chris Paul, New Orl./OK City
2007	Brandon Roy, Portland
2008	Kevin Durant, Seattle
2009	Derrick Rose, Chicago
2010	Tyreke Evans, Sacramento
2011	Blake Griffin, L.A. Clippers
2012	Kyrie Irving, Cleveland
2013	Damian Lillard, Portland
2014	Michael Carter-Williams, Philadelphia
2015	Andrew Wiggins, Minnesota
2016	Karl-Anthony Towns, Minnesota
2017	Malcolm Brogdon, Milwaukee
2018	Ben Simmons, Philadelphia
2019	Luka Dončić, Dallas
2020	Ja Morant, Memphis
2021	LaMelo Ball, Charlotte
2022	Scottie Barnes, Toronto
2023	Paolo Banchero, Orlando
2024	Victor Wembanyama, San Antonio

NBA Sixth Man Award, 1983-2024

Year	Player, team
1983	Bobby Jones, Philadelphia
1984	Kevin McHale, Boston
1985	Kevin McHale, Boston
1986	Bill Walton, Boston
1987	Ricky Pierce, Milwaukee
1988	Roy Tarpley, Dallas
1989	Eddie Johnson, Phoenix
1990	Ricky Pierce, Milwaukee
1991	Detlef Schrempf, Indiana
1992	Detlef Schrempf, Indiana
1993	Clifford Robinson, Portland
1994	Dell Curry, Charlotte
1995	Anthony Mason, New York
1996	Toni Kukoc, Chicago
1997	John Starks, New York
1998	Danny Manning, Phoenix
1999	Darrell Armstrong, Orlando
2000	Rodney Rogers, Phoenix
2001	Aaron McKie, Philadelphia
2002	Corliss Williamson, Detroit
2003	Bobby Jackson, Sacramento
2004	Antawn Jamison, Dallas
2005	Ben Gordon, Chicago
2006	Mike Miller, Memphis
2007	Leandro Barbosa, Phoenix
2008	Manu Ginobili, San Antonio
2009	Jason Terry, Dallas
2010	Jamal Crawford, Atlanta
2011	Lamar Odom, L.A. Lakers
2012	James Harden, Oklahoma City
2013	J.R. Smith, New York
2014	Jamal Crawford, L.A. Clippers
2015	Lou Williams, Toronto
2016	Jamal Crawford, L.A. Clippers
2017	Eric Gordon, Houston
2018	Lou Williams, L.A. Clippers
2019	Lou Williams, L.A. Clippers
2020	Montrezl Harrell, L.A. Clippers
2021	Jordan Clarkson, Utah
2022	Tyler Herro, Miami
2023	Malcolm Brogdon, Boston
2024	Naz Reid, Minnesota

NBA Player Draft First-Round Picks, 2024

(Held June 26, 2024)

Team	Player, position, school/team
1. Atlanta	Zaccharie Risacher, F, JL Bourg (France)
2. Washington	Alex Sarr, C, Perth Wildcats (Australia)
3. Houston[1]	Reed Sheppard, G, Kentucky
4. San Antonio	Stephon Castle, G, UConn
5. Detroit	Ron Holland, F, G League Ignite (NV)
6. Charlotte	Tidjane Salaün, F, Cholet Basket (France)
7. Portland	Donovan Clingan, C, UConn
8. San Antonio[2]	Rob Dillingham, G, Kentucky
9. Memphis	Zach Edey, C, Purdue
10. Utah	Cody Williams, G/F, Colorado
11. Chicago	Matas Buzelis, F, G League Ignite (NV)
12. Oklahoma City[3]	Nikola Topić, G, KK Crvena Zvezda (Serbia)
13. Sacramento	Devin Carter, G, Providence
14. Portland[4]	Carlton Carrington, G, Pittsburgh
15. Miami	Kel'el Ware, C, Indiana
16. Philadelphia	Jared McCain, G, Duke
17. L.A. Lakers	Dalton Knecht, F, Tennessee
18. Orlando	Tristan da Silva, F, Colorado
19. Toronto[5]	Ja'Kobe Walter, G, Baylor
20. Cleveland	Jaylon Tyson, F, California
21. New Orleans[6]	Yves Missi, C, Baylor
22. Phoenix[7]	DaRon Holmes II, F, Dayton
23. Milwaukee[8]	AJ Johnson, G, Illawarra Hawks (Australia)
24. New York[9]	Kyshawn George, G, Miami
25. New York	Pacôme Dadiet, F, Ratiopharm Ulm (Germany)
26. Washington[10]	Dillon Jones, F, Weber State
27. Minnesota	Terrence Shannon Jr., G, Illinois
28. Denver[11]	Ryan Dunn, F, Virginia
29. Utah[12]	Isaiah Collier, G, USC
30. Boston	Baylor Scheierman, G/F, Creighton

(1) From Brooklyn. (2) From Toronto, rights traded to Minnesota. (3) From Houston. (4) From Golden State to Memphis to Boston, rights traded to Washington. (5) From Indiana. (6) From Milwaukee. (7) Rights traded to Denver. (8) From New Orleans. (9) From Dallas, rights traded to Washington. (10) From L.A. Clippers to Oklahoma City to Dallas, rights traded to Oklahoma City via New York. (11) Rights traded to Phoenix. (12) From Oklahoma City to Indiana to Toronto.

Number-One First-Round NBA Draft Picks, 1966-2024

Year	Team	Player, school/team
1966	New York	Cazzie Russell, Michigan
1967	Detroit	Jimmy Walker, Providence
1968	San Diego	Elvin Hayes, Houston
1969	Milwaukee	Lew Alcindor (Kareem Abdul-Jabbar), UCLA
1970	Detroit	Bob Lanier, St. Bonaventure
1971	Cleveland	Austin Carr, Notre Dame
1972	Portland	LaRue Martin, Loyola-Chicago
1973	Philadelphia	Doug Collins, Illinois State
1974	Portland	Bill Walton, UCLA
1975	Atlanta	David Thompson[1], NC State
1976	Houston	John Lucas, Maryland
1977	Milwaukee	Kent Benson, Indiana
1978	Portland	Mychal Thompson, Minnesota
1979	L.A. Lakers	Earvin "Magic" Johnson, Michigan State
1980	Golden State	Joe Barry Carroll, Purdue
1981	Dallas	Mark Aguirre, DePaul
1982	L.A. Lakers	James Worthy, North Carolina
1983	Houston	Ralph Sampson, Virginia
1984	Houston	Hakeem Olajuwon, Houston
1985	New York	Patrick Ewing, Georgetown
1986	Cleveland	Brad Daugherty, North Carolina
1987	San Antonio	David Robinson, Navy
1988	L.A. Clippers	Danny Manning, Kansas
1989	Sacramento	Pervis Ellison, Louisville
1990	New Jersey	Derrick Coleman, Syracuse
1991	Charlotte	Larry Johnson, UNLV
1992	Orlando	Shaquille O'Neal, LSU
1993	Orlando	Chris Webber[2], Michigan
1994	Milwaukee	Glenn Robinson, Purdue
1995	Golden State	Joe Smith, Maryland
1996	Philadelphia	Allen Iverson, Georgetown
1997	San Antonio	Tim Duncan, Wake Forest
1998	L.A. Clippers	Michael Olowokandi, Pacific (CA)
1999	Chicago	Elton Brand, Duke
2000	New Jersey	Kenyon Martin, Cincinnati
2001	Washington	Kwame Brown, Glynn Academy (HS)
2002	Houston	Yao Ming, Shanghai Sharks (China)
2003	Cleveland	LeBron James, St. Vincent-St. Mary (HS)

Year	Team	Player, school/team
2004	Orlando	Dwight Howard, Southwest Atlanta Christian Academy (HS)
2005	Milwaukee	Andrew Bogut, Utah
2006	Toronto	Andrea Bargnani, Benetton Treviso (Italy)
2007	Portland	Greg Oden, Ohio State
2008	Chicago	Derrick Rose, Memphis
2009	L.A. Clippers	Blake Griffin, Oklahoma
2010	Washington	John Wall, Kentucky
2011	Cleveland	Kyrie Irving, Duke
2012	New Orleans	Anthony Davis, Kentucky
2013	Cleveland	Anthony Bennett, UNLV
2014	Cleveland	Andrew Wiggins, Kansas
2015	Minnesota	Karl-Anthony Towns, Kentucky
2016	Philadelphia	Ben Simmons, LSU
2017	Philadelphia	Markelle Fultz, Washington
2018	Phoenix	Deandre Ayton, Arizona
2019	New Orleans	Zion Williamson, Duke
2020	Minnesota	Anthony Edwards, Georgia
2021	Detroit	Cade Cunningham, Oklahoma St.
2022	Orlando	Paolo Banchero, Duke
2023	San Antonio	Victor Wembanyama, Metropolitans 92 (France)
2024	Atlanta	Zaccharie Risacher, JL Bourg (France)

HS = High school. (1) Signed with Denver of the American Basketball Association (ABA). (2) Traded to Golden State for rights to Anfernee Hardaway and three future first-round draft choices.

All-Time NBA Statistical Leaders

(At end of 2023-24 season. * = Active in 2023-24 season. Does not include ABA statistics.)

Scoring Average
(Minimum 400 games or 10,000 points)

	GP	PTS	AVG
Michael Jordan	1,072	32,292	30.1
Wilt Chamberlain	1,045	31,419	30.1
*Luka Dončić	400	11,470	28.7
*Joel Embiid	433	12,071	27.9
Elgin Baylor	846	23,149	27.4
*Kevin Durant	1,061	28,924	27.3
*LeBron James	1,492	40,474	27.1
Jerry West	932	25,192	27.0
Allen Iverson	714	24,368	26.7
Bob Pettit	792	20,880	26.4

3-Point Field Goal Percentage
(Minimum 250 3-point field goals made)

	3-FGM	3-FGA	PCT
Steve Kerr	726	1,599	45.4
Hubert Davis	728	1,651	44.1
*Luke Kennard	790	1,801	43.9
Dražen Petrović	255	583	43.7
*Joe Harris	1,026	2,354	43.6
Jason Kapono	457	1,054	43.4
Tim Legler	260	603	43.1
*Seth Curry	862	2,001	43.1
Steve Novak	575	1,337	43.0
Kyle Korver	2,450	5,715	42.9

Free Throw Percentage
(Minimum 1,200 free throws made)

	FTM	FTA	PCT
*Stephen Curry	3,753	4,125	91.0
Steve Nash	3,060	3,384	90.4
Mark Price	2,135	2,362	90.4
Rick Barry	3,818	4,243	90.0
*Damian Lillard	4,900	5,460	89.7
Peja Stojakovic	2,237	2,500	89.5
Chauncey Billups	4,496	5,029	89.4
Ray Allen	4,398	4,920	89.4
Calvin Murphy	3,445	3,864	89.2
JJ Redick	2,060	2,310	89.2

Field Goal Percentage
(Minimum 2,000 field goals made)

	FGM	FGA	PCT
*DeAndre Jordan	3,765	5,585	67.4
*Rudy Gobert	3,562	5,440	65.5
*Jarrett Allen	2,460	3,902	63.0
*Clint Capela	3,252	5,238	62.1
*Montrezl Harrell	2,506	4,050	61.9
Artis Gilmore	5,732	9,570	59.9
Tyson Chandler	3,558	5,964	59.7
*Mason Plumlee	2,595	4,367	59.4
*Deandre Ayton	2,640	4,458	59.2
Steven Adams	2,713	4,619	58.7

Minutes Played

Kareem Abdul-Jabbar	57,446
*LeBron James	56,597
Karl Malone	54,852
Dirk Nowitzki	51,369
Kevin Garnett	50,418
Jason Kidd	50,110
Elvin Hayes	50,000
Kobe Bryant	48,638
Wilt Chamberlain	47,859
John Stockton	47,764

Games Played

Robert Parish	1,611
Kareem Abdul-Jabbar	1,560
Vince Carter	1,541
Dirk Nowitzki	1,522
John Stockton	1,504
*LeBron James	1,492
Karl Malone	1,476
Kevin Garnett	1,462
Kevin Willis	1,424
Jason Terry	1,410

Personal Fouls

Kareem Abdul-Jabbar	4,657
Karl Malone	4,578
Robert Parish	4,443
Charles Oakley	4,421
Hakeem Olajuwon	4,383
Buck Williams	4,267
Elvin Hayes	4,193
Clifford Robinson	4,175
Kevin Willis	4,172
Shaquille O'Neal	4,146
Otis Thorpe	4,146

Blocked Shots

Hakeem Olajuwon	3,830
Dikembe Mutombo	3,289
Kareem Abdul-Jabbar	3,189
Mark Eaton	3,064
Tim Duncan	3,020
David Robinson	2,954
Patrick Ewing	2,894
Shaquille O'Neal	2,732
Tree Rollins	2,542
Robert Parish	2,361

Field Goals Attempted

*LeBron James	29,313
Kareem Abdul-Jabbar	28,307
Karl Malone	26,210
Kobe Bryant	26,200
Michael Jordan	24,537
Elvin Hayes	24,272
John Havlicek	23,930
Dirk Nowitzki	23,734
Wilt Chamberlain	23,497
Carmelo Anthony	22,643

Field Goals Made

Kareem Abdul-Jabbar	15,837
*LeBron James	14,837
Karl Malone	13,528
Wilt Chamberlain	12,681
Michael Jordan	12,192
Kobe Bryant	11,719
Shaquille O'Neal	11,330
Dirk Nowitzki	11,169
Elvin Hayes	10,976
Hakeem Olajuwon	10,749

3-Point Field Goals Attempted

*Stephen Curry	8,805
*James Harden	8,082
Ray Allen	7,429
*Damian Lillard	7,032
*LeBron James	6,926
Reggie Miller	6,486
Jamal Crawford	6,379
Vince Carter	6,168
Jason Terry	6,010
*Klay Thompson	6,010

3-Point Field Goals Made

*Stephen Curry	3,747
Ray Allen	2,973
*James Harden	2,940
*Damian Lillard	2,607
Reggie Miller	2,560
*Klay Thompson	2,481
Kyle Korver	2,450
*LeBron James	2,410
Vince Carter	2,290
Jason Terry	2,282

Points

*LeBron James	40,474
Kareem Abdul-Jabbar	38,387
Karl Malone	36,928
Kobe Bryant	33,643
Michael Jordan	32,292
Dirk Nowitzki	31,560
Wilt Chamberlain	31,419
*Kevin Durant	28,924
Shaquille O'Neal	28,596
Carmelo Anthony	28,289

Rebounds

Wilt Chamberlain	23,924
Bill Russell	21,620
Kareem Abdul-Jabbar	17,440
Elvin Hayes	16,279
Moses Malone	16,212
Tim Duncan	15,091
Karl Malone	14,968
Robert Parish	14,715
Kevin Garnett	14,662
Dwight Howard	14,627

Assists

John Stockton	15,806
Jason Kidd	12,091
*Chris Paul	11,894
*LeBron James	11,009
Steve Nash	10,335
Mark Jackson	10,334
Magic Johnson	10,141
Oscar Robertson	9,887
*Russell Westbrook	9,468
Isiah Thomas	9,061

Steals

John Stockton	3,265
Jason Kidd	2,684
*Chris Paul	2,614
Michael Jordan	2,514
Gary Payton	2,445
Maurice Cheeks	2,310
Scottie Pippen	2,307
*LeBron James	2,275
Clyde Drexler	2,207
Hakeem Olajuwon	2,162

NBA Coach of the Year, 1963-2024

Year	Coach, team	Year	Coach, team	Year	Coach, team
1963	Harry Gallatin, St. Louis	1984	Frank Layden, Utah	2005	Mike D'Antoni, Phoenix
1964	Alex Hannum, San Francisco	1985	Don Nelson, Milwaukee	2006	Avery Johnson, Dallas
1965	Red Auerbach, Boston	1986	Mike Fratello, Atlanta	2007	Sam Mitchell, Toronto
1966	Dolph Schayes, Philadelphia	1987	Mike Schuler, Portland	2008	Byron Scott, New Orleans
1967	Johnny Kerr, Chicago	1988	Doug Moe, Denver	2009	Mike Brown, Cleveland
1968	Richie Guerin, St. Louis	1989	Cotton Fitzsimmons, Phoenix	2010	Scott Brooks, Oklahoma City
1969	Gene Shue, Baltimore	1990	Pat Riley, L.A. Lakers	2011	Tom Thibodeau, Chicago
1970	Red Holzman, New York	1991	Don Chaney, Houston	2012	Gregg Popovich, San Antonio
1971	Dick Motta, Chicago	1992	Don Nelson, Golden State	2013	George Karl, Denver
1972	Bill Sharman, L.A. Lakers	1993	Pat Riley, New York	2014	Gregg Popovich, San Antonio
1973	Tom Heinsohn, Boston	1994	Lenny Wilkens, Atlanta	2015	Mike Budenholzer, Atlanta
1974	Ray Scott, Detroit	1995	Del Harris, L.A. Lakers	2016	Steve Kerr, Golden State
1975	Phil Johnson, Kansas City-Omaha	1996	Phil Jackson, Chicago	2017	Mike D'Antoni, Houston
1976	Bill Fitch, Cleveland	1997	Pat Riley, Miami	2018	Dwane Casey, Toronto
1977	Tom Nissalke, Houston	1998	Larry Bird, Indiana	2019	Mike Budenholzer, Milwaukee
1978	Hubie Brown, Atlanta	1999	Mike Dunleavy, Portland	2020	Nick Nurse, Toronto
1979	Cotton Fitzsimmons, Kansas City	2000	Glenn "Doc" Rivers, Orlando	2021	Tom Thibodeau, New York
1980	Bill Fitch, Boston	2001	Larry Brown, Philadelphia	2022	Monty Williams, Phoenix
1981	Jack McKinney, Indiana	2002	Rick Carlisle, Detroit	2023	Mike Brown, Sacramento
1982	Gene Shue, Washington	2003	Gregg Popovich, San Antonio	2024	Mark Daignealt, Oklahoma City
1983	Don Nelson, Milwaukee	2004	Hubie Brown, Memphis		

National Basketball Association Franchise Origins

Team, founding year (in NBA, Basketball Assn. of Amer. [BAA], or Amer. Basketball Assn. [ABA]), location, and subsequent history. Neutral sites and arena sites in the same metropolitan area not listed separately.

Atlanta Hawks: 1949, NBA, as Tri-Cities Blackhawks, 1949-51, Moline, IL. Milwaukee Hawks, 1951-55; St. Louis Hawks, 1955-68; Atlanta Hawks, 1968-present.
Boston Celtics: 1946, BAA, Boston, MA, 1946-present.
Brooklyn Nets: 1967, ABA, as New Jersey Americans, 1967-68, Teaneck, NJ. New York Nets, 1968-77; New Jersey Nets, 1977-2012; Brooklyn Nets, 2012-present.
Charlotte Hornets: 2004, NBA, as Charlotte Bobcats, 2004-14, Charlotte, NC. Charlotte Hornets, 2014-present.
Chicago Bulls: 1966, NBA, Chicago, IL, 1966-present.
Cleveland Cavaliers: 1970, NBA, Cleveland, OH, 1970-present.
Dallas Mavericks: 1980, NBA, Dallas, TX, 1980-present.
Denver Nuggets: 1967, ABA, as Denver Rockets, 1967-74, Denver, CO. Denver Nuggets, 1974-present.
Detroit Pistons: 1948, BAA, as Ft. Wayne Pistons, 1948-57, Ft. Wayne, IN. Detroit Pistons, 1957-present.
Golden State Warriors: 1946, BAA, as Philadelphia Warriors, 1946-62, Philadelphia, PA. San Francisco Warriors, 1962-71; Golden State Warriors, 1971-2019, Oakland, CA; 2019-present, San Francisco, CA.
Houston Rockets: 1967, NBA, as San Diego Rockets, 1967-71, San Diego, CA. Houston Rockets, 1971-present.
Indiana Pacers: 1967, ABA, Indianapolis, IN, 1974-present.
L.A. Clippers: 1970, NBA, as Buffalo Braves, 1970-78, Buffalo, NY. San Diego Clippers, 1978-84; L.A. Clippers, 1984-present.
L.A. Lakers: 1948, BAA, as Minneapolis Lakers, 1948-60, Minneapolis, MN. L.A. Lakers, 1960-present.
Memphis Grizzlies: 1995, NBA, as Vancouver Grizzlies, 1995-2001, Vancouver, BC, Canada. Memphis Grizzlies, 2001-present.
Miami Heat: 1988, NBA, Miami, FL, 1988-present.
Milwaukee Bucks: 1968, NBA, Milwaukee, WI, 1968-present.
Minnesota Timberwolves: 1989, NBA, Minneapolis, MN, 1989-present.
New Orleans Pelicans: 1988, NBA, as Charlotte Hornets, 1988-2002, Charlotte, NC. New Orleans Hornets, 2002-13 (Hornets played most home games in Oklahoma City, 2005-07, as city repaired Hurricane Katrina damage); New Orleans Pelicans, 2013-present.
New York Knicks: 1946, BAA, New York, NY, 1946-present.
Oklahoma City Thunder: 1967, NBA, as Seattle SuperSonics, 1967-2008, Seattle, WA. Oklahoma City Thunder, 2008-present.
Orlando Magic: 1989, NBA, Orlando, FL, 1989-present.
Philadelphia 76ers: 1949, NBA, as Syracuse Nationals, 1949-63, Syracuse, NY. Philadelphia 76ers, 1963-present.
Phoenix Suns: 1968, NBA, Phoenix, AZ, 1968-present.
Portland Trail Blazers: 1970, NBA, Portland, OR, 1970-present.
Sacramento Kings: 1948, BAA, as Rochester Royals, 1948-57, Rochester, NY. Cincinnati Royals, 1957-72; Kansas City-Omaha Kings, 1972-75; Kansas City Kings, 1975-85; Sacramento Kings, 1985-present.
San Antonio Spurs: ABA, as Dallas Chaparrals, 1967-73, Dallas, TX. San Antonio Spurs, 1973-present.
Toronto Raptors: 1995, NBA, Toronto, ON, Canada, 1995-present.
Utah Jazz: 1974, NBA, as New Orleans Jazz, 1974-79, New Orleans, LA. Utah Jazz, 1979-present, Salt Lake City.
Washington Wizards: 1961, NBA, as Chicago Packers, 1961-62, Chicago, IL. Chicago Zephyrs, 1962-63; Baltimore Bullets, 1963-73; Capital Bullets, 1973-74, Landover, MD; Washington Bullets, 1974-97; Washington Wizards, 1997-present.

NBA Home Courts

Team	Name (year built)	Capacity[1]	Team	Name (year built)	Capacity[1]
Atlanta	State Farm Arena[2] (1999)	16,888	Miami	Kaseya Center[10] (1999)	19,600
Boston	TD Garden[3] (1995)	19,156	Milwaukee	Fiserv Forum (2018)	17,341
Brooklyn	Barclays Center[4] (2012)	17,732	Minnesota	Target Center (1990)	19,356
Charlotte	Spectrum Center[5] (2005)	19,077	New Orleans	Smoothie King Center[11] (1999)	16,867
Chicago	United Center (1994)	20,917	New York	Madison Square Garden (IV) (1968)	19,812
Cleveland	Rocket Mortgage FieldHouse[6] (1994)	19,432	Oklahoma City	Paycom Center[12] (2002)	18,203
Dallas	American Airlines Center (2001)	19,200	Orlando	Kia Center[13] (2010)	18,500
Denver	Ball Arena[7] (1999)	19,520	Philadelphia	Wells Fargo Center[14] (1996)	19,746
Detroit	Little Caesars Arena (2017)	20,332	Phoenix	Footprint Center[15] (1992)	17,071
Golden State	Chase Center (2019)	18,064	Portland	Moda Center[16] (1995)	19,393
Houston	Toyota Center (2003)	18,055	Sacramento	Golden 1 Center (2016)	17,583
Indiana	Gainbridge Fieldhouse[8] (1999)	17,923	San Antonio	Frost Bank Center[17] (2002)	18,354
L.A. Clippers	Crypto.com Arena[9] (1999)	18,937	Toronto	Scotiabank Arena[18] (1999)	19,800
L.A. Lakers	Crypto.com Arena[9] (1999)	18,910	Utah	Delta Center[19] (1991)	18,300
Memphis	FedExForum (2004)	17,794	Washington	Capital One Arena[20] (1997)	20,362

(1) At the end of the 2023-24 season. (2) Philips Arena, 1999-2018. (3) FleetCenter, 1995-2005; TD Banknorth Garden, 2005-09. (4) The New Jersey Nets relocated to Brooklyn prior to the 2012-13 season. (5) Charlotte Bobcats Arena, 2005-08; Time Warner Cable Arena, 2008-16. (6) Gund Arena, 1994-2005; Quicken Loans Arena, 2005-19. (7) Pepsi Center, 1999-2020. (8) Conseco Fieldhouse, 1999-2011; Bankers Life Fieldhouse, 2011-21. (9) Staples Center, 1999-2021. (10) AmericanAirlines Arena, 1999-2021; FTX Arena 2021-23; Miami-Dade Arena, 2023. (11) New Orleans Arena, 1999-2014; because of damage to New Orleans Arena due to Hurricane, Katrina, the Hornets played 35 games in the Ford Center in Oklahoma City, OK, 3 games in New Orleans Arena, and 3 games at other locations during the 2005-06 season; in 2006-07, the Hornets played 35 games at the Ford Center and 6 games in New Orleans Arena. (12) Ford Center, 2008-11; Chesapeake Energy Arena, 2012-21. (13) Amway Center, 2010-23. (14) CoreStates Center, 1996-98; First Union Center, 1998-2003; Wachovia Center, 2003-10. (15) America West Arena, 1992-2006; US Airways Center, 2006-15; Talking Stick Resort Arena, 2015-19; Phoenix Suns Arena, 2020. (16) The Rose Garden, 1995-2013. (17) SBC Center, 2002-06; AT&T Center, 2006-23. (18) Air Canada Centre, 1999-2018. The Raptors played the 2020-21 season at Amalie Arena in Tampa, FL, due to COVID-19 related travel restrictions. (19) Delta Center, 1991-2006; EnergySolutions Arena, 2006-15; Vivint Arena, 2015-23. (20) MCI Center, 1997-2006; Verizon Center, 2006-17.

All-Time NBA Regular Season Coaching Victories

(At the end of the 2023-24 season, ranked by wins. * = Active in 2023-24 season.)

Coach	W	L	PCT	Coach	W	L	PCT	Coach	W	L	PCT
*Gregg Popovich	1,388	821	.628	*Doc Rivers	1,114	782	.588	Jack Ramsay	864	783	.525
Don Nelson	1,335	1,063	.557	Larry Brown	1,098	904	.548	Cotton Fitzsimmons	832	775	.518
Lenny Wilkens	1,332	1,155	.536	Rick Adelman	1,042	749	.582	Gene Shue	784	861	.477
Jerry Sloan	1,221	803	.603	Bill Fitch	944	1,106	.460	Nate McMillan	760	668	.532
Pat Riley	1,210	694	.636	*Rick Carlisle	943	828	.532	*Erik Spoelstra	750	527	.587
George Karl	1,175	824	.588	Red Auerbach	938	479	.662	John MacLeod	707	657	.518
Phil Jackson	1,155	485	.704	Dick Motta	935	1,017	.479	Red Holzman	696	603	.536

Naismith Memorial Basketball Hall of Fame

* = 2024 inductee. + = Enshrined as both a player and coach. Referee inductees not shown. www.hoophall.com

Players

Abdul-Jabbar, Kareem
Allen, Ray
Archibald, Nate
Arizin, Paul
*Augustus, Seimone
Barkley, Charles
Barlow, Thomas
*Barnett, Dick
Barry, Rick
Baylor, Elgin
Beaty, Zelmo
Beckman, John
Bellamy, Walt
Belov, Sergei
*Billups, Chauncey
Bing, Dave
Bird, Larry
Blazejowski, Carol
Borgmann, Bennie
Bosh, Chris
Boswell, Wyatt "Sonny"
Bradley, Bill
Braun, Carl
Brennan, Joseph
Brown, Roger
Bryant, Kobe
*Carter, Vince
Cash, Swin
Catchings, Tamika
Cervi, Al
Chamberlain, Wilt
Cheeks, Maurice
Clayton, Zack
Cooper, Charles
Cooper, Charles "Chuck"
Cooper, Cynthia
*Cooper, Michael
Cosic, Kresimir
Cousy, Bob
Cowens, Dave
Crawford, Joan
Cunningham, Billy
Curry, Denise
Dalipagic, Drazen
Dampier, Louis
Dandridge, Bob
Daniels, Mel
Dantley, Adrian
Davies, Bob
*Davis, Walter
DeBernardi, Forrest
DeBusschere, Dave
Dehnert, Henry "Dutch"
Divac, Vlade
Donovan, Anne
Drexler, Clyde
Dumars, Joe
Duncan, Tim
Edwards, Teresa
Endacott, Paul
English, Alex
Erving, Julius
Ewing, Patrick
Foster, Bud
Frazier, Walt
Friedman, Max
Fulks, Joe
Gale, Lauren
Galis, Nick
Gallatin, Harry
Garnett, Kevin
Gasol, Pau
Gates, William "Pop"
Gervin, George
Gilmore, Artis
Ginobili, Manu
Gola, Tom
Goodrich, Gail
Greer, Hal
Griffith, Yolanda
Gruenig, Robert "Ace"
Guerin, Richard
Hagan, Cliff
Hammon, Becky
Hanson, Victor
Hardaway, Tim
Harris-Stewart, Lusia
Havlicek, John
Hawkins, Cornelius "Connie"
Hayes, Elvin
Haynes, Marques
Haywood, Spencer
+Heinsohn, Tom
Hill, Grant
Holman, Nat
Houbregs, Bob
Howell, Bailey
Hudson, Lou
Hyatt, Chuck
Isaacs, John
Issel, Dan
Iverson, Allen
Jackson, Inman
Jackson, Lauren
Jeannette, Harry "Buddy"
Jenkins, Clarence "Fats"
Johnson, Dennis
Johnson, Earvin "Magic"
Johnson, Gus
Johnson, William
Johnston, Neil
Jones, Bobby
Jones, K. C.
Jones, Sam
Jordan, Michael
Kidd, Jason
King, Bernard
Krause, Ed "Moose"
Kukoc, Tony
Kurland, Bob
Lanier, Bob
Lapchick, Joe
Leslie, Lisa
Lieberman, Nancy
Lovellette, Clyde
Lucas, Jerry
Luisetti, Angelo "Hank"
Macauley, Ed
Malone, Karl
Malone, Moses
Maravich, Pete
Marcari, Hortencia
Marciulionis, Sarunas
Martin, Slater
McAdoo, Bob
McClain, Katrina
McCracken, Emmett "Branch"
McCracken, Jack
McDermott, Bobby
McGinnis, George
McGrady, Tracy
McGuire, Dick
McHale, Kevin
Meneghin, Dino
Meyers, Ann
Mikan, George
Mikkelsen, Vern
Miller, Cheryl
Miller, Reggie
Ming, Yao
Moncrief, Sidney
Monroe, Earl
Moore, Pearl
Mourning, Alonzo
Mullin, Chris
Murphy, Calvin
Murphy, Charles "Stretch"
Mutombo, Dikembe
Nash, Steve
Nowitzki, Dirk
Olajuwon, Hakeem
O'Neal, Shaquille
Page, Harlan "Pat"
Parish, Robert
Parker, Tony
Payton, Gary
Pereira, Maciel "Ubiratan"
Petrovic, Drazen
Pettit, Bob
Phillip, Andy
Pierce, Paul
Pippen, Scottie
Pollard, Jim
Pollins, Albert "Runt"
Posey, Cumberland
Radivoj, Korac
Radja, Dino
Ramsey, Frank
Reed, Willis
Richmond, Mitch
Risen, Arnie
Robertson, Oscar
Robinson, David
Rodgers, Guy
Rodman, Dennis
Roosma, John
+Russell, Bill
Russell, John "Honey"
*+Ryan, Bo
Sabonis, Arvydas
Sampson, Ralph
Schayes, Adolph
Schmidt, Ernest
Schmidt, Oscar
Schommer, John
Scott, Charlie
Sedran, Barney
Semjonova, Uljana
Shank-Grentz, Theresa
+Sharman, Bill
Sikma, Jack
*+Smith, Charles
Smith, Katie
Staley, Dawn
Steinmetz, Chris
Stockton, John
Stokes, Maurice
Swoopes, Sheryl
Tatum, Reece "Goose"
Thomas, Isiah
Thompson, David
Thompson, John
Thompson, Tina
Thurmond, Nate
*Timms, Michele
Twyman, Jack
Unseld, Wes
Vandivier, Robert "Fuzzy"
Wachter, Ed
Wade, Dwyane
Walker, Chet
Wallace, Ben
Walton, Bill
Wanzer, Bobby
Washington, Ora Mae
Weatherspoon, Teresa
Webber, Chris
West, Jerry
Westphal, Paul
Whalen, Lindsay
White, Jo Jo
White, Nera
+Wilkens, Lenny
Wilkes, Jamaal
Wilkins, Dominique
Woodard, Lynette
+Wooden, John
Worthy, James
Yardley, George

Coaches

Adelman, Rick
Alexeeva, Lidia
Allen, Forrest C. "Phog"
Anderson, Harold
Auerbach, Arnold "Red"
Auriemma, Geno
Barmore, Leon
Barry, Justin "Sam"
Bess, Gene
Blair, Gary
Blood, Ernest
Boeheim, Jim
Brown, Larry
Calhoun, Jim
Calipari, John
Cann, Howard
Carlson, Clifford
Carnesecca, Lou
Carnevale, Ben
Carril, Pete
Case, Everett
Chancellor, Van
Chaney, John
Conradt, Jody
Crum, Denzil "Denny"
Daly, Chuck
Dean, Everett
Diaz-Miguel, Antonio
Diddle, Edgar
Drake, Bruce
Driesell, Charles "Lefty"
Ferrándiz, Pedro
Fitch, Bill
Gaines, Clarence
Gamba, Sandro
Gardner, James "Jack"
Gaze, Lindsay
Gill, Amory "Slats"
Gomelsky, Aleksandr
Gunter, Sue
Hannum, Alex
Harshman, Marv
Haskins, Don
Hatchell, Sylvia
+Heinsohn, Tom
Hickey, Edgar
Hixon, David
Hobson, Howard
Holzman, William "Red"
Huggins, Bob
Hughes, Robert
Hurley, Bob, Sr.
Iba, Hank
Izzo, Tom
Jackson, Phil
Julian, Alvin
Karl, George
Keady, Gene
Keaney, Frank
Keogan, George
Knight, Bob
Krzyzewski, Mike
Kundla, John
Lambert, Ward
Leonard, Bob
Lewis, Guy V.
Litwack, Harry
Loeffler, Kenneth
Lonborg, Arthur "Dutch"
Magee, Herb
McCutchan, Arad
McGraw, Muffet
McGuire, Al
McGuire, Frank
McLendon, John
Meanwell, Dr. Walter
Meyer, Ray
Miller, Ralph
Moore, Billie
Mulkey, Kim
Nelson, Don
Newell, Pete
Nikolic, Aleksandar
Novosel, Mirko
Olson, Robert "Lute"
Pitino, Rick
Popovich, Gregg
Ramsay, John "Jack"
*Redin, Harley
Richardson, Nolan
Riley, Pat
Rubini, Cesare
Rupp, Adolph
Rush, Cathy
+Russell, Bill
*+Ryan, Bo
Sachs, Leonard
Self, Bill
+Sharman, Bill
Shelton, Everett
Sloan, Jerry
*+Smith, Charles
Smith, Dean
Stanley, Marianne
Stevens, Barbara
Stringer, C. Vivian
Summitt, Pat
Sutton, Eddie
Tarkanian, Jerry
Taylor, Fred
Teague, Bertha
Thompson, John R.
Tomjanovich, Rudy
VanDerveer, Tara
Wade, Margaret
Watts, Stan
+Wilkens, Lenny
Williams, Gary
Williams, Roy
Winter, Tex
+Wooden, John
Woolpert, Phil
Wootten, Morgan
Wright, Jay
Yow, Kay

Teams

1948-82 Wayland Baptist (women's teams)
1957-59 Tennessee A&I (men's teams)
1960 USA Men's Olympic Team
1966 Texas Western
1972-73-74 Immaculata Coll.
1976 USA Women's Olympic Team
1992 USA Men's Olympic "Dream Team"
All American Red Heads
Buffalo Germans
First Team
Harlem Globetrotters
New York Renaissance
Original Celtics

Contributors

Abbott, Senda Berenson
Ackerman, Val
Attles, Al
Barksdale, Don
Baumann, Patrick
Bee, Clair
Biasone, Danny
Brown, Hubert "Hubie"
Brown, Walter
Bunn, John
Buss, Jerry
Clifton, Nat
Colangelo, Jerry
*Collins, Doug
Costello, Larry
Davidson, Bill
Douglas, Bob
Duer, Al
Embry, Wayne
Fagan, Cliff
Fisher, Harry
Fitzsimmons, Cotton
Garfinkel, Howard
Fleisher, Larry
Gavitt, David
Gottlieb, Edward
Granik, Russ
Gulick, Dr. Luther
Harris, Del
Harrison, Lester
Hearn, Francis "Chick"
Henderson, E. B.
Hepp, Dr. Ferenc
Hickox, Edward
Hinkle, Tony
Irish, Edward "Ned"
Jackson, Mannie
Jernstedt, Tom
Jones, R. William
Kennedy, Walter
Knight, Phil
Krause, Jerry
Lemon, Meadowlark
Liston, Emil
Lloyd, Earl
Lobo, Rebecca
McLendon, John
Mokray, Bill
Morgan, Ralph
Morgenweck, Frank
Naismith, Dr. James
Newton, C. M.
O'Brien, John
O'Brien, Larry
Olsen, Harold
Podoloff, Maurice
Porter, Henry V.
Raveling, George
Reid, William
Reinsdorf, Jerry
Ripley, Elmer
St. John, Lynn
Sanders, Tom "Satch"
Saperstein, Abe
Schabinger, Arthur
*Simon, Herb
Stagg, Alonzo
Stankovic, Boris
Steitz, Edward
Stern, David
Taylor, Chuck
Thorn, Rod
Tower, Oswald
Trester, Arthur
Valvano, Jim
Vitale, Dick
Wells, Clifford
Welts, Rick
*West, Jerry
Wilke, Lou
Zollner, Fred

Liberty at Last! New York Claims First WNBA Title in 2024

The New York Liberty won their first WNBA championship, holding off the Minnesota Lynx in Game 5 in overtime, 67-62, at Barclays Center in Brooklyn, NY, on Oct. 20, 2024. Liberty center Jonquel Jones scored 17 points in the final game and was named Finals MVP.

All-time leading NCAA scorer Caitlin Clark of Univ. of Iowa, selected first in the WNBA draft by Indiana, was 2024 WNBA Rookie of the Year, finishing with the most assists in the league. She helped Indiana move from sixth to third in the Eastern Conference while setting the league's all-time attendance mark. A'ja Wilson of Las Vegas earned MVP for the third time, becoming the first 1,000-point scorer in league history and the first to crack 450 rebounds. League attendance was up 48 percent, with a summer hiatus for the 2024 Olympics; all 12 WNBA teams saw at least double-digit percentage attendance growth.

WNBA Finals Standings, 2024

(Playoff seeds in parentheses; top eight teams by PCT advance, regardless of conference.)

Eastern Conference	W	L	PCT	GB
New York Liberty (1)	32	8	0.800	—
Connecticut Sun (3)	28	12	0.700	4
Indiana Fever (6)	20	20	0.500	12
Atlanta Dream (8)	15	25	0.375	17
Washington Mystics	14	26	0.350	18
Chicago Sky	13	27	0.325	19

Western Conference	W	L	PCT	GB
Minnesota Lynx (2)	30	10	0.750	—
Las Vegas Aces (4)	27	13	0.675	3
Seattle Storm (5)	25	15	0.625	5
Phoenix Mercury (7)	19	21	0.475	11
Dallas Wings	9	31	0.225	21
Los Angeles Sparks	8	32	0.200	22

WNBA Playoff Results, 2024

First Round (best-of-three)
(1) New York defeated (8) Atlanta, 2 games to 0
(2) Minnesota defeated (7) Phoenix, 2 games to 0
(3) Connecticut defeated (6) Indiana, 2 games to 0
(4) Las Vegas defeated (5) Seattle, 2 games to 0

Semifinals (best-of-five)
(1) New York defeated (4) Las Vegas, 3 games to 1
(2) Minnesota defeated (3) Connecticut, 3 games to 2

WNBA Championship
(1) New York defeated (2) Minnesota, 3 games to 2 (93-95, 80-66, 80-77, 80-82, 67-62 [OT])

WNBA Champions, 1997-2024

	Regular Season		Playoffs		
Year	Eastern champion	Western champion	Champion	Winning coach	Opponent
1997	Houston Comets	Phoenix Mercury	Houston	Van Chancellor	New York
1998	Cleveland Rockers	Houston Comets	Houston	Van Chancellor	Phoenix
1999	New York Liberty	Houston Comets	Houston	Van Chancellor	New York
2000	New York Liberty	Los Angeles Sparks	Houston	Van Chancellor	New York
2001	Cleveland Rockers	Los Angeles Sparks	Los Angeles	Michael Cooper	Charlotte
2002	New York Liberty	Los Angeles Sparks	Los Angeles	Michael Cooper	New York
2003	Detroit Shock	Los Angeles Sparks	Detroit	Bill Laimbeer	Los Angeles
2004	Connecticut Sun	Los Angeles Sparks	Seattle	Anne Donovan	Connecticut
2005	Connecticut Sun	Sacramento Monarchs	Sacramento	John Whisenant	Connecticut
2006	Connecticut Sun	Los Angeles Sparks	Detroit	Bill Laimbeer	Sacramento
2007	Detroit Shock	Phoenix Mercury	Phoenix	Paul Westhead	Detroit
2008	Detroit Shock	San Antonio Silver Stars	Detroit	Bill Laimbeer	San Antonio
2009	Indiana Fever	Phoenix Mercury	Phoenix	Corey Gaines	Indiana
2010	Washington Mystics	Seattle Storm	Seattle	Brian Agler	Atlanta
2011	Indiana Fever	Minnesota Lynx	Minnesota	Cheryl Reeve	Atlanta
2012	Connecticut Sun	Minnesota Lynx	Indiana	Lin Dunn	Minnesota
2013	Chicago Sky	Minnesota Lynx	Minnesota	Cheryl Reeve	Atlanta
2014	Atlanta Dream	Phoenix Mercury	Phoenix	Sandy Brondello	Chicago
2015	New York Liberty	Minnesota Lynx	Minnesota	Cheryl Reeve	Indiana
2016	New York Liberty	Minnesota Lynx	Los Angeles	Brian Agler	Minnesota
2017	New York Liberty	Minnesota Lynx	Minnesota	Cheryl Reeve	Los Angeles
2018	Atlanta Dream	Seattle Storm	Seattle	Dan Hughes	Washington
2019	Washington Mystics	Los Angeles Sparks	Washington	Mike Thibault	Connecticut
2020	Chicago Sky	Las Vegas Aces	Seattle	Gary Kloppenburg[1]	Las Vegas
2021	Connecticut Sun	Las Vegas Aces	Chicago	James Wade	Phoenix
2022	Chicago Sky	Las Vegas Aces	Las Vegas	Becky Hammon	Connecticut
2023	New York Liberty	Las Vegas Aces	Las Vegas	Becky Hammon	New York
2024	New York Liberty	Minnesota Lynx	New York	Sandy Brondello	Minnesota

(1) Seattle head coach Dan Hughes was not medically cleared for the 2020 season.

WNBA Finals MVP, 1997-2024

Year	Player, team	Year	Player, team	Year	Player, team
1997	Cynthia Cooper, Houston	2007	Cappie Pondexter, Phoenix	2016	Candace Parker, Los Angeles
1998	Cynthia Cooper, Houston	2008	Katie Smith, Detroit	2017	Sylvia Fowles, Minnesota
1999	Cynthia Cooper, Houston	2009	Diana Taurasi, Phoenix	2018	Breanna Stewart, Seattle
2000	Cynthia Cooper, Houston	2010	Lauren Jackson, Seattle	2019	Emma Meesseman, Wash.
2001	Lisa Leslie, Los Angeles	2011	Seimone Augustus, Minnesota	2020	Breanna Stewart, Seattle
2002	Lisa Leslie, Los Angeles	2012	Tamika Catchings, Indiana	2021	Kahleah Copper, Chicago
2003	Ruth Riley, Detroit	2013	Maya Moore, Minnesota	2022	Chelsea Gray, Las Vegas
2004	Betty Lennox, Seattle	2014	Diana Taurasi, Phoenix	2023	A'ja Wilson, Las Vegas
2005	Yolanda Griffith, Sacramento	2015	Sylvia Fowles, Minnesota	2024	Jonquel Jones, New York
2006	Deanna Nolan, Detroit				

WNBA Most Valuable Player, 1997-2024

Year	Player, team	Year	Player, team	Year	Player, team
1997	Cynthia Cooper, Houston	2007	Lauren Jackson, Seattle	2016	Nneka Ogwumike, Los Angeles
1998	Cynthia Cooper, Houston	2008	Candace Parker, Los Angeles	2017	Sylvia Fowles, Minnesota
1999	Yolanda Griffith, Sacramento	2009	Diana Taurasi, Phoenix	2018	Breanna Stewart, Seattle
2000	Sheryl Swoopes, Houston	2010	Lauren Jackson, Seattle	2019	Elena Delle Donne, Wash.
2001	Lisa Leslie, Los Angeles	2011	Tamika Catchings, Indiana	2020	A'ja Wilson, Las Vegas
2002	Sheryl Swoopes, Houston	2012	Tina Charles, Connecticut	2021	Jonquel Jones, Connecticut
2003	Lauren Jackson, Seattle	2013	Candace Parker, Los Angeles	2022	A'ja Wilson, Las Vegas
2004	Lisa Leslie, Los Angeles	2014	Maya Moore, Minnesota	2023	Breanna Stewart, New York
2005	Sheryl Swoopes, Houston	2015	Elena Delle Donne, Chicago	2024	A'ja Wilson, Las Vegas
2006	Lisa Leslie, Los Angeles				

WNBA Statistical Leaders, 2024

Minutes played: 1,466, Arike Ogunbowale, Dallas
Total points: 1,021, A'ja Wilson, Las Vegas
Field goal pct.: .579, Brittney Griner, Phoenix
3-point field goal pct.: .474, Emily Engstler, Washington
Free throw pct.: .921, Arike Ogunbowale, Dallas
Rebounds: 451, A'ja Wilson, Las Vegas
Assists: 337, Caitlin Clark, Indiana
Steals: 81, Arike Ogunbowale, Dallas
Blocks: 98, A'ja Wilson, Las Vegas

WNBA Rookie of the Year, 1997-2024

Year	Player, team	Year	Player, team	Year	Player, team
1997	No award	2007	Armintie Price, Chicago	2016	Breanna Stewart, Seattle
1998	Tracy Reid, Charlotte	2008	Candace Parker, Los Angeles	2017	Allisha Gray, Dallas
1999	Chamique Holdsclaw, Washington	2009	Angel McCoughtry, Atlanta	2018	A'ja Wilson, Las Vegas
2000	Betty Lennox, Minnesota	2010	Tina Charles, Connecticut	2019	Napheesa Collier, Minnesota
2001	Jackie Stiles, Portland	2011	Maya Moore, Minnesota	2020	Crystal Dangerfield, Minnesota
2002	Tamika Catchings, Indiana	2012	Nneka Ogwumike, Los Angeles	2021	Michaela Onyenwere, New York
2003	Cheryl Ford, Detroit	2013	Elena Delle Donne, Chicago	2022	Rhyne Howard, Atlanta
2004	Diana Taurasi, Phoenix	2014	Chiney Ogwumike, Connecticut	2023	Aliyah Boston, Indiana
2005	Temeka Johnson, Washington	2015	Jewell Loyd, Seattle	2024	Caitlin Clark, Indiana
2006	Seimone Augustus, Minnesota				

WNBA Scoring Leaders, 1997-2024

(Average points per game; season minimums vary.)

Year	Player, team	PTS	AVG	Year	Player, team	PTS	AVG
1997	Cynthia Cooper, Houston	621	22.2	2011	Diana Taurasi, Phoenix	692	21.6
1998	Cynthia Cooper, Houston	680	22.7	2012	Angel McCoughtry, Atlanta	514	21.4
1999	Cynthia Cooper, Houston	686	22.1	2013	Angel McCoughtry, Atlanta	711	21.5
2000	Sheryl Swoopes, Houston	643	20.7	2014	Maya Moore, Minnesota	812	23.9
2001	Katie Smith, Minnesota	739	23.1	2015	Elena Delle Donne, Chicago	725	23.4
2002	Chamique Holdsclaw, Washington	397	19.9	2016	Tina Charles, New York	688	21.5
2003	Lauren Jackson, Seattle	698	21.2	2017	Brittney Griner, Phoenix	569	21.9
2004	Lauren Jackson, Seattle	634	20.5	2018	Liz Cambage, Dallas	737	23.0
2005	Sheryl Swoopes, Houston	614	18.6	2019	Brittney Griner, Phoenix	642	20.7
2006	Diana Taurasi, Phoenix	860	25.3	2020	Arike Ogunbowale, Dallas	501	22.8
2007	Lauren Jackson, Seattle	739	23.8	2021	Tina Charles, Washington	631	23.4
2008	Diana Taurasi, Phoenix	820	24.1	2022	Breanna Stewart, Seattle	741	21.8
2009	Diana Taurasi, Phoenix	631	20.4	2023	Jewell Loyd, Seattle	939	24.7
2010	Diana Taurasi, Phoenix	702	22.6	2024	A'ja Wilson, Las Vegas	1,021	26.9

WNBA Rebounding Leaders, 1997-2024

(Average rebounds per game; season minimums vary.)

Year	Player, team	REB	RPG	Year	Player, team	REB	RPG
1997	Lisa Leslie, Los Angeles	266	9.5	2011	Tina Charles, Connecticut	374	11.0
1998	Lisa Leslie, Los Angeles	285	10.2	2012	Tina Charles, Connecticut	345	10.5
1999	Yolanda Griffith, Sacramento	329	11.3	2013	Sylvia Fowles, Chicago	369	11.5
2000	Natalie Williams, Utah	336	11.6	2014	Courtney Paris, Tulsa	347	10.2
2001	Yolanda Griffith, Sacramento	357	11.2	2015	Courtney Paris, Tulsa	317	9.3
2002	Chamique Holdsclaw, Washington	232	11.6	2016	Tina Charles, New York	317	9.9
2003	Chamique Holdsclaw, Washington	294	10.9	2017	Jonquel Jones, Connecticut	403	11.9
2004	Lisa Leslie, Los Angeles	336	9.9	2018	Sylvia Fowles, Minnesota	404	11.9
2005	Cheryl Ford, Detroit	322	9.8	2019	Jonquel Jones, Connecticut	330	9.7
2006	Cheryl Ford, Detroit	363	11.3	2020	Candace Parker, Los Angeles	214	9.7
2007	Lauren Jackson, Seattle	300	9.7	2021	Jonquel Jones, Connecticut	303	11.2
2008	Candace Parker, Los Angeles	313	9.5	2022	Sylvia Fowles, Minnesota	294	9.8
2009	Candace Parker, Los Angeles	244	9.8	2023	Alyssa Thomas, Connecticut	394	9.9
2010	Tina Charles, Connecticut	398	11.7	2024	Angel Reese, Chicago	446	13.1

All-Time WNBA Statistical Leaders

(At the end of the 2024 season. * = Active in 2024 season.)

Scoring Average

(Minimum 100 games)

Player	G	PTS	AVG	Player	G	PTS	AVG
*A'ja Wilson	227	4,782	21.1	Lauren Jackson	317	6,007	18.9
Cynthia Cooper	124	2,601	21.0	*Diana Taurasi	565	10,646	18.8
*Breanna Stewart	261	5,419	20.8	Angel McCoughtry	311	5,797	18.6
*Arike Ogunbowale	195	4,014	20.6	Maya Moore	271	4,984	18.4
Elena Delle Donne	241	4,706	19.5	*Tina Charles	430	7,696	17.9

Points		Rebounds		Steals	
*Diana Taurasi	10,646	*Tina Charles	4,014	Tamika Catchings	1,074
*Tina Charles	7,696	Sylvia Fowles	4,006	Ticha Penicheiro	764
Tina Thompson	7,488	Candace Parker	3,467	Sue Bird	724
*DeWanna Bonner	7,482	Rebekkah Brunson	3,356	Alana Beard	710
Tamika Catchings	7,380	Tamika Catchings	3,316	Sheryl Swoopes	657
Candice Dupree	6,895	Lisa Leslie	3,307	Jia Perkins	635
Cappie Pondexter	6,811	Candice Dupree	3,149	Sancho Lyttle	634
Sue Bird	6,803	Tina Thompson	3,070	Angel McCoughtry	627
Candace Parker	6,574	*DeWanna Bonner	3,067	Katie Douglas	623
*Nneka Ogwumike	6,502	Taj McWilliams-Franklin	3,013	DeLisha Milton-Jones	619

3-Point Field Goals Made		Assists		Blocked Shots	
*Diana Taurasi	1,447	Sue Bird	3,234	Margo Dydek	877
Sue Bird	1,001	*Courtney Vandersloot	2,850	Lisa Leslie	822
Katie Smith	906	Ticha Penicheiro	2,599	*Brittney Griner	812
Becky Hammon	829	*Diana Taurasi	2,394	Sylvia Fowles	721
Tina Thompson	748	Lindsay Whalen	2,348	Candace Parker	619
Katie Douglas	727	Becky Hammon	1,708	Lauren Jackson	586
Kristi Toliver	651	Candace Parker	1,634	Tangela Smith	557
*DeWanna Bonner	623	*Chelsea Gray	1,631	Tammy Sutton-Brown	555

Panthers Sneak Past Oilers for First Stanley Cup in 2024

The Florida Panthers won the franchise's first Stanley Cup, defeating the Edmonton Oilers, 2-1, in Game 7 on June 24, 2024, at Amerant Bank Arena in Sunrise, FL. Panthers head coach Paul Maurice, with 1,848 games behind the bench (second most all time), claimed his first Stanley Cup. Florida led off the series with three straight wins, only to see Edmonton win three straight to force a deciding game. Despite being on the losing side, Edmonton's Connor McDavid beat out Florida goalie Sergei Bobrovsky for the Conn Smythe Trophy as the top postseason performer. McDavid piled up a record 34 assists in the playoffs and became the first player in the NHL finals with consecutive four-point games.

Alex Ovechkin of the Washington Capitals set a new career record for most open net goals (57). Toronto Maple Leaf Auston Matthews became the first player since Mario Lemieux in 1995-96 to score 69 goals in a season; Matthews also captained the winning squad in the the All-Star Game Feb. 3, 2024, at his home Scotiabank Arena. Edmonton's McDavid and Nikita Kucherov of Tampa Bay became the fourth and fifth players ever to record 100 assists in a season; it was the first NHL season with two triple-digit assist totals since Wayne Gretzky and Mario Lemieux did it in 1988-89. Kucherov claimed the Art Ross Trophy for most points, Nathan MacKinnon of the Colorado Avalanche won the Hart Trophy as most valuable player, Vancouver Canuck Quinn Hughes received the James Norris Trophy as best defenseman, Connor Hellebuyck of the Winnipeg Jets earned the Vezina Trophy as best goalie, and first overall draft pick Connor Bedard of the Chicago Blackhawks took the Calder Trophy. Rick Tocchet, who was a studio analyst when the Canucks put him behind the bench in Jan. 2023, claimed the Jack Adams Award as top coach.

The Arizona Coyotes and L.A. Kings faced off in the preseason Sept. 23-24, 2023, at Rod Laver Arena in Melbourne for the first NHL games in Australia. Four games were played in Nov. 2023 in Stockholm, Sweden. New Year's Day brought the Winter Classic to T-Mobile Park in Seattle, as the home Kraken blanked the defending Stanley Cup champion Vegas Golden Knights, 3-0. The Oilers beat Calgary in an outdoor game at Commonwealth Stadium in Edmonton Oct. 29, 2023, 5-2. All three New York area teams—plus the Philadelphia Flyers—played at the outdoor MetLife Stadium in New Jersey Feb. 17-18, 2024: the Devils beat the Flyers, 6-3, and the eventual Presidents' Trophy-winning Rangers topped the Islanders in overtime, 6-5.

Final NHL Standings, 2023-24

(* = clinched playoff berth)

Standings are determined by total points; teams earn two points for each win and one point for each game lost in overtime or in a shootout. Ties broken by fewer number of games played (i.e., superior points percentage), then by regulation wins (RW).

Eastern Conference

Metropolitan	W	L	OT	GF	GA	RW	ROW	PTS	PCT
NY Rangers*	55	23	4	282	229	43	51	114	.695
Carolina*	52	23	7	279	216	44	50	111	.677
NY Islanders*	39	27	16	246	263	29	38	94	.573
Washington*	40	31	11	220	257	32	36	91	.555
Pittsburgh	38	32	12	255	251	32	36	88	.537
Philadelphia	38	33	11	235	261	30	34	87	.530
New Jersey	38	39	5	264	283	33	38	81	.494
Columbus	27	43	12	237	300	21	24	66	.402
Atlantic	**W**	**L**	**OT**	**GF**	**GA**	**RW**	**ROW**	**PTS**	**PCT**
Florida*	52	24	6	268	200	42	49	110	.671
Boston*	47	20	15	267	224	36	43	109	.665
Toronto*	46	26	10	303	263	33	41	102	.622
Tampa Bay*	45	29	8	291	268	37	42	98	.598
Detroit	41	32	9	278	274	27	38	91	.555
Buffalo	39	37	6	246	244	33	37	84	.512
Ottawa	37	41	4	255	281	25	32	78	.476
Montréal	30	36	16	236	289	20	26	76	.463

Western Conference

Central	W	L	OT	GF	GA	RW	ROW	PTS	PCT
Dallas*	52	21	9	298	234	40	48	113	.689
Winnipeg*	52	24	6	259	199	46	52	110	.671
Colorado*	50	25	7	304	254	42	48	107	.652
Nashville*	47	30	5	269	248	38	44	99	.604
St. Louis	43	33	6	239	250	31	38	92	.561
Minnesota	39	34	9	251	263	32	36	87	.530
Arizona	36	41	5	256	274	28	34	77	.470
Chicago	23	53	6	179	290	17	22	52	.317
Pacific	**W**	**L**	**OT**	**GF**	**GA**	**RW**	**ROW**	**PTS**	**PCT**
Vancouver*	50	23	9	279	223	44	50	109	.665
Edmonton*	49	27	6	294	237	39	47	104	.634
Los Angeles*	44	27	11	256	215	37	42	99	.604
Vegas*	45	29	8	267	245	34	41	98	.598
Calgary	38	39	5	253	271	32	38	81	.494
Seattle	34	35	13	217	236	28	31	81	.494
Anaheim	27	50	5	204	295	21	26	59	.360
San Jose	19	54	9	181	331	14	18	47	.287

Stanley Cup Playoff Results, 2024

First Round

Florida defeated Tampa Bay, 4-1
Boston defeated Toronto, 4-3
NY Rangers defeated Washington, 4-0
Carolina defeated NY Islanders, 4-1
Dallas defeated Vegas, 4-3
Colorado defeated Winnipeg, 4-1
Vancouver defeated Nashville, 4-2
Edmonton defeated Los Angeles, 4-1

Second Round

Florida defeated Boston, 4-2
NY Rangers defeated Carolina, 4-2
Dallas defeated Colorado, 4-2
Edmonton defeated Vancouver, 4-3

Stanley Cup Semifinals

Florida defeated NY Rangers, 4-2
Edmonton defeated Dallas, 4-2

Stanley Cup Final

Florida defeated Edmonton
(3-0, 4-1, 4-3, 1-8, 3-5, 1-5, 2-1)

Stanley Cup Champions, 1927-2024

Year	Champion	Coach	Final opponent
1927	Ottawa	Dave Gill	Boston
1928	NY Rangers	Lester Patrick	Montréal Maroons
1929	Boston	Art Ross	NY Rangers
1930	Montréal Canadiens	Cecil Hart	Boston
1931	Montréal Canadiens	Cecil Hart	Chicago
1932	Toronto	Dick Irvin	NY Rangers
1933	NY Rangers	Lester Patrick	Toronto
1934	Chicago	Tommy Gorman	Detroit
1935	Montréal Maroons	Tommy Gorman	Toronto
1936	Detroit	Jack Adams	Toronto
1937	Detroit	Jack Adams	NY Rangers
1938	Chicago	Bill Stewart	Toronto
1939	Boston	Art Ross	Toronto
1940	NY Rangers	Frank Boucher	Toronto
1941	Boston	Cooney Weiland	Detroit
1942	Toronto	Hap Day	Detroit
1943	Detroit	Jack Adams	Boston
1944	Montréal	Dick Irvin	Chicago
1945	Toronto	Hap Day	Detroit
1946	Montréal	Dick Irvin	Boston
1947	Toronto	Hap Day	Montréal
1948	Toronto	Hap Day	Detroit
1949	Toronto	Hap Day	Detroit
1950	Detroit	Tommy Ivan	NY Rangers
1951	Toronto	Joe Primeau	Montréal
1952	Detroit	Tommy Ivan	Montréal
1953	Montréal	Dick Irvin	Boston
1954	Detroit	Tommy Ivan	Montréal
1955	Detroit	Jimmy Skinner	Montréal
1956	Montréal	Toe Blake	Detroit
1957	Montréal	Toe Blake	Boston
1958	Montréal	Toe Blake	Boston
1959	Montréal	Toe Blake	Toronto
1960	Montréal	Toe Blake	Toronto
1961	Chicago	Rudy Pilous	Detroit
1962	Toronto	Punch Imlach	Chicago
1963	Toronto	Punch Imlach	Detroit
1964	Toronto	Punch Imlach	Detroit
1965	Montréal	Toe Blake	Chicago
1966	Montréal	Toe Blake	Detroit
1967	Toronto	Punch Imlach	Montréal
1968	Montréal	Toe Blake	St. Louis
1969	Montréal	Claude Ruel	St. Louis
1970	Boston	Harry Sinden	St. Louis
1971	Montréal	Al MacNeil	Chicago

Year	Champion	Coach	Final opponent
1972	Boston	Tom Johnson	NY Rangers
1973	Montréal	Scotty Bowman	Chicago
1974	Philadelphia	Fred Shero	Boston
1975	Philadelphia	Fred Shero	Buffalo
1976	Montréal	Scotty Bowman	Philadelphia
1977	Montréal	Scotty Bowman	Boston
1978	Montréal	Scotty Bowman	Boston
1979	Montréal	Scotty Bowman	NY Rangers
1980	NY Islanders	Al Arbour	Philadelphia
1981	NY Islanders	Al Arbour	Minnesota
1982	NY Islanders	Al Arbour	Vancouver
1983	NY Islanders	Al Arbour	Edmonton
1984	Edmonton	Glen Sather	NY Islanders
1985	Edmonton	Glen Sather	Philadelphia
1986	Montréal	Jean Perron	Calgary
1987	Edmonton	Glen Sather	Philadelphia
1988	Edmonton	Glen Sather	Boston
1989	Calgary	Terry Crisp	Montréal
1990	Edmonton	John Muckler	Boston
1991	Pittsburgh	Bob Johnson	Minnesota
1992	Pittsburgh	Scotty Bowman	Chicago
1993	Montréal	Jacques Demers	Los Angeles
1994	NY Rangers	Mike Keenan	Vancouver
1995	New Jersey	Jacques Lemaire	Detroit
1996	Colorado	Marc Crawford	Florida
1997	Detroit	Scotty Bowman	Philadelphia
1998	Detroit	Scotty Bowman	Washington
1999	Dallas	Ken Hitchcock	Buffalo
2000	New Jersey	Larry Robinson	Dallas
2001	Colorado	Bob Hartley	New Jersey
2002	Detroit	Scotty Bowman	Carolina
2003	New Jersey	Pat Burns	Anaheim
2004	Tampa Bay	John Tortorella	Calgary
2005	No competition (labor dispute; season canceled)		
2006	Carolina	Peter Laviolette	Edmonton
2007	Anaheim	Randy Carlyle	Ottawa
2008	Detroit	Mike Babcock	Pittsburgh
2009	Pittsburgh	Dan Bylsma	Detroit
2010	Chicago	Joel Quenneville	Philadelphia
2011	Boston	Claude Julien	Vancouver
2012	Los Angeles	Darryl Sutter	New Jersey
2013	Chicago	Joel Quenneville	Boston
2014	Los Angeles	Darryl Sutter	NY Rangers
2015	Chicago	Joel Quenneville	Tampa Bay
2016	Pittsburgh	Mike Sullivan	San Jose
2017	Pittsburgh	Mike Sullivan	Nashville
2018	Washington	Barry Trotz	Vegas
2019	St. Louis	Craig Berube	Boston
2020	Tampa Bay	Jon Cooper	Dallas
2021	Tampa Bay	Jon Cooper	Montréal
2022	Colorado	Jared Bednar	Tampa Bay
2023	Vegas	Bruce Cassidy	Florida
2024	Florida	Paul Maurice	Edmonton

Presidents' Trophy, 1986-2024

Awarded annually to club with best regular season record. Records are Win-Loss-Tie, 1986-99; Win-Loss-Tie-Overtime Loss, 2000-04; Win-Loss-Overtime Loss, 2006-present. (Because of a labor dispute, the 2005 season was canceled.)

Year	Team	Record	Points
1986	Edmonton	56-17-7	119
1987	Edmonton	50-24-6	106
1988	Calgary	48-23-9	105
1989	Calgary	54-17-9	117
1990	Boston	46-25-9	101
1991	Chicago	49-23-8	106
1992	NY Rangers	50-25-5	105
1993	Pittsburgh	56-21-7	119
1994	NY Rangers	52-24-8	112
1995	Detroit	33-11-4	70
1996	Detroit	62-13-7	131
1997	Colorado	49-24-9	107
1998	Dallas	49-22-11	109
1999	Dallas	51-19-12	114
2000	St. Louis	51-19-11-1	114
2001	Colorado	52-16-10-4	118
2002	Detroit	51-17-10-4	116
2003	Ottawa	52-21-8-1	113
2004	Detroit	48-21-11-2	109
2006	Detroit	58-16-8	124
2007	Buffalo	53-22-7	113
2008	Detroit	54-21-7	115
2009	San Jose	53-18-11	117
2010	Washington	54-15-13	121
2011	Vancouver	54-19-9	117
2012	Vancouver	51-22-9	111
2013	Chicago	36-7-5	77
2014	Boston	54-19-9	117
2015	NY Rangers	53-22-7	113
2016	Washington	56-18-8	120
2017	Washington	55-19-8	118
2018	Nashville	53-18-11	117
2019	Tampa Bay	62-16-4	128
2020	Boston	44-14-12	100
2021	Colorado	39-13-4	82
2022	Florida	58-18-6	122
2023	Boston	65-12-5	135
2024	NY Rangers	55-23-4	114

Most NHL Goals in a Season

Player	Team	Season	Goals
Wayne Gretzky	Edmonton	1981-82	92
Wayne Gretzky	Edmonton	1983-84	87
Brett Hull	St. Louis	1990-91	86
Mario Lemieux	Pittsburgh	1988-89	85
Phil Esposito	Boston	1970-71	76
Alexander Mogilny	Buffalo	1992-93	76
Teemu Selanne	Winnipeg	1992-93	76
Wayne Gretzky	Edmonton	1984-85	73
Brett Hull	St. Louis	1989-90	72
Wayne Gretzky	Edmonton	1982-83	71
Jari Kurri	Edmonton	1984-85	71
Mario Lemieux	Pittsburgh	1987-88	70
Bernie Nicholls	Los Angeles	1988-89	70
Brett Hull	St. Louis	1991-92	70
Mike Bossy	NY Islanders	1978-79	69
Mario Lemieux	Pittsburgh	1992-93	69
Mario Lemieux	Pittsburgh	1995-96	69
Auston Matthews	Toronto	2023-24	69

NHL Regular Season Career Scoring Leaders

(Through end of 2023-24 season. * = Active in 2023-24 season.)

Player	Goals	Assists	Points
Wayne Gretzky	894	1,963	2,857
Jaromir Jagr	766	1,155	1,921
Mark Messier	694	1,193	1,887
Gordie Howe	801	1,049	1,850
Ron Francis	549	1,249	1,798
Marcel Dionne	731	1,040	1,771
Steve Yzerman	692	1,063	1,755
Mario Lemieux	690	1,033	1,723
Joe Sakic	625	1,016	1,641
*Sidney Crosby	592	1,004	1,596
Phil Esposito	717	873	1,590
Ray Bourque	410	1,169	1,579
*Alex Ovechkin	853	697	1,550
Joe Thornton	430	1,109	1,539
Mark Recchi	577	956	1,533
Paul Coffey	396	1,135	1,531
Stan Mikita	541	926	1,467
Teemu Selanne	684	773	1,457
Bryan Trottier	524	901	1,425
Adam Oates	341	1,079	1,420
Doug Gilmour	450	964	1,414
Dale Hawerchuk	518	891	1,409
Jari Kurri	601	797	1,398
Luc Robitaille	668	726	1,394
Brett Hull	741	650	1,391
Mike Modano	561	813	1,374
Johnny Bucyk	556	813	1,369
Brendan Shanahan	656	698	1,354
Guy Lafleur	560	793	1,353
Mats Sundin	564	785	1,349
Dave Andreychuk	640	698	1,338
Denis Savard	473	865	1,338
Mike Gartner	708	627	1,335
Pierre Turgeon	515	812	1,327
Gilbert Perreault	512	814	1,326
Jarome Iginla	625	675	1,300
*Evgeni Malkin	498	798	1,296
*Patrick Kane	471	813	1,284
Alex Delvecchio	456	825	1,281

Leading NHL Career Goaltenders

(Through end of 2023-24 season. * = Active in 2023-24 season.)

Ranked by Shutouts

Martin Brodeur	125
Terry Sawchuk	103
George Hainsworth	94
Glenn Hall	84
Jacques Plante	82
Alec Connell	81
Tiny Thompson	81
Dominik Hasek	81
Roberto Luongo	77
Ed Belfour	76
Tony Esposito	76
*Marc-André Fleury	75
Lorne Chabot	71
Harry Lumley	71
Roy Worters	67
Patrick Roy	66
Henrik Lundqvist	64
Turk Broda	61
*Jonathan Quick	60
Pekka Rinne	60
Evgeni Nabokov	59
John Ross Roach	58

Ranked by Wins

Martin Brodeur	691
*Marc-André Fleury	561
Patrick Roy	551
Roberto Luongo	489
Ed Belfour	484
Henrik Lundqvist	459
Curtis Joseph	454
Terry Sawchuk	445
Jacques Plante	437
Tony Esposito	423
Glenn Hall	407
Grant Fuhr	403
Chris Osgood	401
*Sergei Bobrovsky	396
*Jonathan Quick	393
Ryan Miller	391
Dominik Hasek	389
Mike Vernon	385
John Vanbiesbrouck	374
Andy Moog	372
Tom Barrasso	369
Pekka Rinne	369

Hart Memorial Trophy (MVP), 1927-2024

Year	Player, team	Year	Player, team	Year	Player, team
1927	Herb Gardiner, Montréal Canadiens	1960	Gordie Howe, Detroit	1992	Mark Messier, NY Rangers
1928	Howie Morenz, Montréal Canadiens	1961	Bernie Geoffrion, Montréal	1993	Mario Lemieux, Pittsburgh
1929	Roy Worters, NY Americans	1962	Jacques Plante, Montréal	1994	Sergei Fedorov, Detroit
1930	Nels Stewart, Montréal Maroons	1963	Gordie Howe, Detroit	1995	Eric Lindros, Philadelphia
1931	Howie Morenz, Montréal Canadiens	1964	Jean Beliveau, Montréal	1996	Mario Lemieux, Pittsburgh
1932	Howie Morenz, Montréal Canadiens	1965	Bobby Hull, Chicago	1997	Dominik Hasek, Buffalo
1933	Eddie Shore, Boston	1966	Bobby Hull, Chicago	1998	Dominik Hasek, Buffalo
1934	Aurel Joliat, Montréal Canadiens	1967	Stan Mikita, Chicago	1999	Jaromir Jagr, Pittsburgh
1935	Eddie Shore, Boston	1968	Stan Mikita, Chicago	2000	Chris Pronger, St. Louis
1936	Eddie Shore, Boston	1969	Phil Esposito, Boston	2001	Joe Sakic, Colorado
1937	Babe Siebert, Montréal Canadiens	1970	Bobby Orr, Boston	2002	Jose Theodore, Montréal
1938	Eddie Shore, Boston	1971	Bobby Orr, Boston	2003	Peter Forsberg, Colorado
1939	Toe Blake, Montréal	1972	Bobby Orr, Boston	2004	Martin St. Louis, Tampa Bay
1940	Ebbie Goodfellow, Detroit	1973	Bobby Clarke, Philadelphia	2006	Joe Thornton, San Jose
1941	Bill Cowley, Boston	1974	Phil Esposito, Boston	2007	Sidney Crosby, Pittsburgh
1942	Tom Anderson, Brooklyn Americans	1975	Bobby Clarke, Philadelphia	2008	Alex Ovechkin, Washington
1943	Bill Cowley, Boston	1976	Bobby Clarke, Philadelphia	2009	Alex Ovechkin, Washington
1944	Babe Pratt, Toronto	1977	Guy Lafleur, Montréal	2010	Henrik Sedin, Vancouver
1945	Elmer Lach, Montréal	1978	Guy Lafleur, Montréal	2011	Corey Perry, Anaheim
1946	Max Bentley, Chicago	1979	Bryan Trottier, NY Islanders	2012	Evgeni Malkin, Pittsburgh
1947	Maurice Richard, Montréal	1980	Wayne Gretzky, Edmonton	2013	Alex Ovechkin, Washington
1948	Buddy O'Connor, NY Rangers	1981	Wayne Gretzky, Edmonton	2014	Sidney Crosby, Pittsburgh
1949	Sid Abel, Detroit	1982	Wayne Gretzky, Edmonton	2015	Carey Price, Montréal
1950	Chuck Rayner, NY Rangers	1983	Wayne Gretzky, Edmonton	2016	Patrick Kane, Chicago
1951	Milt Schmidt, Boston	1984	Wayne Gretzky, Edmonton	2017	Connor McDavid, Edmonton
1952	Gordie Howe, Detroit	1985	Wayne Gretzky, Edmonton	2018	Taylor Hall, New Jersey
1953	Gordie Howe, Detroit	1986	Wayne Gretzky, Edmonton	2019	Nikita Kucherov, Tampa Bay
1954	Al Rollins, Chicago	1987	Wayne Gretzky, Edmonton	2020	Leon Draisaitl, Edmonton
1955	Ted Kennedy, Toronto	1988	Mario Lemieux, Pittsburgh	2021	Connor McDavid, Edmonton
1956	Jean Beliveau, Montréal	1989	Wayne Gretzky, Los Angeles	2022	Auston Matthews, Toronto
1957	Gordie Howe, Detroit	1990	Mark Messier, Edmonton	2023	Connor McDavid, Edmonton
1958	Gordie Howe, Detroit	1991	Brett Hull, St. Louis	2024	Nathan MacKinnon, Colorado
1959	Andy Bathgate, NY Rangers				

Conn Smythe Trophy (MVP in Playoffs), 1965-2024

Year	Player, team	Year	Player, team	Year	Player, team
1965	Jean Beliveau, Montréal	1985	Wayne Gretzky, Edmonton	2006	Cam Ward, Carolina
1966	Roger Crozier, Detroit	1986	Patrick Roy, Montréal	2007	Scott Niedermayer, Anaheim
1967	Dave Keon, Toronto	1987	Ron Hextall, Philadelphia	2008	Henrik Zetterberg, Detroit
1968	Glenn Hall, St. Louis	1988	Wayne Gretzky, Edmonton	2009	Evgeni Malkin, Pittsburgh
1969	Serge Savard, Montréal	1989	Al MacInnis, Calgary	2010	Jonathan Toews, Chicago
1970	Bobby Orr, Boston	1990	Bill Ranford, Edmonton	2011	Tim Thomas, Boston
1971	Ken Dryden, Montréal	1991	Mario Lemieux, Pittsburgh	2012	Jonathan Quick, Los Angeles
1972	Bobby Orr, Boston	1992	Mario Lemieux, Pittsburgh	2013	Patrick Kane, Chicago
1973	Yvan Cournoyer, Montréal	1993	Patrick Roy, Montréal	2014	Justin Williams, Los Angeles
1974	Bernie Parent, Philadelphia	1994	Brian Leetch, NY Rangers	2015	Duncan Keith, Chicago
1975	Bernie Parent, Philadelphia	1995	Claude Lemieux, New Jersey	2016	Sidney Crosby, Pittsburgh
1976	Reggie Leach, Philadelphia	1996	Joe Sakic, Colorado	2017	Sidney Crosby, Pittsburgh
1977	Guy Lafleur, Montréal	1997	Mike Vernon, Detroit	2018	Alex Ovechkin, Washington
1978	Larry Robinson, Montréal	1998	Steve Yzerman, Detroit	2019	Ryan O'Reilly, St. Louis
1979	Bob Gainey, Montréal	1999	Joe Nieuwendyk, Dallas	2020	Victor Hedman, Tampa Bay
1980	Bryan Trottier, NY Islanders	2000	Scott Stevens, New Jersey	2021	Andrei Vasilevskiy, Tampa Bay
1981	Butch Goring, NY Islanders	2001	Patrick Roy, Colorado	2022	Cale Makar, Colorado
1982	Mike Bossy, NY Islanders	2002	Nicklas Lidstrom, Detroit	2023	Jonathan Marchessault, Vegas
1983	Billy Smith, NY Islanders	2003	Jean-Sebastien Giguere, Anaheim	2024	Connor McDavid, Edmonton
1984	Mark Messier, Edmonton	2004	Brad Richards, Tampa Bay		

Calder Memorial Trophy (Best Rookie), 1933-2024

Year	Player, team	Year	Player, team	Year	Player, team
1933	Carl Voss, Detroit	1964	Jacques Laperrière, Montréal	1994	Martin Brodeur, New Jersey
1934	Russ Blinco, Montréal Maroons	1965	Roger Crozier, Detroit	1995	Peter Forsberg, Quebec
1935	Dave Schriner, NY Americans	1966	Brit Selby, Toronto	1996	Daniel Alfredsson, Ottawa
1936	Mike Karakas, Chicago	1967	Bobby Orr, Boston	1997	Bryan Berard, NY Islanders
1937	Syl Apps, Toronto	1968	Derek Sanderson, Boston	1998	Sergei Samsonov, Boston
1938	Cully Dahlstrom, Chicago	1969	Danny Grant, Minnesota	1999	Chris Drury, Colorado
1939	Frank Brimsek, Boston	1970	Tony Esposito, Chicago	2000	Scott Gomez, New Jersey
1940	Kilby MacDonald, NY Rangers	1971	Gilbert Perreault, Buffalo	2001	Evgeni Nabokov, San Jose
1941	John Quilty, Montréal	1972	Ken Dryden, Montréal	2002	Dany Heatley, Atlanta
1942	Grant Warwick, NY Rangers	1973	Steve Vickers, NY Rangers	2003	Barret Jackman, St. Louis
1943	Gaye Stewart, Toronto	1974	Denis Potvin, NY Islanders	2004	Andrew Raycroft, Boston
1944	Gus Bodnar, Toronto	1975	Eric Vail, Atlanta	2006	Alex Ovechkin, Washington
1945	Frank McCool, Toronto	1976	Bryan Trottier, NY Islanders	2007	Evgeni Malkin, Pittsburgh
1946	Edgar Laprade, NY Rangers	1977	Willi Plett, Atlanta	2008	Patrick Kane, Chicago
1947	Howie Meeker, Toronto	1978	Mike Bossy, NY Islanders	2009	Steve Mason, Columbus
1948	Jim McFadden, Detroit	1979	Bobby Smith, Minnesota	2010	Tyler Myers, Buffalo
1949	Pentti Lund, NY Rangers	1980	Ray Bourque, Boston	2011	Jeff Skinner, Carolina
1950	Jack Gelineau, Boston	1981	Peter Stastny, Quebec	2012	Gabriel Landeskog, Colorado
1951	Terry Sawchuk, Detroit	1982	Dale Hawerchuk, Winnipeg	2013	Jonathan Huberdeau, Florida
1952	Bernie Geoffrion, Montréal	1983	Steve Larmer, Chicago	2014	Nathan MacKinnon, Colorado
1953	Gump Worsley, NY Rangers	1984	Tom Barrasso, Buffalo	2015	Aaron Ekblad, Florida
1954	Camille Henry, NY Rangers	1985	Mario Lemieux, Pittsburgh	2016	Artemi Panarin, Chicago
1955	Ed Litzenberger, Chicago	1986	Gary Suter, Calgary	2017	Auston Matthews, Toronto
1956	Glenn Hall, Detroit	1987	Luc Robitaille, Los Angeles	2018	Mathew Barzal, NY Islanders
1957	Larry Regan, Boston	1988	Joe Nieuwendyk, Calgary	2019	Elias Pettersson, Vancouver
1958	Frank Mahovlich, Toronto	1989	Brian Leetch, NY Rangers	2020	Cale Makar, Colorado
1959	Ralph Backstrom, Montréal	1990	Sergei Makarov, Calgary	2021	Kirill Kaprizov, Minnesota
1960	Bill Hay, Chicago	1991	Ed Belfour, Chicago	2022	Moritz Seider, Detroit
1961	Dave Keon, Toronto	1992	Pavel Bure, Vancouver	2023	Matty Beniers, Seattle
1962	Bobby Rousseau, Montréal	1993	Teemu Selanne, Winnipeg	2024	Connor Bedard, Chicago
1963	Kent Douglas, Toronto				

Lady Byng Memorial Trophy (Most Gentlemanly Player), 1925-2024

Year	Player, team	Year	Player, team	Year	Player, team
1925	Frank Nighbor, Ottawa	1958	Camille Henry, NY Rangers	1992	Wayne Gretzky, Los Angeles
1926	Frank Nighbor, Ottawa	1959	Alex Delvecchio, Detroit	1993	Pierre Turgeon, NY Islanders
1927	Billy Burch, NY Americans	1960	Don McKenney, Boston	1994	Wayne Gretzky, Los Angeles
1928	Frank Boucher, NY Rangers	1961	Red Kelly, Toronto	1995	Ron Francis, Pittsburgh
1929	Frank Boucher, NY Rangers	1962	Dave Keon, Toronto	1996	Paul Kariya, Anaheim
1930	Frank Boucher, NY Rangers	1963	Dave Keon, Toronto	1997	Paul Kariya, Anaheim
1931	Frank Boucher, NY Rangers	1964	Ken Wharram, Chicago	1998	Ron Francis, Pittsburgh
1932	Joe Primeau, Toronto	1965	Bobby Hull, Chicago	1999	Wayne Gretzky, NY Rangers
1933	Frank Boucher, NY Rangers	1966	Alex Delvecchio, Detroit	2000	Pavol Demitra, St. Louis
1934	Frank Boucher, NY Rangers	1967	Stan Mikita, Chicago	2001	Joe Sakic, Colorado
1935	Frank Boucher, NY Rangers	1968	Stan Mikita, Chicago	2002	Ron Francis, Carolina
1936	Doc Romnes, Chicago	1969	Alex Delvecchio, Detroit	2003	Alexander Mogilny, Toronto
1937	Marty Barry, Detroit	1970	Phil Goyette, St. Louis	2004	Brad Richards, Tampa Bay
1938	Gordie Drillon, Toronto	1971	John Bucyk, Boston	2006	Pavel Datsyuk, Detroit
1939	Clint Smith, NY Rangers	1972	Jean Ratelle, NY Rangers	2007	Pavel Datsyuk, Detroit
1940	Bobby Bauer, Boston	1973	Gil Perreault, Buffalo	2008	Pavel Datsyuk, Detroit
1941	Bobby Bauer, Boston	1974	John Bucyk, Boston	2009	Pavel Datsyuk, Detroit
1942	Syl Apps, Toronto	1975	Marcel Dionne, Detroit	2010	Martin St. Louis, Tampa Bay
1943	Max Bentley, Chicago	1976	Jean Ratelle, NYR-Boston	2011	Martin St. Louis, Tampa Bay
1944	Clint Smith, Chicago	1977	Marcel Dionne, Los Angeles	2012	Brian Campbell, Florida
1945	Bill Mosienko, Chicago	1978	Butch Goring, Los Angeles	2013	Martin St. Louis, Tampa Bay
1946	Toe Blake, Montréal	1979	Bob MacMillan, Atlanta	2014	Ryan O'Reilly, Colorado
1947	Bobby Bauer, Boston	1980	Wayne Gretzky, Edmonton	2015	Jiri Hudler, Calgary
1948	Buddy O'Connor, NY Rangers	1981	Rick Kehoe, Pittsburgh	2016	Anze Kopitar, Los Angeles
1949	Bill Quackenbush, Detroit	1982	Rick Middleton, Boston	2017	Johnny Gaudreau, Calgary
1950	Edgar Laprade, NY Rangers	1983	Mike Bossy, NY Islanders	2018	William Karlsson, Vegas
1951	Red Kelly, Detroit	1984	Mike Bossy, NY Islanders	2019	Aleksander Barkov, Florida
1952	Sid Smith, Toronto	1985	Jari Kurri, Edmonton	2020	Nathan MacKinnon, Colorado
1953	Red Kelly, Detroit	1986	Mike Bossy, NY Islanders	2021	Jaccob Slavin, Carolina
1954	Red Kelly, Detroit	1987	Joe Mullen, Calgary	2022	Kyle Connor, Winnipeg
1955	Sid Smith, Toronto	1988	Mats Naslund, Montréal	2023	Anze Kopitar, Los Angeles
1956	Dutch Reibel, Detroit	1989	Joe Mullen, Calgary	2024	Jaccob Slavin, Carolina
1957	Andy Hebenton, NY Rangers	1990	Brett Hull, St. Louis		
		1991	Wayne Gretzky, Los Angeles		

James Norris Memorial Trophy (Best Defenseman), 1954-2024

Year	Player, team	Year	Player, team	Year	Player, team
1954	Red Kelly, Detroit	1978	Denis Potvin, NY Islanders	2001	Nicklas Lidstrom, Detroit
1955	Doug Harvey, Montréal	1979	Denis Potvin, NY Islanders	2002	Nicklas Lidstrom, Detroit
1956	Doug Harvey, Montréal	1980	Larry Robinson, Montréal	2003	Nicklas Lidstrom, Detroit
1957	Doug Harvey, Montréal	1981	Randy Carlyle, Pittsburgh	2004	Scott Niedermayer, New Jersey
1958	Doug Harvey, Montréal	1982	Doug Wilson, Chicago	2006	Nicklas Lidstrom, Detroit
1959	Tom Johnson, Montréal	1983	Rod Langway, Washington	2007	Nicklas Lidstrom, Detroit
1960	Doug Harvey, Montréal	1984	Rod Langway, Washington	2008	Nicklas Lidstrom, Detroit
1961	Doug Harvey, Montréal	1985	Paul Coffey, Edmonton	2009	Zdeno Chara, Boston
1962	Doug Harvey, NY Rangers	1986	Paul Coffey, Edmonton	2010	Duncan Keith, Chicago
1963	Pierre Pilote, Chicago	1987	Ray Bourque, Boston	2011	Nicklas Lidstrom, Detroit
1964	Pierre Pilote, Chicago	1988	Ray Bourque, Boston	2012	Erik Karlsson, Ottawa
1965	Pierre Pilote, Chicago	1989	Chris Chelios, Montréal	2013	P. K. Subban, Montréal
1966	Jacques Laperrière, Montréal	1990	Ray Bourque, Boston	2014	Duncan Keith, Chicago
1967	Harry Howell, NY Rangers	1991	Ray Bourque, Boston	2015	Erik Karlsson, Ottawa
1968	Bobby Orr, Boston	1992	Brian Leetch, NY Rangers	2016	Drew Doughty, Los Angeles
1969	Bobby Orr, Boston	1993	Chris Chelios, Chicago	2017	Brent Burns, San Jose
1970	Bobby Orr, Boston	1994	Ray Bourque, Boston	2018	Victor Hedman, Tampa Bay
1971	Bobby Orr, Boston	1995	Paul Coffey, Detroit	2019	Mark Giordano, Calgary
1972	Bobby Orr, Boston	1996	Chris Chelios, Chicago	2020	Roman Josi, Nashville
1973	Bobby Orr, Boston	1997	Brian Leetch, NY Rangers	2021	Adam Fox, NY Rangers
1974	Bobby Orr, Boston	1998	Rob Blake, Los Angeles	2022	Cale Makar, Colorado
1975	Bobby Orr, Boston	1999	Al MacInnis, St. Louis	2023	Erik Karlsson, San Jose
1976	Denis Potvin, NY Islanders	2000	Chris Pronger, St. Louis	2024	Quinn Hughes, Vancouver
1977	Larry Robinson, Montréal				

Art Ross Trophy (Highest Scorer), 1947-2024

Year	Player, team	Year	Player, team	Year	Player, team
1947	Max Bentley, Chicago	1973	Phil Esposito, Boston	1999	Jaromir Jagr, Pittsburgh
1948	Elmer Lach, Montréal	1974	Phil Esposito, Boston	2000	Jaromir Jagr, Pittsburgh
1949	Roy Conacher, Chicago	1975	Bobby Orr, Boston	2001	Jaromir Jagr, Pittsburgh
1950	Ted Lindsay, Detroit	1976	Guy Lafleur, Montréal	2002	Jarome Iginla, Calgary
1951	Gordie Howe, Detroit	1977	Guy Lafleur, Montréal	2003	Peter Forsberg, Colorado
1952	Gordie Howe, Detroit	1978	Guy Lafleur, Montréal	2004	Martin St. Louis, Tampa Bay
1953	Gordie Howe, Detroit	1979	Bryan Trottier, NY Islanders	2006	Joe Thornton, Boston/San Jose
1954	Gordie Howe, Detroit	1980	Marcel Dionne, Los Angeles	2007	Sidney Crosby, Pittsburgh
1955	Bernie Geoffrion, Montréal	1981	Wayne Gretzky, Edmonton	2008	Alex Ovechkin, Washington
1956	Jean Beliveau, Montréal	1982	Wayne Gretzky, Edmonton	2009	Evgeni Malkin, Pittsburgh
1957	Gordie Howe, Detroit	1983	Wayne Gretzky, Edmonton	2010	Henrik Sedin, Vancouver
1958	Dickie Moore, Montréal	1984	Wayne Gretzky, Edmonton	2011	Daniel Sedin, Vancouver
1959	Dickie Moore, Montréal	1985	Wayne Gretzky, Edmonton	2012	Evgeni Malkin, Pittsburgh
1960	Bobby Hull, Chicago	1986	Wayne Gretzky, Edmonton	2013	Martin St. Louis, Tampa Bay
1961	Bernie Geoffrion, Montréal	1987	Wayne Gretzky, Edmonton	2014	Sidney Crosby, Pittsburgh
1962	Bobby Hull, Chicago	1988	Mario Lemieux, Pittsburgh	2015	Jamie Benn, Dallas
1963	Gordie Howe, Detroit	1989	Mario Lemieux, Pittsburgh	2016	Patrick Kane, Chicago
1964	Stan Mikita, Chicago	1990	Wayne Gretzky, Los Angeles	2017	Connor McDavid, Edmonton
1965	Stan Mikita, Chicago	1991	Wayne Gretzky, Los Angeles	2018	Connor McDavid, Edmonton
1966	Bobby Hull, Chicago	1992	Mario Lemieux, Pittsburgh	2019	Nikita Kucherov, Tampa Bay
1967	Stan Mikita, Chicago	1993	Mario Lemieux, Pittsburgh	2020	Leon Draisaitl, Edmonton
1968	Stan Mikita, Chicago	1994	Wayne Gretzky, Los Angeles	2021	Connor McDavid, Edmonton
1969	Phil Esposito, Boston	1995	Jaromir Jagr, Pittsburgh	2022	Connor McDavid, Edmonton
1970	Bobby Orr, Boston	1996	Mario Lemieux, Pittsburgh	2023	Connor McDavid, Edmonton
1971	Phil Esposito, Boston	1997	Mario Lemieux, Pittsburgh	2024	Nikita Kucherov, Tampa Bay
1972	Phil Esposito, Boston	1998	Jaromir Jagr, Pittsburgh		

Vezina Trophy (Best Goaltender), 1927-2024

Year	Player, team	Year	Player, team	Year	Player, team
1927	George Hainsworth, Montréal Canadiens	1929	George Hainsworth, Montréal Canadiens	1932	Charlie Gardiner, Chicago
				1933	Tiny Thompson, Boston
1928	George Hainsworth, Montréal Canadiens	1930	Tiny Thompson, Boston	1934	Charlie Gardiner, Chicago
		1931	Roy Worters, NY Americans	1935	Lorne Chabot, Chicago

Year	Player, team
1936	Tiny Thompson, Boston
1937	Normie Smith, Detroit
1938	Tiny Thompson, Boston
1939	Frank Brimsek, Boston
1940	Dave Kerr, NY Rangers
1941	Turk Broda, Toronto
1942	Frank Brimsek, Boston
1943	Johnny Mowers, Detroit
1944	Bill Durnan, Montréal
1945	Bill Durnan, Montréal
1946	Bill Durnan, Montréal
1947	Bill Durnan, Montréal
1948	Turk Broda, Toronto
1949	Bill Durnan, Montréal
1950	Bill Durnan, Montréal
1951	Al Rollins, Toronto
1952	Terry Sawchuk, Detroit
1953	Terry Sawchuk, Detroit
1954	Harry Lumley, Toronto
1955	Terry Sawchuk, Detroit
1956	Jacques Plante, Montréal
1957	Jacques Plante, Montréal
1958	Jacques Plante, Montréal
1959	Jacques Plante, Montréal
1960	Jacques Plante, Montréal
1961	Johnny Bower, Toronto
1962	Jacques Plante, Montréal
1963	Glenn Hall, Chicago
1964	Charlie Hodge, Montréal
1965	Sawchuk, Bower; Toronto
1966	Lorne Worsley, Hodge; Montréal
1967	Hall, Denis DeJordy; Chicago
1968	Worsley, Rogatien Vachon; Montréal
1969	Hall, Plante; St. Louis
1970	Tony Esposito, Chicago
1971	Ed Giacomin, Gilles Villemure; NY Rangers
1972	Esposito, Gary Smith; Chicago
1973	Ken Dryden, Montréal
1974	Bernie Parent, Philadelphia; Tony Esposito, Chicago
1975	Bernie Parent, Philadelphia
1976	Ken Dryden, Montréal
1977	Dryden, Michel Larocque; Montréal
1978	Dryden, Larocque; Montréal
1979	Dryden, Larocque; Montréal
1980	Bob Sauve, Don Edwards; Buffalo
1981	Richard Sevigny, Michel Larocque, Denis Herron; Montréal
1982	Bill Smith, NY Islanders
1983	Pete Peeters, Boston
1984	Tom Barrasso, Buffalo
1985	Pelle Lindbergh, Philadelphia
1986	John Vanbiesbrouck, NY Rangers
1987	Ron Hextall, Philadelphia
1988	Grant Fuhr, Edmonton
1989	Patrick Roy, Montréal
1990	Patrick Roy, Montréal
1991	Ed Belfour, Chicago
1992	Patrick Roy, Montréal
1993	Ed Belfour, Chicago
1994	Dominik Hasek, Buffalo
1995	Dominik Hasek, Buffalo
1996	Jim Carey, Washington
1997	Dominik Hasek, Buffalo
1998	Dominik Hasek, Buffalo
1999	Dominik Hasek, Buffalo
2000	Olaf Kolzig, Washington
2001	Dominik Hasek, Buffalo
2002	Jose Theodore, Montréal
2003	Martin Brodeur, New Jersey
2004	Martin Brodeur, New Jersey
2006	Miikka Kiprusoff, Calgary
2007	Martin Brodeur, New Jersey
2008	Martin Brodeur, New Jersey
2009	Tim Thomas, Boston
2010	Ryan Miller, Buffalo
2011	Tim Thomas, Boston
2012	Henrik Lundqvist, NY Rangers
2013	Sergei Bobrovsky, Columbus
2014	Tuukka Rask, Boston
2015	Carey Price, Montréal
2016	Braden Holtby, Washington
2017	Sergei Bobrovsky, Columbus
2018	Pekka Rinne, Nashville
2019	Andrei Vasilevskiy, Tampa Bay
2020	Connor Hellebuyck, Winnipeg
2021	Marc-André Fleury, Vegas
2022	Igor Shesterkin, NY Rangers
2023	Linus Ullmark, Boston
2024	Connor Hellebuyck, Winnipeg

National Hockey League Franchise Origins

Team: founding year, league (NHL, World Hockey Association [WHA], or National Hockey Association of Canada [NHA]). Original location; subsequent history. Sites in the same metropolitan area not shown. * = Joined NHL in 1979 from defunct WHA.

Anaheim Ducks: 1993, NHL, as Mighty Ducks of Anaheim. Anaheim, CA, 1993-present. (Ducks, 2006-present.)
Boston Bruins: 1924, NHL. Boston, 1924-present.
Buffalo Sabres: 1970, NHL. Buffalo, NY, 1970-present.
Calgary Flames: 1972, NHL, as Atlanta Flames. Atlanta, GA, 1972-80; Calgary, AB, Canada, 1980-present.
***Carolina Hurricanes:** 1972, WHA, as Hartford Whalers. Hartford, CT, 1979-97; Carolina Hurricanes, Greensboro, NC, 1997-99; Raleigh, NC, 1999-present.
Chicago Blackhawks: 1926, NHL, as Chicago Black Hawks. Chicago, 1926-present. (Blackhawks, 1986-present.)
***Colorado Avalanche:** 1972, WHA, as Quebec Nordiques. Quebec City, QC, Canada, 1979-95; Colorado Avalanche, Denver, 1995-present.
Columbus Blue Jackets: 2000, NHL. Columbus, OH, 2000-present.
Dallas Stars: 1967, NHL, as Minnesota North Stars. Bloomington, MN, 1967-93; Dallas Stars, Dallas, 1993-present.
Detroit Red Wings: 1926, NHL, as Detroit Cougars, 1926-30. Detroit Falcons, 1930-32; Detroit Red Wings, 1932-present.
***Edmonton Oilers:** 1972, WHA. Edmonton, AB, Canada, 1979-present.
Florida Panthers: 1993, NHL. Miami, FL, 1993-98; Sunrise, FL, 1998-present.
Los Angeles Kings: 1967, NHL. Los Angeles, 1967-present.
Minnesota Wild: 2000, NHL. St. Paul, MN, 2000-present.
Montréal Canadiens: 1909, NHA; joined NHL, 1917. Montréal, QC, Canada, 1909-present.
Nashville Predators: 1998, NHL. Nashville, TN, 1998-present.
New Jersey Devils: 1974, NHL, as Kansas City Scouts. Kansas City, MO, 1974-76; Colorado Rockies, Denver, CO, 1976-82; New Jersey Devils, East Rutherford, NJ, 1982-2007; Newark, NJ, 2007-present.
New York Islanders: 1972, NHL. Uniondale, NY, 1972-2015, 2021, and selected games, 2018-20; Brooklyn, NY, 2015-20.
New York Rangers: 1926, NHL. New York City, 1926-present.
Ottawa Senators: 1992, NHL. Ottawa, ON, Canada, 1992-present.
Philadelphia Flyers: 1967, NHL. Philadelphia, 1967-present.
Pittsburgh Penguins: 1967, NHL. Pittsburgh, 1967-present.
St. Louis Blues: 1967, NHL. St. Louis, MO, 1967-present.
San Jose Sharks: 1991, NHL. Daly City, CA, 1991-93; San Jose, CA, 1993-present.
Seattle Kraken: 2021, NHL. Seattle, WA, 2021-present.
Tampa Bay Lightning: 1992, NHL. Tampa, FL, 1992-93; St. Petersburg, FL, 1993-96; Tampa, FL, 1996-present.
Toronto Maple Leafs: 1917, NHL, as Toronto (ON, Canada) Arenas, 1917-19. Toronto St. Patricks, 1919-26; Toronto Maple Leafs, 1926-present.
***Utah Hockey Club:** 1972, WHA, as Winnipeg Jets. Winnipeg, MB, Canada, 1979-96; Phoenix Coyotes, 1996-2014; Arizona Coyotes, Glendale, AZ, 2014-24. Salt Lake City, UT, 2024-present.
Vancouver Canucks: 1970, NHL. Vancouver, BC, Canada, 1970-present.
Vegas Golden Knights: 2017, NHL. Las Vegas, NV, 2017-present.
Washington Capitals: 1974, NHL. Landover, MD, 1974-97; Washington, DC, 1997-present.
Winnipeg Jets: 1999, NHL, as Atlanta Thrashers. Atlanta, GA, 1999-2011; Winnipeg, MB, Canada, 2011-present.

NHL Home Ice

Team	Name (year play began)	Capacity
Anaheim	Honda Center[1] (1993)	17,174
Boston	TD Garden[2] (1995)	17,850
Buffalo	KeyBank Center[3] (1996)	19,070
Calgary	Scotiabank Saddledome[4] (1983)	19,289
Carolina	PNC Arena[5] (1999)	18,700
Chicago	United Center (1994)	19,717
Colorado	Ball Arena[6] (1999)	17,809
Columbus	Nationwide Arena (2000)	18,144
Dallas	American Airlines Center (2001)	18,532
Detroit	Little Caesars Arena (2017)	19,515
Edmonton	Rogers Place (2016)	18,347
Florida	Amerant Bank Arena[7] (1998)	19,250
Los Angeles	Crypto.com Arena[8] (1999)	18,230
Minnesota	Xcel Energy Center (2000)	17,954
Montréal	Centre Bell[9] (1996)	21,105
Nashville	Bridgestone Arena[10] (1997)	17,159
New Jersey	Prudential Center (2007)	16,514
NY Islanders	UBS Arena (2021)	17,255
NY Rangers	Madison Square Garden (IV) (1968)	18,006
Ottawa	Canadian Tire Centre[11] (1996)	18,652
Philadelphia	Wells Fargo Center[12] (1996)	19,173
Pittsburgh	PPG Paints Arena[13] (2010)	18,187
St. Louis	Enterprise Center[14] (1994)	18,096
San Jose	SAP Center at San Jose[15] (1993)	17,470
Seattle	Climate Pledge Arena (2021)	17,100
Tampa Bay	Amalie Arena[16] (1996)	19,092
Toronto	Scotiabank Arena[17] (1999)	18,819
Utah	Delta Center (2024)	16,200
Vancouver	Rogers Arena[18] (1995)	18,870
Vegas	T-Mobile Arena (2017)	17,367
Washington	Capital One Arena[19] (1997)	18,573
Winnipeg	Canada Life Centre[20] (2004)	15,325

Note: Capacity as of the end of the 2023-24 season. (1) The Arrowhead Pond of Anaheim, 1993-2006. (2) FleetCenter, 1995-2005; TD Banknorth Garden, 2005-09. (3) Marine Midland Arena, 1996-99; HSBC Arena, 1999-2011; First Niagara Center, 2011-16. (4) Olympic Saddledome, 1983-96; Canadian Airlines Saddledome, 1996-2000; Pengrowth Saddledome, 2000-10. (5) Raleigh Entertainment and Sports Arena, 1999-2002; RBC Center, 2002-11. (6) Pepsi Center, 1999-2020. (7) National Car Rental Center, 1998-2002; Office Depot Center, 2002-05; BankAtlantic Center, 2005-12; BB&T Center, 2012-21; FLA Live Arena, 2021-23. (8) Staples Center, 1999-2021. (9) Le Centre Molson, 1996-2002. (10) Nashville Arena, 1997-99; Gaylord Entertainment Center, 1999-2007; Sommet Center, 2007-10. (11) Corel Centre, 1996-2006; Scotiabank Place, 2006-13. (12) CoreStates Center, 1996-98; First Union Center, 1998-2003; Wachovia Center, 2003-10. (13) CONSOL Energy Center, 2010-16. (14) Kiel Center, 1994-2000; Savvis Center, 2000-06; Scottrade Center, 2006-18. (15) San Jose Arena, 1993-2001; Compaq Center, 2001-02; HP Pavilion at San Jose, 2002-13. (16) Ice Palace, 1996-2002; St. Pete Times Forum, 2002-12; Tampa Bay Times Forum, 2012-14. (17) Air Canada Centre, 1999-2018. (18) General Motors Place, 1995-2010. (19) MCI Center, 1997-2006; Verizon Center, 2006-17. (20) MTS Centre, 2004-17; Bell MTS Place, 2017-21.

Spain Wins 2023 FIFA Women's World Cup

The Spanish women's national team won its first FIFA World Cup, defeating England, 1-0, on Aug. 20, 2023, at Stadium Australia in Sydney, Australia. The lone goal was scored by Olga Carmona in the 29th minute. Both teams appeared in the title match for the first time; Spain's previous best finish was the round of 16 in 2019. The team's momentous victory was quickly overshadowed by Luis Rubiales, head of the country's soccer federation, who forcibly kissed forward Jennifer Hermoso during the post-game celebration. Rubiales initially refused calls to resign, even after suspension by FIFA, but finally stepped down weeks later.

Spain's Aitana Bonmatí won the Golden Ball as the tournament's best player. The Golden Boot went to top scorer Hinata Miyazawa, who recorded five goals for Japan—two in a 4-0 group-stage drubbing of Spain. The Golden Glove went to English goalkeeper Mary Earps, who lived up to her nickname, "Mary Queen of Stops." Spain's Salma Paralluelo captured Young Player of the Tournament.

The U.S. team, winners of the last two World Cups and four of nine since the event started in 1991, was bounced in the round of 16 on penalty kicks by eventual third-place finisher Sweden. Vlatko Andonovski, coach of the U.S. women since 2019, resigned.

Women's World Cup Results, 2023

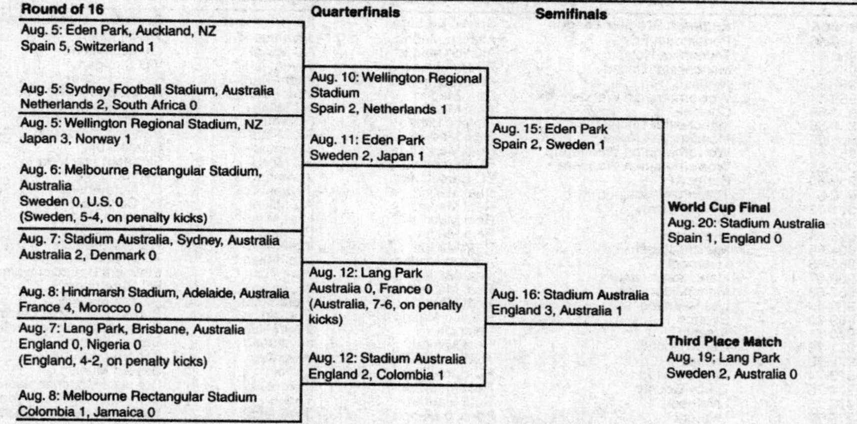

Women's World Cup Results, 1991-2023

Year	Winner	Final opponent	Score	Site
1991	U.S.	Norway	2-1	China
1995	Norway	Germany	2-0	Sweden
1999	U.S.	China	0-0 (5-4)*	Pasadena, CA, U.S.
2003	Germany	Sweden	2-1#	Carson, CA, U.S.
2007	Germany	Brazil	2-0	China
2011	Japan	U.S.	2-2 (3-1)*	Germany
2015	U.S.	Japan	5-2	Canada
2019	U.S.	Netherlands	2-0	France
2023	Spain	England	1-0	Australia

* = Match decided on penalty kicks (shootout score in parentheses). # = Match decided in extra time.

Gotham FC Wins First Title in 2023

One year after finishing in last place, the NJ/NY Gotham Football Club won its first National Women's Soccer League title on Nov. 11, 2023, defeating the OL Reign, 2-1, at Snapdragon Stadium in San Diego, CA. Midge Purce, limited by injury to just two assists all year, assisted on both Gotham FC goals to earn MVP of the championship game. Soccer legend Megan Rapinoe of OL Reign left the match, her final career game, in the sixth minute due to injury. Gotham FC, the sixth and last team to qualify for the NWSL playoffs, upset the defending champion Portland Thorns to reach the final while the Reign defeated the top-ranked San Diego Wave. The North Carolina Courage won the Challenge Cup for the second time.

Women's Professional Soccer Champions

Year	Winner	Final opponent	Score	Site	MVP
		Women's United Soccer Association champions			
2001	Bay Area CyberRays	Atlanta Beat	3-3 (4-2)*	Foxborough, MA	Julie Murray
2002	Carolina Courage	Washington Freedom	3-2	Atlanta, GA	Birgit Prinz
2003	Washington Freedom	Atlanta Beat	2-1	San Diego, CA	Abby Wambach
		Women's Professional Soccer champions			
2009	Sky Blue FC	Los Angeles Sol	1-0	Carson, CA	Heather O'Reilly
2010	FC Gold Pride	Philadelphia Independence	4-1	Hayward, CA	Marta
2011	Western New York Flash	Philadelphia Independence	1-1 (5-4)*	Rochester, NY	Christine Sinclair
		National Women's Soccer League champions			
2013	Portland Thorns FC	Western New York Flash	2-0	Rochester, NY	Tobin Heath
2014	FC Kansas City	Seattle Reign FC	2-1	Tukwila, WA	Lauren Holiday
2015	FC Kansas City	Seattle Reign FC	1-0	Portland, OR	Amy Rodriguez
2016	Western New York Flash	Washington Spirit	2-2 (3-2)*	Houston, TX	Sabrina D'Angelo
2017	Portland Thorns FC	North Carolina Courage	1-0	Orlando, FL	Lindsey Horan
2018	North Carolina Courage	Portland Thorns FC	3-0	Portland, OR	Jess McDonald
2019	North Carolina Courage	Chicago Red Stars	4-0	Cary, NC	Debinha
2020	Houston Dash	Chicago Red Stars	2-0	Sandy, UT	Rachel Daly
2021	Washington Spirit	Chicago Red Stars	2-1#	Louisville, KY	Aubrey Kingsbury
2022	Portland Thorns FC	Kansas City Current	2-0	Washington, DC	Sophia Smith
2023	NJ/NY Gotham FC	OL Reign	2-1	San Diego	Midge Purce

* = Match decided on penalty kicks (shootout score in parentheses). # = Match decided in extra time. **Note:** National Women's Soccer League (NWSL) began play in 2013 with eight teams competing: Boston Breakers, Chicago Red Stars, FC Kansas City, Portland Thorns FC, Seattle Reign FC, Sky Blue FC (New York/New Jersey), Washington Spirit (DC), and Western New York Flash.

UEFA Women's European Football Championship, 1984-2022

Year	Winner	Final opponent	Score	Site
1984	Sweden	England	1-0, 0-1(4-3)*	No fixed host
1987	Norway	Sweden	2-1	Norway
1989	West Germany	Norway	4-1	West Germany
1991	Germany	Norway	3-1#	Denmark
1993	Norway	Italy	1-0	Italy
1995	Germany	Sweden	3-2	No fixed host
1997	Germany	Italy	2-0	Norway, Sweden
2001	Germany	Sweden	1-0+	Germany
2005	Germany	Norway	3-1	England
2009	Germany	England	6-2	Finland
2013	Germany	Norway	1-0	Sweden
2017	Netherlands	Denmark	4-2	Netherlands
2022	England	Germany	2-1#	England

* = Match decided on penalty kicks (shootout in parentheses). # = Match decided in extra time. + = Sudden death (a.k.a. golden goal).
Note: 1984 champion decided by two matches; after each team won one, Sweden won on penalty kicks.

Selected European Soccer League Champions, 1950-2024

Season	England: Premier League[1]	Spain: La Liga	Italy: Serie A	Germany: Bundesliga[2]
1949-50	Portsmouth FC	Atlético Madrid	Juventus	VfB Stuttgart
1950-51	Tottenham Hotspur	Atlético Madrid	AC Milan	Kaiserslautern
1951-52	Manchester United	FC Barcelona	Juventus	VfB Stuttgart
1952-53	Arsenal	FC Barcelona	Inter Milan	Kaiserslautern
1953-54	Wolverhampton Wanderers	Real Madrid	Inter Milan	Hannoverscher SV 96
1954-55	Chelsea	Real Madrid	AC Milan	Rot-Weiss Essen
1955-56	Manchester United	Athletic Bilbao	Fiorentina	Borussia Dortmund
1956-57	Manchester United	Real Madrid	AC Milan	Borussia Dortmund
1957-58	Wolverhampton Wanderers	Real Madrid	Juventus	Schalke 04
1958-59	Wolverhampton Wanderers	FC Barcelona	AC Milan	Eintracht Frankfurt
1959-60	Burnley FC	FC Barcelona	Juventus	Hamburg SV
1960-61	Tottenham Hotspur	Real Madrid	Juventus	FC Nuremberg
1961-62	Ipswich Town	Real Madrid	AC Milan	FC Cologne
1962-63	Everton	Real Madrid	Inter Milan	Borussia Dortmund
1963-64	Liverpool	Real Madrid	Bologna	FC Cologne
1964-65	Manchester United	Real Madrid	Inter Milan	Werder Bremen
1965-66	Liverpool	Atlético Madrid	Inter Milan	TSV 1860 Munich
1966-67	Manchester United	Real Madrid	Juventus	Eintracht Braunschweig
1967-68	Manchester City	Real Madrid	AC Milan	FC Nuremberg
1968-69	Leeds United	Real Madrid	Fiorentina	Bayern Munich
1969-70	Everton	Atlético Madrid	Cagliari	Borussia Mönchengladbach
1970-71	Arsenal	Valencia	Inter Milan	Borussia Mönchengladbach
1971-72	Derby County	Real Madrid	Juventus	Bayern Munich
1972-73	Liverpool	Atlético Madrid	Juventus	Bayern Munich
1973-74	Leeds United	FC Barcelona	Lazio	Bayern Munich
1974-75	Derby County	Real Madrid	Juventus	Borussia Mönchengladbach
1975-76	Liverpool	Real Madrid	Torino	Borussia Mönchengladbach
1976-77	Liverpool	Atlético Madrid	Juventus	Borussia Mönchengladbach
1977-78	Nottingham Forest	Real Madrid	Juventus	FC Cologne
1978-79	Liverpool	Real Madrid	AC Milan	Hamburg SV
1979-80	Liverpool	Real Madrid	Inter Milan	Bayern Munich
1980-81	Aston Villa	Real Sociedad	Juventus	Bayern Munich
1981-82	Liverpool	Real Sociedad	Juventus	Hamburg SV
1982-83	Liverpool	Athletic Bilbao	AS Roma	Hamburg SV
1983-84	Liverpool	Athletic Bilbao	Juventus	VfB Stuttgart
1984-85	Everton	FC Barcelona	Verona	Bayern Munich
1985-86	Liverpool	Real Madrid	Juventus	Bayern Munich
1986-87	Everton	Real Madrid	Napoli	Bayern Munich
1987-88	Liverpool	Real Madrid	AC Milan	Werder Bremen
1988-89	Arsenal	Real Madrid	Inter Milan	Bayern Munich
1989-90	Liverpool	Real Madrid	Napoli	Bayern Munich
1990-91	Arsenal	FC Barcelona	Sampdoria	FC Kaiserslautern
1991-92	Leeds United	FC Barcelona	AC Milan	VfB Stuttgart
1992-93	Manchester United	FC Barcelona	AC Milan	Werder Bremen
1993-94	Manchester United	FC Barcelona	AC Milan	Bayern Munich
1994-95	Blackburn Rovers	Real Madrid	Juventus	Borussia Dortmund
1995-96	Manchester United	Atlético Madrid	AC Milan	Borussia Dortmund
1996-97	Manchester United	Real Madrid	Juventus	Bayern Munich
1997-98	Arsenal	FC Barcelona	Juventus	FC Kaiserslautern
1998-99	Manchester United	FC Barcelona	AC Milan	Bayern Munich
1999-2000	Manchester United	Deportivo Coruña	Lazio	Bayern Munich
2000-01	Manchester United	Real Madrid	AS Roma	Bayern Munich
2001-02	Arsenal	Valencia	Juventus	Borussia Dortmund
2002-03	Manchester United	Real Madrid	Juventus	Bayern Munich
2003-04	Arsenal	Valencia	AC Milan	Werder Bremen
2004-05	Chelsea	FC Barcelona	None[3]	Bayern Munich
2005-06	Chelsea	FC Barcelona	Inter Milan[3]	Bayern Munich
2006-07	Manchester United	Real Madrid	Inter Milan	VfB Stuttgart
2007-08	Manchester United	Real Madrid	Inter Milan	Bayern Munich
2008-09	Manchester United	FC Barcelona	Inter Milan	VfL Wolfsburg
2009-10	Chelsea	FC Barcelona	Inter Milan	Bayern Munich
2010-11	Manchester United	FC Barcelona	AC Milan	Borussia Dortmund
2011-12	Manchester City	Real Madrid	Juventus	Borussia Dortmund
2012-13	Manchester United	FC Barcelona	Juventus	Bayern Munich
2013-14	Manchester City	Atlético Madrid	Juventus	Bayern Munich
2014-15	Chelsea	FC Barcelona	Juventus	Bayern Munich
2015-16	Leicester City	FC Barcelona	Juventus	Bayern Munich
2016-17	Chelsea	Real Madrid	Juventus	Bayern Munich
2017-18	Manchester City	FC Barcelona	Juventus	Bayern Munich
2018-19	Manchester City	FC Barcelona	Juventus	Bayern Munich
2019-20	Liverpool	Real Madrid	Juventus	Bayern Munich
2020-21	Manchester City	Atlético Madrid	Inter Milan	Bayern Munich
2022	Manchester City	Real Madrid	AC Milan	Bayern Munich
2023	Manchester City	FC Barcelona	Napoli	Bayern Munich
2024	Manchester City	Real Madrid	Inter Milan	Bayer Leverkusen

(1) Football League champions are listed prior to 1992-93 season, when the Premier League formed. (2) Regional champions are listed prior to 1963-64 season, when National Bundesliga formed. (3) Juventus was stripped of two titles in 2006 because of match-fixing.

Argentina Wins 2022 FIFA Men's World Cup

Argentina won its third FIFA World Cup men's soccer title Dec. 18, 2022, claiming victory on penalty kicks against defending champion France at Lusail Stadium in Lusail, Qatar. Tied 3-3 after extra time, Argentina dominated France in the penalty kicks, 4-2. France's Kylian Mbappé became the first player since 1966 to record a hat trick in the men's World Cup final, scoring twice in less than two minutes to tie the game in the second half. After Argentina went ahead on a goal by veteran superstar Lionel Messi, playing in his fifth World Cup, Mbappé converted a penalty to force extra time. Mbappé, with a tournament-high eight goals, earned the Golden Boot while Messi took the Golden Ball. Argentina's Emiliano Martínez was awarded the Golden Glove as best goalie and Enzo Fernández received the Young Player Award.

Argentina defeated Australia in the Round of 16 and beat the Netherlands on penalty kicks to reach the semifinals, where they blanked Croatia. The French knocked off Poland and defeated England, 2-1, in the quarterfinals. A 2-0 victory over Morocco, the first African and Arab team to reach the semifinals, put France in the final for the second straight World Cup.

Due to Qatar's hot climate, the tournament was held in Nov. and Dec., one of several controversial issues; other concerns included the host country's record on human rights, including treatment of women, migrant workers, and the LGBT community, plus alleged corruption in the bidding process. For the first time the World Cup allowed a concussion substitution of one per team per game, not counting against the team's regulation maximum of five subs. The total 172 goals scored were the most recorded since the 32-team World Cup format was unveiled in 1998. The field was expanding to 48 teams for the 2026 World Cup, which will be hosted June-July 2026 by the U.S., Canada, and Mexico.

Men's World Cup Results, 2022

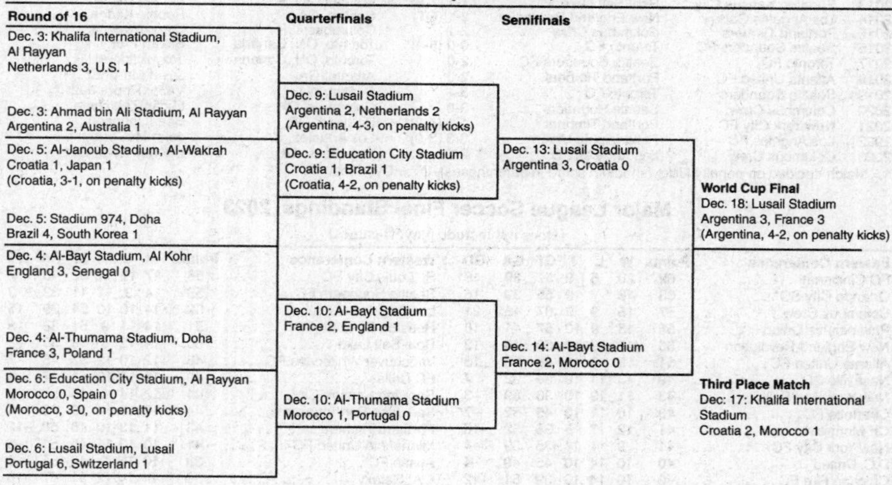

Men's World Cup Group Standings, 2022

(* = advanced to round of 16)

GROUP A	MP	W	D	L	GF	GA	+/–	PTS
Netherlands*	3	2	1	0	5	1	4	7
Senegal*	3	2	0	1	5	4	1	6
Ecuador	3	1	1	1	4	3	1	4
Qatar	3	0	0	3	1	7	–6	0
GROUP B								
England*	3	2	1	0	9	2	7	7
U.S.*	3	1	2	0	2	1	1	5
Iran	3	1	0	2	4	7	–3	3
Wales	3	0	1	2	1	6	–5	1
GROUP C								
Argentina*	3	2	0	1	5	2	3	6
Poland*	3	1	1	1	2	2	0	4
Mexico	3	1	1	1	2	3	–1	4
Saudi Arabia	3	1	0	2	3	5	–2	3
GROUP D								
France*	3	2	0	1	6	3	3	6
Australia*	3	2	0	1	3	4	–1	6
Tunisia	3	1	1	1	1	1	0	4
Denmark	3	0	1	2	1	3	–2	1

GROUP E	MP	W	D	L	GF	GA	+/–	PTS
Japan*	3	2	0	1	4	3	1	6
Spain*	3	1	1	1	9	3	6	4
Germany	3	1	1	1	6	5	1	4
Costa Rica	3	1	0	2	3	11	–8	3
GROUP F								
Morocco*	3	2	1	0	4	1	3	7
Croatia*	3	1	2	0	4	1	3	5
Belgium	3	1	1	1	1	2	–1	4
Canada	3	0	0	3	2	7	–5	0
GROUP G								
Brazil*	3	2	0	1	3	1	2	6
Switzerland*	3	2	0	1	4	3	1	6
Cameroon	3	1	1	1	4	4	0	4
Serbia	3	0	1	2	5	8	–3	1
GROUP H								
Portugal*	3	2	0	1	6	4	2	6
South Korea*	3	1	1	1	4	4	0	4
Uruguay	3	1	1	1	2	2	0	4
Ghana	3	1	0	2	5	7	–2	3

Columbus Cruises to Third MLS Championship in 2023

The Columbus Crew won the Major League Soccer Cup Dec. 9, 2023, defeating defending champion Los Angeles Football Club, 2-1, at Lower.com Field in Columbus, OH. Cucho Hernández, who scored the first goal on a penalty kick, was named MVP of the match. An expanded 18-team playoff field included a single-elimination Wild Card game for the eighth and ninth seeds in each conference, followed by a best-of-three first round, with all subsequent rounds single elimination. St. Louis City SC joined the MLS in 2023 as its 29th team and captured the Western Conference in its first season.

Major League Soccer (MLS) Cup Results, 1996-2023

Year	Winner	Final opponent	Score	Site	MVP
1996	DC United	Los Angeles Galaxy	3-2 (OT)	Foxborough, MA	Marco Etcheverry
1997	DC United	Colorado Rapids	2-1	Washington, DC	Jaime Moreno
1998	Chicago Fire	DC United	2-0	Pasadena, CA	Peter Nowak
1999	DC United	Los Angeles Galaxy	2-0	Foxborough, MA	Ben Olsen
2000	Kansas City Wizards	Chicago Fire	1-0	Washington, DC	Tony Meola
2001	San Jose Earthquakes	Los Angeles Galaxy	2-1 (OT)	Columbus, OH	Dwayne De Rosario
2002	Los Angeles Galaxy	New England Revolution	1-0 (OT)	Foxborough, MA	Carlos Ruiz
2003	San Jose Earthquakes	Chicago Fire	4-2	Carson, CA	Landon Donovan
2004	DC United	Kansas City Wizards	3-2	Carson, CA	Alecko Eskandarian
2005	Los Angeles Galaxy	New England Revolution	1-0 (OT)	Frisco, TX	Guillermo Ramírez
2006	Houston Dynamo	New England Revolution	1-1 (4-3)*	Frisco, TX	Brian Ching
2007	Houston Dynamo	New England Revolution	2-1	Washington, DC	Dwayne De Rosario
2008	Columbus Crew	New York Red Bulls	3-1	Carson, CA	Guillermo Barros Schelotto
2009	Real Salt Lake	Los Angeles Galaxy	1-1 (5-4)*	Seattle, WA	Nick Rimando
2010	Colorado Rapids	FC Dallas	2-1 (OT)	Toronto, ON, Canada	Conor Casey
2011	Los Angeles Galaxy	Houston Dynamo	1-0	Carson, CA	Landon Donovan
2012	Los Angeles Galaxy	Houston Dynamo	3-1	Carson, CA	Omar Gonzalez
2013	Sporting Kansas City	Real Salt Lake	1-1 (7-6)*	Kansas City, KS	Aurelien Collin
2014	Los Angeles Galaxy	New England Revolution	2-1 (OT)	Carson, CA	Robbie Keane
2015	Portland Timbers	Columbus Crew	2-1	Columbus, OH	Diego Valeri
2016	Seattle Sounders FC	Toronto FC	0-0 (5-4)*	Toronto, ON, Canada	Stefan Frei
2017	Toronto FC	Seattle Sounders FC	2-0	Toronto, ON, Canada	Jozy Altidore
2018	Atlanta United FC	Portland Timbers	2-0	Atlanta, GA	Josef Martínez
2019	Seattle Sounders	Toronto FC	3-1	Seattle, WA	Víctor Rodríguez
2020	Columbus Crew	Seattle Sounders	3-0	Columbus, OH	Lucas Zelarayan
2021	New York City FC	Portland Timbers	1-1 (4-2)*	Portland, OR	Sean Johnson
2022	Los Angeles FC	Philadelphia Union	3-3 (3-0)*	Los Angeles, CA	John McCarthy
2023	Columbus Crew	Los Angeles FC	2-1	Columbus, OH	Cucho Hernández

* = Match decided on penalty kicks (shootout score in parentheses). OT = Overtime.

Major League Soccer Final Standings, 2023

(Does not include playoff games)

Eastern Conference	Points	W	L	T	GF	GA	GD
FC Cincinnati	69	20	5	9	57	39	18
Orlando City SC	63	18	7	9	55	39	16
Columbus Crew	57	16	9	9	67	46	21
Philadelphia Union	55	15	9	10	57	41	16
New England Revolution	55	15	9	10	58	46	12
Atlanta United FC	51	13	9	12	66	53	13
Nashville SC	49	13	11	10	39	32	7
New York Red Bulls	43	11	13	10	36	39	–3
Charlotte FC	43	10	11	13	45	52	–7
CF Montréal	41	12	17	5	36	52	–16
New York City FC	41	9	11	14	35	39	–4
D.C. United	40	10	14	10	45	49	–4
Chicago Fire FC	40	10	14	10	39	51	–12
Inter Miami CF	34	9	18	7	41	54	–13
Toronto FC	22	4	20	10	26	59	–33

Western Conference	Points	W	L	T	GF	GA	GD
St. Louis City SC	56	17	12	5	62	45	17
Seattle Sounders FC	53	14	9	11	41	32	9
Los Angeles FC	52	14	10	10	54	39	15
Houston Dynamo FC	51	14	11	9	51	38	13
Real Salt Lake	50	14	12	8	48	50	–2
Vancouver Whitecaps FC	48	12	10	12	55	48	7
FC Dallas	46	11	10	13	41	37	4
Sporting Kansas City	44	12	14	8	48	51	–3
San Jose Earthquakes	44	10	10	14	39	43	–4
Portland Timbers	43	11	13	10	46	58	–12
Minnesota United FC	41	10	13	11	46	51	–5
Austin FC	39	10	15	9	49	55	–6
L.A. Galaxy	36	8	14	12	51	67	–16
Colorado Rapids	27	5	17	12	26	54	–28

Major League Soccer Scoring Leaders, 2023

Player	Club	GP	G
Dénis Bouanga	LAFC	31	20
Luciano Acosta	Cincinnati	32	17
Giorgos Giakoumakis	Atlanta	27	17
Cucho Hernández	Columbus	27	16
Hany Mukhtar	Nashville	34	15
Brian White	Vancouver	32	15
Dániel Gazdag	Philadelphia	32	14
Christian Benteke	DC United	31	14
Julián Carranza	Philadelphia	31	14
Facundo Torres	Orlando	30	14
Alan Pulido	Kansas City	28	14

Landon Donovan MLS Most Valuable Player Award, 1996-2023

(Honda MLS Most Valuable Player Award, 1996-2007; Volkswagen MLS Most Valuable Player Award, 2007-14)

Year	Player, team
1996	Carlos Valderrama, Tampa Bay
1997	Preki, Kansas City
1998	Marco Etcheverry, DC
1999	Jason Kreis, Dallas
2000	Tony Meola, Kansas City
2001	Alex Pineda Chacón, Miami
2002	Carlos Ruiz, L.A. Galaxy
2003	Preki, Kansas City
2004	Amado Guevara, NY/NJ
2005	Taylor Twellman, New England
2006	Christian Gómez, DC
2007	Luciano Emilio, DC
2008	Guillermo Barros Schelotto, Columbus
2009	Landon Donovan, L.A. Galaxy
2010	David Ferreira, Dallas
2011	Dwayne De Rosario, DC
2012	Chris Wondolowski, San Jose
2013	Mike Magee, Chicago
2014	Robbie Keane, L.A. Galaxy
2015	Sebastian Giovinco, Toronto
2016	David Villa, New York City
2017	Diego Valeri, Portland
2018	Josef Martínez, Atlanta
2019	Carlos Vela, LAFC
2020	Alejandro Pozuelo, Toronto
2021	Carles Gil, New England
2022	Hany Mukhtar, Nashville
2023	Luciano Acosta, Cincinnati

Men's World Cup Results, 1930-2022

Year	Winner	Final opponent	Score	Site
1930	Uruguay	Argentina	4-2	Uruguay
1934	Italy	Czechoslovakia	2-1#	Italy
1938	Italy	Hungary	4-2	France
1950	Uruguay	Brazil	2-1	Brazil
1954	W. Germany	Hungary	3-2	Switzerland
1958	Brazil	Sweden	5-2	Sweden
1962	Brazil	Czechoslovakia	3-1	Chile
1966	England	W. Germany	4-2#	England
1970	Brazil	Italy	4-1	Mexico
1974	W. Germany	Netherlands	2-1	W. Germany
1978	Argentina	Netherlands	3-1#	Argentina
1982	Italy	W. Germany	3-1	Spain
1986	Argentina	W. Germany	3-2	Mexico
1990	W. Germany	Argentina	1-0	Italy
1994	Brazil	Italy	0-0 (3-2)*	U.S.
1998	France	Brazil	3-0	France
2002	Brazil	Germany	2-0	Japan/S. Korea
2006	Italy	France	1-1 (5-3)*	Germany
2010	Spain	Netherlands	1-0#	South Africa
2014	Germany	Argentina	1-0#	Brazil
2018	France	Croatia	4-2	Russia
2022	Argentina	France	3-3 (4-2)*	Qatar

* = Match decided on penalty kicks (shootout score in parentheses). # = Match decided in extra time.

UEFA Champions League Results, 1956-2024

Year	Winner	Final opponent	Score
1956	Real Madrid	Reims	4-3
1957	Real Madrid	Fiorentina	2-0
1958	Real Madrid	AC Milan	3-2#
1959	Real Madrid	Reims	2-0
1960	Real Madrid	Eintracht Frankfurt	7-3
1961	Benfica	FC Barcelona	3-2
1962	Benfica	Real Madrid	5-3
1963	AC Milan	Benfica	2-1
1964	Inter Milan	Real Madrid	3-1
1965	Inter Milan	Benfica	1-0
1966	Real Madrid	Partizan	2-1
1967	Celtic	Inter Milan	2-1
1968	Manchester United	Benfica	4-1#
1969	AC Milan	Ajax	4-1
1970	Feyenoord	Celtic	2-1#
1971	Ajax	Panathinaikos	2-0
1972	Ajax	Inter Milan	2-0
1973	Ajax	Juventus	1-0
1974	Bayern Munich	Atlético Madrid	5-1[1]
1975	Bayern Munich	Leeds United	2-0
1976	Bayern Munich	St.-Étienne	1-0
1977	Liverpool	Borussia Mönchengladbach	3-1
1978	Liverpool	Club Brugge	1-0
1979	Nottingham Forest	Malmö	1-0
1980	Nottingham Forest	Hamburg SV	1-0
1981	Liverpool	Real Madrid	1-0
1982	Aston Villa	Bayern Munich	1-0
1983	Hamburg SV	Juventus	1-0
1984	Liverpool	AS Roma	1-1 (4-2)*
1985	Juventus	Liverpool	1-0
1986	Steaua	FC Barcelona	0-0 (2-0)*
1987	Porto	Bayern Munich	2-1
1988	PSV	Benfica	0-0 (6-5)*
1989	AC Milan	Steaua	4-0
1990	AC Milan	Benfica	1-0
1991	Crvena Zvezda	Marseille	0-0 (5-3)*
1992	FC Barcelona	Sampdoria	1-0#
1993	Marseille	AC Milan	1-0
1994	AC Milan	FC Barcelona	4-0
1995	Ajax	AC Milan	1-0
1996	Juventus	Ajax	1-1 (4-2)*
1997	Borussia Dortmund	Juventus	3-1
1998	Real Madrid	Juventus	1-0
1999	Manchester United	Bayern Munich	2-1
2000	Real Madrid	Valencia	3-0
2001	Bayern Munich	Valencia	1-1 (5-4)*
2002	Real Madrid	Leverkusen	2-1
2003	AC Milan	Juventus	0-0 (3-2)*
2004	Porto	Monaco	3-0
2005	Liverpool	AC Milan	3-3 (3-2)*
2006	FC Barcelona	Arsenal	2-1
2007	AC Milan	Liverpool	2-1
2008	Manchester United	Chelsea	1-1 (6-5)*
2009	FC Barcelona	Manchester United	2-0
2010	Inter Milan	Bayern Munich	2-0
2011	FC Barcelona	Manchester United	3-1
2012	Chelsea	Bayern Munich	1-1 (4-3)*
2013	Bayern Munich	Borussia Dortmund	2-1
2014	Real Madrid	Atlético Madrid	4-1#
2015	FC Barcelona	Juventus	3-1
2016	Real Madrid	Atlético Madrid	1-1 (5-3)*
2017	Real Madrid	Juventus	4-1
2018	Real Madrid	Liverpool	3-1
2019	Liverpool	Tottenham	2-0
2020	Bayern Munich	Paris St.-Germain	1-0
2021	Chelsea	Manchester City	1-0
2022	Real Madrid	Liverpool	1-0
2023	Manchester City	Inter Milan	1-0
2024	Real Madrid	Borussia Dortmund	2-0

* = Match decided on penalty kicks (shootout score in parentheses). # = Match decided in extra time. (1) Aggregate score. First game, 1-1; second, 4-0.

UEFA European Football Championships, 1960-2024

Spain claimed its record fourth European Championship with a 2-1 victory over England at Olympiastadion in Berlin, Germany, July 14, 2024. Substitute Mikel Oyarzabal scored the deciding goal in the 86th minute. Spain's Rodri was named Best Player and 17-year-old countryman Lamine Yamal, with a tournament-high four assists, was chosen top Young Player.

Georgia played in its first Euro Championship and reached the Round of 16 before falling to the eventual champions. Spain then defeated Germany and France to reach the final. After England defeated Slovakia (extra time) and Switzerland (shootout), substitute Ollie Watkins scored the winner in injury time against the Netherlands to put the Three Lions in their second consecutive final.

Year	Winner	Final opponent	Score	Site
1960	USSR	Yugoslavia	2-1#	France
1964	Spain	USSR	2-1	Spain
1968	Italy	Yugoslavia	2-0	Italy
1972	W. Germany	USSR	3-0	Belgium
1976	Czechoslovakia	W. Germany	2-2 (5-3)*	Yugoslavia
1980	W. Germany	Belgium	2-1	Italy
1984	France	Spain	2-0	France
1988	Netherlands	USSR	2-0	W. Germany
1992	Denmark	Germany	2-0	Sweden
1996	Germany	Czech Rep.	2-1#	England
2000	France	Italy	2-1#	Belgium/Neth.
2004	Greece	Portugal	1-0	Portugal
2008	Spain	Germany	1-0	Austria/Switz.
2012	Spain	Italy	4-0	Poland/Ukr.
2016	Portugal	France	1-0#	France
2020[1]	Italy	England	1-1 (3-2)	England
2024	Spain	England	2-1	Germany

* = Match decided on penalty kicks (shootout score in parentheses). # = Match decided in extra time. (1) Euro 2020 played in 2021 due to COVID-19 pandemic.

Men's All-Time Leading Major Professional Championship Winners

Through Oct. 2024. * = Active PGA player in 2024; (a) = amateur.

Player	Masters	U.S. Open	British Open	PGA	Total
Jack Nicklaus	1963, '65-'66, '72, '75, '86	1962, '67, '72, '80	1966, '70, '78	1963, '71, '73, '75, '80	18
*Tiger Woods	1997, 2001-02, '05, '19	2000, '02, '08	2000, '05-'06	1999-2000, '06-'07	15
Walter Hagen	—	1914, '19	1922, '24, '28-'29	1921, '24-'27	11
Ben Hogan	1951, '53	1948, '50-'51, '53	1953	1946, '48	9
Gary Player	1961, '74, '78	1965	1959, '68, '74	1962, '72	9
Tom Watson	1977, '81	1982	1975, '77, '80, '82-'83	—	8
Bobby Jones (a)	—	1923, '26, '29-'30	1926-27, '30	—	7
Arnold Palmer	1958, '60, '62, '64	1960	1961-62	—	7
Gene Sarazen	1935	1922, '32	1932	1922-23, '33	7
Sam Snead	1949, '52, '54	—	1946	1942, '49, '51	7
Harry Vardon	—	1900	1896, '98-'99, 1903, '11, '14	—	7
Nick Faldo	1989-90, '96	—	1987, '90, '92	—	6
Lee Trevino	—	1968, '71	1971-72	1974, '84	6
*Phil Mickelson	2004, '06, '10	—	2013	2005, '21	6

Men's All-Time Leading PGA Tournament Winners

Ranked by career wins in PGA Tour co-sponsored and/or approved tournaments through 2023-24 season. * = Active PGA player in 2023-24 season.

Player	Wins	Majors
Sam Snead	82	7
*Tiger Woods	82	15
Jack Nicklaus	73	18
Ben Hogan	64	9
Arnold Palmer	62	7
Byron Nelson	52	5
Billy Casper	51	3
Walter Hagen	45	11
*Phil Mickelson	45	6
Tom Watson	39	8
Cary Middlecoff	39	3
Gene Sarazen	38	7
Lloyd Mangrum	36	1
*Vijay Singh	34	3
Jimmy Demaret	31	3
Horton Smith	30	2
Lee Trevino	29	6
Gene Littler	29	1
Harry Cooper	29	0
Leo Diegel	28	2
Paul Runyan	28	2
*Rory McIlroy	26	4
Henry Picard	26	2
Tommy Armour	25	3
Johnny Miller	25	2
Macdonald Smith	25	0
Gary Player	24	9
*Dustin Johnson	24	2
Jim Barnes	22	4
Raymond Floyd	22	4
Johnny Farrell	22	1
Craig Wood	21	2
*Davis Love III	21	1
Willie Macfarlane	21	1
Lanny Wadkins	21	1
Hale Irwin	20	3
Greg Norman	20	2
Johnny Revolta	20	1
Doug Sanders	20	0

Professional Golfers' Association Leading Money Winners, 1946-2024

Year	Player	Earnings
1946	Ben Hogan	$42,556
1947	Jimmy Demaret	27,936
1948	Ben Hogan	32,112
1949	Sam Snead	31,593
1950	Sam Snead	35,758
1951	Lloyd Mangrum	26,088
1952	Julius Boros	37,032
1953	Lew Worsham	34,002
1954	Bob Toski	65,819
1955	Julius Boros	63,121
1956	Ted Kroll	72,835
1957	Dick Mayer	65,835
1958	Arnold Palmer	42,607
1959	Art Wall Jr.	53,167
1960	Arnold Palmer	75,262
1961	Gary Player	64,540
1962	Arnold Palmer	81,448
1963	Arnold Palmer	128,230
1964	Jack Nicklaus	113,284
1965	Jack Nicklaus	140,752
1966	Billy Casper	121,944
1967	Jack Nicklaus	188,998
1968	Billy Casper	205,168
1969	Frank Beard	164,707
1970	Lee Trevino	157,037
1971	Jack Nicklaus	244,490
1972	Jack Nicklaus	$320,542
1973	Jack Nicklaus	308,362
1974	Johnny Miller	353,021
1975	Jack Nicklaus	298,149
1976	Jack Nicklaus	266,438
1977	Tom Watson	310,653
1978	Tom Watson	362,429
1979	Tom Watson	462,636
1980	Tom Watson	530,808
1981	Tom Kite	375,699
1982	Craig Stadler	446,462
1983	Hal Sutton	426,668
1984	Tom Watson	476,260
1985	Curtis Strange	542,321
1986	Greg Norman	653,296
1987	Curtis Strange	925,941
1988	Curtis Strange	1,147,644
1989	Tom Kite	1,395,278
1990	Greg Norman	1,165,477
1991	Corey Pavin	979,430
1992	Fred Couples	1,344,188
1993	Nick Price	1,478,557
1994	Nick Price	1,499,927
1995	Greg Norman	1,654,959
1996	Tom Lehman	1,780,159
1997	Tiger Woods	2,066,833
1998	David Duval	$2,591,031
1999	Tiger Woods	6,616,585
2000	Tiger Woods	9,188,321
2001	Tiger Woods	5,687,777
2002	Tiger Woods	6,912,625
2003	Vijay Singh	7,573,907
2004	Vijay Singh	10,905,166
2005	Tiger Woods	10,628,024
2006	Tiger Woods	9,941,563
2007	Tiger Woods	10,867,052
2008	Vijay Singh	6,601,094
2009	Tiger Woods	10,508,163
2010	Matt Kuchar	4,910,477
2011	Luke Donald	6,683,214
2012	Rory McIlroy	8,047,952
2013	Tiger Woods	8,553,439
2014	Rory McIlroy	8,280,096
2015	Jordan Spieth	12,030,465
2016	Dustin Johnson	9,365,185
2017	Justin Thomas	9,921,560
2018	Justin Thomas	8,694,821
2019	Brooks Koepka	9,684,006
2020	Justin Thomas	7,344,040
2021	Jon Rahm	7,705,933
2022	Scottie Scheffler	14,046,910
2023	Scottie Scheffler	21,014,342
2024	Scottie Scheffler	29,228,357

Note: The PGA Tour introduced a new split season format in Oct. 2013, which concluded with the FedEx Cup in Sept. 2014. From 2014 on, year shown is the one in which season ended.

FedEx Cup Winners, 2007-24

The FedEx Cup, a season-long competition with points awarded by finishing rank in each tournament, divides the PGA Tour into a regular season consisting of 43 events, combined with a 3-event playoff that ends with the Tour Championship. The coronavirus pandemic reduced the 2019-20 season to a total of 36 tournaments. The winner's share increased to $25 million in 2024.

Year	Winner
2007	Tiger Woods
2008	Vijay Singh
2009	Tiger Woods
2010	Jim Furyk
2011	Bill Haas
2012	Brandt Snedeker
2013	Henrik Stenson
2014	Billy Horschel
2015	Jordan Spieth
2016	Rory McIlroy
2017	Justin Thomas
2018	Justin Rose
2019	Rory McIlroy
2020	Dustin Johnson
2021	Patrick Cantlay
2022	Rory McIlroy
2023	Viktor Hovland
2024	Scottie Scheffler

Masters Golf Tournament Winners, 1940-2024

First contested in 1934 as Augusta National Invitation Tournament (name changed in 1939); not played, 1943-45.

Year	Winner	Year	Winner	Year	Winner	Year	Winner	Year	Winner
1940	Jimmy Demaret	1960	Arnold Palmer	1977	Tom Watson	1993	Bernhard Langer	2009	Angel Cabrera
1941	Craig Wood	1961	Gary Player	1978	Gary Player	1994	José María Olazábal	2010	Phil Mickelson
1942	Byron Nelson	1962	Arnold Palmer	1979	Fuzzy Zoeller	1995	Ben Crenshaw	2011	Charl Schwartzel
1946	Herman Keiser	1963	Jack Nicklaus	1980	Seve Ballesteros	1996	Nick Faldo	2012	Bubba Watson
1947	Jimmy Demaret	1964	Arnold Palmer	1981	Tom Watson	1997	Tiger Woods	2013	Adam Scott
1948	Claude Harmon	1965	Jack Nicklaus	1982	Craig Stadler	1998	Mark O'Meara	2014	Bubba Watson
1949	Sam Snead	1966	Jack Nicklaus	1983	Seve Ballesteros	1999	José María Olazábal	2015	Jordan Spieth
1950	Jimmy Demaret	1967	Gay Brewer Jr.	1984	Ben Crenshaw	2000	Vijay Singh	2016	Danny Willett
1951	Ben Hogan	1968	Bob Goalby	1985	Bernhard Langer	2001	Tiger Woods	2017	Sergio García
1952	Sam Snead	1969	George Archer	1986	Jack Nicklaus	2002	Tiger Woods	2018	Patrick Reed
1953	Ben Hogan	1970	Billy Casper	1987	Larry Mize	2003	Mike Weir	2019	Tiger Woods
1954	Sam Snead	1971	Charles Coody	1988	Sandy Lyle	2004	Phil Mickelson	2020	Dustin Johnson
1955	Cary Middlecoff	1972	Jack Nicklaus	1989	Nick Faldo	2005	Tiger Woods	2021	Hideki Matsuyama
1956	Jack Burke	1973	Tommy Aaron	1990	Nick Faldo	2006	Phil Mickelson	2022	Scottie Scheffler
1957	Doug Ford	1974	Gary Player	1991	Ian Woosnam	2007	Zach Johnson	2023	Jon Rahm
1958	Arnold Palmer	1975	Jack Nicklaus	1992	Fred Couples	2008	Trevor Immelman	2024	Scottie Scheffler
1959	Art Wall Jr.	1976	Ray Floyd						

U.S. Open Winners, 1940-2024

First contested in 1895; not played, 1942-45.

Year	Winner	Year	Winner	Year	Winner	Year	Winner	Year	Winner
1940	Lawson Little	1961	Gene Littler	1977	Hubert Green	1993	Lee Janzen	2009	Lucas Glover
1941	Craig Wood	1962	Jack Nicklaus	1978	Andy North	1994	Ernie Els	2010	Graeme McDowell
1946	Lloyd Mangrum	1963	Julius Boros	1979	Hale Irwin	1995	Corey Pavin	2011	Rory McIlroy
1947	Lew Worsham	1964	Ken Venturi	1980	Jack Nicklaus	1996	Steve Jones	2012	Webb Simpson
1948	Ben Hogan	1965	Gary Player	1981	David Graham	1997	Ernie Els	2013	Justin Rose
1949	Cary Middlecoff	1966	Billy Casper	1982	Tom Watson	1998	Lee Janzen	2014	Martin Kaymer
1950	Ben Hogan	1967	Jack Nicklaus	1983	Larry Nelson	1999	Payne Stewart	2015	Jordan Spieth
1951	Ben Hogan	1968	Lee Trevino	1984	Fuzzy Zoeller	2000	Tiger Woods	2016	Dustin Johnson
1952	Julius Boros	1969	Orville Moody	1985	Andy North	2001	Retief Goosen	2017	Brooks Koepka
1953	Ben Hogan	1970	Tony Jacklin	1986	Ray Floyd	2002	Tiger Woods	2018	Brooks Koepka
1954	Ed Furgol	1971	Lee Trevino	1987	Scott Simpson	2003	Jim Furyk	2019	Gary Woodland
1955	Jack Fleck	1972	Jack Nicklaus	1988	Curtis Strange	2004	Retief Goosen	2020	Bryson DeChambeau
1956	Cary Middlecoff	1973	Johnny Miller	1989	Curtis Strange	2005	Michael Campbell	2021	Jon Rahm
1957	Dick Mayer	1974	Hale Irwin	1990	Hale Irwin	2006	Geoff Ogilvy	2022	Matt Fitzpatrick
1958	Tommy Bolt	1975	Lou Graham	1991	Payne Stewart	2007	Angel Cabrera	2023	Wyndham Clark
1959	Billy Casper	1976	Jerry Pate	1992	Tom Kite	2008	Tiger Woods	2024	Bryson DeChambeau
1960	Arnold Palmer								

British Open Winners, 1946-2024

Officially called the Open Championship. First contested in 1860; not played, 1940-45, 2020.

Year	Winner	Year	Winner	Year	Winner	Year	Winner	Year	Winner
1946	Sam Snead	1962	Arnold Palmer	1978	Jack Nicklaus	1994	Nick Price	2009	Stewart Cink
1947	Fred Daly	1963	Bob Charles	1979	Seve Ballesteros	1995	John Daly	2010	Louis Oosthuizen
1948	Henry Cotton	1964	Tony Lema	1980	Tom Watson	1996	Tom Lehman	2011	Darren Clarke
1949	Bobby Locke	1965	Peter Thomson	1981	Bill Rogers	1997	Justin Leonard	2012	Ernie Els
1950	Bobby Locke	1966	Jack Nicklaus	1982	Tom Watson	1998	Mark O'Meara	2013	Phil Mickelson
1951	Max Faulkner	1967	Roberto de Vicenzo	1983	Tom Watson	1999	Paul Lawrie	2014	Rory McIlroy
1952	Bobby Locke	1968	Gary Player	1984	Seve Ballesteros	2000	Tiger Woods	2015	Zach Johnson
1953	Ben Hogan	1969	Tony Jacklin	1985	Sandy Lyle	2001	David Duval	2016	Henrik Stenson
1954	Peter Thomson	1970	Jack Nicklaus	1986	Greg Norman	2002	Ernie Els	2017	Jordan Spieth
1955	Peter Thomson	1971	Lee Trevino	1987	Nick Faldo	2003	Ben Curtis	2018	Francesco Molinari
1956	Peter Thomson	1972	Lee Trevino	1988	Seve Ballesteros	2004	Todd Hamilton	2019	Shane Lowry
1957	Bobby Locke	1973	Tom Weiskopf	1989	Mark Calcavecchia	2005	Tiger Woods	2021	Collin Morikawa
1958	Peter Thomson	1974	Gary Player	1990	Nick Faldo	2006	Tiger Woods	2022	Cameron Smith
1959	Gary Player	1975	Tom Watson	1991	Ian Baker-Finch	2007	Padraig Harrington	2023	Brian Harman
1960	Kel Nagle	1976	Johnny Miller	1992	Nick Faldo	2008	Padraig Harrington	2024	Xander Schauffele
1961	Arnold Palmer	1977	Tom Watson	1993	Greg Norman				

PGA Championship Winners, 1940-2024

First contested in 1916; not played, 1943.

Year	Winner	Year	Winner	Year	Winner	Year	Winner	Year	Winner
1940	Byron Nelson	1958	Dow Finsterwald	1975	Jack Nicklaus	1992	Nick Price	2009	Y.E. Yang
1941	Victor Ghezzi	1959	Bob Rosburg	1976	Dave Stockton	1993	Paul Azinger	2010	Martin Kaymer
1942	Sam Snead	1960	Jay Hebert	1977	Lanny Wadkins	1994	Nick Price	2011	Keegan Bradley
1944	Bob Hamilton	1961	Jerry Barber	1978	John Mahaffey	1995	Steve Elkington	2012	Rory McIlroy
1945	Byron Nelson	1962	Gary Player	1979	David Graham	1996	Mark Brooks	2013	Jason Dufner
1946	Ben Hogan	1963	Jack Nicklaus	1980	Jack Nicklaus	1997	Davis Love III	2014	Rory McIlroy
1947	Jim Ferrier	1964	Bob Nichols	1981	Larry Nelson	1998	Vijay Singh	2015	Jason Day
1948	Ben Hogan	1965	Dave Marr	1982	Ray Floyd	1999	Tiger Woods	2016	Jimmy Walker
1949	Sam Snead	1966	Al Geiberger	1983	Hal Sutton	2000	Tiger Woods	2017	Justin Thomas
1950	Chandler Harper	1967	Don January	1984	Lee Trevino	2001	David Toms	2018	Brooks Koepka
1951	Sam Snead	1968	Julius Boros	1985	Hubert Green	2002	Rich Beem	2019	Brooks Koepka
1952	James Turnesa	1969	Ray Floyd	1986	Bob Tway	2003	Shaun Micheel	2020	Collin Morikawa
1953	Walter Burkemo	1970	Dave Stockton	1987	Larry Nelson	2004	Vijay Singh	2021	Phil Mickelson
1954	Melvin Harbert	1971	Jack Nicklaus	1988	Jeff Sluman	2005	Phil Mickelson	2022	Justin Thomas
1955	Doug Ford	1972	Gary Player	1989	Payne Stewart	2006	Tiger Woods	2023	Brooks Koepka
1956	Jack Burke	1973	Jack Nicklaus	1990	Wayne Grady	2007	Tiger Woods	2024	Xander Schauffele
1957	Lionel Hebert	1974	Lee Trevino	1991	John Daly	2008	Padraig Harrington		

Ryder Cup, 1927-2023

The Ryder Cup began in 1927 as a biennial team competition between U.S. and British pro male golfers. The British team expanded in 1973 to include players from Ireland and in 1979 to golfers from the rest of Europe.

Year	Winner, score	Year	Winner, score	Year	Winner, score	Year	Winner, score
1927	U.S., 9½-2½	1957	Great Britain, 7½-4½	1979	U.S., 17-11	2002	Europe, 15½-12½
1929	Great Britain, 7-5	1959	U.S., 8½-3½	1981	U.S., 18½-9½	2004	Europe, 18½-9½
1931	U.S., 9-3	1961	U.S., 14½-9½	1983	U.S., 14½-13½	2006	Europe, 18½-9½
1933	Great Britain, 6½-5½	1963	U.S., 23-9	1985	Europe, 16½-11½	2008	U.S., 16½-11½
1935	U.S., 9-3	1965	U.S., 19½-12½	1987	Europe, 15-13	2010	Europe, 14½-13½
1937	U.S., 8-4	1967	U.S., 23½-8½	1989	Draw, 14-14	2012	Europe, 14½-13½
1947	U.S., 11-1	1969	Draw, 16-16	1991	U.S., 14½-13½	2014	Europe, 16½-11½
1949	U.S., 7-5	1971	U.S., 18½-13½	1993	U.S., 15-13	2016	U.S., 17-11
1951	U.S., 9½-2½	1973	U.S., 19-13	1995	Europe, 14½-13½	2018	Europe, 17½-10½
1953	U.S., 6½-5½	1975	U.S., 21-11	1997	Europe, 14½-13½	2021	U.S., 19-9
1955	U.S., 8-4	1977	U.S., 12½-7½	1999	U.S., 14½-13½	2023	Europe, 16½-11½

Women's All-Time Leading Major Professional Championship Winners

Through Oct. 2024. * = Active in 2024 LPGA season.

Player	Chevron Champ.[1]	KPMG Women's PGA[2]	U.S. Women's Open	Women's British Open[3]	Titleholders[4]	Western Open[5]	Total
Patty Berg	—	—	1946	—	1937-39, '48, '53, '55, '57	1941, '43, '48, '51, '55, '57-'58	15
Mickey Wright	—	1958, '60-'61, '63	1958-59, '61, '64	—	1961-62	1962-63, '66	13
Louise Suggs	—	1957	1949, '52	—	1946, '54, '56, '59	1946-47, '49, '53	11
Annika Sorenstam	2001-02, '05	2003-05	1995-96, 2006	2003	—	—	10
Babe Zaharias	—	—	1948, '50, '54	—	1947, '50, '52	1940, '44-'45, '50	10
Betsy Rawls	—	1959, '69	1951, '53, '57, '60	—	—	1952, '59	8
*Juli Inkster	1984, '89	1999-2000	1999, 2002	1984	—	—	7
Inbee Park	2013	2013-15	2008, '13	2015	—	—	7
*Karrie Webb	2000, '06	2001	2000-01	1999, 2002	—	—	7

(1) Formerly the Nabisco Dinah Shore (1982-99), the Nabisco Championship (2000-01), the Kraft Nabisco Championship (2002-14), and the ANA Inspiration (2015-21); designated major in 1983. (2) Formerly the LPGA Championship (1955-2014). (3) In 2001, the British Open replaced the du Maurier Classic as the LPGA's fourth major; wins in column prior to 2001 are for the Peter Jackson (1979-82) or du Maurier (1983-2000) Classic. (4) Titleholders Championship was a major, 1937-72. (5) Western Open was a major, 1930-67.

Ladies Professional Golf Association Leading Money Winners, 1954-2023

Year	Player	Earnings	Year	Player	Earnings	Year	Player	Earnings
1954	Patty Berg	$16,011	1978	Nancy Lopez	$189,814	2001	Annika Sorenstam	$2,105,868
1955	Patty Berg	16,492	1979	Nancy Lopez	197,489	2002	Annika Sorenstam	2,863,904
1956	Marlene Hagge	20,235	1980	Beth Daniel	231,000	2003	Annika Sorenstam	2,029,506
1957	Patty Berg	16,272	1981	Beth Daniel	206,998	2004	Annika Sorenstam	2,544,707
1958	Beverly Hanson	12,639	1982	JoAnne Carner	310,400	2005	Annika Sorenstam	2,588,240
1959	Betsy Rawls	26,774	1983	JoAnne Carner	291,404	2006	Lorena Ochoa	2,592,872
1960	Louise Suggs	16,892	1984	Betsy King	266,771	2007	Lorena Ochoa	4,364,994
1961	Mickey Wright	22,236	1985	Nancy Lopez	416,472	2008	Lorena Ochoa	2,763,193
1962	Mickey Wright	21,641	1986	Pat Bradley	492,021	2009	Jiyai Shin	1,807,334
1963	Mickey Wright	31,269	1987	Ayako Okamoto	466,034	2010	Na Yeon Choi	1,871,166
1964	Mickey Wright	29,800	1988	Sherri Turner	350,851	2011	Yani Tseng	2,921,713
1965	Kathy Whitworth	28,658	1989	Betsy King	654,132	2012	Inbee Park	2,287,080
1966	Kathy Whitworth	33,517	1990	Beth Daniel	863,578	2013	Inbee Park	2,456,619
1967	Kathy Whitworth	32,937	1991	Pat Bradley	763,118	2014	Stacy Lewis	2,539,039
1968	Kathy Whitworth	48,379	1992	Dottie Mochrie	693,335	2015	Lydia Ko	2,800,802
1969	Carol Mann	49,152	1993	Betsy King	595,992	2016	Ariya Jutanugarn	2,550,947
1970	Kathy Whitworth	30,235	1994	Laura Davies	687,201	2017	Sung Hyun Park	2,335,883
1971	Kathy Whitworth	41,181	1995	Annika Sorenstam	666,533	2018	Ariya Jutanugarn	2,743,949
1972	Kathy Whitworth	65,063	1996	Karrie Webb	1,002,000	2019	Jin Young Ko	2,773,894
1973	Kathy Whitworth	82,864	1997	Annika Sorenstam	1,236,789	2020	Jin Young Ko	1,667,925
1974	JoAnne Carner	87,094	1998	Annika Sorenstam	1,092,748	2021	Jin Young Ko	3,502,161
1975	Sandra Palmer	76,374	1999	Karrie Webb	1,591,959	2022	Lydia Ko	4,364,403
1976	Judy Rankin	150,734	2000	Karrie Webb	1,876,853	2023	Lilia Vu	3,502,303
1977	Judy Rankin	122,890						

Women's All-Time Leading LPGA Tournament Winners

Ranked by career tournament wins through Sept. 2024. * = Active LPGA player in 2024.

Player	Wins	Majors	Player	Wins	Majors	Player	Wins	Majors
Kathy Whitworth	88	6	JoAnne Carner	43	2	Betsy King	34	6
Mickey Wright	82	13	Sandra Haynie	42	4	Beth Daniel	33	1
Annika Sorenstam	72	10	Babe Didrikson Zaharias	41	10	*Juli Inkster	31	7
Louise Suggs	61	11	*Karrie Webb	41	7	Pat Bradley	31	6
Patty Berg	60	15	Carol Mann	38	2	Amy Alcott	29	5
Betsy Rawls	55	8	Patty Sheehan	35	6	Lorena Ochoa	27	2
Nancy Lopez	48	3				Jane Blalock	27	0

Chevron Championship Winners, 1983-2024

Began in 1972 and designated a major championship in 1983; formerly the Colgate Dinah Shore (1972-81), the Nabisco Dinah Shore (1982-99), the Nabisco Championship (2000-01), the Kraft Nabisco Championship (2002-14), and the ANA Inspiration (2015-21).

Year	Winner	Year	Winner	Year	Winner	Year	Winner	Year	Winner
1983	Amy Alcott	1992	Dottie Pepper	2001	Annika Sorenstam	2009	Brittany Lincicome	2017	So Yeon Ryu
1984	Juli Inkster	1993	Helen Alfredsson	2002	Annika Sorenstam	2010	Yani Tseng	2018	Pernilla Lindberg
1985	Alice Miller	1994	Donna Andrews	2003	P. Meunier-Lebouc	2011	Stacy Lewis	2019	Jin Young Ko
1986	Pat Bradley	1995	Nanci Bowen	2004	Grace Park	2012	Sun Young Yoo	2020	Mirim Lee
1987	Betsy King	1996	Patty Sheehan	2005	Annika Sorenstam	2013	Inbee Park	2021	Patty Tavatanakit
1988	Amy Alcott	1997	Betsy King	2006	Karrie Webb	2014	Lexi Thompson	2022	Jennifer Kupcho
1989	Juli Inkster	1998	Pat Hurst	2007	Morgan Pressel	2015	Brittany Lincicome	2023	Lilia Vu
1990	Betsy King	1999	Dottie Pepper	2008	Lorena Ochoa	2016	Lydia Ko	2024	Nelly Korda
1991	Amy Alcott	2000	Karrie Webb						

KPMG Women's PGA Championship Winners, 1955-2024

Formerly LPGA Championship (1955-2014).

Year	Winner	Year	Winner	Year	Winner	Year	Winner	Year	Winner
1955	Beverly Hanson	1969	Betsy Rawls	1983	Patty Sheehan	1997	Christa Johnson	2011	Yani Tseng
1956	Marlene Hagge	1970	Shirley Englehorn	1984	Patty Sheehan	1998	Se Ri Pak	2012	Shanshan Feng
1957	Louise Suggs	1971	Kathy Whitworth	1985	Nancy Lopez	1999	Juli Inkster	2013	Inbee Park
1958	Mickey Wright	1972	Kathy Ahern	1986	Pat Bradley	2000	Juli Inkster	2014	Inbee Park
1959	Betsy Rawls	1973	Mary Mills	1987	Jane Geddes	2001	Karrie Webb	2015	Inbee Park
1960	Mickey Wright	1974	Sandra Haynie	1988	Sherri Turner	2002	Se Ri Pak	2016	Brooke Henderson
1961	Mickey Wright	1975	Kathy Whitworth	1989	Nancy Lopez	2003	Annika Sorenstam	2017	Danielle Kang
1962	Judy Kimball	1976	Betty Burfeindt	1990	Beth Daniel	2004	Annika Sorenstam	2018	Sung Hyun Park
1963	Mickey Wright	1977	Chako Higuchi	1991	Meg Mallon	2005	Annika Sorenstam	2019	Hannah Green
1964	Mary Mills	1978	Nancy Lopez	1992	Betsy King	2006	Se Ri Pak	2020	Sei Young Kim
1965	Sandra Haynie	1979	Donna Caponi	1993	Patty Sheehan	2007	Suzann Pettersen	2021	Nelly Korda
1966	Gloria Ehret	1980	Sally Little	1994	Laura Davies	2008	Yani Tseng	2022	In Gee Chun
1967	Kathy Whitworth	1981	Donna Caponi	1995	Kelly Robbins	2009	Anna Nordqvist	2023	Yin Ruoning
1968	Sandra Post	1982	Jan Stephenson	1996	Laura Davies	2010	Cristie Kerr	2024	Amy Yang

U.S. Women's Open Winners, 1946-2024

Year	Winner	Year	Winner	Year	Winner	Year	Winner	Year	Winner
1946	Patty Berg	1962	Murle Lindstrom	1978	Hollis Stacy	1994	Patty Sheehan	2010	Paula Creamer
1947	Betty Jameson	1963	Mary Mills	1979	Jerilyn Britz	1995	Annika Sorenstam	2011	So Yeon Ryu
1948	Babe Zaharias	1964	Mickey Wright	1980	Amy Alcott	1996	Annika Sorenstam	2012	Na Yeon Choi
1949	Louise Suggs	1965	Carol Mann	1981	Pat Bradley	1997	Alison Nicholas	2013	Inbee Park
1950	Babe Zaharias	1966	Sandra Spuzich	1982	Janet Alex	1998	Se Ri Pak	2014	Michelle Wie
1951	Betsy Rawls	1967	Catherine Lacoste	1983	Jan Stephenson	1999	Juli Inkster	2015	In Gee Chun
1952	Louise Suggs	1968	Susie Berning	1984	Hollis Stacy	2000	Karrie Webb	2016	Brittany Lang
1953	Betsy Rawls	1969	Donna Caponi	1985	Kathy Baker	2001	Karrie Webb	2017	Sung Hyun Park
1954	Babe Zaharias	1970	Donna Caponi	1986	Jane Geddes	2002	Juli Inkster	2018	Ariya Jutanugarn
1955	Fay Crocker	1971	JoAnne Carner	1987	Laura Davies	2003	Hilary Lunke	2019	Jeongeun Lee6
1956	Kathy Cornelius	1972	Susie Berning	1988	Liselotte Neumann	2004	Meg Mallon	2020	Kim A-lim
1957	Betsy Rawls	1973	Susie Berning	1989	Betsy King	2005	Birdie Kim	2021	Yuka Saso
1958	Mickey Wright	1974	Sandra Haynie	1990	Betsy King	2006	Annika Sorenstam	2022	Minjee Lee
1959	Mickey Wright	1975	Sandra Palmer	1991	Meg Mallon	2007	Cristie Kerr	2023	Allisen Corpuz
1960	Betsy Rawls	1976	JoAnne Carner	1992	Patty Sheehan	2008	Inbee Park	2024	Yuka Saso
1961	Mickey Wright	1977	Hollis Stacy	1993	Lauri Merten	2009	Eun-Hee Ji		

AIG Women's British Open Winners, 1979-2024

First contested as the Ladies' British Open in 1976; became the LPGA's fourth major championship in 2001, replacing the du Maurier Classic. Winners listed are for the Peter Jackson (1979-82) and du Maurier (1983-2000) Classic.

Year	Winner	Year	Winner	Year	Winner	Year	Winner	Year	Winner
1979	Amy Alcott	1989	Tammie Green	1998	Brandie Burton	2007	Lorena Ochoa	2016	Ariya Jutanugarn
1980	Pat Bradley	1990	Cathy Johnston	1999	Karrie Webb	2008	Jiyai Shin	2017	In-Kyung Kim
1981	Jan Stephenson	1991	Nancy Scranton	2000	Meg Mallon	2009	Catriona Matthew	2018	Georgia Hall
1982	Sandra Haynie	1992	Sherri Steinhauer	2001	Se Ri Pak	2010	Yani Tseng	2019	Hinako Shibuno
1983	Hollis Stacy	1993	Brandie Burton	2002	Karrie Webb	2011	Yani Tseng	2020	Sophia Popov
1984	Juli Inkster	1994	Martha Nause	2003	Annika Sorenstam	2012	Jiyai Shin	2021	Anna Nordqvist
1985	Pat Bradley	1995	Jenny Lidback	2004	Karen Stupples	2013	Stacy Lewis	2022	Ashleigh Buhai
1986	Pat Bradley	1996	Laura Davies	2005	Jeong Jang	2014	Mo Martin	2023	Lilia Vu
1987	Jody Rosenthal	1997	Colleen Walker	2006	Sherri Steinhauer	2015	Inbee Park	2024	Lydia Ko
1988	Sally Little								

Amundi Evian Championship, 2013-24

Began in 1994 as the Evian Masters; became the LPGA's fifth major tournament in 2013.

Year	Winner	Year	Winner	Year	Winner	Year	Winner
2013	Suzann Pettersen	2016	In Gee Chun	2019	Jin Young Ko	2023	Céline Boutier
2014	Hyo Joo Kim	2017	Anna Nordqvist	2021	Minjee Lee	2024	Ayaka Furue
2015	Lydia Ko	2018	Angela Stanford	2022	Brooke Henderson		

Solheim Cup, 1990-2024

The Solheim Cup began in 1990 as a biennial team competition between pro women golfers from the U.S. and Europe. The 2023 competition ended in a tie, so the cup remained in the hands of the previous winner.

Year	Winner, score	Year	Winner, score	Year	Winner, score	Year	Winner, score
1990	U.S., 11½-4½	2000	Europe, 14½-11½	2009	U.S., 16-12	2019	Europe, 14½-13½
1992	Europe, 11½-6½	2002	U.S., 15½-12½	2011	Europe, 15-13	2021	Europe, 15-13
1994	U.S., 13-7	2003	Europe, 17½-10½	2013	Europe, 18-10	2023	Europe, 14-14
1996	U.S., 17-11	2005	U.S., 15½-12½	2015	U.S., 14½-13½	2024	U.S., 15½-12½
1998	U.S., 16-12	2007	U.S., 16-12	2017	U.S., 16½-11½		

TENNIS

Australian Open Champions, 1969-2024

First contested 1905 for men, 1922 for women. Became an open championship in 1969.

Men's Singles

Year	Champion	Final opponent
1969	Rod Laver	Andrés Gimeno
1970	Arthur Ashe	Dick Crealy
1971	Ken Rosewall	Arthur Ashe
1972	Ken Rosewall	Mal Anderson
1973	John Newcombe	Onny Parun
1974	Jimmy Connors	Phil Dent
1975	John Newcombe	Jimmy Connors
1976	Mark Edmondson	John Newcombe
1977	Roscoe Tanner	Guillermo Vilas
	Vitas Gerulaitis	John Lloyd
1978	Guillermo Vilas	John Marks
1979	Guillermo Vilas	John Sadri
1980	Brian Teacher	Kim Warwick
1981	Johan Kriek	Steve Denton
1982	Johan Kriek	Steve Denton
1983	Mats Wilander	Ivan Lendl
1984	Mats Wilander	Kevin Curren
1985	Stefan Edberg	Mats Wilander
1987	Stefan Edberg	Pat Cash
1988	Mats Wilander	Pat Cash
1989	Ivan Lendl	Miloslav Mecir
1990	Ivan Lendl	Stefan Edberg
1991	Boris Becker	Ivan Lendl
1992	Jim Courier	Stefan Edberg
1993	Jim Courier	Stefan Edberg
1994	Pete Sampras	Todd Martin
1995	Andre Agassi	Pete Sampras
1996	Boris Becker	Michael Chang
1997	Pete Sampras	Carlos Moya
1998	Petr Korda	Marcelo Rios
1999	Yevgeny Kafelnikov	Thomas Enqvist
2000	Andre Agassi	Yevgeny Kafelnikov
2001	Andre Agassi	Arnaud Clement
2002	Thomas Johansson	Marat Safin
2003	Andre Agassi	Rainer Schuettler
2004	Roger Federer	Marat Safin
2005	Marat Safin	Lleyton Hewitt
2006	Roger Federer	Marcos Baghdatis
2007	Roger Federer	Fernando Gonzalez
2008	Novak Djokovic	Jo-Wilfried Tsonga
2009	Rafael Nadal	Roger Federer
2010	Roger Federer	Andy Murray
2011	Novak Djokovic	Andy Murray
2012	Novak Djokovic	Rafael Nadal
2013	Novak Djokovic	Andy Murray
2014	Stanislas Wawrinka	Rafael Nadal
2015	Novak Djokovic	Andy Murray
2016	Novak Djokovic	Andy Murray
2017	Roger Federer	Rafael Nadal
2018	Roger Federer	Marin Cilic
2019	Novak Djokovic	Rafael Nadal
2020	Novak Djokovic	Dominic Thiem
2021	Novak Djokovic	Daniil Medvedev
2022	Rafael Nadal	Daniil Medvedev
2023	Novak Djokovic	Stefanos Tsitsipas
2024	Jannik Sinner	Daniil Medvedev

Women's Singles

Year	Champion	Final opponent
1969	Margaret Smith Court	Billie Jean King
1970	Margaret Smith Court	Kerry Melville Reid
1971	Margaret Smith Court	Evonne Goolagong
1972	Virginia Wade	Evonne Goolagong
1973	Margaret Smith Court	Evonne Goolagong
1974	Evonne Goolagong	Chris Evert
1975	Evonne Goolagong	Martina Navratilova
1976	Evonne Goolagong Cawley	Renata Tomanova
1977	Kerry Reid	Dianne Balestrat
	Evonne Goolagong Cawley	Helen Gourlay
1978	Chris O'Neil	Betsy Nagelsen
1979	Barbara Jordan	Sharon Walsh
1980	Hana Mandlikova	Wendy Turnbull
1981	Martina Navratilova	Chris Evert Lloyd
1982	Chris Evert Lloyd	Martina Navratilova
1983	Martina Navratilova	Kathy Jordan
1984	Chris Evert Lloyd	Helena Sukova
1985	Martina Navratilova	Chris Evert Lloyd
1987	Hana Mandlikova	Martina Navratilova
1988	Steffi Graf	Chris Evert
1989	Steffi Graf	Helena Sukova
1990	Steffi Graf	Mary Joe Fernandez
1991	Monica Seles	Jana Novotna
1992	Monica Seles	Mary Joe Fernandez
1993	Monica Seles	Steffi Graf
1994	Steffi Graf	Arantxa Sánchez Vicario
1995	Mary Pierce	Arantxa Sánchez Vicario
1996	Monica Seles	Anke Huber
1997	Martina Hingis	Mary Pierce
1998	Martina Hingis	Conchita Martínez
1999	Martina Hingis	Amélie Mauresmo
2000	Lindsay Davenport	Martina Hingis
2001	Jennifer Capriati	Martina Hingis
2002	Jennifer Capriati	Martina Hingis
2003	Serena Williams	Venus Williams
2004	Justine Henin-Hardenne	Kim Clijsters
2005	Serena Williams	Lindsay Davenport
2006	Amélie Mauresmo	Justine Henin-Hardenne
2007	Serena Williams	Maria Sharapova
2008	Maria Sharapova	Ana Ivanovic
2009	Serena Williams	Dinara Safina
2010	Serena Williams	Justine Henin
2011	Kim Clijsters	Li Na
2012	Victoria Azarenka	Maria Sharapova
2013	Victoria Azarenka	Li Na
2014	Li Na	Dominika Cibulkova
2015	Serena Williams	Maria Sharapova
2016	Angelique Kerber	Serena Williams
2017	Serena Williams	Venus Williams
2018	Caroline Wozniacki	Simona Halep
2019	Naomi Osaka	Petra Kvitova
2020	Sofia Kenin	Garbiñe Muguruza
2021	Naomi Osaka	Jennifer Brady
2022	Ashleigh Barty	Danielle Collins
2023	Aryna Sabalenka	Elena Rybakina
2024	Aryna Sabalenka	Qinwen Zheng

French Open (Roland Garros) Champions, 1968-2024

First contested 1891 for men, 1897 for women. Became an open championship in 1968.

Men's Singles

Year	Champion	Final opponent
1968	Ken Rosewall	Rod Laver
1969	Rod Laver	Ken Rosewall
1970	Jan Kodes	Zeljko Franulovic
1971	Jan Kodes	Ilie Nastase
1972	Andrés Gimeno	Patrick Proisy
1973	Ilie Nastase	Nikki Pilic
1974	Björn Borg	Manuel Orantes
1975	Björn Borg	Guillermo Vilas
1976	Adriano Panatta	Harold Solomon
1977	Guillermo Vilas	Brian Gottfried
1978	Björn Borg	Guillermo Vilas
1979	Björn Borg	Victor Pecci
1980	Björn Borg	Vitas Gerulaitis
1981	Björn Borg	Ivan Lendl
1982	Mats Wilander	Guillermo Vilas
1983	Yannick Noah	Mats Wilander
1984	Ivan Lendl	John McEnroe
1985	Mats Wilander	Ivan Lendl
1986	Ivan Lendl	Mikael Pernfors
1987	Ivan Lendl	Mats Wilander
1988	Mats Wilander	Henri Leconte
1989	Michael Chang	Stefan Edberg
1990	Andres Gomez	Andre Agassi
1991	Jim Courier	Andre Agassi
1992	Jim Courier	Petr Korda
1993	Sergi Bruguera	Jim Courier
1994	Sergi Bruguera	Alberto Berasategui
1995	Thomas Muster	Michael Chang
1996	Yevgeny Kafelnikov	Michael Stich
1997	Gustavo Kuerten	Sergi Bruguera
1998	Carlos Moya	Alex Corretja
1999	Andre Agassi	Andrei Medvedev
2000	Gustavo Kuerten	Magnus Norman
2001	Gustavo Kuerten	Alex Corretja
2002	Albert Costa	Juan Carlos Ferrero
2003	Juan Carlos Ferrero	Martin Verkerk
2004	Gaston Gaudio	Guillermo Coria
2005	Rafael Nadal	Mariano Puerta
2006	Rafael Nadal	Roger Federer
2007	Rafael Nadal	Roger Federer
2008	Rafael Nadal	Roger Federer
2009	Roger Federer	Robin Soderling
2010	Rafael Nadal	Robin Soderling
2011	Rafael Nadal	Roger Federer
2012	Rafael Nadal	Novak Djokovic
2013	Rafael Nadal	David Ferrer
2014	Rafael Nadal	Novak Djokovic
2015	Stan Wawrinka	Novak Djokovic
2016	Novak Djokovic	Andy Murray
2017	Rafael Nadal	Stan Wawrinka
2018	Rafael Nadal	Dominic Thiem
2019	Rafael Nadal	Dominic Thiem
2020	Rafael Nadal	Novak Djokovic
2021	Novak Djokovic	Stefanos Tsitsipas
2022	Rafael Nadal	Casper Ruud
2023	Novak Djokovic	Casper Ruud
2024	Carlos Alcaraz	Alexander Zverev

Women's Singles

Year	Champion	Final opponent
1968	Nancy Richey	Ann Jones
1969	Margaret Smith Court	Ann Jones
1970	Margaret Smith Court	Helga Niessen
1971	Evonne Goolagong	Helen Gourlay
1972	Billie Jean King	Evonne Goolagong

Year	Champion	Final opponent
1973	Margaret Smith Court	Chris Evert
1974	Chris Evert	Olga Morozova
1975	Chris Evert	Martina Navratilova
1976	Sue Barker	Renata Tomanova
1977	Mima Jausovec	Florenta Mihai
1978	Virginia Ruzici	Mima Jausovec
1979	Chris Evert Lloyd	Wendy Turnbull
1980	Chris Evert Lloyd	Virginia Ruzici
1981	Hana Mandlikova	Sylvia Hanika
1982	Martina Navratilova	Andrea Jaeger
1983	Chris Evert Lloyd	Mima Jausovec
1984	Martina Navratilova	Chris Evert Lloyd
1985	Chris Evert Lloyd	Martina Navratilova
1986	Chris Evert Lloyd	Martina Navratilova
1987	Steffi Graf	Martina Navratilova
1988	Steffi Graf	Natalia Zvereva
1989	Arantxa Sánchez Vicario	Steffi Graf
1990	Monica Seles	Steffi Graf
1991	Monica Seles	Arantxa Sánchez Vicario
1992	Monica Seles	Steffi Graf
1993	Steffi Graf	Mary Joe Fernandez
1994	Arantxa Sánchez Vicario	Mary Pierce
1995	Steffi Graf	Arantxa Sánchez Vicario
1996	Steffi Graf	Arantxa Sánchez Vicario
1997	Iva Majoli	Martina Hingis
1998	Arantxa Sánchez Vicario	Monica Seles
1999	Steffi Graf	Martina Hingis
2000	Mary Pierce	Conchita Martínez
2001	Jennifer Capriati	Kim Clijsters
2002	Serena Williams	Venus Williams
2003	Justine Henin-Hardenne	Kim Clijsters
2004	Anastasia Myskina	Elena Dementieva
2005	Justine Henin-Hardenne	Mary Pierce
2006	Justine Henin-Hardenne	Svetlana Kuznetsova
2007	Justine Henin	Ana Ivanovic
2008	Ana Ivanovic	Dinara Safina
2009	Svetlana Kuznetsova	Dinara Safina
2010	Francesca Schiavone	Samantha Stosur
2011	Li Na	Francesca Schiavone
2012	Maria Sharapova	Sara Errani
2013	Serena Williams	Maria Sharapova
2014	Maria Sharapova	Simona Halep
2015	Serena Williams	Lucie Safarova
2016	Garbiñe Muguruza	Serena Williams
2017	Jelena Ostapenko	Simona Halep
2018	Simona Halep	Sloane Stephens
2019	Ashleigh Barty	Marketa Vondrousova
2020	Iga Swiatek	Sofia Kenin
2021	Barbora Krejcikova	Anastasia Pavlyuchenkova
2022	Iga Swiatek	Coco Gauff
2023	Iga Swiatek	Karolina Muchova
2024	Iga Swiatek	Jasmine Paolini

Wimbledon Champions, 1925-2024

First contested 1877 for men, 1884 for women. Became an open championship in 1968. Not held 1940-45, 2020.

Men's Singles

Year	Champion	Final opponent
1925	René Lacoste	Jean Borotra
1926	Jean Borotra	Howard Kinsey
1927	Henri Cochet	Jean Borotra
1928	René Lacoste	Henri Cochet
1929	Henri Cochet	Jean Borotra
1930	Bill Tilden	Wilmer Allison
1931	Sidney B. Wood	Francis X. Shields
1932	Ellsworth Vines	Henry Austin
1933	Jack Crawford	Ellsworth Vines
1934	Fred Perry	Jack Crawford
1935	Fred Perry	Gottfried von Cramm
1936	Fred Perry	Gottfried von Cramm
1937	Donald Budge	Gottfried von Cramm
1938	Donald Budge	Henry Austin
1939	Bobby Riggs	Elwood Cooke
1946	Yvon Petra	Geoff E. Brown
1947	Jack Kramer	Tom P. Brown
1948	Bob Falkenburg	John Bromwich
1949	Ted Schroeder	Jaroslav Drobny
1950	Budge Patty	Frank Sedgman
1951	Dick Savitt	Ken McGregor
1952	Frank Sedgman	Jaroslav Drobny
1953	Vic Seixas	Kurt Nielsen
1954	Jaroslav Drobny	Ken Rosewall
1955	Tony Trabert	Kurt Nielsen
1956	Lew Hoad	Ken Rosewall
1957	Lew Hoad	Ashley Cooper
1958	Ashley Cooper	Neale Fraser
1959	Alex Olmedo	Rod Laver
1960	Neale Fraser	Rod Laver
1961	Rod Laver	Chuck McKinley
1962	Rod Laver	Martin Mulligan
1963	Chuck McKinley	Fred Stolle
1964	Roy Emerson	Fred Stolle
1965	Roy Emerson	Fred Stolle
1966	Manuel Santana	Dennis Ralston
1967	John Newcombe	Wilhelm Bungert
1968	Rod Laver	Tony Roche
1969	Rod Laver	John Newcombe
1970	John Newcombe	Ken Rosewall
1971	John Newcombe	Stan Smith
1972	Stan Smith	Ilie Nastase
1973	Jan Kodes	Alex Metreveli
1974	Jimmy Connors	Ken Rosewall
1975	Arthur Ashe	Jimmy Connors
1976	Björn Borg	Ilie Nastase
1977	Björn Borg	Jimmy Connors
1978	Björn Borg	Jimmy Connors
1979	Björn Borg	Roscoe Tanner
1980	Björn Borg	John McEnroe
1981	John McEnroe	Björn Borg
1982	Jimmy Connors	John McEnroe
1983	John McEnroe	Chris Lewis
1984	John McEnroe	Jimmy Connors
1985	Boris Becker	Kevin Curren
1986	Boris Becker	Ivan Lendl
1987	Pat Cash	Ivan Lendl
1988	Stefan Edberg	Boris Becker
1989	Boris Becker	Stefan Edberg
1990	Stefan Edberg	Boris Becker
1991	Michael Stich	Boris Becker
1992	Andre Agassi	Goran Ivanisevic
1993	Pete Sampras	Jim Courier
1994	Pete Sampras	Goran Ivanisevic
1995	Pete Sampras	Boris Becker
1996	Richard Krajicek	MaliVai "Mai" Washington
1997	Pete Sampras	Cedric Pioline
1998	Pete Sampras	Goran Ivanisevic
1999	Pete Sampras	Andre Agassi
2000	Pete Sampras	Patrick Rafter
2001	Goran Ivanisevic	Patrick Rafter
2002	Lleyton Hewitt	David Nalbandian
2003	Roger Federer	Mark Philippoussis
2004	Roger Federer	Andy Roddick
2005	Roger Federer	Andy Roddick
2006	Roger Federer	Rafael Nadal
2007	Roger Federer	Rafael Nadal
2008	Rafael Nadal	Roger Federer
2009	Roger Federer	Andy Roddick
2010	Rafael Nadal	Tomas Berdych
2011	Novak Djokovic	Rafael Nadal
2012	Roger Federer	Andy Murray
2013	Andy Murray	Novak Djokovic
2014	Novak Djokovic	Roger Federer
2015	Novak Djokovic	Roger Federer
2016	Andy Murray	Milos Raonic
2017	Roger Federer	Marin Cilic
2018	Novak Djokovic	Kevin Anderson
2019	Novak Djokovic	Roger Federer
2021	Novak Djokovic	Matteo Berrettini
2022	Novak Djokovic	Nick Kyrgios
2023	Carlos Alcaraz	Novak Djokovic
2024	Carlos Alcaraz	Novak Djokovic

Women's Singles

Year	Champion	Final opponent
1925	Suzanne Lenglen	Joan Fry
1926	Kathleen McKane Godfree	Lili de Alvarez
1927	Helen Wills	Lili de Alvarez
1928	Helen Wills	Lili de Alvarez
1929	Helen Wills	Helen H. Jacobs
1930	Helen Wills Moody	Elizabeth Ryan
1931	Cilly Aussem	Hilde Krahwinkel
1932	Helen Wills Moody	Helen H. Jacobs
1933	Helen Wills Moody	Dorothy Round
1934	Dorothy Round	Helen H. Jacobs
1935	Helen Wills Moody	Helen H. Jacobs
1936	Helen H. Jacobs	Hilde Krahwinkel Sperling
1937	Dorothy Round	Jadwiga Jedrzejowska
1938	Helen Wills Moody	Helen H. Jacobs
1939	Alice Marble	Kay Stammers
1946	Pauline Betz	Louise Brough
1947	Margaret Osborne	Doris Hart
1948	Louise Brough	Doris Hart
1949	Louise Brough	Margaret Osborne duPont
1950	Louise Brough	Margaret Osborne duPont
1951	Doris Hart	Shirley Fry
1952	Maureen Connolly	Louise Brough
1953	Maureen Connolly	Doris Hart
1954	Maureen Connolly	Louise Brough
1955	Louise Brough	Beverly Fleitz
1956	Shirley Fry	Angela Buxton
1957	Althea Gibson	Darlene Hard
1958	Althea Gibson	Angela Mortimer
1959	Maria Bueno	Darlene Hard
1960	Maria Bueno	Sandra Reynolds
1961	Angela Mortimer	Christine Truman
1962	Karen Hantze-Susman	Vera Sukova
1963	Margaret Smith	Billie Jean Moffitt
1964	Maria Bueno	Margaret Smith

Year	Champion	Final opponent
1965	Margaret Smith	Maria Bueno
1966	Billie Jean King	Maria Bueno
1967	Billie Jean King	Ann Haydon Jones
1968	Billie Jean King	Judy Tegart
1969	Ann Haydon Jones	Billie Jean King
1970	Margaret Smith Court	Billie Jean King
1971	Evonne Goolagong	Margaret Smith Court
1972	Billie Jean King	Evonne Goolagong
1973	Billie Jean King	Chris Evert
1974	Chris Evert	Olga Morozova
1975	Billie Jean King	Evonne Goolagong Cawley
1976	Chris Evert	Evonne Goolagong Cawley
1977	Virginia Wade	Betty Stove
1978	Martina Navratilova	Chris Evert
1979	Martina Navratilova	Chris Evert Lloyd
1980	Evonne Goolagong Cawley	Chris Evert Lloyd
1981	Chris Evert Lloyd	Hana Mandlikova
1982	Martina Navratilova	Chris Evert Lloyd
1983	Martina Navratilova	Andrea Jaeger
1984	Martina Navratilova	Chris Evert Lloyd
1985	Martina Navratilova	Chris Evert Lloyd
1986	Martina Navratilova	Hana Mandlikova
1987	Martina Navratilova	Steffi Graf
1988	Steffi Graf	Martina Navratilova
1989	Steffi Graf	Martina Navratilova
1990	Martina Navratilova	Zina Garrison
1991	Steffi Graf	Gabriela Sabatini
1992	Steffi Graf	Monica Seles
1993	Steffi Graf	Jana Novotna
1994	Conchita Martínez	Martina Navratilova
1995	Steffi Graf	Arantxa Sánchez Vicario
1996	Steffi Graf	Arantxa Sánchez Vicario
1997	Martina Hingis	Jana Novotna
1998	Jana Novotna	Nathalie Tauziat
1999	Lindsay Davenport	Steffi Graf
2000	Venus Williams	Lindsay Davenport
2001	Venus Williams	Justine Henin
2002	Serena Williams	Venus Williams
2003	Serena Williams	Venus Williams
2004	Maria Sharapova	Serena Williams
2005	Venus Williams	Lindsay Davenport
2006	Amélie Mauresmo	Justine Henin-Hardenne
2007	Venus Williams	Marion Bartoli
2008	Venus Williams	Serena Williams
2009	Serena Williams	Venus Williams
2010	Serena Williams	Vera Zvonareva
2011	Petra Kvitova	Maria Sharapova
2012	Serena Williams	Agnieszka Radwanska
2013	Marion Bartoli	Sabine Lisicki
2014	Petra Kvitova	Eugenie Bouchard
2015	Serena Williams	Garbiñe Muguruza
2016	Serena Williams	Angelique Kerber
2017	Garbiñe Muguruza	Venus Williams
2018	Angelique Kerber	Serena Williams
2019	Simona Halep	Serena Williams
2021	Ashleigh Barty	Karolina Pliskova
2022	Elena Rybakina	Ons Jabeur
2023	Marketa Vondrousova	Ons Jabeur
2024	Barbora Krejcikova	Jasmine Paolini

U.S. Open Champions, 1925-2024

First contested 1881 for men, 1887 for women. The former U.S. National Championship became an open championship in 1968.

Men's Singles

Year	Champion	Final opponent
1925	Bill Tilden	William Johnston
1926	René Lacoste	Jean Borotra
1927	René Lacoste	Bill Tilden
1928	Henri Cochet	Francis Hunter
1929	Bill Tilden	Francis Hunter
1930	John Doeg	Francis X. Shields
1931	Ellsworth Vines	George Lott
1932	Ellsworth Vines	Henri Cochet
1933	Fred Perry	John Crawford
1934	Fred Perry	Wilmer Allison
1935	Wilmer Allison	Sidney Wood
1936	Fred Perry	Don Budge
1937	Don Budge	Gottfried von Cramm
1938	Don Budge	C. Gene Mako
1939	Bobby Riggs	S. Welby Van Horn
1940	Don McNeill	Bobby Riggs
1941	Bobby Riggs	F. L. Kovacs
1942	F. R. Schroeder Jr.	Frank Parker
1943	Joseph Hunt	Jack Kramer
1944	Frank Parker	Bill Talbert
1945	Frank Parker	Bill Talbert
1946	Jack Kramer	Tom Brown Jr.
1947	Jack Kramer	Frank Parker
1948	Pancho Gonzales	Eric Sturgess
1949	Pancho Gonzales	F. R. Schroeder Jr.
1950	Arthur Larsen	Herbert Flam
1951	Frank Sedgman	E. Victor Seixas Jr.
1952	Frank Sedgman	Gardnar Mulloy
1953	Tony Trabert	E. Victor Seixas Jr.
1954	E. Victor Seixas Jr.	Rex Hartwig
1955	Tony Trabert	Ken Rosewall
1956	Ken Rosewall	Lewis Hoad
1957	Malcolm Anderson	Ashley Cooper
1958	Ashley Cooper	Malcolm Anderson
1959	Neale A. Fraser	Alejandro Olmedo
1960	Neale A. Fraser	Rod Laver
1961	Roy Emerson	Rod Laver
1962	Rod Laver	Roy Emerson
1963	Rafael Osuna	F. A. Froehling III
1964	Roy Emerson	Fred Stolle
1965	Manuel Santana	Cliff Drysdale
1966	Fred Stolle	John Newcombe
1967	John Newcombe	Clark Graebner
1968	Arthur Ashe	Tom Okker
1969	Rod Laver	Tony Roche
1970	Ken Rosewall	Tony Roche
1971	Stan Smith	Jan Kodes
1972	Ilie Nastase	Arthur Ashe
1973	John Newcombe	Jan Kodes
1974	Jimmy Connors	Ken Rosewall
1975	Manuel Orantes	Jimmy Connors
1976	Jimmy Connors	Björn Borg
1977	Guillermo Vilas	Jimmy Connors
1978	Jimmy Connors	Björn Borg
1979	John McEnroe	Vitas Gerulaitis
1980	John McEnroe	Björn Borg
1981	John McEnroe	Björn Borg
1982	Jimmy Connors	Ivan Lendl
1983	Jimmy Connors	Ivan Lendl
1984	John McEnroe	Ivan Lendl
1985	Ivan Lendl	John McEnroe
1986	Ivan Lendl	Miloslav Mecir
1987	Ivan Lendl	Mats Wilander
1988	Mats Wilander	Ivan Lendl
1989	Boris Becker	Ivan Lendl
1990	Pete Sampras	Andre Agassi
1991	Stefan Edberg	Jim Courier
1992	Stefan Edberg	Pete Sampras
1993	Pete Sampras	Cedric Pioline
1994	Andre Agassi	Michael Stich
1995	Pete Sampras	Andre Agassi
1996	Pete Sampras	Michael Chang
1997	Patrick Rafter	Greg Rusedski
1998	Patrick Rafter	Mark Philippoussis
1999	Andre Agassi	Todd Martin
2000	Marat Safin	Pete Sampras
2001	Lleyton Hewitt	Pete Sampras
2002	Pete Sampras	Andre Agassi
2003	Andy Roddick	Juan Carlos Ferrero
2004	Roger Federer	Lleyton Hewitt
2005	Roger Federer	Andre Agassi
2006	Roger Federer	Andy Roddick
2007	Roger Federer	Novak Djokovic
2008	Roger Federer	Andy Murray
2009	Juan Martín del Potro	Roger Federer
2010	Rafael Nadal	Novak Djokovic
2011	Novak Djokovic	Rafael Nadal
2012	Andy Murray	Novak Djokovic
2013	Rafael Nadal	Novak Djokovic
2014	Marin Cilic	Kei Nishikori
2015	Novak Djokovic	Roger Federer
2016	Stan Wawrinka	Novak Djokovic
2017	Rafael Nadal	Kevin Anderson
2018	Novak Djokovic	Juan Martín del Potro
2019	Rafael Nadal	Daniil Medvedev
2020	Dominic Thiem	Alexander Zverev
2021	Daniil Medvedev	Novak Djokovic
2022	Carlos Alcaraz	Casper Ruud
2023	Novak Djokovic	Daniil Medvedev
2024	Jannik Sinner	Taylor Fritz

Women's Singles

Year	Champion	Final opponent
1925	Helen Willis	Kathleen McKane
1926	Molla B. Mallory	Elizabeth Ryan
1927	Helen Wills	Betty Nuthall
1928	Helen Wills	Helen H. Jacobs
1929	Helen Wills	Phoebe Holcroft-Watson
1930	Betty Nuthall	Anna McCune Harper
1931	Helen Wills Moody	E. B. Whittingstall
1932	Helen H. Jacobs	Carolin A. Babcock
1933	Helen H. Jacobs	Helen Wills Moody
1934	Helen H. Jacobs	Sarah H. Palfrey
1935	Helen H. Jacobs	Sarah Palfrey Fabyan
1936	Alice Marble	Helen H. Jacobs
1937	Anita Lizana	Jadwiga Jedrzejowska
1938	Alice Marble	Nancye Wynne
1939	Alice Marble	Helen H. Jacobs

Year	Champion	Final opponent
1940	Alice Marble	Helen H. Jacobs
1941	Sarah Palfrey Cooke	Pauline Betz
1942	Pauline Betz	Louise Brough
1943	Pauline Betz	Louise Brough
1944	Pauline Betz	Margaret Osborne
1945	Sarah Palfrey Cooke	Pauline Betz
1946	Pauline Betz	Patricia Canning
1947	Louise Brough	Margaret Osborne
1948	Margaret Osborne duPont	Louise Brough
1949	Margaret Osborne duPont	Doris Hart
1950	Margaret Osborne duPont	Doris Hart
1951	Maureen Connolly	Shirley Fry
1952	Maureen Connolly	Doris Hart
1953	Maureen Connolly	Doris Hart
1954	Doris Hart	Louise Brough
1955	Doris Hart	Patricia Ward
1956	Shirley Fry	Althea Gibson
1957	Althea Gibson	Louise Brough
1958	Althea Gibson	Darlene Hard
1959	Maria Bueno	Christine Truman
1960	Darlene Hard	Maria Bueno
1961	Darlene Hard	Ann Haydon
1962	Margaret Smith	Darlene Hard
1963	Maria Bueno	Margaret Smith
1964	Maria Bueno	Carole Caldwell Graebner
1965	Margaret Smith	Billie Jean Moffitt
1966	Maria Bueno	Nancy Richey
1967	Billie Jean King	Ann Haydon Jones
1968	Virginia Wade	Billie Jean King
1969	Margaret Smith Court	Nancy Richey
1970	Margaret Smith Court	Rosemary Casals
1971	Billie Jean King	Rosemary Casals
1972	Billie Jean King	Kerry Melville
1973	Margaret Smith Court	Evonne Goolagong
1974	Billie Jean King	Evonne Goolagong
1975	Chris Evert	Evonne Goolagong Cawley
1976	Chris Evert	Evonne Goolagong Cawley
1977	Chris Evert	Wendy Turnbull
1978	Chris Evert	Pam Shriver
1979	Tracy Austin	Chris Evert Lloyd
1980	Chris Evert Lloyd	Hana Mandlikova
1981	Tracy Austin	Martina Navratilova
1982	Chris Evert Lloyd	Hana Mandlikova
1983	Martina Navratilova	Chris Evert Lloyd
1984	Martina Navratilova	Chris Evert Lloyd
1985	Hana Mandlikova	Martina Navratilova
1986	Martina Navratilova	Helena Sukova
1987	Martina Navratilova	Steffi Graf
1988	Steffi Graf	Gabriela Sabatini
1989	Steffi Graf	Martina Navratilova
1990	Gabriela Sabatini	Steffi Graf
1991	Monica Seles	Martina Navratilova
1992	Monica Seles	Arantxa Sánchez Vicario
1993	Steffi Graf	Helena Sukova
1994	Arantxa Sánchez Vicario	Steffi Graf
1995	Steffi Graf	Monica Seles
1996	Steffi Graf	Monica Seles
1997	Martina Hingis	Venus Williams
1998	Lindsay Davenport	Martina Hingis
1999	Serena Williams	Martina Hingis
2000	Venus Williams	Lindsay Davenport
2001	Venus Williams	Serena Williams
2002	Serena Williams	Venus Williams
2003	Justine Henin-Hardenne	Kim Clijsters
2004	Svetlana Kuznetsova	Elena Dementieva
2005	Kim Clijsters	Mary Pierce
2006	Maria Sharapova	Justine Henin-Hardenne
2007	Justine Henin	Svetlana Kuznetsova
2008	Serena Williams	Jelena Jankovic
2009	Kim Clijsters	Caroline Wozniacki
2010	Kim Clijsters	Vera Zvonareva
2011	Samantha Stosur	Serena Williams
2012	Serena Williams	Victoria Azarenka
2013	Serena Williams	Victoria Azarenka
2014	Serena Williams	Caroline Wozniacki
2015	Flavia Pennetta	Roberta Vinci
2016	Angelique Kerber	Karolina Pliskova
2017	Sloane Stephens	Madison Keys
2018	Naomi Osaka	Serena Williams
2019	Bianca Andreescu	Serena Williams
2020	Naomi Osaka	Victoria Azarenka
2021	Emma Raducanu	Leylah Fernandez
2022	Iga Swiatek	Ons Jabeur
2023	Coco Gauff	Aryna Sabalenka
2024	Aryna Sabalenka	Jessica Pegula

Davis Cup, 1970-2023

The Davis Cup began in 1900 as a competition between the U.S. and Great Britain. Not held, 2020.

Year	Result
1970	U.S. 5, W. Germany 0
1971	U.S. 3, Romania 2
1972	U.S. 3, Romania 2
1973	Australia 5, U.S. 0
1974	South Africa (default by India)
1975	Sweden 3, Czechoslovakia 2
1976	Italy 4, Chile 1
1977	Australia 3, Italy 1
1978	U.S. 4, Great Britain 1
1979	U.S. 5, Italy 0
1980	Czechoslovakia 4, Italy 1
1981	U.S. 3, Argentina 1
1982	U.S. 4, France, 1
1983	Australia 3, Sweden 2
1984	Sweden 4, U.S. 1
1985	Sweden 3, W. Germany 2
1986	Australia 3, Sweden 2
1987	Sweden 5, India 0
1988	W. Germany 4, Sweden 1
1989	W. Germany 3, Sweden 2
1990	U.S. 3, Australia 2
1991	France 3, U.S. 1
1992	U.S. 3, Switzerland 1
1993	Germany 4, Australia 1
1994	Sweden 4, Russia 1
1995	U.S. 3, Russia 2
1996	France 3, Sweden 2
1997	Sweden 5, U.S. 0
1998	Sweden 4, Italy 1
1999	Australia 3, France 2
2000	Spain 3, Australia 1
2001	France 3, Australia 2
2002	Russia 3, France 2
2003	Australia 3, Spain 1
2004	Spain 3, U.S. 2
2005	Croatia 3, Slovakia 2
2006	Russia 3, Argentina 2
2007	U.S. 4, Russia 1
2008	Spain 3, Argentina 1
2009	Spain 5, Czech Republic 0
2010	Serbia 3, France 2
2011	Spain 3, Argentina 1
2012	Czech Republic 3, Spain 2
2013	Czech Republic 3, Serbia 2
2014	Switzerland 3, France 1
2015	Great Britain 3, Belgium 1
2016	Argentina 3, Croatia 2
2017	France 3, Belgium 2
2018	Croatia 3, France 1
2019	Spain 2, Canada 0
2021	Russia 2, Croatia 0
2022	Canada 2, Australia 0
2023	Italy 2, Australia 0

Note: The challenge round format, which guaranteed the previous year's winner a spot in the finals at home, was eliminated in 1972.

All-Time Grand Slam Singles Title Leaders

Men	Australian Open	French Open[1]	Wimbledon	U.S. Open	Total
Novak Djokovic*	2008, '11-'13, '15-'16, '19-'21, '23	2016, '21, '23	2011, '14-'15, '18-'19, '21-'22	2011, '15, '18, '23	24
Rafael Nadal*	2009, '22	2005-08, '10-'14, '17-'20, '22	2008, '10	2010, '13, '17, '19	22
Roger Federer	2004, '06-'07, '10, '17-'18	2009	2003-07, '09, '12, '17	2004-08	20
Pete Sampras	1994, '97	—	1993-95, 1997-2000	1990, '93, '95-'96, 2002	14
Roy Emerson	1961, '63-'67	1963, '67	1964-65	1961, '64	12
Björn Borg	—	1974-75, '78-'81	1976-80	—	11
Rod Laver	1960, '62, '69	1962, '69	1961-62, '68-'69	1962, '69	11
Bill Tilden	—	—	1920-21, '30	1920-25, '29	10
Andre Agassi	1995, 2000-01, '03	1999	1992	1994, '99	8
Jimmy Connors	1974	—	1974, '82	1974, '76, '78, '82-'83	8
Ivan Lendl	1989-90	1984, '86-'87	—	1985-87	8
Fred Perry	1934	1935	1934-36	1933-34, '36	8
Ken Rosewall	1953, '55, '71-'72	1953, '68	—	1956, '70	8

Women	Australian Open	French Open[1]	Wimbledon	U.S. Open	Total
Margaret Smith Court	1960-66, '69-'71, '73	1962, '64, '69-'70, '73	1963, '65, '70	1962, '65, '69-'70, '73	24
Serena Williams	2003, '05, '07, '09-'10, '15, '17	2002, '13, '15	2002-03, '09-'10, '12, '15-'16	1999, 2002, '08, '12-'14	23
Steffi Graf	1988-90, '94	1987-88, '93, '95-'96, '99	1988-89, '91-'93, '95-'96	1988-89, '93, '95-'96	22
Helen Wills Moody	—	1928-30, '32	1927-30, '32-'33, '35, '38	1923-25, '27-'29, '31	19
Chris Evert	1982, '84	1974-75, '79-'80, '83, '85-'86	1974, '76, '81	1975-78, '80, '82	18
Martina Navratilova	1981, '83, '85	1982, '84	1978-79, '82-'87, '90	1983-84, '86-'87	18
Billie Jean King	1968	1972	1966-68, '72-'73, '75	1967, '71-'72, '74	12
Suzanne Lenglen	—	1920-23, '25-'26	1919-23, '25	—	12
Maureen Connolly	1953	1953-54	1952-54	1951-53	9
Monica Seles	1991-93, '96	1990-92	—	1991-92	9

* = Player active in 2024. (1) Prior to 1925, French Open entry was limited to members of French clubs.

AUTO RACING

Indianapolis 500 Winners, 1911-2024

At Indianapolis Motor Speedway in Indianapolis, IN. Not held 1917-18, 1942-45.

Year	Driver(s), car[1]	Avg. mph	Year	Driver(s), car[1]	Avg. mph
1911	Ray Harroun, Marmon	74.602	1971	Al Unser, P.J. Colt-Ford	157.735
1912	Joe Dawson, National	78.719	1972	Mark Donohue, McLaren-Offy	162.962
1913	Jules Goux, Peugeot	75.933	1973	Gordon Johncock, Eagle-Offy	159.036
1914	René Thomas, Delage	82.474	1974	Johnny Rutherford, McLaren-Offy	158.589
1915	Ralph DePalma, Mercedes	89.840	1975	Bobby Unser, Eagle-Offy	149.213
1916	Dario Resta, Peugeot	84.001	1976	Johnny Rutherford, McLaren-Offy	148.725
1919	Howdy Wilcox, Peugeot	88.050	1977	A. J. Foyt, Coyote-Foyt	161.331
1920	Gaston Chevrolet, Frontenac	88.618	1978	Al Unser, Lola-Cosworth	161.363
1921	Tommy Milton, Frontenac	89.621	1979	Rick Mears, Penske-Cosworth	158.899
1922	Jimmy Murphy, Duesenberg-Miller	94.484	1980	Johnny Rutherford, Chaparral-Cosworth	142.862
1923	Tommy Milton, Miller	90.954	1981	Bobby Unser, Penske-Cosworth	139.184
1924	L. L. Corum/Joe Boyer, Duesenberg	98.234	1982	Gordon Johncock, Wildcat-Cosworth	162.029
1925	Peter DePaolo, Duesenberg	101.127	1983	Tom Sneva, March-Cosworth	162.117
1926	Frank Lockhart, Miller	95.904	1984	Rick Mears, March-Cosworth	163.612
1927	George Souders, Duesenberg	97.545	1985	Danny Sullivan, March-Cosworth	152.982
1928	Louis Meyer, Miller	99.482	1986	Bobby Rahal, March-Cosworth	170.722
1929	Ray Keech, Miller	97.585	1987	Al Unser, March-Cosworth	162.175
1930	Billy Arnold, Summers-Miller	100.448	1988	Rick Mears, Penske-Chevy Indy V8	144.809
1931	Louis Schneider, Stevens-Miller	96.629	1989	Emerson Fittipaldi, Penske-Chevy Indy V8	167.581
1932	Fred Frame, Wetteroth-Miller	104.144	1990	Arie Luyendyk, Lola-Chevy Indy V8	185.981
1933	Louis Meyer, Miller	104.162	1991	Rick Mears, Penske-Chevy Indy V8	176.457
1934	Bill Cummings, Miller	104.863	1992	Al Unser Jr., Galmer-Chevy Indy V8A	134.477
1935	Kelly Petillo, Wetteroth-Offy	106.240	1993	Emerson Fittipaldi, Penske-Chevy Indy V8C	157.207
1936	Louis Meyer, Stevens-Miller	109.069	1994	Al Unser Jr., Penske-Mercedes Benz	160.872
1937	Wilbur Shaw, Shaw-Offy	113.580	1995	Jacques Villeneuve, Reynard-Ford Cosworth XB	153.616
1938	Floyd Roberts, Wetteroth-Miller	117.200	1996	Buddy Lazier, Reynard-Ford Cosworth XB	147.956
1939	Wilbur Shaw, Maserati	115.035	1997	Arie Luyendyk, G Force-Aurora	145.827
1940	Wilbur Shaw, Maserati	114.277	1998	Eddie Cheever Jr., Dallara-Aurora	145.155
1941	Floyd Davis/Mauri Rose, Wetteroth-Offy	115.117	1999	Kenny Brack, Dallara-Aurora	153.176
1946	George Robson, Adams-Sparks	114.820	2000	Juan Pablo Montoya, G Force-Oldsmobile	167.607
1947	Mauri Rose, Deidt-Offy	116.338	2001	Helio Castroneves, Dallara-Oldsmobile	141.574
1948	Mauri Rose, Deidt-Offy	119.814	2002	Helio Castroneves, Dallara-Chevrolet	166.499
1949	Bill Holland, Deidt-Offy	121.327	2003	Gil de Ferran, G Force-Toyota	156.291
1950	Johnnie Parsons, Kurtis-Offy	124.002	2004	Buddy Rice, G Force-Honda	138.518
1951	Lee Wallard, Kurtis-Offy	126.244	2005	Dan Wheldon, Dallara-Honda	157.603
1952	Troy Ruttman, Kuzma-Offy	128.922	2006	Sam Hornish Jr., Dallara-Honda	157.085
1953	Bill Vukovich, KK500A-Offy	127.740	2007	Dario Franchitti, Dallara-Honda	151.774
1954	Bill Vukovich, KK500A-Offy	130.840	2008	Scott Dixon, Dallara-Honda	143.567
1955	Bob Sweikert, KK500D-Offy	128.209	2009	Helio Castroneves, Dallara-Honda	150.318
1956	Pat Flaherty, Watson-Offy	128.490	2010	Dario Franchitti, Dallara-Honda	161.623
1957	Sam Hanks, Salih-Offy	135.601	2011	Dan Wheldon, Dallara-Honda	170.265
1958	Jimmy Bryan, Salih-Offy	133.791	2012	Dario Franchitti, Dallara-Honda	167.734
1959	Rodger Ward, Watson-Offy	135.857	2013	Tony Kanaan, Dallara-Chevrolet	187.433
1960	Jim Rathmann, Watson-Offy	138.767	2014	Ryan Hunter-Reay, Dallara-Honda	186.563
1961	A. J. Foyt, Trevis-Offy	139.130	2015	Juan Pablo Montoya, Dallara-Chevrolet	161.341
1962	Rodger Ward, Watson-Offy	140.293	2016	Alexander Rossi, Dallara-Honda	166.634
1963	Parnelli Jones, Watson-Offy	143.137	2017	Takuma Sato, Dallara-Honda	155.395
1964	A. J. Foyt, Watson-Offy	147.350	2018	Will Power, Dallara-Chevrolet	166.935
1965	Jim Clark, Lotus-Ford	150.686	2019	Simon Pagenaud, Dallara-Chevrolet	175.794
1966	Graham Hill, Lola-Ford	144.317	2020	Takuma Sato, Dallara-Honda	157.724
1967	A. J. Foyt, Coyote-Ford	151.207	2021	Helio Castroneves, Dallara-Honda	190.690
1968	Bobby Unser, Eagle-Offy	152.882	2022	Marcus Ericsson, Dallara-Honda	175.428
1969	Mario Andretti, Hawk-Ford	156.867	2023	Josef Newgarden, Dallara-Chevrolet	168.193
1970	Al Unser, P.J. Colt-Ford	155.749	2024	Josef Newgarden, Dallara-Chevrolet	167.763

Note: The race was less than 500 mi in the following years: 1916 (300 mi), 1926 (400 mi), 1950 (345 mi), 1973 (332.5 mi), 1975 (435 mi), 1976 (255 mi), 2004 (450 mi), 2007 (415 mi). (1) Chassis-engine.

IndyCar Series Champions, 1996-2024

A breakaway group of Championship Auto Racing Teams (CART) drivers began the Indy Racing League (IRL) in 1994; it awarded its first championship in 1996. Known as the IndyCar Series in 2003-11 and as IndyCar from 2011 on. Merged with Champ Car World Series, 2008, under the IndyCar name.

Year	Driver	Year	Driver	Year	Driver	Year	Driver	Year	Driver
1996	Scott Sharp; Buzz Calkins (tie)	2001	Sam Hornish Jr.	2007	Dario Franchitti	2013	Scott Dixon	2019	Josef Newgarden
1997	Tony Stewart	2002	Sam Hornish Jr.	2008	Scott Dixon	2014	Will Power	2020	Scott Dixon
1998	Kenny Brack	2003	Scott Dixon	2009	Dario Franchitti	2015	Scott Dixon	2021	Alex Palou
1999	Greg Ray	2004	Tony Kanaan	2010	Dario Franchitti	2016	Simon Pagenaud	2022	Will Power
2000	Buddy Lazier	2005	Dan Wheldon	2011	Dario Franchitti	2017	Josef Newgarden	2023	Alex Palou
		2006	Sam Hornish Jr.	2012	Ryan Hunter-Reay	2018	Scott Dixon	2024	Alex Palou

Champ Car World Series Winners, 1959-2007

Known as U.S. Auto Club, 1959-78; Championship Auto Racing Teams (CART), 1979-2003; Champ Car World Series, 2004-07. The Vanderbilt Cup became the series championship trophy in 2000. Merged with Indy Racing League (now IndyCar) in 2008.

Year	Driver	Year	Driver	Year	Driver	Year	Driver	Year	Driver
1959	Rodger Ward	1969	Mario Andretti	1979	Rick Mears	1989	Emerson Fittipaldi	1999	Juan Montoya
1960	A. J. Foyt	1970	Al Unser	1980	Johnny Rutherford	1990	Al Unser Jr.	2000	Gil de Ferran
1961	A. J. Foyt	1971	Joe Leonard	1981	Rick Mears	1991	Michael Andretti	2001	Gil de Ferran
1962	Rodger Ward	1972	Joe Leonard	1982	Rick Mears	1992	Bobby Rahal	2002	Cristiano da Matta
1963	A. J. Foyt	1973	Roger McCluskey	1983	Al Unser	1993	Nigel Mansell	2003	Paul Tracy
1964	A. J. Foyt	1974	Bobby Unser	1984	Mario Andretti	1994	Al Unser Jr.	2004	Sébastien Bourdais
1965	Mario Andretti	1975	A. J. Foyt	1985	Al Unser	1995	Jacques Villeneuve	2005	Sébastien Bourdais
1966	Mario Andretti	1976	Gordon Johncock	1986	Bobby Rahal	1996	Jimmy Vasser	2006	Sébastien Bourdais
1967	A. J. Foyt	1977	Tom Sneva	1987	Bobby Rahal	1997	Alex Zanardi	2007	Sébastien Bourdais
1968	Bobby Unser	1978	Tom Sneva	1988	Danny Sullivan	1998	Alex Zanardi		

NASCAR Cup Series Champions, 1949-2023

Known as Strictly Stock, 1949; Grand National, 1950-70; Winston Cup, 1971-2003; Nextel Cup, 2004-07; Sprint Cup, 2008-16; Monster Energy NASCAR Cup, 2017-19.

Year	Driver	Year	Driver	Year	Driver	Year	Driver	Year	Driver
1949	Red Byron	1964	Richard Petty	1979	Richard Petty	1994	Dale Earnhardt	2009	Jimmie Johnson
1950	Bill Rexford	1965	Ned Jarrett	1980	Dale Earnhardt	1995	Jeff Gordon	2010	Jimmie Johnson
1951	Herb Thomas	1966	David Pearson	1981	Darrell Waltrip	1996	Terry Labonte	2011	Tony Stewart
1952	Tim Flock	1967	Richard Petty	1982	Darrell Waltrip	1997	Jeff Gordon	2012	Brad Keselowski
1953	Herb Thomas	1968	David Pearson	1983	Bobby Allison	1998	Jeff Gordon	2013	Jimmie Johnson
1954	Lee Petty	1969	David Pearson	1984	Terry Labonte	1999	Dale Jarrett	2014	Kevin Harvick
1955	Tim Flock	1970	Bobby Isaac	1985	Darrell Waltrip	2000	Bobby Labonte	2015	Kyle Busch
1956	Buck Baker	1971	Richard Petty	1986	Dale Earnhardt	2001	Jeff Gordon	2016	Jimmie Johnson
1957	Buck Baker	1972	Richard Petty	1987	Dale Earnhardt	2002	Tony Stewart	2017	Martin Truex Jr.
1958	Lee Petty	1973	Benny Parsons	1988	Bill Elliott	2003	Matt Kenseth	2018	Joey Logano
1959	Lee Petty	1974	Richard Petty	1989	Rusty Wallace	2004	Kurt Busch	2019	Kyle Busch
1960	Rex White	1975	Richard Petty	1990	Dale Earnhardt	2005	Tony Stewart	2020	Chase Elliott
1961	Ned Jarrett	1976	Cale Yarborough	1991	Dale Earnhardt	2006	Jimmie Johnson	2021	Kyle Larson
1962	Joe Weatherly	1977	Cale Yarborough	1992	Alan Kulwicki	2007	Jimmie Johnson	2022	Joey Logano
1963	Joe Weatherly	1978	Cale Yarborough	1993	Dale Earnhardt	2008	Jimmie Johnson	2023	Ryan Blaney

NASCAR Cup Series Rookie of the Year, 1958-2023

Year	Driver	Year	Driver	Year	Driver	Year	Driver	Year	Driver
1958	Shorty Rollins	1972	Larry Smith	1985	Ken Schrader	1998	Kenny Irwin	2011	Andy Lally
1959	Richard Petty	1973	Lennie Pond	1986	Alan Kulwicki	1999	Tony Stewart	2012	Stephen Leicht
1960	David Pearson	1974	Earl Ross	1987	Davey Allison	2000	Matt Kenseth	2013	Ricky Stenhouse Jr.
1961	Woodie Wilson	1975	Bruce Hill	1988	Ken Bouchard	2001	Kevin Harvick	2014	Kyle Larson
1962	Tom Cox	1976	Skip Manning	1989	Dick Trickle	2002	Ryan Newman	2015	Brett Moffitt
1963	Billy Wade	1977	Ricky Rudd	1990	Rob Moroso	2003	Jamie McMurray	2016	Chase Elliott
1964	Doug Cooper	1978	Ronnie Thomas	1991	Bobby Hamilton	2004	Kasey Kahne	2017	Erik Jones
1965	Sam McQuagg	1979	Dale Earnhardt	1992	Jimmy Hensley	2005	Kyle Busch	2018	William Byron
1966	James Hylton	1980	Jody Ridley	1993	Jeff Gordon	2006	Denny Hamlin	2019	Daniel Hemric
1967	Donnie Allison	1981	Ron Bouchard	1994	Jeff Burton	2007	Juan Pablo Montoya	2020	Cole Custer
1968	Pete Hamilton	1982	Geoff Bodine	1995	Ricky Craven	2008	Regan Smith	2021	Chase Briscoe
1969	Dick Brooks	1983	Sterling Marlin	1996	Johnny Benson	2009	Joey Logano	2022	Austin Cindric
1970	Bill Dennis	1984	Rusty Wallace	1997	Mike Skinner	2010	Kevin Conway	2023	Ty Gibbs
1971	Walter Ballard								

Daytona 500 Winners, 1959-2024

At Daytona International Speedway in Daytona Beach, FL.

Year	Driver, car	Avg. mph	Year	Driver, car	Avg. mph	Year	Driver, car	Avg. mph
1959	Lee Petty, Oldsmobile	135.521	1982	Bobby Allison, Buick	153.991	2004	Dale Earnhardt Jr., Chevrolet	156.345
1960	Junior Johnson, Chevrolet	124.740	1983	Cale Yarborough, Pontiac	155.979	2005	Jeff Gordon, Chevrolet	135.173
1961	Marvin Panch, Pontiac	149.601	1984	Cale Yarborough, Chevrolet	150.994	2006	Jimmie Johnson, Chevrolet	142.667
1962	Fireball Roberts, Pontiac	152.529	1985	Bill Elliott, Ford	172.265	2007	Kevin Harvick, Chevrolet	149.335
1963	Tiny Lund, Ford	151.566	1986	Geoff Bodine, Chevrolet	148.124	2008	Ryan Newman, Dodge	152.672
1964	Richard Petty, Plymouth	154.334	1987	Bill Elliott, Ford	176.263	2009	Matt Kenseth, Ford	132.816
1965	Fred Lorenzen, Ford	141.539	1988	Bobby Allison, Buick	137.531	2010	Jamie McMurray, Chevrolet	137.284
1966	Richard Petty, Plymouth	160.627	1989	Darrell Waltrip, Chevrolet	148.466	2011	Trevor Bayne, Ford	130.326
1967	Mario Andretti, Ford	146.926	1990	Derrike Cope, Chevrolet	165.761	2012	Matt Kenseth, Ford	140.256
1968	Cale Yarborough, Mercury	143.251	1991	Ernie Irvan, Chevrolet	148.148	2013	Jimmie Johnson, Chevrolet	159.250
1969	LeeRoy Yarbrough, Ford	157.950	1992	Davey Allison, Ford	160.256	2014	Dale Earnhardt Jr., Chevrolet	145.290
1970	Pete Hamilton, Plymouth	149.601	1993	Dale Jarrett, Chevrolet	154.972	2015	Joey Logano, Ford	161.939
1971	Richard Petty, Plymouth	144.462	1994	Sterling Marlin, Chevrolet	156.931	2016	Denny Hamlin, Toyota	157.549
1972	A. J. Foyt, Mercury	161.550	1995	Sterling Marlin, Chevrolet	141.710	2017	Kurt Busch, Ford	143.187
1973	Richard Petty, Dodge	157.205	1996	Dale Jarrett, Ford	154.308	2018	Austin Dillon, Chevrolet	150.545
1974	Richard Petty, Dodge	140.894	1997	Jeff Gordon, Chevrolet	148.295	2019	Denny Hamlin, Toyota	137.440
1975	Benny Parsons, Chevrolet	153.649	1998	Dale Earnhardt, Chevrolet	172.712	2020	Denny Hamlin, Toyota	141.110
1976	David Pearson, Mercury	152.181	1999	Jeff Gordon, Chevrolet	161.551	2021	Michael McDowell, Ford	144.416
1977	Cale Yarborough, Chevrolet	153.218	2000	Dale Jarrett, Ford	155.669	2022	Austin Cindric, Ford	142.295
1978	Bobby Allison, Ford	159.730	2001	Michael Waltrip, Chevrolet	161.783	2023	Ricky Stenhouse Jr., Chevrolet	145.283
1979	Richard Petty, Oldsmobile	143.977	2002	Ward Burton, Dodge	142.971	2024	William Byron, Chevrolet	157.178
1980	Buddy Baker, Oldsmobile	177.602	2003	Michael Waltrip, Chevrolet	133.870			
1981	Richard Petty, Buick	169.651						

Coca-Cola 600 Winners, 1960-2024

At Charlotte Motor Speedway in Concord, NC. Known as the World 600, 1960-85. * = Rain-shortened.

Year	Driver, car	Avg. mph	Year	Driver, car	Avg. mph	Year	Driver, car	Avg. mph
1960	Joe Lee Johnson, Chevrolet	107.735	1981	Bobby Allison, Buick	129.326	2003	Jimmie Johnson, Chevrolet	126.198*
1961	David Pearson, Pontiac	111.633	1982	Neil Bonnett, Ford	130.058	2004	Jimmie Johnson, Chevrolet	142.763
1962	Nelson Stacy, Ford	125.552	1983	Neil Bonnett, Chevrolet	140.707	2005	Jimmie Johnson, Chevrolet	114.698
1963	Fred Lorenzen, Ford	132.418	1984	Bobby Allison, Buick	129.233	2006	Kasey Kahne, Dodge	128.840
1964	Jim Paschal, Plymouth	125.772	1985	Darrell Waltrip, Chevrolet	141.807	2007	Casey Mears, Chevrolet	130.222
1965	Fred Lorenzen, Ford	121.722	1986	Dale Earnhardt, Chevrolet	140.406	2008	Kasey Kahne, Dodge	135.772
1966	Marvin Panch, Plymouth	135.042	1987	Kyle Petty, Ford	131.483	2009	David Reutimann, Toyota	120.899*
1967	Jim Paschal, Plymouth	135.832	1988	Darrell Waltrip, Chevrolet	124.460	2010	Kurt Busch, Dodge	144.966
1968	Buddy Baker, Dodge	104.207*	1989	Darrell Waltrip, Chevrolet	144.077	2011	Kevin Harvick, Chevrolet	132.414
1969	LeeRoy Yarbrough, Mercury	134.361	1990	Rusty Wallace, Pontiac	137.650	2012	Kasey Kahne, Chevrolet	155.687
1970	Donnie Allison, Ford	129.680	1991	Davey Allison, Ford	138.951	2013	Kevin Harvick, Chevrolet	130.521
1971	Bobby Allison, Mercury	140.422	1992	Dale Earnhardt, Chevrolet	132.980	2014	Jimmie Johnson, Chevrolet	145.484
1972	Buddy Baker, Dodge	142.255	1993	Dale Earnhardt, Chevrolet	145.504	2015	Carl Edwards, Toyota	147.803
1973	Buddy Baker, Dodge	134.890	1994	Jeff Gordon, Chevrolet	139.445	2016	Martin Truex Jr., Toyota	160.655
1974	David Pearson, Mercury	135.720	1995	Bobby Labonte, Chevrolet	151.952	2017	Austin Dillon, Chevrolet	138.800
1975	Richard Petty, Dodge	145.327	1996	Dale Jarrett, Ford	147.581	2018	Kyle Busch, Toyota	136.692
1976	David Pearson, Mercury	137.352	1997	Jeff Gordon, Chevrolet	136.745*	2019	Martin Truex Jr., Toyota	124.074
1977	Richard Petty, Dodge	137.676	1998	Jeff Gordon, Chevrolet	136.424	2020	Brad Keselowski, Ford	135.042
1978	Darrell Waltrip, Chevrolet	138.355	1999	Jeff Burton, Ford	151.367	2021	Kyle Larson, Chevrolet	150.785
1979	Darrell Waltrip, Chevrolet	136.674	2000	Matt Kenseth, Ford	142.640	2022	Denny Hamlin, Toyota	118.703
1980	Benny Parsons, Chevrolet	119.265	2001	Jeff Burton, Ford	138.107	2023	Ryan Blaney, Ford	120.468
			2002	Mark Martin, Ford	137.729	2024	Christopher Bell, Toyota	123.053

NASCAR All-Star Race Winners, 1985-2024

At Charlotte Motor Speedway in Concord, NC, 1985-2019; Bristol Motor Speedway in Bristol, TN, 2020; Texas Motor Speedway in Ft. Worth, TX, 2021-22; North Wilkesboro Speedway in North Wilkesboro, NC, 2023-24.

Year	Driver, car
1985	Darrell Waltrip, Chevrolet
1986	Bill Elliott, Ford
1987	Dale Earnhardt, Chevrolet
1988	Terry Labonte, Chevrolet
1989	Rusty Wallace, Pontiac
1990	Dale Earnhardt, Chevrolet
1991	Davey Allison, Ford
1992	Davey Allison, Ford
1993	Dale Earnhardt, Chevrolet
1994	Geoff Bodine, Ford
1995	Jeff Gordon, Chevrolet
1996	Michael Waltrip, Ford
1997	Jeff Gordon, Chevrolet
1998	Mark Martin, Ford
1999	Terry Labonte, Chevrolet
2000	Dale Earnhardt Jr., Chevrolet
2001	Jeff Gordon, Chevrolet
2002	Ryan Newman, Ford
2003	Jimmie Johnson, Chevrolet
2004	Matt Kenseth, Ford
2005	Mark Martin, Ford
2006	Jimmie Johnson, Chevrolet
2007	Kevin Harvick, Chevrolet
2008	Kasey Kahne, Dodge
2009	Tony Stewart, Chevrolet
2010	Kurt Busch, Dodge
2011	Carl Edwards, Ford
2012	Jimmie Johnson, Chevrolet
2013	Jimmie Johnson, Chevrolet
2014	Jamie McMurray, Chevrolet
2015	Denny Hamlin, Toyota
2016	Joey Logano, Ford
2017	Kyle Busch, Toyota
2018	Kevin Harvick, Ford
2019	Kyle Larson, Chevrolet
2020	Chase Elliott, Chevrolet
2021	Kyle Larson, Chevrolet
2022	Ryan Blaney, Ford
2023	Kyle Larson, Chevrolet
2024	Joey Logano, Ford

Brickyard Race Winners, 1994-2024

At Indianapolis Motor Speedway in Indianapolis, IN. Brickyard 400 (under various sponsors), 1994-2020, 2024; Verizon 200 (200 mi on the combined road course), 2021-23.

Year	Driver, car	Avg. mph
1994	Jeff Gordon, Chevrolet	131.977
1995	Dale Earnhardt, Chevrolet	155.206
1996	Dale Jarrett, Ford	139.508
1997	Ricky Rudd, Ford	130.814
1998	Jeff Gordon, Chevrolet	126.772
1999	Dale Jarrett, Ford	148.194
2000	Bobby Labonte, Pontiac	155.912
2001	Jeff Gordon, Chevrolet	130.790
2002	Bill Elliott, Dodge	125.033
2003	Kevin Harvick, Chevrolet	134.554
2004	Jeff Gordon, Chevrolet	115.037
2005	Tony Stewart, Chevrolet	118.782
2006	Jimmie Johnson, Chevrolet	137.182
2007	Tony Stewart, Chevrolet	117.379
2008	Jimmie Johnson, Chevrolet	115.117
2009	Jimmie Johnson, Chevrolet	145.882
2010	Jamie McMurray, Chevrolet	136.054
2011	Paul Menard, Chevrolet	140.762
2012	Jimmie Johnson, Chevrolet	137.680
2013	Ryan Newman, Chevrolet	153.485
2014	Jeff Gordon, Chevrolet	150.297
2015	Kyle Busch, Toyota	131.656
2016	Kyle Busch, Toyota	128.940
2017	Kasey Kahne, Chevrolet	114.384
2018	Brad Keselowski, Ford	128.629
2019	Kevin Harvick, Ford	119.443
2020	Kevin Harvick, Ford	123.162
2021	AJ Allmendinger, Chevrolet	69.171
2022	Tyler Reddick, Chevrolet	78.511
2023	Michael McDowell, Ford	92.319
2024	Kyle Larson, Chevrolet	119.770

Bass Pro Shops Night Race Winners, 1961-2024

At Bristol Motor Speedway in Bristol, TN. * = Rain-shortened.

Year	Driver, car	Avg. mph
1961	Jack Smith, Pontiac	68.373
1962	Bobby Johns, Pontiac	73.320
1963	Fred Lorenzen, Ford	74.844
1964	Fred Lorenzen, Ford	78.044
1965	Ned Jarrett, Ford	61.826
1966	Paul Goldsmith, Plymouth	77.963
1967	Richard Petty, Plymouth	78.705
1968	David Pearson, Ford	76.310
1969	David Pearson, Ford	79.737
1970	Bobby Allison, Dodge	84.880
1971	Charlie Glotzbach, Chevrolet	101.074
1972	Bobby Allison, Chevrolet	92.735
1973	Benny Parsons, Chevrolet	91.342
1974	Cale Yarborough, Chevrolet	75.430
1975	Richard Petty, Dodge	97.016
1976	Cale Yarborough, Chevrolet	99.175
1977	Cale Yarborough, Chevrolet	79.726
1978	Cale Yarborough, Olds.	88.628
1979	Darrell Waltrip, Chevrolet	91.493
1980	Cale Yarborough, Chevrolet	86.973
1981	Darrell Waltrip, Buick	84.723
1982	Darrell Waltrip, Buick	94.318
1983	Darrell Waltrip, Chevrolet	89.430*
1984	Terry Labonte, Chevrolet	85.365
1985	Dale Earnhardt, Chevrolet	81.388
1986	Darrell Waltrip, Chevrolet	86.934
1987	Dale Earnhardt, Chevrolet	90.373
1988	Dale Earnhardt, Chevrolet	78.775
1989	Darrell Waltrip, Chevrolet	85.554
1990	Ernie Irvan, Chevrolet	91.782
1991	Alan Kulwicki, Ford	82.028
1992	Darrell Waltrip, Chevrolet	91.198
1993	Mark Martin, Ford	88.172
1994	Rusty Wallace, Ford	91.363
1995	Terry Labonte, Chevrolet	81.979
1996	Rusty Wallace, Ford	91.267
1997	Dale Jarrett, Ford	80.013
1998	Mark Martin, Ford	86.949
1999	Dale Earnhardt, Chevrolet	91.276
2000	Rusty Wallace, Ford	85.394
2001	Tony Stewart, Pontiac	85.106
2002	Jeff Gordon, Chevrolet	77.097
2003	Kurt Busch, Ford	77.421
2004	Dale Earnhardt Jr., Chevrolet	88.538
2005	Matt Kenseth, Ford	84.678
2006	Matt Kenseth, Ford	90.025
2007	Carl Edwards, Ford	89.006
2008	Carl Edwards, Ford	91.581
2009	Kyle Busch, Toyota	84.820
2010	Kyle Busch, Toyota	99.071
2011	Brad Keselowski, Dodge	96.753
2012	Denny Hamlin, Toyota	84.402
2013	Matt Kenseth, Toyota	90.279
2014	Joey Logano, Ford	92.965
2015	Joey Logano, Ford	96.890
2016	Kevin Harvick, Chevrolet	77.968
2017	Kyle Busch, Toyota	95.969
2018	Kurt Busch, Ford	89.538
2019	Denny Hamlin, Toyota	94.531
2020	Kevin Harvick, Ford	95.911
2021	Kyle Larson, Chevrolet	87.409
2022	Chris Buescher, Ford	88.286
2023	Denny Hamlin, Toyota	94.990
2024	Kyle Larson, Chevrolet	101.277

Formula One World Drivers' Champions, 1950-2023

Awarded by the Fédération Internationale de l'Automobile (FIA); champions determined through a series of Grand Prix races.

Year	Driver, country
1950	Giuseppe "Nino" Farina, Italy
1951	Juan Manuel Fangio, Argentina
1952	Alberto Ascari, Italy
1953	Alberto Ascari, Italy
1954	Juan Manuel Fangio, Argentina
1955	Juan Manuel Fangio, Argentina
1956	Juan Manuel Fangio, Argentina
1957	Juan Manuel Fangio, Argentina
1958	Mike Hawthorn, England, UK
1959	Jack Brabham, Australia
1960	Jack Brabham, Australia
1961	Phil Hill, United States
1962	Graham Hill, England, UK
1963	Jim Clark, Scotland, UK
1964	John Surtees, England, UK
1965	Jim Clark, Scotland, UK
1966	Jack Brabham, Australia
1967	Denis Hulme, New Zealand
1968	Graham Hill, England, UK
1969	Jackie Stewart, Scotland, UK
1970	Jochen Rindt, Austria
1971	Jackie Stewart, Scotland, UK
1972	Emerson Fittipaldi, Brazil
1973	Jackie Stewart, Scotland, UK
1974	Emerson Fittipaldi, Brazil
1975	Niki Lauda, Austria
1976	James Hunt, England, UK
1977	Niki Lauda, Austria
1978	Mario Andretti, United States
1979	Jody Scheckter, South Africa
1980	Alan Jones, Australia
1981	Nelson Piquet, Brazil
1982	Keke Rosberg, Finland
1983	Nelson Piquet, Brazil
1984	Niki Lauda, Austria
1985	Alain Prost, France
1986	Alain Prost, France
1987	Nelson Piquet, Brazil
1988	Ayrton Senna, Brazil
1989	Alain Prost, France
1990	Ayrton Senna, Brazil
1991	Ayrton Senna, Brazil
1992	Nigel Mansell, England, UK
1993	Alain Prost, France
1994	Michael Schumacher, Germany
1995	Michael Schumacher, Germany
1996	Damon Hill, England, UK
1997	Jacques Villeneuve, Canada
1998	Mika Hakkinen, Finland
1999	Mika Hakkinen, Finland
2000	Michael Schumacher, Germany
2001	Michael Schumacher, Germany
2002	Michael Schumacher, Germany
2003	Michael Schumacher, Germany
2004	Michael Schumacher, Germany
2005	Fernando Alonso, Spain
2006	Fernando Alonso, Spain
2007	Kimi Raikkonen, Finland
2008	Lewis Hamilton, England, UK
2009	Jenson Button, England, UK
2010	Sebastian Vettel, Germany
2011	Sebastian Vettel, Germany
2012	Sebastian Vettel, Germany
2013	Sebastian Vettel, Germany
2014	Lewis Hamilton, England, UK
2015	Lewis Hamilton, England, UK
2016	Nico Rosberg, Germany
2017	Lewis Hamilton, England, UK
2018	Lewis Hamilton, England, UK
2019	Lewis Hamilton, England, UK
2020	Lewis Hamilton, England, UK
2021	Max Verstappen, Netherlands
2022	Max Verstappen, Netherlands
2023	Max Verstappen, Netherlands

BOXING

There are many boxing governing bodies, including the World Boxing Assn. (WBA; known as the National Boxing Assn. [NBA] until 1962), World Boxing Council (WBC), International Boxing Fed. (IBF), World Boxing Org., N. American Boxing Fed., and European Boxing Union. All have their own champions and divisions.

Boxing Champions by Class

Class (weight limit)	WBA Champion	WBC Champion	IBF Champion
Heavyweight (none)	Oleksandr Usyk, Ukraine[1] Maumoud Charr, Germany	Oleksandr Usyk, Ukraine	Daniel Dubois, UK
Cruiserweight (200lbs)	Gilberto Ramírez, Mexico[1]	Noel Mikaelian, Armenia	Jai Opetaia, Australia
Light Heavyweight (175 lbs)	Dmitry Bivol, Russia[1] David Morrell, Cuba	Artur Beterbiev, Russia David Benavidez, U.S.[2]	Artur Beterbiev, Russia
Super Middleweight (168 lbs)	Canelo Álvarez, Mexico[1]	Canelo Álvarez, Mexico	Vacant
Middleweight (160 lbs)	Erislandy Lara, U.S.	Carlos Adames, Dominican Republic	Janibek Alimkhanuly, Kazakhstan
Super Welterweight/Jr. Middleweight (154 lbs)	Terence Crawford, U.S.	Sebastian Fundora, U.S. Vergil Ortiz Jr. U.S.[2]	Bakhram Murtazaliev, Russia
Welterweight (147 lbs)	Eimantas Stanionis, Lithuania	Mario Barrios, U.S.	Jaron Ennis, U.S.
Super Lightweight/Jr. Welterweight (140 lbs)	José Valenzuela, U.S.-Mex. Andy Hiraoka, Japan[2]	Alberto Puello, Dominican Republic	Liam Paro, Australia
Lightweight (135 lbs)	Gervonta Davis, U.S.	Shakur Stevenson, U.S.	Vasily Lomachenko, Ukraine
Super Featherweight/Jr. Lightweight (130 lbs)	Lamont Roach Jr., U.S. Albert Batyrgraziev, Russia[2]	Robson Conceição, Brazil	Anthony Cacace, Ireland
Featherweight (126 lbs)	Nick Ball, UK	Rey Vargas, Mexico Brandon Figueroa, U.S.[2]	Angelo Leo, U.S.
Super Bantamweight/Jr. Featherweight (122 lbs)	Naoya Inoue, Japan[1]	Naoya Inoue, Japan	Naoya Inoue, Japan
Bantamweight (118 lbs)	Takume Inoue, Japan	Junto Nakatani, Japan	Ryosuke Nishida, Japan
Super Flyweight/Jr. Bantamweight (115 lbs)	Fernando Martínez, Argentina David Jiménez, Costa Rico[2]	Jesse Rodriguez, U.S. Pedro Guevara, Mexico[2]	Fernando Martínez, Argentina
Flyweight (112 lbs)	Seigo Yuri Akui, Japan	Vacant	Ángel Ayala, Mexico
Light Flyweight/Jr. Flyweight (108 lbs)	Vacant	Vacant	Sivenathi Nontshinga, South Africa
Strawweight/Mini Flyweight (105 lbs)	Knockout CP Freshmart, Thailand[1]	Melvin Jerusalem, Phillipines	Pedro Taduran, Phillipines

Note: As of Sept. 22, 2024. (1) Super champion. (2) Interim champion.

Ring Champions by Years

* = Abandoned/relinquished the title or was stripped of it. IBF champions listed only for heavyweight division. International Boxing Hall of Fame inductees in *italics*. For years with multiple champions, boxers are listed according to date of earliest title bout.

Heavyweights

Years	Champion
1882-92	*John L. Sullivan*[1]
1892-97	*James J. Corbett*[2]
1897-99	*Bob Fitzsimmons*
1899-1905	*James J. Jeffries**[3]
1905-06	Marvin Hart
1906-08	*Tommy Burns*
1908-15	*Jack Johnson*
1915-19	*Jess Willard*
1919-26	*Jack Dempsey*
1926-28	*Gene Tunney**
1928-30	Vacant
1930-32	*Max Schmeling*
1932-33	*Jack Sharkey*
1933-34	Primo Carnera
1934-35	*Max Baer*
1935-37	*James J. Braddock*
1937-49	*Joe Louis**
1949-51	*Ezzard Charles*
1951-52	*Joe Walcott*
1952-56	*Rocky Marciano**
1956-59	*Floyd Patterson*
1959-60	*Ingemar Johansson*
1960-62	*Floyd Patterson*
1962-64	*Sonny Liston*
1964-67	*Cassius Clay (Muhammad Ali)**[4]
1968-70	Jimmy Ellis[4]
1970-73	*Joe Frazier*
1973-74	*George Foreman*
1974-78	*Muhammad Ali*
1978	Leon Spinks (WBA/WBC*)[5]; *Ken Norton* (WBC)
1978-79	*Muhammad Ali* (WBA*)[5]
1978-83	*Larry Holmes* (WBC*)[6]
1979-80	John Tate (WBA)
1980-82	Mike Weaver (WBA)
1982-83	Michael Dokes (WBA)
1983-84	Gerrie Coetzee (WBA)
1983-85	*Larry Holmes* (IBF)[6]
1984	Tim Witherspoon (WBC)
1984-86	Pinklon Thomas (WBC)
1984-85	Greg Page (WBA)
1985-86	Tony Tubbs (WBA)
1985-87	*Michael Spinks* (IBF*)
1986	Tim Witherspoon (WBA); Trevor Berbick (WBC)
1986-87	*Mike Tyson* (WBC); James "Bonecrusher" Smith (WBA)
1987	Tony Tucker (IBF)
1987-90	*Mike Tyson* (WBA/WBC/IBF)
1990	James "Buster" Douglas (WBA/WBC/IBF)
1990-92	*Evander Holyfield* (WBA/WBC/IBF)
1992-93	*Riddick Bowe* (WBA/WBC*/IBF)
1992-94	*Lennox Lewis* (WBC)
1993-94	*Evander Holyfield* (WBA/IBF)
1994	Michael Moorer (WBA/IBF)
1994-95	Oliver McCall (WBC); *George Foreman* (WBA*/IBF*)
1995-96	Bruce Seldon (WBA); Frank Bruno (WBC)
1995	Frans Botha (IBF*)
1996	*Mike Tyson* (WBA/WBC*)
1996-97	Michael Moorer (IBF)
1996-99	*Evander Holyfield* (WBA/IBF)
1997-99	*Lennox Lewis* (WBC)
1999-2001	*Lennox Lewis* (WBA*/WBC/IBF)
2000-01	*Evander Holyfield* (WBA)
2001-03	John Ruiz (WBA)
2001	Hasim Rahman (WBC/IBF)
2001-02	*Lennox Lewis* (IBF*)
2001-04	*Lennox Lewis* (WBC)
2002-06	Chris Byrd (IBF)
2003	*Roy Jones Jr.* (WBA*)
2004-05	John Ruiz (WBA)[7]; *Vitali Klitschko* (WBC*)
2005-06	Hasim Rahman (WBC)
2005-07	Nicolai Valuev (WBA)
2006-15	*Wladimir Klitschko* (IBF)
2006-08	Oleg Maskaev (WBC)
2007-08	Ruslan Chagaev (WBA)
2008	Samuel Peter (WBC)
2008-09	Nikolai Valuev (WBA)
2008-13	*Vitali Klitschko* (WBC*)
2009-11	David Haye (WBA)
2011-15	*Wladimir Klitschko* (WBA)
2014-15	Bermane Stiverne (WBC)
2015-20	Deontay Wilder (WBC)
2015-16	Tyson Fury (WBA*)
2015	Tyson Fury (IBF*)
2016	Charles Martin (IBF)
2016-19	Anthony Joshua (IBF)
2017-19	Anthony Joshua (WBA)
2019	Andy Ruiz Jr. (WBA/IBF)
2019-21	Anthony Joshua (WBA/IBF)
2020-24	Tyson Fury (WBC)
2021-	Oleksandr Usyk (WBA/WBC/IBF)

(1) London Prize Ring (bare-knuckle champion). (2) First Marquis of Queensberry champion. (3) Jeffries vacated title (1905) and designated Marvin Hart and Jack Root as logical contenders. Hart def. Root in 12 rounds (1905); in turn was def. by Tommy Burns (1906), who claimed the title. Jack Johnson def. Burns (1908) and was recognized as champ. Johnson won the title by defeating Jeffries in the latter's attempted comeback (1910). (4) Title declared vacant by the WBA and others in 1967 after Ali refused military induction for religious reasons during the Vietnam War. Joe Frazier recognized as champ by six states, Mexico, and S. America. Jimmy Ellis won a tournament for the WBA title. (5) After Spinks def. Ali for the WBA title, the WBC recognized Ken Norton as champ. Ali def. Spinks in 1978 rematch for WBA title and retired in 1979. (6) Relinquished WBC title in Dec. 1983 to fight as champ of the new IBF. (7) James Toney def. Ruiz Apr. 30, 2005, to claim the title, but it was rescinded when Toney tested positive for steroids.

Light Heavyweights

1903-05 *Bob Fitzsimmons*
1905-12 *Philadelphia Jack O'Brien**
1912-16 *Jack Dillon*
1916-20 *Battling Levinsky*
1920-22 *Georges Carpentier*
1922-23 Battling Siki
1923-25 Mike McTigue
1925-26 *Paul Berlenbach*
1926-27 *Jack Delaney**
1927-29 *Tommy Loughran**
1930-34 *Maxie Rosenbloom*
1934-35 Bob Olin
1935-39 *John Henry Lewis**
1939 Melio Bettina
1939-41 *Billy Conn**
1941 Anton Christoforidis (NBA)
1941-48 Gus Lesnevich
1948-50 Freddie Mills
1950-52 *Joey Maxim*
1952-62 *Archie Moore*
1962-63 *Harold Johnson*
1963-65 *Willie Pastrano*
1965-66 *José Torres*
1966-68 *Dick Tiger*
1968-74 *Bob Foster**
1974-77 John Conteh (WBC*)
1974-78 *Victor Galindez* (WBA)
1977-78 Miguel Cuello (WBC)
1978 Mate Parlov (WBC)
1978-79 Mike Rossman (WBA); Marvin Johnson (WBC)
1979 *Victor Galindez* (WBA)
1979-81 *Matthew Saad Muhammad* (WBC)
1979-80 Marvin Johnson (WBA)
1980-81 Eddie Mustafa Muhammad (WBA)
1981-85 *Michael Spinks* (WBA)
1981-83 *Dwight Muhammad-Qawi Braxton* (WBC)
1983-85 *Michael Spinks* (WBC*)
1985-86 J. B. Williamson (WBC)
1986-87 Marvin Johnson (WBA); Dennis Andries (WBC)
1987 *Thomas Hearns* (WBC*)
1987 Leslie Stewart (WBA)
1987-91 *Virgil Hill* (WBA)
1987-88 Don Lalonde (WBC)
1988 *Sugar Ray Leonard* (WBC*)
1989 Dennis Andries (WBC)
1989-90 Jeff Harding (WBC)
1990-91 Dennis Andries (WBC)
1991-92 *Thomas Hearns* (WBA)
1991-94 Jeff Harding (WBC)
1992 Iran Barkley (WBA*)
1992-97 *Virgil Hill* (WBA)
1994-95 *Mike McCallum* (WBC)
1995-96 Fabrice Tiozzo (WBC*)
1996-97 *Roy Jones Jr.* (WBC)
1997 Montell Griffin (WBC); Dariusz Michalczewski (WBA*); *Roy Jones Jr.* (WBC)
1997-98 Lou Del Valle (WBA)
1998-2003 *Roy Jones Jr.* (WBA*/WBC*)
2003 Mehdi Sahnoune (WBA); Silvio Branco (WBA); Antonio Tarver (WBC)
2003-04 *Roy Jones Jr.* (WBA/WBC*)
2004 Antonio Tarver (WBA/WBC*)
2004-06 Fabrice Tiozzo (WBA)
2005-07 Tomasz Adamek (WBC)
2006-07 Silvio Branco (WBA)
2007-08 Chad Dawson (WBC*)
2007 Stipe Drews (WBA); Danny Green (WBA)
2008-09 Hugo Hernan Garay (WBA); Adrian Diaconu (WBC)
2009-11 Jean Pascal (WBC)
2009-10 Gabriel Campillo (WBA)
2010-14 Beibut Shumenov (WBA)
2011-12 *Bernard Hopkins* (WBC)
2012-13 Chad Dawson (WBC)
2013-18 Adonis Stevenson (WBC)
2014 *Bernard Hopkins* (WBA)
2014-16 Sergey Kovalev (WBA)
2016-17 *Andre Ward* (WBA)
2017- Dmitry Bivol (WBA)
2018-19 Oleksandr Gvozdyk (WBC)
2019- Artur Beterbiev (WBC)

Middleweights

1884-91 *Jack "Nonpareil" Dempsey*
1891-97 *Bob Fitzsimmons**
1897-1907 *Tommy Ryan**
1907-08 *Stanley Ketchel*; *Billy Papke*
1908-10 *Stanley Ketchel*
1911-13 Vacant
1913 Frank Klaus; George Chip
1914-17 Al McCoy
1917-20 *Mike O'Dowd*
1920-23 Johnny Wilson
1923-26 *Harry Greb*
1926 *Theodore "Tiger" Flowers*
1926-31 *Mickey Walker**
1931-32 *William "Gorilla" Jones* (NBA)
1932-37 *Marcel Thil*
1938 Al Hostak (NBA); Solly Krieger (NBA)
1939-40 Al Hostak (NBA)
1940-47 *Tony Zale*
1947-48 *Rocky Graziano*
1948 *Tony Zale*; *Marcel Cerdan*
1949-51 *Jake LaMotta*
1951 *"Sugar" Ray Robinson*; *Randy Turpin*
1951-52 *"Sugar" Ray Robinson**
1953-55 *Carl "Bobo" Olson*
1955-57 *"Sugar" Ray Robinson*
1957 *Gene Fullmer*; *"Sugar" Ray Robinson*
1957-58 *Carmen Basilio*
1958 *"Sugar" Ray Robinson*
1959 *Gene Fullmer* (NBA); *"Sugar" Ray Robinson* (NY)
1960 *Gene Fullmer* (NBA); Paul Pender (NY/MA)
1961 *Gene Fullmer* (NBA); Terry Downes (NY/MA/Europe)
1962 *Gene Fullmer*; Paul Pender (NY/MA*); *Dick Tiger* (NBA)
1963 *Dick Tiger* (universal)
1963-65 *Joey Giardello*
1965-66 *Dick Tiger*
1966-67 *Emile Griffith*
1967 *Nino Benvenuti*
1967-68 *Emile Griffith*
1968-70 *Nino Benvenuti*
1970-77 *Carlos Monzon**
1977-78 Rodrigo Valdez
1978-79 Hugo Corro
1979-80 Vito Antuofermo
1980 Alan Minter
1980-87 *"Marvelous" Marvin Hagler*
1987 *Sugar Ray Leonard* (WBC*)
1987-89 Sumbu Kalambay (WBA)
1987-88 *Thomas Hearns* (WBC)
1988-89 Iran Barkley (WBC)
1989-90 *Roberto Duran* (WBC*)
1989-91 *Mike McCallum* (WBA*)
1990-93 *Julian Jackson* (WBC)
1992-93 Reggie Johnson (WBA)
1993-95 Gerald McClellan (WBC*)
1993-94 John David Jackson (WBA*)
1994-95 Jorge Castro (WBA)
1995 *Julian Jackson* (WBC)
1995-96 Quincy Taylor (WBC); Shinji Takehara (WBA)
1996-98 Keith Holmes (WBC)
1996-97 William Joppy (WBA)
1997 Julio Cesar Green (WBA)
1998-2001 William Joppy (WBA)
1998-99 Hacine Cherifi (WBC)
1999-2001 Keith Holmes (WBC)
2001 *Felix Trinidad* (WBA)
2001-05 *Bernard Hopkins* (WBC/WBA)
2005-06 Jermain Taylor (WBA)
2005-07 Jermain Taylor (WBC)
2006-07 Javier Castillejo (WBA)[1]
2007-12 Felix Sturm (WBA)
2007-10 Kelly Pavlik (WBC)
2009-11 Sebastian Zbik (WBC)
2010 Sergio Martinez (WBC)
2011-12 Julio Cesar Chavez Jr. (WBC)
2012 Daniel Geale (WBA*)
2012-14 Sergio Martinez (WBC)
2012-18 Gennady Golovkin (WBA)
2014-15 *Miguel Cotto* (WBC)
2015-16 Canelo Álvarez (WBC*)
2016-18 Gennady Golovkin (WBC)
2018-19 Canelo Álvarez (WBA/WBC[2])
2019-21 Canelo Álvarez (WBA)
2019-24 Jermall Charlo (WBC[3])
2021-22 Ryōta Murata (WBA)
2022-23 Gennady Golovkin (WBA)
2023- Erislandy Lara (WBA)
2024 Carlos Adames (WBC)

(1) Castillejo lost title to Mariano Carrera Dec. 2, 2006, but regained it Feb. 23, 2007, after Carrera tested positive for steroids. (2) Canelo Álvarez was reclassified in 2019 as WBC Franchise Champion. (3) WBC stripped Jermall Charlo of WBC title in 2024 after drunk driving accident.

Title-Changing Heavyweight Championship Bouts, 1889-2024

1889: July 8, John L. Sullivan def. Jake Kilrain, 75, Richburg, MS.
1892: Sept. 7, James J. Corbett def. John L. Sullivan, 21, New Orleans.
1897: Mar. 17, Bob Fitzsimmons def. James J. Corbett, 14, Carson City, NV.
1899: June 9, James J. Jeffries def. Bob Fitzsimmons, 11, Coney Island, NY. (Jeffries retired as champion in 1905.)
1905: July 3, Marvin Hart KOd Jack Root, 12, Reno, NV. (James J. Jeffries refereed, gave title to Hart. Jack O'Brien also claimed the title.)
1906: Feb. 23, Tommy Burns def. Marvin Hart, 20, Los Angeles.
1908: Dec. 26, Jack Johnson def. Tommy Burns, 14, Sydney, Australia. (Police halted contest.)
1915: Apr. 5, Jess Willard KOd Jack Johnson, 26, Havana, Cuba.
1919: July 4, Jack Dempsey KOd Jess Willard, Toledo, OH. (Willard failed to answer bell for 4th round.)
1926: Sept. 23, Gene Tunney def. Jack Dempsey, 10, Philadelphia. (Tunney retired as champion in 1928.)
1930: June 12, Max Schmeling def. Jack Sharkey on a foul, 4, New York City. (Resulted in the election of a successor to Gene Tunney.)
1932: June 21, Jack Sharkey def. Max Schmeling, 15, NYC.
1933: June 29, Primo Carnera KOd Jack Sharkey, 6, NYC.
1934: June 14, Max Baer KOd Primo Carnera, 11, NYC.
1935: June 13, James J. Braddock def. Max Baer, 15, NYC.
1937: June 22, Joe Louis KOd James J. Braddock, 8, Chicago. (Louis retired as champion in 1949.)
1949: June 22, Ezzard Charles def. Joe Walcott, 15, Chicago; NBA recognition only.
1951: July 18, Joe Walcott KOd Ezzard Charles, 7, Pittsburgh.
1952: Sept. 23, Rocky Marciano KOd Joe Walcott, 13, Philadelphia. (Marciano retired as champion in 1956.)
1956: Nov. 30, Floyd Patterson KOd Archie Moore, 5, Chicago.
1959: June 26, Ingemar Johansson KOd Floyd Patterson, 3, NYC.
1960: June 20, Floyd Patterson KOd Ingemar Johansson, 5, NYC.
1962: Sept. 25, Sonny Liston KOd Floyd Patterson, 1, Chicago.
1964: Feb. 25, Cassius Clay (Muhammad Ali) KOd Sonny Liston, 7, Miami Beach, FL. (Liston failed to answer bell for 7th round. In 1967, Ali was stripped of title for refusing military service.)
1970: Feb. 16, Joe Frazier KOd Jimmy Ellis, 5, NYC. (Frazier def. Ali, 15, NYC, on Mar. 8, 1971, in "Fight of the Century.")
1973: Jan. 22, George Foreman KOd Joe Frazier, 2, Kingston, Jamaica.
1974: Oct. 30, Muhammad Ali KOd George Foreman, 8, Kinshasa, Zaire (billed as the "Rumble in the Jungle").
1978: Feb. 15, Leon Spinks def. Muhammad Ali, 15, Las Vegas (WBC recognized Ken Norton as champion after Spinks refused to fight him before his rematch with Ali); June 9, (WBC) Larry Holmes def. Ken Norton, 15, Las Vegas; Sept. 15, (WBA) Muhammad Ali def. Leon Spinks, 15, New Orleans. (Ali retired as champion in 1979.)
1979: Oct. 20, (WBA) John Tate def. Gerrie Coetzee, 15, Pretoria, South Africa.
1980: Mar. 31, (WBA) Mike Weaver KOd John Tate, 15, Knoxville, TN.
1982: Dec. 10, (WBA) Michael Dokes KOd Mike Weaver, 1, Las Vegas.
1983: Sept. 23, (WBA) Gerrie Coetzee KOd Michael Dokes, 10, Richfield, OH; in Dec., Larry Holmes relinquished the WBC title and was named champion of the newly formed IBF.
1984: Mar. 9, (WBC) Tim Witherspoon def. Greg Page, 12, Las Vegas; Aug. 31, (WBC) Pinklon Thomas def. Tim Witherspoon, 12, Las Vegas; Dec. 1, (WBA) Greg Page KOd Gerrie Coetzee, 8, Sun City, Bophuthatswana, South Africa.
1985: Apr. 29, (WBA) Tony Tubbs def. Greg Page, 15, Buffalo, NY; Sept. 21, (IBF) Michael Spinks def. Larry Holmes, 15, Las Vegas. (Spinks relinquished title in Feb. 1987.)
1986: Jan. 17, (WBA) Tim Witherspoon def. Tony Tubbs, 15, Atlanta; Mar. 22, (WBC) Trevor Berbick def. Pinklon Thomas, 12, Las Vegas; Nov. 22, (WBC) Mike Tyson KOd Trevor Berbick, 2, Las Vegas; Dec. 12, (WBA) James "Bonecrusher" Smith KOd Tim Witherspoon, 1, NYC.
1987: Mar. 7, (WBA) Mike Tyson def. James "Bonecrusher" Smith, 12, Las Vegas; May 30, (IBF) Tony Tucker KOd James "Buster" Douglas, 10, Las Vegas; Aug. 1, (IBF) Mike Tyson def. Tony Tucker, 12, Las Vegas. (Tyson became undisputed champion.)
1990: Feb. 11, (WBA/WBC/IBF) James "Buster" Douglas KOd Mike Tyson, 10, Tokyo, Japan; Oct. 25, (WBA/WBC/IBF) Evander Holyfield KOd James "Buster" Douglas, 3, Las Vegas.
1992: Nov. 13, (WBA/WBC/IBF) Riddick Bowe def. Evander Holyfield, 12, Las Vegas; in Dec., Lennox Lewis was named WBC champion after Bowe relinquished the WBC title rather than fight Lewis.
1993: Nov. 6, (WBA/IBF) Evander Holyfield def. Riddick Bowe, 12, Las Vegas.
1994: Apr. 22, (WBA/IBF) Michael Moorer def. Evander Holyfield, 12, Las Vegas; Sept. 24, (WBC) Oliver McCall KOd Lennox Lewis, 2, London, Eng.; Nov. 5, (WBA/IBF) George Foreman KOd Michael Moorer, 10, Las Vegas.
1995: In Mar., George Foreman was stripped of his WBA title for refusing to fight challenger Tony Tucker; in June, Foreman relinquished his IBF title rather than submit to a rematch with Axel Schulz; Apr. 8, (WBA) Bruce Seldon TKOd Tony Tucker, 7, Las Vegas; Sept. 2, (WBC) Frank Bruno def. Oliver McCall, 12, London, Eng.; Dec. 9, (IBF) Frans Botha def. Axel Schulz, 12, Stuttgart, Germany (Botha was subsequently stripped of title after testing positive for a steroid).
1996: Mar. 16, (WBC) Mike Tyson KOd Frank Bruno, 3, Las Vegas; June 22, (IBF) Michael Moorer def. Axel Schulz, 12, Dortmund, Germany; Sept. 7, (WBA) Mike Tyson KOd Bruce Seldon, 1, Las Vegas (Tyson was subsequently stripped of WBC title after refusing to fight Lennox Lewis); Nov. 9, (WBA) Evander Holyfield KOd Mike Tyson, 11, Las Vegas.
1997: Feb. 7, (WBC) Lennox Lewis TKOd Oliver McCall, 5, Las Vegas; Nov. 8, (IBF) Evander Holyfield def. Michael Moorer, 8, Las Vegas.
1999: Nov. 13, (IBF) Lennox Lewis def. Evander Holyfield, 12, Las Vegas. (Lewis became undisputed champion.)
2000: In Apr., Lennox Lewis was stripped of his WBA title after refusing to fight challenger John Ruiz; Aug. 12, (WBA) Evander Holyfield def. John Ruiz, 12, Las Vegas.
2001: Mar. 3, (WBA) John Ruiz def. Evander Holyfield, 12, Las Vegas; Apr. 22, (WBC/IBF) Hasim Rahman KOd Lennox Lewis, 5, Brakpan, South Africa; Nov. 17, (WBC/IBF) Lennox Lewis KOd Hasim Rahman, 4, Las Vegas.
2002: In Sept., Lennox Lewis relinquished his IBF title; Dec. 14, (IBF) Chris Byrd def. Evander Holyfield, 12, Atlantic City, NJ.
2003: Mar. 1, (WBA) Roy Jones Jr. def. John Ruiz, 12, Las Vegas.
2004: Feb. 20, (WBA) John Ruiz gained title when Roy Jones Jr. relinquished it; Apr. 24, (WBC) Vitali Klitschko TKOd Corrie Sanders, 8, Los Angeles, to win title vacated by retirement of Lennox Lewis in Feb.
2005: Apr. 30, (WBA) James Toney def. John Ruiz, 12, NYC (title was returned to Ruiz after Toney tested positive for steroids); Nov. 9, (WBC) Hasim Rahman gained title when Vitali Klitschko retired due to an injury; Dec. 17, (WBA) Nikolai Valuev def. John Ruiz, 12, Berlin, Germany.
2006: Apr. 22, (IBF) Wladimir Klitschko TKOd Chris Byrd, 7, Mannheim, Germany; Aug. 12, (WBC) Oleg Maskaev TKOd Hasim Rahman, 12, Las Vegas.
2007: Apr. 14, (WBA) Ruslan Chagaev def. Nikolai Valuev, 12, Stuttgart, Germany. (An injured Chagaev was named champion in recess, July 2008.)
2008: Mar. 8, (WBC) Samuel Peter TKOd Oleg Maskaev, 6, Cancún, Mexico; Aug. 30, (WBA) Nikolai Valuev def. John Ruiz, 12, Berlin, Germany; Oct. 11, (WBC) Vitali Klitschko TKOd Samuel Peter, 8, Berlin, Germany.
2009: Nov. 7, (WBA) David Haye def. Nikolai Valuev, 12, Nuremberg, Germany.
2011: July 2, (WBA) Wladimir Klitschko def. David Haye, 12, Hamburg, Germany.
2014: May 10, (WBC) Bermane Stiverne TKOd Chris Arreola, 6, Los Angeles, to win title vacated in Dec. 2013.
2015: Jan. 17, (WBC) Deontay Wilder def. Bermane Stiverne, 12, Las Vegas; Nov. 28 (WBA/IBF) Tyson Fury def. Wladimir Klitschko, 12, Dusseldorf, Germany; in Dec., Fury was stripped of IBF title for refusing to fight mandatory challenger Vyacheslav Glazkov. (Fury relinquished WBA title Oct. 2016.)
2016: Jan. 16, (IBF) Charles Martin TKOd Vyacheslav Glazkov, 3, Brooklyn, NY; Apr. 9, (IBF) Anthony Joshua KOd Charles Martin, 2, London, Eng., UK.
2017: Apr. 29, (WBA) Anthony Joshua TKOd Wladimir Klitschko, 11, London, Eng., UK.
2019: June 1, (WBA/IBF) Andy Ruiz Jr. TKOd Anthony Joshua, 7, NYC; Dec. 7, (WBA/IBF) Anthony Joshua def. Andy Ruiz Jr., 12, Diriyah, Saudi Arabia.
2020: Feb. 22, (WBC) Tyson Fury TKOd Deontay Wilder, 7, Las Vegas.
2021: Sept. 25, (WBA/WBO/IBF) Oleksandr Usyk def. Anthony Joshua, 12, London, Eng., UK.
2024: May 18, (WBC) Oleksandr Usyk def. Tyson Fury, 12, Riyadh, Saudi Arabia. Usyk became undisputed champion.

THOROUGHBRED RACING

Triple Crown Winners

The Kentucky Derby, Preakness Stakes, and Belmont Stakes make up the Triple Crown. Since 1920, colts have carried 126 lbs in Triple Crown events; fillies, 121 lbs.

Year	Horse	Jockey	Trainer
1919	Sir Barton	J. Loftus	H. G. Bedwell
1930	Gallant Fox	E. Sande	J. Fitzsimmons
1935	Omaha	W. Sanders	J. Fitzsimmons
1937	War Admiral	C. Kurtsinger	G. Conway
1941	Whirlaway	E. Arcaro	B. A. Jones
1943	Count Fleet	J. Longden	G. D. Cameron
1946	Assault	W. Mehrtens	M. Hirsch
1948	Citation	E. Arcaro	H. A. Jones
1973	Secretariat	R. Turcotte	L. Laurin
1977	Seattle Slew	J. Cruguet	W. H. Turner Jr.
1978	Affirmed	S. Cauthen	L. S. Barrera
2015	American Pharoah	V. Espinoza	B. Baffert
2018	Justify	M. Smith	B. Baffert

Kentucky Derby Winners, 1875-2024

Churchill Downs, Louisville, KY. Distance: 1¼ mi; 1½ mi until 1896. 3-year-olds. Best time: 1:59-2/5, Secretariat (1973); 2024 time: 2:03.34. (Until 2001, times were measured in fifths of a second.)

Year	Horse	Jockey
1875	Aristides	O. Lewis
1876	Vagrant	R. Swim
1877	Baden Baden	W. Walker
1878	Day Star	J. Carter
1879	Lord Murphy	C. Schauer
1880	Fonso	G. Lewis
1881	Hindoo	J. McLaughlin
1882	Apollo	B. Hurd
1883	Leonatus	W. Donohue
1884	Buchanan	I. Murphy
1885	Joe Cotton	E. Henderson
1886	Ben Ali	P. Duffy
1887	Montrose	I. Lewis
1888	Macbeth II	G. Covington
1889	Spokane	T. Kiley
1890	Riley	I. Murphy
1891	Kingman	I. Murphy
1892	Azra	A. Clayton
1893	Lookout	E. Kunze
1894	Chant	F. Goodale
1895	Halma	J. Perkins
1896	Ben Brush	W. Simms
1897	Typhoon II	F. Garner
1898	Plaudit	W. Simms
1899	Manuel	F. Taral
1900	Lieut. Gibson	J. Boland
1901	His Eminence	J. Winkfield
1902	Alan-a-Dale	J. Winkfield
1903	Judge Himes	H. Booker
1904	Elwood	F. Prior
1905	Agile	J. Martin
1906	Sir Huon	R. Troxler
1907	Pink Star	A. Minder
1908	Stone Street	A. Pickens
1909	Wintergreen	V. Powers
1910	Donau	F. Herbert
1911	Meridian	G. Archibald
1912	Worth	C. Shilling
1913	Donerail	R. Goose
1914	Old Rosebud	J. McCabe
1915	Regret[1]	J. Notter
1916	George Smith	J. Loftus
1917	Omar Khayyam	C. Borel
1918	Exterminator	W. Knapp
1919	Sir Barton	J. Loftus
1920	Paul Jones	T. Rice
1921	Behave Yourself	C. Thompson
1922	Morvich	A. Johnson
1923	Zev	E. Sande
1924	Black Gold	J. D. Mooney
1925	Flying Ebony	E. Sande
1926	Bubbling Over	A. Johnson
1927	Whiskery	L. McAtee
1928	Reigh Count	C. Lang
1929	Clyde Van Dusen	L. McAtee
1930	Gallant Fox	E. Sande
1931	Twenty Grand	C. Kurtsinger
1932	Burgoo King	E. James
1933	Brokers Tip	D. Meade
1934	Cavalcade	M. Garner
1935	Omaha	W. Saunders
1936	Bold Venture	I. Hanford
1937	War Admiral	C. Kurtsinger
1938	Lawrin	E. Arcaro
1939	Johnstown	J. Stout
1940	Gallahadion	C. Bierman
1941	Whirlaway	E. Arcaro
1942	Shut Out	W. Wright
1943	Count Fleet	J. Longden
1944	Pensive	C. McCreary
1945	Hoop Jr.	E. Arcaro
1946	Assault	W. Mehrtens
1947	Jet Pilot	E. Guerin
1948	Citation	E. Arcaro
1949	Ponder	S. Brooks
1950	Middleground	W. Boland
1951	Count Turf	C. McCreary
1952	Hill Gail	E. Arcaro
1953	Dark Star	H. Moreno
1954	Determine	R. York
1955	Swaps	W. Shoemaker
1956	Needles	D. Erb
1957	Iron Liege	W. Hartack
1958	Tim Tam	I. Valenzuela
1959	Tomy Lee	W. Shoemaker
1960	Venetian Way	W. Hartack
1961	Carry Back	J. Sellers
1962	Decidedly	W. Hartack
1963	Chateaugay	B. Baeza
1964	Northern Dancer	W. Hartack
1965	Lucky Debonair	W. Shoemaker
1966	Kauai King	D. Brumfield
1967	Proud Clarion	R. Ussery
1968	Forward Pass[2]	I. Valenzuela
1969	Majestic Prince	W. Hartack
1970	Dust Commander	M. Manganello
1971	Canonero II	G. Avila
1972	Riva Ridge	R. Turcotte
1973	Secretariat	R. Turcotte
1974	Cannonade	A. Cordero
1975	Foolish Pleasure	J. Vasquez
1976	Bold Forbes	A. Cordero
1977	Seattle Slew	J. Cruguet
1978	Affirmed	S. Cauthen
1979	Spectacular Bid	R. Franklin
1980	Genuine Risk[1]	J. Vasquez
1981	Pleasant Colony	J. Velasquez
1982	Gato Del Sol	E. Delahoussaye
1983	Sunny's Halo	E. Delahoussaye
1984	Swale	L. Pincay
1985	Spend a Buck	A. Cordero
1986	Ferdinand	W. Shoemaker
1987	Alysheba	C. McCarron
1988	Winning Colors[1]	G. Stevens
1989	Sunday Silence	P. Valenzuela
1990	Unbridled	C. Perret
1991	Strike the Gold	C. Antley
1992	Lil E. Tee	P. Day
1993	Sea Hero	J. Bailey
1994	Go for Gin	C. McCarron
1995	Thunder Gulch	G. Stevens
1996	Grindstone	J. Bailey
1997	Silver Charm	G. Stevens
1998	Real Quiet	K. Desormeaux
1999	Charismatic	C. Antley
2000	Fusaichi Pegasus	K. Desormeaux
2001	Monarchos	J. Chavez
2002	War Emblem	V. Espinoza
2003	Funny Cide	J. Santos
2004	Smarty Jones	S. Elliot
2005	Giacomo	M. Smith
2006	Barbaro	E. Prado
2007	Street Sense	C. Borel
2008	Big Brown	K. Desormeaux
2009	Mine That Bird	C. Borel
2010	Super Saver	C. Borel
2011	Animal Kingdom	J. Velazquez
2012	I'll Have Another	M. Gutierrez
2013	Orb	J. Rosario
2014	California Chrome	V. Espinoza
2015	American Pharoah	V. Espinoza
2016	Nyquist	M. Gutierrez
2017	Always Dreaming	J. Velazquez
2018	Justify	M. Smith
2019	Country House[3]	F. Prat
2020	Authentic	J. Velazquez
2021	Mandaloun[4]	F. Geroux
2022	Rich Strike	S. Leon
2023	Mage	J. Castellano
2024	Mystik Dan	B. Hernandez Jr.

Note: Two jockeys have won the Kentucky Derby five times: Eddie Arcaro and Bill Hartack. Willie Shoemaker won four times. (1) Regret, Genuine Risk, and Winning Colors are the only fillies to have won the Derby. (2) Dancer's Image came in first but was disqualified by a drug test. All wagers were paid on Dancer's Image, but Forward Pass was awarded the first-place money. (3) Maximum Security came in first but was disqualified for interference following the race. (4) Medina Spirit came in first but was disqualified due to a positive post-race test for a banned substance; wagers were paid on Medina Spirit, but Mandaloun was awarded the first-place money.

Fastest Winning Times for the Kentucky Derby

Until 2001, Kentucky Derby times were measured in fifths of a second.

Time	Horse	Jockey	Year
1 min., 59-2/5 s.	Secretariat	Ron Turcotte	1973
1 min., 59.97 s.	Monarchos	Jorge Chavez	2001
2 min.	Northern Dancer	Bill Hartack	1964
2 min., 1/5 s.	Spend a Buck	Angel Cordero Jr.	1985
2 min., 2/5 s.	Decidedly	Bill Hartack	1962
2 min., 3/5 s.	Proud Clarion	Robert Ussery	1967
2 min., 0.61 s.	Authentic	John Velazquez	2020
2 min., 1 s.	Fusaichi Pegasus	Kent Desormeaux	2000
	Grindstone	Jerry Bailey	1996
2 min., 1.10 s.	Mandaloun	Florent Geroux	2021
2 min., 1.13 s.	War Emblem	Victor Espinoza	2002
2 min., 1.19 s.	Funny Cide	Jose Santos	2003
2 min., 1-1/5 s.	Thunder Gulch	Gary Stevens	1995
	Affirmed	Steve Cauthen	1978
	Lucky Debonair	Bill Shoemaker	1965
2 min., 1.31 s.	Nyquist	Mario Gutierrez	2016
2 min., 1-2/5 s.	Barbaro	Edgar Prado	2006
	Whirlaway	Eddie Arcaro	1941

Preakness Stakes Winners, 1873-2024

Pimlico Race Course, Baltimore, MD. Distance: 1-3/16 mi. 3-year-olds. * = Horses ran in two divisions. Best time: 1:53, Secretariat (1973); 2024 time: 1:56.82.

Year	Horse	Jockey
1873	Survivor	G. Barbee
1874	Culpepper	M. Donohue
1875	Tom Ochiltree	L. Hughes
1876	Shirley	G. Barbee
1877	Cloverbrook	C. Holloway
1878	Duke of Magenta	C. Holloway
1879	Harold	L. Hughes
1880	Grenada	L. Hughes
1881	Saunterer	W. Costello
1882	Vanguard	W. Costello
1883	Jacobus	G. Barbee
1884	Knight of Ellerslie	S. Fisher
1885	Tecumseh	J. McLaughlin
1886	The Bard	S. Fisher
1887	Dunboyne	W. Donohue
1888	Refund	F. Littlefield
1889	Buddhist	G. Anderson
1890	Montague	W. Martin
1894	Assignee	F. Taral
1895	Belmar	F. Taral
1896	Margrave	H. Griffin
1897	Paul Kauvar	C. Thorpe
1898	Sly Fox	W. Simms
1899	Half Time	R. Clawson
1900	Hindus	H. Spencer
1901	The Parader	F. Landry
1902	Old England	L. Jackson
1903	Flocarline	W. Gannon
1904	Bryn Mawr	E. Hildebrand
1905	Cairngorm	W. Davis
1906	Whimsical	W. Miller
1907	Don Enrique	G. Mountain
1908	Royal Tourist	E. Dugan
1909	Effendi	W. Doyle
1910	Layminster	R. Estep
1911	Watervale	E. Dugan
1912	Colonel Holloway	C. Turner
1913	Buskin	J. Butwell
1914	Holiday	A. Schuttinger
1915	Rhine Maiden	D. Hoffman
1916	Damrosch	L. McAtee
1917	Kalitan	E. Haynes
1918*	War Cloud	J. Loftus
	Jack Hare Jr.	C. Peak
1919	Sir Barton	J. Loftus
1920	Man o' War	C. Kummer
1921	Broomspun	F. Coltiletti
1922	Pillory	L. Morris
1923	Vigil	B. Marinelli
1924	Nellie Morse	J. Merimee
1925	Coventry	C. Kummer
1926	Display	J. Malben
1927	Bostonian	A. Abel
1928	Victorian	R. Workman
1929	Dr. Freeland	L. Schaefer
1930	Gallant Fox	E. Sande
1931	Mate	G. Ellis
1932	Burgoo King	E. James
1933	Head Play	C. Kurtsinger
1934	High Quest	R. Jones
1935	Omaha	W. Saunders
1936	Bold Venture	G. Woolf
1937	War Admiral	C. Kurtsinger
1938	Dauber	M. Peters
1939	Challedon	G. Seabo
1940	Bimelech	F. A. Smith
1941	Whirlaway	E. Arcaro
1942	Alsab	B. James
1943	Count Fleet	J. Longden
1944	Pensive	C. McCreary
1945	Polynesian	W. D. Wright
1946	Assault	W. Mehrtens
1947	Faultless	D. Dodson
1948	Citation	E. Arcaro
1949	Capot	T. Atkinson
1950	Hill Prince	E. Arcaro
1951	Bold	E. Arcaro
1952	Blue Man	C. McCreary
1953	Native Dancer	E. Guerin
1954	Hasty Road	J. Adams
1955	Nashua	E. Arcaro
1956	Fabius	W. Hartack
1957	Bold Ruler	E. Arcaro
1958	Tim Tam	I. Valenzuela
1959	Royal Orbit	W. Harmatz
1960	Bally Ache	R. Ussery
1961	Carry Back	J. Sellers
1962	Greek Money	J. L. Rotz
1963	Candy Spots	W. Shoemaker
1964	Northern Dancer	W. Hartack
1965	Tom Rolfe	R. Turcotte
1966	Kauai King	D. Brumfield
1967	Damascus	W. Shoemaker
1968	Forward Pass	I. Valenzuela
1969	Majestic Prince	W. Hartack
1970	Personality	E. Belmonte
1971	Canonero II	G. Avila
1972	Bee Bee Bee	E. Nelson
1973	Secretariat	R. Turcotte
1974	Little Current	M. Rivera
1975	Master Derby	D. McHargue
1976	Elocutionist	J. Lively
1977	Seattle Slew	J. Cruguet
1978	Affirmed	S. Cauthen
1979	Spectacular Bid	R. Franklin
1980	Codex	A. Cordero
1981	Pleasant Colony	J. Velasquez
1982	Aloma's Ruler	J. Kaenel
1983	Deputed Testamony	D. Miller
1984	Gate Dancer	A. Cordero
1985	Tank's Prospect	P. Day
1986	Snow Chief	A. Solis
1987	Alysheba	C. McCarron
1988	Risen Star	E. Delahoussaye
1989	Sunday Silence	P. Valenzuela
1990	Summer Squall	P. Day
1991	Hansel	J. Bailey
1992	Pine Bluff	C. McCarron
1993	Prairie Bayou	M. Smith
1994	Tabasco Cat	P. Day
1995	Timber Country	P. Day
1996	Louis Quatorze	P. Day
1997	Silver Charm	G. Stevens
1998	Real Quiet	K. Desormeaux
1999	Charismatic	C. Antley
2000	Red Bullet	J. Bailey
2001	Point Given	G. Stevens
2002	War Emblem	V. Espinoza
2003	Funny Cide	J. Santos
2004	Smarty Jones	S. Elliot
2005	Afleet Alex	J. Rose
2006	Bernardini	J. Castellano
2007	Curlin	R. Albarado
2008	Big Brown	K. Desormeaux
2009	Rachel Alexandra	C. Borel
2010	Lookin At Lucky	M. Garcia
2011	Shackleford	J. Castanon
2012	I'll Have Another	M. Gutierrez
2013	Oxbow	G. Stevens
2014	California Chrome	V. Espinoza
2015	American Pharoah	V. Espinoza
2016	Exaggerator	K. Desormeaux
2017	Cloud Computing	J. Castellano
2018	Justify	M. Smith
2019	War of Will	T. Gaffalione
2020	Swiss Skydiver	R. Albarado
2021	Rombauer	F. Prat
2022	Early Voting	J. Ortiz
2023	National Treasure	J. Velazquez
2024	Seize the Grey	J. Torres

Belmont Stakes Winners, 1867-2024

Belmont Park, Elmont, NY. Distance: 1½ mi (2020, 1⅛ mi; 2024, 1¼ mi). 3-year-olds. Best time: 2:24, Secretariat (1973); 2024 time: 2:01.64.

Year	Horse	Jockey
1867	Ruthless	J. Gilpatrick
1868	General Duke	R. Swim
1869	Fenian	C. Miller
1870	Kingfisher	W. Dick
1871	Harry Bassett	W. Miller
1872	Joe Daniels	J. Rowe
1873	Springbok	J. Rowe
1874	Saxon	G. Barbee
1875	Calvin	R. Swim
1876	Algerine	W. Donohue
1877	Cloverbrook	C. Holloway
1878	Duke of Magenta	L. Hughes
1879	Spendthrift	S. Evans
1880	Grenada	L. Hughes
1881	Saunterer	T. Costello
1882	Forester	J. McLaughlin
1883	George Kinney	J. McLaughlin
1884	Panique	J. McLaughlin
1885	Tyrant	P. Duffy
1886	Inspector B	J. McLaughlin
1887	Hanover	J. McLaughlin
1888	Sir Dixon	J. McLaughlin
1889	Eric	W. Hayward
1890	Burlington	S. Barnes
1891	Foxford	E. Garrison
1892	Patron	W. Hayward
1893	Comanche	W. Simms
1894	Henry of Navarre	W. Simms
1895	Belmar	F. Taral
1896	Hastings	H. Griffin
1897	Scottish Chieftain	J. Scherrer
1898	Bowling Brook	F. Littlefield
1899	Jean Bereaud	R. R. Clawson
1900	Ildrim	N. Turner
1901	Commando	H. Spencer
1902	Masterman	J. Bullman
1903	Africander	J. Bullman
1904	Delhi	G. Odom
1905	Tanya	E. Hildebrand
1906	Burgomaster	L. Lyne
1907	Peter Pan	G. Mountain
1908	Colin	J. Notter
1909	Joe Madden	E. Dugan
1910	Sweep	J. Butwell
1913	Prince Eugene	R. Troxler
1914	Luke McLuke	M. Buxton
1915	The Finn	G. Byrne
1916	Friar Rock	E. Haynes
1917	Hourless	J. Butwell
1918	Johren	F. Robinson
1919	Sir Barton	J. Loftus
1920	Man o' War	C. Kummer
1921	Grey Lag	E. Sande
1922	Pillory	C. H. Miller
1923	Zev	E. Sande
1924	Mad Play	E. Sande
1925	American Flag	A. Johnson
1926	Crusader	A. Johnson
1927	Chance Shot	E. Sande
1928	Vito	C. Kummer
1929	Blue Larkspur	M. Garner
1930	Gallant Fox	E. Sande
1931	Twenty Grand	C. Kurtsinger
1932	Faireno	T. Malley
1933	Hurryoff	M. Garner
1934	Peace Chance	W. D. Wright
1935	Omaha	W. Saunders
1936	Granville	J. Stout
1937	War Admiral	C. Kurtsinger
1938	Pasteurized	J. Stout
1939	Johnstown	J. Stout
1940	Bimelech	F. A. Smith
1941	Whirlaway	E. Arcaro
1942	Shut Out	E. Arcaro
1943	Count Fleet	J. Longden
1944	Bounding Home	G. L. Smith
1945	Pavot	E. Arcaro
1946	Assault	W. Mehrtens
1947	Phalanx	R. Donoso
1948	Citation	E. Arcaro
1949	Capot	T. Atkinson
1950	Middleground	W. Boland
1951	Counterpoint	D. Gorman
1952	One Count	E. Arcaro
1953	Native Dancer	E. Guerin
1954	High Gun	E. Guerin
1955	Nashua	E. Arcaro
1956	Needles	D. Erb
1957	Gallant Man	W. Shoemaker
1958	Cavan	P. Anderson
1959	Sword Dancer	W. Shoemaker
1960	Celtic Ash	W. Hartack
1961	Sherluck	B. Baeza
1962	Jaipur	W. Shoemaker
1963	Chateaugay	B. Baeza
1964	Quadrangle	M. Ycaza

Year	Horse	Jockey
1965	Hail to All	J. Sellers
1966	Amberoid	W. Boland
1967	Damascus	W. Shoemaker
1968	Stage Door Johnny	H. Gustines
1969	Arts and Letters	B. Baeza
1970	High Echelon	J. L. Rotz
1971	Pass Catcher	W. Blum
1972	Riva Ridge	R. Turcotte
1973	Secretariat	R. Turcotte
1974	Little Current	M. Rivera
1975	Avatar	W. Shoemaker
1976	Bold Forbes	A. Cordero
1977	Seattle Slew	J. Cruguet
1978	Affirmed	S. Cauthen
1979	Coastal	R. Hernandez
1980	Temperence Hill	E. Maple
1981	Summing	G. Martens
1982	Conquistador Cielo	L. Pincay
1983	Caveat	L. Pincay
1984	Swale	L. Pincay
1985	Creme Fraiche	E. Maple
1986	Danzig Connection	C. McCarron
1987	Bet Twice	C. Perret
1988	Risen Star	E. Delahoussaye
1989	Easy Goer	P. Day
1990	Go and Go	M. Kinane
1991	Hansel	J. Bailey
1992	A.P. Indy	E. Delahoussaye
1993	Colonial Affair	J. Krone
1994	Tabasco Cat	P. Day
1995	Thunder Gulch	G. Stevens
1996	Editor's Note	R. Douglas
1997	Touch Gold	C. McCarron
1998	Victory Gallop	G. Stevens
1999	Lemon Drop Kid	J. Santos
2000	Commendable	P. Day
2001	Point Given	G. Stevens
2002	Sarava	E. Prado
2003	Empire Maker	J. Bailey
2004	Birdstone	E. Prado
2005	Afleet Alex	J. Rose
2006	Jazil	F. Jara
2007	Rags to Riches	J. Velazquez
2008	Da' Tara	A. Garcia
2009	Summer Bird	K. Desormeaux
2010	Drosselmeyer	M. Smith
2011	Ruler On Ice	J. Valdivia Jr.
2012	Union Rags	J. Velazquez
2013	Palace Malice	M. Smith
2014	Tonalist	J. Rosario
2015	American Pharoah	V. Espinoza
2016	Creator	I. Ortiz Jr.
2017	Tapwrit	J. Ortiz
2018	Justify	M. Smith
2019	Sir Winston	J. Rosario
2020	Tiz the Law	M. Franco
2021	Essential Quality	L. Saez
2022	Mo Donegal	I. Ortiz Jr.
2023	Arcangelo	J. Castellano
2024	Dornoch	L. Saez

Annual Leading Jockey by Earnings, 1957-2023

Total purses earned by all horses that jockey raced in year listed; does not reflect what jockey earned.

Year	Jockey	Earnings
1957	Bill Hartack	$3,060,501
1958	Willie Shoemaker	2,961,693
1959	Willie Shoemaker	2,843,133
1960	Willie Shoemaker	2,123,961
1961	Willie Shoemaker	2,690,819
1962	Willie Shoemaker	2,916,844
1963	Willie Shoemaker	2,526,925
1964	Willie Shoemaker	2,649,553
1965	Braulio Baeza	2,582,702
1966	Braulio Baeza	2,951,022
1967	Braulio Baeza	3,088,888
1968	Braulio Baeza	2,835,108
1969	Jorge Velasquez	2,542,315
1970	Laffit Pincay Jr.	2,626,526
1971	Laffit Pincay Jr.	3,784,377
1972	Laffit Pincay Jr.	3,225,827
1973	Laffit Pincay Jr.	4,093,492
1974	Laffit Pincay Jr.	4,251,060
1975	Braulio Baeza	3,695,198
1976	Angel Cordero Jr.	4,709,500
1977	Steve Cauthen	6,151,750
1978	Darrel McHargue	6,029,885
1979	Laffit Pincay Jr.	$8,193,535
1980	Chris McCarron	7,663,300
1981	Chris McCarron	8,397,604
1982	Angel Cordero Jr.	9,483,590
1983	Angel Cordero Jr.	10,116,697
1984	Chris McCarron	12,045,813
1985	Laffit Pincay Jr.	13,353,299
1986	Jose Santos	11,329,297
1987	Jose Santos	12,375,433
1988	Jose Santos	14,877,298
1989	Jose Santos	13,838,389
1990	Gary Stevens	13,881,198
1991	Chris McCarron	14,441,083
1992	Kent Desormeaux	14,193,006
1993	Mike Smith	14,024,815
1994	Mike Smith	15,979,820
1995	Jerry D. Bailey	16,311,876
1996	Jerry D. Bailey	19,465,376
1997	Jerry D. Bailey	18,320,743
1998	Gary Stevens	19,622,855
1999	Pat Day	18,092,845
2000	Pat Day	17,479,838
2001	Jerry D. Bailey	$22,597,720
2002	Jerry D. Bailey	19,271,814
2003	Jerry D. Bailey	23,354,960
2004	John R. Velazquez	22,220,261
2005	John R. Velazquez	20,799,923
2006	Garrett K. Gomez	20,122,592
2007	Garrett K. Gomez	22,800,074
2008	Garrett K. Gomez	23,344,351
2009	Garrett K. Gomez	18,536,105
2010	Ramon A. Dominguez	16,911,880
2011	Ramon A. Dominguez	20,267,032
2012	Ramon A. Dominguez	25,584,852
2013	Javier Castellano	26,214,007
2014	Javier Castellano	25,056,464
2015	Javier Castellano	28,120,809
2016	Javier Castellano	26,826,241
2017	José L. Ortiz	27,318,875
2018	Irad Ortiz Jr.	27,727,039
2019	Irad Ortiz Jr.	34,109,019
2020	Irad Ortiz Jr.	21,050,726
2021	Joel Rosario	32,956,215
2022	Irad Ortiz Jr.	37,075,772
2023	Irad Ortiz Jr.	39,193,365

Breeders' Cup World Thoroughbred Championships, 1984-2024

The Breeders' Cup began in 1984 and through 2006, consisted of seven races at one track on one day. In 2007, it expanded to two days, with new races.

Classic

Year	Horse	Jockey
1984	Wild Again	P. Day
1985	Proud Truth	J. Velasquez
1986	Skywalker	L. Pincay Jr.
1987	Ferdinand	W. Shoemaker
1988	Alysheba	C. McCarron
1989	Sunday Silence	C. McCarron
1990	Unbridled	P. Day
1991	Black Tie Affair	J. Bailey
1992	A.P. Indy	E. Delahoussaye
1993	Arcangues	J. Bailey
1994	Concern	J. Bailey
1995	Cigar	J. Bailey
1996	Alphabet Soup	C. McCarron
1997	Skip Away	M. Smith
1998	Awesome Again	P. Day
1999	Cat Thief	P. Day
2000	Tiznow	C. McCarron
2001	Tiznow	C. McCarron
2002	Volponi	J. Santos
2003	Pleasantly Perfect	A. Solis
2004	Ghostzapper	J. Castellano
2005	Saint Liam	J. Bailey
2006	Invasor	F. Jara
2007	Curlin	R. Albarado
2008	Raven's Pass	F. Dettori
2009	Zenyatta	M. Smith
2010	Blame	G. Gomez
2011	Drosselmeyer	M. Smith
2012	Fort Larned	B. Hernandez
2013	Mucho Macho Man	G. Stevens
2014	Bayern	M. Garcia
2015	American Pharoah	V. Espinoza
2016	Arrogate	M. Smith
2017	Gun Runner	F. Geroux
2018	Accelerate	J. Rosario
2019	Vino Rosso	I. Ortiz Jr.
2020	Authentic	J. Velazquez
2021	Knicks Go	J. Rosario
2022	Flightline	F. Prat
2023	White Abarrio	I. Ortiz Jr.
2024	Sierra Leone	F. Prat

Juvenile

Year	Horse	Jockey
1984	Chief's Crown	D. MacBeth
1985	Tasso	L. Pincay Jr.
1986	Capote	L. Pincay Jr.
1987	Success Express	J. Santos
1988	Is It True	L. Pincay Jr.
1989	Rhythm	C. Perret
1990	Fly So Free	J. Santos
1991	Arazi	P. Valenzuela
1992	Gilded Time	C. McCarron
1993	Brocco	G. Stevens
1994	Timber Country	P. Day
1995	Unbridled's Song	M. Smith
1996	Boston Harbor	J. Bailey
1997	Favorite Trick	P. Day
1998	Answer Lively	J. Bailey
1999	Anees	G. Stevens
2000	Macho Uno	J. Bailey
2001	Johannesburg	M. Kinane
2002	Vindication	M. Smith
2003	Action This Day	D. Flores
2004	Wilko	F. Dettori
2005	Stevie Wonderboy	G. Gomez
2006	Street Sense	C. Borel
2007	War Pass	C. Velasquez
2008	Midshipman	G. Gomez
2009	Vale of York	A. Ajtebi
2010	Uncle Mo	J. Velazquez
2011	Hansen	R. Dominguez
2012	Shanghai Bobby	R. Napravnik
2013	New Year's Day	M. Garcia
2014	Texas Red	K. Desormeaux
2015	Nyquist	M. Gutierrez
2016	Classic Empire	J. Leparoux
2017	Good Magic	J. Ortiz
2018	Game Winner	J. Rosario
2019	Storm the Court	F. Prat
2020	Essential Quality	L. Saez
2021	Corniche	M. Smith
2022	Forte	I. Ortiz Jr.
2023	Fierceness	J. Velazquez
2024	Citizen Bull	M. Garcia

Filly and Mare Sprint

Year	Horse	Jockey
2007	Maryfield	E. Trujillo
2008	Ventura	G. Gomez
2009	Informed Decision	J. Leparoux
2010	Dubai Majesty	J. Theriot
2011	Musical Romance	J. Leyva
2012	Groupie Doll	R. Maragh
2013	Groupie Doll	R. Maragh
2014	Judy the Beauty	M. Smith
2015	Wavell Avenue	J. Rosario
2016	Finest City	M. Smith
2017	Bar of Gold	I. Ortiz Jr.
2018	Shamrock Rose	I. Ortiz Jr.
2019	Covfefe	J. Rosario
2020	Gamine	J. Velazquez
2021	Ce Ce	V. Espinoza
2022	Goodnight Olive	I. Ortiz Jr.
2023	Goodnight Olive	I. Ortiz Jr.
2024	Soul of an Angel	D. Van Dyke

Juvenile Fillies

Year	Horse	Jockey
1984	Outstandingly	W. Guerra
1985	Twilight Ridge	J. Velasquez
1986	Brave Raj	P. Valenzuela
1987	Epitome	P. Day
1988	Open Mind	A. Cordero Jr.
1989	Go for Wand	R. Romero
1990	Meadow Star	J. Santos
1991	Pleasant Stage	E. Delahoussaye
1992	Eliza	P. Valenzuela
1993	Phone Chatter	L. Pincay Jr.
1994	Flanders	P. Day
1995	My Flag	J. Bailey
1996	Storm Song	C. Perret
1997	Countess Diana	S. Sellers
1998	Silverbulletday	G. Stevens
1999	Cash Run	J. Bailey
2000	Caressing	J. Velazquez
2001	Tempera	D. Flores
2002	Storm Flag Flying	J. Velazquez
2003	Halfbridled	J. Krone
2004	Sweet Catomine	C. Nakatani
2005	Folklore	E. Prado
2006	Dreaming of Anna	R. Douglas
2007	Indian Blessing	G. Gomez
2008	Stardom Bound	M. Smith
2009	She Be Wild	J. Leparoux
2010	Awesome Feather	J. Sanchez
2011	My Miss Aurelia	C. Nakatani
2012	Beholder	G. Gomez
2013	Ria Antonia	J. Castellano
2014	Take Charge Brandi	V. Espinoza
2015	Songbird	M. Smith
2016	Champagne Room	M. Gutierrez
2017	Caledonia Road	M. Smith
2018	Jaywalk	J. Rosario
2019	British Idiom	J. Castellano
2020	Vequist	J. Rosario
2021	Echo Zulu	J. Rosario
2022	Wonder Wheel	T. Gaffalione
2023	Just FYI	J. Alvarado
2024	Immersive	M. Franco

Sprint

Year	Horse	Jockey
1984	Eillo	C. Perret
1985	Precisionist	C. McCarron
1986	Smile	J. Vasquez
1987	Very Subtle	P. Valenzuela
1988	Gulch	A. Cordero Jr.
1989	Dancing Spree	A. Cordero Jr.
1990	Safely Kept	C. Perret
1991	Sheikh Albadou	P. Eddery
1992	Thirty Slews	E. Delahoussaye
1993	Cardmania	E. Delahoussaye
1994	Cherokee Run	M. Smith
1995	Desert Stormer	K. Desormeaux
1996	Lit de Justice	C. Nakatani
1997	Elmhurst	C. Nakatani
1998	Reraise	C. Nakatani
1999	Artax	J. Chaves
2000	Kona Gold	A. Solis
2001	Squirtle Squirt	J. Bailey
2002	Orientate	J. Bailey
2003	Cajun Beat	C. Velasquez
2004	Speightstown	J. Velazquez
2005	Silver Train	E. Prado
2006	Thor's Echo	C. Nakatani
2007	Midnight Lute	G. Gomez
2008	Midnight Lute	G. Gomez
2009	Dancing in Silks	J. Rosario
2010	Big Drama	E. Coa
2011	Amazombie	M. Smith
2012	Trinniberg	W. Martinez
2013	Secret Circle	M. Garcia
2014	Work All Week	F. Geroux
2015	Runhappy	E. Prado
2016	Drefong	M. Garcia
2017	Roy H	K. Desormeaux
2018	Roy H	P. Lopez
2019	Mitole	R. Santana Jr.
2020	Whitmore	I. Ortiz Jr.
2021	Aloha West	J. Ortiz
2022	Elite Power	I. Ortiz Jr.
2023	Elite Power	I. Ortiz Jr.
2024	Straight No Chaser	J. Velazquez

Mile

Year	Horse	Jockey
1984	Royal Heroine	F. Toro
1985	Cozzene	W. Guerra
1986	Last Tycoon	Y. St.-Martin
1987	Miesque	F. Head
1988	Miesque	F. Head
1989	Steinlen	J. Santos
1990	Royal Academy	L. Piggott
1991	Opening Verse	P. Valenzuela
1992	Lure	M. Smith
1993	Lure	M. Smith
1994	Barathea	F. Dettori
1995	Ridgewood Pearl	J. Murtagh
1996	Da Hoss	G. Stevens
1997	Spinning World	C. Asmussan
1998	Da Hoss	J. Velazquez
1999	Silic	C. Nakatani
2000	War Chant	G. Stevens
2001	Val Royal	J. Valdivia Jr.
2002	Domedriver	T. Thulliez
2003	Six Perfections	J. Bailey
2004	Singletary	D. Flores
2005	Artie Schiller	G. Gomez
2006	Miesque's Approval	E. Castro
2007	Kip Deville	C. Velasquez
2008	Goldikova	O. Peslier
2009	Goldikova	O. Peslier
2010	Goldikova	O. Peslier
2011	Court Vision	R. Albarado
2012	Wise Dan	J. Velazquez
2013	Wise Dan	J. Lezcano
2014	Karakatonie	S. Pasquier
2015	Tepin	J. Leparoux
2016	Tourist	J. Rosario
2017	World Approval	J. Velazquez
2018	Expert Eye	F. Dettori
2019	Uni	J. Rosario
2020	Order of Australia	P. Boudot
2021	Space Blues	W. Buick
2022	Modern Games	W. Buick
2023	Master of the Seas	W. Buick
2024	More Than Looks	J. Ortiz

Distaff

Year	Horse	Jockey
1984	Princess Rooney	E. Delahoussaye
1985	Life's Magic	A. Cordero Jr.
1986	Lady's Secret	P. Day
1987	Sacahuista	R. Romero
1988	Personal Ensign	R. Romero
1989	Bayakoa	L. Pincay Jr.
1990	Bayakoa	L. Pincay Jr.
1991	Dance Smartly	P. Day
1992	Paseana	C. McCarron
1993	Hollywood Wildcat	E. Delahoussaye
1994	One Dreamer	G. Stevens
1995	Inside Information	M. Smith
1996	Jewel Princess	C. Nakatani
1997	Ajina	M. Smith
1998	Escena	G. Stevens
1999	Beautiful Pleasure	J. Chaves
2000	Spain	V. Espinoza
2001	Unbridled Elaine	P. Day
2002	Azeri	M. Smith
2003	Adoration	P. Valenzuela
2004	Ashado	J. Velazquez
2005	Pleasant Home	C. Velasquez
2006	Round Pond	E. Prado
2007	Ginger Punch	R. Bejarano
2008	Zenyatta	M. Smith
2009	Life Is Sweet	G. Gomez
2010	Unrivaled Belle	K. Desormeaux
2011	Royal Delta	J. Lezcano
2012	Royal Delta	M. Smith
2013	Beholder	G. Stevens
2014	Untapable	R. Napravnik
2015	Stopchargingmaria	J. Castellano
2016	Beholder	G. Stevens
2017	Forever Unbridled	J. Velazquez
2018	Monomoy Girl	F. Geroux
2019	Blue Prize	J. Bravo
2020	Monomoy Girl	F. Geroux
2021	Marche Lorraine	O. Murphy
2022	Malathaat	J. Velazquez
2023	Idiomatic	F. Geroux
2024	Thorpedo Anna	B. Hernandez Jr.

Turf

Year	Horse	Jockey
1984	Lashkari	Y. St.-Martin
1985	Pebbles	P. Eddery
1986	Manila	J. Santos
1987	Theatrical	P. Day
1988	Great Communicator	R. Sibille
1989	Prized	E. Delahoussaye
1990	In the Wings	G. Stevens
1991	Miss Alleged	E. Legrix
1992	Fraise	P. Valenzuela
1993	Kotashaan	K. Desormeaux
1994	Tikkanen	M. Smith
1995	Northern Spur	C. McCarron
1996	Pilsudski	W. Swinburn
1997	Chief Bearhart	J. Santos
1998	Buck's Boy	S. Sellers
1999	Daylami	F. Dettori
2000	Kalanisi	J. Murtagh
2001	Fantastic Light	F. Dettori
2002	High Chaparral	M. Kinane
2003	(tie) High Chaparral	M. Kinane
	Johar	A. Solis
2004	Better Talk Now	R. Dominguez
2005	Shirocco	C. Soumillon
2006	Red Rocks	F. Dettori
2007	English Channel	J. Velasquez
2008	Conduit	R. Moore
2009	Conduit	R. Moore
2010	Dangerous Midge	F. Dettori
2011	St Nicholas Abbey	J. O'Brien
2012	Little Mike	R. Dominguez
2013	Magician	R. Moore
2014	Main Sequence	J. Velazquez
2015	Found	R. Moore
2016	Highland Reel	S. Heffernan
2017	Talismanic	M. Barzalona
2018	Enable	F. Dettori
2019	Bricks and Mortar	I. Ortiz Jr.
2020	Tarnawa	C. Keane
2021	Yibir	W. Buick
2022	Rebel's Romance	J. Doyle
2023	Auguste Rodin	R. Moore
2024	Rebel's Romance	W. Buick

Filly and Mare Turf

Year	Horse	Jockey
1999	Soaring Softly	J. Bailey
2000	Perfect Sting	J. Bailey
2001	Banks Hill	O. Peslier
2002	Starine	J. Velazquez
2003	Islington	K. Fallon
2004	Ouija Board	F. Dettori
2005	Intercontinental	R. Bejarano
2006	Ouija Board	F. Dettori
2007	Lahudood	A. Garcia
2008	Forever Together	J. Leparoux
2009	Midday	T. Queally
2010	Shared Account	E. Prado
2011	Perfect Shirl	J. Velazquez
2012	Zagora	J. Castellano
2013	Dank	R. Moore
2014	Dayatthespa	J. Castellano
2015	Stephanie's Kitten	J. Velazquez
2016	Queen's Trust	F. Dettori
2017	Wuheida	W. Buick
2018	Sistercharlie	J. Velazquez
2019	Iridessa	W. Lordan
2020	Audarya	P. Boudot
2021	Loves Only You	Y. Kawada
2022	Tuesday	R. Moore
2023	Inspiral	F. Dettori
2024	Moira	F. Prat

Juvenile Turf

Year	Horse	Jockey
2007	Nownownow	J. Leparoux
2008	Donativum	F. Dettori
2009	Pounced	F. Dettori
2010	Pluck	G. Gomez
2011	Wrote	R. Moore
2012	George Vancouver	R. Moore
2013	Outstrip	M. Smith
2014	Hootenanny	F. Dettori
2015	Hit It a Bomb	R. Moore
2016	Oscar Performance	J. Ortiz
2017	Mendelssohn	R. Moore
2018	Line of Duty	W. Buick
2019	Structor	J. Ortiz
2020	Fire At Will	R. Santana Jr.
2021	Modern Games	W. Buick
2022	Victoria Road	R. Moore
2023	Unquestionable	R. Moore
2024	Henri Matisse	R. Moore

Dirt Mile

Year	Horse	Jockey
2007	Corinthian	K. Desormeaux
2008	Albertus Maximus	G. Gomez
2009	Furthest Land	J. Leparoux
2010	Dakota Phone	J. Rosario
2011	Caleb's Posse	R. Maragh
2012	Tapizar	C. Nakatani
2013	Goldencents	R. Bejarano
2014	Goldencents	R. Bejarano
2015	Liam's Map	J. Castellano
2016	Tamarkuz	M. Smith
2017	Battle of Midway	F. Prat
2018	City of Light	J. Castellano
2019	Spun to Run	I. Ortiz Jr.
2020	Knicks Go	J. Rosario
2021	Life Is Good	I. Ortiz Jr.
2022	Cody's Wish	J. Alvarado
2023	Cody's Wish	J. Alvarado
2024	Full Serrano	J. Rosario

Turf Sprint

Year	Horse	Jockey
2008	Desert Code	R. Migliore
2009	California Flag	J. Talamo
2010	Chamberlain Bridge	J. Theriot
2011	Regally Ready	C. Nakatani
2012	Mizdirection	M. Smith
2013	Mizdirection	M. Smith
2014	Bobby's Kitten	J. Rosario
2015	Mongolian Saturday	F. Geroux
2016	Obviously	F. Prat
2017	Stormy Liberal	J. Rosario
2018	Stormy Liberal	D. Van Dyke
2019	Belvoir Bay	J. Castellano
2020	Glass Slippers	T. Eaves
2021	Golden Pal	I. Ortiz Jr.
2022	Caravel	T. Gaffalione
2023	Nobals	G. Corrales
2024	Starlust	R. Ryan

Juvenile Fillies Turf

Year	Horse	Jockey
2008	Maram	J. Lezcano
2009	Tapitsfly	R. Albarado
2010	More Than Real	G. Gomez
2011	Stephanie's Kitten	J. Velazquez
2012	Flotilla	C. Lemaire
2013	Chriselliam	R. Hughes
2014	Lady Eli	I. Ortiz Jr.
2015	Catch a Glimpse	F. Geroux
2016	New Money Honey	J. Castellano
2017	Rushing Fall	J. Castellano
2018	Newspaperofrecord	I. Ortiz Jr.
2019	Sharing	M. Franco
2020	Aunt Pearl	F. Geroux
2021	Pizza Bianca	J. Ortiz
2022	Meditate	R. Moore
2023	Hard to Justify	F. Prat
2024	Lake Victoria	R. Moore

Juvenile Turf Sprint

Year	Horse	Jockey
2018	Bulletin	J. Castellano
2019	Four Wheel Drive	I. Ortiz Jr.
2020	Golden Pal	I. Ortiz Jr.
2021	Twilight Gleaming	I. Ortiz Jr.
2022	Mischief Magic	W. Buick
2023	Big Evs	T. Marquand
2024	Magnum Force	C. Keane

Eclipse Awards, 2023

The Eclipse Awards, honoring the Horse of the Year and other champions of thoroughbred racing, began in 1971 and are sponsored by the *Daily Racing Form*, the National Thoroughbred Racing Association, and the National Turf Writers and Broadcasters.

Horse of the year: Cody's Wish
Two-year-old male: Fierceness
Two-year-old filly: Just F Y I
Three-year-old male: Arcangelo
Three-year-old filly: Pretty Mischievous
Older dirt male: Cody's Wish
Older dirt female: Idiomatic
Male sprinter: Elite Power
Female sprinter: Goodnight Olive
Turf male: Up to the Mark
Turf female: Inspiral
Steeplechase horse: Merry Maker
Owner: Godolphin LLC
Breeder: Godolphin LLC
Jockey: Irad Ortiz Jr.
Apprentice jockey: Axel Concepcion
Trainer: Bill Mott

HARNESS RACING

Harness Horse of the Year, 1947-2023

Chosen by the U.S. Trotting Assn. and the U.S. Harness Writers Assn.

Year	Horse
1947	Victory Song
1948	Rodney
1949	Good Time
1950	Proximity
1951	Pronto Don
1952	Good Time
1953	Hi Lo's Forbes
1954	Stenographer
1955	Scott Frost
1956	Scott Frost
1957	Torpid
1958	Emily's Pride
1959	Bye Bye Byrd
1960	Adios Butler
1961	Adios Butler
1962	Su Mac Lad
1963	Speedy Scot
1964	Bret Hanover
1965	Bret Hanover
1966	Bret Hanover
1967	Nevele Pride
1968	Nevele Pride
1969	Nevele Pride
1970	Fresh Yankee
1971	Albatross
1972	Albatross
1973	Sir Dalrae
1974	Delmonica Hanover
1975	Savoir
1976	Keystone Ore
1977	Green Speed
1978	Abercrombie
1979	Niatross
1980	Niatross
1981	Fan Hanover
1982	Cam Fella
1983	Cam Fella
1984	Fancy Crown
1985	Nihilator
1986	Forrest Skipper
1987	Mack Lobell
1988	Mack Lobell
1989	Matt's Scooter
1990	Beach Towel
1991	Precious Bunny
1992	Artsplace
1993	Staying Together
1994	Cam's Card Shark
1995	CR Kay Suzie
1996	Continental Victory
1997	Malabar Man
1998	Moni Maker
1999	Moni Maker
2000	Gallo Blue Chip
2001	Bunny Lake
2002	Real Desire
2003	No Pan Intended
2004	Rainbow Blue
2005	Rocknroll Hanover
2006	Glidemaster
2007	Donato Hanover
2008	Somebeachsomewhere
2009	Muscle Hill
2010	Rock N Roll Heaven
2011	San Pail
2012	Chapter Seven
2013	Bee a Magician
2014	JK She'salady
2015	Wiggle It Jiggleit
2016	Always B Miki
2017	Hannelore Hanover
2018	McWicked
2019	Shartin N
2020	Tall Dark Stranger
2021	Test Of Faith
2022	Bulldog Hanover
2023	Confederate

Hambletonian Winners (3-year-old trotters), 1965-2024

Year	Horse	Driver	Year	Horse	Driver	Year	Horse	Driver
1965	Egyptian Candor	D. Cameron	1985	Prakas	B. O'Donnell	2005	Vivid Photo	R. Hammer
1966	Kerry Way	F. Ervin	1986	Nuclear Kosmos	U. Thoresen	2006	Glidemaster	J. Campbell
1967	Speedy Streak	D. Cameron	1987	Mack Lobell	J. Campbell	2007	Donato Hanover	R. Pierce
1968	Nevele Pride	S. Dancer	1988	Armbro Goal	J. Campbell	2008	Deweycheatumnhowe	R. Schnittker
1969	Lindy's Pride	H. Beissinger	1989	Park Avenue Joe	R. Waples	2009	Muscle Hill	B. Sears
1970	Timothy T	J. Simpson Sr.	1990	Harmonious	J. Campbell	2010	Muscle Massive	R. Pierce
1971	Speedy Crown	H. Beissinger	1991	Giant Victory	J. Moiseyev	2011	Broad Bahn	G. Brennan
1972	Super Bowl	S. Dancer	1992	Alf Palema	M. McNicholl	2012	Market Share	T. Tetrick
1973	Flirth	R. Baldwin	1993	American Winner	R. Pierce	2013	Royalty For Life	B. Sears
1974	Christopher T	B. Haughton	1994	Victory Dream	M. Lachance	2014	Trixton	J. Takter
1975	Bonefish	S. Dancer	1995	Tagliabue	J. Campbell	2015	Pinkman	B. Sears
1976	Steve Lobell	B. Haughton	1996	Continental Victory	M. Lachance	2016	Marion Marauder	S. Zeron
1977	Green Speed	B. Haughton	1997	Malabar Man	M. Burroughs	2017	Perfect Spirit	A. Svanstedt
1978	Speedy Somolli	H. Beissinger	1998	Muscles Yankee	J. Campbell	2018	Atlanta	S. Zeron
1979	Legend Hanover	G. Sholty	1999	Self Possessed	M. Lachance	2019	Forbidden Trade	B. McClure
1980	Burgomeister	B. Haughton	2000	Yankee Paco	T. Ritchie	2020	Ramona Hill	A. McCarthy
1981	Shiaway St. Pat	R. Remmen	2001	Scarlet Knight	S. Melander	2021	Captain Corey	A. Svanstedt
1982	Speed Bowl	T. Haughton	2002	Chip Chip Hooray	E. Ledford	2022	Cool Papa Bell	T. McCarthy
1983	Duenna	S. Dancer	2003	Amigo Hall	M. Lachance	2023	Tactical Approach	S. Zeron
1984	Historic Freight	B. Webster	2004	Windsong's Legacy	T. Smedshammer	2024	Karl	Y. Gingras

BOWLING

Professional Bowlers Association Tournament of Champions, 1965-2024

Year	Winner	Year	Winner	Year	Winner	Year	Winner
1965	Billy Hardwick	1979	George Pappas	1993	George Branham III	2010	Kelly Kulick
1966	Wayne Zahn	1980	Wayne Webb	1994	Norm Duke	2011	Mika Koivuniemi
1967	Jim Stefanich	1981	Steve Cook	1996	Dave D'Entremont	2012	Sean Rash
1968	Dave Davis	1982	Mike Durbin	1997	John Gant	2013	Pete Weber
1969	Jim Godman	1983	Joe Berardi	1998	Bryan Goebel	2014	Jason Belmonte
1970	Don Johnson	1984	Mike Durbin	1999	Jason Couch	2015	Jason Belmonte
1971	Johnny Petraglia	1985	Mark Williams	2000	Jason Couch	2016	Jesper Svensson
1972	Mike Durbin	1986	Marshall Holman	2002	Jason Couch	2017	EJ Tackett
1973	Jim Godman	1987	Pete Weber	2003	Patrick Healey Jr.	2018	Matt O'Grady
1974	Earl Anthony	1988	Mark Williams	2005	Steve Jaros	2019	Jason Belmonte
1975	Dave Davis	1989	Del Ballard Jr.	2006	Chris Barnes	2020	Kris Prather
1976	Marshall Holman	1990	Dave Ferraro	2007	Tommy Jones	2021	François Lavoie
1977	Mike Berlin	1991	David Ozio	2008	Michael Haugen Jr.	2022	Dom Barrett
1978	Earl Anthony	1992	Marc McDowell	2009	Patrick Allen	2023	Jason Belmonte
						2024	Marshall Kent

Note: No tournament held in 2001 or 2004.

Professional Bowlers Association Leading Money Winners, 1962-2023

Total winnings from tournaments only. For 2000-13, year shown is year the PBA season ended.

Year	Bowler	Earnings	Year	Bowler	Earnings	Year	Bowler	Earnings
1962	Don Carter	$49,972	1982	Earl Anthony	$134,760	2003	Walter Ray Williams Jr.	$419,700
1963	Dick Weber	46,333	1983	Earl Anthony	135,605	2004	Mika Koivuniemi	238,590
1964	Bob Strampe	33,592	1984	Mark Roth	158,712	2005	Patrick Allen	350,740
1965	Dick Weber	47,674	1985	Mike Aulby	201,200	2006	Tommy Jones	301,700
1966	Wayne Zahn	54,720	1986	Walter Ray Williams Jr.	145,550	2007	Doug Kent	200,530
1967	Dave Davis	54,165	1987	Pete Weber	175,491	2008	Norm Duke	176,855
1968	Jim Stefanich	67,377	1988	Brian Voss	225,485	2009	Norm Duke	199,130
1969	Billy Hardwick	64,160	1989	Mike Aulby	298,237	2010	Walter Ray Williams Jr.	152,670
1970	Mike McGrath	52,049	1990	Amleto Monacelli	204,775	2011	Mika Koivuniemi	333,040
1971	Johnny Petraglia	85,065	1991	David Ozio	225,585	2012	Sean Rash	140,250
1972	Don Johnson	56,648	1992	Marc McDowell	174,215	2013	Sean Rash	248,317
1973	Don McCune	69,000	1993	Walter Ray Williams Jr.	296,370	2014	Jason Belmonte	163,778
1974	Earl Anthony	99,585	1994	Norm Duke	273,753	2015	Jason Belmonte	178,542
1975	Earl Anthony	107,585	1995	Mike Aulby	219,792	2016	EJ Tackett	168,290
1976	Earl Anthony	110,833	1996	Walter Ray Williams Jr.	241,330	2017	Jason Belmonte	238,912
1977	Mark Roth	105,583	1997	Walter Ray Williams Jr.	240,544	2018	Anthony Simonsen	115,975
1978	Mark Roth	134,500	1998	Walter Ray Williams Jr.	238,225	2019	Jason Belmonte	285,290
1979	Mark Roth	124,517	1999	Parker Bohn III	240,912	2020	Jason Belmonte	293,050
1980	Wayne Webb	116,700	2000	Norm Duke	143,325	2021	Kyle Troup	496,900
1981	Earl Anthony	164,735	2002	Parker Bohn III	245,200	2022	Jason Belmonte	302,525
						2023	EJ Tackett	458,450

World Chess Champions, 1886-2024

Source: U.S. Chess Federation, International Chess Federation (FIDE)
Official world champions since the title was first used.

Years	Champion, country	Years	Champion, country
1886-94	Wilhelm Steinitz, Austria	**1975-85**	Anatoly Karpov, USSR
1894-1921	Emanuel Lasker, Germany	**1985-2000**	Garry Kasparov, USSR/Russia[3,4]
1921-27	Jose R. Capablanca, Cuba	**1993-99**	Anatoly Karpov, Russia (FIDE)[3]
1927-35	Alexander Alekhine, France	**1999-2000**	Alexander Khalifman, Russia (FIDE)
1935-37	Max Euwe, Netherlands	**2000-02**	Viswanathan Anand, India (FIDE)
1937-46	Alexander Alekhine, France[1]	**2000-06**	Vladimir Kramnik, Russia (classical)[4]
1948-57	Mikhail Botvinnik, USSR	**2002-04**	Ruslan Ponomariov, Ukraine (FIDE)
1957-58	Vassily Smyslov, USSR	**2004-05**	Rustam Kasimdzhanov, Uzbekistan (FIDE)
1958-59	Mikhail Botvinnik, USSR	**2005-06**	Veselin Topalov, Bulgaria (FIDE)[5]
1960-61	Mikhail Tal, USSR	**2006-07**	Vladimir Kramnik, Russia[5]
1961-63	Mikhail Botvinnik, USSR	**2007-13**	Viswanathan Anand, India
1963-69	Tigran Petrosian, USSR	**2013-22**	Magnus Carlsen, Norway
1969-72	Boris Spassky, USSR	**2023-**	Ding Liren, China
1972-75	Bobby Fischer, U.S.[2]		

(1) After Alekhine died in 1946, the title was vacant until 1948, when Botvinnik won the first world championship event sanctioned by FIDE. (2) Defaulted championship after refusing to accept FIDE rules for a championship match, Apr. 1975. (3) Kasparov broke with FIDE, Feb. 26, 1993. FIDE stripped Kasparov of his FIDE title Mar. 23. Kasparov defeated Nigel Short (UK) in a world championship match played Sept.-Oct. 1993 under the auspices of the Professional Chess Association (PCA), a new organization the two founded. FIDE held a championship match between Anatoly Karpov (Russia) and Jan Timman (Netherlands), which Karpov won in Nov. 1993. The PCA folded in 1995, but Kasparov was still considered the "classical" world champion. (That is, he defended his title against challengers; FIDE matches are arranged differently.) (4) In Nov. 2000, Kramnik defeated Kasparov for the classical world championship title. (5) Kramnik, the classical world champion since 2000, unified the chess titles by defeating Topalov on Oct. 13, 2006, at a world championship match.

Alpine Skiing Men's World Cup Champions, 1967-2024

Year	Champion, country	Year	Champion, country	Year	Champion, country
1967	Jean Claude Killy, France	1987	Pirmin Zurbriggen, Switzerland	2006	Benjamin Raich, Austria
1968	Jean Claude Killy, France	1988	Pirmin Zurbriggen, Switzerland	2007	Aksel Lund Svindal, Norway
1969	Karl Schranz, Austria	1989	Marc Girardelli, Luxembourg	2008	Bode Miller, U.S.
1970	Karl Schranz, Austria	1990	Pirmin Zurbriggen, Switzerland	2009	Aksel Lund Svindal, Norway
1971	Gustavo Thoeni, Italy	1991	Marc Girardelli, Luxembourg	2010	Carlo Janka, Switzerland
1972	Gustavo Thoeni, Italy	1992	Paul Accola, Switzerland	2011	Ivica Kostelic, Croatia
1973	Gustavo Thoeni, Italy	1993	Marc Girardelli, Luxembourg	2012	Marcel Hirscher, Austria
1974	Piero Gros, Italy	1994	Kjetil André Aamodt, Norway	2013	Marcel Hirscher, Austria
1975	Gustavo Thoeni, Italy	1995	Alberto Tomba, Italy	2014	Marcel Hirscher, Austria
1976	Ingemar Stenmark, Sweden	1996	Lasse Kjus, Norway	2015	Marcel Hirscher, Austria
1977	Ingemar Stenmark, Sweden	1997	Luc Alphand, France	2016	Marcel Hirscher, Austria
1978	Ingemar Stenmark, Sweden	1998	Hermann Maier, Austria	2017	Marcel Hirscher, Austria
1979	Peter Luescher, Switzerland	1999	Lasse Kjus, Norway	2018	Marcel Hirscher, Austria
1980	Andreas Wenzel, Liechtenstein	2000	Hermann Maier, Austria	2019	Marcel Hirscher, Austria
1981	Phil Mahre, U.S.	2001	Hermann Maier, Austria	2020	Aleksander Aamodt Kilde, Norway
1982	Phil Mahre, U.S.	2002	Stephan Eberharter, Austria	2021	Alexis Pinturault, France
1983	Phil Mahre, U.S.	2003	Stephan Eberharter, Austria	2022	Marco Odermatt, Switzerland
1984	Pirmin Zurbriggen, Switzerland	2004	Hermann Maier, Austria	2023	Marco Odermatt, Switzerland
1985	Marc Girardelli, Luxembourg	2005	Bode Miller, U.S.	2024	Marco Odermatt, Switzerland
1986	Marc Girardelli, Luxembourg				

Alpine Skiing Women's World Cup Champions, 1967-2024

Year	Champion, country	Year	Champion, country	Year	Champion, country
1967	Nancy Greene, Canada	1987	Maria Walliser, Switzerland	2006	Janica Kostelic, Croatia
1968	Nancy Greene, Canada	1988	Michela Figini, Switzerland	2007	Nicole Hosp, Austria
1969	Gertrud Gabl, Austria	1989	Vreni Schneider, Switzerland	2008	Lindsey Vonn, U.S.
1970	Michèle Jacot, France	1990	Petra Kronberger, Austria	2009	Lindsey Vonn, U.S.
1971	Annemarie Proell, Austria	1991	Petra Kronberger, Austria	2010	Lindsey Vonn, U.S.
1972	Annemarie Proell, Austria	1992	Petra Kronberger, Austria	2011	Maria Höfl-Riesch, Germany
1973	Annemarie Proell, Austria	1993	Anita Wachter, Austria	2012	Lindsey Vonn, U.S.
1974	Annemarie Proell, Austria	1994	Vreni Schneider, Switzerland	2013	Tina Maze, Slovenia
1975	Annemarie Proell, Austria	1995	Vreni Schneider, Switzerland	2014	Anna Fenninger, Austria
1976	Rosi Mittermaier, W. Germany	1996	Katja Seizinger, Germany	2015	Anna Fenninger, Austria
1977	Lise-Marie Morerod, Switzerland	1997	Pernilla Wiberg, Sweden	2016	Lara Gut, Switzerland
1978	Hanni Wenzel, Liechtenstein	1998	Katja Seizinger, Germany	2017	Mikaela Shiffrin, U.S.
1979	Annemarie Moser-Proell, Austria	1999	Alexandra Meissnitzer, Austria	2018	Mikaela Shiffrin, U.S.
1980	Hanni Wenzel, Liechtenstein	2000	Renate Goetschl, Austria	2019	Mikaela Shiffrin, U.S.
1981	Marie-Theres Nadig, Switzerland	2001	Janica Kostelic, Croatia	2020	Federica Brignone, Italy
1982	Erika Hess, Switzerland	2002	Michaela Dorfmeister, Austria	2021	Petra Vlhova, Slovakia
1983	Tamara McKinney, U.S.	2003	Janica Kostelic, Croatia	2022	Mikaela Shiffrin, U.S.
1984	Erika Hess, Switzerland	2004	Anja Paerson, Sweden	2023	Mikaela Shiffrin, U.S.
1985	Michela Figini, Switzerland	2005	Anja Paerson, Sweden	2024	Lara Gut-Behrami, Switzerland
1986	Maria Walliser, Switzerland				

U.S. and World Figure Skating Champions, 1955-2024

U.S. Champions			World Champions	
Men's winner	Women's winner	Year	Men's winner, country	Women's winner, country
Hayes Jenkins	Tenley Albright	1955	Hayes Jenkins, U.S.	Tenley Albright, U.S.
Hayes Jenkins	Tenley Albright	1956	Hayes Jenkins, U.S.	Carol Heiss, U.S.
David Jenkins	Carol Heiss	1957	David Jenkins, U.S.	Carol Heiss, U.S.
David Jenkins	Carol Heiss	1958	David Jenkins, U.S.	Carol Heiss, U.S.
David Jenkins	Carol Heiss	1959	David Jenkins, U.S.	Carol Heiss, U.S.
David Jenkins	Carol Heiss	1960	Alain Giletti, France	Carol Heiss, U.S.
Bradley Lord	Laurence Owen	1961	No competition[1]	No competition[1]
Monty Hoyt	Barbara Roles Pursley	1962	Don Jackson, Canada	Sjoukje Dijkstra, Netherlands
Tommy Litz	Lorraine Hanlon	1963	Don McPherson, Canada	Sjoukje Dijkstra, Netherlands
Scott Allen	Peggy Fleming	1964	Manfred Schnelldorfer, W. Germany	Sjoukje Dijkstra, Netherlands
Gary Visconti	Peggy Fleming	1965	Alain Calmat, France	Petra Burka, Canada
Scott Allen	Peggy Fleming	1966	Emmerich Danzer, Austria	Peggy Fleming, U.S.
Gary Visconti	Peggy Fleming	1967	Emmerich Danzer, Austria	Peggy Fleming, U.S.
Tim Wood	Peggy Fleming	1968	Emmerich Danzer, Austria	Peggy Fleming, U.S.
Tim Wood	Janet Lynn	1969	Tim Wood, U.S.	Gabriele Seyfert, E. Germany
Tim Wood	Janet Lynn	1970	Tim Wood, U.S.	Gabriele Seyfert, E. Germany
John Misha Petkevich	Janet Lynn	1971	Ondrej Nepela, Czechoslovakia	Beatrix Schuba, Austria
Ken Shelley	Janet Lynn	1972	Ondrej Nepela, Czechoslovakia	Beatrix Schuba, Austria
Gordon McKellen Jr.	Janet Lynn	1973	Ondrej Nepela, Czechoslovakia	Karen Magnussen, Canada
Gordon McKellen Jr.	Dorothy Hamill	1974	Jan Hoffmann, E. Germany	Christine Errath, E. Germany
Gordon McKellen Jr.	Dorothy Hamill	1975	Sergei Volkov, USSR	Dianne de Leeuw, Neth.
Terry Kubicka	Dorothy Hamill	1976	John Curry, UK	Dorothy Hamill, U.S.
Charles Tickner	Linda Fratianne	1977	Vladimir Kovalev, USSR	Linda Fratianne, U.S.
Charles Tickner	Linda Fratianne	1978	Charles Tickner, U.S.	Anett Poetzsch, E. Germany
Charles Tickner	Linda Fratianne	1979	Vladimir Kovalev, USSR	Linda Fratianne, U.S.
Charles Tickner	Linda Fratianne	1980	Jan Hoffmann, E. Germany	Anett Poetzsch, E. Germany
Scott Hamilton	Elaine Zayak	1981	Scott Hamilton, U.S.	Denise Biellmann, Switzerland
Scott Hamilton	Rosalynn Sumners	1982	Scott Hamilton, U.S.	Elaine Zayak, U.S.
Scott Hamilton	Rosalynn Sumners	1983	Scott Hamilton, U.S.	Rosalynn Sumners, U.S.
Scott Hamilton	Rosalynn Sumners	1984	Scott Hamilton, U.S.	Katarina Witt, E. Germany
Brian Boitano	Tiffany Chin	1985	Aleksandr Fadeev, USSR	Katarina Witt, E. Germany
Brian Boitano	Debi Thomas	1986	Brian Boitano, U.S.	Debi Thomas, U.S.
Brian Boitano	Jill Trenary	1987	Brian Orser, Canada	Katarina Witt, E. Germany
Brian Boitano	Debi Thomas	1988	Brian Boitano, U.S.	Katarina Witt, E. Germany
Christopher Bowman	Jill Trenary	1989	Kurt Browning, Canada	Midori Ito, Japan
Todd Eldredge	Jill Trenary	1990	Kurt Browning, Canada	Jill Trenary, U.S.

U.S. Champions			World Champions	
Men's winner	**Women's winner**	**Year**	**Men's winner, country**	**Women's winner, country**
Todd Eldredge	Tonya Harding	**1991**	Kurt Browning, Canada	Kristi Yamaguchi, U.S.
Christopher Bowman	Kristi Yamaguchi	**1992**	Viktor Petrenko, Russia	Kristi Yamaguchi, U.S.
Scott Davis	Nancy Kerrigan	**1993**	Kurt Browning, Canada	Oksana Baiul, Ukraine
Scott Davis	Vacant[2]	**1994**	Elvis Stojko, Canada	Yuka Sato, Japan
Todd Eldredge	Nicole Bobek	**1995**	Elvis Stojko, Canada	Chen Lu, China
Rudy Galindo	Michelle Kwan	**1996**	Todd Eldredge, U.S.	Michelle Kwan, U.S.
Todd Eldredge	Tara Lipinski	**1997**	Elvis Stojko, Canada	Tara Lipinski, U.S.
Todd Eldredge	Michelle Kwan	**1998**	Alexei Yagudin, Russia	Michelle Kwan, U.S.
Michael Weiss	Michelle Kwan	**1999**	Alexei Yagudin, Russia	Maria Butyrskaya, Russia
Michael Weiss	Michelle Kwan	**2000**	Alexei Yagudin, Russia	Michelle Kwan, U.S.
Timothy Goebel	Michelle Kwan	**2001**	Yevgeny Plushenko, Russia	Michelle Kwan, U.S.
Todd Eldredge	Michelle Kwan	**2002**	Alexei Yagudin, Russia	Irina Slutskaya, Russia
Michael Weiss	Michelle Kwan	**2003**	Yevgeny Plushenko, Russia	Michelle Kwan, U.S.
Johnny Weir	Michelle Kwan	**2004**	Yevgeny Plushenko, Russia	Shizuka Arakawa, Japan
Johnny Weir	Michelle Kwan	**2005**	Stéphane Lambiel, Switzerland	Irina Slutskaya, Russia
Johnny Weir	Sasha Cohen	**2006**	Stéphane Lambiel, Switzerland	Kimmie Meissner, U.S.
Evan Lysacek	Kimmie Meissner	**2007**	Brian Joubert, France	Miki Ando, Japan
Evan Lysacek	Mirai Nagasu	**2008**	Jeffrey Buttle, Canada	Mao Asada, Japan
Jeremy Abbott	Alissa Czisny	**2009**	Evan Lysacek, U.S.	Yuna Kim, South Korea
Jeremy Abbott	Rachael Flatt	**2010**	Daisuke Takahashi, Japan	Mao Asada, Japan
Ryan Bradley	Alissa Czisny	**2011**	Patrick Chan, Canada	Miki Ando, Japan
Jeremy Abbott	Ashley Wagner	**2012**	Patrick Chan, Canada	Carolina Kostner, Italy
Max Aaron	Ashley Wagner	**2013**	Patrick Chan, Canada	Yuna Kim, South Korea
Jeremy Abbott	Gracie Gold	**2014**	Yuzuru Hanyu, Japan	Mao Asada, Japan
Jason Brown	Ashley Wagner	**2015**	Javier Fernández, Spain	Elizaveta Tuktamysheva, Russia
Adam Rippon	Gracie Gold	**2016**	Javier Fernández, Spain	Evgenia Medvedeva, Russia
Nathan Chen	Karen Chen	**2017**	Yuzuru Hanyu, Japan	Evgenia Medvedeva, Russia
Nathan Chen	Bradie Tennell	**2018**	Nathan Chen, U.S.	Kaetlyn Osmond, Canada
Nathan Chen	Alysa Liu	**2019**	Nathan Chen, U.S.	Alina Zagitova, Russia
Nathan Chen	Alysa Liu	**2020**[3]	No champion	No champion
Nathan Chen	Bradie Tennell	**2021**	Nathan Chen, U.S.	Anna Shcherbakova, Russia
Nathan Chen	Mariah Bell	**2022**	Shoma Uno, Japan	Kaori Sakamoto, Japan
Ilia Malinin	Isabeau Levito	**2023**	Shoma Uno, Japan	Kaori Sakamoto, Japan
Ilia Malinin	Amber Glenn	**2024**	Ilia Malinin, U.S.	Kaori Sakamoto, Japan

(1) Competition canceled after 18-member U.S. team died in plane crash en route. (2) Tonya Harding was stripped of the title for her involvement in an attack on rival Nancy Kerrigan. (3) World championships canceled due to COVID-19 pandemic.

Tour de France Winners, 1903-2024

The Tour de France was first held in 1903. Sixty cyclists began the 1,509-mi (2,428-km) race at Montgeron, a suburb of Paris, and 21 cyclists finished the six-stage race 17 days later in Paris. The race route changes every year. Race not held, 1915-18, 1940-46.

Year	Winner, country
1903	Maurice Garin, France
1904	Henri Cornet, France
1905	Louis Trousselier, France
1906	René Pottier, France
1907	Lucien Petit-Breton, France
1908	Lucien Petit-Breton, France
1909	François Faber, Luxembourg
1910	Octave Lapize, France
1911	Gustave Garrigou, France
1912	Odile Defraye, Belgium
1913	Philippe Thys, Belgium
1914	Philippe Thys, Belgium
1919	Firmin Lambot, Belgium
1920	Philippe Thys, Belgium
1921	Léon Scieur, Belgium
1922	Firmin Lambot, Belgium
1923	Henri Pélissier, France
1924	Ottavio Bottecchia, Italy
1925	Ottavio Bottecchia, Italy
1926	Lucien Buysse, Belgium
1927	Nicolas Frantz, Luxembourg
1928	Nicolas Frantz, Luxembourg
1929	Maurice Dewaele, Belgium
1930	André Leducq, France
1931	Antonin Magne, France
1932	André Leducq, France
1933	Georges Speicher, France
1934	Antonin Magne, France
1935	Romain Maes, Belgium
1936	Sylvère Maes, Belgium
1937	Roger Lapépie, France
1938	Gino Bartali, Italy
1939	Sylvère Maes, Belgium
1947	Jean Robic, France
1948	Gino Bartali, Italy
1949	Fausto Coppi, Italy
1950	Ferdi Kübler, Switzerland
1951	Hugo Koblet, Switzerland
1952	Fausto Coppi, Italy
1953	Louison Bobet, France
1954	Louison Bobet, France
1955	Louison Bobet, France
1956	Roger Walkowiak, France
1957	Jacques Anquetil, France
1958	Charly Gaul, Luxembourg
1959	Federico Bahamontes, Spain
1960	Gastone Nencini, Italy
1961	Jacques Anquetil, France
1962	Jacques Anquetil, France
1963	Jacques Anquetil, France
1964	Jacques Anquetil, France
1965	Felice Gimondi, Italy
1966	Lucien Aimar, France
1967	Roger Pingeon, France
1968	Jan Janssen, Netherlands
1969	Eddy Merckx, Belgium
1970	Eddy Merckx, Belgium
1971	Eddy Merckx, Belgium
1972	Eddy Merckx, Belgium
1973	Luis Ocaña, Spain
1974	Eddy Merckx, Belgium
1975	Bernard Thévenet, France
1976	Lucien Van Impe, Belgium
1977	Bernard Thévenet, France
1978	Bernard Hinault, France
1979	Bernard Hinault, France
1980	Joop Zoetemelk, Netherlands
1981	Bernard Hinault, France
1982	Bernard Hinault, France
1983	Laurent Fignon, France
1984	Laurent Fignon, France
1985	Bernard Hinault, France
1986	Greg LeMond, U.S.
1987	Stephen Roche, Ireland
1988	Pedro Delgado, Spain
1989	Greg LeMond, U.S.
1990	Greg LeMond, U.S.
1991	Miguel Indurain, Spain
1992	Miguel Indurain, Spain
1993	Miguel Indurain, Spain
1994	Miguel Indurain, Spain
1995	Miguel Indurain, Spain
1996	Bjarne Riis, Denmark
1997	Jan Ullrich, Germany
1998	Marco Pantani, Italy
1999	Vacant[1]
2000	Vacant[1]
2001	Vacant[1]
2002	Vacant[1]
2003	Vacant[1]
2004	Vacant[1]
2005	Vacant[1]
2006	Óscar Pereiro, Spain[2]
2007	Alberto Contador, Spain
2008	Carlos Sastre, Spain
2009	Alberto Contador, Spain
2010	Andy Schleck, Luxembourg[3]
2011	Cadel Evans, Australia
2012	Bradley Wiggins, UK
2013	Chris Froome, UK
2014	Vincenzo Nibali, Italy
2015	Chris Froome, UK
2016	Chris Froome, UK
2017	Chris Froome, UK
2018	Geraint Thomas, UK
2019	Egan Bernal, Colombia
2020	Tadej Pogacar, Slovenia
2021	Tadej Pogacar, Slovenia
2022	Jonas Vingegaard, Denmark
2023	Jonas Vingegaard, Denmark
2024	Tadej Pogacar, Slovenia

(1) Lance Armstrong, U.S., was stripped of his seven Tour titles Oct. 22, 2012; Armstrong had dropped his fight against doping charges Aug. 23, 2012. (2) Floyd Landis, U.S., was stripped of the 2006 title, Sept. 20, 2007, for doping. Landis lost a final appeal of the ruling June 30, 2008. (3) Alberto Contador, Spain, was stripped of the 2010 title, Feb. 6, 2012, for doping.

Swimming World Records

Long course (50-m pools only) records, as of Sept. 2024. All times in minutes:seconds.

Men's Records

Freestyle

Distance	Record	Holder	Country	Location	Date
50 meters	**0:20.91**	César Cielo Filho	Brazil	São Paulo, Brazil	Dec. 18, 2009
100 meters	**0:46.40**	Pan Zhanle	China	Paris, France	July 31, 2024
200 meters	**1:42.00**	Paul Biedermann	Germany	Rome, Italy	July 28, 2009
400 meters	**3:40.07**	Paul Biedermann	Germany	Rome, Italy	July 26, 2009
800 meters	**7:32.12**	Zhang Lin	China	Rome, Italy	July 29, 2009
1,500 meters	**14:30.67**	Bobby Finke	U.S.	Paris, France	Aug. 4, 2024

Backstroke

Distance	Record	Holder	Country	Location	Date
50 meters	**0:23.55**	Kliment Kolesnikov	Russia	Kazan, Russia	July 27, 2023
100 meters	**0:51.60**	Thomas Ceccon	Italy	Budapest, Hungary	June 20, 2022
200 meters	**1:51.92**	Aaron Peirsol	U.S.	Rome, Italy	July 31, 2009

Breaststroke

Distance	Record	Holder	Country	Location	Date
50 meters	**0:25.95**	Adam Peaty	UK	Budapest, Hungary	July 25, 2017
100 meters	**0:56.88**	Adam Peaty	UK	Gwangju, South Korea	July 21, 2019
200 meters	**2:05.48**	Qin Haiyang	China	Fukuoka, Japan	July 28, 2023

Butterfly

Distance	Record	Holder	Country	Location	Date
50 meters	**0:22.27**	Andriy Govorov	Ukraine	Rome, Italy	July 1, 2018
100 meters	**0:49.45**	Caeleb Dressel	U.S.	Tokyo, Japan	July 31, 2021
200 meters	**1:50.34**	Kristof Milak	Hungary	Budapest, Hungary	June 21, 2022

Individual medley

Distance	Record	Holder	Country	Location	Date
200 meters	**1:54.00**	Ryan Lochte	U.S.	Shanghai, China	July 28, 2011
400 meters	**4:02.50**	Leon Marchand	France	Fukuoka, Japan	July 23, 2023

Freestyle relay

Distance	Record	Holder	Country	Location	Date
400 m (4×100)	**3:08.24**	Phelps, Weber-Gale, Jones, Lezak	U.S.	Beijing, China	Aug. 11, 2008
800 m (4×200)	**6:58.55**	Phelps, Berens, Walters, Lochte	U.S.	Rome, Italy	July 31, 2009

Medley relay

Distance	Record	Holder	Country	Location	Date
400 m (4×100)	**3:26.78**	Andrew, Murphy, Dressel, Apple	U.S.	Tokyo, Japan	Aug. 1, 2021

Women's Records

Freestyle

Distance	Record	Holder	Country	Location	Date
50 meters	**0:23.61**	Sarah Sjöström	Sweden	Fukuoka, Japan	July 29, 2023
100 meters	**0:51.71**	Sarah Sjöström	Sweden	Budapest, Hungary	July 23, 2017
200 meters	**1:52.23**	Ariarne Titmus	Australia	Brisbane, Australia	June 12, 2024
400 meters	**3:55.38**	Ariarne Titmus	Australia	Fukuoka, Japan	July 23, 2023
800 meters	**8:04.79**	Katie Ledecky	U.S.	Rio de Janeiro, Brazil	Aug. 12, 2016
1,500 meters	**15:20.48**	Katie Ledecky	U.S.	Indianapolis, IN	May 16, 2018

Backstroke

Distance	Record	Holder	Country	Location	Date
50 meters	**0:26.86**	Kaylee McKeown	Australia	Budapest, Hungary	Oct. 20, 2023
100 meters	**0:57.13**	Regan Smith	U.S.	Indianapolis, IN	June 18, 2024
200 meters	**2:03.14**	Kaylee McKeown	Australia	Sydney, Australia	Mar. 10, 2023

Breaststroke

Distance	Record	Holder	Country	Location	Date
50 meters	**0:29.16**	Ruta Meilutyte	Lithuania	Fukuoka, Japan	July 30, 2023
100 meters	**1:04.13**	Lilly King	U.S.	Budapest, Hungary	July 25, 2017
200 meters	**2:17.55**	Evgeniia Chikunova	Russia	Kazan, Russia	Apr. 21, 2023

Butterfly

Distance	Record	Holder	Country	Location	Date
50 meters	**0:24.43**	Sarah Sjöström	Sweden	Boras, Sweden	July 5, 2014
100 meters	**0:55.18**	Gretchen Walsh	U.S.	Indianapolis, IN	June 15, 2024
200 meters	**2:01.81**	Liu Zige	China	Jinan, China	Oct. 21, 2009

Individual medley

Distance	Record	Holder	Country	Location	Date
200 meters	**2:06.12**	Katinka Hosszú	Hungary	Kazan, Russia	Aug. 3, 2015
400 meters	**4:24.38**	Summer McIntosh	Canada	Toronto, ON, Canada	May 16, 2024

Freestyle relay

Distance	Record	Holder	Country	Location	Date
400 m (4×100)	**3:27.96**	McKeon, O'Callaghan, Harris, Jack	Australia	Fukuoka, Japan	July 23, 2023
800 m (4×200)	**7:37.50**	O'Callaghan, Throssell, Titmus, Jack	Australia	Fukuoka, Japan	July 27, 2023

Medley relay

Distance	Record	Holder	Country	Location	Date
400 m (4×100)	**3:49.63**	Smith, Walsh, King, Huske	U.S.	Paris, France	Aug. 4, 2024

World Track and Field Outdoor Records

The International Association of Athletics Federations (IAAF), the world body of track and field, recognizes only records in metric distances, except for the mile. As of Oct. 2024. * = record confirmation pending.

Men's Records

Running

Event	Record	Holder	Country	Location	Date
100 meters	**9.58 s.**	Usain Bolt	Jamaica	Berlin, Germany	Aug. 16, 2009
200 meters	**19.19 s.**	Usain Bolt	Jamaica	Berlin, Germany	Aug. 20, 2009
400 meters	**43.03 s.**	Wayde Van Niekerk	South Africa	Rio de Janeiro, Brazil	Aug. 14, 2016
800 meters	**1 min., 40.91 s.**	David Rudisha	Kenya	London, England, UK	Aug. 9, 2012
1,000 meters	**2 min., 11.96 s.**	Noah Ngeny	Kenya	Rieti, Italy	Sept. 5, 1999
1,500 meters	**3 min., 26.00 s.**	Hicham El Guerrouj	Morocco	Rome, Italy	July 14, 1998
1 mile	**3 min., 43.13 s.**	Hicham El Guerrouj	Morocco	Rome, Italy	July 7, 1999
2,000 meters	**4 min., 43:13 s.**	Jakob Ingebrigtsen	Norway	Brussels, Belgium	Sept. 8, 2023
3,000 meters	**7 min., 20.67 s.**	Daniel Komen	Kenya	Rieti, Italy	Sept. 1, 1996
3,000-meter stpl.	**7 min., 52.11 s.**	Lamecha Girma	Ethiopia	Paris, France	June 9, 2023
5,000 meters	**12 min., 35.36 s.**	Joshua Cheptegei	Uganda	Monaco	Aug. 14, 2020
10,000 meters	**26 min., 11.00 s.**	Joshua Cheptegei	Uganda	Valencia, Spain	Oct. 7, 2020
Marathon[1]	**2 hr., 35 s.**	Kelvin Kiptum	Kenya	Chicago, IL	Oct. 8, 2023
110-meter hurdles	**12.80 s.**	Aries Merritt	U.S.	Brussels, Belgium	Sept. 7, 2012
400-meter hurdles	**45.94 s.**	Karsten Warholm	Norway	Tokyo, Japan	Aug. 3, 2021
400 m (4×100)	**36.84 s.**	Carter, Frater, Blake, Bolt	Jamaica	London, England, UK	Aug. 11, 2012
800 m (4×200)	**1 min., 18.63 s.**	Ashmeade, Weir, Brown, Blake	Jamaica	Nassau, The Bahamas	May 24, 2014
1,600 m (4×400)	**2 min., 54.29 s.**	Valmon, Watts, Reynolds, Johnson	U.S.	Stuttgart, Germany	Aug. 22, 1993
3,200 m (4×800)	**7 min., 2.43 s.**	Mutua, Yiampoy, Kombich, Bungei	Kenya	Brussels, Belgium	Aug. 25, 2006

Field Events

Event	Record	Holder	Country	Location	Date
High jump	**2.45 m** (8' ½")	Javier Sotomayor	Cuba	Salamanca, Spain	July 27, 1993
Long jump	**8.95 m** (29' 4½")	Mike Powell	U.S.	Tokyo, Japan	Aug. 30, 1991
Triple jump	**18.29 m** (60' ¼")	Jonathan Edwards	UK	Gothenburg, Sweden	Aug. 7, 1995
Pole vault	**6.26 m** (20' 5")*	Armand Duplantis	Sweden	Chorzow, Poland	Aug. 25, 2024
Discus	**74.35 m** (243' 11¼")	Mykolas Alekna	Lithuania	Ramona, OK	Apr. 14, 2024
Hammer	**86.74 m** (284' 7")	Yuriy Sedykh	USSR	Stuttgart, W. Germany	Aug. 30, 1986
Javelin	**98.48 m** (323' 1")	Jan Zelezný	Czech Rep.	Jena, W. Germany	May 25, 1996
Shot put	**23.56 m** (77' 3½")	Ryan Crouser	U.S.	Los Angeles, CA	May 27, 2023
Decathlon	**9,126 pts.**	Kevin Mayer	France	Talence, France	Sept. 16, 2018

(1) Eliud Kipchoge, Kenya, ran a marathon in 1:59:40.2 in Vienna, Austria, Oct. 12, 2019, but the run was ineligible for record consideration per IAAF guidelines.

Women's Records

Running

Event	Record	Holder	Country	Location	Date
100 meters	**10.49 s.**	Florence Griffith-Joyner	U.S.	Indianapolis, IN.	July 16, 1988
200 meters	**21.34 s.**	Florence Griffith-Joyner	U.S.	Seoul, S. Korea	Sept. 29, 1988
400 meters	**47.60 s.**	Marita Koch	E. Germany	Canberra, Australia	Oct. 6, 1985
800 meters	**1 min., 53.28 s.**	Jarmila Kratochvílová	Czechoslovakia	Munich, W. Germany	July 26, 1983
1,000 meters	**2 min., 28.98 s.**	Svetlana Masterkova	Russia	Brussels, Belgium	Aug. 23, 1996
1,500 meters	**3 min., 49.04 s.**	Faith Kipyegon	Kenya	Paris, France	July 7, 2024
1 mile	**4 min., 7.64 s.**	Faith Kipyegon	Kenya	Monaco	July 21, 2023
2,000 meters	**5 min., 19.70 s.***	Jessica Hull	Australia	Monaco	July 12, 2024
3,000 meters	**8 min., 6.11 s.**	Wang Junxia	China	Beijing, China	Sept. 13, 1993
3,000-meter stpl.	**8 min., 44.32 s.**	Beatrice Chepkoech	Kenya	Monaco	July 20, 2018
5,000 meters	**14 min., 0.21 s.**	Gudaf Tsegay	Ethiopia	Eugene, OR	Sept. 17, 2023
10,000 meters	**28 min., 54.14 s.***	Beatrice Chebet	Kenya	Eugene, OR	May 25, 2024
Marathon	**2 hr., 9 min., 56 sec.***	Ruth Chepngetich	Kenya	Chicago, IL	Oct. 13, 2024
100-meter hurdles	**12.12 s.**	Tobi Amusan	Nigeria	Eugene, OR	July 24, 2022
400-meter hurdles	**50.37 s.***	Sydney McLaughlin-Levrone	U.S.	Paris, France	Aug. 8, 2024
400 m (4×100)	**40.82 s.**	Madison, Felix, Knight, Jeter	U.S.	London, England, UK	Aug. 10, 2012
800 m (4×200)	**1 min., 27.46 s.**	Jenkins, Colander, Perry, Jones	U.S.	Philadelphia, PA	Apr. 29, 2000
1,600 m (4×400)	**3 min., 15.17 s.**	Ledovskaya, Nazarova, Pinigina, Bryzgina	USSR	Seoul, S. Korea	Oct. 1, 1988
3,200 m (4×800)	**7 min., 50.17 s.**	Olizarenko, Gurina, Borisova, Podyalovskaya	USSR	Moscow, Russia	Aug. 5, 1984

Field Events

Event	Record	Holder	Country	Location	Date
High jump	**2.10 m** (6' 10¾")*	Yaroslava Mahuchikh	Ukraine	Paris, France	July 7, 2024
Long jump	**7.52 m** (24' 8¼")	Galina Chistyakova	USSR	Leningrad, Russia	June 11, 1988
Triple jump	**15.74 m** (51' 7¾")	Yulimar Rojas	Venezuela	Belgrade, Serbia	Mar. 20, 2022
Pole vault	**5.06 m** (16' 7¾")	Yelena Isinbayeva	Russia	Zürich, Switzerland	Aug. 28, 2009
Discus	**76.80 m** (252' 0")	Gabriele Reinsch	E. Germany	Neubrandenburg, E. Germany	July 9, 1988
Hammer	**82.98 m** (272' 3")	Anita Wlodarczyk	Poland	Warsaw, Poland	Aug. 28, 2016
Javelin	**72.28 m** (237' 1¾")	Barbora Spotáková	Czech Rep.	Stuttgart, Germany	Sept. 13, 2008
Shot put	**22.63 m** (74' 3")	Natalya Lisovskaya	USSR	Moscow, Russia	June 7, 1987
Heptathlon	**7,291 pts.**	Jackie Joyner-Kersee	U.S.	Seoul, S. Korea	Sept. 24, 1988

Westminster Kennel Club Best-In-Show Dogs, 1985-2024

Year	Best-in-Show winner, breed
1985	Braeburn's Close Encounter, Scottish Terrier
1986	Marjetta National Acclaim, Pointer
1987	Covy Tucker Hill's Manhattan, German Shepherd Dog
1988	Great Elms Prince Charming II, Pomeranian
1989	Royal Tudor's Wild As The Wind, Doberman Pinscher
1990	Wendessa Crown Prince, Pekingese
1991	Whisperwind On A Carousel, Poodle (Standard)
1992	Registry's Lonesome Dove, Fox Terrier (Wire)
1993	Salilyn's Condor, Spaniel (English Springer)
1994	Chidley Willum The Conqueror, Norwich Terrier
1995	Gaelforce Post Script, Scottish Terrier
1996	Clussexx Country Sunrise, Spaniel (Clumber)
1997	Parsifal Di Casa Netzer, Standard Schnauzer
1998	Fairewood Frolic, Norwich Terrier
1999	Loteki Supernatural Being, Papillon
2000	Salilyn 'N Erin's Shameless, Spaniel (English Springer)
2001	Special Times Just Right, Bichon Frise
2002	Surrey Spice Girl, Poodle (Miniature)
2003	Torums Scarf Michael, Kerry Blue Terrier
2004	Darbydale's All Rise Pouch Cove, Newfoundland
2005	Kan-Point's VJK Autumn Roses, Pointer (German Shorthaired)
2006	Rocky Top's Sundance Kid, Bull Terrier (Colored)
2007	Felicity's Diamond Jim, Spaniel (English Springer)
2008	K-Run's Park Me In First, Beagle (15 Inch)
2009	Clussexx Three D Grinchy Glee, Spaniel (Sussex)
2010	Roundtown Mercedes Of Maryscot, Scottish Terrier
2011	Foxcliffe Hickory Wind, Scottish Deerhound
2012	Palacegarden Malachy, Pekingese
2013	Banana Joe V Tani Kazari, Affenpinscher
2014	Afterall Painting The Sky, Fox Terrier (Wire)
2015	Tashtins Lookin For Trouble, Beagle (15 Inch)
2016	Vjk-Myst Garbonita's California Journey, Pointer (German Shorthaired)
2017	Lockenhaus' Rumor Has It V Kenlyn, German Shepherd Dog
2018	Belle Creek's All I Care About Is Love, Bichon Frise
2019	Kingarthur Van Foliny Home, Fox Terrier (Wire)
2020	Stone Run Afternoon Tea, Poodle (Standard)
2021	Pequest Wasabi, Pekingese
2022	Flessner's Toot My Own Horn, Bloodhound
2023	Soletrader Buddy Holly, Petit Basset Griffon Vendeen
2024	Surrey Sage, Poodle (Miniature)

World Marathon Majors Winners, 2006-23

Marathoners are awarded points relative to their finish in each race in the series; number of races and time period encompassed by each series varies.

Series	Men's winner, country	Women's winner, country
I: 2006-07	Robert K. Cheruiyot, Kenya	Gete Wami, Ethiopia
II: 2007-08	Martin Lel, Kenya	Irina Mikitenko, Germany
III: 2008-09	Samuel Wanjiru, Kenya	Irina Mikitenko, Germany
IV: 2009-10	Samuel Wanjiru, Kenya	Irina Mikitenko, Germany*
V: 2010-11	Emmanuel Mutai, Kenya	Edna Kiplagat, Kenya*
VI: 2011-12	Geoffrey Mutai, Kenya	Mary Keitany, Kenya
VII: 2012-13	Tsegaye Kebede, Ethiopia	Priscah Jeptoo, Kenya
VIII: 2013-14	Wilson Kipsang, Kenya	Edna Kiplagat, Kenya*
IX: 2015-16	Eliud Kipchoge, Kenya	Mary Keitany, Kenya
X: 2016-17	Eliud Kipchoge, Kenya	Edna Kiplagat, Kenya*
XI: 2017-18	Eliud Kipchoge, Kenya	Mary Keitany, Kenya
XII: 2018-19	Eliud Kipchoge, Kenya	Brigid Kosgei, Kenya
XIII: 2019-21	Albert Korir, Kenya	Peres Jepchirchir, Kenya; Joyciline Jepkosgei, Kenya
XIV: 2021-22	Eliud Kipchoge, Kenya	Gotytom Gebreslase, Ethiopia
XV: 2023	Kelvin Kiptum, Kenya	Sifan Hassan, Netherlands

* = Winner adjusted following doping disqualifications.

Boston Marathon Winners, 1972-2024

All times in hour:minute:second format. * = Course record. The 2020 race was canceled due to the COVID-19 pandemic.

Men's winner, country	Time	Year	Women's winner, country	Time
Olavi Suomalainen, Finland	2:15:39	**1972**	Nina Kuscsik, U.S.	3:10:26
Jon Anderson, U.S.	2:16:03	**1973**	Jacqueline Hansen, U.S.	3:05:59
Neil Cusack, Ireland	2:13:39	**1974**	Miki Gorman, U.S.	2:47:11
Bill Rodgers, U.S.	2:09:55	**1975**	Liane Winter, West Germany	2:42:24
Jack Fultz, U.S.	2:20:19	**1976**	Kim Merritt, U.S.	2:47:10
Jerome Drayton, Canada	2:14:46	**1977**	Miki Gorman, U.S.	2:48:33
Bill Rodgers, U.S.	2:10:13	**1978**	Gayle S. Barron, U.S.	2:44:52
Bill Rodgers, U.S.	2:09:27	**1979**	Joan Benoit, U.S.	2:35:15
Bill Rodgers, U.S.	2:12:11	**1980**	Jacqueline Gareau, Canada	2:34:28
Toshihiko Seko, Japan	2:09:26	**1981**	Allison Roe, New Zealand	2:26:46
Alberto Salazar, U.S.	2:08:52	**1982**	Charlotte Teske, West Germany	2:29:33
Greg Meyer, U.S.	2:09:00	**1983**	Joan Benoit, U.S.	2:22:43
Geoff Smith, England, UK	2:10:34	**1984**	Lorraine Moller, New Zealand	2:29:28
Geoff Smith, England, UK	2:14:05	**1985**	Lisa Larsen Weidenbach, U.S.	2:34:06
Robert de Castella, Australia	2:07:51	**1986**	Ingrid Kristiansen, Norway	2:24:55
Toshihiko Seko, Japan	2:11:50	**1987**	Rosa Mota, Portugal	2:25:21
Ibrahim Hussein, Kenya	2:08:43	**1988**	Rosa Mota, Portugal	2:24:30
Abebe Mekonnen, Ethiopia	2:09:06	**1989**	Ingrid Kristiansen, Norway	2:24:33
Gelindo Bordin, Italy	2:08:19	**1990**	Rosa Mota, Portugal	2:25:24
Ibrahim Hussein, Kenya	2:11:06	**1991**	Wanda Panfil, Poland	2:24:18
Ibrahim Hussein, Kenya	2:08:14	**1992**	Olga Markova, Russia	2:23:43
Cosmas Ndeti, Kenya	2:09:33	**1993**	Olga Markova, Russia	2:25:27
Cosmas Ndeti, Kenya	2:07:15	**1994**	Uta Pippig, Germany	2:21:45
Cosmas Ndeti, Kenya	2:09:22	**1995**	Uta Pippig, Germany	2:25:11
Moses Tanui, Kenya	2:09:15	**1996**	Uta Pippig, Germany	2:27:12
Lameck Aguta, Kenya	2:10:34	**1997**	Fatuma Roba, Ethiopia	2:26:23
Moses Tanui, Kenya	2:07:34	**1998**	Fatuma Roba, Ethiopia	2:23:21
Joseh Chebet, Kenya	2:09:52	**1999**	Fatuma Roba, Ethiopia	2:23:25
Elijah Lagat, Kenya	2:09:47	**2000**	Catherine Ndereba, Kenya	2:26:11
Lee Bong-ju, South Korea	2:09:43	**2001**	Catherine Ndereba, Kenya	2:23:53
Rodgers Rop, Kenya	2:09:02	**2002**	Margaret Okayo, Kenya	2:20:43
Robert Kipkoech Cheruiyot, Kenya	2:10:11	**2003**	Svetlana Zakharova, Russia	2:25:20
Timothy Cherigat, Kenya	2:10:37	**2004**	Catherine Ndereba, Kenya	2:24:27
Hailu Negussie, Ethiopia	2:11:45	**2005**	Catherine Ndereba, Kenya	2:25:13
Robert Kipkoech Cheruiyot, Kenya	2:07:14	**2006**	Rita Jeptoo, Kenya	2:23:38
Robert Kipkoech Cheruiyot, Kenya	2:14:13	**2007**	Lidiya Grigoryeva, Russia	2:29:18
Robert Kipkoech Cheruiyot, Kenya	2:07:46	**2008**	Dire Tune, Ethiopia	2:25:25
Deriba Merga, Ethiopia	2:08:42	**2009**	Salina Kosgei, Kenya	2:32:16
Robert Kiprono Cheruiyot, Kenya	2:05:52	**2010**	Teyba Erkesso, Ethiopia	2:26:11
Geoffrey Mutai, Kenya	2:03:02*	**2011**	Caroline Kilel, Kenya	2:22:36
Wesley Korir, Kenya	2:12:40	**2012**	Sharon Cherop, Kenya	2:31:50
Lelisa Desisa, Ethiopia	2:10:22	**2013**	Rita Jeptoo, Kenya	2:26:25
Meb Keflezighi, U.S.	2:08:37	**2014**	Buzunesh Deba, Ethiopia[1]	2:19:59*
Lelisa Desisa, Ethiopia	2:09:17	**2015**	Caroline Rotich, Kenya	2:24:55
Lemi Berhanu Hayle, Ethiopia	2:12:45	**2016**	Atsede Baysa, Ethiopia	2:29:19
Geoffrey Kirui, Kenya	2:09:37	**2017**	Edna Kiplagat, Kenya	2:21:52
Yuki Kawauchi, Japan	2:15:58	**2018**	Desiree Linden, U.S.	2:39:54
Lawrence Cherono, Kenya	2:07:57	**2019**	Worknesh Degefa, Ethiopia	2:23:31
Benson Kipruto, Kenya	2:09:51	**2021**	Diana Kipyokei, Kenya	2:24:45
Evans Chebet, Kenya	2:06:51	**2022**	Peres Jepchirchir, Kenya	2:21:01
Evans Chebet, Kenya	2:05:54	**2023**	Hellen Obiri, Kenya	2:21:38
Sisay Lemma, Ethiopia	2:06:17	**2024**	Hellen Obiri, Kenya	2:22:37

(1) Kenya's Rita Jeptoo was stripped of the victory in Dec. 2016 due to doping.

New York City Marathon Winners, 1970-2024

All times in hour:minute:second format. * = Course record. Race not held, 2012, 2020.

Men's winner, country	Time	Year	Women's winner, country	Time
Gary Muhrcke, U.S.	2:31:38	1970	No finisher	—
Norman Higgins, U.S.	2:22:54	1971	Beth Bonner, U.S.	2:55:22
Sheldon Karlin, U.S.	2:27:52	1972	Nina Kuscsik, U.S.	3:08:41
Tom Fleming, U.S.	2:19:25	1973	Nina Kuscsik, U.S.	2:57:07
Norbert Sander, U.S.	2:26:30	1974	Katherine Switzer, U.S.	3:07:29
Tom Fleming, U.S.	2:19:27	1975	Kim Merritt, U.S.	2:46:14
Bill Rodgers, U.S.	2:10:10	1976	Miki Gorman, U.S.	2:39:11
Bill Rodgers, U.S.	2:11:28	1977	Miki Gorman, U.S.	2:43:10
Bill Rodgers, U.S.	2:12:12	1978	Grete Waitz, Norway	2:32:30
Bill Rodgers, U.S.	2:11:42	1979	Grete Waitz, Norway	2:27:33
Alberto Salazar, U.S.	2:09:41	1980	Grete Waitz, Norway	2:25:42
Alberto Salazar, U.S.	2:08:13	1981	Allison Roe, New Zealand	2:25:29
Alberto Salazar, U.S.	2:09:29	1982	Grete Waitz, Norway	2:27:14
Rod Dixon, New Zealand	2:08:59	1983	Grete Waitz, Norway	2:27:00
Orlando Pizzolato, Italy	2:14:53	1984	Grete Waitz, Norway	2:29:30
Orlando Pizzolato, Italy	2:11:34	1985	Grete Waitz, Norway	2:28:34
Gianni Poli, Italy	2:11:06	1986	Grete Waitz, Norway	2:28:06
Ibrahim Hussein, Kenya	2:11:01	1987	Priscilla Welch, England, UK	2:30:17
Steve Jones, Wales, UK	2:08:20	1988	Grete Waitz, Norway	2:28:07
Juma Ikangaa, Tanzania	2:08:01	1989	Ingrid Kristiansen, Norway	2:25:30
Douglas Wakiihuri, Kenya	2:12:39	1990	Wanda Panfil, Poland	2:30:45
Salvador García, Mexico	2:09:28	1991	Liz McColgan, Scotland, UK	2:27:32
Willie Mtolo, South Africa	2:09:29	1992	Lisa Ondieki, Australia	2:24:40
Andres Espinosa, Mexico	2:10:04	1993	Uta Pippig, Germany	2:26:24
German Silva, Mexico	2:11:21	1994	Tegla Loroupe, Kenya	2:27:37
German Silva, Mexico	2:11:00	1995	Tegla Loroupe, Kenya	2:28:06
Giacomo Leone, Italy	2:09:54	1996	Anuta Catuna, Romania	2:28:43
John Kagwe, Kenya	2:08:12	1997	F. Rochat-Moser, Switzerland	2:28:43
John Kagwe, Kenya	2:08:45	1998	Franca Fiacconi, Italy	2:25:17
Joseph Chebet, Kenya	2:09:14	1999	Adriana Fernandez, Mexico	2:25:06
Abdelkader El Mouaziz, Morocco	2:10:09	2000	Ludmila Petrova, Russia	2:25:45
Tesfaye Jifar, Ethiopia	2:07:43	2001	Margaret Okayo, Kenya	2:24:21
Rodgers Rop, Kenya	2:08:07	2002	Joyce Chepchumba, Kenya	2:25:56
Martin Lel, Kenya	2:10:30	2003	Margaret Okayo, Kenya	2:22:31*
Hendrik Ramaala, South Africa	2:09:28	2004	Paula Radcliffe, England, UK	2:23:10
Paul Tergat, Kenya	2:09:30	2005	Jelena Prokopcuka, Latvia	2:24:41
Marilson Gomes dos Santos, Brazil	2:09:58	2006	Jelena Prokopcuka, Latvia	2:25:05
Martin Lel, Kenya	2:09:04	2007	Paula Radcliffe, England, UK	2:23:09
Marilson Gomes dos Santos, Brazil	2:08:43	2008	Paula Radcliffe, England, UK	2:23:56
Meb Keflezighi, U.S.	2:09:15	2009	Derartu Tulu, Ethiopia	2:28:52
Gebre Gebremariam, Ethiopia	2:08:14	2010	Edna Kiplagat, Kenya	2:28:20
Geoffrey Mutai, Kenya	2:05:06	2011	Firehiwot Dado, Ethiopia	2:23:15
Geoffrey Mutai, Kenya	2:08:24	2013	Priscah Jeptoo, Kenya	2:25:07
Wilson Kipsang, Kenya	2:10:59	2014	Mary Keitany, Kenya	2:25:07
Stanley Biwott, Kenya	2:10:34	2015	Mary Keitany, Kenya	2:24:25
Ghirmay Ghebreslassie, Eritrea	2:07:51	2016	Mary Keitany, Kenya	2:24.26
Geoffrey Kamworor, Kenya	2:10:53	2017	Shalane Flanagan, U.S.	2:26:53
Lelisa Desisa, Ethiopia	2:05:59	2018	Mary Keitany, Kenya	2:22:48
Geoffrey Kamworor, Kenya	2:08:13	2019	Joyciline Jepkosgei, Kenya	2:22:38
Albert Korir, Kenya	2:08:22	2021	Peres Jepchirchir, Kenya	2:22:39
Evans Chebet, Kenya	2:08:41	2022	Sharon Lokedi, Kenya	2:23:23
Tamirat Tola, Ethiopia	2:04:58*	2023	Hellen Obiri, Kenya	2:27:23
Abdi Nageeye, Netherlands	2:07:39	2024	Sheila Chepkirui, Kenya	2:24:35

Ironman Triathlon World Championships, 1985-2024

A 2.4-mi ocean swim, 112-mi bike ride, and 26.2-mi run. All times in hr.:min.:sec. * = Course record. The 2020 event was not held due to the COVID-19 pandemic.

Men's winner, country	Time	Year	Women's winner, country	Time
Scott Tinley, U.S.	8:50:54	1985	Joanne Ernst, U.S.	10:25:22
Dave Scott, U.S.	8:28:37	1986	Paula Newby-Fraser, Zimbabwe	9:49:14
Dave Scott, U.S.	8:34:13	1987	Erin Baker, New Zealand	9:35:25
Scott Molina, U.S.	8:31:00	1988	Paula Newby-Fraser, Zimbabwe	9:01:01
Mark Allen, U.S.	8:09:15	1989	Paula Newby-Fraser, Zimbabwe	9:00:56
Mark Allen, U.S.	8:28:17	1990	Erin Baker, New Zealand	9:13:42
Mark Allen, U.S.	8:18:32	1991	Paula Newby-Fraser, Zimbabwe	9:07:52
Mark Allen, U.S.	8:09:08	1992	Paula Newby-Fraser, Zimbabwe	8:55:28
Mark Allen, U.S.	8:07:45	1993	Paula Newby-Fraser, Zimbabwe	8:58:23
Greg Welch, Australia	8:20:27	1994	Paula Newby-Fraser, Zimbabwe	9:20:14
Mark Allen, U.S.	8:20:34	1995	Karen Smyers, U.S.	9:16:46
Luc Van Lierde, Belgium	8:04:08	1996	Paula Newby-Fraser, Zimbabwe	9:06:49
Thomas Hellriegel, Germany	8:33:01	1997	Heather Fuhr, Canada	9:31:43
Peter Reid, Canada	8:24:20	1998	Natascha Badmann, Switzerland	9:24:16
Luc Van Lierde, Belgium	8:17:17	1999	Lori Bowden, U.S.	9:13:02
Peter Reid, Canada	8:21:01	2000	Natascha Badmann, Switzerland	9:26:16
Timothy Deboom, U.S.	8:31:18	2001	Natascha Badmann, Switzerland	9:28:37
Timothy Deboom, U.S.	8:29:56	2002	Natascha Badmann, Switzerland	9:07:54
Peter Reid, Canada	8:22:35	2003	Lori Bowden, Canada	9:11:55
Normann Stadler, Germany	8:33:29	2004	Natascha Badmann, Switzerland[1]	9:50:04
Faris al-Sultan, Germany	8:14:17	2005	Natascha Badmann, Switzerland	9:09:30
Normann Stadler, Germany	8:11:56	2006	Michellie Jones, Australia	9:18:31
Chris McCormack, Australia	8:15:34	2007	Chrissie Wellington, UK	9:08:45
Craig Alexander, Australia	8:17:45	2008	Chrissie Wellington, UK	9:06:23
Craig Alexander, Australia	8:20:21	2009	Chrissie Wellington, UK	8:54:02
Chris McCormack, Australia	8:10:37	2010	Mirinda Carfrae, Australia	8:58:36
Craig Alexander, Australia	8:03:56	2011	Chrissie Wellington, UK	8:55:08
Pete Jacobs, Australia	8:18:37	2012	Leanda Cave, U.S.	9:15:54
Frederik Van Lierde, Belgium	8:12:29	2013	Mirinda Carfrae, Australia	8:52:14
Sebastian Kienle, Germany	8:14:18	2014	Mirinda Carfrae, Australia	9:00:55
Jan Frodeno, Germany	8:14:40	2015	Daniela Ryf, Switzerland	8:57:57
Jan Frodeno, Germany	8:06:30	2016	Daniela Ryf, Switzerland	8:46:46
Patrick Lange, Germany	8:01:40	2017	Daniela Ryf, Switzerland	8:50:47
Patrick Lange, Germany	7:52:39	2018	Daniela Ryf, Switzerland	8:26:18
Jan Frodeno, Germany	7:51:13	2019	Anne Haug, Germany	8:40:10
Kristian Blummenfelt, Germany	7:49:16	2021	Daniela Ryf, Switzerland	8:34:59
Gustav Iden, Norway	7:40:24	2022	Chelsea Sodaro, U.S.	8:33:46
Sam Laidlow, France	8:06.22	2023	Lucy Charles-Barclay, UK	8:24:31*
Patrick Lange, Germany	7:35:53*	2024	Laura Philipp, Germany	8:45:15

(1) First-place finisher Nina Kraft, Germany, admitted to using performance-enhancing drugs and was disqualified, Nov. 15, 2004.

GENERAL INDEX

Note: Page numbers in boldface indicate key reference. Page numbers in italics indicate photo or illustration captions.

B

H

I

Q

R

T

U

X

Y

Z

QUICK REFERENCE INDEX

For complete index, see pages 980-1007.